"If you tire of 'too much information' when you consult a Bible dictionary, ***What Does Jesus Say About . . .,*** is for you. It's a handy A to Z reference in the words of Jesus in Scripture. Not a commentary, this is an at-your-fingertips tool presenting both the setting and biblical text of what Jesus said arranged in alphabetic categories. Ingenious and greatly helpful."

— *Dr. Woodrow Kroll, Author and President, Back to the Bible International, Lincoln, Nebraska*

"What could be more important than having available a topically arranged reference guide containing Jesus' words dealing with the basic and vital issues of life and death? Cecil Price, in his volume, ***What Does Jesus Say About . . .***, provides such a handy and valuable source book."

— *Dr. Donald K. Campbell, President Emeritus and Professor Emeritus of Bible Exposition, Dallas Theological Seminary, Dallas, Texas*

"From A to Z, I love this unique, user-friendly reference work for when I need a fresh perspective on the words of Jesus. Thank you, Cecil, for picking up where my trusty concordance leaves off!"

— *June Hunt, Author, Founder and Chief Executive Officer, Hope For The Heart, Dallas, Texas*

"Cecil Price has performed an invaluable service for Christians in this new book, ***What Does Jesus Say About . . .*** Instead of writing about Jesus' teachings, Price allows the reader to experience the power of Jesus' own words on a variety of issues relevant to our lives. This book should be read by every serious student of the Bible and every committed disciple of Jesus Christ."

— *Dr. Robert Jeffress, Author and Senior Pastor, First Baptist Church, Dallas, Texas*

"What Does Jesus Say About . . . is an insightful reference work focusing on the most important words ever spoken. Each entry in this work goes one step further than any other concordance and provides us with the powerful message from our Lord's teaching. ***What Does Jesus Say About . . .*** will be used by pastors and lay people for generations to come."

— *Dr. Jack Graham, Author and Senior Pastor, Prestonwood Baptist Church, Plano, Texas*

"WWJD? (What Would Jesus Do?) is more than just a great sentiment. God calls on Christians to be like Jesus. And yet, it's hard to know what Jesus would *do* in any given situation if we can't remember what He *said*. In ***What Does Jesus Say About . . .***, Cecil Price provides an A-to-Z compendium of Jesus' teachings on a wide variety of issues and topics. This is a handy reference tool for anyone seeking to know what Jesus said about life's crucial issues."

— *Dr. Charles H. Dyer, Provost and Dean of Education, Moody Bible Institute, Chicago, Illinois*

"Now where did Jesus say that? No longer do you have to hunt through the Bible to find the answer to your question. Cecil Price in his book, ***What Does Jesus Say About . . .***, organizes the important teachings of Jesus Christ according to key terms and phrases. A helpful book to put these key verses at your fingertips."

— *Kerby Anderson, National Director, Probe Ministries and Host, Point of View Radio talk show*

"Cecil Price's organization of Jesus' statements helps us not just wonder what Jesus might do, but actually listen as Jesus weighs in on an extensive list of topics common to every day existence. Excellently prepared, this is a must-have resource for anyone wishing to quickly identify many of those things about which Jesus concerned Himself, and those things which should therefore concern us."

— *Matthew R. St. John, Senior Pastor, Scofield Memorial Church, Dallas, Texas*

"***What Does Jesus Say About . . .*** is a handy reference work on how Scripture reports Jesus' sayings and teachings to His disciples, even down to noting the context of His remarks. This tool should prove useful to His disciples in today's world who want to be responsive to Him."

— *Dr. Darrell L. Bock, Author and Research Professor of New Testament Studies, Dallas Theological Seminary, Dallas, Texas*

"What does Jesus *say about..."*

CHRIST SPEAKS TO US TODAY

"What does Jesus say about..."

CHRIST SPEAKS TO US TODAY

CECIL PRICE

Advancing the Ministries of the Gospel
AMG *Publishers*
God's Word to you is our highest calling.

What Did Jesus Say About . . .?

Published by AMG Publishers
6815 Shallowford Rd.
Chattanooga, Tennessee 37421

All Web addresses contained in this book were correct as of time of publication. If you find that a URL is no longer active, please notify AMG Publishers by e-mail at **info@amgpublishers.com**. Thank you.

ISBN: 978-089957611-4

First printing—January 2008

Cover designed by Brightboy Designs, Chattanooga, Tennessee
Interior design and typesetting by Reider Publishing Services, West Hollywood, California
Edited and proofread by Rich Cairnes, Dan Penwell, and Rick Steele

Printed in Canada

14 13 12 11 10 09 08–T– 8 7 6 5 4 3 2 1

To my parents, the late Kenneth and Mary Sue Price,
who, from early childhood, introduced me to the truths of the Bible.

Contents

Acknowledgments

No book about the teachings of the Lord Jesus Christ would be complete without giving tribute to the Giver of life, the God of the Bible, existing in the Father, the Son, and the Holy Spirit. Without His active role throughout this entire process, this work would not have materialized.

A special thanks to AMG Sales Director Joe Suter for recommending I submit this book idea to them. And, I appreciate the cooperation, enthusiasm, and professionalism of the AMG Publishers team including Dale Anderson, Dan Penwell, Warren Baker, Rick Steele, and Trevor Overcash, along with Rich Cairnes, Cheri Mullins, and Andrea Reider.

I remain thankful to Pike Lambeth and The Lockman Foundation for allowing the use of the *New American Standard Bible–Updated Edition* in this project.

And, I would be remiss not to mention Dr. Darrell Bock for *The Bible Knowledge Key Word Study* and Dr. Robert Thomas for *A Harmony of the Gospels*. These notable resources allowed me to verify many of the topical entries.

Furthermore, I acknowledge the insightful lectures that expanded my thinking from the courses entitled "The Life of Christ on Earth" by Dr. Dwight Pentecost and "Gospels" by Dr. Stephen Bramer and Dr. Jay Quine of the Bible Exposition Department at Dallas Theological Seminary.

Additionally, I am grateful for the prayers and encouragement from El and Jeanne Arnold, Rod and Carol Baker, John and Debra Blank, Mary Brooks, Jon Campbell, Alan and Catherine Cole, Clayton Coliz, Eric and Cherie Condreay, Jane Corey, Rhonda Dalton, John Eclarin, Lee and Christy Faulkner, Brian Frost, Ingrim Green, Karen Hammitt, Tom Harris, Deborah Hayhoe, Daniel Heideman, Harold and Jean Hines, Ryan and Laura Ho, Ken and Kathy Horton, John and Cozette Jacobs, Joseph Jikong, Ben and Merri Jones, Winston and Barbara Jones, Dennis Kavanaugh, Don Kirby, David and Kathy Lawrence, Agnes Leung, Jim and Laura Lightfoot, Liz Maxfield, Ty and Rhonda Maxfield, Cord Miller, Cesar Muego, Dale Muirhead, Art and Linda Mullan, Jason Neill, Lloyd and Karen Olsen, John Oliver, Tom and Karolyn Perry, Charlie and Leona Plummer, Basil and Lynn Price, Susan Rainey, Margaret Rheingrover, Al and Brenda Robbins, A.W. and Dee Robbins, Rick Rood, Elizabeth Shepherd, Greg Sheryl, Glenda Simmons, Kevin and Kelly Stern, Greg and Trisha Stovall, W. J. Subach, Radford and Debbie Tarry, Colby Torres, Eric and Susie Weir and Paul and Gwen Wright. And then, the valuable counsel from Bill Peel, Sandra Glahn, and David Bea helped make this concept a reality.

Preface

It's been popular among Christians to ask, "What would Jesus do?" Our Lord gives many answers and insights for us in the Scriptures about our questions concerning life. This book attempts to categorize many of the key words, concepts, and phrases of Jesus Christ from the New Testament on various issues and matters about life on earth, death, and eternity. Not every word that Jesus spoke in the New Testament is reproduced here. And, due to space limitations, you will not find every word categorized from the text. Yet, there are instances when a word, not specifically spoken by Jesus, but prominent in a verse or passage where He does speak, is indexed for clarity in understanding the context. An effort is made to present His words on the myriad of topics that people face today. And, since many of His statements apply to more than one area of life, an attempt has been made to list them according to the subject matters He addresses. Both traditional and contemporary terminologies are utilized in the subject headings.

Many Christians are looking forward to experiencing the great blessings of heaven. Some cannot wait to see Jesus face-to-face. Fellowshipping with Him will undoubtedly afford an opportunity to ask questions about the puzzles that perplex us on earth. But, we may be surprised to hear Him tell us the answers to many of our questions were readily available from His teachings in the New Testament.

By producing this book, the compiler does not purport that the words of Jesus are more important than the rest of the revelation of God in His Word, the Bible. Commentaries and other books are written on individual books of the Bible. The intent of this book is to organize the teachings of Jesus in a topical manner to enhance study, personal growth, and obedience to God's truth.

With ***What Does Jesus Say About . . .*** being a reference book, you probably will not read it cover-to-cover in one sitting. However, as you use this resource, be sure to take time to check out the appendixes detailing "How to Personally Know Jesus" and "Resources for Additional Study," along with the "Map of the Ministry of Jesus."

The Scriptures present a depth of truth the human mind cannot fully comprehend in a lifetime. This work only scratches the surface of God's immense, wonderful revelation to us about His Son, the Lord Jesus Christ. Nevertheless, it is my hope that this book will give you a greater appreciation and understanding of His life, words, work, and wisdom. In addition to personal benefit, may you share these truths of Christ with your family, friends, and others in your spheres of influence. No doubt, you will agree with the statement of the officers in John 7:46: "*. . . Never has a man spoken the way this man speaks.*"

Cecil R. Price, Th. M.
Dallas, Texas

How to Get the Most Out of This Book

What Does Jesus Say About . . . allows the words of Jesus to speak for themselves without commentary. It focuses on the words of the Lord in the New Testament, or "the words in red," as some Bible editions distinguish His words with red letters. The Gospel narratives include statements of others along with commentary and transitions. Again, the words of Jesus are emphasized here. The categories are predominately nouns though some verbs are included. To examine the usage of every single word in a book of the Bible, you may wish to consult an exhaustive concordance or Bible software program.

Distinctions of this resource, not found in a regular concordance, include categorized phrases, compound subjects, and contemporary terminology.

Key Words, Terms, and Phrases

Look up any words you remember from the text of the updated New American Standard Bible or familiar terms that come to mind for the concept you are seeking. For example, if you are looking for Heavenly Father, this resource lists it as: "Father, Heavenly." If you cannot locate anything under a particular term or word, employ a synonym or antonym.

Should you not find what you are looking for in a general category such as NAME, look under a specific entry that follows, such as NAME, MY or under a cross-reference listed such as see NAME, FATHER'S.

As much as possible, the compiler tries to allow the text of the *New American Standard Bible* to determine each entry or subject heading. Below are some sample entries. In the majority of cases, the actual word or phrase is used in the verse or passage within the entry as shown:

ABBA
Setting: Gethsemane on the Mount of Olives, east of the temple in Jerusalem. Jesus agonizes over His impending death, disappointed His disciples keep falling asleep instead of watching and praying with Him.

They came to a place named Gethsemane; and He said to the disciples, "Sit here until I have prayed." And He took with Him Peter and James and John, and began to be very distressed and troubled. And He said to them, "My soul is deeply grieved to the point of death; remain here and keep watch." And He went a little beyond them, and fell to the ground and began to pray that if it were possible, the hour might pass Him by. And He was saying, "Abba! Father! All things are possible for You; remove this cup from Me; yet not what I will, but what You will." And He came and found them sleeping, and said to Peter, "Simon, are you asleep? Could you not keep watch for one hour? Keep watching and praying that you may not come into temptation; the spirit is willing, but the flesh is weak" (Mark 14:32–38; cf. Matthew 26:36–41; Luke 22:41–46; see Romans 8:15; Galatians 4:6).

Sometimes the passage contains a similar word, but the exact key word indexed or listed is not in the text. An entry with a similar word would be:

ALERTNESS
[ALERTNESS from be on guard and keep on the alert]
Setting: Jerusalem. Following a time of ministry in the temple a few days before His crucifixion, after conveying the Parable of the Fig Tree, Jesus warns His disciples to keep alert regarding future events.

"Be on guard, so that your hearts will not be weighted down with dissipation and drunkenness and the worries of life, and that day will not come on you suddenly like a trap; for it will come upon all those who dwell on the face of all the earth. But keep on the alert at all times, praying that you may have strength to escape all these things that are about to take place, and to stand before the Son of Man" (Luke 21:34–36; cf. Mark 13:33; see Matthew 24:42–44).

At other times, the passage contains the concept, though the actual word or similar words are not written:

ACCOUNTABILITY (Also See ACCOUNTING; JUDGMENT; and RESPONSIBILITY, PERSONAL)
[ACCOUNTABILITY inferred]
Setting: Galilee. Following His explanation of the Parable of the Sower to His disciples, Jesus informs them about personal accountability and responsibility.

And He was saying to them, "Take care what you listen to. By your standard of measure it will be measured to you; and more will be given you besides. For whoever has, to him more shall be given; and whoever does not have, even what he has shall be taken away from him" (Mark 4:24, 25; cf. Matthew 13:12; Luke 8:18; see Matthew 7:2).

Setting

The setting or context of the Scripture is given above each verse or passage, along with the location whenever possible. I have attempted to use present tense verbs.

Order

Verses listed under each subject heading occur in the order they appear in the New Testament.

Quotes

The updated *New American Standard Bible* capitalizes Old Testament quotes reproduced in the New Testament. In this reference book, whenever Jesus quotes from an Old Testament book, the source of the quotation is given following the actual reference. For example:

Setting: The temple in Jerusalem. The Sadducees question Jesus about levirate marriage (marriage to a brother-in-law) in order to test Him as He teaches.

But Jesus answered and said to them, "You are mistaken, not understanding the Scriptures nor the power of God. For in the resurrection they neither marry nor are given in marriage, but are like angels in heaven. But regarding the resurrection of the dead, have you not read what was spoken to you by God: 'I AM THE GOD OF ABRAHAM, AND THE GOD OF ISAAC, AND THE GOD OF JACOB'? He is not the God of the dead but of the living" (Matthew 22:29–32, Jesus quotes from Exodus 3:6; cf. Mark 12:18–27; Luke 20:27–38; see Deuteronomy 25:5; John 20:9).

Italicized Words in the Text

The updated *New American Standard Bible* utilizes italicized words to indicate that the particular word is not found in the original Aramaic or Greek, but is inferred in the text. These italicized words are used in the verses. And, many of the words are included in the entries for categorized topics.

Setting: By the Sea of Galilee. After a long day of ministry, Jesus prepares to demonstrate the power of God to His disciples by feeding more than 5,000 people.

But He answered them, "You give them something to eat!" And they said to Him, "Shall we go and spend two hundred denarii on bread and give them *something* to eat? And He said to them, "How many loaves do you have? Go look!" And when they found out, they said, "Five, and two fish" (Mark 6:37, 38; cf. Matthew 14:16, 17; Luke 9:13, 14; John 6:5–9; see Mark 3:20; 6:33–36, 39–44).

Cross-References

Cross-references may be listed from both the Old and New Testaments. The abbreviation cf. (Latin for compare) after a quoted verse directs you to similar Scripture. The word see used after a quoted verse guides you to (1) other helpful verses that may be somewhat similar to the quoted verse(s) or (2) to a verse or verses that will assist in understanding the context.

Setting: Judea beyond the Jordan (Perea). After informing a rich man how righteous believers may have treasure in heaven, Jesus conveys to His disciples the reward of those who sacrifice in this life to follow Him.

Jesus said, "Truly I say to you, there is no one who has left house or brothers or sisters or mother or father or children or farms, for My sake and for the gospel's sake, but that he will received a hundred times as much now in the present age, houses and brothers and sisters and mothers and children and farms, along with persecutions; and in the age to come, eternal life. But many who are first will be last, and the last, first" (Mark 10:29–31; cf. Matthew 19:27–30; Luke 18:28–30; see Matthew 6:33).

In comparative passages, there will be some wording variance as a different human author under the inspiration of the Holy Spirit wrote each Gospel narrative. Also, the updated *New American Standard Bible* is not identical to any other English Bible. Therefore, one Gospel account may be listed under a specific topic, while a parallel account will not contain the same word, so it will not be listed in the same indexed category.

It is possible a particular entry has been inadvertently omitted by the compiler of this work or deleted during the editorial process. Since topical indexing is a subjective endeavor, the reader may think of other terms that should be included in this work.

Notes about the *New American Standard Bible–Updated Edition*

The New American Standard Bible-Updated Edition is one of the finest translations available today with "literal equivalence," or word-for-word translation.

A few noteworthy distinctions of this version include:

1. Pronouns referring to God, Jesus, and the Holy Spirit are capitalized in the text.
2. When the New Testament quotes the Old Testament, the quoted text is capitalized.
3. Italicized words in the scriptural text are not found in the original languages, but are provided by the translators to help convey the intended concept.
4. Verses in brackets are not found in early manuscripts.

My sheep hear My voice, and I know them, and they follow Me . . . (John 21:25).

A

ABANDONMENT

[ABANDONMENT from You do not want to go away also, do you?]

Setting: The synagogue at Capernaum of Galilee. After the Jewish religious leaders argue with one another when Jesus says He will give His flesh to the world to eat, some of His disciples also express difficulty with His statements.

So Jesus said to the twelve, "You do not want to go away also, do you?" (John 6:67).

[ABANDONMENT from leaves the sheep]

Setting: Jerusalem. Following the Pharisees' interrogation and dismissal of the formerly blind man Jesus healed on the Sabbath, the Lord conveys the Parable of the Good Shepherd to the Pharisees using figures of speech they do not understand.

So Jesus said to them again, "Truly, truly, I say to you, I am the door of the sheep. All who came before Me are thieves and robbers, but the sheep did not hear them. I am the door; if anyone enters through Me, he will be saved, and will go in and out and find pasture. The thief comes only to steal and kill and destroy; I came that they may have life, and have *it* abundantly. I am the good shepherd; the good shepherd lays down His life for the sheep. He who is a hired hand, and not a shepherd, who is not the owner of the sheep, sees the wolf coming, and leaves the sheep and flees, and the wolf snatches them and scatters *them. He flees* because he is a hired hand and is not concerned about the sheep. I am the good shepherd, and I know My own and My own know Me, even as the Father knows Me and I know the Father; and I lay down My life for the sheep. I have other sheep, which are not of this fold; I must bring them also, and they will hear My voice; and they will become one flock *with* one shepherd. For this reason the Father loves Me, because I lay down My life so that I may take it again. No one has taken it away from Me, but I lay it down on My own initiative. I have authority to take it up again. This commandment I received from My Father" (John 10:7–18; see Isaiah 40:11; 56:8; Jeremiah 23:1; Matthew 11:27).

[ABANDONMENT from I will not leave you as orphans]

Setting: Jerusalem. Before the Passover, after responding to Philip's request for Him to show His disciples the Father, Jesus conveys the upcoming role of the Holy Spirit in their lives.

"I will not leave you as orphans; I will come to you. After a little while the world will no longer see Me, but you *will* see Me; because I live, you will live also. In that day you will know that I am in the Father, and you in Me, and I in you. He who has My commandments and keeps them is the one who loves Me; and he who loves Me will be loved by My Father, and I will love him and will disclose Myself to him" (John 14:18–21; see John 6:57; 10:37, 38; 16:16, 22).

ABBA

Setting: Gethsemane on the Mount of Olives, east of the temple in Jerusalem. Jesus agonizes over His impending death, disappointed His disciples keep falling asleep instead of watching and praying with Him.

They came to a place named Gethsemane; and He said to the disciples, "Sit here until I have prayed." And He took with Him Peter and James and John, and began to be very distressed and troubled. And He said to them, "My soul is deeply grieved to the point of death; remain here and keep watch." And He went a little beyond *them,* and fell to the ground and *began* to pray that if it were possible, the hour might pass Him by. And He was saying, "Abba! Father! All things are possible for You; remove this cup from Me; yet not what I will, but what You will." And He came and found them sleeping, and said to Peter, "Simon, are you asleep?

Could you not keep watch for one hour? Keep watching and praying that you may not come into temptation; the spirit is willing, but the flesh is weak" (Mark 14:32–38; cf. Matthew 26:36–41; Luke 22:41–46; see Romans 8:15; Galatians 4:6).

ABEL

Setting: The temple in Jerusalem. After the Jewish religious leaders test Him with questions, Jesus pronounces the eighth of eight woes on them in front of the crowds and His disciples.

"Woe to you, scribes and Pharisees, hypocrites! For you build the tombs of the prophets and adorn the monuments of the righteous, and say, 'If we had been *living* in the days of our fathers, we would not have been partners with them in *shedding* the blood of the prophets.' So you testify against yourselves, that you are sons of those who murdered the prophets. Fill up, then, the measure *of the guilt* of your fathers. You serpents, you brood of vipers, how will you escape the sentence of hell? Therefore, behold, I am sending you prophets and wise men and scribes; some of them you will kill and crucify, and some of them you will scourge in your synagogues, and persecute from city to city, so that upon you may fall *the guilt of* all the righteous blood shed on earth, from the blood of righteous Abel to the blood of Zechariah, the son of Berechiah, whom you murdered between the temple and the altar. Truly I say to you, all these things will come upon this generation" (Matthew 23:29–36; cf. 2 Chronicles 24:21; Zechariah 1:1; Matthew 3:7; Luke 11:47–52; see Matthew 10:23).

Setting: On the way from Galilee to Jerusalem. After Jesus pronounces woes upon the Pharisees, a lawyer replies that His remarks insult lawyers, too.

But He said, "Woe to you lawyers as well! For you weigh men down with burdens hard to bear, while you yourselves will not even touch the burdens with one of your fingers. Woe to you! For you build the tombs of the prophets, and it was your fathers who killed them. So you are witnesses and approve the deeds of your fathers; because it was they who killed them, and you build their tombs. For this reason also the wisdom of God said, 'I will send them prophets and apostles, and some of them they will kill and some they will persecute, so that the blood of all the prophets, shed since the foundation of the world, may be charged against this generation, from the blood of Abel to the blood of Zechariah, who was killed between the altar and the house of God; yes, I tell you, it shall be charged against this generation.' Woe to you lawyers! For you have taken away the key of knowledge; you yourselves did not enter, and you hindered those who were entering" (Luke 11:46–52; cf. Matthew 23:29–32; see 2 Chronicles 24:20, 21; Matthew 23:4, 13).

ABIATHAR

Setting: Galilee. Early in His ministry, the Pharisees ask Jesus why He allows His disciples to harvest and eat grain on the Sabbath.

And He said to them, "Have you never read what David did when he was in need and he and his companions became hungry; how he entered the house of God in the time of Abiathar *the* high priest, and ate the consecrated bread, which is not lawful for *anyone* to eat except the priests, and he also gave it to those who were with him?" Jesus said to them, "The Sabbath was made for man, and not man for the Sabbath. So the Son of Man is Lord even of the Sabbath" (Mark 2:25–28; cf. Matthew 12:1–8; Luke 6:1–5; see Exodus 23:12).

ABIDE (Also see ABIDES; and FAITHFULNESS)

[ABIDE from abiding]

Setting: Jerusalem. During the feast of the Jews, Jesus responds to criticism from the Jewish religious leaders by referring to God as His Father (thereby making Himself equal with God) and informing them that God, John the Baptist, and His works all testify to His mission.

"I can do nothing on My own initiative. As I hear, I judge; and My judgment is just, because I do not seek My own will, but the will of Him who sent Me. If I *alone* testify about Myself, My testimony is not true. There is another who testifies of Me, and I know that the testimony which He gives about Me is true. You have sent to John, and he has testified to the truth. But the testimony which I receive is not from man, but I say these things so that you may be saved. He was the lamp that was burning and was shining and you were willing to rejoice for a while in his light. But the testimony which I have is greater than the *testimony of* John; for the works which the Father has given Me to accomplish—the very works that I do—testify about Me, that the Father has sent Me. And the Father who sent Me, He has testified of Me. You have neither heard His voice at any time nor seen His form. You do not have His word abiding in you, for you do not believe Him whom He sent" (John 5:30–38; see Matthew 3:17; Mark 1:4, 5; John 1:7, 15, 32; 4:34; 8:14–16; 10:25, 37, 38).

[ABIDE from abiding]
Setting: Jerusalem. Before the Passover, after answering Thomas's question as to where He is going and how they will know the way, Jesus responds to Philip's request for Him to show His disciples the Father.

Jesus said to him, "Have I been so long with you, and *yet* you have not come to know Me, Philip? He who has seen Me has seen the Father; how *can* you say, 'Show us the Father'? Do you not believe that I am in the Father, and the Father is in Me? The words that I say to you I do not speak on My own initiative, but the Father abiding in Me does His works. Believe Me that I am in the Father and the Father is in Me; otherwise believe because of the works themselves. Truly, truly, I say to you, he who believes in Me, the works that I do, he will do also; and greater *works* than these he will do; because I go to the Father. Whatever you ask in My name, that will I do, so that the Father may be glorified in the Son. If you ask Me anything in My name, I will do *it*" (John 14:9–14; see Matthew 7:7; John 1:14; 5:19, 20, 36; 10:37, 38; 15:16).

[ABIDE from abiding]
Setting: Jerusalem. Before the Passover, after responding to Philip's request for Him to show His disciples the Father, Jesus conveys the upcoming ministry of the Holy Spirit in their lives.

"These things I have spoken to you while abiding with you. But the Helper, the Holy Spirit, whom the Father will send in My name, He will teach you all things, and bring to your remembrance all that I said to you" (John 14:25, 26; see John 16:13).

Setting: Jerusalem. Before the Passover, after He conveys the upcoming ministry of the Holy Spirit in His disciples' lives, with His imminent departure from, Jesus explains He is the vine and they are the branches.

"I am the true vine, and My Father is the vinedresser. Every branch in Me that does not bear fruit, He takes away; and every *branch* that bears fruit, He prunes it so that it may bear more fruit. You are already clean because of the word which I have spoken to you. Abide in Me, and I in you. As the branch cannot bear fruit of itself unless it abides in the vine, so neither *can* you unless you abide in Me. I am the vine, you are the branches; he who abides in Me and I in him, he bears much fruit, for apart from Me you can do nothing. If anyone does not abide in Me, he is thrown away as a branch and dries up; and they gather them, and cast them into the fire and they are burned. If you abide in Me, and My words abide in you, ask whatever you wish, and it will be done for you. My Father is glorified by this, that you bear much fruit, and *so* prove to be My disciples. Just as the Father has loved Me, I have also loved you; abide in My love. If you keep My commandments, you will abide in My love; just as I have kept My Father's commandments and abide in His love. These things I have spoken to you so that My joy may be in you, and *that* your joy may be made full" (John 15:1–11; see Matthew 5:16; 7:7; John 3:29, 35; 6:56; 8:29, 31; 13:10; 15:16).

ABIDES (Also see ABIDE)
Setting: Capernaum of Galilee. After Jesus informs the people whom He miraculously fed with a lad's five loaves and two fish how they might receive the bread out of heaven, the Jewish religious leaders argue with one another when Jesus says He will give His flesh to the world to eat.

So Jesus said to them, "Truly, truly, I say to you, unless you eat the flesh of the Son of Man and drink His blood, you have no life in yourselves. He who eats My flesh and drinks My blood has eternal life, and I will raise him up on the last day. For My flesh is true food, and My blood is true drink. He who eats My flesh and drinks My blood abides in Me, and I in him. As the living Father sent Me, and I live because of the Father, so he who eats Me, he also will live because of Me. This is the bread which came down out of heaven; not as the fathers ate and died; he who eats this bread will live forever" (John 6:53–58; see Matthew 16:16; Luke 4:22; John 3:36; John 6:26–40, 52; 9:16; 15:4).

Setting: Jerusalem. Before the Passover, after responding to Philip's request for Him to show His disciples the Father, Jesus conveys the upcoming role of the Holy Spirit in their lives.

"If you love Me, you will keep My commandments. I will ask the Father, and He will give you another Helper, that He may be with you forever; *that* is the Spirit of truth, whom the world cannot receive, because it does not see Him or know Him, *but* you know Him because He abides with you and will be in you" (John 14:15–17; see John 7:39; 15:26; 1 John 5:3).

Setting: Jerusalem. Before the Passover, after He conveys the upcoming ministry of the Holy Spirit in His disciples' lives, with His imminent departure from them, Jesus explains He is the vine and they are the branches.

"I am the true vine, and My Father is the vinedresser. Every branch in Me that does not bear fruit, He takes away; and every *branch* that bears fruit, He prunes it so that it may bear more fruit. You are already clean because of the word which I have spoken to you. Abide in Me, and I in you. As the branch cannot bear fruit of itself unless it abides in the vine, so neither *can* you unless you abide in Me. I am the vine, you are the branches; he who abides in Me and I in him, he bears much fruit, for apart from Me you can do nothing. If anyone does not abide in Me, he is thrown away as a branch and dries up; and they gather them, and cast them into the fire and they are burned. If you abide in Me, and My words abide in you, ask whatever you wish, and it will be done for you. My Father is glorified by this, that you bear much fruit, and *so* prove to be My disciples. Just as the Father has loved Me, I have also loved you; abide in My love. If you keep My commandments, you will abide in My love; just as I have kept My Father's commandments and abide in His love. These things I have spoken to you so that My joy may be in you, and *that* your joy may be made full" (John 15:1–11; see Matthew 5:16; 7:7; John 3:29, 35; 6:56; 8:29, 31; 13:10; 15:16).

ABILITY

Setting: The Mount of Olives, just east of Jerusalem. During His discourse, after answering His disciples' questions as to when the temple will be destroyed and Jerusalem overrun, along with the signs of His coming and the end of the age, Jesus reemphasizes to His disciples that they should be on the alert for His return.

"For *it is* just like a man *about* to go on a journey, who called his own slaves and entrusted his possessions to them. To one he gave five talents, to another, two, and to another, one, each according to his own ability; and he went on his journey. Immediately the one who had received the five talents went and traded with them, and gained five more talents. In the same manner the one who *had received* the two *talents* gained two more. But he who received the one *talent* went away, and dug a *hole* in the ground and hid his master's money. Now after a long time the master of those slaves came and settled accounts with them. The one who had received the five talents came up and brought five more talents, saying, 'Master, you entrusted five talents to me. See, I have gained five more talents.' His master said to him, 'Well done, good and faithful slave. You were faithful with a few things, I will put you in charge of many things; enter into the joy of your master.' Also the one who *had received* the two talents came up and said, 'Master, you entrusted two talents to me. See, I have gained two more talents.' His master said to him, 'Well done, good and faithful slave. You were faithful with a few things, I will put you in charge of many things; enter into the joy of your master.' And the one also who had received the one talent came up and said, 'Master, I knew you to be a hard man, reaping where you did not sow and gathering where you scattered no *seed.* And I was afraid, and went away and hid your talent in the ground. See, you have what is yours.' But his master answered and said to him, 'You wicked, lazy slave, you knew that I reap where I did not sow and gather where I scattered no *seed.* Then you ought to have put my money in the bank, and on my arrival I would have received my *money* back with interest. 'Therefore take away the talent from him, and give it to the one who has ten talents.' For to everyone who has, *more* shall be given, and he will have an abundance; but from the one who does not have, even what he does have shall be taken away. Throw out the worthless slave into the outer darkness; in that place there will be weeping and gnashing of teeth" (Matthew 25:14–30; cf. Matthew 8:12; 13:12; 24:45–47; see Matthew 18:23, 24; Luke 12:44).

ABODE

Setting: Jerusalem. Before the Passover, after conveying the upcoming ministry of the Holy Spirit in His disciples' lives, Jesus answers Judas's (not Iscariot) question as to why He discloses Himself to them but not the whole world.

Jesus answered and said to him, "If anyone loves Me, he will keep My word; and My Father will love him, and We will come to him and make Our abode with him. He who does not love Me does not keep My words; and the word which you hear is not Mine, but the Father's who sent Me" (John 14:23, 24; see John 7:16; 8:51).

ABOMINATION (See ABOMINATION OF DESOLATION; and DETESTABLE)

ABOMINATION OF DESOLATION (Also see ANTICHRIST)

Setting: The Mount of Olives, just east of Jerusalem. During His discourse, Jesus answers His disciples' questions as to when the temple will be destroyed and Jerusalem overrun, along with the signs of His coming and the end of the age.

"Therefore when you see the ABOMINATION OF DESOLATION which was spoken of through Daniel the prophet, standing in the holy place (let the reader understand), then those who are in Judea must flee to the mountains. Whoever is on the housetop must not go down to get the things that are in his house. Whoever is in the field must not turn back to get his cloak. But woe to those who are pregnant and to those who are nursing babies in those days! But pray that your flight will not be in the winter, or on a Sabbath. For then there will be a great tribulation, such as has not occurred since the beginning of the world until now, nor ever will. Unless those days had been cut short, no life would have been saved; but for the sake of the elect those days will be cut short. Then if anyone says to you, 'Behold, here is the Christ,' or "There *He is,*' do not believe *him.* For false Christs and false prophets will arise and will show great signs and wonders, so as to mislead, if possible, even the elect. Behold, I have told you in advance. So if they say to you, 'Behold, He is in the wilderness,' do not go out, *or,* 'Behold, He is in the inner rooms,' do not believe *them.* For just as the lightning comes from the east and flashes even to the west, so will the coming of the Son of Man be. Wherever a corpse is, there the vultures will gather" (Matthew 24:15–28, Jesus quotes from Daniel 9:27; cf. Daniel 12:1; Mark 13:14–23; Luke 17:22–31; 21:20–24; 23:29; see John 4:48).

Setting: During His discourse on the Mount of Olives east of the temple in Jerusalem, after prophesying the temple's destruction, Jesus responds to questions from Peter, James, John, and Andrew about future events.

"But when you see the ABOMINATION OF DESOLATION standing where it should not be (let the reader understand), then those who are in Judea must flee to the mountains. The one who is on the housetop must not go down, or go in to get anything out of his house; and the one who is in the field must not turn back to get his coat. But woe to those who are pregnant and to those who are nursing babies in those days! But pray that it may not happen in winter. For those days will be a *time of* tribulation such as has not occurred since the beginning of the creation which God created until now, and never will. Unless the Lord had shortened *those* days, no life would have been saved; but for the sake of the elect, whom He chose, He shortened the days. And then if anyone says to you, 'Behold, here is the Christ'; or, 'Behold, *He is* there'; do not believe *him*; for false Christs and false prophets will arise, and will show signs and wonders, in order to lead astray, if possible, the elect. But take heed; behold, I have told you everything in advance" (Mark 13:14–23; cf. Matthew 24:15–28; Luke 21:20–24; see Daniel 9:27; 12:1; Luke 17:31).

ABRAHAM (ABRAHAM, DAUGHTER OF; and ABRAHAM, SON OF are listed as separate entries)

Setting: Capernaum. After the Lord gives the Sermon on the Mount in Galilee and cleanses a leper, a Roman centurion implores Him to heal his servant.

Now when Jesus heard *this,* He marveled, and said to those who were following, "Truly I say to you, I have not found such great faith with anyone in Israel. I say to you that many will come from east and west, and recline *at the table* with Abraham, Isaac and Jacob in the kingdom of heaven; but the sons of the kingdom will be cast out into the outer darkness; in that place there will be weeping and gnashing of teeth." And Jesus said to the centurion, "Go; it shall be done for you as you have believed." And the servant was healed that *very* moment (Matthew 8:10–13; cf. Luke 7:9, 10).

Setting: The temple in Jerusalem. The Sadducees question Jesus about levirate marriage (marriage to a brother-in-law) in order to test Him as He teaches.

But Jesus answered and said to them, "You are mistaken, not understanding the Scriptures nor the power of God. For in the resurrection they neither marry nor are given in marriage, but are like angels in heaven. But regarding the resurrection of the dead, have you not read what was spoken to you by God: 'I AM THE GOD OF ABRAHAM, AND THE GOD OF ISAAC, AND THE GOD OF JACOB'? He is not the God of the dead but of the living" (Matthew 22:29–32, Jesus quotes from Exodus 3:6; cf. Mark 12:18–27; Luke 20:27–38; see Deuteronomy 25:5; John 20:9).

Setting: The temple in Jerusalem. After some of the Pharisees and Herodians attempt to trap Jesus in a statement, some Sadducees question Him about the status of marriage after death.

Jesus said to them, "Is this not the reason you are mistaken, that you do not understand the Scriptures or the power of God? For when they rise from the dead, they neither marry nor are given in marriage, but are like angels in heaven. But regarding the fact that the dead rise again, have you not read in the book of Moses, in the *passage* about *the burning* bush, how God spoke to him, saying, 'I AM THE GOD OF ABRAHAM, AND THE GOD OF ISAAC, and the God of Jacob'? He is not the God of the dead, but of the living; you are greatly mistaken" (Mark 12:24–27, Jesus quotes from Exodus 3:6; cf. Matthew 22:29–33; Luke 20:34–40).

Setting: On the way from Galilee to Jerusalem. While teaching in the cities and villages, Jesus responds to a question about who is saved.

And someone said to Him, "Lord, are here *just* a few who are being saved?" And He said to them, "Strive to enter through the narrow door; for many, I tell you, will seek to enter and will not be able. Once the head of the house gets up and shuts the door, and you begin to stand outside and knock on the door, saying, 'Lord, open up to us!' then He will answer and say to you, 'I do not know where you are from.' Then you will begin to say, 'We ate and drank in Your presence, and You taught in our streets'; and He will say, 'I tell you, I do not know where you are from; DEPART FROM ME, ALL YOU EVILDOERS.' In that place there will be weeping and gnashing of teeth when you see Abraham and Isaac and Jacob and all the prophets in the kingdom of God, but you yourselves being thrown out. And they will come from east and west and from north and south, and will recline *at the table* in the kingdom of God. And behold, *some* are last who will be first and *some* are first who will be last" (Luke 13:23–30, Jesus quotes from Psalm 6:8; cf. Matthew 7:13, 23; 8:11, 12; see Matthew 19:30; Luke 3:8).

Setting: On the way from Galilee to Jerusalem. After He responds to the Pharisees' scoffing at His teaching His disciples about stewardship and the permanence of the Law, Jesus conveys the story of the rich man and Lazarus.

"Now there was a rich man, and he habitually dressed in purple and fine linen, joyously living in splendor every day. And a poor man named Lazarus was laid at his gate, covered with sores, and longing to be fed with the crumbs which were falling from the rich man's table; besides, even the dogs were coming and licking his sores. Now the poor man died and was carried away by the angels to Abraham's bosom; and the rich man also died and was buried. In Hades he lifted up his eyes, being in torment, and saw Abraham far away and Lazarus in his bosom. And he cried out and said, 'Father Abraham, have mercy on me, and send Lazarus so that he may dip the tip of his finger in water and cool off my tongue, for I am in agony in this flame.' But Abraham said, 'Child, remember that during your life you received your good things, and likewise Lazarus bad things; but now he is being comforted here, and you are in agony. And besides all this, between us and you there is a great chasm fixed, so that those who wish to come over from here to you will not be able, and that none may cross over from there to us.' And he said, 'Then I beg you, father, that you send him to my father's house—for I have five brothers—in order that he may warn them, so that they will not also come to this place of torment.' But Abraham said, 'They have Moses and the Prophets; let them hear them.' But he said, 'No, father Abraham, but if someone goes to them from the dead, they will repent!' But he said to him, 'If they do not listen to Moses and the Prophets, they will not be persuaded even if someone rises from the dead'" (Luke 16:19–31; see Luke 3:8; 6:24; 16:1, 14).

Setting: The temple in Jerusalem. While Jesus is ministering a few days before His crucifixion, after the scribes and Pharisees seek to trap Him by questioning Him about paying taxes to Caesar, some Sadducees (who say there is no resurrection) ask Him a question about the resurrection.

Jesus said to them, "The sons of this age marry and are given in marriage, but those who are considered worthy to attain to that age and the resurrection from the dead, neither marry nor are given in marriage; for they cannot even die anymore, because they are like angels, and are sons of God, being sons of the resurrection. But that the dead are raised, even Moses showed, in the passage about the burning bush, where he calls the Lord THE GOD OF ABRAHAM, AND THE GOD OF ISAAC, AND THE GOD OF JACOB. Now He is not the God of the dead but of the living; for all live to Him" (Luke 20:34–38, Jesus quotes from Exodus 3:6; cf. Matthew 22:23–32; Mark 12:18–27).

Setting: The temple treasury in Jerusalem. After the scribes and Pharisees question His testimony about Himself, Jesus interacts with them regarding their ancestry and motives.

They answered and said to Him, "Abraham is our father." Jesus said to them, "If you are Abraham's children, do the deeds of Abraham. But as it is, you are seeking to kill Me, a man who has told you the truth, which I heard from God; this Abraham did not do. You are doing the deeds of your father." They said to Him, "We were not born of fornication; we have one Father: God" (John 8:39–41; see Romans 9:6, 7).

Setting: The temple treasury in Jerusalem. While Jesus is interacting with the scribes and Pharisees, they state their belief that Jesus is a demon-possessed Samaritan because of His statement that anyone who keeps His word will never taste death.

Jesus answered, "If I glorify Myself, My glory is nothing; it is My Father who glorifies Me, of whom you say, 'He is our God'; and you have not come to know Him, but I know Him; and if I say that I do not know Him, I will be a liar like you, but I do know Him and keep His word. Your father Abraham rejoiced to see My day, and he saw *it* and was glad" (John 8:54–56; see Matthew 13:17; John 7:29).

Setting: The temple treasury in Jerusalem. While Jesus is interacting with the scribes and Pharisees, they question how Jesus, not yet fifty years old in their eyes, could claim to have seen Abraham.

Jesus said to them, "Truly, truly, I say to you, before Abraham was born, I am" (John 8:58; see Exodus 3:14).

ABRAHAM, DAUGHTER OF (Also see ABRAHAM, SON OF)

Setting: On the way from Galilee to Jerusalem. Jesus responds to a synagogue official's anger after He heals in the synagogue on the Sabbath a woman who has been sick eighteen years.

But the Lord answered him and said, "You hypocrites, does not each of you on the Sabbath untie his ox or his donkey from the stall and lead him away to water him? And this woman, a daughter of Abraham as she is, whom Satan has bound for eighteen long years, should she not have been released from this bond on the Sabbath day?" (Luke 13:15, 16; see Luke 14:5).

ABRAHAM, SON OF (Also see ABRAHAM, DAUGHTER OF)

Setting: On the way from Galilee to Jerusalem. After taking time to heal a blind man, Jesus comments on Zacheus's response to Him.

And Jesus said to him, "Today salvation has come to this house, because he, too, is a son of Abraham. For the Son of Man has come to seek and to save that which was lost" (Luke 19:9, 10; cf. Matthew 18:11).

ABRAHAM'S CHILDREN (Listed under CHILDREN, ABRAHAM'S)

ABRAHAM'S DESCENDANTS (Listed under DESCENDANTS, ABRAHAM'S)

ABUNDANCE

Setting: By the Sea of Galilee. Jesus responds to His disciples' questions about the Parable of the Sower, which He has just taught from a boat.

Jesus answered them, "To you it has been granted to know the mysteries of the kingdom of heaven, but to them it has not been granted. For whoever has, to him *more* shall be given, and he will have an abundance; but whoever does not have, even what he has shall be taken away from him. Therefore, I speak to them in parables; because while seeing they do not see, and while hearing they do not hear, nor do they understand. In their case the prophecy of Isaiah is being fulfilled, which says, 'YOU WILL KEEP ON HEARING, BUT WILL NOT UNDERSTAND; YOU WILL KEEP ON SEEING, BUT WILL NOT PERCEIVE; FOR THE HEART OF THIS PEOPLE HAS BECOME DULL, WITH THEIR EARS THEY SCARCELY HEAR, AND THEY HAVE CLOSED THEIR EYES, OTHERWISE THEYWOULD SEE WITH THEIR EYES, HEAR WITH THEIR EARS, AND UNDERSTAND WITH THEIR HEART AND RETURN, AND I WOULD HEAL THEM.' But blessed are your eyes, because they see; and your ears, because they hear. For truly I say to you that many prophets and righteous men desired to see what you see, and did not see *it,* and to hear what you hear, and did not hear *it*" (Matthew 13:11–17, Jesus quotes from Isaiah 6:9, 10; cf. Matthew 25:29; Mark 4:11–13; Luke 8:10; see Deuteronomy 29:4; John 8:56).

Setting: The Mount of Olives, just east of Jerusalem. During His discourse, after answering His disciples' questions as to when the temple will be destroyed and Jerusalem overrun, along with the signs of His coming and the end of the age, Jesus reemphasizes to His disciples that they should be on the alert for His return.

"For *it is* just like a man *about* to go on a journey, who called his own slaves and entrusted his possessions to them. To one he gave five talents, to another, two, and to another, one, each according to his own ability; and he went on his journey. Immediately the one who had received the five talents went and traded with them, and gained five more talents. In the same manner the one who *had received* the two *talents* gained two more. But he who received the one *talent* went away, and dug a *hole* in the ground and hid his master's money. Now after a long time the master of those slaves came and settled accounts with them. The one who had received the five talents came up and brought five more talents, saying, 'Master, you entrusted five talents to me. See, I have gained five more talents.' His master said to him, 'Well done, good and faithful slave. You were faithful with a few things, I will put you in charge of many things; enter into the joy of your master.' Also the one who *had received* the two talents came up and said, 'Master, you entrusted two talents to me. See, I have gained two more talents.' His master said to him, 'Well done, good and faithful slave. You were faithful with a few things, I will put you in charge of many things; enter into the joy of your master.' And the one also who had received the one talent came up and said, 'Master, I knew you to be a hard man, reaping where you did not sow and gathering where you scattered no *seed.* And I was afraid, and went away and hid your talent in the ground. See, you have what is yours.' But his master answered and said to him, 'You wicked, lazy slave, you knew that I reap where I did not sow and gather where I scattered no *seed.* Then you ought to have put my money in the bank, and on my arrival I would have received my *money* back with interest. 'Therefore take away the talent from him, and give it to the one who has ten talents.' For to everyone who has, *more* shall be given, and he will have an abundance; but from the one who does not have, even what he does have shall be taken away. Throw out the worthless slave into the outer darkness; in that place there will be weeping and gnashing of teeth" (Matthew 25:14–30; cf. Matthew 8:12; 13:12; 24:45–47; see Matthew 18:23, 24; Luke 12:44).

Setting: On the way from Galilee to Jerusalem. After the scribes and Pharisees turn hostile and question Him in an attempt to catch Him in something He might say, Jesus teaches the crowds and His disciples about greed and possessions.

But He said to him, "Man, who appointed Me a judge or arbitrator over you?" Then He said to them, "Beware, and be on your guard against every form of greed; for not even when one has an abundance does his life consist of his possessions" (Luke 12:14, 15; see 1 Timothy 6:6–10).

ABUNDANT LIFE

[ABUNDANT LIFE from life and abundantly]

Setting: Jerusalem. Following the Pharisees' interrogation and dismissal of the formerly blind man Jesus healed on the Sabbath, the Lord conveys the Parable of the Good Shepherd to the Pharisees, using figures of speech they do not understand.

So Jesus said to them again, "Truly, truly, I say to you, I am the door of the sheep. All who came before Me are thieves and robbers, but the sheep did not hear them. I am the door; if anyone enters through Me, he will be saved, and will go in and out and find pasture. The thief comes only to steal and kill and destroy; I came that they may have life, and have *it* abundantly. I am the good shepherd; the good shepherd lays down His life for the sheep. He who is a hired hand, and not a shepherd, who is not the owner of the sheep, sees the wolf coming, and leaves the sheep and flees, and the wolf snatches them and scatters *them. He flees* because he is a hired hand and is not concerned about the sheep. I am the good shepherd, and I know My own and My own know Me, even as the Father knows Me and I know the Father; and I lay down My life for the sheep. I have other sheep, which are not of this fold; I must bring them also, and they will hear My voice; and they will become one flock *with* one shepherd. For this reason the Father loves Me, because I lay down My life so that I may take it again. No one has taken it away from Me, but I lay it down on My own initiative. I have authority to take it up again. This commandment I received from My Father" (John 10:7–18; see Isaiah 40:11; 56:8; Jeremiah 23:1; Matthew 11:27).

ABUSE (See MISTREATMENT)

ABYSS (See HADES)

ACCEPTANCE

[ACCEPTANCE from the one who comes to Me I will certainly not cast out]

Setting: Capernaum. The day after walking on the Sea of Galilee to join His disciples in a boat, the people He miraculously fed with a lad's five loaves and two fish ask Jesus to always give them this bread out of heaven.

Jesus said to them, "I am the bread of life; he who comes to Me will not hunger, and he who believes in Me will never thirst. But I said to you that you have seen Me, and yet do not believe. All that the Father gives Me will come to Me, and the one who comes to Me I will certainly not cast out. For I have come down from heaven, not to do My own will, but the will of Him who sent Me. This is the will of Him who sent Me, that of all that He has given Me I lose nothing, but raise it up on the last day. For this is the will of My Father, that everyone who beholds the Son and believes in Him will have eternal life, and I Myself will raise him up on the last day" (John 6:35–40; see John 3:13, 16; 4:13, 14).

ACCOUNTABILITY (Also see ACCOUNTING; JUDGMENT; and RESPONSIBILITY, PERSONAL)

[ACCOUNTABILITY inferred]

Setting: The Mount of Olives, just east of Jerusalem. During His discourse, after answering His disciples' questions as to when the temple will be destroyed and Jerusalem overrun, along with the signs of His coming and the end of the age, Jesus reemphasizes to His disciples that they should be on the alert for His return.

"Therefore be on the alert, for you do not know which day your Lord is coming. But be sure of this, that if the head of the house had known at what time of the night the thief was coming, he would have been on the alert and would not have allowed his house to be broken into. For this reason you also must be ready; for the Son of Man is coming at an hour when you do not think *He will.* Who then is the faithful and sensible slave whom his master put in charge of his household to give their food at the proper time? Blessed is that slave whom his master finds so doing when he comes. Truly I say to you that he will put him in charge of all his possessions. But if that evil slave says in his heart, 'My master is not coming for a long time,' and begins to beat his fellow slaves and eat and drink with drunkards; the master of that slave will come on a day when he does not expect *him* and at an hour which he does not know, and will cut him in pieces and assign him a place with the hypocrites; in that place there will be weeping and gnashing of teeth" (Matthew 24:42–51; cf. Mark 13:33–37; Luke 12:39–46; 21:34–36; see Matthew 8:11, 12; 25:21–23).

[ACCOUNTABILITY inferred]

Setting: The Mount of Olives, just east of Jerusalem. During His discourse, after answering His disciples' questions as to when the temple will be destroyed and Jerusalem overrun, along with the signs of His coming and the end of the age, Jesus reemphasizes to His disciples that they should be on the alert for His return.

"For *it is* just like a man *about* to go on a journey, who called his own slaves and entrusted his possessions to them. To one he gave five talents, to another, two, and to another, one, each according to his own ability; and he went on his journey. Immediately the one who had received the five talents went and traded with them, and gained five more talents. In the same manner the one who *had received* the two *talents* gained two more. But he who received the one *talent* went away, and dug a *hole* in the ground and hid his master's money. Now after a long time the master of those slaves came and settled accounts with them. The one who had received the five talents came up and brought five more talents, saying, 'Master, you entrusted five talents to me. See, I have gained five more talents.' His master said to him, 'Well done, good and faithful slave. You were faithful with a few things, I will put you in charge of many things; enter into the joy of your master.' Also the one who *had received* the two talents came up and said, 'Master, you entrusted two talents to me. See, I have gained two more talents.' His master said to him, 'Well done, good and faithful slave. You were faithful with a few things, I will put you in charge of many things; enter into the joy of your master.' And the one also who had received the one talent came up and said, 'Master, I knew you to be a hard man, reaping where you did not sow and gathering where you scattered no *seed.* And I was afraid, and went away and hid your talent in the ground. See, you have what is yours.' But his master answered and said to him, 'You wicked, lazy slave, you knew that I reap where I did not sow and gather where I scattered no *seed.* Then you ought to have put my money in the bank, and on my arrival I would have received my *money* back with interest. 'Therefore take away the talent from him, and give it to the one who has ten talents.' For to everyone who has, *more* shall be given, and he will have an abundance; but from the one who does not have, even what he does have shall be taken away. Throw out the worthless slave into the outer darkness; in that place there will be weeping and gnashing of teeth" (Matthew 25:14–30; cf. Matthew 8:12; 13:12; 24:45–47; see Matthew 18:23, 24; Luke 12:44).

[ACCOUNTABILITY inferred]
Setting: The Mount of Olives, just east of Jerusalem. During His discourse, after answering His disciples' questions as to when the temple will be destroyed and Jerusalem overrun, along with the signs of His coming and the end of the age, Jesus reveals the future judgments following His return.

"But when the Son of Man comes in His glory, and all the angels with Him, then He will sit on His glorious throne. All the nations will be gathered before Him; and He will separate them from one another, as the shepherd separates the sheep from the goats; and He will put the sheep on His right, and the goats on the left. Then the King will say to those on His right, 'Come, you who are blessed of My Father, inherit the kingdom prepared for you from the foundation of the world. 'For I was hungry, and you gave Me *something* to eat; I was thirsty, and you gave Me *something* to drink; I was a stranger, and you invited Me in; naked, and you clothed Me; I was sick, and you visited Me; I was in prison, and you came to Me.' Then the righteous will answer Him, 'Lord, when did we see You hungry and feed You, or thirsty, and give you *something* to drink? And when did we see You a stranger, and invite You in, or naked, and clothe You? When did we see You sick, or in prison, and come to You?' The King will answer and say to them, 'Truly I say to you, to the extent that you did it to one of these brothers of Mine, *even* the least *of them,* you did it to Me.' Then He will also say to those on His left, 'Depart from Me, accursed ones, into the eternal fire which has been prepared for the devil and his angels; for I was hungry, and you gave Me *nothing* to eat; I was thirsty, and you gave Me nothing to drink; I was a stranger, and you did not invite Me in; naked, and you did not clothe Me; sick, and in prison, and you did not visit Me.' Then they themselves also will answer, 'Lord, when did we see You hungry, or thirsty, or a stranger, or naked, or sick, or in prison, and did not take care of You?' Then He will answer them, 'Truly I say to you, to the extent that you did not do it to one of the least of these, you did not do it to Me.' These will go away into eternal punishment, but the righteous into eternal life" (Matthew 25:31–46; see Matthew 7:23; 16:27; 19:29).

[ACCOUNTABILITY inferred]
Setting: Galilee. Following His explanation of the Parable of the Sower to His disciples, Jesus informs them about personal accountability and responsibility.

And He was saying to them, "Take care what you listen to. By your standard of measure it will be measured to you; and more will be given you besides. For whoever has, to him *more* shall be given; and whoever does not have, even what he has shall be taken away from him" (Mark 4:24, 25; cf. Matthew 13:12; Luke 8:18; see Matthew 7:2).

[ACCOUNTABILITY from everyone who has been given much, much will be required]
Setting: On the way from Galilee to Jerusalem. When Jesus uses a parable to challenge the crowd and His disciples to be ready for His return, Peter asks Him whom He is addressing.

And the Lord said, "Who then is the faithful and sensible steward, whom his master will put in charge of his servants, to give them their rations at the proper time? Blessed is that slave whom his master finds so doing when he comes. Truly I say to you that he will put him in charge of all his possessions. But if that slave says in his heart, 'My master will be a long time in coming,' and begins to beat the slaves, both men and women, and to eat and drink and get drunk; the master of that slave will come on a day when he does not expect him and at an hour he does not know, and will cut him in pieces, and assign him a place with the unbelievers. And that slave who knew his master's will and did not get ready or act in accord with his will, will receive many lashes, but the one who did know it, and committed deeds worthy of flogging, will receive but few. From everyone who has been given much, much will be required; and to whom they entrusted much, of him they will ask all the more" (Luke 12:42–48; cf. Matthew 24:45–51; see Leviticus 5:17).

[ACCOUNTABILITY inferred]
Setting: Jericho, on the way to Jerusalem. After commending Zaccheus's faith in Him, Jesus provides a parable about stewardship.

So He said, "A nobleman went to a distant country to receive a kingdom for himself, and then return. And he called ten of his slaves, and gave them ten minas and said to them, 'Do business with this until I come back.' But his citizens hated him and sent a delegation after him, saying, 'We do not want this man to reign over us.' When he returned, after receiving the kingdom, he ordered that these slaves, to whom he had given the money, be called to him so that he might know what business they had done. The first appeared, saying, 'Master, your mina has made ten minas more.' And he said to him, 'Well done, good slave, because you have been faithful in a very little thing, you are to be in authority over ten cities.' The second came, saying, 'Your mina, master, has made five minas.' And he said to him, also, 'And you are to be over five cities.' Another came, saying, 'Master, here is your mina, which I kept put away in a handkerchief; for I was afraid of you, because you are an exacting man; you take up what you did not lay down and reap what you did not sow.' He said to him, 'By your own words I will judge you, you worthless slave. Did you know that I am an exacting man, taking up what I did not lay down and reaping what I did not sow? Then why did you not put my money in the bank, and having come, I would have collected it with interest?' Then he said to the bystanders, 'Take the mina away from him and give it to the one who has the ten minas.' And they said to him, 'Master, he has ten minas already.' I tell you that to everyone who has, more shall be given, but from the one who does not have, even what he does have shall be taken away. But these enemies of mine, who did not want me to reign over them, bring them here and slay them in my presence" (Luke 19:12–27; cf. Matthew 25:14–30; see Matthew 13:12; Luke 16:10).

ACCOUNTING (Also see JUDGMENT)

Setting: Galilee. After Jesus heals a blind, mute, demon-possessed man, the Pharisees accuse Him in front of crowds of being a worker of Satan.

"Either make the tree good and its fruit good, or make the tree bad and its fruit bad; for the tree is known by its fruit. You brood of vipers, how can you, being evil, speak what is good? For the mouth speaks out of that which fills the heart. The good man brings out of *his* good treasure what is good; and the evil man brings out of *his* evil treasure what is evil. But I tell you that every careless word that people speak, they shall give an accounting for it in the day of judgment. For by your words you will be justified, and by your words you will be condemned" (Matthew 12:33–37; cf. Matthew 3:7; 7:16–18).

Setting: On the way from Galilee to Jerusalem. The Lord teaches His disciples about stewardship after giving the story of the prodigal son.

Now He was also saying to the disciples, "There was a rich man who had a manager, and this manager was reported to him as squandering his possessions. And he called him and said to him, 'What is this I hear about you? Give an accounting of your management, for you can no longer be a manager.' The manager said to himself, 'What shall I do, since my master is taking the management away from me? I am not strong enough to dig; I am ashamed to beg. I know what I shall do, so that when I am removed from the management people will welcome me into their homes.' And he summoned each one of his master's debtors, and he began saying to the first, 'How much do you owe my master?' And he said, 'A hundred measures of oil.' And he said to him, 'Take your bill, and sit down quickly and write fifty.' Then he said to another, 'And how much do you owe?' And he said, 'A hundred measures of wheat.' He said to him, 'Take your bill, and write eighty.' And his master praised the unrighteous manager because he had acted shrewdly; for the sons of this age are more shrewd in relation to their own kind than the sons of light. And I say to you, make friends for yourselves by means of the wealth of unrighteousness, so that when it fails, they will receive you into the eternal dwellings. He who is faithful in a very little thing is faithful also in much; and he who is unrighteous in a very little thing is unrighteous also in much. Therefore if you have not been faithful in the use of unrighteous wealth, who will entrust the true riches to you? And if you have not been faithful in the use of that which is another's, who will give you that which is your own? No servant can serve two masters; for either he will hate the one and love the other, or else he will be devoted to one and despise the other. You cannot serve God and wealth" (Luke 16:1–13; cf. Matthew 6:24; see Matthew 25:14–30).

ACCOUNTS

Setting: Capernaum of Galilee. Jesus illustrates forgiveness after Peter asks Him if forgiving someone seven times who has sinned against him is adequate.

"For this reason the kingdom of heaven may be compared to a king who wished to settle accounts with his slaves. When he had begun to settle *them,* one who owed him ten thousand talents was brought to him. But since he did not have *the means* to repay, his lord commanded him to be sold, along with his wife and children and all that he had, and repayment to be made. So the slave fell *to the ground* and prostrated himself before him, saying, 'Have patience with me and I will repay you everything.' And the lord of that slave felt compassion and released him and forgave him the debt. But that slave went out and found one of his fellow slaves who owed him a hundred denarii; and he seized him and *began* to choke *him,* saying, 'Pay back what you owe.' So his fellow slave fell *to the ground* and *began* to plead with him, saying, 'Have patience with me and I will repay you.' But he was unwilling and went and threw him in prison until he should pay back what was owed. So when his fellow slaves saw what had happened, they were deeply grieved and came and reported to their lord all that had happened. Then summoning him, his lord said to him, 'You wicked slave, I forgave you all that debt because you pleaded with me. Should you not also have had mercy on your fellow slave, in the same way that I had mercy on you?' And his lord, moved with anger, handed him over to the torturers until he should repay all that was owed him. My heavenly Father will also do the same to you, if each of you does not forgive his brother from your heart" (Matthew 18:23–35; cf. Matthew 6:12, 14, 15; Luke 7:42; see Matthew 25:19–28).

Setting: The Mount of Olives, just east of Jerusalem. During His discourse, after answering His disciples' questions as to when the temple will be destroyed and Jerusalem overrun , along with the signs of His coming and the end of the age, Jesus reemphasizes to His disciples that they should be on the alert for His return.

"For *it is* just like a man *about* to go on a journey, who called his own slaves and entrusted his possessions to them. To one he gave five talents, to another, two, and to another, one, each according to his own ability; and he went on his journey. Immediately the one who had received the five talents went and traded with them, and gained five more talents. In the same manner the one who *had received* the two *talents* gained two more. But he who received the one *talent* went away, and dug a *hole* in the ground and hid his master's money. Now after a long time the master of those slaves came and settled accounts with them. The one who had received the five talents came up and brought five more talents, saying, 'Master, you entrusted five talents to me. See, I have gained five more talents.' His master said to him, 'Well done, good and faithful slave. You were faithful with a few things, I will put you in charge of many things; enter into the joy of your master.' Also the one who *had received* the two talents came up and said, 'Master, you entrusted two talents to me. See, I have gained two more talents.' His master said to him, 'Well done, good and faithful slave. You were faithful with a few things, I will put you in charge of many things; enter into the joy of your master.' And the one also who had received the one talent came up and said, 'Master, I knew you to be a hard man, reaping where you did not sow and gathering where you scattered no *seed.* And I was afraid, and went away and hid your talent in the ground. See, you have what is yours.' But his master answered and said to him, 'You wicked, lazy slave, you knew that I reap where I did not sow and gather where I scattered no *seed.* Then you ought to have put my money in the bank, and on my arrival I would have received my *money* back with interest. 'Therefore take away the talent from him, and give it to the one who has ten talents.' For to everyone who has, *more* shall be given, and he will have an abundance; but from the one who does not have, even what he does have shall be taken away. Throw out the worthless slave into the outer darkness; in that place there will be weeping and gnashing of teeth" (Matthew 25:14–30; cf. Matthew 8:12; 13:12; 24:45–47; see Matthew 18:23, 24; Luke 12:44).

ACCURSED ONES (Listed under ONES, ACCURSED)

ACCUSATION (Also see CONDEMNATION)

[ACCUSATION from I will accuse you and the one who accuses you is Moses]

Setting: Jerusalem. During the Feast of the Jews, Jesus responds to criticism from the Jewish religious leaders by referring to God as His Father (thereby making Himself equal with God) and informing them that God, John the Baptist, His works, and the Scriptures all testify to His mission.

"You search the Scriptures because you think that in them you have eternal life; it is these that testify about Me; and you are unwilling to come to Me so that you may have life. I do not receive glory from men; but I know you, that you do not have the love of God in yourselves. I have come in My Father's name, and you do not receive Me; if another comes in his own name, you will receive him. How can you believe, when you receive glory from one another and you do not seek the glory that is from the *one and* only God? Do not think that I will accuse you before the Father; the one who accuses you is Moses, in whom you have set your hope. For if you believed Moses, you would believe Me, for he wrote about Me. But if you do not believe his writings, how will you believe My words?" (John 5:39–47; see Matthew 24:5; Luke 16:29, 31; 24:27; John 9:28; 17:3).

ADAM AND EVE (Also see CREATION)

[ADAM AND EVE from male and female as the first created human beings]

Setting: Judea beyond the Jordan (Perea). After Jesus replies to Peter's question about forgiveness, the Pharisees test Jesus with a question about divorce in front of a large crowd.

And He answered and said, "Have you not read that He who created *them* from the beginning MADE THEM MALE AND FEMALE, and said, 'FOR THIS REASON A MAN SHALL LEAVE HIS FATHER AND MOTHER AND BE JOINED TO HIS WIFE, AND THE TWO SHALL BECOME ONE FLESH'? So they are no longer two, but one flesh. What therefore God has joined together, let no man separate" (Matthew 19:4–6, Jesus quotes from Genesis 1:27; 2:24; cf. Mark 10:5–9; see 1 Timothy 2:14).

[ADAM AND EVE from male and female as the first created human beings]

Setting: Judea beyond the Jordan (Perea). Jesus teaches the crowds gathered around Him about divorce after the Pharisees test and question Him about this subject.

And He answered and said to them, "What did Moses command you?" They said, "Moses permitted a *man* TO WRITE A CERTIFICATE OF DIVORCE AND SEND *her* AWAY." But Jesus said to them, "Because of your hardness of heart he wrote you this commandment. But from the beginning of creation, *God* MADE THEM MALE AND FEMALE. FOR THIS REASON A MAN SHALL LEAVE HIS FATHER AND MOTHER, AND THE TWO SHALL BECOME ONE FLESH; so they are no longer two, but one flesh. What therefore God has joined together, let no man separate. In the house the disciples *began* questioning Him about this again. And He said to them, "Whoever divorces his wife and marries another woman commits adultery against her; and if she herself divorces her husband and marries another man, she is committing adultery" (Mark 10:3–12, Jesus quotes from Genesis 1:27; 2:24; cf. Matthew 19:1–9; see Deuteronomy 24:1–3; Matthew 5:32; see Romans 7: 2, 3; 1 Corinthians 7:10, 11, 13, 39; 1 Timothy 2:14).

ADULTERERS (Also see ADULTERY; FORNICATIONS; and SEXUAL SIN)

Setting: On the way from Galilee to Jerusalem. After instructing His disciples about persistence in prayer, Jesus conveys a parable about self-righteousness.

And He also told this parable to some people who trusted in themselves that they were righteous, and viewed others with contempt: "Two men went up into the temple to pray, one a Pharisee and the other a tax collector. The Pharisee stood and was praying this to himself: 'God, I thank You that I am not like other people: swindlers, unjust, adulterers, or even like this tax collector. I fast twice a week; I pay tithes of all that I get.' But the tax collector, standing some distance away, was even unwilling to lift up his eyes to heaven, but was beating his breast, saying, 'God, be merciful to me, the sinner!' I tell you, this man went to his house justified rather than the other; for everyone who exalts himself will be humbled, but he who humbles himself will be exalted" (Luke 18:9–14; see Ezra 9:6; Matthew 6:5, 23:12; Luke 11:42; 16:15; Romans 14:3, 10).

ADULTERIES (Also see ADULTERY)

Setting: Galilee. Jesus explains to the crowd the meaning of His instruction about what defiles a man.

Peter said to Him, "Explain the parable to us." Jesus said, "Are you still lacking in understanding also? Do you not understand that everything that goes into the mouth passes into the stomach and is eliminated? But the things that proceed out of the mouth come from the heart, and those defile the man. For out of the heart come evil thoughts, murders, adulteries, fornications, thefts, false witness, slanders. These are the things which defile a man; but to eat with unwashed hands does not defile the man" (Matthew 15:15–20; cf. Mark 7:18–23; see Galatians 5:19–21).

Setting: Galilee. After the Pharisees and scribes from Jerusalem question His disciples' lack of obedience to the tradition regarding ceremonial cleansing, Jesus speaks to a crowd and explains His teaching to His disciples.

After He called the crowd to Him again, He *began* saying to them, "Listen to Me, all of you, and understand: there is nothing outside the man which can defile him if it goes into him; but the things which proceed out of the man are what defile the man. [If anyone has ears to hear, let him hear."] When he had left the crowd *and* entered the house, His disciples questioned Him about the parable. And He said to them, "Are you so lacking in understanding also? Do you not understand that whatever goes into the man from outside cannot defile him, because it does not go into his heart, but into his stomach, and is eliminated?" (*Thus He* declared all foods clean.) And He was saying, "That which proceeds out of the man, that is what defiles the man. For from within, out of the heart of men, proceed the evil thoughts, fornications, thefts, murders, adulteries, deeds of coveting *and* wickedness, *as well* as deceit, sensuality, envy, slander, pride *and* foolishness. All these evil things proceed from within and defile the man" (Mark 7:14–23; cf. Matthew 15:10–20).

ADULTERY (Also see ADULTERIES; FORNICATIONS and SEXUAL SIN)

Setting: Galilee. During the early part of His ministry, Jesus preaches the Sermon on the Mount to His disciples and the multitudes.

"You have heard that it was said, 'YOU SHALL NOT COMMIT ADULTERY'; but I say to you that everyone who looks at a woman with lust for her has already committed adultery with her in his heart" (Matthew 5:27, 28, Jesus quotes from Exodus 20:14; see 2 Samuel 11:2–5).

Setting: Galilee. During the early part of His ministry, Jesus preaches the Sermon on the Mount to His disciples and the multitudes.

"It was said, 'WHOEVER SENDS HIS WIFE AWAY, LET HIM GIVE HER A CERTIFICATE OF DIVORCE'; but I say to you that everyone who divorces his wife, except for *the* reason of unchastity, makes her commit adultery; and whoever marries a divorced woman commits adultery" (Matthew 5:31, 32, Jesus quotes from Deuteronomy 24: 1, 3; cf. Matthew 19:9; see Romans 7:2, 3; 1 Corinthians 7:10, 39).

Setting: Judea beyond the Jordan (Perea). In front of a large crowd, Jesus responds to the Pharisees' follow-up question about Moses' command regarding a certificate of divorce.

He said to them, "Because of your hardness of heart Moses permitted you to divorce your wives; but from the beginning it has not been this way. And I say to you, whoever divorces his wife, except for immorality, and marries another woman commits adultery" (Matthew 19:8, 9; cf. Deuteronomy 24:1–4; Matthew 5:32; 19:7; Mark 10:1–12; see Romans 7:2, 3; 1 Corinthians 7:10, 39).

Setting: Judea beyond the Jordan (Perea). Jesus shares with a rich, young ruler how he can obtain eternal life.

And He said to him, "Why are you asking Me about what is good? There is *only* One who is good; but if you wish to enter into life, keep the commandments." *Then* he said to Him, 'Which ones?' And Jesus said, "YOU SHALL NOT COMMIT MURDER; YOU SHALL NOT COMMIT ADULTERY; YOU SHALL NOT STEAL; YOU SHALL NOT BEAR FALSE WITNESS; HONOR YOUR FATHER AND MOTHER; and YOU SHALL LOVE YOUR NEIGHBOR AS YOURSELF." The young man said to Him, "All these things I have kept; what am I still lacking?" Jesus said to him, "If you wish to complete go *and* sell your possessions and give to *the* poor, and you will have treasure in heaven; and come, follow Me" (Matthew 19:16–22, Jesus quotes from Exodus 20:13–15; Leviticus 19:18; cf. Leviticus 18:5; Mark 10:17–21; Luke 10:25–28; 12:33; 18:18–24).

Setting: Judea beyond the Jordan (Perea). Jesus teaches the crowds gathered around Him about divorce after the Pharisees test and question Him about this subject.

And He answered and said to them, "What did Moses command you?" They said, "Moses permitted a *man* TO WRITE A CERTIFICATE OF DIVORCE AND SEND *her* AWAY." But Jesus said to them, "Because of your hardness of heart he wrote you this commandment. But from the beginning of creation, *God* MADE THEM MALE AND FEMALE. FOR THIS REASON A MAN SHALL LEAVE HIS FATHER AND MOTHER, AND THE TWO SHALL BECOME ONE FLESH; so they are no longer two, but one flesh. What therefore God has joined together, let no man separate. In the house the disciples *began* questioning Him about this again. And He said to them, "Whoever divorces his wife and marries another woman commits adultery against her; and if she herself divorces her husband and marries another man, she is committing adultery" (Mark 10:3–12, Jesus quotes from Genesis 1:27; Genesis 2:24; cf. Matthew 19:1–9; see Deuteronomy 24:1–3; Matthew 5:32; Romans 7:2, 3, 1 Corinthians 7:10, 11, 13, 39; 1 Timothy 2:14).

Setting: Judea beyond the Jordan (Perea). After demonstrating to His disciples the importance of little children, Jesus encounters a rich man seeking eternal life.

And Jesus said to him, "Why do you call Me good? No one is good except God alone. You know the commandments, 'DO NOT MURDER, DO NOT COMMIT ADULTERY, DO NOT STEAL, DO NOT BEAR FALSE WITNESS, Do not defraud, HONOR YOUR FATHER AND MOTHER.'" And he said to Him, "Teacher, I have kept all these things from my youth up." Looking at him, Jesus felt a love for him and said to him, "One thing you lack: go and sell all you possess and give to the poor, and you will have treasure in heaven; and come, follow Me" (Mark 10:18–21; Jesus quotes from Exodus 20:12–16; cf. Matthew 19:16–22; Luke 18:18–24; see Matthew 6:20).

Setting: On the way from Galilee to Jerusalem. The Lord responds to the Pharisees' scoffing at His teaching His disciples about stewardship with an illustration of the earthly commitment of marriage.

"Everyone who divorces his wife and marries another commits adultery, and he who marries one who is divorced from a husband commits adultery" (Luke 16:18; cf. Matthew 5:31, 32; 19:9; Mark 10:11, 12; see Luke 16:1, 14; Romans 7:2, 3; 1 Corinthians 7:10, 39).

Setting: On the way from Galilee to Jerusalem. After speaking of the importance of children, Jesus responds to a ruler's question about inheriting eternal life.

A ruler questioned Him, saying, "Good Teacher, what shall I do to inherit eternal life?" And Jesus said to him, "Why do you call Me good? No one is good except God alone. You know the commandments, 'DO NOT COMMIT ADULTERY, DO NOT MURDER, DO NOT STEAL, DO NOT BEAR FALSE WITNESS, HONOR YOUR FATHER AND MOTHER.'" And he said, "All these things I have kept from my youth." When Jesus heard this, He said to him, "One thing you still lack; sell all that you possess and distribute it to the poor, and you shall have treasure in heaven; and come, follow Me" (Luke 18:18–22, Jesus quotes from Exodus 20:12–16; cf. Matthew 19:16–22; Mark 10:17–22; see Luke 10:25–28).

[ADULTERY from sin no more]
Setting: The temple in Jerusalem. Following the Feast of Booths, Jesus retires to the Mount of Olives, and returns the next day to teach. The scribes and Pharisees set a woman caught in adultery before Him to test whether He will follow Moses' command to stone her.

This they said, tempting him, that they might have grounds for accusing him. But Jesus stooped down and with His finger wrote on the ground. But when they persisted in asking Him, He straightened up, and said to them, "He who is without sin among you, let him be the first to throw a stone at her." Again He stooped down and wrote on the ground. When they heard it, they *began* to go out one by one, beginning with the older ones, and He was left alone, and the woman, where she was, in the center *of the court.* Straightening up, Jesus said to her, "Woman, where are they? Did no one condemn you?" She said, "No one, Lord." And Jesus said, "I do not condemn you either. Go. From now on sin no more" (John 8:6–11; see John 3:17).

Setting: The island of Patmos (in the Aegean Sea about fifty miles southwest of Ephesus in modern Turkey). On the Lord's Day (Sunday), about fifty years after Jesus' resurrection, the disciple John encounters the Lord Jesus Christ, who communicates a new revelation for the apostle to record for the church in Thyatira and to six other churches in Asia.

"And to the angel of the church in Thyatira write: The Son of God, who has eyes like a flame of fire, and His feet are like burnished bronze, says this: 'I know your deeds, and your love and faith and service and perseverance, and that your deeds of late are greater than at first. But I have *this* against you, that you tolerate the woman Jezebel, who calls herself a prophetess, and she teaches and leads My bond-servants astray so that they commit *acts of* immorality and eat things sacrificed to idols. I gave her time to repent, and she does not want to repent of her immorality. Behold, I will throw her on a bed *of sickness,* and those who commit adultery with her into great tribulation, unless they repent of her deeds. And I will kill her children with pestilence, and all the churches will know that I am He who searches the minds and hearts; and I will give to each one of you according to your deeds. But I say to you, the rest who are in Thyatira, who do not hold this teaching, who have not known the deep things of Satan, as they call them—I place no other burden on you. Nevertheless what you have, hold fast until I come. He who overcomes, and he who keeps My deeds until the end, TO HIM I WILL GIVE AUTHORITY OVER THE NATIONS; AND HE SHALL RULE THEM WITH A ROD OF IRON, AS THE VESSELS OF THE POTTER ARE BROKEN TO PIECES, as I also have received *authority* from My Father; and I will give him the morning star. He who has an ear, let him hear what the Spirit says to the churches' (Revelation 2:18–29; Jesus quotes from Psalm 2:8, 9; Isaiah 30:14; see 1 Kings 16:31; Psalm 7:9; Romans 2:5; 1 Corinthians 2:10; 2 Peter 3:9; Revelation 1:14; 2:7; 3:11; 17:1–20).

ADVANTAGE

Setting: Jerusalem. Before the Passover, after warning His disciples of the persecution they will face after His departure to heaven, Jesus elaborates about the coming ministry of the Holy Spirit.

"But now I am going to Him who sent Me; and none of you asks Me, 'Where are You going?' But because I have said these things to you, sorrow has filled your heart. But I tell you the truth, it is to your advantage that I go away; for if I do not go away, the Helper will not come to you; but if I go, I will send Him to you. And He, when He comes, will convict the world concerning sin and righteousness and judgment; concerning sin, because they do not believe in Me; and concerning righteousness, because I go to the Father and you no longer see Me; and concerning judgment, because the ruler of this world has been judged" (John 16:5–11; see John 7:33; 12:31; 14:1, 16; 15:22, 24).

ADVERSARY (See DEVIL; ENEMY; EVIL ONE; OPPONENT; and SATAN)

ADVERSITY (See ENDURANCE; MINISTRY, DIFFICULTIES IN; PERSECUTION; TRIBULATION; and TROUBLE)

AFFLICTION (Also see PERSECUTION; and SUFFERING)

Setting: By the Sea of Galilee. With the religious leadership rejecting His message, Jesus begins to teach in parables and explains the meaning of the Parable of the Sower to His disciples.

"Hear then the parable of the sower. When anyone hears the word of the kingdom and does not understand it, the evil *one* comes and snatches away what has been sown in his heart. This is the one on whom seed was sown beside the road. The one on whom seed was sown on the rocky places, this is the man who hears the word and immediately receives it with joy; yet he has no *firm* root in himself, but is *only* temporary, and when affliction or persecution arises because of the word, immediately he falls away. And the one on whom seed was sown among the thorns, this is the man who hears the word, and the worry of the world and the deceitfulness of wealth choke the word, and it becomes unfruitful. And the one on whom seed was sown on the good soil, this is the man who hears the word and understands it; who indeed bears fruit and brings forth, some a hundredfold, some sixty, and some thirty" (Matthew 13:18–23; cf. Mark 4:13–20; Luke 8:11–15; see Matthew 13:8).

Setting: By the Sea of Galilee. During the early part of His ministry, after presenting the Parable of the Sower to a very large crowd from a boat, Jesus explains the meaning to His disciples and followers.

And He said to them, "Do you not understand this parable? How will you understand all the parables? The sower sows the word. These are the ones who are beside the road where the word is sown; and when they hear, immediately Satan comes and takes away the word which has been sown in them. In a similar way these are the ones on whom seed was sown on the rocky places, who, when they hear the word, immediately receive it with joy; and they have no *firm* root in themselves, but are *only* temporary; then, when affliction or persecution arises because of the word, immediately they fall away. And others are the ones on whom seed was sown among the thorns; these are the ones who have heard the word, but the worries of the world and the deceitfulness of riches, and the desires for other things enter in and choke the word, and it becomes unfruitful. And those are the ones on whom seed was sown on the good soil; and they hear the word and accept it and bear fruit, thirty, sixty, and a hundredfold" (Mark 4:13–20; cf. Matthew 13:18–23; Luke 8:11–15).

Setting: By the Sea of Galilee. After Jesus and His disciples return from ministry to the Gerasenes across the water, a woman who has had a hemorrhage for twelve years touches Jesus to be healed.

And He said to her, "Daughter, your faith has made you well; go in peace and be healed of your affliction" (Mark 5:34; cf. Matthew 9:22; Luke 8:48; see Mark 5:31–33; Luke 7:50).

AFRAID (See FEAR)

AGAIN, BORN (See BORN AGAIN)

AGE (Specifics such as AGE, END OF THE; and AGE, THIS are separate entries)

Setting: The temple in Jerusalem. While ministering a few days before His crucifixion, after the scribes and Pharisees seek to trap Jesus by questioning Him about paying taxes to Caesar, some Sadducees (who say there is no resurrection) ask Him a question about the resurrection.

Jesus said to them, "The sons of this age marry and are given in marriage, but those who are considered worthy to attain to that age and the resurrection from the dead, neither marry nor are given in marriage; for they cannot even die anymore, because they are like angels, and are sons of God, being sons of the resurrection. But that the dead are raised, even Moses showed, in the passage about the burning bush, where he calls the Lord THE GOD OF ABRAHAM, AND THE GOD OF ISAAC, AND THE GOD OF JACOB. Now He is not the God of the dead but of the living; for all live to Him" (Luke 20:34–38, Jesus quotes from Exodus 3:6; cf. Matthew 22:23–32; Mark 12:18–27).

AGE, END OF THE (END is listed as a separate entry)

Setting: A house near the Sea of Galilee. Jesus explains the meaning of the Parable of the Wheat and the Tares to His disciples.

And He said, "The one who sows the good seed is the Son of Man, and the field is the world; and as *for* the good seed, these are the sons of the kingdom; and the tares are the sons of the evil *one;* and the enemy who sowed them is the devil, and the harvest is the end of the age; and the reapers are angels. So just as the tares are gathered up and burned with fire, so shall it be at the end of the age. The Son of Man will send forth His angels, and they will gather out of His kingdom all stumbling blocks, and those who commit lawlessness, and will throw them into the furnace of fire; in that place there will be weeping and gnashing of teeth. Then THE RIGHTEOUS WILL SHINE FORTH AS THE SUN in the kingdom of their Father. He who has ears, let him hear" (Matthew 13:37–43, Jesus quotes from Daniel 12:3; cf. Matthew 8:12; 13:50).

Setting: By the Sea of Galilee. Because the religious leaders are rejecting His message, Jesus continues teaching His disciples with the Parable of the Dragnet.

"Again, the kingdom of heaven is like a dragnet cast into the sea, and gathering *fish* of every kind; and when it was filled, they drew it up on the beach; and they sat down and gathered the good *fish* into containers, but the bad they threw away. So it will be at the end of the age; the angels will come forth and take out the wicked from among the righteous, and will throw them into the furnace of fire; in that place there will be weeping and gnashing of teeth. Have you understood all these things?" They said to Him, "Yes" (Matthew 13:47–51).

Setting: On a mountain in Galilee. Following His resurrection from the dead in Jerusalem, Jesus conveys the Great Commission to the eleven remaining disciples.

And Jesus came up and spoke to them, saying, "All authority has been given to Me in heaven and on earth. Go therefore and make disciples of all the nations, baptizing them in the name of the Father and the Son and the Holy Spirit, teaching them to observe all that I commanded you; and lo, I am with you always, even to the end of the age" (Matthew 28:18–20; cf. Mark 16:15; see Daniel 7:13).

AGE, PRESENT (Also see AGE, THIS)

Setting: Judea beyond the Jordan (Perea). After informing a rich man how righteous believers may have treasure in heaven, Jesus conveys to His disciples the reward of those who sacrifice in this life to follow Him.

Jesus said, "Truly I say to you, there is no one who has left house or brothers or sisters or mother or father or children or farms, for My sake and for the gospel's sake, but that he will receive a hundred times as much now in the present age, houses and brothers and sisters and mothers and children and farms, along with persecutions; and in the age to come, eternal life. But many *who are* first will be last, and the last, first" (Mark 10:29–31; cf. Matthew 19:27–30; Luke 18:28–30; see Matthew 6:33).

AGE, SONS OF THIS

Setting: On the way from Galilee to Jerusalem. The Lord teaches His disciples about stewardship after giving the story of the Prodigal Son.

Now He was also saying to the disciples, "There was a rich man who had a manager, and this manager was reported to him as squandering his possessions. And he called him and said to him, 'What is this I hear about you? Give an accounting of your management, for you can no longer be a manager.' The manager said to himself, 'What shall I do, since my master is taking the management away from me? I am not strong enough to dig; I am ashamed to beg. I know what I shall do, so that when I am removed from the management people will welcome me into their homes.' And he summoned each one of his master's debtors, and he began saying to the first, 'How much do you owe my master?' And he said, 'A hundred measures of oil.' And he said to him, 'Take your bill, and sit down quickly and write fifty.' Then he said to another, 'And how much do you owe?' And he said, 'A hundred measures of wheat.' He said to him, 'Take your bill, and write eighty.' And his master praised the unrighteous manager because he had acted shrewdly; for the sons of this age are more shrewd in relation to their own kind than the sons of light. And I say to you, make friends for yourselves by means of the wealth of unrighteousness, so that when it fails, they will receive you into the eternal dwellings. He who is faithful in a very little thing is faithful also in much; and he who is unrighteous in a very little thing is unrighteous also in much. Therefore if you have not been faithful in the use of unrighteous wealth, who will entrust the true riches to you? And if you have not been faithful in the use of that which is another's, who will give you that which is your own? No servant can serve two masters; for either he will hate the one and love the other, or else he will be devoted to one and despise the other. You cannot serve God and wealth" (Luke 16:1–13; cf. Matthew 6:24; see Matthew 25:14–30).

Setting: The temple in Jerusalem. While ministering a few days before His crucifixion, after the scribes and Pharisees seek to trap Jesus by questioning Him about paying taxes to Caesar, some Sadducees (who say there is no resurrection) ask Him a question about the resurrection.

Jesus said to them, "The sons of this age marry and are given in marriage, but those who are considered worthy to attain to that age and the resurrection from the dead, neither marry nor are given in marriage; for they cannot even die anymore, because they are like angels, and are sons of God, being sons of the resurrection. But that the dead are raised, even Moses showed, in the passage about the burning bush, where he calls the Lord THE GOD OF ABRAHAM, AND THE GOD OF ISAAC, AND THE GOD OF JACOB. Now He is not the God of the dead but of the living; for all live to Him" (Luke 20:34–38, Jesus quotes from Exodus 3:6; cf. Matthew 22:23–32; Mark 12:18–27).

AGE, THIS (Also see AGE, PRESENT)

Setting: Galilee. After He heals a blind, mute, demon-possessed man, Jesus warns the Pharisees about the unpardonable sin. They accuse Him in front of crowds of being a worker of Satan.

"He who is not with Me is against Me; and he who does not gather with Me scatters. Therefore I say to you, any sin and blasphemy shall be forgiven people, but blasphemy against the Spirit shall not be forgiven. Whoever speaks a word against the Son of Man, it shall be forgiven him; but whoever speaks against the Holy Spirit, it shall not be forgiven him, either in this age or in the *age* to come" (Matthew 12:30–32; cf. Luke 12:10; see Mark 9:40).

Setting: On the way from Galilee to Jerusalem. The Lord teaches His disciples about stewardship after giving the story of the prodigal son.

Now He was also saying to the disciples, "There was a rich man who had a manager, and this manager was reported to him as squandering his possessions. And he called him and said to him, 'What is this I hear about you? Give an accounting of your management, for you can no longer be a manager.' The manager said to himself, 'What shall I do, since my master is taking the management away from me? I am not strong enough to dig; I am ashamed to beg. I know what I shall do, so that when I am removed from the management people will welcome me into their homes.' And he summoned each one of his master's debtors, and he began saying to the first, 'How much do you owe my master?' And he said, 'A hundred measures of oil.' And he said to him, 'Take your bill, and sit down quickly and write fifty.' Then he said to another, 'And how much do you owe?' And he said, 'A hundred measures of wheat.' He said to him, 'Take your bill, and write eighty.' And his master praised the unrighteous manager because he had acted shrewdly; for the sons of this age are more shrewd in relation to their own kind than the sons of light. And I say to you, make friends for yourselves by means of the wealth of unrighteousness, so that when it fails, they will receive you into the eternal dwellings. He who is faithful in a very little thing is faithful also in much; and he who is unrighteous in a very little thing is unrighteous also in much. Therefore if you have not been faithful in the use of unrighteous wealth, who will entrust the true riches to you? And if you have not been faithful in the use of that which is another's, who will give you that which is your own? No servant can serve two masters; for either he will hate the one and love the other, or else he will be devoted to one and despise the other. You cannot serve God and wealth" (Luke 16:1–13; cf. Matthew 6:24; see Matthew 25:14–30).

Setting: The temple in Jerusalem. While ministering a few days before His crucifixion, after the scribes and Pharisees seek to trap Jesus by questioning Him about paying taxes to Caesar, some Sadducees (who say there is no resurrection) ask Him a question about the resurrection.

Jesus said to them, "The sons of this age marry and are given in marriage, but those who are considered worthy to attain to that age and the resurrection from the dead, neither marry nor are given in marriage; for they cannot even die anymore, because they are like angels, and are sons of God, being sons of the resurrection. But that the dead are raised, even Moses showed, in the passage about the burning bush, where he calls the Lord THE GOD OF ABRAHAM, AND THE GOD OF ISAAC, AND THE GOD OF JACOB. Now He is not the God of the dead but of the living; for all live to Him" (Luke 20:34–38, Jesus quotes from Exodus 3:6; cf. Matthew 22:23–32; Mark 12:18–27).

AGE TO COME (Also see FUTURE, PREDICTING THE; and TOMORROW)

Setting: Galilee, In front of crowds, after He heals a blind, mute, demon-possessed man, Jesus warns the Pharisees about the unpardonable sin, as they accuse Him of being a worker of Satan.

"He who is not with Me is against Me; and he who does not gather with Me scatters. Therefore I say to you, any sin and blasphemy shall be forgiven people, but blasphemy against the Spirit shall not be forgiven. Whoever speaks a word against the Son of Man, it shall be forgiven him; but whoever speaks against the Holy Spirit, it shall not be forgiven him, either in this age or in the *age* to come" (Matthew 12:30–32; cf. Luke 12:10; see Mark 9:40).

Setting: Judea beyond the Jordan (Perea). After informing a rich man how righteous believers may have treasure in heaven, Jesus conveys to His disciples the reward of those who sacrifice in this life to follow Him.

Jesus said, "Truly I say to you, there is no one who has left house or brothers or sisters or mother or father or children or farms, for My sake and for the gospel's sake, but that he will receive a hundred times as much now in the present age, houses and brothers and sisters and mothers and children and farms, along with persecutions; and in the age to come, eternal life. But many *who are* first will be last, and the last, first" (Mark 10:29–31; cf. Matthew 19:27–30; Luke 18:28–30; see Matthew 6:33).

Setting: On the way from Galilee to Jerusalem. After responding to His disciples' question about salvation, Jesus replies to Peter's statement about their personal sacrifice.

Peter said, "Behold, we have left our own homes and followed You." And He said to them, "Truly I say to you, there is no one who has left house or wife or brothers or parents or children, for the sake of the kingdom of God, who will not receive many times as much at this time and in the age to come, eternal life" (Luke 18:28–30; cf. Matthew 19:27–29; Mark 10:28–30; see Matthew 6:33; Luke 5:11).

AGONY (Also see TORMENT)

Setting: On the way from Galilee to Jerusalem. After He responds to the Pharisees' scoffing at His teaching His disciples about stewardship and the permanence of the Law, Jesus conveys the story of the rich man and Lazarus.

"Now there was a rich man, and he habitually dressed in purple and fine linen, joyously living in splendor every day. And a poor man named Lazarus was laid at his gate, covered with sores, and longing to be fed with the crumbs which were falling from the rich man's table; besides, even the dogs were coming and licking his sores. Now the poor man died and was carried away by the angels to Abraham's bosom; and the rich man also died and was buried. In Hades he lifted up his eyes, being in torment, and saw Abraham far away and Lazarus in his bosom. And he cried out and said, 'Father Abraham, have mercy on me, and send Lazarus so that he may dip the tip of his finger in water and cool off my tongue, for I am in agony in this flame.' But Abraham said, 'Child, remember that during your life you received your good things, and likewise Lazarus bad things; but now he is being comforted here, and you are in agony. And besides all this, between us and you there is a great chasm fixed, so that those who wish to come over from here to you will not be able, and that none may cross over from there to us.' And he said, 'Then I beg you, father, that you send him to my father's house—for I have five brothers—in order that he may warn them, so that they will not also come to this place of torment.' But Abraham said, 'They have Moses and the Prophets; let them hear them.' But he said, 'No, father Abraham, but if someone goes to them from the dead, they will repent!' But he said to him, 'If they do not listen to Moses and the Prophets, they will not be persuaded even if someone rises from the dead'" (Luke 16:19–31; see Luke 3:8; 6:24; 16:1, 14).

AGREEMENT (Also see CHURCH DISCIPLINE)

[AGREEMENT from if two of you agree]

Setting: Capernaum of Galilee. After conveying to His disciples the value of little ones, Jesus gives instruction about church discipline.

"If your brother sins, go and show him his fault in private; if he listens to you, you have won your brother. But if he does not listen *to you,* take one or two more with you, so that BY THE MOUTH OF TWO OR THREE WITNESSES EVERY FACT MAY BE CONFIRMED. If he refuses to listen to them, tell it to the church; and if he refuses to listen even to the church, let him be to you as a Gentile and a tax collector. Truly I say to you, whatever you bind of earth shall have been bound in heaven; and whatever you loose on earth shall have been loosed in heaven. Again, I say to you, that if two of you agree on earth about anything that they may ask, it shall be done for them by My Father who is in heaven. For there two or three have gathered together in My name, I am there in their midst" (Matthew 18:15–20. Jesus quotes from Deuteronomy 19:15; cf. Matthew 7:7; 16:19; see Leviticus 19:17; Matthew 28:20; 2 Thessalonians 3:6, 14).

[AGREEMENT from agreed and did you not agree with me]
Setting: Judea beyond the Jordan (Perea). Jesus illustrates the kingdom of heaven to His disciples through the story of laborers in the vineyard.

"For the kingdom of heaven is like a landowner who went out early in the morning to hire laborers for his vineyard. When he had agreed with the laborers for a denarius for the day, he sent them into his vineyard. And he went out about the third hour and saw others standing idle in the market place; and to those he said, 'You also go into the vineyard, and whatever is right I will give you.' And *so* they went. Again he went out about the sixth and the ninth hour, and did the same thing. And about the eleventh *hour* he went out and found others standing *around;* and he said to them, 'Why have you been standing idle here all day long?' They said to him, 'Because no one hired us.' He said to them, 'You go into the vineyard too.' When evening came, the owner of the vineyard said to his foreman, 'Call the laborers and pay them their wages, beginning with the last *group* to the first.' When those *hired* about the eleventh hour came, each one received a denarius. When those *hired* first came, they thought that they would receive more; but each of them also received a denarius. When they received it, they grumbled at the landowner, saying, 'These last men have worked *only* one hour, and you have made them equal to us who have borne the burden and the scorching heat of the day.' But he answered and said to one of them, 'Friend, I am doing you no wrong; did you not agree with me for a denarius? Take what is yours and go, but I wish to give to this last man the same as to you. It is not lawful for me to do what I wish with what is my own? Or is your eye envious because I am generous?' So the last shall be first, and the first last" (Matthew 20:1–16; cf. Matthew 19:30).

AIR

Setting: Galilee. During the early part of His ministry, Jesus preaches the Sermon on the Mount to His disciples and the multitudes.

"For this reason I say to you, do not be worried about your life, *as to* what you will eat or what you will drink; nor for your body, *as to* what you will put on. Is not life more than food, and the body more than clothing? Look at the birds of the air, that they do not sow, nor reap nor gather into barns, and *yet* your heavenly Father feeds them. Are you not worth much more than they? And who of you by being worried can add a *single* hour to his life? And why are you worried about clothing? Observe how the lilies of the field grow; they do not toil nor do they spin, yet I say to you that not even Solomon in all his glory clothed himself like one of these. But if God so clothes the grass of the field, which is *alive* today and tomorrow is thrown into the furnace, *will He* not much more *clothe* you? You of little faith! Do not worry then, saying 'What will we eat?' or 'What will we drink?' or 'What will we wear for clothing?" For the Gentiles eagerly seek all these things; for your heavenly Father knows that you need all these things. But seek first His kingdom and His righteousness, and all these things will be added to you. So do not worry about tomorrow; for tomorrow will care for itself. Each day has enough trouble of its own" (Matthew 6:25–34; cf. Luke 12:22–31; see 1 Kings 10:4–7; Job 35:11; Matthew 8:26).

Setting: By the Sea of Galilee. After casting out evil spirits from the demon-possessed and healing the ill in fulfillment of Isaiah 53:4, Jesus lays out to an inquiring scribe the demands of discipleship.

Then a scribe came and said to Him, "Teacher, I will follow You wherever you go." Jesus said to him, "The foxes have holes and the birds of the air *have* nests, but the Son of Man has nowhere to lay His head." Another of the disciples said to Him, "Lord, permit me first to go and bury my father." But Jesus said to him, "Follow Me, and allow the dead to bury their own dead" (Matthew 8:19–22; cf. Luke 9:57–60).

Setting: By the Sea of Galilee. Since the religious leaders are rejecting His message, Jesus continues teaching the crowds with the Parable of the Mustard Seed.

He presented another parable to them, saying, "The kingdom of heaven is like a mustard seed, which a man took and sowed in his field; and this is smaller than all *other* seeds, but when it is full grown, it is larger than the garden plants and becomes a tree, so that THE BIRDS OF THE AIR come and NEST IN ITS BRANCHES" (Matthew 13:31, 32, Jesus quotes from Ezekiel 17:23; cf. Mark 4:30–32; Luke 13:18, 19).

Setting: Galilee. After giving the Parable of the Sower and the Parable of the Seed, Jesus continues teaching in parables by presenting the Parable of the Mustard Seed to His disciples.

And He said, "How shall we picture the kingdom of God, or by what parable shall we present it? *It is* like a mustard seed, which, when sown upon the soil, though it is smaller than all the seeds that are upon the soil, yet when it is sown, it grows up and becomes larger than all the garden plants and forms large branches; so that THE BIRDS OF THE AIR can NEST UNDER ITS SHADE" (Mark 4:30–32, Jesus quotes from Ezekiel 17:23; cf. Matthew 13:31, 32; Luke 13:18, 19).

Setting: Galilee. After His visit in the home of Simon the Pharisee, Jesus goes into the villages and cities proclaiming and preaching the kingdom of God.

When a large crowd was coming together, and those from various cities were journeying to Him, He spoke by way of a parable: "The sower went out to sow his seed; and as he sowed, some fell beside the road, and it was trampled under foot and the birds of the air ate it up. Other seed fell on rocky soil, and as soon as it grew up, it was withered away, because it had no moisture. Other seed fell among the thorns; and the thorns grew up with it and choked it out. Other seed fell into the good soil, and grew up, and produced a crop a hundred times as great." As He said these things, He would call out, "He who has ears to hear, let him hear" (Luke 8:4–8; cf. Matthew 13:2–9; Mark 4:3–9).

Setting: On the way from Galilee to Jerusalem. The Lord responds to someone seeking to follow Him.

And Jesus said to him, "The foxes have holes and the birds of the air have nests, but the Son of Man has nowhere to lay His head" (Luke 9:58; cf. Matthew 8:19–22).

Setting: On the way from Galilee to Jerusalem. After responding to a synagogue official's anger when He healed a woman, sick eighteen years, in the synagogue on the Sabbath, Jesus conveys the Parable of the Mustard Seed and the Parable of the Leaven.

So He was saying, "What is the kingdom of God like, and to what shall I compare it? It is like a mustard seed which a man took and threw into his own garden; and it grew and became a tree, and THE BIRDS OF THE AIR NESTED IN ITS BRANCHES." And again He said, "To what shall I compare the kingdom of God? It is like leaven, which a woman took and hid in three pecks of flour until it was all leavened" (Luke 13:18–21, Jesus quotes from Ezekiel 17:23; cf. Matthew 13:31–34; Mark 4:30–32).

ALERTNESS (Also see PREPAREDNESS; READINESS; and WATCHFULNESS)

[ALERTNESS from be on the alert and be ready]

Setting: The Mount of Olives, just east of Jerusalem. During His discourse, after answering His disciples' questions as to when the temple will be destroyed and Jerusalem overrun, along with the signs of His coming and the end of the age, Jesus reemphasizes to His disciples that they should be on the alert for His return.

"Therefore be on the alert, for you do not know which day your Lord is coming. But be sure of this, that if the head of the house had known at what time of the night the thief was coming, he would have been on the alert and would not have allowed his house to be broken into. For this reason you also must be ready; for the Son of Man is coming at an hour when you do not think *He will.* Who then is the faithful and sensible slave whom his master put in charge of his household to give their food at the proper time? Blessed is that slave whom his master finds so doing when he comes. Truly I say to you that he will put him in charge of all his possessions. But if that evil slave says in his heart, 'My master is not coming for a long time,' and begins to beat his fellow slaves and eat and drink with drunkards; the master of that slave will come on a day when he does not expect *him* and at an hour which he does not know, and will cut him in pieces and assign him a place with the hypocrites; in that place there will be weeping and gnashing of teeth" (Matthew 24:42–51; cf. Mark 13:33–37; Luke 12:39–46; 21:34–36; see Matthew 8:11, 12; 25:21–23).

[ALERTNESS from Be on the alert]
Setting: The Mount of Olives, just east of Jerusalem. During His discourse, after answering His disciples' questions as to when the temple will be destroyed and Jerusalem overrun, along with the signs of His coming and the end of the age, Jesus reemphasizes to His disciples that they should be on the alert for His return.

"Then the kingdom of heaven will be comparable to ten virgins, who took their lamps and went out to meet the bridegroom. Five of them were foolish, and five were prudent. For when the foolish took their lamps, they took no oil with them, but the prudent took oil in flasks along with their lamps. Now while the bridegroom was delaying, they all got drowsy and *began* to sleep. But at midnight there was a shout, 'Behold, the bridegroom! Come out to meet *him.*' Then all those virgins rose and trimmed their lamps. The foolish said to the prudent, 'Give us some of your oil, for our lamps are going out.' But the prudent answered, 'No, there will not be enough for us and you *too;* go instead to the dealers and buy *some* for yourselves.' And while they were going away to make the purchase, the bridegroom came, and those who were ready went in with him to the wedding feast; and the door was shut. Later the other virgins also came, saying, 'Lord, lord, open up for us.' But he answered, 'Truly I say to you, I do not know you.' Be on the alert then, for you do not know the day nor the hour" (Matthew 25:1–13; cf. Matthew 24:42; Luke 12:35; see Matthew 7:21, 24).

[ALERTNESS from be on your guard]
Setting: The Mount of Olives, east of the temple in Jerusalem. During His discourse, after prophesying the temple's destruction, Jesus responds to questions from Peter, James, John, and Andrew about future events.

And Jesus began to say to them, "See to it that no one misleads you. Many will come in My name, saying, 'I am *He!*' and will mislead many. When you hear of wars and rumors of wars, do not be frightened; *those things* must take place; but *that is* not yet the end. For nation will rise up against nation, and kingdom against kingdom; there will be earthquakes in various places; there will *also be* famines. These things are *merely* the beginning of birth pangs. But be on your guard; for they will deliver you to *the* courts, and you will be flogged in *the* synagogues, and you will stand before governors and kings for My sake, as a testimony to them. The gospel must first be preached to all the nations. When they arrest you and hand you over, do not worry beforehand about what you are to say, but say whatever is given you in that hour; for it is not you who speak, but *it is* the Holy Spirit. Brother will betray brother to death, and a father *his* child; and children will rise up against parents and have them put to death. You will be hated by all because of My name, but the one who endures to the end, he will be saved" (Mark 13:5–13; cf. Matthew 24:4–14; Luke 21:7–19; see Matthew 10:17–22).

[ALERTNESS from keep on the alert; stay on the alert; and be on the alert]
Setting: The Mount of Olives, east of the temple in Jerusalem. During His discourse, after prophesying the temple's destruction, Jesus responds to questions from Peter, James, John, and Andrew about future events.

"Take heed, keep on the alert; stay on the alert; for you do not know when the *appointed* time will come. *It is* like a man away on a journey, *who* upon leaving his house and putting his slaves in charge, *assigning* to each one his task, also commanded the doorkeeper to stay on the alert. Therefore, be on the alert—for you do not know when the master of the house is coming, whether in the evening, at midnight, or when the rooster crows, or in the morning—in case he should come suddenly and find you asleep. What I say to you I say to all, 'Be on the alert!'" (Mark 13:33–37; cf. Matthew 24:42–43; Luke 21:34–36; see Luke 12:36–38; Ephesians 6:18).

[ALERTNESS from be on your guard]
Setting: On the way from Galilee to Jerusalem. Jesus teaches the crowds and His disciples about greed and possessions. The scribes and Pharisees turn hostile and question Him in an attempt to catch Him in something He might say.

But He said to him, "Man, who appointed Me a judge or arbitrator over you?" Then He said to them, "Beware, and be on your guard against every form of greed; for not even when one has an abundance does his life consist of his possessions" (Luke 12:14, 15; see 1 Timothy 6:6–10).

[ALERTNESS from Be dressed in readiness; on the alert; be ready]
Setting: On the way from Galilee to Jerusalem. After giving a parable about riches and greed, Jesus uses a parable to challenge the crowd and His disciples to be ready for His return.

"Be dressed in readiness, and keep your lamps lit. Be like men who are waiting for their master when he returns from the wedding feast, so that they may immediately open the door to him when he comes and knocks. Blessed are those slaves whom the master will find on the alert when he comes; truly I say to you, that he will gird himself to serve, and have them recline at the table, and will come up and wait on them. Whether he comes in the second watch, or even in the third and finds them so, blessed are those slaves. But be sure of this, that if the head of the house had known at what hour the thief was coming, he would not have allowed his house to be broken into. You too, be ready; for the Son of Man is coming at an hour that you do not expect" (Luke 12:35–40; cf. Matthew 24:42–44; see Mark 13:33; Ephesians 6:14).

[ALERTNESS from Be on your guard]
Setting: On the way from Galilee to Jerusalem. After conveying the story of the rich man and Lazarus, the Lord gives instruction to His disciples on forgiveness.

He said to His disciples, "It is inevitable that stumbling blocks come, but woe to him through whom they come! It would be better for him if a millstone were hung around his neck and he were thrown into the sea, than that he would cause one of these little ones to stumble. Be on your guard! If your brother sins, rebuke him; and if he repents, forgive him. And if he sins against you seven times a day, and returns to you seven times, saying, 'I repent,' forgive him" (Luke 17:1–4; see Matthew 18:5–7, 15, 21, 22).

[ALERTNESS from Be on guard and keep alert]
Setting: The Mount of Olives, just east of Jerusalem. Following a time of ministry in the temple a few days before His crucifixion, after conveying the Parable of the Fig Tree, Jesus warns His disciples during His Olivet Discourse to keep alert regarding future events.

"Be on guard, so that your hearts will not be weighted down with dissipation and drunkenness and the worries of life, and that day will not come upon you suddenly like a trap; for it will come upon all those who dwell on the face of all the earth. But keep on the alert at all times, praying that you may have strength to escape all these things that are about to take place, and to stand before the Son of Man" (Luke 21:34–36; cf. Mark 13:33; see Matthew 24:42–44).

ALIVE (Also see LIFE; and LIVING)

Setting: Galilee. During the early part of His ministry, Jesus preaches the Sermon on the Mount to His disciples and the multitudes.

"For this reason I say to you, do not be worried about your life, *as to* what you will eat or what you will drink; nor for your body, *as to* what you will put on. Is not life more than food, and the body more than clothing? Look at the birds of the air, that they do not sow, nor reap nor gather into barns, and *yet* your heavenly Father feeds them. Are you not worth much more than they? And who of you by being worried can add a *single* hour to his life? And why are you worried about clothing? Observe how the lilies of the field grow; they do not toil nor do they spin, yet I say to you that not even Solomon in all his glory clothed himself like one of these. But if God so clothes the grass of the field, which is *alive* today and tomorrow is thrown into the furnace, *will He* not much more *clothe* you? You of little faith! Do not worry then, saying 'What will we eat?' or 'What will we drink?' or 'What will be wear for clothing?" For the Gentiles eagerly seek all these things; for your heavenly Father knows that you need all these things. But seek first His kingdom and His righteousness, and all these things will be added to you. So do not worry about tomorrow; for tomorrow will care for itself. Each day has enough trouble of its own" (Matthew 6:25–34; cf. Luke 12:22–31; see 1 Kings 10:4–7; Job 35:11; Matthew 8:26).

Setting: On the way from Galilee to Jerusalem. Jesus comforts the crowd and His disciples after giving a parable about riches and greed. The scribes and Pharisees turn hostile and question Him in an attempt to catch Him in something He might say.

And He said to His disciples, "For this reason I say to you, do not worry about your life, as to what you will eat; nor for your body, as to what you will put on. For life is more than food, and the body more than clothing. Consider the ravens, for they neither sow nor reap; they have no storeroom nor barn, and yet God feeds them; how much more valuable you are than the birds! And which of you by worrying can add a single hour to his life's span? If then you cannot do even a very little thing, why do you worry about other matters? Consider the lilies, how they grow: they neither toil nor spin; but I tell you, not even Solomon in all his glory clothed himself like one of these. But if God so clothes the grass in the field, which is alive today and tomorrow is thrown into the furnace, how much more will He clothe you? You men of little faith! And do not seek what you will eat and what you will drink, and do not keep worrying. For all these things the nations of the world eagerly seek; but your Father knows that you need these things. But seek His kingdom, and these things will be added to you. Do not be afraid, little flock, for your Father has chosen gladly to give you the kingdom" (Luke 12:22–32; cf. Matthew 6:25–33; see 1 Kings 10:4–7; Job 38:41).

Setting: On the island of Patmos (in the Aegean Sea about fifty miles southwest of Ephesus in modern Turkey). On the Lord's Day (Sunday), about fifty years after Jesus' resurrection, the disciple John encounters the Lord Jesus Christ, who communicates a new revelation for the apostle to record for the church in Thyatira and to six other churches in Asia.

When I saw Him, I fell at His feet like a dead man. And He placed His right hand on me, saying, "Do not be afraid; I am the first and the last, and the living One; and I was dead, and behold, I am alive forevermore, and I have the keys of death and of Hades. Therefore write the things which you have seen, and the things which are, and the things which will take place after these things. As for the mystery of the seven stars which you saw in My right hand, and the seven golden lampstands: the seven stars are the angels of the seven churches, and the seven lampstands are the seven churches" (Revelation 1:17–20; see Isaiah 44:6; Luke 24:5; Revelation 2:8).

Setting: On the island of Patmos (in the Aegean Sea about fifty miles southwest of Ephesus in modern Turkey). On the Lord's Day (Sunday), about fifty years after Jesus' resurrection, the disciple John encounters the Lord Jesus Christ, who communicates a new revelation for the apostle to record for the church in Thyatira and to six other churches in Asia.

"To the angel of the church in Sardis write: He who has the seven Spirits of God and the seven stars, says this: 'I know your deeds, that you have a name that you are alive, but you are dead. Wake up, and strengthen the things that remain, which were about to die; for I have not found your deeds completed in the sight of My God. So remember what you have received and heard; and keep *it,* and repent. Therefore if you do not wake up, I will come like a thief, and you will not know at what hour I will come to you. But you have a few people in Sardis who have not soiled their garments; and they will walk with Me in white, for they are worthy. He who overcomes will thus be clothed in white garments; and I will not erase his name from the book of life, and I will confess his name before My Father and before His angels. He who has an ear, let him hear what the Spirit says to the churches'" (Revelation 3:1–6; see Matthew 10:32; Revelation 1:16).

ALLEGIANCE (See COMMITMENT; DEVOTION; DISCIPLE; DISCIPLESHIP; FOLLOWING JESUS CHRIST; and OBEDIENCE)

ALL THINGS (Listed under THINGS, ALL)

ALMIGHTY

Setting: On the small island of Patmos (in the Aegean Sea about fifty miles southwest of Ephesus in modern Turkey). An angel speaks the first words of the revelation of Jesus Christ, approximately fifty years after His resurrection, to His bond-servant, the apostle John.

"I am the Alpha and the Omega," says the Lord God, "who is and who was and who is to come, the Almighty" (Revelation 1:8; see Revelation 21:6).

ALMS (See GIVING; POOR; and POOR, GIVING TO THE)

ALONE

Setting: Judea, near the Jordan River. Following Jesus' baptism, and before He begins His public ministry, the Spirit leads Him into the wilderness for temptation by Satan.

But He answered and said, "It is written, 'MAN SHALL NOT LIVE ON BREAD ALONE, BUT ON EVERY WORD THAT PROCEEDS OUT OF THE MOUTH OF GOD'" (Matthew 4:4, Jesus quotes from Deuteronomy 8:3; cf. Luke 4:4).

Setting: Galilee. Jesus responds to the Pharisees' objection to His disciples picking grain on the Sabbath.

But He said to them, "Have you not read what David did when he became hungry, he and his companions, how they entered the house of God, and ate the consecrated bread, which was not lawful for him to eat nor for those with him, but for the priests alone? Or, have you not read in the Law, that on the Sabbath the priests in the temple break the Sabbath and are innocent? But I say to you that something greater than the temple is here. But if you had known what this means, 'I DESIRE COMPASSION, AND NOT A SACRIFICE,' you would not have condemned the innocent. For the Son of Man is Lord of the Sabbath" (Matthew 12:3–8, Jesus quotes from Hosea 6:6; cf. Mark 2:25–28; Luke 6:3–5; see 1 Samuel 21:6).

Setting: Galilee. Jesus instructs His disciples after rebuking the Pharisees and scribes for questioning their lack of obedience to tradition.

But He answered and said, "Every plant which My heavenly Father did not plant shall be uprooted. Let them alone; they are blind guides of the blind. And if a blind man guides a blind man, both will fall into a pit" (Matthew 15:13, 14; cf. Matthew 23:16; Luke 6:39).

Setting: Judea beyond the Jordan (Perea). Jesus shows His love for children after His disciples rebuke some children who want Jesus' blessing.

But Jesus said, "Let the children alone, and do not hinder them from coming to Me; for the kingdom of heaven belongs to such as these" (Matthew 19:14; cf. Mark 10:13–16; Luke 18:15–17; see Matthew 18:3; 19:13, 15).

Setting: The Mount of Olives, just east of Jerusalem. During His discourse, after answering His disciples' questions as to when the temple will be destroyed and Jerusalem overrun, along with the signs of His coming and the end of the age, Jesus teaches them the Parable of the Fig Tree.

"Now learn the parable from the fig tree: when its branch has already become tender and puts forth its leaves, you know that summer is near; so, you too, when you see all these things, recognize that He is near, *right* at the door. Truly, I say to you, this generation will not pass away until all these things take place. Heaven and earth will pass away, but My words will not pass away. But of that day and hour no one knows, not even the angels of heaven, nor the Son, but the Father alone. For the coming of the Son of Man will be just like the days of Noah. For as in those days before the flood they were eating and drinking, marrying and giving in marriage, until the day that Noah entered the ark, and they did not understand until the flood came and took them all away; so will the coming of the Son of Man be. Then there will be two men in the field; one will be taken and one will be left. Two women *will be* grinding at the mill; one will be taken and one will be left" (Matthew 24:32–41; cf. Mark 13:28–32; Luke 17:34–36; 21:28–33; see Genesis 6:5; 7:7; Matthew 5:18; 10:23; James 5:9).

Setting: Judea beyond the Jordan (Perea). After demonstrating to His disciples the importance of little children, Jesus encounters a rich man seeking eternal life.

And Jesus said to him, "Why do you call Me good? No one is good except God alone. You know the commandments, 'DO NOT MURDER, DO NOT COMMIT ADULTERY, DO NOT STEAL, DO NOT BEAR FALSE WITNESS, Do not defraud, HONOR YOUR FATHER AND MOTHER.' " And he said to Him, "Teacher, I have kept all these things from my youth up." Looking at him, Jesus felt a love for him and said to him, "One thing you lack: go and sell all you possess and give to the poor, and you will have treasure in heaven; and come, follow Me" (Mark 10:18–21; Jesus quotes from Exodus 20:12–16; cf.. Matthew 19:16–22; Luke 18:18–24; see Matthew 6:20).

Setting: The Mount of Olives, east of the temple in Jerusalem. During His discourse, after prophesying the temple's destruction, Jesus responds to questions from Peter, James, John and Andrew about future events.

"Now learn the parable from the fig tree: when its branch has already become tender and puts forth its leaves, you know that summer is near. Even so, you too, when you see these things happening, recognize that He is near, *right* at the door. Truly I say to you, this generation will not pass away until all these things take place. Heaven and earth will pass away, but My words will not pass away. But of the day or hour no one knows, not even the angels in heaven, nor the Son, but the Father *alone*" (Mark 13:28–32; cf. Matthew 24:32–36; Luke 21:28–33).

Setting: The home of Simon the leper in Bethany. Two days before Passover (the Feast of Unleavened Bread), Jesus commends a woman who anoints His head with costly perfume that some thought should have been sold and the proceeds given to the poor.

But Jesus said, "Let her alone; why do you bother her? She has done a good deed to Me. For you always have the poor with you, and whenever you wish you can do good to them; but you do not always have Me. She has done what she could; she has anointed My body beforehand for the burial. Truly I say to you, wherever the gospel is preached in the whole world, what this woman has done will also be spoken of in memory of her" (Mark 14:6–9; cf. Matthew 26:6–13; John 12:2–8; see Deuteronomy 15:11).

Setting: Judea, near the Jordan River. Following Jesus' His baptism, and before He begins His public ministry, the Spirit leads Jesus into the wilderness for forty days of temptation by Satan.

And Jesus answered him, "It is written, 'MAN SHALL NOT LIVE ON BREAD ALONE'" (Luke 4:4, Jesus quotes from Deuteronomy 8:3; cf. Matthew 4:1–4; see Mark 1:12, 13).

Setting: Probably Galilee. As Jesus and His disciples pass through some grain fields, some of the Pharisees ask Jesus why His followers harvest grain on the Sabbath.

And Jesus answering them said, "Have you not even read what David did when he was hungry, he and those who were with him, how he entered the house of God, and took and ate the consecrated bread which is not lawful for any to eat except the priests alone, and gave it to his companions?" And He was saying to them, "The Son of Man is Lord of the Sabbath" (Luke 6:3–5; cf. Matthew 12:1–8; Mark 2:23–28; see Exodus 20:8; Leviticus 24:1–9; Deuteronomy 5:12; 1 Samuel 21:1–6).

Setting: On the way from Galilee to Jerusalem. After some present report to Him about the Galileans whose blood Pilate (Roman governor of Judea) mixed with their sacrifices, Jesus responds to their concern by calling them to repentance and illustrating His point with a parable.

And He began telling this parable: "A man had a fig tree which had been planted in his vineyard; and he came looking for fruit on it and did not find any. And he said to the vineyard-keeper, 'Behold, for three years I have come looking for fruit on this fig tree without finding any. Cut it down! Why does it even use up the ground?' And he answered and said to him, 'Let it alone, sir, for this year too, until I dig around it and put fertilizer; and if it bears fruit next year, fine; but if not, cut it down'" (Luke 13:6–9; see Matthew 3:10).

Setting: On the way from Galilee to Jerusalem. After speaking of the importance of children, Jesus responds to a ruler's question about inheriting eternal life.

A ruler questioned Him, saying, "Good Teacher, what shall I do to inherit eternal life?" And Jesus said to him, "Why do you call Me good? No one is good except God alone. You know the commandments, 'DO NOT COMMIT ADULTERY, DO NOT MURDER, DO NOT STEAL, DO NOT BEAR FALSE WITNESS, HONOR YOUR FATHER AND MOTHER.'" And he said, "All these things I have kept from my youth."

When Jesus heard this, He said to him, "One thing you still lack; sell all that you possess and distribute it to the poor, and you shall have treasure in heaven; and come, follow Me" (Luke 18:18–22, Jesus quotes from Exodus 20:12–16; cf. Matthew 19:16–22; Mark 10:17–22; see Luke 10:25–28).

Setting: Jerusalem. During the Feast of the Jews, Jesus responds to criticism from the Jewish religious leaders by referring to God as His Father (thereby making Himself equal with God) and informing them that God, John the Baptist, and His works all testify to His mission.

"I can do nothing on My own initiative. As I hear, I judge; and My judgment is just, because I do not seek My own will, but the will of Him who sent Me. If I *alone* testify about Myself, My testimony is not true. There is another who testifies of Me, and I know that the testimony which He gives about Me is true. You have sent to John, and he has testified to the truth. But the testimony which I receive is not from man, but I say these things so that you may be saved. He was the lamp that was burning and was shining and you were willing to rejoice for a while in his light. But the testimony which I have is greater than the *testimony of* John; for the works which the Father has given Me to accomplish—the very works that I do—testify about Me, that the Father has sent Me. And the Father who sent Me, He has testified of Me. You have neither heard His voice at any time nor seen His form. You do not have His word abiding in you, for you do not believe Him whom He sent" (John 5:30–38; see Matthew 3:17; Mark 1:4, 5; John 1:7, 15, 32; 4:34; 8:14–16; 10:25, 37, 38).

Setting: The temple in Jerusalem. Following the Feast of Booths and the scribes' and Pharisees' failed attempt to stone a woman for committing adultery, Jesus returns to teach. His enemies question His testimony about Himself.

Jesus answered and said to them, "Even if I testify about Myself, My testimony is true, for I know where I came from and where I am going; but you do not know where I come from or where I am going. You judge according to the flesh; I am not judging anyone. But even if I do judge, My judgment is true; for I am not alone *in it,* but I and the Father who sent Me. Even in your law it has been written that the testimony of two men is true. I am He who testifies about Myself, and the Father who sent Me testifies about Me." So they were saying to Him, "Where is Your Father?" Jesus answered, "You know neither Me nor My Father; if you knew Me, you would know My Father also" (John 8:14–19; see Deuteronomy 17:6; 19:15; Matthew 18:16; John 3:17; 5:30, 37; 7:28; 42).

Setting: The temple treasury in Jerusalem. Following the Feast of Booths and the scribes' and Pharisees' failed attempt to stone a woman for committing adultery, Jesus returns to teach. They question His testimony about Himself.

So Jesus said, "When you lift up the Son of Man, then you will know that I am *He,* and I do nothing on my own initiative, but I speak these things as the Father taught Me. And He who sent Me is with Me; He has not left Me alone, for I always do the things that are pleasing to Him" (John 8:28, 29; see John 3:14).

Setting: Bethany near Jerusalem. Six days before the Passover in Jerusalem, as the chief priests and Pharisees plot to seize Him, Jesus visits Lazarus, Martha, and Mary. Mary anoints the Lord's feet with costly perfume made of pure nard.

Therefore Jesus said, "Let her alone, so that she may keep it for the day of My burial. For you always have the poor with you, but you do not always have Me" (John 12:7, 8; cf. Matthew 26:6–13; Mark 14:3–9; see Deuteronomy 15:11).

Setting: Jerusalem. Just days before the Passover, with the chief priests and Pharisees plotting to seize Him, crowds welcome Jesus to Jerusalem with palm branches and praise, and some Greeks ask to meet Him.

And Jesus answered them, saying, "The hour has come for the Son of Man to be glorified. Truly, truly, I say to you, unless a grain of wheat falls into the earth and dies, it remains alone; but if it dies, it bears much fruit. He who loves his life loses it, and he who hates his life in this world will keep it to life eternal. If anyone serves Me, he must follow Me; and where I am, there My servant will be also; if anyone serves Me, the Father will honor him" (John 12:23–26; see Matthew 10:39).

Setting: Jerusalem. Before the Passover, after conveying promises about praying in His name, Jesus prophesies His disciples' future scattering and gives them hope that in the midst of tribulation they will have His peace.

"Jesus answered them, "Do you now believe? Behold, an hour is coming, and has *already* come, for you to be scattered, each to his own *home,* and to leave Me alone; and *yet* I am not alone, because the Father is with Me. These things I have spoken to you, so that in Me you may have peace. In the world you have tribulation, but take courage, I have overcome the world" (John 16:31–33; see Zechariah 13:7; John 8:29; 14:27; Romans 8:37).

Setting: Jerusalem. Before the Passover, after giving His disciples assurance that in the midst of tribulation they will have His peace, Jesus continues praying His high-priestly prayer.

"But now I come to You; and these things I speak in the world so that they may have My joy made full in themselves. I have given them Your word; and the world has hated them, because they are not of the world, even as I am not of the world. I do not ask You to take them out of the world, but to keep them from the evil *one.* They are not of the world, even as I am not of the world. Sanctify them in the truth; Your word is truth. As You sent Me into the world, I also have sent them into the world. For their sakes I sanctify Myself, that they themselves also may be sanctified in truth. I do not ask on behalf of these alone, but for those also who believe in Me through their word; that they may all be one; even as You, Father, *are* in Me and I in You, that they also maybe in Us, so that the world may believe that You sent Me" (John 17:13–21; see Matthew 10:5, 38; John 7:33; 15:3, 11, 19; 17:1–12).

ALPHA (Also see BEGINNING; and FIRST)

Setting: On the small island of Patmos (in the Aegean Sea about fifty miles southwest of Ephesus in modern Turkey). An angel speaks the first words of the revelation of Jesus Christ, approximately fifty years after His resurrection, to His bond-servant, the apostle John.

"I am the Alpha and the Omega," says the Lord God, "who is and who was and who is to come, the Almighty" (Revelation 1:8; see Revelation 21:6).

Setting: On the small island of Patmos (in the Aegean Sea about fifty miles southwest of Ephesus in modern Turkey). In the final chapter of the Lord Jesus Christ's Revelation via the disciple John, approximately fifty years after His resurrection, the Lord reveals His coming return, reward, and eternality.

"Behold, I am coming quickly, and My reward *is* with Me, to render to every man according to what he has done. I am the Alpha and the Omega, the first and the last, the beginning and the end" (Revelation 22:12, 13; see Isaiah 40:10; 44:6).

ALPHABET (See LETTER)

ALTAR

Setting: Galilee. During the early part of His ministry, Jesus preaches the Sermon on the Mount to His disciples and the multitudes.

"Therefore if you are presenting your offering at the altar, and there remember that your brother has something against you, leave your offering there before the altar and go; first be reconciled to your brother, and then come and present your offering" (Matthew 5:23, 24; see Romans 12:17, 18).

Setting: The temple in Jerusalem. After the Jewish religious leaders test Him with questions, Jesus pronounces the fourth of eight woes on them in front of the crowds and His disciples.

"Woe to you, blind guides, who say, 'Whoever swears by the temple, *that* is nothing; but whoever swears by the gold of the temple is obligated.' You fools and blind men! Which is more important, the gold or the temple that sanctified the gold? And, 'Whoever swears by the altar, *that* is nothing, but whoever swears by the offering on it, he is obligated.' You blind men, which is more important, the offering, or the altar that sanctifies the offering? Therefore, whoever swears by the altar, swears *both* by the altar and by everything on it. And whoever swears by the temple, swears *both* by the temple and by Him who dwells within it. And whoever swears by heaven, swears *both* by the throne of God and by Him who sits upon it" (Matthew 23:16–22; see Exodus 29:37; 1 Kings 8:13; Isaiah 66:1; Matthew 15:14).

Setting: The temple in Jerusalem. After the Jewish religious leaders test Him with questions, Jesus pronounces the fourth of eight woes on them in front of the crowds and His disciples.

"Woe to you, scribes and Pharisees, hypocrites! For you build the tombs of the prophets and adorn the monuments of the righteous, and say, 'If we had been *living* in the days of our fathers, we would not have been partners with them in *shedding* the blood of the prophets.' So you testify against yourselves, that you are sons of those who murdered the prophets. Fill up, then, the measure *of the guilt* of you fathers. You serpents, you brood of vipers, how will you escape the sentence of hell? Therefore, behold, I am sending you prophets and wise men and scribes; some of them you will kill and crucify, and some of them you will scourge in your synagogues, and persecute from city to city, so that upon you may fall *the guilt of* all the righteous blood shed on earth, from the blood of righteous Abel to the blood of Zechariah, the son of Berechiah, whom you murdered between the temple and the altar. Truly I say to you, all these things will come upon this generation" (Matthew 23:29–36; cf. 2 Chronicles 24:21; Zechariah 1:1; Matthew 3:7; Luke 11:47–52; see Matthew 10:23).

Setting: On the way from Galilee to Jerusalem. After Jesus pronounces woes upon the Pharisees, a lawyer replies that His remarks insult lawyers, too.

But He said, "Woe to you lawyers as well! For you weigh men down with burdens hard to bear, while you yourselves will not even touch the burdens with one of your fingers. Woe to you! For you build the tombs of the prophets, and it was your fathers who killed them. So you are witnesses and approve the deeds of your fathers; because it was they who killed them, and you build their tombs. For this reason also the wisdom of God said, 'I will send them prophets and apostles, and some of them they will kill and some they will persecute, so that the blood of all the prophets, shed since the foundation of the world, may be charged against this generation, from the blood of Abel to the blood of Zechariah, who was killed between the altar and the house of God; yes, I tell you, it shall be charged against this generation.' Woe to you lawyers! For you have taken away the key of knowledge; you yourselves did not enter, and you hindered those who were entering" (Luke 11:46–52; cf. Matthew 23:29–32; see 2 Chronicles 24:20, 21; Matthew 23:4, 13).

AMBITION (prideful)

[AMBITION inferred]
Setting: On the way to Jerusalem. The mother of James and John, the sons of Zebedee, asks Jesus to make her sons exalted rulers with Him in His coming kingdom.

And He said to her, "What do you wish?" She said to Him, 'Command that in Your kingdom these two sons of mine may sit one on Your right and one on Your left.' But Jesus answered, "You do not know what you are asking. Are you able to drink the cup that I am about to drink?" They said to Him, 'We are able.' He said to them, "My cup you shall drink; but to sit on My right and on *My* left, this is not Mine to give, but it is for those for whom it has been prepared by My Father" (Matthew 20:21–23; cf. Mark 10:35–40; see Matthew 19:28; Acts 12:2).

[AMBITION inferred]
Setting: On the road to Jerusalem. After Jesus prophesies His persecution, death, and resurrection, James and John ask for special honor and privileges in His coming kingdom.

And He said to them, "What do you want Me to do for you?" They said to Him, "Grant that we may sit, one on Your right and one on *Your* left, in Your glory." But Jesus said to them, "You do not know what you are asking. Are you able to drink the cup that I drink, or to be baptized with the baptism with which I am baptized?" They said to Him, "We are able." And Jesus said to them,

"The cup that I drink you shall drink; and you shall be baptized with the baptism with which I am baptized. But to sit on My right or on *My* left, this is not Mine to give; but it is for those for whom it has been prepared" (Mark 10:36–40; cf. Matthew 20:20–23; see Matthew 19:28; Acts 12:2).

AMEN

Setting: Galilee. During the early part of His ministry, Jesus gives a model prayer to His disciples and the multitudes while conveying The Sermon on the Mount.

"Pray, then, in this way: 'Our Father who is in heaven, hallowed be Your name. Your kingdom come. Your will be done, on earth as it is in heaven. Give us this day our daily bread. And forgive us our debts, as we also have forgiven our debtors. And do not lead us into temptation, but deliver us from evil. [For Yours is the kingdom and the power and the glory forever. Amen]'" (Matthew 6:9–13; cf. Luke 11:2–4; see John 17:15).

Setting: On the island of Patmos (in the Aegean Sea about fifty miles southwest of Ephesus in modern Turkey). On the Lord's Day (Sunday), about fifty years after Jesus' resurrection, the disciple John encounters the Lord Jesus Christ, who communicates a new revelation for the apostle to record for the church in Laodicea and to six other churches in Asia.

"To the angel of the church in Laodicea write: The Amen, the faithful and true Witness, the Beginning of the creation of God, says this: 'I know your deeds, that you are neither cold nor hot; I wish that you were cold or hot. So because you are lukewarm, and neither hot nor cold, I will spit you out of My mouth. Because you say, "I am rich, and have become wealthy, and have need of nothing," and you do not know that you are wretched and miserable and poor and blind and naked, I advise you to buy from Me gold refined by fire so that you may become rich, and white garments so that you may clothe yourself, and *that* the shame of your nakedness will not be revealed; and eye salve to anoint your eyes so that you may see. Those whom I love, I reprove and discipline; therefore be zealous and repent. Behold, I stand at the door and knock; if anyone hears My voice and opens the door, I will come in to him and will dine with him, and he with Me. He who overcomes, I will grant to him to sit down with Me on My throne, as I also overcame and sat down with My Father on His throne. He who has an ear, let him hear what the Spirit says to the churches'" (Revelation 3:14–22; see Proverbs 3:12; Hosea 12:8; John 14:23; 16:33).

Setting: On the island of Patmos (in the Aegean Sea about fifty miles southwest of Ephesus in modern Turkey). In the final chapter of the Lord Jesus Christ's Revelation via the disciple John, approximately fifty years after His resurrection, the Lord reveals His coming return to the earth.

He who testifies to these things says, "Yes, I am coming quickly." Amen. Come, Lord Jesus (Revelation 22:20).

ANANIAS

Setting: Damascus. Luke, writing in Acts, conveys how the Lord Jesus instructs one of His disciples, Ananias, to locate Saul of Tarsus to touch him in order to restore his vision.

Now there was a disciple at Damascus named Ananias; and the Lord said to him in a vision, "Ananias." And he said, "Here I am, Lord." And the Lord *said* to him, "Get up and go to the street called Straight, and inquire at the house of Judas for a man from Tarsus named Saul, for he is praying, and he was seen in a vision a man named Ananias come in and lay his hands on him, so that he might regain his sight" (Acts 9:10–12; see Acts 22:12–14).

ANCESTOR(S) (See ANCIENTS; and DESCENDANT)

ANCIENTS

Setting: Galilee. During the early part of His ministry, Jesus preaches the Sermon on the Mount to His disciples and the multitudes.

"You have heard that the ancients were told, 'YOU SHALL NOT COMMIT MURDER' and "whoever commits murder shall be liable to the court' (Matthew 5:21, Jesus quotes from Exodus 20:13).

Setting: Galilee. During the early part of His ministry, Jesus preaches the Sermon on the Mount to His disciples and the multitudes.

"Again, you have heard that the ancients were told, 'YOU SHALL NOT MAKE FALSE VOWS, BUT SHALL FULFILL YOUR VOWS TO THE LORD.' But I say to you, make no oath at all, either by heaven, for it is the throne of God, or by the earth, for it is the footstool of His feet, or by Jerusalem, for it is THE CITY OF THE GREAT KING. Nor shall you make an oath by your head, for you cannot make one hair white or black. But let your statement be 'Yes, yes' *or* 'No, no'; anything beyond these is of evil" (Matthew 5:33–37, Jesus quotes from Leviticus 19:12, Psalm 48:2; Isaiah 66:1; cf. James 5:12).

ANGEL (Also see ANGELS)

Setting: On the island of Patmos (in the Aegean Sea about fifty miles southwest of Ephesus in modern Turkey). On the Lord's Day (Sunday), about fifty years after Jesus' resurrection, the disciple John encounters the Lord Jesus Christ, who communicates a new revelation for the apostle to record for the church in Ephesus and to six other churches in Asia.

"To the angel of the church in Ephesus write: The One who holds the seven stars in His right hand, the One who walks among the seven golden lampstands, says this: 'I know your deeds and your toil and perseverance, and that you cannot tolerate evil men, and you put to the test those who call themselves apostles, and they are not, and you found them *to be* false; and you have perseverance and have endured for My name's sake, and have not grown weary. But I have *this* against you, that you have left your first love. Therefore remember from where you have fallen, and repent and do the deeds you did at first; or else I am coming to you and will remove your lampstand out of its place—unless you repent. Yet this you do have, that you hate the deeds of the Nicolaitans, which I also hate. He who has an ear, let him hear what the Spirit says to the churches. To him who overcomes, I will grant to eat of the tree of life which is in the Paradise of God'" (Revelation 2:1–7; see Genesis 2:9; Ezekiel 28:13; 1 John 4:1; Revelation 1:10, 11, 19, 20; 2:15, 16).

Setting: On the island of Patmos (in the Aegean Sea about fifty miles southwest of Ephesus in modern Turkey). On the Lord's Day (Sunday), about fifty years after Jesus' resurrection, the disciple John encounters the Lord Jesus Christ, who communicates a new revelation for the apostle to record for the church in Smyrna and to six other churches in Asia.

"And to the angel of the church in Smyrna write: The first and the last, who was dead, and has come to life, says this: 'I know your tribulation and your poverty (but you are rich), and the blasphemy by those who say they are Jews and are not, but are a synagogue of Satan. Do not fear what you are about to suffer. Behold, the devil is about to cast some of you into prison, so that you will be tested, and you will have tribulation for ten days. Be faithful until death, and I will give you the crown of life. He who has an ear, let him hear what the Spirit says to the churches. He who overcomes will not be hurt by the second death' (Revelation 2:8–11; see Isaiah 44:6; Revelation 1:9, 18; 20:6, 14).

Setting: On the island of Patmos (in the Aegean Sea about fifty miles southwest of Ephesus in modern Turkey). On the Lord's Day (Sunday), about fifty years after Jesus' resurrection, the disciple John encounters the Lord Jesus Christ, who communicates a new revelation for the apostle to record for the church in Pergamum and to six other churches in Asia.

"And to the angel of the church in Pergamum write: The One who has the sharp two-edged sword says this: 'I know where you dwell, where Satan's throne is; and you hold fast My name, and did not deny My faith even in the days of Antipas, My witness, My faithful one, who was killed among you, where Satan dwells. But I have a few things against you, because you have there some who hold the teaching of Balaam, who kept teaching Balak to put a stumbling block before the sons of Israel, to eat things sacrificed to idols and to commit *acts of* immorality. So you also have some who in the same way hold the teaching of the Nicolaitans. Therefore repent; or else I am coming to you quickly, and I will make war against them with the sword of My mouth. He who has an ear, let him hear what the Spirit says to the churches. To him who overcomes, to him I will give *some* of the hidden manna, and I will give him a white stone, and a new name written on the stone which no one knows but he who receives it' (Revelation 2:12–17; see Numbers 25:1–3; Isaiah 62:2; Revelation 1:16; 2:5, 6, 16).

Setting: On the island of Patmos (in the Aegean Sea about fifty miles southwest of Ephesus in modern Turkey). On the Lord's Day (Sunday), about fifty years after Jesus' resurrection, the disciple John encounters the Lord Jesus Christ, who communicates a new revelation for the apostle to record for the church in Thyatira and to six other churches in Asia.

"And to the angel of the church in Thyatira write: The Son of God, who has eyes like a flame of fire, and His feet are like burnished bronze, says this: 'I know your deeds, and your love and faith and service and perseverance, and that your deeds of late are greater than at first. But I have *this* against you, that you tolerate the woman Jezebel, who calls herself a prophetess, and she teaches and leads My bond-servants astray so that they commit *acts of* immorality and eat things sacrificed to idols. I gave her time to repent, and she does not want to repent of her immorality. Behold, I will throw her on a bed *of sickness,* and those who commit adultery with her into great tribulation, unless they repent of her deeds. And I will kill her children with pestilence, and all the churches will know that I am He who searches the minds and hearts; and I will give to each one of you according to your deeds. But I say to you, the rest who are in Thyatira, who do not hold this teaching, who have not known the deep things of Satan, as they call them—I place no other burden on you. Nevertheless what you have, hold fast until I come. He who overcomes, and he who keeps My deeds until the end, TO HIM I WILL GIVE AUTHORITY OVER THE NATIONS; AND HE SHALL RULE THEM WITH A ROD OF IRON, AS THE VESSELS OF THE POTTER ARE BROKEN TO PIECES, as I also have received *authority* from My Father; and I will give him the morning star. He who has an ear, let him hear what the Spirit says to the churches' (Revelation 2:18–29; Jesus quotes from Psalm 2:8, 9; Isaiah 30:14; see 1 Kings 16:31; Psalm 7:9; Romans 2:5; 1 Corinthians 2:10; 2 Peter 3:9; Revelation 1:14; 2:7; 3:11; 17:1–20).

Setting: On the island of Patmos (in the Aegean Sea about fifty miles southwest of Ephesus in modern Turkey). On the Lord's Day (Sunday), about fifty years after Jesus' resurrection, the disciple John encounters the Lord Jesus Christ, who communicates a new revelation for the apostle to record for the church in Sardis and to six other churches in Asia.

"To the angel of the church in Sardis write: He who has the seven Spirits of God and the seven stars, says this: 'I know your deeds, that you have a name that you are alive, but you are dead. Wake up, and strengthen the things that remain, which were about to die; for I have not found your deeds completed in the sight of My God. So remember what you have received and heard; and keep *it,* and repent. Therefore if you do not wake up, I will come like a thief, and you will not know at what hour I will come to you. But you have a few people in Sardis who have not soiled their garments; and they will walk with Me in white, for they are worthy. He who overcomes will thus be clothed in white garments; and I will not erase his name from the book of life, and I will confess his name before My Father and before His angels. He who has an ear, let him hear what the Spirit says to the churches'" (Revelation 3:1–6; see Matthew 10:32; Revelation 1:16).

Setting: On the island of Patmos (in the Aegean Sea about fifty miles southwest of Ephesus in modern Turkey). On the Lord's Day (Sunday), about fifty years after Jesus' resurrection, the disciple John encounters the Lord Jesus Christ, who communicates a new revelation for the apostle to record for the church in Philadelphia and to six other churches in Asia.

"And to the angel of the church in Philadelphia write: He who is holy, who is true, who has the key of David, who opens and no one will shut, and who shuts and no one opens, says this: 'I know your deeds. Behold, I have put before you an open door which no one can shut, because you have a little power, and have kept My word, and have not denied My name. Behold, I will cause *those* of the synagogue of Satan, who say they are Jews and are not, but lie—I will make them come and bow down at your feet, and *make them* know that I have loved you. Because you have kept the word of My perseverance, I also will keep you from the hour of testing, that *hour* which is about to come upon the whole world, to test those who dwell on the earth. I am coming quickly;

hold fast what you have, so that no one will take your crown. He who overcomes, I will make him a pillar in the temple of My God, and he will not go out from it anymore; and I will write on him the name of My God, and the name of the city of My God, the new Jerusalem, which comes down out of heaven from My God, and My new name. He who has an ear, let him hear what the Spirit says to the churches'" (Revelation 3:7–13; see Isaiah 22:22; Galatians 2:9; Revelation 2:9, 10, 13, 25; 14:1).

Setting: On the island of Patmos (in the Aegean Sea about fifty miles southwest of Ephesus in modern Turkey). On the Lord's Day (Sunday), about fifty years after Jesus' resurrection, the disciple John encounters the Lord Jesus Christ, who communicates a new revelation for the apostle to record for the church in Laodicea and to six other churches in Asia.

"To the angel of the church in Laodicea write: The Amen, the faithful and true Witness, the Beginning of the creation of God, says this: 'I know your deeds, that you are neither cold nor hot; I wish that you were cold or hot. So because you are lukewarm, and neither hot nor cold, I will spit you out of My mouth. Because you say, "I am rich, and have become wealthy, and have need of nothing," and you do not know that you are wretched and miserable and poor and blind and naked, I advise you to buy from Me gold refined by fire so that you may become rich, and white garments so that you may clothe yourself, and *that* the shame of your nakedness will not be revealed; and eye salve to anoint your eyes so that you may see. Those whom I love, I reprove and discipline; therefore be zealous and repent. Behold, I stand at the door and knock; if anyone hears My voice and opens the door, I will come in to him and will dine with him, and he with Me. He who overcomes, I will grant to him to sit down with Me on My throne, as I also overcame and sat down with My Father on His throne. He who has an ear, let him hear what the Spirit says to the churches'" (Revelation 3:14–22; see Proverbs 3:12; Hosea 12:8; John 14:23; 16:33).

Setting: On the island of Patmos (in the Aegean Sea about fifty miles southwest of Ephesus in modern Turkey). In the final chapter of the Lord Jesus Christ's Revelation via the disciple John, approximately fifty years after His resurrection, the Lord authenticates the truthfulness of His message, along with His earthly lineage through King David.

"I, Jesus, have sent My angel to testify to you these things for the churches. I am the root and the descendant of David, the bright morning star" (Revelation 22:16).

ANGELS **(Specifics such as ANGELS, HIS; and ANGELS, HOLY are listed as separate entries; also see ANGEL)**

Setting: A house near the Sea of Galilee. Jesus explains the meaning of the Parable of the Wheat and the Tares to His disciples.

And He said, "The one who sows the good seed is the Son of Man, and the field is the world; and as *for* the good seed, these are the sons of the kingdom; and the tares are the sons of the evil *one;* and the enemy who sowed them is the devil, and the harvest is the end of the age; and the reapers are angels. So just as the tares are gathered up and burned with fire, so shall it be at the end of the age. The Son of Man will send forth His angels, and they will gather out of His kingdom all stumbling blocks, and those who commit lawlessness, and will throw them into the furnace of fire; in that place there will be weeping and gnashing of teeth. Then THE RIGHTEOUS WILL SHINE FORTH AS THE SUN in the kingdom of their Father. He who has ears, let him hear" (Matthew 13:37–43, Jesus quotes from Daniel 12:3; cf. Matthew 8:12; 13:50).

Setting: By the Sea of Galilee. Because the religious leaders are rejecting His message, Jesus continues teaching His disciples with the Parable of the Dragnet.

"Again, the kingdom of heaven is like a dragnet cast into the sea, and gathering *fish* of every kind; and when it was filled, they drew it up on the beach; and they sat down and gathered the good *fish* into containers, but the bad they threw away. So it will be at the end of the age; the angels will come forth and take out the wicked from among the righteous, and will throw them into the furnace of fire; in that place there will be weeping and gnashing of teeth. Have you understood all these things?" They said to Him, "Yes" (Matthew 13:47–51).

Setting: Capernaum of Galilee. Jesus elaborates about the value of little ones when His disciples ask about greatness in the kingdom of heaven.

"See that you do not despise one of these little ones, for I say to you that their angels in heaven continually see the face of My Father who is in heaven" (Matthew 18:10; see Luke 1:19).

Setting: The temple in Jerusalem. The Sadducees question Jesus about levirate marriage (marriage to a brother-in-law) in order to test Him as He teaches.

But Jesus answered and said to them, "You are mistaken, not understanding the Scriptures nor the power of God. For in the resurrection they neither marry nor are given in marriage, but are like angels in heaven. But regarding the resurrection of the dead, have you not read what was spoken to you by God: 'I AM THE GOD OF ABRAHAM, AND THE GOD OF ISAAC, AND THE GOD OF JACOB'? He is not the God of the dead but of the living" (Matthew 22:29–32, Jesus quotes from Exodus 3:6; cf. Mark 12:18–27; Luke 20:27–38; see Deuteronomy 25:5; John 20:9).

Setting: The Mount of Olives, just east of Jerusalem. During His discourse, after answering His disciples' questions as to when the temple will be destroyed and Jerusalem overrun, along with the signs of His coming and the end of the age, Jesus teaches them the Parable of the Fig Tree.

"Now learn the parable from the fig tree: when its branch has already become tender and puts forth its leaves, you know that summer is near; so, you too, when you see all these things, recognize that He is near, *right* at the door. Truly, I say to you, this generation will not pass away until all these things take place. Heaven and earth will pass away, but My words will not pass away. But of that day and hour no one knows, not even the angels of heaven, nor the Son, but the Father alone. For the coming of the Son of Man will be just like the days of Noah. For as in those days before the flood they were eating and drinking, marrying and giving in marriage, until the day that Noah entered the ark, and they did not understand until the flood came and took them all away; so will the coming of the Son of Man be. Then there will be two men in the field; one will be taken and one will be left. Two women *will be* grinding at the mill; one will be taken and one will be left" (Matthew 24:32–41; cf. Mark 13:28–32; Luke 17:34–36; 21:28–33; see Genesis 6:5; 7:7; Matthew 5:18; 10:23; James 5:9).

Setting: The Mount of Olives, just east of Jerusalem. During His discourse, after answering His disciples' questions as to when the temple will be destroyed and Jerusalem overrun, along with the signs of His coming and the end of the age, Jesus reveals the future judgments following His return.

"But when the Son of Man comes in His glory, and all the angels with Him, then He will sit on His glorious throne. All the nations will be gathered before Him; and He will separate them from one another, as the shepherd separates the sheep from the goats; and He will put the sheep on His right, and the goats on the left. Then the King will say to those on His right, 'Come, you who are blessed of My Father, inherit the kingdom prepared for you from the foundation of the world. 'For I was hungry, and you gave Me *something* to eat; I was thirsty, and you gave Me *something* to drink; I was a stranger, and you invited Me in; naked, and you clothed Me; I was sick, and you visited Me; I was in prison, and you came to Me.' Then the righteous will answer Him, 'Lord, when did we see You hungry and feed You, or thirsty, and give you *something* to drink? And when did we see You a stranger, and invite You in, or naked, and clothe You? When did we see You sick, or in prison, and come to You?' The King will answer and say to them, 'Truly I say to you, to the extent that you did it to one of these brothers of Mine, *even* the least *of them,* you did it to Me.' Then He will also say to those on His left, 'Depart from Me, accursed ones, into the eternal fire which has been prepared for the devil and his angels; for I was hungry, and you gave Me *nothing* to eat; I was thirsty, and you gave Me nothing to drink; I was a stranger, and you did not invite Me in; naked, and you did not clothe Me; sick, and in prison, and you did not visit Me.' Then they themselves also will answer, 'Lord, when did we see You hungry, or thirsty, or a stranger, or naked, or sick, or in prison, and did not take care of You?' Then He will answer them, 'Truly I say to you, to the extent that you did not do it to one of the least of these, you did not do it to Me.' These will go away into eternal punishment, but the righteous into eternal life" (Matthew 25:31–46; see Matthew 7:23; 16:27; 19:29).

Setting: The temple in Jerusalem. After some of the Pharisees and Herodians attempt to trap Jesus in a statement, some Sadducees question Him about the status of marriage after death.

Jesus said to them, "Is this not the reason you are mistaken, that you do not understand the Scriptures or the power of God? For when they rise from the dead, they neither marry nor are given in marriage, but are like angels in heaven. But regarding the fact that the dead rise again, have you not read in the book of Moses, in the *passage* about *the burning* bush, how God spoke to him, saying, 'I AM THE GOD OF ABRAHAM, AND THE GOD OF ISAAC, and the God of Jacob?' He is not the God of the dead, but of the living; you are greatly mistaken" (Mark 12:24–27, Jesus quotes from Exodus 3:6; cf. Matthew 22:29–33; Luke 20:34–40).

Setting: The Mount of Olives, east of the temple in Jerusalem. During His discourse, after prophesying the temple's destruction, Jesus responds to questions from Peter, James, John, and Andrew about future events.

"But in those days, after that tribulation, THE SUN WILL BE DARKENED AND THE MOON WILL NOT GIVE ITS LIGHT, AND THE STARS WILL BE FALLING from heaven, and the powers that are in the heavens will be shaken. Then they will see THE SON OF MAN COMING IN CLOUDS with great power and glory. And then He will send forth the angels, and will gather together His elect from the four winds, from the farthest end of the earth to the farthest end of heaven" (Mark 13:24–27. Jesus quotes from Isaiah 13:10; 34:4; Daniel 7:13; cf. Matthew 24:29–31; Luke 21:25–27).

Setting: The Mount of Olives, east of the temple in Jerusalem. During His discourse, after prophesying the temple's destruction, Jesus responds to questions from Peter, James, John, and Andrew about future events.

"Now learn the parable from the fig tree: when its branch has already become tender and puts forth its leaves, you know that summer is near. Even so, you too, when you see these things happening, recognize that He is near, *right* at the door. Truly I say to you, this generation will not pass away until all these things take place. Heaven and earth will pass away, but My words will not pass away. But of the day or hour no one knows, not even the angels in heaven, nor the Son, but the Father *alone*" (Mark 13:28–32; cf. Matthew 24:32–36; Luke 21:28–33).

Setting: On the way from Galilee to Jerusalem. Jesus warns His disciples of future events, as the scribes and Pharisees turn hostile and question Him in an attempt to catch Him in something He might say.

"And I say to you, everyone who confesses Me before men, the Son of Man will confess him also before the angels of God; but he who denies Me before men will be denied before the angels of God. And everyone who speaks a word against the Son of Man, it will be forgiven him; but he who blasphemes against the Holy Spirit, it will not be forgiven him. When they bring you before the synagogues and the rulers and the authorities, do not worry about how or what you are to speak in your defense, or what you are to say; for the Holy Spirit will teach you in that very hour what you ought to say" (Luke 12:8–12; cf. Matthew 10:32, 33; 12:31, 32; see Matthew 10:20).

Setting: On the way from Galilee to Jerusalem. Jesus conveys the principles of the lost sheep and the lost coin because the Pharisees and scribes complain He associates with tax collectors and sinners.

"So He told them this parable, saying, "What man among you, if he has a hundred sheep and has lost one of them, does not leave the ninety-nine in the open pasture and go after the one which is lost until he finds it? When he has found it, he lays it on his shoulders, rejoicing. And when he comes home, he calls together his friends and his neighbors, saying to them, 'Rejoice with me, for I have found my sheep which was lost!' I tell you that in the same way, there will be more joy in heaven over one sinner who repents than over ninety-nine righteous persons who need no repentance. Or what woman, if she has ten silver coins and loses one coin, does not light a lamp and sweep the house and search carefully until she finds it? When she has found it, she calls together her friends and neighbors, saying, 'Rejoice with me, for I have found the coin which I had lost!' In the same way, I tell you, there is joy in the presence of the angels of God over one sinner who repents" (Luke 15:3–10; cf. Matthew 18:12-14; see Matthew 9:11-13).

Setting: On the way from Galilee to Jerusalem. After He responds to the Pharisees' scoffing at His teaching His disciples about stewardship and the permanence of the Law, Jesus conveys the story of the rich man and Lazarus.

"Now there was a rich man, and he habitually dressed in purple and fine linen, joyously living in splendor every day. And a poor man named Lazarus was laid at his gate, covered with sores, and longing to be fed with the crumbs which were falling from the rich man's table; besides, even the dogs were coming and licking his sores. Now the poor man died and was carried away by the angels to Abraham's bosom; and the rich man also died and was buried. In Hades he lifted up his eyes, being in torment, and saw Abraham far away and Lazarus in his bosom. And he cried out and said, 'Father Abraham, have mercy on me, and send Lazarus so that he may dip the tip of his finger in water and cool off my tongue, for I am in agony in this flame.' But Abraham said, 'Child, remember that during your life you received your good things, and likewise Lazarus bad things; but now he is being comforted here, and you are in agony. And besides all this, between us and you there is a great chasm fixed, so that those who wish to come over from here to you will not be able, and that none may cross over from there to us.' And he said, 'Then I beg you, father, that you send him to my father's house—for I have five brothers—in order that he may warn them, so that they will not also come to this place of torment.' But Abraham said, 'They have Moses and the Prophets; let them hear them.' But he said, 'No, father Abraham, but if someone goes to them from the dead, they will repent!' But he said to him, 'If they do not listen to Moses and the Prophets, they will not be persuaded even if someone rises from the dead'" (Luke 16:19–31; see Luke 3:8; 6:24; 16:1, 14).

Setting: The temple in Jerusalem. While ministering a few days before His crucifixion, after the scribes and Pharisees seek to trap Jesus by questioning Him about paying taxes to Caesar, some Sadducees (who say there is no resurrection) ask Him a question about the resurrection.

Jesus said to them, "The sons of this age marry and are given in marriage, but those who are considered worthy to attain to that age and the resurrection from the dead, neither marry nor are given in marriage; for they cannot even die anymore, because they are like angels, and are sons of God, being sons of the resurrection. But that the dead are raised, even Moses showed, in the passage about the burning bush, where he calls the Lord THE GOD OF ABRAHAM, AND THE GOD OF ISAAC, AND THE GOD OF JACOB. Now He is not the God of the dead but of the living; for all live to Him" (Luke 20:34–38, Jesus quotes from Exodus 3:6; cf. Matthew 22:23–32; Mark 12:18–27).

Setting: Galilee. After beginning His public ministry and choosing His first disciples, Andrew and Simon (Peter) near Bethany beyond the Jordan, and Philip in Galilee, Jesus calls Philip's friend, Nathanael, (some believe he may have been also called Bartholomew) as His next follower.

Jesus saw Nathanael coming to Him, and said of him, "Behold, an Israelite indeed, in whom there is no deceit!" Nathanael said to Him, "How do you know me?" Jesus answered and said to him, "Before Philip called you, when you were under the fig tree, I saw you." Nathanael answered Him, "Rabbi, You are the Son of God; You are the King of Israel." Jesus answered and said to him, "Because I said to you that I saw you under the fig tree, do you believe? You will see greater things than these." And He said to him, "Truly, truly, I say to you, you will see the heavens opened and the angels of God ascending and descending on the Son of Man" (John 1:47–51).

Setting: On the island of Patmos (in the Aegean Sea about fifty miles southwest of Ephesus in modern Turkey). On the Lord's Day (Sunday), approximately fifty years after His resurrection, the disciple John encounters the Lord Jesus Christ, who communicates new revelations for the apostle to record for the seven churches in Asia.

When I saw Him, I fell at His feet like a dead man. And He placed His right hand on me, saying, "Do not be afraid; I am the first and the last, and the living One; and I was dead, and behold, I am alive forevermore, and I have the keys of death and of Hades. Therefore write the things which you have seen, and the things which are, and the things which will take place after these things. As for the mystery of the seven stars which you saw in My right hand, and the seven golden lampstands: the seven stars are the angels of the seven churches, and the seven lampstands are the seven churches" (Revelation 1:17–20; see Isaiah 44:6; Luke 24:5; Revelation 2:8).

ANGELS, FALLEN (See DEMONS)

ANGELS, GUARDIAN (Also see ANGEL)

[GUARDIAN ANGELS from their angels]

Setting: Capernaum of Galilee. Jesus elaborates about the value of little ones after His disciples' ask about greatness in the kingdom of heaven.

"See that you do not despise one of these little ones, for I say to you that their angels in heaven continually see the face of My Father who is in heaven" (Matthew 18:10; see Luke 1:19).

ANGELS, HIS (God's/Jesus')

Setting: A house near the Sea of Galilee. Jesus explains the meaning of the Parable of the Wheat and the Tares to His disciples.

And He said, "The one who sows the good seed is the Son of Man, and the field is the world; and as *for* the good seed, these are the sons of the kingdom; and the tares are the sons of the evil *one;* and the enemy who sowed them is the devil, and the harvest is the end of the age; and the reapers are angels. So just as the tares are gathered up and burned with fire, so shall it be at the end of the age. The Son of Man will send forth His angels, and they will gather out of His kingdom all stumbling blocks, and those who commit lawlessness, and will throw them into the furnace of fire; in that place there will be weeping and gnashing of teeth. Then THE RIGHTEOUS WILL SHINE FORTH AS THE SUN in the kingdom of their Father. He who has ears, let him hear" (Matthew 13:37–43, Jesus quotes from Daniel 12:3; cf. Matthew 8:12; 13:50).

Setting: Near Caesarea Philippi. After He rebukes Peter for trying to forbid Him to accomplish His earthly mission of dying and being resurrected, Jesus teaches His disciples about the costs of discipleship.

Then Jesus said to His disciples, "If anyone wishes to come after Me, he must deny himself, and take up his cross and follow Me. For whoever wishes to save his life will lose it; but whoever loses his life for My sake will find it. For what will it profit a man if he gains the whole world and forfeits his soul? Or what will a man give in exchange for his soul? For the Son of Man is going to come in the glory of His Father with His angels, and WILL THEN REPAY EVERY MAN ACCORDING TO HIS DEEDS. Truly, I say to you, there are some of you who are standing here who will not taste death until they see the Son of Man coming in His kingdom" (Matthew 16:24–28, Jesus quotes from Psalm 62:12; cf. Mark 8:34–37; Luke 9:23–27; see Matthew 10:38, 39).

Setting: The Mount of Olives, just east of Jerusalem. During His discourse, Jesus answers His disciples' questions as to when the temple will be destroyed and Jerusalem overrun, along with the signs of His coming and the end of the age.

"But immediately after the tribulation of those days THE SUN WILL BE DARKENED, AND THE MOON WILL NOT GIVE ITS LIGHT, AND THE STARS WILL FALL from the sky, and the powers of the heavens will be shaken. And then the sign of the Son of Man will appear in the sky, and then all the tribes of the earth will mourn, and they will see the SON OF MAN COMING ON THE CLOUDS OF THE SKY with power and great glory. And He will send forth His angels with A GREAT TRUMPET and THEY WILL GATHER TOGETHER His elect from the four winds, from one end of the sky to the other" (Matthew 24:29–31, Jesus quotes from Isaiah 13:10, Daniel 7:13; Exodus 19:16; cf. Mark 13:24–27; Luke 21:25–27).

Setting: On the island of Patmos (in the Aegean Sea about fifty miles southwest of Ephesus in modern Turkey). On the Lord's Day (Sunday), approximately fifty years after His resurrection, the disciple John encounters the Lord Jesus Christ, who communicates new revelations for the apostle to record for the church in Sardis and to six other churches in Asia.

"To the angel of the church in Sardis write: He who has the seven Spirits of God and the seven stars, says this: 'I know your deeds, that you have a name that you are alive, but you are dead. Wake up, and strengthen the things that remain, which were about to die; for I have not found your deeds completed in the sight of My God. So remember what you have received and heard; and keep *it,* and repent. Therefore if you do not wake up, I will come like a thief, and you will not know at what hour I will come to you. But you have a few people in Sardis who have not soiled their garments; and they will walk with Me in white, for they are worthy. He who overcomes will thus be clothed in white garments; and I will not erase his name from the book of life, and I will confess his name before My Father and before His angels. He who has an ear, let him hear what the Spirit says to the churches'" (Revelation 3:1–6; see Matthew 10:32; Revelation 1:16).

ANGELS, HOLY (Also see ANGELS)

Setting: Caesarea Philippi. After He rebukes Peter for desiring to thwart His mission to the cross, Jesus summons a crowd along with His disciples and informs them of the high costs of following Him.

And He summoned the crowd with His disciples, and said to them, "If anyone wishes to come after Me, he must deny himself, and take up his cross and follow Me. For whoever wishes to save his life will lose it, but whoever loses his life for My sake and the gospel's will save it. For what does it profit a man to gain the whole world, and forfeit his soul? For what will a man give in exchange for his soul? For whoever is ashamed of Me and My words in this adulterous and sinful generation, the Son of Man will also be ashamed of him when He comes in the glory of His Father with the holy angels" (Mark 8:34–38; cf. Matthew 16:24–28; Luke 9:23–27; see Matthew 10:33, 38, 39).

Setting: Galilee following Peter's pronouncement that Jesus is the Christ of God, the Lord conveys the demands of discipleship and the hope regarding the kingdom of God.

And He was saying to them all, "If anyone wishes to come after Me, he must deny himself, and take up his cross daily and follow Me. For whoever wishes to save his life will lose it, but whoever loses his life for My sake, he is the one who will save it. For what is a man profited if he gains the whole world, and loses or forfeits himself? For whoever is ashamed of Me and My words, the Son of Man will be ashamed of him when He comes in His glory, and the glory of the Father and of the holy angels. But I say to you truthfully, there are some of those standing here who will not taste death until they see the kingdom of God" (Luke 9:23–27; cf. Matthew 16:24–26, 28; Mark 8:34–37; see Matthew 10:33, 38, 39).

ANGELS, LEGIONS OF (Also see ANGELS)

Setting: The garden of Gethsemane on the Mount of Olives. As Jesus submits to His Father's will and allows Judas to betray Him, Peter attempts to defend Him, but Jesus does not permit it.

Then Jesus said to him, "Put your sword back into its place; for all those who take up the sword shall perish by the sword. Or do you think that I cannot appeal to My Father, and He will at once put at My disposal more than twelve legions of angels? How then will the Scriptures be fulfilled, *which say* that it must happen this way?" (Matthew 26:52–54; cf. Mark 14:47; Luke 22:50, 51; John 18:10, 11; see Matthew 26:24).

ANGELS, SATAN AND HIS (See ANGELS, THE DEVIL AND HIS)

ANGELS, THE DEVIL AND HIS (Also see DEMONS and SATAN)

Setting: The Mount of Olives, just east of Jerusalem. During His discourse, after answering His disciples' questions as to when the temple will be destroyed and Jerusalem overrun, along with the signs of His coming and the end of the age, Jesus reveals the future judgments following His return.

"But when the Son of Man comes in His glory, and all the angels with Him, then He will sit on His glorious throne. All the nations will be gathered before Him; and He will separate them from one another, as the shepherd separates the sheep from the goats; and He will put the sheep on His right, and the goats on the left. Then the King will say to those on His right, 'Come, you who are blessed of My Father, inherit the kingdom prepared for you from the foundation of the world. 'For I was hungry, and you gave Me *something* to eat; I was thirsty, and you gave Me *something* to drink; I was a stranger, and you invited Me in; naked, and you clothed Me; I was sick, and you visited Me; I was in prison, and you came to Me.' Then the righteous will answer Him, 'Lord, when did we see You hungry and feed You, or thirsty, and give you *something* to drink? And when did we see You a stranger, and invite You in, or naked, and clothe You? When did we see You sick, or in prison, and come to You?' The King will answer and say to them, 'Truly I say to you, to the extent that you did it to one of these brothers of Mine, *even* the least *of them,* you did it to Me.' Then He will also say to those on His left, 'Depart from Me, accursed ones, into the eternal fire which has been prepared for the devil and his angels; for I was hungry, and you gave Me *nothing* to eat; I was thirsty, and you gave Me nothing to drink; I was a stranger, and you did not invite Me in; naked, and you did not clothe Me; sick, and in prison, and you did not visit Me.' Then they themselves also will answer, 'Lord, when did we see You hungry, or thirsty, or a stranger, or naked, or sick, or in prison, and did not take care of You?' Then He will answer them, 'Truly I say to you, to the extent that you did not do it to one of the least of these, you did not do it to Me.' These will go away into eternal punishment, but the righteous into eternal life" (Matthew 25:31–46; see Matthew 7:23; 16:27; 19:29).

ANGER (Also see specific emotions such as ENVY; HATE; and JEALOUSY)

[ANGER from angry]

Setting: Galilee. During the early part of His ministry, Jesus preaches the Sermon on the Mount to His disciples and the multitudes.

"But I say to you that everyone who is angry with his brother shall be guilty before the court; and whoever says to his brother, 'You good-for-nothing,' shall be guilty before the supreme court; and whoever says, 'You fool,' shall be guilty *enough to go* into the fiery hell" (Matthew 5:22).

Setting: Capernaum of Galilee. Jesus illustrates forgiveness after Peter asks Him if forgiving someone seven times who has sinned against him is adequate.

"For this reason the kingdom of heaven may be compared to a king who wished to settle accounts with his slaves. When he had begun to settle *them,* one who owed him ten thousand talents was brought to him. But since he did not have *the means* to repay, his lord commanded him to be sold, along with his wife and children and all that he had, and repayment to be made. So the slave fell *to the ground* and prostrated himself before him, saying, 'Have patience with me and I will repay you everything.' And the lord of that slave felt compassion and released him and forgave him the debt. But that slave went out and found one of his fellow slaves who owed him a hundred denarii; and he seized him and *began* to choke *him,* saying, 'Pay back what you owe.' So his fellow slave fell *to the ground* and *began* to plead with him, saying, 'Have patience with me and I will repay you.' But he was unwilling and went and threw him in prison until he should pay back what was owed. So when his fellow slaves saw what had happened, they were deeply grieved and came and reported to their lord all that had happened. Then summoning him, his lord said to him, 'You wicked slave, I forgave you all that debt because you pleaded with me. Should you not also have had mercy on your fellow slave, in the same way that I had mercy on you?' And his lord, moved with anger, handed him over to the torturers until he should repay all that was owed him. My heavenly Father will also do the same to you, if each of you does not forgive his brother from your heart" (Matthew 18:23–35; cf. Matthew 6:12, 14, 15; Luke 7:42; see Matthew 25:19–28).

[ANGER from angry]

Setting: On the way from Galilee to Jerusalem. After He speaks a parable to the invited guests and the host at a banquet, Jesus responds to a guest's proclamation about the blessings of eating bread in the kingdom of God.

But He said to him, "A man was giving a big dinner, and he invited many; and at the dinner hour he sent his slave to say to those who had been invited, 'Come; for everything is ready now.' But they all alike began to make excuses. The first one said to him, 'I have bought a piece of land and I need to go out and look at it; please consider me excused.' Another one said, 'I have bought five yoke of oxen, and I am going to try them out; please consider me excused.' Another one said, I have married a wife, and for that reason I cannot come.' And the slave came back and reported this to his master. Then the head of the household became angry and said to his slave, 'Go out at once into the streets and lanes of the city and bring in here the poor and crippled and blind and lame.' And the slave said, 'Master, what you commanded has been done, and still there is room.' And the master said to the slave, 'Go out into the highways and along the hedges, and compel them to come in, so that my house may be filled. For I tell you, none of those men who were invited shall taste of my dinner'" (Luke 14:16–24; see Deuteronomy 24:5; Matthew 22:2–14).

[ANGER from angry]
Setting: On the way from Galilee to Jerusalem. Jesus conveys the illustration of the prodigal son because the Pharisees and scribes complain He associates with tax collectors and sinners.

And He said, "A man had two sons. The younger of them said to his father, 'Father, give me the share of the estate that falls to me.' So he divided his wealth between them. And not many days later, the younger son gathered everything together and went on a journey into a distant country, and there he squandered his estate with loose living. Now when he had spent everything, a severe famine occurred in that country, and he began to be impoverished. So he went and hired himself out to one of the citizens of that country, and he sent him into his fields to feed swine. And he would have gladly filled his stomach with the pods that the swine were eating, and no one was giving anything to him. But when he came to his senses, he said, 'How many of my father's hired men have more than enough bread, but I am dying here with hunger! I will get up and go to my father, and will say to him, "Father, I have sinned against heaven, and in your sight; I am no longer worthy to be called your son; make me as one of your hired men."' So he got up and came to his father. But while he was still a long way off, his father saw him and felt compassion for him, and ran and embraced him and kissed him. And the son said to him, "Father, I have sinned against heaven and in your sight; I am no longer worthy to be called your son.' But the father said to his slaves, 'Quickly bring out the best robe and put it on him, and put a ring on his hand and sandals on his feet; and bring the fattened calf, kill it, and let us eat and celebrate; for this son of mine was dead and has come to life again; he was lost and has been found.' And they began to celebrate. Now his older son was in the field, when he came and approached the house, he heard music and dancing. And he summoned one of the servants and began inquiring what these things could be. And he said to him, 'Your brother has come, and your father has killed the fattened calf because he has received him back safe and sound.' But he became angry and was not willing to go in; and his father came out and began pleading with him. But he answered and said to his father, 'Look! For so many years I have been serving you and I have never neglected a command of yours; and yet you have never given me a young goat, so that I might celebrate with my friends; but when this son of yours came, who has devoured your wealth with prostitutes, you killed the fattened calf for him.' And he said to him, 'Son, you have always been with me, and all that is mine is yours. But we had to celebrate and rejoice, for this brother of yours was dead and has begun to live, and was lost and has been found'" (Luke 15:11–32; see Proverbs 29:2; Luke 15:1, 2).

[ANGER from angry]
Setting: The temple in Jerusalem. After receiving encouragement from His blood brothers in Galilee to attend the upcoming Feast of Booths in order to demonstrate His works to His disciples and the world, Jesus goes and teaches, astonishing the Jewish religious leaders.

Jesus answered them, "I did one deed, and you all marvel. For this reason Moses has given you circumcision (not because it is from Moses, but from the fathers), and on *the* Sabbath you circumcise a man. If a man receives circumcision on *the* Sabbath so that the Law of Moses will not be broken, are you angry with Me because I made an entire man well on *the* Sabbath? Do not judge according to appearance, but judge with righteous judgment" (John 7:21–24; see Genesis 17:10–14; Leviticus 12:3; 19:15; Matthew 12:2; John 5:2–16; 7–20; 7:10–15).

ANGUISH (Also see ANXIETY; DESPAIR; FEAR; SADNESS; and WORRY)
Setting: Jerusalem. Before the Passover, after warning His disciples of the persecution they will face after His departure to heaven, empathizing with their sadness over His prophecies, Jesus gives them hope for the future.

"A little while, and you will no longer see Me; and again a little while, and you will see Me." *Some* of His disciples then said to one another, "What is this thing He is telling us, 'A little while, and you will not see Me; and again a little while, and you will see Me'; and, 'because I go to the Father'?" So they were saying, "What is this that He says, 'A little while'? We do not know what He is talking about." Jesus knew that they wished to question Him, and He said to them, "Are you deliberating together about this, that I said, 'A little while, and you will not see Me, and again a little while, and you will see Me'? Truly, truly, I say to you, that you will weep and lament, but the world will rejoice; you will grieve, but your grief will be turned into joy. Whenever a woman is in labor she has pain, because her hour has come; but when she gives birth to the child, she no longer remembers the anguish because of the joy that a child has been born into the world. Therefore you too have grief now; but I will see you again, and your heart will rejoice, and no one *will* take your joy away from you" (John 16:16–22; see Mark 9:32; Luke 23:27; John 14:18–24; 16:5, 6; 20:20).

ANNAS (See HIGH PRIEST)

ANOTHER, ONE (See ONE ANOTHER)

ANOTHER'S

Setting. On the way from Galilee to Jerusalem. After telling the Parable of the Prodigal Son, the Lord teaches His disciples about stewardship.

Now He was also saying to the disciples, "There was a rich man who had a manager, and this manager was reported to him as squandering his possessions. And he called him and said to him, 'What is this I hear about you? Give an accounting of your management, for you can no longer be a manager.' The manager said to himself, 'What shall I do, since my master is taking the management away from me? I am not strong enough to dig; I am ashamed to beg. I know what I shall do, so that when I am removed from the management people will welcome me into their homes.' And he summoned each one of his master's debtors, and he began saying to the first, 'How much do you owe my master?' And he said, 'A hundred measures of oil.' And he said to him, 'Take your bill, and sit down quickly and write fifty.' Then he said to another, 'And how much do you owe?' And he said, 'A hundred measures of wheat.' He said to him, 'Take your bill, and write eighty.' And his master praised the unrighteous manager because he had acted shrewdly; for the sons of this age are more shrewd in relation to their own kind than the sons of light. And I say to you, make friends for yourselves by means of the wealth of unrighteousness, so that when it fails, they will receive you into the eternal dwellings. He who is faithful in a very little thing is faithful also in much; and he who is unrighteous in a very little thing is unrighteous also in much. Therefore if you have not been faithful in the use of unrighteous wealth, who will entrust the true riches to you? And if you have not been faithful in the use of that which is another's, who will give you that which is your own? No servant can serve two masters; for either he will hate the one and love the other, or else he will be devoted to one and despise the other. You cannot serve God and wealth" (Luke 16:1–13; cf. Matthew 6:24; see Matthew 25:14–30).

Setting: Jerusalem. Before the Passover, with His death on the cross nearing, Jesus explains the reason for His vivid example of servanthood in washing His disciples' feet.

So when He had washed their feet, and taken His garments and reclined *at the table* again, He said to them, "Do you know what I have done to you? You call Me Teacher and Lord; and you are right, for *so* I am. If I then, the Lord and the Teacher, washed your feet, you also ought to wash one another's feet. For I gave you an example that you also should do as I did to you. Truly, truly I say to you, a slave is not greater than his master, nor *is* one who is sent greater than the one who sent him. If you know these things, you are blessed if you do them. I do not speak of all of you. I know the ones I have chosen; but *it is* that the Scripture may be fulfilled, 'HE WHO EATS MY BREAD HAS LIFTED UP HIS HEEL AGAINST ME.' From now on I am telling you before *it* comes to pass, so that when it does occur, you may believe that I am *He. Truly,* truly, I say to you, he who receives whomever I send receives Me; and he who receives Me receives Him who sent Me" (John 13:12–20; Jesus quotes from Psalm 41:9; see Matthew 7:24; 10:24, 40; John 8:24; 14:29; 1 Peter 5:3).

ANSWER

[ANSWER from answered]

Setting: Judea beyond the Jordan (Perea). Jesus illustrates the kingdom of heaven to His disciples through the story of laborers in the vineyard.

"For the kingdom of heaven is like a landowner who went out early in the morning to hire laborers for his vineyard. When he had agreed with the laborers for a denarius for the day, he sent them into his vineyard. And he went out about the third hour and saw others standing idle in the market place; and to those he said, 'You also go into the vineyard, and whatever is right I will give you.' And *so* they went. Again he went out about the sixth and the ninth hour, and did the same thing. And about the eleventh *hour* he went out and found others standing *around;* and he said to them, 'Why have you been standing idle here all day long?' They said to him, 'Because no one hired us.' He said to them, 'You go into the vineyard too.' When evening came, the owner of the vineyard said to his foreman, 'Call the laborers and pay them their wages, beginning with the last *group* to the first.' When those *hired* about the eleventh hour came, each one received a denarius. When those *hired* first came, they thought that they would receive more; but each of them also received a denarius. When they received it, they grumbled at the landowner, saying, 'These last men have worked *only* one hour, and you have made them equal to us who have borne the burden and the scorching heat of the day.' But he answered and said to one of them, 'Friend, I am doing you no wrong; did you not agree with me for a denarius? Take what is yours and go, but I wish to give to this last man the same as to you. It is not lawful for me to do what I wish with what is my own? Or is your eye envious because I am generous?' So the last shall be first, and the first last" (Matthew 20:1–16; cf. Matthew 19:30).

[ANSWER from answered]
Setting: The temple in Jerusalem. Jesus delivers a parable to the chief priests and elders after they question His authority.

"But what do you think? A man had two sons, and he came to the first and said, 'Son, go work today in the vineyard.' And he answered, 'I will not'; but afterward he regretted it and went. The man came to the second and said the same thing; and he answered, 'I *will,* sir'; but he did not go. Which of the two sons did the will of his father?" They said, "The first." Jesus said to them, "Truly, I say to you that the tax collectors and prostitutes will get into the kingdom of God before you. For John came to you in the way of righteousness and you did not believe him; but the tax collectors and prostitutes did believe him; and you, seeing *this,* did not even feel remorse afterward so as to believe him" (Matthew 21:28–32; cf. Luke 7:29, 30, 37–50).

[ANSWER from answered]
Setting: The Mount of Olives, just east of Jerusalem. During His discourse, after answering His disciples' questions as to when the temple will be destroyed and Jerusalem overrun, along with the signs of His coming and the end of the age, Jesus reemphasizes to His disciples that they should be on the alert for His return.

"Then the kingdom of heaven will be comparable to ten virgins, who took their lamps and went out to meet the bridegroom. Five of them were foolish, and five were prudent. For when the foolish took their lamps, they took no oil with them, but the prudent took oil in flasks along with their lamps. Now while the bridegroom was delaying, they all got drowsy and *began* to sleep. But at midnight there was a shout, 'Behold, the bridegroom! Come out to meet *him.*' Then all those virgins rose and trimmed their lamps. The foolish said to the prudent, 'Give us some of your oil, for our lamps are going out.' But the prudent answered, 'No, there will not be enough for us and you *too;* go instead to the dealers and buy *some* for yourselves.' And while they were going away to make the purchase, the bridegroom came, and those who were ready went in with him to the wedding feast; and the door was shut. Later the other virgins also came, saying, 'Lord, lord, open up for us.' But he answered, 'Truly I say to you, I do not know you.' Be on the alert then, for you do not know the day nor the hour" (Matthew 25:1–13; cf. Matthew 24:42; Luke 12:35; see Matthew 7:21, 24).

[ANSWER from answered]
Setting: The Mount of Olives, just east of Jerusalem. During His discourse, after answering His disciples' questions as to when the temple will be destroyed and Jerusalem overrun, along with the signs of His coming and the end of the age, Jesus reemphasizes to His disciples that they should be on the alert for His return.

"For *it is* just like a man *about* to go on a journey, who called his own slaves and entrusted his possessions to them. To one he gave five talents, to another, two, and to another, one, each according to his own ability; and he went on his journey. Immediately the one who had received the five talents went and traded with them, and gained five more talents. In the same manner the one who *had received* the two *talents* gained two more. But he who received the one *talent* went away, and dug a *hole* in the ground and hid his master's money. Now after a long time the master of those slaves came and settled accounts with them. The one who had received the five talents came up and brought five more talents, saying, 'Master, you entrusted five talents to me. See, I have gained five more talents.' His master said to him, 'Well done, good and faithful slave. You were faithful with a few things, I will put you in charge of many things; enter into the joy of your master.' Also the one who *had received* the two talents came up and said, 'Master, you entrusted two talents to me. See, I have gained two more talents.' His master said to him, 'Well done, good and faithful slave. You were faithful with a few things, I will put you in charge of many things; enter into the joy of your master.' And the one also who had received the one talent came up and said, 'Master, I knew you to be a hard man, reaping where you did not sow and gathering where you scattered no *seed*. And I was afraid, and went away and hid your talent in the ground. See, you have what is yours.' But his master answered and said to him, 'You wicked, lazy slave, you knew that I reap where I did not sow and gather where I scattered no *seed*. Then you ought to have put my money in the bank, and on my arrival I would have received my *money* back with interest. 'Therefore take away the talent from him, and give it to the one who has ten talents.' For to everyone who has, *more* shall be given, and he will have an abundance; but from the one who does not have, even what he does have shall be taken away. Throw out the worthless slave into the outer darkness; in that place there will be weeping and gnashing of teeth" (Matthew 25:14–30; cf. Matthew 8:12; 13:12; 24:45–47; see Matthew 18:23, 24; Luke 12:44).

Setting: The Mount of Olives, just east of Jerusalem. During His discourse, after answering His disciples' questions as to when the temple will be destroyed and Jerusalem overrun, along with the signs of His coming and the end of the age, Jesus reveals the future judgments following His return.

"But when the Son of Man comes in His glory, and all the angels with Him, then He will sit on His glorious throne. All the nations will be gathered before Him; and He will separate them from one another, as the shepherd separates the sheep from the goats; and He will put the sheep on His right, and the goats on the left. Then the King will say to those on His right, 'Come, you who are blessed of My Father, inherit the kingdom prepared for you from the foundation of the world. 'For I was hungry, and you gave Me *something* to eat; I was thirsty, and you gave Me *something* to drink; I was a stranger, and you invited Me in; naked, and you clothed Me; I was sick, and you visited Me; I was in prison, and you came to Me.' Then the righteous will answer Him, 'Lord, when did we see You hungry and feed You, or thirsty, and give you *something* to drink? And when did we see You a stranger, and invite You in, or naked, and clothe You? When did we see You sick, or in prison, and come to You?' The King will answer and say to them, 'Truly I say to you, to the extent that you did it to one of these brothers of Mine, *even* the least *of them*, you did it to Me.' Then He will also say to those on His left, 'Depart from Me, accursed ones, into the eternal fire which has been prepared for the devil and his angels; for I was hungry, and you gave Me *nothing* to eat; I was thirsty, and you gave Me nothing to drink; I was a stranger, and you did not invite Me in; naked, and you did not clothe Me; sick, and in prison, and you did not visit Me.' Then they themselves also will answer, 'Lord, when did we see You hungry, or thirsty, or a stranger, or naked, or sick, or in prison, and did not take care of You?' Then He will answer them, 'Truly I say to you, to the extent that you did not do it to one of the least of these, you did not do it to Me.' These will go away into eternal punishment, but the righteous into eternal life" (Matthew 25:31–46; see Matthew 7:23; 16:27; 19:29).

Setting: The region of Tyre. After the Pharisees and scribes from Jerusalem question Jesus' disciples' lack of obedience to the tradition regarding ceremonial cleansing, Jesus casts out a demon from the daughter of a Gentile woman (Syrophoenician).

And He was saying to her, "Let the children be satisfied first, for it is not good to take the children's bread and throw it to the dogs." But she answered and said to Him, "Yes, Lord *but* even the dogs under the table feed on the children's crumbs. And He said to her, "Because of this answer go; the demon has gone out of your daughter" (Mark 7:27–29; cf. Matthew 15:21–28).

Setting: The temple in Jerusalem. After Jesus teaches about faith and forgiveness, utilizing the cursed fig tree as an object lesion, His authority is questioned by the chief priests, scribes, and elders.

And Jesus said to them, "I will ask you one question, and you answer Me, and *then* I will tell you by what authority I do these things. Was the baptism of John from heaven, or from men? Answer Me." They *began* reasoning among themselves, saying, "If we say 'From heaven,' He will say, 'Then why did you not believe him?' "But shall we say 'From men'?"—they were afraid of the people, for everyone considered John to have been a real prophet. Answering Jesus, they said, "We do not know." And Jesus said to them, "Nor will I tell you by what authority I do these things" (Mark 11:29–33; cf. Matthew 21:23–27; Luke 20:1–8).

[ANSWER from answered]
Setting: On the way from Galilee to Jerusalem. After Jesus tells His disciples in private the privilege they have of living in the time of the Messiah, a lawyer tests Him.

And a lawyer stood up and put Him to the test, saying, "Teacher, what shall I do to inherit eternal life?" And He said to him, "What is written in the Law? How does it read to you?" And he answered, "YOU SHALL LOVE THE LORD YOUR GOD WITH ALL YOUR

HEART, AND WITH ALL YOUR SOUL, AND WITH ALL YOUR STRENGTH, AND WITH ALL YOUR MIND; AND YOUR NEIGHBOR AS YOURSELF." And He said to him, "You have answered correctly; DO THIS AND YOU WILL LIVE" (Luke 10:25–28, Jesus quotes from Leviticus 18:5; see Deuteronomy 6:5; Matthew 19:16–19).

Setting: On the way from Galilee to Jerusalem. After revealing to His disciples how to pray, Jesus illustrates persistence in prayer.

Then He said to them, "Suppose one of you has a friend, and goes to him at midnight and says to him, 'Friend, lend me three loaves; for a friend of mine has come to me from a journey, and I have nothing to set before him'; and from inside he answers and says, 'Do not bother me; the door has already been shut and my children and I are in bed; I cannot get up and give you anything.' I tell you, even though he will not get up and give him anything because he is his friend, yet because of his persistence he will get up and give him as much as he needs. So I say to you, ask, and it will be given to you; seek, and you will find; knock, and it will be opened to you. For everyone who asks, receives; and he who seeks, finds; and to him who knocks, it will be opened" (Luke 11:5–10; cf. Matthew 7:7, 8; see Luke 18:1–5).

[ANSWER from answered]
Setting: On the way from Galilee to Jerusalem. After some present report to Him about the Galileans whose blood Pilate (Roman governor of Judea) had mixed with their sacrifices, Jesus responds to their concern by calling them to repentance and illustrating His point with a parable.

And He began telling this parable: "A man had a fig tree which had been planted in his vineyard; and he came looking for fruit on it and did not find any. And he said to the vineyard-keeper, 'Behold, for three years I have come looking for fruit on this fig tree without finding any. Cut it down! Why does it even use up the ground?' And he answered and said to him, 'Let it alone, sir, for this year too, until I dig around it and put fertilizer; and if it bears fruit next year, fine; but if not, cut it down'"(Luke 13:6–9; see Matthew 3:10).

Setting: On the way from Galilee to Jerusalem. While teaching in the cities and villages, Jesus responds to a question about who is saved.

And someone said to Him, "Lord, are here *just* a few who are being saved?" And He said to them, "Strive to enter through the narrow door; for many, I tell you, will seek to enter and will not be able. Once the head of the house gets up and shuts the door, and you begin to stand outside and knock on the door, saying, 'Lord, open up to us!' then He will answer and say to you, 'I do not know where you are from.' Then you will begin to say, 'We ate and drank in Your presence, and You taught in our streets'; and He will say, 'I tell you, I do not know where you are from; DEPART FROM ME, ALL YOU EVILDOERS.' In that place there will be weeping and gnashing of teeth when you see Abraham and Isaac and Jacob and all the prophets in the kingdom of God, but you yourselves being thrown out. And they will come from east and west and from north and south, and will recline *at the table* in the kingdom of God. And behold, *some* are last who will be first and *some* are first who will be last" (Luke 13:23–30, Jesus quotes from Psalm 6:8; cf. Matthew 7:13, 23; 8:11, 12; see Matthew 19:30; Luke 3:8).

[ANSWER from answered]
Setting: On the way from Galilee to Jerusalem. Jesus conveys the illustration of the prodigal son because the Pharisees and scribes complain He associates with tax collectors and sinners.

And He said, "A man had two sons. The younger of them said to his father, 'Father, give me the share of the estate that falls to me.' So he divided his wealth between them. And not many days later, the younger son gathered everything together and went on a journey into a distant country, and there he squandered his estate with loose living. Now when he had spent everything, a severe famine occurred in that country, and he began to be impoverished. So he went and hired himself out to one of the citizens of that country, and he sent him into his fields to feed swine. And he would have gladly filled his stomach with the pods that the swine were eating, and no one was giving anything to him. But when he came to his senses, he said, 'How many of my father's hired men have more than enough bread, but I am dying here with hunger! I will get up and go to my father, and will say to him, "Father, I have sinned against heaven, and in your sight; I am no longer worthy to be called your son; make me as one of your hired men."' So he got up and came to his father. But while he was still a long way off, his father saw him and felt compassion for him, and ran and embraced him and kissed him. And the son said to him, "Father, I have sinned against heaven and in your sight; I am no longer worthy to be called your son.' But the father said to his slaves, 'Quickly bring out the best robe and put it on him, and put a ring on his hand and sandals on his feet; and bring the fattened calf, kill it, and let us eat and celebrate; for this son of mine was dead and has come to life again; he was lost and has been found.' And they began to celebrate. Now his older son was in the field, when he came and approached the house, he heard music and dancing. And he summoned one of the servants and began inquiring what these things could be. And he said to him, 'Your brother has come, and your father has killed the fattened calf because he has received him back safe and sound.' But he became angry and was not willing to go in; and his father came out and began pleading with him. But he answered and said to his father, 'Look! For so many years I have been serving you and I have never neglected a command of yours; and yet you have never given me a young goat, so that I might celebrate with my friends; but when this son of yours came, who has devoured your wealth with prostitutes, you killed the fattened calf for him.' And he said to him, 'Son, you have always been with me, and all that is mine is yours. But we had to celebrate and rejoice, for this brother of yours was dead and has begun to live, and was lost and has been found'" (Luke 15:11–32; see Proverbs 29:2; Luke 15:1, 2).

Setting: Jerusalem. After being arrested, denied by Peter, and mocked and beaten, with His crucifixion imminent, Jesus appears before the Sanhedrin.

"If You are the Christ, tell us." But He said to them, "If I tell you, you will not believe; and if I ask you a question, you will not answer. But from now on THE SON OF MAN WILL BE SEATED AT THE RIGHT HAND of the power OF GOD." And they all said, "Are You the Son of God, then? And He said to them, "Yes, I am" (Luke 22:67–70, Jesus quotes from Psalm 110:1; cf. Matthew 26:57–65; Mark 14:55–65).

ANTICHRIST (See ABOMINATION OF DESOLATION)

ANTIPAS, DAYS OF

Setting: On the island of Patmos (in the Aegean Sea about fifty miles southwest of Ephesus in modern Turkey). On the Lord's Day (Sunday), about fifty years after Jesus' resurrection, the disciple John encounters the Lord Jesus Christ, who communicates a new revelation for the apostle to record for the church in Pergamum and to six other churches in Asia.

"And to the angel of the church in Pergamum write: The One who has the sharp two-edged sword says this: 'I know where you dwell, where Satan's throne is; and you hold fast My name, and did not deny My faith even in the days of Antipas, My witness, My faithful one, who was killed among you, where Satan dwells. But I have a few things against you, because you have there some who hold the teaching of Balaam, who kept teaching Balak to put a stumbling block before the sons of Israel, to eat things sacrificed to idols and to commit *acts of* immorality. So you also have some who in the same way hold the teaching of the Nicolaitans. Therefore repent; or else I am coming to you quickly, and I will make war against them with the sword of My mouth. He who has an ear, let him hear what the Spirit says to the churches. To him who overcomes, to him I will give *some* of the hidden manna, and I will give him a white stone, and a new name written on the stone which no one knows but he who receives it' (Revelation 2:12–17; see Numbers 25:1–3; Isaiah 62:2; Revelation 1:16; 2:5, 6, 16).

ANTIPAS, HEROD (See HEROD)

ANXIETY (Also see ANGUISH; DESPAIR; FEAR; GRIEF; and WORRY)

[ANXIETY from My soul is deeply grieved]

Setting: Jerusalem. After celebrating the Passover meal with His disciples, Jesus retreats to the Garden of Gethsemane on the Mount of Olives to pray prior to His betrayal by Judas.

Then Jesus came with them to a place called Gethsemane, and said to His disciples, "Sit here while I go over there and pray." And

He took with Him Peter and the two sons of Zebedee, and began to be grieved and distressed. Then He said to them, "My soul is deeply grieved, to the point of death; remain here and keep watch with Me." And He went a little beyond *them,* and fell on His face and prayed, saying, "My Father, if it is possible, let this cup pass from Me; yet not as I will, but as You will." And He came to the disciples and found them sleeping, and said to Peter, "So, you *men* could not keep watch with Me for one hour? Keep watching and praying that you may not enter into temptation; the spirit is willing, but the flesh is weak." He went away again a second time and prayed, saying, "My Father, if this cannot pass away unless I drink it, Your will be done." Again He came and found them sleeping, for their eyes were heavy. And He left them again, and went away and prayed a third time, saying the same thing once more. Then He came to the disciples and said to them, "Are you still sleeping and resting? Behold the hour is at hand and the Son of Man is being betrayed into the hands of sinners. Get up, let us be going; behold the one who betrays Me is at hand!" (Matthew 26:36–46; cf. Mark 14:32–42; Luke 22:40–46; see Matthew 20:22; John 12:27).

[ANXIETY from my soul is deeply grieved]
Setting: Gethsemane on the Mount of Olives, east of the temple in Jerusalem. Jesus agonizes over His impending death, amazed that His disciples keep falling asleep instead of watching and praying with Him.

They came to a place named Gethsemane; and He said to the disciples, "Sit here until I have prayed." And He took with Him Peter and James and John, and began to be very distressed and troubled. And He said to them, "My soul is deeply grieved to the point of death; remain here and keep watch." And He went a little beyond *them,* and fell to the ground and *began* to pray that if it were possible, the hour might pass Him by. And He was saying, "Abba! Father! All things are possible for You; remove this cup from Me; yet not what I will, but what You will." And He came and found them sleeping, and said to Peter, "Simon, are you asleep? Could you not keep watch for one hour? Keep watching and praying that you may not come into temptation; the spirit is willing, but the flesh is weak" (Mark 14:32–38; cf. Matthew 26:36–41; Luke 22:41–46; see Romans 8:15; Galatians 4:6).

[ANXIETY from how distressed I am]
Setting: On the way from Galilee to Jerusalem. After clarifying a parable for Peter and the crowd, Jesus conveys how a relationship with Him divides families.

"I have come to cast fire upon the earth; and how I wish it were already kindled! But I have a baptism to undergo, and how distressed I am until it is accomplished! Do you suppose that I came to grant peace on earth? I tell you, no, but rather division; for from now on five members in one household will be divided, three against two and two against three. They will be divided, father against son and son against father, mother against daughter, and daughter against mother, mother-in-law against daughter-in-law and daughter-in-law against mother-in-law" (Luke 12:49–53; cf. Matthew 10:34–36; see Micah 7:6; Mark 10:38).

[ANXIETY from become troubled]
Setting: Jerusalem. Just days before the Passover, with the chief priests and Pharisees plotting to seize Him, and crowds welcoming Him with palm branches and praise, Jesus expresses anxiety about His upcoming death by crucifixion.

"Now My soul has become troubled; and what shall I say, 'Father, save Me from this hour'? But for this purpose I came to this hour. Father glorify Your name." Then a voice came out of heaven: "I have glorified it, and will glorify it again." So the crowd *of people* who stood by and heard it were saying that it had thundered; others were saying, "An angel has spoken to Him." Jesus answered and said, "This voice has not come for My sake, but for your sakes. Now judgment is upon this world; now the ruler of this world will be cast out. And I, if I am lifted up from the earth, will draw all men to Myself" (John 12:27–32; see Matthew 3:17; 26:38; John 3:14; 6:44; 11:42; 14:30).

[ANXIETY from be troubled]
Setting: Jerusalem. Before the Passover, after taking issue with Peter's assertion that he would lay down his life for Him, Jesus comforts and gives hope to His disciples regarding their future after His return to heaven.

"Do not let your heart be troubled; believe in God, believe also in Me. In My Father's house are many dwelling places; if it were not so, I would have told you; for I go to prepare a place for you. If I go and prepare a place for you, I will come again and receive you to Myself, that where I am, there you may be also. And you know the way where I am going" (John 14:1–4; see John 13:35; 14:27, 28).

[ANXIETY from be troubled]
Setting: Jerusalem. Before the Passover, after Jesus conveys the upcoming ministry of the Holy Spirit in His disciples' lives, He again relates peace, hope, and comfort to them regarding His return to the Father.

"Peace I leave with you; My peace I give to you; not as the world gives do I give to you. Do not let your heart be troubled, nor let it be fearful. You heard that I said to you, 'I go away, and I will come to you,' If you loved Me, you would have rejoiced because I go to the Father, for the Father is greater than I. Now I have told you before it happens, so that when it happens, you may believe. I will not speak much more with you, for the ruler of the world is coming, and he has nothing in Me; but so that the world may know that I love the Father, I do exactly as the Father commanded Me. Get up, let us go from here" (John 14:27–31; see John 10:18, 29; 12:31; 13:19; 16:33).

ANYONE

Setting: Galilee. During the early part of His ministry, Jesus preaches the Sermon on the Mount to His disciples and the multitudes.

"You are the light of the world. A city set on a hill cannot be hidden; nor does *anyone* light a lamp and put it under a basket, but on the lampstand, and it gives light to all who are in the house. Let your light shine before men in such a way that they may see your good works, and glorify your Father who is in heaven" (Matthew 5:14–16; cf. Mark 4:21; 1 Peter 2:12).

Setting: Galilee. During the early part of His ministry, Jesus preaches the Sermon on the Mount to His disciples and the multitudes.

"If anyone wants to sue you and take your shirt, let him have your coat also" (Matthew 5:40).

Setting: Entering Capernaum. After the Lord gives the Sermon on the Mount and cleanses a leper, a Roman centurion implores Jesus to heal his servant.

Now when Jesus heard *this,* He marveled, and said to those who were following, "Truly I say to you, I have not found such great faith with anyone in Israel. I say to you that many will come from east and west, and recline *at the table* with Abraham, Isaac and Jacob in the kingdom of heaven; but the sons of the kingdom will be cast out into the outer darkness; in that place there will be weeping and gnashing of teeth." And Jesus said to the centurion, "Go; it shall be done for you as you have believed." And the servant was healed that *very* moment (Matthew 8:10–13; cf. Luke 7:9, 10).

Setting: Galilee. While speaking to the crowds, Jesus pays tribute to the ministry of John the Baptist, but emphasizes that the one who is least in the kingdom of heaven is greater than John.

As these men were going *away,* Jesus began to speak to the crowds about John, "What did you go out into the wilderness to see? A reed shaken by the wind? But what did you go out to see? A man dressed in soft *clothing?* Those who wear soft *clothing* are in kings' palaces! But what did you go out to see? A prophet? Yes, I tell you, and the one who is more than a prophet. This is the one about whom it is written, 'BEHOLD, I SEND MY MESSENGER AHEAD OF YOU, WHO WILL PREPARE YOUR WAY BEFORE YOU.' Truly, I say to you, among those born of women there has not arisen *anyone* greater than John the Baptist! Yet the one who is least in the kingdom of heaven is greater than he. From the days of John the Baptist until now the kingdom of heaven suffers violence, and violent men take it by force. For all the prophets and the Law prophesied until John. And, if you are willing to accept *it,* John himself is Elijah who was to come. He who has ears to hear, let him hear" (Matthew 11:7–15, Jesus quotes from Malachi 3:1; cf. Malachi 4:5; Luke 7:24–28; 16:16; see Matthew 14:5).

Setting: Galilee. After pronouncing woes against unrepentant cities as He teaches and preaches, Jesus prays a thanksgiving prayer to His Father in heaven.

At that time Jesus said, "I praise You, Father, Lord of heaven and earth, that you have hidden these things from *the* wise and intelligent and have revealed them to infants. Yes, Father, for this way was well-pleasing in Your sight. All things have been handed over to Me by My Father; and no one knows the Son except the Father; nor does anyone know the Father except the Son, and anyone to whom the Son wills to reveal *Him*" (Matthew 11:25–27; cf. Luke 10:21, 22).

Setting: Galilee. After Jesus heals a blind, mute, demon-possessed man, the Pharisees accuse Him in front of crowds of being a worker of Satan.

And knowing their thoughts Jesus said to them, "Any kingdom divided against itself is laid waste; and any city or house divided against itself will not stand. If Satan casts out Satan, he is divided against himself; how then will his kingdom stand? If I by Beelzebul cast out demons, by whom do your sons cast *them* out? For this reason they will be your judges. But if I cast out demons by the Spirit of God, then the kingdom of God has come upon you. Or how can anyone enter the strong man's house and carry off his property, unless he first binds the strong *man?* And then he will plunder his house" (Matthew 12:25–29; cf. Matthew 9:34; Mark 3:23–27; Luke 11:17–20).

Setting: By the Sea of Galilee. With the religious leadership rejecting His message, Jesus begins to teach in parables and explains the meaning of the Parable of the Sower to His disciples.

"Hear then the parable of the sower. When anyone hears the word of the kingdom and does not understand it, the evil *one* comes and snatches away what has been sown in his heart. This is the one on whom seed was sown beside the road. The one on whom seed was sown on the rocky places, this is the man who hears the word and immediately receives it with joy; yet he has no *firm* root in himself, but is *only* temporary, and when affliction or persecution arises because of the word, immediately he falls away. And the one on whom seed was sown among the thorns, this is the man who hears the word, and the worry of the world and the deceitfulness of wealth choke the word, and it becomes unfruitful. And the one on whom seed was sown on the good soil, this is the man who hears the word and understands it; who indeed bears fruit and brings forth, some a hundredfold, some sixty, and some thirty" (Matthew 13:18–23; cf. Mark 4:13–20; Luke 8:11–15; see Matthew 13:8).

Setting: Near Caesarea Philippi. After rebuking Peter for trying to forbid Him to accomplish His earthly mission of dying and being resurrected, Jesus teaches His disciples about the costs of discipleship.

Then Jesus said to His disciples, "If anyone wishes to come after Me, he must deny himself, and take up his cross and follow Me. For whoever wishes to save his life will lose it; but whoever loses his life for My sake will find it. For what will it profit a man if he gains the whole world and forfeits his soul? Or what will a man give in exchange for his soul? For the Son of Man is going to come in the glory of His Father with His angels, and WILL THEN REPAY EVERY MAN ACCORDING TO HIS DEEDS. Truly, I say to you, there are some of you who are standing here who will not taste death until they see the Son of Man coming in His kingdom" (Matthew 16:24–28, Jesus quotes from Psalm 62:12; cf. Mark 8:34–37; Luke 9:23–27; see Matthew 10:38, 39).

Setting: Bethphage, on the way to Jerusalem for Jesus' crucifixion. After healing some blind men in Jericho, Jesus instructs two disciples to acquire a donkey and colt to be used in His triumphal entry into the city.

When they had approached Jerusalem and had come to Bethphage, at the Mount of Olives, then Jesus sent two disciples, saying to them, "Go into the village opposite you, and immediately you will find a donkey tied *there* and a colt with her; untie them and bring them to Me. If anyone says anything to you, you shall say, 'The Lord has need of them,' and immediately he will send them" (Matthew 21:1–3; cf. Mark 11:1–3; Luke 19:29–31).

Setting: The temple in Jerusalem. Jesus exposes the truth about Pharisaism to the crowds and His disciples after the Jewish religious leaders test Him with questions.

Then Jesus spoke to the crowds and to His disciples, saying: "The scribes and the Pharisees have seated themselves in the chair of Moses; therefore all that they tell you, do and observe, but do not do according to their deeds; for they say *things* and do not do *them.* They tie up heavy burdens and lay them on men's shoulders, but they themselves are unwilling to move them with *so much as* a finger. But they do all their deeds to be noticed by men; for they broaden their phylacteries and lengthen their tassels *of their garments.* They love the place of honor at banquets and the chief seats in the synagogues, and respectful greetings in the market places, and being called Rabbi by men. But do not be called Rabbi; for One is your Teacher, and you are all brothers. Do not call *anyone* on earth your father; for One is your Father, He who is in heaven. Do not be called leaders; for One is your Leader, *that is,* Christ. But the greatest among you shall be your servant. Whoever exalts himself shall be humbled; and whoever humbles himself shall be exalted" (Matthew 23:1–12; cf. Matthew 20:26; Mark 12:38–40; Luke 20:46, 47; see Exodus 13:9; Deuteronomy 33:3; Matthew 6:1, 5, 6, 9, 16; Mark 14:11; Luke 11:43; 14:11).

Setting: The Mount of Olives, just east of Jerusalem. During His discourse, Jesus answers His disciples' questions as to when the temple will be destroyed and Jerusalem overrun, along with the signs of His coming and the end of the age.

"Therefore when you see the ABOMINATION OF DESOLATION which was spoken of through Daniel the prophet, standing in the holy place (let the reader understand), then those who are in Judea must flee to the mountains. Whoever is on the housetop must not go down to get the things that are in his house. Whoever is in the field must not turn back to get his cloak. But woe to those who are pregnant and to those who are nursing babies in those days! But pray that your flight will not be in the winter, or on a Sabbath. For then there will be a great tribulation, such as has not occurred since the beginning of the world until now, nor ever will. Unless those days had been cut short, no life would have been saved; but for the sake of the elect those days will be cut short. Then if anyone says to you, 'Behold, here is the Christ,' or "There *He is,*' do not believe *him.* For false Christs and false prophets will arise and will show great signs and wonders, so as to mislead, if possible, even the elect. Behold, I have told you in advance. So if they say to you, 'Behold, He is in the wilderness,' do not go out, *or,* 'Behold, He is in the inner rooms,' do not believe *them.* For just as the lightning comes from the east and flashes even to the west, so will the coming of the Son of Man be. Wherever the corpse is, there the vultures will gather" (Matthew 24:15–28, Jesus quotes from Daniel 9:27; cf. Daniel 12:1; Mark 13:14–23; Luke 17:22–31; 21:20–24; 23:29; see John 4:48).

Setting: A synagogue in Galilee. As Jesus preaches and casts out demons, a leper beseeches Him for healing.

Moved with compassion, Jesus stretched out His hand and touched him, and said to him, "I am willing; be cleansed." Immediately the leprosy left him and he was cleansed. And He sternly warned him and immediately sent him away, and He said to him, "See that you say nothing to anyone; but go, show yourself to the priest and offer for your cleansing what Moses commanded, as a testimony to them" (Mark 1:41–44; cf. Luke 5:12–14; see Leviticus 14:1–32; Matthew 8:3).

Setting: Galilee. Early in His ministry, the Pharisees ask Jesus why He allows His disciples to harvest and eat grain on the Sabbath.

And He said to them, "Have you never read what David did when he was in need and he and his companions became hungry; how he entered the house of God in the time of Abiathar *the* high priest, and ate the consecrated bread, which is not lawful for *anyone* to eat except the priests, and he also gave it to those who were with him?" Jesus said to them, "The Sabbath was made for man, and not man for the Sabbath. So the Son of Man is Lord even of the Sabbath" (Mark 2:25–28; cf. Matthew 12:1–8; Luke 6:1–5; see Exodus 23:12).

Setting: Galilee. Following His explanation of the Parable of the Sower to His disciples, Jesus illustrates what they should do with this truth.

And He was saying to them, "A lamp is not brought to be put under a basket, is it, or under a bed? Is it not *brought* to be put on the lampstand? For nothing is hidden, except to be revealed; nor has *anything* been secret, but that it would come to light. If anyone has ears to hear, let him hear" (Mark 4:21–23; cf. Luke 8:16, 17; see Matthew 5:14–16; Matthew 10:26).

Setting: Galilee. After the Pharisees and scribes from Jerusalem question Jesus' disciples' lack of obedience to the tradition of ceremonial cleansing, Jesus speaks to a crowd and explains His teaching to His disciples.

After He called the crowd to Him again, He *began* saying to them, "Listen to Me, all of you, and understand: there is nothing outside the man which can defile him if it goes into him; but the things which proceed out of the man are what defile the man. [If anyone has ears to hear, let him hear."] When he had left the crowd *and* entered the house, His disciples questioned Him about the parable. And He said to them, "Are you so lacking in understanding also? Do you not understand that whatever goes into the man from outside cannot defile him, because it does not go into his heart, but into his stomach, and is eliminated?" (*Thus He* declared all foods clean.) And He was saying, "That which proceeds out of the man, that is what defiles the man. For from within, out of the heart of men, proceed the evil thoughts, fornications, thefts, murders, adulteries, deeds of coveting *and* wickedness, *as well* as deceit, sensuality, envy, slander, pride *and* foolishness. All these evil things proceed from within and defile the man" (Mark 7:14–23; cf. Matthew 15:10–20).

Setting: Caesarea Philippi. After rebuking Peter for desiring to thwart His mission to the cross, Jesus summons a crowd along with His disciples and informs them of the high costs of following Him.

And He summoned the crowd with His disciples, and said to them, "If anyone wishes to come after Me, he must deny himself, and take up his cross and follow Me. For whoever wishes to save his life will lose it, but whoever loses his life for My sake and the gospel's will save it. For what does it profit a man to gain the whole world, and forfeit his soul? For what will a man give in exchange for his soul? For whoever is ashamed of Me and My words in this adulterous and sinful generation, the Son of Man will also be ashamed of him when He comes in the glory of His Father with the holy angels" (Mark 8:34–38; cf. Matthew 16:24–28; Luke 9:23–27; see Matthew 10:33, 38, 39).

Setting: Capernaum of Galilee. As Jesus teaches His disciples in private, they ask Him about greatness.

They came to Capernaum; and when He was in the house, He *began* to question them, "What were you discussing on the way?" But they kept silent, for on the way they had discussed with one another which *of them* was the greatest. Sitting down, He called the twelve and said to them, "If anyone wants to be first, he shall be last of all and servant of all." Taking a child, He set him before them, and taking him in His arms, He said to them, "Whoever receives one child like this in My name receives Me; and whoever receives Me does not receive Me, but Him who sent Me" (Mark 9:33–37; cf. Matthew 18:1–5; Luke 9:46–48; see Matthew 20:26; Matthew 10:40).

Setting: Bethphage. As He and His disciples approach Jerusalem for His impending death on the cross, Jesus instructs two of His disciples to obtain a colt for His triumphal entry into the city.

As they approached Jerusalem, at Bethphage and Bethany, near the Mount of Olives, He sent two of His disciples, and said to them, "Go into the village opposite you, and immediately as you enter it, you will find a colt tied *there,* on which no one yet has ever sat; untie it and bring it *here.* If anyone says to you, 'Why are you doing this?' you say, 'The Lord has need of it'; and immediately he will send it back here" (Mark 11:1–3; cf. Matthew 21:1–3; Luke 19:29–31; see Matthew 21:4–7; Luke 19:32–35; John 12:12–15).

Setting: Just outside Jerusalem. Following Jesus' instruction to the money changers while cleansing the temple, Peter draws Jesus' and His disciples' attention to the fig tree He cursed earlier.

And Jesus answered saying to them, "Have faith in God. Truly, I say to you, whoever says to this mountain, 'Be taken up and cast into the sea,' and does not doubt in his heart, but believes that what he says is going to happen, it will be *granted* him. Therefore I say to you, all things for which you pray and ask, believe that you have received them, and they will be *granted* you. Whenever you stand praying, forgive, if you have anything against anyone, so that your Father who is in heaven will also forgive you your transgressions. [But if you do not forgive, neither will your Father who is in heaven forgive your transgressions'] (Mark 11:22–26; cf. Matthew 21:19–22; see Matthew 6:14, 15; 7:7; 17:20).

Setting: The Mount of Olives, east of the temple. During His discourse, after prophesying the temple's destruction, Jesus responds to questions from Peter, James, John, and Andrew about future events.

"But when you see the ABOMINATION OF DESOLATION standing where it should not be (let the reader understand), then those who are in Judea must flee to the mountains. The one who is on the housetop must not go down, or go in to get anything out of his house; and the one who is in the field must not turn back to get his coat. But woe to those who are pregnant and to those who are nursing babies in those days! But pray that it may not happen in winter. For those days will be a *time of* tribulation such as has not occurred since the beginning of the creation which God created until now, and never will. Unless the Lord had shortened *those* days, no life would have been saved; but for the sake of the elect, whom He chose, He shortened the days. And then if anyone says to you, 'Behold, here is the Christ'; or, 'Behold, *He is* there'; do not believe *him*; for false Christs and false prophets will arise, and will show signs and wonders, in order to lead astray, if possible, the elect. But take heed; behold, I have told you everything in advance" (Mark 13:14–23; cf. Matthew 24:15–28; Luke 21:20–24; see Daniel 9:27; 12:1; Luke 17:31).

Setting: Galilee. Following Peter's pronouncement that Jesus is the Christ of God, the Lord conveys the demands of discipleship and the hope regarding the kingdom of God.

And He was saying to them all, "If anyone wishes to come after Me, he must deny himself, and take up his cross daily and follow Me. For whoever wishes to save his life will lose it, but whoever loses his life for My sake, he is the one who will save it. For what is a man profited if he gains the whole world, and loses or forfeits himself? For whoever is ashamed of Me and My words, the Son of Man will be ashamed of him when He comes in His glory, and the glory of the Father and of the holy angels. But I say to you truthfully, there are some of those standing here who will not taste death until they see the kingdom of God" (Luke 9:23–27; cf. Matthew 16:24–26, 28; Mark 8:34–37; see Matthew 10:33, 38, 39).

Setting: On the way from Galilee to Jerusalem. The Lord responds to a report from the seventy sent out in pairs to every place where He Himself would soon visit.

At that very time He rejoiced greatly in the Holy Spirit, and said, "I praise You, O Father, Lord of heaven and earth, that You have hidden these things from the wise and intelligent and have revealed them to infants. Yes, Father, for this way was well-pleasing in Your sight. All things have been handed over to Me by My Father, and no one knows who the Son is except the Father, and who the Father is except the Son, and anyone to whom the Son wills to reveal Him" (Luke 10:21, 22; cf. Matthew 11:25–27; see Luke 10:1, 17; John 3:35; 10:15).

Setting: On the way from Galilee to Jerusalem. After responding to a guest's proclamation about the blessings of eating bread in the kingdom of God, Jesus presents to large crowds the demands of discipleship.

Now large crowds were going along with Him; and He turned and said to them, "If anyone comes to Me, and does not hate his own father and mother and wife and children and brothers and sisters, yes, and even his own life, he cannot be My disciple. Whoever does not carry his own cross and come after Me cannot be My disciple. For which one of you, when he wants to build a tower, does not first sit down and calculate the cost to see if he has enough to complete it? Otherwise, when he has laid a foundation and is not able to finish, all who observe it begin to ridicule him, saying, 'This man began to build and was not able to finish.' Or what king, when he sets out to meet another king in battle, will not first sit down and consider whether he is strong enough with ten thousand *men* to encounter the one coming against him with twenty thousand? Or else, while the other is still far away, he sends a delegation and asks for terms of peace. So then, none of you can be My disciple who does not give up all his possessions. Therefore, salt is good; but if even salt has become tasteless, with what will it be seasoned? It is useless either for the soil or for the manure pile; it is thrown out. He who has ears to hear, let him hear" (Luke 14:25–35; cf. Matthew 5:13; 10:37–39; see Proverbs 20:18; Luke 14:1, 2; Philippians 3:7).

Setting: Jericho. After He provides a parable about stewardship, Jesus and His disciples head to the outskirts of Jerusalem to prepare for His triumphal entry into the city and His upcoming crucifixion.

When He approached Bethphage and Bethany, near the mount that is called Olivet, He sent two of the disciples, saying, "Go into the village ahead of *you;* there, as you enter, you will find a colt tied on which no one yet has ever sat; untie it and bring it *here.* If anyone asks you, 'Why are you untying it?' you shall say, 'The Lord has need of it'" (Luke 19:29–31; cf. Matthew 21:1–3; Mark 11:1–3).

Setting: By the pool of Bethesda in Jerusalem. During the Feast of the Jews, Jesus responds to criticism from the Jewish religious leaders for healing a lame man on the Sabbath and for referring to God as His Father (thereby making Himself equal with God).

Therefore Jesus answered and was saying to them, "Truly, truly, I say to you, the Son can do nothing of Himself, unless *it is* something He sees the Father doing; for whatever the Father does, these things the Son also does in like manner. For the Father loves the Son, and shows Him all things that He Himself is doing; and *the Father* will show Him greater works than these, so that you will marvel. For just as the Father raises the dead and gives them life, even so the Son also gives life to whom He wishes. For not even the Father judges anyone, but He has given all judgment to the Son, so that all will honor the Son even as they honor the Father. He who does not honor the Son does not honor the Father who sent Him" (John 5:19–23; see Luke 10:16; John 3:35; 11:25; 14:12).

Setting: Capernaum of Galilee. After Jesus informs the people whom He miraculously fed with a lad's five loaves and two fish how they might receive the bread out of heaven, the Jewish religious leaders grumble because Jesus claims He came down out of heaven.

Therefore the Jews were grumbling about Him, because He said, "I am the bread that came down out of heaven." They were saying, "Is not this Jesus, the son of Joseph, whose father and mother we know? How does He now say, 'I have come down out of heaven'?" Jesus answered and said to them, "Do not grumble among yourselves. No one can come to Me unless the Father who sent Me draws him; and I will raise him up on the last day. It is written in the prophets, 'AND THEY SHALL ALL BE TAUGHT OF GOD.' Everyone who has heard and learned from the Father, comes to Me. Not that anyone has seen the Father, except the One who is from God; He has seen the Father. Truly, truly, I say to you, he who believes has eternal life. I am the bread of life. Your fathers ate the manna in the wilderness, and they died. This is the bread which comes down out of heaven, so that one may eat of it and not die. I am the living bread that came down out of heaven; if anyone eats of this bread, he will live forever; and the bread also which I will give for the life of the world is My flesh" (John 6:41–51, Jesus quotes from Isaiah 54:13; see John 1:18, 29; 3:36; 7:27)

Setting: The temple in Jerusalem. After receiving encouragement from His blood brothers in Galilee to attend the upcoming Feast of Booths in Jerusalem in order to demonstrate His works to His disciples and the world, Jesus goes and teaches, astonishing the Jewish religious leaders.

So Jesus answered them and said, "My teaching is not Mine, but His who sent Me. If anyone is willing to do His will, he will know of the teaching, whether it is of God or *whether* I speak of Myself. He who speaks from himself seeks his own glory; but He who is seeking the glory of the One who sent Him, He is true, and there is no unrighteousness in Him" (John 7:16–18; see John 5:41).

Setting: Jerusalem. On the last day of the Feast of Booths, after causing discussion whether He is the Christ, while the chief priests and Pharisees attempt to understand where He says He will be going soon, Jesus offers His hearers salvation and the abundant life.

Now on the last day, the great *day* of the feast, Jesus stood and cried out, saying, "If anyone is thirsty, let him come to Me and drink. He who believes in Me, as the Scripture said, 'From his innermost being will flow rivers of living water'" (John 7:37, 38).

Setting: The temple in Jerusalem. Following the Feast of Booths and the scribes' and Pharisees' failed attempt to stone a woman for committing adultery, Jesus returns the next day to teach. His enemies question His testimony about Himself.

Jesus answered and said to them, "Even if I testify about Myself, My testimony is true, for I know where I came from and where I am going; but you do not know where I come from or where I am going. You judge according to the flesh; I am not judging anyone. But even if I do judge, My judgment is true; for I am not alone *in it,* but I and the Father who sent Me. Even in your law it has been written that the testimony of two men is true. I am He who testifies about Myself, and the Father who sent Me testifies about Me." So they were saying to Him, "Where is Your Father?" Jesus answered, "You know neither Me nor My Father; if you knew Me, you would know My Father also" (John 8:14–19; see Deuteronomy 17:6; 19:15; Matthew 18:16; John 3:17; 5:30, 37; 7:28).

Setting: The temple treasury in Jerusalem. While Jesus is interacting with the scribes and Pharisees about His testimony, their ancestry, and their motives, they state their belief He is a demon-possessed Samaritan.

Jesus answered, "I do not have a demon; but I honor My Father, and you dishonor Me. But I do not seek My glory; there is One who seeks and judges. Truly, truly, I say to you, if anyone keeps My word he will never see death" (John 8:49–51; see Matthew 16:28; John 5:41; 7:20).

Setting: The temple treasury in Jerusalem. While Jesus is interacting with the scribes and Pharisees about His testimony, their ancestry, and their motives, they state their belief He is a demon-possessed Samaritan.

Jesus answered, "I do not have a demon; but I honor My Father, and you dishonor Me. But I do not seek My glory; there is One who seeks and judges. Truly, truly, I say to you, if anyone keeps My word he will never see death" (John 8:49–51; see Matthew 16:28; John 5:41; 7:20).

Setting: Jerusalem. Following the Pharisees' interrogation and dismissal of the formerly blind man Jesus healed on the Sabbath, the Lord conveys the Parable of the Good Shepherd to the Pharisees, using figures of speech they do not understand.

So Jesus said to them again, "Truly, truly, I say to you, I am the door of the sheep. All who came before Me are thieves and robbers, but the sheep did not hear them. I am the door; if anyone enters through Me, he will be saved, and will go in and out and find pasture. The thief comes only to steal and kill and destroy; I came that they may have life, and have *it* abundantly. I am the good shepherd; the good shepherd lays down His life for the sheep. He who is a hired hand, and not a shepherd, who is not the owner of the sheep, sees the wolf coming, and leaves the sheep and flees, and the wolf snatches them and scatters *them. He flees* because he is a hired hand and is not concerned about the sheep. I am the good shepherd, and I know My own and My own know Me, even as the Father knows Me and I know the Father; and I lay down My life for the sheep. I have other sheep, which are not of this fold; I must bring them also, and they will hear My voice; and they will become one flock *with* one shepherd. For this reason the Father loves Me, because I lay down My life so that I may take it again. No one has taken it away from Me, but I lay it down on My own initiative. I have authority to take it up again. This commandment I received from My Father" (John 10:7–18; see Isaiah 40:11; 56:8; Jeremiah 23:1; Matthew 11:27).

Setting: Beyond the Jordan While He and His disciples are avoiding the Jerusalem Pharisees, Jesus receives word from Lazarus's sisters in Bethany of His friend's sickness, and decides to go there.

Then after this He said to the disciples, "Let us go to Judea again." The disciples said to Him, "Rabbi, the Jews were just now seeking to stone You, and are You going there again?" Jesus answered, "Are there not twelve hours in the day? If anyone walks in the day, he does not stumble, because he sees the light of this world. But if anyone walks in the night, he stumbles, because the light is not in him." This He said, and after that He said to them, "Our friend Lazarus has fallen asleep; but I go, so that I may awaken him out of sleep" (John 11:7–11; see John 8:59; 10:39).

Setting: Jerusalem. Just days before the Passover, with the chief priests and Pharisees plotting to seize Him, crowds welcome Jesus with palm branches and praise, and some Greeks ask to meet Him.

And Jesus answered them, saying, "The hour has come for the Son of Man to be glorified. Truly, truly, I say to you, unless a grain of wheat falls into the earth and dies, it remains alone; but if it dies, it bears much fruit. He who loves his life loses it, and he who hates his life in this world will keep it to life eternal. If anyone serves Me, he must follow Me; and where I am, there My servant will be also; if anyone serves Me, the Father will honor him" (John 12:23–26; see Matthew 10:39).

Setting: Jerusalem. Just days before the Passover, the chief priests and Pharisees are plotting to seize Jesus, who is expressing anxiety about His upcoming death by crucifixion. Some of the people believe in Him, while others are rejecting His message.

And Jesus cried out and said, "He who believes in Me, does not believe in Me but in Him who sent Me. He who sees Me sees the One who sent Me. I have come *as* Light into the world, so that everyone who believes in Me will not remain in darkness. If anyone hears My sayings and does not keep them, I do not judge him; for I did not come to judge the world, but to save the world. He who rejects Me and does not receive My sayings, has one who judges him; the word I spoke is what will judge him at the last day. For I did not speak on My own initiative, but the Father Himself who sent Me has given Me a commandment *as to* what to say and what to speak. I know that His commandment is eternal life; therefore the things I speak, I speak just as the Father as told Me" (John 12:44–50; see Matthew 10:40; Luke 10:16; John 1:4; 3:17; 5:19; 6:68; 14:9).

Setting: Jerusalem. Before the Passover, after conveying the upcoming ministry of the Holy Spirit in His disciples' lives, Jesus answers Judas's (not Iscariot) question why He discloses Himself to His disciples but not the whole world.

Jesus answered and said to him, "If anyone loves Me, he will keep My word; and My Father will love him, and We will come to him and make Our abode with him. He who does not love Me does not keep My words; and the word which you hear is not Mine, but the Father's who sent Me" (John 14:23, 24; see John 7:16; 8:51).

Setting: Jerusalem. Before the Passover, after He conveys the upcoming ministry of the Holy Spirit in His disciples' lives with His upcoming departure from them, Jesus explains He is the vine and they are the branches.

"I am the true vine, and My Father is the vinedresser. Every branch in Me that does not bear fruit, He takes away; and every *branch* that bears fruit, He prunes it so that it may bear more fruit. You are already clean because of the word which I have spoken to you. Abide in Me, and I in you. As the branch cannot bear fruit of itself unless it abides in the vine, so neither *can* you unless you abide in Me. I am the vine, you are the branches; he who abides in Me and I in him, he bears much fruit, for apart from Me you can do nothing. If anyone does not abide in Me, he is thrown away as a branch and dries up; and they gather them, and cast them into the fire and they are burned. If you abide in Me, and My words abide in you, ask whatever you wish, and it will be done for you. My Father is glorified by this, that you bear much fruit, and *so* prove to be My disciples. Just as the Father has loved Me, I have also loved you; abide in My love. If you keep My commandments, you will abide in My love; just as I have kept My Father's commandments and abide in His love. These things I have spoken to you so that My joy may be in you, and *that* your joy may be made full" (John 15:1–11; see Matthew 5:16; 7:7; John 3:29, 35; 6:56; 8:29, 31; 13:10; 15:16).

Setting: On the island of Patmos (in the Aegean Sea about fifty miles southwest of Ephesus in modern Turkey). On the Lord's Day (Sunday), about fifty years after Jesus' resurrection, the disciple John encounters the Lord Jesus Christ, who communicates new revelations for the apostle to record for the church in Laodicea and to six other churches in Asia.

"To the angel of the church in Laodicea write: The Amen, the faithful and true Witness, the Beginning of the creation of God, says this: 'I know your deeds, that you are neither cold nor hot; I wish that you were cold or hot. So because you are lukewarm, and neither hot nor cold, I will spit you out of My mouth. Because you say, "I am rich, and have become wealthy, and have need of nothing," and you do not know that you are wretched and miserable and poor and blind and naked, I advise you to buy from Me gold refined by fire so that you may become rich, and white garments so that you may clothe yourself, and *that* the shame of your nakedness will not be revealed; and eye salve to anoint your eyes so that you may see. Those whom I love, I reprove and discipline; therefore be zealous and repent. Behold, I stand at the door and knock; if anyone hears My voice and opens the door, I will come in to him and will dine with him, and he with Me. He who overcomes, I will grant to him to sit down with Me on My throne, as I also overcame and sat down with My Father on His throne. He who has an ear, let him hear what the Spirit says to the churches'" (Revelation 3:14–22; see Proverb 3:12; Hosea 12:8; John 14:23; 16:33).

ANYTHING (Also see SOMETHING)

Setting: Galilee. During the early part of His ministry, Jesus preaches the Sermon on the Mount to His disciples and the multitudes.

"You are the salt of the earth; but if the salt has become tasteless, how can it be made salty *again*? It is not longer good for anything, except to be thrown out and trampled under foot by men" (Matthew 5:13; cf. Mark 9:50).

Setting: Galilee. During the early part of His ministry, Jesus preaches the Sermon on the Mount to His disciples and the multitudes.

"Again, you have heard that the ancients were told, 'YOU SHALL NOT MAKE FALSE VOWS, BUT SHALL FULFILL YOUR VOWS TO THE LORD.' But I say to you, make no oath at all, either by heaven, for it is the throne of God, or by the earth, for it is the footstool of His feet, or by Jerusalem, for it is THE CITY OF THE GREAT KING. Nor shall you make an oath by your head, for you cannot make one hair white or black. But let your statement be 'Yes, yes' *or* 'No, no'; anything beyond these is of evil" (Matthew 5:33–37, Jesus quotes from Leviticus 19:12, Psalm 48:2; Isaiah 66:1; cf. James 5:12).

Setting: Capernaum of Galilee. after conveying to His disciples the value of little ones, Jesus gives instruction about church discipline.

"If your brother sins, go and show him his fault in private; if he listens to you, you have won your brother. But if he does not listen *to you,* take one or two more with you, so that BY THE MOUTH OF TWO OR THREE WITNESSES EVERY FACT MAY BE CONFIRMED. If he refuses to listen to them, tell it to the church; and if he refuses to listen even to the church, let him be to you as a Gentile and a tax collector. Truly I say to you, whatever you bind of earth shall have been bound in heaven; and whatever you loose on earth shall have been loosed in heaven. Again, I say to you, that if two of you agree on earth about anything that they may ask, it shall be done for them by My Father who is in heaven. For there two or three have gathered together in My name, I am there in their midst" (Matthew 18:15–20. Jesus quotes from Deuteronomy 19:15; cf. Matthew 7:7; 16:19; see Leviticus 19:17; Matthew 28:20; 2 Thessalonians 3:6, 14).

Setting: Entering Bethphage. After healing some blind men in Jericho, on the way to Jerusalem for His crucifixion, Jesus instructs two disciples to acquire a donkey and colt to be used in His triumphal entry into Jerusalem

When they had approached Jerusalem and had come to Bethphage, at the Mount of Olives, then Jesus sent two disciples, saying to them, "Go into the village opposite you, and immediately you will find a donkey tied *there* and a colt with her; untie them and bring them to Me. If anyone says anything to you, you shall say, 'The Lord has need of them,' and immediately he will send them" (Matthew 21:1–3; cf. Mark 11:1–3; Luke 19:29–31).

Setting: Galilee. Following His explanation of the Parable of the Sower to His disciples, Jesus illustrates what they should do with this truth.

And He was saying to them, "A lamp is not brought to be put under a basket, is it, or under a bed? Is it not *brought* to be put on the lampstand? For nothing is hidden, except to be revealed; nor has *anything* been secret, but that it would come to light. If anyone has ears to hear, let him hear" (Mark 4:21–23; cf. Luke 8:16, 17; see Matthew 5:14–16; Matthew 10:26).

Setting: Galilee. The Pharisees and some of the scribes from Jerusalem question why Jesus' disciples do not follow the tradition of ceremonial hand cleansing before eating bread.

And He said to them, "Rightly did Isaiah prophesy of you hypocrites, as it is written: 'THIS PEOPLE HONORS ME WITH THEIR LIPS, BUT THEIR HEART IS FAR AWAY FROM ME. BUT IN VAIN DO THEY WORSHIP ME, TEACHING AS DOCTRINES THE PRECEPTS OF MEN.' Neglecting the commandment of God, you hold to the tradition of men." He was also saying to them, "You are experts at setting aside the commandment of God in order to keep tradition. For Moses said, 'HONOR YOUR FATHER AND YOUR MOTHER'; and, 'HE WHO SPEAKS EVIL OF FATHER OR MOTHER, IS TO BE PUT TO DEATH'; but you say, 'If a man says to *his* father or *his* mother, whatever I have that would help you is Corban (that is to say, given *to God*),' you no longer permit him to do anything for *his* father or *his* mother; *thus* invalidating the word of God by your tradition which you have handed down; and you do many things such as that" (Mark 7:6–13, Jesus quotes from Exodus 20:12; 21:17; Isaiah 29:13; cf. Matthew 15:1–6).

Setting: Bethsaida of Galilee. After His disciples discuss with one another that they have no bread, Jesus gives sight to a blind man.

Taking the blind man by the hand, He brought him out of the village; and after spitting on his eyes and laying His hands on him, He asked him, "Do you see anything?" (Mark 8:23).

Setting: Galilee. Upon returning from a high mountain (perhaps Mount Hermon) where Jesus was transfigured before Peter, James and John, the four discover the remaining disciples arguing with some scribes.

And He asked them, "What are you discussing with them?" And one of the crowd answered Him, "Teacher, I brought You my son, possessed with a spirit which makes him mute; and whenever it seizes him, it slams him *to the ground* and he foams *at the mouth,* and grinds his teeth and stiffens out. I told Your disciples to cast it out, and they could not *do it.* And He answered them, and said, "O unbelieving generation, how long shall I be with you? How long shall I put up with you? Bring him to Me!" They brought the boy to Him. When he saw Him, immediately the spirit threw him into a convulsion, and falling to the ground, be *began* rolling around and foaming *at the mouth.* And He asked his father, "How long has this been happening to him?" And he said, "From childhood. It has often thrown him both into the fire and into the water to destroy him. But if You can do anything, take pity on us and help us!" And Jesus said to him, "'If You can?' All things are possible to him who believes." Immediately the boy's father cried out and said, "I do believe; help my unbelief." When Jesus saw that a crowd was rapidly gathering, He rebuked the unclean spirit, saying to it, "You deaf and mute spirit, I command you, come out of him and do not enter him again." After crying out and throwing him into terrible convulsions, it came out; and *the boy* became so much like a corpse that most *of them,* said, "He is dead!" But Jesus took him by the hand and raised him; and he got up. When He came into *the* house, His disciples *began* questioning Him privately, "Why could we not drive it out?" And He said to them, "This kind cannot come out by anything but prayer" (Mark 9:16–29; cf. Matthew 17:14–21; Luke 9:37–43; see Matthew 17:20).

Setting: Just outside Jerusalem. After Jesus instructs the money changers while cleansing the temple, Peter draws His and His disciples' attention to the fig tree Jesus cursed earlier.

And Jesus answered saying to them, "Have faith in God. Truly, I say to you, whoever says to this mountain, 'Be taken up and cast into the sea,' and does not doubt in his heart, but believes that what he says is going to happen, it will be *granted* him. Therefore I say to you, all things for which you pray and ask, believe that you have received them, and they will be *granted* you. Whenever you stand praying, forgive, if you have anything against anyone, so that your Father who is in heaven will also forgive you your transgressions. [But if you do not forgive, neither will your Father who is in heaven forgive your transgressions'] (Mark 11:22–26; cf. Matthew 21:19–22; see Matthew 6:14, 15; 7:7; 17:20).

Setting: The Mount of Olives, east of the temple in Jerusalem. During His discourse, after prophesying the temple's destruction, Jesus responds to questions from Peter, James, John, and Andrew about future events.

"But when you see the ABOMINATION OF DESOLATION standing where it should not be (let the reader understand), then those who are in Judea must flee to the mountains. The one who is on the housetop must not go down, or go in to get anything out of his house; and the one who is in the field must not turn back to get his coat. But woe to those who are pregnant and to those who are nursing babies in those days! But pray that it may not happen in winter. For those days will be a *time of* tribulation such as has not occurred since the beginning of the creation which God created until now, and never will. Unless the Lord had shortened *those* days, no life would have been saved; but for the sake of the elect, whom He chose, He shortened the days. And then if anyone says to you, 'Behold, here is the Christ'; or, 'Behold, *He is* there'; do not believe *him*; for false Christs and false prophets will arise, and will show signs and wonders, in order to lead astray, if possible, the elect. But take heed; behold, I have told you everything in advance" (Mark 13:14–23; cf. Matthew 24:15–28; Luke 21:20–24; see Daniel 9:27; 12:1; Luke 17:31).

Setting: Galilee. After explaining the Parable of the Sower to His disciples, Jesus gives the Parable of the Lamp.

"Now no one after lighting a lamp covers it over with a container, or puts it under a bed; but he puts it on a lampstand, so that those who come in may see the light. For nothing is hidden that will not become evident, nor anything secret that will not be known and come to light. So take care how you listen; for whoever has, to him more shall be given; and whoever does not have, even what he thinks he has shall be taken away from him" (Luke 8:16–18; cf. Mark 4:21–23; see Matthew 5:14, 15; 10:26; 13:12).

Setting: On the way from Galilee to Jerusalem. After revealing to His disciples how to pray, Jesus illustrates persistence in prayer.

Then He said to them, "Suppose one of you has a friend, and goes to him at midnight and says to him, 'Friend, lend me three loaves; for a friend of mine has come to me from a journey, and I have nothing to set before him'; and from inside he answers and says, 'Do not bother me; the door has already been shut and my children and I are in bed; I cannot get up and give you anything.' I tell you, even though he will not get up and give him anything because he is his friend, yet because of his persistence he will get up and give him as much as he needs. So I say to you, ask, and it will be given to you; seek, and you will find; knock, and it will be opened to you. For everyone who asks, receives; and he who seeks, finds; and to him who knocks, it will be opened" (Luke 11:5–10; cf. Matthew 7:7, 8; see Luke 18:1–5).

Setting: On the way from Galilee to Jerusalem. Jesus conveys the Parable of the Prodigal Son because the Pharisees and scribes complain He associates with tax collectors and sinners.

And He said, "A man had two sons. The younger of them said to his father, 'Father, give me the share of the estate that falls to me.' So he divided his wealth between them. And not many days later, the younger son gathered everything together and went on a journey into a distant country, and there he squandered his estate with loose living. Now when he had spent everything, a severe famine occurred in that country, and he began to be impoverished. So he went and hired himself out to one of the citizens of that country, and he sent him into his fields to feed swine. And he would have gladly filled his stomach with the pods that the swine were eating, and no one was giving anything to him. But when he came to his senses, he said, 'How many of my father's hired men have more than enough bread, but I am dying here with hunger! I will get up and go to my father, and will say to him, "Father, I have sinned against heaven, and in your sight; I am no longer worthy to be called your son; make me as one of your hired men."' So he got up and came to his father. But while he was still a long way off, his father saw him and felt compassion for him, and ran and embraced him and kissed him. And the son said to him, "Father, I have sinned against heaven and in your sight; I am no longer worthy to be called your son.' But the father said to his slaves, 'Quickly bring out the best robe and put it on him, and put a ring on his hand and sandals on his feet; and bring the fattened calf, kill it, and let us eat and celebrate; for this son of mine was dead and has come to life again; he was lost and has been found.' And they began to celebrate. Now his older son was in the field, when he came and approached the house, he heard music and dancing. And he summoned one of the servants and began inquiring what these things could be. And he said to him, 'Your brother has come, and your father has killed the fattened calf because he has received him back safe and sound.' But he became angry and was not willing to go in; and his father came out and began pleading with him. But he answered and said to his father, 'Look! For so many years I have been serving you and I have never neglected a command of yours; and yet you have never given me a young goat, so that I might celebrate with my friends; but when this son of yours came, who has devoured your wealth with prostitutes, you killed the fattened calf for him.' And he said to him, 'Son, you have always been with me, and all that is mine is yours. But we had to celebrate and rejoice, for this brother of yours was dead and has begun to live, and was lost and has been found'" (Luke 15:11–32; see Proverbs 29:2; Luke 15:1, 2).

Setting: Jerusalem. During the Feast of Unleavened Bread (Passover) just before the crucifixion, while celebrating the Passover meal, instituting the Lord's Supper, and prophesying Peter's denial of Him, Jesus instructs His disciples to prepare to persevere without Him.

And He said to them, "When I sent you out without money belt and bag and sandals, you did not lack anything, did you?" They said, "No, nothing." And He said to them, "But now, whoever has a money belt is to take it along, likewise also a bag, and whoever has no sword is to sell his coat and buy one. For I tell you that this which is written must be fulfilled in Me, 'AND HE WAS NUMBERED WITH TRANSGRESSORS'; for that which refers to Me has its fulfillment." They said, "Lord, look, here are two swords." And He said to them, "It is enough" (Luke 22:35–38, Jesus quotes from Isaiah 53:12; see Matthew 10:5–15; Mark 6:7–11; Luke 9:1–5; 10:1–12; 22:49; John 17:4).

Setting: Jerusalem. After rising from the grave on the third day after being crucified and appearing to two of His followers on the road to Emmaus, Jesus appears to some of His disciples.

While they were telling these things, He Himself stood in their midst and said to them, "Peace be to you." But they were startled and frightened and thought they were seeing a spirit. And He said to them, "Why are you troubled, and why do doubts arise in your hearts? See My hands and My feet, that it is I Myself; touch Me and see, for a spirit does not have flesh and bones as you see that I have." And when He had said this, He showed them His hands and His feet. While they still could not believe it because of their joy and amazement. He said to them, "Have you anything to eat?" They gave Him a piece of a broiled fish; and He took it and ate it before them (Luke 24:36–43; see Mark 16:14; John 20:27; Acts 10:40–41).

Setting: Jerusalem. Before the Passover, after answering Thomas's question where He is going and how His disciples will know the way, Jesus responds to Philip's request for Him to show them the Father.

Jesus said to him, "Have I been so long with you, and *yet* you have not come to know Me, Philip? He who has seen Me has seen the Father; how *can* you say, 'Show us the Father'? Do you not believe that I am in the Father, and the Father is in Me? The words that I say to you I do not speak on My own initiative, but the Father abiding in Me does His works. Believe Me that I am in the Father and the Father is in Me; otherwise believe because of the works themselves. Truly, truly, I say to you, he who believes in Me, the works that I do, he will do also; and greater *works* than these he will do; because I go to the Father. Whatever you ask in My name, that will I do, so that the Father may be glorified in the Son. If you ask Me anything in My name, I will do *it*" (John 14:9–14; see Matthew 7:7; John 1:14; 5:19, 20, 36; 10:37, 38; 15:16).

Setting: Jerusalem. Before the Passover, after empathizing with His disciples' sadness over His prophecies and giving them hope for the future, Jesus conveys promises about praying in His name.

"In that day you will not question Me about anything. Truly, truly, I say to you, if you ask the Father for anything in My name, He will give it to you. Until now you have asked for nothing in My name; ask and you will receive, so that your joy may be made full. These things I have spoken to you in figurative language; an hour is coming when I will no longer speak to you in figurative language, but will tell you plainly of the Father. In that day you will ask in My name, and I do not say to you that I will request of the Father on your behalf; for the Father Himself loves you, because you have loved Me and have believed that I came forth from the Father. I came forth from the Father and have come into the world; I am leaving the world again and going to the Father" (John 16:23–28; see Matthew 13:34; John 8:42; 13:1, 3; 14:14, 21, 23; 15:16).

APART, SET (See SANCTIFICATION)

APOSTLES (Also see APOSTLES, FALSE)

Setting: On the way from Galilee to Jerusalem. After Jesus pronounces woes upon the Pharisees, a lawyer replies that His remarks insult lawyers, too.

But He said, "Woe to you lawyers as well! For you weigh men down with burdens hard to bear, while you yourselves will not even touch the burdens with one of your fingers. Woe to you! For you build the tombs of the prophets, and it was your fathers who killed them. So you are witnesses and approve the deeds of your fathers; because it was they who killed them, and you build their tombs. For this reason also the wisdom of God said, 'I will send them prophets and apostles, and some of them they will kill and some they will persecute, so that the blood of all the prophets, shed since the foundation of the world, may be charged against this generation, from the blood of Abel to the blood of Zechariah, who was killed between the altar and the house of God; yes, I tell you, it shall be charged against this generation.' Woe to you lawyers! For you have taken away the key of knowledge; you yourselves did not enter, and you hindered those who were entering" (Luke 11:46–52; cf. Matthew 23:29–32; see 2 Chronicles 24:20, 21; Matthew 23:4, 13).

APOSTLES, FALSE (Also see TEACHERS, FALSE)

[FALSE APOSTLES from apostles, and they are not, and you found them *to be* false]

Setting: On the island of Patmos (in the Aegean Sea about fifty miles southwest of Ephesus in modern Turkey). On the Lord's Day (Sunday), about fifty years after Jesus' resurrection, the disciple John encounters the Lord Jesus Christ, who communicates a new revelation for the apostle to record for the church in Ephesus and to six other churches in Asia.

"To the angel of the church in Ephesus write: The One who holds the seven stars in His right hand, the One who walks among the seven golden lampstands, says this: 'I know your deeds and your toil and perseverance, and that you cannot tolerate evil men, and you put to the test those who call themselves apostles, and they are not, and you found them *to be* false; and you have perseverance and have endured for My name's sake, and have not grown weary. But I have *this* against you, that you have left your first love. Therefore remember from where you have fallen, and repent and do the deeds you did at first; or else I am coming to you and will remove your lampstand out of its place—unless you repent. Yet this you do have, that you hate the deeds of the Nicolaitans, which I also hate. He who has an ear, let him hear what the Spirit says to the churches. To him who overcomes, I will grant to eat of the tree of life which is in the Paradise of God'" (Revelation 2:1–7; see Genesis 2:9; Ezekiel 28:13; 1 John 4:1; Revelation 1:10,11, 19, 20; 2:15, 16).

APPEARANCE (Also see HYPOCRISY)

Setting: Galilee. During the early part of His ministry, Jesus preaches the Sermon on the Mount to His disciples and the multitudes.

"Whenever you fast, do not put on a gloomy face as the hypocrites *do,* for they neglect their appearance so that they will be noticed by men when they are fasting. Truly I say to you, they have their reward in full. But you, when you fast, anoint your head and wash your face so that your fasting will not be noticed by men, but by your Father who is in secret; and your Father who sees *what is done* in secret will reward you" (Matthew 6:16–18; see Matthew 6:4, 6).

Setting: Magadan of Galilee. The Pharisees and Sadducees, rejecting Jesus' message, continue to test Jesus, by asking Him for a sign from heaven.

But He replied to them, "When it is evening, you say, '*It will be* fair weather, for the sky is red.' And in the morning, '*There will* be a storm today, for the sky is red and threatening.' Do you know how to discern the appearance of the sky, but cannot *discern* the signs of the times? An evil and adulterous generation seeks after a sign; and a sign will not be given it, except the sign of Jonah." And He left them and went away (Matthew 16:2–4; cf. Matthew 12:39; Mark 8:12; Luke 12:54–56).

[APPEARANCE from appear]

Setting: The temple in Jerusalem. After the Jewish religious leaders test Him with questions, Jesus pronounces the seventh of eight woes on them in front of the crowds and His disciples.

"Woe to you, scribes and Pharisees, hypocrites! For you are like whitewashed tombs which on the outside appear beautiful, but inside they are full of dead men's bones and all uncleanness. So you, too, outwardly appear righteous to men, but inwardly you are full of hypocrisy and lawlessness" (Matthew 23:27, 28; cf. Luke 11:44).

[APPEARANCE from appear]
Setting: The Mount of Olives, just east of Jerusalem. During His discourse, Jesus answers His disciples' questions as to when the temple will be destroyed and Jerusalem overrun, along with the signs of His coming and the end of the age.

"But immediately after the tribulation of those days THE SUN WILL BE DARKENED, AND THE MOON WILL NOT GIVE ITS LIGHT, AND THE STARS WILL FALL from the sky, and the powers of the heavens will be shaken. And then the sign of the Son of Man will appear in the sky, and then all the tribes of the earth will mourn, and they will see the SON OF MAN COMING ON THE CLOUDS OF THE SKY with power and great glory. And He will send forth His angels with A GREAT TRUMPET and THEY WILL GATHER TOGETHER His elect from the four winds, from one end of the sky to the other" (Matthew 24:29–31, Jesus quotes from Isaiah 13:10, Daniel 7:13; Exodus 19:16; cf. Mark 13:24–27; Luke 21:25–27).

Setting: On the way from Galilee to Jerusalem. After foretelling how a relationship with Him will divide families, Jesus chastises the crowds for being able to discern the weather but not the present age.

And He was also saying to the crowds, "When you see a cloud rising in the west, immediately you say, 'A shower is coming,' and so it turns out. And when you see a south wind blowing, you say, 'It will be a hot day,' and it turns out that way. You hypocrites! You know how to analyze the appearance of the earth and the sky, but why do you not analyze this present time?" (Luke 12:54–56; cf. Matthew 16:2, 3).

[APPEARANCE from appear]
Setting: On the way from Galilee to Jerusalem. After chastising the crowds for being able to discern the weather but not the present age, Jesus exhorts them to settle any financial disputes outside of court.

"And why do you not even on your own initiative judge what is right? For while you are going with your opponent to appear before the magistrate, on your way there make an effort to settle with him, so that he may not drag you before the judge, and the judge turn you over to the officer, and the officer throw you into prison. I say to you, you will not get out of there until you have paid the very last cent" (Luke 12:57–59; cf. Matthew 5:25, 26).

[APPEARANCE from appeared]
Setting: Jericho, on the way to Jerusalem. After commending Zaccheus's faith in Him, Jesus provides a parable about stewardship.

So He said, "A nobleman went to a distant country to receive a kingdom for himself, and then return. And he called ten of his slaves, and gave them ten minas and said to them, 'Do business with this until I come back.' But his citizens hated him and sent a delegation after him, saying, 'We do not want this man to reign over us.' When he returned, after receiving the kingdom, he ordered that these slaves, to whom he had given the money, be called to him so that he might know what business they had done. The first appeared, saying, 'Master, your mina has made ten minas more.' And he said to him, 'Well done, good slave, because you have been faithful in a very little thing, you are to be in authority over ten cities.' The second came, saying, 'Your mina, master, has made five minas.' And he said to him, also, 'And you are to be over five cities.' Another came, saying, 'Master, here is your mina, which I kept put away in a handkerchief; for I was afraid of you, because you are an exacting man; you take up what you did not lay down and reap what you did not sow.' He said to him, 'By your own words I will judge you, you worthless slave. Did you know that I am an exacting man, taking up what I did not lay down and reaping what I did not sow? Then why did you not put my money in the bank, and having come, I would have collected it with interest?' Then he said to the bystanders, 'Take the mina away from him and give it to the one who has the ten minas.' And they said to him, 'Master, he has ten minas already.' I tell you that to everyone who has, more shall be given, but from the one who does not have, even what he does have shall be taken away. But these enemies of mine, who did not want me to reign over them, bring them here and slay them in my presence" (Luke 19:12–27; cf. Matthew 25:14–30; see Matthew 13:12; Luke 16:10).

Setting: The temple in Jerusalem. After receiving encouragement from His blood brothers in Galilee to attend the upcoming Feast of Booths in order to demonstrate His works to His disciples and the world, Jesus goes and teaches, astonishing the Jewish religious leaders.

Jesus answered them, "I did one deed, and you all marvel. For this reason Moses has given you circumcision (not because it is from Moses, but from the fathers), and on *the* Sabbath you circumcise a man. If a man receives circumcision on *the* Sabbath so that the Law of Moses will not be broken, are you angry with Me because I made an entire man well on *the* Sabbath? Do not judge according to appearance, but judge with righteous judgment" (John 7:21–24; see Genesis 17:10–14; Leviticus 12:3; 19:15; Matthew 12:2; John 5:2–16; 7–20; 7:10–15).

[APPEARANCE from appear and appeared]
Setting: Caesarea. Luke, writing in Acts, gives Paul's retelling of his conversion to Christ as he appears before King Agrippa following his hearing before the Jewish Council in Jerusalem and arrest by the Roman commander (on his way to Rome after the apostle's third missionary journey).

"And when we had fallen to the ground, I heard a voice saying to me in the Hebrew dialect, 'Saul, Saul, why are you persecuting Me? It is hard for you to kick against the goads.' And I said, 'Who are You, Lord?' And the Lord said, 'I am Jesus whom you are persecuting. But get up and stand on your feet; for this purpose I have appeared to you, to appoint you a minister and a witness not only to the things which you have seen, but also to the things in which I will appear to you; rescuing you from the *Jewish* people and from the Gentiles, to whom I am sending you, to open their eyes so that they may turn from darkness to light and from the dominion of Satan to God, that they may receive forgiveness of sins and an inheritance among those who have been sanctified by faith in Me' (Acts 26:14–18; see Isaiah 35:5; Acts 21:40; 22:14).

APPEARANCE'S SAKE (Listed under SAKE, APPEARANCE'S)

APPEARANCES (See APPEARANCE; and HYPOCRISY)

APPEARANCES, JESUS' POST-RESURRECTION (See JESUS' POST-RESURRECTION APPEARANCES)

APPROVAL, GOD'S (See COMMENDATION; FAITHFULNESS; OBEDIENCE; and REWARDS)

APPROVAL, MAN'S (Also see PRAISE (received from others))

[MAN'S APPROVAL from speak well of]
Setting: Galilee. After selecting His twelve disciples, Jesus teaches the Beatitudes (part of the Sermon on the Mount) to His disciples and a great throng of people from Judea, Jerusalem, and the central coastal region of Tyre and Sidon.

"Woe to you when all men speak well of you, for their fathers used to treat the false prophets in the same way" (Luke 6:26; see Matthew 7:15; 24:11, 24).

ARBITRATOR

Setting: On the way from Galilee to Jerusalem. After the scribes and Pharisees turn hostile and question Him in an attempt to catch Him in something He might say, Jesus teaches the crowds and His disciples about greed and possessions.

But He said to him, "Man, who appointed Me a judge or arbitrator over you?" Then He said to them, "Beware, and be on your guard against every form of greed; for not even when one has an abundance does his life consist of his possessions" (Luke 12:14, 15; see 1 Timothy 6:6–10).

ARK (Also see NOAH, DAYS OF)

Setting: The Mount of Olives, just east of Jerusalem. During His discourse, after answering His disciples' questions as to when the temple will be destroyed and Jerusalem overrun, along with the signs of His coming and the end of the age, Jesus teaches them the Parable of the Fig Tree.

"Now learn the parable from the fig tree: when its branch has already become tender and puts forth its leaves, you know that summer is near; so, you too, when you see all these things, recognize that He is near, *right* at the door. Truly, I say to you, this generation will not pass away until all these things take place. Heaven and earth will pass away, but My words will not pass away. But of that day and hour no one knows, not even the angels of heaven, nor the Son, but the Father alone. For the coming of the Son of Man will be just like the days of Noah. For as in those days before the flood they were eating and drinking, marrying and giving in marriage, until the day that Noah entered the ark, and they did not understand until the flood came and took them all away; so will the coming of the Son of Man be. Then there will be two men in the field; one will be taken and one will be left. Two women *will be* grinding at the mill; one will be taken and one will be left" (Matthew 24:32–41; cf. Mark 13:28–32; Luke 17:34–36; 21:28–33; see Genesis 6:5; 7:7; Matthew 5:18; 10:23; James 5:9).

Setting: Samaria, on the way from Galilee to Jerusalem. After the Pharisees question Him about the coming of the kingdom of God, Jesus tells His disciples of His second coming.

And He said to the disciples, "The days will come when you will long to see one of the days of the Son of Man, and you will not see it. They will say to you, 'Look there! Look here!' Do not go away, and do not run after them. For just like the lightning, when it flashes out of one part of the sky, shines to the other part of the sky, so will the Son of Man be in His day. But first He must suffer many things and be rejected by this generation. And just as it happened in the days of Noah, so it will be also in the days of the Son of Man: they were eating, they were drinking, they were marrying, they were being given in marriage, until the day that Noah entered the ark, and the flood came and destroyed them all. It was the same as happened in the days of Lot: they were eating, they were drinking, they were buying, they were selling, they were planting, they were building; but on the day that Lot went out from Sodom it rained fire and brimstone from heaven and destroyed them all. It will be just the same on the day that the Son of Man is revealed. On that day, the one who is on the housetop and whose goods are in the house must not go down to take them out; and likewise the one who is in the field must not turn back. Remember Lot's wife. Whoever seeks to keep his life will lose it, and whoever loses his life will preserve it. I tell you, on that night there will be two in one bed; one will be taken and the other will be left. There will be two women grinding at the same place; one will be taken and the other will be left. [Two men will be in the field; one will be taken and the other will be left."] And answering they said to Him, "Where, Lord?" And He said to them, "Where the body is, there also the vultures will be gathered" (Luke 17:22–37; see Genesis 19; Matthew 10:39; 16:21, 27; 24:17–28, 37–41).

ARMIES

Setting: The temple in Jerusalem. Jesus speaks another parable to the chief priests and elders after they question His authority.

Jesus spoke to them again in parables, saying, "The kingdom of heaven may be compared to a king who gave a wedding feast for his son. And he sent out his slaves to call those who had been invited to the wedding feast, and they were unwilling to come. Again he sent out other slaves saying, 'Tell those who have been invited, "Behold, I have prepared my dinner; my oxen and my fattened livestock are *all* butchered and everything is ready; come to the wedding feast." But they paid no attention and went their way, one to his own farm, another to his business, and the rest seized his slaves and mistreated them and killed them. But the king was enraged, and he sent his armies and destroyed those murderers and set their city on fire. Then he said to his slaves, 'The wedding is ready, but those who were invited were not worthy. 'Go therefore to the main highways, and as many as you find *there,* invite to the wedding feast.' Those slaves went out into the streets and gathered together all they found, both evil and good; and the wedding hall was filled with dinner guests. But when the king came in to look over the dinner guests, he saw a man there who was not dressed in wedding clothes, and he said to him, 'Friend, how did you come in here without wedding clothes?' And the man was speechless. Then the king said to the servants, 'Bind him hand and foot, and throw him into the outer darkness; in that place there will be weeping and gnashing of teeth.' For many are called, but few *are* chosen" (Matthew 22:1–14; cf. Matthew 8:11, 12).

Setting: The Mount of Olives, just east of Jerusalem. During His discourse, following a time of ministry in the temple a few days before His crucifixion, Jesus elaborates more about things to come during His Olivet Discourse.

"But when you see Jerusalem surrounded by armies, then recognize that her desolation is near. Then those who are in Judea must flee to the mountains, and those who are in the midst of the city must leave, and those who are in the country must not enter the city; because these are days of vengeance, so that all things which are written will be fulfilled. Woe to those who are pregnant and to those who are nursing babies in those days; for there will be a great distress upon the land and wrath to this people; and they will fall by the edge of the sword, and will be led captive into all the nations; and Jerusalem will be trampled under foot by the Gentiles until the times of the Gentiles are fulfilled" (Luke 21:20–24; see Matthew 24:15–18; Mark 13:14–16; Luke 19:43).

ARMOR

Setting: On the way from Galilee to Jerusalem. After some in the crowd test Him, demanding a sign from heaven, Jesus illustrates His power over Satan.

"When a strong man, fully armed, guards his own house, his possessions are undisturbed. But when someone stronger than he attacks him and overpowers him, he takes away from him all his armor on which he had relied and distributes his plunder. He who is not with Me is against Me; and he who does not gather with Me, scatters" (Luke 11:21–23; cf. Matthew 12:29, 30).

ARREST (JESUS' ARREST is a separate entry)

Setting: The Mount of Olives, east of the temple in Jerusalem. During His discourse, after prophesying the temple's destruction, Jesus responds to questions from Peter, James, John, and Andrew about future events.

And Jesus began to say to them, "See to it that no one misleads you. Many will come in My name, saying, 'I am *He!*' and will mislead many. When you hear of wars and rumors of wars, do not be frightened; *those things* must take place; but *that is* not yet the end. For nation will rise up against nation, and kingdom against kingdom; there will be earthquakes in various places; there will *also be* famines. These things are *merely* the beginning of birth pangs. But be on your guard; for they will deliver you to *the* courts, and you will be flogged in *the* synagogues, and you will stand before governors and kings for My sake, as a testimony to them. The gospel must first be preached to all the nations. When they arrest you and hand you over, do not worry beforehand about what you are to say, but say whatever is given you in that hour; for it is not you who speak, but *it is* the Holy Spirit. Brother will betray brother to death, and a father *his* child; and children will rise up against parents and have them put to death. You will be hated by all because of My name, but the one who endures to the end, he will be saved" (Mark 13:5–13; cf. Matthew 24:4–14; Luke 21:7–19; see Matthew 10:17–22).

ARREST, JESUS' (See JESUS' ARREST)

ARROGANCE (Also see PRIDE)

[ARROGANCE from God, I thank You that I am not like other people: swindlers, unjust, adulterers, or even like this tax collector]

Setting: On the way from Galilee to Jerusalem. After instructing His disciples about persistence in prayer, Jesus conveys a parable about self-righteousness.

And He also told this parable to some people who trusted in themselves that they were righteous, and viewed others with contempt: "Two men went up into the temple to pray, one a Pharisee and the other a tax collector. The Pharisee stood and was praying this to himself: 'God, I thank You that I am not like other people: swindlers, unjust, adulterers, or even like this tax collector. I fast twice a week; I pay tithes of all that I get.' But the tax collector, standing some distance away, was even unwilling to lift up his eyes to heaven, but was beating his breast, saying, 'God, be merciful to me, the sinner!' I tell you, this man went to his house justified rather than the other; for everyone who exalts himself will be humbled, but he who humbles himself will be exalted" (Luke 18:9–14; see Ezra 9:6; Matthew 6:5, 23:12; Luke 11:42, 16:15; Romans 14:3, 10).

ASCENSION (Also see JESUS' ASCENSION)

[ASCENSION from ascended]

Setting: Jerusalem. Before the Passover of the Jews, after the Lord cleanses the temple, a Pharisee, Nicodemus, asks Him by night the meaning of "born of the Spirit."

Jesus answered and said to him, "Are you the teacher of Israel and do not understand these things? Truly, truly, I say to you, we speak of what we know and testify of what we have seen, and you do not accept our testimony. If I told you earthly things and you do not believe, how will you believe if I tell you heavenly things? No one has ascended into heaven, but He who descended from heaven: the Son of Man. As Moses lifted up the serpent in the wilderness, even so must the Son of Man be lifted up; so that whoever believes will in Him have eternal life" (John 3:10–15; see Numbers 21:9; Proverbs 30:4; John 12:34; 20:30, 31).

ASHAMED (Also see JESUS, ASHAMED OF; and SHAME)

Setting: Caesarea Philippi. Following His rebuke of Peter for desiring to thwart His mission to the cross, Jesus summons a crowd along with His disciples and informs them of the high costs of following Him.

And He summoned the crowd with His disciples, and said to them, "If anyone wishes to come after Me, he must deny himself, and take up his cross and follow Me. For whoever wishes to save his life will lose it, but whoever loses his life for My sake and the gospel's will save it. For what does it profit a man to gain the whole world, and forfeit his soul? For what will a man give in exchange for his soul? For whoever is ashamed of Me and My words in this adulterous and sinful generation, the Son of Man will also be ashamed of him when He comes in the glory of His Father with the holy angels" (Mark 8:34–38; cf. Matthew 16:24–28; Luke 9:23–27; see Matthew 10:33, 38, 39).

Setting: On the way from Galilee to Jerusalem. After giving the Parable of the Prodigal Son, the Lord teaches His disciples about stewardship.

Now He was also saying to the disciples, "There was a rich man who had a manager, and this manager was reported to him as squandering his possessions. And he called him and said to him, 'What is this I hear about you? Give an accounting of your management, for you can no longer be a manager.' The manager said to himself, 'What shall I do, since my master is taking the management away from me? I am not strong enough to dig; I am ashamed to beg. I know what I shall do, so that when I am removed from the management people will welcome me into their homes.' And he summoned each one of his master's debtors, and he began saying to the first, 'How much do you owe my master?' And he said, 'A hundred measures of oil.' And he said to him, 'Take your bill, and sit down quickly and write fifty.' Then he said to another, 'And how much do you owe?' And he said, 'A hundred measures of wheat.' He said to him, 'Take your bill, and write eighty.' And his master praised the unrighteous manager because he had acted shrewdly; for the sons of this age are more shrewd in relation to their own kind than the sons of light. And I say to you, make friends for yourselves by means of the wealth of unrighteousness, so that when it fails, they will receive you into the eternal dwellings. He who is faithful in a very little thing is faithful also in much; and he who is unrighteous in a very little thing is unrighteous also in much. Therefore if you have not been faithful in the use of unrighteous wealth, who will entrust the true riches to you? And if you have not been faithful in the use of that which is another's, who will give you that which is your own? No servant can serve two masters; for either he will hate the one and love the other, or else he will be devoted to one and despise the other. You cannot serve God and wealth" (Luke 16:1–13; cf. Matthew 6:24; see Matthew 25:14–30).

ASHES (Also see SACKCLOTH)

Setting: Galilee. After performing miracles throughout the region, Jesus pronounces woes against those cities who have not repented.

"Woe to you, Chorazin! Woe to you, Bethsaida! For if the miracles had occurred in Tyre and Sidon which occurred in you, they would have repented long ago in sackcloth and ashes. Nevertheless I say to you, it will be more tolerable for Tyre and Sidon in *the* day of judgment than for you. And you, Capernaum, will not be exalted to heaven, will you? You will descend to Hades; for if the miracles had occurred in Sodom which occurred in you, it would have remained to this day. Nevertheless, I say to you that it will be more tolerable for the land of Sodom in *the* day of judgment, than for you" (Matthew 11:21–24; cf. Matthew 10:15; Luke 10:13–15).

Setting: On the way from Galilee to Jerusalem. The Lord pronounces woes on cities who reject the gospel as He appoints seventy followers and sends them out in pairs to every city and place He Himself will soon visit.

"Woe to you, Chorazin! Woe to you, Bethsaida! For if the miracles had been performed in Tyre and Sidon which occurred in you, they would have repented long ago, sitting in sackcloth and ashes. But it will be more tolerable for Tyre and Sidon in the judgment than for you. And you, Capernaum, will not be exalted to heaven, will you? You will be brought down to Hades! The one who listens to you listens to Me, and the one who rejects you rejects Me; and he who rejects Me rejects the One who sent Me" (Luke 10:13–16; cf. Matthew 11:21–23; see Matthew 10:40).

ASIA, CHURCHES IN (See EPHESUS; LAODICEA; PERGAMUM; PHILADELPHIA; SARDIS; SMYRNA; and THYATIRA)

ASKING (Also see BESEECHING; PRAYER; REQUEST; SEEKING; and WISH)

[ASKING from asks]

Setting: Galilee. During the early part of His ministry, Jesus preaches the Sermon on the Mount to His disciples and the multitudes.

"Give to him who asks of you, and do not turn away from him who wants to borrow from you" (Matthew 5:42; see Deuteronomy 15:7–11).

[ASKING from ask]

Setting: Galilee. During the early part of His ministry, Jesus preaches the Sermon on the Mount to His disciples and the multitudes.

"And when you are praying, do not use meaningless repetition as the Gentiles do, for they suppose that they will be heard for their many words. So do not be like them; for your Father knows what you need before you ask Him" (Matthew 6:7, 8; see 1 Kings 18:26–29).

[ASKING from Ask and asks]

Setting: Galilee. During the early part of His ministry, Jesus preaches the Sermon on the Mount to His disciples and the multitudes.

"Ask, and it will be given to you; seek, and you will find; knock, and it will be opened to you. For everyone who asks receives, and he who seeks finds, and to him who knocks it will be opened. Or what man is there among you who, when his son asks for a loaf, will give him a stone? Or if he asks for a fish, he will not give him a snake, will he? If you then, being evil, know how to give good gifts to your children, how much more will your Father who is in heaven give what is good to those who ask Him! In everything, therefore, treat people the same way you want them to treat you, for this is the Law and the Prophets" (Matthew 7:7–12; cf. Matthew 22:40; Luke 6:31; Luke 11:9–13; see Psalm 84:11).

[ASKING from ask]

Setting: Capernaum of Galilee. After conveying to His disciples the value of little ones, Jesus gives instruction about church discipline.

"If your brother sins, go and show him his fault in private; if he listens to you, you have won your brother. But if he does not listen *to you,* take one or two more with you, so that BY THE MOUTH OF TWO OR THREE WITNESSES EVERY FACT MAY BE CONFIRMED. If he refuses to listen to them, tell it to the church; and if he refuses to listen even to the church, let him be to you as a Gentile and a tax collector. Truly I say to you, whatever you bind of earth shall have been bound in heaven; and whatever you loose on earth shall have been loosed in heaven. Again, I say to you, that if two of you agree on earth about anything that they may ask, it shall be done for them by My Father who is in heaven. For there two or three have gathered together in My name, I am there in their midst" (Matthew 18:15–20. Jesus quotes from Deuteronomy 19:15; cf. Matthew 7:7; 16:19; see Leviticus 19:17; Matthew 28:20; 2 Thessalonians 3:6, 14).

Setting: Judea beyond the Jordan (Perea). Jesus shares with a rich, young ruler how he can obtain eternal life.

And He said to him, "Why are you asking Me about what is good? There is only One who is good; but if you wish to enter into life, keep the commandments." Then he said to Him, 'Which ones?' And Jesus said, "YOU SHALL NOT COMMIT MURDER; YOU SHALL NOT COMMIT ADULTERY; YOU SHALL NOT STEAL; YOU SHALL NOT BEAR FALSE WITNESS; HONOR YOUR FATHER AND MOTHER; and YOU SHALL LOVE YOUR NEIGHBOR AS YOURSELF." The young man said to Him, "All these things I have kept; what am I still lacking?" Jesus said to him, "If you wish to complete go and sell your possessions and give to the poor, and you will have treasure in heaven; and come, follow Me" (Matthew 19:16–22, Jesus quotes from Exodus 20:13–15; Leviticus 19:18; cf. Leviticus 18:5; Mark 10:17–21; Luke 10:25–28; 12:33; 18:18–24).

Setting: On the way to Jerusalem. The mother of James and John, the sons of Zebedee, asks Jesus to make her sons exalted rulers with Him in His coming kingdom.

And He said to her, "What do you wish?" She said to Him, 'Command that in Your kingdom these two sons of mine may sit one on Your right and one on Your left.' But Jesus answered, "You do not know what you are asking. Are you able to drink the cup that I am about to drink?" They said to Him, 'We are able.' He said to them, "My cup you shall drink; but to sit on My right and on *My* left, this is not Mine to give, but it is for those for whom it has been prepared by My Father" (Matthew 20:21–23; cf. Mark 10:35–40; see Matthew 19:28; 20:20; Acts 12:2).

[ASKING from ask]
Setting: On the way from Bethany to Jerusalem. Jesus' disciples ask Him how the fig tree He cursed (an illustration of the nation of Israel) so quickly withered.

And Jesus answered and said to them, "Truly I say to you, if you have faith and do not doubt, you will not only do what was done to the fig tree, but even if you say to this mountain, 'Be taken up and cast into the sea,' it will happen. And all things you ask in prayer, believing, you will receive" (Matthew 21:21, 22; cf. Matthew 7:7; 17:20; Mark 11:20–24).

[ASKING from ask]
Setting: The temple in Jerusalem. Having spent the night in Bethany, Jesus returns, and the chief priests and elders question His authority in an effort to challenge His teaching to the nation.

Jesus said to them, "I will also ask you one thing, which if you tell Me, I will also tell you by what authority I do these things. The baptism of John was from what *source*, from heaven or from men?" And they *began* reasoning among themselves, saying, "If we say 'From heaven,' He will say to us, 'Then why did you not believe him?' But if we say, 'From men,' we fear the people; for they all regard John as a prophet." And answering Jesus, they said, "We do not know." He also said to them, "Neither will I tell you by what authority I do these things" (Matthew 21:24–27; cf. Mark 11:29–33; Luke 20:3–8).

Setting: On the road to Jerusalem. After Jesus prophesies His persecution, death, and resurrection, James and John ask for special honor and privileges in His coming kingdom.

And He said to them, "What do you want Me to do for you?" They said to Him, "Grant that we may sit, one on Your right and one on *Your* left, in Your glory." But Jesus said to them, "You do not know what you are asking. Are you able to drink the cup that I drink, or to be baptized with the baptism with which I am baptized?" They said to Him, "We are able." And Jesus said to them, "The cup that I drink you shall drink; and you shall be baptized with the baptism with which I am baptized. But to sit on My right or on *My* left, this is not Mine to give; but it is for those for whom it has been prepared" (Mark 10:36–40; cf. Matthew 20:20–23; see Matthew 19:28; Mark 10:35; Acts 12:2).

[ASKING from ask]
Setting: Just outside Jerusalem. After Jesus instructs the money changers while cleansing the temple, Peter draws His and His disciples' attention to the fig tree He cursed earlier.

And Jesus answered saying to them, "Have faith in God. Truly, I say to you, whoever says to this mountain, 'Be taken up and cast into the sea,' and does not doubt in his heart, but believes that what he says is going to happen, it will be *granted* him. Therefore I say to you, all things for which you pray and ask, believe that you have received them, and they will be *granted* you. Whenever you stand praying, forgive, if you have anything against anyone, so that your Father who is in heaven will also forgive you your transgressions. [But if you do not forgive, neither will your Father who is in heaven forgive your transgressions'] (Mark 11:22–26; cf. Matthew 21:19–22; see Matthew 6:14, 15; 7:7; 17:20).

[ASKING from ask]
Setting: The temple in Jerusalem. After Jesus teaches about faith and forgiveness utilizing a cursed fig tree as an object lesson, His authority is questioned by the chief priests, scribes, and elders.

And Jesus said to them, "I will ask you one question, and you answer Me, and *then* I will tell you by what authority I do these things. Was the baptism of John from heaven, or from men? Answer Me." They *began* reasoning among themselves, saying, "If we say 'From heaven,' He will say, 'Then why did you not believe him?' "But shall we say 'From men'?"—they were afraid of the people, for everyone considered John to have been a real prophet. Answering Jesus, they said, "We do not know." And Jesus said to them, "Nor will I tell you by what authority I do these things" (Mark 11:29–33; cf. Matthew 21:23–27; Luke 20:1–8).

[ASKING from ask]
Setting: A synagogue in Galilee. As Jesus teaches on a Sabbath, the scribes and Pharisees watch to see if He heals a man's withered hand.

But He knew what they were thinking, and He said to the man with the withered hand, "Get up and come forward!" And he got up and came forward. And Jesus said to them, "I ask you, is it lawful to do good or to do harm on the Sabbath, to save a life or destroy it?" And looking around at them all, He said to him, "Stretch out your hand!" And he did so; and his hand was restored (Luke 6:8–10; cf. Matthew 12:9–13; Mark 3:1–5).

[ASKING from asks]
Setting: Galilee. After selecting His twelve disciples, Jesus teaches the Sermon on the Mount to His disciples and a great throng of people from Judea, Jerusalem, and the central coastal region of Tyre and Sidon.

"But I say to you who hear, love your enemies, do good to those who hate you, bless those who curse you, pray for those who mistreat you. Whoever hits you on the cheek, offer him the other also; and whoever takes away your coat, do not withhold your shirt from him either. Give to everyone who asks of you, and whoever takes away what is yours, do not demand it back. Treat others the same way you want them to treat you. If you love those who love you, what credit is that to you? For even sinners love those who love them. If you do good to those who do good to you, what credit is that to you? For even sinners do the same. If you lend to those from whom you expect to receive, what credit is that to you? Even sinners lend to sinners in order to receive back the same amount. But love your enemies, and do good, and lend, expecting nothing in return; and your reward will be great, and you will be sons of the Most High; for He Himself is kind to ungrateful and evil men. Be merciful, just as your Father is merciful" (Luke 6:27–36; cf. Matthew 5:9, 39–48; 7:12).

[ASKING from asks]
Setting: On the way from Galilee to Jerusalem. After revealing to His disciples how to pray, Jesus illustrates persistence in prayer.

Then He said to them, "Suppose one of you has a friend, and goes to him at midnight and says to him, 'Friend, lend me three loaves; for a friend of mine has come to me from a journey, and I have nothing to set before him'; and from inside he answers and says, 'Do not bother me; the door has already been shut and my children and I are in bed; I cannot get up and give you anything.' I tell you, even though he will not get up and give him anything because he is his friend, yet because of his persistence he will get up and give him as much as he needs. So I say to you, ask, and it will be given to you; seek, and you will find; knock, and it will be opened to you. For everyone who asks, receives; and he who seeks, finds; and to him who knocks, it will be opened" (Luke 11:5–10; cf. Matthew 7:7, 8; see Luke 18:1–5).

[ASKING from asked and ask]

Setting: On the way from Galilee to Jerusalem. After revealing to His disciples how to pray, Jesus illustrates God's benevolence in answering prayer and giving the Holy Spirit.

"Now suppose one of you fathers is asked by his son for a fish; he will not give him a snake instead of a fish, will he? Or if he is asked for an egg, he will not give him a scorpion, will he? If you then, being evil, know how to give good gifts to your children, how much more will your heavenly Father give the Holy Spirit to those who ask Him?" (Luke 11:11–13; cf. Matthew 7:9–11).

[ASKING from ask]

Setting: On the way from Galilee to Jerusalem. When Jesus uses a parable to challenge the crowd and His disciples to be ready for His return, Peter asks Him whom He is addressing.

And the Lord said, "Who then is the faithful and sensible steward, whom his master will put in charge of his servants, to give them their rations at the proper time? Blessed is that slave whom his master finds so doing when he comes. Truly I say to you that he will put him in charge of all his possessions. But if that slave says in his heart, 'My master will be a long time in coming,' and begins to beat the slaves, both men and women, and to eat and drink and get drunk; the master of that slave will come on a day when he does not expect him and at an hour he does not know, and will cut him in pieces, and assign him a place with the unbelievers. And that slave who knew his master's will and did not get ready or act in accord with his will, will receive many lashes, but the one who did know it, and committed deeds worthy of flogging, will receive but few. From everyone who has been given much, much will be required; and to whom they entrusted much, of him they will ask all the more" (Luke 12:42–48; cf. Matthew 24:45–51; see Leviticus 5:17; Luke 12:41).

[ASKING from asks]

Setting: On the way from Galilee to Jerusalem. After He responds to a guest's proclamation about the blessings of eating bread in the kingdom of God, Jesus presents to large crowds the demands of discipleship.

Now large crowds were going along with Him; and He turned and said to them, "If anyone comes to Me, and does not hate his own father and mother and wife and children and brothers and sisters, yes, and even his own life, he cannot be My disciple. Whoever does not carry his own cross and come after Me cannot be My disciple. For which one of you, when he wants to build a tower, does not first sit down and calculate the cost to see if he has enough to complete it? Otherwise, when he has laid a foundation and is not able to finish, all who observe it begin to ridicule him, saying, 'This man began to build and was not able to finish.' Or what king, when he sets out to meet another king in battle, will not first sit down and consider whether he is strong enough with ten thousand *men* to encounter the one coming against him with twenty thousand? Or else, while the other is still far away, he sends a delegation and asks for terms of peace. So then, none of you can be My disciple who does not give up all his possessions. Therefore, salt is good; but if even salt has become tasteless, with what will it be seasoned? It is useless either for the soil or for the manure pile; it is thrown out. He who has ears to hear, let him hear" (Luke 14:25–35; cf. Matthew 5:13; 10:37–39; see Proverbs 20:18; Philippians 3:7).

[ASKING from asks]

Setting: Jericho. After He provides a parable about stewardship, Jesus and His disciples head to the outskirts of Jerusalem to prepare for His triumphal entry into the city and His upcoming crucifixion.

When He approached Bethphage and Bethany, near the mount that is called Olivet, He sent two of the disciples, saying, "Go into the village ahead of *you;* there, as you enter, you will find a colt tied on which no one yet has ever sat; untie it and bring it *here.* If anyone asks you, 'Why are you untying it?' you shall say, 'The Lord has need of it'" (Luke 19:29–31; cf. Matthew 21:1–3; Mark 11:1–3).

[ASKING from ask]

Setting: The temple in Jerusalem. While Jesus ministers a few days before His crucifixion, with the conflict with the religious leaders of Israel escalating, the chief priests and the scribes question His authority to teach and preach.

Jesus answered and said to them, "I will also ask you a question, and you tell Me: Was the baptism of John from heaven or from men?" They reasoned among themselves, saying, "If we say, 'From heaven,' He will say, 'Why did you not believe him?' But if we say, 'From men,' all the people will stone us to death, for they are convinced that John was a prophet." So they answered that they did not know where it came from. And Jesus said to them, "Nor will I tell you by what authority I do these things" (Luke 20:3–8; cf. Matthew 21:23–27; Mark 11:27–33).

[ASKING from ask]
Setting: Jerusalem. After being arrested, having Peter deny Him, and being mocked and beaten, with His crucifixion imminent, Jesus appears before the Sanhedrin.

"If You are the Christ, tell us." But He said to them, "If I tell you, you will not believe; and if I ask you a question, you will not answer. But from now on THE SON OF MAN WILL BE SEATED AT THE RIGHT HAND of the power OF GOD." And they all said, "Are You the Son of God, then? And He said to them, "Yes, I am" (Luke 22:67–70, Jesus quotes from Psalm 110:1; cf. Matthew 26:57–65; Mark 14:55–65).

[ASKING from asked]
Setting: Sychar in Samaria, on the way to Galilee. Jesus interacts with a Samaritan woman at Jacob's well while His disciples shop for food.

Jesus answered and said to her, "If you knew the gift of God, and who it is who says to you, 'Give Me a drink,' you would have asked Him, and He would have given you living water" (John 4:10; see John 4:1–9).

[ASKING from ask]
Setting: Jerusalem. Before the Passover, after answering Thomas's question about where He is going and how His disciples will know the way, Jesus responds to Philip's request for Him to show them the Father.

Jesus said to him, "Have I been so long with you, and *yet* you have not come to know Me, Philip? He who has seen Me has seen the Father; how *can* you say, 'Show us the Father'? Do you not believe that I am in the Father, and the Father is in Me? The words that I say to you I do not speak on My own initiative, but the Father abiding in Me does His works. Believe Me that I am in the Father and the Father is in Me; otherwise believe because of the works themselves. Truly, truly, I say to you, he who believes in Me, the works that I do, he will do also; and greater *works* than these he will do; because I go to the Father. Whatever you ask in My name, that will I do, so that the Father may be glorified in the Son. If you ask Me anything in My name, I will do *it*" (John 14:9–14; see Matthew 7:7; John 1:14; 5:19, 20, 36; 10:37, 38; 15:16).

[ASKING from ask]
Setting: Jerusalem. Before the Passover, after responding to Philip's request for Him to show His disciples the Father, Jesus conveys the upcoming role of the Holy Spirit in their lives.

"If you love Me, you will keep My commandments. I will ask the Father, and He will give you another Helper, that He may be with you forever; *that* is the Spirit of truth, whom the world cannot receive, because it does not see Him or know Him, *but* you know Him because He abides with you and will be in you" (John 14:15–17; see John 7:39; 15:26; 1 John 5:3).

[ASKING from ask]
Setting: Jerusalem. Before the Passover, after He conveys the upcoming ministry of the Holy Spirit in His disciples' lives with His upcoming departure from them, Jesus explains He is the vine and His disciples are the branches.

"I am the true vine, and My Father is the vinedresser. Every branch in Me that does not bear fruit, He takes away; and every *branch* that bears fruit, He prunes it so that it may bear more fruit. You are already clean because of the word which I have spoken to you. Abide in Me, and I in you. As the branch cannot bear fruit of itself unless it abides in the vine, so neither *can* you unless you abide in Me. I am the vine, you are the branches; he who abides in Me and I in him, he bears much fruit, for apart from Me you can do nothing. If anyone does not abide in Me, he is thrown away as a branch and dries up; and they gather them, and cast them into the fire and they are burned. If you abide in Me, and My words abide in you, ask whatever you wish, and it will be done for you. My Father is glorified by this, that you bear much fruit, and *so* prove to be My disciples. Just as the Father has loved Me, I have also loved you; abide in My love. If you keep My commandments, you will abide in My love; just as I have kept My Father's commandments and abide in His love. These things I have spoken to you so that My joy may be in you, and *that* your joy may be made full" (John 15:1–11; see Matthew 5:16; 7:7; John 3:29, 35; 6:56; 8:29, 31; 13:10; 15:16).

[ASKING from ask]
Setting: Jerusalem. Before the Passover, with His departure in mind, after explaining He is the vine and His disciples are the branches, Jesus commands them to love one another.

"This is My commandment, that you love one another, just as I have loved you. Greater love has no one than this, that one lay down his life for his friends. You are My friends if you do what I command you. No longer do I call you slaves, for the slave does not know what his master is doing; but I have called you friends, for all things that I have heard from My Father I have made known to you. You did not choose Me but I chose you, and appointed you that you would go and bear fruit, and *that* your fruit would remain, so that whatever you ask of the Father in My name He may give to you. This I command you, that you love one another" (John 15:12–17; see Matthew 12:50; John 6:70; 8:26; 10:11; 13:34).

[ASKING from asks]
Setting: Jerusalem. Before the Passover, after warning His disciples of the persecution they will face after His departure to heaven, Jesus elaborates about the coming ministry of the Holy Spirit.

"But now I am going to Him who sent Me; and none of you asks Me, 'Where are You going?' But because I have said these things to you, sorrow has filled your heart. But I tell you the truth, it is to your advantage that I go away; for if I do not go away, the Helper will not come to you; but if I go, I will send Him to you. And He, when He comes, will convict the world concerning sin and righteousness and judgment; concerning sin, because they do not believe in Me; and concerning righteousness, because I go to the Father and you no longer see Me; and concerning judgment, because the ruler of this world has been judged" (John 16:5–11; see John 7:33; 12:31; 14:1, 16; 15:22, 24).

[ASKING from asked and ask]
Setting: Jerusalem. Before the Passover, after empathizing with His disciples' sadness over His prophecies and giving them hope for the future, Jesus conveys promises about praying in His name.

"In that day you will not question Me about anything. Truly, truly, I say to you, if you ask the Father for anything in My name, He will give it to you. Until now you have asked for nothing in My name; ask and you will receive, so that your joy may be made full. These things I have spoken to you in figurative language; an hour is coming when I will no longer speak to you in figurative language, but will tell you plainly of the Father. In that day you will ask in My name, and I do not say to you that I will request of the Father on your behalf; for the Father Himself loves you, because you have loved Me and have believed that I came forth from the Father. I came forth from the Father and have come into the world; I am leaving the world again and going to the Father" (John 16:23–28; see Matthew 13:34; John 8:42; 13:1, 3; 14:14, 21, 23; 15:16).

[ASKING from ask]
Setting: Jerusalem. Before the Passover, after giving His disciples assurance that in the midst of tribulation they will have His peace, Jesus prays His high-priestly prayer.

Jesus spoke these things; and lifting up His eyes to heaven, He said, "Father, the hour has come; glorify Your Son, that the Son may glorify You, even as You gave Him authority over all flesh, that to all whom You have given Him, He may give eternal life. This is eternal life, that they may know You, the only true God, and Jesus Christ whom You have sent. I glorified You on the earth, having accomplished the work which You have given Me to do. Now, Father, glorify Me together with Yourself, with the glory which I had with You before the world was. I have manifested Your name to the men whom You gave Me out of the world; they were Yours and You gave them to Me, and they have kept Your word. Now they have come to know that everything You have given Me is from You; for the words which You gave Me I have given to them; and they received *them* and truly understood that I came forth from You, and they believed You sent Me. I ask on their behalf; I do not ask on behalf of the world, but of those whom You have given Me; for they are Yours; and all things that are Mine are Yours, and Yours are Mine; and have been glorified in them. I am no longer in the world; and *yet* they themselves are in the world, and I come to You. Holy Father, keep them in Your name, *the name* which You have given Me, that they may be even as We *are.* While I was with them, I was keeping them in Your name which You have given Me; and I guarded them and not one of them perished but the son of perdition, so that the Scripture would be fulfilled" (John 17:1–12; see Luke 22:32; John 1:1; 3:35; 4:34; 5:44; 6:37–39, 70; 8:42; 11:41; 12:49; 13:18, 31; 16:15; 17:20; Philippians 2:9).

[ASKING from ask]

Setting: Jerusalem. Before the Passover, after giving His disciples assurance that in the midst of tribulation they will have His peace, Jesus continues praying His high-priestly prayer.

"But now I come to You; and these things I speak in the world so that they may have My joy made full in themselves. I have given them Your word; and the world has hated them, because they are not of the world, even as I am not of the world. I do not ask You to take them out of the world, but to keep them from the evil *one.* They are not of the world, even as I am not of the world. Sanctify them in the truth; Your word is truth. As You sent Me into the world, I also have sent them into the world. For their sakes I sanctify Myself, that they themselves also may be sanctified in truth. I do not ask on behalf of these alone, but for those also who believe in Me through their word; that they may all be one; even as You, Father, *are* in Me and I in You, that they also maybe in Us, so that the world may believe that You sent Me" (John 17:13–21; see Matthew 10:5, 38; John 7:33; 15:3, 11, 19).

ASLEEP (See SLEEP)

ATTENDANTS (Also see WEDDING)

Setting: Capernaum near the Sea of Galilee. John the Baptist's disciples ask Jesus why His own disciples do not participate in fasting, while they and the Pharisees do.

And Jesus said to them, "The attendants of the bridegroom cannot mourn as long as the bridegroom is with them, can they? But the days will come when the bridegroom is taken away from them, and then they will fast. But no one puts a patch of unshrunk cloth on an old garment; for the patch pulls away from the garment, and a worse tear results. Nor do *people* put new wine into old wineskins; otherwise the wineskins burst, and the wine pours out and the wineskins are ruined; but they put new wine into fresh wineskins, and both are preserved" (Matthew 9:15–17; cf. Mark 2:18–22; Luke 5:33–39).

Setting: Capernaum near the Sea of Galilee. John the Baptist's disciples and the Pharisees question why Jesus' disciples do not fast, while *they* do.

And Jesus said to them, "While the bridegroom is with them, the attendants of the bridegroom cannot fast, can they? So long as they have the bridegroom with them, they cannot fast. But the days will come when the bridegroom is taken away from them, and then they will fast in that day. No one sews a patch of unshrunk cloth on an old garment; otherwise the patch pulls away from it, the new from the old, and a worse tear results. No one puts new wine into old wineskins; otherwise the wine will burst the skins, and the wine is lost and the skins as *well;* but *one puts* new wine into fresh wineskins" (Mark 2:19–22; cf. Matthew 9:14–17; Luke 5:33–38).

Setting: The home of Levi (Matthew) in Capernaum. At a reception for Jesus following Levi's call to be a disciple, the Pharisees and their scribes question Jesus about fasting.

And Jesus said to them, "You cannot make the attendants of the bridegroom fast while the bridegroom is with them, can you? But the days will come; and when the bridegroom is taken away from them, then they will fast in those days" (Luke 5:34, 35; cf. Matthew 9:14, 15; Mark 2:18–20).

ATTITUDE (See GREATNESS; and SERVICE)

AUTHORITIES (Also see AUTHORITY; and RULERS)

Setting: As Jesus and His disciples head toward Jerusalem from Galilee, Jesus warns His disciples of future events as the scribes and Pharisees turn hostile and begin to question Him on many subjects in an attempt to catch Him in something He might say.

"And I say to you, everyone who confesses Me before men, the Son of Man will confess him also before the angels of God; but he who denies Me before men will be denied before the angels of God. And everyone who speaks a word against the Son of Man, it will be forgiven him; but he who blasphemes against the Holy Spirit, it will not be forgiven him. When they bring you before the synagogues and the rulers and the authorities, do not worry about how or what you are to speak in your defense, or what you are to say; for the Holy Spirit will teach you in that very hour what you ought to say" (Luke 12:8–12; cf. Matthew 10:32, 33; 12:31, 32; see Matthew 10:20).

AUTHORITY (Also see AUTHORITIES; KEYS; MOSES, CHAIR OF; POWER; RULERS; STEWARDSHIP; and SUBJECTION)

Setting: Capernaum near the Sea of Galilee. After Jesus heals and forgives a paralytic of his sins in front of crowds, some scribes accuse Him of blasphemy.

And they brought to Him a paralytic lying on a bed. Seeing their faith, Jesus said to the paralytic, "Take courage, son; your sins are forgiven." And some scribes said to themselves. "This *fellow* blasphemes." And Jesus knowing their thoughts said, "Why are you thinking evil in your hearts? Which is easier to say, 'Your sins are forgiven,' or to say, 'Get up, and walk'? But so that you may know that the Son of Man has authority on earth to forgive sins"—then He said to the paralytic, "Get up, pick up your bed and go home" (Matthew 9:2–6; cf. Mark 2:3–12; Luke 5:17–26).

[AUTHORITY from All things have been handed over to Me by My Father]

Setting: Galilee. After pronouncing woes against unrepentant cities as He teaches and preaches, Jesus prays a thanksgiving prayer to His Father in heaven.

At that time Jesus said, "I praise You, Father, Lord of heaven and earth, that you have hidden these things from *the* wise and intelligent and have revealed them to infants. Yes, Father, for this way was well-pleasing in Your sight. All things have been handed over to Me by My Father; and no one knows the Son except the Father; nor does anyone know the Father except the Son, and anyone to whom the Son wills to reveal *Him*" (Matthew 11:25–27; cf. Luke 10:21, 22).

Setting: On the way to Jerusalem for the crucifixion, Jesus teaches His disciples about true greatness after the mother of James and John, the sons of Zebedee, asks Him to make her sons exalted rulers with Him in His coming kingdom.

But Jesus called them to Himself and said, "You know that the rulers of the Gentiles lord it over them, and *their* great men exercise authority over them. It is not this way among you, but whoever wishes to become great among you shall be your servant, and whoever wishes to be first among you shall be your slave; just as the Son of Man did not come to be served, but to serve, and to give His life a ransom for many" (Matthew 20:25–28; cf. Matthew 23:11; 26:28; Mark 10:42–45).

Setting: The temple in Jerusalem. Having spent the night in Bethany, Jesus returns, and the chief priests and elders question His authority in an effort to challenge His teaching to the nation.

Jesus said to them, "I will also ask you one thing, which if you tell Me, I will also tell you by what authority I do these things. The baptism of John was from what *source,* from heaven or from men?" And they *began* reasoning among themselves, saying "If we say 'From heaven,' He will say to us, 'Then why did you not believe him?' But if we say, 'From men,' we fear the people; for they all regard John as a prophet." And answering Jesus, they said, "We do not know." He also said to them, "Neither will I tell you by what authority I do these things" (Matthew 21:24–27; cf. Mark 11:29–33; Luke 20:3–8).

Setting: On a mountain in Galilee. Following His resurrection from the dead in Jerusalem, Jesus conveys the Great Commission to the eleven remaining disciples.

And Jesus came up and spoke to them, saying, "All authority has been given to Me in heaven and on earth. Go therefore and make disciples of all the nations, baptizing them in the name of the Father and the Son and the Holy Spirit, teaching them to observe all that I commanded you; and lo, I am with you always, even to the end of the age" (Matthew 28:18–20; cf. Mark 16:15; see Daniel 7:13).

Setting: Capernaum. When Jesus heals and forgives the sins of a paralytic man, some scribes believe He commits blasphemy.

Immediately Jesus, aware in His spirit that they were reasoning that way within themselves, said to them, "Why are you reasoning about these things in your hearts? Which is easier, to say to the paralytic, 'Your sins are forgiven'; or to say, 'Get up, and pick up your pallet and walk'? "But so that you may know that the Son of Man has authority on earth to forgive sins"—He said to the paralytic, "I say to you, get up, pick up your pallet and go home" (Mark 2:8–11; cf. Matthew 9:4–7; Luke 5:21–24).

Setting: On the road to Jerusalem. When James and John ask Jesus for special honor and privileges in His kingdom, the other disciples become angry, so Jesus uses this moment to teach them about servanthood.

Calling them to Himself, Jesus said to them, "You know that those who are recognized as rulers of the Gentiles lord it over them; and their great men exercise authority over them. But it is not this way among you, but whoever wishes to become great among you shall be your servant; and whoever wishes to be first among you shall be slave of all. For even the Son of Man did not come to be served, but to serve, and to give His life a ransom for many" (Mark 10:42–45; cf. Matthew 20:25–28).

Setting: The temple in Jerusalem. After Jesus teaches about faith and forgiveness utilizing a cursed fig tree as an object lesson, His authority is questioned by the chief priests, scribes, and elders.

And Jesus said to them, "I will ask you one question, and you answer Me, and *then* I will tell you by what authority I do these things. Was the baptism of John from heaven, or from men? Answer Me." They *began* reasoning among themselves, saying, "If we say 'From heaven,' He will say, 'Then why did you not believe him?' "But shall we say 'From men'?"—they were afraid of the people, for everyone considered John to have been a real prophet. Answering Jesus, they said, "We do not know." And Jesus said to them, "Nor will I tell you by what authority I do these things" (Mark 11:29–33; cf. Matthew 21:23–27; Luke 20:1–8).

Setting: Capernaum of Galilee. After Jesus heals and forgives the sins of a paralytic man, some Pharisees and teachers of the law from Galilee and Judea accuse Him of committing blasphemy.

But Jesus, aware of their reasonings, answered and said to them, "Why are you reasoning in your hearts? Which is easier, to say, 'Your sins have been forgiven you,' or to say, 'Get up and walk'? But, so that you may know that the Son of Man has authority on earth to forgive sins,"—He said to the paralytic—"I say to you, get up, and pick up your stretcher and go home" (Luke 5:22–24; cf. Matthew 9:4–8; Mark 2:8–12; see Matthew 4:24).

[AUTHORITY inferred]
Setting: Galilee. After conveying who His true relatives are, Jesus and His disciples set sail on the Sea of Galilee, where He calms a storm.

And He said to them, "Where is your faith?" They were fearful and amazed, saying to one another, "Who then is this, that He commands even the winds and the water, and they obey Him?" (Luke 8:25; cf. Matthew 8:23–27; Mark 4:35–41).

Setting: On the way from Galilee to Jerusalem. The Lord responds to a report from the seventy sent out in pairs to every city and place He Himself will soon visit.

And He said to them, "I was watching Satan fall from heaven like lightning. Behold, I have given you authority to tread on serpents and scorpions, and over all the power of the enemy, and nothing will injure you. Nevertheless do not rejoice in this, that the spirits are subject to you, but rejoice that your names are recorded in heaven" (Luke 10:18–20; see Psalm 91:13; Isaiah 14:12–14; Luke 9:1).

[AUTHORITY from All things have been handed over to Me by My Father]
Setting: On the way from Galilee to Jerusalem. The Lord responds to a report from the seventy sent out in pairs to every city and place He Himself will soon visit.

At that very time He rejoiced greatly in the Holy Spirit, and said, "I praise You, O Father, Lord of heaven and earth, that You have hidden these things from the wise and intelligent and have revealed them to infants. Yes, Father, for this way was well-pleasing in Your sight. All things have been handed over to Me by My Father, and no one knows who the Son is except the Father, and who the Father is except the Son, and anyone to whom the Son wills to reveal Him." (Luke 10:21, 22; cf. Matthew 11:25–27; see Luke 10:1, 17; John 3:35; 10:15).

Setting: On the way from Galilee to Jerusalem. Jesus warns His disciples of future events as the scribes and Pharisees turn hostile and question Him in an attempt to catch Him in something He might say.

Under these circumstances, after so many thousands of people had gathered together that they were stepping on one another, He began saying to His disciples first of all, "Beware of the leaven of the Pharisees, which is hypocrisy. But there is nothing covered up that will not be revealed, and hidden that will not be known. Accordingly, whatever you have said in the dark will be heard in the light, and what you have whispered in the inner rooms will be proclaimed upon the housetops. I say to you, My friends, do not be afraid of those who kill the body and after that have no more that they can do. But I will warn you whom to fear: fear the One who, after He has killed, has authority to cast into hell; yes, I tell you, fear Him! Are not five sparrows sold for two cents? Yet not one of them is forgotten before God. Indeed, the very hairs of your head are all numbered. Do not fear; you are more valuable than many sparrows" (Luke 12:1–7; cf. Matthew 10:26–31; see Matthew 16:6; Hebrews 10:31).

[AUTHORITY also from reign over]
Setting: Jericho, on the way to Jerusalem. After commending Zaccheus's faith in Him, Jesus provides a parable about stewardship.

So He said, "A nobleman went to a distant country to receive a kingdom for himself, and then return. And he called ten of his slaves, and gave them ten minas and said to them, 'Do business with this until I come back.' But his citizens hated him and sent a delegation after him, saying, 'We do not want this man to reign over us.' When he returned, after receiving the kingdom, he ordered that these slaves, to whom he had given the money, be called to him so that he might know what business they had done. The first appeared, saying, 'Master, your mina has made ten minas more.' And he said to him, 'Well done, good slave, because you have been faithful in a very little thing, you are to be in authority over ten cities.' The second came, saying, 'Your mina, master, has made five minas.' And he said to him, also, 'And you are to be over five cities.' Another came, saying, 'Master, here is your mina, which I kept put away in a handkerchief; for I was afraid of you, because you are an exacting man; you take up what you did not lay down and reap what you did not sow.' He said to him, 'By your own words I will judge you, you worthless slave. Did you know that I am an exacting man, taking up what I did not lay down and reaping what I did not sow? Then why did you not put my money in the bank, and having come, I would have collected it with interest?' Then he said to the bystanders, 'Take the mina away from him and give it to the one who has the ten minas.' And they said to him, 'Master, he has ten minas already.' I tell you

that to everyone who has, more shall be given, but from the one who does not have, even what he does have shall be taken away. But these enemies of mine, who did not want me to reign over them, bring them here and slay them in my presence" (Luke 19:12–27; cf. Matthew 25:14–30; see Matthew 13:12; Luke 16:10).

Setting: The temple in Jerusalem. While ministering a few days before His crucifixion, with the conflict with the religious leaders of Israel escalating, the chief priests and the scribes question Jesus' authority to teach and preach.

Jesus answered and said to them, "I will also ask you a question, and you tell Me: Was the baptism of John from heaven or from men?" They reasoned among themselves, saying, "If we say, 'From heaven,' He will say, 'Why did you not believe him?' But if we say, 'From men,' all the people will stone us to death, for they are convinced that John was a prophet." So they answered that they did not know where it came from. And Jesus said to them, "Nor will I tell you by what authority I do these things" (Luke 20:3–8; cf. Matthew 21:23–27; Mark 11:27–33).

Setting: And upper room in Jerusalem. During the Feast of Unleavened Bread (Passover) just before Jesus' crucifixion, while He celebrates the Passover meal with His disciples and institutes the Lord's Supper, the disciples argue over who is the greatest among them.

And He said to them, "The kings of the Gentiles lord it over them; and those who have authority over them are called 'Benefactors.' But it is not this way with you, but the one who is the greatest among you must become like the youngest, and the leader like a servant. For who is greater, the one who reclines at the table or the one who serves? Is it not the one who reclines at the table? But I am among you as the one who serves" (Luke 22:25–27; cf. Matthew 20:25–28; 23:11; Mark 10:42–45).

Setting: Jerusalem. During the Feast of the Jews, Jesus responds to criticism from the Jewish religious leaders by referring to God as His Father (thereby making Himself equal with God) and prophesying His participation in the resurrection and judgment of men.

"Truly, truly, I say to you, an hour is coming and now is, when the dead will hear the voice of the Son of God, and those who hear will live. For just as the Father has life in Himself, even so He gave to the Son also to have life in Himself; and He gave Him authority to execute judgment, because He is *the* Son of Man. Do not marvel at this; for an hour is coming, in which all who are in the tombs will hear His voice, and will come forth; those who did the good *deeds* to a resurrection of life, those who committed the evil *deeds* to a resurrection of judgment" (John 5:25–29; see Daniel 12:2; John 1:4; 11:24).

Setting: Jerusalem. Following the Pharisees' interrogation and dismissal of the formerly blind man Jesus healed on the Sabbath, the Lord conveys the Parable of the Good Shepherd to the Pharisees, using figures of speech they do not understand.

So Jesus said to them again, "Truly, truly, I say to you, I am the door of the sheep. All who came before Me are thieves and robbers, but the sheep did not hear them. I am the door; if anyone enters through Me, he will be saved, and will go in and out and find pasture. The thief comes only to steal and kill and destroy; I came that they may have life, and have *it* abundantly. I am the good shepherd; the good shepherd lays down His life for the sheep. He who is a hired hand, and not a shepherd, who is not the owner of the sheep, sees the wolf coming, and leaves the sheep and flees, and the wolf snatches them and scatters *them. He flees* because he is a hired hand and is not concerned about the sheep. I am the good shepherd, and I know My own and My own know Me, even as the Father knows Me and I know the Father; and I lay down My life for the sheep. I have other sheep, which are not of this fold; I must bring them also, and they will hear My voice; and they will become one flock *with* one shepherd. For this reason the Father loves Me, because I lay down My life so that I may take it again. No one has taken it away from Me, but I lay it down on My own initiative. I have authority to take it up again. This commandment I received from My Father" (John 10:7–18; see Isaiah 40:11; 56:8; Jeremiah 23:1; Matthew 11:27).

Setting: Jerusalem. Before the Passover, after giving His disciples assurance that in the midst of tribulation they will have His peace, Jesus prays His high-priestly prayer.

Jesus spoke these things; and lifting up His eyes to heaven, He said, "Father, the hour has come; glorify Your Son, that the Son may glorify You, even as You gave Him authority over all flesh, that to all whom You have given Him, He may give eternal life. This is eternal life, that they may know You, the only true God, and Jesus Christ whom You have sent. I glorified You on the earth, having accomplished the work which You have given Me to do. Now, Father, glorify Me together with Yourself, with the glory which I had with You before the world was. I have manifested Your name to the men whom You gave Me out of the world; they were Yours and You gave them to Me, and they have kept Your word. Now they have come to know that everything You have given Me is from You; for the words which You gave Me I have given to them; and they received *them* and truly understood that I came forth from You, and they believed You sent Me. I ask on their behalf; I do not ask on behalf of the world, but of those whom You have given Me; for they are Yours; and all things that are Mine are Yours, and Yours are Mine; and have been glorified in them. I am no longer in the world; and *yet* they themselves are in the world, and I come to You. Holy Father, keep them in Your name, *the name* which You have given Me, that they may be even as We *are.* While I was with them, I was keeping them in Your name which You have given Me; and I guarded them and not one of them perished but the son of perdition, so that the Scripture would be fulfilled" (John 17:1–12; see Luke 22:32; John 1:1; 3:35; 4:34; 5:44; 6:37–39, 70; 8:42; 11:41; 12:49; 13:18, 31; 16:15; 17:20; Philippians 2:9).

Setting: Jerusalem. Pontius Pilate (Roman governor of Judea), who continues to find no guilt in Jesus, has Him scourged in an attempt to appease the hostile Jewish religious leaders, and seeks more information as to where the King of the Jews is from.

Jesus answered, "You would have no authority over Me, unless it had been given you from above; for this reason he who delivered Me to you has *the* greater sin" (John 19:11; see Romans 13:1).

Setting: Jerusalem. Luke, writing in Acts, presents quotes from Jesus' post-resurrection appearances, in which He responds to His followers' question if He is about to restore the kingdom to Israel.

He said to them, "It is not for you to know times or epochs which the Father has fixed by His own authority; but you will receive power when the Holy Spirit has come upon you; and you shall be My witnesses both in Jerusalem, and in all Judea and Samaria, and even to the remotest part of the earth" (Acts 1:7, 8; see Luke 24:48, 49; Acts 2:1–4).

Setting: On the island of Patmos (in the Aegean Sea about fifty miles southwest of Ephesus in modern Turkey). On the Lord's Day (Sunday), about fifty years after Jesus' resurrection, the disciple John encounters the Lord Jesus Christ, who communicates a new revelation for the apostle to record for the church in Thyatira and to six other churches in Asia.

"And to the angel of the church in Thyatira write: The Son of God, who has eyes like a flame of fire, and His feet are like burnished bronze, says this: 'I know your deeds, and your love and faith and service and perseverance, and that your deeds of late are greater than at first. But I have *this* against you, that you tolerate the woman Jezebel, who calls herself a prophetess, and she teaches and leads My bond-servants astray so that they commit *acts of* immorality and eat things sacrificed to idols. I gave her time to repent, and she does not want to repent of her immorality. Behold, I will throw her on a bed *of sickness,* and those who commit adultery with her into great tribulation, unless they repent of her deeds. And I will kill her children with pestilence, and all the churches will know that I am He who searches the minds and hearts; and I will give to each one of you according to your deeds. But I say to you, the rest who are in Thyatira, who do not hold this teaching, who have not known the deep things of Satan, as they call them—I place no other burden on you. Nevertheless what you have, hold fast until I come. He who overcomes, and he who keeps My deeds until the end, TO HIM I WILL GIVE AUTHORITY OVER THE NATIONS; AND HE SHALL RULE THEM WITH A ROD OF IRON, AS THE VESSELS OF THE POTTER ARE BROKEN TO PIECES, as I also have received *authority* from My Father; and I will give him the morning star. He who has an ear, let him hear what the Spirit says to the churches' (Revelation 2:18–29; Jesus quotes from Psalm 2:8, 9; Isaiah 30:14; see 1 Kings 16:31; Psalm 7:9; Romans 2:5; 1 Corinthians 2:10; 2 Peter 3:9; Revelation 1:14; 2:7; 3:11; 17:1–20).

Setting: On the way from Galilee to Jerusalem. Jesus warns His disciples of future events as the scribes and Pharisees turn hostile and question Him in an attempt to catch Him in something He might say.

"And I say to you, everyone who confesses Me before men, the Son of Man will confess him also before the angels of God; but he who denies Me before men will be denied before the angels of God. And everyone who speaks a word against the Son of Man, it will be forgiven him; but he who blasphemes against the Holy Spirit, it will not be forgiven him. When they bring you before the synagogues and the rulers and the authorities, do not worry about how or what you are to speak in your defense, or what you are to say; for the Holy Spirit will teach you in that very hour what you ought to say" (Luke 12:8–12; cf. Matthew 10:32, 33; 12:31, 32; see Matthew 10:20).

AWAY, PASS (Also see END)

Setting: Galilee. During the early part of His ministry, Jesus preaches the Sermon on the Mount to His disciples and the multitudes.

"Do not think that I came to abolish the Law or the Prophets; I did not come to abolish but to fulfill. For truly I say to you, until heaven and earth pass away, not the smallest letter or stroke shall pass from the Law until all is accomplished" (Matthew 5:17, 18; cf. Matthew 24:35).

Setting: The Mount of Olives, just east of Jerusalem. During His discourse, after answering His disciples' questions as to when the temple will be destroyed and Jerusalem overrun, along with the signs of His coming and the end of the age, Jesus teaches them the Parable of the Fig Tree.

"Now learn the parable from the fig tree: when its branch has already become tender and puts forth its leaves, you know that summer is near; so, you too, when you see all these things, recognize that He is near, *right* at the door. Truly, I say to you, this generation will not pass away until all these things take place. Heaven and earth will pass away, but My words will not pass away. But of that day and hour no one knows, not even the angels of heaven, nor the Son, but the Father alone. For the coming of the Son of Man will be just like the days of Noah. For as in those days before the flood they were eating and drinking, marrying and giving in marriage, until the day that Noah entered the ark, and they did not understand until the flood came and took them all away; so will the coming of the Son of Man be. Then there will be two men in the field; one will be taken and one will be left. Two women *will be* grinding at the mill; one will be taken and one will be left" (Matthew 24:32–41; cf. Mark 13:28–32; Luke 17:34–36; 21:28–33; see Genesis 6:5; 7:7; Matthew 5:18; 10:23; James 5:9).

Setting: An upper room in Jerusalem. After celebrating the Passover meal with His disciples, Jesus retreats to the Garden of Gethsemane on the Mount of Olives to pray prior to His betrayal by Judas.

Then Jesus came with them to a place called Gethsemane, and said to His disciples, "Sit here while I go over there and pray." And He took with Him Peter and the two sons of Zebedee, and began to be grieved and distressed. Then He said to them, "My soul is deeply grieved, to the point of death; remain here and keep watch with Me." And He went a little beyond *them,* and fell on His face and prayed, saying, "My Father, if it is possible, let this cup pass from Me; yet not as I will, but as You will." And He came to the disciples and found them sleeping, and said to Peter, "So, you *men* could not keep watch with Me for one hour? Keep watching and praying that you may not enter into temptation; the spirit is willing, but the flesh is weak." He went away again a second time and prayed, saying, "My Father, if this cannot pass away unless I drink it, Your will be done." Again He came and found them sleeping, for their eyes were heavy. And He left them again, and went away and prayed a third time, saying the same thing once more. Then He came to the disciples and said to them, "Are you still sleeping and resting? Behold the hour is at hand and the Son of Man is being betrayed into the hands of sinners. Get up, let us be going; behold the one who betrays Me is at hand!" (Matthew 26:36–46; cf. Mark 14:32–42; Luke 22:40–46; see Matthew 20:22; John 12:27).

Setting: The Mount of Olives, east of the temple in Jerusalem. During His discourse, after prophesying the temple's destruction, Jesus responds to questions from Peter, James, John, and Andrew about future events.

"Now learn the parable from the fig tree: when its branch has already become tender and puts forth its leaves, you know that summer is near. Even so, you too, when you see these things happening, recognize that He is near, *right* at the door. Truly I say

to you, this generation will not pass away until all these things take place. Heaven and earth will pass away, but My words will not pass away. But of the day or hour no one knows, not even the angels in heaven, nor the Son, but the Father *alone*" (Mark 13:28–32; cf. Matthew 24:32–36; Luke 21:28–33).

Setting: On the way from Galilee to Jerusalem. The Lord responds to the Pharisees' scoffing at His teaching His disciples about stewardship.

And He said to them, "You are those who justify yourselves in the sight of men, but God knows your hearts; for that which is highly esteemed among men is detestable in the sight of God. The Law and the Prophets were proclaimed until John; since that time the gospel of the kingdom of God has been preached, and everyone is forcing his way into it. But is it easier for heaven and earth to pass away than for one stroke of a letter of the Law to fail" (Luke 16:15–17; cf. Matthew 5:18; see 1 Samuel 16:7; Matthew 4:23; 11:11–14).

Setting: The Mount of Olives, just east of Jerusalem. Following a time of ministry in the temple a few days before His crucifixion, after giving His disciples more details regarding His return, Jesus conveys the Parable of the Fig Tree.

Then He told them a parable: "Behold the fig tree and all the trees; as soon as they put forth leaves, you see it and know for yourselves that summer is now near. So you also, when you see these things happening, recognize that the kingdom of God is near. Truly, I say to you, this generation will not pass away until all things take place. Heaven and earth will pass away, but My words will not pass away" (Luke 21:29–33; cf. Matthew 24:32–35; Mark 13:28–31; see Matthew 5:18).

B

BABIES (See BABIES, NURSING; CHILDREN; INFANTS; and LITTLE ONES)

BABIES, NURSING (Also see INFANTS; and LITTLE ONES)

Setting: In Jerusalem, after cleansing the temple by driving out the money changers and merchants, Jesus responds to the chief priests and scribes, who are indignant about the praises the children render to Him.

But when the chief priests and the scribes saw the wonderful things that He had done, and the children who were shouting in the temple, "Hosanna to the Son of David," they became indignant and said to Him, "Do You hear what these *children* are saying?" And Jesus said to them, "Yes, have you never read, 'OUT OF THE MOUTH OF INFANTS AND NURSING BABIES YOU HAVE PREPARED PRAISE FOR YOURSELF'?" (Matthew 21:15, 16, Jesus quotes from Psalm 8:2; see Matthew 9:27).

Setting: The Mount of Olives, just east of Jerusalem. During His discourse, Jesus answers His disciples' questions as to when the temple will be destroyed and Jerusalem overrun, along with the signs of His coming and the end of the age. During His Olivet Discourse, Jesus comments to His disciples regarding their question as to when the temple will be destroyed, Jerusalem overrun along with the signs of His coming and the end of the age on the Mount of Olives just east of Jerusalem.

"Therefore when you see the ABOMINATION OF DESOLATION which was spoken of through Daniel the prophet, standing in the holy place (let the reader understand), then those who are in Judea must flee to the mountains. Whoever is on the housetop must not go down to get the things that are in his house. Whoever is in the field must not turn back to get his cloak. But woe to those who are pregnant and to those who are nursing babies in those days! But pray that your flight will not be in the winter, or on a Sabbath. For then there will be a great tribulation, such as has not occurred since the beginning of the world until now, nor ever will. Unless those days had been cut short, no life would have been saved; but for the sake of the elect those days will be cut short. Then if anyone says to you, 'Behold, here is the Christ,' or "There *He is,*' do not believe *him.* For false Christs and false prophets will arise and will show great signs and wonders, so as to mislead, if possible, even the elect. Behold, I have told you in advance. So if they say to you, 'Behold, He is in the wilderness,' do not go out, *or,* 'Behold, He is in the inner rooms,' do not believe *them.* For just as the lightning comes from the east and flashes even to the west, so will the coming of the Son of Man be. Wherever the corpse is, there the vultures will gather" (Matthew 24:15–28, Jesus quotes from Daniel 9:27; cf. Daniel 12:1; Mark 13:14–23; Luke 17:22–31; 21:20–24; 23:29; see John 4:48).

Setting: The Mount of Olives, east of the temple in Jerusalem. During His discourse, after prophesying the temple's destruction, Jesus responds to questions from Peter, James, John, and Andrew about future events.

"But when you see the ABOMINATION OF DESOLATION standing where it should not be (let the reader understand), then those who are in Judea must flee to the mountains. The one who is on the housetop must not go down, or go in to get anything out of his house; and the one who is in the field must not turn back to get his coat. But woe to those who are pregnant and to those who are nursing babies in those days! But pray that it may not happen in winter. For those days will be a *time of* tribulation such as has not occurred since the beginning of the creation which God created until now, and never will. Unless the Lord had shortened *those* days, no life would have been saved; but for the sake of the elect, whom He chose, He shortened the days. And then if anyone says to you, 'Behold, here is the Christ'; or, 'Behold, *He is* there'; do not believe *him*; for false Christs and false prophets will arise, and will show signs and wonders, in order to lead astray, if possible, the elect. But take heed; behold, I have told you everything in advance" (Mark 13:14–23; cf. Matthew 24:15–28; Luke 21:20–24; see Daniel 9:27; 12:1; Luke 17:31).

Setting: The Mount of Olives, just east of Jerusalem. After a time of ministry in the temple a few days before His crucifixion, Jesus continues to give His disciples details regarding future events.

"But when you see Jerusalem surrounded by armies, then recognize that her desolation is near. Then those who are in Judea must flee to the mountains, and those who are in the midst of the city must leave, and those who are in the country must not enter the city; because these are days of vengeance, so that all things which are written will be fulfilled. Woe to those who are pregnant and to those who are nursing babies in those days; for there will be a great distress upon the land and wrath to this people; and they will fall by the edge of the sword, and will be led captive into all the nations; and Jerusalem will be trampled under foot by the Gentiles until the times of the Gentiles are fulfilled" (Luke 21:20–24; see Matthew 24:15–18; Mark 13:14–16; Luke 19:43).

BAD FRUIT (Listed under FRUIT, BAD)

BAD THINGS (Listed under THINGS, BAD)

BAD TREE (Listed under TREE, BAD)

BAG

Setting: Galilee. As His twelve disciples observe His ministry, Jesus summons and specifically instructs them about their ministry to the people of Israel.

These twelve Jesus sent out after instructing them: "Do not go in *the* way of *the* Gentiles, and do not enter *any* city of the Samaritans; but rather go to the lost sheep of the house of Israel. And as you go, preach, saying, 'The kingdom of heaven is at hand.' Heal *the* sick, raise *the* dead, cleanse *the* lepers, cast out demons. Freely you received, freely give. Do not acquire gold, or silver, or copper for your money belts, or a bag for *your* journey, or even two coats, or sandals, or a staff; for the worker is worthy of his support. And whatever city or village you enter, inquire who is worthy in it, and stay at his house until you leave *that city*. As you enter the house, give it your greeting. If the house is worthy, give it your *blessing of* peace. But if it is not worthy, take back your *blessing of* peace. Whoever does not receive you, nor heed your words, as you go out of that house or that city, shake the dust off your feet. Truly I say to you, it will be more tolerable for *the* land of Sodom and Gomorrah in the day of judgment than for that city" (Matthew 10:5–15; cf. Mark 6:7–11; Luke 9:1–5; see Matthew 3:2; 11:22, 24; 15:24; Luke 22:35; 1 Corinthians 9:14).

Setting: Galilee. After raising Jairus's daughter from the dead, Jesus calls the Twelve together and gives them power and authority over demons, along with the ability to heal diseases.

And He said to them, "Take nothing for your journey, neither a staff, nor a bag, nor bread, nor money; and do not even have two tunics apiece. Whatever house you enter, stay there until you leave that city. And as for those who do not receive you, go out from that city, shake the dust off your feet as a testimony against them" (Luke 9:3–5; cf. Matthew 10:1–15; Mark 6:7–11; see Luke 10:4–12).

Setting: On the way from Galilee to Jerusalem. The Lord appoints seventy followers and sends them out in pairs to every city and place He Himself will soon visit.

And He was saying to them, "The harvest is plentiful, but the laborers are few; therefore beseech the Lord of the harvest to send out laborers into His harvest. Go; behold, I send you out as lambs in the midst of wolves. Carry no money belt, no bag, no shoes; and greet no one on the way. Whatever house you enter, first say, 'Peace be to this house.' If a man of peace is there, your peace will rest on him; but if not, it will return to you. Stay in that house, eating and drinking what they give you; for the laborer is worthy of his wages. Do not keep moving from house to house. Whatever city you enter and they receive you, eat what is set before you; and heal those in it who are sick, and say to them, 'The kingdom of God has come near to you.' But whatever city you enter and they do not receive you, go out into its streets and say, 'Even the dust of your city which clings to our feet we wipe off in protest against you; yet be sure of this, that the kingdom of God has come near.' I say to you, it will be more tolerable in that day for Sodom than for that city" (Luke 10:2–12; see Genesis 19:24–28; Matthew 9:37, 38, 10:9–14, 16; 1 Corinthians 10:27).

Setting: An upper room in Jerusalem. During the Feast of Unleavened Bread (Passover) just before His crucifixion, while celebrating the Passover meal, instituting the Lord's Supper, and prophesying Peter's denial of Him, Jesus instructs His disciples to prepare to persevere without Him.

And He said to them, "When I sent you out without money belt and bag and sandals, you did not lack anything, did you?" They said, "No, nothing." And He said to them, "But now, whoever has a money belt is to take it along, likewise also a bag, and whoever has no sword is to sell his coat and buy one. For I tell you that this which is written must be fulfilled in Me, 'AND HE WAS NUMBERED WITH TRANSGRESSORS'; for that which refers to Me has its fulfillment." They said, "Lord, look, here are two swords." And He said to them, "It is enough" (Luke 22:35–38, Jesus quotes from Isaiah 53:12; see Matthew 10:5–15; Mark 6:7–11; Luke 9:1–5; 10:1–12; 22:49; John 17:4).

BALAAM (Listed under BALAAM, TEACHING OF)

BALAAM, TEACHING OF

Setting: On the island of Patmos (in the Aegean Sea about fifty miles southwest of Ephesus in modern Turkey). On the Lord's Day (Sunday), about fifty years after Jesus' resurrection, the disciple John encounters the Lord Jesus Christ, who communicates a new revelation for the apostle to record for the church in Pergamum and to six other churches in Asia.

"And to the angel of the church in Pergamum write: The One who has the sharp two-edged sword says this: 'I know where you dwell, where Satan's throne is; and you hold fast My name, and did not deny My faith even in the days of Antipas, My witness, My faithful one, who was killed among you, where Satan dwells. But I have a few things against you, because you have there some who hold the teaching of Balaam, who kept teaching Balak to put a stumbling block before the sons of Israel, to eat things sacrificed to idols and to commit *acts of* immorality. So you also have some who in the same way hold the teaching of the Nicolaitans. Therefore repent; or else I am coming to you quickly, and I will make war against them with the sword of My mouth. He who has an ear, let him hear what the Spirit says to the churches. To him who overcomes, to him I will give *some* of the hidden manna, and I will give him a white stone, and a new name written on the stone which no one knows but he who receives it' (Revelation 2:12–17; see Numbers 25:1–3; Isaiah 62:2; Revelation 1:16).

BALAK

Setting: On the island of Patmos (in the Aegean Sea about fifty miles southwest of Ephesus in modern Turkey). On the Lord's Day (Sunday), about fifty years after Jesus' resurrection, the disciple John encounters the Lord Jesus Christ, who communicates a new revelation for the apostle to record for the church in Pergamum and to six other churches in Asia.

"And to the angel of the church in Pergamum write: The One who has the sharp two-edged sword says this: 'I know where you dwell, where Satan's throne is; and you hold fast My name, and did not deny My faith even in the days of Antipas, My witness, My faithful one, who was killed among you, where Satan dwells. But I have a few things against you, because you have there some who hold the teaching of Balaam, who kept teaching Balak to put a stumbling block before the sons of Israel, to eat things sacrificed to idols and to commit *acts of* immorality. So you also have some who in the same way hold the teaching of the Nicolaitans. Therefore repent; or else I am coming to you quickly, and I will make war against them with the sword of My mouth. He who has an ear, let him hear what the Spirit says to the churches. To him who overcomes, to him I will give *some* of the hidden manna, and I will give him a white stone, and a new name written on the stone which no one knows but he who receives it' (Revelation 2:12–17; see Numbers 25:1–3; Isaiah 62:2; Revelation 1:16; 2:5, 6, 16).

BANK (Also see INTEREST; and MONEY)

Setting: The Mount of Olives, just east of Jerusalem. During His discourse, after answering His disciples' questions as to when the temple will be destroyed and Jerusalem overrun, along with the signs of His coming and the end of the age, Jesus reemphasizes to His disciples that they should be on the alert for His return.

"For *it is* just like a man *about* to go on a journey, who called his own slaves and entrusted his possessions to them. To one he gave five talents, to another, two, and to another, one, each according to his own ability; and he went on his journey. Immediately the one who had received the five talents went and traded with them, and gained five more talents. In the same manner the one who *had received* the two *talents* gained two more. But he who received the one *talent* went away, and dug a *hole* in the ground and hid his master's money. Now after a long time the master of those slaves came and settled accounts with them. The one who had received the five talents came up and brought five more talents, saying, 'Master, you entrusted five talents to me. See, I have gained five more talents.' His master said to him, 'Well done, good and faithful slave. You were faithful with a few things, I will put you in charge of many things; enter into the joy of your master.' Also the one who *had received* the two talents came up and said, 'Master, you entrusted two talents to me. See, I have gained two more talents.' His master said to him, 'Well done, good and faithful slave. You were faithful with a few things, I will put you in charge of many things; enter into the joy of your master.' And the one also who had received the one talent came up and said, 'Master, I knew you to be a hard man, reaping where you did not sow and gathering where you scattered no *seed.* And I was afraid, and went away and hid your talent in the ground. See, you have what is yours.' But his master answered and said to him, 'You wicked, lazy slave, you knew that I reap where I did not sow and gather where I scattered no *seed.* Then you ought to have put my money in the bank, and on my arrival I would have received my *money* back with interest. 'Therefore take away the talent from him, and give it to the one who has ten talents.' For to everyone who has, *more* shall be given, and he will have an abundance; but from the one who does not have, even what he does have shall be taken away. Throw out the worthless slave into the outer darkness; in that place there will be weeping and gnashing of teeth" (Matthew 25:14–30; cf. Matthew 8:12; 13:12; 24:45–47; see Matthew 18:23, 24; Luke 12:44).

Setting: Jericho, on the way to Jerusalem. After commending Zaccheus's faith in Him, Jesus provides a parable about stewardship.

So He said, "A nobleman went to a distant country to receive a kingdom for himself, and then return. And he called ten of his slaves, and gave them ten minas and said to them, 'Do business with this until I come back.' But his citizens hated him and sent a delegation after him, saying, 'We do not want this man to reign over us.' When he returned, after receiving the kingdom, he ordered that these slaves, to whom he had given the money, be called to him so that he might know what business they had done. The first appeared, saying, 'Master, your mina has made ten minas more.' And he said to him, 'Well done, good slave, because you have been faithful in a very little thing, you are to be in authority over ten cities.' The second came, saying, 'Your mina, master, has made five minas.' And he said to him, also, 'And you are to be over five cities.' Another came, saying, 'Master, here is your mina, which I kept put away in a handkerchief; for I was afraid of you, because you are an exacting man; you take up what you did not lay down and reap what you did not sow.' He said to him, 'By your own words I will judge you, you worthless slave. Did you know that I am an exacting man, taking up what I did not lay down and reaping what I did not sow? Then why did you not put my money in the bank, and having come, I would have collected it with interest?' Then he said to the bystanders, 'Take the mina away from him and give it to the one who has the ten minas.' And they said to him, 'Master, he has ten minas already.' I tell you that to everyone who has, more shall be given, but from the one who does not have, even what he does have shall be taken away. But these enemies of mine, who did not want me to reign over them, bring them here and slay them in my presence" (Luke 19:12–27; cf. Matthew 25:14–30; see Matthew 13:12; Luke 16:10).

BANQUET, PARABLE OF THE WEDDING (See FEAST, PARABLE OF THE WEDDING)

BANQUET, WEDDING (See FEAST, WEDDING)

BANQUETS (Also see DINNER)

Setting: The temple in Jerusalem. Jesus exposes the truth about Pharisaism to the crowds and His disciples after the Jewish religious leaders test Him with questions.

Then Jesus spoke to the crowds and to His disciples, saying: "The scribes and the Pharisees have seated themselves in the chair of Moses; therefore all that they tell you, do and observe, but do not do according to their deeds; for they say *things* and do not do *them.* They tie up heavy burdens and lay them on men's shoulders, but they themselves are unwilling to move them with *so much as* a finger. But they do all their deeds to be noticed by men; for they broaden their phylacteries and lengthen their tassels *of their garments.* They love the place of honor at banquets and the chief seats in the synagogues, and respectful greetings in the market places, and being called Rabbi by men. But do not be called Rabbi; for One is your Teacher, and you are all brothers. Do not call *anyone* on earth your father; for One is your Father, He who is in heaven. Do not be called leaders; for One is your Leader, *that is,* Christ. But the greatest among you shall be your servant. Whoever exalts himself shall be humbled; and whoever humbles himself shall be exalted" (Matthew 23:1–12; cf. Matthew 20:26; Mark 12:38–40; Luke 20:46, 47; see Exodus 13:9; Deuteronomy 33:3; Matthew 6:1, 5, 6, 9, 16; Mark 14:11; Luke 11:43; 14:11).

Setting: The temple in Jerusalem. After commending a scribe for his nearness to the kingdom of God, Jesus warns the crowd about the other scribes.

In His teaching He was saying: "Beware of the scribes who like to walk around in long robes, and *like* respectful greetings in the market places, and chief seats in the synagogues and places of honor at banquets, who devour widows' houses, and for appearance's sake offer long prayers; these will receive greater condemnation" (Mark 12:38–40; cf. Matthew 23:1–7; Luke 20:45–47).

Setting: The temple in Jerusalem. While ministering a few days before His crucifixion, after posing a question to the scribes, who do not answer, Jesus warns His disciples about the lifestyle of the scribes.

"Beware of the scribes, who like to walk around in long robes, and love respectful greetings in the market places, and chief seats in the synagogues and places of honor at banquets, who devour widows' houses, and for appearance's sake offer long prayers. These will receive greater condemnation" (Luke 20:46, 47; cf. Matthew 23:1–7; Mark 12:38–40; see Luke 11:43).

BAPTISM (identification in persecution and suffering; also see JESUS, CONFESSING; PERSECUTION; and SUFFERING)

Setting: The temple in Jerusalem. While ministering a few days before His crucifixion, after posing a question to the scribes, who do not answer, Jesus warns On the road to Jerusalem. After Jesus prophesies His persecution, death, and resurrection, James and John ask Him for special honor and privileges in His coming kingdom.

And He said to them, "What do you want Me to do for you?" They said to Him, "Grant that we may sit, one on Your right and one on *Your* left, in Your glory." But Jesus said to them, "You do not know what you are asking. Are you able to drink the cup that I drink, or to be baptized with the baptism with which I am baptized?" They said to Him, "We are able." And Jesus said to them, "The cup that I drink you shall drink; and you shall be baptized with the baptism with which I am baptized. But to sit on My right or on *My* left, this is not Mine to give; but it is for those for whom it has been prepared" (Mark 10:36–40; cf. Matthew 20:20–23; see Matthew 19:28; Mark 10:35; Acts 12:2).

Setting: On the way from Galilee to Jerusalem. After clarifying a parable for Peter and the crowd, Jesus conveys how a relationship with Him divides families.

"I have come to cast fire upon the earth; and how I wish it were already kindled! But I have a baptism to undergo, and how distressed I am until it is accomplished! Do you suppose that I came to grant peace on earth? I tell you, no, but rather division; for from now on five members in one household will be divided, three against two and two against three. They will be divided, father against son and son against father, mother against daughter, and daughter against mother, mother-in-law against daughter-in-law and daughter-in-law against mother-in-law" (Luke 12:49–53; cf. Matthew 10:34–36; see Micah 7:6; Mark 10:38).

BAPTISM (with water; JESUS, BAPTISM OF; and JOHN, BAPTISM OF are separate entries; also see JESUS, CONFESSING)

[BAPTISM from baptizing]

Setting: On a mountain in Galilee. Following His resurrection from the dead in Jerusalem, Jesus conveys the Great Commission to His eleven remaining disciples.

And Jesus came up and spoke to them, saying, "All authority has been given to Me in heaven and on earth. Go therefore and make disciples of all the nations, baptizing them in the name of the Father and the Son and the Holy Spirit, teaching them to observe all that I commanded you; and lo, I am with you always, even to the end of the age" (Matthew 28:18–20; cf. Mark 16:15; see Daniel 7:13).

[BAPTISM from baptized]
Setting: Jerusalem. Following His resurrection from the dead after being crucified, Jesus commissions His disciples to preach His gospel to the world.

And He said to them, "Go into all the world and preach the gospel to all creation. He who has believed and has been baptized shall be saved; but he who has disbelieved shall be condemned. These signs will accompany those who have believed: in My name they will cast out demons, they will speak with new tongues; they will pick up serpents, and if they drink any deadly poison, it will not hurt them; they will lay hands on the sick, and they will recover" (Mark 16:15–18; cf. Matthew 28:16–20; see Mark 9:38; John 3:18, 36; 1 Corinthians 15:6).

[Note: Some scholars question the authenticity of Mark 16:9–20, as these verses do not appear in some early New Testament manuscripts.]

[BAPTISM from baptized]
Setting: Jerusalem. Luke, writing in Acts, presents quotes from Jesus' post-resurrection appearances, in which He informs and instructs His disciples about their imminent baptism with the Holy Spirit.

Gathering them together, He commanded them not to leave Jerusalem, but to wait for what the Father had promised, "Which," *He said,* "you heard of from Me; for John baptized with water, but you will be baptized with the Holy Spirit not many days from now" (Acts 1:4, 5; see Luke 24:49; John 14:16, 26; Acts 2:1–4).

[BAPTISM from baptized]
Setting: Jerusalem. Luke, writing in Acts, records Peter (following a time of ministry to the Gentiles) recalling the words of Jesus regarding the baptism of the Holy Spirit.

And I remembered the word of the Lord, how He used to say, "John baptized with water, but you will be baptized with the Holy Spirit" (Acts 11:16; cf. Acts 1:5).

BAPTISM OF JESUS (Listed under JESUS, BAPTISM OF)

BAPTISM OF JOHN (Listed under JOHN, BAPTISM OF)

BAPTISM OF THE HOLY SPIRIT (Listed under HOLY SPIRIT, BAPTISM OF THE)

BARJONA, SIMON (See SIMON BARJONA)

BARN (Also see BARNS)

Setting: By the Sea of Galilee. Because the religious leaders are rejecting His message, Jesus continues teaching the crowds with the Parable of the Wheat and the Tares.

Jesus presented another parable to them, saying, "The kingdom of heaven may be compared to a man who sowed good seed in his field. But while his men were sleeping, his enemy came and sowed tares among the wheat, and went away. But when the wheat sprouted and bore grain, then the tares became evident also. The slaves of the landowner came and said to him, 'Sir, did you not sow good seed in your field? How then does it have tares?' And he said to them, 'An enemy has done this!' The slaves said to him,

'Do you want us, then, to go and gather them up?' But he said, 'No; for while you are gathering up the tares, you may uproot the wheat with them. Allow both to grow together until the harvest; and in the time of the harvest I will say to the reapers, "First gather up the tares and bind them in bundles to burn them up; but gather the wheat into my barn"'" (Matthew 13:24–30; cf. Matthew 3:12).

Setting: On the way from Galilee to Jerusalem. Jesus comforts the crowd and His disciples after giving them a parable about riches and greed. The scribes and Pharisees turn hostile and question Him in an attempt to catch Him in something He might say.

And He said to His disciples, "For this reason I say to you, do not worry about your life, as to what you will eat; nor for your body, as to what you will put on. For life is more than food, and the body more than clothing. Consider the ravens, for they neither sow nor reap; they have no storeroom nor barn, and yet God feeds them; how much more valuable you are than the birds! And which of you by worrying can add a single hour to his life's span? If then you cannot do even a very little thing, why do you worry about other matters? Consider the lilies, how they grow: they neither toil nor spin; but I tell you, not even Solomon in all his glory clothed himself like one of these. But if God so clothes the grass in the field, which is alive today and tomorrow is thrown into the furnace, how much more will He clothe you? You men of little faith! And do not seek what you will eat and what you will drink, and do not keep worrying. For all these things the nations of the world eagerly seek; but your Father knows that you need these things. But seek His kingdom, and these things will be added to you. Do not be afraid, little flock, for your Father has chosen gladly to give you the kingdom" (Luke 12:22–32; cf. Matthew 6:25–33; see 1 Kings 10:4–7; Job 38:41).

BARNS (Also see BARN)

Setting: Galilee. During the early part of His ministry, Jesus preaches the Sermon on the Mount to His disciples and the multitudes.

"For this reason I say to you, do not be worried about your life, *as to* what you will eat or what you will drink; nor for your body, *as to* what you will put on. Is not life more than food, and the body more than clothing? Look at the birds of the air, that they do not sow, nor reap nor gather into barns, and *yet* your heavenly Father feeds them. Are you not worth much more than they? And who of you by being worried can add a *single* hour to his life? And why are you worried about clothing? Observe how the lilies of the field grow; they do not toil nor do they spin, yet I say to you that not even Solomon in all his glory clothed himself like one of these. But if God so clothes the grass of the field, which is *alive* today and tomorrow is thrown into the furnace, *will He* not much more *clothe* you? You of little faith! Do not worry then, saying 'What will we eat?' or 'What will we drink?' or 'What will be wear for clothing?" For the Gentiles eagerly seek all these things; for your heavenly Father knows that you need all these things. But seek first His kingdom and His righteousness, and all these things will be added to you. So do not worry about tomorrow; for tomorrow will care for itself. Each day has enough trouble of its own" (Matthew 6:25–34; cf. Luke 12:22–31; see 1 Kings 10:4–7; Job 35:11; Matthew 8:26).

Setting: On the way from Galilee to Jerusalem. After the scribes and Pharisees turn hostile and question Him in an attempt to catch Him in something He might say, Jesus responds to a question from the crowd and gives a parable about riches and greed.

And He told them a parable, saying, "The land of a rich man was very productive. And he began reasoning to himself, saying, 'What shall I do, since I have no place to store my crops?' Then he said, 'This is what I will do: I will tear down my barns and build larger ones, and here I will store all my grain and my goods. And I will say to my soul, "Soul, you have many goods laid up for many years to come; take your ease, eat, drink and be merry."' "But God said to him, 'You fool! This very night your soul is required of you; and now who will own what you have prepared?' So is the man who stores up treasure for himself, and is not rich toward God" (Luke 12:16–21; see Job 27:8; Psalm 39:6; Ecclesiastes 12:9; Philippians 2:3).

BARRENNESS

[BARRENNESS from looking for fruit on it and did not find any]
Setting: On the way from Galilee to Jerusalem. After some present report to Him about the Galileans whose blood Pilate (Roman governor of Judea) had mixed with their sacrifices, Jesus responds to their concern by calling them to repentance and illustrating His point with a parable.

And He began telling this parable: "A man had a fig tree which had been planted in his vineyard; and he came looking for fruit on it and did not find any. And he said to the vineyard-keeper, 'Behold, for three years I have come looking for fruit on this fig tree without finding any. Cut it down! Why does it even use up the ground?' And he answered and said to him, 'Let it alone, sir, for this year too, until I dig around it and put fertilizer; and if it bears fruit next year, fine; but if not, cut it down.'" (Luke 13:6–9; see Matthew 3:10)

[BARRENNESS from barren]

Setting: Jerusalem. After being arrested and appearing before the Council of Elders (Sanhedrin), Pontius Pilate (Roman governor of Judea), Herod Antipas (tetrarch of Galilee and Perea), and Pilate a second time (when Pilate bows to the crowd's pressure and grants that Jesus be crucified), the Lord prophesies to the women mourning Him regarding the coming judgment of Jerusalem.

But Jesus turning to them said, "Daughters of Jerusalem, stop weeping for Me, but weep for yourselves and for your children. For behold, the days are coming when they will say, 'Blessed are the barren, and the wombs that never bore, and the breasts that never nursed.' Then they will begin TO SAY TO THE MOUNTAINS, 'FALL ON US,' AND TO THE HILLS, 'COVER US.' For if they do these things when the tree is green, what will happen when it is dry?" (Luke 23:28–31, Jesus quotes from Hosea 10:8; see Matthew 24:19).

BARRICADE

Setting: Approaching Jerusalem. After being praised by the people in a triumphal welcome, the Lord weeps as He sees the city ahead of Him.

When He approached Jerusalem, He saw the city and wept over it, saying, "If you had known in this day, even you, the things which make for peace! But now they have been hidden from your eyes. For the days will come upon you when your enemies will throw up a barricade against you, and surround you and hem you in on every side, and they will level you to the ground and your children within you, and they will not leave in you one stone upon another, because you did not recognize the time of your visitation" (Luke 19:41–44; see Matthew 24:1, 2; Luke 13:34, 35).

BASKET (Also see BASKETS)

Setting: Galilee. During the early part of His ministry, Jesus preaches the Sermon on the Mount to His disciples and the multitudes.

"You are the light of the world. A city set on a hill cannot be hidden; nor does *anyone* light a lamp and put it under a basket, but on the lampstand, and it gives light to all who are in the house. Let your light shine before men in such a way that they may see your good works, and glorify your Father who is in heaven" (Matthew 5:14–16; cf. Mark 4:21; 1 Peter 2:12).

Setting: Galilee. Following His explanation of the Parable of the Sower to His disciples, Jesus illustrates what they should do with this truth.

And He was saying to them, "A lamp is not brought to be put under a basket, is it, or under a bed? Is it not *brought* to be put on the lampstand? For nothing is hidden, except to be revealed; nor has *anything* been secret, but that it would come to light. If anyone has ears to hear, let him hear" (Mark 4:21–23; cf. Luke 8:16, 17; see Matthew 5:14–16; 10:26).

Setting: On the way from Galilee to Jerusalem. After telling the increasing crowds of the sign of Jonah, Jesus illustrates His point by speaking of a lamp.

"No one, after lighting a lamp, puts it away in a cellar nor under a basket, but on the lampstand, so that those who enter may see the light. The eye is the lamp of your body; when your eye is clear, your whole body also is full of light; but when it is bad, your body also is full of darkness. Then watch out that the light in you is not darkness. If therefore your whole body is full of light, with no dark part in it, it will be wholly illumined, as when the lamp illumines you with its rays" (Luke 11:33–36; cf. Matthew 5:15, 6:22, 23).

BASKETS (Also see BASKET)

Setting: By the Sea of Galilee. Jesus repeats the warning to His disciples about the teaching of the religious leaders of the day, the Pharisees and Sadducees.

But Jesus aware of this, said, "You men of little faith, why do you discuss among yourselves that you have no bread? Do you not yet understand or remember the five loaves of the five thousand and how many baskets *full* you picked up? Or the seven loaves of the four thousand, and how many large baskets *full* you picked up? How is it that you do not understand that I did not speak to you concerning bread? But beware of the leaven of the Pharisees and Sadducees" (Matthew 16:8–11; cf. Matthew 14:17–21; 15:34–38; Mark 8:17–21).

Setting: The district of Dalmanutha. After the Pharisees argue with Jesus, seeking a sign from heaven to test Him, Jesus and His disciples cross to the other side of the Sea of Galilee, where His disciples discuss with one another that they have no bread.

And Jesus, aware of this, said to them, "Why do you discuss *the fact* that you have no bread? Do you not yet see or understand? Do you have a hardened heart? HAVING EYES, DO YOU NOT SEE? AND HAVING EARS, DO YOU NOT HEAR? And do you not remember, when I broke the five loaves for the five thousand, how many baskets full of broken pieces you picked you? They said to Him, "Twelve." When *I broke* the seven for the four thousand, how many large baskets full of broken pieces did you pick up?" They said to Him, "Seven." And He was saying to them, "Do you not yet understand?" (Mark 8:17–21, Jesus quotes from Jeremiah 5:21; cf. Matthew 16:5–12; see Matthew 14:19, 20; Mark 6:41–44, 52; 8:6–9).

BATH (Also see WASHING)

[BATH from bathed]

Setting: Jerusalem. Before the Passover, with His crucifixion nearing, Jesus eats supper with His disciples and assumes the role of a servant by washing their feet.

Jesus answered and said to him, "What I do you do not realize now, but you will understand hereafter." Peter said to Him, "Never shall You wash my feet!" Jesus answered him, "If I do not wash you, you have no part with Me." Simon Peter said to Him, "Lord, *then wash* not only my feet, but also my hand and my head." Jesus said to him, "He who has bathed needs only to wash his feet, but is completely clean; and you are clean, but not all *of you*. For He knew the one who was betraying Him; for this reason He said, "Not all of you are clean" (John 13:7–11; see John 6:64; 15:3).

BATTLE

Setting: On the way from Galilee to Jerusalem. After He responds to a guest's proclamation about the blessings of eating bread in the kingdom of God, Jesus presents to large crowds the demands of discipleship.

Now large crowds were going along with Him; and He turned and said to them, "If anyone comes to Me, and does not hate his own father and mother and wife and children and brothers and sisters, yes, and even his own life, he cannot be My disciple. Whoever does not carry his own cross and come after Me cannot be My disciple. For which one of you, when he wants to build a tower, does not first sit down and calculate the cost to see if he has enough to complete it? Otherwise, when he has laid a foundation and is not able to finish, all who observe it begin to ridicule him, saying, 'This man began to build and was not able to finish.' Or what king, when he sets out to meet another king in battle, will not first sit down and consider whether he is strong enough with ten thousand *men* to encounter the one coming against him with twenty thousand? Or else, while the other is still far away, he sends a delegation and asks for terms of peace. So then, none of you can be My disciple who does not give up all his possessions. Therefore, salt is good; but if even salt has become tasteless, with what will it be seasoned? It is useless either for the soil or for the manure pile; it is thrown out. He who has ears to hear, let him hear" (Luke 14:25–35; cf. Matthew 5:13; 10:37–39; see Proverbs 20:18; Philippians 3:7).

BEACH

Setting: By the Sea of Galilee. Because the religious leaders are rejecting His message, Jesus continues teaching His disciples with the Parable of the Dragnet.

"Again, the kingdom of heaven is like a dragnet cast into the sea, and gathering *fish* of every kind; and when it was filled, they drew it up on the beach; and they sat down and gathered the good *fish* into containers, but the bad they threw away. So it will be at the end of the age; the angels will come forth and take out the wicked from among the righteous, and will throw them into the furnace of fire; in that place there will be weeping and gnashing of teeth. Have you understood all these things?" They said to Him, "Yes" (Matthew 13:47–51).

BEAST

Setting: On the way from Galilee to Jerusalem. While being tested by a lawyer, Jesus tells him the Parable of the Good Samaritan.

Jesus replied and said, "A man was going down from Jerusalem to Jericho, and fell among robbers, and they stripped him and beat him, and went away leaving him half dead. And by chance a priest was going down on that road, and when he saw him, he passed by on the other side. Likewise a Levite also, when he came to the place and saw him, passed by on the other side. But a Samaritan, who was on a journey, came upon him; and when he saw him, he felt compassion, and came to him and bandaged up his wounds, pouring oil and wine on them; and he put him on his own beast, and brought him to an inn and took care of him. On the next day he took out two denarii and gave them to the innkeeper and said, 'Take care of him; and whatever more you spend, when I return I will repay you.' Which of these three do you think proved to be a neighbor to the man who fell into the robbers' hands?" And he said, "The one who showed mercy toward him." Then Jesus said to him, "Go and do the same" (Luke 10:30–37).

BEATING (See LASHES)

BEATITUDES, THE (See specific verses in Matthew 5 and Luke 6)

BED (Also see PALLET; and STRETCHER)

Setting: Capernaum near the Sea of Galilee. After Jesus heals and forgives a paralytic of his sins in front of crowds, some scribes accuse Him of blasphemy.

And they brought to Him a paralytic lying on a bed. Seeing their faith, Jesus said to the paralytic, "Take courage, son; your sins are forgiven." And some scribes said to themselves, "This *fellow* blasphemes." And Jesus knowing their thoughts said, "Why are you thinking evil in your hearts? Which is easier to say, 'Your sins are forgiven,' or to say, 'Get up, and walk'? But so that you may know that the Son of Man has authority on earth to forgive sins"—then He said to the paralytic, "Get up, pick up your bed and go home" (Matthew 9:2–6; cf. Mark 2:3–12; Luke 5:17–26).

Setting: Galilee. Following His explanation of the Parable of the Sower to His disciples, Jesus illustrates what they should do with this truth.

And He was saying to them, "A lamp is not brought to be put under a basket, is it, or under a bed? Is it not *brought* to be put on the lampstand? For nothing is hidden, except to be revealed; nor has *anything* been secret, but that it would come to light. If anyone has ears to hear, let him hear" (Mark 4:21–23; cf. Luke 8:16, 17; see Matthew 5:14–16; Matthew 10:26).

Setting: Galilee. Following His explanation of the Parable of the Sower to His disciples, Jesus conveys the Parable of the Seed.

And He was saying, "The kingdom of God is like a man who casts seed upon the soil; and he goes to bed at night and gets up by day, and the seed sprouts and grows—how, he himself does not know. The soil produces crops by itself; first the blade, then the head, then the mature grain in the head. But when the crop permits, he immediately puts in the sickle, because the harvest has come" (Mark 4:26–29; see Joel 3:13).

Setting: Galilee. Following the explanation of the Parable of the Sower to His disciples, Jesus gives the Parable of the Lamp.

"Now no one after lighting a lamp covers it over with a container, or puts it under a bed; but he puts it on a lampstand, so that those who come in may see the light. For nothing is hidden that will not become evident, nor anything secret that will not be known and come to light. So take care how you listen; for whoever has, to him more shall be given; and whoever does not have, even what he thinks he has shall be taken away from him" (Luke 8:16–18; cf. Mark 4:21–23; see Matthew 5:14, 15; 10:26; 13:12).

Setting: On the way from Galilee to Jerusalem. After revealing to His disciples how to pray, Jesus illustrates persistence in prayer.

Then He said to them, "Suppose one of you has a friend, and goes to him at midnight and says to him, 'Friend, lend me three loaves; for a friend of mine has come to me from a journey, and I have nothing to set before him'; and from inside he answers and says, 'Do not bother me; the door has already been shut and my children and I are in bed; I cannot get up and give you anything.' I tell you, even though he will not get up and give him anything because he is his friend, yet because of his persistence he will get up and give him as much as he needs. So I say to you, ask, and it will be given to you; seek, and you will find; knock, and it will be opened to you. For everyone who asks, receives; and he who seeks, finds; and to him who knocks, it will be opened" (Luke 11:5–10; compare Matthew 7:7, 8; see Luke 18:1–5).

Setting: Samaria, on the way from Galilee to Jerusalem. After the Pharisees question Him about the coming of the kingdom of God, Jesus tells His disciples of His second coming.

And He said to the disciples, "The days will come when you will long to see one of the days of the Son of Man, and you will not see it. They will say to you, 'Look there! Look here!' Do not go away, and do not run after them. For just like the lightning, when it flashes out of one part of the sky, shines to the other part of the sky, so will the Son of Man be in His day. But first He must suffer many things and be rejected by this generation. And just as it happened in the days of Noah, so it will be also in the days of the Son of Man: they were eating, they were drinking, they were marrying, they were being given in marriage, until the day that Noah entered the ark, and the flood came and destroyed them all. It was the same as happened in the days of Lot: they were eating, they were drinking, they were buying, they were selling, they were planting, they were building; but on the day that Lot went out from Sodom it rained fire and brimstone from heaven and destroyed them all. It will be just the same on the day that the Son of Man is revealed. On that day, the one who is on the housetop and whose goods are in the house must not go down to take them out; and likewise the one who is in the field must not turn back. Remember Lot's wife. Whoever seeks to keep his life will lose it, and whoever loses his life will preserve it. I tell you, on that night there will be two in one bed; one will be taken and the other will be left. There will be two women grinding at the same place; one will be taken and the other will be left. [Two men will be in the field; one will be taken and the other will be left."] And answering they said to Him, "Where, Lord?" And He said to them, "Where the body is, there also the vultures will be gathered" (Luke 17:22–37; see Genesis 19; Matthew 10:39; 16:21, 27; 24:17–28, 37–41).

Setting: On the island of Patmos (in the Aegean Sea about fifty miles southwest of Ephesus in modern Turkey). On the Lord's Day (Sunday), about fifty years after Jesus' resurrection, the disciple John encounters the Lord Jesus Christ, who communicates a new revelation for the apostle to record for the church in Thyatira and to six other churches in Asia.

"And to the angel of the church in Thyatira write: The Son of God, who has eyes like a flame of fire, and His feet are like burnished bronze, says this: 'I know your deeds, and your love and faith and service and perseverance, and that your deeds of late are greater than at first. But I have this against you, that you tolerate the woman Jezebel, who calls herself a prophetess, and she teaches and leads My bond-servants astray so that they commit acts of immorality and eat things sacrificed to idols. I gave her time to repent, and she does not want to repent of her immorality. Behold, I will throw her on a bed of sickness, and those who commit adultery with her into great tribulation, unless they repent of her deeds. And I will kill her children with pestilence, and all the churches will know that I am He who searches the minds and hearts; and I will give to each one of you according to your deeds. But I say to you, the rest who are in Thyatira, who do not hold this teaching, who have not known the deep things of Satan, as they call them—I place no other burden on you. Nevertheless what you have, hold fast until I come. He who overcomes, and he who keeps My deeds until the end, TO HIM I WILL GIVE AUTHORITY OVER THE NATIONS; AND HE SHALL RULE THEM WITH A ROD OF

IRON, AS THE VESSELS OF THE POTTER ARE BROKEN TO PIECES, as I also have received authority from My Father; and I will give him the morning star. He who has an ear, let him hear what the Spirit says to the churches' (Revelation 2:18–29; Jesus quotes from Psalm 2:8, 9; Isaiah 30:14; see 1 Kings 16:31; Psalm 7:9; Romans 2:5; 1 Corinthians 2:10; 2 Peter 3:9; Revelation 1:14; 2:7; 3:11; 17:1–20).

BEELZEBUB (See BEELZEBUL)

BEELZEBUL (referring to Satan; also see DEVIL; EVIL ONE; and SATAN)

Setting: Galilee. After His disciples observe His ministry, Jesus summons and specifically instructs them about the difficulties ahead involving true discipleship.

"A disciple is not above his teacher, nor a slave above his master. It is enough for the disciple that he become like his teacher, and the slave like his master. If they have called the head of the house Beelzebul, how much more *will they malign* the members of his household!" (Matthew 10:24, 25; compare Luke 6:40; see 2 Kings 1:2).

Setting: Galilee. After Jesus heals a blind, mute, demon-possessed man, the Pharisees accuse Him in front of crowds of being a worker of Satan.

And knowing their thoughts Jesus said to them, "Any kingdom divided against itself is laid waste; and any city or house divided against itself will not stand. If Satan casts out Satan, he is divided against himself; how then will his kingdom stand? If I by Beelzebul cast out demons, by whom do your sons cast *them* out? For this reason they will be your judges. But if I cast out demons by the Spirit of God, then the kingdom of God has come upon you. Or how can anyone enter the strong man's house and carry off his property, unless he first binds the strong *man?* And then he will plunder his house" (Matthew 12:25–29; compare Matthew 9:34; Mark 3:23–27; Luke 11:17–20).

Setting: On the way from Galilee to Jerusalem. After Jesus casts out a demon, some in the crowd test Him, demanding a sign from heaven.

But He knew their thoughts and said to them, "Any kingdom divided against itself is laid waste; and a house divided against itself falls. If Satan also is divided against himself, how will his kingdom stand? For you say that I cast out demons by Beelzebul. And if I by Beelzebul cast out demons, by whom do your sons cast them out? So they will be your judges. But if I cast out demons by the finger of God, then the kingdom of God has come upon you" (Luke 11:17–20; cf. Matthew 12:25–28; Mark 3:23–27; see Exodus 8:19; Matthew 3:2, 10:25).

BEGGING (Also see CHARITY; and POOR, GIVING TO THE)

[BEGGING from beg]

Setting: On the way from Galilee to Jerusalem. After He gives the Parable of the Prodigal Son, the Lord teaches His disciples about stewardship.

Now He was also saying to the disciples, "There was a rich man who had a manager, and this manager was reported to him as squandering his possessions. And he called him and said to him, 'What is this I hear about you? Give an accounting of your management, for you can no longer be a manager.' The manager said to himself, 'What shall I do, since my master is taking the management away from me? I am not strong enough to dig; I am ashamed to beg. I know what I shall do, so that when I am removed from the management people will welcome me into their homes.' And he summoned each one of his master's debtors, and he began saying to the first, 'How much do you owe my master?' And he said, 'A hundred measures of oil.' And he said to him, 'Take your bill, and sit down quickly and write fifty.' Then he said to another, 'And how much do you owe?' And he said, 'A hundred measures of wheat.' He said to him, 'Take your bill, and write eighty.' And his master praised the unrighteous manager because he had acted shrewdly; for the sons of this age are more shrewd in relation to their own kind than the sons of light. And I say to you, make friends for yourselves by means of the wealth of unrighteousness, so that when it fails, they will receive you into the eternal dwellings. He who is faithful in a very little thing is faithful also in much; and he who is unrighteous in a very little thing is unrighteous also in much. Therefore if you have not been faithful in the use of unrighteous wealth, who will entrust the true riches to you? And if you have not been faithful in the use of that which is another's, who will give you that which is your own? No servant can serve two masters; for either he will hate the one and love the other, or else he will be devoted to one and despise the other. You cannot serve God and wealth" (Luke 16:1–13; cf. Matthew 6:24; see Matthew 25:14–30).

[BEGGING from beg]

Setting: On the way from Galilee to Jerusalem. After responding to the Pharisees' scoffing at His teaching His disciples about stewardship and the permanence of the Law, Jesus conveys the story of the rich man and Lazarus.

"Now there was a rich man, and he habitually dressed in purple and fine linen, joyously living in splendor every day. And a poor man named Lazarus was laid at his gate, covered with sores, and longing to be fed with the crumbs which were falling from the rich man's table; besides, even the dogs were coming and licking his sores. Now the poor man died and was carried away by the angels to Abraham's bosom; and the rich man also died and was buried. In Hades he lifted up his eyes, being in torment, and saw Abraham far away and Lazarus in his bosom. And he cried out and said, 'Father Abraham, have mercy on me, and send Lazarus so that he may dip the tip of his finger in water and cool off my tongue, for I am in agony in this flame.' But Abraham said, 'Child, remember that during your life you received your good things, and likewise Lazarus bad things; but now he is being comforted here, and you are in agony. And besides all this, between us and you there is a great chasm fixed, so that those who wish to come over from here to you will not be able, and that none may cross over from there to us.' And he said, 'Then I beg you, father, that you send him to my father's house—for I have five brothers—in order that he may warn them, so that they will not also come to this place of torment.' But Abraham said, 'They have Moses and the Prophets; let them hear them.' But he said, 'No, father Abraham, but if someone goes to them from the dead, they will repent!' But he said to him, 'If they do not listen to Moses and the Prophets, they will not be persuaded even if someone rises from the dead'" (Luke 16:19–31; see Luke 3:8; 6:24; 16:1, 14).

BEGINNING (CREATION, BEGINNING OF; and CREATION, BEGINNING OF THE are separate entries; also see CREATION)

Setting: Judea beyond the Jordan (Perea). After Jesus replies to Peter's question about forgiveness, in front of a large crowd, the Pharisees test Him with a question about divorce.

And He answered and said, "Have you not read that He who created *them* from the beginning MADE THEM MALE AND FEMALE, and said, 'FOR THIS REASON A MAN SHALL LEAVE HIS FATHER AND MOTHER AND BE JOINED TO HIS WIFE, AND THE TWO SHALL BECOME ONE FLESH'? So they are no longer two, but one flesh. What therefore God has joined together, let no man separate" (Matthew 19:4–6, Jesus quotes from Genesis 1:27; 2:24; cf. Mark 10:5–9; see 1 Timothy 2:14).

Setting: Judea beyond the Jordan (Perea). Jesus responds to the Pharisees' follow-up question in front of a large crowd about Moses' command regarding a certificate of divorce.

He said to them. "Because of your hardness of heart Moses permitted you to divorce your wives; but from the beginning it has not been this way. And I say to you, whoever divorces his wife, except for immorality, and marries another woman commits adultery" (Matthew 19:8, 9; cf. Deuteronomy 24:1–4; Matthew 5:32; 19:7; Mark 10:1–12; see Romans 7:2, 3; 1 Corinthians 7:10, 39).

Setting: Judea beyond the Jordan (Perea). Jesus illustrates the kingdom of heaven to His disciples through the story of laborers in the vineyard.

"For the kingdom of heaven is like a landowner who went out early in the morning to hire laborers for his vineyard. When he had agreed with the laborers for a denarius for the day, he sent them into his vineyard. And he went out about the third hour and saw others standing idle in the market place; and to those he said, 'You also go into the vineyard, and whatever is right I will give you.' And *so* they went. Again he went out about the sixth and the ninth hour, and did the same thing. And about the eleventh *hour* he went out and found others standing *around;* and he said to them, 'Why have you been standing idle here all day long?' They said to him, 'Because no one hired us.' He said to them, 'You go into the vineyard too.' When evening came, the owner of the vineyard said to his foreman, 'Call the laborers and pay them their wages, beginning with the last *group* to the first.' When those *hired* about the eleventh hour came, each one received a denarius. When those *hired* first came, they thought that they would receive more; but each of them also received a denarius. When they received it, they grumbled at the landowner, saying, 'These last men have worked *only* one hour, and you have made them equal to us who have borne the burden and the scorching heat of the day.' But he answered and said to one of them, 'Friend, I am doing you no wrong; did you not agree with me for a denarius? Take what is yours and go, but I wish to give to this last man the same as to you. It is not lawful for me to do what I wish with what is my own? Or is your eye envious because I am generous?' So the last shall be first, and the first last" (Matthew 20:1–16; cf. Matthew 19:30).

Setting: The Mount of Olives, just east of Jerusalem. During His discourse, Jesus answers His disciples' questions as to when the temple will be destroyed and Jerusalem overrun, along with the signs of His coming and the end of the age.

And Jesus answered and said to them, "See to it that no one misleads you. For many will come in My name, saying, 'I am the Christ,' and will mislead many. You will be hearing of wars and rumors of wars. See that you are not frightened, for *those things* must take place, but *that* is not yet the end. For nation will rise against nation, and kingdom against kingdom, and in various places there will be famines and earthquakes. But all these things are *merely* the beginning of birth pangs. Then they will deliver you to tribulation, and will kill you, and you will be hated by all nations because of My name. At that time many will fall away and will betray one another and hate one another. Many false prophets will arise and will mislead many. Because lawlessness is increased, most people's love will grow cold. But the one who endures to the end, he will be saved. This gospel of the kingdom shall be preached in the whole world as a testimony to all the nations, and then the end will come" (Matthew 24:4–14; cf. Jeremiah 29:8; Matthew 7:15; 10:17, 22; Mark 13:3–13; Luke 21:7–19; Revelation 6:4).

Setting: The Mount of Olives, east of the temple in Jerusalem. During His discourse, after prophesying the temple's destruction, Jesus responds to questions from Peter, James, John, and Andrew about future events.

And Jesus began to say to them, "See to it that no one misleads you. Many will come in My name, saying, 'I am *He!*' and will mislead many. When you hear of wars and rumors of wars, do not be frightened; *those things* must take place; but *that is* not yet the end. For nation will rise up against nation, and kingdom against kingdom; there will be earthquakes in various places; there will *also be* famines. These things are *merely* the beginning of birth pangs. But be on your guard; for they will deliver you to *the* courts, and you will be flogged in *the* synagogues, and you will stand before governors and kings for My sake, as a testimony to them. The gospel must first be preached to all the nations. When they arrest you and hand you over, do not worry beforehand about what you are to say, but say whatever is given you in that hour; for it is not you who speak, but *it is* the Holy Spirit. Brother will betray brother to death, and a father *his* child; and children will rise up against parents and have them put to death. You will be hated by all because of My name, but the one who endures to the end, he will be saved" (Mark 13:5–13; cf. Matthew 24:4–14; Luke 21:7–19; see Matthew 10:17–22).

Setting: Jerusalem. After rising from the grave on the third day following being crucified, and appearing to two of His followers on the road to Emmaus, Jesus gives instruction to some of the Twelve about His mission on earth and the promise of future power from God.

Now He said to them, "These are My words which I spoke to you while I was still with you, that all things which are written about Me in the Law of Moses and the Prophets and the Psalms must be fulfilled." Then He opened their minds to understand the Scriptures, and He said to them, "Thus it is written, that the Christ would suffer and rise again from the dead the third day, and that repentance for forgiveness of sins would be proclaimed in His name to all the nations, beginning from Jerusalem. You are witnesses of these things. And behold, I am sending forth the promise of My Father upon you; but you are to stay in the city until you are clothed with power from on high" (Luke 24:44–49; see Matthew 28:19, 20; Luke 24:1–43; Acts 1:8).

Setting: The temple treasury in Jerusalem. Following the Feast of Booths and the scribes' and Pharisees' failed attempt to stone a woman for adultery, Jesus returns to teach, as they question His testimony about Himself.

Then He said again to them, "I go away, and you will seek Me, and will die in your sin; where I am going, you cannot come." So the Jews were saying, "Surely He will not kill Himself, will He, since He says, "Where I am going, you cannot come'?" And He was saying to them, "You are from below, I am from above; you are of this world, I am not of this world. Therefore I said to you that you will die in your sins; for unless you believe that I am *He,* you will die in your sins." So they were saying to Him, "Who are You?" Jesus said to them, "What have I been saying to you *from* the beginning? I have many things to speak and to judge concerning you, but He who sent Me is true; and the things which I heard from Him, these I speak to the world" (John 8:21–26; see John 3:31–33; 5:34, 35; 8:1–20, 27; 17:14, 16).

Setting: The temple treasury in Jerusalem. After the scribes and Pharisees question His testimony about Himself, Jesus interacts with them regarding their ancestry and motives.

Jesus said to them, "If God were your Father, you would love Me, for I proceeded forth and have come from God, for I have not even come on My own initiative, but He sent Me. Why do you not understand what I am saying? *It is* because you cannot hear My word. You are of *your* father the devil, and you want to do the desires of your father. He was a murderer from the beginning, and does not stand in the truth because there is no truth in him. Whenever he speaks a lie, he speaks from his own *nature,* for he is a liar and the father of lies. But because I speak the truth, you do not believe Me. Which one of you convicts Me of sin? If I speak truth, why do not believe Me? He who is of God hears the words of God; for this reason you do not hear *them,* because you are not of God" (John 8:42–47; see John 8:1–41; 18:37; 1 John 3:8; 4:6; 5:1).

Setting: Jerusalem. Before the Passover, with His departure in mind, after explaining He is the vine and His disciples are the branches, Jesus elaborates more about the future ministry of the Holy Spirit.

"When the Helper comes, whom I will send to you from the Father, *that is* the Spirit of truth who proceeds from the Father, He will testify about Me, and you *will* testify also, because you have been with Me from the beginning" (John 15:26, 27; see Luke 24:48; John 14:16).

Setting: Jerusalem. Before the Passover, after explaining He is the vine and His disciples are the branches, Jesus warns them of the persecution they will face after His departure to heaven.

"These things I have spoken to you so that you may be kept from stumbling. They will make you outcasts from the synagogue, but an hour is coming for everyone who kills you to think that he is offering service to God. These things they will do because they have not known the Father or Me. But these things I have spoken to you, so that when their hour comes, you may remember that I told you of them. These things I did not say to you at the beginning, because I was with you" (John 16:1–4; see John 8:19, 55; 9:22; 13:19; 15:18–27).

Setting: On the island of Patmos (in the Aegean Sea about fifty miles southwest of Ephesus in modern Turkey). On the Lord's Day (Sunday), about fifty years after Jesus' resurrection, the disciple John encounters the Lord Jesus Christ, who communicates a new revelation for the apostle to record for the church in Laodicea and to six other churches in Asia.

"To the angel of the church in Laodicea write: The Amen, the faithful and true Witness, the Beginning of the creation of God, says this: 'I know your deeds, that you are neither cold nor hot; I wish that you were cold or hot. So because you are lukewarm, and neither hot nor cold, I will spit you out of My mouth. Because you say, "I am rich, and have become wealthy, and have need of nothing," and you do not know that you are wretched and miserable and poor and blind and naked, I advise you to buy from Me gold refined by fire so that you may become rich, and white garments so that you may clothe yourself, and *that* the shame of your nakedness will not be revealed; and eye salve to anoint your eyes so that you may see. Those whom I love, I reprove and discipline; therefore be zealous and repent. Behold, I stand at the door and knock; if anyone hears My voice and opens the door, I will come in to him and will dine with him, and he with Me. He who overcomes, I will grant to him to sit down with Me on My throne, as I also overcame and sat down with My Father on His throne. He who has an ear, let him hear what the Spirit says to the churches'" (Revelation 3:14–22; see Proverbs 3:12; Hosea 12:8; John 14:23; 16:33).

Setting: On the island of Patmos (in the Aegean Sea about fifty miles southwest of Ephesus in modern Turkey). In the final chapter of the Lord Jesus Christ's Revelation via the disciple John, approximately fifty years after His resurrection, the Lord reveals His upcoming return, reward, and eternality.

"Behold, I am coming quickly, and My reward is with Me, to render to every man according to what he has done. I am the Alpha and the Omega, the first and the last, the beginning and the end" (Revelation 22:12, 13; see Isaiah 40:10; 44:6).

BEGINNING OF THE WORLD (Listed under WORLD, BEGINNING OF THE; also see CREATION; CREATION, BEGINNING OF; CREATION, BEGINNING OF THE; and WORLD, FOUNDATION OF THE)

BEHAVIOR, GODLY (See LIVING, GODLY)

BEING, INNERMOST

Setting: Jerusalem. On the last day of the Feast of Booths, after Jesus causes discussion whether He is the Christ, the chief priests and Pharisees attempt to understand where He says He will be going soon. Jesus offers salvation and the abundant life to His hearers.

Now on the last day, the great *day* of the feast, Jesus stood and cried out, saying, "If anyone is thirsty, let him come to Me and drink. He who believes in Me, as the Scripture said, 'From his innermost being will flow rivers of living water'" (John 7:37, 38; see John 7:10–15).

BELIEF (including BELIEVE/BELIEVED/BELIEVES/BELIEVING; also see FAITH; and UNBELIEF)

Setting: Entering Capernaum. After the Lord gives the Sermon on the Mount in Galilee and cleanses a leper, a Roman centurion implores Him to heal his servant.

Now when Jesus heard *this,* He marveled, and said to those who were following, "Truly I say to you, I have not found such great faith with anyone in Israel. I say to you that many will come from east and west, and recline *at the table* with Abraham, Isaac and Jacob in the kingdom of heaven; but the sons of the kingdom will be cast out into the outer darkness; in that place there will be weeping and gnashing of teeth." And Jesus said to the centurion, "Go; it shall be done for you as you have believed." And the servant was healed that *very* moment (Matthew 8:10–13; cf. Luke 7:9, 10).

Setting: Galilee. After healing a woman with internal bleeding and resuscitating a synagogue official's daughter from the dead, Jesus gives sight to two blind men.

When He entered the house, the blind men came up to Him, and Jesus said to them, "Do you believe that I am able to do this?" They said to Him, "Yes, Lord." Then He touched their eyes saying, "It shall be done for you according to your faith." And their eyes were opened. And Jesus sternly warned them: "See that no one knows *about this!*" (Matthew 9:28–30).

Setting: Capernaum of Galilee. Jesus answers His disciples' question about greatness, or rank, in the kingdom of heaven.

And He called a child to Himself and set him before them, and said, "Truly I say to you, unless you are converted and become like children, you will not enter the kingdom of heaven. Whoever then humbles himself as this child, he is the greatest in the kingdom of heaven. And whoever receives one such child in My name receives Me; but whoever causes one of these little ones who believe in Me to stumble, it would be better for him to have a heavy millstone hung around his neck, and to be drowned in the depth of the sea" (Matthew 18:2–6; cf. Matthew 19:14; Mark 9:33–37, 42; Luke 9:47, 48; 17:1, 2).

Setting: On the way from Bethany to Jerusalem. Jesus' disciples ask Jesus how the fig tree He cursed (an illustration of the nation of Israel) so quickly withered.

And Jesus answered and said to them, "Truly I say to you, if you have faith and do not doubt, you will not only do what was done to the fig tree, but even if you say to this mountain, 'Be taken up and cast into the sea,' it will happen. And all things you ask in prayer, believing, you will receive" (Matthew 21:21, 22; cf. Matthew 7:7; 17:20; Mark 11:20–24).

Setting: The temple in Jerusalem. Jesus delivers a parable to the chief priests and elders after they question His authority.

"But what do you think? A man had two sons, and he came to the first and said, 'Son, go work today in the vineyard.' And he answered, 'I will not'; but afterward he regretted it and went. The man came to the second and said the same thing; and he answered, 'I *will,* sir'; but he did not go. Which of the two sons did the will of his father?" They said, "The first." Jesus said to them, "Truly, I say to you that the tax collectors and prostitutes will get into the kingdom of God before you. For John came to you in the way of righteousness and you did not believe him; but the tax collectors and prostitutes did believe him; and you, seeing *this,* did not even feel remorse afterward so as to believe him" (Matthew 21:28–32; cf. Luke 7:29, 30, 37–50).

Setting: The Mount of Olives, just east of Jerusalem. During His discourse, Jesus answers His disciples' question as to when the temple will be destroyed and Jerusalem overrun, along with the signs of His coming and the end of the age.

"Therefore when you see the ABOMINATION OF DESOLATION which was spoken of through Daniel the prophet, standing in the holy place (let the reader understand), then those who are in Judea must flee to the mountains. Whoever is on the housetop must not go down to get the things that are in his house. Whoever is in the field must not turn back to get his cloak. But woe to those who are pregnant and to those who are nursing babies in those days! But pray that your flight will not be in the winter, or on a Sabbath. For then there will be a great tribulation, such as has not occurred since the beginning of the world until now, nor ever will. Unless those days had been cut short, no life would have been saved; but for the sake of the elect those days will be cut short. Then if anyone says to you, 'Behold, here is the Christ,' or "There *He is,*' do not believe *him.* For false Christs and false prophets will arise and will show great signs and wonders, so as to mislead, if possible, even the elect. Behold, I have told you in advance. So if they say to you, 'Behold, He is in the wilderness,' do not go out, *or,* 'Behold, He is in the inner rooms,' do not believe *them.* For just as the lightning comes from the east and flashes even to the west, so will the coming of the Son of Man be. Wherever the corpse is, there the vultures will gather" (Matthew 24:15–28, Jesus quotes from Daniel 9:27; cf. Daniel 12:1; Mark 13:14–23; Luke 17:22–31; 21:20–24; 23:29; see John 4:48).

Setting: Galilee. After being baptized by John the Baptist in the Jordan River, Jesus commences His gospel-preaching ministry shortly after John has been taken into custody by Herod Antipas.

Now after John had been taken into custody, Jesus came into Galilee, preaching the gospel of God, and saying, "The time is fulfilled, and the kingdom of God is at hand; repent and believe in the gospel" (Mark 1:14, 15, cf. Matthew 4:17; Galatians 4:4).

Setting: Capernaum by the Sea of Galilee. Jairus, a synagogue official, after asking Jesus to heal his daughter, receives word she has died.

But Jesus, overhearing what was being spoken, said to the synagogue official, "Do not be afraid *any longer*, only believe" (Mark 5:36; cf. Luke 8:49, 50; see Matthew 19:18, 19; Mark 5:21–24; Luke 8:41, 42).

Setting: Galilee. Upon returning from a high mountain (perhaps Mount Hermon) where Jesus was transfigured before Peter, James, and John, the four discover the remaining disciples arguing with some scribes.

And He asked them, "What are you discussing with them?" And one of the crowd answered Him, "Teacher, I brought You my son, possessed with a spirit which makes him mute; and whenever it seizes him, it slams him *to the ground* and he foams *at the mouth,* and grinds his teeth and stiffens out. I told Your disciples to cast it out, and they could not *do it.* And He answered them, and said, "O unbelieving generation, how long shall I be with you? How long shall I put up with you? Bring him to Me!" They brought the boy to Him. When he saw Him, immediately the spirit threw him into a convulsion, and falling to the ground, be *began* rolling around and foaming *at the mouth.* And He asked his father, "How long has this been happening to him?" And he said, "From childhood. It has often thrown him both into the fire and into the water to destroy him. But if You can do anything, take pity on us and help us!" And Jesus said to him, "'If You can?' All things are possible to him who believes." Immediately the boy's father cried out and said, "I do believe; help my unbelief." When Jesus saw that a crowd was rapidly gathering, He rebuked the unclean spirit, saying to it, "You deaf and mute spirit, I command you, come out of him and do not enter him again." After crying out and throwing him into terrible convulsions, it came out; and *the boy* became so much like a corpse that most *of them,* said, "He is dead!" But Jesus took him by the hand and raised him; and he got up. When He came into *the* house, His disciples *began* questioning Him privately, "Why could we not drive it out?" And He said to them, "This kind cannot come out by anything but prayer" (Mark 9:16–29; cf. Matthew 17:14–21; Luke 9:37–43; see Matthew 17:20).

Setting: Capernaum of Galilee. As Jesus teaches His disciples in private, they ask Him about greatness.

But Jesus said, "Do not hinder him, for there is no one who will perform a miracle in My name, and be able soon afterward to speak evil of Me. For he who is not against us is for us. For whoever gives you a cup of water to drink because of your name as *followers* of Christ, truly I say to you, he will not lose his reward. Whoever causes one of these little ones who believe to stumble, it would be better for him if, with a heavy millstone hung around his neck, he had been cast into the sea. If your hand causes you to stumble, cut it off; it is better for you to enter life crippled, than, having your two hands, to go into hell, into the unquenchable fire, [where THEIR WORM DOES NOT DIE, AND THE FIRE IS NOT QUENCHED.] If your foot causes you to stumble, cut it off; it is better for you to enter life lame, than, having your two feet, to be cast into hell, [where THEIR WORM DOES NOT DIE, AND THE FIRE IS NOT QUENCHED.] If your eye causes you to stumble, throw it out; it is better for you to enter the kingdom of God with one eye, than, having two eyes, to be cast into hell, where THEIR WORM DOES NOT DIE, AND THE FIRE IS NOT QUENCHED. For everyone will be salted with fire. Salt is good; but if the salt becomes unsalty, with what will you make it salty *again?* Have salt in yourselves, and be at peace with one another" (Mark 9:39–50; Jesus quotes from Isaiah 66:24; cf. Matthew 18:6–9; Luke 9:49, 50; see Matthew 5:13, 29, 30; 10:42; 12:30; 18:5, 6).

Setting: Just outside Jerusalem. After Jesus' instruction to the money changers while cleansing the temple, Peter draws Jesus' and His disciples' attention to the earlier-cursed fig tree.

And Jesus answered saying to them, "Have faith in God. Truly, I say to you, whoever says to this mountain, 'Be taken up and cast into the sea,' and does not doubt in his heart, but believes that what he says is going to happen, it will be *granted* him. Therefore I say to you, all things for which you pray and ask, believe that you have received them, and they will be *granted* you. Whenever you stand praying, forgive, if you have anything against anyone, so that your Father who is in heaven will also forgive you your transgressions. [But if you do not forgive, neither will your Father who is in heaven forgive your transgressions'] (Mark 11:22–26; cf. Matthew 21:19–22; see Matthew 6:14, 15; 7:7; 17:20).

Setting: The Mount of Olives, east of the temple in Jerusalem. During His discourse, after prophesying the temple's destruction, Jesus responds to questions from Peter, James, John, and Andrew about future events.

"But when you see the ABOMINATION OF DESOLATION standing where it should not be (let the reader understand), then those who are in Judea must flee to the mountains. The one who is on the housetop must not go down, or go in to get anything out of his house; and the one who is in the field must not turn back to get his coat. But woe to those who are pregnant and to those who are nursing babies in those days! But pray that it may not happen in winter. For those days will be a *time of* tribulation such as has not occurred since the beginning of the creation which God created until now, and never will. Unless the Lord had shortened *those* days, no life would have been saved; but for the sake of the elect, whom He chose, He shortened the days. And then if anyone says to you, 'Behold, here is the Christ'; or, 'Behold, *He is* there'; do not believe *him*; for false Christs and false prophets will arise, and will show signs and wonders, in order to lead astray, if possible, the elect. But take heed; behold, I have told you everything in advance" (Mark 13:14–23; cf. Matthew 24:15–28; Luke 21:20–24; see Daniel 9:27; 12:1; Luke 17:31).

Setting: Jerusalem. Following His resurrection from the dead after being crucified, Jesus commissions His disciples to preach His gospel to the world.

And He said to them, "Go into all the world and preach the gospel to all creation. He who has believed and has been baptized shall be saved; but he who has disbelieved shall be condemned. These signs will accompany those who have believed: in My name they will cast out demons, they will speak with new tongues; they will pick up serpents, and if they drink any deadly poison, it will not hurt them; they will lay hands on the sick, and they will recover" (Mark 16:15–18; cf. Matthew 28:16–20; see Mark 9:38; John 3:18, 36; 1 Corinthians 15:6).

[Note: Some scholars question the authenticity of Mark 16:9–20, as these verses do not appear in some early New Testament manuscripts.]

Setting: Galilee. After Jesus presents the Parable of the Sower to the crowds, His disciples ask Him to explain the parable's meaning.

And He said, "To you it has been granted to know the mysteries of the kingdom of God, but to the rest it is in parables, so that SEEING THEY MAY NOT SEE, AND HEARING THEY MAY NOT UNDERSTAND. Now the parable is this: the seed is the word of God. Those beside the road are those who have heard; then the devil comes and takes away the word from their heart, so that they will not believe and be saved. Those on the rocky soil are those who, when they hear, receive the word with joy; and these have no firm root; they believe for a while, and in time of temptation fall away. The seed which fell among the thorns, these are the ones who have heard, and as they go on their way they are choked with worries and riches and pleasures of this life, and bring no fruit to maturity. But the seed in the good soil, these are the ones who have heard the word in an honest and good heart, and hold it fast, and bear fruit with perseverance" (Luke 8:10–15, Jesus quotes from Isaiah 6:9; cf. Matthew 13:10–23; Mark 4:10–20).

Setting: Capernaum. After healing a woman ill for twelve years, Jesus receives word that the daughter of a Galilee synagogue official has died.

But when Jesus heard this, He answered him, "Do not be afraid any longer; only believe and she will be made well." When He came to the house, He did not allow anyone to enter with Him except Peter and John and James and the girl's father and mother. Now they were all weeping and lamenting for her; but He said, "Stop weeping; for she has not died, but is asleep." And they began laughing at Him, knowing that she had died. He, however, took her by the hand and called, saying, "Child, arise!" And her spirit returned, and she got up immediately; and He gave orders for something to be given her to eat (Luke 8:50–55; cf. Matthew 9:18, 19, 23–26; Mark 5:21–24, 35–43).

Setting: Jerusalem. After being arrested, having Peter deny Him, and being mocked and beaten, with His crucifixion imminent, Jesus appears before the Sanhedrin.

"If You are the Christ, tell us." But He said to them, "If I tell you, you will not believe; and if I ask you a question, you will not answer. But from now on THE SON OF MAN WILL BE SEATED AT THE RIGHT HAND of the power OF GOD." And they all said, "Are You the Son of God, then? And He said to them, "Yes, I am" (Luke 22:67–70, Jesus quotes from Psalm 110:1; cf. Matthew 26:57–65; Mark 14:55–65).

Setting: After rising from the grave on the third day after being crucified, Jesus appears to two of His followers on the road to Emmaus, elaborating on the purpose of His coming to earth. They had heard reports the tomb was empty.

And He said to them, "O foolish men and slow of heart to believe in all that the prophets have spoken! Was it not necessary for the Christ to suffer these things and to enter into His glory?" (Luke 24:25, 26).

Setting: Galilee. After beginning His public ministry and choosing His first disciples, Andrew and Simon (Peter) near Bethany beyond the Jordan, and Philip in Galilee, Jesus calls Philip's friend, Nathanael, (some believe he may have been also called Bartholomew) as His next follower.

Jesus saw Nathanael coming to Him, and said of him, "Behold, an Israelite indeed, in whom there is no deceit!" Nathanael said to Him, "How do you know me?" Jesus answered and said to him, "Before Philip called you, when you were under the fig tree, I saw you." Nathanael answered Him, "Rabbi, You are the Son of God; You are the King of Israel." Jesus answered and said to him, "Because I said to you that I saw you under the fig tree, do you believe? You will see greater things than these." And He said to him, "Truly, truly, I say to you, you will see the heavens opened and the angels of God ascending and descending on the Son of Man" (John 1:47–51).

Setting: Jerusalem. At the time of the Passover of the Jews, after the Lord cleanses the temple, a Pharisee, Nicodemus, asks Him by night the meaning of "born of the Spirit."

Jesus answered and said to him, "Are you the teacher of Israel and do not understand these things? Truly, truly, I say to you, we speak of what we know and testify of what we have seen, and you do not accept our testimony. If I told you earthly things and you do not believe, how will you believe if I tell you heavenly things? No one has ascended into heaven, but He who descended from heaven: the Son of Man. As Moses lifted up the serpent in the wilderness, even so must the Son of Man be lifted up; so that whoever believes will in Him have eternal life" (John 3:10–15; see Numbers 21:9; Proverbs 30:4; John 12:34; 20:30, 31).

Setting: Jerusalem. Before the Passover of the Jews, after the Lord cleanses the temple, a Pharisee, Nicodemus, asks Him by night the meaning of "born again."

"For God so loved the world, that He gave His only begotten Son, that whoever believes in Him shall not perish, but have eternal life. For God did not send the Son into the world to judge the world, but that the world might be saved through Him. He who believes in Him is not judged; he who does not believe has been judged already, because he has not believed in the name of the only begotten Son of God. This is the judgment, that the Light has come into the world, and men loved darkness rather than the Light, for their deeds were evil. For everyone who does evil hates the Light, and does not come to the Light for fear that his deeds will be exposed. But he who practices the truth comes to the Light, so that his deeds may be manifested as having been wrought in God" (John 3:16–21; see Luke 19:10; John 1:4; 1:18; Romans 5:8; 1 John 1:6, 7).

Setting: Sychar in Samaria, on the way to Galilee. Jesus interacts with a Samaritan woman at Jacob's well, while His disciples shop for food.

Jesus said to her, "Woman, believe Me, an hour is coming when neither in this mountain nor in Jerusalem will you worship the Father. You worship what you do not know; we worship what we know, for salvation is from the Jews. But an hour is coming, and now is, when the true worshipers will worship the Father in spirit and truth; for such people the Father seeks to be His worshipers. God is spirit, and those who worship Him must worship in spirit and truth" (John 4:21–24; see Isaiah 2:3; Philippians 3:3).

Setting: Cana of Galilee. After conversing with a Samaritan woman at Jacob's well, and ministering to the Samaritan people for two days, Jesus returns and encounters a royal official seeking healing for his son, sick at the point of death in Capernaum.

So Jesus said to him, "Unless you *people* see signs and wonders, you *simply* will not believe" (John 4:48).

Setting: By the pool of Bethesda in Jerusalem. During the Feast of the Jews, Jesus responds to criticism from the Jewish religious leaders for healing a lame man on the Sabbath and for referring to God as His Father (thereby making Himself equal with God).

"Truly, truly, I say to you, he who hears My word, and believes Him who sent Me, has eternal life, and does not come into judgment, but has passed out of death into life" (John 5:24; see John 3:18; 12:44).

Setting: Jerusalem. During the Feast of the Jews, Jesus responds to criticism from the Jewish religious leaders by referring to God as His Father (thereby making Himself equal with God) and informing them that God, John the Baptist, and His works all testify to His mission.

"I can do nothing on My own initiative. As I hear, I judge; and My judgment is just, because I do not seek My own will, but the will of Him who sent Me. If I *alone* testify about Myself, My testimony is not true. There is another who testifies of Me, and I know that the testimony which He gives about Me is true. You have sent to John, and he has testified to the truth. But the testimony which I receive is not from man, but I say these things so that you may be saved. He was the lamp that was burning and was shining and you were willing to rejoice for a while in his light. But the testimony which I have is greater than the *testimony of* John; for the works which the Father has given Me to accomplish—the very works that I do—testify about Me, that the Father has sent Me. And the Father who sent Me, He has testified of Me. You have neither heard His voice at any time nor seen His form. You do not have His word abiding in you, for you do not believe Him whom He sent" (John 5:30–38; see Matthew 3:17; Mark 1:4–5; John 1:7, 15, 32; 4:34; 8:14–16; 10:25, 37, 38).

Setting: Jerusalem. During the Feast of the Jews, Jesus responds to criticism from the Jewish religious leaders by referring to God as His Father (thereby making Himself equal with God) and informing them that God, John the Baptist, and His works all testify to His mission.

"You search the Scriptures because you think that in them you have eternal life; it is these that testify about Me; and you are unwilling to come to Me so that you may have life. I do not receive glory from men; but I know you, that you do not have the love of God in yourselves. I have come in My Father's name, and you do not receive Me; if another comes in his own name, you will receive him. How can you believe, when you receive glory from one another and you do not seek the glory that is from the *one and* only God? Do not think that I will accuse you before the Father; the one who accuses you is Moses, in whom you have set your hope. For if you believed Moses, you would believe Me, for he wrote about Me. But if you do not believe his writings, how will you believe My words?" (John 5:39–47; see Matthew 24:5; Luke 16:29, 31; 24:27; John 9:28; 17:3).

Setting: Capernaum. The day after Jesus walks on the Sea of Galilee to join His disciples in a boat, the people He miraculously fed with a lad's five loaves and two fish quiz Jesus about how they may do the works of God.

Jesus answered and said to them, "This is the work of God, that you believe in Him whom He has sent" (John 6:29; see 1 Thessalonians 1:3).

Setting: Capernaum. The day after Jesus walks on the Sea of Galilee to join His disciples in a boat, the people He miraculously fed with a lad's five loaves and two fish ask Jesus to always give them this bread out of heaven.

Jesus said to them, "I am the bread of life; he who comes to Me will not hunger, and he who believes in Me will never thirst. But I said to you that you have seen Me, and yet do not believe. All that the Father gives Me will come to Me, and the one who comes to Me I will certainly not cast out. For I have come down from heaven, not to do My own will, but the will of Him who sent Me. This is the will of Him who sent Me, that of all that He has given Me I lose nothing, but raise it up on the last day. For this is the will of My Father, that everyone who beholds the Son and believes in Him will have eternal life, and I Myself will raise him up on the last day" (John 6:35–40; see John 3:13, 16; 4:13, 14).

Setting: Capernaum of Galilee. After Jesus informs the people whom He miraculously fed with a lad's five loaves and two fish how they might receive the bread out of heaven, the Jewish religious leaders grumble because He claims that He came down out of heaven.

Therefore the Jews were grumbling about Him, because He said, "I am the bread that came down out of heaven." They were saying, "Is not this Jesus, the son of Joseph, whose father and mother we know? How does He now say, 'I have come down out of heaven'?" Jesus answered and said to them, "Do not grumble among yourselves. No one can come to Me unless the Father who sent Me draws him; and I will raise him up on the last day. It is written in the prophets, 'AND THEY SHALL ALL BE TAUGHT OF GOD.' Everyone who has heard and learned from the Father, comes to Me. Not that anyone has seen the Father, except the One who is from God; He has seen the Father. Truly, truly, I say to you, he who believes has eternal life. I am the bread of life. Your fathers ate the manna in the wilderness, and they died. This is the bread which comes down out of heaven, so that one may eat of it and not die. I am the living bread that came down out of heaven; if anyone eats of this bread, he will live forever; and the bread also which I will give for the life of the world is My flesh" (John 6:41–51, Jesus quotes from Isaiah 54:13; see John 1:18, 29; 3:36; 7:27).

Setting: The synagogue at Capernaum of Galilee. After the Jewish religious leaders argue with one another about Jesus saying He will give His flesh to the world to eat, some of His disciples also express difficulty with His statements.

But, Jesus, conscious that His disciples grumbled at this, said to them, "Does this cause you to stumble? *What* then if you see the Son of Man ascending to where He was before? It is the Spirit who gives life; the flesh profits nothing; the words that I have spoken to you are spirit and are life. But there are some of you who do not believe." For Jesus knew from the beginning who they were who did not believe, and who it was that would betray Him. And He was saying, "For this reason I have said to you, that no one can come to Me unless it has been granted him from the Father" (John 6:61–65; see Matthew 11:6; 13:11; John 3:13).

Setting: Jerusalem. On the last day of the Feast of Booths, after causing discussion whether He is the Christ, the chief priests and Pharisees attempt to understand where He says He will be going soon. Jesus offers salvation and the abundant life to His hearers.

Now on the last day, the great *day* of the feast, Jesus stood and cried out, saying, "If anyone is thirsty, let him come to Me and drink. He who believes in Me, as the Scripture said, 'From his innermost being will flow rivers of living water'" (John 7:37, 38).

Setting: The temple treasury in Jerusalem. Following the Feast of Booths and the scribes' and Pharisees' failed attempt to stone a woman for adultery, Jesus returns to teach, as they question His testimony about Himself.

Then He said again to them, "I go away, and you will seek Me, and will die in your sin; where I am going, you cannot come." So the Jews were saying, "Surely He will not kill Himself, will He, since He says, "Where I am going, you cannot come'?" And He was saying to them, "You are from below, I am from above; you are of this world, I am not of this world. Therefore I said to you that you will die in your sins; for unless you believe that I am *He,* you will die in your sins." So they were saying to Him, "Who are You?" Jesus said to them, "What have I been saying to you *from* the beginning? I have many things to speak and to judge concerning you, but He who sent Me is true; and the things which I heard from Him, these I speak to the world" (John 8:21–26; see John 3:31–33; 5:34, 35; 17:14, 16).

Setting: The temple treasury in Jerusalem. after the scribes and Pharisees question His testimony about Himself, Jesus interacts with them regarding their ancestry and motives.

Jesus said to them, "If God were your Father, you would love Me, for I proceeded forth and have come from God, for I have not even come on My own initiative, but He sent Me. Why do you not understand what I am saying? *It is* because you cannot hear My word. You are of *your* father the devil, and you want to do the desires of your father. He was a murderer from the beginning, and does not stand in the truth because there is no truth in him. Whenever he speaks a lie, he speaks from his own *nature,* for he is a liar and the father of lies. But because I speak the truth, you do not believe Me. Which one of you convicts Me of sin? If I speak truth, why do not believe Me? He who is of God hears the words of God; for this reason you do not hear *them,* because you are not of God" (John 8:42–47; see John 8:1–41; 18:37; 1 John 3:8; 4:6; 5:1).

Setting: Jerusalem. Following the Pharisees' interrogation and dismissal of the formerly blind man Jesus healed on the Sabbath, the Lord converses with him about believing in the Son of Man.

Jesus heard that they had put him out, and finding him, He said, "Do you believe in the Son of Man?" He answered, "Who is He, Lord, that I may believe in Him?" Jesus said to him, "You have both seen Him, and He is the one who is talking to you" And he said, "Lord, I believe." And he worshiped Him (John 9:35–38; see John 4:26).

Setting: Jerusalem. At the Feast of Dedication, just after conveying the Parable of the Good Shepherd to the Pharisees (who do not understand it), they ask Him plainly if He is the Christ.

Jesus answered them, "I told you, and you do not believe; the works that I do in My Father's name, these testify of Me. But you do not believe because you are not of My sheep. My sheep hear My voice, and I know them, and they follow Me; and I give eternal life to them, and they will never perish; and no one will snatch them out of My hand. My Father, who has given *them* to Me, is greater than all; and no one is able to snatch *them* out of the Father's hand. I and the Father are one" (John 10:25–30; see John 8:47; 10:4, 22–24; 17:1, 2, 20, 21).

Setting: Jerusalem. At the Feast of Dedication, the Pharisees desire to stone Jesus because He claims to be equal with God when they ask plainly whether He is the Christ.

Jesus answered them, "Has it not been written in your Law, 'I SAID, YOU ARE GODS'? If he called them gods, to whom the word of God came (and the Scripture cannot be broken), do you say of Him, whom the Father sanctified and sent into the world, 'You are blaspheming,' because I said, 'I am the Son of God'? If I do not do the works of My Father, do not believe Me; but if I do them, though you do not believe Me, believe the works, so that you may know and understand that the Father is in Me, and I in the Father" (John 10:34–38, Jesus quotes from Psalm 82:6; see John 14:10, 20).

Setting: Beyond the Jordan. While Jesus and His disciples are avoiding the Jerusalem Pharisees, He communicates Lazarus's death to them, deciding to go to Bethany.

So Jesus then said to them plainly, "Lazarus is dead, and I am glad for your sakes that I was not there, so that you may believe; but let us go to him" (John 11:14, 15).

Setting: Beyond the Jordan. Jesus travels with His disciples to Bethany in Judea to see Lazarus's sisters, Martha and Mary, after the death of His friend.

Jesus said to her, "Your brother will rise again." Martha said to Him, "I know that he will rise again in the resurrection on the last day." Jesus said to her, "I am the resurrection and the life; he who believes in Me will live even if he dies, and everyone who lives and believes in Me will never die. Do you believe this?" (John 11:23–26; see Daniel 12:2; John 1:4; 6:47–51).

Setting: Bethany in Judea. After the death of His friend Lazarus, Jesus travels with His disciples from beyond the Jordan to visit Lazarus's sisters, Martha and Mary, and raises Lazarus from the dead.

Jesus said, "Remove the stone." Martha, the sister of the deceased, said to Him, "Lord, by this time there will be a stench, for he has been *dead* four days." Jesus said to her, "Did I not say to you that if you believe, you will see the glory of God?" So they removed the stone. Then Jesus raised His eyes, and said, "Father, I thank You that You have heard Me. I knew that You always hear Me; but because of the people standing around I said it, so that they may believe that you sent Me." When He had said these things, He cried out with a loud voice, "Lazarus, come forth." The man who had died came forth, bound hand and foot with wrappings, and his face was wrapped around with a cloth. Jesus said to them, "Unbind him, and let him go" (John 11:39–44; see Matthew 11:25).

Setting: Jerusalem. Just days before the Passover, the chief priests and Pharisees are plotting to seize Jesus, who is expressing anxiety about His upcoming death by crucifixion. The crowds ask the Lord about the identity of the Son of Man.

The crowd then answered Him, "We have heard out of the Law that the Christ is to remain forever; and how can You say, 'The Son of Man must be lifted up'? Who is this Son of Man?" So Jesus said to them, "For a little while longer the Light is among you. Walk while you have the Light, so that darkness will not overtake you; he who walks in the darkness does not know where he goes. While you have the Light, believe in the Light, so that you may become sons of Light." These things Jesus spoke, and He went away and hid Himself from them (John 12:34–36; see 1 John 1:6).

Setting: Jerusalem. Just days before the Passover, the chief priests and Pharisees are plotting to seize Jesus, who is expressing anxiety about His upcoming death by crucifixion. Some of the people believe in Jesus, while others are rejecting His message.

And Jesus cried out and said, "He who believes in Me, does not believe in Me but in Him who sent Me. He who sees Me sees the One who sent Me. I have come *as* Light into the world, so that everyone who believes in Me will not remain in darkness. If anyone hears My sayings and does not keep them, I do not judge him; for I did not come to judge the world, but to save the world. He who rejects Me and does not receive My sayings, has one who judges him; the word I spoke is what will judge him at the last day. For I did not speak on My own initiative, but the Father Himself who sent Me has given Me a commandment *as to* what to say and what to speak. I know that His commandment is eternal life; therefore the things I speak, I speak just as the Father as told Me" (John 12:44–50; see Matthew 10:40; Luke 10:16; John 1:4; 3:17; 5:19; 6:68; 14:9).

Setting: Jerusalem. Before the Passover, with His death on the cross nearing, Jesus explains the reason for His vivid example of servanthood in washing His disciples' feet.

So when He had washed their feet, and taken His garments and reclined *at the table* again, He said to them, "Do you know what I have done to you? You call Me Teacher and Lord; and you are right, for *so* I am. If I then, the Lord and the Teacher, washed your feet, you also ought to wash one another's feet. For I gave you an example that you also should do as I did to you. Truly, truly I say to you, a slave is not greater than his master, nor *is* one who is sent greater than the one who sent him. If you know these things, you are blessed if you do them. I do not speak of all of you. I know the ones I have chosen; but *it is* that the Scripture may be fulfilled, 'HE WHO EATS MY BREAD HAS LIFTED UP HIS HEEL AGAINST ME.' From now on I am telling you before *it* comes to pass, so that when it does occur, you may believe that I am *He. Truly,* truly, I say to you, he who receives whomever I send receives Me; and he who receives Me receives Him who sent Me" (John 13:12–20; Jesus quotes from Psalm 41:9; see Matthew 7:24; 10:24, 40; John 8:24; 14:29; 1 Peter 5:3).

Setting: Jerusalem. Before the Passover, after taking issue with Peter's assertion that he would lay down his life for Him, Jesus comforts and gives assurance to His disciples regarding their future after He returns to heaven.

"Do not let your heart be troubled; believe in God, believe also in Me. In My Father's house are many dwelling places; if it were not so, I would have told you; for I go to prepare a place for you. If I go and prepare a place for you, I will come again and receive you to Myself, that where I am, *there* you may be also. And you know the way where I am going" (John 14:1–4; see John 13:35; 14:27, 28).

Setting: Jerusalem. Before the Passover, after answering Thomas's question where He is going and how they will know the way, Jesus responds to Philip's request for Him to show His disciples the Father.

Jesus said to him, "Have I been so long with you, and *yet* you have not come to know Me, Philip? He who has seen Me has seen the Father; how *can* you say, 'Show us the Father'? Do you not believe that I am in the Father, and the Father is in Me? The words that I say to you I do not speak on My own initiative, but the Father abiding in Me does His works. Believe Me that I am in the Father and the Father is in Me; otherwise believe because of the works themselves. Truly, truly, I say to you, he who believes in Me, the works that I do, he will do also; and greater *works* than these he will do; because I go to the Father. Whatever you ask in My name, that will I do, so that the Father may be glorified in the Son. If you ask Me anything in My name, I will do *it*" (John 14:9–14; see Matthew 7:7; John 1:14; 5:19, 20, 36; 10:37, 38; 15:16).

Setting: Jerusalem. Before the Passover, after Jesus conveys the upcoming ministry of the Holy Spirit in His disciples' lives, He again relates peace, hope, and comfort to them regarding His return to the Father.

"Peace I leave with you; My peace I give to you; not as the world gives do I give to you. Do not let your heart be troubled, nor let it be fearful. You heard that I said to you, 'I go away, and I will come to you,' If you loved Me, you would have rejoiced because I go to the Father, for the Father is greater than I. Now I have told you before it happens, so that when it happens, you may believe. I will not speak much more with you, for the ruler of the world is coming, and he has nothing in Me; but so that the world may know that I love the Father, I do exactly as the Father commanded Me. Get up, let us go from here" (John 14:27–31; see John 10:18, 29; 12:31; 13:19; 16:33).

Setting: Jerusalem. Before the Passover, after warning His disciples of the persecution they will face after His departure to heaven, Jesus elaborates about the coming ministry of the Holy Spirit.

"But now I am going to Him who sent Me; and none of you asks Me, 'Where are You going?' But because I have said these things to you, sorrow has filled your heart. But I tell you the truth, it is to your advantage that I go away; for if I do not go away, the Helper will not come to you; but if I go, I will send Him to you. And He, when He comes, will convict the world concerning sin and righteousness and judgment; concerning sin, because they do not believe in Me; and concerning righteousness, because I go to the Father and you no longer see Me; and concerning judgment, because the ruler of this world has been judged" (John 16:5–11; see John 7:33; 12:31; 14:1, 16; 15:22, 24).

Setting: Jerusalem. Before the Passover, after empathizing with His disciples' sadness over His prophecies and giving them assurance for the future, Jesus conveys promises about praying in His name.

"In that day you will not question Me about anything. Truly, truly, I say to you, if you ask the Father for anything in My name, He will give it to you. Until now you have asked for nothing in My name; ask and you will receive, so that your joy may be made full. These things I have spoken to you in figurative language; an hour is coming when I will no longer speak to you in figurative language, but will tell you plainly of the Father. In that day you will ask in My name, and I do not say to you that I will request of the Father on your behalf; for the Father Himself loves you, because you have loved Me and have believed that I came forth from the Father. I came forth from the Father and have come into the world; I am leaving the world again and going to the Father" (John 16:23–28; see Matthew 13:34; John 8:42; 13:1, 3; 14:14, 21, 23; 15:16).

Setting: Jerusalem. Before the Passover, after conveying promises about praying in His name, Jesus prophesies His disciples' impending scattering and gives them assurance that in the midst of tribulation they will have His peace.

"Jesus answered them, "Do you now believe? Behold, an hour is coming, and has *already* come, for you to be scattered, each to his own *home,* and to leave Me alone; and *yet* I am not alone, because the Father is with Me. These things I have spoken to you, so that in Me you may have peace. In the world you have tribulation, but take courage, I have overcome the world" (John 16:31–33; see Zechariah 13:7; John 8:29; 14:27; Romans 8:37).

Setting: Jerusalem. Before the Passover, after giving His disciples assurance that in the midst of tribulation they will have His peace, Jesus prays His high-priestly prayer.

Jesus spoke these things; and lifting up His eyes to heaven, He said, "Father, the hour has come; glorify Your Son, that the Son may glorify You, even as You gave Him authority over all flesh, that to all whom You have given Him, He may give eternal life. This is eternal life, that they may know You, the only true God, and Jesus Christ whom You have sent. I glorified You on the earth, having accomplished the work which You have given Me to do. Now, Father, glorify Me together with Yourself, with the glory which I had with You before the world was. I have manifested Your name to the men whom You gave Me out of the world; they were Yours and You gave them to Me, and they have kept Your word. Now they have come to know that everything You have given Me is from You; for the words which You gave Me I have given to them; and they received *them* and truly understood that I came forth from You, and they believed You sent Me. I ask on their behalf; I do not ask on behalf of the world, but of those whom You have given Me; for they are Yours; and all things that are Mine are Yours, and Yours are Mine; and have been glorified in them. I am no longer in the world; and *yet* they themselves are in the world, and I come to You. Holy Father, keep them in Your name, *the name* which You have given Me, that they may be even as We *are.* While I was with them, I was keeping them in Your name which You have given Me; and I guarded them and not one of them perished but the son of perdition, so that the Scripture would be fulfilled" (John 17:1–12; see Luke 22:32; John 1:1; 3:35; 4:34; 5:44; 6:37–39, 70; 8:42; 11:41; 12:49; 13:18, 31; 16:15; 17:20; Philippians 2:9).

Setting: Jerusalem. Before the Passover, after giving His disciples assurance that in the midst of tribulation they will have His peace, Jesus continues praying His high-priestly prayer.

"But now I come to You; and these things I speak in the world so that they may have My joy made full in themselves. I have given them Your word; and the world has hated them, because they are not of the world, even as I am not of the world. I do not ask You to take them out of the world, but to keep them from the evil *one.* They are not of the world, even as I am not of the world. Sanctify them in the truth; Your word is truth. As You sent Me into the world, I also have sent them into the world. For their sakes I sanctify Myself, that they themselves also may be sanctified in truth. I do not ask on behalf of these alone, but for those also who believe in Me through their word; that they may all be one; even as You, Father, *are* in Me and I in You, that they also maybe in Us, so that the world may believe that You sent Me" (John 17:13–21; see Matthew 10:5, 38; John 7:33; 15:3, 11, 19).

Setting: Jerusalem. The risen Jesus meets with His disciple Thomas (Didymus), who has doubts about the testimony of the other disciples claiming to have seen and spoken with the Lord eight days earlier.

After eight days His disciples were again inside, and Thomas with them. Jesus came, the doors having been shut, and stood in their midst and said, "Peace *be* with you." Then He said to Thomas, "Reach here with your finger, and see My hands; and reach here your hand and put it into My side; and do not be unbelieving, but believing." Thomas answered and said to Him, "My Lord and my God!" Jesus said to him, "Because you have seen Me, have you believed? Blessed *are* they who did not see, and *yet* believed" (John 20:26–29; see Luke 24:36, 40; 1 Peter 1:8).

BELLY (Also see STOMACH)

Setting: Galilee. After Jesus warns the Pharisees about the unpardonable sin and their future judgment, some Pharisees and scribes ask Him to perform a miraculous sign for them in front of the crowds.

But He answered and said to them, "An evil and adulterous generation craves for a sign; and *yet* no sign will be given to it but the sign of Jonah the prophet; for just as JONAH WAS THREE DAYS AND THREE NIGHTS IN THE BELLY OF THE SEA MONSTER, so will the Son of Man be three days and three nights in the heart of the earth. The men of Nineveh will stand up with this generation at the judgment, and will condemn it because they repented at the preaching of Jonah; and behold, something greater than Jonah is here. *The* Queen of *the* South will rise up with this generation at the judgment and will condemn it, because she came from the ends of the earth to hear the wisdom of Solomon; and behold, something greater than Solomon is here" (Matthew 12:39–42; Jesus quotes from Jonah 1:17; cf. 1 Kings 10:1; Jonah 3:5; Matthew 16:1, 4; Luke 11:29).

BELOVED SON (Listed under SON, BELOVED)

BELT, MONEY (Also see BELTS, MONEY)

Setting: On the way from Galilee to Jerusalem. The Lord appoints seventy followers and sends them out in pairs to every city and place He Himself will soon visit.

And He was saying to them, "The harvest is plentiful, but the laborers are few; therefore beseech the Lord of the harvest to send out laborers into His harvest. Go; behold, I send you out as lambs in the midst of wolves. Carry no money belt, no bag, no shoes; and greet no one on the way. Whatever house you enter, first say, 'Peace be to this house.' If a man of peace is there, your peace will rest on him; but if not, it will return to you. Stay in that house, eating and drinking what they give you; for the laborer is worthy of his wages. Do not keep moving from house to house. Whatever city you enter and they receive you, eat what is set before you; and heal those in it who are sick, and say to them, 'The kingdom of God has come near to you.' But whatever city you enter and they do not receive you, go out into its streets and say, 'Even the dust of your city which clings to our feet we wipe off in protest against you; yet be sure of this, that the kingdom of God has come near.' I say to you, it will be more tolerable in that day for Sodom than for that city" (Luke 10:2–12; see Genesis 19:24–28; Matthew 9:37, 38, 10:9–14, 16; 1 Corinthians 10:27).

Setting: Jerusalem. During the Feast of Unleavened Bread (Passover) just before the Crucifixion, while celebrating the Passover meal, instituting the Lord's Supper, and prophesying Peter's upcoming denial of Him, Jesus instructs His disciples to prepare to persevere without Him.

And He said to them, "When I sent you out without money belt and bag and sandals, you did not lack anything, did you?" They said, "No, nothing." And He said to them, "But now, whoever has a money belt is to take it along, likewise also a bag, and whoever has no sword is to sell his coat and buy one. For I tell you that this which is written must be fulfilled in Me, 'AND HE WAS NUMBERED WITH

TRANSGRESSORS'; for that which refers to Me has its fulfillment." They said, "Lord, look, here are two swords." And He said to them, "It is enough" (Luke 22:35–38, Jesus quotes from Isaiah 53:12; see Matthew 10:5–15; Mark 6:7–11; Luke 9:1–5; 10:1–12; 22:49; John 17:4).

BELTS, MONEY (Also see BELT, MONEY)

Setting: Galilee. After His twelve disciples observe His ministry, Jesus summons and specifically instructs them about their ministry to the people of Israel.

These twelve Jesus sent out after instructing them: "Do not go in *the* way of *the* Gentiles, and do not enter *any* city of the Samaritans; but rather go to the lost sheep of the house of Israel. And as you go, preach, saying, 'The kingdom of heaven is at hand.' Heal *the* sick, raise *the* dead, cleanse *the* lepers, cast out demons. Freely you received, freely give. Do not acquire gold, or silver, or copper for your money belts, or a bag for *your* journey, or even two coats, or sandals, or a staff; for the worker is worthy of his support. And whatever city or village you enter, inquire who is worthy in it, and stay at his house until you leave *that city*. As you enter the house, give it your greeting. If the house is worthy, give it your *blessing of* peace. But if it is not worthy, take back your *blessing of* peace. Whoever does not receive you, nor heed your words, as you go out of that house or that city, shake the dust off your feet. Truly I say to you, it will be more tolerable for *the* land of Sodom and Gomorrah in the day of judgment than for that city" (Matthew 10:5–15; cf. Mark 6:7–11; Luke 9:1–5; see Matthew 3:2; 11:22, 24; 15:24; Luke 22:35; 1 Corinthians 9:14).

Setting: On the way from Galilee to Jerusalem. After giving a parable about riches and greed, Jesus challenges the crowd and His disciples concerning godly living.

"Sell your possessions and give to charity; make yourselves money belts which do not wear out, an unfailing treasure in heaven, where no thief comes near nor moth destroys. For where your treasure is, there your heart will be also" (Luke 12:33, 34; cf. Matthew 6:19–21; 19:21).

BENEFACTORS

Setting: An upper room in Jerusalem. During the Feast of Unleavened Bread (Passover) just before the Crucifixion, while Jesus celebrates the Passover meal with His disciples and institutes the Lord's Supper, the disciples argue over who is the greatest among them.

And He said to them, "The kings of the Gentiles lord it over them; and those who have authority over them are called 'Benefactors.' But it is not this way with you, but the one who is the greatest among you must become like the youngest, and the leader like a servant. For who is greater, the one who reclines at the table or the one who serves? Is it not the one who reclines at the table? But I am among you as the one who serves" (Luke 22:25–27; cf. Matthew 20:25–28; 23:11; Mark 10:42–45).

BERECHIAH

Setting: The temple in Jerusalem. After the Jewish religious leaders test Him with questions, Jesus pronounces the eighth of eight woes on them in front of the crowds and His disciples.

"Woe to you, scribes and Pharisees, hypocrites! For you build the tombs of the prophets and adorn the monuments of the righteous, and say, 'If we had been *living* in the days of our fathers, we would not have been partners with them in *shedding* the blood of the prophets.' So you testify against yourselves, that you are sons of those who murdered the prophets. Fill up, then, the measure *of the guilt* of you fathers. You serpents, you brood of vipers, how will you escape the sentence of hell? Therefore, behold, I am sending you prophets and wise men and scribes; some of them you will kill and crucify, and some of them you will scourge in your synagogues, and persecute from city to city, so that upon you may fall *the guilt of* all the righteous blood shed on earth, from the blood of righteous Abel to the blood of Zechariah, the son of Berechiah, whom you murdered between the temple and the altar. Truly I say to you, all these things will come upon this generation" (Matthew 23:29–36; cf. 2 Chronicles 24:21; Zechariah 1:1; Matthew 3:7; Luke 11:47–52; see Matthew 10:23).

BESEECHING (Also see ASKING; PRAYER; REQUEST; and WISH)
[BESEECHING from beseech]
Setting: Galilee. While healing the sick, raising the dead, and casting out demons in the villages and cities of the region, Jesus comments on the enormity of the task and the need to ask the Lord of the harvest for additional workers.

Then He said to His disciples, "The harvest is plentiful, but the workers are few. Therefore beseech the Lord of the harvest to send out workers into His harvest" (Matthew 9:37, 38; cf. Luke 10:2).

[BESEECHING from beseech]
Setting: On the way from Galilee to Jerusalem. The Lord appoints seventy followers and sends them out in pairs to every city and place He Himself will soon visit.

And He was saying to them, "The harvest is plentiful, but the laborers are few; therefore beseech the Lord of the harvest to send out laborers into His harvest. Go; behold, I send you out as lambs in the midst of wolves. Carry no money belt, no bag, no shoes; and greet no one on the way. Whatever house you enter, first say, 'Peace be to this house.' If a man of peace is there, your peace will rest on him; but if not, it will return to you. Stay in that house, eating and drinking what they give you; for the laborer is worthy of his wages. Do not keep moving from house to house. Whatever city you enter and they receive you, eat what is set before you; and heal those in it who are sick, and say to them, 'The kingdom of God has come near to you.' But whatever city you enter and they do not receive you, go out into its streets and say, 'Even the dust of your city which clings to our feet we wipe off in protest against you; yet be sure of this, that the kingdom of God has come near.' I say to you, it will be more tolerable in that day for Sodom than for that city" (Luke 10:2–12; see Genesis 19:24–28; Matthew 9:37, 38, 10:9–14, 16; 1 Corinthians 10:27).

BETHSAIDA
Setting: Galilee. After performing miracles throughout the region, Jesus pronounces woes against those cities who did not repent.

"Woe to you, Chorazin! Woe to you, Bethsaida! For if the miracles had occurred in Tyre and Sidon which occurred in you, they would have repented long ago in sackcloth and ashes. Nevertheless I say to you, it will be more tolerable for Tyre and Sidon in *the* day of judgment than for you. And you, Capernaum, will not be exalted to heaven, will you? You will descend to Hades; for if the miracles had occurred in Sodom which occurred in you, it would have remained to this day. Nevertheless, I say to you that it will be more tolerable for the land of Sodom in *the* day of judgment, than for you" (Matthew 11:21–24; cf. Matthew 10:15; Luke 10:13–15).

Setting: On the way from Galilee to Jerusalem. The Lord pronounces woes on cities who reject the gospel as He appoints seventy followers and sends them out in pairs to every city and place He Himself will soon visit.

"Woe to you, Chorazin! Woe to you, Bethsaida! For if the miracles had been performed in Tyre and Sidon which occurred in you, they would have repented long ago, sitting in sackcloth and ashes. But it will be more tolerable for Tyre and Sidon in the judgment than for you. And you, Capernaum, will not be exalted to heaven, will you? You will be brought down to Hades! The one who listens to you listens to Me, and the one who rejects you rejects Me; and he who rejects Me rejects the One who sent Me" (Luke 10:13–16; cf. Matthew 11:21–23; see Matthew 10:40; Luke 10:1).

BETRAYAL (Also see BETRAYAL, PROPHECY OF JESUS'; JUDAS, BETRAYAL OF JESUS BY; and PERSECUTION)
[BETRAYAL from Brother will betray brother]
Setting: Galilee. After His disciples observe His ministry, Jesus summons and specifically instructs them about the upcoming difficulties of *their* ministry to the people of Israel.

"Brother will betray brother to death, and a father *his* child; and children will rise up against parents and cause them to be put to death. You will be hated by all because of My name, but it is the one who has endured to the end who will be saved. But whenever they persecute you in one city, flee to the next; for truly I say to you, you will not finish *going through* the cities of Israel until the Son of Man comes" (Matthew 10:21–23; cf. Matthew 10:35, 36; 16:27, 28; 24:9).

[BETRAYAL from will betray one another]
Setting: The Mount of Olives, just east of Jerusalem. During His discourse, Jesus answers His disciples' questions as to when the temple will be destroyed and Jerusalem overrun, along with the signs of His coming and the end of the age.

And Jesus answered and said to them, "See to it that no one misleads you. For many will come in My name, saying, 'I am the Christ,' and will mislead many. You will be hearing of wars and rumors of wars. See that you are not frightened, for *those things* must take place, but *that* is not yet the end. For nation will rise against nation, and kingdom against kingdom, and in various places there will be famines and earthquakes. But all these things are *merely* the beginning of birth pangs. Then they will deliver you to tribulation, and will kill you, and you will be hated by all nations because of My name. At that time many will fall away and will betray one another and hate one another. Many false prophets will arise and will mislead many. Because lawlessness is increased, most people's love will grow cold. But the one who endures to the end, he will be saved. This gospel of the kingdom shall be preached in the whole world as a testimony to all the nations, and then the end will come" (Matthew 24:4–14; cf. Jeremiah 29:8; Matthew 7:15; 10:17, 22; Mark 13:3–13; Luke 21:7–19; Revelation 6:4).

[BETRAYAL from Brother will betray brother]
Setting: The Mount of Olives, east of the temple in Jerusalem. During His discourse, after prophesying the temple's destruction, Jesus responds to questions from Peter, James, John, and Andrew about future events.

And Jesus began to say to them, "See to it that no one misleads you. Many will come in My name, saying, 'I am *He!*' and will mislead many. When you hear of wars and rumors of wars, do not be frightened; *those things* must take place; but *that is* not yet the end. For nation will rise up against nation, and kingdom against kingdom; there will be earthquakes in various places; there will *also be* famines. These things are *merely* the beginning of birth pangs. But be on your guard; for they will deliver you to *the* courts, and you will be flogged in *the* synagogues, and you will stand before governors and kings for My sake, as a testimony to them. The gospel must first be preached to all the nations. When they arrest you and hand you over, do not worry beforehand about what you are to say, but say whatever is given you in that hour; for it is not you who speak, but *it is* the Holy Spirit. Brother will betray brother to death, and a father *his* child; and children will rise up against parents and have them put to death. You will be hated by all because of My name, but the one who endures to the end, he will be saved" (Mark 13:5–13; cf. Matthew 24:4–14; Luke 21:7–19; see Matthew 10:17–22).

[BETRAYAL from you will be betrayed]
Setting: The temple in Jerusalem. While ministering a few days before His crucifixion, after giving His disciples more details regarding the temple's future destruction, Jesus elaborates about other future events.

Then He continued by saying to them, "Nation will rise against nation and kingdom against kingdom, and there will be great earthquakes, and in various places plagues and famines; and there will be terrors and great signs from heaven. But before all these things, they will lay their hands on you and will persecute you, delivering you to the synagogues and prisons, bringing you before kings and governors for My name's sake. It will lead to an opportunity for your testimony. So make up your minds not to prepare beforehand to defend yourselves; for I will give you utterance and wisdom which none of your opponents will be able to resist or refute. But you will be betrayed even by parents and brothers and relatives and friends, and they will put some of you to death, and you will be hated by all because of My name. Yet not a hair of your head will perish. By your endurance you will gain your lives" (Luke 21:10–19; cf. Matthew 10:19–22; 24:7–14; Mark 13:8–13).

BETRAYAL, PREDICTION OF JESUS' (See BETRAYAL, PROPHECY OF JESUS')

BETRAYAL, PROPHECY OF JESUS' (Also see JUDAS, BETRAYAL OF JESUS BY)

[PROPHECY OF JESUS' BETRAYAL from the one who will betray Me]
Setting: Jerusalem. While celebrating the Passover meal, Jesus surprises His disciples with the revelation that one of them will soon betray Him to His enemies.

As they were eating, He said, "Truly I say to you that one of you will betray Me." Being deeply grieved, they each one began to say to Him, 'Surely not I, Lord?' And He answered, "He who dipped his hand with Me in the bowl is the one who will betray Me. The Son of Man *is to* go, just as it is written of Him; but woe to that man by whom the Son of Man is betrayed! It would have been good for that man if he had not been born." And Judas, who was betraying Him, said, 'Surely it is not I, Rabbi?' Jesus said to him, "You have said *it* yourself" (Matthew 26:21–25; cf. Mark 14:18–21; Luke 22:21–23; John 13:21–30; see Psalm 41:9).

[PROPHECY OF JESUS' BETRAYAL from one of you will betray Me]
Setting: A borrowed upper room in Jerusalem. While Jesus and His twelve disciples are eating the Passover meal, the Lord states that one of them will betray Him.

As they were reclining *at the table* and eating, Jesus said, "Truly I say to you that one of you will betray Me—one who is eating with Me." They began to be grieved and to say to Him one by one, "Surely not I?" And He said to them, "*It is* one of the twelve, one who dips with Me in the bowl. For the Son of Man *is to* go just as it is written of Him; but woe to that man by whom the Son of Man is betrayed! *It would have been* good for that man if he had not been born" (Mark 14:18–21; cf. Matthew 26:21–24; Luke 22:21–23; John 13:21, 22).

[PROPHECY OF JESUS' BETRAYAL from one of you will betray Me]
Setting: Jerusalem. Before the Passover, as His death on the cross nears, Jesus becomes troubled in spirit and acknowledges that one of His disciples will betray Him to the chief priests and Pharisees.

When Jesus had said this, He became troubled in spirit, and testified and said, "Truly, truly I say to you, that one of you will betray Me" (John 13:21; cf. Matthew 26:21; Mark 14:18; Luke 22:21).

BETRAYAL BY JUDAS (See JUDAS, BETRAYAL OF JESUS BY)

BETRAYAL OF JESUS (See JUDAS, BETRAYAL OF JESUS BY)

BEVERAGE (See specifics such as WATER; and WINE)

BIBLE (For an expanded viewpoint, check; OLD TESTAMENT; SCRIPTURE; SCRIPTURES; WORD, MY; WORD, YOUR; WORDS, MY; WORD; WORD, GOD'S; WORD OF GOD; and WRITINGS)

[BIBLE from EVERY WORD THAT PROCEEDS OUT OF THE MOUTH OF GOD]
Setting: Following Jesus' baptism, and before He begins His public ministry, the Spirit leads Him into the Judean wilderness for temptation by Satan.

But He answered and said, "It is written, 'MAN SHALL NOT LIVE ON BREAD ALONE, BUT ON EVERY WORD THAT PROCEEDS OUT OF THE MOUTH OF GOD'" (Matthew 4:4, Jesus quotes from Deuteronomy 8:3; cf. Luke 4:4).

[BIBLE from the Law of Moses and the Prophets and the Psalms]
Setting: Jerusalem. After rising from the grave on the third day following being crucified and appearing to two of His followers on the road to Emmaus, Jesus gives instruction to some of His disciples about His mission on earth and the promise of future power from God.

Now He said to them, "These are My words which I spoke to you while I was still with you, that all things which are written about Me in the Law of Moses and the Prophets and the Psalms must be fulfilled." Then He opened their minds to understand the Scriptures, and He said to them, "Thus it is written, that the Christ would suffer and rise again from the dead the third day, and that repentance for forgiveness of sins would be proclaimed in His name to all the nations, beginning from Jerusalem. You are witnesses of these things. And behold, I am sending forth the promise of My Father upon you; but you are to stay in the city until you are clothed with power from on high" (Luke 24:44–49; see Matthew 28:19, 20; Acts 1:8).

BIBLE SUMMARIZED (See COMMANDMENT, FOREMOST)

BILL

Setting: On the way from Galilee to Jerusalem. After telling the Parable of the Prodigal Son, the Lord teaches His disciples about stewardship.

Now He was also saying to the disciples, "There was a rich man who had a manager, and this manager was reported to him as squandering his possessions. And he called him and said to him, 'What is this I hear about you? Give an accounting of your management, for you can no longer be a manager.' The manager said to himself, 'What shall I do, since my master is taking the management away from me? I am not strong enough to dig; I am ashamed to beg. I know what I shall do, so that when I am removed from the management people will welcome me into their homes.' And he summoned each one of his master's debtors, and he began saying to the first, 'How much do you owe my master?' And he said, 'A hundred measures of oil.' And he said to him, 'Take your bill, and sit down quickly and write fifty.' Then he said to another, 'And how much do you owe?' And he said, 'A hundred measures of wheat.' He said to him, 'Take your bill, and write eighty.' And his master praised the unrighteous manager because he had acted shrewdly; for the sons of this age are more shrewd in relation to their own kind than the sons of light. And I say to you, make friends for yourselves by means of the wealth of unrighteousness, so that when it fails, they will receive you into the eternal dwellings. He who is faithful in a very little thing is faithful also in much; and he who is unrighteous in a very little thing is unrighteous also in much. Therefore if you have not been faithful in the use of unrighteous wealth, who will entrust the true riches to you? And if you have not been faithful in the use of that which is another's, who will give you that which is your own? No servant can serve two masters; for either he will hate the one and love the other, or else he will be devoted to one and despise the other. You cannot serve God and wealth" (Luke 16:1–13; cf. Matthew 6:24; see Matthew 25:14–30).

BIRDS (Also see specific birds such as DOVES; RAVENS; and SPARROWS)

Setting: Galilee. During the early part of His ministry, Jesus preaches the Sermon on the Mount to His disciples and the multitudes.

"For this reason I say to you, do not be worried about your life, *as to* what you will eat or what you will drink; nor for your body, *as to* what you will put on. Is not life more than food, and the body more than clothing? Look at the birds of the air, that they do not sow, nor reap nor gather into barns, and *yet* your heavenly Father feeds them. Are you not worth much more than they? And who of you by being worried can add a *single* hour to his life? And why are you worried about clothing? Observe how the lilies of the field grow; they do not toil nor do they spin, yet I say to you that not even Solomon in all his glory clothed himself like one of these. But if God so clothes the grass of the field, which is *alive* today and tomorrow is thrown into the furnace, *will He* not much more *clothe* you? You of little faith! Do not worry then, saying 'What will we eat?' or 'What will we drink?' or 'What will be wear for clothing?" For the Gentiles eagerly seek all these things; for your heavenly Father knows that you need all these things. But seek first His kingdom and His righteousness, and all these things will be added to you. So do not worry about tomorrow; for tomorrow will care for itself. Each day has enough trouble of its own" (Matthew 6:25–34; cf. Luke 12:22–31; see 1 Kings 10:4–7; Job 35:11; Matthew 8:26).

Setting: By the Sea of Galilee. After casting out evil spirits from the demon-possessed and healing the ill, in fulfillment of Isaiah 53:4, Jesus lays out to an inquiring scribe the demands of discipleship.

Then a scribe came and said to Him, "Teacher, I will follow You wherever you go." Jesus said to him, "The foxes have holes and the birds of the air *have* nests, but the Son of Man has nowhere to lay His head." Another of the disciples said to Him, "Lord, permit me first to go and bury my father." But Jesus said to him, "Follow Me, and allow the dead to bury their own dead" (Matthew 8:19–22; cf. Luke 9:57–60).

Setting: By the Sea of Galilee. While teaching and preaching to the crowds from a boat, Jesus conveys the Parable of the Sower.

And He spoke many things to them in parables, saying, "Behold, the sower went out to sow; and as he sowed, some *seeds* fell beside the road, and the birds came and ate them up. Others fell on the rocky places, where they did not have much soil; and immediately they sprang up, because they had no depth of soil. But when the sun had risen, they were scorched; and because they had no root, they withered away. Others fell among the thorns, and the thorns came up and choked them out. And others fell on the good soil and yielded a crop, some a hundredfold, some sixty, and some thirty. He who has ears, let him hear" (Matthew 13:3–9; cf. Mark 4:3–9; Luke 8:4–8).

Setting: By the Sea of Galilee. Because the religious leaders are rejecting His message, Jesus continues teaching the crowds with the Parable of the Mustard Seed.

He presented another parable to them, saying, "The kingdom of heaven is like a mustard seed, which a man took and sowed in his field; and this is smaller than all *other* seeds, but when it is full grown, it is larger than the garden plants and becomes a tree, so that THE BIRDS OF THE AIR come and NEST IN ITS BRANCHES" (Matthew 13:31, 32, Jesus quotes from Ezekiel 17:23; cf. Mark 4:30–32; Luke 13:18, 19).

Setting: By the Sea of Galilee. During the early part of His ministry, just after a visit from his mother and brothers, Jesus instructs a very large crowd with the Parable of the Sower from a boat.

"Listen *to this!* Behold, the sower went out to sow; as he was sowing, some *seed* fell beside the road, and the birds came and ate it up. Other *seed* fell on the rocky *ground* where it did not have much soil; and immediately it sprang up because it had no depth of soil. And after the sun had risen, it was scorched; and because it had no root, it withered away. Other *seed* fell among the thorns, and the thorns came up and choked it, and it yielded no crop. Other *seeds* fell into the good soil, and as the grew up and increased, they yielded a crop and produced thirty, sixty, and a hundredfold." And He was saying, "He who has ears to hear, let him hear" (Mark 4:3–9; cf. Matthew 13:3–9; Luke 8:5–8).

Setting: Galilee. After giving the Parable of the Sower and the Parable of the Seed, Jesus continues teaching by presenting the Parable of the Mustard Seed to His disciples.

And He said, "How shall we picture the kingdom of God, or by what parable shall we present it? *It is* like a mustard seed, which, when sown upon the soil, though it is smaller than all the seeds that are upon the soil, yet when it is sown, it grows up and becomes larger than all the garden plants and forms large branches; so that THE BIRDS OF THE AIR can NEST UNDER ITS SHADE" (Mark 4:30–32, Jesus quotes from Ezekiel 17:23; cf. Matthew 13:31, 32; Luke 13:18, 19).

Setting: Galilee. After His visit in the home of Simon the Pharisee, Jesus goes into the villages and cities of the region proclaiming and preaching the kingdom of God.

When a large crowd was coming together, and those from various cities were journeying to Him, He spoke by way of a parable: "The sower went out to sow his seed; and as he sowed, some fell beside the road, and it was trampled under foot and the birds of the air ate it up. Other seed fell on rocky soil, and as soon as it grew up, it was withered away, because it had no moisture. Other seed fell among the thorns; and the thorns grew up with it and choked it out. Other seed fell into the good soil, and grew up, and produced a crop a hundred times as great." As He said these things, He would call out, "He who has ears to hear, let him hear" (Luke 8:4–8; cf. Matthew 13:2–9; Mark 4:3–9).

Setting: On the way from Galilee to Jerusalem. The Lord responds to someone seeking to follow Him.

And Jesus said to him, "The foxes have holes and the birds of the air have nests, but the Son of Man has nowhere to lay His head" (Luke 9:58; cf. Matthew 8:19–22).

Setting: On the way from Galilee to Jerusalem. Jesus comforts the crowd and His disciples after giving a parable about riches and greed. The scribes and Pharisees turn hostile and question Him in an attempt to catch Him in something He might say.

And He said to His disciples, "For this reason I say to you, do not worry about your life, as to what you will eat; nor for your body, as to what you will put on. For life is more than food, and the body more than clothing. Consider the ravens, for they neither sow nor reap; they have no storeroom nor barn, and yet God feeds them; how much more valuable you are than the birds! And which of you by worrying can add a single hour to his life's span? If then you cannot do even a very little thing, why do you worry about other matters? Consider the lilies, how they grow: they neither toil nor spin; but I tell you, not even Solomon in all his glory clothed himself like one of these. But if God so clothes the grass in the field, which is alive today and tomorrow is thrown into the furnace, how much more will He clothe you? You men of little faith! And do not seek what you will eat and what you will drink, and do not keep worrying. For all these things the nations of the world eagerly seek; but your Father knows that you need these things. But seek His kingdom, and these things will be added to you. Do not be afraid, little flock, for your Father has chosen gladly to give you the kingdom" (Luke 12:22–32; cf. Matthew 6:25–33; see 1 Kings 10:4–7; Job 38:41).

Setting: On the way from Galilee to Jerusalem. Jesus conveys the Parable of the Mustard Seed and the Parable of the Leaven after responding to a synagogue official's anger for healing a woman, sick eighteen years, in a synagogue on the Sabbath.

So He was saying, "What is the kingdom of God like, and to what shall I compare it? It is like a mustard seed which a man took and threw into his own garden; and it grew and became a tree, and THE BIRDS OF THE AIR NESTED IN ITS BRANCHES." And again He said, "To what shall I compare the kingdom of God? It is like leaven, which a woman took and hid in three pecks of flour until it was all leavened" (Luke 13:18–21, Jesus quotes from Ezekiel 17:23; cf. Matthew 13:31–34; Mark 4:30–32).

BIRTH (Also see BORN; and PANGS, BIRTH)

Setting: Jerusalem. Before the Passover, after warning His disciples of the persecution they will face after His departure to heaven, empathizing with their sadness over His prophecies, Jesus gives them hope for the future.

"A little while, and you will no longer see Me; and again a little while, and you will see Me." *Some* of His disciples then said to one another, "What is this thing He is telling us, 'A little while, and you will not see Me; and again a little while, and you will see Me'; and, 'because I go to the Father'?" So they were saying, "What is this that He says, 'A little while'? We do not know what He is talking about." Jesus knew that they wished to question Him, and He said to them, "Are you deliberating together about this, that I said, 'A little while, and you will not see Me, and again a little while, and you will see Me'? Truly, truly, I say to you, that you will weep and lament, but the world will rejoice; you will grieve, but your grief will be turned into joy. Whenever a woman is in labor she has pain, because her hour has come; but when she gives birth to the child, she no longer remembers the anguish because of the joy that a child has been born into the world. Therefore you too have grief now; but I will see you again, and your heart will rejoice, and no one *will* take your joy away from you" (John 16:16–22; see Mark 9:32; Luke 23:27; John 14:18–24; 16:5–6; 20:20).

BIRTH, SPIRITUAL (See BORN AGAIN)

BIRTH PAINS (See PANGS, BIRTH)

BIRTH PANGS (Listed under PANGS, BIRTH)

BITTERNESS (See GRUDGES)

BLADE (grain; also see CROP; CROPS; and WHEAT)

Setting: Galilee. Following His explanation of the Parable of the Sower to His disciples, Jesus conveys the Parable of the Seed.

And He was saying, "The kingdom of God is like a man who casts seed upon the soil; and he goes to bed at night and gets up by day, and the seed sprouts and grows—how, he himself does not know. The soil produces crops by itself; first the blade, then the head, then the mature grain in the head. But when the crop permits, he immediately puts in the sickle, because the harvest has come" (Mark 4:26–29; see Joel 3:13).

BLASPHEMES (See BLASPHEMY; and HOLY SPIRIT, BLASPHEMY AGAINST THE)

BLASPHEMIES (Also see BLASPHEMY; and HOLY SPIRIT, BLASPHEMY AGAINST THE)

Setting: Galilee. After Jesus selects His twelve disciples, scribes from Jerusalem attribute His miraculous powers to Beelzebul (Satan).

And He called them to Himself and began speaking to them in parables, "How can Satan cast out Satan? If a kingdom is divided against itself, that kingdom cannot stand. If a house is divided against itself, that house will not be able to stand. If Satan has risen up against himself and is divided, he cannot stand, but he is finished! But no one can enter the strong man's house and plunder his property unless he first binds the strong man, and then he will plunder his house. Truly I say to you, all sins shall be forgiven the sons of men, and whatever blasphemies they utter; but whoever blasphemes against the Holy Spirit never has forgiveness, but is guilty of an eternal sin"—because they were saying, "He has an unclean spirit" (Mark 3:23–30; cf. Matthew 12:25–32; Luke 12:10).

BLASPHEMY (HOLY SPIRIT, BLASPHEMY AGAINST THE is a separate entry; also see BLASPHEMIES)

[BLASPHEMY from blaspheming]

Setting: Jerusalem. At the Feast of Dedication, the Pharisees desire to stone Jesus for claiming to be equal with God when they ask Him plainly whether He is the Christ.

Jesus answered them, "Has it not been written in your Law, 'I SAID, YOU ARE GODS'? If he called them gods, to whom the word of God came (and the Scripture cannot be broken), do you say of Him, whom the Father sanctified and sent into the world, 'You are blaspheming,' because I said, 'I am the Son of God'? If I do not do the works of My Father, do not believe Me; but if I do them, though you do not believe Me, believe the works, so that you may know and understand that the Father is in Me, and I in the Father" (John 10:34–38, Jesus quotes from Psalm 82:6; see John 14:10, 20).

Setting: On the island of Patmos (in the Aegean Sea about fifty miles southwest of Ephesus in modern Turkey). On the Lord's Day (Sunday), about fifty years after Jesus' resurrection, the disciple John encounters the Lord Jesus Christ, who communicates a new revelation for the apostle to record for the church in Smyrna and to six other churches in Asia.

"And to the angel of the church in Smyrna write: The first and the last, who was dead, and has come to life, says this: 'I know your tribulation and your poverty (but you are rich), and the blasphemy by those who say they are Jews and are not, but are a synagogue of Satan. Do not fear what you are about to suffer. Behold, the devil is about to cast some of you into prison, so that you will be tested, and you will have tribulation for ten days. Be faithful until death, and I will give you the crown of life. He who has an ear, let him hear what the Spirit says to the churches. He who overcomes will not be hurt by the second death' (Revelation 2:8–11; see Isaiah 44:6; Revelation 1:9, 18; 2:13; 20:6, 14).

BLASPHEMY AGAINST THE HOLY SPIRIT (Listed under HOLY SPIRIT, BLASPHEMY AGAINST THE; also see SIN, UNFORGIVABLE and SIN, UNPARDONABLE)

BLASPHEMY AGAINST THE SPIRIT (See HOLY SPIRIT, BLASPHEMY AGAINST THE; SIN, UNFORGIVABLE)

BLESSED (Also see BLESSING; GOD, GIFTS FROM; and GIFTS, GOOD)

Setting: Galilee. Early in His ministry, Jesus presents the Beatitudes (part of the Sermon on the Mount) to His disciples and the gathered crowds from Galilee, Decapolis, Jerusalem, Judea, and beyond the Jordan.

He opened His mouth and *began* to teach them, saying, "Blessed are the poor in spirit, for theirs is the kingdom of heaven" (Matthew 5:2, 3; see Matthew 13:35).

Setting: Galilee. Early in His ministry, Jesus presents the Beatitudes (part of the Sermon on the Mount) to His disciples and the gathered crowds from Galilee, Decapolis, Jerusalem, Judea, and beyond the Jordan.

"Blessed are those who mourn, for they shall be comforted" (Matthew 5:4; see Isaiah 61:2; Matthew 13:35).

Setting: Galilee. Early in His ministry, Jesus presents the Beatitudes (part of the Sermon on the Mount) to His disciples and the gathered crowds from Galilee, Decapolis, Jerusalem, Judea, and beyond the Jordan.

"Blessed are the gentle, for they shall inherit the earth" (Matthew 5:5; cf. Psalm 37:11; see Matthew 13:35).

Setting: Galilee. Early in His ministry, Jesus presents the Beatitudes (part of the Sermon on the Mount) to His disciples and the gathered crowds from Galilee, Decapolis, Jerusalem, Judea, and beyond the Jordan.

"Blessed are those who hunger and thirst for righteousness, for they shall be satisfied" (Matthew 5:6; see Matthew 13:35).

Galilee. Early in His ministry, Jesus presents the Beatitudes (part of the Sermon on the Mount) to His disciples and the gathered crowds from Galilee, Decapolis, Jerusalem, Judea, and beyond the Jordan.

"Blessed are the merciful, for they shall receive mercy" (Matthew 5:7; cf. Proverbs 11:17; see Matthew 13:35).

Setting: Galilee. Early in His ministry, Jesus presents the Beatitudes (part of the Sermon on the Mount) to His disciples and the gathered crowds from Galilee, Decapolis, Jerusalem, Judea, and beyond the Jordan.

"Blessed are the pure in heart, for they shall see God" (Matthew 5:8; see Matthew 13:35).

Setting: Galilee. Early in His ministry, Jesus presents the Beatitudes (part of the Sermon on the Mount) to His disciples and the gathered crowds from Galilee, Decapolis, Jerusalem, Judea, and beyond the Jordan.

"Blessed are the peacemakers, for they shall be called sons of God" (Matthew 5:9; see Matthew 13:35).

Setting: Galilee. Early in His ministry, Jesus presents the Beatitudes (part of the Sermon on the Mount) to His disciples and the gathered crowds from Galilee, Decapolis, Jerusalem, Judea, and beyond the Jordan.

"Blessed are those who have been persecuted for the sake of righteousness, for theirs is the kingdom of heaven" (Matthew 5:10; cf. Luke 6:22; 1 Peter 3:14; see Matthew 13:35).

Setting: Galilee. Early in His ministry, Jesus presents the Beatitudes (part of the Sermon on the Mount) to His disciples and the gathered crowds from Galilee, Decapolis, Jerusalem, Judea, and beyond the Jordan.

"Blessed are you when *people* insult you and persecute you, and falsely say all kinds of evil against you because of Me. Rejoice and be glad, for your reward in heaven is great; for in the same way they persecuted the prophets who were before you" (Matthew 5:11, 12; cf. 2 Chronicles 36:16; Luke 6:22, 23; 1 Peter 4:14; see Matthew 13:35).

Setting: Galilee. As He teaches and preaches, Jesus responds to John the Baptist's question (asked by John's disciples) whether He is Israel's promised Messiah.

Jesus answered and said to them, "Go and report to John what you hear and see: *the* BLIND RECEIVE SIGHT and *the* lame walk, *the* lepers are cleansed and *the* deaf hear, *the* dead are raised up, and *the* POOR HAVE THE GOSPEL PREACHED TO THEM. And blessed is he who does not take offense at Me" (Matthew 11:4–6, Jesus quotes from Isaiah 35:5f; cf. Luke 7:22, 23).

Setting: By the Sea of Galilee. Jesus responds to His disciples' questions about the Parable of the Sower, which He has just taught from a boat.

Jesus answered them, "To you it has been granted to know the mysteries of the kingdom of heaven, but to them it has not been granted. For whoever has, to him *more* shall be given, and he will have an abundance; but whoever does not have, even what he has shall be taken away from him. Therefore, I speak to them in parables; because while seeing they do not see, and while hearing they do not hear, nor do they understand. In their case the prophecy of Isaiah is being fulfilled, which says, 'YOU WILL KEEP ON HEARING, BUT WILL NOT UNDERSTAND; YOU WILL KEEP ON SEEING, BUT WILL NOT PERCEIVE; FOR THE HEART OF THIS PEOPLE HAS BECOME DULL, WITH THEIR EARS THEY SCARCELY HEAR, AND THEY HAVE CLOSED THEIR EYES, OTHERWISE THEYWOULD SEE WITH THEIR EYES, HEAR WITH THEIR EARS, AND UNDERSTAND WITH THEIR HEART AND RETURN, AND I WOULD HEAL THEM.' But blessed are your eyes, because they see; and your ears, because they hear. For truly I say to you that many prophets and righteous men desired to see what you see, and did not see *it,* and to hear what you hear, and did not hear *it*" (Matthew 13:11–17, Jesus quotes from Isaiah 6:9, 10; cf. Matthew 25:29; Mark 4:11–13; Luke 8:10; see Deuteronomy 29:4; John 8:56).

Setting: Caesarea Philippi. Jesus responds to Simon Peter's declaration that He is the Christ, the Son of the living God.

And Jesus said to him, "Blessed are you, Simon Barjona, because flesh and blood did not reveal *this* to you, but My Father who is in heaven. I also say to you that you are Peter, and upon this rock I will build My church; and the gates of Hades will not overpower it. I will give you the keys of the kingdom of heaven; and whatever you bind on earth shall have been bound in heaven, and whatever you loose on earth shall have been loosed in heaven" (Matthew 16:17–19; cf. Matthew 18:18; Mark 8:29; Luke 9:20).

Setting: The temple in Jerusalem. With His death on the cross just days away, Jesus laments over Jerusalem's hardheartedness and lack of repentance.

"Jerusalem, Jerusalem, who kills the prophets and stones those who are sent to her! How often I wanted to gather your children together, the way a hen gathers her chicks under her wings, and you were unwilling. Behold, your house is being left to you desolate! For I say to you, from now on you will not see Me until you say, 'BLESSED IS HE WHO COMES IN THE NAME OF THE LORD!'" (Matthew 23:37–39, Jesus quotes from Psalm 118:26; cf. 1 Kings 9:7; Luke 13:34, 35).

Setting: The Mount of Olives, just east of Jerusalem. During His discourse, after answering His disciples' questions as to when the temple will be destroyed and Jerusalem overrun, along with the signs of His coming and the end of the age, Jesus reemphasizes to His disciples that they should be on the alert for His return.

"Therefore be on the alert, for you do not know which day your Lord is coming. But be sure of this, that if the head of the house had known at what time of the night the thief was coming, he would have been on the alert and would not have allowed his house to be broken into. For this reason you also must be ready; for the Son of Man is coming at an hour when you do not think *He will.* Who then is the faithful and sensible slave whom his master put in charge of his household to give their food at the proper time? Blessed is that slave whom his master finds so doing when he comes. Truly I say to you that he will put him in charge of all his possessions. But if that evil slave says in his heart, 'My master is not coming for a long time,' and begins to beat his fellow slaves and eat and drink with drunkards; the master of that slave will come on a day when he does not expect *him* and at an hour which he does not know, and will cut him in pieces and assign him a place with the hypocrites; in that place there will be weeping and gnashing of teeth" (Matthew 24:42–51; cf. Mark 13:33–37; Luke 12:39–46; 21:34–36; see Matthew 8:11, 12; 25:21–23).

Setting: The Mount of Olives, just east of Jerusalem. During His discourse, after answering His disciples' questions as to when the temple will be destroyed and Jerusalem overrun, along with the signs of His coming and the end of the age, Jesus reveals the future judgments following His return.

"But when the Son of Man comes in His glory, and all the angels with Him, then He will sit on His glorious throne. All the nations will be gathered before Him; and He will separate them from one another, as the shepherd separates the sheep from the goats; and He will put the sheep on His right, and the goats on the left. Then the King will say to those on His right, 'Come, you who are blessed of My Father, inherit the kingdom prepared for you from the foundation of the world. 'For I was hungry, and you gave Me *something* to eat; I was thirsty, and you gave Me *something* to drink; I was a stranger, and you invited Me in; naked, and you clothed Me; I was sick, and you visited Me; I was in prison, and you came to Me.' Then the righteous will answer Him, 'Lord, when did we see You hungry and feed You, or thirsty, and give you *something* to drink? And when did we see You a stranger, and invite You in, or naked, and clothe You? When did we see You sick, or in prison, and come to You?' The King will answer and say to them, 'Truly I say to you, to the extent that you did it to one of these brothers of Mine, *even* the least *of them,* you did it to Me.' Then He will also say to those on His left, 'Depart from Me, accursed ones, into the eternal fire which has been prepared for the devil and his angels; for I was hungry, and you gave Me *nothing* to eat; I was thirsty, and you gave Me nothing to drink; I was a stranger, and you did not invite Me in; naked, and you did not clothe Me; sick, and in prison, and you did not visit Me.' Then they themselves also will answer, 'Lord, when did we see You hungry, or thirsty, or a stranger, or naked, or sick, or in prison, and did not take care of You?' Then He will answer them, 'Truly I say to you, to the extent that you did not do it to one of the least of these, you did not do it to Me.' These will go away into eternal punishment, but the righteous into eternal life" (Matthew 25:31–46; see Matthew 7:23; 16:27; 19:29).

Setting: Galilee. After selecting His twelve disciples, Jesus teaches the Beatitudes (part of the Sermon on the Mount) to His disciples and a great throng of people from Judea, Jerusalem, and the central coastal region of Tyre and Sidon.

And turning His gaze toward His disciples, He began to say, "Blessed are you who are poor, for yours is the kingdom of God" (Luke 6:20; cf. Matthew 5:3).

Setting: Galilee. After selecting His twelve disciples, Jesus teaches the Beatitudes to His disciples and a great throng from Judea, Jerusalem, and the central coastal region of Tyre and Sidon.

"Blessed are you who hunger now, for you shall be satisfied. Blessed are you who weep now, for you shall laugh" (Luke 6:21; cf. Matthew 5:4, 6).

Setting: On a mountain in Galilee. After selecting His twelve disciples, Jesus teaches the Beatitudes to His disciples and a great throng from Judea, Jerusalem, and the central coastal region of Tyre and Sidon.

"Blessed are you when men hate you, and ostracize you, and insult you, and scorn your name as evil, for the sake of the Son of Man. Be glad in that day and leap for joy, for behold, your reward is great in heaven. For in the same way their fathers used to treat the prophets" (Luke 6:22, 23; cf. Matthew 5:10–12; see 2 Chronicles 36:16).

Setting: Galilee. After Jesus raises a woman's son from the dead in Nain, the disciples of John the Baptist inquire whether He is the promised Messiah.

And He answered and said to them, "Go and report to John what you have seen and heard: the BLIND RECEIVE SIGHT, the lame walk, the lepers are cleansed, and the deaf hear, the dead are raised up, the POOR HAVE THE GOSPEL PREACHED TO THEM. Blessed is he who does not take offense at Me" (Luke 7:22, 23, Jesus quotes from Isaiah 35:5; 61:1; cf. Matthew 11:2–6).

Setting: On the way from Galilee to Jerusalem. After responding to a report from the seventy sent out in pairs to every city and place He Himself will soon visit, the Lord addresses His disciples in private.

Turning to the disciples, He said privately, "Blessed are the eyes which see the things you see, for I say to you, that many prophets and kings wished to see the things you see, and did not see them, and to hear the things which you hear, and did not hear them" (Luke 10:23, 24; cf. Matthew 13:16, 17; see Luke 10:17).

Setting: On the way from Galilee to Jerusalem. After revealing a problem with exorcism, Jesus responds to a blessing from a woman in the crowd.

But He said, "On the contrary, blessed are those who hear the word of God and observe it" (Luke 11:28).

Setting: On the way from Galilee to Jerusalem. After giving a parable about riches and greed, Jesus uses a parable to challenge the crowd and His disciples to be ready for His return.

"Be dressed in readiness, and keep your lamps lit. Be like men who are waiting for their master when he returns from the wedding feast, so that they may immediately open the door to him when he comes and knocks. Blessed are those slaves whom the master will find on the alert when he comes; truly I say to you, that he will gird himself to serve, and have them recline at the table, and will come up and wait on them. Whether he comes in the second watch, or even in the third and finds them so, blessed are those slaves. But be sure of this, that if the head of the house had known at what hour the thief was coming, he would not have allowed his house to be broken into. You too, be ready; for the Son of Man is coming at an hour that you do not expect" (Luke 12:35–40; cf. Matthew 24:42–44; see Mark 13:33; Ephesians 6:14).

Setting: On the way from Galilee to Jerusalem. When Jesus uses a parable to challenge the crowd and His disciples to be ready for His return, Peter asks Him whom He is addressing.

And the Lord said, "Who then is the faithful and sensible steward, whom his master will put in charge of his servants, to give them their rations at the proper time? Blessed is that slave whom his master finds so doing when he comes. Truly I say to you that he will put him in charge of all his possessions. But if that slave says in his heart, 'My master will be a long time in coming,' and begins to beat the slaves, both men and women, and to eat and drink and get drunk; the master of that slave will come on a day when he does not expect him and at an hour he does not know, and will cut him in pieces, and assign him a place with the unbelievers. And that slave who knew his master's will and did not get ready or act in accord with his will, will receive many lashes, but the one who did know it, and committed deeds worthy of flogging, will receive but few. From everyone who has been given much, much will be required; and to whom they entrusted much, of him they will ask all the more" (Luke 12:42–48; cf. Matthew 24:45–51; see Leviticus 5:17).

Setting: On the way from Galilee to Jerusalem. While teaching in the cities and villages, after Jesus responds to a question about who is saved, some Pharisees ask Him to leave, claiming Herod Antipas (tetrarch of Galilee and Perea) seeks to kill Him.

And He said to them, "Go and tell that fox, 'Behold, I cast out demons and perform cures today and tomorrow, and the third day I reach My goal.' Nevertheless I must journey on today and tomorrow and the next day; for it cannot be that a prophet would perish outside of Jerusalem. O Jerusalem, Jerusalem, the city that kills the prophets and stones those sent to her! How often I wanted to gather your children together, just as a hen gathers her brood under her wings, and you would not have it! Behold, your house is left to you desolate; and I say to you, you will not see Me until the time comes when you say, 'BLESSED IS HE WHO COMES IN THE NAME OF THE LORD!'" (Luke 13:32–35, Jesus quotes from Psalm 118:26; cf. Matthew 23:37).

Setting: On the way from Galilee to Jerusalem. Jesus speaks a parable to the guests of a Pharisee leader on the Sabbath. As He observes the guests selecting places of honor at the table, Jesus comments to the host about the people to invite in the future.

And He also went on to say to the one who had invited Him, "When you give a luncheon or a dinner, do not invite your friends or your brothers or your relatives or rich neighbors, otherwise they may also invite you in return and that will be your repayment. But when you give a reception, invite the poor, the crippled, the lame, the blind, and you will be blessed, since they do not have the means to repay you; for you will be repaid at the resurrection of the righteous" (Luke 14:12–14; see Luke 14:1, 2, 15; John 5:28, 29).

Setting: Jerusalem. After being arrested and appearing before the Council of Elders (Sanhedrin), Pontius Pilate (Roman governor of Judea), Herod Antipas (tetrarch of Galilee and Perea), and Pilate a second time (when Pilate bows to the crowd's pressure and grants that Jesus be crucified), the Lord prophesies to the women mourning Him regarding the coming judgment of Jerusalem.

But Jesus turning to them said, "Daughters of Jerusalem, stop weeping for Me, but weep for yourselves and for your children. For behold, the days are coming when they will say, 'Blessed are the barren, and the wombs that never bore, and the breasts that never nursed.' Then they will begin TO SAY TO THE MOUNTAINS, 'FALL ON US,' AND TO THE HILLS, 'COVER US.' For it they do these things when the tree is green, what will happen when it is dry?" (Luke 23:28–31, Jesus quotes from Hosea 10:8; see Matthew 24:19).

Setting: Jerusalem. Before the Passover, with His death on the cross nearing, Jesus explains the reason for His vivid example of servanthood in washing His disciples' feet.

So when He had washed their feet, and taken His garments and reclined *at the table* again, He said to them, "Do you know what I have done to you? You call Me Teacher and Lord; and you are right, for *so* I am. If I then, the Lord and the Teacher, washed your feet, you also ought to wash one another's feet. For I gave you an example that you also should do as I did to you. Truly, truly I say to you, a slave is not greater than his master, nor *is* one who is sent greater than the one who sent him. If you know these things, you are blessed if you do them. I do not speak of all of you. I know the ones I have chosen; but *it is* that the Scripture may be fulfilled, 'HE WHO EATS MY BREAD HAS LIFTED UP HIS HEEL AGAINST ME.' From now on I am telling you before *it* comes to pass, so that when it does occur, you may believe that I am *He. Truly,* truly, I say to you, he who receives whomever I send receives Me; and he who receives Me receives Him who sent Me" (John 13:12–20; Jesus quotes from Psalm 41:9; see Matthew 7:24; 10:24, 40; John 8:24; 14:29; 1 Peter 5:3).

Setting: Jerusalem. The risen Jesus meets with His disciple Thomas (Didymus), who has been having doubts about the testimony of the other disciples claiming to have seen and spoken with the Lord eight days earlier.

After eight days His disciples were again inside, and Thomas with them. Jesus came, the doors having been shut, and stood in their midst and said, "Peace be with you." Then He said to Thomas, "Reach here with your finger, and see My hands; and reach here your hand and put it into My side; and do not be unbelieving, but believing." Thomas answered and said to Him, "My Lord and my God!" Jesus said to him, "Because you have seen Me, have you believed? Blessed are they who did not see, and yet believed" (John 20:26–29; see Luke 24:36, 40; 1 Peter 1:8).

Setting: Ephesus. Luke, writing in Acts, gives Paul's recollection of Jesus' words regarding giving and receiving. This occurs during Paul's farewell address to the elders of the church at Ephesus during his third missionary journey just before leaving for Jerusalem.

"In everything I showed you that working hard in this manner you must help the weak and remember the words of the Lord Jesus, that He Himself said, "It is more blessed to give than to receive'" (Acts 20:35; see Matthew 10:8).

Setting: On the island of Patmos (in the Aegean Sea about fifty miles southwest of Ephesus in modern Turkey). In the final chapter of the Lord Jesus Christ's Revelation via the disciple John, approximately fifty years after His resurrection, the Lord reveals His coming return and the blessing to those who heed the words of the prophecy of this book.

"And behold, I am coming quickly. Blessed is he who heeds the words of the prophecy of this book" (Revelation 22:7; see Revelation 1:3).

BLESSING (Also see BLESSED; PERSECUTION; and SERVICE)

[BLESSING from Truly I say to you, to the extent that you did it to one of these brothers of Mine, *even* the least *of them,* you did it to Me]

Setting: The Mount of Olives, just east of Jerusalem. During His discourse, after answering His disciples' questions as to when the temple will be destroyed and Jerusalem overrun, along with the signs of His coming and the end of the age, Jesus reveals the future judgments following His return.

"But when the Son of Man comes in His glory, and all the angels with Him, then He will sit on His glorious throne. All the nations will be gathered before Him; and He will separate them from one another, as the shepherd separates the sheep from the goats; and He will put the sheep on His right, and the goats on the left. Then the King will say to those on His right, 'Come, you who are blessed of My Father, inherit the kingdom prepared for you from the foundation of the world. 'For I was hungry, and you gave Me *something* to eat; I was thirsty, and you gave Me *something* to drink; I was a stranger, and you invited Me in; naked, and you clothed Me; I was sick, and you visited Me; I was in prison, and you came to Me.' Then the righteous will answer Him, 'Lord, when did we see You hungry and feed You, or thirsty, and give you *something* to drink? And when did we see You a stranger, and invite You in, or naked, and clothe You? When did we see You sick, or in prison, and come to You?' The King will answer and say to them, 'Truly I say to you, to the extent that you did it to one of these brothers of Mine, *even* the least *of them,* you did it to Me.' Then He will also say to those on His left, 'Depart from Me, accursed ones, into the eternal fire which has been prepared for the devil and his angels; for I was hungry, and you gave Me *nothing* to eat; I was thirsty, and you gave Me nothing to drink; I was a stranger, and you did not invite Me in; naked, and you did not clothe Me; sick, and in prison, and you did not visit Me.' Then they themselves also will answer, 'Lord, when did we see You hungry, or thirsty, or a stranger, or naked, or sick, or in prison, and did not take care of You?' Then He will answer them, 'Truly I say to you, to the extent that you did not do it to one of the least of these, you did not do it to Me.' These will go away into eternal punishment, but the righteous into eternal life" (Matthew 25:31–46; Matthew 7:23; 16:27; 19:29).

[BLESSING from bless]
Setting: Galilee. After selecting His twelve disciples, Jesus teaches the Sermon on the Mount to His disciples and a great throng from Judea, Jerusalem, and the central coastal region of Tyre and Sidon.

"But I say to you who hear, love your enemies, do good to those who hate you, bless those who curse you, pray for those who mistreat you. Whoever hits you on the cheek, offer him the other also; and whoever takes away your coat, do not withhold your shirt from him either. Give to everyone who asks of you, and whoever takes away what is yours, do not demand it back. Treat others the same way you want them to treat you. If you love those who love you, what credit is that to you? For even sinners love those who love them. If you do good to those who do good to you, what credit is that to you? For even sinners do the same. If you lend to those from whom you expect to receive, what credit is that to you? Even sinners lend to sinners in order to receive back the same amount. But love your enemies, and do good, and lend, expecting nothing in return; and your reward will be great, and you will be sons of the Most High; for He Himself is kind to ungrateful and evil men. Be merciful, just as your Father is merciful" (Luke 6:27–36; cf. Matthew 5:9, 39–48; Matthew 7:12).

BLESSING OF PEACE (Listed under PEACE, BLESSING OF)

BLIND GUIDES (Listed under GUIDES, BLIND)

BLIND MEN (physically; see MEN, PHYSICALLY BLIND; also see BLINDNESS)

BLIND MEN (spiritually; see MEN, SPIRITUALLY BLIND)

BLINDNESS (GUIDES, BLIND; HEALING; MEN, PHYSICALLY BLIND; MEN, SPIRITUALLY BLIND; and PHARISEE, BLIND are separate entries)

[BLINDNESS from BLIND]
Setting: Galilee. As He teaches and preaches, Jesus responds to John the Baptist's question (posed by John's disciples) whether He is Israel's promised Messiah.

Jesus answered and said to them, "Go and report to John what you hear and see: *the* BLIND RECEIVE SIGHT and *the* lame walk, *the* lepers are cleansed and *the* deaf hear, *the* dead are raised up, and *the* POOR HAVE THE GOSPEL PREACHED TO THEM. And blessed is he who does not take offense at Me" (Matthew 11:4–6, Jesus quotes from Isaiah 35:5f; cf. Luke 7:22, 23).

[BLINDNESS from BLIND]
Setting: The synagogue in Jesus' hometown of Nazareth in Galilee. At the beginning of Jesus' public ministry, He reads on the Sabbath from the book of the prophet Isaiah.

And the book of the prophet Isaiah was handed to Him. And He opened the book and found the place where it was written, "THE SPIRIT OF THE LORD IS UPON ME, BECAUSE HE ANOINTED ME TO PREACH THE GOSPEL TO THE POOR. HE HAS SENT ME TO PROCLAIM

RELEASE TO THE CAPTIVES, AND RECOVERY OF SIGHT TO THE BLIND, TO SET FREE THOSE WHO ARE OPPRESSED, TO PROCLAIM THE FAVORABLE YEAR OF THE LORD." And He closed the book, gave it back to the attendant and sat down; and the eyes of all in the synagogue were fixed on Him. And He began to say to them, "Today this Scripture has been fulfilled in your hearing" (Luke 4:17–21, Jesus quotes from Isaiah 61:1, 2).

[BLINDNESS from BLIND]
Setting: Galilee. After Jesus raises a woman's son from the dead in Nain, the disciples of John the Baptist inquire whether He is the promised Messiah.

And He answered and said to them, "Go and report to John what you have seen and heard: the BLIND RECEIVE SIGHT, the lame walk, the lepers are cleansed, and the deaf hear, the dead are raised up, the POOR HAVE THE GOSPEL PREACHED TO THEM. Blessed is he who does not take offense at Me" (Luke 7:22, 23, Jesus quotes from Isaiah 35:5; 61:1; cf. Matthew 11:2–6).

[BLINDNESS from BLIND]
Setting: On the way from Galilee to Jerusalem. Jesus speaks a parable to the guests of a Pharisee leader on the Sabbath. As He observes the guests selecting places of honor at the table, Jesus comments to the host about the people to invite in the future.

And He also went on to say to the one who had invited Him, "When you give a luncheon or a dinner, do not invite your friends or your brothers or your relatives or rich neighbors, otherwise they may also invite you in return and that will be your repayment. But when you give a reception, invite the poor, the crippled, the lame, the blind, and you will be blessed, since they do not have the means to repay you; for you will be repaid at the resurrection of the righteous" (Luke 14:12–14; see John 5:28, 29).

[BLINDNESS from BLIND]
Setting: On the way from Galilee to Jerusalem. After He speaks a parable to the invited guests and the host at a banquet, Jesus responds to a guest's proclamation about the blessings of eating bread in the kingdom of God.

But He said to him, "A man was giving a big dinner, and he invited many; and at the dinner hour he sent his slave to say to those who had been invited, 'Come; for everything is ready now.' But they all alike began to make excuses. The first one said to him, 'I have bought a piece of land and I need to go out and look at it; please consider me excused.' Another one said, 'I have bought five yoke of oxen, and I am going to try them out; please consider me excused.' Another one said, I have married a wife, and for that reason I cannot come.' And the slave came back and reported this to his master. Then the head of the household became angry and said to his slave, 'Go out at once into the streets and lanes of the city and bring in here the poor and crippled and blind and lame.' And the slave said, 'Master, what you commanded has been done, and still there is room.' And the master said to the slave, 'Go out into the highways and along the hedges, and compel them to come in, so that my house may be filled. For I tell you, none of those men who were invited shall taste of my dinner'" (Luke 14:16–24; see Deuteronomy 24:5; Matthew 22:2–14; Luke 14:1, 2).

[BLINDNESS from BLIND]
Setting: Jerusalem. Following the Pharisees' interrogation and dismissal of the formerly blind man Jesus healed on the Sabbath, the Lord addresses them about His mission in this world.

And Jesus said, "For judgment I came into this world, so that those who do not see may see, and that those who see may become blind" (John 9:39; see Luke 4:18; John 5:22, 27).

[BLINDNESS from BLIND]
Setting: Jerusalem. Following the Pharisees' interrogation and dismissal of the formerly blind man Jesus healed on the Sabbath, the Lord responds to their question whether they are spiritually blind.

Jesus said to them, "If you were blind, you would have no sin; but since you say, 'We see,' your sin remains" (John 9:41; see John 15:22–24).

[BLINDNESS from BLIND]

Setting: On the island of Patmos (in the Aegean Sea about fifty miles southwest of Ephesus in modern Turkey). On the Lord's Day (Sunday), about fifty years after Jesus' resurrection, the disciple John encounters the Lord Jesus Christ, who communicates a new revelation for the apostle to record for the church in Laodicea and to six other churches in Asia.

"To the angel of the church in Laodicea write: The Amen, the faithful and true Witness, the Beginning of the creation of God, says this: 'I know your deeds, that you are neither cold nor hot; I wish that you were cold or hot. So because you are lukewarm, and neither hot nor cold, I will spit you out of My mouth. Because you say, "I am rich, and have become wealthy, and have need of nothing," and you do not know that you are wretched and miserable and poor and blind and naked, I advise you to buy from Me gold refined by fire so that you may become rich, and white garments so that you may clothe yourself, and *that* the shame of your nakedness will not be revealed; and eye salve to anoint your eyes so that you may see. Those whom I love, I reprove and discipline; therefore be zealous and repent. Behold, I stand at the door and knock; if anyone hears My voice and opens the door, I will come in to him and will dine with him, and he with Me. He who overcomes, I will grant to him to sit down with Me on My throne, as I also overcame and sat down with My Father on His throne. He who has an ear, let him hear what the Spirit says to the churches'" (Revelation 3:14–22; see Proverbs 3:12; Hosea 12:8; John 14:23; 16:33).

BLINDNESS, SPIRITUAL (See MEN, SPIRITUALLY BLIND)

BLOCK (See STUMBLING BLOCK; and STUMBLING BLOCKS)

BLOCKS (See STUMBLING BLOCK; and STUMBLING BLOCKS)

BLOOD (BLOOD, NEW COVENANT IN MY; BLOOD, MY; COVENANT, BLOOD OF THE; and PROPHETS, BLOOD OF THE are separate entries)

Setting: The temple in Jerusalem. After the Jewish religious leaders test Him with questions, Jesus pronounces the eighth of eight woes on them in front of the crowds and His disciples.

"Woe to you, scribes and Pharisees, hypocrites! For you build the tombs of the prophets and adorn the monuments of the righteous, and say, 'If we had been *living* in the days of our fathers, we would not have been partners with them in *shedding* the blood of the prophets.' So you testify against yourselves, that you are sons of those who murdered the prophets. Fill up, then, the measure *of the guilt* of you fathers. You serpents, you brood of vipers, how will you escape the sentence of hell? Therefore, behold, I am sending you prophets and wise men and scribes; some of them you will kill and crucify, and some of them you will scourge in your synagogues, and persecute from city to city, so that upon you may fall *the guilt of* all the righteous blood shed on earth, from the blood of righteous Abel to the blood of Zechariah, the son of Berechiah, whom you murdered between the temple and the altar. Truly I say to you, all these things will come upon this generation" (Matthew 23:29–36; cf. 2 Chronicles 24:21; Zechariah 1:1; Matthew 3:7; Luke 11:47–52; see Matthew 10:23).

Setting: On the way from Galilee to Jerusalem. After Jesus pronounces woes upon the Pharisees, a lawyer replies that Jesus' remarks insult lawyers, too.

But He said, "Woe to you lawyers as well! For you weigh men down with burdens hard to bear, while you yourselves will not even touch the burdens with one of your fingers. Woe to you! For you build the tombs of the prophets, and it was your fathers who killed them. So you are witnesses and approve the deeds of your fathers; because it was they who killed them, and you build their tombs. For this reason also the wisdom of God said, 'I will send them prophets and apostles, and some of them they will kill and some they will persecute, so that the blood of all the prophets, shed since the foundation of the world, may be charged against this generation, from the blood of Abel to the blood of Zechariah, who was killed between the altar and the house of God; yes, I tell you, it shall be charged against this generation.' Woe to you lawyers! For you have taken away the key of knowledge; you yourselves did not enter, and you hindered those who were entering" (Luke 11:46–52; cf. Matthew 23:29–32; see 2 Chronicles

24:20, 21; Matthew 23:4, 13).

BLOOD, FLESH AND

Setting: Caesarea Philippi. Jesus responds to Simon Peter's declaration that He is the Christ, the Son of the living God.

And Jesus said to him, "Blessed are you, Simon Barjona, because flesh and blood did not reveal *this* to you, but My Father who is in heaven. I also say to you that you are Peter, and upon this rock I will build My church; and the gates of Hades will not overpower it. I will give you the keys of the kingdom of heaven; and whatever you bind on earth shall have been bound in heaven, and whatever you loose on earth shall have been loosed in heaven" (Matthew 16:17–19; cf. Matthew 18:18; Mark 8:29; Luke 9:20).

BLOOD, HIS (Jesus')

Setting: Capernaum of Galilee. After Jesus informs the people whom He miraculously fed with a lad's five loaves and two fish how they might receive the bread out of heaven, the Jewish religious leaders argue with one another about Jesus saying He will give His flesh to the world to eat.

So Jesus said to them, "Truly, truly, I say to you, unless you eat the flesh of the Son of Man and drink His blood, you have no life in yourselves. He who eats My flesh and drinks My blood has eternal life, and I will raise him up on the last day. For My flesh is true food, and My blood is true drink. He who eats My flesh and drinks My blood abides in Me, and I in him. As the living Father sent Me, and I live because of the Father, so he who eats Me, he also will live because of Me. This is the bread which came down out of heaven; not as the fathers ate and died; he who eats this bread will live forever" (John 6:53–58; see Matthew 16:16; Luke 4:22; John 3:36; John 6:26–40; 9:16; 15:4).

BLOOD, JESUS' (See BLOOD, HIS; BLOOD, MY; BLOOD, NEW COVENANT IN MY; and COVENANT, BLOOD OF THE)

BLOOD, MY (Jesus'; also see BLOOD, NEW COVENANT IN MY and COVENANT, BLOOD OF THE)

Setting: Capernaum of Galilee. After Jesus informs the people whom He miraculously fed with a lad's five loaves and two fish how they might receive the bread out of heaven, the Jewish religious leaders argue with one another when Jesus says He will give His flesh to the world to eat.

So Jesus said to them, "Truly, truly, I say to you, unless you eat the flesh of the Son of Man and drink His blood, you have no life in yourselves. He who eats My flesh and drinks My blood has eternal life, and I will raise him up on the last day. For My flesh is true food, and My blood is true drink. He who eats My flesh and drinks My blood abides in Me, and I in him. As the living Father sent Me, and I live because of the Father, so he who eats Me, he also will live because of Me. This is the bread which came down out of heaven; not as the fathers ate and died; he who eats this bread will live forever" (John 6:53–58; see Matthew 16:16; Luke 4:22; John 3:36; John 9:16; 15:4).

BLOOD, NEW COVENANT IN MY (Also see BLOOD, HIS; BLOOD, MY; and COVENANT, BLOOD OF THE)

Setting: An upper room in Jerusalem. During the Feast of Unleavened Bread (Passover) just before Jesus' crucifixion, while celebrating the Passover meal with His disciples, Jesus institutes the Lord's Supper.

And when He had taken a cup and given thanks, He said, "Take this and share it among yourselves; for I say to you, I will not drink of the fruit of the vine from now on until the kingdom of God comes." And when he had taken some bread and given thanks, He broke it and gave it to them, saying, "This is My body which is given for you; do this in remembrance of Me." And in the same way He took the cup after they had eaten, saying, "This cup which is poured out for you is the new covenant in My blood. But behold, the hand of the one betraying Me is with Mine on the table. For indeed, the Son of Man is going as it has been determined; but woe to that man by whom He is betrayed!" (Luke 22:17–22; cf. Matthew 26:26–29; Mark 14:22–25; 1 Corinthians 11:23–26; see Psalm 41:9; Luke 14:15; 1 Corinthians 10:16).

Setting: An upper room in Jerusalem. During his third missionary journey, writing from Ephesus to the church at Corinth, the Apostle Paul recounts the Lord Jesus' words as He institutes the Lord's Supper.

For I received from the Lord that which I also delivered to you, that the Lord Jesus in the night in which He was betrayed took bread; and when He had given thanks, He broke it and said, "This is My body, which is for you; do this in remembrance of Me." In the same way *He took* the cup also after supper, saying, "This cup is the new covenant in My blood; do this, as often as you drink *it,* in remembrance of Me" (1 Corinthians 11:23–25; cf. Matthew 26:26–28; Mark 14:22–24; Luke 22:17–20).

BLOOD OF THE COVENANT (Listed under COVENANT, BLOOD OF THE)

BLOOD OF THE PROPHETS (Listed under PROPHETS, BLOOD OF THE; also see MARTYRS; and MARTYRDOM)

BOAT

Setting: By the Sea of Galilee (Tiberias). During His third post-resurrection appearance to His disciples, Jesus directs them to a great catch of fish following their unsuccessful night of fishing.

So Jesus said to them, "Children, you do not have any fish, do you?" They answered Him, "No." And He said to them, "Cast the net on the right-hand side of the boat and you will find a *catch.*" So they cast, and then they were not able to haul it in because of the great number of fish (John 21:5–6; see Luke 5:4).

BODY (BODY, MY is a separate entry; also see FLESH)

Setting: Galilee. During the early part of His ministry, Jesus preaches the Sermon on the Mount to His disciples and the multitudes.

"If your right eye makes you stumble, tear it out and throw it from you; for it is better for you to lose one of the parts of your body, than for your whole body to be thrown into hell. If your right hand makes you stumble, cut it off and throw it from you; for it is better for you to lose one of the parts of your body, than for your whole body to go into hell" (Matthew 5:29, 30; cf. Matthew 18:8, 9).

Setting: Galilee. During the early part of His ministry, Jesus preaches the Sermon on the Mount to His disciples and the multitudes.

"The eye is the lamp of the body; so then if your eye is clear, your whole body will be full of light. But if your eye is bad, your whole body will be full of darkness. If then the light that is in you is darkness, how great is the darkness!" (Matthew 6:22, 23; cf. Luke 11:34, 35).

Setting: Galilee. During the early part of His ministry, Jesus preaches the Sermon on the Mount to His disciples and the multitudes.

"For this reason I say to you, do not be worried about your life, *as to* what you will eat or what you will drink; nor for your body, *as to* what you will put on. Is not life more than food, and the body more than clothing? Look at the birds of the air, that they do not sow, nor reap nor gather into barns, and *yet* your heavenly Father feeds them. Are you not worth much more than they? And who of you by being worried can add a *single* hour to his life? And why are you worried about clothing? Observe how the lilies of the field grow; they do not toil nor do they spin, yet I say to you that not even Solomon in all his glory clothed himself like one of these. But if God so clothes the grass of the field, which is *alive* today and tomorrow is thrown into the furnace, *will He* not much more *clothe* you? You of little faith! Do not worry then, saying 'What will we eat?' or 'What will we drink?' or 'What will be wear for clothing?" For the Gentiles eagerly seek all these things; for your heavenly Father knows that you need all these things. But seek first His kingdom and His righteousness, and all these things will be added to you. So do not worry about tomorrow; for tomorrow will care for itself. Each day has enough trouble of its own" (Matthew 6:25–34; cf. Luke 12:22–31; see 1 Kings 10:4–7; Job 35:11; Matthew 8:26).

Setting: Galilee. After His disciples observe His ministry, Jesus summons and specifically instructs them about their ministry ahead involving true discipleship.

"Therefore do not fear them, for there is nothing concealed that will not be revealed, or hidden that will not be known. What I tell you in the darkness, speak in the light; and what you hear *whispered* in your ear, proclaim upon the housetops. Do not fear those who kill the body but are unable to kill the soul; but rather fear Him who is able to destroy both soul and body in hell" (Matthew 10:26–28; cf. Mark 4:22; Luke 12:3; see Hebrews 10:31).

Setting: On the way from Galilee to Jerusalem. After telling the increasing crowds of the sign of Jonah, Jesus illustrates His point by speaking of a lamp.

"No one, after lighting a lamp, puts it away in a cellar nor under a basket, but on the lampstand, so that those who enter may see the light. The eye is the lamp of your body; when your eye is clear, your whole body also is full of light; but when it is bad, your body also is full of darkness. Then watch out that the light in you is not darkness. If therefore your whole body is full of light, with no dark part in it, it will be wholly illumined, as when the lamp illumines you with its rays" (Luke 11:33–36; cf. Matthew 5:15, 6:22, 23).

Setting: On the way from Galilee to Jerusalem. Jesus warns His disciples of future events as the scribes and Pharisees turn hostile and question Him in an attempt to catch Him in something He might say.

Under these circumstances, after so many thousands of people had gathered together that they were stepping on one another, He began saying to His disciples first of all, "Beware of the leaven of the Pharisees, which is hypocrisy. But there is nothing covered up that will not be revealed, and hidden that will not be known. Accordingly, whatever you have said in the dark will be heard in the light, and what you have whispered in the inner rooms will be proclaimed upon the housetops. I say to you, My friends, do not be afraid of those who kill the body and after that have no more that they can do. But I will warn you whom to fear: fear the One who, after He has killed, has authority to cast into hell; yes, I tell you, fear Him! Are not five sparrows sold for two cents? Yet not one of them is forgotten before God. Indeed, the very hairs of your head are all numbered. Do not fear; you are more valuable than many sparrows" (Luke 12:1–7; cf. Matthew 10:26–31; see Matthew 16:6; Hebrews 10:31).

Setting: On the way from Galilee to Jerusalem. After giving a parable about riches and greed, Jesus comforts the crowd and His disciples. The scribes and Pharisees turn hostile and question Him in an attempt to catch Him in something He might say.

And He said to His disciples, "For this reason I say to you, do not worry about your life, as to what you will eat; nor for your body, as to what you will put on. For life is more than food, and the body more than clothing. Consider the ravens, for they neither sow nor reap; they have no storeroom nor barn, and yet God feeds them; how much more valuable you are than the birds! And which of you by worrying can add a single hour to his life's span? If then you cannot do even a very little thing, why do you worry about other matters? Consider the lilies, how they grow: they neither toil nor spin; but I tell you, not even Solomon in all his glory clothed himself like one of these. But if God so clothes the grass in the field, which is alive today and tomorrow is thrown into the furnace, how much more will He clothe you? You men of little faith! And do not seek what you will eat and what you will drink, and do not keep worrying. For all these things the nations of the world eagerly seek; but your Father knows that you need these things. But seek His kingdom, and these things will be added to you. Do not be afraid, little flock, for your Father has chosen gladly to give you the kingdom" (Luke 12:22–32; cf. Matthew 6:25–33; see 1 Kings 10:4–7; Job 38:41).

Setting: Samaria, on the way from Galilee to Jerusalem. After the Pharisees question Him about the coming of the kingdom of God, Jesus tells His disciples of His second coming.

And He said to the disciples, "The days will come when you will long to see one of the days of the Son of Man, and you will not see it. They will say to you, 'Look there! Look here!' Do not go away, and do not run after them. For just like the lightning, when it flashes out of one part of the sky, shines to the other part of the sky, so will the Son of Man be in His day. But first He must suffer many things and be rejected by this generation. And just as it happened in the days of Noah, so it will be also in the days of the Son of Man: they were eating, they were drinking, they were marrying, they were being given in marriage, until the day that Noah entered the ark, and the flood came and destroyed them all. It was the same as happened in the days of Lot: they were eating, they were drinking, they were buying, they were selling, they were planting, they were building; but on the day that Lot went out from Sodom it rained fire and brimstone from heaven and destroyed them all. It will be just the same on the day that the Son of Man is revealed. On that day, the one who is on the housetop and whose goods are in the house must not go down to take them out; and likewise the one who is in the field must not turn back. Remember Lot's wife. Whoever seeks to keep his life will lose it, and whoever loses his life will preserve it. I tell you, on that night there will be two in one bed; one will be taken and the other will be left. There will be two women grinding at the same place; one will be taken and the other will be left. [Two men will be in the field; one will be taken and the other will be left."] And answering they said to Him, "Where, Lord?" And He said to them, "Where the body is, there also the vultures will be gathered" (Luke 17:22–37; see Genesis 19; Matthew 10:39; 16:21, 27; 24:17–28, 37–41).

[BODY from temple and John 2:21]

Setting: Jerusalem. After Jesus cleanses the temple during the Passover of the Jews, the Jewish religious leaders question Jesus' authority to do these things.

Jesus answered them, "Destroy this temple, and in three days I will raise it up" (John 2:19; cf. Matthew 26:61).

BODY, MY (Jesus')

Setting: The home of Simon the leper in Bethany. Jesus rebukes His disciples after they criticize a woman for pouring a vial of costly perfume on Jesus' head in preparation for His burial.

But Jesus, aware of this, said to them, "Why do you bother the woman? For she has done a good deed to Me. For you always have the poor with you; but you do not always have Me. For when she poured this perfume on My body, she did it to prepare Me for burial. Truly I say to you, wherever this gospel is preached in the whole world, what this woman has done will also be spoken of in memory of her" (Matthew 26:10–13; cf. Mark 14:3–9; Luke 7:37–39; John 12:2–8; see Deuteronomy 15:11).

Setting: An upper room in Jerusalem. While celebrating the Passover meal with His disciples, Jesus institutes the Lord's Supper ordinance before being arrested by His enemies.

While they were eating, Jesus took *some* bread, and after a blessing, He broke *it* and gave *it* to the disciples, and said, "Take, eat; this is My body." And when He had taken a cup and given thanks, He gave *it* to them saying, "Drink from it, all of you; for this is My blood of the covenant, which is poured out for many for forgiveness of sins. But I say to you, I will not drink of this fruit of the vine from now on until that day when I drink it new with you in My Father's kingdom" (Matthew 26:26–29; cf. Mark 14:22–25; Luke 22:17–20; 1 Corinthians 11:23–26; see 1 Corinthians 10:16).

Setting: The home of Simon the leper in Bethany. Two days before the Feast of Unleavened Bread (Passover), Jesus commends a woman who anoints His head with costly perfume that some thought should have been sold and the proceeds given to the poor.

But Jesus said, "Let her alone; why do you bother her? She has done a good deed to Me. For you always have the poor with you, and whenever you wish you can do good to them; but you do not always have Me. She has done what she could; she has anointed My body beforehand for the burial. Truly I say to you, wherever the gospel is preached in the whole world, what this woman has done will also be spoken of in memory of her" (Mark 14:6–9; cf. Matthew 26:6–13; John 12:2–8; see Deuteronomy 15:11).

Setting: An upper room in Jerusalem. While celebrating the Feast of Unleavened Bread (Passover) with His disciples, Jesus institutes the ordinance of the Lord's Supper.

While they were eating, He took *some* bread, and after a blessing He broke *it*, and gave *it* to them, and said, "Take *it;* this is My body." And when He had taken a cup *and* given thanks, He gave *it* to them, and they all drank from it. And He said to them, "This is My blood of the covenant, which is poured out for many. Truly I say to you, I will never again drink of the fruit of the vine until that day when I drink it new in the kingdom of God" (Mark 14:22–25; cf. Matthew 26:26–29; Luke 22:17–20; 1 Corinthians 11:23–26; see Exodus 24:8).

Setting: An upper room in Jerusalem. During the Feast of Unleavened Bread (Passover) just before Jesus' crucifixion, while celebrating the Passover meal with His disciples, Jesus institutes the Lord's Supper.

And when He had taken a cup and given thanks, He said, "Take this and share it among yourselves; for I say to you, I will not drink of the fruit of the vine from now on until the kingdom of God comes." And when he had taken some bread and given thanks, He broke it and gave it to them, saying, "This is My body which is given for you; do this in remembrance of Me." And in the same way He took the cup after they had eaten, saying, "This cup which is poured out for you is the new covenant in My blood. But behold, the hand of the one betraying Me is with Mine on the table. For indeed, the Son of Man is going as it has been determined; but woe to that man by whom He is betrayed!" (Luke 22:17–22; cf. Matthew 26:26–29; Mark 14:22–25; 1 Corinthians 11:23–26; see Psalm 41:9; Luke 14:15; 1 Corinthians 10:16).

Setting: An upper room in Jerusalem. During his third missionary journey, writing from Ephesus to the church at Corinth, the Apostle Paul recounts the Lord Jesus' words as He institutes the Lord's Supper.

For I received from the Lord that which I also delivered to you, that the Lord Jesus in the night in which He was betrayed took bread; and when He had given thanks, He broke it and said, "This is My body, which is for you; do this in remembrance of Me." In the same way *He took* the cup also after supper, saying, "This cup is the new covenant in My blood; do this, as often as you drink *it,* in remembrance of Me" (1 Corinthians 11:23–25; cf. Matthew 26:26–28; Mark 14:22–24; Luke 22:17–20).

BOND

Setting: On the way from Galilee to Jerusalem. Jesus responds to a synagogue official's anger for healing a woman, sick eighteen years, in the synagogue on the Sabbath.

But the Lord answered him and said, "You hypocrites, does not each of you on the Sabbath untie his ox or his donkey from the stall and lead him away to water him? And this woman, a daughter of Abraham as she is, whom Satan has bound for eighteen long years, should she not have been released from this bond on the Sabbath day?" (Luke 13:15, 16; see Luke 13:10–14, 17; 14:5).

BOND-SERVANTS

Setting: On the island of Patmos (in the Aegean Sea about fifty miles southwest of Ephesus in modern Turkey). On the Lord's Day (Sunday), about fifty years after Jesus' resurrection, the disciple John encounters the Lord Jesus Christ, who communicates a new revelation for the apostle to record for the church in Thyatira and to six other churches in Asia.

"And to the angel of the church in Thyatira write: The Son of God, who has eyes like a flame of fire, and His feet are like burnished bronze, says this: 'I know your deeds, and your love and faith and service and perseverance, and that your deeds of late are greater than at first. But I have *this* against you, that you tolerate the woman Jezebel, who calls herself a prophetess, and she teaches and leads My bond-servants astray so that they commit *acts of* immorality and eat things sacrificed to idols. I gave her time to repent, and she does not want to repent of her immorality. Behold, I will throw her on a bed *of sickness,* and those who commit adultery with her into great tribulation, unless they repent of her deeds. And I will kill her children with pestilence, and all the churches will know that I am He who searches the minds and hearts; and I will give to each one of you according to your deeds. But I say to you, the rest who are in Thyatira, who do not hold this teaching, who have not known the deep things of Satan, as they call them—I place no other burden on you. Nevertheless what you have, hold fast until I come. He who overcomes, and he who keeps My deeds until the end, TO HIM I WILL GIVE AUTHORITY OVER THE NATIONS; AND HE SHALL RULE THEM WITH A ROD OF IRON, AS THE VESSELS OF THE POTTER ARE BROKEN TO PIECES, as I also have received *authority* from My Father; and I will give him the morning star. He who has an ear, let him hear what the Spirit says to the churches' (Revelation 2:18–29; Jesus quotes from Psalm 2:8, 9; Isaiah 30:14; see 1 Kings 16:31, Psalm 7:9; Romans 2:5; 1 Corinthians 2:10; 2 Peter 3:9; Revelation 1:14; 2:7; 3:11; 17:1–20).

BOLDNESS IN PRAYER (Listed under PRAYER, BOLDNESS IN)

BONES (BONES, DEAD MEN'S is a separate entry)

Setting: Jerusalem. After rising from the grave on the third day after being crucified, and appearing to two of His followers on the road to Emmaus, Jesus appears to some of His disciples.

While they were telling these things, He Himself stood in their midst and said to them, "Peace be to you." But they were startled and frightened and thought they were seeing a spirit. And He said to them, "Why are you troubled, and why do doubts arise in your hearts? See My hands and My feet, that it is I Myself; touch Me and see, for a spirit does not have flesh and bones as you see that I have." And when He had said this, He showed them His hands and His feet. While they still could not believe it because of their joy and amazement. He said to them, "Have you anything to eat?" They gave Him a piece of a broiled fish; and He took it and ate it before them (Luke 24:36–43; see Mark 16:14; John 20:27; Acts 10:40, 41).

BONES, DEAD MEN'S (Also see TOMBS)

Setting: The temple in Jerusalem. After the Jewish religious leaders test Him with questions, Jesus pronounces the seventh of eight woes on them in front of the crowds and His disciples.

"Woe to you, scribes and Pharisees, hypocrites! For you are like whitewashed tombs which on the outside appear beautiful, but inside they are full of dead men's bones and all uncleanness. So you, too, outwardly appear righteous to men, but inwardly you are full of hypocrisy and lawlessness" (Matthew 23:27, 28; cf. Luke 11:44).

BOOK (LIFE, BOOK OF is a separate entry)

Setting: On the island of Patmos (in the Aegean Sea about fifty miles southwest of Ephesus in modern Turkey). On the Lord's Day (Sunday), approximately fifty years after His resurrection, the disciple John encounters the Lord Jesus Christ, who communicates new revelations for the apostle to record for the seven churches in Asia.

I was in the Spirit on the Lord's day, and I heard behind me a loud voice like *the sound* of a trumpet, saying, "Write in a book what you see, and send *it* to the seven churches: to Ephesus and to Smyrna and to Pergamum and to Thyatira and to Sardis and to Philadelphia and to Laodicea" (Revelation 1:10, 11).

Setting: On the island of Patmos (in the Aegean Sea about fifty miles southwest of Ephesus in modern Turkey). In the final chapter of the Lord Jesus Christ's Revelation via the disciple John, approximately fifty years after His resurrection, the Lord reveals His coming return and the blessing to those who heed the words of the prophecy of this book.

"And behold, I am coming quickly. Blessed is he who heeds the words of the prophecy of this book" (Revelation 22:7; see Revelation 1:3).

BOOK OF LIFE (Listed as LIFE, BOOK OF)

BOOK OF MOSES (Listed as MOSES, BOOK OF)

BOOK OF PSALMS (Listed under PSALMS)

BOOTHS, FEAST OF

[FEAST OF BOOTHS from feast and John 7:2]

Setting: Capernaum of Galilee. Jesus' blood brothers, who do not yet believe in Him, encourage Him to attend the upcoming Feast of Booths in Jerusalem in order to demonstrate His works to His disciples and the world.

So Jesus said to them, "My time is not yet here, but your time is always opportune. The world cannot hate you, but it hates Me because I testify of it, that its deeds are evil. Go up to the feast yourselves; I do not go up to this feast because My time has not yet fully come" (John 7:6–8; see John 3:18, 19; 15:18–20).

[FEAST OF BOOTHS from feast]
Setting: Jerusalem. On the last day of the Feast of Booths, after Jesus causes discussion whether He is the Christ, the chief priests and Pharisees attempt to understand where He says He will be going soon. Jesus offers salvation and the abundant life to His hearers.

Now on the last day, the great *day* of the feast, Jesus stood and cried out, saying, "If anyone is thirsty, let him come to Me and drink. He who believes in Me, as the Scripture said, 'From his innermost being will flow rivers of living water'" (John 7:37–38; see John 7:10–15).

BORN (Also see BIRTH)

Setting: Galilee. While speaking to the crowds, Jesus pays tribute to the ministry of John the Baptist, but emphasizes that the one who is least in the kingdom of heaven is greater than John.

As these men were going *away,* Jesus began to speak to the crowds about John, "What did you go out into the wilderness to see? A reed shaken by the wind? But what did you go out to see? A man dressed in soft *clothing?* Those who wear soft *clothing* are in kings' palaces! But what did you go out to see? A prophet? Yes, I tell you, and the one who is more than a prophet. This is the one about whom it is written, 'BEHOLD, I SEND MY MESSENGER AHEAD OF YOU, WHO WILL PREPARE YOUR WAY BEFORE YOU.' Truly, I say to you, among those born of women there has not arisen *anyone* greater than John the Baptist! Yet the one who is least in the kingdom of heaven is greater than he. From the days of John the Baptist until now the kingdom of heaven suffers violence, and violent men take it by force. For all the prophets and the Law prophesied until John. And, if you are willing to accept *it,* John himself is Elijah who was to come. He who has ears to hear, let him hear" (Matthew 11:7–15, Jesus quotes from Malachi 3:1; cf. Malachi 4:5; Luke 7:24–28; 16:16; see Matthew 14:5).

Setting: Judea beyond the Jordan (Perea). Jesus answers His disciples' private question following His response to the Pharisees' question about Moses' command regarding a certificate of divorce.

But He said to them, "Not all men *can* accept this statement, but *only* those to whom it has been given. For there are eunuchs who were born that way from their mother's womb; and there are eunuchs who were made eunuchs by men; and there are *also* eunuchs who made themselves eunuchs for the sake of the kingdom of heaven. He who is able to accept *this,* let him accept *it*" (Matthew 19:11, 12; cf. 1 Corinthians 7:7).

Setting: An upper room in Jerusalem. While celebrating the Passover meal, Jesus surprises His disciples with the revelation that one of them will soon betray Him to His enemies.

As they were eating, He said, "Truly I say to you that one of you will betray Me." Being deeply grieved, they each one began to say to Him, 'Surely not I, Lord?' And He answered, "He who dipped his hand with Me in the bowl is the one who will betray Me. The Son of Man *is to* go, just as it is written of Him; but woe to that man by whom the Son of Man is betrayed! It would have been good for that man if he had not been born." And Judas, who was betraying Him, said, 'Surely it is not I, Rabbi?' Jesus said to him, "You have said *it* yourself" (Matthew 26:21–25; cf. Mark 14:18–21; Luke 22:21–23; John 13:21–30; see Psalm 41:9).

Setting: A borrowed upper room in Jerusalem. While Jesus and His twelve disciples are eating the Passover meal, the Lord states that one of His disciples will betray Him.

As they were reclining *at the table* and eating, Jesus said, "Truly I say to you that one of you will betray Me—one who is eating with Me." They began to be grieved and to say to Him one by one, "Surely not I?" And He said to them, "*It is* one of the twelve, one who dips with Me in the bowl. For the Son of Man *is to* go just as it is written of Him; but woe to that man by whom the Son of Man is betrayed! *It would have been* good for that man if he had not been born" (Mark 14:18–21; cf. Matthew 26:21–24; Luke 22:21–23; John 13:21, 22).

Setting: Galilee. After He responds to the disciples of John the Baptist whether He is the promised Messiah, Jesus speaks to the crowds about John.

When the messengers of John had left, He began to speak to the crowds about John, "What did you go out into the wilderness to see? A reed shaken by the wind? But what did you go out to see? A man dressed in soft clothing? Those who are splendidly clothed and live in luxury are found in royal palaces! But what did you go out to see? A prophet? Yes, I say to you, and one who is more than a prophet. This is the one about whom it is written, 'BEHOLD, I SEND MY MESSENGER AHEAD OF YOU, WHO WILL PREPARE YOUR WAY BEFORE YOU.' I say to you, among those born of women there is no one greater than John; yet he who is least in the kingdom of God is greater than he" (Luke 7:24–28, Jesus quotes from Malachi 3:1; cf. Matthew 11:7–11).

Setting: Jerusalem. At the time of the Passover of the Jews, after the Lord cleanses the temple, a Pharisee, Nicodemus, comes to Him by night to converse with Him.

Jesus answered and said to him, "Truly, truly, I say to you, unless one is born again he cannot see the kingdom of God" (John 3:3; see 2 Corinthians 5:17).

Setting: Jerusalem. At the time of the Passover of the Jews, after the Lord cleanses the temple, a Pharisee, Nicodemus, asks Him by night the meaning of "born again."

Jesus answered, "Truly, truly, I say to you, unless one is born of water and the Spirit he cannot enter into the kingdom of God. That which is born of the flesh is flesh, and that which is born of the Spirit is spirit. Do not be amazed that I said to you, 'You must be born again.' The wind blows where it wishes and you hear the sound of it, but do not know where it comes from and where it is going; so is everyone who is born of the Spirit" (John 3:5–8; see Psalm 135:7; John 1:13).

Setting: The temple treasury in Jerusalem. While Jesus interacts with the scribes and Pharisees, they question how He, not yet fifty years old in their eyes, can claim to have seen Abraham.

Jesus said to them, "Truly, truly, I say to you, before Abraham was born, I am" (John 8:58; see Exodus 3:14).

Setting: Jerusalem. Before the Passover, after warning His disciples of the persecution they will face after His departure to heaven, empathizing with their sadness over His prophecies, Jesus gives them assurance for the future.

"A little while, and you will no longer see Me; and again a little while, and you will see Me." *Some* of His disciples then said to one another, "What is this thing He is telling us, 'A little while, and you will not see Me; and again a little while, and you will see Me'; and, 'because I go to the Father'?" So they were saying, "What is this that He says, 'A little while'? We do not know what He is talking about." Jesus knew that they wished to question Him, and He said to them, "Are you deliberating together about this, that I said, 'A little while, and you will not see Me, and again a little while, and you will see Me'? Truly, truly, I say to you, that you will weep and lament, but the world will rejoice; you will grieve, but your grief will be turned into joy. Whenever a woman is in labor she has pain, because her hour has come; but when she gives birth to the child, she no longer remembers the anguish because of the joy that a child has been born into the world. Therefore you too have grief now; but I will see you again, and your heart will rejoice, and no one *will* take your joy away from you" (John 16:16–22; see Mark 9:32; Luke 23:27; John 14:18–24; 16:5–6; 20:20).

Setting: Jerusalem. After the previous and current high priests (Annas and Caiaphas) question Jesus, and Peter denies the second and third times being the Lord's disciple, Pontius Pilate (Roman governor of Judea), asks Jesus if He is a king.

Therefore Pilate said to Him, "So You are a king?" Jesus answered, "You say *correctly* that I am a king. For this I have been born, and for this I have come into the world, to testify to the truth. Everyone who is of the truth hears my voice" (John 18:37; cf. Matthew 27:11; Mark 15:2; Luke 23:3).

BORN AGAIN (Also see BELIEF; ETERNAL LIFE; FAITH; and SALVATION)

Setting: Jerusalem. Before the Passover of the Jews, after the Lord cleanses the temple, a Pharisee, Nicodemus, comes to Jesus by night to converse with Him.

Jesus answered and said to him, "Truly, truly, I say to you, unless one is born again he cannot see the kingdom of God" (John 3:3; see 2 Corinthians 5:17).

Setting: Jerusalem. Before the Passover of the Jews, after the Lord cleanses the temple, a Pharisee, Nicodemus, asks Him by night the meaning of "born again."

Jesus answered, "Truly, truly, I say to you, unless one is born of water and the Spirit he cannot enter into the kingdom of God. That which is born of the flesh is flesh, and that which is born of the Spirit is spirit. Do not be amazed that I said to you, 'You must be born again.' The wind blows where it wishes and you hear the sound of it, but do not know where it comes from and where it is going; so is everyone who is born of the Spirit" (John 3:5–8; see Psalm 135:7; John 1:13).

BOSOM (See BOSOM, ABRAHAM'S)

BOSOM, ABRAHAM'S (Also see BREAST)

Setting: On the way from Galilee to Jerusalem. After He responds to the Pharisees' scoffing at His teaching His disciples about stewardship and the permanence of the Law, Jesus conveys the story of the rich man and Lazarus.

"Now there was a rich man, and he habitually dressed in purple and fine linen, joyously living in splendor every day. And a poor man named Lazarus was laid at his gate, covered with sores, and longing to be fed with the crumbs which were falling from the rich man's table; besides, even the dogs were coming and licking his sores. Now the poor man died and was carried away by the angels to Abraham's bosom; and the rich man also died and was buried. In Hades he lifted up his eyes, being in torment, and saw Abraham far away and Lazarus in his bosom. And he cried out and said, 'Father Abraham, have mercy on me, and send Lazarus so that he may dip the tip of his finger in water and cool off my tongue, for I am in agony in this flame.' But Abraham said, 'Child, remember that during your life you received your good things, and likewise Lazarus bad things; but now he is being comforted here, and you are in agony. And besides all this, between us and you there is a great chasm fixed, so that those who wish to come over from here to you will not be able, and that none may cross over from there to us.' And he said, 'Then I beg you, father, that you send him to my father's house—for I have five brothers—in order that he may warn them, so that they will not also come to this place of torment.' But Abraham said, 'They have Moses and the Prophets; let them hear them.' But he said, 'No, father Abraham, but if someone goes to them from the dead, they will repent!' But he said to him, 'If they do not listen to Moses and the Prophets, they will not be persuaded even if someone rises from the dead'" (Luke 16:19–31; see Luke 3:8; 6:24; 16:1, 14).

BOWL

Setting: An upper room in Jerusalem. While celebrating the Passover meal, Jesus surprises His disciples with the revelation that one of them will soon betray Him to His enemies.

As they were eating, He said, "Truly I say to you that one of you will betray Me." Being deeply grieved, they each one began to say to Him, 'Surely not I, Lord?' And He answered, "He who dipped his hand with Me in the bowl is the one who will betray Me. The Son of Man *is to* go, just as it is written of Him; but woe to that man by whom the Son of Man is betrayed! It would have been good for that man if he had not been born." And Judas, who was betraying Him, said, 'Surely it is not I, Rabbi?' Jesus said to him,

"You have said *it yourself*" (Matthew 26:21–25; cf. Mark 14:18–21; Luke 22:21–23; John 13:21–30; see Psalm 41:9).

Setting: A borrowed upper room in Jerusalem. While Jesus and His twelve disciples are eating the Passover meal, the Lord states that one of His disciples will betray Him.

As they were reclining *at the table* and eating, Jesus said, "Truly I say to you that one of you will betray Me—one who is eating with Me." They began to be grieved and to say to Him one by one, "Surely not I?" And He said to them, "*It is* one of the twelve, one who dips with Me in the bowl. For the Son of Man *is to* go just as it is written of Him; but woe to that man by whom the Son of Man is betrayed! *It would have been* good for that man if he had not been born" (Mark 14:18–21; cf. Matthew 26:21–24; Luke 22:21–23; John 13:21, 22).

BOY, JESUS AS A (See JESUS AS A BOY)

BRANCH (Also see BRANCHES; LEAVES; ROOT; and TREE)

Setting: The Mount of Olives, just east of Jerusalem. During His discourse, after answering His disciples' questions as to when the temple will be destroyed and Jerusalem overrun, along with the signs of His coming and the end of the age, Jesus teaches them the Parable of the Fig Tree.

"Now learn the parable from the fig tree: when its branch has already become tender and puts forth its leaves, you know that summer is near; so, you too, when you see all these things, recognize that He is near, *right* at the door. Truly, I say to you, this generation will not pass away until all these things take place. Heaven and earth will pass away, but My words will not pass away. But of that day and hour no one knows, not even the angels of heaven, nor the Son, but the Father alone. For the coming of the Son of Man will be just like the days of Noah. For as in those days before the flood they were eating and drinking, marrying and giving in marriage, until the day that Noah entered the ark, and they did not understand until the flood came and took them all away; so will the coming of the Son of Man be. Then there will be two men in the field; one will be taken and one will be left. Two women *will be* grinding at the mill; one will be taken and one will be left" (Matthew 24:32–41; cf. Mark 13:28–32; Luke 17:34–36; 21:28–33; see Genesis 6:5; 7:7; Matthew 5:18; 10:23; James 5:9).

Setting: During His discourse on the Mount of Olives, east of the temple in Jerusalem, after prophesying the temple's destruction, Jesus responds to questions from Peter, James, John, and Andrew about future events.

"Now learn the parable from the fig tree: when its branch has already become tender and puts forth its leaves, you know that summer is near. Even so, you too, when you see these things happening, recognize that He is near, *right* at the door. Truly I say to you, this generation will not pass away until all these things take place. Heaven and earth will pass away, but My words will not pass away. But of the day or hour no one knows, not even the angels in heaven, nor the Son, but the Father *alone*" (Mark 13:28–32; cf. Matthew 24:32–36; Luke 21:28–33).

Setting: Jerusalem. Before the Passover, after He conveys the upcoming ministry of the Holy Spirit in His disciples' lives, with His impending departure from them, Jesus explains He is the vine and they are the branches.

"I am the true vine, and My Father is the vinedresser. Every branch in Me that does not bear fruit, He takes away; and every *branch* that bears fruit, He prunes it so that it may bear more fruit. You are already clean because of the word which I have spoken to you. Abide in Me, and I in you. As the branch cannot bear fruit of itself unless it abides in the vine, so neither *can* you unless you abide in Me. I am the vine, you are the branches; he who abides in Me and I in him, he bears much fruit, for apart from Me you can do nothing. If anyone does not abide in Me, he is thrown away as a branch and dries up; and they gather them, and cast them into the fire and they are burned. If you abide in Me, and My words abide in you, ask whatever you wish, and it will be done for you. My Father is glorified by this, that you bear much fruit, and *so* prove to be My disciples. Just as the Father has loved Me, I have also loved you; abide in My love. If you keep My commandments, you will abide in My love; just as I have kept My Father's commandments and abide in His love. These things I have spoken to you so that My joy may be in you, and *that* your joy may be made full" (John 15:1–11; see Matthew 5:16; 7:7; John 3:29, 35; 6:56; 8:29, 31; 13:10; 15:16).

BRANCHES (BRANCHES, LARGE is a separate entry; also see BRANCH; LEAVES; ROOT; and TREE)

Setting: By the Sea of Galilee. Because the religious leaders are rejecting His message, Jesus continues teaching the crowds with the Parable of the Mustard Seed.

He presented another parable to them, saying, "The kingdom of heaven is like a mustard seed, which a man took and sowed in his field; and this is smaller than all *other* seeds, but when it is full grown, it is larger than the garden plants and becomes a tree, so that THE BIRDS OF THE AIR come and NEST IN ITS BRANCHES" (Matthew 13:31, 32, Jesus quotes from Ezekiel 17:23; cf. Mark 4:30–32; Luke 13:18, 19).

Setting: On the way from Galilee to Jerusalem. After responding to a synagogue official's anger for healing a woman, sick eighteen years, in the synagogue on the Sabbath, Jesus conveys the Parable of the Mustard Seed and the Parable of the Leaven.

So He was saying, "What is the kingdom of God like, and to what shall I compare it? It is like a mustard seed which a man took and threw into his own garden; and it grew and became a tree, and THE BIRDS OF THE AIR NESTED IN ITS BRANCHES." And again He said, "To what shall I compare the kingdom of God? It is like leaven, which a woman took and hid in three pecks of flour until it was all leavened" (Luke 13:18–21, Jesus quotes from Ezekiel 17:23; cf. Matthew 13:31–34; Mark 4:30–32).

Setting: Jerusalem. Before the Passover, after He conveys the upcoming ministry of the Holy Spirit in His disciples' lives, with His impending departure from them, Jesus explains He is the vine and they are the branches.

"I am the true vine, and My Father is the vinedresser. Every branch in Me that does not bear fruit, He takes away; and every *branch* that bears fruit, He prunes it so that it may bear more fruit. You are already clean because of the word which I have spoken to you. Abide in Me, and I in you. As the branch cannot bear fruit of itself unless it abides in the vine, so neither *can* you unless you abide in Me. I am the vine, you are the branches; he who abides in Me and I in him, he bears much fruit, for apart from Me you can do nothing. If anyone does not abide in Me, he is thrown away as a branch and dries up; and they gather them, and cast them into the fire and they are burned. If you abide in Me, and My words abide in you, ask whatever you wish, and it will be done for you. My Father is glorified by this, that you bear much fruit, and *so* prove to be My disciples. Just as the Father has loved Me, I have also loved you; abide in My love. If you keep My commandments, you will abide in My love; just as I have kept My Father's commandments and abide in His love. These things I have spoken to you so that My joy may be in you, and *that* your joy may be made full" (John 15:1–11; see Matthew 5:16; 7:7; John 3:29, 35; 6:56; 8:29, 31; 13:10; 15:16).

BRANCHES, LARGE

Setting: Galilee. After giving the Parable of the Sower and the Parable of the Seed, Jesus continues teaching by presenting the Parable of the Mustard Seed to His disciples.

And He said, "How shall we picture the kingdom of God, or by what parable shall we present it? *It is* like a mustard seed, which, when sown upon the soil, though it is smaller than all the seeds that are upon the soil, yet when it is sown, it grows up and becomes larger than all the garden plants and forms large branches; so that THE BIRDS OF THE AIR can NEST UNDER ITS SHADE" (Mark 4:30–32, Jesus quotes from Ezekiel 17:23; cf. Matthew 13:31, 32; Luke 13:18, 19).

BREAD (Specifics such as BREAD, CHILDREN'S; and BREAD, DAILY are separate entries; also see CRUMBS; FLOUR; FOOD; LOAF; LOAVES; MORSEL; and WHEAT)

Setting: Judea, near the Jordan River. Following Jesus' baptism, and before He begins His public ministry, the Spirit leads Him into the wilderness for temptation by Satan.

But He answered and said, "It is written, 'MAN SHALL NOT LIVE ON BREAD ALONE, BUT ON EVERY WORD THAT PROCEEDS OUT OF THE MOUTH OF GOD'" (Matthew 4:4, Jesus quotes from Deuteronomy 8:3; cf. Luke 4:4).

Setting: By the Sea of Galilee. Jesus repeats the warning to His disciples about the teaching of the religious leaders of the day, the Pharisees and Sadducees.

But Jesus aware of this, said, "You men of little faith, why do you discuss among yourselves that you have no bread? Do you not yet understand or remember the five loaves of the five thousand and how many baskets *full* you picked up? Or the seven loaves of the four thousand, and how many large baskets *full* you picked up? How is it that you do not understand that I did not speak to you concerning bread? But beware of the leaven of the Pharisees and Sadducees" (Matthew 16:8–11; cf. Matthew 14:17–21; 15:34–38; Mark 8:17–21).

Setting: Across the Sea of Galilee from the district of Dalmanutha. After the Pharisees argue with Him, seeking a sign from heaven to test Him, Jesus and His disciples cross to the other side, where His disciples discuss with one another that they have no bread.

And Jesus, aware of this, said to them, "Why do you discuss *the fact* that you have no bread? Do you not yet see or understand? Do you have a hardened heart? HAVING EYES, DO YOU NOT SEE? AND HAVING EARS, DO YOU NOT HEAR? And do you not remember, when I broke the five loaves for the five thousand, how many baskets full of broken pieces you picked up? They said to Him, "Twelve." When *I broke* the seven for the four thousand, how many large baskets full of broken pieces did you pick up?" They said to Him, "Seven." And He was saying to them, "Do you not yet understand?" (Mark 8:17–21, Jesus quotes from Jeremiah 5:21; cf. Matthew 16:5–12; see Matthew 14:19, 20; Mark 6:41–44, 52; 8:6–9).

Setting: Judea, near the Jordan River. Following His baptism, and before He begins His public ministry, Jesus is led by the Spirit into the wilderness for forty days of temptation by Satan.

And Jesus answered him, "It is written, 'MAN SHALL NOT LIVE ON BREAD ALONE'" (Luke 4:4, Jesus quotes from Deuteronomy 8:3; cf. Matthew 4:1–4; see Mark 1:12, 13).

Setting: Galilee. After praising John the Baptist to the crowds, Jesus criticizes the Pharisees and lawyers, who reject God's purpose and John's message.

"To what then shall I compare the men of this generation, and what are they like? They are like children who sit in the market place and call to one another, and they say, 'We played the flute for you, and you did not dance; we sang a dirge, and you did not weep.' For John the Baptist has come eating no bread and drinking no wine, and you say, 'He has a demon!' The Son of Man has come eating and drinking, and you say, 'Behold, a gluttonous man and a drunkard, a friend of tax collectors and sinners!' Yet wisdom is vindicated by all her children" (Luke 7:31–35; cf. Matthew 11:16–19; see Luke 1:15).

Setting: Galilee. After raising Jairus's daughter from the dead, Jesus calls the twelve disciples together and gives them power and authority over demons, along with the ability to heal diseases.

And He said to them, "Take nothing for your journey, neither a staff, nor a bag, nor bread, nor money; and do not even have two tunics apiece. Whatever house you enter, stay there until you leave that city. And as for those who do not receive you, go out from that city, shake the dust off your feet as a testimony against them" (Luke 9:3–5; cf. Matthew 10:1–15; Mark 6:7–11; see Luke 10:4–12).

Setting: On the way from Galilee to Jerusalem. Jesus conveys the Parable of The Prodigal Son because the Pharisees and scribes complain He associates with tax collectors and sinners.

And He said, "A man had two sons. The younger of them said to his father, 'Father, give me the share of the estate that falls to me.' So he divided his wealth between them. And not many days later, the younger son gathered everything together and went on a journey into a distant country, and there he squandered his estate with loose living. Now when he had spent everything, a severe famine occurred in that country, and he began to be impoverished. So he went and hired himself out to one of the citizens of that country, and he sent him into his fields to feed swine. And he would have gladly filled his stomach with the pods that the swine were eating, and no one was giving anything to him. But when he came to his senses, he said, 'How many of my father's hired men have more than enough bread, but I am dying here with hunger! I will get up and go to my father, and will say to him, "Father, I have sinned against heaven, and in your sight; I am no longer worthy to be called your son; make me as one of your hired men."' So he got up and came to his father. But while he was still a long way off, his father saw him and felt compassion for him, and ran and embraced him and kissed him. And the son said to him, "Father, I have sinned against heaven and in your sight; I am no longer worthy to be called your son.' But the father said to his slaves, 'Quickly bring out the best robe and put it on him, and put a ring on his hand and sandals on his feet; and bring the fattened calf, kill it, and let us eat and celebrate; for this son of mine was dead and has come to life again; he was lost and has been found.' And they began to celebrate. Now his older son was in the field, when he came and approached the house, he heard music and dancing. And he summoned one of the servants and began inquiring what these things could be. And he said to him, 'Your brother has come, and your father has killed the fattened calf because he has received him back safe and sound.' But he became angry and was not willing to go in; and his father came out and began pleading with him. But he answered and said to his father, 'Look! For so many years I have been serving you and I have never neglected a command of yours; and yet you have never given me a young goat, so that I might celebrate with my friends; but when this son of yours came, who has devoured your wealth with prostitutes, you killed the fattened calf for him.' And he said to him, 'Son, you have always been with me, and all that is mine is yours. But we had to celebrate and rejoice, for this brother of yours was dead and has begun to live, and was lost and has been found'" (Luke 15:11–32; see Proverbs 29:2; Luke 15:1, 2).

Setting: By the Sea of Galilee. After revealing to the Jewish religious leadership during the Feast of the Jews in Jerusalem that God, John the Baptist, His works, and the Scriptures testify to His mission, Jesus returns to Galilee, where He ministers to a large crowd.

Therefore Jesus, lifting up His eyes and seeing that a large crowd was coming to Him, said to Philip, "Where are we to buy bread, so that these may eat?" (John 6:5; cf. Matthew 14:13–16; Mark 6:35–37; Luke 9:12, 13).

Setting: Capernaum. The day after Jesus walks on the Sea of Galilee to join His disciples in a boat, the people He miraculously fed with a lad's five loaves and two fish quiz Him about the signs and works He performs, so they may believe in Him.

Jesus then said to them, "Truly, truly, I say to you, it is not Moses who has given you the bread out of heaven, but it is My Father who gives you the true bread out of heaven. For the bread of God is that which comes down out of heaven, and gives life to the world" (John 6:32, 33).

Setting: Capernaum. The day after Jesus walks on the Sea of Galilee to join His disciples in a boat, the people He miraculously fed with a lad's five loaves and two fish ask Him to always give them this bread out of heaven.

Jesus said to them, "I am the bread of life; he who comes to Me will not hunger, and he who believes in Me will never thirst. But I said to you that you have seen Me, and yet do not believe. All that the Father gives Me will come to Me, and the one who comes to Me I will certainly not cast out. For I have come down from heaven, not to do My own will, but the will of Him who sent Me. This is the will of Him who sent Me, that of all that He has given Me I lose nothing, but raise it up on the last day. For this is the will of My Father, that everyone who beholds the Son and believes in Him will have eternal life, and I Myself will raise him up on the last day" (John 6:35–40; see John 3:13, 16; 4:13, 14; 6: 48, 51).

Setting: Capernaum of Galilee. After Jesus informs the people whom He miraculously fed with a lad's five loaves and two fish how they might receive the bread out of heaven, the Jewish religious leaders grumble because He claims that He came down out of heaven.

Therefore the Jews were grumbling about Him, because He said, "I am the bread that came down out of heaven." They were saying, "Is not this Jesus, the son of Joseph, whose father and mother we know? How does He now say, 'I have come down out of heaven'?" Jesus answered and said to them, "Do not grumble among yourselves. No one can come to Me unless the Father who sent Me draws him; and I will raise him up on the last day. It is written in the prophets, 'AND THEY SHALL ALL BE TAUGHT OF GOD.' Everyone who has heard and learned from the Father, comes to Me. Not that anyone has seen the Father, except the One who is from God; He has seen the Father. Truly, truly, I say to you, he who believes has eternal life. I am the bread of life. Your fathers ate the manna in the wilderness, and they died. This is the bread which comes down out of heaven, so that one may eat of it and not die. I am the living bread that came down out of heaven; if anyone eats of this bread, he will live forever; and the bread also which I will give for the life of the world is My flesh" (John 6:41–51, Jesus quotes from Isaiah 54:13; see John 1:18, 29; 3:36; 7:27).

Setting: Capernaum of Galilee. After Jesus informs the people whom He miraculously fed with a lad's five loaves and two fish how they might receive the bread out of heaven, the Jewish religious leaders argue with one another about Jesus' saying He will give His flesh to the world to eat.

So Jesus said to them, "Truly, truly, I say to you, unless you eat the flesh of the Son of Man and drink His blood, you have no life in yourselves. He who eats My flesh and drinks My blood has eternal life, and I will raise him up on the last day. For My flesh is true food, and My blood is true drink. He who eats My flesh and drinks My blood abides in Me, and I in him. As the living Father sent Me, and I live because of the Father, so he who eats Me, he also will live because of Me. This is the bread which came down out of heaven; not as the fathers ate and died; he who eats this bread will live forever" (John 6:53–58; see Matthew 16:16; Luke 4:22; John 3:36; John 9:16; 15:4).

Setting: Jerusalem. Before the Passover, with His death on the cross nearing, Jesus explains the reason for His vivid example of servanthood in washing His disciples' feet.

So when He had washed their feet, and taken His garments and reclined *at the table* again, He said to them, "Do you know what I have done to you? You call Me Teacher and Lord; and you are right, for *so* I am. If I then, the Lord and the Teacher, washed your feet, you also ought to wash one another's feet. For I gave you an example that you also should do as I did to you. Truly, truly I say to you, a slave is not greater than his master, nor *is* one who is sent greater than the one who sent him. If you know these things, you are blessed if you do them. I do not speak of all of you. I know the ones I have chosen; but *it is* that the Scripture may be fulfilled, 'HE WHO EATS MY BREAD HAS LIFTED UP HIS HEEL AGAINST ME.' From now on I am telling you before *it* comes to pass, so that when it does occur, you may believe that I am *He. Truly,* truly, I say to you, he who receives whomever I send receives Me; and he who receives Me receives Him who sent Me" (John 13:12–20; Jesus quotes from Psalm 41:9; see Matthew 7:24; 10:24, 40; John 8:24; 14:29; 1 Peter 5:3).

BREAD, CHILDREN'S

Setting: The district of Tyre and Sidon. A Canaanite woman appeals to Jesus to heal her demon-possessed daughter.

But He answered and said, "I was sent only to the lost sheep of the house of Israel." But she came and *began* to bow down before Him, saying, "Lord, help me!" And He answered and said, "It is not good to take the children's bread and throw it to the dogs." But she said, "Yes, Lord; but even the dogs feed from the crumbs which fall from their masters' table." Then Jesus said to her, "O woman, your faith is great; it shall be done for you as you wish." And her daughter was healed at once (Matthew 15:24–28; cf. Mark 7: 24–30; see Matthew 9:22; 10:5, 6).

Setting: The region of Tyre. After the Pharisees and scribes from Jerusalem question Jesus' disciples' lack of obedience in Galilee to the tradition regarding ceremonial cleansing, Jesus casts a demon from the daughter of a Gentile (Syrophoenician) woman.

And He was saying to her, "Let the children be satisfied first, for it is not good to take the children's bread and throw it to the dogs." But she answered and said to Him, "Yes, Lord *but* even the dogs under the table feed on the children's crumbs. And He said to her, "Because of this answer go; the demon has gone out of your daughter" (Mark 7:27–29; cf. Matthew 15:21–28).

BREAD, CONSECRATED

Setting: Galilee. Jesus responds to the Pharisees' objection to His disciples' picking grain from the fields on the

Sabbath.

But He said to them, "Have you not read what David did when he became hungry, he and his companions, how they entered the house of God, and ate the consecrated bread, which was not lawful for him to eat nor for those with him, but for the priests alone? Or, have you not read in the Law, that on the Sabbath the priests in the temple break the Sabbath and are innocent? But I say to you that something greater than the temple is here. But if you had known what this means, 'I DESIRE COMPASSION, AND NOT A SACRIFICE,' you would not have condemned the innocent. For the Son of Man is Lord of the Sabbath" (Matthew 12:3–8, Jesus quotes from Hosea 6:6; cf. Mark 2:25–28; Luke 6:3–5; see 1 Samuel 21:6).

Setting: Galilee. Early in His ministry, the Pharisees ask Jesus why He allows His disciples to harvest and eat grain on the Sabbath.

And He said to them, "Have you never read what David did when he was in need and he and his companions became hungry; how he entered the house of God in the time of Abiathar *the* high priest, and ate the consecrated bread, which is not lawful for *any-one* to eat except the priests, and he also gave it to those who were with him?" Jesus said to them, "The Sabbath was made for man, and not man for the Sabbath. So the Son of Man is Lord even of the Sabbath" (Mark 2:25–28; cf. Matthew 12:1–8; Luke 6:1–5; see Exodus 23:12).

Setting: Probably in Galilee. As Jesus and His disciples pass through some grain fields, some of the Pharisees question why His followers harvest and eat grain on the Sabbath.

And Jesus answering them said, "Have you not even read what David did when he was hungry, he and those who were with him, how he entered the house of God, and took and ate the consecrated bread which is not lawful for any to eat except the priests alone, and gave it to his companions?" And He was saying to them, "The Son of Man is Lord of the Sabbath" (Luke 6:3–5; cf. Matthew 12:1–8; Mark 2:23–28; see Exodus 20:8; Leviticus 24:1–9; Deuteronomy 5:12; 1 Samuel 21:1–6).

BREAD, DAILY (Also see GOD, DEPENDENCE ON; NEEDS; and PROVISION, GOD'S)

Setting: Galilee. During the early part of His ministry, Jesus gives a model prayer to His disciples and the multitudes while conveying The Sermon on the Mount.

"Pray, then, in this way: 'Our Father who is in heaven, hallowed be Your name. Your kingdom come. Your will be done, on earth as it is in heaven. Give us this day our daily bread. And forgive us our debts, as we also have forgiven our debtors. And do not lead us into temptation, but deliver us from evil. [For Yours is the kingdom and the power and the glory forever. Amen]'" (Matthew 6:9–13; cf. Luke 11:2–4; see John 17:15).

Setting: On the way from Galilee to Jerusalem. After Jesus visits in the home of Martha and Mary of Bethany, a disciple asks Him to teach them to pray.

And He said to them, "When you pray, say: 'Father, hallowed be Your name. Your kingdom come. Give us each day our daily bread. And forgive us our sins, for we ourselves also forgive everyone who is indebted to us. And lead us not into temptation'" (Luke 11:2–4; cf. Matthew 6:9–13).

BREAD, FEAST OF UNLEAVENED (See PASSOVER)

BREAD, LIVING

Setting: Capernaum of Galilee. After Jesus informs the people whom He miraculously fed with a lad's five loaves and two fish how they might receive the bread out of heaven, the Jewish religious leaders grumble because He claims that He came down out of heaven.

Therefore the Jews were grumbling about Him, because He said, "I am the bread that came down out of heaven." They were saying, "Is not this Jesus, the son of Joseph, whose father and mother we know? How does He now say, 'I have come down out of heaven'?" Jesus answered and said to them, "Do not grumble among yourselves. No one can come to Me unless the Father who sent Me draws him; and I will raise him up on the last day. It is written in the prophets, 'AND THEY SHALL ALL BE TAUGHT OF GOD.' Everyone who has heard and learned from the Father, comes to Me. Not that anyone has seen the Father, except the One who is from God; He has seen the Father. Truly, truly, I say to you, he who believes has eternal life. I am the bread of life. Your fathers ate the manna in the wilderness, and they died. This is the bread which comes down out of heaven, so that one may eat of it and not die. I am the living bread that came down out of heaven; if anyone eats of this bread, he will live forever; and the bread also which I will give for the life of the world is My flesh" (John 6:41–51, Jesus quotes from Isaiah 54:13; see John 1:18, 29; 3:36; 6:58; 7:27).

BREAD, TRUE

Setting: Capernaum. The day after Jesus walks on the Sea of Galilee to join His disciples in a boat, the people He miraculously fed with a lad's five loaves and two fish quiz Him about the signs and works He performs, so they may believe in Him.

Jesus then said to them, "Truly, truly, I say to you, it is not Moses who has given you the bread out of heaven, but it is My Father who gives you the true bread out of heaven. For the bread of God is that which comes down out of heaven, and gives life to the world" (John 6:32, 33; see John 6:50).

BREAD OF GOD (Listed under GOD, BREAD OF)

BREAD OF LIFE (Listed under LIFE, BREAD OF)

BREAD OUT OF HEAVEN (Listed under HEAVEN, BREAD OUT OF)

BREAKFAST

Setting: By the Sea of Galilee. In His third post-resurrection appearance to His disciples, after providing a great catch of fish following their unsuccessful night of fishing, Jesus invites them to have breakfast with Him.

Jesus said to them, "Come *and* have breakfast." None of the disciples ventured to question Him, "Who are You?" knowing that it was the Lord (John 21:12).

BREAST (Also see BOSOM, ABRAHAM'S; and BREASTS)

Setting: On the way from Galilee to Jerusalem. After instructing His disciples about persistence in prayer, Jesus conveys a parable about self-righteousness.

And He also told this parable to some people who trusted in themselves that they were righteous, and viewed others with contempt: "Two men went up into the temple to pray, one a Pharisee and the other a tax collector. The Pharisee stood and was praying this to himself: 'God, I thank You that I am not like other people: swindlers, unjust, adulterers, or even like this tax collector. I fast twice a week; I pay tithes of all that I get.' But the tax collector, standing some distance away, was even unwilling to lift up his eyes to heaven, but was beating his breast, saying, 'God, be merciful to me, the sinner!' I tell you, this man went to his house justified rather than the other; for everyone who exalts himself will be humbled, but he who humbles himself will be exalted" (Luke 18:9–14; see Ezra 9:6; Matthew 6:5, 23:12; Luke 11:42; 16:15; Romans 14:3, 10).

BREASTS (Also see BREAST)

Setting: Jerusalem. After being arrested and appearing before the Council of Elders (Sanhedrin), Pontius Pilate (Roman governor of Judea), Herod Antipas (tetrarch of Galilee and Perea), and Pilate a second time (when Pilate bows to the crowd's pressure and grants that Jesus be crucified), the Lord prophesies to the women mourning Him regarding the coming judgment of Jerusalem.

But Jesus turning to them said, "Daughters of Jerusalem, stop weeping for Me, but weep for yourselves and for your children. For behold, the days are coming when they will say, 'Blessed are the barren, and the wombs that never bore, and the breasts that never nursed.' Then they will begin TO SAY TO THE MOUNTAINS, 'FALL ON US,' AND TO THE HILLS, 'COVER US.' For it they do these things when the tree is green, what will happen when it is dry?" (Luke 23:28–31, Jesus quotes from Hosea 10:8; see Matthew 24:19).

BRETHREN, MY (Also see BROTHERS)

Setting: Jerusalem. The day after the Sabbath, after rising from the dead, Jesus appears to Mary Magdalene and the other Mary with instructions for His disciples.

Then Jesus said to them, "Do not be afraid; go and take word to My brethren to leave for Galilee, and there they will see Me" (Matthew 28:10; see John 20:17).

Setting: In Jerusalem, the risen Jesus first appears to Mary Magdalene after she tells Simon Peter and John about the empty tomb where Jesus had been after dying on the cross for the sins of the world.

Jesus said to her, "Woman, why are you weeping? Whom are you seeking?" Supposing Him to be the gardener, she said to Him, "Sir, if you have carried Him away, tell me where you have laid Him, and I will take Him away." Jesus said to her, "Mary!" She turned and said to Him in Hebrew "Rabboni!" (which means, Teacher). Jesus said to her, "Stop clinging to Me, for I have not yet ascended to the Father; but go to My brethren and say to them, 'I ascend to My Father and your Father, and My God and Your God'" (John 20:15–17; see Mark 16:9–11; John 7:33; 19:31–42).

BRIAR BUSH (Listed under BUSH, BRIAR)

BRIDEGROOM (Also see WEDDING)

Setting: Capernaum near the Sea of Galilee. John the Baptist's disciples ask Jesus why His own disciples do not participate in fasting, while they and the Pharisees do.

And Jesus said to them, "The attendants of the bridegroom cannot mourn as long as the bridegroom is with them, can they? But the days will come when the bridegroom is taken away from them, and then they will fast. But no one puts a patch of unshrunk cloth on an old garment; for the patch pulls away from the garment, and a worse tear results. Nor do *people* put new wine into old wineskins; otherwise the wineskins burst, and the wine pours out and the wineskins are ruined; but they put new wine into fresh wineskins, and both are preserved" (Matthew 9:15–17; cf. Mark 2:18–22; Luke 5:33–39).

Setting: The Mount of Olives, just east of Jerusalem. During His discourse, after answering His disciples' questions as to when the temple will be destroyed and Jerusalem overrun, along with the signs of His coming and the end of the age, Jesus reemphasizes to His disciples that they should be on the alert for His return.

"Then the kingdom of heaven will be comparable to ten virgins, who took their lamps and went out to meet the bridegroom. Five of them were foolish, and five were prudent. For when the foolish took their lamps, they took no oil with them, but the prudent took oil in flasks along with their lamps. Now while the bridegroom was delaying, they all got drowsy and *began* to sleep. But at midnight there was a shout, 'Behold, the bridegroom! Come out to meet *him*.' Then all those virgins rose and trimmed their lamps. The foolish said to the prudent, 'Give us some of your oil, for our lamps are going out.' But the prudent answered, 'No, there will not be enough for us and you *too;* go instead to the dealers and buy *some* for yourselves.' And while they were going away to make the purchase, the bridegroom came, and those who were ready went in with him to the wedding feast; and the door was shut. Later the other virgins also came, saying, 'Lord, lord, open up for us.' But he answered, 'Truly I say to you, I do not know you.' Be on the alert then, for you do not know the day nor the hour" (Matthew 25:1–13; cf. Matthew 24:42; Luke 12:35; see Matthew 7:21, 24).

Setting: Capernaum. John's disciples and the Pharisees question why Jesus' disciples do not fast when they do.

And Jesus said to them, "While the bridegroom is with them, the attendants of the bridegroom cannot fast, can they? So long as they have the bridegroom with them, they cannot fast. But the days will come when the bridegroom is taken away from them, and then they will fast in that day. No one sews a patch of unshrunk cloth on an old garment; otherwise the patch pulls away from it, the new from the old, and a worse tear results. No one puts new wine into old wineskins; otherwise the wine will burst the skins, and the wine is lost and the skins as *well;* but *one puts* new wine into fresh wineskins" (Mark 2:19–22; cf. Matthew 9:14–17; Luke 5:33–38).

Setting: The home of Levi (Matthew) in Capernaum. At a reception for Jesus following Levi's call to be a disciple, the Pharisees and their scribes question Jesus about fasting.

And Jesus said to them, "You cannot make the attendants of the bridegroom fast while the bridegroom is with them, can you? But the days will come; and when the bridegroom is taken away from them, then they will fast in those days" (Luke 5:34, 35; cf. Matthew 9:14, 15; Mark 2:18–20).

BRIMSTONE (Also see FIRE)

Setting: Samaria, on the way from Galilee to Jerusalem. After the Pharisees question Him about the coming of the kingdom of God, Jesus tells His disciples of His second coming.

And He said to the disciples, "The days will come when you will long to see one of the days of the Son of Man, and you will not see it. They will say to you, 'Look there! Look here!' Do not go away, and do not run after them. For just like the lightning, when it flashes out of one part of the sky, shines to the other part of the sky, so will the Son of Man be in His day. But first He must suffer many things and be rejected by this generation. And just as it happened in the days of Noah, so it will be also in the days of the Son of Man: they were eating, they were drinking, they were marrying, they were being given in marriage, until the day that Noah entered the ark, and the flood came and destroyed them all. It was the same as happened in the days of Lot: they were eating, they were drinking, they were buying, they were selling, they were planting, they were building; but on the day that Lot went out from Sodom it rained fire and brimstone from heaven and destroyed them all. It will be just the same on the day that the Son of Man is revealed. On that day, the one who is on the housetop and whose goods are in the house must not go down to take them out, and likewise the one who is in the field must not turn back. Remember Lot's wife. Whoever seeks to keep his life will lose it, and whoever loses his life will preserve it. I tell you, on that night there will be two in one bed; one will be taken and the other will be left. There will be two women grinding at the same place; one will be taken and the other will be left. [Two men will be in the field; one will be taken and the other will be left."] And answering they said to Him, "Where, Lord?" And He said to them, "Where the body is, there also the vultures will be gathered" (Luke 17:22–37; see Genesis 19; Matthew 10:39; 16:21, 27; 24:17–28, 37–41).

BROAD WAY

[BROAD WAY from the way is broad]

Setting: Galilee. During the early part of His ministry, Jesus preaches the Sermon on the Mount to His disciples and the multitudes.

"Enter through the narrow gate; for the gate is wide and the way is broad that leads to destruction, and there are many who enter through it. For the gate is small and the way is narrow that leads to life, and there are few who find it" (Matthew 7:13, 14; cf. Luke 13:24).

BROKEN PIECES (Listed under PIECES, BROKEN)

BROKEN TO PIECES (Listed under PIECES, BROKEN TO)

BRONZE, BURNISHED

Setting: On the island of Patmos (in the Aegean Sea about fifty miles southwest of Ephesus in modern Turkey). On the Lord's Day (Sunday), about fifty years after Jesus' resurrection, the disciple John encounters the Lord Jesus Christ, who communicates a new revelation for the apostle to record for the church in Thyatira and to six other churches in Asia.

"And to the angel of the church in Thyatira write: The Son of God, who has eyes like a flame of fire, and His feet are like burnished bronze, says this: 'I know your deeds, and your love and faith and service and perseverance, and that your deeds of late are greater than at first. But I have *this* against you, that you tolerate the woman Jezebel, who calls herself a prophetess, and she teaches and leads My bond-servants astray so that they commit *acts of* immorality and eat things sacrificed to idols. I gave her time to repent, and she does not want to repent of her immorality. Behold, I will throw her on a bed *of sickness,* and those who commit adultery with her into great tribulation, unless they repent of her deeds. And I will kill her children with pestilence, and all the churches will know that I am He who searches the minds and hearts; and I will give to each one of you according to your deeds. But I say to you, the rest who are in Thyatira, who do not hold this teaching, who have not known the deep things of Satan, as they call them—I place no other burden on you. Nevertheless what you have, hold fast until I come. He who overcomes, and he who keeps My deeds until the end, TO HIM I WILL GIVE AUTHORITY OVER THE NATIONS; AND HE SHALL RULE THEM WITH A ROD OF IRON, AS THE VESSELS OF THE POTTER ARE BROKEN TO PIECES, as I also have received *authority* from My Father; and I will give him the morning star. He who has an ear, let him hear what the Spirit says to the churches' (Revelation 2:18–29; Jesus quotes from Psalm 2:8, 9; Isaiah 30:14; see 1 Kings 16:31; Psalm 7:9; Romans 2:5; 1 Corinthians 2:10; 2 Peter 3:9; Revelation 1:14; 2:7; 3:11; 17:1–20).

BROOD (VIPERS, BROOD OF is a separate entry)

Setting: On the way from Galilee to Jerusalem. While teaching in the cities and villages, after Jesus responds to a question about who is saved, some Pharisees ask Him to leave, claiming Herod seeks His life.

And He said to them, "Go and tell that fox, 'Behold, I cast out demons and perform cures today and tomorrow, and the third day I reach My goal.' Nevertheless I must journey on today and tomorrow and the next day; for it cannot be that a prophet would perish outside of Jerusalem. O Jerusalem, Jerusalem, the city that kills the prophets and stones those sent to her! How often I wanted to gather your children together, just as a hen gathers her brood under her wings, and you would not have it! Behold, your house is left to you desolate; and I say to you, you will not see Me until the time comes when you say, 'BLESSED IS HE WHO COMES IN THE NAME OF THE LORD!'" (Luke 13:32–35, Jesus quotes from Psalm 118:26; cf. Matthew 23:37).

BROOD OF VIPERS (Listed under VIPERS, BROOD OF; also see SERPENTS; SNAKE; and SNAKES)

BROTHER (Also see BROTHERS)

Setting: Galilee. During the early part of His ministry, Jesus preaches the Sermon on the Mount to His disciples and the multitudes.

"But I say to you that everyone who is angry with his brother shall be guilty before the court; and whoever says to his brother, 'You good-for-nothing,' shall be guilty before the supreme court; and whoever says, 'You fool,' shall be guilty *enough to go* into the fiery hell" (Matthew 5:22).

Setting: Galilee. During the early part of His ministry, Jesus preaches the Sermon on the Mount to His disciples and the multitudes.

"Therefore if you are presenting your offering at the altar, and there remember that your brother has something against you, leave your offering there before the altar and go; first be reconciled to your brother, and then come and present your offering" (Matthew 5:23, 24; see Romans 12:17, 18).

Setting: Galilee. During the early part of His ministry, Jesus preaches the Sermon on the Mount to His disciples and the multitudes.

"Do not judge so that you will not be judged. For in the way you judge, you will be judged; and by your standard of measure, it will be measured to you. Why do you look at the speck that is in your brother's eye, but do not notice the log that is in your own eye? Or how can you say to your brother, 'Let me take the speck out of your eye, and behold, the log is in your own eye? You hypocrite, first take the log out of your own eye, and then you will see clearly to take the speck out of your brother's eye" (Matthew 7:1–5; cf. Mark 4:24; Luke 6:37–42; Romans 2:1; 14:10, 13).

Setting: Galilee. After His disciples observe His ministry, Jesus summons and specifically instructs them about the upcoming difficulties of *their* ministry to the people of Israel.

"Brother will betray brother to death, and a father *his* child; and children will rise up against parents and cause them to be put to death. You will be hated by all because of My name, but it is the one who has endured to the end who will be saved. But whenever they persecute you in one city, flee to the next; for truly I say to you, you will not finish *going through* the cities of Israel until the Son of Man comes" (Matthew 10:21–23; cf. Matthew 10:35, 36; 16:27, 28; 24:9).

Setting: Galilee. Jesus' mother, Mary, and His brothers are waiting to see Him as He teaches and preaches.

But Jesus answered the one who was telling Him and said, "Who is My mother and who are My brothers?" And stretching out His hand toward His disciples, He said, "Behold, My mother and My brothers! For whoever does the will of My Father who is in heaven, he is My brother and sister and mother" (Matthew 12:48–50; cf. Mark 3:31–35; Luke 8:19–21).

Setting: Capernaum of Galilee. After conveying to His disciples the value of little ones, Jesus gives instruction about church discipline.

"If your brother sins, go and show him his fault in private; if he listens to you, you have won your brother. But if he does not listen *to you,* take one or two more with you, so that BY THE MOUTH OF TWO OR THREE WITNESSES EVERY FACT MAY BE CONFIRMED. If he refuses to listen to them, tell it to the church; and if he refuses to listen even to the church, let him be to you as a Gentile and a tax collector. Truly I say to you, whatever you bind of earth shall have been bound in heaven; and whatever you loose on earth shall have been loosed in heaven. Again, I say to you, that if two of you agree on earth about anything that they may ask, it shall be done for them by My Father who is in heaven. For there two or three have gathered together in My name, I am there in their midst" (Matthew 18:15–20. Jesus quotes from Deuteronomy 19:15; cf. Matthew 7:7; 16:19; see Leviticus 19:17; Matthew 28:20; 2 Thessalonians 3:6, 14).

Setting: Capernaum of Galilee. Jesus illustrates forgiveness after Peter asks Him if forgiving someone seven times who has sinned against him is adequate.

"For this reason the kingdom of heaven may be compared to a king who wished to settle accounts with his slaves. When he had begun to settle *them,* one who owed him ten thousand talents was brought to him. But since he did not have *the means* to repay, his lord commanded him to be sold, along with his wife and children and all that he had, and repayment to be made. So the slave fell *to the ground* and prostrated himself before him, saying, 'Have patience with me and I will repay you everything.' And the lord of that slave felt compassion and released him and forgave him the debt. But that slave went out and found one of his fellow slaves who owed him a hundred denarii; and he seized him and *began* to choke *him,* saying, 'Pay back what you owe.' So his fellow slave fell *to the ground* and *began* to plead with him, saying, 'Have patience with me and I will repay you.' But he was unwilling and went and threw him in prison until he should pay back what was owed. So when his fellow slaves saw what had happened, they were deeply grieved and came and reported to their lord all that had happened. Then summoning him, his lord said to him, 'You wicked slave, I forgave you all that debt because you pleaded with me. Should you not also have had mercy on your fellow slave, in the same way that I had mercy on you?' And his lord, moved with anger, handed him over to the torturers until he should repay all that was owed him. My heavenly Father will also do the same to you, if each of you does not forgive his brother from your heart" (Matthew 18:23–35; cf. Matthew 6:12, 14, 15; Luke 7:42; see Matthew 25:19–28).

Setting: Galilee. During the early part of His ministry, just after selecting His twelve disciples, Jesus is informed that his mother and brothers are waiting to see Him. He explains to the crowd who His true relatives are.

Answering them, He said, "Who are My mother and My brothers?" Looking about at those who were sitting around Him, He said, "Behold My mother and My brothers! For whoever does the will of God, he is My brother and sister and mother" (Mark 3:33–35; cf. Matthew 12:46–50; Luke 8:19–21).

Setting: The Mount of Olives, east of the temple in Jerusalem. During His discourse, after prophesying the temple's destruction, Jesus responds to questions from Peter, James, John, and Andrew about future events.

And Jesus began to say to them, "See to it that no one misleads you. Many will come in My name, saying, 'I am *He!*' and will mislead many. When you hear of wars and rumors of wars, do not be frightened; *those things* must take place; but *that is* not yet the end. For nation will rise up against nation, and kingdom against kingdom; there will be earthquakes in various places; there will *also be* famines. These things are *merely* the beginning of birth pangs. But be on your guard; for they will deliver you to *the* courts, and you will be flogged in *the* synagogues, and you will stand before governors and kings for My sake, as a testimony to them. The gospel must first be preached to all the nations. When they arrest you and hand you over, do not worry beforehand about what you are to say, but say whatever is given you in that hour; for it is not you who speak, but *it is* the Holy Spirit. Brother will betray brother to death, and a father *his* child; and children will rise up against parents and have them put to death. You will be hated by all because of My name, but the one who endures to the end, he will be saved" (Mark 13:5–13; cf. Matthew 24:4–14; Luke 21:7–19; see Matthew 10:17–22).

Setting: Galilee. After selecting His twelve disciples, Jesus teaches the Beatitudes (part of the Sermon on the Mount) to His disciples and a great throng of people from Judea, Jerusalem, and the central coastal region of Tyre and Sidon.

And He also spoke a parable to them: "A blind man cannot guide a blind man, can he? Will they not both fall into a pit? A pupil is not above his teacher; but everyone, after he has been fully trained, will be like his teacher. Why do you look at the speck that is in your brother's eye, but do not notice the log that is in your own eye? Or how can you say to your brother, 'Brother, let me take out the speck that is in your eye,' when you yourself do not see the log that is in your own eye? You hypocrite, first take the log out of your own eye, and then you will see clearly to take out the speck that is in your brother's eye. For there is no good tree which produces bad fruit, nor, on the other hand, a bad tree which produces good fruit. For each tree is known by its own fruit. For men do not gather figs from thorns, nor do they pick grapes from a briar bush. The good man out of the good treasure of his heart brings forth what is good; and the evil man out of the evil treasure brings forth what is evil; for his mouth speaks from that which fills his heart" (Luke 6:39–45; cf. Matthew 7:3–6. 16, 18, 20; 12:35; see Matthew 10:24; 15:14; Luke 6:12–19).

Setting: On the way from Galilee to Jerusalem. Jesus conveys the Parable of The Prodigal Son because the Pharisees and scribes complain He associates with tax collectors and sinners.

And He said, "A man had two sons. The younger of them said to his father, 'Father, give me the share of the estate that falls to me.' So he divided his wealth between them. And not many days later, the younger son gathered everything together and went on a journey into a distant country, and there he squandered his estate with loose living. Now when he had spent everything, a severe famine occurred in that country, and he began to be impoverished. So he went and hired himself out to one of the citizens of that country, and he sent him into his fields to feed swine. And he would have gladly filled his stomach with the pods that the swine were eating, and no one was giving anything to him. But when he came to his senses, he said, 'How many of my father's hired men have more than enough bread, but I am dying here with hunger! I will get up and go to my father, and will say to him, "Father, I have sinned against heaven, and in your sight; I am no longer worthy to be called your son; make me as one of your hired men."' So he got up and came to his father. But while he was still a long way off, his father saw him and felt compassion for him, and ran and embraced him and kissed him. And the son said to him, "Father, I have sinned against heaven and in your sight; I am no longer worthy to be called your son.' But the father said to his slaves, 'Quickly bring out the best robe and put it on him, and put a ring on his hand and sandals on his feet; and bring the fattened calf, kill it, and let us eat and celebrate; for this son of mine was dead and has come to life again; he was lost and has been found.' And they began to celebrate. Now his older son was in the field, when he came and approached the house, he heard music and dancing. And he summoned one of the servants and began inquiring what these things could be. And he said to him, 'Your brother has come, and your father has killed the fattened calf because he has received him back safe and sound.' But he became angry and was not willing to go in; and his father came out and began pleading with him. But he answered and said to his father, 'Look! For so many years I have been serving you and I have never neglected a command of yours; and yet you have never given me a young goat, so that I might celebrate with my friends; but when this son of yours came, who has devoured your wealth with prostitutes, you killed the fattened calf for him.' And he said to him, 'Son, you have always been with me, and all that is mine is yours. But we had to celebrate and rejoice, for this brother of yours was dead and has begun to live, and was lost and has been found'" (Luke 15:11–32; see Proverbs 29:2;

Luke 15:1, 2).

Setting: On the way from Galilee to Jerusalem. After conveying the story of the rich man and Lazarus, the Lord gives instruction to His disciples on forgiveness.

He said to His disciples, "It is inevitable that stumbling blocks come, but woe to him through whom they come! It would be better for him if a millstone were hung around his neck and he were thrown into the sea, than that he would cause one of these little ones to stumble. Be on your guard! If your brother sins, rebuke him; and if he repents, forgive him. And if he sins against you seven times a day, and returns to you seven times, saying, 'I repent,' forgive him" (Luke 17:1–4; see Matthew 18:5–7, 15, 21, 22).

Setting: Bethany near Jerusalem. After the death of Lazarus, Jesus travels with His disciples to Bethany in Judea to see His friend's sisters, Martha and Mary.

Jesus said to her, "Your brother will rise again." Martha said to Him, "I know that he will rise again in the resurrection on the last day." Jesus said to her, "I am the resurrection and the life; he who believes in Me will live even if he dies, and everyone who lives and believes in Me will never die. Do you believe this?" (John 11:23–26; see Daniel 12:2; John 1:4; 6:47–51).

BROTHER'S EYE (Listed under EYE, BROTHER'S)

BROTHERS (Also see BRETHREN; BROTHER; and RELATIVES)

Setting: Galilee. During the early part of His ministry, Jesus preaches the Sermon on the Mount to His disciples and the multitudes.

"You have heard that it was said, 'YOU SHALL LOVE YOUR NEIGHBOR and hate your enemy.' But I say to you, love your enemies and pray for those who persecute you, so that you may be sons of your Father who is in heaven; for He causes His sun to rise on *the* evil and *the* good, and sends rain on *the* righteous and *the* unrighteous. For if you love those who love you, what reward do you have? Do not even the tax collectors do the same? If you greet only your brothers, what more are you doing *than others?* Do not even the Gentiles do the same? Therefore, you are to be perfect, as your heavenly Father is perfect" (Matthew 5:43–48, Jesus quotes from Leviticus 19:18; cf. Leviticus 19:2; Luke 6:27–36).

Setting: Galilee. Jesus' mother, Mary, and His brothers are waiting to see Him as He teaches and preaches.

But Jesus answered the one who was telling Him and said, "Who is My mother and who are My brothers?" And stretching out His hand toward His disciples, He said, "Behold, My mother and My brothers! For whoever does the will of My Father who is in heaven, he is My brother and sister and mother" (Matthew 12:48–50; cf. Mark 3:31–35; Luke 8:19–21).

Setting: Judea beyond the Jordan (Perea). Jesus promises rewards to His disciples for their personal sacrifice and commitment to following Him.

And Jesus said to them, "Truly I say to you, that you who have followed Me, in the regeneration when the Son of Man will sit on His glorious throne, you also shall sit upon twelve thrones, judging the twelve tribes of Israel. And everyone who has left houses or brothers or sisters or father or mother or children or farms for My name's sake, will receive many times as much, and will inherit eternal life. But many *who* are first will be last; and *the* last, first" (Matthew 19:28–30; cf. Matthew 6:33; 20:15; Mark 10:29, 30; Luke 18:29, 30; 22:30).

Setting: The temple in Jerusalem. Jesus exposes the truth about Pharisaism to the crowds and His disciples after the Jewish religious leaders test Him with questions.

Then Jesus spoke to the crowds and to His disciples, saying: "The scribes and the Pharisees have seated themselves in the chair of Moses; therefore all that they tell you, do and observe, but do not do according to their deeds; for they say *things* and do not do *them.* They tie up heavy burdens and lay them on men's shoulders, but they themselves are unwilling to move them with *so much as* a finger. But they do all their deeds to be noticed by men; for they broaden their phylacteries and lengthen their tassels *of their garments.* They love the place of honor at banquets and the chief seats in the synagogues, and respectful greetings in the market places, and being called Rabbi by men. But do not be called Rabbi; for One is your Teacher, and you are all brothers. Do not call *anyone* on earth your father; for One is your Father, He who is in heaven. Do not be called leaders; for One is your Leader, *that is,* Christ. But the greatest among you shall be your servant. Whoever exalts himself shall be humbled; and whoever humbles himself shall be exalted" (Matthew 23:1–12; cf. Matthew 20:26; Mark 12:38–40; Luke 20:46, 47; see Exodus 13:9; Deuteronomy 33:3; Matthew 6:1, 5, 6, 9, 16; Mark 14:11; Luke 11:43; 14:11).

Setting: The Mount of Olives, just east of Jerusalem. During His discourse, after answering His disciples' questions as to when the temple will be destroyed and Jerusalem overrun, along with the signs of His coming and the end of the age, Jesus reveals the future judgments following His return.

"But when the Son of Man comes in His glory, and all the angels with Him, then He will sit on His glorious throne. All the nations will be gathered before Him; and He will separate them from one another, as the shepherd separates the sheep from the goats; and He will put the sheep on His right, and the goats on the left. Then the King will say to those on His right, 'Come, you who are blessed of My Father, inherit the kingdom prepared for you from the foundation of the world. 'For I was hungry, and you gave Me *something* to eat; I was thirsty, and you gave Me *something* to drink; I was a stranger, and you invited Me in; naked, and you clothed Me; I was sick, and you visited Me; I was in prison, and you came to Me.' Then the righteous will answer Him, 'Lord, when did we see You hungry and feed You, or thirsty, and give you *something* to drink? And when did we see You a stranger, and invite You in, or naked, and clothe You? When did we see You sick, or in prison, and come to You?' The King will answer and say to them, 'Truly I say to you, to the extent that you did it to one of these brothers of Mine, *even* the least *of them,* you did it to Me.' Then He will also say to those on His left, 'Depart from Me, accursed ones, into the eternal fire which has been prepared for the devil and his angels; for I was hungry, and you gave Me *nothing* to eat; I was thirsty, and you gave Me nothing to drink; I was a stranger, and you did not invite Me in; naked, and you did not clothe Me; sick, and in prison, and you did not visit Me.' Then they themselves also will answer, 'Lord, when did we see You hungry, or thirsty, or a stranger, or naked, or sick, or in prison, and did not take care of You?' Then He will answer them, 'Truly I say to you, to the extent that you did not do it to one of the least of these, you did not do it to Me.' These will go away into eternal punishment, but the righteous into eternal life" (Matthew 25:31–46; see Matthew 7:23; 16:27; 19:29).

Setting: Galilee. During the early part of His ministry, just after selecting His twelve disciples, Jesus is informed his mother and brothers are waiting to see Him. He explains to the crowd who His true relatives are.

Answering them, He said, "Who are My mother and My brothers?" Looking about at those who were sitting around Him, He said, "Behold My mother and My brothers! For whoever does the will of God, he is My brother and sister and mother" (Mark 3:33–35; cf. Matthew 12:46–50; Luke 8:19–21).

Setting: Judea beyond the Jordan (Perea). After informing a rich man how to inherit eternal life, Jesus conveys to His disciples the reward of those who sacrifice in this life to follow Him.

Jesus said, "Truly I say to you, there is no one who has left house or brothers or sisters or mother or father or children or farms, for My sake and for the gospel's sake, but that he will receive a hundred times as much now in the present age, houses and brothers and sisters and mothers and children and farms, along with persecutions; and in the age to come, eternal life. But many *who are* first will be last, and the last, first" (Mark 10:29–31; cf. Matthew 19:27–30; Luke 18:28–30; see Matthew 6:33).

Setting: Galilee. After giving of the Parable of the Lamp to His disciples, Jesus is informed His mother and brothers are seeking Him. He conveys who His true relatives are.

But He answered and said to them, "My mother and My brothers are these who hear the word of God and do it" (Luke 8:21; cf. Matthew 12:26–50; Mark 3:31–35).

Setting: On the way from Galilee to Jerusalem. Jesus speaks a parable to the guests of a Pharisee leader on the Sabbath. As He observes the guests selecting places of honor at the table, Jesus comments to the host about the people to invite in the future.

And He also went on to say to the one who had invited Him, "When you give a luncheon or a dinner, do not invite your friends or your brothers or your relatives or rich neighbors, otherwise they may also invite you in return and that will be your repayment. But when you give a reception, invite the poor, the crippled, the lame, the blind, and you will be blessed, since they do not have the means to repay you; for you will be repaid at the resurrection of the righteous" (Luke 14:12–14; see Luke 14:1, 2; John 5:28, 29).

Setting: On the way from Galilee to Jerusalem. After He responds to a guest's proclamation about the blessings of eating bread in the kingdom of God, Jesus presents to large crowds the demands of discipleship.

Now large crowds were going along with Him; and He turned and said to them, "If anyone comes to Me, and does not hate his own father and mother and wife and children and brothers and sisters, yes, and even his own life, he cannot be My disciple. Whoever does not carry his own cross and come after Me cannot be My disciple. For which one of you, when he wants to build a tower, does not first sit down and calculate the cost to see if he has enough to complete it? Otherwise, when he has laid a foundation and is not able to finish, all who observe it begin to ridicule him, saying, 'This man began to build and was not able to finish.' Or what king, when he sets out to meet another king in battle, will not first sit down and consider whether he is strong enough with ten thousand *men* to encounter the one coming against him with twenty thousand? Or else, while the other is still far away, he sends a delegation and asks for terms of peace. So then, none of you can be My disciple who does not give up all his possessions. Therefore, salt is good; but if even salt has become tasteless, with what will it be seasoned? It is useless either for the soil or for the manure pile; it is thrown out. He who has ears to hear, let him hear" (Luke 14:25–35; cf. Matthew 5:13; 10:37–39; see Proverbs 20:18; Luke 14:1, 2; Philippians 3:7).

Setting: On the way from Galilee to Jerusalem. After He responds to the Pharisees' scoffing at His teaching His disciples about stewardship and the permanence of the Law, Jesus conveys the story of the rich man and Lazarus.

"Now there was a rich man, and he habitually dressed in purple and fine linen, joyously living in splendor every day. And a poor man named Lazarus was laid at his gate, covered with sores, and longing to be fed with the crumbs which were falling from the rich man's table; besides, even the dogs were coming and licking his sores. Now the poor man died and was carried away by the angels to Abraham's bosom; and the rich man also died and was buried. In Hades he lifted up his eyes, being in torment, and saw Abraham far away and Lazarus in his bosom. And he cried out and said, 'Father Abraham, have mercy on me, and send Lazarus so that he may dip the tip of his finger in water and cool off my tongue, for I am in agony in this flame.' But Abraham said, 'Child, remember that during your life you received your good things, and likewise Lazarus bad things; but now he is being comforted here, and you are in agony. And besides all this, between us and you there is a great chasm fixed, so that those who wish to come over from here to you will not be able, and that none may cross over from there to us.' And he said, 'Then I beg you, father, that you send him to my father's house—for I have five brothers—in order that he may warn them, so that they will not also come to this place of torment.' But Abraham said, 'They have Moses and the Prophets; let them hear them.' But he said, 'No, father Abraham, but if someone goes to them from the dead, they will repent!' But he said to him, 'If they do not listen to Moses and the Prophets, they will not be persuaded even if someone rises from the dead'" (Luke 16:19–31; see Luke 3:8; 6:24; 16:1, 14).

Setting: On the way from Galilee to Jerusalem. After responding to His disciples' question about salvation, Jesus responds to Peter's statement about their personal sacrifice.

Peter said, "Behold, we have left our own homes and followed You." And He said to them, "Truly I say to you, there is no one who has left house or wife or brothers or parents or children, for the sake of the kingdom of God, who will not receive many times as much at this time and in the age to come, eternal life" (Luke 18:28–30; cf. Matthew 19:27–29; Mark 10:28–30; see Matthew 6:33; Luke 5:11).

Setting: The Mount of Olives, east of the temple in Jerusalem. During His discourse, a few days before His crucifixion, after giving His disciples more details regarding the temple's future destruction, Jesus elaborates about other future events.

Then He continued by saying to them, "Nation will rise against nation and kingdom against kingdom, and there will be great earthquakes, and in various places plagues and famines; and there will be terrors and great signs from heaven. But before all these things, they will lay their hands on you and will persecute you, delivering you to the synagogues and prisons, bringing you before kings and governors for My name's sake. It will lead to an opportunity for your testimony. So make up your minds not to prepare beforehand to defend yourselves; for I will give you utterance and wisdom which none of your opponents will be able to resist or refute. But you will be betrayed even by parents and brothers and relatives and friends, and they will put some of you to death, and you will be hated by all because of My name. Yet not a hair of your head will perish. By your endurance you will gain your lives" (Luke 21:10–19; cf. Matthew 10:19–22; 24:7–14; Mark 13:8–13).

Setting: Jerusalem. During the Feast of Unleavened Bread (Passover) just before the Crucifixion, while Jesus celebrates the Passover meal and institutes the Lord's Supper, His disciples argue over who is the greatest among them. Jesus prophesies Peter's upcoming denial of Him.

"Simon, Simon, behold, Satan has demanded permission to sift you like wheat; but I have prayed for you, that your faith may not fail; and you, when once you have turned again, strengthen your brothers." But he said to Him, "Lord, with You I am ready to go both to prison and to death!" And He said, "I say to you, Peter, the rooster will not crow today until you have denied three times that you know Me" (Luke 22:31–34; cf. Matthew 26:33–35; John 13:36–38; see Job 1:6–12; John 17:15).

BROTHERS, FIVE (See BROTHERS)

BUILDERS (Also see BUILDINGS; CONSTRUCTION; and FOUNDATION)

Setting: The temple in Jerusalem. Jesus delivers a prophecy to the chief priests and elders after they question His authority.

Jesus said to them, "Did you never read in the Scriptures, 'THE STONE WHICH THE BUILDERS REJECTED, THIS BECAME THE CHIEF CORNER stone; THIS CAME ABOUT FROM THE LORD, AND IT IS MARVELOUS IN OUR EYES'? Therefore I say to you, the kingdom of God will be taken away from you and given to a people, producing the fruit of it. And he who falls on this stone will be broken to pieces; but on whomever it falls, it will scatter him like dust" (Matthew 21:42–44, Jesus quotes from Psalm 118:22; cf. Isaiah 8:14, 15; Mark 12:10, 11; Luke 20:17, 18).

Setting: The temple in Jerusalem. Having His authority questioned by the chief priests, scribes, and elders, Jesus begins to teach them in parables.

And He began to speak to them in parables: "A man PLANTED A VINEYARD AND PUT A WALL AROUND IT, AND DUG A VAT UNDER THE WINE PRESS AND BUILT A TOWER, and rented it out to vine-growers and went on a journey. At the harvest time he sent a slave to the vine-growers, in order to receive some of the produce of the vineyard from the vine-growers. They took him, and beat him and sent him away empty-handed. Again he sent them another slave, and they wounded him in the head, and treated him shamefully. And he sent another, and that one they killed; and so with many others, beating some and killing others. He had one more to send, a beloved son; he sent him last of all to them, saying, 'They will respect my son.' But those vine-growers said to one another, 'This is the heir; come, let us kill him, and the inheritance will be ours!' They took him, and killed him and threw him out of the vineyard. What will the owner of the vineyard do? He will come and destroy the vine-growers, and will give the vineyard to others. Have you not even read this Scripture: 'THE STONE WHICH THE BUILDERS REJECTED, THIS BECAME THE CHIEF CORNER stone; THIS CAME ABOUT FROM THE LORD, AND IT IS MARVELOUS IN OUR EYES'?" (Mark 12:1–11, Jesus quotes from Psalm 118:22, 23; Isaiah 5:1, 2; cf. Matthew 21:33–46; Luke 20:9–19).

Setting: The temple in Jerusalem. While ministering a few days before His crucifixion, after the chief priests and the scribes question His authority to teach and preach, Jesus conveys the Parable of the Vine-Growers to the people.

And He began to tell the people this parable: "A man planted a vineyard and rented it out to vine-growers, and went on a journey for a long time. At the harvest time he sent a slave to the vine-growers, so that they would give him some of the produce of the vineyard; but the vine-growers beat him and sent him away empty-handed. And he proceeded to send another slave; and they beat him also and treated him shamefully and sent him away empty-handed. And he proceeded to send a third; and this one also they wounded and cast out. The owner of the vineyard said, 'What shall I do? I will send my beloved son; perhaps they will respect him.' But when the vine-growers saw him, they reasoned with one another, saying, 'This is the heir; let us kill him so that the inheritance will be ours.' So they threw him out of the vineyard and killed him. What, then, will the owner of the vineyard do to them? He will come and destroy these vine-growers and will give the vineyard to others." When they heard it, they said, "May it never be!" But Jesus looked at them and said, "What then is this that is written: 'THE STONE WHICH THE BUILDERS REJECTED, THIS BECAME THE CHIEF CORNER stone'? Everyone who falls on that stone will be broken to pieces; but on whomever it falls, it will scatter him like dust" (Luke 20:9–18, Jesus quotes from Psalm 118:22; cf. Matthew 21:33–44; Mark 12:1–11; see Ephesians 2:20).

BUILDINGS, GREAT (Also see BUILDERS; CONSTRUCTION; and FOUNDATION)

Setting: The temple treasury in Jerusalem. Following the teaching moment with His disciples regarding a poor widow's offering, Jesus prophesies the coming destruction of the temple.

And Jesus said to him, "Do you see these great buildings? Not one stone will be left upon another which will not be torn down" (Mark 13:2; cf. Matthew 24:1, 2; Luke 21:5, 6; see Luke 19:44).

BUNDLES

Setting: By the Sea of Galilee. Because the religious leaders are rejecting His message, Jesus continues teaching the crowds with the Parable of the Wheat and the Tares.

Jesus presented another parable to them, saying, "The kingdom of heaven may be compared to a man who sowed good seed in his field. But while his men were sleeping, his enemy came and sowed tares among the wheat, and went away. But when the wheat sprouted and bore grain, then the tares became evident also. The slaves of the landowner came and said to him, 'Sir, did you not sow good seed in your field? How then does it have tares?' And he said to them, 'An enemy has done this!' The slaves said to him, 'Do you want us, then, to go and gather them up?' But he said, 'No; for while you are gathering up the tares, you may uproot the wheat with them. Allow both to grow together until the harvest; and in the time of the harvest I will say to the reapers, "First gather up the tares and bind them in bundles to burn them up; but gather the wheat into my barn" '" (Matthew 13:24–30; cf. Matthew 3:12).

BURDEN (Also see BURDENED; and HEAVY LADEN)

Setting: Galilee. After rendering a thanksgiving prayer to His Father in heaven, Jesus offers rest to all who are weary and heavy-laden as He preaches and teaches.

"Come to Me, all who are weary and heavy-laden, and I will give you rest. Take My yoke upon you and learn from Me, for I am gentle and humble in heart, and YOU WILL FIND REST FOR YOUR SOULS. For My yoke is easy and My burden is light" (Matthew 11:28–30, Jesus quotes from Jeremiah 6:16; see Jeremiah 31:35; 1 John 5:3).

Setting: Judea beyond the Jordan (Perea). Jesus illustrates the kingdom of heaven to His disciples through the story of laborers in the vineyard.

"For the kingdom of heaven is like a landowner who went out early in the morning to hire laborers for his vineyard. When he had agreed with the laborers for a denarius for the day, he sent them into his vineyard. And he went out about the third hour and saw others standing idle in the market place; and to those he said, 'You also go into the vineyard, and whatever is right I will give you.' And *so* they went. Again he went out about the sixth and the ninth hour, and did the same thing. And about the eleventh *hour* he went out and found others standing *around;* and he said to them, 'Why have you been standing idle here all day long?' They said to him, 'Because no one hired us.' He said to them, 'You go into the vineyard too.' When evening came, the owner of the vineyard said to his foreman, 'Call the laborers and pay them their wages, beginning with the last *group* to the first.' When those *hired* about the eleventh hour came, each one received a denarius. When those *hired* first came, they thought that they would receive more; but each of them also received a denarius. When they received it, they grumbled at the landowner, saying, 'These

last men have worked *only* one hour, and you have made them equal to us who have borne the burden and the scorching heat of the day.' But he answered and said to one of them, 'Friend, I am doing you no wrong; did you not agree with me for a denarius? Take what is yours and go, but I wish to give to this last man the same as to you. It is not lawful for me to do what I wish with what is my own? Or is your eye envious because I am generous?' So the last shall be first, and the first last" (Matthew 20:1–16; cf. Matthew 19:30).

Setting: The island of Patmos (in the Aegean Sea about fifty miles southwest of Ephesus in modern Turkey). On the Lord's Day (Sunday), about fifty years after Jesus' resurrection, the disciple John encounters the Lord Jesus Christ. Jesus communicates a new revelation for the apostle to record for the church in Thyatira and to six other churches in Asia.

"And to the angel of the church in Thyatira write: The Son of God, who has eyes like a flame of fire, and His feet are like burnished bronze, says this: 'I know your deeds, and your love and faith and service and perseverance, and that your deeds of late are greater than at first. But I have *this* against you, that you tolerate the woman Jezebel, who calls herself a prophetess, and she teaches and leads My bond-servants astray so that they commit *acts of* immorality and eat things sacrificed to idols. I gave her time to repent, and she does not want to repent of her immorality. Behold, I will throw her on a bed *of sickness,* and those who commit adultery with her into great tribulation, unless they repent of her deeds. And I will kill her children with pestilence, and all the churches will know that I am He who searches the minds and hearts; and I will give to each one of you according to your deeds. But I say to you, the rest who are in Thyatira, who do not hold this teaching, who have not known the deep things of Satan, as they call them—I place no other burden on you. Nevertheless what you have, hold fast until I come. He who overcomes, and he who keeps My deeds until the end, TO HIM I WILL GIVE AUTHORITY OVER THE NATIONS; AND HE SHALL RULE THEM WITH A ROD OF IRON, AS THE VESSELS OF THE POTTER ARE BROKEN TO PIECES, as I also have received *authority* from My Father; and I will give him the morning star. He who has an ear, let him hear what the Spirit says to the churches' (Revelation 2:18–29; Jesus quotes from Psalm 2:8, 9; Isaiah 30:14; see 1 Kings 16:31; Psalm 7:9; Romans 2:5; 1 Corinthians 2:10; 2 Peter 3:9; Revelation 1:14; 2:7; 3:11; 17:1–20).

BURDENS (BURDENS, HEAVY is a separate entry; also see BURDEN; BURDENED; and HEAVY-LADEN)

Setting: On the way from Galilee to Jerusalem. After Jesus pronounces woes upon the Pharisees, a lawyer replies that His remarks insult lawyers, too.

But He said, "Woe to you lawyers as well! For you weigh men down with burdens hard to bear, while you yourselves will not even touch the burdens with one of your fingers. Woe to you! For you build the tombs of the prophets, and it was your fathers who killed them. So you are witnesses and approve the deeds of your fathers; because it was they who killed them, and you build their tombs. For this reason also the wisdom of God said, 'I will send them prophets and apostles, and some of them they will kill and some they will persecute, so that the blood of all the prophets, shed since the foundation of the world, may be charged against this generation, from the blood of Abel to the blood of Zechariah, who was killed between the altar and the house of God; yes, I tell you, it shall be charged against this generation.' Woe to you lawyers! For you have taken away the key of knowledge; you yourselves did not enter, and you hindered those who were entering" (Luke 11:46–52; cf. Matthew 23:29–32; see 2 Chronicles 24:20, 21; Matthew 23:4, 13).

BURDENS, HEAVY (Also see BURDEN; and HEAVY-LADEN)

Setting: The temple in Jerusalem. After the Jewish religious leaders test Him with questions, Jesus exposes the truth about Pharisaism to the crowds and His disciples.

Then Jesus spoke to the crowds and to His disciples, saying: "The scribes and the Pharisees have seated themselves in the chair of Moses; therefore all that they tell you, do and observe, but do not do according to their deeds; for they say *things* and do not do *them.* They tie up heavy burdens and lay them on men's shoulders, but they themselves are unwilling to move them with *so much as* a finger. But they do all their deeds to be noticed by men; for they broaden their phylacteries and lengthen their tassels *of their garments.* They love the place of honor at banquets and the chief seats in the synagogues, and respectful greetings in the market places, and being called Rabbi by men. But do not be called Rabbi; for One is your Teacher, and you are all brothers. Do not call *anyone* on earth your father; for One is your Father, He who is in heaven. Do not be called leaders; for One is your Leader, *that is,* Christ. But the greatest among you shall be your servant. Whoever exalts himself shall be humbled; and whoever humbles himself shall be exalted" (Matthew 23:1–12; cf. Matthew 20:26; Mark 12:38–40; Luke 20:46, 47; see Exodus 13:9; Deuteronomy 33:3; Matthew 6:1, 5, 6, 9, 16; Mark 14:11; Luke 11:43; 14:11).

BURGLARY (Also see ROBBER; ROBBERY; STEALING; and THEFT)

[BURGLARY from house to be broken into]

Setting: The Mount of Olives, just east of Jerusalem. During His discourse, after answering His disciples' questions as to when the temple will be destroyed and Jerusalem overrun, along with the signs of His coming and the end of the age, Jesus reemphasizes to His disciples that they should be on the alert for His return.

"Therefore be on the alert, for you do not know which day your Lord is coming. But be sure of this, that if the head of the house had known at what time of the night the thief was coming, he would have been on the alert and would not have allowed his house to be broken into. For this reason you also must be ready; for the Son of Man is coming at an hour when you do not think *He will.* Who then is the faithful and sensible slave whom his master put in charge of his household to give their food at the proper time? Blessed is that slave whom his master finds so doing when he comes. Truly I say to you that he will put him in charge of all his possessions. But if that evil slave says in his heart, 'My master is not coming for a long time,' and begins to beat his fellow slaves and eat and drink with drunkards; the master of that slave will come on a day when he does not expect *him* and at an hour which he does not know, and will cut him in pieces and assign him a place with the hypocrites; in that place there will be weeping and gnashing of teeth" (Matthew 24:42–51; cf. Mark 13:33–37; Luke 12:39–46; 21:34–36; see Matthew 8:11, 12; 25:21–23).

[BURGLARY from house to be broken into]

Setting: On the way from Galilee to Jerusalem. After giving a parable about riches and greed, Jesus uses a parable to challenge the crowd and His disciples to be ready for His return.

"Be dressed in readiness, and keep your lamps lit. Be like men who are waiting for their master when he returns from the wedding feast, so that they may immediately open the door to him when he comes and knocks. Blessed are those slaves whom the master will find on the alert when he comes; truly I say to you, that he will gird himself to serve, and have them recline at the table, and will come up and wait on them. Whether he comes in the second watch, or even in the third and finds them so, blessed are those slaves. But be sure of this, that if the head of the house had known at what hour the thief was coming, he would not have allowed his house to be broken into. You too, be ready; for the Son of Man is coming at an hour that you do not expect" (Luke 12:35–40; cf. Matthew 24:42–44; see Mark 13:33; Ephesians 6:14).

BURIAL (Also see DEATH; and DIRGE)

Setting: The home of Simon the Leper in Bethany. Jesus rebukes His disciples after they criticize a woman for pouring a vial of costly perfume on Jesus' head in preparation for His burial.

But Jesus, aware of this, said to them, "Why do you bother the woman? For she has done a good deed to Me. For you always have the poor with you; but you do not always have Me. For when she poured this perfume on My body, she did it to prepare Me for burial. Truly I say to you, wherever this gospel is preached in the whole world, what this woman has done will also be spoken of in memory of her" (Matthew 26:10–13; cf. Mark 14:3–9; Luke 7:37–39; John 12:2–8; see Deuteronomy 15:11).

Setting: The home of Simon the leper in Bethany. Two days before the Feast of Unleavened Bread (Passover), Jesus commends a woman who anoints His head with costly perfume, which some thought should have been sold and the proceeds given to the poor.

But Jesus said, "Let her alone; why do you bother her? She has done a good deed to Me. For you always have the poor with you, and whenever you wish you can do good to them; but you do not always have Me. She has done what she could; she has anointed My body beforehand for the burial. Truly I say to you, wherever the gospel is preached in the whole world, what this woman has done will also be spoken of in memory of her" (Mark 14:6–9; cf. Matthew 26:6–13; John 12:2–8; see Deuteronomy 15:11).

Setting: Bethany near Jerusalem. Six days before the Passover in Jerusalem, as the chief priests and Pharisees plot to seize Him, Jesus visits Lazarus, Martha and Mary. Mary anoints the Lord's feet with costly perfume made of pure nard.

Therefore Jesus said, "Let her alone, so that she may keep it for the day of My burial. For you always have the poor with you, but you do not always have Me" (John 12:7–8; cf. Matthew 26:6–13; Mark 14:3–9; see Deuteronomy 15:11).

BURNING BUSH (Listed as BUSH, BURNING)

BUSH, BRIAR

Setting: Galilee. After selecting His twelve disciples, Jesus teaches the Beatitudes (part of the Sermon on the Mount) to His disciples and a great throng of people from Judea, Jerusalem, and the central coastal region of Tyre and Sidon.

And He also spoke a parable to them: "A blind man cannot guide a blind man, can he? Will they not both fall into a pit? A pupil is not above his teacher; but everyone, after he has been fully trained, will be like his teacher. Why do you look at the speck that is in your brother's eye, but do not notice the log that is in your own eye? Or how can you say to your brother, 'Brother, let me take out the speck that is in your eye,' when you yourself do not see the log that is in your own eye? You hypocrite, first take the log out of your own eye, and then you will see clearly to take out the speck that is in your brother's eye. For there is no good tree which produces bad fruit, nor, on the other hand, a bad tree which produces good fruit. For each tree is known by its own fruit. For men do not gather figs from thorns, nor do they pick grapes from a briar bush. The good man out of the good treasure of his heart brings forth what is good; and the evil man out of the evil treasure brings forth what is evil; for his mouth speaks from that which fills his heart" (Luke 6:39–45; cf. Matthew 7:3–6. 16, 18, 20; 12:35; see Matthew 10:24; 15:14; Luke 6:12–19).

BUSH, BURNING

Setting: The temple in Jerusalem. After some of the Pharisees and Herodians attempt to trap Jesus in a statement, some Sadducees question Him about the status of marriage after death.

Jesus said to them, "Is this not the reason you are mistaken, that you do not understand the Scriptures or the power of God? For when they rise from the dead, they neither marry nor are given in marriage, but are like angels in heaven. But regarding the fact that the dead rise again, have you not read in the book of Moses, in the *passage* about *the burning* bush, how God spoke to him, saying, 'I AM THE GOD OF ABRAHAM, AND THE GOD OF ISAAC, and the God of Jacob?' He is not the God of the dead, but of the living; you are greatly mistaken" (Mark 12:24–27, Jesus quotes from Exodus 3:6; cf. Matthew 22:29–33; Luke 20:34–40).

Setting: The temple in Jerusalem. While ministering a few days before His crucifixion, after the scribes and Pharisees seek to trap Jesus by questioning Him about paying taxes to Caesar, some Sadducees (who say there is no resurrection) ask Him a question about the resurrection.

Jesus said to them, "The sons of this age marry and are given in marriage, but those who are considered worthy to attain to that age and the resurrection from the dead, neither marry nor are given in marriage; for they cannot even die anymore, because they are like angels, and are sons of God, being sons of the resurrection. But that the dead are raised, even Moses showed, in the passage about the burning bush, where he calls the Lord THE GOD OF ABRAHAM, AND THE GOD OF ISAAC, AND THE GOD OF JACOB. Now He is not the God of the dead but of the living; for all live to Him" (Luke 20:34–38, Jesus quotes from Exodus 3:6; cf. Matthew 22:23–32; Mark 12:18–27).

BUSINESS (Also see PLACES, MARKET)

Setting: The temple in Jerusalem. Jesus speaks another parable to the chief priests and elders after they question His authority.

Jesus spoke to them again in parables, saying, "The kingdom of heaven may be compared to a king who gave a wedding feast for his son. And he sent out his slaves to call those who had been invited to the wedding feast, and they were unwilling to come.

Again he sent out other slaves saying, 'Tell those who have been invited, "Behold, I have prepared my dinner; my oxen and my fattened livestock are *all* butchered and everything is ready; come to the wedding feast." But they paid no attention and went their way, one to his own farm, another to his business, and the rest seized his slaves and mistreated them and killed them. But the king was enraged, and he sent his armies and destroyed those murderers and set their city on fire. Then he said to his slaves, 'The wedding is ready, but those who were invited were not worthy. 'Go therefore to the main highways, and as many as you find *there,* invite to the wedding feast.' Those slaves went out into the streets and gathered together all they found, both evil and good; and the wedding hall was filled with dinner guests. But when the king came in to look over the dinner guests, he saw a man there who was not dressed in wedding clothes, and he said to him, 'Friend, how did you come in here without wedding clothes?' And the man was speechless. Then the king said to the servants, 'Bind him hand and foot, and throw him into the outer darkness; in that place there will be weeping and gnashing of teeth.' For many are called, but few *are* chosen" (Matthew 22:1–14; cf. Matthew 8:11, 12).

Setting: Jericho, on the way to Jerusalem. After commending Zaccheus's faith in Him, Jesus provides a parable about stewardship.

So He said, "A nobleman went to a distant country to receive a kingdom for himself, and then return. And he called ten of his slaves, and gave them ten minas and said to them, 'Do business with this until I come back.' But his citizens hated him and sent a delegation after him, saying, 'We do not want this man to reign over us.' When he returned, after receiving the kingdom, he ordered that these slaves, to whom he had given the money, be called to him so that he might know what business they had done. The first appeared, saying, 'Master, your mina has made ten minas more.' And he said to him, 'Well done, good slave, because you have been faithful in a very little thing, you are to be in authority over ten cities.' The second came, saying, 'Your mina, master, has made five minas.' And he said to him, also, 'And you are to be over five cities.' Another came, saying, 'Master, here is your mina, which I kept put away in a handkerchief; for I was afraid of you, because you are an exacting man; you take up what you did not lay down and reap what you did not sow.' He said to him, 'By your own words I will judge you, you worthless slave. Did you know that I am an exacting man, taking up what I did not lay down and reaping what I did not sow? Then why did you not put my money in the bank, and having come, I would have collected it with interest?' Then he said to the bystanders, 'Take the mina away from him and give it to the one who has the ten minas.' And they said to him, 'Master, he has ten minas already.' I tell you that to everyone who has, more shall be given, but from the one who does not have, even what he does have shall be taken away. But these enemies of mine, who did not want me to reign over them, bring them here and slay them in my presence" (Luke 19:12–27; cf. Matthew 25:14–30; see Matthew 13:12; Luke 16:10).

Setting: The temple in Jerusalem. After beginning His ministry in Galilee by selecting His disciples and performing a miracle at a wedding in Cana, Jesus attends the Passover of the Jews, and confronts those perverting the temple for business.

And He made a scourge of cords, and drove them all out of the temple, with the sheep and the oxen; and He poured out the coins of the money changers and overturned their tables; and to those who were selling the doves He said, "Take these things away; stop making My Father's house a place of business" (John 2:15, 16; cf. Matthew 21:12, 13; see Deuteronomy 16:1–6; John 1:11–14, 17).

BUSINESS, MIND YOUR OWN

[MIND YOUR OWN BUSINESS from what *is that* to you]

Setting: By the Sea of Galilee. During His third post-resurrection appearance to His disciples, after quizzing Peter regarding his love for Him, Jesus responds to Peter's inquiry about the future of John the disciple.

Jesus said to him, "If I want him to remain until I come, what *is that* to you? You follow Me!" Therefore this saying went out among the brethren that that disciple would not die; yet Jesus did not say to him that he would not die, but *only*, "If I want him to remain until I come, what *is that* to you?" (John 21:22, 23; see Matthew 8:22; 16:27).

BYSTANDERS

Setting: Jericho, on the way to Jerusalem. After commending Zaccheus's faith in Him, Jesus provides a parable about stewardship.

So He said, "A nobleman went to a distant country to receive a kingdom for himself, and then return. And he called ten of his slaves, and gave them ten minas and said to them, 'Do business with this until I come back.' But his citizens hated him and sent a delegation after him, saying, 'We do not want this man to reign over us.' When he returned, after receiving the kingdom, he ordered that these slaves, to whom he had given the money, be called to him so that he might know what business they had done. The first appeared, saying, 'Master, your mina has made ten minas more.' And he said to him, 'Well done, good slave, because you have been faithful in a very little thing, you are to be in authority over ten cities.' The second came, saying, 'Your mina, master, has made five minas.' And he said to him, also, 'And you are to be over five cities.' Another came, saying, 'Master, here is your mina, which I kept put away in a handkerchief; for I was afraid of you, because you are an exacting man; you take up what you did not lay down and reap what you did not sow.' He said to him, 'By your own words I will judge you, you worthless slave. Did you know that I am an exacting man, taking up what I did not lay down and reaping what I did not sow? Then why did you not put my money in the bank, and having come, I would have collected it with interest?' Then he said to the bystanders, 'Take the mina away from him and give it to the one who has the ten minas.' And they said to him, 'Master, he has ten minas already.' I tell you that to everyone who has, more shall be given, but from the one who does not have, even what he does have shall be taken away. But these enemies of mine, who did not want me to reign over them, bring them here and slay them in my presence" (Luke 19:12–27; cf. Matthew 25:14–30; see Matthew 13:12; Luke 16:10).

C

CAESAR/CAESAR'S

Setting: The temple in Jerusalem. While Jesus teaches, the Pharisees send their disciples and the Herodians to test Jesus about the poll-tax, in order to trap Him.

But Jesus perceived their malice, and said, "Why are you testing Me, you hypocrites? Show Me the coin *used* for the poll-tax." And they brought Him a denarius. And He said to them, "Whose likeness and inscription is this?" They said to Him, "Caesar's." Then He said to them, "Then render to Caesar the things that are Caesar's; and to God the things that are God's" (Matthew 22:18–21; cf. Matthew 17:25; Mark 12:15–17; Luke 20:22–25).

Setting: The temple in Jerusalem. After Jesus teaches the chief priests, scribes, and elders in parables, they send some of the Pharisees and Herodians in an attempt to trap Him in a statement.

"Shall we pay or shall we not pay?" But He, knowing their hypocrisy, said to them, "Why are you testing Me? Bring Me a denarius to look at." They brought *one.* And He said to them, "Whose likeness and inscription is this?" And they said to Him, "Caesar's." And Jesus said to them, "Render to Caesar the things that are Caesar's, and to God the things that are God's." And they were amazed at Him (Mark 12:15–17; cf. Matthew 22:15–22; Luke 20:20–26).

Setting: The temple in Jerusalem. A few days before His crucifixion, after Jesus conveys the Parable of the Vine-Growers to the people, the scribes and Pharisees seek to trap Him by questioning Him about paying taxes to Caesar.

But He detected their trickery and said to them, "Show Me a denarius. Whose likeness and inscription does it have?" They said "Caesar's." And He said to them, "Then render to Caesar the things that are Caesar's, and to God the things that are God's" (Luke 20:23–25; cf. Matthew 22:15–21; Mark 12:13–17).

CAIAPHAS (Also see HIGH PRIEST)

[CAIAPHAS from he who delivered Me to you]

Setting: Jerusalem. Pontius Pilate (Roman governor of Judea) continues to find no guilt in Jesus, but has Him scourged in an attempt to appease the hostile Jewish religious leaders, and seeks more information as to where the King of the Jews is from.

Jesus answered, "You would have no authority over Me, unless it had been given you from above; for this reason he who delivered Me to you has *the* greater sin" (John 19:11; see Romans 13:1).

CALF, FATTENED

Setting: On the way from Galilee to Jerusalem. Jesus conveys the Parable of The Prodigal Son, because the Pharisees and scribes complain He associates with tax collectors and sinners.

And He said, "A man had two sons. The younger of them said to his father, 'Father, give me the share of the estate that falls to me.' So he divided his wealth between them. And not many days later, the younger son gathered everything together and went on a journey into a distant country, and there he squandered his estate with loose living. Now when he had spent everything, a severe famine occurred in that country, and he began to be impoverished. So he went and hired himself out to one of the citizens of that country, and he sent him into his fields to feed swine. And he would have gladly filled his stomach with the pods that the swine were eating, and no one was giving anything to him. But when he came to his senses, he said, 'How many of my father's hired men have more than enough bread, but I am dying here with hunger! I will get up and go to my father, and will say to him, "Father, I have sinned against heaven, and in your sight; I am no longer worthy to be called your son; make me as one of your hired men."' So he got up and came to his father. But while he was still a long way off, his father saw him and felt compassion for him, and ran and embraced him and kissed him. And the son said to him, "Father, I have sinned against heaven and in your sight; I am no longer worthy to be called your son.' But the father said to his slaves, 'Quickly bring out the best robe and put it on him, and put a ring on his hand and sandals on his feet; and bring the fattened calf, kill it, and let us eat and celebrate; for this son of mine was dead and has come to life again; he was lost and has been found.' And they began to celebrate. Now his older son was in the field, when he came and approached the house, he heard music and dancing. And he summoned one of the servants and began inquiring what these things could be. And he said to him, 'Your brother has come, and your father has killed the fattened calf because he has received him back safe and sound.' But he became angry and was not willing to go in; and his father came out and began pleading with him. But he answered and said to his father, 'Look! For so many years I have been serving you and I have never neglected a command of yours; and yet you have never given me a young goat, so that I might celebrate with my friends; but when this son of yours came, who has devoured your wealth with prostitutes, you killed the fattened calf for him.' And he said to him, 'Son, you have always been with me, and all that is mine is yours. But we had to celebrate and rejoice, for this brother of yours was dead and has begun to live, and was lost and has been found'" (Luke 15:11–32; see Proverbs 29:2; Luke 15:1, 2).

CALL/CALLS (Also see CALLED)

Setting: Capernaum near the Sea of Galilee. While in the home of Levi (Matthew), Jesus calls him to be His disciple.

But when Jesus heard this, He said, "It is not those who are healthy who need a physician, but those who are sick. But go and learn what this means: 'I DESIRE COMPASSION, AND NOT SACRIFICE,' for I did not come to call the righteous, but sinners" (Matthew 9:12, 13, Jesus quotes from Hosea 6:6; cf. Mark 2:17; Luke 5:31, 32; see Mark 2:15, 16).

Setting: Galilee. After praising John the Baptist as His forerunner, Jesus demonstrates the foolish thinking of the current generation of Jewish religious leaders by repeating what they say about John's ascetic lifestyle and ministry along with His own.

"But to what shall I compare this generation? It is like children sitting in the market places, who call out to the other *children,* and say, 'We played the flute for you, and you did not dance; we sang a dirge, and you did not mourn.' For John came neither eating nor drinking, and they say, 'He has a demon!' The Son of Man came eating and drinking, and they say, 'Behold, a gluttonous man and a drunkard, a friend of tax collectors and sinners! Yet wisdom is vindicated by her deeds" (Matthew 11:16–19; cf. Luke 7:31–35; see Matthew 9:11, 34; Luke 1:15).

Setting: Judea beyond the Jordan (Perea). Jesus illustrates the kingdom of heaven to His disciples through the story of laborers in the vineyard.

"For the kingdom of heaven is like a landowner who went out early in the morning to hire laborers for his vineyard. When he had agreed with the laborers for a denarius for the day, he sent them into his vineyard. And he went out about the third hour and saw others standing idle in the market place; and to those he said, 'You also go into the vineyard, and whatever is right I will give you.' And *so* they went. Again he went out about the sixth and the ninth hour, and did the same thing. And about the eleventh *hour* he went out and found others standing *around;* and he said to them, 'Why have you been standing idle here all day long?' They said to him, 'Because no one hired us.' He said to them, 'You go into the vineyard too.' When evening came, the owner of the vineyard said to his foreman, 'Call the laborers and pay them their wages, beginning with the last *group* to the first.' When those *hired* about the eleventh hour came, each one received a denarius. When those *hired* first came, they thought that they would receive more; but each of them also received a denarius. When they received it, they grumbled at the landowner, saying, 'These last men have worked *only* one hour, and you have made them equal to us who have borne the burden and the scorching heat of the day.' But he answered and said to one of them, 'Friend, I am doing you no wrong; did you not agree with me for a denarius? Take what is yours and go, but I wish to give to this last man the same as to you. It is not lawful for me to do what I wish with

what is my own? Or is your eye envious because I am generous?' So the last shall be first, and the first last" (Matthew 20:1–16; cf. Matthew 19:30).

Setting: The temple in Jerusalem. Jesus speaks another parable to the chief priests and elders after they question His authority.

Jesus spoke to them again in parables, saying, "The kingdom of heaven may be compared to a king who gave a wedding feast for his son. And he sent out his slaves to call those who had been invited to the wedding feast, and they were unwilling to come. Again he sent out other slaves saying, 'Tell those who have been invited, "Behold, I have prepared my dinner; my oxen and my fattened livestock are *all* butchered and everything is ready; come to the wedding feast." But they paid no attention and went their way, one to his own farm, another to his business, and the rest seized his slaves and mistreated them and killed them. But the king was enraged, and he sent his armies and destroyed those murderers and set their city on fire. Then he said to his slaves, 'The wedding is ready, but those who were invited were not worthy. 'Go therefore to the main highways, and as many as you find *there,* invite to the wedding feast.' Those slaves went out into the streets and gathered together all they found, both evil and good; and the wedding hall was filled with dinner guests. But when the king came in to look over the dinner guests, he saw a man there who was not dressed in wedding clothes, and he said to him, 'Friend, how did you come in here without wedding clothes?' And the man was speechless. Then the king said to the servants, 'Bind him hand and foot, and throw him into the outer darkness; in that place there will be weeping and gnashing of teeth.' For many are called, but few *are* chosen" (Matthew 22:1–14; cf. Matthew 8:11, 12).

Setting: The temple in Jerusalem. Following the Sadducees' and Pharisees' unsuccessful attempts to test Him with questions, with the crowds listening, Jesus poses a question to some of the Pharisees.

"What do you think about the Christ, whose son is He?" They said to Him, "The *son* of David." He said to them, "Then how does David in the Spirit call Him 'Lord,' saying, 'THE LORD SAID TO MY LORD, SIT AT MY RIGHT HAND, UNTIL I PUT YOUR ENEMIES BENEATH YOUR FEET"'? "If David then calls Him 'Lord," how is He his son?" (Matthew 22:42–45; Jesus quotes from Psalm 110:1; cf. Mark 12:35–37; Luke 20:41–44; see 2 Samuel 23:2).

Setting: The temple in Jerusalem. Jesus exposes the truth about Pharisaism to the crowds and His disciples after the Jewish religious leaders test Him with questions.

Then Jesus spoke to the crowds and to His disciples, saying: "The scribes and the Pharisees have seated themselves in the chair of Moses; therefore all that they tell you, do and observe, but do not do according to their deeds; for they say *things* and do not do *them.* They tie up heavy burdens and lay them on men's shoulders, but they themselves are unwilling to move them with *so much as* a finger. But they do all their deeds to be noticed by men; for they broaden their phylacteries and lengthen their tassels *of their garments.* They love the place of honor at banquets and the chief seats in the synagogues, and respectful greetings in the market places, and being called Rabbi by men. But do not be called Rabbi; for One is your Teacher, and you are all brothers. Do not call *anyone* on earth your father; for One is your Father, He who is in heaven. Do not be called leaders; for One is your Leader, *that is,* Christ. But the greatest among you shall be your servant. Whoever exalts himself shall be humbled; and whoever humbles himself shall be exalted" (Matthew 23:1–12; cf. Matthew 20:26; Mark 12:38–40; Luke 20:46, 47; see Exodus 13:9; Deuteronomy 33:3; Matthew 6:1, 5, 6, 9, 16; Mark 14:11; Luke 11:43; 14:11).

Setting: The home of Levi (Matthew) in Capernaum by the Sea of Galilee. The scribes of the Pharisees question Jesus' association with sinners and tax collectors after He calls Levi (Matthew) the tax collector to be His disciple.

And hearing *this,* Jesus said to them, "*It is* not those who are healthy who need a physician, but those who are sick; I did not come to call the righteous, but sinners" (Mark 2:17; cf. Matthew 9:12, 13; Luke 5:29–32).

Setting: Judea beyond the Jordan (Perea). After demonstrating to His disciples the importance of little children, Jesus encounters a rich man seeking eternal life.

And Jesus said to him, "Why do you call Me good? No one is good except God alone. You know the commandments, 'DO NOT MURDER, DO NOT COMMIT ADULTERY, DO NOT STEAL, DO NOT BEAR FALSE WITNESS, Do not defraud, HONOR YOUR FATHER AND MOTHER.'" And he said to Him, "Teacher, I have kept all these things from my youth up." Looking at him, Jesus felt a love for him and said to him, "One thing you lack: go and sell all you possess and give to the poor, and you will have treasure in heaven; and come, follow Me" (Mark 10:18–21; Jesus quotes from Exodus 20:12–16; cf. Matthew 19:16–22; Luke 18:18–24; see Matthew 6:20).

Setting: Jericho, on the way to Jerusalem. A blind beggar named Bartimaeus cries out to Jesus for healing.

And Jesus stopped and said, "Call him *here*." So they called the blind man, saying to him, "Take courage, stand up! He is calling for you." Throwing aside his cloak, he jumped up and came to Jesus. And answering him, Jesus said, "What do you want Me to do for you?" And the blind man said to him, "Rabboni, *I want* to regain my sight!" And Jesus said to him, "Go; your faith has made you well." Immediately he regained his sight and *began* following Him on the road (Mark 10:49–52; cf. Matthew 20:29–34; Luke 18:35–43; see Matthew 9:2, 22).

Setting: The temple in Jerusalem. Jesus teaches the crowd after commending a scribe for his nearness to the kingdom of God.

And Jesus *began* to say, as He taught in the temple, "How *is it that* the scribes say that the Christ is the son of David? David himself said in the Holy Spirit, 'THE LORD SAID TO MY LORD, SIT AT MY RIGHT HAND, UNTIL I PUT YOUR ENEMIES BENEATH YOUR FEET.'" David himself calls Him 'Lord'; so in what sense is He his son?" And the large crowd enjoyed listening to Him (Mark 12:35–37, Jesus quotes from Psalm 110:1; cf. Matthew 22:41–46; Luke 20:41–44).

Setting: The home of Levi (Matthew) in Capernaum. At a reception for Jesus, after He calls Levi (Matthew) to become His disciple, the Pharisees and their scribes ask Jesus why He associates with tax collectors and sinners.

And Jesus answered and said to them, "It is not those who are well who need a physician, but those who are sick. I have not come to call the righteous but sinners to repentance" (Luke 5:31, 32; cf. Matthew 9:10–13; Mark 2:15–17).

Setting: Galilee. After selecting His twelve disciples, Jesus teaches the Beatitudes (part of the Sermon on the Mount) to His disciples and a great throng of people from Judea, Jerusalem, and the central coastal region of Tyre and Sidon.

"Why do you call Me, 'Lord, Lord,' and do not do what I say? Everyone who comes to Me and hears My words and acts on them, I will show you whom he is like; he is like a man building a house, who dug deep and laid a foundation on the rock; and when a flood occurred, the torrent burst against that house and could not shake it, because it had been well built. But the one who has heard and has not acted accordingly, is like a man who built a house on the ground without any foundation; and the torrent burst against it and immediately it collapsed, and the ruin of that house was great" (Luke 6:46–49; cf. Matthew 7:24–27; see Luke 6:12–19; James 1:22).

Setting: Galilee. Jesus praises John the Baptist to the crowds, then criticizes the Pharisees and lawyers who reject God's purpose and John's message.

"To what then shall I compare the men of this generation, and what are they like? They are like children who sit in the market place and call to one another, and they say, 'We played the flute for you, and you did not dance; we sang a dirge, and you did not weep.' For John the Baptist has come eating no bread and drinking no wine, and you say, 'He has a demon!' The Son of Man has come eating and drinking, and you say, 'Behold, a gluttonous man and a drunkard, a friend of tax collectors and sinners!' Yet wisdom is vindicated by all her children" (Luke 7:31–35; cf. Matthew 11:16–19; see Luke 1:15).

Setting: On the way from Galilee to Jerusalem. After Jesus presents to large crowds the demands of discipleship, the Pharisees and scribes complain He associates with tax collectors and sinners.

So He told them this parable, saying, "What man among you, if he has a hundred sheep and has lost one of them, does not leave the ninety-nine in the open pasture and go after the one which is lost until he finds it? When he has found it, he lays it on his shoulders, rejoicing. And when he comes home, he calls together his friends and his neighbors, saying to them, 'Rejoice with me, for I have found my sheep which was lost!' I tell you that in the same way, there will be more joy in heaven over one sinner who repents than over ninety-nine righteous persons who need no repentance" (Luke 15:3–7; cf. Matthew 18:12–14; see Matthew 9:11–13; Luke 5:29–32).

Setting: On the way from Galilee to Jerusalem. Jesus conveys the principles of the lost sheep and the lost coin because the Pharisees and scribes complain He associates with tax collectors and sinners.

"So He told them this parable, saying, "What man among you, if he has a hundred sheep and has lost one of them, does not leave the ninety-nine in the open pasture and go after the one which is lost until he finds it? When he has found it, he lays it on his shoulders, rejoicing. And when he comes home, he calls together his friends and his neighbors, saying to them, 'Rejoice with me, for I have found my sheep which was lost!' I tell you that in the same way, there will be *more* joy in heaven over one sinner who repents than over ninety-nine righteous persons who need no repentance. Or what woman, if she has ten silver coins and loses one coin, does not light a lamp and sweep the house and search carefully until she finds it? When she has found it, she calls together her friends and neighbors, saying, 'Rejoice with me, for I have found the coin which I had lost!' In the same way, I tell you, there is joy in the presence of the angels of God over one sinner who repents" (Luke 15:3–10; cf. Matthew 18:12-14; see Matthew 9:11-13).

Setting: On the way from Galilee to Jerusalem via Samaria. After speaking of the importance of children, Jesus responds to a ruler's question about inheriting eternal life.

A ruler questioned Him, saying, "Good Teacher, what shall I do to inherit eternal life?" And Jesus said to him, "Why do you call Me good? No one is good except God alone. You know the commandments, 'DO NOT COMMIT ADULTERY, DO NOT MURDER, DO NOT STEAL, DO NOT BEAR FALSE WITNESS, HONOR YOUR FATHER AND MOTHER.'" And he said, "All these things I have kept from my youth." When Jesus heard this, He said to him, "One thing you still lack; sell all that you possess and distribute it to the poor, and you shall have treasure in heaven; and come, follow Me" (Luke 18:18–22, Jesus quotes from Exodus 20:12–16; cf. Matthew 19:16–22; Mark 10:17–22; see Luke 10:25–28).

Setting: The temple in Jerusalem. A few days before Jesus' crucifixion, after the scribes and Pharisees seek to trap Him with questions about paying taxes to Caesar, some Sadducees (who say there is no resurrection) ask Him a question about the resurrection.

Jesus said to them, "The sons of this age marry and are given in marriage, but those who are considered worthy to attain to that age and the resurrection from the dead, neither marry nor are given in marriage; for they cannot even die anymore, because they are like angels, and are sons of God, being sons of the resurrection. But that the dead are raised, even Moses showed, in the passage about the burning bush, where he calls the Lord THE GOD OF ABRAHAM, AND THE GOD OF ISAAC, AND THE GOD OF JACOB. Now He is not the God of the dead but of the living; for all live to Him" (Luke 20:34–38, Jesus quotes from Exodus 3:6; cf. Matthew 22:23–32; Mark 12:18–27).

Setting: The temple in Jerusalem. A few days before His crucifixion, after some of the Sadducees question Him about the resurrection, Jesus poses a question to the scribes, who say He answered well.

Then He said to them, "How is it that they say the Christ is David's son? For David himself says in the book of Psalms, 'THE LORD SAID TO MY LORD, SIT AT MY RIGHT HAND, UNTIL I MAKE YOUR ENEMIES A FOOTSTOOL FOR YOUR FEET.' Therefore David calls Him 'Lord,' and how is He his son?" (Luke 20:41–44, Jesus quotes from Psalm 110:1; cf. Matthew 22:41–46; Mark 12:35–37).

Setting: Sychar in Samaria, on the way to Galilee. Jesus interacts with a Samaritan woman at Jacob's well while His disciples shop for food.

He said to her, "Go, call your husband and come here." The woman answered and said, "I have no husband." Jesus said to her, "You have correctly said, 'I have no husband'; for you have had five husbands, and the one whom you now have is not your husband; this you have said truly" (John 4:16–18; see John 6:35).

Setting: Jerusalem. Following the Pharisees' interrogation and dismissal of the formerly blind man Jesus healed on the Sabbath, the Lord speaks to the Pharisees using parabolic language they do not understand.

"Truly, truly, I say to you, he who does not enter by the door into the fold of the sheep, but climbs up some other way, he is a thief and a robber. But he who enters by the door is a shepherd of the sheep. To him the doorkeeper opens, and the sheep hear his voice, and he calls his own sheep by name and leads them out. When he puts forth all his own, he goes ahead of them, and the sheep follow him because they know his voice. A stranger they simply will not follow, but will flee from him, because they do not know the voice of strangers" (John 10:1–5; see John 10:6–8, 11, 16, 27).

Setting: An upper room in Jerusalem. Before the Passover meal, with His death on the cross nearing, Jesus explains to his disciples the reason for His vivid example of servanthood in washing their feet.

So when He had washed their feet, and taken His garments and reclined *at the table* again, He said to them, "Do you know what I have done to you? You call Me Teacher and Lord; and you are right, for *so* I am. If I then, the Lord and the Teacher, washed your feet, you also ought to wash one another's feet. For I gave you an example that you also should do as I did to you. Truly, truly I say to you, a slave is not greater than his master, nor *is* one who is sent greater than the one who sent him. If you know these things, you are blessed if you do them. I do not speak of all of you. I know the ones I have chosen; but *it is* that the Scripture may be fulfilled, 'HE WHO EATS MY BREAD HAS LIFTED UP HIS HEEL AGAINST ME.' From now on I am telling you before *it* comes to pass, so that when it does occur, you may believe that I am *He. Truly,* truly, I say to you, he who receives whomever I send receives Me; and he who receives Me receives Him who sent Me" (John 13:12–20; Jesus quotes from Psalm 41:9; see Matthew 7:24; 10:24, 40; John 8:24; 14:29; 1 Peter 5:3).

Setting: Jerusalem. Before the Passover, with His departure in mind, after explaining He is the vine and His disciples are the branches, Jesus informs them they should love one another.

"This is My commandment, that you love one another, just as I have loved you. Greater love has no one than this, that one lay down his life for his friends. You are My friends if you do what I command you. No longer do I call you slaves, for the slave does not know what his master is doing; but I have called you friends, for all things that I have heard from My Father I have made known to you. You did not choose Me but I chose you, and appointed you that you would go and bear fruit, and *that* your fruit would remain, so that whatever you ask of the Father in My name He may give to you. This I command you, that you love one another" (John 15:12–17; see Matthew 12:50; John 6:70; 8:26; 10:11; 13:34).

Setting: The island of Patmos (in the Aegean Sea about fifty miles southwest of Ephesus in modern Turkey). On the Lord's Day (Sunday), about fifty years after Jesus' resurrection, the disciple John encounters the Lord Jesus Christ. Jesus communicates a new revelation for the apostle to record for the church in Ephesus and to six other churches in Asia.

"To the angel of the church in Ephesus write: The One who holds the seven stars in His right hand, the One who walks among the seven golden lampstands, says this: 'I know your deeds and your toil and perseverance, and that you cannot tolerate evil men, and you put to the test those who call themselves apostles, and they are not, and you found them *to be* false; and you have perseverance and have endured for My name's sake, and have not grown weary. But I have *this* against you, that you have left your first love. Therefore remember from where you have fallen, and repent and do the deeds you did at first; or else I am coming to you and will remove your lampstand out of its place—unless you repent. Yet this you do have, that you hate the deeds of the Nicolaitans, which I also hate. He who has an ear, let him hear what the Spirit says to the churches. To him who overcomes, I will grant to eat of the tree of life which is in the Paradise of God'" (Revelation 2:1–7; see Genesis 2:9; Ezekiel 28:13; 1 John 4:1; Revelation 1:10, 11, 19, 20; 2:15, 16).

Setting: The island of Patmos (in the Aegean Sea about fifty miles southwest of Ephesus in modern Turkey). On the Lord's Day (Sunday), about fifty years after Jesus' resurrection, the disciple John encounters the Lord Jesus Christ. Jesus communicates a new revelation for the apostle to record for the church in Thyatira and to six other churches in Asia.

"And to the angel of the church in Thyatira write: The Son of God, who has eyes like a flame of fire, and His feet are like burnished bronze, says this: 'I know your deeds, and your love and faith and service and perseverance, and that your deeds of late are greater than at first. But I have this against you, that you tolerate the woman Jezebel, who calls herself a prophetess, and she teaches and leads My bond-servants astray so that they commit acts of immorality and eat things sacrificed to idols. I gave her time to repent, and she does not want to repent of her immorality. Behold, I will throw her on a bed of sickness, and those who commit adultery with her into great tribulation, unless they repent of her deeds. And I will kill her children with pestilence, and all the churches will know that I am He who searches the minds and hearts; and I will give to each one of you according to your deeds. But I say to you, the rest who are in Thyatira, who do not hold this teaching, who have not known the deep things of Satan, as they call them—I place no other burden on you. Nevertheless what you have, hold fast until I come. He who overcomes, and he who keeps My deeds until the end, TO HIM I WILL GIVE AUTHORITY OVER THE NATIONS; AND HE SHALL RULE THEM WITH A ROD OF IRON, AS THE VESSELS OF THE POTTER ARE BROKEN TO PIECES, as I also have received authority from My Father; and I will give him the morning star. He who has an ear, let him hear what the Spirit says to the churches' (Revelation 2:18–29; Jesus quotes from Psalm 2:8, 9; Isaiah 30:14; see 1 Kings 16:31; Psalm 7:9; Romans 2:5; 1 Corinthians 2:10; 2 Peter 3:9; Revelation 1:14; 2:7; 3:11; 17:1–20).

CALLED (Also see CALL/CALLS)

Setting: Galilee. Early in His ministry, Jesus presents the Beatitudes (part of the Sermon on the Mount) to His disciples and the gathered crowds from Galilee, Decapolis, Jerusalem, Judea, and beyond the Jordan.

"Blessed are the peacemakers, for they shall be called sons of God" (Matthew 5:9; see Matthew 5:1; 13:35).

Setting: Galilee. During the early part of His ministry, Jesus preaches the Sermon on the Mount to His disciples and the multitudes.

"Whoever then annuls one of the least of these commandments, and teaches others *to do* the same, shall be called least in the kingdom of heaven; but whoever keeps and teaches *them*, he shall be called great in the kingdom of heaven" (Matthew 5:19; cf. Matthew 11:11).

Setting: Galilee. After His disciples observe His ministry, Jesus summons and specifically instructs them about the difficulties ahead involving true discipleship.

"A disciple is not above his teacher, nor a slave above his master. It is enough for the disciple that he become like his teacher, and the slave like his master. If they have called the head of the house Beelzebul, how much more *will they malign* the members of his household!" (Matthew 10:24, 25; cf. Luke 6:40; see 2 Kings 1:2).

Setting: Jerusalem. After being welcomed with blessings from the crowds, Jesus cleanses the temple by driving out the money changers and merchants.

And He said to them, "It is written, 'MY HOUSE SHALL BE CALLED A HOUSE OF PRAYER'; but you are making it a ROBBERS' DEN" (Matthew 21:13; Jesus quotes from Isaiah 56:7; Jeremiah 7:11; cf. Mark 11:15–18; Luke 19:46).

Setting: The temple in Jerusalem. Jesus speaks another parable to the chief priests and elders after they question His authority.

Jesus spoke to them again in parables, saying, "The kingdom of heaven may be compared to a king who gave a wedding feast for his son. And he sent out his slaves to call those who had been invited to the wedding feast, and they were unwilling to come. Again he sent out other slaves saying, 'Tell those who have been invited, "Behold, I have prepared my dinner; my oxen and my fattened livestock are *all* butchered and everything is ready; come to the wedding feast." But they paid no attention and went their way, one to his own farm, another to his business, and the rest seized his slaves and mistreated them and killed them. But the king was enraged, and he sent his armies and destroyed those murderers and set their city on fire. Then he said to his slaves, 'The wedding is ready, but those who were invited were not worthy. 'Go therefore to the main highways, and as many as you find *there,* invite to the wedding feast.' Those slaves went out into the streets and gathered together all they found, both evil and good; and the wedding hall was filled with dinner guests. But when the king came in to look over the dinner guests, he saw a man there who was not dressed in wedding clothes, and he said to him, 'Friend, how did you come in here without wedding clothes?' And the man was speechless. Then the king said to the servants, 'Bind him hand and foot, and throw him into the outer darkness; in that place there will be weeping and gnashing of teeth.' For many are called, but few *are* chosen" (Matthew 22:1–14; cf. Matthew 8:11, 12).

Setting: The temple in Jerusalem. Jesus exposes the truth about Pharisaism to the crowds and His disciples after the Jewish religious leaders test Him with questions.

Then Jesus spoke to the crowds and to His disciples, saying: "The scribes and the Pharisees have seated themselves in the chair of Moses; therefore all that they tell you, do and observe, but do not do according to their deeds; for they say *things* and do not do *them.* They tie up heavy burdens and lay them on men's shoulders, but they themselves are unwilling to move them with *so much as* a finger. But they do all their deeds to be noticed by men; for they broaden their phylacteries and lengthen their tassels *of their garments.* They love the place of honor at banquets and the chief seats in the synagogues, and respectful greetings in the market places, and being called Rabbi by men. But do not be called Rabbi; for One is your Teacher, and you are all brothers. Do not call *anyone* on earth your father; for One is your Father, He who is in heaven. Do not be called leaders; for One is your Leader, *that is,* Christ. But the greatest among you shall be your servant. Whoever exalts himself shall be humbled; and whoever humbles himself shall be exalted" (Matthew 23:1–12; cf. Matthew 20:26; Mark 12:38–40; Luke 20:46, 47; see Exodus 13:9; Deuteronomy 33:3; Matthew 6:1, 5, 6, 9, 16; Mark 14:11; Luke 11:43; 14:11).

Setting: The Mount of Olives, just east of Jerusalem. During His discourse, after answering His disciples' questions as to when the temple will be destroyed and Jerusalem overrun, along with the signs of His coming and the end of the age, Jesus reemphasizes to His disciples that they should be on the alert for His return.

"For *it is* just like a man *about* to go on a journey, who called his own slaves and entrusted his possessions to them. To one he gave five talents, to another, two, and to another, one, each according to his own ability; and he went on his journey. Immediately the one who had received the five talents went and traded with them, and gained five more talents. In the same manner the one who *had received* the two *talents* gained two more. But he who received the one *talent* went away, and dug a *hole* in the ground and hid his master's money. Now after a long time the master of those slaves came and settled accounts with them. The one who had received the five talents came up and brought five more talents, saying, 'Master, you entrusted five talents to me. See, I have gained five more talents.' His master said to him, 'Well done, good and faithful slave. You were faithful with a few things, I will put you in charge of many things; enter into the joy of your master.' Also the one who *had received* the two talents came up and said, 'Master, you entrusted two talents to me. See, I have gained two more talents.' His master said to him, 'Well done, good and faithful slave. You were faithful with a few things, I will put you in charge of many things; enter into the joy of your master.' And the one also who had received the one talent came up and said, 'Master, I knew you to be a hard man, reaping where you did not sow and gathering where you scattered no *seed.* And I was afraid, and went away and hid your talent in the ground. See, you have what is yours.' But his master answered and said to him, 'You wicked, lazy slave, you knew that I reap where I did not sow and gather where I scattered no *seed.* Then you ought to have put my money in the bank, and on my arrival I would have received my *money* back with interest. 'Therefore take away the talent from him, and give it to the one who has ten talents.' For to everyone who has, *more* shall be given, and he will have an abundance; but from the one who does not have, even what he does have shall be taken away. Throw out the worthless slave into the outer darkness; in that place there will be weeping and gnashing of teeth" (Matthew 25:14–30; cf. Matthew 8:12; 13:12; 24:45–47; see Matthew 18:23, 24; Luke 12:44).

Setting: Jerusalem. Following His triumphal entry, cursing of a fig tree, and cleansing the temple of the money changers, Jesus rebukes the Jewish religious leaders for the corrupt practices they permit in His Father's house.

And He *began* to teach and say to them, "Is it not written, 'MY HOUSE SHALL BE CALLED A HOUSE OF PRAYER FOR ALL THE NATIONS'? But you have made it a ROBBERS' DEN" (Mark 11:17, Jesus quotes from Isaiah 56:7; Jeremiah 7:11; cf. Matthew 21:12, 13; Luke 19:45–48).

Setting: On the way from Galilee to Jerusalem. Jesus conveys the illustration of the prodigal son because the Pharisees and scribes complain He associates with tax collectors and sinners.

And He said, "A man had two sons. The younger of them said to his father, 'Father, give me the share of the estate that falls to me.' So he divided his wealth between them. And not many days later, the younger son gathered everything together and went on a journey into a distant country, and there he squandered his estate with loose living. Now when he had spent everything, a severe famine occurred in that country, and he began to be impoverished. So he went and hired himself out to one of the citizens of that country, and he sent him into his fields to feed swine. And he would have gladly filled his stomach with the pods that the swine were eating, and no one was giving anything to him. But when he came to his senses, he said, 'How many of my father's hired men have more than enough bread, but I am dying here with hunger! I will get up and go to my father, and will say to him, "Father, I have sinned against heaven, and in your sight; I am no longer worthy to be called your son; make me as one of your hired men."' So he got up and came to his father. But while he was still a long way off, his father saw him and felt compassion for him, and ran and embraced him and kissed him. And the son said to him, "Father, I have sinned against heaven and in your sight; I am no longer worthy to be called your son.' But the father said to his slaves, 'Quickly bring out the best robe and put it on him, and put a ring on his hand and sandals on his feet; and bring the fattened calf, kill it, and let us eat and celebrate; for this son of mine was dead and has come to life again; he was lost and has been found.' And they began to celebrate. Now his older son was in the field, when he came and approached the house, he heard music and dancing. And he summoned one of the servants and began inquiring what these things could be. And he said to him, 'Your brother has come, and your father has killed the fattened calf because he has received him back safe and sound.' But he became angry and was not willing to go in; and his father came out and began pleading with him. But he answered and said to his father, 'Look! For so many years I have been serving you and I have never neglected a command of yours; and yet you have never given me a young goat, so that I might celebrate with my friends; but when this son of yours came, who has devoured your wealth with prostitutes, you killed the fattened calf for him.' And he said to him, 'Son, you have always been with me, and all that is mine is yours. But we had to celebrate and rejoice, for this brother of yours was dead and has begun to live, and was lost and has been found'"(Luke 15:11–32; see Proverbs 29:2).

Setting: On the way from Galilee to Jerusalem. After giving the story of the Prodigal Son, the Lord teaches His disciples about stewardship.

Now He was also saying to the disciples, "There was a rich man who had a manager, and this manager was reported to him as squandering his possessions. And he called him and said to him, 'What is this I hear about you? Give an accounting of your management, for you can no longer be a manager.' The manager said to himself, 'What shall I do, since my master is taking the management away from me? I am not strong enough to dig; I am ashamed to beg. I know what I shall do, so that when I am removed from the management people will welcome me into their homes.' And he summoned each one of his master's debtors, and he began saying to the first, 'How much do you owe my master?' And he said, 'A hundred measures of oil.' And he said to him, 'Take your bill, and sit down quickly and write fifty.' Then he said to another, 'And how much do you owe?' And he said, 'A hundred measures of wheat.' He said to him, 'Take your bill, and write eighty.' And his master praised the unrighteous manager because he had acted shrewdly; for the sons of this age are more shrewd in relation to their own kind than the sons of light. And I say to you, make friends for yourselves by means of the wealth of unrighteousness, so that when it fails, they will receive you into the eternal dwellings. He who is faithful in a very little thing is faithful also in much; and he who is unrighteous in a very little thing is unrighteous also in much. Therefore if you have not been faithful in the use of unrighteous wealth, who will entrust the true riches to you? And if you have not been faithful in the use of that which is another's, who will give you that which is your own? No servant can serve two masters; for either he will hate the one and love the other, or else he will be devoted to one and despise the other. You cannot serve God and wealth" (Luke 16:1–13; cf. Matthew 6:24; see Matthew 25:14–30).

Setting: Jericho, on the way to Jerusalem. After commending Zaccheus's faith in Him, Jesus provides a parable about stewardship.

So He said, "A nobleman went to a distant country to receive a kingdom for himself, and then return. And he called ten of his slaves, and gave them ten minas and said to them, 'Do business with this until I come back.' But his citizens hated him and sent a delegation after him, saying, 'We do not want this man to reign over us.' When he returned, after receiving the kingdom, he ordered that these slaves, to whom he had given the money, be called to him so that he might know what business they had done. The first appeared, saying, 'Master, your mina has made ten minas more.' And he said to him, 'Well done, good slave, because you have been faithful in a very little thing, you are to be in authority over ten cities.' The second came, saying, 'Your mina, master, has made five minas.' And he said to him, also, 'And you are to be over five cities.' Another came, saying, 'Master, here is your mina, which I kept put away in a handkerchief; for I was afraid of you, because you are an exacting man; you take up what you did not lay down and reap what you did not sow.' He said to him, 'By your own words I will judge you, you worthless slave. Did you know that I am an exacting man, taking up what I did not lay down and reaping what I did not sow? Then why did you not put my money in the bank, and having come, I would have collected it with interest?' Then he said to the bystanders, 'Take the mina away from him and give it to the one who has the ten minas.' And they said to him, 'Master, he has ten minas already.' I tell you that to everyone who has, more shall be given, but from the one who does not have, even what he does have shall be taken away. But these enemies of mine, who did not want me to reign over them, bring them here and slay them in my presence" (Luke 19:12–27; cf. Matthew 25:14–30; see Matthew 13:12; Luke 16:10).

Setting: An upper room in Jerusalem. During the Feast of Unleavened Bread (Passover) just before Jesus' crucifixion, while Jesus celebrates the Passover meal with His disciples and institutes the Lord's Supper, the disciples argue over who is the greatest among them.

And He said to them, "The kings of the Gentiles lord it over them; and those who have authority over them are called 'Benefactors.' But it is not this way with you, but the one who is the greatest among you must become like the youngest, and the leader like a servant. For who is greater, the one who reclines at the table or the one who serves? Is it not the one who reclines at the table? But I am among you as the one who serves" (Luke 22:25–27; cf. Matthew 20:25–28; 23:11; Mark 10:42–45).

Setting: Bethany beyond the Jordan. After being baptized in the Jordan River, Jesus begins His public ministry and chooses His first disciples, Andrew and Simon (Peter), who believe He is the Messiah.

He brought him to Jesus. Jesus looked at him and said, "You are Simon the son of John; you shall be called Cephas" (which is translated Peter) (John 1:42).

Setting: Galilee. After beginning His public ministry and choosing His first disciples, Andrew and Simon (Peter) near Bethany beyond the Jordan, and Philip in Galilee, Jesus calls Philip's friend, Nathanael, (some believe he may have been also called Bartholomew) as His next follower.

Jesus saw Nathanael coming to Him, and said of him, "Behold, an Israelite indeed, in whom there is no deceit!" Nathanael said to Him, "How do you know me?" Jesus answered and said to him, "Before Philip called you, when you were under the fig tree, I saw you." Nathanael answered Him, "Rabbi, You are the Son of God; You are the King of Israel." Jesus answered and said to him, "Because I said to you that I saw you under the fig tree, do you believe? You will see greater things than these." And He said to him, "Truly, truly, I say to you, you will see the heavens opened and the angels of God ascending and descending on the Son of Man" (John 1:47–51).

Setting: Jerusalem. At the Feast of Dedication, the Pharisees desire to stone Jesus when He claims to be equal with God after they ask Him plainly whether He is the Christ.

Jesus answered them, "Has it not been written in your Law, 'I SAID, YOU ARE GODS'? If he called them gods, to whom the word of God came (and the Scripture cannot be broken), do you say of Him, whom the Father sanctified and sent into the world, 'You are blaspheming,' because I said, 'I am the Son of God'? If I do not do the works of My Father, do not believe Me; but if I do them, though you do not believe Me, believe the works, so that you may know and understand that the Father is in Me, and I in the Father" (John 10:34–38, Jesus quotes from Psalm 82:6; see John 14:10, 20).

Setting: Jerusalem. Before the Passover, with His departure in mind, after explaining He is the vine and His disciples are the branches, Jesus instructs them to love one another.

"This is My commandment, that you love one another, just as I have loved you. Greater love has no one than this, that one lay down his life for his friends. You are My friends if you do what I command you. No longer do I call you slaves, for the slave does not know what his master is doing; but I have called you friends, for all things that I have heard from My Father I have made known to you. You did not choose Me but I chose you, and appointed you that you would go and bear fruit, and *that* your fruit would remain, so that whatever you ask of the Father in My name He may give to you. This I command you, that you love one another" (John 15:12–17; see Matthew 12:50; John 6:70; 8:26; 10:11; 13:34).

CALLOUSNESS (See HEART, HARDNESS OF)

CALMING THE SEA (Listed under SEA, CALMING THE)

CALMING THE STORM (See SEA, CALMING THE)

CAMEL

Setting: Judea beyond the Jordan (Perea). Jesus comments to His disciples about the rich, young ruler who asked how he might obtain eternal life but rejected Jesus' instructions to sell his possessions and give the proceeds to the poor.

And Jesus said to His disciples, "Truly I say to you, it is hard for a rich man to enter the kingdom of heaven. Again, I say to you, it is easier for a camel to go through the eye of a needle, than for a rich man to enter the kingdom of God" (Matthew 19:23, 24; cf. Matthew 13:22; Mark 10:23–25; Luke 18:24).

Setting: The temple in Jerusalem. After the Jewish religious leaders test Him with questions, Jesus pronounces the fifth of eight woes on them in front of the crowds and His disciples.

"Woe to you, scribes and Pharisees, hypocrites! For you tithe mint and dill and cummin, and have neglected the weightier provisions of the law: justice and mercy and faithfulness; but these are things you should have done without neglecting the others. You blind guides, who strain out a gnat and swallow a camel!" (Matthew 23:23, 24).

Setting: Judea beyond the Jordan (Perea). After informing a rich man how righteous believers may have treasure in heaven, Jesus conveys to His disciples the difficulty the wealthy have entering the kingdom of God.

And Jesus, looking around, said to His disciples, "How hard it will be for those who are wealthy to enter the kingdom of God!" The disciples were amazed at His words. But Jesus answered again and said to them, "Children, how hard it is to enter the kingdom of God! It is easier for a camel to go through the eye of a needle than for a rich man to enter the kingdom of God." They were even more astonished and said to Him, "Then who can be saved?" Looking at them, Jesus said, "With people it is impossible, but not with God; for all things are possible with God" (Mark 10:23–27; cf. Matthew 19:23–26; Luke 18:24, 25).

Setting: Judea beyond the Jordan (Perea). After responding to a ruler's question about inheriting eternal life, Jesus comments to him about the challenge of being wealthy and saved.

And Jesus looked at him and said, "How hard it is for those who are wealthy to enter the kingdom of God! For it is easier for a camel to go through the eye of a needle than for a rich man to enter the kingdom of God" (Luke 18:24, 25; cf. Matthew 19:23, 24; Mark 10:25).

CAPERNAUM

Setting: Galilee. Having performed many miracles, Jesus pronounces woes against those cities who did not repent.

"Woe to you, Chorazin! Woe to you, Bethsaida! For if the miracles had occurred in Tyre and Sidon which occurred in you, they would have repented long ago in sackcloth and ashes. Nevertheless I say to you, it will be more tolerable for Tyre and Sidon in *the* day of judgment than for you. And you, Capernaum, will not be exalted to heaven, will you? You will descend to Hades; for if the miracles had occurred in Sodom which occurred in you, it would have remained to this day. Nevertheless, I say to you that it will be more tolerable for the land of Sodom in *the* day of judgment, than for you" (Matthew 11:21–24; cf. Matthew 10:15; Luke 10:13–15).

Setting: The synagogue in Jesus' hometown of Nazareth in Galilee. At the beginning of Jesus' public ministry, He comments to the congregation after reading on the Sabbath from the book of the prophet Isaiah.

And He said to them, "No doubt you will quote this proverb to Me, 'Physician, heal yourself! Whatever we heard was done at Capernaum, do here in your hometown as well.'" And He said, "Truly I say to you, no prophet is welcome in his hometown. But I say to you in truth, there were many widows in Israel in the days of Elijah, when the sky was shut up for three years and six months, when a great famine came over all the land; and yet Elijah was sent to none of them, but only to Zarephath, *in the land* of Sidon, to a woman who was a widow. And there were many lepers in Israel in the time of Elisha the prophet; and none of them was cleansed, but only Naaman the Syrian" (Luke 4:23–27; Jesus refers to 1 Kings 17:1, 9; 2 Kings 5:1–14; see Matthew 13:53–58).

Setting: On the way from Galilee to Jerusalem. The Lord pronounces woes on cities who reject the gospel as He appoints seventy followers and sends them out in pairs to every city and place He Himself will soon visit.

"Woe to you, Chorazin! Woe to you, Bethsaida! For if the miracles had been performed in Tyre and Sidon which occurred in you, they would have repented long ago, sitting in sackcloth and ashes. But it will be more tolerable for Tyre and Sidon in the judgment than for you. And you, Capernaum, will not be exalted to heaven, will you? You will be brought down to Hades! The one who listens to you listens to Me, and the one who rejects you rejects Me; and he who rejects Me rejects the One who sent Me" (Luke 10:13–16; cf. Matthew 11:21–23; see Matthew 10:40; Luke 10:1).

CAPTIVE (Also see CAPTIVES)

Setting: The Mount of Olives, just east of Jerusalem. During His discourse, after ministering in the temple a few days before His crucifixion, Jesus elaborates more about future events.

"But when you see Jerusalem surrounded by armies, then recognize that her desolation is near. Then those who are in Judea must flee to the mountains, and those who are in the midst of the city must leave, and those who are in the country must not enter the city; because these are days of vengeance, so that all things which are written will be fulfilled. Woe to those who are pregnant and to those who are nursing babies in those days; for there will be a great distress upon the land and wrath to this people; and they will fall by the edge of the sword, and will be led captive into all the nations; and Jerusalem will be trampled under foot by the Gentiles until the times of the Gentiles are fulfilled" (Luke 21:20–24; see Matthew 24:15–18; Mark 13:14–16; Luke 19:43).

CAPTIVES (Also see CAPTIVE)

Setting: The synagogue in Jesus' hometown of Nazareth in Galilee. At the beginning of Jesus' public ministry, He reads from the book of the prophet Isaiah on the Sabbath.

And the book of the prophet Isaiah was handed to Him. And He opened the book and found the place where it was written, "THE SPIRIT OF THE LORD IS UPON ME, BECAUSE HE ANOINTED ME TO PREACH THE GOSPEL TO THE POOR. HE HAS SENT ME TO PROCLAIM RELEASE TO THE CAPTIVES, AND RECOVERY OF SIGHT TO THE BLIND, TO SET FREE THOSE WHO ARE OPPRESSED, TO PROCLAIM THE FAVORABLE YEAR OF THE LORD." And He closed the book, gave it back to the attendant and sat down; and the eyes of all in the synagogue were fixed on Him. And He began to say to them, "Today this Scripture has been fulfilled in your hearing" (Luke 4:17–21, Jesus quotes from Isaiah 61:1, 2).

CARE, GOD'S (See PROVISION, GOD'S)

CARELESS WORD (Listed as WORD, CARELESS)

CASTING OUT DEMONS (Listed as DEMONS, CASTING OUT)

CASTRATED MAN (Listed under MAN, CASTRATED; also see CELIBACY; EUNUCH; and EUNUCHS)

CATCH (fish)

Setting: By the Sea of Galilee (Tiberias). After teaching the people from Simon's (Peter) boat, Jesus calls Peter, James, and John to follow Him. (This appears to be a permanent call, as Simon and other companions were with Him earlier in Mark 1:35–39 and Luke 4:38–39.)

When He had finished speaking, He said to Simon, "Put out into the deep water and let down your nets for a catch." ". . . and so also *were* James and John, sons of Zebedee, who were partners with Simon. And Jesus said to Simon, "Do not fear, from now on you will be catching men" (Luke 5:4, 10; see John 21:6).

Setting: By the Sea of Galilee (Tiberias). During His third post-resurrection appearance to His disciples, Jesus directs them to a great catch of fish following their unsuccessful night of fishing.

So Jesus said to them, "Children, you do not have any fish, do you?" They answered Him, "No." And He said to them, "Cast the net on the right-hand side of the boat and you will find a *catch*." So they cast, and then they were not able to haul it in because of the great number of fish (John 21:5, 6; see Luke 5:4).

[CATCH from caught]
Setting: By the Sea of Galilee. In His third post-resurrection appearance to His disciples, after providing a great catch of fish following their unsuccessful night of fishing, Jesus asks them to bring Him some of the fish.

Jesus said to them, "Bring some of the fish which you have now caught" (John 21:10).

CAUSE (Also see REASON)

Setting: Jerusalem. Before the Passover, with His departure in mind, after explaining He is the vine and His disciples are the branches, Jesus prepares them for future hatred by the world.

"He who hates Me hates My Father also. If I had not done among them the works which no one else did, they would not have sin; but now they have both seen and hated Me and My Father as well. But *they have done this* to fulfill the word that is written in their Law, 'THEY HATED ME WITHOUT A CAUSE'" (John 15:23–25, Jesus quotes from Psalm 35:19; see John 9:41).

Setting: Jerusalem. Luke, writing in Acts, presents Jesus' encouraging words to Paul in the Roman barracks following Paul's hearing before the Jewish Council and arrest by the Roman commander (after the apostle's third missionary journey).

But on the night *immediately* following, the Lord stood at his side and said, "Take courage; for as you have solemnly witnessed to My cause at Jerusalem, so you must witness at Rome also" (Acts 23:11; see Acts 19:21).

CELEBRATION (Also see BANQUETS; FEAST, WEDDING; and REJOICING)

[CELEBRATION from celebrate]
Setting: On the way from Galilee to Jerusalem. Jesus conveys the illustration of the prodigal son because the Pharisees and scribes complain He associates with tax collectors and sinners.

And He said, "A man had two sons. The younger of them said to his father, 'Father, give me the share of the estate that falls to me.' So he divided his wealth between them. And not many days later, the younger son gathered everything together and went

on a journey into a distant country, and there he squandered his estate with loose living. Now when he had spent everything, a severe famine occurred in that country, and he began to be impoverished. So he went and hired himself out to one of the citizens of that country, and he sent him into his fields to feed swine. And he would have gladly filled his stomach with the pods that the swine were eating, and no one was giving anything to him. But when he came to his senses, he said, 'How many of my father's hired men have more than enough bread, but I am dying here with hunger! I will get up and go to my father, and will say to him, "Father, I have sinned against heaven, and in your sight; I am no longer worthy to be called your son; make me as one of your hired men."' So he got up and came to his father. But while he was still a long way off, his father saw him and felt compassion for him, and ran and embraced him and kissed him. And the son said to him, "Father, I have sinned against heaven and in your sight; I am no longer worthy to be called your son.' But the father said to his slaves, 'Quickly bring out the best robe and put it on him, and put a ring on his hand and sandals on his feet; and bring the fattened calf, kill it, and let us eat and celebrate; for this son of mine was dead and has come to life again; he was lost and has been found.' And they began to celebrate. Now his older son was in the field, when he came and approached the house, he heard music and dancing. And he summoned one of the servants and began inquiring what these things could be. And he said to him, 'Your brother has come, and your father has killed the fattened calf because he has received him back safe and sound.' But he became angry and was not willing to go in; and his father came out and began pleading with him. But he answered and said to his father, 'Look! For so many years I have been serving you and I have never neglected a command of yours; and yet you have never given me a young goat, so that I might celebrate with my friends; but when this son of yours came, who has devoured your wealth with prostitutes, you killed the fattened calf for him.' And he said to him, 'Son, you have always been with me, and all that is mine is yours. But we had to celebrate and rejoice, for this brother of yours was dead and has begun to live, and was lost and has been found'" (Luke 15:11–32; see Proverbs 29:2; Luke 15:1, 2).

CELIBACY (Also see EUNUCHS)

[CELIBACY from there are *also* eunuchs who made themselves eunuchs for the sake of the kingdom of heaven]
Setting: Judea beyond the Jordan (Perea). After responding to the Pharisees' question about Moses' command regarding a certificate of divorce, Jesus answers a private question from His disciples.

But He said to them, "Not all men *can* accept this statement, but *only* those to whom it has been given. For there are eunuchs who were born that way from their mother's womb; and there are eunuchs who were made eunuchs by men; and there are *also* eunuchs who made themselves eunuchs for the sake of the kingdom of heaven. He who is able to accept *this,* let him accept *it*" (Matthew 19:11, 12; cf. 1 Corinthians 7:7).

CELIBATE (See EUNUCHS)

CELLAR

Setting: On the way from Galilee to Jerusalem. After telling the increasing crowds about the sign of Jonah, Jesus illustrates His point by speaking of a lamp.

"No one, after lighting a lamp, puts it away in a cellar nor under a basket, but on the lampstand, so that those who enter may see the light. The eye is the lamp of your body; when your eye is clear, your whole body also is full of light; but when it is bad, your body also is full of darkness. Then watch out that the light in you is not darkness. If therefore your whole body is full of light, with no dark part in it, it will be wholly illumined, as when the lamp illumines you with its rays" (Luke 11:33–36; cf. Matthew 5:15, 6:22, 23).

CENT (Also see CENTS; COIN; and PENNY)

Setting: Galilee. During the early part of His ministry, Jesus preaches the Sermon on the Mount to His disciples and the multitudes.

"Make friends quickly with your opponent at law while you are with him on the way, so that your opponent may not hand you over to the judge, and the judge to the officer, and you be thrown into prison. Truly I say to you, you will not come out of there until you have paid up the last cent" (Matthew 5:25, 26; cf. Luke 12:58, 59).

Setting: Galilee. After His disciples observe His ministry, Jesus summons and specifically instructs them about their ministry ahead involving true discipleship.

"Are not two sparrows sold for a cent? And *yet* not one of them will fall to the ground apart from your Father. But the very hairs of your head are all numbered. So do not fear; you are more valuable than many sparrows" (Matthew 10:29–31; cf. Luke 12:6; see Matthew 12:12).

Setting: On the way from Galilee to Jerusalem. After chastising the crowds for being able to discern the weather but not the present age, Jesus exhorts them to settle any financial disputes outside of court.

"And why do you not even on your own initiative judge what is right? For while you are going with your opponent to appear before the magistrate, on your way there make an effort to settle with him, so that he may not drag you before the judge, and the judge turn you over to the officer, and the officer throw you into prison. I say to you, you will not get out of there until you have paid the very last cent" (Luke 12:57–59; cf. Matthew 5:25, 26).

CENTS (Also see CENT; COIN; and MONEY)

Setting: On the way from Galilee to Jerusalem. Jesus warns His disciples of future events, as the scribes and Pharisees turn hostile and question Him in an attempt to catch Him in something He might say.

Under these circumstances, after so many thousands of people had gathered together that they were stepping on one another, He began saying to His disciples first of all, "Beware of the leaven of the Pharisees, which is hypocrisy. But there is nothing covered up that will not be revealed, and hidden that will not be known. Accordingly, whatever you have said in the dark will be heard in the light, and what you have whispered in the inner rooms will be proclaimed upon the housetops. I say to you, My friends, do not be afraid of those who kill the body and after that have no more that they can do. But I will warn you whom to fear: fear the One who, after He has killed, has authority to cast into hell; yes, I tell you, fear Him! Are not five sparrows sold for two cents? Yet not one of them is forgotten before God. Indeed, the very hairs of your head are all numbered. Do not fear; you are more valuable than many sparrows" (Luke 12:1–7; cf. Matthew 10:26–31; see Matthew 16:6; Hebrews 10:31).

CEPHAS (See PETER; SIMON; and SIMON BARJONA)

Setting: Bethany beyond the Jordan. After being baptized in the Jordan River, Jesus begins His public ministry and chooses His first disciples, Andrew and Simon (Peter), who believe He is the Messiah.

He brought him to Jesus. Jesus looked at him and said, "You are Simon the son of John; you shall be called Cephas." (which is translated Peter) (John 1:42).

CERTIFICATE

Setting: Galilee. During the early part of His ministry, Jesus preaches the Sermon on the Mount to His disciples and the multitudes.

"It was said, 'WHOEVER SENDS HIS WIFE AWAY, LET HIM GIVE HER A CERTIFICATE OF DIVORCE'; but I say to you that everyone who divorces his wife, except for *the* reason of unchastity, makes her commit adultery; and whoever marries a divorced woman commits adultery" (Matthew 5:31, 32, Jesus quotes from Deuteronomy 24: 1, 3; cf. Matthew 19:9; see Romans 7:2, 3; 1 Corinthians 7:10, 39).

Setting: Judea beyond the Jordan (Perea). Jesus teaches the crowds gathered around Him about divorce after the Pharisees test and question Him about this subject.

And He answered and said to them, "What did Moses command you?" They said, "Moses permitted a *man* TO WRITE A CERTIFICATE OF DIVORCE AND SEND *her* AWAY." But Jesus said to them, "Because of your hardness of heart he wrote you this commandment. But from the beginning of creation, *God* MADE THEM MALE AND FEMALE. FOR THIS REASON A MAN SHALL LEAVE HIS FATHER

AND MOTHER, AND THE TWO SHALL BECOME ONE FLESH; so they are no longer two, but one flesh. What therefore God has joined together, let no man separate. In the house the disciples *began* questioning Him about this again. And He said to them, "Whoever divorces his wife and marries another woman commits adultery against her; and if she herself divorces her husband and marries another man, she is committing adultery" (Mark 10:3–12, Jesus quotes from Genesis 1:27; 2:24; cf. Matthew 19:1–9; see Deuteronomy 24:1–3; Matthew 5:32: see Romans 7:2, 3; 1 Corinthians 7:10, 11, 39; 1, 13; 1 Timothy 2:14).

CHAIR OF MOSES (Listed under MOSES, CHAIR OF)

CHANCE

Setting: On the way from Galilee to Jerusalem. While being tested by a lawyer, Jesus tells him the story of the good Samaritan.

Jesus replied and said, "A man was going down from Jerusalem to Jericho, and fell among robbers, and they stripped him and beat him, and went away leaving him half dead. And by chance a priest was going down on that road, and when he saw him, he passed by on the other side. Likewise a Levite also, when he came to the place and saw him, passed by on the other side. But a Samaritan, who was on a journey, came upon him; and when he saw him, he felt compassion, and came to him and bandaged up his wounds, pouring oil and wine on them; and he put him on his own beast, and brought him to an inn and took care of him. On the next day he took out two denarii and gave them to the innkeeper and said, 'Take care of him; and whatever more you spend, when I return I will repay you.' Which of these three do you think proved to be a neighbor to the man who fell into the robbers' hands?" And he said, "The one who showed mercy toward him." Then Jesus said to him, "Go and do the same" (Luke 10:30–37).

CHANCES, SECOND

[SECOND CHANCES from Let it alone, sir, for this year too, until I dig around it and put fertilizer; and if it bears fruit next year, fine; but if not, cut it down]

Setting: On the way from Galilee to Jerusalem. After some report to Him about the Galileans whose blood Pilate (Roman governor of Judea) had mixed with their sacrifices, Jesus responds to their concern by calling them to repentance and illustrating His point with a parable.

And He began telling this parable: "A man had a fig tree which had been planted in his vineyard; and he came looking for fruit on it and did not find any. And he said to the vineyard-keeper, 'Behold, for three years I have come looking for fruit on this fig tree without finding any. Cut it down! Why does it even use up the ground?' And he answered and said to him, 'Let it alone, sir, for this year too, until I dig around it and put fertilizer; and if it bears fruit next year, fine; but if not, cut it down'"(Luke 13:6–9; see Matthew 3:10; Luke 13:1).

CHANGERS, MONEY (See ROBBERS' DEN)

CHARITY (Also see GIVING; POOR; and POOR, GIVING TO THE)

Setting: On the way from Galilee to Jerusalem. After speaking of how a lamp illuminates, the Lord has lunch with a Pharisee who is surprised He doesn't wash before eating.

But the Lord said to him, "Now you Pharisees clean the outside of the cup and of the platter; but inside of you, you are full of robbery and wickedness. You foolish ones, did not He who made the outside make the inside also? But give that which is within as charity, and then all things are clean for you. But woe to you Pharisees! You pay tithe of mint and rue and every kind of garden herb, and yet disregard justice and the love of God; but these are the things you should have done without neglecting the others. Woe to you Pharisees! For you love the chief seats in the synagogues and the respectful greetings in the market places. Woe to you! For you are like concealed tombs, and the people who walk over them are unaware of it" (Luke 11:39–44; cf. Matthew 23:6–7, 23–27; see Matthew 15:2; Titus 1:15).

Setting: On the way from Galilee to Jerusalem. After giving the crowd and His disciples a parable about riches and greed, Jesus challenges them concerning godly living.

"Sell your possessions and give to charity; make yourselves money belts which do not wear out, an unfailing treasure in heaven, where no thief comes near nor moth destroys. For where your treasure is, there your heart will be also" (Luke 12:33, 34; cf. Matthew 6:19–21; 19:21).

CHASM, GREAT

Setting: On the way from Galilee to Jerusalem. After He responds to the Pharisees' scoffing at His teaching His disciples about stewardship and the permanence of the Law, Jesus conveys the story of the rich man and Lazarus.

"Now there was a rich man, and he habitually dressed in purple and fine linen, joyously living in splendor every day. And a poor man named Lazarus was laid at his gate, covered with sores, and longing to be fed with the crumbs which were falling from the rich man's table; besides, even the dogs were coming and licking his sores. Now the poor man died and was carried away by the angels to Abraham's bosom; and the rich man also died and was buried. In Hades he lifted up his eyes, being in torment, and saw Abraham far away and Lazarus in his bosom. And he cried out and said, 'Father Abraham, have mercy on me, and send Lazarus so that he may dip the tip of his finger in water and cool off my tongue, for I am in agony in this flame.' But Abraham said, 'Child, remember that during your life you received your good things, and likewise Lazarus bad things; but now he is being comforted here, and you are in agony. And besides all this, between us and you there is a great chasm fixed, so that those who wish to come over from here to you will not be able, and that none may cross over from there to us.' And he said, 'Then I beg you, father, that you send him to my father's house—for I have five brothers—in order that he may warn them, so that they will not also come to this place of torment.' But Abraham said, 'They have Moses and the Prophets; let them hear them.' But he said, 'No, father Abraham, but if someone goes to them from the dead, they will repent!' But he said to him, 'If they do not listen to Moses and the Prophets, they will not be persuaded even if someone rises from the dead'" (Luke 16:19–31; see Luke 3:8; 6:24; 16:1, 14).

CHEEK (Also see FACE)

Setting: Galilee. During the early part of His ministry, Jesus preaches the Sermon on the Mount to His disciples and the multitudes.

"You have heard that it was said, 'AN EYE FOR AN EYE, AND A TOOTH FOR A TOOTH.' But I say to you, do not resist an evil person; but whoever slaps you on your right cheek, turn the other to him also" (Matthew 5:38, 39, Jesus quotes from Exodus 21:24; cf. Leviticus 24:20).

Setting: Galilee. After selecting His twelve disciples, Jesus teaches the Sermon on the Mount to His disciples and a great throng from Judea, Jerusalem, and the central coastal region of Tyre and Sidon.

"But I say to you who hear, love your enemies, do good to those who hate you, bless those who curse you, pray for those who mistreat you. Whoever hits you on the cheek, offer him the other also; and whoever takes away your coat, do not withhold your shirt from him either. Give to everyone who asks of you, and whoever takes away what is yours, do not demand it back. Treat others the same way you want them to treat you. If you love those who love you, what credit is that to you? For even sinners love those who love them. If you do good to those who do good to you, what credit is that to you? For even sinners do the same. If you lend to those from whom you expect to receive, what credit is that to you? Even sinners lend to sinners in order to receive back the same amount. But love your enemies, and do good, and lend, expecting nothing in return; and your reward will be great, and you will be sons of the Most High; for He Himself is kind to ungrateful and evil men. Be merciful, just as your Father is merciful" (Luke 6:27–36; cf. Matthew 5:9, 39–48; Matthew 7:12; see Luke 6:12–19).

CHEEK, RIGHT (See CHEEK)

CHICKS (Also see HEN; and ROOSTER)

Setting: The temple in Jerusalem. With His death on the cross just days away, Jesus laments over Jerusalem's hard-heartedness and lack of repentance.

"Jerusalem, Jerusalem, who kills the prophets and stones those who are sent to her! How often I wanted to gather your children together, the way a hen gathers her chicks under her wings, and you were unwilling. Behold, your house is being left to you desolate! For I say to you, from now on you will not see Me until you say, 'BLESSED IS HE WHO COMES IN THE NAME OF THE LORD!'" (Matthew 23:37–39, Jesus quotes from Psalm 118:26; cf. 1 Kings 9:7; Luke 13:34, 35).

CHIEF CORNERSTONE (Listed under CORNER STONE, CHIEF)

CHIEF PRIESTS (Also see ELDERS; PRIESTS; SCRIBES; and SEATS, CHIEF)

Setting: On the road to Jerusalem. Before going to Jerusalem, Jesus again tells His disciples of His impending death and resurrection.

As Jesus was about to go up to Jerusalem, He took the twelve *disciples* aside by themselves, and on the way He said to them, "Behold, we are going up to Jerusalem; and the Son of Man will be delivered to the chief priests and scribes, and they will condemn Him to death, and will hand Him over to the Gentiles to mock and scourge and crucify *Him,* and on the third day, He will be raised up" (Matthew 20:17–19; cf. Matthew 16:21; Mark 10:32–34; Luke 18:31–33).

Setting: On the road to Jerusalem. After encouraging His disciples with a revelation of their future reward, Jesus prophesies His persecution, death, and resurrection.

They were on the road going up to Jerusalem, and Jesus was walking on ahead of them; and they were amazed, and those who followed were fearful. And again He took the twelve aside and began to tell them what was going to happen to Him, saying, "Behold, we are going up to Jerusalem, and the Son of Man will be delivered to the chief priests and the scribes; and they will condemn Him to death and will hand Him over to the Gentiles. They will mock Him and spit on Him, and scourge Him and kill Him, and three days later He will rise again" (Mark 10:32–34; cf. Matthew 20:17–19; Luke 18:31–34; see Matthew 16:21; Mark 8:31).

Setting: Galilee. Following Peter's pronouncement that Jesus is the Christ of God, the Lord warns His disciples not to reveal His identity to anyone.

But He warned them and instructed them not to tell this to anyone, saying, "The Son of Man must suffer many things and be rejected by the elders and chief priests and scribes, and be killed and be raised up on the third day" (Luke 9:21, 22; cf. Matthew 16:21; Mark 8:31).

CHIEF SEATS (Listed under SEATS, CHIEF; also see SYNAGOGUES)

CHILD (Also see BABIES; CHILDREN; INFANTS; and LITTLE ONES)

Setting: Galilee. After His disciples observe His ministry, Jesus summons and specifically instructs them about the upcoming difficulties of *their* ministry to the people of Israel.

"Brother will betray brother to death, and a father *his* child; and children will rise up against parents and cause them to be put to death. You will be hated by all because of My name, but it is the one who has endured to the end who will be saved. But whenever they persecute you in one city, flee to the next; for truly I say to you, you will not finish *going through* the cities of Israel until the Son of Man comes" (Matthew 10:21–23; cf. Matthew 10.35, 36; 16:27, 28; 24:9).

Setting: Capernaum of Galilee. Jesus answers His disciples' question about greatness, or rank, in the kingdom of heaven.

And He called a child to Himself and set him before them, and said, "Truly I say to you, unless you are converted and become like children, you will not enter the kingdom of heaven. Whoever then humbles himself as this child, he is the greatest in the kingdom of heaven. And whoever receives one such child in My name receives Me; but whoever causes one of these little ones who believe in Me to stumble, it would be better for him to have a heavy millstone hung around his neck, and to be drowned in the depth of the sea" (Matthew 18:2–6; cf. Matthew 19:14; Mark 9:33–37, 42; Luke 9:47, 48; 17:1, 2).

Setting: Home of Jairus (a synagogue official) in Capernaum. Jesus assures those present that Jairus's daughter has not died, but is asleep.

And entering in, He said to them, "Why make a commotion and weep? The child has not died, but is asleep" (Mark 5:39; cf. Matthew 9:24; Luke 8:52).

Setting: Capernaum of Galilee. As Jesus teaches His disciples in private, they ask Him about greatness.

They came to Capernaum; and when He was in the house, He *began* to question them, "What were you discussing on the way?" But they kept silent, for on the way they had discussed with one another which *of them* was the greatest. Sitting down, He called the twelve and said to them, "If anyone wants to be first, he shall be last of all and servant of all." Taking a child, He set him before them, and taking him in His arms, He said to them, "Whoever receives one child like this in My name receives Me; and whoever receives Me does not receive Me, but Him who sent Me" (Mark 9:33–37; cf. Matthew 18:1–5; Luke 9:46–48; see Matthew 20:26; 10:40).

Setting: Judea beyond the Jordan (Perea). After the Pharisees test and question Jesus about divorce, He demonstrates to His disciples the importance of little children.

But when Jesus saw this, He was indignant and said to them, "Permit the children to come to Me; do not hinder them; for the kingdom of God belongs to such as these. Truly I say to you, whoever does not receive the kingdom of God like a child will not enter it *at all*" (Mark 10:14, 15; cf. Matthew 19:13–15; Luke 18:15–17; see Matthew 18:3).

Setting: The Mount of Olives, east of the temple in Jerusalem. During His discourse, after prophesying the temple's destruction, Jesus responds to questions from Peter, James, John, and Andrew about future events.

And Jesus began to say to them, "See to it that no one misleads you. Many will come in My name, saying, 'I am *He!*' and will mislead many. When you hear of wars and rumors of wars, do not be frightened; *those things* must take place; but *that is* not yet the end. For nation will rise up against nation, and kingdom against kingdom; there will be earthquakes in various places; there will *also be* famines. These things are *merely* the beginning of birth pangs. But be on your guard; for they will deliver you to *the* courts, and you will be flogged in *the* synagogues, and you will stand before governors and kings for My sake, as a testimony to them. The gospel must first be preached to all the nations. When they arrest you and hand you over, do not worry beforehand about what you are to say, but say whatever is given you in that hour; for it is not you who speak, but *it is* the Holy Spirit. Brother will betray brother to death, and a father *his* child; and children will rise up against parents and have them put to death. You will be hated by all because of My name, but the one who endures to the end, he will be saved" (Mark 13:5–13; cf. Matthew 24:4–14; Luke 21:7–19; see Matthew 10:17–22)

Setting: Capernaum in Galilee. After healing a woman ill for twelve years, Jesus receives word that the daughter of synagogue official Jairus has died.

But when Jesus heard this, He answered him, "Do not be afraid any longer; only believe and she will be made well." When He came to the house, He did not allow anyone to enter with Him except Peter and John and James and the girl's father and mother. Now they were all weeping and lamenting for her; but He said, "Stop weeping; for she has not died, but is asleep." And they began laughing at Him, knowing that she had died. He, however, took her by the hand and called, saying, "Child, arise!" And her spirit returned, and she got up immediately; and He gave orders for something to be given her to eat (Luke 8:50–55; cf. Matthew 9:18, 19, 23–26; Mark 5:21–24, 35–43; see Luke 8:41, 42).

Setting: Galilee. After Jesus prophesies His death, an argument arises among His disciples as to who is the greatest. The Lord solves the matter by using a child as a teaching illustration.

But Jesus, knowing what they were thinking in their heart, took a child and stood him by His side, and said to them, "Whoever receives this child in My name receives Me, and whoever receives Me receives Him who sent Me; for the one who is least among all of you, this is the one who is great" (Luke 9:47, 48; cf. Matthew 18:1–5; Mark 9:33–47; see Matthew 10:40; Luke 22:24).

Setting: On the way from Galilee to Jerusalem. After He responds to the Pharisees' scoffing at His teaching His disciples about stewardship and the permanence of the Law, Jesus conveys the story of the rich man and Lazarus.

"Now there was a rich man, and he habitually dressed in purple and fine linen, joyously living in splendor every day. And a poor man named Lazarus was laid at his gate, covered with sores, and longing to be fed with the crumbs which were falling from the rich man's table; besides, even the dogs were coming and licking his sores. Now the poor man died and was carried away by the angels to Abraham's bosom; and the rich man also died and was buried. In Hades he lifted up his eyes, being in torment, and saw Abraham far away and Lazarus in his bosom. And he cried out and said, 'Father Abraham, have mercy on me, and send Lazarus so that he may dip the tip of his finger in water and cool off my tongue, for I am in agony in this flame.' But Abraham said, 'Child, remember that during your life you received your good things, and likewise Lazarus bad things; but now he is being comforted here, and you are in agony. And besides all this, between us and you there is a great chasm fixed, so that those who wish to come over from here to you will not be able, and that none may cross over from there to us.' And he said, 'Then I beg you, father, that you send him to my father's house—for I have five brothers—in order that he may warn them, so that they will not also come to this place of torment.' But Abraham said, 'They have Moses and the Prophets; let them hear them.' But he said, 'No, father Abraham, but if someone goes to them from the dead, they will repent!' But he said to him, 'If they do not listen to Moses and the Prophets, they will not be persuaded even if someone rises from the dead.'" (Luke 16:19–31; see Luke 3:8; 6:24; 16:1, 14)

Setting: On the way from Galilee to Jerusalem. After giving a parable about self-righteousness, Jesus speaks of the importance of children.

But Jesus called for them, saying, "Permit the children to come to Me, and do not hinder them, for the kingdom of God belongs to such as these. Truly I say to you, whoever does not receive the kingdom of God like a child will not enter it *at all*" (Luke 18:16, 17; cf. Matthew 19:13–15; Mark 10:13–16; see Matthew 18:3).

Setting: Jerusalem. Before the Passover, after warning His disciples of the persecution they will face after His departure to heaven, empathizing with their sadness over His prophecies, Jesus gives them assurance for the future.

"A little while, and you will no longer see Me; and again a little while, and you will see Me." *Some* of His disciples then said to one another, "What is this thing He is telling us, 'A little while, and you will not see Me; and again a little while, and you will see Me'; and, 'because I go to the Father'?" So they were saying, "What is this that He says, 'A little while'? We do not know what He is talking about." Jesus knew that they wished to question Him, and He said to them, "Are you deliberating together about this, that I said, 'A little while, and you will not see Me, and again a little while, and you will see Me'? Truly, truly, I say to you, that you will weep and lament, but the world will rejoice; you will grieve, but your grief will be turned into joy. Whenever a woman is in labor she has pain, because her hour has come; but when she gives birth to the child, she no longer remembers the anguish because of the joy that a child has been born into the world. Therefore you too have grief now; but I will see you again, and your heart will rejoice, and no one *will* take your joy away from you" (John 16:16–22; see Mark 9:32; Luke 23:27; John 14:18–24; 16:5, 6; 20:20).

CHILDLESSNESS (See BARRENNESS)

CHILDREN (CHILDREN, ABRAHAM'S is a separate entry; also see BABIES, NURSING; CHILD; INFANTS; and LITTLE ONES)

Setting: Galilee. During the early part of His ministry, Jesus preaches the Sermon on the Mount to His disciples and the multitudes.

"Ask, and it will be given to you; seek, and you will find; knock, and it will be opened to you. For everyone who asks receives, and he who seeks finds, and to him who knocks it will be opened. Or what man is there among you who, when his son asks for a loaf, will give him a stone? Or if he asks for a fish, he will not give him a snake, will he? If you then, being evil, know how to give good gifts to your children, how much more will your Father who is in heaven give what is good to those who ask Him! In everything, therefore, treat people the same way you want them to treat you, for this is the Law and the Prophets" (Matthew 7:7–12; cf. Matthew 22:40; Luke 6:31; 11:9–13; see Psalm 84:11).

Setting: Galilee. After His disciples observe His ministry, Jesus summons and specifically instructs them about the upcoming difficulties of *their* ministry to the people of Israel.

"Brother will betray brother to death, and a father *his* child; and children will rise up against parents and cause them to be put to death. You will be hated by all because of My name, but it is the one who has endured to the end who will be saved. But whenever they persecute you in one city, flee to the next; for truly I say to you, you will not finish *going through* the cities of Israel until the Son of Man comes" (Matthew 10:21–23; cf. Matthew 10:35, 36; 16:27, 28; 24:9).

Setting: Galilee. After praising John the Baptist as His forerunner, Jesus demonstrates the foolish thinking of the current generation of Jewish religious leaders by repeating what they say about John's ascetic lifestyle and ministry along with His own.

"But to what shall I compare this generation? It is like children sitting in the market places, who call out to the other *children,* and say, 'We played the flute for you, and you did not dance; we sang a dirge, and you did not mourn.' For John came neither eating nor drinking, and they say, 'He has a demon!' The Son of Man came eating and drinking, and they say, 'Behold, a gluttonous man and a drunkard, a friend of tax collectors and sinners! Yet wisdom is vindicated by her deeds" (Matthew 11:16–19; cf. Luke 7:31–35; see Matthew 9:11, 34; Luke 1:15).

Setting: Capernaum in Galilee. Jesus answers His disciples' question about greatness, or rank, in the kingdom of heaven.

And He called a child to Himself and set him before them, and said, "Truly I say to you, unless you are converted and become like children, you will not enter the kingdom of heaven. Whoever then humbles himself as this child, he is the greatest in the kingdom of heaven. And whoever receives one such child in My name receives Me; but whoever causes one of these little ones who believe in Me to stumble, it would be better for him to have a heavy millstone hung around his neck, and to be drowned in the depth of the sea"
(Matthew 18:2–6; cf. Matthew 19:14; Mark 9:33–37, 42; Luke 9:47, 48; Luke 17:1, 2).

Setting: Capernaum in Galilee. Jesus illustrates forgiveness after Peter asks Him if forgiving someone seven times who has sinned against him is adequate.

"For this reason the kingdom of heaven may be compared to a king who wished to settle accounts with his slaves. When he had begun to settle *them,* one who owed him ten thousand talents was brought to him. But since he did not have *the means* to repay, his lord commanded him to be sold, along with his wife and children and all that he had, and repayment to be made. So the slave fell *to the ground* and prostrated himself before him, saying, 'Have patience with me and I will repay you everything.' And the lord of that slave felt compassion and released him and forgave him the debt. But that slave went out and found one of his fellow slaves who owed him a hundred denarii; and he seized him and *began* to choke *him,* saying, 'Pay back what you owe.' So his fellow slave fell *to the ground* and *began* to plead with him, saying, 'Have patience with me and I will repay you.' But he was unwilling and went and threw him in prison until he should pay back what was owed. So when his fellow slaves saw what had happened, they were deeply grieved and came and reported to their lord all that had happened. Then summoning him, his lord said to him, 'You wicked slave, I forgave you all that debt because you pleaded with me. Should you not also have had mercy on your fellow slave, in the same way that I had mercy on you?' And his lord, moved with anger, handed him over to the torturers until he should repay all that was owed him. My heavenly Father will also do the same to you, if each of you does not forgive his brother from your heart" (Matthew 18:23–35; cf. Matthew 6:12, 14, 15; Luke 7:42; see Matthew 25:19–28).

Setting: Judea beyond the Jordan (Perea). Jesus shows His love for children after His disciples rebuke some children who wanted Jesus' blessing.

But Jesus said, "Let the children alone, and do not hinder them from coming to Me; for the kingdom of heaven belongs to such as these" (Matthew 19:14; cf. Mark 10:13–16; Luke 18:15–17; see Matthew 18:3).

Setting: Judea beyond the Jordan (Perea). Jesus promises rewards to His disciples for their personal sacrifice and commitment to following Him.

And Jesus said to them, "Truly I say to you, that you who have followed Me, in the regeneration when the Son of Man will sit on His glorious throne, you also shall sit upon twelve thrones, judging the twelve tribes of Israel. And everyone who has left houses or brothers or sisters or father or mother or children or farms for My name's sake, will receive many times as much, and will inherit eternal life. But many *who* are first will be last; and *the* last, first" (Matthew 19:28–30; cf. Matthew 6:33; 20:15; Mark 10:29, 30; Luke 18:29, 30; 22:30).

Setting: The temple in Jerusalem. With His death on the cross just days away, Jesus laments over the city's hard-heartedness and lack of repentance.

"Jerusalem, Jerusalem, who kills the prophets and stones those who are sent to her! How often I wanted to gather your children together, the way a hen gathers her chicks under her wings, and you were unwilling. Behold, your house is being left to you desolate! For I say to you, from now on you will not see Me until you say, 'BLESSED IS HE WHO COMES IN THE NAME OF THE LORD!'" (Matthew 23:37–39, Jesus quotes from Psalm 118:26; cf. 1 Kings 9:7; Luke 13:34, 35).

Setting: The region of Tyre. After the Pharisees and scribes from Jerusalem question Jesus' disciples' lack of obedience in Galilee to the tradition of ceremonial cleansing, Jesus casts out a demon from the daughter of a Gentile (Syrophoenician) woman.

And He was saying to her, "Let the children be satisfied first, for it is not good to take the children's bread and throw it to the dogs." But she answered and said to Him, "Yes, Lord *but* even the dogs under the table feed on the children's crumbs. And He said to her, "Because of this answer go; the demon has gone out of your daughter" (Mark 7:27–29; cf. Matthew 15:21–28).

Setting: Judea beyond the Jordan (Perea). After the Pharisees test and question Him about divorce, Jesus demonstrates to His disciples the importance of little children.

But when Jesus saw this, He was indignant and said to them, "Permit the children to come to Me; do not hinder them; for the kingdom of God belongs to such as these. Truly I say to you, whoever does not receive the kingdom of God like a child will not enter it *at all*" (Mark 10:14, 15; cf. Matthew 19:13–15; Luke 18:15–17; see Matthew 18:3).

Setting: After informing a rich man how righteous believers may have treasure in heaven, Jesus conveys to His disciples the difficulty the wealthy have entering the kingdom of God.

And Jesus, looking around, said to His disciples, "How hard it will be for those who are wealthy to enter the kingdom of God!" The disciples were amazed at His words. But Jesus answered again and said to them, "Children, how hard it is to enter the kingdom of God! It is easier for a camel to go through the eye of a needle than for a rich man to enter the kingdom of God." They were even more astonished and said to Him, "Then who can be saved?" Looking at them, Jesus said, "With people it is impossible, but not with God; for all things are possible with God" (Mark 10:23–27; cf. Matthew 19:23–26; Luke 18:24, 25).

Setting: After informing a rich man how righteous believers may have treasure in heaven, Jesus conveys to His disciples the reward of those who sacrifice in this life to follow Him.

Jesus said, "Truly I say to you, there is no one who has left house or brothers or sisters or mother or father or children or farms, for My sake and for the gospel's sake, but that he will receive a hundred times as much now in the present age, houses and brothers and sisters and mothers and children and farms, along with persecutions; and in the age to come, eternal life. But many *who are* first will be last, and the last, first" (Mark 10:29–31; cf. Matthew 19:27–30; Luke 18:28–30; see Matthew 6:33).

Setting: The Mount of Olives, east of the temple in Jerusalem. During His discourse, after prophesying the temple's destruction, Jesus responds to questions from Peter, James, John, and Andrew about future events.

And Jesus began to say to them, "See to it that no one misleads you. Many will come in My name, saying, 'I am *He!*' and will mislead many. When you hear of wars and rumors of wars, do not be frightened; *those things* must take place; but *that is* not yet the end. For nation will rise up against nation, and kingdom against kingdom; there will be earthquakes in various places; there will *also be* famines. These things are *merely* the beginning of birth pangs. But be on your guard; for they will deliver you to *the* courts, and you will be flogged in *the* synagogues, and you will stand before governors and kings for My sake, as a testimony to them. The gospel must first be preached to all the nations. When they arrest you and hand you over, do not worry beforehand about what you are to say, but say whatever is given you in that hour; for it is not you who speak, but *it is* the Holy Spirit. Brother will betray brother to death, and a father *his* child; and children will rise up against parents and have them put to death. You will be hated by all because of My name, but the one who endures to the end, he will be saved" (Mark 13:5–13; cf. Matthew 24:4–14; Luke 21:7–19; see Matthew 10:17–22).

Setting: Galilee. After praising John the Baptist to the crowds, Jesus criticizes the Pharisees and lawyers who reject God's purpose and John's message.

"To what then shall I compare the men of this generation, and what are they like? They are like children who sit in the market place and call to one another, and they say, 'We played the flute for you, and you did not dance; we sang a dirge, and you did not weep.' For John the Baptist has come eating no bread and drinking no wine, and you say, 'He has a demon!' The Son of Man has come eating and drinking, and you say, 'Behold, a gluttonous man and a drunkard, a friend of tax collectors and sinners!' Yet wisdom is vindicated by all her children" (Luke 7:31–35; cf. Matthew 11:16–19; see Luke 1:15).

Setting: On the way from Galilee to Jerusalem. After revealing to His disciples how to pray, Jesus illustrates persistence in prayer.

Then He said to them, "Suppose one of you has a friend, and goes to him at midnight and says to him, 'Friend, lend me three loaves; for a friend of mine has come to me from a journey, and I have nothing to set before him'; and from inside he answers and says, 'Do not bother me; the door has already been shut and my children and I are in bed; I cannot get up and give you anything.' I tell you, even though he will not get up and give him anything because he is his friend, yet because of his persistence he will get up and give him as much as he needs. So I say to you, ask, and it will be given to you; seek, and you will find; knock, and it will be opened to you. For everyone who asks, receives; and he who seeks, finds; and to him who knocks, it will be opened" (Luke 11:5–10; cf. Matthew 7:7, 8; see Luke 18:1–5).

Setting: On the way from Galilee to Jerusalem. After revealing to His disciples how to pray, Jesus illustrates God's benevolence in answering prayer and giving the Holy Spirit.

"Now suppose one of you fathers is asked by his son for a fish; he will not give him a snake instead of a fish, will he? Or if he is asked for an egg, he will not give him a scorpion, will he? If you then, being evil, know how to give good gifts to your children, how much more will your heavenly Father give the Holy Spirit to those who ask Him?" (Luke 11:11–13; cf. Matthew 7:9–11).

Setting: On the way from Galilee to Jerusalem. While teaching in the cities and villages, Jesus responds to a question about who is saved. Some Pharisees ask Him to leave, claiming Herod Antipas (tetrarch of Galilee and Perea) seeks to kill Him.

And He said to them, "Go and tell that fox, 'Behold, I cast out demons and perform cures today and tomorrow, and the third day I reach My goal.' Nevertheless I must journey on today and tomorrow and the next day; for it cannot be that a prophet would perish outside of Jerusalem. O Jerusalem, Jerusalem, the city that kills the prophets and stones those sent to her! How often I wanted to gather your children together, just as a hen gathers her brood under her wings, and you would not have it! Behold, your house is left to you desolate; and I say to you, you will not see Me until the time comes when you say, 'BLESSED IS HE WHO COMES IN THE NAME OF THE LORD!'" (Luke 13:32–35, Jesus quotes from Psalm 118:26; cf. Matthew 23:37).

Setting: On the way from Galilee to Jerusalem. After responding to a guest's proclamation about the blessings of eating bread in the kingdom of God, Jesus presents to large crowds the demands of discipleship.

Now large crowds were going along with Him; and He turned and said to them, "If anyone comes to Me, and does not hate his own father and mother and wife and children and brothers and sisters, yes, and even his own life, he cannot be My disciple. Whoever does not carry his own cross and come after Me cannot be My disciple. For which one of you, when he wants to build a tower, does not first sit down and calculate the cost to see if he has enough to complete it? Otherwise, when he has laid a foundation and is not able to finish, all who observe it begin to ridicule him, saying, 'This man began to build and was not able to finish.' Or what king, when he sets out to meet another king in battle, will not first sit down and consider whether he is strong enough with ten thousand *men* to encounter the one coming against him with twenty thousand? Or else, while the other is still far away, he sends a delegation and asks for terms of peace. So then, none of you can be My disciple who does not give up all his possessions. Therefore, salt is good; but if even salt has become tasteless, with what will it be seasoned? It is useless either for the soil or for the manure pile; it is thrown out. He who has ears to hear, let him hear" (Luke 14:25–35; cf. Matthew 5:13; 10:37–39; see Proverbs 20:18; Luke 14:1, 2, 15; Philippians 3:7).

Setting: On the way from Galilee to Jerusalem. After giving a parable about self-righteousness, Jesus speaks of the importance of children.

But Jesus called for them, saying, "Permit the children to come to Me, and do not hinder them, for the kingdom of God belongs to such as these. Truly I say to you, whoever does not receive the kingdom of God like a child will not enter it at all" (Luke 18:16, 17; cf. Matthew 19:13–15; Mark 10:13–16; see Matthew 18:3).

Setting: On the way from Galilee to Jerusalem. After responding to His disciples' question about salvation, Jesus replies to Peter's statement about their personal sacrifice.

Peter said, "Behold, we have left our own homes and followed You." And He said to them, "Truly I say to you, there is no one who has left house or wife or brothers or parents or children, for the sake of the kingdom of God, who will not receive many times as much at this time and in the age to come, eternal life" (Luke 18:28–30; cf. Matthew 19:27–29; Mark 10:28–30; see Matthew 6:33; Luke 5:11).

Setting: Approaching Jerusalem. After being praised by the people in a triumphal welcome, the Lord weeps as He sees the city ahead of Him.

When He approached Jerusalem, He saw the city and wept over it, saying, "If you had known in this day, even you, the things which make for peace! But now they have been hidden from your eyes. For the days will come upon you when your enemies will throw up a barricade against you, and surround you and hem you in on every side, and they will level you to the ground and your children within you, and they will not leave in you one stone upon another, because you did not recognize the time of your visitation" (Luke 19:41–44; see Matthew 24:1, 2; Luke 13:34, 35).

Setting: Jerusalem. After being arrested and appearing before the Council of Elders (Sanhedrin), Pontius Pilate (Roman governor of Judea), Herod Antipas (tetrarch of Galilee and Perea), and Pilate a second time (when Pilate bows to the crowd's pressure and grants that Jesus be crucified), the Lord prophesies to the women mourning Him regarding the coming judgment of Jerusalem.

But Jesus turning to them said, "Daughters of Jerusalem, stop weeping for Me, but weep for yourselves and for your children. For behold, the days are coming when they will say, 'Blessed are the barren, and the wombs that never bore, and the breasts that never nursed.' Then they will begin TO SAY TO THE MOUNTAINS, 'FALL ON US,' AND TO THE HILLS, 'COVER US.' For if they do these things when the tree is green, what will happen when it is dry?" (Luke 23:28–31, Jesus quotes from Hosea 10:8; see Matthew 24:19).

Setting: Jerusalem. Before the Passover, after revealing to His disciples that Judas will betray Him to the chief priests and Pharisees, Jesus conveys how He will soon be glorified in His death, and commands them to love one another.

Therefore when he had gone out, Jesus said, "Now is the Son of Man glorified, and God is glorified in Him; if God is glorified in Him, God will also glorify Him in Himself, and will glorify Him immediately. Little children, I am with you a little while longer. You will seek Me; and as I said to the Jews, now I also say to you, 'Where I am going, you cannot come.' A new commandment I give to you, that you love one another, even as I have loved you, that you also love one another. By this all men will know that you are My disciples, if you have love for one another" (John 13:31–35; see Leviticus 19:18; John 7:33, 34; 13:1–30; 17:1; 1 John 3:14).

Setting: By the Sea of Galilee (Tiberias). During His third post-resurrection appearance to His disciples, Jesus directs them to a great catch of fish following their unsuccessful night of fishing.

So Jesus said to them, "Children, you do not have any fish, do you?" They answered Him, "No." And He said to them, "Cast the net on the right-hand side of the boat and you will find a *catch*." So they cast, and then they were not able to haul it in because of the great number of fish (John 21:5, 6; see Luke 5:4).

Setting: The island of Patmos (in the Aegean Sea about fifty miles southwest of Ephesus in modern Turkey). On the Lord's Day (Sunday), about fifty years after Jesus' resurrection, the disciple John encounters the Lord Jesus Christ. Jesus communicates a new revelation for the apostle to record for the church in Thyatira and to six other churches in Asia.

"And to the angel of the church in Thyatira write: The Son of God, who has eyes like a flame of fire, and His feet are like burnished bronze, says this: 'I know your deeds, and your love and faith and service and perseverance, and that your deeds of late are greater than at first. But I have *this* against you, that you tolerate the woman Jezebel, who calls herself a prophetess, and she teaches and leads My bond-servants astray so that they commit *acts of* immorality and eat things sacrificed to idols. I gave her time to repent, and she does not want to repent of her immorality. Behold, I will throw her on a bed *of sickness,* and those who commit adultery with her into great tribulation, unless they repent of her deeds. And I will kill her children with pestilence, and all the churches will know that I am He who searches the minds and hearts; and I will give to each one of you according to your deeds. But I say to you, the rest who are in Thyatira, who do not hold this teaching, who have not known the deep things of Satan, as they call them—I place no other burden on you. Nevertheless what you have, hold fast until I come. He who overcomes, and he who keeps My deeds until the end, TO HIM I WILL GIVE AUTHORITY OVER THE NATIONS; AND HE SHALL RULE THEM WITH A ROD OF IRON, AS THE VESSELS OF THE POTTER ARE BROKEN TO PIECES, as I also have received *authority* from My Father; and I will give him the morning star. He who has an ear, let him hear what the Spirit says to the churches' (Revelation 2:18–29; Jesus quotes from Psalm 2:8, 9; Isaiah 30:14; see 1 Kings 16:31; Psalm 7:9; Romans 2:5, 1 Corinthians 2:10; 2 Peter 3:9; Revelation 1:14; 2:7; 3:11; 17:1–20).

CHILDREN, ABRAHAM'S (Also see DESCENDANTS, ABRAHAM'S)

Setting: The temple treasury in Jerusalem. After the scribes and Pharisees question His testimony about Himself, Jesus interacts with them regarding their ancestry and motives.

They answered and said to Him, "Abraham is our father." Jesus said to them, "If you are Abraham's children, do the deeds of Abraham. But as it is, you are seeking to kill Me, a man who has told you the truth, which I heard from God; this Abraham did not do. You are doing the deeds of your father." They said to Him, "We were not born of fornication; we have one Father: God" (John 8:39–41; see Romans 9:6, 7).

CHILDREN'S BREAD (Listed under BREAD, CHILDREN'S)

CHILDREN'S CRUMBS (See BREAD, CHILDREN'S)

CHORAZIN

Setting: Galilee. Having performed many miracles throughout the region, Jesus pronounces woes against those cities who did not repent.

"Woe to you, Chorazin! Woe to you, Bethsaida! For if the miracles had occurred in Tyre and Sidon which occurred in you, they would have repented long ago in sackcloth and ashes. Nevertheless I say to you, it will be more tolerable for Tyre and Sidon in *the* day of judgment than for you. And you, Capernaum, will not be exalted to heaven, will you? You will descend to Hades; for if the miracles had occurred in Sodom which occurred in you, it would have remained to this day. Nevertheless, I say to you that it will be more tolerable for the land of Sodom in *the* day of judgment, than for you" (Matthew 11:21–24; cf. Matthew 10:15; Luke 10:13–15).

Setting: On the way from Galilee to Jerusalem. The Lord pronounces woes on cities who reject the gospel as He appoints seventy followers and sends them out in pairs to every city and place He Himself will soon visit.

"Woe to you, Chorazin! Woe to you, Bethsaida! For if the miracles had been performed in Tyre and Sidon which occurred in you, they would have repented long ago, sitting in sackcloth and ashes. But it will be more tolerable for Tyre and Sidon in the judgment than for you. And you, Capernaum, will not be exalted to heaven, will you? You will be brought down to Hades! The one who listens to you listens to Me, and the one who rejects you rejects Me; and he who rejects Me rejects the One who sent Me" (Luke 10:13–16; cf. Matthew 11:21–23; see Matthew 10:40; Luke 10:1).

CHOSEN

Setting: The temple in Jerusalem. Jesus speaks another parable to the chief priests and elders after they question His authority.

Jesus spoke to them again in parables, saying, "The kingdom of heaven may be compared to a king who gave a wedding feast for his son. And he sent out his slaves to call those who had been invited to the wedding feast, and they were unwilling to come. Again he sent out other slaves saying, 'Tell those who have been invited, "Behold, I have prepared my dinner; my oxen and my fattened livestock are *all* butchered and everything is ready; come to the wedding feast." But they paid no attention and went their way, one to his own farm, another to his business, and the rest seized his slaves and mistreated them and killed them. But the king was enraged, and he sent his armies and destroyed those murderers and set their city on fire. Then he said to his slaves, 'The wedding is ready, but those who were invited were not worthy. 'Go therefore to the main highways, and as many as you find *there,* invite to the wedding feast.' Those slaves went out into the streets and gathered together all they found, both evil and good; and the wedding hall was filled with dinner guests. But when the king came in to look over the dinner guests, he saw a man there who was not dressed in wedding clothes, and he said to him, 'Friend, how did you come in here without wedding clothes?' And the man was speechless. Then the king said to the servants, 'Bind him hand and foot, and throw him into the outer darkness; in that place there will be weeping and gnashing of teeth.' For many are called, but few *are* chosen" (Matthew 22:1–14; cf. Matthew 8:11, 12).

Setting: Bethany, on the way from Galilee to Jerusalem. After being tested by a lawyer, the Lord and His disciples are welcomed into the home of Mary and Martha.

But the Lord answered and said to her, "Martha, Martha, you are worried and bothered about so many things; but only one thing is necessary, for Mary has chosen the good part, which shall not be taken away from her" (Luke 10:41, 42; see Matthew 6:25).

Setting: On the way from Galilee to Jerusalem. Jesus comforts the crowd and His disciples after giving a parable about riches and greed, while the scribes and Pharisees turn hostile and question Him in an attempt to catch Him in something He might say.

And He said to His disciples, "For this reason I say to you, do not worry about your life, as to what you will eat; nor for your body, as to what you will put on. For life is more than food, and the body more than clothing. Consider the ravens, for they neither sow nor reap; they have no storeroom nor barn, and yet God feeds them; how much more valuable you are than the birds! And which of you by worrying can add a single hour to his life's span? If then you cannot do even a very little thing, why do you worry about other matters? Consider the lilies, how they grow: they neither toil nor spin; but I tell you, not even Solomon in all his glory clothed himself like one of these. But if God so clothes the grass in the field, which is alive today and tomorrow is thrown into the furnace, how much more will He clothe you? You men of little faith! And do not seek what you will eat and what you will drink, and

do not keep worrying. For all these things the nations of the world eagerly seek; but your Father knows that you need these things. But seek His kingdom, and these things will be added to you. Do not be afraid, little flock, for your Father has chosen gladly to give you the kingdom" (Luke 12:22–32; cf. Matthew 6:25–33; see 1 Kings 10:4–7; Job 38:41).

Setting: Jerusalem. Before the Passover, with His death on the cross nearing, Jesus explains the reason for His vivid example of servanthood in washing His disciples' feet.

So when He had washed their feet, and taken His garments and reclined *at the table* again, He said to them, "Do you know what I have done to you? You call Me Teacher and Lord; and you are right, for *so* I am. If I then, the Lord and the Teacher, washed your feet, you also ought to wash one another's feet. For I gave you an example that you also should do as I did to you. Truly, truly I say to you, a slave is not greater than his master, nor *is* one who is sent greater than the one who sent him. If you know these things, you are blessed if you do them. I do not speak of all of you. I know the ones I have chosen; but *it is* that the Scripture may be fulfilled, 'HE WHO EATS MY BREAD HAS LIFTED UP HIS HEEL AGAINST ME.' From now on I am telling you before *it* comes to pass, so that when it does occur, you may believe that I am *He. Truly,* truly, I say to you, he who receives whomever I send receives Me; and he who receives Me receives Him who sent Me" (John 13:12–20; Jesus quotes from Psalm 41:9; see Matthew 7:24; 10:24, 40; John 8:24; 14:29; 1 Peter 5:3).

CHRIST, CONFESSING JESUS (See JESUS, CONFESSING)

CHRIST, DENYING JESUS (See JESUS, DENYING)

CHRIST, FOLLOWING JESUS (See FOLLOWING JESUS CHRIST)

CHRIST, JESUS (See JESUS CHRIST)

CHRIST, PETER'S DECLARATION OF JESUS AS THE (See PETER'S DECLARATION OF JESUS AS THE CHRIST)

CHRIST, THE (Also see DAVID, SON OF; GOD, JESUS AS; SON OF GOD; JESUS; JESUS CHRIST; KING, JESUS AS; KING OF THE JEWS; LORD; MESSIAH; and SON OF MAN)

[THE CHRIST from *the* BLIND RECEIVE SIGHT and *the* lame walk, *the* lepers are cleansed and *the* deaf hear, *the* dead are raised up]
Setting: Galilee. As He teaches and preaches, Jesus responds to John the Baptist's question (posed by John's disciples) whether He is Israel's promised Messiah.

Jesus answered and said to them, "Go and report to John what you hear and see: *the* BLIND RECEIVE SIGHT and *the* lame walk, *the* lepers are cleansed and *the* deaf hear, *the* dead are raised up, and *the* POOR HAVE THE GOSPEL PREACHED TO THEM. And blessed is he who does not take offense at Me" (Matthew 11:4–6, Jesus quotes from Isaiah 35:5f; cf. Luke 7:22, 23).

Setting: The temple in Jerusalem. After the Sadducees and Pharisees unsuccessfully attempt to test Jesus with questions, with the crowds listening, He poses a question to some of the Pharisees.

"What do you think about the Christ, whose son is He?" They said to Him, "The *son* of David." He said to them, "Then how does David in the Spirit call Him 'Lord,' saying, 'THE LORD SAID TO MY LORD, SIT AT MY RIGHT HAND, UNTIL I PUT YOUR ENEMIES BENEATH YOUR FEET'"? "If David then calls Him 'Lord,' how is He his son?" (Matthew 22:42–45; Jesus quotes from Psalm 110:1; cf. Mark 12:35–37; Luke 20:41–44; see 2 Samuel 23:2).

[THE CHRIST from Christ]
Setting: The temple in Jerusalem. After the Jewish religious leaders test Him with questions, Jesus exposes the truth about Pharisaism to the crowds and His disciples.

Then Jesus spoke to the crowds and to His disciples, saying: "The scribes and the Pharisees have seated themselves in the chair of Moses; therefore all that they tell you, do and observe, but do not do according to their deeds; for they say *things* and do not do *them.* They tie up heavy burdens and lay them on men's shoulders, but they themselves are unwilling to move them with *so much as* a finger. But they do all their deeds to be noticed by men; for they broaden their phylacteries and lengthen their tassels *of their garments.* They love the place of honor at banquets and the chief seats in the synagogues, and respectful greetings in the market places, and being called Rabbi by men. But do not be called Rabbi; for One is your Teacher, and you are all brothers. Do not call *anyone* on earth your father; for One is your Father, He who is in heaven. Do not be called leaders; for One is your Leader, *that is,* Christ. But the greatest among you shall be your servant. Whoever exalts himself shall be humbled; and whoever humbles himself shall be exalted" (Matthew 23:1–12; cf. Matthew 20:26; Mark 12:38–40; Luke 20:46, 47; see Exodus 13:9; Deuteronomy 33:3; Matthew 6:1, 5, 6, 9, 16; Mark 14:11; Luke 11:43; 14:11).

Setting: The Mount of Olives, just east of Jerusalem. During His discourse, Jesus answers His disciples' questions as to when the temple will be destroyed and Jerusalem overrun, along with the signs of His coming and the end of the age.

And Jesus answered and said to them, "See to it that no one misleads you. For many will come in My name, saying, 'I am the Christ,' and will mislead many. You will be hearing of wars and rumors of wars. See that you are not frightened, for *those things* must take place, but *that* is not yet the end. For nation will rise against nation, and kingdom against kingdom, and in various places there will be famines and earthquakes. But all these things are *merely* the beginning of birth pangs. Then they will deliver you to tribulation, and will kill you, and you will be hated by all nations because of My name. At that time many will fall away and will betray one another and hate one another. Many false prophets will arise and will mislead many. Because lawlessness is increased, most people's love will grow cold. But the one who endures to the end, he will be saved. This gospel of the kingdom shall be preached in the whole world as a testimony to all the nations, and then the end will come" (Matthew 24:4–14; cf. Jeremiah 29:8; Matthew 7:15; 10:17, 22; Mark 13:3–13; Luke 21:7–19; Revelation 6:4).

Setting: The Mount of Olives, just east of Jerusalem. During His discourse, Jesus answers His disciples' questions as to when the temple will be destroyed and Jerusalem overrun, along with the signs of His coming and the end of the age.

"Therefore when you see the ABOMINATION OF DESOLATION which was spoken of through Daniel the prophet, standing in the holy place (let the reader understand), then those who are in Judea must flee to the mountains. Whoever is on the housetop must not go down to get the things that are in his house. Whoever is in the field must not turn back to get his cloak. But woe to those who are pregnant and to those who are nursing babies in those days! But pray that your flight will not be in the winter, or on a Sabbath. For then there will be a great tribulation, such as has not occurred since the beginning of the world until now, nor ever will. Unless those days had been cut short, no life would have been saved; but for the sake of the elect those days will be cut short. Then if anyone says to you, 'Behold, here is the Christ,' or "There *He is,*' do not believe *him.* For false Christs and false prophets will arise and will show great signs and wonders, so as to mislead, if possible, even the elect. Behold, I have told you in advance. So if they say to you, 'Behold, He is in the wilderness,' do not go out, *or,* 'Behold, He is in the inner rooms,' do not believe *them.* For just as the lightning comes from the east and flashes even to the west, so will the coming of the Son of Man be. Wherever the corpse is, there the vultures will gather" (Matthew 24:15–28, Jesus quotes from Daniel 9:27; cf. Daniel 12:1; Mark 13:14–23; Luke 17:22–31; 21:20–24; 23:29; see John 4:48).

[THE CHRIST from You have said it *yourself*]
Setting: Jerusalem. After being betrayed by Judas and arrested, Jesus appears before Caiaphas (the high priest) and the Council for interrogation in an attempt to entrap Him.

Jesus said to him, "You have said it *yourself;* nevertheless I tell you, hereafter you will see THE SON OF MAN SITTING AT THE RIGHT HAND OF POWER, AND COMING ON THE CLOUDS OF HEAVEN" (Matthew 26:64, Jesus quotes from Daniel 7:13; cf. Mark 14:62).

[THE CHRIST from "It is as you say."]
Setting: Jesus' verifies His true identity while before the Roman governor of Judea, Pilate, in Jerusalem prior to the crucifixion.

Now Jesus stood before the governor, and the governor questioned Him, saying, "Are You the King of the Jews?" And Jesus said to him, "*It is as* you say" (Matthew 27:11; cf. Mark 15:2, Luke 23:3; John 18:33, 34).

Setting: In Capernaum of Galilee, as Jesus teaches His disciples in private, they ask Him about greatness.

But Jesus said, "Do not hinder him, for there is no one who will perform a miracle in My name, and be able soon afterward to speak evil of Me. For he who is not against us is for us. For whoever gives you a cup of water to drink because of your name as *followers* of Christ, truly I say to you, he will not lose his reward. Whoever causes one of these little ones who believe to stumble, it would be better for him if, with a heavy millstone hung around his neck, he had been cast into the sea. If your hand causes you to stumble, cut it off; it is better for you to enter life crippled, than, having your two hands, to go into hell, into the unquenchable fire, [where THEIR WORM DOES NOT DIE, AND THE FIRE IS NOT QUENCHED.] If your foot causes you to stumble, cut it off; it is better for you to enter life lame, than, having your two feet, to be cast into hell, [where THEIR WORM DOES NOT DIE, AND THE FIRE IS NOT QUENCHED.] If your eye causes you to stumble, throw it out; it is better for you to enter the kingdom of God with one eye, than, having two eyes, to be cast into hell, where THEIR WORM DOES NOT DIE, AND THE FIRE IS NOT QUENCHED. For everyone will be salted with fire. Salt is good; but if the salt becomes unsalty, with what will you make it salty *again?* Have salt in yourselves, and be at peace with one another" (Mark 9:39–50; Jesus quotes from Isaiah 66:24; cf. Matthew 18:6–9; Luke 9:49–50; see Matthew 5:13, 29, 30; 10:42; 12:30; 18:5, 6).

Setting: The temple in Jerusalem. After commending a scribe for his nearness to the kingdom of God, Jesus teaches the crowd.

And Jesus *began* to say, as He taught in the temple, "How *is it that* the scribes say that the Christ is the son of David? David himself said in the Holy Spirit, 'THE LORD SAID TO MY LORD, SIT AT MY RIGHT HAND, UNTIL I PUT YOUR ENEMIES BENEATH YOUR FEET.'" David himself calls Him 'Lord'; so in what sense is He his son?" And the large crowd enjoyed listening to Him (Mark 12:35–37, Jesus quotes from Psalm 110:1; cf. Matthew 22:41–46; Luke 20:41–44).

Setting: The Mount of Olives, east of the temple in Jerusalem. During His discourse, after prophesying the temple's destruction, Jesus responds to questions from Peter, James, John, and Andrew about future events.

"But when you see the ABOMINATION OF DESOLATION standing where it should not be (let the reader understand), then those who are in Judea must flee to the mountains. The one who is on the housetop must not go down, or go in to get anything out of his house; and the one who is in the field must not turn back to get his coat. But woe to those who are pregnant and to those who are nursing babies in those days! But pray that it may not happen in winter. For those days will be a *time of* tribulation such as has not occurred since the beginning of the creation which God created until now, and never will. Unless the Lord had shortened *those* days, no life would have been saved; but for the sake of the elect, whom He chose, He shortened the days. And then if anyone says to you, 'Behold, here is the Christ'; or, 'Behold, *He is* there'; do not believe *him*; for false Christs and false prophets will arise, and will show signs and wonders, in order to lead astray, if possible, the elect. But take heed; behold, I have told you everything in advance" (Mark 13:14–23; cf. Matthew 24:15–28; Luke 21:20–24; see Daniel 9:27; 12:1; Luke 17:31).

[THE CHRIST from I am]

Setting: Jerusalem. Following His betrayal by Judas and His arrest, Jesus confirms He is the Christ to the high priest and all the chief priests, as they seek evidence to put Him to death.

And Jesus said, "I am; and you shall see THE SON OF MAN SITTING AT THE RIGHT HAND OF POWER, and COMING WITH THE CLOUDS OF HEAVEN" (Mark 14:62, Jesus quotes from Psalm 110:1; Daniel 7:13; cf. Matthew 26:57–68; see Luke 22:54).

[THE CHRIST from *It is as* you say]

Setting: Jerusalem. Following Jesus' betrayal by Judas and His arrest, after interrogating Him, the chief priests, elders, and scribes deliver Him to Pilate (Roman governor of Judea) for further questioning.

Pilate questioned Him, "Are You the King of the Jews?" And He answered him, "*It is as* you say" (Mark 15:2; cf. Matthew 27:2, 11–14; Luke 23:1–5; John 18:28–38).

[THE CHRIST from THE SPIRIT OF THE LORD IS UPON ME, BECAUSE HE ANOINTED ME TO PREACH THE GOSPEL TO THE POOR. HE HAS SENT ME TO PROCLAIM RELEASE TO THE CAPTIVES, AND RECOVERY OF SIGHT TO THE BLIND, TO SET FREE THOSE WHO ARE OPPRESSED, TO PROCLAIM THE FAVORABLE YEAR OF THE LORD]

Setting: The synagogue in Jesus' hometown of Nazareth in Galilee. At the beginning of Jesus' public ministry, He reads on the Sabbath from the book of the prophet Isaiah.

And the book of the prophet Isaiah was handed to Him. And He opened the book and found the place where it was written, "THE SPIRIT OF THE LORD IS UPON ME, BECAUSE HE ANOINTED ME TO PREACH THE GOSPEL TO THE POOR. HE HAS SENT ME TO PROCLAIM RELEASE TO THE CAPTIVES, AND RECOVERY OF SIGHT TO THE BLIND, TO SET FREE THOSE WHO ARE OPPRESSED, TO PROCLAIM THE FAVORABLE YEAR OF THE LORD." And He closed the book, gave it back to the attendant and sat down; and the eyes of all in the synagogue were fixed on Him. And He began to say to them, "Today this Scripture has been fulfilled in your hearing" (Luke 4:17–21, Jesus quotes from Isaiah 61:1, 2).

[THE CHRIST from Go and report to John what you have seen and heard: the BLIND RECEIVE SIGHT, the lame walk, the lepers are cleansed, and the deaf hear, the dead are raised up, the POOR HAVE THE GOSPEL PREACHED TO THEM.]

Setting: Galilee. After Jesus raises a woman's son from the dead in Nain, the disciples of John the Baptist inquire whether He is the promised Messiah.

And He answered and said to them, "Go and report to John what you have seen and heard: the BLIND RECEIVE SIGHT, the lame walk, the lepers are cleansed, and the deaf hear, the dead are raised up, the POOR HAVE THE GOSPEL PREACHED TO THEM. Blessed is he who does not take offense at Me" (Luke 7:22, 23, Jesus quotes from Isaiah 35:5; 61:1; cf. Matthew 11:2–6).

Setting: The temple in Jerusalem. A few days before His crucifixion, after some of the Sadducees question Him about the resurrection, Jesus poses a question to the scribes, who say He answered well.

Then He said to them, "How is it that they say the Christ is David's son? For David himself says in the book of Psalms, 'THE LORD SAID TO MY LORD, SIT AT MY RIGHT HAND, UNTIL I MAKE YOUR ENEMIES A FOOTSTOOL FOR YOUR FEET.' Therefore David calls Him 'Lord,' and how is He his son?" (Luke 20:41–44, Jesus quotes from Psalm 110:1; cf. Matthew 22:41–46; Mark 12:35–37).

Setting: Jerusalem. After being arrested, having Peter deny Him, and being mocked and beaten, with His crucifixion imminent, Jesus appears before the Sanhedrin.

"If You are the Christ, tell us." But He said to them, "If I tell you, you will not believe; and if I ask you a question, you will not answer. But from now on THE SON OF MAN WILL BE SEATED AT THE RIGHT HAND of the power OF GOD." And they all said, "Are You the Son of God, then? And He said to them, "Yes, I am" (Luke 22:67–70, Jesus quotes from Psalm 110:1; cf. Matthew 26:57–65; Mark 14:55–65).

[THE CHRIST from It is as you say]

Setting: Jerusalem. After being arrested, mocked, and beaten, and appearing before the Council of Elders (Sanhedrin), with His crucifixion imminent, Jesus is brought before Pilate (Roman governor of Judea).

So Pilate asked Him, saying, "Are You the King of the Jews?" And He answered him and said, "It is as you say" (Luke 23:3; cf. Matthew 27:11–14; Mark 15:2–5; John 18:33–38; see Luke 22:70).

Setting: On the way from Jerusalem to Emmaus. After rising from the grave on the third day after being crucified, Jesus appears to two of His followers, who had heard reports the tomb was empty. He elaborates on the purpose of His coming to earth.

And He said to them, "O foolish men and slow of heart to believe in all that the prophets have spoken! Was it not necessary for the Christ to suffer these things and to enter into His glory?" (Luke 24:25, 26).

Setting: Jerusalem. After rising from the grave on the third day following being crucified and appearing to two of His followers on the road to Emmaus, Jesus gives instruction to some of His disciples about His mission on earth and the promise of future power from God.

Now He said to them, "These are My words which I spoke to you while I was still with you, that all things which are written about Me in the Law of Moses and the Prophets and the Psalms must be fulfilled." Then He opened their minds to understand the Scriptures, and He said to them, "Thus it is written, that the Christ would suffer and rise again from the dead the third day, and that repentance for forgiveness of sins would be proclaimed in His name to all the nations, beginning from Jerusalem. You are witnesses of these things. And behold, I am sending forth the promise of My Father upon you; but you are to stay in the city until you are clothed with power from on high" (Luke 24:44–49; see Matthew 28:19, 20; Acts 1:8).

[THE CHRIST from I who speak to you am *He*]
Setting: Sychar in Samaria, on the way to Galilee. Jesus interacts with a Samaritan woman at Jacob's well, while His disciples shop for food.

The woman said to Him, "I know that Messiah is coming (He who is called Christ); when that One comes, He will declare all things to us." Jesus said to her, "I who speak to you am *He*" (John 4:25, 26; see Matthew 1:16; John 8:28, 58).

[THE CHRIST from I am *He*]
Setting: The temple treasury in Jerusalem. Following the Feast of Booths and the scribes' and Pharisees' failed attempt to stone a woman for adultery, Jesus returns the next day to teach as they question His testimony about Himself.

Then He said again to them, "I go away, and you will seek Me, and will die in your sin; where I am going, you cannot come." So the Jews were saying, "Surely He will not kill Himself, will He, since He says, 'Where I am going, you cannot come'?" And He was saying to them, "You are from below, I am from above; you are of this world, I am not of this world. Therefore I said to you that you will die in your sins; for unless you believe that I am *He,* you will die in your sins." So they were saying to Him, "Who are You?" Jesus said to them, "What have I been saying to you *from* the beginning? I have many things to speak and to judge concerning you, but He who sent Me is true; and the things which I heard from Him, these I speak to the world" (John 8:21–26; see John 3:31–33; 5:34, 35; 17:14, 16).

[THE CHRIST from I am *He*]
Setting: The temple treasury in Jerusalem. Following the Feast of Booths and the scribes' and Pharisees' failed attempt to stone a woman for adultery, Jesus returns the next day to teach, as they question His testimony about Himself.

So Jesus said, "When you lift up the Son of Man, then you will know that I am *He,* and I do nothing on my own initiative, but I speak these things as the Father taught Me. And He who sent Me is with Me; He has not left Me alone, for I always do the things that are pleasing to Him" (John 8:28, 29; see John 3:14).

[THE CHRIST from I am *He*]
Setting: An upper room in Jerusalem. Before the Passover, with His death on the cross nearing, Jesus explains the reason for His vivid example of servanthood in washing His disciples' feet.

So when He had washed their feet, and taken His garments and reclined *at the table* again, He said to them, "Do you know what I have done to you? You call Me Teacher and Lord; and you are right, for *so* I am. If I then, the Lord and the Teacher, washed your feet, you also ought to wash one another's feet. For I gave you an example that you also should do as I did to you. Truly, truly I say to you, a slave is not greater than his master, nor *is* one who is sent greater than the one who sent him. If you know these things, you are blessed if you do them. I do not speak of all of you. I know the ones I have chosen; but *it is* that the Scripture may be fulfilled, 'HE WHO EATS MY BREAD HAS LIFTED UP HIS HEEL AGAINST ME.' From now on I am telling you before *it* comes to pass, so that when it does occur, you may believe that I am *He*. Truly, truly, I say to you, he who receives whomever I send receives Me; and he who receives Me receives Him who sent Me" (John 13:12–20; Jesus quotes from Psalm 41:9; see Matthew 7:24; 10:24, 40; John 8:24; 14:29; 1 Peter 5:3).

CHRIST'S SAKE (See SAKE, MY)

CHRISTIAN MANDATE (See GREAT COMMISSION)

CHRISTS, FALSE (Also see DECEPTION; and PROPHETS, FALSE)

[FALSE CHRISTS from For many will come in My name and false prophets]

Setting: The Mount of Olives, just east of Jerusalem. During His discourse, Jesus answers His disciples' questions as to when the temple will be destroyed and Jerusalem overrun, along with the signs of His coming and the end of the age.

And Jesus answered and said to them, "See to it that no one misleads you. For many will come in My name, saying, 'I am the Christ,' and will mislead many. You will be hearing of wars and rumors of wars. See that you are not frightened, for *those things* must take place, but *that* is not yet the end. For nation will rise against nation, and kingdom against kingdom, and in various places there will be famines and earthquakes. But all these things are *merely* the beginning of birth pangs. Then they will deliver you to tribulation, and will kill you, and you will be hated by all nations because of My name. At that time many will fall away and will betray one another and hate one another. Many false prophets will arise and will mislead many. Because lawlessness is increased, most people's love will grow cold. But the one who endures to the end, he will be saved. This gospel of the kingdom shall be preached in the whole world as a testimony to all the nations, and then the end will come" (Matthew 24:4–14; cf. Jeremiah 29:8; Matthew 7:15; 10:17, 22; Mark 13:3–13; Luke 21:7–19; Revelation 6:4).

Setting: The Mount of Olives, just east of Jerusalem. During His discourse, Jesus answers His disciples' questions as to when the temple will be destroyed and Jerusalem overrun, along with the signs of His coming and the end of the age.

"Therefore when you see the ABOMINATION OF DESOLATION which was spoken of through Daniel the prophet, standing in the holy place (let the reader understand), then those who are in Judea must flee to the mountains. Whoever is on the housetop must not go down to get the things that are in his house. Whoever is in the field must not turn back to get his cloak. But woe to those who are pregnant and to those who are nursing babies in those days! But pray that your flight will not be in the winter, or on a Sabbath. For then there will be a great tribulation, such as has not occurred since the beginning of the world until now, nor ever will. Unless those days had been cut short, no life would have been saved; but for the sake of the elect those days will be cut short. Then if anyone says to you, 'Behold, here is the Christ,' or "There *He is,*' do not believe *him.* For false Christs and false prophets will arise and will show great signs and wonders, so as to mislead, if possible, even the elect. Behold, I have told you in advance. So if they say to you, 'Behold, He is in the wilderness,' do not go out, *or,* 'Behold, He is in the inner rooms,' do not believe *them.* For just as the lightning comes from the east and flashes even to the west, so will the coming of the Son of Man be. Wherever the corpse is, there the vultures will gather" (Matthew 24:15–28, Jesus quotes from Daniel 9:27; cf. Daniel 12:1; Mark 13:14–23; Luke 17:22–31; 21:20–24; 23:29; see John 4:48).

[FALSE CHRISTS from Many will come in My name, saying, 'I am *He*'!]

Setting: The Mount of Olives, east of the temple in Jerusalem. During His discourse, after prophesying the temple's destruction, Jesus responds to questions from Peter, James, John, and Andrew about future events.

And Jesus began to say to them, "See to it that no one misleads you. Many will come in My name, saying, 'I am *He!*' and will mislead many. When you hear of wars and rumors of wars, do not be frightened; *those things* must take place; but *that is* not yet the end. For nation will rise up against nation, and kingdom against kingdom; there will be earthquakes in various places; there will *also be* famines. These things are *merely* the beginning of birth pangs. But be on your guard; for they will deliver you to *the* courts, and you will be flogged in *the* synagogues, and you will stand before governors and kings for My sake, as a testimony to them. The gospel must first be preached to all the nations. When they arrest you and hand you over, do not worry beforehand about what you are to say, but say whatever is given you in that hour; for it is not you who speak, but *it is* the Holy Spirit. Brother will betray brother to death, and a father *his* child; and children will rise up against parents and have them put to death. You will be hated by all because of My name, but the one who endures to the end, he will be saved" (Mark 13:5–13; cf. Matthew 24:4–14; Luke 21:7–19; see Matthew 10:17–22).

Setting: The Mount of Olives, east of the temple in Jerusalem. During His discourse, after prophesying the temple's destruction, Jesus responds to questions from Peter, James, John, and Andrew about future events.

"But when you see the ABOMINATION OF DESOLATION standing where it should not be (let the reader understand), then those who are in Judea must flee to the mountains. The one who is on the housetop must not go down, or go in to get anything out of his house; and the one who is in the field must not turn back to get his coat. But woe to those who are pregnant and to those who are nursing babies in those days! But pray that it may not happen in winter. For those days will be a *time of* tribulation such as has not occurred since the beginning of the creation which God created until now, and never will. Unless the Lord had shortened *those* days, no life would have been saved; but for the sake of the elect, whom He chose, He shortened the days. And then if anyone says to you, 'Behold, here is the Christ'; or, 'Behold, *He is* there'; do not believe *him*; for false Christs and false prophets will arise, and will show signs and wonders, in order to lead astray, if possible, the elect. But take heed; behold, I have told you everything in advance" (Mark 13:14–23; cf. Matthew 24:15–28; Luke 21:20–24; see Daniel 9:27; 12:1; Luke 17:31).

[FALSE CHRISTS from many will come in My name]
Setting: The temple in Jerusalem. While ministering a few days before Jesus' crucifixion, after prophesying the destruction of the temple during His Olivet Discourse, His disciples ask Him when this will happen.

And He said, "See to it that you are not misled; for many will come in My name, saying, "I am He,' and, 'The time is near.' Do not go after them. When you hear of wars and disturbances, do not be terrified; for these things must take place first, but the end does not follow immediately" (Luke 21:8, 9; cf. Matthew 24:4–8; Mark 13:5–8).

[FALSE CHRISTS from All who came before Me]
Setting: Jerusalem. Following the Pharisees' interrogation and dismissal of the formerly blind man Jesus healed on the Sabbath, the Lord conveys the Parable of the Good Shepherd to the Pharisees using figures of speech they do not understand.

So Jesus said to them again, "Truly, truly, I say to you, I am the door of the sheep. All who came before Me are thieves and robbers, but the sheep did not hear them. I am the door; if anyone enters through Me, he will be saved, and will go in and out and find pasture. The thief comes only to steal and kill and destroy; I came that they may have life, and have *it* abundantly. I am the good shepherd; the good shepherd lays down His life for the sheep. He who is a hired hand, and not a shepherd, who is not the owner of the sheep, sees the wolf coming, and leaves the sheep and flees, and the wolf snatches them and scatters *them. He flees* because he is a hired hand and is not concerned about the sheep. I am the good shepherd, and I know My own and My own know Me, even as the Father knows Me and I know the Father; and I lay down My life for the sheep. I have other sheep, which are not of this fold; I must bring them also, and they will hear My voice; and they will become one flock *with* one shepherd. For this reason the Father loves Me, because I lay down My life so that I may take it again. No one has taken it away from Me, but I lay it down on My own initiative. I have authority to take it up again. This commandment I received from My Father" (John 10:7–18; see Isaiah 40:11; 56:8; Jeremiah 23:1; Matthew 11:27).

CHURCH (Also see CHURCHES)
Setting: Caesarea Philippi. Jesus responds to Simon Peter's declaration that He is the Christ, the Son of the living God.

And Jesus said to him, "Blessed are you, Simon Barjona, because flesh and blood did not reveal *this* to you, but My Father who is in heaven. I also say to you that you are Peter, and upon this rock I will build My church; and the gates of Hades will not overpower it. I will give you the keys of the kingdom of heaven; and whatever you bind on earth shall have been bound in heaven, and whatever you loose on earth shall have been loosed in heaven" (Matthew 16:17–19; cf. Matthew 18:18; Mark 8:29; Luke 9:20).

Setting: Capernaum of Galilee. After conveying to His disciples the value of little ones, Jesus gives instruction about church discipline.

"If your brother sins, go and show him his fault in private; if he listens to you, you have won your brother. But if he does not listen *to you,* take one or two more with you, so that BY THE MOUTH OF TWO OR THREE WITNESSES EVERY FACT MAY BE CONFIRMED. If he refuses to listen to them, tell it to the church; and if he refuses to listen even to the church, let him be to you as a Gentile and a tax collector. Truly I say to you, whatever you bind of earth shall have been bound in heaven; and whatever you loose on earth shall have been loosed in heaven. Again, I say to you, that if two of you agree on earth about anything that they may ask, it shall be done for them by My Father who is in heaven. For there two or three have gathered together in My name, I am there in their midst" (Matthew 18:15–20. Jesus quotes from Deuteronomy 19:15; cf. Matthew 7:7; 16:19; see Leviticus 19:17; Matthew 28:20; 2 Thessalonians 3:6, 14).

Setting: The island of Patmos (in the Aegean Sea about fifty miles southwest of Ephesus in modern Turkey). On the Lord's Day (Sunday), about fifty years after Jesus' resurrection, the disciple John encounters the Lord Jesus Christ. Jesus communicates a new revelation for the apostle to record for the church in Ephesus and to six other churches in Asia.

"To the angel of the church in Ephesus write: The One who holds the seven stars in His right hand, the One who walks among the seven golden lampstands, says this: 'I know your deeds and your toil and perseverance, and that you cannot tolerate evil men, and you put to the test those who call themselves apostles, and they are not, and you found them *to be* false; and you have perseverance and have endured for My name's sake, and have not grown weary. But I have *this* against you, that you have left your first love. Therefore remember from where you have fallen, and repent and do the deeds you did at first; or else I am coming to you and will remove your lampstand out of its place—unless you repent. Yet this you do have, that you hate the deeds of the Nicolaitans, which I also hate. He who has an ear, let him hear what the Spirit says to the churches. To him who overcomes, I will grant to eat of the tree of life which is in the Paradise of God'" (Revelation 2:1–7; see Genesis 2:9; Ezekiel 28:13; 1 John 4:1; Revelation 1:10, 11, 19, 20; 2:15, 16).

Setting: The island of Patmos (in the Aegean Sea about fifty miles southwest of Ephesus in modern Turkey). On the Lord's Day (Sunday), about fifty years after Jesus' resurrection, the disciple John encounters the Lord Jesus Christ. Jesus communicates a new revelation for the apostle to record for the church in Smyrna and to six other churches in Asia.

"And to the angel of the church in Smyrna write: The first and the last, who was dead, and has come to life, says this: 'I know your tribulation and your poverty (but you are rich), and the blasphemy by those who say they are Jews and are not, but are a synagogue of Satan. Do not fear what you are about to suffer. Behold, the devil is about to cast some of you into prison, so that you will be tested, and you will have tribulation for ten days. Be faithful until death, and I will give you the crown of life. He who has an ear, let him hear what the Spirit says to the churches. He who overcomes will not be hurt by the second death' (Revelation 2:8–11; see Isaiah 44:6; Revelation 1:9, 18; 20:6, 14).

Setting: The island of Patmos (in the Aegean Sea about fifty miles southwest of Ephesus in modern Turkey). On the Lord's Day (Sunday), about fifty years after Jesus' resurrection, the disciple John encounters the Lord Jesus Christ. Jesus communicates a new revelation for the apostle to record for the church in Pergamum and to six other churches in Asia.

"And to the angel of the church in Pergamum write: The One who has the sharp two-edged sword says this: 'I know where you dwell, where Satan's throne is; and you hold fast My name, and did not deny My faith even in the days of Antipas, My witness,

My faithful one, who was killed among you, where Satan dwells. But I have a few things against you, because you have there some who hold the teaching of Balaam, who kept teaching Balak to put a stumbling block before the sons of Israel, to eat things sacrificed to idols and to commit *acts of* immorality. So you also have some who in the same way hold the teaching of the Nicolaitans. Therefore repent; or else I am coming to you quickly, and I will make war against them with the sword of My mouth. He who has an ear, let him hear what the Spirit says to the churches. To him who overcomes, to him I will give *some* of the hidden manna, and I will give him a white stone, and a new name written on the stone which no one knows but he who receives it' (Revelation 2:12–17; see Numbers 25:1–3; Isaiah 62:2; Revelation 1:16).

Setting: The island of Patmos (in the Aegean Sea about fifty miles southwest of Ephesus in modern Turkey). On the Lord's Day (Sunday), about fifty years after Jesus' resurrection, the disciple John encounters the Lord Jesus Christ. Jesus communicates a new revelation for the apostle to record for the church in Thyatira and to six other churches in Asia.

"And to the angel of the church in Thyatira write: The Son of God, who has eyes like a flame of fire, and His feet are like burnished bronze, says this: 'I know your deeds, and your love and faith and service and perseverance, and that your deeds of late are greater than at first. But I have *this* against you, that you tolerate the woman Jezebel, who calls herself a prophetess, and she teaches and leads My bond-servants astray so that they commit *acts of* immorality and eat things sacrificed to idols. I gave her time to repent, and she does not want to repent of her immorality. Behold, I will throw her on a bed *of sickness,* and those who commit adultery with her into great tribulation, unless they repent of her deeds. And I will kill her children with pestilence, and all the churches will know that I am He who searches the minds and hearts; and I will give to each one of you according to your deeds. But I say to you, the rest who are in Thyatira, who do not hold this teaching, who have not known the deep things of Satan, as they call them—I place no other burden on you. Nevertheless what you have, hold fast until I come. He who overcomes, and he who keeps My deeds until the end, TO HIM I WILL GIVE AUTHORITY OVER THE NATIONS; AND HE SHALL RULE THEM WITH A ROD OF IRON, AS THE VESSELS OF THE POTTER ARE BROKEN TO PIECES, as I also have received *authority* from My Father; and I will give him the morning star. He who has an ear, let him hear what the Spirit says to the churches' (Revelation 2:18–29; Jesus quotes from Psalm 2:8, 9; Isaiah 30:14; see 1 Kings 16:31; Psalm 7:9; Romans 2:5; 1 Corinthians 2:10; 2 Peter 3:9; Revelation 1:14; 2:7; 3:11; 17:1–20).

Setting: The island of Patmos (in the Aegean Sea about fifty miles southwest of Ephesus in modern Turkey). On the Lord's Day (Sunday), about fifty years after Jesus' resurrection, the disciple John encounters the Lord Jesus Christ. Jesus communicates a new revelation for the apostle to record for the church in Sardis and to six other churches in Asia.

"To the angel of the church in Sardis write: He who has the seven Spirits of God and the seven stars, says this: 'I know your deeds, that you have a name that you are alive, but you are dead. Wake up, and strengthen the things that remain, which were about to die; for I have not found your deeds completed in the sight of My God. So remember what you have received and heard; and keep *it,* and repent. Therefore if you do not wake up, I will come like a thief, and you will not know at what hour I will come to you. But you have a few people in Sardis who have not soiled their garments; and they will walk with Me in white, for they are worthy. He who overcomes will thus be clothed in white garments; and I will not erase his name from the book of life, and I will confess his name before My Father and before His angels. He who has an ear, let him hear what the Spirit says to the churches'" (Revelation 3:1–6; see Matthew 10:32; Revelation 1:16).

Setting: The island of Patmos (in the Aegean Sea about fifty miles southwest of Ephesus in modern Turkey). On the Lord's Day (Sunday), about fifty years after Jesus' resurrection, the disciple John encounters the Lord Jesus Christ. Jesus communicates a new revelation for the apostle to record for the church in Philadelphia and to six other churches in Asia.

"And to the angel of the church in Philadelphia write: He who is holy, who is true, who has the key of David, who opens and no one will shut, and who shuts and no one opens, says this: 'I know your deeds. Behold, I have put before you an open door which no one can shut, because you have a little power, and have kept My word, and have not denied My name. Behold, I will cause *those* of the synagogue of Satan, who say that they are Jews and are not, but lie—I will make them come and bow down at your feet, and *make them* know that I have loved you. Because you have kept the word of My perseverance, I also will keep you from the hour of testing, that *hour* which is about to come upon the whole world, to test those who dwell on the earth. I am coming quickly; hold fast what you have, so that no one will take your crown. He who overcomes, I will make him a pillar in the temple of My God, and he will not go out from it anymore; and I will write on him the name of My God, and the name of the city of My God, the new Jerusalem, which comes down out of heaven from My God, and My new name. He who has an ear, let him hear what the Spirit says to the churches'" (Revelation 3:7–13; see Isaiah 22:22; Galatians 2:9; Revelation 2:9, 10, 13, 25; 14:1).

Setting: The island of Patmos (in the Aegean Sea about fifty miles southwest of Ephesus in modern Turkey). On the Lord's Day (Sunday), about fifty years after Jesus' resurrection, the disciple John encounters the Lord Jesus Christ. Jesus communicates a new revelation for the apostle to record for the church in Laodicea and to six other churches in Asia.

"To the angel of the church in Laodicea write: The Amen, the faithful and true Witness, the Beginning of the creation of God, says this: 'I know your deeds, that you are neither cold nor hot; I wish that you were cold or hot. So because you are lukewarm, and neither hot nor cold, I will spit you out of My mouth. Because you say, "I am rich, and have become wealthy, and have need of nothing," and you do not know that you are wretched and miserable and poor and blind and naked, I advise you to buy from Me gold refined by fire so that you may become rich, and white garments so that you may clothe yourself, and *that* the shame of your nakedness will not be revealed; and eye salve to anoint your eyes so that you may see. Those whom I love, I reprove and discipline; therefore be zealous and repent. Behold, I stand at the door and knock; if anyone hears My voice and opens the door, I will come in to him and will dine with him, and he with Me. He who overcomes, I will grant to him to sit down with Me on My throne, as I also overcame and sat down with My Father on His throne. He who has an ear, let him hear what the Spirit says to the churches'" (Revelation 3:14–22; see Proverbs 3:12; Hosea 12:8; John 14:23; 16:33).

CHURCH AGE (See GENTILES, TIMES OF THE)

CHURCH DISCIPLINE

[CHURCH DISCIPLINE from If he refuses to listen to them, tell it to the church; and if he refuses to listen even to the church, let him be to you as a Gentile and a tax collector]

Setting: Capernaum of Galilee. After conveying to His disciples the value of little ones, Jesus gives instruction about church discipline.

"If your brother sins, go and show him his fault in private; if he listens to you, you have won your brother. But if he does not listen *to you,* take one or two more with you, so that BY THE MOUTH OF TWO OR THREE WITNESSES EVERY FACT MAY BE CONFIRMED. If he refuses to listen to them, tell it to the church; and if he refuses to listen even to the church, let him be to you as a Gentile and a tax collector. Truly I say to you, whatever you bind of earth shall have been bound in heaven; and whatever you loose on earth shall have been loosed in heaven. Again, I say to you, that if two of you agree on earth about anything that they may ask, it shall be done for them by My Father who is in heaven. For there two or three have gathered together in My name, I am there in their midst" (Matthew 18:15–20. Jesus quotes from Deuteronomy 19:15; cf. Matthew 7:7; 16:19; see Leviticus 19:17; Matthew 28:20; 2 Thessalonians 3:6, 14).

CHURCH, PREDICTION OF THE (See CHURCH, PROPHECY OF THE)]

CHURCH, PROPHECY OF THE

[PROPHECY OF THE CHURCH from upon this rock I will build My church]

Setting: Caesarea Philippi. Jesus responds to Simon Peter's declaration that He is the Christ, the Son of the living God.

And Jesus said to him, "Blessed are you, Simon Barjona, because flesh and blood did not reveal *this* to you, but My Father who is in heaven. I also say to you that you are Peter, and upon this rock I will build My church; and the gates of Hades will not overpower it. I will give you the keys of the kingdom of heaven; and whatever you bind on earth shall have been bound in heaven, and whatever you loose on earth shall have been loosed in heaven" (Matthew 16:17–19; cf. Matthew 18:18; Mark 8:29; Luke 9:20).

[PROPHECY OF THE CHURCH from THE STONE WHICH THE BUILDERS REJECTED, THIS BECAME THE CHIEF CORNER *stone*]
Setting: The temple in Jerusalem. Jesus delivers a prophecy to the chief priests and elders after they question His authority.

Jesus said to them, "Did you never read in the Scriptures, 'THE STONE WHICH THE BUILDERS REJECTED, THIS BECAME THE CHIEF CORNER stone; THIS CAME ABOUT FROM THE LORD, AND IT IS MARVELOUS IN OUR EYES'? Therefore I say to you, the kingdom of God will be taken away from you and given to a people, producing the fruit of it. And he who falls on this stone will be broken to pieces; but on whomever it falls, it will scatter him like dust" (Matthew 21:42–44, Jesus quotes from Psalm 118:22; cf. Isaiah 8:14, 15; Mark 12:10, 11; Luke 20:17, 18).

[PROPHECY OF THE CHURCH from THE STONE WHICH THE BUILDERS REJECTED, THIS BECAME THE CHIEF CORNER *stone*]
Setting: The temple in Jerusalem. Having His authority questioned by the chief priests, scribes, and elders, Jesus begins to teach them in parables.

And He began to speak to them in parables: "A man PLANTED A VINEYARD AND PUT A WALL AROUND IT, AND DUG A VAT UNDER THE WINE PRESS AND BUILT A TOWER, and rented it out to vine-growers and went on a journey. At the harvest time he sent a slave to the vine-growers, in order to receive some of the produce of the vineyard from the vine-growers. They took him, and beat him and sent him away empty-handed. Again he sent them another slave, and they wounded him in the head, and treated him shamefully. And he sent another, and that one they killed; and so with many others, beating some and killing others. He had one more to send, a beloved son; he sent him last of all to them, saying, 'They will respect my son.' But those vine-growers said to one another, 'This is the heir; come, let us kill him, and the inheritance will be ours!' They took him, and killed him and threw him out of the vineyard. What will the owner of the vineyard do? He will come and destroy the vine-growers, and will give the vineyard to others. Have you not even read this Scripture: 'THE STONE WHICH THE BUILDERS REJECTED, THIS BECAME THE CHIEF CORNER stone; THIS CAME ABOUT FROM THE LORD, AND IT IS MARVELOUS IN OUR EYES'?" (Mark 12:1–11, Jesus quotes from Psalm 118:22, 23; Isaiah 5:1, 2; cf. Matthew 21:33–46; Luke 20:9–19).

[PROPHECY OF THE CHURCH from THE STONE WHICH THE BUILDERS REJECTED, THIS BECAME THE CHIEF CORNER stone]
Setting: The temple in Jerusalem. A few days before His crucifixion, after the chief priests and scribes question His authority to teach and preach, Jesus conveys the Parable of the Vine-Growers to the people.

And He began to tell the people this parable: "A man planted a vineyard and rented it out to vine-growers, and went on a journey for a long time. At the harvest time he sent a slave to the vine-growers, so that they would give him some of the produce of the vineyard; but the vine-growers beat him and sent him away empty-handed. And he proceeded to send another slave; and they beat him also and treated him shamefully and sent him away empty-handed. And he proceeded to send a third; and this one also they wounded and cast out. The owner of the vineyard said, 'What shall I do? I will send my beloved son; perhaps they will respect him.' But when the vine-growers saw him, they reasoned with one another, saying, 'This is the heir; let us kill him so that the inheritance will be ours.' So they threw him out of the vineyard and killed him. What, then, will the owner of the vineyard do to them? He will come and destroy these vine-growers and will give the vineyard to others." When they heard it, they said, "May it never be!" But Jesus looked at them and said, "What then is this that is written: 'THE STONE WHICH THE BUILDERS REJECTED, THIS BECAME THE CHIEF CORNER stone'? Everyone who falls on that stone will be broken to pieces; but on whomever it falls, it will scatter him like dust" (Luke 20:9–18, Jesus quotes from Psalm 118:22; cf. Matthew 21:33–44; Mark 12:1–11; see Ephesians 2:20).

CHURCHES (Also see CHURCH)

Setting: The island of Patmos (in the Aegean Sea about fifty miles southwest of Ephesus in modern Turkey). On the Lord's Day (Sunday), the Apostle John hears the voice of the Lord Jesus Christ about fifty years after Jesus' resurrection, communicating new revelations for the apostle to record for the seven churches in Asia.

I was in the Spirit on the Lord's day, and I heard behind me a loud voice like *the sound* of a trumpet, saying, "Write in a book what you see, and send *it* to the seven churches: to Ephesus and to Smyrna and to Pergamum and to Thyatira and to Sardis and to Philadelphia and to Laodicea" (Revelation 1:10, 11; see Revelation 4:1).

Setting: The island of Patmos (in the Aegean Sea about fifty miles southwest of Ephesus in modern Turkey). On the Lord's Day (Sunday), the disciple John encounters the Lord Jesus Christ about fifty years after His resurrection, communicating new revelations for the apostle to record for the seven churches in Asia.

When I saw Him, I fell at His feet like a dead man. And He placed His right hand on me, saying, "Do not be afraid; I am the first and the last, and the living One; and I was dead, and behold, I am alive forevermore, and I have the keys of death and of Hades. Therefore write the things which you have seen, and the things which are, and the things which will take place after these things. As for the mystery of the seven stars which you saw in My right hand, and the seven golden lampstands: the seven stars are the angels of the seven churches, and the seven lampstands are the seven churches" (Revelation 1:17–20; see Isaiah 44:6; Luke 24:5; Revelation 2:8).

Setting: The island of Patmos (in the Aegean Sea about fifty miles southwest of Ephesus in modern Turkey). On the Lord's Day (Sunday), about fifty years after Jesus' resurrection, the disciple John encounters the Lord Jesus Christ. Jesus communicates a new revelation for the apostle to record for the church in Ephesus and to six other churches in Asia.

"To the angel of the church in Ephesus write: The One who holds the seven stars in His right hand, the One who walks among the seven golden lampstands, says this: 'I know your deeds and your toil and perseverance, and that you cannot tolerate evil men, and you put to the test those who call themselves apostles, and they are not, and you found them *to be* false; and you have perseverance and have endured for My name's sake, and have not grown weary. But I have *this* against you, that you have left your first love. Therefore remember from where you have fallen, and repent and do the deeds you did at first; or else I am coming to you and will remove your lampstand out of its place—unless you repent. Yet this you do have, that you hate the deeds of the Nicolaitans, which I also hate. He who has an ear, let him hear what the Spirit says to the churches. To him who overcomes, I will grant to eat of the tree of life which is in the Paradise of God'" (Revelation 2:1–7; see Genesis 2:9; Ezekiel 28:13; 1 John 4:1; Revelation 1:10, 11, 19, 20).

Setting: The island of Patmos (in the Aegean Sea about fifty miles southwest of Ephesus in modern Turkey). On the Lord's Day (Sunday), about fifty years after Jesus' resurrection, the disciple John encounters the Lord Jesus Christ. Jesus communicates a new revelation for the apostle to record for the church in Smyrna and to six other churches in Asia.

"And to the angel of the church in Smyrna write: The first and the last, who was dead, and has come to life, says this: 'I know your tribulation and your poverty (but you are rich), and the blasphemy by those who say they are Jews and are not, but are a synagogue of Satan. Do not fear what you are about to suffer. Behold, the devil is about to cast some of you into prison, so that you will be tested, and you will have tribulation for ten days. Be faithful until death, and I will give you the crown of life. He who has an ear, let him hear what the Spirit says to the churches. He who overcomes will not be hurt by the second death' (Revelation 2:8–11; see Isaiah 44:6; Revelation 1:9, 18; 2:13; 20:6, 14).

Setting: The island of Patmos (in the Aegean Sea about fifty miles southwest of Ephesus in modern Turkey). On the Lord's Day (Sunday), about fifty years after Jesus' resurrection, the disciple John encounters the Lord Jesus Christ. Jesus communicates a new revelation for the apostle to record for the church in Pergamum and to six other churches in Asia.

"And to the angel of the church in Pergamum write: The One who has the sharp two-edged sword says this: 'I know where you dwell, where Satan's throne is; and you hold fast My name, and did not deny My faith even in the days of Antipas, My witness, My faithful one, who was killed among you, where Satan dwells. But I have a few things against you, because you have there some who hold the teaching of Balaam, who kept teaching Balak to put a stumbling block before the sons of Israel, to eat things sacrificed to idols and to commit *acts of* immorality. So you also have some who in the same way hold the teaching of the Nicolaitans. Therefore repent; or else I am coming to you quickly, and I will make war against them with the sword of My mouth. He who has an ear, let him hear what the Spirit says to the churches. To him who overcomes, to him I will give *some* of the hidden manna, and I will give him a white stone, and a new name written on the stone which no one knows but he who receives it' (Revelation 2:12–17; see Numbers 25:1–3; Isaiah 62:2; Revelation 1:16; 2:5, 6, 16).

Setting: The island of Patmos (in the Aegean Sea about fifty miles southwest of Ephesus in modern Turkey). On the Lord's Day (Sunday), about fifty years after Jesus' resurrection, the disciple John encounters the Lord Jesus Christ. Jesus communicates a new revelation for the apostle to record for the church in Thyatira and to six other churches in Asia.

"And to the angel of the church in Thyatira write: The Son of God, who has eyes like a flame of fire, and His feet are like burnished bronze, says this: 'I know your deeds, and your love and faith and service and perseverance, and that your deeds of late are greater than at first. But I have *this* against you, that you tolerate the woman Jezebel, who calls herself a prophetess, and she teaches and leads My bond-servants astray so that they commit *acts of* immorality and eat things sacrificed to idols. I gave her time to repent, and she does not want to repent of her immorality. Behold, I will throw her on a bed *of sickness,* and those who commit adultery with her into great tribulation, unless they repent of her deeds. And I will kill her children with pestilence, and all the churches will know that I am He who searches the minds and hearts; and I will give to each one of you according to your deeds. But I say to you, the rest who are in Thyatira, who do not hold this teaching, who have not known the deep things of Satan, as they call them—I place no other burden on you. Nevertheless what you have, hold fast until I come. He who overcomes, and he who keeps My deeds until the end, TO HIM I WILL GIVE AUTHORITY OVER THE NATIONS; AND HE SHALL RULE THEM WITH A ROD OF IRON, AS THE VESSELS OF THE POTTER ARE BROKEN TO PIECES, as I also have received *authority* from My Father; and I will give him the morning star. He who has an ear, let him hear what the Spirit says to the churches' (Revelation 2:18–29; Jesus quotes from Psalm 2:8, 9; Isaiah 30:14; see 1 Kings 16:31; Psalm 7:9; Romans 2:5; 1 Corinthians 2:10; 2 Peter 3:9; Revelation 1:14; 2:7; 3:11; 17:1–20).

Setting: The island of Patmos (in the Aegean Sea about fifty miles southwest of Ephesus in modern Turkey). On the Lord's Day (Sunday), about fifty years after Jesus' resurrection, the disciple John encounters the Lord Jesus Christ. Jesus communicates a new revelation for the apostle to record for the church in Sardis and to six other churches in Asia.

"To the angel of the church in Sardis write: He who has the seven Spirits of God and the seven stars, says this: 'I know your deeds, that you have a name that you are alive, but you are dead. Wake up, and strengthen the things that remain, which were about to die; for I have not found your deeds completed in the sight of My God. So remember what you have received and heard; and keep *it,* and repent. Therefore if you do not wake up, I will come like a thief, and you will not know at what hour I will come to you. But you have a few people in Sardis who have not soiled their garments; and they will walk with Me in white, for they are worthy. He who overcomes will thus be clothed in white garments; and I will not erase his name from the book of life, and I will confess his name before My Father and before His angels. He who has an ear, let him hear what the Spirit says to the churches'" (Revelation 3:1–6; see Matthew 10:32; Revelation 1:16).

Setting: The island of Patmos (in the Aegean Sea about fifty miles southwest of Ephesus in modern Turkey). On the Lord's Day (Sunday), about fifty years after Jesus' resurrection, the disciple John encounters the Lord Jesus Christ. Jesus communicates a new revelation for the apostle to record for the church in Philadelphia and to six other churches in Asia.

"And to the angel of the church in Philadelphia write: He who is holy, who is true, who has the key of David, who opens and no one will shut, and who shuts and no one opens, says this: 'I know your deeds. Behold, I have put before you an open door which no one can shut, because you have a little power, and have kept My word, and have not denied My name. Behold, I will cause *those* of the synagogue of Satan, who say that they are Jews and are not, but lie—I will make them come and bow down at your feet, and *make them* know that I have loved you. Because you have kept the word of My perseverance, I also will keep you from the hour of testing, that *hour* which is about to come upon the whole world, to test those who dwell on the earth. I am coming quickly; hold fast what you have, so that no one will take your crown. He who overcomes, I will make him a pillar in the temple of My God, and he will not go out from it anymore; and I will write on him the name of My God, and the name of the city of My God, the new Jerusalem, which comes down out of heaven from My God, and My new name. He who has an ear, let him hear what the Spirit says to the churches'" (Revelation 3:7–13; see Isaiah 22:22; Galatians 2:9; Revelation 2:9, 10, 13, 25; 14:1).

Setting: The island of Patmos (in the Aegean Sea about fifty miles southwest of Ephesus in modern Turkey). On the Lord's Day (Sunday), approximately fifty years after Jesus' resurrection, the disciple John encounters the Lord Jesus Christ. Jesus communicates a new revelation for the apostle to record for the church in Laodicea and to six other churches in Asia.

"To the angel of the church in Laodicea write: The Amen, the faithful and true Witness, the Beginning of the creation of God, says this: 'I know your deeds, that you are neither cold nor hot; I wish that you were cold or hot. So because you are lukewarm, and neither hot nor cold, I will spit you out of My mouth. Because you say, "I am rich, and have become wealthy, and have need of nothing," and you do not know that you are wretched and miserable and poor and blind and naked, I advise you to buy from Me gold refined by fire so that you may become rich, and white garments so that you may clothe yourself, and *that* the shame of your nakedness will not be revealed; and eye salve to anoint your eyes so that you may see. Those whom I love, I reprove and discipline; therefore be zealous and repent. Behold, I stand at the door and knock; if anyone hears My voice and opens the door, I will come in to him and will dine with him, and he with Me. He who overcomes, I will grant to him to sit down with Me on My throne, as I also overcame and sat down with My Father on His throne. He who has an ear, let him hear what the Spirit says to the churches'" (Revelation 3:14–22; see Proverbs 3:12; Hosea 12:8; John 14:23; 16:33).

Setting: The island of Patmos (in the Aegean Sea about fifty miles southwest of Ephesus in modern Turkey). In the final chapter of the Lord Jesus Christ's revelation via the disciple John, approximately fifty years after His resurrection, the Lord authenticates the truthfulness of His message, along with His earthly lineage through King David.

"I, Jesus, have sent My angel to testify to you these things for the churches. I am the root and the descendant of David, the bright morning star" (Revelation 22:16).

CHURCHES, SEVEN

Setting: The island of Patmos (in the Aegean Sea about fifty miles southwest of Ephesus in modern Turkey). On the Lord's Day (Sunday), the Apostle John hears the voice of the Lord Jesus Christ approximately fifty years after His resurrection giving him new revelations to record for the seven churches in Asia.

I was in the Spirit on the Lord's day, and I heard behind me a loud voice like *the sound* of a trumpet, saying, "Write in a book what you see, and send *it* to the seven churches: to Ephesus and to Smyrna and to Pergamum and to Thyatira and to Sardis and to Philadelphia and to Laodicea" (Revelation 1:10, 11; see Revelation 4:1).

Setting: The island of Patmos (in the Aegean Sea about fifty miles southwest of Ephesus in modern Turkey). On the Lord's Day (Sunday), the disciple John encounters the Lord Jesus Christ around fifty years after His resurrection for the purpose of the Lord communicating new revelations for the apostle to record for the seven churches in Asia.

When I saw Him, I fell at His feet like a dead man. And He placed His right hand on me, saying, "Do not be afraid; I am the first and the last, and the living One; and I was dead, and behold, I am alive forevermore, and I have the keys of death and of Hades. Therefore write the things which you have seen, and the things which are, and the things which will take place after these things.

As for the mystery of the seven stars which you saw in My right hand, and the seven golden lampstands: the seven stars are the angels of the seven churches, and the seven lampstands are the seven churches" (Revelation 1:17–20; see Isaiah 44:6; Luke 24:5; Revelation 2:8).

CHURCHES IN ASIA (See EPHESUS; LAODICEA; PERGAMUM; PHILADELPHIA; SARDIS; SMYRNA; and THYATIRA)

CIRCUMCISION

Setting: The temple in Jerusalem. After receiving encouragement from His blood brothers in Galilee to attend the upcoming Feast of Booths in order to demonstrate His works to His disciples and the world, Jesus goes and teaches, astonishing the Jewish religious leaders.

Jesus answered them, "I did one deed, and you all marvel. For this reason Moses has given you circumcision (not because it is from Moses, but from the fathers), and on *the* Sabbath you circumcise a man. If a man receives circumcision on *the* Sabbath so that the Law of Moses will not be broken, are you angry with Me because I made an entire man well on *the* Sabbath? Do not judge according to appearance, but judge with righteous judgment" (John 7:21–24; see Genesis 17:10–14; Leviticus 12:3; 19:15; Matthew 12:2; John 5:2–16; 7–20; 7:10–15).

CITIES (The New Testament text contains locations inside and outside Israel not indexed in this book. Check each location under the specific name such as DAMASCUS; EPHESUS; and JERUSALEM; CITIES, FIVE; and CITIES, TEN are listed under separate entries; also see CITY; and TOWNS)

Setting: Galilee. After His disciples observe His ministry, Jesus summons and specifically instructs them about the upcoming difficulties of *their* ministry to the people of Israel.

"Brother will betray brother to death, and a father *his* child; and children will rise up against parents and cause them to be put to death. You will be hated by all because of My name, but it is the one who has endured to the end who will be saved. But whenever they persecute you in one city, flee to the next; for truly I say to you, you will not finish *going through* the cities of Israel until the Son of Man comes" (Matthew 10:21–23; cf. Matthew 10:35, 36; 16:27, 28; 24:9).

Setting: Capernaum in Galilee. After healing Simon's (Peter) mother-in-law from a high fever, Jesus tries to retreat to a secluded place, but the crowds locate Him, and He proclaims His mission.

But He said to them, "I must preach the kingdom of God to the other cities also, for I was sent for this purpose" (Luke 4:43; cf. Matthew 4:23, 24; Mark 1:35–39).

Setting: Jericho, on the way to Jerusalem. After commending Zaccheus's faith in Him, Jesus provides a parable about stewardship.

So He said, "A nobleman went to a distant country to receive a kingdom for himself, and then return. And he called ten of his slaves, and gave them ten minas and said to them, 'Do business with this until I come back.' But his citizens hated him and sent a delegation after him, saying, 'We do not want this man to reign over us.' When he returned, after receiving the kingdom, he ordered that these slaves, to whom he had given the money, be called to him so that he might know what business they had done. The first appeared, saying, 'Master, your mina has made ten minas more.' And he said to him, 'Well done, good slave, because you have been faithful in a very little thing, you are to be in authority over ten cities.' The second came, saying, 'Your mina, master, has made five minas.' And he said to him, also, 'And you are to be over five cities.' Another came, saying, 'Master, here is your mina, which I kept put away in a handkerchief; for I was afraid of you, because you are an exacting man; you take up what you did not lay down and reap what you did not sow.' He said to him, 'By your own words I will judge you, you worthless slave. Did you know that I am an exacting man, taking up what I did not lay down and reaping what I did not sow? Then why did you not put my money in the bank, and having come, I would have collected it with interest?' Then he said to the bystanders, 'Take the mina away from him and give it to the one who has the ten minas.' And they said to him, 'Master, he has ten minas already.' I tell you

that to everyone who has, more shall be given, but from the one who does not have, even what he does have shall be taken away. But these enemies of mine, who did not want me to reign over them, bring them here and slay them in my presence" (Luke 19:12–27; cf. Matthew 25:14–30; see Matthew 13:12; Luke 16:10).

CITIES, FIVE (See CITIES)

CITIES, TEN (See CITIES)

CITIES OF ISRAEL (Listed under ISRAEL, CITIES OF; also check individual city names)

CITIZENS

Setting: As Jesus and His disciples head toward Jerusalem from Galilee, Jesus conveys the illustration of the prodigal son since the Pharisees and scribes complain He associates with tax collectors and sinners.

And He said, "A man had two sons. The younger of them said to his father, 'Father, give me the share of the estate that falls to me.' So he divided his wealth between them. And not many days later, the younger son gathered everything together and went on a journey into a distant country, and there he squandered his estate with loose living. Now when he had spent everything, a severe famine occurred in that country, and he began to be impoverished. So he went and hired himself out to one of the citizens of that country, and he sent him into his fields to feed swine. And he would have gladly filled his stomach with the pods that the swine were eating, and no one was giving anything to him. But when he came to his senses, he said, 'How many of my father's hired men have more than enough bread, but I am dying here with hunger! I will get up and go to my father, and will say to him, "Father, I have sinned against heaven, and in your sight; I am no longer worthy to be called your son; make me as one of your hired men."' So he got up and came to his father. But while he was still a long way off, his father saw him and felt compassion for him, and ran and embraced him and kissed him. And the son said to him, "Father, I have sinned against heaven and in your sight; I am no longer worthy to be called your son.' But the father said to his slaves, 'Quickly bring out the best robe and put it on him, and put a ring on his hand and sandals on his feet; and bring the fattened calf, kill it, and let us eat and celebrate; for this son of mine was dead and has come to life again; he was lost and has been found.' And they began to celebrate. Now his older son was in the field, when he came and approached the house, he heard music and dancing. And he summoned one of the servants and began inquiring what these things could be. And he said to him, 'Your brother has come, and your father has killed the fattened calf because he has received him back safe and sound.' But he became angry and was not willing to go in; and his father came out and began pleading with him. But he answered and said to his father, 'Look! For so many years I have been serving you and I have never neglected a command of yours; and yet you have never given me a young goat, so that I might celebrate with my friends; but when this son of yours came, who has devoured your wealth with prostitutes, you killed the fattened calf for him.' And he said to him, 'Son, you have always been with me, and all that is mine is yours. But we had to celebrate and rejoice, for this brother of yours was dead and has begun to live, and was lost and has been found'" (Luke 15:11–32; see Proverb 29:2).

Setting: As Jesus and His disciples head toward Jerusalem, while in Jericho, after commending Zaccheus's faith in Him, He provides a parable about stewardship.

So He said, "A nobleman went to a distant country to receive a kingdom for himself, and then return. And he called ten of his slaves, and gave them ten minas and said to them, 'Do business with this until I come back.' But his citizens hated him and sent a delegation after him, saying, 'We do not want this man to reign over us.' When he returned, after receiving the kingdom, he ordered that these slaves, to whom he had given the money, be called to him so that he might know what business they had done. The first appeared, saying, 'Master, your mina has made ten minas more.' And he said to him, 'Well done, good slave, because you have been faithful in a very little thing, you are to be in authority over ten cities.' The second came, saying, 'Your mina, master, has made five minas.' And he said to him, also, 'And you are to be over five cities.' Another came, saying, 'Master, here is your mina, which I kept put away in a handkerchief; for I was afraid of you, because you are an exacting man; you take up what you did not lay down and reap what you did not sow.' He said to him, 'By your own words I will judge you, you worthless slave. Did you know that I am an exacting man, taking up what I did not lay down and reaping what I did not sow? Then why did you not put my money in the bank, and having come, I would have collected it with interest?' Then he said to the bystanders, 'Take the mina away from him and give it to the one who has the ten minas.' And they said to him, 'Master, he has ten minas already.' I tell you that to everyone who has, more shall be given, but from the one who does not have, even what he does have shall be taken away. But these enemies of mine, who did not want me to reign over them, bring them here and slay them in my presence" (Luke 19:12–27; compare Matthew 25:14–30; see Matthew 13:12; Luke 16:10).

CITY (Also see TOWN; and VILLAGE)

Setting: Jesus proclaims this part of The Sermon on the Mount as they are on a mountain in Galilee during the early part of His ministry with His disciples and the multitudes as recipients.

"You are the light of the world. A city set on a hill cannot be hidden; nor does *anyone* light a lamp and put it under a basket, but on the lampstand, and it gives light to all who are in the house. Let your light shine before men in such a way that they may see your good works, and glorify your Father who is in heaven" (Matthew 5:14–16; compare Mark 4:21; 1 Peter 2:12).

Setting: Jesus proclaims The Sermon on the Mount as they are on a mountain in Galilee during the early part of His ministry with His disciples and the multitudes as recipients.

"Again, you have heard that the ancients were told, 'YOU SHALL NOT MAKE FALSE VOWS, BUT SHALL FULFILL YOUR VOWS TO THE LORD.' But I say to you, make no oath at all, either by heaven, for it is the throne of God, or by the earth, for it is the footstool of His feet, or by Jerusalem, for it is THE CITY OF THE GREAT KING. Nor shall you make an oath by your head, for you cannot make one hair white or black. But let your statement be 'Yes, yes' *or* 'No, no'; anything beyond these is of evil" (Matthew 5:33–37, Jesus quotes from Leviticus 19:12, Psalm 48:2; Isaiah 66:1; compare James 5:12).

Setting: While in Galilee, after His disciples observe His own ministry, Jesus summons and specifically instructs His twelve disciples about their ministry to the people of Israel.

These twelve Jesus sent out after instructing them: "Do not go in *the* way of *the* Gentiles, and do not enter *any* city of the Samaritans; but rather go to the lost sheep of the house of Israel. And as you go, preach, saying, 'The kingdom of heaven is at hand.' Heal *the* sick, raise *the* dead, cleanse *the* lepers, cast out demons. Freely you received, freely give. Do not acquire gold, or silver, or copper for your money belts, or a bag for *your* journey, or even two coats, or sandals, or a staff; for the worker is worthy of his support. And whatever city or village you enter, inquire who is worthy in it, and stay at his house until you leave *that city*. As you enter the house, give it your greeting. If the house is worthy, give it your *blessing of* peace. But if it is not worthy, take back your *blessing of* peace. Whoever does not receive you, nor heed your words, as you go out of that house or that city, shake the dust off your feet. Truly I say to you, it will be more tolerable for *the* land of Sodom and Gomorrah in the day of judgment than for that city" (Matthew 10:5–15; cf. Mark 6:7–11; Luke 9:1–5; see Matthew 3:2; 11:22, 24; 15:24; Luke 22:35; 1 Corinthians 9:14).

Setting: Galilee. After His disciples observe His ministry, Jesus summons and specifically instructs them about the upcoming difficulties of their ministry to the people of Israel.

"Brother will betray brother to death, and a father *his* child; and children will rise up against parents and cause them to be put to death. You will be hated by all because of My name, but it is the one who has endured to the end who will be saved. But whenever they persecute you in one city, flee to the next; for truly I say to you, you will not finish *going through* the cities of Israel until the Son of Man comes" (Matthew 10:21–23; cf. Matthew 10:35, 36; 16:27, 28; 24:9).

Setting: Galilee. After Jesus heals a blind, mute, demon-possessed man, the Pharisees accuse Jesus in front of crowds of being a worker of Satan.

And knowing their thoughts Jesus said to them, "Any kingdom divided against itself is laid waste; and any city or house divided against itself will not stand. If Satan casts out Satan, he is divided against himself; how then will his kingdom stand? If I by Beelzebul cast out demons, by whom do your sons cast *them* out? For this reason they will be your judges. But if I cast out demons by the Spirit of God, then the kingdom of God has come upon you. Or how can anyone enter the strong man's house and carry off his property, unless he first binds the strong *man?* And then he will plunder his house" (Matthew 12:25–29; cf. Matthew 9:34; Mark 3:23–27; Luke 11:17–20).

Setting: The temple in Jerusalem. Jesus speaks another parable to the chief priests and elders after they question His authority.

Jesus spoke to them again in parables, saying, "The kingdom of heaven may be compared to a king who gave a wedding feast for his son. And he sent out his slaves to call those who had been invited to the wedding feast, and they were unwilling to come. Again he sent out other slaves saying, 'Tell those who have been invited, "Behold, I have prepared my dinner; my oxen and my fattened livestock are *all* butchered and everything is ready; come to the wedding feast." But they paid no attention and went their way, one to his own farm, another to his business, and the rest seized his slaves and mistreated them and killed them. But the king was enraged, and he sent his armies and destroyed those murderers and set their city on fire. Then he said to his slaves, 'The wedding is ready, but those who were invited were not worthy. 'Go therefore to the main highways, and as many as you find *there,* invite to the wedding feast.' Those slaves went out into the streets and gathered together all they found, both evil and good; and the wedding hall was filled with dinner guests. But when the king came in to look over the dinner guests, he saw a man there who was not dressed in wedding clothes, and he said to him, 'Friend, how did you come in here without wedding clothes?' And the man was speechless. Then the king said to the servants, 'Bind him hand and foot, and throw him into the outer darkness; in that place there will be weeping and gnashing of teeth.' For many are called, but few *are* chosen" (Matthew 22:1–14; cf. Matthew 8:11, 12).

Setting: The temple in Jerusalem. After the Jewish religious leaders test Him with questions, Jesus pronounces the eighth of eight woes on them in front of the crowds and His disciples.

"Woe to you, scribes and Pharisees, hypocrites! For you build the tombs of the prophets and adorn the monuments of the righteous, and say, 'If we had been *living* in the days of our fathers, we would not have been partners with them in *shedding* the blood of the prophets.' So you testify against yourselves, that you are sons of those who murdered the prophets. Fill up, then, the measure *of the guilt* of you fathers. You serpents, you brood of vipers, how will you escape the sentence of hell? Therefore, behold, I am sending you prophets and wise men and scribes; some of them you will kill and crucify, and some of them you will scourge in your synagogues, and persecute from city to city, so that upon you may fall *the guilt of* all the righteous blood shed on earth, from the blood of righteous Abel to the blood of Zechariah, the son of Berechiah, whom you murdered between the temple and the altar. Truly I say to you, all these things will come upon this generation" (Matthew 23:29–36; cf. 2 Chronicles 24:21; Zechariah 1:1; Matthew 3:7; Luke 11:47–52; see Matthew 10:23).

Setting: Jerusalem. Just after Judas makes arrangements with the chief priests to betray Jesus, on the first day of the Feast of Unleavened Bread, Jesus informs His disciples where they will celebrate the Passover.

And He said, "Go into the city to a certain man, and say to him, 'The Teacher says, "My time is near; I *am to* keep the Passover at your house with My disciples"'" (Matthew 26:18; cf. Mark 14:13–15; Luke 22:7–13).

Setting: Jerusalem. On the first day of the Feast of Unleavened Bread, when the Passover lamb is to be sacrificed, Jesus responds to His disciples' questions about His plans for the Passover meal.

And He sent two of His disciples and said to them, "Go into the city, and a man will meet you carrying a pitcher of water; follow him; and wherever he enters, say to the owner of the house, 'The Teacher says, "Where is My guest room in which I may eat the Passover with My disciples?"' And he himself will show you a large upper room furnished *and* ready; prepare for us there" (Mark 14:13–15; cf. Matthew 26:17–19; Luke 22:7–13).

Setting: Galilee. After raising Jairus's daughter from the dead, Jesus calls the twelve disciples together and gives them power and authority over demons, along with the ability to heal diseases.

And He said to them, "Take nothing for your journey, neither a staff, nor a bag, nor bread, nor money; and do not even have two tunics apiece. Whatever house you enter, stay there until you leave that city. And as for those who do not receive you, go out from that city, shake the dust off your feet as a testimony against them" (Luke 9:3–5; cf. Matthew 10:1–15; Mark 6:7–11; see Luke 10:4–12).

Setting: On the way from Galilee to Jerusalem. The Lord appoints seventy followers and sends them out in pairs to every city and place He Himself will soon visit.

And He was saying to them, "The harvest is plentiful, but the laborers are few; therefore beseech the Lord of the harvest to send out laborers into His harvest. Go; behold, I send you out as lambs in the midst of wolves. Carry no money belt, no bag, no shoes; and greet no one on the way. Whatever house you enter, first say, 'Peace be to this house.' If a man of peace is there, your peace will rest on him; but if not, it will return to you. Stay in that house, eating and drinking what they give you; for the laborer is worthy of his wages. Do not keep moving from house to house. Whatever city you enter and they receive you, eat what is set before you; and heal those in it who are sick, and say to them, 'The kingdom of God has come near to you.' But whatever city you enter and they do not receive you, go out into its streets and say, 'Even the dust of your city which clings to our feet we wipe off in protest against you; yet be sure of this, that the kingdom of God has come near.' I say to you, it will be more tolerable in that day for Sodom than for that city" (Luke 10:2–12; see Genesis 19:24–28; Matthew 9:37, 38, 10:9–14, 16; 1 Corinthians 10:27).

Setting: On the way from Galilee to Jerusalem. While teaching in the cities and villages, after Jesus responds to a question about who is saved, some Pharisees ask Him to leave, claiming Herod Antipas (tetrarch of Galilee and Perea) seeks to kill Him.

And He said to them, "Go and tell that fox, 'Behold, I cast out demons and perform cures today and tomorrow, and the third day I reach My goal.' Nevertheless I must journey on today and tomorrow and the next day; for it cannot be that a prophet would perish outside of Jerusalem. O Jerusalem, Jerusalem, the city that kills the prophets and stones those sent to her! How often I wanted to gather your children together, just as a hen gathers her brood under her wings, and you would not have it! Behold, your house is left to you desolate; and I say to you, you will not see Me until the time comes when you say, 'BLESSED IS HE WHO COMES IN THE NAME OF THE LORD!'" (Luke 13:32–35, Jesus quotes from Psalm 118:26; cf. Matthew 23:37).

Setting: On the way from Galilee to Jerusalem. After Jesus speaks a parable to the invited guests and the host at a banquet, He responds to a guest's proclamation about the blessings of eating bread in the kingdom of God.

But He said to him, "A man was giving a big dinner, and he invited many; and at the dinner hour he sent his slave to say to those who had been invited, 'Come; for everything is ready now.' But they all alike began to make excuses. The first one said to him, 'I have bought a piece of land and I need to go out and look at it; please consider me excused.' Another one said, 'I have bought five yoke of oxen, and I am going to try them out; please consider me excused.' Another one said, I have married a wife, and for that reason I cannot come.' And the slave came back and reported this to his master. Then the head of the household became angry and said to his slave, 'Go out at once into the streets and lanes of the city and bring in here the poor and crippled and blind and lame.' And the slave said, 'Master, what you commanded has been done, and still there is room.' And the master said to the slave, 'Go out into the highways and along the hedges, and compel them to come in, so that my house may be filled. For I tell you, none of those men who were invited shall taste of my dinner'" (Luke 14:16–24; see Deuteronomy 24:5; Matthew 22:2–14).

Setting: On the way from Galilee to Jerusalem. After telling His disciples of His second coming, Jesus instructs them about persistence in prayer.

Now He was telling them a parable to show that at all times they ought to pray and not to lose heart, saying, "In a certain city there was a judge who did not fear God and did not respect man. There was a widow in that city, and she kept coming to him, saying, 'Give me legal protection from my opponent.' For a while he was unwilling; but afterward he said to himself, 'Even though I do not fear God nor respect man, yet because this woman bothers me, I will give her legal protection, otherwise by continually coming she will wear me out.'" And the Lord said, "Hear what the unrighteous judge said; now, will not God bring about justice for His elect who cry to Him day and night, and will He delay long over them? I tell you that He will bring about justice for them quickly. However, when the Son of Man comes, will He find faith on the earth?" (Luke 18:1–8; see Luke 11:5–10).

Setting: The Mount of Olives, just east of Jerusalem. During His discourse, following a time of ministry in the temple a few days before His crucifixion, Jesus elaborates about future events.

"But when you see Jerusalem surrounded by armies, then recognize that her desolation is near. Then those who are in Judea must flee to the mountains, and those who are in the midst of the city must leave, and those who are in the country must not enter the city; because these are days of vengeance, so that all things which are written will be fulfilled. Woe to those who are pregnant and to those who are nursing babies in those days; for there will be a great distress upon the land and wrath to this people; and they will fall by the edge of the sword, and will be led captive into all the nations; and Jerusalem will be trampled under foot by the Gentiles until the times of the Gentiles are fulfilled" (Luke 21:20–24; see Matthew 24:15–18; Mark 13:14–16; Luke 19:43).

Setting: Jerusalem. With the Passover (Feast of Unleavened Bread) approaching, Jesus informs His disciples where they will celebrate the feast, as the chief priests and scribes seek to kill Him, and Satan enters Judas Iscariot in order to betray the Lord.

And Jesus sent Peter and John, saying, "Go and prepare the Passover for us, so that we may eat it." They said to Him, "Where do You want us to prepare it?" And He said to them, "When you have entered the city, a man will meet you carrying a pitcher of water; follow him into the house that he enters. And you shall say to the owner of the house, 'The Teacher says to you, "Where is the guest room in which I may eat the Passover with My disciples?"' And he will show you a large, furnished upper room; prepare it there" (Luke 22:8–12; cf. Matthew 26:17–19; Mark 14:12–16).

Setting: Jerusalem. After rising from the grave on the third day following being crucified and appearing to two of His followers on the road to Emmaus, Jesus gives instruction to some of His disciples about His mission on earth and the promise of future power from God.

Now He said to them, "These are My words which I spoke to you while I was still with you, that all things which are written about Me in the Law of Moses and the Prophets and the Psalms must be fulfilled." Then He opened their minds to understand the Scriptures, and He said to them, "Thus it is written, that the Christ would suffer and rise again from the dead the third day, and that repentance for forgiveness of sins would be proclaimed in His name to all the nations, beginning from Jerusalem. You are witnesses of these things. And behold, I am sending forth the promise of My Father upon you; but you are to stay in the city until you are clothed with power from on high" (Luke 24:44–49; see Matthew 28:19, 20; Acts 1:8).

Setting: On the way from Jerusalem to Damascus. Luke, writing in Acts, reveals how Saul of Tarsus (who will later have the name Paul), a persecutor of the disciples of Jesus, receives the Lord's calling, and is temporarily blinded.

As he was traveling, it happened that he was approaching Damascus, and suddenly a light from heaven flashed around him; and he fell to the ground and heard a voice saying to him. "Saul, Saul, why are you persecuting Me?" And he said, "Who are You, Lord?" And He *said,* "I am Jesus whom you are persecuting, but get up and enter the city, and it will be told you what you must do" (Acts 9:3–6; see Acts 22:7, 8).

Setting: Corinth. Luke, writing in Acts, records the Lord Jesus' comforting revelation through a vision to Paul as he works among the Jews and Gentiles, testifying that Jesus is the Christ (Messiah) during his second missionary journey.

And the Lord said to Paul in the night by a vision, "Do not be afraid *any longer,* but go on speaking and do not be silent; for I am with you, and no man will attack you in order to harm you, for I have many people in this city" (Acts 18:9,10).

Setting: The island of Patmos (in the Aegean Sea about fifty miles southwest of Ephesus in modern Turkey). On the Lord's Day (Sunday), about fifty years after Jesus' resurrection, the disciple John encounters the Lord Jesus Christ. Jesus communicates a new revelation for the apostle to record for the church in Philadelphia and to six other churches in Asia.

"And to the angel of the church in Philadelphia write: He who is holy, who is true, who has the key of David, who opens and no one will shut, and who shuts and no one opens, says this: 'I know your deeds. Behold, I have put before you an open door which no one can shut, because you have a little power, and have kept My word, and have not denied My name. Behold, I will cause *those* of the synagogue of Satan, who say that they are Jews and are not, but lie—I will make them come and bow down at your feet, and *make them* know that I have loved you. Because you have kept the word of My perseverance, I also will keep you from the hour of testing, that *hour* which is about to come upon the whole world, to test those who dwell on the earth. I am coming quickly; hold fast what you have, so that no one will take your crown. He who overcomes, I will make him a pillar in the temple of My God, and he will not go out from it anymore; and I will write on him the name of My God, and the name of the city of My God, the new Jerusalem, which comes down out of heaven from My God, and My new name. He who has an ear, let him hear what the Spirit says to the churches'" (Revelation 3:7–13; see Isaiah 22:22; Galatians 2:9; Revelation 2:9, 10, 13, 25; 14:1).

CITY OF MY GOD (Listed under GOD, CITY OF MY)

CLEANLINESS (Also see CLEANSING)

[CLEANLINESS from clean]

Setting: The temple in Jerusalem. After the Jewish religious leaders test Him with questions, Jesus pronounces the sixth of eight woes on them in front of the crowds and His disciples.

"Woe to you, scribes and Pharisees, hypocrites! For you clean the outside of the cup and of the dish, but inside they are full of robbery and self-indulgence. You blind Pharisee, first clean the inside of the cup and of the dish, so that the outside of it may become clean also" (Matthew 23:25, 26; see Mark 7:4).

[CLEANLINESS from clean]

Setting: On the way from Galilee to Jerusalem. After speaking of how a lamp illuminates, the Lord has lunch with a Pharisee who is surprised He doesn't wash before eating.

But the Lord said to him, "Now you Pharisees clean the outside of the cup and of the platter; but inside of you, you are full of robbery and wickedness. You foolish ones, did not He who made the outside make the inside also? But give that which is within as charity, and then all things are clean for you. But woe to you Pharisees! You pay tithe of mint and rue and every kind of garden herb, and yet disregard justice and the love of God; but these are the things you should have done without neglecting the others. Woe to you Pharisees! For you love the chief seats in the synagogues and the respectful greetings in the market places. Woe to you! For you are like concealed tombs, and the people who walk over them are unaware of it" (Luke 11:39–44; cf. Matthew 23:6–7, 23–27; see Matthew 15:2; Titus 1:15).

[CLEANLINESS from clean]

Setting: An upper room in Jerusalem. With His crucifixion nearing, while He eats the Passover meal with His disciples, Jesus assumes the role of a servant and washes their feet.

Jesus answered and said to him, "What I do you do not realize now, but you will understand hereafter." Peter said to Him, "Never shall You wash my feet!" Jesus answered him, "If I do not wash you, you have no part with Me." Simon Peter said to Him, "Lord, then wash not only my feet, but also my hand and my head." Jesus said to him, "He who has bathed needs only to wash his feet, but is completely clean; and you are clean, but not all of you. For He knew the one who was betraying Him; for this reason He said, "Not all of you are clean" (John 13:7–11; see John 6:64; 15:3).

[CLEANLINESS from clean]
Setting: Jerusalem. Before the Passover, after He conveys the upcoming ministry of the Holy Spirit in His disciples' lives, with His imminent departure from them, Jesus explains He is the vine and they are the branches.

"I am the true vine, and My Father is the vinedresser. Every branch in Me that does not bear fruit, He takes away; and every *branch* that bears fruit, He prunes it so that it may bear more fruit. You are already clean because of the word which I have spoken to you. Abide in Me, and I in you. As the branch cannot bear fruit of itself unless it abides in the vine, so neither *can* you unless you abide in Me. I am the vine, you are the branches; he who abides in Me and I in him, he bears much fruit, for apart from Me you can do nothing. If anyone does not abide in Me, he is thrown away as a branch and dries up; and they gather them, and cast them into the fire and they are burned. If you abide in Me, and My words abide in you, ask whatever you wish, and it will be done for you. My Father is glorified by this, that you bear much fruit, and *so* prove to be My disciples. Just as the Father has loved Me, I have also loved you; abide in My love. If you keep My commandments, you will abide in My love; just as I have kept My Father's commandments and abide in His love. These things I have spoken to you so that My joy may be in you, and *that* your joy may be made full" (John 15:1–11; see Matthew 5:16; 7:7; John 3:29, 35; 6:56; 8:29, 31; 13:10).

CLEANSING (See LEPROSY, CLEANSING FROM; also see LEPERS)

CLEANSING A LEPER (See LEPROSY, CLEANSING FROM)

CLEANSING THE TEMPLE (Listed under TEMPLE, CLEANSING THE)

CLOAK (Also see CLOTHING; COAT; and GARMENT)

Setting: The Mount of Olives, just east of Jerusalem. During His discourse, Jesus answers His disciples' questions as to when the temple will be destroyed and Jerusalem overrun, along with the signs of His coming and the end of the age.

"Therefore when you see the ABOMINATION OF DESOLATION which was spoken of through Daniel the prophet, standing in the holy place (let the reader understand), then those who are in Judea must flee to the mountains. Whoever is on the housetop must not go down to get the things that are in his house. Whoever is in the field must not turn back to get his cloak. But woe to those who are pregnant and to those who are nursing babies in those days! But pray that your flight will not be in the winter, or on a Sabbath. For then there will be a great tribulation, such as has not occurred since the beginning of the world until now, nor ever will. Unless those days had been cut short, no life would have been saved; but for the sake of the elect those days will be cut short. Then if anyone says to you, 'Behold, here is the Christ,' or "There *He is,*' do not believe *him.* For false Christs and false prophets will arise and will show great signs and wonders, so as to mislead, if possible, even the elect. Behold, I have told you in advance. So if they say to you, 'Behold, He is in the wilderness,' do not go out, *or,* 'Behold, He is in the inner rooms,' do not believe *them.* For just as the lightning comes from the east and flashes even to the west, so will the coming of the Son of Man be. Wherever the corpse is, there the vultures will gather" (Matthew 24:15–28, Jesus quotes from Daniel 9:27; cf. Daniel 12:1; Mark 13:14–23; Luke 17:22–31; 21:20–24; 23:29; see John 4:48).

CLOTII, PARABLE OF THE NEW (unshrunk)

Setting: Capernaum near the Sea of Galilee. John the Baptist's disciples ask Jesus why His disciples do not participate in fasting, while they and the Pharisees do.

And Jesus said to them, "The attendants of the bridegroom cannot mourn as long as the bridegroom is with them, can they? But the days will come when the bridegroom is taken away from them, and then they will fast. But no one puts a patch of unshrunk cloth on an old garment; for the patch pulls away from the garment, and a worse tear results. Nor do *people* put new wine into old wineskins; otherwise the wineskins burst, and the wine pours out and the wineskins are ruined; but they put new wine into fresh wineskins, and both are preserved" (Matthew 9:15–17; cf. Mark 2:18–22; Luke 5:33–39).

Setting: Capernaum. John's disciples and the Pharisees question why Jesus' disciples do not fast when they do.

And Jesus said to them, "While the bridegroom is with them, the attendants of the bridegroom cannot fast, can they? So long as they have the bridegroom with them, they cannot fast. But the days will come when the bridegroom is taken away from them, and then they will fast in that day. No one sews a patch of unshrunk cloth on an old garment; otherwise the patch pulls away from it, the new from the old, and a worse tear results. No one puts new wine into old wineskins; otherwise the wine will burst the skins, and the wine is lost and the skins as *well;* but *one puts* new wine into fresh wineskins" (Mark 2:19–22; cf. Matthew 9:14–17; Luke 5:33–38).

[PARABLE OF THE NEW CLOTH from parable and a piece of cloth from a new garment]
Setting: The home of Levi (Matthew) in Capernaum. At a reception for Jesus following Levi's call to be a disciple, the Lord tells a parable to the Pharisees and their scribes, who question His association with tax collectors and sinners.

And He was also telling them a parable: "No one tears a piece of cloth from a new garment and puts it on an old garment; otherwise he will both tear the new, and the piece from the new will not match the old. And no one puts new wine into old wineskins; otherwise the new wine will burst the skins and it will be spilled out, and the skins will be ruined. But new wine must be put into fresh wineskins. And no one, after drinking old wine wishes for new; for he says, 'The old is good enough.'" (Luke 5:36–39; cf. Matthew 9:16, 17; Mark 2:21, 22).

CLOTH, UNSHRUNK

Setting: Capernaum near the Sea of Galilee. John the Baptist's disciples ask Jesus why His disciples do not participate in fasting, while they and the Pharisees do.

And Jesus said to them, "The attendants of the bridegroom cannot mourn as long as the bridegroom is with them, can they? But the days will come when the bridegroom is taken away from them, and then they will fast. But no one puts a patch of unshrunk cloth on an old garment; for the patch pulls away from the garment, and a worse tear results. Nor do *people* put new wine into old wineskins; otherwise the wineskins burst, and the wine pours out and the wineskins are ruined; but they put new wine into fresh wineskins, and both are preserved" (Matthew 9:15–17; cf. Mark 2:18–22; Luke 5:33–39).

Setting: Capernaum. John's disciples and the Pharisees question why Jesus' disciples do not fast when they do.

And Jesus said to them, "While the bridegroom is with them, the attendants of the bridegroom cannot fast, can they? So long as they have the bridegroom with them, they cannot fast. But the days will come when the bridegroom is taken away from them, and then they will fast in that day. No one sews a patch of unshrunk cloth on an old garment; otherwise the patch pulls away from it, the new from the old, and a worse tear results. No one puts new wine into old wineskins; otherwise the wine will burst the skins, and the wine is lost and the skins as *well;* but *one puts* new wine into fresh wineskins" (Mark 2:19–22; cf. Matthew 9:14–17; Luke 5:33–38).

CLOTHES, WEDDING

Setting: The temple in Jerusalem. Jesus speaks another parable to the chief priests and elders after they question His authority.

Jesus spoke to them again in parables, saying, "The kingdom of heaven may be compared to a king who gave a wedding feast for his son. And he sent out his slaves to call those who had been invited to the wedding feast, and they were unwilling to come. Again he sent out other slaves saying, 'Tell those who have been invited, "Behold, I have prepared my dinner; my oxen and my fattened livestock are *all* butchered and everything is ready; come to the wedding feast." But they paid no attention and went their way, one to his own farm, another to his business, and the rest seized his slaves and mistreated them and killed them. But the king was enraged, and he sent his armies and destroyed those murderers and set their city on fire. Then he said to his slaves, 'The wedding is ready, but those who were invited were not worthy. 'Go therefore to the main highways, and as many as you find *there,* invite to the wedding feast.' Those slaves went out into the streets and gathered together all they found, both evil and good; and the wedding hall was filled with dinner guests. But when the king came in to look over the dinner guests, he saw a man there who was not dressed in wedding clothes, and he said to him, 'Friend, how did you come in here without wedding clothes?' And the man was speechless. Then the king said to the servants, 'Bind him hand and foot, and throw him into the outer darkness; in that place there will be weeping and gnashing of teeth.' For many are called, but few *are* chosen" (Matthew 22:1–14; cf. Matthew 8:11, 12).

CLOTHING (CLOTHING, SOFT; and CLOTHING, SHEEP'S are separate entries; also see GARMENTS and specific words for clothing, such as COAT; and SHIRT)

Setting: Galilee. During the early part of His ministry, Jesus preaches the Sermon on the Mount to His disciples and the multitudes.

"For this reason I say to you, do not be worried about your life, *as to* what you will eat or what you will drink; nor for your body, *as to* what you will put on. Is not life more than food, and the body more than clothing? Look at the birds of the air, that they do not sow, nor reap nor gather into barns, and *yet* your heavenly Father feeds them. Are you not worth much more than they? And who of you by being worried can add a *single* hour to his life? And why are you worried about clothing? Observe how the lilies of the field grow; they do not toil nor do they spin, yet I say to you that not even Solomon in all his glory clothed himself like one of these. But if God so clothes the grass of the field, which is *alive* today and tomorrow is thrown into the furnace, *will He* not much more *clothe* you? You of little faith! Do not worry then, saying 'What will we eat?' or 'What will we drink?' or 'What will be wear for clothing?" For the Gentiles eagerly seek all these things; for your heavenly Father knows that you need all these things. But seek first His kingdom and His righteousness, and all these things will be added to you. So do not worry about tomorrow; for tomorrow will care for itself. Each day has enough trouble of its own" (Matthew 6:25–34; cf. Luke 12:22–31; see 1 Kings 10:4–7; Job 35:11; Matthew 8:26).

[CLOTHING from what you will put on]

Setting: On the way from Galilee to Jerusalem. Jesus comforts the crowd and His disciples after giving a parable about riches and greed, while the scribes and Pharisees turn hostile and question Him in an attempt to catch Him in something He might say.

And He said to His disciples, "For this reason I say to you, do not worry about your life, as to what you will eat; nor for your body, as to what you will put on. For life is more than food, and the body more than clothing. Consider the ravens, for they neither sow nor reap; they have no storeroom nor barn, and yet God feeds them; how much more valuable you are than the birds! And which of you by worrying can add a single hour to his life's span? If then you cannot do even a very little thing, why do you worry about other matters? Consider the lilies, how they grow: they neither toil nor spin; but I tell you, not even Solomon in all his glory clothed himself like one of these. But if God so clothes the grass in the field, which is alive today and tomorrow is thrown into the furnace, how much more will He clothe you? You men of little faith! And do not seek what you will eat and what you will drink, and do not keep worrying. For all these things the nations of the world eagerly seek; but your Father knows that you need these things. But seek His kingdom, and these things will be added to you. Do not be afraid, little flock, for your Father has chosen gladly to give you the kingdom" (Luke 12:22–32; cf. Matthew 6:25–33; see 1 Kings 10:4–7; Job 38:41).

CLOTHING, SHEEP'S (Also see DECEPTION; and DISCERNMENT)

Setting: Galilee. During the early part of His ministry, Jesus preaches the Sermon on the Mount to His disciples and the multitudes.

"Beware of the false prophets, who come to you in sheep's clothing, but inwardly are ravenous wolves. You will know them by their fruits. Grapes are not gathered from *bushes* nor figs from thistles, are they? So every good tree bears good fruit, but the bad tree bears bad fruit. A good tree cannot produce bad fruit, nor can a bad tree produce good fruit. Every tree that does not bear good fruit is cut down and thrown into the fire. So then, you will know them by their fruits" (Matthew 7:15–20; cf. Matthew 3:10; 12:33, 35; 24:11, 24; Luke 6:43, 44).

CLOTHING, SOFT

Setting: Galilee. While speaking to the crowds, Jesus pays tribute to the ministry of John the Baptist, but emphasizes that the one who is least in the kingdom of heaven is greater than John.

As these men were going *away,* Jesus began to speak to the crowds about John, "What did you go out into the wilderness to see? A reed shaken by the wind? But what did you go out to see? A man dressed in soft *clothing?* Those who wear soft *clothing* are in kings' palaces! But what did you go out to see? A prophet? Yes, I tell you, and the one who is more than a prophet. This is the one about whom it is written, 'BEHOLD, I SEND MY MESSENGER AHEAD OF YOU, WHO WILL PREPARE YOUR WAY BEFORE YOU.' Truly, I say to you, among those born of women there has not arisen *anyone* greater than John the Baptist! Yet the one who is least in the kingdom of heaven is greater than he. From the days of John the Baptist until now the kingdom of heaven suffers violence, and violent men take it by force. For all the prophets and the Law prophesied until John. And, if you are willing to accept *it,* John himself is Elijah who was to come. He who has ears to hear, let him hear" (Matthew 11:7–15, Jesus quotes from Malachi 3:1; cf. Malachi 4:5; Luke 7:24–28; 16:16; see Matthew 14:5).

Setting: Galilee. After He responds to the disciples of John the Baptist whether He is the promised Messiah, Jesus speaks to the crowds about John.

When the messengers of John had left, He began to speak to the crowds about John, "What did you go out into the wilderness to see? A reed shaken by the wind? But what did you go out to see? A man dressed in soft clothing? Those who are splendidly clothed and live in luxury are found in royal palaces! But what did you go out to see? A prophet? Yes, I say to you, and one who is more than a prophet. This is the one about whom it is written, 'BEHOLD, I SEND MY MESSENGER AHEAD OF YOU, WHO WILL PREPARE YOUR WAY BEFORE YOU.' I say to you, among those born of women there is no one greater than John; yet he who is least in the kingdom of God is greater than he" (Luke 7:24–28, Jesus quotes from Malachi 3:1; cf. Matthew 11:7–11).

CLOUD (Also see CLOUDS; SKY; and WEATHER)

Setting: On the way from Galilee to Jerusalem. After telling how a relationship with Him will divide families, Jesus chastises the crowds for being able to discern the weather but not the present age.

And He was also saying to the crowds, "When you see a cloud rising in the west, immediately you say, 'A shower is coming,' and so it turns out. And when you see a south wind blowing, you say, 'It will be a hot day,' and it turns out that way. You hypocrites! You know how to analyze the appearance of the earth and the sky, but why do you not analyze this present time?" (Luke 12:54–56; cf. Matthew 16:2, 3).

Setting: The Mount of Olives, just east of Jerusalem. During His discourse, following a time of ministry in the temple a few days before His crucifixion, Jesus elaborates about future events.

"There will be signs in sun and moon and stars, and on the earth dismay among the nations, in perplexity at the roaring of the sea and the waves, men fainting from fear and the expectation of the things which are coming upon the world; for the powers of the heavens will be shaken. Then they will see THE SON OF MAN COMING IN A CLOUD with power and great glory. But when these things begin to take place, straighten up and lift up your heads, because your redemption is drawing near" (Luke 21:25–28, Jesus quotes from Daniel 7:13; cf. Matthew 24:29–31; Mark 13:24–27).

CLOUDS (HEAVEN, CLOUDS OF is a separate entry; also see CLOUD; SKY; and WEATHER)

Setting: The Mount of Olives, just east of Jerusalem. During His discourse, Jesus answers His disciples' questions as to when the temple will be destroyed and Jerusalem overrun, along with the signs of His coming and the end of the age.

"But immediately after the tribulation of those days THE SUN WILL BE DARKENED, AND THE MOON WILL NOT GIVE ITS LIGHT, AND THE STARS WILL FALL from the sky, and the powers of the heavens will be shaken. And then the sign of the Son of Man will appear in the sky, and then all the tribes of the earth will mourn, and they will see the SON OF MAN COMING ON THE CLOUDS OF THE SKY with power and great glory. And He will send forth His angels with A GREAT TRUMPET and THEY WILL GATHER TOGETHER His elect from the four winds, from one end of the sky to the other" (Matthew 24:29–31, Jesus quotes from Isaiah 13:10, Daniel 7:13; Exodus 19:16; cf. Mark 13:24–27; Luke 21:25–27).

Setting: The Mount of Olives, east of the temple in Jerusalem. During His discourse, after prophesying the temple's destruction, Jesus responds to questions from Peter, James, John, and Andrew about future events.

"But in those days, after that tribulation, THE SUN WILL BE DARKENED AND THE MOON WILL NOT GIVE ITS LIGHT, AND THE STARS WILL BE FALLING from heaven, and the powers that are in the heavens will be shaken. Then they will see THE SON OF MAN COMING IN CLOUDS with great power and glory. And then He will send forth the angels, and will gather together His elect from the four winds, from the farthest end of the earth to the farthest end of heaven" (Mark 13:24–27. Jesus quotes from Isaiah 13:10; 34:4; Daniel 7:13; cf. Matthew 24:29–31; Luke 21:25–27).

CLOUDS OF HEAVEN (Listed under HEAVEN, CLOUDS OF; also see CLOUDS)

CLUBS (weapons)

Setting: Gethsemane on the Mount of Olives, just east of Jerusalem. As He submits to His Father's will and allows Judas to betray Him, Jesus reveals that this incident is a fulfillment of prophecy.

At that time Jesus said to the crowds, "Have you come out with swords and clubs to arrest Me as *you would* against a robber? Every day I used to sit in the temple teaching and you did not seize Me. But all this has taken place to fulfill the Scriptures of the prophets" (Matthew 26:55, 56; cf. Mark 14:48, 49; Luke 22:52, 53).

Setting: Gethsemane on the Mount of Olives, just east of Jerusalem. Judas betrays Jesus with a kiss in front of the crowd of chief priests, scribes, and elders seeking to seize Jesus with swords and clubs.

And Jesus said to them, "Have you come out with swords and clubs to arrest Me, as *you would* against a robber? Every day I was with you in the temple teaching, and you did not seize Me; but *this has taken place* to fulfill the Scriptures" (Mark 14:48, 49; cf. Matthew 26:55, 56; Luke 22:52, 53).

Setting: Gethsemane on the Mount of Olives, just east of Jerusalem. After praying for deliverance, with His crucifixion imminent, Jesus chastises the religious leaders after Judas betrays Him and the hostile crowd surrounds Him.

Then Jesus said to the chief priests and officers of the temple and elders who had come against Him, "Have you come out with swords and clubs as you would against a robber? While I was with you daily in the temple, you did not lay hands on Me; but this hour and the power of darkness are yours" (Luke 22:52, 53; cf. Matthew 26:47–56; Mark 14:43–50).

CLUBS, SWORDS AND (See SWORDS; also see SWORD)

COAT (Also see CLOAK; CLOTHING; GARMENTS; and ROBE)

Setting: The Mount of Olives, just east of Jerusalem. During His discourse, Jesus answers His disciples' questions as to when the temple will be destroyed and Jerusalem overrun, along with the signs of His coming and the end of the age.

"If anyone wants to sue you and take your shirt, let him have your coat also" (Matthew 5:40).

Setting: The Mount of Olives, east of the temple in Jerusalem. During His discourse, after prophesying the temple's destruction, Jesus responds to questions from Peter, James, John, and Andrew about future events.

"But when you see the ABOMINATION OF DESOLATION standing where it should not be (let the reader understand), then those who are in Judea must flee to the mountains. The one who is on the housetop must not go down, or go in to get anything out of his house; and the one who is in the field must not turn back to get his coat. But woe to those who are pregnant and to those who are nursing babies in those days! But pray that it may not happen in winter. For those days will be a *time of* tribulation such as has not occurred since the beginning of the creation which God created until now, and never will. Unless the Lord had shortened *those* days, no life would have been saved; but for the sake of the elect, whom He chose, He shortened the days. And then if anyone says to you, 'Behold, here is the Christ'; or, 'Behold, *He is* there'; do not believe *him*; for false Christs and false prophets will arise, and will show signs and wonders, in order to lead astray, if possible, the elect. But take heed; behold, I have told you everything in advance" (Mark 13:14–23; cf. Matthew 24:15–28; Luke 21:20–24; see Daniel 9:27; 12:1; Luke 17:31).

Setting: Galilee. After selecting His twelve disciples, Jesus teaches the Sermon on the Mount to His disciples and a great throng from Judea, Jerusalem, and the central coastal region of Tyre and Sidon.

"But I say to you who hear, love your enemies, do good to those who hate you, bless those who curse you, pray for those who mistreat you. Whoever hits you on the cheek, offer him the other also; and whoever takes away your coat, do not withhold your shirt from him either. Give to everyone who asks of you, and whoever takes away what is yours, do not demand it back. Treat others the same way you want them to treat you. If you love those who love you, what credit is that to you? For even sinners love those who love them. If you do good to those who do good to you, what credit is that to you? For even sinners do the same. If you lend to those from whom you expect to receive, what credit is that to you? Even sinners lend to sinners in order to receive back the same amount. But love your enemies, and do good, and lend, expecting nothing in return; and your reward will be great, and you will be sons of the Most High; for He Himself is kind to ungrateful and evil men. Be merciful, just as your Father is merciful" (Luke 6:27–36; cf. Matthew 5:9, 39–48; Matthew 7:12; see Luke 6:12–19, 25).

Setting: Jerusalem. During the Feast of Unleavened Bread (Passover) just before His crucifixion, while celebrating the Passover meal, instituting the Lord's Supper, and prophesying Peter's upcoming denial of Him, Jesus instructs His disciples to prepare to persevere without Him.

And He said to them, "When I sent you out without money belt and bag and sandals, you did not lack anything, did you?" They said, "No, nothing." And He said to them, "But now, whoever has a money belt is to take it along, likewise also a bag, and whoever has no sword is to sell his coat and buy one. For I tell you that this which is written must be fulfilled in Me, 'AND HE WAS NUMBERED WITH TRANSGRESSORS'; for that which refers to Me has its fulfillment." They said, "Lord, look, here are two swords." And He said to them, "It is enough" (Luke 22:35–38, Jesus quotes from Isaiah 53:12; see Matthew 10:5–15; Mark 6:7–11; Luke 9:1–5; 10:1–12; 22:49; John 17:4).

COATS (Also see COAT)

Setting: Galilee. After His disciples observe His ministry, Jesus summons and specifically instructs them about their ministry to the people of Israel.

These twelve Jesus sent out after instructing them: "Do not go in *the* way of *the* Gentiles, and do not enter *any* city of the Samaritans; but rather go to the lost sheep of the house of Israel. And as you go, preach, saying, 'The kingdom of heaven is at hand.' Heal *the* sick, raise *the* dead, cleanse *the* lepers, cast out demons. Freely you received, freely give. Do not acquire gold, or silver, or copper for your money belts, or a bag for *your* journey, or even two coats, or sandals, or a staff; for the worker is worthy of his support. And whatever city or village you enter, inquire who is worthy in it, and stay at his house until you leave *that city*. As you enter the house, give it your greeting. If the house is worthy, give it your *blessing of* peace. But if it is not worthy, take back your *blessing of* peace. Whoever does not receive you, nor heed your words, as you go out of that house or that city, shake the dust off your feet. Truly I say to you, it will be more tolerable for *the* land of Sodom and Gomorrah in the day of judgment than for that city" (Matthew 10:5–15; cf. Mark 6:7–11; Luke 9:1–5; see Matthew 3:2; 11:22, 24; 15:24; Luke 22:35; 1 Corinthians 9:14).

COHABITATION (See SEXUAL SIN)

COIN (Also see CENT; COINS; DENARII; DENARIUS; MONEY; and SHEKEL)

Setting: The temple in Jerusalem. The Pharisees' disciples and the Herodians test Jesus about the poll-tax, in order to trap Him.

But Jesus perceived their malice, and said, "Why are you testing Me, you hypocrites? Show Me the coin *used* for the poll-tax." And they brought Him a denarius. And He said to them, "Whose likeness and inscription is this?" They said to Him, "Caesar's." Then He said to them, "Then render to Caesar the things that are Caesar's; and to God the things that are God's" (Matthew 22:18–21; cf. Matthew 17:25; Mark 12:15–17; Luke 20:22–25).

Setting: On the way from Galilee to Jerusalem. Jesus conveys the principles of the lost sheep and the lost coin because the Pharisees and scribes complain He associates with tax collectors and sinners.

"So He told them this parable, saying, "What man among you, if he has a hundred sheep and has lost one of them, does not leave the ninety-nine in the open pasture and go after the one which is lost until he finds it? When he has found it, he lays it on his shoulders, rejoicing. And when he comes home, he calls together his friends and his neighbors, saying to them, 'Rejoice with me, for I have found my sheep which was lost!' I tell you that in the same way, there will be more joy in heaven over one sinner who repents than over ninety-nine righteous persons who need no repentance. Or what woman, if she has ten silver coins and loses one coin, does not light a lamp and sweep the house and search carefully until she finds it? When she has found it, she calls together her friends and neighbors, saying, 'Rejoice with me, for I have found the coin which I had lost!' In the same way, I tell you, there is joy in the presence of the angels of God over one sinner who repents" (Luke 15:3–10; cf. Matthew 18:12-14; see Matthew 9:11-13).

COIN, PARABLE OF THE LOST

[PARABLE OF THE LOST COIN from loses one coin]

Setting: On the way from Galilee to Jerusalem. Jesus conveys the principles of the lost sheep and the lost coin because the Pharisees and scribes complain He associates with tax collectors and sinners.

"So He told them this parable, saying, "What man among you, if he has a hundred sheep and has lost one of them, does not leave the ninety-nine in the open pasture and go after the one which is lost until he finds it? When he has found it, he lays it on his shoulders, rejoicing. And when he comes home, he calls together his friends and his neighbors, saying to them, 'Rejoice with me, for I have found my sheep which was lost!' I tell you that in the same way, there will be more joy in heaven over one sinner who repents than over ninety-nine righteous persons who need no repentance. Or what woman, if she has ten silver coins and loses one coin, does not light a lamp and sweep the house and search carefully until she finds it? When she has found it, she calls together her friends and neighbors, saying, 'Rejoice with me, for I have found the coin which I had lost!' In the same way, I tell you, there is joy in the presence of the angels of God over one sinner who repents" (Luke 15:3–10; cf. Matthew 18:12-14; see Matthew 9:11-13).

COINS (Also see CENT; COIN; DENNARII; DENARIUS; MONEY; and SHEKEL)

Setting: On the way from Galilee to Jerusalem. Jesus conveys the principles of the lost sheep and the lost coin because the Pharisees and scribes complain He associates with tax collectors and sinners.

"So He told them this parable, saying, "What man among you, if he has a hundred sheep and has lost one of them, does not leave the ninety-nine in the open pasture and go after the one which is lost until he finds it? When he has found it, he lays it on his shoulders, rejoicing. And when he comes home, he calls together his friends and his neighbors, saying to them, 'Rejoice with me, for I have found my sheep which was lost!' I tell you that in the same way, there will be more joy in heaven over one sinner who repents than over ninety-nine righteous persons who need no repentance. Or what woman, if she has ten silver coins and loses one coin, does not light a lamp and sweep the house and search carefully until she finds it? When she has found it, she calls together her friends and neighbors, saying, 'Rejoice with me, for I have found the coin which I had lost!' In the same way, I tell you, there is joy in the presence of the angels of God over one sinner who repents" (Luke 15:3–10; cf. Matthew 18:12-14; see Matthew 9:11-13).

COINS, SILVER (See COINS)

CO-LABORERS (See CO-WORKERS)

COLD

Setting: The Mount of Olives, just east of Jerusalem. During His discourse, Jesus answers His disciples' questions as to when the temple will be destroyed and Jerusalem overrun, along with the signs of His coming and the end of the age.

And Jesus answered and said to them, "See to it that no one misleads you. For many will come in My name, saying, 'I am the Christ,' and will mislead many. You will be hearing of wars and rumors of wars. See that you are not frightened, for *those things* must take place, but *that* is not yet the end. For nation will rise against nation, and kingdom against kingdom, and in various places there will be famines and earthquakes. But all these things are *merely* the beginning of birth pangs. Then they will deliver you to tribulation, and will kill you, and you will be hated by all nations because of My name. At that time many will fall away and will betray one another and hate one another. Many false prophets will arise and will mislead many. Because lawlessness is increased, most people's love will grow cold. But the one who endures to the end, he will be saved. This gospel of the kingdom shall be preached in the whole world as a testimony to all the nations, and then the end will come" (Matthew 24:4–14; cf. Jeremiah 29:8; Matthew 7:15; 10:17, 22; Mark 13:3–13; Luke 21:7–19; Revelation 6:4).

Setting: The island of Patmos (in the Aegean Sea about fifty miles southwest of Ephesus in modern Turkey). On the Lord's Day (Sunday), about fifty years after Jesus' resurrection, the disciple John encounters the Lord Jesus Christ. Jesus communicates a new revelation for the apostle to record for the church in Laodicea and to six other churches in Asia.

"To the angel of the church in Laodicea write: The Amen, the faithful and true Witness, the Beginning of the creation of God, says this: 'I know your deeds, that you are neither cold nor hot; I wish that you were cold or hot. So because you are lukewarm, and neither hot nor cold, I will spit you out of My mouth. Because you say, "I am rich, and have become wealthy, and have need of nothing," and you do not know that you are wretched and miserable and poor and blind and naked, I advise you to buy from Me gold refined by fire so that you may become rich, and white garments so that you may clothe yourself, and *that* the shame of your nakedness will not be revealed; and eye salve to anoint your eyes so that you may see. Those whom I love, I reprove and discipline; therefore be zealous and repent. Behold, I stand at the door and knock; if anyone hears My voice and opens the door, I will come in to him and will dine with him, and he with Me. He who overcomes, I will grant to him to sit down with Me on My throne, as I also overcame and sat down with My Father on His throne. He who has an ear, let him hear what the Spirit says to the churches'" (Revelation 3:14–22; see Proverbs 3:12; Hosea 12:8; John 14:23; 16:33).

COLLECTOR, PARABLE OF THE PHARISEE AND THE TAX

[PARABLE OF THE PHARISEE AND THE TAX COLLECTOR from parable; Pharisee; and tax collector]
Setting: On the way from Galilee to Jerusalem. After instructing His disciples about persistence in prayer, Jesus conveys a parable about self-righteousness.

And He also told this parable to some people who trusted in themselves that they were righteous, and viewed others with contempt: "Two men went up into the temple to pray, one a Pharisee and the other a tax collector. The Pharisee stood and was praying this to himself: 'God, I thank You that I am not like other people: swindlers, unjust, adulterers, or even like this tax collector. I fast twice a week; I pay tithes of all that I get.' But the tax collector, standing some distance away, was even unwilling to lift up his eyes to heaven, but was beating his breast, saying, 'God, be merciful to me, the sinner!' I tell you, this man went to his house justified rather than the other; for everyone who exalts himself will be humbled, but he who humbles himself will be exalted" (Luke 18:9–14; see Ezra 9:6; Matthew 6:5, 23:12; Luke 11:42, 16:15; Romans 14:3, 10).

COLLECTOR, TAX (See TAX COLLECTOR)

COLLECTORS, TAX (See TAX COLLECTORS)

COLT

Setting: Bethphage, just outside Jerusalem. On the way to Jerusalem for His crucifixion, after healing some blind men in Jericho, Jesus instructs two disciples to acquire a donkey and colt to be used in His triumphal entry into the city.

When they had approached Jerusalem and had come to Bethphage, at the Mount of Olives, then Jesus sent two disciples, saying to them, "Go into the village opposite you, and immediately you will find a donkey tied *there* and a colt with her; untie them and bring them to Me. If anyone says anything to you, you shall say, 'The Lord has need of them,' and immediately he will send them" (Matthew 21:1–3; cf. Mark 11:1–3; Luke 19:29–31).

Setting: Bethphage, just outside Jerusalem. On the way to Jerusalem for His crucifixion, after healing some blind men in Jericho, Jesus instructs two disciples to acquire a donkey and colt to be used in His triumphal entry into the city.

As they approached Jerusalem, at Bethphage and Bethany, near the Mount of Olives, He sent two of His disciples, and said to them, "Go into the village opposite you, and immediately as you enter it, you will find a colt tied *there,* on which no one yet has ever sat; untie it and bring it *here.* If anyone says to you, 'Why are you doing this?' you say, 'The Lord has need of it'; and immediately he will send it back here" (Mark 11:1–3; cf. Matthew 21:1–3; Luke 19:29–31; see Matthew 21:4–7; Luke 19:32–35; John 12:12–15).

Setting: On the way to Jerusalem. After Jesus provides a parable about stewardship, He and His disciples head to the outskirts of Jerusalem to prepare for His triumphal entry into the city and His upcoming crucifixion.

When He approached Bethphage and Bethany, near the mount that is called Olivet, He sent two of the disciples, saying, "Go into the village ahead of *you;* there, as you enter, you will find a colt tied on which no one yet has ever sat; untie it and bring it *here.* If anyone asks you, 'Why are you untying it?' you shall say, 'The Lord has need of it'" (Luke 19:29–31; cf. Matthew 21:1–3; Mark 11:1–3).

COMFORT

[COMFORT from comforted]

Setting: Galilee. Early in His ministry, Jesus presents the Beatitudes (part of the Sermon on the Mount) to His disciples and the gathered crowds from Galilee, Decapolis, Jerusalem, Judea, and beyond the Jordan.

"Blessed are those who mourn, for they shall be comforted" (Matthew 5:4; see Isaiah 61:2; Matthew 13:35).

Setting: Galilee. After selecting His twelve disciples, Jesus teaches the Beatitudes (part of the Sermon on the Mount) to His disciples and a great throng from Judea, Jerusalem, and the central coastal region of Tyre and Sidon.

"But woe to you who are rich, for you are receiving your comfort in full" (Luke 6:24).

[COMFORT from well-fed now]

Setting: Galilee. After selecting His twelve disciples, Jesus teaches the Beatitudes (part of the Sermon on the Mount) to His disciples and a great throng from Judea, Jerusalem, and the central coastal region of Tyre and Sidon.

"Woe to you who are well fed now, for you shall be hungry. Woe to you who laugh now, for you shall mourn and weep" (Luke 6:25; cf. Matthew 5:4).

[COMFORT from comforted]

Setting: On the way from Galilee to Jerusalem. After He responds to the Pharisees' scoffing at His teaching His disciples about stewardship and the permanence of the Law, Jesus conveys the story of the rich man and Lazarus.

"Now there was a rich man, and he habitually dressed in purple and fine linen, joyously living in splendor every day. And a poor man named Lazarus was laid at his gate, covered with sores, and longing to be fed with the crumbs which were falling from the rich man's table; besides, even the dogs were coming and licking his sores. Now the poor man died and was carried away by the angels to Abraham's bosom; and the rich man also died and was buried. In Hades he lifted up his eyes, being in torment, and saw Abraham far away and Lazarus in his bosom. And he cried out and said, 'Father Abraham, have mercy on me, and send Lazarus so that he may dip the tip of his finger in water and cool off my tongue, for I am in agony in this flame.' But Abraham said, 'Child, remember that during your life you received your good things, and likewise Lazarus bad things; but now he is being comforted here, and you are in agony. And besides all this, between us and you there is a great chasm fixed, so that those who wish to come over from here to you will not be able, and that none may cross over from there to us.' And he said, 'Then I beg you, father, that you send him to my father's house—for I have five brothers—in order that he may warn them, so that they will not also come to this place of torment.' But Abraham said, 'They have Moses and the Prophets; let them hear them.' But he said, 'No, father Abraham, but if someone goes to them from the dead, they will repent!' But he said to him, 'If they do not listen to Moses and the Prophets, they will not be persuaded even if someone rises from the dead'" (Luke 16:19–31; see Luke 3:8; 6:24).

COMING OF THE LORD (Listed under LORD, COMING OF THE; also see JESUS' RETURN; and SON OF MAN, COMING OF THE)

COMING OF THE SON OF MAN (Listed under SON OF MAN, COMING OF THE; also see JESUS' RETURN)

COMING, SECOND (See JESUS' RETURN; LORD, COMING OF THE; and SON OF MAN, COMING OF THE)

COMMAND (Also see COMMANDMENTS; and COMMANDS)

[COMMAND from commanded]

Setting: Capernaum of Galilee. Jesus illustrates forgiveness after Peter asks Him if forgiving someone seven times who has sinned against him is adequate.

"For this reason the kingdom of heaven may be compared to a king who wished to settle accounts with his slaves. When he had begun to settle *them,* one who owed him ten thousand talents was brought to him. But since he did not have *the means* to repay, his lord commanded him to be sold, along with his wife and children and all that he had, and repayment to be made. So the slave fell *to the ground* and prostrated himself before him, saying, 'Have patience with me and I will repay you everything.' And the lord of that slave felt compassion and released him and forgave him the debt. But that slave went out and found one of his fellow slaves who owed him a hundred denarii; and he seized him and *began* to choke *him,* saying, 'Pay back what you owe.' So his fellow slave fell *to the ground* and *began* to plead with him, saying, 'Have patience with me and I will repay you.' But he was unwilling and went and threw him in prison until he should pay back what was owed. So when his fellow slaves saw what had happened, they were deeply grieved and came and reported to their lord all that had happened. Then summoning him, his lord said to him, 'You wicked slave, I forgave you all that debt because you pleaded with me. Should you not also have had mercy on your fellow slave, in the same way that I had mercy on you?' And his lord, moved with anger, handed him over to the torturers until he should repay all that was owed him. My heavenly Father will also do the same to you, if each of you does not forgive his brother from your heart" (Matthew 18:23–35; cf. Matthew 6:12, 14, 15; Luke 7:42; see Matthew 25:19–28).

Setting: Galilee. Upon returning from a high mountain (perhaps Mount Hermon) where Jesus has just been transfigured in front of Peter, James, and John, the four discover the remaining disciples arguing with some scribes.

And He asked them, "What are you discussing with them?" And one of the crowd answered Him, "Teacher, I brought You my son, possessed with a spirit which makes him mute; and whenever it seizes him, it slams him *to the ground* and he foams *at the mouth,* and grinds his teeth and stiffens out. I told Your disciples to cast it out, and they could not *do it.* And He answered them, and said, "O unbelieving generation, how long shall I be with you? How long shall I put up with you? Bring him to Me!" They brought the boy to Him. When he saw Him, immediately the spirit threw him into a convulsion, and falling to the ground, be *began* rolling around and foaming *at the mouth.* And He asked his father, "How long has this been happening to him?" And he said, "From childhood. It has often thrown him both into the fire and into the water to destroy him. But if You can do anything, take pity on us and help us!" And Jesus said to him, "'If You can?' All things are possible to him who believes." Immediately the boy's father cried out and said, "I do believe; help my unbelief." When Jesus saw that a crowd was rapidly gathering, He rebuked the unclean spirit, saying to it, "You deaf and mute spirit, I command you, come out of him and do not enter him again." After crying out and throwing him into terrible convulsions, it came out; and *the boy* became so much like a corpse that most *of them,* said, "He is dead!" But Jesus took him by the hand and raised him; and he got up. When He came into *the* house, His disciples *began* questioning Him privately, "Why could we not drive it out?" And He said to them, "This kind cannot come out by anything but prayer" (Mark 9:16–29; cf. Matthew 17:14–21; Luke 9:37–43; see Matthew 17:20).

Setting: Judea beyond the Jordan (Perea). Jesus teaches the crowds gathered around Him about divorce after the Pharisees test and question Him about this subject.

And He answered and said to them, "What did Moses command you?" They said, "Moses permitted a *man* TO WRITE A CERTIFICATE OF DIVORCE AND SEND *her* AWAY." But Jesus said to them, "Because of your hardness of heart he wrote you this commandment. But from the beginning of creation, *God* MADE THEM MALE AND FEMALE. FOR THIS REASON A MAN SHALL LEAVE HIS FATHER AND MOTHER, AND THE TWO SHALL BECOME ONE FLESH; so they are no longer two, but one flesh. What therefore God has joined together, let no man separate. In the house the disciples *began* questioning Him about this again. And He said to them, "Whoever divorces his wife and marries another woman commits adultery against her; and if she herself divorces her husband and marries another man, she is committing adultery" (Mark 10:3–12, Jesus quotes from Genesis 1:27; 2:24; cf. Matthew 19:1–9; see Deuteronomy 24:1–3; Matthew 5:32; see Romans 7:2, 3; 1 Corinthians 7:10, 11, 39; 1, 13; 1 Timothy 2:14).

[COMMAND from commanded]
Setting: The Mount of Olives, east of the temple in Jerusalem. During His discourse, after prophesying the temple's destruction, Jesus responds to questions from Peter, James, John, and Andrew about future events.

"Take heed, keep on the alert; for you do not know when the *appointed* time will come. *It is* like a man away on a journey, *who* upon leaving his house and putting his slaves in charge, *assigning* to each one his task, also commanded the doorkeeper to stay on the alert. Therefore, be on the alert—for you do not know when the master of the house is coming, whether in the evening, at midnight, or when the rooster crows, or in the morning—in case he should come suddenly and find you asleep. What I say to you I say to all, 'Be on the alert!'" (Mark 13:33–37; cf. Matthew 24:42, 43; Luke 21:34–36; see Luke 12:36–38; Ephesians 6:18).

[COMMAND from commanded]
Setting: Jerusalem. Before the Passover, after Jesus conveys the upcoming ministry of the Holy Spirit in His disciples' lives, He again relates peace, hope, and comfort to them regarding His return to the Father.

"Peace I leave with you; My peace I give to you; not as the world gives do I give to you. Do not let your heart be troubled, nor let it be fearful. You heard that I said to you, 'I go away, and I will come to you,' If you loved Me, you would have rejoiced because I go to the Father, for the Father is greater than I. Now I have told you before it happens, so that when it happens, you may believe. I will not speak much more with you, for the ruler of the world is coming, and he has nothing in Me; but so that the world may know that I love the Father, I do exactly as the Father commanded Me. Get up, let us go from here" (John 14:27–31; see John 10:18, 29; 12:31; 13:19; 16:33).

[COMMAND from commanded]
Setting: On the way from Galilee to Jerusalem. After Jesus speaks a parable to the invited guests and the host at a banquet, He responds to a guest's proclamation about the blessings of eating bread in the kingdom of God.

But He said to him, "A man was giving a big dinner, and he invited many; and at the dinner hour he sent his slave to say to those who had been invited, 'Come; for everything is ready now.' But they all alike began to make excuses. The first one said to him, 'I have bought a piece of land and I need to go out and look at it; please consider me excused.' Another one said, 'I have bought five yoke of oxen, and I am going to try them out; please consider me excused.' Another one said, I have married a wife, and for that reason I cannot come.' And the slave came *back* and reported this to his master. Then the head of the household became angry and said to his slave, 'Go out at once into the streets and lanes of the city and bring in here the poor and crippled and blind and lame.' And the slave said, 'Master, what you commanded has been done, and still there is room.' And the master said to the slave, 'Go out into the highways and along the hedges, and compel *them* to come in, so that my house may be filled. For I tell you, none of those men who were invited shall taste of my dinner'" (Luke 14:16–24; see Deuteronomy 24:5; Matthew 22:2–14).

Setting: On the way from Galilee to Jerusalem. Jesus conveys the illustration of the prodigal son because the Pharisees and scribes complain He associates with tax collectors and sinners.

And He said, "A man had two sons. The younger of them said to his father, 'Father, give me the share of the estate that falls to me.' So he divided his wealth between them. And not many days later, the younger son gathered everything together and went on a journey into a distant country, and there he squandered his estate with loose living. Now when he had spent everything, a severe famine occurred in that country, and he began to be impoverished. So he went and hired himself out to one of the citizens of that country, and he sent him into his fields to feed swine. And he would have gladly filled his stomach with the pods that the swine were eating, and no one was giving anything to him. But when he came to his senses, he said, 'How many of my father's hired men have more than enough bread, but I am dying here with hunger! I will get up and go to my father, and will say to him, "Father, I have sinned against heaven, and in your sight; I am no longer worthy to be called your son; make me as one of your hired men."' So he got up and came to his father. But while he was still a long way off, his father saw him and felt compassion for him, and ran and embraced him and kissed him. And the son said to him, "Father, I have sinned against heaven and in your sight; I am no longer worthy to be called your son.' But the father said to his slaves, 'Quickly bring out the best robe and put it on him, and put a ring on his hand and sandals on his feet; and bring the fattened calf, kill it, and let us eat and celebrate; for this son of mine was dead and has come to life again; he was lost and has been found.' And they began to celebrate. Now his older son was in the field, when he came and approached the house, he heard music and dancing. And he summoned one of the servants and began inquiring what these things could be. And he said to him, 'Your brother has come, and your father has killed the fattened calf because he has received him back safe and sound.' But he became angry and was not willing to go in; and his father came out and began pleading with him. But he answered and said to his father, 'Look! For so many years I have been serving you and I have never neglected a command of yours; and yet you have never given me a young goat, so that I might celebrate with my friends; but when this son of yours came, who has devoured your wealth with prostitutes, you killed the fattened calf for him.' And he said to him, 'Son, you have always been with me, and all that is mine is yours. But we had to celebrate and rejoice, for this brother of yours was dead and has begun to live, and was lost and has been found'" (Luke 15:11–32; see Proverbs 29:2; Luke 15:1, 2).

Setting: Jerusalem. Before the Passover, with His departure in mind, after explaining that He is the vine and His disciples are the branches, Jesus instructs them to love one another.

"This is My commandment, that you love one another, just as I have loved you. Greater love has no one than this, that one lay down his life for his friends. You are My friends if you do what I command you. No longer do I call you slaves, for the slave does not know what his master is doing; but I have called you friends, for all things that I have heard from My Father I have made known to you. You did not choose Me but I chose you, and appointed you that you would go and bear fruit, and *that* your fruit would remain, so that whatever you ask of the Father in My name He may give to you. This I command you, that you love one another" (John 15:12–17; see Matthew 12:50; John 6:70; 8:26; 10:11; 13:34).

COMMANDMENT (Specifics such as COMMANDMENT, MY; COMMANDMENT, NEW; and GOD, COMMANDMENT OF are separate entries; also see COMMANDMENTS)

Setting: Judea beyond the Jordan (Perea). Jesus teaches the crowds gathered around Him about divorce after the Pharisees test and question Him about this subject.

And He answered and said to them, "What did Moses command you?" They said, "Moses permitted a *man* TO WRITE A CERTIFICATE OF DIVORCE AND SEND *her* AWAY." But Jesus said to them, "Because of your hardness of heart he wrote you this commandment. But from the beginning of creation, *God* MADE THEM MALE AND FEMALE. FOR THIS REASON A MAN SHALL LEAVE HIS FATHER AND MOTHER, AND THE TWO SHALL BECOME ONE FLESH; so they are no longer two, but one flesh. What therefore God has joined together, let no man separate. In the house the disciples *began* questioning Him about this again. And He said to them, "Whoever divorces his wife and marries another woman commits adultery against her; and if she herself divorces her husband and marries another man, she is committing adultery" (Mark 10:3–12, Jesus quotes from Genesis 1:27; 2:24; cf. Matthew 19:1–9; see Deuteronomy 24:1–3; Matthew 5:32; see Romans 7:2, 3; 1 Corinthians 7:10, 11, 13, 39; 1 Timothy 2:14).

Setting: The temple in Jerusalem. With the Pharisees and Herodians failing to trap Jesus in a statement, one of the scribes asks Him which commandment is foremost.

Jesus answered, "The foremost is, 'HEAR, O ISRAEL! THE LORD OUR GOD IS ONE LORD; AND YOU SHALL LOVE THE LORD YOUR GOD WITH ALL YOUR HEART, AND WITH ALL YOUR SOUL, AND WITH ALL YOUR MIND AND WITH ALL YOUR STRENGTH.' The second is this, 'YOU SHALL LOVE YOUR NEIGHBOR AS YOURSELF.' There is no other commandment greater than these" (Mark 12:29–31, Jesus quotes from Deuteronomy 6:4, 5; Leviticus 19:18; cf. Matthew 22:34–40).

Setting: Jerusalem. Following the Pharisees' interrogation and dismissal of the formerly blind man Jesus healed on the Sabbath, the Lord conveys the Parable of the Good Shepherd to the Pharisees using figures of speech they do not understand.

So Jesus said to them again, "Truly, truly, I say to you, I am the door of the sheep. All who came before Me are thieves and robbers, but the sheep did not hear them. I am the door; if anyone enters through Me, he will be saved, and will go in and out and find pasture. The thief comes only to steal and kill and destroy; I came that they may have life, and have *it* abundantly. I am the good shepherd; the good shepherd lays down His life for the sheep. He who is a hired hand, and not a shepherd, who is not the owner of the sheep, sees the wolf coming, and leaves the sheep and flees, and the wolf snatches them and scatters *them. He flees* because he is a hired hand and is not concerned about the sheep. I am the good shepherd, and I know My own and My own know Me, even as the Father knows Me and I know the Father; and I lay down My life for the sheep. I have other sheep, which are not of this fold; I must bring them also, and they will hear My voice; and they will become one flock *with* one shepherd. For this reason the Father loves Me, because I lay down My life so that I may take it again. No one has taken it away from Me, but I lay it down on My own initiative. I have authority to take it up again. This commandment I received from My Father" (John 10:7–18; see Isaiah 40:11; 56:8; Jeremiah 23:1; Matthew 11:27).

Setting: Jerusalem. Just days before the Passover, with the chief priests and Pharisees plotting to seize Jesus, who is expressing anxiety about His upcoming death by crucifixion, some believe in Jesus, while others are rejecting His message.

And Jesus cried out and said, "He who believes in Me, does not believe in Me but in Him who sent Me. He who sees Me sees the One who sent Me. I have come *as* Light into the world, so that everyone who believes in Me will not remain in darkness. If anyone hears My sayings and does not keep them, I do not judge him; for I did not come to judge the world, but to save the world. He who rejects Me and does not receive My sayings, has one who judges him; the word I spoke is what will judge him at the last day. For I did not speak on My own initiative, but the Father Himself who sent Me has given Me a commandment *as to* what to say and what to speak. I know that His commandment is eternal life; therefore the things I speak, I speak just as the Father as told Me" (John 12:44–50; see Matthew 10:40; Luke 10:16; John 1:4; 3:17; 5:19; 6:68; 14:9).

COMMANDMENT, FOREMOST

Setting: The temple in Jerusalem. As Jesus teaches, a Pharisee lawyer asks Him which is the great commandment of the Law in order to test Him.

And He said to him, " 'YOU SHALL LOVE THE LORD YOUR GOD WITH ALL YOUR HEART, AND WITH ALL YOUR SOUL, AND WITH ALL YOUR MIND.' This is the great and foremost commandment. The second is like it, 'YOU SHALL LOVE YOUR NEIGHBOR AS YOURSELF.' On these two commandments depend the whole Law and the Prophets" (Matthew 22:37–40; Jesus quotes from Leviticus 19:18; Deuteronomy 6:5; cf. Mark 12:28–34; see Matthew 7:12).

[FOREMOST COMMANDMENT from foremost and no other commandment greater]

Setting: The temple in Jerusalem. With the Pharisees and Herodians failing to trap Jesus in a statement, one of the scribes asks Him which commandment is foremost.

Jesus answered, "The foremost is, 'HEAR, O ISRAEL! THE LORD OUR GOD IS ONE LORD; AND YOU SHALL LOVE THE LORD YOUR GOD WITH ALL YOUR HEART, AND WITH ALL YOUR SOUL, AND WITH ALL YOUR MIND AND WITH ALL YOUR STRENGTH.' The second is this, 'YOU SHALL LOVE YOUR NEIGHBOR AS YOURSELF.' There is no other commandment greater than these" (Mark 12:29–31, Jesus quotes from Deuteronomy 6:4, 5; Leviticus 19:18; cf. Matthew 22:34–40).

COMMANDMENT, GREAT AND FOREMOST

Setting: The temple in Jerusalem. As Jesus teaches, a Pharisee lawyer asks Him which is the great commandment of the Law in order to test Him.

And He said to him, " 'YOU SHALL LOVE THE LORD YOUR GOD WITH ALL YOUR HEART, AND WITH ALL YOUR SOUL, AND WITH ALL YOUR MIND.' This is the great and foremost commandment. The second is like it, 'YOU SHALL LOVE YOUR NEIGHBOR AS YOURSELF.' On these two commandments depend the whole Law and the Prophets" (Matthew 22:37–40; Jesus quotes from Leviticus 19:18; Deuteronomy 6:5; cf. Mark 12:28–34; see Matthew 7:12).

COMMANDMENT, GREATEST (See COMMANDMENT, FOREMOST)

COMMANDMENT, MY

Setting: Jerusalem. Before the Passover, with His departure in mind, after explaining He is the vine and His disciples are the branches, Jesus instructs them to love one another.

"This is My commandment, that you love one another, just as I have loved you. Greater love has no one than this, that one lay down his life for his friends. You are My friends if you do what I command you. No longer do I call you slaves, for the slave does not know what his master is doing; but I have called you friends, for all things that I have heard from My Father I have made known to you. You did not choose Me but I chose you, and appointed you that you would go and bear fruit, and *that* your fruit would remain, so that whatever you ask of the Father in My name He may give to you. This I command you, that you love one another" (John 15:12–17; see Matthew 12:50; John 6:70; 8:26; 10:11; 13:34).

COMMANDMENT, NEW

Setting: Jerusalem. Before the Passover, after revealing to His disciples that Judas will betray Him to the chief priests and Pharisees, Jesus conveys how He will soon be glorified in His death, and commands them to love one another.

Therefore when he had gone out, Jesus said, "Now is the Son of Man glorified, and God is glorified in Him; if God is glorified in Him, God will also glorify Him in Himself, and will glorify Him immediately. Little children, I am with you a little while longer. You will seek Me; and as I said to the Jews, now I also say to you, 'Where I am going, you cannot come.' A new commandment I give to you, that you love one another, even as I have loved you, that you also love one another. By this all men will know that you are My disciples, if you have love for one another" (John 13:31–35; see Leviticus 19:18; John 7:33, 34; 13:1–30; 17:1; 1 John 3:14).

COMMANDMENT OF GOD (Listed under GOD, COMMANDMENT OF)

COMMANDMENTS (COMMANDMENTS, MY; and COMMANDMENTS, MY FATHER'S are separate entries; also see COMMANDMENT; and COMMANDMENTS, QUOTATIONS FROM THE TEN)

Setting: Galilee. During the early part of His ministry, Jesus preaches the Sermon on the Mount to His disciples and the multitudes.

"Whoever then annuls one of the least of these commandments, and teaches others *to do* the same, shall be called least in the kingdom of heaven; but whoever keeps and teaches *them*, he shall be called great in the kingdom of heaven" (Matthew 5:19; cf. Matthew 11:11).

Setting: Judea beyond the Jordan (Perea). Jesus shares with a rich, young ruler how he can obtain eternal life.

And He said to him, "Why are you asking Me about what is good? There is *only* One who is good; but if you wish to enter into life, keep the commandments." *Then* he said to Him, 'Which ones?' And Jesus said, "YOU SHALL NOT COMMIT MURDER; YOU SHALL NOT COMMIT ADULTERY; YOU SHALL NOT STEAL; YOU SHALL NOT BEAR FALSE WITNESS; HONOR YOUR FATHER AND MOTHER; and YOU SHALL LOVE YOUR NEIGHBOR AS YOURSELF." The young man said to Him, "All these things I have kept; what am I still lacking?" Jesus said to him, "If you wish to complete go *and* sell your possessions and give to *the* poor, and you will have treasure in heaven; and come, follow Me" (Matthew 19:16–22, Jesus quotes from Exodus 20:13–15; Leviticus 19:18; cf. Leviticus 18:5; Mark 10:17–21; Luke 10:25–28; 12:33; 18:18–24).

Setting: The temple in Jerusalem. As Jesus teaches, a Pharisee lawyer asks Him which is the great commandment of the Law in order to test Him.

And He said to him, " 'YOU SHALL LOVE THE LORD YOUR GOD WITH ALL YOUR HEART, AND WITH ALL YOUR SOUL, AND WITH ALL YOUR MIND.' This is the great and foremost commandment. The second is like it, 'YOU SHALL LOVE YOUR NEIGHBOR AS YOURSELF.' On these two commandments depend the whole Law and the Prophets" (Matthew 22:37–40; Jesus quotes from Leviticus 19:18; Deuteronomy 6:5; cf. Mark 12:28–34; see Matthew 7:12).

Setting: Judea beyond the Jordan (Perea). After demonstrating to His disciples the importance of little children, Jesus encounters a rich man seeking eternal life.

And Jesus said to him, "Why do you call Me good? No one is good except God alone. You know the commandments, 'DO NOT MURDER, DO NOT COMMIT ADULTERY, DO NOT STEAL, DO NOT BEAR FALSE WITNESS, Do not defraud, HONOR YOUR FATHER AND MOTHER.'" And he said to Him, "Teacher, I have kept all these things from my youth up." Looking at him, Jesus felt a love for him and said to him, "One thing you lack: go and sell all you possess and give to the poor, and you will have treasure in heaven; and come, follow Me" (Mark 10:18–21; Jesus quotes from Exodus 20:12–16; cf. Matthew 19:16–22; Luke 18:18–24; see Matthew 6:20).

Setting: On the way from Galilee to Jerusalem. After speaking of the importance of children, Jesus responds to a ruler's question about inheriting eternal life.

A ruler questioned Him, saying, "Good Teacher, what shall I do to inherit eternal life?" And Jesus said to him, "Why do you call Me good? No one is good except God alone. You know the commandments, 'DO NOT COMMIT ADULTERY, DO NOT MURDER, DO NOT STEAL, DO NOT BEAR FALSE WITNESS, HONOR YOUR FATHER AND MOTHER.'" And he said, "All these things I have kept from my youth." When Jesus heard this, He said to him, "One thing you still lack; sell all that you possess and distribute it to the poor, and you shall have treasure in heaven; and come, follow Me" (Luke 18:18–22, Jesus quotes from Exodus 20:12–16; cf. Matthew 19:16–22; Mark 10:17–22; see Luke 10:25–28).

COMMANDMENTS, MY (Also see COMMANDMENTS)

Setting: Jerusalem. Before the Passover, after responding to Philip's request for Him to show His disciples the Father, Jesus conveys the upcoming role of the Holy Spirit in their lives.

"If you love Me, you will keep My commandments. I will ask the Father, and He will give you another Helper, that He may be with you forever; *that* is the Spirit of truth, whom the world cannot receive, because it does not see Him or know Him, *but* you know Him because He abides with you and will be in you" (John 14:15–17; see John 7:39; 15:26; 1 John 5:3).

Setting: Jerusalem. Before the Passover, after responding to Philip's request for Him to show His disciples the Father, Jesus conveys the upcoming role of the Holy Spirit in their lives.

"I will not leave you as orphans; I will come to you. After a little while the world will no longer see Me, but you *will* see Me; because I live, you will live also. In that day you will know that I am in the Father, and you in Me, and I in you. He who has My commandments and keeps them is the one who loves Me; and he who loves Me will be loved by My Father, and I will love him and will disclose Myself to him" (John 14:18–21; see John 6:57; 10:37, 38; 16:16, 22).

Setting: Jerusalem. Before the Passover, after Jesus conveys the upcoming ministry of the Holy Spirit in His disciples' lives with His impending departure from them, He explains He is the vine and they are the branches.

"I am the true vine, and My Father is the vinedresser. Every branch in Me that does not bear fruit, He takes away; and every *branch* that bears fruit, He prunes it so that it may bear more fruit. You are already clean because of the word which I have spoken to you. Abide in Me, and I in you. As the branch cannot bear fruit of itself unless it abides in the vine, so neither *can* you unless you abide in Me. I am the vine, you are the branches; he who abides in Me and I in him, he bears much fruit, for apart from Me you can do nothing. If anyone does not abide in Me, he is thrown away as a branch and dries up; and they gather them, and cast them into the fire and they are burned. If you abide in Me, and My words abide in you, ask whatever you wish, and it will be done for you. My Father is glorified by this, that you bear much fruit, and *so* prove to be My disciples. Just as the Father has loved Me, I have also loved you; abide in My love. If you keep My commandments, you will abide in My love; just as I have kept My Father's commandments and abide in His love. These things I have spoken to you so that My joy may be in you, and *that* your joy may be made full" (John 15:1–11; see Matthew 5:16; 7:7; John 3:29, 35; 6:56; 8:29, 31; 13:10; 15:16).

COMMANDMENTS, MY FATHER'S (Also see COMMANDMENTS)

Setting: Jerusalem. Before the Passover, after Jesus conveys the upcoming ministry of the Holy Spirit in His disciples' lives with His impending departure from them, He explains He is the vine and they are the branches.

"I am the true vine, and My Father is the vinedresser. Every branch in Me that does not bear fruit, He takes away; and every *branch* that bears fruit, He prunes it so that it may bear more fruit. You are already clean because of the word which I have spoken to you. Abide in Me, and I in you. As the branch cannot bear fruit of itself unless it abides in the vine, so neither *can* you unless you abide in Me. I am the vine, you are the branches; he who abides in Me and I in him, he bears much fruit, for apart from Me you can do nothing. If anyone does not abide in Me, he is thrown away as a branch and dries up; and they gather them, and cast them into the fire and they are burned. If you abide in Me, and My words abide in you, ask whatever you wish, and it will be done for you. My Father is glorified by this, that you bear much fruit, and *so* prove to be My disciples. Just as the Father has loved Me, I have also loved you; abide in My love. If you keep My commandments, you will abide in My love; just as I have kept My Father's commandments and abide in His love. These things I have spoken to you so that My joy may be in you, and *that* your joy may be made full" (John 15:1–11; see Matthew 5:16; 7:7; John 3:29, 35; 6:56; 8:29, 31; 13:10; 15:16).

COMMANDMENTS, QUOTATIONS FROM THE TEN (See COMMANDMENT, FOREMOST; COMMANDMENT, GREAT AND FOREMOST; COMMANDMENTS; and specific commandments listed under ADULTERY; COVETING, DEEDS OF; GOD, LOVING; HONORING FATHER AND MOTHER; MURDER; NEIGHBOR; STEALING; and WITNESS, FALSE)

COMMANDS (Also see COMMAND)

[COMMANDS from commanded]

Setting: Galilee. When Jesus comes down after preaching The Sermon on the Mount, large crowds follow Him as a leper approaches Him asking for cleansing.

Jesus stretched out His hand and touched him, saying, "I am willing, be cleansed." And immediately his leprosy was cleansed. And Jesus said to him, "See that you tell no one; but go, show yourself to the priest and present the offering that Moses commanded, as a testimony to them" (Matthew 8:3, 4; cf. Mark 1:40–44; Luke 5:12–14; see Matthew 8:1, 2).

[COMMANDS from commanded]

Setting: On a mountain in Galilee. Following His resurrection from the dead in Jerusalem, Jesus conveys the Great Commission to the eleven remaining disciples.

And Jesus came up and spoke to them, saying, "All authority has been given to Me in heaven and on earth. Go therefore and make disciples of all the nations, baptizing them in the name of the Father and the Son and the Holy Spirit, teaching them to observe all that I commanded you; and lo, I am with you always, even to the end of the age" (Matthew 28:18–20; cf. Mark 16:15; see Daniel 7:13).

[COMMANDS from commanded]

Setting: Galilee. Early in His ministry, as Jesus preaches and casts out demons in the synagogues, a leper beseeches the Lord to heal him.

Moved with compassion, Jesus stretched out His hand and touched him, and said to him, "I am willing; be cleansed." Immediately the leprosy left him and he was cleansed. And He sternly warned him and immediately sent him away, and He said to him, "See that you say nothing to anyone; but go, show yourself to the priest and offer for your cleansing what Moses commanded, as a testimony to them" (Mark 1:41–44; cf. Luke 5:12–14; see Leviticus 14:1–32; Matthew 8:3).

[COMMANDS from commanded]
Setting: Galilee. Early in His ministry, after calling Simon (Peter), James, and John to follow Him, Jesus heals a leper.

And He stretched out His hand and touched Him, saying, "I am willing; be cleansed." And immediately the leprosy left him. And He ordered him to tell no one, "But go and show yourself to the priest and make an offering for your cleansing, just as Moses commanded, as a testimony to them" (Luke 5:13, 14; cf. Matthew 8:2–4; Mark 1:40–45; see Leviticus 13:49).

[COMMANDS from commanded]
Setting: On the way from Galilee to Jerusalem. After His disciples ask that their faith be increased following His instruction on forgiveness, the Lord illustrates with the mustard seed and an obedient slave.

And the Lord said, "If you had faith like a mustard seed, you would say to this mulberry tree, 'Be uprooted and be planted in the sea'; and it would obey you. Which of you, having a slave plowing or tending sheep, will say to him when he has come from the field, 'Come immediately and sit down to eat'? But will he not say to him, "Prepare something for me to eat, and properly clothe yourself and serve me while I eat and drink; and afterward you may eat and drink'? He does not thank the slave because he did the things which were commanded, does he? So you too, when you do all the things which are commanded you, say, 'We are unworthy slaves; we have done only that which we ought to have done'" (Luke 17:6–10; see Matthew 13:31; Luke 12:37).

COMMENDATION (Also see FAITHFULNESS; and OBEDIENCE)

[COMMENDATION from Well done]
Setting: The Mount of Olives, just east of Jerusalem. During His discourse, after answering His disciples' questions as to when the temple will be destroyed and Jerusalem overrun, along with the signs of His coming and the end of the age, Jesus reemphasizes to His disciples that they should be on the alert for His return.

"For it is just like a man about to go on a journey, who called his own slaves and entrusted his possessions to them. To one he gave five talents, to another, two, and to another, one, each according to his own ability; and he went on his journey. Immediately the one who had received the five talents went and traded with them, and gained five more talents. In the same manner the one who had received the two talents gained two more. But he who received the one talent went away, and dug a hole in the ground and hid his master's money. Now after a long time the master of those slaves came and settled accounts with them. The one who had received the five talents came up and brought five more talents, saying, 'Master, you entrusted five talents to me. See, I have gained five more talents.' His master said to him, 'Well done, good and faithful slave. You were faithful with a few things, I will put you in charge of many things; enter into the joy of your master.' Also the one who had received the two talents came up and said, 'Master, you entrusted two talents to me. See, I have gained two more talents.' His master said to him, 'Well done, good and faithful slave. You were faithful with a few things, I will put you in charge of many things; enter into the joy of your master.' And the one also who had received the one talent came up and said, 'Master, I knew you to be a hard man, reaping where you did not sow and gathering where you scattered no seed. And I was afraid, and went away and hid your talent in the ground. See, you have what is yours.' But his master answered and said to him, 'You wicked, lazy slave, you knew that I reap where I did not sow and gather where I scattered no seed. Then you ought to have put my money in the bank, and on my arrival I would have received my money back with interest. 'Therefore take away the talent from him, and give it to the one who has ten talents.' For to everyone who has, more shall be given, and he will have an abundance; but from the one who does not have, even what he does have shall be taken away. Throw out the worthless slave into the outer darkness; in that place there will be weeping and gnashing of teeth" (Matthew 25:14–30; cf. Matthew 8:12; 13:12; 24:45–47; see Matthew 18:23, 24; Luke 12:44).

[COMMENDATION from his master praised]
Setting: On the way from Galilee to Jerusalem. After conveying the Parable of the Prodigal Son, the Lord teaches His disciples about stewardship.

Now He was also saying to the disciples, "There was a rich man who had a manager, and this manager was reported to him as squandering his possessions. And he called him and said to him, 'What is this I hear about you? Give an accounting of your management, for you can no longer be a manager.' The manager said to himself, 'What shall I do, since my master is taking the management away from me? I am not strong enough to dig; I am ashamed to beg. I know what I shall do, so that when I am removed from the management people will welcome me into their homes.' And he summoned each one of his master's debtors, and he began saying to the first, 'How much do you owe my master?' And he said, 'A hundred measures of oil.' And he said to him, 'Take your bill, and sit down quickly and write fifty.' Then he said to another, 'And how much do you owe?' And he said, 'A hundred measures of wheat.' He said to him, 'Take your bill, and write eighty.' And his master praised the unrighteous manager because he had acted shrewdly; for the sons of this age are more shrewd in relation to their own kind than the sons of light. And I say to you, make friends for yourselves by means of the wealth of unrighteousness, so that when it fails, they will receive you into the eternal dwellings. He who is faithful in a very little thing is faithful also in much; and he who is unrighteous in a very little thing is unrighteous also in much. Therefore if you have not been faithful in the use of unrighteous wealth, who will entrust the true riches to you? And if you have not been faithful in the use of that which is another's, who will give you that which is your own? No servant can serve two masters; for either he will hate the one and love the other, or else he will be devoted to one and despise the other. You cannot serve God and wealth" (Luke 16:1–13; cf. Matthew 6:24; see Matthew 25:14–30).

[COMMENDATION from Well done]
Setting: On the way to Jerusalem. After commending Zaccheus's faith in Him, Jesus provides a parable about stewardship.

So He said, "A nobleman went to a distant country to receive a kingdom for himself, and then return. And he called ten of his slaves, and gave them ten minas and said to them, 'Do business with this until I come back.' But his citizens hated him and sent a delegation after him, saying, 'We do not want this man to reign over us.' When he returned, after receiving the kingdom, he ordered that these slaves, to whom he had given the money, be called to him so that he might know what business they had done. The first appeared, saying, 'Master, your mina has made ten minas more.' And he said to him, 'Well done, good slave, because you have been faithful in a very little thing, you are to be in authority over ten cities.' The second came, saying, 'Your mina, master, has made five minas.' And he said to him, also, 'And you are to be over five cities.' Another came, saying, 'Master, here is your mina, which I kept put away in a handkerchief; for I was afraid of you, because you are an exacting man; you take up what you did not lay down and reap what you did not sow.' He said to him, 'By your own words I will judge you, you worthless slave. Did you know that I am an exacting man, taking up what I did not lay down and reaping what I did not sow? Then why did you not put my money in the bank, and having come, I would have collected it with interest?' Then he said to the bystanders, 'Take the mina away from him and give it to the one who has the ten minas.' And they said to him, 'Master, he has ten minas already.' I tell you that to everyone who has, more shall be given, but from the one who does not have, even what he does have shall be taken away. But these enemies of mine, who did not want me to reign over them, bring them here and slay them in my presence" (Luke 19:12–27; cf. Matthew 25:14–30; see Matthew 13:12; Luke 16:10).

COMMERCE (Also see DEALERS; and MERCHANT)

[COMMERCE from they were buying, they were selling]
Setting: Samaria, on the way from Galilee to Jerusalem. After the Pharisees question Him about the coming of the kingdom of God, Jesus tells His disciples of His second coming.

And He said to the disciples, "The days will come when you will long to see one of the days of the Son of Man, and you will not see it. They will say to you, 'Look there! Look here!' Do not go away, and do not run after them. For just like the lightning, when it flashes out of one part of the sky, shines to the other part of the sky, so will the Son of Man be in His day. But first He must suffer many things and be rejected by this generation. And just as it happened in the days of Noah, so it will be also in the days of the Son of Man: they were eating, they were drinking, they were marrying, they were being given in marriage, until the day that Noah entered the ark, and the flood came and destroyed them all. It was the same as happened in the days of Lot: they were eating, they were drinking, they were buying, they were selling, they were planting, they were building; but on the day that Lot went out from Sodom it rained fire and brimstone from heaven and destroyed them all. It will be just the same on the day that the Son of Man is revealed. On that day, the one who is on the housetop and whose goods are in the house must not go down to take them out; and likewise the one who is in the field must not turn back. Remember Lot's wife. Whoever seeks to keep his life will lose it, and whoever loses his life will preserve it. I tell you, on that night there will be two in one bed; one will be taken and the other will be left. There will be two women grinding at the same place; one will be taken and the other will be left. [Two men will be in the field; one will be taken and the other will be left."] And answering they said to Him, "Where, Lord?" And He said to them, "Where the body is, there also the vultures will be gathered" (Luke 17:22–37; see Genesis 19; Matthew 10:39; 16:21, 27; 24:17–28, 37–41).

COMMISSION, GREAT (See GREAT COMMISSION)

COMMISSIONING, DISCIPLES' (Also see DISCIPLESHIP; FOLLOWING JESUS CHRIST; and PERSECUTION)

[DISCIPLES' COMMISSIONING from Do not go in *the* way of *the* Gentiles]
Setting: Galilee. After His disciples observe His ministry, Jesus summons and specifically instructs them about their ministry to the people of Israel.

These twelve Jesus sent out after instructing them: "Do not go in *the* way of *the* Gentiles, and do not enter *any* city of the Samaritans; but rather go to the lost sheep of the house of Israel. And as you go, preach, saying, 'The kingdom of heaven is at hand.' Heal *the* sick, raise *the* dead, cleanse *the* lepers, cast out demons. Freely you received, freely give. Do not acquire gold, or silver, or copper for your money belts, or a bag for *your* journey, or even two coats, or sandals, or a staff; for the worker is worthy of his support. And whatever city or village you enter, inquire who is worthy in it, and stay at his house until you leave *that city*. As you enter the house, give it your greeting. If the house is worthy, give it your *blessing of* peace. But if it is not worthy, take back your *blessing of* peace. Whoever does not receive you, nor heed your words, as you go out of that house or that city, shake the dust off your feet. Truly I say to you, it will be more tolerable for *the* land of Sodom and Gomorrah in the day of judgment than for that city" (Matthew 10:5–15; cf. Mark 6:7–11; Luke 9:1–5; see Matthew 3:2; 11:22, 24; 15:24; Luke 22:35; 1 Corinthians 9:14).

[DISCIPLES' COMMISSIONING from I send you out as sheep in the midst of wolves]
Setting: Galilee. After His disciples observe His ministry, Jesus summons and specifically instructs them about the upcoming hardships of *their* ministry to the people of Israel.

"Behold, I send you out as sheep in the midst of wolves; so be shrewd as serpents and innocent as doves. But beware of men, for they will hand you over to *the* courts and scourge you in their synagogues; and you will even be brought before governors and kings for My sake, as a testimony to them and to the Gentiles. But when they hand you over, do not worry about how or what you are to say; for it will be given you in that hour what you are to say. For it is not you who speak, but *it* is the Spirit of your Father who speaks in you" (Matthew 10:16–20; cf. Luke 10:3).

[DISCIPLES' COMMISSIONING from Do not put on two tunics]
Setting: The villages of Galilee. After encountering unbelief in His hometown of Nazareth, Jesus sends the Twelve out in pairs with authority and instructions about ministry.

And He summoned the twelve and began to send them out in pairs, and gave them authority over the unclean spirits; and He instructed them that they should take nothing for *their* journey, except a mere staff—no bread, no bag, no money in their belt—but to wear sandals; and *He added,* "Do not put on two tunics." And He said to them, "Wherever you enter a house, stay there until you leave town. Any place that does not receive you or listen to you, as you go out from there, shake the dust off the soles of your feet for a testimony against them" (Mark 6:7–11; cf. Matthew 10:1–14; Luke 9:1–5).

[DISCIPLES' COMMISSIONING from Take nothing for your journey]
Setting: Galilee. After raising Jairus's daughter from the dead, Jesus calls His disciples together and gives them power and authority over demons, along with the ability to heal diseases.

And He said to them, "Take nothing for your journey, neither a staff, nor a bag, nor bread, nor money; and do not even have two tunics apiece. Whatever house you enter, stay there until you leave that city. And as for those who do not receive you, go out from that city, shake the dust off your feet as a testimony against them" (Luke 9:3–5; cf. Matthew 10:1–15; Mark 6:7–11; see Luke 10:4–12).

[DISCIPLES' COMMISSIONING from I send you out as lambs in the midst of wolves]
Setting: On the way from Galilee to Jerusalem. The Lord appoints seventy followers and sends them out in pairs to every city and place He Himself will soon visit.

And He was saying to them, "The harvest is plentiful, but the laborers are few; therefore beseech the Lord of the harvest to send out laborers into His harvest. Go; behold, I send you out as lambs in the midst of wolves. Carry no money belt, no bag, no shoes; and greet no one on the way. Whatever house you enter, first say, 'Peace be to this house.' If a man of peace is there, your peace will rest on him; but if not, it will return to you. Stay in that house, eating and drinking what they give you; for the laborer is worthy of his wages. Do not keep moving from house to house. Whatever city you enter and they receive you, eat what is set before you; and heal those in it who are sick, and say to them, 'The kingdom of God has come near to you.' But whatever city you enter and they do not receive you, go out into its streets and say, 'Even the dust of your city which clings to our feet we wipe off in protest against you; yet be sure of this, that the kingdom of God has come near.' I say to you, it will be more tolerable in that day for Sodom than for that city" (Luke 10:2–12; see Genesis 19:24–28; Matthew 9:37, 38, 10:9–14, 16; 1 Corinthians 10:27).

COMMITMENT (Also see COMMITMENTS; DEVOTION; DISCIPLE; DISCIPLESHIP; FOLLOWING JESUS CHRIST; OBEDIENCE; and SACRIFICE, PERSONAL)

[COMMITMENT from And he who does not take his cross and follow after Me is not worthy of Me]
Setting: Galilee. After His twelve disciples observe His ministry, Jesus summons and specifically instructs them about their ministry ahead involving true discipleship.

"He who loves father or mother more than Me is not worthy of Me; and he who loves son or daughter more than Me is not worthy of Me. And he who does not take his cross and follow after Me is not worthy of Me. He who has found his life will lose it, and he who has lost his life for My sake will find it" (Matthew 10:37–39; cf. Matthew 16:24, 25).

[COMMITMENT from If anyone wishes to come after Me, he must deny himself, and take up his cross and follow Me]
Setting: Near Caesarea Philippi. After rebuking Peter for attempting to forbid Him to accomplish His earthly mission of dying and being resurrected, Jesus teaches His disciples about the costs of discipleship.

Then Jesus said to His disciples, "If anyone wishes to come after Me, he must deny himself, and take up his cross and follow Me. For whoever wishes to save his life will lose it; but whoever loses his life for My sake will find it. For what will it profit a man if he gains the whole world and forfeits his soul? Or what will a man give in exchange for his soul? For the Son of Man is going to come in the glory of His Father with His angels, and WILL THEN REPAY EVERY MAN ACCORDING TO HIS DEEDS. Truly, I say to you, there are some of you who are standing here who will not taste death until they see the Son of Man coming in His kingdom" (Matthew 16:24–28, Jesus quotes from Psalm 62:12; cf. Mark 8:34–37; Luke 9:23–27; see Matthew 10:38, 39).

[COMMITMENT from If anyone wishes to come after Me, he must deny himself, and take up his cross and follow Me]
Setting: Caesarea Philippi. After Jesus rebukes Peter for desiring to thwart His mission to the cross, Jesus summons a crowd along with His disciples and informs them of the high costs of following Him.

And He summoned the crowd with His disciples, and said to them, "If anyone wishes to come after Me, he must deny himself, and take up his cross and follow Me. For whoever wishes to save his life will lose it, but whoever loses his life for My sake and the gospel's will save it. For what does it profit a man to gain the whole world, and forfeit his soul? For what will a man give in exchange for his soul? For whoever is ashamed of Me and My words in this adulterous and sinful generation, the Son of Man will also be ashamed of him when He comes in the glory of His Father with the holy angels" (Mark 8:34–38; cf. Matthew 16:24–28; Luke 9:23–27; see Matthew 10:33, 38, 39).

[COMMITMENT from If anyone wishes to come after Me, he must deny himself, and take up his cross daily and follow Me]
Setting: Galilee. Following Peter's pronouncement that Jesus is the Christ of God, the Lord conveys the demands of discipleship and the hope regarding the kingdom of God.

And He was saying to them all, "If anyone wishes to come after Me, he must deny himself, and take up his cross daily and follow Me. For whoever wishes to save his life will lose it, but whoever loses his life for My sake, he is the one who will save it. For what is a man profited if he gains the whole world, and loses or forfeits himself? For whoever is ashamed of Me and My words, the Son of Man will be ashamed of him when He comes in His glory, and the glory of the Father and of the holy angels. But I say to you truthfully, there are some of those standing here who will not taste death until they see the kingdom of God" (Luke 9:23–27; cf. Matthew 16:24–26, 28; Mark 8:34–37; see Matthew 10:33, 38, 39).

[COMMITMENT from none of you can be My disciple who does not give up all his possessions]
Setting: On the way from Galilee to Jerusalem. After He responds to a guest's proclamation about the blessings of eating bread in the kingdom of God, Jesus presents to large crowds the demands of discipleship.

Now large crowds were going along with Him; and He turned and said to them, "If anyone comes to Me, and does not hate his own father and mother and wife and children and brothers and sisters, yes, and even his own life, he cannot be My disciple. Whoever does not carry his own cross and come after Me cannot be My disciple. For which one of you, when he wants to build a tower, does not first sit down and calculate the cost to see if he has enough to complete it? Otherwise, when he has laid a foundation and is not able to finish, all who observe it begin to ridicule him, saying, 'This man began to build and was not able to finish.' Or what king, when he sets out to meet another king in battle, will not first sit down and consider whether he is strong enough with ten thousand *men* to encounter the one coming against him with twenty thousand? Or else, while the other is still far away, he sends a delegation and asks for terms of peace. So then, none of you can be My disciple who does not give up all his possessions. Therefore, salt is good; but if even salt has become tasteless, with what will it be seasoned? It is useless either for the soil or for the manure pile; it is thrown out. He who has ears to hear, let him hear" (Luke 14:25–35; cf. Matthew 5:13; 10:37–39; see Proverbs 20:18; Philippians 3:7).

COMMITMENTS (Also see COMMITMENT)

[COMMITMENTS from But let your statement be 'Yes, yes' or 'No, no'; anything beyond these is of evil]
Setting: Galilee. During the early part of His ministry, Jesus preaches the Sermon on the Mount to His disciples and the multitudes.

"Again, you have heard that the ancients were told, 'YOU SHALL NOT MAKE FALSE VOWS, BUT SHALL FULFILL YOUR VOWS TO THE LORD.' But I say to you, make no oath at all, either by heaven, for it is the throne of God, or by the earth, for it is the footstool of His feet, or by Jerusalem, for it is THE CITY OF THE GREAT KING. Nor shall you make an oath by your head, for you cannot make one hair white or black. But let your statement be 'Yes, yes' or 'No, no'; anything beyond these is of evil" (Matthew 5:33–37, Jesus quotes from Leviticus 19:12, Psalm 48:2; Isaiah 66:1; cf. James 5:12).

COMMOTION (Also see GRIEF; LAMENT; MOURNING; and WEEPING)

Setting: The home of Jairus (a synagogue official) in Capernaum by the Sea of Galilee. Jesus assures those present that Jairus's daughter has not died, but is asleep.

And entering in, He said to them, "Why make a commotion and weep? The child has not died, but is asleep" (Mark 5:39; cf. Matthew 9:24; Luke 8:52).

COMMUNICATION WITH GOD (See PRAYER)

COMMUNION (See LORD'S SUPPER)

COMPANIONS (Also see FRIEND; and FRIENDS)

Setting: Galilee. Jesus responds to the Pharisees' objection to His disciples' picking grain from the fields on the Sabbath.

But He said to them, "Have you not read what David did when he became hungry, he and his companions, how they entered the house of God, and ate the consecrated bread, which was not lawful for him to eat nor for those with him, but for the priests alone? Or, have you not read in the Law, that on the Sabbath the priests in the temple break the Sabbath and are innocent? But I say to you that something greater than the temple is here. But if you had known what this means, 'I DESIRE COMPASSION, AND NOT A SACRIFICE,' you would not have condemned the innocent. For the Son of Man is Lord of the Sabbath" (Matthew 12:3–8, Jesus quotes from Hosea 6:6; cf. Mark 2:25–28; Luke 6:3–5: see 1 Samuel 21:6; Matthew 12:1, 2).

Setting: Galilee. Early in His ministry, the Pharisees ask Jesus why He allows His disciples to harvest and eat grain on the Sabbath.

And He said to them, "Have you never read what David did when he was in need and he and his companions became hungry; how he entered the house of God in the time of Abiathar *the* high priest, and ate the consecrated bread, which is not lawful for *anyone* to eat except the priests, and he also gave it to those who were with him?" Jesus said to them, "The Sabbath was made for man, and not man for the Sabbath. So the Son of Man is Lord even of the Sabbath" (Mark 2:25–28; cf. Matthew 12:1–8; Luke 6:1–5; see Exodus 23:12).

Setting: Probably in Galilee. As Jesus and His disciples pass through some grain fields, some of the Pharisees ask why His followers harvest and eat grain on the Sabbath.

And Jesus answering them said, "Have you not even read what David did when he was hungry, he and those who were with him, how he entered the house of God, and took and ate the consecrated bread which is not lawful for any to eat except the priests alone, and gave it to his companions?" And He was saying to them, "The Son of Man is Lord of the Sabbath" (Luke 6:3–5; cf. Matthew 12:1–8; Mark 2:23–28; see Exodus 20:8; Leviticus 24:1–9; Deuteronomy 5:12; 1 Samuel 21:1–6).

COMPASSION (Also see LOVE; MERCY; NEIGHBOR; SAMARITAN; and SERVICE)

Setting: The home of Matthew in Capernaum near the Sea of Galilee. Jesus calls Matthew the tax collector to be His disciple.

But when Jesus heard *this*, He said, "*It is* not those who are healthy who need a physician, but those who are sick. But go and learn what this means: 'I DESIRE COMPASSION, AND NOT SACRIFICE,' for I did not come to call the righteous, but sinners" (Matthew 9:12, 13, Jesus quotes from Hosea 6:6; cf. Mark 2:17; Luke 5:31, 32; see Mark 2:15, 16).

Setting: Galilee. Jesus responds to the Pharisees' objection to His disciples' picking grain from the fields on the Sabbath.

But He said to them, "Have you not read what David did when he became hungry, he and his companions, how they entered the house of God, and ate the consecrated bread, which was not lawful for him to eat nor for those with him, but for the priests alone? Or, have you not read in the Law, that on the Sabbath the priests in the temple break the Sabbath and are innocent? But I say to you that something greater than the temple is here. But if you had known what this means, 'I DESIRE COMPASSION, AND NOT A SACRIFICE,' you would not have condemned the innocent. For the Son of Man is Lord of the Sabbath" (Matthew 12:3–8, Jesus quotes from Hosea 6:6; cf. Mark 2:25–28; Luke 6:3–5: see 1 Samuel 21:6; Matthew 12:1, 2).

Setting: Near the Sea of Galilee. After being impressed by a Canaanite woman's faith, Jesus cures her daughter from demon possession, then feeds more than 4,000 primarily Gentile people following Him.

And Jesus called His disciples to Him, and said, "I feel compassion for the people, because they have remained with Me now three days and have nothing to eat; and I do not want to send them away hungry, for they might faint on the way." The disciples said to Him, "Where would we get so many loaves in *this* desolate place to satisfy a large crowd?" And Jesus said to them, "How many loaves do you have?" And they said, "Seven and a few small fish" (Matthew 15:32–34; cf. Mark 8:1–9).

Setting: Capernaum of Galilee. Jesus illustrates forgiveness after Peter asks Him if forgiving someone seven times who has sinned against him is adequate.

"For this reason the kingdom of heaven may be compared to a king who wished to settle accounts with his slaves. When he had begun to settle *them,* one who owed him ten thousand talents was brought to him. But since he did not have *the means* to repay, his lord commanded him to be sold, along with his wife and children and all that he had, and repayment to be made. So the slave fell *to the ground* and prostrated himself before him, saying, 'Have patience with me and I will repay you everything.' And the lord of that slave felt compassion and released him and forgave him the debt. But that slave went out and found one of his fellow slaves who owed him a hundred denarii; and he seized him and *began* to choke *him,* saying, 'Pay back what you owe.' So his fellow slave fell *to the ground* and *began* to plead with him, saying, 'Have patience with me and I will repay you.' But he was unwilling and went and threw him in prison until he should pay back what was owed. So when his fellow slaves saw what had happened, they were deeply grieved and came and reported to their lord all that had happened. Then summoning him, his lord said to him, 'You wicked slave, I forgave you all that debt because you pleaded with me. Should you not also have had mercy on your fellow slave, in the same way that I had mercy on you?' And his lord, moved with anger, handed him over to the torturers until he should repay all that was owed him. My heavenly Father will also do the same to you, if each of you does not forgive his brother from your heart" (Matthew 18:23–35; cf. Matthew 6:12, 14, 15; Luke 7:42; see Matthew 25:19–28).

Setting: Decapolis near the Sea of Galilee. Jesus miraculously feeds more than 4,000 primarily Gentile people.

In those days, when there was again a large crowd and they had nothing to eat, Jesus called His disciples and said to them, "I feel compassion for the people because they have remained with Me now three days and have nothing to eat. If I send them away hungry to their homes, they will faint on their way; and some of them have come a great distance" (Mark 8:1–3; cf. Matthew 15:32–38; see Matthew 9:36).

Setting: On the way from Galilee to Jerusalem. While being tested by a lawyer, Jesus tells him the story of the good Samaritan.

Jesus replied and said, "A man was going down from Jerusalem to Jericho, and fell among robbers, and they stripped him and beat him, and went away leaving him half dead. And by chance a priest was going down on that road, and when he saw him, he passed by on the other side. Likewise a Levite also, when he came to the place and saw him, passed by on the other side. But a Samaritan, who was on a journey, came upon him; and when he saw him, he felt compassion, and came to him and bandaged up his wounds, pouring oil and wine on them; and he put him on his own beast, and brought him to an inn and took care of him. On the next day he took out two denarii and gave them to the innkeeper and said, 'Take care of him; and whatever more you spend, when I return I will repay you.' Which of these three do you think proved to be a neighbor to the man who fell into the robbers' hands?" And he said, "The one who showed mercy toward him." Then Jesus said to him, "Go and do the same" (Luke 10:30–37).

Setting: On the way from Galilee to Jerusalem. Jesus conveys the illustration of the prodigal son because the Pharisees and scribes complain He associates with tax collectors and sinners.

And He said, "A man had two sons. The younger of them said to his father, 'Father, give me the share of the estate that falls to me.' So he divided his wealth between them. And not many days later, the younger son gathered everything together and went on a journey into a distant country, and there he squandered his estate with loose living. Now when he had spent everything, a severe famine occurred in that country, and he began to be impoverished. So he went and hired himself out to one of the citizens of that country, and he sent him into his fields to feed swine. And he would have gladly filled his stomach with the pods that the swine were eating, and no one was giving anything to him. But when he came to his senses, he said, 'How many of my father's hired men have more than enough bread, but I am dying here with hunger! I will get up and go to my father, and will say to him, "Father, I have sinned against heaven, and in your sight; I am no longer worthy to be called your son; make me as one of your hired men."' So he got up and came to his father. But while he was still a long way off, his father saw him and felt compassion for him, and ran and embraced him and kissed him. And the son said to him, "Father, I have sinned against heaven and in your sight; I am no longer worthy to be called your son.' But the father said to his slaves, 'Quickly bring out the best robe and put it on him, and put a ring on his hand and sandals on his feet; and bring the fattened calf, kill it, and let us eat and celebrate; for this son of mine was dead and has come to life again; he was lost and has been found.' And they began to celebrate. Now his older son was in the field, when he came and approached the house, he heard music and dancing. And he summoned one of the servants and began inquiring what these things could be. And he said to him, 'Your brother has come, and your father has killed the fattened calf because he has received him back safe and sound.' But he became angry and was not willing to go in; and his father came out and began pleading with him. But he answered and said to his father, 'Look! For so many years I have been serving you and I have never neglected a command of yours; and yet you have never given me a young goat, so that I might celebrate with my friends; but when this son of yours came, who has devoured your wealth with prostitutes, you killed the fattened calf for him.' And he said to him, 'Son, you have always been with me, and all that is mine is yours. But we had to celebrate and rejoice, for this brother of yours was dead and has begun to live, and was lost and has been found'" (Luke 15:11–32; see Proverbs 29:2).

COMPENSATION (See DENARIUS; MONEY; PAY; and WAGES)

COMPLIMENTS

[COMPLIMENTS from men speak well of you]

Setting: Galilee. After selecting His twelve disciples, Jesus teaches the Beatitudes (part of the Sermon on the Mount) to His disciples and a great throng of people from Judea, Jerusalem, and the central coastal region of Tyre and Sidon.

"Woe to you when all men speak well of you, for their fathers used to treat the false prophets in the same way" (Luke 6:26; see Matthew 7:15; 24:11, 24; Luke 6:12–19).

COMPREHENSION (See UNDERSTANDING)

CONCERN FOR THE LOST (Listed under LOST, CONCERN FOR THE)

CONDEMNATION (CONDEMNATION, GREATER; and CONDEMNATION, HUMAN are separate entries; also see JUDGMENT, DAY OF; JUDGMENT, DIVINE; and PUNISHMENT, ETERNAL)

[CONDEMNATION from condemned]

Setting: Galilee. After Jesus heals a blind, mute, demon-possessed man, the Pharisees accuse Jesus in front of crowds of being a worker of Satan.

"Either make the tree good and its fruit good, or make the tree bad and its fruit bad; for the tree is known by its fruit. You brood of vipers, how can you, being evil, speak what is good? For the mouth speaks out of that which fills the heart. The good man brings out of *his* good treasure what is good; and the evil man brings out of *his* evil treasure what is evil. But I tell you that every careless word that people speak, they shall give an accounting for it in the day of judgment. For by your words you will be justified, and by your words you will be condemned" (Matthew 12:33–37; cf. Matthew 3:7; 7:16–18).

[CONDEMNATION from condemn]

Setting: Galilee. After Jesus warns the Pharisees about the unpardonable sin and their future judgment, some Pharisees and scribes ask Him to perform a miraculous sign for them in front of the crowds.

But He answered and said to them, "An evil and adulterous generation craves for a sign; and *yet* no sign will be given to it but the sign of Jonah the prophet; for just as JONAH WAS THREE DAYS AND THREE NIGHTS IN THE BELLY OF THE SEA MONSTER, so will the Son of Man be three days and three nights in the heart of the earth. The men of Nineveh will stand up with this generation at the

judgment, and will condemn it because they repented at the preaching of Jonah; and behold, something greater than Jonah is here. *The* Queen of *the* South will rise up with this generation at the judgment and will condemn it, because she came from the ends of the earth to hear the wisdom of Solomon; and behold, something greater than Solomon is here" (Matthew 12:39–42; Jesus quotes from Jonah 1:17; cf. 1 Kings 10:1; Jonah 3:5; Matthew 16:1, 4; 12:38; Luke 11:29).

[CONDEMNATION from condemned]
Setting: Following His resurrection from the dead after being crucified, Jesus commissions His disciples to preach His gospel to the world.

And He said to them, "Go into all the world and preach the gospel to all creation. He who has believed and has been baptized shall be saved; but he who has disbelieved shall be condemned. These signs will accompany those who have believed: in My name they will cast out demons, they will speak with new tongues; they will pick up serpents, and if they drink any deadly poison, it will not hurt them; they will lay hands on the sick, and they will recover" (Mark 16:15–18; cf. Matthew 28:16–20; see Mark 9:38; John 3:18, 36; 1 Corinthians 15:6).

[Note: Some scholars question the authenticity of Mark 16:9–20, as these verses do not appear in some early New Testament manuscripts.]

[CONDEMNATION from condemned]
Setting: Galilee. After selecting His twelve disciples, Jesus teaches the Beatitudes (part of the Sermon on the Mount) to His disciples and a great throng of people from Judea, Jerusalem, and the central coastal region of Tyre and Sidon.

"Do not judge, and you will not be judged; and do not condemn, and you will not be condemned; pardon, and you will be pardoned. Give and it will be given to you. They will pour into your lap a good measure—pressed down, shaken together, and running over. For by your standard of measure it will be measured to you in return" (Luke 6:37, 38; cf. Matthew 7:1–5; Mark 4:24; see Luke 6:12–19).

[CONDEMNATION from condemn]
Setting: On the way from Galilee to Jerusalem. After revealing a problem with exorcism and responding to a blessing from a woman in the crowd, Jesus tells the increasing crowds of the sign of Jonah.

As the crowds were increasing, He began to say, "This generation is a wicked generation; it seeks for a sign, and yet no sign will be given to it but the sign of Jonah. For just as Jonah became a sign to the Ninevites, so will the Son of Man be to this generation. The Queen of the South will rise up with the men of this generation at the judgment and condemn them, because she came from the ends of the earth to hear the wisdom of Solomon; and behold, something greater than Solomon is here. The men of Nineveh will stand up with this generation at the judgment and condemn it, because they repented at the preaching of Jonah; and behold, something greater than Jonah is here" (Luke 11:29–32; cf. Matthew 16:4; see 1 Kings 10:1–10; Jonah 3:4, 5).

[CONDEMNATION from condemn]
Setting: The temple in Jerusalem. Following the Feast of Booths in Jerusalem, Jesus retires to the Mount of Olives, and returns the next day to teach. The scribes and Pharisees set a woman caught in adultery before Him to test whether He will follow Moses' command to stone her.

They were saying this, testing Him, so that they might have grounds for accusing Him. But Jesus stooped down and with His finger wrote on the ground. But when they persisted in asking Him, He straightened up, and said to them, "He who is without sin among you, let him *be the* first to throw a stone at her." Again He stooped down and wrote on the ground. When they heard it, they *began* to go out one by one, beginning with the older ones, and He was left alone, and the woman, where she was, in the center *of the court*. Straightening up, Jesus said to her, "Woman, where are they? Did no one condemn you?" She said, "No one, Lord." And Jesus said, "I do not condemn you either. Go. From now on sin no more" (John 8:6–11; see John 3:17; 8:1–9).

CONDEMNATION, GREATER (Also see JUDGMENT, DIVINE; PUNISHMENT, ETERNAL; and SIN, GREATER)

Setting: The temple in Jerusalem. After the Jewish religious leaders test Him with questions, Jesus pronounces the second of eight woes on them in front of the crowds and His disciples.

["Woe to you, scribes and Pharisees, hypocrites, because you devour widows' houses, and for a pretense you make long prayers; therefore you will receive greater condemnation] (Matthew 23:14; cf. Mark 12:40; Luke 20:47).

Setting: The temple in Jerusalem. After commending one scribe for his nearness to the kingdom of God, Jesus warns the crowd about the other scribes.

In His teaching He was saying: "Beware of the scribes who like to walk around in long robes, and *like* respectful greetings in the market places, and chief seats in the synagogues and places of honor at banquets, who devour widows' houses, and for appearance's sake offer long prayers; these will receive greater condemnation" (Mark 12:38–40; cf. Matthew 23:1–7; Luke 20:45–47).

Setting: The temple in Jerusalem. A few days before His crucifixion, after posing a question to the scribes, who do not answer, Jesus warns His disciples about the scribes' lifestyle.

"Beware of the scribes, who like to walk around in long robes, and love respectful greetings in the market places, and chief seats in the synagogues and places of honor at banquets, who devour widows' houses, and for appearance's sake offer long prayers. These will receive greater condemnation" (Luke 20:46, 47; cf. Matthew 23:1–7; Mark 12:38–40; see Luke 11:43).

CONDEMNATION, HUMAN (Also see CONDEMNATION)

[HUMAN CONDEMNATION from condemned]

Setting: Galilee. Jesus responds to the Pharisees' objection to His disciples' picking grain from the fields on the Sabbath.

But He said to them, "Have you not read what David did when he became hungry, he and his companions, how they entered the house of God, and ate the consecrated bread, which was not lawful for him to eat nor for those with him, but for the priests alone? Or, have you not read in the Law, that on the Sabbath the priests in the temple break the Sabbath and are innocent? But I say to you that something greater than the temple is here. But if you had known what this means, 'I DESIRE COMPASSION, AND NOT A SACRIFICE,' you would not have condemned the innocent. For the Son of Man is Lord of the Sabbath" (Matthew 12:3–8, Jesus quotes from Hosea 6:6; cf. Mark 2:25–28; Luke 6:3–5; see 1 Samuel 21:6).

[HUMAN CONDEMNATION from condemn]

Setting: On the road to Jerusalem. Before going to Jerusalem, Jesus again tells His disciples of His impending death and resurrection.

As Jesus was about to go up to Jerusalem, He took the twelve *disciples* aside by themselves, and on the way He said to them, "Behold, we are going up to Jerusalem; and the Son of Man will be delivered to the chief priests and scribes, and they will condemn Him to death, and will hand Him over to the Gentiles to mock and scourge and crucify *Him,* and on the third day, He will be raised up" (Matthew 20:17–19; cf. Matthew 16:21; Mark 10:32–34; Luke 18:31–33).

[HUMAN CONDEMNATION from condemn]

Setting: On the way to Jerusalem. After encouraging His disciples with a revelation of their future reward, Jesus prophesies His persecution, death, and resurrection.

They were on the road going up to Jerusalem, and Jesus was walking on ahead of them; and they were amazed, and those who followed were fearful. And again He took the twelve aside and began to tell them what was going to happen to Him, *saying,* "Behold, we are going up to Jerusalem, and the Son of Man will be delivered to the chief priests and the scribes; and they will condemn Him to death and will hand Him over to the Gentiles. They will mock Him and spit on Him, and scourge Him and kill *Him,* and three days later He will rise again" (Mark 10:32–34; cf. Matthew 20:17–19; Luke 18:31–34; see Matthew 16:21; Mark 8:31).

[HUMAN CONDEMNATION from do not condemn]
Setting: Galilee. After selecting His twelve disciples, Jesus teaches the Beatitudes (part of the Sermon on the Mount) to His disciples and a great throng of people from Judea, Jerusalem, and the central coastal region of Tyre and Sidon.

"Do not judge, and you will not be judged; and do not condemn, and you will not be condemned; pardon, and you will be pardoned. Give and it will be given to you. They will pour into your lap a good measure—pressed down, shaken together, *and* running over. For by your standard of measure it will be measured to you in return" (Luke 6:37, 38; cf. Matthew 7:1–5; Mark 4:24; see Luke 6:12–19).

[HUMAN CONDEMNATION from condemn]
Setting: The temple in Jerusalem. Following the Feast of Booths, Jesus retires to the Mount of Olives, and returns the next day to teach. The scribes and Pharisees set a woman caught in adultery before Him to test whether He will follow Moses' command to stone her.

They were saying this, testing Him, so that they might have grounds for accusing Him. But Jesus stooped down and with His finger wrote on the ground. But when they persisted in asking Him, He straightened up, and said to them, "He who is without sin among you, let him *be the* first to throw a stone at her." Again He stooped down and wrote on the ground. When they heard it, they *began* to go out one by one, beginning with the older ones, and He was left alone, and the woman, where she was, in the center *of the court.* Straightening up, Jesus said to her, "Woman, where are they? Did no one condemn you?" She said, "No one, Lord." And Jesus said, "I do not condemn you either. Go. From now on sin no more" (John 8:6–11; see John 3:17; 8:1–9).

CONDITION (See STATE)

CONFESSING JESUS CHRIST (See JESUS, CONFESSING)

CONFLICT, FAMILY (See DIVISION)

CONFRONTATION, PRIVATE

[PRIVATE CONFRONTATION from show him his fault in private]
Setting: Capernaum of Galilee. After conveying to His disciples the value of little ones, Jesus gives instruction about church discipline.

"If your brother sins, go and show him his fault in private; if he listens to you, you have won your brother. But if he does not listen *to you,* take one or two more with you, so that BY THE MOUTH OF TWO OR THREE WITNESSES EVERY FACT MAY BE CONFIRMED. If he refuses to listen to them, tell it to the church; and if he refuses to listen even to the church, let him be to you as a Gentile and a tax collector. Truly I say to you, whatever you bind of earth shall have been bound in heaven; and whatever you loose on earth shall have been loosed in heaven. Again, I say to you, that if two of you agree on earth about anything that they may ask, it shall be done for them by My Father who is in heaven. For there two or three have gathered together in My name, I am there in their midst" (Matthew 18:15–20. Jesus quotes from Deuteronomy 19:15; cf. Matthew 7:7; 16:19; see Leviticus 19:17; Matthew 28:20; 2 Thessalonians 3:6, 14).

CONSECRATED BREAD (Listed under BREAD, CONSECRATED)

CONSTRUCTION (Also see BUILDERS; BUILDINGS; FOUNDATION; and LABOR, MANUAL)

[CONSTRUCTION from built his house]
Setting: Galilee. During the early part of His ministry, Jesus preaches the Sermon on the Mount to His disciples and the multitudes.

"Therefore everyone who hears these words of Mine and acts on them, may be compared to a wise man who built his house on the rock. And the rain fell, and the floods came, and the winds blew and slammed against that house; and *yet* it did not fall, for it had been founded on the rock. Everyone who hears these words of Mine and does not act on them, will be like a foolish man who built his house on the sand. The rain fell, and the floods came, and the winds blew and slammed against that house; and it fell—and great was its fall" (Matthew 7:24–28; cf. Luke 6:47–49).

[CONSTRUCTION from I will build]
Setting: Caesarea Philippi. Jesus responds to Simon Peter's declaration that He is the Christ, the Son of the living God.

And Jesus said to him, "Blessed are you, Simon Barjona, because flesh and blood did not reveal *this* to you, but My Father who is in heaven. I also say to you that you are Peter, and upon this rock I will build My church; and the gates of Hades will not overpower it. I will give you the keys of the kingdom of heaven; and whatever you bind on earth shall have been bound in heaven, and whatever you loose on earth shall have been loosed in heaven" (Matthew 16:17–19; cf. Matthew 18:18; Mark 8:29; Luke 9:20).

[CONSTRUCTION from BUILT A TOWER]
Setting: The temple in Jerusalem. Jesus delivers another parable to the chief priests and elders after they question His authority.

"Listen to another parable. There was a landowner who PLANTED A VINEYARD AND PUT A WALL AROUND IT AND DUG A WINE PRESS IN IT, AND BUILT A TOWER, and rented it out to vine-growers and went on a journey. When the harvest time approached, he sent his slaves to the vine-growers to receive his produce. The vine-growers took his slaves and beat one, and killed another, and stoned a third. Again he sent another group of slaves larger than the first; and they did the same thing to them. But afterward he sent his son to them, saying, 'They will respect my son.' But when the vine-growers saw the son, they said among themselves, 'This is the heir; come, let us kill him and seize his inheritance.' They took him, and threw him out of the vineyard and killed him. Therefore when the owner of the vineyard comes, what will he do to those vine-growers?" (Matthew 21:33–40; Jesus quotes from Isaiah 5:1, 2; cf. Mark 12:1–9; Luke 20:9–15).

[CONSTRUCTION from build the tombs]
Setting: The temple in Jerusalem. After the Jewish religious leaders test Him with questions, Jesus pronounces the eighth of eight woes on them in front of the crowds and His disciples.

"Woe to you, scribes and Pharisees, hypocrites! For you build the tombs of the prophets and adorn the monuments of the righteous, and say, 'If we had been *living* in the days of our fathers, we would not have been partners with them in *shedding* the blood of the prophets.' So you testify against yourselves, that you are sons of those who murdered the prophets. Fill up, then, the measure *of the guilt* of you fathers. You serpents, you brood of vipers, how will you escape the sentence of hell? Therefore, behold, I am sending you prophets and wise men and scribes; some of them you will kill and crucify, and some of them you will scourge in your synagogues, and persecute from city to city, so that upon you may fall *the guilt of* all the righteous blood shed on earth, from the blood of righteous Abel to the blood of Zechariah, the son of Berechiah, whom you murdered between the temple and the altar. Truly I say to you, all these things will come upon this generation" (Matthew 23:29–36; cf. 2 Chronicles 24:21; Zechariah 1:1; Matthew 3:7; Luke 11:47–52; see Matthew 10:23).

[CONSTRUCTION from BUILT A TOWER]
Setting: The temple in Jerusalem. Having His authority questioned by the chief priests, scribes, and elders, Jesus begins to teach them in parables.

And He began to speak to them in parables: "A man PLANTED A VINEYARD AND PUT A WALL AROUND IT, AND DUG A VAT UNDER THE WINE PRESS AND BUILT A TOWER, and rented it out to vine-growers and went on a journey. At the *harvest* time he sent a slave to the vine-growers, in order to receive *some* of the produce of the vineyard from the vine-growers. They took him, and beat him and sent him away empty-handed. Again he sent them another slave, and they wounded him in the head, and treated him shamefully. And he sent another, and that one they killed; and *so with* many others, beating some and killing others. He had one more to *send*, a beloved son; he sent him last *of all* to them, saying, 'They will respect my son.' But those vine-growers said to one another, 'This is the heir; come, let us kill him, and the inheritance will be ours!' They took him, and killed him and threw him out of the vineyard. What will the owner of the vineyard do? He will come and destroy the vine-growers, and will give the vineyard to others. Have you not even read this Scripture: 'THE STONE WHICH THE BUILDERS REJECTED, THIS BECAME THE CHIEF CORNER *stone;* THIS CAME ABOUT FROM THE LORD, AND IT IS MARVELOUS IN OUR EYES'?" (Mark 12:1–11, Jesus quotes from Psalm 118:22, 23; Isaiah 5:1, 2; cf. Matthew 21:33–46; Luke 20:9–19).

[CONSTRUCTION from building a house; well built]
Setting: Galilee. After selecting His twelve disciples, Jesus teaches the Beatitudes (part of the Sermon on the Mount) to His disciples and a great throng of people from Judea, Jerusalem, and the central coastal region of Tyre and Sidon.

"Why do you call Me, 'Lord, Lord,' and do not do what I say? Everyone who comes to Me and hears My words and acts on them, I will show you whom he is like; he is like a man building a house, who dug deep and laid a foundation on the rock; and when a flood occurred, the torrent burst against that house and could not shake it, because it had been well built. But the one who has heard and has not acted accordingly, is like a man who built a house on the ground without any foundation; and the torrent burst against it and immediately it collapsed, and the ruin of that house was great" (Luke 6:46–49; cf. Matthew 7:24–27; see Luke 6:12–19; James 1:22).

[CONSTRUCTION from build the tombs and build their tombs]
Setting: On the way from Galilee to Jerusalem. After Jesus pronounces woes upon the Pharisees, a lawyer replies that His remarks are an insult to lawyers, too.

But He said, "Woe to you lawyers as well! For you weigh men down with burdens hard to bear, while you yourselves will not even touch the burdens with one of your fingers. Woe to you! For you build the tombs of the prophets, and it was your fathers who killed them. So you are witnesses and approve the deeds of your fathers; because it was they who killed them, and you build their tombs. For this reason also the wisdom of God said, 'I will send them prophets and apostles, and some of them they will kill and some they will persecute, so that the blood of all the prophets, shed since the foundation of the world, may be charged against this generation, from the blood of Abel to the blood of Zechariah, who was killed between the altar and the house of God; yes, I tell you, it shall be charged against this generation.' Woe to you lawyers! For you have taken away the key of knowledge; you yourselves did not enter, and you hindered those who were entering" (Luke 11:46–52; cf. Matthew 23:29–32; see 2 Chronicles 24:20, 21; Matthew 23:4, 13).

[CONSTRUCTION from build larger ones]
Setting: On the way from Galilee to Jerusalem. After the scribes and Pharisees turn hostile and question Him in an attempt to catch Him in something He might say, Jesus responds to a question from the crowd and gives a parable about riches and greed.

And He told them a parable, saying, "The land of a rich man was very productive. And he began reasoning to himself, saying, 'What shall I do, since I have no place to store my crops?' Then he said, 'This is what I will do: I will tear down my barns and build larger ones, and here I will store all my grain and my goods. And I will say to my soul, "Soul, you have many goods laid up for many years to come; take your ease, eat, drink and be merry."' "But God said to him, 'You fool! This very night your soul is required of you; and now who will own what you have prepared?' So is the man who stores up treasure for himself, and is not rich toward God" (Luke 12:16–21; see Job 27:8; Psalm 39:6; Ecclesiastes 12:9; Philippians 2:3).

[CONSTRUCTION from build a tower and to build]
Setting: On the way from Galilee to Jerusalem. After He responds to a banquet guest's proclamation about the blessings of eating bread in the kingdom of God, Jesus presents to large crowds the demands of discipleship.

Now large crowds were going along with Him; and He turned and said to them, "If anyone comes to Me, and does not hate his own father and mother and wife and children and brothers and sisters, yes, and even his own life, he cannot be My disciple. Whoever does not carry his own cross and come after Me cannot be My disciple. For which one of you, when he wants to build a tower, does not first sit down and calculate the cost to see if he has enough to complete it? Otherwise, when he has laid a foundation and is not able to finish, all who observe it begin to ridicule him, saying, 'This man began to build and was not able to finish.' Or what king, when he sets out to meet another king in battle, will not first sit down and consider whether he is strong enough with ten thousand *men* to encounter the one coming against him with twenty thousand? Or else, while the other is still far away, he sends a delegation and asks for terms of peace. So then, none of you can be My disciple who does not give up all his possessions. Therefore, salt is good; but if even salt has become tasteless, with what will it be seasoned? It is useless either for the soil or for the manure pile; it is thrown out. He who has ears to hear, let him hear" (Luke 14:25–35; cf. Matthew 5:13; 10:37–39; see Proverbs 20:18; Philippians 3:7).

[CONSTRUCTION from building]
Setting: Samaria, on the way from Galilee to Jerusalem. After the Pharisees question Him about the coming of the kingdom of God, Jesus tells His disciples of His second coming.

And He said to the disciples, "The days will come when you will long to see one of the days of the Son of Man, and you will not see it. They will say to you, 'Look there! Look here!' Do not go away, and do not run after them. For just like the lightning, when it flashes out of one part of the sky, shines to the other part of the sky, so will the Son of Man be in His day. But first He must suffer many things and be rejected by this generation. And just as it happened in the days of Noah, so it will be also in the days of the Son of Man: they were eating, they were drinking, they were marrying, they were being given in marriage, until the day that Noah entered the ark, and the flood came and destroyed them all. It was the same as happened in the days of Lot: they were eating, they were drinking, they were buying, they were selling, they were planting, they were building; but on the day that Lot went out from Sodom it rained fire and brimstone from heaven and destroyed them all. It will be just the same on the day that the Son of Man is revealed. On that day, the one who is on the housetop and whose goods are in the house must not go down to take them out; and likewise the one who is in the field must not turn back. Remember Lot's wife. Whoever seeks to keep his life will lose it, and whoever loses his life will preserve it. I tell you, on that night there will be two in one bed; one will be taken and the other will be left. There will be two women grinding at the same place; one will be taken and the other will be left. [Two men will be in the field; one will be taken and the other will be left."] And answering they said to Him, "Where, Lord?" And He said to them, "Where the body is, there also the vultures will be gathered" (Luke 17:22–37; see Genesis 19; Matthew 10:39; 16:21, 27; 24:17–28, 37–41).

CONTAINER (Also see CONTAINERS)
Setting: Galilee. After explaining the Parable of the Sower to His disciples, Jesus gives the Parable of the Lamp.

"Now no one after lighting a lamp covers it over with a container, or puts it under a bed; but he puts it on a lampstand, so that those who come in may see the light. For nothing is hidden that will not become evident, nor anything secret that will not be known and come to light. So take care how you listen; for whoever has, to him more shall be given; and whoever does not have, even what he thinks he has shall be taken away from him" (Luke 8:16–18; cf. Mark 4:21–23; see Matthew 5:14, 15; 10:26; 13:12).

CONTAINERS (Also see CONTAINER)
Setting: By the Sea of Galilee. Because the religious leaders are rejecting His message, Jesus continues teaching His disciples with the Parable of the Dragnet.

"Again, the kingdom of heaven is like a dragnet cast into the sea, and gathering *fish* of every kind; and when it was filled, they drew it up on the beach; and they sat down and gathered the good *fish* into containers, but the bad they threw away. So it will be at the end of the age; the angels will come forth and take out the wicked from among the righteous, and will throw them into the furnace of fire; in that place there will be weeping and gnashing of teeth. Have you understood all these things?" They said to Him, "Yes" (Matthew 13:47–51).

CONTEMPT

Setting: Possibly Mount Hermon. After informing a crowd and His disciples of the hope involving the coming kingdom of God, Jesus takes Peter, James, and John to a high mountain, where He reveals His glory through the Transfiguration and answers their question about Elijah.

And He said to them, "Elijah does first come and restore all things. And *yet* how is it written of the Son of Man that He will suffer many things and be treated with contempt? But I say to you that Elijah has indeed come, and they did to him whatever they wished, just as it is written of him" (Mark 9:12, 13; cf. Matthew 17:1–13; Luke 9:28–36; see Malachi 4:5, 6; Matthew 16:21).

CONTENTMENT (See BLESSED; FULFILLMENT; GLADNESS; JOY; PROVISION, GOD'S; and SATISFACTION)

CONTRIBUTIONS (See GIVING; and POOR, GIVING TO THE)

CONTRIBUTORS

Setting: Opposite the treasury near the temple in Jerusalem. Jesus focuses His disciples' attention on the monetary sacrifice of a widow.

Calling His disciples to Him, He said to them, "Truly I say to you, this poor widow put in more than all the contributors to the treasury; for they all put in out of their surplus, but she, out of her poverty, put in all she owned, all she had to live on" (Mark 12:43, 44; cf. Luke 21:1–4).

CONVERSATION

[CONVERSATION from words that you are exchanging]

Setting: On the way from Jerusalem to Emmaus. After dying on the cross the day before the Sabbath and being buried in a tomb by Joseph of Arimathea, Jesus rises from the grave on the third day and appears to two of His followers.

And He said to them, "What are these words that you are exchanging with one another as you are walking?" And they stood still, looking sad (Luke 24:17; see Mark 16:12, 13).

CONVERSION (Also see SALVATION)

[CONVERSION from converted]

Setting: Capernaum of Galilee. Jesus answers His disciples' question about greatness, or rank, in the kingdom of heaven.

And He called a child to Himself and set him before them, and said, "Truly I say to you, unless you are converted and become like children, you will not enter the kingdom of heaven. Whoever then humbles himself as this child, he is the greatest in the kingdom of heaven. And whoever receives one such child in My name receives Me; but whoever causes one of these little ones who believe in Me to stumble, it would be better for him to have a heavy millstone hung around his neck, and to be drowned in the depth of the sea"

(Matthew 18:2–6; cf. Matthew 19:14; Mark 9:33–37, 42; Luke 9:47, 48; Luke 17:1, 2).

CONVERSION, PAUL'S (See PAUL'S CONVERSION)

CONVICTION

[CONVICTION from convicts]

Setting: The temple treasury in Jerusalem. After the scribes and Pharisees question His testimony about Himself, Jesus interacts with them regarding their ancestry and motives.

Jesus said to them, "If God were your Father, you would love Me, for I proceeded forth and have come from God, for I have not even come on My own initiative, but He sent Me. Why do you not understand what I am saying? It is because you cannot hear My word. You are of your father the devil, and you want to do the desires of your father. He was a murderer from the beginning, and does not stand in the truth because there is no truth in him. Whenever he speaks a lie, he speaks from his own nature, for he is a liar and the father of lies. But because I speak the truth, you do not believe Me. Which one of you convicts Me of sin? If I speak truth, why do not believe Me? He who is of God hears the words of God; for this reason you do not hear them, because you are not of God" (John 8:42–47; see John 8:1–41; 18:37; 1 John 3:8; 4:6; 5:1).

[CONVICTION from convict]
Setting: Jerusalem. Before the Passover, after warning His disciples of the persecution they will face after His departure to heaven, Jesus elaborates about the coming ministry of the Holy Spirit.

"But now I am going to Him who sent Me; and none of you asks Me, 'Where are You going?' But because I have said these things to you, sorrow has filled your heart. But I tell you the truth, it is to your advantage that I go away; for if I do not go away, the Helper will not come to you; but if I go, I will send Him to you. And He, when He comes, will convict the world concerning sin and righteousness and judgment; concerning sin, because they do not believe in Me; and concerning righteousness, because I go to the Father and you no longer see Me; and concerning judgment, because the ruler of this world has been judged" (John 16:5–11; see John 7:33; 12:31; 14:1, 16; 15:22, 24).

COPPER

Setting: Galilee. After His disciples observe His ministry, Jesus summons and specifically instructs them about their ministry to the people of Israel.

These twelve Jesus sent out after instructing them: "Do not go in *the* way of *the* Gentiles, and do not enter *any* city of the Samaritans; but rather go to the lost sheep of the house of Israel. And as you go, preach, saying, 'The kingdom of heaven is at hand.' Heal *the* sick, raise *the* dead, cleanse *the* lepers, cast out demons. Freely you received, freely give. Do not acquire gold, or silver, or copper for your money belts, or a bag for *your* journey, or even two coats, or sandals, or a staff; for the worker is worthy of his support. And whatever city or village you enter, inquire who is worthy in it, and stay at his house until you leave *that city*. As you enter the house, give it your greeting. If the house is worthy, give it your *blessing of* peace. But if it is not worthy, take back your *blessing of* peace. Whoever does not receive you, nor heed your words, as you go out of that house or that city, shake the dust off your feet. Truly I say to you, it will be more tolerable for *the* land of Sodom and Gomorrah in the day of judgment than for that city" (Matthew 10:5–15; cf. Mark 6:7–11; Luke 9:1–5; see Matthew 3:2; 11:22, 24; 15:24; Luke 22:35; 1 Corinthians 9:14).

CORBAN

Setting: Galilee. The Pharisees and some of the scribes from Jerusalem question why Jesus' disciples do not follow the tradition of ceremonial hand cleansing before eating bread.

And He said to them, "Rightly did Isaiah prophesy of you hypocrites, as it is written: 'THIS PEOPLE HONORS ME WITH THEIR LIPS, BUT THEIR HEART IS FAR AWAY FROM ME. BUT IN VAIN DO THEY WORSHIP ME, TEACHING AS DOCTRINES THE PRECEPTS OF MEN.' Neglecting the commandment of God, you hold to the tradition of men." He was also saying to them, "You are experts at setting aside the commandment of God in order to keep tradition. For Moses said, 'HONOR YOUR FATHER AND YOUR MOTHER'; and, 'HE WHO SPEAKS EVIL OF FATHER OR MOTHER, IS TO BE PUT TO DEATH'; but you say, 'If a man says to *his* father or *his* mother, whatever I have that would help you is Corban (that is to say, given *to God*),' you no longer permit him to do anything for *his* father or *his* mother; *thus* invalidating the word of God by your tradition which you have handed down; and you do many things such as that" (Mark 7:6–13, Jesus quotes from Exodus 20:12; 21:17; Isaiah 29:13; cf. Matthew 15:1–6).

CORINTH

[CORINTH from Acts 18:1, 8 and city]
Setting: Corinth. Luke, writing in Acts, records the Lord Jesus' comforting revelation through a vision to Paul as he works among the Jews and Gentiles during his second missionary journey, testifying that Jesus is the Christ (Messiah).

And the Lord said to Paul in the night by a vision, "Do not be afraid *any longer,* but go on speaking and do not be silent; for I am with you, and no man will attack you in order to harm you, for I have many people in this city" (Acts 18:9, 10).

CORNER STONE, CHIEF (Jesus Christ)

Setting: The temple in Jerusalem. Jesus delivers a prophecy to the chief priests and elders after they question His authority.

Jesus said to them, "Did you never read in the Scriptures, 'THE STONE WHICH THE BUILDERS REJECTED, THIS BECAME THE CHIEF CORNER stone; THIS CAME ABOUT FROM THE LORD, AND IT IS MARVELOUS IN OUR EYES'? Therefore I say to you, the kingdom of God will be taken away from you and given to a people, producing the fruit of it. And he who falls on this stone will be broken to pieces; but on whomever it falls, it will scatter him like dust" (Matthew 21:42–44, Jesus quotes from Psalm 118:22; cf. Isaiah 8:14, 15; Mark 12:10, 11; Luke 20:17, 18).

Setting: The temple in Jerusalem. Having His authority questioned by the chief priests, scribes, and elders, Jesus begins to teach them in parables.

And He began to speak to them in parables: "A man PLANTED A VINEYARD AND PUT A WALL AROUND IT, AND DUG A VAT UNDER THE WINE PRESS AND BUILT A TOWER, and rented it out to vine-growers and went on a journey. At the harvest time he sent a slave to the vine-growers, in order to receive some of the produce of the vineyard from the vine-growers. They took him, and beat him and sent him away empty-handed. Again he sent them another slave, and they wounded him in the head, and treated him shamefully. And he sent another, and that one they killed; and so with many others, beating some and killing others. He had one more to send, a beloved son; he sent him last of all to them, saying, 'They will respect my son.' But those vine-growers said to one another, 'This is the heir; come, let us kill him, and the inheritance will be ours!' They took him, and killed him and threw him out of the vineyard. What will the owner of the vineyard do? He will come and destroy the vine-growers, and will give the vineyard to others. Have you not even read this Scripture: 'THE STONE WHICH THE BUILDERS REJECTED, THIS BECAME THE CHIEF CORNER stone; THIS CAME ABOUT FROM THE LORD, AND IT IS MARVELOUS IN OUR EYES'?" (Mark 12:1–11, Jesus quotes from Psalm 118:22, 23; Isaiah 5:1, 2; cf. Matthew 21:33–46; Luke 20:9–19).

Setting: The temple in Jerusalem. While ministering a few days before His crucifixion, after the chief priests and the scribes question His authority to teach and preach, Jesus conveys the Parable of the Vine-Growers to the people.

And He began to tell the people this parable: "A man planted a vineyard and rented it out to vine-growers, and went on a journey for a long time. At the harvest time he sent a slave to the vine-growers, so that they would give him some of the produce of the vineyard; but the vine-growers beat him and sent him away empty-handed. And he proceeded to send another slave; and they beat him also and treated him shamefully and sent him away empty-handed. And he proceeded to send a third; and this one also they wounded and cast out. The owner of the vineyard said, 'What shall I do? I will send my beloved son; perhaps they will respect him.' But when the vine-growers saw him, they reasoned with one another, saying, 'This is the heir; let us kill him so that the inheritance will be ours.' So they threw him out of the vineyard and killed him. What, then, will the owner of the vineyard do to them? He will come and destroy these vine-growers and will give the vineyard to others." When they heard it, they said, "May it never be!" But Jesus looked at them and said, "What then is this that is written: 'THE STONE WHICH THE BUILDERS REJECTED, THIS BECAME THE CHIEF CORNER stone'? Everyone who falls on that stone will be broken to pieces; but on whomever it falls, it will scatter him like dust" (Luke 20:9–18, Jesus quotes from Psalm 118:22; cf. Matthew 21:33–44; Mark 12:1–11; see Ephesians 2:20).

CORNERS, STREET (See STREET CORNERS)

CORPSE

Setting: The Mount of Olives, just east of Jerusalem. During His discourse, Jesus answers His disciples' questions as to when the temple will be destroyed and Jerusalem overrun, along with the signs of His coming and the end of the age.

"Therefore when you see the ABOMINATION OF DESOLATION which was spoken of through Daniel the prophet, standing in the holy place (let the reader understand), then those who are in Judea must flee to the mountains. Whoever is on the housetop must not go down to get the things that are in his house. Whoever is in the field must not turn back to get his cloak. But woe to those who are pregnant and to those who are nursing babies in those days! But pray that your flight will not be in the winter, or on a Sabbath. For then there will be a great tribulation, such as has not occurred since the beginning of the world until now, nor ever will. Unless those days had been cut short, no life would have been saved; but for the sake of the elect those days will be cut short. Then if anyone says to you, 'Behold, here is the Christ,' or 'There *He is,*' do not believe *him.* For false Christs and false prophets will arise and will show great signs and wonders, so as to mislead, if possible, even the elect. Behold, I have told you in advance. So if they say to you, 'Behold, He is in the wilderness,' do not go out, *or,* 'Behold, He is in the inner rooms,' do not believe *them.* For just as the lightning comes from the east and flashes even to the west, so will the coming of the Son of Man be. Wherever the corpse is, there the vultures will gather" (Matthew 24:15–28, Jesus quotes from Daniel 9:27; cf. Daniel 12:1; Mark 13:14–23; Luke 17:22–31; 21:20–24; 23:29; see John 4:48).

COST

Setting: On the way from Galilee to Jerusalem. After He responds to a guest's proclamation about the blessings of eating bread in the kingdom of God, Jesus presents to large crowds the demands of discipleship.

Now large crowds were going along with Him; and He turned and said to them, "If anyone comes to Me, and does not hate his own father and mother and wife and children and brothers and sisters, yes, and even his own life, he cannot be My disciple. Whoever does not carry his own cross and come after Me cannot be My disciple. For which one of you, when he wants to build a tower, does not first sit down and calculate the cost to see if he has enough to complete it? Otherwise, when he has laid a foundation and is not able to finish, all who observe it begin to ridicule him, saying, 'This man began to build and was not able to finish.' Or what king, when he sets out to meet another king in battle, will not first sit down and consider whether he is strong enough with ten thousand *men* to encounter the one coming against him with twenty thousand? Or else, while the other is still far away, he sends a delegation and asks for terms of peace. So then, none of you can be My disciple who does not give up all his possessions. Therefore, salt is good; but if even salt has become tasteless, with what will it be seasoned? It is useless either for the soil or for the manure pile; it is thrown out. He who has ears to hear, let him hear" (Luke 14:25–35; cf. Matthew 5:13; 10:37–39; see Proverbs 20:18; Philippians 3:7).

COSTS OF DISCIPLESHIP (See DISCIPLESHIP; FOLLOWING JESUS CHRIST; and SACRIFICE, PERSONAL)

COSTS OF FOLLOWING CHRIST (See FOLLOWING JESUS CHRIST; and DISCIPLESHIP)

COUNCIL OF ELDERS (See ELDERS)

COUNTRY (COUNTRY, DISTANT is a separate entry; also see NATION)

Setting: On the way from Galilee to Jerusalem. Jesus conveys the illustration of the prodigal son because the Pharisees and scribes complain He associates with tax collectors and sinners.

And He said, "A man had two sons. The younger of them said to his father, 'Father, give me the share of the estate that falls to me.' So he divided his wealth between them. And not many days later, the younger son gathered everything together and went on a journey into a distant country, and there he squandered his estate with loose living. Now when he had spent everything, a severe famine occurred in that country, and he began to be impoverished. So he went and hired himself out to one of the citizens of that country, and he sent him into his fields to feed swine. And he would have gladly filled his stomach with the pods that the swine were eating, and no one was giving anything to him. But when he came to his senses, he said, 'How many of my father's hired men have more than enough bread, but I am dying here with hunger! I will get up and go to my father, and will say to him, "Father, I have sinned against heaven, and in your sight; I am no longer worthy to be called your son; make me as one of your hired men."' So he got up and came to his father. But while he was still a long way off, his father saw him and felt compassion for him, and ran and embraced him and kissed him. And the son said to him, "Father, I have sinned against heaven and in your sight; I am no longer worthy to be called your son.' But the father said to his slaves, 'Quickly bring out the best robe and put it on him, and put a ring on his hand and sandals on his feet; and bring the fattened calf, kill it, and let us eat and celebrate;

for this son of mine was dead and has come to life again; he was lost and has been found.' And they began to celebrate. Now his older son was in the field, when he came and approached the house, he heard music and dancing. And he summoned one of the servants and began inquiring what these things could be. And he said to him, 'Your brother has come, and your father has killed the fattened calf because he has received him back safe and sound.' But he became angry and was not willing to go in; and his father came out and began pleading with him. But he answered and said to his father, 'Look! For so many years I have been serving you and I have never neglected a command of yours; and yet you have never given me a young goat, so that I might celebrate with my friends; but when this son of yours came, who has devoured your wealth with prostitutes, you killed the fattened calf for him.' And he said to him, 'Son, you have always been with me, and all that is mine is yours. But we had to celebrate and rejoice, for this brother of yours was dead and has begun to live, and was lost and has been found'" (Luke 15:11–32; see Proverbs 29:2).

Setting: The Mount of Olives, just east of Jerusalem. During His discourse, following a time of ministry in the temple a few days before His crucifixion, Jesus elaborates about future events.

"But when you see Jerusalem surrounded by armies, then recognize that her desolation is near. Then those who are in Judea must flee to the mountains, and those who are in the midst of the city must leave, and those who are in the country must not enter the city; because these are days of vengeance, so that all things which are written will be fulfilled. Woe to those who are pregnant and to those who are nursing babies in those days; for there will be a great distress upon the land and wrath to this people; and they will fall by the edge of the sword, and will be led captive into all the nations; and Jerusalem will be trampled under foot by the Gentiles until the times of the Gentiles are fulfilled" (Luke 21:20–24; see Matthew 24:15–18; Mark 13:14–16; Luke 19:43).

COUNTRY, DISTANT

Setting: On the way from Galilee to Jerusalem. Jesus conveys the illustration of the prodigal son because the Pharisees and scribes complain He associates with tax collectors and sinners.

And He said, "A man had two sons. The younger of them said to his father, 'Father, give me the share of the estate that falls to me.' So he divided his wealth between them. And not many days later, the younger son gathered everything together and went on a journey into a distant country, and there he squandered his estate with loose living. Now when he had spent everything, a severe famine occurred in that country, and he began to be impoverished. So he went and hired himself out to one of the citizens of that country, and he sent him into his fields to feed swine. And he would have gladly filled his stomach with the pods that the swine were eating, and no one was giving anything to him. But when he came to his senses, he said, 'How many of my father's hired men have more than enough bread, but I am dying here with hunger! I will get up and go to my father, and will say to him, "Father, I have sinned against heaven, and in your sight; I am no longer worthy to be called your son; make me as one of your hired men."' So he got up and came to his father. But while he was still a long way off, his father saw him and felt compassion for him, and ran and embraced him and kissed him. And the son said to him, "Father, I have sinned against heaven and in your sight; I am no longer worthy to be called your son.' But the father said to his slaves, 'Quickly bring out the best robe and put it on him, and put a ring on his hand and sandals on his feet; and bring the fattened calf, kill it, and let us eat and celebrate; for this son of mine was dead and has come to life again; he was lost and has been found.' And they began to celebrate. Now his older son was in the field, when he came and approached the house, he heard music and dancing. And he summoned one of the servants and began inquiring what these things could be. And he said to him, 'Your brother has come, and your father has killed the fattened calf because he has received him back safe and sound.' But he became angry and was not willing to go in; and his father came out and began pleading with him. But he answered and said to his father, 'Look! For so many years I have been serving you and I have never neglected a command of yours; and yet you have never given me a young goat, so that I might celebrate with my friends; but when this son of yours came, who has devoured your wealth with prostitutes, you killed the fattened calf for him.' And he said to him, 'Son, you have always been with me, and all that is mine is yours. But we had to celebrate and rejoice, for this brother of yours was dead and has begun to live, and was lost and has been found'" (Luke 15:11–32; see Proverbs 29:2).

Setting: On the way to Jerusalem. After commending Zaccheus's faith in Him, Jesus provides a parable about stewardship.

So He said, "A nobleman went to a distant country to receive a kingdom for himself, and then return. And he called ten of his slaves, and gave them ten minas and said to them, 'Do business with this until I come back.' But his citizens hated him and sent a delegation after him, saying, 'We do not want this man to reign over us.' When he returned, after receiving the kingdom, he ordered that these slaves, to whom he had given the money, be called to him so that he might know what business they had done. The first appeared, saying, 'Master, your mina has made ten minas more.' And he said to him, 'Well done, good slave, because you have been faithful in a very little thing, you are to be in authority over ten cities.' The second came, saying, 'Your mina, master, has made five minas.' And he said to him, also, 'And you are to be over five cities.' Another came, saying, 'Master, here is your mina, which I kept put away in a handkerchief; for I was afraid of you, because you are an exacting man; you take up what you did not lay down and reap what you did not sow.' He said to him, 'By your own words I will judge you, you worthless slave. Did you know that I am an exacting man, taking up what I did not lay down and reaping what I did not sow? Then why did you not put my money in the bank, and having come, I would have collected it with interest?' Then he said to the bystanders, 'Take the mina away from him and give it to the one who has the ten minas.' And they said to him, 'Master, he has ten minas already.' I tell you that to everyone who has, more shall be given, but from the one who does not have, even what he does have shall be taken away. But these enemies of mine, who did not want me to reign over them, bring them here and slay them in my presence" (Luke 19:12–27; cf. Matthew 25:14–30; see Matthew 13:12; Luke 16:10).

COURAGE

Setting: Capernaum near the Sea of Galilee. After Jesus heals and forgives a paralytic of his sins in front of crowds, some scribes accuse Him of blasphemy.

And they brought to Him a paralytic lying on a bed. Seeing their faith, Jesus said to the paralytic, "Take courage, son; your sins are forgiven." And some scribes said to themselves. "This *fellow* blasphemes." And Jesus knowing their thoughts said, "Why are you thinking evil in your hearts? Which is easier to say, 'Your sins are forgiven,' or to say, 'Get up, and walk'? But so that you may know that the Son of Man has authority on earth to forgive sins"—then He said to the paralytic, "Get up, pick up your bed and go home" (Matthew 9:2–6; cf. Mark 2:3–12; Luke 5:17–26).

Setting: Capernaum near the Sea of Galilee. Jesus heals a woman who has been suffering with internal bleeding for twelve years.

But Jesus turning and seeing her said, "Daughter, take courage; your faith has made you well." At once the woman was made well (Matthew 9:22; cf. Mark 5:34; Luke 8:48).

Setting: The Sea of Galilee. Following the miraculous feeding of more than 5,000 of His countrymen, in order to take an opportunity to pray, Jesus makes His disciples get into a boat, where He joins them later by walking on the water during a storm.

But immediately Jesus spoke to them, saying, "Take courage, it is I; do not be afraid." Peter said to Him, "Lord, if it is You, command me to come to You on the water." And He said, "Come!" And Peter got out of the boat, and walked on the water and came toward Jesus. But seeing the wind, he became frightened, and beginning to sink, he cried out, "Lord, save me!" Immediately Jesus stretched out His hand and took hold of him, and said to him, "You of little faith, why did you doubt?" (Matthew 14:27–31; cf. Mark 6:47–52; John 6:16–21).

Setting: A boat on the Sea of Galilee, en route to Bethsaida. After feeding more than 5,000 people through God's miraculous provision and returning from a time of prayer on a mountain, Jesus startles His disciples by walking on the water.

But when they saw Him walking on the sea, they supposed that it was a ghost, and cried out; for they all saw Him and were terrified. But immediately He spoke with them and said to them, "Take courage; it is I, do not be afraid" (Mark 6:49, 50; cf. Matthew 14:26, 27; John 6:19, 20).

Setting: Jerusalem. Before the Passover, after conveying promises about praying in His name, Jesus prophesies

His disciples' future scattering and gives them assurance that in the midst of tribulation they will have His peace.

"Jesus answered them, "Do you now believe? Behold, an hour is coming, and has *already* come, for you to be scattered, each to his own *home,* and to leave Me alone; and *yet* I am not alone, because the Father is with Me. These things I have spoken to you, so that in Me you may have peace. In the world you have tribulation, but take courage, I have overcome the world" (John 16:31–33; see Zechariah 13:7; John 8:29; 14:27; Romans 8:37).

Setting: The Roman barracks in Jerusalem. Luke, writing in Acts, presents Jesus' encouraging words to Paul following his hearing before the Jewish Council in Jerusalem and arrest by the Roman commander (after the apostle's third missionary journey).

But on the night *immediately* following, the Lord stood at his side and said, "Take courage; for as you have solemnly witnessed to My cause at Jerusalem, so you must witness at Rome also" (Acts 23:11; see Acts 19:21).

COURT (Also see COURTS; JUDGE; and LAWSUIT)

Setting: Galilee. During the early part of His ministry, Jesus preaches the Sermon on the Mount to His disciples and the multitudes.

"You have heard that the ancients were told, 'YOU SHALL NOT COMMIT MURDER' and "whoever commits murder shall be liable to the court' (Matthew 5:21, Jesus quotes from Exodus 20:13).

Setting: Galilee. During the early part of His ministry, Jesus preaches the Sermon on the Mount to His disciples and the multitudes.

"But I say to you that everyone who is angry with his brother shall be guilty before the court; and whoever says to his brother, 'You good-for-nothing,' shall be guilty before the supreme court; and whoever says, 'You fool,' shall be guilty *enough to go* into the fiery hell" (Matthew 5:22).

COURT, SUPREME (Also see JUDGE, JESUS AS; and JUDGMENT)

Setting: Galilee. During the early part of His ministry, Jesus preaches the Sermon on the Mount to His disciples and the multitudes.

"But I say to you that everyone who is angry with his brother shall be guilty before the court; and whoever says to his brother, 'You good-for-nothing,' shall be guilty before the supreme court; and whoever says, 'You fool,' shall be guilty *enough to go* into the fiery hell" (Matthew 5:22).

[SUPREME COURT from to stand before the Son of Man]

Setting: Jerusalem. Following a time of ministry in the temple a few days before His crucifixion, after conveying the Parable of the Fig Tree, Jesus warns His disciples to keep alert regarding future events.

"Be on guard, so that your hearts will not be weighted down with dissipation and drunkenness and the worries of life, and that day will not come upon you suddenly like a trap; for it will come upon all those who dwell on the face of all the earth. But keep on the alert at all times, praying that you may have strength to escape all these things that are about to take place, and to stand before the Son of Man" (Luke 21:34–36; cf. Mark 13:33; see Matthew 24:42–44).

COURTS (Also see COURT)

Setting: Galilee. After His disciples observe His ministry, Jesus summons and specifically instructs them about the upcoming hardships of *their* ministry to the people of Israel.

"Behold, I send you out as sheep in the midst of wolves; so be shrewd as serpents and innocent as doves. But beware of men, for they will hand you over to *the* courts and scourge you in their synagogues; and you will even be brought before governors and kings for My sake, as a testimony to them and to the Gentiles. But when they hand you over, do not worry about how or what you are to say; for it will be given you in that hour what you are to say. For it is not you who speak, but *it* is the Spirit of your Father who speaks in you" (Matthew 10:16–20; cf. Luke 10:3).

Setting: The Mount of Olives, east of the temple in Jerusalem. During His discourse, after prophesying the temple's destruction, Jesus responds to questions from Peter, James, John, and Andrew about future events.

And Jesus began to say to them, "See to it that no one misleads you. Many will come in My name, saying, 'I am *He!*' and will mislead many. When you hear of wars and rumors of wars, do not be frightened; *those things* must take place; but *that is* not yet the end. For nation will rise up against nation, and kingdom against kingdom; there will be earthquakes in various places; there will *also be* famines. These things are *merely* the beginning of birth pangs. But be on your guard; for they will deliver you to *the* courts, and you will be flogged in *the* synagogues, and you will stand before governors and kings for My sake, as a testimony to them. The gospel must first be preached to all the nations. When they arrest you and hand you over, do not worry beforehand about what you are to say, but say whatever is given you in that hour; for it is not you who speak, but *it is* the Holy Spirit. Brother will betray brother to death, and a father *his* child; and children will rise up against parents and have them put to death. You will be hated by all because of My name, but the one who endures to the end, he will be saved" (Mark 13:5–13; cf. Matthew 24:4–14; Luke 21:7–19; see Matthew 10:17–22).

COVENANT (See COVENANT, BLOOD OF THE; and COVENANT, NEW)

COVENANT, BLOOD OF THE (Also see BLOOD; and BLOOD, COVENANT IN MY)

Setting: An upper room in Jerusalem. While celebrating the Passover meal with His disciples, Jesus institutes the Lord's Supper ordinance before being arrested by His enemies.

While they were eating, Jesus took *some* bread, and after a blessing, He broke *it* and gave *it* to the disciples, and said, "Take, eat; this is My body." And when He had taken a cup and given thanks, He gave *it* to them saying, "Drink from it, all of you; for this is My blood of the covenant, which is poured out for many for forgiveness of sins. But I say to you, I will not drink of this fruit of the vine from now on until that day when I drink it new with you in My Father's kingdom" (Matthew 26:26–29; cf. Mark 14:22–25; Luke 22:17–20; 1 Corinthians 11:23–26; see 1 Corinthians 10:16).

Setting: Jerusalem. While celebrating the Feast of Unleavened Bread (Passover) with His disciples, Jesus institutes the ordinance of the Lord's Supper.

While they were eating, He took *some* bread, and after a blessing He broke *it*, and gave *it* to them, and said, "Take *it;* this is My body." And when He had taken a cup *and* given thanks, He gave *it* to them, and they all drank from it. And He said to them, "This is My blood of the covenant, which is poured out for many. Truly I say to you, I will never again drink of the fruit of the vine until that day when I drink it new in the kingdom of God" (Mark 14:22–25; cf. Matthew 26:26–29; Luke 22:17–20; 1 Corinthians 11:23–26; see Exodus 24:8).

COVENANT, NEW

Setting: An upper room in Jerusalem. During the Feast of Unleavened Bread (Passover) just before His crucifixion, while celebrating the Passover meal with His disciples, Jesus institutes the Lord's Supper.

And when He had taken a cup and given thanks, He said, "Take this and share it among yourselves; for I say to you, I will not drink of the fruit of the vine from now on until the kingdom of God comes." And when he had taken some bread and given thanks, He broke it and gave it to them, saying, "This is My body which is given for you; do this in remembrance of Me." And in the same way He took the cup after they had eaten, saying, "This cup which is poured out for you is the new covenant in My blood. But behold, the hand of the one betraying Me is with Mine on the table. For indeed, the Son of Man is going as it has been determined; but woe to that man by whom He is betrayed!" (Luke 22:17–22; cf. Matthew 26:26–29; Mark 14:22–25; 1 Corinthians 11:23–26; see

Psalm 41:9; Luke 14:15; 1 Corinthians 10:16).

Setting: An upper room in Jerusalem. During his third missionary journey, writing from Ephesus to the church at Corinth, the apostle Paul recounts the Lord Jesus' words as He institutes the Lord's Supper.

For I received from the Lord that which I also delivered to you, that the Lord Jesus in the night in which He was betrayed took bread; and when He had given thanks, He broke it and said, "This is My body, which is for you; do this in remembrance of Me." In the same way *He took* the cup also after supper, saying, "This cup is the new covenant in My blood; do this, as often as you drink *it,* in remembrance of Me" (1 Corinthians 11:23–25; cf. Matthew 26:26–28; Mark 14:22–24; Luke 22:17–20).

COVETING, DEEDS OF

Setting: Galilee. After the Pharisees and scribes from Jerusalem question Jesus' disciples' lack of obedience to the tradition of ceremonial cleansing, Jesus speaks to a crowd and explains His teaching to His disciples.

After He called the crowd to Him again, He *began* saying to them, "Listen to Me, all of you, and understand: there is nothing outside the man which can defile him if it goes into him; but the things which proceed out of the man are what defile the man. [If anyone has ears to hear, let him hear."] When he had left the crowd *and* entered the house, His disciples questioned Him about the parable. And He said to them, "Are you so lacking in understanding also? Do you not understand that whatever goes into the man from outside cannot defile him, because it does not go into his heart, but into his stomach, and is eliminated?" (*Thus He* declared all foods clean.) And He was saying, "That which proceeds out of the man, that is what defiles the man. For from within, out of the heart of men, proceed the evil thoughts, fornications, thefts, murders, adulteries, deeds of coveting *and* wickedness, *as well* as deceit, sensuality, envy, slander, pride *and* foolishness. All these evil things proceed from within and defile the man" (Mark 7:14–23; cf. Matthew 15:10–20).

COVETOUSNESS (See COVETING, DEEDS OF)

CO-WORKERS (Also see HARVEST)

[CO-WORKERS from For he who is not against us is for us]

Setting: Capernaum of Galilee. As Jesus teaches His disciples in private, they ask Him about greatness.

But Jesus said, "Do not hinder him, for there is no one who will perform a miracle in My name, and be able soon afterward to speak evil of Me. For he who is not against us is for us. For whoever gives you a cup of water to drink because of your name as *followers* of Christ, truly I say to you, he will not lose his reward. Whoever causes one of these little ones who believe to stumble, it would be better for him if, with a heavy millstone hung around his neck, he had been cast into the sea. If your hand causes you to stumble, cut it off; it is better for you to enter life crippled, than, having your two hands, to go into hell, into the unquenchable fire, [where THEIR WORM DOES NOT DIE, AND THE FIRE IS NOT QUENCHED.] If your foot causes you to stumble, cut it off; it is better for you to enter life lame, than, having your two feet, to be cast into hell, [where THEIR WORM DOES NOT DIE, AND THE FIRE IS NOT QUENCHED.] If your eye causes you to stumble, throw it out; it is better for you to enter the kingdom of God with one eye, than, having two eyes, to be cast into hell, where THEIR WORM DOES NOT DIE, AND THE FIRE IS NOT QUENCHED. For everyone will be salted with fire. Salt is good; but if the salt becomes unsalty, with what will you make it salty *again?* Have salt in yourselves, and be at peace with one another" (Mark 9:39–50; Jesus quotes from Isaiah 66:24; cf. Matthew 18:6–9; Luke 9:49–50; see Matthew 5:13, 29, 30; 10:42; 12:30; 18:5, 6).

[CO-WORKERS from he who is not against you is for you]

Setting: Galilee. Following His illustration about true greatness with a child as an object lesson, Jesus gives His disciples insights who their co-laborers in ministry are.

But Jesus said to him, "Do not hinder him; for he who is not against you is for you" (Luke 9:50; cf. Matthew 12:30; Mark 9:38–40; see Luke 9:49).

CREATION (CREATION, BEGINNING OF; and CREATION, BEGINNING OF THE are separate entries; also

see ADAM AND EVE; WORLD, BEGINNING OF THE; and WORLD, FOUNDATION OF THE)
[CREATION from created]
Setting: Judea beyond the Jordan (Perea). After Jesus replies to Peter's question about forgiveness, the Pharisees test Him in front of a large crowd with a question about divorce.

And He answered and said, "Have you not read that He who created *them* from the beginning MADE THEM MALE AND FEMALE, and said, 'FOR THIS REASON A MAN SHALL LEAVE HIS FATHER AND MOTHER AND BE JOINED TO HIS WIFE, AND THE TWO SHALL BECOME ONE FLESH'? So they are no longer two, but one flesh. What therefore God has joined together, let no man separate" (Matthew 19:4–6, Jesus quotes from Genesis 1:27; 2:24; cf. Mark 10:5–9; see 1 Timothy 2:14).

Setting: During His discourse on the Mount of Olives, east of the temple in Jerusalem, after prophesying the temple's destruction, Jesus responds to questions from Peter, James, John, and Andrew about future events.

"But when you see the ABOMINATION OF DESOLATION standing where it should not be (let the reader understand), then those who are in Judea must flee to the mountains. The one who is on the housetop must not go down, or go in to get anything out of his house; and the one who is in the field must not turn back to get his coat. But woe to those who are pregnant and to those who are nursing babies in those days! But pray that it may not happen in winter. For those days will be a *time of* tribulation such as has not occurred since the beginning of the creation which God created until now, and never will. Unless the Lord had shortened *those* days, no life would have been saved; but for the sake of the elect, whom He chose, He shortened the days. And then if anyone says to you, 'Behold, here is the Christ'; or, 'Behold, *He is* there'; do not believe *him*; for false Christs and false prophets will arise, and will show signs and wonders, in order to lead astray, if possible, the elect. But take heed; behold, I have told you everything in advance" (Mark 13:14–23; cf. Matthew 24:15–28; Luke 21:20–24; see Daniel 9:27; 12:1; Luke 17:31).

Setting: On a mountain in Galilee. Following His resurrection from the dead after being crucified, Jesus commissions His disciples to preach His gospel to the world.

And He said to them, "Go into all the world and preach the gospel to all creation. He who has believed and has been baptized shall be saved; but he who has disbelieved shall be condemned. These signs will accompany those who have believed: in My name they will cast out demons, they will speak with new tongues; they will pick up serpents, and if they drink any deadly poison, it will not hurt them; they will lay hands on the sick, and they will recover" (Mark 16:15–18; cf. Matthew 28:16–20; see Mark 9:38, John 3:18, 36; 1 Corinthians 15:6).

[Note: Some scholars question the authenticity of Mark 16:9–20, as these verses do not appear in some early New Testament manuscripts.]

CREATION, BEGINNING OF (Also see CREATION; CREATION, BEGINNING OF THE; WORLD, BEGINNING OF THE; and WORLD, FOUNDATION OF THE)
Setting: Judea beyond the Jordan (Perea). Jesus teaches the crowds gathered around Him about divorce after the Pharisees test and question Him about this subject.

And He answered and said to them, "What did Moses command you?" They said, "Moses permitted a *man* TO WRITE A CERTIFICATE OF DIVORCE AND SEND *her* AWAY." But Jesus said to them, "Because of your hardness of heart he wrote you this commandment. But from the beginning of creation, *God* MADE THEM MALE AND FEMALE. FOR THIS REASON A MAN SHALL LEAVE HIS FATHER AND MOTHER, AND THE TWO SHALL BECOME ONE FLESH; so they are no longer two, but one flesh. What therefore God has joined together, let no man separate. In the house the disciples *began* questioning Him about this again. And He said to them, "Whoever divorces his wife and marries another woman commits adultery against her; and if she herself divorces her husband and marries another man, she is committing adultery" (Mark 10:3–12, Jesus quotes from Genesis 1:27; 2:24; cf. Matthew 19:1–9; see Deuteronomy 24:1–3; Matthew 5:32; see Romans 7:2, 3; 1 Corinthians 7:10, 11, 13, 39; 1 Timothy 2:14).

CREATION, BEGINNING OF THE (Also see CREATION; CREATION, BEGINNING OF; WORLD, BEGINNING OF THE; and WORLD, FOUNDATION OF THE)

Setting: The Mount of Olives, east of the temple in Jerusalem. During His discourse, after prophesying the temple's destruction, Jesus responds to questions from Peter, James, John, and Andrew about future events.

"But when you see the ABOMINATION OF DESOLATION standing where it should not be (let the reader understand), then those who are in Judea must flee to the mountains. The one who is on the housetop must not go down, or go in to get anything out of his house; and the one who is in the field must not turn back to get his coat. But woe to those who are pregnant and to those who are nursing babies in those days! But pray that it may not happen in winter. For those days will be a *time of* tribulation such as has not occurred since the beginning of the creation which God created until now, and never will. Unless the Lord had shortened *those* days, no life would have been saved; but for the sake of the elect, whom He chose, He shortened the days. And then if anyone says to you, 'Behold, here is the Christ'; or, 'Behold, *He is* there'; do not believe *him*; for false Christs and false prophets will arise, and will show signs and wonders, in order to lead astray, if possible, the elect. But take heed; behold, I have told you everything in advance" (Mark 13:14–23; cf. Matthew 24:15–28; Luke 21:20–24; see Daniel 9:27; 12:1; Luke 17:31).

Setting: The island of Patmos (in the Aegean Sea about fifty miles southwest of Ephesus in modern Turkey). On the Lord's Day (Sunday), about fifty years after Jesus' resurrection, the disciple John encounters the Lord Jesus Christ. Jesus communicates a new revelation for the apostle to record for the church in Laodicea and to six other churches in Asia.

"To the angel of the church in Laodicea write: The Amen, the faithful and true Witness, the Beginning of the creation of God, says this: 'I know your deeds, that you are neither cold nor hot; I wish that you were cold or hot. So because you are lukewarm, and neither hot nor cold, I will spit you out of My mouth. Because you say, "I am rich, and have become wealthy, and have need of nothing," and you do not know that you are wretched and miserable and poor and blind and naked, I advise you to buy from Me gold refined by fire so that you may become rich, and white garments so that you may clothe yourself, and *that* the shame of your nakedness will not be revealed; and eye salve to anoint your eyes so that you may see. Those whom I love, I reprove and discipline; therefore be zealous and repent. Behold, I stand at the door and knock; if anyone hears My voice and opens the door, I will come in to him and will dine with him, and he with Me. He who overcomes, I will grant to him to sit down with Me on My throne, as I also overcame and sat down with My Father on His throne. He who has an ear, let him hear what the Spirit says to the churches'" (Revelation 3:14–22; see Proverbs 3:12; Hosea 12:8; John 14:23; 16:33).

CREATOR (Also see WORLD, BEGINNING OF THE; and WORLD, FOUNDATION OF THE)

[CREATOR from Did not He who made the outside make the inside also]

Setting: On the way from Galilee to Jerusalem. After speaking of how a lamp illuminates, the Lord has lunch with a Pharisee who is surprised He doesn't wash before eating.

But the Lord said to him, "Now you Pharisees clean the outside of the cup and of the platter; but inside of you, you are full of robbery and wickedness. You foolish ones, did not He who made the outside make the inside also? But give that which is within as charity, and then all things are clean for you. But woe to you Pharisees! You pay tithe of mint and rue and every kind of garden herb, and yet disregard justice and the love of God; but these are the things you should have done without neglecting the others. Woe to you Pharisees! For you love the chief seats in the synagogues and the respectful greetings in the market places. Woe to you! For you are like concealed tombs, and the people who walk over them are unaware of it" (Luke 11:39–44; cf. Matthew 23:6–7, 23–27; see Matthew 15:2; Titus 1:15).

CREATURES, GOD'S CARE FOR

[GOD'S CARE FOR CREATURES from your heavenly Father feeds them]

Setting: Galilee. During the early part of His ministry, Jesus preaches the Sermon on the Mount to His disciples and the multitudes.

"For this reason I say to you, do not be worried about your life, *as to* what you will eat or what you will drink; nor for your body, *as to* what you will put on. Is not life more than food, and the body more than clothing? Look at the birds of the air, that they do not sow, nor reap nor gather into barns, and *yet* your heavenly Father feeds them. Are you not worth much more than they?

And who of you by being worried can add a *single* hour to his life? And why are you worried about clothing? Observe how the lilies of the field grow; they do not toil nor do they spin, yet I say to you that not even Solomon in all his glory clothed himself like one of these. But if God so clothes the grass of the field, which is *alive* today and tomorrow is thrown into the furnace, *will He* not much more *clothe* you? You of little faith! Do not worry then, saying 'What will we eat?' or 'What will we drink?' or 'What will be wear for clothing?" For the Gentiles eagerly seek all these things; for your heavenly Father knows that you need all these things. But seek first His kingdom and His righteousness, and all these things will be added to you. So do not worry about tomorrow; for tomorrow will care for itself. Each day has enough trouble of its own" (Matthew 6:25–34; cf. Luke 12:22–31; see 1 Kings 10:4–7; Job 35:11; Matthew 8:26).

[GOD'S CARE FOR CREATURES from God feeds them]

Setting: On the way from Galilee to Jerusalem. Jesus comforts the crowd and His disciples after giving a parable about riches and greed, while the scribes and Pharisees turn hostile and question Him in an attempt to catch Him in something He might say.

And He said to His disciples, "For this reason I say to you, do not worry about your life, as to what you will eat; nor for your body, as to what you will put on. For life is more than food, and the body more than clothing. Consider the ravens, for they neither sow nor reap; they have no storeroom nor barn, and yet God feeds them; how much more valuable you are than the birds! And which of you by worrying can add a single hour to his life's span? If then you cannot do even a very little thing, why do you worry about other matters? Consider the lilies, how they grow: they neither toil nor spin; but I tell you, not even Solomon in all his glory clothed himself like one of these. But if God so clothes the grass in the field, which is alive today and tomorrow is thrown into the furnace, how much more will He clothe you? You men of little faith! And do not seek what you will eat and what you will drink, and do not keep worrying. For all these things the nations of the world eagerly seek; but your Father knows that you need these things. But seek His kingdom, and these things will be added to you. Do not be afraid, little flock, for your Father has chosen gladly to give you the kingdom" (Luke 12:22–32; cf. Matthew 6:25–33; see 1 Kings 10:4–7; Job 38:41).

CRIPPLED (Also see LAME)

Setting: Capernaum of Galilee. Jesus elaborates about stumbling blocks after His disciples ask about greatness in the kingdom of heaven.

"Woe to the world because of *its* stumbling blocks! For it is inevitable that stumbling blocks come; but woe to that man through whom the stumbling block comes! If your hand or your foot causes you to stumble, cut it off and throw it from you; it is better for you to enter life crippled or lame, than to have two hands or two feet and be cast into the eternal fire. If your eye causes you to stumble, pluck it out and throw it from you. It is better for you to enter life with one eye, than to have two eyes and be cast into the fiery hell" (Matthew 18:7–9; cf. Matthew 5:29, 30; Mark 9:43–48; Luke 17:1).

Setting: Capernaum of Galilee. As Jesus teaches His disciples in private, they ask Him about greatness.

But Jesus said, "Do not hinder him, for there is no one who will perform a miracle in My name, and be able soon afterward to speak evil of Me. For he who is not against us is for us. For whoever gives you a cup of water to drink because of your name as *followers* of Christ, truly I say to you, he will not lose his reward. Whoever causes one of these little ones who believe to stumble, it would be better for him if, with a heavy millstone hung around his neck, he had been cast into the sea. If your hand causes you to stumble, cut it off; it is better for you to enter life crippled, than, having your two hands, to go into hell, into the unquenchable fire, [where THEIR WORM DOES NOT DIE, AND THE FIRE IS NOT QUENCHED.] If your foot causes you to stumble, cut it off; it is better for you to enter life lame, than, having your two feet, to be cast into hell, [where THEIR WORM DOES NOT DIE, AND THE FIRE IS NOT QUENCHED.] If your eye causes you to stumble, throw it out; it is better for you to enter the kingdom of God with one eye, than, having two eyes, to be cast into hell, where THEIR WORM DOES NOT DIE, AND THE FIRE IS NOT QUENCHED. For everyone will be salted with fire. Salt is good; but if the salt becomes unsalty, with what will you make it salty *again?* Have salt in yourselves, and be at peace with one another" (Mark 9:39–50; Jesus quotes from Isaiah 66:24; cf. Matthew 18:6–9; Luke 9:49, 50; see Matthew 5:13, 29, 30; 10:42; 12:30; 18:5, 6; Mark 9:38).

Setting: On the way from Galilee to Jerusalem. Jesus speaks a parable to the guests of a Pharisee leader on the

Sabbath. As He observes the guests selecting places of honor at the table, Jesus comments to the host about the people to invite in the future.

And He also went on to say to the one who had invited Him, "When you give a luncheon or a dinner, do not invite your friends or your brothers or your relatives or rich neighbors, otherwise they may also invite you in return and that will be your repayment. But when you give a reception, invite the poor, the crippled, the lame, the blind, and you will be blessed, since they do not have the means to repay you; for you will be repaid at the resurrection of the righteous" (Luke 14:12–14; see Luke 14:1, 2; John 5:28, 29).

Setting: On the way from Galilee to Jerusalem. After He speaks a parable to the invited guests and the host at a banquet, Jesus responds to a guest's proclamation about the blessings of eating bread in the kingdom of God.

But He said to him, "A man was giving a big dinner, and he invited many; and at the dinner hour he sent his slave to say to those who had been invited, 'Come; for everything is ready now.' But they all alike began to make excuses. The first one said to him, 'I have bought a piece of land and I need to go out and look at it; please consider me excused.' Another one said, 'I have bought five yoke of oxen, and I am going to try them out; please consider me excused.' Another one said, I have married a wife, and for that reason I cannot come.' And the slave came back and reported this to his master. Then the head of the household became angry and said to his slave, 'Go out at once into the streets and lanes of the city and bring in here the poor and crippled and blind and lame.' And the slave said, 'Master, what you commanded has been done, and still there is room.' And the master said to the slave, 'Go out into the highways and along the hedges, and compel them to come in, so that my house may be filled. For I tell you, none of those men who were invited shall taste of my dinner'" (Luke 14:16–24; see Deuteronomy 24:5; Matthew 22:2–14).

CROP (Also see CROPS; FARM; and HARVEST)

Setting: By the Sea of Galilee. While teaching and preaching to the crowds from a boat, Jesus conveys the Parable of the Sower.

And He spoke many things to them in parables, saying, "Behold, the sower went out to sow; and as he sowed, some *seeds* fell beside the road, and the birds came and ate them up. Others fell on the rocky places, where they did not have much soil; and immediately they sprang up, because they had no depth of soil. But when the sun had risen, they were scorched; and because they had no root, they withered away. Others fell among the thorns, and the thorns came up and choked them out. And others fell on the good soil and yielded a crop, some a hundredfold, some sixty, and some thirty. He who has ears, let him hear" (Matthew 13:3–9; cf. Mark 4:3–9; Luke 8:4–8).

Setting: By the Sea of Galilee. During the early part of His ministry, just after a visit from his mother and brothers, Jesus instructs a very large crowd from a boat with the Parable of the Sower.

"Listen *to this!* Behold, the sower went out to sow; as he was sowing, some *seed* fell beside the road, and the birds came and ate it up. Other *seed* fell on the rocky *ground* where it did not have much soil; and immediately it sprang up because it had no depth of soil. And after the sun had risen, it was scorched; and because it had no root, it withered away. Other *seed* fell among the thorns, and the thorns came up and choked it, and it yielded no crop. Other *seeds* fell into the good soil, and as the grew up and increased, they yielded a crop and produced thirty, sixty, and a hundredfold." And He was saying, "He who has ears to hear, let him hear" (Mark 4:3–9; cf. Matthew 13:3–9; Luke 8:5–8).

Setting: Galilee. Following His explanation of the Parable of the Sower to His disciples, Jesus conveys the Parable of the Seed.

And He was saying, "The kingdom of God is like a man who casts seed upon the soil; and he goes to bed at night and gets up by day, and the seed sprouts and grows—how, he himself does not know. The soil produces crops by itself; first the blade, then the head, then the mature grain in the head. But when the crop permits, he immediately puts in the sickle, because the harvest has come" (Mark 4:26–29; see Joel 3:13).

Setting: The villages and cities of Galilee. After His visit in the home of Simon the Pharisee, Jesus proclaims and preaches the kingdom of God.

When a large crowd was coming together, and those from various cities were journeying to Him, He spoke by way of a parable: "The sower went out to sow his seed; and as he sowed, some fell beside the road, and it was trampled under foot and the birds of the air ate it up. Other seed fell on rocky soil, and as soon as it grew up, it was withered away, because it had no moisture. Other seed fell among the thorns; and the thorns grew up with it and choked it out. Other seed fell into the good soil, and grew up, and produced a crop a hundred times as great." As He said these things, He would call out, "He who has ears to hear, let him hear" (Luke 8:4–8; cf. Matthew 13:2–9; Mark 4:3–9).

CROPS (Also see CROP)

Setting: Galilee. Following His explanation of the Parable of the Sower to His disciples, Jesus conveys the Parable of the Seed.

And He was saying, "The kingdom of God is like a man who casts seed upon the soil; and he goes to bed at night and gets up by day, and the seed sprouts and grows—how, he himself does not know. The soil produces crops by itself; first the blade, then the head, then the mature grain in the head. But when the crop permits, he immediately puts in the sickle, because the harvest has come" (Mark 4:26–29; see Joel 3:13).

Setting: On the way from Galilee to Jerusalem. After the scribes and Pharisees turn hostile and question Him in an attempt to catch Him in something He might say, Jesus responds to a question from the crowd and gives a parable about riches and greed.

And He told them a parable, saying, "The land of a rich man was very productive. And he began reasoning to himself, saying, 'What shall I do, since I have no place to store my crops?' Then he said, 'This is what I will do: I will tear down my barns and build larger ones, and here I will store all my grain and my goods. And I will say to my soul, "Soul, you have many goods laid up for many years to come; take your ease, eat, drink and be merry."' "But God said to him, 'You fool! This very night your soul is required of you; and now who will own what you have prepared?' So is the man who stores up treasure for himself, and is not rich toward God" (Luke 12:16–21; see Job 27:8; Psalm 39:6; Ecclesiastes 12:9; Philippians 2:3).

CROSS (JESUS' WORDS WHILE ON THE CROSS is a separate entry; also see CRUCIFIXION)

Setting: Galilee. After His twelve disciples observe His ministry, Jesus summons and specifically instructs them about their ministry ahead involving true discipleship.

"He who loves father or mother more than Me is not worthy of Me; and he who loves son or daughter more than Me is not worthy of Me. And he who does not take his cross and follow after Me is not worthy of Me. He who has found his life will lose it, and he who has lost his life for My sake will find it" (Matthew 10:37–39; cf. Matthew 16:24, 25).

Setting: Near Caesarea Philippi. Jesus teaches His disciples about the costs of discipleship following His rebuke of Peter for forbidding Him to accomplish His earthly mission of dying and being resurrected.

Then Jesus said to His disciples, "If anyone wishes to come after Me, he must deny himself, and take up his cross and follow Me. For whoever wishes to save his life will lose it; but whoever loses his life for My sake will find it. For what will it profit a man if he gains the whole world and forfeits his soul? Or what will a man give in exchange for his soul? For the Son of Man is going to come in the glory of His Father with His angels, and WILL THEN REPAY EVERY MAN ACCORDING TO HIS DEEDS. Truly, I say to you, there are some of you who are standing here who will not taste death until they see the Son of Man coming in His kingdom" (Matthew 16:24–28, Jesus quotes from Psalm 62:12; cf. Mark 8:34–37; Luke 9:23–27; see Matthew 10:38, 39).

Setting: Caesarea Philippi. After He rebukes Peter for desiring to thwart His mission to the cross, Jesus summons a crowd along with His disciples and informs them of the high costs of following Him.

And He summoned the crowd with His disciples, and said to them, "If anyone wishes to come after Me, he must deny himself, and take up his cross and follow Me. For whoever wishes to save his life will lose it, but whoever loses his life for My sake and the gospel's will save it. For what does it profit a man to gain the whole world, and forfeit his soul? For what will a man give in exchange for his soul? For whoever is ashamed of Me and My words in this adulterous and sinful generation, the Son of Man will also be ashamed of him when He comes in the glory of His Father with the holy angels" (Mark 8:34–38; cf. Matthew 16:24–28; Luke 9:23–27; see Matthew 10:33, 38, 39).

Setting: Galilee. Following Peter's pronouncement that Jesus is the Christ of God, the Lord conveys the demands of discipleship and the hope regarding the kingdom of God.

And He was saying to them all, "If anyone wishes to come after Me, he must deny himself, and take up his cross daily and follow Me. For whoever wishes to save his life will lose it, but whoever loses his life for My sake, he is the one who will save it. For what is a man profited if he gains the whole world, and loses or forfeits himself? For whoever is ashamed of Me and My words, the Son of Man will be ashamed of him when He comes in His glory, and the glory of the Father and of the holy angels. But I say to you truthfully, there are some of those standing here who will not taste death until they see the kingdom of God" (Luke 9:23–27; cf. Matthew 16:24–26, 28; Mark 8:34–37; see Matthew 10:33, 38, 39).

Setting: On the way from Galilee to Jerusalem. After He responds to a guest's proclamation about the blessings of eating bread in the kingdom of God, Jesus presents to large crowds the demands of discipleship.

Now large crowds were going along with Him; and He turned and said to them, "If anyone comes to Me, and does not hate his own father and mother and wife and children and brothers and sisters, yes, and even his own life, he cannot be My disciple. Whoever does not carry his own cross and come after Me cannot be My disciple. For which one of you, when he wants to build a tower, does not first sit down and calculate the cost to see if he has enough to complete it? Otherwise, when he has laid a foundation and is not able to finish, all who observe it begin to ridicule him, saying, 'This man began to build and was not able to finish.' Or what king, when he sets out to meet another king in battle, will not first sit down and consider whether he is strong enough with ten thousand *men* to encounter the one coming against him with twenty thousand? Or else, while the other is still far away, he sends a delegation and asks for terms of peace. So then, none of you can be My disciple who does not give up all his possessions. Therefore, salt is good; but if even salt has become tasteless, with what will it be seasoned? It is useless either for the soil or for the manure pile; it is thrown out. He who has ears to hear, let him hear" (Luke 14:25–35; cf. Matthew 5:13; 10:37–39; see Proverbs 20:18; Philippians 3:7).

[CROSS from be lifted up]
Setting: Jerusalem. During the time of the Passover of the Jews, after the Lord cleanses the temple, a Pharisee, Nicodemus, asks Him by night the meaning of "born of the Spirit."

Jesus answered and said to him, "Are you the teacher of Israel and do not understand these things? Truly, truly, I say to you, we speak of what we know and testify of what we have seen, and you do not accept our testimony. If I told you earthly things and you do not believe, how will you believe if I tell you heavenly things? No one has ascended into heaven, but He who descended from heaven: the Son of Man. As Moses lifted up the serpent in the wilderness, even so must the Son of Man be lifted up; so that whoever believes will in Him have eternal life" (John 3:10–15; see Numbers 21:9; Proverbs 30:4; John 12:34; 20:30, 31).

[CROSS from I am lifted up]
Setting: Jerusalem. Just days before the Passover, with the chief priests and Pharisees plotting to seize Him and crowds welcoming Him with palm branches and praise, Jesus expresses anxiety about His upcoming death by crucifixion.

"Now My soul has become troubled; and what shall I say, 'Father, save Me from this hour'? But for this purpose I came to this hour. Father glorify Your name." Then a voice came out of heaven: "I have glorified it, and will glorify it again." So the crowd *of people* who stood by and heard it were saying that it had thundered; others were saying, "An angel has spoken to Him." Jesus answered and said, "This voice has not come for My sake, but for your sakes. Now judgment is upon this world; now the ruler of this world will be cast out. And I, if I am lifted up from the earth, will draw all men to Myself" (John 12:27–32; see Matthew 3:17; 26:38; John 3:14; 6:44; 11:42; 12:9–22; 14:30).

[CROSS from be lifted up]
Setting: Jerusalem. Just days before the Passover, with the chief priests and Pharisees plotting to seize Jesus, who is expressing anxiety about His upcoming death by crucifixion, the crowds ask the Lord about the identity of the Son of Man.

The crowd then answered Him, "We have heard out of the Law that the Christ is to remain forever; and how can You say, 'The Son of Man must be lifted up'? Who is this Son of Man?" So Jesus said to them, "For a little while longer the Light is among you. Walk while you have the Light, so that darkness will not overtake you; he who walks in the darkness does not know where he goes. While you have the Light, believe in the Light, so that you may become sons of Light." These things Jesus spoke, and He went away and hid Himself from them (John 12:34–36; see 1 John 1:6).

CROSS, JESUS' WORDS WHILE ON THE (See JESUS' WORDS WHILE ON THE CROSS)

CROWD (See PEOPLE)

CROWDS (See PEOPLE)

CROWN (LIFE, CROWN OF is a separate entry; also see REWARDS]

Setting: The island of Patmos (in the Aegean Sea about fifty miles southwest of Ephesus in modern Turkey). On the Lord's Day (Sunday), about fifty years after Jesus' resurrection, the disciple John encounters the Lord Jesus Christ. Jesus communicates a new revelation for the apostle to record for the church in Philadelphia and to six other churches in Asia.

"And to the angel of the church in Philadelphia write: He who is holy, who is true, who has the key of David, who opens and no one will shut, and who shuts and no one opens, says this: 'I know your deeds. Behold, I have put before you an open door which no one can shut, because you have a little power, and have kept My word, and have not denied My name. Behold, I will cause *those* of the synagogue of Satan, who say that they are Jews and are not, but lie—I will make them come and bow down at your feet, and *make them* know that I have loved you. Because you have kept the word of My perseverance, I also will keep you from the hour of testing, that *hour* which is about to come upon the whole world, to test those who dwell on the earth. I am coming quickly; hold fast what you have, so that no one will take your crown. He who overcomes, I will make him a pillar in the temple of My God, and he will not go out from it anymore; and I will write on him the name of My God, and the name of the city of My God, the new Jerusalem, which comes down out of heaven from My God, and My new name. He who has an ear, let him hear what the Spirit says to the churches'" (Revelation 3:7–13; see Isaiah 22:22; Galatians 2:9; Revelation 2:9, 10, 13, 25; 14:1).

CROWN OF LIFE (Listed under LIFE, CROWN OF)

CRUCIFIXION (Also see CROSS; JESUS' DEATH; JESUS' WORDS WHILE ON THE CROSS; and PROPHECY OF JESUS' DEATH)

[CRUCIFIXION from crucify]
Setting: On the road to Jerusalem. Before going to Jerusalem, Jesus again tells His disciples of His impending death and resurrection.

As Jesus was about to go up to Jerusalem, He took the twelve *disciples* aside by themselves, and on the way He said to them,

"Behold, we are going up to Jerusalem; and the Son of Man will be delivered to the chief priests and scribes, and they will condemn Him to death, and will hand Him over to the Gentiles to mock and scourge and crucify *Him,* and on the third day, He will be raised up" (Matthew 20:17–19; cf. Matthew 16:21; Mark 10:32–34; Luke 18:31–33).

[CRUCIFIXION from crucify]
Setting: The temple in Jerusalem. After the Jewish religious leaders test Him with questions, Jesus pronounces the eighth of eight woes on them in front of the crowds and His disciples.

"Woe to you, scribes and Pharisees, hypocrites! For you build the tombs of the prophets and adorn the monuments of the righteous, and say, 'If we had been *living* in the days of our fathers, we would not have been partners with them in *shedding* the blood of the prophets.' So you testify against yourselves, that you are sons of those who murdered the prophets. Fill up, then, the measure *of the guilt* of you fathers. You serpents, you brood of vipers, how will you escape the sentence of hell? Therefore, behold, I am sending you prophets and wise men and scribes; some of them you will kill and crucify, and some of them you will scourge in your synagogues, and persecute from city to city, so that upon you may fall *the guilt of* all the righteous blood shed on earth, from the blood of righteous Abel to the blood of Zechariah, the son of Berechiah, whom you murdered between the temple and the altar. Truly I say to you, all these things will come upon this generation" (Matthew 23:29–36; cf. 2 Chronicles 24:21; Zechariah 1:1; Matthew 3:7; Luke 11:47–52; see Matthew 10:23).

Setting: The Mount of Olives, just east of Jerusalem. During His discourse, after answering His disciples' questions as to when the temple will be destroyed and Jerusalem overrun, along with the signs of His coming and the end of the age, Jesus prophesies His crucifixion to them.

When Jesus had finished all these words, He said to His disciples, "You know that after two days the Passover is coming, and the Son of Man is *to be* handed over for crucifixion" (Matthew 26:1, 2; see Mark 14:1, 2; Luke 22:1, 2).

[CRUCIFIXION from be lifted up]
Setting: Jerusalem. During the time of the Passover of the Jews, after the Lord cleanses the temple, a Pharisee, Nicodemus, asks Him by night the meaning of "born of the Spirit."

Jesus answered and said to him, "Are you the teacher of Israel and do not understand these things? Truly, truly, I say to you, we speak of what we know and testify of what we have seen, and you do not accept our testimony. If I told you earthly things and you do not believe, how will you believe if I tell you heavenly things? No one has ascended into heaven, but He who descended from heaven: the Son of Man. As Moses lifted up the serpent in the wilderness, even so must the Son of Man be lifted up; so that whoever believes will in Him have eternal life" (John 3:10–15; see Numbers 21:9; Proverbs 30:4; John 12:34; 20:30, 31).

[CRUCIFIXION from when you lift up the Son of Man]
Setting: The temple treasury in Jerusalem. Following the Feast of Booths and the scribes' and Pharisees' failed attempt to stone a woman for adultery, Jesus returns the next day to teach as they question His testimony about Himself.

So Jesus said, "When you lift up the Son of Man, then you will know that I am *He,* and I do nothing on my own initiative, but I speak these things as the Father taught Me. And He who sent Me is with Me; He has not left Me alone, for I always do the things that are pleasing to Him" (John 8:28, 29; see John 3:14).

[CRUCIFIXION from I am lifted up from the earth]
Setting: Jerusalem. Just days before the Passover, with the chief priests and Pharisees plotting to seize Him and crowds welcoming Him with palm branches and praise, Jesus expresses anxiety about His upcoming death by crucifixion.

"Now My soul has become troubled; and what shall I say, 'Father, save Me from this hour'? But for this purpose I came to this hour. Father glorify Your name." Then a voice came out of heaven: "I have glorified it, and will glorify it again." So the crowd *of people* who stood by and heard it were saying that it had thundered; others were saying, "An angel has spoken to Him." Jesus answered and said, "This voice has not come for My sake, but for your sakes. Now judgment is upon this world; now the ruler of this world will be cast out. And I, if I am lifted up from the earth, will draw all men to Myself" (John 12:27–32; see Matthew 3:17; 26:38; John 3:14; 6:44; 11:42; 14:30).

[CRUCIFIXION from The Son of Man must be lifted up]
Setting: Jerusalem. Just days before the Passover, with the chief priests and Pharisees plotting to seize Jesus, who is expressing anxiety about His upcoming death by crucifixion, the crowds ask the Lord about the identity of the Son of Man.

The crowd then answered Him, "We have heard out of the Law that the Christ is to remain forever; and how can You say, 'The Son of Man must be lifted up'? Who is this Son of Man?" So Jesus said to them, "For a little while longer the Light is among you. Walk while you have the Light, so that darkness will not overtake you; he who walks in the darkness does not know where he goes. While you have the Light, believe in the Light, so that you may become sons of Light." These things Jesus spoke, and He went away and hid Himself from them (John 12:34–36; see 1 John 1:6).

CRUCIFIXION, JESUS' WORDS DURING HIS (See JESUS' WORDS WHILE ON THE CROSS)

CRUMBS (Also see BREAD)
Setting: On the way from Galilee to Jerusalem. After He responds to the Pharisees' scoffing at His teaching His disciples about stewardship and the permanence of the Law, Jesus conveys the story of the rich man and Lazarus.

"Now there was a rich man, and he habitually dressed in purple and fine linen, joyously living in splendor every day. And a poor man named Lazarus was laid at his gate, covered with sores, and longing to be fed with the crumbs which were falling from the rich man's table; besides, even the dogs were coming and licking his sores. Now the poor man died and was carried away by the angels to Abraham's bosom; and the rich man also died and was buried. In Hades he lifted up his eyes, being in torment, and saw Abraham far away and Lazarus in his bosom. And he cried out and said, 'Father Abraham, have mercy on me, and send Lazarus so that he may dip the tip of his finger in water and cool off my tongue, for I am in agony in this flame.' But Abraham said, 'Child, remember that during your life you received your good things, and likewise Lazarus bad things; but now he is being comforted here, and you are in agony. And besides all this, between us and you there is a great chasm fixed, so that those who wish to come over from here to you will not be able, and that none may cross over from there to us.' And he said, 'Then I beg you, father, that you send him to my father's house—for I have five brothers—in order that he may warn them, so that they will not also come to this place of torment.' But Abraham said, 'They have Moses and the Prophets; let them hear them.' But he said, 'No, father Abraham, but if someone goes to them from the dead, they will repent!' But he said to him, 'If they do not listen to Moses and the Prophets, they will not be persuaded even if someone rises from the dead'" (Luke 16:19–31; see Luke 3:8; 6:24).

CRYING (See WEEPING)

CULPRITS
Setting: On the way from Galilee to Jerusalem., After some present report to Him about the Galileans whose blood Pilate (Roman governor of Judea) had mixed with their sacrifices, Jesus responds to their concern by calling them to repentance.

And Jesus said to them, "Do you suppose that these Galileans were greater sinners than all other Galileans because they suffered this fate? I tell you, no, but unless you repent, you will all likewise perish. Or do you suppose that those eighteen on whom the tower in Siloam fell and killed them were worse culprits than all the men who live in Jerusalem? I tell you, no, but unless you repent, you will all likewise perish" (Luke 13:2–5; John 9:2, 3).

CUMMIN (Also see other spices such as DILL; and MINT)

Setting: The temple in Jerusalem. After the Jewish religious leaders test Him with questions, Jesus pronounces the fifth of eight woes on them in front of the crowds and His disciples.

"Woe to you, scribes and Pharisees, hypocrites! For you tithe mint and dill and cummin, and have neglected the weightier provisions of the law: justice and mercy and faithfulness; but these are things you should have done without neglecting the others. You blind guides, who strain out a gnat and swallow a camel!" (Matthew 23:23, 24).

CUP (WATER, CUP OF; and WATER, CUP OF COLD are separate entries; also see SUFFERING)

Setting: On the way to Jerusalem. The mother of James and John, the sons of Zebedee, asks Jesus to make her sons exalted rulers with Him in His coming kingdom.

And He said to her, "What do you wish?" She said to Him, 'Command that in Your kingdom these two sons of mine may sit one on Your right and one on Your left.' But Jesus answered, "You do not know what you are asking. Are you able to drink the cup that I am about to drink?" They said to Him, 'We are able.' He said to them, "My cup you shall drink; but to sit on My right and on *My* left, this is not Mine to give, but it is for those for whom it has been prepared by My Father" (Matthew 20:21–23; cf. Mark 10:35–40; see Matthew 19:28; Acts 12:2).

Setting: The temple in Jerusalem. After the Jewish religious leaders test Him with questions, Jesus pronounces the sixth of eight woes on them in front of the crowds and His disciples.

"Woe to you, scribes and Pharisees, hypocrites! For you clean the outside of the cup and of the dish, but inside they are full of robbery and self-indulgence. You blind Pharisee, first clean the inside of the cup and of the dish, so that the outside of it may become clean also" (Matthew 23:25, 26; see Mark 7:4).

Setting: An upper room in Jerusalem. After celebrating the Passover meal with His disciples, Jesus retreats to the Garden of Gethsemane on the Mount of Olives to pray prior to His betrayal by Judas.

Then Jesus came with them to a place called Gethsemane, and said to His disciples, "Sit here while I go over there and pray." And He took with Him Peter and the two sons of Zebedee, and began to be grieved and distressed. Then He said to them, "My soul is deeply grieved, to the point of death; remain here and keep watch with Me." And He went a little beyond *them,* and fell on His face and prayed, saying, "My Father, if it is possible, let this cup pass from Me; yet not as I will, but as You will." And He came to the disciples and found them sleeping, and said to Peter, "So, you *men* could not keep watch with Me for one hour? Keep watching and praying that you may not enter into temptation; the spirit is willing, but the flesh is weak." He went away again a second time and prayed, saying, "My Father, if this cannot pass away unless I drink it, Your will be done." Again He came and found them sleeping, for their eyes were heavy. And He left them again, and went away and prayed a third time, saying the same thing once more. Then He came to the disciples and said to them, "Are you still sleeping and resting? Behold the hour is at hand and the Son of Man is being betrayed into the hands of sinners. Get up, let us be going; behold the one who betrays Me is at hand!" (Matthew 26:36–46; cf. Mark 14:32–42; Luke 22:40–46; see Matthew 20:22; John 12:27).

Setting: On the way to Jerusalem. After Jesus prophesies His persecution, death, and resurrection, James and John ask for special honor and privileges in His coming kingdom.

And He said to them, "What do you want Me to do for you?" They said to Him, "Grant that we may sit, one on Your right and one on *Your* left, in Your glory." But Jesus said to them, "You do not know what you are asking. Are you able to drink the cup that I drink, or to be baptized with the baptism with which I am baptized?" They said to Him, "We are able." And Jesus said to them, "The cup that I drink you shall drink; and you shall be baptized with the baptism with which I am baptized. But to sit on My right or on *My* left, this is not Mine to give; but it is for those for whom it has been prepared" (Mark 10:36–40; cf. Matthew 20:20–23; see Matthew 19:28; Acts 12:2).

Setting: Mount of Olives, just east of Jerusalem. At a place called Gethsemane, Jesus agonizes over His impending death, disappointed His disciples keep falling asleep instead of watching and praying with Him.

They came to a place named Gethsemane; and He said to the disciples, "Sit here until I have prayed." And He took with Him Peter and James and John, and began to be very distressed and troubled. And He said to them, "My soul is deeply grieved to the point of death; remain here and keep watch." And He went a little beyond *them,* and fell to the ground and *began* to pray that if it were possible, the hour might pass Him by. And He was saying, "Abba! Father! All things are possible for You; remove this cup from Me; yet not what I will, but what You will." And He came and found them sleeping, and said to Peter, "Simon, are you asleep? Could you not keep watch for one hour? Keep watching and praying that you may not come into temptation; the spirit is willing, but the flesh is weak" (Mark 14:32–38; cf. Matthew 26:36–41; Luke 22:41–46; see Romans 8:15; Galatians 4:6).

Setting: On the way from Galilee to Jerusalem. After speaking of how a lamp illuminates, the Lord has lunch with a Pharisee who is surprised He doesn't wash before eating.

But the Lord said to him, "Now you Pharisees clean the outside of the cup and of the platter; but inside of you, you are full of robbery and wickedness. You foolish ones, did not He who made the outside make the inside also? But give that which is within as charity, and then all things are clean for you. But woe to you Pharisees! You pay tithe of mint and rue and every kind of garden herb, and yet disregard justice and the love of God; but these are the things you should have done without neglecting the others. Woe to you Pharisees! For you love the chief seats in the synagogues and the respectful greetings in the market places. Woe to you! For you are like concealed tombs, and the people who walk over them are unaware of it" (Luke 11:39–44; cf. Matthew 23:6–7, 23–27; see Matthew 15:2; Titus 1:15).

Setting: An upper room in Jerusalem. During the Feast of Unleavened Bread (Passover) just before His crucifixion, while celebrating the Passover meal with His disciples, Jesus institutes the Lord's Supper.

And when He had taken a cup and given thanks, He said, "Take this and share it among yourselves; for I say to you, I will not drink of the fruit of the vine from now on until the kingdom of God comes." And when he had taken some bread and given thanks, He broke it and gave it to them, saying, "This is My body which is given for you; do this in remembrance of Me." And in the same way He took the cup after they had eaten, saying, "This cup which is poured out for you is the new covenant in My blood. But behold, the hand of the one betraying Me is with Mine on the table. For indeed, the Son of Man is going as it has been determined; but woe to that man by whom He is betrayed!" (Luke 22:17–22; cf. Matthew 26:26–29; Mark 14:22–25; 1 Corinthians 11:23–26; see Psalm 41:9; Luke 14:15; 22:1–16, 23; 1 Corinthians 10:16).

Setting: Jerusalem. After celebrating the Passover meal and instructing His disciples to prepare to persevere without Him, with His crucifixion imminent, Jesus proceeds to the Mount of Olives to pray.

And He came out and proceeded as was His custom to the Mount of Olives; and the disciples also followed Him. When He arrived at the place, He said to them, "Pray that you may not enter into temptation." And He withdrew from them about a stone's throw, and He knelt down and began to pray, saying, "Father, if You are willing, remove this cup from Me; yet not My will, but Yours be done" (Luke 22:39–42; cf. Matthew 26:36–42; Mark 14:32–49; see Luke 21:37).

Setting: The garden (Gethsemane) over the ravine of the Kidron. Simon Peter attempts to defend Jesus with a sword during Judas's betrayal with a Roman cohort and officers from the chief priests and the Pharisees.

So Jesus said to Peter, "Put the sword into the sheath; the cup which the Father has given Me, shall I not drink it?" (John 18:11; see Matthew 20:22; 26:52; Luke 22:51).

Setting: An upper room in Jerusalem. During his third missionary journey, writing from Ephesus to the church at Corinth, the Apostle Paul recounts the Lord Jesus' words as He institutes the Lord's Supper.

For I received from the Lord that which I also delivered to you, that the Lord Jesus in the night in which He was betrayed took bread; and when He had given thanks, He broke it and said, "This is My body, which is for you; do this in remembrance of Me." In the same way *He took* the cup also after supper, saying, "This cup is the new covenant in My blood; do this, as often as you drink *it,* in remembrance of Me" (1 Corinthians 11:23–25; cf. Matthew 26:26–28; Mark 14:22–24; Luke 22:17–20).

CUP OF COLD WATER (Listed under WATER, CUP OF COLD)

CURES (Also see HEALING)

Setting: On the way from Galilee to Jerusalem. While teaching in the cities and villages, after Jesus responds to a question about who is saved, some Pharisees ask Him to leave, claiming Herod Antipas (tetrarch of Galilee and Perea) seeks to kill Him.

And He said to them, "Go and tell that fox, 'Behold, I cast out demons and perform cures today and tomorrow, and the third day I reach My goal.' Nevertheless I must journey on today and tomorrow and the next day; for it cannot be that a prophet would perish outside of Jerusalem. O Jerusalem, Jerusalem, the city that kills the prophets and stones those sent to her! How often I wanted to gather your children together, just as a hen gathers her brood under her wings, and you would not have it! Behold, your house is left to you desolate; and I say to you, you will not see Me until the time comes when you say, 'BLESSED IS HE WHO COMES IN THE NAME OF THE LORD!'" (Luke 13:32–35, Jesus quotes from Psalm 118:26; cf. Matthew 23:37).

CURES, PERFORMING (See HEALING)

CURSE

[CURSE from No longer shall there ever be *any* fruit from you]

Setting: Having spent the night in Bethany, after cleansing the temple by driving out the money changers and merchants the day before, Jesus becomes hungry while returning and notices a barren fig tree.

Seeing a lone fig tree by the road, He came to it and found nothing on it except leaves only; and He said to it, "No longer shall there ever be *any* fruit from you." And at once the fig tree withered (Matthew 21:19; cf. Mark 11:12–14; see Luke 13:6–9).

[CURSE from May no one ever eat fruit from you again]

Setting: Following His triumphal entry into Jerusalem, days before His impending death on the cross, Jesus curses a fig tree that had no fruit on it near the town of Bethany.

He said to it, "May no one ever eat fruit from you again!" And His disciples were listening (Mark 11:14; cf. Matthew 21:18, 19).

CURSE (profanity)

Setting: Galilee. After selecting His twelve disciples, Jesus teaches the Beatitudes (part of the Sermon on the Mount) to His disciples and a great throng of people from Judea, Jerusalem, and the central coastal region of Tyre and Sidon.

"But I say to you who hear, love your enemies, do good to those who hate you, bless those who curse you, pray for those who mistreat you. Whoever hits you on the cheek, offer him the other also; and whoever takes away your coat, do not withhold your shirt from him either. Give to everyone who asks of you, and whoever takes away what is yours, do not demand it back. Treat others the same way you want them to treat you. If you love those who love you, what credit is that to you? For even sinners love those who love them. If you do good to those who do good to you, what credit is that to you? For even sinners do the same. If you lend to those from whom you expect to receive, what credit is that to you? Even sinners lend to sinners in order to receive back the same amount. But love your enemies, and do good, and lend, expecting nothing in return; and your reward will be great, and you will be sons of the Most High; for He Himself is kind to ungrateful and evil men. Be merciful, just as your Father is merciful" (Luke 6:27–36; cf. Matthew 5:9, 39–48; Matthew 7:12).

CUSTOM (See TRADITION)

CUSTOMS (Also see TAXES)

Setting: Jesus pays the two drachma temple tax for Peter and Himself in an incredible manner while in Capernaum of Galilee.

He said, "Yes." And when he came into the house, Jesus spoke to him first, saying, "What do you think, Simon? From whom do the kings of the earth collect customs or poll-tax, from their sons or from strangers?" When Peter said, "From strangers," Jesus said to him, "Then the sons are exempt. However, so that we do not offend them, go to the sea and throw in a hook, and take the first fish that comes up; and when you open its mouth, you will find a shekel. Take that and give it to them for you and Me" (Matthew 17:25–27; see Exodus 30:11–16; Matthew 22:17–19; Romans 13:7).

D

DAILY (BREAD, DAILY is a separate entry; also see DAY)
Setting: Galilee. Following Peter's pronouncement that Jesus is the Christ of God, the Lord conveys the demands of discipleship and the hope regarding the kingdom of God.

And He was saying to them all, "If anyone wishes to come after Me, he must deny himself, and take up his cross daily and follow Me. For whoever wishes to save his life will lose it, but whoever loses his life for My sake, he is the one who will save it. For what is a man profited if he gains the whole world, and loses or forfeits himself? For whoever is ashamed of Me and My words, the Son of Man will be ashamed of him when He comes in His glory, and the glory of the Father and of the holy angels. But I say to you truthfully, there are some of those standing here who will not taste death until they see the kingdom of God" (Luke 9:23–27; cf. Matthew 16:24–26, 28; Mark 8:34–37; see Matthew 10:33, 38, 39).

Setting: Mount of Olives, just east of Jerusalem. After praying for deliverance, with His crucifixion imminent, Jesus chastises the religious leaders after Judas betrays Him and a hostile crowd surrounds Him.

Then Jesus said to the chief priests and officers of the temple and elders who had come against Him, "Have you come out with swords and clubs as you would against a robber? While I was with you daily in the temple, you did not lay hands on Me; but this hour and the power of darkness are yours" (Luke 22:52, 53; cf. Matthew 26:47–56; Mark 14:43–50; see Luke 22:1–4; 47–51).

DAILY BREAD (Listed under BREAD, DAILY; also see PROVISION, GOD'S)

DAMASCUS
Setting: Jerusalem. Luke, writing in Acts, presents the account of Paul's speech (following his third missionary journey) to a hostile Jewish crowd about His divine encounter with Jesus on the road to Damascus.

"But it happened that as I was on my way, approaching Damascus about noontime, a very bright light suddenly flashed from heaven all around me, and I fell to the ground, and heard a voice saying to me, 'Saul, Saul, why are you persecuting Me?' And I answered, 'Who are You, Lord?' And He said to me, 'I am Jesus the Nazarene, whom you are persecuting.' And those who were with me saw the light, to be sure, but did not understand the voice of the One who was speaking to me. And I said, 'What shall I do, Lord?' And the Lord said to me, 'Get up and go on into Damascus, and there you will be told of all that has been appointed for you to do' (Acts 22:6–10; see Acts 9:7; 26:9).

DAMNATION, ETERNAL (See DEATH, ETERNAL; FIRE, ETERNAL; FIRE, FURNACE OF; GOD, SEPARATION FROM; HELL; JUDGMENT; and PUNISHMENT, ETERNAL)

DANCE (Also see DANCING; and MUSIC)
Setting: Galilee. After praising John the Baptist as His forerunner, Jesus demonstrates the foolish thinking of the current generation of Jewish religious leaders by repeating what they say about John's ascetic lifestyle and ministry along with His own.

"But to what shall I compare this generation? It is like children sitting in the market places, who call out to the other *children,* and say, 'We played the flute for you, and you did not dance; we sang a dirge, and you did not mourn.' For John came neither eating nor drinking, and they say, 'He has a demon!' The Son of Man came eating and drinking, and they say, 'Behold, a gluttonous man and a drunkard, a friend of tax collectors and sinners! Yet wisdom is vindicated by her deeds" (Matthew 11:16–19; cf. Luke 7:31–35; see Matthew 9:11, 34; Luke 1:15).

Setting: Galilee. After praising John the Baptist to the crowds, Jesus criticizes the Pharisees and lawyers who reject God's purpose and John's message.

"To what then shall I compare the men of this generation, and what are they like? They are like children who sit in the market place and call to one another, and they say, 'We played the flute for you, and you did not dance; we sang a dirge, and you did not weep.' For John the Baptist has come eating no bread and drinking no wine, and you say, 'He has a demon!' The Son of Man has come eating and drinking, and you say, 'Behold, a gluttonous man and a drunkard, a friend of tax collectors and sinners!' Yet wisdom is vindicated by all her children" (Luke 7:31–35; cf. Matthew 11:16–19; see Luke 1:15, 7:29, 30).

DANCING (Also see CELEBRATE; DANCE; and MUSIC)

Setting: On the way from Galilee to Jerusalem. Jesus conveys the illustration of the prodigal son because the Pharisees and scribes complain He associates with tax collectors and sinners.

And He said, "A man had two sons. The younger of them said to his father, 'Father, give me the share of the estate that falls to me.' So he divided his wealth between them. And not many days later, the younger son gathered everything together and went on a journey into a distant country, and there he squandered his estate with loose living. Now when he had spent everything, a severe famine occurred in that country, and he began to be impoverished. So he went and hired himself out to one of the citizens of that country, and he sent him into his fields to feed swine. And he would have gladly filled his stomach with the pods that the swine were eating, and no one was giving anything to him. But when he came to his senses, he said, 'How many of my father's hired men have more than enough bread, but I am dying here with hunger! I will get up and go to my father, and will say to him, "Father, I have sinned against heaven, and in your sight; I am no longer worthy to be called your son; make me as one of your hired men."' So he got up and came to his father. But while he was still a long way off, his father saw him and felt compassion for him, and ran and embraced him and kissed him. And the son said to him, "Father, I have sinned against heaven and in your sight; I am no longer worthy to be called your son.' But the father said to his slaves, 'Quickly bring out the best robe and put it on him, and put a ring on his hand and sandals on his feet; and bring the fattened calf, kill it, and let us eat and celebrate; for this son of mine was dead and has come to life again; he was lost and has been found.' And they began to celebrate. Now his older son was in the field, when he came and approached the house, he heard music and dancing. And he summoned one of the servants and began inquiring what these things could be. And he said to him, 'Your brother has come, and your father has killed the fattened calf because he has received him back safe and sound.' But he became angry and was not willing to go in; and his father came out and began pleading with him. But he answered and said to his father, 'Look! For so many years I have been serving you and I have never neglected a command of yours; and yet you have never given me a young goat, so that I might celebrate with my friends; but when this son of yours came, who has devoured your wealth with prostitutes, you killed the fattened calf for him.' And he said to him, 'Son, you have always been with me, and all that is mine is yours. But we had to celebrate and rejoice, for this brother of yours was dead and has begun to live, and was lost and has been found'" (Luke 15:11–32; see Proverbs 29:2; Luke 15:1, 2).

DANIEL (Old Testament Prophet; also see PROPHET; and PROPHETS)

Setting: The Mount of Olives, just east of Jerusalem. During His discourse, Jesus answers His disciples' questions as to when the temple will be destroyed and Jerusalem overrun, along with the signs of His coming and the end of the age.

"Therefore when you see the ABOMINATION OF DESOLATION which was spoken of through Daniel the prophet, standing in the holy place (let the reader understand), then those who are in Judea must flee to the mountains. Whoever is on the housetop must not go down to get the things that are in his house. Whoever is in the field must not turn back to get his cloak. But woe to those who are pregnant and to those who are nursing babies in those days! But pray that your flight will not be in the winter, or on a Sabbath. For then there will be a great tribulation, such as has not occurred since the beginning of the world until now, nor ever will. Unless those days had been cut short, no life would have been saved; but for the sake of the elect those days will be cut short. Then if anyone says to you, 'Behold, here is the Christ,' or "There *He is*,' do not believe *him.* For false Christs and false prophets will arise and will show great signs and wonders, so as to mislead, if possible, even the elect. Behold, I have told you in advance. So if they say to you, 'Behold, He is in the wilderness,' do not go out, *or*, 'Behold, He is in the inner rooms,' do not believe *them*. For just as the lightning comes from the east and flashes even to the west, so will the coming of the Son of Man be. Wherever the corpse is, there the vultures will gather" (Matthew 24:15–28, Jesus quotes from Daniel 9:27; cf. Daniel 12:1; Mark 13:14–23; Luke 17:22–31; 21:20–24; 23:29; see John 4:48).

DARK (Also see DARKNESS)

Setting: On the way from Galilee to Jerusalem. After telling the increasing crowds of the sign of Jonah, Jesus illustrates His point by speaking of a lamp.

"No one, after lighting a lamp, puts it away in a cellar nor under a basket, but on the lampstand, so that those who enter may see the light. The eye is the lamp of your body; when your eye is clear, your whole body also is full of light; but when it is bad, your body also is full of darkness. Then watch out that the light in you is not darkness. If therefore your whole body is full of light, with no dark part in it, it will be wholly illumined, as when the lamp illumines you with its rays" (Luke 11:33–36; cf. Matthew 5:15, 6:22, 23).

Setting: On the way from Galilee to Jerusalem. Jesus warns His disciples of future events, as the scribes and Pharisees turn hostile and question Him in an attempt to catch Him in something He might say.

Under these circumstances, after so many thousands of people had gathered together that they were stepping on one another, He began saying to His disciples first of all, "Beware of the leaven of the Pharisees, which is hypocrisy. But there is nothing covered up that will not be revealed, and hidden that will not be known. Accordingly, whatever you have said in the dark will be heard in the light, and what you have whispered in the inner rooms will be proclaimed upon the housetops. I say to you, My friends, do not be afraid of those who kill the body and after that have no more that they can do. But I will warn you whom to fear: fear the One who, after He has killed, has authority to cast into hell; yes, I tell you, fear Him! Are not five sparrows sold for two cents? Yet not one of them is forgotten before God. Indeed, the very hairs of your head are all numbered. Do not fear; you are more valuable than many sparrows" (Luke 12:1–7; cf. Matthew 10:26–31; see Matthew 16:6; Hebrews 10:31).

DARKNESS (DARKNESS, FULL OF; DARKNESS, OUTER; and DARKNESS, POWER OF are separate entries; also see DARK)

Setting: Galilee. During the early part of His ministry, Jesus preaches the Sermon on the Mount to His disciples and the multitudes.

"The eye is the lamp of the body; so then if your eye is clear, your whole body will be full of light. But if your eye is bad, your whole body will be full of darkness. If then the light that is in you is darkness, how great is the darkness!" (Matthew 6:22, 23; cf. Luke 11:34, 35).

Setting: Galilee. After His disciples observe His ministry, Jesus summons and specifically instructs them about their ministry ahead involving true discipleship.

"Therefore do not fear them, for there is nothing concealed that will not be revealed, or hidden that will not be known. What I tell you in the darkness, speak in the light; and what you hear *whispered* in your ear, proclaim upon the housetops. Do not fear those who kill the body but are unable to kill the soul; but rather fear Him who is able to destroy both soul and body in hell" (Matthew 10:26–28; cf. Mark 4:22; Luke 12:3; see Hebrews 10:31).

Setting: On the way from Galilee to Jerusalem. After telling the increasing crowds of the sign of Jonah, Jesus illustrates His point by speaking of a lamp.

"No one, after lighting a lamp, puts it away in a cellar nor under a basket, but on the lampstand, so that those who enter may see the light. The eye is the lamp of your body; when your eye is clear, your whole body also is full of light; but when it is bad, your body also is full of darkness. Then watch out that the light in you is not darkness. If therefore your whole body is full of light, with no dark part in it, it will be wholly illumined, as when the lamp illumines you with its rays" (Luke 11:33–36; cf. Matthew 5:15, 6:22, 23).

Setting: Jerusalem. During the time for the Passover of the Jews, after the Lord cleanses the temple, a Pharisee, Nicodemus, asks Him by night the meaning of "born again."

"For God so loved the world, that He gave His only begotten Son, that whoever believes in Him shall not perish, but have eternal life. For God did not send the Son into the world to judge the world, but that the world might be saved through Him. He who believes in Him is not judged; he who does not believe has been judged already, because he has not believed in the name of the only begotten Son of God. This is the judgment, that the Light has come into the world, and men loved darkness rather than the Light, for their deeds were evil. For everyone who does evil hates the Light, and does not come to the Light for fear that his deeds will be exposed. But he who practices the truth comes to the Light, so that his deeds may be manifested as having been wrought in God" (John 3:16–21; see Luke 19:10; John 1:4; 1:18; Romans 5:8; 1 John 1:6, 7).

Setting: The temple in Jerusalem. Following the Feast of Booths, Jesus retires to the Mount of Olives, and returns the next day to the temple to teach. He addresses the scribes and Pharisees after their failed attempt to stone a woman caught in adultery.

Then Jesus again spoke to them, saying, "I am the Light of the world; he who follows Me will not walk in the darkness, but will have the Light of life" (John 8:12; see John 1:4; 8:1–11).

Setting: Jerusalem. Just days before the Passover, with the chief priests and Pharisees plotting to seize Jesus, who is expressing anxiety about His upcoming death by crucifixion, the crowds ask the Lord about the identity of the Son of Man.

The crowd then answered Him, "We have heard out of the Law that the Christ is to remain forever; and how can You say, 'The Son of Man must be lifted up'? Who is this Son of Man?" So Jesus said to them, "For a little while longer the Light is among you. Walk while you have the Light, so that darkness will not overtake you; he who walks in the darkness does not know where he goes. While you have the Light, believe in the Light, so that you may become sons of Light." These things Jesus spoke, and He went away and hid Himself from them (John 12:34–36; see John 12:23–33; 1 John 1:6).

Setting: Jerusalem. Just days before the Passover, with the chief priests and Pharisees plotting to seize Jesus, who is expressing anxiety about His upcoming death by crucifixion, some believe in Jesus, while others are rejecting His message.

And Jesus cried out and said, "He who believes in Me, does not believe in Me but in Him who sent Me. He who sees Me sees the One who sent Me. I have come *as* Light into the world, so that everyone who believes in Me will not remain in darkness. If anyone hears My sayings and does not keep them, I do not judge him; for I did not come to judge the world, but to save the world. He who rejects Me and does not receive My sayings, has one who judges him; the word I spoke is what will judge him at the last day. For I did not speak on My own initiative, but the Father Himself who sent Me has given Me a commandment *as to* what to say and what to speak. I know that His commandment is eternal life; therefore the things I speak, I speak just as the Father as told Me" (John 12:44–50; see Matthew 10:40; Luke 10:16; John 1:4; 3:17; 5:19; 6:68; 14:9).

Setting: Caesarea. Luke, writing in Acts, gives Paul's retelling of his conversion to Christ as he appears before King Agrippa following his hearing before the Jewish Council in Jerusalem and arrest by the Roman commander (on his way to Rome after the apostle's third missionary journey).

"And when we had fallen to the ground, I heard a voice saying to me in the Hebrew dialect, 'Saul, Saul, why are you persecuting Me? It is hard for you to kick against the goads.' And I said, 'Who are You, Lord?' And the Lord said, 'I am Jesus whom you are persecuting. But get up and stand on your feet; for this purpose I have appeared to you, to appoint you a minister and a witness not only to the things which you have seen, but also to the things in which I will appear to you; rescuing you from the *Jewish* people and from the Gentiles, to whom I am sending you, to open their eyes so that they may turn from darkness to light and from the dominion of Satan to God, that they may receive forgiveness of sins and an inheritance among those who have been sanctified by faith in Me' (Acts 26:14–18; see Isaiah 35:5; Acts 21:40; 22:14).

DARKNESS, FULL OF

Setting: Galilee. During the early part of His ministry, Jesus preaches the Sermon on the Mount to His disciples and the multitudes.

"The eye is the lamp of the body; so then if your eye is clear, your whole body will be full of light. But if your eye is bad, your whole body will be full of darkness. If then the light that is in you is darkness, how great is the darkness!" (Matthew 6:22, 23; cf. Luke 11:34, 35).

Setting: On the way from Galilee to Jerusalem. After telling the increasing crowds of the sign of Jonah, Jesus illustrates His point by speaking of a lamp.

"No one, after lighting a lamp, puts it away in a cellar nor under a basket, but on the lampstand, so that those who enter may see the light. The eye is the lamp of your body; when your eye is clear, your whole body also is full of light; but when it is bad, your body also is full of darkness. Then watch out that the light in you is not darkness. If therefore your whole body is full of light, with no dark part in it, it will be wholly illumined, as when the lamp illumines you with its rays" (Luke 11:33–36; cf. Matthew 5:15, 6:22, 23).

DARKNESS, OUTER

Setting: Capernaum. After Jesus gives the Sermon on the Mount and cleanses a leper, a Roman centurion implores Him to heal his servant.

Now when Jesus heard *this,* He marveled, and said to those who were following, "Truly I say to you, I have not found such great faith with anyone in Israel. I say to you that many will come from east and west, and recline *at the table* with Abraham, Isaac and Jacob in the kingdom of heaven; but the sons of the kingdom will be cast out into the outer darkness; in that place there will be weeping and gnashing of teeth." And Jesus said to the centurion, "Go; it shall be done for you as you have believed." And the servant was healed that *very* moment (Matthew 8:10–13; cf. Luke 7:9, 10; see Matthew 8:1–9).

Setting: The temple in Jerusalem. Jesus speaks another parable to the chief priests and elders after they question His authority.

Jesus spoke to them again in parables, saying, "The kingdom of heaven may be compared to a king who gave a wedding feast for his son. And he sent out his slaves to call those who had been invited to the wedding feast, and they were unwilling to come. Again he sent out other slaves saying, 'Tell those who have been invited, "Behold, I have prepared my dinner; my oxen and my fattened livestock are *all* butchered and everything is ready; come to the wedding feast." But they paid no attention and went their way, one to his own farm, another to his business, and the rest seized his slaves and mistreated them and killed them. But the king was enraged, and he sent his armies and destroyed those murderers and set their city on fire. Then he said to his slaves, 'The wedding is ready, but those who were invited were not worthy. 'Go therefore to the main highways, and as many as you find *there,* invite to the wedding feast.' Those slaves went out into the streets and gathered together all they found, both evil and good; and the wedding hall was filled with dinner guests. But when the king came in to look over the dinner guests, he saw a man there who was not dressed in wedding clothes, and he said to him, 'Friend, how did you come in here without wedding clothes?' And the man was speechless. Then the king said to the servants, 'Bind him hand and foot, and throw him into the outer darkness; in that place there will be weeping and gnashing of teeth.' For many are called, but few *are* chosen" (Matthew 22:1–14; cf. Matthew 8:11, 12).

Setting: The Mount of Olives, just east of Jerusalem. During His discourse, after answering His disciples' questions as to when the temple will be destroyed and Jerusalem overrun, along with the signs of His coming and the end of the age, Jesus reemphasizes to His disciples that they should be on the alert for His return.

"For *it is* just like a man *about* to go on a journey, who called his own slaves and entrusted his possessions to them. To one he gave five talents, to another, two, and to another, one, each according to his own ability; and he went on his journey. Immediately the one who had received the five talents went and traded with them, and gained five more talents. In the same manner the one who *had received* the two *talents* gained two more. But he who received the one *talent* went away, and dug a *hole* in the ground and hid his master's money. Now after a long time the master of those slaves came and settled accounts with them. The one who had received the five talents came up and brought five more talents, saying, 'Master, you entrusted five talents to me. See, I have gained five more talents.' His master said to him, 'Well done, good and faithful slave. You were faithful with a few things, I will put you in charge of many things; enter into the joy of your master.' Also the one who *had received* the two talents came up and said, 'Master, you entrusted two talents to me. See, I have gained two more talents.' His master said to him, 'Well done, good and faithful slave. You were faithful with a few things, I will put you in charge of many things; enter into the joy of your master.' And the one also who had received the one talent came up and said, 'Master, I knew you to be a hard man, reaping where you did not sow and gathering where you scattered no *seed.* And I was afraid, and went away and hid your talent in the ground. See, you have what is yours.' But his master answered and said to him, 'You wicked, lazy slave, you knew that I reap where I did not sow and gather where I scattered no *seed.* Then you ought to have put my money in the bank, and on my arrival I would have received my *money* back with interest. 'Therefore take away the talent from him, and give it to the one who has ten talents.' For to everyone who has, *more* shall be given, and he will have an abundance; but from the one who does not have, even what he does have shall be taken away. Throw out the worthless slave into the outer darkness; in that place there will be weeping and gnashing of teeth" (Matthew 25:14–30; cf. Matthew 8:12; 3:12; 24:45–47; see Matthew 18:23, 24; Luke 12:44).

DARKNESS, POWER OF (Also see EVIL)

Setting: Gethsemane on the Mount of Olives, just east of Jerusalem. After praying for deliverance, with His crucifixion imminent, Jesus chastises the religious leaders after Judas betrays Him and the hostile crowd surrounds Him.

Then Jesus said to the chief priests and officers of the temple and elders who had come against Him, "Have you come out with swords and clubs as you would against a robber? While I was with you daily in the temple, you did not lay hands on Me; but this hour and the power of darkness are yours" (Luke 22:52, 53; cf. Matthew 26:47–56; Mark 14:43–50; see Luke 22:1–4; 47–51).

DAUGHTER (Also see DAUGHTERS)

Setting: Capernaum near the Sea of Galilee. Jesus heals a woman who has been suffering with internal bleeding for twelve years.

But Jesus turning and seeing her said, "Daughter, take courage; your faith has made you well." At once the woman was made well (Matthew 9:22; cf. Mark 5:34; Luke 8:48).

Setting: Galilee. After His disciples observe His ministry, Jesus summons and specifically instructs them about their ministry hardships ahead involving true discipleship.

"Do not think that I came to bring peace on the earth; I did not come to bring peace, but a sword. For I came to SET A MAN AGAINST HIS FATHER, AND A DAUGHTER AGAINST HER MOTHER, AND A DAUGHTER-IN-LAW AGAINST HER MOTHER-IN-LAW; and A MAN'S ENEMIES WILL BE THE MEMBERS OF HIS HOUSEHOLD" (Matthew 10:34–36; Jesus quotes from Micah 7:6; cf. Luke 12:51–53).

Setting: Galilee. After His twelve disciples observe His ministry, Jesus summons and specifically instructs them about their ministry hardships ahead involving true discipleship.

"He who loves father or mother more than Me is not worthy of Me; and he who loves son or daughter more than Me is not worthy of Me. And he who does not take his cross and follow after Me is not worthy of Me. He who has found his life will lose it, and he who has lost his life for My sake will find it" (Matthew 10:37–39; cf. Matthew 16:24, 25).

Setting: Capernaum by the Sea of Galilee. After Jesus returns from ministry to the Gerasenes, a woman who has had a hemorrhage for twelve years touches Him in order to be healed.

And He said to her, "Daughter, your faith has made you well; go in peace and be healed of your affliction" (Mark 5:34; cf. Matthew 9:22; Luke 8:48; see Mark 5:31–33; Luke 7:50).

Setting: The region of Tyre. After the Pharisees and scribes from Jerusalem question Jesus' disciples' lack of obedience to tradition in Galilee, Jesus casts out a demon from the daughter of a Gentile (Syrophoenician) woman.

And He was saying to her, "Let the children be satisfied first, for it is not good to take the children's bread and throw it to the dogs." But she answered and said to Him, "Yes, Lord *but* even the dogs under the table feed on the children's crumbs. And He said to her, "Because of this answer go; the demon has gone out of your daughter" (Mark 7:27–29; cf. Matthew 15:21–28; see Mark 7:24–26).

Setting: Capernaum. After Jesus returns from ministering in the country of the Gerasenes (across the Sea of Galilee), a woman, ill for 12 years, receives healing by touching His garment.

And Jesus said, "Who is the one who touched Me?" And while they were all denying it, Peter said, "Master, the people are crowding and pressing in on You." But Jesus said, "Someone did touch Me, for I was aware, that power had gone out of Me." When the woman saw that she had not escaped notice, she came trembling and fell down before Him, and declared in the presence of all the people the reason why she had touched Him, and how she had been immediately healed. And He said to her, "Daughter, your faith has made you well; go in peace" (Luke 8:45–48; cf. Matthew 9:20; Mark 5:25–34; see Luke 8:43, 44).

Setting: On the way from Galilee to Jerusalem. After clarifying a parable for Peter and the crowd, Jesus conveys how a relationship with Him divides families.

"I have come to cast fire upon the earth; and how I wish it were already kindled! But I have a baptism to undergo, and how distressed I am until it is accomplished! Do you suppose that I came to grant peace on earth? I tell you, no, but rather division; for from now on five members in one household will be divided, three against two and two against three. They will be divided, father against son and son against father, mother against daughter, and daughter against mother, mother-in-law against daughter-in-law and daughter-in-law against mother-in-law" (Luke 12:49–53; cf. Matthew 10:34–36; see Micah 7:6; Mark 10:38).

Setting: On the way from Galilee to Jerusalem. After healing a woman, sick for eighteen years, in one of the synagogues on the Sabbath, Jesus responds to a synagogue official's anger.

But the Lord answered him and said, "You hypocrites, does not each of you on the Sabbath untie his ox or his donkey from the stall and lead him away to water him? And this woman, a daughter of Abraham as she is, whom Satan has bound for eighteen long years, should she not have been released from this bond on the Sabbath day?" (Luke 13:15, 16; see Luke 13:10–14, 17; 14:5).

DAUGHTER-IN-LAW

Setting: Galilee. After His disciples observe His ministry, Jesus summons and specifically instructs them about their ministry hardships ahead involving true discipleship.

"Do not think that I came to bring peace on the earth; I did not come to bring peace, but a sword. For I came to SET A MAN AGAINST HIS FATHER, AND A DAUGHTER AGAINST HER MOTHER, AND A DAUGHTER-IN-LAW AGAINST HER MOTHER-IN-LAW; and A MAN'S ENEMIES WILL BE THE MEMBERS OF HIS HOUSEHOLD" (Matthew 10:34–36; Jesus quotes from Micah 7:6; cf. Luke 12:51–53).

Setting: On the way from Galilee to Jerusalem. After clarifying a parable for Peter and the crowd, Jesus conveys how a relationship with Him divides families.

"I have come to cast fire upon the earth; and how I wish it were already kindled! But I have a baptism to undergo, and how distressed I am until it is accomplished! Do you suppose that I came to grant peace on earth? I tell you, no, but rather division; for from now on five members in one household will be divided, three against two and two against three. They will be divided, father

against son and son against father, mother against daughter, and daughter against mother, mother-in-law against daughter-in-law and daughter-in-law against mother-in-law" (Luke 12:49–53; cf. Matthew 10:34–36; see Micah 7:6; Mark 10:38).

DAUGHTER OF ABRAHAM (Listed as ABRAHAM, DAUGHTER OF)

DAUGHTERS (See DAUGHTER; and JERUSALEM, DAUGHTERS OF)

DAUGHTERS OF JERUSALEM (Listed under JERUSALEM, DAUGHTERS OF)

DAVID (Specifics such as DAVID, SON OF are separate entries; also see KING; and KINGS)

Setting: Galilee. Jesus responds to the Pharisees' objection to His disciples' picking grain from the fields on the Sabbath.

But He said to them, "Have you not read what David did when he became hungry, he and his companions, how they entered the house of God, and ate the consecrated bread, which was not lawful for him to eat nor for those with him, but for the priests alone? Or, have you not read in the Law, that on the Sabbath the priests in the temple break the Sabbath and are innocent? But I say to you that something greater than the temple is here. But if you had known what this means, 'I DESIRE COMPASSION, AND NOT A SACRIFICE,' you would not have condemned the innocent. For the Son of Man is Lord of the Sabbath" (Matthew 12:3–8, Jesus quotes from Hosea 6:6; cf. Mark 2:25–28; Luke 6:3–5; see 1 Samuel 21:6; Matthew 12:1, 2).

Setting: The temple in Jerusalem. Following the Sadducees' and Pharisees' unsuccessful attempts to test Him with questions, with the crowds listening, Jesus poses a question to some of the Pharisees.

"What do you think about the Christ, whose son is He?" They said to Him, "The *son* of David." He said to them, "Then how does David in the Spirit call Him 'Lord,' saying, 'THE LORD SAID TO MY LORD, SIT AT MY RIGHT HAND, UNTIL I PUT YOUR ENEMIES BENEATH YOUR FEET"'? "If David then calls Him 'Lord," how is He his son?" (Matthew 22:42–45; Jesus quotes from Psalm 110:1; cf. Mark 12:35–37; Luke 20:41–44; see 2 Samuel 23:2).

Setting: Galilee. Early in Jesus' ministry, the Pharisees ask Him why He allows His disciples to harvest and eat grain on the Sabbath.

And He said to them, "Have you never read what David did when he was in need and he and his companions became hungry; how he entered the house of God in the time of Abiathar *the* high priest, and ate the consecrated bread, which is not lawful for *anyone* to eat except the priests, and he also gave it to those who were with him?" Jesus said to them, "The Sabbath was made for man, and not man for the Sabbath. So the Son of Man is Lord even of the Sabbath" (Mark 2:25–28; cf. Matthew 12:1–8; Luke 6:1–5; see Exodus 23:12; Mark 2:23, 24).

Setting: The temple in Jerusalem. Jesus teaches the crowd after commending a scribe for his nearness to the kingdom of God.

And Jesus *began* to say, as He taught in the temple, "How *is it that* the scribes say that the Christ is the son of David? David himself said in the Holy Spirit, 'THE LORD SAID TO MY LORD, SIT AT MY RIGHT HAND, UNTIL I PUT YOUR ENEMIES BENEATH YOUR FEET."' David himself calls Him 'Lord'; so in what sense is He his son?" And the large crowd enjoyed listening to Him (Mark 12:35–37, Jesus quotes from Psalm 110:1; cf. Matthew 22:41–46; Luke 20:41–44).

Setting: Probably Galilee. As Jesus and His disciples pass through some grain fields, some of the Pharisees question why His followers harvest and eat grain on the Sabbath.

And Jesus answering them said, "Have you not even read what David did when he was hungry, he and those who were with him, how he entered the house of God, and took and ate the consecrated bread which is not lawful for any to eat except the priests alone, and gave it to his companions?" And He was saying to them, "The Son of Man is Lord of the Sabbath" (Luke 6:3–5; cf. Matthew 12:1–8; Mark 2:23–28; see Exodus 20:8; Leviticus 24:1–9; Deuteronomy 5:12; 1 Samuel 21:1–6; Luke 6:1, 2).

Setting: The temple in Jerusalem. A few days before His crucifixion, after some of the Sadducees question Him about the resurrection, Jesus poses a question to the scribes, who say He answered well.

Then He said to them, "How is it that they say the Christ is David's son? For David himself says in the book of Psalms, 'THE LORD SAID TO MY LORD, SIT AT MY RIGHT HAND, UNTIL I MAKE YOUR ENEMIES A FOOTSTOOL FOR YOUR FEET.' Therefore David calls Him 'Lord,' and how is He his son?" (Luke 20:41–44, Jesus quotes from Psalm 110:1; cf. Matthew 22:41–46; Mark 12:35–37).

DAVID, DESCENDANT OF

Setting: The island of Patmos (in the Aegean Sea about fifty miles southwest of Ephesus in modern Turkey). In the final chapter of the Lord Jesus Christ's revelation via the disciple John, about fifty years after His resurrection, the Lord authenticates the truthfulness of His message along with His earthly lineage through King David.

"I, Jesus, have sent My angel to testify to you these things for the churches. I am the root and the descendant of David, the bright morning star" (Revelation 22:16; see Revelation 22:17–19).

DAVID, KEY OF

Setting: The island of Patmos (in the Aegean Sea about fifty miles southwest of Ephesus in modern Turkey). On the Lord's Day (Sunday), about fifty years after Jesus' resurrection, the disciple John encounters the Lord Jesus Christ. Jesus communicates a new revelation for the apostle to record for the church in Philadelphia and to six other churches in Asia.

"And to the angel of the church in Philadelphia write: He who is holy, who is true, who has the key of David, who opens and no one will shut, and who shuts and no one opens, says this: 'I know your deeds. Behold, I have put before you an open door which no one can shut, because you have a little power, and have kept My word, and have not denied My name. Behold, I will cause *those* of the synagogue of Satan, who say that they are Jews and are not, but lie—I will make them come and bow down at your feet, and *make them* know that I have loved you. Because you have kept the word of My perseverance, I also will keep you from the hour of testing, that *hour* which is about to come upon the whole world, to test those who dwell on the earth. I am coming quickly; hold fast what you have, so that no one will take your crown. He who overcomes, I will make him a pillar in the temple of My God, and he will not go out from it anymore; and I will write on him the name of My God, and the name of the city of My God, the new Jerusalem, which comes down out of heaven from My God, and My new name. He who has an ear, let him hear what the Spirit says to the churches'" (Revelation 3:7–13; see Isaiah 22:22; Galatians 2:9; Revelation 2:9, 10, 13, 25; 14:1).

DAVID, SON OF (Also see CHRIST, THE; MESSIAH; and SON, DAVID'S)

Setting: The temple in Jerusalem. Jesus teaches the crowd after commending a scribe for his nearness to the kingdom of God.

And Jesus *began* to say, as He taught in the temple, "How *is it that* the scribes say that the Christ is the son of David? David himself said in the Holy Spirit, 'THE LORD SAID TO MY LORD, SIT AT MY RIGHT HAND, UNTIL I PUT YOUR ENEMIES BENEATH YOUR FEET.'" David himself calls Him 'Lord'; so in what sense is He his son?" And the large crowd enjoyed listening to Him (Mark 12:35–37, Jesus quotes from Psalm 110:1; cf. Matthew 22:41–46; Luke 20:41–44).

DAVID'S SON (Listed under SON, DAVID'S; also see DAVID, SON OF)

DAY (Specifics such as DAY, LAST; DAY, THIRD; and JUDGMENT, DAY OF are separate entries; also see DAILY; and DAYS)

Setting: Galilee. During the early part of His ministry, Jesus preaches the Sermon on the Mount to His disciples and the multitudes.

"Pray, then, in this way: 'Our Father who is in heaven, hallowed be Your name. Your kingdom come. Your will be done, on earth as it is in heaven. Give us this day our daily bread. And forgive us our debts, as we also have forgiven our debtors. And do not lead us into temptation, but deliver us from evil. [For Yours is the kingdom and the power and the glory forever. Amen]'" (Matthew 6:9–13; cf. Luke 11:2–4; see John 17:15).

Setting: Galilee. During the early part of His ministry, Jesus preaches the Sermon on the Mount to His disciples and the multitudes.

"Not everyone who says to Me, 'Lord, Lord,' will enter the kingdom of heaven, but he who does the will of My Father who is in heaven *will enter.* Many will say to Me on that day, 'Lord, Lord, did we not prophesy in Your name, and in Your name cast out demons, and in Your name perform many miracles?' And then I will declare to them, 'I never knew you, DEPART FROM ME, YOU WHO PRACTICE LAWLESSNESS'" (Matthew 7:21–23, Jesus quotes from Psalm 6:8; cf. Matthew 25:11–13; see Luke 6:46).

Setting: Galilee. After performing miracles throughout the region, Jesus pronounces woes against those cities who did not repent.

"Woe to you, Chorazin! Woe to you, Bethsaida! For if the miracles had occurred in Tyre and Sidon which occurred in you, they would have repented long ago in sackcloth and ashes. Nevertheless I say to you, it will be more tolerable for Tyre and Sidon in *the* day of judgment than for you. And you, Capernaum, will not be exalted to heaven, will you? You will descend to Hades; for if the miracles had occurred in Sodom which occurred in you, it would have remained to this day. Nevertheless, I say to you that it will be more tolerable for the land of Sodom in *the* day of judgment, than for you" (Matthew 11:21–24; cf. Matthew 10:15; Luke 10:13–15; see Matthew 11:20).

Setting: Judea beyond the Jordan (Perea). Jesus illustrates the kingdom of heaven to His disciples through the story of laborers in the vineyard.

"For the kingdom of heaven is like a landowner who went out early in the morning to hire laborers for his vineyard. When he had agreed with the laborers for a denarius for the day, he sent them into his vineyard. And he went out about the third hour and saw others standing idle in the market place; and to those he said, 'You also go into the vineyard, and whatever is right I will give you.' And *so* they went. Again he went out about the sixth and the ninth hour, and did the same thing. And about the eleventh *hour* he went out and found others standing *around;* and he said to them, 'Why have you been standing idle here all day long?' They said to him, 'Because no one hired us.' He said to them, 'You go into the vineyard too.' When evening came, the owner of the vineyard said to his foreman, 'Call the laborers and pay them their wages, beginning with the last *group* to the first.' When those *hired* about the eleventh hour came, each one received a denarius. When those *hired* first came, they thought that they would receive more; but each of them also received a denarius. When they received it, they grumbled at the landowner, saying, 'These last men have worked *only* one hour, and you have made them equal to us who have borne the burden and the scorching heat of the day.' But he answered and said to one of them, 'Friend, I am doing you no wrong; did you not agree with me for a denarius? Take what is yours and go, but I wish to give to this last man the same as to you. It is not lawful for me to do what I wish with what is my own? Or is your eye envious because I am generous?' So the last shall be first, and the first last" (Matthew 20:1–16; cf. Matthew 19:30).

Setting: The Mount of Olives, just east of Jerusalem. During His discourse, after answering His disciples' questions as to when the temple will be destroyed and Jerusalem overrun, along with the signs of His coming and the end of the age, Jesus teaches them the Parable of the Fig Tree.

"Now learn the parable from the fig tree: when its branch has already become tender and puts forth its leaves, you know that summer is near; so, you too, when you see all these things, recognize that He is near, *right* at the door. Truly, I say to you, this generation will not pass away until all these things take place. Heaven and earth will pass away, but My words will not pass away. But of that day and hour no one knows, not even the angels of heaven, nor the Son, but the Father alone. For the coming of the Son of Man will be just like the days of Noah. For as in those days before the flood they were eating and drinking, marrying and giving in marriage, until the day that Noah entered the ark, and they did not understand until the flood came and took them all away; so will the coming of the Son of Man be. Then there will be two men in the field; one will be taken and one will be left. Two women *will be* grinding at the mill; one will be taken and one will be left" (Matthew 24:32–41; cf. Mark 13:28–32; Luke 17:34–36; 21:28–33; see Genesis 6:5; 7:7; Matthew 5:18; 10:23; James 5:9).

Setting: The Mount of Olives, just east of Jerusalem. During His discourse, after answering His disciples' questions as to when the temple will be destroyed and Jerusalem overrun, along with the signs of His coming and the end of the age, Jesus reemphasizes to His disciples that they should be on the alert for His return.

"Therefore be on the alert, for you do not know which day your Lord is coming. But be sure of this, that if the head of the house had known at what time of the night the thief was coming, he would have been on the alert and would not have allowed his house to be broken into. For this reason you also must be ready; for the Son of Man is coming at an hour when you do not think *He will.* Who then is the faithful and sensible slave whom his master put in charge of his household to give their food at the proper time? Blessed is that slave whom his master finds so doing when he comes. Truly I say to you that he will put him in charge of all his possessions. But if that evil slave says in his heart, 'My master is not coming for a long time,' and begins to beat his fellow slaves and eat and drink with drunkards; the master of that slave will come on a day when he does not expect *him* and at an hour which he does not know, and will cut him in pieces and assign him a place with the hypocrites; in that place there will be weeping and gnashing of teeth" (Matthew 24:42–51; cf. Mark 13:33–37; Luke 12:39–46; 21:34–36; see Matthew 8:11, 12; 25:21–23).

Setting: An upper room in Jerusalem. While celebrating the Passover meal with His disciples, Jesus institutes the Lord's Supper ordinance before being arrested by His enemies.

While they were eating, Jesus took *some* bread, and after a blessing, He broke *it* and gave *it* to the disciples, and said, "Take, eat; this is My body." And when He had taken a cup and given thanks, He gave *it* to them saying, "Drink from it, all of you; for this is My blood of the covenant, which is poured out for many for forgiveness of sins. But I say to you, I will not drink of this fruit of the vine from now on until that day when I drink it new with you in My Father's kingdom" (Matthew 26:26–29; cf. Mark 14:22–25; Luke 22:17–20; 1 Corinthians 11:23–26; see Matthew 26:30; 1 Corinthians 10:16).

Setting: Capernaum. John's disciples and the Pharisees question why Jesus' disciples do not fast when they do.

And Jesus said to them, "While the bridegroom is with them, the attendants of the bridegroom cannot fast, can they? So long as they have the bridegroom with them, they cannot fast. But the days will come when the bridegroom is taken away from them, and then they will fast in that day. No one sews a patch of unshrunk cloth on an old garment; otherwise the patch pulls away from it, the new from the old, and a worse tear results. No one puts new wine into old wineskins; otherwise the wine will burst the skins, and the wine is lost and the skins as *well;* but *one puts* new wine into fresh wineskins" (Mark 2:19–22; cf. Matthew 9:14–17; Luke 5:33–38; see Mark 2:18).

Setting: Galilee. After explaining the Parable of the Sower to His disciples, Jesus conveys the Parable of the Seed.

And He was saying, "The kingdom of God is like a man who casts seed upon the soil; and he goes to bed at night and gets up by day, and the seed sprouts and grows—how, he himself does not know. The soil produces crops by itself; first the blade, then the head, then the mature grain in the head. But when the crop permits, he immediately puts in the sickle, because the harvest has come" (Mark 4:26–29; see Joel 3:13).

Setting: An upper room in Jerusalem. While celebrating the Feast of Unleavened Bread (Passover) with His disciples, Jesus institutes the ordinance of the Lord's Supper.

While they were eating, He took *some* bread, and after a blessing He broke *it*, and gave *it* to them, and said, "Take *it;* this is My body." And when He had taken a cup *and* given thanks, He gave *it* to them, and they all drank from it. And He said to them, "This is My blood of the covenant, which is poured out for many. Truly I say to you, I will never again drink of the fruit of the vine until that day when I drink it new in the kingdom of God" (Mark 14:22–25; cf. Matthew 26:26–29; Luke 22:17–20; 1 Corinthians 11:23–26; see Exodus 24:8).

Setting: Galilee. After selecting His twelve disciples, Jesus teaches the Beatitudes (part of the Sermon on the Mount) to His disciples and a great throng of people from Judea, Jerusalem, and the central coastal region of Tyre and Sidon.

"Blessed are you when men hate you, and ostracize you, and insult you, and scorn your name as evil, for the sake of the Son of Man. Be glad in that day and leap for joy, for behold, your reward is great in heaven. For in the same way their fathers used to treat the prophets" (Luke 6:22, 23; cf. Matthew 5:10–12; see 2 Chronicles 36:16; Luke 6:12–19).

Setting: On the way from Galilee to Jerusalem. The Lord appoints seventy followers and sends them out in pairs to every place He Himself will soon visit.

And He was saying to them, "The harvest is plentiful, but the laborers are few; therefore beseech the Lord of the harvest to send out laborers into His harvest. Go; behold, I send you out as lambs in the midst of wolves. Carry no money belt, no bag, no shoes; and greet no one on the way. Whatever house you enter, first say, 'Peace be to this house.' If a man of peace is there, your peace will rest on him; but if not, it will return to you. Stay in that house, eating and drinking what they give you; for the laborer is worthy of his wages. Do not keep moving from house to house. Whatever city you enter and they receive you, eat what is set before you; and heal those in it who are sick, and say to them, 'The kingdom of God has come near to you.' But whatever city you enter and they do not receive you, go out into its streets and say, 'Even the dust of your city which clings to our feet we wipe off in protest against you; yet be sure of this, that the kingdom of God has come near.' I say to you, it will be more tolerable in that day for Sodom than for that city" (Luke 10:2–12; see Genesis 19:24–28; Matthew 9:37, 38, 10:9–14, 16; Luke 10:1; 1 Corinthians 10:27).

Setting: On the way from Galilee to Jerusalem. When Jesus uses a parable to challenge the crowd and His disciples to be ready for His return, Peter asks Him whom He is addressing.

And the Lord said, "Who then is the faithful and sensible steward, whom his master will put in charge of his servants, to give them their rations at the proper time? Blessed is that slave whom his master finds so doing when he comes. Truly I say to you that he will put him in charge of all his possessions. But if that slave says in his heart, 'My master will be a long time in coming,' and begins to beat the slaves, both men and women, and to eat and drink and get drunk; the master of that slave will come on a day when he does not expect him and at an hour he does not know, and will cut him in pieces, and assign him a place with the unbelievers. And that slave who knew his master's will and did not get ready or act in accord with his will, will receive many lashes, but the one who did know it, and committed deeds worthy of flogging, will receive but few. From everyone who has been given much, much will be required; and to whom they entrusted much, of him they will ask all the more" (Luke 12:42–48; cf. Matthew 24:45–51; see Leviticus 5:17; Luke 12:41).

Setting: On the way from Galilee to Jerusalem. After conveying the story of the rich man and Lazarus, the Lord gives His disciples instruction on forgiveness.

He said to His disciples, "It is inevitable that stumbling blocks come, but woe to him through whom they come! It would be better for him if a millstone were hung around his neck and he were thrown into the sea, than that he would cause one of these little ones to stumble. Be on your guard! If your brother sins, rebuke him; and if he repents, forgive him. And if he sins against you seven times a day, and returns to you seven times, saying, 'I repent,' forgive him" (Luke 17:1–4; see Matthew 18:5–7, 15, 21, 22).

Setting: Samaria, on the way from Galilee to Jerusalem. After the Pharisees question Him about the coming of the kingdom of God, Jesus tells His disciples of His second coming.

And He said to the disciples, "The days will come when you will long to see one of the days of the Son of Man, and you will not see it. They will say to you, 'Look there! Look here!' Do not go away, and do not run after them. For just like the lightning, when it flashes out of one part of the sky, shines to the other part of the sky, so will the Son of Man be in His day. But first He must suffer many things and be rejected by this generation. And just as it happened in the days of Noah, so it will be also in the days of the Son of Man: they were eating, they were drinking, they were marrying, they were being given in marriage, until the day that Noah entered the ark, and the flood came and destroyed them all. It was the same as happened in the days of Lot: they were eating, they were drinking, they were buying, they were selling, they were planting, they were building; but on the day that Lot went out from Sodom it rained fire and brimstone from heaven and destroyed them all. It will be just the same on the day that the Son of Man is revealed. On that day, the one who is on the housetop and whose goods are in the house must not go down to take them out; and likewise the one who is in the field must not turn back. Remember Lot's wife. Whoever seeks to keep his life will lose it, and whoever loses his life will preserve it. I tell you, on that night there will be two in one bed; one will be taken and the other will be left. There will be two women grinding at the same place; one will be taken and the other will be left. [Two men will be in the field; one will be taken and the other will be left."] And answering they said to Him, "Where, Lord?" And He said to them, "Where the body is, there also the vultures will be gathered" (Luke 17:22–37; see Genesis 19; Matthew 10:39; 16:21, 27; 24:17–28, 37–41).

Setting: On the way from Galilee to Jerusalem. After telling His disciples of His second coming, Jesus instructs them about persistence in prayer.

Now He was telling them a parable to show that at all times they ought to pray and not to lose heart, saying, "In a certain city there was a judge who did not fear God and did not respect man. There was a widow in that city, and she kept coming to him, saying, 'Give me legal protection from my opponent.' For a while he was unwilling; but afterward he said to himself, 'Even though I do not fear God nor respect man, yet because this woman bothers me, I will give her legal protection, otherwise by continually coming she will wear me out.'" And the Lord said, "Hear what the unrighteous judge said; now, will not God bring about justice for His elect who cry to Him day and night, and will He delay long over them? I tell you that He will bring about justice for them quickly. However, when the Son of Man comes, will He find faith on the earth?" (Luke 18:1–8; see Luke 11:5–10).

Setting: Approaching Jerusalem. After being praised by the people in a triumphal welcome, the Lord weeps as He sees the city ahead of Him.

When He approached Jerusalem, He saw the city and wept over it, saying, "If you had known in this day, even you, the things which make for peace! But now they have been hidden from your eyes. For the days will come upon you when your enemies will throw up a barricade against you, and surround you and hem you in on every side, and they will level you to the ground and your children within you, and they will not leave in you one stone upon another, because you did not recognize the time of your visitation" (Luke 19:41–44; see Matthew 24:1–2; Luke 13:34, 35; 19:28–40).

Setting: Jerusalem. Following a time of ministry in the temple a few days before Jesus' crucifixion, after conveying the Parable of the Fig Tree, He warns His disciples to keep alert regarding future events.

"Be on guard, so that your hearts will not be weighted down with dissipation and drunkenness and the worries of life, and that day will not come upon you suddenly like a trap; for it will come upon all those who dwell on the face of all the earth. But keep on the alert at all times, praying that you may have strength to escape all these things that are about to take place, and to stand before the Son of Man" (Luke 21:34–36; cf. Mark 13:33; see Matthew 24:42–44; Luke 21:10–33).

Setting: The temple treasury in Jerusalem. After Jesus avoids stoning by the scribes and Pharisees while interacting with them, His disciples wonder if blindness is caused by sin, as the Lord heals a man born blind.

Jesus answered, "*It was* neither *that* this man sinned, nor his parents; but *it was* so that the works of God might be displayed in him. We must work the works of Him who sent Me as long as it is day; night is coming when no one can work. While I am in the world, I am the Light of the world." When He had said this, He spat on the ground, and made clay of the spittle, and applied the clay to his eyes, and said to him, "Go, wash in the pool of Siloam" (which is translated, Sent). So he went away and washed, and came *back* seeing (John 9:3–7; see John 8:12; 9:1, 2; 11:4; 12:46).

Setting: Beyond the Jordan. Avoiding the Jerusalem Pharisees, Jesus receives word from Lazarus's sisters in Bethany of His friend's sickness, and decides to go there.

Then after this He said to the disciples, "Let us go to Judea again." The disciples said to Him, "Rabbi, the Jews were just now seeking to stone You, and are You going there again?" Jesus answered, "Are there not twelve hours in the day? If anyone walks in the day, he does not stumble, because he sees the light of this world. But if anyone walks in the night, he stumbles, because the light is not in him." This He said, and after that He said to them, "Our friend Lazarus has fallen asleep; but I go, so that I may awaken him out of sleep" (John 11:7–11; see John 8:59; 10:39).

Setting: Bethany near Jerusalem. Six days before the Passover in Jerusalem, as the chief priests and Pharisees plot to seize Him, Jesus visits Lazarus, Martha, and Mary, who anoints the Lord's feet with costly perfume made of pure nard.

Therefore Jesus said, "Let her alone, so that she may keep it for the day of My burial. For you always have the poor with you, but you do not always have Me" (John 12:7, 8; cf. Matthew 26:6–13; Mark 14:3–9; see Deuteronomy 15:11; John 12:1–6).

Setting: Jerusalem. Before the Passover, after responding to Philip's request for Him to show His disciples the Father, Jesus conveys the upcoming role of the Holy Spirit in their lives.

"I will not leave you as orphans; I will come to you. After a little while the world will no longer see Me, but you *will* see Me; because I live, you will live also. In that day you will know that I am in the Father, and you in Me, and I in you. He who has My commandments and keeps them is the one who loves Me; and he who loves Me will be loved by My Father, and I will love him and will disclose Myself to him" (John 14:18–21; see John 6:57; 10:37, 38; 14:1–17, 23, 28; 16:16, 22).

Setting: Jerusalem. Before the Passover, after empathizing with His disciples' sadness over His prophecies and giving them assurance for the future, Jesus conveys promises about praying in His name.

"In that day you will not question Me about anything. Truly, truly, I say to you, if you ask the Father for anything in My name, He will give it to you. Until now you have asked for nothing in My name; ask and you will receive, so that your joy may be made full. These things I have spoken to you in figurative language; an hour is coming when I will no longer speak to you in figurative language, but will tell you plainly of the Father. In that day you will ask in My name, and I do not say to you that I will request of the Father on your behalf; for the Father Himself loves you, because you have loved Me and have believed that I came forth from the Father. I came forth from the Father and have come into the world; I am leaving the world again and going to the Father" (John 16:23–28; see Matthew 13:34; John 8:42; 13:1, 3; 14:14, 21, 23; 15:16; 16:19, 30).

DAY, EACH

Setting: Galilee. During the early part of His ministry, Jesus preaches the Sermon on the Mount to His disciples and the multitudes.

"For this reason I say to you, do not be worried about your life, *as to* what you will eat or what you will drink; nor for your body, *as to* what you will put on. Is not life more than food, and the body more than clothing? Look at the birds of the air, that they do not sow, nor reap nor gather into barns, and *yet* your heavenly Father feeds them. Are you not worth much more than they? And who of you by being worried can add a *single* hour to his life? And why are you worried about clothing? Observe how the lilies of the field grow; they do not toil nor do they spin, yet I say to you that not even Solomon in all his glory clothed himself like one of these. But if God so clothes the grass of the field, which is *alive* today and tomorrow is thrown into the furnace, *will He* not much more *clothe* you? You of little faith! Do not worry then, saying 'What will we eat?' or 'What will we drink?' or 'What will be wear for clothing?" For the Gentiles eagerly seek all these things; for your heavenly Father knows that you need all these things. But seek first His kingdom and His righteousness, and all these things will be added to you. So do not worry about tomorrow; for tomorrow will care for itself. Each day has enough trouble of its own" (Matthew 6:25–34; cf. Luke 12:22–31; see 1 Kings 10:4–7; Job 35:11; Matthew 8:26).

Setting: On the way from Galilee to Jerusalem. After Jesus visits in the home of Martha and Mary in Bethany, a disciple asks Him to teach them to pray.

And He said to them, "When you pray, say: 'Father, hallowed be Your name. Your kingdom come. Give us each day our daily bread. And forgive us our sins, for we ourselves also forgive everyone who is indebted to us. And lead us not into temptation'" (Luke 11:2–4; cf. Matthew 6:9–13; see Luke 11:1).

DAY, EVERY

Setting: Gethsemane on the Mount of Olives, just east of Jerusalem. As He submits to His Father's will and allows Judas to betray Him, Jesus reveals that this incident is a fulfillment of prophecy.

At that time Jesus said to the crowds, "Have you come out with swords and clubs to arrest Me as *you would* against a robber? Every day I used to sit in the temple teaching and you did not seize Me. But all this has taken place to fulfill the Scriptures of the prophets" (Matthew 26:55, 56; cf. Mark 14:48, 49; Luke 22:52, 53; see Matthew 26:24).

Setting: Gethsemane on the Mount of Olives, just east of Jerusalem. Judas betrays Jesus with a kiss in front of a crowd of the chief priests, scribes, and elders seeking to seize Jesus with swords and clubs.

And Jesus said to them, "Have you come out with swords and clubs to arrest Me, as *you would* against a robber? Every day I was with you in the temple teaching, and you did not seize Me; but *this has taken place* to fulfill the Scriptures" (Mark 14:48, 49; cf. Matthew 26:55, 56; Luke 22:52, 53; see Mark 14: 26–47).

Setting: On the way from Galilee to Jerusalem. After responding to the Pharisees' scoffing at His teaching His disciples about stewardship and the permanence of the Law, Jesus conveys the story of the rich man and Lazarus.

"Now there was a rich man, and he habitually dressed in purple and fine linen, joyously living in splendor every day. And a poor man named Lazarus was laid at his gate, covered with sores, and longing to be fed with the crumbs which were falling from the rich man's table; besides, even the dogs were coming and licking his sores. Now the poor man died and was carried away by the angels to Abraham's bosom; and the rich man also died and was buried. In Hades he lifted up his eyes, being in torment, and saw Abraham far away and Lazarus in his bosom. And he cried out and said, 'Father Abraham, have mercy on me, and send Lazarus so that he may dip the tip of his finger in water and cool off my tongue, for I am in agony in this flame.' But Abraham said, 'Child, remember that during your life you received your good things, and likewise Lazarus bad things; but now he is being comforted here, and you are in agony. And besides all this, between us and you there is a great chasm fixed, so that those who wish to come over from here to you will not be able, and that none may cross over from there to us.' And he said, 'Then I beg you, father, that you send him to my father's house—for I have five brothers—in order that he may warn them, so that they will not also come to this place of torment.' But Abraham said, 'They have Moses and the Prophets; let them hear them.' But he said, 'No, father Abraham, but if someone goes to them from the dead, they will repent!' But he said to him, 'If they do not listen to Moses and the Prophets, they will not be persuaded even if someone rises from the dead'" (Luke 16:19–31; see Luke 3:8; 6:24; 16:1, 14).

DAY, HOT

Setting: On the way from Galilee to Jerusalem. After telling how a relationship with Him will divide families, Jesus chastises the crowds for being able to discern the weather but not the present age.

And He was also saying to the crowds, "When you see a cloud rising in the west, immediately you say, 'A shower is coming,' and so it turns out. And when you see a south wind blowing, you say, 'It will be a hot day,' and it turns out that way. You hypocrites! You know how to analyze the appearance of the earth and the sky, but why do you not analyze this present time?" (Luke 12:54–56; cf. Matthew 16:2, 3).

DAY, JUDGMENT (See JUDGMENT, DAY OF)

DAY, LAST (Also see JUDGMENT; and JUDGMENT, DAY OF)

Setting: On the way to Capernaum. The day after walking on the Sea of Galilee to join His disciples in a boat, the people He miraculously fed with a lad's five loaves and two fish ask Jesus to always give them this bread out of heaven.

Jesus said to them, "I am the bread of life; he who comes to Me will not hunger, and he who believes in Me will never thirst. But I said to you that you have seen Me, and yet do not believe. All that the Father gives Me will come to Me, and the one who comes to Me I will certainly not cast out. For I have come down from heaven, not to do My own will, but the will of Him who sent Me. This is the will of Him who sent Me, that of all that He has given Me I lose nothing, but raise it up on the last day. For this is the will of My Father, that everyone who beholds the Son and believes in Him will have eternal life, and I Myself will raise him up on the last day" (John 6:35–40; see John 3:13, 16; 4:13, 14; 6:25–34, 48, 51).

Setting: Capernaum of Galilee. After Jesus informs the people whom He miraculously fed with a lad's five loaves and two fish how they might receive the bread out of heaven, the Jewish religious leaders grumble because He claims that He came down out of heaven.

Therefore the Jews were grumbling about Him, because He said, "I am the bread that came down out of heaven." They were saying, "Is not this Jesus, the son of Joseph, whose father and mother we know? How does He now say, 'I have come down out of heaven'?" Jesus answered and said to them, "Do not grumble among yourselves. No one can come to Me unless the Father who sent Me draws him; and I will raise him up on the last day. It is written in the prophets, 'AND THEY SHALL ALL BE TAUGHT OF GOD.' Everyone who has heard and learned from the Father, comes to Me. Not that anyone has seen the Father, except the One who is from God; He has seen the Father. Truly, truly, I say to you, he who believes has eternal life. I am the bread of life. Your fathers ate the manna in the wilderness, and they died. This is the bread which comes down out of heaven, so that one may eat of it and not die. I am the living bread that came down out of heaven; if anyone eats of this bread, he will live forever; and the bread also which I will give for the life of the world is My flesh" (John 6:41–51, Jesus quotes from Isaiah 54:13; see John 1:18, 29; 3:36; 6:26–40, 58; 7:27).

Setting: Capernaum of Galilee. After informing the people whom He miraculously fed with a lad's five loaves and two fish how they might receive the bread out of heaven, the Jewish religious leaders argue with one another when Jesus says He will give His flesh to the world to eat.

So Jesus said to them, "Truly, truly, I say to you, unless you eat the flesh of the Son of Man and drink His blood, you have no life in yourselves. He who eats My flesh and drinks My blood has eternal life, and I will raise him up on the last day. For My flesh is true food, and My blood is true drink. He who eats My flesh and drinks My blood abides in Me, and I in him. As the living Father sent Me, and I live because of the Father, so he who eats Me, he also will live because of Me. This is the bread which came down out of heaven; not as the fathers ate and died; he who eats this bread will live forever" (John 6:53–58; see Matthew 16:16; Luke 4:22; John 3:36; John 6:26–40, 52; 9:16; 15:4).

Setting: Jerusalem. Just days before the Passover, with the chief priests and Pharisees plotting to seize Jesus, who is expressing anxiety about His upcoming death by crucifixion, some of the people believe in Jesus, while others are rejecting His message.

And Jesus cried out and said, "He who believes in Me, does not believe in Me but in Him who sent Me. He who sees Me sees the One who sent Me. I have come *as* Light into the world, so that everyone who believes in Me will not remain in darkness. If anyone hears My sayings and does not keep them, I do not judge him; for I did not come to judge the world, but to save the world. He who rejects Me and does not receive My sayings, has one who judges him; the word I spoke is what will judge him at the last day. For I did not speak on My own initiative, but the Father Himself who sent Me has given Me a commandment *as to* what to say and what to speak. I know that His commandment is eternal life; therefore the things I speak, I speak just as the Father as told Me" (John 12:44–50; see Matthew 10:40; Luke 10:16; John 1:4; 3:17; 5:19; 6:68; 14:9).

DAY, MY (Jesus')

Setting: The temple treasury in Jerusalem. While Jesus interacts with the scribes and Pharisees, they state their belief that Jesus is a demon-possessed Samaritan because of His statement that anyone who keeps His word will never taste death.

Jesus answered, "If I glorify Myself, My glory is nothing; it is My Father who glorifies Me, of whom you say, 'He is our God'; and you have not come to know Him, but I know Him; and if I say that I do not know Him, I will be a liar like you, but I do know Him and keep His word. Your father Abraham rejoiced to see My day, and he saw *it* and was glad" (John 8:54–56; see Matthew 13:17; John 7:29; 8:1–53).

DAY, NEXT

Setting: On the way from Galilee to Jerusalem. While being tested by a lawyer, Jesus tells him the story of the good Samaritan.

Jesus replied and said, "A man was going down from Jerusalem to Jericho, and fell among robbers, and they stripped him and beat him, and went away leaving him half dead. And by chance a priest was going down on that road, and when he saw him, he passed by on the other side. Likewise a Levite also, when he came to the place and saw him, passed by on the other side. But a Samaritan, who was on a journey, came upon him; and when he saw him, he felt compassion, and came to him and bandaged up his wounds, pouring oil and wine on them; and he put him on his own beast, and brought him to an inn and took care of him. On the next day he took out two denarii and gave them to the innkeeper and said, 'Take care of him; and whatever more you spend, when I return I will repay you.' Which of these three do you think proved to be a neighbor to the man who fell into the robbers' hands?" And he said, "The one who showed mercy toward him." Then Jesus said to him, "Go and do the same" (Luke 10:30–37).

Setting: On the way from Galilee to Jerusalem. While teaching in the cities and villages, after Jesus responds to a question about who is saved, some Pharisees ask Him to leave, claiming Herod Antipas (tetrarch of Galilee and Perea) seeks to kill Him.

And He said to them, "Go and tell that fox, 'Behold, I cast out demons and perform cures today and tomorrow, and the third day I reach My goal.' Nevertheless I must journey on today and tomorrow and the next day; for it cannot be that a prophet would perish outside of Jerusalem. O Jerusalem, Jerusalem, the city that kills the prophets and stones those sent to her! How often I wanted to gather your children together, just as a hen gathers her brood under her wings, and you would not have it! Behold, your house is left to you desolate; and I say to you, you will not see Me until the time comes when you say, 'BLESSED IS HE WHO COMES IN THE NAME OF THE LORD!'" (Luke 13:32–35, Jesus quotes from Psalm 118:26; cf. Matthew 23:37; see Luke 13:31).

DAY, SABBATH (See SABBATH DAY)

DAY, THIRD (Also see DAYS, THREE)

Setting: Galilee. Following the Transfiguration, Jesus repeats to His disciples that He must suffer, die, and be raised from the dead.

And while they were gathering together in Galilee, Jesus said to them, "The Son of Man is going to be delivered into the hands of men; and they will kill Him, and He will be raised on the third day." And they were deeply grieved (Matthew 17:22, 23; cf. Matthew 16:21; Mark 9:30–32; Luke 9:44, 45).

Setting: On the road to Jerusalem. Before going to Jerusalem, Jesus again tells His disciples of His impending death and resurrection.

As Jesus was about to go up to Jerusalem, He took the twelve *disciples* aside by themselves, and on the way He said to them, "Behold, we are going up to Jerusalem; and the Son of Man will be delivered to the chief priests and scribes, and they will condemn Him to death, and will hand Him over to the Gentiles to mock and scourge and crucify *Him,* and on the third day, He will be raised up" (Matthew 20:17–19; cf. Matthew 16:21; Mark 10:32–34; Luke 18:31–33).

Setting: Galilee. Following Peter's pronouncement that Jesus is the Christ of God, the Lord warns His disciples not to reveal His identity to anyone.

But He warned them and instructed them not to tell this to anyone, saying, "The Son of Man must suffer many things and be rejected by the elders and chief priests and scribes, and be killed and be raised up on the third day" (Luke 9:21, 22; cf. Matthew 16:21; Mark 8:31).

Setting: On the way from Galilee to Jerusalem. After Jesus, while teaching in the cities and villages, responds to a question about who is saved, some Pharisees ask Him to leave, claiming Herod Antipas (tetrarch of Galilee and Perea) seeks to kill Him.

And He said to them, "Go and tell that fox, 'Behold, I cast out demons and perform cures today and tomorrow, and the third day I reach My goal.' Nevertheless I must journey on today and tomorrow and the next day; for it cannot be that a prophet would perish outside of Jerusalem. O Jerusalem, Jerusalem, the city that kills the prophets and stones those sent to her! How often I wanted to gather your children together, just as a hen gathers her brood under her wings, and you would not have it! Behold, your house is left to you desolate; and I say to you, you will not see Me until the time comes when you say, 'BLESSED IS HE WHO COMES IN THE NAME OF THE LORD!'" (Luke 13:32–35, Jesus quotes from Psalm 118:26; cf. Matthew 23:37; see Luke 13:31).

Setting: On the way from Galilee to Jerusalem. After responding to Peter's statement about His disciples' personal sacrifice in following Him, Jesus tells them of the upcoming sacrifice He will make in Jerusalem.

Then He took the twelve aside and said to them, "Behold, we are going up to Jerusalem, and all things which are written through the prophets about the Son of Man will be accomplished. For He will be handed over to the Gentiles, and will be mocked and mistreated and spit upon, and after they have scourged Him, they will kill Him; and the third day He will rise again" (Luke 18:31–33; cf. Matthew 20:17–19; Mark 10:32–34).

Setting: Jerusalem. After rising from the grave on the third day following being crucified, and appearing to two of His followers on the road to Emmaus, Jesus gives instruction to some of His disciples about His mission on earth and the promise of future power from God.

Now He said to them, "These are My words which I spoke to you while I was still with you, that all things which are written about Me in the Law of Moses and the Prophets and the Psalms must be fulfilled." Then He opened their minds to understand the Scriptures, and He said to them, "Thus it is written, that the Christ would suffer and rise again from the dead the third day, and that repentance for forgiveness of sins would be proclaimed in His name to all the nations, beginning from Jerusalem. You are witnesses of these things. And behold, I am sending forth the promise of My Father upon you; but you are to stay in the city until you are clothed with power from on high" (Luke 24:44–49; see Matthew 28:19, 20; Luke 24:1–43; Acts 1:8).

DAY AND HOUR (Listed under HOUR, DAY AND)

DAY OF JUDGMENT (Listed under JUDGMENT, DAY OF)

DAYS (Specifics such as DAYS, THREE; and DAYS, TWO are separate entries; also see DAY)

Setting: Capernaum near the Sea of Galilee. John the Baptist's disciples ask Jesus why His own disciples do not participate in fasting, while they and the Pharisees do.

And Jesus said to them, "The attendants of the bridegroom cannot mourn as long as the bridegroom is with them, can they? But the days will come when the bridegroom is taken away from them, and then they will fast. But no one puts a patch of unshrunk cloth on an old garment; for the patch pulls away from the garment, and a worse tear results. Nor do *people* put new wine into old wineskins; otherwise the wineskins burst, and the wine pours out and the wineskins are ruined; but they put new wine into fresh wineskins, and both are preserved" (Matthew 9:15–17; cf. Mark 2:18–22; Luke 5:33–39; see Matthew 9:14).

Setting: Galilee. While speaking to the crowds, Jesus pays tribute to the ministry of John the Baptist, but emphasizes that the one who is least in the kingdom of heaven is greater than John.

As these men were going *away,* Jesus began to speak to the crowds about John, "What did you go out into the wilderness to see? A reed shaken by the wind? But what did you go out to see? A man dressed in soft *clothing?* Those who wear soft *clothing* are in kings' palaces! But what did you go out to see? A prophet? Yes, I tell you, and the one who is more than a prophet. This is the one about whom it is written, 'BEHOLD, I SEND MY MESSENGER AHEAD OF YOU, WHO WILL PREPARE YOUR WAY BEFORE YOU.' Truly, I say to you, among those born of women there has not arisen *anyone* greater than John the Baptist! Yet the one who is least in the kingdom of heaven is greater than he. From the days of John the Baptist until now the kingdom of heaven suffers violence, and violent men take it by force. For all the prophets and the Law prophesied until John. And, if you are willing to accept *it,* John himself is Elijah who was to come. He who has ears to hear, let him hear" (Matthew 11:7–15, Jesus quotes from Malachi 3:1; cf. Malachi 4:5; Luke 7:24–28; 16:16; see Matthew 14:5).

Setting: The Mount of Olives, just east of Jerusalem. During His discourse, Jesus answers His disciples' questions as to when the temple will be destroyed and Jerusalem overrun, along with the signs of His coming and the end of the age.

"Therefore when you see the ABOMINATION OF DESOLATION which was spoken of through Daniel the prophet, standing in the holy place (let the reader understand), then those who are in Judea must flee to the mountains. Whoever is on the housetop must not go down to get the things that are in his house. Whoever is in the field must not turn back to get his cloak. But woe to those who are pregnant and to those who are nursing babies in those days! But pray that your flight will not be in the winter, or on a Sabbath. For then there will be a great tribulation, such as has not occurred since the beginning of the world until now, nor ever will. Unless those days had been cut short, no life would have been saved; but for the sake of the elect those days will be cut short. Then if anyone says to you, 'Behold, here is the Christ,' or "There *He is,'* do not believe *him.* For false Christs and false prophets will arise and will show great signs and wonders, so as to mislead, if possible, even the elect. Behold, I have told you in advance. So if they say to you, 'Behold, He is in the wilderness,' do not go out, *or,* 'Behold, He is in the inner rooms,' do not believe *them.* For just as the lightning comes from the east and flashes even to the west, so will the coming of the Son of Man be. Wherever a corpse is, there the vultures will gather" (Matthew 24:15–28, Jesus quotes from Daniel 9:27; cf. Daniel 12:1; Mark 13:14–23; Luke 17:22–31; 21:20–24; 23:29; see Matthew 24:4–14; John 4:48).

Setting: The Mount of Olives, just east of Jerusalem. During His discourse, Jesus answers His disciples' questions as to when the temple will be destroyed and Jerusalem overrun, along with the signs of His coming and the end of the age.

"But immediately after the tribulation of those days THE SUN WILL BE DARKENED, AND THE MOON WILL NOT GIVE ITS LIGHT, AND THE STARS WILL FALL from the sky, and the powers of the heavens will be shaken. And then the sign of the Son of Man will appear in the sky, and then all the tribes of the earth will mourn, and they will see the SON OF MAN COMING ON THE CLOUDS OF THE SKY with power and great glory. And He will send forth His angels with A GREAT TRUMPET and THEY WILL GATHER TOGETHER His elect from the four winds, from one end of the sky to the other" (Matthew 24:29–31, Jesus quotes from Isaiah 13:10, Daniel 7:13; Exodus 19:16; cf. Mark 13:24–27; Luke 21:25–27; see Matthew 24:1–28).

Setting: The Mount of Olives, just east of Jerusalem. During His discourse, after answering His disciples' questions as to when the temple will be destroyed and Jerusalem overrun, along with the signs of His coming and the end of the age, Jesus teaches them the Parable of the Fig Tree.

"Now learn the parable from the fig tree: when its branch has already become tender and puts forth its leaves, you know that summer is near; so, you too, when you see all these things, recognize that He is near, *right* at the door. Truly, I say to you, this generation will not pass away until all these things take place. Heaven and earth will pass away, but My words will not pass away. But of that day and hour no one knows, not even the angels of heaven, nor the Son, but the Father alone. For the coming of the Son of Man will be just like the days of Noah. For as in those days before the flood they were eating and drinking, marrying and giving in marriage, until the day that Noah entered the ark, and they did not understand until the flood came and took them all away; so will the coming of the Son of Man be. Then there will be two men in the field; one will be taken and one will be left. Two women *will be* grinding at the mill; one will be taken and one will be left" (Matthew 24:32–41; cf. Mark 13:28–32; Luke 17:34–36; 21:28–33; see Genesis 6:5; 7:7; Matthew 5:18; 10:23; James 5:9).

Setting: Capernaum. John's disciples and the Pharisees question why Jesus' disciples do not fast when they do.

And Jesus said to them, "While the bridegroom is with them, the attendants of the bridegroom cannot fast, can they? So long as they have the bridegroom with them, they cannot fast. But the days will come when the bridegroom is taken away from them, and then they will fast in that day. No one sews a patch of unshrunk cloth on an old garment; otherwise the patch pulls away from it, the new from the old, and a worse tear results. No one puts new wine into old wineskins; otherwise the wine will burst the skins, and the wine is lost and the skins as *well;* but *one puts* new wine into fresh wineskins" (Mark 2:19–22; cf. Matthew 9:14–17; Luke 5:33–38).

Setting: During His discourse on the Mount of Olives, east of the temple in Jerusalem, after prophesying the temple's destruction, Jesus responds to questions from Peter, James, John, and Andrew about future events.

"But when you see the ABOMINATION OF DESOLATION standing where it should not be (let the reader understand), then those who are in Judea must flee to the mountains. The one who is on the housetop must not go down, or go in to get anything out of his house; and the one who is in the field must not turn back to get his coat. But woe to those who are pregnant and to those who are nursing babies in those days! But pray that it may not happen in winter. For those days will be a *time of* tribulation such as has not occurred since the beginning of the creation which God created until now, and never will. Unless the Lord had shortened *those* days, no life would have been saved; but for the sake of the elect, whom He chose, He shortened the days. And then if anyone says to you, 'Behold, here is the Christ'; or, 'Behold, *He is* there'; do not believe *him;* for false Christs and false prophets will arise, and will show signs and wonders, in order to lead astray, if possible, the elect. But take heed; behold, I have told you everything in advance" (Mark 13:14–23; cf. Matthew 24:15–28; Luke 21:20–24; see Daniel 9:27; 12:1; Luke 17:31).

Setting: The Mount of Olives, east of the temple in Jerusalem. During His discourse, after prophesying the temple's destruction, Jesus responds to questions from Peter, James, John, and Andrew about future events.

"But in those days, after that tribulation, THE SUN WILL BE DARKENED AND THE MOON WILL NOT GIVE ITS LIGHT, AND THE STARS WILL BE FALLING from heaven, and the powers that are in the heavens will be shaken. Then they will see THE SON OF MAN COMING IN CLOUDS with great power and glory. And then He will send forth the angels, and will gather together His elect from the four winds, from the farthest end of the earth to the farthest end of heaven" (Mark 13:24–27. Jesus quotes from Isaiah 13:10; 34:4; Daniel 7:13; cf. Matthew 24:29–31; Luke 21:25–27).

Setting: Jesus' hometown of Nazareth in Galilee. At the beginning of His public ministry, after reading from the book of the prophet Isaiah on the Sabbath, Jesus comments to the congregation in the synagogue.

And He said to them, "No doubt you will quote this proverb to Me, 'Physician, heal yourself! Whatever we heard was done at Capernaum, do here in your hometown as well.'" And He said, "Truly I say to you, no prophet is welcome in his hometown. But I say to you in truth, there were many widows in Israel in the days of Elijah, when the sky was shut up for three years and six months, when a great famine came over all the land; and yet Elijah was sent to none of them, but only to Zarephath, *in the land* of Sidon, to a woman who was a widow. And there were many lepers in Israel in the time of Elisha the prophet; and none of them was cleansed, but only Naaman the Syrian" (Luke 4:23–27; Jesus refers to 1 Kings 17:1, 9; 2 Kings 5:1–14; see Matthew 13:53–58).

Setting: The home of Levi (Matthew) in Capernaum. At a reception for Jesus following Levi's call to be a disciple, the Pharisees and their scribes question Him about fasting.

And Jesus said to them, "You cannot make the attendants of the bridegroom fast while the bridegroom is with them, can you? But the days will come; and when the bridegroom is taken away from them, then they will fast in those days" (Luke 5:34, 35; cf. Matthew 9:14, 15; Mark 2:18–20).

Setting: On the way from Galilee to Jerusalem. Jesus conveys the illustration of the prodigal son because the Pharisees and scribes complain He associates with tax collectors and sinners.

And He said, "A man had two sons. The younger of them said to his father, 'Father, give me the share of the estate that falls to me.' So he divided his wealth between them. And not many days later, the younger son gathered everything together and went on a journey into a distant country, and there he squandered his estate with loose living. Now when he had spent everything, a severe famine occurred in that country, and he began to be impoverished. So he went and hired himself out to one of the citizens of that country, and he sent him into his fields to feed swine. And he would have gladly filled his stomach with the pods that the swine were eating, and no one was giving anything to him. But when he came to his senses, he said, 'How many of my father's hired men have more than enough bread, but I am dying here with hunger! I will get up and go to my father, and will say to him, "Father, I have sinned against heaven, and in your sight; I am no longer worthy to be called your son; make me as one of your hired men."' So he got up and came to his father. But while he was still a long way off, his father saw him and felt compassion for him, and ran and embraced him and kissed him. And the son said to him, "Father, I have sinned against heaven and in your sight; I am no longer worthy to be called your son.' But the father said to his slaves, 'Quickly bring out the best robe and put it on him, and put a ring on his hand and sandals on his feet; and bring the fattened calf, kill it, and let us eat and celebrate; for this son of mine was dead and has come to life again; he was lost and has been found.' And they began to celebrate. Now his older son was in the field, when he came and approached the house, he heard music and dancing. And he summoned one of the servants and began inquiring what these things could be. And he said to him, 'Your brother has come, and your father has killed the fattened calf because he has received him back safe and sound.' But he became angry and was not willing to go in; and his father came out and began pleading with him. But he answered and said to his father, 'Look! For so many years I have been serving you and I have never neglected a command of yours; and yet you have never given me a young goat, so that I might celebrate with my friends; but when this son of yours came, who has devoured your wealth with prostitutes, you killed the fattened calf for him.' And he said to him, 'Son, you have always been with me, and all that is mine is yours. But we had to celebrate and rejoice, for this brother of yours was dead and has begun to live, and was lost and has been found'" (Luke 15:11–32; see Proverbs 29:2; Luke 15:1, 2).

Setting: Samaria, on the way from Galilee to Jerusalem. After the Pharisees question Him about the coming of the kingdom of God, Jesus tells His disciples of His second coming.

And He said to the disciples, "The days will come when you will long to see one of the days of the Son of Man, and you will not see it. They will say to you, 'Look there! Look here!' Do not go away, and do not run after them. For just like the lightning, when it flashes out of one part of the sky, shines to the other part of the sky, so will the Son of Man be in His day. But first He must suffer many things and be rejected by this generation. And just as it happened in the days of Noah, so it will be also in the days of the Son of Man: they were eating, they were drinking, they were marrying, they were being given in marriage, until the day that Noah entered the ark, and the flood came and destroyed them all. It was the same as happened in the days of Lot: they were eating, they were drinking, they were buying, they were selling, they were planting, they were building; but on the day that Lot went out from Sodom it rained fire and brimstone from heaven and destroyed them all. It will be just the same on the day that the Son of Man is revealed. On that day, the one who is on the housetop and whose goods are in the house must not go down to take them out; and likewise the one who is in the field must not turn back. Remember Lot's wife. Whoever seeks to keep his life will lose it, and whoever loses his life will preserve it. I tell you, on that night there will be two in one bed; one will be taken and the other will be left. There will be two women grinding at the same place; one will be taken and the other will be left. [Two men will be in the field; one will be taken and the other will be left."] And answering they said to Him, "Where, Lord?" And He said to them, "Where the body is, there also the vultures will be gathered" (Luke 17:22–37; see Genesis 19; Matthew 10:39; 16:21, 27; 24:17–28, 37–41).

Setting: Approaching Jerusalem. After being praised by the people in a triumphal welcome, the Lord weeps as He sees the city ahead of Him.

When He approached Jerusalem, He saw the city and wept over it, saying, "If you had known in this day, even you, the things which make for peace! But now they have been hidden from your eyes. For the days will come upon you when your enemies will throw up a barricade against you, and surround you and hem you in on every side, and they will level you to the ground and your children within you, and they will not leave in you one stone upon another, because you did not recognize the time of your visitation" (Luke 19:41–44; see Matthew 24:1, 2; Luke 13:34, 35).

Setting: The Mount of Olives, just east of Jerusalem. A few days before His crucifixion, after pointing out the sacrificial giving to the temple treasury of a poor widow, Jesus predicts the future destruction of the temple during His Olivet Discourse.

"As for these things which you are looking at, the days will come in which there will not be left one stone upon another which will not be torn down" (Luke 21:6; cf. Matthew 24:1, 2; Mark 13:1, 2).

Setting: The Mount of Olives, just east of Jerusalem. A few days before His crucifixion, after giving the disciples more details regarding future events, Jesus elaborates more about things to come during His Olivet Discourse.

"But when you see Jerusalem surrounded by armies, then recognize that her desolation is near. Then those who are in Judea must flee to the mountains, and those who are in the midst of the city must leave, and those who are in the country must not enter the city; because these are days of vengeance, so that all things which are written will be fulfilled. Woe to those who are pregnant and to those who are nursing babies in those days; for there will be a great distress upon the land and wrath to this people; and they will fall by the edge of the sword, and will be led captive into all the nations; and Jerusalem will be trampled under foot by the Gentiles until the times of the Gentiles are fulfilled" (Luke 21:20–24; see Matthew 24:15–18; Mark 13:14–16; Luke 19:43).

Setting: Jerusalem. After being arrested and appearing before the Council of Elders (Sanhedrin), Pontius Pilate (the Roman governor of Judea), Herod Antipas (tetrarch of Galilee and Perea), and Pilate a second time (when Pilate bows to the crowd's pressure and grants that Jesus be crucified), the Lord prophesies to the women mourning Him regarding the coming judgment of Jerusalem.

But Jesus turning to them said, "Daughters of Jerusalem, stop weeping for Me, but weep for yourselves and for your children. For behold, the days are coming when they will say, 'Blessed are the barren, and the wombs that never bore, and the breasts that never nursed.' Then they will begin TO SAY TO THE MOUNTAINS, 'FALL ON US,' AND TO THE HILLS, 'COVER US.' For it they do these things when the tree is green, what will happen when it is dry?" (Luke 23:28–31, Jesus quotes from Hosea 10:8; see Matthew 24:19).

Setting: Luke, writing in Acts, presents quotes from Jesus' post-resurrection appearances, in which He informs and instructs His disciples about their imminent baptism with the Holy Spirit.

Gathering them together, He commanded them not to leave Jerusalem, but to wait for what the Father had promised, "Which," *He said,* "you heard of from Me; for John baptized with water, but you will be baptized with the Holy Spirit not many days from now" (Acts 1:4, 5; see Luke 24:49; John 14:16, 26; Acts 2:1–4).

Setting: The island of Patmos (in the Aegean Sea about fifty miles southwest of Ephesus in modern Turkey). On the Lord's Day (Sunday), about fifty years after Jesus' resurrection, the disciple John encounters the Lord Jesus Christ. Jesus communicates a new revelation for the apostle to record for the church in Pergamum and to six other churches in Asia.

"And to the angel of the church in Pergamum write: The One who has the sharp two-edged sword says this: 'I know where you dwell, where Satan's throne is; and you hold fast My name, and did not deny My faith even in the days of Antipas, My witness, My faithful one, who was killed among you, where Satan dwells. But I have a few things against you, because you have there some who hold the teaching of Balaam, who kept teaching Balak to put a stumbling block before the sons of Israel, to eat things sacrificed to idols and to commit *acts of* immorality. So you also have some who in the same way hold the teaching of the Nicolaitans. Therefore repent; or else I am coming to you quickly, and I will make war against them with the sword of My mouth. He who has an ear, let him hear what the Spirit says to the churches. To him who overcomes, to him I will give *some* of the hidden manna,

and I will give him a white stone, and a new name written on the stone which no one knows but he who receives it' (Revelation 2:12–17; see Numbers 25:1–3; Isaiah 62:2; Revelation 1:16; 2:5, 6, 16).

DAYS, TEN

Setting: The island of Patmos (in the Aegean Sea about fifty miles southwest of Ephesus in modern Turkey). On the Lord's Day (Sunday), about fifty years after Jesus' resurrection, the disciple John encounters the Lord Jesus Christ. Jesus communicates a new revelation for the apostle to record for the church in Smyrna and to six other churches in Asia.

"And to the angel of the church in Smyrna write: The first and the last, who was dead, and has come to life, says this: 'I know your tribulation and your poverty (but you are rich), and the blasphemy by those who say they are Jews and are not, but are a synagogue of Satan. Do not fear what you are about to suffer. Behold, the devil is about to cast some of you into prison, so that you will be tested, and you will have tribulation for ten days. Be faithful until death, and I will give you the crown of life. He who has an ear, let him hear what the Spirit says to the churches. He who overcomes will not be hurt by the second death' (Revelation 2:8–11; see Isaiah 44:6; Revelation 1:9, 18; 2:13; 20:6, 14).

DAYS, THREE (Also see DAY, THIRD)

Setting: Galilee. After Jesus warns the Pharisees about the unpardonable sin and their future judgment, some of the Pharisees and scribes ask Him to perform a miraculous sign for them in front of the crowds.

But He answered and said to them, "An evil and adulterous generation craves for a sign; and *yet* no sign will be given to it but the sign of Jonah the prophet; for just as JONAH WAS THREE DAYS AND THREE NIGHTS IN THE BELLY OF THE SEA MONSTER, so will the Son of Man be three days and three nights in the heart of the earth. The men of Nineveh will stand up with this generation at the judgment, and will condemn it because they repented at the preaching of Jonah; and behold, something greater than Jonah is here. *The* Queen of *the* South will rise up with this generation at the judgment and will condemn it, because she came from the ends of the earth to hear the wisdom of Solomon; and behold, something greater than Solomon is here" (Matthew 12:39–42; Jesus quotes from Jonah 1:17; cf. 1 Kings 10:1; Jonah 3:5; Matthew 16:1, 4; Luke 11:29).

Setting: Near the Sea of Galilee. Impressed by the faith of a Canaanite woman, Jesus restores her daughter from demon possession, then feeds more than 4,000 people, primarily Gentiles, following Him.

And Jesus called His disciples to Him, and said, "I feel compassion for the people, because they have remained with Me now three days and have nothing to eat; and I do not want to send them away hungry, for they might faint on the way." The disciples said to Him, "Where would we get so many loaves in *this* desolate place to satisfy a large crowd?" And Jesus said to them, "How many loaves do you have?" And they said, "Seven and a few small fish" (Matthew 15:32–34; cf. Mark 8:1–9).

Setting: Decapolis, near the Sea of Galilee. Jesus miraculously feeds more than 4,000 people, primarily Gentiles

In those days, when there was again a large crowd and they had nothing to eat, Jesus called His disciples and said to them, "I feel compassion for the people because they have remained with Me now three days and have nothing to eat. If I send them away hungry to their homes, they will faint on their way; and some of them have come a great distance" (Mark 8:1–3; cf. Matthew 15:32–38; see Matthew 9:36).

Setting: Galilee. After casting out an unclean spirit from a young boy, Jesus teaches His disciples in secret about His coming death and resurrection.

From there they went out and *began* to go through Galilee, and He did not want anyone to know *about it.* For He was teaching His disciples and telling them, "The Son of Man is to be delivered into the hands of men, and they will kill Him; and when He has been killed, He will rise three days later." But they did not understand *this* statement, and they were afraid to ask Him (Mark 9:30–32; cf. Matthew 17:22, 23; Luke 9:43–45; see Matthew 16:21).

Setting: On the way to Jerusalem. Jesus prophesies His coming persecution, death, and resurrection after encouraging His disciples with a revelation of their future reward.

They were on the road going up to Jerusalem, and Jesus was walking on ahead of them; and they were amazed, and those who followed were fearful. And again He took the twelve aside and began to tell them what was going to happen to Him, *saying*, "Behold, we are going up to Jerusalem, and the Son of Man will be delivered to the chief priests and the scribes; and they will condemn Him to death and will hand Him over to the Gentiles. They will mock Him and spit on Him, and scourge Him and kill *Him*, and three days later He will rise again" (Mark 10:32–34; cf. Matthew 20:17–19; Luke 18:31–34; see Matthew 16:21; Mark 8:31).

Setting: Jerusalem. After Jesus cleanses the temple during the Passover of the Jews, the Jewish religious leaders question His authority to do these things.

Jesus answered them, "Destroy this temple, and in three days I will raise it up" (John 2:19; cf. Matthew 26:61).

DAYS, TWO

Setting: The Mount of Olives, just east of Jerusalem. During His discourse, after answering His disciples' questions as to when the temple will be destroyed and Jerusalem overrun, along with the signs of His coming and the end of the age, Jesus prophesies His crucifixion to His disciples.

When Jesus had finished all these words, He said to His disciples, "You know that after two days the Passover is coming, and the Son of Man is *to be* handed over for crucifixion" (Matthew 26:1, 2; see Mark 14:1, 2; Luke 22:1, 2).

DAYS OF NOAH (See NOAH)

DAYS OF OUR FATHERS (Listed under FATHERS, DAYS OF OUR)

DEAD (Specifics such as DEAD, GOD OF THE; and RESURRECTION OF THE DEAD are separate entries; also see DEATH; and TOMBS)

Setting: By the Sea of Galilee. Following a time of casting out evil spirits from the demon-possessed and healing the ill in fulfillment of Isaiah 53:4, Jesus lays out to an inquiring scribe the demands of discipleship.

Then a scribe came and said to Him, "Teacher, I will follow You wherever you go." Jesus said to him, "The foxes have holes and the birds of the air *have* nests, but the Son of Man has nowhere to lay His head." Another of the disciples said to Him, "Lord, permit me first to go and bury my father." But Jesus said to him, "Follow Me, and allow the dead to bury their own dead" (Matthew 8:19–22; cf. Luke 9:57–60).

Setting: Galilee. After His disciples observe His ministry, Jesus summons and specifically instructs them about their ministry to the people of Israel.

These twelve Jesus sent out after instructing them: "Do not go in *the* way of *the* Gentiles, and do not enter *any* city of the Samaritans; but rather go to the lost sheep of the house of Israel. And as you go, preach, saying, 'The kingdom of heaven is at hand.' Heal *the* sick, raise *the* dead, cleanse *the* lepers, cast out demons. Freely you received, freely give. Do not acquire gold, or silver, or copper for your money belts, or a bag for *your* journey, or even two coats, or sandals, or a staff; for the worker is worthy of his support. And whatever city or village you enter, inquire who is worthy in it, and stay at his house until you leave *that city*. As you enter the house, give it your greeting. If the house is worthy, give it your *blessing of* peace. But if it is not worthy, take back your *blessing of* peace. Whoever does not receive you, nor heed your words, as you go out of that house or that city, shake the dust off your feet. Truly I say to you, it will be more tolerable for *the* land of Sodom and Gomorrah in the day of judgment than for that city" (Matthew 10:5–15; cf. Mark 6:7–11; Luke 9:1–5; see Matthew 3:2; 11:22, 24; 15:24; Luke 22:35; 1 Corinthians 9:14).

Setting: Galilee. As He teaches and preaches, Jesus responds to John the Baptist's question as to whether He is Israel's promised Messiah.

Jesus answered and said to them, "Go and report to John what you hear and see: *the* BLIND RECEIVE SIGHT and *the* lame walk, *the* lepers are cleansed and *the* deaf hear, *the* dead are raised up, and *the* POOR HAVE THE GOSPEL PREACHED TO THEM. And blessed is he who does not take offense at Me" (Matthew 11:4–6, Jesus quotes from Isaiah 35:5f; cf. Luke 7:22, 23).

Setting: Galilee. Jesus instructs Peter, James, and John to keep the Transfiguration, which has just occurred on a high mountain, secret until after His resurrection.

As they were coming down from the mountain, Jesus commanded them, saying, "Tell the vision to no one until the Son of Man has risen from the dead" (Matthew 17:9; cf. Mark 9:9–13; Luke 9:28–36).

Setting: The temple in Jerusalem. After the Jewish religious leaders test Him with questions, Jesus pronounces the seventh of eight woes on them in front of the crowds and His disciples.

"Woe to you, scribes and Pharisees, hypocrites! For you are like whitewashed tombs which on the outside appear beautiful, but inside they are full of dead men's bones and all uncleanness. So you, too, outwardly appear righteous to men, but inwardly you are full of hypocrisy and lawlessness" (Matthew 23:27, 28; cf. Luke 11:44)

Setting: The temple in Jerusalem. After some of the Pharisees and Herodians attempt to trap Jesus in a statement, some Sadducees question Him about the status of marriage after death.

Jesus said to them, "Is this not the reason you are mistaken, that you do not understand the Scriptures or the power of God? For when they rise from the dead, they neither marry nor are given in marriage, but are like angels in heaven. But regarding the fact that the dead rise again, have you not read in the book of Moses, in the *passage* about *the burning* bush, how God spoke to him, saying, 'I AM THE GOD OF ABRAHAM, AND THE GOD OF ISAAC, and the God of Jacob?' He is not the God of the dead, but of the living; you are greatly mistaken" (Mark 12:24–27, Jesus quotes from Exodus 3:6; cf. Matthew 22:29–33; Luke 20:34–40).

Setting: Galilee. After Jesus raises a woman's son from the dead in Nain, the disciples of John the Baptist inquire whether He is the promised Messiah.

And He answered and said to them, "Go and report to John what you have seen and heard: the BLIND RECEIVE SIGHT, the lame walk, the lepers are cleansed, and the deaf hear, the dead are raised up, the POOR HAVE THE GOSPEL PREACHED TO THEM. Blessed is he who does not take offense at Me" (Luke 7:22, 23, Jesus quotes from Isaiah 35:5; 61:1; cf. Matthew 11:2–6).

Setting: On the way from Galilee to Jerusalem. The Lord responds to several men seeking to follow Him.

And He said to another, "Follow Me." But he said, "Lord, permit me first to go and bury my father," But He said to him, "Allow the dead to bury their own dead; but as for you, go and proclaim everywhere the kingdom of God" (Luke 9:59, 60; cf. Matthew 8:19–22).

Setting: On the way from Galilee to Jerusalem. Jesus conveys the illustration of the prodigal son because the Pharisees and scribes complain He associates with tax collectors and sinners.

And He said, "A man had two sons. The younger of them said to his father, 'Father, give me the share of the estate that falls to me.' So he divided his wealth between them. And not many days later, the younger son gathered everything together and went on a journey into a distant country, and there he squandered his estate with loose living. Now when he had spent everything, a severe famine occurred in that country, and he began to be impoverished. So he went and hired himself out to one of the citizens of that country, and he sent him into his fields to feed swine. And he would have gladly filled his stomach with the pods that the swine were eating, and no one was giving anything to him. But when he came to his senses, he said, 'How many of my father's hired men have more than enough bread, but I am dying here with hunger! I will get up and go to my father, and will say to him, "Father, I have sinned against heaven, and in your sight; I am no longer worthy to be called your son; make me as one of your hired men."' So he got up and came to his father. But while he was still a long way off, his father saw him and felt compassion for him, and ran and embraced him and kissed him. And the son said to him, "Father, I have sinned against heaven and in your sight; I am no longer worthy to be called your son.' But the father said to his slaves, 'Quickly bring out the best robe and put it on him, and put a ring on his hand and sandals on his feet; and bring the fattened calf, kill it, and let us eat and celebrate; for this son of mine was dead and has come to life again; he was lost and has been found.' And they began to celebrate. Now his older son was in the field, when he came and approached the house, he heard music and dancing. And he summoned one of the servants and began inquiring what these things could be. And he said to him, 'Your brother has come, and your father has killed the fattened calf because he has received him back safe and sound.' But he became angry and was not willing to go in; and his father came out and began pleading with him. But he answered and said to his father, 'Look! For so many years I have been serving you and I have never neglected a command of yours; and yet you have never given me a young goat, so that I might celebrate with my friends; but when this son of yours came, who has devoured your wealth with prostitutes, you killed the fattened calf for him.' And he said to him, 'Son, you have always been with me, and all that is mine is yours. But we had to celebrate and rejoice, for this brother of yours was dead and has begun to live, and was lost and has been found'" (Luke 15:11–32; see Proverbs 29:2; Luke 15:1, 2).

Setting: On the way from Galilee to Jerusalem. After responding to the Pharisees' scoffing at His teaching His disciples about stewardship and the permanence of the Law, Jesus conveys the story of the rich man and Lazarus.

"Now there was a rich man, and he habitually dressed in purple and fine linen, joyously living in splendor every day. And a poor man named Lazarus was laid at his gate, covered with sores, and longing to be fed with the crumbs which were falling from the rich man's table; besides, even the dogs were coming and licking his sores. Now the poor man died and was carried away by the angels to Abraham's bosom; and the rich man also died and was buried. In Hades he lifted up his eyes, being in torment, and saw Abraham far away and Lazarus in his bosom. And he cried out and said, 'Father Abraham, have mercy on me, and send Lazarus so that he may dip the tip of his finger in water and cool off my tongue, for I am in agony in this flame.' But Abraham said, 'Child, remember that during your life you received your good things, and likewise Lazarus bad things; but now he is being comforted here, and you are in agony. And besides all this, between us and you there is a great chasm fixed, so that those who wish to come over from here to you will not be able, and that none may cross over from there to us.' And he said, 'Then I beg you, father, that you send him to my father's house—for I have five brothers—in order that he may warn them, so that they will not also come to this place of torment.' But Abraham said, 'They have Moses and the Prophets; let them hear them.' But he said, 'No, father Abraham, but if someone goes to them from the dead, they will repent!' But he said to him, 'If they do not listen to Moses and the Prophets, they will not be persuaded even if someone rises from the dead'" (Luke 16:19–31; see Luke 3:8; 6:24; 16:1, 14).

Setting: The temple in Jerusalem. A few days before His crucifixion, after the scribes and Pharisees seek to trap Jesus by questioning Him about paying taxes to Caesar, some Sadducees (who say there is no resurrection) ask Him a question about the resurrection.

Jesus said to them, "The sons of this age marry and are given in marriage, but those who are considered worthy to attain to that age and the resurrection from the dead, neither marry nor are given in marriage; for they cannot even die anymore, because they are like angels, and are sons of God, being sons of the resurrection. But that the dead are raised, even Moses showed, in the passage about the burning bush, where he calls the Lord THE GOD OF ABRAHAM, AND THE GOD OF ISAAC, AND THE GOD OF JACOB. Now He is not the God of the dead but of the living; for all live to Him" (Luke 20:34–38, Jesus quotes from Exodus 3:6; cf. Matthew 22:23–32; Mark 12:18–27).

Setting: Jerusalem. After rising from the grave on the third day following being crucified, and appearing to two of His followers on the road to Emmaus, Jesus gives instruction to some of His disciples about His mission on earth and the promise of future power from God.

Now He said to them, "These are My words which I spoke to you while I was still with you, that all things which are written about Me in the Law of Moses and the Prophets and the Psalms must be fulfilled." Then He opened their minds to understand the Scriptures, and He said to them, "Thus it is written, that the Christ would suffer and rise again from the dead the third day, and that repentance for forgiveness of sins would be proclaimed in His name to all the nations, beginning from Jerusalem. You are witnesses of these things. And behold, I am sending forth the promise of My Father upon you; but you are to stay in the city until you are clothed with power from on high" (Luke 24:44–49; see Matthew 28:19, 20; Acts 1:8).

Setting: By the pool of Bethesda in Jerusalem. During the Feast of the Jews, Jesus responds to criticism from the Jewish religious leaders for healing a lame man on the Sabbath and for referring to God as His Father (thereby making Himself equal with God).

Therefore Jesus answered and was saying to them, "Truly, truly, I say to you, the Son can do nothing of Himself, unless *it is* something He sees the Father doing; for whatever the Father does, these things the Son also does in like manner. For the Father loves the Son, and shows Him all things that He Himself is doing; and *the Father* will show Him greater works than these, so that you will marvel. For just as the Father raises the dead and gives them life, even so the Son also gives life to whom He wishes. For not even the Father judges anyone, but He has given all judgment to the Son, so that all will honor the Son even as they honor the Father. He who does not honor the Son does not honor the Father who sent Him" (John 5:19–23; see Luke 10:16; John 3:35; 11:25; 14:12).

Setting: Jerusalem. During the Feast of the Jews, Jesus responds to criticism from the Jewish religious leaders for referring to God as His Father (thereby making Himself equal with God) and prophesying His participation in the resurrection and judgment of men.

"Truly, truly, I say to you, an hour is coming and now is, when the dead will hear the voice of the Son of God, and those who hear will live. For just as the Father has life in Himself, even so He gave to the Son also to have life in Himself; and He gave Him authority to execute judgment, because He is *the* Son of Man. Do not marvel at this; for an hour is coming, in which all who are in the tombs will hear His voice, and will come forth; those who did the good *deeds* to a resurrection of life, those who committed the evil *deeds* to a resurrection of judgment" (John 5:25–29; see Daniel 12:2; John 1:4; 11:24).

Setting: Beyond the Jordan. While Jesus and His disciples avoid the Jerusalem Pharisees, He communicates Lazarus's death to them, and decides to go to Bethany.

So Jesus then said to them plainly, "Lazarus is dead, and I am glad for your sakes that I was not there, so that you may believe; but let us go to him" (John 11:14, 15).

Setting: The island of Patmos (in the Aegean Sea about fifty miles southwest of Ephesus in modern Turkey). On the Lord's Day (Sunday), the disciple John encounters the Lord Jesus Christ approximately fifty years after His resurrection for the purpose of the Lord communicating new revelations for the apostle to record for the seven churches in Asia.

When I saw Him, I fell at His feet like a dead man. And He placed His right hand on me, saying, "Do not be afraid; I am the first and the last, and the living One; and I was dead, and behold, I am alive forevermore, and I have the keys of death and of Hades. Therefore write the things which you have seen, and the things which are, and the things which will take place after these things. As for the mystery of the seven stars which you saw in My right hand, and the seven golden lampstands: the seven stars are the angels of the seven churches, and the seven lampstands are the seven churches" (Revelation 1:17–20; see Isaiah 44:6; Luke 24:5; Revelation 2:8).

Setting: The island of Patmos (in the Aegean Sea about fifty miles southwest of Ephesus in modern Turkey). On the Lord's Day (Sunday), about fifty years after Jesus' resurrection, the disciple John encounters the Lord Jesus Christ. Jesus communicates a new revelation for the apostle to record for the church in Smyrna and to six other churches in Asia.

"And to the angel of the church in Smyrna write: The first and the last, who was dead, and has come to life, says this: 'I know your tribulation and your poverty (but you are rich), and the blasphemy by those who say they are Jews and are not, but are a synagogue of Satan. Do not fear what you are about to suffer. Behold, the devil is about to cast some of you into prison, so that you will be tested, and you will have tribulation for ten days. Be faithful until death, and I will give you the crown of life. He who has an ear, let him hear what the Spirit says to the churches. He who overcomes will not be hurt by the second death' (Revelation 2:8–11; see Isaiah 44:6; Revelation 1:9, 18; 20:6, 14).

Setting: The island of Patmos (in the Aegean Sea about fifty miles southwest of Ephesus in modern Turkey). On the Lord's Day (Sunday), about fifty years after Jesus' resurrection, the disciple John encounters the Lord Jesus Christ. Jesus communicates a new revelation for the apostle to record for the church in Sardis and to six other churches in Asia.

"To the angel of the church in Sardis write: He who has the seven Spirits of God and the seven stars, says this: 'I know your deeds, that you have a name that you are alive, but you are dead. Wake up, and strengthen the things that remain, which were about to die; for I have not found your deeds completed in the sight of My God. So remember what you have received and heard; and keep *it,* and repent. Therefore if you do not wake up, I will come like a thief, and you will not know at what hour I will come to you. But you have a few people in Sardis who have not soiled their garments; and they will walk with Me in white, for they are worthy. He who overcomes will thus be clothed in white garments; and I will not erase his name from the book of life, and I will confess his name before My Father and before His angels. He who has an ear, let him hear what the Spirit says to the churches'" (Revelation 3:1–6; see Matthew 10:32; Revelation 1:16).

DEAD, GOD OF THE

Setting: The temple in Jerusalem. As Jesus teaches, the Sadducees question Him about levirate marriage (marriage to a brother-in law) in order to test Him.

But Jesus answered and said to them, "You are mistaken, not understanding the Scriptures nor the power of God. For in the resurrection they neither marry nor are given in marriage, but are like angels in heaven. But regarding the resurrection of the dead, have you not read what was spoken to you by God: 'I AM THE GOD OF ABRAHAM, AND THE GOD OF ISAAC, AND THE GOD OF JACOB'? He is not the God of the dead but of the living" (Matthew 22:29–32, Jesus quotes from Exodus 3:6; cf. Mark 12:18–27; Luke 20:27–38; see Deuteronomy 25:5; John 20:9).

Setting: The temple in Jerusalem. After some of the Pharisees and Herodians attempt to trap Jesus in a statement, some Sadducees question Him about the status of marriage after death.

Jesus said to them, "Is this not the reason you are mistaken, that you do not understand the Scriptures or the power of God? For when they rise from the dead, they neither marry nor are given in marriage, but are like angels in heaven. But regarding the fact that the dead rise again, have you not read in the book of Moses, in the *passage* about *the burning* bush, how God spoke to him, saying, 'I AM THE GOD OF ABRAHAM, AND THE GOD OF ISAAC, and the God of Jacob?' He is not the God of the dead, but of the living; you are greatly mistaken" (Mark 12:24–27, Jesus quotes from Exodus 3:6; cf. Matthew 22:29–33; Luke 20:34–40).

Setting: The temple in Jerusalem. A few days before His crucifixion, after the scribes and Pharisees seek to trap Jesus by questioning Him about paying taxes to Caesar, some Sadducees (who say there is no resurrection) ask Him a question about the resurrection.

Jesus said to them, "The sons of this age marry and are given in marriage, but those who are considered worthy to attain to that age and the resurrection from the dead, neither marry nor are given in marriage; for they cannot even die anymore, because they are like angels, and are sons of God, being sons of the resurrection. But that the dead are raised, even Moses showed, in the passage about the burning bush, where he calls the Lord THE GOD OF ABRAHAM, AND THE GOD OF ISAAC, AND THE GOD OF JACOB. Now He is not the God of the dead but of the living; for all live to Him" (Luke 20:34–38, Jesus quotes from Exodus 3:6; cf. Matthew 22:23–32; Mark 12:18–27).

DEAD, HALF

Setting: On the way from Galilee to Jerusalem. While being tested by a lawyer, Jesus tells him the story of the good Samaritan.

Jesus replied and said, "A man was going down from Jerusalem to Jericho, and fell among robbers, and they stripped him and beat him, and went away leaving him half dead. And by chance a priest was going down on that road, and when he saw him, he passed by on the other side. Likewise a Levite also, when he came to the place and saw him, passed by on the other side. But a Samaritan, who was on a journey, came upon him; and when he saw him, he felt compassion, and came to him and bandaged up his wounds, pouring oil and wine on them; and he put him on his own beast, and brought him to an inn and took care of him. On the next day he took out two denarii and gave them to the innkeeper and said, 'Take care of him; and whatever more you spend, when I return I will repay you.' Which of these three do you think proved to be a neighbor to the man who fell into the robbers' hands?" And he said, "The one who showed mercy toward him." Then Jesus said to him, "Go and do the same" (Luke 10:30–37).

DEAD, RAISING THE (See RESUSCITATION; and RESURRECTION)

DEAD, RESURRECTION FROM THE (See RESURRECTION FROM THE DEAD)

DEAD, RESURRECTION OF THE (See RESURRECTION OF THE DEAD)

DEAD MEN'S BONES (Listed under BONES, DEAD MEN'S)

DEAF

Setting: Galilee. As He teaches and preaches, Jesus responds to John the Baptist's question as to whether He is Israel's promised Messiah.

Jesus answered and said to them, "Go and report to John what you hear and see: *the* BLIND RECEIVE SIGHT and *the* lame walk, *the* lepers are cleansed and *the* deaf hear, *the* dead are raised up, and *the* POOR HAVE THE GOSPEL PREACHED TO THEM. And blessed is he who does not take offense at Me" (Matthew 11:4–6, Jesus quotes from Isaiah 35:5f; cf. Luke 7:22, 23).

Setting: Galilee. After Jesus raises a woman's son from the dead in Nain, the disciples of John the Baptist inquire whether He is the promised Messiah.

And He answered and said to them, "Go and report to John what you have seen and heard: the BLIND RECEIVE SIGHT, the lame walk, the lepers are cleansed, and the deaf hear, the dead are raised up, the POOR HAVE THE GOSPEL PREACHED TO THEM. Blessed is he who does not take offense at Me" (Luke 7:22, 23, Jesus quotes from Isaiah 35:5; 61:1; cf. Matthew 11:2–6).

DEAF AND MUTE (Listed under MUTE, DEAF AND)

DEALERS (Also see MERCHANTS)

Setting: The Mount of Olives, just east of Jerusalem. During His discourse, after answering His disciples' questions as to when the temple will be destroyed and Jerusalem overrun, along with the signs of His coming and the end of the age, Jesus reemphasizes to His disciples that they should be on the alert for His return.

"Then the kingdom of heaven will be comparable to ten virgins, who took their lamps and went out to meet the bridegroom. Five of them were foolish, and five were prudent. For when the foolish took their lamps, they took no oil with them, but the prudent took oil in flasks along with their lamps. Now while the bridegroom was delaying, they all got drowsy and *began* to sleep. But at midnight there was a shout, 'Behold, the bridegroom! Come out to meet *him*.' Then all those virgins rose and trimmed their lamps. The foolish said to the prudent, 'Give us some of your oil, for our lamps are going out.' But the prudent answered, 'No, there will not be enough for us and you *too;* go instead to the dealers and buy *some* for yourselves.' And while they were going away to make the purchase, the bridegroom came, and those who were ready went in with him to the wedding feast; and the door was shut. Later the other virgins also came, saying, 'Lord, lord, open up for us.' But he answered, 'Truly I say to you, I do not know you.' Be on the alert then, for you do not know the day nor the hour" (Matthew 25:1–13; cf. Matthew 24:42; Luke 12:35; see Matthew 7:21, 24).

DEATH (Specifics such as DEATH, POINT OF; and PROPHECY OF JESUS' DEATH are separate entries; also see DEAD)

[DEATH from the girl has not died, but is asleep]

Setting: Capernaum near the Sea of Galilee. After healing a woman who has been suffering with internal bleeding for twelve years, Jesus brings a synagogue official's daughter back from death.

When Jesus came into the official's house, and saw the flute-players and the crowd in noisy disorder, He said, "Leave; for the girl has not died, but is asleep." And they *began* laughing at Him. But when the crowd had been sent out, He entered and took her by the hand, and the girl got up (Matthew 9:23–25; cf. Mark 5:21–24, 35–43; Luke 8:41–42, 49–56).

Setting: Galilee. After His disciples observe His ministry, Jesus summons and specifically instructs them about the upcoming difficulties of *their* ministry to the people of Israel.

"Brother will betray brother to death, and a father *his* child; and children will rise up against parents and cause them to be put to death. You will be hated by all because of My name, but it is the one who has endured to the end who will be saved. But whenever they persecute you in one city, flee to the next; for truly I say to you, you will not finish *going through* the cities of Israel until the Son of Man comes" (Matthew 10:21–23; cf. Matthew 10:35, 36; 16:27, 28; 24:9).

Setting: Galilee. Pharisees and scribes from Jerusalem question Jesus about His disciples' lack of obedience to tradition and the commandments.

And He answered and said to them, "Why do you yourselves transgress the commandment of God for the sake of tradition? For God said, 'HONOR YOUR FATHER AND MOTHER,' and, 'HE WHO SPEAKS EVIL OF FATHER OR MOTHER IS TO BE PUT TO DEATH.' But you say, 'Whoever says to *his* father or mother, "Whatever I have that would help you has been given *to God*," he is not to honor his father or mother.' And *by this* you invalidated the word of God for the sake of your tradition. You hypocrites, rightly did Isaiah prophesy of you: 'THIS PEOPLE HONORS ME WITH THEIR LIPS, BUT THEIR HEART IS FAR AWAY FROM ME. BUT IN VAIN DO THEY WORSHIP ME, TEACHING AS DOCTRINES THE PRECEPTS OF MEN'" (Matthew 15:3–9, Jesus quotes from Exodus 20:12, 21:17, Leviticus 20:9; Isaiah 29:13; cf. Mark 7:5–7; see Colossians 2:22).

Setting: Near Caesarea Philippi. Jesus teaches His disciples about the costs of discipleship following His rebuke of Peter for attempting to forbid Him to accomplish His earthly mission of dying and being resurrected.

Then Jesus said to His disciples, "If anyone wishes to come after Me, he must deny himself, and take up his cross and follow Me. For whoever wishes to save his life will lose it; but whoever loses his life for My sake will find it. For what will it profit a man if he gains the whole world and forfeits his soul? Or what will a man give in exchange for his soul? For the Son of Man is going to come in the glory of His Father with His angels, and WILL THEN REPAY EVERY MAN ACCORDING TO HIS DEEDS. Truly, I say to you, there are some of you who are standing here who will not taste death until they see the Son of Man coming in His kingdom" (Matthew 16:24–28, Jesus quotes from Psalm 62:12; cf. Mark 8:34–37; Luke 9:23–27; see Matthew 10:38, 39).

[DEATH from died]

Setting: The home of Jairus, a synagogue official in Capernaum by the Sea of Galilee. Jesus assures those present that Jairus's daughter has not died, but is asleep.

And entering in, He said to them, "Why make a commotion and weep? The child has not died, but is asleep" (Mark 5:39; cf. Matthew 9:24; Luke 8:52).

Setting: Galilee. The Pharisees and some of the scribes from Jerusalem question why Jesus' disciples do not follow the tradition of ceremonial hand cleansing before eating bread.

And He said to them, "Rightly did Isaiah prophesy of you hypocrites, as it is written: 'THIS PEOPLE HONORS ME WITH THEIR LIPS, BUT THEIR HEART IS FAR AWAY FROM ME. BUT IN VAIN DO THEY WORSHIP ME, TEACHING AS DOCTRINES THE PRECEPTS OF MEN.' Neglecting the commandment of God, you hold to the tradition of men." He was also saying to them, "You are experts at setting aside the commandment of God in order to keep tradition. For Moses said, 'HONOR YOUR FATHER AND YOUR MOTHER'; and, 'HE WHO SPEAKS EVIL OF FATHER OR MOTHER, IS TO BE PUT TO DEATH'; but you say, 'If a man says to *his* father or *his* mother, whatever I have that would help you is Corban (that is to say, given *to God*),' you no longer permit him to do anything for *his* father or *his* mother; *thus* invalidating the word of God by your tradition which you have handed down; and you do many things such as that" (Mark 7:6–13, Jesus quotes from Exodus 20:12; 21:17; Isaiah 29:13; cf. Matthew 15:1–6).

Setting: Caesarea Philippi. Following His rebuke of Peter for desiring to thwart His mission to the cross, Jesus summons a crowd, along with His disciples, and informs them of the hope involving the coming kingdom of God.

And Jesus was saying to them, "Truly I say to you, there are some of those who are standing here who will not taste death until they see the kingdom of God after it has come with power" (Mark 9:1; cf. Matthew 16:28; Luke 9:27).

[DEATH from die]
Setting: Capernaum of Galilee. As Jesus teaches His disciples in private, they ask Him about greatness.

But Jesus said, "Do not hinder him, for there is no one who will perform a miracle in My name, and be able soon afterward to speak evil of Me. For he who is not against us is for us. For whoever gives you a cup of water to drink because of your name as *followers* of Christ, truly I say to you, he will not lose his reward. Whoever causes one of these little ones who believe to stumble, it would be better for him if, with a heavy millstone hung around his neck, he had been cast into the sea. If your hand causes you to stumble, cut it off; it is better for you to enter life crippled, than, having your two hands, to go into hell, into the unquenchable fire, [where THEIR WORM DOES NOT DIE, AND THE FIRE IS NOT QUENCHED.] If your foot causes you to stumble, cut it off; it is better for you to enter life lame, than, having your two feet, to be cast into hell, [where THEIR WORM DOES NOT DIE, AND THE FIRE IS NOT QUENCHED.] If your eye causes you to stumble, throw it out; it is better for you to enter the kingdom of God with one eye, than, having two eyes, to be cast into hell, where THEIR WORM DOES NOT DIE, AND THE FIRE IS NOT QUENCHED. For everyone will be salted with fire. Salt is good; but if the salt becomes unsalty, with what will you make it salty *again?* Have salt in yourselves, and be at peace with one another" (Mark 9:39–50; Jesus quotes from Isaiah 66:24; cf. Matthew 18:6–9; Luke 9:49, 50; see Matthew 5:13, 29, 30; 10:42; 12:30; 18:5, 6).

Setting: During His discourse on the Mount of Olives, east of the temple in Jerusalem, after prophesying the temple's destruction, Jesus responds to questions from Peter, James, John, and Andrew about future events.

And Jesus began to say to them, "See to it that no one misleads you. Many will come in My name, saying, 'I am *He!*' and will mislead many. When you hear of wars and rumors of wars, do not be frightened; *those things* must take place; but *that is* not yet the end. For nation will rise up against nation, and kingdom against kingdom; there will be earthquakes in various places; there will *also be* famines. These things are *merely* the beginning of birth pangs. But be on your guard; for they will deliver you to *the* courts, and you will be flogged in *the* synagogues, and you will stand before governors and kings for My sake, as a testimony to them. The gospel must first be preached to all the nations. When they arrest you and hand you over, do not worry beforehand about what you are to say, but say whatever is given you in that hour; for it is not you who speak, but *it is* the Holy Spirit. Brother will betray brother to death, and a father *his* child; and children will rise up against parents and have them put to death. You will be hated by all because of My name, but the one who endures to the end, he will be saved" (Mark 13:5–13; cf. Matthew 24:4–14; Luke 21:7–19; see Matthew 10:17–22).

Setting: Gethsemane on the Mount of Olives, just east of Jerusalem. Jesus agonizes over His impending death, disappointed that His disciples keep falling asleep instead of watching and praying with Him.

They came to a place named Gethsemane; and He said to the disciples, "Sit here until I have prayed." And He took with Him Peter and James and John, and began to be very distressed and troubled. And He said to them, "My soul is deeply grieved to the point of death; remain here and keep watch." And He went a little beyond *them,* and fell to the ground and *began* to pray that if it were possible, the hour might pass Him by. And He was saying, "Abba! Father! All things are possible for You; remove this cup from Me; yet not what I will, but what You will." And He came and found them sleeping, and said to Peter, "Simon, are you asleep? Could you not keep watch for one hour? Keep watching and praying that you may not come into temptation; the spirit is willing, but the flesh is weak" (Mark 14:32–38; cf. Matthew 26:36–41, Luke 22:41–46; see Romans 8:15; Galatians 4:6).

[DEATH from died]
Setting: Capernaum. After healing a woman ill for twelve years, Jesus receives word a Galilee synagogue official's daughter has died.

But when Jesus heard this, He answered him, "Do not be afraid any longer; only believe and she will be made well." When He came to the house, He did not allow anyone to enter with Him except Peter and John and James and the girl's father and mother. Now they were all weeping and lamenting for her; but He said, "Stop weeping; for she has not died, but is asleep." And they began laughing at Him, knowing that she had died. He, however, took her by the hand and called, saying, "Child, arise!" And her spirit returned, and she got up immediately; and He gave orders for something to be given her to eat (Luke 8:50–55; cf. Matthew 9:18, 19, 23–26; Mark 5:21–24, 35–43).

Setting: Galilee. Following Peter's pronouncement that Jesus is the Christ of God, the Lord conveys the demands of discipleship and the hope regarding the kingdom of God.

And He was saying to them all, "If anyone wishes to come after Me, he must deny himself, and take up his cross daily and follow Me. For whoever wishes to save his life will lose it, but whoever loses his life for My sake, he is the one who will save it. For what is a man profited if he gains the whole world, and loses or forfeits himself? For whoever is ashamed of Me and My words, the Son of Man will be ashamed of him when He comes in His glory, and the glory of the Father and of the holy angels. But I say to you truthfully, there are some of those standing here who will not taste death until they see the kingdom of God" (Luke 9:23–27; cf. Matthew 16:24–26, 28; Mark 8:34–37; see Matthew 10:33, 38, 39).

[DEATH from died]
Setting: On the way from Galilee to Jerusalem. After responding to the Pharisees' scoffing at His teaching His disciples about stewardship and the permanence of the Law, Jesus conveys the story of the rich man and Lazarus.

"Now there was a rich man, and he habitually dressed in purple and fine linen, joyously living in splendor every day. And a poor man named Lazarus was laid at his gate, covered with sores, and longing to be fed with the crumbs which were falling from the rich man's table; besides, even the dogs were coming and licking his sores. Now the poor man died and was carried away by the angels to Abraham's bosom; and the rich man also died and was buried. In Hades he lifted up his eyes, being in torment, and saw Abraham far away and Lazarus in his bosom. And he cried out and said, 'Father Abraham, have mercy on me, and send Lazarus so that he may dip the tip of his finger in water and cool off my tongue, for I am in agony in this flame.' But Abraham said, 'Child, remember that during your life you received your good things, and likewise Lazarus bad things; but now he is being comforted here, and you are in agony. And besides all this, between us and you there is a great chasm fixed, so that those who wish to come over from here to you will not be able, and that none may cross over from there to us.' And he said, 'Then I beg you, father, that you send him to my father's house—for I have five brothers—in order that he may warn them, so that they will not also come to this place of torment.' But Abraham said, 'They have Moses and the Prophets; let them hear them.' But he said, 'No, father Abraham, but if someone goes to them from the dead, they will repent!' But he said to him, 'If they do not listen to Moses and the Prophets, they will not be persuaded even if someone rises from the dead'" (Luke 16:19–31; see Luke 3:8; 6:24; 16:1, 14).

[DEATH from die]
Setting: The temple in Jerusalem. A few days before His crucifixion, after the scribes and Pharisees seek to trap Jesus by questioning Him about paying taxes to Caesar, some Sadducees (who say there is no resurrection) ask

Him a question about the resurrection.

Jesus said to them, "The sons of this age marry and are given in marriage, but those who are considered worthy to attain to that age and the resurrection from the dead, neither marry nor are given in marriage; for they cannot even die anymore, because they are like angels, and are sons of God, being sons of the resurrection. But that the dead are raised, even Moses showed, in the passage about the burning bush, where he calls the Lord THE GOD OF ABRAHAM, AND THE GOD OF ISAAC, AND THE GOD OF JACOB. Now He is not the God of the dead but of the living; for all live to Him" (Luke 20:34–38, Jesus quotes from Exodus 3:6; cf. Matthew 22:23–32; Mark 12:18–27).

Setting: The Mount of Olives, east of the temple in Jerusalem. After giving His disciples more details about the temple's coming destruction, Jesus elaborates about other future events during His Olivet Discourse.

Then He continued by saying to them, "Nation will rise against nation and kingdom against kingdom, and there will be great earthquakes, and in various places plagues and famines; and there will be terrors and great signs from heaven. But before all these things, they will lay their hands on you and will persecute you, delivering you to the synagogues and prisons, bringing you before kings and governors for My name's sake. It will lead to an opportunity for your testimony. So make up your minds not to prepare beforehand to defend yourselves; for I will give you utterance and wisdom which none of your opponents will be able to resist or refute. But you will be betrayed even by parents and brothers and relatives and friends, and they will put some of you to death, and you will be hated by all because of My name. Yet not a hair of your head will perish. By your endurance you will gain your lives" (Luke 21:10–19; cf. Matthew 10:19–22; 24:7–14; Mark 13:8–13).

Setting: An upper room in Jerusalem. During the Feast of Unleavened Bread (Passover) just before His crucifixion, Jesus celebrates the Passover meal with His disciples and institutes the Lord's Supper. Later, His disciples argue over who is the greatest among them, and Jesus prophesies Peter's upcoming denial of Him.

"Simon, Simon, behold, Satan has demanded permission to sift you like wheat; but I have prayed for you, that your faith may not fail; and you, when once you have turned again, strengthen your brothers." But he said to Him, "Lord, with You I am ready to go both to prison and to death!" And He said, "I say to you, Peter, the rooster will not crow today until you have denied three times that you know Me" (Luke 22:31–34; cf. Matthew 26:33–35; John 13:36–38; see Job 1:6–12; John 17:15).

Setting: By the pool of Bethesda in Jerusalem. During the Feast of the Jews, Jesus responds to criticism from the Jewish religious leaders for healing a lame man on the Sabbath, and for referring to God as His Father (thereby making Himself equal with God).

"Truly, truly, I say to you, he who hears My word, and believes Him who sent Me, has eternal life, and does not come into judgment, but has passed out of death into life" (John 5:24; see John 3:18; 12:44).

[DEATH from died]

Setting: Capernaum of Galilee. After Jesus informs the people whom He miraculously fed with a lad's five loaves and two fish how they might receive the bread out of heaven, the Jewish religious leaders grumble because He claims that He came down out of heaven.

Therefore the Jews were grumbling about Him, because He said, "I am the bread that came down out of heaven." They were saying, "Is not this Jesus, the son of Joseph, whose father and mother we know? How does He now say, 'I have come down out of heaven'?" Jesus answered and said to them, "Do not grumble among yourselves. No one can come to Me unless the Father who sent Me draws him; and I will raise him up on the last day. It is written in the prophets, 'AND THEY SHALL ALL BE TAUGHT OF GOD.' Everyone who has heard and learned from the Father, comes to Me. Not that anyone has seen the Father, except the One who is from God; He has seen the Father. Truly, truly, I say to you, he who believes has eternal life. I am the bread of life. Your fathers ate the manna in the wilderness, and they died. This is the bread which comes down out of heaven, so that one may eat of it and not die. I am the living bread that came down out of heaven; if anyone eats of this bread, he will live forever; and the bread also which I will give for the life of the world is My flesh" (John 6:41–51, Jesus quotes from Isaiah 54:13; see John 1:18, 29; 3:36; 7:27).

[DEATH from died]
Setting: Capernaum of Galilee. After Jesus informs the people whom He miraculously fed with a lad's five loaves and two fish how they might receive the bread out of heaven, the Jewish religious leaders argue with one another when Jesus says He will give His flesh to the world to eat.

So Jesus said to them, "Truly, truly, I say to you, unless you eat the flesh of the Son of Man and drink His blood, you have no life in yourselves. He who eats My flesh and drinks My blood has eternal life, and I will raise him up on the last day. For My flesh is true food, and My blood is true drink. He who eats My flesh and drinks My blood abides in Me, and I in him. As the living Father sent Me, and I live because of the Father, so he who eats Me, he also will live because of Me. This is the bread which came down out of heaven; not as the fathers ate and died; he who eats this bread will live forever" (John 6:53–58; see Matthew 16:16; Luke 4:22; John 3:36; John 6:26–40; 9:16; 15:4).

[DEATH from will die]
Setting: The temple treasury in Jerusalem. Following the Feast of Booths and the scribes' and Pharisees' failed attempt to stone a woman for adultery, Jesus returns the next day to teach. They question His testimony about Himself.

Then He said again to them, "I go away, and you will seek Me, and will die in your sin; where I am going, you cannot come." So the Jews were saying, "Surely He will not kill Himself, will He, since He says, "Where I am going, you cannot come'?" And He was saying to them, "You are from below, I am from above; you are of this world, I am not of this world. Therefore I said to you that you will die in your sins; for unless you believe that I am *He,* you will die in your sins." So they were saying to Him, "Who are You?" Jesus said to them, "What have I been saying to you *from* the beginning? I have many things to speak and to judge concerning you, but He who sent Me is true; and the things which I heard from Him, these I speak to the world" (John 8:21–26; see John 3:31–33; 5:34, 35; 17:14, 16).

Setting: The temple treasury in Jerusalem. While Jesus interacts with the scribes and Pharisees about His testimony, their ancestry, and their motives, they state their belief He is a demon-possessed Samaritan.

Jesus answered, "I do not have a demon; but I honor My Father, and you dishonor Me. But I do not seek My glory; there is One who seeks and judges. Truly, truly, I say to you, if anyone keeps My word he will never see death" (John 8:49–51; see Matthew 16:28; John 5:41; 7:20).

Setting: The temple treasury in Jerusalem. While Jesus interacts with the scribes and Pharisees, they state their belief Jesus is a demon-possessed Samaritan because of His statement that anyone who keeps His word will never taste death.

The Jews said to Him, "Now we know that You have a demon. Abraham died, and the prophets *also;* and You say, 'If anyone keeps My word, he will never taste of death'" (John 8:52).

Setting: Beyond the Jordan. Following the Feast of Dedication and the Pharisees' desire to stone Him while in Jerusalem, Jesus hears of the sickness of Lazarus of Bethany.

But when Jesus heard *this,* He said, "This sickness is not to end in death, but for the glory of God, so that the Son of God may be glorified by it" (John 11:4).

[DEATH from fallen asleep]
Setting: Beyond the Jordan. While Jesus and His disciples are avoiding the Jerusalem Pharisees, He receives word

from Lazarus's sisters in Bethany of His friend's sickness and decides to go there.

Then after this He said to the disciples, "Let us go to Judea again." The disciples said to Him, "Rabbi, the Jews were just now seeking to stone You, and are You going there again?" Jesus answered, "Are there not twelve hours in the day? If anyone walks in the day, he does not stumble, because he sees the light of this world. But if anyone walks in the night, he stumbles, because the light is not in him." This He said, and after that He said to them, "Our friend Lazarus has fallen asleep; but I go, so that I may awaken him out of sleep" (John 11:7–11; see John 8:59; 10:39).

[DEATH from dies]
Setting: Bethany near Jerusalem. Jesus travels with His disciples to Bethany in Judea to see Lazarus's sisters, Martha and Mary, after the death of His friend.

Jesus said to her, "Your brother will rise again." Martha said to Him, "I know that he will rise again in the resurrection on the last day." Jesus said to her, "I am the resurrection and the life; he who believes in Me will live even if he dies, and everyone who lives and believes in Me will never die. Do you believe this?" (John 11:23–26; see Daniel 12:2; John 1:4; 6:47–51).

[DEATH from dies]
Setting: Jerusalem. Just days before the Passover, with the chief priests and Pharisees plotting to seize Jesus, crowds welcome Him to Jerusalem with palm branches and praise, and some Greeks ask to meet Him.

And Jesus answered them, saying, "The hour has come for the Son of Man to be glorified. Truly, truly, I say to you, unless a grain of wheat falls into the earth and dies, it remains alone; but if it dies, it bears much fruit. He who loves his life loses it, and he who hates his life in this world will keep it to life eternal. If anyone serves Me, he must follow Me; and where I am, there My servant will be also; if anyone serves Me, the Father will honor him" (John 12:23–26; see Matthew 10:39).

Setting: The island of Patmos (in the Aegean Sea about fifty miles southwest of Ephesus in modern Turkey). On the Lord's Day (Sunday), about fifty years after Jesus' resurrection, the disciple John encounters the Lord Jesus Christ. Jesus communicates a new revelation for the apostle to record for the church in Smyrna and to six other churches in Asia.

"And to the angel of the church in Smyrna write: The first and the last, who was dead, and has come to life, says this: 'I know your tribulation and your poverty (but you are rich), and the blasphemy by those who say they are Jews and are not, but are a synagogue of Satan. Do not fear what you are about to suffer. Behold, the devil is about to cast some of you into prison, so that you will be tested, and you will have tribulation for ten days. Be faithful until death, and I will give you the crown of life. He who has an ear, let him hear what the Spirit says to the churches. He who overcomes will not be hurt by the second death' (Revelation 2:8–11; see Isaiah 44:6; Revelation 1:9, 18; 2:13; 20:6, 14).

[DEATH from about to die]
Setting: The island of Patmos (in the Aegean Sea about fifty miles southwest of Ephesus in modern Turkey). On the Lord's Day (Sunday), about fifty years after Jesus' resurrection, the disciple John encounters the Lord Jesus Christ. Jesus communicates a new revelation for the apostle to record for the church in Sardis and to six other churches in Asia.

"To the angel of the church in Sardis write: He who has the seven Spirits of God and the seven stars, says this: 'I know your deeds, that you have a name that you are alive, but you are dead. Wake up, and strengthen the things that remain, which were about to die; for I have not found your deeds completed in the sight of My God. So remember what you have received and heard; and keep *it,* and repent. Therefore if you do not wake up, I will come like a thief, and you will not know at what hour I will come to you. But you have a few people in Sardis who have not soiled their garments; and they will walk with Me in white, for they are worthy. He who overcomes will thus be clothed in white garments; and I will not erase his name from the book of life, and I will confess his name before My Father and before His angels. He who has an ear, let him hear what the Spirit says to the churches'"

(Revelation 3:1–6; see Matthew 10:32; Revelation 1:16).

DEATH, ETERNAL (Also see FIRE, ETERNAL; FIRE, FURNACE OF; GOD, SEPARATION FROM; HELL; JUDGMENT; and PUNISHMENT, ETERNAL)

[ETERNAL DEATH from the gate is wide and the way is broad that leads to destruction]
Setting: Galilee. During the early part of His ministry, Jesus preaches the Sermon on the Mount to His disciples and the multitudes.

"Enter through the narrow gate; for the gate is wide and the way is broad that leads to destruction, and there are many who enter through it. For the gate is small and the way is narrow that leads to life, and there are few who find it" (Matthew 7:13, 14; cf. Luke 13:24).

DEATH, JESUS' (See CROSS; CRUCIFIXION; JESUS' WORDS WHILE ON THE CROSS; and SALVATION)

DEATH, KEYS OF

Setting: The island of Patmos (in the Aegean Sea about fifty miles southwest of Ephesus in modern Turkey). On the Lord's Day (Sunday), the disciple John encounters the Lord Jesus Christ approximately fifty years after His resurrection for the purpose of the Lord communicating new revelations for the apostle to record for the seven churches in Asia.

When I saw Him, I fell at His feet like a dead man. And He placed His right hand on me, saying, "Do not be afraid; I am the first and the last, and the living One; and I was dead, and behold, I am alive forevermore, and I have the keys of death and of Hades. Therefore write the things which you have seen, and the things which are, and the things which will take place after these things. As for the mystery of the seven stars which you saw in My right hand, and the seven golden lampstands: the seven stars are the angels of the seven churches, and the seven lampstands are the seven churches" (Revelation 1:17–20; see Isaiah 44:6; Luke 24:5; Revelation 2:8).

DEATH, POINT OF

Setting: Jerusalem. After celebrating the Passover meal with His disciples, Jesus retreats to the Garden of Gethsemane on the Mount of Olives to pray prior to His betrayal by Judas.

Then Jesus came with them to a place called Gethsemane, and said to His disciples, "Sit here while I go over there and pray." And He took with Him Peter and the two sons of Zebedee, and began to be grieved and distressed. Then He said to them, "My soul is deeply grieved, to the point of death; remain here and keep watch with Me." And He went a little beyond *them,* and fell on His face and prayed, saying, "My Father, if it is possible, let this cup pass from Me; yet not as I will, but as You will." And He came to the disciples and found them sleeping, and said to Peter, "So, you *men* could not keep watch with Me for one hour? Keep watching and praying that you may not enter into temptation; the spirit is willing, but the flesh is weak." He went away again a second time and prayed, saying, "My Father, if this cannot pass away unless I drink it, Your will be done." Again He came and found them sleeping, for their eyes were heavy. And He left them again, and went away and prayed a third time, saying the same thing once more. Then He came to the disciples and said to them, "Are you still sleeping and resting? Behold the hour is at hand and the Son of Man is being betrayed into the hands of sinners. Get up, let us be going; behold the one who betrays Me is at hand!" (Matthew 26:36–46; cf. Mark 14:32–42; Luke 22:40–46; see Matthew 20:22; John 12:27).

Setting: Gethsemane on the Mount of Olives, just east of Jerusalem. Jesus agonizes over His impending death, disappointed that His disciples keep falling asleep instead of watching and praying with Him.

They came to a place named Gethsemane; and He said to the disciples, "Sit here until I have prayed." And He took with Him Peter and James and John, and began to be very distressed and troubled. And He said to them, "My soul is deeply grieved to the point of death; remain here and keep watch." And He went a little beyond *them,* and fell to the ground and *began* to pray that if it were possible, the hour might pass Him by. And He was saying, "Abba! Father! All things are possible for You; remove this cup from Me; yet not what I will, but what You will." And He came and found them sleeping, and said to Peter, "Simon, are you asleep? Could you not keep watch for one hour? Keep watching and praying that you may not come into temptation; the spirit is willing, but the flesh is weak" (Mark 14:32–38; cf. Matthew 26:36–41; Luke 22:41–46; see Romans 8:15; Galatians 4:6).

DEATH, PREDICTION OF JESUS' (See PROPHECY OF JESUS' DEATH)

DEATH, PROPHECY OF JESUS' (See PROPHECY OF JESUS' DEATH)

DEATH, PUT TO

Setting: Galilee. After His disciples observe His ministry, Jesus summons and specifically instructs them about the upcoming difficulties of *their* ministry to the people of Israel.

"Brother will betray brother to death, and a father *his* child; and children will rise up against parents and cause them to be put to death. You will be hated by all because of My name, but it is the one who has endured to the end who will be saved. But whenever they persecute you in one city, flee to the next; for truly I say to you, you will not finish *going through* the cities of Israel until the Son of Man comes" (Matthew 10:21–23; cf. Matthew 10:35, 36; 16:27, 28; 24:9).

Setting: Galilee. Pharisees and scribes from Jerusalem question Jesus about His disciples' lack of obedience to tradition.

And He answered and said to them, "Why do you yourselves transgress the commandment of God for the sake of tradition? For God said, 'HONOR YOUR FATHER AND MOTHER,' and, 'HE WHO SPEAKS EVIL OF FATHER OR MOTHER IS TO BE PUT TO DEATH.' But you say, 'Whoever says to *his* father or mother, "Whatever I have that would help you has been given *to God*," he is not to honor his father or mother.' And *by this* you invalidated the word of God for the sake of your tradition. You hypocrites, rightly did Isaiah prophesy of you: 'THIS PEOPLE HONORS ME WITH THEIR LIPS, BUT THEIR HEART IS FAR AWAY FROM ME. BUT IN VAIN DO THEY WORSHIP ME, TEACHING AS DOCTRINES THE PRECEPTS OF MEN'" (Matthew 15:3–9, Jesus quotes from Exodus 20:12, 21:17, Leviticus 20:9; Isaiah 29:13; cf. Mark 7:5–7; see Colossians 2:22).

Setting: Galilee. The Pharisees and some of the scribes from Jerusalem question why Jesus' disciples do not follow the tradition of ceremonial hand cleansing before eating bread.

And He said to them, "Rightly did Isaiah prophesy of you hypocrites, as it is written: 'THIS PEOPLE HONORS ME WITH THEIR LIPS, BUT THEIR HEART IS FAR AWAY FROM ME. BUT IN VAIN DO THEY WORSHIP ME, TEACHING AS DOCTRINES THE PRECEPTS OF MEN.' Neglecting the commandment of God, you hold to the tradition of men." He was also saying to them, "You are experts at setting aside the commandment of God in order to keep tradition. For Moses said, 'HONOR YOUR FATHER AND YOUR MOTHER'; and, 'HE WHO SPEAKS EVIL OF FATHER OR MOTHER, IS TO BE PUT TO DEATH'; but you say, 'If a man says to *his* father or *his* mother, whatever I have that would help you is Corban (that is to say, given *to God*),' you no longer permit him to do anything for *his* father or *his* mother; *thus* invalidating the word of God by your tradition which you have handed down; and you do many things such as that" (Mark 7:6–13, Jesus quotes from Exodus 20:12; 21:17; Isaiah 29:13; cf. Matthew 15:1–6).

Setting: During His discourse on the Mount of Olives, east of the temple in Jerusalem, after prophesying the temple's destruction, Jesus responds to questions from Peter, James, John, and Andrew about future events.

And Jesus began to say to them, "See to it that no one misleads you. Many will come in My name, saying, 'I am *He!*' and will mislead many. When you hear of wars and rumors of wars, do not be frightened; *those things* must take place; but *that is* not yet the end. For nation will rise up against nation, and kingdom against kingdom; there will be earthquakes in various places; there will *also be* famines. These things are *merely* the beginning of birth pangs. But be on your guard; for they will deliver you to *the* courts, and you will be flogged in *the* synagogues, and you will stand before governors and kings for My sake, as a testimony to them. The gospel must first be preached to all the nations. When they arrest you and hand you over, do not worry beforehand about what you are to say, but say whatever is given you in that hour; for it is not you who speak, but *it is* the Holy Spirit. Brother will betray brother to death, and a father *his* child; and children will rise up against parents and have them put to death. You will be hated by all because of My name, but the one who endures to the end, he will be saved" (Mark 13:5–13; cf. Matthew 24:4–14; Luke 21:7–19; see Matthew 10:17–22).

[PUT TO DEATH from put some of you to death]
Setting: The Mount of Olives, just east of Jerusalem. While ministering in the temple, Jesus has given His disciples more details regarding the temple's future destruction. Now, He elaborates about things to come during His Olivet Discourse.

Then He continued by saying to them, "Nation will rise against nation and kingdom against kingdom, and there will be great earthquakes, and in various places plagues and famines; and there will be terrors and great signs from heaven. But before all these things, they will lay their hands on you and will persecute you, delivering you to the synagogues and prisons, bringing you before kings and governors for My name's sake. It will lead to an opportunity for your testimony. So make up your minds not to prepare beforehand to defend yourselves; for I will give you utterance and wisdom which none of your opponents will be able to resist or refute. But you will be betrayed even by parents and brothers and relatives and friends, and they will put some of you to death, and you will be hated by all because of My name. Yet not a hair of your head will perish. By your endurance you will gain your lives" (Luke 21:10–19; cf. Matthew 10:19–22; 24:7–14; Mark 13:8–13).

DEATH, RESTORATION OF A PHYSICAL BODY AFTER (See RESUSCITATION)

DEATH, SECOND

Setting: The island of Patmos (in the Aegean Sea about fifty miles southwest of Ephesus in modern Turkey). On the Lord's Day (Sunday), about fifty years after Jesus' resurrection, the disciple John encounters the Lord Jesus Christ. Jesus communicates a new revelation for the apostle to record for the church in Smyrna and to six other churches in Asia.

"And to the angel of the church in Smyrna write: The first and the last, who was dead, and has come to life, says this: 'I know your tribulation and your poverty (but you are rich), and the blasphemy by those who say they are Jews and are not, but are a synagogue of Satan. Do not fear what you are about to suffer. Behold, the devil is about to cast some of you into prison, so that you will be tested, and you will have tribulation for ten days. Be faithful until death, and I will give you the crown of life. He who has an ear, let him hear what the Spirit says to the churches. He who overcomes will not be hurt by the second death' (Revelation 2:8–11; see Isaiah 44:6; Revelation 1:9, 18; 2:13; 20:6, 14).

DEATH, SPIRITUAL

[SPIRITUAL DEATH from not die]
Setting: Capernaum of Galilee. After Jesus informs the people whom He miraculously fed with a lad's five loaves and two fish how they might receive the bread out of heaven, the Jewish religious leaders grumble because He claims that He came down out of heaven.

Therefore the Jews were grumbling about Him, because He said, "I am the bread that came down out of heaven." They were saying, "Is not this Jesus, the son of Joseph, whose father and mother we know? How does He now say, 'I have come down out of heaven'?" Jesus answered and said to them, "Do not grumble among yourselves. No one can come to Me unless the Father who sent Me draws him; and I will raise him up on the last day. It is written in the prophets, 'AND THEY SHALL ALL BE TAUGHT OF GOD.' Everyone who has heard and learned from the Father, comes to Me. Not that anyone has seen the Father, except the One who is from God; He has seen the Father. Truly, truly, I say to you, he who believes has eternal life. I am the bread of life. Your fathers ate the manna in the wilderness, and they died. This is the bread which comes down out of heaven, so that one may eat of it and not die. I am the living bread that came down out of heaven; if anyone eats of this bread, he will live forever; and the bread also which I will give for the life of the world is My flesh" (John 6:41–51, Jesus quotes from Isaiah 54:13; see John 1:18, 29; 3:36; 6:26–40, 58; 7:27).

[SPIRITUAL DEATH inferred from never die]

Setting: Bethany near Jerusalem. Jesus travels with His disciples to Bethany in Judea to see Lazarus's sisters, Martha and Mary, after the death of His friend.

Jesus said to her, "Your brother will rise again." Martha said to Him, "I know that he will rise again in the resurrection on the last day." Jesus said to her, "I am the resurrection and the life; he who believes in Me will live even if he dies, and everyone who lives and believes in Me will never die. Do you believe this?" (John 11:23–26; see Daniel 12:2; John 1:4; 6:47–51).

DEATH PENALTY (Listed under PENALTY, DEATH)

DEBT (Also see DEBTS; INTEREST; LOANS; and REPAYMENT)

[DEBT from paid up the last cent]

Setting: Galilee. During the early part of His ministry, Jesus preaches the Sermon on the Mount to His disciples and the multitudes.

"Make friends quickly with your opponent at law while you are with him on the way, so that your opponent may not hand you over to the judge, and the judge to the officer, and you be thrown into prison. Truly I say to you, you will not come out of there until you have paid up the last cent" (Matthew 5:25, 26; cf. Luke 12:58, 59).

Setting: Capernaum of Galilee. Jesus illustrates forgiveness after Peter asks Him if forgiving someone seven times who has sinned against him is adequate.

"For this reason the kingdom of heaven may be compared to a king who wished to settle accounts with his slaves. When he had begun to settle *them,* one who owed him ten thousand talents was brought to him. But since he did not have *the means* to repay, his lord commanded him to be sold, along with his wife and children and all that he had, and repayment to be made. So the slave fell *to the ground* and prostrated himself before him, saying, 'Have patience with me and I will repay you everything.' And the lord of that slave felt compassion and released him and forgave him the debt. But that slave went out and found one of his fellow slaves who owed him a hundred denarii; and he seized him and *began* to choke *him,* saying, 'Pay back what you owe.' So his fellow slave fell *to the ground* and *began* to plead with him, saying, 'Have patience with me and I will repay you.' But he was unwilling and went and threw him in prison until he should pay back what was owed. So when his fellow slaves saw what had happened, they were deeply grieved and came and reported to their lord all that had happened. Then summoning him, his lord said to him, 'You wicked slave, I forgave you all that debt because you pleaded with me. Should you not also have had mercy on your fellow slave, in the same way that I had mercy on you?' And his lord, moved with anger, handed him over to the torturers until he should repay all that was owed him. My heavenly Father will also do the same to you, if each of you does not forgive his brother from your heart" (Matthew 18:23–35; cf. Matthew 6:12, 14, 15; Luke 7:42; see Matthew 25:19–28).

[DEBT from paid the very last cent]

Setting: On the way from Galilee to Jerusalem. After chastising the crowds for being able to discern the weather but not the present age, Jesus exhorts them to settle any financial disputes outside of court.

"And why do you not even on your own initiative judge what is right? For while you are going with your opponent to appear before the magistrate, on your way there make an effort to settle with him, so that he may not drag you before the judge, and the judge turn you over to the officer, and the officer throw you into prison. I say to you, you will not get out of there until you have paid the very last cent" (Luke 12:57–59; cf. Matthew 5:25, 26).

DEBTORS (Also see DEBT; DEBTS; and INDEBTEDNESS)

Setting: Galilee. During the early part of His ministry, Jesus gives a model prayer to His disciples and the multitudes while conveying The Sermon on the Mount.

"Pray, then, in this way: 'Our Father who is in heaven, hallowed be Your name. Your kingdom come. Your will be done, on earth as it is in heaven. Give us this day our daily bread. And forgive us our debts, as we also have forgiven our debtors. And do not lead us into temptation, but deliver us from evil. [For Yours is the kingdom and the power and the glory forever. Amen]'" (Matthew

6:9–13; cf. Luke 11:2–4; see John 17:15).

Setting: Galilee. After Jesus praises John the Baptist to the crowds, Simon, a Pharisee, invites Him to dinner. A sinful woman anoints His feet with perfume, prompting the Lord to convey a parable.

And Jesus answered him, "Simon, I have something to say to you." And he replied, "Say it, Teacher." "A moneylender had two debtors: one owed five hundred denarii, and the other fifty. When they were unable to repay, he graciously forgave them both. So which of them will love him more?" Simon answered and said, "I suppose the one whom he forgave more." And He said to him, "You have judged correctly" (Luke 7:40–43; see Matthew 18:23–35).

Setting: On the way from Galilee to Jerusalem. After giving the story of the prodigal son, the Lord teaches His disciples about stewardship.

Now He was also saying to the disciples, "There was a rich man who had a manager, and this manager was reported to him as squandering his possessions. And he called him and said to him, 'What is this I hear about you? Give an accounting of your management, for you can no longer be a manager.' The manager said to himself, 'What shall I do, since my master is taking the management away from me? I am not strong enough to dig; I am ashamed to beg. I know what I shall do, so that when I am removed from the management people will welcome me into their homes.' And he summoned each one of his master's debtors, and he began saying to the first, 'How much do you owe my master?' And he said, 'A hundred measures of oil.' And he said to him, 'Take your bill, and sit down quickly and write fifty.' Then he said to another, 'And how much do you owe?' And he said, 'A hundred measures of wheat.' He said to him, 'Take your bill, and write eighty.' And his master praised the unrighteous manager because he had acted shrewdly; for the sons of this age are more shrewd in relation to their own kind than the sons of light. And I say to you, make friends for yourselves by means of the wealth of unrighteousness, so that when it fails, they will receive you into the eternal dwellings. He who is faithful in a very little thing is faithful also in much; and he who is unrighteous in a very little thing is unrighteous also in much. Therefore if you have not been faithful in the use of unrighteous wealth, who will entrust the true riches to you? And if you have not been faithful in the use of that which is another's, who will give you that which is your own? No servant can serve two masters; for either he will hate the one and love the other, or else he will be devoted to one and despise the other. You cannot serve God and wealth" (Luke 16:1–13; cf. Matthew 6:24; see Matthew 25:14–30).

DEBTORS, PARABLE OF TWO

Setting: Galilee. After Jesus praises John the Baptist to the crowds, Simon, a Pharisee, invites Jesus to dinner. A sinful woman anoints His feet with perfume, prompting the Lord to convey a parable.

And Jesus answered him, "Simon, I have something to say to you." And he replied, "Say it, Teacher." "A moneylender had two debtors: one owed five hundred denarii, and the other fifty. When they were unable to repay, he graciously forgave them both. So which of them will love him more?" Simon answered and said, "I suppose the one whom he forgave more." And He said to him, "You have judged correctly" (Luke 7:40–43; see Matthew 18:23–35).

DEBTS (Also see DEBT; DEBTORS; INDEBTEDNESS; and LOANS)

Setting: Galilee. During the early part of His ministry, Jesus gives a model prayer to His disciples and the multitudes while conveying The Sermon on the Mount.

"Pray, then, in this way: 'Our Father who is in heaven, hallowed be Your name. Your kingdom come. Your will be done, on earth as it is in heaven. Give us this day our daily bread. And forgive us our debts, as we also have forgiven our debtors. And do not lead us into temptation, but deliver us from evil. [For Yours is the kingdom and the power and the glory forever. Amen]'" (Matthew 6:9–13; cf. Luke 11:2–4; see John 17:15).

DECALOGUE (See COMMANDMENTS)

DECEIT (Also see DECEITFULNESS; and DECEPTION)

Setting: Galilee. After the Pharisees and scribes from Jerusalem question Jesus' disciples' lack of obedience to the tradition regarding ceremonial cleansing, Jesus speaks to a crowd in Galilee and explains His teaching to His disciples.

After He called the crowd to Him again, He *began* saying to them, "Listen to Me, all of you, and understand: there is nothing outside the man which can defile him if it goes into him; but the things which proceed out of the man are what defile the man. [If anyone has ears to hear, let him hear."] When he had left the crowd *and* entered the house, His disciples questioned Him about the parable. And He said to them, "Are you so lacking in understanding also? Do you not understand that whatever goes into the man from outside cannot defile him, because it does not go into his heart, but into his stomach, and is eliminated?" (*Thus He* declared all foods clean.) And He was saying, "That which proceeds out of the man, that is what defiles the man. For from within, out of the heart of men, proceed the evil thoughts, fornications, thefts, murders, adulteries, deeds of coveting *and* wickedness, *as well* as deceit, sensuality, envy, slander, pride *and* foolishness. All these evil things proceed from within and defile the man" (Mark 7:14–23; cf. Matthew 15:10–20).

Setting: Galilee. After beginning His public ministry and choosing His first disciples, Andrew and Simon (Peter) near Bethany beyond the Jordan, and Philip in Galilee, Jesus calls Philip's friend, Nathanael, (some believe he may have been also called Bartholomew) as His next follower.

Jesus saw Nathanael coming to Him, and said of him, "Behold, an Israelite indeed, in whom there is no deceit!" Nathanael said to Him, "How do you know me?" Jesus answered and said to him, "Before Philip called you, when you were under the fig tree, I saw you." Nathanael answered Him, "Rabbi, You are the Son of God; You are the King of Israel." Jesus answered and said to him, "Because I said to you that I saw you under the fig tree, do you believe? You will see greater things than these." And He said to him, "Truly, truly, I say to you, you will see the heavens opened and the angels of God ascending and descending on the Son of Man" (John 1:47–51).

DECEITFULNESS (Also see DECEIT; and DECEPTION)

Setting: By the Sea of Galilee. With the Jewish religious leadership rejecting His message, Jesus begins to teach in parables and explains to His disciples the meaning of the Parable of the Sower.

"Hear then the parable of the sower. When anyone hears the word of the kingdom and does not understand it, the evil *one* comes and snatches away what has been sown in his heart. This is the one on whom seed was sown beside the road. The one on whom seed was sown on the rocky places, this is the man who hears the word and immediately receives it with joy; yet he has no *firm* root in himself, but is *only* temporary, and when affliction or persecution arises because of the word, immediately he falls away. And the one on whom seed was sown among the thorns, this is the man who hears the word, and the worry of the world and the deceitfulness of wealth choke the word, and it becomes unfruitful. And the one on whom seed was sown on the good soil, this is the man who hears the word and understands it; who indeed bears fruit and brings forth, some a hundredfold, some sixty, and some thirty" (Matthew 13:18–23; cf. Mark 4:13–20; Luke 8:11–15; see Matthew 13:8).

Setting: By the Sea of Galilee. During the early part of His ministry, after presenting the Parable of the Sower to a very large crowd from a boat, Jesus explains the meaning of the parable to His disciples and followers.

And He said to them, "Do you not understand this parable? How will you understand all the parables? The sower sows the word. These are the ones who are beside the road where the word is sown; and when they hear, immediately Satan comes and takes away the word which has been sown in them. In a similar way these are the ones on whom seed was sown on the rocky places, who, when they hear the word, immediately receive it with joy; and they have no firm root in themselves, but are only temporary; then, when affliction or persecution arises because of the word, immediately they fall away. And others are the ones on whom seed was sown among the thorns; these are the ones who have heard the word, but the worries of the world and the deceitfulness of riches, and the desires for other things enter in and choke the word, and it becomes unfruitful. And those are the ones on whom seed was sown on the good soil; and they hear the word and accept it and bear fruit, thirty, sixty, and a hundredfold" (Mark 4:13–20; cf. Matthew 13:18–23; Luke 8:11–15).

DECEPTION (**Also see DECEIT; DECEITFULNESS; DISCERNMENT; and LYING**)

[DECEPTION from Beware of the false prophets]

Setting: Galilee. During the early part of His ministry, Jesus preaches the Sermon on the Mount to His disciples and the multitudes.

"Beware of the false prophets, who come to you in sheep's clothing, but inwardly are ravenous wolves. You will know them by their fruits. Grapes are not gathered from *bushes* nor figs from thistles, are they? So every good tree bears good fruit, but the bad tree bears bad fruit. A good tree cannot produce bad fruit, nor can a bad tree produce good fruit. Every tree that does not bear good fruit is cut down and thrown into the fire. So then, you will know them by their fruits" (Matthew 7:15–20; cf. Matthew 3:10; 12:33, 35; 24:11, 24; Luke 6:43, 44).

[DECEPTION from misleads you]

Setting: The Mount of Olives, just east of Jerusalem. During His discourse, Jesus answers His disciples' questions as to when the temple will be destroyed and Jerusalem overrun, along with the signs of His coming and the end of the age.

And Jesus answered and said to them, "See to it that no one misleads you. For many will come in My name, saying, 'I am the Christ,' and will mislead many. You will be hearing of wars and rumors of wars. See that you are not frightened, for *those things* must take place, but *that* is not yet the end. For nation will rise against nation, and kingdom against kingdom, and in various places there will be famines and earthquakes. But all these things are *merely* the beginning of birth pangs. Then they will deliver you to tribulation, and will kill you, and you will be hated by all nations because of My name. At that time many will fall away and will betray one another and hate one another. Many false prophets will arise and will mislead many. Because lawlessness is increased, most people's love will grow cold. But the one who endures to the end, he will be saved. This gospel of the kingdom shall be preached in the whole world as a testimony to all the nations, and then the end will come" (Matthew 24:4–14; cf. Jeremiah 29:8; Matthew 7:15; 10:17, 22; Mark 13:3–13; Luke 21:7–19; Revelation 6:4).

[DECEPTION from so as to mislead]

Setting: The Mount of Olives, just east of Jerusalem. During His discourse, Jesus answers His disciples' questions as to when the temple will be destroyed and Jerusalem overrun, along with the signs of His coming and the end of the age.

"Therefore when you see the ABOMINATION OF DESOLATION which was spoken of through Daniel the prophet, standing in the holy place (let the reader understand), then those who are in Judea must flee to the mountains. Whoever is on the housetop must not go down to get the things that are in his house. Whoever is in the field must not turn back to get his cloak. But woe to those who are pregnant and to those who are nursing babies in those days! But pray that your flight will not be in the winter, or on a Sabbath. For then there will be a great tribulation, such as has not occurred since the beginning of the world until now, nor ever will. Unless those days had been cut short, no life would have been saved; but for the sake of the elect those days will be cut short. Then if anyone says to you, 'Behold, here is the Christ,' or 'There *He is,*' do not believe *him.* For false Christs and false prophets will arise and will show great signs and wonders, so as to mislead, if possible, even the elect. Behold, I have told you in advance. So if they say to you, 'Behold, He is in the wilderness,' do not go out, *or,* 'Behold, He is in the inner rooms,' do not believe *them.* For just as the lightning comes from the east and flashes even to the west, so will the coming of the Son of Man be. Wherever a corpse is, there the vultures will gather" (Matthew 24:15–28, Jesus quotes from Daniel 9:27; cf. Daniel 12:1; Mark 13:14–23; Luke 17:22–31; 21:20–24; 23:29; see John 4:48).

[DECEPTION from misleads you]

Setting: During His discourse on the Mount of Olives, east of the temple in Jerusalem, after prophesying the temple's destruction, Jesus responds to questions from Peter, James, John, and Andrew about future events.

And Jesus began to say to them, "See to it that no one misleads you. Many will come in My name, saying, 'I am *He!*' and will mislead many. When you hear of wars and rumors of wars, do not be frightened; *those things* must take place; but *that is* not yet the end. For nation will rise up against nation, and kingdom against kingdom; there will be earthquakes in various places; there will *also be* famines. These things are *merely* the beginning of birth pangs. But be on your guard; for they will deliver you to *the* courts, and you will be flogged in *the* synagogues, and you will stand before governors and kings for My sake, as a testimony to them. The gospel must first be preached to all the nations. When they arrest you and hand you over, do not worry beforehand about what you are to say, but say whatever is given you in that hour; for it is not you who speak, but *it is* the Holy Spirit. Brother will betray brother to death, and a father *his* child; and children will rise up against parents and have them put to death. You will be hated by all because of My name, but the one who endures to the end, he will be saved" (Mark 13:5–13; cf. Matthew 24:4–14; Luke 21:7–19; see Matthew 10:17–22).

[DECEPTION from in order to lead astray]
Setting: During His discourse on the Mount of Olives, east of the temple in Jerusalem, after prophesying the temple's destruction, Jesus responds to questions from Peter, James, John, and Andrew about future events.

"But when you see the ABOMINATION OF DESOLATION standing where it should not be (let the reader understand), then those who are in Judea must flee to the mountains. The one who is on the housetop must not go down, or go in to get anything out of his house; and the one who is in the field must not turn back to get his coat. But woe to those who are pregnant and to those who are nursing babies in those days! But pray that it may not happen in winter. For those days will be a *time of* tribulation such as has not occurred since the beginning of the creation which God created until now, and never will. Unless the Lord had shortened *those* days, no life would have been saved; but for the sake of the elect, whom He chose, He shortened the days. And then if anyone says to you, 'Behold, here is the Christ'; or, 'Behold, *He is* there'; do not believe *him*; for false Christs and false prophets will arise, and will show signs and wonders, in order to lead astray, if possible, the elect. But take heed; behold, I have told you everything in advance" (Mark 13:14–23; cf. Matthew 24:15–28; Luke 21:20–24; see Daniel 9:27; 12:1; Luke 17:31).

[DECEPTION from misled]
Setting: The temple in Jerusalem. While Jesus ministers a few days before His crucifixion, after prophesying the future destruction of the temple during His Olivet Discourse, His disciples ask Him when this will happen.

And He said, "See to it that you are not misled; for many will come in My name, saying, 'I am He,' and, 'The time is near.' Do not go after them. When you hear of wars and disturbances, do not be terrified; for these things must take place first, but the end does not follow immediately" (Luke 21:8, 9; cf. Matthew 24:4–8; Mark 13:5–8).

[DECEPTION from leads My bond-servants astray]
Setting: The island of Patmos (in the Aegean Sea about fifty miles southwest of Ephesus in modern Turkey). On the Lord's Day (Sunday), about fifty years after Jesus' resurrection, the disciple John encounters the Lord Jesus Christ. Jesus communicates a new revelation for the apostle to record for the church in Thyatira and to six other churches in Asia.

"And to the angel of the church in Thyatira write: The Son of God, who has eyes like a flame of fire, and His feet are like burnished bronze, says this: 'I know your deeds, and your love and faith and service and perseverance, and that your deeds of late are greater than at first. But I have *this* against you, that you tolerate the woman Jezebel, who calls herself a prophetess, and she teaches and leads My bond-servants astray so that they commit *acts of* immorality and eat things sacrificed to idols. I gave her time to repent, and she does not want to repent of her immorality. Behold, I will throw her on a bed *of sickness,* and those who commit adultery with her into great tribulation, unless they repent of her deeds. And I will kill her children with pestilence, and all the churches will know that I am He who searches the minds and hearts; and I will give to each one of you according to your deeds. But I say to you, the rest who are in Thyatira, who do not hold this teaching, who have not known the deep things of Satan, as they call them—I place no other burden on you. Nevertheless what you have, hold fast until I come. He who overcomes, and he who keeps My deeds until the end, TO HIM I WILL GIVE AUTHORITY OVER THE NATIONS; AND HE SHALL RULE THEM WITH A ROD OF IRON, AS THE VESSELS OF THE POTTER ARE BROKEN TO PIECES, as I also have received *authority* from My Father; and I will give him the morning star. He who has an ear, let him hear what the Spirit says to the churches' (Revelation 2:18–29; Jesus quotes from Psalm 2:8, 9; Isaiah 30:14; see 1 Kings 16:31; Psalm 7:9; Romans 2:5; 1 Corinthians 2:10; 2 Peter 3:9; Revelation 1:14; 2:7; 3:11; 17:1–20).

DECISIVENESS

[DECISIVENESS from let your statement be 'Yes, yes' or 'No, no']

Setting: Galilee. During the early part of His ministry, Jesus preaches the Sermon on the Mount to His disciples and the multitudes.

"Again, you have heard that the ancients were told, 'YOU SHALL NOT MAKE FALSE VOWS, BUT SHALL FULFILL YOUR VOWS TO THE LORD.' But I say to you, make no oath at all, either by heaven, for it is the throne of God, or by the earth, for it is the footstool of His feet, or by Jerusalem, for it is THE CITY OF THE GREAT KING. Nor shall you make an oath by your head, for you cannot make one hair white or black. But let your statement be 'Yes, yes' *or* 'No, no'; anything beyond these is of evil" (Matthew 5:33–37, Jesus quotes from Leviticus 19:12, Psalm 48:2; Isaiah 66:1; cf. James 5:12).

DEDICATED TO GOD (See CORBAN)

DEDICATION (See DEVOTION)

DEED (DEED, GOOD is a separate entry; also see DEEDS)

Setting: The temple in Jerusalem. After receiving encouragement from His blood brothers in Galilee to attend the upcoming Feast of Booths to demonstrate His works to His disciples and the world, Jesus goes and teaches, astonishing the Jewish religious leaders.

Jesus answered them, "I did one deed, and you all marvel. For this reason Moses has given you circumcision (not because it is from Moses, but from the fathers), and on *the* Sabbath you circumcise a man. If a man receives circumcision on *the* Sabbath so that the Law of Moses will not be broken, are you angry with Me because I made an entire man well on *the* Sabbath? Do not judge according to appearance, but judge with righteous judgment" (John 7:21–24; see Genesis 17:10–14; Leviticus 12:3; 19:15; Matthew 12:2; John 5:2–16; 7–20; 7:10–15).

DEED, GOOD (Also see DEEDS, GOOD; GOOD, DOING; and WORKS, GOOD)

Setting: The home of Simon the leper in Bethany. Jesus rebukes His disciples after they criticize a woman for pouring a costly vial of perfume on Jesus' head in preparation for His burial.

But Jesus, aware of this, said to them, "Why do you bother the woman? For she has done a good deed to Me. For you always have the poor with you; but you do not always have Me. For when she poured this perfume on My body, she did it to prepare Me for burial. Truly I say to you, wherever this gospel is preached in the whole world, what this woman has done will also be spoken of in memory of her" (Matthew 26:10–13; cf. Mark 14:3–9; Luke 7:37–39; John 12:2–8; see Deuteronomy 15:11; Matthew 26:6–9).

Setting: The home of Simon the Leper in Bethany. Two days before the Feast of Unleavened Bread (Passover), Jesus commends a woman who anoints His head with costly perfume, which some there think should have been sold and the proceeds given to the poor.

But Jesus said, "Let her alone; why do you bother her? She has done a good deed to Me. For you always have the poor with you, and whenever you wish you can do good to them; but you do not always have Me. She has done what she could; she has anointed My body beforehand for the burial. Truly I say to you, wherever the gospel is preached in the whole world, what this woman has done will also be spoken of in memory of her" (Mark 14:6–9; cf. Matthew 26:6–13; John 12:2–8; see Deuteronomy 15:11; Mark 14:1–5).

DEEDS (Specifics such as DEEDS, EVIL; and DEEDS, GOOD are separate entries; also see DEED; FRUIT; and WORKS)

[DEEDS from practicing your righteousness]

Setting: On a mountain in Galilee. During the early part of His ministry, Jesus preaches the Sermon on the Mount to His disciples and the multitudes.

"Beware of practicing your righteousness before men to be noticed by them; otherwise you have no reward with your Father who is in heaven" (Matthew 6:1; cf. Matthew 6:5, 16).

[DEEDS from did we not prophesy in Your name, and in Your name cast out demons, and in Your name perform many miracles]

Setting: On a mountain in Galilee. During the early part of His ministry, Jesus preaches the Sermon on the Mount to His disciples and the multitudes.

"Not everyone who says to Me, 'Lord, Lord,' will enter the kingdom of heaven, but he who does the will of My Father who is in heaven *will enter.* Many will say to Me on that day, 'Lord, Lord, did we not prophesy in Your name, and in Your name cast out demons, and in Your name perform many miracles?' And then I will declare to them, 'I never knew you, DEPART FROM ME, YOU WHO PRACTICE LAWLESSNESS'"(Matthew 7:21–23, Jesus quotes from Psalm 6:8; cf. Matthew 25:11–13; see Luke 6:46).

Setting: After praising John the Baptist as His forerunner, Jesus demonstrates the foolish thinking of the current generation of Jewish religious leaders by repeating what they say about John's ascetic lifestyle and ministry along with His own.

"But to what shall I compare this generation? It is like children sitting in the market places, who call out to the other *children,* and say, 'We played the flute for you, and you did not dance; we sang a dirge, and you did not mourn.' For John came neither eating nor drinking, and they say, 'He has a demon!' The Son of Man came eating and drinking, and they say, 'Behold, a gluttonous man and a drunkard, a friend of tax collectors and sinners! Yet wisdom is vindicated by her deeds" (Matthew 11:16–19; cf. Luke 7:31–35; see Matthew 9:11, 34; Luke 1:15).

Setting: Near Caesarea Philippi. After rebuking Peter for trying to forbid Him to accomplish His earthly mission of dying and being resurrected, Jesus teaches His disciples about the costs of discipleship.

Then Jesus said to His disciples, "If anyone wishes to come after Me, he must deny himself, and take up his cross and follow Me. For whoever wishes to save his life will lose it; but whoever loses his life for My sake will find it. For what will it profit a man if he gains the whole world and forfeits his soul? Or what will a man give in exchange for his soul? For the Son of Man is going to come in the glory of His Father with His angels, and WILL THEN REPAY EVERY MAN ACCORDING TO HIS DEEDS. Truly, I say to you, there are some of you who are standing here who will not taste death until they see the Son of Man coming in His kingdom" (Matthew 16:24–28, Jesus quotes from Psalm 62:12; cf. Mark 8:34–37; Luke 9:23–27; see Matthew 10:38, 39).

Setting: The temple in Jerusalem. Jesus exposes to the crowds and His disciples the truth about Pharisaism after the Jewish religious leaders test Him with questions.

Then Jesus spoke to the crowds and to His disciples, saying: "The scribes and the Pharisees have seated themselves in the chair of Moses; therefore all that they tell you, do and observe, but do not do according to their deeds; for they say *things* and do not do *them.* They tie up heavy burdens and lay them on men's shoulders, but they themselves are unwilling to move them with *so much as* a finger. But they do all their deeds to be noticed by men; for they broaden their phylacteries and lengthen their tassels *of their garments.* They love the place of honor at banquets and the chief seats in the synagogues, and respectful greetings in the market places, and being called Rabbi by men. But do not be called Rabbi; for One is your Teacher, and you are all brothers. Do not call *anyone* on earth your father; for One is your Father, He who is in heaven. Do not be called leaders; for One is your Leader, *that is,* Christ. But the greatest among you shall be your servant. Whoever exalts himself shall be humbled; and whoever humbles himself shall be exalted" (Matthew 23:1–12; cf. Matthew 20:26; Mark 12:38–40; Luke 20:46, 47; see Exodus 13:9; Deuteronomy 33:3; Matthew 6:1, 5, 6, 9, 16; Mark 14:11; Luke 11:43; 14:11).

Setting: Galilee. After the Pharisees and scribes from Jerusalem question Jesus' disciples' lack of obedience to the tradition regarding ceremonial cleansing, Jesus speaks to a crowd and explains His teaching to His disciples.

After He called the crowd to Him again, He *began* saying to them, "Listen to Me, all of you, and understand: there is nothing outside the man which can defile him if it goes into him; but the things which proceed out of the man are what defile the man. [If anyone has ears to hear, let him hear."] When he had left the crowd *and* entered the house, His disciples questioned Him about the parable. And He said to them, "Are you so lacking in understanding also? Do you not understand that whatever goes into the man from outside cannot defile him, because it does not go into his heart, but into his stomach, and is eliminated?" (*Thus He* declared all foods clean.) And He was saying, "That which proceeds out of the man, that is what defiles the man. For from within, out of the heart of men, proceed the evil thoughts, fornications, thefts, murders, adulteries, deeds of coveting *and* wickedness, *as well* as deceit, sensuality, envy, slander, pride *and* foolishness. All these evil things proceed from within and defile the man" (Mark 7:14–23; cf. Matthew 15:10–20).

Setting: On the way from Galilee to Jerusalem. After Jesus pronounces woes upon the Pharisees, a lawyer replies that His remarks are an insult to lawyers, too.

But He said, "Woe to you lawyers as well! For you weigh men down with burdens hard to bear, while you yourselves will not even touch the burdens with one of your fingers. Woe to you! For you build the tombs of the prophets, and it was your fathers who killed them. So you are witnesses and approve the deeds of your fathers; because it was they who killed them, and you build their tombs. For this reason also the wisdom of God said, 'I will send them prophets and apostles, and some of them they will kill and some they will persecute, so that the blood of all the prophets, shed since the foundation of the world, may be charged against this generation, from the blood of Abel to the blood of Zechariah, who was killed between the altar and the house of God; yes, I tell you, it shall be charged against this generation.' Woe to you lawyers! For you have taken away the key of knowledge; you yourselves did not enter, and you hindered those who were entering" (Luke 11:46–52; cf. Matthew 23:29–32; see 2 Chronicles 24:20, 21Matthew 23:4, 13; Luke 11:45, 53–54).

Setting: On the way from Galilee to Jerusalem. When Jesus uses a parable to challenge the crowd and His disciples to be ready for His return, Peter asks Him whom He is addressing.

And the Lord said, "Who then is the faithful and sensible steward, whom his master will put in charge of his servants, to give them their rations at the proper time? Blessed is that slave whom his master finds so doing when he comes. Truly I say to you that he will put him in charge of all his possessions. But if that slave says in his heart, 'My master will be a long time in coming,' and begins to beat the slaves, both men and women, and to eat and drink and get drunk; the master of that slave will come on a day when he does not expect him and at an hour he does not know, and will cut him in pieces, and assign him a place with the unbelievers. And that slave who knew his master's will and did not get ready or act in accord with his will, will receive many lashes, but the one who did know it, and committed deeds worthy of flogging, will receive but few. From everyone who has been given much, much will be required; and to whom they entrusted much, of him they will ask all the more" (Luke 12:42–48; cf. Matthew 24:45–51; see Leviticus 5:17).

Setting: Jerusalem. Before the Passover of the Jews, after the Lord cleanses the temple, a Pharisee, Nicodemus, asks Him by night the meaning of "born again."

"For God so loved the world, that He gave His only begotten Son, that whoever believes in Him shall not perish, but have eternal life. For God did not send the Son into the world to judge the world, but that the world might be saved through Him. He who believes in Him is not judged; he who does not believe has been judged already, because he has not believed in the name of the only begotten Son of God. This is the judgment, that the Light has come into the world, and men loved darkness rather than the Light, for their deeds were evil. For everyone who does evil hates the Light, and does not come to the Light for fear that his deeds will be exposed. But he who practices the truth comes to the Light, so that his deeds may be manifested as having been wrought in God" (John 3:16–21; see Luke 19:10; John 1:4; 1:18; 3:1–15; Romans 5:8; 1 John 1:6, 7).

Setting: The temple treasury in Jerusalem. After the scribes and Pharisees question His testimony about Himself, Jesus interacts with them regarding their ancestry and motives.

They answered and said to Him, "Abraham is our father." Jesus said to them, "If you are Abraham's children, do the deeds of Abraham. But as it is, you are seeking to kill Me, a man who has told you the truth, which I heard from God; this Abraham did not do. You are doing the deeds of your father." They said to Him, "We were not born of fornication; we have one Father: God" (John 8:39–41; see John 8:1–38; Romans 9:6, 7).

Setting: The island of Patmos (in the Aegean Sea about fifty miles southwest of Ephesus in modern Turkey). On the Lord's Day (Sunday), about fifty years after Jesus' resurrection, the disciple John encounters the Lord Jesus Christ. Jesus communicates a new revelation for the apostle to record for the church in Ephesus and to six other churches in Asia.

"To the angel of the church in Ephesus write: The One who holds the seven stars in His right hand, the One who walks among the seven golden lampstands, says this: 'I know your deeds and your toil and perseverance, and that you cannot tolerate evil men, and you put to the test those who call themselves apostles, and they are not, and you found them *to be* false; and you have perseverance and have endured for My name's sake, and have not grown weary. But I have *this* against you, that you have left your first love. Therefore remember from where you have fallen, and repent and do the deeds you did at first; or else I am coming to you and will remove your lampstand out of its place—unless you repent. Yet this you do have, that you hate the deeds of the Nicolaitans, which I also hate. He who has an ear, let him hear what the Spirit says to the churches. To him who overcomes, I will grant to eat of the tree of life which is in the Paradise of God'" (Revelation 2:1–7; see Genesis 2:9; Ezekiel 28:13; 1 John 4:1; Revelation 1:10, 11, 19, 20; 2:15, 16).

Setting: The island of Patmos (in the Aegean Sea about fifty miles southwest of Ephesus in modern Turkey). On the Lord's Day (Sunday), about fifty years after Jesus' resurrection, the disciple John encounters the Lord Jesus Christ. Jesus communicates a new revelation for the apostle to record for the church in Thyatira and to six other churches in Asia.

"And to the angel of the church in Thyatira write: The Son of God, who has eyes like a flame of fire, and His feet are like burnished bronze, says this: 'I know your deeds, and your love and faith and service and perseverance, and that your deeds of late are greater than at first. But I have this against you, that you tolerate the woman Jezebel, who calls herself a prophetess, and she teaches and leads My bond-servants astray so that they commit acts of immorality and eat things sacrificed to idols. I gave her time to repent, and she does not want to repent of her immorality. Behold, I will throw her on a bed of sickness, and those who commit adultery with her into great tribulation, unless they repent of her deeds. And I will kill her children with pestilence, and all the churches will know that I am He who searches the minds and hearts; and I will give to each one of you according to your deeds. But I say to you, the rest who are in Thyatira, who do not hold this teaching, who have not known the deep things of Satan, as they call them—I place no other burden on you. Nevertheless what you have, hold fast until I come. He who overcomes, and he who keeps My deeds until the end, TO HIM I WILL GIVE AUTHORITY OVER THE NATIONS; AND HE SHALL RULE THEM WITH A ROD OF IRON, AS THE VESSELS OF THE POTTER ARE BROKEN TO PIECES, as I also have received authority from My Father; and I will give him the morning star. He who has an ear, let him hear what the Spirit says to the churches' (Revelation 2:18–29; Jesus quotes from Psalm 2:8, 9; Isaiah 30:14; see 1 Kings 16:31; Psalm 7:9; Romans 2:5; 1 Corinthians 2:10; 2 Peter 3:9; Revelation 1:14; 2:7; 3:11; 17:1–20).

Setting: The island of Patmos (in the Aegean Sea about fifty miles southwest of Ephesus in modern Turkey). On the Lord's Day (Sunday), about fifty years after Jesus' resurrection, the disciple John encounters the Lord Jesus Christ. Jesus communicates a new revelation for the apostle to record for the church in Sardis and to six other churches in Asia.

"To the angel of the church in Sardis write: He who has the seven Spirits of God and the seven stars, says this: 'I know your deeds, that you have a name that you are alive, but you are dead. Wake up, and strengthen the things that remain, which were about to die; for I have not found your deeds completed in the sight of My God. So remember what you have received and heard; and keep *it,* and repent. Therefore if you do not wake up, I will come like a thief, and you will not know at what hour I will come to you. But you have a few people in Sardis who have not soiled their garments; and they will walk with Me in white, for they are worthy. He who overcomes will thus be clothed in white garments; and I will not erase his name from the book of life, and I will confess his name before My Father and before His angels. He who has an ear, let him hear what the Spirit says to the churches'" (Revelation 3:1–6; see Matthew 10:32; Revelation 1:16).

Setting: The island of Patmos (in the Aegean Sea about fifty miles southwest of Ephesus in modern Turkey). On the Lord's Day (Sunday), about fifty years after Jesus' resurrection, the disciple John encounters the Lord Jesus Christ. Jesus communicates a new revelation for the apostle to record for the church in Philadelphia and to six other churches in Asia.

"And to the angel of the church in Philadelphia write: He who is holy, who is true, who has the key of David, who opens and no one will shut, and who shuts and no one opens, says this: 'I know your deeds. Behold, I have put before you an open door which no one can shut, because you have a little power, and have kept My word, and have not denied My name. Behold, I will cause *those* of the synagogue of Satan, who say that they are Jews and are not, but lie—I will make them come and bow down at your feet, and *make them* know that I have loved you. Because you have kept the word of My perseverance, I also will keep you from the hour of testing, that *hour* which is about to come upon the whole world, to test those who dwell on the earth. I am coming quickly; hold fast what you have, so that no one will take your crown. He who overcomes, I will make him a pillar in the temple of My God, and he will not go out from it anymore; and I will write on him the name of My God, and the name of the city of My God, the new Jerusalem, which comes down out of heaven from My God, and My new name. He who has an ear, let him hear what the Spirit says to the churches'" (Revelation 3:7–13; see Isaiah 22:22; Galatians 2:9; Revelation 2:9, 10, 13, 25; 14:1).

Setting: The island of Patmos (in the Aegean Sea about fifty miles southwest of Ephesus in modern Turkey). On the Lord's Day (Sunday), about fifty years after Jesus' resurrection, the disciple John encounters the Lord Jesus Christ. Jesus communicates a new revelation for the apostle to record for the church in Laodicea and to six other churches in Asia.

"To the angel of the church in Laodicea write: The Amen, the faithful and true Witness, the Beginning of the creation of God, says this: 'I know your deeds, that you are neither cold nor hot; I wish that you were cold or hot. So because you are lukewarm, and neither hot nor cold, I will spit you out of My mouth. Because you say, "I am rich, and have become wealthy, and have need of nothing," and you do not know that you are wretched and miserable and poor and blind and naked, I advise you to buy from Me gold refined by fire so that you may become rich, and white garments so that you may clothe yourself, and *that* the shame of your nakedness will not be revealed; and eye salve to anoint your eyes so that you may see. Those whom I love, I reprove and discipline; therefore be zealous and repent. Behold, I stand at the door and knock; if anyone hears My voice and opens the door, I will come in to him and will dine with him, and he with Me. He who overcomes, I will grant to him to sit down with Me on My throne, as I also overcame and sat down with My Father on His throne. He who has an ear, let him hear what the Spirit says to the churches'" (Revelation 3:14–22; see Proverbs 3:12; Hosea 12:8; John 14:23; 16:33).

DEEDS, EVIL

Setting: Jerusalem. During the Feast of the Jews, Jesus responds to criticism from the Jewish religious leaders by referring to God as His Father (thereby making Himself equal with God) and prophesying His participation in the resurrection and judgment of men.

"Truly, truly, I say to you, an hour is coming and now is, when the dead will hear the voice of the Son of God, and those who hear will live. For just as the Father has life in Himself, even so He gave to the Son also to have life in Himself; and He gave Him authority to execute judgment, because He is *the* Son of Man. Do not marvel at this; for an hour is coming, in which all who are in the tombs will hear His voice, and will come forth; those who did the good *deeds* to a resurrection of life, those who committed the evil *deeds* to a resurrection of judgment" (John 5:25–29; see Daniel 12:2; John 1:4; 5:18–24; 11:24).

[EVIL DEEDS from deeds are evil]

Setting: Capernaum of Galilee. Jesus' blood brothers, who do not yet believe in Him, encourage Him to attend the upcoming Feast of Booths in Jerusalem in order to demonstrate His works to His disciples and the world.

So Jesus said to them, "My time is not yet here, but your time is always opportune. The world cannot hate you, but it hates Me because I testify of it, that its deeds are evil. Go up to the feast yourselves; I do not go up to this feast because My time has not yet fully come" (John 7:6–8; see John 3:19, 20; 7:1–5; 15:18–20).

DEEDS, GOOD (Also see DEED, GOOD; GOOD, DOING; and WORKS, GOOD)

Setting: Jerusalem. During the Feast of the Jews, Jesus responds to criticism from the Jewish religious leaders by referring to God as His Father (thereby making Himself equal with God) and prophesying His participation in the resurrection and judgment of men.

"Truly, truly, I say to you, an hour is coming and now is, when the dead will hear the voice of the Son of God, and those who hear will live. For just as the Father has life in Himself, even so He gave to the Son also to have life in Himself; and He gave Him authority to execute judgment, because He is *the* Son of Man. Do not marvel at this; for an hour is coming, in which all who are in the tombs will hear His voice, and will come forth; those who did the good *deeds* to a resurrection of life, those who committed the evil *deeds* to a resurrection of judgment" (John 5:25–29; see Daniel 12:2; John 1:4; 5:18–24; 11:24).

DEEDS OF COVETING (Listed under COVETING, DEEDS OF)

DEEP THINGS (Listed under THINGS, DEEP)

DEFENSE

Setting: On the way from Galilee to Jerusalem. Jesus warns His disciples of future events as the scribes and Pharisees turn hostile and question Him in an attempt to catch Him in something He might say.

"And I say to you, everyone who confesses Me before men, the Son of Man will confess him also before the angels of God; but he who denies Me before men will be denied before the angels of God. And everyone who speaks a word against the Son of Man, it will be forgiven him; but he who blasphemes against the Holy Spirit, it will not be forgiven him. When they bring you before the synagogues and the rulers and the authorities, do not worry about how or what you are to speak in your defense, or what you are to say; for the Holy Spirit will teach you in that very hour what you ought to say" (Luke 12:8–12; cf. Matthew 10:32, 33; 12:31, 32; see Matthew 10:20).

[DEFENSE from defend yourselves]

Setting: The Mount of Olives, east of the temple in Jerusalem. After giving His disciples more details about the temple's coming destruction, Jesus elaborates about other future events during His Olivet Discourse.

Then He continued by saying to them, "Nation will rise against nation and kingdom against kingdom, and there will be great earthquakes, and in various places plagues and famines; and there will be terrors and great signs from heaven. But before all these things, they will lay their hands on you and will persecute you, delivering you to the synagogues and prisons, bringing you before kings and governors for My name's sake. It will lead to an opportunity for your testimony. So make up your minds not to prepare beforehand to defend yourselves; for I will give you utterance and wisdom which none of your opponents will be able to resist or refute. But you will be betrayed even by parents and brothers and relatives and friends, and they will put some of you to death, and you will be hated by all because of My name. Yet not a hair of your head will perish. By your endurance you will gain your lives" (Luke 21:10–19; cf. Matthew 10:19–22; 24:7–14; Mark 13:8–13; see Luke 21:5–9).

DEFILEMENT

[DEFILEMENT from defiles]

Setting: Galilee. Jesus instructs the crowd after the Pharisees and scribes ask Him about His disciples' lack of obedience to tradition and the commandments.

After Jesus called the crowd to Him, He said to them, "Hear and understand. *It is* not what enters into the mouth *that* defiles the man, but what proceeds out of the mouth, this defiles the man" (Matthew 15:10, 11; cf. Matthew 15:18).

[DEFILEMENT from defile]
Setting: Galilee. Jesus explains the meaning of His instruction to the crowd about what defiles a man.

Peter said to Him, "Explain the parable to us." Jesus said, "Are you still lacking in understanding also? Do you not understand that everything that goes into the mouth passes into the stomach and is eliminated? But the things that proceed out of the mouth come from the heart, and those defile the man. For out of the heart come evil thoughts, murders, adulteries, fornications, thefts, false witness, slanders. These are the things which defile a man; but to eat with unwashed hands does not defile the man" (Matthew 15:15–20; cf. Mark 7:18–23; see Galatians 5:19–21).

[DEFILEMENT from defile and defiles]
Setting: Galilee. After the Pharisees and scribes from Jerusalem question Jesus' disciples' lack of obedience to the tradition regarding ceremonial cleansing, Jesus speaks to a crowd and explains His teaching to His disciples.

After He called the crowd to Him again, He *began* saying to them, "Listen to Me, all of you, and understand: there is nothing outside the man which can defile him if it goes into him; but the things which proceed out of the man are what defile the man. [If anyone has ears to hear, let him hear."] When he had left the crowd *and* entered the house, His disciples questioned Him about the parable. And He said to them, "Are you so lacking in understanding also? Do you not understand that whatever goes into the man from outside cannot defile him, because it does not go into his heart, but into his stomach, and is eliminated?" (*Thus He* declared all foods clean.) And He was saying, "That which proceeds out of the man, that is what defiles the man. For from within, out of the heart of men, proceed the evil thoughts, fornications, thefts, murders, adulteries, deeds of coveting *and* wickedness, *as well* as deceit, sensuality, envy, slander, pride *and* foolishness. All these evil things proceed from within and defile the man" (Mark 7:14–23; cf. Matthew 15:10–20).

DEFRAUD

Setting: Judea beyond the Jordan (Perea). After demonstrating to His disciples the importance of little children, Jesus encounters a rich man seeking eternal life.

And Jesus said to him, "Why do you call Me good? No one is good except God alone. You know the commandments, 'DO NOT MURDER, DO NOT COMMIT ADULTERY, DO NOT STEAL, DO NOT BEAR FALSE WITNESS, Do not defraud, HONOR YOUR FATHER AND MOTHER.'" And he said to Him, "Teacher, I have kept all these things from my youth up." Looking at him, Jesus felt a love for him and said to him, "One thing you lack: go and sell all you possess and give to the poor, and you will have treasure in heaven; and come, follow Me" (Mark 10:18–21; Jesus quotes from Exodus 20:12–16; cf. Matthew 19:16–22; Luke 18:18–24; see Matthew 6:20; Mark 10:17, 22).

DEGREES OF PUNISHMENT (Listed under PUNISHMENT, DEGREES OF)

DELEGATION

Setting: On the way from Galilee to Jerusalem. After responding to a guest's proclamation about the blessings of eating bread in the kingdom of God, Jesus presents to large crowds the demands of discipleship.

Now large crowds were going along with Him; and He turned and said to them, "If anyone comes to Me, and does not hate his own father and mother and wife and children and brothers and sisters, yes, and even his own life, he cannot be My disciple. Whoever does not carry his own cross and come after Me cannot be My disciple. For which one of you, when he wants to build a tower, does not first sit down and calculate the cost to see if he has enough to complete it? Otherwise, when he has laid a foundation and is not able to finish, all who observe it begin to ridicule him, saying, 'This man began to build and was not able to finish.' Or what king, when he sets out to meet another king in battle, will not first sit down and consider whether he is strong enough with ten thousand *men* to encounter the one coming against him with twenty thousand? Or else, while the other is still far away, he sends a delegation and asks for terms of peace. So then, none of you can be My disciple who does not give up all his possessions. Therefore, salt is good; but if even salt has become tasteless, with what will it be seasoned? It is useless either for the soil or for the manure pile; it is thrown out. He who has ears to hear, let him hear" (Luke 14:25–35; cf. Matthew 5:13; 10:37–39; see Proverbs 20:18; Luke 14:1, 2, 15, 25; Philippians 3:7).

Setting: Jericho, on the way to Jerusalem. After commending Zaccheus's faith in Him, Jesus provides a parable about stewardship.

So He said, "A nobleman went to a distant country to receive a kingdom for himself, and then return. And he called ten of his slaves, and gave them ten minas and said to them, 'Do business with this until I come back.' But his citizens hated him and sent a delegation after him, saying, 'We do not want this man to reign over us.' When he returned, after receiving the kingdom, he ordered that these slaves, to whom he had given the money, be called to him so that he might know what business they had done. The first appeared, saying, 'Master, your mina has made ten minas more.' And he said to him, 'Well done, good slave, because you have been faithful in a very little thing, you are to be in authority over ten cities.' The second came, saying, 'Your mina, master, has made five minas.' And he said to him, also, 'And you are to be over five cities.' Another came, saying, 'Master, here is your mina, which I kept put away in a handkerchief; for I was afraid of you, because you are an exacting man; you take up what you did not lay down and reap what you did not sow.' He said to him, 'By your own words I will judge you, you worthless slave. Did you know that I am an exacting man, taking up what I did not lay down and reaping what I did not sow? Then why did you not put my money in the bank, and having come, I would have collected it with interest?' Then he said to the bystanders, 'Take the mina away from him and give it to the one who has the ten minas.' And they said to him, 'Master, he has ten minas already.' I tell you that to everyone who has, more shall be given, but from the one who does not have, even what he does have shall be taken away. But these enemies of mine, who did not want me to reign over them, bring them here and slay them in my presence" (Luke 19:12–27; cf. Matthew 25:14–30; see Matthew 13:12; Luke 16:10).

DELIBERATION

[DELIBERATION from Are you deliberating]

Setting: Jerusalem. Before the Passover, after warning His disciples of the persecution they will face after His departure to heaven, empathizing with their sadness over His prophecies, Jesus gives them assurance for the future.

"A little while, and you will no longer see Me; and again a little while, and you will see Me." *Some* of His disciples then said to one another, "What is this thing He is telling us, 'A little while, and you will not see Me; and again a little while, and you will see Me'; and, 'because I go to the Father'?" So they were saying, "What is this that He says, 'A little while'? We do not know what He is talking about." Jesus knew that they wished to question Him, and He said to them, "Are you deliberating together about this, that I said, 'A little while, and you will not see Me, and again a little while, and you will see Me'? Truly, truly, I say to you, that you will weep and lament, but the world will rejoice; you will grieve, but your grief will be turned into joy. Whenever a woman is in labor she has pain, because her hour has come; but when she gives birth to the child, she no longer remembers the anguish because of the joy that a child has been born into the world. Therefore you too have grief now; but I will see you again, and your heart will rejoice, and no one *will* take your joy away from you" (John 16:16–22; see Mark 9:32; Luke 23:27; John 14:18–24; 16:5–6; 20:20).

DELIVERANCE FROM EVIL (Listed under EVIL, DELIVERANCE FROM)

DELIVERANCE FROM PERIL (See ENDURANCE)

DEMANDS OF DISCIPLESHIP (See DISCIPLESHIP; FOLLOWING JESUS CHRIST; and SACRIFICE, PERSONAL)

DEMON (Also see DEMONS; SPIRIT, EVIL; SPIRIT, UNCLEAN; and SPIRITS, EVIL)

Setting: Galilee. After praising John the Baptist as His forerunner, Jesus demonstrates the foolish thinking of the current generation of Jewish religious leaders by repeating what they say about John's ascetic lifestyle and ministry along with His own.

"But to what shall I compare this generation? It is like children sitting in the market places, who call out to the other *children,* and say, 'We played the flute for you, and you did not dance; we sang a dirge, and you did not mourn.' For John came neither eating nor drinking, and they say, 'He has a demon!' The Son of Man came eating and drinking, and they say, 'Behold, a gluttonous man and a drunkard, a friend of tax collectors and sinners! Yet wisdom is vindicated by her deeds" (Matthew 11:16–19; cf. Luke 7:31–35; see Matthew 9:11, 34; Luke 1:15).

Setting: The region of Tyre. After the Pharisees and scribes from Jerusalem question Jesus' disciples' lack of obedience to tradition in Galilee, Jesus casts out a demon from the daughter of a Gentile (Syrophoenician) woman.

And He was saying to her, "Let the children be satisfied first, for it is not good to take the children's bread and throw it to the dogs." But she answered and said to Him, "Yes, Lord *but* even the dogs under the table feed on the children's crumbs. And He said to her, "Because of this answer go; the demon has gone out of your daughter" (Mark 7:27–29; cf. Matthew 15:21–28; see Mark 7:24–26).

Setting: Galilee. After praising John the Baptist to the crowds, Jesus criticizes the Pharisees and lawyers who reject God's purpose and John's message.

"To what then shall I compare the men of this generation, and what are they like? They are like children who sit in the market place and call to one another, and they say, 'We played the flute for you, and you did not dance; we sang a dirge, and you did not weep.' For John the Baptist has come eating no bread and drinking no wine, and you say, 'He has a demon!' The Son of Man has come eating and drinking, and you say, 'Behold, a gluttonous man and a drunkard, a friend of tax collectors and sinners!' Yet wisdom is vindicated by all her children" (Luke 7:31–35; cf. Matthew 11:16–19; see Luke 1:15, 7:29, 30).

Setting: The temple treasury in Jerusalem. While Jesus interacts with the scribes and Pharisees about His testimony, their ancestry, and their motives, they state their belief He is a demon-possessed Samaritan.

Jesus answered, "I do not have a demon; but I honor My Father, and you dishonor Me. But I do not seek My glory; there is One who seeks and judges. Truly, truly, I say to you, if anyone keeps My word he will never see death" (John 8:49–51; see Matthew 16:28; John 5:41; 7:20; 8:1–48).

DEMON POSSESSION (Also see DEMON; DEMONS; DEMONS, CASTING OUT: SPIRIT, EVIL; and SPIRIT, UNCLEAN)

[DEMON POSSESSION from this kind does not go out except by prayer and fasting]

Setting: Galilee, near the mountain where the Transfiguration took place. Jesus reveals to His disciples why they could not cure a demon-possessed boy.

And He said to them, "Because of the littleness of your faith; for truly I say to you, if you have faith the size of a mustard seed, you will say to this mountain, 'Move from here to there,' and it will move; and nothing will be impossible to you. ["But this kind does not go out except by prayer and fasting"] (Matthew 17:20, 21; cf. Matthew 21:21, 22; Mark 9:28, 29).

[DEMON POSSESSION from do not enter him again]

Setting: Galilee. Upon returning from a high mountain (perhaps Mount Hermon) where Jesus was transfigured in front of Peter, James, and John, the four discover the remaining disciples arguing with some scribes.

And He asked them, "What are you discussing with them?" And one of the crowd answered Him, "Teacher, I brought You my son, possessed with a spirit which makes him mute; and whenever it seizes him, it slams him *to the ground* and he foams *at the mouth,* and grinds his teeth and stiffens out. I told Your disciples to cast it out, and they could not *do it.* And He answered them, and said, "O unbelieving generation, how long shall I be with you? How long shall I put up with you? Bring him to Me!" They brought the boy to Him. When he saw Him, immediately the spirit threw him into a convulsion, and falling to the ground, be *began* rolling around and foaming *at the mouth.* And He asked his father, "How long has this been happening to him?" And he said, "From childhood. It has often thrown him both into the fire and into the water to destroy him. But if You can do anything, take pity on us and help us!" And Jesus said to him, "'If You can?' All things are possible to him who believes." Immediately the boy's father cried out and said, "I do believe; help my unbelief." When Jesus saw that a crowd was rapidly gathering, He rebuked the unclean spirit, saying to it, "You deaf and mute spirit, I command you, come out of him and do not enter him again." After crying out and throwing him into terrible convulsions, it came out; and *the boy* became so much like a corpse that most *of them,* said, "He is dead!" But Jesus took him by the hand and raised him; and he got up. When He came into *the* house, His disciples *began* questioning Him privately, "Why could we not drive it out?" And He said to them, "This kind cannot come out by anything but prayer" (Mark 9:16–29; cf. Matthew 17:14–21; Luke 9:37–43; see Matthew 17:20).

DEMONS (DEMONS, CASTING OUT is a separate entry; also see DEMON; SPIRIT, UNCLEAN; and SPIRITS)
[DEMONS from the devil and his angels]
Setting: The Mount of Olives, just east of Jerusalem. During His discourse, after answering His disciples' questions as to when the temple will be destroyed and Jerusalem overrun, along with the signs of His coming and the end of the age, Jesus reveals the future judgments following His return.

"But when the Son of Man comes in His glory, and all the angels with Him, then He will sit on His glorious throne. All the nations will be gathered before Him; and He will separate them from one another, as the shepherd separates the sheep from the goats; and He will put the sheep on His right, and the goats on the left. Then the King will say to those on His right, 'Come, you who are blessed of My Father, inherit the kingdom prepared for you from the foundation of the world. 'For I was hungry, and you gave Me *something* to eat; I was thirsty, and you gave Me *something* to drink; I was a stranger, and you invited Me in; naked, and you clothed Me; I was sick, and you visited Me; I was in prison, and you came to Me.' Then the righteous will answer Him, 'Lord, when did we see You hungry and feed You, or thirsty, and give you *something* to drink? And when did we see You a stranger, and invite You in, or naked, and clothe You? When did we see You sick, or in prison, and come to You?' The King will answer and say to them, 'Truly I say to you, to the extent that you did it to one of these brothers of Mine, *even* the least *of them,* you did it to Me.' Then He will also say to those on His left, 'Depart from Me, accursed ones, into the eternal fire which has been prepared for the devil and his angels; for I was hungry, and you gave Me *nothing* to eat; I was thirsty, and you gave Me nothing to drink; I was a stranger, and you did not invite Me in; naked, and you did not clothe Me; sick, and in prison, and you did not visit Me.' Then they themselves also will answer, 'Lord, when did we see You hungry, or thirsty, or a stranger, or naked, or sick, or in prison, and did not take care of You?' Then He will answer them, 'Truly I say to you, to the extent that you did not do it to one of the least of these, you did not do it to Me.' These will go away into eternal punishment, but the righteous into eternal life" (Matthew 25:31–46; see Matthew 7:23; 16:27; 19:29).

DEMONS, CASTING OUT (Also see DEMON; DEMON POSSESSION; DEMONS; MIRACLES; and SIGNS AND WONDERS)
[CASTING OUT DEMONS from cast out demons]
Setting: Galilee. During the early part of His ministry, Jesus preaches the Sermon on the Mount to His disciples and the multitudes.

"Not everyone who says to Me, 'Lord, Lord,' will enter the kingdom of heaven, but he who does the will of My Father who is in heaven *will enter.* Many will say to Me on that day, 'Lord, Lord, did we not prophesy in Your name, and in Your name cast out demons, and in Your name perform many miracles?' And then I will declare to them, 'I never knew you, DEPART FROM ME, YOU WHO PRACTICE LAWLESSNESS'" (Matthew 7:21–23, Jesus quotes from Psalm 6:8; cf. Matthew 25:11–13; see Luke 6:46).

[CASTING OUT DEMONS from Go]
Setting: The country of the Gadarenes. After Jesus calms a great storm on the Sea of Galilee with His voice, He casts demons out of two men into a herd of swine.

And He said to them, "Go!" And they came out and went into the swine, and the whole herd rushed down the steep bank into the sea and perished in the waters (Matthew 8:32; see Mark 5:1–14; Luke 8:26–35).

[CASTING OUT DEMONS from cast out demons]
Setting: Galilee. After His disciples observe His ministry, Jesus summons and specifically instructs them about their ministry to the people of Israel.

These twelve Jesus sent out after instructing them: "Do not go in *the* way of *the* Gentiles, and do not enter *any* city of the Samaritans; but rather go to the lost sheep of the house of Israel. And as you go, preach, saying, 'The kingdom of heaven is at hand.' Heal *the* sick, raise *the* dead, cleanse *the* lepers, cast out demons. Freely you received, freely give. Do not acquire gold, or silver, or copper for your money belts, or a bag for *your* journey, or even two coats, or sandals, or a staff; for the worker is worthy of his support. And whatever city or village you enter, inquire who is worthy in it, and stay at his house until you leave *that city*. As you enter the house, give it your greeting. If the house is worthy, give it your *blessing of* peace. But if it is not worthy, take back your *blessing of* peace. Whoever does not receive you, nor heed your words, as you go out of that house or that city, shake the dust off your feet. Truly I say to you, it will be more tolerable for *the* land of Sodom and Gomorrah in the day of judgment than for that city" (Matthew 10:5–15; cf. Mark 6:7–11; Luke 9:1–5; see Matthew 3:2; 10:1–4; 11:22, 24; 15:24; Luke 22:35; 1 Corinthians 9:14).

[CASTING OUT DEMONS from cast out demons]
Setting: Galilee. After Jesus heals a blind, mute, demon-possessed man, the Pharisees accuse Him in front of crowds of being a worker of Satan.

And knowing their thoughts Jesus said to them, "Any kingdom divided against itself is laid waste; and any city or house divided against itself will not stand. If Satan casts out Satan, he is divided against himself; how then will his kingdom stand? If I by Beelzebul cast out demons, by whom do your sons cast *them* out? For this reason they will be your judges. But if I cast out demons by the Spirit of God, then the kingdom of God has come upon you. Or how can anyone enter the strong man's house and carry off his property, unless he first binds the strong *man?* And then he will plunder his house" (Matthew 12:25–29; cf. Matthew 9:34; Mark 3:23–27; Luke 11:17–20; see Matthew 12:22–24).

[CASTING OUT DEMONS from O woman, your faith is great; it shall be done for you as you wish]
Setting: The district of Tyre and Sidon. A Canaanite woman appeals to Jesus to heal her demon-possessed daughter.

But He answered and said, "I was sent only to the lost sheep of the house of Israel." But she came and *began* to bow down before Him, saying, "Lord, help me!" And He answered and said, "It is not good to take the children's bread and throw it to the dogs." But she said, "Yes, Lord; but even the dogs feed from the crumbs which fall from their masters' table." Then Jesus said to her, "O woman, your faith is great; it shall be done for you as you wish." And her daughter was healed at once (Matthew 15:24 28; cf. Mark 7: 24–30; see Matthew 9:22; 10:5, 6).

[CASTING OUT DEMONS from You unbelieving and perverted generation, how long shall I be with you? How long shall I put up with you? Bring him here to Me]
Setting: Galilee, near the mountain where Jesus was transfigured with Moses and Elijah. After responding to His disciples' question about Elijah's future coming, Jesus expresses dismay over the disciples inability to heal a man's demon-possessed son.

And Jesus answered and said, "You unbelieving and perverted generation, how long shall I be with you? How long shall I put up with you? Bring him here to Me." And Jesus rebuked him, and the demon came out of him, and the boy was cured at once (Matthew 17:17, 18; cf. Mark 9:19–29; Luke 9:41–43; see Matthew 17:14–16).

[CASTING OUT DEMONS from But this kind does not go out except by prayer and fasting
Setting: Galilee, near the mountain where Jesus was transfigured with Moses and Elijah. Jesus reveals to His disciples why they are unable to cure a demon-possessed boy.

And He said to them, "Because of the littleness of your faith; for truly I say to you, if you have faith the size of a mustard seed, you will say to this mountain, 'Move from here to there,' and it will move; and nothing will be impossible to you. ["But this kind does not go out except by prayer and fasting"] (Matthew 17:20, 21; cf. Matthew 21:21, 22; Mark 9:28, 29).

[CASTING OUT DEMONS from Be quiet, and come out of him]
Setting: Capernaum in Galilee. In the beginning of His ministry, after calling some of His disciples, Jesus removes a demon from a man in the synagogue.

And Jesus rebuked him, saying, "Be quiet, and come out of him!" (Mark 1:25; cf. Luke 4:33–35).

[CASTING OUT DEMONS from Come out of the man, you unclean spirit]
Setting: The country of the Gerasenes, across the Sea of Galilee from Capernaum. Jesus encounters and heals a demon-possessed man.

For He had been saying to him, "Come out of the man, you unclean spirit!" And He was asking him, "What is your name?" And he said to Him, "My name is Legion; for we are many" (Mark 5:8, 9; cf. Luke 8:30; see Matthew 8:28–32; Luke 8:26–33).

[CASTING OUT DEMONS from the demon has gone out of your daughter]
Setting: The region of Tyre. After the Pharisees and scribes from Jerusalem question Jesus' disciples' lack of obedience to tradition in Galilee, Jesus casts out a demon from the daughter of a Gentile (Syrophoenician) woman.

And He was saying to her, "Let the children be satisfied first, for it is not good to take the children's bread and throw it to the dogs." But she answered and said to Him, "Yes, Lord *but* even the dogs under the table feed on the children's crumbs. And He said to her, "Because of this answer go; the demon has gone out of your daughter" (Mark 7:27–29; cf. Matthew 15:21–28; see Mark 7:24–26).

[CASTING OUT DEMONS from You deaf and mute spirit, I command you, come out of him and do not enter him again]
Setting: Galilee. After Jesus returns from a high mountain (perhaps Mount Hermon), where He was transfigured before Peter, James, and John, the four discover the remaining disciples arguing with some scribes.

And He asked them, "What are you discussing with them?" And one of the crowd answered Him, "Teacher, I brought You my son, possessed with a spirit which makes him mute; and whenever it seizes him, it slams him *to the ground* and he foams *at the mouth,* and grinds his teeth and stiffens out. I told Your disciples to cast it out, and they could not *do it.* And He answered them, and said, "O unbelieving generation, how long shall I be with you? How long shall I put up with you? Bring him to Me!" They brought the boy to Him. When he saw Him, immediately the spirit threw him into a convulsion, and falling to the ground, be *began* rolling around and foaming *at the mouth.* And He asked his father, "How long has this been happening to him?" And he said, "From childhood. It has often thrown him both into the fire and into the water to destroy him. But if You can do anything, take pity on us and help us!" And Jesus said to him, "'If You can?' All things are possible to him who believes." Immediately the boy's father cried out and said, "I do believe; help my unbelief." When Jesus saw that a crowd was rapidly gathering, He rebuked the unclean spirit, saying to it, "You deaf and mute spirit, I command you, come out of him and do not enter him again." After crying out and throwing him into terrible convulsions, it came out; and *the boy* became so much like a corpse that most *of them,* said, "He is dead!" But Jesus took him by the hand and raised him; and he got up. When He came into *the* house, His disciples *began* questioning Him privately, "Why could we not drive it out?" And He said to them, "This kind cannot come out by anything but prayer" (Mark 9:16–29; cf. Matthew 17:14–21; Luke 9:37–43; see Matthew 17:20).

[CASTING OUT DEMONS from cast out demons]
Setting: Following His resurrection from the dead after being crucified, Jesus commissions His disciples to preach His gospel to the world.

And He said to them, "Go into all the world and preach the gospel to all creation. He who has believed and has been baptized shall be saved; but he who has disbelieved shall be condemned. These signs will accompany those who have believed: in My name they will cast out demons, they will speak with new tongues; they will pick up serpents, and if they drink any deadly poison, it will not hurt them; they will lay hands on the sick, and they will recover" (Mark 16:15–18; cf. Matthew 28:16–20; see Mark 9:38; John 3:18, 36; 1 Corinthians 15:6).

[Note: Some scholars question the authenticity of Mark 16:9–20, as these verses do not appear in some early New Testament manuscripts.]

[CASTING OUT DEMONS from Be quiet and come out of him]
Setting: The synagogue in Capernaum in Galilee. Jesus heals a demon-possessed man.

But Jesus rebuked him, saying, "Be quiet and come out of him!" And when the demon had thrown him down in the midst *of the people,* he came out of him without doing him any harm (Luke 4:35; cf. Mark 1:21–28).

[CASTING OUT DEMONS from cast out demons]
Setting: On the way from Galilee to Jerusalem. After Jesus casts out a demon, some in the crowd test Him, demanding a sign from heaven.

But He knew their thoughts and said to them, "Any kingdom divided against itself is laid waste; and a house divided against itself falls. If Satan also is divided against himself, how will his kingdom stand? For you say that I cast out demons by Beelzebul. And if I by Beelzebul cast out demons, by whom do your sons cast them out? So they will be your judges. But if I cast out demons by the finger of God, then the kingdom of God has come upon you". (Luke 11:17–20; cf. Matthew 12:25–28; Mark 3:23–27; see Exodus 8:19; Matthew 3:2, 10:25).

[CASTING OUT DEMONS from cast out demons]
Setting: On the way from Galilee to Jerusalem. While teaching in the cities and villages, after Jesus responds to a question about who is saved, some Pharisees ask Him to leave, claiming Herod Antipas (tetrarch of Galilee and Perea) seeks to kill Him.

And He said to them, "Go and tell that fox, 'Behold, I cast out demons and perform cures today and tomorrow, and the third day I reach My goal.' Nevertheless I must journey on today and tomorrow and the next day; for it cannot be that a prophet would perish outside of Jerusalem. O Jerusalem, Jerusalem, the city that kills the prophets and stones those sent to her! How often I wanted to gather your children together, just as a hen gathers her brood under her wings, and you would not have it! Behold, your house is left to you desolate; and I say to you, you will not see Me until the time comes when you say, 'BLESSED IS HE WHO COMES IN THE NAME OF THE LORD!'" (Luke 13:32–35, Jesus quotes from Psalm 118:26; cf. Matthew 23:37).

DEN, ROBBERS' (See ROBBERS' DEN)

DENARII (Also see COIN; DENARIUS; and MONEY)
Setting: Capernaum of Galilee. Jesus illustrates forgiveness after Peter asks Him if forgiving someone seven times who has sinned against him is adequate.

"For this reason the kingdom of heaven may be compared to a king who wished to settle accounts with his slaves. When he had begun to settle *them,* one who owed him ten thousand talents was brought to him. But since he did not have *the means* to repay, his lord commanded him to be sold, along with his wife and children and all that he had, and repayment to be made. So the slave fell *to the ground* and prostrated himself before him, saying, 'Have patience with me and I will repay you everything.' And the lord of that slave felt compassion and released him and forgave him the debt. But that slave went out and found one of his fellow slaves who owed him a hundred denarii; and he seized him and *began* to choke *him,* saying, 'Pay back what you owe.' So his fellow slave fell *to the ground* and *began* to plead with him, saying, 'Have patience with me and I will repay you.' But he was unwilling and went and threw him in prison until he should pay back what was owed. So when his fellow slaves saw what had happened, they were deeply grieved and came and reported to their lord all that had happened. Then summoning him, his lord said to him, 'You wicked slave, I forgave you all that debt because you pleaded with me. Should you not also have had mercy on your fellow slave, in the same way that I had mercy on you?' And his lord, moved with anger, handed him over to the torturers until he should repay all that was owed him. My heavenly Father will also do the same to you, if each of you does not forgive his brother from your heart" (Matthew 18:23–35; cf. Matthew 6:12, 14, 15; Luke 7:42; see Matthew 25:19–28).

Setting: By the Sea of Galilee. After a long day of ministry, Jesus prepares to demonstrate the power of God to His disciples by feeding more than 5,000 people.

But He answered them, "You give them *something* to eat!" And they said to Him, "Shall we go and spend two hundred denarii on bread and give them *something* to eat? And He said to them, "How many loaves do you have? Go look!" And when they found out, they said, "Five, and two fish" (Mark 6:37, 38; cf. Matthew 14:16, 17; Luke 9:13, 14; John 6:5–9; see Mark 3:20).

Setting: Galilee. After Jesus praises John the Baptist to the crowds, Simon, a Pharisee, invites Jesus to dinner. A sinful woman anoints His feet with perfume, prompting the Lord to convey a parable.

And Jesus answered him, "Simon, I have something to say to you." And he replied, "Say it, Teacher." "A moneylender had two debtors: one owed five hundred denarii, and the other fifty. When they were unable to repay, he graciously forgave them both. So which of them will love him more?" Simon answered and said, "I suppose the one whom he forgave more." And He said to him, "You have judged correctly" (Luke 7:40–43; see Matthew 18:23–35).

Setting: On the way from Galilee to Jerusalem. While being tested by a lawyer, Jesus tells him the story of the good Samaritan.

Jesus replied and said, "A man was going down from Jerusalem to Jericho, and fell among robbers, and they stripped him and beat him, and went away leaving him half dead. And by chance a priest was going down on that road, and when he saw him, he passed by on the other side. Likewise a Levite also, when he came to the place and saw him, passed by on the other side. But a Samaritan, who was on a journey, came upon him; and when he saw him, he felt compassion, and came to him and bandaged up his wounds, pouring oil and wine on them; and he put him on his own beast, and brought him to an inn and took care of him. On the next day he took out two denarii and gave them to the innkeeper and said, 'Take care of him; and whatever more you spend, when I return I will repay you.' Which of these three do you think proved to be a neighbor to the man who fell into the robbers' hands?" And he said, "The one who showed mercy toward him." Then Jesus said to him, "Go and do the same" (Luke 10:30–37).

DENARIUS (Also see COIN, DENARII; and MONEY)

Setting: Judea beyond the Jordan (Perea). Jesus illustrates the kingdom of heaven to His disciples through the story of laborers in the vineyard.

"For the kingdom of heaven is like a landowner who went out early in the morning to hire laborers for his vineyard. When he had agreed with the laborers for a denarius for the day, he sent them into his vineyard. And he went out about the third hour and saw others standing idle in the market place; and to those he said,' You also go into the vineyard, and whatever is right I will give you.' And *so* they went. Again he went out about the sixth and the ninth hour, and did the same thing. And about the eleventh *hour* he went out and found others standing *around;* and he said to them, 'Why have you been standing idle here all day long?' They said to him, 'Because no one hired us.' He said to them, 'You go into the vineyard too.' When evening came, the owner of the vineyard said to his foreman, 'Call the laborers and pay them their wages, beginning with the last *group* to the first.' When those *hired* about the eleventh hour came, each one received a denarius. When those *hired* first came, they thought that they would receive more; but each of them also received a denarius. When they received it, they grumbled at the landowner, saying, 'These last men have worked *only* one hour, and you have made them equal to us who have borne the burden and the scorching heat of the day.' But he answered and said to one of them, 'Friend, I am doing you no wrong; did you not agree with me for a denarius? Take what is yours and go, but I wish to give to this last man the same as to you. It is not lawful for me to do what I wish with what is my own? Or is your eye envious because I am generous?' So the last shall be first, and the first last" (Matthew 20:1–16; cf. Matthew 19:30)

Setting: The temple in Jerusalem. After Jesus teaches the chief priests, scribes, and elders in parables, they send some of the Pharisees and Herodians in an attempt to trap Him in a statement.

"Shall we pay or shall we not pay?" But He, knowing their hypocrisy, said to them, "Why are you testing Me? Bring Me a denarius to look at." They brought *one.* And He said to them, "Whose likeness and inscription is this?" And they said to Him, "Caesar's."

And Jesus said to them, "Render to Caesar the things that are Caesar's, and to God the things that are God's." And they were amazed at Him (Mark 12:15–17; cf. Matthew 22:15–22; Luke 20:20–26).

Setting: Jerusalem. While Jesus ministers in the temple a few days before His crucifixion, after He conveys to the people the Parable of the Vine-Growers, the scribes and Pharisees seek to trap Him by questioning Him about paying taxes to Caesar.

But He detected their trickery and said to them, "Show Me a denarius. Whose likeness and inscription does it have?" They said "Caesar's." And He said to them, "Then render to Caesar the things that are Caesar's, and to God the things that are God's" (Luke 20:23–25; cf. Matthew 22:15–21; Mark 12:13–17).

DENIAL (See PROPHECY OF PETER'S DENIAL; and JESUS, DENYING)

DENIAL, PETER'S (See PETER'S DENIAL; also see PROPHECY OF PETER'S DENIAL)

DENIAL OF SELF (See SELF-DENIAL)

DENYING JESUS CHRIST (See JESUS, DENYING)

DEPENDENCE ON GOD (Listed under GOD, DEPENDENCE ON)

DEPENDENCE ON JESUS (Listed under JESUS, DEPENDENCE ON)

DEPRAVITY (Also see SINS)

[DEPRAVITY from evil thoughts, murders, adulteries, fornications, thefts, false witness, slanders]
Setting: Galilee. Jesus explains to the crowd the meaning of His instruction about what defiles a man.

Peter said to Him, "Explain the parable to us." Jesus said, "Are you still lacking in understanding also? Do you not understand that everything that goes into the mouth passes into the stomach and is eliminated? But the things that proceed out of the mouth come from the heart, and those defile the man. For out of the heart come evil thoughts, murders, adulteries, fornications, thefts, false witness, slanders. These are the things which defile a man; but to eat with unwashed hands does not defile the man" (Matthew 15:15–20; cf. Mark 7:18–23; see Galatians 5:19–21).

[DEPRAVITY from evil thoughts, fornications, thefts, murders, adulteries, deeds of coveting *and* wickedness, *as well* as deceit, sensuality, envy, slander, pride *and* foolishness]
Setting: Galilee. After the Pharisees and scribes from Jerusalem question Jesus' disciples' lack of obedience to the tradition regarding ceremonial cleansing, Jesus speaks to a crowd and explains His teaching to His disciples.

After He called the crowd to Him again, He began saying to them, "Listen to Me, all of you, and understand: there is nothing outside the man which can defile him if it goes into him; but the things which proceed out of the man are what defile the man. [If anyone has ears to hear, let him hear."] When he had left the crowd and entered the house, His disciples questioned Him about the parable. And He said to them, "Are you so lacking in understanding also? Do you not understand that whatever goes into the man from outside cannot defile him, because it does not go into his heart, but into his stomach, and is eliminated?" (Thus He declared all foods clean.) And He was saying, "That which proceeds out of the man, that is what defiles the man. For from within, out of the heart of men, proceed the evil thoughts, fornications, thefts, murders, adulteries, deeds of coveting and wickedness, as well as deceit, sensuality, envy, slander, pride and foolishness. All these evil things proceed from within and defile the man" (Mark 7:14–23; cf. Matthew 15:10–20).

DESCENDANT OF DAVID (Listed under DAVID, DESCENDANT OF)

DESCENDANTS, ABRAHAM'S (Also see CHILDREN, ABRAHAM'S)

Setting: The temple treasury in Jerusalem. After the scribes and Pharisees question His testimony about Himself, Jesus reveals to those Jews who believe in Him how He will make them free.

So Jesus was saying to those Jews who had believed Him, "If you continue in My word, *then* you are truly disciples of Mine; and you will know the truth, and the truth will make you free." They answered Him, "We are Abraham's descendants and have never yet been enslaved to anyone; how is it that You say, 'You will become free'?" Jesus answered them, "Truly, truly, I say to you, everyone who commits sin is the slave of sin. The slave does not remain in the house forever; the son does remain forever. So if the Son makes you free, you will be free indeed. I know that you are Abraham's descendants; yet you seek to kill Me, because My word has no place in you. I speak the things which I have seen with *My* Father; therefore you also do the things which you heard from *your* father" (John 8:31–38; see John 8:1–30, 36, 41, 44; Romans 6:16).

DESIRE, SEXUAL (See SEXUAL DESIRE)

DESIRES

Setting: By the Sea of Galilee. During the early part of His ministry, after presenting the Parable of the Sower to a very large crowd from a boat, Jesus explains the meaning of the parable to His disciples and followers.

And He said to them, "Do you not understand this parable? How will you understand all the parables? The sower sows the word. These are the ones who are beside the road where the word is sown; and when they hear, immediately Satan comes and takes away the word which has been sown in them. In a similar way these are the ones on whom seed was sown on the rocky places, who, when they hear the word, immediately receive it with joy; and they have no *firm* root in themselves, but are *only* temporary; then, when affliction or persecution arises because of the word, immediately they fall away. And others are the ones on whom seed was sown among the thorns; these are the ones who have heard the word, but the worries of the world and the deceitfulness of riches, and the desires for other things enter in and choke the word, and it becomes unfruitful. And those are the ones on whom seed was sown on the good soil; and they hear the word and accept it and bear fruit, thirty, sixty, and a hundredfold" (Mark 4:13–20; cf. Matthew 13:18–23; Luke 8:11–15).

Setting: The temple treasury in Jerusalem. After the scribes and Pharisees question His testimony about Himself, Jesus interacts with them regarding their ancestry and motives.

Jesus said to them, "If God were your Father, you would love Me, for I proceeded forth and have come from God, for I have not even come on My own initiative, but He sent Me. Why do you not understand what I am saying? *It is* because you cannot hear My word. You are of *your* father the devil, and you want to do the desires of your father. He was a murderer from the beginning, and does not stand in the truth because there is no truth in him. Whenever he speaks a lie, he speaks from his own *nature,* for he is a liar and the father of lies. But because I speak the truth, you do not believe Me. Which one of you convicts Me of sin? If I speak truth, why do not believe Me? He who is of God hears the words of God; for this reason you do not hear *them,* because you are not of God" (John 8:42–47; see John 8:1–41; 18:37; 1 John 3:8; 4:6; 5:1).

DESOLATION (ABOMINATION OF DESOLATION is a separate entry; also see DESTRUCTION)

Setting: The Mount of Olives, just east of Jerusalem. During His discourse, following a time of ministry in the temple a few days before His crucifixion, Jesus elaborates about future events.

"But when you see Jerusalem surrounded by armies, then recognize that her desolation is near. Then those who are in Judea must flee to the mountains, and those who are in the midst of the city must leave, and those who are in the country must not enter the city; because these are days of vengeance, so that all things which are written will be fulfilled. Woe to those who are pregnant and to those who are nursing babies in those days; for there will be a great distress upon the land and wrath to this people; and they will fall by the edge of the sword, and will be led captive into all the nations; and Jerusalem will be trampled under foot by the Gentiles until the times of the Gentiles are fulfilled" (Luke 21:20–24; see Matthew 24:15–18; Mark 13:14–16; Luke 19:43; 21:10–19).

DESPAIR (Also see ANGUISH; ANXIETY; FEAR; SADNESS; and WORRY)

[DESPAIR from WHY HAVE YOU FORSAKEN ME]

Setting: Golgotha, just outside Jerusalem. Jesus speaks words of despair while dying on a cross for the sins of the world.

About the ninth hour Jesus cried out with a loud voice, saying, "ELI, ELI, LAMA SABACHTHANI?" that is, "MY GOD, MY GOD, WHY HAVE YOU FORSAKEN ME?" (Matthew 27:46, Jesus quotes from Psalm 22:1; cf. Mark 15:34; see Matthew 27:33–45, 47–50).

[DESPAIR from WHY HAVE YOU FORSAKEN ME]

Setting: Golgotha, just outside Jerusalem. While on the cross, Jesus cries out at the ninth hour (3 p.m.).

At the ninth hour Jesus cried out with a loud voice, "ELOI, ELOI, LAMA SABACHTHANI?" which is translated, "MY GOD, MY GOD, WHY HAVE YOU FORSAKEN ME?" (Mark 15:34, Jesus quotes from Psalm 22:1; cf. Matthew 27:46).

DESTROYER (See DEVIL; EVIL ONE; and SATAN)

DESTRUCTION (Also see DESOLATION)

[DESTRUCTION from destroy and destroys]

Setting: Galilee. During the early part of His ministry, Jesus preaches the Sermon on the Mount to His disciples and the multitudes.

"Do not store up for yourselves treasures on earth, where moth and rust destroy, and where thieves break in and steal. But store up for yourselves treasures in heaven, where neither moth nor rust destroys, and where thieves do not break in or steal; for where your treasure is, there your heart will be also" (Matthew 6:19–21; cf. Luke 12:34; see Proverbs 23:4; Matthew 19:21).

Setting: Galilee. During the early part of His ministry, Jesus preaches the Sermon on the Mount to His disciples and the multitudes.

"Enter through the narrow gate; for the gate is wide and the way is broad that leads to destruction, and there are many who enter through it. For the gate is small and the way is narrow that leads to life, and there are few who find it" (Matthew 7:13, 14; cf. Luke 13:24).

[DESTRUCTION from destroy]

Setting: Galilee. After His disciples observe His ministry, Jesus summons and specifically instructs them about their ministry ahead involving true discipleship.

"Therefore do not fear them, for there is nothing concealed that will not be revealed, or hidden that will not be known. What I tell you in the darkness, speak in the light; and what you hear *whispered* in your ear, proclaim upon the housetops. Do not fear those who kill the body but are unable to kill the soul; but rather fear Him who is able to destroy both soul and body in hell" (Matthew 10:26–28; cf. Mark 4:22; Luke 12:3; see Hebrews 10:31).

[DESTRUCTION from destroyed]

Setting: The temple in Jerusalem. Jesus speaks another parable to the chief priests and elders after they question His authority.

Jesus spoke to them again in parables, saying, "The kingdom of heaven may be compared to a king who gave a wedding feast for his son. And he sent out his slaves to call those who had been invited to the wedding feast, and they were unwilling to come. Again he sent out other slaves saying, 'Tell those who have been invited, "Behold, I have prepared my dinner; my oxen and my fattened livestock are *all* butchered and everything is ready; come to the wedding feast." But they paid no attention and went their way, one to his own farm, another to his business, and the rest seized his slaves and mistreated them and killed them. But the king was enraged, and he sent his armies and destroyed those murderers and set their city on fire. Then he said to his slaves, 'The wedding is ready, but those who were invited were not worthy. 'Go therefore to the main highways, and as many as you find *there,* invite to the wedding feast.' Those slaves went out into the streets and gathered together all they found, both evil and good; and the wedding hall was filled with dinner guests. But when the king came in to look over the dinner guests, he saw a man there who was not dressed in wedding clothes, and he said to him, 'Friend, how did you come in here without wedding clothes?' And the man was speechless. Then the king said to the servants, 'Bind him hand and foot, and throw him into the outer darkness; in that place there will be weeping and gnashing of teeth.' For many are called, but few *are* chosen" (Matthew 22:1–14; cf. Matthew 8:11, 12).

[DESTRUCTION from destroy]
Setting: The temple in Jerusalem. Having His authority questioned by the chief priests, scribes, and elders, Jesus begins to teach them in parables.

And He began to speak to them in parables: "A man PLANTED A VINEYARD AND PUT A WALL AROUND IT, AND DUG A VAT UNDER THE WINE PRESS AND BUILT A TOWER, and rented it out to vine-growers and went on a journey. At the *harvest* time he sent a slave to the vine-growers, in order to receive *some* of the produce of the vineyard from the vine-growers. They took him, and beat him and sent him away empty-handed. Again he sent them another slave, and they wounded him in the head, and treated him shamefully. And he sent another, and that one they killed; and *so with* many others, beating some and killing others. He had one more to *send*, a beloved son; he sent him last *of all* to them, saying, 'They will respect my son.' But those vine-growers said to one another, 'This is the heir; come, let us kill him, and the inheritance will be ours!' They took him, and killed him and threw him out of the vineyard. What will the owner of the vineyard do? He will come and destroy the vine-growers, and will give the vineyard to others. Have you not even read this Scripture: 'THE STONE WHICH THE BUILDERS REJECTED, THIS BECAME THE CHIEF CORNER *stone;* THIS CAME ABOUT FROM THE LORD, AND IT IS MARVELOUS IN OUR EYES'?" (Mark 12:1–11, Jesus quotes from Psalm 118:22, 23; Isaiah 5:1, 2; cf. Matthew 21:33–46; Luke 20:9–19; see Mark 12:12).

[DESTRUCTION from destroy]
Setting: A synagogue in Galilee. As Jesus teaches on the Sabbath, the scribes and Pharisees watch to see if He heals a man's withered hand.

But He knew what they were thinking, and He said to the man with the withered hand, "Get up and come forward!" And he got up and came forward. And Jesus said to them, "I ask you, is it lawful to do good or to do harm on the Sabbath, to save a life or destroy it?" And looking around at them all, He said to him, "Stretch out your hand!" And he did so; and his hand was restored (Luke 6:8–10; cf. Matthew 12:9–13; Mark 3:1–5).

[DESTRUCTION from destroy]
Setting: Galilee. After Jesus clarifies who His disciples' co-laborers are, He prepares to go to Jerusalem by sending messengers ahead to Samaria, where they experience rejection and seek retribution.

But He turned and rebuked them, [and said, "You do not know what kind of spirit you are of; for the Son of Man did not come to destroy men's lives, but to save them."] And they went on to another village (Luke 9:55, 56; see 2 Kings 1:9–14; Luke 13:22).

[DESTRUCTION from destroys]
Setting: On the way from Galilee to Jerusalem. After giving a parable about riches and greed, Jesus challenges the crowd and His disciples concerning godly living.

"Sell your possessions and give to charity; make yourselves money belts which do not wear out, an unfailing treasure in heaven, where no thief comes near nor moth destroys. For where your treasure is, there your heart will be also" (Luke 12:33, 34; cf. Matthew 6:19–21; 19:21).

[DESTRUCTION from destroyed]
Setting: Samaria, on the way from Galilee to Jerusalem. After the Pharisees question Him about the coming of the kingdom of God, Jesus tells His disciples of His second coming.

And He said to the disciples, "The days will come when you will long to see one of the days of the Son of Man, and you will not see it. They will say to you, 'Look there! Look here!' Do not go away, and do not run after them. For just like the lightning, when it flashes out of one part of the sky, shines to the other part of the sky, so will the Son of Man be in His day. But first He must suffer many things and be rejected by this generation. And just as it happened in the days of Noah, so it will be also in the days of the Son of Man: they were eating, they were drinking, they were marrying, they were being given in marriage, until the day that Noah entered the ark, and the flood came and destroyed them all. It was the same as happened in the days of Lot: they were eating, they were drinking, they were buying, they were selling, they were planting, they were building; but on the day that Lot went out from Sodom it rained fire and brimstone from heaven and destroyed them all. It will be just the same on the day that the Son of Man is revealed. On that day, the one who is on the housetop and whose goods are in the house must not go down to take them out; and likewise the one who is in the field must not turn back. Remember Lot's wife. Whoever seeks to keep his life will lose it, and whoever loses his life will preserve it. I tell you, on that night there will be two in one bed; one will be taken and the other will be left. There will be two women grinding at the same place; one will be taken and the other will be left. [Two men will be in the field; one will be taken and the other will be left."] And answering they said to Him, "Where, Lord?" And He said to them, "Where the body is, there also the vultures will be gathered" (Luke 17:22–37; see Genesis 19; Matthew 10:39; 16:21, 27; 24:17–28, 37–41).

[DESTRUCTION from destroy]
Setting: Jerusalem. While ministering in the temple a few days before His crucifixion, after the chief priests and the scribes question His authority to teach and preach, Jesus conveys the Parable of the Vine-Growers to the people.

And He began to tell the people this parable: "A man planted a vineyard and rented it out to vine-growers, and went on a journey for a long time. At the harvest time he sent a slave to the vine-growers, so that they would give him some of the produce of the vineyard; but the vine-growers beat him and sent him away empty-handed. And he proceeded to send another slave; and they beat him also and treated him shamefully and sent him away empty-handed. And he proceeded to send a third; and this one also they wounded and cast out. The owner of the vineyard said, 'What shall I do? I will send my beloved son; perhaps they will respect him.' But when the vine-growers saw him, they reasoned with one another, saying, 'This is the heir; let us kill him so that the inheritance will be ours.' So they threw him out of the vineyard and killed him. What, then, will the owner of the vineyard do to them? He will come and destroy these vine-growers and will give the vineyard to others." When they heard it, they said, "May it never be!" But Jesus looked at them and said, "What then is this that is written: 'THE STONE WHICH THE BUILDERS REJECTED, THIS BECAME THE CHIEF CORNER stone'? Everyone who falls on that stone will be broken to pieces; but on whomever it falls, it will scatter him like dust" (Luke 20:9–18, Jesus quotes from Psalm 118:22; cf. Matthew 21:33–44; Mark 12:1–11; see Ephesians 2:20).

[DESTRUCTION from Destroy]
Setting: Jerusalem. After Jesus cleanses the temple during the Passover of the Jews, the Jewish religious leaders question His authority to do these things.

Jesus answered them, "Destroy this temple, and in three days I will raise it up" (John 2:19; cf. Matthew 26:61).

[DESTRUCTION from destroy]
Setting: Jerusalem. After the Pharisees interrogate and dismiss the formerly blind man Jesus healed on the Sabbath, the Lord conveys the Parable of the Good Shepherd to the Pharisees using figures of speech they do not understand.

So Jesus said to them again, "Truly, truly, I say to you, I am the door of the sheep. All who came before Me are thieves and robbers, but the sheep did not hear them. I am the door; if anyone enters through Me, he will be saved, and will go in and out and find pasture. The thief comes only to steal and kill and destroy; I came that they may have life, and have *it* abundantly. I am the good shepherd; the good shepherd lays down His life for the sheep. He who is a hired hand, and not a shepherd, who is not the owner of the sheep, sees the wolf coming, and leaves the sheep and flees, and the wolf snatches them and scatters *them. He flees* because he is a hired hand and is not concerned about the sheep. I am the good shepherd, and I know My own and My own know Me, even as the Father knows Me and I know the Father; and I lay down My life for the sheep. I have other sheep, which are not of this fold; I must bring them also, and they will hear My voice; and they will become one flock *with* one shepherd. For this reason the Father loves Me, because I lay down My life so that I may take it again. No one has taken it away from Me, but I lay it down on My own initiative. I have authority to take it up again. This commandment I received from My Father" (John 10:7–18; see Isaiah 40:11; 56:8; Jeremiah 23:1; Matthew 11:27).

DESTRUCTION, PROPHECY OF JERUSALEM'S (See PROPHECY OF THE DESTRUCTION OF JERUSALEM)

DETESTABLE

Setting: On the way from Galilee to Jerusalem. The Lord responds to the Pharisees' scoffing at His teaching His disciples about stewardship.

And He said to them, "You are those who justify yourselves in the sight of men, but God knows your hearts; for that which is highly esteemed among men is detestable in the sight of God. The Law and the Prophets were proclaimed until John; since that time the gospel of the kingdom of God has been preached, and everyone is forcing his way into it. But is it easier for heaven and earth to pass away than for one stroke of a letter of the Law to fail" (Luke 16:15–17; cf. Matthew 5:18; see 1 Samuel 16:7; Matthew 4:23; 11:11–14; Luke 16:1, 14).

DEVIL (Also see BEELZEBUL; EVIL ONE; SATAN; and TEMPTATION OF JESUS)

Setting: In a house near the Sea of Galilee. Jesus explains the meaning of the Parable of the Wheat and the Tares to His disciples.

And He said, "The one who sows the good seed is the Son of Man, and the field is the world; and as *for* the good seed, these are the sons of the kingdom; and the tares are the sons of the evil *one;* and the enemy who sowed them is the devil, and the harvest is the end of the age; and the reapers are angels. So just as the tares are gathered up and burned with fire, so shall it be at the end of the age. The Son of Man will send forth His angels, and they will gather out of His kingdom all stumbling blocks, and those who commit lawlessness, and will throw them into the furnace of fire; in that place there will be weeping and gnashing of teeth. Then THE RIGHTEOUS WILL SHINE FORTH AS THE SUN in the kingdom of their Father. He who has ears, let him hear" (Matthew 13:37–43, Jesus quotes from Daniel 12:3; cf. Matthew 8:12; 13:50).

Setting: The Mount of Olives, just east of Jerusalem. During His discourse, after answering His disciples' questions as to when the temple will be destroyed and Jerusalem overrun, along with the signs of His coming and the end of the age, Jesus reveals the future judgments following His return.

"But when the Son of Man comes in His glory, and all the angels with Him, then He will sit on His glorious throne. All the nations will be gathered before Him; and He will separate them from one another, as the shepherd separates the sheep from the goats; and He will put the sheep on His right, and the goats on the left. Then the King will say to those on His right, 'Come, you who are blessed of My Father, inherit the kingdom prepared for you from the foundation of the world. 'For I was hungry, and you gave Me *something* to eat; I was thirsty, and you gave Me *something* to drink; I was a stranger, and you invited Me in; naked, and you clothed Me; I was sick, and you visited Me; I was in prison, and you came to Me.' Then the righteous will answer Him, 'Lord, when did we see You hungry and feed You, or thirsty, and give you *something* to drink? And when did we see You a stranger, and invite You in, or naked, and clothe You? When did we see You sick, or in prison, and come to You?' The King will answer and say to them, 'Truly I say to you, to the extent that you did it to one of these brothers of Mine, *even* the least *of them,* you did it to Me.' Then He will also say to those on His left, 'Depart from Me, accursed ones, into the eternal fire which has been prepared for the devil and his angels; for I was hungry, and you gave Me *nothing* to eat; I was thirsty, and you gave Me nothing to drink; I was a stranger, and you did not invite Me in; naked, and you did not clothe Me; sick, and in prison, and you did not visit Me.' Then they themselves also will answer, 'Lord, when did we see You hungry, or thirsty, or a stranger, or naked, or sick, or in prison, and did not take care of You?' Then He will answer them, 'Truly I say to you, to the extent that you did not do it to one of the least of these, you did not do it to Me.' These will go away into eternal punishment, but the righteous into eternal life" (Matthew 25:31–46; see Matthew 7:23; 16:27; 19:29).

Setting: Galilee. After Jesus presents the Parable of the Sower to the crowds, His disciples ask Him to explain the parable's meaning.

And He said, "To you it has been granted to know the mysteries of the kingdom of God, but to the rest it is in parables, so that SEEING THEY MAY NOT SEE, AND HEARING THEY MAY NOT UNDERSTAND. Now the parable is this: the seed is the word of God. Those beside the road are those who have heard; then the devil comes and takes away the word from their heart, so that they will not believe and be saved. Those on the rocky soil are those who, when they hear, receive the word with joy; and these have no firm root; they believe for a while, and in time of temptation fall away. The seed which fell among the thorns, these are the ones who have heard, and as they go on their way they are choked with worries and riches and pleasures of this life, and bring no fruit to maturity. But the seed in the good soil, these are the ones who have heard the word in an honest and good heart, and hold it fast, and bear fruit with perseverance" (Luke 8:10–15, Jesus quotes from Isaiah 6:9; cf. Matthew 13:10–23; Mark 4:10–20).

Setting: The synagogue at Capernaum of Galilee. After some of His disciples express difficulty with Jesus' statements about eating His flesh, Simon Peter tells Jesus He has words of eternal life.

Jesus answered them, "Did I Myself not choose you, the twelve, and *yet* one of you is a devil?" (John 6:70; see John 15:16, 19).

[DEVIL from your father]
Setting: The temple treasury in Jerusalem. After the scribes and Pharisees question His testimony about Himself, Jesus reveals to those Jews who believe in Him how He will make them free.

So Jesus was saying to those Jews who had believed Him, "If you continue in My word, *then* you are truly disciples of Mine; and you will know the truth, and the truth will make you free." They answered Him, "We are Abraham's descendants and have never yet been enslaved to anyone; how is it that You say, 'You will become free'?" Jesus answered them, "Truly, truly, I say to you, everyone who commits sin is the slave of sin. The slave does not remain in the house forever; the son does remain forever. So if the Son makes you free, you will be free indeed. I know that you are Abraham's descendants; yet you seek to kill Me, because My word has no place in you. I speak the things which I have seen with *My* Father; therefore you also do the things which you heard from *your* father" (John 8:31–38; see Romans 6:16).

[DEVIL from your father]
Setting: The temple treasury in Jerusalem. After the scribes and Pharisees question His testimony about Himself, Jesus interacts with them regarding their ancestry and motives.

They answered and said to Him, "Abraham is our father." Jesus said to them, "If you are Abraham's children, do the deeds of Abraham. But as it is, you are seeking to kill Me, a man who has told you the truth, which I heard from God; this Abraham did not do. You are doing the deeds of your father." They said to Him, "We were not born of fornication; we have one Father: God" (John 8:39–41; see Romans 9:6, 7).

Setting: The temple treasury in Jerusalem. After the scribes and Pharisees question His testimony about Himself, Jesus interacts with them regarding their ancestry and motives.

Jesus said to them, "If God were your Father, you would love Me, for I proceeded forth and have come from God, for I have not even come on My own initiative, but He sent Me. Why do you not understand what I am saying? *It is* because you cannot hear My word. You are of *your* father the devil, and you want to do the desires of your father. He was a murderer from the beginning, and does not stand in the truth because there is no truth in him. Whenever he speaks a lie, he speaks from his own *nature,* for he is a liar and the father of lies. But because I speak the truth, you do not believe Me. Which one of you convicts Me of sin? If I speak truth, why do not believe Me? He who is of God hears the words of God; for this reason you do not hear *them,* because you are not of God" (John 8:42–47; see John 18:37; 1 John 3:8; 4:6; 5:1).

Setting: The island of Patmos (in the Aegean Sea about fifty miles southwest of Ephesus in modern Turkey). On the Lord's Day (Sunday), about fifty years after Jesus' resurrection, the disciple John encounters the Lord Jesus Christ. Jesus communicates a new revelation for the apostle to record for the church in Smyrna and to six other churches in Asia.

"And to the angel of the church in Smyrna write: The first and the last, who was dead, and has come to life, says this: 'I know your tribulation and your poverty (but you are rich), and the blasphemy by those who say they are Jews and are not, but are a synagogue of Satan. Do not fear what you are about to suffer. Behold, the devil is about to cast some of you into prison, so that you will be tested, and you will have tribulation for ten days. Be faithful until death, and I will give you the crown of life. He who has an ear, let him hear what the Spirit says to the churches. He who overcomes will not be hurt by the second death' (Revelation 2:8–11; see Isaiah 44:6; Revelation 1:9, 18; 2:13; 20:6, 14).

DEVOTION (Also see COMMITMENT; DISCIPLE; DISCIPLESHIP; FOLLOWING JESUS CHRIST; OBEDIENCE; SACRIFICE, PERSONAL; and WORSHIP)
[DEVOTION from devoted]
Setting: Galilee. During the early part of His ministry, Jesus preaches the Sermon on the Mount to His disciples and the multitudes.

"No one can serve two masters; for either he will hate the one and love the other, or he will be devoted to one and despise the other. You cannot serve God and wealth (Matthew 6:24).

[DEVOTION from And he who does not take his cross and follow after Me is not worthy of Me]
Setting: Galilee. After His twelve disciples observe His ministry, Jesus summons and specifically instructs them about their ministry ahead involving true discipleship.

"He who loves father or mother more than Me is not worthy of Me; and he who loves son or daughter more than Me is not worthy of Me. And he who does not take his cross and follow after Me is not worthy of Me. He who has found his life will lose it, and he who has lost his life for My sake will find it" (Matthew 10:37–39; cf. Matthew 16:24, 25).

[DEVOTION from If anyone wishes to come after Me, he must deny himself, and take up his cross and follow Me]
Setting: Near Caesarea Philippi. After rebuking Peter for trying to forbid Him to accomplish His earthly mission of dying and being resurrected, Jesus teaches His disciples about the costs of discipleship.

Then Jesus said to His disciples, "If anyone wishes to come after Me, he must deny himself, and take up his cross and follow Me. For whoever wishes to save his life will lose it; but whoever loses his life for My sake will find it. For what will it profit a man if he gains the whole world and forfeits his soul? Or what will a man give in exchange for his soul? For the Son of Man is going to come in the glory of His Father with His angels, and WILL THEN REPAY EVERY MAN ACCORDING TO HIS DEEDS. Truly, I say to you, there are some of you who are standing here who will not taste death until they see the Son of Man coming in His kingdom" (Matthew 16:24–28, Jesus quotes from Psalm 62:12; cf. Mark 8:34–37; Luke 9:23–27; see Matthew 10:38, 39).

[DEVOTION from For she has done a good deed to Me]
Setting: The home of Simon the leper in Bethany. Jesus rebukes His disciples after they criticize a woman for pouring a vial of costly perfume on Jesus' head in preparation for His burial.

But Jesus, aware of this, said to them, "Why do you bother the woman? For she has done a good deed to Me. For you always have the poor with you; but you do not always have Me. For when she poured this perfume on My body, she did it to prepare Me for burial. Truly I say to you, wherever this gospel is preached in the whole world, what this woman has done will also be spoken of in memory of her" (Matthew 26:10–13; cf. Mark 14:3–9; Luke 7:37–39; John 12:2–8; see Deuteronomy 15:11).

[DEVOTION from If anyone wishes to come after Me, he must deny himself, and take up his cross and follow Me.]
Setting: Caesarea Philippi. After rebuking Peter for desiring to thwart His mission to the cross, Jesus summons a crowd, along with His disciples, and informs them of the high costs of following Him.

And He summoned the crowd with His disciples, and said to them, "If anyone wishes to come after Me, he must deny himself, and take up his cross and follow Me. For whoever wishes to save his life will lose it, but whoever loses his life for My sake and the gospel's will save it. For what does it profit a man to gain the whole world, and forfeit his soul? For what will a man give in exchange for his soul? For whoever is ashamed of Me and My words in this adulterous and sinful generation, the Son of Man will also be ashamed of him when He comes in the glory of His Father with the holy angels" (Mark 8:34–38; cf. Matthew 16:24–28; Luke 9:23–27; see Matthew 10:33, 38, 39).

[DEVOTION from She has done a good deed to Me]
Setting: The home of Simon the leper in Bethany. Two days before the Feast of Unleavened Bread (Passover), Jesus commends a woman who anoints His head with costly perfume, which some there think should have been sold and the proceeds given to the poor.

But Jesus said, "Let her alone; why do you bother her? She has done a good deed to Me. For you always have the poor with you, and whenever you wish you can do good to them; but you do not always have Me. She has done what she could; she has anointed My body beforehand for the burial. Truly I say to you, wherever the gospel is preached in the whole world, what this woman has done will also be spoken of in memory of her" (Mark 14:6–9; cf. Matthew 26:6–13; John 12:2–8; see Deuteronomy 15:11).

[DEVOTION from If anyone wishes to come after Me, he must deny himself, and take up his cross daily and follow Me.]
Setting: Galilee. Following Peter's pronouncement that Jesus is the Christ of God, the Lord conveys the demands of discipleship and the hope regarding the kingdom of God.

And He was saying to them all, "If anyone wishes to come after Me, he must deny himself, and take up his cross daily and follow Me. For whoever wishes to save his life will lose it, but whoever loses his life for My sake, he is the one who will save it. For what is a man profited if he gains the whole world, and loses or forfeits himself? For whoever is ashamed of Me and My words, the Son of Man will be ashamed of him when He comes in His glory, and the glory of the Father and of the holy angels. But I say to you truthfully, there are some of those standing here who will not taste death until they see the kingdom of God" (Luke 9:23–27; cf. Matthew 16:24–26, 28; Mark 8:34–37; see Matthew 10:33, 38, 39).

[DEVOTION from devoted]
Setting: On the way from Galilee to Jerusalem. After giving the story of the prodigal son, the Lord teaches His disciples about stewardship.

Now He was also saying to the disciples, "There was a rich man who had a manager, and this manager was reported to him as squandering his possessions. And he called him and said to him, 'What is this I hear about you? Give an accounting of your management, for you can no longer be a manager.' The manager said to himself, 'What shall I do, since my master is taking the management away from me? I am not strong enough to dig; I am ashamed to beg. I know what I shall do, so that when I am removed from the management people will welcome me into their homes.' And he summoned each one of his master's debtors, and he began saying to the first, 'How much do you owe my master?' And he said, 'A hundred measures of oil.' And he said to him, 'Take your bill, and sit down quickly and write fifty.' Then he said to another, 'And how much do you owe?' And he said, 'A hundred measures of wheat.' He said to him, 'Take your bill, and write eighty.' And his master praised the unrighteous manager because he had acted shrewdly; for the sons of this age are more shrewd in relation to their own kind than the sons of light. And I say to you, make friends for yourselves by means of the wealth of unrighteousness, so that when it fails, they will receive you into the eternal dwellings. He who is faithful in a very little thing is faithful also in much; and he who is unrighteous in a very little thing is unrighteous also in much. Therefore if you have not been faithful in the use of unrighteous wealth, who will entrust the true riches to you? And if you have not been faithful in the use of that which is another's, who will give you that which is your own? No servant can serve two masters; for either he will hate the one and love the other, or else he will be devoted to one and despise the other. You cannot serve God and wealth" (Luke 16:1–13; cf. Matthew 6:24; see Matthew 25:14–30).

DIFFICULTIES IN MINISTRY (Listed under MINISTRY, DIFFICULTIES IN; also see ADVERSITY; TRIBULATION; and TROUBLE)

DIFFICULTY, HEARING

[HEARING DIFFICULTY from "Ephphatha!" that is, "Be opened!"]

Setting: Decapolis near the Sea of Galilee. After casting out a demon from a Gentile woman's daughter in Tyre, Jesus restores a man's hearing and speech.

Jesus took him aside from the crowd, by himself, and put His fingers into his ears, and after spitting, He touched his tongue *with the saliva*; and looking up to heaven with a deep sigh, He said to him, "Ephphatha!" that is, "Be opened!" (Mark 7:33, 34; see Matthew 15:29–31; Mark 8:23).

DIGGING (See LABOR, MANUAL)

DILL (Also see other spices such as CUMMIN; and MINT)

Setting: The temple in Jerusalem. After the Jewish religious leaders test Him with questions, Jesus pronounces the fifth of eight woes on them in front of the crowds and His disciples.

"Woe to you, scribes and Pharisees, hypocrites! For you tithe mint and dill and cummin, and have neglected the weightier provisions of the law: justice and mercy and faithfulness; but these are things you should have done without neglecting the others. You blind guides, who strain out a gnat and swallow a camel!" (Matthew 23:23, 24).

DINNER (GUESTS, DINNER is a separate entry; also see BANQUETS; FEAST; HOSPITALITY; LUNCHEON; and RECEPTION)

Setting: The temple in Jerusalem. Jesus speaks another parable to the chief priests and elders after they question His authority.

Jesus spoke to them again in parables, saying, "The kingdom of heaven may be compared to a king who gave a wedding feast for his son. And he sent out his slaves to call those who had been invited to the wedding feast, and they were unwilling to come. Again he sent out other slaves saying, 'Tell those who have been invited, "Behold, I have prepared my dinner; my oxen and my fattened livestock are *all* butchered and everything is ready; come to the wedding feast." But they paid no attention and went their way, one to his own farm, another to his business, and the rest seized his slaves and mistreated them and killed them. But the king was enraged, and he sent his armies and destroyed those murderers and set their city on fire. Then he said to his slaves, 'The wedding is ready, but those who were invited were not worthy. 'Go therefore to the main highways, and as many as you find *there,* invite to the wedding feast.' Those slaves went out into the streets and gathered together all they found, both evil and good; and the wedding hall was filled with dinner guests. But when the king came in to look over the dinner guests, he saw a man there who was not dressed in wedding clothes, and he said to him, 'Friend, how did you come in here without wedding clothes?' And the man was speechless. Then the king said to the servants, 'Bind him hand and foot, and throw him into the outer darkness; in that place there will be weeping and gnashing of teeth.' For many are called, but few *are* chosen" (Matthew 22:1–14; cf. Matthew 8:11, 12).

Setting: On the way from Galilee to Jerusalem. Jesus speaks a parable to the guests of a Pharisee leader on the Sabbath. As He observes the guests selecting places of honor at the table, He comments to the host about the people to invite in the future.

And He also went on to say to the one who had invited Him, "When you give a luncheon or a dinner, do not invite your friends or your brothers or your relatives or rich neighbors, otherwise they may also invite you in return and that will be your repayment. But when you give a reception, invite the poor, the crippled, the lame, the blind, and you will be blessed, since they do not have the means to repay you; for you will be repaid at the resurrection of the righteous" (Luke 14:12–14; see Luke 14:1, 2, 15; John 5:28, 29).

Setting: On the way from Galilee to Jerusalem. At a banquet, after Jesus speaks a parable to the invited guests and the host, He responds to a guest's proclamation about the blessings of eating bread in the kingdom of God.

But He said to him, "A man was giving a big dinner, and he invited many; and at the dinner hour he sent his slave to say to those who had been invited, 'Come; for everything is ready now.' But they all alike began to make excuses. The first one said to him, 'I have bought a piece of land and I need to go out and look at it; please consider me excused.' Another one said, 'I have bought five yoke of oxen, and I am going to try them out; please consider me excused.' Another one said, I have married a wife, and for that reason I cannot come.' And the slave came back and reported this to his master. Then the head of the household became angry and said to his slave, 'Go out at once into the streets and lanes of the city and bring in here the poor and crippled and blind and lame.' And the slave said, 'Master, what you commanded has been done, and still there is room.' And the master said to the slave, 'Go out into the highways and along the hedges, and compel them to come in, so that my house may be filled. For I tell you, none of those men who were invited shall taste of my dinner'" (Luke 14:16–24; see Deuteronomy 24:5; Matthew 22:2–14; Luke 14:1, 2).

DINNER, BIG (See DINNER)

DINNER, PARABLE OF THE

Setting: On the way from Galilee to Jerusalem. At a banquet, after Jesus speaks a parable to the invited guests and the host, He responds to a guest's proclamation about the blessings of eating bread in the kingdom of God.

But He said to him, "A man was giving a big dinner, and he invited many; and at the dinner hour he sent his slave to say to those who had been invited, 'Come; for everything is ready now.' But they all alike began to make excuses. The first one said to him, 'I have bought a piece of land and I need to go out and look at it; please consider me excused.' Another one said, 'I have bought five yoke of oxen, and I am going to try them out; please consider me excused.' Another one said, I have married a wife, and for that reason I cannot come.' And the slave came back and reported this to his master. Then the head of the household became angry and said to his slave, 'Go out at once into the streets and lanes of the city and bring in here the poor and crippled and blind and lame.' And the slave said, 'Master, what you commanded has been done, and still there is room.' And the master said to the slave, 'Go out into the highways and along the hedges, and compel them to come in, so that my house may be filled. For I tell you, none of those men who were invited shall taste of my dinner'" (Luke 14:16–24; see Deuteronomy 24:5; Matthew 22:2–14; Luke 14:1, 2).

DINNER GUESTS (Listed under GUESTS, DINNER)

DINNER HOUR (Listed under HOUR, DINNER)

DIRGE (funeral hymn)

Setting: Galilee. After praising John the Baptist as His forerunner, Jesus demonstrates the foolish thinking of the current generation of Jewish religious leaders by repeating what they say about John's ascetic lifestyle and ministry along with His own.

"But to what shall I compare this generation? It is like children sitting in the market places, who call out to the other *children,* and say, 'We played the flute for you, and you did not dance; we sang a dirge, and you did not mourn.' For John came neither eating nor drinking, and they say, 'He has a demon!' The Son of Man came eating and drinking, and they say, 'Behold, a gluttonous man and a drunkard, a friend of tax collectors and sinners! Yet wisdom is vindicated by her deeds" (Matthew 11:16–19; cf. Luke 7:31–35; see Matthew 9:11, 34; Luke 1:15).

Setting: Galilee. After praising John the Baptist to the crowds, Jesus criticizes the Pharisees and lawyers who reject God's purpose and John's message.

"To what then shall I compare the men of this generation, and what are they like? They are like children who sit in the market place and call to one another, and they say, 'We played the flute for you, and you did not dance; we sang a dirge, and you did not weep.' For John the Baptist has come eating no bread and drinking no wine, and you say, 'He has a demon!' The Son of Man has come eating and drinking, and you say, 'Behold, a gluttonous man and a drunkard, a friend of tax collectors and sinners!' Yet wisdom is vindicated by all her children" (Luke 7:31–35; cf. Matthew 11:16–19; see Luke 1:15).

DISABLED (See CRIPPLED; and LAME)

DISSOCIATION (Also see REJECTION)

[DISSOCIATION from shake the dust off your feet]
Setting: Galilee. After His twelve disciples observe His ministry, Jesus summons and specifically instructs them about their ministry to the people of Israel.

These twelve Jesus sent out after instructing them: "Do not go in *the* way of *the* Gentiles, and do not enter *any* city of the Samaritans; but rather go to the lost sheep of the house of Israel. And as you go, preach, saying, 'The kingdom of heaven is at hand.' Heal *the* sick, raise *the* dead, cleanse *the* lepers, cast out demons. Freely you received, freely give. Do not acquire gold, or silver, or copper for your money belts, or a bag for *your* journey, or even two coats, or sandals, or a staff; for the worker is worthy of his support. And whatever city or village you enter, inquire who is worthy in it, and stay at his house until you leave *that city*. As you enter the house, give it your greeting. If the house is worthy, give it your *blessing of* peace. But if it is not worthy, take back your *blessing of* peace. Whoever does not receive you, nor heed your words, as you go out of that house or that city, shake the dust off your feet. Truly I say to you, it will be more tolerable for *the* land of Sodom and Gomorrah in the day of judgment than for that city" (Matthew 10:5–15; cf. Mark 6:7–11; Luke 9:1–5; see Matthew 3:2; 11:22, 24; 15:24; Luke 22:35; 1 Corinthians 9:14).

[DISSOCIATION from shake the dust off the soles of your feet for a testimony against them]
Setting: Jesus' hometown of Nazareth. After encountering unbelief, Jesus sends His disciples out in pairs with authority and instructions about ministry.

And He summoned the twelve and began to send them out in pairs, and gave them authority over the unclean spirits; and He instructed them that they should take nothing for *their* journey, except a mere staff—no bread, no bag, no money in their belt—but to wear sandals; and *He added,* "Do not put on two tunics." And He said to them, "Wherever you enter a house, stay there until you leave town. Any place that does not receive you or listen to you, as you go out from there, shake the dust off the soles of your feet for a testimony against them" (Mark 6:7–11; cf. Matthew 10:1–14; Luke 9:1–5).

[DISSOCIATION from shake the dust off your feet as a testimony against them]
Setting: Galilee. After raising Jairus's daughter from the dead, Jesus calls His disciples together and gives them power and authority over demons, along with the ability to heal diseases.

And He said to them, "Take nothing for your journey, neither a staff, nor a bag, nor bread, nor money; and do not even have two tunics apiece. Whatever house you enter, stay there until you leave that city. And as for those who do not receive you, go out from that city, shake the dust off your feet as a testimony against them" (Luke 9:3–5; cf. Matthew 10:1–15; Mark 6:7–11; see Luke 10:4–12).

DISASTERS, NATURAL (See specifics such as FAMINES; EARTHQUAKES; PESTILENCE; and PLAGUES)

DISBELIEF (Also see UNBELIEF)

[DISBELIEF from disbelieved]
Setting: Following His resurrection from the dead after being crucified, Jesus commissions His disciples to preach His gospel to the world.

And He said to them, "Go into all the world and preach the gospel to all creation. He who has believed and has been baptized shall be saved; but he who has disbelieved shall be condemned. These signs will accompany those who have believed: in My name they will cast out demons, they will speak with new tongues; they will pick up serpents, and if they drink any deadly poison, it will not hurt them; they will lay hands on the sick, and they will recover" (Mark 16:15–18; cf. Matthew 28:16–20; see Mark 9:38; John 3:18, 36; 1 Corinthians 15:6).

[Note: Some scholars question the authenticity of Mark 16:9–20, as these verses do not appear in some early New Testament manuscripts.]

DISCERNMENT (Also see DECEPTION; PHARISEES, LEAVEN OF THE; and WISDOM)

[DISCERNMENT from Beware of the false prophets]
Setting: Galilee. During the early part of His ministry, Jesus preaches the Sermon on the Mount to His disciples and the multitudes.

"Beware of the false prophets, who come to you in sheep's clothing, but inwardly are ravenous wolves. You will know them by their fruits. Grapes are not gathered from *bushes* nor figs from thistles, are they? So every good tree bears good fruit, but the bad tree bears bad fruit. A good tree cannot produce bad fruit, nor can a bad tree produce good fruit. Every tree that does not bear good fruit is cut down and thrown into the fire. So then, you will know them by their fruits" (Matthew 7:15–20; cf. Matthew 3:10; 12:33, 35; 24:11, 24; Luke 6:43, 44).

[DISCERNMENT from discern]
Setting: Magadan of Galilee. While rejecting His message, the Pharisees and Sadducees continue to test Jesus by asking Him for a sign from heaven.

But He replied to them, "When it is evening, you say, '*It will be* fair weather, for the sky is red.' And in the morning, '*There will* be a storm today, for the sky is red and threatening.' Do you know how to discern the appearance of the sky, but cannot *discern* the signs of the times? An evil and adulterous generation seeks after a sign; and a sign will not be given it, except the sign of Jonah." And He left them and went away (Matthew 16:2–4; cf. Matthew 12:39; Mark 8:12; Luke 12:54–56).

[DISCERNMENT from analyze the appearance of the earth and the sky, but why do you not analyze this present time]
Setting: On the way from Galilee to Jerusalem. After foretelling how a relationship with Him will divide families, Jesus chastises the crowds for being able to discern the weather but not the present age.

And He was also saying to the crowds, "When you see a cloud rising in the west, immediately you say, 'A shower is coming,' and so it turns out. And when you see a south wind blowing, you say, 'It will be a hot day,' and it turns out that way. You hypocrites! You know how to analyze the appearance of the earth and the sky, but why do you not analyze this present time?" (Luke 12:54–56; cf. Matthew 16:2, 3).

[DISCERNMENT from you put to the test those who call themselves apostles]
Setting: The island of Patmos (in the Aegean Sea about fifty miles southwest of Ephesus in modern Turkey). On the Lord's Day (Sunday), about fifty years after Jesus' resurrection, the disciple John encounters the Lord Jesus Christ. Jesus communicates a new revelation for the apostle to record for the church in Ephesus and to six other churches in Asia.

"To the angel of the church in Ephesus write: The One who holds the seven stars in His right hand, the One who walks among the seven golden lampstands, says this: 'I know your deeds and your toil and perseverance, and that you cannot tolerate evil men, and you put to the test those who call themselves apostles, and they are not, and you found them *to be* false; and you have perseverance and have endured for My name's sake, and have not grown weary. But I have *this* against you, that you have left your first love. Therefore remember from where you have fallen, and repent and do the deeds you did at first; or else I am coming to you and will remove your lampstand out of its place—unless you repent. Yet this you do have, that you hate the deeds of the Nicolaitans, which I also hate. He who has an ear, let him hear what the Spirit says to the churches. To him who overcomes, I will grant to eat of the tree of life which is in the Paradise of God'" (Revelation 2:1–7; see Genesis 2:9; Ezekiel 28:13; 1 John 4:1; Revelation 1:10, 11, 19, 20; 2:15, 16).

DISCERNMENT IN MINISTRY (Listed under MINISTRY, DISCERNMENT IN)

DISCIPLE (Also see DISCIPLES; FOLLOWING JESUS CHRIST; and PUPIL)

Setting: Galilee. After His disciples observe His ministry, Jesus summons and specifically instructs them about the difficulties ahead involving true discipleship.

"A disciple is not above his teacher, nor a slave above his master. It is enough for the disciple that he become like his teacher, and the slave like his master. If they have called the head of the house Beelzebul, how much more *will they malign* the members of his household!" (Matthew 10:24, 25; cf. Luke 6:40; see 2 Kings 1:2).

Setting: Galilee. After His twelve disciples observe His ministry, Jesus summons and specifically instructs them about their ministry ahead, which will include rewards.

"He who receives you receives Me, and he who receives Me receives Him who sent me. He who receives a prophet in the name of a prophet shall receive a prophet's reward; and he who receives a righteous man in the name of a righteous man shall receive a righteous man's reward. And whoever in the name of a disciple gives to one of these little ones even a cup of cold water to drink, truly I say to you, he shall not lose his reward" (Matthew 10:40–42; cf. Matthew 25:40, 44, 45; see Mark 9:37).

Setting: By the Sea of Galilee. Jesus teaches the Parable of the Head of a Household to His disciples.

And Jesus said to them, "Therefore every scribe who has become a disciple of the kingdom of heaven is like a head of a household, who brings out of his treasure things new and old" (Matthew 13:52; see Matthew 13:47–51).

Setting: On the way from Galilee to Jerusalem. After responding to a guest's proclamation about the blessings of eating bread in the kingdom of God, Jesus presents to large crowds the demands of discipleship.

Now large crowds were going along with Him; and He turned and said to them, "If anyone comes to Me, and does not hate his own father and mother and wife and children and brothers and sisters, yes, and even his own life, he cannot be My disciple. Whoever does not carry his own cross and come after Me cannot be My disciple. For which one of you, when he wants to build a tower, does not first sit down and calculate the cost to see if he has enough to complete it? Otherwise, when he has laid a foundation and is not able to finish, all who observe it begin to ridicule him, saying, 'This man began to build and was not able to finish.' Or what king, when he sets out to meet another king in battle, will not first sit down and consider whether he is strong enough with ten thousand *men* to encounter the one coming against him with twenty thousand? Or else, while the other is still far away, he sends a delegation and asks for terms of peace. So then, none of you can be My disciple who does not give up all his possessions. Therefore, salt is good; but if even salt has become tasteless, with what will it be seasoned? It is useless either for the soil or for the manure pile; it is thrown out. He who has ears to hear, let him hear" (Luke 14:25–35; cf. Matthew 5:13; 10:37–39; see Proverbs 20:18; Luke 14:1, 2, 15, 25; Philippians 3:7).

DISCIPLES' PRAYER (See LORD'S PRAYER)

DISCIPLES (Also see APOSTLES; DISCIPLE; and FOLLOWING JESUS CHRIST)

Setting: Near Jerusalem. On the first day of Unleavened Bread, just after Judas makes arrangements with the chief priests to betray Him, Jesus informs His disciples where they will celebrate the Passover.

And He said, "Go into the city to a certain man, and say to him, 'The Teacher says, "My time is near; I *am to* keep the Passover at your house with My disciples"'" (Matthew 26:18; cf. Mark 14:13–15; Luke 22:7–13).

Setting: On a mountain in Galilee. Following His resurrection from the dead in Jerusalem, Jesus conveys the Great Commission to the eleven remaining disciples.

And Jesus came up and spoke to them, saying, "All authority has been given to Me in heaven and on earth. Go therefore and make disciples of all the nations, baptizing them in the name of the Father and the Son and the Holy Spirit, teaching them to observe all that I commanded you; and lo, I am with you always, even to the end of the age" (Matthew 28:18–20; cf. Mark 16:15; see Daniel 7:13).

[DISCIPLES from *followers* of Christ]
Setting: Capernaum of Galilee. As Jesus teaches His disciples in private, they ask Him about greatness.

But Jesus said, "Do not hinder him, for there is no one who will perform a miracle in My name, and be able soon afterward to speak evil of Me. For he who is not against us is for us. For whoever gives you a cup of water to drink because of your name as *followers* of Christ, truly I say to you, he will not lose his reward. Whoever causes one of these little ones who believe to stumble, it would be better for him if, with a heavy millstone hung around his neck, he had been cast into the sea. If your hand causes you to stumble, cut it off; it is better for you to enter life crippled, than, having your two hands, to go into hell, into the unquenchable fire, [where THEIR WORM DOES NOT DIE, AND THE FIRE IS NOT QUENCHED.] If your foot causes you to stumble, cut it off; it is better for you to enter life lame, than, having your two feet, to be cast into hell, [where THEIR WORM DOES NOT DIE, AND THE FIRE IS NOT QUENCHED.] If your eye causes you to stumble, throw it out; it is better for you to enter the kingdom of God with one eye, than, having two eyes, to be cast into hell, where THEIR WORM DOES NOT DIE, AND THE FIRE IS NOT QUENCHED. For everyone will be salted with fire. Salt is good; but if the salt becomes unsalty, with what will you make it salty *again?* Have salt in yourselves, and be at peace with one another" (Mark 9:39–50; Jesus quotes from Isaiah 66:24; cf. Matthew 18:6–9; Luke 9:49–50; see Matthew 5:13, 29, 30; 10:42; 12:30; 18:5, 6).

Setting: Jerusalem. On the first day of Unleavened Bread, when the Passover lamb is to be sacrificed, Jesus responds to His disciples' question about His plans for the Passover meal.

And He sent two of His disciples and said to them, "Go into the city, and a man will meet you carrying a pitcher of water; follow him; and wherever he enters, say to the owner of the house, 'The Teacher says, "Where is My guest room in which I may eat the Passover with My disciples?"' And he himself will show you a large upper room furnished *and* ready; prepare for us there" (Mark 14:13–15; cf. Matthew 26:17–19; Luke 22:7–13).

[DISCIPLES from the twelve]
Setting: A borrowed upper room in Jerusalem. While Jesus and His disciples are eating the Passover meal, the Lord states that one of them will betray Him.

As they were reclining *at the table* and eating, Jesus said, "Truly I say to you that one of you will betray Me—one who is eating with Me." They began to be grieved and to say to Him one by one, "Surely not I?" And He said to them, "*It is* one of the twelve, one who dips with Me in the bowl. For the Son of Man *is to* go just as it is written of Him; but woe to that man by whom the Son of Man is betrayed! *It would have been* good for that man if he had not been born" (Mark 14:18–21; cf. Matthew 26:21–24; Luke 22:21–23; John 13:21, 22).

Setting: Jerusalem. With the Passover (Feast of Unleavened Bread) (Passover) approaching, Jesus informs His disciples where they will celebrate the feast, as the chief priests and scribes seek to kill Him, and Satan enters Judas Iscariot and causes him to betray the Lord.

And Jesus sent Peter and John, saying, "Go and prepare the Passover for us, so that we may eat it." They said to Him, "Where do You want us to prepare it?" And He said to them, "When you have entered the city, a man will meet you carrying a pitcher of water; follow him into the house that he enters. And you shall say to the owner of the house, 'The Teacher says to you, "Where is the guest room in which I may eat the Passover with My disciples?"'

And he will show you a large, furnished upper room; prepare it there" (Luke 22:8–12; cf. Matthew 26:17–19; Mark 14:12–16).

[DISCIPLES from the twelve]
Setting: The synagogue at Capernaum of Galilee., After some of His disciples express difficulty with Jesus' statements about eating His flesh, Simon Peter tells Jesus He has words of eternal life.

Jesus answered them, "Did I Myself not choose you, the twelve, and *yet* one of you is a devil?" (John 6:70; see John 15:16, 19).

Setting: The temple treasury in Jerusalem. After the scribes and Pharisees question His testimony about Himself, Jesus reveals to those Jews who believe in Him how He will make them free.

So Jesus was saying to those Jews who had believed Him, "If you continue in My word, *then* you are truly disciples of Mine; and you will know the truth, and the truth will make you free." They answered Him, "We are Abraham's descendants and have never yet been enslaved to anyone; how is it that You say, 'You will become free'?" Jesus answered them, "Truly, truly, I say to you, everyone who commits sin is the slave of sin. The slave does not remain in the house forever; the son does remain forever. So if the Son makes you free, you will be free indeed. I know that you are Abraham's descendants; yet you seek to kill Me, because My word has no place in you. I speak the things which I have seen with *My* Father; therefore you also do the things which you heard from *your* father" (John 8:31–38; see Romans 6:16).

Setting: Jerusalem. Before the Passover, after revealing to His disciples that Judas will betray Him to the chief priests and Pharisees, Jesus conveys how He will soon be glorified in His death, and commands them to love one another.

Therefore when he had gone out, Jesus said, "Now is the Son of Man glorified, and God is glorified in Him; if God is glorified in Him, God will also glorify Him in Himself, and will glorify Him immediately. Little children, I am with you a little while longer. You will seek Me; and as I said to the Jews, now I also say to you, 'Where I am going, you cannot come.' A new commandment I give to you, that you love one another, even as I have loved you, that you also love one another. By this all men will know that you are My disciples, if you have love for one another" (John 13:31–35; see Leviticus 19:18; John 7:33, 34; 17:1; 1 John 3:14).

Setting: Jerusalem. Before the Passover, after conveying the upcoming ministry of the Holy Spirit in His disciples' lives with His impending departure from them, Jesus explains He is the vine and His disciples are the branches.

"I am the true vine, and My Father is the vinedresser. Every branch in Me that does not bear fruit, He takes away; and every *branch* that bears fruit, He prunes it so that it may bear more fruit. You are already clean because of the word which I have spoken to you. Abide in Me, and I in you. As the branch cannot bear fruit of itself unless it abides in the vine, so neither *can* you unless you abide in Me. I am the vine, you are the branches; he who abides in Me and I in him, he bears much fruit, for apart from Me you can do nothing. If anyone does not abide in Me, he is thrown away as a branch and dries up; and they gather them, and cast them into the fire and they are burned. If you abide in Me, and My words abide in you, ask whatever you wish, and it will be done for you. My Father is glorified by this, that you bear much fruit, and *so* prove to be My disciples. Just as the Father has loved Me, I have also loved you; abide in My love. If you keep My commandments, you will abide in My love; just as I have kept My Father's commandments and abide in His love. These things I have spoken to you so that My joy may be in you, and *that* your joy may be made full" (John 15:1–11; see Matthew 5:16; 7:7; John 3:29, 35; 6:56; 8:29, 31; 13:10; 15:16).

DISCIPLES' COMMISSIONING (Listed under COMMISSIONING, DISCIPLES')

DISCIPLES' PRAYER (See LORD'S PRAYER)

DISCIPLES' REWARD (Listed under REWARD, DISCIPLES')

DISCIPLESHIP (Also see DISCIPLE; DISCIPLES; FOLLOWING JESUS CHRIST; and SACRIFICE, PERSONAL)
[DISCIPLESHIP from If anyone wishes to come after Me]
Setting: Near Caesarea Philippi. After rebuking Peter for trying to forbid Him to accomplish His earthly mission of dying and being resurrected, Jesus teaches His disciples about the costs of discipleship.

Then Jesus said to His disciples, "If anyone wishes to come after Me, he must deny himself, and take up his cross and follow Me. For whoever wishes to save his life will lose it; but whoever loses his life for My sake will find it. For what will it profit a man if he gains the whole world and forfeits his soul? Or what will a man give in exchange for his soul? For the Son of Man is going to come in the glory of His Father with His angels, and WILL THEN REPAY EVERY MAN ACCORDING TO HIS DEEDS. Truly, I say to you, there are some of you who are standing here who will not taste death until they see the Son of Man coming in His kingdom" (Matthew 16:24–28, Jesus quotes from Psalm 62:12; cf. Mark 8:34–37; Luke 9:23–27; see Matthew 10:38, 39).

[DISCIPLESHIP from teaching them]
Setting: On a mountain in Galilee. Following His resurrection from the dead in Jerusalem, Jesus conveys the Great Commission to the eleven remaining disciples.

And Jesus came up and spoke to them, saying, "All authority has been given to Me in heaven and on earth. Go therefore and make disciples of all the nations, baptizing them in the name of the Father and the Son and the Holy Spirit, teaching them to observe all that I commanded you; and lo, I am with you always, even to the end of the age" (Matthew 28:18–20; cf. Mark 16:15; see Daniel 7:13).

[DISCIPLESHIP from If anyone wishes to come after Me, he must deny himself, and take up his cross and follow Me]
Setting: Caesarea Philippi. After rebuking Peter for desiring to thwart His mission to the cross, Jesus summons a crowd, along with His disciples, and informs them of the high costs of following Him.

And He summoned the crowd with His disciples, and said to them, "If anyone wishes to come after Me, he must deny himself, and take up his cross and follow Me. For whoever wishes to save his life will lose it, but whoever loses his life for My sake and the gospel's will save it. For what does it profit a man to gain the whole world, and forfeit his soul? For what will a man give in exchange for his soul? For whoever is ashamed of Me and My words in this adulterous and sinful generation, the Son of Man will also be ashamed of him when He comes in the glory of His Father with the holy angels" (Mark 8:34–38; cf. Matthew 16:24–28; Luke 9:23–27; see Matthew 10:33, 38, 39).

[DISCIPLESHIP from no one who has left house or brothers or sisters or mother or father or children or farms, for My sake and for the gospel's sake]
Setting: Judea beyond the Jordan (Perea). After informing a rich man how righteous believers may have treasure in heaven, Jesus conveys to His disciples the reward of those who sacrifice in this life to follow Him.

Jesus said, "Truly I say to you, there is no one who has left house or brothers or sisters or mother or father or children or farms, for My sake and for the gospel's sake, but that he will receive a hundred times as much now in the present age, houses and brothers and sisters and mothers and children and farms, along with persecutions; and in the age to come, eternal life. But many *who are* first will be last, and the last, first" (Mark 10:29–31; cf. Matthew 19:27–30; Luke 18:28–30; see Matthew 6:33).

[DISCIPLESHIP from If anyone wishes to come after Me]
Setting: Galilee. Following Peter's pronouncement that Jesus is the Christ of God, the Lord conveys the demands of discipleship and the hope regarding the kingdom of God.

And He was saying to them all, "If anyone wishes to come after Me, he must deny himself, and take up his cross daily and follow Me. For whoever wishes to save his life will lose it, but whoever loses his life for My sake, he is the one who will save it. For what is a man profited if he gains the whole world, and loses or forfeits himself? For whoever is ashamed of Me and My words, the Son of Man will be ashamed of him when He comes in His glory, and the glory of the Father and of the holy angels. But I say to you truthfully, there are some of those standing here who will not taste death until they see the kingdom of God" (Luke 9:23–27; cf. Matthew 16:24–26, 28; Mark 8:34–37; see Matthew 10:33, 38, 39).

[DISCIPLESHIP from after putting his hand to the plow and looking back]
Setting: On the way from Galilee to Jerusalem. The Lord responds to several men seeking to follow Him.

But Jesus said to him, "No one, after putting his hand to the plow and looking back, is fit for the kingdom of God" (Luke 9:62; cf. Matthew 8:19–22; see Philippians 3:13).

[DISCIPLESHIP from Whoever does not carry his own cross and come after Me cannot be My disciple]
Setting: On the way from Galilee to Jerusalem. After responding to a guest's proclamation about the blessings of eating bread in the kingdom of God, Jesus presents to large crowds the demands of discipleship.

Now large crowds were going along with Him; and He turned and said to them, "If anyone comes to Me, and does not hate his own father and mother and wife and children and brothers and sisters, yes, and even his own life, he cannot be My disciple. Whoever does not carry his own cross and come after Me cannot be My disciple. For which one of you, when he wants to build a tower, does not first sit down and calculate the cost to see if he has enough to complete it? Otherwise, when he has laid a foundation and is not able to finish, all who observe it begin to ridicule him, saying, 'This man began to build and was not able to finish.' Or what king, when he sets out to meet another king in battle, will not first sit down and consider whether he is strong enough with ten thousand *men* to encounter the one coming against him with twenty thousand? Or else, while the other is still far away, he sends a delegation and asks for terms of peace. So then, none of you can be My disciple who does not give up all his possessions. Therefore, salt is good; but if even salt has become tasteless, with what will it be seasoned? It is useless either for the soil or for the manure pile; it is thrown out. He who has ears to hear, let him hear" (Luke 14:25–35; cf. Matthew 5:13; 10:37–39; see Proverbs 20:18; Luke 14:1, 2, 15; Philippians 3:7).

DISCIPLESHIP, COSTS OF (See DISCIPLESHIP; FOLLOWING JESUS CHRIST; and SACRIFICE, PERSONAL)

DISCIPLESHIP, DEMANDS OF (See DISCIPLESHIP; FOLLOWING JESUS CHRIST; and SACRIFICE, PERSONAL)

DISCIPLINE (CHURCH DISCIPLINE is a separate entry)

Setting: The island of Patmos (in the Aegean Sea about fifty miles southwest of Ephesus in modern Turkey). On the Lord's Day (Sunday), about fifty years after Jesus' resurrection, the disciple John encounters the Lord Jesus Christ. Jesus communicates a new revelation for the apostle to record for the church in Laodicea and to six other churches in Asia.

"To the angel of the church in Laodicea write: The Amen, the faithful and true Witness, the Beginning of the creation of God, says this: 'I know your deeds, that you are neither cold nor hot; I wish that you were cold or hot. So because you are lukewarm, and neither hot nor cold, I will spit you out of My mouth. Because you say, "I am rich, and have become wealthy, and have need of nothing," and you do not know that you are wretched and miserable and poor and blind and naked, I advise you to buy from Me gold refined by fire so that you may become rich, and white garments so that you may clothe yourself, and *that* the shame of your nakedness will not be revealed; and eye salve to anoint your eyes so that you may see. Those whom I love, I reprove and discipline; therefore be zealous and repent. Behold, I stand at the door and knock; if anyone hears My voice and opens the door, I will come in to him and will dine with him, and he with Me. He who overcomes, I will grant to him to sit down with Me on My throne, as I also overcame and sat down with My Father on His throne. He who has an ear, let him hear what the Spirit says to the churches'" (Revelation 3:14–22; see Proverbs 3:12; Hosea 12:8; John 14:23; 16:33).

DISCIPLINE, CHURCH (See CHURCH DISCIPLINE)

DISCLOSURE

[DISCLOSURE from disclose]

Setting: Jerusalem. Before the Passover, after responding to Philip's request for Him to show His disciples the Father, Jesus conveys the upcoming role of the Holy Spirit in their lives.

"I will not leave you as orphans; I will come to you. After a little while the world will no longer see Me, but you *will* see Me; because I live, you will live also. In that day you will know that I am in the Father, and you in Me, and I in you. He who has My commandments and keeps them is the one who loves Me; and he who loves Me will be loved by My Father, and I will love him and will disclose Myself to him" (John 14:18–21; see John 6:57; 10:37, 38; 16:16, 22).

[DISCLOSURE from disclose]

Setting: Jerusalem. Before the Passover, after warning His disciples of the persecution they will face after His departure to heaven, Jesus elaborates about the coming ministry of the Holy Spirit.

"I have many more things to say to you, but you cannot bear *them* now. But when He, the Spirit of truth, comes, He will guide you into all the truth; for He will not speak on His own initiative, but whatever He hears, He will speak; and He will disclose to you what is to come. He will glorify Me, for He will take of Mine and will disclose *it* to you. All things that the Father has are Mine; therefore I said that He takes of Mine and will disclose *it* to you (John 16:12–15; see John 7:39; 14:17, 26; 17:10).

DISCOURSE, UPPER ROOM (See specific verses from John 13:1–16:33)

DISEASE, HEALING FROM (See HEALING)

DISEASE, INFECTIOUS SKIN (See LEPROSY)

DISEASE, SKIN (See LEPROSY)

DISGRACE (Also see DISHONOR)

Setting: On the way from Galilee to Jerusalem. Jesus speaks a parable to the guests of a Pharisee leader on the Sabbath as He observes the guests selecting places of honor at the table.

And He *began* speaking a parable to the invited guests when He noticed how they had been picking out the places of honor *at the table,* saying to them, "When you are invited by someone to a wedding feast, do not take the place of honor, for someone more distinguished than you may have been invited by him, and he who invited you both will come and say to you, 'Give *your* place to this man, and then in disgrace you proceed to occupy the last place. But when you are invited, go and recline at the last place, so that when the one who has invited you comes, he may say to you, 'Friend, move up higher'; then you will have honor in the sight of all who are at the table with you. For everyone who exalts himself will be humbled, and he who humbles himself will be exalted" (Luke 14:7–11; see 2 Samuel 22:28; Proverbs 25:6, 7; Matthew 23:6).

DISH

Setting: The temple in Jerusalem. After the Jewish religious leaders test Him with questions, Jesus pronounces the sixth of eight woes on them in front of the crowds and His disciples.

"Woe to you, scribes and Pharisees, hypocrites! For you clean the outside of the cup and of the dish, but inside they are full of robbery and self-indulgence. You blind Pharisee, first clean the inside of the cup and of the dish, so that the outside of it may become clean also" (Matthew 23:25, 26; see Mark 7:4).

DISHONEST MANAGER (See MANAGER)

DISHONOR (Also see DISGRACE)

[DISHONOR from without honor]
Setting: Jesus' hometown of Nazareth. The residents take offense at the Lord's teaching in their synagogue.

And they took offense at Him. But Jesus said to them, "A prophet is not without honor except in his hometown and in his *own* household" (Matthew 13:57; cf. Mark 6:4; see Matthew 11:6).

[DISHONOR from without honor]
Setting: The synagogue in Jesus' hometown of Nazareth. While Jesus is ministering throughout Galilee, the Nazarenes become offended and question His teaching, wisdom, and ability to perform miracles.

Jesus said to them, "A prophet is not without honor except in his hometown and among his *own* relatives and in his *own* household" (Mark 6:4; cf. Matthew 13:54–58).

Setting: The temple treasury in Jerusalem. While Jesus interacts with the scribes and Pharisees about His testimony, their ancestry, and their motives, they state their belief He is a demon-possessed Samaritan.

Jesus answered, "I do not have a demon; but I honor My Father, and you dishonor Me. But I do not seek My glory; there is One who seeks and judges. Truly, truly, I say to you, if anyone keeps My word he will never see death" (John 8:49–51; see Matthew 16:28; John 5:41; 7:20).

DISMAY (Also see DISTRESS)

Setting: The Mount of Olives, east of the temple in Jerusalem. After ministering in the temple a few days before His crucifixion and giving His disciples more details regarding future events, Jesus speaks of His own return in His Olivet Discourse.

"There will be signs in sun and moon and stars, and on the earth dismay among the nations, in perplexity at the roaring of the sea and the waves, men fainting from fear and the expectation of the things which are coming upon the world; for the powers of the heavens will be shaken. Then they will see THE SON OF MAN COMING IN A CLOUD with power and great glory. But when these things begin to take place, straighten up and lift up your heads, because your redemption is drawing near" (Luke 21:25–28, Jesus quotes from Daniel 7:13; cf. Matthew 24:29–31; Mark 13:24–27).

DISOBEDIENCE (Also see OBEDIENCE)

[DISOBEDIENCE from Whoever then annuls one of the least of these commandments]
Setting: Galilee. During the early part of His ministry, Jesus preaches the Sermon on the Mount to His disciples and the multitudes.

"Whoever then annuls one of the least of these commandments, and teaches others *to do* the same, shall be called least in the kingdom of heaven; but whoever keeps and teaches *them*, he shall be called great in the kingdom of heaven" (Matthew 5:19; cf. Matthew 11:11).

[DISOBEDIENCE from do not do what I say]
Setting: Galilee. After selecting His twelve disciples, Jesus preaches the Sermon on the Mount to His disciples and a great throng from Judea, Jerusalem, and the central coastal region of Tyre and Sidon.

"Why do you call Me, 'Lord, Lord,' and do not do what I say? Everyone who comes to Me and hears My words and acts on them, I will show you whom he is like; he is like a man building a house, who dug deep and laid a foundation on the rock; and when a flood occurred, the torrent burst against that house and could not shake it, because it had been well built. But the one who has heard and has not acted accordingly, is like a man who built a house on the ground without any foundation; and the torrent burst against it and immediately it collapsed, and the ruin of that house was great" (Luke 6:46–49; cf. Matthew 7:24–27; see Luke 6:12–19; James 1:22).

[DISOBEDIENCE from does not keep My words]
Setting: Jerusalem. Before the Passover, after conveying the upcoming ministry of the Holy Spirit in His disciples' lives, Jesus answers Judas' (not Iscariot) question as to why He discloses Himself to His disciples and not the whole world.

Jesus answered and said to him, "If anyone loves Me, he will keep My word; and My Father will love him, and We will come to him and make Our abode with him. He who does not love Me does not keep My words; and the word which you hear is not Mine, but the Father's who sent Me" (John 14:23, 24; see John 7:16; 8:51).

DISSIPATION (Also see PLEASURES)

Setting: The Mount of Olives, just east of Jerusalem. During His discourse, a few days before Jesus' crucifixion, after conveying the Parable of the Fig Tree, Jesus warns His disciples to keep alert regarding future events.

"Be on guard, so that your hearts will not be weighted down with dissipation and drunkenness and the worries of life, and that day will not come upon you suddenly like a trap; for it will come upon all those who dwell on the face of all the earth. But keep on the alert at all times, praying that you may have strength to escape all these things that are about to take place, and to stand before the Son of Man" (Luke 21:34–36; cf. Mark 13:33; see Matthew 24:42–44).

DISTANCE

Setting: Decapolis near the Sea of Galilee. Jesus miraculously feeds more than 4,000 people, primarily Gentiles.

In those days, when there was again a large crowd and they had nothing to eat, Jesus called His disciples and said to them, "I feel compassion for the people because they have remained with Me now three days and have nothing to eat. If I send them away hungry to their homes, they will faint on their way; and some of them have come a great distance" (Mark 8:1–3; cf. Matthew 15:32–38; see Matthew 9:36; Mark 8:1, 4–9).

Setting: On the way from Galilee to Jerusalem. After instructing His disciples about persistence in prayer, Jesus conveys a parable about self-righteousness.

And He also told this parable to some people who trusted in themselves that they were righteous, and viewed others with contempt: "Two men went up into the temple to pray, one a Pharisee and the other a tax collector. The Pharisee stood and was praying this to himself: 'God, I thank You that I am not like other people: swindlers, unjust, adulterers, or even like this tax collector. I fast twice a week; I pay tithes of all that I get.' But the tax collector, standing some distance away, was even unwilling to lift up his eyes to heaven, but was beating his breast, saying, 'God, be merciful to me, the sinner!' I tell you, this man went to his house justified rather than the other; for everyone who exalts himself will be humbled, but he who humbles himself will be exalted" (Luke 18:9–14; see Ezra 9:6; Matthew 6:5; 23:12; Luke 11:42, 16:15; Romans 14:3, 10).

DISTANT COUNTRY (Listed under COUNTRY, DISTANT)

DISTRESS (Also see ANGUISH; ANXIETY; DESPAIR; and WORRY)

[DISTRESS from distressed]
Setting: On the way from Galilee to Jerusalem. After clarifying a parable for Peter and the crowd, Jesus conveys how a relationship with Him divides families.

"I have come to cast fire upon the earth; and how I wish it were already kindled! But I have a baptism to undergo, and how distressed I am until it is accomplished! Do you suppose that I came to grant peace on earth? I tell you, no, but rather division; for from now on five members in one household will be divided, three against two and two against three. They will be divided, father

against son and son against father, mother against daughter, and daughter against mother, mother-in-law against daughter-in-law and daughter-in-law against mother-in-law" (Luke 12:49–53; cf. Matthew 10:34–36; see Micah 7:6; Mark 10:38).

Setting: The Mount of Olives, just east of Jerusalem. After ministering in the temple a few days before His crucifixion and giving His disciples more details regarding future events, Jesus elaborates more about things to come during His Olivet Discourse.

"But when you see Jerusalem surrounded by armies, then recognize that her desolation is near. Then those who are in Judea must flee to the mountains, and those who are in the midst of the city must leave, and those who are in the country must not enter the city; because these are days of vengeance, so that all things which are written will be fulfilled. Woe to those who are pregnant and to those who are nursing babies in those days; for there will be a great distress upon the land and wrath to this people; and they will fall by the edge of the sword, and will be led captive into all the nations; and Jerusalem will be trampled under foot by the Gentiles until the times of the Gentiles are fulfilled" (Luke 21:20–24; see Matthew 24:15–18; Mark 13:14–16; Luke 19:43).

DISTRESS, GREAT (See DISTRESS)

DISTURBANCES

Setting: The temple in Jerusalem. A few days before His crucifixion, after Jesus prophesies the destruction of the temple during His Olivet Discourse, His disciples ask Him when this will happen.

And He said, "See to it that you are not misled; for many will come in My name, saying, "I am He,' and, 'The time is near.' Do not go after them. When you hear of wars and disturbances, do not be terrified; for these things must take place first, but the end does not follow immediately" (Luke 21:8, 9; cf. Matthew 24:4–8; Mark 13:5–8).

DIVIDED FAMILIES (See DIVISION; and HOUSE, DIVIDED)

DIVIDED KINGDOM (Listed under KINGDOM, DIVIDED)

DIVINE JUDGMENT (See JUDGMENT, DIVINE)

DIVINE REVELATION (Listed under REVELATION, DIVINE)

DIVISION (Also see HOUSE, DIVIDED)

[DIVISION from SET A MAN AGAINST HIS FATHER]

Setting: Galilee. After His disciples observe His ministry, Jesus summons and specifically instructs them about their ministry hardships ahead involving true discipleship.

"Do not think that I came to bring peace on the earth; I did not come to bring peace, but a sword. For I came to SET A MAN AGAINST HIS FATHER, AND A DAUGHTER AGAINST HER MOTHER, AND A DAUGHTER-IN-LAW AGAINST HER MOTHER-IN-LAW; and A MAN'S ENEMIES WILL BE THE MEMBERS OF HIS HOUSEHOLD" (Matthew 10:34–36; Jesus quotes from Micah 7:6; cf. Luke 12:51–53).

[DIVISION from divided]

Setting: Galilee. After He heals a blind, mute, demon-possessed man, the Pharisees accuse Jesus in front of crowds of being a worker of Satan.

And knowing their thoughts Jesus said to them, "Any kingdom divided against itself is laid waste; and any city or house divided against itself will not stand. If Satan casts out Satan, he is divided against himself; how then will his kingdom stand? If I by Beelzebul cast out demons, by whom do your sons cast *them* out? For this reason they will be your judges. But if I cast out demons by the Spirit of God, then the kingdom of God has come upon you. Or how can anyone enter the strong man's house and carry off his property, unless he first binds the strong *man?* And then he will plunder his house" (Matthew 12:25–29; cf. Matthew 9:34; Mark 3:23–27; Luke 11:17–20).

[DIVISION from divided]
Setting: Galilee. After Jesus selects His twelve disciples, scribes from Jerusalem attribute His miraculous powers to Beelzebul (Satan).

And He called them to Himself and began speaking to them in parables, "How can Satan cast out Satan? If a kingdom is divided against itself, that kingdom cannot stand. If a house is divided against itself, that house will not be able to stand. If Satan has risen up against himself and is divided, he cannot stand, but he is finished! But no one can enter the strong man's house and plunder his property unless he first binds the strong man, and then he will plunder his house. Truly I say to you, all sins shall be forgiven the sons of men, and whatever blasphemies they utter; but whoever blasphemes against the Holy Spirit never has forgiveness, but is guilty of an eternal sin"—because they were saying, "He has an unclean spirit" (Mark 3:23–30; cf. Matthew 12:25–32; Luke 12:10).

[DIVISION from divided]
Setting: On the way from Galilee to Jerusalem. After Jesus casts out a demon, some in the crowd test Him, demanding a sign from heaven.

But He knew their thoughts and said to them, "Any kingdom divided against itself is laid waste; and a house divided against itself falls. If Satan also is divided against himself, how will his kingdom stand? For you say that I cast out demons by Beelzebul. And if I by Beelzebul cast out demons, by whom do your sons cast them out? So they will be your judges. But if I cast out demons by the finger of God, then the kingdom of God has come upon you" (Luke 11:17–20; cf. Matthew 12:25–28; Mark 3:23–27; see Exodus 8:19; Matthew 3:2, 10:25).

[DIVISION also from divided]
Setting: On the way from Galilee to Jerusalem. After clarifying a parable for Peter and the crowd, Jesus conveys how a relationship with Him divides families.

"I have come to cast fire upon the earth; and how I wish it were already kindled! But I have a baptism to undergo, and how distressed I am until it is accomplished! Do you suppose that I came to grant peace on earth? I tell you, no, but rather division; for from now on five members in one household will be divided, three against two and two against three. They will be divided, father against son and son against father, mother against daughter, and daughter against mother, mother-in-law against daughter-in-law and daughter-in-law against mother-in-law" (Luke 12:49–53; cf. Matthew 10:34–36; see Micah 7:6; Mark 10:38).

[DIVISION from divided]
Setting: On the way from Galilee to Jerusalem. Jesus conveys the illustration of the prodigal son because the Pharisees and scribes complain He associates with tax collectors and sinners.

And He said, "A man had two sons. The younger of them said to his father, 'Father, give me the share of the estate that falls to me.' So he divided his wealth between them. And not many days later, the younger son gathered everything together and went on a journey into a distant country, and there he squandered his estate with loose living. Now when he had spent everything, a severe famine occurred in that country, and he began to be impoverished. So he went and hired himself out to one of the citizens of that country, and he sent him into his fields to feed swine. And he would have gladly filled his stomach with the pods that the swine were eating, and no one was giving anything to him. But when he came to his senses, he said, 'How many of my father's hired men have more than enough bread, but I am dying here with hunger! I will get up and go to my father, and will say to him, "Father, I have sinned against heaven, and in your sight; I am no longer worthy to be called your son; make me as one of your hired men."' So he got up and came to his father. But while he was still a long way off, his father saw him and felt compassion for him, and ran and embraced him and kissed him. And the son said to him, "Father, I have sinned against heaven and in your sight; I am no longer worthy to be called your son.' But the father said to his slaves, 'Quickly bring out the best robe and put it on him, and put a ring on his hand and sandals on his feet; and bring the fattened calf, kill it, and let us eat and celebrate; for this son of mine was dead and has come to life again; he was lost and has been found.' And they began to celebrate. Now his older son was in the field, when he came and approached the house, he heard music and dancing. And he summoned one of the servants and began inquiring what these things could be. And he said to him, 'Your brother has come, and your father has killed the fattened calf because he has received him back safe and sound.' But he became angry and was not willing to go in; and his father came out and began pleading with him. But he answered and said to his father, 'Look! For so many years I have been serving you and I have never neglected a command of yours; and yet you have never given me a young goat, so that I might celebrate with my friends; but when this son of yours came, who has devoured your wealth with prostitutes, you killed the fattened calf for him.' And he said to him, 'Son, you have always been with me, and all that is mine is yours. But we had to celebrate and rejoice, for this brother of yours was dead and has begun to live, and was lost and has been found'" (Luke 15:11–32; see Proverbs 29:2; Luke 15:1, 2).

DIVORCE (Also see MARRIAGE; and REMARRIAGE)

Setting: Galilee. During the early part of His ministry, Jesus preaches the Sermon on the Mount to His disciples and the multitudes.

"It was said, 'WHOEVER SENDS HIS WIFE AWAY, LET HIM GIVE HER A CERTIFICATE OF DIVORCE'; but I say to you that everyone who divorces his wife, except for *the* reason of unchastity, makes her commit adultery; and whoever marries a divorced woman commits adultery" (Matthew 5:31, 32, Jesus quotes from Deuteronomy 24: 1, 3; cf. Matthew 19:9; see Romans 7:2, 3; 1 Corinthians 7:10, 39).

[DIVORCE from let no man separate]

Setting: Judea beyond the Jordan (Perea). After He replies to Peter's question about forgiveness, the Pharisees test Jesus in front of a large crowd with a question about divorce.

And He answered and said, "Have you not read that He who created *them* from the beginning MADE THEM MALE AND FEMALE, and said, 'FOR THIS REASON A MAN SHALL LEAVE HIS FATHER AND MOTHER AND BE JOINED TO HIS WIFE, AND THE TWO SHALL BECOME ONE FLESH'? So they are no longer two, but one flesh. What therefore God has joined together, let no man separate" (Matthew 19:4–6, Jesus quotes from Genesis 1:27; 2:24; cf. Mark 10:5–9; see 1 Timothy 2:14).

Setting: Judea beyond the Jordan (Perea). In front of a large crowd, Jesus responds to the Pharisees' follow-up question about Moses' command regarding a certificate of divorce.

He said to them, "Because of your hardness of heart Moses permitted you to divorce your wives; but from the beginning it has not been this way. And I say to you, whoever divorces his wife, except for immorality, and marries another woman commits adultery" (Matthew 19:8, 9; cf. Deuteronomy 24:1–4; Matthew 5:32; 19:7; Mark 10:1–12; see Romans 7:2, 3; 1 Corinthians 7:10, 39).

Setting: Judea beyond the Jordan (Perea). Jesus teaches the crowds gathered around Him about divorce after the Pharisees test and question Him about this subject.

And He answered and said to them, "What did Moses command you?" They said, "Moses permitted a *man* TO WRITE A CERTIFICATE OF DIVORCE AND SEND *her* AWAY." But Jesus said to them, "Because of your hardness of heart he wrote you this commandment. But from the beginning of creation, *God* MADE THEM MALE AND FEMALE. FOR THIS REASON A MAN SHALL LEAVE HIS FATHER AND MOTHER, AND THE TWO SHALL BECOME ONE FLESH; so they are no longer two, but one flesh. What therefore God has joined together, let no man separate. In the house the disciples *began* questioning Him about this again. And He said to them, "Whoever divorces his wife and marries another woman commits adultery against her; and if she herself divorces her husband and marries another man, she is committing adultery" (Mark 10:3–12, Jesus quotes from Genesis 1:27; 2:24; cf. Matthew 19:1–9; see Deuteronomy 24:1–3; Matthew 5:32; Romans 7:2, 3; 1 Corinthians 7:10, 11, 39; 1, 13; 1 Timothy 2:14).

[DIVORCE from divorces and divorced]

Setting: On the way from Galilee to Jerusalem. The Lord responds to the Pharisees' scoffing at His teaching His disciples about stewardship with an illustration of the earthly commitment of marriage.

"Everyone who divorces his wife and marries another commits adultery, and he who marries one who is divorced from a husband commits adultery" (Luke 16:18; cf. Matthew 5:31, 32; 19:9; Mark 10:11, 12; see Luke 16:1, 14; Romans 7:2, 3; 1 Corinthians 7:10, 39).

DIVORCE, CERTIFICATE OF (See CERTIFICATE)

DIVORCED (See DIVORCE)

DIVORCES (See DIVORCE)

DOCTOR (See PHYSICIAN)

DOCTRINE (See DOCTRINES; PRECEPTS; and TEACHING)

DOCTRINES (Also see PRECEPTS; and TEACHING)

Setting: Galilee. Pharisees and scribes from Jerusalem question Jesus about His disciples' lack of obedience to tradition and the commandments.

And He answered and said to them, "Why do you yourselves transgress the commandment of God for the sake of tradition? For God said, 'HONOR YOUR FATHER AND MOTHER,' and, 'HE WHO SPEAKS EVIL OF FATHER OR MOTHER IS TO BE PUT TO DEATH.' But you say, 'Whoever says to *his* father or mother, "Whatever I have that would help you has been given *to God*," he is not to honor his father or mother.' And *by this* you invalidated the word of God for the sake of your tradition. You hypocrites, rightly did Isaiah prophesy of you: 'THIS PEOPLE HONORS ME WITH THEIR LIPS, BUT THEIR HEART IS FAR AWAY FROM ME. BUT IN VAIN DO THEY WORSHIP ME, TEACHING AS DOCTRINES THE PRECEPTS OF MEN'" (Matthew 15:3–9, Jesus quotes from Exodus 20:12, 21:17, Leviticus 20:9; Isaiah 29:13; cf. Mark 7:5–7; see Matthew 15:1, 2; Colossians 2:22).

Setting: Galilee. The Pharisees and some of the scribes from Jerusalem question why Jesus' disciples do not follow the tradition of ceremonial hand cleansing before eating bread.

And He said to them, "Rightly did Isaiah prophesy of you hypocrites, as it is written: 'THIS PEOPLE HONORS ME WITH THEIR LIPS, BUT THEIR HEART IS FAR AWAY FROM ME. BUT IN VAIN DO THEY WORSHIP ME, TEACHING AS DOCTRINES THE PRECEPTS OF MEN.' Neglecting the commandment of God, you hold to the tradition of men." He was also saying to them, "You are experts at setting aside the commandment of God in order to keep tradition. For Moses said, 'HONOR YOUR FATHER AND YOUR MOTHER'; and, 'HE WHO SPEAKS EVIL OF FATHER OR MOTHER, IS TO BE PUT TO DEATH'; but you say, 'If a man says to *his* father or *his* mother, whatever I have that would help you is Corban (that is to say, given *to God*),' you no longer permit him to do anything for *his* father or *his* mother; *thus* invalidating the word of God by your tradition which you have handed down; and you do many things such as that" (Mark 7:6–13, Jesus quotes from Exodus 20:12; 21:17; Isaiah 29:13; cf. Matthew 15:1–6).

DOERS, EVIL (Also see DEEDS, EVIL; WICKED; and WICKEDNESS)

[EVIL DOERS from everyone who does evil]

Setting: While in Jerusalem for the Passover of the Jews, after the Lord cleanses the temple, a man of the Pharisees, Nicodemus, asks Him by night what He means by being born again.

"For God so loved the world, that He gave His only begotten Son, that whoever believes in Him shall not perish, but have eternal life. For God did not send the Son into the world to judge the world, but that the world might be saved through Him. He who believes in Him is not judged; he who does not believe has been judged already, because he has not believed in the name of the only begotten Son of God. This is the judgment, that the Light has come into the world, and men loved darkness rather than the Light, for their deeds were evil. For everyone who does evil hates the Light, and does not come to the Light for fear that his deeds will be exposed. But he who practices the truth comes to the Light, so that his deeds may be manifested as having been wrought in God" (John 3:16–21; see Luke 19:10; John 1:4; 1:18; Romans 5:8; 1 John 1:6, 7).

DOGS (canines)

Setting: On the way from Galilee to Jerusalem. After responding to the Pharisees' scoffing at His teaching His disciples about stewardship and the permanence of the Law, Jesus conveys the story of the rich man and Lazarus.

"Now there was a rich man, and he habitually dressed in purple and fine linen, joyously living in splendor every day. And a poor man named Lazarus was laid at his gate, covered with sores, and longing to be fed with the crumbs which were falling from the rich man's table; besides, even the dogs were coming and licking his sores. Now the poor man died and was carried away by the angels to Abraham's bosom; and the rich man also died and was buried. In Hades he lifted up his eyes, being in torment, and saw Abraham far away and Lazarus in his bosom. And he cried out and said, 'Father Abraham, have mercy on me, and send Lazarus so that he may dip the tip of his finger in water and cool off my tongue, for I am in agony in this flame.' But Abraham said, 'Child, remember that during your life you received your good things, and likewise Lazarus bad things; but now he is being comforted here, and you are in agony. And besides all this, between us and you there is a great chasm fixed, so that those who wish to come over from here to you will not be able, and that none may cross over from there to us.' And he said, 'Then I beg you, father, that you send him to my father's house—for I have five brothers—in order that he may warn them, so that they will not also come to this place of torment.' But Abraham said, 'They have Moses and the Prophets; let them hear them.' But he said, 'No, father Abraham, but if someone goes to them from the dead, they will repent!' But he said to him, 'If they do not listen to Moses and the Prophets, they will not be persuaded even if someone rises from the dead.'" (Luke 16:19–31; see Luke 3:8; 6:24; 16:1, 14).

DOGS (Gentiles)

Setting: Galilee. During the early part of His ministry, Jesus preaches the Sermon on the Mount to His disciples and the multitudes.

"Do not give what is holy to dogs, and do not throw your pearls before swine, or they will trample them under their feet, and turn and tear you to pieces" (Matthew 7:6; see Matthew 15:26).

Setting: The district of Tyre and Sidon. A Canaanite woman appeals to Jesus to heal her demon-possessed daughter.

But He answered and said, "I was sent only to the lost sheep of the house of Israel." But she came and *began* to bow down before Him, saying, "Lord, help me!" And He answered and said, "It is not good to take the children's bread and throw it to the dogs." But she said, "Yes, Lord; but even the dogs feed from the crumbs which fall from their masters' table." Then Jesus said to her, "O woman, your faith is great; it shall be done for you as you wish." And her daughter was healed at once (Matthew 15:24–28; cf. Mark 7: 24–30; see Matthew 9:22; 10:5, 6).

Setting: The region of Tyre. After the Pharisees and scribes from Jerusalem question His disciples' lack of obedience to tradition in Galilee, Jesus casts out a demon from the daughter of a Gentile (Syrophoenician) woman.

And He was saying to her, "Let the children be satisfied first, for it is not good to take the children's bread and throw it to the dogs." But she answered and said to Him, "Yes, Lord *but* even the dogs under the table feed on the children's crumbs. And He said to her, "Because of this answer go; the demon has gone out of your daughter" (Mark 7:27–29; cf. Matthew 15:21–28).

DOMINATION (Also see GREAT)

[DOMINATION from lord it over them]

Setting: On the way to Jerusalem, where Jesus will die on the cross. Jesus teaches His disciples about true greatness after the mother of James and John, the sons of Zebedee, asks Him to make her sons exalted rulers with Him in His coming kingdom.

But Jesus called them to Himself and said, "You know that the rulers of the Gentiles lord it over them, and *their* great men exercise authority over them. It is not this way among you, but whoever wishes to become great among you shall be your servant, and whoever wishes to be first among you shall be your slave; just as the Son of Man did not come to be served, but to serve, and to give His life a ransom for many" (Matthew 20:25–28; cf. Matthew 23:11; 26:28; Mark 10:42–45).

[DOMINATION from lord it over them]
Setting: On the road to Jerusalem. When James and John ask Jesus for special honor and privileges in His kingdom, the other disciples become angry, so He uses this moment to teach them about servanthood.

Calling them to Himself, Jesus said to them, "You know that those who are recognized as rulers of the Gentiles lord it over them; and their great men exercise authority over them. But it is not this way among you, but whoever wishes to become great among you shall be your servant; and whoever wishes to be first among you shall be slave of all. For even the Son of Man did not come to be served, but to serve, and to give His life a ransom for many" (Mark 10:42–45; cf. Matthew 20:25–28).

[DOMINATION from lord it over them]
Setting: An upper room in Jerusalem. During the Feast of Unleavened Bread (Passover) just before His crucifixion, while Jesus celebrates the Passover meal with His disciples and institutes the Lord's Supper, the disciples argue over who is the greatest among them.

And He said to them, "The kings of the Gentiles lord it over them; and those who have authority over them are called 'Benefactors.' But it is not this way with you, but the one who is the greatest among you must become like the youngest, and the leader like a servant. For who is greater, the one who reclines at the table or the one who serves? Is it not the one who reclines at the table? But I am among you as the one who serves" (Luke 22:25–27; cf. Matthew 20:25–28; 23:11; Mark 10:42–45; Luke 22:1–24).

DOMINION

[DOMINION from All things have been handed over to Me by My Father]
Setting: Galilee. After pronouncing woes against unrepentant cities, Jesus prays a thanksgiving prayer to His Father in heaven.

At that time Jesus said, "I praise You, Father, Lord of heaven and earth, that you have hidden these things from *the* wise and intelligent and have revealed them to infants. Yes, Father, for this way was well pleasing in Your sight. All things have been handed over to Me by My Father; and no one knows the Son except the Father; nor does anyone know the Father except the Son, and anyone to whom the Son wills to reveal *Him*" (Matthew 11:25–27; cf. Luke 10:21, 22).

[DOMINION from All things have been handed over to Me by My Father]
Setting: On the way from Galilee to Jerusalem. The Lord responds to a report from the seventy sent out in pairs to every place He Himself will soon visit.

At that very time He rejoiced greatly in the Holy Spirit, and said, "I praise You, O Father, Lord of heaven and earth, that You have hidden these things from the wise and intelligent and have revealed them to infants. Yes, Father, for this way was well-pleasing in Your sight. All things have been handed over to Me by My Father, and no one knows who the Son is except the Father, and who the Father is except the Son, and anyone to whom the Son wills to reveal Him" (Luke 10:21, 22; cf. Matthew 11:25–27; see Luke 10:1, 17; John 3:35; 10:15).

Setting: Caesarea. Luke, writing in Acts, gives Paul's retelling of his conversion to Christ as he appears before King Agrippa following his hearing before the Jewish Council in Jerusalem and arrest by a Roman commander (on his way to Rome after the apostle's third missionary journey).

"And when we had fallen to the ground, I heard a voice saying to me in the Hebrew dialect, 'Saul, Saul, why are you persecuting Me? It is hard for you to kick against the goads.' And I said, 'Who are You, Lord?' And the Lord said, 'I am Jesus whom you are persecuting. But get up and stand on your feet; for this purpose I have appeared to you, to appoint you a minister and a witness not only to the things which you have seen, but also to the things in which I will appear to you; rescuing you from the *Jewish* people and from the Gentiles, to whom I am sending you, to open their eyes so that they may turn from darkness to light and from the dominion of Satan to God, that they may receive forgiveness of sins and an inheritance among those who have been sanctified by faith in Me' (Acts 26:14–18; see Isaiah 35:5; Acts 21:40; 22:14).

DOMINION OF SATAN (Listed under SATAN, DOMINION OF)

DONATIONS (See GIVING; POOR, GIVING TO THE)

DONKEY

Setting: Entering Bethphage, near Jerusalem. On the way to Jerusalem for His crucifixion, just after healing some blind men in Jericho, Jesus instructs two disciples to acquire a donkey and colt to be used in His triumphal entry into the city.

When they had approached Jerusalem and had come to Bethphage, at the Mount of Olives, then Jesus sent two disciples, saying to them, "Go into the village opposite you, and immediately you will find a donkey tied *there* and a colt with her; untie them and bring them to Me. If anyone says anything to you, you shall say, 'The Lord has need of them,' and immediately he will send them" (Matthew 21:1–3; cf. Mark 11:1–3; Luke 19:29–31).

Setting: A synagogue on the way from Galilee to Jerusalem. After healing a woman, sick for eighteen years, on the Sabbath, Jesus responds to a synagogue official's anger.

But the Lord answered him and said, "You hypocrites, does not each of you on the Sabbath untie his ox or his donkey from the stall and lead him away to water him? And this woman, a daughter of Abraham as she is, whom Satan has bound for eighteen long years, should she not have been released from this bond on the Sabbath day?" (Luke 13:15, 16; see Luke 14:5).

DOOR (DOOR, NARROW; and DOOR, OPEN are separate entries; also see GATE; and KNOCKING)

Setting: Galilee. During the early part of His ministry, Jesus preaches the Sermon on the Mount to His disciples and the multitudes.

"When you pray, you are not to be like the hypocrites; for they love to stand and pray in the synagogues and on the street corners so that they may be seen by men. Truly I say to you, they have their reward in full. But you, when you pray, go into your inner room, close your door and pray to your Father who is in secret, and your Father who sees *what is done* in secret will reward you" (Matthew 6:5, 6; see Mark 11:25).

Setting: The Mount of Olives, just east of Jerusalem. During His discourse, after answering His disciples' questions as to when the temple will be destroyed and Jerusalem overrun, along with the signs of His coming and the end of the age, Jesus teaches them the Parable of the Fig Tree.

"Now learn the parable from the fig tree: when its branch has already become tender and puts forth its leaves, you know that summer is near; so, you too, when you see all these things, recognize that He is near, *right* at the door. Truly, I say to you, this generation will not pass away until all these things take place. Heaven and earth will pass away, but My words will not pass away. But of that day and hour no one knows, not even the angels of heaven, nor the Son, but the Father alone. For the coming of the Son of Man will be just like the days of Noah. For as in those days before the flood they were eating and drinking, marrying and giving in marriage, until the day that Noah entered the ark, and they did not understand until the flood came and took them all away; so will the coming of the Son of Man be. Then there will be two men in the field; one will be taken and one will be left. Two women *will be* grinding at the mill; one will be taken and one will be left" (Matthew 24:32–41; cf. Mark 13:28–32; Luke 17:34–36; 21:28–33; see Genesis 6:5; 7:7; Matthew 5:18; 10:23; James 5:9).

Setting: The Mount of Olives, just east of Jerusalem. During His discourse, after answering His disciples' questions as to when the temple will be destroyed and Jerusalem overrun, along with the signs of His coming and the end of the age, Jesus reemphasizes to His disciples that they should be on the alert for His return.

"Then the kingdom of heaven will be comparable to ten virgins, who took their lamps and went out to meet the bridegroom. Five of them were foolish, and five were prudent. For when the foolish took their lamps, they took no oil with them, but the prudent took oil in flasks along with their lamps. Now while the bridegroom was delaying, they all got drowsy and *began* to sleep. But at midnight there was a shout, 'Behold, the bridegroom! Come out to meet *him*.' Then all those virgins rose and trimmed their lamps. The foolish said to the prudent, 'Give us some of your oil, for our lamps are going out.' But the prudent answered, 'No, there will not be enough for us and you *too;* go instead to the dealers and buy *some* for yourselves.' And while they were going away to make the purchase, the bridegroom came, and those who were ready went in with him to the wedding feast; and the door was shut. Later the other virgins also came, saying, 'Lord, lord, open up for us.' But he answered, 'Truly I say to you, I do not know you.' Be on the alert then, for you do not know the day nor the hour" (Matthew 25:1–13; cf. Matthew 24:42; Luke 12:35; see Matthew 7:21, 24).

Setting: On the Mount of Olives, east of the temple in Jerusalem. During His discourse, after prophesying the temple's destruction, Jesus responds to questions from Peter, James, John, and Andrew about future events.

"Now learn the parable from the fig tree: when its branch has already become tender and puts forth its leaves, you know that summer is near. Even so, you too, when you see these things happening, recognize that He is near, *right* at the door. Truly I say to you, this generation will not pass away until all these things take place. Heaven and earth will pass away, but My words will not pass away. But of the day or hour no one knows, not even the angels in heaven, nor the Son, but the Father *alone*" (Mark 13:28–32; cf. Matthew 24:32–36; Luke 21:28–33).

Setting: On the way from Galilee to Jerusalem. After revealing to His disciples how to pray, Jesus illustrates persistence in prayer.

Then He said to them, "Suppose one of you has a friend, and goes to him at midnight and says to him, 'Friend, lend me three loaves; for a friend of mine has come to me from a journey, and I have nothing to set before him'; and from inside he answers and says, 'Do not bother me; the door has already been shut and my children and I are in bed; I cannot get up and give you anything.' I tell you, even though he will not get up and give him anything because he is his friend, yet because of his persistence he will get up and give him as much as he needs. So I say to you, ask, and it will be given to you; seek, and you will find; knock, and it will be opened to you. For everyone who asks, receives; and he who seeks, finds; and to him who knocks, it will be opened" (Luke 11:5–10; cf. Matthew 7:7, 8; see Luke 18:1–5).

Setting: On the way from Galilee to Jerusalem. After giving a parable about riches and greed, Jesus uses a parable to challenge the crowd and His disciples to be ready for His return.

"Be dressed in readiness, and keep your lamps lit. Be like men who are waiting for their master when he returns from the wedding feast, so that they may immediately open the door to him when he comes and knocks. Blessed are those slaves whom the master will find on the alert when he comes; truly I say to you, that he will gird himself to serve, and have them recline at the table, and will come up and wait on them. Whether he comes in the second watch, or even in the third and finds them so, blessed are those slaves. But be sure of this, that if the head of the house had known at what hour the thief was coming, he would not have allowed his house to be broken into. You too, be ready; for the Son of Man is coming at an hour that you do not expect" (Luke 12:35–40; cf. Matthew 24:42–44; see Mark 13:33; Ephesians 6:14).

Setting: On the way from Galilee to Jerusalem. While teaching in the cities and villages, Jesus responds to a question about who is saved.

And someone said to Him, "Lord, are there *just* a few who are being saved?" And He said to them, "Strive to enter through the narrow door; for many, I tell you, will seek to enter and will not be able. Once the head of the house gets up and shuts the door, and you begin to stand outside and knock on the door, saying, 'Lord, open up to us!' then He will answer and say to you, 'I do not know where you are from.' Then you will begin to say, 'We ate and drank in Your presence, and You taught in our streets'; and He will say, 'I tell you, I do not know where you are from; DEPART FROM ME, ALL YOU EVILDOERS.' In that place there will be weeping and gnashing of teeth when you see Abraham and Isaac and Jacob and all the prophets in the kingdom of God, but you yourselves being thrown out. And they will come from east and west and from north and south, and will recline *at the table* in the kingdom of God. And behold, *some* are last who will be first and *some* are first who will be last" (Luke 13:23–30, Jesus quotes from Psalm 6:8; cf. Matthew 7:13, 23; 8:11, 12; see Matthew 19:30; Luke 3:8; 13:22, 23).

Setting: Jerusalem. Following the Pharisees' interrogation and dismissal of the formerly blind man Jesus healed on the Sabbath, the Lord speaks to the Pharisees using parabolic language they do not understand.

"Truly, truly, I say to you, he who does not enter by the door into the fold of the sheep, but climbs up some other way, he is a thief and a robber. But he who enters by the door is a shepherd of the sheep. To him the doorkeeper opens, and the sheep hear his voice, and he calls his own sheep by name and leads them out. When he puts forth all his own, he goes ahead of them, and the sheep follow him because they know his voice. A stranger they simply will not follow, but will flee from him, because they do not know the voice of strangers" (John 10:1–5).

Setting: Jerusalem. Following the Pharisees' interrogation and dismissal of the formerly blind man Jesus healed on the Sabbath, the Lord conveys the Parable of the Good Shepherd to the Pharisees using figures of speech they do not understand.

So Jesus said to them again, "Truly, truly, I say to you, I am the door of the sheep. All who came before Me are thieves and robbers, but the sheep did not hear them. I am the door; if anyone enters through Me, he will be saved, and will go in and out and find pasture. The thief comes only to steal and kill and destroy; I came that they may have life, and have *it* abundantly. I am the good shepherd; the good shepherd lays down His life for the sheep. He who is a hired hand, and not a shepherd, who is not the owner of the sheep, sees the wolf coming, and leaves the sheep and flees, and the wolf snatches them and scatters *them. He flees* because he is a hired hand and is not concerned about the sheep. I am the good shepherd, and I know My own and My own know Me, even as the Father knows Me and I know the Father; and I lay down My life for the sheep. I have other sheep, which are not of this fold; I must bring them also, and they will hear My voice; and they will become one flock *with* one shepherd. For this reason the Father loves Me, because I lay down My life so that I may take it again. No one has taken it away from Me, but I lay it down on My own initiative. I have authority to take it up again. This commandment I received from My Father" (John 10:7–18; see Isaiah 40:11; 56:8; Jeremiah 23:1; Matthew 11:27).

Setting: The island of Patmos (in the Aegean Sea about fifty miles southwest of Ephesus in modern Turkey). On the Lord's Day (Sunday), about fifty years after Jesus' resurrection, the disciple John encounters the Lord Jesus Christ. Jesus communicates a new revelation for the apostle to record for the church in Laodicea and to six other churches in Asia.

"To the angel of the church in Laodicea write: The Amen, the faithful and true Witness, the Beginning of the creation of God, says this: 'I know your deeds, that you are neither cold nor hot; I wish that you were cold or hot. So because you are lukewarm, and neither hot nor cold, I will spit you out of My mouth. Because you say, "I am rich, and have become wealthy, and have need of nothing," and you do not know that you are wretched and miserable and poor and blind and naked, I advise you to buy from Me gold refined by fire so that you may become rich, and white garments so that you may clothe yourself, and *that* the shame of your nakedness will not be revealed; and eye salve to anoint your eyes so that you may see. Those whom I love, I reprove and discipline; therefore be zealous and repent. Behold, I stand at the door and knock; if anyone hears My voice and opens the door, I will come in to him and will dine with him, and he with Me. He who overcomes, I will grant to him to sit down with Me on My throne, as I also overcame and sat down with My Father on His throne. He who has an ear, let him hear what the Spirit says to the churches'" (Revelation 3:14–22; see Proverbs 3:12; Hosea 12:8; John 14:23; 16:33).

DOOR, NARROW

Setting: On the way from Galilee to Jerusalem. While teaching in the cities and villages, Jesus responds to a question about who is saved.

And someone said to Him, "Lord, are here *just* a few who are being saved?" And He said to them, "Strive to enter through the narrow door; for many, I tell you, will seek to enter and will not be able. Once the head of the house gets up and shuts the door, and you begin to stand outside and knock on the door, saying, 'Lord, open up to us!' then He will answer and say to you, 'I do not know where you are from.' Then you will begin to say, 'We ate and drank in Your presence, and You taught in our streets'; and He will say, 'I tell you, I do not know where you are from; DEPART FROM ME, ALL YOU EVILDOERS.' In that place there will be weeping and gnashing of teeth when you see Abraham and Isaac and Jacob and all the prophets in the kingdom of God, but you yourselves being thrown out. And they will come from east and west and from north and south, and will recline *at the table* in the kingdom of God. And behold, *some* are last who will be first and *some* are first who will be last" (Luke 13:23–30, Jesus quotes from Psalm 6:8; cf. Matthew 7:13, 23; 8:11, 12; see Matthew 19:30; Luke 3:8).

DOOR, OPEN

Setting: The island of Patmos (in the Aegean Sea about fifty miles southwest of Ephesus in modern Turkey). On the Lord's Day (Sunday), about fifty years after Jesus' resurrection, the disciple John encounters the Lord Jesus Christ. Jesus communicates a new revelation for the apostle to record for the church in Philadelphia and to six other churches in Asia.

"And to the angel of the church in Philadelphia write: He who is holy, who is true, who has the key of David, who opens and no one will shut, and who shuts and no one opens, says this: 'I know your deeds. Behold, I have put before you an open door which no one can shut, because you have a little power, and have kept My word, and have not denied My name. Behold, I will cause *those* of the synagogue of Satan, who say that they are Jews and are not, but lie—I will make them come and bow down at your feet, and *make them* know that I have loved you. Because you have kept the word of My perseverance, I also will keep you from the hour of testing, that *hour* which is about to come upon the whole world, to test those who dwell on the earth. I am coming quickly; hold fast what you have, so that no one will take your crown. He who overcomes, I will make him a pillar in the temple of My God, and he will not go out from it anymore; and I will write on him the name of My God, and the name of the city of My God, the new Jerusalem, which comes down out of heaven from My God, and My new name. He who has an ear, let him hear what the Spirit says to the churches'" (Revelation 3:7–13; see Isaiah 22:22; Galatians 2:9; Revelation 2:9, 10, 13, 25; 14:1).

DOORKEEPER

Setting: The Mount of Olives, east of the temple in Jerusalem. During His discourse, after prophesying the temple's destruction, Jesus responds to questions from Peter, James, John, and Andrew about future events.

"Take heed, keep on the alert; for you do not know when the *appointed* time will come. *It is* like a man away on a journey, *who* upon leaving his house and putting his slaves in charge, *assigning* to each one his task, also commanded the doorkeeper to stay on the alert. Therefore, be on the alert—for you do not know when the master of the house is coming, whether in the evening, at midnight, or when the rooster crows, or in the morning—in case he should come suddenly and find you asleep. What I say to you I say to all, 'Be on the alert!'" (Mark 13:33–37; cf. Matthew 24:42, 43; Luke 21:34–36; see Luke 12:36–38; Ephesians 6:18).

Setting: Jerusalem. Following the Pharisees' interrogation and dismissal of the formerly blind man Jesus healed on the Sabbath, the Lord speaks to the Pharisees using parabolic language they do not understand.

"Truly, truly, I say to you, he who does not enter by the door into the fold of the sheep, but climbs up some other way, he is a thief and a robber. But he who enters by the door is a shepherd of the sheep. To him the doorkeeper opens, and the sheep hear his voice, and he calls his own sheep by name and leads them out. When he puts forth all his own, he goes ahead of them, and the sheep follow him because they know his voice. A stranger they simply will not follow, but will flee from him, because they do not know the voice of strangers" (John 10:1–5).

DOUBLE-MINDEDNESS (Also see DEVOTION)

[DOUBLE-MINDEDNESS from No one can serve two masters]

Setting: Galilee. During the early part of His ministry, Jesus preaches the Sermon on the Mount to His disciples and the multitudes.

"No one can serve two masters; for either he will hate the one and love the other, or he will be devoted to one and despise the other. You cannot serve God and wealth (Matthew 6:24).

[DOUBLE-MINDEDNESS from after putting his hand to the plow and looking back]
Setting: On the way from Galilee to Jerusalem. The Lord responds to several men seeking to follow Him.

But Jesus said to him, "No one, after putting his hand to the plow and looking back, is fit for the kingdom of God" (Luke 9:62; cf. Matthew 8:19–22; see Philippians 3:13).

[DOUBLE-MINDEDNESS from No servant can serve two masters]
Setting: On the way from Galilee to Jerusalem. The Lord teaches His disciples about stewardship after giving them the story of the prodigal son.

Now He was also saying to the disciples, "There was a rich man who had a manager, and this manager was reported to him as squandering his possessions. And he called him and said to him, 'What is this I hear about you? Give an accounting of your management, for you can no longer be a manager.' The manager said to himself, 'What shall I do, since my master is taking the management away from me? I am not strong enough to dig; I am ashamed to beg. I know what I shall do, so that when I am removed from the management people will welcome me into their homes.' And he summoned each one of his master's debtors, and he began saying to the first, 'How much do you owe my master?' And he said, 'A hundred measures of oil.' And he said to him, 'Take your bill, and sit down quickly and write fifty.' Then he said to another, 'And how much do you owe?' And he said, 'A hundred measures of wheat.' He said to him, 'Take your bill, and write eighty.' And his master praised the unrighteous manager because he had acted shrewdly; for the sons of this age are more shrewd in relation to their own kind than the sons of light. And I say to you, make friends for yourselves by means of the wealth of unrighteousness, so that when it fails, they will receive you into the eternal dwellings. He who is faithful in a very little thing is faithful also in much; and he who is unrighteous in a very little thing is unrighteous also in much. Therefore if you have not been faithful in the use of unrighteous wealth, who will entrust the true riches to you? And if you have not been faithful in the use of that which is another's, who will give you that which is your own? No servant can serve two masters; for either he will hate the one and love the other, or else he will be devoted to one and despise the other. You cannot serve God and wealth" (Luke 16:1–13; cf. Matthew 6:24; see Matthew 25:14–30).

DOUBT (Also see DOUBTS; FAITH; and UNBELIEF)

Setting: On the Sea of Galilee. Following His miraculous feeding of more than 5,000 of His countrymen, in order to take an opportunity to pray, Jesus makes His disciples get into a boat, where He joins them later by walking on the water during a storm.

But immediately Jesus spoke to them, saying, "Take courage, it is I; do not be afraid." Peter said to Him, "Lord, if it is You, command me to come to You on the water." And He said, "Come!" And Peter got out of the boat, and walked on the water and came toward Jesus. But seeing the wind, he became frightened, and beginning to sink, he cried out, "Lord, save me!" Immediately Jesus stretched out His hand and took hold of him, and said to him, "You of little faith, why did you doubt?" (Matthew 14:27–31; cf. Mark 6:47–52; John 6:16–21).

Setting: On the way from Bethany to Jerusalem. The disciples ask Jesus how the fig tree He cursed (an illustration of the nation of Israel) so quickly withered.

And Jesus answered and said to them, "Truly I say to you, if you have faith and do not doubt, you will not only do what was done to the fig tree, but even if you say to this mountain, 'Be taken up and cast into the sea,' it will happen. And all things you ask in prayer, believing, you will receive" (Matthew 21:21, 22; cf. Matthew 7:7; 17:20; Mark 11:20–24; see Matthew 21:20).

Setting: Jerusalem. Following Jesus' instruction to the money changers while cleansing the temple, Peter draws His and His disciples' attention to the earlier-cursed fig tree.

And Jesus answered saying to them, "Have faith in God. Truly, I say to you, whoever says to this mountain, 'Be taken up and cast into the sea,' and does not doubt in his heart, but believes that what he says is going to happen, it will be *granted* him. Therefore I say to you, all things for which you pray and ask, believe that you have received them, and they will be *granted* you. Whenever you stand praying, forgive, if you have anything against anyone, so that your Father who is in heaven will also forgive you your transgressions. [But if you do not forgive, neither will your Father who is in heaven forgive your transgressions'] (Mark 11:22–26; cf. Matthew 21:19–22; see Matthew 6:14, 15; 7:7; 17:20).

Setting: The synagogue in Jesus' hometown of Nazareth in Galilee. At the beginning of Jesus' public ministry, He comments to the congregation after reading on the Sabbath from the book of the prophet Isaiah.

And He said to them, "No doubt you will quote this proverb to Me, 'Physician, heal yourself! Whatever we heard was done at Capernaum, do here in your hometown as well.'" And He said, "Truly I say to you, no prophet is welcome in his hometown. But I say to you in truth, there were many widows in Israel in the days of Elijah, when the sky was shut up for three years and six months, when a great famine came over all the land; and yet Elijah was sent to none of them, but only to Zarephath, *in the land* of Sidon, to a woman who was a widow. And there were many lepers in Israel in the time of Elisha the prophet; and none of them was cleansed, but only Naaman the Syrian" (Luke 4:23–27; Jesus refers to 1 Kings 17:1, 9; 2 Kings 5:1–14; see Matthew 13:53–58).

DOUBTS (Also see DOUBT)

Setting: Jerusalem. After rising from the grave on the third day after being crucified, and appearing to two of His followers on the road to Emmaus, Jesus appears to some other disciples.

While they were telling these things, He Himself stood in their midst and said to them, "Peace be to you." But they were startled and frightened and thought they were seeing a spirit. And He said to them, "Why are you troubled, and why do doubts arise in your hearts? See My hands and My feet, that it is I Myself; touch Me and see, for a spirit does not have flesh and bones as you see that I have." And when He had said this, He showed them His hands and His feet. While they still could not believe it because of their joy and amazement. He said to them, "Have you anything to eat?" They gave Him a piece of a broiled fish; and He took it and ate it before them (Luke 24:36–43; see Mark 16:14; John 20:27; Acts 10:40, 41).

DOVES (Also see BIRDS; RAVENS; and SPARROWS)

Setting: Galilee. After His disciples observe His ministry, Jesus summons and specifically instructs them about the upcoming hardships of *their* ministry to the people of Israel.

"Behold, I send you out as sheep in the midst of wolves; so be shrewd as serpents and innocent as doves. But beware of men, for they will hand you over to *the* courts and scourge you in their synagogues; and you will even be brought before governors and kings for My sake, as a testimony to them and to the Gentiles. But when they hand you over, do not worry about how or what you are to say; for it will be given you in that hour what you are to say. For it is not you who speak, but *it* is the Spirit of your Father who speaks in you" (Matthew 10:16–20; cf. Luke 10:3).

DRAGNET (Listed under DRAGNET, PARABLE OF THE)

DRAGNET, PARABLE OF THE

Setting: By the Sea of Galilee. Because the religious leaders are rejecting His message, Jesus continues teaching His disciples with the Parable of the Dragnet.

"Again, the kingdom of heaven is like a dragnet cast into the sea, and gathering *fish* of every kind; and when it was filled, they drew it up on the beach; and they sat down and gathered the good *fish* into containers, but the bad they threw away. So it will be at the end of the age; the angels will come forth and take out the wicked from among the righteous, and will throw them into the furnace of fire; in that place there will be weeping and gnashing of teeth. Have you understood all these things?" They said to Him, "Yes" (Matthew 13:47–51).

DRINKING (figurative)

[DRINKING from Are you able to drink the cup that I am about to drink]

Setting: On the way to Jerusalem. The mother of James and John, the sons of Zebedee, asks Jesus to make her sons exalted rulers with Him in His coming kingdom.

And He said to her, "What do you wish?" She said to Him, 'Command that in Your kingdom these two sons of mine may sit one on Your right and one on Your left.' But Jesus answered, "You do not know what you are asking. Are you able to drink the cup that I am about to drink?" They said to Him, 'We are able.' He said to them, "My cup you shall drink; but to sit on My right and on *My* left, this is not Mine to give, but it is for those for whom it has been prepared by My Father" (Matthew 20:21–23; cf. Mark 10:35–40; see Matthew 19:28; Matthew 20:20; Acts 12:2).

[DRINKING from drink]

Setting: An upper room in Jerusalem. After celebrating the Passover meal with His disciples, Jesus retreats to the Garden of Gethsemane on the Mount of Olives to pray prior to His betrayal by Judas.

Then Jesus came with them to a place called Gethsemane, and said to His disciples, "Sit here while I go over there and pray." And He took with Him Peter and the two sons of Zebedee, and began to be grieved and distressed. Then He said to them, "My soul is deeply grieved, to the point of death; remain here and keep watch with Me." And He went a little beyond *them,* and fell on His face and prayed, saying, "My Father, if it is possible, let this cup pass from Me; yet not as I will, but as You will." And He came to the disciples and found them sleeping, and said to Peter, "So, you *men* could not keep watch with Me for one hour? Keep watching and praying that you may not enter into temptation; the spirit is willing, but the flesh is weak." He went away again a second time and prayed, saying, "My Father, if this cannot pass away unless I drink it, Your will be done." Again He came and found them sleeping, for their eyes were heavy. And He left them again, and went away and prayed a third time, saying the same thing once more. Then He came to the disciples and said to them, "Are you still sleeping and resting? Behold the hour is at hand and the Son of Man is being betrayed into the hands of sinners. Get up, let us be going; behold the one who betrays Me is at hand!" (Matthew 26:36–46; cf. Mark 14:32–42; Luke 22:40–46; see Matthew 20:22; John 12:27).

[DRINKING from Are you able to drink the cup that I drink, or to be baptized with the baptism with which I am baptized]

Setting: On the road to Jerusalem. After Jesus prophesies His persecution, death, and resurrection, James and John ask Him for special honor and privileges in His coming kingdom.

And He said to them, "What do you want Me to do for you?" They said to Him, "Grant that we may sit, one on Your right and one on *Your* left, in Your glory." But Jesus said to them, "You do not know what you are asking. Are you able to drink the cup that I drink, or to be baptized with the baptism with which I am baptized?" They said to Him, "We are able." And Jesus said to them, "The cup that I drink you shall drink; and you shall be baptized with the baptism with which I am baptized. But to sit on My right or on *My* left, this is not Mine to give; but it is for those for whom it has been prepared" (Mark 10:36–40; cf. Matthew 20:20–23; see Matthew 19:28; Mark 10:35; Acts 12:2).

[DRINKING from drinks]

Setting: Sychar in Samaria, on the way to Galilee. Jesus interacts with a Samaritan woman at Jacob's well, while His disciples shop for food.

Jesus answered and said to her, "Everyone who drinks of this water will thirst again; but whoever drinks of the water that I will give him shall never thirst; but the water that I will give him will become in him a well of water springing up to eternal life" (John 4:13, 14).

[DRINKING from drinks]

Setting: Capernaum of Galilee. After Jesus informs the people whom He miraculously fed with a lad's five loaves and two fish how they might receive the bread out of heaven, the Jewish religious leaders argue with one another when He says He will give His flesh to the world to eat.

So Jesus said to them, "Truly, truly, I say to you, unless you eat the flesh of the Son of Man and drink His blood, you have no life in yourselves. He who eats My flesh and drinks My blood has eternal life, and I will raise him up on the last day. For My flesh is true food, and My blood is true drink. He who eats My flesh and drinks My blood abides in Me, and I in him. As the living Father sent Me, and I live because of the Father, so he who eats Me, he also will live because of Me. This is the bread which came down out of heaven; not as the fathers ate and died; he who eats this bread will live forever" (John 6:53–58; see Matthew 16:16; Luke 4:22; John 3:36; 15:4).

[DRINKING from drink]
Setting: Jerusalem. On the last day of the Feast of Booths, Jesus causes discussion whether or not He is the Christ. While the chief priests and Pharisees attempt to understand where He says He will be going soon, Jesus offers salvation and the abundant life to His hearers.

Now on the last day, the great *day* of the feast, Jesus stood and cried out, saying, "If anyone is thirsty, let him come to Me and drink. He who believes in Me, as the Scripture said, 'From his innermost being will flow rivers of living water'" (John 7:37, 38; see John 7:10–15).

[DRINKING from the cup which the Father has given Me, shall I not drink it]
Setting: The garden across the ravine of the Kidron. Simon Peter attempts to defend Jesus with a sword when Judas betrays him with a Roman cohort, officers from the chief priests, and the Pharisees.

So Jesus said to Peter, "Put the sword into the sheath; the cup which the Father has given Me, shall I not drink it?" (John 18:11; see Matthew 20:22; 26:52; Luke 22:51).

DRINKING (literal; also see THIRST; WATER; and WINE)
[DRINKING from drink]
Setting: Galilee. During the early part of His ministry, Jesus preaches the Sermon on the Mount to His disciples and the multitudes.

"For this reason I say to you, do not be worried about your life, *as to* what you will eat or what you will drink; nor for your body, *as to* what you will put on. Is not life more than food, and the body more than clothing? Look at the birds of the air, that they do not sow, nor reap nor gather into barns, and *yet* your heavenly Father feeds them. Are you not worth much more than they? And who of you by being worried can add a *single* hour to his life? And why are you worried about clothing? Observe how the lilies of the field grow; they do not toil nor do they spin, yet I say to you that not even Solomon in all his glory clothed himself like one of these. But if God so clothes the grass of the field, which is *alive* today and tomorrow is thrown into the furnace, *will He* not much more *clothe* you? You of little faith! Do not worry then, saying 'What will we eat?' or 'What will we drink?' or 'What will be wear for clothing?" For the Gentiles eagerly seek all these things; for your heavenly Father knows that you need all these things. But seek first His kingdom and His righteousness, and all these things will be added to you. So do not worry about tomorrow; for tomorrow will care for itself. Each day has enough trouble of its own" (Matthew 6:25–34; cf. Luke 12:22–31; see 1 Kings 10:4–7; Job 35:11; Matthew 8:26).

[DRINKING from drink]
Setting: Galilee. After His twelve disciples observe His ministry, Jesus summons and specifically instructs them about their ministry ahead, which will include rewards.

"He who receives you receives Me, and he who receives Me receives Him who sent me. He who receives a prophet in the name of a prophet shall receive a prophet's reward; and he who receives a righteous man in the name of a righteous man shall receive a righteous man's reward. And whoever in the name of a disciple gives to one of these little ones even a cup of cold water to drink, truly I say to you, he shall not lose his reward" (Matthew 10:40–42; cf. Matthew 25:40, 44, 45; see Mark 9:37).

Setting: Galilee. After praising John the Baptist as His forerunner, Jesus demonstrates the foolish thinking of the current generation of Jewish religious leaders by repeating what they say about John's ascetic lifestyle and ministry along with His own.

"But to what shall I compare this generation? It is like children sitting in the market places, who call out to the other *children,* and say, 'We played the flute for you, and you did not dance; we sang a dirge, and you did not mourn.' For John came neither eating nor drinking, and they say, 'He has a demon!' The Son of Man came eating and drinking, and they say, 'Behold, a gluttonous man and a drunkard, a friend of tax collectors and sinners! Yet wisdom is vindicated by her deeds" (Matthew 11:16–19; cf. Luke 7:31–35; see Matthew 9:11, 34; Luke 1:15).

Setting: The Mount of Olives, just east of Jerusalem. During His discourse, after answering His disciples' questions as to when the temple will be destroyed and Jerusalem overrun, along with the signs of His coming and the end of the age, Jesus teaches them the Parable of the Fig Tree.

"Now learn the parable from the fig tree: when its branch has already become tender and puts forth its leaves, you know that summer is near; so, you too, when you see all these things, recognize that He is near, *right* at the door. Truly, I say to you, this generation will not pass away until all these things take place. Heaven and earth will pass away, but My words will not pass away. But of that day and hour no one knows, not even the angels of heaven, nor the Son, but the Father alone. For the coming of the Son of Man will be just like the days of Noah. For as in those days before the flood they were eating and drinking, marrying and giving in marriage, until the day that Noah entered the ark, and they did not understand until the flood came and took them all away; so will the coming of the Son of Man be. Then there will be two men in the field; one will be taken and one will be left. Two women *will be* grinding at the mill; one will be taken and one will be left" (Matthew 24:32–41; cf. Mark 13:28–32; Luke 17:34–36; 21:28–33; see Genesis 6:5; 7:7; Matthew 5:18; 10:23; James 5:9).

[DRINKING from drink]
Setting: The Mount of Olives, just east of Jerusalem. During His discourse, after answering His disciples' questions as to when the temple will be destroyed and Jerusalem overrun, along with the signs of His coming and the end of the age, Jesus reemphasizes to His disciples they should be on the alert for His return.

"Therefore be on the alert, for you do not know which day your Lord is coming. But be sure of this, that if the head of the house had known at what time of the night the thief was coming, he would have been on the alert and would not have allowed his house to be broken into. For this reason you also must be ready; for the Son of Man is coming at an hour when you do not think *He will.* Who then is the faithful and sensible slave whom his master put in charge of his household to give their food at the proper time? Blessed is that slave whom his master finds so doing when he comes. Truly I say to you that he will put him in charge of all his possessions. But if that evil slave says in his heart, 'My master is not coming for a long time,' and begins to beat his fellow slaves and eat and drink with drunkards; the master of that slave will come on a day when he does not expect *him* and at an hour which he does not know, and will cut him in pieces and assign him a place with the hypocrites; in that place there will be weeping and gnashing of teeth" (Matthew 24:42–51; cf. Mark 13:33–37; Luke 12:39–46; 21:34–36; see Matthew 8:11, 12; 25:21–23).

[DRINKING from drink]
Setting: The Mount of Olives, just east of Jerusalem. During His discourse, after answering His disciples' questions as to when the temple will be destroyed and Jerusalem overrun, along with the signs of His coming and the end of the age, Jesus reveals the future judgments following His return.

"But when the Son of Man comes in His glory, and all the angels with Him, then He will sit on His glorious throne. All the nations will be gathered before Him; and He will separate them from one another, as the shepherd separates the sheep from the goats; and He will put the sheep on His right, and the goats on the left. Then the King will say to those on His right, 'Come, you who are blessed of My Father, inherit the kingdom prepared for you from the foundation of the world. 'For I was hungry, and you gave Me *something* to eat; I was thirsty, and you gave Me *something* to drink; I was a stranger, and you invited Me in; naked, and you clothed Me; I was sick, and you visited Me; I was in prison, and you came to Me.' Then the righteous will answer Him, 'Lord, when did we see You hungry and feed You, or thirsty, and give you *something* to drink? And when did we see You a stranger, and invite You in, or naked, and clothe You? When did we see You sick, or in prison, and come to You?' The King will answer and say to them, 'Truly I say to you, to the extent that you did it to one of these brothers of Mine, *even* the least *of them,* you did it to Me.' Then He will also say to those on His left, 'Depart from Me, accursed ones, into the eternal fire which has been prepared for the devil

and his angels; for I was hungry, and you gave Me *nothing* to eat; I was thirsty, and you gave Me nothing to drink; I was a stranger, and you did not invite Me in; naked, and you did not clothe Me; sick, and in prison, and you did not visit Me.' Then they themselves also will answer, 'Lord, when did we see You hungry, or thirsty, or a stranger, or naked, or sick, or in prison, and did not take care of You?' Then He will answer them, 'Truly I say to you, to the extent that you did not do it to one of the least of these, you did not do it to Me.' These will go away into eternal punishment, but the righteous into eternal life" (Matthew 25:31–46; see Matthew 7:23; 16:27; 19:29).

[DRINKING from drink]
Setting: An upper room in Jerusalem. While celebrating the Passover meal with His disciples, Jesus institutes the Lord's Supper ordinance before being arrested by His enemies.

While they were eating, Jesus took *some* bread, and after a blessing, He broke *it* and gave *it* to the disciples, and said, "Take, eat; this is My body." And when He had taken a cup and given thanks, He gave *it* to them saying, "Drink from it, all of you; for this is My blood of the covenant, which is poured out for many for forgiveness of sins. But I say to you, I will not drink of this fruit of the vine from now on until that day when I drink it new with you in My Father's kingdom" (Matthew 26:26–29; cf. Mark 14:22–25; Luke 22:17–20; 1 Corinthians 11:23–26; see Matthew 26:30; 1 Corinthians 10:16).

[DRINKING from drink]
Setting: Capernaum of Galilee. As Jesus teaches His disciples in private, they ask Him about greatness.

But Jesus said, "Do not hinder him, for there is no one who will perform a miracle in My name, and be able soon afterward to speak evil of Me. For he who is not against us is for us. For whoever gives you a cup of water to drink because of your name as *followers* of Christ, truly I say to you, he will not lose his reward. Whoever causes one of these little ones who believe to stumble, it would be better for him if, with a heavy millstone hung around his neck, he had been cast into the sea. If your hand causes you to stumble, cut it off; it is better for you to enter life crippled, than, having your two hands, to go into hell, into the unquenchable fire, [where THEIR WORM DOES NOT DIE, AND THE FIRE IS NOT QUENCHED.] If your foot causes you to stumble, cut it off; it is better for you to enter life lame, than, having your two feet, to be cast into hell, [where THEIR WORM DOES NOT DIE, AND THE FIRE IS NOT QUENCHED.] If your eye causes you to stumble, throw it out; it is better for you to enter the kingdom of God with one eye, than, having two eyes, to be cast into hell, where THEIR WORM DOES NOT DIE, AND THE FIRE IS NOT QUENCHED. For everyone will be salted with fire. Salt is good; but if the salt becomes unsalty, with what will you make it salty *again?* Have salt in yourselves, and be at peace with one another" (Mark 9:39–50; Jesus quotes from Isaiah 66:24; cf. Matthew 18:6–9; Luke 9:49–50; see Matthew 5:13, 29, 30; Matthew 10:42; 12:30; 18:5, 6; Mark 9:38).

[DRINKING from drink]
Setting: An upper room in Jerusalem. While celebrating the Feast of Unleavened Bread (Passover) with His disciples, Jesus institutes the ordinance of the Lord's Supper.

While they were eating, He took *some* bread, and after a blessing He broke *it*, and gave *it* to them, and said, "Take *it;* this is My body." And when He had taken a cup *and* given thanks, He gave *it* to them, and they all drank from it. And He said to them, "This is My blood of the covenant, which is poured out for many. Truly I say to you, I will never again drink of the fruit of the vine until that day when I drink it new in the kingdom of God" (Mark 14:22–25; cf. Matthew 26:26–29; Luke 22:17–20; 1 Corinthians 11:23–26; see Exodus 24:8).

[DRINKING from drink]
Setting: Following His resurrection from the dead after being crucified, Jesus commissions His disciples to preach His gospel to the world.

And He said to them, "Go into all the world and preach the gospel to all creation. He who has believed and has been baptized shall be saved; but he who has disbelieved shall be condemned. These signs will accompany those who have believed: in My name they will cast out demons, they will speak with new tongues; they will pick up serpents, and if they drink any deadly poison, it

will not hurt them; they will lay hands on the sick, and they will recover" (Mark 16:15–18; cf. Matthew 28:16–20; see Mark 9:38; John 3:18, 36; 1 Corinthians 15:6).

[Note: Some scholars question the authenticity of Mark 16:9–20, as these verses do not appear in some early New Testament manuscripts.]

Setting: The home of Levi (Matthew) in Capernaum. At a reception for Jesus following Levi's call to be a disciple, the Lord tells a parable to the Pharisees and their scribes, who question His association with tax collectors and sinners.

And He was also telling them a parable: "No one tears a piece of cloth from a new garment and puts it on an old garment; otherwise he will both tear the new, and the piece from the new will not match the old. And no one puts new wine into old wineskins; otherwise the new wine will burst the skins and it will be spilled out, and the skins will be ruined. But new wine must be put into fresh wineskins. And no one, after drinking old wine wishes for new; for he says, 'The old is good enough'" (Luke 5:36–39; cf. Matthew 9:16, 17; Mark 2:21, 22).

Setting: Galilee. After praising John the Baptist to the crowds, Jesus criticizes the Pharisees and lawyers who reject God's purpose and John's message.

"To what then shall I compare the men of this generation, and what are they like? They are like children who sit in the market place and call to one another, and they say, 'We played the flute for you, and you did not dance; we sang a dirge, and you did not weep.' For John the Baptist has come eating no bread and drinking no wine, and you say, 'He has a demon!' The Son of Man has come eating and drinking, and you say, 'Behold, a gluttonous man and a drunkard, a friend of tax collectors and sinners!' Yet wisdom is vindicated by all her children" (Luke 7:31–35; cf. Matthew 11:16–19; see Luke 1:15).

Setting: On the way from Galilee to Jerusalem. The Lord appoints seventy followers and sends them out in pairs to every place He Himself will soon visit.

And He was saying to them, "The harvest is plentiful, but the laborers are few; therefore beseech the Lord of the harvest to send out laborers into His harvest. Go; behold, I send you out as lambs in the midst of wolves. Carry no money belt, no bag, no shoes; and greet no one on the way. Whatever house you enter, first say, 'Peace be to this house.' If a man of peace is there, your peace will rest on him; but if not, it will return to you. Stay in that house, eating and drinking what they give you; for the laborer is worthy of his wages. Do not keep moving from house to house. Whatever city you enter and they receive you, eat what is set before you; and heal those in it who are sick, and say to them, 'The kingdom of God has come near to you.' But whatever city you enter and they do not receive you, go out into its streets and say, 'Even the dust of your city which clings to our feet we wipe off in protest against you; yet be sure of this, that the kingdom of God has come near.' I say to you, it will be more tolerable in that day for Sodom than for that city" (Luke 10:2–12; see Genesis 19:24–28; Matthew 9:37, 38, 10:9–14, 16; Luke 10:1; 1 Corinthians 10:27).

[DRINKING from drink]

Setting: On the way from Galilee to Jerusalem. After the scribes and Pharisees turn hostile, questioning Him in an attempt to catch Him in something He might say, Jesus responds to a question from the crowd and gives a parable about riches and greed

And He told them a parable, saying, "The land of a rich man was very productive. And he began reasoning to himself, saying, 'What shall I do, since I have no place to store my crops?' Then he said, 'This is what I will do: I will tear down my barns and build larger ones, and here I will store all my grain and my goods. And I will say to my soul, "Soul, you have many goods laid up for many years to come; take your ease, eat, drink and be merry."' "But God said to him, 'You fool! This very night your soul is required of you; and now who will own what you have prepared?' So is the man who stores up treasure for himself, and is not rich toward God" (Luke 12:16–21; see Job 27:8; Psalm 39:6; Ecclesiastes 12:9; Philippians 2:3).

[DRINKING from drink]

Setting: On the way from Galilee to Jerusalem. Jesus comforts the crowd and His disciples after giving a parable about riches and greed, while the scribes and Pharisees turn hostile and question Him in an attempt to catch Him in something He might say.

And He said to His disciples, "For this reason I say to you, do not worry about your life, as to what you will eat; nor for your body, as to what you will put on. For life is more than food, and the body more than clothing. Consider the ravens, for they neither sow nor reap; they have no storeroom nor barn, and yet God feeds them; how much more valuable you are than the birds! And which of you by worrying can add a single hour to his life's span? If then you cannot do even a very little thing, why do you worry about other matters? Consider the lilies, how they grow: they neither toil nor spin; but I tell you, not even Solomon in all his glory clothed himself like one of these. But if God so clothes the grass in the field, which is alive today and tomorrow is thrown into the furnace, how much more will He clothe you? You men of little faith! And do not seek what you will eat and what you will drink, and do not keep worrying. For all these things the nations of the world eagerly seek; but your Father knows that you need these things. But seek His kingdom, and these things will be added to you. Do not be afraid, little flock, for your Father has chosen gladly to give you the kingdom" (Luke 12:22–32; cf. Matthew 6:25–33; see 1 Kings 10:4–7; Job 38:41).

[DRINKING from drink]

Setting: On the way from Galilee to Jerusalem. When Jesus uses a parable to challenge the crowd and His disciples to be ready for His return, Peter asks Him whom He is addressing.

And the Lord said, "Who then is the faithful and sensible steward, whom his master will put in charge of his servants, to give them their rations at the proper time? Blessed is that slave whom his master finds so doing when he comes. Truly I say to you that he will put him in charge of all his possessions. But if that slave says in his heart, 'My master will be a long time in coming,' and begins to beat the slaves, both men and women, and to eat and drink and get drunk; the master of that slave will come on a day when he does not expect him and at an hour he does not know, and will cut him in pieces, and assign him a place with the unbelievers. And that slave who knew his master's will and did not get ready or act in accord with his will, will receive many lashes, but the one who did know it, and committed deeds worthy of flogging, will receive but few. From everyone who has been given much, much will be required; and to whom they entrusted much, of him they will ask all the more" (Luke 12:42–48; cf. Matthew 24:45–51; see Leviticus 5:17; Luke 12:41).

[DRINKING from drink]

Setting: On the way from Galilee to Jerusalem. After the Lord's instruction to His disciples on forgiveness, they ask that their faith be increased, He illustrates with the mustard seed and an obedient slave.

And the Lord said, "If you had faith like a mustard seed, you would say to this mulberry tree, 'Be uprooted and be planted in the sea'; and it would obey you. Which of you, having a slave plowing or tending sheep, will say to him when he has come from the field, 'Come immediately and sit down to eat'? But will he not say to him, "Prepare something for me to eat, and properly clothe yourself and serve me while I eat and drink; and afterward you may eat and drink'? He does not thank the slave because he did the things which were commanded, does he? So you too, when you do all the things which are commanded you, say, 'We are unworthy slaves; we have done only that which we ought to have done'" (Luke 17:6–10; see Matthew 13:31; Luke 12:37; 17:5).

Setting: Samaria, on the way from Galilee to Jerusalem. After the Pharisees question Him about the coming of the kingdom of God, Jesus tells His disciples of His second coming.

And He said to the disciples, "The days will come when you will long to see one of the days of the Son of Man, and you will not see it. They will say to you, 'Look there! Look here!' Do not go away, and do not run after them. For just like the lightning, when it flashes out of one part of the sky, shines to the other part of the sky, so will the Son of Man be in His day. But first He must suffer many things and be rejected by this generation. And just as it happened in the days of Noah, so it will be also in the days of the Son of Man: they were eating, they were drinking, they were marrying, they were being given in marriage, until the day that Noah entered the ark, and the flood came and destroyed them all. It was the same as happened in the days of Lot: they were eating, they were drinking, they were buying, they were selling, they were planting, they were building; but on the day that Lot went out from Sodom it rained fire and brimstone from heaven and destroyed them all. It will be just the same on the day that the Son of Man is revealed. On that day, the one who is on the housetop and whose goods are in the house must not go down to take them out; and likewise the one who is in the field must not turn back. Remember Lot's wife. Whoever seeks to keep his life will lose it, and whoever loses his life will preserve it. I tell you, on that night there will be two in one bed; one will be taken and the other will be left. There will be two women grinding at the same place; one will be taken and the other will be left. [Two men will be in the field; one will be taken and the other will be left."] And answering they said to Him, "Where, Lord?" And He said to them, "Where the body is, there also the vultures will be gathered" (Luke 17:22–37; see Genesis 19; Matthew 10:39; 16:21, 27; 24:17–28, 37–41).

[DRINKING from drink]
Setting: An upper room in Jerusalem. During the Feast of Unleavened Bread (Passover) just before His crucifixion, while celebrating the Passover meal with His disciples, Jesus institutes the Lord's Supper.

And when He had taken a cup and given thanks, He said, "Take this and share it among yourselves; for I say to you, I will not drink of the fruit of the vine from now on until the kingdom of God comes." And when he had taken some bread and given thanks, He broke it and gave it to them, saying, "This is My body which is given for you; do this in remembrance of Me." And in the same way He took the cup after they had eaten, saying, "This cup which is poured out for you is the new covenant in My blood. But behold, the hand of the one betraying Me is with Mine on the table. For indeed, the Son of Man is going as it has been determined; but woe to that man by whom He is betrayed!" (Luke 22:17–22; cf. Matthew 26:26–29; Mark 14:22–25; 1 Corinthians 11:23–26; see Psalm 41:9; Luke 14:15; 22:1–16, 23; 1 Corinthians 10:16).

[DRINKING from drink]
Setting: An upper room in Jerusalem. During the Feast of Unleavened Bread (Passover) just before Jesus' crucifixion, Jesus celebrates the Passover meal and institutes the Lord's Supper. After His disciples argue over who is the greatest among them, He details the kingdom benefits His disciples will experience.

"You are those who have stood by Me in My trials; for just as My Father has granted Me a kingdom, I grant you that you may eat and drink at My table in My kingdom, and you will sit on thrones judging the twelve tribes of Israel" (Luke 22:28–30; cf. Matthew 19:28).

[DRINKING from drink]
Setting: Sychar in Samaria, on the way to Galilee. After the Pharisees hear Jesus is making more disciples than John the Baptist, He encounters a Samaritan woman at Jacob's well, while His disciples are buying food.

There came a woman of Samaria to draw water. Jesus said to her, "Give Me a drink" (John 4:7; see John 4:1–4).

[DRINKING from drink]
Setting: Sychar in Samaria, on the way from Jerusalem to Galilee. Jesus interacts with a Samaritan woman at Jacob's well, while His disciples buy food.

Jesus answered and said to her, "If you knew the gift of God, and who it is who says to you, 'Give Me a drink,' you would have asked Him, and He would have given you living water" (John 4:10).

[DRINKING from drinks]
Setting: Sychar in Samaria, on the way to Galilee. Jesus interacts with a Samaritan woman at Jacob's well, while His disciples buy food.

Jesus answered and said to her, "Everyone who drinks of this water will thirst again; but whoever drinks of the water that I will give him shall never thirst; but the water that I will give him will become in him a well of water springing up to eternal life" (John 4:13, 14).

[DRINKING from drink]
Setting: An upper room in Jerusalem. During his third missionary journey, writing from Ephesus to the church at Corinth, the apostle Paul recounts the Lord Jesus' words as He instituted the Lord's Supper.

For I received from the Lord that which I also delivered to you, that the Lord Jesus in the night in which He was betrayed took bread; and when He had given thanks, He broke it and said, "This is My body, which is for you; do this in remembrance of Me." In the same way *He took* the cup also after supper, saying, "This cup is the new covenant in My blood; do this, as often as you drink *it,* in remembrance of Me" (1 Corinthians 11:23–25; cf. Matthew 26:26–28; Mark 14:22–24; Luke 22:17–20).

DRUNKARD (Also see DRUNKARDS; and WINE)

Setting: Galilee. After praising John the Baptist as His forerunner, Jesus demonstrates the foolish thinking of the current generation of Jewish religious leaders by repeating what they say about John's ascetic lifestyle and ministry along with His own.

"But to what shall I compare this generation? It is like children sitting in the market places, who call out to the other *children,* and say, 'We played the flute for you, and you did not dance; we sang a dirge, and you did not mourn.' For John came neither eating nor drinking, and they say, 'He has a demon!' The Son of Man came eating and drinking, and they say, 'Behold, a gluttonous man and a drunkard, a friend of tax collectors and sinners! Yet wisdom is vindicated by her deeds" (Matthew 11:16–19; cf. Luke 7:31–35; see Matthew 9:11, 34; Luke 1:15).

Setting: Galilee. After praising John the Baptist to the crowds, Jesus criticizes the Pharisees and lawyers who reject God's purpose and John's message.

"To what then shall I compare the men of this generation, and what are they like? They are like children who sit in the market place and call to one another, and they say, 'We played the flute for you, and you did not dance; we sang a dirge, and you did not weep.' For John the Baptist has come eating no bread and drinking no wine, and you say, 'He has a demon!' The Son of Man has come eating and drinking, and you say, 'Behold, a gluttonous man and a drunkard, a friend of tax collectors and sinners!' Yet wisdom is vindicated by all her children" (Luke 7:31–35; cf. Matthew 11:16–19; see Luke 1:15).

DRUNKARDS (Also see DRUNKARD; and WINE)

Setting: The Mount of Olives, just east of Jerusalem. During His discourse, after answering His disciples' questions as to when the temple will be destroyed and Jerusalem overrun, along with the signs of His coming and the end of the age, Jesus reemphasizes to the disciples they should be on the alert for His return.

"Therefore be on the alert, for you do not know which day your Lord is coming. But be sure of this, that if the head of the house had known at what time of the night the thief was coming, he would have been on the alert and would not have allowed his house to be broken into. For this reason you also must be ready; for the Son of Man is coming at an hour when you do not think *He will.* Who then is the faithful and sensible slave whom his master put in charge of his household to give their food at the proper time? Blessed is that slave whom his master finds so doing when he comes. Truly I say to you that he will put him in charge of all his possessions. But if that evil slave says in his heart, 'My master is not coming for a long time,' and begins to beat his fellow slaves and eat and drink with drunkards; the master of that slave will come on a day when he does not expect *him* and at an hour which he does not know, and will cut him in pieces and assign him a place with the hypocrites; in that place there will be weeping and gnashing of teeth" (Matthew 24:42–51; cf. Mark 13:33–37; Luke 12:39–46; Luke 21:34–36; see Matthew 8:11, 12; Matthew 25:21–23).

DRUNKENNESS (Also see DRUNKARD; and WINE)

Setting: The Mount of Olives, just east of Jerusalem. During His discourse, following a time of ministry in the temple and conveying the Parable of the Fig Tree, Jesus warns His disciples to keep alert regarding future events.

"Be on guard, so that your hearts will not be weighted down with dissipation and drunkenness and the worries of life, and that day will not come upon you suddenly like a trap; for it will come upon all those who dwell on the face of all the earth. But keep on the alert at all times, praying that you may have strength to escape all these things that are about to take place, and to stand before the Son of Man" (Luke 21:34–36; cf. Mark 13:33; see Matthew 24:42–44).

DRY

Setting: Jerusalem. After being arrested and appearing before the Council of Elders (Sanhedrin), Pontius Pilate (Roman governor of Judea), Herod Antipas (tetrarch of Galilee and Perea), and Pilate a second time (when Pilate bows to the crowd's pressure and grants that Jesus be crucified), the Lord prophesies to the women mourning Him regarding the coming judgment of Jerusalem.

But Jesus turning to them said, "Daughters of Jerusalem, stop weeping for Me, but weep for yourselves and for your children. For behold, the days are coming when they will say, 'Blessed are the barren, and the wombs that never bore, and the breasts that never nursed.' Then they will begin TO SAY TO THE MOUNTAINS, 'FALL ON US,' AND TO THE HILLS, 'COVER US.' For if they do these things when the tree is green, what will happen when it is dry?" (Luke 23:28–31, Jesus quotes from Hosea 10:8; see Matthew 24:19).

DUST

Setting: Galilee. After His disciples observe His ministry, Jesus summons and specifically instructs them about their ministry to the people of Israel.

These twelve Jesus sent out after instructing them: "Do not go in *the* way of *the* Gentiles, and do not enter *any* city of the Samaritans; but rather go to the lost sheep of the house of Israel. And as you go, preach, saying, 'The kingdom of heaven is at hand.' Heal *the* sick, raise *the* dead, cleanse *the* lepers, cast out demons. Freely you received, freely give. Do not acquire gold, or silver, or copper for your money belts, or a bag for *your* journey, or even two coats, or sandals, or a staff; for the worker is worthy of his support. And whatever city or village you enter, inquire who is worthy in it, and stay at his house until you leave *that city*. As you enter the house, give it your greeting. If the house is worthy, give it your *blessing of* peace. But if it is not worthy, take back your *blessing of* peace. Whoever does not receive you, nor heed your words, as you go out of that house or that city, shake the dust off your feet. Truly I say to you, it will be more tolerable for *the* land of Sodom and Gomorrah in the day of judgment than for that city" (Matthew 10:5–15; cf. Mark 6:7–11; Luke 9:1–5; see Matthew 3:2; 11:22, 24; 15:24; Luke 22:35; 1 Corinthians 9:14).

Setting: The temple in Jerusalem. Jesus delivers a prophecy to the chief priests and elders after they question His authority.

Jesus said to them, "Did you never read in the Scriptures, 'THE STONE WHICH THE BUILDERS REJECTED, THIS BECAME THE CHIEF CORNER stone; THIS CAME ABOUT FROM THE LORD, AND IT IS MARVELOUS IN OUR EYES'? Therefore I say to you, the kingdom of God will be taken away from you and given to a people, producing the fruit of it. And he who falls on this stone will be broken to pieces; but on whomever it falls, it will scatter him like dust" (Matthew 21:42–44, Jesus quotes from Psalm 118:22; cf. Isaiah 8:14, 15; Mark 12:10, 11; Luke 20:17, 18; see Matthew 21:45, 46).

Setting: Jesus' hometown of Nazareth. After encountering unbelief, Jesus sends His disciples out in pairs with authority and instructions about ministry.

And He summoned the twelve and began to send them out in pairs, and gave them authority over the unclean spirits; and He instructed them that they should take nothing for their journey, except a mere staff—no bread, no bag, no money in their belt—but to wear sandals; and He added, "Do not put on two tunics." And He said to them, "Wherever you enter a house, stay there until you leave town. Any place that does not receive you or listen to you, as you go out from there, shake the dust off the soles of your feet for a testimony against them" (Mark 6:7–11; cf. Matthew 10:1–14; Luke 9:1–5).

Setting: Galilee. After raising Jairus's daughter from the dead, Jesus calls His disciples together and gives them power and authority over demons, along with the ability to heal diseases.

And He said to them, "Take nothing for your journey, neither a staff, nor a bag, nor bread, nor money; and do not even have two tunics apiece. Whatever house you enter, stay there until you leave that city. And as for those who do not receive you, go out from that city, shake the dust off your feet as a testimony against them" (Luke 9:3–5; cf. Matthew 10:1–15; Mark 6:7–11; see Luke 10:4–12).

Setting: On the way from Galilee to Jerusalem. The Lord appoints seventy followers and sends them out in pairs to every place He Himself will soon visit.

And He was saying to them, "The harvest is plentiful, but the laborers are few; therefore beseech the Lord of the harvest to send out laborers into His harvest. Go; behold, I send you out as lambs in the midst of wolves. Carry no money belt, no bag, no shoes; and greet no one on the way. Whatever house you enter, first say, 'Peace be to this house.' If a man of peace is there, your peace will rest on him; but if not, it will return to you. Stay in that house, eating and drinking what they give you; for the laborer is worthy of his wages. Do not keep moving from house to house. Whatever city you enter and they receive you, eat what is set before you; and heal those in it who are sick, and say to them, 'The kingdom of God has come near to you.' But whatever city you enter and they do not receive you, go out into its streets and say, 'Even the dust of your city which clings to our feet we wipe off in protest against you; yet be sure of this, that the kingdom of God has come near.' I say to you, it will be more tolerable in that day for Sodom than for that city" (Luke 10:2–12; see Genesis 19:24–28; Matthew 9:37–38, 10:9–14, 16; Luke 10:1; 1 Corinthians 10:27).

Setting: The temple in Jerusalem. A few days before His crucifixion, after the chief priests and the scribes question His authority to teach and preach, Jesus conveys the Parable of the Vine-Growers to the people.

And He began to tell the people this parable: "A man planted a vineyard and rented it out to vine-growers, and went on a journey for a long time. At the harvest time he sent a slave to the vine-growers, so that they would give him some of the produce of the vineyard; but the vine-growers beat him and sent him away empty-handed. And he proceeded to send another slave; and they beat him also and treated him shamefully and sent him away empty-handed. And he proceeded to send a third; and this one also they wounded and cast out. The owner of the vineyard said, 'What shall I do? I will send my beloved son; perhaps they will respect him.' But when the vine-growers saw him, they reasoned with one another, saying, 'This is the heir; let us kill him so that the inheritance will be ours.' So they threw him out of the vineyard and killed him. What, then, will the owner of the vineyard do to them? He will come and destroy these vine-growers and will give the vineyard to others." When they heard it, they said, "May it never be!" But Jesus looked at them and said, "What then is this that is written: 'THE STONE WHICH THE BUILDERS REJECTED, THIS BECAME THE CHIEF CORNER stone'? Everyone who falls on that stone will be broken to pieces; but on whomever it falls, it will scatter him like dust" (Luke 20:9–18, Jesus quotes from Psalm 118:22; cf. Matthew 21:33–44; Mark 12:1–11; see Ephesians 2:20).

DWELLING PLACES (Also see HOMES; and HOUSES)

Setting: Jerusalem. Before the Passover, after taking issue with Peter's assertion that he would lay down his life for Him, Jesus comforts and gives hope to His disciples regarding their future after He returns to heaven.

"Do not let your heart be troubled; believe in God, believe also in Me. In My Father's house are many dwelling places; if it were not so, I would have told you; for I go to prepare a place for you. If I go and prepare a place for you, I will come again and receive you to Myself, that where I am, there you may be also. And you know the way where I am going" (John 14:1–4; see John 13:35; 14:27, 28).

DWELLINGS, ETERNAL

Setting: On the way from Galilee to Jerusalem. The Lord teaches His disciples about stewardship after giving them the story of the prodigal son.

Now He was also saying to the disciples, "There was a rich man who had a manager, and this manager was reported to him as squandering his possessions. And he called him and said to him, 'What is this I hear about you? Give an accounting of your management, for you can no longer be a manager.' The manager said to himself, 'What shall I do, since my master is taking the management away from me? I am not strong enough to dig; I am ashamed to beg. I know what I shall do, so that when I am removed from the management people will welcome me into their homes.' And he summoned each one of his master's debtors, and he began saying to the first, 'How much do you owe my master?' And he said, 'A hundred measures of oil.' And he said to him, 'Take your bill, and sit down quickly and write fifty.' Then he said to another, 'And how much do you owe?' And he said, 'A hundred measures of wheat.' He said to him, 'Take your bill, and write eighty.' And his master praised the unrighteous manager because he had acted shrewdly; for the sons of this age are more shrewd in relation to their own kind than the sons of light. And I say to you, make friends for yourselves by means of the wealth of unrighteousness, so that when it fails, they will receive you into the eternal dwellings. He who is faithful in a very little thing is faithful also in much; and he who is unrighteous in a very little thing is unrighteous also in much. Therefore if you have not been faithful in the use of unrighteous wealth, who will entrust the true riches to you? And if you have not been faithful in the use of that which is another's, who will give you that which is your own? No servant can serve two masters; for either he will hate the one and love the other, or else he will be devoted to one and despise the other. You cannot serve God and wealth" (Luke 16:1–13; cf. Matthew 6:24; see Matthew 25:14–30).

E

EACH

Setting: Galilee. During the early part of His ministry, Jesus preaches the Sermon on the Mount to His disciples and the multitudes.

"For this reason I say to you, do not be worried about your life, *as to* what you will eat or what you will drink; nor for your body, *as to* what you will put on. Is not life more than food, and the body more than clothing? Look at the birds of the air, that they do not sow, nor reap nor gather into barns, and *yet* your heavenly Father feeds them. Are you not worth much more than they? And who of you by being worried can add a *single* hour to his life? And why are you worried about clothing? Observe how the lilies of the field grow; they do not toil nor do they spin, yet I say to you that not even Solomon in all his glory clothed himself like one of these. But if God so clothes the grass of the field, which is *alive* today and tomorrow is thrown into the furnace, *will He* not much more *clothe* you? You of little faith! Do not worry then, saying 'What will we eat?' or 'What will we drink?' or 'What will be wear for clothing?" For the Gentiles eagerly seek all these things; for your heavenly Father knows that you need all these things. But seek first His kingdom and His righteousness, and all these things will be added to you. So do not worry about tomorrow; for tomorrow will care for itself. Each day has enough trouble of its own" (Matthew 6:25–34; cf. Luke 12:22–31; see 1 Kings 10:4–7; Job 35:11; Matthew 8:26).

Setting: Capernaum of Galilee. Jesus illustrates forgiveness after Peter asks Him if forgiving someone seven times who has sinned against him is adequate.

"For this reason the kingdom of heaven may be compared to a king who wished to settle accounts with his slaves. When he had begun to settle *them,* one who owed him ten thousand talents was brought to him. But since he did not have *the means* to repay, his lord commanded him to be sold, along with his wife and children and all that he had, and repayment to be made. So the slave fell *to the ground* and prostrated himself before him, saying, 'Have patience with me and I will repay you everything.' And the lord of that slave felt compassion and released him and forgave him the debt. But that slave went out and found one of his fellow slaves who owed him a hundred denarii; and he seized him and *began* to choke *him,* saying, 'Pay back what you owe.' So his fellow slave fell *to the ground* and *began* to plead with him, saying, 'Have patience with me and I will repay you.' But he was unwilling and went and threw him in prison until he should pay back what was owed. So when his fellow slaves saw what had happened, they were deeply grieved and came and reported to their lord all that had happened. Then summoning him, his lord said to him, 'You wicked slave, I forgave you all that debt because you pleaded with me. Should you not also have had mercy on your fellow slave, in the same way that I had mercy on you?' And his lord, moved with anger, handed him over to the torturers until he should repay all that was owed him. My heavenly Father will also do the same to you, if each of you does not forgive his brother from your heart" (Matthew 18:23–35; cf. Matthew 6:12, 14, 15; Luke 7:42; see Matthew 25:19–28).

Setting: Judea beyond the Jordan (Perea). Jesus illustrates the kingdom of heaven to His disciples through the story of laborers in the vineyard.

"For the kingdom of heaven is like a landowner who went out early in the morning to hire laborers for his vineyard. When he had agreed with the laborers for a denarius for the day, he sent them into his vineyard. And he went out about the third hour and saw others standing idle in the market place; and to those he said, 'You also go into the vineyard, and whatever is right I will give you.' And *so* they went. Again he went out about the sixth and the ninth hour, and did the same thing. And about the eleventh *hour* he went out and found others standing *around;* and he said to them, 'Why have you been standing idle here all day long?' They said to him, 'Because no one hired us.' He said to them, 'You go into the vineyard too.' When evening came, the owner of the vineyard said to his foreman, 'Call the laborers and pay them their wages, beginning with the last *group* to the first.' When those *hired* about the eleventh hour came, each one received a denarius. When those *hired* first came, they thought that they would receive more; but each of them also received a denarius. When they received it, they grumbled at the landowner, saying, 'These last men have worked *only* one hour, and you have made them equal to us who have borne the burden and the scorching heat of the day.' But he answered and said to one of them, 'Friend, I am doing you no wrong; did you not agree with me for a denarius? Take what is yours and go, but I wish to give to this last man the same as to you. It is not lawful for me to do what I wish with what is my own? Or is your eye envious because I am generous?' So the last shall be first, and the first last" (Matthew 20:1–16; cf. Matthew 19:30).

Setting: The Mount of Olives, just east of Jerusalem. During His discourse, after answering His disciples' questions as to when the temple will be destroyed and Jerusalem overrun, along with the signs of His coming and the end of the age, Jesus reemphasizes to the disciples they should be on the alert for His return.

"For *it is* just like a man *about* to go on a journey, who called his own slaves and entrusted his possessions to them. To one he gave five talents, to another, two, and to another, one, each according to his own ability; and he went on his journey. Immediately the one who had received the five talents went and traded with them, and gained five more talents. In the same manner the one who *had received* the two *talents* gained two more. But he who received the one *talent* went away, and dug a *hole* in the ground and hid his master's money. Now after a long time the master of those slaves came and settled accounts with them. The one who had received the five talents came up and brought five more talents, saying, 'Master, you entrusted five talents to me. See, I have gained five more talents.' His master said to him, 'Well done, good and faithful slave. You were faithful with a few things, I will put you in charge of many things; enter into the joy of your master.' Also the one who *had received* the two talents came up and said, 'Master, you entrusted two talents to me. See, I have gained two more talents.' His master said to him, 'Well done, good and faithful slave. You were faithful with a few things, I will put you in charge of many things; enter into the joy of your master.' And the one also who had received the one talent came up and said, 'Master, I knew you to be a hard man, reaping where you did not sow and gathering where you scattered no *seed.* And I was afraid, and went away and hid your talent in the ground. See, you have what is yours.' But his master answered and said to him, 'You wicked, lazy slave, you knew that I reap where I did not sow and gather where I scattered no *seed.* Then you ought to have put my money in the bank, and on my arrival I would have received my *money* back with interest. 'Therefore take away the talent from him, and give it to the one who has ten talents.' For to everyone who has, *more* shall be given, and he will have an abundance; but from the one who does not have, even what he does have shall be taken away. Throw out the worthless slave into the outer darkness; in that place there will be weeping and gnashing of teeth" (Matthew 25:14–30; cf. Matthew 8:12; 3:12; 24:45–47; see Matthew 18:23, 24; Luke 12:44).

Setting: The Mount of Olives, east of the temple in Jerusalem. During His discourse, after prophesying the temple's destruction, Jesus responds to questions from Peter, James, John, and Andrew about future events.

"Take heed, keep on the alert; for you do not know when the *appointed* time will come. *It is* like a man away on a journey, *who* upon leaving his house and putting his slaves in charge, *assigning* to each one his task, also commanded the doorkeeper to stay on the alert. Therefore, be on the alert—for you do not know when the master of the house is coming, whether in the evening, at midnight, or when the rooster crows, or in the morning—in case he should come suddenly and find you asleep. What I say to you I say to all, 'Be on the alert!'" (Mark 13:33–37; cf. Matthew 24:42–43; Luke 21:34–36; see Luke 12:36–38; Ephesians 6:18).

Setting: Galilee. After selecting His twelve disciples, Jesus teaches the Sermon on the Mount to His disciples and a great throng from Judea, Jerusalem, and the central coastal region of Tyre and Sidon.

And He also spoke a parable to them: "A blind man cannot guide a blind man, can he? Will they not both fall into a pit? A pupil is not above his teacher; but everyone, after he has been fully trained, will be like his teacher. Why do you look at the speck that is in your brother's eye, but do not notice the log that is in your own eye? Or how can you say to your brother, 'Brother, let me take out the speck that is in your eye,' when you yourself do not see the log that is in your own eye? You hypocrite, first take the log out of your own eye, and then you will see clearly to take out the speck that is in your brother's eye. For there is no good tree which produces bad fruit, nor, on the other hand, a bad tree which produces good fruit. For each tree is known by its own fruit. For men do not gather figs from thorns, nor do they pick grapes from a briar bush. The good man out of the good treasure of his heart brings forth what is good; and the evil man out of the evil treasure brings forth what is evil; for his mouth speaks from that which fills his heart" (Luke 6:39–45; cf. Matthew 7:3–6. 16, 18, 20; 12:35; see Matthew 10:24; 15:14).

Setting: Bethsaida in Galilee. Following a day of ministry, Jesus and His disciples try to withdraw from the large crowds, but the crowds, having listened to His teaching about the kingdom of God all day, must be fed physically, too.

But He said to them, "You give them something to eat!" And they said, "We have no more than five loaves and two fish, unless perhaps we go and buy food for all these people." (For there were about five thousand men.) And He said to His disciples, "Have them sit down to eat in groups of about fifty each" (Luke 9:13, 14; cf. Matthew 14:15–21; Mark 6:35–44; John 6:4–13; see Luke 9:12, 15–17).

Setting: On the way from Bethany to Jerusalem. After visiting in the home of Martha and Mary, a disciple asks Jesus to teach them to pray.

And He said to them, "When you pray, say: 'Father, hallowed be Your name. Your kingdom come. Give us each day our daily bread. And forgive us our sins, for we ourselves also forgive everyone who is indebted to us. And lead us not into temptation'" (Luke 11:2–4; cf. Matthew 6:9–13).

Setting: On the way from Galilee to Jerusalem. After healing a woman, sick for eighteen years, in a synagogue on the Sabbath, Jesus responds to a synagogue official's anger.

But the Lord answered him and said, "You hypocrites, does not each of you on the Sabbath untie his ox or his donkey from the stall and lead him away to water him? And this woman, a daughter of Abraham as she is, whom Satan has bound for eighteen long years, should she not have been released from this bond on the Sabbath day?" (Luke 13:15, 16; see Luke 13:10–14, 17; 14:5).

Setting: On the way from Galilee to Jerusalem. The Lord teaches His disciples about stewardship after giving them the story of the prodigal son.

Now He was also saying to the disciples, "There was a rich man who had a manager, and this manager was reported to him as squandering his possessions. And he called him and said to him, 'What is this I hear about you? Give an accounting of your management, for you can no longer be a manager.' The manager said to himself, 'What shall I do, since my master is taking the management away from me? I am not strong enough to dig; I am ashamed to beg. I know what I shall do, so that when I am removed from the management people will welcome me into their homes.' And he summoned each one of his master's debtors, and he began saying to the first, 'How much do you owe my master?' And he said, 'A hundred measures of oil.' And he said to him, 'Take your bill, and sit down quickly and write fifty.' Then he said to another, 'And how much do you owe?' And he said, 'A hundred measures of wheat.' He said to him, 'Take your bill, and write eighty.' And his master praised the unrighteous manager because he had acted shrewdly; for the sons of this age are more shrewd in relation to their own kind than the sons of light. And I say to you, make friends for yourselves by means of the wealth of unrighteousness, so that when it fails, they will receive you into the eternal dwellings. He who is faithful in a very little thing is faithful also in much; and he who is unrighteous in a very little thing is unrighteous also in much. Therefore if you have not been faithful in the use of unrighteous wealth, who will entrust the true riches to you? And if you have not been faithful in the use of that which is another's, who will give you that which is your own? No servant can serve two masters; for either he will hate the one and love the other, or else he will be devoted to one and despise the other. You cannot serve God and wealth" (Luke 16:1–13; cf. Matthew 6:24; see Matthew 25:14–30).

Setting: Jerusalem. Before the Passover, after conveying promises about praying in His name, Jesus prophesies His disciples' future scattering and gives them assurance that in the midst of tribulation they will have His peace.

"Jesus answered them, "Do you now believe? Behold, an hour is coming, and has *already* come, for you to be scattered, each to his own *home,* and to leave Me alone; and *yet* I am not alone, because the Father is with Me. These things I have spoken to you, so that in Me you may have peace. In the world you have tribulation, but take courage, I have overcome the world" (John 16:31–33; see Zechariah 13:7; John 8:29; 14:27; 16:29, 30; Romans 8:37).

Setting: The island of Patmos (in the Aegean Sea about fifty miles southwest of Ephesus in modern Turkey). On the Lord's Day (Sunday), about fifty years after Jesus' resurrection, the disciple John encounters the Lord Jesus Christ. Jesus communicates a new revelation for the apostle to record for the church in Thyatira and to six other churches in Asia.

"And to the angel of the church in Thyatira write: The Son of God, who has eyes like a flame of fire, and His feet are like burnished bronze, says this: 'I know your deeds, and your love and faith and service and perseverance, and that your deeds of late are greater than at first. But I have *this* against you, that you tolerate the woman Jezebel, who calls herself a prophetess, and she teaches and leads My bond-servants astray so that they commit *acts of* immorality and eat things sacrificed to idols. I gave her time to repent, and she does not want to repent of her immorality. Behold, I will throw her on a bed *of sickness,* and those who commit adultery with her into great tribulation, unless they repent of her deeds. And I will kill her children with pestilence, and all the churches will know that I am He who searches the minds and hearts; and I will give to each one of you according to your deeds. But I say to you, the rest who are in Thyatira, who do not hold this teaching, who have not known the deep things of Satan, as they call them—I place no other burden on you. Nevertheless what you have, hold fast until I come. He who overcomes, and he who keeps My deeds until the end, TO HIM I WILL GIVE AUTHORITY OVER THE NATIONS; AND HE SHALL RULE THEM WITH A ROD OF IRON, AS THE VESSELS OF THE POTTER ARE BROKEN TO PIECES, as I also have received *authority* from My Father; and I will give him the morning star. He who has an ear, let him hear what the Spirit says to the churches' (Revelation 2:18–29; Jesus quotes from Psalm 2:8, 9; Isaiah 30:14; see 1 Kings 16:31; Psalm 7:9; Romans 2:5; 1 Corinthians 2:10; 2 Peter 3:9; Revelation 1:14; 2:7; 3:11; 17:1–20).

EAR (Also see EARS; HEARING; and LISTENING)

Setting: Galilee. After His disciples observe His ministry, Jesus summons and specifically instructs them about their ministry ahead involving true discipleship.

"Therefore do not fear them, for there is nothing concealed that will not be revealed, or hidden that will not be known. What I tell you in the darkness, speak in the light; and what you hear *whispered* in your ear, proclaim upon the housetops. Do not fear those who kill the body but are unable to kill the soul; but rather fear Him who is able to destroy both soul and body in hell" (Matthew 10:26–28; cf. Mark 4:22; Luke 12:3; see Hebrews 10:31).

Setting: The island of Patmos (in the Aegean Sea about fifty miles southwest of Ephesus in modern Turkey). On the Lord's Day (Sunday), about fifty years after Jesus' resurrection, the disciple John encounters the Lord Jesus Christ. Jesus communicates a new revelation for the apostle to record for the church in Ephesus and to six other churches in Asia.

"To the angel of the church in Ephesus write: The One who holds the seven stars in His right hand, the One who walks among the seven golden lampstands, says this: 'I know your deeds and your toil and perseverance, and that you cannot tolerate evil men, and you put to the test those who call themselves apostles, and they are not, and you found them *to be* false; and you have perseverance and have endured for My name's sake, and have not grown weary. But I have *this* against you, that you have left your first love. Therefore remember from where you have fallen, and repent and do the deeds you did at first; or else I am coming to you and will remove your lampstand out of its place—unless you repent. Yet this you do have, that you hate the deeds of the Nicolaitans, which I also hate. He who has an ear, let him hear what the Spirit says to the churches. To him who overcomes, I will grant to eat of the tree of life which is in the Paradise of God'" (Revelation 2:1–7; see Genesis 2:9; Ezekiel 28:13; 1 John 4:1; Revelation 1:10, 11, 19, 20; 2:15, 16).

Setting: The island of Patmos (in the Aegean Sea about fifty miles southwest of Ephesus in modern Turkey). On the Lord's Day (Sunday), about fifty years after Jesus' resurrection, the disciple John encounters the Lord Jesus Christ. Jesus communicates a new revelation for the apostle to record for the church in Smyrna and to six other churches in Asia.

"And to the angel of the church in Smyrna write: The first and the last, who was dead, and has come to life, says this: 'I know your tribulation and your poverty (but you are rich), and the blasphemy by those who say they are Jews and are not, but are a synagogue of Satan. Do not fear what you are about to suffer. Behold, the devil is about to cast some of you into prison, so that you will be tested, and you will have tribulation for ten days. Be faithful until death, and I will give you the crown of life. He who has an ear, let him hear what the Spirit says to the churches. He who overcomes will not be hurt by the second death' (Revelation 2:8–11; see Isaiah 44:6; Revelation 1:9, 18; 2:13; 20:6, 14).

Setting: The island of Patmos (in the Aegean Sea about fifty miles southwest of Ephesus in modern Turkey). On the Lord's Day (Sunday), about fifty years after Jesus' resurrection, the disciple John encounters the Lord Jesus Christ. Jesus communicates a new revelation for the apostle to record for the church in Pergamum and to six other churches in Asia.

"And to the angel of the church in Pergamum write: The One who has the sharp two-edged sword says this: 'I know where you dwell, where Satan's throne is; and you hold fast My name, and did not deny My faith even in the days of Antipas, My witness, My faithful one, who was killed among you, where Satan dwells. But I have a few things against you, because you have there some who hold the teaching of Balaam, who kept teaching Balak to put a stumbling block before the sons of Israel, to eat things sacrificed to idols and to commit *acts of* immorality. So you also have some who in the same way hold the teaching of the Nicolaitans. Therefore repent; or else I am coming to you quickly, and I will make war against them with the sword of My mouth. He who has an ear, let him hear what the Spirit says to the churches. To him who overcomes, to him I will give *some* of the hidden manna, and I will give him a white stone, and a new name written on the stone which no one knows but he who receives it' (Revelation 2:12–17; see Numbers 25:1–3; Isaiah 62:2; Revelation 1:16; 2:5, 6, 16).

Setting: The island of Patmos (in the Aegean Sea about fifty miles southwest of Ephesus in modern Turkey). On the Lord's Day (Sunday), about fifty years after Jesus' resurrection, the disciple John encounters the Lord Jesus Christ. Jesus communicates a new revelation for the apostle to record for the church in Thyatira and to six other churches in Asia.

"And to the angel of the church in Thyatira write: The Son of God, who has eyes like a flame of fire, and His feet are like burnished bronze, says this: 'I know your deeds, and your love and faith and service and perseverance, and that your deeds of late are greater than at first. But I have this against you, that you tolerate the woman Jezebel, who calls herself a prophetess, and she teaches and leads My bond-servants astray so that they commit acts of immorality and eat things sacrificed to idols. I gave her time to repent, and she does not want to repent of her immorality. Behold, I will throw her on a bed of sickness, and those who commit adultery with her into great tribulation, unless they repent of her deeds. And I will kill her children with pestilence, and all the churches will know that I am He who searches the minds and hearts; and I will give to each one of you according to your deeds. But I say to you, the rest who are in Thyatira, who do not hold this teaching, who have not known the deep things of Satan, as they call them—I place no other burden on you. Nevertheless what you have, hold fast until I come. He who overcomes, and he who keeps My deeds until the end, TO HIM I WILL GIVE AUTHORITY OVER THE NATIONS; AND HE SHALL RULE THEM WITH A ROD OF IRON, AS THE VESSELS OF THE POTTER ARE BROKEN TO PIECES, as I also have received authority from My Father; and I will give him the morning star. He who has an ear, let him hear what the Spirit says to the churches' (Revelation 2:18–29; Jesus quotes from Psalm 2:8, 9; Isaiah 30:14; see 1 Kings 16:31; Psalm 7:9; Romans 2:5; 1 Corinthians 2:10; 2 Peter 3:9; Revelation 1:14; 2:7; 3:11; 17:1–20).

Setting: The island of Patmos (in the Aegean Sea about fifty miles southwest of Ephesus in modern Turkey). On the Lord's Day (Sunday), about fifty years after Jesus' resurrection, the disciple John encounters the Lord Jesus Christ. Jesus communicates a new revelation for the apostle to record for the church in Sardis and to six other churches in Asia.

"To the angel of the church in Sardis write: He who has the seven Spirits of God and the seven stars, says this: 'I know your deeds, that you have a name that you are alive, but you are dead. Wake up, and strengthen the things that remain, which were about to die; for I have not found your deeds completed in the sight of My God. So remember what you have received and heard; and keep *it,* and repent. Therefore if you do not wake up, I will come like a thief, and you will not know at what hour I will come to you. But you have a few people in Sardis who have not soiled their garments; and they will walk with Me in white, for they are worthy. He who overcomes will thus be clothed in white garments; and I will not erase his name from the book of life, and I will confess his name before My Father and before His angels. He who has an ear, let him hear what the Spirit says to the churches'" (Revelation 3:1–6; see Matthew 10:32; Revelation 1:16).

Setting: The island of Patmos (in the Aegean Sea about fifty miles southwest of Ephesus in modern Turkey). On the Lord's Day (Sunday), about fifty years after Jesus' resurrection, the disciple John encounters the Lord Jesus Christ. Jesus communicates a new revelation for the apostle to record for the church in Philadelphia and to six other churches in Asia.

"And to the angel of the church in Philadelphia write: He who is holy, who is true, who has the key of David, who opens and no one will shut, and who shuts and no one opens, says this: 'I know your deeds. Behold, I have put before you an open door which no one can shut, because you have a little power, and have kept My word, and have not denied My name. Behold, I will cause *those* of the synagogue of Satan, who say that they are Jews and are not, but lie—I will make them come and bow down at your feet, and *make them* know that I have loved you. Because you have kept the word of My perseverance, I also will keep you from the hour of testing, that *hour* which is about to come upon the whole world, to test those who dwell on the earth. I am coming quickly; hold fast what you have, so that no one will take your crown. He who overcomes, I will make him a pillar in the temple of My God, and he will not go out from it anymore; and I will write on him the name of My God, and the name of the city of My God, the new Jerusalem, which comes down out of heaven from My God, and My new name. He who has an ear, let him hear what the Spirit says to the churches'" (Revelation 3:7–13; see Isaiah 22:22; Galatians 2:9; Revelation 2:9, 10, 13, 25; 14:1).

Setting: The island of Patmos (in the Aegean Sea about fifty miles southwest of Ephesus in modern Turkey). On the Lord's Day (Sunday), about fifty years after Jesus' resurrection, the disciple John encounters the Lord Jesus Christ. Jesus communicates a new revelation for the apostle to record for the church in Laodicea and to six other churches in Asia.

"To the angel of the church in Laodicea write: The Amen, the faithful and true Witness, the Beginning of the creation of God, says this: 'I know your deeds, that you are neither cold nor hot; I wish that you were cold or hot. So because you are lukewarm, and neither hot nor cold, I will spit you out of My mouth. Because you say, "I am rich, and have become wealthy, and have need of nothing," and you do not know that you are wretched and miserable and poor and blind and naked, I advise you to buy from Me gold refined by fire so that you may become rich, and white garments so that you may clothe yourself, and *that* the shame of your nakedness will not be revealed; and eye salve to anoint your eyes so that you may see. Those whom I love, I reprove and discipline; therefore be zealous and repent. Behold, I stand at the door and knock; if anyone hears My voice and opens the door, I will come in to him and will dine with him, and he with Me. He who overcomes, I will grant to him to sit down with Me on My throne, as I also overcame and sat down with My Father on His throne. He who has an ear, let him hear what the Spirit says to the churches'" (Revelation 3:14–22; see Proverbs 3:12; Hosea 12:8; John 14:23; 16:33).

EARS (Also see EAR; HEARING; and LISTENING)

Setting: Galilee. While speaking to the crowds, Jesus pays tribute to the ministry of John the Baptist, but emphasizes that the one who is least in the kingdom of heaven is greater than John.

As these men were going *away,* Jesus began to speak to the crowds about John, "What did you go out into the wilderness to see? A reed shaken by the wind? But what did you go out to see? A man dressed in soft *clothing?* Those who wear soft *clothing* are in kings' palaces! But what did you go out to see? A prophet? Yes, I tell you, and the one who is more than a prophet. This is the one about whom it is written, 'BEHOLD, I SEND MY MESSENGER AHEAD OF YOU, WHO WILL PREPARE YOUR WAY BEFORE YOU.' Truly, I say to you, among those born of women there has not arisen *anyone* greater than John the Baptist! Yet the one who is least in the kingdom of heaven is greater than he. From the days of John the Baptist until now the kingdom of heaven suffers violence, and violent men take it by force. For all the prophets and the Law prophesied until John. And, if you are willing to accept *it,* John himself is Elijah who was to come. He who has ears to hear, let him hear" (Matthew 11:7–15, Jesus quotes from Malachi 3:1; cf. Malachi 4:5; Luke 7:24–28; 16:16; see Matthew 14:5).

Setting: By the Sea of Galilee. While teaching and preaching to the crowds from a boat, Jesus conveys the Parable of the Sower.

And He spoke many things to them in parables, saying, "Behold, the sower went out to sow; and as he sowed, some *seeds* fell beside the road, and the birds came and ate them up. Others fell on the rocky places, where they did not have much soil; and immediately they sprang up, because they had no depth of soil. But when the sun had risen, they were scorched; and because they had no root, they withered away. Others fell among the thorns, and the thorns came up and choked them out. And others fell on the good soil and yielded a crop, some a hundredfold, some sixty, and some thirty. He who has ears, let him hear" (Matthew 13:3–9; cf. Mark 4:3–9; Luke 8:4–8).

Setting: By the Sea of Galilee. Jesus responds to His disciples' questions about the Parable of the Sower, which He has just taught from a boat.

Jesus answered them, "To you it has been granted to know the mysteries of the kingdom of heaven, but to them it has not been granted. For whoever has, to him *more* shall be given, and he will have an abundance; but whoever does not have, even what he has shall be taken away from him. Therefore, I speak to them in parables; because while seeing they do not see, and while hearing they do not hear, nor do they understand. In their case the prophecy of Isaiah is being fulfilled, which says, 'YOU WILL KEEP ON HEARING, BUT WILL NOT UNDERSTAND; YOU WILL KEEP ON SEEING, BUT WILL NOT PERCEIVE; FOR THE HEART OF THIS PEOPLE HAS BECOME DULL, WITH THEIR EARS THEY SCARCELY HEAR, AND THEY HAVE CLOSED THEIR EYES, OTHERWISE THEYWOULD SEE WITH THEIR EYES, HEAR WITH THEIR EARS, AND UNDERSTAND WITH THEIR HEART AND RETURN, AND I WOULD HEAL THEM.' But blessed are your eyes, because they see; and your ears, because they hear. For truly I say to you that many prophets and righteous men desired to see what you see, and did not see *it*, and to hear what you hear, and did not hear *it*" (Matthew 13:11–17, Jesus quotes from Isaiah 6:9–10; cf. Matthew 25:29; Mark 4:11–13; Luke 8:10; see Deuteronomy 29:4; John 8:56).

Setting: A house near the Sea of Galilee. Jesus explains the meaning of the Parable of the Wheat and the Tares to His disciples.

And He said, "The one who sows the good seed is the Son of Man, and the field is the world; and as *for* the good seed, these are the sons of the kingdom; and the tares are the sons of the evil *one;* and the enemy who sowed them is the devil, and the harvest is the end of the age; and the reapers are angels. So just as the tares are gathered up and burned with fire, so shall it be at the end of the age. The Son of Man will send forth His angels, and they will gather out of His kingdom all stumbling blocks, and those who commit lawlessness, and will throw them into the furnace of fire; in that place there will be weeping and gnashing of teeth. Then THE RIGHTEOUS WILL SHINE FORTH AS THE SUN in the kingdom of their Father. He who has ears, let him hear" (Matthew 13:37–43, Jesus quotes from Daniel 12:3; cf. Matthew 8:12; 13:50).

Setting: By the Sea of Galilee. During the early part of His ministry, just after a visit from his mother and brothers, Jesus instructs a very large crowd from a boat with the Parable of the Sower.

"Listen to this! Behold, the sower went out to sow; as he was sowing, some seed fell beside the road, and the birds came and ate it up. Other seed fell on the rocky ground where it did not have much soil; and immediately it sprang up because it had no depth of soil. And after the sun had risen, it was scorched; and because it had no root, it withered away. Other seed fell among the thorns, and the thorns came up and choked it, and it yielded no crop. Other seeds fell into the good soil, and as the grew up and increased, they yielded a crop and produced thirty, sixty, and a hundredfold." And He was saying, "He who has ears to hear, let him hear" (Mark 4:3–9; cf. Matthew 13:3–9; Luke 8:5–8).

Setting: Galilee. Following His explanation of the Parable of the Sower to His disciples, Jesus illustrates what they should do with this truth.

And He was saying to them, "A lamp is not brought to be put under a basket, is it, or under a bed? Is it not *brought* to be put on the lampstand? For nothing is hidden, except to be revealed; nor has *anything* been secret, but that it would come to light. If anyone has ears to hear, let him hear" (Mark 4:21–23; cf. Luke 8:16, 17; see Matthew 5:14–16; 10:26).

Setting: Galilee. After the Pharisees and scribes from Jerusalem take issue with His disciples' lack of obedience to tradition, Jesus speaks to a crowd and explains His teaching to His disciples.

After He called the crowd to Him again, He *began* saying to them, "Listen to Me, all of you, and understand: there is nothing outside the man which can defile him if it goes into him; but the things which proceed out of the man are what defile the man. [If anyone has ears to hear, let him hear."] When he had left the crowd *and* entered the house, His disciples questioned Him about the parable. And He said to them, "Are you so lacking in understanding also? Do you not understand that whatever goes into the man from outside cannot defile him, because it does not go into his heart, but into his stomach, and is eliminated?" (*Thus He* declared all foods clean.) And He was saying, "That which proceeds out of the man, that is what defiles the man. For from within, out of the heart of men, proceed the evil thoughts, fornications, thefts, murders, adulteries, deeds of coveting *and* wickedness, *as well* as deceit, sensuality, envy, slander, pride *and* foolishness. All these evil things proceed from within and defile the man" (Mark 7:14–23; cf. Matthew 15:10–20).

Setting: The district of Dalmanutha. After the Pharisees argue with Him, seeking a sign from heaven to test Him, Jesus and His disciples cross to the other side of the Sea of Galilee, where His disciples discuss with one another that they have no bread.

And Jesus, aware of this, said to them, "Why do you discuss *the fact* that you have no bread? Do you not yet see or understand? Do you have a hardened heart? HAVING EYES, DO YOU NOT SEE? AND HAVING EARS, DO YOU NOT HEAR? And do you not remember, when I broke the five loaves for the five thousand, how many baskets full of broken pieces you picked you? They said to Him, "Twelve." When *I broke* the seven for the four thousand, how many large baskets full of broken pieces did you pick up?" They said to Him, "Seven." And He was saying to them, "Do you not yet understand?" (Mark 8:17–21, Jesus quotes from Jeremiah 5:21; cf. Matthew 16:5–12; see Matthew 14:18, 19; Mark 6:41–44, 52; 8:6–9).

Setting: The villages and cities of Galilee. After His visit in the home of Simon the Pharisee, Jesus proclaims and preaches the kingdom of God.

When a large crowd was coming together, and those from various cities were journeying to Him, He spoke by way of a parable: "The sower went out to sow his seed; and as he sowed, some fell beside the road, and it was trampled under foot and the birds of the air ate it up. Other seed fell on rocky soil, and as soon as it grew up, it was withered away, because it had no moisture. Other seed fell among the thorns; and the thorns grew up with it and choked it out. Other seed fell into the good soil, and grew up, and produced a crop a hundred times as great." As He said these things, He would call out, "He who has ears to hear, let him hear" (Luke 8:4–8; cf. Matthew 13:2–9; Mark 4:3–9).

Setting: Galilee. After healing the demon-possessed son of a man in the crowd, the Lord prophesies His upcoming death.

"Let these words sink into your ears; for the Son of Man is going to be delivered into the hands of men" (Luke 9:44; cf. Matthew 17:22, 23; Mark 9:31–32; see Luke 9:22).

Setting: On the way from Galilee to Jerusalem. After Jesus responds to a guest's proclamation about the blessings of eating bread in the kingdom of God, He presents to large crowds the demands of discipleship.

Now large crowds were going along with Him; and He turned and said to them, "If anyone comes to Me, and does not hate his own father and mother and wife and children and brothers and sisters, yes, and even his own life, he cannot be My disciple. Whoever does not carry his own cross and come after Me cannot be My disciple. For which one of you, when he wants to build a tower, does not first sit down and calculate the cost to see if he has enough to complete it? Otherwise, when he has laid a foundation and is not able to finish, all who observe it begin to ridicule him, saying, 'This man began to build and was not able to finish.' Or what king, when he sets out to meet another king in battle, will not first sit down and consider whether he is strong enough with ten thousand *men* to encounter the one coming against him with twenty thousand? Or else, while the other is still far away, he sends a delegation and asks for terms of peace. So then, none of you can be My disciple who does not give up all his possessions. Therefore, salt is good; but if even salt has become tasteless, with what will it be seasoned? It is useless either for the soil or for the manure pile; it is thrown out. He who has ears to hear, let him hear" (Luke 14:25–35; cf. Matthew 5:13; 10:37–39; see Proverbs 20:18; Luke 14:1, 2, 15; Philippians 3:7).

EARTH (Specifics such as EARTH, END OF THE; and EARTH, HEAVEN AND, etc., are separate entries; also see GROUND)

Setting: Galilee. Early in His ministry, Jesus presents the Beatitudes (part of the Sermon on the Mount) to His disciples and the gathered crowds from Galilee, Decapolis, Jerusalem, Judea, and beyond the Jordan.

"Blessed are the gentle, for they shall inherit the earth" (Matthew 5:5; cf. Psalm 37:11; see Matthew 5:1; 13:35).

Setting: Galilee. During the early part of His ministry, Jesus preaches the Sermon on the Mount to His disciples and the multitudes.

"Again, you have heard that the ancients were told, 'YOU SHALL NOT MAKE FALSE VOWS, BUT SHALL FULFILL YOUR VOWS TO THE LORD.' But I say to you, make no oath at all, either by heaven, for it is the throne of God, or by the earth, for it is the footstool of His feet, or by Jerusalem, for it is THE CITY OF THE GREAT KING. Nor shall you make an oath by your head, for you cannot make one hair white or black. But let your statement be 'Yes, yes' *or* 'No, no'; anything beyond these is of evil" (Matthew 5:33–37, Jesus quotes from Leviticus 19:12, Psalm 48:2; Isaiah 66:1; cf. James 5:12).

Setting: Galilee. During the early part of His ministry, Jesus gives a model prayer to His disciples and the multitudes while conveying The Sermon on the Mount.

"Pray, then, in this way: 'Our Father who is in heaven, hallowed be Your name. Your kingdom come. Your will be done, on earth as it is in heaven. Give us this day our daily bread. And forgive us our debts, as we also have forgiven our debtors. And do not lead us into temptation, but deliver us from evil. [For Yours is the kingdom and the power and the glory forever. Amen]'" (Matthew 6:9–13; cf. Luke 11:2–4; see John 17:15).

Setting: Galilee. During the early part of His ministry, Jesus preaches the Sermon on the Mount to His disciples and the multitudes.

"Do not store up for yourselves treasures on earth, where moth and rust destroy, and where thieves break in and steal. But store up for yourselves treasures in heaven, where neither moth nor rust destroys, and where thieves do not break in or steal; for where your treasure is, there your heart will be also" (Matthew 6:19–21; cf. Luke 12:34; see Proverbs 23:4; Matthew 19:21).

Setting: Capernaum near the Sea of Galilee. After Jesus heals and forgives a paralytic of his sins in front of crowds, some scribes accuse Him of blasphemy.

And they brought to Him a paralytic lying on a bed. Seeing their faith, Jesus said to the paralytic, "Take courage, son; your sins are forgiven." And some scribes said to themselves. "This *fellow* blasphemes." And Jesus knowing their thoughts said, "Why are you thinking evil in your hearts? Which is easier to say, 'Your sins are forgiven,' or to say, 'Get up, and walk'? But so that you may know that the Son of Man has authority on earth to forgive sins"—then He said to the paralytic, "Get up, pick up your bed and go home" (Matthew 9:2–6; cf. Mark 2:3–12; Luke 5:17–26; see Matthew 9:1).

Setting: Caesarea Philippi. Jesus responds to Simon Peter's declaration that He is the Christ, the Son of the living God.

And Jesus said to him, "Blessed are you, Simon Barjona, because flesh and blood did not reveal *this* to you, but My Father who is in heaven. I also say to you that you are Peter, and upon this rock I will build My church; and the gates of Hades will not overpower it. I will give you the keys of the kingdom of heaven; and whatever you bind on earth shall have been bound in heaven, and whatever you loose on earth shall have been loosed in heaven" (Matthew 16:17–19; cf. Matthew 18:18; Mark 8:29; Luke 9:20).

Setting: Capernaum of Galilee. After conveying to His disciples the value of little ones, Jesus gives instruction about church discipline.

"If your brother sins, go and show him his fault in private; if he listens to you, you have won your brother. But if he does not listen *to you,* take one or two more with you, so that BY THE MOUTH OF TWO OR THREE WITNESSES EVERY FACT MAY BE CONFIRMED. If he refuses to listen to them, tell it to the church; and if he refuses to listen even to the church, let him be to you as a Gentile and a tax collector. Truly I say to you, whatever you bind of earth shall have been bound in heaven; and whatever you loose on earth shall have been loosed in heaven. Again, I say to you, that if two of you agree on earth about anything that they may ask, it shall be done for them by My Father who is in heaven. For there two or three have gathered together in My name, I am there in their midst" (Matthew 18:15–20. Jesus quotes from Deuteronomy 19:15; cf. Matthew 7:7; 16:19; see Leviticus 19:17; Matthew 28:20; 2 Thessalonians 3:6, 14).

Setting: The temple in Jerusalem. Jesus exposes the truth about Pharisaism to the crowds and His disciples after the Jewish religious leaders test Him with questions.

Then Jesus spoke to the crowds and to His disciples, saying: "The scribes and the Pharisees have seated themselves in the chair of Moses; therefore all that they tell you, do and observe, but do not do according to their deeds; for they say *things* and do not do *them.* They tie up heavy burdens and lay them on men's shoulders, but they themselves are unwilling to move them with *so much as* a finger. But they do all their deeds to be noticed by men; for they broaden their phylacteries and lengthen their tassels *of their garments.* They love the place of honor at banquets and the chief seats in the synagogues, and respectful greetings in the market places, and being called Rabbi by men. But do not be called Rabbi; for One is your Teacher, and you are all brothers. Do not call *anyone* on earth your father; for One is your Father, He who is in heaven. Do not be called leaders; for One is your Leader, *that is,* Christ. But the greatest among you shall be your servant. Whoever exalts himself shall be humbled; and whoever humbles himself shall be exalted" (Matthew 23:1–12; cf. Matthew 20:26; Mark 12:38–40; Luke 20:46, 47; see Exodus 13:9; Deuteronomy 33:3; Matthew 6:1, 5, 6, 9, 16; Mark 14:11; Luke 11:43; 14:11).

Setting: The temple in Jerusalem. After the Jewish religious leaders test Him with questions, Jesus pronounces the eighth of eight woes on them in front of the crowds and His disciples.

"Woe to you, scribes and Pharisees, hypocrites! For you build the tombs of the prophets and adorn the monuments of the righteous, and say, 'If we had been *living* in the days of our fathers, we would not have been partners with them in *shedding* the blood of the prophets.' So you testify against yourselves, that you are sons of those who murdered the prophets. Fill up, then, the measure *of the guilt* of you fathers. You serpents, you brood of vipers, how will you escape the sentence of hell? Therefore, behold, I am sending you prophets and wise men and scribes; some of them you will kill and crucify, and some of them you will scourge in your synagogues, and persecute from city to city, so that upon you may fall *the guilt of* all the righteous blood shed on earth, from the blood of righteous Abel to the blood of Zechariah, the son of Berechiah, whom you murdered between the temple and the altar. Truly I say to you, all these things will come upon this generation" (Matthew 23:29–36; cf. 2 Chronicles 24:21; Zechariah 1:1; Matthew 3:7; Luke 11:47–52; see Matthew 10:23).

Setting: On a mountain in Galilee. Following His resurrection from the dead in Jerusalem, Jesus conveys the Great Commission to the eleven remaining disciples.

And Jesus came up and spoke to them, saying, "All authority has been given to Me in heaven and on earth. Go therefore and make disciples of all the nations, baptizing them in the name of the Father and the Son and the Holy Spirit, teaching them to observe all that I commanded you; and lo, I am with you always, even to the end of the age" (Matthew 28:18–20; cf. Mark 16:15; see Daniel 7:13).

Setting: Capernaum. When Jesus heals and forgives the sins of a paralytic man, some scribes believe He commits blasphemy.

Immediately Jesus, aware in His spirit that they were reasoning that way within themselves, said to them, "Why are you reasoning about these things in your hearts? Which is easier, to say to the paralytic, 'Your sins are forgiven'; or to say, 'Get up, and pick up your pallet and walk'? "But so that you may know that the Son of Man has authority on earth to forgive sins"—He said to the paralytic, "I say to you, get up, pick up your pallet and go home" (Mark 2:8–11; cf. Matthew 9:4–7; Luke 5:21–24).

Setting: Capernaum of Galilee. After Jesus heals and forgives the sins of a paralytic man, some Pharisees and teachers of the law from Galilee and Judea accuse Him of blasphemy.

But Jesus, aware of their reasonings, answered and said to them, "Why are you reasoning in your hearts? Which is easier, to say, 'Your sins have been forgiven you,' or to say, 'Get up and walk'? But, so that you may know that the Son of Man has authority on earth to forgive sins,"—He said to the paralytic—"I say to you, get up, and pick up your stretcher and go home" (Luke 5:22–24; cf. Matthew 9:4–8; Mark 2:8–12; see Matthew 4:24).

Setting: On the way from Galilee to Jerusalem. After clarifying a parable for Peter and the crowd, Jesus conveys how a relationship with Him divides families.

"I have come to cast fire upon the earth; and how I wish it were already kindled! But I have a baptism to undergo, and how distressed I am until it is accomplished! Do you suppose that I came to grant peace on earth? I tell you, no, but rather division; for from now on five members in one household will be divided, three against two and two against three. They will be divided, father against son and son against father, mother against daughter, and daughter against mother, mother-in-law against daughter-in-law and daughter-in-law against mother-in-law" (Luke 12:49–53; cf. Matthew 10:34–36; see Micah 7:6; Mark 10:38).

Setting: On the way from Galilee to Jerusalem. After telling how a relationship with Him will divide families, Jesus chastises the crowds for being able to discern the weather but not the present age.

And He was also saying to the crowds, "When you see a cloud rising in the west, immediately you say, 'A shower is coming,' and so it turns out. And when you see a south wind blowing, you say, 'It will be a hot day,' and it turns out that way. You hypocrites! You know how to analyze the appearance of the earth and the sky, but why do you not analyze this present time?" (Luke 12:54–56; cf. Matthew 16:2–3).

Setting: On the way from Galilee to Jerusalem. After telling His disciples of His second coming, Jesus instructs them about persistence in prayer.

Now He was telling them a parable to show that at all times they ought to pray and not to lose heart, saying, "In a certain city there was a judge who did not fear God and did not respect man. There was a widow in that city, and she kept coming to him, saying, 'Give me legal protection from my opponent.' For a while he was unwilling; but afterward he said to himself, 'Even though I do not fear God nor respect man, yet because this woman bothers me, I will give her legal protection, otherwise by continually coming she will wear me out.'" And the Lord said, "Hear what the unrighteous judge said; now, will not God bring about justice for His elect who cry to Him day and night, and will He delay long over them? I tell you that He will bring about justice for them quickly. However, when the Son of Man comes, will He find faith on the earth?" (Luke 18:1–8; see Luke 11:5–10).

Setting: The Mount of Olives, just east of Jerusalem. During His discourse, following a time of ministry in the temple and giving His disciples more details regarding future events, Jesus speaks of His own return.

"There will be signs in sun and moon and stars, and on the earth dismay among the nations, in perplexity at the roaring of the sea and the waves, men fainting from fear and the expectation of the things which are coming upon the world; for the powers of the heavens will be shaken. Then they will see THE SON OF MAN COMING IN A CLOUD with power and great glory. But when these things begin to take place, straighten up and lift up your heads, because your redemption is drawing near" (Luke 21:25–28, Jesus quotes from Daniel 7:13; cf. Matthew 24:29–31; Mark 13:24–27).

Setting: The Mount of Olives, just east of Jerusalem. During His discourse, following a time of ministry in the temple and conveying the Parable of the Fig Tree, Jesus warns His disciples to keep alert regarding future events.

"Be on guard, so that your hearts will not be weighted down with dissipation and drunkenness and the worries of life, and that day will not come upon you suddenly like a trap; for it will come upon all those who dwell on the face of all the earth. But keep on the alert at all times, praying that you may have strength to escape all these things that are about to take place, and to stand before the Son of Man" (Luke 21:34–36; cf. Mark 13:33; see Matthew 24:42–44).

[EARTH from from below]

Setting: The temple treasury in Jerusalem. Following the Feast of Booths and the scribes' and Pharisees' failed attempt to stone a woman for adultery, Jesus returns the next day to teach. The scribes and Pharisees question His testimony about Himself.

Then He said again to them, "I go away, and you will seek Me, and will die in your sin; where I am going, you cannot come." So the Jews were saying, "Surely He will not kill Himself, will He, since He says, "Where I am going, you cannot come'?" And He was saying to them, "You are from below, I am from above; you are of this world, I am not of this world. Therefore I said to you that you will die in your sins; for unless you believe that I am *He,* you will die in your sins." So they were saying to Him, "Who are You?" Jesus said to them, "What have I been saying to you *from* the beginning? I have many things to speak and to judge concerning you, but He who sent Me is true; and the things which I heard from Him, these I speak to the world" (John 8:21–26; see John 3:31–33; 5:34, 35; 17:14, 16).

Setting: Jerusalem. Just days before the Passover, with the chief priests and Pharisees plotting to seize Him, crowds welcome Jesus to Jerusalem with palm branches and praise, and some Greeks ask to meet Him.

And Jesus answered them, saying, "The hour has come for the Son of Man to be glorified. Truly, truly, I say to you, unless a grain of wheat falls into the earth and dies, it remains alone; but if it dies, it bears much fruit. He who loves his life loses it, and he who hates his life in this world will keep it to life eternal. If anyone serves Me, he must follow Me; and where I am, there My servant will be also; if anyone serves Me, the Father will honor him" (John 12:23–26; see Matthew 10:39).

Setting: Jerusalem. Just days before the Passover, with the chief priests and Pharisees plotting to seize Him and crowds welcoming Him with palm branches and praise, Jesus expresses anxiety about His upcoming death by crucifixion.

"Now My soul has become troubled; and what shall I say, 'Father, save Me from this hour'? But for this purpose I came to this hour. Father glorify Your name." Then a voice came out of heaven: "I have glorified it, and will glorify it again." So the crowd of people who stood by and heard it were saying that it had thundered; others were saying, "An angel has spoken to Him." Jesus answered and said, "This voice has not come for My sake, but for your sakes. Now judgment is upon this world; now the ruler of this world will be cast out. And I, if I am lifted up from the earth, will draw all men to Myself" (John 12:27–32; see Matthew 3:17; 26:38; John 3:14; 6:44; 11:42; 14:30).

Setting: Jerusalem. Before the Passover, after giving His disciples assurance that in the midst of tribulation they will have His peace, Jesus prays His high-priestly prayer.

Jesus spoke these things; and lifting up His eyes to heaven, He said, "Father, the hour has come; glorify Your Son, that the Son may glorify You, even as You gave Him authority over all flesh, that to all whom You have given Him, He may give eternal life. This is eternal life, that they may know You, the only true God, and Jesus Christ whom You have sent. I glorified You on the earth, having accomplished the work which you have given Me to do. Now, Father, glorify Me together with Yourself, with the glory which

I had with You before the world was. I have manifested Your name to the men whom You gave Me out of the world; they were Yours and You gave them to Me, and they have kept Your word. Now they have come to know that everything You have given Me is from You; for the words which You gave Me I have given to them; and they received *them* and truly understood that I came forth from You, and they believed You sent Me. I ask on their behalf; I do not ask on behalf of the world, but of those whom You have given Me; for they are Yours; and all things that are Mine are Yours, and Yours are Mine; and I have been glorified in them. I am no longer in the world; and yet they themselves are in the world, and I come to You. Holy Father, keep them in Your name, *the name* which You have given Me, that they may be even as We *are*. While I was with them, I was keeping them in Your name which You have given Me; and I guarded them and not one of them perished but the son of perdition, so that the Scripture would be fulfilled" (John 17:1–12; see Luke 22:32; John 1:1; 3:35; 4:34; 5:44; 6:37–39, 70; 8:42; 11:41; 12:49; 13:18, 31; 16:15; 17:20; Philippians 2:9).

Setting: **Jerusalem. Luke, writing in Acts, presents quotes from Jesus' post-resurrection appearances, in which He responds to their question if He is about to restore the kingdom to Israel.**

He said to them, "It is not for you to know times or epochs which the Father has fixed by His own authority; but you will receive power when the Holy Spirit has come upon you; and you shall be My witnesses both in Jerusalem, and in all Judea and Samaria, and even to the remotest part of the earth" (Acts 1:7, 8; see Luke 24:48, 49; 2:1–4).

Setting: **The island of Patmos (in the Aegean Sea about fifty miles southwest of Ephesus in modern Turkey). On the Lord's Day (Sunday), about fifty years after Jesus' resurrection, the disciple John encounters the Lord Jesus Christ. Jesus communicates a new revelation for the apostle to record for the church in Philadelphia and to six other churches in Asia.**

"And to the angel of the church in Philadelphia write: He who is holy, who is true, who has the key of David, who opens and no one will shut, and who shuts and no one opens, says this: 'I know your deeds. Behold, I have put before you an open door which no one can shut, because you have a little power, and have kept My word, and have not denied My name. Behold, I will cause *those* of the synagogue of Satan, who say that they are Jews and are not, but lie—I will make them come and bow down at your feet, and *make them* know that I have loved you. Because you have kept the word of My perseverance, I also will keep you from the hour of testing, that *hour* which is about to come upon the whole world, to test those who dwell on the earth. I am coming quickly; hold fast what you have, so that no one will take your crown. He who overcomes, I will make him a pillar in the temple of My God, and he will not go out from it anymore; and I will write on him the name of My God, and the name of the city of My God, the new Jerusalem, which comes down out of heaven from My God, and My new name. He who has an ear, let him hear what the Spirit says to the churches'" (Revelation 3:7–13; see Isaiah 22:22; Galatians 2:9; Revelation 2:9, 10, 13, 25; 14:1).

EARTH, END OF THE (Also see EARTH, ENDS OF THE)

Setting: **The Mount of Olives, east of the temple in Jerusalem. During His discourse, after prophesying the temple's destruction, Jesus responds to questions from Peter, James, John, and Andrew about future events.**

"But in those days, after that tribulation, THE SUN WILL BE DARKENED AND THE MOON WILL NOT GIVE ITS LIGHT, AND THE STARS WILL BE FALLING from heaven, and the powers that are in the heavens will be shaken. Then they will see THE SON OF MAN COMING IN CLOUDS with great power and glory. And then He will send forth the angels, and will gather together His elect from the four winds, from the farthest end of the earth to the farthest end of heaven" (Mark 13:24–27. Jesus quotes from Isaiah 13:10; 34:4; Daniel 7:13; cf. Matthew 24:29–31; Luke 21:25–27).

EARTH, ENDS OF THE (Also see EARTH, END OF THE)

Setting: **Galilee. After Jesus warns the Pharisees about the unpardonable sin and their future judgment, some Pharisees and scribes ask Him to perform a miraculous sign for them in front of the crowds.**

But He answered and said to them, "An evil and adulterous generation craves for a sign; and *yet* no sign will be given to it but the sign of Jonah the prophet; for just as JONAH WAS THREE DAYS AND THREE NIGHTS IN THE BELLY OF THE SEA MONSTER, so will the Son of Man be three days and three nights in the heart of the earth. The men of Nineveh will stand up with this generation at the

judgment, and will condemn it because they repented at the preaching of Jonah; and behold, something greater than Jonah is here. *The* Queen of *the* South will rise up with this generation at the judgment and will condemn it, because she came from the ends of the earth to hear the wisdom of Solomon; and behold, something greater than Solomon is here" (Matthew 12:39–42; Jesus quotes from Jonah 1:17; cf. 1 Kings 10:1; Jonah 3:5; Matthew 16:1, 4; 12:38; Luke 11:29).

Setting: On the way from Galilee to Jerusalem. After revealing a problem with exorcism and responding to a blessing from a woman in the crowd, Jesus tells the increasing crowds of the sign of Jonah.

As the crowds were increasing, He began to say, "This generation is a wicked generation; it seeks for a sign, and yet no sign will be given to it but the sign of Jonah. For just as Jonah became a sign to the Ninevites, so will the Son of Man be to this generation. The Queen of the South will rise up with the men of this generation at the judgment and condemn them, because she came from the ends of the earth to hear the wisdom of Solomon; and behold, something greater than Solomon is here. The men of Nineveh will stand up with this generation at the judgment and condemn it, because they repented at the preaching of Jonah; and behold, something greater than Jonah is here" (Luke 11:29–32; cf. Matthew 16:4; see 1 Kings 10:1–10; Jonah 3:4, 5).

EARTH, HEART OF THE

Setting: Galilee. After Jesus warns the Pharisees about the unpardonable sin and their future judgment, some Pharisees and scribes ask Him to perform a miraculous sign for them in front of the crowds.

But He answered and said to them, "An evil and adulterous generation craves for a sign; and *yet* no sign will be given to it but the sign of Jonah the prophet; for just as JONAH WAS THREE DAYS AND THREE NIGHTS IN THE BELLY OF THE SEA MONSTER, so will the Son of Man be three days and three nights in the heart of the earth. The men of Nineveh will stand up with this generation at the judgment, and will condemn it because they repented at the preaching of Jonah; and behold, something greater than Jonah is here. *The* Queen of *the* South will rise up with this generation at the judgment and will condemn it, because she came from the ends of the earth to hear the wisdom of Solomon; and behold, something greater than Solomon is here" (Matthew 12:39–42; Jesus quotes from Jonah 1:17; cf. 1 Kings 10:1; Jonah 3:5; Matthew 16:1, 4; 12:38; Luke 11:29).

EARTH, HEAVEN AND (EARTH, LORD OF HEAVEN AND is a separate entry)

Setting: Galilee. During the early part of His ministry, Jesus preaches the Sermon on the Mount to His disciples and the multitudes.

"Do not think that I came to abolish the Law or the Prophets; I did not come to abolish but to fulfill. For truly I say to you, until heaven and earth pass away, not the smallest letter or stroke shall pass from the Law until all is accomplished" (Matthew 5:17, 18; cf. Matthew 24:35).

Setting: The Mount of Olives, just east of Jerusalem. During His discourse, after answering His disciples' questions as to when the temple will be destroyed and Jerusalem overrun, along with the signs of His coming and the end of the age, Jesus teaches them the Parable of the Fig Tree.

"Now learn the parable from the fig tree: when its branch has already become tender and puts forth its leaves, you know that summer is near; so, you too, when you see all these things, recognize that He is near, *right* at the door. Truly, I say to you, this generation will not pass away until all these things take place. Heaven and earth will pass away, but My words will not pass away. But of that day and hour no one knows, not even the angels of heaven, nor the Son, but the Father alone. For the coming of the Son of Man will be just like the days of Noah. For as in those days before the flood they were eating and drinking, marrying and giving in marriage, until the day that Noah entered the ark, and they did not understand until the flood came and took them all away; so will the coming of the Son of Man be. Then there will be two men in the field; one will be taken and one will be left. Two women *will be* grinding at the mill; one will be taken and one will be left" (Matthew 24:32–41; cf. Mark 13:28–32; Luke 17:34–36; 21:28–33; see Genesis 6:5; 7:7; Matthew 5:18; 10:23; James 5:9).

[HEAVEN AND EARTH from in heaven and on earth]

Setting: On a mountain in Galilee. Following His resurrection from the dead in Jerusalem, Jesus conveys the Great Commission to the eleven remaining disciples.

And Jesus came up and spoke to them, saying, "All authority has been given to Me in heaven and on earth. Go therefore and make disciples of all the nations, baptizing them in the name of the Father and the Son and the Holy Spirit, teaching them to observe all that I commanded you; and lo, I am with you always, even to the end of the age" (Matthew 28:18–20; cf. Mark 16:15; see Daniel 7:13).

Setting: The Mount of Olives, east of the temple in Jerusalem. During His discourse, after prophesying the temple's destruction, Jesus responds to questions from Peter, James, John, and Andrew about future events.

"Now learn the parable from the fig tree: when its branch has already become tender and puts forth its leaves, you know that summer is near. Even so, you too, when you see these things happening, recognize that He is near, *right* at the door. Truly I say to you, this generation will not pass away until all these things take place. Heaven and earth will pass away, but My words will not pass away. But of the day or hour no one knows, not even the angels in heaven, nor the Son, but the Father *alone*" (Mark 13:28–32; cf. Matthew 24:32–36; Luke 21:28–33).

Setting: On the way from Galilee to Jerusalem. The Lord responds to the Pharisees' scoffing at His teaching His disciples about stewardship.

And He said to them, "You are those who justify yourselves in the sight of men, but God knows your hearts; for that which is highly esteemed among men is detestable in the sight of God. The Law and the Prophets were proclaimed until John; since that time the gospel of the kingdom of God has been preached, and everyone is forcing his way into it. But is it easier for heaven and earth to pass away than for one stroke of a letter of the Law to fail" (Luke 16:15–17; cf. Matthew 5:18; see 1 Samuel 16:7; Matthew 4:23; 11:11–14).

Setting: The Mount of Olives, just east of Jerusalem. During His discourse, following a time of ministry in the temple when He gave His disciples more details regarding His own return, Jesus conveys the Parable of the Fig Tree.

Then He told them a parable: "Behold the fig tree and all the trees; as soon as they put forth leaves, you see it and know for yourselves that summer is now near. So you also, when you see these things happening, recognize that the kingdom of God is near. Truly, I say to you, this generation will not pass away until all things take place. Heaven and earth will pass away, but My words will not pass away" (Luke 21:29–33; cf. Matthew 24:32–35; Mark 13:28–31; see Matthew 5:18).

EARTH, KINGS OF THE

Setting: Capernaum of Galilee. Jesus pays the two-drachma temple tax for Peter and Himself in a miraculous manner.

He said, "Yes." And when he came into the house, Jesus spoke to him first, saying, "What do you think, Simon? From whom do the kings of the earth collect customs or poll-tax, from their sons or from strangers?" When Peter said, "From strangers," Jesus said to him, "Then the sons are exempt. However, so that we do not offend them, go to the sea and throw in a hook, and take the first fish that comes up; and when you open its mouth, you will find a shekel. Take that and give it to them for you and Me" (Matthew 17:25–27; see Exodus 30:11–16; Matthew 17:24; 22:17–19; Romans 13:7).

EARTH, LORD OF HEAVEN AND

Setting: Galilee. After pronouncing woes against unrepentant cities as He teaches and preaches, Jesus prays a thanksgiving prayer to His Father in heaven.

At that time Jesus said, "I praise You, Father, Lord of heaven and earth, that you have hidden these things from *the* wise and intelligent and have revealed them to infants. Yes, Father, for this way was well-pleasing in Your sight. All things have been handed over to Me by My Father; and no one knows the Son except the Father; nor does anyone know the Father except the Son, and anyone to whom the Son wills to reveal *Him*" (Matthew 11:25–27; cf. Luke 10:21, 22).

[LORD OF HEAVEN AND EARTH from All authority has been given to Me in heaven and on earth]
Setting: On a mountain in Galilee. Following His resurrection from the dead in Jerusalem, Jesus conveys the Great Commission to His eleven remaining disciples.

And Jesus came up and spoke to them, saying, "All authority has been given to Me in heaven and on earth. Go therefore and make disciples of all the nations, baptizing them in the name of the Father and the Son and the Holy Spirit, teaching them to observe all that I commanded you; and lo, I am with you always, even to the end of the age" (Matthew 28:18–20; cf. Mark 16:15; see Daniel 7:13).

Setting: On the way from Galilee to Jerusalem, The Lord responds to a report from the seventy sent out in pairs to every place He Himself would soon visit.

At that very time He rejoiced greatly in the Holy Spirit, and said, "I praise You, O Father, Lord of heaven and earth, that You have hidden these things from the wise and intelligent and have revealed them to infants. Yes, Father, for this way was well-pleasing in Your sight. All things have been handed over to Me by My Father, and no one knows who the Son is except the Father, and who the Father is except the Son, and anyone to whom the Son wills to reveal Him" (Luke 10:21, 22; cf. Matthew 11:25–27; see Luke 10:1, 17; John 3:35; 10:15).

EARTH, PEACE ON (Also see EARTH, PEACE ON THE)
Setting: On the way from Galilee to Jerusalem, After clarifying a parable for Peter and the crowd, Jesus conveys how a relationship with Him divides families.

"I have come to cast fire upon the earth; and how I wish it were already kindled! But I have a baptism to undergo, and how distressed I am until it is accomplished! Do you suppose that I came to grant peace on earth? I tell you, no, but rather division; for from now on five members in one household will be divided, three against two and two against three. They will be divided, father against son and son against father, mother against daughter, and daughter against mother, mother-in-law against daughter-in-law and daughter-in-law against mother-in-law" (Luke 12:49–53; cf. Matthew 10:34–36; see Micah 7:6; Mark 10:38).

EARTH, PEACE ON THE (Also see EARTH, PEACE ON)
Setting: Galilee. After His disciples observe His ministry, Jesus summons and specifically instructs them about their ministry hardships ahead involving true discipleship.

"Do not think that I came to bring peace on the earth; I did not come to bring peace, but a sword. For I came to SET A MAN AGAINST HIS FATHER, AND A DAUGHTER AGAINST HER MOTHER, AND A DAUGHTER-IN-LAW AGAINST HER MOTHER-IN-LAW; and A MAN'S ENEMIES WILL BE THE MEMBERS OF HIS HOUSEHOLD" (Matthew 10:34–36; Jesus quotes from Micah 7:6; cf. Luke 12:51–53).

EARTH, SALT OF THE
Setting: Galilee. During the early part of His ministry, Jesus preaches the Sermon on the Mount to His disciples and the multitudes.

"You are the salt of the earth; but if the salt has become tasteless, how can it be made salty *again*? It is not longer good for anything, except to be thrown out and trampled under foot by men" (Matthew 5:13; cf. Mark 9:50).

EARTH, TRIBES OF THE (Also see ISRAEL, TWELVE TRIBES OF)
Setting: The Mount of Olives, just east of Jerusalem. During His discourse, Jesus answers His disciples' questions as to when the temple will be destroyed and Jerusalem overrun, along with the signs of His coming and the end of the age.

"But immediately after the tribulation of those days THE SUN WILL BE DARKENED, AND THE MOON WILL NOT GIVE ITS LIGHT, AND THE STARS WILL FALL from the sky, and the powers of the heavens will be shaken. And then the sign of the Son of Man will appear

in the sky, and then all the tribes of the earth will mourn, and they will see the SON OF MAN COMING ON THE CLOUDS OF THE SKY with power and great glory. And He will send forth His angels with A GREAT TRUMPET and THEY WILL GATHER TOGETHER His elect from the four winds, from one end of the sky to the other" (Matthew 24:29–31, Jesus quotes from Isaiah 13:10, Daniel 7:13; Exodus 19:16; cf. Mark 13:24–27; Luke 21:25–27).

EARTHLY THINGS (Listed under THINGS, EARTHLY)

EARTHLY TREASURE (Listed under TREASURE, EARTHLY)

EARTHQUAKES

Setting: The Mount of Olives, just east of Jerusalem. During His discourse, Jesus answers His disciples' questions as to when the temple will be destroyed and Jerusalem overrun, along with the signs of His coming and the end of the age.

And Jesus answered and said to them, "See to it that no one misleads you. For many will come in My name, saying, 'I am the Christ,' and will mislead many. You will be hearing of wars and rumors of wars. See that you are not frightened, for *those things* must take place, but *that* is not yet the end. For nation will rise against nation, and kingdom against kingdom, and in various places there will be famines and earthquakes. But all these things are *merely* the beginning of birth pangs. Then they will deliver you to tribulation, and will kill you, and you will be hated by all nations because of My name. At that time many will fall away and will betray one another and hate one another. Many false prophets will arise and will mislead many. Because lawlessness is increased, most people's love will grow cold. But the one who endures to the end, he will be saved. This gospel of the kingdom shall be preached in the whole world as a testimony to all the nations, and then the end will come" (Matthew 24:4–14; cf. Jeremiah 29:8; Matthew 7:15; 10:17, 22; Mark 13:3–13; Luke 21:7–19; Revelation 6:4).

Setting: The Mount of Olives, east of the temple in Jerusalem. During His discourse, after prophesying the temple's destruction, Jesus responds to questions from Peter, James, John, and Andrew about future events.

And Jesus began to say to them, "See to it that no one misleads you. Many will come in My name, saying, 'I am *He!*' and will mislead many. When you hear of wars and rumors of wars, do not be frightened; *those things* must take place; but *that is* not yet the end. For nation will rise up against nation, and kingdom against kingdom; there will be earthquakes in various places; there will *also be* famines. These things are *merely* the beginning of birth pangs. But be on your guard; for they will deliver you to *the* courts, and you will be flogged in *the* synagogues, and you will stand before governors and kings for My sake, as a testimony to them. The gospel must first be preached to all the nations. When they arrest you and hand you over, do not worry beforehand about what you are to say, but say whatever is given you in that hour; for it is not you who speak, but *it is* the Holy Spirit. Brother will betray brother to death, and a father *his* child; and children will rise up against parents and have them put to death. You will be hated by all because of My name, but the one who endures to the end, he will be saved" (Mark 13:5–13; cf. Matthew 24:4–14; Luke 21:7–19; see Matthew 10:17–22).

Setting: The Mount of Olives, just east of Jerusalem. During His discourse, After a time of ministering in the temple and giving His disciples more details regarding the temple's future destruction, Jesus elaborates about more things to come.

Then He continued by saying to them, "Nation will rise against nation and kingdom against kingdom, and there will be great earthquakes, and in various places plagues and famines; and there will be terrors and great signs from heaven. But before all these things, they will lay their hands on you and will persecute you, delivering you to the synagogues and prisons, bringing you before kings and governors for My name's sake. It will lead to an opportunity for your testimony. So make up your minds not to prepare beforehand to defend yourselves; for I will give you utterance and wisdom which none of your opponents will be able to resist or refute. But you will be betrayed even by parents and brothers and relatives and friends, and they will put some of you to death, and you will be hated by all because of My name. Yet not a hair of your head will perish. By your endurance you will gain your lives" (Luke 21:10–19; cf. Matthew 10:19–22; 24:7–14; Mark 13:8–13).

EARTHQUAKES, GREAT (See EARTHQUAKES)

EAST (Also see NORTH; SOUTH; and WEST)

Setting: Entering Capernaum. After the Lord gives the Sermon on the Mount and cleanses a leper, a Roman centurion implores Jesus to heal his servant.

Now when Jesus heard *this,* He marveled, and said to those who were following, "Truly I say to you, I have not found such great faith with anyone in Israel. I say to you that many will come from east and west, and recline *at the table* with Abraham, Isaac and Jacob in the kingdom of heaven; but the sons of the kingdom will be cast out into the outer darkness; in that place there will be weeping and gnashing of teeth." And Jesus said to the centurion, "Go; it shall be done for you as you have believed." And the servant was healed that *very* moment (Matthew 8:10–13; cf. Luke 7:9, 10).

Setting: The Mount of Olives, just east of Jerusalem. During His discourse, Jesus answers His disciples' questions as to when the temple will be destroyed and Jerusalem overrun, along with the signs of His coming and the end of the age.

"Therefore when you see the ABOMINATION OF DESOLATION which was spoken of through Daniel the prophet, standing in the holy place (let the reader understand), then those who are in Judea must flee to the mountains. Whoever is on the housetop must not go down to get the things that are in his house. Whoever is in the field must not turn back to get his cloak. But woe to those who are pregnant and to those who are nursing babies in those days! But pray that your flight will not be in the winter, or on a Sabbath. For then there will be a great tribulation, such as has not occurred since the beginning of the world until now, nor ever will. Unless those days had been cut short, no life would have been saved; but for the sake of the elect those days will be cut short. Then if anyone says to you, 'Behold, here is the Christ,' or "There *He is,*' do not believe *him.* For false Christs and false prophets will arise and will show great signs and wonders, so as to mislead, if possible, even the elect. Behold, I have told you in advance. So if they say to you, 'Behold, He is in the wilderness,' do not go out, *or,* 'Behold, He is in the inner rooms,' do not believe *them.* For just as the lightning comes from the east and flashes even to the west, so will the coming of the Son of Man be. Wherever a corpse is, there the vultures will gather" (Matthew 24:15–28, Jesus quotes from Daniel 9:27; cf. Daniel 12:1; Mark 13:14–23; Luke 17:22–31; 21:20–24; 23:29; see John 4:48).

Setting: On the way from Galilee to Jerusalem. While teaching in the cities and villages, Jesus responds to a question about who is saved.

And someone said to Him, "Lord, are here *just* a few who are being saved?" And He said to them, "Strive to enter through the narrow door; for many, I tell you, will seek to enter and will not be able. Once the head of the house gets up and shuts the door, and you begin to stand outside and knock on the door, saying, 'Lord, open up to us!' then He will answer and say to you, 'I do not know where you are from.' Then you will begin to say, 'We ate and drank in Your presence, and You taught in our streets'; and He will say, 'I tell you, I do not know where you are from; DEPART FROM ME, ALL YOU EVILDOERS.' In that place there will be weeping and gnashing of teeth when you see Abraham and Isaac and Jacob and all the prophets in the kingdom of God, but you yourselves being thrown out. And they will come from east and west and from north and south, and will recline *at the table* in the kingdom of God. And behold, *some* are last who will be first and *some* are first who will be last" (Luke 13:23–30, Jesus quotes from Psalm 6:8; cf. Matthew 7:13, 23; 8:11, 12; see Matthew 19:30; Luke 3:8).

EASY

Setting: Galilee. After rendering a thanksgiving prayer to His Father in heaven, Jesus offers rest to all who are weary and heavy-laden as He preaches and teaches.

"Come to Me, all who are weary and heavy-laden, and I will give you rest. Take My yoke upon you and learn from Me, for I am gentle and humble in heart, and YOU WILL FIND REST FOR YOUR SOULS. For My yoke is easy and My burden is light" (Matthew 11:28–30, Jesus quotes from Jeremiah 6:16; see Jeremiah 31:35; 1 John 5:3).

EATING (See BREAD, DAILY; and FOOD)

EDGE

Setting: The Mount of Olives, just east of Jerusalem. During His discourse, following a time of ministry in the temple and giving the disciples more details regarding future events, Jesus elaborates more about things to come.

"But when you see Jerusalem surrounded by armies, then recognize that her desolation is near. Then those who are in Judea must flee to the mountains, and those who are in the midst of the city must leave, and those who are in the country must not enter the city; because these are days of vengeance, so that all things which are written will be fulfilled. Woe to those who are pregnant and to those who are nursing babies in those days; for there will be a great distress upon the land and wrath to this people; and they will fall by the edge of the sword, and will be led captive into all the nations; and Jerusalem will be trampled under foot by the Gentiles until the times of the Gentiles are fulfilled" (Luke 21:20–24; see Matthew 24:15–18; Mark 13:14–16; Luke 19:43).

EGG

Setting: On the way from Galilee to Jerusalem. After revealing to His disciples how to pray, Jesus illustrates God's benevolence in answering prayer and giving the Holy Spirit.

"Now suppose one of you fathers is asked by his son for a fish; he will not give him a snake instead of a fish, will he? Or if he is asked for an egg, he will not give him a scorpion, will he? If you then, being evil, know how to give good gifts to your children, how much more will your heavenly Father give the Holy Spirit to those who ask Him?" (Luke 11:11–13; cf. Matthew 7:9–11).

EIGHTEEN

Setting: On the way from Galilee to Jerusalem. After some present report to Him about the Galileans whose blood Pilate (Roman governor of Judea) had mixed with their sacrifices, Jesus responds to their concern by calling them to repentance.

And Jesus said to them, "Do you suppose that these Galileans were greater sinners than all other Galileans because they suffered this fate? I tell you, no, but unless you repent, you will all likewise perish. Or do you suppose that those eighteen on whom the tower in Siloam fell and killed them were worse culprits than all the men who live in Jerusalem? I tell you, no, but unless you repent, you will all likewise perish" (Luke 13:2–5; see John 9:2, 3).

Setting: On the way from Galilee to Jerusalem. After healing a woman sick for eighteen years in a synagogue on the Sabbath, Jesus responds to a synagogue official's anger.

But the Lord answered him and said, "You hypocrites, does not each of you on the Sabbath untie his ox or his donkey from the stall and lead him away to water him? And this woman, a daughter of Abraham as she is, whom Satan has bound for eighteen long years, should she not have been released from this bond on the Sabbath day?" (Luke 13:15, 16; see Luke 14:5).

EIGHTY

Setting: On the way from Galilee to Jerusalem, After giving His disciples the story of the prodigal son, the Lord teaches them about stewardship.

Now He was also saying to the disciples, "There was a rich man who had a manager, and this manager was reported to him as squandering his possessions. And he called him and said to him, 'What is this I hear about you? Give an accounting of your management, for you can no longer be a manager.' The manager said to himself, 'What shall I do, since my master is taking the management away from me? I am not strong enough to dig; I am ashamed to beg. I know what I shall do, so that when I am removed from the management people will welcome me into their homes.' And he summoned each one of his master's debtors, and he began saying to the first, 'How much do you owe my master?' And he said, 'A hundred measures of oil.' And he said to him, 'Take your bill, and sit down quickly and write fifty.' Then he said to another, 'And how much do you owe?' And he said, 'A hundred measures of wheat.' He said to him, 'Take your bill, and write eighty.' And his master praised the unrighteous manager because he had acted shrewdly; for the sons of this age are more shrewd in relation to their own kind than the sons of light. And I say to you, make friends for yourselves by means of the wealth of unrighteousness, so that when it fails, they will receive you into the eternal dwellings. He who is faithful in a very little thing is faithful also in much; and he who is unrighteous in a very little thing is unrighteous also in much. Therefore if you have not been faithful in the use of unrighteous wealth, who will entrust the true riches to you? And if you have not been faithful in the use of that which is another's, who will give you that which is your own? No servant can serve two masters; for either he will hate the one and love the other, or else he will be devoted to one and despise the other. You cannot serve God and wealth" (Luke 16:1–13; cf. Matthew 6:24; see Matthew 25:14–30).

ELDERS (Also see CHIEF PRIESTS; PHARISEES; SADDUCEES; and SCRIBES)

Setting: Galilee. Following Peter's pronouncement that Jesus is the Christ of God, the Lord warns His disciples not to reveal His identity to anyone.

But He warned them and instructed them not to tell this to anyone, saying, "The Son of Man must suffer many things and be rejected by the elders and chief priests and scribes, and be killed and be raised up on the third day" (Luke 9:21, 22; cf. Matthew 16:21; Mark 8:31).

ELECT

Setting: The Mount of Olives, just east of Jerusalem. During His discourse, Jesus answers His disciples' questions as to when the temple will be destroyed and Jerusalem overrun, along with the signs of His coming and the end of the age.

"Therefore when you see the ABOMINATION OF DESOLATION which was spoken of through Daniel the prophet, standing in the holy place (let the reader understand), then those who are in Judea must flee to the mountains. Whoever is on the housetop must not go down to get the things that are in his house. Whoever is in the field must not turn back to get his cloak. But woe to those who are pregnant and to those who are nursing babies in those days! But pray that your flight will not be in the winter, or on a Sabbath. For then there will be a great tribulation, such as has not occurred since the beginning of the world until now, nor ever will. Unless those days had been cut short, no life would have been saved; but for the sake of the elect those days will be cut short. Then if anyone says to you, 'Behold, here is the Christ,' or 'There *He is,*' do not believe *him.* For false Christs and false prophets will arise and will show great signs and wonders, so as to mislead, if possible, even the elect. Behold, I have told you in advance. So if they say to you, 'Behold, He is in the wilderness,' do not go out, *or,* 'Behold, He is in the inner rooms,' do not believe *them.* For just as the lightning comes from the east and flashes even to the west, so will the coming of the Son of Man be. Wherever a corpse is, there the vultures will gather" (Matthew 24:15–28, Jesus quotes from Daniel 9:27; cf. Daniel 12:1; Mark 13:14–23; Luke 17:22–31; 21:20–24; 23:29; see John 4:48).

Setting: The Mount of Olives, just east of Jerusalem. During His discourse, Jesus answers His disciples' questions as to when the temple will be destroyed and Jerusalem overrun, along with the signs of His coming and the end of the age.

"But immediately after the tribulation of those days THE SUN WILL BE DARKENED, AND THE MOON WILL NOT GIVE ITS LIGHT, AND THE STARS WILL FALL from the sky, and the powers of the heavens will be shaken. And then the sign of the Son of Man will appear in the sky, and then all the tribes of the earth will mourn, and they will see the SON OF MAN COMING ON THE CLOUDS OF THE SKY with power and great glory. And He will send forth His angels with A GREAT TRUMPET and THEY WILL GATHER TOGETHER His elect from the four winds, from one end of the sky to the other" (Matthew 24:29–31, Jesus quotes from Isaiah 13:10, Daniel 7:13; Exodus 19:16; cf. Mark 13:24–27; Luke 21:25–27).

Setting: The Mount of Olives, east of the temple in Jerusalem. During His discourse, after prophesying the temple's destruction, Jesus responds to questions from Peter, James, John, and Andrew about future events.

"But when you see the ABOMINATION OF DESOLATION standing where it should not be (let the reader understand), then those who are in Judea must flee to the mountains. The one who is on the housetop must not go down, or go in to get anything out of his house; and the one who is in the field must not turn back to get his coat. But woe to those who are pregnant and to those who are nursing babies in those days! But pray that it may not happen in winter. For those days will be a *time of* tribulation such as has not occurred since the beginning of the creation which God created until now, and never will. Unless the Lord had shortened *those* days, no life would have been saved; but for the sake of the elect, whom He chose, He shortened the days. And then if anyone says to you, 'Behold, here is the Christ'; or, 'Behold, *He is* there'; do not believe *him*; for false Christs and false prophets will arise, and will show signs and wonders, in order to lead astray, if possible, the elect. But take heed; behold, I have told you everything in advance" (Mark 13:14–23; cf. Matthew 24:15–28; Luke 21:20–24; see Daniel 9:27; 12:1; Luke 17:31).

Setting: The Mount of Olives, east of the temple in Jerusalem. During His discourse, after prophesying the temple's destruction, Jesus responds to questions from Peter, James, John, and Andrew about future events.

"But in those days, after that tribulation, THE SUN WILL BE DARKENED AND THE MOON WILL NOT GIVE ITS LIGHT, AND THE STARS WILL BE FALLING from heaven, and the powers that are in the heavens will be shaken. Then they will see THE SON OF MAN COMING IN CLOUDS with great power and glory. And then He will send forth the angels, and will gather together His elect from the four winds, from the farthest end of the earth to the farthest end of heaven" (Mark 13:24–27. Jesus quotes from Isaiah 13:10; 34:4; Daniel 7:13; cf. Matthew 24:29–31; Luke 21:25–27).

Setting: On the way from Galilee to Jerusalem. After telling His disciples of His second coming, Jesus instructs them about persistence in prayer.

Now He was telling them a parable to show that at all times they ought to pray and not to lose heart, saying, "In a certain city there was a judge who did not fear God and did not respect man. There was a widow in that city, and she kept coming to him, saying, 'Give me legal protection from my opponent.' For a while he was unwilling; but afterward he said to himself, 'Even though I do not fear God nor respect man, yet because this woman bothers me, I will give her legal protection, otherwise by continually coming she will wear me out.'" And the Lord said, "Hear what the unrighteous judge said; now, will not God bring about justice for His elect who cry to Him day and night, and will He delay long over them? I tell you that He will bring about justice for them quickly. However, when the Son of Man comes, will He find faith on the earth?" (Luke 18:1–8; see Luke 11:5–10).

ELI (Also see ELOI)

Setting: Golgotha, just outside Jerusalem. Jesus utters words of despair while dying on the cross for the sins of the world.

About the ninth hour Jesus cried out with a loud voice, saying, "ELI, ELI, LAMA SABACHTHANI?" that is, "MY GOD, MY GOD, WHY HAVE YOU FORSAKEN ME?" (Matthew 27:46, Jesus quotes from Psalm 22:1; cf. Mark 15:34).

ELIJAH (referring to John the Baptist; also see JOHN THE BAPTIST; JOHN; and JOHN, BAPTISM OF)

Setting: Galilee. While speaking to the crowds, Jesus pays tribute to the ministry of John the Baptist, but emphasizes that the one who is least in the kingdom of heaven is greater than John.

As these men were going *away,* Jesus began to speak to the crowds about John, "What did you go out into the wilderness to see? A reed shaken by the wind? But what did you go out to see? A man dressed in soft *clothing?* Those who wear soft *clothing* are in kings' palaces! But what did you go out to see? A prophet? Yes, I tell you, and the one who is more than a prophet. This is the one about whom it is written, 'BEHOLD, I SEND MY MESSENGER AHEAD OF YOU, WHO WILL PREPARE YOUR WAY BEFORE YOU.' Truly, I say to you, among those born of women there has not arisen *anyone* greater than John the Baptist! Yet the one who is least in the kingdom of heaven is greater than he. From the days of John the Baptist until now the kingdom of heaven suffers violence, and violent men take it by force. For all the prophets and the Law prophesied until John. And, if you are willing to accept *it,* John himself is Elijah who was to come. He who has ears to hear, let him hear" (Matthew 11:7–15, Jesus quotes from Malachi 3:1; cf. Malachi 4:5; Luke 7:24–28; 16:16; see Matthew 14:5).

Setting: Coming down a mountain in Galilee. After Jesus is transfigured in front of Peter, James, and John, they ask Him why Elijah must come before the Messiah.

And He answered and said, "Elijah is coming and will restore all things; but I say to you that Elijah already came, and they did not recognize him, but did to him whatever they wished. So also the Son of Man is going to suffer at their hands" (Matthew 17:11, 12; cf. Mark 9:11–13).

Setting: Galilee. After informing a crowd and His disciples of the hope involving the coming kingdom of God, Jesus takes Peter, James, and John to a high mountain (some think Mount Hermon), where He reveals His glory through the Transfiguration and answers their question about Elijah.

And He said to them, "Elijah does first come and restore all things. And *yet* how is it written of the Son of Man that He will suffer many things and be treated with contempt? But I say to you that Elijah has indeed come, and they did to him whatever they wished, just as it is written of him" (Mark 9:12, 13; cf. Matthew 17:1–13; Luke 9:28–36; see Malachi 4:5, 6; Matthew 16:21.

ELIJAH (Old Testament prophet; also see PROPHETS)

Setting: The synagogue in Jesus' hometown of Nazareth in Galilee. At the beginning of Jesus' public ministry, He comments to the congregation after reading on the Sabbath from the book of the prophet Isaiah.

And He said to them, "No doubt you will quote this proverb to Me, 'Physician, heal yourself! Whatever we heard was done at Capernaum, do here in your hometown as well.'" And He said, "Truly I say to you, no prophet is welcome in his hometown. But I say to you in truth, there were many widows in Israel in the days of Elijah, when the sky was shut up for three years and six months, when a great famine came over all the land; and yet Elijah was sent to none of them, but only to Zarephath, *in the land* of Sidon, to a woman who was a widow. And there were many lepers in Israel in the time of Elisha the prophet; and none of them was cleansed, but only Naaman the Syrian" (Luke 4:23–27; Jesus refers to 1 Kings 17:1, 9; 2 Kings 5:1–14; see Matthew 13:53–58).

ELISHA (Old Testament prophet; also see PROPHETS)

Setting: The synagogue in Jesus' hometown of Nazareth in Galilee. At the beginning of Jesus' public ministry, He comments to the congregation after reading on the Sabbath from the book of the prophet Isaiah.

And He said to them, "No doubt you will quote this proverb to Me, 'Physician, heal yourself! Whatever we heard was done at Capernaum, do here in your hometown as well.'" And He said, "Truly I say to you, no prophet is welcome in his hometown. But I say to you in truth, there were many widows in Israel in the days of Elijah, when the sky was shut up for three years and six months, when a great famine came over all the land; and yet Elijah was sent to none of them, but only to Zarephath, *in the land* of Sidon, to a woman who was a widow. And there were many lepers in Israel in the time of Elisha the prophet; and none of them was cleansed, but only Naaman the Syrian" (Luke 4:23–27; Jesus refers to 1 Kings 17:1, 9; 2 Kings 5:1–14; see Matthew 13:53–58).

ELOI (Also see ELI)

Setting: Golgotha, just outside Jerusalem. Hanging on the cross, Jesus cries out at the ninth hour (3 p.m.).

At the ninth hour Jesus cried out with a loud voice, "ELOI, ELOI, LAMA SABACHTHANI?" which is translated, "MY GOD, MY GOD, WHY HAVE YOU FORSAKEN ME?" (Mark 15:34, Jesus quotes from Psalm 22:1; cf. Matthew 27:46).

EMBARRASSMENT (See ASHAMED)

EMOTION, EMOTIONS (See specifics such as ANGER; JEALOUSY; and HEART)

EMPTY-HANDED

Setting: The temple in Jerusalem. Having His authority questioned by the chief priests, scribes, and elders, Jesus begins to teach them in parables.

And He began to speak to them in parables: "A man PLANTED A VINEYARD AND PUT A WALL AROUND IT, AND DUG A VAT UNDER THE WINE PRESS AND BUILT A TOWER, and rented it out to vine-growers and went on a journey. At the *harvest* time he sent a slave to the vine-growers, in order to receive *some* of the produce of the vineyard from the vine-growers. They took him, and beat him and sent him away empty-handed. Again he sent them another slave, and they wounded him in the head, and treated him shamefully. And he sent another, and that one they killed; and *so with* many others, beating some and killing others. He had one more to *send*, a beloved son; he sent him last *of all* to them, saying, 'They will respect my son.' But those vine-growers said to one another, 'This is the heir; come, let us kill him, and the inheritance will be ours!' They took him, and killed him and threw him out of the vineyard. What will the owner of the vineyard do? He will come and destroy the vine-growers, and will give the vineyard to others. Have you not even read this Scripture: 'THE STONE WHICH THE BUILDERS REJECTED, THIS BECAME THE CHIEF CORNER *stone;* THIS CAME ABOUT FROM THE LORD, AND IT IS MARVELOUS IN OUR EYES'?" (Mark 12:1–11, Jesus quotes from Psalm 118:22, 23; Isaiah 5:1, 2; cf. Matthew 21:33–46; Luke 20:9–19).

Setting: The temple in Jerusalem. A few days before His crucifixion, after the chief priests and scribes question His authority to teach and preach, Jesus conveys to the people the Parable of the Vine-Growers.

And He began to tell the people this parable: "A man planted a vineyard and rented it out to vine-growers, and went on a journey for a long time. At the harvest time he sent a slave to the vine-growers, so that they would give him some of the produce of the vineyard; but the vine-growers beat him and sent him away empty-handed. And he proceeded to send another slave; and they beat him also and treated him shamefully and sent him away empty-handed. And he proceeded to send a third; and this one also they wounded and cast out. The owner of the vineyard said, 'What shall I do? I will send my beloved son; perhaps they will respect him.' But when the vine-growers saw him, they reasoned with one another, saying, 'This is the heir; let us kill him so that the inheritance will be ours.' So they threw him out of the vineyard and killed him. What, then, will the owner of the vineyard do to them? He will come and destroy these vine-growers and will give the vineyard to others." When they heard it, they said, "May it never be!" But Jesus looked at them and said, "What then is this that is written: 'THE STONE WHICH THE BUILDERS REJECTED, THIS BECAME THE CHIEF CORNER stone'? Everyone who falls on that stone will be broken to pieces; but on whomever it falls, it will scatter him like dust" (Luke 20:9–18, Jesus quotes from Psalm 118:22; cf. Matthew 21:33–44; Mark 12:1–11; see Ephesians 2:20).

END (AGE, END OF THE; and EARTH, END OF THE are separate entries; also see AWAY, PASS; OMEGA; and PROPHECY)

Setting: Galilee. After His disciples observe His ministry, Jesus summons and specifically instructs them about the upcoming difficulties of *their* ministry to the people of Israel.

"Brother will betray brother to death, and a father *his* child; and children will rise up against parents and cause them to be put to death. You will be hated by all because of My name, but it is the one who has endured to the end who will be saved. But whenever they persecute you in one city, flee to the next; for truly I say to you, you will not finish *going through* the cities of Israel until the Son of Man comes" (Matthew 10:21–23; cf. Matthew 10:35, 36; 16:27, 28; 24:9).

Setting: The Mount of Olives, just east of Jerusalem. During His discourse, Jesus answers His disciples' questions as to when the temple will be destroyed and Jerusalem overrun, along with the signs of His coming and the end of the age.

And Jesus answered and said to them, "See to it that no one misleads you. For many will come in My name, saying, 'I am the Christ,' and will mislead many. You will be hearing of wars and rumors of wars. See that you are not frightened, for *those things* must take place, but *that* is not yet the end. For nation will rise against nation, and kingdom against kingdom, and in various places there will be famines and earthquakes. But all these things are *merely* the beginning of birth pangs. Then they will deliver you to tribulation, and will kill you, and you will be hated by all nations because of My name. At that time many will fall away and will betray one another and hate one another. Many false prophets will arise and will mislead many. Because lawlessness is increased, most people's love will grow cold. But the one who endures to the end, he will be saved. This gospel of the kingdom shall be preached in the whole world as a testimony to all the nations, and then the end will come" (Matthew 24:4–14; cf. Jeremiah 29:8; Matthew 7:15; 10:17, 22; Mark 13:3–13; Luke 21:7–19; Revelation 6:4).

Setting: The Mount of Olives, just east of Jerusalem. During His discourse, Jesus answers His disciples' questions as to when the temple will be destroyed and Jerusalem overrun, along with the signs of His coming and the end of the age.

"But immediately after the tribulation of those days THE SUN WILL BE DARKENED, AND THE MOON WILL NOT GIVE ITS LIGHT, AND THE STARS WILL FALL from the sky, and the powers of the heavens will be shaken. And then the sign of the Son of Man will appear in the sky, and then all the tribes of the earth will mourn, and they will see the SON OF MAN COMING ON THE CLOUDS OF THE SKY with power and great glory. And He will send forth His angels with A GREAT TRUMPET and THEY WILL GATHER TOGETHER His elect from the four winds, from one end of the sky to the other" (Matthew 24:29–31, Jesus quotes from Isaiah 13:10, Daniel 7:13; Exodus 19:16; cf. Mark 13:24–27; Luke 21:25–27).

Setting: The Mount of Olives, east of the temple in Jerusalem. During His discourse, after prophesying the temple's destruction, Jesus responds to questions from Peter, James, John, and Andrew about future events.

And Jesus began to say to them, "See to it that no one misleads you. Many will come in My name, saying, 'I am *He!*' and will mislead many. When you hear of wars and rumors of wars, do not be frightened; *those things* must take place; but *that is* not yet the end. For nation will rise up against nation, and kingdom against kingdom; there will be earthquakes in various places; there will *also be* famines. These things are *merely* the beginning of birth pangs. But be on your guard; for they will deliver you to *the* courts, and you will be flogged in *the* synagogues, and you will stand before governors and kings for My sake, as a testimony to them. The gospel must first be preached to all the nations. When they arrest you and hand you over, do not worry beforehand about what you are to say, but say whatever is given you in that hour; for it is not you who speak, but *it is* the Holy Spirit. Brother will betray brother to death, and a father *his* child; and children will rise up against parents and have them put to death. You will be hated by all because of My name, but the one who endures to the end, he will be saved" (Mark 13:5–13; cf. Matthew 24:4–14; Luke 21:7–19; see Matthew 10:17–22).

Setting: The temple in Jerusalem. A few days before Jesus' crucifixion, after prophesying during His Olivet Discourse the destruction of the temple, His disciples ask Him when this will happen.

And He said, "See to it that you are not misled; for many will come in My name, saying, "I am He,' and, 'The time is near.' Do not go after them. When you hear of wars and disturbances, do not be terrified; for these things must take place first, but the end does not follow immediately" (Luke 21:8, 9; cf. Matthew 24:4–8; Mark 13:5–8).

Setting: Beyond the Jordan. Following the Feast of Dedication and the Pharisees' desire to stone Him while in Jerusalem, Jesus hears of the sickness of Lazarus of Bethany.

But when Jesus heard *this,* He said, "This sickness is not to end in death, but for the glory of God, so that the Son of God may be glorified by it" (John 11:4).

Setting: The island of Patmos (in the Aegean Sea about fifty miles southwest of Ephesus in modern Turkey). On the Lord's Day (Sunday), about fifty years after Jesus' resurrection, the disciple John encounters the Lord Jesus Christ. Jesus communicates a new revelation for the apostle to record for the church in Thyatira and to six other churches in Asia.

"And to the angel of the church in Thyatira write: The Son of God, who has eyes like a flame of fire, and His feet are like burnished bronze, says this: 'I know your deeds, and your love and faith and service and perseverance, and that your deeds of late are greater than at first. But I have *this* against you, that you tolerate the woman Jezebel, who calls herself a prophetess, and she teaches and leads My bond-servants astray so that they commit *acts of* immorality and eat things sacrificed to idols. I gave her time to repent, and she does not want to repent of her immorality. Behold, I will throw her on a bed *of sickness,* and those who commit adultery with her into great tribulation, unless they repent of her deeds. And I will kill her children with pestilence, and all the churches will know that I am He who searches the minds and hearts; and I will give to each one of you according to your deeds. But I say to you, the rest who are in Thyatira, who do not hold this teaching, who have not known the deep things of Satan, as they call them—I place no other burden on you. Nevertheless what you have, hold fast until I come. He who overcomes, and he who keeps My deeds until the end, TO HIM I WILL GIVE AUTHORITY OVER THE NATIONS; AND HE SHALL RULE THEM WITH A ROD OF IRON, AS THE VESSELS OF THE POTTER ARE BROKEN TO PIECES, as I also have received *authority* from My Father; and I will give him the morning star. He who has an ear, let him hear what the Spirit says to the churches' (Revelation 2:18–29; Jesus quotes from Psalm 2:8, 9; Isaiah 30:14; see 1 Kings 16:31; Psalm 7:9; Romans 2:5; 1 Corinthians 2:10; 2 Peter 3:9; Revelation 1:14; 2:7; 3:11; 17:1–20).

Setting: On the island of Patmos (in the Aegean Sea about fifty miles southwest of Ephesus in modern Turkey). Approximately fifty years after His resurrection, in the final chapter of His revelation via the disciple John, the Lord Jesus Christ reveals His upcoming return, reward, and eternality.

"Behold, I am coming quickly, and My reward is with Me, to render to every man according to what he has done. I am the Alpha and the Omega, the first and the last, the beginning and the end" (Revelation 22:12, 13; see Isaiah 40:10; 44:6).

END OF THE AGE (Listed under AGE, END OF THE)

ENDS OF THE EARTH (Listed under EARTH, ENDS OF THE)

ENDURANCE (Also see PERSEVERANCE)

[ENDURANCE from endured]

Setting: Galilee. After His disciples observe His ministry, Jesus summons and specifically instructs them about the upcoming difficulties of *their* ministry to the people of Israel.

"Brother will betray brother to death, and a father *his* child; and children will rise up against parents and cause them to be put to death. You will be hated by all because of My name, but it is the one who has endured to the end who will be saved. But whenever they persecute you in one city, flee to the next; for truly I say to you, you will not finish *going through* the cities of Israel until the Son of Man comes" (Matthew 10:21–23; cf. Matthew 10:35, 36; 16:27, 28; 24:9).

[ENDURANCE from endures]

Setting: The Mount of Olives, just east of Jerusalem. During His discourse, Jesus answers His disciples' questions as to when the temple will be destroyed and Jerusalem overrun, along with the signs of His coming and the end of the age.

And Jesus answered and said to them, "See to it that no one misleads you. For many will come in My name, saying, 'I am the Christ,' and will mislead many. You will be hearing of wars and rumors of wars. See that you are not frightened, for *those things* must take place, but *that* is not yet the end. For nation will rise against nation, and kingdom against kingdom, and in various places there will be famines and earthquakes. But all these things are *merely* the beginning of birth pangs. Then they will deliver you to tribulation, and will kill you, and you will be hated by all nations because of My name. At that time many will fall away and will betray one another and hate one another. Many false prophets will arise and will mislead many. Because lawlessness is increased, most people's love will grow cold. But the one who endures to the end, he will be saved. This gospel of the kingdom shall be preached in the whole world as a testimony to all the nations, and then the end will come" (Matthew 24:4–14; cf. Jeremiah 29:8; Matthew 7:15; 10:17, 22; Mark 13:3–13; Luke 21:7–19; Revelation 6:4).

[ENDURANCE from endures]

Setting: The Mount of Olives, east of the temple in Jerusalem. During His discourse, after prophesying the temple's destruction, Jesus responds to questions from Peter, James, John, and Andrew about future events.

And Jesus began to say to them, "See to it that no one misleads you. Many will come in My name, saying, 'I am *He!*' and will mislead many. When you hear of wars and rumors of wars, do not be frightened; *those things* must take place; but *that is* not yet the end. For nation will rise up against nation, and kingdom against kingdom; there will be earthquakes in various places; there will *also be* famines. These things are *merely* the beginning of birth pangs. But be on your guard; for they will deliver you to *the* courts, and you will be flogged in *the* synagogues, and you will stand before governors and kings for My sake, as a testimony to them. The gospel must first be preached to all the nations. When they arrest you and hand you over, do not worry beforehand about what you are to say, but say whatever is given you in that hour; for it is not you who speak, but *it is* the Holy Spirit. Brother will betray brother to death, and a father *his* child; and children will rise up against parents and have them put to death. You will be hated by all because of My name, but the one who endures to the end, he will be saved" (Mark 13:5–13; cf. Matthew 24:4–14; Luke 21:7–19; see Matthew 10:17–22).

Setting: The Mount of Olives, east of the temple in Jerusalem. After ministering in the temple and giving His disciples more details regarding the temple's future destruction, Jesus elaborates about future events during His Olivet Discourse.

Then He continued by saying to them, "Nation will rise against nation and kingdom against kingdom, and there will be great earthquakes, and in various places plagues and famines; and there will be terrors and great signs from heaven. But before all these things, they will lay their hands on you and will persecute you, delivering you to the synagogues and prisons, bringing you before kings and governors for My name's sake. It will lead to an opportunity for your testimony. So make up your minds not to prepare beforehand to defend yourselves; for I will give you utterance and wisdom which none of your opponents will be able to resist or refute. But you will be betrayed even by parents and brothers and relatives and friends, and they will put some of you to death, and you will be hated by all because of My name. Yet not a hair of your head will perish. By your endurance you will gain your lives" (Luke 21:10–19; cf. Matthew 10:19–22; 24:7–14; Mark 13:8–13).

[ENDURANCE from endures]
Setting: Capernaum. The day after Jesus walks on the Sea of Galilee to join His disciples in a boat, the people He had miraculously fed with a lad's five loaves and two fish ask Jesus how He crossed the water, as He had not entered the boat from land with His disciples.

Jesus answered them and said, "Truly, truly, I say to you, you seek Me, not because you saw signs, but because you ate of the loaves and were filled. Do not work for the food which perishes, but for the food which endures to eternal life, which the Son of Man will give to you, for on Him the Father, God, has set His seal" (John 6:26, 27; see John 3:33).

[ENDURANCE from endured]
Setting: The island of Patmos (in the Aegean Sea about fifty miles southwest of Ephesus in modern Turkey). On the Lord's Day (Sunday), about fifty years after Jesus' resurrection, the disciple John encounters the Lord Jesus Christ. Jesus communicates a new revelation for the apostle to record for the church in Ephesus and to six other churches in Asia.

"To the angel of the church in Ephesus write: The One who holds the seven stars in His right hand, the One who walks among the seven golden lampstands, says this: 'I know your deeds and your toil and perseverance, and that you cannot tolerate evil men, and you put to the test those who call themselves apostles, and they are not, and you found them *to be* false; and you have perseverance and have endured for My name's sake, and have not grown weary. But I have *this* against you, that you have left your first love. Therefore remember from where you have fallen, and repent and do the deeds you did at first; or else I am coming to you and will remove your lampstand out of its place—unless you repent. Yet this you do have, that you hate the deeds of the Nicolaitans, which I also hate. He who has an ear, let him hear what the Spirit says to the churches. To him who overcomes, I will grant to eat of the tree of life which is in the Paradise of God'" (Revelation 2:1–7; see Genesis 2:9; Ezekiel 28:13; 1 John 4:1; Revelation 1:10, 11, 19, 20; 2:15, 16).

ENEMIES (Also see ENEMY; OPPONENT; and OPPONENTS)
Setting: Galilee. During the early part of His ministry, Jesus preaches the Sermon on the Mount to His disciples and the multitudes.

"You have heard that it was said, 'YOU SHALL LOVE YOUR NEIGHBOR and hate your enemy.' But I say to you, love your enemies and pray for those who persecute you, so that you may be sons of your Father who is in heaven; for He causes His sun to rise on *the* evil and *the* good, and sends rain on *the* righteous and *the* unrighteous. For if you love those who love you, what reward do you have? Do not even the tax collectors do the same? If you greet only your brothers, what more are you doing *than others?* Do not even the Gentiles do the same? Therefore, you are to be perfect, as your heavenly Father is perfect" (Matthew 5:43–48, Jesus quotes from Leviticus 19:18; cf. Leviticus 19:2; Luke 6:27–36).

Setting: **Galilee. After His disciples observe His ministry, Jesus summons and specifically instructs them about their ministry hardships ahead involving true discipleship.**

"Do not think that I came to bring peace on the earth; I did not come to bring peace, but a sword. For I came to SET A MAN AGAINST HIS FATHER, AND A DAUGHTER AGAINST HER MOTHER, AND A DAUGHTER-IN-LAW AGAINST HER MOTHER-IN-LAW; and A MAN'S ENEMIES WILL BE THE MEMBERS OF HIS HOUSEHOLD" (Matthew 10:34–36; Jesus quotes from Micah 7:6; cf. Luke 12:51–53).

Setting: **The temple in Jerusalem. Following the Sadducees' and Pharisees' unsuccessful attempts to test Him with questions, with the crowds listening, Jesus poses a question to some of the Pharisees.**

"What do you think about the Christ, whose son is He?" They said to Him, "The *son* of David." He said to them, "Then how does David in the Spirit call Him 'Lord,' saying, 'THE LORD SAID TO MY LORD, SIT AT MY RIGHT HAND, UNTIL I PUT YOUR ENEMIES BENEATH YOUR FEET'"? "If David then calls Him 'Lord," how is He his son?" (Matthew 22:42–45; Jesus quotes from Psalm 110:1; cf. Mark 12:35–37; Luke 20:41–44; see 2 Samuel 23:2).

Setting: **The temple in Jerusalem. Jesus teaches the crowd after commending a scribe for his nearness to the kingdom of God.**

And Jesus *began* to say, as He taught in the temple, "How *is it that* the scribes say that the Christ is the son of David? David himself said in the Holy Spirit, 'THE LORD SAID TO MY LORD, SIT AT MY RIGHT HAND, UNTIL I PUT YOUR ENEMIES BENEATH YOUR FEET.'" David himself calls Him 'Lord'; so in what sense is He his son?" And the large crowd enjoyed listening to Him (Mark 12:35–37, Jesus quotes from Psalm 110:1; cf. Matthew 22:41–46; Luke 20:41–44).

Setting: **Galilee. After selecting His twelve disciples, Jesus teaches the Sermon on the Mount to His disciples and a great throng from Judea, Jerusalem, and the central coastal region of Tyre and Sidon.**

"But I say to you who hear, love your enemies, do good to those who hate you, bless those who curse you, pray for those who mistreat you. Whoever hits you on the cheek, offer him the other also; and whoever takes away your coat, do not withhold your shirt from him either. Give to everyone who asks of you, and whoever takes away what is yours, do not demand it back. Treat others the same way you want them to treat you. If you love those who love you, what credit is that to you? For even sinners love those who love them. If you do good to those who do good to you, what credit is that to you? For even sinners do the same. If you lend to those from whom you expect to receive, what credit is that to you? Even sinners lend to sinners in order to receive back the same amount. But love your enemies, and do good, and lend, expecting nothing in return; and your reward will be great, and you will be sons of the Most High; for He Himself is kind to ungrateful and evil men. Be merciful, just as your Father is merciful" (Luke 6:27–36; cf. Matthew 5:9, 39–48; Matthew 7:12).

Setting: **Jericho, on the way to Jerusalem. After commending Zaccheus's faith in Him, Jesus provides a parable about stewardship.**

So He said, "A nobleman went to a distant country to receive a kingdom for himself, and then return. And he called ten of his slaves, and gave them ten minas and said to them, 'Do business with this until I come back.' But his citizens hated him and sent a delegation after him, saying, 'We do not want this man to reign over us.' When he returned, after receiving the kingdom, he ordered that these slaves, to whom he had given the money, be called to him so that he might know what business they had done.

The first appeared, saying, 'Master, your mina has made ten minas more.' And he said to him, 'Well done, good slave, because you have been faithful in a very little thing, you are to be in authority over ten cities.' The second came, saying, 'Your mina, master, has made five minas.' And he said to him, also, 'And you are to be over five cities.' Another came, saying, 'Master, here is your mina, which I kept put away in a handkerchief; for I was afraid of you, because you are an exacting man; you take up what you did not lay down and reap what you did not sow.' He said to him, 'By your own words I will judge you, you worthless slave. Did you know that I am an exacting man, taking up what I did not lay down and reaping what I did not sow? Then why did you not put my money in the bank, and having come, I would have collected it with interest?' Then he said to the bystanders, 'Take the mina away from him and give it to the one who has the ten minas.' And they said to him, 'Master, he has ten minas already.' I tell you that to everyone who has, more shall be given, but from the one who does not have, even what he does have shall be taken away. But these enemies of mine, who did not want me to reign over them, bring them here and slay them in my presence" (Luke 19:12–27; cf. Matthew 25:14–30; see Matthew 13:12; Luke 16:10).

Setting: Approaching Jerusalem. After being praised by the people in a triumphal welcome, the Lord Jesus weeps as He sees the city ahead of Him.

When He approached Jerusalem, He saw the city and wept over it, saying, "If you had known in this day, even you, the things which make for peace! But now they have been hidden from your eyes. For the days will come upon you when your enemies will throw up a barricade against you, and surround you and hem you in on every side, and they will level you to the ground and your children within you, and they will not leave in you one stone upon another, because you did not recognize the time of your visitation" (Luke 19:41–44; see Matthew 24:1, 2; Luke 13:34, 35).

Setting: The temple in Jerusalem. A few days before His crucifixion, after some of the Sadducees question Him about the resurrection, Jesus poses a question to the scribes, who say He answered well.

Then He said to them, "How is it that they say the Christ is David's son? For David himself says in the book of Psalms, 'THE LORD SAID TO MY LORD, SIT AT MY RIGHT HAND, UNTIL I MAKE YOUR ENEMIES A FOOTSTOOL FOR YOUR FEET.' Therefore David calls Him 'Lord,' and how is He his son?" (Luke 20:41–44, Jesus quotes from Psalm 110:1; cf. Matthew 22:41–46; Mark 12:35–37).

ENEMIES, LOVE OF (See ENEMIES)

ENEMY (Also see ENEMIES; OPPONENT; and OPPONENTS)

Setting: Galilee. During the early part of His ministry, Jesus preaches the Sermon on the Mount to His disciples and the multitudes.

"You have heard that it was said, 'YOU SHALL LOVE YOUR NEIGHBOR and hate your enemy.' But I say to you, love your enemies and pray for those who persecute you, so that you may be sons of your Father who is in heaven; for He causes His sun to rise on the evil and the good, and sends rain on the righteous and the unrighteous. For if you love those who love you, what reward do you have? Do not even the tax collectors do the same? If you greet only your brothers, what more are you doing than others? Do not even the Gentiles do the same? Therefore, you are to be perfect, as your heavenly Father is perfect" (Matthew 5:43–48, Jesus quotes from Leviticus 19:18; cf. Leviticus 19:2; Luke 6:27–36).

Setting: By the Sea of Galilee (Tiberias). Because the religious leaders are rejecting His message, Jesus continues teaching the crowds with the Parable of the Wheat and the Tares.

Jesus presented another parable to them, saying, "The kingdom of heaven may be compared to a man who sowed good seed in his field. But while his men were sleeping, his enemy came and sowed tares among the wheat, and went away. But when the wheat sprouted and bore grain, then the tares became evident also. The slaves of the landowner came and said to him, 'Sir, did you not sow good seed in your field? How then does it have tares?' And he said to them, 'An enemy has done this!' The slaves said to him, 'Do you want us, then, to go and gather them up?' But he said, 'No; for while you are gathering up the tares, you may uproot the wheat with them. Allow both to grow together until the harvest; and in the time of the harvest I will say to the reapers, "First gather up the tares and bind them in bundles to burn them up; but gather the wheat into my barn" '" (Matthew 13:24–30; cf. Matthew 3:12).

Setting: A house near the Sea of Galilee. Jesus explains the meaning of the Parable of the Wheat and the Tares to His disciples.

And He said, "The one who sows the good seed is the Son of Man, and the field is the world; and as *for* the good seed, these are the sons of the kingdom; and the tares are the sons of the evil *one;* and the enemy who sowed them is the devil, and the harvest is the end of the age; and the reapers are angels. So just as the tares are gathered up and burned with fire, so shall it be at the end of the age. The Son of Man will send forth His angels, and they will gather out of His kingdom all stumbling blocks, and those who commit lawlessness, and will throw them into the furnace of fire; in that place there will be weeping and gnashing of teeth. Then THE RIGHTEOUS WILL SHINE FORTH AS THE SUN in the kingdom of their Father. He who has ears, let him hear" (Matthew 13:37–43, Jesus quotes from Daniel 12:3; cf. Matthew 8:12; 13:50).

Setting: On the way from Galilee to Jerusalem. The Lord responds to a report from the seventy sent out in pairs to every place He Himself will soon visit.

And He said to them, "I was watching Satan fall from heaven like lightning. Behold, I have given you authority to tread on serpents and scorpions, and over all the power of the enemy, and nothing will injure you. Nevertheless do not rejoice in this, that the spirits are subject to you, but rejoice that your names are recorded in heaven" (Luke 10:18–20; see Psalm 91:13; Isaiah 14:12–14; Luke 9:1).

ENLIGHTENMENT (Also see SIGHT)

[ENLIGHTENMENT from We see]

Setting: Jerusalem. Following the Pharisees' interrogation and dismissal of the formerly blind man Jesus healed on the Sabbath, the Lord responds to the Pharisees' question whether they are spiritually blind.

Jesus said to them, "If you were blind, you would have no sin; but since you say, 'We see,' your sin remains" (John 9:41; see John 15:22–24).

ENOUGH

Setting: Galilee. During the early part of His ministry, Jesus preaches the Sermon on the Mount to His disciples and the multitudes.

"But I say to you that everyone who is angry with his brother shall be guilty before the court; and whoever says to his brother, 'You good-for-nothing,' shall be guilty before the supreme court; and whoever says, 'You fool,' shall be guilty *enough to go* into the fiery hell" (Matthew 5:22).

Setting: Galilee. During the early part of His ministry, Jesus preaches the Sermon on the Mount to His disciples and the multitudes.

"For this reason I say to you, do not be worried about your life, *as to* what you will eat or what you will drink; nor for your body, *as to* what you will put on. Is not life more than food, and the body more than clothing? Look at the birds of the air, that they do not sow, nor reap nor gather into barns, and *yet* your heavenly Father feeds them. Are you not worth much more than they? And who of you by being worried can add a *single* hour to his life? And why are you worried about clothing? Observe how the lilies of the field grow; they do not toil nor do they spin, yet I say to you that not even Solomon in all his glory clothed himself like one of these. But if God so clothes the grass of the field, which is *alive* today and tomorrow is thrown into the furnace, *will He* not much more *clothe* you? You of little faith! Do not worry then, saying 'What will we eat?' or 'What will we drink?' or 'What will be wear for clothing?" For the Gentiles eagerly seek all these things; for your heavenly Father knows that you need all these things. But seek first His kingdom and His righteousness, and all these things will be added to you. So do not worry about tomorrow; for tomorrow will care for itself. Each day has enough trouble of its own" (Matthew 6:25–34; cf. Luke 12:22–31; see 1 Kings 10:4–7; Job 35:11; Matthew 8:26).

Setting: Galilee. After His disciples observe His ministry, Jesus summons and specifically instructs them about the difficulties ahead involving true discipleship.

"A disciple is not above his teacher, nor a slave above his master. It is enough for the disciple that he become like his teacher, and the slave like his master. If they have called the head of the house Beelzebul, how much more *will they malign* the members of his household!" (Matthew 10:24, 25; cf. Luke 6:40; see 2 Kings 1:2).

Setting: The Mount of Olives, just east of Jerusalem. During His discourse, after answering His disciples' questions as to when the temple will be destroyed and Jerusalem overrun, along with the signs of His coming and the end of the age, Jesus reemphasizes to the disciples they should be on the alert for His return.

"Then the kingdom of heaven will be comparable to ten virgins, who took their lamps and went out to meet the bridegroom. Five of them were foolish, and five were prudent. For when the foolish took their lamps, they took no oil with them, but the prudent took oil in flasks along with their lamps. Now while the bridegroom was delaying, they all got drowsy and *began* to sleep. But at midnight there was a shout, 'Behold, the bridegroom! Come out to meet *him*.' Then all those virgins rose and trimmed their lamps. The foolish said to the prudent, 'Give us some of your oil, for our lamps are going out.' But the prudent answered, 'No, there will not be enough for us and you *too;* go instead to the dealers and buy *some* for yourselves.' And while they were going away to make the purchase, the bridegroom came, and those who were ready went in with him to the wedding feast; and the door was shut. Later the other virgins also came, saying, 'Lord, lord, open up for us.' But he answered, 'Truly I say to you, I do not know you.' Be on the alert then, for you do not know the day nor the hour" (Matthew 25:1–13; cf. Matthew 24:42; Luke 12:35; see Matthew 7:21, 24).

Setting: Gethsemane on the Mount of Olives, east of the temple in Jerusalem. Jesus prepares to meet Judas the betrayer, while His other disciples keep falling asleep instead of watching and praying with Him.

And He came the third time, and said to them, "Are you still sleeping and resting? It is enough; the hour has come; behold, the Son of Man is being betrayed into the hands of sinners. Get up, let us be going; behold, the one who betrays Me is at hand!" (Mark 14:41, 42; cf. Matthew 26:45, 46).

Setting: The home of Levi (Matthew) in Capernaum. At a reception for Jesus following Levi's call to be a disciple, the Lord tells a parable to the Pharisees and their scribes, who question His association with tax collectors and sinners.

And He was also telling them a parable: "No one tears a piece of cloth from a new garment and puts it on an old garment; otherwise he will both tear the new, and the piece from the new will not match the old. And no one puts new wine into old wineskins; otherwise the new wine will burst the skins and it will be spilled out, and the skins will be ruined. But new wine must be put into fresh wineskins. And no one, after drinking old wine wishes for new; for he says, 'The old is good enough'" (Luke 5:36–39; cf. Matthew 9:16, 17; Mark 2:21, 22).

Setting: On the way from Galilee to Jerusalem. After responding to a guest's proclamation about the blessings of eating bread in the kingdom of God, Jesus presents to large crowds the demands of discipleship.

Now large crowds were going along with Him; and He turned and said to them, "If anyone comes to Me, and does not hate his own father and mother and wife and children and brothers and sisters, yes, and even his own life, he cannot be My disciple. Whoever does not carry his own cross and come after Me cannot be My disciple. For which one of you, when he wants to build a tower, does not first sit down and calculate the cost to see if he has enough to complete it? Otherwise, when he has laid a foundation and is not able to finish, all who observe it begin to ridicule him, saying, 'This man began to build and was not able to finish.' Or what king, when he sets out to meet another king in battle, will not first sit down and consider whether he is strong enough with ten thousand *men* to encounter the one coming against him with twenty thousand? Or else, while the other is still far away, he sends a delegation and asks for terms of peace. So then, none of you can be My disciple who does not give up all his possessions. Therefore, salt is good; but if even salt has become tasteless, with what will it be seasoned? It is useless either for the soil or for the manure pile; it is thrown out. He who has ears to hear, let him hear" (Luke 14:25–35; cf. Matthew 5:13; 10:37–39; see Proverbs 20:18; Luke 14:1, 2, 15; Philippians 3:7).

Setting: On the way from Galilee to Jerusalem. Jesus conveys the illustration of the prodigal son because the Pharisees and scribes complain He associates with tax collectors and sinners.

And He said, "A man had two sons. The younger of them said to his father, 'Father, give me the share of the estate that falls to me.' So he divided his wealth between them. And not many days later, the younger son gathered everything together and went on a journey into a distant country, and there he squandered his estate with loose living. Now when he had spent everything, a severe famine occurred in that country, and he began to be impoverished. So he went and hired himself out to one of the citizens of that country, and he sent him into his fields to feed swine. And he would have gladly filled his stomach with the pods that the swine were eating, and no one was giving anything to him. But when he came to his senses, he said, 'How many of my father's hired men have more than enough bread, but I am dying here with hunger! I will get up and go to my father, and will say to him, "Father, I have sinned against heaven, and in your sight; I am no longer worthy to be called your son; make me as one of your hired men."' So he got up and came to his father. But while he was still a long way off, his father saw him and felt compassion for him, and ran and embraced him and kissed him. And the son said to him, "Father, I have sinned against heaven and in your sight; I am no longer worthy to be called your son.' But the father said to his slaves, 'Quickly bring out the best robe and put it on him, and put a ring on his hand and sandals on his feet; and bring the fattened calf, kill it, and let us eat and celebrate; for this son of mine was dead and has come to life again; he was lost and has been found.' And they began to celebrate. Now his older son was in the field, when he came and approached the house, he heard music and dancing. And he summoned one of the servants and began inquiring what these things could be. And he said to him, 'Your brother has come, and your father has killed the fattened calf because he has received him back safe and sound.' But he became angry and was not willing to go in; and his father came out and began pleading with him. But he answered and said to his father, 'Look! For so many years I have been serving you and I have never neglected a command of yours; and yet you have never given me a young goat, so that I might celebrate with my friends; but when this son of yours came, who has devoured your wealth with prostitutes, you killed the fattened calf for him.' And he said to him, 'Son, you have always been with me, and all that is mine is yours. But we had to celebrate and rejoice, for this brother of yours was dead and has begun to live, and was lost and has been found'" (Luke 15:11–32; see Proverbs 29:2; Luke 15:1, 2).

Setting: On the way from Galilee to Jerusalem. The Lord teaches His disciples about stewardship after giving them the story of the prodigal son.

Now He was also saying to the disciples, "There was a rich man who had a manager, and this manager was reported to him as squandering his possessions. And he called him and said to him, 'What is this I hear about you? Give an accounting of your management, for you can no longer be a manager.' The manager said to himself, 'What shall I do, since my master is taking the management away from me? I am not strong enough to dig; I am ashamed to beg. I know what I shall do, so that when I am removed from the management people will welcome me into their homes.' And he summoned each one of his master's debtors, and he began saying to the first, 'How much do you owe my master?' And he said, 'A hundred measures of oil.' And he said to him, 'Take your bill, and sit down quickly and write fifty.' Then he said to another, 'And how much do you owe?' And he said, 'A hundred measures of wheat.' He said to him, 'Take your bill, and write eighty.' And his master praised the unrighteous manager because he had acted shrewdly; for the sons of this age are more shrewd in relation to their own kind than the sons of light. And I say to you, make friends for yourselves by means of the wealth of unrighteousness, so that when it fails, they will receive you into the eternal dwellings. He who is faithful in a very little thing is faithful also in much; and he who is unrighteous in a very little thing is unrighteous also in much. Therefore if you have not been faithful in the use of unrighteous wealth, who will entrust the true riches to you? And if you have not been faithful in the use of that which is another's, who will give you that which is your own? No servant can serve two masters; for either he will hate the one and love the other, or else he will be devoted to one and despise the other. You cannot serve God and wealth" (Luke 16:1–13; cf. Matthew 6:24; see Matthew 25:14–30).

Setting: Jerusalem. During the Feast of Unleavened Bread (Passover) just before Jesus' crucifixion, while celebrating the Passover meal, instituting the Lord's Supper, and prophesying Peter's upcoming denial of Him, Jesus instructs His disciples to prepare to persevere without Him.

And He said to them, "When I sent you out without money belt and bag and sandals, you did not lack anything, did you?" They said, "No, nothing." And He said to them, "But now, whoever has a money belt is to take it along, likewise also a bag, and whoever has no sword is to sell his coat and buy one. For I tell you that this which is written must be fulfilled in Me, 'AND HE WAS NUMBERED WITH TRANSGRESSORS'; for that which refers to Me has its fulfillment." They said, "Lord, look, here are two swords." And He said to them, "It is enough" (Luke 22:35–38, Jesus quotes from Isaiah 53:12; see Matthew 10:5–15; Mark 6:7–11; Luke 9:1–5; 10:1–12; 22:49; John 17:4).

ENVY (Also see ANGER; HATE; HATRED; and JEALOUSY)

[ENVY from envious]

Setting: Judea beyond the Jordan (Perea). Jesus illustrates the kingdom of heaven to His disciples through the story of laborers in the vineyard.

"For the kingdom of heaven is like a landowner who went out early in the morning to hire laborers for his vineyard. When he had agreed with the laborers for a denarius for the day, he sent them into his vineyard. And he went out about the third hour and saw others standing idle in the market place; and to those he said, 'You also go into the vineyard, and whatever is right I will give you.' And *so* they went. Again he went out about the sixth and the ninth hour, and did the same thing. And about the eleventh *hour* he went out and found others standing *around;* and he said to them, 'Why have you been standing idle here all day long?' They said to him, 'Because no one hired us.' He said to them, 'You go into the vineyard too.' When evening came, the owner of the vineyard said to his foreman, 'Call the laborers and pay them their wages, beginning with the last *group* to the first.' When those *hired* about the eleventh hour came, each one received a denarius. When those *hired* first came, they thought that they would receive more; but each of them also received a denarius. When they received it, they grumbled at the landowner, saying, 'These last men have worked *only* one hour, and you have made them equal to us who have borne the burden and the scorching heat of the day.' But he answered and said to one of them, 'Friend, I am doing you no wrong; did you not agree with me for a denarius? Take what is yours and go, but I wish to give to this last man the same as to you. It is not lawful for me to do what I wish with what is my own? Or is your eye envious because I am generous?' So the last shall be first, and the first last" (Matthew 20:1–16; cf. Matthew 19:30).

Setting: Galilee. After the Pharisees and scribes from Jerusalem question Jesus' disciples' lack of obedience to tradition, Jesus speaks to a crowd and explains His teaching to His disciples.

After He called the crowd to Him again, He *began* saying to them, "Listen to Me, all of you, and understand: there is nothing outside the man which can defile him if it goes into him; but the things which proceed out of the man are what defile the man. [If anyone has ears to hear, let him hear."] When he had left the crowd *and* entered the house, His disciples questioned Him about the parable. And He said to them, "Are you so lacking in understanding also? Do you not understand that whatever goes into the man from outside cannot defile him, because it does not go into his heart, but into his stomach, and is eliminated?" (*Thus He* declared all foods clean.) And He was saying, "That which proceeds out of the man, that is what defiles the man. For from within, out of the heart of men, proceed the evil thoughts, fornications, thefts, murders, adulteries, deeds of coveting *and* wickedness, *as well* as deceit, sensuality, envy, slander, pride *and* foolishness. All these evil things proceed from within and defile the man" (Mark 7:14–23; cf. Matthew 15:10–20).

EPHESUS

Setting: On the island of Patmos (in the Aegean Sea about fifty miles southwest of Ephesus in modern Turkey). On the Lord's Day (Sunday), approximately fifty years after His resurrection, the disciple John encounters the Lord Jesus Christ, who communicates new revelations for the apostle to record for the seven churches in Asia.

I was in the Spirit on the Lord's day, and I heard behind me a loud voice like *the sound* of a trumpet, saying, "Write in a book what you see, and send *it* to the seven churches: to Ephesus and to Smyrna and to Pergamum and to Thyatira and to Sardis and to Philadelphia and to Laodicea" (Revelation 1:10, 11).

Setting: On the island of Patmos (in the Aegean Sea about fifty miles southwest of Ephesus in modern Turkey). On the Lord's Day (Sunday), about fifty years after Jesus' resurrection, the disciple John encounters the Lord Jesus Christ. Jesus communicates a new revelation for the apostle to record for the church in Ephesus and to six other churches in Asia.

"To the angel of the church in Ephesus write: The One who holds the seven stars in His right hand, the One who walks among the seven golden lampstands, says this: 'I know your deeds and your toil and perseverance, and that you cannot tolerate evil men, and you put to the test those who call themselves apostles, and they are not, and you found them *to be* false; and you have perseverance and have endured for My name's sake, and have not grown weary. But I have *this* against you, that you have left your first love. Therefore remember from where you have fallen, and repent and do the deeds you did at first; or else I am coming to you and will remove your lampstand out of its place—unless you repent. Yet this you do have, that you hate the deeds of the Nicolaitans, which I also hate. He who has an ear, let him hear what the Spirit says to the churches. To him who overcomes, I will grant to eat of the tree of life which is in the Paradise of God'" (Revelation 2:1–7; see Genesis 2:9; Ezekiel 28:13; 1 John 4:1; Revelation 1:10, 11, 19, 20; 2:15, 16).

EPHPHATHA

Setting: Decapolis near the Sea of Galilee. After casting out a demon from a Gentile woman's daughter in Tyre, Jesus restores a man's hearing and speech.

Jesus took him aside from the crowd, by himself, and put His fingers into his ears, and after spitting, He touched his tongue *with the saliva*; and looking up to heaven with a deep sigh, He said to him, "Ephphatha!" that is, "Be opened!" (Mark 7:33, 34; see Matthew 15:29–31; Mark 8:23).

EPOCHS (Also see TIMES)

Setting: Jerusalem. Luke, writing in Acts, presents quotes from Jesus' post-resurrection appearances, in which He responds to their question if He is about to restore the kingdom to Israel.

He said to them, "It is not for you to know times or epochs which the Father has fixed by His own authority; but you will receive power when the Holy Spirit has come upon you; and you shall be My witnesses both in Jerusalem, and in all Judea and Samaria, and even to the remotest part of the earth" (Acts 1:7, 8; see Luke 24:48, 49; Acts 2:1–4).

ESTATE (Also see INHERITANCE)

Setting: On the way from Galilee to Jerusalem. Jesus conveys the illustration of the prodigal son because the Pharisees and scribes complain He associates with tax collectors and sinners.

And He said, "A man had two sons. The younger of them said to his father, 'Father, give me the share of the estate that falls to me.' So he divided his wealth between them. And not many days later, the younger son gathered everything together and went on a journey into a distant country, and there he squandered his estate with loose living. Now when he had spent everything, a severe famine occurred in that country, and he began to be impoverished. So he went and hired himself out to one of the citizens of that country, and he sent him into his fields to feed swine. And he would have gladly filled his stomach with the pods that the swine were eating, and no one was giving anything to him. But when he came to his senses, he said, 'How many of my father's hired men have more than enough bread, but I am dying here with hunger! I will get up and go to my father, and will say to him, "Father, I have sinned against heaven, and in your sight; I am no longer worthy to be called your son; make me as one of your hired men."' So he got up and came to his father. But while he was still a long way off, his father saw him and felt compassion for him, and ran and embraced him and kissed him. And the son said to him, "Father, I have sinned against heaven and in your sight; I am no longer worthy to be called your son.' But the father said to his slaves, 'Quickly bring out the best robe and put it on him, and put a ring on his hand and sandals on his feet; and bring the fattened calf, kill it, and let us eat and celebrate; for this son of mine was dead and has come to life again; he was lost and has been found.' And they began to celebrate. Now his older son was in the field, when he came and approached the house, he heard music and dancing. And he summoned one of the servants and began inquiring what these things could be. And he said to him, 'Your brother has come, and your father has killed the fattened calf because he has received him back safe and sound.' But he became angry and was not willing to go in; and his father came out and began pleading with him. But he answered and said to his father, 'Look! For so many years I have been serving you and I have never neglected a command of yours; and yet you have never given me a young goat, so that I might celebrate with my friends; but when this son of yours came, who has devoured your wealth with prostitutes, you killed the fattened calf for him.' And he said to him, 'Son, you have always been with me, and all that is mine is yours. But we had to celebrate and rejoice, for this brother of yours was dead and has begun to live, and was lost and has been found'" (Luke 15:11–32; see Proverbs 29:2; Luke 15:1, 2).

ESTEEM

[ESTEEM from esteemed]

Setting: On the way from Galilee to Jerusalem. The Lord responds to the Pharisees' scoffing at His teaching His disciples about stewardship.

And He said to them, "You are those who justify yourselves in the sight of men, but God knows your hearts; for that which is highly esteemed among men is detestable in the sight of God. The Law and the Prophets were proclaimed until John; since that time the gospel of the kingdom of God has been preached, and everyone is forcing his way into it. But is it easier for heaven and earth to pass away than for one stroke of a letter of the Law to fail" (Luke 16:15–17; cf. Matthew 5:18; see 1 Samuel 16:7; Matthew 4:23; 11:11–14).

ETERNAL DAMNATION (See DEATH, ETERNAL; FIRE, ETERNAL; FIRE, FURNACE OF; GOD, SEPARATION FROM; HELL; JUDGMENT; and PUNISHMENT, ETERNAL)

ETERNAL DEATH (Listed under DEATH, ETERNAL; also see HELL; and GOD, SEPARATION FROM)

ETERNAL DWELLINGS (Listed under DWELLINGS, ETERNAL)

ETERNAL FIRE (Listed under FIRE, ETERNAL; also see HELL; and GOD, SEPARATION FROM)

ETERNAL LIFE (Also see JESUS' PURPOSE; KINGDOM OF GOD; KINGDOM OF HEAVEN; and SALVATION)

[ETERNAL LIFE from life]

Setting: Galilee. During the early part of His ministry, Jesus preaches the Sermon on the Mount to His disciples and the multitudes.

"Enter through the narrow gate; for the gate is wide and the way is broad that leads to destruction, and there are many who enter through it. For the gate is small and the way is narrow that leads to life, and there are few who find it" (Matthew 7:13, 14; cf. Luke 13:24).

[ETERNAL LIFE from life]

Setting: Capernaum of Galilee. Jesus elaborates about stumbling blocks after His disciples ask about greatness in the kingdom of heaven.

"Woe to the world because of *its* stumbling blocks! For it is inevitable that stumbling blocks come; but woe to that man through whom the stumbling block comes! If your hand or your foot causes you to stumble, cut if off and throw it from you; it is better for you to enter life crippled or lame, than to have two hands or two feet and be cast into the eternal fire. If your eye causes you to stumble, pluck it out and throw it from you. It is better for you to enter life with one eye, than to have two eyes and be cast into the fiery hell" (Matthew 18:7–9; cf. Matthew 5:29, 30; Mark 9:43–48; Luke 17:1).

[ETERNAL LIFE from life]

Setting: Judea beyond the Jordan (Perea). Jesus shares with a rich, young ruler how he can obtain eternal life.

And He said to him, "Why are you asking Me about what is good? There is *only* One who is good; but if you wish to enter into life, keep the commandments." *Then* he said to Him, 'Which ones?' And Jesus said, "YOU SHALL NOT COMMIT MURDER; YOU SHALL NOT COMMIT ADULTERY; YOU SHALL NOT STEAL; YOU SHALL NOT BEAR FALSE WITNESS; HONOR YOUR FATHER AND MOTHER; and YOU SHALL LOVE YOUR NEIGHBOR AS YOURSELF." The young man said to Him, "All these things I have kept; what am I still lacking?" Jesus said to him, "If you wish to complete go *and* sell your possessions and give to *the* poor, and you will have treasure in heaven; and come, follow Me" (Matthew 19:16–22, Jesus quotes from Exodus 20:13–15; Leviticus 19:18; cf. Leviticus 18:5; Mark 10:17–21; Luke 10:25–28; 12:33; 18:18–24).

Setting: Judea beyond the Jordan (Perea). Jesus promises rewards to His disciples for their personal sacrifice and commitment to following Him.

And Jesus said to them, "Truly I say to you, that you who have followed Me, in the regeneration when the Son of Man will sit on His glorious throne, you also shall sit upon twelve thrones, judging the twelve tribes of Israel. And everyone who has left houses or brothers or sisters or father or mother or children or farms for My name's sake, will receive many times as much, and will inherit eternal life. But many *who* are first will be last; and *the* last, first" (Matthew 19:28–30; cf. Matthew 6:33; 20:15; Mark 10:29, 30; Luke 18:29, 30; Luke 22:30).

Setting: On the Mount of Olives, just east of Jerusalem. During His discourse, after answering His disciples' questions as to when the temple will be destroyed and Jerusalem overrun, along with the signs of His coming and the end of the age, Jesus reveals the future judgments following His return.

"But when the Son of Man comes in His glory, and all the angels with Him, then He will sit on His glorious throne. All the nations will be gathered before Him; and He will separate them from one another, as the shepherd separates the sheep from the goats; and He will put the sheep on His right, and the goats on the left. Then the King will say to those on His right, 'Come, you who are blessed of My Father, inherit the kingdom prepared for you from the foundation of the world. 'For I was hungry, and you gave Me *something* to eat; I was thirsty, and you gave Me *something* to drink; I was a stranger, and you invited Me in; naked, and you clothed Me; I was sick, and you visited Me; I was in prison, and you came to Me.' Then the righteous will answer Him, 'Lord, when did we see You hungry and feed You, or thirsty, and give you *something* to drink? And when did we see You a stranger, and invite You in, or naked, and clothe You? When did we see You sick, or in prison, and come to You?' The King will answer and say to them, 'Truly I say to you, to the extent that you did it to one of these brothers of Mine, *even* the least *of them,* you did it to Me.' Then He will also say to those on His left, 'Depart from Me, accursed ones, into the eternal fire which has been prepared for the devil and his angels; for I was hungry, and you gave Me *nothing* to eat; I was thirsty, and you gave Me nothing to drink; I was a stranger, and you did not invite Me in; naked, and you did not clothe Me; sick, and in prison, and you did not visit Me.' Then they themselves also will answer, 'Lord, when did we see You hungry, or thirsty, or a stranger, or naked, or sick, or in prison, and did not take care of You?' Then He will answer them, 'Truly I say to you, to the extent that you did not do it to one of the least of these, you did not do it to Me.' These will go away into eternal punishment, but the righteous into eternal life" (Matthew 25:31–46; see Matthew 7:23; 16:27; 19:29).

[ETERNAL LIFE from life]

Setting: Capernaum of Galilee. As Jesus teaches His disciples in private, they ask Him about greatness.

But Jesus said, "Do not hinder him, for there is no one who will perform a miracle in My name, and be able soon afterward to speak evil of Me. For he who is not against us is for us. For whoever gives you a cup of water to drink because of your name as *followers* of Christ, truly I say to you, he will not lose his reward. Whoever causes one of these little ones who believe to stumble, it would be better for him if, with a heavy millstone hung around his neck, he had been cast into the sea. If your hand causes you to stumble, cut it off; it is better for you to enter life crippled, than, having your two hands, to go into hell, into the unquenchable fire, [where THEIR WORM DOES NOT DIE, AND THE FIRE IS NOT QUENCHED.] If your foot causes you to stumble, cut it off; it is better for you to enter life lame, than, having your two feet, to be cast into hell, [where THEIR WORM DOES NOT DIE, AND THE FIRE IS NOT QUENCHED.] If your eye causes you to stumble, throw it out; it is better for you to enter the kingdom of God with one eye, than, having two eyes, to be cast into hell, where THEIR WORM DOES NOT DIE, AND THE FIRE IS NOT QUENCHED.

For everyone will be salted with fire. Salt is good; but if the salt becomes unsalty, with what will you make it salty *again?* Have salt in yourselves, and be at peace with one another" (Mark 9:39–50; Jesus quotes from Isaiah 66:24; cf. Matthew 18:6–9; Luke 9:49, 50; see Matthew 5:13, 29, 30; 10:42; 12:30; 18:5, 6).

Setting: Judea beyond the Jordan (Perea). After informing a rich man how righteous believers may have treasure in heaven, Jesus conveys to His disciples the reward of those who sacrifice in this life to follow Him.

Jesus said, "Truly I say to you, there is no one who has left house or brothers or sisters or mother or father or children or farms, for My sake and for the gospel's sake, but that he will receive a hundred times as much now in the present age, houses and brothers and sisters and mothers and children and farms, along with persecutions; and in the age to come, eternal life. But many *who are* first will be last, and the last, first" (Mark 10:29–31; cf. Matthew 19:27–30; Luke 18:28–30; see Matthew 6:33).

Setting: On the way from Galilee to Jerusalem. After responding to His disciples' question about salvation, Jesus replies to Peter's statement about their personal sacrifice.

Peter said, "Behold, we have left our own homes and followed You." And He said to them, "Truly I say to you, there is no one who has left house or wife or brothers or parents or children, for the sake of the kingdom of God, who will not receive many times as much at this time and in the age to come, eternal life" (Luke 18:28–30; cf. Matthew 19:27–29; Mark 10:28–30; see Matthew 6:33; Luke 5:11).

Setting: Jerusalem. At the time for the Passover of the Jews, after the Lord cleanses the temple, a Pharisee, Nicodemus, asks Him by night the meaning of "born of the Spirit."

Jesus answered and said to him, "Are you the teacher of Israel and do not understand these things? Truly, truly, I say to you, we speak of what we know and testify of what we have seen, and you do not accept our testimony. If I told you earthly things and you do not believe, how will you believe if I tell you heavenly things? No one has ascended into heaven, but He who descended from heaven: the Son of Man. As Moses lifted up the serpent in the wilderness, even so must the Son of Man be lifted up; so that whoever believes will in Him have eternal life" (John 3:10–15; see Numbers 21:9; Proverbs 30:4; John 20:30, 31).

Setting: Jerusalem. At the time for the Passover of the Jews, after the Lord cleanses the temple, a Pharisee, Nicodemus, asks Him by night the meaning of "born again."

"For God so loved the world, that He gave His only begotten Son, that whoever believes in Him shall not perish, but have eternal life. For God did not send the Son into the world to judge the world, but that the world might be saved through Him. He who believes in Him is not judged; he who does not believe has been judged already, because he has not believed in the name of the only begotten Son of God. This is the judgment, that the Light has come into the world, and men loved darkness rather than the Light, for their deeds were evil. For everyone who does evil hates the Light, and does not come to the Light for fear that his deeds will be exposed. But he who practices the truth comes to the Light, so that his deeds may be manifested as having been wrought in God" (John 3:16–21; see Luke 19:10; John 1:4; 1:18; Romans 5:8; 1 John 1:6, 7).

Setting: Sychar in Samaria, on the way to Galilee. Jesus interacts with a Samaritan woman at Jacob's well, while His disciples are buying food.

Jesus answered and said to her, "Everyone who drinks of this water will thirst again; but whoever drinks of the water that I will give him shall never thirst; but the water that I will give him will become in him a well of water springing up to eternal life" (John 4:13, 14).

[ETERNAL LIFE from life eternal]
Setting: Sychar in Samaria. After Jesus converses with a Samaritan woman at Jacob's well, His disciples return with food. They try to get Jesus to eat but are surprised when He speaks of other food.

Jesus said to them, "My food is to do the will of Him who sent Me and to accomplish His work. Do you not say, 'There are yet four months, and *then* comes the harvest'? Behold, I say to you, lift up your eyes and look on the fields, that they are white for harvest. Already he who reaps is receiving wages and is gathering fruit for life eternal; so that he who sows and he who reaps may rejoice together. For in this *case* the saying is true, 'One sows and another reaps.' I sent you to reap that for which you have not labored; others have labored and you have entered into their labor" (John 4:34–38; see Matthew 9:37, 38; John 5:36).

[ETERNAL LIFE from life]

Setting: By the pool of Bethesda in Jerusalem. During the Feast of the Jews, Jesus responds to criticism from the Jewish religious leaders for healing a lame man on the Sabbath and for referring to God as His Father (thereby making Himself equal with God).

Therefore Jesus answered and was saying to them, "Truly, truly, I say to you, the Son can do nothing of Himself, unless *it is* something He sees the Father doing; for whatever the Father does, these things the Son also does in like manner. For the Father loves the Son, and shows Him all things that He Himself is doing; and *the Father* will show Him greater works than these, so that you will marvel. For just as the Father raises the dead and gives them life, even so the Son also gives life to whom He wishes. For not even the Father judges anyone, but He has given all judgment to the Son, so that all will honor the Son even as they honor the Father. He who does not honor the Son does not honor the Father who sent Him" (John 5:19–23; see Luke 10:16; John 3:35; 11:25; 14:12).

Setting: By the pool of Bethesda in Jerusalem. During the Feast of the Jews, Jesus responds to criticism from the Jewish religious leaders for healing a lame man on the Sabbath and for referring to God as His Father (thereby making Himself equal with God).

"Truly, truly, I say to you, he who hears My word, and believes Him who sent Me, has eternal life, and does not come into judgment, but has passed out of death into life" (John 5:24; see John 3:18; 12:44).

Setting: Jerusalem. During the feast of the Jews, Jesus responds to criticism from the Jewish religious leaders by referring to God as His Father (thereby making Himself equal with God) and informing them that God, John the Baptist, the Scriptures, and His works all testify to His mission.

"You search the Scriptures because you think that in them you have eternal life; it is these that testify about Me; and you are unwilling to come to Me so that you may have life. I do not receive glory from men; but I know you, that you do not have the love of God in yourselves. I have come in My Father's name, and you do not receive Me; if another comes in his own name, you will receive him. How can you believe, when you receive glory from one another and you do not seek the glory that is from the *one and* only God? Do not think that I will accuse you before the Father; the one who accuses you is Moses, in whom you have set your hope. For if you believed Moses, you would believe Me, for he wrote about Me. But if you do not believe his writings, how will you believe My words?" (John 5:39–47; see Matthew 24:5; Luke 16:29, 31; 24:27; 9:28; 17:3)

Setting: Capernaum. The day after Jesus walks on the Sea of Galilee to join His disciples in a boat, the people He miraculously fed with a lad's five loaves and two fish ask the Lord how He had crossed the water, since He had not entered the boat from land with His disciples.

Jesus answered them and said, "Truly, truly, I say to you, you seek Me, not because you saw signs, but because you ate of the loaves and were filled. Do not work for the food which perishes, but for the food which endures to eternal life, which the Son of Man will give to you, for on Him the Father, God, has set His seal" (John 6:26, 27; see John 3:33).

Setting: Capernaum. The day after Jesus walks on the Sea of Galilee to join His disciples in a boat, the people He miraculously fed with a lad's five loaves and two fish ask the Lord to always give them this bread out of heaven.

Jesus said to them, "I am the bread of life; he who comes to Me will not hunger, and he who believes in Me will never thirst. But I said to you that you have seen Me, and yet do not believe. All that the Father gives Me will come to Me, and the one who comes to Me I will certainly not cast out. For I have come down from heaven, not to do My own will, but the will of Him who sent Me. This

is the will of Him who sent Me, that of all that He has given Me I lose nothing, but raise it up on the last day. For this is the will of My Father, that everyone who beholds the Son and believes in Him will have eternal life, and I Myself will raise him up on the last day" (John 6:35–40; see John 3:13, 16; 4:13, 14).

Setting: Capernaum of Galilee. After Jesus informs the people whom He miraculously fed with a lad's five loaves and two fish how they might receive the bread out of heaven, the Jewish religious leaders grumble because the Lord claims that He came down out of heaven.

Therefore the Jews were grumbling about Him, because He said, "I am the bread that came down out of heaven." They were saying, "Is not this Jesus, the son of Joseph, whose father and mother we know? How does He now say, 'I have come down out of heaven'?" Jesus answered and said to them, "Do not grumble among yourselves. No one can come to Me unless the Father who sent Me draws him; and I will raise him up on the last day. It is written in the prophets, 'AND THEY SHALL ALL BE TAUGHT OF GOD.' Everyone who has heard and learned from the Father, comes to Me. Not that anyone has seen the Father, except the One who is from God; He has seen the Father. Truly, truly, I say to you, he who believes has eternal life. I am the bread of life. Your fathers ate the manna in the wilderness, and they died. This is the bread which comes down out of heaven, so that one may eat of it and not die. I am the living bread that came down out of heaven; if anyone eats of this bread, he will live forever; and the bread also which I will give for the life of the world is My flesh" (John 6:41–51, Jesus quotes from Isaiah 54:13; see John 1:18, 29; 3:36; 7:27).

Setting: Capernaum of Galilee. After informing the people whom He miraculously fed with a lad's five loaves and two fish how they might receive the bread out of heaven, the Jewish religious leaders argue with one another when Jesus says He will give His flesh to the world to eat.

So Jesus said to them, "Truly, truly, I say to you, unless you eat the flesh of the Son of Man and drink His blood, you have no life in yourselves. He who eats My flesh and drinks My blood has eternal life, and I will raise him up on the last day. For My flesh is true food, and My blood is true drink. He who eats My flesh and drinks My blood abides in Me, and I in him. As the living Father sent Me, and I live because of the Father, so he who eats Me, he also will live because of Me. This is the bread which came down out of heaven; not as the fathers ate and died; he who eats this bread will live forever" (John 6:53–58; see Matthew 16:16; Luke 4:22; John 3:36; John 9:16; 15:4).

[ETERNAL LIFE from life]
Setting: The synagogue at Capernaum of Galilee. After the Jewish religious leaders argue with one another when Jesus says He will give His flesh to the world to eat, some of His disciples also express difficulty with His statements.

But, Jesus, conscious that His disciples grumbled at this, said to them, "Does this cause you to stumble? *What* then if you see the Son of Man ascending to where He was before? It is the Spirit who gives life; the flesh profits nothing; the words that I have spoken to you are spirit and are life. But there are some of you who do not believe." For Jesus knew from the beginning who they were who did not believe, and who it was that would betray Him. And He was saying, "For this reason I have said to you, that no one can come to Me unless it has been granted him from the Father" (John 6:61–65; see Matthew 11:6; 13:11; John 3:13).

[ETERNAL LIFE from he will never see death]
Setting: The temple treasury in Jerusalem. While Jesus is interacting with the scribes and Pharisees about His testimony, their ancestry, and their motives, they state their belief Jesus is a demon-possessed Samaritan.

Jesus answered, "I do not have a demon; but I honor My Father, and you dishonor Me. But I do not seek My glory; there is One who seeks and judges. Truly, truly, I say to you, if anyone keeps My word he will never see death" (John 8:49–51; see Matthew 16:28; John 5:41; 7:20).

[ETERNAL LIFE from life]
Setting: Jerusalem. Following the Pharisees' interrogation and dismissal of the formerly blind man Jesus healed on the Sabbath, the Lord conveys the Parable of the Good Shepherd to the Pharisees, using figures of speech they do not understand.

So Jesus said to them again, "Truly, truly, I say to you, I am the door of the sheep. All who came before Me are thieves and robbers, but the sheep did not hear them. I am the door; if anyone enters through Me, he will be saved, and will go in and out and find pasture. The thief comes only to steal and kill and destroy; I came that they may have life, and have *it* abundantly. I am the good shepherd; the good shepherd lays down His life for the sheep. He who is a hired hand, and not a shepherd, who is not the owner of the sheep, sees the wolf coming, and leaves the sheep and flees, and the wolf snatches them and scatters *them. He flees* because he is a hired hand and is not concerned about the sheep. I am the good shepherd, and I know My own and My own know Me, even as the Father knows Me and I know the Father; and I lay down My life for the sheep. I have other sheep, which are not of this fold; I must bring them also, and they will hear My voice; and they will become one flock *with* one shepherd. For this reason the Father loves Me, because I lay down My life so that I may take it again. No one has taken it away from Me, but I lay it down on My own initiative. I have authority to take it up again. This commandment I received from My Father" (John 10:7–18; see Isaiah 40:11; 56:8; Jeremiah 23:1; Matthew 11:27).

Setting: Jerusalem. At the Feast of Dedication, just after Jesus conveys the Parable of the Good Shepherd to the Pharisees (who do not understand it), they ask Him plainly if He is the Christ.

Jesus answered them, "I told you, and you do not believe; the works that I do in My Father's name, these testify of Me. But you do not believe because you are not of My sheep. My sheep hear My voice, and I know them, and they follow Me; and I give eternal life to them, and they will never perish; and no one will snatch them out of My hand. My Father, who has given *them* to Me, is greater than all; and no one is able to snatch *them* out of the Father's hand. I and the Father are one" (John 10:25–30; see John 8:47; 17:1, 2, 20, 21).

[ETERNAL LIFE from will never die]
Setting: Bethany near Jerusalem. Jesus travels with His disciples to Bethany in Judea to see Lazarus's sisters, Martha and Mary, after the death of His friend.

Jesus said to her, "Your brother will rise again." Martha said to Him, "I know that he will rise again in the resurrection on the last day." Jesus said to her, "I am the resurrection and the life; he who believes in Me will live even if he dies, and everyone who lives and believes in Me will never die. Do you believe this?" (John 11:23–26; see Daniel 12:2; John 1:4; 6:47–51).

[ETERNAL LIFE from life eternal]
Setting: Jerusalem. Just days before the Passover, with the chief priests and Pharisees plotting to seize Jesus, crowds welcome Him to Jerusalem with palm branches and praise, and some Greeks ask to meet Him.

And Jesus answered them, saying, "The hour has come for the Son of Man to be glorified. Truly, truly, I say to you, unless a grain of wheat falls into the earth and dies, it remains alone; but if it dies, it bears much fruit. He who loves his life loses it, and he who hates his life in this world will keep it to life eternal. If anyone serves Me, he must follow Me; and where I am, there My servant will be also; if anyone serves Me, the Father will honor him" (John 12:23–26; see Matthew 10:39).

Setting: Jerusalem. Just days before the Passover, with the chief priests and Pharisees plotting to seize the Lord, who is expressing anxiety about His upcoming death by crucifixion, some of the Jews believe in Jesus, while others are rejecting His message.

And Jesus cried out and said, "He who believes in Me, does not believe in Me but in Him who sent Me. He who sees Me sees the One who sent Me. I have come *as* Light into the world, so that everyone who believes in Me will not remain in darkness. If anyone hears My sayings and does not keep them, I do not judge him; for I did not come to judge the world, but to save the world. He who rejects Me and does not receive My sayings, has one who judges him; the word I spoke is what will judge him at the last day. For I did not speak on My own initiative, but the Father Himself who sent Me has given Me a commandment *as to* what to say and what to speak. I know that His commandment is eternal life; therefore the things I speak, I speak just as the Father as told Me" (John 12:44–50; see Matthew 10:40; Luke 10:16; John 1:4; 3:17; 5:19; 6:68; 14:9).

[ETERNAL LIFE from life]
Setting: Jerusalem. Before the Passover, as Jesus comforts and gives hope to His disciples regarding their future after He returns to heaven, Thomas asks where He is going and how they will know the way.

Jesus said to him, "I am the way, and the truth, and the life; no one comes to the Father but through Me. If you had known Me, you would have known My Father also; from now on you know Him, and have seen Him" (John 14:6, 7; see John 8:19; 10:9; 11:25).

Setting: Jerusalem. Before the Passover, after giving His disciples assurance that in the midst of tribulation they will have His peace, Jesus prays His high-priestly prayer.

Jesus spoke these things; and lifting up His eyes to heaven, He said, "Father, the hour has come; glorify Your Son, that the Son may glorify You, even as You gave Him authority over all flesh, that to all whom You have given Him, He may give eternal life. This is eternal life, that they may know You, the only true God, and Jesus Christ whom You have sent. I glorified You on the earth, having accomplished the work which You have given Me to do. Now, Father, glorify Me together with Yourself, with the glory which I had with You before the world was. I have manifested Your name to the men whom You gave Me out of the world; they were Yours and You gave them to Me, and they have kept Your word. Now they have come to know that everything You have given Me is from You; for the words which You gave Me I have given to them; and they received *them* and truly understood that I came forth from You, and they believed You sent Me. I ask on their behalf; I do not ask on behalf of the world, but of those whom You have given Me; for they are Yours; and all things that are Mine are Yours, and Yours are Mine; and I have been glorified in them. I am no longer in the world; and *yet* they themselves are in the world, and I come to You. Holy Father, keep them in Your name, *the name* which You have given Me, that they may be even as We *are.* While I was with them, I was keeping them in Your name which You have given Me; and I guarded them and not one of them perished but the son of perdition, so that the Scripture would be fulfilled" (John 17:1–12; see Luke 22:32; John 1:1; 3:35; 4:34; 5:44; 6:37–39, 70; 8:42; 11:41; 12:49; 13:18, 31; 16:15; Philippians 2:9).

ETERNAL PUNISHMENT (Listed under PUNISHMENT, ETERNAL; also see GOD, SEPARATION FROM; HELL; and JUDGMENT)

ETERNAL SECURITY

[ETERNAL SECURITY from no one will snatch them out of My hand and no one is able to snatch them out of the Father's hand]
Setting: Jerusalem. At the Feast of Dedication, just after Jesus conveys the Parable of the Good Shepherd to the Pharisees (who do not understand it), they ask Him plainly if He is the Christ.

Jesus answered them, "I told you, and you do not believe; the works that I do in My Father's name, these testify of Me. But you do not believe because you are not of My sheep. My sheep hear My voice, and I know them, and they follow Me; and I give eternal life to them, and they will never perish; and no one will snatch them out of My hand. My Father, who has given *them* to Me, is greater than all; and no one is able to snatch *them* out of the Father's hand. I and the Father are one" (John 10:25–30; see John 8:47; 17:1, 2, 20, 21).

ETERNAL SIN (Listed under SIN, ETERNAL)

ETERNALITY, JESUS' (See JESUS' PREEXISTENCE)

ETERNITY (See DEATH, SECOND; ETERNAL LIFE; FIRE, ETERNAL; FOREVER; GOD, SEPARATION FROM; HEAVEN; HELL; JUDGMENT; and PUNISHMENT, ETERNAL)

EUCHARIST (See LORD'S SUPPER)

EUNUCHS

Setting: Judea beyond the Jordan (Perea). Jesus answers His disciples' private question following His response to the Pharisees' question about Moses' command regarding a certificate of divorce.

But He said to them, "Not all men *can* accept this statement, but *only* those to whom it has been given. For there are eunuchs who were born that way from their mother's womb; and there are eunuchs who were made eunuchs by men; and there are *also* eunuchs who made themselves eunuchs for the sake of the kingdom of heaven. He who is able to accept *this*, let him accept *it*" (Matthew 19:11, 12; cf. 1 Corinthians 7:7).

EVANGELISM (Also see GOSPEL; GREAT COMMISSION; HARVEST; HARVEST, LORD OF THE; PREACHING; PROCLAMATION; SALVATION; and TESTIMONY)

[EVANGELISM from fishers of men]

Setting: By the Sea of Galilee. As Jesus commences His public ministry, He calls two brothers who are fishermen, Simon (Peter) and Andrew, to be His disciples.

And He said to them, "Follow Me, and I will make you fishers of men" (Matthew 4:19; cf. Mark 4:17).

[EVANGELISM from workers into His harvest]

Setting: The villages and cities of Galilee. While healing the sick, raising the dead, and casting out demons, Jesus comments on the enormity of the task and the need to ask the Lord of the harvest for additional workers.

Then He said to His disciples, "The harvest is plentiful, but the workers are few. Therefore beseech the Lord of the harvest to send out workers into His harvest" (Matthew 9:37, 38; cf. Luke 10:2).

[EVANGELISM from This gospel of the kingdom shall be preached in the whole world as a testimony to all the nations]

Setting: The Mount of Olives, just east of Jerusalem. During His discourse, Jesus answers His disciples' questions as to when the temple will be destroyed and Jerusalem overrun, along with the signs of His coming and the end of the age.

And Jesus answered and said to them, "See to it that no one misleads you. For many will come in My name, saying, 'I am the Christ,' and will mislead many. You will be hearing of wars and rumors of wars. See that you are not frightened, for *those things* must take place, but *that* is not yet the end. For nation will rise against nation, and kingdom against kingdom, and in various places there will be famines and earthquakes. But all these things are *merely* the beginning of birth pangs. Then they will deliver you to tribulation, and will kill you, and you will be hated by all nations because of My name. At that time many will fall away and will betray one another and hate one another. Many false prophets will arise and will mislead many. Because lawlessness is increased, most people's love will grow cold. But the one who endures to the end, he will be saved. This gospel of the kingdom shall be preached in the whole world as a testimony to all the nations, and then the end will come" (Matthew 24:4–14; cf. Jeremiah 29:8; Matthew 7:15; 10:17, 22; Mark 13:3–13; Luke 21:7–19; Revelation 6:4).

[EVANGELISM from Go therefore and make disciples of all the nations]

Setting: On a mountain in Galilee. Following His resurrection from the dead in Jerusalem, Jesus conveys the Great Commission to His eleven remaining disciples.

And Jesus came up and spoke to them, saying, "All authority has been given to Me in heaven and on earth. Go therefore and make disciples of all the nations, baptizing them in the name of the Father and the Son and the Holy Spirit, teaching them to observe all that I commanded you; and lo, I am with you always, even to the end of the age" (Matthew 28:18–20; cf. Mark 16:15; see Daniel 7:13).

[EVANGELISM from fishers of men]

Setting: By the Sea of Galilee. Jesus calls Simon (Peter) and his brother, Andrew, to be His disciples.

And Jesus said to them, "Follow Me, and I will make you become fishers of men" (Mark 1:17; cf. Matthew 4:19).

[EVANGELISM from Do not fear, from now on you will be catching men]
Setting: By the Sea of Galilee. After teaching the people from Simon's (Peter) boat, Jesus calls Peter, James, and John to follow Him. (This appears to be a permanent call, as Simon and other companions are with Him earlier in Mark 1:35–39 and Luke 4:38–39).

When He had finished speaking, He said to Simon, "Put out into the deep water and let down your nets for a catch." ". . . and so also *were* James and John, sons of Zebedee, who were partners with Simon. And Jesus said to Simon, "Do not fear, from now on you will be catching men" (Luke 5:4, 10; see John 21:6).

[EVANGELISM from harvest]
Setting: On the way from Galilee to Jerusalem. The Lord appoints seventy followers and sends them out in pairs to every place He Himself will soon visit.

And He was saying to them, "The harvest is plentiful, but the laborers are few; therefore beseech the Lord of the harvest to send out laborers into His harvest. Go; behold, I send you out as lambs in the midst of wolves. Carry no money belt, no bag, no shoes; and greet no one on the way. Whatever house you enter, first say, 'Peace be to this house.' If a man of peace is there, your peace will rest on him; but if not, it will return to you. Stay in that house, eating and drinking what they give you; for the laborer is worthy of his wages. Do not keep moving from house to house. Whatever city you enter and they receive you, eat what is set before you; and heal those in it who are sick, and say to them, 'The kingdom of God has come near to you.' But whatever city you enter and they do not receive you, go out into its streets and say, 'Even the dust of your city which clings to our feet we wipe off in protest against you; yet be sure of this, that the kingdom of God has come near.' I say to you, it will be more tolerable in that day for Sodom than for that city" (Luke 10:2–12; see Genesis 19:24–28; Matthew 9:37, 38, 10:9–14, 16; 1 Corinthians 10:27).

[EVANGELISM from look on the fields, that they are white for harvest]
Setting: Sychar in Samaria, on the way to Galilee. After Jesus converses with a Samaritan woman at Jacob's well, His disciples return with food. They try to get Jesus to eat but are surprised when He speaks of other food.

Jesus said to them, "My food is to do the will of Him who sent Me and to accomplish His work. Do you not say, 'There are yet four months, and *then* comes the harvest'? Behold, I say to you, lift up your eyes and look on the fields, that they are white for harvest. Already he who reaps is receiving wages and is gathering fruit for life eternal; so that he who sows and he who reaps may rejoice together. For in this *case* the saying is true, 'One sows and another reaps.' I sent you to reap that for which you have not labored; others have labored and you have entered into their labor" (John 4:34–38; see Matthew 9:37, 38; John 5:36).

[EVANGELISM from witnesses]
Setting: Jerusalem. Luke, writing in Acts, presents quotes from Jesus' post-resurrection appearances, in which He responds to His disciples' question if He is about to restore the kingdom to Israel.

He said to them, "It is not for you to know times or epochs which the Father has fixed by His own authority; but you will receive power when the Holy Spirit has come upon you; and you shall be My witnesses both in Jerusalem, and in all Judea and Samaria, and even to the remotest part of the earth" (Acts 1:7, 8; see Luke 24:48, 49; Acts 2:1–4).

EVE, ADAM AND (See ADAM AND EVE)

EVENING (Also see NIGHT)
Setting: Magadan of Galilee. The Pharisees and Sadducees, rejecting Jesus' message, continue to test Him by asking Him for a sign from heaven.

But He replied to them, "When it is evening, you say, '*It will be* fair weather, for the sky is red.' And in the morning, '*There will* be a storm today, for the sky is red and threatening.' Do you know how to discern the appearance of the sky, but cannot *discern* the signs of the times? An evil and adulterous generation seeks after a sign; and a sign will not be given it, except the sign of Jonah." And He left them and went away (Matthew 16:2–4; cf. Matthew 12:39; Mark 8:12; Luke 12:54–56).

Setting: Judea beyond the Jordan (Perea). Jesus illustrates the kingdom of heaven to His disciples through the story of laborers in the vineyard.

"For the kingdom of heaven is like a landowner who went out early in the morning to hire laborers for his vineyard. When he had agreed with the laborers for a denarius for the day, he sent them into his vineyard. And he went out about the third hour and saw others standing idle in the market place; and to those he said, 'You also go into the vineyard, and whatever is right I will give you.' And *so* they went. Again he went out about the sixth and the ninth hour, and did the same thing. And about the eleventh *hour* he went out and found others standing *around;* and he said to them, 'Why have you been standing idle here all day long?' They said to him, 'Because no one hired us.' He said to them, 'You go into the vineyard too.' When evening came, the owner of the vineyard said to his foreman, 'Call the laborers and pay them their wages, beginning with the last *group* to the first.' When those *hired* about the eleventh hour came, each one received a denarius. When those *hired* first came, they thought that they would receive more; but each of them also received a denarius. When they received it, they grumbled at the landowner, saying, 'These last men have worked *only* one hour, and you have made them equal to us who have borne the burden and the scorching heat of the day.' But he answered and said to one of them, 'Friend, I am doing you no wrong; did you not agree with me for a denarius? Take what is yours and go, but I wish to give to this last man the same as to you. It is not lawful for me to do what I wish with what is my own? Or is your eye envious because I am generous?' So the last shall be first, and the first last" (Matthew 20:1–16; cf. Matthew 19:30).

Setting: The Mount of Olives, east of the temple in Jerusalem. During His discourse, after prophesying the temple's destruction, Jesus responds to questions from Peter, James, John, and Andrew about future events.

"Take heed, keep on the alert; for you do not know when the *appointed* time will come. *It is* like a man away on a journey, *who* upon leaving his house and putting his slaves in charge, *assigning* to each one his task, also commanded the doorkeeper to stay on the alert. Therefore, be on the alert—for you do not know when the master of the house is coming, whether in the evening, at midnight, or when the rooster crows, or in the morning—in case he should come suddenly and find you asleep. What I say to you I say to all, 'Be on the alert!'" (Mark 13:33–37; cf. Matthew 24:42–43; Luke 21:34–36; see Luke 12:36–38; Ephesians 6:18).

EVERLASTING LIFE (See ETERNAL LIFE)

EVERYONE

Setting: Galilee. During the early part of His ministry, Jesus preaches the Sermon on the Mount to His disciples and the multitudes.

"But I say to you that everyone who is angry with his brother shall be guilty before the court; and whoever says to his brother, 'You good-for-nothing,' shall be guilty before the supreme court; and whoever says, 'You fool,' shall be guilty *enough to go* into the fiery hell" (Matthew 5:22).

Setting: Galilee. During the early part of His ministry, Jesus preaches the Sermon on the Mount to His disciples and the multitudes.

"You have heard that it was said, 'YOU SHALL NOT COMMIT ADULTERY'; but I say to you that everyone who looks at a woman with lust for her has already committed adultery with her in his heart" (Matthew 5:27, 28, Jesus quotes from Exodus 20:14; see 2 Samuel 11:2–5).

Setting: Galilee. During the early part of His ministry, Jesus preaches the Sermon on the Mount to His disciples and the multitudes.

"It was said, 'WHOEVER SENDS HIS WIFE AWAY, LET HIM GIVE HER A CERTIFICATE OF DIVORCE'; but I say to you that everyone who divorces his wife, except for *the* reason of unchastity, makes her commit adultery; and whoever marries a divorced woman commits adultery" (Matthew 5:31, 32, Jesus quotes from Deuteronomy 24: 1, 3; cf. Matthew 19:9; see Romans 7:2, 3; 1 Corinthians 7:10, 39).

Setting: Galilee. During the early part of His ministry, Jesus preaches the Sermon on the Mount to His disciples and the multitudes.

"Ask, and it will be given to you; seek, and you will find; knock, and it will be opened to you. For everyone who asks receives, and he who seeks finds, and to him who knocks it will be opened. Or what man is there among you who, when his son asks for a loaf, will give him a stone? Or if he asks for a fish, he will not give him a snake, will he? If you then, being evil, know how to give good gifts to your children, how much more will your Father who is in heaven give what is good to those who ask Him! In everything, therefore, treat people the same way you want them to treat you, for this is the Law and the Prophets" (Matthew 7:7–12; cf. Matthew 22:40; Luke 6:31; Luke 11:9–13; see Psalm 84:11).

Setting: Galilee. During the early part of His ministry, Jesus preaches the Sermon on the Mount to His disciples and the multitudes.

"Not everyone who says to Me, 'Lord, Lord,' will enter the kingdom of heaven, but he who does the will of My Father who is in heaven *will enter.* Many will say to Me on that day, 'Lord, Lord, did we not prophesy in Your name, and in Your name cast out demons, and in Your name perform many miracles?' And then I will declare to them, 'I never knew you, DEPART FROM ME, YOU WHO PRACTICE LAWLESSNESS'"(Matthew 7:21–23, Jesus quotes from Psalm 6:8; cf. Matthew 25:11–13; see Luke 6:46).

Setting: Galilee. During the early part of His ministry, Jesus preaches the Sermon on the Mount to His disciples and the multitudes.

"Therefore everyone who hears these words of Mine and acts on them, may be compared to a wise man who built his house on the rock. And the rain fell, and the floods came, and the winds blew and slammed against that house; and *yet* it did not fall, for it had been founded on the rock. Everyone who hears these words of Mine and does not act on them, will be like a foolish man who built his house on the sand. The rain fell, and the floods came, and the winds blew and slammed against that house; and it fell—and great was its fall" (Matthew 7:24–28; cf. Luke 6:47–49).

Setting: Galilee. Jesus explains the meaning of discipleship as He commissions His twelve disciples for ministry.

"Therefore everyone who confesses Me before men, I will also confess him before My Father who is in heaven. But whoever denies Me before men, I will also deny him before My Father who is in heaven" (Matthew 10:32, 33; cf. Mark 8:38; Luke 12:8).

Setting: Judea beyond the Jordan (Perea). Jesus promises rewards to His disciples for their personal sacrifice and commitment to following Him.

And Jesus said to them, "Truly I say to you, that you who have followed Me, in the regeneration when the Son of Man will sit on His glorious throne, you also shall sit upon twelve thrones, judging the twelve tribes of Israel. And everyone who has left houses or brothers or sisters or father or mother or children or farms for My name's sake, will receive many times as much, and will inherit eternal life. But many *who* are first will be last; and *the* last, first" (Matthew 19:28–30; cf. Matthew 6:33; 20:15; Mark 10:29, 30; Luke 18:29, 30; 22:30).

Setting: The Mount of Olives, just east of Jerusalem. During His discourse, after answering His disciples' questions as to when the temple will be destroyed and Jerusalem overrun, along with the signs of His coming and the end of the age, Jesus reemphasizes to the disciples they should be on the alert for His return.

"For *it is* just like a man *about* to go on a journey, who called his own slaves and entrusted his possessions to them. To one he gave five talents, to another, two, and to another, one, each according to his own ability; and he went on his journey. Immediately the one who had received the five talents went and traded with them, and gained five more talents. In the same manner the one who *had received* the two *talents* gained two more. But he who received the one *talent* went away, and dug a *hole* in the ground and hid his master's money. Now after a long time the master of those slaves came and settled accounts with them. The one who had received the five talents came up and brought five more talents, saying, 'Master, you entrusted five talents to me. See, I have gained five more talents.' His master said to him, 'Well done, good and faithful slave. You were faithful with a few things, I will put you in charge of many things; enter into the joy of your master.' Also the one who *had received* the two talents came up and said, 'Master, you entrusted two talents to me. See, I have gained two more talents.' His master said to him, 'Well done, good and faithful slave. You were faithful with a few things, I will put you in charge of many things; enter into the joy of your master.' And the one also who had received the one talent came up and said, 'Master, I knew you to be a hard man, reaping where you did not sow and gathering where you scattered no *seed.* And I was afraid, and went away and hid your talent in the ground. See, you have what is yours.' But his master answered and said to him, 'You wicked, lazy slave, you knew that I reap where I did not sow and gather where I scattered no *seed.* Then you ought to have put my money in the bank, and on my arrival I would have received my *money* back with interest. 'Therefore take away the talent from him, and give it to the one who has ten talents.' For to everyone who has, *more* shall be given, and he will have an abundance; but from the one who does not have, even what he does have shall be taken away. Throw out the worthless slave into the outer darkness; in that place there will be weeping and gnashing of teeth" (Matthew 25:14–30; cf. Matthew 8:12; 13:12; 24:45–47; see Matthew 18:23, 24; Luke 12:44).

Setting: Capernaum of Galilee. As Jesus teaches His disciples in private, they ask Him about greatness.

But Jesus said, "Do not hinder him, for there is no one who will perform a miracle in My name, and be able soon afterward to speak evil of Me. For he who is not against us is for us. For whoever gives you a cup of water to drink because of your name as *followers* of Christ, truly I say to you, he will not lose his reward. Whoever causes one of these little ones who believe to stumble, it would be better for him if, with a heavy millstone hung around his neck, he had been cast into the sea. If your hand causes you to stumble, cut it off; it is better for you to enter life crippled, than, having your two hands, to go into hell, into the unquenchable fire, [where THEIR WORM DOES NOT DIE, AND THE FIRE IS NOT QUENCHED.] If your foot causes you to stumble, cut it off; it is better for you to enter life lame, than, having your two feet, to be cast into hell, [where THEIR WORM DOES NOT DIE, AND THE FIRE IS NOT QUENCHED.] If your eye causes you to stumble, throw it out; it is better for you to enter the kingdom of God with one eye, than, having two eyes, to be cast into hell, where THEIR WORM DOES NOT DIE, AND THE FIRE IS NOT QUENCHED. For everyone will be salted with fire. Salt is good; but if the salt becomes unsalty, with what will you make it salty *again?* Have salt in yourselves, and be at peace with one another" (Mark 9:39–50; Jesus quotes from Isaiah 66:24; cf. Matthew 18:6–9; Luke 9:49–50; see Matthew 5:13, 29, 30; 10:42; 12:30; 18:5, 6).

Setting: Galilee. After selecting His twelve disciples, Jesus teaches the Sermon on the Mount to His disciples and a great throng from Judea, Jerusalem, and the central coastal region of Tyre and Sidon.

"But I say to you who hear, love your enemies, do good to those who hate you, bless those who curse you, pray for those who mistreat you. Whoever hits you on the cheek, offer him the other also; and whoever takes away your coat, do not withhold your shirt from him either. Give to everyone who asks of you, and whoever takes away what is yours, do not demand it back. Treat others the same way you want them to treat you. If you love those who love you, what credit is that to you? For even sinners love those who love them. If you do good to those who do good to you, what credit is that to you? For even sinners do the same. If you lend to those from whom you expect to receive, what credit is that to you? Even sinners lend to sinners in order to receive back the same amount. But love your enemies, and do good, and lend, expecting nothing in return; and your reward will be great, and you will be sons of the Most High; for He Himself is kind to ungrateful and evil men. Be merciful, just as your Father is merciful" (Luke 6:27–36; cf. Matthew 5:9, 39–48; Matthew 7:12).

Setting: Galilee. After selecting His twelve disciples, Jesus teaches the Sermon on the Mount to His disciples and a great throng from Judea, Jerusalem, and the central coastal region of Tyre and Sidon.

And He also spoke a parable to them: "A blind man cannot guide a blind man, can he? Will they not both fall into a pit? A pupil is not above his teacher; but everyone, after he has been fully trained, will be like his teacher. Why do you look at the speck that is in your brother's eye, but do not notice the log that is in your own eye? Or how can you say to your brother, 'Brother, let me take out the speck that is in your eye,' when you yourself do not see the log that is in your own eye? You hypocrite, first take the log out of your own eye, and then you will see clearly to take out the speck that is in your brother's eye. For there is no good tree which produces bad fruit, nor, on the other hand, a bad tree which produces good fruit. For each tree is known by its own fruit. For men do not gather figs from thorns, nor do they pick grapes from a briar bush. The good man out of the good treasure of his heart brings forth what is good; and the evil man out of the evil treasure brings forth what is evil; for his mouth speaks from that which fills his heart" (Luke 6:39–45; cf. Matthew 7:3–6. 16, 18, 20; 12:35; see Matthew 10:24; 15:14).

Setting: Galilee. After selecting His twelve disciples, Jesus teaches the Sermon on the Mount to His disciples and a great throng from Judea, Jerusalem, and the central coastal region of Tyre and Sidon.

"Why do you call Me, 'Lord, Lord,' and do not do what I say? Everyone who comes to Me and hears My words and acts on them, I will show you whom he is like; he is like a man building a house, who dug deep and laid a foundation on the rock; and when a flood occurred, the torrent burst against that house and could not shake it, because it had been well built. But the one who has heard and has not acted accordingly, is like a man who built a house on the ground without any foundation; and the torrent burst against it and immediately it collapsed, and the ruin of that house was great" (Luke 6:46–49; cf. Matthew 7:24–27; see James 1:22).

Setting: On the way from Galilee to Jerusalem via Bethany. After Jesus visits the home of Martha and Mary, a disciple asks Him to teach His disciples to pray.

And He said to them, "When you pray, say: 'Father, hallowed be Your name. Your kingdom come. Give us each day our daily bread. And forgive us our sins, for we ourselves also forgive everyone who is indebted to us. And lead us not into temptation'" (Luke 11:2–4; cf. Matthew 6:9–13).

Setting: On the way from Galilee to Jerusalem. After revealing to His disciples how to pray, Jesus illustrates persistence in prayer.

Then He said to them, "Suppose one of you has a friend, and goes to him at midnight and says to him, 'Friend, lend me three loaves; for a friend of mine has come to me from a journey, and I have nothing to set before him'; and from inside he answers and says, 'Do not bother me; the door has already been shut and my children and I are in bed; I cannot get up and give you anything.' I tell you, even though he will not get up and give him anything because he is his friend, yet because of his persistence he will get up and give him as much as he needs. So I say to you, ask, and it will be given to you; seek, and you will find; knock, and it will be opened to you. For everyone who asks, receives; and he who seeks, finds; and to him who knocks, it will be opened" (Luke 11:5–10; cf. Matthew 7:7, 8; see Luke 18:1–5).

Setting: On the way from Galilee to Jerusalem. Jesus warns His disciples of future events as the scribes and Pharisees turn hostile and question Him in an attempt to catch Him in something He might say.

"And I say to you, everyone who confesses Me before men, the Son of Man will confess him also before the angels of God; but he who denies Me before men will be denied before the angels of God. And everyone who speaks a word against the Son of Man, it will be forgiven him; but he who blasphemes against the Holy Spirit, it will not be forgiven him. When they bring you before the synagogues and the rulers and the authorities, do not worry about how or what you are to speak in your defense, or what you are to say; for the Holy Spirit will teach you in that very hour what you ought to say" (Luke 12:8–12; cf. Matthew 10:32, 33; 12:31, 32; see Matthew 10:20).

Setting: On the way from Galilee to Jerusalem. When Jesus uses a parable to challenge the crowd and His disciples to be ready for His return, Peter asks Him whom He is addressing.

And the Lord said, "Who then is the faithful and sensible steward, whom his master will put in charge of his servants, to give them their rations at the proper time? Blessed is that slave whom his master finds so doing when he comes. Truly I say to you that he will put him in charge of all his possessions. But if that slave says in his heart, 'My master will be a long time in coming,' and begins to beat the slaves, both men and women, and to eat and drink and get drunk; the master of that slave will come on a day when he does not expect him and at an hour he does not know, and will cut him in pieces, and assign him a place with the unbelievers. And that slave who knew his master's will and did not get ready or act in accord with his will, will receive many lashes, but the one who did know it, and committed deeds worthy of flogging, will receive but few. From everyone who has been given much, much will be required; and to whom they entrusted much, of him they will ask all the more" (Luke 12:42–48; cf. Matthew 24:45–51; see Leviticus 5:17).

Setting: On the way from Galilee to Jerusalem. Jesus speaks a parable to the guests of a Pharisee leader on the Sabbath as He observes the guests selecting places of honor at the table.

And He *began* speaking a parable to the invited guests when He noticed how they had been picking out the places of honor *at the table,* saying to them, "When you are invited by someone to a wedding feast, do not take the place of honor, for someone more distinguished than you may have been invited by him, and he who invited you both will come and say to you, 'Give *your* place to this man, and then in disgrace you proceed to occupy the last place. But when you are invited, go and recline at the last place, so that when the one who has invited you comes, he may say to you, 'Friend, move up higher'; then you will have honor in the sight of all who are at the table with you. For everyone who exalts himself will be humbled, and he who humbles himself will be exalted" (Luke 14:7–11; see 2 Samuel 22:28; Proverbs 25:6, 7; Matthew 23:6).

Setting: On the way from Galilee to Jerusalem. The Lord responds to the Pharisees' scoffing at His teaching His disciples about stewardship.

And He said to them, "You are those who justify yourselves in the sight of men, but God knows your hearts; for that which is highly esteemed among men is detestable in the sight of God. The Law and the Prophets were proclaimed until John; since that time the gospel of the kingdom of God has been preached, and everyone is forcing his way into it. But is it easier for heaven and earth to pass away than for one stroke of a letter of the Law to fail" (Luke 16:15–17; cf. Matthew 5:18; see 1 Samuel 16:7; Matthew 4:23; 11:11–14).

Setting: On the way from Galilee to Jerusalem. The Lord responds to the Pharisees' scoffing at His teaching His disciples about stewardship with an illustration of the earthly commitment of marriage.

"Everyone who divorces his wife and marries another commits adultery, and he who marries one who is divorced from a husband commits adultery" (Luke 16:18; cf. Matthew 5:31, 32; 19:9; Mark 10:11, 12; see Romans 7:2, 3; 1 Corinthians 7:10, 39).

Setting: On the way from Galilee to Jerusalem. After instructing His disciples about persistence in prayer, Jesus conveys a parable about self-righteousness.

And He also told this parable to some people who trusted in themselves that they were righteous, and viewed others with contempt: "Two men went up into the temple to pray, one a Pharisee and the other a tax collector. The Pharisee stood and was praying this to himself: 'God, I thank You that I am not like other people: swindlers, unjust, adulterers, or even like this tax collector. I fast twice a week; I pay tithes of all that I get.' But the tax collector, standing some distance away, was even unwilling to lift up his eyes to heaven, but was beating his breast, saying, 'God, be merciful to me, the sinner!' I tell you, this man went to his house justified rather than the other; for everyone who exalts himself will be humbled, but he who humbles himself will be exalted" (Luke 18:9–14; see Ezra 9:6; Matthew 6:5, 23:12; Luke 11:42, 16:15; Romans 14:3, 10).

Setting: Jericho, on the way to Jerusalem. After commending Zaccheus's faith in Him, Jesus provides a parable about stewardship.

So He said, "A nobleman went to a distant country to receive a kingdom for himself, and then return. And he called ten of his slaves, and gave them ten minas and said to them, 'Do business with this until I come back.' But his citizens hated him and sent a delegation after him, saying, 'We do not want this man to reign over us.' When he returned, after receiving the kingdom, he ordered that these slaves, to whom he had given the money, be called to him so that he might know what business they had done. The first appeared, saying, 'Master, your mina has made ten minas more.' And he said to him, 'Well done, good slave, because you have been faithful in a very little thing, you are to be in authority over ten cities.' The second came, saying, 'Your mina, master, has made five minas.' And he said to him, also, 'And you are to be over five cities.' Another came, saying, 'Master, here is your mina, which I kept put away in a handkerchief; for I was afraid of you, because you are an exacting man; you take up what you did not lay down and reap what you did not sow.' He said to him, 'By your own words I will judge you, you worthless slave. Did you know that I am an exacting man, taking up what I did not lay down and reaping what I did not sow? Then why did you not put my money in the bank, and having come, I would have collected it with interest?' Then he said to the bystanders, 'Take the mina away from him and give it to the one who has the ten minas.' And they said to him, 'Master, he has ten minas already.' I tell you that to everyone who has, more shall be given, but from the one who does not have, even what he does have shall be taken away. But these enemies of mine, who did not want me to reign over them, bring them here and slay them in my presence" (Luke 19:12–27; cf. Matthew 25:14–30; see Matthew 13:12; Luke 16:10).

Setting: The temple in Jerusalem. A few days before His crucifixion, after the chief priests and the scribes question His authority to teach and preach, Jesus conveys to the people the Parable of the Vine-Growers.

And He began to tell the people this parable: "A man planted a vineyard and rented it out to vine-growers, and went on a journey for a long time. At the harvest time he sent a slave to the vine-growers, so that they would give him some of the produce of the vineyard; but the vine-growers beat him and sent him away empty-handed. And he proceeded to send another slave; and they beat him also and treated him shamefully and sent him away empty-handed. And he proceeded to send a third; and this one also they wounded and cast out. The owner of the vineyard said, 'What shall I do? I will send my beloved son; perhaps they will respect him.' But when the vine-growers saw him, they reasoned with one another, saying, 'This is the heir; let us kill him so that the inheritance will be ours.' So they threw him out of the vineyard and killed him. What, then, will the owner of the vineyard do to them? He will come and destroy these vine-growers and will give the vineyard to others." When they heard it, they said, "May it never be!" But Jesus looked at them and said, "What then is this that is written: 'THE STONE WHICH THE BUILDERS REJECTED, THIS BECAME THE CHIEF CORNER stone'? Everyone who falls on that stone will be broken to pieces; but on whomever it falls, it will scatter him like dust" (Luke 20:9–18, Jesus quotes from Psalm 118:22; cf. Matthew 21:33–44; Mark 12:1–11; see Ephesians 2:20).

Setting: Jerusalem. At the time of the Passover of the Jews, after the Lord cleanses the temple, a Pharisee, Nicodemus, asks Him by night the meaning of "born again."

Jesus answered, "Truly, truly, I say to you, unless one is born of water and the Spirit he cannot enter into the kingdom of God. That which is born of the flesh is flesh, and that which is born of the Spirit is spirit. Do not be amazed that I said to you, 'You must be born again.' The wind blows where it wishes and you hear the sound of it, but do not know where it comes from and where it is going; so is everyone who is born of the Spirit" (John 3:5–8; see Psalm 135:7; John 1:13).

Setting: Jerusalem. At the time of the Passover of the Jews, after the Lord cleanses the temple, a Pharisee, Nicodemus, asks Him by night the meaning of "born again."

"For God so loved the world, that He gave His only begotten Son, that whoever believes in Him shall not perish, but have eternal life. For God did not send the Son into the world to judge the world, but that the world might be saved through Him. He who believes in Him is not judged; he who does not believe has been judged already, because he has not believed in the name of the only begotten Son of God. This is the judgment, that the Light has come into the world, and men loved darkness rather than the Light, for their deeds were evil. For everyone who does evil hates the Light, and does not come to the Light for fear that his deeds will be exposed. But he who practices the truth comes to the Light, so that his deeds may be manifested as having been wrought in God" (John 3:16–21; see Luke 19:10; John 1:4; 1:18; 3:1–15; Romans 5:8; 1 John 1:6, 7).

Setting: Sychar in Samaria, on the way to Galilee. Jesus interacts with a Samaritan woman at Jacob's well, while His disciples buy food.

Jesus answered and said to her, "Everyone who drinks of this water will thirst again; but whoever drinks of the water that I will give him shall never thirst; but the water that I will give him will become in him a well of water springing up to eternal life" (John 4:13, 14).

Setting: Capernaum. The day after Jesus walks on the Sea of Galilee to join His disciples in a boat, the people He miraculously fed with a lad's five loaves and two fish ask Him to always give them this bread out of heaven.

Jesus said to them, "I am the bread of life; he who comes to Me will not hunger, and he who believes in Me will never thirst. But I said to you that you have seen Me, and yet do not believe. All that the Father gives Me will come to Me, and the one who comes to Me I will certainly not cast out. For I have come down from heaven, not to do My own will, but the will of Him who sent Me. This is the will of Him who sent Me, that of all that He has given Me I lose nothing, but raise it up on the last day. For this is the will of My Father, that everyone who beholds the Son and believes in Him will have eternal life, and I Myself will raise him up on the last day" (John 6:35–40; see John 3:13, 16; 4:13, 14).

Setting: Capernaum of Galilee. After Jesus informs the people whom He miraculously fed with a lad's five loaves and two fish how they might receive the bread out of heaven, the Jewish religious leaders grumble because He claims that He came down out of heaven.

Therefore the Jews were grumbling about Him, because He said, "I am the bread that came down out of heaven." They were saying, "Is not this Jesus, the son of Joseph, whose father and mother we know? How does He now say, 'I have come down out of heaven'?" Jesus answered and said to them, "Do not grumble among yourselves. No one can come to Me unless the Father who sent Me draws him; and I will raise him up on the last day. It is written in the prophets, 'AND THEY SHALL ALL BE TAUGHT OF GOD.' Everyone who has heard and learned from the Father, comes to Me. Not that anyone has seen the Father, except the One who is from God; He has seen the Father. Truly, truly, I say to you, he who believes has eternal life. I am the bread of life. Your fathers ate the manna in the wilderness, and they died. This is the bread which comes down out of heaven, so that one may eat of it and not die. I am the living bread that came down out of heaven; if anyone eats of this bread, he will live forever; and the bread also which I will give for the life of the world is My flesh" (John 6:41–51, Jesus quotes from Isaiah 54:13; see John 1:18, 29; 3:36; 7:27).

Setting: The temple treasury in Jerusalem. After the scribes and Pharisees question His testimony about Himself, Jesus reveals to those Jews who believe in Him how He will make them free.

So Jesus was saying to those Jews who had believed Him, "If you continue in My word, *then* you are truly disciples of Mine; and you will know the truth, and the truth will make you free." They answered Him, "We are Abraham's descendants and have never yet been enslaved to anyone; how is it that You say, 'You will become free'?" Jesus answered them, "Truly, truly, I say to you, everyone who commits sin is the slave of sin. The slave does not remain in the house forever; the son does remain forever. So if the Son makes you free, you will be free indeed. I know that you are Abraham's descendants; yet you seek to kill Me, because My word has no place in you. I speak the things which I have seen with *My* Father; therefore you also do the things which you heard from *your* father" (John 8:31–38; see Romans 6:16).

Setting: Bethany near Jerusalem. Jesus travels with His disciples to Bethany in Judea to see Lazarus's sisters, Martha and Mary, after the death of His friend.

Jesus said to her, "Your brother will rise again." Martha said to Him, "I know that he will rise again in the resurrection on the last day." Jesus said to her, "I am the resurrection and the life; he who believes in Me will live even if he dies, and everyone who lives and believes in Me will never die. Do you believe this?" (John 11:23–26; see Daniel 12:2; John 1:4; 6:47–51).

Setting: Jerusalem. Just days before the Passover, with the chief priests and Pharisees plotting to seize Jesus, who is expressing anxiety about His upcoming death by crucifixion, some believe in Jesus, while others are rejecting His message.

And Jesus cried out and said, "He who believes in Me, does not believe in Me but in Him who sent Me. He who sees Me sees the One who sent Me. I have come *as* Light into the world, so that everyone who believes in Me will not remain in darkness. If anyone hears My sayings and does not keep them, I do not judge him; for I did not come to judge the world, but to save the world. He who rejects Me and does not receive My sayings, has one who judges him; the word I spoke is what will judge him at the last day. For I did not speak on My own initiative, but the Father Himself who sent Me has given Me a commandment *as to* what to say and what to speak. I know that His commandment is eternal life; therefore the things I speak, I speak just as the Father as told Me" (John 12:44–50; see Matthew 10:40; Luke 10:16; John 1:4; 3:17; 5:19; 6:68; 14:9).

Setting: Jerusalem. Before the Passover, after explaining He is the vine and His disciples are the branches, Jesus warns them of the persecution they will face after His departure to heaven.

"These things I have spoken to you so that you may be kept from stumbling. They will make you outcasts from the synagogue, but an hour is coming for everyone who kills you to think that he is offering service to God. These things they will do because they have not known the Father or Me. But these things I have spoken to you, so that when their hour comes, you may remember that I told you of them. These things I did not say to you at the beginning, because I was with you" (John 16:1–4; see John 8:19, 55; 9:22; 13:19; 15:18–27).

Setting: Jerusalem. After the previous and current high priest (Annas and Caiaphas) question Jesus, and Peter denies a second and third time being His disciple, Pilate (Roman governor of Judea) questions Jesus in an attempt to determine if He is a king.

Therefore Pilate said to Him, "So You are a king?" Jesus answered, "You say *correctly* that I am a king. For this I have been born, and for this I have come into the world, to testify to the truth. Everyone who is of the truth hears my voice" (John 18:37; cf. Matthew 27:11; Mark 15:2; Luke 23:3 see John 18:28–36).

EVERYTHING

Setting: Galilee. During the early part of His ministry, Jesus preaches the Sermon on the Mount to His disciples and the multitudes.

"Ask, and it will be given to you; seek, and you will find; knock, and it will be opened to you. For everyone who asks receives, and he who seeks finds, and to him who knocks it will be opened. Or what man is there among you who, when his son asks for a loaf, will give him a stone? Or if he asks for a fish, he will not give him a snake, will he? If you then, being evil, know how to give good gifts to your children, how much more will your Father who is in heaven give what is good to those who ask Him! In everything, therefore, treat people the same way you want them to treat you, for this is the Law and the Prophets" (Matthew 7:7–12; cf. Matthew 22:40; Luke 6:31; 11:9–13; see Psalm 84:11).

Setting: Galilee. Jesus explains the meaning of His instruction to the crowd about what defiles a man.

Peter said to Him, "Explain the parable to us." Jesus said, "Are you still lacking in understanding also? Do you not understand that everything that goes into the mouth passes into the stomach and is eliminated? But the things that proceed out of the mouth come from the heart, and those defile the man. For out of the heart come evil thoughts, murders, adulteries, fornications, thefts, false witness, slanders. These are the things which defile a man; but to eat with unwashed hands does not defile the man" (Matthew 15:15–20; cf. Mark 7:18–23; see Galatians 5:19–21).

Setting: Capernaum of Galilee. Jesus illustrates forgiveness after Peter asks Him if forgiving someone seven times who has sinned against him is adequate.

"For this reason the kingdom of heaven may be compared to a king who wished to settle accounts with his slaves. When he had begun to settle *them,* one who owed him ten thousand talents was brought to him. But since he did not have *the means* to repay, his lord commanded him to be sold, along with his wife and children and all that he had, and repayment to be made. So the slave fell *to the ground* and prostrated himself before him, saying, 'Have patience with me and I will repay you everything.' And the lord of that slave felt compassion and released him and forgave him the debt. But that slave went out and found one of his fellow slaves who owed him a hundred denarii; and he seized him and *began* to choke *him,* saying, 'Pay back what you owe.' So his fellow slave fell *to the ground* and *began* to plead with him, saying, 'Have patience with me and I will repay you.' But he was unwilling and went and threw him in prison until he should pay back what was owed. So when his fellow slaves saw what had happened, they were deeply grieved and came and reported to their lord all that had happened. Then summoning him, his lord said to him, 'You wicked slave, I forgave you all that debt because you pleaded with me. Should you not also have had mercy on your fellow slave, in the same way that I had mercy on you?' And his lord, moved with anger, handed him over to the torturers until he should repay all that was owed him. My heavenly Father will also do the same to you, if each of you does not forgive his brother from your heart" (Matthew 18:23–35; cf. Matthew 6:12, 14, 15; Luke 7:42; see Matthew 25:19–28).

Setting: The temple in Jerusalem. Jesus speaks another parable to the chief priests and elders after they question His authority.

Jesus spoke to them again in parables, saying, "The kingdom of heaven may be compared to a king who gave a wedding feast for his son. And he sent out his slaves to call those who had been invited to the wedding feast, and they were unwilling to come. Again he sent out other slaves saying, 'Tell those who have been invited, "Behold, I have prepared my dinner; my oxen and my fattened livestock are *all* butchered and everything is ready; come to the wedding feast." But they paid no attention and went their way, one to his own farm, another to his business, and the rest seized his slaves and mistreated them and killed them. But the king was enraged, and he sent his armies and destroyed those murderers and set their city on fire. Then he said to his slaves, 'The wedding is ready, but those who were invited were not worthy. 'Go therefore to the main highways, and as many as you find *there,* invite to the wedding feast.' Those slaves went out into the streets and gathered together all they found, both evil and good; and the wedding hall was filled with dinner guests. But when the king came in to look over the dinner guests, he saw a man there who was not dressed in wedding clothes, and he said to him, 'Friend, how did you come in here without wedding clothes?' And the man was speechless. Then the king said to the servants, 'Bind him hand and foot, and throw him into the outer darkness; in that place there will be weeping and gnashing of teeth.' For many are called, but few *are* chosen" (Matthew 22:1–14; cf. Matthew 8:11, 12).

Setting: The temple in Jerusalem. After the Jewish religious leaders test Him with questions, Jesus pronounces the fourth of eight woes on them in front of the crowds and His disciples.

"Woe to you, blind guides, who say, "Whoever swears by the temple, *that* is nothing; but whoever swears by the gold of the temple is obligated.' You fools and blind men! Which is more important, the gold or the temple that sanctified the gold? And, 'Whoever swears by the altar, *that* is nothing, but whoever swears by the offering on it, he is obligated.' You blind men, which is more important, the offering, or the altar that sanctifies the offering? Therefore, whoever swears by the altar, swears *both* by the altar and by everything on it. And whoever swears by the temple, swears *both* by the temple and by Him who dwells within it. And whoever swears by heaven, swears *both* by the throne of God and by Him who sits upon it" (Matthew 23:16–22; see Exodus 29:37; 1 Kings 8:13; Isaiah 66:1; Matthew 15:14).

Setting: By the Sea of Galilee. After Jesus conveys the Parable of the Sower to a crowd from a boat, His disciples question Him about it.

And He was saying to them, "To you has been given the mystery of the kingdom of God, but those who are outside get everything in parables, so that WHILE SEEING, THEY MAY SEE AND NOT PERCEIVE, AND WHILE HEARING, THEY MAY HEAR AND NOT UNDERSTAND, OTHERWISE THEY MIGHT RETURN AND BE FORGIVEN" (Mark 4:11, 12, Jesus quotes from Isaiah 6:9, 10; cf. Matthew 13:10–17).

Setting: The Mount of Olives, east of the temple in Jerusalem. During His discourse, after prophesying the temple's destruction, Jesus responds to questions from Peter, James, John, and Andrew about future events.

"But when you see the ABOMINATION OF DESOLATION standing where it should not be (let the reader understand), then those who are in Judea must flee to the mountains. The one who is on the housetop must not go down, or go in to get anything out of his house; and the one who is in the field must not turn back to get his coat. But woe to those who are pregnant and to those who are nursing babies in those days! But pray that it may not happen in winter. For those days will be a *time of* tribulation such as has not occurred since the beginning of the creation which God created until now, and never will. Unless the Lord had shortened *those* days, no life would have been saved; but for the sake of the elect, whom He chose, He shortened the days. And then if anyone says to you, 'Behold, here is the Christ'; or, 'Behold, *He is* there'; do not believe *him*; for false Christs and false prophets will arise, and will show signs and wonders, in order to lead astray, if possible, the elect. But take heed; behold, I have told you everything in advance" (Mark 13:14–23; cf. Matthew 24:15–28; Luke 21:20–24; see Daniel 9:27; 12:1; Luke 17:31).

Setting: On the way from Galilee to Jerusalem. After speaking a parable to the invited guests and the host at a banquet, Jesus responds to a guest's proclamation about the blessings of eating bread in the kingdom of God.

But He said to him, "A man was giving a big dinner, and he invited many; and at the dinner hour he sent his slave to say to those who had been invited, 'Come; for everything is ready now.' But they all alike began to make excuses. The first one said to him, 'I have bought a piece of land and I need to go out and look at it; please consider me excused.' Another one said, 'I have bought five yoke of oxen, and I am going to try them out; please consider me excused.' Another one said, I have married a wife, and for that reason I cannot come.' And the slave came *back* and reported this to his master. Then the head of the household became angry and said to his slave, 'Go out at once into the streets and lanes of the city and bring in here the poor and crippled and blind and lame.' And the slave said, 'Master, what you commanded has been done, and still there is room.' And the master said to the slave, 'Go out into the highways and along the hedges, and compel *them* to come in, so that my house may be filled. For I tell you, none of those men who were invited shall taste of my dinner'" (Luke 14:16–24; see Deuteronomy 24:5; Matthew 22:2–14).

Setting: On the way from Galilee to Jerusalem. Jesus conveys the illustration of the prodigal son because the Pharisees and scribes complain He associates with tax collectors and sinners.

And He said, "A man had two sons. The younger of them said to his father, 'Father, give me the share of the estate that falls to me.' So he divided his wealth between them. And not many days later, the younger son gathered everything together and went on a journey into a distant country, and there he squandered his estate with loose living. Now when he had spent everything, a severe famine occurred in that country, and he began to be impoverished. So he went and hired himself out to one of the citizens of that country, and he sent him into his fields to feed swine. And he would have gladly filled his stomach with the pods that the swine were eating, and no one was giving anything to him. But when he came to his senses, he said, 'How many of my father's hired men have more than enough bread, but I am dying here with hunger! I will get up and go to my father, and will say to him, "Father, I have sinned against heaven, and in your sight; I am no longer worthy to be called your son; make me as one of your hired men."' So he got up and came to his father. But while he was still a long way off, his father saw him and felt compassion for him, and ran and embraced him and kissed him. And the son said to him, "Father, I have sinned against heaven and in your sight; I am no longer worthy to be called your son.' But the father said to his slaves, 'Quickly bring out the best robe and put it on him, and put a ring on his hand and sandals on his feet; and bring the fattened calf, kill it, and let us eat and celebrate; for this son of mine was dead and has come to life again; he was lost and has been found.' And they began to celebrate. Now his older son was in the field, when he came and approached the house, he heard music and dancing. And he summoned one of the servants and began inquiring what these things could be. And he said to him, 'Your brother has come, and your father has killed the fattened calf because he has received him back safe and sound.' But he became angry and was not willing to go in; and his father came out and began pleading with him. But he answered and said to his father, 'Look! For so many years I have been serving you and I have never neglected a command of yours; and yet you have never given me a young goat, so that I might celebrate with my friends; but when this son of yours came, who has devoured your wealth with prostitutes, you killed the fattened calf for him.' And he said to him, 'Son, you have always been with me, and all that is mine is yours. But we had to celebrate and rejoice, for this brother of yours was dead and has begun to live, and was lost and has been found'" (Luke 15:11–32; see Proverbs 29:2).

Setting: Jerusalem. Before the Passover, after giving His disciples assurance that in the midst of tribulation they will have His peace, Jesus prays His high-priestly prayer.

Jesus spoke these things; and lifting up His eyes to heaven, He said, "Father, the hour has come; glorify Your Son, that the Son may glorify You, even as You gave Him authority over all flesh, that to all whom You have given Him, He may give eternal life. This is eternal life, that they may know You, the only true God, and Jesus Christ whom You have sent. I glorified You on the earth, having accomplished the work which you have given Me to do. Now, Father, glorify Me together with Yourself, with the glory which I had with You before the world was. I have manifested Your name to the men whom You gave Me out of the world; they were Yours and You gave them to Me, and they have kept Your word. Now they have come to know that everything You have given Me is from You; for the words which You gave Me I have given to them; and they received *them* and truly understood that I came forth from You, and they believed You sent Me. I ask on their behalf; I do not ask on behalf of the world, but of those whom You have given Me; for they are Yours; and all things that are Mine are Yours, and Yours are Mine; and I have been glorified in them. I am no longer in the world; and yet they themselves are in the world, and I come to You. Holy Father, keep them in Your name, *the name* which You have given Me, that they may be even as We *are.* While I was with them, I was keeping them in Your name which You have given Me; and I guarded them and not one of them perished but the son of perdition, so that the Scripture would be fulfilled" (John 17:1–12; see Luke 22:32; John 1:1; 3:35; 4:34; 5:44; 6:37–39, 70; 8:42; 11:41; 12:49; 13:18, 31; 16:15; 17:20; Philippians 2:9).

EVERYWHERE

Setting: On the way from Galilee to Jerusalem. The Lord Jesus responds to several men seeking to follow Him.

And He said to another, "Follow Me." But he said, "Lord, permit me first to go and bury my father," But He said to him, "Allow the dead to bury their own dead; but as for you, go and proclaim everywhere the kingdom of God" (Luke 9:59, 60; cf. Matthew 8:19–22).

EVIL (Specifics such as DEEDS, EVIL; EVIL, DELIVERANCE FROM; EVIL, SPEAKING; EVIL ONE; and MAN, EVIL etc., are listed as separate entries)

Setting: Galilee. Early in His ministry, Jesus presents the Beatitudes (part of the Sermon on the Mount) to His disciples and the gathered crowds from Galilee, Decapolis, Jerusalem, Judea, and beyond the Jordan.

"Blessed are you when *people* insult you and persecute you, and falsely say all kinds of evil against you because of Me. Rejoice and be glad, for your reward in heaven is great; for in the same way they persecuted the prophets who were before you" (Matthew 5:11, 12; cf. 2 Chronicles 36:16; Luke 6:22, 23; 1 Peter 4:14; see Matthew 5:1; 13:35).

Setting: Galilee. During the early part of His ministry, Jesus preaches the Sermon on the Mount to His disciples and the multitudes.

"Again, you have heard that the ancients were told, 'YOU SHALL NOT MAKE FALSE VOWS, BUT SHALL FULFILL YOUR VOWS TO THE LORD.' But I say to you, make no oath at all, either by heaven, for it is the throne of God, or by the earth, for it is the footstool of His feet, or by Jerusalem, for it is THE CITY OF THE GREAT KING. Nor shall you make an oath by your head, for you cannot make one hair white or black. But let your statement be 'Yes, yes' *or* 'No, no'; anything beyond these is of evil" (Matthew 5:33–37, Jesus quotes from Leviticus 19:12, Psalm 48:2; Isaiah 66:1; cf. James 5:12).

Setting: Galilee. During the early part of His ministry, Jesus preaches the Sermon on the Mount to His disciples and the multitudes.

"You have heard that it was said, 'YOU SHALL LOVE YOUR NEIGHBOR and hate your enemy.' But I say to you, love your enemies and pray for those who persecute you, so that you may be sons of your Father who is in heaven; for He causes His sun to rise on *the* evil and *the* good, and sends rain on *the* righteous and *the* unrighteous. For if you love those who love you, what reward do you have? Do not even the tax collectors do the same? If you greet only your brothers, what more are you doing *than others?* Do not even the Gentiles do the same? Therefore, you are to be perfect, as your heavenly Father is perfect" (Matthew 5:43–48, Jesus quotes from Leviticus 19:18; cf. Leviticus 19:2; Luke 6:27–36).

Setting: Galilee. During the early part of His ministry, Jesus preaches the Sermon on the Mount to His disciples and the multitudes.

"Ask, and it will be given to you; seek, and you will find; knock, and it will be opened to you. For everyone who asks receives, and he who seeks finds, and to him who knocks it will be opened. Or what man is there among you who, when his son asks for a loaf, will give him a stone? Or if he asks for a fish, he will not give him a snake, will he? If you then, being evil, know how to give good gifts to your children, how much more will your Father who is in heaven give what is good to those who ask Him! In everything, therefore, treat people the same way you want them to treat you, for this is the Law and the Prophets" (Matthew 7:7–12; cf. Matthew 22:40; Luke 6:31; 11:9–13; see Psalm 84:11).

Setting: Capernaum near the Sea of Galilee. After Jesus heals and forgives a paralytic of his sins in front of crowds, some scribes accuse the Lord of blasphemy.

And they brought to Him a paralytic lying on a bed. Seeing their faith, Jesus said to the paralytic, "Take courage, son; your sins are forgiven." And some scribes said to themselves. "This *fellow* blasphemes." And Jesus knowing their thoughts said, "Why are you thinking evil in your hearts? Which is easier to say, 'Your sins are forgiven,' or to say, 'Get up, and walk'? But so that you may know that the Son of Man has authority on earth to forgive sins"—then He said to the paralytic, "Get up, pick up your bed and go home" (Matthew 9:2–6; cf. Mark 2:3–12; Luke 5:17–26).

Setting: Galilee. After Jesus heals a blind, mute, demon-possessed man, the Pharisees accuse Him in front of crowds of being a worker of Satan.

"Either make the tree good and its fruit good, or make the tree bad and its fruit bad; for the tree is known by its fruit. You brood of vipers, how can you, being evil, speak what is good? For the mouth speaks out of that which fills the heart. The good man brings out of *his* good treasure what is good; and the evil man brings out of *his* evil treasure what is evil. But I tell you that every careless word that people speak, they shall give an accounting for it in the day of judgment. For by your words you will be justified, and by your words you will be condemned" (Matthew 12:33–37; cf. Matthew 3:7; 7:16–18).

Setting: The temple in Jerusalem. Jesus speaks another parable to the chief priests and elders after they question His authority.

Jesus spoke to them again in parables, saying, "The kingdom of heaven may be compared to a king who gave a wedding feast for his son. And he sent out his slaves to call those who had been invited to the wedding feast, and they were unwilling to come. Again he sent out other slaves saying, 'Tell those who have been invited, "Behold, I have prepared my dinner; my oxen and my fattened livestock are *all* butchered and everything is ready; come to the wedding feast." But they paid no attention and went their way, one to his own farm, another to his business, and the rest seized his slaves and mistreated them and killed them. But the king was enraged, and he sent his armies and destroyed those murderers and set their city on fire. Then he said to his slaves, 'The wedding is ready, but those who were invited were not worthy. 'Go therefore to the main highways, and as many as you find *there,* invite to the wedding feast.' Those slaves went out into the streets and gathered together all they found, both evil and good; and the wedding hall was filled with dinner guests. But when the king came in to look over the dinner guests, he saw a man there who was not dressed in wedding clothes, and he said to him, 'Friend, how did you come in here without wedding clothes?' And the man was speechless. Then the king said to the servants, 'Bind him hand and foot, and throw him into the outer darkness; in that place there will be weeping and gnashing of teeth.' For many are called, but few *are* chosen" (Matthew 22:1–14; cf. Matthew 8:11, 12).

Setting: Capernaum of Galilee. As Jesus teaches His disciples in private, they ask Him about greatness.

But Jesus said, "Do not hinder him, for there is no one who will perform a miracle in My name, and be able soon afterward to speak evil of Me. For he who is not against us is for us. For whoever gives you a cup of water to drink because of your name as *followers* of Christ, truly I say to you, he will not lose his reward. Whoever causes one of these little ones who believe to stumble, it would be better for him if, with a heavy millstone hung around his neck, he had been cast into the sea. If your hand causes you to stumble, cut it off; it is better for you to enter life crippled, than, having your two hands, to go into hell, into the unquenchable fire, [where THEIR WORM DOES NOT DIE, AND THE FIRE IS NOT QUENCHED.] If your foot causes you to stumble, cut it off; it is better for you to enter life lame, than, having your two feet, to be cast into hell, [where THEIR WORM DOES NOT DIE, AND THE FIRE IS NOT QUENCHED.] If your eye causes you to stumble, throw it out; it is better for you to enter the kingdom of God with one eye, than, having two eyes, to be cast into hell, where THEIR WORM DOES NOT DIE, AND THE FIRE IS NOT QUENCHED. For everyone will be salted with fire. Salt is good; but if the salt becomes unsalty, with what will you make it salty *again?* Have salt in yourselves, and be at peace with one another" (Mark 9:39–50; Jesus quotes from Isaiah 66:24; cf. Matthew 18:6–9; Luke 9:49–50; see Matthew 5:13, 29, 30; 10:42; 12:30; 18:5, 6).

Setting: Galilee. After selecting His twelve disciples, Jesus teaches the Beatitudes (part of the Sermon on the Mount) to His disciples and a great throng of people from Judea, Jerusalem, and the central coastal region of Tyre and Sidon.

"Blessed are you when men hate you, and ostracize you, and insult you, and scorn your name as evil, for the sake of the Son of Man. Be glad in that day and leap for joy, for behold, your reward is great in heaven. For in the same way their fathers used to treat the prophets" (Luke 6:22, 23; cf. Matthew 5:10–12; see 2 Chronicles 36:16).

Setting: Galilee. After selecting His twelve disciples, Jesus teaches the Sermon on the Mount to His disciples and a great throng from Judea, Jerusalem, and the central coastal region of Tyre and Sidon.

And He also spoke a parable to them: "A blind man cannot guide a blind man, can he? Will they not both fall into a pit? A pupil is not above his teacher; but everyone, after he has been fully trained, will be like his teacher. Why do you look at the speck that is in your brother's eye, but do not notice the log that is in your own eye? Or how can you say to your brother, 'Brother, let me take out the speck that is in your eye,' when you yourself do not see the log that is in your own eye? You hypocrite, first take the log out of your own eye, and then you will see clearly to take out the speck that is in your brother's eye. For there is no good tree which produces bad fruit, nor, on the other hand, a bad tree which produces good fruit. For each tree is known by its own fruit. For men do not gather figs from thorns, nor do they pick grapes from a briar bush. The good man out of the good treasure of his heart brings forth what is good; and the evil man out of the evil treasure brings forth what is evil; for his mouth speaks from that which fills his heart" (Luke 6:39–45; cf. Matthew 7:3–6. 16, 18, 20; 12:35; see Matthew 10:24; 15:14; Luke 6:12–19).

Setting: On the way from Galilee to Jerusalem. After revealing to His disciples how to pray, Jesus illustrates God's benevolence in answering prayer and giving the Holy Spirit.

"Now suppose one of you fathers is asked by his son for a fish; he will not give him a snake instead of a fish, will he? Or if he is asked for an egg, he will not give him a scorpion, will he? If you then, being evil, know how to give good gifts to your children, how much more will your heavenly Father give the Holy Spirit to those who ask Him?" (Luke 11:11–13; cf. Matthew 7:9–11).

Setting: On the way from Galilee to Jerusalem. After some in the crowd test Him, demanding a sign from heaven, Jesus illustrates His power over Satan.

"When the unclean spirit goes out of a man, it passes through waterless places seeking rest, and not finding any, it says, 'I will return to my house from which I came.' And when it comes, it finds it swept clean and put in order. Then it goes and takes along seven other spirits more evil than itself, and they go in and live there; and the last state of that man becomes worse than the first" (Luke 11:24–26; cf. Matthew 12:43–45; see Luke 11:14–16).

Setting: Jerusalem. At the time of the Passover of the Jews, after the Lord cleanses the temple, a Pharisee, Nicodemus, asks Him by night the meaning of "born again."

"For God so loved the world, that He gave His only begotten Son, that whoever believes in Him shall not perish, but have eternal life. For God did not send the Son into the world to judge the world, but that the world might be saved through Him. He who believes in Him is not judged; he who does not believe has been judged already, because he has not believed in the name of the only begotten Son of God. This is the judgment, that the Light has come into the world, and men loved darkness rather than the Light, for their deeds were evil. For everyone who does evil hates the Light, and does not come to the Light for fear that his deeds will be exposed. But he who practices the truth comes to the Light, so that his deeds may be manifested as having been wrought in God" (John 3:16–21; see Luke 19:10; John 1:4; 1:18; 3:1–15; Romans 5:8; 1 John 1:6, 7).

Setting: Capernaum of Galilee. Jesus' blood brothers, who do not yet believe in Him, encourage Him to attend the upcoming Feast of Booths in Jerusalem in order to demonstrate His works to His disciples and the world.

So Jesus said to them, "My time is not yet here, but your time is always opportune. The world cannot hate you, but it hates Me because I testify of it, that its deeds are evil. Go up to the feast yourselves; I do not go up to this feast because My time has not yet fully come" (John 7:6–8; see John 3:19, 20; 15:18–20).

EVIL, DELIVERANCE FROM

[DELIVERANCE FROM EVIL from deliver us from evil]

Setting: Galilee. During the early part of His ministry, Jesus gives a model prayer to His disciples and the multitudes while conveying The Sermon on the Mount.

"Pray, then, in this way: 'Our Father who is in heaven, hallowed be Your name. Your kingdom come. Your will be done, on earth as it is in heaven. Give us this day our daily bread. And forgive us our debts, as we also have forgiven our debtors. And do not lead us into temptation, but deliver us from evil. [For Yours is the kingdom and the power and the glory forever. Amen]'" (Matthew 6:9–13; cf. Luke 11:2–4; see John 17:15).

EVIL, SPEAKING (Also see EVIL; and HONORING FATHER AND MOTHER)

[SPEAKING EVIL from SPEAKS EVIL]

Setting: Galilee. Pharisees and scribes from Jerusalem question Jesus about His disciples' lack of obedience to tradition and the commandments.

And He answered and said to them, "Why do you yourselves transgress the commandment of God for the sake of tradition? For God said, 'HONOR YOUR FATHER AND MOTHER,' and, 'HE WHO SPEAKS EVIL OF FATHER OR MOTHER IS TO BE PUT TO DEATH.' But you say, 'Whoever says to *his* father or mother, "Whatever I have that would help you has been given *to God*," he is not to honor his father or mother.' And *by this* you invalidated the word of God for the sake of your tradition. You hypocrites, rightly did Isaiah prophesy of you: 'THIS PEOPLE HONORS ME WITH THEIR LIPS, BUT THEIR HEART IS FAR AWAY FROM ME. BUT IN VAIN DO THEY WORSHIP ME, TEACHING AS DOCTRINES THE PRECEPTS OF MEN'" (Matthew 15:3–9, Jesus quotes from Exodus 20:12, 21:17, Leviticus 20:9; Isaiah 29:13; cf. Mark 7:5–7; see Colossians 2:22).

[SPEAKING EVIL from SPEAKS EVIL]

Setting: Galilee. The Pharisees and some of the scribes from Jerusalem question why Jesus' disciples do not follow the tradition of ceremonial hand cleansing before eating bread.

And He said to them, "Rightly did Isaiah prophesy of you hypocrites, as it is written: 'THIS PEOPLE HONORS ME WITH THEIR LIPS, BUT THEIR HEART IS FAR AWAY FROM ME. BUT IN VAIN DO THEY WORSHIP ME, TEACHING AS DOCTRINES THE PRECEPTS OF MEN.' Neglecting the commandment of God, you hold to the tradition of men." He was also saying to them, "You are experts at setting aside the commandment of God in order to keep tradition. For Moses said, 'HONOR YOUR FATHER AND YOUR MOTHER'; and, 'HE WHO SPEAKS EVIL OF FATHER OR MOTHER, IS TO BE PUT TO DEATH'; but you say, 'If a man says to *his* father or *his* mother, whatever I have that would help you is Corban (that is to say, given *to God*),' you no longer permit him to do anything for *his* father or *his* mother; *thus* invalidating the word of God by your tradition which you have handed down; and you do many things such as that" (Mark 7:6–13, Jesus quotes from Exodus 20:12; 21:17; Isaiah 29:13; cf. Matthew 15:1–6).

EVIL DEEDS (Listed under DEEDS, EVIL)

EVIL MAN (Listed under MAN, EVIL)

EVIL MEN (Listed under MEN, EVIL)

EVIL ONE (Also see BEELZEBUL; DEVIL; EVIL ONE, SONS OF THE; and SATAN)

Setting: By the Sea of Galilee. With the religious leaders rejecting His message, Jesus begins to teach in parables and gives the meaning of the Parable of the Sower to His disciples.

"Hear then the parable of the sower. When anyone hears the word of the kingdom and does not understand it, the evil *one* comes and snatches away what has been sown in his heart. This is the one on whom seed was sown beside the road. The one on whom seed was sown on the rocky places, this is the man who hears the word and immediately receives it with joy; yet he has no *firm* root in himself, but is *only* temporary, and when affliction or persecution arises because of the word, immediately he falls away. And the one on whom seed was sown among the thorns, this is the man who hears the word, and the worry of the world and the deceitfulness of wealth choke the word, and it becomes unfruitful. And the one on whom seed was sown on the good soil, this is the man who hears the word and understands it; who indeed bears fruit and brings forth, some a hundredfold, some sixty, and some thirty" (Matthew 13:18–23; cf. Mark 4:13–20; Luke 8:11–15; see Matthew 13:8).

Setting: Jerusalem. Before the Passover, after giving His disciples hope that in the midst of tribulation they will have His peace, Jesus continues praying His high-priestly prayer.

"But now I come to You; and these things I speak in the world so that they may have My joy made full in themselves. I have given them Your word; and the world has hated them, because they are not of the world, even as I am not of the world. I do not ask You to take them out of the world, but to keep them from the evil *one.* They are not of the world, even as I am not of the world. Sanctify them in the truth; Your word is truth. As You sent Me into the world, I also have sent them into the world. For their sakes I sanctify Myself, that they themselves also may be sanctified in truth. I do not ask on behalf of these alone, but for those also who believe in Me through their word; that they may all be one; even as You, Father, *are* in Me and I in You, that they also maybe in Us, so that the world may believe that You sent Me" (John 17:13–21; see Matthew 10:5, 38; John 7:33; 15:3, 11, 19; 17:1–12).

EVIL ONE, SONS OF THE

Setting: A house near the Sea of Galilee. Jesus explains the meaning of the Parable of the Wheat and the Tares to His disciples.

And He said, "The one who sows the good seed is the Son of Man, and the field is the world; and as *for* the good seed, these are the sons of the kingdom; and the tares are the sons of the evil *one;* and the enemy who sowed them is the devil, and the harvest is the end of the age; and the reapers are angels. So just as the tares are gathered up and burned with fire, so shall it be at the end of the age. The Son of Man will send forth His angels, and they will gather out of His kingdom all stumbling blocks, and those who commit lawlessness, and will throw them into the furnace of fire; in that place there will be weeping and gnashing of teeth. Then THE RIGHTEOUS WILL SHINE FORTH AS THE SUN in the kingdom of their Father. He who has ears, let him hear" (Matthew 13:37–43, Jesus quotes from Daniel 12:3; cf. Matthew 8:12; 13:50).

EVIL PERSON (Listed under PERSON, EVIL)

EVIL SLAVE (Listed under SLAVE, EVIL)

EVIL SPIRITS (Listed under SPIRITS, EVIL; also see DEMON; and DEMONS)

EVIL THINGS (Listed under THINGS, EVIL)

EVIL THOUGHTS (Listed under THOUGHTS, EVIL)

EVIL TREASURE (Listed under TREASURE, EVIL)

EVILDOERS (Also see DEEDS, EVIL; WICKED; and WICKEDNESS)

Setting: On the way from Galilee to Jerusalem. While teaching in the cities and villages, Jesus responds to a question about who is saved.

And someone said to Him, "Lord, are here just a few who are being saved?" And He said to them, "Strive to enter through the narrow door; for many, I tell you, will seek to enter and will not be able. Once the head of the house gets up and shuts the door, and you begin to stand outside and knock on the door, saying, 'Lord, open up to us!' then He will answer and say to you, 'I do not know where you are from.' Then you will begin to say, 'We ate and drank in Your presence, and You taught in our streets'; and He will say, 'I tell you, I do not know where you are from; DEPART FROM ME, ALL YOU EVILDOERS.' In that place there will be weeping and gnashing of teeth when you see Abraham and Isaac and Jacob and all the prophets in the kingdom of God, but you yourselves being thrown out. And they will come from east and west and from north and south, and will recline at the table in the kingdom of God. And behold, some are last who will be first and some are first who will be last" (Luke 13:23–30, Jesus quotes from Psalm 6:8; cf. Matthew 7:13, 23; 8:11, 12; see Matthew 19:30; Luke 3:8).

[EVILDOERS from everyone who does evil]
Setting: Jerusalem. At the time of the Passover of the Jews, after the Lord cleanses the temple, a Pharisee, Nicodemus, asks Him by night the meaning of "born again."

"For God so loved the world, that He gave His only begotten Son, that whoever believes in Him shall not perish, but have eternal life. For God did not send the Son into the world to judge the world, but that the world might be saved through Him. He who believes in Him is not judged; he who does not believe has been judged already, because he has not believed in the name of the only begotten Son of God. This is the judgment, that the Light has come into the world, and men loved darkness rather than the Light, for their deeds were evil. For everyone who does evil hates the Light, and does not come to the Light for fear that his deeds will be exposed. But he who practices the truth comes to the Light, so that his deeds may be manifested as having been wrought in God" (John 3:16–21; see Luke 19:10; John 1:4; 1:18; 3:1–15; Romans 5:8; 1 John 1:6, 7).

EXALTATION (Also see HUMILITY)

[EXALTATION from exalted]
Setting: Galilee. After performing miracles throughout the region, Jesus pronounces woes against those cities who did not repent.

"Woe to you, Chorazin! Woe to you, Bethsaida! For if the miracles had occurred in Tyre and Sidon which occurred in you, they would have repented long ago in sackcloth and ashes. Nevertheless I say to you, it will be more tolerable for Tyre and Sidon in *the* day of judgment than for you. And you, Capernaum, will not be exalted to heaven, will you? You will descend to Hades; for if the miracles had occurred in Sodom which occurred in you, it would have remained to this day. Nevertheless, I say to you that it will be more tolerable for the land of Sodom in *the* day of judgment, than for you" (Matthew 11:21–24; cf. Matthew 10:15; Luke 10:13–15).

[EXALTATION from exalts and exalted]
Setting: The temple in Jerusalem. Jesus exposes the truth about Pharisaism to the crowds and His disciples after the Jewish religious leaders test Him with questions.

Then Jesus spoke to the crowds and to His disciples, saying: "The scribes and the Pharisees have seated themselves in the chair of Moses; therefore all that they tell you, do and observe, but do not do according to their deeds; for they say *things* and do not do *them.* They tie up heavy burdens and lay them on men's shoulders, but they themselves are unwilling to move them with *so much as* a finger. But they do all their deeds to be noticed by men; for they broaden their phylacteries and lengthen their tassels *of their garments.* They love the place of honor at banquets and the chief seats in the synagogues, and respectful greetings in the market places, and being called Rabbi by men. But do not be called Rabbi; for One is your Teacher, and you are all brothers. Do not call *anyone* on earth your father; for One is your Father, He who is in heaven. Do not be called leaders; for One is your Leader, *that is,* Christ. But the greatest among you shall be your servant. Whoever exalts himself shall be humbled; and whoever humbles himself shall be exalted" (Matthew 23:1–12; cf. Matthew 20:26; Mark 12:38–40; Luke 20:46, 47; see Exodus 13:9; Deuteronomy 33:3; Matthew 6:1, 5, 6, 9, 16; Mark 14:11; Luke 11:43; 14:11).

[EXALTATION from exalted]
Setting: On the way from Galilee to Jerusalem. The Lord pronounces woes on cities who reject the gospel as He appoints seventy followers and sends them out in pairs to every place He Himself will soon visit.

"Woe to you, Chorazin! Woe to you, Bethsaida! For if the miracles had been performed in Tyre and Sidon which occurred in you, they would have repented long ago, sitting in sackcloth and ashes. But it will be more tolerable for Tyre and Sidon in the judgment than for you. And you, Capernaum, will not be exalted to heaven, will you? You will be brought down to Hades! The one who listens to you listens to Me, and the one who rejects you rejects Me; and he who rejects Me rejects the One who sent Me" (Luke 10:13–16; cf. Matthew 11:21–23; see Matthew 10:40).

[EXALTATION from exalts; exalted]
Setting: On the way from Galilee to Jerusalem. Jesus speaks a parable to the guests of a Pharisee leader on the Sabbath as He observes the guests selecting places of honor at the table.

And He *began* speaking a parable to the invited guests when He noticed how they had been picking out the places of honor *at the table,* saying to them, "When you are invited by someone to a wedding feast, do not take the place of honor, for someone more distinguished than you may have been invited by him, and he who invited you both will come and say to you, 'Give *your* place to this man, and then in disgrace you proceed to occupy the last place. But when you are invited, go and recline at the last place, so that when the one who has invited you comes, he may say to you, 'Friend, move up higher'; then you will have honor in the sight of all who are at the table with you. For everyone who exalts himself will be humbled, and he who humbles himself will be exalted" (Luke 14:7–11; see 2 Samuel 22:28; Proverbs 25:6, 7; Matthew 23:6).

[EXALTATION from exalts and exalted]
Setting: On the way from Galilee to Jerusalem. After instructing His disciples about persistence in prayer, Jesus conveys a parable about self-righteousness.

And He also told this parable to some people who trusted in themselves that they were righteous, and viewed others with contempt: "Two men went up into the temple to pray, one a Pharisee and the other a tax collector. The Pharisee stood and was praying this to himself: 'God, I thank You that I am not like other people: swindlers, unjust, adulterers, or even like this tax collector. I fast twice a week; I pay tithes of all that I get.' But the tax collector, standing some distance away, was even unwilling to lift up his eyes to heaven, but was beating his breast, saying, 'God, be merciful to me, the sinner!' I tell you, this man went to his house justified rather than the other; for everyone who exalts himself will be humbled, but he who humbles himself will be exalted" (Luke 18:9–14; see Ezra 9:6; Matthew 6:5, 23:12; Luke 11:42, 16:15; Romans 14:3, 10).

EXAMPLE
Setting: An upper room in Jerusalem. Before the Passover meal, with His death on the cross nearing, Jesus explains the reason for His vivid example of servanthood in washing His disciples' feet.

So when He had washed their feet, and taken His garments and reclined *at the table* again, He said to them, "Do you know what I have done to you? You call Me Teacher and Lord; and you are right, for *so* I am. If I then, the Lord and the Teacher, washed your feet, you also ought to wash one another's feet. For I gave you an example that you also should do as I did to you. Truly, truly I say to you, a slave is not greater than his master, nor *is* one who is sent greater than the one who sent him. If you know these things, you are blessed if you do them. I do not speak of all of you. I know the ones I have chosen; but *it is* that the Scripture may be fulfilled, 'HE WHO EATS MY BREAD HAS LIFTED UP HIS HEEL AGAINST ME.' From now on I am telling you before *it* comes to pass, so that when it does occur, you may believe that I am *He*. Truly, truly, I say to you, he who receives whomever I send receives Me; and he who receives Me receives Him who sent Me" (John 13:12–20; Jesus quotes from Psalm 41:9; see Matthew 7:24; 10:24, 40; John 8:24; 14:29; 1 Peter 5:3).

EXCLUSIVITY, JESUS' (See JESUS' EXCLUSIVITY)

EXCUSE (Also see EXCUSES)
Setting: Jerusalem. Before the Passover, with His departure in mind, after explaining He is the vine and His disciples are the branches, Jesus prepares them for persecution from the world.

"If the world hates you, you know that it has hated Me before *it hated* you. If you were of the world, the world would love its own; but because you are not of the world, but I chose you out of the world, because of this the world hates you. Remember the word that I said to you, 'A slave is not greater than his master.' If they persecuted Me, they will also persecute you; if they kept My word, they will keep yours also. But all these things they will do to you for My name's sake, because they do not know the One who sent Me. If I had not come and spoken to them, they would not have sin, but now they have no excuse for their sin" (John 15:18–22; see Matthew 10:22; John 7:7; 8:19, 55; 9:41; 1 Corinthians 4:12).

EXCUSES (Also see EXCUSE)

Setting: On the way from Galilee to Jerusalem. After He speaks a parable to the invited guests and the host at a banquet, Jesus responds to a guest's proclamation about the blessings of eating bread in the kingdom of God.

But He said to him, "A man was giving a big dinner, and he invited many; and at the dinner hour he sent his slave to say to those who had been invited, 'Come; for everything is ready now.' But they all alike began to make excuses. The first one said to him, 'I have bought a piece of land and I need to go out and look at it; please consider me excused.' Another one said, 'I have bought five yoke of oxen, and I am going to try them out; please consider me excused.' Another one said, I have married a wife, and for that reason I cannot come.' And the slave came back and reported this to his master. Then the head of the household became angry and said to his slave, 'Go out at once into the streets and lanes of the city and bring in here the poor and crippled and blind and lame.' And the slave said, 'Master, what you commanded has been done, and still there is room.' And the master said to the slave, 'Go out into the highways and along the hedges, and compel them to come in, so that my house may be filled. For I tell you, none of those men who were invited shall taste of my dinner'" (Luke 14:16–24; see Deuteronomy 24:5; Matthew 22:2–14).

EXECUTED (See DEATH, PUT TO)

EXEMPTION

[EXEMPTION from exempt]

Setting: Capernaum of Galilee. Jesus pays the two-drachma temple tax for Peter and Himself in a miraculous manner.

He said, "Yes." And when he came into the house, Jesus spoke to him first, saying, "What do you think, Simon? From whom do the kings of the earth collect customs or poll-tax, from their sons or from strangers?" When Peter said, "From strangers," Jesus said to him, "Then the sons are exempt. However, so that we do not offend them, go to the sea and throw in a hook, and take the first fish that comes up; and when you open its mouth, you will find a shekel. Take that and give it to them for you and Me" (Matthew 17:25–27; see Exodus 30:11–16; Matthew 22:17–19; Romans 13:7).

EXORCISM (See DEMONS, CASTING OUT)

EXPECTATION (Also see EXPECTATIONS)

[EXPECTATION from expect]

Setting: The Mount of Olives, just east of Jerusalem. During His discourse, after answering His disciples' questions as to when the temple will be destroyed and Jerusalem overrun, along with the signs of His coming and the end of the age, Jesus reemphasizes to His disciples they should be on the alert for His return.

"Therefore be on the alert, for you do not know which day your Lord is coming. But be sure of this, that if the head of the house had known at what time of the night the thief was coming, he would have been on the alert and would not have allowed his house to be broken into. For this reason you also must be ready; for the Son of Man is coming at an hour when you do not think *He will.* Who then is the faithful and sensible slave whom his master put in charge of his household to give their food at the proper time? Blessed is that slave whom his master finds so doing when he comes. Truly I say to you that he will put him in charge of all his possessions. But if that evil slave says in his heart, 'My master is not coming for a long time,' and begins to beat his fellow slaves and eat and drink with drunkards; the master of that slave will come on a day when he does not expect *him* and at an hour which he does not know, and will cut him in pieces and assign him a place with the hypocrites; in that place there will be weeping and gnashing of teeth" (Matthew 24:42–51; cf. Mark 13:33–37; Luke 12:39–46; 21:34–36; see Matthew 8:11, 12; Matthew 25:21–23).

[EXPECTATION from expect and expecting]
Setting: Galilee. After selecting His twelve disciples, Jesus teaches the Sermon on the Mount to His disciples and a great throng from Judea, Jerusalem, and the central coastal region of Tyre and Sidon.

"But I say to you who hear, love your enemies, do good to those who hate you, bless those who curse you, pray for those who mistreat you. Whoever hits you on the cheek, offer him the other also; and whoever takes away your coat, do not withhold your shirt from him either. Give to everyone who asks of you, and whoever takes away what is yours, do not demand it back. Treat others the same way you want them to treat you. If you love those who love you, what credit is that to you? For even sinners love those who love them. If you do good to those who do good to you, what credit is that to you? For even sinners do the same. If you lend to those from whom you expect to receive, what credit is that to you? Even sinners lend to sinners in order to receive back the same amount. But love your enemies, and do good, and lend, expecting nothing in return; and your reward will be great, and you will be sons of the Most High; for He Himself is kind to ungrateful and evil men. Be merciful, just as your Father is merciful" (Luke 6:27–36; cf. Matthew 5:9, 39–48; Matthew 7:12).

[EXPECTATION from expect]
Setting: On the way from Galilee to Jerusalem. After giving a parable about riches and greed, Jesus uses a parable to challenge the crowd and His disciples to be ready for His return.

"Be dressed in readiness, and keep your lamps lit. Be like men who are waiting for their master when he returns from the wedding feast, so that they may immediately open the door to him when he comes and knocks. Blessed are those slaves whom the master will find on the alert when he comes; truly I say to you, that he will gird himself to serve, and have them recline at the table, and will come up and wait on them. Whether he comes in the second watch, or even in the third and finds them so, blessed are those slaves. But be sure of this, that if the head of the house had known at what hour the thief was coming, he would not have allowed his house to be broken into. You too, be ready; for the Son of Man is coming at an hour that you do not expect" (Luke 12:35–40; cf. Matthew 24:42–44; see Mark 13:33; Ephesians 6:14).

Setting: The Mount of Olives, just east of Jerusalem. Following a time of ministry in the temple and giving His disciples more details regarding future events, Jesus speaks of His own return.

"There will be signs in sun and moon and stars, and on the earth dismay among the nations, in perplexity at the roaring of the sea and the waves, men fainting from fear and the expectation of the things which are coming upon the world; for the powers of the heavens will be shaken. Then they will see THE SON OF MAN COMING IN A CLOUD with power and great glory. But when these things begin to take place, straighten up and lift up your heads, because your redemption is drawing near" (Luke 21:25–28, Jesus quotes from Daniel 7:13; cf. Matthew 24:29–31; Mark 13:24–27).

EXPECTATIONS (Also see EXPECTATION; REWARDS; and STEWARDSHIP)

EXPERTS
Setting: Galilee. The Pharisees and some of the scribes from Jerusalem question why Jesus' disciples do not follow the tradition of ceremonial hand cleansing before eating bread.

And He said to them, "Rightly did Isaiah prophesy of you hypocrites, as it is written: 'THIS PEOPLE HONORS ME WITH THEIR LIPS, BUT THEIR HEART IS FAR AWAY FROM ME. BUT IN VAIN DO THEY WORSHIP ME, TEACHING AS DOCTRINES THE PRECEPTS OF MEN.' Neglecting the commandment of God, you hold to the tradition of men." He was also saying to them, "You are experts at setting aside the commandment of God in order to keep tradition. For Moses said, 'HONOR YOUR FATHER AND YOUR MOTHER'; and, 'HE WHO SPEAKS EVIL OF FATHER OR MOTHER, IS TO BE PUT TO DEATH'; but you say, 'If a man says to *his* father or *his* mother, whatever I have that would help you is Corban (that is to say, given *to God*),' you no longer permit him to do anything for *his* father or *his* mother; *thus*

invalidating the word of God by your tradition which you have handed down; and you do many things such as that" (Mark 7:6–13, Jesus quotes from Exodus 20:12; 21:17; Isaiah 29:13; cf. Matthew 15:1–6).

EXPLANATION OF THE PARABLE OF THE SOWER (Listed under SOWER, EXPLANATION OF THE PARABLE OF THE)

EXPLANATION OF THE PARABLE OF THE WHEAT AND THE TARES (Listed under TARES, EXPLANATION OF THE PARABLE OF THE WHEAT AND THE)

EXTERNALS (See HYPOCRISY; and OUTSIDE)

EXTRA MILE (Listed under MILE, EXTRA)

EYE (Specifics such as EYE, BROTHER'S; EYE, RIGHT; NEEDLE, EYE OF A and SALVE, EYE are separate entries; also see EYES; SIGHT; and VISION)

Setting: Galilee. During the early part of His ministry, Jesus preaches the Sermon on the Mount to His disciples and the multitudes.

"You have heard that it was said, 'AN EYE FOR AN EYE, AND A TOOTH FOR A TOOTH.' But I say to you, do not resist an evil person; but whoever slaps you on your right cheek, turn the other to him also" (Matthew 5:38, 39, Jesus quotes from Exodus 21:24; cf. Leviticus 24:20).

Setting: Galilee. During the early part of His ministry, Jesus preaches the Sermon on the Mount to His disciples and the multitudes.

"The eye is the lamp of the body; so then if your eye is clear, your whole body will be full of light. But if your eye is bad, your whole body will be full of darkness. If then the light that is in you is darkness, how great is the darkness!" (Matthew 6:22, 23; cf. Luke 11:34, 35).

Setting: Galilee. During the early part of His ministry, Jesus preaches the Sermon on the Mount to His disciples and the multitudes.

"Do not judge so that you will not be judged. For in the way you judge, you will be judged; and by your standard of measure, it will be measured to you. Why do you look at the speck that is in your brother's eye, but do not notice the log that is in your own eye? Or how can you say to your brother, 'Let me take the speck out of your eye, and behold, the log is in your own eye? You hypocrite, first take the log out of your own eye, and then you will see clearly to take the speck out of your brother's eye" (Matthew 7:1–5; cf. Mark 4:24; Luke 6:37–42; Romans 2:1; 14:10, 13).

Setting: Capernaum of Galilee. Jesus elaborates about stumbling blocks following His disciples' question about greatness in the kingdom of heaven.

"Woe to the world because of *its* stumbling blocks! For it is inevitable that stumbling blocks come; but woe to that man through whom the stumbling block comes! If your hand or your foot causes you to stumble, cut if off and throw it from you; it is better for you to enter life crippled or lame, than to have two hands or two feet and be cast into the eternal fire. If your eye causes you to stumble, pluck it out and throw it from you. It is better for you to enter life with one eye, than to have two eyes and be cast into the fiery hell" (Matthew 18:7–9; cf. Matthew 5:29, 30; Mark 9:43–48; Luke 17:1).

Setting: Judea beyond the Jordan (Perea). Jesus illustrates the kingdom of heaven to His disciples through the story of laborers in the vineyard.

"For the kingdom of heaven is like a landowner who went out early in the morning to hire laborers for his vineyard. When he had agreed with the laborers for a denarius for the day, he sent them into his vineyard. And he went out about the third hour and saw others standing idle in the market place; and to those he said, 'You also go into the vineyard, and whatever is right I will give you.' And *so* they went. Again he went out about the sixth and the ninth hour, and did the same thing. And about the eleventh *hour* he went out and found others standing *around;* and he said to them, 'Why have you been standing idle here all day long?' They said to him, 'Because no one hired us.' He said to them, 'You go into the vineyard too.' When evening came, the owner of the vineyard said to his foreman, 'Call the laborers and pay them their wages, beginning with the last *group* to the first.' When those *hired* about the eleventh hour came, each one received a denarius. When those *hired* first came, they thought that they would receive more; but each of them also received a denarius. When they received it, they grumbled at the landowner, saying, 'These last men have worked *only* one hour, and you have made them equal to us who have borne the burden and the scorching heat of the day.' But he answered and said to one of them, 'Friend, I am doing you no wrong; did you not agree with me for a denarius? Take what is yours and go, but I wish to give to this last man the same as to you. It is not lawful for me to do what I wish with what is my own? Or is your eye envious because I am generous?' So the last shall be first, and the first last" (Matthew 20:1–16; cf. Matthew 19:30).

Setting: Capernaum of Galilee. As Jesus teaches His disciples in private, they ask Him about greatness.

But Jesus said, "Do not hinder him, for there is no one who will perform a miracle in My name, and be able soon afterward to speak evil of Me. For he who is not against us is for us. For whoever gives you a cup of water to drink because of your name as *followers* of Christ, truly I say to you, he will not lose his reward. Whoever causes one of these little ones who believe to stumble, it would be better for him if, with a heavy millstone hung around his neck, he had been cast into the sea. If your hand causes you to stumble, cut it off; it is better for you to enter life crippled, than, having your two hands, to go into hell, into the unquenchable fire, [where THEIR WORM DOES NOT DIE, AND THE FIRE IS NOT QUENCHED.] If your foot causes you to stumble, cut it off; it is better for you to enter life lame, than, having your two feet, to be cast into hell, [where THEIR WORM DOES NOT DIE, AND THE FIRE IS NOT QUENCHED.] If your eye causes you to stumble, throw it out; it is better for you to enter the kingdom of God with one eye, than, having two eyes, to be cast into hell, where THEIR WORM DOES NOT DIE, AND THE FIRE IS NOT QUENCHED. For everyone will be salted with fire. Salt is good; but if the salt becomes unsalty, with what will you make it salty *again?* Have salt in yourselves, and be at peace with one another" (Mark 9:39–50; Jesus quotes from Isaiah 66:24; cf. Matthew 18:6–9; Luke 9:49, 50; see Matthew 5:13, 29, 30; 10:42; 12:30; 18:5, 6).

Setting: On a mountain in Galilee. After selecting His twelve disciples, Jesus teaches the Sermon on the Mount to the disciples and a great throng from Judea, Jerusalem, and the central coastal region of Tyre and Sidon.

And He also spoke a parable to them: "A blind man cannot guide a blind man, can he? Will they not both fall into a pit? A pupil is not above his teacher; but everyone, after he has been fully trained, will be like his teacher. Why do you look at the speck that is in your brother's eye, but do not notice the log that is in your own eye? Or how can you say to your brother, 'Brother, let me take out the speck that is in your eye,' when you yourself do not see the log that is in your own eye? You hypocrite, first take the log out of your own eye, and then you will see clearly to take out the speck that is in your brother's eye. For there is no good tree which produces bad fruit, nor, on the other hand, a bad tree which produces good fruit. For each tree is known by its own fruit. For men do not gather figs from thorns, nor do they pick grapes from a briar bush. The good man out of the good treasure of his heart brings forth what is good; and the evil man out of the evil treasure brings forth what is evil; for his mouth speaks from that which fills his heart" (Luke 6:39–45; cf. Matthew 7:3–6. 16, 18, 20; 12:35; see Matthew 10:24; 15:14; Luke 6:12–19).

Setting: On the way from Galilee to Jerusalem. After telling the increasing crowds of the sign of Jonah, Jesus illustrates His point by speaking of a lamp.

"No one, after lighting a lamp, puts it away in a cellar nor under a basket, but on the lampstand, so that those who enter may see the light. The eye is the lamp of your body; when your eye is clear, your whole body also is full of light; but when it is bad, your body also is full of darkness. Then watch out that the light in you is not darkness. If therefore your whole body is full of light, with no dark part in it, it will be wholly illumined, as when the lamp illumines you with its rays" (Luke 11:33–36; cf. Matthew 5:15, 6:22, 23).

EYE, BROTHER'S

Setting: On a mountain in Galilee. During the early part of His ministry, Jesus preaches the Sermon on the Mount to His disciples and the multitudes.

"Do not judge so that you will not be judged. For in the way you judge, you will be judged; and by your standard of measure, it will be measured to you. Why do you look at the speck that is in your brother's eye, but do not notice the log that is in your own eye? Or how can you say to your brother, 'Let me take the speck out of your eye, and behold, the log is in your own eye? You hypocrite, first take the log out of your own eye, and then you will see clearly to take the speck out of your brother's eye" (Matthew 7:1–5; cf. Mark 4:24; Luke 6:37–42; Romans 2:1; 14:10, 13).

Setting: Galilee. After selecting His twelve disciples, Jesus teaches the Sermon on the Mount to His disciples and a great throng from Judea, Jerusalem, and the central coastal region of Tyre and Sidon.

And He also spoke a parable to them: "A blind man cannot guide a blind man, can he? Will they not both fall into a pit? A pupil is not above his teacher; but everyone, after he has been fully trained, will be like his teacher. Why do you look at the speck that is in your brother's eye, but do not notice the log that is in your own eye? Or how can you say to your brother, 'Brother, let me take out the speck that is in your eye,' when you yourself do not see the log that is in your own eye? You hypocrite, first take the log out of your own eye, and then you will see clearly to take out the speck that is in your brother's eye. For there is no good tree which produces bad fruit, nor, on the other hand, a bad tree which produces good fruit. For each tree is known by its own fruit. For men do not gather figs from thorns, nor do they pick grapes from a briar bush. The good man out of the good treasure of his heart brings forth what is good; and the evil man out of the evil treasure brings forth what is evil; for his mouth speaks from that which fills his heart" (Luke 6:39–45; cf. Matthew 7:3–6. 16, 18, 20; 12:35; see Matthew 10:24; 15:14; Luke 6:12–19).

EYE, RIGHT

Setting: Galilee. During the early part of His ministry, Jesus preaches the Sermon on the Mount to His disciples and the multitudes.

"If your right eye makes you stumble, tear it out and throw it from you; for it is better for you to lose one of the parts of your body, than for your whole body to be thrown into hell. If your right hand makes you stumble, cut it off and throw it from you; for it is better for you to lose one of the parts of your body, than for your whole body to go into hell" (Matthew 5:29, 30; cf. Matthew 18:8, 9).

EYE OF A NEEDLE **(Listed under NEEDLE, EYE OF A)**

EYE SALVE **(Listed under SALVE, EYE)**

EYES **(EYES, TWO is a separate entry; also see EYE; SIGHT; and VISION)**

Setting: By the Sea of Galilee. Jesus responds to His disciples' questions about the Parable of the Sower, which He has just taught from a boat.

Jesus answered them, "To you it has been granted to know the mysteries of the kingdom of heaven, but to them it has not been granted. For whoever has, to him *more* shall be given, and he will have an abundance; but whoever does not have, even what he has shall be taken away from him. Therefore, I speak to them in parables; because while seeing they do not see, and while hearing they do not hear, nor do they understand. In their case the prophecy of Isaiah is being fulfilled, which says, 'YOU WILL KEEP ON HEARING, BUT WILL NOT UNDERSTAND; YOU WILL KEEP ON SEEING, BUT WILL NOT PERCEIVE; FOR THE HEART OF THIS PEOPLE HAS BECOME DULL, WITH THEIR EARS THEY SCARCELY HEAR, AND THEY HAVE CLOSED THEIR EYES, OTHERWISE THEYWOULD SEE WITH THEIR EYES, HEAR WITH THEIR EARS, AND UNDERSTAND WITH THEIR HEART AND RETURN, AND I WOULD HEAL THEM.' But blessed are your eyes, because they see; and your ears, because they hear. For truly I say to you that many prophets and righteous men desired to see what you see, and did not see *it,* and to hear what you hear, and did not hear *it*" (Matthew 13:11–17, Jesus quotes from Isaiah 6:9, 10; cf. Matthew 25:29; Mark 4:11–13; Luke 8:10; see Deuteronomy 29:4; John 8:56).

Setting: The temple in Jerusalem. Jesus delivers a prophecy to the chief priests and elders after they question His authority.

Jesus said to them, "Did you never read in the Scriptures, 'THE STONE WHICH THE BUILDERS REJECTED, THIS BECAME THE CHIEF CORNER stone; THIS CAME ABOUT FROM THE LORD, AND IT IS MARVELOUS IN OUR EYES'? Therefore I say to you, the kingdom of God will be taken away from you and given to a people, producing the fruit of it. And he who falls on this stone will be broken to pieces; but on whomever it falls, it will scatter him like dust" (Matthew 21:42–44, Jesus quotes from Psalm 118:22; cf. Isaiah 8:14, 15; Mark 12:10, 11; Luke 20:17,18).

Setting: The district of Dalmanutha. After the Pharisees argue with Jesus, seeking a sign from heaven to test Him, Jesus and His disciples cross to the other side of the Sea of Galilee, where His disciples discuss with one another that they have no bread.

And Jesus, aware of this, said to them, "Why do you discuss the fact that you have no bread? Do you not yet see or understand? Do you have a hardened heart? HAVING EYES, DO YOU NOT SEE? AND HAVING EARS, DO YOU NOT HEAR? And do you not remember, when I broke the five loaves for the five thousand, how many baskets full of broken pieces you picked up? They said to Him, "Twelve." When I broke the seven for the four thousand, how many large baskets full of broken pieces did you pick up?" They said to Him, "Seven." And He was saying to them, "Do you not yet understand?" (Mark 8:17–21, Jesus quotes from Jeremiah 5:21; cf. Matthew 16:5–12; see Matthew 14:18, 19; Mark 6:41–44, 52; 8:6–9).

Setting: The temple in Jerusalem. Having His authority questioned by the chief priests, scribes, and elders, Jesus begins to teach them in parables.

And He began to speak to them in parables: "A man PLANTED A VINEYARD AND PUT A WALL AROUND IT, AND DUG A VAT UNDER THE WINE PRESS AND BUILT A TOWER, and rented it out to vine-growers and went on a journey. At the harvest time he sent a slave to the vine-growers, in order to receive some of the produce of the vineyard from the vine-growers. They took him, and beat him and sent him away empty-handed. Again he sent them another slave, and they wounded him in the head, and treated him shamefully. And he sent another, and that one they killed; and so with many others, beating some and killing others. He had one more to send, a beloved son; he sent him last of all to them, saying, 'They will respect my son.' But those vine-growers said to one another, 'This is the heir; come, let us kill him, and the inheritance will be ours!' They took him, and killed him and threw him out of the vineyard. What will the owner of the vineyard do? He will come and destroy the vine-growers, and will give the vineyard to others. Have you not even read this Scripture: 'THE STONE WHICH THE BUILDERS REJECTED, THIS BECAME THE CHIEF CORNER stone; THIS CAME ABOUT FROM THE LORD, AND IT IS MARVELOUS IN OUR EYES'?" (Mark 12:1–11, Jesus quotes from Psalm 118:22, 23; Isaiah 5:1, 2; cf. Matthew 21:33–46; Luke 20:9–19).

Setting: On the way from Galilee to Jerusalem. After responding to a report from the seventy sent out in pairs to every place He Himself will soon visit, the Lord addresses His disciples in private.

Turning to the disciples, He said privately, "Blessed are the eyes which see the things you see, for I say to you, that many prophets and kings wished to see the things you see, and did not see them, and to hear the things which you hear, and did not hear them" (Luke 10:23, 24; cf. Matthew 13:16, 17; see Luke 10:17).

Setting: On the way from Galilee to Jerusalem. After responding to the Pharisees' scoffing at His teaching His disciples about stewardship and the permanence of the Law, Jesus conveys the story of the rich man and Lazarus.

"Now there was a rich man, and he habitually dressed in purple and fine linen, joyously living in splendor every day. And a poor man named Lazarus was laid at his gate, covered with sores, and longing to be fed with the crumbs which were falling from the rich man's table; besides, even the dogs were coming and licking his sores. Now the poor man died and was carried away by the angels to Abraham's bosom; and the rich man also died and was buried. In Hades he lifted up his eyes, being in torment, and saw Abraham far away and Lazarus in his bosom. And he cried out and said, 'Father Abraham, have mercy on me, and send

Lazarus so that he may dip the tip of his finger in water and cool off my tongue, for I am in agony in this flame.' But Abraham said, 'Child, remember that during your life you received your good things, and likewise Lazarus bad things; but now he is being comforted here, and you are in agony. And besides all this, between us and you there is a great chasm fixed, so that those who wish to come over from here to you will not be able, and that none may cross over from there to us.' And he said, 'Then I beg you, father, that you send him to my father's house—for I have five brothers—in order that he may warn them, so that they will not also come to this place of torment.' But Abraham said, 'They have Moses and the Prophets; let them hear them.' But he said, 'No, father Abraham, but if someone goes to them from the dead, they will repent!' But he said to him, 'If they do not listen to Moses and the Prophets, they will not be persuaded even if someone rises from the dead'" (Luke 16:19–31; see Luke 3:8; 6:24; 16:1, 14).

Setting: On the way from Galilee to Jerusalem. After instructing His disciples about persistence in prayer, Jesus conveys a parable about self-righteousness.

And He also told this parable to some people who trusted in themselves that they were righteous, and viewed others with contempt: "Two men went up into the temple to pray, one a Pharisee and the other a tax collector. The Pharisee stood and was praying this to himself: 'God, I thank You that I am not like other people: swindlers, unjust, adulterers, or even like this tax collector. I fast twice a week; I pay tithes of all that I get.' But the tax collector, standing some distance away, was even unwilling to lift up his eyes to heaven, but was beating his breast, saying, 'God, be merciful to me, the sinner!' I tell you, this man went to his house justified rather than the other; for everyone who exalts himself will be humbled, but he who humbles himself will be exalted" (Luke 18:9–14; see Ezra 9:6; Matthew 6:5, 23:12; Luke 11:42, 16:15; Romans 14:3, 10).

Setting: Approaching Jerusalem. After being praised by the people in a triumphal welcome, the Lord weeps as He sees the city ahead of Him.

When He approached Jerusalem, He saw the city and wept over it, saying, "If you had known in this day, even you, the things which make for peace! But now they have been hidden from your eyes. For the days will come upon you when your enemies will throw up a barricade against you, and surround you and hem you in on every side, and they will level you to the ground and your children within you, and they will not leave in you one stone upon another, because you did not recognize the time of your visitation" (Luke 19:41–44; see Matthew 24:1–2; Luke 13:34, 35).

Setting: Sychar in Samaria, on the way to Galilee. After Jesus converses with a Samaritan woman at Jacob's well, His disciples return with food. They try to get Jesus to eat but are surprised when He speaks of other food.

Jesus said to them, "My food is to do the will of Him who sent Me and to accomplish His work. Do you not say, 'There are yet four months, and *then* comes the harvest'? Behold, I say to you, lift up your eyes and look on the fields, that they are white for harvest. Already he who reaps is receiving wages and is gathering fruit for life eternal; so that he who sows and he who reaps may rejoice together. For in this *case* the saying is true, 'One sows and another reaps.' I sent you to reap that for which you have not labored; others have labored and you have entered into their labor" (John 4:34–38; see Matthew 9:37, 38; John 5:36).

Setting: Caesarea. Luke, writing in Acts, gives Paul's retelling of his conversion to Christ as he appears before King Agrippa in Caesarea following his hearing before the Jewish Council in Jerusalem and arrest by the Roman commander (on his way to Rome after the apostle's third missionary journey).

"And when we had fallen to the ground, I heard a voice saying to me in the Hebrew dialect, 'Saul, Saul, why are you persecuting Me? It is hard for you to kick against the goads.' And I said, 'Who are You, Lord?' And the Lord said, 'I am Jesus whom you are persecuting. But get up and stand on your feet; for this purpose I have appeared to you, to appoint you a minister and a witness not only to the things which you have seen, but also to the things in which I will appear to you; rescuing you from the *Jewish* people and from the Gentiles, to whom I am sending you, to open their eyes so that they may turn from darkness to light and from the dominion of Satan to God, that they may receive forgiveness of sins and an inheritance among those who have been sanctified by faith in Me' (Acts 26:14–18; see Isaiah 35:5; Acts 21:40; 22:14).

Setting: On the island of Patmos (in the Aegean Sea about fifty miles southwest of Ephesus in modern Turkey). On the Lord's Day (Sunday), the disciple John encounters the Lord Jesus Christ about fifty years after His resurrection. Jesus communicates a new revelation for the apostle to record for the church in Thyatira and to six other churches in Asia.

"And to the angel of the church in Thyatira write: The Son of God, who has eyes like a flame of fire, and His feet are like burnished bronze, says this: 'I know your deeds, and your love and faith and service and perseverance, and that your deeds of late are greater than at first. But I have *this* against you, that you tolerate the woman Jezebel, who calls herself a prophetess, and she teaches and leads My bond-servants astray so that they commit *acts of* immorality and eat things sacrificed to idols. I gave her time to repent, and she does not want to repent of her immorality. Behold, I will throw her on a bed *of sickness,* and those who commit adultery with her into great tribulation, unless they repent of her deeds. And I will kill her children with pestilence, and all the churches will know that I am He who searches the minds and hearts; and I will give to each one of you according to your deeds. But I say to you, the rest who are in Thyatira, who do not hold this teaching, who have not known the deep things of Satan, as they call them—I place no other burden on you. Nevertheless what you have, hold fast until I come. He who overcomes, and he who keeps My deeds until the end, TO HIM I WILL GIVE AUTHORITY OVER THE NATIONS; AND HE SHALL RULE THEM WITH A ROD OF IRON, AS THE VESSELS OF THE POTTER ARE BROKEN TO PIECES, as I also have received *authority* from My Father; and I will give him the morning star. He who has an ear, let him hear what the Spirit says to the churches' (Revelation 2:18–29; Jesus quotes from Psalm 2:8, 9; Isaiah 30:14; see 1 Kings 16:31; Psalm 7:9; Romans 2:5; 1 Corinthians 2:10; 2 Peter 3:9; Revelation 1:14; 2:7; 3:11; 17:1–20).

Setting: On the island of Patmos (in the Aegean Sea about fifty miles southwest of Ephesus in modern Turkey). On the Lord's Day (Sunday), the disciple John encounters the Lord Jesus Christ about fifty years after His resurrection. Jesus communicates a new revelation for the apostle to record for the church in Laodicea and to six other churches in Asia.

"To the angel of the church in Laodicea write: The Amen, the faithful and true Witness, the Beginning of the creation of God, says this: 'I know your deeds, that you are neither cold nor hot; I wish that you were cold or hot. So because you are lukewarm, and neither hot nor cold, I will spit you out of My mouth. Because you say, "I am rich, and have become wealthy, and have need of nothing," and you do not know that you are wretched and miserable and poor and blind and naked, I advise you to buy from Me gold refined by fire so that you may become rich, and white garments so that you may clothe yourself, and *that* the shame of your nakedness will not be revealed; and eye salve to anoint your eyes so that you may see. Those whom I love, I reprove and discipline; therefore be zealous and repent. Behold, I stand at the door and knock; if anyone hears My voice and opens the door, I will come in to him and will dine with him, and he with Me. He who overcomes, I will grant to him to sit down with Me on My throne, as I also overcame and sat down with My Father on His throne. He who has an ear, let him hear what the Spirit says to the churches'" (Revelation 3:14–22; see Proverbs 3:12; Hosea 12:8; John 14:23; 16:33).

EYES, TWO

Setting: Capernaum of Galilee. Jesus elaborates about stumbling blocks following His disciples' question about greatness in the kingdom of heaven.

"Woe to the world because of *its* stumbling blocks! For it is inevitable that stumbling blocks come; but woe to that man through whom the stumbling block comes! If your hand or your foot causes you to stumble, cut if off and throw it from you; it is better for you to enter life crippled or lame, than to have two hands or two feet and be cast into the eternal fire. If your eye causes you to stumble, pluck it out and throw it from you. It is better for you to enter life with one eye, than to have two eyes and be cast into the fiery hell" (Matthew 18:7–9; cf. Matthew 5:29, 30; Mark 9:43–48; Luke 17:1).

Setting: Capernaum of Galilee. As Jesus teaches His disciples in private, they ask Him about greatness.

But Jesus said, "Do not hinder him, for there is no one who will perform a miracle in My name, and be able soon afterward to speak evil of Me. For he who is not against us is for us. For whoever gives you a cup of water to drink because of your name as *followers* of Christ, truly I say to you, he will not lose his reward. Whoever causes one of these little ones who believe to stumble, it would be better for him if, with a heavy millstone hung around his neck, he had been cast into the sea. If your hand causes you to stumble, cut it off; it is better for you to enter life crippled, than, having your two hands, to go into hell, into the unquenchable fire, [where THEIR WORM DOES NOT DIE, AND THE FIRE IS NOT QUENCHED.] If your foot causes you to stumble, cut it off; it is better for you to enter life lame, than, having your two feet, to be cast into hell, [where THEIR WORM DOES NOT DIE, AND THE FIRE IS NOT QUENCHED.] If your eye causes you to stumble, throw it out; it is better for you to enter the kingdom of God with one eye, than, having two eyes, to be cast into hell, where THEIR WORM DOES NOT DIE, AND THE FIRE IS NOT QUENCHED. For everyone will be salted with fire. Salt is good; but if the salt becomes unsalty, with what will you make it salty *again?* Have salt in yourselves, and be at peace with one another" (Mark 9:39–50; Jesus quotes from Isaiah 66:24; cf. Matthew 18:6; Luke 9:49, 50; see Matthew 5:13, 29, 30; 10:42; 12:30; 18:5, 6; Mark 9:38).

F

FACE (Also see specifics such as CHEEK)

Setting: Galilee. During the early part of His ministry, Jesus preaches the Sermon on the Mount to His disciples and the multitudes.

"Whenever you fast, do not put on a gloomy face as the hypocrites *do,* for they neglect their appearance so that they will be noticed by men when they are fasting. Truly I say to you, they have their reward in full. But you, when you fast, anoint your head and wash your face so that your fasting will not be noticed by men, but by your Father who is in secret; and your Father who sees *what is done* in secret will reward you" (Matthew 6:16–18; see Matthew 6:4, 6).

Setting: Capernaum of Galilee. Jesus elaborates about the value of little ones following His disciples' question about greatness in the kingdom of heaven.

"See that you do not despise one of these little ones, for I say to you that their angels in heaven continually see the face of My Father who is in heaven" (Matthew 18:10; see Luke 1:19).

Setting: The Mount of Olives, just east of Jerusalem. During His discourse, following a time of ministry in the temple a few days before His crucifixion, after conveying the Parable of the Fig Tree, Jesus warns His disciples to keep alert regarding future events.

"Be on guard, so that your hearts will not be weighted down with dissipation and drunkenness and the worries of life, and that day will not come upon you suddenly like a trap; for it will come upon all those who dwell on the face of all the earth. But keep on the alert at all times, praying that you may have strength to escape all these things that are about to take place, and to stand before the Son of Man" (Luke 21:34–36; cf. Mark 13:33; see Matthew 24:42–44).

FACE, GOD'S (See FACE)

FACT

Setting: Capernaum of Galilee. Jesus gives instruction about church discipline after conveying to His disciples the value of little ones.

"If your brother sins, go and show him his fault in private; if he listens to you, you have won your brother. But if he does not listen *to you,* take one or two more with you, so that BY THE MOUTH OF TWO OR THREE WITNESSES EVERY FACT MAY BE CONFIRMED. If he refuses to listen to them, tell it to the church; and if he refuses to listen even to the church, let him be to you as a Gentile and a tax collector. Truly I say to you, whatever you bind of earth shall have been bound in heaven; and whatever you loose on earth shall have been loosed in heaven. Again, I say to you, that if two of you agree on earth about anything that they may ask, it shall be done for them by My Father who is in heaven. For there two or three have gathered together in My name, I am there in their midst" (Matthew 18:15–20. Jesus quotes from Deuteronomy 19:15; cf. Matthew 7:7; 16:19; see Leviticus 19:17; Matthew 28:20; 2 Thessalonians 3:6, 14).

Setting: The district of Dalmanutha. After the Pharisees argue with Jesus, seeking a sign from heaven to test Him, Jesus and His disciples cross to the other side of the Sea of Galilee, where His disciples discuss with one another that they have no bread.

And Jesus, aware of this, said to them, "Why do you discuss *the fact* that you have no bread? Do you not yet see or understand?

Do you have a hardened heart? HAVING EYES, DO YOU NOT SEE? AND HAVING EARS, DO YOU NOT HEAR? And do you not remember, when I broke the five loaves for the five thousand, how many baskets full of broken pieces you picked you? They said to Him, "Twelve." When *I broke* the seven for the four thousand, how many large baskets full of broken pieces did you pick up?" They said to Him, "Seven." And He was saying to them, "Do you not yet understand?" (Mark 8:17–21, Jesus quotes from Jeremiah 5:21; cf. Matthew 16:5–12; see Matthew 14:18, 19; Mark 6:41–44, 52; 8:6–9).

Setting: The temple in Jerusalem. After some of the Pharisees and Herodians attempt to trap Jesus in a statement, some Sadducees question Him about the status of marriage after death.

Jesus said to them, "Is this not the reason you are mistaken, that you do not understand the Scriptures or the power of God? For when they rise from the dead, they neither marry nor are given in marriage, but are like angels in heaven. But regarding the fact that the dead rise again, have you not read in the book of Moses, in the *passage* about *the burning* bush, how God spoke to him, saying, 'I AM THE GOD OF ABRAHAM, AND THE GOD OF ISAAC, and the God of Jacob?' He is not the God of the dead, but of the living; you are greatly mistaken" (Mark 12:24–27, Jesus quotes from Exodus 3:6; cf. Matthew 22:29–33; Luke 20:34–40).

FAIL

Setting: On the way from Galilee to Jerusalem, The Lord responds to the Pharisees' scoffing at His teaching His disciples about stewardship.

And He said to them, "You are those who justify yourselves in the sight of men, but God knows your hearts; for that which is highly esteemed among men is detestable in the sight of God. The Law and the Prophets *were proclaimed* until John; since that time the gospel of the kingdom of God has been preached, and everyone is forcing his way into it. But is it easier for heaven and earth to pass away than for one stroke of a letter of the Law to fail" (Luke 16:15–17; cf. Matthew 5:18; see 1 Samuel 16:7; Matthew 4:23; 11:11–14; Luke 16:1, 14).

Setting: An upper room in Jerusalem. During the Feast of Unleavened Bread (Passover) just before His crucifixion, Jesus celebrates the Passover meal and institutes the Lord's Supper. His disciples later argue over who is the greatest among them, and Jesus prophesies Peter's upcoming denial of Him.

"Simon, Simon, behold, Satan has demanded *permission* to sift you like wheat; but I have prayed for you, that your faith may not fail; and you, when once you have turned again, strengthen your brothers." But he said to Him, "Lord, with You I am ready to go both to prison and to death!" And He said, "I say to you, Peter, the rooster will not crow today until you have denied three times that you know Me" (Luke 22:31–34; cf. Matthew 26:33–35; John 13:36–38; see Job 1:6–12; John 17:15).

FAITH **(Specifics such as FAITH, GREAT; and FAITH, LITTLE are separate entries; also see BELIEF; GOSPEL; and SALVATION)**

Setting: Capernaum near the Sea of Galilee. Jesus heals a woman suffering with internal bleeding for twelve years.

But Jesus turning and seeing her said, "Daughter, take courage; your faith has made you well." At once the woman was made well (Matthew 9:22; cf. Mark 5:34; Luke 8:48).

Setting: Somewhere in Galilee. After healing a woman with internal bleeding and resuscitating a synagogue official's daughter from the dead, Jesus gives sight to two blind men.

When He entered the house, the blind men came up to Him, and Jesus said to them, "Do you believe that I am able to do this?" They said to Him, "Yes, Lord." Then He touched their eyes saying, "It shall be done for you according to your faith." And their eyes were opened. And Jesus sternly warned them: "See that no one knows *about this!*" (Matthew 9:28–30).

Setting: The district of Tyre and Sidon. A Canaanite woman appeals to Jesus to heal her demon-possessed daughter.

But He answered and said, "I was sent only to the lost sheep of the house of Israel." But she came and *began* to bow down before

Him, saying, "Lord, help me!" And He answered and said, "It is not good to take the children's bread and throw it to the dogs." But she said, "Yes, Lord; but even the dogs feed from the crumbs which fall from their masters' table." Then Jesus said to her, "O woman, your faith is great; it shall be done for you as you wish." And her daughter was healed at once (Matthew 15:24–28; cf. Mark 7:24–30; see Matthew 9:22; 10:5, 6).

Setting: Near the mountain where the Transfiguration occurred. Jesus reveals to His disciples why they have been unable to cure a demon-possessed boy.

And He said to them, "Because of the littleness of your faith; for truly I say to you, if you have faith the size of a mustard seed, you will say to this mountain, 'Move from here to there,' and it will move; and nothing will be impossible to you. ["But this kind does not go out except by prayer and fasting"] (Matthew 17:20, 21; cf. Matthew 21:21, 22; Mark 9:28, 29).

Setting: Returning to Jerusalem from Bethany. His disciples ask Jesus how the fig tree He cursed (an illustration of the nation of Israel) so quickly withered.

And Jesus answered and said to them, "Truly I say to you, if you have faith and do not doubt, you will not only do what was done to the fig tree, but even if you say to this mountain, 'Be taken up and cast into the sea,' it will happen. And all things you ask in prayer, believing, you will receive" (Matthew 21:21, 22; cf. Matthew 7:7; 17:20; Mark 11:20–24).

Setting: On the Sea of Galilee. In a boat with His disciples, Jesus calms the sea in the midst of a storm.

And He got up and rebuked the wind and said to the sea, "Hush, be still." And the wind died down and it became perfectly calm. And He said to them, "Why are you afraid? Do you still have no faith?" (Mark 4:39, 40: cf. Matthew 13:26; Luke 8:25; see Psalm 65:7; Matthew 14:31).

Setting: Capernaum by the Sea of Galilee. After Jesus returns from ministry to the Gerasenes, a woman who has had a hemorrhage for twelve years touches Jesus in order to be healed.

And He said to her, "Daughter, your faith has made you well; go in peace and be healed of your affliction" (Mark 5:34; cf. Matthew 9:22; Luke 8:48; see Luke 7:50).

Setting: Jericho, on the road to Jerusalem. A blind beggar named Bartimaeus cries out to Jesus for healing.

And Jesus stopped and said, "Call him *here*." So they called the blind man, saying to him, "Take courage, stand up! He is calling for you." Throwing aside his cloak, he jumped up and came to Jesus. And answering him, Jesus said, "What do you want Me to do for you?" And the blind man said to him, "Rabboni, *I want* to regain my sight!" And Jesus said to him, "Go; your faith has made you well." Immediately he regained his sight and *began* following Him on the road (Mark 10:49–52; cf. Matthew 20:29–34; Luke 18:35–43; see Matthew 9:2, 22).

Setting: Jerusalem. Following Jesus' instruction to the money changers while cleansing the temple, Peter draws Jesus' and His disciples' attention to an earlier-cursed fig tree.

And Jesus answered saying to them, "Have faith in God. Truly, I say to you, whoever says to this mountain, 'Be taken up and cast into the sea,' and does not doubt in his heart, but believes that what he says is going to happen, it will be *granted* him. Therefore I say to you, all things for which you pray and ask, believe that you have received them, and they will be *granted* you. Whenever you stand praying, forgive, if you have anything against anyone, so that your Father who is in heaven will also forgive you your transgressions. [But if you do not forgive, neither will your Father who is in heaven forgive your transgressions'] (Mark 11:22–26; cf. Matthew 21:19–22; see Matthew 6:14, 15; 7:7; 17:20).

Setting: Galilee. After Jesus praises John the Baptist to the crowds, Simon, a Pharisee, invites the Lord to dinner, where a sinful woman anoints His feet with perfume, prompting Him to instruct His host about forgiveness.

Turning toward the woman, He said to Simon, "Do you see this woman? I entered your house; you gave Me no water for My feet, but she has wet My feet with her tears and wiped them with her hair. You gave Me no kiss; but she, since the time I came in, has not ceased to kiss My feet. You did not anoint My head with oil, but she anointed My feet with perfume. For this reason I say to you, her sins, which are many, have been forgiven, for she loved much; but he who is forgiven little, loves little." Then He said to her, "Your sins have been forgiven." Those who were reclining *at the table* with Him began to say to themselves, "Who is this *man* who even forgives sins?" And He said to the woman, "Your faith has saved you; go in peace" (Luke 7:44–50; see Matthew 9:2; Mark 5:34; Luke 5:21).

Setting: Galilee. After conveying who His true relatives are, Jesus sets sail with His disciples on the Sea of Galilee, where He calms a storm.

And He said to them, "Where is your faith?" They were fearful and amazed, saying to one another, "Who then is this, that He commands even the winds and the water, and they obey Him?" (Luke 8:25; cf. Matthew 8:23–27; Mark 4:35–41).

Setting: Capernaum of Galilee. After ministering in the country of the Gerasenes, opposite Galilee, Jesus returns. A woman, ill for twelve years, receives healing by touching His garment.

And Jesus said, "Who is the one who touched Me?" And while they were all denying it, Peter said, "Master, the people are crowding and pressing in on You." But Jesus said, "Someone did touch Me, for I was aware, that power had gone out of Me." When the woman saw that she had not escaped notice, she came trembling and fell down before Him, and declared in the presence of all the people the reason why she had touched Him, and how she had been immediately healed. And He said to her, "Daughter, your faith has made you well; go in peace" (Luke 8:45–48; cf. Matthew 9:20; Mark 5:25–34).

Setting: On the way from Galilee to Jerusalem. After His disciples ask that their faith be increased following His instruction on forgiveness, Jesus illustrates with the mustard seed and an obedient slave.

And the Lord said, "If you had faith like a mustard seed, you would say to this mulberry tree, 'Be uprooted and be planted in the sea'; and it would obey you. Which of you, having a slave plowing or tending sheep, will say to him when he has come from the field, 'Come immediately and sit down to eat'? But will he not say to him, "Prepare something for me to eat, and *properly* clothe yourself and serve me while I eat and drink; and afterward you may eat and drink'? He does not thank the slave because he did the things which were commanded, does he? So you too, when you do all the things which are commanded you, say, 'We are unworthy slaves; we have done *only* that which we ought to have done'" (Luke 17:6–10; see Matthew 13:31; Luke 12:37; 17:5).

Setting: Samaria, on the way from Galilee to Jerusalem. The Lord stops to heal ten lepers who ask for cleansing.

When He saw them, He said to them, "Go and show yourselves to the priests." And as they were going, they were cleansed. Now one of them, when he saw that he had been healed, turned back, glorifying God with a loud voice, and he fell on his face at His feet, giving thanks to Him. And he was a Samaritan. Then Jesus answered and said, "Were there not ten cleansed? But the nine—where are they? Was no one found who returned to give glory to God, except this foreigner?" And He said to him, "Stand up and go; your faith has made you well" (Luke 17:14–19; see Leviticus 14:1–32).

Setting: On the way from Galilee to Jerusalem. After telling His disciples of His second coming, Jesus instructs them about persistence in prayer.

Now He was telling them a parable to show that at all times they ought to pray and not to lose heart, saying, "In a certain city there was a judge who did not fear God and did not respect man. There was a widow in that city, and she kept coming to him, saying, 'Give me legal protection from my opponent.' For a while he was unwilling; but afterward he said to himself, 'Even though

I do not fear God nor respect man, yet because this woman bothers me, I will give her legal protection, otherwise by continually coming she will wear me out.'" And the Lord said, "Hear what the unrighteous judge said; now, will not God bring about justice for His elect who cry to Him day and night, and will He delay long over them? I tell you that He will bring about justice for them quickly. However, when the Son of Man comes, will He find faith on the earth?" (Luke 18:1–8; see Luke 11:5–10).

Setting: Approaching Jericho, on the way to Jerusalem. After telling His disciples of the upcoming sacrifice He will make in Jerusalem, Jesus takes time to heal a blind man.

And Jesus stopped and commanded that he be brought to Him; and when he came near, He questioned him, "What do you want Me to do for you?" And he said, "Lord, *I want* to regain my sight!" And Jesus said to him, "Receive your sight; your faith has made you well" (Luke 18:40–42; cf. Matthew 20:29–34; Mark 10:46–52).

Setting: An upper room in Jerusalem. During the Feast of Unleavened Bread (Passover) just before His crucifixion, Jesus celebrates the Passover meal with His disciples and institutes the Lord's Supper. Later, the disciples argue over who is the greatest among them, and Jesus prophesies Peter's denial of Him.

"Simon, Simon, behold, Satan has demanded *permission* to sift you like wheat; but I have prayed for you, that your faith may not fail; and you, when once you have turned again, strengthen your brothers." But he said to Him, "Lord, with You I am ready to go both to prison and to death!" And He said, "I say to you, Peter, the rooster will not crow today until you have denied three times that you know Me" (Luke 22:31–34; cf. Matthew 26:33–35; John 13:36–38; see Job 1:6–12; John 17:15).

Setting: Caesarea. Luke, writing in Acts, gives Paul's retelling of his conversion to Christ as he appears before King Agrippa, following his hearing before the Jewish Council in Jerusalem and arrest by the Roman commander (on his way to Rome after the apostle's third missionary journey).

"And when we had fallen to the ground, I heard a voice saying to me in the Hebrew dialect, 'Saul, Saul, why are you persecuting Me? It is hard for you to kick against the goads.' And I said, 'Who are You, Lord?' And the Lord said, 'I am Jesus whom you are persecuting. But get up and stand on your feet; for this purpose I have appeared to you, to appoint you a minister and a witness not only to the things which you have seen, but also to the things in which I will appear to you; rescuing you from the *Jewish* people and from the Gentiles, to whom I am sending you, to open their eyes so that they may turn from darkness to light and from the dominion of Satan to God, that they may receive forgiveness of sins and an inheritance among those who have been sanctified by faith in Me' (Acts 26:14–18; see Isaiah 35:5; Acts 21:40; 22:14).

Setting: On the island of Patmos (in the Aegean Sea about fifty miles southwest of Ephesus in modern Turkey). On the Lord's Day (Sunday), the disciple John encounters the Lord Jesus Christ about fifty years after His resurrection. Jesus communicates a new revelation for the apostle to record for the church in Pergamum and to six other churches in Asia.

"And to the angel of the church in Pergamum write: The One who has the sharp two-edged sword says this: 'I know where you dwell, where Satan's throne is; and you hold fast My name, and did not deny My faith even in the days of Antipas, My witness, My faithful one, who was killed among you, where Satan dwells. But I have a few things against you, because you have there some who hold the teaching of Balaam, who kept teaching Balak to put a stumbling block before the sons of Israel, to eat things sacrificed to idols and to commit *acts of* immorality. So you also have some who in the same way hold the teaching of the Nicolaitans. Therefore repent; or else I am coming to you quickly, and I will make war against them with the sword of My mouth. He who has an ear, let him hear what the Spirit says to the churches. To him who overcomes, to him I will give *some* of the hidden manna, and I will give him a white stone, and a new name written on the stone which no one knows but he who receives it' (Revelation 2:12–17; see Numbers 25:1–3; Isaiah 62:2; Revelation 1:16; 2:5, 6, 16).

Setting: On the island of Patmos (in the Aegean Sea about fifty miles southwest of Ephesus in modern Turkey). On the Lord's Day (Sunday), the disciple John encounters the Lord Jesus Christ about fifty years after His resurrection. Jesus communicates a new revelation for the apostle to record for the church in Thyatira and to six other churches in Asia.

"And to the angel of the church in Thyatira write: The Son of God, who has eyes like a flame of fire, and His feet are like burnished bronze, says this: 'I know your deeds, and your love and faith and service and perseverance, and that your deeds of late are greater than at first. But I have *this* against you, that you tolerate the woman Jezebel, who calls herself a prophetess, and she teaches and leads My bond-servants astray so that they commit *acts of* immorality and eat things sacrificed to idols. I gave her time to repent, and she does not want to repent of her immorality. Behold, I will throw her on a bed *of sickness,* and those who commit adultery with her into great tribulation, unless they repent of her deeds. And I will kill her children with pestilence, and all the churches will know that I am He who searches the minds and hearts; and I will give to each one of you according to your deeds. But I say to you, the rest who are in Thyatira, who do not hold this teaching, who have not known the deep things of Satan, as they call them—I place no other burden on you. Nevertheless what you have, hold fast until I come. He who overcomes, and he who keeps My deeds until the end, TO HIM I WILL GIVE AUTHORITY OVER THE NATIONS; AND HE SHALL RULE THEM WITH A ROD OF IRON, AS THE VESSELS OF THE POTTER ARE BROKEN TO PIECES, as I also have received *authority* from My Father; and I will give him the morning star. He who has an ear, let him hear what the Spirit says to the churches' (Revelation 2:18–29; Jesus quotes from Psalm 2:8, 9; Isaiah 30:14; see 1 Kings 16:31; Psalm 7:9; Romans 2:5; 1 Corinthians 2:10; 2 Peter 3:9; Revelation 1:14; 2:7; 3:11; 17:1–20).

FAITH, GREAT

Setting: Entering Capernaum. After the Lord gives the Sermon on the Mount and cleanses a leper, a Roman centurion implores Jesus to heal his servant.

Now when Jesus heard *this,* He marveled, and said to those who were following, "Truly I say to you, I have not found such great faith with anyone in Israel. I say to you that many will come from east and west, and recline *at the table* with Abraham, Isaac and Jacob in the kingdom of heaven; but the sons of the kingdom will be cast out into the outer darkness; in that place there will be weeping and gnashing of teeth." And Jesus said to the centurion, "Go; it shall be done for you as you have believed." And the servant was healed that *very* moment (Matthew 8:10–13; cf. Luke 7:9, 10).

Setting: Entering Capernaum. After Jesus completes His Sermon on the Mount, a Roman centurion asks that He heal his gravely ill slave.

Now when Jesus heard this, He marveled at him, and turned and said to the crowd that was following Him, "I say to you, not even in Israel have I found such great faith" (Luke 7:9; cf. Matthew 8:1–10).

FAITH, LACK OF (See UNBELIEF)

FAITH, LITTLE

Setting: Galilee. During the early part of His ministry, Jesus preaches the Sermon on the Mount to His disciples and the multitudes.

"For this reason I say to you, do not be worried about your life, *as to* what you will eat or what you will drink; nor for your body, *as to* what you will put on. Is not life more than food, and the body more than clothing? Look at the birds of the air, that they do not sow, nor reap nor gather into barns, and *yet* your heavenly Father feeds them. Are you not worth much more than they? And who of you by being worried can add a *single* hour to his life? And why are you worried about clothing? Observe how the lilies of the field grow; they do not toil nor do they spin, yet I say to you that not even Solomon in all his glory clothed himself like one of these. But if God so clothes the grass of the field, which is *alive* today and tomorrow is thrown into the furnace, *will He* not much more *clothe* you? You of little faith! Do not worry then, saying 'What will we eat?' or 'What will we drink?' or 'What will be wear for clothing?" For the Gentiles eagerly seek all these things; for your heavenly Father knows that you need all these things. But seek first His kingdom and His righteousness, and all these things will be added to you. So do not worry about tomorrow; for tomorrow will care for itself. Each day has enough trouble of its own" (Matthew 6:25–34; cf. Luke 12:22–31; see 1 Kings 10:4–7; Job 35:11; Matthew 8:26).

Setting: On the Sea of Galilee. After detailing the demands of discipleship to a scribe and one of His disciples, Jesus calms a great storm when His disciples fear for their lives.

He said to them, "Why are you afraid, you men of little faith?" Then He got up and rebuked the winds and the sea, and it became perfectly calm (Matthew 8:26; see Mark 4:35–41; Luke 8:22–25).

Setting: On the Sea of Galilee. Following the miraculous feeding of more than 5,000 of His countrymen, in order to take an opportunity to pray, Jesus makes His disciples get into a boat, where He joins them later by walking on the water during a storm.

But immediately Jesus spoke to them, saying, "Take courage, it is I; do not be afraid." Peter said to Him, "Lord, if it is You, command me to come to You on the water." And He said, "Come!" And Peter got out of the boat, and walked on the water and came toward Jesus. But seeing the wind, he became frightened, and beginning to sink, he cried out, "Lord, save me!" Immediately Jesus stretched out His hand and took hold of him, and said to him, "You of little faith, why did you doubt?" (Matthew 14:27–31; cf. Mark 6:47–52; John 6:16–21).

Setting: By the Sea of Galilee. Jesus repeats His warning to His disciples about the teaching of the Pharisees and Sadducees.

But Jesus aware of this, said, "You men of little faith, why do you discuss among yourselves that you have no bread? Do you not yet understand or remember the five loaves of the five thousand and how many baskets *full* you picked up? Or the seven loaves of the four thousand, and how many large baskets *full* you picked up? How is it that you do not understand that I did not speak to you concerning bread? But beware of the leaven of the Pharisees and Sadducees" (Matthew 16:8–11; cf. Matthew 14:17–21; 15:34–38; Mark 8:17–21).

[LITTLE FAITH from littleness of your faith]
Setting: Near the mountain where the Transfiguration occurred. Jesus reveals to His disciples why they have been unable to cure a demon-possessed boy.

And He said to them, "Because of the littleness of your faith; for truly I say to you, if you have faith the size of a mustard seed, you will say to this mountain, 'Move from here to there,' and it will move; and nothing will be impossible to you. ["But this kind does not go out except by prayer and fasting"] (Matthew 17:20, 21; cf. Matthew 21:21, 22; Mark 9:28, 29).

Setting: On the way from Galilee to Jerusalem. Jesus comforts the crowd and His disciples after giving a parable about riches and greed. The scribes and Pharisees turn hostile and question Him in an attempt to catch Him in something He might say.

And He said to His disciples, "For this reason I say to you, do not worry about *your* life, *as to* what you will eat; nor for your body, *as to* what you will put on. For life is more than food, and the body more than clothing. Consider the ravens, for they neither sow nor reap; they have no storeroom nor barn, and *yet* God feeds them; how much more valuable you are than the birds! And which of you by worrying can add a *single* hour to his life's span? If then you cannot do even a very little thing, why do you worry about other matters? Consider the lilies, how they grow: they neither toil nor spin; but I tell you, not even Solomon in all his glory clothed himself like one of these. But if God so clothes the grass in the field, which is *alive* today and tomorrow is thrown into the furnace, how much more *will He clothe* you? You men of little faith! And do not seek what you will eat and what you will drink, and do not keep worrying. For all these things the nations of the world eagerly seek; but your Father knows that you need these things. But seek His kingdom, and these things will be added to you. Do not be afraid, little flock, for your Father has chosen gladly to give you the kingdom" (Luke 12:22–32; cf. Matthew 6:25–33; see 1 Kings 10:4–7; Job 38:41).

FAITHFUL AND SENSIBLE SLAVE (Listed under SLAVE, FAITHFUL AND SENSIBLE)

FAITHFUL SERVICE (See FAITHFULNESS; REWARDS; and SERVICE)

FAITHFULNESS (Also see ABIDE; COMMENDATION; REWARDS; and STEWARDSHIP)

Setting: The temple in Jerusalem. After the Jewish religious leaders test Him with questions, Jesus pronounces the fifth of eight woes on them in front of the crowds and His disciples.

"Woe to you, scribes and Pharisees, hypocrites! For you tithe mint and dill and cummin, and have neglected the weightier provisions of the law: justice and mercy and faithfulness; but these are things you should have done without neglecting the others. You blind guides, who strain out a gnat and swallow a camel!" (Matthew 23:23, 24).

[FAITHFULNESS from faithful]

Setting: The Mount of Olives, just east of Jerusalem. During His discourse, after answering His disciples' questions as to when the temple will be destroyed and Jerusalem overrun, along with the signs of His coming and the end of the age, Jesus reemphasizes to the disciples they should be on the alert for His return.

"Therefore be on the alert, for you do not know which day your Lord is coming. But be sure of this, that if the head of the house had known at what time of the night the thief was coming, he would have been on the alert and would not have allowed his house to be broken into. For this reason you also must be ready; for the Son of Man is coming at an hour when you do not think *He will.* Who then is the faithful and sensible slave whom his master put in charge of his household to give their food at the proper time? Blessed is that slave whom his master finds so doing when he comes. Truly I say to you that he will put him in charge of all his possessions. But if that evil slave says in his heart, 'My master is not coming for a long time,' and begins to beat his fellow slaves and eat and drink with drunkards; the master of that slave will come on a day when he does not expect *him* and at an hour which he does not know, and will cut him in pieces and assign him a place with the hypocrites; in that place there will be weeping and gnashing of teeth" (Matthew 24:42–51; cf. Mark 13:33–37; Luke 12:39–46; 21:34–36; see Matthew 8:11, 12; 25:21–23).

[FAITHFULNESS from faithful]

Setting: The Mount of Olives, just east of Jerusalem. During His discourse, after answering His disciples' questions as to when the temple will be destroyed and Jerusalem overrun, along with the signs of His coming and the end of the age, Jesus reemphasizes to the disciples they should be on the alert for His return.

"For *it is* just like a man *about* to go on a journey, who called his own slaves and entrusted his possessions to them. To one he gave five talents, to another, two, and to another, one, each according to his own ability; and he went on his journey. Immediately the one who had received the five talents went and traded with them, and gained five more talents. In the same manner the one who *had received* the two *talents* gained two more. But he who received the one *talent* went away, and dug a *hole* in the ground and hid his master's money. Now after a long time the master of those slaves came and settled accounts with them. The one who had received the five talents came up and brought five more talents, saying, 'Master, you entrusted five talents to me. See, I have gained five more talents.' His master said to him, 'Well done, good and faithful slave. You were faithful with a few things, I will put you in charge of many things; enter into the joy of your master.' Also the one who *had received* the two talents came up and said, 'Master, you entrusted two talents to me. See, I have gained two more talents.' His master said to him, 'Well done, good and faithful slave. You were faithful with a few things, I will put you in charge of many things; enter into the joy of your master.' And the one also who had received the one talent came up and said, 'Master, I knew you to be a hard man, reaping where you did not sow and gathering where you scattered no *seed.* And I was afraid, and went away and hid your talent in the ground. See, you have what is yours.' But his master answered and said to him, 'You wicked, lazy slave, you knew that I reap where I did not sow and gather where I scattered no *seed.* Then you ought to have put my money in the bank, and on my arrival I would have received my *money* back with interest. 'Therefore take away the talent from him, and give it to the one who has ten talents.' For to everyone who has, *more* shall be given, and he will have an abundance; but from the one who does not have, even what he does have shall be taken away. Throw out the worthless slave into the outer darkness; in that place there will be weeping and gnashing of teeth" (Matthew 25:14–30; cf. Matthew 8:12; 3:12; 24:45–47; see Matthew 18:23, 24; Luke 12:44).

[FAITHFULNESS from faithful]
Setting: On the way from Galilee to Jerusalem. When Jesus uses a parable to challenge the crowd and His disciples to be ready for His return, Peter asks Him whom He is addressing.

And the Lord said, "Who then is the faithful and sensible steward, whom his master will put in charge of his servants, to give them their rations at the proper time? Blessed is that slave whom his master finds so doing when he comes. Truly I say to you that he will put him in charge of all his possessions. But if that slave says in his heart, 'My master will be a long time in coming,' and begins to beat the slaves, *both* men and women, and to eat and drink and get drunk; the master of that slave will come on a day when he does not expect *him* and at an hour he does not know, and will cut him in pieces, and assign him a place with the unbelievers. And that slave who knew his master's will and did not get ready or act in accord with his will, will receive many lashes, but the one who did know *it,* and committed deeds worthy of flogging, will receive but few. From everyone who has been given much, much will be required; and to whom they entrusted much, of him they will ask all the more" (Luke 12:42–48; cf. Matthew 24:45–51; see Leviticus 5:17).

[FAITHFULNESS from faithful]
Setting: On the way from Galilee to Jerusalem. The Lord teaches His disciples about stewardship after giving the story of the prodigal son.

Now He was also saying to the disciples, "There was a rich man who had a manager, and this *manager* was reported to him as squandering his possessions. And he called him and said to him, 'What is this I hear about you? Give an accounting of your management, for you can no longer be a manager.' The manager said to himself, 'What shall I do, since my master is taking the management away from me? I am not strong enough to dig; I am ashamed to beg. I know what I shall do, so that when I am removed from the management people will welcome me into their homes.' And he summoned each one of his master's debtors, and he *began* saying to the first, 'How much do you owe my master?' And he said, 'A hundred measures of oil.' And he said to him, 'Take your bill, and sit down quickly and write fifty.' Then he said to another, 'And how much do you owe?' And he said, 'A hundred measures of wheat.' He said to him, 'Take your bill, and write eighty.' And his master praised the unrighteous manager because he had acted shrewdly; for the sons of this age are more shrewd in relation to their own kind than the sons of light. And I say to you, make friends for yourselves by means of the wealth of unrighteousness, so that when it fails, they will receive you into the eternal dwellings. He who is faithful in a very little thing is faithful also in much; and he who is unrighteous in a very little thing is unrighteous also in much. Therefore if you have not been faithful in the *use of* unrighteous wealth, who will entrust the *true riches* to you? And if you have not been faithful in *the use of* that which is another's, who will give you that which is your own? No servant can serve two masters; for either he will hate the one and love the other, or else he will be devoted to one and despise the other. You cannot serve God and wealth" (Luke 16:1–13; cf. Matthew 6:24; see Matthew 25:14–30).

[FAITHFULNESS from faithful]
Setting: Jericho, on the way to Jerusalem. After commending Zaccheus's faith in Him, Jesus provides a parable about stewardship.

So He said, "A nobleman went to a distant country to receive a kingdom for himself, and *then* return. And he called ten of his slaves, and gave them ten minas and said to them, 'Do business *with this* until I come *back.*' But his citizens hated him and sent a delegation after him, saying, 'We do not want this man to reign over us.' When he returned, after receiving the kingdom, he ordered that these slaves, to whom he had given the money, be called to him so that he might know what business they had done. The first appeared, saying, 'Master, your mina has made ten minas more.' And he said to him, 'Well done, good slave, because you have been faithful in a very little thing, you are to be in authority over ten cities.' The second came, saying, 'Your mina, master, has made five minas.' And he said to him, also, 'And you are to be over five cities.' Another came, saying, 'Master, here is your mina, which I kept put away in a handkerchief; for I was afraid of you, because you are an exacting man; you take up what you did not lay down and reap what you did not sow.' He said to him, 'By your own words I will judge you, you worthless slave. Did you know that I am an exacting man, taking up what I did not lay down and reaping what I did not sow? Then why did you not put my money in the bank, and having come, I would have collected it with interest?' Then he said to the bystanders, 'Take the mina away from him and give it to the one who has the ten minas.' And they said to him, 'Master, he has ten minas *already.*' I tell you

that to everyone who has, more shall be given, but from the one who does not have, even what he does have shall be taken away. But these enemies of mine, who did not want me to reign over them, bring them here and slay them in my presence" (Luke 19:12–27; cf. Matthew 25:14–30; see Matthew 13:12; Luke 16:10).

[FAITHFULNESS from If you continue in My word]
Setting: The temple treasury in Jerusalem. After the scribes and Pharisees question His testimony about Himself, Jesus reveals to those Jews who believe in Him how He will make them free.

So Jesus was saying to those Jews who had believed Him, "If you continue in My word, *then* you are truly disciples of Mine; and you will know the truth, and the truth will make you free." They answered Him, "We are Abraham's descendants and have never yet been enslaved to anyone; how is it that You say, 'You will become free'?" Jesus answered them, "Truly, truly, I say to you, everyone who commits sin is the slave of sin. The slave does not remain in the house forever; the son does remain forever. So if the Son makes you free, you will be free indeed. I know that you are Abraham's descendants; yet you seek to kill Me, because My word has no place in you. I speak the things which I have seen with *My* Father; therefore you also do the things which you heard from *your* father" (John 8:31–38; see Romans 6:16).

[FAITHFULNESS from faithful]
Setting: On the island of Patmos (in the Aegean Sea about fifty miles southwest of Ephesus in modern Turkey). On the Lord's Day (Sunday), the disciple John encounters the Lord Jesus Christ about fifty years after His resurrection. Jesus communicates a new revelation for the apostle to record for the church in Smyrna and to six other churches in Asia.

"And to the angel of the church in Smyrna write: The first and the last, who was dead, and has come to life, says this: 'I know your tribulation and your poverty (but you are rich), and the blasphemy by those who say they are Jews and are not, but are a synagogue of Satan. Do not fear what you are about to suffer. Behold, the devil is about to cast some of you into prison, so that you will be tested, and you will have tribulation for ten days. Be faithful until death, and I will give you the crown of life. He who has an ear, let him hear what the Spirit says to the churches. He who overcomes will not be hurt by the second death' (Revelation 2:8–11; see Isaiah 44:6; Revelation 1:9, 18; 2:13; 20:6, 14).

[FAITHFULNESS from My faithful one]
Setting: On the island of Patmos (in the Aegean Sea about fifty miles southwest of Ephesus in modern Turkey). On the Lord's Day (Sunday), the disciple John encounters the Lord Jesus Christ about fifty years after His resurrection. Jesus communicates a new revelation for the apostle to record for the church in Pergamum and to six other churches in Asia.

"And to the angel of the church in Pergamum write: The One who has the sharp two-edged sword says this: 'I know where you dwell, where Satan's throne is; and you hold fast My name, and did not deny My faith even in the days of Antipas, My witness, My faithful one, who was killed among you, where Satan dwells. But I have a few things against you, because you have there some who hold the teaching of Balaam, who kept teaching Balak to put a stumbling block before the sons of Israel, to eat things sacrificed to idols and to commit *acts of* immorality. So you also have some who in the same way hold the teaching of the Nicolaitans. Therefore repent; or else I am coming to you quickly, and I will make war against them with the sword of My mouth. He who has an ear, let him hear what the Spirit says to the churches. To him who overcomes, to him I will give *some* of the hidden manna, and I will give him a white stone, and a new name written on the stone which no one knows but he who receives it' (Revelation 2:12–17; see Numbers 25:1–3; Isaiah 62:2; Revelation 1:16; 2:5, 6, 16).

[FAITHFULNESS from faithful]
Setting: On the island of Patmos (in the Aegean Sea about fifty miles southwest of Ephesus in modern Turkey). On the Lord's Day (Sunday), the disciple John encounters the Lord Jesus Christ about fifty years after His resurrection. Jesus communicates a new revelation for the apostle to record for the church in Laodicea and to six other churches in Asia.

"To the angel of the church in Laodicea write: The Amen, the faithful and true Witness, the Beginning of the creation of God, says this: 'I know your deeds, that you are neither cold nor hot; I wish that you were cold or hot. So because you are lukewarm, and neither hot nor cold, I will spit you out of My mouth. Because you say, "I am rich, and have become wealthy, and have need of nothing," and you do not know that you are wretched and miserable and poor and blind and naked, I advise you to buy from Me gold refined by fire so that you may become rich, and white garments so that you may clothe yourself, and *that* the shame of your nakedness will not be revealed; and eye salve to anoint your eyes so that you may see. Those whom I love, I reprove and discipline; therefore be zealous and repent. Behold, I stand at the door and knock; if anyone hears My voice and opens the door, I will come in to him and will dine with him, and he with Me. He who overcomes, I will grant to him to sit down with Me on My throne, as I also overcame and sat down with My Father on His throne. He who has an ear, let him hear what the Spirit says to the churches'" (Revelation 3:14–22; see Proverbs 3:12; Hosea 12:8; John 14:23; 16:33).

FALLEN ANGELS (See DEMONS)

FALSE APOSTLES (Listed under APOSTLES, FALSE)

FALSE CHRISTS (Listed under CHRISTS, FALSE; also see DECEPTION)

FALSE MESSIAHS (See CHRISTS, FALSE; also see DECEPTION)

FALSE PROPHETS (Listed under PROPHETS, FALSE; also see DECEPTION)

FALSE TEACHERS (Listed under TEACHERS, FALSE; also see CHRISTS, FALSE and DECEPTION)

FALSE WITNESS (Listed under WITNESS, FALSE)

FAMILIES, DIVIDED (See DIVISION and HOUSE, DIVIDED)

FAMILY, EARTHLY (See specifics such as BROTHERS; FATHER; HOUSEHOLD; MOTHER; PARENTS; RELATIVES; and SISTERS)

FAMILY, SPIRITUAL (Also see BRETHREN; and BROTHERS)

[SPIRITUAL FAMILY from For whoever does the will of My Father who is in heaven, he is My brother and sister and mother]
Setting: Galilee. Jesus' mother, Mary, and His brothers wait to see Him as He teaches and preaches.

But Jesus answered the one who was telling Him and said, "Who is My mother and who are My brothers?" And stretching out His hand toward His disciples, He said, "Behold, My mother and My brothers! For whoever does the will of My Father who is in heaven, he is My brother and sister and mother" (Matthew 12:48–50; cf. Mark 3:31–35; Luke 8:19–21).

[SPIRITUAL FAMILY from whoever does the will of God, he is My brother and sister and mother]
Setting: Galilee. During the early part of His ministry, having just selected His twelve disciples, after being informed his mother and brothers are waiting to see Him, Jesus explains to the crowd who His true relatives are.

Answering them, He said, "Who are My mother and My brothers?" Looking about at those who were sitting around Him, He said, "Behold My mother and My brothers! For whoever does the will of God, he is My brother and sister and mother" (Mark 3:33–35; cf. Matthew 12:46–50; Luke 8:19–21).

FAMILY CONFLICT (See DIVISION)

FAMINE (Also see FAMINES)

Setting: The synagogue in Jesus' hometown of Nazareth. At the beginning of Jesus' public ministry, He comments to the congregation after reading on the Sabbath from the book of the prophet Isaiah.

And He said to them, "No doubt you will quote this proverb to Me, 'Physician, heal yourself! Whatever we heard was done at Capernaum, do here in your hometown as well.'" And He said, "Truly I say to you, no prophet is welcome in his hometown. But I say to you in truth, there were many widows in Israel in the days of Elijah, when the sky was shut up for three years and six months, when a great famine came over all the land; and yet Elijah was sent to none of them, but only to Zarephath, *in the land* of Sidon, to a woman who was a widow. And there were many lepers in Israel in the time of Elisha the prophet; and none of them was cleansed, but only Naaman the Syrian" (Luke 4:23–27; Jesus refers to 1 Kings 17:1, 9; 2 Kings 5:1–14; see Matthew 13:53–58).

Setting: On the way from Galilee to Jerusalem. Jesus conveys the illustration of the prodigal son because the Pharisees and scribes complain He associates with tax collectors and sinners.

And He said, "A man had two sons. The younger of them said to his father, 'Father, give me the share of the estate that falls to me.' So he divided his wealth between them. And not many days later, the younger son gathered everything together and went on a journey into a distant country, and there he squandered his estate with loose living. Now when he had spent everything, a severe famine occurred in that country, and he began to be impoverished. So he went and hired himself out to one of the citizens of that country, and he sent him into his fields to feed swine. And he would have gladly filled his stomach with the pods that the swine were eating, and no one was giving *anything* to him. But when he came to his senses, he said, 'How many of my father's hired men have more than enough bread, but I am dying here with hunger! I will get up and go to my father, and will say to him, "Father, I have sinned against heaven, and in your sight; I am no longer worthy to be called your son; make me as one of your hired men."' So he got up and came to his father. But while he was still a long way off, his father saw him and felt compassion *for him,* and ran and embraced him and kissed him. And the son said to him, "Father, I have sinned against heaven and in your sight; I am no longer worthy to be called your son.' But the father said to his slaves, 'Quickly bring out the best robe and put it on him, and put a ring on his hand and sandals on his feet; and bring the fattened calf, kill it, and let us eat and celebrate; for this son of mine was dead and has come to life again; he was lost and has been found.' And they began to celebrate. Now his older son was in the field, when he came and approached the house, he heard music and dancing. And he summoned one of the servants and *began* inquiring what these things could be. And he said to him, 'Your brother has come, and your father has killed the fattened calf because he has received him back safe and sound.' But he became angry and was not willing to go in; and his father came out and *began* pleading with him. But he answered and said to his father, 'Look! For so many years I have been serving you and I have never neglected a command of yours; and *yet* you have never given me a young goat, so that I might celebrate with my friends; but when this son of yours came, who has devoured your wealth with prostitutes, you killed the fattened calf for him.' And he said to him, 'Son, you have always been with me, and all that is mine is yours. But we had to celebrate and rejoice, for this brother of yours was dead and *has begun* to live, and was lost and has been found' " (Luke 15:11–32; see Proverbs 29:2).

FAMINE, GREAT (See FAMINE)

FAMINE, SEVERE (See FAMINE)

FAMINES (Also see DISASTERS, NATURAL; and FAMINE)

Setting: The Mount of Olives, just east of Jerusalem. During His discourse, Jesus answers His disciples' questions as to when the temple will be destroyed and Jerusalem overrun, along with the signs of His coming and the end of the age.

And Jesus answered and said to them, "See to it that no one misleads you. For many will come in My name, saying, 'I am the Christ,' and will mislead many. You will be hearing of wars and rumors of wars. See that you are not frightened, for *those things* must take place, but *that* is not yet the end. For nation will rise against nation, and kingdom against kingdom, and in various places there will be famines and earthquakes. But all these things are *merely* the beginning of birth pangs. Then they will deliver you to tribulation, and will kill you, and you will be hated by all nations because of My name. At that time many will fall away and will betray one another and hate one another. Many false prophets will arise and will mislead many. Because lawlessness is increased, most people's love will grow cold. But the one who endures to the end, he will be saved. This gospel of the kingdom shall be preached in the whole world as a testimony to all the nations, and then the end will come" (Matthew 24:4–14; cf. Jeremiah 29:8; Matthew 7:15; 10:17, 22; Mark 13:3–13; Luke 21:7–19; Revelation 6:4).

Setting: The Mount of Olives, east of the temple in Jerusalem. During His discourse, after prophesying the temple's destruction, Jesus responds to questions from Peter, James, John, and Andrew about future events.

And Jesus began to say to them, "See to it that no one misleads you. Many will come in My name, saying, 'I am *He!*' and will mislead many. When you hear of wars and rumors of wars, do not be frightened; *those things* must take place; but *that is* not yet the end. For nation will rise up against nation, and kingdom against kingdom; there will be earthquakes in various places; there will *also be* famines. These things are *merely* the beginning of birth pangs. But be on your guard; for they will deliver you to *the* courts, and you will be flogged in *the* synagogues, and you will stand before governors and kings for My sake, as a testimony to them. The gospel must first be preached to all the nations. When they arrest you and hand you over, do not worry beforehand about what you are to say, but say whatever is given you in that hour; for it is not you who speak, but *it is* the Holy Spirit. Brother will betray brother to death, and a father *his* child; and children will rise up against parents and have them put to death. You will be hated by all because of My name, but the one who endures to the end, he will be saved" (Mark 13:5–13; cf. Matthew 24:4–14; Luke 21:7–19; see Matthew 10:17–22).

Setting: The Mount of Olives, east of the temple in Jerusalem. After ministering in the temple and giving His disciples more details regarding the temple's future destruction, Jesus elaborates about things to come during His Olivet Discourse.

Then He continued by saying to them, "Nation will rise against nation and kingdom against kingdom, and there will be great earthquakes, and in various places plagues and famines; and there will be terrors and great signs from heaven. But before all these things, they will lay their hands on you and will persecute you, delivering you to the synagogues and prisons, bringing you before kings and governors for My name's sake. It will lead to an opportunity for your testimony. So make up your minds not to prepare beforehand to defend yourselves; for I will give you utterance and wisdom which none of your opponents will be able to resist or refute. But you will be betrayed even by parents and brothers and relatives and friends, and they will put *some* of you to death, and you will be hated by all because of My name. Yet not a hair of your head will perish. By your endurance you will gain your lives" (Luke 21:10–19; cf. Matthew 10:19–22; 24:7–14; Mark 13:8–13).

FARM (Also see CROP; and FARMS)

Setting: The temple in Jerusalem. Jesus speaks another parable to the chief priests and elders after they question His authority.

Jesus spoke to them again in parables, saying, "The kingdom of heaven may be compared to a king who gave a wedding feast for his son. And he sent out his slaves to call those who had been invited to the wedding feast, and they were unwilling to come. Again he sent out other slaves saying, 'Tell those who have been invited, "Behold, I have prepared my dinner; my oxen and my fattened livestock are *all* butchered and everything is ready; come to the wedding feast." But they paid no attention and went their way, one to his own farm, another to his business, and the rest seized his slaves and mistreated them and killed them. But the king was enraged, and he sent his armies and destroyed those murderers and set their city on fire. Then he said to his slaves, 'The wedding is ready, but those who were invited were not worthy. 'Go therefore to the main highways, and as many as you find *there,* invite to the wedding feast.' Those slaves went out into the streets and gathered together all they found, both evil and good; and the wedding hall was filled with dinner guests. But when the king came in to look over the dinner guests, he saw a man there who was not dressed in wedding clothes, and he said to him, 'Friend, how did you come in here without wedding clothes?' And the man was speechless. Then the king said to the servants, 'Bind him hand and foot, and throw him into the outer darkness; in that place there will be weeping and gnashing of teeth.' For many are called, but few *are* chosen" (Matthew 22:1–14; cf. Matthew 8:11, 12).

FARMING (See CROP; HARVEST; and PLANTING)

FARMS (Also see CROP; FARM; and REWARDS)

Setting: Judea beyond the Jordan (Perea). Jesus promises rewards to His disciples for their personal sacrifice and commitment to following Him.

And Jesus said to them, "Truly I say to you, that you who have followed Me, in the regeneration when the Son of Man will sit on His glorious throne, you also shall sit upon twelve thrones, judging the twelve tribes of Israel. And everyone who has left houses or brothers or sisters or father or mother or children or farms for My name's sake, will receive many times as much, and will inherit eternal life. But many *who* are first will be last; and *the* last, first" (Matthew 19:28–30; cf. Matthew 6:33; 20:15; Mark 10:29, 30; Luke 18:29, 30; Luke 22:30).

Setting: Judea beyond the Jordan (Perea). After informing a rich man how righteous believers may have treasure in heaven, Jesus conveys to His disciples the reward of those who sacrifice in this life to follow Him.

Jesus said, "Truly I say to you, there is no one who has left house or brothers or sisters or mother or father or children or farms, for My sake and for the gospel's sake, but that he will receive a hundred times as much now in the present age, houses and brothers and sisters and mothers and children and farms, along with persecutions; and in the age to come, eternal life. But many *who are* first will be last, and the last, first" (Mark 10:29–31; cf. Matthew 19:27–30; Luke 18:28–30; see Matthew 6:33).

FAST (See FASTING)

FASTING (FASTING, PRAYER AND is a separate entry; also see FOOD; and HUNGER)

Setting: Galilee. During the early part of His ministry, Jesus preaches the Sermon on the Mount to His disciples and the multitudes.

"Whenever you fast, do not put on a gloomy face as the hypocrites *do,* for they neglect their appearance so that they will be noticed by men when they are fasting. Truly I say to you, they have their reward in full. But you, when you fast, anoint your head and wash your face so that your fasting will not be noticed by men, but by your Father who is in secret; and your Father who sees *what is done* in secret will reward you" (Matthew 6:16–18; see Matthew 6:4, 6).

[FASTING from fast]

Setting: Capernaum near the Sea of Galilee. John the Baptist's disciples ask Jesus why His disciples do not participate in fasting, while they and the Pharisees do.

And Jesus said to them, "The attendants of the bridegroom cannot mourn as long as the bridegroom is with them, can they? But the days will come when the bridegroom is taken away from them, and then they will fast. But no one puts a patch of unshrunk cloth on an old garment; for the patch pulls away from the garment, and a worse tear results. Nor do *people* put new wine into old wineskins; otherwise the wineskins burst, and the wine pours out and the wineskins are ruined; but they put new wine into fresh wineskins, and both are preserved" (Matthew 9:15–17; cf. Mark 2:18–22; Luke 5:33–39).

[FASTING from fast]

Setting: Capernaum. John's disciples and the Pharisees question why Jesus' disciples do not fast when they do.

And Jesus said to them, "While the bridegroom is with them, the attendants of the bridegroom cannot fast, can they? So long as they have the bridegroom with them, they cannot fast. But the days will come when the bridegroom is taken away from them, and then they will fast in that day. No one sews a patch of unshrunk cloth on an old garment; otherwise the patch pulls away from it, the new from the old, and a worse tear results. No one puts new wine into old wineskins; otherwise the wine will burst the skins, and the wine is lost and the skins as *well;* but *one puts* new wine into fresh wineskins" (Mark 2:19–22; cf. Matthew 9:14–17; Luke 5:33–38).

[FASTING from fast]
Setting: The home of Levi (Matthew) in Capernaum. At a reception for Jesus following Levi's call to be a disciple, the Pharisees and their scribes question the Lord about fasting.

And Jesus said to them, "You cannot make the attendants of the bridegroom fast while the bridegroom is with them, can you? But *the* days will come; and when the bridegroom is taken away from them, then they will fast in those days" (Luke 5:34, 35; cf. Matthew 9:14, 15; Mark 2:18–20).

[FASTING from fast]
Setting: On the way from Galilee to Jerusalem. After instructing His disciples about persistence in prayer, Jesus conveys a parable about self-righteousness.

And He also told this parable to some people who trusted in themselves that they were righteous, and viewed others with contempt: "Two men went up into the temple to pray, one a Pharisee and the other a tax collector. The Pharisee stood and was praying this to himself: 'God, I thank You that I am not like other people: swindlers, unjust, adulterers, or even like this tax collector. I fast twice a week; I pay tithes of all that I get.' But the tax collector, standing some distance away, was even unwilling to lift up his eyes to heaven, but was beating his breast, saying, 'God, be merciful to me, the sinner!' I tell you, this man went to his house justified rather than the other; for everyone who exalts himself will be humbled, but he who humbles himself will be exalted" (Luke 18:9–14; see Ezra 9:6; Matthew 6:5, 23:12; Luke 11:42, 16:15; Romans 14:3, 10).

FASTING, PRAYER AND

Setting: Near the mountain where the Transfiguration occurred. Jesus reveals to His disciples why they could not cure a demon-possessed boy.

And He said to them, "Because of the littleness of your faith; for truly I say to you, if you have faith the size of a mustard seed, you will say to this mountain, 'Move from here to there,' and it will move; and nothing will be impossible to you. ["But this kind does not go out except by prayer and fasting"] (Matthew 17:20, 21; cf. Matthew 21:21, 22; Mark 9:28, 29).

FATHER (God; specifics such as FATHER, HEAVENLY; FATHER, MY; and FATHER, YOUR are separate entries)

[FATHER from Him who sent me]
Setting: Galilee. After His twelve disciples observe His ministry, Jesus summons and specifically instructs them about their ministry ahead, which will include rewards.

"He who receives you receives Me, and he who receives Me receives Him who sent me. He who receives a prophet in the name of a prophet shall receive a prophet's reward; and he who receives a righteous man in the name of a righteous man shall receive a righteous man's reward. And whoever in the name of a disciple gives to one of these little ones even a cup of cold water to drink, truly I say to you, he shall not lose his reward" (Matthew 10:40–42; cf. Matthew 25:40, 44, 45; see Mark 9:37).

Setting: Galilee. After pronouncing woes against unrepentant cities as He teaches and preaches, Jesus prays a thanksgiving prayer to His Father in heaven.

At that time Jesus said, "I praise You, Father, Lord of heaven and earth, that you have hidden these things from *the* wise and intelligent and have revealed them to infants. Yes, Father, for this way was well-pleasing in Your sight. All things have been handed over to Me by My Father; and no one knows the Son except the Father; nor does anyone know the Father except the Son, and anyone to whom the Son wills to reveal *Him*" (Matthew 11:25–27; cf. Luke 10:21, 22).

Setting: A house near the Sea of Galilee. Jesus explains the meaning of the Parable of the Wheat and the Tares to His disciples.

And He said, "The one who sows the good seed is the Son of Man, and the field is the world; and as *for* the good seed, these are the sons of the kingdom; and the tares are the sons of the evil *one;* and the enemy who sowed them is the devil, and the harvest is the end of the age; and the reapers are angels. So just as the tares are gathered up and burned with fire, so shall it be at the end of the age. The Son of Man will send forth His angels, and they will gather out of His kingdom all stumbling blocks, and those who commit lawlessness, and will throw them into the furnace of fire; in that place there will be weeping and gnashing of teeth. Then THE RIGHTEOUS WILL SHINE FORTH AS THE SUN in the kingdom of their Father. He who has ears, let him hear" (Matthew 13:37–43, Jesus quotes from Daniel 12:3; cf. Matthew 8:12; 13:50).

Setting: The Mount of Olives, just east of Jerusalem. During His discourse, after answering His disciples' questions as to when the temple will be destroyed and Jerusalem overrun, along with the signs of His coming and the end of the age, Jesus teaches them the Parable of the Fig Tree.

"Now learn the parable from the fig tree: when its branch has already become tender and puts forth its leaves, you know that summer is near; so, you too, when you see all these things, recognize that He is near, *right* at the door. Truly, I say to you, this generation will not pass away until all these things take place. Heaven and earth will pass away, but My words will not pass away. But of that day and hour no one knows, not even the angels of heaven, nor the Son, but the Father alone. For the coming of the Son of Man will be just like the days of Noah. For as in those days before the flood they were eating and drinking, marrying and giving in marriage, until the day that Noah entered the ark, and they did not understand until the flood came and took them all away; so will the coming of the Son of Man be. Then there will be two men in the field; one will be taken and one will be left. Two women *will be* grinding at the mill; one will be taken and one will be left" (Matthew 24:32–41; cf. Mark 13:28–32; Luke 17:34–36; 21:28–33; see Genesis 6:5; 7:7; Matthew 5:18; 10:23; James 5:9).

Setting: On a mountain in Galilee. After rising from the dead and spending some days with His eleven remaining disciples, Jesus conveys the Great Commission to them.

And Jesus came up and spoke to them, saying, "All authority has been given to Me in heaven and on earth. Go therefore and make disciples of all the nations, baptizing them in the name of the Father and the Son and the Holy Spirit, teaching them to observe all that I commanded you; and lo, I am with you always, even to the end of the age" (Matthew 28:18–20; cf. Mark 16:15; see Daniel 7:13).

[FATHER from Him who sent Me]
Setting: Capernaum of Galilee. As Jesus teaches His disciples in private, they ask Him about greatness.

They came to Capernaum; and when He was in the house, He *began* to question them, "What were you discussing on the way?" But they kept silent, for on the way they had discussed with one another which *of them* was the greatest. Sitting down, He called the twelve and said to them, "If anyone wants to be first, he shall be last of all and servant of all." Taking a child, He set him before them, and taking him in His arms, He said to them, "Whoever receives one child like this in My name receives Me; and whoever receives Me does not receive Me, but Him who sent Me" (Mark 9:33–37; cf. Matthew 18:1–5; Luke 9:46–48; see Matthew 20:26; 10:40).

Setting: The Mount of Olives, east of the temple in Jerusalem. During His discourse, after prophesying the temple's destruction, Jesus responds to questions from Peter, James, John, and Andrew about future events.

"Now learn the parable from the fig tree: when its branch has already become tender and puts forth its leaves, you know that summer is near. Even so, you too, when you see these things happening, recognize that He is near, *right* at the door. Truly I say to you, this generation will not pass away until all these things take place. Heaven and earth will pass away, but My words will not pass away. But of the day or hour no one knows, not even the angels in heaven, nor the Son, but the Father *alone*" (Mark 13:28–32; cf. Matthew 24:32–36; Luke 21:28–33).

Setting: Gethsemane on the Mount of Olives, east of the temple in Jerusalem. Jesus agonizes over His impending death, disappointed that His disciples keep falling asleep instead of watching and praying with Him.

They came to a place named Gethsemane; and He said to the disciples, "Sit here until I have prayed." And He took with Him Peter and James and John, and began to be very distressed and troubled. And He said to them, "My soul is deeply grieved to the point of death; remain here and keep watch." And He went a little beyond *them,* and fell to the ground and *began* to pray that if it were possible, the hour might pass Him by. And He was saying, "Abba! Father! All things are possible for You; remove this cup from Me; yet not what I will, but what You will." And He came and found them sleeping, and said to Peter, "Simon, are you asleep? Could you not keep watch for one hour? Keep watching and praying that you may not come into temptation; the spirit is willing, but the flesh is weak" (Mark 14:32–38; cf. Matthew 26:36–41; Luke 22:41–46; see Romans 8:15; Galatians 4:6).

Setting: Galilee. Following Peter's pronouncement that Jesus is the Christ of God, the Lord conveys the demands of discipleship and the hope regarding the kingdom of God.

And He was saying to *them* all, "If anyone wishes to come after Me, he must deny himself, and take up his cross daily and follow Me. For whoever wishes to save his life will lose it, but whoever loses his life for My sake, he is the one who will save it. For what is a man profited if he gains the whole world, and loses or forfeits himself? For whoever is ashamed of Me and My words, the Son of Man will be ashamed of him when He comes in His glory, and *the glory* of the Father and of the holy angels. But I say to you truthfully, there are some of those standing here who will not taste death until they see the kingdom of God" (Luke 9:23–27; cf. Matthew 16:24–26, 28; Mark 8:34–37; see Matthew 10:33, 38, 39).

[FATHER from Him who sent Me]

Setting: Galilee. After Jesus prophesies His death, an argument arises among His disciples as to who is the greatest. The Lord solves the matter by using a child as a teaching illustration.

But Jesus, knowing what they were thinking in their heart, took a child and stood him by His side, and said to them, "Whoever receives this child in My name receives Me, and whoever receives Me receives Him who sent Me; for the one who is least among all of you, this is the one who is great" (Luke 9:47, 48; cf. Matthew 18:1–5; Mark 9:33–47; see Matthew 10:40; Luke 22:24).

Setting: On the way from Galilee to Jerusalem. The Lord responds to a report from the seventy sent out in pairs to every place He Himself will soon visit.

At that very time He rejoiced greatly in the Holy Spirit, and said, "I praise You, O Father, Lord of heaven and earth, that You have hidden these things from *the* wise and intelligent and have revealed them to infants. Yes, Father, for this way was well-pleasing in Your sight. All things have been handed over to Me by My Father, and no one knows who the Son is except the Father, and who the Father is except the Son, and anyone to whom the Son wills to reveal *Him*" (Luke 10:21, 22; cf. Matthew 11:25–27; see Luke 10:1, 17; John 3:35; 10:15).

Setting: On the way from Galilee to Jerusalem via Bethany. After Jesus visits the home of Martha and Mary, one of the disciples asks Him to teach them to pray.

And He said to them, "When you pray, say: 'Father, hallowed be Your name. Your kingdom come. Give us each day our daily bread. And forgive us our sins, for we ourselves also forgive everyone who is indebted to us. And lead us not into temptation'" (Luke 11:2–4; cf. Matthew 6:9–13).

Setting: An upper room in Jerusalem. After celebrating the Passover meal and instructing His disciples to prepare to persevere without Him, with His crucifixion imminent, Jesus proceeds to the Mount of Olives to pray.

And He came out and proceeded as was His custom to the Mount of Olives; and the disciples also followed Him. When He arrived at the place, He said to them, "Pray that you may not enter into temptation." And He withdrew from them about a stone's throw, and He knelt down and *began* to pray, saying, "Father, if You are willing, remove this cup from Me; yet not My will, but Yours be done" (Luke 22:39–42; cf. Matthew 26:36–42; Mark 14:32–49; see Luke 21:37).

Setting: Calvary (Golgotha), just outside Jerusalem. After being arrested, tried, and sentenced to death by crucifixion by Pontius Pilate (Roman governor of Judea), the Lord Jesus, while hanging between two criminals, requests from His Father forgiveness for the crucifiers.

But Jesus was saying, "Father, forgive them; for they do not know what they are doing." And they cast lots, dividing up His garments among themselves (Luke 23:34; see Psalm 22:18; Matthew 27:33–36; Mark 15:22–24; John 19:23–25).

Setting: Golgotha, just outside Jerusalem. While being mocked on the cross, after granting forgiveness to one of the criminals being crucified with Him, who asks to be remembered in Christ's kingdom, Jesus dies.

And Jesus, crying out with a loud voice, said, "Father, INTO YOUR HANDS I COMMIT MY SPIRIT." Having said this, He breathed His last (Luke 23:46, Jesus quotes from Psalm 31:5; cf. Matthew 27:45–50; Mark 15:33–37; John 19:28–30).

Setting: Sychar in Samaria, on the way to Galilee. Jesus interacts with a Samaritan woman at Jacob's well, while His disciples buy food.

Jesus said to her, "Woman, believe Me, an hour is coming when neither in this mountain nor in Jerusalem will you worship the Father. You worship what you do not know; we worship what we know, for salvation is from the Jews. But an hour is coming, and now is, when the true worshipers will worship the Father in spirit and truth; for such people the Father seeks to be His worshipers. God is spirit, and those who worship Him must worship in spirit and truth" (John 4:21–24; see Isaiah 2:3; Philippians 3:3).

[FATHER from Him who sent Me]
Setting: Sychar in Samaria. After Jesus converses with a Samaritan woman at Jacob's well, His disciples return with food. They try to get Jesus to eat but are surprised when He speaks of other food.

Jesus said to them, "My food is to do the will of Him who sent Me and to accomplish His work. Do you not say, 'There are yet four months, and *then* comes the harvest'? Behold, I say to you, lift up your eyes and look on the fields, that they are white for harvest. Already he who reaps is receiving wages and is gathering fruit for life eternal; so that he who sows and he who reaps may rejoice together. For in this *case* the saying is true, 'One sows and another reaps.' I sent you to reap that for which you have not labored; others have labored and you have entered into their labor" (John 4:34–38; see Matthew 9:37, 38; 5:36).

Setting: By the pool of Bethesda in Jerusalem. During the Feast of the Jews, Jesus responds to criticism from the Jewish religious leaders for healing a lame man on the Sabbath and for referring to God as His Father (thereby making Himself equal with God).

Therefore Jesus answered and was saying to them, "Truly, truly, I say to you, the Son can do nothing of Himself, unless *it is* something He sees the Father doing; for whatever the Father does, these things the Son also does in like manner. For the Father loves the Son, and shows Him all things that He Himself is doing; and *the Father* will show Him greater works than these, so that you will marvel. For just as the Father raises the dead and gives them life, even so the Son also gives life to whom He wishes. For not even the Father judges anyone, but He has given all judgment to the Son, so that all will honor the Son even as they honor the Father. He who does not honor the Son does not honor the Father who sent Him" (John 5:19–23; see Luke 10:16; John 3:35; 11:25; 14:12).

[FATHER from Him who sent Me]
Setting: By the pool of Bethesda in Jerusalem. During the Feast of the Jews, Jesus responds to criticism from the Jewish religious leaders for healing a lame man on the Sabbath and for referring to God as His Father (thereby making Himself equal with God).

"Truly, truly, I say to you, he who hears My word, and believes Him who sent Me, has eternal life, and does not come into judgment, but has passed out of death into life" (John 5:24; see John 3:18;12:44).

Setting: Jerusalem. During the Feast of the Jews, Jesus responds to criticism from the Jewish religious leaders by referring to God as His Father (thereby making Himself equal with God) and prophesying His participation in the resurrection and judgment of men.

"Truly, truly, I say to you, an hour is coming and now is, when the dead will hear the voice of the Son of God, and those who hear will live. For just as the Father has life in Himself, even so He gave to the Son also to have life in Himself; and He gave Him authority to execute judgment, because He is *the* Son of Man. Do not marvel at this; for an hour is coming, in which all who are in the tombs will hear His voice, and will come forth; those who did the good *deeds* to a resurrection of life, those who committed the evil *deeds* to a resurrection of judgment" (John 5:25–29; see Daniel 12:2; John 1:4; 11:24).

Setting: Jerusalem. During the Feast of the Jews, Jesus responds to criticism from the Jewish religious leaders by referring to God as His Father (thereby making Himself equal with God) and informing them that God, John the Baptist, and His works all testify to His mission.

"I can do nothing on My own initiative. As I hear, I judge; and My judgment is just, because I do not seek My own will, but the will of Him who sent Me. If I *alone* testify about Myself, My testimony is not true. There is another who testifies of Me, and I know that the testimony which He gives about Me is true. You have sent to John, and he has testified to the truth. But the testimony which I receive is not from man, but I say these things so that you may be saved. He was the lamp that was burning and was shining and you were willing to rejoice for a while in his light. But the testimony which I have is greater than the *testimony of* John; for the works which the Father has given Me to accomplish—the very works that I do—testify about Me, that the Father has sent Me. And the Father who sent Me, He has testified of Me. You have neither heard His voice at any time nor seen His form. You do not have His word abiding in you, for you do not believe Him whom He sent" (John 5:30–38; see Matthew 3:17; Mark 1:4, 5; John 1:7, 15, 32; 4:34; 8:14–16; 10:25, 37, 38).

Setting: Jerusalem. During the Feast of the Jews, Jesus responds to criticism from the Jewish religious leaders by referring to God as His Father (thereby making Himself equal with God) and informing them that God, John the Baptist, His works, and the Scriptures all testify to His mission.

"You search the Scriptures because you think that in them you have eternal life; it is these that testify about Me; and you are unwilling to come to Me so that you may have life. I do not receive glory from men; but I know you, that you do not have the love of God in yourselves. I have come in My Father's name, and you do not receive Me; if another comes in his own name, you will receive him. How can you believe, when you receive glory from one another and you do not seek the glory that is from the *one and* only God? Do not think that I will accuse you before the Father; the one who accuses you is Moses, in whom you have set your hope. For if you believed Moses, you would believe Me, for he wrote about Me. But if you do not believe his writings, how will you believe My words?" (John 5:39–47; see Matthew 24:5; Luke 16:29, 31; 24:27; 9:28; 17:3).

Setting: Capernaum of Galilee. The day after Jesus walks on the Sea of Galilee to join His disciples in a boat, the people He miraculously fed with a lad's five loaves and two fish ask Him how He crossed the water, since He had not entered the boat from land with His disciples.

Jesus answered them and said, "Truly, truly, I say to you, you seek Me, not because you saw signs, but because you ate of the loaves and were filled. Do not work for the food which perishes, but for the food which endures to eternal life, which the Son of Man will give to you, for on Him the Father, God, has set His seal" (John 6:26, 27; see John 3:33).

[FATHER also from Him who sent Me]
Setting: Capernaum. The day after Jesus walks on the Sea of Galilee to join His disciples in a boat, the people He miraculously fed with a lad's five loaves and two fish ask Him to always give them this bread out of heaven.

Jesus said to them, "I am the bread of life; he who comes to Me will not hunger, and he who believes in Me will never thirst. But I said to you that you have seen Me, and yet do not believe. All that the Father gives Me will come to Me, and the one who comes to Me I will certainly not cast out. For I have come down from heaven, not to do My own will, but the will of Him who sent Me. This is the will of Him who sent Me, that of all that He has given Me I lose nothing, but raise it up on the last day. For this is the will of My Father, that everyone who beholds the Son and believes in Him will have eternal life, and I Myself will raise him up on the last day" (John 6:35–40; see John 3:13, 16; 4:13, 14).

Setting: Capernaum of Galilee. After Jesus informs the people He miraculously fed with a lad's five loaves and two fish how they might receive the bread out of heaven, the Jewish religious leaders grumble because Jesus claims He came down out of heaven.

Therefore the Jews were grumbling about Him, because He said, "I am the bread that came down out of heaven." They were saying, "Is not this Jesus, the son of Joseph, whose father and mother we know? How does He now say, 'I have come down out of heaven'?" Jesus answered and said to them, "Do not grumble among yourselves. No one can come to Me unless the Father who sent Me draws him; and I will raise him up on the last day. It is written in the prophets, 'AND THEY SHALL ALL BE TAUGHT OF GOD.' Everyone who has heard and learned from the Father, comes to Me. Not that anyone has seen the Father, except the One who is from God; He has seen the Father. Truly, truly, I say to you, he who believes has eternal life. I am the bread of life. Your fathers ate the manna in the wilderness, and they died. This is the bread which comes down out of heaven, so that one may eat of it and not die. I am the living bread that came down out of heaven; if anyone eats of this bread, he will live forever; and the bread also which I will give for the life of the world is My flesh" (John 6:41–51, Jesus quotes from Isaiah 54:13; see John 1:18, 29; 3:36; 7:27).

Setting: Capernaum of Galilee. After informing the people He miraculously fed with a lad's five loaves and two fish how they might receive the bread out of heaven, the Jewish religious leaders argue with one another when Jesus says He will give His flesh to the world to eat.

So Jesus said to them, "Truly, truly, I say to you, unless you eat the flesh of the Son of Man and drink His blood, you have no life in yourselves. He who eats My flesh and drinks My blood has eternal life, and I will raise him up on the last day. For My flesh is true food, and My blood is true drink. He who eats My flesh and drinks My blood abides in Me, and I in him. As the living Father sent Me, and I live because of the Father, so he who eats Me, he also will live because of Me. This is the bread which came down out of heaven; not as the fathers ate and died; he who eats this bread will live forever" (John 6:53–58; see Matthew 16:16; Luke 4:22; John 3:36; 9:16; 15:4).

Setting: The synagogue at Capernaum of Galilee. After the Jewish religious leaders argue with one another because Jesus says He will give His flesh to the world to eat, some of His disciples also express difficulty with His statements.

But, Jesus, conscious that His disciples grumbled at this, said to them, "Does this cause you to stumble? *What* then if you see the Son of Man ascending to where He was before? It is the Spirit who gives life; the flesh profits nothing; the words that I have spoken to you are spirit and are life. But there are some of you who do not believe." For Jesus knew from the beginning who they were who did not believe, and who it was that would betray Him. And He was saying, "For this reason I have said to you, that no one can come to Me unless it has been granted him from the Father" (John 6:61–65; see Matthew 11:6; 13:11; John 3:13).

[FATHER from Him who sent Me]
Setting: The temple in Jerusalem. While Jesus teaches during the Feast of Booths and causes discussion as to whether He is the Christ, many believe in Him, while the chief priests and Pharisees plan to seize Him.

Therefore Jesus said, "For a little while longer I am with you, then I go to Him who sent Me. You will seek Me, and will not find Me; and where I am, you cannot come" (John 7:33, 34; see John 12:35).

Setting: The temple in Jerusalem. Following the Feast of Booths and the scribes' and Pharisees' failed attempt to stone a woman for adultery, Jesus returns the next day to teach. His enemies question His testimony about Himself.

Jesus answered and said to them, "Even if I testify about Myself, My testimony is true, for I know where I came from and where I am going; but you do not know where I come from or where I am going. You judge according to the flesh; I am not judging anyone. But even if I do judge, My judgment is true; for I am not alone *in it,* but I and the Father who sent Me. Even in your law it has been written that the testimony of two men is true. I am He who testifies about Myself, and the Father who sent Me testifies about Me." So they were saying to Him, "Where is Your Father?" Jesus answered, "You know neither Me nor My Father; if you knew Me, you would know My Father also" (John 8:14–19; see Deuteronomy 17:6; 19:15; Matthew 18:16; John 3:17; 5:30, 37; 7:28).

Setting: The temple treasury in Jerusalem. Following the Feast of Booths and the scribes' and Pharisees' failed attempt to stone a woman for adultery, Jesus returns the next day to teach. They question His testimony about Himself.

So Jesus said, "When you lift up the Son of Man, then you will know that I am *He,* and I do nothing on my own initiative, but I speak these things as the Father taught Me. And He who sent Me is with Me; He has not left Me alone, for I always do the things that are pleasing to Him" (John 8:28, 29; see John 3:14).

[FATHER from Him who sent Me]
Setting: The temple treasury in Jerusalem. After avoiding being stoned by the scribes and Pharisees, Jesus' disciples wonder if blindness is caused by sin as the Lord heals a man born blind.

Jesus answered, "*It was* neither *that* this man sinned, nor his parents; but *it was* so that the works of God might be displayed in him. We must work the works of Him who sent Me as long as it is day; night is coming when no one can work. While I am in the world, I am the Light of the world." When He had said this, He spat on the ground, and made clay of the spittle, and applied the clay to his eyes, and said to him, "Go, wash in the pool of Siloam" (which is translated, Sent). So he went away and washed, and came *back* seeing (John 9:3–7; see John 8:12; 11:4; 12:46).

Setting: Jerusalem. Following the Pharisees' interrogation and dismissal of the formerly blind man Jesus healed on the Sabbath, the Lord conveys the Parable of the Good Shepherd to the Pharisees using figures of speech they do not understand.

So Jesus said to them again, "Truly, truly, I say to you, I am the door of the sheep. All who came before Me are thieves and robbers, but the sheep did not hear them. I am the door; if anyone enters through Me, he will be saved, and will go in and out and find pasture. The thief comes only to steal and kill and destroy; I came that they may have life, and have *it* abundantly. I am the good shepherd; the good shepherd lays down His life for the sheep. He who is a hired hand, and not a shepherd, who is not the owner of the sheep, sees the wolf coming, and leaves the sheep and flees, and the wolf snatches them and scatters *them. He flees* because he is a hired hand and is not concerned about the sheep. I am the good shepherd, and I know My own and My own know Me, even as the Father knows Me and I know the Father; and I lay down My life for the sheep. I have other sheep, which are not of this fold; I must bring them also, and they will hear My voice; and they will become one flock *with* one shepherd. For this reason the Father loves Me, because I lay down My life so that I may take it again. No one has taken it away from Me, but I lay it down on My own initiative. I have authority to take it up again. This commandment I received from My Father" (John 10:7–18; see Isaiah 40:11; 56:8; Jeremiah 23:1; Matthew 11:27).

Setting: Jerusalem. At the Feast of Dedication, just after Jesus conveys the Parable of the Good Shepherd to the Pharisees (who do not understand it), they ask Him plainly if He is the Christ.

Jesus answered them, "I told you, and you do not believe; the works that I do in My Father's name, these testify of Me. But you do not believe because you are not of My sheep. My sheep hear My voice, and I know them, and they follow Me; and I give eternal life to them, and they will never perish; and no one will snatch them out of My hand. My Father, who has given *them* to Me, is greater than all; and no one is able to snatch *them* out of the Father's hand. I and the Father are one" (John 10:25–30; see John 8:47; 17:1, 2, 20, 21).

Setting: Jerusalem. At the Feast of Dedication, the Pharisees desire to stone Him when, in response to the question they pose to Him plainly whether He is the Christ, Jesus claims to be equal with God.

Jesus answered them, "I showed you many good works from the Father; for which of them are you stoning Me?" (John 10:32).

Setting: Jerusalem. At the Feast of Dedication, the Pharisees desire to stone Jesus when, in response to the question they pose to Him plainly whether He is the Christ, He claims to be equal with God.

Jesus answered them, "Has it not been written in your Law, 'I SAID, YOU ARE GODS'? If he called them gods, to whom the word of God came (and the Scripture cannot be broken), do you say of Him, whom the Father sanctified and sent into the world, 'You are blaspheming,' because I said, 'I am the Son of God'? If I do not do the works of My Father, do not believe Me; but if I do them, though you do not believe Me, believe the works, so that you may know and understand that the Father is in Me, and I in the Father" (John 10:34–38, Jesus quotes from Psalm 82:6; see John 14:10, 20).

Setting: Bethany near Jerusalem. After the death of His friend Lazarus, Jesus travels with His disciples from beyond the Jordan to visit Lazarus's sisters, Martha and Mary, and raises Lazarus from the dead.

Jesus said, "Remove the stone." Martha, the sister of the deceased, said to Him, "Lord, by this time there will be a stench, for he has been *dead* four days." Jesus said to her, "Did I not say to you that if you believe, you will see the glory of God?" So they removed the stone. Then Jesus raised His eyes, and said, "Father, I thank You that You have heard Me. I knew that You always hear Me; but because of the people standing around I said it, so that they may believe that you sent Me." When He had said these things, He cried out with a loud voice, "Lazarus, come forth." The man who had died came forth, bound hand and foot with wrappings, and his face was wrapped around with a cloth. Jesus said to them, "Unbind him, and let him go" (John 11:39–44; see Matthew 11:25).

Setting: Jerusalem. Just days before the Passover, with the chief priests and Pharisees plotting to seize Jesus, crowds welcome Him with palm branches and praise, and some Greeks ask to meet Him.

And Jesus answered them, saying, "The hour has come for the Son of Man to be glorified. Truly, truly, I say to you, unless a grain of wheat falls into the earth and dies, it remains alone; but if it dies, it bears much fruit. He who loves his life loses it, and he who hates his life in this world will keep it to life eternal. If anyone serves Me, he must follow Me; and where I am, there My servant will be also; if anyone serves Me, the Father will honor him" (John 12:23–26; see Matthew 10:39).

Setting: Jerusalem. Just days before the Passover, with the chief priests and Pharisees plotting to seize Him, and crowds welcoming Him with palm branches and praise, Jesus expresses anxiety about His upcoming death by crucifixion.

"Now My soul has become troubled; and what shall I say, 'Father, save Me from this hour'? But for this purpose I came to this hour. Father glorify Your name." Then a voice came out of heaven: "I have glorified it, and will glorify it again." So the crowd *of people* who stood by and heard it were saying that it had thundered; others were saying, "An angel has spoken to Him." Jesus answered and said, "This voice has not come for My sake, but for your sakes. Now judgment is upon this world; now the ruler of this world will be cast out. And I, if I am lifted up from the earth, will draw all men to Myself" (John 12:27–32; see Matthew 3:17; 26:38; John 3:14; 6:44; 11:42;14:30).

Setting: Jerusalem. Just days before the Passover, with the chief priests and Pharisees plotting to seize Jesus, who is expressing anxiety about His upcoming death by crucifixion, some believe in Him, while others are rejecting His message.

And Jesus cried out and said, "He who believes in Me, does not believe in Me but in Him who sent Me. He who sees Me sees the One who sent Me. I have come *as* Light into the world, so that everyone who believes in Me will not remain in darkness. If anyone hears My sayings and does not keep them, I do not judge him; for I did not come to judge the world, but to save the world. He who rejects Me and does not receive My sayings, has one who judges him; the word I spoke is what will judge him at the last day. For I did not speak on My own initiative, but the Father Himself who sent Me has given Me a commandment *as to* what to say and what to speak. I know that His commandment is eternal life; therefore the things I speak, I speak just as the Father as told Me" (John 12:44–50; see Matthew 10:40; Luke 10:16; John 1:4; 3:17; 5:19; 6:68; 14:9).

[FATHER from Him who sent me]
Setting: An upper room in Jerusalem. Before the Passover, with His death on the cross nearing, Jesus explains the reason for His vivid example of servanthood in washing His disciples' feet.

So when He had washed their feet, and taken His garments and reclined *at the table* again, He said to them, "Do you know what I have done to you? You call Me Teacher and Lord; and you are right, for *so* I am. If I then, the Lord and the Teacher, washed your feet, you also ought to wash one another's feet. For I gave you an example that you also should do as I did to you. Truly, truly I say to you, a slave is not greater than his master, nor *is* one who is sent greater than the one who sent him. If you know these things, you are blessed if you do them. I do not speak of all of you. I know the ones I have chosen; but *it is* that the Scripture may be fulfilled, 'HE WHO EATS MY BREAD HAS LIFTED UP HIS HEEL AGAINST ME.' From now on I am telling you before *it* comes to pass, so that when it does occur, you may believe that I am *He*. Truly, truly, I say to you, he who receives whomever I send receives Me; and he who receives Me receives Him who sent Me" (John 13:12–20; Jesus quotes from Psalm 41:9; see Matthew 7:24; 10:24, 40; John 8:24; 14:29; 1 Peter 5:3).

Setting: Jerusalem. Before the Passover, as Jesus comforts and gives hope to His disciples regarding their future after He returns to heaven, Thomas asks where He is going and how they will know the way.

Jesus said to him, "I am the way, and the truth, and the life; no one comes to the Father but through Me. If you had known Me, you would have known My Father also; from now on you know Him, and have seen Him" (John 14:6, 7; see John 8:19; 10:9; 11:25).

Setting: Jerusalem. Before the Passover, after answering Thomas' question as to where He is going and how His disciples will know the way, Jesus responds to Philip's request for Him to show them the Father.

Jesus said to him, "Have I been so long with you, and *yet* you have not come to know Me, Philip? He who has seen Me has seen the Father; how *can* you say, 'Show us the Father'? Do you not believe that I am in the Father, and the Father is in Me? The words that I say to you I do not speak on My own initiative, but the Father abiding in Me does His works. Believe Me that I am in the Father and the Father is in Me; otherwise believe because of the works themselves. Truly, truly, I say to you, he who believes in Me, the works that I do, he will do also; and greater *works* than these he will do; because I go to the Father. Whatever you ask in My name, that will I do, so that the Father may be glorified in the Son. If you ask Me anything in My name, I will do *it*" (John 14:9–14; see Matthew 7:7; John 1:14; 5:19, 20, 36; 10:37, 38;15:16).

Setting: Jerusalem. Before the Passover, after responding to Philip's request for Him to show His disciples the Father, Jesus conveys the upcoming role of the Holy Spirit in their lives.

"If you love Me, you will keep My commandments. I will ask the Father, and He will give you another Helper, that He may be with you forever; *that* is the Spirit of truth, whom the world cannot receive, because it does not see Him or know Him, *but* you know Him because He abides with you and will be in you" (John 14:15–17; see John 7:39; 15:26; 1 John 5:3).

Setting: Jerusalem. Before the Passover, after responding to Philip's request for Him to show His disciples the Father, Jesus conveys the upcoming role of the Holy Spirit in their lives.

"I will not leave you as orphans; I will come to you. After a little while the world will no longer see Me, but you *will* see Me; because I live, you will live also. In that day you will know that I am in the Father, and you in Me, and I in you. He who has My commandments and keeps them is the one who loves Me; and he who loves Me will be loved by My Father, and I will love him and will disclose Myself to him" (John 14:18–21; see John 6:57; 10:37, 38; 16:16, 22).

Setting: Jerusalem. Before the Passover, after responding to Philip's request for Him to show His disciples the Father, Jesus conveys the upcoming ministry of the Holy Spirit in their lives.

"These things I have spoken to you while abiding with you. But the Helper, the Holy Spirit, whom the Father will send in My name, He will teach you all things, and bring to your remembrance all that I said to you" (John 14:25, 26; see John 16:13).

Setting: Jerusalem. Before the Passover, after conveying the upcoming ministry of the Holy Spirit in His disciples' lives, Jesus again relates peace, hope, and comfort to them regarding His return to the Father.

"Peace I leave with you; My peace I give to you; not as the world gives do I give to you. Do not let your heart be troubled, nor let it be fearful. You heard that I said to you, 'I go away, and I will come to you.' If you loved Me, you would have rejoiced because I go to the Father, for the Father is greater than I. Now I have told you before it happens, so that when it happens, you may believe. I will not speak much more with you, for the ruler of the world is coming, and he has nothing in Me; but so that the world may know that I love the Father, I do exactly as the Father commanded Me. Get up, let us go from here" (John 14:27–31; see John 10:18, 29; 12:31; 13:19; 16:33).

Setting: Jerusalem. Before the Passover, after conveying the upcoming ministry of the Holy Spirit in His disciples' lives with His imminent departure from them, Jesus explains He is the vine and they are the branches.

"I am the true vine, and My Father is the vinedresser. Every branch in Me that does not bear fruit, He takes away; and every *branch* that bears fruit, He prunes it so that it may bear more fruit. You are already clean because of the word which I have spoken to you. Abide in Me, and I in you. As the branch cannot bear fruit of itself unless it abides in the vine, so neither *can* you unless you abide in Me. I am the vine, you are the branches; he who abides in Me and I in him, he bears much fruit, for apart from Me you can do nothing. If anyone does not abide in Me, he is thrown away as a branch and dries up; and they gather them, and cast them into the fire and they are burned. If you abide in Me, and My words abide in you, ask whatever you wish, and it will be done for you. My Father is glorified by this, that you bear much fruit, and *so* prove to be My disciples. Just as the Father has loved Me, I have also loved you; abide in My love. If you keep My commandments, you will abide in My love; just as I have kept My Father's commandments and abide in His love. These things I have spoken to you so that My joy may be in you, and *that* your joy may be made full" (John 15:1–11; see Matthew 5:16; 7:7; John 3:29, 35; 6:56; 8:29, 31; 13:10; 15:16).

Setting: Jerusalem. Before the Passover, with His upcoming departure in mind, after explaining He is the vine and His disciples are the branches, Jesus instructs them to love one another.

"This is My commandment, that you love one another, just as I have loved you. Greater love has no one than this, that one lay down his life for his friends. You are My friends if you do what I command you. No longer do I call you slaves, for the slave does not know what his master is doing; but I have called you friends, for all things that I have heard from My Father I have made known to you. You did not choose Me but I chose you, and appointed you that you would go and bear fruit, and *that* your fruit would remain, so that whatever you ask of the Father in My name He may give to you. This I command you, that you love one another" (John 15:12–17; see Matthew 12:50; John 6:70; 8:26; 10:11; 13:34).

Setting: Jerusalem. Before the Passover, with His upcoming departure in mind, after explaining He is the vine and His disciples are the branches, Jesus elaborates more about the future ministry of the Holy Spirit.

"When the Helper comes, whom I will send to you from the Father, *that is* the Spirit of truth who proceeds from the Father, He will testify about Me, and you *will* testify also, because you have been with Me from the beginning" (John 15:26, 27; see Luke 24:48; John 14:16).

Setting: Jerusalem. Before the Passover, after explaining He is the vine and His disciples are the branches, Jesus warns His disciples of the persecution they will face after His departure to heaven.

"These things I have spoken to you so that you may be kept from stumbling. They will make you outcasts from the synagogue, but an hour is coming for everyone who kills you to think that he is offering service to God. These things they will do because they have not known the Father or Me. But these things I have spoken to you, so that when their hour comes, you may remember that

I told you of them. These things I did not say to you at the beginning, because I was with you" (John 16:1–4; see John 8:19, 55; 9:22; 13:19; 15:18–27).

Setting: Jerusalem. Before the Passover, after warning His disciples of the persecution they will face after His departure to heaven, Jesus elaborates about the coming ministry of the Holy Spirit.

"But now I am going to Him who sent Me; and none of you asks Me, 'Where are You going?' But because I have said these things to you, sorrow has filled your heart. But I tell you the truth, it is to your advantage that I go away; for if I do not go away, the Helper will not come to you; but if I go, I will send Him to you. And He, when He comes, will convict the world concerning sin and righteousness and judgment; concerning sin, because they do not believe in Me; and concerning righteousness, because I go to the Father and you no longer see Me; and concerning judgment, because the ruler of this world has been judged" (John 16:5–11; see John 7:33; 12:31; 14:1, 16; 15:22, 24).

Setting: Jerusalem. Before the Passover, after warning His disciples of the persecution they will face after His departure to heaven, Jesus elaborates about the upcoming ministry of the Holy Spirit.

"I have many more things to say to you, but you cannot bear *them* now. But when He, the Spirit of truth, comes, He will guide you into all the truth; for He will not speak on His own initiative, but whatever He hears, He will speak; and He will disclose to you what is to come. He will glorify Me, for He will take of Mine and will disclose *it* to you. All things that the Father has are Mine; therefore I said that He takes of Mine and will disclose *it* to you (John 16:12–15; see John 7:39; 14:17, 26; 17:10).

Setting: Jerusalem. Before the Passover, after warning His disciples of the persecution they will face after His departure to heaven, empathizing with their sadness over His prophecies, Jesus gives them hope for the future.

"A little while, and you will no longer see Me; and again a little while, and you will see Me." *Some* of His disciples then said to one another, "What is this thing He is telling us, 'A little while, and you will not see Me; and again a little while, and you will see Me'; and, 'because I go to the Father'?" So they were saying, "What is this that He says, 'A little while'? We do not know what He is talking about." Jesus knew that they wished to question Him, and He said to them, "Are you deliberating together about this, that I said, 'A little while, and you will not see Me, and again a little while, and you will see Me'? Truly, truly, I say to you, that you will weep and lament, but the world will rejoice; you will grieve, but your grief will be turned into joy. Whenever a woman is in labor she has pain, because her hour has come; but when she gives birth to the child, she no longer remembers the anguish because of the joy that a child has been born into the world. Therefore you too have grief now; but I will see you again, and your heart will rejoice, and no one *will* take your joy away from you" (John 16:16–22; see Mark 9:32; Luke 23:27; John 14:18–24; 16:5, 6; 20:20).

Setting: Jerusalem. Before the Passover, after empathizing with His disciples' sadness over His prophecies and giving them the hope for the future, Jesus conveys promises about praying in His name.

"In that day you will not question Me about anything. Truly, truly, I say to you, if you ask the Father for anything in My name, He will give it to you. Until now you have asked for nothing in My name; ask and you will receive, so that your joy may be made full. These things I have spoken to you in figurative language; an hour is coming when I will no longer speak to you in figurative language, but will tell you plainly of the Father. In that day you will ask in My name, and I do not say to you that I will request of the Father on your behalf; for the Father Himself loves you, because you have loved Me and have believed that I came forth from the Father. I came forth from the Father and have come into the world; I am leaving the world again and going to the Father" (John 16:23–28; see Matthew 13:34; John 8:42; 13:1, 3; 14:14, 21, 23; 15:16).

Setting: Jerusalem. Before the Passover, after conveying promises about praying in His name, Jesus prophesies His disciples' scattering and gives them assurance that in the midst of tribulation they will have His peace.

"Jesus answered them, "Do you now believe? Behold, an hour is coming, and has *already* come, for you to be scattered, each to his own *home,* and to leave Me alone; and *yet* I am not alone, because the Father is with Me. These things I have spoken to you, so that in Me you may have peace. In the world you have tribulation, but take courage, I have overcome the world" (John 16:31–33; see Zechariah 13:7; John 8:29; 14:27; Romans 8:37).

Setting: Jerusalem. Before the Passover, after giving His disciples assurance that in the midst of tribulation they will have His peace, Jesus prays His high-priestly prayer.

Jesus spoke these things; and lifting up His eyes to heaven, He said, "Father, the hour has come; glorify Your Son, that the Son may glorify You, even as You gave Him authority over all flesh, that to all whom You have given Him, He may give eternal life. This is eternal life, that they may know You, the only true God, and Jesus Christ whom You have sent. I glorified You on the earth, having accomplished the work which you have given Me to do. Now, Father, glorify Me together with Yourself, with the glory which I had with You before the world was. I have manifested Your name to the men whom You gave Me out of the world; they were Yours and You gave them to Me, and they have kept Your word. Now they have come to know that everything You have given Me is from You; for the words which You gave Me I have given to them; and they received *them* and truly understood that I came forth from You, and they believed You sent Me. I ask on their behalf; I do not ask on behalf of the world, but of those whom You have given Me; for they are Yours; and all things that are Mine are Yours, and Yours are Mine; and I have been glorified in them. I am no longer in the world; and yet they themselves are in the world, and I come to You. Holy Father, keep them in Your name, *the name* which You have given Me, that they may be even as We *are.* While I was with them, I was keeping them in Your name which You have given Me; and I guarded them and not one of them perished but the son of perdition, so that the Scripture would be fulfilled" (John 17:1–12; see Luke 22:32; John 1:1; 3:35; 4:34; 5:44; 6:37–39, 70; 8:42; 11:41; 12:49; 13:18, 31; 16:15; 17:20; Philippians 2:9).

Setting: Jerusalem. Before the Passover, after giving His disciples assurance that in the midst of tribulation they will have His peace, Jesus continues praying His high-priestly prayer.

"But now I come to You; and these things I speak in the world so that they may have My joy made full in themselves. I have given them Your word; and the world has hated them, because they are not of the world, even as I am not of the world. I do not ask You to take them out of the world, but to keep them from the evil *one.* They are not of the world, even as I am not of the world. Sanctify them in the truth; Your word is truth. As You sent Me into the world, I also have sent them into the world. For their sakes I sanctify Myself, that they themselves also may be sanctified in truth. I do not ask on behalf of these alone, but for those also who believe in Me through their word; that they may all be one; even as You, Father, *are* in Me and I in You, that they also maybe in Us, so that the world may believe that You sent Me" (John 17:13–21; see Matthew 10:5, 38; John 7:33; 15:3, 11, 19).

Setting: Jerusalem. Before the Passover, after giving His disciples assurance that in the midst of tribulation they will have His peace, Jesus continues praying His high-priestly prayer.

"The glory which You have given Me I have given to them, that they may be one, just as We are one; I in them and You in Me, that they may be perfected in unity, so that the world may know that you sent Me, and loved them, even as You have loved Me. Father, I desire that they also, whom You have given Me, be with Me where I am, so that they may see My glory which You have given Me, for You loved Me before the foundation of the world. O righteous Father, although the world has not known You, yet I have known You; and these have known that You sent Me; and I have made Your name known to them, and will make it known, so that the love with which You loved Me may be in them, and I in them" (John 17:22–26; see Matthew 25:34; John 1:14, 10.38, 15.9, 16:27).

Setting: The garden across the ravine of the Kidron. Simon Peter attempts to defend Jesus with a sword during Judas' betrayal accompanied by a Roman cohort, officers from the chief priests, and the Pharisees.

So Jesus said to Peter, "Put the sword into the sheath; the cup which the Father has given Me, shall I not drink it?" (John 18:11; see Matthew 20:22; 26:52; Luke 22:51).

Setting: In Jerusalem, the risen Jesus first appears to Mary Magdalene after she tells Simon Peter and John about the empty tomb where Jesus had been the day before the Sabbath. He had died on the cross for the sins of the world.

Jesus said to her, "Woman, why are you weeping? Whom are you seeking?" Supposing Him to be the gardener, she said to Him, "Sir, if you have carried Him away, tell me where you have laid Him, and I will take Him away." Jesus said to her, "Mary!" She turned and said to Him in Hebrew "Rabboni!" (which means, Teacher). Jesus said to her, "Stop clinging to Me, for I have not yet ascended to the Father; but go to My brethren and say to them, 'I ascend to My Father and your Father, and My God and Your God'" (John 20:15–17; see Mark 16:9–11; John 7:33; 19:31–42).

Setting: Jerusalem. After Mary Magdalene encounters the risen Jesus in the morning, that evening He stands in the midst of His disciples (with the exception of Thomas), in hiding behind closed doors due to fear of the Jewish religious leadership.

So when it was evening on that day, the first *day* of the week, and when the doors were shut where the disciples were, for fear of the Jews, Jesus came and stood in their midst and said to them, "Peace *be* with you." And when He had said this, He showed them both His hands and His side. The disciples then rejoiced when they saw the Lord. So Jesus said to them again, "Peace *be* with you; as the Father has sent Me, I also send you." And when He had said this, He breathed on them and said to them, "Receive the Holy Spirit. If you forgive the sins of any, *their sins* have been forgiven them; if you retain the *sins* of any, they have been retained" (John 20:19–23; cf. Luke 24:36–43; see Matthew 16:19; Mark 16:14).

Setting: Jerusalem. Luke, writing in Acts, presents quotes from Jesus' post-resurrection appearances, in which He responds to His disciples' question if He is about to restore the kingdom to Israel.

He said to them, "It is not for you to know times or epochs which the Father has fixed by His own authority; but you will receive power when the Holy Spirit has come upon you; and you shall be My witnesses both in Jerusalem, and in all Judea and Samaria, and even to the remotest part of the earth" (Acts 1:7, 8; see Luke 24:48, 49; Acts 2:1–4).

FATHER (human; also see FATHERS)

Setting: Galilee. After His disciples observe His ministry, Jesus summons and specifically instructs them about the upcoming difficulties of *their* ministry to the people of Israel.

"Brother will betray brother to death, and a father *his* child; and children will rise up against parents and cause them to be put to death. You will be hated by all because of My name, but it is the one who has endured to the end who will be saved. But whenever they persecute you in one city, flee to the next; for truly I say to you, you will not finish *going through* the cities of Israel until the Son of Man comes" (Matthew 10:21–23; cf. Matthew 10:35, 36; 16:27, 28; 24:9).

Setting: Galilee. After His disciples observe His ministry, Jesus summons and specifically instructs them about their ministry hardships ahead involving true discipleship.

"Do not think that I came to bring peace on the earth; I did not come to bring peace, but a sword. For I came to SET A MAN AGAINST HIS FATHER, AND A DAUGHTER AGAINST HER MOTHER, AND A DAUGHTER-IN-LAW AGAINST HER MOTHER-IN-LAW; and A MAN'S ENEMIES WILL BE THE MEMBERS OF HIS HOUSEHOLD" (Matthew 10:34–36; Jesus quotes from Micah 7:6; cf. Luke 12:51–53).

Setting: Galilee. After His twelve disciples observe His ministry, Jesus summons and specifically instructs them about their ministry ahead involving true discipleship.

"He who loves father or mother more than Me is not worthy of Me; and he who loves son or daughter more than Me is not worthy of Me. And he who does not take his cross and follow after Me is not worthy of Me. He who has found his life will lose it, and he who has lost his life for My sake will find it" (Matthew 10:37–39; cf. Matthew 16:24, 25).

Setting: Galilee. Pharisees and scribes from Jerusalem question Jesus about His disciples' lack of obedience to tradition and the commandments.

And He answered and said to them, "Why do you yourselves transgress the commandment of God for the sake of tradition? For God said, 'HONOR YOUR FATHER AND MOTHER,' and, 'HE WHO SPEAKS EVIL OF FATHER OR MOTHER IS TO BE PUT TO DEATH.' But you say, 'Whoever says to *his* father or mother, "Whatever I have that would help you has been given *to God*," he is not to honor his father or mother.' And *by this* you invalidated the word of God for the sake of your tradition. You hypocrites, rightly did Isaiah prophesy of you: 'THIS PEOPLE HONORS ME WITH THEIR LIPS, BUT THEIR HEART IS FAR AWAY FROM ME. BUT IN VAIN DO THEY WORSHIP ME, TEACHING AS DOCTRINES THE PRECEPTS OF MEN' "(Matthew 15:3–9, Jesus quotes from Exodus 20:12, 21:17, Leviticus 20:9; Isaiah 29:13; cf. Mark 7:5–7; see Colossians 2:22).

Setting: Judea beyond the Jordan (Perea). After Jesus replies to Peter's question about forgiveness, the Pharisees test Jesus in front of a large crowd with a question about divorce.

And He answered and said, "Have you not read that He who created *them* from the beginning MADE THEM MALE AND FEMALE, and said, 'FOR THIS REASON A MAN SHALL LEAVE HIS FATHER AND MOTHER AND BE JOINED TO HIS WIFE, AND THE TWO SHALL BECOME ONE FLESH'? So they are no longer two, but one flesh. What therefore God has joined together, let no man separate" (Matthew 19:4–6, Jesus quotes from Genesis 1:27; 2:24; cf. Mark 10:5–9; see 1 Timothy 2:14).

Setting: Judea beyond the Jordan (Perea). Jesus shares with a rich, young ruler how he can obtain eternal life.

And He said to him, "Why are you asking Me about what is good? There is *only* One who is good; but if you wish to enter into life, keep the commandments." *Then* he said to Him, 'Which ones?' And Jesus said, "YOU SHALL NOT COMMIT MURDER; YOU SHALL NOT COMMIT ADULTERY; YOU SHALL NOT STEAL; YOU SHALL NOT BEAR FALSE WITNESS; HONOR YOUR FATHER AND MOTHER; and YOU SHALL LOVE YOUR NEIGHBOR AS YOURSELF." The young man said to Him, "All these things I have kept; what am I still lacking?" Jesus said to him, "If you wish to complete go *and* sell your possessions and give to *the* poor, and you will have treasure in heaven; and come, follow Me" (Matthew 19:16–22, Jesus quotes from Exodus 20:13–15; Leviticus 19:18; cf. Leviticus 18:5; Mark 10:17–21; Luke 10:25–28; 12:33; 18:18–24).

Setting: Judea beyond the Jordan (Perea). Jesus promises rewards to His disciples for their personal sacrifice and commitment to following Him.

And Jesus said to them, "Truly I say to you, that you who have followed Me, in the regeneration when the Son of Man will sit on His glorious throne, you also shall sit upon twelve thrones, judging the twelve tribes of Israel. And everyone who has left houses or brothers or sisters or father or mother or children or farms for My name's sake, will receive many times as much, and will inherit eternal life. But many *who* are first will be last; and *the* last, first" (Matthew 19:28–30; cf. Matthew 6:33; 20:15; Mark 10:29, 30; Luke 18:29, 30; 22:30).

Setting: The temple in Jerusalem. Jesus delivers a parable to the chief priests and elders after they question His authority.

"But what do you think? A man had two sons, and he came to the first and said, 'Son, go work today in the vineyard.' And he answered, 'I will not'; but afterward he regretted it and went. The man came to the second and said the same thing; and he answered, 'I *will*, sir'; but he did not go. Which of the two sons did the will of his father?" They said, "The first." Jesus said to them, "Truly, I say to you that the tax collectors and prostitutes will get into the kingdom of God before you. For John came to you in the way of righteousness and you did not believe him; but the tax collectors and prostitutes did believe him; and you, seeing *this*, did not even feel remorse afterward so as to believe him" (Matthew 21:28–32; cf. Luke 7:29, 30, 37–50).

Setting: The temple in Jerusalem. Jesus exposes the truth about Pharisaism to the crowds and His disciples after the Jewish religious leaders test Him with questions.

Then Jesus spoke to the crowds and to His disciples, saying: "The scribes and the Pharisees have seated themselves in the chair of Moses; therefore all that they tell you, do and observe, but do not do according to their deeds; for they say *things* and do not do *them.* They tie up heavy burdens and lay them on men's shoulders, but they themselves are unwilling to move them with *so much as* a finger. But they do all their deeds to be noticed by men; for they broaden their phylacteries and lengthen their tassels *of their garments.* They love the place of honor at banquets and the chief seats in the synagogues, and respectful greetings in the market places, and being called Rabbi by men. But do not be called Rabbi; for One is your Teacher, and you are all brothers. Do not call *anyone* on earth your father; for One is your Father, He who is in heaven. Do not be called leaders; for One is your Leader, *that is,* Christ. But the greatest among you shall be your servant. Whoever exalts himself shall be humbled; and whoever humbles himself shall be exalted" (Matthew 23:1–12; cf. Matthew 20:26; Mark 12:38–40; Luke 20:46, 47; see Exodus 13:9; Deuteronomy 33:3; Matthew 6:1, 5, 6, 9, 16; Mark 14:11; Luke 11:43; 14:11).

Setting: Galilee. The Pharisees and some of the scribes from Jerusalem question why Jesus' disciples do not follow the tradition of ceremonial hand cleansing before eating bread.

And He said to them, "Rightly did Isaiah prophesy of you hypocrites, as it is written: 'THIS PEOPLE HONORS ME WITH THEIR LIPS, BUT THEIR HEART IS FAR AWAY FROM ME. BUT IN VAIN DO THEY WORSHIP ME, TEACHING AS DOCTRINES THE PRECEPTS OF MEN.' Neglecting the commandment of God, you hold to the tradition of men." He was also saying to them, "You are experts at setting aside the commandment of God in order to keep tradition. For Moses said, 'HONOR YOUR FATHER AND YOUR MOTHER'; and, 'HE WHO SPEAKS EVIL OF FATHER OR MOTHER, IS TO BE PUT TO DEATH'; but you say, 'If a man says to *his* father or *his* mother, whatever I have that would help you is Corban (that is to say, given *to God*),' you no longer permit him to do anything for *his* father or *his* mother; *thus* invalidating the word of God by your tradition which you have handed down; and you do many things such as that" (Mark 7:6–13, Jesus quotes from Exodus 20:12; 21:17; Isaiah 29:13; cf. Matthew 15:1–6).

Setting: Judea beyond the Jordan (Perea). Jesus teaches the crowds gathered around Him about divorce after the Pharisees test Him with questions about this subject.

And He answered and said to them, "What did Moses command you?" They said, "Moses permitted a *man* TO WRITE A CERTIFICATE OF DIVORCE AND SEND *her* AWAY." But Jesus said to them, "Because of your hardness of heart he wrote you this commandment. But from the beginning of creation, *God* MADE THEM MALE AND FEMALE. FOR THIS REASON A MAN SHALL LEAVE HIS FATHER AND MOTHER, AND THE TWO SHALL BECOME ONE FLESH; so they are no longer two, but one flesh. What therefore God has joined together, let no man separate. In the house the disciples *began* questioning Him about this again. And He said to them, "Whoever divorces his wife and marries another woman commits adultery against her; and if she herself divorces her husband and marries another man, she is committing adultery" (Mark 10:3–12, Jesus quotes from Genesis 1:27; 2:24; cf. Matthew 19:1–9; see Deuteronomy 24:1–3; Matthew 5:32; see Romans 7:2, 3; 1 Corinthians 7:10, 11, 13, 39; 1 Timothy 2:14).

Setting: Galilee. After His disciples observe His ministry, Jesus summons and specifically instructs them about the upcoming difficulties of *their* ministry to the people of Israel.

"Brother will betray brother to death, and a father *his* child; and children will rise up against parents and cause them to be put to death. You will be hated by all because of My name, but it is the one who has endured to the end who will be saved. But whenever they persecute you in one city, flee to the next; for truly I say to you, you will not finish *going through* the cities of Israel until the Son of Man comes" (Matthew 10:21–23; cf. Matthew 10:35, 36; 16:27, 28; 24:9).

Setting: Judea beyond the Jordan (Perea). After demonstrating to His disciples the importance of little children, Jesus encounters a rich man seeking eternal life.

And Jesus said to him, "Why do you call Me good? No one is good except God alone. You know the commandments, 'DO NOT MURDER, DO NOT COMMIT ADULTERY, DO NOT STEAL, DO NOT BEAR FALSE WITNESS, Do not defraud, HONOR YOUR FATHER AND MOTHER.'" And he said to Him, "Teacher, I have kept all these things from my youth up." Looking at him, Jesus felt a love for him and said to him, "One thing you lack: go and sell all you possess and give to the poor, and you will have treasure in heaven; and come, follow Me" (Mark 10:18–21; Jesus quotes from Exodus 20:12–16; cf. Matthew 19:16–22; Luke 18:18–24; see Matthew 6:20; Mark 10:17, 22).

Setting: Judea beyond the Jordan (Perea). After informing a rich man how righteous believers may have treasure in heaven, Jesus conveys to His disciples the reward of those who sacrifice in this life to follow Him.

Jesus said, "Truly I say to you, there is no one who has left house or brothers or sisters or mother or father or children or farms, for My sake and for the gospel's sake, but that he will receive a hundred times as much now in the present age, houses and brothers and sisters and mothers and children and farms, along with persecutions; and in the age to come, eternal life. But many *who are* first will be last, and the last, first" (Mark 10:29–31; cf. Matthew 19:27–30; Luke 18:28–30; see Matthew 6:33).

Setting: The Mount of Olives, east of the temple in Jerusalem. During His discourse, after prophesying the temple's destruction, Jesus responds to questions from Peter, James, John, and Andrew about future events.

And Jesus began to say to them, "See to it that no one misleads you. Many will come in My name, saying, 'I am *He!*' and will mislead many. When you hear of wars and rumors of wars, do not be frightened; *those things* must take place; but *that is* not yet the end. For nation will rise up against nation, and kingdom against kingdom; there will be earthquakes in various places; there will *also be* famines. These things are *merely* the beginning of birth pangs. But be on your guard; for they will deliver you to *the* courts, and you will be flogged in *the* synagogues, and you will stand before governors and kings for My sake, as a testimony to them. The gospel must first be preached to all the nations. When they arrest you and hand you over, do not worry beforehand about what you are to say, but say whatever is given you in that hour; for it is not you who speak, but *it is* the Holy Spirit. Brother will betray brother to death, and a father *his* child; and children will rise up against parents and have them put to death. You will be hated by all because of My name, but the one who endures to the end, he will be saved" (Mark 13:5–13; cf. Matthew 24:4–14; Luke 21:7–19; see Matthew 10:17–22; Mark 13:3, 4).

Setting: On the way from Galilee to Jerusalem. After clarifying a parable for Peter and the crowd, Jesus conveys how a relationship with Him divides families.

"I have come to cast fire upon the earth; and how I wish it were already kindled! But I have a baptism to undergo, and how distressed I am until it is accomplished! Do you suppose that I came to grant peace on earth? I tell you, no, but rather division; for from now on five *members* in one household will be divided, three against two and two against three. They will be divided, father against son and son against father, mother against daughter, and daughter against mother, mother-in-law against daughter-in-law and daughter-in-law against mother-in-law" (Luke 12:49–53; cf. Matthew 10:34–36; see Micah 7:6; Mark 10:38).

Setting: On the way from Galilee to Jerusalem. After responding to a guest's proclamation about the blessings of eating bread in the kingdom of God, Jesus presents to large crowds the demands of discipleship.

Now large crowds were going along with Him; and He turned and said to them, "If anyone comes to Me, and does not hate his own father and mother and wife and children and brothers and sisters, yes, and even his own life, he cannot be My disciple. Whoever does not carry his own cross and come after Me cannot be My disciple. For which one of you, when he wants to build a tower, does not first sit down and calculate the cost to see if he has enough to complete it? Otherwise, when he has laid a foundation and is not able to finish, all who observe it begin to ridicule him, saying, 'This man began to build and was not able to finish.' Or what king, when he sets out to meet another king in battle, will not first sit down and consider whether he is strong enough with ten thousand *men* to encounter the one coming against him with twenty thousand? Or else, while the other is still far away, he sends a delegation and asks for terms of peace. So then, none of you can be My disciple who does not give up all his possessions. Therefore, salt is good; but if even salt has become tasteless, with what will it be seasoned? It is useless either for the soil or for the manure pile; it is thrown out. He who has ears to hear, let him hear" (Luke 14:25–35; cf. Matthew 5:13; 10:37–39; see Proverbs 20:18; Philippians 3:7).

Setting: On the way from Galilee to Jerusalem. Jesus conveys the illustration of the prodigal son because the Pharisees and scribes complain He associates with tax collectors and sinners.

And He said, "A man had two sons. The younger of them said to his father, 'Father, give me the share of the estate that falls to me.' So he divided his wealth between them. And not many days later, the younger son gathered everything together and went

on a journey into a distant country, and there he squandered his estate with loose living. Now when he had spent everything, a severe famine occurred in that country, and he began to be impoverished. So he went and hired himself out to one of the citizens of that country, and he sent him into his fields to feed swine. And he would have gladly filled his stomach with the pods that the swine were eating, and no one was giving *anything* to him. But when he came to his senses, he said, 'How many of my father's hired men have more than enough bread, but I am dying here with hunger! I will get up and go to my father, and will say to him, "Father, I have sinned against heaven, and in your sight; I am no longer worthy to be called your son; make me as one of your hired men."' So he got up and came to his father. But while he was still a long way off, his father saw him and felt compassion *for him,* and ran and embraced him and kissed him. And the son said to him, "Father, I have sinned against heaven and in your sight; I am no longer worthy to be called your son.' But the father said to his slaves, 'Quickly bring out the best robe and put it on him, and put a ring on his hand and sandals on his feet; and bring the fattened calf, kill it, and let us eat and celebrate; for this son of mine was dead and has come to life again; he was lost and has been found.' And they began to celebrate. Now his older son was in the field, when he came and approached the house, he heard music and dancing. And he summoned one of the servants and *began* inquiring what these things could be. And he said to him, 'Your brother has come, and your father has killed the fattened calf because he has received him back safe and sound.' But he became angry and was not willing to go in; and his father came out and *began* pleading with him. But he answered and said to his father, 'Look! For so many years I have been serving you and I have never neglected a command of yours; and *yet* you have never given me a young goat, so that I might celebrate with my friends; but when this son of yours came, who has devoured your wealth with prostitutes, you killed the fattened calf for him.' And he said to him, 'Son, you have always been with me, and all that is mine is yours. But we had to celebrate and rejoice, for this brother of yours was dead and *has begun* to live, and was lost and has been found' " Luke 15:11–32; see Proverbs 29:2).

Setting: On the way from Galilee to Jerusalem. After responding to the Pharisees' scoffing at His teaching His disciples about stewardship and the permanence of the Law, Jesus conveys the story of the rich man and Lazarus.

"Now there was a rich man, and he habitually dressed in purple and fine linen, joyously living in splendor every day. And a poor man named Lazarus was laid at his gate, covered with sores, and longing to be fed with the *crumbs* which were falling from the rich man's table; besides, even the dogs were coming and licking his sores. Now the poor man died and was carried away by the angels to Abraham's bosom; and the rich man also died and was buried. In Hades he lifted up his eyes, being in torment, and saw Abraham far away and Lazarus in his bosom. And he cried out and said, 'Father Abraham, have mercy on me, and send Lazarus so that he may dip the tip of his finger in water and cool off my tongue, for I am in agony in this flame.' But Abraham said, 'Child, remember that during your life you received your good things, and likewise Lazarus bad things; but now he is being comforted here, and you are in agony. And besides all this, between us and you there is a great chasm fixed, so that those who wish to come over from here to you will not be able, and *that* none may cross over from there to us.' And he said, 'Then I beg you, father, that you send him to my father's house—for I have five brothers—in order that he may warn them, so that they will not also come to this place of torment.' But Abraham said, 'They have Moses and the Prophets; let them hear them.' But he said, 'No, father Abraham, but if someone goes to them from the dead, they will repent!' But he said to him, 'If they do not listen to Moses and the Prophets, they will not be persuaded even if someone rises from the dead' " (Luke 16:19–31; see Luke 3:8; 6:24; 16:1, 14).

Setting: On the way from Galilee to Jerusalem. After speaking of the importance of children, Jesus responds to a ruler's question about inheriting eternal life.

A ruler questioned Him, saying, "Good Teacher, what shall I do to inherit eternal life?" And Jesus said to him, "Why do you call Me good? No one is good except God alone. You know the commandments, 'DO NOT COMMIT ADULTERY, DO NOT MURDER, DO NOT STEAL, DO NOT BEAR FALSE WITNESS, HONOR YOUR FATHER AND MOTHER.' '" And he said "All these things I have kept from *my* youth." When Jesus heard *this,* He said to him, "One thing you still lack; sell all that you possess and distribute it to the poor, and you shall have treasure in heaven; and come, follow Me" (Luke 18:18–22, Jesus quotes from Exodus 20:12–16; cf. Matthew 19:16–22; Mark 10:17–22; see Luke 10:25–28).

Setting: The temple treasury in Jerusalem. While Jesus interacts with the scribes and Pharisees, they state their belief that Jesus is a demon-possessed Samaritan because of His statement that anyone who keeps His word will never taste death.

Jesus answered, "If I glorify Myself, My glory is nothing; it is My Father who glorifies Me, of whom you say, 'He is our God'; and you have not come to know Him, but I know Him; and if I say that I do not know Him, I will be a liar like you, but I do know Him and keep His word. Your father Abraham rejoiced to see My day, and he saw *it* and was glad" (John 8:54–56; see Matthew 13:17; John 7:29).

FATHER AND/OR MOTHER (FATHER; and MOTHER are a separate entries; also see FAMILY; and PARENTS)

Setting: Galilee. After His twelve disciples observe His ministry, Jesus summons and specifically instructs them about their ministry ahead involving true discipleship.

"He who loves father or mother more than Me is not worthy of Me; and he who loves son or daughter more than Me is not worthy of Me. And he who does not take his cross and follow after Me is not worthy of Me. He who has found his life will lose it, and he who has lost his life for My sake will find it" (Matthew 10:37–39; cf. Matthew 16:24, 25).

Setting: Galilee. Pharisees and scribes from Jerusalem question Jesus about His disciples' lack of obedience to tradition and the commandments.

And He answered and said to them, "Why do you yourselves transgress the commandment of God for the sake of tradition? For God said, 'HONOR YOUR FATHER AND MOTHER,' and, 'HE WHO SPEAKS EVIL OF FATHER OR MOTHER IS TO BE PUT TO DEATH.' But you say, 'Whoever says to *his* father or mother, "Whatever I have that would help you has been given *to God*," he is not to honor his father or mother.' And *by this* you invalidated the word of God for the sake of your tradition. You hypocrites, rightly did Isaiah prophesy of you: 'THIS PEOPLE HONORS ME WITH THEIR LIPS, BUT THEIR HEART IS FAR AWAY FROM ME. BUT IN VAIN DO THEY WORSHIP ME, TEACHING AS DOCTRINES THE PRECEPTS OF MEN'" (Matthew 15:3–9, Jesus quotes from Exodus 20:12, 21:17, Leviticus 20:9; Isaiah 29:13; cf. Mark 7:5–7; see Colossians 2:22).

Setting: Judea beyond the Jordan (Perea). After Jesus replies to Peter's question about forgiveness, in front of a large crowd, the Pharisees test the Lord with a question about divorce.

And He answered and said, "Have you not read that He who created *them* from the beginning MADE THEM MALE AND FEMALE, and said, 'FOR THIS REASON A MAN SHALL LEAVE HIS FATHER AND MOTHER AND BE JOINED TO HIS WIFE, AND THE TWO SHALL BECOME ONE FLESH'? So they are no longer two, but one flesh. What therefore God has joined together, let no man separate" (Matthew 19:4–6, Jesus quotes from Genesis 1:27; 2:24; cf. Mark 10:5–9; see 1 Timothy 2:14).

Setting: Judea beyond the Jordan (Perea). Jesus promises rewards to His disciples for their personal sacrifice and commitment to following Him.

And Jesus said to them, "Truly I say to you, that you who have followed Me, in the regeneration when the Son of Man will sit on His glorious throne, you also shall sit upon twelve thrones, judging the twelve tribes of Israel. And everyone who has left houses or brothers or sisters or father or mother or children or farms for My name's sake, will receive many times as much, and will inherit eternal life. But many *who* are first will be last; and *the* last, first" (Matthew 19:28–30; cf. Matthew 6:33; 20:15; Mark 10:29, 30; Luke 18:29, 30; 22:30).

Setting: Galilee. The Pharisees and some of the scribes from Jerusalem ask Jesus why His disciples do not follow the tradition of ceremonial hand cleansing before eating bread.

And He said to them, "Rightly did Isaiah prophesy of you hypocrites, as it is written: 'THIS PEOPLE HONORS ME WITH THEIR LIPS, BUT THEIR HEART IS FAR AWAY FROM ME. BUT IN VAIN DO THEY WORSHIP ME, TEACHING AS DOCTRINES THE PRECEPTS OF MEN.' Neglecting the commandment of God, you hold to the tradition of men." He was also saying to them, "You are experts at setting aside the commandment of God in order to keep tradition. For Moses said, 'HONOR YOUR FATHER AND YOUR MOTHER'; and, 'HE WHO SPEAKS EVIL OF FATHER OR MOTHER, IS TO BE PUT TO DEATH'; but you say, 'If a man says to *his* father or *his* mother, whatever I have that would help you is Corban (that is to say, given *to God*),' you no longer permit him to do anything for *his* father or *his* mother; *thus*

invalidating the word of God by your tradition which you have handed down; and you do many things such as that" (Mark 7:6–13, Jesus quotes from Exodus 20:12; 21:17; Isaiah 29:13; cf. Matthew 15:1–6).

Setting: Judea beyond the Jordan (Perea). Jesus teaches the crowds gathered around Him about divorce after the Pharisees test and question Him on the subject.

And He answered and said to them, "What did Moses command you?" They said, "Moses permitted a *man* TO WRITE A CERTIFICATE OF DIVORCE AND SEND *her* AWAY." But Jesus said to them, "Because of your hardness of heart he wrote you this commandment. But from the beginning of creation, *God* MADE THEM MALE AND FEMALE. FOR THIS REASON A MAN SHALL LEAVE HIS FATHER AND MOTHER, AND THE TWO SHALL BECOME ONE FLESH; so they are no longer two, but one flesh. What therefore God has joined together, let no man separate. In the house the disciples *began* questioning Him about this again. And He said to them, "Whoever divorces his wife and marries another woman commits adultery against her; and if she herself divorces her husband and marries another man, she is committing adultery" (Mark 10:3–12, Jesus quotes from Genesis 1:27; 2:24; cf. Matthew 19:1–9; see Deuteronomy 24:1–3; Matthew 5:32; Romans 7:2, 3; 1 Corinthians 7:10, 11, 13, 39; 1 Timothy 2:14).

Setting: Judea beyond the Jordan (Perea). After demonstrating to His disciples the importance of little children, Jesus encounters a rich man seeking eternal life.

And Jesus said to him, "Why do you call Me good? No one is good except God alone. You know the commandments, 'DO NOT MURDER, DO NOT COMMIT ADULTERY, DO NOT STEAL, DO NOT BEAR FALSE WITNESS, Do not defraud, HONOR YOUR FATHER AND MOTHER.'" And he said to Him, "Teacher, I have kept all these things from my youth up." Looking at him, Jesus felt a love for him and said to him, "One thing you lack: go and sell all you possess and give to the poor, and you will have treasure in heaven; and come, follow Me" (Mark 10:18–21; Jesus quotes from Exodus 20:12–16; cf. Matthew 19:16–22; Luke 18:18–24; see Matthew 6:20; Mark 10:17, 22).

Setting: Judea beyond the Jordan (Perea). After informing a rich man how righteous believers may have treasure in heaven, Jesus tells His disciples about the reward of those who sacrifice in this life to follow Him.

Jesus said, "Truly I say to you, there is no one who has left house or brothers or sisters or mother or father or children or farms, for My sake and for the gospel's sake, but that he will receive a hundred times as much now in the present age, houses and brothers and sisters and mothers and children and farms, along with persecutions; and in the age to come, eternal life. But many *who are* first will be last, and the last, first" (Mark 10:29–31; cf. Matthew 19:27–30; Luke 18:28–30; see Matthew 6:33; Mark 10:28).

Setting: On the way from Galilee to Jerusalem. After He responds to a guest's proclamation about the blessings of eating bread in the kingdom of God, Jesus presents to large crowds the demands of discipleship.

Now large crowds were going along with Him; and He turned and said to them, "If anyone comes to Me, and does not hate his own father and mother and wife and children and brothers and sisters, yes, and even his own life, he cannot be My disciple. Whoever does not carry his own cross and come after Me cannot be My disciple. For which one of you, when he wants to build a tower, does not first sit down and calculate the cost to see if he has enough to complete it? Otherwise, when he has laid a foundation and is not able to finish, all who observe it begin to ridicule him, saying, 'This man began to build and was not able to finish.' Or what king, when he sets out to meet another king in battle, will not first sit down and consider whether he is strong enough with ten thousand *men* to encounter the one coming against him with twenty thousand? Or else, while the other is still far away, he sends a delegation and asks for terms of peace. So then, none of you can be My disciple who does not give up all his possessions. Therefore, salt is good; but if even salt has become tasteless, with what will it be seasoned? It is useless either for the soil or for the manure pile; it is thrown out. He who has ears to hear, let him hear" (Luke 14:25–35; cf. Matthew 5:13; 10:37–39; see Proverb 20:18; Philippians 3:7).

FATHER AND THE SON AND THE HOLY SPIRIT (See HOLY SPIRIT, NAME OF THE FATHER AND THE SON AND THE; and TRINITY)

FATHER, GLORY OF HIS (Also see GLORIFICATION, GOD'S)

Setting: Near Caesarea Philippi. After rebuking Peter for trying to forbid Him to accomplish His earthly mission of dying and being resurrected, Jesus teaches His disciples about the costs of discipleship.

Then Jesus said to His disciples, "If anyone wishes to come after Me, he must deny himself, and take up his cross and follow Me. For whoever wishes to save his life will lose it; but whoever loses his life for My sake will find it. For what will it profit a man if he gains the whole world and forfeits his soul? Or what will a man give in exchange for his soul? For the Son of Man is going to come in the glory of His Father with His angels, and WILL THEN REPAY EVERY MAN ACCORDING TO HIS DEEDS. Truly, I say to you, there are some of you who are standing here who will not taste death until they see the Son of Man coming in His kingdom" (Matthew 16:24–28, Jesus quotes from Psalm 62:12; cf. Mark 8:34–37; Luke 9:23–27; see Matthew 10:38, 39).

Setting: Caesarea Philippi. After rebuking Peter for desiring to thwart His mission to the cross, Jesus summons a crowd, along with His disciples, and informs them of the high costs of following Him.

And He summoned the crowd with His disciples, and said to them, "If anyone wishes to come after Me, he must deny himself, and take up his cross and follow Me. For whoever wishes to save his life will lose it, but whoever loses his life for My sake and the gospel's will save it. For what does it profit a man to gain the whole world, and forfeit his soul? For what will a man give in exchange for his soul? For whoever is ashamed of Me and My words in this adulterous and sinful generation, the Son of Man will also be ashamed of him when He comes in the glory of His Father with the holy angels" (Mark 8:34–38; cf. Matthew 16:24–28; Luke 9:23–27; see Matthew 10:33, 38, 39).

Setting: Galilee. Following Peter's pronouncement that Jesus is the Christ of God, the Lord conveys to the Twelve the demands of discipleship and the hope regarding the kingdom of God.

And He was saying to *them* all, "If anyone wishes to come after Me, he must deny himself, and take up his cross daily and follow Me. For whoever wishes to save his life will lose it, but whoever loses his life for My sake, he is the one who will save it. For what is a man profited if he gains the whole world, and loses or forfeits himself? For whoever is ashamed of Me and My words, the Son of Man will be ashamed of him when He comes in His glory, and *the glory* of the Father and of the holy angels. But I say to you truthfully, there are some of those standing here who will not taste death until they see the kingdom of God" (Luke 9:23–27; cf. Matthew 16:24–26, 28; Mark 8:34–37; see Matthew 10:33, 38, 39).

FATHER, HEAVENLY

[HEAVENLY FATHER from Father who is in heaven]

Setting: Galilee. During the early part of His ministry, Jesus preaches the Sermon on the Mount to His disciples and the multitudes.

"You are the light of the world. A city set on a hill cannot be hidden; nor does *anyone* light a lamp and put it under a basket, but on the lampstand, and it gives light to all who are in the house. Let your light shine before men in such a way that they may see your good works, and glorify your Father who is in heaven" (Matthew 5:14–16; cf. Mark 4:21; 1 Peter 2:12).

Setting: Galilee. During the early part of His ministry, Jesus preaches the Sermon on the Mount to His disciples and the multitudes.

"You have heard that it was said, 'YOU SHALL LOVE YOUR NEIGHBOR and hate your enemy.' But I say to you, love your enemies and pray for those who persecute you, so that you may be sons of your Father who is in heaven; for He causes His sun to rise on *the* evil and *the* good, and sends rain on *the* righteous and *the* unrighteous. For if you love those who love you, what reward do you have? Do not even the tax collectors do the same? If you greet only your brothers, what more are you doing *than others?* Do not even the Gentiles do the same? Therefore, you are to be perfect, as your heavenly Father is perfect" (Matthew 5:43–48, Jesus quotes from Leviticus 19:18; cf. Leviticus 19:2; Luke 6:27–36).

[HEAVENLY FATHER from Father who is in heaven]
Setting: Galilee. During the early part of His ministry, Jesus preaches the Sermon on the Mount to His disciples and the multitudes.

"Beware of practicing your righteousness before men to be noticed by them; otherwise you have no reward with your Father who is in heaven" (Matthew 6:1; cf. Matthew 6:5, 16).

[HEAVENLY FATHER from Our Father who is in heaven]
Setting: Galilee. During the early part of His ministry, Jesus gives a model prayer to His disciples and the multitudes while conveying The Sermon on the Mount.

"Pray, then, in this way: 'Our Father who is in heaven, hallowed be Your name. Your kingdom come. Your will be done, on earth as it is in heaven. Give us this day our daily bread. And forgive us our debts, as we also have forgiven our debtors. And do not lead us into temptation, but deliver us from evil. [For Yours is the kingdom and the power and the glory forever. Amen]'" (Matthew 6:9–13; cf. Luke 11:2–4; see John 17:15).

Setting: Galilee. During the early part of His ministry, Jesus preaches the Sermon on the Mount to His disciples and the multitudes.

"For if you forgive others for their transgressions, your heavenly Father will also forgive you. But if you do not forgive others, then your Father will not forgive your transgressions" (Matthew 6:14, 15; cf. Matthew 18:15; see Mark 7:2).

Setting: Galilee. During the early part of His ministry, Jesus preaches the Sermon on the Mount to His disciples and the multitudes.

"For this reason I say to you, do not be worried about your life, *as to* what you will eat or what you will drink; nor for your body, *as to* what you will put on. Is not life more than food, and the body more than clothing? Look at the birds of the air, that they do not sow, nor reap nor gather into barns, and *yet* your heavenly Father feeds them. Are you not worth much more than they? And who of you by being worried can add a *single* hour to his life? And why are you worried about clothing? Observe how the lilies of the field grow; they do not toil nor do they spin, yet I say to you that not even Solomon in all his glory clothed himself like one of these. But if God so clothes the grass of the field, which is *alive* today and tomorrow is thrown into the furnace, *will He* not much more *clothe* you? You of little faith! Do not worry then, saying 'What will we eat?' or 'What will we drink?' or 'What will be wear for clothing?" For the Gentiles eagerly seek all these things; for your heavenly Father knows that you need all these things. But seek first His kingdom and His righteousness, and all these things will be added to you. So do not worry about tomorrow; for tomorrow will care for itself. Each day has enough trouble of its own" (Matthew 6:25–34; cf. Luke 12:22–31; see 1 Kings 10:4–7; Job 35:11; Matthew 8:26).

[HEAVENLY FATHER from Father who is in heaven]
Setting: Galilee. During the early part of His ministry, Jesus preaches the Sermon on the Mount to His disciples and the multitudes.

"Ask, and it will be given to you; seek, and you will find; knock, and it will be opened to you. For everyone who asks receives, and he who seeks finds, and to him who knocks it will be opened. Or what man is there among you who, when his son asks for a loaf, will give him a stone? Or if he asks for a fish, he will not give him a snake, will he? If you then, being evil, know how to give good gifts to your children, how much more will your Father who is in heaven give what is good to those who ask Him! In everything, therefore, treat people the same way you want them to treat you, for this is the Law and the Prophets" (Matthew 7:7–12; cf. Matthew 22:40; Luke 6:31; 11:9–13; see Psalm 84:11).

[HEAVENLY FATHER from Father who is in heaven]
Setting: Galilee. During the early part of His ministry, Jesus preaches the Sermon on the Mount to His disciples and the multitudes.

"Not everyone who says to Me, 'Lord, Lord,' will enter the kingdom of heaven, but he who does the will of My Father who is in heaven *will enter.* Many will say to Me on that day, 'Lord, Lord, did we not prophesy in Your name, and in Your name cast out demons, and in Your name perform many miracles?' And then I will declare to them, 'I never knew you, DEPART FROM ME, YOU WHO PRACTICE LAWLESSNESS'"(Matthew 7:21–23, Jesus quotes from Psalm 6:8; cf. Matthew 25:11–13; see Luke 6:46).

[HEAVENLY FATHER from Father who is in heaven]
Setting: Galilee. Jesus explains the meaning of discipleship as He commissions the Twelve for ministry.

"Therefore everyone who confesses Me before men, I will also confess him before My Father who is in heaven. But whoever denies Me before men, I will also deny him before My Father who is in heaven" (Matthew 10:32, 33; cf. Mark 8:38; Luke 12:8).

[HEAVENLY FATHER from Father who is in heaven]
Setting: Galilee. Jesus' mother, Mary, and His brothers are waiting to see Him as He teaches and preaches.

But Jesus answered the one who was telling Him and said, "Who is My mother and who are My brothers?" And stretching out His hand toward His disciples, He said, "Behold, My mother and My brothers! For whoever does the will of My Father who is in heaven, he is My brother and sister and mother" (Matthew 12:48–50; cf. Mark 3:31–35; Luke 8:19–21).

Setting: Galilee. Jesus instructs His disciples following His rebuke of the Pharisees and scribes for questioning the disciples' lack of obedience to tradition and the commandments.

But He answered and said, "Every plant which My heavenly Father did not plant shall be uprooted. Let them alone; they are blind guides of the blind. And if a blind man guides a blind man, both will fall into a pit" (Matthew 15:13, 14; cf. Matthew 23:16; Luke 6:39).

[HEAVENLY FATHER from Father who is in heaven]
Setting: Caesarea Philippi. Jesus responds to Simon Peter's declaration that He is the Christ, the Son of the living God.

And Jesus said to him, "Blessed are you, Simon Barjona, because flesh and blood did not reveal *this* to you, but My Father who is in heaven. I also say to you that you are Peter, and upon this rock I will build My church; and the gates of Hades will not overpower it. I will give you the keys of the kingdom of heaven; and whatever you bind on earth shall have been bound in heaven, and whatever you loose on earth shall have been loosed in heaven" (Matthew 16:17–19; cf. Matthew 18:18; Mark 8:29; Luke 9:20).

[HEAVENLY FATHER from Father who is in heaven]
Setting: Capernaum of Galilee. After His disciples ask about greatness in the kingdom of heaven, Jesus elaborates about the value of little ones.

"See that you do not despise one of these little ones, for I say to you that their angels in heaven continually see the face of My Father who is in heaven" (Matthew 18:10; see Luke 1:19).

[HEAVENLY FATHER from Father who is in heaven]
Setting: Capernaum of Galilee. Jesus illustrates to His disciples the value of little ones.

"What do you think? If any man has a hundred sheep, and one of them has gone astray, does he not leave the ninety-nine on the mountains and go and search for the one that is straying? If it turns out that he finds it, truly I say to you, he rejoices over it more than the ninety-nine which have not gone astray. So it is not *the* will of your Father who is in heaven that one of these little ones perish" (Matthew 18:12–14; cf. Luke 15:4–7).

[HEAVENLY FATHER from Father who is in heaven]
Setting: Capernaum of Galilee. After conveying to His disciples the value of little ones, Jesus gives instruction about church discipline.

"If your brother sins, go and show him his fault in private; if he listens to you, you have won your brother. But if he does not listen *to you,* take one or two more with you, so that BY THE MOUTH OF TWO OR THREE WITNESSES EVERY FACT MAY BE CONFIRMED. If he refuses to listen to them, tell it to the church; and if he refuses to listen even to the church, let him be to you as a Gentile and a tax collector. Truly I say to you, whatever you bind of earth shall have been bound in heaven; and whatever you loose on earth shall have been loosed in heaven. Again, I say to you, that if two of you agree on earth about anything that they may ask, it shall be done for them by My Father who is in heaven. For there two or three have gathered together in My name, I am there in their midst" (Matthew 18:15–20. Jesus quotes from Deuteronomy 19:15; cf. Matthew 7:7; 16:19; see Leviticus 19:17; Matthew 28:20; 2 Thessalonians 3:6, 14).

Setting: Capernaum of Galilee. Jesus illustrates forgiveness after Peter asks Him if forgiving someone seven times who has sinned against him is adequate.

"For this reason the kingdom of heaven may be compared to a king who wished to settle accounts with his slaves. When he had begun to settle *them,* one who owed him ten thousand talents was brought to him. But since he did not have *the means* to repay, his lord commanded him to be sold, along with his wife and children and all that he had, and repayment to be made. So the slave fell *to the ground* and prostrated himself before him, saying, 'Have patience with me and I will repay you everything.' And the lord of that slave felt compassion and released him and forgave him the debt. But that slave went out and found one of his fellow slaves who owed him a hundred denarii; and he seized him and *began* to choke *him,* saying, 'Pay back what you owe.' So his fellow slave fell *to the ground* and *began* to plead with him, saying, 'Have patience with me and I will repay you.' But he was unwilling and went and threw him in prison until he should pay back what was owed. So when his fellow slaves saw what had happened, they were deeply grieved and came and reported to their lord all that had happened. Then summoning him, his lord said to him, 'You wicked slave, I forgave you all that debt because you pleaded with me. Should you not also have had mercy on your fellow slave, in the same way that I had mercy on you?' And his lord, moved with anger, handed him over to the torturers until he should repay all that was owed him. My heavenly Father will also do the same to you, if each of you does not forgive his brother from your heart" (Matthew 18:23–35; cf. Matthew 6:12, 14, 15; Luke 7:42; see Matthew 25:19–28).

[HEAVENLY FATHER from One is your Father, He who is in heaven]
Setting: The temple in Jerusalem. Jesus exposes the truth about Pharisaism to the crowds and His disciples after the Jewish religious leaders test Him with questions.

Then Jesus spoke to the crowds and to His disciples, saying. "The scribes and the Pharisees have seated themselves in the chair of Moses; therefore all that they tell you, do and observe, but do not do according to their deeds; for they say *things* and do not do *them.* They tie up heavy burdens and lay them on men's shoulders, but they themselves are unwilling to move them with *so much as* a finger. But they do all their deeds to be noticed by men; for they broaden their phylacteries and lengthen their tassels *of their garments.* They love the place of honor at banquets and the chief seats in the synagogues, and respectful greetings in the market places, and being called Rabbi by men. But do not be called Rabbi; for One is your Teacher, and you are all brothers. Do not call *anyone* on earth your father; for One is your Father, He who is in heaven. Do not be called leaders; for One is your Leader, *that is,* Christ. But the greatest among you shall be your servant. Whoever exalts himself shall be humbled; and whoever humbles himself shall be exalted" (Matthew 23:1–12; cf. Matthew 20:26; Mark 12:38–40; Luke 20:46, 47; see Exodus 13:9; Deuteronomy 33:3; Matthew 6:1, 5, 6, 9, 16; Mark 14:11; Luke 11:43; 14:11).

[HEAVENLY FATHER from Father who is in heaven]
Setting: Between Jerusalem and Bethany. After Jesus instructs the money changers while cleansing the temple, Peter draws His and His disciples' attention to an earlier-cursed fig tree.

And Jesus answered saying to them, "Have faith in God. Truly, I say to you, whoever says to this mountain, 'Be taken up and cast into the sea,' and does not doubt in his heart, but believes that what he says is going to happen, it will be *granted* him. Therefore I say to you, all things for which you pray and ask, believe that you have received them, and they will be *granted* you. Whenever you stand praying, forgive, if you have anything against anyone, so that your Father who is in heaven will also forgive you your transgressions. [But if you do not forgive, neither will your Father who is in heaven forgive your transgressions'] (Mark 11:22–26; cf. Matthew 21:19–22; see Matthew 6:14, 15; 7:7; 17:20).

Setting: On the way from Galilee to Jerusalem. After revealing to His disciples how to pray, Jesus illustrates God's benevolence in answering prayer and giving the Holy Spirit.

"Now suppose one of you fathers is asked by his son for a fish; he will not give him a snake instead of a fish, will he? Or *if* he is asked for an egg, he will not give him a scorpion, will he? If you then, being evil, know how to give good gifts to your children, how much more will *your* heavenly Father give the Holy Spirit to those who ask Him?" (Luke 11:11–13; cf. Matthew 7:9–11).

FATHER, HIS (Jesus'; see FATHER, GLORY OF HIS)

FATHER, HOLY

Setting: Jerusalem. Before the Passover, after giving His disciples assurance that in the midst of tribulation they will have His peace, Jesus prays His high-priestly prayer.

Jesus spoke these things; and lifting up His eyes to heaven, He said, "Father, the hour has come; glorify Your Son, that the Son may glorify You, even as You gave Him authority over all flesh, that to all whom You have given Him, He may give eternal life. This is eternal life, that they may know You, the only true God, and Jesus Christ whom You have sent. I glorified You on the earth, having accomplished the work which you have given Me to do. Now, Father, glorify Me together with Yourself, with the glory which I had with You before the world was. I have manifested Your name to the men whom You gave Me out of the world; they were Yours and You gave them to Me, and they have kept Your word. Now they have come to know that everything You have given Me is from You; for the words which You gave Me I have given to them; and they received *them* and truly understood that I came forth from You, and they believed You sent Me. I ask on their behalf; I do not ask on behalf of the world, but of those whom You have given Me; for they are Yours; and all things that are Mine are Yours, and Yours are Mine; and I have been glorified in them. I am no longer in the world; and yet they themselves are in the world, and I come to You. Holy Father, keep them in Your name, *the name* which You have given Me, that they may be even as We *are.* While I was with them, I was keeping them in Your name which You have given Me; and I guarded them and not one of them perished but the son of perdition, so that the Scripture would be fulfilled" (John 17:1–12; see Luke 22:32; John 1:1; 3:35; 4:34; 5:44; 6:37–39, 70; 8:42; 11:41; 12:49; 13:18, 31; 16:15; 17:20; Philippians 2:9).

FATHER, JESUS PRAISING HIS

[JESUS PRAISING HIS FATHER from I praise You, Father]

Setting: Galilee. After pronouncing woes against unrepentant cities as He teaches and preaches, Jesus prays a thanksgiving prayer to His Father in heaven.

At that time Jesus said, "I praise You, Father, Lord of heaven and earth, that you have hidden these things from *the* wise and intelligent and have revealed them to infants. Yes, Father, for this way was well-pleasing in Your sight. All things have been handed over to Me by My Father; and no one knows the Son except the Father; nor does anyone know the Father except the Son, and anyone to whom the Son wills to reveal *Him*" (Matthew 11:25–27; cf. Luke 10:21, 22).

[JESUS PRAISING HIS FATHER from I praise You, O Father]

Setting: On the way from Galilee to Jerusalem. The Lord responds to a report from the seventy sent out in pairs to every place He Himself will soon visit.

At that very time He rejoiced greatly in the Holy Spirit, and said, "I praise You, O Father, Lord of heaven and earth, that You have hidden these things from *the* wise and intelligent and have revealed them to infants. Yes, Father, for this way was well-pleasing in Your sight. All things have been handed over to Me by My Father, and no one knows who the Son is except the Father, and who the Father is except the Son, and anyone to whom the Son wills to reveal *Him*" (Luke 10:21, 22; cf. Matthew 11:25–27; see Luke 10:1, 17; John 3:35; John 10:15).

FATHER, KINGDOM OF THEIR

Setting: A house near the Sea of Galilee (Tiberias). Jesus explains to His disciples the meaning of the Parable of the Wheat and the Tares.

And He said, "The one who sows the good seed is the Son of Man, and the field is the world; and as *for* the good seed, these are the sons of the kingdom; and the tares are the sons of the evil *one;* and the enemy who sowed them is the devil, and the harvest is the end of the age; and the reapers are angels. So just as the tares are gathered up and burned with fire, so shall it be at the end of the age. The Son of Man will send forth His angels, and they will gather out of His kingdom all stumbling blocks, and those who commit lawlessness, and will throw them into the furnace of fire; in that place there will be weeping and gnashing of teeth. Then THE RIGHTEOUS WILL SHINE FORTH AS THE SUN in the kingdom of their Father. He who has ears, let him hear" (Matthew 13:37–43, Jesus quotes from Daniel 12:3; cf. Matthew 8:12; 13:50).

FATHER, MY (Jesus')

Setting: Galilee. During the early part of His ministry, Jesus preaches the Sermon on the Mount to His disciples and the multitudes.

"Not everyone who says to Me, 'Lord, Lord,' will enter the kingdom of heaven, but he who does the will of My Father who is in heaven *will enter.* Many will say to Me on that day, 'Lord, Lord, did we not prophesy in Your name, and in Your name cast out demons, and in Your name perform many miracles?' And then I will declare to them, 'I never knew you, DEPART FROM ME, YOU WHO PRACTICE LAWLESSNESS'"(Matthew 7:21–23, Jesus quotes from Psalm 6:8; cf. Matthew 25:11–13; see Luke 6:46).

Setting: Galilee. Jesus explains the meaning of discipleship as He commissions the Twelve for ministry.

"Therefore everyone who confesses Me before men, I will also confess him before My Father who is in heaven. But whoever denies Me before men, I will also deny him before My Father who is in heaven" (Matthew 10:32, 33; cf. Mark 8:38; Luke 12:8).

Setting: Galilee. After pronouncing woes against unrepentant cities as He teaches and preaches, Jesus prays a thanksgiving prayer to His Father in heaven.

At that time Jesus said, "I praise You, Father, Lord of heaven and earth, that you have hidden these things from *the* wise and intelligent and have revealed them to infants. Yes, Father, for this way was well-pleasing in Your sight. All things have been handed over to Me by My Father; and no one knows the Son except the Father; nor does anyone know the Father except the Son, and anyone to whom the Son wills to reveal *Him*" (Matthew 11:25–27; cf. Luke 10:21, 22).

Setting: Galilee. Jesus' mother, Mary, and His brothers are waiting to see Him as He teaches and preaches.

But Jesus answered the one who was telling Him and said, "Who is My mother and who are My brothers?" And stretching out His hand toward His disciples, He said, "Behold, My mother and My brothers! For whoever does the will of My Father who is in heaven, he is My brother and sister and mother" (Matthew 12:48–50; cf. Mark 3:31–35; Luke 8:19–21).

Setting: Caesarea Philippi. Jesus responds to Simon Peter's declaration that He is the Christ, the Son of the living God.

And Jesus said to him, "Blessed are you, Simon Barjona, because flesh and blood did not reveal *this* to you, but My Father who is in heaven. I also say to you that you are Peter, and upon this rock I will build My church; and the gates of Hades will not overpower it. I will give you the keys of the kingdom of heaven; and whatever you bind on earth shall have been bound in heaven, and whatever you loose on earth shall have been loosed in heaven" (Matthew 16:17–19; cf. Matthew 18:18; Mark 8:29; Luke 9:20).

Setting: Capernaum of Galilee. After His disciples ask about greatness in the kingdom of heaven, Jesus elaborates about the value of little ones.

"See that you do not despise one of these little ones, for I say to you that their angels in heaven continually see the face of My Father who is in heaven" (Matthew 18:10; see Luke 1:19).

Setting: **Capernaum of Galilee. After conveying to His disciples the value of little ones, Jesus gives instruction about church discipline.**

"If your brother sins, go and show him his fault in private; if he listens to you, you have won your brother. But if he does not listen *to you,* take one or two more with you, so that BY THE MOUTH OF TWO OR THREE WITNESSES EVERY FACT MAY BE CONFIRMED. If he refuses to listen to them, tell it to the church; and if he refuses to listen even to the church, let him be to you as a Gentile and a tax collector. Truly I say to you, whatever you bind of earth shall have been bound in heaven; and whatever you loose on earth shall have been loosed in heaven. Again, I say to you, that if two of you agree on earth about anything that they may ask, it shall be done for them by My Father who is in heaven. For there two or three have gathered together in My name, I am there in their midst" (Matthew 18:15–20. Jesus quotes from Deuteronomy 19:15; cf. Matthew 7:7; 16:19; see Leviticus 19:17; Matthew 28:20; 2 Thessalonians 3:6, 14).

Setting: **On the way to Jerusalem. The mother of James and John, the sons of Zebedee, asks Jesus to make her sons exalted rulers with Him in His coming kingdom.**

And He said to her, "What do you wish?" She said to Him, 'Command that in Your kingdom these two sons of mine may sit one on Your right and one on Your left.' But Jesus answered, "You do not know what you are asking. Are you able to drink the cup that I am about to drink?" They said to Him, 'We are able.' He said to them, "My cup you shall drink; but to sit on My right and on *My* left, this is not Mine to give, but it is for those for whom it has been prepared by My Father" (Matthew 20:21–23; cf. Mark 10:35–40; see Matthew 19:28; 20:20; Acts 12:2).

Setting: **The Mount of Olives, just east of Jerusalem. During His discourse, after answering His disciples' questions as to when the temple will be destroyed and Jerusalem overrun, along with the signs of His coming and the end of the age, Jesus reveals the future judgments following His return.**

"But when the Son of Man comes in His glory, and all the angels with Him, then He will sit on His glorious throne. All the nations will be gathered before Him; and He will separate them from one another, as the shepherd separates the sheep from the goats; and He will put the sheep on His right, and the goats on the left. Then the King will say to those on His right, 'Come, you who are blessed of My Father, inherit the kingdom prepared for you from the foundation of the world. 'For I was hungry, and you gave Me *something* to eat; I was thirsty, and you gave Me *something* to drink; I was a stranger, and you invited Me in; naked, and you clothed Me; I was sick, and you visited Me; I was in prison, and you came to Me.' Then the righteous will answer Him, 'Lord, when did we see You hungry and feed You, or thirsty, and give you *something* to drink? And when did we see You a stranger, and invite You in, or naked, and clothe You? When did we see You sick, or in prison, and come to You?' The King will answer and say to them, 'Truly I say to you, to the extent that you did it to one of these brothers of Mine, *even* the least *of them,* you did it to Me.' Then He will also say to those on His left, 'Depart from Me, accursed ones, into the eternal fire which has been prepared for the devil and his angels; for I was hungry, and you gave Me *nothing* to eat; I was thirsty, and you gave Me nothing to drink; I was a stranger, and you did not invite Me in; naked, and you did not clothe Me; sick, and in prison, and you did not visit Me.' Then they themselves also will answer, 'Lord, when did we see You hungry, or thirsty, or a stranger, or naked, or sick, or in prison, and did not take care of You?' Then He will answer them, 'Truly I say to you, to the extent that you did not do it to one of the least of these, you did not do it to Me.' These will go away into eternal punishment, but the righteous into eternal life" (Matthew 25:31–46; see Matthew 7:23; 16:27; 19:29).

Setting: **An upper room in Jerusalem. After celebrating the Passover meal with His disciples, Jesus retreats to the Garden of Gethsemane on the Mount of Olives to pray prior to His betrayal by Judas.**

Then Jesus came with them to a place called Gethsemane, and said to His disciples, "Sit here while I go over there and pray." And He took with Him Peter and the two sons of Zebedee, and began to be grieved and distressed. Then He said to them, "My soul is deeply grieved, to the point of death; remain here and keep watch with Me." And He went a little beyond *them,* and fell on His face and prayed, saying, "My Father, if it is possible, let this cup pass from Me; yet not as I will, but as You will." And He came to the disciples and found them sleeping, and said to Peter, "So, you *men* could not keep watch with Me for one hour? Keep watching and praying that you may not enter into temptation; the spirit is willing, but the flesh is weak." He went away again a second time and prayed, saying, "My Father, if this cannot pass away unless I drink it, Your will be done." Again He came and found them sleeping, for their eyes were heavy. And He left them again, and went away and prayed a third time, saying the same thing once more. Then He came to the disciples and said to them, "Are you still sleeping and resting? Behold the hour is at hand and the Son of Man is being betrayed into the hands of sinners. Get up, let us be going; behold the one who betrays Me is at hand!" (Matthew 26:36–46; cf. Mark 14:32–42; Luke 22:40–46; see Matthew 20:22; John 12:27).

Setting: Gethsemane on the Mount of Olives, just east of Jerusalem. As Jesus submits to His Father's will and allows Judas to betray Him, Peter attempts to defend Him by force, but Jesus does not permit it.

Then Jesus said to him, "Put your sword back into its place; for all those who take up the sword shall perish by the sword. Or do you think that I cannot appeal to My Father, and He will at once put at My disposal more than twelve legions of angels? How then will the Scriptures be fulfilled, *which say* that it must happen this way?" (Matthew 26:52–54; cf. Mark 14:47; Luke 22:50, 51; John 18:10, 11; see Matthew 26:24, 51).

Setting: On the way from Galilee to Jerusalem. The Lord responds to a report from the seventy sent out in pairs to every place He Himself will soon visit.

At that very time He rejoiced greatly in the Holy Spirit, and said, "I praise You, O Father, Lord of heaven and earth, that You have hidden these things from *the* wise and intelligent and have revealed them to infants. Yes, Father, for this way was well-pleasing in Your sight. All things have been handed over to Me by My Father, and no one knows who the Son is except the Father, and who the Father is except the Son, and anyone to whom the Son wills to reveal *Him*" (Luke 10:21, 22; cf. Matthew 11:25–27; see Luke 10:1, 17; John 3:35; 10:15).

Setting: An upper room in Jerusalem. During the Feast of Unleavened Bread (Passover) just before Jesus' crucifixion, while Jesus celebrates the Passover meal and institutes the Lord's Supper, His disciples argue over who is the greatest among them.

"You are those who have stood by Me in My trials; for just as My Father has granted Me a kingdom, I grant you that you may eat and drink at My table in My kingdom, and you will sit on thrones judging the twelve tribes of Israel" (Luke 22:28–30; cf. Matthew 19:28).

Setting: In Jerusalem, after rising from the grave on the third day following being crucified and appearing to two of His followers on the road to Emmaus, Jesus gives instruction to His disciples about His mission on earth and the promise of future power from God.

Now He said to them, "These are My words which I spoke to you while I was still with you, that all things which are written about Me in the Law of Moses and the Prophets and the Psalms must be fulfilled." Then He opened their minds to understand the Scriptures, and He said to them, "Thus it is written, that the Christ would suffer and rise again from the dead the third day, and that repentance for forgiveness of sins would be proclaimed in His name to all the nations, beginning from Jerusalem. You are witnesses of these things. And behold, I am sending forth the promise of My Father upon you; but you are to stay in the city until you are clothed with power from on high" (Luke 24:44–49; see Matthew 28:19, 20; Acts 1:8).

Setting: By the pool of Bethesda in Jerusalem. During the Feast of the Jews, Jesus responds to criticism from the Jewish religious leaders for healing a lame man on the Sabbath.

But He answered them, "My Father is working until now, and I Myself am working" (John 5:17).

Setting: Capernaum. The day after Jesus walks on the Sea of Galilee to join His disciples in a boat, the people He miraculously fed with a lad's five loaves and two fish quiz Him about the signs and works He performs so they may believe in Him.

Jesus then said to them, "Truly, truly, I say to you, it is not Moses who has given you the bread out of heaven, but it is My Father who gives you the true bread out of heaven. For the bread of God is that which comes down out of heaven, and gives life to the world" (John 6:32, 33).

Setting: The temple in Jerusalem. Following the Feast of Booths and the scribes' and Pharisees' failed attempt to stone a woman for adultery, Jesus returns the next day to teach; His enemies question His testimony about Himself.

Jesus answered and said to them, "Even if I testify about Myself, My testimony is true, for I know where I came from and where I am going; but you do not know where I come from or where I am going. You judge according to the flesh; I am not judging anyone. But even if I do judge, My judgment is true; for I am not alone *in it,* but I and the Father who sent Me. Even in your law it has been written that the testimony of two men is true. I am He who testifies about Myself, and the Father who sent Me testifies about Me." So they were saying to Him, "Where is Your Father?" Jesus answered, "You know neither Me nor My Father; if you knew Me, you would know My Father also" (John 8:14–19; see Deuteronomy 17:6; 19:15; Matthew 18:16; John 3:17; 5:30, 37; 7:28; 8:42).

Setting: The temple treasury in Jerusalem. After the scribes and Pharisees question His testimony about Himself, Jesus reveals to those Jews who believe in Him how He will make them free.

So Jesus was saying to those Jews who had believed Him, "If you continue in My word, *then* you are truly disciples of Mine; and you will know the truth, and the truth will make you free." They answered Him, "We are Abraham's descendants and have never yet been enslaved to anyone; how is it that You say, 'You will become free'?" Jesus answered them, "Truly, truly, I say to you, everyone who commits sin is the slave of sin. The slave does not remain in the house forever; the son does remain forever. So if the Son makes you free, you will be free indeed. I know that you are Abraham's descendants; yet you seek to kill Me, because My word has no place in you. I speak the things which I have seen with *My* Father; therefore you also do the things which you heard from *your* father" (John 8:31–38; see Romans 6:16).

Setting: The temple treasury in Jerusalem. While interacting with the scribes and Pharisees about His testimony, and their ancestry and motives, they state their belief Jesus is a demon-possessed Samaritan.

Jesus answered, "I do not have a demon; but I honor My Father, and you dishonor Me. But I do not seek My glory; there is One who seeks and judges. Truly, truly, I say to you, if anyone keeps My word he will never see death" (John 8:49–51; see Matthew 16:28; John 5:41; 7:20).

Setting: The temple treasury in Jerusalem. While Jesus interacts with the scribes and Pharisees, they state their belief that Jesus is a demon-possessed Samaritan because of His statement that anyone who keeps His word will never taste death.

Jesus answered, "If I glorify Myself, My glory is nothing; it is My Father who glorifies Me, of whom you say, 'He is our God'; and you have not come to know Him, but I know Him; and if I say that I do not know Him, I will be a liar like you, but I do know Him and keep His word. Your father Abraham rejoiced to see My day, and he saw *it* and was glad" (John 8:54–56; see Matthew 13:17; John 7:29).

Setting: Jerusalem. Following the Pharisees' interrogation and dismissal of the formerly blind man Jesus healed on the Sabbath, the Lord conveys the Parable of the Good Shepherd to the Pharisees using figures of speech they do not understand.

So Jesus said to them again, "Truly, truly, I say to you, I am the door of the sheep. All who came before Me are thieves and robbers, but the sheep did not hear them. I am the door; if anyone enters through Me, he will be saved, and will go in and out and find pasture. The thief comes only to steal and kill and destroy; I came that they may have life, and have *it* abundantly. I am the good shepherd; the good shepherd lays down His life for the sheep. He who is a hired hand, and not a shepherd, who is not the owner of the sheep, sees the wolf coming, and leaves the sheep and flees, and the wolf snatches them and scatters *them. He*

flees because he is a hired hand and is not concerned about the sheep. I am the good shepherd, and I know My own and My own know Me, even as the Father knows Me and I know the Father; and I lay down My life for the sheep. I have other sheep, which are not of this fold; I must bring them also, and they will hear My voice; and they will become one flock *with* one shepherd. For this reason the Father loves Me, because I lay down My life so that I may take it again. No one has taken it away from Me, but I lay it down on My own initiative. I have authority to take it up again. This commandment I received from My Father" (John 10:7–18; see Isaiah 40:11; 56:8; Jeremiah 23:1; Matthew 11:27).

Setting: Jerusalem. Following the Pharisees' interrogation and dismissal of the formerly blind man Jesus healed on the Sabbath, the Lord conveys the Parable of the Good Shepherd to the Pharisees using figures of speech they do not understand.

So Jesus said to them again, "Truly, truly, I say to you, I am the door of the sheep. All who came before Me are thieves and robbers, but the sheep did not hear them. I am the door; if anyone enters through Me, he will be saved, and will go in and out and find pasture. The thief comes only to steal and kill and destroy; I came that they may have life, and have *it* abundantly. I am the good shepherd; the good shepherd lays down His life for the sheep. He who is a hired hand, and not a shepherd, who is not the owner of the sheep, sees the wolf coming, and leaves the sheep and flees, and the wolf snatches them and scatters *them. He flees* because he is a hired hand and is not concerned about the sheep. I am the good shepherd, and I know My own and My own know Me, even as the Father knows Me and I know the Father; and I lay down My life for the sheep. I have other sheep, which are not of this fold; I must bring them also, and they will hear My voice; and they will become one flock *with* one shepherd. For this reason the Father loves Me, because I lay down My life so that I may take it again. No one has taken it away from Me, but I lay it down on My own initiative. I have authority to take it up again. This commandment I received from My Father" (John 10:7–18; see Isaiah 40:11; 56:8; Jeremiah 23:1; Matthew 11:27).

Setting: Jerusalem. At the Feast of Dedication, just after Jesus conveys the Parable of the Good Shepherd to the Pharisees (who do not understand it), they ask Him plainly if He is the Christ.

Jesus answered them, "I told you, and you do not believe; the works that I do in My Father's name, these testify of Me. But you do not believe because you are not of My sheep. My sheep hear My voice, and I know them, and they follow Me; and I give eternal life to them, and they will never perish; and no one will snatch them out of My hand. My Father, who has given *them* to Me, is greater than all; and no one is able to snatch *them* out of the Father's hand. I and the Father are one" (John 10:25–30; see John 8:47, 10:4; 17:1, 2, 20, 21).

Setting: Jerusalem. At the Feast of Dedication, the Pharisees desire to stone Jesus because He claims to be equal with God when they ask Him plainly whether He is the Christ.

Jesus answered them, "Has it not been written in your Law, 'I SAID, YOU ARE GODS'? If he called them gods, to whom the word of God came (and the Scripture cannot be broken), do you say of Him, whom the Father sanctified and sent into the world, 'You are blaspheming,' because I said, 'I am the Son of God'? If I do not do the works of My Father, do not believe Me; but if I do them, though you do not believe Me, believe the works, so that you may know and understand that the Father is in Me, and I in the Father" (John 10:34–38, Jesus quotes from Psalm 82:6; see John 14:10, 20).

Setting: Jerusalem. Before the Passover, as Jesus comforts and gives hope to His disciples regarding their future after He returns to heaven, Thomas asks where He is going and how they will know the way.

Jesus said to him, "I am the way, and the truth, and the life; no one comes to the Father but through Me. If you had known Me, you would have known My Father also; from now on you know Him, and have seen Him" (John 14:6, 7; see John 8:19; 10:9; 11:25).

Setting: Jerusalem. Before the Passover, after responding to Philip's request for Him to show His disciples the Father, Jesus conveys the upcoming role of the Holy Spirit in their lives.

"I will not leave you as orphans; I will come to you. After a little while the world will no longer see Me, but you *will* see Me; because I live, you will live also. In that day you will know that I am in the Father, and you in Me, and I in you. He who has My commandments and keeps them is the one who loves Me; and he who loves Me will be loved by My Father, and I will love him and will disclose Myself to him" (John 14:18–21; see John 6:57; 10:37, 38; 16:16, 22).

Setting: Jerusalem. Before the Passover, after conveying the upcoming ministry of the Holy Spirit in His disciples' lives, Jesus answers Judas' (not Iscariot) question why He will disclose Himself to His disciples but not the whole world.

Jesus answered and said to him, "If anyone loves Me, he will keep My word; and My Father will love him, and We will come to him and make Our abode with him. He who does not love Me does not keep My words; and the word which you hear is not Mine, but the Father's who sent Me" (John 14:23, 24; see John 7:16; 8:51).

Setting: Jerusalem. Before the Passover, after conveying the upcoming ministry of the Holy Spirit in His disciples' lives with His imminent departure, Jesus explains He is the vine and His disciples are the branches.

"I am the true vine, and My Father is the vinedresser. Every branch in Me that does not bear fruit, He takes away; and every *branch* that bears fruit, He prunes it so that it may bear more fruit. You are already clean because of the word which I have spoken to you. Abide in Me, and I in you. As the branch cannot bear fruit of itself unless it abides in the vine, so neither *can* you unless you abide in Me. I am the vine, you are the branches; he who abides in Me and I in him, he bears much fruit, for apart from Me you can do nothing. If anyone does not abide in Me, he is thrown away as a branch and dries up; and they gather them, and cast them into the fire and they are burned. If you abide in Me, and My words abide in you, ask whatever you wish, and it will be done for you. My Father is glorified by this, that you bear much fruit, and *so* prove to be My disciples. Just as the Father has loved Me, I have also loved you; abide in My love. If you keep My commandments, you will abide in My love; just as I have kept My Father's commandments and abide in His love. These things I have spoken to you so that My joy may be in you, and *that* your joy may be made full" (John 15:1–11; see Matthew 5:16; 7:7; John 3:29, 35; 6:56; 8:29, 31; 13:10; 15:16).

Setting: Jerusalem. Before the Passover, with His departure in mind, after explaining He is the vine and His disciples are the branches, Jesus instructs them to love one another.

"This is My commandment, that you love one another, just as I have loved you. Greater love has no one than this, that one lay down his life for his friends. You are My friends if you do what I command you. No longer do I call you slaves, for the slave does not know what his master is doing; but I have called you friends, for all things that I have heard from My Father I have made known to you. You did not choose Me but I chose you, and appointed you that you would go and bear fruit, and *that* your fruit would remain, so that whatever you ask of the Father in My name He may give to you. This I command you, that you love one another" (John 15:12–17; see Matthew 12:50; John 6:70; 8:26; 10:11; 13:34).

Setting: Jerusalem. Before the Passover, with His departure in mind, after explaining He is the vine and His disciples are the branches, Jesus prepares them to be hated by the world.

"He who hates Me hates My Father also. If I had not done among them the works which no one else did, they would not have sin; but now they have both seen and hated Me and My Father as well. But *they have done this* to fulfill the word that is written in their Law, 'THEY HATED ME WITHOUT A CAUSE'" (John 15:23–25, Jesus quotes from Psalm 35:19; see John 9:41).

Setting: Jerusalem. The risen Jesus first appears to Mary Magdalene after she tells Simon Peter and John about the empty tomb where Jesus had been the day before the Sabbath. He had died on the cross for the sins of the world.

Jesus said to her, "Woman, why are you weeping? Whom are you seeking?" Supposing Him to be the gardener, she said to Him, "Sir, if you have carried Him away, tell me where you have laid Him, and I will take Him away." Jesus said to her, "Mary!" She turned and said to Him in Hebrew "Rabboni!" (which means, Teacher). Jesus said to her, "Stop clinging to Me, for I have not yet ascended to the Father; but go to My brethren and say to them, 'I ascend to My Father and your Father, and My God and Your God'" (John 20:15–17; see Mark 16:9–11; John 7:33; 19:31–42).

Setting: On the island of Patmos (in the Aegean Sea about fifty miles southwest of Ephesus in modern Turkey). On the Lord's Day (Sunday), about fifty years after Jesus' resurrection, the disciple John encounters the Lord Jesus Christ, who communicates a new revelation for the apostle to record for the church in Thyatira and to six other churches in Asia.

"And to the angel of the church in Thyatira write: The Son of God, who has eyes like a flame of fire, and His feet are like burnished bronze, says this: 'I know your deeds, and your love and faith and service and perseverance, and that your deeds of late are greater than at first. But I have *this* against you, that you tolerate the woman Jezebel, who calls herself a prophetess, and she teaches and leads My bond-servants astray so that they commit *acts of* immorality and eat things sacrificed to idols. I gave her time to repent, and she does not want to repent of her immorality. Behold, I will throw her on a bed *of sickness,* and those who commit adultery with her into great tribulation, unless they repent of her deeds. And I will kill her children with pestilence, and all the churches will know that I am He who searches the minds and hearts; and I will give to each one of you according to your deeds. But I say to you, the rest who are in Thyatira, who do not hold this teaching, who have not known the deep things of Satan, as they call them—I place no other burden on you. Nevertheless what you have, hold fast until I come. He who overcomes, and he who keeps My deeds until the end, TO HIM I WILL GIVE AUTHORITY OVER THE NATIONS; AND HE SHALL RULE THEM WITH A ROD OF IRON, AS THE VESSELS OF THE POTTER ARE BROKEN TO PIECES, as I also have received *authority* from My Father; and I will give him the morning star. He who has an ear, let him hear what the Spirit says to the churches' (Revelation 2:18–29; Jesus quotes from Psalm 2:8, 9; Isaiah 30:14; see 1 Kings 16:31; Psalm 7:9; Romans 2:5; 1 Corinthians 2:10; 2 Peter 3:9; Revelation 1:14; 2:7; 3:11; 17:1–20).

Setting: On the island of Patmos (in the Aegean Sea about fifty miles southwest of Ephesus in modern Turkey). On the Lord's Day (Sunday), about fifty years after Jesus' resurrection, the disciple John encounters the Lord Jesus Christ, who communicates a new revelation for the apostle to record for the church in Sardis and to six other churches in Asia.

"To the angel of the church in Sardis write: He who has the seven Spirits of God and the seven stars, says this: 'I know your deeds, that you have a name that you are alive, but you are dead. Wake up, and strengthen the things that remain, which were about to die; for I have not found your deeds completed in the sight of My God. So remember what you have received and heard; and keep *it,* and repent. Therefore if you do not wake up, I will come like a thief, and you will not know at what hour I will come to you. But you have a few people in Sardis who have not soiled their garments; and they will walk with Me in white, for they are worthy. He who overcomes will thus be clothed in white garments; and I will not erase his name from the book of life, and I will confess his name before My Father and before His angels. He who has an ear, let him hear what the Spirit says to the churches' " (Revelation 3:1–6; see Matthew 10:32; Revelation 1:16).

Setting: On the island of Patmos (in the Aegean Sea about fifty miles southwest of Ephesus in modern Turkey). On the Lord's Day (Sunday), about fifty years after Jesus' resurrection, the disciple John encounters the Lord Jesus Christ, who communicates a new revelation for the apostle to record for the church in Laodicea and to six other churches in Asia.

"To the angel of the church in Laodicea write: The Amen, the faithful and true Witness, the Beginning of the creation of God, says this: 'I know your deeds, that you are neither cold nor hot; I wish that you were cold or hot. So because you are lukewarm, and neither hot nor cold, I will spit you out of My mouth. Because you say, "I am rich, and have become wealthy, and have need of nothing," and you do not know that you are wretched and miserable and poor and blind and naked, I advise you to buy from Me gold refined by fire so that you may become rich, and white garments so that you may clothe yourself, and *that* the shame of your nakedness will not be revealed; and eye salve to anoint your eyes so that you may see. Those whom I love, I reprove and discipline; therefore be zealous and repent. Behold, I stand at the door and knock; if anyone hears My voice and opens the door, I will come in to him and will dine with him, and he with Me. He who overcomes, I will grant to him to sit down with Me on My throne, as I also overcame and sat down with My Father on His throne. He who has an ear, let him hear what the Spirit says to the churches'" (Revelation 3:14–22; see Proverbs 3:12; Hosea 12:8; John 14:23; 16:33).

FATHER, OUR (God)

Setting: Galilee. During the early part of His ministry, Jesus gives a model prayer to His disciples and the multitudes while conveying The Sermon on the Mount.

"Pray, then, in this way: 'Our Father who is in heaven, hallowed be Your name. Your kingdom come. Your will be done, on earth as it is in heaven. Give us this day our daily bread. And forgive us our debts, as we also have forgiven our debtors. And do not lead us into temptation, but deliver us from evil. [For Yours is the kingdom and the power and the glory forever. Amen]'" (Matthew 6:9–13; cf. Luke 11:2–4; see John 17:15).

FATHER, PARABLE OF THE LOVING (See SON, PARABLE OF THE PRODIGAL)

FATHER, RIGHTEOUS

Setting: Jerusalem. Before the Passover, after giving His disciples assurance that in the midst of tribulation they will have His peace, Jesus continues praying His high-priestly prayer.

"The glory which You have given Me I have given to them, that they may be one, just as We are one; I in them and You in Me, that they may be perfected in unity, so that the world may know that you sent Me, and loved them, even as You have loved Me. Father, I desire that they also, whom You have given Me, be with Me where I am, so that they may see My glory which You have given Me, for You loved Me before the foundation of the world. O righteous Father, although the world has not known You, yet I have known You; and these have known that You sent Me; and I have made Your name known to them, and will make it known, so that the love with which You loved Me may be in them, and I in them" (John 17:22–26; see Matthew 25:34; John 1:14; 10:38; 15:9; 16:27).

FATHER, SONS OF YOUR

Setting: Galilee. During the early part of His ministry, Jesus preaches the Sermon on the Mount to His disciples and the multitudes.

"You have heard that it was said, 'YOU SHALL LOVE YOUR NEIGHBOR and hate your enemy.' But I say to you, love your enemies and pray for those who persecute you, so that you may be sons of your Father who is in heaven; for He causes His sun to rise on *the* evil and *the* good, and sends rain on *the* righteous and *the* unrighteous. For if you love those who love you, what reward do you have? Do not even the tax collectors do the same? If you greet only your brothers, what more are you doing *than others?* Do not even the Gentiles do the same? Therefore, you are to be perfect, as your heavenly Father is perfect" (Matthew 5:43–48, Jesus quotes from Leviticus 19:18; cf. Leviticus 19:2; Luke 6:27–36).

FATHER, WILL OF HIS (human)

Setting: The temple in Jerusalem. Jesus delivers a parable to the chief priests and elders after they question His authority.

"But what do you think? A man had two sons, and he came to the first and said, 'Son, go work today in the vineyard.' And he answered, 'I will not'; but afterward he regretted it and went. The man came to the second and said the same thing; and he answered, 'I *will,* sir'; but he did not go. Which of the two sons did the will of his father?" They said, "The first." Jesus said to them, "Truly, I say to you that the tax collectors and prostitutes will get into the kingdom of God before you. For John came to you in the way of righteousness and you did not believe him; but the tax collectors and prostitutes did believe him; and you, seeing *this,* did not even feel remorse afterward so as to believe him" (Matthew 21:28–32; cf. Luke 7:29, 30, 37–50).

FATHER, WILL OF MY (Also see FATHER, WILL OF YOUR; and WILL OF GOD)

[WILL OF MY FATHER from Your will be done]

Setting: Galilee. During the early part of His ministry, Jesus gives a model prayer to His disciples and the multitudes while conveying the Sermon on the Mount.

"Pray, then, in this way: 'Our Father who is in heaven, hallowed be Your name. Your kingdom come. Your will be done, on earth as it is in heaven. Give us this day our daily bread. And forgive us our debts, as we also have forgiven our debtors. And do not lead us into temptation, but deliver us from evil. [For Yours is the kingdom and the power and the glory forever. Amen]'" (Matthew 6:9–13; cf. Luke 11:2–4; see John 17:15).

Setting: Galilee. During the early part of His ministry, Jesus preaches the Sermon on the Mount to His disciples and the multitudes.

"Not everyone who says to Me, 'Lord, Lord,' will enter the kingdom of heaven, but he who does the will of My Father who is in heaven *will enter.* Many will say to Me on that day, 'Lord, Lord, did we not prophesy in Your name, and in Your name cast out demons, and in Your name perform many miracles?' And then I will declare to them, 'I never knew you, DEPART FROM ME, YOU WHO PRACTICE LAWLESSNESS'"(Matthew 7:21–23, Jesus quotes from Psalm 6:8; cf. Matthew 25:11–13; see Luke 6:46).

Setting: Galilee. Jesus' mother, Mary, and His brothers are waiting to see Him as He teaches and preaches.

But Jesus answered the one who was telling Him and said, "Who is My mother and who are My brothers?" And stretching out His hand toward His disciples, He said, "Behold, My mother and My brothers! For whoever does the will of My Father who is in heaven, he is My brother and sister and mother" (Matthew 12:48–50; cf. Mark 3:31–35; Luke 8:19–21).

[WILL OF MY FATHER from not as I will, but as You will and Your will be done]
Setting: An upper room in Jerusalem. After celebrating the Passover meal with His disciples, Jesus retreats to the Garden of Gethsemane on the Mount of Olives to pray prior to His betrayal by Judas.

Then Jesus came with them to a place called Gethsemane, and said to His disciples, "Sit here while I go over there and pray." And He took with Him Peter and the two sons of Zebedee, and began to be grieved and distressed. Then He said to them, "My soul is deeply grieved, to the point of death; remain here and keep watch with Me." And He went a little beyond *them,* and fell on His face and prayed, saying, "My Father, if it is possible, let this cup pass from Me; yet not as I will, but as You will." And He came to the disciples and found them sleeping, and said to Peter, "So, you *men* could not keep watch with Me for one hour? Keep watching and praying that you may not enter into temptation; the spirit is willing, but the flesh is weak." He went away again a second time and prayed, saying, "My Father, if this cannot pass away unless I drink it, Your will be done." Again He came and found them sleeping, for their eyes were heavy. And He left them again, and went away and prayed a third time, saying the same thing once more. Then He came to the disciples and said to them, "Are you still sleeping and resting? Behold the hour is at hand and the Son of Man is being betrayed into the hands of sinners. Get up, let us be going; behold the one who betrays Me is at hand!" (Matthew 26:36–46; cf. Mark 14:32–42; Luke 22:40–46; see Matthew 20:22; John 12:27).

[WILL OF MY FATHER from yet not what I will, but what You will]
Setting: Gethsemane on the Mount of Olives, east of the temple in Jerusalem. Jesus agonizes over His impending death, disappointed that His disciples keep falling asleep instead of watching and praying with Him.

They came to a place named Gethsemane; and He said to the disciples, "Sit here until I have prayed." And He took with Him Peter and James and John, and began to be very distressed and troubled. And He said to them, "My soul is deeply grieved to the point of death; remain here and keep watch." And He went a little beyond *them,* and fell to the ground and *began* to pray that if it were possible, the hour might pass Him by. And He was saying, "Abba! Father! All things are possible for You; remove this cup from Me; yet not what I will, but what You will." And He came and found them sleeping, and said to Peter, "Simon, are you asleep? Could you not keep watch for one hour? Keep watching and praying that you may not come into temptation; the spirit is willing, but the flesh is weak" (Mark 14:32–38; cf. Matthew 26:36–41; Luke 22:41–46; see Romans 8:15; Galatians 4:6).

[WILL OF MY FATHER from not My will, but Yours be done]
Setting: An upper room in Jerusalem. After celebrating the Passover meal and instructing His disciples to prepare to persevere without Him, with His crucifixion imminent, Jesus proceeds to the Mount of Olives to pray.

And He came out and proceeded as was His custom to the Mount of Olives; and the disciples also followed Him. When He arrived at the place, He said to them, "Pray that you may not enter into temptation." And He withdrew from them about a stone's throw, and He knelt down and *began* to pray, saying, "Father, if You are willing, remove this cup from Me; yet not My will, but Yours be done" (Luke 22:39–42; cf. Matthew 26:36–42; Mark 14:32–49; see Luke 21:37).

[WILL OF MY FATHER from the will of Him who sent Me]
Setting: Sychar in Samaria. After Jesus converses with a Samaritan woman at Jacob's well, His disciples return with food. They try to get Jesus to eat but are surprised when He speaks of other food.

Jesus said to them, "My food is to do the will of Him who sent Me and to accomplish His work. Do you not say, 'There are yet four months, and *then* comes the harvest'? Behold, I say to you, lift up your eyes and look on the fields, that they are white for harvest. Already he who reaps is receiving wages and is gathering fruit for life eternal; so that he who sows and he who reaps may rejoice together. For in this *case* the saying is true, 'One sows and another reaps.' I sent you to reap that for which you have not labored; others have labored and you have entered into their labor" (John 4:34–38; see Matthew 9:37, 38; John 5:36).

[WILL OF MY FATHER from will of Him who sent Me]
Setting: Jerusalem. During the Feast of the Jews, Jesus responds to criticism from the Jewish religious leaders by referring to God as His Father (thereby making Himself equal with God) and informing them that God, John the Baptist, and His works all testify to His mission.

"I can do nothing on My own initiative. As I hear, I judge; and My judgment is just, because I do not seek My own will, but the will of Him who sent Me. If I *alone* testify about Myself, My testimony is not true. There is another who testifies of Me, and I know that the testimony which He gives about Me is true. You have sent to John, and he has testified to the truth. But the testimony which I receive is not from man, but I say these things so that you may be saved. He was the lamp that was burning and was shining and you were willing to rejoice for a while in his light. But the testimony which I have is greater than the *testimony of* John; for the works which the Father has given Me to accomplish—the very works that I do—testify about Me, that the Father has sent Me. And the Father who sent Me, He has testified of Me. You have neither heard His voice at any time nor seen His form. You do not have His word abiding in you, for you do not believe Him whom He sent" (John 5:30–38; see Matthew 3:17; Mark 1:4, 5; John 1:7, 15, 32; 4:34; 8:14–16; 10:25, 37, 38).

[WILL OF MY FATHER also from will of Him who sent Me]
Setting: On the way to Capernaum. The day after walking on the Sea of Galilee to join His disciples in a boat, the people He miraculously fed with a lad's five loaves and two fish ask Jesus to always give them this bread out of heaven.

Jesus said to them, "I am the bread of life; he who comes to Me will not hunger, and he who believes in Me will never thirst. But I said to you that you have seen Me, and yet do not believe. All that the Father gives Me will come to Me, and the one who comes to Me I will certainly not cast out. For I have come down from heaven, not to do My own will, but the will of Him who sent Me. This is the will of Him who sent Me, that of all that He has given Me I lose nothing, but raise it up on the last day. For this is the will of My Father, that everyone who beholds the Son and believes in Him will have eternal life, and I Myself will raise him up on the last day" (John 6:35–40; see John 3:13, 16; 4:13, 14).

[WILL OF MY FATHER from His will]
Setting: The temple in Jerusalem. After receiving encouragement from His blood brothers in Galilee to attend the upcoming Feast of Booths in Jerusalem in order to demonstrate His works to His disciples and the world, Jesus goes and teaches, astonishing the Jewish religious leaders.

So Jesus answered them and said, "My teaching is not Mine, but His who sent Me. If anyone is willing to do His will, he will know of the teaching, whether it is of God or *whether* I speak of Myself. He who speaks from himself seeks his own glory; but He who is seeking the glory of the One who sent Him, He is true, and there is no unrighteousness in Him" (John 7:16–18; see John 5:41).

FATHER, WILL OF YOUR (Also see FATHER, WILL OF MY; and WILL OF GOD)

Setting: Capernaum of Galilee. Jesus illustrates to His disciples the value of little ones.

"What do you think? If any man has a hundred sheep, and one of them has gone astray, does he not leave the ninety-nine on the mountains and go and search for the one that is straying? If it turns out that he finds it, truly I say to you, he rejoices over it more than the ninety-nine which have not gone astray. So it is not *the* will of your Father who is in heaven that one of these little ones perish" (Matthew 18:12–14; cf. Luke 15:4–7).

FATHER, WORKS OF MY (Also see JESUS' WORK)

[WORKS OF MY FATHER from His work]

Setting: Sychar in Samaria. After Jesus converses with a Samaritan woman at Jacob's well, His disciples return with food. They try to get Jesus to eat but are surprised when He speaks of other food.

Jesus said to them, "My food is to do the will of Him who sent Me and to accomplish His work. Do you not say, 'There are yet four months, and *then* comes the harvest'? Behold, I say to you, lift up your eyes and look on the fields, that they are white for harvest. Already he who reaps is receiving wages and is gathering fruit for life eternal; so that he who sows and he who reaps may rejoice together. For in this *case* the saying is true, 'One sows and another reaps.' I sent you to reap that for which you have not labored; others have labored and you have entered into their labor" (John 4:34–38; see Matthew 9:37, 38; John 5:36).

[WORKS OF MY FATHER from My Father is working until now]

Setting: By the pool of Bethesda in Jerusalem. During the Feast of the Jews, Jesus responds to criticism from the Jewish religious leaders for healing a lame man on the Sabbath.

But He answered them, "My Father is working until now, and I Myself am working" (John 5:17).

[WORKS OF MY FATHER from He sees the Father doing]

Setting: By the pool of Bethesda in Jerusalem. During the Feast of the Jews, Jesus responds to criticism from the Jewish religious leaders for healing a lame man on the Sabbath and for referring to God as His Father (thereby making Himself equal with God).

Therefore Jesus answered and was saying to them, "Truly, truly, I say to you, the Son can do nothing of Himself, unless *it is* something He sees the Father doing; for whatever the Father does, these things the Son also does in like manner. For the Father loves the Son, and shows Him all things that He Himself is doing; and *the Father* will show Him greater works than these, so that you will marvel. For just as the Father raises the dead and gives them life, even so the Son also gives life to whom He wishes. For not even the Father judges anyone, but He has given all judgment to the Son, so that all will honor the Son even as they honor the Father. He who does not honor the Son does not honor the Father who sent Him" (John 5:19–23; see Luke 10:16; John 3:35; 11:25; 14:12).

[WORKS OF MY FATHER from works of Him who sent Me]

Setting: The temple treasury in Jerusalem. After Jesus avoids being stoned by the scribes and Pharisees, His disciples wonder if blindness is caused by sin as the Lord heals a man born blind.

Jesus answered, "*It was* neither *that* this man sinned, nor his parents; but *it was* so that the works of God might be displayed in him. We must work the works of Him who sent Me as long as it is day; night is coming when no one can work. While I am in the world, I am the Light of the world." When He had said this, He spat on the ground, and made clay of the spittle, and applied the clay to his eyes, and said to him, "Go, wash in the pool of Siloam" (which is translated, Sent). So he went away and washed, and came *back* seeing (John 9:3–7; see John 8:12; 11:4; 12:46).

Setting: Jerusalem. At the Feast of Dedication, the Pharisees desire to stone Jesus because He claims to be equal with God when they ask Him plainly whether He is the Christ.

Jesus answered them, "Has it not been written in your Law, 'I SAID, YOU ARE GODS'? If he called them gods, to whom the word of God came (and the Scripture cannot be broken), do you say of Him, whom the Father sanctified and sent into the world, 'You are blaspheming,' because I said, 'I am the Son of God'? If I do not do the works of My Father, do not believe Me; but if I do them, though you do not believe Me, believe the works, so that you may know and understand that the Father is in Me, and I in the Father" (John 10:34–38, Jesus quotes from Psalm 82:6; see John 10, 20).

[WORKS OF MY FATHER from His works]

Setting: Jerusalem. Before the Passover, after answering Thomas' question as to where He is going and how His disciples will know the way, Jesus responds to Philip's request for Him to show His disciples the Father.

Jesus said to him, "Have I been so long with you, and *yet* you have not come to know Me, Philip? He who has seen Me has seen the Father; how *can* you say, 'Show us the Father'? Do you not believe that I am in the Father, and the Father is in Me? The words that I say to you I do not speak on My own initiative, but the Father abiding in Me does His works. Believe Me that I am in the Father and the Father is in Me; otherwise believe because of the works themselves. Truly, truly, I say to you, he who believes in Me, the works that I do, he will do also; and greater *works* than these he will do; because I go to the Father. Whatever you ask in My name, that will I do, so that the Father may be glorified in the Son. If you ask Me anything in My name, I will do *it*" (John 14:9–14; see Matthew 7:7; John 1:14; 5:19, 20, 36; 10:37, 38; 15:16).

FATHER, YOUR (God, humans, and Satan)

Setting: Galilee. During the early part of His ministry, Jesus preaches the Sermon on the Mount to His disciples and the multitudes.

"You are the light of the world. A city set on a hill cannot be hidden; nor does *anyone* light a lamp and put it under a basket, but on the lampstand, and it gives light to all who are in the house. Let your light shine before men in such a way that they may see your good works, and glorify your Father who is in heaven" (Matthew 5:14–16; cf. Mark 4:21; 1 Peter 2:12).

Setting: Galilee. During the early part of His ministry, Jesus preaches the Sermon on the Mount to His disciples and the multitudes.

"You have heard that it was said, 'YOU SHALL LOVE YOUR NEIGHBOR and hate your enemy.' But I say to you, love your enemies and pray for those who persecute you, so that you may be sons of your Father who is in heaven; for He causes His sun to rise on *the* evil and *the* good, and sends rain on *the* righteous and *the* unrighteous. For if you love those who love you, what reward do you have? Do not even the tax collectors do the same? If you greet only your brothers, what more are you doing *than others?* Do not even the Gentiles do the same? Therefore, you are to be perfect, as your heavenly Father is perfect" (Matthew 5:43–48, Jesus quotes from Leviticus 19:18; cf. Leviticus 19:2; Luke 6:27–36).

Setting: Galilee. During the early part of His ministry, Jesus preaches the Sermon on the Mount to His disciples and the multitudes.

"Beware of practicing your righteousness before men to be noticed by them; otherwise you have no reward with your Father who is in heaven" (Matthew 6:1; cf. Matthew 6:5, 16).

Setting: Galilee. During the early part of His ministry, Jesus preaches the Sermon on the Mount to His disciples and the multitudes.

"So when you give to the poor, do not sound a trumpet before you, as the hypocrites do in the synagogues and in the streets, so that they may be honored by men. Truly I say to you, they have their reward in full. But when you give to the poor, do not let your left hand know what your right hand is doing, so that your giving will be in secret; and your Father who sees *what is done* in secret will reward you" (Matthew 6:2–4; see Jeremiah 17:10; Matthew 6:16).

Setting: Galilee. During the early part of His ministry, Jesus preaches the Sermon on the Mount to His disciples and the multitudes.

"When you pray, you are not to be like the hypocrites; for they love to stand and pray in the synagogues and on the street corners so that they may be seen by men. Truly I say to you, they have their reward in full. But you, when you pray, go into your inner room, close your door and pray to your Father who is in secret, and your Father who sees *what is done* in secret will reward you" (Matthew 6:5, 6; see Mark 11:25).

Setting: Galilee. During the early part of His ministry, Jesus preaches the Sermon on the Mount to His disciples and the multitudes.

"And when you are praying, do not use meaningless repetition as the Gentiles do, for they suppose that they will be heard for their many words. So do not be like them; for your Father knows what you need before you ask Him" (Matthew 6:7, 8; see 1 Kings 18:26–29).

Setting: Galilee. During the early part of His ministry, Jesus preaches the Sermon on the Mount to His disciples and the multitudes.

"For if you forgive others for their transgressions, your heavenly Father will also forgive you. But if you do not forgive others, then your Father will not forgive your transgressions" (Matthew 6:14, 15; cf. Matthew 18:15; see Mark 7:2).

Setting: Galilee. During the early part of His ministry, Jesus preaches the Sermon on the Mount to His disciples and the multitudes.

"Whenever you fast, do not put on a gloomy face as the hypocrites *do,* for they neglect their appearance so that they will be noticed by men when they are fasting. Truly I say to you, they have their reward in full. But you, when you fast, anoint your head and wash your face so that your fasting will not be noticed by men, but by your Father who is in secret; and your Father who sees *what is done* in secret will reward you" (Matthew 6:16–18; see Matthew 6:4, 6).

Setting: Galilee. During the early part of His ministry, Jesus preaches the Sermon on the Mount to His disciples and the multitudes.

"Ask, and it will be given to you; seek, and you will find; knock, and it will be opened to you. For everyone who asks receives, and he who seeks finds, and to him who knocks it will be opened. Or what man is there among you who, when his son asks for a loaf, will give him a stone? Or if he asks for a fish, he will not give him a snake, will he? If you then, being evil, know how to give good gifts to your children, how much more will your Father who is in heaven give what is good to those who ask Him! In everything, therefore, treat people the same way you want them to treat you, for this is the Law and the Prophets" (Matthew 7:7–12; cf. Matthew 22:40; Luke 6:31; 11:9–13; see Psalm 84:11).

Setting: Galilee. After His disciples observe His ministry, Jesus summons and specifically instructs them about the upcoming hardships of *their* ministry to the people of Israel.

"Behold, I send you out as sheep in the midst of wolves; so be shrewd as serpents and innocent as doves. But beware of men, for they will hand you over to *the* courts and scourge you in their synagogues; and you will even be brought before governors and kings for My sake, as a testimony to them and to the Gentiles. But when they hand you over, do not worry about how or what you are to say; for it will be given you in that hour what you are to say. For it is not you who speak, but *it* is the Spirit of your Father who speaks in you" (Matthew 10:16–20; cf. Luke 10:3).

Setting: Galilee. After His disciples observe His ministry, Jesus summons and specifically instructs them about their ministry ahead involving true discipleship.

"Are not two sparrows sold for a cent? And *yet* not one of them will fall to the ground apart from your Father. But the very hairs of your head are all numbered. So do not fear; you are more valuable than many sparrows" (Matthew 10:29–31; cf. Luke 12:6; see Matthew 12:12).

Setting: Galilee. Pharisees and scribes from Jerusalem question Jesus about His disciples' lack of obedience to tradition and the commandments.

And He answered and said to them, "Why do you yourselves transgress the commandment of God for the sake of tradition? For God said, 'HONOR YOUR FATHER AND MOTHER,' and, 'HE WHO SPEAKS EVIL OF FATHER OR MOTHER IS TO BE PUT TO DEATH.' But you say, 'Whoever says to *his* father or mother, "Whatever I have that would help you has been given *to God*," he is not to honor his father or mother.' And *by this* you invalidated the word of God for the sake of your tradition. You hypocrites, rightly did Isaiah prophesy of you: 'THIS PEOPLE HONORS ME WITH THEIR LIPS, BUT THEIR HEART IS FAR AWAY FROM ME. BUT IN VAIN DO THEY WORSHIP ME, TEACHING AS DOCTRINES THE PRECEPTS OF MEN' "(Matthew 15:3–9, Jesus quotes from Exodus 20:12, 21:17, Leviticus 20:9; Isaiah 29:13; cf. Mark 7:5–7; see Colossians 2:22).

Setting: Capernaum of Galilee. Jesus illustrates to His disciples the value of little ones.

"What do you think? If any man has a hundred sheep, and one of them has gone astray, does he not leave the ninety-nine on the mountains and go and search for the one that is straying? If it turns out that he finds it, truly I say to you, he rejoices over it more than the ninety-nine which have not gone astray. So it is not *the* will of your Father who is in heaven that one of these little ones perish" (Matthew 18:12–14; cf. Luke 15:4–7).

Setting: Judea beyond the Jordan (Perea). Jesus shares with a rich, young ruler how he can obtain eternal life.

And He said to him, "Why are you asking Me about what is good? There is *only* One who is good; but if you wish to enter into life, keep the commandments." *Then* he said to Him, 'Which ones?' And Jesus said, "YOU SHALL NOT COMMIT MURDER; YOU SHALL NOT COMMIT ADULTERY; YOU SHALL NOT STEAL; YOU SHALL NOT BEAR FALSE WITNESS; HONOR YOUR FATHER AND MOTHER; and YOU SHALL LOVE YOUR NEIGHBOR AS YOURSELF." The young man said to Him, "All these things I have kept; what am I still lacking?" Jesus said to him, "If you wish to complete go *and* sell your possessions and give to *the* poor, and you will have treasure in heaven; and come, follow Me" (Matthew 19:16–22, Jesus quotes from Exodus 20:13–15; Leviticus 19:18; cf. Leviticus 18:5; Mark 10:17–21; Luke 10:25–28; 12:33; 18:18–24).

Setting: The temple in Jerusalem. Jesus exposes the truth about Pharisaism to the crowds and His disciples after the Jewish religious leaders test Him with questions.

Then Jesus spoke to the crowds and to His disciples, saying: "The scribes and the Pharisees have seated themselves in the chair of Moses; therefore all that they tell you, do and observe, but do not do according to their deeds; for they say *things* and do not do *them.* They tie up heavy burdens and lay them on men's shoulders, but they themselves are unwilling to move them with *so much as* a finger. But they do all their deeds to be noticed by men; for they broaden their phylacteries and lengthen their tassels *of their garments.* They love the place of honor at banquets and the chief seats in the synagogues, and respectful greetings in the market places, and being called Rabbi by men. But do not be called Rabbi; for One is your Teacher, and you are all brothers. Do not call *anyone* on earth your father; for One is your Father, He who is in heaven. Do not be called leaders; for One is your Leader, *that is,* Christ. But the greatest among you shall be your servant. Whoever exalts himself shall be humbled; and whoever humbles himself shall be exalted" (Matthew 23:1–12; cf. Matthew 20:26; Mark 12:38–40; Luke 20:46, 47; see Exodus 13:9; Deuteronomy 33:3; Matthew 6:1, 5, 6, 9, 16; Mark 14:11; Luke 11:43; 14:11).

Setting: Galilee. The Pharisees and some of the scribes from Jerusalem question why Jesus' disciples do not follow the tradition of ceremonial hand cleansing before eating bread.

And He said to them, "Rightly did Isaiah prophesy of you hypocrites, as it is written: 'THIS PEOPLE HONORS ME WITH THEIR LIPS, BUT THEIR HEART IS FAR AWAY FROM ME. BUT IN VAIN DO THEY WORSHIP ME, TEACHING AS DOCTRINES THE PRECEPTS OF MEN.' Neglecting the commandment of God, you hold to the tradition of men." He was also saying to them, "You are experts at setting aside the commandment of God in order to keep tradition. For Moses said, 'HONOR YOUR FATHER AND YOUR MOTHER'; and, 'HE WHO SPEAKS EVIL OF FATHER OR MOTHER, IS TO BE PUT TO DEATH'; but you say, 'If a man says to *his* father or *his* mother, whatever I have that would help you is Corban (that is to say, given *to God*),' you no longer permit him to do anything for *his* father or *his* mother; *thus* invalidating the word of God by your tradition which you have handed down; and you do many things such as that" (Mark 7:6–13, Jesus quotes from Exodus 20:12; 21:17; Isaiah 29:13; cf. Matthew 15:1–6).

Setting: Judea beyond the Jordan (Perea). After demonstrating to His disciples the importance of little children, Jesus encounters a rich man seeking eternal life.

And Jesus said to him, "Why do you call Me good? No one is good except God alone. You know the commandments, 'DO NOT MURDER, DO NOT COMMIT ADULTERY, DO NOT STEAL, DO NOT BEAR FALSE WITNESS, Do not defraud, HONOR YOUR FATHER AND MOTHER.'" And he said to Him, "Teacher, I have kept all these things from my youth up." Looking at him, Jesus felt a love for him and said to him, "One thing you lack: go and sell all you possess and give to the poor, and you will have treasure in heaven; and come, follow Me" (Mark 10:18–21; Jesus quotes from Exodus 20:12–16; cf. Matthew 19:16–22; Luke 18:18–24; see Matthew 6:20).

Setting: Jerusalem. After Jesus instructs the money changers while cleansing the temple, Peter draws His and His disciples' attention to the earlier-cursed fig tree.

And Jesus answered saying to them, "Have faith in God. Truly, I say to you, whoever says to this mountain, 'Be taken up and cast into the sea,' and does not doubt in his heart, but believes that what he says is going to happen, it will be *granted* him. Therefore I say to you, all things for which you pray and ask, believe that you have received them, and they will be *granted* you. Whenever you stand praying, forgive, if you have anything against anyone, so that your Father who is in heaven will also forgive you your transgressions. [But if you do not forgive, neither will your Father who is in heaven forgive your transgressions'] (Mark 11:22–26; cf. Matthew 21:19–22; see Matthew 6:14, 15; 7:7; 17:20).

Setting: Galilee. After selecting His twelve disciples, Jesus teaches the Sermon on the Mount to His disciples and a great throng from Judea, Jerusalem, and the central coastal region of Tyre and Sidon.

"But I say to you who hear, love your enemies, do good to those who hate you, bless those who curse you, pray for those who mistreat you. Whoever hits you on the cheek, offer him the other also; and whoever takes away your coat, do not withhold your shirt from him either. Give to everyone who asks of you, and whoever takes away what is yours, do not demand it back. Treat others the same way you want them to treat you. If you love those who love you, what credit is *that* to you? For even sinners love those who love them. If you do good to those who do good to you, what credit is *that* to you? For even sinners do the same. If you lend to those from whom you expect to receive, what credit is *that* to you? Even sinners lend to sinners in order to receive back the same *amount*. But love your enemies, and do good, and lend, expecting nothing in return; and your reward will be great, and you will be sons of the Most High; for He Himself is kind to ungrateful and evil *men*. Be merciful, just as your Father is merciful" (Luke 6:27–36; cf. Matthew 5:9, 39–48; Matthew 7:12).

Setting: On the way from Galilee to Jerusalem. Jesus comforts the crowd and His disciples after giving a parable about riches and greed. The scribes and Pharisees turn hostile and question Him repeatedly in an attempt to catch Him in something He might say.

And He said to His disciples, "For this reason I say to you, do not worry about *your* life, *as to* what you will eat; nor for your body, *as to* what you will put on. For life is more than food, and the body more than clothing. Consider the ravens, for they neither sow nor reap; they have no storeroom nor barn, and *yet* God feeds them; how much more valuable you are than the birds! And which of you by worrying can add a *single* hour to his life's span? If then you cannot do even a very little thing, why do you worry about other matters? Consider the lilies, how they grow: they neither toil nor spin; but I tell you, not even Solomon in all his glory clothed himself like one of these. But if God so clothes the grass in the field, which is *alive* today and tomorrow is thrown into the furnace, how much more *will He clothe* you? You men of little faith! And do not seek what you will eat and what you will drink, and

do not keep worrying. For all these things the nations of the world eagerly seek; but your Father knows that you need these things. But seek His kingdom, and these things will be added to you. Do not be afraid, little flock, for your Father has chosen gladly to give you the kingdom" (Luke 12:22–32; cf. Matthew 6:25–33; see 1 Kings 10:4–7; Job 38:41).

Setting: On the way from Galilee to Jerusalem. Jesus conveys the illustration of the prodigal son because the Pharisees and scribes complain He associates with tax collectors and sinners.

And He said, "A man had two sons. The younger of them said to his father, 'Father, give me the share of the estate that falls to me.' So he divided his wealth between them. And not many days later, the younger son gathered everything together and went on a journey into a distant country, and there he squandered his estate with loose living. Now when he had spent everything, a severe famine occurred in that country, and he began to be impoverished. So he went and hired himself out to one of the citizens of that country, and he sent him into his fields to feed swine. And he would have gladly filled his stomach with the pods that the swine were eating, and no one was giving *anything* to him. But when he came to his senses, he said, 'How many of my father's hired men have more than enough bread, but I am dying here with hunger! I will get up and go to my father, and will say to him, "Father, I have sinned against heaven, and in your sight; I am no longer worthy to be called your son; make me as one of your hired men."' So he got up and came to his father. But while he was still a long way off, his father saw him and felt compassion *for him,* and ran and embraced him and kissed him. And the son said to him, "Father, I have sinned against heaven and in your sight; I am no longer worthy to be called your son.' But the father said to his slaves, 'Quickly bring out the best robe and put it on him, and put a ring on his hand and sandals on his feet; and bring the fattened calf, kill it, and let us eat and celebrate; for this son of mine was dead and has come to life again; he was lost and has been found.' And they began to celebrate. Now his older son was in the field, when he came and approached the house, he heard music and dancing. And he summoned one of the servants and *began* inquiring what these things could be. And he said to him, 'Your brother has come, and your father has killed the fattened calf because he has received him back safe and sound.' But he became angry and was not willing to go in; and his father came out and *began* pleading with him. But he answered and said to his father, 'Look! For so many years I have been serving you and I have never neglected a command of yours; and *yet* you have never given me a young goat, so that I might celebrate with my friends; but when this son of yours came, who has devoured your wealth with prostitutes, you killed the fattened calf for him.' And he said to him, 'Son, you have always been with me, and all that is mine is yours. But we had to celebrate and rejoice, for this brother of yours was dead and *has begun* to live, and was lost and has been found' " (Luke 15:11–32; see Proverbs 29:2).

Setting: Judea beyond the Jordan (Perea). After speaking of the importance of children, Jesus responds to a ruler's question about inheriting eternal life.

A ruler questioned Him, saying, "Good Teacher, what shall I do to inherit eternal life?" And Jesus said to him, "Why do you call Me good? No one is good except God alone. You know the commandments, 'DO NOT COMMIT ADULTERY, DO NOT MURDER, DO NOT STEAL, DO NOT BEAR FALSE WITNESS, HONOR YOUR FATHER AND MOTHER.'" And he said "All these things I have kept from *my* youth." When Jesus heard *this,* He said to him, "One thing you still lack; sell all that you possess and distribute it to the poor, and you shall have treasure in heaven; and come, follow Me" (Luke 18:18–22, Jesus quotes from Exodus 20:12–16; cf. Matthew 19:16–22; Mark 10:17–22; see Luke 10:25–28).

Setting: The temple in Jerusalem. Following the Feast of Booths and the scribes' and Pharisees' failed attempt to stone a woman for adultery, Jesus returns the next day to teach. His enemies question His testimony about Himself.

Jesus answered and said to them, "Even if I testify about Myself, My testimony is true, for I know where I came from and where I am going; but you do not know where I come from or where I am going. You judge according to the flesh; I am not judging anyone. But even if I do judge, My judgment is true; for I am not alone *in it,* but I and the Father who sent Me. Even in your law it has been written that the testimony of two men is true. I am He who testifies about Myself, and the Father who sent Me testifies about Me." So they were saying to Him, "Where is Your Father?" Jesus answered, "You know neither Me nor My Father; if you knew Me, you would know My Father also" (John 8:14–19; see Deuteronomy 17:6; 19:15; Matthew 18:16; John 3:17; 5:30, 37; 7:28; 8:42).

Setting: The temple treasury in Jerusalem. After the scribes and Pharisees question His testimony about Himself, Jesus reveals to those Jews who believe in Him how He will make them free.

So Jesus was saying to those Jews who had believed Him, "If you continue in My word, *then* you are truly disciples of Mine; and you will know the truth, and the truth will make you free." They answered Him, "We are Abraham's descendants and have never yet been enslaved to anyone; how is it that You say, 'You will become free'?" Jesus answered them, "Truly, truly, I say to you, everyone who commits sin is the slave of sin. The slave does not remain in the house forever; the son does remain forever. So if the Son makes you free, you will be free indeed. I know that you are Abraham's descendants; yet you seek to kill Me, because My word has no place in you. I speak the things which I have seen with *My* Father; therefore you also do the things which you heard from *your* father" (John 8:31–38; see Romans 6:16).

Setting: The temple treasury in Jerusalem. After the scribes and Pharisees question His testimony about Himself, Jesus interacts with them regarding their ancestry and motives.

They answered and said to Him, "Abraham is our father." Jesus said to them, "If you are Abraham's children, do the deeds of Abraham. But as it is, you are seeking to kill Me, a man who has told you the truth, which I heard from God; this Abraham did not do. You are doing the deeds of your father." They said to Him, "We were not born of fornication; we have one Father: God" (John 8:39–41; see John 8:1–38; Romans 9:6, 7).

Setting: The temple treasury in Jerusalem. After the scribes and Pharisees question His testimony about Himself, Jesus interacts with them regarding their ancestry and motives.

Jesus said to them, "If God were your Father, you would love Me, for I proceeded forth and have come from God, for I have not even come on My own initiative, but He sent Me. Why do you not understand what I am saying? *It is* because you cannot hear My word. You are of *your* father the devil, and you want to do the desires of your father. He was a murderer from the beginning, and does not stand in the truth because there is no truth in him. Whenever he speaks a lie, he speaks from his own *nature,* for he is a liar and the father of lies. But because I speak the truth, you do not believe Me. Which one of you convicts Me of sin? If I speak truth, why do not believe Me? He who is of God hears the words of God; for this reason you do not hear *them,* because you are not of God" (John 8:42–47; see John 18:37; 1 John 3:8; 4:6; 5:1).

Setting: The temple treasury in Jerusalem. While Jesus is interacting with the scribes and Pharisees, they state their belief Jesus is a demon-possessed Samaritan because of His statement that anyone who keeps His word will never taste death.

Jesus answered, "If I glorify Myself, My glory is nothing; it is My Father who glorifies Me, of whom you say, 'He is our God'; and you have not come to know Him, but I know Him; and if I say that I do not know Him, I will be a liar like you, but I do know Him and keep His word. Your father Abraham rejoiced to see My day, and he saw *it* and was glad" (John 8:54–56; see Matthew 13:17; John 7:29).

Setting: In Jerusalem, the risen Jesus first appears to Mary Magdalene after she tells Simon Peter and John about the empty tomb where Jesus' body had been laid the day before the Sabbath. He had died on the cross for the sins of the world.

Jesus said to her, "Woman, why are you weeping? Whom are you seeking?" Supposing Him to be the gardener, she said to Him, "Sir, if you have carried Him away, tell me where you have laid Him, and I will take Him away." Jesus said to her, "Mary!" She turned and said to Him in Hebrew "Rabboni!" (which means, Teacher). Jesus said to her, "Stop clinging to Me, for I have not yet ascended to the Father; but go to My brethren and say to them, 'I ascend to My Father and your Father, and My God and Your God'" (John 20:15–17; see Mark 16:9–11; John 7:33; 19:31–42).

FATHER'S HAND (Listed under HAND, FATHER'S)

FATHER'S HOUSE (Listed under HOUSE, FATHER'S)

FATHER'S NAME (Listed under NAME, FATHER'S)

FATHER'S KINGDOM (Listed under KINGDOM, FATHER'S)

FATHER'S WILL (Listed under WILL, FATHER'S; also see FATHER, WILL OF MY; and WILL OF GOD)

FATHERS (Also see FATHER)

Setting: The temple in Jerusalem. After the Jewish religious leaders test Him with questions, Jesus pronounces the eighth of eight woes on them in front of the crowds and His disciples.

"Woe to you, scribes and Pharisees, hypocrites! For you build the tombs of the prophets and adorn the monuments of the righteous, and say, 'If we had been *living* in the days of our fathers, we would not have been partners with them in *shedding* the blood of the prophets.' So you testify against yourselves, that you are sons of those who murdered the prophets. Fill up, then, the measure *of the guilt* of you fathers. You serpents, you brood of vipers, how will you escape the sentence of hell? Therefore, behold, I am sending you prophets and wise men and scribes; some of them you will kill and crucify, and some of them you will scourge in your synagogues, and persecute from city to city, so that upon you may fall *the guilt of* all the righteous blood shed on earth, from the blood of righteous Abel to the blood of Zechariah, the son of Berechiah, whom you murdered between the temple and the altar. Truly I say to you, all these things will come upon this generation" (Matthew 23:29–36; cf. 2 Chronicles 24:21; Zechariah 1:1; Matthew 3:7; Luke 11:47–52; see Matthew 10:23).

Setting: Galilee. After selecting His twelve disciples, Jesus teaches the Beatitudes (part of the Sermon on the Mount) to His disciples and a great throng from Judea, Jerusalem, and the central coastal region of Tyre and Sidon.

"Blessed are you when men hate you, and ostracize you, and insult you, and scorn your name as evil, for the sake of the Son of Man. Be glad in that day and leap *for joy*, for behold, your reward is great in heaven. For in the same way their fathers used to treat the prophets" (Luke 6:22, 23; cf. Matthew 5:10–12; see 2 Chronicles 36:16).

Setting: Galilee. After selecting His twelve disciples, Jesus teaches the Beatitudes (part of the Sermon on the Mount) to His disciples and a great throng from Judea, Jerusalem, and the central coastal region of Tyre and Sidon.

"Woe *to you* when all men speak well of you, for their fathers used to treat the false prophets in the same way" (Luke 6:26; see Matthew 7:15; 24:11, 24).

Setting: On the way from Galilee to Jerusalem. After revealing to His disciples how to pray, Jesus illustrates God's benevolence in answering prayer and giving the Holy Spirit.

"Now suppose one of you fathers is asked by his son for a fish; he will not give him a snake instead of a fish, will he? Or *if* he is asked for an egg, he will not give him a scorpion, will he? If you then, being evil, know how to give good gifts to your children, how much more will *your* heavenly Father give the Holy Spirit to those who ask Him?" (Luke 11:11–13; cf. Matthew 7:9–11).

Setting: On the way from Galilee to Jerusalem. After Jesus pronounces woes upon the Pharisees, a lawyer replies that His remarks are an insult to lawyers, too.

But He said, "Woe to you lawyers as well! For you weigh men down with burdens hard to bear, while you yourselves will not even touch the burdens with one of your fingers. Woe to you! For you build the tombs of the prophets, and *it was* your fathers *who* killed them. So you are witnesses and approve the deeds of your fathers; because it was they who killed them, and you build *their tombs*. For this reason also the wisdom of God said, 'I will send them prophets and apostles, and *some* of them they will kill and *some* they will persecute, so that the blood of all the prophets, shed since the foundation of the world, may be charged against this generation, from the blood of Abel to the blood of Zechariah, who was killed between the altar and the house *of God*; yes, I tell you, it shall be charged against this generation.' Woe to you lawyers! For you have taken away the key of knowledge; you yourselves did not enter, and you hindered those who were entering" (Luke 11:46–52; cf. Matthew 23:29–32; see 2 Chronicles 24:20, 21; Matthew 23:4, 13).

Setting: Capernaum of Galilee. After Jesus informs the people whom He miraculously fed with a lad's five loaves and two fish how they might receive the bread out of heaven, the Jewish religious leaders grumble because Jesus claims He came down out of heaven.

Therefore the Jews were grumbling about Him, because He said, "I am the bread that came down out of heaven." They were saying, "Is not this Jesus, the son of Joseph, whose father and mother we know? How does He now say, 'I have come down out of heaven'?" Jesus answered and said to them, "Do not grumble among yourselves. No one can come to Me unless the Father who sent Me draws him; and I will raise him up on the last day. It is written in the prophets, 'AND THEY SHALL ALL BE TAUGHT OF GOD.' Everyone who has heard and learned from the Father, comes to Me. Not that anyone has seen the Father, except the One who is from God; He has seen the Father. Truly, truly, I say to you, he who believes has eternal life. I am the bread of life. Your fathers ate the manna in the wilderness, and they died. This is the bread which comes down out of heaven, so that one may eat of it and not die. I am the living bread that came down out of heaven; if anyone eats of this bread, he will live forever; and the bread also which I will give for the life of the world is My flesh" (John 6:41–51, Jesus quotes from Isaiah 54:13; see John 1:18, 29; 3:36; 7:27).

Setting: Capernaum of Galilee. After Jesus informs the people whom He miraculously fed with a lad's five loaves and two fish how they might receive the bread out of heaven, the Jewish religious leaders argue with one another when Jesus says He will give His flesh to the world to eat.

So Jesus said to them, "Truly, truly, I say to you, unless you eat the flesh of the Son of Man and drink His blood, you have no life in yourselves. He who eats My flesh and drinks My blood has eternal life, and I will raise him up on the last day. For My flesh is true food, and My blood is true drink. He who eats My flesh and drinks My blood abides in Me, and I in him. As the living Father sent Me, and I live because of the Father, so he who eats Me, he also will live because of Me. This is the bread which came down out of heaven; not as the fathers ate and died; he who eats this bread will live forever" (John 6:53–58; see Matthew 16:16; Luke 4:22; John 3:36; 9:16; 15:4).

Setting: The temple in Jerusalem. After receiving encouragement from His blood brothers in Galilee to attend the upcoming Feast of Booths in order to demonstrate His works to His disciples and the world, Jesus goes and teaches, astonishing the Jewish religious leaders.

Jesus answered them, "I did one deed, and you all marvel. For this reason Moses has given you circumcision (not because it is from Moses, but from the fathers), and on *the* Sabbath you circumcise a man. If a man receives circumcision on *the* Sabbath so that the Law of Moses will not be broken, are you angry with Me because I made an entire man well on *the* Sabbath? Do not judge according to appearance, but judge with righteous judgment" (John 7:21–24; see Genesis 17:10–14; Leviticus 12:3; 19:15; Matthew 12:2; John 5:2–16; 7–20; 7:10–15).

FATHERS, DAYS OF OUR (See FATHERS)

FATTENED CALF (Listed under CALF, FATTENED)

FATTENED LIVESTOCK (Listed under LIVESTOCK, FATTENED)

FAULT

Setting: Capernaum of Galilee. Jesus gives instruction about church discipline after conveying to His disciples the value of little ones.

"If your brother sins, go and show him his fault in private; if he listens to you, you have won your brother. But if he does not listen *to you,* take one or two more with you, so that BY THE MOUTH OF TWO OR THREE WITNESSES EVERY FACT MAY BE CONFIRMED. If he refuses to listen to them, tell it to the church; and if he refuses to listen even to the church, let him be to you as a Gentile and a tax collector. Truly I say to you, whatever you bind of earth shall have been bound in heaven; and whatever you loose on earth shall have been loosed in heaven. Again, I say to you, that if two of you agree on earth about anything that they may ask, it shall be done for them by My Father who is in heaven. For there two or three have gathered together in My name, I am there in their midst" (Matthew 18:15–20. Jesus quotes from Deuteronomy 19:15; cf. Matthew 7:7; 16:19; see Leviticus 19:17; Matthew 28:20; 2 Thessalonians 3:6, 14).

FAVORITISM (Also see PRIVILEGE)

[FAVORITISM from but to sit on My right and on *My* left, this is not Mine to give]

Setting: On the way to Jerusalem. The mother of James and John, the sons of Zebedee, asks Jesus to make her sons exalted rulers with Him in His coming kingdom.

And He said to her, "What do you wish?" She said to Him, 'Command that in Your kingdom these two sons of mine may sit one on Your right and one on Your left.' But Jesus answered, "You do not know what you are asking. Are you able to drink the cup that I am about to drink?" They said to Him, 'We are able.' He said to them, "My cup you shall drink; but to sit on My right and on *My* left, this is not Mine to give, but it is for those for whom it has been prepared by My Father" (Matthew 20:21–23; cf. Mark 10:35–40; see Matthew 19:28; Acts 12:2).

[FAVORITISM from But to sit on My right or on *My* left, this is not Mine to give]

Setting: On the road to Jerusalem. After Jesus prophesies His persecution, death, and resurrection, James and John ask for special honor and privileges in His coming kingdom.

And He said to them, "What do you want Me to do for you?" They said to Him, "Grant that we may sit, one on Your right and one on *Your* left, in Your glory." But Jesus said to them, "You do not know what you are asking. Are you able to drink the cup that I drink, or to be baptized with the baptism with which I am baptized?" They said to Him, "We are able." And Jesus said to them, "The cup that I drink you shall drink; and you shall be baptized with the baptism with which I am baptized. But to sit on My right or on *My* left, this is not Mine to give; but it is for those for whom it has been prepared" (Mark 10:36–40; cf. Matthew 20:20–23; see Matthew 19:28; Acts 12:2).

FEAR (FEARING GOD is a separate entry; also see ANXIETY; and WORRY)

[FEAR from afraid]

Setting: On the Sea of Galilee. After giving the demands of discipleship to a scribe and one of His disciples, Jesus calms a great storm when His disciples fear for their lives.

He said to them, "Why are you afraid, you men of little faith?" Then He got up and rebuked the winds and the sea, and it became perfectly calm (Matthew 8:26; see Mark 4:35–41; Luke 8:22–25).

Setting: Galilee. After His disciples observe His ministry, Jesus summons and specifically instructs them about their ministry ahead involving true discipleship.

"Therefore do not fear them, for there is nothing concealed that will not be revealed, or hidden that will not be known. What I tell you in the darkness, speak in the light; and what you hear *whispered* in your ear, proclaim upon the housetops. Do not fear those who kill the body but are unable to kill the soul; but rather fear Him who is able to destroy both soul and body in hell" (Matthew 10:26–28; cf. Mark 4:22; Luke 12:3; see Hebrews 10:31).

Setting: Galilee. After His disciples observe His ministry, Jesus summons and specifically instructs them about their ministry ahead involving true discipleship.

"Are not two sparrows sold for a cent? And *yet* not one of them will fall to the ground apart from your Father. But the very hairs of your head are all numbered. So do not fear; you are more valuable than many sparrows" (Matthew 10:29–31; cf. Luke 12:6; see Matthew 12:12).

[FEAR from afraid]
Setting: On the Sea of Galilee. Following the miraculous feeding of more than 5,000 of His countrymen, in order to take an opportunity to pray, Jesus makes His disciples get into a boat, where He joins them later by walking on the water during a storm.

But immediately Jesus spoke to them, saying, "Take courage, it is I; do not be afraid." Peter said to Him, "Lord, if it is You, command me to come to You on the water." And He said, "Come!" And Peter got out of the boat, and walked on the water and came toward Jesus. But seeing the wind, he became frightened, and beginning to sink, he cried out, "Lord, save me!" Immediately Jesus stretched out His hand and took hold of him, and said to him, "You of little faith, why did you doubt?" (Matthew 14:27–31; cf. Mark 6:47–52; John 6:16–21).

[FEAR from afraid]
Setting: Caesarea Philippi. After teaching His disciples about the costs of discipleship, Jesus takes Peter, James, and John up to a high mountain. He gives them a glimpse of His true glory in the Transfiguration, as Moses and Elijah appear with Him.

And Jesus came to *them* and touched them and said, "Get up, and do not be afraid" (Matthew 17:7; see Matthew 14:27; 16:1–6, 8, 9; Mark 9:2–8; Luke 9:28–36).

[FEAR from frightened]
Setting: The Mount of Olives, just east of Jerusalem. During His discourse, Jesus answers His disciples' questions as to when the temple will be destroyed and Jerusalem overrun, along with the signs of His coming and the end of the age.

And Jesus answered and said to them, "See to it that no one misleads you. For many will come in My name, saying, 'I am the Christ,' and will mislead many. You will be hearing of wars and rumors of wars. See that you are not frightened, for *those things* must take place, but *that* is not yet the end. For nation will rise against nation, and kingdom against kingdom, and in various places there will be famines and earthquakes. But all these things are *merely* the beginning of birth pangs. Then they will deliver you to tribulation, and will kill you, and you will be hated by all nations because of My name. At that time many will fall away and will betray one another and hate one another. Many false prophets will arise and will mislead many. Because lawlessness is increased, most people's love will grow cold. But the one who endures to the end, he will be saved. This gospel of the kingdom shall be preached in the whole world as a testimony to all the nations, and then the end will come" (Matthew 24:4–14; cf. Jeremiah 29:8; Matthew 7:15; 10:17, 22; Mark 13:3–13; Luke 21:7–19; Revelation 6:4).

[FEAR from afraid]
Setting: The Mount of Olives, just east of Jerusalem. During His discourse, after answering His disciples' questions as to when the temple will be destroyed and Jerusalem overrun, along with the signs of His coming and the end of the age, Jesus reemphasizes to His disciples that they should be on the alert for His return.

"For *it is* just like a man *about* to go on a journey, who called his own slaves and entrusted his possessions to them. To one he gave five talents, to another, two, and to another, one, each according to his own ability; and he went on his journey. Immediately the one who had received the five talents went and traded with them, and gained five more talents. In the same manner the one who *had received* the two *talents* gained two more. But he who received the one *talent* went away, and dug a *hole* in the ground and hid his master's money. Now after a long time the master of those slaves came and settled accounts with them. The one who had received the five talents came up and brought five more talents, saying, 'Master, you entrusted five talents to me. See, I have gained five more talents.' His master said to him, 'Well done, good and faithful slave. You were faithful with a few things, I will put you in charge of many things; enter into the joy of your master.' Also the one who *had received* the two talents came up and said, 'Master, you entrusted two talents to me. See, I have gained two more talents.' His master said to him, 'Well done, good and faithful slave. You were faithful with a few things, I will put you in charge of many things; enter into the joy of your master.' And the one also who had received the one talent came up and said, 'Master, I knew you to be a hard man, reaping where you did not sow and gathering where you scattered no *seed.* And I was afraid, and went away and hid your talent in the ground. See, you have what is yours.' But his master answered and said to him, 'You wicked, lazy slave, you knew that I reap where I did not sow and gather where I scattered no *seed.* Then you ought to have put my money in the bank, and on my arrival I would have received my *money* back with interest. 'Therefore take away the talent from him, and give it to the one who has ten talents.' For to everyone who has, *more* shall be given, and he will have an abundance; but from the one who does not have, even what he does have shall be taken away. Throw out the worthless slave into the outer darkness; in that place there will be weeping and gnashing of teeth" (Matthew 25:14–30; cf. Matthew 8:12; 13:12; 24:45–47; see Matthew 18:23, 24; Luke 12:44).

[FEAR from afraid]
Setting: Jerusalem. The day after the Sabbath, after rising from the dead, Jesus appears to Mary Magdalene and the other Mary with instructions for His disciples.

Then Jesus said to them, "Do not be afraid; go and take word to My brethren to leave for Galilee, and there they will see Me" (Matthew 28:10; see John 20:17).

[FEAR from afraid]
Setting: On the Sea of Galilee. In a boat with His disciples, Jesus calms the sea in the midst of a raging storm.

And He got up and rebuked the wind and said to the sea, "Hush, be still." And the wind died down and it became perfectly calm. And He said to them, "Why are you afraid? Do you still have no faith?" (Mark 4:39, 40: cf. Matthew 13:26; Luke 8:25; see Psalm 65:7; Matthew 14:31).

[FEAR from afraid]
Setting: Capernaum by the Sea of Galilee. Jairus, a synagogue official, receives word that his daughter has died after he asked Jesus to heal her.

But Jesus, overhearing what was being spoken, said to the synagogue official, "Do not be afraid *any longer*, only believe" (Mark 5:36; cf. Luke 8:49, 50; see Matthew 19:18, 19; Mark 5:21–24; Luke 8:41, 42).

[FEAR from afraid]
Setting: On the Sea of Galilee, en route to Bethsaida. After feeding more than 5,000 people through God's miraculous provision and returning from a time of prayer on a mountain, Jesus startles His disciples by walking on the water to their boat.

But when they saw Him walking on the sea, they supposed that it was a ghost, and cried out; for they all saw Him and were terrified. But immediately He spoke with them and said to them, "Take courage; it is I, do not be afraid" (Mark 6:49, 50; cf. Matthew 14:26, 27; John 6:19, 20).

[FEAR from frightened]
Setting: The Mount of Olives, east of the temple in Jerusalem. During His discourse, after prophesying the temple's destruction, Jesus responds to questions from Peter, James, John, and Andrew about future events.

And Jesus began to say to them, "See to it that no one misleads you. Many will come in My name, saying, 'I am *He!*' and will mislead many. When you hear of wars and rumors of wars, do not be frightened; *those things* must take place; but *that is* not yet the end. For nation will rise up against nation, and kingdom against kingdom; there will be earthquakes in various places; there will *also be* famines. These things are *merely* the beginning of birth pangs. But be on your guard; for they will deliver you to *the* courts, and you will be flogged in *the* synagogues, and you will stand before governors and kings for My sake, as a testimony to them. The gospel must first be preached to all the nations. When they arrest you and hand you over, do not worry beforehand about what you are to say, but say whatever is given you in that hour; for it is not you who speak, but *it is* the Holy Spirit. Brother will betray brother to death, and a father *his* child; and children will rise up against parents and have them put to death. You will be hated by all because of My name, but the one who endures to the end, he will be saved" (Mark 13:5–13; cf. Matthew 24:4–14; Luke 21:7–19; see Matthew 10:17–22).

Setting: By the Sea of Galilee. After teaching the people from Simon's (Peter) boat, Jesus calls Peter, James, and John to follow Him. [This appears to be a permanent call, as Simon and other companions are with Him earlier in Mark 1:35–39 and Luke 4:38–39.]

When He had finished speaking, He said to Simon, "Put out into the deep water and let down your nets for a catch." ". . . and so also *were* James and John, sons of Zebedee, who were partners with Simon. And Jesus said to Simon, "Do not fear, from now on you will be catching men" (Luke 5:4, 10; see John 21:6).

[FEAR from afraid]
Setting: Capernaum in Galilee. After healing a woman who has been ill for twelve years, Jesus receives word that a synagogue official's daughter has died.

But when Jesus heard *this,* He answered him, "Do not be afraid *any longer;* only believe and she will be made well." When He came to the house, He did not allow anyone to enter with Him except Peter and John and James and the girl's father and mother. Now they were all weeping and lamenting for her; but He said, "Stop weeping; for she has not died, but is asleep." And they *began* laughing at Him, knowing that she had died. He, however, took her by the hand and called, saying, "Child, arise!" And her spirit returned, and she got up immediately; and He gave orders for *something* to be given her to eat (Luke 8:50–55; cf. Matthew 9:18, 19, 23–26; Mark 5:21–24, 35–43).

Setting: On the way from Galilee to Jerusalem, Jesus warns His disciples of future events. The scribes and Pharisees turn hostile and question Him repeatedly in an attempt to catch Him in something He might say.

Under these circumstances, after so many thousands of people had gathered together that they were stepping on one another, He began saying to His disciples first *of all,* "Beware of the leaven of the Pharisees, which is hypocrisy. But there is nothing covered up that will not be revealed, and hidden that will not be known. Accordingly, whatever you have said in the dark will be heard in the light, and what you have whispered in the inner rooms will be proclaimed upon the housetops. I say to you, My friends, do not be afraid of those who kill the body and after that have no more that they can do. But I will warn you whom to fear: fear the One who, after He has killed, has authority to cast into hell; yes, I tell you, fear Him! Are not five sparrows sold for two cents? *Yet* not one of them is forgotten before God. Indeed, the very hairs of your head are all numbered. Do not fear; you are more valuable than many sparrows" (Luke 12:1–7; cf. Matthew 10:26–31; see Matthew 16:6; Hebrews 10:31).

[FEAR from afraid]
Setting: On the way from Galilee to Jerusalem. Jesus comforts the crowd and His disciples after giving a parable about riches and greed. The scribes and Pharisees turn hostile and question Him repeatedly in an attempt to catch Him in something He might say.

And He said to His disciples, "For this reason I say to you, do not worry about *your* life, *as to* what you will eat; nor for your body, *as to* what you will put on. For life is more than food, and the body more than clothing. Consider the ravens, for they neither sow nor reap; they have no storeroom nor barn, and *yet* God feeds them; how much more valuable you are than the birds! And which of you by worrying can add a *single* hour to his life's span? If then you cannot do even a very little thing, why do you worry about other matters? Consider the lilies, how they grow: they neither toil nor spin; but I tell you, not even Solomon in all his glory clothed himself like one of these. But if God so clothes the grass in the field, which is *alive* today and tomorrow is thrown into the furnace, how much more *will He clothe* you? You men of little faith! And do not seek what you will eat and what you will drink, and do not keep worrying. For all these things the nations of the world eagerly seek; but your Father knows that you need these things. But seek His kingdom, and these things will be added to you. Do not be afraid, little flock, for your Father has chosen gladly to give you the kingdom" (Luke 12:22–32; cf. Matthew 6:25–33; see 1 Kings 10:4–7; Job 38:41).

[FEAR from afraid]
Setting: Jericho, on the way to Jerusalem. After commending Zaccheus's faith in Him, Jesus provides a parable about stewardship.

So He said, "A nobleman went to a distant country to receive a kingdom for himself, and *then* return. And he called ten of his slaves, and gave them ten minas and said to them, 'Do business *with this* until I come *back.*' But his citizens hated him and sent a delegation after him, saying, 'We do not want this man to reign over us.' When he returned, after receiving the kingdom, he ordered that these slaves, to whom he had given the money, be called to him so that he might know what business they had done. The first appeared, saying, 'Master, your mina has made ten minas more.' And he said to him, 'Well done, good slave, because you have been faithful in a very little thing, you are to be in authority over ten cities.' The second came, saying, 'Your mina, master, has made five minas.' And he said to him, also, 'And you are to be over five cities.' Another came, saying, 'Master, here is your mina, which I kept put away in a handkerchief; for I was afraid of you, because you are an exacting man; you take up what you did not lay down and reap what you did not sow.' He said to him, 'By your own words I will judge you, you worthless slave. Did you know that I am an exacting man, taking up what I did not lay down and reaping what I did not sow? Then why did you not put my money in the bank, and having come, I would have collected it with interest?' Then he said to the bystanders, 'Take the mina away from him and give it to the one who has the ten minas.' And they said to him, 'Master, he has ten minas *already.*' I tell you that to everyone who has, more shall be given, but from the one who does not have, even what he does have shall be taken away. But these enemies of mine, who did not want me to reign over them, bring them here and slay them in my presence" (Luke 19:12–27; cf. Matthew 25:14–30; see Matthew 13:12; Luke 16:10).

[FEAR from terrified]
Setting: The temple in Jerusalem. A few days before His crucifixion, after Jesus prophesies the destruction of the temple during His Olivet Discourse, His disciples ask Him when this will happen.

And He said, "See to it that you are not misled; for many will come in My name, saying, 'I am *He,*' and, 'The time is near.' Do not go after them. When you hear of wars and disturbances, do not be terrified; for these things must take place first, but the end *does* not *follow* immediately" (Luke 21:8–9; cf. Matthew 24:4–8; Mark 13:5–8).

Setting: The Mount of Olives, just east of Jerusalem. After ministering in the temple and giving His disciples more details regarding future events, Jesus speaks of His own return during His Olivet Discourse.

"There will be signs in sun and moon and stars, and on the earth dismay among the nations, in perplexity at the roaring of the sea and the waves, men fainting from fear and the expectation of the things which are coming upon the world; for the powers of the heavens will be shaken. Then they will see THE SON OF MAN COMING IN A CLOUD with power and great glory. But when these things begin to take place, straighten up and lift up your heads, because your redemption is drawing near" (Luke 21:25–28, Jesus quotes from Daniel 7:13; cf. Matthew 24:29–31; Mark 13:24–27).

Setting: Jerusalem. During the time for the Passover of the Jews, after the Lord cleanses the temple, a Pharisee, Nicodemus, asks Him by night the meaning of "born again."

"For God so loved the world, that He gave His only begotten Son, that whoever believes in Him shall not perish, but have eternal life. For God did not send the Son into the world to judge the world, but that the world might be saved through Him. He who believes in Him is not judged; he who does not believe has been judged already, because he has not believed in the name of the only begotten Son of God. This is the judgment, that the Light has come into the world, and men loved darkness rather than the Light, for their deeds were evil. For everyone who does evil hates the Light, and does not come to the Light for fear that his deeds will be exposed. But he who practices the truth comes to the Light, so that his deeds may be manifested as having been wrought in God" (John 3:16–21; see Luke 19:10; John 1:4; 1:18; Romans 5:8; 1 John 1:6, 7).

[FEAR from afraid]
Setting: Galilee. Knowing the people want to make Him king after He miraculously feeds more than 5,000 of them, Jesus withdraws to a mountain. His disciples board a boat and start across the Sea of Galilee, where He will join them by walking on water during a storm.

But He said to them, "It is I; do not be afraid" (John 6:20; cf. Matthew 14:27; Mark 6:50).

[FEAR from fearful]
Setting: Jerusalem. Before the Passover, after Jesus conveys the upcoming ministry of the Holy Spirit in His disciples' lives, He again relates peace, hope, and comfort to them regarding His return to the Father.

"Peace I leave with you; My peace I give to you; not as the world gives do I give to you. Do not let your heart be troubled, nor let it be fearful. You heard that I said to you, 'I go away, and I will come to you,' If you loved Me, you would have rejoiced because I go to the Father, for the Father is greater than I. Now I have told you before it happens, so that when it happens, you may believe. I will not speak much more with you, for the ruler of the world is coming, and he has nothing in Me; but so that the world may know that I love the Father, I do exactly as the Father commanded Me. Get up, let us go from here" (John 14:27–31; see John 10:18, 29; 12:31; 13:19; 16:33).

[FEAR from afraid]
Setting: Corinth in Greece. Luke, writing in Acts, records the Lord Jesus' comforting revelation through a vision to Paul as he works among the Jews and Gentiles during his second missionary journey, testifying that Jesus is the Christ (Messiah).

And the Lord said to Paul in the night by a vision, "Do not be afraid *any longer,* but go on speaking and do not be silent; for I am with you, and no man will attack you in order to harm you, for I have many people in this city" (Acts 18:9, 10).

[FEAR from afraid]
Setting: On the island of Patmos (in the Aegean Sea about fifty miles southwest of Ephesus in modern Turkey). On the Lord's Day (Sunday), the disciple John encounters the Lord Jesus Christ approximately fifty years after His resurrection. The Lord communicates new revelations for the apostle to record for the seven churches in Asia.

When I saw Him, I fell at His feet like a dead man. And He placed His right hand on me, saying, "Do not be afraid; I am the first and the last, and the living One; and I was dead, and behold, I am alive forevermore, and I have the keys of death and of Hades. Therefore write the things which you have seen, and the things which are, and the things which will take place after these things. As for the mystery of the seven stars which you saw in My right hand, and the seven golden lampstands: the seven stars are the angels of the seven churches, and the seven lampstands are the seven churches" (Revelation 1:17–20; see Isaiah 44:6; Luke 24:5; Revelation 2:8).

Setting: On the island of Patmos (in the Aegean Sea about fifty miles southwest of Ephesus in modern Turkey). On the Lord's Day (Sunday), about fifty years after Jesus' resurrection, the disciple John encounters the Lord Jesus Christ, who communicates a new revelation for the apostle to record for the church in Smyrna and to six other churches in Asia.

"And to the angel of the church in Smyrna write: The first and the last, who was dead, and has come to life, says this: 'I know your tribulation and your poverty (but you are rich), and the blasphemy by those who say they are Jews and are not, but are a synagogue of Satan. Do not fear what you are about to suffer. Behold, the devil is about to cast some of you into prison, so that you will be tested, and you will have tribulation for ten days. Be faithful until death, and I will give you the crown of life. He who has an ear, let him hear what the Spirit says to the churches. He who overcomes will not be hurt by the second death' (Revelation 2:8–11; see Isaiah 44:6; Revelation 1:9, 18; 2:13; 20:6, 14).

FEARING GOD

[FEARING GOD from fear Him who is able to destroy both soul and body in hell]
Setting: Galilee. After His disciples observe His ministry, Jesus summons and specifically instructs them about their ministry ahead involving true discipleship.

"Therefore do not fear them, for there is nothing concealed that will not be revealed, or hidden that will not be known. What I tell you in the darkness, speak in the light; and what you hear *whispered* in your ear, proclaim upon the housetops. Do not fear those who kill the body but are unable to kill the soul; but rather fear Him who is able to destroy both soul and body in hell" (Matthew 10:26–28; cf. Mark 4:22; Luke 12:3; see Hebrews 10:31).

[FEARING GOD from fear the One who, after He has killed, has authority to cast into hell and fear Him]
Setting: On the way from Galilee to Jerusalem. Jesus warns His disciples of future events, as the scribes and Pharisees turn hostile and question Him repeatedly in an attempt to catch Him in something He might say.

Under these circumstances, after so many thousands of people had gathered together that they were stepping on one another, He began saying to His disciples first *of all,* "Beware of the leaven of the Pharisees, which is hypocrisy. But there is nothing covered up that will not be revealed, and hidden that will not be known. Accordingly, whatever you have said in the dark will be heard in the light, and what you have whispered in the inner rooms will be proclaimed upon the housetops. I say to you, My friends, do not be afraid of those who kill the body and after that have no more that they can do. But I will warn you whom to fear: fear the One who, after He has killed, has authority to cast into hell; yes, I tell you, fear Him! Are not five sparrows sold for two cents? *Yet* not one of them is forgotten before God. Indeed, the very hairs of your head are all numbered. Do not fear; you are more valuable than many sparrows" (Luke 12:1–7; cf. Matthew 10:26–31; see Matthew 16:6; Hebrews 10:31).

[FEARING GOD from fear God]
Setting: On the way from Jerusalem. After telling His disciples of His second coming, Jesus instructs them about persistence in prayer.

Now He was telling them a parable to show that at all times they ought to pray and not to lose heart, saying, "In a certain city there was a judge who did not fear God and did not respect man. There was a widow in that city, and she kept coming to him, saying, 'Give me legal protection from my opponent.' For a while he was unwilling; but afterward he said to himself, 'Even though I do not fear God nor respect man, yet because this woman bothers me, I will give her legal protection, otherwise by continually coming she will wear me out.'" And the Lord said, "Hear what the unrighteous judge said; now, will not God bring about justice for His elect who cry to Him day and night, and will He delay long over them? I tell you that He will bring about justice for them quickly. However, when the Son of Man comes, will He find faith on the earth?" (Luke 18:1–8; see Luke 11:5–10).

FEAST (FEAST, WEDDING is a separate entry)

Setting: Capernaum of Galilee. Jesus' blood brothers, who do not yet believe in Him, encourage Him to attend the upcoming Feast of Booths in Jerusalem in order to demonstrate His works to His disciples and the world.

So Jesus said to them, "My time is not yet here, but your time is always opportune. The world cannot hate you, but it hates Me because I testify of it, that its deeds are evil. Go up to the feast yourselves; I do not go up to this feast because My time has not yet fully come" (John 7:6–8; see John 3:19, 20; 15:18–20).

FEAST, PARABLE OF THE MARRIAGE (See FEAST, PARABLE OF THE WEDDING)

FEAST, PARABLE OF THE WEDDING

[PARABLE OF THE WEDDING FEAST from parables and wedding feast]
Setting: The temple in Jerusalem, Jesus speaks another parable to the chief priests and elders after they question His authority.

Jesus spoke to them again in parables, saying, "The kingdom of heaven may be compared to a king who gave a wedding feast for his son. And he sent out his slaves to call those who had been invited to the wedding feast, and they were unwilling to come. Again he sent out other slaves saying, 'Tell those who have been invited, "Behold, I have prepared my dinner; my oxen and my fattened livestock are *all* butchered and everything is ready; come to the wedding feast." But they paid no attention and went their way, one to his own farm, another to his business, and the rest seized his slaves and mistreated them and killed them. But the king was enraged, and he sent his armies and destroyed those murderers and set their city on fire. Then he said to his slaves, 'The wedding is ready, but those who were invited were not worthy. 'Go therefore to the main highways, and as many as you find *there,* invite to the wedding feast.' Those slaves went out into the streets and gathered together all they found, both evil and good; and the wedding hall was filled with dinner guests. But when the king came in to look over the dinner guests, he saw a man there who was not dressed in wedding clothes, and he said to him, 'Friend, how did you come in here without wedding clothes?' And the man was speechless. Then the king said to the servants, 'Bind him hand and foot, and throw him into the outer darkness; in that place there will be weeping and gnashing of teeth.' For many are called, but few *are* chosen" (Matthew 22:1–14; cf. Matthew 8:11, 12).

FEAST, WEDDING (FEAST, PARABLE OF THE WEDDING is a separate entry; also see BANQUETS and FEAST)

Setting: The Mount of Olives, just east of Jerusalem. During His discourse, after answering His disciples' questions as to when the temple will be destroyed and Jerusalem overrun, along with the signs of His coming and the end of the age, Jesus reemphasizes to the disciples that they should be on the alert for His return.

"Then the kingdom of heaven will be comparable to ten virgins, who took their lamps and went out to meet the bridegroom. Five of them were foolish, and five were prudent. For when the foolish took their lamps, they took no oil with them, but the prudent took oil in flasks along with their lamps. Now while the bridegroom was delaying, they all got drowsy and *began* to sleep. But at midnight there was a shout, 'Behold, the bridegroom! Come out to meet *him*.' Then all those virgins rose and trimmed their lamps. The foolish said to the prudent, 'Give us some of your oil, for our lamps are going out.' But the prudent answered, 'No, there will not be enough for us and you *too;* go instead to the dealers and buy *some* for yourselves.' And while they were going away to make the purchase, the bridegroom came, and those who were ready went in with him to the wedding feast; and the door was shut. Later the other virgins also came, saying, 'Lord, lord, open up for us.' But he answered, 'Truly I say to you, I do not know you.' Be on the alert then, for you do not know the day nor the hour" (Matthew 25:1–13; cf. Matthew 24:42; Luke 12:35; see Matthew 7:21, 24).

Setting: On the way from Galilee to Jerusalem. After giving a parable about riches and greed, Jesus uses a parable to challenge the crowd and His disciples to be ready for His return.

"Be dressed in readiness, and *keep* your lamps lit. Be like men who are waiting for their master when he returns from the wedding feast, so that they may immediately open *the door* to him when he comes and knocks. Blessed are those slaves whom the master will find on the alert when he comes; truly I say to you, that he will gird himself *to serve,* and have them recline *at the table,* and will come up and wait on them. Whether he comes in the second watch, or even in the third and finds *them* so, blessed are those *slaves*. But be sure of this, that if the head of the house had known at what hour the thief was coming, he would not have allowed his house to be broken into. You too, be ready; for the Son of Man is coming at an hour that you do not expect" (Luke 12:35–40; cf. Matthew 24:42–44; see Mark 13:33; Ephesians 6:14).

Setting: On the way from Galilee to Jerusalem. Jesus speaks a parable to the guests of a Pharisee leader on the Sabbath as He observes the guests selecting places of honor at the table.

And He *began* speaking a parable to the invited guests when He noticed how they had been picking out the places of honor *at the table,* saying to them, "When you are invited by someone to a wedding feast, do not take the place of honor, for someone more distinguished than you may have been invited by him, and he who invited you both will come and say to you, 'Give *your* place to this man,' and then in disgrace you proceed to occupy the last place. But when you are invited, go and recline at the last place, so that when the one who has invited you comes, he may say to you, 'Friend, move up higher'; then you will have honor in the sight of all who are at the table with you. For everyone who exalts himself will be humbled, and he who humbles himself will be exalted" (Luke 14:7–11; see 2 Samuel 22:28; Proverbs 25:6, 7; Matthew 23:6).

FEAST OF BOOTHS **(Listed under BOOTHS, FEAST OF)**

FEAST OF UNLEAVENED BREAD **(See PASSOVER)**

FEET (Also see FOOT; and HEEL)

Setting: Galilee. During the early part of His ministry, Jesus preaches the Sermon on the Mount to His disciples and the multitudes.

"Again, you have heard that the ancients were told, 'YOU SHALL NOT MAKE FALSE VOWS, BUT SHALL FULFILL YOUR VOWS TO THE LORD.' But I say to you, make no oath at all, either by heaven, for it is the throne of God, or by the earth, for it is the footstool of His feet, or by Jerusalem, for it is THE CITY OF THE GREAT KING. Nor shall you make an oath by your head, for you cannot make one hair white or black. But let your statement be 'Yes, yes' *or* 'No, no'; anything beyond these is of evil" (Matthew 5:33–37, Jesus quotes from Leviticus 19:12, Psalm 48:2; Isaiah 66:1; cf. James 5:12).

Setting: Galilee. During the early part of His ministry, Jesus preaches the Sermon on the Mount to His disciples and the multitudes.

"Do not give what is holy to dogs, and do not throw your pearls before swine, or they will trample them under their feet, and turn and tear you to pieces" (Matthew 7:6; see Matthew 15:26).

Setting: Galilee. After His twelve disciples observe His ministry, Jesus summons and specifically instructs them about their ministry to the people of Israel.

These twelve Jesus sent out after instructing them: "Do not go in *the* way of *the* Gentiles, and do not enter *any* city of the Samaritans; but rather go to the lost sheep of the house of Israel. And as you go, preach, saying, 'The kingdom of heaven is at hand.' Heal *the* sick, raise *the* dead, cleanse *the* lepers, cast out demons. Freely you received, freely give. Do not acquire gold, or silver, or copper for your money belts, or a bag for *your* journey, or even two coats, or sandals, or a staff; for the worker is worthy of his support. And whatever city or village you enter, inquire who is worthy in it, and stay at his house until you leave *that city*. As you enter the house, give it your greeting. If the house is worthy, give it your *blessing of* peace. But if it is not worthy, take back your *blessing of* peace. Whoever does not receive you, nor heed your words, as you go out of that house or that city, shake the dust off your feet. Truly I say to you, it will be more tolerable for *the* land of Sodom and Gomorrah in the day of judgment than for that city" (Matthew 10:5–15; cf. Mark 6:7–11; Luke 9:1–5; see Matthew 3:2; 11:22, 24; 15:24; Luke 22:35; 1 Corinthians 9:14).

Setting: Capernaum of Galilee. Jesus elaborates about stumbling blocks following His disciples' question about greatness in the kingdom of heaven.

"Woe to the world because of *its* stumbling blocks! For it is inevitable that stumbling blocks come; but woe to that man through whom the stumbling block comes! If your hand or your foot causes you to stumble, cut it off and throw it from you; it is better for you to enter life crippled or lame, than to have two hands or two feet and be cast into the eternal fire. If your eye causes you to stumble, pluck it out and throw it from you. It is better for you to enter life with one eye, than to have two eyes and be cast into the fiery hell" (Matthew 18:7–9; cf. Matthew 5:29, 30; Mark 9:43–48; Luke 17:1).

Setting: The temple in Jerusalem. Following the Sadducees' and Pharisees' unsuccessful attempts to test Him with questions, with the crowds listening, Jesus poses a question to some of the Pharisees.

"What do you think about the Christ, whose son is He?" They said to Him, "The *son* of David." He said to them, "Then how does David in the Spirit call Him 'Lord,' saying, 'THE LORD SAID TO MY LORD, SIT AT MY RIGHT HAND, UNTIL I PUT YOUR ENEMIES BENEATH YOUR FEET"'? "If David then calls Him 'Lord," how is He his son?" (Matthew 22:42–45; Jesus quotes from Psalm 110:1; cf. Mark 12:35–37; Luke 20:41–44; see 2 Samuel 23:2).

Setting: Jesus' hometown of Nazareth. After encountering unbelief, Jesus sends the Twelve out in pairs with authority and instructions about ministry.

And He summoned the twelve and began to send them out in pairs, and gave them authority over the unclean spirits; and He instructed them that they should take nothing for *their* journey, except a mere staff—no bread, no bag, no money in their belt—

but to wear sandals; and *He added,* "Do not put on two tunics." And He said to them, "Wherever you enter a house, stay there until you leave town. Any place that does not receive you or listen to you, as you go out from there, shake the dust off the soles of your feet for a testimony against them" (Mark 6:7–11; cf. Matthew 10:1–14; Luke 9:1–5).

Setting: Capernaum of Galilee. As Jesus teaches His disciples in private, they ask Him about greatness.

But Jesus said, "Do not hinder him, for there is no one who will perform a miracle in My name, and be able soon afterward to speak evil of Me. For he who is not against us is for us. For whoever gives you a cup of water to drink because of your name as *followers* of Christ, truly I say to you, he will not lose his reward. Whoever causes one of these little ones who believe to stumble, it would be better for him if, with a heavy millstone hung around his neck, he had been cast into the sea. If your hand causes you to stumble, cut it off; it is better for you to enter life crippled, than, having your two hands, to go into hell, into the unquenchable fire, [where THEIR WORM DOES NOT DIE, AND THE FIRE IS NOT QUENCHED.] If your foot causes you to stumble, cut it off; it is better for you to enter life lame, than, having your two feet, to be cast into hell, [where THEIR WORM DOES NOT DIE, AND THE FIRE IS NOT QUENCHED.] If your eye causes you to stumble, throw it out; it is better for you to enter the kingdom of God with one eye, than, having two eyes, to be cast into hell, where THEIR WORM DOES NOT DIE, AND THE FIRE IS NOT QUENCHED. For everyone will be salted with fire. Salt is good; but if the salt becomes unsalty, with what will you make it salty *again?* Have salt in yourselves, and be at peace with one another" (Mark 9:39–50; Jesus quotes from Isaiah 66:24; cf. Matthew 18:6–9; Luke 9:49–50; see Matthew 5:13, 29, 30; 10:42; 12:30; 18:5, 6).

Setting: The temple in Jerusalem. Jesus teaches the crowd after commending a scribe for his nearness to the kingdom of God.

And Jesus *began* to say, as He taught in the temple, "How *is it that* the scribes say that the Christ is the son of David? David himself said in the Holy Spirit, 'THE LORD SAID TO MY LORD, SIT AT MY RIGHT HAND, UNTIL I PUT YOUR ENEMIES BENEATH YOUR FEET.'" David himself calls Him 'Lord'; so in what sense is He his son?" And the large crowd enjoyed listening to Him (Mark 12:35–37, Jesus quotes from Psalm 110:1; cf. Matthew 22:41–46; Luke 20:41–44).

Setting: Galilee. After Jesus praises John the Baptist to the crowds, Simon, a Pharisee, invites Him to dinner. A sinful woman anoints His feet with perfume, prompting the Lord to instruct His host about forgiveness.

Turning toward the woman, He said to Simon, "Do you see this woman? I entered your house; you gave Me no water for My feet, but she has wet My feet with her tears and wiped them with her hair. You gave Me no kiss; but she, since the time I came in, has not ceased to kiss My feet. You did not anoint My head with oil, but she anointed My feet with perfume. For this reason I say to you, her sins, which are many, have been forgiven, for she loved much; but he who is forgiven little, loves little." Then He said to her, "Your sins have been forgiven." Those who were reclining *at the table* with Him began to say to themselves, "Who is this *man* who even forgives sins?" And He said to the woman, "Your faith has saved you; go in peace" (Luke 7:44–50; see Matthew 9:2; Mark 5:34; Luke 5:21).

Setting: Galilee. After raising Jairus's daughter from the dead, Jesus calls the Twelve together and gives them power and authority over demons, along with the ability to heal diseases.

And He said to them, "Take nothing for *your* journey, neither a staff, nor a bag, nor bread, nor money; and do not *even* have two tunics apiece. Whatever house you enter, stay there until you leave that city. And as for those who do not receive you, go out from that city, shake the dust off your feet as a testimony against them" (Luke 9:3–5; cf. Matthew 10:1–15; Mark 6:7–11; see Luke 10:4–12).

Setting: On the way from Galilee to Jerusalem. The Lord appoints seventy followers and sends them out in pairs to every place He Himself will soon visit.

And He was saying to them, "The harvest is plentiful, but the laborers are few; therefore beseech the Lord of the harvest to send out laborers into His harvest. Go; behold, I send you out as lambs in the midst of wolves. Carry no money belt, no bag, no shoes;

and greet no one on the way. Whatever house you enter, first say, 'Peace be to this house.' If a man of peace is there, your peace will rest on him; but if not, it will return to you. Stay in that house, eating and drinking what they give you; for the laborer is worthy of his wages. Do not keep moving from house to house. Whatever city you enter and they receive you, eat what is set before you; and heal those in it who are sick, and say to them, 'The kingdom of God has come near to you.' But whatever city you enter and they do not receive you, go out into its streets and say, 'Even the dust of your city which clings to our feet we wipe off *in protest* against you; yet be sure of this, that the kingdom of God has come near.' I say to you, it will be more tolerable in that day for Sodom than for that city" (Luke 10:2–12; see Genesis 19:24–28; Matthew 9:37, 38, 10:9–14, 16; 1 Corinthians 10:27).

Setting: On the way from Galilee to Jerusalem. Jesus conveys the illustration of the prodigal son because the Pharisees and scribes complain He associates with tax collectors and sinners.

And He said, "A man had two sons. The younger of them said to his father, 'Father, give me the share of the estate that falls to me.' So he divided his wealth between them. And not many days later, the younger son gathered everything together and went on a journey into a distant country, and there he squandered his estate with loose living. Now when he had spent everything, a severe famine occurred in that country, and he began to be impoverished. So he went and hired himself out to one of the citizens of that country, and he sent him into his fields to feed swine. And he would have gladly filled his stomach with the pods that the swine were eating, and no one was giving *anything* to him. But when he came to his senses, he said, 'How many of my father's hired men have more than enough bread, but I am dying here with hunger! I will get up and go to my father, and will say to him, "Father, I have sinned against heaven, and in your sight; I am no longer worthy to be called your son; make me as one of your hired men."' So he got up and came to his father. But while he was still a long way off, his father saw him and felt compassion *for him,* and ran and embraced him and kissed him. And the son said to him, "Father, I have sinned against heaven and in your sight; I am no longer worthy to be called your son.' But the father said to his slaves, 'Quickly bring out the best robe and put it on him, and put a ring on his hand and sandals on his feet; and bring the fattened calf, kill it, and let us eat and celebrate; for this son of mine was dead and has come to life again; he was lost and has been found.' And they began to celebrate. Now his older son was in the field, when he came and approached the house, he heard music and dancing. And he summoned one of the servants and *began* inquiring what these things could be. And he said to him, 'Your brother has come, and your father has killed the fattened calf because he has received him back safe and sound.' But he became angry and was not willing to go in; and his father came out and *began* pleading with him. But he answered and said to his father, 'Look! For so many years I have been serving you and I have never neglected a command of yours; and *yet* you have never given me a young goat, so that I might celebrate with my friends; but when this son of yours came, who has devoured your wealth with prostitutes, you killed the fattened calf for him.' And he said to him, 'Son, you have always been with me, and all that is mine is yours. But we had to celebrate and rejoice, for this brother of yours was dead and *has begun* to live, and was lost and has been found' " (Luke 15:11–32; see Proverbs 29:2).

Setting: The temple in Jerusalem. A few days before His crucifixion, after some of the Sadducees question Him about the resurrection, Jesus poses a question to the scribes, who say He answered well.

Then He said to them, "How *is it that* they say the Christ is David's son? For David himself says in the book of Psalms, 'THE LORD SAID TO MY LORD, SIT AT MY RIGHT HAND, UNTIL I MAKE YOUR ENEMIES A FOOTSTOOL FOR YOUR FEET.' Therefore David calls Him 'Lord,' and how is He his son?" (Luke 20:41–44, Jesus quotes from Psalm 110:1; cf. Matthew 22:41–46; Mark 12:35–37).

Setting: Jerusalem. After rising from the grave on the third day after being crucified, and appearing to two of His followers on the road to Emmaus, Jesus appears to His disciples (except Thomas).

While they were telling these things, He Himself stood in their midst and said to them, "Peace be to you." But they were startled and frightened and thought they were seeing a spirit. And He said to them, "Why are you troubled, and why do doubts arise in your hearts? See My hands and My feet, that it is I Myself; touch Me and see, for a spirit does not have flesh and bones as you see that I have." And when He had said this, He showed them His hands and His feet. While they still could not believe *it* because of their joy and amazement. He said to them, "Have you anything to eat?" They gave Him a piece of a broiled fish; and He took it and ate *it* before them (Luke 24:36–43; see Mark 16:14; John 20:27; Acts 10:40, 41).

Setting: Jerusalem. Before the Passover, with His crucifixion nearing, Jesus eats supper with His disciples and assumes the role of a servant by washing their feet.

Jesus answered and said to him, "What I do you do not realize now, but you will understand hereafter." Peter said to Him, "Never shall You wash my feet!" Jesus answered him, "If I do not wash you, you have no part with Me." Simon Peter said to Him, "Lord, *then wash* not only my feet, but also my hand and my head." Jesus said to him, "He who has bathed needs only to wash his feet, but is completely clean; and you are clean, but not all *of you*. For He knew the one who was betraying Him; for this reason He said, "Not all of you are clean" (John 13:7–11; see John 6:64; 15:3).

Setting: Jerusalem. Before the Passover, with His death on the cross nearing, Jesus explains the reason for His vivid example of servanthood in washing His disciples' feet.

So when He had washed their feet, and taken His garments and reclined *at the table* again, He said to them, "Do you know what I have done to you? You call Me Teacher and Lord; and you are right, for *so* I am. If I then, the Lord and the Teacher, washed your feet, you also ought to wash one another's feet. For I gave you an example that you also should do as I did to you. Truly, truly I say to you, a slave is not greater than his master, nor *is* one who is sent greater than the one who sent him. If you know these things, you are blessed if you do them. I do not speak of all of you. I know the ones I have chosen; but *it is* that the Scripture may be fulfilled, 'HE WHO EATS MY BREAD HAS LIFTED UP HIS HEEL AGAINST ME.' From now on I am telling you before *it* comes to pass, so that when it does occur, you may believe that I am *He*. Truly, truly, I say to you, he who receives whomever I send receives Me; and he who receives Me receives Him who sent Me" (John 13:12–20; Jesus quotes from Psalm 41:9; see Matthew 7:24; 10:24, 40; John 8:24; 14:29; 1 Peter 5:3).

Setting: Caesarea. Luke, writing in Acts, gives Paul's retelling of his conversion to Christ as he appears before King Agrippa following his hearing before the Jewish Council in Jerusalem and arrest by the Roman commander (on his way to Rome after the apostle's third missionary journey).

"And when we had fallen to the ground, I heard a voice saying to me in the Hebrew dialect, 'Saul, Saul, why are you persecuting Me? It is hard for you to kick against the goads.' And I said, 'Who are You, Lord?' And the Lord said, 'I am Jesus whom you are persecuting. But get up and stand on your feet; for this purpose I have appeared to you, to appoint you a minister and a witness not only to the things which you have seen, but also to the things in which I will appear to you; rescuing you from the *Jewish* people and from the Gentiles, to whom I am sending you, to open their eyes so that they may turn from darkness to light and from the dominion of Satan to God, that they may receive forgiveness of sins and an inheritance among those who have been sanctified by faith in Me' (Acts 26:14–18; see Isaiah 35:5; Acts 21:40; 22:14).

Setting: On the island of Patmos (in the Aegean Sea about fifty miles southwest of Ephesus in modern Turkey). On the Lord's Day (Sunday), about fifty years after Jesus' resurrection, the disciple John encounters the Lord Jesus Christ, who communicates a new revelation for the apostle to record for the church in Thyatira and to six other churches in Asia.

"And to the angel of the church in Thyatira write: The Son of God, who has eyes like a flame of fire, and His feet are like burnished bronze, says this: 'I know your deeds, and your love and faith and service and perseverance, and that your deeds of late are greater than at first. But I have *this* against you, that you tolerate the woman Jezebel, who calls herself a prophetess, and she teaches and leads My bond-servants astray so that they commit *acts of* immorality and eat things sacrificed to idols. I gave her time to repent, and she does not want to repent of her immorality. Behold, I will throw her on a bed *of sickness,* and those who commit adultery with her into great tribulation, unless they repent of her deeds. And I will kill her children with pestilence, and all the churches will know that I am He who searches the minds and hearts; and I will give to each one of you according to your deeds. But I say to you, the rest who are in Thyatira, who do not hold this teaching, who have not known the deep things of Satan, as they call them—I place no other burden on you. Nevertheless what you have, hold fast until I come. He who overcomes, and he who keeps My deeds until the end, TO HIM I WILL GIVE AUTHORITY OVER THE NATIONS; AND HE SHALL RULE THEM WITH A ROD OF IRON, AS THE VESSELS OF THE POTTER ARE BROKEN TO PIECES, as I also have received *authority* from My Father; and I will give him the morning star. He who has an ear, let him hear what the Spirit says to the churches' (Revelation 2:18–29; Jesus quotes from Psalm 2:8, 9; Isaiah 30:14; see 1 Kings 16:31; Psalm 7:9; Romans 2:5; 1 Corinthians 2:10; 2 Peter 3:9; Revelation 1:14; 2:7; 3:11; 17:1–20).

Setting: On the island of Patmos (in the Aegean Sea about fifty miles southwest of Ephesus in modern Turkey). On the Lord's Day (Sunday), about fifty years after Jesus' resurrection, the disciple John encounters the Lord Jesus Christ, who communicates a new revelation for the apostle to record for the church in Philadelphia and to six other churches in Asia.

"And to the angel of the church in Philadelphia write: He who is holy, who is true, who has the key of David, who opens and no one will shut, and who shuts and no one opens, says this: 'I know your deeds. Behold, I have put before you an open door which no one can shut, because you have a little power, and have kept My word, and have not denied My name. Behold, I will cause *those* of the synagogue of Satan, who say that they are Jews and are not, but lie—I will make them come and bow down at your feet, and *make them* know that I have loved you. Because you have kept the word of My perseverance, I also will keep you from the hour of testing, that *hour* which is about to come upon the whole world, to test those who dwell on the earth. I am coming quickly; hold fast what you have, so that no one will take your crown. He who overcomes, I will make him a pillar in the temple of My God, and he will not go out from it anymore; and I will write on him the name of My God, and the name of the city of My God, the new Jerusalem, which comes down out of heaven from My God, and My new name. He who has an ear, let him hear what the Spirit says to the churches' " (Revelation 3:7–13; see Isaiah 22:22; Galatians 2:9; Revelation 2:9, 10, 13, 25; 14:1).

FELLOWSHIP

[FELLOWSHIP from I am with you always]

Setting: On a mountain in Galilee. Following His resurrection from the dead in Jerusalem, Jesus conveys the Great Commission to His eleven remaining disciples.

And Jesus came up and spoke to them, saying, "All authority has been given to Me in heaven and on earth. Go therefore and make disciples of all the nations, baptizing them in the name of the Father and the Son and the Holy Spirit, teaching them to observe all that I commanded you; and lo, I am with you always, even to the end of the age" (Matthew 28:18–20; cf. Mark 16:15; see Daniel 7:13).

[FELLOWSHIP from will disclose Myself to him]

Setting: Jerusalem. Before the Passover, after responding to Philip's request for Him to show His disciples the Father, Jesus conveys the upcoming role of the Holy Spirit in their lives.

"I will not leave you as orphans; I will come to you. After a little while the world will no longer see Me, but you *will* see Me; because I live, you will live also. In that day you will know that I am in the Father, and you in Me, and I in you. He who has My commandments and keeps them is the one who loves Me; and he who loves Me will be loved by My Father, and I will love him and will disclose Myself to him" (John 14:18–21; see John 6:57; 10:37, 38; 16:16, 22).

[FELLOWSHIP from will dine with him, and he with Me]

Setting: On the island of Patmos (in the Aegean Sea about fifty miles southwest of Ephesus in modern Turkey). On the Lord's Day (Sunday), about fifty years after Jesus' resurrection, the disciple John encounters the Lord Jesus Christ, who communicates a new revelation for the apostle to record for the church in Laodicea and to six other churches in Asia.

"To the angel of the church in Laodicea write: The Amen, the faithful and true Witness, the Beginning of the creation of God, says this: 'I know your deeds, that you are neither cold nor hot; I wish that you were cold or hot. So because you are lukewarm, and neither hot nor cold, I will spit you out of My mouth. Because you say, "I am rich, and have become wealthy, and have need of nothing," and you do not know that you are wretched and miserable and poor and blind and naked, I advise you to buy from Me gold refined by fire so that you may become rich, and white garments so that you may clothe yourself, and *that* the shame of

your nakedness will not be revealed; and eye salve to anoint your eyes so that you may see. Those whom I love, I reprove and discipline; therefore be zealous and repent. Behold, I stand at the door and knock; if anyone hears My voice and opens the door, I will come in to him and will dine with him, and he with Me. He who overcomes, I will grant to him to sit down with Me on My throne, as I also overcame and sat down with My Father on His throne. He who has an ear, let him hear what the Spirit says to the churches'" (Revelation 3:14–22; see Proverbs 3:12; Hosea 12:8; John 14:23; 16:33).

FEMALE (Also see WOMAN; and WOMEN)

Setting: Judea beyond the Jordan (Perea). After Jesus replies to Peter's question about forgiveness, the Pharisees test Jesus in front of a large crowd with a question about divorce.

And He answered and said, "Have you not read that He who created *them* from the beginning MADE THEM MALE AND FEMALE, and said, 'FOR THIS REASON A MAN SHALL LEAVE HIS FATHER AND MOTHER AND BE JOINED TO HIS WIFE, AND THE TWO SHALL BECOME ONE FLESH'? So they are no longer two, but one flesh. What therefore God has joined together, let no man separate" (Matthew 19:4–6, Jesus quotes from Genesis 1:27; 2:24; cf. Mark 10:5–9; see 1 Timothy 2:14).

Setting: Judea beyond the Jordan (Perea). Jesus teaches the crowds gathered around Him about divorce after the Pharisees test and question Him about this subject.

And He answered and said to them, "What did Moses command you?" They said, "Moses permitted a *man* TO WRITE A CERTIFICATE OF DIVORCE AND SEND *her* AWAY." But Jesus said to them, "Because of your hardness of heart he wrote you this commandment. But from the beginning of creation, *God* MADE THEM MALE AND FEMALE. FOR THIS REASON A MAN SHALL LEAVE HIS FATHER AND MOTHER, AND THE TWO SHALL BECOME ONE FLESH; so they are no longer two, but one flesh. What therefore God has joined together, let no man separate. In the house the disciples *began* questioning Him about this again. And He said to them, "Whoever divorces his wife and marries another woman commits adultery against her; and if she herself divorces her husband and marries another man, she is committing adultery" (Mark 10:3–12, Jesus quotes from Genesis 1:27; 2:24; cf. Matthew 19:1–9; see Deuteronomy 24:1–3; Matthew 5:32; see Romans 7:2, 3; 1 Corinthians 7:10, 11, 13, 39; 1 Timothy 2:14).

FERTILIZER

Setting: On the way from Galilee to Jerusalem. After some present report to Him about the Galileans whose blood Pilate (Roman governor of Judea) had mixed with their sacrifices, Jesus responds to their concern by calling them to repentance and illustrating His point with a parable.

And He *began* telling this parable: "A man had a fig tree which had been planted in his vineyard; and he came looking for fruit on it and did not find any. And he said to the vineyard-keeper, 'Behold, for three years I have come looking for fruit on this fig tree without finding any. Cut it down! Why does it even use up the ground?' And he answered and said to him, 'Let it alone, sir, for this year too, until I dig around it and put fertilizer; and if it bears fruit next year, *fine*; but if not, cut it down.'"(Luke 13:6–9; see Matthew 3:10).

[FERTILIZER from manure pile]

Setting: On the way from Galilee to Jerusalem. After responding to a guest's proclamation about the blessings of eating bread in the kingdom of God, Jesus presents to large crowds the demands of discipleship.

Now large crowds were going along with Him; and He turned and said to them, "If anyone comes to Me, and does not hate his own father and mother and wife and children and brothers and sisters, yes, and even his own life, he cannot be My disciple. Whoever does not carry his own cross and come after Me cannot be My disciple. For which one of you, when he wants to build a tower, does not first sit down and calculate the cost to see if he has enough to complete it? Otherwise, when he has laid a foundation and is not able to finish, all who observe it begin to ridicule him, saying, 'This man began to build and was not able to finish.' Or what king, when he sets out to meet another king in battle, will not first sit down and consider whether he is strong enough with ten thousand *men* to encounter the one coming against him with twenty thousand? Or else, while the other is still far away, he sends a delegation and asks for terms of peace. So then, none of you can be My disciple who does not give up all his possessions.

Therefore, salt is good; but if even salt has become tasteless, with what will it be seasoned? It is useless either for the soil or for the manure pile; it is thrown out. He who has ears to hear, let him hear" (Luke 14:25–35; cf. Matthew 5:13; 10:37–39; see Proverbs 20:18; Philippians 3:7).

FEW THINGS (Listed under THINGS, FEW)

FIELD (Also see FIELDS)

Setting: Galilee. During the early part of His ministry, Jesus preaches the Sermon on the Mount to His disciples and the multitudes.

"For this reason I say to you, do not be worried about your life, *as to* what you will eat or what you will drink; nor for your body, *as to* what you will put on. Is not life more than food, and the body more than clothing? Look at the birds of the air, that they do not sow, nor reap nor gather into barns, and *yet* your heavenly Father feeds them. Are you not worth much more than they? And who of you by being worried can add a *single* hour to his life? And why are you worried about clothing? Observe how the lilies of the field grow; they do not toil nor do they spin, yet I say to you that not even Solomon in all his glory clothed himself like one of these. But if God so clothes the grass of the field, which is *alive* today and tomorrow is thrown into the furnace, *will He* not much more *clothe* you? You of little faith! Do not worry then, saying 'What will we eat?' or 'What will we drink?' or 'What will be wear for clothing?" For the Gentiles eagerly seek all these things; for your heavenly Father knows that you need all these things. But seek first His kingdom and His righteousness, and all these things will be added to you. So do not worry about tomorrow; for tomorrow will care for itself. Each day has enough trouble of its own" (Matthew 6:25–34; cf. Luke 12:22–31; see 1 Kings 10:4–7; Job 35:11; Matthew 8:26).

Setting: By the Sea of Galilee (Tiberias). Because the religious leaders are rejecting His message, Jesus continues teaching the crowds with the Parable of the Wheat and the Tares.

Jesus presented another parable to them, saying, "The kingdom of heaven may be compared to a man who sowed good seed in his field. But while his men were sleeping, his enemy came and sowed tares among the wheat, and went away. But when the wheat sprouted and bore grain, then the tares became evident also. The slaves of the landowner came and said to him, 'Sir, did you not sow good seed in your field? How then does it have tares?' And he said to them, 'An enemy has done this!' The slaves said to him, 'Do you want us, then, to go and gather them up?' But he said, 'No; for while you are gathering up the tares, you may uproot the wheat with them. Allow both to grow together until the harvest; and in the time of the harvest I will say to the reapers, "First gather up the tares and bind them in bundles to burn them up; but gather the wheat into my barn"'" (Matthew 13:24–30; cf. Matthew 3:12).

Setting: By the Sea of Galilee (Tiberias). Because the religious leaders are rejecting His message, Jesus continues teaching the crowds with the Parable of the Mustard Seed.

He presented another parable to them, saying, "The kingdom of heaven is like a mustard seed, which a man took and sowed in his field; and this is smaller than all *other* seeds, but when it is full grown, it is larger than the garden plants and becomes a tree, so that THE BIRDS OF THE AIR come and NEST IN ITS BRANCHES" (Matthew 13:31, 32, Jesus quotes from Ezekiel 17:23; cf. Mark 4:30–32; Luke 13:18, 19).

Setting: A house near the Sea of Galilee. Jesus explains to His disciples the meaning of the Parable of the Wheat and the Tares.

And He said, "The one who sows the good seed is the Son of Man, and the field is the world; and as *for* the good seed, these are the sons of the kingdom; and the tares are the sons of the evil *one;* and the enemy who sowed them is the devil, and the harvest is the end of the age; and the reapers are angels. So just as the tares are gathered up and burned with fire, so shall it be at the end of the age. The Son of Man will send forth His angels, and they will gather out of His kingdom all stumbling blocks, and those who commit lawlessness, and will throw them into the furnace of fire; in that place there will be weeping and gnashing of teeth.

Then THE RIGHTEOUS WILL SHINE FORTH AS THE SUN in the kingdom of their Father. He who has ears, let him hear" (Matthew 13:37–43, Jesus quotes from Daniel 12:3; cf. Matthew 8:12; 13:50).

Setting: By the Sea of Galilee (Tiberias). Because the religious leaders are rejecting His message, Jesus continues teaching the crowds with the Parable of the Hidden Treasure.

"The kingdom of heaven is like a treasure hidden in the field, which a man found and hid *again;* and from joy over it he goes and sells all that he has and buys that field" (Matthew 13:44).

Setting: The Mount of Olives, just east of Jerusalem. During His discourse, Jesus answers His disciples' questions as to when the temple will be destroyed and Jerusalem overrun, along with the signs of His coming and the end of the age.

"Therefore when you see the ABOMINATION OF DESOLATION which was spoken of through Daniel the prophet, standing in the holy place (let the reader understand), then those who are in Judea must flee to the mountains. Whoever is on the housetop must not go down to get the things that are in his house. Whoever is in the field must not turn back to get his cloak. But woe to those who are pregnant and to those who are nursing babies in those days! But pray that your flight will not be in the winter, or on a Sabbath. For then there will be a great tribulation, such as has not occurred since the beginning of the world until now, nor ever will. Unless those days had been cut short, no life would have been saved; but for the sake of the elect those days will be cut short. Then if anyone says to you, 'Behold, here is the Christ,' or "There *He is,'* do not believe *him.* For false Christs and false prophets will arise and will show great signs and wonders, so as to mislead, if possible, even the elect. Behold, I have told you in advance. So if they say to you, 'Behold, He is in the wilderness,' do not go out, *or,* 'Behold, He is in the inner rooms,' do not believe *them.* For just as the lightning comes from the east and flashes even to the west, so will the coming of the Son of Man be. Wherever a corpse is, there the vultures will gather" (Matthew 24:15–28, Jesus quotes from Daniel 9:27; cf. Daniel 12:1; Mark 13:14–23; Luke 17:22–31; 21:20–24; 23:29; see John 4:48).

Setting: The Mount of Olives, just east of Jerusalem. During His discourse, after answering His disciples' questions as to when the temple will be destroyed and Jerusalem overrun, along with the signs of His coming and the end of the age, Jesus teaches them the Parable of the Fig Tree.

"Now learn the parable from the fig tree: when its branch has already become tender and puts forth its leaves, you know that summer is near; so, you too, when you see all these things, recognize that He is near, *right* at the door. Truly, I say to you, this generation will not pass away until all these things take place. Heaven and earth will pass away, but My words will not pass away. But of that day and hour no one knows, not even the angels of heaven, nor the Son, but the Father alone. For the coming of the Son of Man will be just like the days of Noah. For as in those days before the flood they were eating and drinking, marrying and giving in marriage, until the day that Noah entered the ark, and they did not understand until the flood came and took them all away; so will the coming of the Son of Man be. Then there will be two men in the field; one will be taken and one will be left. Two women *will be* grinding at the mill; one will be taken and one will be left" (Matthew 24:32–41; cf. Mark 13:28–32; Luke 17:34–36; 21:28–33; see Genesis 6:5; 7:7; Matthew 5:18; 10:23; James 5:9).

Setting: The Mount of Olives, east of the temple in Jerusalem. During His discourse, after prophesying the temple's destruction, Jesus responds to questions from Peter, James, John, and Andrew about future events.

"But when you see the ABOMINATION OF DESOLATION standing where it should not be (let the reader understand), then those who are in Judea must flee to the mountains. The one who is on the housetop must not go down, or go in to get anything out of his house; and the one who is in the field must not turn back to get his coat. But woe to those who are pregnant and to those who are nursing babies in those days! But pray that it may not happen in winter. For those days will be a *time of* tribulation such as has not occurred since the beginning of the creation which God created until now, and never will. Unless the Lord had shortened *those* days, no life would have been saved; but for the sake of the elect, whom He chose, He shortened the days. And then if anyone says to you, 'Behold, here is the Christ'; or, 'Behold, *He is* there'; do not believe *him;* for false Christs and false prophets will arise, and will show signs and wonders, in order to lead astray, if possible, the elect. But take heed; behold, I have told you everything in advance" (Mark 13:14–23; cf. Matthew 24:15–28; Luke 21:20–24; see Daniel 9:27; 12:1; Luke 17:31).

Setting: On the way from Galilee to Jerusalem. Jesus comforts the crowd and His disciples after giving a parable about riches and greed. The scribes and Pharisees turn hostile and question Him repeatedly in an attempt to catch Him in something He might say.

And He said to His disciples, "For this reason I say to you, do not worry about *your* life, *as to* what you will eat; nor for your body, *as to* what you will put on. For life is more than food, and the body more than clothing. Consider the ravens, for they neither sow nor reap; they have no storeroom nor barn, and *yet* God feeds them; how much more valuable you are than the birds! And which of you by worrying can add a *single* hour to his life's span? If then you cannot do even a very little thing, why do you worry about other matters? Consider the lilies, how they grow: they neither toil nor spin; but I tell you, not even Solomon in all his glory clothed himself like one of these. But if God so clothes the grass in the field, which is *alive* today and tomorrow is thrown into the furnace, how much more *will He clothe* you? You men of little faith! And do not seek what you will eat and what you will drink, and do not keep worrying. For all these things the nations of the world eagerly seek; but your Father knows that you need these things. But seek His kingdom, and these things will be added to you. Do not be afraid, little flock, for your Father has chosen gladly to give you the kingdom" (Luke 12:22–32; cf. Matthew 6:25–33; see 1 Kings 10:4–7; Job 38:41).

Setting: On the way from Galilee to Jerusalem. Jesus conveys the illustration of the prodigal son because the Pharisees and scribes complain He associates with tax collectors and sinners.

And He said, "A man had two sons. The younger of them said to his father, 'Father, give me the share of the estate that falls to me.' So he divided his wealth between them. And not many days later, the younger son gathered everything together and went on a journey into a distant country, and there he squandered his estate with loose living. Now when he had spent everything, a severe famine occurred in that country, and he began to be impoverished. So he went and hired himself out to one of the citizens of that country, and he sent him into his fields to feed swine. And he would have gladly filled his stomach with the pods that the swine were eating, and no one was giving *anything* to him. But when he came to his senses, he said, 'How many of my father's hired men have more than enough bread, but I am dying here with hunger! I will get up and go to my father, and will say to him, "Father, I have sinned against heaven, and in your sight; I am no longer worthy to be called your son; make me as one of your hired men."' So he got up and came to his father. But while he was still a long way off, his father saw him and felt compassion *for him,* and ran and embraced him and kissed him. And the son said to him, "Father, I have sinned against heaven and in your sight; I am no longer worthy to be called your son.' But the father said to his slaves, 'Quickly bring out the best robe and put it on him, and put a ring on his hand and sandals on his feet; and bring the fattened calf, kill it, and let us eat and celebrate; for this son of mine was dead and has come to life again; he was lost and has been found.' And they began to celebrate. Now his older son was in the field, when he came and approached the house, he heard music and dancing. And he summoned one of the servants and *began* inquiring what these things could be. And he said to him, 'Your brother has come, and your father has killed the fattened calf because he has received him back safe and sound.' But he became angry and was not willing to go in; and his father came out and *began* pleading with him. But he answered and said to his father, 'Look! For so many years I have been serving you and I have never neglected a command of yours; and *yet* you have never given me a young goat, so that I might celebrate with my friends; but when this son of yours came, who has devoured your wealth with prostitutes, you killed the fattened calf for him.' And he said to him, 'Son, you have always been with me, and all that is mine is yours. But we had to celebrate and rejoice, for this brother of yours was dead and *has begun* to live, and was lost and has been found' " Luke 15:11–32; see Proverbs 29:2; Luke 15:1, 2).

Setting: On the way from Galilee to Jerusalem. After His disciples ask that their faith be increased following His instruction on forgiveness, the Lord Jesus illustrates with the mustard seed and an obedient slave.

And the Lord said, "If you had faith like a mustard seed, you would say to this mulberry tree, 'Be uprooted and be planted in the sea'; and it would obey you. Which of you, having a slave plowing or tending sheep, will say to him when he has come from the field, 'Come immediately and sit down to eat'? But will he not say to him, "Prepare something for me to eat, and *properly* clothe yourself and serve me while I eat and drink; and afterward you may eat and drink'? He does not thank the slave because he did the things which were commanded, does he? So you too, when you do all the things which are commanded you, say, 'We are unworthy slaves; we have done *only* that which we ought to have done' " (Luke 17:6–10; see Matthew 13:31; Luke 12:37; 17:5).

Setting: Samaria, on the way from Galilee to Jerusalem. After the Pharisees question Him about the coming of the kingdom of God, Jesus tells His disciples of His second coming.

And He said to the disciples, "The days will come when you will long to see one of the days of the Son of Man, and you will not see it. They will say to you, 'Look there! Look here!' Do not go away, and do not run after *them*. For just like the lightning, when it flashes out of one part of the sky, shines to the other part of the sky, so will the Son of Man be in His day. But first He must suffer many things and be rejected by this generation. And just as it happened in the days of Noah, so it will be also in the days of the Son of Man: they were eating, they were drinking, they were marrying, they were being given in marriage, until the day that Noah entered the ark, and the flood came and destroyed them all. It was the same as happened in the days of Lot: they were eating, they were drinking, they were buying, they were selling, they were planting, they were building; but on the day that Lot went out from Sodom it rained fire and brimstone from heaven and destroyed them all. It will be just the same on the day that the Son of Man is revealed. On that day, the one who is on the housetop and whose goods are in the house must not go down to take them out; and likewise the one who is in the field must not turn back. Remember Lot's wife. Whoever seeks to keep his life will lose it, and whoever loses *his life* will preserve it. I tell you, on that night there will be two in one bed; one will be taken and the other will be left. There will be two women grinding at the same place; one will be taken and the other will be left. [Two men will be in the field; one will be taken and the other will be left."] And answering they said to Him, "Where, Lord?" And He said to them, "Where the body *is*, there also the vultures will be gathered" (Luke 17:22–37; see Genesis 19; Matthew 10:39; 16:21, 27; 24:17–28, 37–41).

FIELDS (Also see FIELD)

Setting: On the way from Galilee to Jerusalem. Jesus conveys the illustration of the prodigal son because the Pharisees and scribes complain He associates with tax collectors and sinners.

And He said, "A man had two sons. The younger of them said to his father, 'Father, give me the share of the estate that falls to me.' So he divided his wealth between them. And not many days later, the younger son gathered everything together and went on a journey into a distant country, and there he squandered his estate with loose living. Now when he had spent everything, a severe famine occurred in that country, and he began to be impoverished. So he went and hired himself out to one of the citizens of that country, and he sent him into his fields to feed swine. And he would have gladly filled his stomach with the pods that the swine were eating, and no one was giving *anything* to him. But when he came to his senses, he said, 'How many of my father's hired men have more than enough bread, but I am dying here with hunger! I will get up and go to my father, and will say to him, "Father, I have sinned against heaven, and in your sight; I am no longer worthy to be called your son; make me as one of your hired men."' So he got up and came to his father. But while he was still a long way off, his father saw him and felt compassion *for him,* and ran and embraced him and kissed him. And the son said to him, "Father, I have sinned against heaven and in your sight; I am no longer worthy to be called your son.' But the father said to his slaves, 'Quickly bring out the best robe and put it on him, and put a ring on his hand and sandals on his feet; and bring the fattened calf, kill it, and let us eat and celebrate; for this son of mine was dead and has come to life again; he was lost and has been found.' And they began to celebrate. Now his older son was in the field, when he came and approached the house, he heard music and dancing. And he summoned one of the servants and *began* inquiring what these things could be. And he said to him, 'Your brother has come, and your father has killed the fattened calf because he has received him back safe and sound.' But he became angry and was not willing to go in; and his father came out and *began* pleading with him. But he answered and said to his father, 'Look! For so many years I have been serving you and I have never neglected a command of yours; and *yet* you have never given me a young goat, so that I might celebrate with my friends; but when this son of yours came, who has devoured your wealth with prostitutes, you killed the fattened calf for him.' And he said to him, 'Son, you have always been with me, and all that is mine is yours. But we had to celebrate and rejoice, for this brother of yours was dead and *has begun* to live, and was lost and has been found' " (Luke 15:11–32; see Proverbs 29:2; Luke 15:1, 2).

Setting: Sychar in Samaria. After Jesus converses with a Samaritan woman at Jacob's well, His disciples return with food. They try to get Jesus to eat but are surprised when He speaks of other food.

Jesus said to them, "My food is to do the will of Him who sent Me and to accomplish His work. Do you not say, 'There are yet four months, and *then* comes the harvest'? Behold, I say to you, lift up your eyes and look on the fields, that they are white for harvest. Already he who reaps is receiving wages and is gathering fruit for life eternal; so that he who sows and he who reaps may rejoice together. For in this *case* the saying is true, 'One sows and another reaps.' I sent you to reap that for which you have not labored; others have labored and you have entered into their labor" (John 4:34–38; see Matthew 9:37, 38; John 5:36).

FIFTY

Setting: Galilee. After Jesus praises John the Baptist to the crowds, Simon, a Pharisee, invites Him to dinner. A sinful woman anoints Jesus' feet with perfume, prompting the Lord to convey a parable.

And Jesus answered him, "Simon, I have something to say to you." And he replied, "Say it, Teacher." "A moneylender had two debtors: one owed five hundred denarii, and the other fifty. When they were unable to repay, he graciously forgave them both. So which of them will love him more?" Simon answered and said, "I suppose the one whom he forgave more." And He said to him, "You have judged correctly" (Luke 7:40–43; see Matthew 18:23–35).

Setting: Bethsaida in Galilee. Following a day of ministry, Jesus and His disciples try to withdraw from the large crowds, but the crowds, having listened to His teaching about the kingdom of God all day, must be fed physically, too.

But He said to them, "You give them *something* to eat!" And they said, "We have no more than five loaves and two fish, unless perhaps we go and buy food for all these people." (For there were about five thousand men.) And He said to His disciples, "Have them sit down *to eat* in groups of about fifty each" (Luke 9:13, 14; cf. Matthew 14:15–21; Mark 6:35–44; John 6:4–13).

Setting: On the way from Galilee to Jerusalem. The Lord teaches His disciples about stewardship after giving them the story of the prodigal son.

Now He was also saying to the disciples, "There was a rich man who had a manager, and this *manager* was reported to him as squandering his possessions. And he called him and said to him, 'What is this I hear about you? Give an accounting of your management, for you can no longer be a manager.' The manager said to himself, 'What shall I do, since my master is taking the management away from me? I am not strong enough to dig; I am ashamed to beg. I know what I shall do, so that when I am removed from the management people will welcome me into their homes.' And he summoned each one of his master's debtors, and he *began* saying to the first, 'How much do you owe my master?' And he said, 'A hundred measures of oil.' And he said to him, 'Take your bill, and sit down quickly and write fifty.' Then he said to another, 'And how much do you owe?' And he said, 'A hundred measures of wheat.' He said to him, 'Take your bill, and write eighty.' And his master praised the unrighteous manager because he had acted shrewdly; for the sons of this age are more shrewd in relation to their own kind than the sons of light. And I say to you, make friends for yourselves by means of the wealth of unrighteousness, so that when it fails, they will receive you into the eternal dwellings. He who is faithful in a very little thing is faithful also in much; and he who is unrighteous in a very little thing is unrighteous also in much. Therefore if you have not been faithful in the *use of* unrighteous wealth, who will entrust the *true riches* to you? And if you have not been faithful in *the use of* that which is another's, who will give you that which is your own? No servant can serve two masters; for either he will hate the one and love the other, or else he will be devoted to one and despise the other. You cannot serve God and wealth" (Luke 16:1–13; cf. Matthew 6:24; see Matthew 25:14–30).

FIG (See FIGS; and TREE, FIG)

FIG TREE (Listed under TREE, FIG; also see FIGS)

FIGS (Also see TREE, FIG)

Setting: Galilee. During the early part of His ministry, Jesus preaches the Sermon on the Mount to His disciples and the multitudes.

"Beware of the false prophets, who come to you in sheep's clothing, but inwardly are ravenous wolves. You will know them by their fruits. Grapes are not gathered from *bushes* nor figs from thistles, are they? So every good tree bears good fruit, but the bad tree bears bad fruit. A good tree cannot produce bad fruit, nor can a bad tree produce good fruit. Every tree that does not bear good fruit is cut down and thrown into the fire. So then, you will know them by their fruits" (Matthew 7:15–20; cf. Matthew 3:10; Matthew 12:33, 35; Matthew 24:11, 24; Luke 6:43, 44).

Setting: Galilee. After selecting His twelve disciples, Jesus teaches the Sermon on the Mount to the disciples and a great throng from Judea, Jerusalem, and the central coastal region of Tyre and Sidon.

And He also spoke a parable to them: "A blind man cannot guide a blind man, can he? Will they not both fall into a pit? A pupil is not above his teacher; but everyone, after he has been fully trained, will be like his teacher. Why do you look at the speck that is in your brother's eye, but do not notice the log that is in your own eye? Or how can you say to your brother, 'Brother, let me take out the speck that is in your eye,' when you yourself do not see the log that is in your own eye? You hypocrite, first take the log out of your own eye, and then you will see clearly to take out the speck that is in your brother's eye. For there is no good tree which produces bad fruit, nor, on the other hand, a bad tree which produces good fruit. For each tree is known by its own fruit. For men do not gather figs from thorns, nor do they pick grapes from a briar bush. The good man out of the good treasure of his heart brings forth what is good; and the evil *man* out of the evil *treasure* brings forth what is evil; for his mouth speaks from that which fills his heart" (Luke 6:39–45; cf. Matthew 7:3–6. 16, 18, 20; 12:35; see Matthew 10:24; 15:14; Luke 6:12–19).

FINGER (GOD, FINGER OF is a separate listing; also see FINGERS; HAND; and HANDS)

Setting: The temple in Jerusalem. Jesus exposes the truth about Pharisaism to the crowds and His disciples after the Jewish religious leaders test Him with questions.

Then Jesus spoke to the crowds and to His disciples, saying: "The scribes and the Pharisees have seated themselves in the chair of Moses; therefore all that they tell you, do and observe, but do not do according to their deeds; for they say *things* and do not do *them.* They tie up heavy burdens and lay them on men's shoulders, but they themselves are unwilling to move them with *so much as* a finger. But they do all their deeds to be noticed by men; for they broaden their phylacteries and lengthen their tassels *of their garments.* They love the place of honor at banquets and the chief seats in the synagogues, and respectful greetings in the market places, and being called Rabbi by men. But do not be called Rabbi; for One is your Teacher, and you are all brothers. Do not call *anyone* on earth your father; for One is your Father, He who is in heaven. Do not be called leaders; for One is your Leader, *that is,* Christ. But the greatest among you shall be your servant. Whoever exalts himself shall be humbled; and whoever humbles himself shall be exalted" (Matthew 23:1–12; cf. Matthew 20:26; Mark 12:38–40; Luke 20:46, 47; see Exodus 13:9; Deuteronomy 33:3; Matthew 6:1, 5, 6, 9, 16; Mark 14:11; Luke 11:43; 14:11).

Setting: On the way from Galilee to Jerusalem. After responding to the Pharisees' scoffing at His teaching His disciples about stewardship and the permanence of the Law, Jesus conveys the story of the rich man and Lazarus.

"Now there was a rich man, and he habitually dressed in purple and fine linen, joyously living in splendor every day. And a poor man named Lazarus was laid at his gate, covered with sores, and longing to be fed with the *crumbs* which were falling from the rich man's table; besides, even the dogs were coming and licking his sores. Now the poor man died and was carried away by the angels to Abraham's bosom; and the rich man also died and was buried. In Hades he lifted up his eyes, being in torment, and saw Abraham far away and Lazarus in his bosom. And he cried out and said, 'Father Abraham, have mercy on me, and send Lazarus so that he may dip the tip of his finger in water and cool off my tongue, for I am in agony in this flame.' But Abraham said, 'Child, remember that during your life you received your good things, and likewise Lazarus bad things; but now he is being comforted here, and you are in agony. And besides all this, between us and you there is a great chasm fixed, so that those who wish to come over from here to you will not be able, and *that* none may cross over from there to us.' And he said, 'Then I beg you, father, that you send him to my father's house—for I have five brothers—in order that he may warn them, so that they will not also come to this place of torment.' But Abraham said, 'They have Moses and the Prophets; let them hear them.' But he said, 'No, father Abraham, but if someone goes to them from the dead, they will repent!' But he said to him, 'If they do not listen to Moses and the Prophets, they will not be persuaded even if someone rises from the dead' " (Luke 16:19–31; see Luke 3:8; 6:24; 16:1, 14).

Setting: Jerusalem. The risen Jesus meets with His disciple Thomas (Didymus), who has had doubts when the other disciples claim to have seen and spoken with the Lord eight days earlier.

After eight days His disciples were again inside, and Thomas with them. Jesus came, the doors having been shut, and stood in their midst and said, "Peace *be* with you." Then He said to Thomas, "Reach here with your finger, and see My hands; and reach here your hand and put it into My side; and do not be unbelieving, but believing." Thomas answered and said to Him, "My Lord and my God!" Jesus said to him, "Because you have seen Me, have you believed? Blessed *are* they who did not see, and *yet* believed" (John 20:26–29; see Luke 24:36, 40; 1 Peter 1:8).

FINGER OF GOD (Listed under GOD, FINGER OF)

FINGERS (Also see FINGER; HAND; and HANDS)

Setting: On the way from Galilee to Jerusalem. After Jesus pronounces woes upon the Pharisees, a lawyer replies that Jesus' remarks are an insult to lawyers, too.

But He said, "Woe to you lawyers as well! For you weigh men down with burdens hard to bear, while you yourselves will not even touch the burdens with one of your fingers. Woe to you! For you build the tombs of the prophets, and *it was* your fathers *who* killed them. So you are witnesses and approve the deeds of your fathers; because it was they who killed them, and you build *their tombs*. For this reason also the wisdom of God said, 'I will send them prophets and apostles, and *some* of them they will kill and *some* they will persecute, so that the blood of all the prophets, shed since the foundation of the world, may be charged against this generation, from the blood of Abel to the blood of Zechariah, who was killed between the altar and the house *of God*; yes, I tell you, it shall be charged against this generation.' Woe to you lawyers! For you have taken away the key of knowledge; you yourselves did not enter, and you hindered those who were entering" (Luke 11:46–52; cf. Matthew 23:29–32; see 2 Chronicles 24:20, 21; Matthew 23:4, 13).

FIRE (Specifics such as FIRE, ETERNAL; FIRE, FURNACE OF; etc. are separate entries; also see FLAME)

Setting: Galilee. During the early part of His ministry, Jesus preaches the Sermon on the Mount to His disciples and the multitudes.

"Beware of the false prophets, who come to you in sheep's clothing, but inwardly are ravenous wolves. You will know them by their fruits. Grapes are not gathered from *bushes* nor figs from thistles, are they? So every good tree bears good fruit, but the bad tree bears bad fruit. A good tree cannot produce bad fruit, nor can a bad tree produce good fruit. Every tree that does not bear good fruit is cut down and thrown into the fire. So then, you will know them by their fruits" (Matthew 7:15–20; cf. Matthew 3:10; 12:33, 35; 24:11, 24; Luke 6:43, 44).

Setting: A house near the Sea of Galilee. Jesus explains to His disciples the meaning of the Parable of the Wheat and the Tares.

And He said, "The one who sows the good seed is the Son of Man, and the field is the world; and as *for* the good seed, these are the sons of the kingdom; and the tares are the sons of the evil *one*; and the enemy who sowed them is the devil, and the harvest is the end of the age; and the reapers are angels. So just as the tares are gathered up and burned with fire, so shall it be at the end of the age. The Son of Man will send forth His angels, and they will gather out of His kingdom all stumbling blocks, and those who commit lawlessness, and will throw them into the furnace of fire; in that place there will be weeping and gnashing of teeth. Then THE RIGHTEOUS WILL SHINE FORTH AS THE SUN in the kingdom of their Father. He who has ears, let him hear" (Matthew 13:37–43, Jesus quotes from Daniel 12:3; cf. Matthew 8:12; 13:50).

Setting: The temple in Jerusalem. Jesus speaks another parable to the chief priests and elders after they question His authority.

Jesus spoke to them again in parables, saying, "The kingdom of heaven may be compared to a king who gave a wedding feast for his son. And he sent out his slaves to call those who had been invited to the wedding feast, and they were unwilling to come.

Again he sent out other slaves saying, 'Tell those who have been invited, "Behold, I have prepared my dinner; my oxen and my fattened livestock are *all* butchered and everything is ready; come to the wedding feast." But they paid no attention and went their way, one to his own farm, another to his business, and the rest seized his slaves and mistreated them and killed them. But the king was enraged, and he sent his armies and destroyed those murderers and set their city on fire. Then he said to his slaves, 'The wedding is ready, but those who were invited were not worthy. 'Go therefore to the main highways, and as many as you find *there,* invite to the wedding feast.' Those slaves went out into the streets and gathered together all they found, both evil and good; and the wedding hall was filled with dinner guests. But when the king came in to look over the dinner guests, he saw a man there who was not dressed in wedding clothes, and he said to him, 'Friend, how did you come in here without wedding clothes?' And the man was speechless. Then the king said to the servants, 'Bind him hand and foot, and throw him into the outer darkness; in that place there will be weeping and gnashing of teeth.' For many are called, but few *are* chosen" (Matthew 22:1–14; cf. Matthew 8:11, 12).

Setting: Capernaum of Galilee. As Jesus teaches His disciples in private, they ask Him about greatness.

But Jesus said, "Do not hinder him, for there is no one who will perform a miracle in My name, and be able soon afterward to speak evil of Me. For he who is not against us is for us. For whoever gives you a cup of water to drink because of your name as *followers* of Christ, truly I say to you, he will not lose his reward. Whoever causes one of these little ones who believe to stumble, it would be better for him if, with a heavy millstone hung around his neck, he had been cast into the sea. If your hand causes you to stumble, cut it off; it is better for you to enter life crippled, than, having your two hands, to go into hell, into the unquenchable fire, [where THEIR WORM DOES NOT DIE, AND THE FIRE IS NOT QUENCHED.] If your foot causes you to stumble, cut it off; it is better for you to enter life lame, than, having your two feet, to be cast into hell, [where THEIR WORM DOES NOT DIE, AND THE FIRE IS NOT QUENCHED.] If your eye causes you to stumble, throw it out; it is better for you to enter the kingdom of God with one eye, than, having two eyes, to be cast into hell, where THEIR WORM DOES NOT DIE, AND THE FIRE IS NOT QUENCHED. For everyone will be salted with fire. Salt is good; but if the salt becomes unsalty, with what will you make it salty *again?* Have salt in yourselves, and be at peace with one another" (Mark 9:39–50; Jesus quotes from Isaiah 66:24; cf. Matthew 18:6–9; Luke 9:49–50; see Matthew 5:13, 29, 30; 10:42; 12:30; 18:5, 6).

Setting: On the way from Galilee to Jerusalem. After clarifying a parable for Peter and the crowd, Jesus conveys how a relationship with Him divides families.

"I have come to cast fire upon the earth; and how I wish it were already kindled! But I have a baptism to undergo, and how distressed I am until it is accomplished! Do you suppose that I came to grant peace on earth? I tell you, no, but rather division; for from now on five *members* in one household will be divided, three against two and two against three. They will be divided, father against son and son against father, mother against daughter, and daughter against mother, mother-in-law against daughter-in-law and daughter-in-law against mother-in-law" (Luke 12:49–53; cf. Matthew 10:34–36; see Micah 7:6; Mark 10:38).

Setting: Samaria, on the way from Galilee to Jerusalem. After the Pharisees question Him about the coming of the kingdom of God, Jesus tells His disciples of His second coming.

And He said to the disciples, "The days will come when you will long to see one of the days of the Son of Man, and you will not see it. They will say to you, 'Look there! Look here!' Do not go away, and do not run after *them.* For just like the lightning, when it flashes out of one part of the sky, shines to the other part of the sky, so will the Son of Man be in His day. But first He must suffer many things and be rejected by this generation. And just as it happened in the days of Noah, so it will be also in the days of the Son of Man: they were eating, they were drinking, they were marrying, they were being given in marriage, until the day that Noah entered the ark, and the flood came and destroyed them all. It was the same as happened in the days of Lot: they were eating, they were drinking, they were buying, they were selling, they were planting, they were building; but on the day that Lot went out from Sodom it rained fire and brimstone from heaven and destroyed them all. It will be just the same on the day that the Son of Man is revealed. On that day, the one who is on the housetop and whose goods are in the house must not go down to take them out; and likewise the one who is in the field must not turn back. Remember Lot's wife. Whoever seeks to keep his life will lose it, and whoever loses *his life* will preserve it. I tell you, on that night there will be two in one bed; one will be taken and the other will be left. There will be two women grinding at the same place; one will be taken and the other will be left. [Two men will be in the field; one will be taken and the other will be left."] And answering they said to Him, "Where, Lord?" And He said to them, "Where the body *is*, there also the vultures will be gathered" (Luke 17:22–37; see Genesis 19; Matthew 10:39; 16:21, 27; 24:17–28, 37–41).

Setting: Jerusalem. Before the Passover, after conveying the upcoming ministry of the Holy Spirit in His disciples' lives with His imminent departure from them, Jesus explains He is the vine and His disciples are the branches.

"I am the true vine, and My Father is the vinedresser. Every branch in Me that does not bear fruit, He takes away; and every *branch* that bears fruit, He prunes it so that it may bear more fruit. You are already clean because of the word which I have spoken to you. Abide in Me, and I in you. As the branch cannot bear fruit of itself unless it abides in the vine, so neither *can* you unless you abide in Me. I am the vine, you are the branches; he who abides in Me and I in him, he bears much fruit, for apart from Me you can do nothing. If anyone does not abide in Me, he is thrown away as a branch and dries up; and they gather them, and cast them into the fire and they are burned. If you abide in Me, and My words abide in you, ask whatever you wish, and it will be done for you. My Father is glorified by this, that you bear much fruit, and *so* prove to be My disciples. Just as the Father has loved Me, I have also loved you; abide in My love. If you keep My commandments, you will abide in My love; just as I have kept My Father's commandments and abide in His love. These things I have spoken to you so that My joy may be in you, and *that* your joy may be made full" (John 15:1–11; see Matthew 5:16; 7:7; John 3:29, 35; 6:56; 8:29, 31; 13:10; 15:16).

Setting: On the island of Patmos (in the Aegean Sea about fifty miles southwest of Ephesus in modern Turkey). On the Lord's Day (Sunday), about fifty years after Jesus' resurrection, the disciple John encounters the Lord Jesus Christ, who communicates a new revelation for the apostle to record for the church in Laodicea and to six other churches in Asia.

"To the angel of the church in Laodicea write: The Amen, the faithful and true Witness, the Beginning of the creation of God, says this: 'I know your deeds, that you are neither cold nor hot; I wish that you were cold or hot. So because you are lukewarm, and neither hot nor cold, I will spit you out of My mouth. Because you say, "I am rich, and have become wealthy, and have need of nothing," and you do not know that you are wretched and miserable and poor and blind and naked, I advise you to buy from Me gold refined by fire so that you may become rich, and white garments so that you may clothe yourself, and *that* the shame of your nakedness will not be revealed; and eye salve to anoint your eyes so that you may see. Those whom I love, I reprove and discipline; therefore be zealous and repent. Behold, I stand at the door and knock; if anyone hears My voice and opens the door, I will come in to him and will dine with him, and he with Me. He who overcomes, I will grant to him to sit down with Me on My throne, as I also overcame and sat down with My Father on His throne. He who has an ear, let him hear what the Spirit says to the churches'" (Revelation 3:14–22; see Proverbs 3:12; Hosea 12:8; John 14:23; 16:33).

FIRE, ETERNAL (Also see FIRE, FURNACE OF; GOD, SEPARATION FROM; HELL; and PUNISHMENT, ETERNAL)

Setting: Capernaum of Galilee. Jesus elaborates about stumbling blocks following His disciples' question about greatness in the kingdom of heaven.

"Woe to the world because of *its* stumbling blocks! For it is inevitable that stumbling blocks come; but woe to that man through whom the stumbling block comes! If your hand or your foot causes you to stumble, cut if off and throw it from you; it is better for you to enter life crippled or lame, than to have two hands or two feet and be cast into the eternal fire. If your eye causes you to stumble, pluck it out and throw it from you. It is better for you to enter life with one eye, than to have two eyes and be cast into the fiery hell" (Matthew 18:7–9; cf. Matthew 5:29, 30; Mark 9:43–48 and Luke 17:1).

Setting: The Mount of Olives, just east of Jerusalem. During His discourse, after answering His disciples' questions as to when the temple will be destroyed and Jerusalem overrun, along with the signs of His coming and the end of the age, Jesus reveals the future judgments following His return.

"But when the Son of Man comes in His glory, and all the angels with Him, then He will sit on His glorious throne. All the nations will be gathered before Him; and He will separate them from one another, as the shepherd separates the sheep from the goats; and He will put the sheep on His right, and the goats on the left. Then the King will say to those on His right, 'Come, you who are blessed of My Father, inherit the kingdom prepared for you from the foundation of the world. 'For I was hungry, and you gave Me *something* to eat; I was thirsty, and you gave Me *something* to drink; I was a stranger, and you invited Me in; naked, and you clothed Me; I was sick, and you visited Me; I was in prison, and you came to Me.' Then the righteous will answer Him, 'Lord, when did we see You hungry and feed You, or thirsty, and give you *something* to drink? And when did we see You a stranger, and invite You in, or naked, and clothe You? When did we see You sick, or in prison, and come to You?' The King will answer and say to them, 'Truly I say to you, to the extent that you did it to one of these brothers of Mine, *even* the least *of them,* you did it to Me.' Then He will also say to those on His left, 'Depart from Me, accursed ones, into the eternal fire which has been prepared for the devil and his angels; for I was hungry, and you gave Me *nothing* to eat; I was thirsty, and you gave Me nothing to drink; I was a stranger, and you did not invite Me in; naked, and you did not clothe Me; sick, and in prison, and you did not visit Me.' Then they themselves also will answer, 'Lord, when did we see You hungry, or thirsty, or a stranger, or naked, or sick, or in prison, and did not take care of You?' Then He will answer them, 'Truly I say to you, to the extent that you did not do it to one of the least of these, you did not do it to Me.' These will go away into eternal punishment, but the righteous into eternal life" (Matthew 25:31–46; see Matthew 7:23; 16:27; 19:29).

FIRE, FLAME OF

Setting: On the island of Patmos (in the Aegean Sea about fifty miles southwest of Ephesus in modern Turkey). On the Lord's Day (Sunday), about fifty years after Jesus' resurrection, the disciple John encounters the Lord Jesus Christ, who communicates a new revelation for the apostle to record for the church in Thyatira and to six other churches in Asia.

"And to the angel of the church in Thyatira write: The Son of God, who has eyes like a flame of fire, and His feet are like burnished bronze, says this: 'I know your deeds, and your love and faith and service and perseverance, and that your deeds of late are greater than at first. But I have *this* against you, that you tolerate the woman Jezebel, who calls herself a prophetess, and she teaches and leads My bond-servants astray so that they commit *acts of* immorality and eat things sacrificed to idols. I gave her time to repent, and she does not want to repent of her immorality. Behold, I will throw her on a bed *of sickness,* and those who commit adultery with her into great tribulation, unless they repent of her deeds. And I will kill her children with pestilence, and all the churches will know that I am He who searches the minds and hearts; and I will give to each one of you according to your deeds. But I say to you, the rest who are in Thyatira, who do not hold this teaching, who have not known the deep things of Satan, as they call them—I place no other burden on you. Nevertheless what you have, hold fast until I come. He who overcomes, and he who keeps My deeds until the end, TO HIM I WILL GIVE AUTHORITY OVER THE NATIONS; AND HE SHALL RULE THEM WITH A ROD OF IRON, AS THE VESSELS OF THE POTTER ARE BROKEN TO PIECES, as I also have received *authority* from My Father; and I will give him the morning star. He who has an ear, let him hear what the Spirit says to the churches' (Revelation 2:18–29; Jesus quotes from Psalm 2:8, 9; Isaiah 30:14; see 1 Kings 16:31; Psalm 7:9; Romans 2:5; 1 Corinthians 2:10; 2 Peter 3:9; Revelation 1:14; 2:7; 3:11; 17:1–20).

FIRE, FURNACE OF (Also see FIRE, ETERNAL; FIRE, UNQUENCHABLE; GOD, SEPARATION FROM; HELL; and PUNISHMENT, ETERNAL)

Setting: A house near the Sea of Galilee. Jesus explains to His disciples the meaning of the Parable of the Wheat and the Tares.

And He said, "The one who sows the good seed is the Son of Man, and the field is the world; and as *for* the good seed, these are the sons of the kingdom; and the tares are the sons of the evil *one;* and the enemy who sowed them is the devil, and the harvest is the end of the age; and the reapers are angels. So just as the tares are gathered up and burned with fire, so shall it be at the end of the age. The Son of Man will send forth His angels, and they will gather out of His kingdom all stumbling blocks, and those who commit lawlessness, and will throw them into the furnace of fire; in that place there will be weeping and gnashing of teeth. Then THE RIGHTEOUS WILL SHINE FORTH AS THE SUN in the kingdom of their Father. He who has ears, let him hear" (Matthew 13:37–43, Jesus quotes from Daniel 12:3; cf. Matthew 8:12; 13:50).

Setting: By the sea of Galilee. Because the religious leaders are rejecting His message, Jesus continues teaching His disciples with the Parable of the Dragnet.

"Again, the kingdom of heaven is like a dragnet cast into the sea, and gathering *fish* of every kind; and when it was filled, they drew it up on the beach; and they sat down and gathered the good *fish* into containers, but the bad they threw away. So it will be at the end of the age; the angels will come forth and take out the wicked from among the righteous, and will throw them into the furnace of fire; in that place there will be weeping and gnashing of teeth. Have you understood all these things?" They said to Him, "Yes" (Matthew 13:47–51).

FIRE, UNQUENCHABLE (Also see FIRE, ETERNAL; FIRE, FURNACE OF; HELL; and PUNISHMENT, ETERNAL)

Setting: Capernaum of Galilee. As Jesus teaches His disciples in private, they ask Him about greatness.

But Jesus said, "Do not hinder him, for there is no one who will perform a miracle in My name, and be able soon afterward to speak evil of Me. For he who is not against us is for us. For whoever gives you a cup of water to drink because of your name as *followers* of Christ, truly I say to you, he will not lose his reward. Whoever causes one of these little ones who believe to stumble, it would be better for him if, with a heavy millstone hung around his neck, he had been cast into the sea. If your hand causes you to stumble, cut it off; it is better for you to enter life crippled, than, having your two hands, to go into hell, into the unquenchable fire, [where THEIR WORM DOES NOT DIE, AND THE FIRE IS NOT QUENCHED.] If your foot causes you to stumble, cut it off; it is better for you to enter life lame, than, having your two feet, to be cast into hell, [where THEIR WORM DOES NOT DIE, AND THE FIRE IS NOT QUENCHED.] If your eye causes you to stumble, throw it out; it is better for you to enter the kingdom of God with one eye, than, having two eyes, to be cast into hell, where THEIR WORM DOES NOT DIE, AND THE FIRE IS NOT QUENCHED. For everyone will be salted with fire. Salt is good; but if the salt becomes unsalty, with what will you make it salty *again?* Have salt in yourselves, and be at peace with one another" (Mark 9:39–50; Jesus quotes from Isaiah 66:24; cf. Matthew 18:6–9; Luke 9:49, 50; see Matthew 5:13, 29, 30; 10:42; 12:30; 18:5, 6).

FIRST (Also see ALPHA; BEGINNING; and PRIORITIES)

Setting: Galilee. During the early part of His ministry, Jesus preaches the Sermon on the Mount to His disciples and the multitudes.

"Therefore if you are presenting your offering at the altar, and there remember that your brother has something against you, leave your offering there before the altar and go; first be reconciled to your brother, and then come and present your offering" (Matthew 5:23, 24; see Romans 12:17, 18).

Setting: Galilee. During the early part of His ministry, Jesus preaches the Sermon on the Mount to His disciples and the multitudes.

"For this reason I say to you, do not be worried about your life, *as to* what you will eat or what you will drink; nor for your body, *as to* what you will put on. Is not life more than food, and the body more than clothing? Look at the birds of the air, that they do not sow, nor reap nor gather into barns, and *yet* your heavenly Father feeds them. Are you not worth much more than they? And who of you by being worried can add a *single* hour to his life? And why are you worried about clothing? Observe how the lilies of the field grow; they do not toil nor do they spin, yet I say to you that not even Solomon in all his glory clothed himself like one of these. But if God so clothes the grass of the field, which is *alive* today and tomorrow is thrown into the furnace, *will He* not much more *clothe* you? You of little faith! Do not worry then, saying 'What will we eat?' or 'What will we drink?' or 'What will be wear for clothing?" For the Gentiles eagerly seek all these things; for your heavenly Father knows that you need all these things. But seek first His kingdom and His righteousness, and all these things will be added to you. So do not worry about tomorrow; for tomorrow will care for itself. Each day has enough trouble of its own" (Matthew 6:25–34; cf. Luke 12:22–31; see 1 Kings 10:4–7; Job 35:11; Matthew 8:26).

Setting: Galilee. During the early part of His ministry, Jesus preaches the Sermon on the Mount to His disciples and the multitudes.

"Do not judge so that you will not be judged. For in the way you judge, you will be judged; and by your standard of measure, it will be measured to you. Why do you look at the speck that is in your brother's eye, but do not notice the log that is in your own eye? Or how can you say to your brother, 'Let me take the speck out of your eye, and behold, the log is in your own eye? You hypocrite, first take the log out of your own eye, and then you will see clearly to take the speck out of your brother's eye" (Matthew 7:1–5; cf. Mark 4:24; Luke 6:37–42; Romans 2:1; Romans 14:10, 13).

Setting: Galilee. After He heals a blind, mute, demon-possessed man, the Pharisees accuse Jesus in front of crowds of being a worker of Satan.

And knowing their thoughts Jesus said to them, "Any kingdom divided against itself is laid waste; and any city or house divided against itself will not stand. If Satan casts out Satan, he is divided against himself; how then will his kingdom stand? If I by Beelzebul cast out demons, by whom do your sons cast *them* out? For this reason they will be your judges. But if I cast out demons by the Spirit of God, then the kingdom of God has come upon you. Or how can anyone enter the strong man's house and carry off his property, unless he first binds the strong *man?* And then he will plunder his house" (Matthew 12:25–29; cf. Matthew 9:34; Mark 3:23–27; Luke 11:17–20).

Setting: Galilee. Jesus responds to some Pharisees and scribes who ask Him for a miraculous sign.

"Now when the unclean spirit goes out of a man, it passes through waterless places seeking rest, and does not find *it.* Then it says, 'I will return to my house from which I came'; and when it comes, it finds *it* unoccupied, swept, and put in order. Then it goes and takes along with it seven other spirits more wicked than itself, and they go in and live there; and the last state of that man becomes worse than the first. That is the way it will also be for this evil generation" (Matthew 12:43–45; cf. Luke 11:24–26; see Matthew 12:38; Mark 5:9).

Setting: By the Sea of Galilee. Because the religious leaders are rejecting His message, Jesus continues teaching the crowds with the Parable of the Wheat and the Tares.

Jesus presented another parable to them, saying, "The kingdom of heaven may be compared to a man who sowed good seed in his field. But while his men were sleeping, his enemy came and sowed tares among the wheat, and went away. But when the wheat sprouted and bore grain, then the tares became evident also. The slaves of the landowner came and said to him, 'Sir, did you not sow good seed in your field? How then does it have tares?' And he said to them, 'An enemy has done this!' The slaves said to him, 'Do you want us, then, to go and gather them up?' But he said, 'No; for while you are gathering up the tares, you may uproot the wheat with them. Allow both to grow together until the harvest; and in the time of the harvest I will say to the reapers, "First gather up the tares and bind them in bundles to burn them up; but gather the wheat into my barn"'" (Matthew 13:24–30; cf. Matthew 3:12).

Setting: Capernaum of Galilee. Jesus pays the two-drachma temple tax for Peter and Himself in a miraculous manner.

He said, "Yes." And when he came into the house, Jesus spoke to him first, saying, "What do you think, Simon? From whom do the kings of the earth collect customs or poll-tax, from their sons or from strangers?" When Peter said, "From strangers," Jesus said to him, "Then the sons are exempt. However, so that we do not offend them, go to the sea and throw in a hook, and take the first fish that comes up; and when you open its mouth, you will find a shekel. Take that and give it to them for you and Me" (Matthew 17:25–27; see Exodus 30:11–16; Matthew 17:24; 22:17–19; Romans 13:7).

Setting: Judea beyond the Jordan (Perea). Jesus promises rewards to His disciples for their personal sacrifice and commitment to following Him.

And Jesus said to them, "Truly I say to you, that you who have followed Me, in the regeneration when the Son of Man will sit on His glorious throne, you also shall sit upon twelve thrones, judging the twelve tribes of Israel. And everyone who has left houses or brothers or sisters or father or mother or children or farms for My name's sake, will receive many times as much, and will inherit eternal life. But many *who* are first will be last; and *the* last, first" (Matthew 19:28–30; cf. Matthew 6:33; 20:15; Mark 10:29, 30; Luke 18:29, 30; 22:30).

Setting: Judea beyond the Jordan (Perea). Jesus illustrates the kingdom of heaven to His disciples through the story of laborers in the vineyard.

"For the kingdom of heaven is like a landowner who went out early in the morning to hire laborers for his vineyard. When he had agreed with the laborers for a denarius for the day, he sent them into his vineyard. And he went out about the third hour and saw others standing idle in the market place; and to those he said, 'You also go into the vineyard, and whatever is right I will give you.' And *so* they went. Again he went out about the sixth and the ninth hour, and did the same thing. And about the eleventh *hour* he went out and found others standing *around;* and he said to them, 'Why have you been standing idle here all day long?' They said to him, 'Because no one hired us.' He said to them, 'You go into the vineyard too.' When evening came, the owner of the vineyard said to his foreman, 'Call the laborers and pay them their wages, beginning with the last *group* to the first.' When those *hired* about the eleventh hour came, each one received a denarius. When those *hired* first came, they thought that they would receive more; but each of them also received a denarius. When they received it, they grumbled at the landowner, saying, 'These last men have worked *only* one hour, and you have made them equal to us who have borne the burden and the scorching heat of the day.' But he answered and said to one of them, 'Friend, I am doing you no wrong; did you not agree with me for a denarius? Take what is yours and go, but I wish to give to this last man the same as to you. It is not lawful for me to do what I wish with what is my own? Or is your eye envious because I am generous?' So the last shall be first, and the first last" (Matthew 20:1–16; cf. Matthew 19:30).

Setting: On the way to Jerusalem, where Jesus will die on the cross. Jesus teaches His disciples about true greatness after the mother of James and John, the sons of Zebedee, asks Him to make her sons exalted rulers with Him in His coming kingdom.

But Jesus called them to Himself and said, "You know that the rulers of the Gentiles lord it over them, and *their* great men exercise authority over them. It is not this way among you, but whoever wishes to become great among you shall be your servant, and whoever wishes to be first among you shall be your slave; just as the Son of Man did not come to be served, but to serve, and to give His life a ransom for many" (Matthew 20:25–28; cf. Matthew 23:11; 26:28; Mark 10:42–45).

Setting: The temple in Jerusalem. Jesus delivers a parable to the chief priests and elders after they question His authority.

"But what do you think? A man had two sons, and he came to the first and said, 'Son, go work today in the vineyard.' And he answered, 'I will not'; but afterward he regretted it and went. The man came to the second and said the same thing; and he answered, 'I *will,* sir'; but he did not go. Which of the two sons did the will of his father?" They said, "The first." Jesus said to them, "Truly, I say to you that the tax collectors and prostitutes will get into the kingdom of God before you. For John came to you in the way of righteousness and you did not believe him; but the tax collectors and prostitutes did believe him; and you, seeing *this,* did not even feel remorse afterward so as to believe him" (Matthew 21:28–32; cf. Luke 7:29, 30, 37–50).

Setting: The temple in Jerusalem. Jesus delivers another parable to the chief priests and elders after they question His authority.

"Listen to another parable. There was a landowner who PLANTED A VINEYARD AND PUT A WALL AROUND IT AND DUG A WINE PRESS IN IT, AND BUILT A TOWER, and rented it out to vine-growers and went on a journey. When the harvest time approached, he sent his slaves to the vine-growers to receive his produce. The vine-growers took his slaves and beat one, and killed another, and stoned a third. Again he sent another group of slaves larger than the first; and they did the same thing to them. But afterward he sent his son to them, saying, 'They will respect my son.' But when the vine-growers saw the son, they said among themselves, 'This is the heir; come, let us kill him and seize his inheritance.' They took him, and threw him out of the vineyard and killed him. Therefore when the owner of the vineyard comes, what will he do to those vine-growers?" (Matthew 21:33–40; Jesus quotes from Isaiah 5:1, 2; cf. Mark 12:1–9; Luke 20:9–15).

Setting: The temple in Jerusalem. After the Jewish religious leaders test Him with questions, Jesus pronounces the sixth of eight woes on them in front of the crowds and His disciples.

"Woe to you, scribes and Pharisees, hypocrites! For you clean the outside of the cup and of the dish, but inside they are full of robbery and self-indulgence. You blind Pharisee, first clean the inside of the cup and of the dish, so that the outside of it may become clean also" (Matthew 23:25, 26; see Mark 7:4).

Setting: Galilee. After Jesus selects His twelve disciples, scribes from Jerusalem attribute His miraculous powers to Beelzebul (Satan).

And He called them to Himself and began speaking to them in parables, "How can Satan cast out Satan? If a kingdom is divided against itself, that kingdom cannot stand. If a house is divided against itself, that house will not be able to stand. If Satan has risen up against himself and is divided, he cannot stand, but he is finished! But no one can enter the strong man's house and plunder his property unless he first binds the strong man, and then he will plunder his house. Truly I say to you, all sins shall be forgiven the sons of men, and whatever blasphemies they utter; but whoever blasphemes against the Holy Spirit never has forgiveness, but is guilty of an eternal sin"—because they were saying, "He has an unclean spirit" (Mark 3:23–30; cf. Matthew 12:25–32; Luke 12:10).

Setting: Galilee. Following His explanation of the Parable of the Sower to His disciples, Jesus conveys the Parable of the Seed.

And He was saying, "The kingdom of God is like a man who casts seed upon the soil; and he goes to bed at night and gets up by day, and the seed sprouts and grows—how, he himself does not know. The soil produces crops by itself; first the blade, then the head, then the mature grain in the head. But when the crop permits, he immediately puts in the sickle, because the harvest has come" (Mark 4:26–29; see Joel 3:13).

Setting: The region of Tyre. After the Pharisees and scribes from Jerusalem question His disciples' lack of obedience to tradition in Galilee, Jesus casts out a demon from the daughter of a Gentile (Syrophoenician) woman.

And He was saying to her, "Let the children be satisfied first, for it is not good to take the children's bread and throw it to the dogs." But she answered and said to Him, "Yes, Lord *but* even the dogs under the table feed on the children's crumbs. And He said to her, "Because of this answer go; the demon has gone out of your daughter" (Mark 7:27–29; cf. Matthew 15:21–28).

Setting: Galilee. After informing a crowd and His disciples of the hope involving the coming kingdom of God, Jesus takes Peter, James, and John to a high mountain (some think Mount Hermon). There He reveals His glory through the Transfiguration and answers their question about Elijah.

And He said to them, "Elijah does first come and restore all things. And *yet* how is it written of the Son of Man that He will suffer many things and be treated with contempt? But I say to you that Elijah has indeed come, and they did to him whatever they wished, just as it is written of him" (Mark 9:12, 13; cf. Matthew 17:1–13; Luke 9:28–36; see Malachi 4:5, 6; Matthew 16:21).

Setting: Capernaum of Galilee. As Jesus teaches His disciples in private, they ask Him about greatness.

They came to Capernaum; and when He was in the house, He *began* to question them, "What were you discussing on the way?" But they kept silent, for on the way they had discussed with one another which *of them* was the greatest. Sitting down, He called the twelve and said to them, "If anyone wants to be first, he shall be last of all and servant of all." Taking a child, He set him before them, and taking him in His arms, He said to them, "Whoever receives one child like this in My name receives Me; and whoever receives Me does not receive Me, but Him who sent Me" (Mark 9:33–37; cf. Matthew 18:1–5; Luke 9:46–48; see Matthew 20:26; 10:40).

Setting: Judea beyond the Jordan (Perea). After informing a rich man how righteous believers may have treasure in heaven, Jesus conveys to His disciples the reward of those who sacrifice in this life to follow Him.

Jesus said, "Truly I say to you, there is no one who has left house or brothers or sisters or mother or father or children or farms, for My sake and for the gospel's sake, but that he will receive a hundred times as much now in the present age, houses and brothers and sisters and mothers and children and farms, along with persecutions; and in the age to come, eternal life. But many *who are* first will be last, and the last, first" (Mark 10:29–31; cf. Matthew 19:27–30; Luke 18:28–30; see Matthew 6:33).

Setting: On the road to Jerusalem. When James and John ask Jesus for special honor and privileges in His kingdom, the other disciples become angry. Jesus uses this moment to teach them about servanthood.

Calling them to Himself, Jesus said to them, "You know that those who are recognized as rulers of the Gentiles lord it over them; and their great men exercise authority over them. But it is not this way among you, but whoever wishes to become great among you shall be your servant; and whoever wishes to be first among you shall be slave of all. For even the Son of Man did not come to be served, but to serve, and to give His life a ransom for many" (Mark 10:42–45; cf. Matthew 20:25–28).

Setting: The Mount of Olives, east of the temple in Jerusalem. During His discourse, after prophesying the temple's destruction, Jesus responds to questions from Peter, James, John, and Andrew about future events.

And Jesus began to say to them, "See to it that no one misleads you. Many will come in My name, saying, 'I am *He!*' and will mislead many. When you hear of wars and rumors of wars, do not be frightened; *those things* must take place; but *that is* not yet the end. For nation will rise up against nation, and kingdom against kingdom; there will be earthquakes in various places; there will *also be* famines. These things are *merely* the beginning of birth pangs. But be on your guard; for they will deliver you to *the* courts, and you will be flogged in *the* synagogues, and you will stand before governors and kings for My sake, as a testimony to them. The gospel must first be preached to all the nations. When they arrest you and hand you over, do not worry beforehand about what you are to say, but say whatever is given you in that hour; for it is not you who speak, but *it is* the Holy Spirit. Brother will betray brother to death, and a father *his* child; and children will rise up against parents and have them put to death. You will be hated by all because of My name, but the one who endures to the end, he will be saved" (Mark 13:5–13; cf. Matthew 24:4–14; Luke 21:7–19; see Matthew 10:17–22).

Setting: Galilee. After selecting His twelve disciples, Jesus teaches the Sermon on the Mount to the disciples and a great throng from Judea, Jerusalem, and the central coastal region of Tyre and Sidon.

And He also spoke a parable to them: "A blind man cannot guide a blind man, can he? Will they not both fall into a pit? A pupil is not above his teacher; but everyone, after he has been fully trained, will be like his teacher. Why do you look at the speck that is in your brother's eye, but do not notice the log that is in your own eye? Or how can you say to your brother, 'Brother, let me take out the speck that is in your eye,' when you yourself do not see the log that is in your own eye? You hypocrite, first take the log out of your own eye, and then you will see clearly to take out the speck that is in your brother's eye. For there is no good tree which produces bad fruit, nor, on the other hand, a bad tree which produces good fruit. For each tree is known by its own fruit. For men do not gather figs from thorns, nor do they pick grapes from a briar bush. The good man out of the good treasure of his heart brings forth what is good; and the evil *man* out of the evil *treasure* brings forth what is evil; for his mouth speaks from that which fills his heart" (Luke 6:39–45; cf. Matthew 7:3–6. 16, 18, 20; 12:35; see Matthew 10:24; 15:14; Luke 6:12–19).

Setting: On the way from Galilee to Jerusalem. The Lord appoints seventy followers and sends them out in pairs to every place He Himself will soon visit.

And He was saying to them, "The harvest is plentiful, but the laborers are few; therefore beseech the Lord of the harvest to send out laborers into His harvest. Go; behold, I send you out as lambs in the midst of wolves. Carry no money belt, no bag, no shoes; and greet no one on the way. Whatever house you enter, first say, 'Peace be to this house.' If a man of peace is there, your peace will rest on him; but if not, it will return to you. Stay in that house, eating and drinking what they give you; for the laborer is worthy of his wages. Do not keep moving from house to house. Whatever city you enter and they receive you, eat what is set before you; and heal those in it who are sick, and say to them, 'The kingdom of God has come near to you.' But whatever city you enter and they do not receive you, go out into its streets and say, 'Even the dust of your city which clings to our feet we wipe off *in protest* against you; yet be sure of this, that the kingdom of God has come near.' I say to you, it will be more tolerable in that day for Sodom than for that city" (Luke 10:2–12; see Genesis 19:24–28; Matthew 9:37, 38, 10:9–14, 16; 1 Corinthians 10:27).

Setting: On the way from Galilee to Jerusalem. After some in the crowd test Him, demanding a sign from heaven, Jesus illustrates His power over Satan.

"When the unclean spirit goes out of a man, it passes through waterless places seeking rest, and not finding any, it says, 'I will return to my house from which I came.' And when it comes, it finds it swept clean and put in order. Then it goes and takes *along* seven other spirits more evil than itself, and they go in and live there; and the last state of that man becomes worse than the first" (Luke 11:24–26; cf. Matthew 12:43–45; see Luke 11:14–16).

Setting: On the way from Galilee to Jerusalem. While teaching in the cities and villages, Jesus responds to a question about who is saved.

And someone said to Him, "Lord, are here *just* a few who are being saved?" And He said to them, "Strive to enter through the narrow door; for many, I tell you, will seek to enter and will not be able. Once the head of the house gets up and shuts the door, and you begin to stand outside and knock on the door, saying, 'Lord, open up to us!' then He will answer and say to you, 'I do not know where you are from.' Then you will begin to say, 'We ate and drank in Your presence, and You taught in our streets'; and He will say, 'I tell you, I do not know where you are from; DEPART FROM ME, ALL YOU EVILDOERS.' In that place there will be weeping and gnashing of teeth when you see Abraham and Isaac and Jacob and all the prophets in the kingdom of God, but you yourselves being thrown out. And they will come from east and west and from north and south, and will recline *at the table* in the kingdom of God. And behold, *some* are last who will be first and *some* are first who will be last" (Luke 13:23–30, Jesus quotes from Psalm 6:8; cf. Matthew 7:13, 23; 8:11, 12; see Matthew 19:30; Luke 3:8).

Setting: On the way to Galilee from Jerusalem. After speaking a parable to the invited guests and the host at a banquet, Jesus responds to a guest's proclamation about the blessings of eating bread in the kingdom of God.

But He said to him, "A man was giving a big dinner, and he invited many; and at the dinner hour he sent his slave to say to those who had been invited, 'Come; for everything is ready now.' But they all alike began to make excuses. The first one said to him, 'I have bought a piece of land and I need to go out and look at it; please consider me excused.' Another one said, 'I have bought five yoke of oxen, and I am going to try them out; please consider me excused.' Another one said, I have married a wife, and for that reason I cannot come.' And the slave came *back* and reported this to his master. Then the head of the household became angry and said to his slave, 'Go out at once into the streets and lanes of the city and bring in here the poor and crippled and blind and lame.' And the slave said, 'Master, what you commanded has been done, and still there is room.' And the master said to the slave, 'Go out into the highways and along the hedges, and compel *them* to come in, so that my house may be filled. For I tell you, none of those men who were invited shall taste of my dinner'" (Luke 14:16–24; see Deuteronomy 24:5; Matthew 22:2–14; Luke 14:1, 2).

Setting: On the way from Galilee to Jerusalem. After responding to a guest's proclamation about the blessings of eating bread in the kingdom of God, Jesus presents to large crowds the demands of discipleship.

Now large crowds were going along with Him; and He turned and said to them, "If anyone comes to Me, and does not hate his own father and mother and wife and children and brothers and sisters, yes, and even his own life, he cannot be My disciple. Whoever does not carry his own cross and come after Me cannot be My disciple. For which one of you, when he wants to build a tower, does not first sit down and calculate the cost to see if he has enough to complete it? Otherwise, when he has laid a foundation and is not able to finish, all who observe it begin to ridicule him, saying, 'This man began to build and was not able to finish.' Or what king, when he sets out to meet another king in battle, will not first sit down and consider whether he is strong enough with ten thousand *men* to encounter the one coming against him with twenty thousand? Or else, while the other is still far away, he

sends a delegation and asks for terms of peace. So then, none of you can be My disciple who does not give up all his possessions. Therefore, salt is good; but if even salt has become tasteless, with what will it be seasoned? It is useless either for the soil or for the manure pile; it is thrown out. He who has ears to hear, let him hear" (Luke 14:25–35; cf. Matthew 5:13; 10:37–39; see Proverbs 20:18; Luke 14:1, 2; Philippians 3:7).

Setting: On the way from Galilee to Jerusalem. The Lord teaches His disciples about stewardship after giving the story of the prodigal son.

Now He was also saying to the disciples, "There was a rich man who had a manager, and this *manager* was reported to him as squandering his possessions. And he called him and said to him, 'What is this I hear about you? Give an accounting of your management, for you can no longer be a manager.' The manager said to himself, 'What shall I do, since my master is taking the management away from me? I am not strong enough to dig; I am ashamed to beg. I know what I shall do, so that when I am removed from the management people will welcome me into their homes.' And he summoned each one of his master's debtors, and he *began* saying to the first, 'How much do you owe my master?' And he said, 'A hundred measures of oil.' And he said to him, 'Take your bill, and sit down quickly and write fifty.' Then he said to another, 'And how much do you owe?' And he said, 'A hundred measures of wheat.' He said to him, 'Take your bill, and write eighty.' And his master praised the unrighteous manager because he had acted shrewdly; for the sons of this age are more shrewd in relation to their own kind than the sons of light. And I say to you, make friends for yourselves by means of the wealth of unrighteousness, so that when it fails, they will receive you into the eternal dwellings. He who is faithful in a very little thing is faithful also in much; and he who is unrighteous in a very little thing is unrighteous also in much. Therefore if you have not been faithful in the *use of* unrighteous wealth, who will entrust the *true riches* to you? And if you have not been faithful in *the use of* that which is another's, who will give you that which is your own? No servant can serve two masters; for either he will hate the one and love the other, or else he will be devoted to one and despise the other. You cannot serve God and wealth" (Luke 16:1–13; cf. Matthew 6:24; see Matthew 25:14–30).

Setting: Samaria, on the way from Galilee to Jerusalem. After the Pharisees question Him about the coming of the kingdom of God, Jesus tells His disciples of His second coming.

And He said to the disciples, "The days will come when you will long to see one of the days of the Son of Man, and you will not see it. They will say to you, 'Look there! Look here!' Do not go away, and do not run after *them*. For just like the lightning, when it flashes out of one part of the sky, shines to the other part of the sky, so will the Son of Man be in His day. But first He must suffer many things and be rejected by this generation. And just as it happened in the days of Noah, so it will be also in the days of the Son of Man: they were eating, they were drinking, they were marrying, they were being given in marriage, until the day that Noah entered the ark, and the flood came and destroyed them all. It was the same as happened in the days of Lot: they were eating, they were drinking, they were buying, they were selling, they were planting, they were building; but on the day that Lot went out from Sodom it rained fire and brimstone from heaven and destroyed them all. It will be just the same on the day that the Son of Man is revealed. On that day, the one who is on the housetop and whose goods are in the house must not go down to take them out; and likewise the one who is in the field must not turn back. Remember Lot's wife. Whoever seeks to keep his life will lose it, and whoever loses *his life* will preserve it. I tell you, on that night there will be two in one bed; one will be taken and the other will be left. There will be two women grinding at the same place; one will be taken and the other will be left. [Two men will be in the field; one will be taken and the other will be left."] And answering they said to Him, "Where, Lord?" And He said to them, "Where the body *is*, there also the vultures will be gathered" (Luke 17:22–37; see Genesis 19; Matthew 10:39; 16:21, 27; 24:17–28, 37–41).

Setting: Jericho, on the way to Jerusalem. After commending Zaccheus's faith in Him, Jesus provides a parable about stewardship.

So He said, "A nobleman went to a distant country to receive a kingdom for himself, and *then* return. And he called ten of his slaves, and gave them ten minas and said to them, 'Do business *with this* until I come *back*.' But his citizens hated him and sent a delegation after him, saying, 'We do not want this man to reign over us.' When he returned, after receiving the kingdom, he ordered that these slaves, to whom he had given the money, be called to him so that he might know what business they had done. The first appeared, saying, 'Master, your mina has made ten minas more.' And he said to him, 'Well done, good slave, because you have been faithful in a very little thing, you are to be in authority over ten cities.' The second came, saying, 'Your mina, master, has made five minas.' And he said to him, also, 'And you are to be over five cities.' Another came, saying, 'Master, here is your mina, which I kept put away in a handkerchief; for I was afraid of you, because you are an exacting man; you take up what you did not lay down and reap what you did not sow.' He said to him, 'By your own words I will judge you, you worthless slave. Did you know that I am an exacting man, taking up what I did not lay down and reaping what I did not sow? Then why did you not put my money in the bank, and having come, I would have collected it with interest?' Then he said to the bystanders, 'Take the mina away from him and give it to the one who has the ten minas.' And they said to him, 'Master, he has ten minas *already.*' I tell you that to everyone who has, more shall be given, but from the one who does not have, even what he does have shall be taken away. But these enemies of mine, who did not want me to reign over them, bring them here and slay them in my presence" (Luke 19:12–27; cf. Matthew 25:14–30; see Matthew 13:12; Luke 16:10).

Setting: The temple in Jerusalem. A few days before His crucifixion, after Jesus prophesies the future destruction of the temple during His Olivet Discourse, His disciples ask Him when this will happen.

And He said, "See to it that you are not misled; for many will come in My name, saying, "I am *He*,' and, 'The time is near.' Do not go after them. When you hear of wars and disturbances, do not be terrified; for these things must take place first, but the end *does* not *follow* immediately" (Luke 21:8, 9; cf. Matthew 24:4–8; Mark 13:5–8).

Setting: The temple in Jerusalem. Following the Feast of Booths in Jerusalem, Jesus returns from the Mount of Olives to teach. The scribes and Pharisees set a woman caught in adultery before Him to test whether He will follow Moses' command to stone her.

They were saying this, testing Him, so that they might have grounds for accusing Him. But Jesus stooped down and with His finger wrote on the ground. But when they persisted in asking Him, He straightened up, and said to them, "He who is without sin among you, let him *be the* first to throw a stone at her. Again He stooped down and wrote on the ground. When they heard it, they *began* to go out one by one, beginning with the older ones, and He was left alone, and the woman, where she was, in the center *of the court.* Straightening up, Jesus said to her, "Woman, where are they? Did no one condemn you?" She said, "No one, Lord ." And Jesus said, "I do not condemn you, either. Go. From now on sin no more" (John 8:6–11; see Deuteronomy 17:2–7).

Setting: On the island of Patmos (in the Aegean Sea about fifty miles southwest of Ephesus in modern Turkey). On the Lord's Day (Sunday), approximately fifty years after Jesus' resurrection, the disciple John encounters the Lord Jesus Christ, who communicates new revelations for the apostle to record for the seven churches in Asia.

When I saw Him, I fell at His feet like a dead man. And He placed His right hand on me, saying, "Do not be afraid; I am the first and the last, and the living One; and I was dead, and behold, I am alive forevermore, and I have the keys of death and of Hades. Therefore write the things which you have seen, and the things which are, and the things which will take place after these things. As for the mystery of the seven stars which you saw in My right hand, and the seven golden lampstands: the seven stars are the angels of the seven churches, and the seven lampstands are the seven churches" (Revelation 1:17–20; see Isaiah 44:6; Luke 24:5; Revelation 2:8).

Setting: On the island of Patmos (in the Aegean Sea about fifty miles southwest of Ephesus in modern Turkey). On the Lord's Day (Sunday), about fifty years after Jesus' resurrection, the disciple John encounters the Lord Jesus Christ, who communicates a new revelation for the apostle to record for the church in Ephesus and to six other churches in Asia.

"To the angel of the church in Ephesus write: The One who holds the seven stars in His right hand, the One who walks among the seven golden lampstands, says this: 'I know your deeds and your toil and perseverance, and that you cannot tolerate evil men, and you put to the test those who call themselves apostles, and they are not, and you found them *to be* false; and you have perseverance and have endured for My name's sake, and have not grown weary. But I have *this* against you, that you have left your first love. Therefore remember from where you have fallen, and repent and do the deeds you did at first; or else I am coming to you and will remove your lampstand out of its place—unless you repent. Yet this you do have, that you hate the deeds of the Nicolaitans, which I also hate. He who has an ear, let him hear what the Spirit says to the churches. To him who overcomes, I will grant to eat of the tree of life which is in the Paradise of God' " (Revelation 2:1–7; see Genesis 2:9; Ezekiel 28:13; 1 John 4:1; Revelation 1:10, 11, 19, 20; 2:15, 16).

Setting: On the island of Patmos (in the Aegean Sea about fifty miles southwest of Ephesus in modern Turkey). On the Lord's Day (Sunday), about fifty years after Jesus' resurrection, the disciple John encounters the Lord Jesus Christ, who communicates a new revelation for the apostle to record for the church in Smyrna and to six other churches in Asia.

"And to the angel of the church in Smyrna write: The first and the last, who was dead, and has come to life, says this: 'I know your tribulation and your poverty (but you are rich), and the blasphemy by those who say they are Jews and are not, but are a synagogue of Satan. Do not fear what you are about to suffer. Behold, the devil is about to cast some of you into prison, so that you will be tested, and you will have tribulation for ten days. Be faithful until death, and I will give you the crown of life. He who has an ear, let him hear what the Spirit says to the churches. He who overcomes will not be hurt by the second death' (Revelation 2:8–11; see Isaiah 44:6; Revelation 1:9, 18; 20:6, 14).

Setting: On the island of Patmos (in the Aegean Sea about fifty miles southwest of Ephesus in modern Turkey). On the Lord's Day (Sunday), about fifty years after Jesus' resurrection, the disciple John encounters the Lord Jesus Christ, who communicates a new revelation for the apostle to record for the church in Thyatira and to six other churches in Asia.

"And to the angel of the church in Thyatira write: The Son of God, who has eyes like a flame of fire, and His feet are like burnished bronze, says this: 'I know your deeds, and your love and faith and service and perseverance, and that your deeds of late are greater than at first. But I have *this* against you, that you tolerate the woman Jezebel, who calls herself a prophetess, and she teaches and leads My bond-servants astray so that they commit *acts of* immorality and eat things sacrificed to idols. I gave her time to repent, and she does not want to repent of her immorality. Behold, I will throw her on a bed *of sickness,* and those who commit adultery with her into great tribulation, unless they repent of her deeds. And I will kill her children with pestilence, and all the churches will know that I am He who searches the minds and hearts; and I will give to each one of you according to your deeds. But I say to you, the rest who are in Thyatira, who do not hold this teaching, who have not known the deep things of Satan, as they call them—I place no other burden on you. Nevertheless what you have, hold fast until I come. He who overcomes, and he who keeps My deeds until the end, TO HIM I WILL GIVE AUTHORITY OVER THE NATIONS; AND HE SHALL RULE THEM WITH A ROD OF IRON, AS THE VESSELS OF THE POTTER ARE BROKEN TO PIECES, as I also have received *authority* from My Father; and I will give him the morning star. He who has an ear, let him hear what the Spirit says to the churches' (Revelation 2:18–29; Jesus quotes from Psalm 2:8–9 and Isaiah 30:14; see 1 Kings 16:31; Psalm 7:9; Romans 2:5; 1 Corinthians 2:10; 2 Peter 3:9; Revelation 1:14; 2:7; 3:11; 17:1–20).

Setting: On the island of Patmos (in the Aegean Sea about fifty miles southwest of Ephesus in modern Turkey). In the final chapter of the Lord Jesus Christ's revelation via the disciple John, approximately fifty years after His resurrection, the Lord reveals His upcoming return, reward, and eternality.

"Behold, I am coming quickly, and My reward *is* with Me, to render to every man according to what he has done. I am the Alpha and the Omega, the first and the last, the beginning and the end" (Revelation 22:12, 13; see Isaiah 40:10; 44:6).

FIRST LOVE (Listed under LOVE, FIRST)

FIRST MIRACLE (Listed under MIRACLE, FIRST)

FISH (Also see CATCH; FISHING; and HOOK)

Setting: Galilee. During the early part of His ministry, Jesus preaches the Sermon on the Mount to His disciples

and the multitudes.

"Ask, and it will be given to you; seek, and you will find; knock, and it will be opened to you. For everyone who asks receives, and he who seeks finds, and to him who knocks it will be opened. Or what man is there among you who, when his son asks for a loaf, will give him a stone? Or if he asks for a fish, he will not give him a snake, will he? If you then, being evil, know how to give good gifts to your children, how much more will your Father who is in heaven give what is good to those who ask Him! In everything, therefore, treat people the same way you want them to treat you, for this is the Law and the Prophets" (Matthew 7:7–12; cf. Matthew 22:40; Luke 6:31; 11:9–13; see Psalm 84:11).

Setting: By the Sea of Galilee. Because the religious leaders are rejecting His message, Jesus continues teaching His disciples with the Parable of the Dragnet.

"Again, the kingdom of heaven is like a dragnet cast into the sea, and gathering *fish* of every kind; and when it was filled, they drew it up on the beach; and they sat down and gathered the good *fish* into containers, but the bad they threw away. So it will be at the end of the age; the angels will come forth and take out the wicked from among the righteous, and will throw them into the furnace of fire; in that place there will be weeping and gnashing of teeth. Have you understood all these things?" They said to Him, "Yes" (Matthew 13:47–51).

Setting: Capernaum of Galilee. Jesus pays the two-drachma temple tax for Peter and Himself in a miraculous manner.

He said, "Yes." And when he came into the house, Jesus spoke to him first, saying, "What do you think, Simon? From whom do the kings of the earth collect customs or poll-tax, from their sons or from strangers?" When Peter said, "From strangers," Jesus said to him, "Then the sons are exempt. However, so that we do not offend them, go to the sea and throw in a hook, and take the first fish that comes up; and when you open its mouth, you will find a shekel. Take that and give it to them for you and Me" (Matthew 17:25–27; see Exodus 30:11–16; Matthew 22:17–19; Romans 13:7).

Setting: On the way from Galilee to Jerusalem. After revealing to His disciples how to pray, Jesus illustrates God's benevolence in answering prayer and giving the Holy Spirit.

"Now suppose one of you fathers is asked by his son for a fish; he will not give him a snake instead of a fish, will he? Or *if* he is asked for an egg, he will not give him a scorpion, will he? If you then, being evil, know how to give good gifts to your children, how much more will *your* heavenly Father give the Holy Spirit to those who ask Him?" (Luke 11:11–13; cf. Matthew 7:9–11).

Setting: By the Sea of Galilee (Tiberias). During His third post-resurrection appearance to His disciples, Jesus directs them to a great catch of fish following their unsuccessful night of fishing.

So Jesus said to them, "Children, you do not have any fish, do you?" They answered Him, "No." And He said to them, "Cast the net on the right-hand side of the boat and you will find a *catch*." So they cast, and then they were not able to haul it in because of the great number of fish (John 21:5, 6; see Luke 5:4).

Setting: By the Sea of Galilee (Tiberias). In His third post-resurrection appearance to His disciples, after providing a great catch of fish following their unsuccessful night of fishing, Jesus asks them to bring Him some of the fish.

Jesus said to them, "Bring some of the fish which you have now caught" (John 21:10).

FISHERS (Also see FISH; and FISHING)

Setting: By the Sea of Galilee. As Jesus commences His public ministry, He calls two brothers who are fishermen,

Simon (Peter) and Andrew, to be His disciples.

And He said to them, "Follow Me, and I will make you fishers of men" (Matthew 4:19; cf. Mark 4:17).

Setting: Along the Sea of Galilee. Jesus calls Simon (Peter) and his brother, Andrew, to be His disciples.

And Jesus said to them, "Follow Me, and I will make you become fishers of men" (Mark 1:17; cf. Matthew 4:19).

FISHING (Also see CATCH; FISH; and FISHERS)

[FISHING from let down your nets for a catch]
Setting: By the Sea of Galilee. After teaching the people from Simon's (Peter) boat, Jesus calls Peter, James, and John to follow Him. [This appears to be a permanent call, as Simon and his companions are with Him earlier in Mark 1:35–39 and Luke 4:38–39.]

When He had finished speaking, He said to Simon, "Put out into the deep water and let down your nets for a catch." ". . . and so also *were* James and John, sons of Zebedee, who were partners with Simon. And Jesus said to Simon, "Do not fear, from now on you will be catching men" (Luke 5:4, 10; see John 21:6).

[FISHING from you will find a *catch*]
Setting: By the Sea of Galilee (Tiberias). During His third post-resurrection appearance to His disciples, Jesus directs them to a great catch of fish following their unsuccessful night of fishing.

So Jesus said to them, "Children, you do not have any fish, do you?" They answered Him, "No." And He said to them, "Cast the net on the right-hand side of the boat and you will find a *catch*." So they cast, and then they were not able to haul it in because of the great number of fish (John 21:5, 6; see Luke 5:4).

FISHNET (See DRAGNET)

FIVE CITIES (See CITIES, FIVE)

FIVE HUNDRED (Listed under HUNDRED, FIVE)

FIVE LOAVES (Listed under LOAVES, FIVE; also see BREAD)

FIVE THOUSAND (Listed under THOUSAND, FIVE)

FLAME (FIRE, FLAME OF is a separate entry; also see FIRE)

Setting: On the way from Galilee to Jerusalem. After responding to the Pharisees' scoffing at His teaching His disciples about stewardship and the permanence of the Law, Jesus conveys the story of the rich man and Lazarus.

"Now there was a rich man, and he habitually dressed in purple and fine linen, joyously living in splendor every day. And a poor man named Lazarus was laid at his gate, covered with sores, and longing to be fed with the *crumbs* which were falling from the rich man's table; besides, even the dogs were coming and licking his sores. Now the poor man died and was carried away by the angels to Abraham's bosom; and the rich man also died and was buried. In Hades he lifted up his eyes, being in torment, and saw Abraham far away and Lazarus in his bosom. And he cried out and said, 'Father Abraham, have mercy on me, and send Lazarus so that he may dip the tip of his finger in water and cool off my tongue, for I am in agony in this flame.' But Abraham said, 'Child, remember that during your life you received your good things, and likewise Lazarus bad things; but now he is being comforted here, and you are in agony. And besides all this, between us and you there is a great chasm fixed, so that those who wish to come over from here to you will not be able, and *that* none may cross over from there to us.' And he said, 'Then I beg you, father, that you send him to my father's house—for I have five brothers—in order that he may warn them, so that they will not also come to this place of torment.' But Abraham said, 'They have Moses and the Prophets; let them hear them.' But he said, 'No, father Abraham, but if someone goes to them from the dead, they will repent!' But he said to him, 'If they do not listen to Moses and the Prophets, they will not be persuaded even if someone rises from the dead' " (Luke 16:19–31; see Luke 3:8; 6:24; 16:1, 14).

FLAME OF FIRE (Listed under FIRE, FLAME OF)

FLESH (FLESH, ONE is a separate entry; also see BODY)

Setting: Caesarea Philippi. Jesus responds to Simon Peter's declaration that He is the Christ, the Son of the living God.

And Jesus said to him, "Blessed are you, Simon Barjona, because flesh and blood did not reveal *this* to you, but My Father who is in heaven. I also say to you that you are Peter, and upon this rock I will build My church; and the gates of Hades will not overpower it. I will give you the keys of the kingdom of heaven; and whatever you bind on earth shall have been bound in heaven, and whatever you loose on earth shall have been loosed in heaven" (Matthew 16:17–19; cf. Matthew 18:18; Mark 8:29; Luke 9:20).

Setting: Jerusalem. After celebrating the Passover meal with His disciples, Jesus retreats to the Garden of Gethsemane on the Mount of Olives to pray prior to His betrayal by Judas.

Then Jesus came with them to a place called Gethsemane, and said to His disciples, "Sit here while I go over there and pray." And He took with Him Peter and the two sons of Zebedee, and began to be grieved and distressed. Then He said to them, "My soul is deeply grieved, to the point of death; remain here and keep watch with Me." And He went a little beyond *them,* and fell on His face and prayed, saying, "My Father, if it is possible, let this cup pass from Me; yet not as I will, but as You will." And He came to the disciples and found them sleeping, and said to Peter, "So, you *men* could not keep watch with Me for one hour? Keep watching and praying that you may not enter into temptation; the spirit is willing, but the flesh is weak." He went away again a second time and prayed, saying, "My Father, if this cannot pass away unless I drink it, Your will be done." Again He came and found them sleeping, for their eyes were heavy. And He left them again, and went away and prayed a third time, saying the same thing once more. Then He came to the disciples and said to them, "Are you still sleeping and resting? Behold the hour is at hand and the Son of Man is being betrayed into the hands of sinners. Get up, let us be going; behold the one who betrays Me is at hand!" (Matthew 26:36–46; cf. Mark 14:32–42; Luke 22:40–46; see Matthew 20:22; John 12:27).

Setting: Gethsemane on the Mount of Olives, east of the temple in Jerusalem. Jesus agonizes over His impending death, disappointed that His disciples keep falling asleep instead of watching and praying with Him.

They came to a place named Gethsemane; and He said to the disciples, "Sit here until I have prayed." And He took with Him Peter and James and John, and began to be very distressed and troubled. And He said to them, "My soul is deeply grieved to the point of death; remain here and keep watch." And He went a little beyond *them,* and fell to the ground and *began* to pray that if it were possible, the hour might pass Him by. And He was saying, "Abba! Father! All things are possible for You; remove this cup from Me; yet not what I will, but what You will." And He came and found them sleeping, and said to Peter, "Simon, are you asleep? Could you not keep watch for one hour? Keep watching and praying that you may not come into temptation; the spirit is willing, but the flesh is weak" (Mark 14:32–38; cf. Matthew 26:36–41; Luke 22:41–46; see Romans 8:15; Galatians 4:6).

Setting: Jerusalem. After rising from the grave on the third day after being crucified, and appearing to two of His followers on the road to Emmaus, Jesus appears to His disciples (except Thomas).

While they were telling these things, He Himself stood in their midst and said to them, "Peace be to you." But they were startled and frightened and thought they were seeing a spirit. And He said to them, "Why are you troubled, and why do doubts arise in your hearts? See My hands and My feet, that it is I Myself; touch Me and see, for a spirit does not have flesh and bones as you see that I have." And when He had said this, He showed them His hands and His feet. While they still could not believe *it* because of their joy and amazement. He said to them, "Have you anything to eat?" They gave Him a piece of a broiled fish; and He took it and ate *it* before them (Luke 24:36–43; see Mark 16:14; John 20:27; Acts 10:40, 41).

Setting: Jerusalem. At the time of the Passover of the Jews, after the Lord cleanses the temple, a Pharisee, Nicodemus, asks Him by night the meaning of "born again."

Jesus answered, "Truly, truly, I say to you, unless one is born of water and the Spirit he cannot enter into the kingdom of God. That which is born of the flesh is flesh, and that which is born of the Spirit is spirit. Do not be amazed that I said to you, 'You must be born again.' The wind blows where it wishes and you hear the sound of it, but do not know where it comes from and where it is going; so is everyone who is born of the Spirit" (John 3:5–8; see Psalm 135:7; John 1:13).

Setting: Capernaum of Galilee. After Jesus informs the people whom He miraculously fed with a lad's five loaves and two fish how they can receive the bread out of heaven, the Jewish religious leaders grumble because Jesus claims He came down out of heaven.

Therefore the Jews were grumbling about Him, because He said, "I am the bread that came down out of heaven." They were saying, "Is not this Jesus, the son of Joseph, whose father and mother we know? How does He now say, 'I have come down out of heaven'?" Jesus answered and said to them, "Do not grumble among yourselves. No one can come to Me unless the Father who sent Me draws him; and I will raise him up on the last day. It is written in the prophets, 'AND THEY SHALL ALL BE TAUGHT OF GOD.' Everyone who has heard and learned from the Father, comes to Me. Not that anyone has seen the Father, except the One who is from God; He has seen the Father. Truly, truly, I say to you, he who believes has eternal life. I am the bread of life. Your fathers ate the manna in the wilderness, and they died. This is the bread which comes down out of heaven, so that one may eat of it and not die. I am the living bread that came down out of heaven; if anyone eats of this bread, he will live forever; and the bread also which I will give for the life of the world is My flesh" (John 6:41–51, Jesus quotes from Isaiah 54:13; see John 1:18, 29; 3:36; 7:27).

Setting: Capernaum of Galilee. After Jesus informs the people whom He miraculously fed with a lad's five loaves and two fish how they can receive the bread out of heaven, the Jewish religious leaders argue with one another when Jesus says He will give His flesh to the world to eat.

So Jesus said to them, "Truly, truly, I say to you, unless you eat the flesh of the Son of Man and drink His blood, you have no life in yourselves. He who eats My flesh and drinks My blood has eternal life, and I will raise him up on the last day. For My flesh is true food, and My blood is true drink. He who eats My flesh and drinks My blood abides in Me, and I in him. As the living Father sent Me, and I live because of the Father, so he who eats Me, he also will live because of Me. This is the bread which came down out of heaven; not as the fathers ate and died; he who eats this bread will live forever" (John 6:53–58; see Matthew 16:16; Luke 4:22; John 3:36; 9:16; 15:4).

Setting: The synagogue at Capernaum of Galilee. After the Jewish religious leaders argue with one another when Jesus says He will give His flesh to the world to eat, some of His disciples also express difficulty with His statements.

But, Jesus, conscious that His disciples grumbled at this, said to them, "Does this cause you to stumble? *What* then if you see the Son of Man ascending to where He was before? It is the Spirit who gives life; the flesh profits nothing; the words that I have spoken to you are spirit and are life. But there are some of you who do not believe." For Jesus knew from the beginning who they were who did not believe, and who it was that would betray Him. And He was saying, "For this reason I have said to you, that no one can come to Me unless it has been granted him from the Father" (John 6:61–65; see Matthew 11:6; 13:11; John 3:13).

Setting: The temple in Jerusalem. Following the Feast of Booths and the scribes' and Pharisees' failed attempt to stone a woman for adultery, Jesus returns the next day to teach. His enemies question His testimony about Himself.

Jesus answered and said to them, "Even if I testify about Myself, My testimony is true, for I know where I came from and where I am going; but you do not know where I come from or where I am going. You judge according to the flesh; I am not judging anyone.

But even if I do judge, My judgment is true; for I am not alone *in it,* but I and the Father who sent Me. Even in your law it has been written that the testimony of two men is true. I am He who testifies about Myself, and the Father who sent Me testifies about Me." So they were saying to Him, "Where is Your Father?" Jesus answered, "You know neither Me nor My Father; if you knew Me, you would know My Father also" (John 8:14–19; see Deuteronomy 17:6; 19:15; Matthew 18:16; John 3:17; 5:30, 37; 7:28; 8:42).

Setting: Jerusalem. Before the Passover, after giving His disciples assurance that in the midst of tribulation they will have His peace, Jesus prays His high-priestly prayer.

Jesus spoke these things; and lifting up His eyes to heaven, He said, "Father, the hour has come; glorify Your Son, that the Son may glorify You, even as You gave Him authority over all flesh, that to all whom You have given Him, He may give eternal life. This is eternal life, that they may know You, the only true God, and Jesus Christ whom You have sent. I glorified You on the earth, having accomplished the work which you have given Me to do. Now, Father, glorify Me together with Yourself, with the glory which I had with You before the world was. I have manifested Your name to the men whom You gave Me out of the world; they were Yours and You gave them to Me, and they have kept Your word. Now they have come to know that everything You have given Me is from You; for the words which You gave Me I have given to them; and they received *them* and truly understood that I came forth from You, and they believed You sent Me. I ask on their behalf; I do not ask on behalf of the world, but of those whom You have given Me; for they are Yours; and all things that are Mine are Yours, and Yours are Mine; and I have been glorified in them. I am no longer in the world; and yet they themselves are in the world, and I come to You. Holy Father, keep them in Your name, *the name* which You have given Me, that they may be even as We *are.* While I was with them, I was keeping them in Your name which You have given Me; and I guarded them and not one of them perished but the son of perdition, so that the Scripture would be fulfilled" (John 17:1–12; see Luke 22:32; John 1:1; 3:35; 4:34; 5:44; 6:37–39, 70; 8:42; 11:41; 12:49; 13:18, 31; 16:15; 17:20; Philippians 2:9).

FLESH AND BLOOD (Listed under BLOOD, FLESH AND)

FLESH, ONE (Also see MARRIAGE)

Setting: Judea beyond the Jordan (Perea). After Jesus replies to Peter's question about forgiveness, the Pharisees test Jesus in front of a large crowd with a question about divorce.

And He answered and said, "Have you not read that He who created *them* from the beginning MADE THEM MALE AND FEMALE, and said, 'FOR THIS REASON A MAN SHALL LEAVE HIS FATHER AND MOTHER AND BE JOINED TO HIS WIFE, AND THE TWO SHALL BECOME ONE FLESH'? So they are no longer two, but one flesh. What therefore God has joined together, let no man separate" (Matthew 19:4–6, Jesus quotes from Genesis 1:27; 2:24; cf. Mark 10:5–9; see 1 Timothy 2:14).

Setting: Judea beyond the Jordan (Perea). Jesus teaches the crowds gathered around Him about divorce after the Pharisees test and question Him on this subject.

And He answered and said to them, "What did Moses command you?" They said, "Moses permitted a *man* TO WRITE A CERTIFICATE OF DIVORCE AND SEND *her* AWAY." But Jesus said to them, "Because of your hardness of heart he wrote you this commandment. But from the beginning of creation, *God* MADE THEM MALE AND FEMALE. FOR THIS REASON A MAN SHALL LEAVE HIS FATHER AND MOTHER, AND THE TWO SHALL BECOME ONE FLESH; so they are no longer two, but one flesh. What therefore God has joined together, let no man separate. In the house the disciples *began* questioning Him about this again. And He said to them, "Whoever divorces his wife and marries another woman commits adultery against her; and if she herself divorces her husband and marries another man, she is committing adultery" (Mark 10:3–12, Jesus quotes from Genesis 1:27; 2:24; cf. Matthew 19:1–9; see Deuteronomy 24:1–3; Matthew 5:32; see Romans 7: 2, 3; 1 Corinthians 7:10, 11, 13, 39; 1 Timothy 2:14).

FLIGHT

Setting: The Mount of Olives, just east of Jerusalem. During His discourse, Jesus answers His disciples' questions as to when the temple will be destroyed and Jerusalem overrun, along with the signs of His coming and the end of the age.

"Therefore when you see the ABOMINATION OF DESOLATION which was spoken of through Daniel the prophet, standing in the holy place (let the reader understand), then those who are in Judea must flee to the mountains. Whoever is on the housetop must not go down to get the things that are in his house. Whoever is in the field must not turn back to get his cloak. But woe to those who are pregnant and to those who are nursing babies in those days! But pray that your flight will not be in the winter, or on a Sabbath. For then there will be a great tribulation, such as has not occurred since the beginning of the world until now, nor ever will. Unless those days had been cut short, no life would have been saved; but for the sake of the elect those days will be cut short. Then if anyone says to you, 'Behold, here is the Christ,' or "There *He is,*' do not believe *him.* For false Christs and false prophets will arise and will show great signs and wonders, so as to mislead, if possible, even the elect. Behold, I have told you in advance. So if they say to you, 'Behold, He is in the wilderness,' do not go out, *or,* 'Behold, He is in the inner rooms,' do not believe *them.* For just as the lightning comes from the east and flashes even to the west, so will the coming of the Son of Man be. Wherever a corpse is, there the vultures will gather" (Matthew 24:15–28, Jesus quotes from Daniel 9:27; cf. Daniel 12:1; Mark 13:14–23; Luke 17:22–31; 21:20–24; 23:29; see John 4:48).

FLOCK (Also see FOLD; SHEEP; and SHEPHERD)

Setting: Jerusalem. After celebrating the Passover meal, as they go out to the Mount of Olives prior to His betrayal by Judas, Jesus states that all His disciples will deny Him that very day.

Then Jesus said to them, "You will all fall away because of Me this night, for it is written, 'I WILL STRIKE DOWN THE SHEPHERD, AND THE SHEEP OF THE FLOCK SHALL BE SCATTERED.' But after I have been raised, I will go ahead of you to Galilee." But Peter said to Him, '*Even* though all may fall away because of You, I will never fall away.' Jesus said to him, "Truly I say to you that this *very* night, before a rooster crows, you will deny Me three times" (Matthew 26:31–34, Jesus quotes from Zechariah 13:7; cf. Mark 14:26–31; see Matthew 28:7, 10, 16; John 13:37).

Setting: On the way from Galilee to Jerusalem. Jesus comforts the crowd and His disciples after giving a parable about riches and greed. The scribes and Pharisees turn hostile and question Him repeatedly in an attempt to catch Him in something He might say.

And He said to His disciples, "For this reason I say to you, do not worry about *your* life, *as to* what you will eat; nor for your body, *as to* what you will put on. For life is more than food, and the body more than clothing. Consider the ravens, for they neither sow nor reap; they have no storeroom nor barn, and *yet* God feeds them; how much more valuable you are than the birds! And which of you by worrying can add a *single* hour to his life's span? If then you cannot do even a very little thing, why do you worry about other matters? Consider the lilies, how they grow: they neither toil nor spin; but I tell you, not even Solomon in all his glory clothed himself like one of these. But if God so clothes the grass in the field, which is *alive* today and tomorrow is thrown into the furnace, how much more *will He clothe* you? You men of little faith! And do not seek what you will eat and what you will drink, and do not keep worrying. For all these things the nations of the world eagerly seek; but your Father knows that you need these things. But seek His kingdom, and these things will be added to you. Do not be afraid, little flock, for your Father has chosen gladly to give you the kingdom" (Luke 12:22–32; cf. Matthew 6:25–33; see 1 Kings 10:4–7; Job 38:41).

Setting: Jerusalem. Following the Pharisees' interrogation and dismissal of the formerly blind man Jesus healed on the Sabbath, the Lord conveys the Parable of the Good Shepherd to the Pharisees using figures of speech they do not understand.

So Jesus said to them again, "Truly, truly, I say to you, I am the door of the sheep. All who came before Me are thieves and robbers, but the sheep did not hear them. I am the door; if anyone enters through Me, he will be saved, and will go in and out and find pasture. The thief comes only to steal and kill and destroy; I came that they may have life, and have *it* abundantly. I am the good shepherd; the good shepherd lays down His life for the sheep. He who is a hired hand, and not a shepherd, who is not the owner of the sheep, sees the wolf coming, and leaves the sheep and flees, and the wolf snatches them and scatters *them. He flees* because he is a hired hand and is not concerned about the sheep. I am the good shepherd, and I know My own and My own know Me, even as the Father knows Me and I know the Father; and I lay down My life for the sheep. I have other sheep, which are not of this fold; I must bring them also, and they will hear My voice; and they will become one flock *with* one shepherd. For this reason the Father loves Me, because I lay down My life so that I may take it again. No one has taken it away from Me, but I lay it down on My own initiative. I have authority to take it up again. This commandment I received from My Father" (John 10:7–18;

see Isaiah 40:11; 56:8; Jeremiah 23:1; Matthew 11:27).

FLOCK, LITTLE (See FLOCK)

FLOOD (Also see FLOODS; and TORRENT)

Setting: The Mount of Olives, just east of Jerusalem. During His discourse, after answering His disciples' questions as to when the temple will be destroyed and Jerusalem overrun, along with the signs of His coming and the end of the age, Jesus teaches them the Parable of the Fig Tree.

"Now learn the parable from the fig tree: when its branch has already become tender and puts forth its leaves, you know that summer is near; so, you too, when you see all these things, recognize that He is near, *right* at the door. Truly, I say to you, this generation will not pass away until all these things take place. Heaven and earth will pass away, but My words will not pass away. But of that day and hour no one knows, not even the angels of heaven, nor the Son, but the Father alone. For the coming of the Son of Man will be just like the days of Noah. For as in those days before the flood they were eating and drinking, marrying and giving in marriage, until the day that Noah entered the ark, and they did not understand until the flood came and took them all away; so will the coming of the Son of Man be. Then there will be two men in the field; one will be taken and one will be left. Two women *will be* grinding at the mill; one will be taken and one will be left" (Matthew 24:32–41; cf. Mark 13:28–32; Luke 17:34–36; 21:28–33; see Genesis 6:5; 7:7; Matthew 5:18; 10:23; James 5:9).

Setting: Galilee. After selecting His twelve disciples, Jesus teaches the Sermon on the Mount to the disciples and a great throng from Judea, Jerusalem, and the central coastal region of Tyre and Sidon.

"Why do you call Me, 'Lord, Lord,' and do not do what I say? Everyone who comes to Me and hears My words and acts on them, I will show you whom he is like; he is like a man building a house, who dug deep and laid a foundation on the rock; and when a flood occurred, the torrent burst against that house and could not shake it, because it had been well built. But the one who has heard and has not acted *accordingly,* is like a man who built a house on the ground without any foundation; and the torrent burst against it and immediately it collapsed, and the ruin of that house was great" (Luke 6:46–49; cf. Matthew 7:24–27; see Luke 6:12–19; James 1:22).

Setting: Samaria, on the way from Galilee to Jerusalem. After the Pharisees question Him about the coming of the kingdom of God, Jesus tells His disciples of His second coming.

And He said to the disciples, "The days will come when you will long to see one of the days of the Son of Man, and you will not see it. They will say to you, 'Look there! Look here!' Do not go away, and do not run after *them.* For just like the lightning, when it flashes out of one part of the sky, shines to the other part of the sky, so will the Son of Man be in His day. But first He must suffer many things and be rejected by this generation. And just as it happened in the days of Noah, so it will be also in the days of the Son of Man: they were eating, they were drinking, they were marrying, they were being given in marriage, until the day that Noah entered the ark, and the flood came and destroyed them all. It was the same as happened in the days of Lot: they were eating, they were drinking, they were buying, they were selling, they were planting, they were building; but on the day that Lot went out from Sodom it rained fire and brimstone from heaven and destroyed them all. It will be just the same on the day that the Son of Man is revealed. On that day, the one who is on the housetop and whose goods are in the house must not go down to take them out; and likewise the one who is in the field must not turn back. Remember Lot's wife. Whoever seeks to keep his life will lose it, and whoever loses *his life* will preserve it. I tell you, on that night there will be two in one bed; one will be taken and the other will be left. There will be two women grinding at the same place; one will be taken and the other will be left. [Two men will be in the field; one will be taken and the other will be left."] And answering they said to Him, "Where, Lord?" And He said to them, "Where the body *is,* there also the vultures will be gathered" (Luke 17:22–37; see Genesis 19; Matthew 10:39; 16:21, 27; 24:17–28, 37–41).

FLOODS (Also see FLOOD; and TORRENT)

Setting: Galilee. During the early part of His ministry, Jesus preaches the Sermon on the Mount to His disciples

and the multitudes.

"Therefore everyone who hears these words of Mine and acts on them, may be compared to a wise man who built his house on the rock. And the rain fell, and the floods came, and the winds blew and slammed against that house; and7, for it had been founded on the rock. Everyone who hears these words of Mine and does not act on them, will be like a foolish man who built his house on the sand. The rain fell, and the floods came, and the winds blew and slammed against that house; and it fell—and great was its fall" (Matthew 7:24–28; cf. Luke 6:47–49).

FLOUR (Also see BREAD; and WHEAT)

Setting: By the Sea of Galilee (Tiberias). Because the religious leaders are rejecting His message, Jesus continues teaching the crowd with the Parable of the Leaven.

He spoke another parable to them, "The kingdom of heaven is like leaven, which a woman took and hid in three pecks of flour until it was all leavened" (Matthew 13:33).

Setting: On the way from Galilee to Jerusalem. After responding to a synagogue official's anger for healing a woman, sick eighteen years, in the synagogue on the Sabbath, Jesus conveys the Parable of the Mustard Seed and the Parable of the Leaven.

So He was saying, "What is the kingdom of God like, and to what shall I compare it? It is like a mustard seed which a man took and threw into his own garden; and it grew and became a tree, and THE BIRDS OF THE AIR NESTED IN ITS BRANCHES." And again He said, "To what shall I compare the kingdom of God? It is like leaven, which a woman took and hid in three pecks of flour until it was all leavened" (Luke 13:18–21, Jesus quotes from Ezekiel 17:23; cf. Matthew 13:31–34; Mark 4:30–32).

FLOWERS (See specifics like LILIES)

FLUTE (Also see MUSIC)

Setting: Galilee. After praising John the Baptist as His forerunner, Jesus demonstrates the foolish thinking of the current generation of Jewish religious leaders by repeating what they say about John's ascetic lifestyle and ministry along with His own.

"But to what shall I compare this generation? It is like children sitting in the market places, who call out to the other *children,* and say, 'We played the flute for you, and you did not dance; we sang a dirge, and you did not mourn.' For John came neither eating nor drinking, and they say, 'He has a demon!' The Son of Man came eating and drinking, and they say, 'Behold, a gluttonous man and a drunkard, a friend of tax collectors and sinners! Yet wisdom is vindicated by her deeds" (Matthew 11:16–19; cf. Luke 7:31–35; see Matthew 9:11, 34; Luke 1:15).

Setting: Galilee. After praising John the Baptist to the crowds, Jesus criticizes the Pharisees and lawyers who reject God's purpose and John's message.

"To what then shall I compare the men of this generation, and what are they like? They are like children who sit in the market place and call to one another, and they say, 'We played the flute for you, and you did not dance; we sang a dirge, and you did not weep.' For John the Baptist has come eating no bread and drinking no wine, and you say, 'He has a demon!' The Son of Man has come eating and drinking, and you say, 'Behold, a gluttonous man and a drunkard, a friend of tax collectors and sinners!' Yet wisdom is vindicated by all her children" (Luke 7:31–35; cf. Matthew 11:16–19; see Luke 1:15).

FOLD (Also see FLOCK)

Setting: Jerusalem. Following the Pharisees' interrogation and dismissal of the formerly blind man Jesus healed on the Sabbath, the Lord speaks to the Pharisees using parabolic language they do not understand.

"Truly, truly, I say to you, he who does not enter by the door into the fold of the sheep, but climbs up some other way, he is a thief and a robber. But he who enters by the door is a shepherd of the sheep. To him the doorkeeper opens, and the sheep hear his voice, and he calls his own sheep by name and leads them out. When he puts forth all his own, he goes ahead of them, and the sheep follow him because they know his voice. A stranger they simply will not follow, but will flee from him, because they do not know the voice of strangers" (John 10:1–5; see John 10:27).

Setting: Jerusalem. Following the Pharisees' interrogation and dismissal of the formerly blind man Jesus healed on the Sabbath, the Lord conveys the Parable of the Good Shepherd to the Pharisees using figures of speech they do not understand.

So Jesus said to them again, "Truly, truly, I say to you, I am the door of the sheep. All who came before Me are thieves and robbers, but the sheep did not hear them. I am the door; if anyone enters through Me, he will be saved, and will go in and out and find pasture. The thief comes only to steal and kill and destroy; I came that they may have life, and have *it* abundantly. I am the good shepherd; the good shepherd lays down His life for the sheep. He who is a hired hand, and not a shepherd, who is not the owner of the sheep, sees the wolf coming, and leaves the sheep and flees, and the wolf snatches them and scatters *them. He flees* because he is a hired hand and is not concerned about the sheep. I am the good shepherd, and I know My own and My own know Me, even as the Father knows Me and I know the Father; and I lay down My life for the sheep. I have other sheep, which are not of this fold; I must bring them also, and they will hear My voice; and they will become one flock *with* one shepherd. For this reason the Father loves Me, because I lay down My life so that I may take it again. No one has taken it away from Me, but I lay it down on My own initiative. I have authority to take it up again. This commandment I received from My Father" (John 10:7–18; see Isaiah 40:11; 56:8; Jeremiah 23:1; Matthew 11:27; John 10:27).

FOLLOWER (See DISCIPLE; and FOLLOWING JESUS CHRIST)

FOLLOWERS (Also see DISCIPLES)

Setting: Capernaum of Galilee. As Jesus teaches His disciples in private, they ask Him about greatness.

But Jesus said, "Do not hinder him, for there is no one who will perform a miracle in My name, and be able soon afterward to speak evil of Me. For he who is not against us is for us. For whoever gives you a cup of water to drink because of your name as *followers* of Christ, truly I say to you, he will not lose his reward. Whoever causes one of these little ones who believe to stumble, it would be better for him if, with a heavy millstone hung around his neck, he had been cast into the sea. If your hand causes you to stumble, cut it off; it is better for you to enter life crippled, than, having your two hands, to go into hell, into the unquenchable fire, [where THEIR WORM DOES NOT DIE, AND THE FIRE IS NOT QUENCHED.] If your foot causes you to stumble, cut it off; it is better for you to enter life lame, than, having your two feet, to be cast into hell, [where THEIR WORM DOES NOT DIE, AND THE FIRE IS NOT QUENCHED.] If your eye causes you to stumble, throw it out; it is better for you to enter the kingdom of God with one eye, than, having two eyes, to be cast into hell, where THEIR WORM DOES NOT DIE, AND THE FIRE IS NOT QUENCHED. For everyone will be salted with fire. Salt is good; but if the salt becomes unsalty, with what will you make it salty *again?* Have salt in yourselves, and be at peace with one another" (Mark 9:39–50; Jesus quotes from Isaiah 66:24; cf. Matthew 18:6–9; Luke 9:49–50; see Matthew 5:13, 29, 30; 10:42; 12:30; 18:5, 6).

FOLLOWING JESUS CHRIST (Also see COMMITMENT; DEVOTION; DISCIPLE; DISCIPLES; DISCIPLESHIP; OBEDIENCE; PRIORITIES; REWARDS; SACRIFICE, PERSONAL; SAKE, GOSPEL'S; and SAKE, MY)

[FOLLOWING JESUS CHRIST from Follow Me]
Setting: By the Sea of Galilee. As Jesus commences His public ministry, He calls two brothers who are fishermen, Simon (Peter) and Andrew, to be His disciples.

And He said to them, "Follow Me, and I will make you fishers of men" (Matthew 4:19; cf. Mark 4:17).

[FOLLOWING JESUS CHRIST from Follow Me]
Setting: By the Sea of Galilee. After casting out evil spirits from the demon-possessed and healing the ill in fulfillment of Isaiah 53:4, Jesus lays out for an inquiring scribe the demands of discipleship.

Then a scribe came and said to Him, "Teacher, I will follow You wherever you go." Jesus said to him, "The foxes have holes and the birds of the air *have* nests, but the Son of Man has nowhere to lay His head." Another of the disciples said to Him, "Lord, permit me first to go and bury my father." But Jesus said to him, "Follow Me, and allow the dead to bury their own dead" (Matthew 8:19–22; cf. Luke 9:57–60).

[FOLLOWING JESUS CHRIST from Follow Me]
Setting: Capernaum near the Sea of Galilee. After healing and forgiving a paralytic of his sins, Jesus calls Matthew, a tax collector, to follow Him as a disciple.

As Jesus went on from there, He saw a man called Matthew, sitting in the tax collector's booth; and He said to him, "Follow Me!" And he got up and followed Him (Matthew 9:9; cf. Mark 2:13, 14; Luke 5:27, 28).

[FOLLOWING JESUS CHRIST from And he who does not take his cross and follow after Me is not worthy of Me]
Setting: While in Galilee, after His twelve disciples observe His own ministry, Jesus summons and specifically instructs them about the ministry ahead involving true discipleship.

"He who loves father or mother more than Me is not worthy of Me; and he who loves son or daughter more than Me is not worthy of Me. And he who does not take his cross and follow after Me is not worthy of Me. He who has found his life will lose it, and he who has lost his life for My sake will find it" (Matthew 10:37–39; compare Matthew 16:24, 25).

[FOLLOWING JESUS CHRIST from follow Me]
Setting: Near Caesarea Philippi. Jesus teaches His disciples about the costs of discipleship following His rebuke of Peter forbidding Him to accomplish His earthly mission of dying and resurrecting from the grave.

Then Jesus said to His disciples, "If anyone wishes to come after Me, he must deny himself, and take up his cross and follow Me. For whoever wishes to save his life will lose it; but whoever loses his life for My sake will find it. For what will it profit a man if he gains the whole world and forfeits his soul? Or what will a man give in exchange for his soul? For the Son of Man is going to come in the glory of His Father with His angels, and WILL THEN REPAY EVERY MAN ACCORDING TO HIS DEEDS. Truly, I say to you, there are some of you who are standing here who will not taste death until they see the Son of Man coming in His kingdom" (Matthew 16:24–28, Jesus quotes from Psalm 62:12; cf. Mark 8:34–37; Luke 9:23–27; see Matthew 10:38, 39).

[FOLLOWING JESUS CHRIST from follow Me]
Setting: Judea beyond the Jordan (Perea). Jesus shares with the rich, young ruler how he can obtain eternal life.

And He said to him, "Why are you asking Me about what is good? There is *only* One who is good; but if you wish to enter into life, keep the commandments." *Then* he said to Him, 'Which ones?' And Jesus said, "YOU SHALL NOT COMMIT MURDER; YOU SHALL NOT COMMIT ADULTERY; YOU SHALL NOT STEAL; YOU SHALL NOT BEAR FALSE WITNESS; HONOR YOUR FATHER AND MOTHER; and YOU SHALL LOVE YOUR NEIGHBOR AS YOURSELF." The young man said to Him, "All these things I have kept; what am I still lacking?" Jesus said to him, "If you wish to complete go *and* sell your possessions and give to *the* poor, and you will have treasure in heaven; and come, follow Me" (Matthew 19:16–22, Jesus quotes from Exodus 20:13–15; Leviticus 19:18; cf. Leviticus 18:5; Mark 10:17–21; Luke 10:25–28; Luke 12:33; 18:18–24).

[FOLLOWING JESUS CHRIST from you who have followed Me]
Setting: Judea beyond the Jordan (Perea). Jesus promises rewards to His disciples for their personal sacrifice and commitment to following Him.

And Jesus said to them, "Truly I say to you, that you who have followed Me, in the regeneration when the Son of Man will sit on His glorious throne, you also shall sit upon twelve thrones, judging the twelve tribes of Israel. And everyone who has left houses or brothers or sisters or father or mother or children or farms for My name's sake, will receive many times as much, and will inherit eternal life. But many *who* are first will be last; and *the* last, first" (Matthew 19:28–30; cf. Matthew 6:33; 20:15; Mark 10:29, 30; Luke 18:29, 30; Luke 22:30).

[FOLLOWING JESUS CHRIST from Follow Me]
Setting: Along the Sea of Galilee (Tiberias). Jesus calls Simon (Peter) and his brother, Andrew, to be His disciples.

And Jesus said to them, "Follow Me, and I will make you become fishers of men" (Mark 1:17; cf. Matthew 4:19).

[FOLLOWING JESUS CHRIST from Follow Me]
Setting: Capernaum near the Sea of Galilee. Jesus calls Levi (Matthew) the tax collector to be His disciple.

As He passed by, He saw Levi the *son* of Alphaeus sitting in the tax booth, and He said to him, "Follow Me!" And he got up and followed Him (Mark 2:14; cf. Matthew 9:9; Luke 5:27, 28).

[FOLLOWING JESUS CHRIST from If anyone wishes to come after Me, he must deny himself, and take up his cross and follow Me]
Setting: Caesarea Philippi. After rebuking Peter for desiring to thwart His mission to the cross, Jesus summons a crowd along with His disciples and informs them of the high costs of following Him.

And He summoned the crowd with His disciples, and said to them, "If anyone wishes to come after Me, he must deny himself, and take up his cross and follow Me. For whoever wishes to save his life will lose it, but whoever loses his life for My sake and the gospel's will save it. For what does it profit a man to gain the whole world, and forfeit his soul? For what will a man give in exchange for his soul? For whoever is ashamed of Me and My words in this adulterous and sinful generation, the Son of Man will also be ashamed of him when He comes in the glory of His Father with the holy angels" (Mark 8:34–38; cf. Matthew 16:24–28; Luke 9:23–27; see Matthew 10:33, 38, 39).

[FOLLOWING JESUS CHRIST from *followers* of Christ]
Setting: Capernaum of Galilee. As Jesus teaches His disciples in private, they ask Him about greatness.

But Jesus said, "Do not hinder him, for there is no one who will perform a miracle in My name, and be able soon afterward to speak evil of Me. For he who is not against us is for us. For whoever gives you a cup of water to drink because of your name as *followers* of Christ, truly I say to you, he will not lose his reward. Whoever causes one of these little ones who believe to stumble, it would be better for him if, with a heavy millstone hung around his neck, he had been cast into the sea. If your hand causes you to stumble, cut it off; it is better for you to enter life crippled, than, having your two hands, to go into hell, into the unquenchable fire, ⌈where THEIR WORM DOES NOT DIE, AND THE FIRE IS NOT QUENCHED.⌉ If your foot causes you to stumble, cut it off; it is better for you to enter life lame, than, having your two feet, to be cast into hell, ⌈where THEIR WORM DOES NOT DIE, AND THE FIRE IS NOT QUENCHED.⌉ If your eye causes you to stumble, throw it out; it is better for you to enter the kingdom of God with one eye, than, having two eyes, to be cast into hell, where THEIR WORM DOES NOT DIE, AND THE FIRE IS NOT QUENCHED. For everyone will be salted with fire. Salt is good; but if the salt becomes unsalty, with what will you make it salty *again?* Have salt in yourselves, and be at peace with one another" (Mark 9:39–50; Jesus quotes from Isaiah 66:24; cf. Matthew 18:6; Luke 9:49, 50; see Matthew 5:13, 29, 30; 10:42; 12:30; 18:5, 6).

[FOLLOWING JESUS CHRIST from follow Me]
Setting: Judea beyond the Jordan (Perea). After demonstrating to His disciples the importance of little children, Jesus encounters a rich man seeking eternal life.

And Jesus said to him, "Why do you call Me good? No one is good except God alone. You know the commandments, 'DO NOT MURDER, DO NOT COMMIT ADULTERY, DO NOT STEAL, DO NOT BEAR FALSE WITNESS, Do not defraud, HONOR YOUR FATHER AND MOTHER.'" And he said to Him, "Teacher, I have kept all these things from my youth up." Looking at him, Jesus felt a love for him and said to him, "One thing you lack: go and sell all you possess and give to the poor, and you will have treasure in heaven; and come, follow Me" (Mark 10:18–21; Jesus quotes from Exodus 20:12–16; cf. Matthew 19:16–22; Luke 18:18–24; see Matthew 6:20).

[FOLLOWING JESUS CHRIST from Follow Me]
Setting: Capernaum of Galilee. After amazing the crowd and being accused of blasphemy by some Pharisees and teachers of the law from Galilee and Judea for healing a paralytic man, Jesus calls Levi (Matthew) to be His disciple.

After that He went out and noticed a tax collector named Levi sitting in the tax booth, and He said to him, "Follow Me." And he left everything behind, and got up and *began* to follow Him (Luke 5:27, 28; cf. Matthew 9:9–13; Mark 2:13, 14).

[FOLLOWING JESUS CHRIST from come after Me and follow Me]
Setting: Galilee. Following Peter's pronouncement that Jesus is the Christ of God, the Lord conveys the demands of discipleship and the hope regarding the kingdom of God.

And He was saying to *them* all, "If anyone wishes to come after Me, he must deny himself, and take up his cross daily and follow Me. For whoever wishes to save his life will lose it, but whoever loses his life for My sake, he is the one who will save it. For what is a man profited if he gains the whole world, and loses or forfeits himself? For whoever is ashamed of Me and My words, the Son of Man will be ashamed of him when He comes in His glory, and *the glory* of the Father and of the holy angels. But I say to you truthfully, there are some of those standing here who will not taste death until they see the kingdom of God" (Luke 9:23–27; cf. Matthew 16:24–26, 28; Mark 8:34–37; see Matthew 10:33, 38, 39).

[FOLLOWING JESUS CHRIST from Follow Me]
Setting: On the way from Galilee to Jerusalem. The Lord responds to several men seeking to follow Him.

And He said to another, "Follow Me." But he said, "Lord, permit me first to go and bury my father," But He said to him, "Allow the dead to bury their own dead; but as for you, go and proclaim everywhere the kingdom of God" (Luke 9:59, 60; cf. Matthew 8:19–22).

[FOLLOWING JESUS CHRIST from come after Me]
Setting: On the way from Galilee to Jerusalem. After responding to a guest's proclamation about the blessings of eating bread in the kingdom of God, Jesus presents to large crowds the demands of discipleship.

Now large crowds were going along with Him; and He turned and said to them, "If anyone comes to Me, and does not hate his own father and mother and wife and children and brothers and sisters, yes, and even his own life, he cannot be My disciple. Whoever does not carry his own cross and come after Me cannot be My disciple. For which one of you, when he wants to build a tower, does not first sit down and calculate the cost to see if he has enough to complete it? Otherwise, when he has laid a foundation and is not able to finish, all who observe it begin to ridicule him, saying, 'This man began to build and was not able to finish.' Or what king, when he sets out to meet another king in battle, will not first sit down and consider whether he is strong enough with ten thousand *men* to encounter the one coming against him with twenty thousand? Or else, while the other is still far away, he sends a delegation and asks for terms of peace. So then, none of you can be My disciple who does not give up all his possessions. Therefore, salt is good; but if even salt has become tasteless, with what will it be seasoned? It is useless either for the soil or for the manure pile; it is thrown out. He who has ears to hear, let him hear" (Luke 14:25–35; cf. Matthew 5:13; 10:37–39; see Proverbs 20:18; Luke 14:1, 2, 15, 25; Philippians 3:7).

[FOLLOWING JESUS CHRIST from follow Me]
Setting: On the way from Galilee to Jerusalem. After speaking of the importance of children, Jesus responds to a ruler's question about inheriting eternal life.

A ruler questioned Him, saying, "Good Teacher, what shall I do to inherit eternal life?" And Jesus said to him, "Why do you call Me good? No one is good except God alone. You know the commandments, 'DO NOT COMMIT ADULTERY, DO NOT MURDER, DO NOT STEAL, DO NOT BEAR FALSE WITNESS, HONOR YOUR FATHER AND MOTHER.'" And he said, "All these things I have kept from *my* youth." When Jesus heard *this,* He said to him, "One thing you still lack; sell all that you possess and distribute it to the poor, and you shall have treasure in heaven; and come, follow Me" (Luke 18:18–22, Jesus quotes from Exodus 20:12–16; cf. Matthew 19:16–22; Mark 10:17–22; see Luke 10:25–28).

[FOLLOWING JESUS CHRIST from Follow Me]
Setting: Bethany beyond the Jordan. After beginning His public ministry and choosing His first disciples, Andrew and Simon (Peter) near Bethany beyond the Jordan, the next day, Jesus selects Philip as a disciple.

The next day He purposed to go into Galilee, and He found Philip. And Jesus said to him, "Follow Me" (John 1:43).

[FOLLOWING JESUS CHRIST from he who follows Me]
Setting: The temple in Jerusalem. Following the Feast of Booths, Jesus retires to the Mount of Olives, and returns the next day, when He addresses the scribes and Pharisees after their failed attempt to stone a woman caught in adultery.

Then Jesus again spoke to them, saying, "I am the Light of the world; he who follows Me will not walk in the darkness, but will have the Light of life" (John 8:12; see John 1:4).

[FOLLOWING JESUS CHRIST from they follow Me]
Setting: Jerusalem. At the Feast of Dedication, just after Jesus conveys the Parable of the Good Shepherd to the Pharisees (who do not understand it), they ask Him plainly if He is the Christ.

Jesus answered them, "I told you, and you do not believe; the works that I do in My Father's name, these testify of Me. But you do not believe because you are not of My sheep. My sheep hear My voice, and I know them, and they follow Me; and I give eternal life to them, and they will never perish; and no one will snatch them out of My hand. My Father, who has given *them* to Me, is greater than all; and no one is able to snatch *them* out of the Father's hand. I and the Father are one" (John 10:25–30; see John 8:47; 10:4, 22–24; 17:1, 2, 20, 21).

[FOLLOWING JESUS CHRIST from he must follow Me]
Setting: Jerusalem. Just days before the Passover, with the chief priests and Pharisees plotting to seize Jesus, crowds welcome Him with palm branches and praise, and some Greeks ask to meet Him.

And Jesus answered them, saying, "The hour has come for the Son of Man to be glorified. Truly, truly, I say to you, unless a grain of wheat falls into the earth and dies, it remains alone; but if it dies, it bears much fruit. He who loves his life loses it, and he who hates his life in this world will keep it to life eternal. If anyone serves Me, he must follow Me; and where I am, there My servant will be also; if anyone serves Me, the Father will honor him" (John 12:23–26; see Matthew 10:39).

[FOLLOWING JESUS CHRIST from you will follow later]
Setting: Jerusalem. Before the Passover, after revealing to His disciples that they cannot follow Him back to heaven, Jesus takes issue with Peter's assertion that he would lay down his life for Jesus.

Simon Peter said to Him, "Lord, where are You going?" Jesus answered, "Where I go, you cannot follow Me now; but you will follow later." Peter said to Him, "Lord, why can I not follow You right now? I will lay down my life for You." Jesus answered, "Will you lay down your life for Me? Truly, truly, I say to you, a rooster will not crow until you deny Me three times" (John 13:36–38; see Matthew 26:34; Mark 14:30, 72; Luke 22:33, 34).

[FOLLOWING JESUS CHRIST from Follow Me]
Setting: By the Sea of Galilee. During the Lord's third post-resurrection appearance to His disciples, after quizzing Peter regarding his love for Him, Jesus gives this disciple details about his aging and his eventual death.

"Truly, truly, I say to you, when you were younger, you used to gird yourself and walk wherever you wished; but when you grow old, you will stretch out your hands and someone else will gird you, and bring you where you do not wish to *go*." Now this He said, signifying by what kind of death he would glorify God. And when He had spoken this, He said to him, "Follow Me!" (John 21:18, 19).

[FOLLOWING JESUS CHRIST from You follow Me]
Setting: By the Sea of Galilee. During His third post-resurrection appearance to His disciples, after quizzing Peter regarding his love for Him, Jesus responds to his inquiry about the future of John the disciple.

Jesus said to him, "If I want him to remain until I come, what *is that* to you? You follow Me!" Therefore this saying went out among the brethren that that disciple would not die; yet Jesus did not say to him that he would not die, but *only*, "If I want him to remain until I come, what *is that* to you?" (John 21:22, 23; see Matthew 8:22; 16:27).

FOOD (Also see BREAD; BREAD, DAILY; FASTING; HUNGER; LOAF; LOAVES; and RATIONS)

Setting: Galilee. During the early part of His ministry, Jesus preaches the Sermon on the Mount to His disciples and the multitudes.

"For this reason I say to you, do not be worried about your life, *as to* what you will eat or what you will drink; nor for your body, *as to* what you will put on. Is not life more than food, and the body more than clothing? Look at the birds of the air, that they do not sow, nor reap nor gather into barns, and *yet* your heavenly Father feeds them. Are you not worth much more than they? And who of you by being worried can add a *single* hour to his life? And why are you worried about clothing? Observe how the lilies of the field grow; they do not toil nor do they spin, yet I say to you that not even Solomon in all his glory clothed himself like one of these. But if God so clothes the grass of the field, which is *alive* today and tomorrow is thrown into the furnace, *will He* not much more *clothe* you? You of little faith! Do not worry then, saying 'What will we eat?' or 'What will we drink?' or 'What will be wear for clothing?" For the Gentiles eagerly seek all these things; for your heavenly Father knows that you need all these things. But seek first His kingdom and His righteousness, and all these things will be added to you. So do not worry about tomorrow; for tomorrow will care for itself. Each day has enough trouble of its own" (Matthew 6:25–34; cf. Luke 12:22–31; see 1 Kings 10:4–7; Job 35:11; Matthew 8:26).

[FOOD from *something* to eat]

Setting: By the Sea of Galilee. Late in the day, after hearing the news of John the Baptist's beheading and healing the sick from the crowd following Him, Jesus miraculously feeds more than 5,000 of His countrymen.

But Jesus said to them, "They do not need to go away; you give them *something* to eat!" They said to Him, "We have here only five loaves and two fish." And He said, "Bring them here to Me" (Matthew 14:16–18; cf. Mark 6:35–44; Luke 9:12–17; John 6:4–13; see Matthew 16:9).

[FOOD from what enters into the mouth]

Setting: Galilee. Jesus instructs the crowd after the Pharisees and scribes ask Him about His disciples' lack of obedience to tradition and the commandments.

After Jesus called the crowd to Him, He said to them, "Hear and understand. *It is* not what enters into the mouth *that* defiles the man, but what proceeds out of the mouth, this defiles the man" (Matthew 15:10, 11; cf. Matthew 15:18).

[FOOD from everything that goes into the mouth passes into the stomach]

Setting: Galilee. Jesus explains to the crowd the meaning of His instruction about what defiles a man.

Peter said to Him, "Explain the parable to us." Jesus said, "Are you still lacking in understanding also? Do you not understand that everything that goes into the mouth passes into the stomach and is eliminated? But the things that proceed out of the mouth come from the heart, and those defile the man. For out of the heart come evil thoughts, murders, adulteries, fornications, thefts, false witness, slanders. These are the things which defile a man; but to eat with unwashed hands does not defile the man" (Matthew 15:15–20; cf. Mark 7:18–23; see Galatians 5:19–21).

[FOOD from nothing to eat]

Setting: Near the Sea of Galilee. After being impressed by a Canaanite woman's faith, Jesus cures her daughter from demon possession, then feeds more than 4,000 primarily Gentile people following Him.

And Jesus called His disciples to Him, and said, "I feel compassion for the people, because they have remained with Me now three days and have nothing to eat; and I do not want to send them away hungry, for they might faint on the way." The disciples said to Him, "Where would we get so many loaves in *this* desolate place to satisfy a large crowd?" And Jesus said to them, "How many loaves do you have?" And they said, "Seven and a few small fish" (Matthew 15:32–34; cf. Mark 8:1–9).

Setting: The Mount of Olives, just east of Jerusalem. During His discourse, after answering His disciples' questions as to when the temple will be destroyed and Jerusalem overrun, along with the signs of His coming and the end of the age, Jesus reemphasizes to the disciples that they should be on the alert for His return.

"Therefore be on the alert, for you do not know which day your Lord is coming. But be sure of this, that if the head of the house had known at what time of the night the thief was coming, he would have been on the alert and would not have allowed his house to be broken into. For this reason you also must be ready; for the Son of Man is coming at an hour when you do not think *He will.* Who then is the faithful and sensible slave whom his master put in charge of his household to give their food at the proper time? Blessed is that slave whom his master finds so doing when he comes. Truly I say to you that he will put him in charge of all his possessions. But if that evil slave says in his heart, 'My master is not coming for a long time,' and begins to beat his fellow slaves and eat and drink with drunkards; the master of that slave will come on a day when he does not expect *him* and at an hour which he does not know, and will cut him in pieces and assign him a place with the hypocrites; in that place there will be weeping and gnashing of teeth" (Matthew 24:42–51; cf. Mark 13:33–37; Luke 12:39–46; 21:34–36; see Matthew 8:11, 12; 25:21–23).

[FOOD from *something* to eat]
Setting: The Mount of Olives, just east of Jerusalem. During His discourse, after answering His disciples' questions as to when the temple will be destroyed and Jerusalem overrun, along with the signs of His coming and the end of the age, Jesus reveals the future judgments following His return.

"But when the Son of Man comes in His glory, and all the angels with Him, then He will sit on His glorious throne. All the nations will be gathered before Him; and He will separate them from one another, as the shepherd separates the sheep from the goats; and He will put the sheep on His right, and the goats on the left. Then the King will say to those on His right, 'Come, you who are blessed of My Father, inherit the kingdom prepared for you from the foundation of the world. 'For I was hungry, and you gave Me *something* to eat; I was thirsty, and you gave Me *something* to drink; I was a stranger, and you invited Me in; naked, and you clothed Me; I was sick, and you visited Me; I was in prison, and you came to Me.' Then the righteous will answer Him, 'Lord, when did we see You hungry and feed You, or thirsty, and give you *something* to drink? And when did we see You a stranger, and invite You in, or naked, and clothe You? When did we see You sick, or in prison, and come to You?' The King will answer and say to them, 'Truly I say to you, to the extent that you did it to one of these brothers of Mine, *even* the least *of them,* you did it to Me.' Then He will also say to those on His left, 'Depart from Me, accursed ones, into the eternal fire which has been prepared for the devil and his angels; for I was hungry, and you gave Me *nothing* to eat; I was thirsty, and you gave Me nothing to drink; I was a stranger, and you did not invite Me in; naked, and you did not clothe Me; sick, and in prison, and you did not visit Me.' Then they themselves also will answer, 'Lord, when did we see You hungry, or thirsty, or a stranger, or naked, or sick, or in prison, and did not take care of You?' Then He will answer them, 'Truly I say to you, to the extent that you did not do it to one of the least of these, you did not do it to Me.' These will go away into eternal punishment, but the righteous into eternal life" (Matthew 25:31–46; see Matthew 7:23; 16:27; 19:29).

[FOOD from nothing to eat]
Setting: Decapolis near the Sea of Galilee. Jesus miraculously feeds more than 4,000 primarily Gentile people.

In those days, when there was again a large crowd and they had nothing to eat, Jesus called His disciples and said to them, "I feel compassion for the people because they have remained with Me now three days and have nothing to eat. If I send them away hungry to their homes, they will faint on their way; and some of them have come a great distance" (Mark 8:1–3; cf. Matthew 15:32–38; see Matthew 9:36).

[FOOD from You give them *something* to eat]
Setting: By the Sea of Galilee. After a long day of ministry, Jesus prepares to demonstrate the power of God to His disciples by feeding more than 5,000 people.

But He answered them, "You give them *something* to eat!" And they said to Him, "Shall we go and spend two hundred denarii on bread and give them *something* to eat? And He said to them, "How many loaves do you have? Go look!" And when they found out, they said, "Five, and two fish" (Mark 6:37, 38; cf. Matthew 14:16, 17; Luke 9:13, 14; John 6:5–9; see Mark 3:20).

[FOOD from whatever goes into the man from outside cannot defile him]
Setting: Galilee. After the Pharisees and scribes from Jerusalem question His disciples' lack of obedience to the tradition of ceremonial cleansing, Jesus speaks to a crowd and explains His teaching to the disciples.

After He called the crowd to Him again, He *began* saying to them, "Listen to Me, all of you, and understand: there is nothing outside the man which can defile him if it goes into him; but the things which proceed out of the man are what defile the man. [If anyone has ears to hear, let him hear."] When he had left the crowd *and* entered the house, His disciples questioned Him about the parable. And He said to them, "Are you so lacking in understanding also? Do you not understand that whatever goes into the man from outside cannot defile him, because it does not go into his heart, but into his stomach, and is eliminated?" (*Thus He* declared all foods clean.) And He was saying, "That which proceeds out of the man, that is what defiles the man. For from within, out of the heart of men, proceed the evil thoughts, fornications, thefts, murders, adulteries, deeds of coveting *and* wickedness, *as well* as deceit, sensuality, envy, slander, pride *and* foolishness. All these evil things proceed from within and defile the man" (Mark 7:14–23; cf. Matthew 15:10–20).

[FOOD from You give them *something* to eat]
Setting: Bethsaida in Galilee. Following a day of ministry, Jesus and His disciples try to withdraw from the large crowds, but the crowds, having listened to His teaching about the kingdom of God all day, must be fed physically, too.

But He said to them, "You give them *something* to eat!" And they said, "We have no more than five loaves and two fish, unless perhaps we go and buy food for all these people." (For there were about five thousand men.) And He said to His disciples, "Have them sit down *to eat* in groups of about fifty each" (Luke 9:13, 14; cf. Matthew 14:15–21; Mark 6:35–44; John 6:4–13).

Setting: On the way from Galilee to Jerusalem. Jesus comforts the crowd and His disciples after giving a parable about riches and greed. The scribes and Pharisees turn hostile and question Him repeatedly in an attempt to catch Him in something He might say.

And He said to His disciples, "For this reason I say to you, do not worry about *your* life, *as to* what you will eat; nor for your body, *as to* what you will put on. For life is more than food, and the body more than clothing. Consider the ravens, for they neither sow nor reap; they have no storeroom nor barn, and *yet* God feeds them; how much more valuable you are than the birds! And which of you by worrying can add a *single* hour to his life's span? If then you cannot do even a very little thing, why do you worry about other matters? Consider the lilies, how they grow: they neither toil nor spin; but I tell you, not even Solomon in all his glory clothed himself like one of these. But if God so clothes the grass in the field, which is *alive* today and tomorrow is thrown into the furnace, how much more *will He clothe* you? You men of little faith! And do not seek what you will eat and what you will drink, and do not keep worrying. For all these things the nations of the world eagerly seek; but your Father knows that you need these things. But seek His kingdom, and these things will be added to you. Do not be afraid, little flock, for your Father has chosen gladly to give you the kingdom" (Luke 12:22–32; cf. Matthew 6:25–33; see 1 Kings 10:4–7; Job 38:41).

[FOOD from Prepare something for me to eat]
Setting: On the way from Galilee to Jerusalem. After His disciples ask that their faith be increased following His instruction on forgiveness, the Lord illustrates with the mustard seed and an obedient slave.

And the Lord said, "If you had faith like a mustard seed, you would say to this mulberry tree, 'Be uprooted and be planted in the sea'; and it would obey you. Which of you, having a slave plowing or tending sheep, will say to him when he has come from the field, 'Come immediately and sit down to eat'? But will he not say to him, "Prepare something for me to eat, and *properly* clothe yourself and serve me while I eat and drink; and afterward you may eat and drink'? He does not thank the slave because he did the things which were commanded, does he? So you too, when you do all the things which are commanded you, say, 'We are unworthy slaves; we have done *only* that which we ought to have done'" (Luke 17:6–10; see Matthew 13:31; Luke 12:37).

[FOOD from Have you anything to eat]
Setting: Jerusalem. After rising from the grave on the third day after being crucified, and appearing to two of His

followers on the road to Emmaus, Jesus appears to His disciples (except Thomas).

While they were telling these things, He Himself stood in their midst and said to them, "Peace be to you." But they were startled and frightened and thought they were seeing a spirit. And He said to them, "Why are you troubled, and why do doubts arise in your hearts? See My hands and My feet, that it is I Myself; touch Me and see, for a spirit does not have flesh and bones as you see that I have." And when He had said this, He showed them His hands and His feet. While they still could not believe *it* because of their joy and amazement. He said to them, "Have you anything to eat?" They gave Him a piece of a broiled fish; and He took it and ate *it* before them (Luke 24:36–43; see Mark 16:14; John 20:27; Acts 10:40, 41).

Setting: Sychar of Samaria, on the way to Galilee. After Jesus converses with a Samaritan woman at Jacob's well, His disciples return with food and try to get Jesus to eat.

But He said to them, "I have food to eat that you do not know about" (John 4:32).

Setting: Sychar of Samaria. After Jesus converses with a Samaritan woman at Jacob's well, His disciples return with food. They try to get Jesus to eat but are surprised when He speaks of other food.

Jesus said to them, "My food is to do the will of Him who sent Me and to accomplish His work. Do you not say, 'There are yet four months, and *then* comes the harvest'? Behold, I say to you, lift up your eyes and look on the fields, that they are white for harvest. Already he who reaps is receiving wages and is gathering fruit for life eternal; so that he who sows and he who reaps may rejoice together. For in this *case* the saying is true, 'One sows and another reaps.' I sent you to reap that for which you have not labored; others have labored and you have entered into their labor" (John 4:34–38; see Matthew 9:37, 38; John 5:36).

[FOOD from leftover fragments]
Setting: By the Sea of Galilee. After revealing to the Jewish religious leadership during the Feast of the Jews that God, John the Baptist, His works, and the Scriptures all testify to His mission, Jesus returns to the Sea of Galilee. He miraculously feeds more than 5,000 people with a lad's five barley loaves and two fish.

Jesus said, "Have the people sit down." Now there was much grass in the place. So the men sat down, in number about five thousand. Jesus took the loaves, and having given thanks, He distributed to those who were seated; likewise also of the fish as much as they wanted. When they were filled, He said to the disciples, "Gather up the leftover fragments so that nothing will be lost" (John 6:10–12; cf. Matthew 14:17–21; Mark 6:38–44; Luke 9:14–17; see Matthew 15:32–38).

Setting: Capernaum. The day after walking on the Sea of Galilee to join His disciples in a boat, the people Jesus miraculously fed ask Him how He crossed the water, since He had not entered the boat from land with His disciples.

Jesus answered them and said, "Truly, truly, I say to you, you seek Me, not because you saw signs, but because you ate of the loaves and were filled. Do not work for the food which perishes, but for the food which endures to eternal life, which the Son of Man will give to you, for on Him the Father, God, has set His seal" (John 6:26, 27; see John 3:33).

Setting: Capernaum of Galilee. After Jesus informs the people whom He miraculously fed with a lad's five loaves and two fish how they might receive the bread out of heaven, the Jewish religious leaders argue with one another when Jesus says He will give His flesh to the world to eat.

So Jesus said to them, "Truly, truly, I say to you, unless you eat the flesh of the Son of Man and drink His blood, you have no life in yourselves. He who eats My flesh and drinks My blood has eternal life, and I will raise him up on the last day. For My flesh is true food, and My blood is true drink. He who eats My flesh and drinks My blood abides in Me, and I in him. As the living Father sent Me, and I live because of the Father, so he who eats Me, he also will live because of Me. This is the bread which came down out of heaven; not as the fathers ate and died; he who eats this bread will live forever" (John 6:53–58; see Matthew 16:16; Luke

4:22; John 3:36; 9:16; 15:4).

[FOOD from to eat things sacrificed to idols]
Setting: On the island of Patmos (in the Aegean Sea about fifty miles southwest of Ephesus in modern Turkey). On the Lord's Day (Sunday), about fifty years after Jesus' resurrection, the disciple John encounters the Lord Jesus Christ, who communicates a new revelation for the apostle to record for the church in Pergamum and to six other churches in Asia.

"And to the angel of the church in Pergamum write: The One who has the sharp two-edged sword says this: 'I know where you dwell, where Satan's throne is; and you hold fast My name, and did not deny My faith even in the days of Antipas, My witness, My faithful one, who was killed among you, where Satan dwells. But I have a few things against you, because you have there some who hold the teaching of Balaam, who kept teaching Balak to put a stumbling block before the sons of Israel, to eat things sacrificed to idols and to commit *acts of* immorality. So you also have some who in the same way hold the teaching of the Nicolaitans. Therefore repent; or else I am coming to you quickly, and I will make war against them with the sword of My mouth. He who has an ear, let him hear what the Spirit says to the churches. To him who overcomes, to him I will give *some* of the hidden manna, and I will give him a white stone, and a new name written on the stone which no one knows but he who receives it'" (Revelation 2:12–17; see Numbers 25:1–3; Isaiah 62:2; Revelation 1:16; 2:5, 6).

FOOD, ABSTAINING FROM (See FASTING)

FOOL (FOOLISHNESS; FOOLS; and MAN, FOOLISH are separate entries)
Setting: Galilee. During the early part of His ministry, Jesus preaches the Sermon on the Mount to His disciples and the multitudes.

"But I say to you that everyone who is angry with his brother shall be guilty before the court; and whoever says to his brother, 'You good-for-nothing,' shall be guilty before the supreme court; and whoever says, 'You fool,' shall be guilty *enough to go* into the fiery hell" (Matthew 5:22).

Setting: On the way from Galilee to Jerusalem, After the scribes and Pharisees turn hostile and question Him repeatedly, Jesus responds to a question from the crowd and gives a parable about riches and greed.

And He told them a parable, saying, "The land of a rich man was very productive. And he began reasoning to himself, saying, 'What shall I do, since I have no place to store my crops?' Then he said, 'This is what I will do: I will tear down my barns and build larger ones, and here I will store all my grain and my goods. And I will say to my soul, "Soul, you have many goods laid up for many years *to come;* take your ease, eat, drink *and* be merry."' "But God said to him, 'You fool! This *very* night your soul is required of you; and *now* who will own what you have prepared?' So is the man who stores up treasure for himself, and is not rich toward God" (Luke 12:16–21; see Job 27:8; Psalm 39:6; Ecclesiastes 12:9; Philippians 2:3).

FOOL, PARABLE OF THE RICH (See MAN, PARABLE OF THE RICH)

FOOLISH MAN (Listed under MAN, FOOLISH; also see FOOL; FOOLISHNESS; FOOLS; and MEN, FOOLISH)

FOOLISH MEN (Listed under MEN, FOOLISH; also see FOOL; FOOLISHNESS; FOOLS; and MAN, FOOLISH)

FOOLISHNESS (Also see FOOL; FOOLS; and MAN, FOOLISH)
[FOOLISHNESS from foolish]
Setting: The Mount of Olives, just east of Jerusalem. During His discourse, after answering His disciples' questions as to when the temple will be destroyed and Jerusalem overrun, along with the signs of His coming and the end of the age, Jesus reemphasizes to the disciples that they should be on the alert for His return.

"Then the kingdom of heaven will be comparable to ten virgins, who took their lamps and went out to meet the bridegroom. Five of them were foolish, and five were prudent. For when the foolish took their lamps, they took no oil with them, but the prudent took oil in flasks along with their lamps. Now while the bridegroom was delaying, they all got drowsy and *began* to sleep. But at midnight there was a shout, 'Behold, the bridegroom! Come out to meet *him*.' Then all those virgins rose and trimmed their lamps. The foolish said to the prudent, 'Give us some of your oil, for our lamps are going out.' But the prudent answered, 'No, there will not be enough for us and you *too;* go instead to the dealers and buy *some* for yourselves.' And while they were going away to make the purchase, the bridegroom came, and those who were ready went in with him to the wedding feast; and the door was shut. Later the other virgins also came, saying, 'Lord, lord, open up for us.' But he answered, 'Truly I say to you, I do not know you.' Be on the alert then, for you do not know the day nor the hour" (Matthew 25:1–13; cf. Matthew 24:42; Luke 12:35; see Matthew 7:21, 24).

Setting: Galilee. After the Pharisees and scribes from Jerusalem question His disciples' lack of obedience to the tradition of ceremonial cleansing, Jesus speaks to a crowd and explains His teaching to the disciples.

After He called the crowd to Him again, He *began* saying to them, "Listen to Me, all of you, and understand: there is nothing outside the man which can defile him if it goes into him; but the things which proceed out of the man are what defile the man. [If anyone has ears to hear, let him hear."] When he had left the crowd *and* entered the house, His disciples questioned Him about the parable. And He said to them, "Are you so lacking in understanding also? Do you not understand that whatever goes into the man from outside cannot defile him, because it does not go into his heart, but into his stomach, and is eliminated?" (*Thus He* declared all foods clean.) And He was saying, "That which proceeds out of the man, that is what defiles the man. For from within, out of the heart of men, proceed the evil thoughts, fornications, thefts, murders, adulteries, deeds of coveting *and* wickedness, *as well* as deceit, sensuality, envy, slander, pride *and* foolishness. All these evil things proceed from within and defile the man" (Mark 7:14–23; cf. Matthew 15:10–20).

FOOLS (Also see FOOL; FOOLISHNESS; and MAN, FOOLISH)

Setting: The temple in Jerusalem. After the Jewish religious leaders test Him with questions, Jesus pronounces the fourth of eight woes on them in front of the crowds and His disciples.

"Woe to you, blind guides, who say, "Whoever swears by the temple, *that* is nothing; but whoever swears by the gold of the temple is obligated.' You fools and blind men! Which is more important, the gold or the temple that sanctified the gold? And, 'Whoever swears by the altar, *that* is nothing, but whoever swears by the offering on it, he is obligated.' You blind men, which is more important, the offering, or the altar that sanctifies the offering? Therefore, whoever swears by the altar, swears *both* by the altar and by everything on it. And whoever swears by the temple, swears *both* by the temple and by Him who dwells within it. And whoever swears by heaven, swears *both* by the throne of God and by Him who sits upon it" (Matthew 23:16–22; see Exodus 29:37; 1 Kings 8:13; Isaiah 66:1; Matthew 15:14).

[FOOLS from foolish ones]

Setting: On the way from Galilee to Jerusalem. After speaking of how a lamp illuminates, the Lord has lunch with a Pharisee, who is surprised He doesn't wash before eating.

But the Lord said to him, "Now you Pharisees clean the outside of the cup and of the platter; but inside of you, you are full of robbery and wickedness. You foolish ones, did not He who made the outside make the inside also? But give that which is within as charity, and then all things are clean for you. But woe to you Pharisees! You pay tithe of mint and rue and every *kind of* garden herb, and *yet* disregard justice and the love of God; but these are the things you should have done without neglecting the others. Woe to you Pharisees! For you love the chief seats in the synagogues and the respectful greetings in the market places. Woe to you! For you are like concealed tombs, and the people who walk over *them* are unaware *of it*" (Luke 11:39–44; cf. Matthew 23:6–7, 23–27; see Matthew 15:2; Titus 1:15).

FOOT (Also see FEET; and HEEL)

Setting: Galilee. During the early part of His ministry, Jesus preaches the Sermon on the Mount to His disciples

and the multitudes.

"You are the salt of the earth; but if the salt has become tasteless, how can it be made salty *again*? It is not longer good for anything, except to be thrown out and trampled under foot by men" (Matthew 5:13; cf. Mark 9:50).

Setting: Capernaum of Galilee. Jesus elaborates about stumbling blocks following His disciples' question about greatness in the kingdom of heaven.

"Woe to the world because of *its* stumbling blocks! For it is inevitable that stumbling blocks come; but woe to that man through whom the stumbling block comes! If your hand or your foot causes you to stumble, cut if off and throw it from you; it is better for you to enter life crippled or lame, than to have two hands or two feet and be cast into the eternal fire. If your eye causes you to stumble, pluck it out and throw it from you. It is better for you to enter life with one eye, than to have two eyes and be cast into the fiery hell" (Matthew 18:7–9; cf. Matthew 5:29, 30; Mark 9:43–48; Luke 17:1).

Setting: The temple in Jerusalem. Jesus speaks another parable to the chief priests and elders after they question His authority.

Jesus spoke to them again in parables, saying, "The kingdom of heaven may be compared to a king who gave a wedding feast for his son. And he sent out his slaves to call those who had been invited to the wedding feast, and they were unwilling to come. Again he sent out other slaves saying, 'Tell those who have been invited, "Behold, I have prepared my dinner; my oxen and my fattened livestock are *all* butchered and everything is ready; come to the wedding feast." But they paid no attention and went their way, one to his own farm, another to his business, and the rest seized his slaves and mistreated them and killed them. But the king was enraged, and he sent his armies and destroyed those murderers and set their city on fire. Then he said to his slaves, 'The wedding is ready, but those who were invited were not worthy. 'Go therefore to the main highways, and as many as you find *there,* invite to the wedding feast.' Those slaves went out into the streets and gathered together all they found, both evil and good; and the wedding hall was filled with dinner guests. But when the king came in to look over the dinner guests, he saw a man there who was not dressed in wedding clothes, and he said to him, 'Friend, how did you come in here without wedding clothes?' And the man was speechless. Then the king said to the servants, 'Bind him hand and foot, and throw him into the outer darkness; in that place there will be weeping and gnashing of teeth.' For many are called, but few *are* chosen" (Matthew 22:1–14; cf. Matthew 8:11, 12).

Setting: Capernaum of Galilee. As Jesus teaches His disciples in private, they ask Him about greatness.

But Jesus said, "Do not hinder him, for there is no one who will perform a miracle in My name, and be able soon afterward to speak evil of Me. For he who is not against us is for us. For whoever gives you a cup of water to drink because of your name as *followers* of Christ, truly I say to you, he will not lose his reward. Whoever causes one of these little ones who believe to stumble, it would be better for him if, with a heavy millstone hung around his neck, he had been cast into the sea. If your hand causes you to stumble, cut it off; it is better for you to enter life crippled, than, having your two hands, to go into hell, into the unquenchable fire, [where THEIR WORM DOES NOT DIE, AND THE FIRE IS NOT QUENCHED.] If your foot causes you to stumble, cut it off; it is better for you to enter life lame, than, having your two feet, to be cast into hell, [where THEIR WORM DOES NOT DIE, AND THE FIRE IS NOT QUENCHED.] If your eye causes you to stumble, throw it out; it is better for you to enter the kingdom of God with one eye, than, having two eyes, to be cast into hell, where THEIR WORM DOES NOT DIE, AND THE FIRE IS NOT QUENCHED. For everyone will be salted with fire. Salt is good; but if the salt becomes unsalty, with what will you make it salty *again?* Have salt in yourselves, and be at peace with one another" (Mark 9:39–50; Jesus quotes from Isaiah 66:24; cf. Matthew 18:6–9; Luke 9:49, 50; see Matthew 5:13, 29, 30; 10:42; 12:30; 18:5, 6).

Setting: The villages and cities of Galilee. After His visit in the home of Simon the Pharisee, Jesus proclaims and preaches the kingdom of God.

When a large crowd was coming together, and those from various cities were journeying to Him, He spoke by way of a parable: "The sower went out to sow his seed; and as he sowed, some fell beside the road, and it was trampled under foot and the birds of the air ate it up. Other *seed* fell on rocky *soil,* and as soon as it grew up, it was withered away, because it had no moisture. Other *seed* fell among the thorns; and the thorns grew up with it and choked it out. Other *seed* fell into the good soil, and grew up, and produced a crop a hundred times as great." As He said these things, He would call out, "He who has ears to hear, let him hear" (Luke 8:4–8; cf. Matthew 13:2–9; Mark 4:3–9).

Setting: The Mount of Olives, east of the temple in Jerusalem. After ministering in the temple and giving the disciples more details regarding future events, Jesus elaborates more about things to come during His Olivet Discourse.

"But when you see Jerusalem surrounded by armies, then recognize that her desolation is near. Then those who are in Judea must flee to the mountains, and those who are in the midst of the city must leave, and those who are in the country must not enter the city; because these are days of vengeance, so that all things which are written will be fulfilled. Woe to those who are pregnant and to those who are nursing babies in those days; for there will be a great distress upon the land and wrath to this people; and they will fall by the edge of the sword, and will be led captive into all the nations; and Jerusalem will be trampled under foot by the Gentiles until the times of the Gentiles are fulfilled" (Luke 21:20–24; see Matthew 24:15–18; Mark 13:14–16; Luke 19:43).

FOOTSTOOL

Setting: Galilee. During the early part of His ministry, Jesus preaches the Sermon on the Mount to His disciples and the multitudes.

"Again, you have heard that the ancients were told, 'YOU SHALL NOT MAKE FALSE VOWS, BUT SHALL FULFILL YOUR VOWS TO THE LORD.' But I say to you, make no oath at all, either by heaven, for it is the throne of God, or by the earth, for it is the footstool of His feet, or by Jerusalem, for it is THE CITY OF THE GREAT KING. Nor shall you make an oath by your head, for you cannot make one hair white or black. But let your statement be 'Yes, yes' *or* 'No, no'; anything beyond these is of evil" (Matthew 5:33–37, Jesus quotes from Leviticus 19:12, Psalm 48:2; Isaiah 66:1; cf. James 5:12).

Setting: The temple in Jerusalem. A few days before His crucifixion, after some of the Sadducees question Him about the resurrection, Jesus poses a question to the scribes, who say He answered well.

Then He said to them, "How *is it that* they say the Christ is David's son? For David himself says in the book of Psalms, 'THE LORD SAID TO MY LORD, SIT AT MY RIGHT HAND, UNTIL I MAKE YOUR ENEMIES A FOOTSTOOL FOR YOUR FEET.' Therefore David calls Him 'Lord,' and how is He his son?" (Luke 20:41–44, Jesus quotes from Psalm 110:1; cf. Matthew 22:41–46; Mark 12:35–37).

FOOTWASHING (See HUMILITY; and SERVICE)

[FOOTWASHING from wash his feet]

Setting: Jerusalem. Before the Passover, with His crucifixion nearing, Jesus eats supper with His disciples and assumes the role of a servant by washing His followers' feet.

Jesus answered and said to him, "What I do you do not realize now, but you will understand hereafter." Peter said to Him, "Never shall You wash my feet!" Jesus answered him, "If I do not wash you, you have no part with Me." Simon Peter said to Him, "Lord, *then wash* not only my feet, but also my hand and my head." Jesus said to him, "He who has bathed needs only to wash his feet, but is completely clean; and you are clean, but not all *of you.* For He knew the one who was betraying Him; for this reason He said, "Not all of you are clean" (John 13:7–11; see John 6:64: 15:3).

[FOOTWASHING from washed your feet]

Setting: Jerusalem. Before the Passover, with His death on the cross nearing, Jesus explains the reason for His vivid example of servanthood in washing His disciples' feet.

So when He had washed their feet, and taken His garments and reclined *at the table* again, He said to them, "Do you know what I have done to you? You call Me Teacher and Lord; and you are right, for *so* I am. If I then, the Lord and the Teacher, washed your feet, you also ought to wash one another's feet. For I gave you an example that you also should do as I did to you. Truly, truly I say to you, a slave is not greater than his master, nor *is* one who is sent greater than the one who sent him. If you know these things, you are blessed if you do them. I do not speak of all of you. I know the ones I have chosen; but *it is* that the Scripture may be fulfilled, 'HE WHO EATS MY BREAD HAS LIFTED UP HIS HEEL AGAINST ME.' From now on I am telling you before *it* comes to pass, so that when it does occur, you may believe that I am *He*. Truly, truly, I say to you, he who receives whomever I send receives Me; and he who receives Me receives Him who sent Me" (John 13:12–20; Jesus quotes from Psalm 41:9; see Matthew 7:24; 10:24, 40; John 8:24; 13:1–11; 14:29; 1 Peter 5:3).

FOREIGNER

Setting: Samaria, on the way from Galilee to Jerusalem. The Lord stops to heal ten lepers who ask for cleansing.

When He saw them, He said to them, "Go and show yourselves to the priests." And as they were going, they were cleansed. Now one of them, when he saw that he had been healed, turned back, glorifying God with a loud voice, and he fell on his face at His feet, giving thanks to Him. And he was a Samaritan. Then Jesus answered and said, "Were there not ten cleansed? But the nine—where are they? Was no one found who returned to give glory to God, except this foreigner?" And He said to him, "Stand up and go; your faith has made you well" (Luke 17:14–19; see Leviticus 14:1–32).

FOREMAN (Also see LABORERS; LANDOWNER; and WORKERS)

Setting: Judea beyond the Jordan (Perea). Jesus illustrates the kingdom of heaven to His disciples through the story of laborers in the vineyard.

"For the kingdom of heaven is like a landowner who went out early in the morning to hire laborers for his vineyard. When he had agreed with the laborers for a denarius for the day, he sent them into his vineyard. And he went out about the third hour and saw others standing idle in the market place; and to those he said, 'You also go into the vineyard, and whatever is right I will give you.' And *so* they went. Again he went out about the sixth and the ninth hour, and did the same thing. And about the eleventh *hour* he went out and found others standing *around;* and he said to them, 'Why have you been standing idle here all day long?' They said to him, 'Because no one hired us.' He said to them, 'You go into the vineyard too.' When evening came, the owner of the vineyard said to his foreman, 'Call the laborers and pay them their wages, beginning with the last *group* to the first.' When those *hired* about the eleventh hour came, each one received a denarius. When those *hired* first came, they thought that they would receive more; but each of them also received a denarius. When they received it, they grumbled at the landowner, saying, 'These last men have worked *only* one hour, and you have made them equal to us who have borne the burden and the scorching heat of the day.' But he answered and said to one of them, 'Friend, I am doing you no wrong; did you not agree with me for a denarius? Take what is yours and go, but I wish to give to this last man the same as to you. It is not lawful for me to do what I wish with what is my own? Or is your eye envious because I am generous?' So the last shall be first, and the first last" (Matthew 20:1–16; cf. Matthew 19:30).

FOREMOST COMMANDMENT (Listed under COMMANDMENT, FOREMOST; also see COMMANDMENT, GREAT)

FORETELLING THE FUTURE (See PROPHECY)

FOREVER (Also see ETERNITY; and FOREVERMORE)

Setting: Galilee. During the early part of His ministry, Jesus gives a model prayer to His disciples and the multitudes while conveying The Sermon on the Mount.

"Pray, then, in this way: 'Our Father who is in heaven, hallowed be Your name. Your kingdom come. Your will be done, on earth as it is in heaven. Give us this day our daily bread. And forgive us our debts, as we also have forgiven our debtors. And do not lead us into temptation, but deliver us from evil. [For Yours is the kingdom and the power and the glory forever. Amen.]'" (Matthew 6:9–13; cf. Luke 11:2–4; see John 17:15).

Setting: Capernaum of Galilee. After Jesus informs the people whom He miraculously fed with a lad's five loaves and two fish how they might receive the bread out of heaven, the Jewish religious leaders grumble when Jesus claims He came down out of heaven.

Therefore the Jews were grumbling about Him, because He said, "I am the bread that came down out of heaven." They were saying, "Is not this Jesus, the son of Joseph, whose father and mother we know? How does He now say, 'I have come down out of heaven'?" Jesus answered and said to them, "Do not grumble among yourselves. No one can come to Me unless the Father who sent Me draws him; and I will raise him up on the last day. It is written in the prophets, 'AND THEY SHALL ALL BE TAUGHT OF GOD.' Everyone who has heard and learned from the Father, comes to Me. Not that anyone has seen the Father, except the One who is from God; He has seen the Father. Truly, truly, I say to you, he who believes has eternal life. I am the bread of life. Your fathers ate the manna in the wilderness, and they died. This is the bread which comes down out of heaven, so that one may eat of it and not die. I am the living bread that came down out of heaven; if anyone eats of this bread, he will live forever; and the bread also which I will give for the life of the world is My flesh" (John 6:41–51, Jesus quotes from Isaiah 54:13; see John 1:18, 29; 3:36; 7:27).

Setting: Capernaum of Galilee. After Jesus informs the people whom He miraculously fed with a lad's five loaves and two fish how they might receive the bread out of heaven, the Jewish religious leaders argue with one another when He says He will give His flesh to the world to eat.

So Jesus said to them, "Truly, truly, I say to you, unless you eat the flesh of the Son of Man and drink His blood, you have no life in yourselves. He who eats My flesh and drinks My blood has eternal life, and I will raise him up on the last day. For My flesh is true food, and My blood is true drink. He who eats My flesh and drinks My blood abides in Me, and I in him. As the living Father sent Me, and I live because of the Father, so he who eats Me, he also will live because of Me. This is the bread which came down out of heaven; not as the fathers ate and died; he who eats this bread will live forever" (John 6:53–58; see Matthew 16:16; Luke 4:22; John 3:36; 9:16; 15:4).

Setting: The temple treasury in Jerusalem. After the scribes and Pharisees question His testimony about Himself, Jesus reveals to those Jews who believe in Him how He will make them free.

So Jesus was saying to those Jews who had believed Him, "If you continue in My word, *then* you are truly disciples of Mine; and you will know the truth, and the truth will make you free." They answered Him, "We are Abraham's descendants and have never yet been enslaved to anyone; how is it that You say, 'You will become free'?" Jesus answered them, "Truly, truly, I say to you, everyone who commits sin is the slave of sin. The slave does not remain in the house forever; the son does remain forever. So if the Son makes you free, you will be free indeed. I know that you are Abraham's descendants; yet you seek to kill Me, because My word has no place in you. I speak the things which I have seen with *My* Father; therefore you also do the things which you heard from *your* father" (John 8:31–38; see Romans 6:16).

Setting: Jerusalem. Before the Passover, after responding to Philip's request for Him to show His disciples the Father, Jesus conveys the upcoming role of the Holy Spirit in their lives.

"If you love Me, you will keep My commandments. I will ask the Father, and He will give you another Helper, that He may be with you forever; *that* is the Spirit of truth, whom the world cannot receive, because it does not see Him or know Him, *but* you know Him because He abides with you and will be in you" (John 14:15–17; see John 7:39; 15:26; 1 John 5:3).

FOREVERMORE (Also see FOREVER)

Setting: On the island of Patmos (in the Aegean Sea about fifty miles southwest of Ephesus in modern Turkey). On the Lord's Day, approximately fifty years after Jesus' resurrection, the disciple John encounters the Lord, who communicates new revelations for the apostle to record for the seven churches in Asia.

When I saw Him, I fell at His feet like a dead man. And He placed His right hand on me, saying, "Do not be afraid; I am the first and the last, and the living One; and I was dead, and behold, I am alive forevermore, and I have the keys of death and of Hades. Therefore write the things which you have seen, and the things which are, and the things which will take place after these things. As for the mystery of the seven stars which you saw in My right hand, and the seven golden lampstands: the seven stars are the angels of the seven churches, and the seven lampstands are the seven churches" (Revelation 1:17–20; see Isaiah 44:6; Luke

24:5; Revelation 2:8).

FORGIVENESS (FORGIVENESS OF SINS is a separate entry; also see PEACEMAKERS; and RECONCILIATION)

[FORGIVENESS from forgive and forgiven]

Setting: Galilee. During the early part of His ministry, Jesus gives a model prayer to His disciples and the multitudes while conveying The Sermon on the Mount.

"Pray, then, in this way: 'Our Father who is in heaven, hallowed be Your name. Your kingdom come. Your will be done, on earth as it is in heaven. Give us this day our daily bread. And forgive us our debts, as we also have forgiven our debtors. And do not lead us into temptation, but deliver us from evil. [For Yours is the kingdom and the power and the glory forever. Amen.]'" (Matthew 6:9–13; cf. Luke 11:2–4; see John 17:15).

[FORGIVENESS from forgive]

Setting: Galilee. During the early part of His ministry, Jesus preaches the Sermon on the Mount to His disciples and the multitudes.

"For if you forgive others for their transgressions, your heavenly Father will also forgive you. But if you do not forgive others, then your Father will not forgive your transgressions" (Matthew 6:14, 15; cf. Matthew 18:15; see Mark 7:2).

[FORGIVENESS from forgiven]

Setting: Galilee. After He heals a blind, mute, demon-possessed man, the Pharisees accuse Jesus of being a worker of Satan. Jesus warns them about the unpardonable sin.

"He who is not with Me is against Me; and he who does not gather with Me scatters. Therefore I say to you, any sin and blasphemy shall be forgiven people, but blasphemy against the Spirit shall not be forgiven. Whoever speaks a word against the Son of Man, it shall be forgiven him; but whoever speaks against the Holy Spirit, it shall not be forgiven him, either in this age or in the *age* to come" (Matthew 12:30–32; cf. Luke 12:10; see Mark 9:40).

[FORGIVENESS from forgave and forgive]

Setting: Capernaum of Galilee. Jesus illustrates forgiveness after Peter asks Him if forgiving someone seven times who has sinned against him is adequate.

"For this reason the kingdom of heaven may be compared to a king who wished to settle accounts with his slaves. When he had begun to settle *them,* one who owed him ten thousand talents was brought to him. But since he did not have *the means* to repay, his lord commanded him to be sold, along with his wife and children and all that he had, and repayment to be made. So the slave fell *to the ground* and prostrated himself before him, saying, 'Have patience with me and I will repay you everything.' And the lord of that slave felt compassion and released him and forgave him the debt. But that slave went out and found one of his fellow slaves who owed him a hundred denarii; and he seized him and *began* to choke *him,* saying, 'Pay back what you owe.' So his fellow slave fell *to the ground* and *began* to plead with him, saying, 'Have patience with me and I will repay you.' But he was unwilling and went and threw him in prison until he should pay back what was owed. So when his fellow slaves saw what had happened, they were deeply grieved and came and reported to their lord all that had happened. Then summoning him, his lord said to him, 'You wicked slave, I forgave you all that debt because you pleaded with me. Should you not also have had mercy on your fellow slave, in the same way that I had mercy on you?' And his lord, moved with anger, handed him over to the torturers until he should repay all that was owed him. My heavenly Father will also do the same to you, if each of you does not forgive his brother from your heart" (Matthew 18:23–35; cf. Matthew 6:12, 14, 15; Luke 7:42; see Matthew 25:19–28).

Setting: Galilee. After Jesus selects His twelve disciples, scribes from Jerusalem attribute His miraculous powers to Beelzebul (Satan).

And He called them to Himself and began speaking to them in parables, "How can Satan cast out Satan? If a kingdom is divided against itself, that kingdom cannot stand. If a house is divided against itself, that house will not be able to stand. If Satan has risen up against himself and is divided, he cannot stand, but he is finished! But no one can enter the strong man's house and plunder his property unless he first binds the strong man, and then he will plunder his house. Truly I say to you, all sins shall be forgiven the sons of men, and whatever blasphemies they utter; but whoever blasphemes against the Holy Spirit never has forgiveness, but is guilty of an eternal sin"—because they were saying, "He has an unclean spirit" (Mark 3:23–30; cf. Matthew 12:25–32; Luke 12:10).

[FORGIVENESS from FORGIVEN]
Setting: By the Sea of Galilee. After Jesus conveys the Parable of the Sower to a crowd from a boat, His disciples ask Him questions about it.

And He was saying to them, "To you has been given the mystery of the kingdom of God, but those who are outside get everything in parables, so that WHILE SEEING, THEY MAY SEE AND NOT PERCEIVE, AND WHILE HEARING, THEY MAY HEAR AND NOT UNDERSTAND, OTHERWISE THEY MIGHT RETURN AND BE FORGIVEN" (Mark 4:11, 12, Jesus quotes from Isaiah 6:9, 10; cf. Matthew 13:10–17).

[FORGIVENESS from forgive]
Setting: Jerusalem. Following Jesus' instruction to the money changers while cleansing the temple, Peter draws His and His disciples' attention to the earlier-cursed fig tree.

And Jesus answered saying to them, "Have faith in God. Truly, I say to you, whoever says to this mountain, 'Be taken up and cast into the sea,' and does not doubt in his heart, but believes that what he says is going to happen, it will be *granted* him. Therefore I say to you, all things for which you pray and ask, believe that you have received them, and they will be *granted* you. Whenever you stand praying, forgive, if you have anything against anyone, so that your Father who is in heaven will also forgive you your transgressions. [But if you do not forgive, neither will your Father who is in heaven forgive your transgressions'] (Mark 11:22–26; cf. Matthew 21:19–22; see Matthew 6:14, 15; 7:7; 17:20).

[FORGIVENESS from forgave]
Setting: Galilee. After Jesus praises John the Baptist to the crowds, Simon, a Pharisee, invites Jesus to dinner. A sinful woman anoints the Lord's feet with perfume, prompting Him to convey a parable.

And Jesus answered him, "Simon, I have something to say to you." And he replied, "Say it, Teacher." "A moneylender had two debtors: one owed five hundred denarii, and the other fifty. When they were unable to repay, he graciously forgave them both. So which of them will love him more?" Simon answered and said, "I suppose the one whom he forgave more." And He said to him, "You have judged correctly" (Luke 7:40–43; see Matthew 18:23–35).

[FORGIVENESS from forgiven and forgives]
Setting: Galilee. After Jesus praises John the Baptist to the crowds, Simon, a Pharisee, invites Jesus to dinner. A sinful woman anoints the Lord's feet with perfume, prompting Him to instruct His host about forgiveness.

Turning toward the woman, He said to Simon, "Do you see this woman? I entered your house; you gave Me no water for My feet, but she has wet My feet with her tears and wiped them with her hair. You gave Me no kiss; but she, since the time I came in, has not ceased to kiss My feet. You did not anoint My head with oil, but she anointed My feet with perfume. For this reason I say to you, her sins, which are many, have been forgiven, for she loved much; but he who is forgiven little, loves little." Then He said to her, "Your sins have been forgiven." Those who were reclining *at the table* with Him began to say to themselves, "Who is this *man* who even forgives sins?" And He said to the woman, "Your faith has saved you; go in peace" (Luke 7:44–50; see Matthew 9:2; Mark 5:34; Luke 5:21).

[FORGIVENESS from forgive]
Setting: On the way from Galilee to Jerusalem via Bethany. After Jesus visits in the home of Martha and Mary, one of the disciples asks Jesus to teach them to pray.

And He said to them, "When you pray, say: 'Father, hallowed be Your name. Your kingdom come. Give us each day our daily bread. And forgive us our sins, for we ourselves also forgive everyone who is indebted to us. And lead us not into temptation'" (Luke 11:2–4; cf. Matthew 6:9–13).

[FORGIVENESS from forgiven]
Setting: On the way from Galilee to Jerusalem. Jesus warns His disciples of future events as the scribes and Pharisees turn hostile and question Him repeatedly in an attempt to catch Him in something He might say.

"And I say to you, everyone who confesses Me before men, the Son of Man will confess him also before the angels of God; but he who denies Me before men will be denied before the angels of God. And everyone who speaks a word against the Son of Man, it will be forgiven him; but he who blasphemes against the Holy Spirit, it will not be forgiven him. When they bring you before the synagogues and the rulers and the authorities, do not worry about how or what you are to speak in your defense, or what you are to say; for the Holy Spirit will teach you in that very hour what you ought to say" (Luke 12:8–12; cf. Matthew 10:32, 33; 12:31, 32; see Matthew 10:20).

[FORGIVENESS from forgive]
Setting: On the way from Galilee to Jerusalem. After conveying the story of the rich man and Lazarus, the Lord gives instruction to His disciples on forgiveness.

He said to His disciples, "It is inevitable that stumbling blocks come, but woe to him through whom they come! It would be better for him if a millstone were hung around his neck and he were thrown into the sea, than that he would cause one of these little ones to stumble. Be on your guard! If your brother sins, rebuke him; and if he repents, forgive him. And if he sins against you seven times a day, and returns to you seven times, saying, 'I repent,' forgive him" (Luke 17:1–4; see Matthew 18:5–7, 15, 21, 22).

[FORGIVENESS from forgive]
Setting: Golgotha (Calvary), just outside Jerusalem. After being arrested, tried, and sentenced to crucifixion by Pontius Pilate (Roman governor of Judea), while hanging between two criminals, the Lord requests from His Father forgiveness for the crucifiers.

But Jesus was saying, "Father, forgive them; for they do not know what they are doing." And they cast lots, dividing up His garments among themselves (Luke 23:34; see Psalm 22:18; Matthew 27:33–36; Mark 15:22–24; John 19:23–25).

[FORGIVENESS from Truly I say to you, today you shall be with Me in Paradise]
Setting: Golgotha (Calvary), just outside Jerusalem. While Jesus is being mocked on the cross, one of the criminals being crucified with Him asks to be remembered in Christ's kingdom. Jesus grants his plea with forgiveness and entrance into Paradise.

And He said to him, "Truly I say to you, today you shall be with Me in Paradise" (Luke 23:43; see Matthew 27:39–44; Mark 15:29–32).

[FORGIVENESS from I do not condemn you either]
Setting: The temple in Jerusalem. Following the Feast of Booths, Jesus retires to the Mount of Olives, and returns the next day to teach. The scribes and Pharisees set a woman caught in adultery before Him to test whether He will follow Moses' command to stone her.

They were saying this, testing Him, so that they might have grounds for accusing Him. But Jesus stooped down and with His finger wrote on the ground. But when they persisted in asking Him, He straightened up, and said to them, "He who is without sin among you, let him *be the* first to throw a stone at her." Again He stooped down and wrote on the ground. When they heard it, they *began* to go out one by one, beginning with the older ones, and He was left alone, and the woman, where she was, in the center *of the court.* Straightening up, Jesus said to her, "Woman, where are they? Did no one condemn you?" She said, "No one, Lord." And Jesus said, "I do not condemn you either. Go. From now on sin no more" (John 8:6–11; see John 3:17).

[FORGIVENESS from forgiven]
Setting: Jerusalem. After Mary Magdalene encounters the risen Jesus in the morning, He appears that evening in the midst of His disciples (with the exception of Thomas) in hiding behind closed doors for fear of the Jewish religious leaders.

So when it was evening on that day, the first *day* of the week, and when the doors were shut where the disciples were, for fear of the Jews, Jesus came and stood in their midst and said to them, "Peace *be* with you." And when He had said this, He showed them both His hands and His side. The disciples then rejoiced when they saw the Lord. So Jesus said to them again, "Peace *be* with you; as the Father has sent Me, I also send you." And when He had said this, He breathed on them and said to them, "Receive the Holy Spirit. If you forgive the sins of any, *their sins* have been forgiven them; if you retain the *sins* of any, they have been retained" (John 20:19–23; cf. Luke 24:36–43; see Matthew 16:19; Mark 16:14).

FORGIVENESS OF SINS (Also see FORGIVENESS; GOSPEL; and SALVATION)
[FORGIVENESS OF SINS from your sins are forgiven and forgive sins]
Setting: Capernaum, near the Sea of Galilee. After Jesus heals a paralytic and forgives his sins in front of crowds, some scribes accuse the Lord of blasphemy.

And they brought to Him a paralytic lying on a bed. Seeing their faith, Jesus said to the paralytic, "Take courage, son; your sins are forgiven." And some scribes said to themselves. "This *fellow* blasphemes." And Jesus knowing their thoughts said, "Why are you thinking evil in your hearts? Which is easier to say, 'Your sins are forgiven,' or to say, 'Get up, and walk'? But so that you may know that the Son of Man has authority on earth to forgive sins"—then He said to the paralytic, "Get up, pick up your bed and go home" (Matthew 9:2–6; cf. Mark 2:3–12; Luke 5:17–26).

Setting: An upper room in Jerusalem. While celebrating the Passover meal with His disciples, Jesus institutes the Lord's Supper ordinance before being arrested by His enemies.

While they were eating, Jesus took *some* bread, and after a blessing, He broke it and gave *it* to the disciples, and said, "Take, eat; this is My body." And when He had taken a cup and given thanks, He gave *it* to them saying, "Drink from it, all of you; for this is My blood of the covenant, which is poured out for many for forgiveness of sins. But I say to you, I will not drink of this fruit of the vine from now on until that day when I drink it new with you in My Father's kingdom" (Matthew 26:26–29; cf. Mark 14:22–25; Luke 22:17–20; 1 Corinthians 11:23–26; see 1 Corinthians 10:16).

[FORGIVENESS OF SINS from sins are forgiven]
Setting: Galilee. Early in Jesus' gospel-preaching ministry, word of His healing abilities spreads, so some friends bring a paralytic man to Him for healing.

And Jesus seeing their faith said to the paralytic, "Son, your sins are forgiven" (Mark 2:5; cf. Matthew 9:1–3; Luke 5:17–20).

[FORGIVENESS OF SINS from Your sins are forgiven and forgives sins]
Setting: Capernaum. When Jesus heals a paralytic man and forgives his sins, some scribes believe the Lord commits blasphemy.

Immediately Jesus, aware in His spirit that they were reasoning that way within themselves, said to them, "Why are you reasoning about these things in your hearts? Which is easier, to say to the paralytic, 'Your sins are forgiven'; or to say, 'Get up, and pick up your pallet and walk'? "But so that you may know that the Son of Man has authority on earth to forgive sins"—He said to the paralytic, "I say to you, get up, pick up your pallet and go home" (Mark 2:8–11; cf. Matthew 9:4–7; Luke 5:21–24).

[FORGIVENESS OF SINS from sins shall be forgiven]
Setting: Galilee. After Jesus selects His twelve disciples, scribes from Jerusalem attribute His miraculous powers to Beelzebul (Satan).

And He called them to Himself and began speaking to them in parables, "How can Satan cast out Satan? If a kingdom is divided against itself, that kingdom cannot stand. If a house is divided against itself, that house will not be able to stand. If Satan has risen up against himself and is divided, he cannot stand, but he is finished! But no one can enter the strong man's house and plunder his property unless he first binds the strong man, and then he will plunder his house. Truly I say to you, all sins shall be forgiven the sons of men, and whatever blasphemies they utter; but whoever blasphemes against the Holy Spirit never has forgiveness, but is guilty of an eternal sin"—because they were saying, "He has an unclean spirit" (Mark 3:23–30; cf. Matthew 12:25–32; Luke 12:10).

[FORGIVENESS OF SINS from sins are forgiven]
Setting: Galilee. While some Pharisees and teachers of the law from Galilee and Judea observe, several men lower a paralyzed man through the roof in front of Jesus.

Seeing their faith, He said, "Friend, your sins are forgiven you" (Luke 5:20; cf. Mark 2:2–12; see Matthew 9:1–8).

[FORGIVENESS OF SINS from sins have been forgiven and to forgive sins]
Setting: Capernaum of Galilee. When Jesus heals a paralytic man and forgives his sins, some Pharisees and teachers of the law from Galilee and Judea accuse the Lord of committing blasphemy.

But Jesus, aware of their reasonings, answered and said to them, "Why are you reasoning in your hearts? Which is easier, to say, 'Your sins have been forgiven you,' or to say, 'Get up and walk'? But, so that you may know that the Son of Man has authority on earth to forgive sins,"—He said to the paralytic—"I say to you, get up, and pick up your stretcher and go home" (Luke 5:22–24; cf. Matthew 9:4–8; Mark 2:8–12; see Matthew 4:24).

[FORGIVENESS OF SINS from her sins, which are many, have been forgiven; Your sins have been forgiven; and forgives sins]
Setting: Galilee. After Jesus praises John the Baptist to the crowds, Simon, a Pharisee, invites the Lord to dinner. A sinful woman anoints His feet with perfume, prompting Him to instruct His host about forgiveness.

Turning toward the woman, He said to Simon, "Do you see this woman? I entered your house; you gave Me no water for My feet, but she has wet My feet with her tears and wiped them with her hair. You gave Me no kiss; but she, since the time I came in, has not ceased to kiss My feet. You did not anoint My head with oil, but she anointed My feet with perfume. For this reason I say to you, her sins, which are many, have been forgiven, for she loved much; but he who is forgiven little, loves little." Then He said to her, "Your sins have been forgiven." Those who were reclining *at the table* with Him began to say to themselves, "Who is this *man* who even forgives sins?" And He said to the woman, "Your faith has saved you; go in peace" (Luke 7:44–50; see Matthew 9:2; Mark 5:34; Luke 5:21).

[FORGIVENESS OF SINS from today you shall be with Me in Paradise]
Setting: On the hill called Golgotha (Calvary), just outside Jerusalem. While Jesus, hanging nailed to a cross, is being mocked and ridiculed, one of the criminals being crucified with Him asks to be remembered in Christ's kingdom, which Jesus grants with forgiveness and entrance into Paradise.

And He said to him, "Truly I say to you, today you shall be with Me in Paradise" (Luke 23:43; see Matthew 27:39–44; Mark 15:29–32).

Setting: Jerusalem. After rising from the tomb on the third day after being crucified, and appearing to two of His followers on the road to Emmaus, Jesus gives instruction to His disciples (except Thomas) about His mission on earth and the promise of future power from God.

Now He said to them, "These are My words which I spoke to you while I was still with you, that all things which are written about Me in the Law of Moses and the Prophets and the Psalms must be fulfilled." Then He opened their minds to understand the Scriptures, and He said to them, "Thus it is written, that the Christ would suffer and rise again from the dead the third day, and that repentance for forgiveness of sins would be proclaimed in His name to all the nations, beginning from Jerusalem. You are witnesses of these things. And behold, I am sending forth the promise of My Father upon you; but you are to stay in the city until you are clothed with power from on high" (Luke 24:44–49; see Matthew 28:19, 20; Acts 1:8).

[FORGIVENESS OF SINS from forgive the sins]
Setting: Jerusalem. After Mary Magdalene encounters the risen Jesus in the morning, He appears that evening in the midst of His disciples (except Thomas), who are in hiding behind closed doors for fear of the Jewish religious leaders.

So when it was evening on that day, the first *day* of the week, and when the doors were shut where the disciples were, for fear of the Jews, Jesus came and stood in their midst and said to them, "Peace *be* with you." And when He had said this, He showed them both His hands and His side. The disciples then rejoiced when they saw the Lord. So Jesus said to them again, "Peace *be* with you; as the Father has sent Me, I also send you." And when He had said this, He breathed on them and said to them, "Receive the Holy Spirit. If you forgive the sins of any, *their sins* have been forgiven them; if you retain the *sins* of any, they have been retained" (John 20:19–23; cf. Luke 24:36–43; see Matthew 16:19; Mark 16:14).

Setting: Caesarea. Luke, writing in Acts, gives Paul's retelling of his conversion to Christ as he appears before King Agrippa following his hearing before the Jewish Council in Jerusalem and arrest by the Roman commander (on his way to Rome after the apostle's third missionary journey).

"And when we had fallen to the ground, I heard a voice saying to me in the Hebrew dialect, 'Saul, Saul, why are you persecuting Me? It is hard for you to kick against the goads.' And I said, 'Who are You, Lord?' And the Lord said, 'I am Jesus whom you are persecuting. But get up and stand on your feet; for this purpose I have appeared to you, to appoint you a minister and a witness not only to the things which you have seen, but also to the things in which I will appear to you; rescuing you from the *Jewish* people and from the Gentiles, to whom I am sending you, to open their eyes so that they may turn from darkness to light and from the dominion of Satan to God, that they may receive forgiveness of sins and an inheritance among those who have been sanctified by faith in Me' (Acts 26:14–18; see Isaiah 35:5; Acts 21:40; 22:14).

FORM

Setting: On the way from Galilee to Jerusalem. After the scribes and Pharisees turn hostile and question Him repeatedly in an attempt to catch Him in something He might say, Jesus teaches the crowds and His disciples about greed and possessions.

But He said to him, "Man, who appointed Me a judge or arbitrator over you?" Then He said to them, "Beware, and be on your guard against every form of greed; for not *even* when one has an abundance does his life consist of his possessions" (Luke 12:14, 15; see 1 Timothy 6:6–10).

Setting: Jerusalem. During the Feast of the Jews, Jesus responds to criticism from the Jewish religious leaders by referring to God as His Father (thereby making Himself equal with God) and informing them that God, John the Baptist, and His works all testify to His mission.

"I can do nothing on My own initiative. As I hear, I judge; and My judgment is just, because I do not seek My own will, but the will of Him who sent Me. If I *alone* testify about Myself, My testimony is not true. There is another who testifies of Me, and I know that the testimony which He gives about Me is true. You have sent to John, and he has testified to the truth. But the testimony which I receive is not from man, but I say these things so that you may be saved. He was the lamp that was burning and was shining and you were willing to rejoice for a while in his light. But the testimony which I have is greater than the *testimony of* John; for the works which the Father has given Me to accomplish—the very works that I do—testify about Me, that the Father has sent Me. And the Father who sent Me, He has testified of Me. You have neither heard His voice at any time nor seen His form. You do not have His word abiding in you, for you do not believe Him whom He sent" (John 5:30–38; see Matthew 3:17; Mark 1:4–5; John 1:7, 15, 32; 4:34; 8:14–16; 10:25, 37, 38).

FORNICATIONS (Also see ADULTERIES; ADULTERY; IMMORALITY; and SEXUAL SIN)

Setting: Galilee. Jesus explains to the crowd the meaning of His instruction about what defiles a man.

Peter said to Him, "Explain the parable to us." Jesus said, "Are you still lacking in understanding also? Do you not understand that everything that goes into the mouth passes into the stomach and is eliminated? But the things that proceed out of the mouth come from the heart, and those defile the man. For out of the heart come evil thoughts, murders, adulteries, fornications, thefts, false witness, slanders. These are the things which defile a man; but to eat with unwashed hands does not defile the man" (Matthew 15:15–20; cf. Mark 7:18–23; see Galatians 5:19–21).

Setting: Galilee. After the Pharisees and scribes from Jerusalem question Jesus' disciples' lack of obedience to the tradition regarding ceremonial cleansing, the Lord speaks to a crowd and explains His teaching to His disciples.

After He called the crowd to Him again, He *began* saying to them, "Listen to Me, all of you, and understand: there is nothing outside the man which can defile him if it goes into him; but the things which proceed out of the man are what defile the man. [If anyone has ears to hear, let him hear."] When he had left the crowd *and* entered the house, His disciples questioned Him about the parable. And He said to them, "Are you so lacking in understanding also? Do you not understand that whatever goes into the man from outside cannot defile him, because it does not go into his heart, but into his stomach, and is eliminated?" (*Thus He* declared all foods clean.) And He was saying, "That which proceeds out of the man, that is what defiles the man. For from within, out of the heart of men, proceed the evil thoughts, fornications, thefts, murders, adulteries, deeds of coveting *and* wickedness, *as well* as deceit, sensuality, envy, slander, pride *and* foolishness. All these evil things proceed from within and defile the man" (Mark 7:14–23; cf. Matthew 15:10–20).

FORSAKEN

Setting: Golgotha (Calvary), just outside Jerusalem. Jesus utters words of despair while dying on the cross for the sins of the world.

About the ninth hour Jesus cried out with a loud voice, saying, "ELI, ELI, LAMA SABACHTHANI?" that is, "MY GOD, MY GOD, WHY HAVE YOU FORSAKEN ME?" (Matthew 27:46, Jesus quotes from Psalm 22:1; cf. Mark 15:34).

Setting: Golgotha (Calvary), just outside Jerusalem. While on the cross, Jesus cries out at the ninth hour (3 p.m.).

At the ninth hour Jesus cried out with a loud voice, "ELOI, ELOI, LAMA SABACHTHANI?" which is translated, "MY GOD, MY GOD, WHY HAVE YOU FORSAKEN ME?" (Mark 15:34, Jesus quotes from Psalm 22:1; cf. Matthew 27:46).

FOUND

Setting: Capernaum of Galilee. After the Lord gives the Sermon on the Mount and cleanses a leper, a Roman centurion implores Jesus to heal his servant.

Now when Jesus heard *this,* He marveled, and said to those who were following, "Truly I say to you, I have not found such great faith with anyone in Israel. I say to you that many will come from east and west, and recline *at the table* with Abraham, Isaac and Jacob in the kingdom of heaven; but the sons of the kingdom will be cast out into the outer darkness; in that place there will be weeping and gnashing of teeth." And Jesus said to the centurion, "Go; it shall be done for you as you have believed." And the servant was healed that *very* moment (Matthew 8:10–13; cf. Luke 7:9, 10).

Setting: Galilee. After His twelve disciples observe His ministry, Jesus summons and specifically instructs them

about their ministry ahead involving true discipleship.

"He who loves father or mother more than Me is not worthy of Me; and he who loves son or daughter more than Me is not worthy of Me. And he who does not take his cross and follow after Me is not worthy of Me. He who has found his life will lose it, and he who has lost his life for My sake will find it" (Matthew 10:37–39; cf. Matthew 16:24, 25).

Setting: By the Sea of Galilee. Because the religious leaders are rejecting His message, Jesus continues teaching the crowds with the Parable of the Hidden Treasure.

"The kingdom of heaven is like a treasure hidden in the field, which a man found and hid *again;* and from joy over it he goes and sells all that he has and buys that field" (Matthew 13:44).

Setting: Capernaum of Galilee. Jesus illustrates forgiveness after Peter asks Him if forgiving someone seven times who has sinned against him is adequate.

"For this reason the kingdom of heaven may be compared to a king who wished to settle accounts with his slaves. When he had begun to settle *them,* one who owed him ten thousand talents was brought to him. But since he did not have *the means* to repay, his lord commanded him to be sold, along with his wife and children and all that he had, and repayment to be made. So the slave fell *to the ground* and prostrated himself before him, saying, 'Have patience with me and I will repay you everything.' And the lord of that slave felt compassion and released him and forgave him the debt. But that slave went out and found one of his fellow slaves who owed him a hundred denarii; and he seized him and *began* to choke *him,* saying, 'Pay back what you owe.' So his fellow slave fell *to the ground* and *began* to plead with him, saying, 'Have patience with me and I will repay you.' But he was unwilling and went and threw him in prison until he should pay back what was owed. So when his fellow slaves saw what had happened, they were deeply grieved and came and reported to their lord all that had happened. Then summoning him, his lord said to him, 'You wicked slave, I forgave you all that debt because you pleaded with me. Should you not also have had mercy on your fellow slave, in the same way that I had mercy on you?' And his lord, moved with anger, handed him over to the torturers until he should repay all that was owed him. My heavenly Father will also do the same to you, if each of you does not forgive his brother from your heart" (Matthew 18:23–35; cf. Matthew 6:12, 14, 15; Luke 7:42; see Matthew 25:19–28).

Setting: Judea beyond the Jordan (Perea). Jesus illustrates the kingdom of heaven to His disciples through the story of laborers in the vineyard.

"For the kingdom of heaven is like a landowner who went out early in the morning to hire laborers for his vineyard. When he had agreed with the laborers for a denarius for the day, he sent them into his vineyard. And he went out about the third hour and saw others standing idle in the market place; and to those he said, 'You also go into the vineyard, and whatever is right I will give you.' And *so* they went. Again he went out about the sixth and the ninth hour, and did the same thing. And about the eleventh *hour* he went out and found others standing *around;* and he said to them, 'Why have you been standing idle here all day long?' They said to him, 'Because no one hired us.' He said to them, 'You go into the vineyard too.' When evening came, the owner of the vineyard said to his foreman, 'Call the laborers and pay them their wages, beginning with the last *group* to the first.' When those *hired* about the eleventh hour came, each one received a denarius. When those *hired* first came, they thought that they would receive more; but each of them also received a denarius. When they received it, they grumbled at the landowner, saying, 'These last men have worked *only* one hour, and you have made them equal to us who have borne the burden and the scorching heat of the day.' But he answered and said to one of them, 'Friend, I am doing you no wrong; did you not agree with me for a denarius? Take what is yours and go, but I wish to give to this last man the same as to you. It is not lawful for me to do what I wish with what is my own? Or is your eye envious because I am generous?' So the last shall be first, and the first last" (Matthew 20:1–16; cf. Matthew 19:30).

Setting: The temple in Jerusalem. Jesus speaks another parable to the chief priests and elders after they question His authority.

Jesus spoke to them again in parables, saying, "The kingdom of heaven may be compared to a king who gave a wedding feast for his son. And he sent out his slaves to call those who had been invited to the wedding feast, and they were unwilling to come. Again he sent out other slaves saying, 'Tell those who have been invited, "Behold, I have prepared my dinner; my oxen and my fattened livestock are *all* butchered and everything is ready; come to the wedding feast." But they paid no attention and went their way, one to his own farm, another to his business, and the rest seized his slaves and mistreated them and killed them. But the king was enraged, and he sent his armies and destroyed those murderers and set their city on fire. Then he said to his slaves, 'The wedding is ready, but those who were invited were not worthy. 'Go therefore to the main highways, and as many as you find *there,* invite to the wedding feast.' Those slaves went out into the streets and gathered together all they found, both evil and good; and the wedding hall was filled with dinner guests. But when the king came in to look over the dinner guests, he saw a man there who was not dressed in wedding clothes, and he said to him, 'Friend, how did you come in here without wedding clothes?' And the man was speechless. Then the king said to the servants, 'Bind him hand and foot, and throw him into the outer darkness; in that place there will be weeping and gnashing of teeth.' For many are called, but few *are* chosen" (Matthew 22:1–14; cf. Matthew 8:11, 12).

Setting: **Capernaum in Galilee. After Jesus completes His Sermon on the Mount, a Roman centurion asks Him to heal his gravely ill slave.**

Now when Jesus heard this, He marveled at him, and turned and said to the crowd that was following Him, "I say to you, not even in Israel have I found such great faith" (Luke 7:9; cf. Matthew 8:1–10).

Setting: **Galilee. After responding to the disciples of John the Baptist whether He is the promised Messiah, Jesus speaks to the crowds about John.**

When the messengers of John had left, He began to speak to the crowds about John, "What did you go out into the wilderness to see? A reed shaken by the wind? But what did you go out to see? A man dressed in soft clothing? Those who are splendidly clothed and live in luxury are *found* in royal palaces! But what did you go out to see? A prophet? Yes, I say to you, and one who is more than a prophet. This is the one about whom it is written, 'BEHOLD, I SEND MY MESSENGER AHEAD OF YOU, WHO WILL PREPARE YOUR WAY BEFORE YOU.' I say to you, among those born of women there is no one greater than John; yet he who is least in the kingdom of God is greater than he" (Luke 7:24–28, Jesus quotes from Malachi 3:1; cf. Matthew 11:7–11).

Setting: **On the way from Galilee to Jerusalem. After Jesus presents to large crowds the demands of discipleship, the Pharisees and scribes complain He associates with tax collectors and sinners.**

So He told them this parable, saying, "What man among you, if he has a hundred sheep and has lost one of them, does not leave the ninety-nine in the open pasture and go after the one which is lost until he finds it? When he has found it, he lays it on his shoulders, rejoicing. And when he comes home, he calls together his friends and his neighbors, saying to them, 'Rejoice with me, for I have found my sheep which was lost!' I tell you that in the same way, there will be *more* joy in heaven over one sinner who repents than over ninety-nine righteous persons who need no repentance" (Luke 15:3–7; cf. Matthew 18:12–14; see Matthew 9:11–13; Luke 5:29–32).

Setting: **On the way from Galilee to Jerusalem. Jesus conveys the principles of the lost sheep and the lost coin because the Pharisees and scribes complain He associates with tax collectors and sinners.**

"So He told them this parable, saying, "What man among you, if he has a hundred sheep and has lost one of them, does not leave the ninety-nine in the open pasture and go after the one which is lost until he finds it? When he has found it, he lays it on his shoulders, rejoicing. And when he comes home, he calls together his friends and his neighbors, saying to them, 'Rejoice with me, for I have found my sheep which was lost!' I tell you that in the same way, there will be more joy in heaven over one sinner who repents than over ninety-nine righteous persons who need no repentance. Or what woman, if she has ten silver coins and loses one coin, does not light a lamp and sweep the house and search carefully until she finds it? When she has found it, she calls together her friends and neighbors, saying, 'Rejoice with me, for I have found the coin which I had lost!' In the same way, I tell you, there is joy in the presence of the angels of God over one sinner who repents" (Luke 15:3–10; cf. Matthew 18:12-14; see Matthew 9:11-13).

Setting: On the way from Galilee to Jerusalem. Jesus conveys the illustration of the prodigal son because the Pharisees and scribes complain He associates with tax collectors and sinners.

And He said, "A man had two sons. The younger of them said to his father, 'Father, give me the share of the estate that falls to me.' So he divided his wealth between them. And not many days later, the younger son gathered everything together and went on a journey into a distant country, and there he squandered his estate with loose living. Now when he had spent everything, a severe famine occurred in that country, and he began to be impoverished. So he went and hired himself out to one of the citizens of that country, and he sent him into his fields to feed swine. And he would have gladly filled his stomach with the pods that the swine were eating, and no one was giving *anything* to him. But when he came to his senses, he said, 'How many of my father's hired men have more than enough bread, but I am dying here with hunger! I will get up and go to my father, and will say to him, "Father, I have sinned against heaven, and in your sight; I am no longer worthy to be called your son; make me as one of your hired men."' So he got up and came to his father. But while he was still a long way off, his father saw him and felt compassion *for him,* and ran and embraced him and kissed him. And the son said to him, "Father, I have sinned against heaven and in your sight; I am no longer worthy to be called your son.' But the father said to his slaves, 'Quickly bring out the best robe and put it on him, and put a ring on his hand and sandals on his feet; and bring the fattened calf, kill it, and let us eat and celebrate; for this son of mine was dead and has come to life again; he was lost and has been found.' And they began to celebrate. Now his older son was in the field, when he came and approached the house, he heard music and dancing. And he summoned one of the servants and *began* inquiring what these things could be. And he said to him, 'Your brother has come, and your father has killed the fattened calf because he has received him back safe and sound.' But he became angry and was not willing to go in; and his father came out and *began* pleading with him. But he answered and said to his father, 'Look! For so many years I have been serving you and I have never neglected a command of yours; and *yet* you have never given me a young goat, so that I might celebrate with my friends; but when this son of yours came, who has devoured your wealth with prostitutes, you killed the fattened calf for him.' And he said to him, 'Son, you have always been with me, and all that is mine is yours. But we had to celebrate and rejoice, for this brother of yours was dead and *has begun* to live, and was lost and has been found' " (Luke 15:11–32; see Proverbs 29:2).

Setting: Samaria, on the way from Galilee to Jerusalem. The Lord stops to heal ten lepers who ask for cleansing.

When He saw them, He said to them, "Go and show yourselves to the priests." And as they were going, they were cleansed. Now one of them, when he saw that he had been healed, turned back, glorifying God with a loud voice, and he fell on his face at His feet, giving thanks to Him. And he was a Samaritan. Then Jesus answered and said, "Were there not ten cleansed? But the nine—where are they? Was no one found who returned to give glory to God, except this foreigner?" And He said to him, "Stand up and go; your faith has made you well" (Luke 17:14–19; see Leviticus 14:1–32).

Setting: On the island of Patmos (in the Aegean Sea about fifty miles southwest of Ephesus in modern Turkey). On the Lord's Day (Sunday), about fifty years after Jesus' resurrection, the disciple John encounters the Lord Jesus Christ, who communicates a new revelation for the apostle to record for the church in Ephesus and to six other churches in Asia.

"To the angel of the church in Ephesus write: The One who holds the seven stars in His right hand, the One who walks among the seven golden lampstands, says this: 'I know your deeds and your toil and perseverance, and that you cannot tolerate evil men, and you put to the test those who call themselves apostles, and they are not, and you found them *to be* false; and you have perseverance and have endured for My name's sake, and have not grown weary. But I have *this* against you, that you have left your first love. Therefore remember from where you have fallen, and repent and do the deeds you did at first; or else I am coming to you and will remove your lampstand out of its place—unless you repent. Yet this you do have, that you hate the deeds of the Nicolaitans, which I also hate. He who has an ear, let him hear what the Spirit says to the churches. To him who overcomes, I will grant to eat of the tree of life which is in the Paradise of God' " (Revelation 2:1–7; see Genesis 2:9; Ezekiel 28:13; 1 John 4:1; Revelation 1:10, 11, 19, 20; 2:15, 16).

Setting: On the island of Patmos (in the Aegean Sea about fifty miles southwest of Ephesus in modern Turkey). On the Lord's Day (Sunday), about fifty years after Jesus' resurrection, the disciple John encounters the Lord Jesus

Christ, who communicates a new revelation for the apostle to record for the church in Sardis and to six other churches in Asia.

"To the angel of the church in Sardis write: He who has the seven Spirits of God and the seven stars, says this: 'I know your deeds, that you have a name that you are alive, but you are dead. Wake up, and strengthen the things that remain, which were about to die; for I have not found your deeds completed in the sight of My God. So remember what you have received and heard; and keep *it,* and repent. Therefore if you do not wake up, I will come like a thief, and you will not know at what hour I will come to you. But you have a few people in Sardis who have not soiled their garments; and they will walk with Me in white, for they are worthy. He who overcomes will thus be clothed in white garments; and I will not erase his name from the book of life, and I will confess his name before My Father and before His angels. He who has an ear, let him hear what the Spirit says to the churches' " (Revelation 3:1–6; see Matthew 10:32; Revelation 1:16).

FOUNDATION (WORLD, FOUNDATION OF THE is a separate entry; also see BUILDERS; BUILDINGS; and CONSTRUCTION)

[FOUNDATION from founded on the rock]

Setting: Galilee. During the early part of His ministry, Jesus preaches the Sermon on the Mount to His disciples and the multitudes.

"Therefore everyone who hears these words of Mine and acts on them, may be compared to a wise man who built his house on the rock. And the rain fell, and the floods came, and the winds blew and slammed against that house; and *yet* it did not fall, for it had been founded on the rock. Everyone who hears these words of Mine and does not act on them, will be like a foolish man who built his house on the sand. The rain fell, and the floods came, and the winds blew and slammed against that house; and it fell—and great was its fall" (Matthew 7:24–28; cf. Luke 6:47–49).

Setting: Galilee. After selecting His twelve disciples, Jesus teaches the Sermon on the Mount to the disciples and a great throng from Judea, Jerusalem, and the central coastal region of Tyre and Sidon.

"Why do you call Me, 'Lord, Lord,' and do not do what I say? Everyone who comes to Me and hears My words and acts on them, I will show you whom he is like; he is like a man building a house, who dug deep and laid a foundation on the rock; and when a flood occurred, the torrent burst against that house and could not shake it, because it had been well built. But the one who has heard and has not acted *accordingly,* is like a man who built a house on the ground without any foundation; and the torrent burst against it and immediately it collapsed, and the ruin of that house was great" (Luke 6:46–49; cf. Matthew 7:24–27; see Luke 6:12–19; James 1:22).

Setting: On the way from Galilee to Jerusalem. After responding to a guest's proclamation about the blessings of eating bread in the kingdom of God, Jesus presents to large crowds the demands of discipleship.

Now large crowds were going along with Him; and He turned and said to them, "If anyone comes to Me, and does not hate his own father and mother and wife and children and brothers and sisters, yes, and even his own life, he cannot be My disciple. Whoever does not carry his own cross and come after Me cannot be My disciple. For which one of you, when he wants to build a tower, does not first sit down and calculate the cost to see if he has enough to complete it? Otherwise, when he has laid a foundation and is not able to finish, all who observe it begin to ridicule him, saying, 'This man began to build and was not able to finish.' Or what king, when he sets out to meet another king in battle, will not first sit down and consider whether he is strong enough with ten thousand *men* to encounter the one coming against him with twenty thousand? Or else, while the other is still far away, he sends a delegation and asks for terms of peace. So then, none of you can be My disciple who does not give up all his possessions. Therefore, salt is good; but if even salt has become tasteless, with what will it be seasoned? It is useless either for the soil or for the manure pile; it is thrown out. He who has ears to hear, let him hear" (Luke 14:25–35; cf. Matthew 5:13; 10:37–39; see Proverbs 20:18; Philippians 3:7).

FOUNDATION OF THE WORLD (Listed under WORLD, FOUNDATION OF THE; also see CREATION; and WORLD, BEGINNING OF THE)

FOUNDATION, SOLID (See FOUNDATION)

FOUR THOUSAND (Listed under THOUSAND, FOUR)

FOUR WINDS (Listed under WINDS, FOUR)

FOX (referring to Herod Antipas)

Setting: On the way toward Jerusalem from Galilee. After Jesus responds to a question about who is saved while teaching in the cities and villages some Pharisees ask Him to leave claiming Herod Antipas (tetrarch of Galilee and Perea) seeks to kill Him.

And He said to them, "Go and tell that fox, 'Behold, I cast out demons and perform cures today and tomorrow, and the third *day* I reach My goal.' Nevertheless I must journey on today and tomorrow and the next *day*; for it cannot be that a prophet would perish outside of Jerusalem. O Jerusalem, Jerusalem, *the city* that kills the prophets and stones those sent to her! How often I wanted to gather your children together, just as a hen *gathers* her brood under her wings, and you would not *have it*! Behold, your house is left to you *desolate*; and I say to you, you will not see Me until *the time* comes when you say, 'BLESSED IS HE WHO COMES IN THE NAME OF THE LORD!'" (Luke 13:32-35, Jesus quotes from Psalm 118:26; compare Matthew 23:37).

FOXES

Setting: By the Sea of Galilee. Following a time of casting out evil spirits from the demon-possessed and healing the ill in fulfillment of Isaiah 53:4, Jesus lays out the demands of discipleship to an inquiring scribe.

Then a scribe came and said to Him, "Teacher, I will follow You wherever you go." Jesus said to him, "The foxes have holes and the birds of the air *have* nests, but the Son of Man has nowhere to lay His head." Another of the disciples said to Him, "Lord, permit me first to go and bury my father." But Jesus said to him, "Follow Me, and allow the dead to bury their own dead" (Matthew 8:19-22; compare Luke 9:57-60).

FRAGMENTS

Setting: Near the Sea of Galilee. After revealing to the Jewish religious leadership during the Feast of the Jews that God, John the Baptist, His works, and the Scriptures all testify to His mission, Jesus returns to the Sea of Galilee. He miraculously feeds more than 5,000 people with a lad's five barley loaves and two fish.

Jesus said, "Have the people sit down." Now there was much grass in the place. So the men sat down, in number about five thousand. Jesus took the loaves, and having given thanks, He distributed to those who were seated; likewise also of the fish as much as they wanted. When they were filled, He said to the disciples, "Gather up the leftover fragments so that nothing will be lost" (John 6:10–12; cf. Matthew 14:17–21; Mark 6:38–44; Luke 9:14–17; see Matthew 15:32–38).

FREEDOM (Also see RELEASE)

[FREEDOM from SET FREE]

Setting: The synagogue in Jesus' hometown of Nazareth in Galilee. Early in His public ministry, Jesus reads on the Sabbath from the book of the prophet Isaiah.

And the book of the prophet Isaiah was handed to Him. And He opened the book and found the place where it was written, "THE SPIRIT OF THE LORD IS UPON ME, BECAUSE HE ANOINTED ME TO PREACH THE GOSPEL TO THE POOR. HE HAS SENT ME TO PROCLAIM RELEASE TO THE CAPTIVES, AND RECOVERY OF SIGHT TO THE BLIND, TO SET FREE THOSE WHO ARE OPPRESSED, TO PROCLAIM THE FAVORABLE YEAR OF THE LORD." And He closed the book, gave it back to the attendant and sat down; and the eyes of all in the synagogue were fixed on Him. And He began to say to them, "Today this Scripture has been fulfilled in your hearing" (Luke 4:17–21, Jesus quotes from Isaiah 61:1, 2).

[FREEDOM from FREE]

Setting: The temple treasury in Jerusalem. After the scribes and Pharisees question His testimony about Himself, Jesus reveals to those Jews who believe in Him how He will make them free.

So Jesus was saying to those Jews who had believed Him, "If you continue in My word, *then* you are truly disciples of Mine; and you will know the truth, and the truth will make you free." They answered Him, "We are Abraham's descendants and have never yet been enslaved to anyone; how is it that You say, 'You will become free'?" Jesus answered them, "Truly, truly, I say to you, everyone who commits sin is the slave of sin. The slave does not remain in the house forever; the son does remain forever. So if the Son makes you free, you will be free indeed. I know that you are Abraham's descendants; yet you seek to kill Me, because My word has no place in you. I speak the things which I have seen with *My* Father; therefore you also do the things which you heard from *your* father" (John 8:31–38; see Romans 6:16).

FRIEND (Also see COMPANIONS; and FRIENDS)

Setting: Galilee. After praising John the Baptist as His forerunner, Jesus demonstrates the foolish thinking of the current generation of Jewish religious leaders by comparing what they say about John's ascetic lifestyle and ministry along with His own.

"But to what shall I compare this generation? It is like children sitting in the market places, who call out to the other *children,* and say, 'We played the flute for you, and you did not dance; we sang a dirge, and you did not mourn.' For John came neither eating nor drinking, and they say, 'He has a demon!' The Son of Man came eating and drinking, and they say, 'Behold, a gluttonous man and a drunkard, a friend of tax collectors and sinners! Yet wisdom is vindicated by her deeds" (Matthew 11:16–19; cf. Luke 7:31–35; see Matthew 9:11, 34; Luke 1:15).

Setting: Judea beyond the Jordan (Perea). Jesus illustrates the kingdom of heaven to His disciples through the story of laborers in the vineyard.

"For the kingdom of heaven is like a landowner who went out early in the morning to hire laborers for his vineyard. When he had agreed with the laborers for a denarius for the day, he sent them into his vineyard. And he went out about the third hour and saw others standing idle in the market place; and to those he said, 'You also go into the vineyard, and whatever is right I will give you.' And *so* they went. Again he went out about the sixth and the ninth hour, and did the same thing. And about the eleventh *hour* he went out and found others standing *around;* and he said to them, 'Why have you been standing idle here all day long?' They said to him, 'Because no one hired us.' He said to them, 'You go into the vineyard too.' When evening came, the owner of the vineyard said to his foreman, 'Call the laborers and pay them their wages, beginning with the last *group* to the first.' When those *hired* about the eleventh hour came, each one received a denarius. When those *hired* first came, they thought that they would receive more; but each of them also received a denarius. When they received it, they grumbled at the landowner, saying, 'These last men have worked *only* one hour, and you have made them equal to us who have borne the burden and the scorching heat of the day.' But he answered and said to one of them, 'Friend, I am doing you no wrong; did you not agree with me for a denarius? Take what is yours and go, but I wish to give to this last man the same as to you. It is not lawful for me to do what I wish with what is my own? Or is your eye envious because I am generous?' So the last shall be first, and the first last" (Matthew 20:1–16; cf. Matthew 19:30).

Setting: The temple in Jerusalem. Jesus speaks another parable to the chief priests and elders after they question His authority.

Jesus spoke to them again in parables, saying, "The kingdom of heaven may be compared to a king who gave a wedding feast for his son. And he sent out his slaves to call those who had been invited to the wedding feast, and they were unwilling to come. Again he sent out other slaves saying, 'Tell those who have been invited, "Behold, I have prepared my dinner; my oxen and my fattened livestock are *all* butchered and everything is ready; come to the wedding feast." But they paid no attention and went their way, one to his own farm, another to his business, and the rest seized his slaves and mistreated them and killed them. But the king was enraged, and he sent his armies and destroyed those murderers and set their city on fire. Then he said to his slaves, 'The wedding is ready, but those who were invited were not worthy. 'Go therefore to the main highways, and as many as you find *there,* invite to the wedding feast.' Those slaves went out into the streets and gathered together all they found, both evil and good; and the wedding hall was filled with dinner guests. But when the king came in to look over the dinner guests, he saw a man there who was not dressed in wedding clothes, and he said to him, 'Friend, how did you come in here without wedding clothes?' And the man was speechless. Then the king said to the servants, 'Bind him hand and foot, and throw him into the outer darkness; in that place there will be weeping and gnashing of teeth.' For many are called, but few *are* chosen" (Matthew 22:1–14; cf. Matthew 8:11, 12).

Setting: The Garden of Gethsemane, east of the temple in Jerusalem. After praying for God's will to be done, Jesus submits to His Father's will and allows Judas to betray Him.

And Jesus said to him, "Friend, *do* what you have come for." Then they came and laid hands on Jesus and seized Him. (Matthew 26:50; cf. Mark 14:43–46; Luke 22:47–48; John 18:2–9).

Setting: Galilee. As some Pharisees and teachers of the law from Galilee and Judea look on, several men lower a paralyzed man through the roof in front of Jesus.

Seeing their faith, He said, "Friend, your sins are forgiven you" (Luke 5:20; cf. Mark 2:2–12; see Matthew 9:1–8).

Setting: Galilee. After praising John the Baptist to the crowds, Jesus criticizes the Pharisees and lawyers who reject God's purpose and John's message.

"To what then shall I compare the men of this generation, and what are they like? They are like children who sit in the market place and call to one another, and they say, 'We played the flute for you, and you did not dance; we sang a dirge, and you did not weep.' For John the Baptist has come eating no bread and drinking no wine, and you say, 'He has a demon!' The Son of Man has come eating and drinking, and you say, 'Behold, a gluttonous man and a drunkard, a friend of tax collectors and sinners!' Yet wisdom is vindicated by all her children" (Luke 7:31–35; cf. Matthew 11:16–19; see Luke 1:15).

Setting: On the way from Galilee to Jerusalem. After revealing to His disciples how to pray, Jesus illustrates persistence in prayer.

Then He said to them, "Suppose one of you has a friend, and goes to him at midnight and says to him, 'Friend, lend me three loaves; for a friend of mine has come to me from a journey, and I have nothing to set before him'; and from inside he answers and says, 'Do not bother me; the door has already been shut and my children and I are in bed; I cannot get up and give you *anything.*' I tell you, even though he will not get up and give him *anything* because he is his friend, yet because of his persistence he will get up and give him as much as he needs. So I say to you, ask, and it will be given to you; seek, and you will find; knock, and it will be opened to you. For everyone who asks, receives; and he who seeks, finds; and to him who knocks, it will be opened" (Luke 11:5–10; cf. Matthew 7:7, 8; see Luke 18:1–5).

Setting: On the way from Galilee to Jerusalem. Observing the guests of a Pharisee leader selecting places of honor at the dinner table on the Sabbath, Jesus relates to them a parable.

And He *began* speaking a parable to the invited guests when He noticed how they had been picking out the places of honor *at the table,* saying to them, "When you are invited by someone to a wedding feast, do not take the place of honor, for someone more distinguished than you may have been invited by him, and he who invited you both will come and say to you, 'Give *your* place to this man, and then in disgrace you proceed to occupy the last place. But when you are invited, go and recline at the last place, so that when the one who has invited you comes, he may say to you, 'Friend, move up higher'; then you will have honor in the sight of all who are at the table with you. For everyone who exalts himself will be humbled, and he who humbles himself will be exalted" (Luke 14:7–11; see 2 Samuel 22:28; Proverbs 25:6, 7; Matthew 23:6; Luke 14:1, 2).

Setting: Beyond the Jordan. While Jesus and His disciples are avoiding the Jerusalem Pharisees, He receives word from Lazarus's sisters in Bethany of His friend's sickness and decides to go there.

Then after this He said to the disciples, "Let us go to Judea again." The disciples said to Him, "Rabbi, the Jews were just now seeking to stone You, and are You going there again?" Jesus answered, "Are there not twelve hours in the day? If anyone walks in the day, he does not stumble, because he sees the light of this world. But if anyone walks in the night, he stumbles, because the light is not in him." This He said, and after that He said to them, "Our friend Lazarus has fallen asleep; but I go, so that I may awaken him out of sleep" (John 11:7–11; see John 8:59; 10:39).

FRIENDS (Also see COMPANIONS; and FRIEND)

Setting: Galilee. During the early part of His ministry, Jesus preaches the Sermon on the Mount to His disciples and the multitudes.

"Make friends quickly with your opponent at law while you are with him on the way, so that your opponent may not hand you over to the judge, and the judge to the officer, and you be thrown into prison. Truly I say to you, you will not come out of there until you have paid up the last cent'" (Matthew 5:25, 26; cf. Luke 12:58, 59).

Setting: On the way from Galilee to Jerusalem. Jesus warns His disciples of future events. The scribes and Pharisees turn hostile and question Him repeatedly in an attempt to catch Him in something He might say.

Under these circumstances, after so many thousands of people had gathered together that they were stepping on one another, He began saying to His disciples first *of all,* "Beware of the leaven of the Pharisees, which is hypocrisy. But there is nothing covered up that will not be revealed, and hidden that will not be known. Accordingly, whatever you have said in the dark will be heard in the light, and what you have whispered in the inner rooms will be proclaimed upon the housetops. I say to you, My friends, do not be afraid of those who kill the body and after that have no more that they can do. But I will warn you whom to fear: fear the One who, after He has killed, has authority to cast into hell; yes, I tell you, fear Him! Are not five sparrows sold for two cents? *Yet* not one of them is forgotten before God. Indeed, the very hairs of your head are all numbered. Do not fear; you are more valuable than many sparrows" (Luke 12:1–7; cf. Matthew 10:26–31; see Matthew 16:6; Hebrews 10:31).

Setting: On the way from Galilee to Jerusalem. Observing the guests of a Pharisee leader selecting places of honor at the dinner table on the Sabbath, Jesus relates to them a parable. Then He comments to the host about the people to invite in the future.

And He also went on to say to the one who had invited Him, "When you give a luncheon or a dinner, do not invite your friends or your brothers or your relatives or rich neighbors, otherwise they may also invite you in return and *that* will be your repayment. But when you give a reception, invite *the* poor, *the* crippled, *the* lame, *the* blind, and you will be blessed, since they do not have *the means* to repay you; for you will be repaid at the resurrection of the righteous" (Luke 14:12–14; see Luke 14:1–2, 15; John 5:28, 29).

Setting: On the way from Galilee to Jerusalem. After Jesus presents to large crowds the demands of discipleship, the Pharisees and scribes complain He associates with tax collectors and sinners.

So He told them this parable, saying, "What man among you, if he has a hundred sheep and has lost one of them, does not leave the ninety-nine in the open pasture and go after the one which is lost until he finds it? When he has found it, he lays it on his shoulders, rejoicing. And when he comes home, he calls together his friends and his neighbors, saying to them, 'Rejoice with me, for I have found my sheep which was lost!' I tell you that in the same way, there will be *more* joy in heaven over one sinner who repents than over ninety-nine righteous persons who need no repentance" (Luke 15:3–7; cf. Matthew 18:12–14; see Matthew 9:11–13; Luke 5:29–32).

Setting: On the way from Galilee to Jerusalem. Jesus conveys the principles of the lost sheep and the lost coin because the Pharisees and scribes complain He associates with tax collectors and sinners.

"So He told them this parable, saying, "What man among you, if he has a hundred sheep and has lost one of them, does not leave the ninety-nine in the open pasture and go after the one which is lost until he finds it? When he has found it, he lays it on his shoulders, rejoicing. And when he comes home, he calls together his friends and his neighbors, saying to them, 'Rejoice with me, for I have found my sheep which was lost!' I tell you that in the same way, there will be more joy in heaven over one sinner who repents than over ninety-nine righteous persons who need no repentance. Or what woman, if she has ten silver coins and loses one coin, does not light a lamp and sweep the house and search carefully until she finds it? When she has found it, she calls together her friends and neighbors, saying, 'Rejoice with me, for I have found the coin which I had lost!' In the same way, I tell you, there is joy in the presence of the angels of God over one sinner who repents" (Luke 15:3–10; cf. Matthew 18:12-14; see Matthew 9:11-13).

Setting: On the way from Galilee to Jerusalem. Jesus conveys the illustration of the prodigal son because the Pharisees and scribes complain He associates with tax collectors and sinners.

And He said, "A man had two sons. The younger of them said to his father, 'Father, give me the share of the estate that falls to me.' So he divided his wealth between them. And not many days later, the younger son gathered everything together and went on a journey into a distant country, and there he squandered his estate with loose living. Now when he had spent everything, a severe famine occurred in that country, and he began to be impoverished. So he went and hired himself out to one of the citizens of that country, and he sent him into his fields to feed swine. And he would have gladly filled his stomach with the pods that the swine were eating, and no one was giving *anything* to him. But when he came to his senses, he said, 'How many of my father's hired men have more than enough bread, but I am dying here with hunger! I will get up and go to my father, and will say to him, "Father, I have sinned against heaven, and in your sight; I am no longer worthy to be called your son; make me as one of your hired men."' So he got up and came to his father. But while he was still a long way off, his father saw him and felt compassion *for him,* and ran and embraced him and kissed him. And the son said to him, "Father, I have sinned against heaven and in your sight; I am no longer worthy to be called your son.' But the father said to his slaves, 'Quickly bring out the best robe and put it on him, and put a ring on his hand and sandals on his feet; and bring the fattened calf, kill it, and let us eat and celebrate; for this son of mine was dead and has come to life again; he was lost and has been found.' And they began to celebrate. Now his older son was in the field, when he came and approached the house, he heard music and dancing. And he summoned one of the servants and *began* inquiring what these things could be. And he said to him, 'Your brother has come, and your father has killed the fattened calf because he has received him back safe and sound.' But he became angry and was not willing to go in; and his father came out and *began* pleading with him. But he answered and said to his father, 'Look! For so many years I have been serving you and I have never neglected a command of yours; and *yet* you have never given me a young goat, so that I might celebrate with my friends; but when this son of yours came, who has devoured your wealth with prostitutes, you killed the fattened calf for him.' And he said to him, 'Son, you have always been with me, and all that is mine is yours. But we had to celebrate and rejoice, for this brother of yours was dead and *has begun* to live, and was lost and has been found' " Luke 15:11–32; see Proverbs 29:2; Luke 15:1, 2).

Setting: On the way from Galilee to Jerusalem. After giving them the story of the prodigal son, the Lord teaches His disciples about stewardship.

Now He was also saying to the disciples, "There was a rich man who had a manager, and this *manager* was reported to him as squandering his possessions. And he called him and said to him, 'What is this I hear about you? Give an accounting of your management, for you can no longer be a manager.' The manager said to himself, 'What shall I do, since my master is taking the management away from me? I am not strong enough to dig; I am ashamed to beg. I know what I shall do, so that when I am removed from the management people will welcome me into their homes.' And he summoned each one of his master's debtors, and he *began* saying to the first, 'How much do you owe my master?' And he said, 'A hundred measures of oil.' And he said to him, 'Take your bill, and sit down quickly and write fifty.' Then he said to another, 'And how much do you owe?' And he said, 'A hundred measures of wheat.' He said to him, 'Take your bill, and write eighty.' And his master praised the unrighteous manager because he had acted shrewdly; for the sons of this age are more shrewd in relation to their own kind than the sons of light. And I say to you, make friends for yourselves by means of the wealth of unrighteousness, so that when it fails, they will receive you into the eternal dwellings. He who is faithful in a very little thing is faithful also in much; and he who is unrighteous in a very little thing is unrighteous also in much. Therefore if you have not been faithful in the *use of* unrighteous wealth, who will entrust the *true riches* to you? And if you have not been faithful in *the use of* that which is another's, who will give you that which is your own? No servant can serve two masters; for either he will hate the one and love the other, or else he will be devoted to one and despise the other. You cannot serve God and wealth" (Luke 16:1–13; cf. Matthew 6:24; see Matthew 25:14–30).

Setting: The Mount of Olives, east of the temple in Jerusalem. After ministering in the temple and giving the disciples more details regarding the temple's future destruction, Jesus elaborates about other things to come during His Olivet Discourse.

Then He continued by saying to them, "Nation will rise against nation and kingdom against kingdom, and there will be great earthquakes, and in various places plagues and famines; and there will be terrors and great signs from heaven. But before all these things, they will lay their hands on you and will persecute you, delivering you to the synagogues and prisons, bringing you before kings and governors for My name's sake. It will lead to an opportunity for your testimony. So make up your minds not to prepare beforehand to defend yourselves; for I will give you utterance and wisdom which none of your opponents will be able to resist or refute. But you will be betrayed even by parents and brothers and relatives and friends, and they will put *some* of you to death, and you will be hated by all because of My name. Yet not a hair of your head will perish. By your endurance you will gain your lives" (Luke 21:10–19; cf. Matthew 10:19–22; 24:7–14; Mark 13:8–13; see Luke 21:5–9).

Setting: Jerusalem. Before the Passover, with His departure in mind, after explaining He is the vine and His disciples are the branches, Jesus instructs them to love one another.

"This is My commandment, that you love one another, just as I have loved you. Greater love has no one than this, that one lay down his life for his friends. You are My friends if you do what I command you. No longer do I call you slaves, for the slave does not know what his master is doing; but I have called you friends, for all things that I have heard from My Father I have made known to you. You did not choose Me but I chose you, and appointed you that you would go and bear fruit, and *that* your fruit would remain, so that whatever you ask of the Father in My name He may give to you. This I command you, that you love one another" (John 15:12–17; see Matthew 12:50; John 6:70; 8:26; 10:11; 13:34).

FRUIT (FRUIT, BAD; FRUIT, GOOD; FRUIT-BEARING; and FRUIT OF THE VINE are separate entries; also see DEEDS; and FRUITS)

Setting: Galilee. After He heals a blind, mute, demon-possessed man, the Pharisees accuse Jesus in front of crowds of being a worker of Satan.

"Either make the tree good and its fruit good, or make the tree bad and its fruit bad; for the tree is known by its fruit. You brood of vipers, how can you, being evil, speak what is good? For the mouth speaks out of that which fills the heart. The good man brings out of *his* good treasure what is good; and the evil man brings out of *his* evil treasure what is evil. But I tell you that every careless word that people speak, they shall give an accounting for it in the day of judgment. For by your words you will be justified, and by your words you will be condemned" (Matthew 12:33–37; cf. Matthew 3:7; 7:16–18).

Setting: By the Sea of Galilee. With the Jewish religious leaders rejecting His message, Jesus begins to teach in parables, then explains to His disciples the meaning of the Parable of the Sower.

"Hear then the parable of the sower. When anyone hears the word of the kingdom and does not understand it, the evil *one* comes and snatches away what has been sown in his heart. This is the one on whom seed was sown beside the road. The one on whom seed was sown on the rocky places, this is the man who hears the word and immediately receives it with joy; yet he has no *firm* root in himself, but is *only* temporary, and when affliction or persecution arises because of the word, immediately he falls away. And the one on whom seed was sown among the thorns, this is the man who hears the word, and the worry of the world and the deceitfulness of wealth choke the word, and it becomes unfruitful. And the one on whom seed was sown on the good soil, this is the man who hears the word and understands it; who indeed bears fruit and brings forth, some a hundredfold, some sixty, and some thirty" (Matthew 13:18–23; cf. Mark 4:13–20; Luke 8:11–15).

Setting: On the way from Bethany to Jerusalem. After cleansing the temple by driving out the money changers and merchants, Jesus spends the night in Bethany, The next day, He becomes hungry and notices a barren fig tree.

Seeing a lone fig tree by the road, He came to it and found nothing on it except leaves only; and He said to it, "No longer shall there ever be *any* fruit from you." And at once the fig tree withered (Matthew 21:19; cf. Mark 11:12–14; see Luke 13:6–9).

Setting: The temple in Jerusalem. Jesus delivers a prophecy to the chief priests and elders after they question His authority.

Jesus said to them, "Did you never read in the Scriptures, 'THE STONE WHICH THE BUILDERS REJECTED, THIS BECAME THE CHIEF CORNER *stone;* THIS CAME ABOUT FROM THE LORD, AND IT IS MARVELOUS IN OUR EYES'? Therefore I say to you, the kingdom of God will be taken away from you and given to a people, producing the fruit of it. And he who falls on this stone will be broken to pieces; but on whomever it falls, it will scatter him like dust" (Matthew 21:42–44, Jesus quotes from Psalm 118:22; cf. Isaiah 8:14, 15; Mark 12:10, 11; Luke 20:17, 18).

Setting: By the Sea of Galilee. During the early part of His ministry, after presenting the Parable of the Sower from a boat to a very large crowd, Jesus explains the meaning to His disciples and followers.

And He said to them, "Do you not understand this parable? How will you understand all the parables? The sower sows the word. These are the ones who are beside the road where the word is sown; and when they hear, immediately Satan comes and takes away the word which has been sown in them. In a similar way these are the ones on whom seed was sown on the rocky places, who, when they hear the word, immediately receive it with joy; and they have no *firm* root in themselves, but are *only* temporary; then, when affliction or persecution arises because of the word, immediately they fall away. And others are the ones on whom seed was sown among the thorns; these are the ones who have heard the word, but the worries of the world and the deceitfulness of riches, and the desires for other things enter in and choke the word, and it becomes unfruitful. And those are the ones on whom seed was sown on the good soil; and they hear the word and accept it and bear fruit, thirty, sixty, and a hundredfold" (Mark 4:13–20; cf. Matthew 13:18–23; Luke 8:11–15).

Setting: Between Bethany and Jerusalem. The day after His triumphal entry into Jerusalem, just days before His impending death on the cross, Jesus curses a fig tree that has no fruit on it.

He said to it, "May no one ever eat fruit from you again!" And His disciples were listening (Mark 11:14; cf. Matthew 21:18, 19).

Setting: Galilee. After selecting His twelve disciples, Jesus teaches the Sermon on the Mount to those disciples and a great throng from Judea, Jerusalem, and the central coastal region of Tyre and Sidon.

And He also spoke a parable to them: "A blind man cannot guide a blind man, can he? Will they not both fall into a pit? A pupil is not above his teacher; but everyone, after he has been fully trained, will be like his teacher. Why do you look at the speck that is in your brother's eye, but do not notice the log that is in your own eye? Or how can you say to your brother, 'Brother, let me take out the speck that is in your eye,' when you yourself do not see the log that is in your own eye? You hypocrite, first take the log out of your own eye, and then you will see clearly to take out the speck that is in your brother's eye. For there is no good tree which produces bad fruit, nor, on the other hand, a bad tree which produces good fruit. For each tree is known by its own fruit. For men do not gather figs from thorns, nor do they pick grapes from a briar bush. The good man out of the good treasure of his heart brings forth what is good; and the evil *man* out of the evil *treasure* brings forth what is evil; for his mouth speaks from that which fills his heart" (Luke 6:39–45; cf. Matthew 7:3–6. 16, 18, 20; 12:35; see Matthew 10:24; 15:14; Luke 6:12–19).

Setting: On the way from Galilee to Jerusalem. After some present report to Him about the Galileans whose blood Pilate (Roman governor of Judea) had mixed with their sacrifices, Jesus responds to their concern by calling them to repentance and illustrating His point with a parable.

And He *began* telling this parable: "A man had a fig tree which had been planted in his vineyard; and he came looking for fruit on it and did not find any. And he said to the vineyard-keeper, 'Behold, for three years I have come looking for fruit on this fig tree without finding any. Cut it down! Why does it even use up the ground?' And he answered and said to him, 'Let it alone, sir, for this year too, until I dig around it and put fertilizer; and if it bears fruit next year, *fine*; but if not, cut it down'" (Luke 13:6–9; see Matthew 3:10).

Setting: Sychar in Samaria. After Jesus converses with a Samaritan woman at Jacob's well, His disciples return with food. They try to get Jesus to eat but are surprised when He speaks of other food.

Jesus said to them, "My food is to do the will of Him who sent Me and to accomplish His work. Do you not say, 'There are yet four months, and *then* comes the harvest'? Behold, I say to you, lift up your eyes and look on the fields, that they are white for harvest. Already he who reaps is receiving wages and is gathering fruit for life eternal; so that he who sows and he who reaps may rejoice together. For in this *case* the saying is true, 'One sows and another reaps.' I sent you to reap that for which you have not labored; others have labored and you have entered into their labor" (John 4:34–38; see Matthew 9:37, 38; John 5:36).

Setting: Jerusalem. Before the Passover, with His departure in mind, after explaining He is the vine and His disciples are the branches, Jesus instructs them to love one another.

"This is My commandment, that you love one another, just as I have loved you. Greater love has no one than this, that one lay down his life for his friends. You are My friends if you do what I command you. No longer do I call you slaves, for the slave does not know what his master is doing; but I have called you friends, for all things that I have heard from My Father I have made known to you. You did not choose Me but I chose you, and appointed you that you would go and bear fruit, and *that* your fruit would remain, so that whatever you ask of the Father in My name He may give to you. This I command you, that you love one another" (John 15:12–17; see Matthew 12:50; John 6:70; 8:26; 10:11; 13:34).

FRUIT, BAD

Setting: Galilee. During the early part of His ministry, Jesus preaches the Sermon on the Mount to His disciples and the multitudes.

"Beware of the false prophets, who come to you in sheep's clothing, but inwardly are ravenous wolves. You will know them by their fruits. Grapes are not gathered from *bushes* nor figs from thistles, are they? So every good tree bears good fruit, but the bad tree bears bad fruit. A good tree cannot produce bad fruit, nor can a bad tree produce good fruit. Every tree that does not bear good fruit is cut down and thrown into the fire. So then, you will know them by their fruits" (Matthew 7:15–20; cf. Matthew 3:10; 12:33, 35; 24:11, 24; Luke 6:43, 44).

Setting: Galilee. After He heals a blind, mute, demon-possessed man, the Pharisees accuse Jesus in front of crowds of being a worker of Satan.

"Either make the tree good and its fruit good, or make the tree bad and its fruit bad; for the tree is known by its fruit. You brood of vipers, how can you, being evil, speak what is good? For the mouth speaks out of that which fills the heart. The good man brings out of *his* good treasure what is good; and the evil man brings out of *his* evil treasure what is evil. But I tell you that every careless word that people speak, they shall give an accounting for it in the day of judgment. For by your words you will be justified, and by your words you will be condemned" (Matthew 12:33–37; cf. Matthew 3:7; 7:16–18).

Setting: Galilee. After selecting His twelve disciples, Jesus teaches the Sermon on the Mount to those disciples and a great throng from Judea, Jerusalem, and the central coastal region of Tyre and Sidon.

And He also spoke a parable to them: "A blind man cannot guide a blind man, can he? Will they not both fall into a pit? A pupil is not above his teacher; but everyone, after he has been fully trained, will be like his teacher. Why do you look at the speck that is in your brother's eye, but do not notice the log that is in your own eye? Or how can you say to your brother, 'Brother, let me take out the speck that is in your eye,' when you yourself do not see the log that is in your own eye? You hypocrite, first take the log out of your own eye, and then you will see clearly to take out the speck that is in your brother's eye. For there is no good tree which produces bad fruit, nor, on the other hand, a bad tree which produces good fruit. For each tree is known by its own fruit. For men do not gather figs from thorns, nor do they pick grapes from a briar bush. The good man out of the good treasure of his heart brings forth what is good; and the evil *man* out of the evil *treasure* brings forth what is evil; for his mouth speaks from that which fills his heart" (Luke 6:39–45; cf. Matthew 7:3–6. 16, 18, 20; 12:35; see Matthew 10:24; 15:14; Luke 6:12–19).

FRUIT, GOOD

Setting: Galilee. During the early part of His ministry, Jesus preaches the Sermon on the Mount to His disciples and the multitudes.

"Beware of the false prophets, who come to you in sheep's clothing, but inwardly are ravenous wolves. You will know them by their fruits. Grapes are not gathered from *bushes* nor figs from thistles, are they? So every good tree bears good fruit, but the bad tree bears bad fruit. A good tree cannot produce bad fruit nor can a bad tree produce good fruit. Every tree that does not bear good fruit is cut down and thrown into the fire. So then, you will know them by their fruits" (Matthew 7:15–20; cf. Matthew 3:10; 12:33, 35; 24:11, 24; Luke 6:43, 44).

[GOOD FRUIT from fruit good]

Setting: Galilee. After He heals a blind, mute, demon-possessed man, the Pharisees accuse Jesus in front of crowds of being a worker of Satan.

"Either make the tree good and its fruit good, or make the tree bad and its fruit bad; for the tree is known by its fruit. You brood of vipers, how can you, being evil, speak what is good? For the mouth speaks out of that which fills the heart. The good man brings out of *his* good treasure what is good; and the evil man brings out of *his* evil treasure what is evil. But I tell you that every careless word that people speak, they shall give an accounting for it in the day of judgment. For by your words you will be justified, and by your words you will be condemned" (Matthew 12:33–37; cf. Matthew 3:7; 7:16–18).

Setting: Galilee. After selecting His twelve disciples, Jesus teaches the Sermon on the Mount to those disciples and a great throng from Judea, Jerusalem, and the central coastal region of Tyre and Sidon.

And He also spoke a parable to them: "A blind man cannot guide a blind man, can he? Will they not both fall into a pit? A pupil is not above his teacher; but everyone, after he has been fully trained, will be like his teacher. Why do you look at the speck that is in your brother's eye, but do not notice the log that is in your own eye? Or how can you say to your brother, 'Brother, let me take out the speck that is in your eye,' when you yourself do not see the log that is in your own eye? You hypocrite, first take the log out of your own eye, and then you will see clearly to take out the speck that is in your brother's eye. For there is no good tree which produces bad fruit, nor, on the other hand, a bad tree which produces good fruit. For each tree is known by its own fruit. For men do not gather figs from thorns, nor do they pick grapes from a briar bush. The good man out of the good treasure of his heart brings forth what is good; and the evil *man* out of the evil *treasure* brings forth what is evil; for his mouth speaks from that which fills his heart" (Luke 6:39–45; cf. Matthew 7:3–6. 16, 18, 20; 12:35; see Matthew 10:24; 15:14; Luke 6:12–19).

FRUIT, NO

[NO FRUIT from No longer shall there ever be *any* fruit from you]

Setting: On the way from Bethany to Jerusalem. After cleansing the temple by driving out the money changers and merchants, Jesus spends the night in Bethany. The next day, He becomes hungry and notices a barren fig tree.

Seeing a lone fig tree by the road, He came to it and found nothing on it except leaves only; and He said to it, "No longer shall there ever be *any* fruit from you." And at once the fig tree withered (Matthew 21:19; cf. Mark 11:12–14; see Matthew 21:18; Luke 13:6–9).

[NO FRUIT from May no one ever eat fruit from you again]

Setting: Between Bethany and Jerusalem. The day after His triumphal entry into Jerusalem, just days before His impending death on the cross, Jesus curses a fig tree that has no fruit on it.

He said to it, "May no one ever eat fruit from you again!" And His disciples were listening (Mark 11:14; cf. Matthew 21:18, 19).

Setting: Galilee. After Jesus presents the Parable of the Sower to the crowds, His disciples ask Him to explain the parable's meaning.

And He said, "To you it has been granted to know the mysteries of the kingdom of God, but to the rest *it is* in parables, so that SEEING THEY MAY NOT SEE, AND HEARING THEY MAY NOT UNDERSTAND. Now the parable is this: the seed is the word of God. Those beside the road are those who have heard; then the devil comes and takes away the word from their heart, so that they will not believe and be saved. Those on the rocky *soil* are those who, when they hear, receive the word with joy; and these have no *firm* root; they believe for a while, and in time of temptation fall away. The *seed* which fell among the thorns, these are the ones who have heard, and as they go on their way they are choked with worries and riches and pleasures of *this* life, and bring no fruit to maturity. But the *seed* in the good soil, these are the ones who have heard the word in an honest and good heart, and hold it fast, and bear fruit with perseverance" (Luke 8:10–15, Jesus quotes from Isaiah 6:9; cf. Matthew 13:10–23; Mark 4:10–20).

FRUIT OF THE VINE (Also see GRAPES; VINE; and WINE)

Setting: An upper room in Jerusalem. While celebrating the Passover meal in Jerusalem with His disciples, Jesus institutes the Lord's Supper ordinance before being arrested by His enemies.

While they were eating, Jesus took *some* bread, and after a blessing, He broke *it* and gave *it* to the disciples, and said, "Take, eat; this is My body." And when He had taken a cup and given thanks, He gave *it* to them saying, "Drink from it, all of you; for this is My blood of the covenant, which is poured out for many for forgiveness of sins. But I say to you, I will not drink of this fruit of the vine from now on until that day when I drink it new with you in My Father's kingdom" (Matthew 26:26–29; cf. Mark 14:22–25; Luke 22:17–20; 1 Corinthians 11:23–26; see 1 Corinthians 10:16).

Setting: An upper room in Jerusalem. While celebrating the Feast of Unleavened Bread (Passover) with His disciples, Jesus institutes the ordinance of the Lord's Supper.

While they were eating, He took *some* bread, and after a blessing He broke *it,* and gave *it* to them, and said, "Take *it;* this is My body." And when He had taken a cup *and* given thanks, He gave *it* to them, and they all drank from it. And He said to them, "This is My blood of the covenant, which is poured out for many. Truly I say to you, I will never again drink of the fruit of the vine until that day when I drink it new in the kingdom of God" (Mark 14:22–25; cf. Matthew 26:26–29; Luke 22:17–20; 1 Corinthians 11:23–26; see Exodus 24:8).

Setting: An upper room in Jerusalem. During the Feast of Unleavened Bread (Passover) just before His crucifixion, while celebrating the Passover meal with His disciples, Jesus institutes the Lord's Supper.

And when He had taken a cup *and* given thanks, He said, "Take this and share it among yourselves; for I say to you, I will not drink of the fruit of the vine from now on until the kingdom of God comes." And when he had taken *some* bread and given thanks, He broke it and gave it to them, saying, "This is My body which is given for you; do this in remembrance of Me." And in the same way *He took* the cup after they had eaten, saying, "This cup which is poured out for you is the new covenant in My blood. But behold, the hand of the one betraying Me is with Mine on the table. For indeed, the Son of Man is going as it has been determined; but woe to that man by whom He is betrayed!" (Luke 22:17–22; cf. Matthew 26:26–29; Mark 14:22–25; 1 Corinthians 11:23–26; see Psalm 41:9; Luke 14:15; 1 Corinthians 10:16).

FRUIT-BEARING (Also see FRUIT)

[FRUIT-BEARING from bears fruit]

Setting: By the Sea of Galilee. With the religious leadership rejecting His message, Jesus begins to teach in parables, and explains to His disciples the meaning of the Parable of the Sower.

"Hear then the parable of the sower. When anyone hears the word of the kingdom and does not understand it, the evil *one* comes and snatches away what has been sown in his heart. This is the one on whom seed was sown beside the road. The one on whom seed was sown on the rocky places, this is the man who hears the word and immediately receives it with joy; yet he has no *firm* root in himself, but is *only* temporary, and when affliction or persecution arises because of the word, immediately he falls away. And the one on whom seed was sown among the thorns, this is the man who hears the word, and the worry of the world and the deceitfulness of wealth choke the word, and it becomes unfruitful. And the one on whom seed was sown on the good soil, this is the man who hears the word and understands it; who indeed bears fruit and brings forth, some a hundredfold, some sixty, and some thirty" (Matthew 13:18–23; cf. Mark 4:13–20; Luke 8:11–15; see Matthew 13:8).

[FRUIT-BEARING from bear fruit]
Setting: By the Sea of Galilee. During the early part of His ministry, after presenting the Parable of the Sower from a boat to a very large crowd, Jesus explains to His disciples and followers the meaning of the parable.

And He said to them, "Do you not understand this parable? How will you understand all the parables? The sower sows the word. These are the ones who are beside the road where the word is sown; and when they hear, immediately Satan comes and takes away the word which has been sown in them. In a similar way these are the ones on whom seed was sown on the rocky places, who, when they hear the word, immediately receive it with joy; and they have no *firm* root in themselves, but are *only* temporary; then, when affliction or persecution arises because of the word, immediately they fall away. And others are the ones on whom seed was sown among the thorns; these are the ones who have heard the word, but the worries of the world and the deceitfulness of riches, and the desires for other things enter in and choke the word, and it becomes unfruitful. And those are the ones on whom seed was sown on the good soil; and they hear the word and accept it and bear fruit, thirty, sixty, and a hundredfold" (Mark 4:13–20; cf. Matthew 13:18–23; Luke 8:11–15).

[FRUIT-BEARING from bear fruit]
Setting: Galilee. After Jesus presents the Parable of the Sower to the crowds, His disciples ask Him to explain the parable's meaning.

And He said, "To you it has been granted to know the mysteries of the kingdom of God, but to the rest *it is* in parables, so that SEEING THEY MAY NOT SEE, AND HEARING THEY MAY NOT UNDERSTAND. Now the parable is this: the seed is the word of God. Those beside the road are those who have heard; then the devil comes and takes away the word from their heart, so that they will not believe and be saved. Those on the rocky *soil* are those who, when they hear, receive the word with joy; and these have no *firm* root; they believe for a while, and in time of temptation fall away. The *seed* which fell among the thorns, these are the ones who have heard, and as they go on their way they are choked with worries and riches and pleasures of *this* life, and bring no fruit to maturity. But the *seed* in the good soil, these are the ones who have heard the word in an honest and good heart, and hold it fast, and bear fruit with perseverance" (Luke 8:10–15, Jesus quotes from Isaiah 6:9; cf. Matthew 13:10–23; Mark 4:10–20).

[FRUIT-BEARING from bears fruit]
Setting: On the way from Galilee to Jerusalem. After some present report to Him about the Galileans whose blood Pilate (Roman governor of Judea) had mixed with their sacrifices, Jesus responds to their concern by calling them to repentance and illustrating His point with a parable.

And He *began* telling this parable: "A man had a fig tree which had been planted in his vineyard; and he came looking for fruit on it and did not find any. And he said to the vineyard-keeper, 'Behold, for three years I have come looking for fruit on this fig tree without finding any. Cut it down! Why does it even use up the ground?' And he answered and said to him, 'Let it alone, sir, for this year too, until I dig around it and put fertilizer; and if it bears fruit next year, *fine*; but if not, cut it down'" (Luke 13:6–9; see Matthew 3:10).

[FRUIT-BEARING from bears much fruit]
Setting: Jerusalem. Just days before the Passover, with the chief priests and Pharisees plotting to seize Him, crowds welcome Jesus with palm branches and praise, and some Greeks ask to meet Him.

And Jesus answered them, saying, "The hour has come for the Son of Man to be glorified. Truly, truly, I say to you, unless a grain of wheat falls into the earth and dies, it remains alone; but if it dies, it bears much fruit. He who loves his life loses it, and he who hates his life in this world will keep it to life eternal. If anyone serves Me, he must follow Me; and where I am, there My servant will be also; if anyone serves Me, the Father will honor him" (John 12:23–26; see Matthew 10:39).

[FRUIT-BEARING from bear fruit; bears fruit; bear more fruit; bears much fruit; and bear much fruit]
Setting: Jerusalem. Before the Passover, after conveying the upcoming ministry of the Holy Spirit in His disciples' lives with His imminent departure from them, Jesus explains He is the vine and they are the branches.

"I am the true vine, and My Father is the vinedresser. Every branch in Me that does not bear fruit, He takes away; and every *branch* that bears fruit, He prunes it so that it may bear more fruit. You are already clean because of the word which I have spoken to you. Abide in Me, and I in you. As the branch cannot bear fruit of itself unless it abides in the vine, so neither *can* you unless you abide in Me. I am the vine, you are the branches; he who abides in Me and I in him, he bears much fruit, for apart from Me you can do nothing. If anyone does not abide in Me, he is thrown away as a branch and dries up; and they gather them, and cast them into the fire and they are burned. If you abide in Me, and My words abide in you, ask whatever you wish, and it will be done for you. My Father is glorified by this, that you bear much fruit, and *so* prove to be My disciples. Just as the Father has loved Me, I have also loved you; abide in My love. If you keep My commandments, you will abide in My love; just as I have kept My Father's commandments and abide in His love. These things I have spoken to you so that My joy may be in you, and *that* your joy may be made full" (John 15:1–11; see Matthew 5:16; 7:7; John 3:29, 35; 6:56; 8:29, 31; 13:10).

[FRUIT-BEARING from bear fruit]
Setting: Jerusalem. Before the Passover, with His departure in mind, after explaining He is the vine and His disciples are the branches, Jesus instructs them to love one another.

"This is My commandment, that you love one another, just as I have loved you. Greater love has no one than this, that one lay down his life for his friends. You are My friends if you do what I command you. No longer do I call you slaves, for the slave does not know what his master is doing; but I have called you friends, for all things that I have heard from My Father I have made known to you. You did not choose Me but I chose you, and appointed you that you would go and bear fruit, and *that* your fruit would remain, so that whatever you ask of the Father in My name He may give to you. This I command you, that you love one another" (John 15:12–17; see Matthew 12:50; John 6:70; 8:26; 10:11; 13:34).

FRUITFULNESS (See FRUIT; and FRUIT-BEARING)

FRUITS (Also see FRUIT)
Setting: Galilee. During the early part of His ministry, Jesus preaches the Sermon on the Mount to His disciples and the multitudes.

"Beware of the false prophets, who come to you in sheep's clothing, but inwardly are ravenous wolves. You will know them by their fruits. Grapes are not gathered from *bushes* nor figs from thistles, are they? So every good tree bears good fruit, but the bad tree bears bad fruit. A good tree cannot produce bad fruit, nor can a bad tree produce good fruit. Every tree that does not bear good fruit is cut down and thrown into the fire. So then, you will know them by their fruits" (Matthew 7:15–20; cf. Matthew 3:10; 12:33, 35; 24:11, 24; Luke 6:43–44).

FULFILLMENT (Also see GLADNESS; HAPPINESS; and SATISFACTION)
[FULFILLMENT from fulfilled]
Setting: Galilee. After being baptized by John the Baptist in the Jordan River, Jesus commences His gospel-preaching ministry shortly after John is taken into custody by Herod Antipas.

Now after John had been taken into custody, Jesus came into Galilee, preaching the gospel of God, and saying, "The time is fulfilled, and the kingdom of God is at hand; repent and believe in the gospel" (Mark 1:14, 15, cf. Matthew 4:17; Galatians 4:4).

Setting: An upper room in Jerusalem. During the Feast of Unleavened Bread (Passover) just before His crucifixion, while celebrating the Passover meal, instituting the Lord's Supper, and prophesying Peter's upcoming denial of Him, Jesus instructs His disciples to prepare to persevere without Him.

And He said to them, "When I sent you out without money belt and bag and sandals, you did not lack anything, did you?" They said, "*No*, nothing." And He said to them, "But now, whoever has a money belt is to take it along, likewise also a bag, and whoever has no sword is to sell his coat and buy one. For I tell you that this which is written must be fulfilled in Me, 'AND HE WAS NUMBERED WITH TRANSGRESSORS'; for that which refers to Me has *its* fulfillment." They said, "Lord, look, here are two swords." And He said to them, "It is enough" (Luke 22:35–38, Jesus quotes from Isaiah 53:12; see Matthew 10:5–15; Mark 6:7–11; Luke 9:1–5; 10:1–12; 22:49; John 17:4).

FULFILLMENT OF PROPHECY (Listed under PROPHECY, FULFILLMENT OF)

FULFILLMENT OF SCRIPTURE (Listed under SCRIPTURE, FULFILLMENT OF)

FULFILLMENT OF THE LAW (Listed under LAW, FULFILLMENT OF THE)

FUNERAL HYMN (See DIRGE)

FURNACE (FIRE, FURNACE OF is a separate entry)

Setting: Galilee. During the early part of His ministry, Jesus preaches the Sermon on the Mount to His disciples and the multitudes.

"For this reason I say to you, do not be worried about your life, *as to* what you will eat or what you will drink; nor for your body, *as to* what you will put on. Is not life more than food, and the body more than clothing? Look at the birds of the air, that they do not sow, nor reap nor gather into barns, and *yet* your heavenly Father feeds them. Are you not worth much more than they? And who of you by being worried can add a *single* hour to his life? And why are you worried about clothing? Observe how the lilies of the field grow; they do not toil nor do they spin, yet I say to you that not even Solomon in all his glory clothed himself like one of these. But if God so clothes the grass of the field, which is *alive* today and tomorrow is thrown into the furnace, *will He* not much more *clothe* you? You of little faith! Do not worry then, saying 'What will we eat?' or 'What will we drink?' or 'What will be wear for clothing?" For the Gentiles eagerly seek all these things; for your heavenly Father knows that you need all these things. But seek first His kingdom and His righteousness, and all these things will be added to you. So do not worry about tomorrow; for tomorrow will care for itself. Each day has enough trouble of its own" (Matthew 6:25–34; cf. Luke 12:22–31; see 1 Kings 10:4–7; Job 35:11; Matthew 8:26).

Setting: On the way from Galilee to Jerusalem. Jesus comforts the crowd and His disciples after giving a parable about riches and greed. The scribes and Pharisees turn hostile and question Him repeatedly in an attempt to catch Him in something He might say.

And He said to His disciples, "For this reason I say to you, do not worry about *your* life, *as to* what you will eat; nor for your body, *as to* what you will put on. For life is more than food, and the body more than clothing. Consider the ravens, for they neither sow nor reap; they have no storeroom nor barn, and *yet* God feeds them; how much more valuable you are than the birds! And which of you by worrying can add a *single* hour to his life's span? If then you cannot do even a very little thing, why do you worry about other matters? Consider the lilies, how they grow: they neither toil nor spin; but I tell you, not even Solomon in all his glory clothed himself like one of these. But if God so clothes the grass in the field, which is *alive* today and tomorrow is thrown into the furnace, how much more *will He clothe* you? You men of little faith! And do not seek what you will eat and what you will drink, and do not keep worrying. For all these things the nations of the world eagerly seek; but your Father knows that you need these things. But seek His kingdom, and these things will be added to you. Do not be afraid, little flock, for your Father has chosen gladly to give you the kingdom" (Luke 12:22–32; cf. Matthew 6:25–33; see 1 Kings 10:4–7; Job 38:41).

FURNACE OF FIRE (Listed under FIRE, FURNACE OF; also see FIRE, ETERNAL; GOD, SEPARATION FROM; and HELL)

FUTURE, PREDICTING THE (Also see AGE TO COME; BETRAYAL; CHURCH, PROPHECY OF THE; PETER'S DENIAL; PROPHECY; PROPHECY, FULFILLMENT OF;PROPHECY OF JESUS' DEATH; PROPHECY OF JESUS' RESURRECTION; PROPHECY OF THE DESTRUCTION OF JERUSALEM; PROPHECY OF THE DESTRUCTION OF THE TEMPLE; PROPHESY)

[PREDICTING THE FUTURE from must take place]

Setting: The Mount of Olives, just east of Jerusalem. During His discourse, Jesus answers His disciples' questions as to when the temple will be destroyed and Jerusalem overrun, along with the signs of His coming and the end of the age.

And Jesus answered and said to them, "See to it that no one misleads you. For many will come in My name, saying, 'I am the Christ,' and will mislead many. You will be hearing of wars and rumors of wars. See that you are not frightened, for *those things* must take place, but *that* is not yet the end. For nation will rise against nation, and kingdom against kingdom, and in various places there will be famines and earthquakes. But all these things are *merely* the beginning of birth pangs. Then they will deliver you to tribulation, and will kill you, and you will be hated by all nations because of My name. At that time many will fall away and will betray one another and hate one another. Many false prophets will arise and will mislead many. Because lawlessness is increased, most people's love will grow cold. But the one who endures to the end, he will be saved. This gospel of the kingdom shall be preached in the whole world as a testimony to all the nations, and then the end will come" (Matthew 24:4–14; cf. Jeremiah 29:8; Matthew 7:15; 10:17, 22; Mark 13:3–13; Luke 21:7–19; Revelation 6:4).

[PREDICTING THE FUTURE from until all these things take place]

Setting: The Mount of Olives, just east of Jerusalem. During His discourse, after answering His disciples' questions as to when the temple will be destroyed and Jerusalem overrun, along with the signs of His coming and the end of the age, Jesus teaches them the Parable of the Fig Tree.

"Now learn the parable from the fig tree: when its branch has already become tender and puts forth its leaves, you know that summer is near; so, you too, when you see all these things, recognize that He is near, *right* at the door. Truly, I say to you, this generation will not pass away until all these things take place. Heaven and earth will pass away, but My words will not pass away. But of that day and hour no one knows, not even the angels of heaven, nor the Son, but the Father alone. For the coming of the Son of Man will be just like the days of Noah. For as in those days before the flood they were eating and drinking, marrying and giving in marriage, until the day that Noah entered the ark, and they did not understand until the flood came and took them all away; so will the coming of the Son of Man be. Then there will be two men in the field; one will be taken and one will be left. Two women *will be* grinding at the mill; one will be taken and one will be left" (Matthew 24:32–41; cf. Mark 13:28–32; Luke 17:34–36; 21:28–33; see Genesis 6:5; 7:7; Matthew 5:18; 10:23; James 5:9).

[PREDICTING THE FUTURE from must take place]

Setting: The Mount of Olives, east of the temple in Jerusalem. After predicting the temple's destruction, Jesus responds during His Olivet Discourse to questions from Peter, James, John, and Andrew about future events.

And Jesus began to say to them, "See to it that no one misleads you. Many will come in My name, saying, 'I am *He!*' and will mislead many. When you hear of wars and rumors of wars, do not be frightened; *those things* must take place; but *that is* not yet the end. For nation will rise up against nation, and kingdom against kingdom; there will be earthquakes in various places; there will *also be* famines. These things are *merely* the beginning of birth pangs. But be on your guard; for they will deliver you to *the* courts, and you will be flogged in *the* synagogues, and you will stand before governors and kings for My sake, as a testimony to them. The gospel must first be preached to all the nations. When they arrest you and hand you over, do not worry beforehand about what you are to say, but say whatever is given you in that hour; for it is not you who speak, but *it is* the Holy Spirit. Brother will betray brother to death, and a father *his* child; and children will rise up against parents and have them put to death. You will be hated by all because of My name, but the one who endures to the end, he will be saved" (Mark 13:5–13; cf. Matthew 24:4–14; Luke 21:7–19; see Matthew 10:17–22).

[PREDICTING THE FUTURE from until all these things take place]
Setting: The Mount of Olives, east of the temple in Jerusalem. After predicting the temple's destruction, Jesus responds during His Olivet Discourse to questions from Peter, James, John, and Andrew about future events.

"Now learn the parable from the fig tree: when its branch has already become tender and puts forth its leaves, you know that summer is near. Even so, you too, when you see these things happening, recognize that He is near, *right* at the door. Truly I say to you, this generation will not pass away until all these things take place. Heaven and earth will pass away, but My words will not pass away. But of the day or hour no one knows, not even the angels in heaven, nor the Son, but the Father *alone*" (Mark 13:28–32; cf. Matthew 24:32–36; Luke 21:28–33).

[PREDICTING THE FUTURE from must take place]
Setting: The temple in Jerusalem. A few days before His crucifixion, after Jesus prophesies during His Olivet Discourse the destruction of the temple, His disciples ask Him when this will happen.

And He said, "See to it that you are not misled; for many will come in My name, saying, "I am *He*,' and, 'The time is near.' Do not go after them. When you hear of wars and disturbances, do not be terrified; for these things must take place first, but the end *does* not *follow* immediately" (Luke 21:8, 9; cf. Matthew 24:4–8; Mark 13:5–8).

[PREDICTING THE FUTURE from these things begin to take place]
Setting: The Mount of Olives, east of the temple in Jerusalem. After ministering in the temple a few days before His crucifixion, and giving His disciples more details regarding future events, Jesus speaks during His Olivet Discourse of His return.

"There will be signs in sun and moon and stars, and on the earth dismay among the nations, in perplexity at the roaring of the sea and the waves, men fainting from fear and the expectation of the things which are coming upon the world; for the powers of the heavens will be shaken. Then they will see THE SON OF MAN COMING IN A CLOUD with power and great glory. But when these things begin to take place, straighten up and lift up your heads, because your redemption is drawing near" (Luke 21:25–28, Jesus quotes from Daniel 7:13; cf. Matthew 24:29–31; Mark 13:24–27).

[PREDICTING THE FUTURE from until all things take place]
Setting: The Mount of Olives, east of the temple in Jerusalem. After ministering in the temple a few days before His crucifixion, and giving the disciples more details regarding His return, Jesus conveys the Parable of the Fig Tree during His Olivet Discourse.

Then He told them a parable: "Behold the fig tree and all the trees; as soon as they put forth *leaves*, you see it and know for yourselves that summer is now near. So you also, when you see these things happening, recognize that the kingdom of God is near. Truly, I say to you, this generation will not pass away until all things take place. Heaven and earth will pass away, but My words will not pass away" (Luke 21:29–33; cf. Matthew 24:32–35; Mark 13:28–31; see Matthew 5:18).

[PREDICTING THE FUTURE from all these things that are about to take place]
Setting: The Mount of Olives, east of the temple in Jerusalem. After ministering in the temple a few days before His crucifixion, after conveying the Parable of the Fig Tree, Jesus warns His disciples during His Olivet Discourse to keep alert regarding future events.

"Be on guard, so that your hearts will not be weighted down with dissipation and drunkenness and the worries of life, and that day will not come upon you suddenly like a trap; for it will come upon all those who dwell on the face of all the earth. But keep on the alert at all times, praying that you may have strength to escape all these things that are about to take place, and to stand before the Son of Man" (Luke 21:34–36; cf. Mark 13:33; see Matthew 24:42–44).

[PREDICTING THE FUTURE from I am telling you before *it* comes to pass]

Setting: Jerusalem. Before the Passover, with His death on the cross nearing, Jesus explains the reason for His vivid example of servanthood in washing His disciples' feet.

So when He had washed their feet, and taken His garments and reclined *at the table* again, He said to them, "Do you know what I have done to you? You call Me Teacher and Lord; and you are right, for *so* I am. If I then, the Lord and the Teacher, washed your feet, you also ought to wash one another's feet. For I gave you an example that you also should do as I did to you. Truly, truly I say to you, a slave is not greater than his master, nor *is* one who is sent greater than the one who sent him. If you know these things, you are blessed if you do them. I do not speak of all of you. I know the ones I have chosen; but *it is* that the Scripture may be fulfilled, 'HE WHO EATS MY BREAD HAS LIFTED UP HIS HEEL AGAINST ME.' From now on I am telling you before *it* comes to pass, so that when it does occur, you may believe that I am *He*. Truly, truly, I say to you, he who receives whomever I send receives Me; and he who receives Me receives Him who sent Me" (John 13:12–20; Jesus quotes from Psalm 41:9; see Matthew 7:24; 10:24, 40; John 8:24; 14:29; 1 Peter 5:3).

[PREDICTING THE FUTURE from Now I have told you before it happens]
Setting: Jerusalem. Before the Passover, after conveying the upcoming ministry of the Holy Spirit in His disciples' lives, Jesus again relates peace, hope, and comfort to them regarding His return to the Father.

"Peace I leave with you; My peace I give to you; not as the world gives do I give to you. Do not let your heart be troubled, nor let it be fearful. You heard that I said to you, 'I go away, and I will come to you.' If you loved Me, you would have rejoiced because I go to the Father, for the Father is greater than I. Now I have told you before it happens, so that when it happens, you may believe. I will not speak much more with you, for the ruler of the world is coming, and he has nothing in Me; but so that the world may know that I love the Father, I do exactly as the Father commanded Me. Get up, let us go from here" (John 14:27–31; see John 10:18, 29; 12:31; 13:19; 16:33).

[PREDICTING THE FUTURE from these things I have spoken to you, so that when their hour comes]
Setting: Jerusalem. Before the Passover, after explaining He is the vine and His disciples are the branches, Jesus warns them of the persecution they will face after His departure to heaven.

"These things I have spoken to you so that you may be kept from stumbling. They will make you outcasts from the synagogue, but an hour is coming for everyone who kills you to think that he is offering service to God. These things they will do because they have not known the Father or Me. But these things I have spoken to you, so that when their hour comes, you may remember that I told you of them. These things I did not say to you at the beginning, because I was with you" (John 16:1–4; see John 8:19, 55; 9:22; 13:19; 15:18–27).

[PREDICTING THE FUTURE from the things which will take place]
Setting: On the island of Patmos (in the Aegean Sea about fifty miles southwest of Ephesus in modern Turkey). On the Lord's Day (Sunday), approximately fifty years after His resurrection, the disciple John encounters the Lord Jesus Christ, who communicates new revelations for the apostle to record for the seven churches in Asia.

When I saw Him, I fell at His feet like a dead man. And He placed His right hand on me, saying, "Do not be afraid; I am the first and the last, and the living One; and I was dead, and behold, I am alive forevermore, and I have the keys of death and of Hades. Therefore write the things which you have seen, and the things which are, and the things which will take place after these things. As for the mystery of the seven stars which you saw in My right hand, and the seven golden lampstands: the seven stars are the angels of the seven churches, and the seven lampstands are the seven churches" (Revelation 1:17–20; see Isaiah 44:6; Luke 24:5; Revelation 2:8).

G

GALILEANS (Also see GALILEE)

Setting: On the way from Galilee to Jerusalem. After some present report to Him about the Galileans whose blood Pilate (Roman governor of Judea) mixed with their sacrifices, Jesus responds to their concern by calling them to repentance.

And Jesus said to them, "Do you suppose that these Galileans were *greater* sinners than all *other* Galileans because they suffered this *fate*? I tell you, no, but unless you repent, you will all likewise perish. Or do you suppose that those eighteen on whom the tower in Siloam fell and killed them were *worse* culprits than all the men who live in Jerusalem? I tell you, no, but unless you repent, you will all likewise perish" (Luke 13:2–5; John 9:2, 3).

GALILEE

Setting: Jerusalem. After celebrating the Passover meal, as they go out to the Mount of Olives prior to His betrayal by Judas, Jesus states that all His disciples will deny Him that very day.

Then Jesus said to them, "You will all fall away because of Me this night, for it is written, 'I WILL STRIKE DOWN THE SHEPHERD, AND THE SHEEP OF THE FLOCK SHALL BE SCATTERED.' But after I have been raised, I will go ahead of you to Galilee." But Peter said to Him, '*Even* though all may fall away because of You, I will never fall away.' Jesus said to him, "Truly I say to you that this *very* night, before a rooster crows, you will deny Me three times" (Matthew 26:31–34, Jesus quotes from Zechariah 13:7; cf. Mark 14:26–31; see Matthew 28:7, 10, 16; John 13:37).

Setting: Jerusalem. The day after the Sabbath, after rising from the dead, Jesus appears to Mary Magdalene and the other Mary with instructions for His disciples.

Then Jesus said to them, "Do not be afraid; go and take word to My brethren to leave for Galilee, and there they will see Me" (Matthew 28:10; see John 20:17).

Setting: A borrowed upper room in Jerusalem. After Jesus and His twelve disciples celebrate the Passover and the Lord's Supper, they go to the Mount of Olives.

And Jesus said to them, "You will all fall away, because it is written, 'I WILL STRIKE DOWN THE SHEPHERD, AND THE SHEEP SHALL BE SCATTERED.' But after I have been raised, I will go ahead of you to Galilee." But Peter said to Him, "*Even* though all may fall away, yet I will not." And Jesus said to him, "Truly I say to you, that this very night, before a rooster crows twice, you yourself will deny Me three times" (Mark 14:27–30, Jesus quotes from Zechariah 13:7; cf. Matthew 26:30–34; see Mark 14:72).

GALILEE, CALMING THE STORM ON THE SEA OF (See SEA, CALMING THE)

GALILEE, LAKE OF (See GALILEE, SEA OF)

GALILEE, SEA OF

[SEA OF GALILEE from lake]

Setting: Galilee. After conveying who His true relatives are, Jesus sets sail with His disciples on the Sea of Galilee, where He calms a storm.

Now on one of *those* days Jesus and His disciples got into a boat, and He said to them, "Let us go over to the other side of the lake." So they launched out (Luke 8:22; cf. Mark 4:35; see Matthew 8:18).

GARDEN (Also see HERB, GARDEN; PLANT; and PLANTS, GARDEN)

Setting: On the way from Galilee to Jerusalem. After responding to a synagogue official's anger for healing a woman, sick eighteen years, in the synagogue on the Sabbath, Jesus conveys the Parable of the Mustard Seed and the Parable of the Leaven.

So He was saying, "What is the kingdom of God like, and to what shall I compare it? It is like a mustard seed which a man took and threw into his own garden; and it grew and became a tree, and THE BIRDS OF THE AIR NESTED IN ITS BRANCHES." And again He said, "To what shall I compare the kingdom of God? It is like leaven, which a woman took and hid in three pecks of flour until it was all leavened" (Luke 13:18–21, Jesus quotes from Ezekiel 17:23; cf. Matthew 13:31–34; Mark 4:30–32).

GARDEN HERB (Listed under HERB, GARDEN)

GARDEN PLANTS (Listed under PLANTS, GARDEN)

GARDENER (See VINEDRESSER)

GARMENT, NEW (Also see CLOTHING; and GARMENT, OLD)

Setting: The home of Levi (Matthew) in Capernaum. At a reception for Jesus following Levi's call to be a disciple, the Lord tells a parable to the Pharisees and their scribes, who question His association with tax collectors and sinners.

And He was also telling them a parable: "No one tears a piece of cloth from a new garment and puts it on an old garment; otherwise he will both tear the new, and the piece from the new will not match the old. And no one puts new wine into old wineskins; otherwise the new wine will burst the skins and it will be spilled out, and the skins will be ruined. But new wine must be put into fresh wineskins. And no one, after drinking old *wine* wishes for new; for he says, 'The old is good *enough*.'" (Luke 5:36–39; cf. Matthew 9:16, 17; Mark 2:21, 22)

GARMENT, OLD (Also see CLOTHING; and GARMENT, NEW)

Setting: Capernaum near the Sea of Galilee. John the Baptist's disciples ask Jesus why His disciples do not participate in fasting, while they and the Pharisees do.

And Jesus said to them, "The attendants of the bridegroom cannot mourn as long as the bridegroom is with them, can they? But the days will come when the bridegroom is taken away from them, and then they will fast. But no one puts a patch of unshrunk cloth on an old garment; for the patch pulls away from the garment, and a worse tear results. Nor do *people* put new wine into old wineskins; otherwise the wineskins burst, and the wine pours out and the wineskins are ruined; but they put new wine into fresh wineskins, and both are preserved" (Matthew 9:15–17; cf. Mark 2:18–22; Luke 5:33–39).

Setting: Capernaum. John the Baptist's disciples and the Pharisees question why Jesus' disciples do not fast when they do.

And Jesus said to them, "While the bridegroom is with them, the attendants of the bridegroom cannot fast, can they? So long as they have the bridegroom with them, they cannot fast. But the days will come when the bridegroom is taken away from them, and then they will fast in that day. No one sews a patch of unshrunk cloth on an old garment; otherwise the patch pulls away from it, the new from the old, and a worse tear results. No one puts new wine into old wineskins; otherwise the wine will burst the skins, and the wine is lost and the skins as *well;* but *one puts* new wine into fresh wineskins" (Mark 2:19–22; cf. Matthew 9:14–17; Luke 5:33–38).

Setting: The home of Levi (Matthew) in Capernaum. At a reception for Jesus following Levi's call to be a disciple, the Lord tells a parable to the Pharisees and their scribes, who question His association with tax collectors and

And He was also telling them a parable: "No one tears a piece of cloth from a new garment and puts it on an old garment; otherwise he will both tear the new, and the piece from the new will not match the old. And no one puts new wine into old wineskins; otherwise the new wine will burst the skins and it will be spilled out, and the skins will be ruined. But new wine must be put into fresh wineskins. And no one, after drinking old *wine* wishes for new; for he says, 'The old is good *enough.*'" (Luke 5:36–39; cf. Matthew 9:16, 17; Mark 2:21, 22)

GARMENTS (Also see CLOAK; CLOTHING, and specific items such as SHIRT)

Setting: The temple in Jerusalem. Jesus exposes the truth about Pharisaism to the crowds and His disciples after the Jewish religious leaders test Him with questions.

Then Jesus spoke to the crowds and to His disciples, saying: "The scribes and the Pharisees have seated themselves in the chair of Moses; therefore all that they tell you, do and observe, but do not do according to their deeds; for they say *things* and do not do *them.* They tie up heavy burdens and lay them on men's shoulders, but they themselves are unwilling to move them with *so much as* a finger. But they do all their deeds to be noticed by men; for they broaden their phylacteries and lengthen their tassels *of their garments.* They love the place of honor at banquets and the chief seats in the synagogues, and respectful greetings in the market places, and being called Rabbi by men. But do not be called Rabbi; for One is your Teacher, and you are all brothers. Do not call *anyone* on earth your father; for One is your Father, He who is in heaven. Do not be called leaders; for One is your Leader, *that is,* Christ. But the greatest among you shall be your servant. Whoever exalts himself shall be humbled; and whoever humbles himself shall be exalted" (Matthew 23:1–12; cf. Matthew 20:26; Mark 12:38–40; Luke 20:46, 47; see Exodus 13:9; Deuteronomy 33:3; Matthew 6:1, 5, 6, 9, 16; Mark 14:11; Luke 11:43; 14:11).

Setting: By the Sea of Galilee. After Jesus returns from ministry to the Gerasenes, a woman who has had a hemorrhage for twelve years touches the hem of His garment in order to be healed.

Immediately Jesus, perceiving in Himself that the power *proceeding* from Him had gone forth, turned around in the crowd and said, "Who touched My garments?" (Mark 5:30; see Matthew 9:20, 21; Luke 8:43–48).

Setting: On the island of Patmos (in the Aegean Sea about fifty miles southwest of Ephesus in modern Turkey). On the Lord's Day (Sunday), about fifty years after Jesus' resurrection, the disciple John encounters the Lord Jesus Christ, who communicates a new revelation for the apostle to record for the church in Sardis and to six other churches in Asia.

"To the angel of the church in Sardis write: He who has the seven Spirits of God and the seven stars, says this: 'I know your deeds, that you have a name that you are alive, but you are dead. Wake up, and strengthen the things that remain, which were about to die; for I have not found your deeds completed in the sight of My God. So remember what you have received and heard; and keep *it,* and repent. Therefore if you do not wake up, I will come like a thief, and you will not know at what hour I will come to you. But you have a few people in Sardis who have not soiled their garments; and they will walk with Me in white, for they are worthy. He who overcomes will thus be clothed in white garments; and I will not erase his name from the book of life, and I will confess his name before My Father and before His angels. He who has an ear, let him hear what the Spirit says to the churches' " (Revelation 3:1–6; see Matthew 10:32; Revelation 1:16).

Setting: On the island of Patmos (in the Aegean Sea about fifty miles southwest of Ephesus in modern Turkey). On the Lord's Day (Sunday), about fifty years after Jesus' resurrection, the disciple John encounters the Lord Jesus Christ, who communicates a new revelation for the apostle to record for the church in Laodicea and to six other churches in Asia.

"To the angel of the church in Laodicea write: The Amen, the faithful and true Witness, the Beginning of the creation of God, says this: 'I know your deeds, that you are neither cold nor hot; I wish that you were cold or hot. So because you are lukewarm, and neither hot nor cold, I will spit you out of My mouth. Because you say, "I am rich, and have become wealthy, and have need of nothing," and you do not know that you are wretched and miserable and poor and blind and naked, I advise you to buy from Me gold refined by fire so that you may become rich, and white garments so that you may clothe yourself, and *that* the shame of your nakedness will not be revealed; and eye salve to anoint your eyes so that you may see. Those whom I love, I reprove and discipline; therefore be zealous and repent. Behold, I stand at the door and knock; if anyone hears My voice and opens the door, I will come in to him and will dine with him, and he with Me. He who overcomes, I will grant to him to sit down with Me on My throne, as I also overcame and sat down with My Father on His throne. He who has an ear, let him hear what the Spirit says to the churches'" (Revelation 3:14–22; see Proverbs 3:12; Hosea 12:8; John 14:23; 16:33).

GARMENTS, WHITE (Listed under GARMENTS)

GATE (Also see DOOR)

Setting: Galilee. During the early part of His ministry, Jesus preaches the Sermon on the Mount to His disciples and the multitudes.

"Enter through the narrow gate; for the gate is wide and the way is broad that leads to destruction, and there are many who enter through it. For the gate is small and the way is narrow that leads to life, and there are few who find it" (Matthew 7:13, 14; cf. Luke 13:24).

Setting: On the way from Galilee to Jerusalem. After He responds to the Pharisees' scoffing at His teaching His disciples about stewardship and the permanence of the Law, Jesus conveys the story of the rich man and Lazarus.

"Now there was a rich man, and he habitually dressed in purple and fine linen, joyously living in splendor every day. And a poor man named Lazarus was laid at his gate, covered with sores, and longing to be fed with the *crumbs* which were falling from the rich man's table; besides, even the dogs were coming and licking his sores. Now the poor man died and was carried away by the angels to Abraham's bosom; and the rich man also died and was buried. In Hades he lifted up his eyes, being in torment, and saw Abraham far away and Lazarus in his bosom. And he cried out and said, 'Father Abraham, have mercy on me, and send Lazarus so that he may dip the tip of his finger in water and cool off my tongue, for I am in agony in this flame.' But Abraham said, 'Child, remember that during your life you received your good things, and likewise Lazarus bad things; but now he is being comforted here, and you are in agony. And besides all this, between us and you there is a great chasm fixed, so that those who wish to come over from here to you will not be able, and *that* none may cross over from there to us.' And he said, 'Then I beg you, father, that you send him to my father's house—for I have five brothers—in order that he may warn them, so that they will not also come to this place of torment.' But Abraham said, 'They have Moses and the Prophets; let them hear them.' But he said, 'No, father Abraham, but if someone goes to them from the dead, they will repent!' But he said to him, 'If they do not listen to Moses and the Prophets, they will not be persuaded even if someone rises from the dead' " (Luke 16:19–31; see Luke 3:8; 6:24; 16:1, 14).

GATE, NARROW (Listed under GATE)

GATES OF HADES (Listed under HADES, GATES OF)

GATHERING (collecting; also see CROP; CROPS; HARVEST; PRODUCE; REAPERS; and REAPING)

[GATHERING from gather]

Setting: Galilee. During the early part of His ministry, Jesus preaches the Sermon on the Mount to His disciples and the multitudes.

"For this reason I say to you, do not be worried about your life, *as to* what you will eat or what you will drink; nor for your body, *as to* what you will put on. Is not life more than food, and the body more than clothing? Look at the birds of the air, that they do not sow, nor reap nor gather into barns, and *yet* your heavenly Father feeds them. Are you not worth much more than they? And who of you by being worried can add a *single* hour to his life? And why are you worried about clothing? Observe how the lilies of the field grow; they do not toil nor do they spin, yet I say to you that not even Solomon in all his glory clothed himself like one of these. But if God so clothes the grass of the field, which is *alive* today and tomorrow is thrown into the furnace, *will He* not much more *clothe* you? You of little faith! Do not worry then, saying 'What will we eat?' or 'What will we drink?' or 'What will be wear for clothing?" For the Gentiles eagerly seek all these things; for your heavenly Father knows that you need all these things. But seek first His kingdom and His righteousness, and all these things will be added to you. So do not worry about tomorrow; for tomorrow will care for itself. Each day has enough trouble of its own" (Matthew 6:25–34; cf. Luke 12:22–31; see 1 Kings 10:4–7; Job 35:11; Matthew 8:26).

[GATHERING from gathered]
Setting: Galilee. During the early part of His ministry, Jesus preaches the Sermon on the Mount to His disciples and the multitudes.

"Beware of the false prophets, who come to you in sheep's clothing, but inwardly are ravenous wolves. You will know them by their fruits. Grapes are not gathered from *bushes* nor figs from thistles, are they? So every good tree bears good fruit, but the bad tree bears bad fruit. A good tree cannot produce bad fruit, nor can a bad tree produce good fruit. Every tree that does not bear good fruit is cut down and thrown into the fire. So then, you will know them by their fruits" (Matthew 7:15–20; cf. Matthew 3:10; 12:33, 35; 24:11, 24; Luke 6:43–44).

[GATHERING from gather]
Setting: Galilee. After Jesus heals a blind, mute, demon-possessed man, the Pharisees accuse Him of being a worker of Satan. Jesus warns them about the unpardonable sin.

"He who is not with Me is against Me; and he who does not gather with Me scatters. Therefore I say to you, any sin and blasphemy shall be forgiven people, but blasphemy against the Spirit shall not be forgiven. Whoever speaks a word against the Son of Man, it shall be forgiven him; but whoever speaks against the Holy Spirit, it shall not be forgiven him, either in this age or in the *age* to come" (Matthew 12:30–32; cf. Luke 12:10; see Mark 9:40).

Setting: By the Sea of Galilee. Because the religious leaders are rejecting His message, Jesus continues teaching the crowds with the Parable of the Wheat and the Tares.

Jesus presented another parable to them, saying, "The kingdom of heaven may be compared to a man who sowed good seed in his field. But while his men were sleeping, his enemy came and sowed tares among the wheat, and went away. But when the wheat sprouted and bore grain, then the tares became evident also. The slaves of the landowner came and said to him, 'Sir, did you not sow good seed in your field? How then does it have tares?' And he said to them, 'An enemy has done this!' The slaves said to him, 'Do you want us, then, to go and gather them up?' But he said, 'No; for while you are gathering up the tares, you may uproot the wheat with them. Allow both to grow together until the harvest; and in the time of the harvest I will say to the reapers, "First gather up the tares and bind them in bundles to burn them up; but gather the wheat into my barn"'" (Matthew 13:24–30; cf. Matthew 3:12).

[GATHERING from gathered and gather]
Setting: A house near the Sea of Galilee. Jesus explains to His disciples the meaning of the Parable of the Wheat and the Tares.

And He said, "The one who sows the good seed is the Son of Man, and the field is the world; and as *for* the good seed, these are the sons of the kingdom; and the tares are the sons of the evil *one;* and the enemy who sowed them is the devil, and the harvest is the end of the age; and the reapers are angels. So just as the tares are gathered up and burned with fire, so shall it be at the end of the age. The Son of Man will send forth His angels, and they will gather out of His kingdom all stumbling blocks, and those who commit lawlessness, and will throw them into the furnace of fire; in that place there will be weeping and gnashing of teeth. Then THE RIGHTEOUS WILL SHINE FORTH AS THE SUN in the kingdom of their Father. He who has ears, let him hear" (Matthew 13:37–43, Jesus quotes from Daniel 12:3; cf. Matthew 8:12; 13:50).

[GATHERING from gathered]
Setting: By the Sea of Galilee. Because the religious leaders are rejecting His message, Jesus continues teaching His disciples with the Parable of the Dragnet.

"Again, the kingdom of heaven is like a dragnet cast into the sea, and gathering *fish* of every kind; and when it was filled, they drew it up on the beach; and they sat down and gathered the good *fish* into containers, but the bad they threw away. So it will be at the end of the age; the angels will come forth and take out the wicked from among the righteous, and will throw them into the furnace of fire; in that place there will be weeping and gnashing of teeth. Have you understood all these things?" They said to Him, "Yes" (Matthew 13:47–51).

[GATHERING from gathered]
Setting: Capernaum of Galilee. After conveying to His disciples the value of little ones, Jesus gives instruction about church discipline.

"If your brother sins, go and show him his fault in private; if he listens to you, you have won your brother. But if he does not listen *to you,* take one or two more with you, so that BY THE MOUTH OF TWO OR THREE WITNESSES EVERY FACT MAY BE CONFIRMED. If he refuses to listen to them, tell it to the church; and if he refuses to listen even to the church, let him be to you as a Gentile and a tax collector. Truly I say to you, whatever you bind of earth shall have been bound in heaven; and whatever you loose on earth shall have been loosed in heaven. Again, I say to you, that if two of you agree on earth about anything that they may ask, it shall be done for them by My Father who is in heaven. For there two or three have gathered together in My name, I am there in their midst" (Matthew 18:15–20. Jesus quotes from Deuteronomy 19:15; cf. Matthew 7:7; 16:19; see Leviticus 19:17; Matthew 28:20; 2 Thessalonians 3:6, 14).

[GATHERING from gathered]
Setting: The temple in Jerusalem. Jesus speaks another parable to the chief priests and elders after they question His authority.

Jesus spoke to them again in parables, saying, "The kingdom of heaven may be compared to a king who gave a wedding feast for his son. And he sent out his slaves to call those who had been invited to the wedding feast, and they were unwilling to come. Again he sent out other slaves saying, 'Tell those who have been invited, "Behold, I have prepared my dinner; my oxen and my fattened livestock are *all* butchered and everything is ready; come to the wedding feast." But they paid no attention and went their way, one to his own farm, another to his business, and the rest seized his slaves and mistreated them and killed them. But the king was enraged, and he sent his armies and destroyed those murderers and set their city on fire. Then he said to his slaves, 'The wedding is ready, but those who were invited were not worthy. 'Go therefore to the main highways, and as many as you find *there,* invite to the wedding feast.' Those slaves went out into the streets and gathered together all they found, both evil and good; and the wedding hall was filled with dinner guests. But when the king came in to look over the dinner guests, he saw a man there who was not dressed in wedding clothes, and he said to him, 'Friend, how did you come in here without wedding clothes?' And the man was speechless. Then the king said to the servants, 'Bind him hand and foot, and throw him into the outer darkness; in that place there will be weeping and gnashing of teeth.' For many are called, but few *are* chosen" (Matthew 22:1–14; cf. Matthew 8:11, 12).

[GATHERING from gather and gathers]
Setting: The temple in Jerusalem. With His death on the cross just days away, Jesus laments over Jerusalem's hardheartedness and lack of repentance.

"Jerusalem, Jerusalem, who kills the prophets and stones those who are sent to her! How often I wanted to gather your children together, the way a hen gathers her chicks under her wings, and you were unwilling. Behold, your house is being left to you desolate! For I say to you, from now on you will not see Me until you say, 'BLESSED IS HE WHO COMES IN THE NAME OF THE LORD!'" (Matthew 23:37–39, Jesus quotes from Psalm 118:26; cf. 1 Kings 9:7; Luke 13:34, 35).

[GATHERING from gather]
Setting: The Mount of Olives, just east of Jerusalem. During His discourse, Jesus answers His disciples' questions as to when the temple will be destroyed and Jerusalem overrun, along with the signs of His coming and the end of the age.

"Therefore when you see the ABOMINATION OF DESOLATION which was spoken of through Daniel the prophet, standing in the holy place (let the reader understand), then those who are in Judea must flee to the mountains. Whoever is on the housetop must not go down to get the things that are in his house. Whoever is in the field must not turn back to get his cloak. But woe to those who are pregnant and to those who are nursing babies in those days! But pray that your flight will not be in the winter, or on a Sabbath. For then there will be a great tribulation, such as has not occurred since the beginning of the world until now, nor ever will. Unless those days had been cut short, no life would have been saved; but for the sake of the elect those days will be cut short. Then if anyone says to you, 'Behold, here is the Christ,' or "There *He is,*' do not believe *him.* For false Christs and false prophets will arise and will show great signs and wonders, so as to mislead, if possible, even the elect. Behold, I have told you in advance. So if they say to you, 'Behold, He is in the wilderness,' do not go out, *or,* 'Behold, He is in the inner rooms,' do not believe *them.* For just as the lightning comes from the east and flashes even to the west, so will the coming of the Son of Man be. Wherever a corpse is, there the vultures will gather" (Matthew 24:15–28, Jesus quotes from Daniel 9:27; cf. Daniel 12:1; Mark 13:14–23; Luke 17:22–31; 21:20–24; 23:29; see John 4:48).

[GATHERING from GATHER]
Setting: The Mount of Olives, just east of Jerusalem. During His discourse, Jesus answers His disciples' questions as to when the temple will be destroyed and Jerusalem overrun, along with the signs of His coming and the end of the age.

"But immediately after the tribulation of those days THE SUN WILL BE DARKENED, AND THE MOON WILL NOT GIVE ITS LIGHT, AND THE STARS WILL FALL from the sky, and the powers of the heavens will be shaken. And then the sign of the Son of Man will appear in the sky, and then all the tribes of the earth will mourn, and they will see the SON OF MAN COMING ON THE CLOUDS OF THE SKY with power and great glory. And He will send forth His angels with A GREAT TRUMPET and THEY WILL GATHER TOGETHER His elect from the four winds, from one end of the sky to the other" (Matthew 24:29–31, Jesus quotes from Isaiah 13:10, Daniel 7:13; Exodus 19:16; cf. Mark 13:24–27; Luke 21:25–27).

Setting: The Mount of Olives, just east of Jerusalem. During His discourse, after answering His disciples' questions as to when the temple will be destroyed and Jerusalem overrun, along with the signs of His coming and the end of the age, Jesus reemphasizes to His disciples that they should be on the alert for His return.

"For *it is* just like a man *about* to go on a journey, who called his own slaves and entrusted his possessions to them. To one he gave five talents, to another, two, and to another, one, each according to his own ability; and he went on his journey. Immediately the one who had received the five talents went and traded with them, and gained five more talents. In the same manner the one who *had received* the two *talents* gained two more. But he who received the one *talent* went away, and dug a *hole* in the ground and hid his master's money. Now after a long time the master of those slaves came and settled accounts with them. The one who had received the five talents came up and brought five more talents, saying, 'Master, you entrusted five talents to me. See, I have gained five more talents.' His master said to him, 'Well done, good and faithful slave. You were faithful with a few things, I will put you in charge of many things; enter into the joy of your master.' Also the one who *had received* the two talents came up and said, 'Master, you entrusted two talents to me. See, I have gained two more talents.' His master said to him, 'Well done, good and faithful slave. You were faithful with a few things, I will put you in charge of many things; enter into the joy of your master.' And the one also who had received the one talent came up and said, 'Master, I knew you to be a hard man, reaping where you did not sow and gathering where you scattered no *seed.* And I was afraid, and went away and hid your talent in the ground. See, you have what is yours.' But his master answered and said to him, 'You wicked, lazy slave, you knew that I reap where I did not sow and gather where I scattered no *seed.* Then you ought to have put my money in the bank, and on my arrival I would have received my *money* back with interest. 'Therefore take away the talent from him, and give it to the one who has ten talents.' For to everyone who has, *more* shall be given, and he will have an abundance; but from the one who does not have, even what he does have shall be taken away. Throw out the worthless slave into the outer darkness; in that place there will be weeping and gnashing of teeth" (Matthew 25:14–30; cf. Matthew 8:12; 13:12; 24:45–47; see Matthew 18:23, 24; Luke 12:44).

[GATHERING from gathered]
Setting: The Mount of Olives, just east of Jerusalem. During His discourse, after answering His disciples' questions as to when the temple will be destroyed and Jerusalem overrun, along with the signs of His coming and the end of the age, Jesus reveals the future judgments following His return.

"But when the Son of Man comes in His glory, and all the angels with Him, then He will sit on His glorious throne. All the nations will be gathered before Him; and He will separate them from one another, as the shepherd separates the sheep from the goats; and He will put the sheep on His right, and the goats on the left. Then the King will say to those on His right, 'Come, you who are blessed of My Father, inherit the kingdom prepared for you from the foundation of the world. 'For I was hungry, and you gave Me *something* to eat; I was thirsty, and you gave Me *something* to drink; I was a stranger, and you invited Me in; naked, and you clothed Me; I was sick, and you visited Me; I was in prison, and you came to Me.' Then the righteous will answer Him, 'Lord, when did we see You hungry and feed You, or thirsty, and give you *something* to drink? And when did we see You a stranger, and invite You in, or naked, and clothe You? When did we see You sick, or in prison, and come to You?' The King will answer and say to them, 'Truly I say to you, to the extent that you did it to one of these brothers of Mine, *even* the least *of them,* you did it to Me.' Then He will also say to those on His left, 'Depart from Me, accursed ones, into the eternal fire which has been prepared for the devil and his angels; for I was hungry, and you gave Me *nothing* to eat; I was thirsty, and you gave Me nothing to drink; I was a stranger, and you did not invite Me in; naked, and you did not clothe Me; sick, and in prison, and you did not visit Me.' Then they themselves also will answer, 'Lord, when did we see You hungry, or thirsty, or a stranger, or naked, or sick, or in prison, and did not take care of You?' Then He will answer them, 'Truly I say to you, to the extent that you did not do it to one of the least of these, you did not do it to Me.' These will go away into eternal punishment, but the righteous into eternal life" (Matthew 25:31–46; see Matthew 7:23; 16:27; 19:29).

[GATHERING from gather]
Setting: On the Mount of Olives, east of the temple in Jerusalem. After predicting the temple's destruction, during His Olivet Discourse, Jesus responds to questions from Peter, James, John, and Andrew about future events.

"But in those days, after that tribulation, THE SUN WILL BE DARKENED AND THE MOON WILL NOT GIVE ITS LIGHT, AND THE STARS WILL BE FALLING from heaven, and the powers that are in the heavens will be shaken. Then they will see THE SON OF MAN COMING IN CLOUDS with great power and glory. And then He will send forth the angels, and will gather together His elect from the four winds, from the farthest end of the earth to the farthest end of heaven" (Mark 13:24–27. Jesus quotes from Isaiah 13:10; 34:4; Daniel 7:13; cf. Matthew 24:29–31; Luke 21:25–27).

[GATHERING from gather]
Setting: Galilee. After selecting His twelve disciples, Jesus teaches the Sermon on the Mount to those disciples and a great throng from Judea, Jerusalem, and the central coastal region of Tyre and Sidon.

And He also spoke a parable to them: "A blind man cannot guide a blind man, can he? Will they not both fall into a pit? A pupil is not above his teacher; but everyone, after he has been fully trained, will be like his teacher. Why do you look at the speck that is in your brother's eye, but do not notice the log that is in your own eye? Or how can you say to your brother, 'Brother, let me take out the speck that is in your eye,' when you yourself do not see the log that is in your own eye? You hypocrite, first take the log out of your own eye, and then you will see clearly to take out the speck that is in your brother's eye. For there is no good tree which produces bad fruit, nor, on the other hand, a bad tree which produces good fruit. For each tree is known by its own fruit. For men do not gather figs from thorns, nor do they pick grapes from a briar bush. The good man out of the good treasure of his heart brings forth what is good; and the evil *man* out of the evil *treasure* brings forth what is evil; for his mouth speaks from that which fills his heart" (Luke 6:39–45; cf. Matthew 7:3–6. 16, 18, 20; 12:35; see Matthew 10:24; 15:14; Luke 6:12–19).

[GATHERING from gather]
Setting: On the way from Galilee to Jerusalem. After some in the crowd test Him, demanding a sign from heaven, Jesus illustrates His power over Satan.

"When a strong *man*, fully armed, guards his own house, his possessions are undisturbed. But when someone stronger than he attacks him and overpowers him, he takes away from him all his armor on which he had relied and distributes his plunder. He who is not with Me is against Me; and he who does not gather with Me, scatters" (Luke 11:21–23; cf. Matthew 12:29, 30).

[GATHERING from gather and gathers]
Setting: On the way from Galilee to Jerusalem. While teaching in the cities and villages, after Jesus responds to a question about who is saved, some Pharisees ask Him to leave, claiming Herod Antipas (tetrarch of Galilee and Perea) seeks to kill Him.

And He said to them, "Go and tell that fox, 'Behold, I cast out demons and perform cures today and tomorrow, and the third *day* I reach My goal.' Nevertheless I must journey on today and tomorrow and the next *day*; for it cannot be that a prophet would perish outside of Jerusalem. O Jerusalem, Jerusalem, *the city* that kills the prophets and stones those sent to her! How often I wanted to gather your children together, just as a hen *gathers* her brood under her wings, and you would not *have it*! Behold, your house is left to you *desolate*; and I say to you, you will not see Me until *the time* comes when you say, 'BLESSED IS HE WHO COMES IN THE NAME OF THE LORD!'" (Luke 13:32–35, Jesus quotes from Psalm 118:26; cf. Matthew 23:37).

[GATHERING from gathered]
Setting: On the way from Galilee to Jerusalem. Jesus conveys the illustration of the prodigal son because the Pharisees and scribes complain He associates with tax collectors and sinners.

And He said, "A man had two sons. The younger of them said to his father, 'Father, give me the share of the estate that falls to me.' So he divided his wealth between them. And not many days later, the younger son gathered everything together and went on a journey into a distant country, and there he squandered his estate with loose living. Now when he had spent everything, a severe famine occurred in that country, and he began to be impoverished. So he went and hired himself out to one of the citizens of that country, and he sent him into his fields to feed swine. And he would have gladly filled his stomach with the pods that the swine were eating, and no one was giving *anything* to him. But when he came to his senses, he said, 'How many of my father's hired men have more than enough bread, but I am dying here with hunger! I will get up and go to my father, and will say to him, "Father, I have sinned against heaven, and in your sight; I am no longer worthy to be called your son; make me as one of your hired men."' So he got up and came to his father. But while he was still a long way off, his father saw him and felt compassion *for him,* and ran and embraced him and kissed him. And the son said to him, "Father, I have sinned against heaven and in your sight; I am no longer worthy to be called your son.' But the father said to his slaves, 'Quickly bring out the best robe and put it on him, and put a ring on his hand and sandals on his feet; and bring the fattened calf, kill it, and let us eat and celebrate; for this son of mine was dead and has come to life again; he was lost and has been found.' And they began to celebrate. Now his older son was in the field, when he came and approached the house, he heard music and dancing. And he summoned one of the servants and *began* inquiring what these things could be. And he said to him, 'Your brother has come, and your father has killed the fattened calf because he has received him back safe and sound.' But he became angry and was not willing to go in; and his father came out and *began* pleading with him. But he answered and said to his father, 'Look! For so many years I have been serving you and I have never neglected a command of yours; and *yet* you have never given me a young goat, so that I might celebrate with my friends; but when this son of yours came, who has devoured your wealth with prostitutes, you killed the fattened calf for him.' And he said to him, 'Son, you have always been with me, and all that is mine is yours. But we had to celebrate and rejoice, for this brother of yours was dead and *has begun* to live, and *was* lost and has been found'" (Luke 15:11–32; see Proverbs 29:2; Luke 15:1, 2).

[GATHERING from gathered]
Setting: Samaria, on the way from Galilee to Jerusalem. After the Pharisees question Him about the coming of the kingdom of God, Jesus tells His disciples of His second coming.

And He said to the disciples, "The days will come when you will long to see one of the days of the Son of Man, and you will not see it. They will say to you, 'Look there! Look here!' Do not go away, and do not run after *them*. For just like the lightning, when it flashes out of one part of the sky, shines to the other part of the sky, so will the Son of Man be in His day. But first He must suffer many things and be rejected by this generation. And just as it happened in the days of Noah, so it will be also in the days of the Son of Man: they were eating, they were drinking, they were marrying, they were being given in marriage, until the day that Noah entered the ark, and the flood came and destroyed them all. It was the same as happened in the days of Lot: they were eating, they were drinking, they were buying, they were selling, they were planting, they were building; but on the day that Lot went out from Sodom it rained fire and brimstone from heaven and destroyed them all. It will be just the same on the day that the Son of Man is revealed. On that day, the one who is on the housetop and whose goods are in the house must not go down to take them out; and likewise the one who is in the field must not turn back. Remember Lot's wife. Whoever seeks to keep his life will lose it, and whoever loses *his life* will preserve it. I tell you, on that night there will be two in one bed; one will be taken and the other will be left. There will be two women grinding at the same place; one will be taken and the other will be left. [Two men will be in the field; one will be taken and the other will be left."] And answering they said to Him, "Where, Lord?" And He said to them, "Where the body *is*, there also the vultures will be gathered" (Luke 17:22–37; see Genesis 19; Matthew 10:39; 16:21, 27; 24:17–28, 37–41).

Setting: Sychar in Samaria. After Jesus converses with a Samaritan woman at Jacob's well, His disciples return with food. They try to get Jesus to eat but are surprised when He speaks of other food.

Jesus said to them, "My food is to do the will of Him who sent Me and to accomplish His work. Do you not say, 'There are yet four months, and *then* comes the harvest'? Behold, I say to you, lift up your eyes and look on the fields, that they are white for harvest. Already he who reaps is receiving wages and is gathering fruit for life eternal; so that he who sows and he who reaps may rejoice together. For in this *case* the saying is true, 'One sows and another reaps.' I sent you to reap that for which you have not labored; others have labored and you have entered into their labor" (John 4:34–38; see Matthew 9:37, 38; John 5:36).

[GATHERING from gather]
Setting: Near the Sea of Galilee. After revealing to the Jewish religious leaders during the Feast of the Jews in Jerusalem that God, John the Baptist, His works, and the Scriptures all testify to His mission, Jesus miraculously feeds more than 5,000 people with a lad's five barley loaves and two fish.

Jesus said, "Have the people sit down." Now there was much grass in the place. So the men sat down, in number about five thousand. Jesus took the loaves, and having given thanks, He distributed to those who were seated; likewise also of the fish as much as they wanted. When they were filled, He said to the disciples, "Gather up the leftover fragments so that nothing will be lost" (John 6:10–12; cf. Matthew 14:17–21; Mark 6:38–44; Luke 9:14–17; see Matthew 15:32–38).

[GATHERING from gather]
Setting: Jerusalem. Before the Passover, after He conveys the upcoming ministry of the Holy Spirit in His disciples' lives with His imminent departure from them, Jesus explains He is the vine and they are the branches.

"I am the true vine, and My Father is the vinedresser. Every branch in Me that does not bear fruit, He takes away; and every *branch* that bears fruit, He prunes it so that it may bear more fruit. You are already clean because of the word which I have spoken to you. Abide in Me, and I in you. As the branch cannot bear fruit of itself unless it abides in the vine, so neither *can* you unless you abide in Me. I am the vine, you are the branches; he who abides in Me and I in him, he bears much fruit, for apart from Me you can do nothing. If anyone does not abide in Me, he is thrown away as a branch and dries up; and they gather them, and cast them into the fire and they are burned. If you abide in Me, and My words abide in you, ask whatever you wish, and it will be done for you. My Father is glorified by this, that you bear much fruit, and *so* prove to be My disciples. Just as the Father has loved Me, I have also loved you; abide in My love. If you keep My commandments, you will abide in My love; just as I have kept My Father's commandments and abide in His love. These things I have spoken to you so that My joy may be in you, and *that* your joy may be made full" (John 15:1–11; see Matthew 5:16; 7:7; John 3:29, 35; 6:56; 8:29, 31; 13:10; 15:16).

GENERATION (Specifics such as GENERATION, EVIL are separate entries)

Setting: Galilee. After praising John the Baptist as His forerunner, Jesus demonstrates the foolish thinking of the current generation of Jewish religious leaders by repeating what they say about John's ascetic lifestyle and ministry along with His own.

"But to what shall I compare this generation? It is like children sitting in the market places, who call out to the other *children,* and say, 'We played the flute for you, and you did not dance; we sang a dirge, and you did not mourn.' For John came neither eating nor drinking, and they say, 'He has a demon!' The Son of Man came eating and drinking, and they say, 'Behold, a gluttonous man and a drunkard, a friend of tax collectors and sinners! Yet wisdom is vindicated by her deeds" (Matthew 11:16–19; cf. Luke 7:31–35; see Matthew 9:11, 34; Luke 1:15).

Setting: Galilee. After Jesus warns the Pharisees about the unpardonable sin and their future judgment, some Pharisees and scribes ask Him to perform a miraculous sign for them in front of the crowds.

But He answered and said to them, "An evil and adulterous generation craves for a sign; and *yet* no sign will be given to it but the sign of Jonah the prophet; for just as JONAH WAS THREE DAYS AND THREE NIGHTS IN THE BELLY OF THE SEA MONSTER, so will the Son of Man be three days and three nights in the heart of the earth. The men of Nineveh will stand up with this generation at the judgment, and will condemn it because they repented at the preaching of Jonah; and behold, something greater than Jonah is here. *The* Queen of *the* South will rise up with this generation at the judgment and will condemn it, because she came from the ends of the earth to hear the wisdom of Solomon; and behold, something greater than Solomon is here" (Matthew 12:39–42; Jesus quotes from Jonah 1:17; cf. 1 Kings 10:1; Jonah 3:5; Matthew 16:1, 4; Luke 11:29).

Setting: The temple in Jerusalem. After the Jewish religious leaders test Him with questions, Jesus pronounces the eighth of eight woes on them in front of the crowds and His disciples.

"Woe to you, scribes and Pharisees, hypocrites! For you build the tombs of the prophets and adorn the monuments of the righteous, and say, 'If we had been *living* in the days of our fathers, we would not have been partners with them in *shedding* the blood of the prophets.' So you testify against yourselves, that you are sons of those who murdered the prophets. Fill up, then, the measure *of the guilt* of you fathers. You serpents, you brood of vipers, how will you escape the sentence of hell? Therefore, behold, I am sending you prophets and wise men and scribes; some of them you will kill and crucify, and some of them you will scourge in your synagogues, and persecute from city to city, so that upon you may fall *the guilt of* all the righteous blood shed on earth, from the blood of righteous Abel to the blood of Zechariah, the son of Berechiah, whom you murdered between the temple and the altar. Truly I say to you, all these things will come upon this generation" (Matthew 23:29–36; cf. 2 Chronicles 24:21; Zechariah 1:1; Matthew 3:7; Luke 11:47–52; see Matthew 10:23).

Setting: The Mount of Olives, just east of Jerusalem. During His discourse, after answering His disciples' questions as to when the temple will be destroyed and Jerusalem overrun, along with the signs of His coming and the end of the age, Jesus teaches them the Parable of the Fig Tree.

"Now learn the parable from the fig tree: when its branch has already become tender and puts forth its leaves, you know that summer is near; so, you too, when you see all these things, recognize that He is near, *right* at the door. Truly, I say to you, this generation will not pass away until all these things take place. Heaven and earth will pass away, but My words will not pass away. But of that day and hour no one knows, not even the angels of heaven, nor the Son, but the Father alone. For the coming of the Son of Man will be just like the days of Noah. For as in those days before the flood they were eating and drinking, marrying and giving in marriage, until the day that Noah entered the ark, and they did not understand until the flood came and took them all away; so will the coming of the Son of Man be. Then there will be two men in the field; one will be taken and one will be left. Two women *will be* grinding at the mill; one will be taken and one will be left" (Matthew 24:32–41; cf. Mark 13:28–32; Luke 17:34–36; 21:28–33; see Genesis 6:5; 7:7; Matthew 5:18; 10:23; James 5:9).

Setting: The district of Dalmanutha. After Jesus miraculously feeds 4,000 people, the Pharisees argue with Him, seeking a sign from heaven to test Him.

Sighing deeply in His spirit, He said, "Why does this generation seek for a sign? Truly I say to you, no sign will be given to this generation" (Mark 8:12; cf. Matthew 16:1–4; see Matthew 12:39, 40).

Setting: On the Mount of Olives, east of the temple in Jerusalem. After predicting the temple's destruction, during His Olivet Discourse, Jesus responds to questions from Peter, James, John, and Andrew about future events.

"Now learn the parable from the fig tree: when its branch has already become tender and puts forth its leaves, you know that summer is near. Even so, you too, when you see these things happening, recognize that He is near, *right* at the door. Truly I say to you, this generation will not pass away until all these things take place. Heaven and earth will pass away, but My words will not pass away. But of the day or hour no one knows, not even the angels in heaven, nor the Son, but the Father *alone*" (Mark 13:28–32; cf. Matthew 24:32–36; Luke 21:28–33).

Setting: Galilee. After praising John the Baptist to the crowds, Jesus criticizes the Pharisees and lawyers who reject God's purpose and John's message.

"To what then shall I compare the men of this generation, and what are they like? They are like children who sit in the market place and call to one another, and they say, 'We played the flute for you, and you did not dance; we sang a dirge, and you did not weep.' For John the Baptist has come eating no bread and drinking no wine, and you say, 'He has a demon!' The Son of Man has come eating and drinking, and you say, 'Behold, a gluttonous man and a drunkard, a friend of tax collectors and sinners!' Yet wisdom is vindicated by all her children." (Luke 7:31–35; cf. Matthew 11:16–19; see Luke 1:15).

Setting: On the way from Galilee to Jerusalem. After revealing a problem with exorcism and responding to a blessing from a woman in the crowd, Jesus tells the increasing crowds of the sign of Jonah.

As the crowds were increasing, He began to say, "This generation is a wicked generation; it seeks for a sign, and *yet* no sign will be given to it but the sign of Jonah. For just as Jonah became a sign to the Ninevites, so will the Son of Man be to this generation. The Queen of the South will rise up with the men of this generation at the judgment and condemn them, because she came from the ends of the earth to hear the wisdom of Solomon; and behold, something greater than Solomon is here. The men of Nineveh will stand up with this generation at the judgment and condemn it, because they repented at the preaching of Jonah; and behold, something greater than Jonah is here" (Luke 11:29–32; cf. Matthew 16:4; see 1 Kings 10:1–10; Jonah 3:4, 5).

Setting: On the way from Galilee to Jerusalem. After Jesus pronounces woes upon the Pharisees, a lawyer replies that His remarks are an insult to lawyers, too.

But He said, "Woe to you lawyers as well! For you weigh men down with burdens hard to bear, while you yourselves will not even touch the burdens with one of your fingers. Woe to you! For you build the tombs of the prophets, and *it was* your fathers *who* killed them. So you are witnesses and approve the deeds of your fathers; because it was they who killed them, and you build *their tombs*. For this reason also the wisdom of God said, 'I will send them prophets and apostles, and *some* of them they will kill and *some* they will persecute, so that the blood of all the prophets, shed since the foundation of the world, may be charged against this generation, from the blood of Abel to the blood of Zechariah, who was killed between the altar and the house *of God*; yes, I tell you, it shall be charged against this generation.' Woe to you lawyers! For you have taken away the key of knowledge; you yourselves did not enter, and you hindered those who were entering." (Luke 11:46–52; cf. Matthew 23:29–32; see 2 Chronicles 24:20, 21; Matthew 23:4, 13).

Setting: Samaria, on the way from Galilee to Jerusalem. After the Pharisees question Him about the coming of the kingdom of God, Jesus tells His disciples of His second coming.

And He said to the disciples, "The days will come when you will long to see one of the days of the Son of Man, and you will not see it. They will say to you, 'Look there! Look here!' Do not go away, and do not run after *them*. For just like the lightning, when it flashes out of one part of the sky, shines to the other part of the sky, so will the Son of Man be in His day. But first He must suffer many things and be rejected by this generation. And just as it happened in the days of Noah, so it will be also in the days of the Son of Man: they were eating, they were drinking, they were marrying, they were being given in marriage, until the day that Noah entered the ark, and the flood came and destroyed them all. It was the same as happened in the days of Lot: they were eating, they were drinking, they were buying, they were selling, they were planting, they were building; but on the day that Lot went out from Sodom it rained fire and brimstone from heaven and destroyed them all. It will be just the same on the day that the Son of Man is revealed. On that day, the one who is on the housetop and whose goods are in the house must not go down to take them out; and likewise the one who is in the field must not turn back. Remember Lot's wife. Whoever seeks to keep his life will lose it, and whoever loses *his life* will preserve it. I tell you, on that night there will be two in one bed; one will be taken and the other will be left. There will be two women grinding at the same place; one will be taken and the other will be left. [Two men will be in the field; one will be taken and the other will be left."] And answering they said to Him, "Where, Lord?" And He said to them, "Where the body *is*, there also the vultures will be gathered" (Luke 17:22–37; see Genesis 19; Matthew 10:39; 16:21, 27; 24:17–28, 37–41).

Setting: On the Mount of Olives, just east of Jerusalem. After ministering in the temple a few days before His crucifixion and giving His disciples more details regarding His return, Jesus conveys the Parable of the Fig Tree during His Olivet Discourse.

Then He told them a parable: "Behold the fig tree and all the trees; as soon as they put forth *leaves*, you see it and know for yourselves that summer is now near. So you also, when you see these things happening, recognize that the kingdom of God is near. Truly, I say to you, this generation will not pass away until all things take place. Heaven and earth will pass away, but My words will not pass away" (Luke 21:29–33; cf. Matthew 24:32–35; Mark 13:28–31; see Matthew 5:18).

GENERATION, ADULTEROUS AND SINFUL (Also see GENERATION, EVIL AND ADULTEROUS)

Setting: Caesarea Philippi. After rebuking Peter for desiring to thwart His mission to the cross, Jesus summons a crowd, along with His disciples, and informs them of the high costs of following Him.

And He summoned the crowd with His disciples, and said to them, "If anyone wishes to come after Me, he must deny himself, and take up his cross and follow Me. For whoever wishes to save his life will lose it, but whoever loses his life for My sake and the gospel's will save it. For what does it profit a man to gain the whole world, and forfeit his soul? For what will a man give in exchange for his soul? For whoever is ashamed of Me and My words in this adulterous and sinful generation, the Son of Man will also be ashamed of him when He comes in the glory of His Father with the holy angels" (Mark 8:34–38; cf. Matthew 16:24–28; Luke 9:23–27; see Matthew 10:33, 38, 39).

GENERATION, EVIL (Also see GENERATION, WICKED)

Setting: Galilee. Jesus responds to some Pharisees and scribes who ask Him for a miraculous sign.

"Now when the unclean spirit goes out of a man, it passes through waterless places seeking rest, and does not find *it*. Then it says, 'I will return to my house from which I came'; and when it comes, it finds *it* unoccupied, swept, and put in order. Then it goes and takes along with it seven other spirits more wicked than itself, and they go in and live there; and the last state of that man becomes worse than the first. That is the way it will also be for this evil generation" (Matthew 12:43–45; cf. Luke 11:24–26; see Matthew 12:38; Mark 5:9).

GENERATION, EVIL AND ADULTEROUS (Also see GENERATION, ADULTEROUS AND SINFUL)

Setting: Galilee. After Jesus warns the Pharisees about the unpardonable sin and their future judgment, some of the Pharisees and scribes ask Him to perform a miraculous sign for them before the crowds.

But He answered and said to them, "An evil and adulterous generation craves for a sign; and *yet* no sign will be given to it but the sign of Jonah the prophet; for just as JONAH WAS THREE DAYS AND THREE NIGHTS IN THE BELLY OF THE SEA MONSTER, so will the Son of Man be three days and three nights in the heart of the earth. The men of Nineveh will stand up with this generation at the judgment, and will condemn it because they repented at the preaching of Jonah; and behold, something greater than Jonah is here. *The* Queen of *the* South will rise up with this generation at the judgment and will condemn it, because she came from the ends of the earth to hear the wisdom of Solomon; and behold, something greater than Solomon is here" (Matthew 12:39–42; Jesus quotes from Jonah 1:17; cf. 1 Kings 10:1; Jonah 3:5; Matthew 16:1, 4; 12:38; Luke 11:29).

Setting: Magadan of Galilee. After the Pharisees and Sadducees reject Jesus' message; these enemies continue to test Him by asking Him for a sign from heaven.

But He replied to them, "When it is evening, you say, '*It will be* fair weather, for the sky is red.' And in the morning, '*There will* be a storm today, for the sky is red and threatening.' Do you know how to discern the appearance of the sky, but cannot *discern* the signs of the times? An evil and adulterous generation seeks after a sign; and a sign will not be given it, except the sign of Jonah." And He left them and went away (Matthew 16:2–4; cf. Matthew 12:39; Mark 8:12; Luke 12:54–56).

GENERATION, UNBELIEVING

Setting: Galilee. When Jesus, Peter, James, and John return from a high mountain (perhaps Mount Hermon) where Jesus was transfigured, they discover the remaining disciples arguing with some scribes.

And He asked them, "What are you discussing with them?" And one of the crowd answered Him, "Teacher, I brought You my son, possessed with a spirit which makes him mute; and whenever it seizes him, it slams him *to the ground* and he foams *at the mouth,* and grinds his teeth and stiffens out. I told Your disciples to cast it out, and they could not *do it.* And He answered them, and said, "O unbelieving generation, how long shall I be with you? How long shall I put up with you? Bring him to Me!" They brought the boy to Him. When he saw Him, immediately the spirit threw him into a convulsion, and falling to the ground, be *began* rolling around and foaming *at the mouth.* And He asked his father, "How long has this been happening to him?" And he said, "From childhood. It has often thrown him both into the fire and into the water to destroy him. But if You can do anything, take pity on us and help us!" And Jesus said to him, "'If You can?' All things are possible to him who believes." Immediately the boy's father cried out and said, "I do believe; help my unbelief." When Jesus saw that a crowd was rapidly gathering, He rebuked the unclean spirit, saying to it, "You deaf and mute spirit, I command you, come out of him and do not enter him again." After crying out and throwing him into terrible convulsions, it came out; and *the boy* became so much like a corpse that most *of them,* said, "He is dead!" But Jesus took him by the hand and raised him; and he got up. When He came into *the* house, His disciples *began* questioning Him privately, "Why could we not drive it out?" And He said to them, "This kind cannot come out by anything but prayer" (Mark 9:16–29; cf. Matthew 17:14–21; Luke 9:37–43; see Matthew 17:20; Mark 9:14, 15).

GENERATION, UNBELIEVING AND PERVERTED

Setting: Galilee. Jesus, Peter, James, and John descend the mountain where Jesus was transfigured with Moses and Elijah. After responding to His disciples' question about Elijah's future coming, Jesus expresses dismay over their inability to heal a man's demon-possessed son.

And Jesus answered and said, "You unbelieving and perverted generation, how long shall I be with you? How long shall I put up with you? Bring him here to Me." And Jesus rebuked him, and the demon came out of him, and the boy was cured at once (Matthew 17:17, 18; cf. Mark 9:19–29; Luke 9:41–43).

Setting: On a mountain in Galilee. A day after Jesus' transfiguration, a man from a large crowd begs Him to look at his demon-possessed son.

And Jesus answered and said, "You unbelieving and perverted generation, how long shall I be with you and put up with you? Bring your son here" (Luke 9:41; cf. Matthew 17:14–18; Mark 9:14–27).

GENERATION, WICKED (Also see GENERATION, EVIL)

Setting: On the way from Galilee to Jerusalem. After revealing a problem with exorcism and responding to a blessing from a woman in the crowd, Jesus tells the increasing crowds of the sign of Jonah.

As the crowds were increasing, He began to say, "This generation is a wicked generation; it seeks for a sign, and *yet* no sign will be given to it but the sign of Jonah. For just as Jonah became a sign to the Ninevites, so will the Son of Man be to this generation. The Queen of the South will rise up with the men of this generation at the judgment and condemn them, because she came from the ends of the earth to hear the wisdom of Solomon; and behold, something greater than Solomon is here. The men of Nineveh will stand up with this generation at the judgment and condemn it, because they repented at the preaching of Jonah; and behold, something greater than Jonah is here" (Luke 11:29–32; cf. Matthew 16:4; see 1 Kings 10:1–10; Jonah 3:4, 5).

GENEROSITY (Also see GIFTS TO OTHER PEOPLE)

[GENEROSITY from generous]

Setting: Judea beyond the Jordan (Perea). Jesus illustrates the kingdom of heaven to His disciples through the story of laborers in the vineyard.

"For the kingdom of heaven is like a landowner who went out early in the morning to hire laborers for his vineyard. When he had agreed with the laborers for a denarius for the day, he sent them into his vineyard. And he went out about the third hour and saw others standing idle in the market place; and to those he said,' You also go into the vineyard, and whatever is right I will give you.' And *so* they went. Again he went out about the sixth and the ninth hour, and did the same thing. And about the eleventh *hour* he went out and found others standing *around;* and he said to them, 'Why have you been standing idle here all day long?' They said to him, 'Because no one hired us.' He said to them, 'You go into the vineyard too.' When evening came, the owner of the vineyard said to his foreman, 'Call the laborers and pay them their wages, beginning with the last *group* to the first.' When those *hired* about the eleventh hour came, each one received a denarius. When those *hired* first came, they thought that they would receive more; but each of them also received a denarius. When they received it, they grumbled at the landowner, saying, 'These last men have worked *only* one hour, and you have made them equal to us who have borne the burden and the scorching heat of the day.' But he answered and said to one of them, 'Friend, I am doing you no wrong; did you not agree with me for a denarius? Take what is yours and go, but I wish to give to this last man the same as to you. It is not lawful for me to do what I wish with what is my own? Or is your eye envious because I am generous?' So the last shall be first, and the first last" (Matthew 20:1–16; cf. Matthew 19:30).

GENNESARET, LAKE OF (See GALILEE, SEA OF)

GENTILE (Also see GENTILES)

Setting: Capernaum of Galilee. After conveying to His disciples the value of little ones, Jesus gives instruction about church discipline.

"If your brother sins, go and show him his fault in private; if he listens to you, you have won your brother. But if he does not listen *to you,* take one or two more with you, so that BY THE MOUTH OF TWO OR THREE WITNESSES EVERY FACT MAY BE CONFIRMED. If he refuses to listen to them, tell it to the church; and if he refuses to listen even to the church, let him be to you as a Gentile and a tax collector. Truly I say to you, whatever you bind of earth shall have been bound in heaven; and whatever you loose on earth shall have been loosed in heaven. Again, I say to you, that if two of you agree on earth about anything that they may ask, it shall be done for them by My Father who is in heaven. For there two or three have gathered together in My name, I am there in their midst" (Matthew 18:15–20. Jesus quotes from Deuteronomy 19:15; cf. Matthew 7:7; 16:19; see Leviticus 19:17; Matthew 28:20; 2 Thessalonians 3:6, 14).

GENTILES (GENTILES, TIMES OF THE is a separate entry; also see GENTILE)

Setting: Galilee. During the early part of His ministry, Jesus preaches the Sermon on the Mount to His disciples and the multitudes.

"You have heard that it was said, 'YOU SHALL LOVE YOUR NEIGHBOR and hate your enemy.' But I say to you, love your enemies and pray for those who persecute you, so that you may be sons of your Father who is in heaven; for He causes His sun to rise on *the* evil and *the* good, and sends rain on *the* righteous and *the* unrighteous. For if you love those who love you, what reward do you have? Do not even the tax collectors do the same? If you greet only your brothers, what more are you doing *than others?* Do not even the Gentiles do the same? Therefore, you are to be perfect, as your heavenly Father is perfect" (Matthew 5:43–48, Jesus quotes from Leviticus 19:18; cf. Leviticus 19:2; Luke 6:27–36).

Setting: Galilee. During the early part of His ministry, Jesus preaches the Sermon on the Mount to His disciples and the multitudes.

"And when you are praying, do not use meaningless repetition as the Gentiles do, for they suppose that they will be heard for their many words. So do not be like them; for your Father knows what you need before you ask Him" (Matthew 6:7, 8; see 1 Kings 18:26–29).

Setting: Galilee. During the early part of His ministry, Jesus preaches the Sermon on the Mount to His disciples and the multitudes.

"For this reason I say to you, do not be worried about your life, *as to* what you will eat or what you will drink; nor for your body, *as to* what you will put on. Is not life more than food, and the body more than clothing? Look at the birds of the air, that they do not sow, nor reap nor gather into barns, and *yet* your heavenly Father feeds them. Are you not worth much more than they? And who of you by being worried can add a *single* hour to his life? And why are you worried about clothing? Observe how the lilies of the field grow; they do not toil nor do they spin, yet I say to you that not even Solomon in all his glory clothed himself like one of these. But if God so clothes the grass of the field, which is *alive* today and tomorrow is thrown into the furnace, *will He* not much more *clothe* you? You of little faith! Do not worry then, saying 'What will we eat?' or 'What will we drink?' or 'What will be wear for clothing?" For the Gentiles eagerly seek all these things; for your heavenly Father knows that you need all these things. But seek first His kingdom and His righteousness, and all these things will be added to you. So do not worry about tomorrow; for tomorrow will care for itself. Each day has enough trouble of its own" (Matthew 6:25–34; cf. Luke 12:22–31; see 1 Kings 10:4–7; Job 35:11; Matthew 8:26).

Setting: Galilee. After His twelve disciples observe His ministry, Jesus summons and specifically instructs them about their ministry to the people of Israel.

These twelve Jesus sent out after instructing them: "Do not go in *the* way of *the* Gentiles, and do not enter *any* city of the Samaritans; but rather go to the lost sheep of the house of Israel. And as you go, preach, saying, 'The kingdom of heaven is at hand.' Heal *the* sick, raise *the* dead, cleanse *the* lepers, cast out demons. Freely you received, freely give. Do not acquire gold, or silver, or copper for your money belts, or a bag for *your* journey, or even two coats, or sandals, or a staff; for the worker is worthy of his support. And whatever city or village you enter, inquire who is worthy in it, and stay at his house until you leave *that city*. As you enter the house, give it your greeting. If the house is worthy, give it your *blessing of* peace. But if it is not worthy, take back your *blessing of* peace. Whoever does not receive you, nor heed your words, as you go out of that house or that city, shake the dust off your feet. Truly I say to you, it will be more tolerable for *the* land of Sodom and Gomorrah in the day of judgment than for that city" (Matthew 10:5–15; cf. Mark 6:7–11; Luke 9:1–5; see Matthew 3:2; 10:1–4; 11:22, 24; 15:24; Luke 22:35; 1 Corinthians 9:14).

Setting: Galilee. After His disciples observe His ministry, Jesus summons and specifically instructs them about the upcoming hardships of *their* ministry to the people of Israel.

"Behold, I send you out as sheep in the midst of wolves; so be shrewd as serpents and innocent as doves. But beware of men, for they will hand you over to *the* courts and scourge you in their synagogues; and you will even be brought before governors and kings for My sake, as a testimony to them and to the Gentiles. But when they hand you over, do not worry about how or what you are to say; for it will be given you in that hour what you are to say. For it is not you who speak, but *it* is the Spirit of your Father who speaks in you" (Matthew 10:16–20; cf. Luke 10:3).

[GENTILES from dogs]
Setting: The district of Tyre and Sidon. A Canaanite woman appeals to Jesus to heal her demon-possessed daughter.

But He answered and said, "I was sent only to the lost sheep of the house of Israel." But she came and *began* to bow down before Him, saying, "Lord, help me!" And He answered and said, "It is not good to take the children's bread and throw it to the dogs." But she said, "Yes, Lord; but even the dogs feed from the crumbs which fall from their masters' table." Then Jesus said to her, "O woman, your faith is great; it shall be done for you as you wish." And her daughter was healed at once (Matthew 15:24–28; cf. Mark 7: 24–30; see Matthew 9:22; 10:5, 6).

Setting: Judea beyond the Jordan (Perea). Before going to Jerusalem, Jesus again tells His disciples of His impending death and resurrection.

As Jesus was about to go up to Jerusalem, He took the twelve *disciples* aside by themselves, and on the way He said to them, "Behold, we are going up to Jerusalem; and the Son of Man will be delivered to the chief priests and scribes, and they will condemn Him to death, and will hand Him over to the Gentiles to mock and scourge and crucify *Him,* and on the third day, He will be raised up" (Matthew 20:17–19; cf. Matthew 16:21; Mark 10:32–34; Luke 18:31–33).

Setting: On the way to Jerusalem, where Jesus will die on the cross. Jesus teaches His disciples about true greatness after the mother of James and John, the sons of Zebedee, asks Him to make her sons exalted rulers with Him in His coming kingdom.

But Jesus called them to Himself and said, "You know that the rulers of the Gentiles lord it over them, and *their* great men exercise authority over them. It is not this way among you, but whoever wishes to become great among you shall be your servant, and whoever wishes to be first among you shall be your slave; just as the Son of Man did not come to be served, but to serve, and to give His life a ransom for many" (Matthew 20:25–28; cf. Matthew 23:11; 26:28; Mark 10:42–45).

[GENTILES from dogs]

Setting: The region of Tyre. After the Pharisees and scribes from Jerusalem question Jesus' disciples' lack of obedience to tradition in Galilee, Jesus casts out a demon from the daughter of a Gentile (Syrophoenician) woman.

And He was saying to her, "Let the children be satisfied first, for it is not good to take the children's bread and throw it to the dogs." But she answered and said to Him, "Yes, Lord *but* even the dogs under the table feed on the children's crumbs. And He said to her, "Because of this answer go; the demon has gone out of your daughter" (Mark 7:27–29; cf. Matthew 15:21–28).

Setting: On the road to Jerusalem, Jesus prophesies His persecution, death, and resurrection after encouraging His disciples with revelation of their future reward.

Saying, "Behold, we are going up to Jerusalem, and the Son of Man will be delivered to the chief priests and the scribes; and they will condemn Him to death and will hand Him over to the Gentiles. They will mock Him and spit on Him, and scourge Him and kill *Him,* and three days later He will rise again" (Mark 10:32–34; cf. Matthew 20:17–19; Luke 18:31–34; see Matthew 16:21; Mark 8:31).

Setting: On the road to Jerusalem. James and John ask Jesus for special honor and privileges in His kingdom. The other disciples become angry, so Jesus uses this moment to teach them about servanthood.

Calling them to Himself, Jesus said to them, "You know that those who are recognized as rulers of the Gentiles lord it over them; and their great men exercise authority over them. But it is not this way among you, but whoever wishes to become great among you shall be your servant; and whoever wishes to be first among you shall be slave of all. For even the Son of Man did not come to be served, but to serve, and to give His life a ransom for many" (Mark 10:42–45; cf. Matthew 20:25–28).

Setting: On the way from Galilee to Jerusalem. After responding to Peter's statement about His disciples' personal sacrifice in following Him, Jesus tells them of the upcoming sacrifice He will make in Jerusalem.

Then He took the twelve aside and said to them, "Behold, we are going up to Jerusalem, and all things which are written through the prophets about the Son of Man will be accomplished. For He will be handed over to the Gentiles, and will be mocked and mistreated and spit upon, and after they have scourged Him, they will kill Him; and the third day He will rise again" (Luke 18:31–33; cf. Matthew 20:17–19; Mark 10:32–34).

Setting: The Mount of Olives, east of the temple in Jerusalem. After ministering in the temple a few days before His crucifixion, and giving the disciples more details regarding future events, Jesus elaborates more about things to come during His Olivet Discourse.

"But when you see Jerusalem surrounded by armies, then recognize that her desolation is near. Then those who are in Judea must flee to the mountains, and those who are in the midst of the city must leave, and those who are in the country must not enter the city; because these are days of vengeance, so that all things which are written will be fulfilled. Woe to those who are pregnant and to those who are nursing babies in those days; for there will be a great distress upon the land and wrath to this people; and they will fall by the edge of the sword, and will be led captive into all the nations; and Jerusalem will be trampled under foot by the Gentiles until the times of the Gentiles are fulfilled" (Luke 21:20–24; see Matthew 24:15–18; Mark 13:14–16; Luke 19:43).

Setting: An upper room in Jerusalem. During the Feast of Unleavened Bread (Passover) just before Jesus' crucifixion, while the Lord is celebrating the Passover meal and instituting the Lord's Supper, His disciples argue over who is the greatest among them.

And He said to them, "The kings of the Gentiles lord it over them; and those who have authority over them are called 'Benefactors.' But *it is* not this way with you, but the one who is the greatest among you must become like the youngest, and the leader like a servant. For who is greater, the one who reclines *at the table* or the one who serves? Is it not the one who reclines *at the table?* But I am among you as the one who serves" (Luke 22:25–27; cf. Matthew 20:25–28; 23:11; Mark 10:42–45; Luke 22:1–24).

Setting: Damascus. Luke, writing in Acts, describes the reluctance of Ananias, a follower of Jesus, to locate Saul of Tarsus (a known enemy of the church) in order to restore Saul's vision.

But the Lord said to him, "Go, for he is a chosen instrument of Mine, to bear My name before the Gentiles and kings and the sons of Israel; for I will show him how much he must suffer for My name's sake" (Acts 9:15, 16; see Acts 13:2; 20:22–24).

Setting: Jerusalem. Luke, writing in Acts, recounts Paul's speech to a hostile Jewish crowd (after his third missionary journey). Paul recounts his instructions from the Lord Jesus following his conversion on the road to Damascus.

"And He said to me, 'Go! For I will send you far away to the Gentiles'" (Acts 22:21; see Acts 9:15).

Setting: Caesarea. Luke, writing in Acts, gives Paul's retelling of his conversion to Christ as he appeared before King Agrippa following his hearing before the Jewish Council in Jerusalem and arrest by the Roman commander (on his way to Rome after the apostle's third missionary journey).

"And when we had fallen to the ground, I heard a voice saying to me in the Hebrew dialect, 'Saul, Saul, why are you persecuting Me? It is hard for you to kick against the goads.' And I said, 'Who are You, Lord?' And the Lord said, 'I am Jesus whom you are persecuting. But get up and stand on your feet; for this purpose I have appeared to you, to appoint you a minister and a witness not only to the things which you have seen, but also to the things in which I will appear to you; rescuing you from the *Jewish* people and from the Gentiles, to whom I am sending you, to open their eyes so that they may turn from darkness to light and from the dominion of Satan to God, that they may receive forgiveness of sins and an inheritance among those who have been sanctified by faith in Me' (Acts 26:14–18; see Isaiah 35:5; Acts 21:40; 22:14).

GENTILES, TIMES OF THE (Also see GENTILES)

Setting: On the Mount of Olives, east of the temple in Jerusalem. After ministering in the temple a few days before His crucifixion, and giving the disciples more details regarding future events, Jesus elaborates more about things to come during His Olivet Discourse.

"But when you see Jerusalem surrounded by armies, then recognize that her desolation is near. Then those who are in Judea must flee to the mountains, and those who are in the midst of the city must leave, and those who are in the country must not enter the city; because these are days of vengeance, so that all things which are written will be fulfilled. Woe to those who are pregnant and to those who are nursing babies in those days; for there will be a great distress upon the land and wrath to this people; and they will fall by the edge of the sword, and will be led captive into all the nations; and Jerusalem will be trampled under foot by the Gentiles until the times of the Gentiles are fulfilled" (Luke 21:20–24; see Matthew 24:15–18; Mark 13:14–16; Luke 19:43).

GENTLENESS

[GENTLENESS from gentle]

Setting: Galilee. Early in His ministry, Jesus presents the Beatitudes (part of the Sermon on the Mount) to His disciples and the gathered crowds from Galilee, Decapolis, Jerusalem, Judea, and beyond the Jordan.

"Blessed are the gentle, for they shall inherit the earth" (Matthew 5:5; cf. Psalm 37:11; see Matthew 5:1; 13:35).

[GENTLENESS from gentle]

Setting: Throughout Galilee. After rendering a thanksgiving prayer to His Father in heaven, as He preaches and teaches, Jesus offers rest to all who are weary and heavy-laden.

"Come to Me, all who are weary and heavy-laden, and I will give you rest. Take My yoke upon you and learn from Me, for I am gentle and humble in heart, and YOU WILL FIND REST FOR YOUR SOULS. For My yoke is easy and My burden is light" (Matthew 11:28–30, Jesus quotes from Jeremiah 6:16; see Jeremiah 31:35; 1 John 5:3).

GIFT OF GOD (Listed under GOD, GIFT OF)

GIFTS, GOOD (Also see GENEROSITY; GIFTS TO OTHER PEOPLE and GIVING)

Setting: Galilee. During the early part of His ministry, Jesus preaches the Sermon on the Mount to His disciples and the multitudes.

"Ask, and it will be given to you; seek, and you will find; knock, and it will be opened to you. For everyone who asks receives, and he who seeks finds, and to him who knocks it will be opened. Or what man is there among you who, when his son asks for a loaf, will give him a stone? Or if he asks for a fish, he will not give him a snake, will he? If you then, being evil, know how to give good gifts to your children, how much more will your Father who is in heaven give what is good to those who ask Him! In everything, therefore, treat people the same way you want them to treat you, for this is the Law and the Prophets" (Matthew 7:7–12; cf. Matthew 22:40; Luke 6:31; 11:9–13; see Psalm 84:11).

Setting: On the way from Galilee to Jerusalem. After revealing to His disciples how to pray, Jesus illustrates God's benevolence in answering prayer and giving the Holy Spirit.

"Now suppose one of you fathers is asked by his son for a fish; he will not give him a snake instead of a fish, will he? Or *if* he is asked for an egg, he will not give him a scorpion, will he? If you then, being evil, know how to give good gifts to your children, how much more will *your* heavenly Father give the Holy Spirit to those who ask Him?" (Luke 11:11–13; cf. Matthew 7:9–11).

GIFTS FROM GOD (Listed under GOD, GIFTS FROM)

GIFTS TO OTHER PEOPLE (Also see GENEROSITY; GIFTS, GOOD; OFFERING; STEWARDSHIP; and TITHE)

[GIFTS TO OTHER PEOPLE from Give to him who asks of you]

Setting: Galilee. During the early part of His ministry, Jesus preaches the Sermon on the Mount to His disciples and the multitudes.

"Give to him who asks of you, and do not turn away from him who wants to borrow from you" (Matthew 5:42; see Deuteronomy 15:7–11).

[GIFTS TO OTHER PEOPLE from give to the poor and your giving]

Setting: Galilee. During the early part of His ministry, Jesus preaches the Sermon on the Mount to His disciples and the multitudes.

"So when you give to the poor, do not sound a trumpet before you, as the hypocrites do in the synagogues and in the streets, so that they may be honored by men. Truly I say to you, they have their reward in full. But when you give to the poor, do not let your left hand know what your right hand is doing, so that your giving will be in secret; and your Father who sees *what is done* in secret will reward you" (Matthew 6:2–4; see Jeremiah 17:10; Matthew 6:16).

[GIFTS TO OTHER PEOPLE from freely give]
Setting: Galilee. After His twelve disciples observe His ministry, Jesus summons and specifically instructs them about their ministry to the people of Israel.

These twelve Jesus sent out after instructing them: "Do not go in *the* way of *the* Gentiles, and do not enter *any* city of the Samaritans; but rather go to the lost sheep of the house of Israel. And as you go, preach, saying, 'The kingdom of heaven is at hand.' Heal *the* sick, raise *the* dead, cleanse *the* lepers, cast out demons. Freely you received, freely give. Do not acquire gold, or silver, or copper for your money belts, or a bag for *your* journey, or even two coats, or sandals, or a staff; for the worker is worthy of his support. And whatever city or village you enter, inquire who is worthy in it, and stay at his house until you leave *that city*. As you enter the house, give it your greeting. If the house is worthy, give it your *blessing of* peace. But if it is not worthy, take back your *blessing of* peace. Whoever does not receive you, nor heed your words, as you go out of that house or that city, shake the dust off your feet. Truly I say to you, it will be more tolerable for *the* land of Sodom and Gomorrah in the day of judgment than for that city" (Matthew 10:5–15; cf. Mark 6:7–11; Luke 9:1–5; see Matthew 3:2; 11:22, 24; 15:24; Luke 22:35; 1 Corinthians 9:14).

[GIFTS TO OTHER PEOPLE from gives to one of these little ones even a cup of cold water to drink]
Setting: Galilee. After His twelve disciples observe His ministry, Jesus summons and specifically instructs them about their ministry ahead that will include rewards.

"He who receives you receives Me, and he who receives Me receives Him who sent me. He who receives a prophet in the name of a prophet shall receive a prophet's reward; and he who receives a righteous man in the name of a righteous man shall receive a righteous man's reward. And whoever in the name of a disciple gives to one of these little ones even a cup of cold water to drink, truly I say to you, he shall not lose his reward" (Matthew 10:40–42; cf. Matthew 25:40, 44, 45; see Mark 9:37).

[GIFTS TO OTHER PEOPLE from you give them *something* to eat]
Setting: By the Sea of Galilee. Late in the day, after He hears the news of John the Baptist's beheading and heals the sick from the crowd following Him, Jesus miraculously feeds more than 5,000 of His countrymen.

But Jesus said to them, "They do not need to go away; you give them *something* to eat!" They said to Him, "We have here only five loaves and two fish." And He said, "Bring them here to Me" (Matthew 14:16–18; cf. Mark 6:35–44; Luke 9:12–17; John 6:4–13; see Matthew 16:9).

[GIFTS TO OTHER PEOPLE from give to *the* poor]
Setting: Judea beyond the Jordan (Perea). Jesus shares with a rich, young ruler how to obtain eternal life.

And He said to him, "Why are you asking Me about what is good? There is *only* One who is good; but if you wish to enter into life, keep the commandments." *Then* he said to Him, 'Which ones?' And Jesus said, "YOU SHALL NOT COMMIT MURDER; YOU SHALL NOT COMMIT ADULTERY; YOU SHALL NOT STEAL; YOU SHALL NOT BEAR FALSE WITNESS; HONOR YOUR FATHER AND MOTHER; and YOU SHALL LOVE YOUR NEIGHBOR AS YOURSELF." The young man said to Him, "All these things I have kept; what am I still lacking?" Jesus said to him, "If you wish to complete go *and* sell your possessions and give to *the* poor, and you will have treasure in heaven; and come, follow Me" (Matthew 19:16–22, Jesus quotes from Exodus 20:13–15; Leviticus 19:18; cf. Leviticus 18:5; Mark 10:17–21; Luke 10:25–28; 12:33; 18:18–24).

[GIFTS TO OTHER PEOPLE from Truly I say to you, to the extent that you did not do it to one of the least of these, you did not do it to Me]

Setting: On the Mount of Olives, just east of Jerusalem. During His Olivet Discourse, after answering His disciples' questions as to when the temple will be destroyed and Jerusalem overrun, along with the signs of His coming and the end of the age, Jesus reveals the future judgments following His return.

"But when the Son of Man comes in His glory, and all the angels with Him, then He will sit on His glorious throne. All the nations will be gathered before Him; and He will separate them from one another, as the shepherd separates the sheep from the goats; and He will put the sheep on His right, and the goats on the left. Then the King will say to those on His right, 'Come, you who are blessed of My Father, inherit the kingdom prepared for you from the foundation of the world. 'For I was hungry, and you gave Me *something* to eat; I was thirsty, and you gave Me *something* to drink; I was a stranger, and you invited Me in; naked, and you clothed Me; I was sick, and you visited Me; I was in prison, and you came to Me.' Then the righteous will answer Him, 'Lord, when did we see You hungry and feed You, or thirsty, and give you *something* to drink? And when did we see You a stranger, and invite You in, or naked, and clothe You? When did we see You sick, or in prison, and come to You?' The King will answer and say to them, 'Truly I say to you, to the extent that you did it to one of these brothers of Mine, *even* the least *of them,* you did it to Me.' Then He will also say to those on His left, 'Depart from Me, accursed ones, into the eternal fire which has been prepared for the devil and his angels; for I was hungry, and you gave Me *nothing* to eat; I was thirsty, and you gave Me nothing to drink; I was a stranger, and you did not invite Me in; naked, and you did not clothe Me; sick, and in prison, and you did not visit Me.' Then they themselves also will answer, 'Lord, when did we see You hungry, or thirsty, or a stranger, or naked, or sick, or in prison, and did not take care of You?' Then He will answer them, 'Truly I say to you, to the extent that you did not do it to one of the least of these, you did not do it to Me.' These will go away into eternal punishment, but the righteous into eternal life" (Matthew 25:31–46; see Matthew 7:23; 16:27; 19:29).

[GIFTS TO OTHER PEOPLE from You give them *something* to eat]
Setting: By the Sea of Galilee. After a long day of ministry, Jesus prepares to demonstrate to His disciples the power of God by feeding more than 5,000 people.

But He answered them, "You give them *something* to eat!" And they said to Him, "Shall we go and spend two hundred denarii on bread and give them *something* to eat? And He said to them, "How many loaves do you have? Go look!" And when they found out, they said, "Five, and two fish" (Mark 6:37, 38; cf. Matthew 14:16, 17; Luke 9:13, 14; John 6:5–9; see Mark 3:20).

[GIFTS TO OTHER PEOPLE from give to the poor]
Setting: Judea beyond the Jordan (Perea). After demonstrating to His disciples the importance of little children, Jesus encounters a rich man seeking eternal life.

And Jesus said to him, "Why do you call Me good? No one is good except God alone. You know the commandments, 'DO NOT MURDER, DO NOT COMMIT ADULTERY, DO NOT STEAL, DO NOT BEAR FALSE WITNESS, Do not defraud, HONOR YOUR FATHER AND MOTHER.'" And he said to Him, "Teacher, I have kept all these things from my youth up." Looking at him, Jesus felt a love for him and said to him, "One thing you lack: go and sell all you possess and give to the poor, and you will have treasure in heaven; and come, follow Me" (Mark 10:18–21; Jesus quotes from Exodus 20:12–16; cf. Matthew 19:16–22; Luke 18:18–24; see Matthew 6:20).

[GIFTS TO OTHER PEOPLE from Give to everyone who asks of you]
Setting: Galilee. After selecting His twelve disciples, Jesus teaches the Sermon on the Mount to those disciples and a great throng of people from Judea, Jerusalem, and the central coastal region of Tyre and Sidon.

"But I say to you who hear, love your enemies, do good to those who hate you, bless those who curse you, pray for those who mistreat you. Whoever hits you on the cheek, offer him the other also; and whoever takes away your coat, do not withhold your shirt from him either. Give to everyone who asks of you, and whoever takes away what is yours, do not demand it back. Treat others the same way you want them to treat you. If you love those who love you, what credit is *that* to you? For even sinners love those who love them. If you do good to those who do good to you, what credit is *that* to you? For even sinners do the same. If you lend to those from whom you expect to receive, what credit is *that* to you? Even sinners lend to sinners in order to receive back the same *amount.* But love your enemies, and do good, and lend, expecting nothing in return; and your reward will be great, and you will be sons of the Most High; for He Himself is kind to ungrateful and evil *men*. Be merciful, just as your Father is merciful" (Luke 6:27–36; cf. Matthew 5:9, 39–48; 7:12).

[GIFTS TO OTHER PEOPLE from Give and it will be given to you]
Setting: Galilee. After selecting His twelve disciples, Jesus teaches the Sermon on the Mount to those disciples and a great throng of people from Judea, Jerusalem, and the central coastal region of Tyre and Sidon.

"Do not judge, and you will not be judged; and do not condemn, and you will not be condemned; pardon, and you will be pardoned. Give and it will be given to you. They will pour into your lap a good measure—pressed down, shaken together, *and* running over. For by your standard of measure it will be measured to you in return" (Luke 6:37, 38; cf. Matthew 7:1–5; Mark 4:24; see Luke 6:12–19).

[GIFTS TO OTHER PEOPLE from You give them *something* to eat]
Setting: Galilee. Following a day of ministry, Jesus and His disciples try to withdraw to Bethsaida, but the large crowds have been relishing His teaching about the kingdom of God all day, so they must be fed physically, too.

But He said to them, "You give them *something* to eat!" And they said, "We have no more than five loaves and two fish, unless perhaps we go and buy food for all these people." (For there were about five thousand men.) And He said to His disciples, "Have them sit down *to eat* in groups of about fifty each" (Luke 9:13, 14; cf. Matthew 14:15–21; Mark 6:35–44; John 6:4–13).

[GIFTS TO OTHER PEOPLE from what they give you]
Setting: On the way from Galilee to Jerusalem. The Lord appoints seventy followers and sends them out in pairs to every place He Himself will soon visit.

And He was saying to them, "The harvest is plentiful, but the laborers are few; therefore beseech the Lord of the harvest to send out laborers into His harvest. Go; behold, I send you out as lambs in the midst of wolves. Carry no money belt, no bag, no shoes; and greet no one on the way. Whatever house you enter, first say, 'Peace be to this house.' If a man of peace is there, your peace will rest on him; but if not, it will return to you. Stay in that house, eating and drinking what they give you; for the laborer is worthy of his wages. Do not keep moving from house to house. Whatever city you enter and they receive you, eat what is set before you; and heal those in it who are sick, and say to them, 'The kingdom of God has come near to you.' But whatever city you enter and they do not receive you, go out into its streets and say, 'Even the dust of your city which clings to our feet we wipe off *in protest* against you; yet be sure of this, that the kingdom of God has come near.' I say to you, it will be more tolerable in that day for Sodom than for that city" (Luke 10:2–12; see Genesis 19:24–28; Matthew 9:37, 38, 10:9–14, 16; 1 Corinthians 10:27).

[GIFTS TO OTHER PEOPLE from give him as much as he needs]
Setting: On the way from Galilee to Jerusalem. After revealing to His disciples how to pray, Jesus illustrates persistence in prayer.

Then He said to them, "Suppose one of you has a friend, and goes to him at midnight and says to him, 'Friend, lend me three loaves; for a friend of mine has come to me from a journey, and I have nothing to set before him'; and from inside he answers and says, 'Do not bother me; the door has already been shut and my children and I are in bed; I cannot get up and give you *anything.*' I tell you, even though he will not get up and give him *anything* because he is his friend, yet because of his persistence he will get up and give him as much as he needs. So I say to you, ask, and it will be given to you; seek, and you will find; knock, and it will be opened to you. For everyone who asks, receives; and he who seeks, finds; and to him who knocks, it will be opened" (Luke 11:5–10; cf. Matthew 7:7, 8; see Luke 18:1–5).

[GIFTS TO OTHER PEOPLE from give to charity]
Setting: On the way from Galilee to Jerusalem. After giving a parable about riches and greed, Jesus challenges the crowd and His disciples concerning godly living.

"Sell your possessions and give to charity; make yourselves money belts which do not wear out, an unfailing treasure in heaven, where no thief comes near nor moth destroys. For where your treasure is, there your heart will be also" (Luke 12:33, 34; cf. Matthew 6:19–21; 19:21).

[GIFTS TO OTHER PEOPLE from When you give a luncheon or a dinner]
Setting: On the way from Galilee to Jerusalem. After Jesus, observing the invited guests of a Pharisee leader selecting places of honor at the table, speaks a parable to them, He comments to the host about the people to invite in the future.

And He also went on to say to the one who had invited Him, "When you give a luncheon or a dinner, do not invite your friends or your brothers or your relatives or rich neighbors, otherwise they may also invite you in return and *that* will be your repayment. But when you give a reception, invite *the* poor, *the* crippled, *the* lame, *the* blind, and you will be blessed, since they do not have *the means* to repay you; for you will be repaid at the resurrection of the righteous" (Luke 14:12–14; see John 5:28, 29).

[GIFTS TO OTHER PEOPLE from giving a big dinner]
Setting: On the way from Galilee to Jerusalem. After speaking a parable to the invited guests and the host at a banquet, Jesus responds to a guest's proclamation about the blessings of eating bread in the kingdom of God.

But He said to him, "A man was giving a big dinner, and he invited many; and at the dinner hour he sent his slave to say to those who had been invited, 'Come; for everything is ready now.' But they all alike began to make excuses. The first one said to him, 'I have bought a piece of land and I need to go out and look at it; please consider me excused.' Another one said, 'I have bought five yoke of oxen, and I am going to try them out; please consider me excused.' Another one said, I have married a wife, and for that reason I cannot come.' And the slave came *back* and reported this to his master. Then the head of the household became angry and said to his slave, 'Go out at once into the streets and lanes of the city and bring in here the poor and crippled and blind and lame.' And the slave said, 'Master, what you commanded has been done, and still there is room.' And the master said to the slave, 'Go out into the highways and along the hedges, and compel *them* to come in, so that my house may be filled. For I tell you, none of those men who were invited shall taste of my dinner'" (Luke 14:16–24; see Deuteronomy 24:5; Matthew 22:2–14).

[GIFTS TO OTHER PEOPLE from give up all his possessions]
Setting: On the way from Galilee to Jerusalem. After He responds to a guest's proclamation about the blessings of eating bread in the kingdom of God, Jesus presents to large crowds the demands of discipleship.

Now large crowds were going along with Him; and He turned and said to them, "If anyone comes to Me, and does not hate his own father and mother and wife and children and brothers and sisters, yes, and even his own life, he cannot be My disciple. Whoever does not carry his own cross and come after Me cannot be My disciple. For which one of you, when he wants to build a tower, does not first sit down and calculate the cost to see if he has enough to complete it? Otherwise, when he has laid a foundation and is not able to finish, all who observe it begin to ridicule him, saying, 'This man began to build and was not able to finish.' Or what king, when he sets out to meet another king in battle, will not first sit down and consider whether he is strong enough with ten thousand *men* to encounter the one coming against him with twenty thousand? Or else, while the other is still far away, he sends a delegation and asks for terms of peace. So then, none of you can be My disciple who does not give up all his possessions. Therefore, salt is good; but if even salt has become tasteless, with what will it be seasoned? It is useless either for the soil or for the manure pile; it is thrown out. He who has ears to hear, let him hear" (Luke 14:25–35; cf. Matthew 5:13; 10:37–39; see Proverb 20:18; Philippians 3:7).

[GIFTS TO OTHER PEOPLE from Give Me a drink]
Setting: Jerusalem. When the Pharisees hear Jesus is making more disciples than John the Baptist, the Lord leaves the city for Galilee. He and His disciples pass through Sychar in Samaria, where He encounters a woman at Jacob's well.

There came a woman of Samaria to draw water. Jesus said to her, "Give Me a drink" (John 4:7).

[GIFTS TO OTHER PEOPLE from It is more blessed to give than to receive]
Setting: Ephesus. Luke, writing in Acts, recounts Paul's recollection of Jesus' words regarding giving and receiving during the apostle's farewell address to the elders of the church during his third missionary journey, just before leaving for Jerusalem.

"In everything I showed you that working hard in this manner you must help the weak and remember the words of the Lord Jesus, that He Himself said, "It is more blessed to give than to receive'" (Acts 20:35; see Matthew 10:8).

GIRL

Setting: Capernaum near the Sea of Galilee. Following the healing of a woman suffering with internal bleeding for twelve years, Jesus brings a synagogue official's daughter back from death.

When Jesus came into the official's house, and saw the flute-players and the crowd in noisy disorder, He said, "Leave; for the girl has not died, but is asleep." And they *began* laughing at Him. But when the crowd had been sent out, He entered and took her by the hand, and the girl got up (Matthew 9:23–25; cf. Mark 5:21–24, 35–43; Luke 8:41, 42, 49–56).

Setting: Capernaum by the Sea of Galilee. In the home of Jairus, a synagogue official, Jesus revives Jairus's daughter, who had died.

Taking the child by the hand, He said to her, "Talitha kum!" (which translated means, "Little girl, I say to you, get up!") (Mark 5:41; cf. Matthew 9:25; Luke 8:54; see Luke 8:55, 56; Luke 7:14).

GIVING BACK TO GOD (See SERVICE; STEWARDSHIP: TITHE; and WORKS, GOOD)

GIVING TO OTHER PEOPLE (See GIFTS TO OTHER PEOPLE)

GIVING TO THE POOR (Listed under POOR, GIVING TO THE; also see CHARITY and POOR)

GLADNESS (Also see FULFILLMENT; HAPPINESS; JOY; and SATISFACTION)

[GLADNESS from glad]
Setting: Galilee. Early in His ministry, Jesus presents the Beatitudes (part of the Sermon on the Mount) to His disciples and the gathered crowds from Galilee, Decapolis, Jerusalem, Judea, and beyond the Jordan.

"Blessed are you when *people* insult you and persecute you, and falsely say all kinds of evil against you because of Me. Rejoice and be glad, for your reward in heaven is great; for in the same way they persecuted the prophets who were before you" (Matthew 5:11, 12; cf. 2 Chronicles 36:16; Luke 6:22, 23; 1 Peter 4:14; see Matthew 5:1; 13:35).

[GLADNESS from glad]
Setting: Galilee. After selecting His twelve disciples, Jesus teaches the Beatitudes (part of the Sermon on the Mount) to those disciples and a great throng of people from Judea, Jerusalem, and the central coastal region of Tyre and Sidon.

"Blessed are you when men hate you, and ostracize you, and insult you, and scorn your name as evil, for the sake of the Son of Man. Be glad in that day and leap *for joy*, for behold, your reward is great in heaven. For in the same way their fathers used to treat the prophets." (Luke 6:22, 23; cf. Matthew 5:10–12; see 2 Chronicles 36:16; Luke 6:12–19).

[GLADNESS from glad]
Setting: The temple treasury in Jerusalem. While Jesus is interacting with the scribes and Pharisees, they state their belief that He is a demon-possessed Samaritan because of His statement that anyone who keeps His word will never taste death.

Jesus answered, "If I glorify Myself, My glory is nothing; it is My Father who glorifies Me, of whom you say, 'He is our God'; and you have not come to know Him, but I know Him; and if I say that I do not know Him, I will be a liar like you, but I do know Him and keep His word. Your father Abraham rejoiced to see My day, and he saw *it* and was glad" (John 8:54–56; see Matthew 13:17; John 7:29).

[GLADNESS from glad]
Setting: Beyond the Jordan. While Jesus and His disciples are avoiding the Jerusalem Pharisees, Jesus communicates Lazarus's death to them and decides to go to Bethany.

So Jesus then said to them plainly, "Lazarus is dead, and I am glad for your sakes that I was not there, so that you may believe; but let us go to him" (John 11:14, 15).

GLORIFICATION, GOD'S (Also see FATHER, GLORY OF HIS; GLORIFYING GOD; and JESUS' GLORIFICATION)

[GOD'S GLORIFICATION from Father, glorify Your name]
Setting: Jerusalem. Just days before the Passover, with the chief priests and Pharisees plotting to seize Him and crowds welcoming Him to Jerusalem with palm branches and praise, Jesus expresses anxiety about His upcoming death by crucifixion.

"Now My soul has become troubled; and what shall I say, 'Father, save Me from this hour'? But for this purpose I came to this hour. "Father, glorify Your name." Then a voice came out of heaven: "I have glorified it, and will glorify it again." So the crowd *of people* who stood by and heard it were saying that it had thundered; others were saying, "An angel has spoken to Him." Jesus answered and said, "This voice has not come for My sake, but for your sakes. Now judgment is upon this world; now the ruler of this world will be cast out. And I, if I am lifted up from the earth, will draw all men to Myself" (John 12:27–32; see Matthew 3:17; 26:38; John 3:14; 6:44; 11:42; 14:30).

[GOD'S GLORIFICATION from God is glorified in Him]
Setting: Jerusalem. Before the Passover, after revealing to His disciples that Judas will betray Him to the chief priests and Pharisees, Jesus conveys how He will soon be glorified in His death, and commands the disciples to love one another.

Therefore when he had gone out, Jesus said, "Now is the Son of Man glorified, and God is glorified in Him; if God is glorified in Him, God will also glorify Him in Himself, and will glorify Him immediately. Little children, I am with you a little while longer. You will seek Me; and as I said to the Jews, now I also say to you, 'Where I am going, you cannot come.' A new commandment I give to you, that you love one another, even as I have loved you, that you also love one another. By this all men will know that you are My disciples, if you have love for one another" (John 13:31–35; see Leviticus 19:18; John 7:33, 34; 17:1; 1 John 3:14).

[GOD'S GLORIFICATION from so that the Father may be glorified in the Son]
Setting: Jerusalem. Before the Passover, after answering Thomas' question where He is going and how they will know the way, Jesus responds to Philip's request for Him to show His disciples the Father.

Jesus said to him, "Have I been so long with you, and *yet* you have not come to know Me, Philip? He who has seen Me has seen the Father; how *can* you say, 'Show us the Father'? Do you not believe that I am in the Father, and the Father is in Me? The words that I say to you I do not speak on My own initiative, but the Father abiding in Me does His works. Believe Me that I am in the Father and the Father is in Me; otherwise believe because of the works themselves. Truly, truly, I say to you, he who believes in Me, the works that I do, he will do also; and greater *works* than these he will do; because I go to the Father. Whatever you ask in My name, that will I do, so that the Father may be glorified in the Son. If you ask Me anything in My name, I will do *it*" (John 14:9–14; see Matthew 7:7; John 1:14; 5:19, 20, 36; 10:37, 38; 15:16).

[GOD'S GLORIFICATION from My Father is glorified by this]
Setting: Jerusalem. Before the Passover, after He conveys the upcoming ministry of the Holy Spirit in His disciples' lives with His imminent departure from them, Jesus explains He is the vine and His disciples are the branches.

"I am the true vine, and My Father is the vinedresser. Every branch in Me that does not bear fruit, He takes away; and every *branch* that bears fruit, He prunes it so that it may bear more fruit. You are already clean because of the word which I have spoken to you. Abide in Me, and I in you. As the branch cannot bear fruit of itself unless it abides in the vine, so neither *can* you unless you abide in Me. I am the vine, you are the branches; he who abides in Me and I in him, he bears much fruit, for apart from Me you can do nothing. If anyone does not abide in Me, he is thrown away as a branch and dries up; and they gather them, and cast them into the fire and they are burned. If you abide in Me, and My words abide in you, ask whatever you wish, and it will be done for you. My Father is glorified by this, that you bear much fruit, and *so* prove to be My disciples. Just as the Father has loved Me, I have also loved you; abide in My love. If you keep My commandments, you will abide in My love; just as I have kept My Father's commandments and abide in His love. These things I have spoken to you so that My joy may be in you, and *that* your joy may be made full" (John 15:1–11; see Matthew 5:16; 7:7; John 3:29, 35; 6:56; 8:29, 31; 13:10; 15:16).

[GOD'S GLORIFICATION from the Son may glorify You and I glorified You on the earth]
Setting: Jerusalem. Before the Passover, after giving His disciples assurance that in the midst of tribulation they will have His peace, Jesus prays His high-priestly prayer.

Jesus spoke these things; and lifting up His eyes to heaven, He said, "Father, the hour has come; glorify Your Son, that the Son may glorify You, even as You gave Him authority over all flesh, that to all whom You have given Him, He may give eternal life. This is eternal life, that they may know You, the only true God, and Jesus Christ whom You have sent. I glorified You on the earth, having accomplished the work which you have given Me to do. Now, Father, glorify Me together with Yourself, with the glory which I had with You before the world was. I have manifested Your name to the men whom You gave Me out of the world; they were Yours and You gave them to Me, and they have kept Your word. Now they have come to know that everything You have given Me is from You; for the words which You gave Me I have given to them; and they received *them* and truly understood that I came forth from You, and they believed You sent Me. I ask on their behalf; I do not ask on behalf of the world, but of those whom You have given Me; for they are Yours; and all things that are Mine are Yours, and Yours are Mine; and I have been glorified in them. I am no longer in the world; and yet they themselves are in the world, and I come to You. Holy Father, keep them in Your name, *the name* which You have given Me, that they may be even as We *are*. While I was with them, I was keeping them in Your name which You have given Me; and I guarded them and not one of them perished but the son of perdition, so that the Scripture would be fulfilled" (John 17:1–12; see Luke 22:32; John 1:1; 3:35; 4:34; 5:44; 6:37–39, 70; 8:42; 11:41; 12:49; 13:18, 31; 16:15; 17:20; Philippians 2:9).

GLORIFICATION, JESUS' (See JESUS' GLORIFICATION)

GLORIFY (See GLORIFICATION, GOD'S; GLORIFYING GOD; GLORY; and JESUS' GLORIFICATION)

GLORIFYING GOD (Also see GLORIFICATION, GOD's; GOD, GLORY TO; and JESUS' GLORIFICATION)

[GLORIFYING GOD from glorify your Father who is in heaven]
Setting: Galilee: During the early part of His ministry, Jesus preaches the Sermon on the Mount to His disciples and the multitudes.

"You are the light of the world. A city set on a hill cannot be hidden; nor does *anyone* light a lamp and put it under a basket, but on the lampstand, and it gives light to all who are in the house. Let your light shine before men in such a way that they may see your good works, and glorify your Father who is in heaven" (Matthew 5:14–16; cf. Mark 4:21; 1 Peter 2:12).

[GLORIFYING GOD from describe what great things God has done for you]
Setting: The country of the Gerasenes, opposite Galilee. Jesus heals a demon-possessed man who then desires to join His ministry, but the Lord sends him home.

"Return to your house and describe what great things God has done for you." So he went away, proclaiming throughout the whole city what great things Jesus had done for him (Luke 8:39; cf. Matthew 8:28–34; Mark 5:1–20).

Setting: Samaria, on the way from Galilee to Jerusalem. The Lord stops to heal ten lepers who ask for cleansing.

When He saw them, He said to them, "Go and show yourselves to the priests." And as they were going, they were cleansed. Now one of them, when he saw that he had been healed, turned back, glorifying God with a loud voice, and he fell on his face at His feet, giving thanks to Him. And he was a Samaritan. Then Jesus answered and said, "Were there no ten cleansed? But the nine—where are they? Was no one found who returned to give glory to God, except this foreigner?" And He said to him, "Stand up and go; you faith has made you well" (Luke 17:14–19; see Leviticus 14:1–32).

GLORIOUS THRONE (Listed under THRONE, GLORIOUS)

GLORY (GLORY, GREAT; and GLORY, MY are separate entries; also see GLORIFY)

Setting: Galilee. During the early part of His ministry, Jesus gives a model prayer to His disciples and the multitudes while conveying The Sermon on the Mount.

"Pray, then, in this way: 'Our Father who is in heaven, hallowed be Your name. Your kingdom come. Your will be done, on earth as it is in heaven. Give us this day our daily bread. And forgive us our debts, as we also have forgiven our debtors. And do not lead us into temptation, but deliver us from evil. [For Yours is the kingdom and the power and the glory forever. Amen]'" (Matthew 6:9–13; cf. Luke 11:2–4; see John 17:15).

Setting: Galilee. During the early part of His ministry, Jesus preaches the Sermon on the Mount to His disciples and the multitudes.

"For this reason I say to you, do not be worried about your life, *as to* what you will eat or what you will drink; nor for your body, *as to* what you will put on. Is not life more than food, and the body more than clothing? Look at the birds of the air, that they do not sow, nor reap nor gather into barns, and *yet* your heavenly Father feeds them. Are you not worth much more than they? And who of you by being worried can add a *single* hour to his life? And why are you worried about clothing? Observe how the lilies of the field grow; they do not toil nor do they spin, yet I say to you that not even Solomon in all his glory clothed himself like one of these. But if God so clothes the grass of the field, which is *alive* today and tomorrow is thrown into the furnace, *will He* not much more *clothe* you? You of little faith! Do not worry then, saying 'What will we eat?' or 'What will we drink?' or 'What will be wear for clothing?" For the Gentiles eagerly seek all these things; for your heavenly Father knows that you need all these things. But seek first His kingdom and His righteousness, and all these things will be added to you. So do not worry about tomorrow; for tomorrow will care for itself. Each day has enough trouble of its own" (Matthew 6:25–34; cf. Luke 12:22–31; see 1 Kings 10:4–7; Job 35:11; Matthew 8:26).

Setting: Near Caesarea Philippi. After rebuking Peter for trying to forbid Him to accomplish His earthly mission of dying and being resurrected, Jesus teaches His disciples about the costs of discipleship.

Then Jesus said to His disciples, "If anyone wishes to come after Me, he must deny himself, and take up his cross and follow Me. For whoever wishes to save his life will lose it; but whoever loses his life for My sake will find it. For what will it profit a man if he gains the whole world and forfeits his soul? Or what will a man give in exchange for his soul? For the Son of Man is going to come in the glory of His Father with His angels, and WILL THEN REPAY EVERY MAN ACCORDING TO HIS DEEDS. Truly, I say to you, there are some of you who are standing here who will not taste death until they see the Son of Man coming in His kingdom" (Matthew 16:24–28, Jesus quotes from Psalm 62:12; cf. Mark 8:34–37; Luke 9:23–27; see Matthew 10:38, 39).

Setting: The Mount of Olives, just east of Jerusalem. During His discourse, after answering His disciples' questions as to when the temple will be destroyed and Jerusalem overrun, along with the signs of His coming and the end of the age, Jesus reveals the future judgments following His return.

"But when the Son of Man comes in His glory, and all the angels with Him, then He will sit on His glorious throne. All the nations will be gathered before Him; and He will separate them from one another, as the shepherd separates the sheep from the goats;

and He will put the sheep on His right, and the goats on the left. Then the King will say to those on His right, 'Come, you who are blessed of My Father, inherit the kingdom prepared for you from the foundation of the world. 'For I was hungry, and you gave Me *something* to eat; I was thirsty, and you gave Me *something* to drink; I was a stranger, and you invited Me in; naked, and you clothed Me; I was sick, and you visited Me; I was in prison, and you came to Me.' Then the righteous will answer Him, 'Lord, when did we see You hungry and feed You, or thirsty, and give you *something* to drink? And when did we see You a stranger, and invite You in, or naked, and clothe You? When did we see You sick, or in prison, and come to You?' The King will answer and say to them, 'Truly I say to you, to the extent that you did it to one of these brothers of Mine, *even* the least *of them,* you did it to Me.' Then He will also say to those on His left, 'Depart from Me, accursed ones, into the eternal fire which has been prepared for the devil and his angels; for I was hungry, and you gave Me *nothing* to eat; I was thirsty, and you gave Me nothing to drink; I was a stranger, and you did not invite Me in; naked, and you did not clothe Me; sick, and in prison, and you did not visit Me.' Then they themselves also will answer, 'Lord, when did we see You hungry, or thirsty, or a stranger, or naked, or sick, or in prison, and did not take care of You?' Then He will answer them, 'Truly I say to you, to the extent that you did not do it to one of the least of these, you did not do it to Me.' These will go away into eternal punishment, but the righteous into eternal life" (Matthew 25:31–46; see Matthew 7:23; 16:27; 19:29).

Setting: Caesarea Philippi. After rebuking Peter for desiring to thwart His mission to the cross, Jesus summons a crowd, along with His disciples, and informs them of the high costs of following Him.

And He summoned the crowd with His disciples, and said to them, "If anyone wishes to come after Me, he must deny himself, and take up his cross and follow Me. For whoever wishes to save his life will lose it, but whoever loses his life for My sake and the gospel's will save it. For what does it profit a man to gain the whole world, and forfeit his soul? For what will a man give in exchange for his soul? For whoever is ashamed of Me and My words in this adulterous and sinful generation, the Son of Man will also be ashamed of him when He comes in the glory of His Father with the holy angels" (Mark 8:34–38; cf. Matthew 16:24–28; Luke 9:23–27; see Matthew 10:33, 38, 39).

Setting: On the Mount of Olives, east of the temple in Jerusalem. After predicting the temple's destruction, during His Olivet Discourse, Jesus responds to questions from Peter, James, John, and Andrew about future events.

"But in those days, after that tribulation, THE SUN WILL BE DARKENED AND THE MOON WILL NOT GIVE ITS LIGHT, AND THE STARS WILL BE FALLING from heaven, and the powers that are in the heavens will be shaken. Then they will see THE SON OF MAN COMING IN CLOUDS with great power and glory. And then He will send forth the angels, and will gather together His elect from the four winds, from the farthest end of the earth to the farthest end of heaven" (Mark 13:24–27. Jesus quotes from Isaiah 13:10; 34:4; Daniel 7:13; cf. Matthew 24:29–31; Luke 21:25–27).

Setting: Galilee. Following Peter's pronouncement that Jesus is the Christ of God, the Lord conveys the demands of discipleship and the hope regarding the kingdom of God.

And He was saying to *them* all, "If anyone wishes to come after Me, he must deny himself, and take up his cross daily and follow Me. For whoever wishes to save his life will lose it, but whoever loses his life for My sake, he is the one who will save it. For what is a man profited if he gains the whole world, and loses or forfeits himself? For whoever is ashamed of Me and My words, the Son of Man will be ashamed of him when He comes in His glory, and *the glory* of the Father and of the holy angels. But I say to you truthfully, there are some of those standing here who will not taste death until they see the kingdom of God" (Luke 9:23–27; cf. Matthew 16:24–26, 28; Mark 8:34–37; see Matthew 10:33, 38, 39).

Setting: On the way from Galilee to Jerusalem. Jesus comforts the crowd and His disciples after giving a parable about riches and greed. The scribes and Pharisees turn hostile and question Him repeatedly in an attempt to catch Him in something He might say.

And He said to His disciples, "For this reason I say to you, do not worry about *your* life, *as to* what you will eat; nor for your body, *as to* what you will put on. For life is more than food, and the body more than clothing. Consider the ravens, for they neither sow nor reap; they have no storeroom nor barn, and *yet* God feeds them; how much more valuable you are than the birds! And which of you by worrying can add a *single* hour to his life's span? If then you cannot do even a very little thing, why do you worry about other matters? Consider the lilies, how they grow: they neither toil nor spin; but I tell you, not even Solomon in all his glory clothed himself like one of these. But if God so clothes the grass in the field, which is *alive* today and tomorrow is thrown into the furnace, how much more *will He clothe* you? You men of little faith! And do not seek what you will eat and what you will drink, and do not keep worrying. For all these things the nations of the world eagerly seek; but your Father knows that you need these things. But seek His kingdom, and these things will be added to you. Do not be afraid, little flock, for your Father has chosen gladly to give you the kingdom" (Luke 12:22–32; cf. Matthew 6:25–33; see 1 Kings 10:4–7; Job 38:41).

Setting: Samaria, on the way from Galilee to Jerusalem. The Lord stops and heals ten lepers who ask for cleansing.

When He saw them, He said to them, "Go and show yourselves to the priests." And as they were going, they were cleansed. Now one of them, when he saw that he had been healed, turned back, glorifying God with a loud voice, and he fell on his face at His feet, giving thanks to Him. And he was a Samaritan. Then Jesus answered and said, "Were there not ten cleansed? But the nine—where are they? Was no one found who returned to give glory to God, except this foreigner? "And He said to him, "Stand up and go; your faith has made you well" (Luke 17:14–19; see Leviticus 14:1–32).

Setting: On the road to Emmaus from Jerusalem. After rising from the grave on the third day after being crucified, Jesus appears to two of His followers, who had heard that the tomb was empty. He elaborates on the purpose of His coming to earth.

And He said to them, "O foolish men and slow of heart to believe in all that the prophets have spoken! Was it not necessary for the Christ to suffer these things and to enter into His glory?" (Luke 24:25, 26).

Setting: Jerusalem. During the Feast of the Jews, Jesus responds to criticism from the Jewish religious leaders by referring to God as His Father (thereby making Himself equal with God), and informing them that God, John the Baptist, His works, and the Scriptures all testify to His mission.

"You search the Scriptures because you think that in them you have eternal life; it is these that testify about Me; and you are unwilling to come to Me so that you may have life. I do not receive glory from men, but I know you, that you do not have the love of God in yourselves. I have come in My Father's name, and you do not receive Me; if another comes in his own name, you will receive him. How can you believe, when you receive glory from one another and you do not seek the glory that is from the *one and* only God? Do not think that I will accuse you before the Father; the one who accuses you is Moses, in whom you have set your hope. For if you believed Moses, you would believe Me, for he wrote about Me. But if you do not believe his writings, how will you believe My words?" (John 5:39–47; see Matthew 24:5; Luke 16:29, 31; 24:27; John 9:28; 17:3).

Setting: The temple in Jerusalem. After receiving encouragement from His blood brothers in Galilee to attend the upcoming Feast of Booths in order to demonstrate His works to His disciples and the world, Jesus goes and teaches, astonishing the Jewish religious leaders.

So Jesus answered them and said, "My teaching is not Mine, but His who sent Me. If anyone is willing to do His will, he will know of the teaching, whether it is of God or *whether* I speak of Myself. He who speaks from himself seeks his own glory; but He who is seeking the glory of the One who sent Him, He is true, and there is no unrighteousness in Him" (John 7:16–18; see John 5:41).

Setting: Jerusalem. Following the Feast of Dedication and the Pharisees' desire to stone Him, Jesus goes beyond the Jordan, where He hears of the sickness of Lazarus of Bethany.

But when Jesus heard *this,* He said, "This sickness is not to end in death, but for the glory of God, so that the Son of God may be glorified by it" (John 11:4).

Setting: Bethany near Jerusalem. After the death of His friend Lazarus, Jesus travels with His disciples from beyond the Jordan in Judea to visit Lazarus's sisters, Martha and Mary. Jesus raises Lazarus from the dead.

Jesus said, "Remove the stone." Martha, the sister of the deceased, said to Him, "Lord, by this time there will be a stench, for he has been *dead* four days." Jesus said to her, "Did I not say to you that if you believe, you will see the glory of God?" So they removed the stone. Then Jesus raised His eyes, and said, "Father, I thank You that You have heard Me. I knew that You always hear Me; but because of the people standing around I said it, so that they may believe that you sent Me." When He had said these things, He cried out with a loud voice, "Lazarus, come forth." The man who had died came forth, bound hand and foot with wrappings, and his face was wrapped around with a cloth. Jesus said to them, "Unbind him, and let him go" (John 11:39–44; see Matthew 11:25).

Setting: Jerusalem. Before the Passover, after giving His disciples assurance that in the midst of tribulation they will have His peace, Jesus prays His high-priestly prayer.

Jesus spoke these things; and lifting up His eyes to heaven, He said, "Father, the hour has come; glorify Your Son, that the Son may glorify You, even as You gave Him authority over all flesh, that to all whom You have given Him, He may give eternal life. This is eternal life, that they may know You, the only true God, and Jesus Christ whom You have sent. I glorified You on the earth, having accomplished the work which you have given Me to do. Now, Father, glorify Me together with Yourself, with the glory which I had with You before the world was. I have manifested Your name to the men whom You gave Me out of the world; they were Yours and You gave them to Me, and they have kept Your word. Now they have come to know that everything You have given Me is from You; for the words which You gave Me I have given to them; and they received *them* and truly understood that I came forth from You, and they believed You sent Me. I ask on their behalf; I do not ask on behalf of the world, but of those whom You have given Me; for they are Yours; and all things that are Mine are Yours, and Yours are Mine; and I have been glorified in them. I am no longer in the world; and yet they themselves are in the world, and I come to You. Holy Father, keep them in Your name, *the name* which You have given Me, that they may be even as We *are.* While I was with them, I was keeping them in Your name which You have given Me; and I guarded them and not one of them perished but the son of perdition, so that the Scripture would be fulfilled" (John 17:1–12; see Luke 22:32; John 1:1; 3:35; 4:34; 5:44; 6:37–39, 70; 8:42; 11:41; 12:49; 13:18, 31; 16:15; 17:20; Philippians 2:9).

Setting: Jerusalem. Before the Passover, after giving His disciples assurance that in the midst of tribulation they will have His peace, Jesus continues praying His high-priestly prayer.

"The glory which You have given Me I have given to them, that they may be one, just as We are one; I in them and You in Me, that they may be perfected in unity, so that the world may know that you sent Me, and loved them, even as You have loved Me. Father, I desire that they also, whom You have given Me, be with Me where I am, so that they may see My glory which You have given Me, for You loved Me before the foundation of the world. O righteous Father, although the world has not known You, yet I have known You; and these have known that You sent Me; and I have made Your name known to them, and will make it known, so that the love with which You loved Me may be in them, and I in them" (John 17:22–26; see Matthew 25:34; John 1:14; 10:38; 15:9; 16:27).

GLORY, GREAT

Setting: The Mount of Olives, just east of Jerusalem. During His discourse, Jesus answers His disciples' questions as to when the temple will be destroyed and Jerusalem overrun, along with the signs of His coming and the end of the age.

"But immediately after the tribulation of those days THE SUN WILL BE DARKENED, AND THE MOON WILL NOT GIVE ITS LIGHT, AND THE STARS WILL FALL from the sky, and the powers of the heavens will be shaken. And then the sign of the Son of Man will appear in the sky, and then all the tribes of the earth will mourn, and they will see the SON OF MAN COMING ON THE CLOUDS OF THE SKY with power and great glory. And He will send forth His angels with A GREAT TRUMPET and THEY WILL GATHER TOGETHER His elect from the four winds, from one end of the sky to the other" (Matthew 24:29–31, Jesus quotes from Isaiah 13:10, Daniel 7:13; Exodus 19:16; cf. Mark 13:24–27; Luke 21:25–27).

Setting: On the Mount of Olives, just east of Jerusalem. After ministering in the temple a few days before His crucifixion, and giving His disciples more details regarding future events, Jesus speaks during His discourse of His return

"There will be signs in sun and moon and stars, and on the earth dismay among the nations, in perplexity at the roaring of the sea and the waves, men fainting from fear and the expectation of the things which are coming upon the world; for the powers of the heavens will be shaken. Then they will see THE SON OF MAN COMING IN A CLOUD with power and great glory. But when these things begin to take place, straighten up and lift up your heads, because your redemption is drawing near" (Luke 21:25–28, Jesus quotes from Daniel 7:13; cf. Matthew 24:29–31; Mark 13:24–27).

GLORY, MY (Jesus')

Setting: The temple treasury in Jerusalem. While Jesus is interacting with the scribes and Pharisees about His testimony, their ancestry, and their motives, they state their belief that Jesus is a demon-possessed Samaritan.

Jesus answered, "I do not have a demon; but I honor My Father, and you dishonor Me. But I do not seek My glory; there is One who seeks and judges. Truly, truly, I say to you, if anyone keeps My word he will never see death" (John 8:49–51; see Matthew 16:28; John 5:41; 7:20).

Setting: The temple treasury in Jerusalem. While Jesus is interacting with the scribes and Pharisees, they state their belief Jesus is a demon-possessed Samaritan because of His statement that anyone who keeps His word will never taste death.

Jesus answered, "If I glorify Myself, My glory is nothing; it is My Father who glorifies Me, of whom you say, 'He is our God'; and you have not come to know Him, but I know Him; and if I say that I do not know Him, I will be a liar like you, but I do know Him and keep His word. Your father Abraham rejoiced to see My day, and he saw *it* and was glad" (John 8:54–56; see Matthew 13:17; John 7:29).

Setting: Jerusalem. Before the Passover, after giving His disciples assurance that in the midst of tribulation they will have His peace, Jesus continues praying His high-priestly prayer.

"The glory which You have given Me I have given to them, that they may be one, just as We are one; I in them and You in Me, that they may be perfected in unity, so that the world may know that you sent Me, and loved them, even as You have loved Me. Father, I desire that they also, whom You have given Me, be with Me where I am, so that they may see My glory which You have given Me, for You loved Me before the foundation of the world. O righteous Father, although the world has not known You, yet I have known You; and these have known that You sent Me; and I have made Your name known to them, and will make it known, so that the love with which You loved Me may be in them, and I in them" (John 17:22–26; see Matthew 25:34; John 1:14; 10:38; 15:9; 16:27).

GLORY OF GOD (Also see GLORIFICATION, GOD'S; and JESUS' GLORIFICATION)

Setting: Jerusalem. Following the Feast of Dedication and the Pharisees' desire to stone Him, Jesus goes beyond the Jordan, where He hears of the sickness of Lazarus of Bethany.

But when Jesus heard *this,* He said, "This sickness is not to end in death, but for the glory of God, so that the Son of God may be glorified by it" (John 11:4).

Setting: Bethany near Jerusalem. After the death of His friend Lazarus, Jesus travels with His disciples from beyond the Jordan to visit Lazarus's sisters, Martha and Mary. The Lord raises Lazarus from the dead.

Jesus said, "Remove the stone." Martha, the sister of the deceased, said to Him, "Lord, by this time there will be a stench, for he has been *dead* four days." Jesus said to her, "Did I not say to you that if you believe, you will see the glory of God?" So they removed the stone. Then Jesus raised His eyes, and said, "Father, I thank You that You have heard Me. I knew that You always hear Me; but because of the people standing around I said it, so that they may believe that you sent Me." When He had said these things, He cried out with a loud voice, "Lazarus, come forth." The man who had died came forth, bound hand and foot with wrappings, and his face was wrapped around with a cloth. Jesus said to them, "Unbind him, and let him go" (John 11:39–44; see Matthew 11:25; John 11:1–38).

GLORY OF HIS FATHER (Listed under FATHER, GLORY OF HIS)

GLUTTONOUS MAN (Listed under MAN, GLUTTONOUS)

GNAT

Setting: The temple in Jerusalem. After the Jewish religious leaders test Him with questions, Jesus pronounces the fifth of eight woes on them in front of the crowds and His disciples.

"Woe to you, scribes and Pharisees, hypocrites! For you tithe the mint and dill and cummin, and have neglected the weightier provisions of the law: justice and mercy and faithfulness; but these are things you should have done without neglecting the others. You blind guides, who strain out a gnat and swallow a camel!" (Matthew 23:23, 24).

GOADS (sticks or prods used for driving animals)

Setting: Caesarea. Luke, writing in Acts, gives Paul's retelling of his conversion to Christ as he appears before King Agrippa in Caesarea following his hearing before the Jewish Council in Jerusalem and arrest by the Roman commander (on his way to Rome after the apostle's third missionary journey).

"And when we had fallen to the ground, I heard a voice saying to me in the Hebrew dialect, 'Saul, Saul, why are you persecuting Me? It is hard for you to kick against the goads.' And I said, 'Who are You, Lord?' And the Lord said, 'I am Jesus whom you are persecuting. But get up and stand on your feet; for this purpose I have appeared to you, to appoint you a minister and a witness not only to the things which you have seen, but also to the things in which I will appear to you; rescuing you from the *Jewish* people and from the Gentiles, to whom I am sending you, to open their eyes so that they may turn from darkness to light and from the dominion of Satan to God, that they may receive forgiveness of sins and an inheritance among those who have been sanctified by faith in Me' (Acts 26:14–18; see Isaiah 35:5; Acts 21:40; 22:14).

GOAL (Also see JESUS' MISSION; and JESUS' PURPOSE)

Setting: On the way from Galilee to Jerusalem. After Jesus, while teaching in the cities and villages, responds to a question about who is saved, some Pharisees ask Him to leave, claiming Herod Antipas (tetrarch of Galilee and Perea) seeks to kill Him.

And He said to them, "Go and tell that fox, 'Behold, I cast out demons and perform cures today and tomorrow, and the third *day* I reach My goal.' Nevertheless I must journey on today and tomorrow and the next *day*; for it cannot be that a prophet would perish outside of Jerusalem. O Jerusalem, Jerusalem, *the city* that kills the prophets and stones those sent to her! How often I wanted to gather your children together, just as a hen *gathers* her brood under her wings, and you would not *have it*! Behold, your house is left to you *desolate*; and I say to you, you will not see Me until *the time* comes when you say, 'BLESSED IS HE WHO COMES IN THE NAME OF THE LORD!'" (Luke 13:32–35, Jesus quotes from Psalm 118:26; cf. Matthew 23:37).

GOAT (Also see GOATS)

Setting: On the way from Galilee to Jerusalem. Jesus conveys the illustration of the prodigal son because the Pharisees and scribes complain He associates with tax collectors and sinners.

And He said, "A man had two sons. The younger of them said to his father, 'Father, give me the share of the estate that falls to me.' So he divided his wealth between them. And not many days later, the younger son gathered everything together and went on a journey into a distant country, and there he squandered his estate with loose living. Now when he had spent everything, a severe famine occurred in that country, and he began to be impoverished. So he went and hired himself out to one of the citizens of that country, and he sent him into his fields to feed swine. And he would have gladly filled his stomach with the pods that the swine were eating, and no one was giving *anything* to him. But when he came to his senses, he said, 'How many of my father's hired men have more than enough bread, but I am dying here with hunger! I will get up and go to my father, and will say to him, "Father, I have sinned against heaven, and in your sight; I am no longer worthy to be called your son; make me as one of your hired men."' So he got up and came to his father. But while he was still a long way off, his father saw him and felt compassion *for him,* and ran and embraced him and kissed him. And the son said to him, "Father, I have sinned against heaven and in your sight; I am no longer worthy to be called your son.' But the father said to his slaves, 'Quickly bring out the best robe and put it on him, and put a ring on his hand and sandals on his feet; and bring the fattened calf, kill it, and let us eat and celebrate; for this son of mine was dead and has come to life again; he was lost and has been found.' And they began to celebrate. Now his older son was in the field, when he came and approached the house, he heard music and dancing. And he summoned one of the servants and *began* inquiring what these things could be. And he said to him, 'Your brother has come, and your father has killed the fattened calf because he has received him back safe and sound.' But he became angry and was not willing to go in; and his father came out and *began* pleading with him. But he answered and said to his father, 'Look! For so many years I have been serving you and I have never neglected a command of yours; and *yet* you have never given me a young goat, so that I might celebrate with my friends; but when this son of yours came, who has devoured your wealth with prostitutes, you killed the fattened calf for him.' And he said to him, 'Son, you have always been with me, and all that is mine is yours. But we had to celebrate and rejoice, for this brother of yours was dead and *has begun* to live, and was lost and has been found'" Luke 15:11–32; see Proverbs 29:2).

GOATS (Also see GOAT)

Setting: The Mount of Olives, just east of Jerusalem. During His discourse, after answering His disciples' questions as to when the temple will be destroyed and Jerusalem overrun, along with the signs of His coming and the end of the age, Jesus reveals the future judgments following His return. During His Olivet Discourse, Jesus reveals to His disciples the future judgments following His return after answering their question as to when the temple will be destroyed, Jerusalem overrun along with the signs of His coming and the end of the age on the Mount of Olives just east of Jerusalem.

"But when the Son of Man comes in His glory, and all the angels with Him, then He will sit on His glorious throne. All the nations will be gathered before Him; and He will separate them from one another, as the shepherd separates the sheep from the goats; and He will put the sheep on His right, and the goats on the left. Then the King will say to those on His right, 'Come, you who are blessed of My Father, inherit the kingdom prepared for you from the foundation of the world. 'For I was hungry, and you gave Me *something* to eat; I was thirsty, and you gave Me *something* to drink; I was a stranger, and you invited Me in; naked, and you clothed Me; I was sick, and you visited Me; I was in prison, and you came to Me.' Then the righteous will answer Him, 'Lord, when did we see You hungry and feed You, or thirsty, and give you *something* to drink? And when did we see You a stranger, and invite You in, or naked, and clothe You? When did we see You sick, or in prison, and come to You?' The King will answer and say to them, 'Truly I say to you, to the extent that you did it to one of these brothers of Mine, *even* the least *of them,* you did it to Me.' Then He will also say to those on His left, 'Depart from Me, accursed ones, into the eternal fire which has been prepared for the devil and his angels; for I was hungry, and you gave Me *nothing* to eat; I was thirsty, and you gave Me nothing to drink; I was a stranger, and you did not invite Me in; naked, and you did not clothe Me; sick, and in prison, and you did not visit Me.' Then they themselves also will answer, 'Lord, when did we see You hungry, or thirsty, or a stranger, or naked, or sick, or in prison, and did not take care of You?' Then He will answer them, 'Truly I say to you, to the extent that you did not do it to one of the least of these, you did not do it to Me.' These will go away into eternal punishment, but the righteous into eternal life" (Matthew 25:31–46; see Matthew 7:23; 16:27; 19:29).

GOD (KINGDOM OF GOD and other specifics about GOD are separate entries; also see FATHER, HEAVENLY; GODS; HOLY SPIRIT; JESUS; and TRINITY)

Setting: Galilee. During the early part of His ministry, Jesus preaches the Sermon on the Mount to His disciples and the multitudes.

"For this reason I say to you, do not be worried about your life, *as to* what you will eat or what you will drink; nor for your body, *as to* what you will put on. Is not life more than food, and the body more than clothing? Look at the birds of the air, that they do not sow, nor reap nor gather into barns, and *yet* your heavenly Father feeds them. Are you not worth much more than they? And who of you by being worried can add a *single* hour to his life? And why are you worried about clothing? Observe how the lilies of the field grow; they do not toil nor do they spin, yet I say to you that not even Solomon in all his glory clothed himself like one of these. But if God so clothes the grass of the field, which is *alive* today and tomorrow is thrown into the furnace, *will He* not much more *clothe* you? You of little faith! Do not worry then, saying 'What will we eat?' or 'What will we drink?' or 'What will be wear for clothing?" For the Gentiles eagerly seek all these things; for your heavenly Father knows that you need all these things. But seek first His kingdom and His righteousness, and all these things will be added to you. So do not worry about tomorrow; for tomorrow will care for itself. Each day has enough trouble of its own" (Matthew 6:25–34; cf. Luke 12:22–31; see 1 Kings 10:4–7; Job 35:11; Matthew 8:26).

Setting: Galilee. Pharisees and scribes from Jerusalem question Jesus about His disciples' lack of obedience to tradition and the commandments.

And He answered and said to them, "Why do you yourselves transgress the commandment of God for the sake of tradition? For God said, 'HONOR YOUR FATHER AND MOTHER,' and, 'HE WHO SPEAKS EVIL OF FATHER OR MOTHER IS TO BE PUT TO DEATH.' But you say, 'Whoever says to *his* father or mother, "Whatever I have that would help you has been given *to God*," he is not to honor his father or mother.' And *by this* you invalidated the word of God for the sake of your tradition. You hypocrites, rightly did Isaiah prophesy of you: 'THIS PEOPLE HONORS ME WITH THEIR LIPS, BUT THEIR HEART IS FAR AWAY FROM ME. BUT IN VAIN DO THEY WORSHIP ME, TEACHING AS DOCTRINES THE PRECEPTS OF MEN' "(Matthew 15:3–9, Jesus quotes from Exodus 20:12, 21:17, Leviticus 20:9; Isaiah 29:13; cf. Mark 7:5–7; see Colossians 2:22).

Setting: Judea beyond the Jordan (Perea). After Jesus replies to Peter's question about forgiveness, the Pharisees test Him in front of a large crowd with a question about divorce.

And He answered and said, "Have you not read that He who created *them* from the beginning MADE THEM MALE AND FEMALE, and said, 'FOR THIS REASON A MAN SHALL LEAVE HIS FATHER AND MOTHER AND BE JOINED TO HIS WIFE, AND THE TWO SHALL BECOME ONE FLESH'? So they are no longer two, but one flesh. What therefore God has joined together, let no man separate" (Matthew 19:4–6, Jesus quotes from Genesis 1:27; 2:24; cf. Mark 10:5–9; see 1 Timothy 2:14).

Setting: The temple in Jerusalem. The Pharisees send their disciples and the Herodians to test Jesus about the poll-tax, in order to trap Him.

But Jesus perceived their malice, and said, "Why are you testing Me, you hypocrites? Show Me the coin *used* for the poll-tax." And they brought Him a denarius. And He said to them, "Whose likeness and inscription is this?" They said to Him, "Caesar's." Then He said to them, "Then render to Caesar the things that are Caesar's; and to God the things that are God's" (Matthew 22:18–21; cf. Matthew 17:25; Mark 12:15–17; Luke 20:22–25).

Setting: The temple in Jerusalem. The Sadducees question Jesus about Levirate marriage (marriage to a brother-in-law), in order to test Him.

But Jesus answered and said to them, "You are mistaken, not understanding the Scriptures nor the power of God. For in the resurrection they neither marry nor are given in marriage, but are like angels in heaven. But regarding the resurrection of the dead, have you not read what was spoken to you by God: 'I AM THE GOD OF ABRAHAM, AND THE GOD OF ISAAC, AND THE GOD OF JACOB'? He is not the God of the dead but of the living" (Matthew 22:29–32, Jesus quotes from Exodus 3:6; cf. Mark 12:18–27; Luke 20:27–38; see Deuteronomy 25:5; John 20:9).

Setting: The temple in Jerusalem. A Pharisee lawyer asks Jesus which is the great commandment of the Law, in order to test Him.

And He said to him, " 'YOU SHALL LOVE THE LORD YOUR GOD WITH ALL YOUR HEART, AND WITH ALL YOUR SOUL, AND WITH ALL YOUR MIND.' This is the great and foremost commandment. The second is like it, 'YOU SHALL LOVE YOUR NEIGHBOR AS YOURSELF.' On these two commandments depend the whole Law and the Prophets" (Matthew 22:37–40; Jesus quotes from Leviticus 19:18; Deuteronomy 6:5; cf. Mark 12:28–34; see Matthew 7:12).

Setting: Judea beyond the Jordan (Perea). Jesus teaches the crowds gathered around Him about divorce after the Pharisees test and question Him about this subject.

And He answered and said to them, "What did Moses command you?" They said, "Moses permitted a *man* TO WRITE A CERTIFICATE OF DIVORCE AND SEND *her* AWAY." But Jesus said to them, "Because of your hardness of heart he wrote you this commandment. But from the beginning of creation, *God* MADE THEM MALE AND FEMALE. FOR THIS REASON A MAN SHALL LEAVE HIS FATHER AND MOTHER, AND THE TWO SHALL BECOME ONE FLESH; so they are no longer two, but one flesh. What therefore God has joined together, let no man separate. In the house the disciples *began* questioning Him about this again. And He said to them, "Whoever divorces his wife and marries another woman commits adultery against her; and if she herself divorces her husband and marries another man, she is committing adultery" (Mark 10:3–12, Jesus quotes from Genesis 1:27; 2:24; cf. Matthew 19:1–9; see Deuteronomy 24:1–3; Matthew 5:32; see Romans 7: 2, 3; 1 Corinthians 7:10, 11, 13, 39; 1 Timothy 2:14).

Setting: Judea beyond the Jordan (Perea). After demonstrating to His disciples the importance of little children, Jesus encounters a rich man seeking eternal life.

And Jesus said to him, "Why do you call Me good? No one is good except God alone. You know the commandments, 'DO NOT MURDER, DO NOT COMMIT ADULTERY, DO NOT STEAL, DO NOT BEAR FALSE WITNESS, Do not defraud, HONOR YOUR FATHER AND MOTHER.'" And he said to Him, "Teacher, I have kept all these things from my youth up." Looking at him, Jesus felt a love for him and said to him, "One thing you lack: go and sell all you possess and give to the poor, and you will have treasure in heaven; and come, follow Me" (Mark 10:18–21; Jesus quotes from Exodus 20:12–16; cf. Matthew 19:16–22; Luke 18:18–24; see Matthew 6:20).

Setting: On the road to Bethany, just outside Jerusalem. After Jesus instructs the money changers while cleansing the temple, Peter draws Jesus' and His disciples' attention to an earlier-cursed fig tree.

And Jesus answered saying to them, "Have faith in God. Truly, I say to you, whoever says to this mountain, 'Be taken up and cast into the sea,' and does not doubt in his heart, but believes that what he says is going to happen, it will be *granted* him. Therefore I say to you, all things for which you pray and ask, believe that you have received them, and they will be *granted* you. Whenever you stand praying, forgive, if you have anything against anyone, so that your Father who is in heaven will also forgive you your transgressions. [But if you do not forgive, neither will your Father who is in heaven forgive your transgressions'] (Mark 11:22–26; cf. Matthew 21:19–22; see Matthew 6:14, 15; 7:7; 17:20).

Setting: The temple in Jerusalem. After Jesus teaches the chief priests, scribes, and elders in parables, they send some of the Pharisees and Herodians in an attempt to trap Him in a statement.

"Shall we pay or shall we not pay?" But He, knowing their hypocrisy, said to them, "Why are you testing Me? Bring Me a denarius to look at." They brought *one.* And He said to them, "Whose likeness and inscription is this?" And they said to Him, "Caesar's." And Jesus said to them, "Render to Caesar the things that are Caesar's, and to God the things that are God's." And they were amazed at Him (Mark 12:15–17; cf. Matthew 22:15–22; Luke 20:20–26).

Setting: The temple in Jerusalem. After some of the Pharisees and Herodians attempt to trap Jesus in a statement, some Sadducees question Him about the status of marriage after death.

Jesus said to them, "Is this not the reason you are mistaken, that you do not understand the Scriptures or the power of God? For when they rise from the dead, they neither marry nor are given in marriage, but are like angels in heaven. But regarding the fact that the dead rise again, have you not read in the book of Moses, in the *passage* about *the burning* bush, how God spoke to him, saying, 'I AM THE GOD OF ABRAHAM, AND THE GOD OF ISAAC, AND THE GOD OF JACOB?' He is not the God of the dead, but of the living; you are greatly mistaken" (Mark 12:24–27, Jesus quotes from Exodus 3:6; cf. Matthew 22:29–33; Luke 20:34–40).

Setting: The temple in Jerusalem. When the Pharisees and Herodians fail to trap Jesus in a statement, one of the scribes asks Him which commandment is foremost.

Jesus answered, "The foremost is, 'HEAR, O ISRAEL! THE LORD OUR GOD IS ONE LORD; AND YOU SHALL LOVE THE LORD YOUR GOD WITH ALL YOUR HEART, AND WITH ALL YOUR SOUL, AND WITH ALL YOUR MIND AND WITH ALL YOUR STRENGTH.' The second is this, 'YOU SHALL LOVE YOUR NEIGHBOR AS YOURSELF.' There is no other commandment greater than these" (Mark 12:29–31, Jesus quotes from Deuteronomy 6:4, 5; Leviticus 19:18; cf. Matthew 22:34–40).

Setting: On the Mount of Olives, east of the temple in Jerusalem. After predicting the temple's destruction, Jesus responds during His Olivet Discourse to questions from Peter, James, John, and Andrew about future events.

"But when you see the ABOMINATION OF DESOLATION standing where it should not be (let the reader understand), then those who are in Judea must flee to the mountains. The one who is on the housetop must not go down, or go in to get anything out of his house; and the one who is in the field must not turn back to get his coat. But woe to those who are pregnant and to those who are nursing babies in those days! But pray that it may not happen in winter. For those days will be a *time of* tribulation such as has not occurred since the beginning of the creation which God created until now, and never will. Unless the Lord had shortened *those* days, no life would have been saved; but for the sake of the elect, whom He chose, He shortened the days. And then if anyone says to you, 'Behold, here is the Christ'; or, 'Behold, *He is* there'; do not believe *him*; for false Christs and false prophets will arise, and will show signs and wonders, in order to lead astray, if possible, the elect. But take heed; behold, I have told you everything in advance" (Mark 13:14–23; cf. Matthew 24:15–28; Luke 21:20–24; see Daniel 9:27; 12:1; Luke 17:31).

Setting: Judea, near the Jordan River. Following His baptism, and before He begins His public ministry, Jesus is led by the Spirit into the wilderness for forty days of temptation by Satan.

Jesus answered him, "It is written, 'YOU SHALL WORSHIP THE LORD YOUR GOD AND SERVE HIM ONLY'" (Luke 4:8, Jesus quotes from Deuteronomy 6:13; cf. Matthew 4:10).

Setting: The country of the Gerasenes, opposite Galilee. Jesus heals a demon-possessed man who then desires to join His ministry, but the Lord sends him home.

"Return to your house and describe what great things God has done for you." So he went away, proclaiming throughout the whole city what great things Jesus had done for him (Luke 8:39; cf. Matthew 8:28–34; Mark 5:1–20).

Setting: On the way from Galilee to Jerusalem. Jesus warns His disciples of future events as the scribes and Pharisees turn hostile and question Him in an attempt to catch Him in something He might say.

Under these circumstances, after so many thousands of people had gathered together that they were stepping on one another, He began saying to His disciples first *of all,* "Beware of the leaven of the Pharisees, which is hypocrisy. But there is nothing covered up that will not be revealed, and hidden that will not be known. Accordingly, whatever you have said in the dark will be heard in the light, and what you have whispered in the inner rooms will be proclaimed upon the housetops. I say to you, My friends, do not be afraid of those who kill the body and after that have no more that they can do. But I will warn you whom to fear: fear the One who, after He has killed, has authority to cast into hell; yes, I tell you, fear Him! Are not five sparrows sold for two cents? *Yet* not one of them is forgotten before God. Indeed, the very hairs of your head are all numbered. Do not fear; you are more valuable than many sparrows" (Luke 12:1–7; cf. Matthew 10:26–31; see Matthew 16:6; Hebrews 10:31).

Setting: On the way from Galilee to Jerusalem. After the scribes and Pharisees turn hostile and question Him in an attempt to catch Him in something He might say, Jesus responds to a question from the crowd and gives a parable about riches and greed.

And He told them a parable, saying, "The land of a rich man was very productive. And he began reasoning to himself, saying, 'What shall I do, since I have no place to store my crops?' Then he said, 'This is what I will do: I will tear down my barns and build larger ones, and here I will store all my grain and my goods. And I will say to my soul, "Soul, you have many goods laid up for many years *to come;* take your ease, eat, drink *and* be merry."' "But God said to him, 'You fool! This *very* night your soul is required of you; and *now* who will own what you have prepared?' So is the man who stores up treasure for himself, and is not rich toward God" (Luke 12:16–21; see Job 27:8; Psalm 39:6; Ecclesiastes 12:9; Philippians 2:3).

Setting: On the way from Galilee to Jerusalem. After giving a parable about riches and greed, Jesus comforts the crowd and His disciples. The scribes and Pharisees turn hostile and question Him in an attempt to catch Him in something He might say.

And He said to His disciples, "For this reason I say to you, do not worry about *your* life, *as to* what you will eat; nor for your body, *as to* what you will put on. For life is more than food, and the body more than clothing. Consider the ravens, for they neither sow nor reap; they have no storeroom nor barn, and *yet* God feeds them; how much more valuable you are than the birds! And which of you by worrying can add a *single* hour to his life's span? If then you cannot do even a very little thing, why do you worry about other matters? Consider the lilies, how they grow: they neither toil nor spin; but I tell you, not even Solomon in all his glory clothed himself like one of these. But if God so clothes the grass in the field, which is *alive* today and tomorrow is thrown into the furnace, how much more *will He clothe* you? You men of little faith! And do not seek what you will eat and what you will drink, and do not keep worrying. For all these things the nations of the world eagerly seek; but your Father knows that you need these things. But seek His kingdom, and these things will be added to you. Do not be afraid, little flock, for your Father has chosen gladly to give you the kingdom." (Luke 12:22–32; cf. Matthew 6:25–33; see 1 Kings 10:4–7; Job 38:41).

Setting: On the way from Galilee to Jerusalem. The Lord teaches His disciples about stewardship after giving them the story of the prodigal son.

Now He was also saying to the disciples, "There was a rich man who had a manager, and this *manager* was reported to him as squandering his possessions. And he called him and said to him, 'What is this I hear about you? Give an accounting of your management, for you can no longer be a manager.' The manager said to himself, 'What shall I do, since my master is taking the management away from me? I am not strong enough to dig; I am ashamed to beg. I know what I shall do, so that when I am removed from the management people will welcome me into their homes.' And he summoned each one of his master's debtors, and he *began* saying to the first, 'How much do you owe my master?' And he said, 'A hundred measures of oil.' And he said to him, 'Take your bill, and sit down quickly and write fifty.' Then he said to another, 'And how much do you owe?' And he said, 'A hundred measures of wheat.' He said to him, 'Take your bill, and write eighty.' And his master praised the unrighteous manager because he had acted shrewdly; for the sons of this age are more shrewd in relation to their own kind than the sons of light. And I say to you, make friends for yourselves by means of the wealth of unrighteousness, so that when it fails, they will receive you into the eternal dwellings. He who is faithful in a very little thing is faithful also in much; and he who is unrighteous in a very little thing is unrighteous also in much. Therefore if you have not been faithful in the *use of* unrighteous wealth, who will entrust the *true riches* to you? And if you have not been faithful in *the use of* that which is another's, who will give you that which is your own? No servant can serve two masters; for either he will hate the one and love the other, or else he will be devoted to one and despise the other. You cannot serve God and wealth" (Luke 16:1–13; cf. Matthew 6:24; see Matthew 25:14–30).

Setting: On the way from Galilee to Jerusalem. The Lord responds to the Pharisees' scoffing at His teaching His disciples about stewardship.

And He said to them, "You are those who justify yourselves in the sight of men, but God knows your hearts; for that which is highly esteemed among men is detestable in the sight of God. The Law and the Prophets *were proclaimed* until John; since that time the gospel of the kingdom of God has been preached, and everyone is forcing his way into it. But is it easier for heaven and earth to pass away than for one stroke of a letter of the Law to fail" (Luke 16:15–17; cf. Matthew 5:18; see 1 Samuel 16:7; Matthew 4:23; 11:11–14).

Setting: On the way from Galilee to Jerusalem. After telling His disciples of His second coming, Jesus instructs them about persistence in prayer.

Now He was telling them a parable to show that at all times they ought to pray and not to lose heart, saying, "In a certain city there was a judge who did not fear God and did not respect man. There was a widow in that city, and she kept coming to him, saying, 'Give me legal protection from my opponent.' For a while he was unwilling; but afterward he said to himself, 'Even though I do not fear God nor respect man, yet because this woman bothers me, I will give her legal protection, otherwise by continually coming she will wear me out.'" And the Lord said, "Hear what the unrighteous judge said; now, will not God bring about justice for His elect who cry to Him day and night, and will He delay long over them? I tell you that He will bring about justice for them quickly. However, when the Son of Man comes, will He find faith on the earth?" (Luke 18:1–8; see Luke 11:5–10).

Setting: On the way from Galilee to Jerusalem. After instructing His disciples about persistence in prayer, Jesus conveys a parable about self-righteousness.

And He also told this parable to some people who trusted in themselves that they were righteous, and viewed others with contempt: "Two men went up into the temple to pray, one a Pharisee and the other a tax collector. The Pharisee stood and was praying this to himself: 'God, I thank You that I am not like other people: swindlers, unjust, adulterers, or even like this tax collector. I fast twice a week; I pay tithes of all that I get.' But the tax collector, standing some distance away, was even unwilling to lift up his eyes to heaven, but was beating his breast, saying, 'God, be merciful to me, the sinner!' I tell you, this man went to his house justified rather than the other; for everyone who exalts himself will be humbled, but he who humbles himself will be exalted" (Luke 18:9–14; see Ezra 9:6; Matthew 6:5, 23:12; Luke 11:42, 16:15; Romans 14:3, 10).

Setting: On the way from Galilee to Jerusalem. After speaking of the importance of children, Jesus responds to a ruler's question about inheriting eternal life.

A ruler questioned Him, saying, "Good Teacher, what shall I do to inherit eternal life?" And Jesus said to him, "Why do you call Me good? No one is good except God alone. You know the commandments, 'DO NOT COMMIT ADULTERY, DO NOT MURDER, DO NOT STEAL, DO NOT BEAR FALSE WITNESS, HONOR YOUR FATHER AND MOTHER.'" And he said, "All these things I have kept from *my* youth." When Jesus heard *this,* He said to him, "One thing you still lack; sell all that you possess and distribute it to the poor, and you shall have treasure in heaven; and come, follow Me" (Luke 18:18–22, Jesus quotes from Exodus 20:12–16; cf. Matthew 19:16–22; Mark 10:17–22; see Luke 10:25–28).

Setting: The temple in Jerusalem. A few days before His crucifixion, after Jesus conveys the Parable of the Vine-Growers to the people, the scribes and Pharisees seek to trap Him by questioning Him about paying taxes to Caesar.

But He detected their trickery and said to them, "Show Me a denarius. Whose likeness and inscription does it have?" They said "Caesar's." And He said to them, "Then render to Caesar the things that are Caesar's, and to God the things that are God's" (Luke 20:23–25; cf. Matthew 22:15–21; Mark 12:13–17).

Setting: The temple in Jerusalem. A few days before His crucifixion, after the scribes and Pharisees seek to trap Jesus by questioning Him about paying taxes to Caesar, some Sadducees (who say there is no resurrection) ask Him a question about the resurrection.

Jesus said to them, "The sons of this age marry and are given in marriage, but those who are considered worthy to attain to that age and the resurrection from the dead, neither marry nor are given in marriage; for they cannot even die anymore, because they are like angels, and are sons of God, being sons of the resurrection. But that the dead are raised, even Moses showed, in the *passage about the burning* bush, where he calls the Lord THE GOD OF ABRAHAM, AND THE GOD OF ISAAC, AND THE GOD OF JACOB. Now He is not the God of the dead but of the living; for all live to Him" (Luke 20:34–38, Jesus quotes from Exodus 3:6; cf. Matthew 22:23–32; Mark 12:18–27).

Setting: Jerusalem. At the time for the Passover of the Jews, after the Lord cleanses the temple, a Pharisee, Nicodemus, asks Him by night the meaning of "born again."

"For God so loved the world, that He gave His only begotten Son, that whoever believes in Him shall not perish, but have eternal life. For God did not send the Son into the world to judge the world, but that the world might be saved through Him. He who believes in Him is not judged; he who does not believe has been judged already, because he has not believed in the name of the only begotten Son of God. This is the judgment, that the Light has come into the world, and men loved darkness rather than the Light, for their deeds were evil. For everyone who does evil hates the Light, and does not come to the Light for fear that his deeds will be exposed. But he who practices the truth comes to the Light, so that his deeds may be manifested as having been wrought in God" (John 3:16–21; see Luke 19:10; John 1:4; 1:18; Romans 5:8; 1 John 1:6, 7).

Setting: Sychar in Samaria, on the way to Galilee. Jesus interacts with a Samaritan woman at Jacob's well, while His disciples shop for food.

Jesus said to her, "Woman, believe Me, an hour is coming when neither in this mountain nor in Jerusalem will you worship the Father. You worship what you do not know; we worship what we know, for salvation is from the Jews. But an hour is coming, and now is, when the true worshipers will worship the Father in spirit and truth; for such people the Father seeks to be His worshipers. God is spirit, and those who worship Him must worship in spirit and truth" (John 4:21–24; see Isaiah 2:3; Philippians 3:3).

Setting: Jerusalem. During the Feast of the Jews, Jesus responds to criticism from the Jewish religious leaders by referring to God as His Father (thereby making Himself equal with God) and informing them that God, John the Baptist, His works, and the Scriptures all testify to His mission.

"You search the Scriptures because you think that in them you have eternal life; it is these that testify about Me; and you are unwilling to come to Me so that you may have life. I do not receive glory from men; but I know you, that you do not have the love of God in yourselves. I have come in My Father's name, and you do not receive Me; if another comes in his own name, you will receive him. How can you believe, when you receive glory from one another and you do not seek the glory that is from the *one and* only God? Do not think that I will accuse you before the Father; the one who accuses you is Moses, in whom you have set your hope. For if you believed Moses, you would believe Me, for he wrote about Me. But if you do not believe his writings, how will you believe My words?" (John 5:39–47; see Matthew 24:5; Luke 16:29, 31; 24:27; John 9:28; 17:3).

Setting: Capernaum. The day after Jesus walks on the Sea of Galilee to join His disciples in a boat, the people He miraculously fed with a lad's five loaves and two fish ask Him how He crossed the water, since He had not entered the boat from land with His disciples.

Jesus answered them and said, "Truly, truly, I say to you, you seek Me, not because you saw signs, but because you ate of the loaves and were filled. Do not work for the food which perishes, but for the food which endures to eternal life, which the Son of Man will give to you, for on Him the Father, God, has set His seal" (John 6:26, 27; see John 3:33).

Setting: Capernaum of Galilee. After informing the people whom He miraculously fed with a lad's five loaves and two fish how they might receive the bread out of heaven, the Jewish religious leaders grumble because Jesus claims that He came down out of heaven.

Therefore the Jews were grumbling about Him, because He said, "I am the bread that came down out of heaven." They were saying, "Is not this Jesus, the son of Joseph, whose father and mother we know? How does He now say, 'I have come down out of heaven'?" Jesus answered and said to them, "Do not grumble among yourselves. No one can come to Me unless the Father who sent Me draws him; and I will raise him up on the last day. It is written in the prophets, 'AND THEY SHALL ALL BE TAUGHT OF GOD.' Everyone who has heard and learned from the Father, comes to Me. Not that anyone has seen the Father, except the One who is from God; He has seen the Father. Truly, truly, I say to you, he who believes has eternal life. I am the bread of life. Your fathers ate the manna in the wilderness, and they died. This is the bread which comes down out of heaven, so that one may eat of it and not die. I am the living bread that came down out of heaven; if anyone eats of this bread, he will live forever; and the bread also which I will give for the life of the world is My flesh" (John 6:41–51, Jesus quotes from Isaiah 54:13; see John 1:18, 29; 3:36; 7:27).

Setting: The temple in Jerusalem. After receiving encouragement from His blood brothers in Galilee to attend the upcoming Feast of Booths in order to demonstrate His works to His disciples and the world, Jesus goes and teaches, astonishing the Jewish religious leaders.

So Jesus answered them and said, "My teaching is not Mine, but His who sent Me. If anyone is willing to do His will, he will know of the teaching, whether it is of God or *whether* I speak of Myself. He who speaks from himself seeks his own glory; but He who is seeking the glory of the One who sent Him, He is true, and there is no unrighteousness in Him" (John 7:16–18; see John 5:41).

Setting: The temple treasury in Jerusalem. After the scribes and Pharisees question His testimony about Himself, Jesus interacts with them regarding their ancestry and motives.

They answered and said to Him, "Abraham is our father." Jesus said to them, "If you are Abraham's children, do the deeds of Abraham. But as it is, you are seeking to kill Me, a man who has told you the truth, which I heard from God; this Abraham did not do. You are doing the deeds of your father." They said to Him, "We were not born of fornication; we have one Father: God" (John 8:39–41; see Romans 9:6, 7).

Setting: The temple treasury in Jerusalem. After the scribes and Pharisees question His testimony about Himself, Jesus interacts with them regarding their ancestry and motives.

Jesus said to them, "If God were your Father, you would love Me, for I proceeded forth and have come from God, for I have not even come on My own initiative, but He sent Me. Why do you not understand what I am saying? *It is* because you cannot hear My word. You are of *your* father the devil, and you want to do the desires of your father. He was a murderer from the beginning, and does not stand in the truth because there is no truth in him. Whenever he speaks a lie, he speaks from his own *nature,* for he is a liar and the father of lies. But because I speak the truth, you do not believe Me. Which one of you convicts Me of sin? If I speak truth, why do not believe Me? He who is of God hears the words of God; for this reason you do not hear *them,* because you are not of God" (John 8:42–47; see John 18:37; 1 John 3:8; 4:6; 5:1).

Setting: The temple treasury in Jerusalem. While Jesus is interacting with the scribes and Pharisees, they state their belief Jesus is a demon-possessed Samaritan because of His statement that anyone who keeps His word will never taste death.

Jesus answered, "If I glorify Myself, My glory is nothing; it is My Father who glorifies Me, of whom you say, 'He is our God'; and you have not come to know Him, but I know Him; and if I say that I do not know Him, I will be a liar like you, but I do know Him and keep His word. Your father Abraham rejoiced to see My day, and he saw *it* and was glad" (John 8:54–56; see Matthew 13:17; John 7:29).

Setting: Jerusalem. Before the Passover, after taking issue with Peter's assertion he would lay down his life for Jesus, Jesus comforts and gives hope to His disciples regarding their future after He returns to heaven.

"Do not let your heart be troubled; believe in God, believe also in Me. In My Father's house are many dwelling places; if it were not so, I would have told you; for I go to prepare a place for you. If I go and prepare a place for you, I will come again and receive you to Myself, that where I am, *there* you may be also. And you know the way where I am going" (John 14:1–4; see John 13:35; 14:27, 28).

Setting: Jerusalem. Before the Passover, after explaining He is the vine and His disciples are the branches, Jesus warns His disciples of the persecution they will face after His departure to heaven.

"These things I have spoken to you so that you may be kept from stumbling. They will make you outcasts from the synagogue, but an hour is coming for everyone who kills you to think that he is offering service to God. These things they will do because they have not known the Father or Me. But these things I have spoken to you, so that when their hour comes, you may remember that

I told you of them. These things I did not say to you at the beginning, because I was with you" (John 16:1–4; see John 8:19, 55; 9:22; 13:19; 15:18–27).

[GOD from from above]

Setting: Jerusalem. Pontius Pilate (Roman governor of Judea) continues to find no guilt in Jesus. He has Jesus scourged in an attempt to appease the hostile Jewish religious leaders, but seeks more information as to where the King of the Jews is from.

Jesus answered, "You would have no authority over Me, unless it had been given you from above; for this reason he who delivered Me to you has *the* greater sin" (John 19:11; see Romans 13:1).

Setting: In Jerusalem, the risen Jesus first appears to Mary Magdalene after she tells Simon Peter and John about the empty tomb where Jesus had been the day before the Sabbath. He had died on the cross for the sins of the world.

Jesus said to her, "Woman, why are you weeping? Whom are you seeking?" Supposing Him to be the gardener, she said to Him, "Sir, if you have carried Him away, tell me where you have laid Him, and I will take Him away." Jesus said to her, "Mary!" She turned and said to Him in Hebrew "Rabboni!" (which means, Teacher). Jesus said to her, "Stop clinging to Me, for I have not yet ascended to the Father; but go to My brethren and say to them, 'I ascend to My Father and your Father, and My God and Your God'" (John 20:15–17; see Mark 16:9–11; John 7:33; 19:31–42).

Setting: Caesarea. Luke, writing in Acts, gives Paul's retelling of his conversion to Christ as he appears before King Agrippa following his hearing before the Jewish Council in Jerusalem and arrest by the Roman commander (on his way to Rome after the apostle's third missionary journey).

"And when we had fallen to the ground, I heard a voice saying to me in the Hebrew dialect, 'Saul, Saul, why are you persecuting Me? It is hard for you to kick against the goads.' And I said, 'Who are You, Lord?' And the Lord said, 'I am Jesus whom you are persecuting. But get up and stand on your feet; for this purpose I have appeared to you, to appoint you a minister and a witness not only to the things which you have seen, but also to the things in which I will appear to you; rescuing you from the *Jewish* people and from the Gentiles, to whom I am sending you, to open their eyes so that they may turn from darkness to light and from the dominion of Satan to God, that they may receive forgiveness of sins and an inheritance among those who have been sanctified by faith in Me' (Acts 26:14–18; see Isaiah 35:5; Acts 21:40; 22:14).

Setting: On the island of Patmos (in the Aegean Sea about fifty miles southwest of Ephesus in modern Turkey). On the Lord's Day (Sunday), about fifty years after Jesus' resurrection, the disciple John encounters the Lord Jesus Christ, who communicates a new revelation for the apostle to record for the church in Laodicea and to six other churches in Asia.

"To the angel of the church in Laodicea write: The Amen, the faithful and true Witness, the Beginning of the creation of God, says this: 'I know your deeds, that you are neither cold nor hot; I wish that you were cold or hot. So because you are lukewarm, and neither hot nor cold, I will spit you out of My mouth. Because you say, "I am rich, and have become wealthy, and have need of nothing," and you do not know that you are wretched and miserable and poor and blind and naked, I advise you to buy from Me gold refined by fire so that you may become rich, and white garments so that you may clothe yourself, and *that* the shame of your nakedness will not be revealed; and eye salve to anoint your eyes so that you may see. Those whom I love, I reprove and discipline; therefore be zealous and repent. Behold, I stand at the door and knock; if anyone hears My voice and opens the door, I will come in to him and will dine with him, and he with Me. He who overcomes, I will grant to him to sit down with Me on My throne, as I also overcame and sat down with My Father on His throne. He who has an ear, let him hear what the Spirit says to the churches'" (Revelation 3:14–22; see Proverbs 3:12; Hosea 12:8; John 14:23; 16:33).

GOD, ANGELS OF (Also see ANGEL; and ANGELS)

Setting: On the way from Galilee to Jerusalem. Jesus warns His disciples of future events, as the scribes and Pharisees turn hostile and question Him repeatedly in an attempt to catch Him in something He might say.

"And I say to you, everyone who confesses Me before men, the Son of Man will confess him also before the angels of God; but he who denies Me before men will be denied before the angels of God. And everyone who speaks a word against the Son of Man, it will be forgiven him; but he who blasphemes against the Holy Spirit, it will not be forgiven him. When they bring you before the synagogues and the rulers and the authorities, do not worry about how or what you are to speak in your defense, or what you are to say; for the Holy Spirit will teach you in that very hour what you ought to say" (Luke 12:8–12; cf. Matthew 10:32, 33; 12:31, 32; see Matthew 10:20).

Setting: On the way from Galilee to Jerusalem. Jesus conveys the principles of the lost sheep and the lost coin because the Pharisees and scribes complain He associates with tax collectors and sinners.

"So He told them this parable, saying, "What man among you, if he has a hundred sheep and has lost one of them, does not leave the ninety-nine in the open pasture and go after the one which is lost until he finds it? When he has found it, he lays it on his shoulders, rejoicing. And when he comes home, he calls together his friends and his neighbors, saying to them, 'Rejoice with me, for I have found my sheep which was lost!' I tell you that in the same way, there will be more joy in heaven over one sinner who repents than over ninety-nine righteous persons who need no repentance. Or what woman, if she has ten silver coins and loses one coin, does not light a lamp and sweep the house and search carefully until she finds it? When she has found it, she calls together her friends and neighbors, saying, 'Rejoice with me, for I have found the coin which I had lost!' In the same way, I tell you, there is joy in the presence of the angels of God over one sinner who repents" (Luke 15:3–10; cf. Matthew 18:12-14; see Matthew 9:11-13).

Setting: Galilee. After beginning His public ministry and choosing His first disciples, Andrew and Simon (Peter) near Bethany beyond the Jordan and Philip in Galilee, Jesus calls Philip's friend, Nathanael, (some believe he may have been also called Bartholomew) as His next follower.

Jesus saw Nathanael coming to Him, and said of him, "Behold, an Israelite indeed, in whom there is no deceit!" Nathanael said to Him, "How do you know me?" Jesus answered and said to him, "Before Philip called you, when you were under the fig tree, I saw you." Nathanael answered Him, "Rabbi, You are the Son of God; You are the King of Israel." Jesus answered and said to him, "Because I said to you that I saw you under the fig tree, do you believe? You will see greater things than these." And He said to him, "Truly, truly, I say to you, you will see the heavens opened and the angels of God ascending and descending on the Son of Man" (John 1:47–51).

GOD, BREAD OF

Setting: Capernaum. The day after Jesus walks on the Sea of Galilee to join His disciples in a boat, the people He miraculously fed with a lad's five loaves and two fish quiz Him about the signs and works He performs so they may believe in Him.

Jesus then said to them, "Truly, truly, I say to you, it is not Moses who has given you the bread out of heaven, but it is My Father who gives you the true bread out of heaven. For the bread of God is that which comes down out of heaven, and gives life to the world" (John 6:32, 33).

GOD, CITY OF MY

Setting: On the island of Patmos (in the Aegean Sea about fifty miles southwest of Ephesus in modern Turkey). On the Lord's Day (Sunday), about fifty years after Jesus' resurrection, the disciple John encounters the Lord Jesus Christ, who communicates a new revelation for the apostle to record for the church in Philadelphia and to six other churches in Asia.

"And to the angel of the church in Philadelphia write: He who is holy, who is true, who has the key of David, who opens and no one will shut, and who shuts and no one opens, says this: 'I know your deeds. Behold, I have put before you an open door which no one can shut, because you have a little power, and have kept My word, and have not denied My name. Behold, I will cause *those* of the synagogue of Satan, who say that they are Jews and are not, but lie—I will make them come and bow down at your feet, and *make them* know that I have loved you. Because you have kept the word of My perseverance, I also will keep you from the hour of testing, that *hour* which is about to come upon the whole world, to test those who dwell on the earth. I am coming quickly; hold fast what you have, so that no one will take your crown. He who overcomes, I will make him a pillar in the temple of My God, and he will not go out from it anymore; and I will write on him the name of My God, and the name of the city of My God, the new Jerusalem, which comes down out of heaven from My God, and My new name. He who has an ear, let him hear what the Spirit says to the churches' " (Revelation 3:7–13; see Isaiah 22:22; Galatians 2:9; Revelation 2:9, 10, 13, 25; 14:1).

GOD, COMMANDMENT OF (Also see COMMANDMENT; and COMMANDMENTS)

Setting: Galilee. Pharisees and scribes from Jerusalem question Jesus about His disciples' lack of obedience to tradition and the commandments.

And He answered and said to them, "Why do you yourselves transgress the commandment of God for the sake of tradition? For God said, 'HONOR YOUR FATHER AND MOTHER,' and, 'HE WHO SPEAKS EVIL OF FATHER OR MOTHER IS TO BE PUT TO DEATH.' But you say, 'Whoever says to *his* father or mother, "Whatever I have that would help you has been given *to God*," he is not to honor his father or mother.' And *by this* you invalidated the word of God for the sake of your tradition. You hypocrites, rightly did Isaiah prophesy of you: 'THIS PEOPLE HONORS ME WITH THEIR LIPS, BUT THEIR HEART IS FAR AWAY FROM ME. BUT IN VAIN DO THEY WORSHIP ME, TEACHING AS DOCTRINES THE PRECEPTS OF MEN' "(Matthew 15:3–9, Jesus quotes from Exodus 20:12, 21:17, Leviticus 20:9; Isaiah 29:13; cf. Mark 7:5–7; see Colossians 2:22).

Setting: Galilee. The Pharisees and some of the scribes from Jerusalem question why Jesus' disciples do not follow the tradition of ceremonial hand cleansing before eating bread.

And He said to them, "Rightly did Isaiah prophesy of you hypocrites, as it is written: 'THIS PEOPLE HONORS ME WITH THEIR LIPS, BUT THEIR HEART IS FAR AWAY FROM ME. BUT IN VAIN DO THEY WORSHIP ME, TEACHING AS DOCTRINES THE PRECEPTS OF MEN.' Neglecting the commandment of God, you hold to the tradition of men." He was also saying to them, "You are experts at setting aside the commandment of God in order to keep tradition. For Moses said, 'HONOR YOUR FATHER AND YOUR MOTHER'; and, 'HE WHO SPEAKS EVIL OF FATHER OR MOTHER, IS TO BE PUT TO DEATH'; but you say, 'If a man says to *his* father or *his* mother, whatever I have that would help you is Corban (that is to say, given *to God*),' you no longer permit him to do anything for *his* father or *his* mother; *thus* invalidating the word of God by your tradition which you have handed down; and you do many things such as that" (Mark 7:6–13, Jesus quotes from Exodus 20:12; 21:17; Isaiah 29:13; cf. Matthew 15:1–6).

GOD, COMMUNICATION WITH (See PRAYER)

GOD, DEDICATED TO (See CORBAN)

GOD, DEPENDENCE ON (Also see BREAD, DAILY; JESUS, DEPENDENCE ON; NEEDS; and PROVISION, GOD'S)

[DEPENDENCE ON GOD from they should take nothing for *their* journey]

Setting: Jesus' hometown of Nazareth. After encountering unbelief, Jesus sends the Twelve out in pairs, with authority and instructions about ministry.

And He summoned the twelve and began to send them out in pairs, and gave them authority over the unclean spirits; and He instructed them that they should take nothing for *their* journey, except a mere staff—no bread, no bag, no money in their belt—but to wear sandals; and *He added,* "Do not put on two tunics." And He said to them, "Wherever you enter a house, stay there until you leave town. Any place that does not receive you or listen to you, as you go out from there, shake the dust off the soles of your feet for a testimony against them" (Mark 6:7–11; cf. Matthew 10:1–14; Luke 9:1–5).

[DEPENDENCE ON GOD from Take nothing for *your* journey]

Setting: Galilee. After raising Jairus's daughter from the dead, Jesus calls the Twelve together and gives them power and authority over demons, along with the ability to cure diseases.

And He said to them, "Take nothing for *your* journey, neither a staff, nor a bag, nor bread, nor money; and do not *even* have two tunics apiece. Whatever house you enter, stay there until you leave that city. And as for those who do not receive you, go out from that city, shake the dust off your feet as a testimony against them" (Luke 9:3–5; cf. Matthew 10:1–15; Mark 6:7–11; see Luke 10:4–12).

GOD, FEARING (See FEARING GOD)

GOD, FINGER OF

Setting: On the way from Galilee to Jerusalem. After Jesus casts out a demon, some in the crowd test Him, demanding a sign from heaven.

But He knew their thoughts and said to them, "Any kingdom divided against itself is laid waste; and a house *divided* against itself falls. If Satan also is divided against himself, how will his kingdom stand? For you say that I cast out demons by Beelzebul. And if I by Beelzebul cast out demons, by whom do your sons cast them out? So they will be your judges. But if I cast out demons by the finger of God, then the kingdom of God has come upon you" (Luke 11:17–20; cf. Matthew 12:25–28; Mark 3:23–27; see Exodus 8:19; Matthew 3:2, 10:25).

GOD, GIFT OF

Setting: Sychar in Samaria, on the way to Galilee. Jesus interacts with a Samaritan woman at Jacob's well, while His disciples shop for food.

Jesus answered and said to her, "If you knew the gift of God, and who it is who says to you, 'Give Me a drink,' you would have asked Him, and He would have given you living water" (John 4:10).

GOD, GIFTS FROM (Also see GIFTS, GOOD; and GOD, GIFT OF)

[GIFTS FROM GOD from Give us this day our daily bread]
Setting: Galilee. During the early part of His ministry, Jesus gives a model prayer to His disciples and the multitudes while conveying The Sermon on the Mount.

"Pray, then, in this way: 'Our Father who is in heaven, hallowed be Your name. Your kingdom come. Your will be done, on earth as it is in heaven. Give us this day our daily bread. And forgive us our debts, as we also have forgiven our debtors. And do not lead us into temptation, but deliver us from evil. [For Yours is the kingdom and the power and the glory forever. Amen]'" (Matthew 6:9–13; cf. Luke 11:2–4; see John 17:15).

[GIFTS FROM GOD from your Father who is in heaven give what is good to those who ask Him]
Setting: Galilee. During the early part of His ministry, Jesus preaches the Sermon on the Mount to His disciples and the multitudes.

"Ask, and it will be given to you; seek, and you will find; knock, and it will be opened to you. For everyone who asks receives, and he who seeks finds, and to him who knocks it will be opened. Or what man is there among you who, when his son asks for a loaf, will give him a stone? Or if he asks for a fish, he will not give him a snake, will he? If you then, being evil, know how to give good gifts to your children, how much more will your Father who is in heaven give what is good to those who ask Him! In everything, therefore, treat people the same way you want them to treat you, for this is the Law and the Prophets" (Matthew 7:7–12; cf. Matthew 22:40; Luke 6:31; 11:9–13; see Psalm 84:11).

[GIFTS FROM GOD from rest]
Setting: Galilee. After rendering a thanksgiving prayer to His Father in heaven, Jesus offers rest to all who are weary and heavy-laden as He preaches and teaches throughout the region.

"Come to Me, all who are weary and heavy-laden, and I will give you rest. Take My yoke upon you and learn from Me, for I am gentle and humble in heart, and YOU WILL FIND REST FOR YOUR SOULS. For My yoke is easy and My burden is light" (Matthew 11:28–30, Jesus quotes from Jeremiah 6:16; see Jeremiah 31:35; 1 John 5:3).

[GIFTS FROM GOD from I will give]
Setting: Caesarea Philippi. Jesus responds to Simon Peter's declaration that He is the Christ, the Son of the living God.

And Jesus said to him, "Blessed are you, Simon Barjona, because flesh and blood did not reveal *this* to you, but My Father who is in heaven. I also say to you that you are Peter, and upon this rock I will build My church; and the gates of Hades will not overpower it. I will give you the keys of the kingdom of heaven; and whatever you bind on earth shall have been bound in heaven, and whatever you loose on earth shall have been loosed in heaven" (Matthew 16:17–19; cf. Matthew 18:18; Mark 8:29; Luke 9:20).

[GIFTS FROM GOD from this is not Mine to give]
Setting: On the way to Jerusalem. The mother of James and John, the sons of Zebedee, asks Jesus to make her sons exalted rulers with Him in His coming kingdom.

And He said to her, "What do you wish?" She said to Him, 'Command that in Your kingdom these two sons of mine may sit one on Your right and one on Your left.' But Jesus answered, "You do not know what you are asking. Are you able to drink the cup that I am about to drink?" They said to Him, 'We are able.' He said to them, "My cup you shall drink; but to sit on My right and on *My* left, this is not Mine to give, but it is for those for whom it has been prepared by My Father" (Matthew 20:21–23; cf. Mark 10:35–40; see Matthew 19:28; 20:20; Acts 12:2).

[GIFTS FROM GOD from to give His life a ransom for many]
Setting: On the way to Jerusalem, where Jesus will die on the cross. Jesus teaches His disciples about true greatness after the mother of James and John, the sons of Zebedee, asks Him to make her sons exalted rulers with Him in His coming kingdom.

But Jesus called them to Himself and said, "You know that the rulers of the Gentiles lord it over them, and *their* great men exercise authority over them. It is not this way among you, but whoever wishes to become great among you shall be your servant, and whoever wishes to be first among you shall be your slave; just as the Son of Man did not come to be served, but to serve, and to give His life a ransom for many" (Matthew 20:25–28; cf. Matthew 23:11; 26:28; Mark 10:42–45).

[GIFTS FROM GOD from this is not Mine to give]
Setting: On the road to Jerusalem. Jesus prophesies His persecution, death, and resurrection, while James and John ask for special honor and privileges in His coming kingdom.

And He said to them, "What do you want Me to do for you?" They said to Him, "Grant that we may sit, one on Your right and one on *Your* left, in Your glory." But Jesus said to them, "You do not know what you are asking. Are you able to drink the cup that I drink, or to be baptized with the baptism with which I am baptized?" They said to Him, "We are able." And Jesus said to them, "The cup that I drink you shall drink; and you shall be baptized with the baptism with which I am baptized. But to sit on My right or on *My* left, this is not Mine to give; but it is for those for whom it has been prepared" (Mark 10:36–40; cf. Matthew 20:20–23; see Matthew 19:28; Acts 12:2).

[GIFTS FROM GOD from give His life a ransom for many]
Setting: On the road to Jerusalem. James and John ask Jesus for special honor and privileges in His kingdom. The other disciples become angry, so the Lord uses this moment to teach them about servanthood.

Calling them to Himself, Jesus said to them, "You know that those who are recognized as rulers of the Gentiles lord it over them; and their great men exercise authority over them. But it is not this way among you, but whoever wishes to become great among you shall be your servant; and whoever wishes to be first among you shall be slave of all. For even the Son of Man did not come to be served, but to serve, and to give His life a ransom for many" (Mark 10:42–45; cf. Matthew 20:25–28).

[GIFTS FROM GOD from Give us each day our daily bread]
Setting: On the way from Galilee to Jerusalem via Bethany. After Jesus visits in the home of Martha and Mary, a disciple asks Him to teach His disciples to pray.

And He said to them, "When you pray, say: 'Father, hallowed be Your name. Your kingdom come. Give us each day our daily bread. And forgive us our sins, for we ourselves also forgive everyone who is indebted to us. And lead us not into temptation'" (Luke 11:2–4; cf. Matthew 6:9–13).

[GIFTS FROM GOD from give the Holy Spirit to those who ask Him]
Setting: On the way from Galilee to Jerusalem. After revealing to His disciples how to pray, Jesus illustrates God's benevolence in answering prayer and giving the Holy Spirit.

"Now suppose one of you fathers is asked by his son for a fish; he will not give him a snake instead of a fish, will he? Or *if* he is asked for an egg, he will not give him a scorpion, will he? If you then, being evil, know how to give good gifts to your children, how much more will *your* heavenly Father give the Holy Spirit to those who ask Him?" (Luke 11:11–13; cf. Matthew 7:9–11).

[GIFTS FROM GOD from to give you the kingdom]
Setting: On the way from Galilee to Jerusalem. Jesus comforts the crowd and His disciples after giving a parable about riches and greed. The scribes and Pharisees turn hostile and question Him in an attempt to catch Him in something He might say.

And He said to His disciples, "For this reason I say to you, do not worry about *your* life, *as to* what you will eat; nor for your body, *as to* what you will put on. For life is more than food, and the body more than clothing. Consider the ravens, for they neither sow nor reap; they have no storeroom nor barn, and *yet* God feeds them; how much more valuable you are than the birds! And which of you by worrying can add a *single* hour to his life's span? If then you cannot do even a very little thing, why do you worry about other matters? Consider the lilies, how they grow: they neither toil nor spin; but I tell you, not even Solomon in all his glory clothed himself like one of these. But if God so clothes the grass in the field, which is *alive* today and tomorrow is thrown into the furnace, how much more *will He clothe* you? You men of little faith! And do not seek what you will eat and what you will drink, and do not keep worrying. For all these things the nations of the world eagerly seek; but your Father knows that you need these things. But seek His kingdom, and these things will be added to you. Do not be afraid, little flock, for your Father has chosen gladly to give you the kingdom" (Luke 12:22–32; cf. Matthew 6:25–33; see 1 Kings 10:4–7; Job 38:41).

[GIFTS FROM GOD from He would have given you living water]
Setting: Sychar in Samaria, on the way to Galilee. Jesus interacts with a Samaritan woman at Jacob's well, while His disciples shop for food.

Jesus answered and said to her, "If you knew the gift of God, and who it is who says to you, 'Give Me a drink,' you would have asked Him, and He would have given you living water" (John 4:10).

[GIFTS FROM GOD from the Son of Man will give to you]
Setting: Capernaum. The day after Jesus walks on the Sea of Galilee to join His disciples in a boat, the people He miraculously fed with a lad's five loaves and two fish ask Jesus how He crossed the water, since He had not entered the boat from land with His disciples.

Jesus answered them and said, "Truly, truly, I say to you, you seek Me, not because you saw signs, but because you ate of the loaves and were filled. Do not work for the food which perishes, but for the food which endures to eternal life, which the Son of Man will give to you, for on Him the Father, God, has set His seal" (John 6:26, 27; see John 3:33).

[GIFTS FROM GOD from I will give for the life of the world]
Setting: Capernaum of Galilee. After informing the people whom He miraculously fed with a lad's five loaves and two fish how they might receive the bread out of heaven, the Jewish religious leaders grumble because Jesus claims that He came down out of heaven.

Therefore the Jews were grumbling about Him, because He said, "I am the bread that came down out of heaven." They were saying, "Is not this Jesus, the son of Joseph, whose father and mother we know? How does He now say, 'I have come down out of heaven'?" Jesus answered and said to them, "Do not grumble among yourselves. No one can come to Me unless the Father who sent Me draws him; and I will raise him up on the last day. It is written in the prophets, 'AND THEY SHALL ALL BE TAUGHT OF GOD.' Everyone who has heard and learned from the Father, comes to Me. Not that anyone has seen the Father, except the One who is from God; He has seen the Father. Truly, truly, I say to you, he who believes has eternal life. I am the bread of life. Your fathers ate the manna in the wilderness, and they died. This is the bread which comes down out of heaven, so that one may eat of it and not die. I am the living bread that came down out of heaven; if anyone eats of this bread, he will live forever; and the bread also which I will give for the life of the world is My flesh" (John 6:41–51, Jesus quotes from Isaiah 54:13; see John 1:18, 29; 3:36; 7:27).

[GIFTS FROM GOD from I give eternal life to them]
Setting: Jerusalem. At the Feast of Dedication, just after Jesus conveys the Parable of the Good Shepherd to the Pharisees (who do not understand it), they ask Him plainly if He is the Christ.

Jesus answered them, "I told you, and you do not believe; the works that I do in My Father's name, these testify of Me. But you do not believe because you are not of My sheep. My sheep hear My voice, and I know them, and they follow Me; and I give eternal life to them, and they will never perish; and no one will snatch them out of My hand. My Father, who has given *them* to Me, is greater than all; and no one is able to snatch *them* out of the Father's hand. I and the Father are one" (John 10:25 30; see John 8:47; 10:4, 17:1, 2, 20, 21).

[GIFTS FROM GOD from He will give you another Helper]
Setting: Jerusalem. Before the Passover, after responding to Philip's request for Him to show His disciples the Father, Jesus conveys the upcoming role of the Holy Spirit in their lives.

"If you love Me, you will keep My commandments. I will ask the Father, and He will give you another Helper, that He may be with you forever; *that* is the Spirit of truth, whom the world cannot receive, because it does not see Him or know Him, *but* you know Him because He abides with you and will be in you" (John 14:15–17; see John 7:39; 15:26; 1 John 5:3).

[GIFTS FROM GOD from My peace I give to you]
Setting: Jerusalem. Before the Passover, after He conveys the upcoming ministry of the Holy Spirit in His disciples' lives, Jesus again relates peace, hope, and comfort to them regarding His return to the Father.

"Peace I leave with you; My peace I give to you; not as the world gives do I give to you. Do not let your heart be troubled, nor let it be fearful. You heard that I said to you, 'I go away, and I will come to you,' If you loved Me, you would have rejoiced because I go to the Father, for the Father is greater than I. Now I have told you before it happens, so that when it happens, you may believe. I will not speak much more with you, for the ruler of the world is coming, and he has nothing in Me; but so that the world may know that I love the Father, I do exactly as the Father commanded Me. Get up, let us go from here" (John 14:27–31; see John 10:18, 29; 12:31; 13:19; 16:33).

[GIFTS FROM GOD from He may give to you]
Setting: Jerusalem. Before the Passover, with His departure in mind, after explaining He is the vine and His disciples are the branches, Jesus instructs them to love one another.

"This is My commandment, that you love one another, just as I have loved you. Greater love has no one than this, that one lay down his life for his friends. You are My friends if you do what I command you. No longer do I call you slaves, for the slave does not know what his master is doing; but I have called you friends, for all things that I have heard from My Father I have made known to you. You did not choose Me but I chose you, and appointed you that you would go and bear fruit, and *that* your fruit would remain, so that whatever you ask of the Father in My name He may give to you. This I command you, that you love one another" (John 15:12–17; see Matthew 12:50; John 6:70; 8:26; 10:11; 13:34).

[GIFTS FROM GOD from He will give it to you]
Setting: Jerusalem. Before the Passover, after empathizing with His disciples' sadness over His prophecies and giving them hope for the future, Jesus conveys promises about praying in His name.

"In that day you will not question Me about anything. Truly, truly, I say to you, if you ask the Father for anything in My name, He will give it to you. Until now you have asked for nothing in My name; ask and you will receive, so that your joy may be made full. These things I have spoken to you in figurative language; an hour is coming when I will no longer speak to you in figurative language, but will tell you plainly of the Father. In that day you will ask in My name, and I do not say to you that I will request of the Father on your behalf; for the Father Himself loves you, because you have loved Me and have believed that I came forth from the Father. I came forth from the Father and have come into the world; I am leaving the world again and going to the Father" (John 16:23–28; see Matthew 13:34; John 8:42; 13:1, 3; 14:14, 21, 23; 15:16).

[GIFTS FROM GOD from I will give you]
Setting: On the island of Patmos (in the Aegean Sea about fifty miles southwest of Ephesus in modern Turkey). On the Lord's Day (Sunday), about fifty years after Jesus' resurrection, the disciple John encounters the Lord Jesus Christ, who communicates a new revelation for the apostle to record for the church in Smyrna and to six other churches in Asia.

"And to the angel of the church in Smyrna write: The first and the last, who was dead, and has come to life, says this: 'I know your tribulation and your poverty (but you are rich), and the blasphemy by those who say they are Jews and are not, but are a synagogue of Satan. Do not fear what you are about to suffer. Behold, the devil is about to cast some of you into prison, so that you will be tested, and you will have tribulation for ten days. Be faithful until death, and I will give you the crown of life. He who has an ear, let him hear what the Spirit says to the churches. He who overcomes will not be hurt by the second death' (Revelation 2:8–11; see Isaiah 44:6; Revelation 1:9, 18; 2:13; 20:6, 14).

[GIFTS FROM GOD from I will give him]
Setting: On the island of Patmos (in the Aegean Sea about fifty miles southwest of Ephesus in modern Turkey). On the Lord's Day (Sunday), about fifty years after Jesus' resurrection, the disciple John encounters the Lord Jesus Christ, who communicates a new revelation for the apostle to record for the church in Pergamum and to six other churches in Asia.

"And to the angel of the church in Pergamum write: The One who has the sharp two-edged sword says this: 'I know where you dwell, where Satan's throne is; and you hold fast My name, and did not deny My faith even in the days of Antipas, My witness, My faithful one, who was killed among you, where Satan dwells. But I have a few things against you, because you have there some who hold the teaching of Balaam, who kept teaching Balak to put a stumbling block before the sons of Israel, to eat things sacrificed to idols and to commit *acts of* immorality. So you also have some who in the same way hold the teaching of the Nicolaitans. Therefore repent; or else I am coming to you quickly, and I will make war against them with the sword of My mouth. He who has an ear, let him hear what the Spirit says to the churches. To him who overcomes, to him I will give *some* of the hidden manna, and I will give him a white stone, and a new name written on the stone which no one knows but he who receives it' (Revelation 2:12–17; see Numbers 25:1–3; Isaiah 62:2; Revelation 1:16; 2:5, 6, 16).

[GIFTS FROM GOD from I will give to each one]
Setting: On the island of Patmos (in the Aegean Sea about fifty miles southwest of Ephesus in modern Turkey). On the Lord's Day (Sunday), about fifty years after Jesus' resurrection, the disciple John encounters the Lord Jesus Christ, who communicates a new revelation for the apostle to record for the church in Thyatira and to six other churches in Asia.

"And to the angel of the church in Thyatira write: The Son of God, who has eyes like a flame of fire, and His feet are like burnished bronze, says this: 'I know your deeds, and your love and faith and service and perseverance, and that your deeds of late are greater than at first. But I have *this* against you, that you tolerate the woman Jezebel, who calls herself a prophetess, and she teaches and leads My bond-servants astray so that they commit *acts of* immorality and eat things sacrificed to idols. I gave her time to repent, and she does not want to repent of her immorality. Behold, I will throw her on a bed *of sickness,* and those who commit adultery with her into great tribulation, unless they repent of her deeds. And I will kill her children with pestilence, and all the churches will know that I am He who searches the minds and hearts; and I will give to each one of you according to your deeds. But I say to you, the rest who are in Thyatira, who do not hold this teaching, who have not known the deep things of Satan, as they call them—I place no other burden on you. Nevertheless what you have, hold fast until I come. He who overcomes, and he who keeps My deeds until the end, TO HIM I WILL GIVE AUTHORITY OVER THE NATIONS; AND HE SHALL RULE THEM WITH A ROD OF IRON, AS THE VESSELS OF THE POTTER ARE BROKEN TO PIECES, as I also have received *authority* from My Father; and I will give him the morning star. He who has an ear, let him hear what the Spirit says to the churches' (Revelation 2:18–29; Jesus quotes from Psalm 2:8, 9; Isaiah 30:14; see 1 Kings 16:31; Psalm 7:9; Romans 2:5; 1 Corinthians 2:10; 2 Peter 3:9; Revelation 1:14; 2:7; 3:11; 17:1–20).

GOD, GIVING BACK TO (See SERVICE; TITHE; and WORKS, GOOD)

GOD, GLORIFYING (Listed under GLORIFYING GOD)

GOD, GLORY OF (Listed under GLORY OF GOD)

GOD, GOODNESS OF (See BLESSED; GOD, GIFTS FROM; and GIFTS, GOOD)

GOD, HATRED OF (Also see JESUS, HATRED OF)

[HATRED OF GOD from He who hates Me hates My Father also]
Setting: Jerusalem. Before the Passover, with His departure in mind, after explaining He is the vine and His disciples are the branches, Jesus prepares them for future hatred by the world.

"He who hates Me hates My Father also. If I had not done among them the works which no one else did, they would not have sin; but now they have both seen and hated Me and My Father as well. But *they have done this* to fulfill the word that is written in their Law, 'THEY HATED ME WITHOUT A CAUSE'" (John 15:23–25, Jesus quotes from Psalm 35:19, see John 9:41).

GOD, HOUSE OF (See HOUSE OF GOD)

GOD, JESUS AS (Also see GOD, SEEING; JUDGMENT; MIRACLE; MIRACLES; POWER, RIGHT HAND OF; and SIGNS AND WONDERS)

[JESUS AS GOD from your sins are forgiven]
Setting: Capernaum, near the Sea of Galilee. After Jesus heals a paralytic and forgives his sins in front of crowds, some scribes accuse the Lord of blasphemy.

And they brought to Him a paralytic lying on a bed. Seeing their faith, Jesus said to the paralytic, "Take courage, son; your sins are forgiven." And some scribes said to themselves. "This *fellow* blasphemes." And Jesus knowing their thoughts said, "Why are you thinking evil in your hearts? Which is easier to say, 'Your sins are forgiven,' or to say, 'Get up, and walk'? But so that you may know that the Son of Man has authority on earth to forgive sins"—then He said to the paralytic, "Get up, pick up your bed and go home" (Matthew 9:2–6; cf. Mark 2:3–12; Luke 5:17–26).

[JESUS AS GOD from your sins are forgiven]
Setting: Galilee. Early in Jesus' gospel-preaching ministry, word of His healing abilities spreads, so some friends bring a paralytic man to Him for healing.

And Jesus seeing their faith said to the paralytic, "Son, your sins are forgiven" (Mark 2:5; cf. Matthew 9:1–3; Luke 5:17–20).

[JESUS AS GOD from Friend, your sins are forgiven you]
Setting: Galilee. As some Pharisees and teachers of the law from Galilee and Judea look on, several men lower a paralyzed man through the roof in front of Jesus.

Seeing their faith, He said, "Friend, your sins are forgiven you" (Luke 5:20; cf. Mark 2:2–12; see Matthew 9:1–8).

[JESUS AS GOD from Yes, I am]
Setting: Jerusalem. After being arrested, having Peter deny Him, and being mocked and beaten, with His crucifixion imminent, Jesus appears before the Sanhedrin (Council of Elders).

"If You are the Christ, tell us." But He said to them, "If I tell you, you will not believe; and if I ask you a question, you will not answer. But from now on THE SON OF MAN WILL BE SEATED AT THE RIGHT HAND of the power OF GOD." And they all said, "Are You the Son of God, then? And He said to them, "Yes, I am" (Luke 22:67–70, Jesus quotes from Psalm 110:1; cf. Matthew 26:57–65; Mark 14:55–65).

[JESUS AS GOD from the Son also gives life to whom He wishes]
Setting: Jerusalem, by the pool of Bethesda. During the Feast of the Jews, Jesus responds to criticism from the Jewish religious leaders for healing a lame man on the Sabbath and for referring to God as His Father (thereby making Himself equal with God).

Therefore Jesus answered and was saying to them, "Truly, truly, I say to you, the Son can do nothing of Himself, unless *it is* something He sees the Father doing; for whatever the Father does, these things the Son also does in like manner. For the Father loves the Son, and shows Him all things that He Himself is doing; and *the Father* will show Him greater works than these, so that you will marvel. For just as the Father raises the dead and gives them life, even so the Son also gives life to whom He wishes. For not even the Father judges anyone, but He has given all judgment to the Son, so that all will honor the Son even as they honor the Father. He who does not honor the Son does not honor the Father who sent Him" (John 5:19–23; see Luke 10:16; John 3:35; 11:25; 14:12).

[JESUS AS GOD from I am]
Setting: The temple treasury in Jerusalem. While Jesus interacts with the scribes and Pharisees, they question how He, not yet fifty years old in their eyes, could claim to have seen Abraham.

Jesus said to them, "Truly, truly, I say to you, before Abraham was born, I am" (John 8:58; see Exodus 3:14).

[JESUS AS GOD from I and the Father are one]
Setting: Jerusalem. At the Feast of Dedication, just after Jesus conveys the Parable of the Good Shepherd to the Pharisees (who do not understand it), they ask Him plainly if He is the Christ.

Jesus answered them, "I told you, and you do not believe; the works that I do in My Father's name, these testify of Me. But you do not believe because you are not of My sheep. My sheep hear My voice, and I know them, and they follow Me; and I give eternal life to them, and they will never perish; and no one will snatch them out of My hand. My Father, who has given *them* to Me, is greater than all; and no one is able to snatch *them* out of the Father's hand. I and the Father are one" (John 10:25–30; see John 8:47; 10:4; 17:1, 2, 20, 21).

[JESUS AS GOD from who is and who was and who is to come, the Almighty]
Setting: On the small island of Patmos (in the Aegean Sea about fifty miles southwest of Ephesus in modern Turkey). Approximately fifty years after Jesus' resurrection, His angel speaks the first words of His revelation to His bond-servant, the Apostle John.

"I am the Alpha and the Omega," says the Lord God, "who is and who was and who is to come, the Almighty" (Revelation 1:8; see Revelation 21:6).

[JESUS AS GOD from I am]
Setting: On the island of Patmos (in the Aegean Sea about fifty miles southwest of Ephesus in modern Turkey). On the Lord's Day (Sunday), approximately fifty years after His resurrection, the disciple John encounters the Lord Jesus Christ, who communicates new revelations for the apostle to record for the seven churches in Asia.

When I saw Him, I fell at His feet like a dead man. And He placed His right hand on me, saying, "Do not be afraid; *I am* the first and the last, and the living One; and I was dead, and behold, I am alive forevermore, and I have the keys of death and of Hades. Therefore write the things which you have seen, and the things which are, and the things which will take place after these things. As for the mystery of the seven stars which you saw in My right hand, and the seven golden lampstands: the seven stars are the angels of the seven churches, and the seven lampstands are the seven churches" (Revelation 1:17–20; see Isaiah 44:6; Luke 24:5; Revelation 2:8).

[JESUS AS GOD from I am the Alpha and the Omega, the first and the last, the beginning and the end]
Setting: On the island of Patmos (in the Aegean Sea about fifty miles southwest of Ephesus in modern Turkey). Approximately fifty years after the Lord Jesus Christ's resurrection, in the final chapter of His revelation via the disciple John, He reveals His upcoming return, reward, and eternality.

"Behold, I am coming quickly, and My reward *is* with Me, to render to every man according to what he has done. I am the Alpha and the Omega, the first and the last, the beginning and the end" (Revelation 22:12, 13; see Isaiah 40:10; 44:6).

GOD, KINGDOM OF (Listed under KINGDOM OF GOD)

GOD, KNOWING (Also see JESUS, KNOWING)

[KNOWING GOD from they may know You, the only true God, and Jesus Christ whom You have sent]
Setting: Jerusalem. Before the Passover, after giving His disciples assurance that in the midst of tribulation they will have His peace, Jesus prays His high-priestly prayer.

Jesus spoke these things; and lifting up His eyes to heaven, He said, "Father, the hour has come; glorify Your Son, that the Son may glorify You, even as You gave Him authority over all flesh, that to all whom You have given Him, He may give eternal life. This is eternal life, that they may know You, the only true God, and Jesus Christ whom You have sent. I glorified You on the earth, having accomplished the work which you have given Me to do. Now, Father, glorify Me together with Yourself, with the glory which I had with You before the world was. I have manifested Your name to the men whom You gave Me out of the world; they were Yours and You gave them to Me, and they have kept Your word. Now they have come to know that everything You have given Me is from You; for the words which You gave Me I have given to them; and they received *them* and truly understood that I came forth from You, and they believed You sent Me. I ask on their behalf; I do not ask on behalf of the world, but of those whom You have given Me; for they are Yours; and all things that are Mine are Yours, and Yours are Mine; and I have been glorified in them. I am no longer in the world; and yet they themselves are in the world, and I come to You. Holy Father, keep them in Your name, *the name* which You have given Me, that they may be even as We *are*. While I was with them, I was keeping them in Your name which You have given Me; and I guarded them and not one of them perished but the son of perdition, so that the Scripture would be fulfilled" (John 17:1–12; see Luke 22:32; John 1:1; 3:35; 4:34; 5:44; 6:37–39, 70; 8:42; 11:41; 12:49; 13:18, 31; 16:15; 17:20; Philippians 2:9).

GOD, LOVE OF (Listed under LOVE OF GOD)

GOD, LOVING (Listed under LOVING GOD)

GOD, MOUTH OF

Setting: Judea near the Jordan. Following Jesus' baptism, and before He begins His public ministry, the Spirit leads Him into the Judean wilderness for temptation by Satan.

But He answered and said, "It is written, 'MAN SHALL NOT LIVE ON BREAD ALONE, BUT ON EVERY WORD THAT PROCEEDS OUT OF THE MOUTH OF GOD'" (Matthew 4:4, Jesus quotes from Deuteronomy 8:3; cf. Luke 4:4).

GOD, MY

Setting: Golgotha (Calvary), just outside Jerusalem. Jesus utters words of despair while dying on the cross for the sins of the world.

About the ninth hour Jesus cried out with a loud voice, saying, "ELI, ELI, LAMA SABACHTHANI?" that is, "MY GOD, MY GOD, WHY HAVE YOU FORSAKEN ME?" (Matthew 27:46, Jesus quotes from Psalm 22:1; cf. Mark 15:34).

Setting: Golgotha (Calvary), just outside Jerusalem. Jesus utters words of despair from the cross at the ninth hour (3 p.m.).

At the ninth hour Jesus cried out with a loud voice, "ELOI, ELOI, LAMA SABACHTHANI?" which is translated, "MY GOD, MY GOD, WHY HAVE YOU FORSAKEN ME?" (Mark 15:34, Jesus quotes from Psalm 22:1; cf. Matthew 27:46).

Setting: In Jerusalem, the risen Jesus first appears to Mary Magdalene after she tells Simon Peter and John about the now-empty tomb where Jesus' body had been laid the day before the Sabbath. He had just died on the cross for the sins of the world.

Jesus said to her, "Woman, why are you weeping? Whom are you seeking?" Supposing Him to be the gardener, she said to Him, "Sir, if you have carried Him away, tell me where you have laid Him, and I will take Him away." Jesus said to her, "Mary!" She turned and said to Him in Hebrew "Rabboni!" (which means, Teacher). Jesus said to her, "Stop clinging to Me, for I have not yet ascended to the Father; but go to My brethren and say to them, 'I ascend to My Father and your Father, and My God and Your God'" (John 20:15–17; see Mark 16:9–11; John 7:33; 19:31–42).

Setting: On the Lord's Day (Sunday), about fifty years after Jesus' resurrection, the disciple John, on the island of Patmos (in the Aegean Sea about fifty miles southwest of Ephesus in modern Turkey) encounters the Lord Jesus Christ. Jesus communicates a new revelation for the apostle to record for the church in Sardis and to six other churches in Asia.

"To the angel of the church in Sardis write: He who has the seven Spirits of God and the seven stars, says this: 'I know your deeds, that you have a name that you are alive, but you are dead. Wake up, and strengthen the things that remain, which were about to die; for I have not found your deeds completed in the sight of My God. So remember what you have received and heard; and keep *it*, and repent. Therefore if you do not wake up, I will come like a thief, and you will not know at what hour I will come to you. But you have a few people in Sardis who have not soiled their garments; and they will walk with Me in white, for they are worthy. He who overcomes will thus be clothed in white garments; and I will not erase his name from the book of life, and I will confess his name before My Father and before His angels. He who has an ear, let him hear what the Spirit says to the churches' " (Revelation 3:1–6; see Matthew 10:32; Revelation 1:16).

Setting: On the Lord's Day (Sunday), about fifty years after Jesus' resurrection, the disciple John, on the island of Patmos (in the Aegean Sea about fifty miles southwest of Ephesus in modern Turkey) encounters the Lord Jesus Christ. Jesus communicates a new revelation for the apostle to record for the church in Philadelphia and to six other churches in Asia.

"And to the angel of the church in Philadelphia write: He who is holy, who is true, who has the key of David, who opens and no one will shut, and who shuts and no one opens, says this: 'I know your deeds. Behold, I have put before you an open door which no one can shut, because you have a little power, and have kept My word, and have not denied My name. Behold, I will cause *those* of the synagogue of Satan, who say that they are Jews and are not, but lie—I will make them come and bow down at your feet, and *make them* know that I have loved you. Because you have kept the word of My perseverance, I also will keep you from the hour of testing, that *hour* which is about to come upon the whole world, to test those who dwell on the earth. I am coming quickly; hold fast what you have, so that no one will take your crown. He who overcomes, I will make him a pillar in the temple of My God, and he will not go out from it anymore; and I will write on him the name of My God, and the name of the city of My God, the new Jerusalem, which comes down out of heaven from My God, and My new name. He who has an ear, let him hear what the Spirit says to the churches' " (Revelation 3:7–13; see Isaiah 22:22; Galatians 2:9; Revelation 2:9, 10, 13, 25; 14:1).

GOD, PARADISE OF (See PARADISE OF GOD)

GOD, POSSIBILITIES WITH (Also see POWER OF GOD)

[POSSIBILITIES WITH GOD from with God all things are possible]

Setting: Judea beyond the Jordan (Perea). Jesus makes a pronouncement to His disciples following their astonishment over His statement on the difficulty of a rich man obtaining eternal life.

And looking at them, Jesus said to them, "With people this is impossible, but with God all things are possible" (Matthew 19:26; cf. Genesis 18:14; Mark 10:27; Luke 18:27).

[POSSIBILITIES WITH GOD from All things are possible to him who believes]

Setting: Returning from a high mountain in Galilee (perhaps Mount Hermon). After Jesus is transfigured before Peter, James, and John, the four discover the remaining disciples arguing with some scribes.

And He asked them, "What are you discussing with them?" And one of the crowd answered Him, "Teacher, I brought You my son, possessed with a spirit which makes him mute; and whenever it seizes him, it slams him *to the ground* and he foams *at the mouth,* and grinds his teeth and stiffens out. I told Your disciples to cast it out, and they could not *do it.* And He answered them, and said, "O unbelieving generation, how long shall I be with you? How long shall I put up with you? Bring him to Me!" They brought the boy to Him. When he saw Him, immediately the spirit threw him into a convulsion, and falling to the ground, be *began* rolling around and foaming *at the mouth.* And He asked his father, "How long has this been happening to him?" And he said, "From childhood. It has often thrown him both into the fire and into the water to destroy him. But if You can do anything, take pity on us and help us!" And Jesus said to him, "'If You can?' All things are possible to him who believes." Immediately the boy's father cried out and said, "I do believe; help my unbelief." When Jesus saw that a crowd was rapidly gathering, He rebuked the unclean spirit, saying to it, "You deaf and mute spirit, I command you, come out of him and do not enter him again." After crying out and throwing him into terrible convulsions, it came out; and *the boy* became so much like a corpse that most *of them,* said, "He is dead!" But Jesus took him by the hand and raised him; and he got up. When He came into *the* house, His disciples *began* questioning Him privately, "Why could we not drive it out?" And He said to them, "This kind cannot come out by anything but prayer" (Mark 9:16–29; cf. Matthew 17:14–21; Luke 9:37–43; see Matthew 17:20).

[POSSIBILITIES WITH GOD from all things are possible with God]

Setting: Judea beyond the Jordan (Perea). After informing a rich man how righteous believers may have treasure in heaven, Jesus conveys to His disciples the difficulty the wealthy have entering the kingdom of God.

And Jesus, looking around, said to His disciples, "How hard it will be for those who are wealthy to enter the kingdom of God!" The disciples were amazed at His words. But Jesus answered again and said to them, "Children, how hard it is to enter the kingdom of God! It is easier for a camel to go through the eye of a needle than for a rich man to enter the kingdom of God." They were even more astonished and said to Him, "Then who can be saved?" Looking at them, Jesus said, "With people it is impossible, but not with God; for all things are possible with God" (Mark 10:23–27; cf. Matthew 19:23–26; Luke 18:24, 25).

[POSSIBILITIES WITH GOD from All things are possible for You]

Setting: Gethsemane on the Mount of Olives, east of the temple in Jerusalem. Jesus agonizes over His impending death, disappointed that His disciples keep falling asleep instead of watching and praying with Him.

They came to a place named Gethsemane; and He said to the disciples, "Sit here until I have prayed." And He took with Him Peter and James and John, and began to be very distressed and troubled. And He said to them, "My soul is deeply grieved to the point of death; remain here and keep watch." And He went a little beyond *them,* and fell to the ground and *began* to pray that if it were possible, the hour might pass Him by. And He was saying, "Abba! Father! All things are possible for You; remove this cup from Me; yet not what I will, but what You will." And He came and found them sleeping, and said to Peter, "Simon, are you asleep? Could you not keep watch for one hour? Keep watching and praying that you may not come into temptation; the spirit is willing, but the flesh is weak" (Mark 14:32–38; cf. Matthew 26:36–41; Luke 22:41–46; see Romans 8:15; Galatians 4:6).

[POSSIBILITIES WITH GOD from are possible with God]
Setting: On the way from Galilee to Jerusalem. After answering a ruler's question about inheriting eternal life, Jesus responds to His disciples' confusion about being saved.

But He said, "The things that are impossible with people are possible with God" (Luke 18:27; cf. Matthew 19:26).

GOD, POWER OF (See POWER OF GOD)

GOD, PRAISING (See PRAISING GOD; and WORSHIP)

GOD, REJECTION OF (See JESUS, REJECTING)

GOD, RESPONDING TO (See DISOBEDIENCE; and OBEDIENCE)

GOD, SEEING (Also see GOD, JESUS AS)

[SEEING GOD from see God]
Setting: Galilee. Early in His ministry, Jesus presents the Beatitudes (part of the Sermon on the Mount) to His disciples and the gathered crowds from Galilee, Decapolis, Jerusalem, Judea, and beyond the Jordan.

"Blessed are the pure in heart, for they shall see God" (Matthew 5:8; see Matthew 5:1; 13:35).

[SEEING GOD from Not that anyone has seen the Father, except the One who is from God; He has seen the Father]
Setting: Capernaum of Galilee. After Jesus informs the people He miraculously fed with a lad's five loaves and two fish how they might receive the bread out of heaven, the Jewish religious leaders grumble because Jesus claims that He came down out of heaven.

Therefore the Jews were grumbling about Him, because He said, "I am the bread that came down out of heaven." They were saying, "Is not this Jesus, the son of Joseph, whose father and mother we know? How does He now say, 'I have come down out of heaven'?" Jesus answered and said to them, "Do not grumble among yourselves. No one can come to Me unless the Father who sent Me draws him; and I will raise him up on the last day. It is written in the prophets, 'AND THEY SHALL ALL BE TAUGHT OF GOD.' Everyone who has heard and learned from the Father, comes to Me. Not that anyone has seen the Father, except the One who is from God; He has seen the Father. Truly, truly, I say to you, he who believes has eternal life. I am the bread of life. Your fathers ate the manna in the wilderness, and they died. This is the bread which comes down out of heaven, so that one may eat of it and not die. I am the living bread that came down out of heaven; if anyone eats of this bread, he will live forever; and the bread also which I will give for the life of the world is My flesh" (John 6:41–51, Jesus quotes from Isaiah 54:13; see John 1:18, 29; 3:36; 7:27).

[SEEING GOD from He who has seen Me has seen the Father]
Setting: Jerusalem. Before the Passover, after answering Thomas's question as to where He is going and how they will know the way, Jesus responds to Philip's request for Him to show His disciples the Father.

Jesus said to him, "Have I been so long with you, and *yet* you have not come to know Me, Philip? He who has seen Me has seen the Father; how *can* you say, 'Show us the Father'? Do you not believe that I am in the Father, and the Father is in Me? The words that I say to you I do not speak on My own initiative, but the Father abiding in Me does His works. Believe Me that I am in the Father and the Father is in Me; otherwise believe because of the works themselves. Truly, truly, I say to you, he who believes in Me, the works that I do, he will do also; and greater *works* than these he will do; because I go to the Father. Whatever you ask in My name, that will I do, so that the Father may be glorified in the Son. If you ask Me anything in My name, I will do *it*" (John 14:9–14; see Matthew 7:7; John 1:14; 5:19, 20, 36; 10:37, 38; 15:16).

GOD, SEPARATION FROM (See DAMNATION, ETERNAL; DEATH, ETERNAL; FIRE, ETERNAL; FIRE, FURNACE OF; PUNISHMENT, ETERNAL; HELL; and HELL, SENTENCE OF)

GOD, SERVING (See SERVING GOD)

GOD, SIGHT OF (Also see GOD, SIGHT OF MY; and SIGHT, GOD'S)

Setting: On the way from Galilee to Jerusalem. The Lord responds to the Pharisees' scoffing at His teaching His disciples about stewardship.

And He said to them, "You are those who justify yourselves in the sight of men, but God knows your hearts; for that which is highly esteemed among men is detestable in the sight of God. The Law and the Prophets *were proclaimed* until John; since that time the gospel of the kingdom of God has been preached, and everyone is forcing his way into it. But is it easier for heaven and earth to pass away than for one stroke of a letter of the Law to fail" (Luke 16:15–17; cf. Matthew 5:18; see 1 Samuel 16:7; Matthew 4:23; 11:11–14).

GOD, SIGHT OF MY (Also see GOD, SIGHT OF)

Setting: On the island of Patmos (in the Aegean Sea about fifty miles southwest of Ephesus in modern Turkey). On the Lord's Day (Sunday), about fifty years after Jesus' resurrection, the disciple John encounters the Lord Jesus Christ, who communicates a new revelation for the apostle to record for the church in Sardis and to six other churches in Asia.

"To the angel of the church in Sardis write: He who has the seven Spirits of God and the seven stars, says this: 'I know your deeds, that you have a name that you are alive, but you are dead. Wake up, and strengthen the things that remain, which were about to die; for I have not found your deeds completed in the sight of My God. So remember what you have received and heard; and keep *it*, and repent. Therefore if you do not wake up, I will come like a thief, and you will not know at what hour I will come to you. But you have a few people in Sardis who have not soiled their garments; and they will walk with Me in white, for they are worthy. He who overcomes will thus be clothed in white garments; and I will not erase his name from the book of life, and I will confess his name before My Father and before His angels. He who has an ear, let him hear what the Spirit says to the churches' " (Revelation 3:1–6; see Matthew 10:32; Revelation 1:16).

GOD, SON OF (See SON OF GOD)

GOD, SONS OF (See SONS OF GOD)

GOD, SPIRIT OF (See HOLY SPIRIT; and SPIRIT (God))

GOD, TEMPLE OF MY (Also see TEMPLE)

Setting: On the island of Patmos (in the Aegean Sea about fifty miles southwest of Ephesus in modern Turkey). On the Lord's Day (Sunday), about fifty years after Jesus' resurrection, the disciple John encounters the Lord Jesus Christ, who communicates a new revelation for the apostle to record for the church in Philadelphia and to six other churches in Asia.

"And to the angel of the church in Philadelphia write: He who is holy, who is true, who has the key of David, who opens and no one will shut, and who shuts and no one opens, says this: 'I know your deeds. Behold, I have put before you an open door which no one can shut, because you have a little power, and have kept My word, and have not denied My name. Behold, I will cause *those* of the synagogue of Satan, who say that they are Jews and are not, but lie—I will make them come and bow down at your feet, and *make them* know that I have loved you. Because you have kept the word of My perseverance, I also will keep you from the hour of testing, that *hour* which is about to come upon the whole world, to test those who dwell on the earth. I am coming quickly; hold fast what you have, so that no one will take your crown. He who overcomes, I will make him a pillar in the temple of My God, and he will not go out from it anymore; and I will write on him the name of My God, and the name of the city of My God, the new Jerusalem, which comes down out of heaven from My God, and My new name. He who has an ear, let him hear what the Spirit says to the churches' " (Revelation 3:7–13; see Isaiah 22:22; Galatians 2:9; Revelation 2:9, 10, 13, 25; 14:1).

GOD, TESTING

[TESTING GOD from YOU SHALL NOT PUT THE LORD YOUR GOD TO THE TEST]
Setting: Judea near the Jordan River. Following His baptism, and before He begins His public ministry, Jesus is led by the Spirit into the Judean wilderness for forty days of temptation by Satan.

Jesus said to him, "On the other hand, it is written, 'YOU SHALL NOT PUT THE LORD YOUR GOD TO THE TEST'" (Matthew 4:7, Jesus quotes from Deuteronomy 6:16; cf. Luke 4:12).

[TESTING GOD from YOU SHALL NOT PUT THE LORD YOUR GOD TO THE TEST]
Setting: Judea, near the Jordan River. Following His baptism, and before He begins His public ministry, Jesus is led by the Spirit into the wilderness for forty days of temptation by Satan.

And Jesus answered and said to him, "It is said, 'YOU SHALL NOT PUT THE LORD YOUR GOD TO THE TEST'" (Luke 4:12, Jesus quotes from Deuteronomy 6:16; cf. Matthew 4:7).

GOD, THRONE OF (See THRONE OF GOD)

GOD, TRIUNE (See TRINITY)

GOD, TRUE

Setting: Jerusalem. Before the Passover, after giving His disciples assurance that in the midst of tribulation they will have His peace, Jesus prays His high-priestly prayer.

Jesus spoke these things; and lifting up His eyes to heaven, He said, "Father, the hour has come; glorify Your Son, that the Son may glorify You, even as You gave Him authority over all flesh, that to all whom You have given Him, He may give eternal life. This is eternal life, that they may know You, the only true God, and Jesus Christ whom You have sent. I glorified You on the earth, having accomplished the work which You have given Me to do. Now, Father, glorify Me together with Yourself, with the glory which I had with You before the world was. I have manifested Your name to the men whom You gave Me out of the world; they were Yours and You gave them to Me, and they have kept Your word. Now they have come to know that everything You have given Me is from You; for the words which You gave Me I have given to them; and they received *them* and truly understood that I came forth from You, and they believed You sent Me. I ask on their behalf; I do not ask on behalf of the world, but of those whom You have given Me; for they are Yours; and all things that are Mine are Yours, and Yours are Mine; and have been glorified in them. I am no longer in the world; and *yet* they themselves are in the world, and I come to You. Holy Father, keep them in Your name, *the name* which You have given Me, that they may be even as We *are.* While I was with them, I was keeping them in Your name which You have given Me; and I guarded them and not one of them perished but the son of perdition, so that the Scripture would be fulfilled" (John 17:1–12; see Luke 22:32; John 1:1; 3:35; 4:34; 5:44; 6:37–39, 70; 8:42; 11:41; 12:49; 13:18, 31; 16:15; 17:20; Philippians 2:9).

GOD, TRUSTING (See GOD, DEPENDENCE ON; NEEDS; PROVISION, GOD'S; and WORRY)

GOD, VISITATION FROM (See VISION)

GOD, WILL OF (See WILL OF GOD)

GOD, WISDOM OF

Setting: On the way from Galilee to Jerusalem. After Jesus pronounces woes upon the Pharisees, a lawyer replies that His remarks are an insult to lawyers, too.

But He said, "Woe to you lawyers as well! For you weigh men down with burdens hard to bear, while you yourselves will not even touch the burdens with one of your fingers. Woe to you! For you build the tombs of the prophets, and *it was* your fathers *who* killed them. So you are witnesses and approve the deeds of your fathers; because it was they who killed them, and you build *their tombs*. For this reason also the wisdom of God said, 'I will send them prophets and apostles, and *some* of them they will kill and *some* they will persecute, so that the blood of all the prophets, shed since the foundation of the world, may be charged against this generation, from the blood of Abel to the blood of Zechariah, who was killed between the altar and the house *of God*; yes, I tell you, it shall be charged against this generation.' Woe to you lawyers! For you have taken away the key of knowledge; you yourselves did not enter, and you hindered those who were entering." (Luke 11:46–52; cf. Matthew 23:29–32; see 2 Chronicles 24:20, 21; Matthew 23:4, 13).

GOD, WORD OF (See WORD OF GOD)

GOD, WORDS OF (See WORDS OF GOD)

GOD, WORK OF (Also see GOD, WORKS OF; and JESUS' WORK)

[WORK OF GOD from His work]

Setting: Sychar in Samaria, on the way to Galilee. After Jesus converses with a Samaritan woman at Jacob's well, His disciples return with food. They try to get Jesus to eat but are surprised when He speaks of other food.

Jesus said to them, "My food is to do the will of Him who sent Me and to accomplish His work. Do you not say, 'There are yet four months, and *then* comes the harvest'? Behold, I say to you, lift up your eyes and look on the fields, that they are white for harvest. Already he who reaps is receiving wages and is gathering fruit for life eternal; so that he who sows and he who reaps may rejoice together. For in this *case* the saying is true, 'One sows and another reaps.' I sent you to reap that for which you have not labored; others have labored and you have entered into their labor" (John 4:34–38; see Matthew 9:37, 38; John 5:36).

[WORK OF GOD from My Father is working]

Setting: By the pool of Bethesda in Jerusalem. During the Feast of the Jews, Jesus responds to criticism from the Jewish religious leaders for healing a lame man on the Sabbath.

But He answered them, "My Father is working until now, and I Myself am working" (John 5:17).

Setting: Capernaum. The day after Jesus walks on the Sea of Galilee to join His disciples in a boat, the people He miraculously fed with a lad's five loaves and two fish quiz Him about how they may do the works of God.

Jesus answered and said to them, "This is the work of God, that you believe in Him whom He has sent" (John 6:29; see 1 Thessalonians 1:3).

GOD, WORKS OF (Also see FATHER, WORKS OF MY; GOD, WORK OF; and JESUS' WORK)

Setting: The temple treasury in Jerusalem. After Jesus avoids being stoned by the scribes and Pharisees, His disciples wonder if blindness is caused by sin as the Lord heals a man born blind.

Jesus answered, "*It was* neither *that* this man sinned, nor his parents; but *it was* so that the works of God might be displayed in him. We must work the works of Him who sent Me as long as it is day; night is coming when no one can work. While I am in the world, I am the Light of the world." When He had said this, He spat on the ground, and made clay of the spittle, and applied the clay to his eyes, and said to him, "Go, wash in the pool of Siloam" (which is translated, Sent). So he went away and washed, and came *back* seeing (John 9:3–7; see John 8:12; 11:4; 12:46).

GOD, WORSHIPING (See WORSHIP)

GOD OF THE DEAD (Listed under DEAD, GOD OF THE)

GOD OF THE LIVING (Listed under LIVING, GOD OF THE)

GOD'S APPROVAL (Listed under APPROVAL, GOD'S)

GOD'S CARE FOR CREATURES (Listed under CREATURES, GOD'S CARE FOR)

GOD'S FACE (Listed under FACE, GOD'S)

GOD'S GLORIFICATION (Listed under GLORIFICATION, GOD'S)

GOD'S GOODNESS (Listed under GOODNESS, GOD'S)

GOD'S GREATNESS (Listed under GREATNESS, GOD'S)

GOD'S GUIDANCE (Listed under GUIDANCE, GOD'S)

GOD'S INTERESTS (Listed under INTERESTS, GOD'S)

GOD'S INVISIBILITY (Listed under INVISIBILITY, GOD'S)

GOD'S LOVE (See LOVE OF GOD)

GOD'S OMNISCIENCE (Listed under OMNISCIENCE, GOD'S)

GOD'S POWER (Listed under POWER OF GOD)

GOD'S PROVISION (Listed under PROVISION, GOD'S; also see BREAD, DAILY)

GOD'S SIGHT (Listed under SIGHT, GOD'S)

GOD'S THINGS (Listed under THINGS, GOD'S)

GOD'S THRONE (See THRONE OF GOD)

GOD'S WILL (See FATHER, WILL OF MY; and WILL OF GOD)

GOD'S WORD (See BIBLE; OLD TESTAMENT; SCRIPTURES and WORD OF GOD)

GOD'S WORK (See under GOD, WORK OF)

GODHEAD (See TRINITY)

GODLINESS (See RIGHTEOUSNESS)

GODLY LIVING (Listed under LIVING, GODLY)

GODS (Also see GOD)

Setting: Jerusalem. At the Feast of Dedication, the Pharisees desire to stone Jesus because He claims to be equal with God when they ask Him plainly whether He is the Christ.

Jesus answered them, "Has it not been written in your Law, 'I SAID, YOU ARE GODS'? If he called them gods, to whom the word of God came (and the Scripture cannot be broken), do you say of Him, whom the Father sanctified and sent into the world, 'You are blaspheming,' because I said, 'I am the Son of God'? If I do not do the works of My Father, do not believe Me; but if I do them, though you do not believe Me, believe the works, so that you may know and understand that the Father is in Me, and I in the Father" (John 10:34–38, Jesus quotes from Psalm 82:6; see John 14:10, 20).

GOLD

Setting: Galilee. After His twelve disciples observe His ministry, Jesus summons and specifically instructs them about their ministry to the people of Israel.

These twelve Jesus sent out after instructing them: "Do not go in *the* way of *the* Gentiles, and do not enter *any* city of the Samaritans; but rather go to the lost sheep of the house of Israel. And as you go, preach, saying, 'The kingdom of heaven is at hand.' Heal *the* sick, raise *the* dead, cleanse *the* lepers, cast out demons. Freely you received, freely give. Do not acquire gold, or silver, or copper for your money belts, or a bag for *your* journey, or even two coats, or sandals, or a staff; for the worker is worthy of his support. And whatever city or village you enter, inquire who is worthy in it, and stay at his house until you leave *that city*. As you enter the house, give it your greeting. If the house is worthy, give it your *blessing of* peace. But if it is not worthy, take back your *blessing of* peace. Whoever does not receive you, nor heed your words, as you go out of that house or that city, shake the dust off your feet. Truly I say to you, it will be more tolerable for *the* land of Sodom and Gomorrah in the day of judgment than for that city" (Matthew 10:5–15; cf. Mark 6:7–11; Luke 9:1–5; see Matthew 3:2; 11:22, 24; 15:24; Luke 22:35; 1 Corinthians 9:14).

Setting: The temple in Jerusalem. After the Jewish religious leaders test Him with questions, Jesus pronounces the fourth of eight woes on them in front of the crowds and His disciples.

"Woe to you, blind guides, who say, "Whoever swears by the temple, *that* is nothing; but whoever swears by the gold of the temple is obligated.' You fools and blind men! Which is more important, the gold or the temple that sanctified the gold? And, 'Whoever swears by the altar, *that* is nothing, but whoever swears by the offering on it, he is obligated.' You blind men, which is more important, the offering, or the altar that sanctifies the offering? Therefore, whoever swears by the altar, swears *both* by the altar and by everything on it. And whoever swears by the temple, swears *both* by the temple and by Him who dwells within it. And whoever swears by heaven, swears *both* by the throne of God and by Him who sits upon it" (Matthew 23:16–22; see Exodus 29:37; 1 Kings 8:13; Isaiah 66:1; Matthew 15:14).

Setting: On the island of Patmos (in the Aegean Sea about fifty miles southwest of Ephesus in modern Turkey). On the Lord's Day (Sunday), about fifty years after Jesus' resurrection, the disciple John encounters the Lord Jesus Christ, who communicates a new revelation for the apostle to record for the church in Laodicea and to six other churches in Asia.

"To the angel of the church in Laodicea write: The Amen, the faithful and true Witness, the Beginning of the creation of God, says this: 'I know your deeds, that you are neither cold nor hot; I wish that you were cold or hot. So because you are lukewarm, and neither hot nor cold, I will spit you out of My mouth. Because you say, "I am rich, and have become wealthy, and have need of nothing," and you do not know that you are wretched and miserable and poor and blind and naked, I advise you to buy from Me gold refined by fire so that you may become rich, and white garments so that you may clothe yourself, and *that* the shame of your nakedness will not be revealed; and eye salve to anoint your eyes so that you may see. Those whom I love, I reprove and discipline; therefore be zealous and repent. Behold, I stand at the door and knock; if anyone hears My voice and opens the door, I will come in to him and will dine with him, and he with Me. He who overcomes, I will grant to him to sit down with Me on My throne, as I also overcame and sat down with My Father on His throne. He who has an ear, let him hear what the Spirit says to the churches'" (Revelation 3:14–22; see Proverbs 3:12; Hosea 12:8; John 14:23; 16:33).

GOLDEN RULE (Also see NEIGHBOR)

[GOLDEN RULE from treat people the same way you want them to treat you]

Setting: Galilee. During the early part of His ministry, Jesus preaches the Sermon on the Mount to His disciples and the multitudes.

"In everything, therefore, treat people the same way you want them to treat you, for this is the Law and the Prophets" (Matthew 7:12; cf. Matthew 22:20; Luke 6:31).

[GOLDEN RULE from Treat others the same way you want them to treat you]

Setting: Galilee. After selecting His twelve disciples, Jesus teaches the Sermon on the Mount to those disciples and a great throng of people from Judea, Jerusalem, and the central coastal region of Tyre and Sidon.

"But I say to you who hear, love your enemies, do good to those who hate you, bless those who curse you, pray for those who mistreat you. Whoever hits you on the cheek, offer him the other also; and whoever takes away your coat, do not withhold your shirt from him either. Give to everyone who asks of you, and whoever takes away what is yours, do not demand it back. Treat others the same way you want them to treat you. If you love those who love you, what credit is *that* to you? For even sinners love those who love them. If you do good to those who do good to you, what credit is *that* to you? For even sinners do the same. If you lend to those from whom you expect to receive, what credit is *that* to you? Even sinners lend to sinners in order to receive back the same *amount.* But love your enemies, and do good, and lend, expecting nothing in return; and your reward will be great, and you will be sons of the Most High; for He Himself is kind to ungrateful and evil *men*. Be merciful, just as your Father is merciful" (Luke 6:27–36; cf. Matthew 5:9, 39–48; 7:12).

GOMORRAH

Setting: Galilee. After His twelve disciples observe His ministry, Jesus summons and specifically instructs them about their ministry to the people of Israel.

These twelve Jesus sent out after instructing them: "Do not go in *the* way of *the* Gentiles, and do not enter *any* city of the Samaritans; but rather go to the lost sheep of the house of Israel. And as you go, preach, saying, 'The kingdom of heaven is at hand.' Heal *the* sick, raise *the* dead, cleanse *the* lepers, cast out demons. Freely you received, freely give. Do not acquire gold, or silver, or copper for your money belts, or a bag for *your* journey, or even two coats, or sandals, or a staff; for the worker is worthy of his support. And whatever city or village you enter, inquire who is worthy in it, and stay at his house until you leave *that city*. As you enter the house, give it your greeting. If the house is worthy, give it your *blessing of* peace. But if it is not worthy, take back your *blessing of* peace. Whoever does not receive you, nor heed your words, as you go out of that house or that city, shake the dust off your feet. Truly I say to you, it will be more tolerable for *the* land of Sodom and Gomorrah in the day of judgment than for that city" (Matthew 10:5–15; cf. Mark 6:7–11; Luke 9:1–5; see Matthew 3:2; 11:22, 24; 15:24; Luke 22:35; 1 Corinthians 9:14).

GOOD (Specifics such as DEED, GOOD; FRUIT, GOOD; and WORKS, GOOD are separate entries)

Setting: Galilee. During the early part of His ministry, Jesus preaches the Sermon on the Mount to His disciples and the multitudes.

"You are the salt of the earth; but if the salt has become tasteless, how can it be made salty *again*? It is not longer good for anything, except to be thrown out and trampled under foot by men" (Matthew 5:13; cf. Mark 9:50).

Setting: Galilee. During the early part of His ministry, Jesus preaches the Sermon on the Mount to His disciples and the multitudes.

"You have heard that it was said, 'YOU SHALL LOVE YOUR NEIGHBOR and hate your enemy.' But I say to you, love your enemies and pray for those who persecute you, so that you may be sons of your Father who is in heaven; for He causes His sun to rise on *the* evil and *the* good, and sends rain on *the* righteous and *the* unrighteous. For if you love those who love you, what reward do you have? Do not even the tax collectors do the same? If you greet only your brothers, what more are you doing *than others?* Do not even the Gentiles do the same? Therefore, you are to be perfect, as your heavenly Father is perfect" (Matthew 5:43–48, Jesus quotes from Leviticus 19:18; cf. Leviticus 19:2; Luke 6:27–36).

Setting: Galilee. During the early part of His ministry, Jesus preaches the Sermon on the Mount to His disciples and the multitudes.

"Ask, and it will be given to you; seek, and you will find; knock, and it will be opened to you. For everyone who asks receives, and he who seeks finds, and to him who knocks it will be opened. Or what man is there among you who, when his son asks for a loaf, will give him a stone? Or if he asks for a fish, he will not give him a snake, will he? If you then, being evil, know how to give good gifts to your children, how much more will your Father who is in heaven give what is good to those who ask Him! In everything, therefore, treat people the same way you want them to treat you, for this is the Law and the Prophets" (Matthew 7:7–12; cf. Matthew 22:40; Luke 6:31; 11:9–13; see Psalm 84:11).

Setting: A synagogue in Galilee. Jesus answers questions the Pharisees pose about the Sabbath.

And He said to them, "What man is there among you who has a sheep, and if it falls into a pit on the Sabbath, will he not take hold of it and lift it out? How much more valuable then is a man than a sheep! So then, it is lawful to do good on the Sabbath." Then He said to the man, "Stretch out your hand!" He stretched it out, and it was restored to normal, like the other (Matthew 12:11–13; cf. Matthew 10:31; Mark 3:4–5; Luke 6:9, 10; 14:5; see Matthew 8:3).

Setting: Galilee. After He heals a blind, mute, demon-possessed man, the Pharisees accuse Jesus in front of crowds of being a worker of Satan.

"Either make the tree good and its fruit good, or make the tree bad and its fruit bad; for the tree is known by its fruit. You brood of vipers, how can you, being evil, speak what is good? For the mouth speaks out of that which fills the heart. The good man brings out of *his* good treasure what is good; and the evil man brings out of *his* evil treasure what is evil. But I tell you that every careless word that people speak, they shall give an accounting for it in the day of judgment. For by your words you will be justified, and by your words you will be condemned" (Matthew 12:33–37; cf. Matthew 3:7; 7:16–18).

Setting: The district of Tyre and Sidon. A Canaanite woman appeals to Jesus to heal her demon-possessed daughter.

But He answered and said, "I was sent only to the lost sheep of the house of Israel." But she came and *began* to bow down before Him, saying, "Lord, help me!" And He answered and said, "It is not good to take the children's bread and throw it to the dogs." But she said, "Yes, Lord; but even the dogs feed from the crumbs which fall from their masters' table." Then Jesus said to her, "O woman, your faith is great; it shall be done for you as you wish." And her daughter was healed at once (Matthew 15:24–28; cf. Mark 7: 24–30; see Matthew 9:22; 10:5–6).

Setting: Judea beyond the Jordan (Perea). Jesus shares with a rich, young ruler how he can obtain eternal life.

And He said to him, "Why are you asking Me about what is good? There is *only* One who is good; but if you wish to enter into life, keep the commandments." *Then* he said to Him, 'Which ones?' And Jesus said, "YOU SHALL NOT COMMIT MURDER; YOU SHALL NOT COMMIT ADULTERY; YOU SHALL NOT STEAL; YOU SHALL NOT BEAR FALSE WITNESS; HONOR YOUR FATHER AND MOTHER; and YOU SHALL LOVE YOUR NEIGHBOR AS YOURSELF." The young man said to Him, "All these things I have kept; what am I still lacking?" Jesus said to him, "If you wish to complete go *and* sell your possessions and give to *the* poor, and you will have treasure in heaven; and come, follow Me" (Matthew 19:16–22, Jesus quotes from Exodus 20:13–15; Leviticus 19:18; cf. Leviticus 18:5; Mark 10:17–21; Luke 10:25–28; 12:33; 18:18–24).

Setting: The temple in Jerusalem. Jesus speaks another parable to the chief priests and elders after they question His authority.

Jesus spoke to them again in parables, saying, "The kingdom of heaven may be compared to a king who gave a wedding feast for his son. And he sent out his slaves to call those who had been invited to the wedding feast, and they were unwilling to come. Again he sent out other slaves saying, 'Tell those who have been invited, "Behold, I have prepared my dinner; my oxen and my fattened livestock are *all* butchered and everything is ready; come to the wedding feast." But they paid no attention and went their way, one to his own farm, another to his business, and the rest seized his slaves and mistreated them and killed them. But the king was enraged, and he sent his armies and destroyed those murderers and set their city on fire. Then he said to his slaves, 'The wedding is ready, but those who were invited were not worthy. 'Go therefore to the main highways, and as many as you find *there,* invite to the wedding feast.' Those slaves went out into the streets and gathered together all they found, both evil and good; and the wedding hall was filled with dinner guests. But when the king came in to look over the dinner guests, he saw a man there who was not dressed in wedding clothes, and he said to him, 'Friend, how did you come in here without wedding clothes?' And the man was speechless. Then the king said to the servants, 'Bind him hand and foot, and throw him into the outer darkness; in that place there will be weeping and gnashing of teeth.' For many are called, but few *are* chosen" (Matthew 22:1–14; cf. Matthew 8:11, 12).

Setting: An upper room in Jerusalem. While celebrating the Passover meal, Jesus shocks His disciples with the revelation that one of them will soon betray Him to His enemies.

As they were eating, He said, "Truly I say to you that one of you will betray Me." Being deeply grieved, they each one began to say to Him, 'Surely not I, Lord?' And He answered, "He who dipped his hand with Me in the bowl is the one who will betray Me. The Son of Man *is to* go, just as it is written of Him; but woe to that man by whom the Son of Man is betrayed! It would have been good for that man if he had not been born." And Judas, who was betraying Him, said, 'Surely it is not I, Rabbi?' Jesus said to him, "You have said *it* yourself" (Matthew 26:21–25; cf. Mark 14:18–21; Luke 22:21, 23; John 13:21–30; see Psalm 41:9).

Setting: A synagogue in Galilee. Early in His ministry, Jesus heals a man's withered hand on the Sabbath while the Pharisees observe.

He said to the man with the withered hand, "Get up and come forward!" And He said to them, "Is it lawful to do good or do harm on the Sabbath, to save a life or to kill?" But they kept silent. After looking around at them with anger, grieved at their hardness of heart, He said to the man, "Stretch out your hand." And he stretched it out, and his hand was restored (Mark 3:3–5; cf. Matthew 12:9–14; Luke 6:6–11).

Setting: The region of Tyre. After the Pharisees and scribes from Jerusalem question His disciples' lack of obedience to the tradition in Galilee, Jesus casts a demon out from the daughter of a Gentile (Syrophoenician) woman from Tyre.

And He was saying to her, "Let the children be satisfied first, for it is not good to take the children's bread and throw it to the dogs." But she answered and said to Him, "Yes, Lord *but* even the dogs under the table feed on the children's crumbs. And He said to her, "Because of this answer go; the demon has gone out of your daughter" (Mark 7:27–29; cf. Matthew 15:21–28).

Setting: Capernaum of Galilee. As Jesus teaches His disciples in private, they ask Him about greatness.

But Jesus said, "Do not hinder him, for there is no one who will perform a miracle in My name, and be able soon afterward to speak evil of Me. For he who is not against us is for us. For whoever gives you a cup of water to drink because of your name as *followers* of Christ, truly I say to you, he will not lose his reward. Whoever causes one of these little ones who believe to stumble, it would be better for him if, with a heavy millstone hung around his neck, he had been cast into the sea. If your hand causes you to stumble, cut it off; it is better for you to enter life crippled, than, having your two hands, to go into hell, into the unquenchable fire, [where THEIR WORM DOES NOT DIE, AND THE FIRE IS NOT QUENCHED.] If your foot causes you to stumble, cut it off; it is better for you to enter life lame, than, having your two feet, to be cast into hell, [where THEIR WORM DOES NOT DIE, AND THE FIRE IS NOT QUENCHED.] If your eye causes you to stumble, throw it out; it is better for you to enter the kingdom of God with one eye, than, having two eyes, to be cast into hell, where THEIR WORM DOES NOT DIE, AND THE FIRE IS NOT QUENCHED. For everyone will be salted with fire. Salt is good; but if the salt becomes unsalty, with what will you make it salty *again?* Have salt in yourselves, and be at peace with one another" (Mark 9:39–50; Jesus quotes from Isaiah 66:24; cf. Matthew 18:6–9; Luke 9:49, 50; see Matthew 5:13, 29, 30; 10:42; 12:30; 18:5, 6).

Setting: Judea beyond the Jordan (Perea). After demonstrating to His disciples the importance of little children, Jesus encounters a rich man seeking eternal life.

And Jesus said to him, "Why do you call Me good? No one is good except God alone. You know the commandments, 'DO NOT MURDER, DO NOT COMMIT ADULTERY, DO NOT STEAL, DO NOT BEAR FALSE WITNESS, Do not defraud, HONOR YOUR FATHER AND MOTHER.'" And he said to Him, "Teacher, I have kept all these things from my youth up." Looking at him, Jesus felt a love for him and said to him, "One thing you lack: go and sell all you possess and give to the poor, and you will have treasure in heaven; and come, follow Me" (Mark 10:18–21; Jesus quotes from Exodus 20:12–16; cf. Matthew 19:16–22; Luke 18:18–24; see Matthew 6:20).

Setting: The home of Simon the leper in Bethany. Two days before the Feast of Unleavened Bread (Passover), Jesus commends a woman who anoints His head with costly perfume, which some there think should have been sold and the proceeds given to the poor.

But Jesus said, "Let her alone; why do you bother her? She has done a good deed to Me. For you always have the poor with you, and whenever you wish you can do good to them; but you do not always have Me. She has done what she could; she has anointed My body beforehand for the burial. Truly I say to you, wherever the gospel is preached in the whole world, what this woman has done will also be spoken of in memory of her" (Mark 14:6–9; cf. Matthew 26:6–13; John 12:2–8; see Deuteronomy 15:11).

Setting: A borrowed upper room in Jerusalem. While Jesus and His twelve disciples are eating the Passover meal, the Lord states one of His disciples will betray Him.

As they were reclining *at the table* and eating, Jesus said, "Truly I say to you that one of you will betray Me—one who is eating with Me." They began to be grieved and to say to Him one by one, "Surely not I?" And He said to them, "*It is* one of the twelve, one who dips with Me in the bowl. For the Son of Man *is to* go just as it is written of Him; but woe to that man by whom the Son of Man is betrayed! *It would have been* good for that man if he had not been born" (Mark 14:18–21; cf. Matthew 26:21–24; Luke 22:21–23; John 13:21, 22).

Setting: The home of Levi (Matthew) in Capernaum. At a reception for Jesus following Levi's call to be a disciple, the Lord tells a parable to the Pharisees and their scribes, who question His association with tax collectors and sinners.

And He was also telling them a parable: "No one tears a piece of cloth from a new garment and puts it on an old garment; otherwise he will both tear the new, and the piece from the new will not match the old. And no one puts new wine into old wineskins; otherwise the new wine will burst the skins and it will be spilled out, and the skins will be ruined. But new wine must be put into fresh wineskins. And no one, after drinking old *wine* wishes for new; for he says, 'The old is good *enough.*'" (Luke 5:36–39; cf. Matthew 9:16, 17; Mark 2:21, 22).

Setting: A synagogue in Galilee. As Jesus teaches on the Sabbath, the scribes and Pharisees watch to see if He heals a man's withered hand.

But He knew what they were thinking, and He said to the man with the withered hand, "Get up and come forward!" And he got up and came forward. And Jesus said to them, "I ask you, is it lawful to do good or to do harm on the Sabbath, to save a life or destroy it?" And looking around at them all, He said to him, "Stretch out your hand!" And he did *so;* and his hand was restored (Luke 6:8–10; cf. Matthew 12:9–13; Mark 3:1–5).

Setting: Galilee. After selecting His twelve disciples, Jesus teaches the Sermon on the Mount to those disciples and a great throng from Judea, Jerusalem, and the central coastal region of Tyre and Sidon.

"But I say to you who hear, love your enemies, do good to those who hate you, bless those who curse you, pray for those who mistreat you. Whoever hits you on the cheek, offer him the other also; and whoever takes away your coat, do not withhold your shirt from him either. Give to everyone who asks of you, and whoever takes away what is yours, do not demand it back. Treat others the same way you want them to treat you. If you love those who love you, what credit is *that* to you? For even sinners love those who love them. If you do good to those who do good to you, what credit is *that* to you? For even sinners do the same. If you lend to those from whom you expect to receive, what credit is *that* to you? Even sinners lend to sinners in order to receive back the same *amount.* But love your enemies, and do good, and lend, expecting nothing in return; and your reward will be great, and you will be sons of the Most High; for He Himself is kind to ungrateful and evil *men.* Be merciful, just as your Father is merciful" (Luke 6:27–36; cf. Matthew 5:9, 39–48; Matthew 7:12).

Setting: Galilee. After selecting His twelve disciples, Jesus teaches the Sermon on the Mount to those disciples and a great throng from Judea, Jerusalem, and the central coastal region of Tyre and Sidon.

And He also spoke a parable to them: "A blind man cannot guide a blind man, can he? Will they not both fall into a pit? A pupil is not above his teacher; but everyone, after he has been fully trained, will be like his teacher. Why do you look at the speck that is in your brother's eye, but do not notice the log that is in your own eye? Or how can you say to your brother, 'Brother, let me take out the speck that is in your eye,' when you yourself do not see the log that is in your own eye? You hypocrite, first take the log out of your own eye, and then you will see clearly to take out the speck that is in your brother's eye. For there is no good tree which produces bad fruit, nor, on the other hand, a bad tree which produces good fruit. For each tree is known by its own fruit. For men do not gather figs from thorns, nor do they pick grapes from a briar bush. The good man out of the good treasure of his heart brings forth what is good; and the evil *man* out of the evil *treasure* brings forth what is evil; for his mouth speaks from that which fills his heart" (Luke 6:39–45; cf. Matthew 7:3–6. 16, 18, 20; 12:35; see Matthew 10:24; 15:14).

Setting: On the way from Galilee to Jerusalem. After He responds to a guest's proclamation about the blessings of eating bread in the kingdom of God, Jesus presents to large crowds the demands of discipleship.

Now large crowds were going along with Him; and He turned and said to them, "If anyone comes to Me, and does not hate his own father and mother and wife and children and brothers and sisters, yes, and even his own life, he cannot be My disciple. Whoever does not carry his own cross and come after Me cannot be My disciple. For which one of you, when he wants to build a tower, does not first sit down and calculate the cost to see if he has enough to complete it? Otherwise, when he has laid a foundation and is not able to finish, all who observe it begin to ridicule him, saying, 'This man began to build and was not able to finish.' Or what king, when he sets out to meet another king in battle, will not first sit down and consider whether he is strong enough with ten thousand *men* to encounter the one coming against him with twenty thousand? Or else, while the other is still far away, he sends a delegation and asks for terms of peace. So then, none of you can be My disciple who does not give up all his possessions. Therefore, salt is good; but if even salt has become tasteless, with what will it be seasoned? It is useless either for the soil or for the manure pile; it is thrown out. He who has ears to hear, let him hear" (Luke 14:25–35; cf. Matthew 5:13; 10:37–39; see Proverbs 20:18; Philippians 3:7).

Setting: On the way from Galilee to Jerusalem. After speaking of the importance of children, Jesus responds to a ruler's question about inheriting eternal life.

A ruler questioned Him, saying, "Good Teacher, what shall I do to inherit eternal life?" And Jesus said to him, "Why do you call Me good? No one is good except God alone. You know the commandments, 'DO NOT COMMIT ADULTERY, DO NOT MURDER, DO NOT STEAL, DO NOT BEAR FALSE WITNESS, HONOR YOUR FATHER AND MOTHER.'" And he said, "All these things I have kept from *my* youth." When Jesus heard *this,* He said to him, "One thing you still lack; sell all that you possess and distribute it to the poor, and you shall have treasure in heaven; and come, follow Me" (Luke 18:18–22, Jesus quotes from Exodus 20:12–16; cf. Matthew 19:16–22; Mark 10:17–22; see Luke 10:25–28).

GOOD, DOING (Also see DEED, GOOD; DEEDS, GOOD; and WORKS, GOOD)

[DOING GOOD from do good]
Setting: A synagogue in Galilee. Jesus answers questions the Pharisees pose about the Sabbath.

And He said to them, "What man is there among you who has a sheep, and if it falls into a pit on the Sabbath, will he not take hold of it and lift it out? How much more valuable then is a man than a sheep! So then, it is lawful to do good on the Sabbath." Then He said to the man, "Stretch out your hand!" He stretched it out, and it was restored to normal, like the other (Matthew 12:11–13; cf. Matthew 10:31; Mark 3:4–5; Luke 6:9, 10; Luke 14:5; see Matthew 8:3).

[DOING GOOD from do good]
Setting: A synagogue in Galilee. Early in His ministry, Jesus heals a man's withered hand on the Sabbath, with the Pharisees looking on.

He said to the man with the withered hand, "Get up and come forward!" And He said to them, "Is it lawful to do good or do harm on the Sabbath, to save a life or to kill?" But they kept silent. After looking around at them with anger, grieved at their hardness of heart, He said to the man, "Stretch out your hand." And he stretched it out, and his hand was restored (Mark 3:3–5; cf. Matthew 12:9–14; Luke 6:6–11).

[DOING GOOD from do good]
Setting: A synagogue in Galilee. As Jesus teaches on the Sabbath, the scribes and Pharisees watch to see if He heals a man's withered hand.

But He knew what they were thinking, and He said to the man with the withered hand, "Get up and come forward!" And he got up and came forward. And Jesus said to them, "I ask you, is it lawful to do good or to do harm on the Sabbath, to save a life or destroy it?" And looking around at them all, He said to him, "Stretch out your hand!" And he did *so;* and his hand was restored. (Luke 6:8–10; cf. Matthew 12:9–13; Mark 3:1–5).

[DOING GOOD from do good]
Setting: Galilee. After selecting His twelve disciples, Jesus teaches the Sermon on the Mount to those disciples and a great throng from Judea, Jerusalem, and the central coastal region of Tyre and Sidon.

"But I say to you who hear, love your enemies, do good to those who hate you, bless those who curse you, pray for those who mistreat you. Whoever hits you on the cheek, offer him the other also; and whoever takes away your coat, do not withhold your shirt from him either. Give to everyone who asks of you, and whoever takes away what is yours, do not demand it back. Treat others the same way you want them to treat you. If you love those who love you, what credit is *that* to you? For even sinners love those who love them. If you do good to those who do good to you, what credit is *that* to you? For even sinners do the same. If you lend to those from whom you expect to receive, what credit is *that* to you? Even sinners lend to sinners in order to receive back the same *amount.* But love your enemies, and do good, and lend, expecting nothing in return; and your reward will be great, and you will be sons of the Most High; for He Himself is kind to ungrateful and evil *men.* Be merciful, just as your Father is merciful" (Luke 6:27–36; cf. Matthew 5:9, 39–48; Matthew 7:12).

GOOD AND FAITHFUL SLAVE (Listed under SLAVE, GOOD AND FAITHFUL; also see STEWARDSHIP)

GOOD DEED (Listed under DEED, GOOD; also see DEEDS, GOOD; FRUIT, GOOD; and WORKS, GOOD)

GOOD DEEDS (Listed under DEEDS, GOOD; also see DEED, GOOD; FRUIT, GOOD; GOOD, DOING; and WORKS, GOOD)

GOOD FRUIT (Listed under FRUIT, GOOD)

GOOD GIFTS (Listed under GIFTS, GOOD)

GOOD HEART (Listed under HEART, GOOD)

GOOD MAN (Listed under MAN, GOOD)

GOOD MEASURE (Listed under MEASURE, GOOD)

GOOD SAMARITAN (See SAMARITAN)

GOOD SEED (Listed under SEED, GOOD)

GOOD SHEPHERD (Listed under SHEPHERD, GOOD)

GOOD SOIL (Listed under SOIL, GOOD)

GOOD THINGS (Listed under THINGS, GOOD)

GOOD TREASURE (Listed under TREASURE, GOOD)

GOOD TREE (Listed under TREE, GOOD)

GOOD WORKS (Listed under WORKS, GOOD; also see DEEDS, GOOD and FRUIT, GOOD)

GOODNESS, GOD'S (See GOD, GOODNESS OF)

GOODNESS OF GOD (Listed under GOD, GOODNESS OF)

GOODS (Also see POSSESSIONS; and WEALTH)

Setting: On the way from Galilee to Jerusalem. After the scribes and Pharisees turn hostile and question Him in an attempt to catch Him in something He might say, Jesus responds to a question from the crowd and gives a parable about riches and greed.

And He told them a parable, saying, "The land of a rich man was very productive. And he began reasoning to himself, saying, 'What shall I do, since I have no place to store my crops?' Then he said, 'This is what I will do: I will tear down my barns and build larger ones, and here I will store all my grain and my goods. And I will say to my soul, "Soul, you have many goods laid up for many years *to come;* take your ease, eat, drink *and* be merry."' "But God said to him, 'You fool! This *very* night your soul is required of you; and *now* who will own what you have prepared?' So is the man who stores up treasure for himself, and is not rich toward God" (Luke 12:16–21; see Job 27:8; Psalm 39:6; Ecclesiastes 12:9; Philippians 2:3).

Setting: Samaria, on the way from Galilee to Jerusalem. After the Pharisees question Him about the coming of the kingdom of God, Jesus tells His disciples of His second coming.

And He said to the disciples, "The days will come when you will long to see one of the days of the Son of Man, and you will not see it. They will say to you, 'Look there! Look here!' Do not go away, and do not run after *them*. For just like the lightning, when it flashes out of one part of the sky, shines to the other part of the sky, so will the Son of Man be in His day. But first He must suffer many things and be rejected by this generation. And just as it happened in the days of Noah, so it will be also in the days of the Son of Man: they were eating, they were drinking, they were marrying, they were being given in marriage, until the day that Noah entered the ark, and the flood came and destroyed them all. It was the same as happened in the days of Lot: they were eating, they were drinking, they were buying, they were selling, they were planting, they were building; but on the day that Lot went out from Sodom it rained fire and brimstone from heaven and destroyed them all. It will be just the same on the day that the Son of Man is revealed. On that day, the one who is on the housetop and whose goods are in the house must not go down to take them out; and likewise the one who is in the field must not turn back. Remember Lot's wife. Whoever seeks to keep his life will lose it, and whoever loses *his life* will preserve it. I tell you, on that night there will be two in one bed; one will be taken and the other will be left. There will be two women grinding at the same place; one will be taken and the other will be left. [Two men will be in the field; one will be taken and the other will be left."] And answering they said to Him, "Where, Lord?" And He said to them, "Where the body *is*, there also the vultures will be gathered" (Luke 17:22–37; see Genesis 19; Matthew 10:39; 16:21, 27; 24:17–28, 37–41).

GOSPEL (Also see ETERNAL LIFE; FAITH; GREAT COMMISSION; PREACHING; and SALVATION)

Setting: Galilee. As He teaches and preaches in Galilee, Jesus responds to John the Baptist's question (asked by John's disciples) whether He is Israel's promised Messiah.

Jesus answered and said to them, "Go and report to John what you hear and see: *the* BLIND RECEIVE SIGHT and *the* lame walk, *the* lepers are cleansed and *the* deaf hear, *the* dead are raised up, and *the* POOR HAVE THE GOSPEL PREACHED TO THEM. And blessed is he who does not take offense at Me" (Matthew 11:4–6, Jesus quotes from Isaiah 35:5f; cf. Luke 7:22, 23).

Setting: The Mount of Olives, just east of Jerusalem. During His discourse, Jesus answers His disciples' questions as to when the temple will be destroyed and Jerusalem overrun, along with the signs of His coming and the end of the age.

And Jesus answered and said to them, "See to it that no one misleads you. For many will come in My name, saying, 'I am the Christ,' and will mislead many. You will be hearing of wars and rumors of wars. See that you are not frightened, for *those things* must take place, but *that* is not yet the end. For nation will rise against nation, and kingdom against kingdom, and in various places there will be famines and earthquakes. But all these things are *merely* the beginning of birth pangs. Then they will deliver you to tribulation, and will kill you, and you will be hated by all nations because of My name. At that time many will fall away and will betray one another and hate one another. Many false prophets will arise and will mislead many. Because lawlessness is increased, most people's love will grow cold. But the one who endures to the end, he will be saved. This gospel of the kingdom shall be preached in the whole world as a testimony to all the nations, and then the end will come" (Matthew 24:4–14; cf. Jeremiah 29:8; Matthew 7:15; 10:17, 22; Mark 13:3–13; Luke 21:7–19; Revelation 6:4).

Setting: The home of Simon the leper in Bethany. Jesus rebukes His disciples after they criticize a woman for pouring a vial of costly perfume on His head in preparation for His burial.

But Jesus, aware of this, said to them, "Why do you bother the woman? For she has done a good deed to Me. For you always have the poor with you; but you do not always have Me. For when she poured this perfume on My body, she did it to prepare Me for burial. Truly I say to you, wherever this gospel is preached in the whole world, what this woman has done will also be spoken of in memory of her" (Matthew 26:10–13; cf. Mark 14:3–9; Luke 7:37–39; John 12:2–8; see Deuteronomy 15:11).

Setting: Galilee. After being baptized by John in the Jordan River, Jesus commences His gospel-preaching ministry shortly after John is taken into custody by Herod Antipas.

Now after John had been taken into custody, Jesus came into Galilee, preaching the gospel of God, and saying, "The time is fulfilled, and the kingdom of God is at hand; repent and believe in the gospel" (Mark 1:14, 15, cf. Matthew 4:17; Galatians 4:4).

Setting: On the Mount of Olives, east of the temple. After predicting the temple's destruction, Jesus responds during His Olivet Discourse to questions from Peter, James, John, and Andrew about future events.

And Jesus began to say to them, "See to it that no one misleads you. Many will come in My name, saying, 'I am *He!*' and will mislead many. When you hear of wars and rumors of wars, do not be frightened; *those things* must take place; but *that is* not yet the end. For nation will rise up against nation, and kingdom against kingdom; there will be earthquakes in various places; there will *also be* famines. These things are *merely* the beginning of birth pangs. But be on your guard; for they will deliver you to *the* courts, and you will be flogged in *the* synagogues, and you will stand before governors and kings for My sake, as a testimony to them. The gospel must first be preached to all the nations. When they arrest you and hand you over, do not worry beforehand about what you are to say, but say whatever is given you in that hour; for it is not you who speak, but *it is* the Holy Spirit. Brother will betray brother to death, and a father *his* child; and children will rise up against parents and have them put to death. You will be hated by all because of My name, but the one who endures to the end, he will be saved" (Mark 13:5–13; cf. Matthew 24:4–14; Luke 21:7–19; see Matthew 10:17–22).

Setting: The home of Simon the leper in Bethany. Two days before the Feast of Unleavened Bread (Passover), Jesus commends a woman who anoints His head with costly perfume that some there think should have been sold and the proceeds given to the poor.

But Jesus said, "Let her alone; why do you bother her? She has done a good deed to Me. For you always have the poor with you, and whenever you wish you can do good to them; but you do not always have Me. She has done what she could; she has anointed My body beforehand for the burial. Truly I say to you, wherever the gospel is preached in the whole world, what this woman has done will also be spoken of in memory of her" (Mark 14:6–9; cf. Matthew 26:6–13; John 12:2–8; see Deuteronomy 15:11).

Setting: Following His resurrection from the dead after being crucified, Jesus commissions His disciples to preach His gospel to the world.

And He said to them, "Go into all the world and preach the gospel to all creation. He who has believed and has been baptized shall be saved; but he who has disbelieved shall be condemned. These signs will accompany those who have believed: in My name they will cast out demons, they will speak with new tongues; they will pick up serpents, and if they drink any deadly *poison,* it will not hurt them; they will lay hands on the sick, and they will recover" (Mark 16:15–18; cf. Matthew 28:16–20; see Mark 9:38; John 3:18, 36; 1 Corinthians 15:6).

[Note: Some scholars question the authenticity of Mark 16:9–20, as these verses do not appear in some early New Testament manuscripts.]

Setting: The synagogue in Jesus' hometown of Nazareth in Galilee. At the beginning of His public ministry, Jesus reads on the Sabbath from the book of the prophet Isaiah.

And the book of the prophet Isaiah was handed to Him. And He opened the book and found the place where it was written, "THE SPIRIT OF THE LORD IS UPON ME, BECAUSE HE ANOINTED ME TO PREACH THE GOSPEL TO THE POOR. HE HAS SENT ME TO PROCLAIM RELEASE TO THE CAPTIVES, AND RECOVERY OF SIGHT TO THE BLIND, TO SET FREE THOSE WHO ARE OPPRESSED, TO PROCLAIM THE FAVORABLE YEAR OF THE LORD." And He closed the book, gave it back to the attendant and sat down; and the eyes of all in the synagogue were fixed on Him. And He began to say to them, "Today this Scripture has been fulfilled in your hearing" (Luke 4:17–21, Jesus quotes from Isaiah 61:1, 2).

Setting: Galilee. After Jesus raises a woman's son from the dead in Nain, the disciples of John the Baptist ask Him whether He is the promised Messiah.

And He answered and said to them, "Go and report to John what you have seen and heard: *the* BLIND RECEIVE SIGHT, *the* lame walk, *the* lepers are cleansed, and *the* deaf hear, *the* dead are raised up, *the* POOR HAVE THE GOSPEL PREACHED TO THEM. Blessed is he who does not take offense at Me" (Luke 7:22, 23, Jesus quotes from Isaiah 35:5; 61:1; cf. Matthew 11:2–6).

Setting: On the way from Galilee to Jerusalem. The Lord responds to the Pharisees' scoffing at His teaching His disciples about stewardship.

And He said to them, "You are those who justify yourselves in the sight of men, but God knows your hearts; for that which is highly esteemed among men is detestable in the sight of God. The Law and the Prophets *were proclaimed* until John; since that time the gospel of the kingdom of God has been preached, and everyone is forcing his way into it. But is it easier for heaven and earth to pass away than for one stroke of a letter of the Law to fail" (Luke 16:15–17; cf. Matthew 5:18; see 1 Samuel 16:7; Matthew 4:23; 11:11–14).

[GOSPEL from whoever believes in Him shall not perish, but have eternal life]
Setting: Jerusalem. At the time for the Passover of the Jews, after the Lord cleanses the temple, a Pharisee, Nicodemus, asks Him by night the meaning of "born again."

"For God so loved the world, that He gave His only begotten Son, that whoever believes in Him shall not perish, but have eternal life. For God did not send the Son into the world to judge the world, but that the world might be saved through Him. He who believes in Him is not judged; he who does not believe has been judged already, because he has not believed in the name of the only begotten Son of God. This is the judgment, that the Light has come into the world, and men loved darkness rather than the Light, for their deeds were evil. For everyone who does evil hates the Light, and does not come to the Light for fear that his deeds will be exposed. But he who practices the truth comes to the Light, so that his deeds may be manifested as having been wrought in God" (John 3:16–21; see Luke 19:10; John 1:4; 1:18; Romans 5:8; 1 John 1:6, 7).

GOSPEL, REJECTING THE (Also see JESUS, REJECTING; JUDGMENT; REJECTION; and UNWELCOME)

[REJECTING THE GOSPEL from Do not give what is holy to dogs]
Setting: Galilee. During the early part of His ministry, Jesus preaches the Sermon on the Mount to His disciples and the multitudes.

"Do not give what is holy to dogs, and do not throw your pearls before swine, or they will trample them under their feet, and turn and tear you to pieces." (Matthew 7:6; see Matthew 15:26).

[REJECTING THE GOSPEL from Whoever does not receive you, nor heed your words]
Setting: Galilee. After His twelve disciples observe His ministry, Jesus summons and specifically instructs them about their ministry to the people of Israel.

These twelve Jesus sent out after instructing them: "Do not go in *the* way of *the* Gentiles, and do not enter *any* city of the Samaritans; but rather go to the lost sheep of the house of Israel. And as you go, preach, saying, 'The kingdom of heaven is at hand.' Heal *the* sick, raise *the* dead, cleanse *the* lepers, cast out demons. Freely you received, freely give. Do not acquire gold, or silver, or copper for your money belts, or a bag for *your* journey, or even two coats, or sandals, or a staff; for the worker is worthy of his support. And whatever city or village you enter, inquire who is worthy in it, and stay at his house until you leave *that city*. As you enter the house, give it your greeting. If the house is worthy, give it your *blessing of* peace. But if it is not worthy, take back your *blessing of* peace. Whoever does not receive you, nor heed your words, as you go out of that house or that city, shake the dust off your feet. Truly I say to you, it will be more tolerable for *the* land of Sodom and Gomorrah in the day of judgment than for that city" (Matthew 10:5–15; cf. Mark 6:7–11; Luke 9:1–5; see Matthew 3:2; 11:22, 24; 15:24; Luke 22:35; 1 Corinthians 9:14).

[REJECTING THE GOSPEL from Any place that does not receive you or listen to you]
Setting: Jesus' hometown of Nazareth. After encountering unbelief, Jesus sends the Twelve out in pairs with authority and instructions about ministry.

And He summoned the twelve and began to send them out in pairs, and gave them authority over the unclean spirits; and He instructed them that they should take nothing for *their* journey, except a mere staff—no bread, no bag, no money in their belt—but to wear sandals; and *He added,* "Do not put on two tunics." And He said to them, "Wherever you enter a house, stay there until you leave town. Any place that does not receive you or listen to you, as you go out from there, shake the dust off the soles of your feet for a testimony against them" (Mark 6:7–11; cf. Matthew 10:1–14; Luke 9:1–5).

[REJECTING THE GOSPEL from he who rejects Me rejects the One who sent Me]
Setting: On the way from Galilee to Jerusalem. The Lord pronounces woes on cities who reject the gospel as He appoints seventy followers and sends them out in pairs to every place He Himself will soon visit.

"Woe to you, Chorazin! Woe to you, Bethsaida! For if the miracles had been performed in Tyre and Sidon which occurred in you, they would have repented long ago, sitting in sackcloth and ashes. But it will be more tolerable for Tyre and Sidon in the judgment than for you. And you, Capernaum, will not be exalted to heaven, will you? You will be brought down to Hades! The one who listens to you listens to Me, and the one who rejects you rejects Me; and he who rejects Me rejects the One who sent Me" (Luke 10:13–16; cf. Matthew 11:21–23; see Matthew 10:40).

GOSPEL'S SAKE (Listed under SAKE, GOSPEL'S)

GOVERNORS

Setting: Galilee. After His disciples observe His ministry, Jesus summons and specifically instructs them about the upcoming hardships of *their* ministry to the people of Israel.

"Behold, I send you out as sheep in the midst of wolves; so be shrewd as serpents and innocent as doves. But beware of men, for they will hand you over to *the* courts and scourge you in their synagogues; and you will even be brought before governors and kings for My sake, as a testimony to them and to the Gentiles. But when they hand you over, do not worry about how or what you are to say; for it will be given you in that hour what you are to say. For it is not you who speak, but *it* is the Spirit of your Father who speaks in you" (Matthew 10:16–20; cf. Luke 10:3).

Setting: On the Mount of Olives, east of the temple in Jerusalem. After predicting the temple's destruction, Jesus responds during His Olivet Discourse to questions from Peter, James, John, and Andrew about future events.

And Jesus began to say to them, "See to it that no one misleads you. Many will come in My name, saying, 'I am *He!*' and will mislead many. When you hear of wars and rumors of wars, do not be frightened; *those things* must take place; but *that is* not yet the end. For nation will rise up against nation, and kingdom against kingdom; there will be earthquakes in various places; there will *also be* famines. These things are *merely* the beginning of birth pangs. But be on your guard; for they will deliver you to *the* courts, and you will be flogged in *the* synagogues, and you will stand before governors and kings for My sake, as a testimony to them. The gospel must first be preached to all the nations. When they arrest you and hand you over, do not worry beforehand about what you are to say, but say whatever is given you in that hour; for it is not you who speak, but *it is* the Holy Spirit. Brother will betray brother to death, and a father *his* child; and children will rise up against parents and have them put to death. You will be hated by all because of My name, but the one who endures to the end, he will be saved" (Mark 13:5–13; cf. Matthew 24:4–14; Luke 21:7–19; see Matthew 10:17–22).

Setting: The Mount of Olives, just east of Jerusalem. A few days before His crucifixion, after giving His disciples more details regarding the temple's future destruction, Jesus elaborates during His Olivet Discourse about future events.

Then He continued by saying to them, "Nation will rise against nation and kingdom against kingdom, and there will be great earthquakes, and in various places plagues and famines; and there will be terrors and great signs from heaven. But before all these things, they will lay their hands on you and will persecute you, delivering you to the synagogues and prisons, bringing you before kings and governors for My name's sake. It will lead to an opportunity for your testimony. So make up your minds not to

prepare beforehand to defend yourselves; for I will give you utterance and wisdom which none of your opponents will be able to resist or refute. But you will be betrayed even by parents and brothers and relatives and friends, and they will put *some* of you to death, and you will be hated by all because of My name. Yet not a hair of your head will perish. By your endurance you will gain your lives" (Luke 21:10–19; cf. Matthew 10:19–22; 24:7–14; Mark 13:8–13).

GRACE (Also see GRACIOUSNESS)

Setting: Macedonia. During his third missionary journey, writing a second letter to the church at Corinth, the Apostle Paul recounts the Lord Jesus' response to his three requests to remove the thorn in his flesh from Satan.

And He has said to me, "My grace is sufficient for you, for power is perfected in weakness." Most gladly, therefore, I will rather boast about my weaknesses, so that the power of Christ may dwell in me (2 Corinthians 12:9; see 1 Corinthians 2:1–5).

GRACIOUSNESS (Also see GRACE; KINDNESS; LOVE; and MERCY)

[GRACIOUSNESS from Truly I say to you, to the extent that you did not do it to one of the least of these, you did not do it to Me]

Setting: The Mount of Olives, just east of Jerusalem. During His discourse, after answering His disciples' questions as to when the temple will be destroyed and Jerusalem overrun, along with the signs of His coming and the end of the age, Jesus reveals the future judgments following His return.

"But when the Son of Man comes in His glory, and all the angels with Him, then He will sit on His glorious throne. All the nations will be gathered before Him; and He will separate them from one another, as the shepherd separates the sheep from the goats; and He will put the sheep on His right, and the goats on the left. Then the King will say to those on His right, 'Come, you who are blessed of My Father, inherit the kingdom prepared for you from the foundation of the world. 'For I was hungry, and you gave Me *something* to eat; I was thirsty, and you gave Me *something* to drink; I was a stranger, and you invited Me in; naked, and you clothed Me; I was sick, and you visited Me; I was in prison, and you came to Me.' Then the righteous will answer Him, 'Lord, when did we see You hungry and feed You, or thirsty, and give you *something* to drink? And when did we see You a stranger, and invite You in, or naked, and clothe You? When did we see You sick, or in prison, and come to You?' The King will answer and say to them, 'Truly I say to you, to the extent that you did it to one of these brothers of Mine, *even* the least *of them,* you did it to Me.' Then He will also say to those on His left, 'Depart from Me, accursed ones, into the eternal fire which has been prepared for the devil and his angels; for I was hungry, and you gave Me *nothing* to eat; I was thirsty, and you gave Me nothing to drink; I was a stranger, and you did not invite Me in; naked, and you did not clothe Me; sick, and in prison, and you did not visit Me.' Then they themselves also will answer, 'Lord, when did we see You hungry, or thirsty, or a stranger, or naked, or sick, or in prison, and did not take care of You?' Then He will answer them, 'Truly I say to you, to the extent that you did not do it to one of the least of these, you did not do it to Me.' These will go away into eternal punishment, but the righteous into eternal life" (Matthew 25:31–46; see Matthew 7:23; 16:27; 19:29).

[GRACIOUSNESS from love your enemies, do good to those who hate you, bless those who curse you, pray for those who mistreat you]

Setting: Galilee. After selecting His twelve disciples, Jesus teaches the Sermon on the Mount to those disciples and a great throng from Judea, Jerusalem, and the central coastal region of Tyre and Sidon.

"But I say to you who hear, love your enemies, do good to those who hate you, bless those who curse you, pray for those who mistreat you. Whoever hits you on the cheek, offer him the other also; and whoever takes away your coat, do not withhold your shirt from him either. Give to everyone who asks of you, and whoever takes away what is yours, do not demand it back. Treat others the same way you want them to treat you. If you love those who love you, what credit is *that* to you? For even sinners love those who love them. If you do good to those who do good to you, what credit is *that* to you? For even sinners do the same. If you lend to those from whom you expect to receive, what credit is *that* to you? Even sinners lend to sinners in order to receive back the same *amount.* But love your enemies, and do good, and lend, expecting nothing in return; and your reward will be great, and you will be sons of the Most High; for He Himself is kind to ungrateful and evil *men*. Be merciful, just as your Father is merciful" (Luke 6:27–36; cf. Matthew 5:9, 39–48; Matthew 7:12).

GRAIN (Also see BREAD; CROPS; HARVEST; and WHEAT)

Setting: By the Sea of Galilee. Because the religious leaders are rejecting His message, Jesus continues teaching the crowds with the Parable of the Wheat and the Tares.

Jesus presented another parable to them, saying, "The kingdom of heaven may be compared to a man who sowed good seed in his field. But while his men were sleeping, his enemy came and sowed tares among the wheat, and went away. But when the wheat sprouted and bore grain, then the tares became evident also. The slaves of the landowner came and said to him, 'Sir, did you not sow good seed in your field? How then does it have tares?' And he said to them, 'An enemy has done this!' The slaves said to him, 'Do you want us, then, to go and gather them up?' But he said, 'No; for while you are gathering up the tares, you may uproot the wheat with them. Allow both to grow together until the harvest; and in the time of the harvest I will say to the reapers, "First gather up the tares and bind them in bundles to burn them up; but gather the wheat into my barn"'" (Matthew 13:24–30; cf. Matthew 3:12).

Setting: Galilee. Following His explanation of the Parable of the Sower to His disciples, Jesus conveys the Parable of the Seed.

And He was saying, "The kingdom of God is like a man who casts seed upon the soil; and he goes to bed at night and gets up by day, and the seed sprouts and grows—how, he himself does not know. The soil produces crops by itself; first the blade, then the head, then the mature grain in the head. But when the crop permits, he immediately puts in the sickle, because the harvest has come" (Mark 4:26–29; see Joel 3:13).

Setting: On the way from Galilee to Jerusalem. After the scribes and Pharisees turn hostile and question Him in an attempt to catch Him in something He might say, Jesus responds to a question from the crowd and gives a parable about riches and greed.

And He told them a parable, saying, "The land of a rich man was very productive. And he began reasoning to himself, saying, 'What shall I do, since I have no place to store my crops?' Then he said, 'This is what I will do: I will tear down my barns and build larger ones, and here I will store all my grain and my goods. And I will say to my soul, "Soul, you have many goods laid up for many years *to come;* take your ease, eat, drink *and* be merry."' "But God said to him, 'You fool! This *very* night your soul is required of you; and *now* who will own what you have prepared?' So is the man who stores up treasure for himself, and is not rich toward God" (Luke 12:16–21; see Job 27:8; Psalm 39:6; Ecclesiastes 12:9; Philippians 2:3).

Setting: Jerusalem. Just days before the Passover, with the chief priests and Pharisees plotting to seize Him, crowds welcome Jesus with palm branches and praise, and some Greeks ask to meet Him.

And Jesus answered them, saying, "The hour has come for the Son of Man to be glorified. Truly, truly, I say to you, unless a grain of wheat falls into the earth and dies, it remains alone; but if it dies, it bears much fruit. He who loves his life loses it, and he who hates his life in this world will keep it to life eternal. If anyone serves Me, he must follow Me; and where I am, there My servant will be also; if anyone serves Me, the Father will honor him" (John 12:23–26; see Matthew 10:39).

GRAIN, HARVESTING (Also see HARVEST)

[HARVESTING GRAIN from puts in the sickle]

Setting: Galilee. Following His explanation of the Parable of the Sower to His disciples, Jesus conveys the Parable of the Seed.

And He was saying, "The kingdom of God is like a man who casts seed upon the soil; and he goes to bed at night and gets up by day, and the seed sprouts and grows—how, he himself does not know. The soil produces crops by itself; first the blade, then the head, then the mature grain in the head. But when the crop permits, he immediately puts in the sickle, because the harvest has come" (Mark 4:26–29; see Joel 3:13).

GRAPES (Also see FRUIT OF THE VINE; and WINE)

Setting: Galilee. During the early part of His ministry, Jesus preaches the Sermon on the Mount to His disciples and the multitudes.

"Beware of the false prophets, who come to you in sheep's clothing, but inwardly are ravenous wolves. You will know them by their fruits. Grapes are not gathered from *bushes* nor figs from thistles, are they? So every good tree bears good fruit, but the bad tree bears bad fruit. A good tree cannot produce bad fruit, nor can a bad tree produce good fruit. Every tree that does not bear good fruit is cut down and thrown into the fire. So then, you will know them by their fruits" (Matthew 7:15–20; cf. Matthew 3:10; 12:33, 35; 24:11, 24; Luke 6:43, 44).

Setting: Galilee. After selecting His twelve disciples, Jesus teaches the Sermon on the Mount to those disciples and a great throng from Judea, Jerusalem, and the central coastal region of Tyre and Sidon.

And He also spoke a parable to them: "A blind man cannot guide a blind man, can he? Will they not both fall into a pit? A pupil is not above his teacher; but everyone, after he has been fully trained, will be like his teacher. Why do you look at the speck that is in your brother's eye, but do not notice the log that is in your own eye? Or how can you say to your brother, 'Brother, let me take out the speck that is in your eye,' when you yourself do not see the log that is in your own eye? You hypocrite, first take the log out of your own eye, and then you will see clearly to take out the speck that is in your brother's eye. For there is no good tree which produces bad fruit, nor, on the other hand, a bad tree which produces good fruit. For each tree is known by its own fruit. For men do not gather figs from thorns, nor do they pick grapes from a briar bush. The good man out of the good treasure of his heart brings forth what is good; and the evil *man* out of the evil *treasure* brings forth what is evil; for his mouth speaks from that which fills his heart" (Luke 6:39–45; cf. Matthew 7:3–6. 16, 18, 20; 12:35; see Matthew 10:24; 15:14; Luke 6:12–19).

GRASS

Setting: Galilee. During the early part of His ministry, Jesus preaches the Sermon on the Mount to His disciples and the multitudes.

"For this reason I say to you, do not be worried about your life, *as to* what you will eat or what you will drink; nor for your body, *as to* what you will put on. Is not life more than food, and the body more than clothing? Look at the birds of the air, that they do not sow, nor reap nor gather into barns, and *yet* your heavenly Father feeds them. Are you not worth much more than they? And who of you by being worried can add a *single* hour to his life? And why are you worried about clothing? Observe how the lilies of the field grow; they do not toil nor do they spin, yet I say to you that not even Solomon in all his glory clothed himself like one of these. But if God so clothes the grass of the field, which is *alive* today and tomorrow is thrown into the furnace, *will He* not much more *clothe* you? You of little faith! Do not worry then, saying 'What will we eat?' or 'What will we drink?' or 'What will be wear for clothing?" For the Gentiles eagerly seek all these things; for your heavenly Father knows that you need all these things. But seek first His kingdom and His righteousness, and all these things will be added to you. So do not worry about tomorrow; for tomorrow will care for itself. Each day has enough trouble of its own" (Matthew 6:25–34; cf. Luke 12:22–31; see 1 Kings 10:4–7; Job 35:11; Matthew 8:26).

Setting: On the way from Galilee to Jerusalem. After giving a parable about riches and greed, Jesus comforts the crowd and His disciples. The scribes and Pharisees turn hostile and question Him in an attempt to catch Him in something He might say.

And He said to His disciples, "For this reason I say to you, do not worry about *your* life, *as to* what you will eat; nor for your body, *as to* what you will put on. For life is more than food, and the body more than clothing. Consider the ravens, for they neither sow nor reap; they have no storeroom nor barn, and *yet* God feeds them; how much more valuable you are than the birds! And which of you by worrying can add a *single* hour to his life's span? If then you cannot do even a very little thing, why do you worry about other matters? Consider the lilies, how they grow: they neither toil nor spin; but I tell you, not even Solomon in all his glory clothed himself like one of these. But if God so clothes the grass in the field, which is *alive* today and tomorrow is thrown into the furnace, how much more *will He clothe* you? You men of little faith! And do not seek what you will eat and what you will drink, and

do not keep worrying. For all these things the nations of the world eagerly seek; but your Father knows that you need these things. But seek His kingdom, and these things will be added to you. Do not be afraid, little flock, for your Father has chosen gladly to give you the kingdom" (Luke 12:22–32; cf. Matthew 6:25–33; see 1 Kings 10:4–7; Job 38:41).

GRATITUDE

[GRATITUDE from Was no one found who returned to give glory to God, except this foreigner]

Setting: Samaria, on the way from Galilee to Jerusalem. The Lord stops to heal ten lepers who ask for cleansing.

When He saw them, He said to them, "Go and show yourselves to the priests." And as they were going, they were cleansed. Now one of them, when he saw that he had been healed, turned back, glorifying God with a loud voice, and he fell on his face at His feet, giving thanks to Him. And he was a Samaritan. Then Jesus answered and said, "Were there not ten cleansed? But the nine—where are they? Was no one found who returned to give glory to God, except this foreigner? "And He said to him, "Stand up and go; your faith has made you well" (Luke 17:14–19; see Leviticus 14:1–32).

GRAVES (See BONES, DEAD MEN'S; and TOMBS, WHITEWASHED)

GREAT (GREATEST; and GREATNESS along with specifics such as MEN, GREAT; and THINGS, GREAT are separate entries; also see GREATEST; and GREATNESS)

Setting: Galilee. Early in His ministry, Jesus presents the Beatitudes (part of the Sermon on the Mount) to His disciples and the gathered crowds from Galilee, Decapolis, Jerusalem, Judea, and beyond the Jordan.

"Blessed are you when *people* insult you and persecute you, and falsely say all kinds of evil against you because of Me. Rejoice and be glad, for your reward in heaven is great; for in the same way they persecuted the prophets who were before you" (Matthew 5:11, 12; cf. 2 Chronicles 36:16; Luke 6:22, 23; 1 Peter 4:14; see Matthew 5:1; 13:35).

Setting: Galilee. During the early part of His ministry, Jesus preaches the Sermon on the Mount to His disciples and the multitudes.

"The eye is the lamp of the body; so then if your eye is clear, your whole body will be full of light. But if your eye is bad, your whole body will be full of darkness. If then the light that is in you is darkness, how great is the darkness!" (Matthew 6:22, 23; cf. Luke 11:34, 35).

Setting: Galilee. During the early part of His ministry, Jesus preaches the Sermon on the Mount to His disciples and the multitudes.

"Therefore everyone who hears these words of Mine and acts on them, may be compared to a wise man who built his house on the rock. And the rain fell, and the floods came, and the winds blew and slammed against that house; and *yet* it did not fall, for it had been founded on the rock. Everyone who hears these words of Mine and does not act on them, will be like a foolish man who built his house on the sand. The rain fell, and the floods came, and the winds blew and slammed against that house; and it fell—and great was its fall" (Matthew 7:24–28; cf. Luke 6:47–49).

Setting: The district of Tyre and Sidon. A Canaanite woman appeals to Jesus to heal her demon-possessed daughter.

But He answered and said, "I was sent only to the lost sheep of the house of Israel." But she came and *began* to bow down before Him, saying, "Lord, help me!" And He answered and said, "It is not good to take the children's bread and throw it to the dogs." But she said, "Yes, Lord; but even the dogs feed from the crumbs which fall from their masters' table." Then Jesus said to her, "O woman, your faith is great; it shall be done for you as you wish." And her daughter was healed at once (Matthew 15:24–28; cf. Mark 7: 24–30; see Matthew 9:22; 10:5, 6).

Setting: Galilee. After selecting His twelve disciples, Jesus teaches the Beatitudes (part of the Sermon on the Mount) to His disciples and a great throng of people from Judea, Jerusalem, and the central coastal region of Tyre and Sidon.

"Blessed are you when men hate you, and ostracize you, and insult you, and scorn your name as evil, for the sake of the Son of Man. Be glad in that day and leap *for joy*, for behold, your reward is great in heaven. For in the same way their fathers used to treat the prophets" (Luke 6:22, 23; cf. Matthew 5:10–12; see 2 Chronicles 36:16).

Setting: Galilee. After selecting His twelve disciples, Jesus teaches the Beatitudes (part of the Sermon on the Mount) to His disciples and a great throng of people from Judea, Jerusalem, and the central coastal region of Tyre and Sidon.

"But I say to you who hear, love your enemies, do good to those who hate you, bless those who curse you, pray for those who mistreat you. Whoever hits you on the cheek, offer him the other also; and whoever takes away your coat, do not withhold your shirt from him either. Give to everyone who asks of you, and whoever takes away what is yours, do not demand it back. Treat others the same way you want them to treat you. If you love those who love you, what credit is *that* to you? For even sinners love those who love them. If you do good to those who do good to you, what credit is *that* to you? For even sinners do the same. If you lend to those from whom you expect to receive, what credit is *that* to you? Even sinners lend to sinners in order to receive back the same *amount*. But love your enemies, and do good, and lend, expecting nothing in return; and your reward will be great, and you will be sons of the Most High; for He Himself is kind to ungrateful and evil *men*. Be merciful, just as your Father is merciful" (Luke 6:27–36; cf. Matthew 5:9, 39–48; 7:12).

Setting: Galilee. After selecting His twelve disciples, Jesus teaches the Beatitudes (part of the Sermon on the Mount) to His disciples and a great throng of people from Judea, Jerusalem, and the central coastal region of Tyre and Sidon.

"Why do you call Me, 'Lord, Lord,' and do not do what I say? Everyone who comes to Me and hears My words and acts on them, I will show you whom he is like; he is like a man building a house, who dug deep and laid a foundation on the rock; and when a flood occurred, the torrent burst against that house and could not shake it, because it had been well built. But the one who has heard and has not acted *accordingly,* is like a man who built a house on the ground without any foundation; and the torrent burst against it and immediately it collapsed, and the ruin of that house was great" (Luke 6:46–49; cf. Matthew 7:24–27; see Luke 6:12–19; James 1:22).

Setting: The villages and cities of Galilee. After His visit in the home of Simon the Pharisee, Jesus proclaims and preaches the kingdom of God.

When a large crowd was coming together, and those from various cities were journeying to Him, He spoke by way of a parable: "The sower went out to sow his seed; and as he sowed, some fell beside the road, and it was trampled under foot and the birds of the air ate it up. Other *seed* fell on rocky *soil,* and as soon as it grew up, it was withered away, because it had no moisture. Other *seed* fell among the thorns; and the thorns grew up with it and choked it out. Other *seed* fell into the good soil, and grew up, and produced a crop a hundred times as great." As He said these things, He would call out, "He who has ears to hear, let him hear" (Luke 8:4–8; cf. Matthew 13:2–9; Mark 4:3–9).

Setting: Galilee. After Jesus prophesies His death, an argument arises among His disciples as to who is the greatest. The Lord solves the matter by using a child as a teaching illustration.

But Jesus, knowing what they were thinking in their heart, took a child and stood him by His side, and said to them, "Whoever receives this child in My name receives Me, and whoever receives Me receives Him who sent Me; for the one who is least among all of you, this is the one who is great" (Luke 9:47, 48; cf. Matthew 18:1–5; Mark 9:33–47; see Matthew 10:40; Luke 22:24).

GREAT BUILDINGS **(Listed as BUILDINGS, GREAT)**

GREAT COMMANDMENT **(See COMMANDMENT, GREAT AND FOREMOST and COMMANDMENT, FOREMOST)**

GREAT COMMISSION **(Also see DISCIPLESHIP; EVANGELISM; GOSPEL; HARVEST; and SALVATION)**

[GREAT COMMISSION from Go therefore and make disciples of all the nations, baptizing them in the name of the Father and the Son and the Holy Spirit, teaching them to observe all that I commanded you]

Setting: On a mountain in Galilee. Following His resurrection from the dead in Jerusalem, Jesus conveys the Great Commission to His eleven remaining disciples.

And Jesus came up and spoke to them, saying, "All authority has been given to Me in heaven and on earth. Go therefore and make disciples of all the nations, baptizing them in the name of the Father and the Son and the Holy Spirit, teaching them to observe all that I commanded you; and lo, I am with you always, even to the end of the age" (Matthew 28:18–20; cf. Mark 16:15; see Daniel 7:13).

[GREAT COMMISSION from Go into all the world and preach the gospel to all creation]

Setting: On a mountain in Galilee. Following His resurrection from the dead after being crucified, Jesus commissions His eleven remaining disciples to preach His gospel to the world.

And He said to them, "Go into all the world and preach the gospel to all creation. He who has believed and has been baptized shall be saved; but he who has disbelieved shall be condemned. These signs will accompany those who have believed: in My name they will cast out demons, they will speak with new tongues; they will pick up serpents, and if they drink any deadly *poison,* it will not hurt them; they will lay hands on the sick, and they will recover" (Mark 16:15–18; cf. Matthew 28:16–20; see Mark 9:38, John 3:18, 36; 1 Corinthians 15:6).

[Note: Some scholars question the authenticity of Mark 16:9–20, as these verses do not appear in some early New Testament manuscripts.]

[GREAT COMMISSION from you shall be My witnesses both in Jerusalem, and in all Judea and Samaria, and even to the remotest part of the earth]

Setting: Jerusalem. Luke, writing in Acts, quotes Jesus prior to His return to heaven. He responds to His disciples' question if He is about to restore the kingdom to Israel.

He said to them, "It is not for you to know times or epochs which the Father has fixed by His own authority; but you will receive power when the Holy Spirit has come upon you; and you shall be My witnesses both in Jerusalem, and in all Judea and Samaria, and even to the remotest part of the earth" (Acts 1:7, 8; see Luke 24:48, 49; Acts 2:1–4).

GREAT FAITH **(Listed under FAITH, GREAT)**

GREAT GLORY **(Listed under GLORY, GREAT)**

GREAT MEN **(Listed under MEN, GREAT)**

GREAT THINGS **(Listed under THINGS, GREAT)**

GREAT TRIBULATION **(Also see TRIBULATION)**

Setting: The Mount of Olives, just east of Jerusalem. During His Olivet Discourse, Jesus answers His disciples' questions as to when the temple will be destroyed and Jerusalem overrun, along with the signs of His coming and the end of the age.

"Therefore when you see the ABOMINATION OF DESOLATION which was spoken of through Daniel the prophet, standing in the holy place (let the reader understand), then those who are in Judea must flee to the mountains. Whoever is on the housetop must not go down to get the things that are in his house. Whoever is in the field must not turn back to get his cloak. But woe to those who are pregnant and to those who are nursing babies in those days! But pray that your flight will not be in the winter, or on a Sabbath. For then there will be a great tribulation, such as has not occurred since the beginning of the world until now, nor ever will. Unless those days had been cut short, no life would have been saved; but for the sake of the elect those days will be cut short. Then if anyone says to you, 'Behold, here is the Christ,' or "There *He is,'* do not believe *him.* For false Christs and false prophets will arise and will show great signs and wonders, so as to mislead, if possible, even the elect. Behold, I have told you in advance. So if they say to you, 'Behold, He is in the wilderness,' do not go out, *or,* 'Behold, He is in the inner rooms,' do not believe *them.* For just as the lightning comes from the east and flashes even to the west, so will the coming of the Son of Man be. Wherever the corpse is, there the vultures will gather" (Matthew 24:15–28, Jesus quotes from Daniel 9:27; cf. Daniel 12:1; Mark 13:14–23; Luke 17:22–31; 21:20–24; 23:29; see John 4:48).

[GREAT TRIBULATION from context]
Setting: On the Mount of Olives, east of the temple in Jerusalem. After prophesying the temple's destruction, Jesus responds during His Olivet Discourse to questions from Peter, James, John, and Andrew about other future events.

"But when you see the ABOMINATION OF DESOLATION standing where it should not be (let the reader understand), then those who are in Judea must flee to the mountains. The one who is on the housetop must not go down, or go in to get anything out of his house; and the one who is in the field must not turn back to get his coat. But woe to those who are pregnant and to those who are nursing babies in those days! But pray that it may not happen in winter. For those days will be a *time of* tribulation such as has not occurred since the beginning of the creation which God created until now, and never will. Unless the Lord had shortened *those* days, no life would have been saved; but for the sake of the elect, whom He chose, He shortened the days. And then if anyone says to you, 'Behold, here is the Christ'; or, 'Behold, *He is* there'; do not believe *him*; for false Christs and false prophets will arise, and will show signs and wonders, in order to lead astray, if possible, the elect. But take heed; behold, I have told you everything in advance" (Mark 13:14–23; cf. Matthew 24:15–28; Luke 21:20–24; see Daniel 9:27; 12:1; Luke 17:31).

[GREAT TRIBULATION from context]
Setting: On the Mount of Olives, east of the temple in Jerusalem. After ministering in the temple a few days before His crucifixion, and giving the disciples more details regarding future events, Jesus elaborates during His Olivet Discourse about things to come.

"But when you see Jerusalem surrounded by armies, then recognize that her desolation is near. Then those who are in Judea must flee to the mountains, and those who are in the midst of the city must leave, and those who are in the country must not enter the city; because these are days of vengeance, so that all things which are written will be fulfilled. Woe to those who are pregnant and to those who are nursing babies in those days; for there will be a great distress upon the land and wrath to this people; and they will fall by the edge of the sword, and will be led captive into all the nations; and Jerusalem will be trampled under foot by the Gentiles until the times of the Gentiles are fulfilled" (Luke 21:20–24; see Matthew 24:15–18; Mark 13:14–16; Luke 19:43).

Setting: On the island of Patmos (in the Aegean Sea about fifty miles southwest of Ephesus in modern Turkey). On the Lord's Day (Sunday), approximately fifty years after the Resurrection, the disciple John encounters the Lord Jesus Christ, who communicates a new revelation for the apostle to record for the church in Thyatira and to six other churches in Asia.

"And to the angel of the church in Thyatira write: The Son of God, who has eyes like a flame of fire, and His feet are like burnished bronze, says this: 'I know your deeds, and your love and faith and service and perseverance, and that your deeds of late are greater than at first. But I have *this* against you, that you tolerate the woman Jezebel, who calls herself a prophetess, and she teaches and leads My bond-servants astray so that they commit *acts of* immorality and eat things sacrificed to idols. I gave her time to repent, and she does not want to repent of her immorality. Behold, I will throw her on a bed *of sickness,* and those who commit adultery with her into great tribulation, unless they repent of her deeds. And I will kill her children with pestilence, and all the churches will know that I am He who searches the minds and hearts; and I will give to each one of you according to your deeds. But I say to you, the rest who are in Thyatira, who do not hold this teaching, who have not known the deep things of Satan, as they call them—I place no other burden on you. Nevertheless what you have, hold fast until I come. He who overcomes, and he who keeps My deeds until the end, TO HIM I WILL GIVE AUTHORITY OVER THE NATIONS; AND HE SHALL RULE THEM WITH A ROD OF IRON, AS THE VESSELS OF THE POTTER ARE BROKEN TO PIECES, as I also have received *authority* from My Father; and I will give him the morning star. He who has an ear, let him hear what the Spirit says to the churches' (Revelation 2:18–29; Jesus quotes from Psalm 2:8, 9; Isaiah 30:14; see 1 Kings 16:31; Psalm 7:9; Romans 2:5; 1 Corinthians 2:10; 2 Peter 3:9; Revelation 1:14; 2:7; 3:11; 17:1–20).

GREAT TRUMPET (Listed under TRUMPET, GREAT)

GREATER CONDEMNATION (Listed under CONDEMNATION, GREATER; also see JUDGMENT)

GREATER LOVE (Listed under LOVE, GREATER)

GREATER THINGS (Listed under THINGS, GREATER)

GREATER WORKS (Listed under WORKS, GREATER)

GREATEST (Also see GREAT; GREATNESS; GREATNESS, GOD'S; and MEN, GREAT)

Setting: Capernaum of Galilee. Jesus answers His disciples' question about greatness, or rank, in the kingdom of heaven.

And He called a child to Himself and set him before them, and said, "Truly I say to you, unless you are converted and become like children, you will not enter the kingdom of heaven. Whoever then humbles himself as this child, he is the greatest in the kingdom of heaven. And whoever receives one such child in My name receives Me; but whoever causes one of these little ones who believe in Me to stumble, it would be better for him to have a heavy millstone hung around his neck, and to be drowned in the depth of the sea"

(Matthew 18:2–6; cf. Matthew 19:14; Mark 9:33–37, 42; Luke 9:47, 48; 17:1, 2).

Setting: The temple in Jerusalem. Jesus exposes the truth about Pharisaism to the crowds and His disciples after the Jewish religious leaders test Him with questions.

Then Jesus spoke to the crowds and to His disciples, saying: "The scribes and the Pharisees have seated themselves in the chair of Moses; therefore all that they tell you, do and observe, but do not do according to their deeds; for they say *things* and do not do *them*. They tie up heavy burdens and lay them on men's shoulders, but they themselves are unwilling to move them with *so much as* a finger. But they do all their deeds to be noticed by men; for they broaden their phylacteries and lengthen their tassels *of their garments*. They love the place of honor at banquets and the chief seats in the synagogues, and respectful greetings in the market places, and being called Rabbi by men. But do not be called Rabbi; for One is your Teacher, and you are all brothers. Do not call *anyone* on earth your father; for One is your Father, He who is in heaven. Do not be called leaders; for One is your Leader, *that is,* Christ. But the greatest among you shall be your servant. Whoever exalts himself shall be humbled; and whoever humbles himself shall be exalted" (Matthew 23:1–12; cf. Matthew 20:26; Mark 12:38–40; Luke 20:46, 47; see Exodus 13:9; Deuteronomy 33:3; Matthew 6:1, 5, 6, 9, 16; Mark 14:11; Luke 11:43; 14:11).

Setting: In Capernaum of Galilee. As Jesus teaches His disciples in private, they ask Him about greatness.

They came to Capernaum; and when He was in the house, He *began* to question them, "What were you discussing on the way?" But they kept silent, for on the way they had discussed with one another which *of them* was the greatest. Sitting down, He called the twelve and said to them, "If anyone wants to be first, he shall be last of all and servant of all." Taking a child, He set him before them, and taking him in His arms, He said to them, "Whoever receives one child like this in My name receives Me; and whoever receives Me does not receive Me, but Him who sent Me" (Mark 9:33–37; cf. Matthew 18:1–5; Luke 9:46–48; see Matthew

20:26; Mark 10:40).

Setting: An upper room in Jerusalem. During the Feast of Unleavened Bread (Passover) just before Jesus' crucifixion, while Jesus and His disciples celebrate the Passover meal and He institutes the Lord's Supper, the disciples argue over who is the greatest among them.

And He said to them, "The kings of the Gentiles lord it over them; and those who have authority over them are called 'Benefactors.' But *it is* not this way with you, but the one who is the greatest among you must become like the youngest, and the leader like a servant. For who is greater, the one who reclines *at the table* or the one who serves? Is it not the one who reclines *at the table?* But I am among you as the one who serves" (Luke 22:25–27; cf. Matthew 20:25–28; 23:11; Mark 10:42–45; Luke 22:1–24).

GREATNESS (Also see GREAT; GREATEST; GREATNESS, GOD'S; HUMILITY; MEN, GREAT; and SERVANT)

[GREATNESS from great]

Setting: Galilee. During the early part of His ministry, Jesus preaches the Sermon on the Mount to His disciples and the multitudes.

"Whoever then annuls one of the least of these commandments, and teaches others *to do* the same, shall be called least in the kingdom of heaven; but whoever keeps and teaches *them,* he shall be called great in the kingdom of heaven" (Matthew 5:19; cf. Matthew 11:11).

[GREATNESS from greater than John the Baptist]

Setting: Galilee. While speaking to the crowds, Jesus pays tribute to the ministry of John the Baptist, but emphasizes that the one who is least in the kingdom of heaven is greater than John.

As these men were going *away,* Jesus began to speak to the crowds about John, "What did you go out into the wilderness to see? A reed shaken by the wind? But what did you go out to see? A man dressed in soft *clothing?* Those who wear soft *clothing* are in kings' palaces! But what did you go out to see? A prophet? Yes, I tell you, and the one who is more than a prophet. This is the one about whom it is written, 'BEHOLD, I SEND MY MESSENGER AHEAD OF YOU, WHO WILL PREPARE YOUR WAY BEFORE YOU.' Truly, I say to you, among those born of women there has not arisen *anyone* greater than John the Baptist! Yet the one who is least in the kingdom of heaven is greater than he. From the days of John the Baptist until now the kingdom of heaven suffers violence, and violent men take it by force. For all the prophets and the Law prophesied until John. And, if you are willing to accept *it,* John himself is Elijah who was to come. He who has ears to hear, let him hear" (Matthew 11:7–15, Jesus quotes from Malachi 3:1; cf. Malachi 4:5; Luke 7:24–28; 16:16; see Matthew 14:5).

[GREATNESS from greater than Jonah and greater than Solomon]

Setting: Galilee. After Jesus warns the Pharisees about the unpardonable sin and their future judgment, some of the Pharisees and scribes ask Him in front of the crowds to perform a miraculous sign for them.

But He answered and said to them, "An evil and adulterous generation craves for a sign; and *yet* no sign will be given to it but the sign of Jonah the prophet; for just as JONAH WAS THREE DAYS AND THREE NIGHTS IN THE BELLY OF THE SEA MONSTER, so will the Son of Man be three days and three nights in the heart of the earth. The men of Nineveh will stand up with this generation at the judgment, and will condemn it because they repented at the preaching of Jonah; and behold, something greater than Jonah is here. *The* Queen of *the* South will rise up with this generation at the judgment and will condemn it, because she came from the ends of the earth to hear the wisdom of Solomon; and behold, something greater than Solomon is here" (Matthew 12:39–42; Jesus quotes from Jonah 1:17; cf. 1 Kings 10:1; Jonah 3:5; Matthew 16:1, 4; 12:38; Luke 11:29).

[GREATNESS from whoever wishes to become great]

Setting: On the way to Jerusalem, where Jesus will die on the cross. After the mother of James and John, the sons of Zebedee, asks Jesus to make her sons exalted rulers with Him in His coming kingdom, the Lord teaches His disciples about true greatness.

But Jesus called them to Himself and said, "You know that the rulers of the Gentiles lord it over them, and *their* great men exercise authority over them. It is not this way among you, but whoever wishes to become great among you shall be your servant, and whoever wishes to be first among you shall be your slave; just as the Son of Man did not come to be served, but to serve, and to give His life a ransom for many" (Matthew 20:25–28; cf. Matthew 23:11; 26:28; Mark 10:42–45).

[GREATNESS from If anyone wants to be first, he shall be last of all]
Setting: In Capernaum of Galilee., As Jesus teaches His disciples in private, they ask Him about greatness.

They came to Capernaum; and when He was in the house, He *began* to question them, "What were you discussing on the way?" But they kept silent, for on the way they had discussed with one another which *of them* was the greatest. Sitting down, He called the twelve and said to them, "If anyone wants to be first, he shall be last of all and servant of all." Taking a child, He set him before them, and taking him in His arms, He said to them, "Whoever receives one child like this in My name receives Me; and whoever receives Me does not receive Me, but Him who sent Me" (Mark 9:33–37; cf. Matthew 18:1–5; Luke 9:46–48; see Matthew 20:26; Mark 10:40).

[GREATNESS from whoever wishes to become great]
Setting: On the road to Jerusalem. James and John ask Jesus for special honor and privileges in His kingdom. The other disciples become angry, so the Lord uses this moment to teach them about servanthood.

Calling them to Himself, Jesus said to them, "You know that those who are recognized as rulers of the Gentiles lord it over them; and their great men exercise authority over them. But it is not this way among you, but whoever wishes to become great among you shall be your servant; and whoever wishes to be first among you shall be slave of all. For even the Son of Man did not come to be served, but to serve, and to give His life a ransom for many" (Mark 10:42–45; cf. Matthew 20:25–28).

[GREATNESS from no one greater than John]
Setting: Galilee. After He responds to the disciples of John the Baptist whether He is the promised Messiah, Jesus speaks to the crowds about John.

When the messengers of John had left, He began to speak to the crowds about John, "What did you go out into the wilderness to see? A reed shaken by the wind? But what did you go out to see? A man dressed in soft clothing? Those who are splendidly clothed and live in luxury are *found* in royal palaces! But what did you go out to see? A prophet? Yes, I say to you, and one who is more than a prophet. This is the one about whom it is written, 'BEHOLD, I SEND MY MESSENGER AHEAD OF YOU, WHO WILL PREPARE YOUR WAY BEFORE YOU.' I say to you, among those born of women there is no one greater than John; yet he who is least in the kingdom of God is greater than he" (Luke 7:24–28, Jesus quotes from Malachi 3:1; cf. Matthew 11:7–11).

[GREATNESS from is the one who is great]
Setting: Galilee. After Jesus prophesies His death, an argument arises among His disciples as to who is the greatest. The Lord resolves the matter by using a child as a teaching illustration.

But Jesus, knowing what they were thinking in their heart, took a child and stood him by His side, and said to them, "Whoever receives this child in My name receives Me, and whoever receives Me receives Him who sent Me; for the one who is least among all of you, this is the one who is great" (Luke 9:47, 48; cf. Matthew 18:1–5; Mark 9:33–47; see Matthew 10:40; Luke 22:24).

[GREATNESS from something greater than Solomon and something greater than Jonah]
Setting: On the way from Galilee to Jerusalem. After revealing a problem with exorcism and responding to a blessing from a woman in the crowd, Jesus tells the increasing crowds of the sign of Jonah.

As the crowds were increasing, He began to say, "This generation is a wicked generation; it seeks for a sign, and *yet* no sign will be given to it but the sign of Jonah. For just as Jonah became a sign to the Ninevites, so will the Son of Man be to this generation. The Queen of the South will rise up with the men of this generation at the judgment and condemn them, because she came from the ends of the earth to hear the wisdom of Solomon; and behold, something greater than Solomon is here. The men of Nineveh will stand up with this generation at the judgment and condemn it, because they repented at the preaching of Jonah; and behold, something greater than Jonah is here" (Luke 11:29–32; cf. Matthew 16:4; see 1 Kings 10:1–10; Jonah 3:4, 5).

[GREATNESS from But I am among you as the one who serves]
Setting: An upper room in Jerusalem. During the Feast of Unleavened Bread (Passover) just before Jesus' crucifixion, while Jesus and His disciples celebrate the Passover meal and He institutes the Lord's Supper, the disciples argue over who is the greatest among them.

And He said to them, "The kings of the Gentiles lord it over them; and those who have authority over them are called 'Benefactors.' But *it is* not this way with you, but the one who is the greatest among you must become like the youngest, and the leader like a servant. For who is greater, the one who reclines *at the table* or the one who serves? Is it not the one who reclines *at the table?* But I am among you as the one who serves" (Luke 22:25–27; cf. Matthew 20:25–28; 23:11; Mark 10:42–45; Luke 22:1–24).

[GREATNESS from a slave is not greater than his master and one who is sent greater than the one who sent him]
Setting: Jerusalem. Before the Passover, with His death on the cross nearing, Jesus explains the reason for His vivid example of servanthood in washing His disciples' feet.

So when He had washed their feet, and taken His garments and reclined *at the table* again, He said to them, "Do you know what I have done to you? You call Me Teacher and Lord; and you are right, for *so* I am. If I then, the Lord and the Teacher, washed your feet, you also ought to wash one another's feet. For I gave you an example that you also should do as I did to you. Truly, truly I say to you, a slave is not greater than his master, nor *is* one who is sent greater than the one who sent him. If you know these things, you are blessed if you do them. I do not speak of all of you. I know the ones I have chosen; but *it is* that the Scripture may be fulfilled, 'HE WHO EATS MY BREAD HAS LIFTED UP HIS HEEL AGAINST ME.' From now on I am telling you before *it* comes to pass, so that when it does occur, you may believe that I am *He*. Truly, truly, I say to you, he who receives whomever I send receives Me; and he who receives Me receives Him who sent Me" (John 13:12–20; Jesus quotes from Psalm 41:9; see Matthew 7:24; 10:24, 40; John 8:24; 14:29; 1 Peter 5:3).

[GREATNESS from A slave is not greater than his master]
Setting: Jerusalem. Before the Passover, with His departure in mind, after explaining He is the vine and His disciples are the branches, Jesus prepares them for persecution from the world.

"If the world hates you, you know that it has hated Me before *it hated* you. If you were of the world, the world would love its own; but because you are not of the world, but I chose you out of the world, because of this the world hates you. Remember the word that I said to you, 'A slave is not greater than his master.' If they persecuted Me, they will also persecute you; if they kept My word, they will keep yours also. But all these things they will do to you for My name's sake, because they do not know the One who sent Me. If I had not come and spoken to them, they would not have sin, but now they have no excuse for their sin" (John 15:18–22; see Matthew 10:22; John 7:7; 8:19, 55; 9:41; 1 Corinthians 4:12).

GREATNESS, GOD'S

[GOD'S GREATNESS from My Father, who has given *them* to Me, is greater than all]
Setting: Jerusalem. At the Feast of Dedication, just after Jesus conveys the Parable of the Good Shepherd to the Pharisees (who do not understand it), they ask Him plainly if He is the Christ.

Jesus answered them, "I told you, and you do not believe; the works that I do in My Father's name, these testify of Me. But you do not believe because you are not of My sheep. My sheep hear My voice, and I know them, and they follow Me; and I give eternal life to them, and they will never perish; and no one will snatch them out of My hand. My Father, who has given *them* to Me, is greater than all; and no one is able to snatch *them* out of the Father's hand. I and the Father are one" (John 10:25–30; see John 8:47; 17:1, 2, 20, 21).

[GOD'S GREATNESS from the Father is greater than I]

Setting: Jerusalem. Before the Passover. after He conveys the upcoming ministry of the Holy Spirit in His disciples' lives, Jesus again relates peace, hope, and comfort to them regarding His return to the Father.

"Peace I leave with you; My peace I give to you; not as the world gives do I give to you. Do not let your heart be troubled, nor let it be fearful. You heard that I said to you, 'I go away, and I will come to you,' If you loved Me, you would have rejoiced because I go to the Father, for the Father is greater than I. Now I have told you before it happens, so that when it happens, you may believe. I will not speak much more with you, for the ruler of the world is coming, and he has nothing in Me; but so that the world may know that I love the Father, I do exactly as the Father commanded Me. Get up, let us go from here" (John 14:27–31; see John 10:18, 29; 12:31; 13:19; 16:33).

GREED (Also see MONEY; POSSESSIONS; and WEALTH)

Setting: On the way from Galilee to Jerusalem. After the scribes and Pharisees turn hostile and question Him in an attempt to catch Him in something He might say, Jesus teaches the crowds and His disciples about greed and possessions.

But He said to him, "Man, who appointed Me a judge or arbitrator over you?" Then He said to them, "Beware, and be on your guard against every form of greed; for not *even* when one has an abundance does his life consist of his possessions" (Luke 12:14, 15; see 1 Timothy 6:6–10).

[GREED from I will tear down my barns and build larger ones]
Setting: On the way from Galilee to Jerusalem. After the scribes and Pharisees turn hostile and question Him in an attempt to catch Him in something He might say, Jesus responds to a question from the crowd and gives a parable about riches and greed.

And He told them a parable, saying, "The land of a rich man was very productive. And he began reasoning to himself, saying, 'What shall I do, since I have no place to store my crops?' Then he said, 'This is what I will do: I will tear down my barns and build larger ones, and here I will store all my grain and my goods. And I will say to my soul, "Soul, you have many goods laid up for many years *to come;* take your ease, eat, drink *and* be merry."' "But God said to him, 'You fool! This *very* night your soul is required of you; and *now* who will own what you have prepared?' So is the man who stores up treasure for himself, and is not rich toward God" (Luke 12:16–21; see Job 27:8; Psalm 39:6; Ecclesiastes 12:9; Philippians 2:3).

GREEN

Setting: Jerusalem. After being arrested and appearing before the Council of Elders (Sanhedrin), Pontius Pilate (Roman governor of Judea), Herod Antipas (tetrarch of Galilee and Perea), and Pilate a second time (when Pilate bows to the crowd's pressure and grants that Jesus be crucified), the Lord prophesies to the women mourning Him regarding the coming judgment of Jerusalem.

But Jesus turning to them said, "Daughters of Jerusalem, stop weeping for Me, but weep for yourselves and for your children. For behold, the days are coming when they will say, 'Blessed are the barren, and the wombs that never bore, and the breasts that never nursed.' Then they will begin TO SAY TO THE MOUNTAINS, 'FALL ON US,' AND TO THE HILLS, 'COVER US.' For it they do these things when the tree is green, what will happen when it is dry?" (Luke 23:28–31, Jesus quotes from Hosea 10:8; see Matthew 24:19).

GREETING

[GREETING from greet]
Setting: Galilee. During the early part of His ministry, Jesus preaches the Sermon on the Mount to His disciples and the multitudes.

"You have heard that it was said, 'YOU SHALL LOVE YOUR NEIGHBOR and hate your enemy.' But I say to you, love your enemies and pray for those who persecute you, so that you may be sons of your Father who is in heaven; for He causes His sun to rise on *the* evil and *the* good, and sends rain on *the* righteous and *the* unrighteous. For if you love those who love you, what reward do you have? Do not even the tax collectors do the same? If you greet only your brothers, what more are you doing *than others?* Do not even the Gentiles do the same? Therefore, you are to be perfect, as your heavenly Father is perfect" (Matthew 5:43–48, Jesus quotes from Leviticus 19:18; cf. Leviticus 19:2; Luke 6:27–36).

Setting: Galilee. After His disciples observe His ministry, Jesus summons and specifically instructs them about their ministry to the people of Israel.

These twelve Jesus sent out after instructing them: "Do not go in *the* way of *the* Gentiles, and do not enter *any* city of the Samaritans; but rather go to the lost sheep of the house of Israel. And as you go, preach, saying, 'The kingdom of heaven is at hand.' Heal *the* sick, raise *the* dead, cleanse *the* lepers, cast out demons. Freely you received, freely give. Do not acquire gold, or silver, or copper for your money belts, or a bag for *your* journey, or even two coats, or sandals, or a staff; for the worker is worthy of his support. And whatever city or village you enter, inquire who is worthy in it, and stay at his house until you leave *that city*. As you enter the house, give it your greeting. If the house is worthy, give it your *blessing of* peace. But if it is not worthy, take back your *blessing of* peace. Whoever does not receive you, nor heed your words, as you go out of that house or that city, shake the dust off your feet. Truly I say to you, it will be more tolerable for *the* land of Sodom and Gomorrah in the day of judgment than for that city" (Matthew 10:5–15; cf. Mark 6:7–11; Luke 9:1–5; see Matthew 3:2; 11:22, 24; 15:24; Luke 22:35; 1 Corinthians 9:14).

[GREETING from greet no one]
Setting: On the way from Galilee to Jerusalem. The Lord appoints seventy followers and sends them out in pairs to every place He Himself will soon visit.

And He was saying to them, "The harvest is plentiful, but the laborers are few; therefore beseech the Lord of the harvest to send out laborers into His harvest. Go; behold, I send you out as lambs in the midst of wolves. Carry no money belt, no bag, no shoes; and greet no one on the way. Whatever house you enter, first say, 'Peace be to this house.' If a man of peace is there, your peace will rest on him; but if not, it will return to you. Stay in that house, eating and drinking what they give you; for the laborer is worthy of his wages. Do not keep moving from house to house. Whatever city you enter and they receive you, eat what is set before you; and heal those in it who are sick, and say to them, 'The kingdom of God has come near to you.' But whatever city you enter and they do not receive you, go out into its streets and say, 'Even the dust of your city which clings to our feet we wipe off *in protest* against you; yet be sure of this, that the kingdom of God has come near.' I say to you, it will be more tolerable in that day for Sodom than for that city" (Luke 10:2–12; see Genesis 19:24–28; Matthew 9:37, 38, 10:9–14, 16; 1 Corinthians 10:27).

GREETINGS, RESPECTFUL

Setting: The temple in Jerusalem. Jesus exposes the truth about Pharisaism to the crowds and His disciples after the Jewish religious leaders test Him with questions.

Then Jesus spoke to the crowds and to His disciples, saying: "The scribes and the Pharisees have seated themselves in the chair of Moses; therefore all that they tell you, do and observe, but do not do according to their deeds; for they say *things* and do not do *them.* They tie up heavy burdens and lay them on men's shoulders, but they themselves are unwilling to move them with *so much as* a finger. But they do all their deeds to be noticed by men; for they broaden their phylacteries and lengthen their tassels *of their garments.* They love the place of honor at banquets and the chief seats in the synagogues, and respectful greetings in the market places, and being called Rabbi by men. But do not be called Rabbi; for One is your Teacher, and you are all brothers. Do not call *anyone* on earth your father; for One is your Father, He who is in heaven. Do not be called leaders; for One is your Leader, *that is,* Christ. But the greatest among you shall be your servant. Whoever exalts himself shall be humbled; and whoever humbles himself shall be exalted" (Matthew 23:1–12; cf. Matthew 20:26; Mark 12:38–40; Luke 20:46, 47; see Exodus 13:9; Deuteronomy 33:3; Matthew 6:1, 5, 6, 9, 16; Mark 14:11; Luke 11:43; 14:11).

Setting: The temple in Jerusalem. Jesus warns the crowd about the scribes, after commending one scribe for his nearness to the kingdom of God.

In His teaching He was saying: "Beware of the scribes who like to walk around in long robes, and *like* respectful greetings in the market places, and chief seats in the synagogues and places of honor at banquets, who devour widows' houses, and for appearance's sake offer long prayers; these will receive greater condemnation" (Mark 12:38–40; cf. Matthew 23:1–7; Luke 20:45–47).

Setting: On the way from Galilee to Jerusalem. After speaking of how a lamp illuminates, the Lord has lunch with a Pharisee who is surprised He doesn't wash before eating.

But the Lord said to him, "Now you Pharisees clean the outside of the cup and of the platter; but inside of you, you are full of robbery and wickedness. You foolish ones, did not He who made the outside make the inside also? But give that which is within as charity, and then all things are clean for you. But woe to you Pharisees! You pay tithe of mint and rue and every *kind of* garden herb, and *yet* disregard justice and the love of God; but these are the things you should have done without neglecting the others. Woe to you Pharisees! For you love the chief seats in the synagogues and the respectful greetings in the market places. Woe to you! For you are like concealed tombs, and the people who walk over *them* are unaware *of it*." (Luke 11:39–44; cf. Matthew 23:6, 7, 23–27; see Matthew 15:2; Titus 1:15).

Setting: The temple in Jerusalem. A few days before His crucifixion, after posing a question to the scribes, who do not answer, Jesus warns His disciples about the lifestyle of the scribes.

"Beware of the scribes, who like to walk around in long robes, and love respectful greetings in the market places, and chief seats in the synagogues and places of honor at banquets, who devour widows' houses, and for appearance's sake offer long prayers. These will receive greater condemnation" (Luke 20:46, 47; cf. Matthew 23:1–7; Mark 12:38–40; see Luke 11:43).

GRIEF (Also see LAMENT; MOURNING; SORROW; and WEEPING)

[GRIEF from grieved]

Setting: Capernaum of Galilee. Jesus illustrates forgiveness after Peter asks Him if forgiving someone seven times who has sinned against him is adequate.

"For this reason the kingdom of heaven may be compared to a king who wished to settle accounts with his slaves. When he had begun to settle *them,* one who owed him ten thousand talents was brought to him. But since he did not have *the means* to repay, his lord commanded him to be sold, along with his wife and children and all that he had, and repayment to be made. So the slave fell *to the ground* and prostrated himself before him, saying, 'Have patience with me and I will repay you everything.' And the lord of that slave felt compassion and released him and forgave him the debt. But that slave went out and found one of his fellow slaves who owed him a hundred denarii; and he seized him and *began* to choke *him,* saying, 'Pay back what you owe.' So his fellow slave fell *to the ground* and *began* to plead with him, saying, 'Have patience with me and I will repay you.' But he was unwilling and went and threw him in prison until he should pay back what was owed. So when his fellow slaves saw what had happened, they were deeply grieved and came and reported to their lord all that had happened. Then summoning him, his lord said to him, 'You wicked slave, I forgave you all that debt because you pleaded with me. Should you not also have had mercy on your fellow slave, in the same way that I had mercy on you?' And his lord, moved with anger, handed him over to the torturers until he should repay all that was owed him. My heavenly Father will also do the same to you, if each of you does not forgive his brother from your heart" (Matthew 18:23–35; cf. Matthew 6:12, 14, 15; Luke 7:42; see Matthew 25:19–28).

[GRIEF from grieved]

Setting: Jerusalem. After celebrating the Passover meal with His disciples, Jesus retreats to the Garden of Gethsemane on the Mount of Olives to pray prior to His betrayal by Judas.

Then Jesus came with them to a place called Gethsemane, and said to His disciples, "Sit here while I go over there and pray." And He took with Him Peter and the two sons of Zebedee, and began to be grieved and distressed. Then He said to them, "My soul is deeply grieved, to the point of death; remain here and keep watch with Me." And He went a little beyond *them,* and fell on His face and prayed, saying, "My Father, if it is possible, let this cup pass from Me; yet not as I will, but as You will." And He came to the disciples and found them sleeping, and said to Peter, "So, you *men* could not keep watch with Me for one hour? Keep watching and praying that you may not enter into temptation; the spirit is willing, but the flesh is weak." He went away again a second time and prayed, saying, "My Father, if this cannot pass away unless I drink it, Your will be done." Again He came and found them sleeping, for their eyes were heavy. And He left them again, and went away and prayed a third time, saying the same thing once more. Then He came to the disciples and said to them, "Are you still sleeping and resting? Behold the hour is at hand and the Son of Man is being betrayed into the hands of sinners. Get up, let us be going; behold the one who betrays Me is at hand!" (Matthew 26:36–46; cf. Mark 14:32–42; Luke 22:40–46; see Matthew 20:22; John 12:27).

[GRIEF from make a commotion]
Setting: The home of Jairus, a synagogue official in Capernaum. Jesus assures those present that Jairus's daughter has not died, but is asleep.

And entering in, He said to them, "Why make a commotion and weep? The child has not died, but is asleep" (Mark 5:39; cf. Matthew 9:24 and Luke 8:52).

[GRIEF from grieved]
Setting: Gethsemane on the Mount of Olives, east of the temple in Jerusalem. Jesus agonizes over His impending death, disappointed that His disciples keep falling asleep instead of watching and praying with Him.

They came to a place named Gethsemane; and He said to the disciples, "Sit here until I have prayed." And He took with Him Peter and James and John, and began to be very distressed and troubled. And He said to them, "My soul is deeply grieved to the point of death; remain here and keep watch." And He went a little beyond *them,* and fell to the ground and *began* to pray that if it were possible, the hour might pass Him by. And He was saying, "Abba! Father! All things are possible for You; remove this cup from Me; yet not what I will, but what You will." And He came and found them sleeping, and said to Peter, "Simon, are you asleep? Could you not keep watch for one hour? Keep watching and praying that you may not come into temptation; the spirit is willing, but the flesh is weak" (Mark 14:32–38; cf. Matthew 26:36–41; Luke 22:41–46; see Romans 8:15; Galatians 4:6).

Setting: Jerusalem. Before the Passover, after warning His disciples of the persecution they will face after His departure to heaven, empathizing with their sadness over His prophecies, Jesus gives them the hope for the future.

"A little while, and you will no longer see Me, and again a little while, and you will see Me." *Some* of His disciples then said to one another, "What is this thing He is telling us, 'A little while, and you will not see Me; and again a little while, and you will see Me'; and, 'because I go to the Father'?" So they were saying, "What is this that He says, 'A little while'? We do not know what He is talking about." Jesus knew that they wished to question Him, and He said to them, "Are you deliberating together about this, that I said, 'A little while, and you will not see Me, and again a little while, and you will see Me'? Truly, truly, I say to you, that you will weep and lament, but the world will rejoice; you will grieve, but your grief will be turned into joy. Whenever a woman is in labor she has pain, because her hour has come; but when she gives birth to the child, she no longer remembers the anguish because of the joy that a child has been born into the world. Therefore you too have grief now; but I will see you again, and your heart will rejoice, and no one *will* take your joy away from you" (John 16:16–22; see Mark 9:32; Luke 23:27; John 14:18–24; 16:5, 6; 20:20).

GROOM (See BRIDEGROOM)

GROUND (GROUND, ROCKY is a separate entry; also see EARTH; and SOIL)

Setting: Galilee. After His disciples observe His ministry, Jesus summons and specifically instructs them about their ministry ahead involving true discipleship.

"Are not two sparrows sold for a cent? And *yet* not one of them will fall to the ground apart from your Father. But the very hairs of your head are all numbered. So do not fear; you are more valuable than many sparrows" (Matthew 10:29–31; cf. Luke 12:6; see Matthew 12:12).

Setting: Capernaum of Galilee. Jesus illustrates the matter of forgiveness after Peter asks Him if forgiving someone seven times who has sinned against him is adequate.

"For this reason the kingdom of heaven may be compared to a king who wished to settle accounts with his slaves. When he had begun to settle *them,* one who owed him ten thousand talents was brought to him. But since he did not have *the means* to repay, his lord commanded him to be sold, along with his wife and children and all that he had, and repayment to be made. So the slave fell *to the ground* and prostrated himself before him, saying, 'Have patience with me and I will repay you everything.' And the lord of that slave felt compassion and released him and forgave him the debt. But that slave went out and found one of his fellow slaves who owed him a hundred denarii; and he seized him and *began* to choke *him,* saying, 'Pay back what you owe.' So his fellow slave fell *to the ground* and *began* to plead with him, saying, 'Have patience with me and I will repay you.' But he was unwilling and went and threw him in prison until he should pay back what was owed. So when his fellow slaves saw what had happened, they were deeply grieved and came and reported to their lord all that had happened. Then summoning him, his lord said to him, 'You wicked slave, I forgave you all that debt because you pleaded with me. Should you not also have had mercy on your fellow slave, in the same way that I had mercy on you?' And his lord, moved with anger, handed him over to the torturers until he should repay all that was owed him. My heavenly Father will also do the same to you, if each of you does not forgive his brother from your heart" (Matthew 18:23–35; cf. Matthew 6:12, 14, 15; Luke 7:42; see Matthew 25:19–28).

Setting: The Mount of Olives, just east of Jerusalem. During His discourse, after answering His disciples' questions as to when the temple will be destroyed and Jerusalem overrun, along with the signs of His coming and the end of the age, Jesus reemphasizes to His disciples that they should be on the alert for His return.

"For *it is* just like a man *about* to go on a journey, who called his own slaves and entrusted his possessions to them. To one he gave five talents, to another, two, and to another, one, each according to his own ability; and he went on his journey. Immediately the one who had received the five talents went and traded with them, and gained five more talents. In the same manner the one who *had received* the two *talents* gained two more. But he who received the one *talent* went away, and dug a *hole* in the ground and hid his master's money. Now after a long time the master of those slaves came and settled accounts with them. The one who had received the five talents came up and brought five more talents, saying, 'Master, you entrusted five talents to me. See, I have gained five more talents.' His master said to him, 'Well done, good and faithful slave. You were faithful with a few things, I will put you in charge of many things; enter into the joy of your master.' Also the one who *had received* the two talents came up and said, 'Master, you entrusted two talents to me. See, I have gained two more talents.' His master said to him, 'Well done, good and faithful slave. You were faithful with a few things, I will put you in charge of many things; enter into the joy of your master.' And the one also who had received the one talent came up and said, 'Master, I knew you to be a hard man, reaping where you did not sow and gathering where you scattered no *seed.* And I was afraid, and went away and hid your talent in the ground. See, you have what is yours.' But his master answered and said to him, 'You wicked, lazy slave, you knew that I reap where I did not sow and gather where I scattered no *seed.* Then you ought to have put my money in the bank, and on my arrival I would have received my *money* back with interest. 'Therefore take away the talent from him, and give it to the one who has ten talents.' For to everyone who has, *more* shall be given, and he will have an abundance; but from the one who does not have, even what he does have shall be taken away. Throw out the worthless slave into the outer darkness; in that place there will be weeping and gnashing of teeth" (Matthew 25:14–30; cf. Matthew 8:12; 13:12; 24:45–47; see Matthew 18:23, 24; Luke 12:44).

Setting: Galilee. After selecting His twelve disciples, Jesus teaches the Sermon on the Mount to those disciples and a great throng of people from Judea, Jerusalem, and the central coastal region of Tyre and Sidon.

"Why do you call Me, 'Lord, Lord,' and do not do what I say? Everyone who comes to Me and hears My words and acts on them, I will show you whom he is like; he is like a man building a house, who dug deep and laid a foundation on the rock; and when a flood occurred, the torrent burst against that house and could not shake it, because it had been well built. But the one who has heard and has not acted *accordingly,* is like a man who built a house on the ground without any foundation; and the torrent burst against it and immediately it collapsed, and the ruin of that house was great" (Luke 6:46–49; cf. Matthew 7:24–27; see Luke 6:12–19; James 1:22).

Setting: On the way from Galilee to Jerusalem. After some present report to Him about the Galileans whose blood

Pilate (Roman governor of Judea) mixed with their sacrifices, Jesus responds to their concern by calling them to repentance and illustrating His point with a parable.

And He *began* telling this parable: "A man had a fig tree which had been planted in his vineyard; and he came looking for fruit on it and did not find any. And he said to the vineyard-keeper, 'Behold, for three years I have come looking for fruit on this fig tree without finding any. Cut it down! Why does it even use up the ground?' And he answered and said to him, 'Let it alone, sir, for this year too, until I dig around it and put fertilizer; and if it bears fruit next year, *fine*; but if not, cut it down.'" (Luke 13:6–9; see Matthew 3:10).

Setting: Approaching Jerusalem. After being praised by the people in a triumphal welcome, the Lord weeps as He sees the city ahead of Him.

When He approached *Jerusalem,* He saw the city and wept over it, saying, "If you had known in this day, even you, the things which make for peace! But now they have been hidden from your eyes. For the days will come upon you when your enemies will throw up a barricade against you, and surround you and hem you in on every side, and they will level you to the ground and your children within you, and they will not leave in you one stone upon another, because you did not recognize the time of your visitation." (Luke 19:41–44; see Matthew 24:1–2; Luke 13:34, 35).

GROUND, ROCKY (Also see GROUND)

Setting: By the Sea of Galilee. During the early part of His ministry, just after a visit from his mother and brothers, Jesus instructs a very large crowd from a boat with the Parable of the Sower.

"Listen *to this!* Behold, the sower went out to sow; as he was sowing, some *seed* fell beside the road, and the birds came and ate it up. Other *seed* fell on the rocky *ground* where it did not have much soil; and immediately it sprang up because it had no depth of soil. And after the sun had risen, it was scorched; and because it had no root, it withered away. Other *seed* fell among the thorns, and the thorns came up and choked it, and it yielded no crop. Other *seeds* fell into the good soil, and as the grew up and increased, they yielded a crop and produced thirty, sixty, and a hundredfold." And He was saying, "He who has ears to hear, let him hear" (Mark 4:3–9; cf. Matthew 13:3–9; Luke 8:5–8).

GROUP (Also see GROUPS)

Setting: Judea beyond the Jordan (Perea). Jesus illustrates the kingdom of heaven to His disciples through the story of laborers in the vineyard.

"For the kingdom of heaven is like a landowner who went out early in the morning to hire laborers for his vineyard. When he had agreed with the laborers for a denarius for the day, he sent them into his vineyard. And he went out about the third hour and saw others standing idle in the market place; and to those he said,' You also go into the vineyard, and whatever is right I will give you.' And *so* they went. Again he went out about the sixth and the ninth hour, and did the same thing. And about the eleventh *hour* he went out and found others standing *around;* and he said to them, 'Why have you been standing idle here all day long?' They said to him, 'Because no one hired us.' He said to them, 'You go into the vineyard too.' When evening came, the owner of the vineyard said to his foreman, 'Call the laborers and pay them their wages, beginning with the last *group* to the first.' When those *hired* about the eleventh hour came, each one received a denarius. When those *hired* first came, they thought that they would receive more; but each of them also received a denarius. When they received it, they grumbled at the landowner, saying, 'These last men have worked *only* one hour, and you have made them equal to us who have borne the burden and the scorching heat of the day.' But he answered and said to one of them, 'Friend, I am doing you no wrong; did you not agree with me for a denarius? Take what is yours and go, but I wish to give to this last man the same as to you. It is not lawful for me to do what I wish with what is my own? Or is your eye envious because I am generous?' So the last shall be first, and the first last" (Matthew 20:1–16; cf. Matthew 19:30).

Setting: The temple in Jerusalem. Jesus delivers another parable to the chief priests and elders after they question His authority.

"Listen to another parable. There was a landowner who PLANTED A VINEYARD AND PUT A WALL AROUND IT AND DUG A WINE PRESS

IN IT, AND BUILT A TOWER, and rented it out to vine-growers and went on a journey. When the harvest time approached, he sent his slaves to the vine-growers to receive his produce. The vine-growers took his slaves and beat one, and killed another, and stoned a third. Again he sent another group of slaves larger than the first; and they did the same thing to them. But afterward he sent his son to them, saying, 'They will respect my son.' But when the vine-growers saw the son, they said among themselves, 'This is the heir; come, let us kill him and seize his inheritance.' They took him, and threw him out of the vineyard and killed him. Therefore when the owner of the vineyard comes, what will he do to those vine-growers?" (Matthew 21:33–40; Jesus quotes from Isaiah 5:1, 2; cf. Mark 12:1–9; Luke 20:9–15).

GROUPS (Also see GROUP)

Setting: Bethsaida in Galilee. Following a day of ministry, Jesus and His disciples try to withdraw from the large crowds, but the crowds, having listened to His teaching about the kingdom of God all day, must be fed physically, too.

But He said to them, "You give them *something* to eat!" And they said, "We have no more than five loaves and two fish, unless perhaps we go and buy food for all these people." (For there were about five thousand men.) And He said to His disciples, "Have them sit down *to eat* in groups of about fifty each" (Luke 9:13, 14; cf. Matthew 14:15–21; Mark 6:35–44; John 6:4–13).

GRUDGES (Also see FORGIVENESS; and RECONCILIATION)

[GRUDGES from if you have anything against anyone]

Setting: On the road to Bethany. After Jesus instructs the money changers while cleansing the temple, Peter draws Jesus' and His disciples' attention to an earlier-cursed fig tree.

And Jesus answered saying to them, "Have faith in God. Truly, I say to you, whoever says to this mountain, 'Be taken up and cast into the sea,' and does not doubt in his heart, but believes that what he says is going to happen, it will be *granted* him. Therefore I say to you, all things for which you pray and ask, believe that you have received them, and they will be *granted* you. Whenever you stand praying, forgive, if you have anything against anyone, so that your Father who is in heaven will also forgive you your transgressions. [But if you do not forgive, neither will your Father who is in heaven forgive your transgressions'] (Mark 11:22–26; cf. Matthew 21:19–22; see Matthew 6:14, 15; Matthew 7:7; 17:20).

GRUMBLING

[GRUMBLING from they grumbled at the landowner]

Setting: Judea beyond the Jordan (Perea). Jesus illustrates the kingdom of heaven to His disciples through the story of laborers in the vineyard.

"For the kingdom of heaven is like a landowner who went out early in the morning to hire laborers for his vineyard. When he had agreed with the laborers for a denarius for the day, he sent them into his vineyard. And he went out about the third hour and saw others standing idle in the market place; and to those he said,' You also go into the vineyard, and whatever is right I will give you.' And *so* they went. Again he went out about the sixth and the ninth hour, and did the same thing. And about the eleventh *hour* he went out and found others standing *around;* and he said to them, 'Why have you been standing idle here all day long?' They said to him, 'Because no one hired us.' He said to them, 'You go into the vineyard too.' When evening came, the owner of the vineyard said to his foreman, 'Call the laborers and pay them their wages, beginning with the last *group* to the first.' When those *hired* about the eleventh hour came, each one received a denarius. When those *hired* first came, they thought that they would receive more; but each of them also received a denarius. When they received it, they grumbled at the landowner, saying, 'These last men have worked *only* one hour, and you have made them equal to us who have borne the burden and the scorching heat of the day.' But he answered and said to one of them, 'Friend, I am doing you no wrong; did you not agree with me for a denarius? Take what is yours and go, but I wish to give to this last man the same as to you. It is not lawful for me to do what I wish with what is my own? Or is your eye envious because I am generous?' So the last shall be first, and the first last" (Matthew 20:1–16; cf. Matthew 19:30).

[GRUMBLING from grumble]

Setting: Capernaum of Galilee. After Jesus informs the people whom He miraculously fed with a lad's five loaves and two fish how they might receive the bread out of heaven, the Jewish religious leaders grumble because Jesus claims that He came down out of heaven.

Therefore the Jews were grumbling about Him, because He said, "I am the bread that came down out of heaven." They were saying, "Is not this Jesus, the son of Joseph, whose father and mother we know? How does He now say, 'I have come down out of heaven'?" Jesus answered and said to them, "Do not grumble among yourselves. No one can come to Me unless the Father who sent Me draws him; and I will raise him up on the last day. It is written in the prophets, 'AND THEY SHALL ALL BE TAUGHT OF GOD.' Everyone who has heard and learned from the Father, comes to Me. Not that anyone has seen the Father, except the One who is from God; He has seen the Father. Truly, truly, I say to you, he who believes has eternal life. I am the bread of life. Your fathers ate the manna in the wilderness, and they died. This is the bread which comes down out of heaven, so that one may eat of it and not die. I am the living bread that came down out of heaven; if anyone eats of this bread, he will live forever; and the bread also which I will give for the life of the world is My flesh" (John 6:41–51, Jesus quotes from Isaiah 54:13; see John 1:18, 29; 3:36; 7:27).

GUARD, BE ON YOUR (Also see ALERTNESS; READINESS; WARNING; and WATCHFULNESS)

Setting: On the Mount of Olives, east of the temple in Jerusalem. After predicting the temple's destruction, Jesus responds during His Olivet Discourse to questions from Peter, James, John, and Andrew about future events.

And Jesus began to say to them, "See to it that no one misleads you. Many will come in My name, saying, 'I am *He!*' and will mislead many. When you hear of wars and rumors of wars, do not be frightened; *those things* must take place; but *that is* not yet the end. For nation will rise up against nation, and kingdom against kingdom; there will be earthquakes in various places; there will *also be* famines. These things are *merely* the beginning of birth pangs. But be on your guard; for they will deliver you to *the* courts, and you will be flogged in *the* synagogues, and you will stand before governors and kings for My sake, as a testimony to them. The gospel must first be preached to all the nations. When they arrest you and hand you over, do not worry beforehand about what you are to say, but say whatever is given you in that hour; for it is not you who speak, but *it is* the Holy Spirit. Brother will betray brother to death, and a father *his* child; and children will rise up against parents and have them put to death. You will be hated by all because of My name, but the one who endures to the end, he will be saved" (Mark 13:5–13; cf. Matthew 24:4–14; Luke 21:7–19; see Matthew 10:17–22).

Setting: On the way from Galilee to Jerusalem. After the scribes and Pharisees turn hostile and question Him repeatedly in an attempt to catch Him in something He might say, Jesus teaches the crowds and His disciples about greed and possessions.

But He said to him, "Man, who appointed Me a judge or arbitrator over you?" Then He said to them, "Beware, and be on your guard against every form of greed; for not *even* when one has an abundance does his life consist of his possessions" (Luke 12:14, 15; see 1 Timothy 6:6–10).

Setting: On the way from Galilee to Jerusalem. After conveying the story of the rich man and Lazarus, the Lord gives instruction to His disciples on forgiveness.

He said to His disciples, "It is inevitable that stumbling blocks come, but woe to him through whom they come! It would be better for him if a millstone were hung around his neck and he were thrown into the sea, than that he would cause one of these little ones to stumble. Be on your guard! If your brother sins, rebuke him; and if he repents, forgive him. And if he sins against you seven times a day, and returns to you seven times, saying, 'I repent,' forgive him" (Luke 17:1–4; see Matthew 18:5–7, 15, 21, 22).

Setting: The Mount of Olives, just east of Jerusalem. Following a time of ministry in the temple a few days before His crucifixion, after conveying the Parable of the Fig Tree, Jesus warns His disciples during His Olivet Discourse to keep alert regarding future events.

"Be on guard, so that your hearts will not be weighted down with dissipation and drunkenness and the worries of life, and that day will not come upon you suddenly like a trap; for it will come upon all those who dwell on the face of all the earth. But keep on the alert at all times, praying that you may have strength to escape all these things that are about to take place, and to stand before the Son of Man" (Luke 21:34–36; cf. Mark 13:33; see Matthew 24:42–44; Luke 21:10–33).

GUARDIAN ANGELS (Listed under ANGELS, GUARDIAN; also see ANGELS)

GUEST ROOM (Listed under ROOM, GUEST)

GUESTS, DINNER (Also see HOSPITALITY; and INVITATION)

Setting: The temple in Jerusalem. Jesus speaks another parable to the chief priests and elders after they question His authority.

Jesus spoke to them again in parables, saying, "The kingdom of heaven may be compared to a king who gave a wedding feast for his son. And he sent out his slaves to call those who had been invited to the wedding feast, and they were unwilling to come. Again he sent out other slaves saying, 'Tell those who have been invited, "Behold, I have prepared my dinner; my oxen and my fattened livestock are *all* butchered and everything is ready; come to the wedding feast." But they paid no attention and went their way, one to his own farm, another to his business, and the rest seized his slaves and mistreated them and killed them. But the king was enraged, and he sent his armies and destroyed those murderers and set their city on fire. Then he said to his slaves, 'The wedding is ready, but those who were invited were not worthy. 'Go therefore to the main highways, and as many as you find *there,* invite to the wedding feast.' Those slaves went out into the streets and gathered together all they found, both evil and good; and the wedding hall was filled with dinner guests. But when the king came in to look over the dinner guests, he saw a man there who was not dressed in wedding clothes, and he said to him, 'Friend, how did you come in here without wedding clothes?' And the man was speechless. Then the king said to the servants, 'Bind him hand and foot, and throw him into the outer darkness; in that place there will be weeping and gnashing of teeth.' For many are called, but few *are* chosen" (Matthew 22:1–14; cf. Matthew 8:11, 12).

GUESTS, PARABLE OF THE

[PARABLE OF THE GUESTS from invited by someone to a wedding feast]

Setting: On the way from Galilee to Jerusalem. As He observes them selecting places of honor at the table, Jesus speaks a parable to the guests of a Pharisee leader on the Sabbath.

And He *began* speaking a parable to the invited guests when He noticed how they had been picking out the places of honor *at the table,* saying to them, "When you are invited by someone to a wedding feast, do not take the place of honor, for someone more distinguished than you may have been invited by him, and he who invited you both will come and say to you, 'Give *your* place to this man, and then in disgrace you proceed to occupy the last place. But when you are invited, go and recline at the last place, so that when the one who has invited you comes, he may say to you, 'Friend, move up higher'; then you will have honor in the sight of all who are at the table with you. For everyone who exalts himself will be humbled, and he who humbles himself will be exalted" (Luke 14:7–11; see 2 Samuel 22:28; Proverbs 25:6, 7; Matthew 23:6).

[PARABLE OF THE GUESTS from But when you give a reception]

Setting: On the way from Galilee to Jerusalem.. After He speaks a parable to the invited guests in the house of a Pharisee leader on the Sabbath, Jesus comments to the host about the people to invite in the future.

And He also went on to say to the one who had invited Him, "When you give a luncheon or a dinner, do not invite your friends or your brothers or your relatives or rich neighbors, otherwise they may also invite you in return and *that* will be your repayment. But when you give a reception, invite *the* poor, *the* crippled, *the* lame, *the* blind, and you will be blessed, since they do not have *the means* to repay you; for you will be repaid at the resurrection of the righteous" (Luke 14:12–14; see John 5:28, 29).

GUIDANCE, GOD'S (Also see WILL OF GOD; and WISDOM)

[GOD'S GUIDANCE from guide]
Setting: Jerusalem. Before the Passover, after warning His disciples of the persecution they will face after His departure to heaven, Jesus elaborates about the coming ministry of the Holy Spirit.

"I have many more things to say to you, but you cannot bear *them* now. But when He, the Spirit of truth, comes, He will guide you into all the truth; for He will not speak on His own initiative, but whatever He hears, He will speak; and He will disclose to you what is to come. He will glorify Me, for He will take of Mine and will disclose *it* to you. All things that the Father has are Mine; therefore I said that He takes of Mine and will disclose *it* to you (John 16:12–15; see John 7:39; 14:17, 26; 17:10).

GUIDANCE, HUMAN

[HUMAN GUIDANCE from A blind man cannot guide a blind man]
Setting: Galilee. After selecting His twelve disciples, Jesus teaches the Sermon on the Mount to those disciples and a great throng of people from Judea, Jerusalem, and the central coastal region of Tyre and Sidon.

And He also spoke a parable to them: "A blind man cannot guide a blind man, can he? Will they not both fall into a pit? A pupil is not above his teacher; but everyone, after he has been fully trained, will be like his teacher. Why do you look at the speck that is in your brother's eye, but do not notice the log that is in your own eye? Or how can you say to your brother, 'Brother, let me take out the speck that is in your eye,' when you yourself do not see the log that is in your own eye? You hypocrite, first take the log out of your own eye, and then you will see clearly to take out the speck that is in your brother's eye. For there is no good tree which produces bad fruit, nor, on the other hand, a bad tree which produces good fruit. For each tree is known by its own fruit. For men do not gather figs from thorns, nor do they pick grapes from a briar bush. The good man out of the good treasure of his heart brings forth what is good; and the evil *man* out of the evil *treasure* brings forth what is evil; for his mouth speaks from that which fills his heart" (Luke 6:39–45; cf. Matthew 7:3–6. 16, 18, 20; 12:35; see Matthew 10:24; 15:14).

GUIDES, BLIND (Also see MEN, SPIRITUALLY BLIND; PHARISEES; SADDUCEES; and SCRIBES)

Setting: Galilee. Jesus instructs His disciples after rebuking the Pharisees and scribes for questioning the disciples' lack of obedience to tradition and the commandments.

But He answered and said, "Every plant which My heavenly Father did not plant shall be uprooted. Let them alone; they are blind guides of the blind. And if a blind man guides a blind man, both will fall into a pit." (Matthew 15:13, 14; cf. Matthew 23:16; Luke 6:39).

Setting: The temple in Jerusalem. After the Jewish religious leaders test Him with questions, Jesus pronounces the fourth of eight woes on them in front of the crowds and His disciples.

"Woe to you, blind guides, who say, "Whoever swears by the temple, *that* is nothing; but whoever swears by the gold of the temple is obligated.' You fools and blind men! Which is more important, the gold or the temple that sanctified the gold? And, 'Whoever swears by the altar, *that* is nothing, but whoever swears by the offering on it, he is obligated.' You blind men, which is more important, the offering, or the altar that sanctifies the offering? Therefore, whoever swears by the altar, swears *both* by the altar and by everything on it. And whoever swears by the temple, swears *both* by the temple and by Him who dwells within it. And whoever swears by heaven, swears *both* by the throne of God and by Him who sits upon it" (Matthew 23:16–22; see Exodus 29:37; 1 Kings 8:13; Isaiah 66:1; Matthew 15:14).

Setting: The temple in Jerusalem. After the Jewish religious leaders test Him with questions, Jesus pronounces the fifth of eight woes on them in front of the crowds and His disciples.

"Woe to you, scribes and Pharisees, hypocrites! For you tithe mint and dill and cummin, and have neglected the weightier provisions of the law: justice and mercy and faithfulness; but these are things you should have done without neglecting the others. You blind guides, who strain out a gnat and swallow a camel!" (Matthew 23:23, 24).

GUILT

[GUILT from guilty]
Setting: Galilee. During the early part of His ministry, Jesus preaches the Sermon on the Mount to His disciples and the multitudes.

"But I say to you that everyone who is angry with his brother shall be guilty before the court; and whoever says to his brother, 'You good-for-nothing,' shall be guilty before the supreme court; and whoever says, 'You fool,' shall be guilty *enough to go* into the fiery hell" (Matthew 5:22).

Setting: The temple in Jerusalem. After the Jewish religious leaders test Him with questions, Jesus pronounces the eighth of eight woes upon them in front of the crowds and His disciples.

"Woe to you, scribes and Pharisees, hypocrites! For you build the tombs of the prophets and adorn the monuments of the righteous, and say, 'If we had been *living* in the days of our fathers, we would not have been partners with them in *shedding* the blood of the prophets.' So you testify against yourselves, that you are sons of those who murdered the prophets. Fill up, then, the measure *of the guilt* of you fathers. You serpents, you brood of vipers, how will you escape the sentence of hell? Therefore, behold, I am sending you prophets and wise men and scribes; some of them you will kill and crucify, and some of them you will scourge in your synagogues, and persecute from city to city, so that upon you may fall *the guilt of* all the righteous blood shed on earth, from the blood of righteous Abel to the blood of Zechariah, the son of Berechiah, whom you murdered between the temple and the altar. Truly I say to you, all these things will come upon this generation" (Matthew 23:29–36; cf. 2 Chronicles 24:21; Zechariah 1:1; Matthew 3:7; Luke 11:47–52; see Matthew 10:23).

[GUILT from guilty]
Setting: Galilee. After Jesus selects His twelve disciples, scribes from Jerusalem attribute His miraculous powers to Beelzebul, or Satan.

And He called them to Himself and began speaking to them in parables, "How can Satan cast out Satan? If a kingdom is divided against itself, that kingdom cannot stand. If a house is divided against itself, that house will not be able to stand. If Satan has risen up against himself and is divided, he cannot stand, but he is finished! But no one can enter the strong man's house and plunder his property unless he first binds the strong man, and then he will plunder his house. Truly I say to you, all sins shall be forgiven the sons of men, and whatever blasphemies they utter; but whoever blasphemes against the Holy Spirit never has forgiveness, but is guilty of an eternal sin"—because they were saying, "He has an unclean spirit" (Mark 3:23–30; cf. Matthew 12:25–32; Luke 12:10).

H

HADES (HADES, GATES OF is a separate entry; also see HELL)

Setting: Galilee. After performing miracles throughout the region, Jesus pronounces woes against those cities who did not repent.

"Woe to you, Chorazin! Woe to you, Bethsaida! For if the miracles had occurred in Tyre and Sidon which occurred in you, they would have repented long ago in sackcloth and ashes. Nevertheless I say to you, it will be more tolerable for Tyre and Sidon in *the* day of judgment than for you. And you, Capernaum, will not be exalted to heaven, will you? You will descend to Hades; for if the miracles had occurred in Sodom which occurred in you, it would have remained to this day. Nevertheless, I say to you that it will be more tolerable for the land of Sodom in *the* day of judgment, than for you" (Matthew 11:21–24; cf. Matthew 10:15; Luke 10:13–15).

Setting: On the way from Galilee to Jerusalem. The Lord pronounces woes on cities who reject the gospel, as He appoints seventy followers and sends them out in pairs to every place He Himself will soon visit.

"Woe to you, Chorazin! Woe to you, Bethsaida! For if the miracles had been performed in Tyre and Sidon which occurred in you, they would have repented long ago, sitting in sackcloth and ashes. But it will be more tolerable for Tyre and Sidon in the judgment than for you. And you, Capernaum, will not be exalted to heaven, will you? You will be brought down to Hades! The one who listens to you listens to Me, and the one who rejects you rejects Me; and he who rejects Me rejects the One who sent Me" (Luke 10:13–16; cf. Matthew 11:21–23; see Matthew 10:40; Luke 10:1).

Setting: On the way from Galilee to Jerusalem. After He responds to the Pharisees' scoffing at His teaching His disciples about stewardship and the permanence of the Law, Jesus conveys the story of the rich man and Lazarus.

"Now there was a rich man, and he habitually dressed in purple and fine linen, joyously living in splendor every day. And a poor man named Lazarus was laid at his gate, covered with sores, and longing to be fed with the *crumbs* which were falling from the rich man's table; besides, even the dogs were coming and licking his sores. Now the poor man died and was carried away by the angels to Abraham's bosom; and the rich man also died and was buried. In Hades he lifted up his eyes, being in torment, and saw Abraham far away and Lazarus in his bosom. And he cried out and said, 'Father Abraham, have mercy on me, and send Lazarus so that he may dip the tip of his finger in water and cool off my tongue, for I am in agony in this flame.' But Abraham said, 'Child, remember that during your life you received your good things, and likewise Lazarus bad things; but now he is being comforted here, and you are in agony. And besides all this, between us and you there is a great chasm fixed, so that those who wish to come over from here to you will not be able, and *that* none may cross over from there to us.' And he said, 'Then I beg you, father, that you send him to my father's house—for I have five brothers—in order that he may warn them, so that they will not also come to this place of torment.' But Abraham said, 'They have Moses and the Prophets; let them hear them.' But he said, 'No, father Abraham, but if someone goes to them from the dead, they will repent!' But he said to him, 'If they do not listen to Moses and the Prophets, they will not be persuaded even if someone rises from the dead.' " (Luke 16:19–31; see Luke 3:8; 6:24; 16:1, 14).

Setting: On the island of Patmos (in the Aegean Sea about fifty miles southwest of Ephesus in modern Turkey). On the Lord's Day (Sunday), approximately fifty years after His resurrection, the disciple John encounters the Lord Jesus Christ, who communicates new revelations for the apostle to record for the seven churches in Asia.

When I saw Him, I fell at His feet like a dead man. And He placed His right hand on me, saying, "Do not be afraid; I am the first and the last, and the living One; and I was dead, and behold, I am alive forevermore, and I have the keys of death and of Hades. Therefore write the things which you have seen, and the things which are, and the things which will take place after these things.

As for the mystery of the seven stars which you saw in My right hand, and the seven golden lampstands: the seven stars are the angels of the seven churches, and the seven lampstands are the seven churches" (Revelation 1:17–20; see Isaiah 44:6; Luke 24:5; Revelation 2:8).

HADES, GATES OF (Also see HADES)

Setting: Caesarea Philippi. Jesus responds to Simon Peter's declaration that He is the Christ, the Son of the living God.

And Jesus said to him, "Blessed are you, Simon Barjona, because flesh and blood did not reveal *this* to you, but My Father who is in heaven. I also say to you that you are Peter, and upon this rock I will build My church; and the gates of Hades will not overpower it. I will give you the keys of the kingdom of heaven; and whatever you bind on earth shall have been bound in heaven, and whatever you loose on earth shall have been loosed in heaven" (Matthew 16:17–19; cf. Matthew 18:18; Mark 8:29; Luke 9:20).

HAIR (Also see HAIRS; and HEAD)

Setting: Galilee. During the early part of His ministry, Jesus preaches the Sermon on the Mount to His disciples and the multitudes.

"Again, you have heard that the ancients were told, 'YOU SHALL NOT MAKE FALSE VOWS, BUT SHALL FULFILL YOUR VOWS TO THE LORD.' But I say to you, make no oath at all, either by heaven, for it is the throne of God, or by the earth, for it is the footstool of His feet, or by Jerusalem, for it is THE CITY OF THE GREAT KING. Nor shall you make an oath by your head, for you cannot make one hair white or black. But let your statement be 'Yes, yes' *or* 'No, no'; anything beyond these is of evil" (Matthew 5:33–37, Jesus quotes from Leviticus 19:12, Psalm 48:2; Isaiah 66:1; cf. James 5:12).

Setting: Galilee. After Jesus praises John the Baptist to the crowds, Simon, a Pharisee, invites Him to dinner. A sinful woman anoints His feet with perfume, prompting the Lord to instruct His host about forgiveness.

Turning toward the woman, He said to Simon, "Do you see this woman? I entered your house; you gave Me no water for My feet, but she has wet My feet with her tears and wiped them with her hair. You gave Me no kiss; but she, since the time I came in, has not ceased to kiss My feet. You did not anoint My head with oil, but she anointed My feet with perfume. For this reason I say to you, her sins, which are many, have been forgiven, for she loved much; but he who is forgiven little, loves little." Then He said to her, "Your sins have been forgiven." Those who were reclining *at the table* with Him began to say to themselves, "Who is this *man* who even forgives sins?" And He said to the woman, "Your faith has saved you; go in peace" (Luke 7:44–50; see Matthew 9:2; Mark 5:34; Luke 5:21).

Setting: The Mount of Olives, east of the temple in Jerusalem. After ministering in the temple a few days before His crucifixion, and giving His disciples more details regarding the temple's future destruction, Jesus elaborates during His Olivet Discourse about things to come.

Then He continued by saying to them, "Nation will rise against nation and kingdom against kingdom, and there will be great earthquakes, and in various places plagues and famines; and there will be terrors and great signs from heaven. But before all these things, they will lay their hands on you and will persecute you, delivering you to the synagogues and prisons, bringing you before kings and governors for My name's sake. It will lead to an opportunity for your testimony. So make up your minds not to prepare beforehand to defend yourselves; for I will give you utterance and wisdom which none of your opponents will be able to resist or refute. But you will be betrayed even by parents and brothers and relatives and friends, and they will put *some* of you to death, and you will be hated by all because of My name. Yet not a hair of your head will perish. By your endurance you will gain your lives" (Luke 21:10–19; cf. Matthew 10:19–22; 24:7–14; Mark 13:8–13).

HAIRS (Also see HAIR; and HEAD)

Setting: Galilee. After His disciples observe His ministry, Jesus summons and specifically instructs them about their ministry ahead involving true discipleship.

"Are not two sparrows sold for a cent? And *yet* not one of them will fall to the ground apart from your Father. But the very hairs of your head are all numbered. So do not fear; you are more valuable than many sparrows" (Matthew 10:29–31; cf. Luke 12:6; see Matthew 12:12).

Setting: On the way from Galilee to Jerusalem. Jesus warns His disciples of future events, as the scribes and Pharisees turn hostile and question Him repeatedly in an attempt to catch Him in something He might say.

Under these circumstances, after so many thousands of people had gathered together that they were stepping on one another, He began saying to His disciples first *of all,* "Beware of the leaven of the Pharisees, which is hypocrisy. But there is nothing covered up that will not be revealed, and hidden that will not be known. Accordingly, whatever you have said in the dark will be heard in the light, and what you have whispered in the inner rooms will be proclaimed upon the housetops. I say to you, My friends, do not be afraid of those who kill the body and after that have no more that they can do. But I will warn you whom to fear: fear the One who, after He has killed, has authority to cast into hell; yes, I tell you, fear Him! Are not five sparrows sold for two cents? *Yet* not one of them is forgotten before God. Indeed, the very hairs of your head are all numbered. Do not fear; you are more valuable than many sparrows". (Luke 12:1–7; cf. Matthew 10:26–31; see Matthew 16:6; Hebrews 10:31)

HALL, WEDDING

Setting: The temple in Jerusalem. Jesus speaks another parable to the chief priests and elders after they question His authority.

Jesus spoke to them again in parables, saying, "The kingdom of heaven may be compared to a king who gave a wedding feast for his son. And he sent out his slaves to call those who had been invited to the wedding feast, and they were unwilling to come. Again he sent out other slaves saying, 'Tell those who have been invited, "Behold, I have prepared my dinner; my oxen and my fattened livestock are *all* butchered and everything is ready; come to the wedding feast." But they paid no attention and went their way, one to his own farm, another to his business, and the rest seized his slaves and mistreated them and killed them. But the king was enraged, and he sent his armies and destroyed those murderers and set their city on fire. Then he said to his slaves, 'The wedding is ready, but those who were invited were not worthy. 'Go therefore to the main highways, and as many as you find *there,* invite to the wedding feast.' Those slaves went out into the streets and gathered together all they found, both evil and good; and the wedding hall was filled with dinner guests. But when the king came in to look over the dinner guests, he saw a man there who was not dressed in wedding clothes, and he said to him, 'Friend, how did you come in here without wedding clothes?' And the man was speechless. Then the king said to the servants, 'Bind him hand and foot, and throw him into the outer darkness; in that place there will be weeping and gnashing of teeth.' For many are called, but few *are* chosen" (Matthew 22:1–14; cf. Matthew 8:11, 12).

HALLOWED

Setting: Galilee. During the early part of His ministry, Jesus gives a model prayer to His disciples and the multitudes while conveying The Sermon on the Mount.

"Pray, then, in this way: 'Our Father who is in heaven, hallowed be Your name. Your kingdom come. Your will be done, on earth as it is in heaven. Give us this day our daily bread. And forgive us our debts, as we also have forgiven our debtors. And do not lead us into temptation, but deliver us from evil. [For Yours is the kingdom and the power and the glory forever. Amen]'" (Matthew 6:9–13; cf. Luke 11:2–4; see John 17:15).

Setting: On the way from Galilee to Jerusalem via Bethany. After Jesus visits in the home of Martha and Mary, one of his disciples asks Him to teach them to pray.

And He said to them, "When you pray, say: 'Father, hallowed be Your name. Your kingdom come. Give us each day our daily bread. And forgive us our sins, for we ourselves also forgive everyone who is indebted to us. And lead us not into temptation'" (Luke 11:2–4; cf. Matthew 6:9–13).

HAND (Specifics such as HAND, RIGHT are separate entries; also see FINGER; and HANDS)
Setting: Judea, near the Jordan River. Following His baptism, and before He begins His public ministry, Jesus is led by the Spirit into the wilderness for forty days of temptation by Satan.

Jesus said to him, "On the other hand, it is written, 'YOU SHALL NOT PUT THE LORD YOUR GOD TO THE TEST'" (Matthew 4:7, Jesus quotes from Deuteronomy 6:16; cf. Luke 4:12).

Setting: A synagogue in Galilee. Jesus answers questions posed by the Pharisees about the Sabbath.

And He said to them, "What man is there among you who has a sheep, and if it falls into a pit on the Sabbath, will he not take hold of it and lift it out? How much more valuable then is a man than a sheep! So then, it is lawful to do good on the Sabbath." Then He said to the man, "Stretch out your hand!" He stretched it out, and it was restored to normal, like the other (Matthew 12:11–13; cf. Matthew 10:31; Mark 3:4, 5; Luke 6:9, 10; 14:5; see Matthew 8:3).

Setting: Capernaum of Galilee. Jesus elaborates about stumbling blocks after His disciples ask about greatness in the kingdom of heaven.

"Woe to the world because of *its* stumbling blocks! For it is inevitable that stumbling blocks come; but woe to that man through whom the stumbling block comes! If your hand or your foot causes you to stumble, cut if off and throw it from you; it is better for you to enter life crippled or lame, than to have two hands or two feet and be cast into the eternal fire. If your eye causes you to stumble, pluck it out and throw it from you. It is better for you to enter life with one eye, than to have two eyes and be cast into the fiery hell" (Matthew 18:7–9; cf. Matthew 5:29, 30; Mark 9:43–48; Luke 17:1).

Setting: The temple in Jerusalem. Jesus speaks another parable to the chief priests and elders after they question His authority.

Jesus spoke to them again in parables, saying, "The kingdom of heaven may be compared to a king who gave a wedding feast for his son. And he sent out his slaves to call those who had been invited to the wedding feast, and they were unwilling to come. Again he sent out other slaves saying, 'Tell those who have been invited, "Behold, I have prepared my dinner; my oxen and my fattened livestock are *all* butchered and everything is ready; come to the wedding feast." But they paid no attention and went their way, one to his own farm, another to his business, and the rest seized his slaves and mistreated them and killed them. But the king was enraged, and he sent his armies and destroyed those murderers and set their city on fire. Then he said to his slaves, 'The wedding is ready, but those who were invited were not worthy. 'Go therefore to the main highways, and as many as you find *there,* invite to the wedding feast.' Those slaves went out into the streets and gathered together all they found, both evil and good; and the wedding hall was filled with dinner guests. But when the king came in to look over the dinner guests, he saw a man there who was not dressed in wedding clothes, and he said to him, 'Friend, how did you come in here without wedding clothes?' And the man was speechless. Then the king said to the servants, 'Bind him hand and foot, and throw him into the outer darkness; in that place there will be weeping and gnashing of teeth.' For many are called, but few *are* chosen" (Matthew 22:1–14; cf. Matthew 8:11, 12).

Setting: An upper room in Jerusalem. While celebrating the Passover meal with His disciples, Jesus shocks them with the revelation that one of them will soon betray Him to His enemies.

As they were eating, He said, "Truly I say to you that one of you will betray Me." Being deeply grieved, they each one began to say to Him, 'Surely not I, Lord?' And He answered, "He who dipped his hand with Me in the bowl is the one who will betray Me. The Son of Man *is to* go, just as it is written of Him; but woe to that man by whom the Son of Man is betrayed! It would have been good for that man if he had not been born." And Judas, who was betraying Him, said, 'Surely it is not I, Rabbi?' Jesus said to him, "You have said *it yourself*" (Matthew 26:21–25; cf. Mark 14:18–21; Luke 22:21–23; John 13:21–30; see Psalm 41:9).

Setting: A synagogue in Galilee. Early in His ministry, Jesus heals a man's withered hand on the Sabbath while the Pharisees observe.

He said to the man with the withered hand, "Get up and come forward!" And He said to them, "Is it lawful to do good or do harm on the Sabbath, to save a life or to kill?" But they kept silent. After looking around at them with anger, grieved at their hardness of heart, He said to the man, "Stretch out your hand." And he stretched it out, and his hand was restored (Mark 3:3–5; cf. Matthew 12:9–14; Luke 6:6–11).

Setting: Capernaum of Galilee. As Jesus teaches His disciples in private, they ask Him about greatness.

But Jesus said, "Do not hinder him, for there is no one who will perform a miracle in My name, and be able soon afterward to speak evil of Me. For he who is not against us is for us. For whoever gives you a cup of water to drink because of your name as *followers* of Christ, truly I say to you, he will not lose his reward. Whoever causes one of these little ones who believe to stumble, it would be better for him if, with a heavy millstone hung around his neck, he had been cast into the sea. If your hand causes you to stumble, cut it off; it is better for you to enter life crippled, than, having your two hands, to go into hell, into the unquenchable fire, [where THEIR WORM DOES NOT DIE, AND THE FIRE IS NOT QUENCHED.] If your foot causes you to stumble, cut it off; it is better for you to enter life lame, than, having your two feet, to be cast into hell, [where THEIR WORM DOES NOT DIE, AND THE FIRE IS NOT QUENCHED.] If your eye causes you to stumble, throw it out; it is better for you to enter the kingdom of God with one eye, than, having two eyes, to be cast into hell, where THEIR WORM DOES NOT DIE, AND THE FIRE IS NOT QUENCHED. For everyone will be salted with fire. Salt is good; but if the salt becomes unsalty, with what will you make it salty *again?* Have salt in yourselves, and be at peace with one another" (Mark 9:39–50; Jesus quotes from Isaiah 66:24; cf. Matthew 18:6–9; Luke 9:49, 50; see Matthew 5:13, 29, 30; 10:42; 12:30; 18:5, 6).

Setting: A synagogue in Galilee. As Jesus teaches on a Sabbath, the scribes and Pharisees watch to see if He heals a man's withered hand.

But He knew what they were thinking, and He said to the man with the withered hand, "Get up and come forward!" And he got up and came forward. And Jesus said to them, "I ask you, is it lawful to do good or to do harm on the Sabbath, to save a life or destroy it?" And looking around at them all, He said to him, "Stretch out your hand!" And he did *so;* and his hand was restored (Luke 6:8–10; cf. Matthew 12:9–13; Mark 3:1–5).

Setting: Galilee. After selecting His twelve disciples, Jesus teaches the Sermon on the Mount to those disciples and a great throng of people from Judea, Jerusalem, and the central coastal region of Tyre and Sidon.

And He also spoke a parable to them: "A blind man cannot guide a blind man, can he? Will they not both fall into a pit? A pupil is not above his teacher; but everyone, after he has been fully trained, will be like his teacher. Why do you look at the speck that is in your brother's eye, but do not notice the log that is in your own eye? Or how can you say to your brother, 'Brother, let me take out the speck that is in your eye,' when you yourself do not see the log that is in your own eye? You hypocrite, first take the log out of your own eye, and then you will see clearly to take out the speck that is in your brother's eye. For there is no good tree which produces bad fruit, nor, on the other hand, a bad tree which produces good fruit. For each tree is known by its own fruit. For men do not gather figs from thorns, nor do they pick grapes from a briar bush. The good man out of the good treasure of his heart brings forth what is good; and the evil *man* out of the evil *treasure* brings forth what is evil; for his mouth speaks from that which fills his heart" (Luke 6:39–45; cf. Matthew 7:3–6. 16, 18, 20; 12:35; see Matthew 10:24; 15:14; Luke 6:12–19).

Setting: On the way from Galilee to Jerusalem. The Lord responds to several men seeking to follow Him.

But Jesus said to him, "No one, after putting his hand to the plow and looking back, is fit for the kingdom of God" (Luke 9:62; cf. Matthew 8:19–22; see Philippians 3:13).

Setting: On the way from Galilee to Jerusalem. Jesus conveys the illustration of the prodigal son because the Pharisees and scribes complain He associates with tax collectors and sinners.

And He said, "A man had two sons. The younger of them said to his father, 'Father, give me the share of the estate that falls to me.' So he divided his wealth between them. And not many days later, the younger son gathered everything together and went

on a journey into a distant country, and there he squandered his estate with loose living. Now when he had spent everything, a severe famine occurred in that country, and he began to be impoverished. So he went and hired himself out to one of the citizens of that country, and he sent him into his fields to feed swine. And he would have gladly filled his stomach with the pods that the swine were eating, and no one was giving *anything* to him. But when he came to his senses, he said, 'How many of my father's hired men have more than enough bread, but I am dying here with hunger! I will get up and go to my father, and will say to him, "Father, I have sinned against heaven, and in your sight; I am no longer worthy to be called your son; make me as one of your hired men."' So he got up and came to his father. But while he was still a long way off, his father saw him and felt compassion *for him,* and ran and embraced him and kissed him. And the son said to him, "Father, I have sinned against heaven and in your sight; I am no longer worthy to be called your son.' But the father said to his slaves, 'Quickly bring out the best robe and put it on him, and put a ring on his hand and sandals on his feet; and bring the fattened calf, kill it, and let us eat and celebrate; for this son of mine was dead and has come to life again; he was lost and has been found.' And they began to celebrate. Now his older son was in the field, when he came and approached the house, he heard music and dancing. And he summoned one of the servants and *began* inquiring what these things could be. And he said to him, 'Your brother has come, and your father has killed the fattened calf because he has received him back safe and sound.' But he became angry and was not willing to go in; and his father came out and *began* pleading with him. But he answered and said to his father, 'Look! For so many years I have been serving you and I have never neglected a command of yours; and *yet* you have never given me a young goat, so that I might celebrate with my friends; but when this son of yours came, who has devoured your wealth with prostitutes, you killed the fattened calf for him.' And he said to him, 'Son, you have always been with me, and all that is mine is yours. But we had to celebrate and rejoice, for this brother of yours was dead and *has begun* to live, and *was* lost and has been found'" (Luke 15:11–32; see Proverbs 29:2; Luke 15:1, 2).

Setting: An upper room in Jerusalem. During the Feast of Unleavened Bread (Passover) just before Jesus' crucifixion, while celebrating the Passover meal with His disciples, Jesus institutes the Lord's Supper.

And when He had taken a cup *and* given thanks, He said, "Take this and share it among yourselves; for I say to you, I will not drink of the fruit of the vine from now on until the kingdom of God comes." And when he had taken *some* bread and given thanks, He broke it and gave it to them, saying, "This is My body which is given for you; do this in remembrance of Me." And in the same way *He took* the cup after they had eaten, saying, "This cup which is poured out for you is the new covenant in My blood. But behold, the hand of the one betraying Me is with Mine on the table. For indeed, the Son of Man is going as it has been determined; but woe to that man by whom He is betrayed!" (Luke 22:17–22; cf. Matthew 26:26–29; Mark 14:22–25; 1 Corinthians 11:23–26; see Psalm 41:9; Luke 14:15; 1 Corinthians 10:16).

Setting: Jerusalem. The risen Jesus meets with His disciple Thomas (Didymus), who had doubts about the other disciples' testimony claiming to have seen and spoken with the Lord eight days earlier.

After eight days His disciples were again inside, and Thomas with them. Jesus came, the doors having been shut, and stood in their midst and said, "Peace *be* with you." Then He said to Thomas, "Reach here with your finger, and see My hands; and reach here your hand and put it into My side; and do not be unbelieving, but believing." Thomas answered and said to Him, "My Lord and my God!" Jesus said to him, "Because you have seen Me, have you believed? Blessed *are* they who did not see, and *yet* believed" (John 20:26–29; see Luke 24:36, 40; 1 Peter 1:8).

HAND, AT (near)

Setting: Galilee. After hearing that John the Baptist has been taken into custody, Jesus begins His ministry, settling in Capernaum by the Sea of Galilee in fulfillment of Isaiah 9:1, 2.

From that time Jesus began to preach and say, "Repent, for the kingdom of heaven is at hand" (Matthew 4:17; cf. Mark 1:15).

Setting: Galilee. After His disciples observe His ministry, Jesus summons and specifically instructs them about their ministry to the people of Israel.

These twelve Jesus sent out after instructing them: "Do not go in *the* way of *the* Gentiles, and do not enter *any* city of the Samaritans; but rather go to the lost sheep of the house of Israel. And as you go, preach, saying, 'The kingdom of heaven is at hand.'

Heal *the* sick, raise *the* dead, cleanse *the* lepers, cast out demons. Freely you received, freely give. Do not acquire gold, or silver, or copper for your money belts, or a bag for *your* journey, or even two coats, or sandals, or a staff; for the worker is worthy of his support. And whatever city or village you enter, inquire who is worthy in it, and stay at his house until you leave *that city*. As you enter the house, give it your greeting. If the house is worthy, give it your *blessing of* peace. But if it is not worthy, take back your *blessing of* peace. Whoever does not receive you, nor heed your words, as you go out of that house or that city, shake the dust off your feet. Truly I say to you, it will be more tolerable for *the* land of Sodom and Gomorrah in the day of judgment than for that city" (Matthew 10:5–15; cf. Mark 6:7–11; Luke 9:1–5; see Matthew 3:2; 11:22, 24; 15:24; Luke 22:35; 1 Corinthians 9:14).

Setting: Jerusalem. After celebrating the Passover meal with His disciples, Jesus retreats to the Garden of Gethsemane on the Mount of Olives to pray prior to His betrayal by Judas.

Then Jesus came with them to a place called Gethsemane, and said to His disciples, "Sit here while I go over there and pray." And He took with Him Peter and the two sons of Zebedee, and began to be grieved and distressed. Then He said to them, "My soul is deeply grieved, to the point of death; remain here and keep watch with Me." And He went a little beyond *them,* and fell on His face and prayed, saying, "My Father, if it is possible, let this cup pass from Me; yet not as I will, but as You will." And He came to the disciples and found them sleeping, and said to Peter, "So, you *men* could not keep watch with Me for one hour? Keep watching and praying that you may not enter into temptation; the spirit is willing, but the flesh is weak." He went away again a second time and prayed, saying, "My Father, if this cannot pass away unless I drink it, Your will be done." Again He came and found them sleeping, for their eyes were heavy. And He left them again, and went away and prayed a third time, saying the same thing once more. Then He came to the disciples and said to them, "Are you still sleeping and resting? Behold the hour is at hand and the Son of Man is being betrayed into the hands of sinners. Get up, let us be going; behold the one who betrays Me is at hand!" (Matthew 26:36–46; cf. Mark 14:32–42; Luke 22:40–46; see Matthew 20:22; John 12:27).

Setting: Galilee. After being baptized by John in the Jordan River, Jesus commences His gospel-preaching ministry shortly after John is taken into custody by Herod Antipas.

Now after John had been taken into custody, Jesus came into Galilee, preaching the gospel of God, and saying, "The time is fulfilled, and the kingdom of God is at hand; repent and believe in the gospel" (Mark 1:14, 15, cf. Matthew 4:17; Galatians 4:4).

Setting: Gethsemane on the Mount of Olives, east of the temple in Jerusalem. Jesus prepares to meet Judas the betrayer while His other disciples keep falling asleep instead of watching and praying with Him.

And He came the third time, and said to them, "Are you still sleeping and resting? It is enough; the hour has come; behold, the Son of Man is being betrayed into the hands of sinners. Get up, let us be going; behold, the one who betrays Me is at hand!" (Mark 14:41, 42; cf. Matthew 26:45, 46).

HAND, FATHER'S

Setting: Jerusalem. At the Feast of Dedication, just after Jesus conveys the Parable of the Good Shepherd to the Pharisees (who do not understand it), they ask Him plainly if He is the Christ.

Jesus answered them, "I told you, and you do not believe; the works that I do in My Father's name, these testify of Me. But you do not believe because you are not of My sheep. My sheep hear My voice, and I know them, and they follow Me; and I give eternal life to them, and they will never perish; and no one will snatch them out of My hand. My Father, who has given *them* to Me, is greater than all; and no one is able to snatch *them* out of the Father's hand. I and the Father are one" (John 10:25–30; see John 8:47; 10:4, 17:1–2, 20, 21).

HAND, HIRED

Setting: Jerusalem. Following the Pharisees' interrogation and dismissal of the formerly blind man Jesus healed on the Sabbath, the Lord conveys the Parable of the Good Shepherd to the Pharisees, using figures of speech they do not understand.

So Jesus said to them again, "Truly, truly, I say to you, I am the door of the sheep. All who came before Me are thieves and robbers, but the sheep did not hear them. I am the door; if anyone enters through Me, he will be saved, and will go in and out and find pasture. The thief comes only to steal and kill and destroy; I came that they may have life, and have *it* abundantly. I am the good shepherd; the good shepherd lays down His life for the sheep. He who is a hired hand, and not a shepherd, who is not the owner of the sheep, sees the wolf coming, and leaves the sheep and flees, and the wolf snatches them and scatters *them. He flees* because he is a hired hand and is not concerned about the sheep. I am the good shepherd, and I know My own and My own know Me, even as the Father knows Me and I know the Father; and I lay down My life for the sheep. I have other sheep, which are not of this fold; I must bring them also, and they will hear My voice; and they will become one flock *with* one shepherd. For this reason the Father loves Me, because I lay down My life so that I may take it again. No one has taken it away from Me, but I lay it down on My own initiative. I have authority to take it up again. This commandment I received from My Father" (John 10:7–18; see Isaiah 40:11; 56:8; Jeremiah 23:1; Matthew 11:27).

HAND, LEFT

Setting: Galilee. During the early part of His ministry, Jesus preaches the Sermon on the Mount to His disciples and the multitudes.

"So when you give to the poor, do not sound a trumpet before you, as the hypocrites do in the synagogues and in the streets, so that they may be honored by men. Truly I say to you, they have their reward in full. But when you give to the poor, do not let your left hand know what your right hand is doing, so that your giving will be in secret; and your Father who sees *what is done* in secret will reward you" (Matthew 6:2–4; see Jeremiah 17:10; Matthew 6:5, 16).

HAND, MY (Jesus')

Setting: Jerusalem. At the Feast of Dedication, just after Jesus conveys the Parable of the Good Shepherd to the Pharisees (who do not understand it), they ask Him plainly if He is the Christ.

Jesus answered them, "I told you, and you do not believe; the works that I do in My Father's name, these testify of Me. But you do not believe because you are not of My sheep. My sheep hear My voice, and I know them, and they follow Me; and I give eternal life to them, and they will never perish; and no one will snatch them out of My hand. My Father, who has given *them* to Me, is greater than all; and no one is able to snatch *them* out of the Father's hand. I and the Father are one" (John 10:25–30; see John 8:47; 17:1–2, 20, 21).

HAND, RIGHT (Also see POWER; and POWER, RIGHT HAND OF)

Setting: Galilee. During the early part of His ministry, Jesus preaches the Sermon on the Mount to His disciples and the multitudes.

"If your right eye makes you stumble, tear it out and throw it from you; for it is better for you to lose one of the parts of your body, than for your whole body to be thrown into hell. If your right hand makes you stumble, cut it off and throw it from you; for it is better for you to lose one of the parts of your body, than for your whole body to go into hell" (Matthew 5:29, 30; cf. Matthew 18:8, 9).

Setting: Galilee. During the early part of His ministry, Jesus preaches the Sermon on the Mount to His disciples and the multitudes.

"So when you give to the poor, do not sound a trumpet before you, as the hypocrites do in the synagogues and in the streets, so that they may be honored by men. Truly I say to you, they have their reward in full. But when you give to the poor, do not let your left hand know what your right hand is doing, so that your giving will be in secret; and your Father who sees *what is done* in secret will reward you" (Matthew 6:2–4; see Jeremiah 17:10; Matthew 6:5, 16).

Setting: The temple in Jerusalem. Following the Sadducees' and Pharisees' unsuccessful attempts to test Him with questions, with the crowds listening, Jesus poses a question to some of the Pharisees.

"What do you think about the Christ, whose son is He?" They said to Him, "The *son* of David." He said to them, "Then how does David in the Spirit call Him 'Lord,' saying, 'THE LORD SAID TO MY LORD, SIT AT MY RIGHT HAND, UNTIL I PUT YOUR ENEMIES BENEATH YOUR FEET"'? "If David then calls Him 'Lord," how is He his son?" (Matthew 22:42–45; Jesus quotes from Psalm 110:1; cf. Mark 12:35–37; Luke 20:41–44; see 2 Samuel 23:2).

Setting: Jerusalem. After being betrayed by Judas and arrested, Jesus appears before Caiaphas the high priest and the Council, who interrogate and try to entrap Him.

Jesus said to him, "You have said it *yourself;* nevertheless I tell you, hereafter you will see THE SON OF MAN SITTING AT THE RIGHT HAND OF POWER, AND COMING ON THE CLOUDS OF HEAVEN" (Matthew 26:64, Jesus quotes from Daniel 7:13; cf. Mark 14:62).

Setting: The temple in Jerusalem. Jesus teaches the crowd after commending a scribe for his nearness to the kingdom of God.

And Jesus *began* to say, as He taught in the temple, "How *is it that* the scribes say that the Christ is the son of David? David himself said in the Holy Spirit, 'THE LORD SAID TO MY LORD, SIT AT MY RIGHT HAND, UNTIL I PUT YOUR ENEMIES BENEATH YOUR FEET."' David himself calls Him 'Lord'; so in what sense is He his son?" And the large crowd enjoyed listening to Him (Mark 12:35–37, Jesus quotes from Psalm 110:1; cf. Matthew 22:41–46; Luke 20:40–44).

Setting: Following His betrayal by Judas and arrest, Jesus confirms that He is the Christ to the high priest and all the chief priests in Jerusalem as they seek evidence so they might find reason to put Him to death.

And Jesus said, "I am; and you shall see THE SON OF MAN SITTING AT THE RIGHT HAND OF POWER, and COMING WITH THE CLOUDS OF HEAVEN" (Mark 14:62, Jesus quotes from Psalm 110:1 and Daniel 7:13; cf. Matthew 26:57–68; see Luke 22:54).

Setting: The temple in Jerusalem. A few days before His crucifixion, after some of the Sadducees question Him about the resurrection, Jesus poses a question to the scribes, who say He answered well.

Then He said to them, "How *is it that* they say the Christ is David's son? For David himself says in the book of Psalms, 'THE LORD SAID TO MY LORD, SIT AT MY RIGHT HAND, UNTIL I MAKE YOUR ENEMIES A FOOTSTOOL FOR YOUR FEET.' Therefore David calls Him 'Lord,' and how is He his son?" (Luke 20:41–44, Jesus quotes from Psalm 110:1; cf. Matthew 22:41–46; Mark 12:35–37).

Setting: Jerusalem. After being arrested, having Peter deny Him, and being mocked and beaten, with His crucifixion imminent, Jesus appears in front of the Sanhedrin (Council of Elders).

"If You are the Christ, tell us." But He said to them, "If I tell you, you will not believe; and if I ask you a question, you will not answer. But from now on THE SON OF MAN WILL BE SEATED AT THE RIGHT HAND of the power OF GOD." And they all said, "Are You the Son of God, then? And He said to them, "Yes, I am" (Luke 22:67–70, Jesus quotes from Psalm 110:1; cf. Matthew 26:57–65; Mark 14:55–65).

Setting: By the Sea of Galilee (Tiberias). During His third post-resurrection appearance to His disciples, Jesus directs them to a great catch of fish following their unsuccessful night of fishing.

So Jesus said to them, "Children, you do not have any fish, do you?" They answered Him, "No." And He said to them, "Cast the net on the right-hand side of the boat and you will find a *catch*." So they cast, and then they were not able to haul it in because of the great number of fish (John 21:5, 6; see Luke 5:4).

Setting: On the island of Patmos (in the Aegean Sea about fifty miles southwest of Ephesus in modern Turkey). On the Lord's Day (Sunday), approximately fifty years after His resurrection, the disciple John encounters the Lord Jesus Christ, who communicates new revelations for the apostle to record for the seven churches in Asia.

When I saw Him, I fell at His feet like a dead man. And He placed His right hand on me, saying, "Do not be afraid; I am the first and the last, and the living One; and I was dead, and behold, I am alive forevermore, and I have the keys of death and of Hades. Therefore write the things which you have seen, and the things which are, and the things which will take place after these things. As for the mystery of the seven stars which you saw in My right hand, and the seven golden lampstands: the seven stars are the angels of the seven churches, and the seven lampstands are the seven churches" (Revelation 1:17–20; see Isaiah 44:6; Luke 24:5; Revelation 2:8).

Setting: On the island of Patmos (in the Aegean Sea about fifty miles southwest of Ephesus in modern Turkey). On the Lord's Day (Sunday), about fifty years after Jesus' resurrection, the disciple John encounters the Lord Jesus Christ, who communicates a new revelation for the apostle to record for the church at Ephesus and to six other churches in Asia.

"To the angel of the church in Ephesus write: The One who holds the seven stars in His right hand, the One who walks among the seven golden lampstands, says this: 'I know your deeds and your toil and perseverance, and that you cannot tolerate evil men, and you put to the test those who call themselves apostles, and they are not, and you found them *to be* false; and you have perseverance and have endured for My name's sake, and have not grown weary. But I have *this* against you, that you have left your first love. Therefore remember from where you have fallen, and repent and do the deeds you did at first; or else I am coming to you and will remove your lampstand out of its place—unless you repent. Yet this you do have, that you hate the deeds of the Nicolaitans, which I also hate. He who has an ear, let him hear what the Spirit says to the churches. To him who overcomes, I will grant to eat of the tree of life which is in the Paradise of God' " (Revelation 2:1–7; see Genesis 2:9; Ezekiel 28:13; 1 John 4:1; Revelation 1:10, 11, 19, 20; 2:15, 16).

HAND OF POWER, RIGHT (Listed under POWER, RIGHT HAND OF)

HAND WASHING (See WASHING)

HANDED, EMPTY (Listed under EMPTY-HANDED)

HANDICAPPED (See CRIPPLED; and LAME)

HANDKERCHIEF

Setting: Jericho, on the way to Jerusalem. After commending Zaccheus's faith in Him, Jesus provides a parable about stewardship.

So He said, "A nobleman went to a distant country to receive a kingdom for himself, and *then* return. And he called ten of his slaves, and gave them ten minas and said to them, 'Do business *with this* until I come *back.*' But his citizens hated him and sent a delegation after him, saying, 'We do not want this man to reign over us.' When he returned, after receiving the kingdom, he ordered that these slaves, to whom he had given the money, be called to him so that he might know what business they had done. The first appeared, saying, 'Master, your mina has made ten minas more.' And he said to him, 'Well done, good slave, because you have been faithful in a very little thing, you are to be in authority over ten cities.' The second came, saying, 'Your mina, master, has made five minas.' And he said to him, also, 'And you are to be over five cities.' Another came, saying, 'Master, here is your mina, which I kept put away in a handkerchief; for I was afraid of you, because you are an exacting man; you take up what you did not lay down and reap what you did not sow.' He said to him, 'By your own words I will judge you, you worthless slave. Did you know that I am an exacting man, taking up what I did not lay down and reaping what I did not sow? Then why did you not put my money in the bank, and having come, I would have collected it with interest?' Then he said to the bystanders, 'Take the mina away from him and give it to the one who has the ten minas.' And they said to him, 'Master, he has ten minas *already.*' I tell you that to everyone who has, more shall be given, but from the one who does not have, even what he does have shall be taken away. But these enemies of mine, who did not want me to reign over them, bring them here and slay them in my presence" (Luke 19:12–27; cf. Matthew 25:14–30; see Matthew 13:12; Luke 16:10).

HANDS (Specifics such as HANDS, TWO are separate entries; also see FINGER; and HAND)

Setting: In the area of Caesarea Philippi. Following the Transfiguration, coming down the mountain, Peter, James, and John ask Jesus why Elijah must come before the Messiah.

And He answered and said, "Elijah is coming and will restore all things; but I say to you that Elijah already came, and they did not recognize him, but did to him whatever they wished. So also the Son of Man is going to suffer at their hands" (Matthew 17:11, 12; cf. Mark 9:11–13).

Setting: Galilee. Following the Transfiguration, Jesus repeats to His disciples that He must suffer, die, and be raised.

And while they were gathering together in Galilee, Jesus said to them, "The Son of Man is going to be delivered into the hands of men; and they will kill Him, and He will be raised on the third day." And they were deeply grieved (Matthew 17:22, 23; cf. Matthew 16:21; Mark 9:30–32; Luke 9:44, 45).

Setting: Jerusalem. After celebrating the Passover meal with His disciples, Jesus retreats to the Garden of Gethsemane on the Mount of Olives to pray prior to His betrayal by Judas.

Then Jesus came with them to a place called Gethsemane, and said to His disciples, "Sit here while I go over there and pray." And He took with Him Peter and the two sons of Zebedee, and began to be grieved and distressed. Then He said to them, "My soul is deeply grieved, to the point of death; remain here and keep watch with Me." And He went a little beyond *them,* and fell on His face and prayed, saying, "My Father, if it is possible, let this cup pass from Me; yet not as I will, but as You will." And He came to the disciples and found them sleeping, and said to Peter, "So, you *men* could not keep watch with Me for one hour? Keep watching and praying that you may not enter into temptation; the spirit is willing, but the flesh is weak." He went away again a second time and prayed, saying, "My Father, if this cannot pass away unless I drink it, Your will be done." Again He came and found them sleeping, for their eyes were heavy. And He left them again, and went away and prayed a third time, saying the same thing once more. Then He came to the disciples and said to them, "Are you still sleeping and resting? Behold the hour is at hand and the Son of Man is being betrayed into the hands of sinners. Get up, let us be going; behold the one who betrays Me is at hand!" (Matthew 26:36–46; cf. Mark 14:32–42; Luke 22:40–46; see Matthew 20:22; John 12:27).

Setting: Galilee. After casting out an unclean spirit from a young boy, Jesus teaches His disciples in secret about His coming death and resurrection.

From there they went out and *began* to go through Galilee, and He did not want anyone to know *about it.* For He was teaching His disciples and telling them, "The Son of Man is to be delivered into the hands of men, and they will kill Him; and when He has been killed, He will rise three days later." But they did not understand *this* statement, and they were afraid to ask Him (Mark 9:30–32; cf. Matthew 17:22, 23; Luke 9:43–45; see Matthew 16:21).

Setting: Gethsemane on the Mount of Olives, east of the temple in Jerusalem. Jesus prepares to meet Judas the betrayer while His other disciples keep falling asleep instead of watching and praying with Him.

And He came the third time, and said to them, "Are you still sleeping and resting? It is enough; the hour has come; behold, the Son of Man is being betrayed into the hands of sinners. Get up, let us be going; behold, the one who betrays Me is at hand!" (Mark 14:41, 42; cf. Matthew 26:45, 46).

Setting: Following His resurrection from the dead after being crucified, Jesus commissions His disciples to preach His gospel to the world.

And He said to them, "Go into all the world and preach the gospel to all creation. He who has believed and has been baptized shall be saved; but he who has disbelieved shall be condemned. These signs will accompany those who have believed: in My name they will cast out demons, they will speak with new tongues; they will pick up serpents, and if they drink any deadly *poison,* it

will not hurt them; they will lay hands on the sick, and they will recover" (Mark 16:15–18; cf. Matthew 28:16–20; see Mark 9:38; John 3:18, 36; 1 Corinthians 15:6).

[Note: Some scholars question the authenticity of Mark 16:9–20, as these verses do not appear in some early New Testament manuscripts.]

Setting: Galilee. After healing the demon-possessed son of a man from the crowd, the Lord prophesies His death.

"Let these words sink into your ears; for the Son of Man is going to be delivered into the hands of men" (Luke 9:44; cf. Matthew 17:22, 23; Mark 9:31, 32).

Setting: The Mount of Olives, east of the temple in Jerusalem. After ministering in the temple a few days before His crucifixion, and giving His disciples more details regarding the temple's future destruction, Jesus elaborates during His Olivet Discourse about things to come.

Then He continued by saying to them, "Nation will rise against nation and kingdom against kingdom, and there will be great earthquakes, and in various places plagues and famines; and there will be terrors and great signs from heaven. But before all these things, they will lay their hands on you and will persecute you, delivering you to the synagogues and prisons, bringing you before kings and governors for My name's sake. It will lead to an opportunity for your testimony. So make up your minds not to prepare beforehand to defend yourselves; for I will give you utterance and wisdom which none of your opponents will be able to resist or refute. But you will be betrayed even by parents and brothers and relatives and friends, and they will put *some* of you to death, and you will be hated by all because of My name. Yet not a hair of your head will perish. By your endurance you will gain your lives" (Luke 21:10–19; cf. Matthew 10:19–22; 24:7–14; Mark 13:8–13).

Setting: Golgotha (Calvary), just outside Jerusalem. While being mocked and ridiculed on the cross, after granting forgiveness to one of the criminals being crucified with Him who asks to be remembered in His kingdom, Jesus dies.

And Jesus, crying out with a loud voice, said, "Father, INTO YOUR HANDS I COMMIT MY SPIRIT." Having said this, He breathed His last (Luke 23:46, Jesus quotes from Psalm 31:5; cf. Matthew 27:45–50; Mark 15:33–37; John 19:28–30).

Setting: Jerusalem. After rising from the grave on the third day after being crucified, and appearing to two of His followers on the road to Emmaus, Jesus appears to His disciples (except Thomas).

While they were telling these things, He Himself stood in their midst and said to them, "Peace be to you." But they were startled and frightened and thought they were seeing a spirit. And He said to them, "Why are you troubled, and why do doubts arise in your hearts? See My hands and My feet, that it is I Myself; touch Me and see, for a spirit does not have flesh and bones as you see that I have." And when He had said this, He showed them His hands and His feet. While they still could not believe *it* because of their joy and amazement. He said to them, "Have you anything to eat?" They gave Him a piece of a broiled fish; and He took it and ate *it* before them (Luke 24:36–43; see Mark 16:14; John 20:27; Acts 10:40, 41).

Setting: Jerusalem. The risen Jesus meets with His disciple Thomas (Didymus), who had doubts about the other disciples' testimony claiming to have seen and spoken with the Lord eight days earlier.

After eight days His disciples were again inside, and Thomas with them. Jesus came, the doors having been shut, and stood in their midst and said, "Peace *be* with you." Then He said to Thomas, "Reach here with your finger, and see My hands; and reach here your hand and put it into My side; and do not be unbelieving, but believing." Thomas answered and said to Him, "My Lord and my God!" Jesus said to him, "Because you have seen Me, have you believed? Blessed *are* they who did not see, and *yet* believed" (John 20:26–29; see Luke 24:36, 40; 1 Peter 1:8).

Setting: By the Sea of Galilee. During the Lord's third post-resurrection appearance to His disciples, after quizzing Peter regarding his love for Him, Jesus gives this disciple details about his aging and eventual death

"Truly, truly, I say to you, when you were younger, you used to gird yourself and walk wherever you wished; but when you grow old, you will stretch out your hands and someone else will gird you, and bring you where you do not wish to *go*." Now this He said, signifying by what kind of death he would glorify God. And when He had spoken this, He said to him, "Follow Me!" (John 21:18, 19).

HANDS, LAYING ON OF

[LAYING ON OF HANDS from lay hands on]
Setting: Following His resurrection from the dead after being crucified, Jesus commissions His disciples to preach His gospel to the world.

And He said to them, "Go into all the world and preach the gospel to all creation. He who has believed and has been baptized shall be saved; but he who has disbelieved shall be condemned. These signs will accompany those who have believed: in My name they will cast out demons, they will speak with new tongues; they will pick up serpents, and if they drink any deadly *poison*, it will not hurt them; they will lay hands on the sick, and they will recover" (Mark 16:15–18; cf. Matthew 28:16–20; see Mark 9:38; John 3:18, 36; 1 Corinthians 15:6).

[Note: Some scholars question the authenticity of Mark 16:9–20, as these verses do not appear in some early New Testament manuscripts.]

[LAYING ON OF HANDS from lay hands on]
Setting: On the Mount of Olives, east of the temple in Jerusalem. After praying for deliverance, with His crucifixion imminent, Jesus chastises the religious leaders after Judas betrays Him and the hostile crowd surround Him.

Then Jesus said to the chief priests and officers of the temple and elders who had come against Him, "Have you come out with swords and clubs as you would against a robber? While I was with you daily in the temple, you did not lay hands on Me; but this hour and the power of darkness are yours" (Luke 22:52, 53; cf. Matthew 26:47–56; Mark 14:43–50).

[LAYING ON OF HANDS from lay his hands on him]
Setting: Damascus. Luke, writing in Acts, conveys how the Lord Jesus instructs one of His disciples, Ananias, to locate Saul of Tarsus to touch him in order to restore his vision.

Now there was a disciple at Damascus named Ananias; and the Lord said to him in a vision, "Ananias." And he said, "Here I am, Lord." And the Lord *said* to him, "Get up and go to the street called Straight, and inquire at the house of Judas for a man from Tarsus named Saul, for he is praying, and he was seen in a vision a man named Ananias come in and lay his hands on him, so that he might regain his sight" (Acts 9:10–12; see Acts 22:12–14).

HANDS, ROBBERS'

Setting: On the way from Galilee to Jerusalem. While being tested by a lawyer, Jesus tells him the story of the good Samaritan.

Jesus replied and said, "A man was going down from Jerusalem to Jericho, and fell among robbers, and they stripped him and beat him, and went away leaving him half dead. And by chance a priest was going down on that road, and when he saw him, he passed by on the other side. Likewise a Levite also, when he came to the place and saw him, passed by on the other side. But a Samaritan, who was on a journey, came upon him; and when he saw him, he felt compassion, and came to him and bandaged up his wounds, pouring oil and wine on *them;* and he put him on his own beast, and brought him to an inn and took care of him. On the next day he took out two denarii and gave them to the innkeeper and said, 'Take care of him; and whatever more you spend, when I return I will repay you.' Which of these three do you think proved to be a neighbor to the man who fell into the robbers' *hands?*" And he said, "The one who showed mercy toward him." Then Jesus said to him, "Go and do the same" (Luke 10:30–37).

HANDS, TWO

Setting: Capernaum of Galilee. Jesus elaborates about stumbling blocks after His disciples ask about greatness in the kingdom of heaven.

"Woe to the world because of *its* stumbling blocks! For it is inevitable that stumbling blocks come; but woe to that man through whom the stumbling block comes! If your hand or your foot causes you to stumble, cut it off and throw it from you; it is better for you to enter life crippled or lame, than to have two hands or two feet and be cast into the eternal fire. If your eye causes you to stumble, pluck it out and throw it from you. It is better for you to enter life with one eye, than to have two eyes and be cast into the fiery hell" (Matthew 18:7–9; cf. Matthew 5:29, 30; Mark 9:43–48; Luke 17:1).

Setting: Capernaum of Galilee. As Jesus teaches His disciples in private, they ask Him about greatness.

But Jesus said, "Do not hinder him, for there is no one who will perform a miracle in My name, and be able soon afterward to speak evil of Me. For he who is not against us is for us. For whoever gives you a cup of water to drink because of your name as *followers* of Christ, truly I say to you, he will not lose his reward. Whoever causes one of these little ones who believe to stumble, it would be better for him if, with a heavy millstone hung around his neck, he had been cast into the sea. If your hand causes you to stumble, cut it off; it is better for you to enter life crippled, than, having your two hands, to go into hell, into the unquenchable fire, [where THEIR WORM DOES NOT DIE, AND THE FIRE IS NOT QUENCHED.] If your foot causes you to stumble, cut it off; it is better for you to enter life lame, than, having your two feet, to be cast into hell, [where THEIR WORM DOES NOT DIE, AND THE FIRE IS NOT QUENCHED.] If your eye causes you to stumble, throw it out; it is better for you to enter the kingdom of God with one eye, than, having two eyes, to be cast into hell, where THEIR WORM DOES NOT DIE, AND THE FIRE IS NOT QUENCHED. For everyone will be salted with fire. Salt is good; but if the salt becomes unsalty, with what will you make it salty *again?* Have salt in yourselves, and be at peace with one another" (Mark 9:39–50; Jesus quotes from Isaiah 66:24; cf. Matthew 18:6–9; Luke 9:49–50; see Matthew 5:13, 29, 30; 10:42; 12:30; 8:5, 6).

HANDS, UNWASHED

Setting: Galilee. Jesus explains the meaning of His instruction to the crowd about what defiles a man.

Peter said to Him, "Explain the parable to us." Jesus said, "Are you still lacking in understanding also? Do you not understand that everything that goes into the mouth passes into the stomach and is eliminated? But the things that proceed out of the mouth come from the heart, and those defile the man. For out of the heart come evil thoughts, murders, adulteries, fornications, thefts, false witness, slanders. These are the things which defile a man; but to eat with unwashed hands does not defile the man" (Matthew 15:15–20; cf. Mark 7:18–23; see Galatians 5:19–21).

HANDS OF MEN (Listed under MEN, HANDS OF; also see HANDS)

HANDS OF SINNERS (Listed under SINNERS, HANDS OF; also see HANDS)

HAPPINESS (See BLESSED; FULFILLMENT; GLADNESS; and SATISFACTION)

HARD TIMES (See PERSECUTION; SUFFERING; TRIBULATION; and TROUBLE)

HARDNESS OF HEART (Listed under HEART, HARDNESS OF)

HARDSHIP (See MINISTRY, DIFFICULTIES IN; PERSECUTION; SUFFERING; TRIBULATION; and TROUBLE)

HARM

Setting: A synagogue in Galilee. Early in His ministry, Jesus heals a man's withered hand on the Sabbath while the Pharisees observe.

He said to the man with the withered hand, "Get up and come forward!" And He said to them, "Is it lawful to do good or do harm on the Sabbath, to save a life or to kill?" But they kept silent. After looking around at them with anger, grieved at their hardness of heart, He said to the man, "Stretch out your hand." And he stretched it out, and his hand was restored (Mark 3:3–5; cf. Matthew 12:9–14; Luke 6:6–11).

Setting: A synagogue in Galilee. As Jesus teaches on the Sabbath, the scribes and Pharisees watch to see if He heals a man's withered hand.

But He knew what they were thinking, and He said to the man with the withered hand, "Get up and come forward!" And he got up and came forward. And Jesus said to them, "I ask you, is it lawful to do good or to do harm on the Sabbath, to save a life or destroy it?" And looking around at them all, He said to him, "Stretch out your hand!" And he did *so;* and his hand was restored (Luke 6:8–10; cf. Matthew 12:9–13; Mark 3:1–5).

Setting: Corinth. Luke, writing in Acts, records the Lord Jesus' comforting revelation through a vision to Paul during his second missionary journey as he works among the Jews and Gentiles, testifying that Jesus is the Christ (Messiah).

And the Lord said to Paul in the night by a vision, "Do not be afraid *any longer,* but go on speaking and do not be silent; for I am with you, and no man will attack you in order to harm you, for I have many people in this city" (Acts 18:9, 10).

HARVEST (HARVEST, LORD OF THE and HARVEST TIME are separate entries; also see CROP; CROPS; GATHERING; GREAT COMMISSION; PRODUCE; REAPERS; REAPING; SEED; and SOWING)

Setting: Villages and cities in Galilee. While healing the sick, raising the dead, and casting out demons, Jesus comments on the enormity of the task and the need to ask the Lord of the harvest for additional workers.

Then He said to His disciples, "The harvest is plentiful, but the workers are few. Therefore beseech the Lord of the harvest to send out workers into His harvest" (Matthew 9:37, 38; cf. Luke 10:2).

Setting: By the Sea of Galilee. Because the religious leaders are rejecting His message, Jesus continues teaching the crowds with the Parable of the Wheat and the Tares.

Jesus presented another parable to them, saying, "The kingdom of heaven may be compared to a man who sowed good seed in his field. But while his men were sleeping, his enemy came and sowed tares among the wheat, and went away. But when the wheat sprouted and bore grain, then the tares became evident also. The slaves of the landowner came and said to him, 'Sir, did you not sow good seed in your field? How then does it have tares?' And he said to them, 'An enemy has done this!' The slaves said to him, 'Do you want us, then, to go and gather them up?' But he said, 'No; for while you are gathering up the tares, you may uproot the wheat with them. Allow both to grow together until the harvest; and in the time of the harvest I will say to the reapers, "First gather up the tares and bind them in bundles to burn them up; but gather the wheat into my barn"'" (Matthew 13:24–30; cf. Matthew 3:12).

Setting: A house near the Sea of Galilee. Jesus explains the meaning of the Parable of the Wheat and the Tares to His disciples.

And He said, "The one who sows the good seed is the Son of Man, and the field is the world; and as *for* the good seed, these are the sons of the kingdom; and the tares are the sons of the evil *one;* and the enemy who sowed them is the devil, and the harvest is the end of the age; and the reapers are angels. So just as the tares are gathered up and burned with fire, so shall it be at the end of the age. The Son of Man will send forth His angels, and they will gather out of His kingdom all stumbling blocks, and those who commit lawlessness, and will throw them into the furnace of fire; in that place there will be weeping and gnashing of teeth. Then THE RIGHTEOUS WILL SHINE FORTH AS THE SUN in the kingdom of their Father. He who has ears, let him hear" (Matthew 13:37–43, Jesus quotes from Daniel 12:3; cf. Matthew 8:12; 13:50).

Setting: Galilee. Following His explanation of the Parable of the Sower to His disciples, Jesus conveys the Parable of the Seed.

And He was saying, "The kingdom of God is like a man who casts seed upon the soil; and he goes to bed at night and gets up by day, and the seed sprouts and grows—how, he himself does not know. The soil produces crops by itself; first the blade, then the head, then the mature grain in the head. But when the crop permits, he immediately puts in the sickle, because the harvest has come" (Mark 4:26–29; see Joel 3:13).

Setting: On the way from Galilee to Jerusalem. The Lord appoints seventy followers and sends them out in pairs to every place He Himself will soon visit.

And He was saying to them, "The harvest is plentiful, but the laborers are few; therefore beseech the Lord of the harvest to send out laborers into His harvest. Go; behold, I send you out as lambs in the midst of wolves. Carry no money belt, no bag, no shoes; and greet no one on the way. Whatever house you enter, first say, 'Peace be to this house.' If a man of peace is there, your peace will rest on him; but if not, it will return to you. Stay in that house, eating and drinking what they give you; for the laborer is worthy of his wages. Do not keep moving from house to house. Whatever city you enter and they receive you, eat what is set before you; and heal those in it who are sick, and say to them, 'The kingdom of God has come near to you.' But whatever city you enter and they do not receive you, go out into its streets and say, 'Even the dust of your city which clings to our feet we wipe off *in protest* against you; yet be sure of this, that the kingdom of God has come near.' I say to you, it will be more tolerable in that day for Sodom than for that city" (Luke 10:2–12; see Genesis 19:24–28; Matthew 9:37, 38, 10:9–14, 16; 1 Corinthians 10:27).

Setting: Sychar in Samaria. After Jesus converses with a Samaritan woman at Jacob's well, His disciples return with food. They try to get Jesus to eat but are surprised when He speaks of other food.

Jesus said to them, "My food is to do the will of Him who sent Me and to accomplish His work. Do you not say, 'There are yet four months, and *then* comes the harvest'? Behold, I say to you, lift up your eyes and look on the fields, that they are white for harvest. Already he who reaps is receiving wages and is gathering fruit for life eternal; so that he who sows and he who reaps may rejoice together. For in this *case* the saying is true, 'One sows and another reaps.' I sent you to reap that for which you have not labored; others have labored and you have entered into their labor" (John 4:34–38; see Matthew 9:37, 38; John 5:36).

HARVEST, LORD OF THE (Also see GREAT COMMISSION; and HARVEST)

Setting: The villages and cities of Galilee. While healing the sick, raising the dead, and casting out demons, Jesus comments on the enormity of the task and the need to ask the Lord of the harvest for additional workers.

Then He said to His disciples, "The harvest is plentiful, but the workers are few. Therefore beseech the Lord of the harvest to send out workers into His harvest" (Matthew 9:37, 38; cf. Luke 10:2).

Setting: On the way from Galilee to Jerusalem. The Lord appoints seventy followers and sends them out in pairs to every place He Himself will soon visit.

And He was saying to them, "The harvest is plentiful, but the laborers are few; therefore beseech the Lord of the harvest to send out laborers into His harvest. Go; behold, I send you out as lambs in the midst of wolves. Carry no money belt, no bag, no shoes; and greet no one on the way. Whatever house you enter, first say, 'Peace be to this house.' If a man of peace is there, your peace will rest on him; but if not, it will return to you. Stay in that house, eating and drinking what they give you; for the laborer is worthy of his wages. Do not keep moving from house to house. Whatever city you enter and they receive you, eat what is set before you; and heal those in it who are sick, and say to them, 'The kingdom of God has come near to you.' But whatever city you enter and they do not receive you, go out into its streets and say, 'Even the dust of your city which clings to our feet we wipe off *in protest* against you; yet be sure of this, that the kingdom of God has come near.' I say to you, it will be more tolerable in that day for Sodom than for that city" (Luke 10:2–12; see Genesis 19:24–28; Matthew 9:37, 38, 10:9–14, 16; 1 Corinthians 10:27).

HARVEST TIME (Also see HARVEST)

[HARVEST TIME from time of the harvest]

Setting: By the Sea of Galilee. Because the religious leaders are rejecting His message, Jesus continues teaching the crowds with the Parable of the Wheat and the Tares.

Jesus presented another parable to them, saying, "The kingdom of heaven may be compared to a man who sowed good seed in his field. But while his men were sleeping, his enemy came and sowed tares among the wheat, and went away. But when the wheat sprouted and bore grain, then the tares became evident also. The slaves of the landowner came and said to him, 'Sir, did you not sow good seed in your field? How then does it have tares?' And he said to them, 'An enemy has done this!' The slaves said to him, 'Do you want us, then, to go and gather them up?' But he said, 'No; for while you are gathering up the tares, you may uproot the wheat with them. Allow both to grow together until the harvest; and in the time of the harvest I will say to the reapers, "First gather up the tares and bind them in bundles to burn them up; but gather the wheat into my barn"'" (Matthew 13:24–30; cf. Matthew 3:12).

Setting: The temple in Jerusalem. Jesus delivers another parable to the chief priests and elders after they question His authority.

"Listen to another parable. There was a landowner who PLANTED A VINEYARD AND PUT A WALL AROUND IT AND DUG A WINE PRESS IN IT, AND BUILT A TOWER, and rented it out to vine-growers and went on a journey. When the harvest time approached, he sent his slaves to the vine-growers to receive his produce. The vine-growers took his slaves and beat one, and killed another, and stoned a third. Again he sent another group of slaves larger than the first; and they did the same thing to them. But afterward he sent his son to them, saying, 'They will respect my son.' But when the vine-growers saw the son, they said among themselves, 'This is the heir; come, let us kill him and seize his inheritance.' They took him, and threw him out of the vineyard and killed him. Therefore when the owner of the vineyard comes, what will he do to those vine-growers?" (Matthew 21:33–40; Jesus quotes from Isaiah 5:1, 2; cf. Mark 12:1–9; Luke 20:9–15).

Setting: The temple in Jerusalem. Having His authority questioned by the chief priests, scribes, and elders, Jesus begins to teach them in parables.

And He began to speak to them in parables: "A man PLANTED A VINEYARD AND PUT A WALL AROUND IT, AND DUG A VAT UNDER THE WINE PRESS AND BUILT A TOWER, and rented it out to vine-growers and went on a journey. At the *harvest* time he sent a slave to the vine-growers, in order to receive *some* of the produce of the vineyard from the vine-growers. They took him, and beat him and sent him away empty-handed. Again he sent them another slave, and they wounded him in the head, and treated him shamefully. And he sent another, and that one they killed; and *so with* many others, beating some and killing others. He had one more to *send*, a beloved son; he sent him last *of all* to them, saying, 'They will respect my son.' But those vine-growers said to one another, 'This is the heir; come, let us kill him, and the inheritance will be ours!' They took him, and killed him and threw him out of the vineyard. What will the owner of the vineyard do? He will come and destroy the vine-growers, and will give the vineyard to others. Have you not even read this Scripture: 'THE STONE WHICH THE BUILDERS REJECTED, THIS BECAME THE CHIEF CORNER *stone;* THIS CAME ABOUT FROM THE LORD, AND IT IS MARVELOUS IN OUR EYES'?" (Mark 12:1–11, Jesus quotes from Psalm 118:22, 23; Isaiah 5:1, 2; cf. Matthew 21:33–46; Luke 20:9–19).

Setting: The temple in Jerusalem. While ministering a few days before His crucifixion, after the chief priests and the scribes question His authority to teach and preach, Jesus conveys the Parable of the Vine-Growers to the people.

And He began to tell the people this parable: "A man planted a vineyard and rented it out to vine-growers, and went on a journey for a long time. At the *harvest* time he sent a slave to the vine-growers, so that they would give him *some* of the produce of the vineyard; but the vine-growers beat him and sent him away empty-handed. And he proceeded to send another slave; and they beat him also and treated him shamefully and sent him away empty-handed. And he proceeded to send a third; and this one also they wounded and cast out. The owner of the vineyard said, 'What shall I do? I will send my beloved son; perhaps they will respect him.' But when the vine-growers saw him, they reasoned with one another, saying, 'This is the heir; let us kill him so that the inheritance will be ours.' So they threw him out of the vineyard and killed him. What, then, will the owner of the vineyard do to them? He will come and destroy these vine-growers and will give the vineyard to others." When they heard it, they said, "May it never be!" But Jesus looked at them and said, "What then is this that is written: 'THE STONE WHICH THE BUILDERS REJECTED, THIS BECAME THE CHIEF CORNER *stone*'? Everyone who falls on that stone will be broken to pieces; but on whomever it falls, it will scatter him like dust" (Luke 20:9–18, Jesus quotes from Psalm 118:22; cf. Matthew 21:33–44; Mark 12:1–11; see Ephesians 2:20).

HARVESTING GRAIN (Listed under GRAIN, HARVESTING)

HATE (Also see other emotions such as ANGER; ENVY; and JEALOUSY)

Setting: Galilee. During the early part of His ministry, Jesus preaches the Sermon on the Mount to His disciples and the multitudes.

"You have heard that it was said, 'YOU SHALL LOVE YOUR NEIGHBOR and hate your enemy.' But I say to you, love your enemies and pray for those who persecute you, so that you may be sons of your Father who is in heaven; for He causes His sun to rise on *the* evil and *the* good, and sends rain on *the* righteous and *the* unrighteous. For if you love those who love you, what reward do you have? Do not even the tax collectors do the same? If you greet only your brothers, what more are you doing *than others?* Do not even the Gentiles do the same? Therefore, you are to be perfect, as your heavenly Father is perfect" (Matthew 5:43–48, Jesus quotes from Leviticus 19:18; cf. Leviticus 19:2; Luke 6:27–36).

Setting: Galilee. During the early part of His ministry, Jesus preaches the Sermon on the Mount to His disciples and the multitudes.

"No one can serve two masters; for either he will hate the one and love the other, or he will be devoted to one and despise the other. You cannot serve God and wealth (Matthew 6:24).

[HATE from hated]

Setting: Galilee. After His disciples observe His ministry, Jesus summons and specifically instructs them about the upcoming difficulties of *their* ministry to the people of Israel.

"Brother will betray brother to death, and a father *his* child; and children will rise up against parents and cause them to be put to death. You will be hated by all because of My name, but it is the one who has endured to the end who will be saved. But whenever they persecute you in one city, flee to the next; for truly I say to you, you will not finish *going through* the cities of Israel until the Son of Man comes" (Matthew 10:21–23; cf. Matthew 10:35, 36; 16:27, 28; 24:9).

Setting: The Mount of Olives, just east of Jerusalem. During His discourse, Jesus answers His disciples' questions as to when the temple will be destroyed and Jerusalem overrun, along with the signs of His coming and the end of the age.

And Jesus answered and said to them, "See to it that no one misleads you. For many will come in My name, saying, 'I am the Christ,' and will mislead many. You will be hearing of wars and rumors of wars. See that you are not frightened, for *those things* must take place, but *that* is not yet the end. For nation will rise against nation, and kingdom against kingdom, and in various places there will be famines and earthquakes. But all these things are *merely* the beginning of birth pangs. Then they will deliver you to tribulation, and will kill you, and you will be hated by all nations because of My name. At that time many will fall away and will betray one another and hate one another. Many false prophets will arise and will mislead many. Because lawlessness is increased, most people's love will grow cold. But the one who endures to the end, he will be saved. This gospel of the kingdom shall be preached in the whole world as a testimony to all the nations, and then the end will come" (Matthew 24:4–14; cf. Jeremiah 29:8; Matthew 7:15; 10:17, 22; Mark 13:3–13; Luke 21:7–19; Revelation 6:4).

[HATE from hated]

Setting: On the Mount of Olives, east of the temple in Jerusalem. After predicting the temple's destruction, Jesus responds during His Olivet Discourse to questions from Peter, James, John, and Andrew about future events.

And Jesus began to say to them, "See to it that no one misleads you. Many will come in My name, saying, 'I am *He!*' and will mislead many. When you hear of wars and rumors of wars, do not be frightened; *those things* must take place; but *that is* not yet the end. For nation will rise up against nation, and kingdom against kingdom; there will be earthquakes in various places; there will *also be* famines. These things are *merely* the beginning of birth pangs. But be on your guard; for they will deliver you to *the* courts, and you will be flogged in *the* synagogues, and you will stand before governors and kings for My sake, as a testimony to them. The gospel must first be preached to all the nations. When they arrest you and hand you over, do not worry beforehand about what you are to say, but say whatever is given you in that hour; for it is not you who speak, but *it is* the Holy Spirit. Brother will betray brother to death, and a father *his* child; and children will rise up against parents and have them put to death. You will be hated by all because of My name, but the one who endures to the end, he will be saved" (Mark 13:5–13; cf. Matthew 24:4–14; Luke 21:7–19; see Matthew 10:17–22).

Setting: Galilee. After selecting His twelve disciples, Jesus teaches the Beatitudes (part of the Sermon on the Mount) to those disciples and a great throng of people from Judea, Jerusalem, and the central coastal region of Tyre and Sidon.

"Blessed are you when men hate you, and ostracize you, and insult you, and scorn your name as evil, for the sake of the Son of Man. Be glad in that day and leap *for joy*, for behold, your reward is great in heaven. For in the same way their fathers used to treat the prophets" (Luke 6:22, 23; cf. Matthew 5:10–12; see 2 Chronicles 36:16).

Setting: Galilee. After selecting His twelve disciples, Jesus teaches the Beatitudes (part of the Sermon on the Mount) to those disciples and a great throng of people from Judea, Jerusalem, and the central coastal region of Tyre and Sidon.

"But I say to you who hear, love your enemies, do good to those who hate you, bless those who curse you, pray for those who mistreat you. Whoever hits you on the cheek, offer him the other also; and whoever takes away your coat, do not withhold your shirt from him either. Give to everyone who asks of you, and whoever takes away what is yours, do not demand it back. Treat others the same way you want them to treat you. If you love those who love you, what credit is *that* to you? For even sinners love those who love them. If you do good to those who do good to you, what credit is *that* to you? For even sinners do the same. If you lend to those from whom you expect to receive, what credit is *that* to you? Even sinners lend to sinners in order to receive back the same *amount*. But love your enemies, and do good, and lend, expecting nothing in return; and your reward will be great, and you will be sons of the Most High; for He Himself is kind to ungrateful and evil *men*. Be merciful, just as your Father is merciful" (Luke 6:27–36; cf. Matthew 5:9, 39–48; 7:12).

Setting: On the way from Galilee to Jerusalem. After He responds to a guest's proclamation about the blessings of eating bread in the kingdom of God, Jesus presents to large crowds the demands of discipleship.

Now large crowds were going along with Him; and He turned and said to them, "If anyone comes to Me, and does not hate his own father and mother and wife and children and brothers and sisters, yes, and even his own life, he cannot be My disciple. Whoever does not carry his own cross and come after Me cannot be My disciple. For which one of you, when he wants to build a tower, does not first sit down and calculate the cost to see if he has enough to complete it? Otherwise, when he has laid a foundation and is not able to finish, all who observe it begin to ridicule him, saying, 'This man began to build and was not able to finish.' Or what king, when he sets out to meet another king in battle, will not first sit down and consider whether he is strong enough with ten thousand *men* to encounter the one coming against him with twenty thousand? Or else, while the other is still far away, he

sends a delegation and asks for terms of peace. So then, none of you can be My disciple who does not give up all his possessions. Therefore, salt is good; but if even salt has become tasteless, with what will it be seasoned? It is useless either for the soil or for the manure pile; it is thrown out. He who has ears to hear, let him hear" (Luke 14:25–35; cf. Matthew 5:13; 10:37–39; see Proverbs 20:18; Philippians 3:7).

Setting: On the way from Galilee to Jerusalem. The Lord teaches His disciples about stewardship after giving them the story of the prodigal son.

Now He was also saying to the disciples, "There was a rich man who had a manager, and this *manager* was reported to him as squandering his possessions. And he called him and said to him, 'What is this I hear about you? Give an accounting of your management, for you can no longer be a manager.' The manager said to himself, 'What shall I do, since my master is taking the management away from me? I am not strong enough to dig; I am ashamed to beg. I know what I shall do, so that when I am removed from the management people will welcome me into their homes.' And he summoned each one of his master's debtors, and he *began* saying to the first, 'How much do you owe my master?' And he said, 'A hundred measures of oil.' And he said to him, 'Take your bill, and sit down quickly and write fifty.' Then he said to another, 'And how much do you owe?' And he said, 'A hundred measures of wheat.' He said to him, 'Take your bill, and write eighty.' And his master praised the unrighteous manager because he had acted shrewdly; for the sons of this age are more shrewd in relation to their own kind than the sons of light. And I say to you, make friends for yourselves by means of the wealth of unrighteousness, so that when it fails, they will receive you into the eternal dwellings. He who is faithful in a very little thing is faithful also in much; and he who is unrighteous in a very little thing is unrighteous also in much. Therefore if you have not been faithful in the *use of* unrighteous wealth, who will entrust the *true riches* to you? And if you have not been faithful in *the use of* that which is another's, who will give you that which is your own? No servant can serve two masters; for either he will hate the one and love the other, or else he will be devoted to one and despise the other. You cannot serve God and wealth" (Luke 16:1–13; cf. Matthew 6:24; see Matthew 25:14–30).

[HATE from hated]
Setting: Jericho, on the way to Jerusalem. After commending Zaccheus's faith in Him, Jesus provides a parable about stewardship.

So He said, "A nobleman went to a distant country to receive a kingdom for himself, and *then* return. And he called ten of his slaves, and gave them ten minas and said to them, 'Do business *with this* until I come *back.*' But his citizens hated him and sent a delegation after him, saying, 'We do not want this man to reign over us.' When he returned, after receiving the kingdom, he ordered that these slaves, to whom he had given the money, be called to him so that he might know what business they had done. The first appeared, saying, 'Master, your mina has made ten minas more.' And he said to him, 'Well done, good slave, because you have been faithful in a very little thing, you are to be in authority over ten cities.' The second came, saying, 'Your mina, master, has made five minas.' And he said to him, also, 'And you are to be over five cities.' Another came, saying, 'Master, here is your mina, which I kept put away in a handkerchief; for I was afraid of you, because you are an exacting man; you take up what you did not lay down and reap what you did not sow.' He said to him, 'By your own words I will judge you, you worthless slave. Did you know that I am an exacting man, taking up what I did not lay down and reaping what I did not sow? Then why did you not put my money in the bank, and having come, I would have collected it with interest?' Then he said to the bystanders, 'Take the mina away from him and give it to the one who has the ten minas.' And they said to him, 'Master, he has ten minas *already.*' I tell you that to everyone who has, more shall be given, but from the one who does not have, even what he does have shall be taken away. But these enemies of mine, who did not want me to reign over them, bring them here and slay them in my presence" (Luke 19:12–27; cf. Matthew 25:14–30; see Matthew 13:12; Luke 16:10).

[HATE from hated]
Setting: The Mount of Olives, east of the temple in Jerusalem. After giving His disciples more details about the temple's coming destruction, Jesus elaborates during His Olivet Discourse about other future events.

Then He continued by saying to them, "Nation will rise against nation and kingdom against kingdom, and there will be great earthquakes, and in various places plagues and famines; and there will be terrors and great signs from heaven. But before all these things, they will lay their hands on you and will persecute you, delivering you to the synagogues and prisons, bringing you before kings and governors for My name's sake. It will lead to an opportunity for your testimony. So make up your minds not to prepare beforehand to defend yourselves; for I will give you utterance and wisdom which none of your opponents will be able to resist or refute. But you will be betrayed even by parents and brothers and relatives and friends, and they will put *some* of you to death, and you will be hated by all because of My name. Yet not a hair of your head will perish. By your endurance you will gain your lives" (Luke 21:10–19; cf. Matthew 10:19–22; 24:7–14; Mark 13:8–13).

[HATE from hates]
Setting: Jerusalem. At the time for the Passover of the Jews, after the Lord cleanses the temple, a Pharisee, Nicodemus, asks Him by night the meaning of "born again."

"For God so loved the world, that He gave His only begotten Son, that whoever believes in Him shall not perish, but have eternal life. For God did not send the Son into the world to judge the world, but that the world might be saved through Him. He who believes in Him is not judged; he who does not believe has been judged already, because he has not believed in the name of the only begotten Son of God. This is the judgment, that the Light has come into the world, and men loved darkness rather than the Light, for their deeds were evil. For everyone who does evil hates the Light, and does not come to the Light for fear that his deeds will be exposed. But he who practices the truth comes to the Light, so that his deeds may be manifested as having been wrought in God" (John 3:16–21; see Luke 19:10; John 1:4; 1:18; Romans 5:8; 1 John 1:6, 7).

Setting: Capernaum of Galilee. Jesus' blood brothers, who do not yet believe in Him, encourage Him to attend the upcoming Feast of Booths in Jerusalem in order to demonstrate His works to His disciples and the world.

So Jesus said to them, "My time is not yet here, but your time is always opportune. The world cannot hate you, but it hates Me because I testify of it, that its deeds are evil. Go up to the feast yourselves; I do not go up to this feast because My time has not yet fully come" (John 7:6–8; see John 3:19, 20; 15:18–20).

[HATE from hates]
Setting: Jerusalem. Just days before the Passover, with the chief priests and Pharisees plotting to seize Him, crowds welcome Jesus to Jerusalem with palm branches and praise, and some Greeks ask to meet Him.

And Jesus answered them, saying, "The hour has come for the Son of Man to be glorified. Truly, truly, I say to you, unless a grain of wheat falls into the earth and dies, it remains alone; but if it dies, it bears much fruit. He who loves his life loses it, and he who hates his life in this world will keep it to life eternal. If anyone serves Me, he must follow Me; and where I am, there My servant will be also; if anyone serves Me, the Father will honor him" (John 12:23–26; see Matthew 10:39).

[HATE from hates]
Setting: Jerusalem. Before the Passover, with His departure in mind, after explaining He is the vine and His disciples are the branches, Jesus prepares them for persecution from the world.

"If the world hates you, you know that it has hated Me before *it hated* you. If you were of the world, the world would love its own; but because you are not of the world, but I chose you out of the world, because of this the world hates you. Remember the word that I said to you, 'A slave is not greater than his master.' If they persecuted Me, they will also persecute you; if they kept My word, they will keep yours also. But all these things they will do to you for My name's sake, because they do not know the One who sent Me. If I had not come and spoken to them, they would not have sin, but now they have no excuse for their sin" (John 15:18–22; see Matthew 10:22; John 7:7; 8:19, 55; 9:41; 1 Corinthians 4:12).

[HATE from hates and hated]
Setting: Jerusalem. Before the Passover, with His departure in mind, after explaining He is the vine and His disciples are the branches, Jesus prepares them for hatred by the world.

"He who hates Me hates My Father also. If I had not done among them the works which no one else did, they would not have sin;

but now they have both seen and hated Me and My Father as well. But *they have done this* to fulfill the word that is written in their Law, 'THEY HATED ME WITHOUT A CAUSE'" (John 15:23–25, Jesus quotes from Psalm 35:19; see John 9:41).

[HATE from hated]

Setting: Jerusalem. Before the Passover, after giving His disciples assurance that in the midst of tribulation they will have His peace, Jesus continues praying His high-priestly prayer.

"But now I come to You; and these things I speak in the world so that they may have My joy made full in themselves. I have given them Your word; and the world has hated them, because they are not of the world, even as I am not of the world. I do not ask You to take them out of the world, but to keep them from the evil *one.* They are not of the world, even as I am not of the world. Sanctify them in the truth; Your word is truth. As You sent Me into the world, I also have sent them into the world. For their sakes I sanctify Myself, that they themselves also may be sanctified in truth. I do not ask on behalf of these alone, but for those also who believe in Me through their word; that they may all be one; even as You, Father, *are* in Me and I in You, that they also maybe in Us, so that the world may believe that You sent Me" (John 17:13–21; see Matthew 10:5, 38; John 7:33; 15:3, 11, 19).

Setting: On the island of Patmos (in the Aegean Sea about fifty miles southwest of Ephesus in modern Turkey). On the Lord's Day (Sunday), about fifty years after Jesus' resurrection, the disciple John encounters the Lord Jesus Christ, who communicates a new revelation for the apostle to record for the church in Ephesus and to six other churches in Asia.

"To the angel of the church in Ephesus write: The One who holds the seven stars in His right hand, the One who walks among the seven golden lampstands, says this: 'I know your deeds and your toil and perseverance, and that you cannot tolerate evil men, and you put to the test those who call themselves apostles, and they are not, and you found them *to be* false; and you have perseverance and have endured for My name's sake, and have not grown weary. But I have *this* against you, that you have left your first love. Therefore remember from where you have fallen, and repent and do the deeds you did at first; or else I am coming to you and will remove your lampstand out of its place—unless you repent. Yet this you do have, that you hate the deeds of the Nicolaitans, which I also hate. He who has an ear, let him hear what the Spirit says to the churches. To him who overcomes, I will grant to eat of the tree of life which is in the Paradise of God' " (Revelation 2:1–7; see Genesis 2:9; Ezekiel 28:13; 1 John 4:1; Revelation 1:10, 11, 19, 20; 2:15, 16).

HATING GOD (Listed under GOD, HATING)

HATRED (See HATE; also check other emotions such as ANGER; ENVY; and JEALOUSY)

HATRED OF JESUS (Listed under JESUS, HATRED OF)

HEAD (HOUSE, HEAD OF THE; HOUSEHOLD, HEAD OF A; and JESUS' HEAD are separate entries; also see HAIR; and HEADS)

Setting: Galilee. During the early part of His ministry, Jesus preaches the Sermon on the Mount to His disciples and the multitudes.

"Again, you have heard that the ancients were told, 'YOU SHALL NOT MAKE FALSE VOWS, BUT SHALL FULFILL YOUR VOWS TO THE LORD.' But I say to you, make no oath at all, either by heaven, for it is the throne of God, or by the earth, for it is the footstool of His feet, or by Jerusalem, for it is THE CITY OF THE GREAT KING. Nor shall you make an oath by your head, for you cannot make one hair white or black. But let your statement be 'Yes, yes' *or* 'No, no'; anything beyond these is of evil" (Matthew 5:33–37, Jesus quotes from Leviticus 19:12, Psalm 48:2; Isaiah 66:1; cf. James 5:12).

Setting: Galilee. During the early part of His ministry, Jesus preaches the Sermon on the Mount to His disciples and the multitudes.

"Whenever you fast, do not put on a gloomy face as the hypocrites *do,* for they neglect their appearance so that they will be noticed by men when they are fasting. Truly I say to you, they have their reward in full. But you, when you fast, anoint your head and wash your face so that your fasting will not be noticed by men, but by your Father who is in secret; and your Father who sees *what is done* in secret will reward you" (Matthew 6:16–18; see Matthew 6:4, 6).

Setting: Galilee. After His disciples observe His ministry, Jesus summons and specifically instructs them about their ministry ahead involving true discipleship.

"Are not two sparrows sold for a cent? And *yet* not one of them will fall to the ground apart from your Father. But the very hairs of your head are all numbered. So do not fear; you are more valuable than many sparrows" (Matthew 10:29–31; cf. Luke 12:6; see Matthew 12:12).

Setting: The temple in Jerusalem. Having His authority questioned by the chief priests, scribes, and elders, Jesus begins to teach them in parables.

And He began to speak to them in parables: "A man PLANTED A VINEYARD AND PUT A WALL AROUND IT, AND DUG A VAT UNDER THE WINE PRESS AND BUILT A TOWER, and rented it out to vine-growers and went on a journey. At the *harvest* time he sent a slave to the vine-growers, in order to receive *some* of the produce of the vineyard from the vine-growers. They took him, and beat him and sent him away empty-handed. Again he sent them another slave, and they wounded him in the head, and treated him shamefully. And he sent another, and that one they killed; and *so with* many others, beating some and killing others. He had one more to *send*, a beloved son; he sent him last *of all* to them, saying, 'They will respect my son.' But those vine-growers said to one another, 'This is the heir; come, let us kill him, and the inheritance will be ours!' They took him, and killed him and threw him out of the vineyard. What will the owner of the vineyard do? He will come and destroy the vine-growers, and will give the vineyard to others. Have you not even read this Scripture: 'THE STONE WHICH THE BUILDERS REJECTED, THIS BECAME THE CHIEF CORNER *stone;* THIS CAME ABOUT FROM THE LORD, AND IT IS MARVELOUS IN OUR EYES'?" (Mark 12:1–11, Jesus quotes from Psalm 118:22, 23; Isaiah 5:1, 2; cf. Matthew 21:33–46; Luke 20:9–19).

Setting: On the way from Galilee to Jerusalem. Jesus warns His disciples of future events as the scribes and Pharisees turn hostile and question Him repeatedly in an attempt to catch Him in something He might say.

Under these circumstances, after so many thousands of people had gathered together that they were stepping on one another, He began saying to His disciples first *of all*, "Beware of the leaven of the Pharisees, which is hypocrisy. But there is nothing covered up that will not be revealed, and hidden that will not be known. Accordingly, whatever you have said in the dark will be heard in the light, and what you have whispered in the inner rooms will be proclaimed upon the housetops. I say to you, My friends, do not be afraid of those who kill the body and after that have no more that they can do. But I will warn you whom to fear: fear the One who, after He has killed, has authority to cast into hell; yes, I tell you, fear Him! Are not five sparrows sold for two cents? *Yet* not one of them is forgotten before God. Indeed, the very hairs of your head are all numbered. Do not fear; you are more valuable than many sparrows" (Luke 12:1–7; cf. Matthew 10:26–31; see Matthew 16:6; Hebrews 10:31).

Setting: The Mount of Olives, east of the temple in Jerusalem. After giving His disciples more details about the temple's coming destruction, Jesus elaborates during His Olivet Discourse about other future events.

Then He continued by saying to them, "Nation will rise against nation and kingdom against kingdom, and there will be great earthquakes, and in various places plagues and famines; and there will be terrors and great signs from heaven. But before all these things, they will lay their hands on you and will persecute you, delivering you to the synagogues and prisons, bringing you before kings and governors for My name's sake. It will lead to an opportunity for your testimony. So make up your minds not to prepare beforehand to defend yourselves; for I will give you utterance and wisdom which none of your opponents will be able to resist or refute. But you will be betrayed even by parents and brothers and relatives and friends, and they will put *some* of you to death, and you will be hated by all because of My name. Yet not a hair of your head will perish. By your endurance you will gain your lives" (Luke 21:10–19; cf. Matthew 10:19–22; 24:7–14; Mark 13:8–13).

HEAD (grain)

Setting: Galilee. After explaining the Parable of the Sower to His disciples, Jesus conveys the Parable of the Seed.

And He was saying, "The kingdom of God is like a man who casts seed upon the soil; and he goes to bed at night and gets up by day, and the seed sprouts and grows—how, he himself does not know. The soil produces crops by itself; first the blade, then the head, then the mature grain in the head. But when the crop permits, he immediately puts in the sickle, because the harvest has come" (Mark 4:26–29; see Joel 3:13).

HEAD, JESUS' (See JESUS' HEAD)

HEAD OF A HOUSEHOLD (Listed under HOUSEHOLD, HEAD OF A; also see HOUSE, HEAD OF THE)

HEAD OF THE HOUSE (Listed under HOUSE, HEAD OF THE; also see HOUSEHOLD, HEAD OF A)

HEADS (Also see HEAD)

Setting: The Mount of Olives, east of the temple in Jerusalem. After ministering in the temple a few days before His crucifixion, and giving His disciples more details regarding future events, Jesus speaks during His Olivet Discourse of His return.

"There will be signs in sun and moon and stars, and on the earth dismay among the nations, in perplexity at the roaring of the sea and the waves, men fainting from fear and the expectation of the things which are coming upon the world; for the powers of the heavens will be shaken. Then they will see THE SON OF MAN COMING IN A CLOUD with power and great glory. But when these things begin to take place, straighten up and lift up your heads, because your redemption is drawing near" (Luke 21:25–28, Jesus quotes from Daniel 7:13; cf. Matthew 24:29–31; Mark 13:24–27).

HEADWAITER

Setting: Cana of Galilee. On the third day of His public ministry, after choosing Andrew, Peter, Philip, and Nathanael to be His disciples, Jesus attends a wedding. His mother prompts Him to perform His first miracle, turning water into wine.

Jesus said to them, "Fill the waterpots with water." So they filled them up to the brim. And He said to them, "Draw *some* out now and take it to the headwaiter." So they took it *to him* (John 2:7, 8).

HEALING (Also see CURES; DEMONS, CASTING OUT; LEPROSY, CLEANSING FROM; MIRACLE; MIRACLES; RESUSCITATION; SIGNS AND WONDERS; and WELLNESS)

[HEALING from heal]

Setting: Capernaum of Galilee. After cleansing a leper, the Lord marvels at the faith of a Roman centurion who implores Him to heal his servant.

Jesus said to him, "I will come and heal him" (Matthew 8:7; see Luke 7:1–10).

[HEALING from "Go; it shall be done for you as you have believed."]

Setting: Entering Capernaum. After the Lord Jesus gives the Sermon on the Mount and cleanses a leper, a Roman centurion implores Him to heal his servant.

Now when Jesus heard *this,* He marveled, and said to those who were following, "Truly I say to you, I have not found such great faith with anyone in Israel. I say to you that many will come from east and west, and recline *at the table* with Abraham, Isaac and Jacob in the kingdom of heaven; but the sons of the kingdom will be cast out into the outer darkness; in that place there will be weeping and gnashing of teeth." And Jesus said to the centurion, "Go; it shall be done for you as you have believed." And the servant was healed that *very* moment (Matthew 8:10–13; cf. Luke 7:9, 10).

[HEALING from "Get up, pick up your bed and go home."]
Setting: Capernaum, near the Sea of Galilee. After Jesus heals and forgives a paralytic of his sins in front of crowds, some scribes accuse the Lord of blasphemy.

And they brought to Him a paralytic lying on a bed. Seeing their faith, Jesus said to the paralytic, "Take courage, son; your sins are forgiven." And some scribes said to themselves. "This *fellow* blasphemes." And Jesus knowing their thoughts said, "Why are you thinking evil in your hearts? Which is easier to say, 'Your sins are forgiven,' or to say, 'Get up, and walk'? But so that you may know that the Son of Man has authority on earth to forgive sins"—then He said to the paralytic, "Get up, pick up your bed and go home" (Matthew 9:2–6; cf. Mark 2:3–12; Luke 5:17–26).

[HEALING from your faith has made you well]
Setting: Capernaum, near the Sea of Galilee. Jesus heals a woman who has been suffering with internal bleeding for twelve years.

But Jesus turning and seeing her said, "Daughter, take courage; your faith has made you well." At once the woman was made well (Matthew 9:22; cf. Mark 5:34; Luke 8:48).

[HEALING from "It shall be done for you according to your faith."]
Setting: Somewhere in Galilee. After healing a woman with internal bleeding and resuscitating a synagogue official's daughter from the dead, Jesus gives sight to two blind men.

When He entered the house, the blind men came up to Him, and Jesus said to them, "Do you believe that I am able to do this?" They said to Him, "Yes, Lord." Then He touched their eyes saying, "It shall be done for you according to your faith." And their eyes were opened. And Jesus sternly warned them: "See that no one knows *about this!*" (Matthew 9:28–30).

[HEALING from heal]
Setting: Galilee. After His twelve disciples observe His ministry, Jesus summons and specifically instructs them about their ministry to the people of Israel.

These twelve Jesus sent out after instructing them: "Do not go in *the* way of *the* Gentiles, and do not enter *any* city of the Samaritans; but rather go to the lost sheep of the house of Israel. And as you go, preach, saying, 'The kingdom of heaven is at hand.' Heal *the* sick, raise *the* dead, cleanse *the* lepers, cast out demons. Freely you received, freely give. Do not acquire gold, or silver, or copper for your money belts, or a bag for *your* journey, or even two coats, or sandals, or a staff; for the worker is worthy of his support. And whatever city or village you enter, inquire who is worthy in it, and stay at his house until you leave *that city*. As you enter the house, give it your greeting. If the house is worthy, give it your *blessing of* peace. But if it is not worthy, take back your *blessing of* peace. Whoever does not receive you, nor heed your words, as you go out of that house or that city, shake the dust off your feet. Truly I say to you, it will be more tolerable for *the* land of Sodom and Gomorrah in the day of judgment than for that city" (Matthew 10:5–15; cf. Mark 6:7–11; Luke 9:1–5; see Matthew 3:2; 11:22, 24; 15:24; Luke 22:35; 1 Corinthians 9:14).

[HEALING from "Stretch out your hand!"]
Setting: A synagogue in Galilee. Jesus answers questions posed by the Pharisees about the Sabbath.

And He said to them, "What man is there among you who has a sheep, and if it falls into a pit on the Sabbath, will he not take hold of it and lift it out? How much more valuable then is a man than a sheep! So then, it is lawful to do good on the Sabbath." Then He said to the man, "Stretch out your hand!" He stretched it out, and it was restored to normal, like the other (Matthew 12:11–13; cf. Matthew 10:31; Mark 3:4, 5; Luke 6:9, 10; Luke 14:5; see Matthew 8:3).

[HEALING from HEAL]
Setting: By the Sea of Galilee. Jesus' responds to His disciples' questions about the Parable of the Sower, which He has just taught from a boat.

Jesus answered them, "To you it has been granted to know the mysteries of the kingdom of heaven, but to them it has not been granted. For whoever has, to him *more* shall be given, and he will have an abundance; but whoever does not have, even what he has shall be taken away from him. Therefore, I speak to them in parables; because while seeing they do not see, and while hearing they do not hear, nor do they understand. In their case the prophecy of Isaiah is being fulfilled, which says, 'YOU WILL KEEP ON HEARING, BUT WILL NOT UNDERSTAND; YOU WILL KEEP ON SEEING, BUT WILL NOT PERCEIVE; FOR THE HEART OF THIS PEOPLE HAS BECOME DULL, WITH THEIR EARS THEY SCARCELY HEAR, AND THEY HAVE CLOSED THEIR EYES, OTHERWISE THEYWOULD SEE WITH THEIR EYES, HEAR WITH THEIR EARS, AND UNDERSTAND WITH THEIR HEART AND RETURN, AND I WOULD HEAL THEM.' But blessed are your eyes, because they see; and your ears, because they hear. For truly I say to you that many prophets and righteous men desired to see what you see, and did not see *it,* and to hear what you hear, and did not hear *it*" (Matthew 13:11–17, Jesus quotes from Isaiah 6:9, 10; cf. Matthew 25:29; Mark 4:11–13; Luke 8:10; see Deuteronomy 29:4; John 8:56).

[HEALING from "O woman, your faith is great; it shall be done for you as you wish."]
Setting: The district of Tyre and Sidon. A Canaanite woman appeals to Jesus to heal her demon-possessed daughter.

But He answered and said, "I was sent only to the lost sheep of the house of Israel." But she came and *began* to bow down before Him, saying, "Lord, help me!" And He answered and said, "It is not good to take the children's bread and throw it to the dogs." But she said, "Yes, Lord; but even the dogs feed from the crumbs which fall from their masters' table." Then Jesus said to her, "O woman, your faith is great; it shall be done for you as you wish." And her daughter was healed at once (Matthew 15:24–28; cf. Mark 7:24–30; see Matthew 9:22; 10:5, 6).

[HEALING from Lord, we want our eyes to be opened]
Setting: Leaving Jericho, on the way to Jerusalem. Two blind men sitting by the road loudly cry out for the Lord to restore their sight.

And Jesus stopped and called them, and said, "What do you want Me to do for you?" They said to Him, "Lord, *we want* our eyes to be opened." Moved with compassion, Jesus touched their eyes; and immediately they regained their sight and followed Him (Matthew 20:32–34; cf. Mark 10:49–52; Luke 18:40–43).

[HEALING from your sins are forgiven]
Setting: Galilee. During the beginning of His gospel-preaching ministry, word of Jesus' healing abilities spreads, so some friends bring a paralytic man to Him for healing.

And Jesus seeing their faith said to the paralytic, "Son, your sins are forgiven" (Mark 2:5; cf. Matthew 9:1–3; Luke 5:17–20).

[HEALING from "I say to you, get up, pick up your pallet and go home."]
Setting: Capernaum. When He heals and forgives the sins of a paralytic man, some scribes believe Jesus commits blasphemy.

Immediately Jesus, aware in His spirit that they were reasoning that way within themselves, said to them, "Why are you reasoning about these things in your hearts? Which is easier, to say to the paralytic, 'Your sins are forgiven'; or to say, 'Get up, and pick up your pallet and walk'? "But so that you may know that the Son of Man has authority on earth to forgive sins"—He said to the paralytic, "I say to you, get up, pick up your pallet and go home" (Mark 2:8–11; cf. Matthew 9:4–7; Luke 5:21–24).

[HEALING FROM "Stretch our your hand."]
Setting: A synagogue in Galilee. Early in His ministry, Jesus heals a man's withered hand on the Sabbath while the Pharisees observe.

He said to the man with the withered hand, "Get up and come forward!" And He said to them, "Is it lawful to do good or do harm on the Sabbath, to save a life or to kill?" But they kept silent. After looking around at them with anger, grieved at their hardness of heart, He said to the man, "Stretch out your hand." And he stretched it out, and his hand was restored (Mark 3:3–5; cf. Matthew 12:9–14; Luke 6:6–11).

[HEALING from "Go home to your people and report to them what great things the Lord has done for you, and *how* He had mercy on you"]
Setting: The country of the Gerasenes, across the Sea of Galilee from Capernaum. Jesus encounters and heals a man possessed by a legion of demons.

And He did not let him, but He said to him, "Go home to your people and report to them what great things the Lord has done for you, and *how* He had mercy on you" (Mark 5:19; cf. Luke 8:39; see Matthew 8:33, 34; Luke 8:36–38).

[HEALING from "Who touched My garments?"]
Setting: By the Sea of Galilee. After Jesus returns from ministry to the Gerasenes, a woman who has had a hemorrhage for twelve years touches His clothes in order to be healed.

Immediately Jesus, perceiving in Himself that the power *proceeding* from Him had gone forth, turned around in the crowd and said, "Who touched My garments?" (Mark 5:30; see Matthew 9:20, 21; Mark 5:25–29, 31–34; Luke 8:43–48).

[HEALING from your faith has made you well]
Setting: By the Sea of Galilee. After Jesus returns from ministry to the Gerasenes, a woman who has had a hemorrhage for twelve years touches His clothes in order to be healed.

And He said to her, "Daughter, your faith has made you well; go in peace and be healed of your affliction" (Mark 5:34; cf. Matthew 9:22; Luke 8:48; see Mark 5:31–33; Luke 7:50).

[HEALING from "Be opened!"]
Setting: Decapolis, near the Sea of Galilee. After casting out a demon from a Gentile woman's daughter in Tyre, Jesus restores a man's hearing and speech.

Jesus took him aside from the crowd, by himself, and put His fingers into his ears, and after spitting, He touched his tongue *with the saliva*; and looking up to heaven with a deep sigh, He said to him, "Ephphatha!" that is, "Be opened!" (Mark 7:33, 34; see Matthew 15:29–31; Mark 7:31, 32, 35–37; Mark 8:23).

[HEALING from "Do you see anything?"]
Setting: Bethsaida of Galilee. After Jesus' disciples discuss with one another that they have no bread, Jesus gives sight to a blind man.

Taking the blind man by the hand, He brought him out of the village; and after spitting on his eyes and laying His hands on him, He asked him, "Do you see anything?" (Mark 8:23).

[HEALING from "Go; your faith has made you well."]
Setting: Jericho, on the road to Jerusalem. A blind beggar named Bartimaeus cries out to Jesus for healing.

And Jesus stopped and said, "Call him *here*." So they called the blind man, saying to him, "Take courage, stand up! He is calling for you." Throwing aside his cloak, he jumped up and came to Jesus. And answering him, Jesus said, "What do you want Me to do for you?" And the blind man said to him, "Rabboni, *I want* to regain my sight!" And Jesus said to him, "Go; your faith has made you well." Immediately he regained his sight and *began* following Him on the road (Mark 10:49–52; cf. Matthew 20:29–34; Luke 18:35–43; see Matthew 9:2, 22).

[HEALING from lay hands on the sick]
Setting: Following His resurrection from the dead after being crucified, Jesus commissions His disciples to preach His gospel to the world.

And He said to them, "Go into all the world and preach the gospel to all creation. He who has believed and has been baptized shall be saved; but he who has disbelieved shall be condemned. These signs will accompany those who have believed: in My name they will cast out demons, they will speak with new tongues; they will pick up serpents, and if they drink any deadly *poison,* it will not hurt them; they will lay hands on the sick, and they will recover" (Mark 16:15–18; cf. Matthew 28:16–20; see Mark 9:38; John 3:18, 36; 1 Corinthians 15:6).

[Note: Some scholars question the authenticity of Mark 16:9–20, as these verses do not appear in some early New Testament manuscripts.]

[HEALING from heal]
Setting: The synagogue in Jesus' hometown of Nazareth. At the beginning of Jesus' public ministry, He comments to the congregation after reading on the Sabbath from the book of the prophet Isaiah.

And He said to them, "No doubt you will quote this proverb to Me, 'Physician, heal yourself! Whatever we heard was done at Capernaum, do here in your hometown as well.'" And He said, "Truly I say to you, no prophet is welcome in his hometown. But I say to you in truth, there were many widows in Israel in the days of Elijah, when the sky was shut up for three years and six months, when a great famine came over all the land; and yet Elijah was sent to none of them, but only to Zarephath, *in the land* of Sidon, to a woman who was a widow. And there were many lepers in Israel in the time of Elisha the prophet; and none of them was cleansed, but only Naaman the Syrian" (Luke 4:23–27; Jesus refers to 1 Kings 17:1, 9; 2 Kings 5:1–14; see Matthew 13:53–58).

[HEALING from "I say to you, get up, and pick up your stretcher and go home."]
Setting: Capernaum of Galilee. After Jesus heals and forgives the sins of a paralytic man, some Pharisees and teachers of the law from Galilee and Judea accuse Him of committing blasphemy.

But Jesus, aware of their reasonings, answered and said to them, "Why are you reasoning in your hearts? Which is easier, to say, 'Your sins have been forgiven you,' or to say, 'Get up and walk'? But, so that you may know that the Son of Man has authority on earth to forgive sins,"—He said to the paralytic—"I say to you, get up, and pick up your stretcher and go home" (Luke 5:22–24; cf. Matthew 9:4–8; Mark 2:8–12; see Matthew 4:24).

[HEALING from "Stretch out your hand!"]
Setting: A synagogue in Galilee. As Jesus teaches on the Sabbath, the scribes and Pharisees watch to see if He heals a man's withered hand.

But He knew what they were thinking, and He said to the man with the withered hand, "Get up and come forward!" And he got up and came forward. And Jesus said to them, "I ask you, is it lawful to do good or to do harm on the Sabbath, to save a life or destroy it?" And looking around at them all, He said to him, "Stretch out your hand!" And he did *so;* and his hand was restored (Luke 6:8–10; cf. Matthew 12:9–13; Mark 3:1–5).

[HEALING from "Return to your house and describe what great things God has done for you."]
Setting: The country of the Gerasenes, opposite Galilee. Jesus heals a demon-possessed man who then desires to join His ministry, but the Lord sends him home.

"Return to your house and describe what great things God has done for you." So he went away, proclaiming throughout the whole city what great things Jesus had done for him (Luke 8:39; cf. Matthew 8:28–34; Mark 5:1–20).

[HEALING from Daughter, your faith made you well]
Setting: Galilee. Jesus returns after ministering in the country of the Gerasenes, and a woman, ill for twelve years, receives healing by touching His garment.

And Jesus said, "Who is the one who touched Me?" And while they were all denying it, Peter said, "Master, the people are crowding and pressing in on You." But Jesus said, "Someone did touch Me, for I was aware, that power had gone out of Me." When the woman saw that she had not escaped notice, she came trembling and fell down before Him, and declared in the presence of all the people the reason why she had touched Him, and how she had been immediately healed. And He said to her, "Daughter, your faith has made you well; go in peace" (Luke 8:45–48; cf. Matthew 9:20; Mark 5:25–34).

[HEALING from heal]
Setting: On the way from Galilee to Jerusalem. The Lord appoints seventy followers and sends them out in pairs to every place He Himself will soon visit.

And He was saying to them, "The harvest is plentiful, but the laborers are few; therefore beseech the Lord of the harvest to send out laborers into His harvest. Go; behold, I send you out as lambs in the midst of wolves. Carry no money belt, no bag, no shoes; and greet no one on the way. Whatever house you enter, first say, 'Peace be to this house.' If a man of peace is there, your peace will rest on him; but if not, it will return to you. Stay in that house, eating and drinking what they give you; for the laborer is worthy of his wages. Do not keep moving from house to house. Whatever city you enter and they receive you, eat what is set before you; and heal those in it who are sick, and say to them, 'The kingdom of God has come near to you.' But whatever city you enter and they do not receive you, go out into its streets and say, 'Even the dust of your city which clings to our feet we wipe off *in protest* against you; yet be sure of this, that the kingdom of God has come near.' I say to you, it will be more tolerable in that day for Sodom than for that city" (Luke 10:2–12; see Genesis 19:24–28; Matthew 9:37, 38, 10:9–14, 16; 1 Corinthians 10:27).

[HEALING from you are freed from your sickness]
Setting: On the way from Galilee to Jerusalem. While Jesus is teaching in the synagogue on the Sabbath, a woman who has been sick eighteen years seeks healing.

When Jesus saw her, He called her over and said to her, "Woman, you are freed from your sickness" (Luke 13:12).

[HEALING from released]
Setting: On the way from Galilee to Jerusalem. Jesus responds to a synagogue official's anger for healing a woman, sick for eighteen years, in the synagogue on the Sabbath.

But the Lord answered him and said, "You hypocrites, does not each of you on the Sabbath untie his ox or his donkey from the stall and lead him away to water *him?* And this woman, a daughter of Abraham as she is, whom Satan has bound for eighteen long years, should she not have been released from this bond on the Sabbath day?" (Luke 13:15, 16; see Luke 14:5).

[HEALING from heal and healed]
Setting: On the way from Galilee to Jerusalem. Jesus goes on the Sabbath to eat bread in the house of a Pharisee leader, where a man suffering from dropsy sits.

And Jesus answered and spoke to the lawyers and Pharisees, saying, "Is it lawful to heal on the Sabbath, or not?" But they kept silent. And He took hold of him and healed him, and sent him away. And He said to them, "Which one of you will have a son or an ox fall into a well, and will not immediately pull him out on a Sabbath day?" And they could make no reply to this (Luke 14:3–6, cf. Matthew 12:11–13).

[HEALING from Receive your sight]
Setting: Approaching Jericho, on the way from Galilee to Jerusalem. After telling His disciples of the sacrifice He will make in Jerusalem, Jesus takes time to heal a blind man.

And Jesus stopped and commanded that he be brought to Him; and when he came near, He questioned him, "What do you want Me to do for you?" And he said, "Lord, *I want* to regain my sight!" And Jesus said to him, "Receive your sight; your faith has made you well" (Luke 18:40–42; cf. Matthew 20:29–34; Mark 10:46–52).

[HEALING from "Friend, your sins are forgiven you."]
Setting: Galilee. While some Pharisees and teachers of the law from Galilee and Judea observe, several men lower a paralyzed man through the roof in front of Jesus.

Seeing their faith, He said, "Friend, your sins are forgiven you" (Luke 5:20; cf. Mark 2:2–12; see Matthew 9:1–8).

[HEALING from He touched his ear and healed him]
Setting: Gethsemane on the Mount of Olives, east of the temple in Jerusalem. As Judas betrays Jesus to a crowd of His enemies with a kiss, one of the Lord's disciples (Peter, according to John 18:10) cuts off the right ear of a slave of the high priest. Jesus commands His disciples not to resist His arrest with violence.

But Jesus answered and said, "Stop! No more of this." And He touched his ear and healed him (Luke 22:51; see Matthew 26:51–53; Mark 14:46, 47; John 18:10, 11).

[HEALING from "Go; your son lives."]
Setting: Cana of Galilee. After ministering to the Samaritan people for two days, Jesus encounters a royal official pleading for healing of his son, who is at the point of death in Capernaum.

Jesus said to him, "Go; your son lives." The man believed the word that Jesus spoke to him and started off (John 4:50; see Matthew 8:5–13).

[HEALING from "Get up, pick up your pallet and walk."]
Setting: By the pool of Bethesda. After healing the son of a royal official from Capernaum, Jesus returns to Jerusalem for the Feast of the Jews, where He heals a man, disabled for thirty-eight years, on the Sabbath.

Jesus said to him, "Get up, pick up your pallet and walk" (John 5:8; see Matthew 9:6).

[HEALING from I did one deed and I made an entire man well]
Setting: The temple in Jerusalem. After receiving encouragement from His blood brothers in Galilee to attend the upcoming Feast of Booths in order to demonstrate His works to His disciples and the world, Jesus goes and teaches, astonishing the Jewish religious leaders.

Jesus answered them, "I did one deed, and you all marvel. For this reason Moses has given you circumcision (not because it is from Moses, but from the fathers), and on *the* Sabbath you circumcise a man. If a man receives circumcision on *the* Sabbath so that the Law of Moses will not be broken, are you angry with Me because I made an entire man well on *the* Sabbath? Do not judge according to appearance, but judge with righteous judgment" (John 7:21–24; see Genesis 17:10–14; Leviticus 12:3; 19:15; Matthew 12:2; John 5:2–16; 7–20).

[HEALING from "Go, wash in the pool of Siloam."]
Setting: The temple treasury in Jerusalem. After Jesus avoids being stoned by the scribes and Pharisees, His disciples wonder if blindness is caused by sin as the Lord heals a man born blind.

Jesus answered, "*It was* neither *that* this man sinned, nor his parents; but *it was* so that the works of God might be displayed in him. We must work the works of Him who sent Me as long as it is day; night is coming when no one can work. While I am in the world, I am the Light of the world." When He had said this, He spat on the ground, and made clay of the spittle, and applied the clay to his eyes, and said to him, "Go, wash in the pool of Siloam" (which is translated, Sent). So he went away and washed, and came *back* seeing (John 9:3–7; see John 8:12; 11:4; 12:46).

HEALTH (Also see WELLNESS)

[HEALTH from healthy]

Setting: Matthew's home in Capernaum, near the Sea of Galilee. Jesus calls Matthew the tax collector to be His disciple.

But when Jesus heard *this,* He said, "*It is* not those who are healthy who need a physician, but those who are sick. But go and learn what this means: 'I DESIRE COMPASSION, AND NOT SACRIFICE,' for I did not come to call the righteous, but sinners" (Matthew 9:12, 13, Jesus quotes from Hosea 6:6; cf. Mark 2:17; Luke 5:31–32; see Mark 2:15, 16).

[HEALTH from healthy]

Setting: The home of Levi (Matthew) in Capernaum. The scribes of the Pharisees question Jesus associating with sinners and tax collectors after He calls Levi (Matthew) the tax collector to be His disciple.

And hearing *this,* Jesus said to them, "*It is* not those who are healthy who need a physician, but those who are sick; I did not come to call the righteous, but sinners" (Mark 2:17; cf. Matthew 9:12, 13; Luke 5:29–32).

HEARING (Also see EAR; EARS; and LISTENING)

[HEARING from hears]

Setting: Galilee. During the early part of His ministry, Jesus preaches the Sermon on the Mount to His disciples and the multitudes.

"Therefore everyone who hears these words of Mine and acts on them, may be compared to a wise man who built his house on the rock. And the rain fell, and the floods came, and the winds blew and slammed against that house; and *yet* it did not fall, for it had been founded on the rock. Everyone who hears these words of Mine and does not act on them, will be like a foolish man who built his house on the sand. The rain fell, and the floods came, and the winds blew and slammed against that house; and it fell—and great was its fall" (Matthew 7:24–28; cf. Luke 6:47–49 and see Matthew 7:29).

[HEARING from hear]

Setting: Galilee After His disciples observe His ministry, Jesus summons and specifically instructs them about their ministry ahead involving true discipleship.

"Therefore do not fear them, for there is nothing concealed that will not be revealed, or hidden that will not be known. What I tell you in the darkness, speak in the light; and what you hear *whispered* in your ear, proclaim upon the housetops. Do not fear those who kill the body but are unable to kill the soul; but rather fear Him who is able to destroy both soul and body in hell" (Matthew 10:26–28; cf. Mark 4:22; Luke 12:3; see Hebrews 10:31).

[HEARING from hear]

Setting: Galilee. As He teaches and preaches, Jesus responds to John the Baptist's question (relayed by John's disciples) whether He is Israel's promised Messiah.

Jesus answered and said to them, "Go and report to John what you hear and see: *the* BLIND RECEIVE SIGHT and *the* lame walk, *the* lepers are cleansed and *the* deaf hear, *the* dead are raised up, and *the* POOR HAVE THE GOSPEL PREACHED TO THEM. And blessed is he who does not take offense at Me" (Matthew 11:4–6, Jesus quotes from Isaiah 35:5f; cf. Luke 7:22, 23).

[HEARING from hear]

Setting: Galilee. While speaking to the crowds, Jesus pays tribute to the ministry of John the Baptist, but emphasizes that the one who is least in the kingdom of heaven is greater than John.

As these men were going *away,* Jesus began to speak to the crowds about John, "What did you go out into the wilderness to see? A reed shaken by the wind? But what did you go out to see? A man dressed in soft *clothing?* Those who wear soft *clothing* are in kings' palaces! But what did you go out to see? A prophet? Yes, I tell you, and the one who is more than a prophet. This is the one about whom it is written, 'BEHOLD, I SEND MY MESSENGER AHEAD OF YOU, WHO WILL PREPARE YOUR WAY BEFORE YOU.' Truly, I say to you, among those born of women there has not arisen *anyone* greater than John the Baptist! Yet the one who is least in the kingdom of heaven is greater than he. From the days of John the Baptist until now the kingdom of heaven suffers violence, and violent men take it by force. For all the prophets and the Law prophesied until John. And, if you are willing to accept *it,* John himself is Elijah who was to come. He who has ears to hear, let him hear" (Matthew 11:7–15, Jesus quotes from Malachi 3:1; cf. Malachi 4:5; Luke 7:24–28; 16:16; see Matthew 14:5).

[HEARING from hear]
Setting: Galilee. After Jesus warns the Pharisees about the unpardonable sin and their future judgment, some of the Pharisees and scribes ask Him to perform a miraculous sign for them in front of the crowds.

But He answered and said to them, "An evil and adulterous generation craves for a sign; and *yet* no sign will be given to it but the sign of Jonah the prophet; for just as JONAH WAS THREE DAYS AND THREE NIGHTS IN THE BELLY OF THE SEA MONSTER, so will the Son of Man be three days and three nights in the heart of the earth. The men of Nineveh will stand up with this generation at the judgment, and will condemn it because they repented at the preaching of Jonah; and behold, something greater than Jonah is here. *The* Queen of *the* South will rise up with this generation at the judgment and will condemn it, because she came from the ends of the earth to hear the wisdom of Solomon; and behold, something greater than Solomon is here" (Matthew 12:39–42; Jesus quotes from Jonah 1:17; cf. 1 Kings 10:1; Jonah 3:5; Matthew 16:1, 4; Luke 11:29).

[HEARING from hear]
Setting: By the Sea of Galilee. While teaching and preaching to the crowds, Jesus conveys from a boat the Parable of the Sower.

And He spoke many things to them in parables, saying, "Behold, the sower went out to sow; and as he sowed, some *seeds* fell beside the road, and the birds came and ate them up. Others fell on the rocky places, where they did not have much soil; and immediately they sprang up, because they had no depth of soil. But when the sun had risen, they were scorched; and because they had no root, they withered away. Others fell among the thorns, and the thorns came up and choked them out. And others fell on the good soil and yielded a crop, some a hundredfold, some sixty, and some thirty. He who has ears, let him hear" (Matthew 13:3–9; cf. Mark 4:3–9; Luke 8:4–8).

Setting: By the Sea of Galilee. Jesus responds to His disciples' questions about the Parable of the Sower, which He has just taught from a boat.

Jesus answered them, "To you it has been granted to know the mysteries of the kingdom of heaven, but to them it has not been granted. For whoever has, to him *more* shall be given, and he will have an abundance; but whoever does not have, even what he has shall be taken away from him. Therefore, I speak to them in parables; because while seeing they do not see, and while hearing they do not hear, nor do they understand. In their case the prophecy of Isaiah is being fulfilled, which says, 'YOU WILL KEEP ON HEARING, BUT WILL NOT UNDERSTAND; YOU WILL KEEP ON SEEING, BUT WILL NOT PERCEIVE; FOR THE HEART OF THIS PEOPLE HAS BECOME DULL, WITH THEIR EARS THEY SCARCELY HEAR, AND THEY HAVE CLOSED THEIR EYES, OTHERWISE THEYWOULD SEE WITH THEIR EYES, HEAR WITH THEIR EARS, AND UNDERSTAND WITH THEIR HEART AND RETURN, AND I WOULD HEAL THEM.' But blessed are your eyes, because they see; and your ears, because they hear. For truly I say to you that many prophets and righteous men desired to see what you see, and did not see *it,* and to hear what you hear, and did not hear *it*" (Matthew 13:11–17, Jesus quotes from Isaiah 6:9–10; cf. Matthew 25:29; Mark 4:11–13; Luke 8:10; see Deuteronomy 29:4; John 8:56).

[HEARING from hear and hears]
Setting: By the Sea of Galilee. With the religious leaders rejecting His message, Jesus begins to teach in parables, and explains the meaning of the Parable of the Sower to His disciples.

"Hear then the parable of the sower. When anyone hears the word of the kingdom and does not understand it, the evil *one* comes and snatches away what has been sown in his heart. This is the one on whom seed was sown beside the road. The one on whom seed was sown on the rocky places, this is the man who hears the word and immediately receives it with joy; yet he has no *firm* root in himself, but is *only* temporary, and when affliction or persecution arises because of the word, immediately he falls away. And the one on whom seed was sown among the thorns, this is the man who hears the word, and the worry of the world and the deceitfulness of wealth choke the word, and it becomes unfruitful. And the one on whom seed was sown on the good soil, this is the man who hears the word and understands it; who indeed bears fruit and brings forth, some a hundredfold, some sixty, and some thirty" (Matthew 13:18–23; cf. Mark 4:13–20; Luke 8:11–15).

[HEARING from hear]

Setting: A house near the Sea of Galilee. Jesus explains to His disciples the meaning of the Parable of the Wheat and the Tares.

And He said, "The one who sows the good seed is the Son of Man, and the field is the world; and as *for* the good seed, these are the sons of the kingdom; and the tares are the sons of the evil *one;* and the enemy who sowed them is the devil, and the harvest is the end of the age; and the reapers are angels. So just as the tares are gathered up and burned with fire, so shall it be at the end of the age. The Son of Man will send forth His angels, and they will gather out of His kingdom all stumbling blocks, and those who commit lawlessness, and will throw them into the furnace of fire; in that place there will be weeping and gnashing of teeth. Then THE RIGHTEOUS WILL SHINE FORTH AS THE SUN in the kingdom of their Father. He who has ears, let him hear" (Matthew 13:37–43, Jesus quotes from Daniel 12:3; cf. Matthew 8:12; 13:50).

[HEARING from hear]

Setting: Galilee. After the Pharisees and scribes question Him about His disciples' lack of obedience to tradition and the commandments, Jesus instructs the crowd.

After Jesus called the crowd to Him, He said to them, "Hear and understand. *It* is not what enters into the mouth *that* defiles the man, but what proceeds out of the mouth, this defiles the man" (Matthew 15:10, 11; cf. Matthew 15:18).

Setting: The Mount of Olives, just east of Jerusalem. During His discourse, Jesus answers His disciples' questions as to when the temple will be destroyed and Jerusalem overrun, along with the signs of His coming and the end of the age.

And Jesus answered and said to them, "See to it that no one misleads you. For many will come in My name, saying, 'I am the Christ,' and will mislead many. You will be hearing of wars and rumors of wars. See that you are not frightened, for *those things* must take place, but *that* is not yet the end. For nation will rise against nation, and kingdom against kingdom, and in various places there will be famines and earthquakes. But all these things are *merely* the beginning of birth pangs. Then they will deliver you to tribulation, and will kill you, and you will be hated by all nations because of My name. At that time many will fall away and will betray one another and hate one another. Many false prophets will arise and will mislead many. Because lawlessness is increased, most people's love will grow cold. But the one who endures to the end, he will be saved. This gospel of the kingdom shall be preached in the whole world as a testimony to all the nations, and then the end will come" (Matthew 24:4–14; cf. Jeremiah 29:8; Matthew 7:15; 10:17, 22; Mark 13:3–13; Luke 21:7–19; Revelation 6:4).

[HEARING from hear]

Setting: By the Sea of Galilee. During the early part of His ministry, just after a visit from his mother and brothers, Jesus, while in a boat, instructs a very large crowd with the Parable of the Sower.

"Listen *to this!* Behold, the sower went out to sow; as he was sowing, some *seed* fell beside the road, and the birds came and ate it up. Other *seed* fell on the rocky *ground* where it did not have much soil; and immediately it sprang up because it had no depth of soil. And after the sun had risen, it was scorched; and because it had no root, it withered away. Other *seed* fell among the thorns, and the thorns came up and choked it, and it yielded no crop. Other *seeds* fell into the good soil, and as the grew up and increased, they yielded a crop and produced thirty, sixty, and a hundredfold." And He was saying, "He who has ears to hear, let him hear" (Mark 4:3–9; cf. Matthew 13:3–9; Luke 8:5–8).

Setting: By the Sea of Galilee. After Jesus conveys the Parable of the Sower to a crowd from a boat, His disciples asks Him questions about it.

And He was saying to them, "To you has been given the mystery of the kingdom of God, but those who are outside get everything in parables, so that WHILE SEEING, THEY MAY SEE AND NOT PERCEIVE, AND WHILE HEARING, THEY MAY HEAR AND NOT UNDERSTAND, OTHERWISE THEY MIGHT RETURN AND BE FORGIVEN" (Mark 4:11, 12, Jesus quotes from Isaiah 6:9–10; cf. Matthew 13:10–17).

[HEARING from hear]
Setting: By the Sea of Galilee. During the early part of His ministry, after presenting to a very large crowd the Parable of the Sower from a boat, Jesus explains the meaning of the parable to His disciples and followers.

And He said to them, "Do you not understand this parable? How will you understand all the parables? The sower sows the word. These are the ones who are beside the road where the word is sown; and when they hear, immediately Satan comes and takes away the word which has been sown in them. In a similar way these are the ones on whom seed was sown on the rocky places, who, when they hear the word, immediately receive it with joy; and they have no *firm* root in themselves, but are *only* temporary; then, when affliction or persecution arises because of the word, immediately they fall away. And others are the ones on whom seed was sown among the thorns; these are the ones who have heard the word, but the worries of the world and the deceitfulness of riches, and the desires for other things enter in and choke the word, and it becomes unfruitful. And those are the ones on whom seed was sown on the good soil; and they hear the word and accept it and bear fruit, thirty, sixty, and a hundredfold" (Mark 4:13–20; cf. Matthew 13:18–23; Luke 8:11–15).

[HEARING from hear]
Setting: Galilee. Following His explanation of the Parable of the Sower to His disciples, Jesus illustrates what they should do with this truth.

And He was saying to them, "A lamp is not brought to be put under a basket, is it, or under a bed? Is it not *brought* to be put on the lampstand? For nothing is hidden, except to be revealed; nor has *anything* been secret, but that it would come to light. If anyone has ears to hear, let him hear" (Mark 4:21–23; cf. Luke 8:16, 17; see Matthew 5:14–16; 10:26).

[HEARING from hear]
Setting: Galilee. After the Pharisees and scribes from Jerusalem question His disciples' lack of obedience to tradition, Jesus speaks to a crowd and explains His teaching to His disciples.

After He called the crowd to Him again, He *began* saying to them, "Listen to Me, all of you, and understand: there is nothing outside the man which can defile him if it goes into him; but the things which proceed out of the man are what defile the man. [If anyone has ears to hear, let him hear."] When he had left the crowd *and* entered the house, His disciples questioned Him about the parable. And He said to them, "Are you so lacking in understanding also? Do you not understand that whatever goes into the man from outside cannot defile him, because it does not go into his heart, but into his stomach, and is eliminated?" (*Thus He* declared all foods clean.) And He was saying, "That which proceeds out of the man, that is what defiles the man. For from within, out of the heart of men, proceed the evil thoughts, fornications, thefts, murders, adulteries, deeds of coveting *and* wickedness, *as well* as deceit, sensuality, envy, slander, pride *and* foolishness. All these evil things proceed from within and defile the man" (Mark 7:14–23; cf. Matthew 15:10–20).

[HEARING from HEAR]
Setting: Opposite the district of Dalmanutha. After the Pharisees argue with Jesus, seeking a sign from heaven to test Him, He and His disciples cross to the other side of the Sea of Galilee, where His disciples discuss with one another that they have no bread.

And Jesus, aware of this, said to them, "Why do you discuss *the fact* that you have no bread? Do you not yet see or understand? Do you have a hardened heart? HAVING EYES, DO YOU NOT SEE? AND HAVING EARS, DO YOU NOT HEAR? And do you not remember, when I broke the five loaves for the five thousand, how many baskets full of broken pieces you picked you? They said to Him, "Twelve." When *I broke* the seven for the four thousand, how many large baskets full of broken pieces did you pick up?" They said to Him, "Seven." And He was saying to them, "Do you not yet understand?" (Mark 8:17–21, Jesus quotes from Jeremiah 5:21; cf. Matthew 16:5–12; see Matthew 14:18, 19; Mark 6:41–44, 52; 8:6–9).

[HEARING from HEAR]
Setting: The temple in Jerusalem. With the Pharisees and Herodians failing to trap Jesus in a statement, one of the scribes asks Him which commandment is foremost.

Jesus answered, "The foremost is, 'HEAR, O ISRAEL! THE LORD OUR GOD IS ONE LORD; AND YOU SHALL LOVE THE LORD YOUR GOD WITH ALL YOUR HEART, AND WITH ALL YOUR SOUL, AND WITH ALL YOUR MIND AND WITH ALL YOUR STRENGTH.' The second is this, 'YOU SHALL LOVE YOUR NEIGHBOR AS YOURSELF.' There is no other commandment greater than these" (Mark 12:29–31, Jesus quotes from Deuteronomy 6:4–5; Leviticus 19:18; cf. Matthew 22:34–40).

[HEARING from hear]
Setting: On the Mount of Olives, east of the temple in Jerusalem. After predicting the temple's destruction, Jesus responds during His Olivet Discourse to questions from Peter, James, John, and Andrew about future events.

And Jesus began to say to them, "See to it that no one misleads you. Many will come in My name, saying, 'I am *He!*' and will mislead many. When you hear of wars and rumors of wars, do not be frightened; *those things* must take place; but *that is* not yet the end. For nation will rise up against nation, and kingdom against kingdom; there will be earthquakes in various places; there will *also be* famines. These things are *merely* the beginning of birth pangs. But be on your guard; for they will deliver you to *the* courts, and you will be flogged in *the* synagogues, and you will stand before governors and kings for My sake, as a testimony to them. The gospel must first be preached to all the nations. When they arrest you and hand you over, do not worry beforehand about what you are to say, but say whatever is given you in that hour; for it is not you who speak, but *it is* the Holy Spirit. Brother will betray brother to death, and a father *his* child; and children will rise up against parents and have them put to death. You will be hated by all because of My name, but the one who endures to the end, he will be saved" (Mark 13:5–13; cf. Matthew 24:4–14; Luke 21:7–19; see Matthew 10:17–22).

Setting: The synagogue in Jesus' hometown of Nazareth in Galilee. At the beginning of Jesus' public ministry, He reads on the Sabbath from the book of the prophet Isaiah.

And the book of the prophet Isaiah was handed to Him. And He opened the book and found the place where it was written, "THE SPIRIT OF THE LORD IS UPON ME, BECAUSE HE ANOINTED ME TO PREACH THE GOSPEL TO THE POOR. HE HAS SENT ME TO PROCLAIM RELEASE TO THE CAPTIVES, AND RECOVERY OF SIGHT TO THE BLIND, TO SET FREE THOSE WHO ARE OPPRESSED, TO PROCLAIM THE FAVORABLE YEAR OF THE LORD." And He closed the book, gave it back to the attendant and sat down; and the eyes of all in the synagogue were fixed on Him. And He began to say to them, "Today this Scripture has been fulfilled in your hearing" (Luke 4:17–21, Jesus quotes from Isaiah 61:1, 2).

[HEARING from hear]
Setting: Galilee. After selecting His twelve disciples, Jesus teaches the Sermon on the Mount to those disciples and a great throng of people from Judea, Jerusalem, and the central coastal region of Tyre and Sidon.

"But I say to you who hear, love your enemies, do good to those who hate you, bless those who curse you, pray for those who mistreat you. Whoever hits you on the cheek, offer him the other also; and whoever takes away your coat, do not withhold your shirt from him either. Give to everyone who asks of you, and whoever takes away what is yours, do not demand it back. Treat others the same way you want them to treat you. If you love those who love you, what credit is *that* to you? For even sinners love those who love them. If you do good to those who do good to you, what credit is *that* to you? For even sinners do the same. If you lend to those from whom you expect to receive, what credit is *that* to you? Even sinners lend to sinners in order to receive back the same *amount.* But love your enemies, and do good, and lend, expecting nothing in return; and your reward will be great, and you will be sons of the Most High; for He Himself is kind to ungrateful and evil *men.* Be merciful, just as your Father is merciful" (Luke 6:27–36; cf. Matthew 5:9, 39–48; 7:12).

[HEARING from hears]
Setting: Galilee. After selecting His twelve disciples, Jesus teaches the Sermon on the Mount to those disciples and a great throng of people from Judea, Jerusalem, and the central coastal region of Tyre and Sidon.

"Why do you call Me, 'Lord, Lord,' and do not do what I say? Everyone who comes to Me and hears My words and acts on them, I will show you whom he is like; he is like a man building a house, who dug deep and laid a foundation on the rock; and when a flood occurred, the torrent burst against that house and could not shake it, because it had been well built. But the one who has heard and has not acted *accordingly,* is like a man who built a house on the ground without any foundation; and the torrent burst against it and immediately it collapsed, and the ruin of that house was great" (Luke 6:46–49; cf. Matthew 7:24–27; see Luke 6:12–19; James 1:22).

[HEARING from hear]
Setting: Galilee. After Jesus raises a woman's son from the dead in Nain, the disciples of John the Baptist inquire whether He is the promised Messiah.

And He answered and said to them, "Go and report to John what you have seen and heard: *the* BLIND RECEIVE SIGHT, *the* lame walk, *the* lepers are cleansed, and *the* deaf hear, *the* dead are raised up, *the* POOR HAVE THE GOSPEL PREACHED TO THEM. Blessed is he who does not take offense at Me" (Luke 7:22, 23, Jesus quotes from Isaiah 35:5; 61:1; cf. Matthew 11:2–6).

[HEARING from hear]
Setting: The villages and cities of Galilee. After visiting the home of Simon the Pharisee, Jesus proclaims and preaches the kingdom of God.

When a large crowd was coming together, and those from various cities were journeying to Him, He spoke by way of a parable: "The sower went out to sow his seed; and as he sowed, some fell beside the road, and it was trampled under foot and the birds of the air ate it up. Other *seed* fell on rocky *soil,* and as soon as it grew up, it was withered away, because it had no moisture. Other *seed* fell among the thorns; and the thorns grew up with it and choked it out. Other *seed* fell into the good soil, and grew up, and produced a crop a hundred times as great." As He said these things, He would call out, "He who has ears to hear, let him hear" (Luke 8:4–8; cf. Matthew 13:2–9; Mark 4:3–9).

Setting: Galilee. After Jesus presents the Parable of the Sower to the crowds, His disciples ask Him to give them the parable's meaning.

And He said, "To you it has been granted to know the mysteries of the kingdom of God, but to the rest *it is* in parables, so that SEEING THEY MAY NOT SEE, AND HEARING THEY MAY NOT UNDERSTAND. Now the parable is this: the seed is the word of God. Those beside the road are those who have heard; then the devil comes and takes away the word from their heart, so that they will not believe and be saved. Those on the rocky *soil* are those who, when they hear, receive the word with joy; and these have no *firm* root; they believe for a while, and in time of temptation fall away. The *seed* which fell among the thorns, these are the ones who have heard, and as they go on their way they are choked with worries and riches and pleasures of *this* life, and bring no fruit to maturity. But the *seed* in the good soil, these are the ones who have heard the word in an honest and good heart, and hold it fast, and bear fruit with perseverance" (Luke 8:10–15, Jesus quotes from Isaiah 6:9; cf. Matthew 13:10–23; Mark 4:10–20).

[HEARING from hear]
Setting: Galilee. After giving the Parable of the Lamp to His disciples, Jesus conveys who His true relatives are after being informed that His mother and brothers are seeking Him.

But He answered and said to them, "My mother and My brothers are these who hear the word of God and do it" (Luke 8:21; cf. Matthew 12:26–50; Mark 3:31–35).

[HEARING from hear]
Setting: On the way from Galilee to Jerusalem. After responding to a report from the seventy sent out in pairs to every place He Himself will soon visit, the Lord addresses His disciples in private.

Turning to the disciples, He said privately, "Blessed *are* the eyes which see the things you see, for I say to you, that many prophets and kings wished to see the things you see, and did not see *them*, and to hear the things which you hear, and did not hear *them*" (Luke 10:23, 24; cf. Matthew 13:16, 17; see Luke 10:17).

[HEARING from hear]
Setting: On the way from Galilee to Jerusalem. After revealing a problem with exorcism, Jesus responds to a blessing from a woman in the crowd.

But He said, "On the contrary, blessed are those who hear the word of God and observe it" (Luke 11:28).

[HEARING from hear]
Setting: On the way from Galilee to Jerusalem. After revealing a problem with exorcism and responding to a blessing from a woman in the crowd, Jesus tells the increasing crowds of the sign of Jonah.

As the crowds were increasing, He began to say, "This generation is a wicked generation; it seeks for a sign, and *yet* no sign will be given to it but the sign of Jonah. For just as Jonah became a sign to the Ninevites, so will the Son of Man be to this generation. The Queen of the South will rise up with the men of this generation at the judgment and condemn them, because she came from the ends of the earth to hear the wisdom of Solomon; and behold, something greater than Solomon is here. The men of Nineveh will stand up with this generation at the judgment and condemn it, because they repented at the preaching of Jonah; and behold, something greater than Jonah is here" (Luke 11:29–32; cf. Matthew 16:4; see 1 Kings 10:1–10; Jonah 3:4, 5).

[HEARING from hear]
Setting: On the way from Galilee to Jerusalem. After responding to a guest's proclamation about the blessings of eating bread in the kingdom of God, Jesus presents to large crowds the demands of discipleship.

Now large crowds were going along with Him; and He turned and said to them, "If anyone comes to Me, and does not hate his own father and mother and wife and children and brothers and sisters, yes, and even his own life, he cannot be My disciple. Whoever does not carry his own cross and come after Me cannot be My disciple. For which one of you, when he wants to build a tower, does not first sit down and calculate the cost to see if he has enough to complete it? Otherwise, when he has laid a foundation and is not able to finish, all who observe it begin to ridicule him, saying, 'This man began to build and was not able to finish.' Or what king, when he sets out to meet another king in battle, will not first sit down and consider whether he is strong enough with ten thousand *men* to encounter the one coming against him with twenty thousand? Or else, while the other is still far away, he sends a delegation and asks for terms of peace. So then, none of you can be My disciple who does not give up all his possessions. Therefore, salt is good; but if even salt has become tasteless, with what will it be seasoned? It is useless either for the soil or for the manure pile; it is thrown out. He who has ears to hear, let him hear" (Luke 14:25–35; cf. Matthew 5:13; 10:37–39; see Proverbs 20:18; Philippians 3:7).

[HEARING from hear]
Setting: On the way from Galilee to Jerusalem. The Lord teaches His disciples about stewardship after giving the story of the prodigal son.

Now He was also saying to the disciples, "There was a rich man who had a manager, and this *manager* was reported to him as squandering his possessions. And he called him and said to him, 'What is this I hear about you? Give an accounting of your management, for you can no longer be a manager.' The manager said to himself, 'What shall I do, since my master is taking the management away from me? I am not strong enough to dig; I am ashamed to beg. I know what I shall do, so that when I am removed from the management people will welcome me into their homes.' And he summoned each one of his master's debtors, and he *began* saying to the first, 'How much do you owe my master?' And he said, 'A hundred measures of oil.' And he said to him, 'Take your bill, and sit down quickly and write fifty.' Then he said to another, 'And how much do you owe?' And he said, 'A hundred measures of wheat.' He said to him, 'Take your bill, and write eighty.' And his master praised the unrighteous manager because he had acted shrewdly; for the sons of this age are more shrewd in relation to their own kind than the sons of light. And I say to you, make friends for yourselves by means of the wealth of unrighteousness, so that when it fails, they will receive you into the eternal dwellings. He who is faithful in a very little thing is faithful also in much; and he who is unrighteous in a very little thing is unrighteous also in much. Therefore if you have not been faithful in the *use of* unrighteous wealth, who will entrust the *true riches* to you? And if you have not been faithful in *the use of* that which is another's, who will give you that which is your own? No servant can serve two masters; for either he will hate the one and love the other, or else he will be devoted to one and despise the other. You cannot serve God and wealth" (Luke 16:1–13; cf. Matthew 6:24; see Matthew 25:14–30).

[HEARING from hear]
Setting: On the way from Galilee to Jerusalem. After He responds to the Pharisees' scoffing at His teaching His disciples about stewardship and the permanence of the Law, Jesus conveys the story of the rich man and Lazarus.

"Now there was a rich man, and he habitually dressed in purple and fine linen, joyously living in splendor every day. And a poor man named Lazarus was laid at his gate, covered with sores, and longing to be fed with the *crumbs* which were falling from the rich man's table; besides, even the dogs were coming and licking his sores. Now the poor man died and was carried away by the angels to Abraham's bosom; and the rich man also died and was buried. In Hades he lifted up his eyes, being in torment, and saw Abraham far away and Lazarus in his bosom. And he cried out and said, 'Father Abraham, have mercy on me, and send Lazarus so that he may dip the tip of his finger in water and cool off my tongue, for I am in agony in this flame.' But Abraham said, 'Child, remember that during your life you received your good things, and likewise Lazarus bad things; but now he is being comforted here, and you are in agony. And besides all this, between us and you there is a great chasm fixed, so that those who wish to come over from here to you will not be able, and *that* none may cross over from there to us.' And he said, 'Then I beg you, father, that you send him to my father's house—for I have five brothers—in order that he may warn them, so that they will not also come to this place of torment.' But Abraham said, 'They have Moses and the Prophets; let them hear them.' But he said, 'No, father Abraham, but if someone goes to them from the dead, they will repent!' But he said to him, 'If they do not listen to Moses and the Prophets, they will not be persuaded even if someone rises from the dead' " (Luke 16:19–31; see Luke 3:8; 6:24; 16:1, 14).

[HEARING from hear]
Setting: On the way from Galilee to Jerusalem. After telling His disciples of His second coming, Jesus instructs them about persistence in prayer.

Now He was telling them a parable to show that at all times they ought to pray and not to lose heart, saying, "In a certain city there was a judge who did not fear God and did not respect man. There was a widow in that city, and she kept coming to him, saying, 'Give me legal protection from my opponent.' For a while he was unwilling; but afterward he said to himself, 'Even though I do not fear God nor respect man, yet because this woman bothers me, I will give her legal protection, otherwise by continually coming she will wear me out.'" And the Lord said, "Hear what the unrighteous judge said; now, will not God bring about justice for His elect who cry to Him day and night, and will He delay long over them? I tell you that He will bring about justice for them quickly. However, when the Son of Man comes, will He find faith on the earth?" (Luke 18:1–8; see Luke 11:5–10).

[HEARING from hear]
Setting: The temple in Jerusalem. A few days before His crucifixion, after Jesus prophesies the destruction of the temple during His Olivet Discourse, His disciples ask Him when this will happen.

And He said, "See to it that you are not misled; for many will come in My name, saying, "I am *He*,' and, 'The time is near.' Do not go after them. When you hear of wars and disturbances, do not be terrified; for these things must take place first, but the end *does* not *follow* immediately" (Luke 21:8, 9; cf. Matthew 24:4–8; Mark 13:5–8).

[HEARING from hear]
Setting: Jerusalem. At the time for the Passover of the Jews, after the Lord cleanses the temple, a Pharisee, Nicodemus, asks Him by night the meaning of "born again."

Jesus answered, "Truly, truly, I say to you, unless one is born of water and the Spirit he cannot enter into the kingdom of God. That which is born of the flesh is flesh, and that which is born of the Spirit is spirit. Do not be amazed that I said to you, 'You must be born again.' The wind blows where it wishes and you hear the sound of it, but do not know where it comes from and where it is going; so is everyone who is born of the Spirit" (John 3:5–8; see Psalm 135:7; John 1:13).

[HEARING from hears]
Setting: Jerusalem, by the pool of Bethesda. During the Feast of the Jews, Jesus responds to criticism from the Jewish religious leaders for healing a lame man on the Sabbath and for referring to God as His Father (thereby making Himself equal with God).

"Truly, truly, I say to you, he who hears My word, and believes Him who sent Me, has eternal life, and does not come into judgment, but has passed out of death into life" (John 5:24; see John 3:18; 12:44).

[HEARING from hear]
Setting: Jerusalem. During the Feast of the Jews, Jesus responds to criticism from the Jewish religious leaders by referring to God as His Father (thereby making Himself equal with God) and stating He will someday participate in the resurrection and judgment of men.

"Truly, truly, I say to you, an hour is coming and now is, when the dead will hear the voice of the Son of God, and those who hear will live. For just as the Father has life in Himself, even so He gave to the Son also to have life in Himself; and He gave Him authority to execute judgment, because He is *the* Son of Man. Do not marvel at this; for an hour is coming, in which all who are in the tombs will hear His voice, and will come forth; those who did the good *deeds* to a resurrection of life, those who committed the evil *deeds* to a resurrection of judgment" (John 5:25–29; see Daniel 12:2; John 1:4; 11:24).

[HEARING from hear]
Setting: Jerusalem. During the Feast of the Jews, Jesus responds to criticism from the Jewish religious leaders by referring to God as His Father (thereby making Himself equal with God) and informing them that God, John the Baptist, and His works all testify to His mission.

"I can do nothing on My own initiative. As I hear, I judge; and My judgment is just, because I do not seek My own will, but the will of Him who sent Me. If I *alone* testify about Myself, My testimony is not true. There is another who testifies of Me, and I know that the testimony which He gives about Me is true. You have sent to John, and he has testified to the truth. But the testimony which I receive is not from man, but I say these things so that you may be saved. He was the lamp that was burning and was shining and you were willing to rejoice for a while in his light. But the testimony which I have is greater than the *testimony of* John; for the works which the Father has given Me to accomplish—the very works that I do—testify about Me, that the Father has sent Me. And the Father who sent Me, He has testified of Me. You have neither heard His voice at any time nor seen His form. You do not have His word abiding in you, for you do not believe Him whom He sent" (John 5:30–38; see Matthew 3:17; Mark 1:4–5; John 1:7, 15, 32; 4:34; 8:14–16; 10:25, 37, 38).

[HEARING from hear and hears]
Setting: The temple treasury in Jerusalem. After the scribes and Pharisees question His testimony about Himself, Jesus interacts with them regarding their ancestry and motives.

Jesus said to them, "If God were your Father, you would love Me, for I proceeded forth and have come from God, for I have not even come on My own initiative, but He sent Me. Why do you not understand what I am saying? *It is* because you cannot hear My word. You are of *your* father the devil, and you want to do the desires of your father. He was a murderer from the beginning, and does not stand in the truth because there is no truth in him. Whenever he speaks a lie, he speaks from his own *nature,* for he is a liar and the father of lies. But because I speak the truth, you do not believe Me. Which one of you convicts Me of sin? If I speak truth, why do not believe Me? He who is of God hears the words of God; for this reason you do not hear *them,* because you are not of God" (John 8:42–47; see John 8:1–41; 18:37; 1 John 3:8; 4:6; 5:1).

[HEARING from hear]
Setting: Jerusalem. Following the Pharisees' interrogation and dismissal of the formerly blind man Jesus healed on the Sabbath, the Lord speaks to the Pharisees using parabolic language they do not understand.

"Truly, truly, I say to you, he who does not enter by the door into the fold of the sheep, but climbs up some other way, he is a thief and a robber. But he who enters by the door is a shepherd of the sheep. To him the doorkeeper opens, and the sheep hear his voice, and he calls his own sheep by name and leads them out. When he puts forth all his own, he goes ahead of them, and the sheep follow him because they know his voice. A stranger they simply will not follow, but will flee from him, because they do not know the voice of strangers" (John 10:1–5).

Setting: Jerusalem. Following the Pharisees' interrogation and dismissal of the formerly blind man Jesus healed on the Sabbath, the Lord conveys the Parable of the Good Shepherd to the Pharisees using figures of speech they do not understand.

[HEARING from hear]
So Jesus said to them again, "Truly, truly, I say to you, I am the door of the sheep. All who came before Me are thieves and robbers, but the sheep did not hear them. I am the door; if anyone enters through Me, he will be saved, and will go in and out and find pasture. The thief comes only to steal and kill and destroy; I came that they may have life, and have *it* abundantly. I am the good shepherd; the good shepherd lays down His life for the sheep. He who is a hired hand, and not a shepherd, who is not the owner of the sheep, sees the wolf coming, and leaves the sheep and flees, and the wolf snatches them and scatters *them. He flees* because he is a hired hand and is not concerned about the sheep. I am the good shepherd, and I know My own and My own know Me, even as the Father knows Me and I know the Father; and I lay down My life for the sheep. I have other sheep, which are not of this fold; I must bring them also, and they will hear My voice; and they will become one flock *with* one shepherd. For this reason the Father loves Me, because I lay down My life so that I may take it again. No one has taken it away from Me, but I lay it down on My own initiative. I have authority to take it up again. This commandment I received from My Father" (John 10:7–18; see Isaiah 40:11; 56:8; Jeremiah 23:1; Matthew 11:27).

[HEARING from hear]
Setting: Jerusalem. At the Feast of Dedication, just after Jesus conveys the Parable of the Good Shepherd to the Pharisees (who do not understand it), they ask Him plainly if He is the Christ.

Jesus answered them, "I told you, and you do not believe; the works that I do in My Father's name, these testify of Me. But you do not believe because you are not of My sheep. My sheep hear My voice, and I know them, and they follow Me; and I give eternal life to them, and they will never perish; and no one will snatch them out of My hand. My Father, who has given *them* to Me, is greater than all; and no one is able to snatch *them* out of the Father's hand. I and the Father are one" (John 10:25–30; see John 8:47; 10:4, 17:1–2, 20, 21).

[HEARING from hear]
Setting: Bethany in Judea. After the death of His friend Lazarus, Jesus travels with His disciples from beyond the Jordan to visit Lazarus's sisters, Martha and Mary, and raises Lazarus from the dead.

Jesus said, "Remove the stone." Martha, the sister of the deceased, said to Him, "Lord, by this time there will be a stench, for he has been *dead* four days." Jesus said to her, "Did I not say to you that if you believe, you will see the glory of God?" So they removed the stone. Then Jesus raised His eyes, and said, "Father, I thank You that You have heard Me. I knew that You always hear Me; but because of the people standing around I said it, so that they may believe that you sent Me." When He had said these things, He cried out with a loud voice, "Lazarus, come forth." The man who had died came forth, bound hand and foot with wrappings, and his face was wrapped around with a cloth. Jesus said to them, "Unbind him, and let him go" (John 11:39–44; see Matthew 11:25; John 11:1–38).

[HEARING from hears]
Setting: Jerusalem. Just days before the Passover, with the chief priests and Pharisees plotting to seize Jesus, who is expressing anxiety about His upcoming death by crucifixion, some people believe in Jesus, while others are rejecting His message.

And Jesus cried out and said, "He who believes in Me, does not believe in Me but in Him who sent Me. He who sees Me sees the One who sent Me. I have come *as* Light into the world, so that everyone who believes in Me will not remain in darkness. If anyone hears My sayings and does not keep them, I do not judge him; for I did not come to judge the world, but to save the world. He who rejects Me and does not receive My sayings, has one who judges him; the word I spoke is what will judge him at the last day. For I did not speak on My own initiative, but the Father Himself who sent Me has given Me a commandment *as to* what to say and what to speak. I know that His commandment is eternal life; therefore the things I speak, I speak just as the Father as told Me" (John 12:44–50; see Matthew 10:40; Luke 10:16; John 1:4; 3:17; 5:19; 6:68; 14:9).

[HEARING from hear]
Setting: Jerusalem. Before the Passover, after conveying the upcoming ministry of the Holy Spirit in His disciples' lives, Jesus answers Judas' (not Iscariot) question as to why He discloses Himself to His disciples but not the whole world.

Jesus answered and said to him, "If anyone loves Me, he will keep My word; and My Father will love him, and We will come to him and make Our abode with him. He who does not love Me does not keep My words; and the word which you hear is not Mine, but the Father's who sent Me" (John 14:23, 24; see John 7:16; 8:51).

[HEARING from hears]
Setting: Jerusalem. Before the Passover, after warning His disciples of the persecution they will face after His departure to heaven, Jesus elaborates about the coming ministry of the Holy Spirit.

"I have many more things to say to you, but you cannot bear *them* now. But when He, the Spirit of truth, comes, He will guide you into all the truth; for He will not speak on His own initiative, but whatever He hears, He will speak; and He will disclose to you what is to come. He will glorify Me, for He will take of Mine and will disclose *it* to you. All things that the Father has are Mine; therefore I said that He takes of Mine and will disclose *it* to you (John 16:12–15; see John 7:39; 14:17, 26; 17:10).

[HEARING from hears]
Setting: After the previous and current high priests (Annas and Caiaphas) question Jesus, and Peter denies a second and third time being His disciple, Pilate (Roman governor of Judea) questions Jesus in an attempt to determine if He is a king.

Therefore Pilate said to Him, "So You are a king?" Jesus answered, "You say *correctly* that I am a king. For this I have been born, and for this I have come into the world, to testify to the truth. Everyone who is of the truth hears my voice" (John 18:37; cf. Matthew 27:11; Mark 15:2; Luke 23:3 see John 18:28–36).

[HEARING from hear]
Setting: On the island of Patmos (in the Aegean Sea about fifty miles southwest of Ephesus in modern Turkey). On the Lord's Day (Sunday), about fifty years after Jesus' resurrection, the disciple John encounters the Lord Jesus Christ, who communicates a new revelation for the apostle to record for the church in Ephesus and to six other churches in Asia.

"To the angel of the church in Ephesus write: The One who holds the seven stars in His right hand, the One who walks among the seven golden lampstands, says this: 'I know your deeds and your toil and perseverance, and that you cannot tolerate evil men, and you put to the test those who call themselves apostles, and they are not, and you found them *to be* false; and you have perseverance and have endured for My name's sake, and have not grown weary. But I have *this* against you, that you have left your first love. Therefore remember from where you have fallen, and repent and do the deeds you did at first; or else I am coming to you and will remove your lampstand out of its place—unless you repent. Yet this you do have, that you hate the deeds of the Nicolaitans, which I also hate. He who has an ear, let him hear what the Spirit says to the churches. To him who overcomes, I will grant to eat of the tree of life which is in the Paradise of God' " (Revelation 2:1–7; see Genesis 2:9; Ezekiel 28:13; 1 John 4:1; Revelation 1:10, 11, 19, 20; 2:15, 16).

[HEARING from hear]
Setting: On the island of Patmos (in the Aegean Sea about fifty miles southwest of Ephesus in modern Turkey). On the Lord's Day (Sunday), about fifty years after Jesus' resurrection, the disciple John encounters the Lord Jesus Christ, who communicates a new revelation for the apostle to record for the church in Smyrna and to six other churches in Asia.

"And to the angel of the church in Smyrna write: The first and the last, who was dead, and has come to life, says this: 'I know your tribulation and your poverty (but you are rich), and the blasphemy by those who say they are Jews and are not, but are a synagogue of Satan. Do not fear what you are about to suffer. Behold, the devil is about to cast some of you into prison, so that you will be tested, and you will have tribulation for ten days. Be faithful until death, and I will give you the crown of life. He who has an ear, let him hear what the Spirit says to the churches. He who overcomes will not be hurt by the second death' (Revelation 2:8–11; see Isaiah 44:6; Revelation 1:9, 18; 2:13; 20:6, 14).

[HEARING from hear]
Setting: On the island of Patmos (in the Aegean Sea about fifty miles southwest of Ephesus in modern Turkey). On the Lord's Day (Sunday), about fifty years after Jesus' resurrection, the disciple John encounters the Lord Jesus Christ, who communicates a new revelation for the apostle to record for the church in Pergamum and to six other churches in Asia.

"And to the angel of the church in Pergamum write: The One who has the sharp two-edged sword says this: 'I know where you dwell, where Satan's throne is; and you hold fast My name, and did not deny My faith even in the days of Antipas, My witness, My faithful one, who was killed among you, where Satan dwells. But I have a few things against you, because you have there some who hold the teaching of Balaam, who kept teaching Balak to put a stumbling block before the sons of Israel, to eat things sacrificed to idols and to commit *acts of* immorality. So you also have some who in the same way hold the teaching of the Nicolaitans. Therefore repent; or else I am coming to you quickly, and I will make war against them with the sword of My mouth. He who has an ear, let him hear what the Spirit says to the churches. To him who overcomes, to him I will give *some* of the hidden manna, and I will give him a white stone, and a new name written on the stone which no one knows but he who receives it' (Revelation 2:12–17; see Numbers 25:1–3; Isaiah 62:2; Revelation 1:16; 2:5, 6, 16).

[HEARING from hear]
Setting: On the island of Patmos (in the Aegean Sea about fifty miles southwest of Ephesus in modern Turkey). On the Lord's Day (Sunday), about fifty years after Jesus' resurrection, the disciple John encounters the Lord Jesus Christ, who communicates a new revelation for the apostle to record for the church in Thyatira and to six other churches in Asia.

"And to the angel of the church in Thyatira write: The Son of God, who has eyes like a flame of fire, and His feet are like burnished bronze, says this: 'I know your deeds, and your love and faith and service and perseverance, and that your deeds of late are greater than at first. But I have *this* against you, that you tolerate the woman Jezebel, who calls herself a prophetess, and she teaches and leads My bond-servants astray so that they commit *acts of* immorality and eat things sacrificed to idols. I gave her time to repent, and she does not want to repent of her immorality. Behold, I will throw her on a bed *of sickness,* and those who commit adultery with her into great tribulation, unless they repent of her deeds. And I will kill her children with pestilence, and all the churches will know that I am He who searches the minds and hearts; and I will give to each one of you according to your deeds. But I say to you, the rest who are in Thyatira, who do not hold this teaching, who have not known the deep things of Satan, as they call them—I place no other burden on you. Nevertheless what you have, hold fast until I come. He who overcomes, and he who keeps My deeds until the end, TO HIM I WILL GIVE AUTHORITY OVER THE NATIONS; AND HE SHALL RULE THEM WITH A ROD OF IRON, AS THE VESSELS OF THE POTTER ARE BROKEN TO PIECES, as I also have received *authority* from My Father; and I will give him the morning star. He who has an ear, let him hear what the Spirit says to the churches' (Revelation 2:18–29; Jesus quotes from Psalm 2:8, 9; Isaiah 30:14; see 1 Kings 16:31; Psalm 7:9; Romans 2:5; 1 Corinthians 2:10; 2 Peter 3:9; Revelation 1:14; 2:7; 3:11; 17:1–20).

[HEARING from hear]
Setting: On the island of Patmos (in the Aegean Sea about fifty miles southwest of Ephesus in modern Turkey). On the Lord's Day (Sunday), about fifty years after Jesus' resurrection, the disciple John encounters the Lord Jesus Christ, who communicates a new revelation for the apostle to record for the church in Sardis and to six other churches in Asia.

"To the angel of the church in Sardis write: He who has the seven Spirits of God and the seven stars, says this: 'I know your deeds, that you have a name that you are alive, but you are dead. Wake up, and strengthen the things that remain, which were about to die; for I have not found your deeds completed in the sight of My God. So remember what you have received and heard; and keep *it,* and repent. Therefore if you do not wake up, I will come like a thief, and you will not know at what hour I will come to you. But you have a few people in Sardis who have not soiled their garments; and they will walk with Me in white, for they are worthy. He who overcomes will thus be clothed in white garments; and I will not erase his name from the book of life, and I will confess his name before My Father and before His angels. He who has an ear, let him hear what the Spirit says to the churches' " (Revelation 3:1–6; see Matthew 10:32; Revelation 1:16).

[HEARING from hear]
Setting: The island of Patmos (in the Aegean Sea about fifty miles southwest of Ephesus in modern Turkey). On the Lord's Day (Sunday), about fifty years after Jesus' resurrection, the disciple John encounters the Lord Jesus Christ, who communicates a new revelation for the apostle to record for the church in Thyatira and to six other churches in Asia.

"And to the angel of the church in Thyatira write: The Son of God, who has eyes like a flame of fire, and His feet are like burnished bronze, says this: 'I know your deeds, and your love and faith and service and perseverance, and that your deeds of late are greater than at first. But I have *this* against you, that you tolerate the woman Jezebel, who calls herself a prophetess, and she teaches and leads My bond-servants astray so that they commit *acts of* immorality and eat things sacrificed to idols. I gave her time to repent, and she does not want to repent of her immorality. Behold, I will throw her on a bed *of sickness,* and those who commit adultery with her into great tribulation, unless they repent of her deeds. And I will kill her children with pestilence, and all the churches will know that I am He who searches the minds and hearts; and I will give to each one of you according to your deeds. But I say to you, the rest who are in Thyatira, who do not hold this teaching, who have not known the deep things of Satan, as they call them—I place no other burden on you. Nevertheless what you have, hold fast until I come. He who overcomes, and he who keeps My deeds until the end, TO HIM I WILL GIVE AUTHORITY OVER THE NATIONS; AND HE SHALL RULE THEM WITH A ROD OF IRON, AS THE VESSELS OF THE POTTER ARE BROKEN TO PIECES, as I also have received *authority* from My Father; and I will give him the morning star. He who has an ear, let him hear what the Spirit says to the churches' (Revelation 2:18–29; Jesus quotes from Psalm 2:8, 9; Isaiah 30:14; see 1 Kings 16:31; Psalm 7:9; Romans 2:5; 1 Corinthians 2:10; 2 Peter 3:9; Revelation 1:14; 2:7; 3:11; 17:1–20).

[HEARING from hears and hear]
Setting: On the island of Patmos (in the Aegean Sea about fifty miles southwest of Ephesus in modern Turkey). On the Lord's Day (Sunday), about fifty years after Jesus' resurrection, the disciple John encounters the Lord Jesus Christ, who communicates a new revelation for the apostle to record for the church in Laodicea and to six other churches in Asia.

"To the angel of the church in Laodicea write: The Amen, the faithful and true Witness, the Beginning of the creation of God, says this: 'I know your deeds, that you are neither cold nor hot; I wish that you were cold or hot. So because you are lukewarm, and neither hot nor cold, I will spit you out of My mouth. Because you say, "I am rich, and have become wealthy, and have need of nothing," and you do not know that you are wretched and miserable and poor and blind and naked, I advise you to buy from Me gold refined by fire so that you may become rich, and white garments so that you may clothe yourself, and *that* the shame of your nakedness will not be revealed; and eye salve to anoint your eyes so that you may see. Those whom I love, I reprove and discipline; therefore be zealous and repent. Behold, I stand at the door and knock; if anyone hears My voice and opens the door, I will come in to him and will dine with him, and he with Me. He who overcomes, I will grant to him to sit down with Me on My throne, as I also overcame and sat down with My Father on His throne. He who has an ear, let him hear what the Spirit says to the churches'" (Revelation 3:14–22; see Proverbs 3:12; Hosea 12:8; John 14:23; 16:33).

HEARING DIFFICULTY (Listed as DIFFICULTY, HEARING)

HEART (Specifics such as EARTH, HEART OF THE; and HEART, HARDNESS OF are separate entries; also see HEARTS; and MIND)

Setting: Galilee. During the early part of His ministry, Jesus preaches the Sermon on the Mount to His disciples and the multitudes.

"You have heard that it was said, 'YOU SHALL NOT COMMIT ADULTERY'; but I say to you that everyone who looks at a woman with lust for her has already committed adultery with her in his heart" (Matthew 5:27, 28, Jesus quotes from Exodus 20:14; see 2 Samuel 11:2–5).

Setting: Galilee. During the early part of His ministry, Jesus preaches the Sermon on the Mount to His disciples and the multitudes.

"Do not store up for yourselves treasures on earth, where moth and rust destroy, and where thieves break in and steal. But store up for yourselves treasures in heaven, where neither moth nor rust destroys, and where thieves do not break in or steal; for where your treasure is, there your heart will be also" (Matthew 6:19–21; cf. Luke 12:34; see Proverbs 23:4; Matthew 19:21).

Setting: Galilee. After He heals a blind, mute, demon-possessed man, the Pharisees accuse Jesus in front of crowds of being a worker of Satan.

"Either make the tree good and its fruit good, or make the tree bad and its fruit bad; for the tree is known by its fruit. You brood of vipers, how can you, being evil, speak what is good? For the mouth speaks out of that which fills the heart. The good man brings out of *his* good treasure what is good; and the evil man brings out of *his* evil treasure what is evil. But I tell you that every careless word that people speak, they shall give an accounting for it in the day of judgment. For by your words you will be justified, and by your words you will be condemned" (Matthew 12:33–37; cf. Matthew 3:7; 7:16–18).

Setting: By the Sea of Galilee. Jesus responds to His disciples' questions about the Parable of the Sower, which He has just taught from a boat.

Jesus answered them, "To you it has been granted to know the mysteries of the kingdom of heaven, but to them it has not been granted. For whoever has, to him *more* shall be given, and he will have an abundance; but whoever does not have, even what he has shall be taken away from him. Therefore, I speak to them in parables; because while seeing they do not see, and while hearing they do not hear, nor do they understand. In their case the prophecy of Isaiah is being fulfilled, which says, 'YOU WILL KEEP ON HEARING, BUT WILL NOT UNDERSTAND; YOU WILL KEEP ON SEEING, BUT WILL NOT PERCEIVE; FOR THE HEART OF THIS PEOPLE HAS BECOME DULL, WITH THEIR EARS THEY SCARCELY HEAR, AND THEY HAVE CLOSED THEIR EYES, OTHERWISE THEY WOULD SEE WITH THEIR EYES, HEAR WITH THEIR EARS, AND UNDERSTAND WITH THEIR HEART AND RETURN, AND I WOULD HEAL THEM.' But blessed are your eyes, because they see; and your ears, because they hear. For truly I say to you that many prophets and righteous men desired to see what you see, and did not see *it*, and to hear what you hear, and did not hear *it*" (Matthew 13:11–17, Jesus quotes from Isaiah 6:9, 10; cf. Matthew 25:29; Mark 4:11–13; Luke 8:10; see Deuteronomy 29:4; Matthew 13:10; John 8:56).

Setting: By the Sea of Galilee. With the religious leaders rejecting His message, Jesus begins to teach in parables, and explains the meaning of the Parable of the Sower to His disciples.

"Hear then the parable of the sower. When anyone hears the word of the kingdom and does not understand it, the evil *one* comes and snatches away what has been sown in his heart. This is the one on whom seed was sown beside the road. The one on whom seed was sown on the rocky places, this is the man who hears the word and immediately receives it with joy; yet he has no *firm* root in himself, but is *only* temporary, and when affliction or persecution arises because of the word, immediately he falls away. And the one on whom seed was sown among the thorns, this is the man who hears the word, and the worry of the world and the deceitfulness of wealth choke the word, and it becomes unfruitful. And the one on whom seed was sown on the good soil, this is the man who hears the word and understands it; who indeed bears fruit and brings forth, some a hundredfold, some sixty, and some thirty" (Matthew 13:18–23; cf. Mark 4:13–20; Luke 8:11–15; see Matthew 13:8).

Setting: Galilee. Pharisees and scribes from Jerusalem question Jesus about His disciples' lack of obedience to tradition and the commandments.

And He answered and said to them, "Why do you yourselves transgress the commandment of God for the sake of tradition? For God said, 'HONOR YOUR FATHER AND MOTHER,' and, 'HE WHO SPEAKS EVIL OF FATHER OR MOTHER IS TO BE PUT TO DEATH.' But you say, 'Whoever says to *his* father or mother, "Whatever I have that would help you has been given *to God*," he is not to honor his father or mother.' And *by this* you invalidated the word of God for the sake of your tradition. You hypocrites, rightly did Isaiah prophesy of you: 'THIS PEOPLE HONORS ME WITH THEIR LIPS, BUT THEIR HEART IS FAR AWAY FROM ME. BUT IN VAIN DO THEY WORSHIP ME, TEACHING AS DOCTRINES THE PRECEPTS OF MEN' "(Matthew 15:3–9, Jesus quotes from Exodus 20:12, 21:17, Leviticus 20:9; Isaiah 29:13; cf. Mark 7:5–7; see Colossians 2:22).

Setting: Galilee. Jesus explains the meaning of His instruction to the crowd about what defiles a man.

Peter said to Him, "Explain the parable to us." Jesus said, "Are you still lacking in understanding also? Do you not understand that everything that goes into the mouth passes into the stomach and is eliminated? But the things that proceed out of the mouth come from the heart, and those defile the man. For out of the heart come evil thoughts, murders, adulteries, fornications, thefts, false witness, slanders. These are the things which defile a man; but to eat with unwashed hands does not defile the man" (Matthew 15:15–20; cf. Mark 7:18–23; see Galatians 5:19–21).

Setting: Capernaum of Galilee. Jesus illustrates forgiveness after Peter asks Him if forgiving someone seven times who has sinned against him is adequate.

"For this reason the kingdom of heaven may be compared to a king who wished to settle accounts with his slaves. When he had begun to settle *them,* one who owed him ten thousand talents was brought to him. But since he did not have *the means* to repay, his lord commanded him to be sold, along with his wife and children and all that he had, and repayment to be made. So the slave fell *to the ground* and prostrated himself before him, saying, 'Have patience with me and I will repay you everything.' And the lord of that slave felt compassion and released him and forgave him the debt. But that slave went out and found one of his fellow slaves who owed him a hundred denarii; and he seized him and *began* to choke *him,* saying, 'Pay back what you owe.' So his fellow slave fell *to the ground* and *began* to plead with him, saying, 'Have patience with me and I will repay you.' But he was unwilling and went and threw him in prison until he should pay back what was owed. So when his fellow slaves saw what had happened, they were deeply grieved and came and reported to their lord all that had happened. Then summoning him, his lord said to him, 'You wicked slave, I forgave you all that debt because you pleaded with me. Should you not also have had mercy on your fellow slave, in the same way that I had mercy on you?' And his lord, moved with anger, handed him over to the torturers until he should repay all that was owed him. My heavenly Father will also do the same to you, if each of you does not forgive his brother from your heart" (Matthew 18:23–35; cf. Matthew 6:12, 14, 15; Luke 7:42; see Matthew 25:19–28).

Setting: The temple in Jerusalem. As Jesus teaches, a Pharisee lawyer asks Jesus which is the great commandment of the Law, in order to test Him.

And He said to him, " 'YOU SHALL LOVE THE LORD YOUR GOD WITH ALL YOUR HEART, AND WITH ALL YOUR SOUL, AND WITH ALL YOUR

MIND.' This is the great and foremost commandment. The second is like it, 'YOU SHALL LOVE YOUR NEIGHBOR AS YOURSELF.' On these two commandments depend the whole Law and the Prophets" (Matthew 22:37–40; Jesus quotes from Leviticus 19:18; Deuteronomy 6:5; cf. Mark 12:28–34; see Matthew 7:12).

Setting: The Mount of Olives, just east of Jerusalem. During His discourse, after answering His disciples' questions as to when the temple will be destroyed and Jerusalem overrun, along with the signs of His coming and the end of the age, Jesus reemphasizes to His disciples that they should be on the alert for His return.

"Therefore be on the alert, for you do not know which day your Lord is coming. But be sure of this, that if the head of the house had known at what time of the night the thief was coming, he would have been on the alert and would not have allowed his house to be broken into. For this reason you also must be ready; for the Son of Man is coming at an hour when you do not think *He will.* Who then is the faithful and sensible slave whom his master put in charge of his household to give their food at the proper time? Blessed is that slave whom his master finds so doing when he comes. Truly I say to you that he will put him in charge of all his possessions. But if that evil slave says in his heart, 'My master is not coming for a long time,' and begins to beat his fellow slaves and eat and drink with drunkards; the master of that slave will come on a day when he does not expect *him* and at an hour which he does not know, and will cut him in pieces and assign him a place with the hypocrites; in that place there will be weeping and gnashing of teeth" (Matthew 24:42–51; cf. Mark 13:33–37; Luke 12:39–46; 21:34–36; see Matthew 8:11, 12; 25:21–23).

Setting: Galilee. The Pharisees and some of the scribes from Jerusalem question why Jesus' disciples do not follow the tradition of ceremonial hand cleansing before eating bread.

And He said to them, "Rightly did Isaiah prophesy of you hypocrites, as it is written: 'THIS PEOPLE HONORS ME WITH THEIR LIPS, BUT THEIR HEART IS FAR AWAY FROM ME. BUT IN VAIN DO THEY WORSHIP ME, TEACHING AS DOCTRINES THE PRECEPTS OF MEN.' Neglecting the commandment of God, you hold to the tradition of men." He was also saying to them, "You are experts at setting aside the commandment of God in order to keep tradition. For Moses said, 'HONOR YOUR FATHER AND YOUR MOTHER'; and, 'HE WHO SPEAKS EVIL OF FATHER OR MOTHER, IS TO BE PUT TO DEATH'; but you say, 'If a man says to *his* father or *his* mother, whatever I have that would help you is Corban (that is to say, given *to God*),' you no longer permit him to do anything for *his* father or *his* mother; *thus* invalidating the word of God by your tradition which you have handed down; and you do many things such as that" (Mark 7:6–13, Jesus quotes from Exodus 20:12; 21:17; Isaiah 29:13; cf. Matthew 15:1–6).

Setting: Galilee. After the Pharisees and scribes from Jerusalem question His disciples' lack of obedience to tradition, Jesus speaks to a crowd and explains His teaching to His disciples.

After He called the crowd to Him again, He *began* saying to them, "Listen to Me, all of you, and understand: there is nothing outside the man which can defile him if it goes into him; but the things which proceed out of the man are what defile the man. [If anyone has ears to hear, let him hear."] When he had left the crowd *and* entered the house, His disciples questioned Him about the parable. And He said to them, "Are you so lacking in understanding also? Do you not understand that whatever goes into the man from outside cannot defile him, because it does not go into his heart, but into his stomach, and is eliminated?" (*Thus He* declared all foods clean.) And He was saying, "That which proceeds out of the man, that is what defiles the man. For from within, out of the heart of men, proceed the evil thoughts, fornications, thefts, murders, adulteries, deeds of coveting *and* wickedness, *as well* as deceit, sensuality, envy, slander, pride *and* foolishness. All these evil things proceed from within and defile the man" (Mark 7:14–23; cf. Matthew 15:10–20).

Setting: On the road from Jerusalem to Bethany. After Jesus instructs the money changers while cleansing the temple, Peter draws the Lord's and His disciples' attention to an earlier-cursed fig tree.

And Jesus answered saying to them, "Have faith in God. Truly, I say to you, whoever says to this mountain, 'Be taken up and cast into the sea,' and does not doubt in his heart, but believes that what he says is going to happen, it will be *granted* him. Therefore I say to you, all things for which you pray and ask, believe that you have received them, and they will be *granted* you. Whenever you stand praying, forgive, if you have anything against anyone, so that your Father who is in heaven will also forgive you your transgressions. [But if you do not forgive, neither will your Father who is in heaven forgive your transgressions'] (Mark 11:22–26; cf. Matthew 21:19–22; see Matthew 6:14, 15; 7:7; 17:20).

Setting: The temple in Jerusalem. With the Pharisees and Herodians failing to trap Jesus in a statement, one of the scribes asks Him which commandment is foremost.

Jesus answered, "The foremost is, 'HEAR, O ISRAEL! THE LORD OUR GOD IS ONE LORD; AND YOU SHALL LOVE THE LORD YOUR GOD WITH ALL YOUR HEART, AND WITH ALL YOUR SOUL, AND WITH ALL YOUR MIND AND WITH ALL YOUR STRENGTH.' The second is this, 'YOU SHALL LOVE YOUR NEIGHBOR AS YOURSELF.' There is no other commandment greater than these" (Mark 12:29–31, Jesus quotes from Deuteronomy 6:4, 5; Leviticus 19:18; cf. Matthew 22:34–40).

Setting: Galilee. After selecting His twelve disciples, Jesus teaches the Sermon on the Mount to those disciples and a great throng of people from Judea, Jerusalem, and the central coastal region of Tyre and Sidon.

And He also spoke a parable to them: "A blind man cannot guide a blind man, can he? Will they not both fall into a pit? A pupil is not above his teacher; but everyone, after he has been fully trained, will be like his teacher. Why do you look at the speck that is in your brother's eye, but do not notice the log that is in your own eye? Or how can you say to your brother, 'Brother, let me take out the speck that is in your eye,' when you yourself do not see the log that is in your own eye? You hypocrite, first take the log out of your own eye, and then you will see clearly to take out the speck that is in your brother's eye. For there is no good tree which produces bad fruit, nor, on the other hand, a bad tree which produces good fruit. For each tree is known by its own fruit. For men do not gather figs from thorns, nor do they pick grapes from a briar bush. The good man out of the good treasure of his heart brings forth what is good; and the evil *man* out of the evil *treasure* brings forth what is evil; for his mouth speaks from that which fills his heart" (Luke 6:39–45; cf. Matthew 7:3–6. 16, 18, 20; 12:35; see Matthew 10:24; 15:14; Luke 6:12–19).

Setting: Galilee. After Jesus presents the Parable of the Sower to the crowds, His disciples ask Him to explain the parable's meaning.

And He said, "To you it has been granted to know the mysteries of the kingdom of God, but to the rest *it is* in parables, so that SEEING THEY MAY NOT SEE, AND HEARING THEY MAY NOT UNDERSTAND. Now the parable is this: the seed is the word of God. Those beside the road are those who have heard; then the devil comes and takes away the word from their heart, so that they will not believe and be saved. Those on the rocky *soil* are those who, when they hear, receive the word with joy; and these have no *firm* root, they believe for a while, and in time of temptation fall away. The *seed* which fell among the thorns, these are the ones who have heard, and as they go on their way they are choked with worries and riches and pleasures of *this* life, and bring no fruit to maturity. But the *seed* in the good soil, these are the ones who have heard the word in an honest and good heart, and hold it fast, and bear fruit with perseverance" (Luke 8:10–15, Jesus quotes from Isaiah 6:9; cf. Matthew 13:10–23; Mark 4:10–20; see Luke 8:4–8).

Setting: On the way from Galilee to Jerusalem. After giving a parable about riches and greed, Jesus challenges the crowd and His disciples concerning godly living.

"Sell your possessions and give to charity; make yourselves money belts which do not wear out, an unfailing treasure in heaven, where no thief comes near nor moth destroys. For where your treasure is, there your heart will be also" (Luke 12:33, 34; cf. Matthew 6:19–21; 19:21).

Setting: On the way from Galilee to Jerusalem. When Jesus uses a parable to challenge the crowd and His disciples to be ready for His return, Peter asks Him whom He is addressing.

And the Lord said, "Who then is the faithful and sensible steward, whom his master will put in charge of his servants, to give them their rations at the proper time? Blessed is that slave whom his master finds so doing when he comes. Truly I say to you that he will put him in charge of all his possessions. But if that slave says in his heart, 'My master will be a long time in coming,' and begins to beat the slaves, *both* men and women, and to eat and drink and get drunk; the master of that slave will come on a day when he does not expect *him* and at an hour he does not know, and will cut him in pieces, and assign him a place with the unbelievers. And that slave who knew his master's will and did not get ready or act in accord with his will, will receive many lashes, but the one who did know *it*, and committed deeds worthy of flogging, will receive but few. From everyone who has been given much, much will be required; and to whom they entrusted much, of him they will ask all the more" (Luke 12:42–48; cf. Matthew 24:45–51; see Leviticus 5:17).

Setting: Jerusalem. Before the Passover, after taking issue with Peter's assertion he would lay down his life for Jesus, the Lord comforts and gives hope to His disciples regarding their future after He returns to heaven.

"Do not let your heart be troubled; believe in God, believe also in Me. In My Father's house are many dwelling places; if it were not so, I would have told you; for I go to prepare a place for you. If I go and prepare a place for you, I will come again and receive you to Myself, that where I am, *there* you may be also. And you know the way where I am going" (John 14:1–4; see John 13:35; 14:27, 28).

Setting: Jerusalem. Before the Passover, after He conveys the upcoming ministry of the Holy Spirit in His disciples' lives, Jesus again relates peace, hope, and comfort to them regarding His return to the Father.

"Peace I leave with you; My peace I give to you; not as the world gives do I give to you. Do not let your heart be troubled, nor let it be fearful. You heard that I said to you, 'I go away, and I will come to you,' If you loved Me, you would have rejoiced because I go to the Father, for the Father is greater than I. Now I have told you before it happens, so that when it happens, you may believe. I will not speak much more with you, for the ruler of the world is coming, and he has nothing in Me; but so that the world may know that I love the Father, I do exactly as the Father commanded Me. Get up, let us go from here" (John 14:27–31; see John 10:18, 29; 12:31; 13:19; 16:33).

Setting: Jerusalem. Before the Passover, after warning His disciples of the persecution they will face after His departure to heaven, Jesus elaborates about the coming ministry of the Holy Spirit.

"But now I am going to Him who sent Me; and none of you asks Me, 'Where are You going?' But because I have said these things to you, sorrow has filled your heart. But I tell you the truth, it is to your advantage that I go away; for if I do not go away, the Helper will not come to you; but if I go, I will send Him to you. And He, when He comes, will convict the world concerning sin and righteousness and judgment; concerning sin, because they do not believe in Me; and concerning righteousness, because I go to the Father and you no longer see Me; and concerning judgment, because the ruler of this world has been judged" (John 16:5–11; see John 7:33; 12:31; 14:1, 16; 15:22, 24).

Setting: Jerusalem. Before the Passover, after warning His disciples of the persecution they will face after His departure to heaven, empathizing with their sadness over His prophecies, Jesus gives them hope for the future.

"A little while, and you will no longer see Me; and again a little while, and you will see Me." *Some* of His disciples then said to one another, "What is this thing He is telling us, 'A little while, and you will not see Me; and again a little while, and you will see Me'; and, 'because I go to the Father'?" So they were saying, "What is this that He says, 'A little while'? We do not know what He is talking about." Jesus knew that they wished to question Him, and He said to them, "Are you deliberating together about this, that I said, 'A little while, and you will not see Me, and again a little while, and you will see Me'? Truly, truly, I say to you, that you will weep and lament, but the world will rejoice; you will grieve, but your grief will be turned into joy. Whenever a woman is in labor she has pain, because her hour has come; but when she gives birth to the child, she no longer remembers the anguish because of the joy that a child has been born into the world. Therefore you too have grief now; but I will see you again, and your heart will rejoice, and no one *will* take your joy away from you" (John 16:16–22; see Mark 9:32; Luke 23:27; John 14:18–24; 16:5, 6; 20:20).

HEART, GOOD

Setting: Galilee. After Jesus presents the Parable of the Sower to the crowds, His disciples ask Him to give them the parable's meaning.

And He said, "To you it has been granted to know the mysteries of the kingdom of God, but to the rest *it is* in parables, so that SEEING THEY MAY NOT SEE, AND HEARING THEY MAY NOT UNDERSTAND. Now the parable is this: the seed is the word of God. Those beside the road are those who have heard; then the devil comes and takes away the word from their heart, so that they will not believe and be saved. Those on the rocky *soil* are those who, when they hear, receive the word with joy; and these have no *firm* root; they believe for a while, and in time of temptation fall away. The *seed* which fell among the thorns, these are the ones who have heard, and as they go on their way they are choked with worries and riches and pleasures of *this* life, and bring no fruit to maturity. But the *seed* in the good soil, these are the ones who have heard the word in an honest and good heart, and hold it fast, and bear fruit with perseverance" (Luke 8:10–15, Jesus quotes from Isaiah 6:9; cf. Matthew 13:10–23; Mark 4:10–20).

HEART, HARDENED (Also see HEART, HARDNESS OF)

Setting: Opposite Dalmanutha. After the Pharisees argue with Him, seeking a sign from heaven to test Him, Jesus and His disciples cross to the other side of the Sea of Galilee, where His disciples discuss with one another that they have no bread.

And Jesus, aware of this, said to them, "Why do you discuss *the fact* that you have no bread? Do you not yet see or understand? Do you have a hardened heart? HAVING EYES, DO YOU NOT SEE? AND HAVING EARS, DO YOU NOT HEAR? And do you not remember, when I broke the five loaves for the five thousand, how many baskets full of broken pieces you picked you? They said to Him, "Twelve." When *I broke* the seven for the four thousand, how many large baskets full of broken pieces did you pick up?" They said to Him, "Seven." And He was saying to them, "Do you not yet understand?" (Mark 8:17–21, Jesus quotes from Jeremiah 5:21, cf. Matthew 16:5–12; see Matthew 14:19, 20; Mark 6:41–44, 52; 8:6–9).

HEART, HARDNESS OF (Also see HEART, HARDENED)

Setting: Judea beyond the Jordan (Perea). Jesus responds to the Pharisees' follow-up question before a large crowd about Moses' command regarding a certificate of divorce.

He said to them, "Because of your hardness of heart Moses permitted you to divorce your wives; but from the beginning it has not been this way. And I say to you, whoever divorces his wife, except for immorality, and marries another woman commits adultery" (Matthew 19:8, 9; cf. Deuteronomy 24:1–4; Matthew 5:32; Mark 10:1–12; see Romans 7:2, 3; 1 Corinthians 7:10, 39).

Setting: A synagogue in Galilee. Early in His ministry, Jesus heals a man's withered hand on the Sabbath while the Pharisees observe.

He said to the man with the withered hand, "Get up and come forward!" And He said to them, "Is it lawful to do good or do harm on the Sabbath, to save a life or to kill?" But they kept silent. After looking around at them with anger, grieved at their hardness of heart, He said to the man, "Stretch out your hand." And he stretched it out, and his hand was restored (Mark 3:3–5; cf. Matthew 12:9–14; Luke 6:6–11).

Setting: Judea beyond the Jordan (Perea). Jesus teaches the crowds gathered around Him about divorce after the Pharisees test and question Him on the subject.

And He answered and said to them, "What did Moses command you?" They said, "Moses permitted a *man* TO WRITE A CERTIFICATE OF DIVORCE AND SEND *her* AWAY." But Jesus said to them, "Because of your hardness of heart he wrote you this commandment. But from the beginning of creation, *God* MADE THEM MALE AND FEMALE. FOR THIS REASON A MAN SHALL LEAVE HIS FATHER AND MOTHER, AND THE TWO SHALL BECOME ONE FLESH; so they are no longer two, but one flesh. What therefore God has joined together, let no man separate. In the house the disciples *began* questioning Him about this again. And He said to them, "Whoever divorces his wife and marries another woman commits adultery against her; and if she herself divorces her husband and marries another man, she is committing adultery" (Mark 10:3–12, Jesus quotes from Genesis 1:27; 2:24; cf. Matthew 19:1–9; see

Deuteronomy 24:1–3; Matthew 5:32; see Romans 7:2, 3; 1 Corinthians 7:10, 11, 13, 39; 1 Timothy 2:14).

HEART, HUMBLE IN (Also see HUMILITY)

Setting: Galilee. After rendering a thanksgiving prayer to His Father in heaven, as He preaches and teaches, Jesus offers rest to all who are weary and heavy-laden.

"Come to Me, all who are weary and heavy-laden, and I will give you rest. Take My yoke upon you and learn from Me, for I am gentle and humble in heart, and YOU WILL FIND REST FOR YOUR SOULS. For My yoke is easy and My burden is light" (Matthew 11:28–30, Jesus quotes from Jeremiah 6:16; see Jeremiah 31:35; 1 John 5:3).

HEART OF THE EARTH (Listed under EARTH, HEART OF THE)

HEART, PURE IN

Setting: On a mountain in Galilee. Early in His ministry, Jesus presents the Beatitudes (part of the Sermon on the Mount) to His disciples and the gathered crowds from Galilee, Decapolis, Jerusalem, Judea, and beyond the Jordan.

"Blessed are the pure in heart, for they shall see God" (Matthew 5:8; see Matthew 5:1; 13:35).

HEART, SLOW OF

Setting: On the road to Emmaus. After rising from the grave on the third day after being crucified, Jesus appears to two of His followers, who had heard that His tomb was empty, elaborating on the purpose of His coming to earth.

And He said to them, "O foolish men and slow of heart to believe in all that the prophets have spoken! Was it not necessary for the Christ to suffer these things and to enter into His glory?" (Luke 24:25, 26).

HEARTS (Also see HEART)

Setting: Capernaum near the Sea of Galilee. After Jesus, in front of crowds, heals and forgives a paralytic of his sins, some scribes accuse Him of blasphemy.

And they brought to Him a paralytic lying on a bed. Seeing their faith, Jesus said to the paralytic, "Take courage, son; your sins are forgiven." And some scribes said to themselves. "This *fellow* blasphemes." And Jesus knowing their thoughts said, "Why are you thinking evil in your hearts? Which is easier to say, 'Your sins are forgiven,' or to say, 'Get up, and walk'? But so that you may know that the Son of Man has authority on earth to forgive sins"—then He said to the paralytic, "Get up, pick up your bed and go home" (Matthew 9:2–6; cf. Mark 2:3–12; Luke 5:17–26).

Setting: Capernaum. When Jesus heals and forgives the sins of a paralytic man, some scribes believe He commits blasphemy.

Immediately Jesus, aware in His spirit that they were reasoning that way within themselves, said to them, "Why are you reasoning about these things in your hearts? Which is easier, to say to the paralytic, 'Your sins are forgiven'; or to say, 'Get up, and pick up your pallet and walk'? "But so that you may know that the Son of Man has authority on earth to forgive sins"—He said to the paralytic, "I say to you, get up, pick up your pallet and go home" (Mark 2:8–11; cf. Matthew 9:4–7; Luke 5:21–24).

Setting: Capernaum of Galilee. After Jesus heals and forgives the sins of a paralytic man, some Pharisees and teachers of the law from Galilee and Judea accuse Him of blasphemy.

But Jesus, aware of their reasonings, answered and said to them, "Why are you reasoning in your hearts? Which is easier, to say,

'Your sins have been forgiven you,' or to say, 'Get up and walk'? But, so that you may know that the Son of Man has authority on earth to forgive sins,"—He said to the paralytic—"I say to you, get up, and pick up your stretcher and go home" (Luke 5:22–24; cf. Matthew 9:4–8; Mark 2:8–12; see Matthew 4:24).

Setting: On the way from Galilee to Jerusalem. The Lord responds to the Pharisees' scoffing at His teaching His disciples about stewardship.

And He said to them, "You are those who justify yourselves in the sight of men, but God knows your hearts; for that which is highly esteemed among men is detestable in the sight of God. The Law and the Prophets *were proclaimed* until John; since that time the gospel of the kingdom of God has been preached, and everyone is forcing his way into it. But is it easier for heaven and earth to pass away than for one stroke of a letter of the Law to fail" (Luke 16:15–17; cf. Matthew 5:18; see 1 Samuel 16:7; Matthew 4:23; 11:11–14).

Setting: The Mount of Olives, east of the temple in Jerusalem. After ministering in the temple a few days before His crucifixion, after conveying the Parable of the Fig Tree, Jesus warns His disciples during His Olivet Discourse to keep alert regarding future events.

"Be on guard, so that your hearts will not be weighted down with dissipation and drunkenness and the worries of life, and that day will not come upon you suddenly like a trap; for it will come upon all those who dwell on the face of all the earth. But keep on the alert at all times, praying that you may have strength to escape all these things that are about to take place, and to stand before the Son of Man" (Luke 21:34–36; cf. Mark 13:33; see Matthew 24:42–44).

Setting: Jerusalem After rising from the grave on the third day after being crucified, and appearing to two of His followers on the road to Emmaus, Jesus appears to His disciples (except Thomas).

While they were telling these things, He Himself stood in their midst and said to them, "Peace be to you." But they were startled and frightened and thought they were seeing a spirit. And He said to them, "Why are you troubled, and why do doubts arise in your hearts? See My hands and My feet, that it is I Myself; touch Me and see, for a spirit does not have flesh and bones as you see that I have." And when He had said this, He showed them His hands and His feet. While they still could not believe *it* because of their joy and amazement. He said to them, "Have you anything to eat?" They gave Him a piece of a broiled fish; and He took it and ate *it* before them (Luke 24:36–43; see Mark 16:14; John 20:27; Acts 10:40–41).

Setting: On the island of Patmos (in the Aegean Sea about fifty miles southwest of Ephesus in modern Turkey). On the Lord's Day (Sunday), about fifty years after Jesus' resurrection, the disciple John encounters the Lord Jesus Christ, who communicates a new revelation for the apostle to record for the church in Thyatira and to six other churches in Asia.

"And to the angel of the church in Thyatira write: The Son of God, who has eyes like a flame of fire, and His feet are like burnished bronze, says this: 'I know your deeds, and your love and faith and service and perseverance, and that your deeds of late are greater than at first. But I have *this* against you, that you tolerate the woman Jezebel, who calls herself a prophetess, and she teaches and leads My bond-servants astray so that they commit *acts of* immorality and eat things sacrificed to idols. I gave her time to repent, and she does not want to repent of her immorality. Behold, I will throw her on a bed *of sickness,* and those who commit adultery with her into great tribulation, unless they repent of her deeds. And I will kill her children with pestilence, and all the churches will know that I am He who searches the minds and hearts; and I will give to each one of you according to your deeds. But I say to you, the rest who are in Thyatira, who do not hold this teaching, who have not known the deep things of Satan, as they call them—I place no other burden on you. Nevertheless what you have, hold fast until I come. He who overcomes, and he who keeps My deeds until the end, TO HIM I WILL GIVE AUTHORITY OVER THE NATIONS; AND HE SHALL RULE THEM WITH A ROD OF IRON, AS THE VESSELS OF THE POTTER ARE BROKEN TO PIECES, as I also have received *authority* from My Father; and I will give him the morning star. He who has an ear, let him hear what the Spirit says to the churches' (Revelation 2:18–29; Jesus quotes from Psalm 2:8, 9; Isaiah 30:14; see 1 Kings 16:31; Psalm 7:9; Romans 2:5; 1 Corinthians 2:10; 2 Peter 3:9; Revelation 1:14; 2:7; 3:11;

17:1–20).

HEAT, SCORCHING (Also see SUN)

Setting: Judea beyond the Jordan (Perea). Jesus illustrates the kingdom of heaven to His disciples through the story of laborers in the vineyard.

"For the kingdom of heaven is like a landowner who went out early in the morning to hire laborers for his vineyard. When he had agreed with the laborers for a denarius for the day, he sent them into his vineyard. And he went out about the third hour and saw others standing idle in the market place; and to those he said,' You also go into the vineyard, and whatever is right I will give you.' And *so* they went. Again he went out about the sixth and the ninth hour, and did the same thing. And about the eleventh *hour* he went out and found others standing *around;* and he said to them, 'Why have you been standing idle here all day long?' They said to him, 'Because no one hired us.' He said to them, 'You go into the vineyard too.' When evening came, the owner of the vineyard said to his foreman, 'Call the laborers and pay them their wages, beginning with the last *group* to the first.' When those *hired* about the eleventh hour came, each one received a denarius. When those *hired* first came, they thought that they would receive more; but each of them also received a denarius. When they received it, they grumbled at the landowner, saying, 'These last men have worked *only* one hour, and you have made them equal to us who have borne the burden and the scorching heat of the day.' But he answered and said to one of them, 'Friend, I am doing you no wrong; did you not agree with me for a denarius? Take what is yours and go, but I wish to give to this last man the same as to you. It is not lawful for me to do what I wish with what is my own? Or is your eye envious because I am generous?' So the last shall be first, and the first last" (Matthew 20:1–16; cf. Matthew 19:30).

HEAVEN (Specifics such as HEAVEN, TREASURE IN; and KINGDOM OF HEAVEN are separate entries; also see ETERNAL LIFE; HEAVENS; PARADISE; and PARADISE OF GOD)

Setting: Galilee. Early in His ministry, Jesus presents the Beatitudes (part of the Sermon on the Mount) to His disciples and the gathered crowds from Galilee, Decapolis, Jerusalem, Judea, and beyond the Jordan.

"Blessed are you when *people* insult you and persecute you, and falsely say all kinds of evil against you because of Me. Rejoice and be glad, for your reward in heaven is great; for in the same way they persecuted the prophets who were before you" (Matthew 5:11, 12; cf. 2 Chronicles 36:16; Luke 6:22, 23; 1 Peter 4:14; see Matthew 5:1; 13:35).

Setting: Galilee. During the early part of His ministry, Jesus preaches the Sermon on the Mount to His disciples and the multitudes.

"You are the light of the world. A city set on a hill cannot be hidden; nor does *anyone* light a lamp and put it under a basket, but on the lampstand, and it gives light to all who are in the house. Let your light shine before men in such a way that they may see your good works, and glorify your Father who is in heaven" (Matthew 5:14–16; cf. Mark 4:21; 1 Peter 2:12).

Setting: Galilee. During the early part of His ministry, Jesus preaches the Sermon on the Mount to His disciples and the multitudes.

"Do not think that I came to abolish the Law or the Prophets; I did not come to abolish but to fulfill. For truly I say to you, until heaven and earth pass away, not the smallest letter or stroke shall pass from the Law until all is accomplished" (Matthew 5:17, 18; cf. Matthew 24:35).

Setting: Galilee. During the early part of His ministry, Jesus preaches the Sermon on the Mount to His disciples and the multitudes.

"Again, you have heard that the ancients were told, 'YOU SHALL NOT MAKE FALSE VOWS, BUT SHALL FULFILL YOUR VOWS TO THE LORD.' But I say to you, make no oath at all, either by heaven, for it is the throne of God, or by the earth, for it is the footstool of His feet, or by Jerusalem, for it is THE CITY OF THE GREAT KING. Nor shall you make an oath by your head, for you cannot make one hair white or black. But let your statement be 'Yes, yes' *or* 'No, no'; anything beyond these is of evil" (Matthew 5:33–37, Jesus quotes from Leviticus 19:12, Psalm 48:2; Isaiah 66:1; cf. James 5:12).

Setting: Galilee. During the early part of His ministry, Jesus preaches the Sermon on the Mount to His disciples and the multitudes.

"You have heard that it was said, 'YOU SHALL LOVE YOUR NEIGHBOR and hate your enemy.' But I say to you, love your enemies and pray for those who persecute you, so that you may be sons of your Father who is in heaven; for He causes His sun to rise on *the* evil and *the* good, and sends rain on *the* righteous and *the* unrighteous. For if you love those who love you, what reward do you have? Do not even the tax collectors do the same? If you greet only your brothers, what more are you doing *than others?* Do not even the Gentiles do the same? Therefore, you are to be perfect, as your heavenly Father is perfect" (Matthew 5:43–48, Jesus quotes from Leviticus 19:18; cf. Leviticus 19:2; Luke 6:27–36).

Setting: Galilee. During the early part of His ministry, Jesus preaches the Sermon on the Mount to His disciples and the multitudes.

"Beware of practicing your righteousness before men to be noticed by them; otherwise you have no reward with your Father who is in heaven" (Matthew 6:1; cf. Matthew 6:5, 16).

Setting: Galilee. During the early part of His ministry, Jesus gives a model prayer to His disciples and the multitudes while conveying The Sermon on the Mount.

"Pray, then, in this way: 'Our Father who is in heaven, hallowed be Your name. Your kingdom come. Your will be done, on earth as it is in heaven. Give us this day our daily bread. And forgive us our debts, as we also have forgiven our debtors. And do not lead us into temptation, but deliver us from evil. [For Yours is the kingdom and the power and the glory forever. Amen]'" (Matthew 6:9–13; cf. Luke 11:2–4; see John 17:15).

Setting: Galilee. During the early part of His ministry, Jesus preaches the Sermon on the Mount to His disciples and the multitudes.

"Ask, and it will be given to you; seek, and you will find; knock, and it will be opened to you. For everyone who asks receives, and he who seeks finds, and to him who knocks it will be opened. Or what man is there among you who, when his son asks for a loaf, will give him a stone? Or if he asks for a fish, he will not give him a snake, will he? If you then, being evil, know how to give good gifts to your children, how much more will your Father who is in heaven give what is good to those who ask Him! In everything, therefore, treat people the same way you want them to treat you, for this is the Law and the Prophets" (Matthew 7:7–12; cf. Matthew 22:40; Luke 6:31; 11:9–13; see Psalm 84:11).

Setting: Galilee. During the early part of His ministry, Jesus preaches the Sermon on the Mount to His disciples and the multitudes.

"Not everyone who says to Me, 'Lord, Lord,' will enter the kingdom of heaven, but he who does the will of My Father who is in heaven *will enter.* Many will say to Me on that day, 'Lord, Lord, did we not prophesy in Your name, and in Your name cast out demons, and in Your name perform many miracles?' And then I will declare to them, 'I never knew you, DEPART FROM ME, YOU WHO PRACTICE LAWLESSNESS'" (Matthew 7:21–23, Jesus quotes from Psalm 6:8; cf. Matthew 25:11–13; see Luke 6:46).

Setting: Galilee. Jesus explains the meaning of discipleship as He commissions His twelve disciples for ministry.

"Therefore everyone who confesses Me before men, I will also confess him before My Father who is in heaven. But whoever denies Me before men, I will also deny him before My Father who is in heaven" (Matthew 10:32, 33; cf. Mark 8:38; Luke 12:8).

Setting: Galilee. After performing miracles throughout the region, Jesus pronounces woes against those cities who did not repent.

"Woe to you, Chorazin! Woe to you, Bethsaida! For if the miracles had occurred in Tyre and Sidon which occurred in you, they would have repented long ago in sackcloth and ashes. Nevertheless I say to you, it will be more tolerable for Tyre and Sidon in *the* day of judgment than for you. And you, Capernaum, will not be exalted to heaven, will you? You will descend to Hades; for if the miracles had occurred in Sodom which occurred in you, it would have remained to this day. Nevertheless, I say to you that it will be more tolerable for the land of Sodom in *the* day of judgment, than for you" (Matthew 11:21–24; cf. Matthew 10:15; Luke 10:13–15).

Setting: Galilee. After pronouncing woes against unrepentant cities as He teaches and preaches, Jesus prays a thanksgiving prayer to His Father in heaven.

At that time Jesus said, "I praise You, Father, Lord of heaven and earth, that you have hidden these things from *the* wise and intelligent and have revealed them to infants. Yes, Father, for this way was well-pleasing in Your sight. All things have been handed over to Me by My Father; and no one knows the Son except the Father; nor does anyone know the Father except the Son, and anyone to whom the Son wills to reveal *Him*" (Matthew 11:25–27; cf. Luke 10:21, 22).

Setting: Galilee. Jesus' mother, Mary, and His brothers are waiting to see Him as He teaches and preaches.

But Jesus answered the one who was telling Him and said, "Who is My mother and who are My brothers?" And stretching out His hand toward His disciples, He said, "Behold, My mother and My brothers! For whoever does the will of My Father who is in heaven, he is My brother and sister and mother" (Matthew 12:48–50; cf. Mark 3:31–35; Luke 8:19–21).

Setting: Caesarea Philippi. Jesus responds to Simon Peter's declaration that He is the Christ, the Son of the living God.

And Jesus said to him, "Blessed are you, Simon Barjona, because flesh and blood did not reveal *this* to you, but My Father who is in heaven. I also say to you that you are Peter, and upon this rock I will build My church; and the gates of Hades will not overpower it. I will give you the keys of the kingdom of heaven; and whatever you bind on earth shall have been bound in heaven, and whatever you loose on earth shall have been loosed in heaven" (Matthew 16:17–19; cf. Matthew 18:18; Mark 8:29; Luke 9:20).

Setting: Capernaum of Galilee. Jesus elaborates about the value of little ones after His disciples ask about greatness in the kingdom of heaven.

"See that you do not despise one of these little ones, for I say to you that their angels in heaven continually see the face of My Father who is in heaven" (Matthew 18:10; see Luke 1:19).

Setting: Capernaum of Galilee. Jesus illustrates to His disciples the value of little ones.

"What do you think? If any man has a hundred sheep, and one of them has gone astray, does he not leave the ninety-nine on the mountains and go and search for the one that is straying? If it turns out that he finds it, truly I say to you, he rejoices over it more than the ninety-nine which have not gone astray. So it is not *the* will of your Father who is in heaven that one of these little ones perish" (Matthew 18:12–14; cf. Luke 15:4–7).

Setting: Capernaum of Galilee. Jesus gives instruction about church discipline after conveying to His disciples the value of little ones.

"If your brother sins, go and show him his fault in private; if he listens to you, you have won your brother. But if he does not listen *to you,* take one or two more with you, so that BY THE MOUTH OF TWO OR THREE WITNESSES EVERY FACT MAY BE CONFIRMED. If he refuses to listen to them, tell it to the church; and if he refuses to listen even to the church, let him be to you as a Gentile and a tax collector. Truly I say to you, whatever you bind of earth shall have been bound in heaven; and whatever you loose on earth shall have been loosed in heaven. Again, I say to you, that if two of you agree on earth about anything that they may ask, it shall be done for them by My Father who is in heaven. For there two or three have gathered together in My name, I am there in their midst" (Matthew 18:15–20. Jesus quotes from Deuteronomy 19:15; cf. Matthew 7:7; 16:19; see Leviticus 19:17; Matthew 28:20; 2 Thessalonians 3:6, 14).

Setting: The temple in Jerusalem. Having spent the night in Bethany, Jesus returns, and the chief priests and elders question His authority in an effort to challenge His teaching to the nation.

Jesus said to them, "I will also ask you one thing, which if you tell Me, I will also tell you by what authority I do these things. The baptism of John was from what *source,* from heaven or from men?" And they *began* reasoning among themselves, saying "If we say 'From heaven,' He will say to us, 'Then why did you not believe him?' But if we say, 'From men,' we fear the people; for they all regard John as a prophet." And answering Jesus, they said, "We do not know." He also said to them, "Neither will I tell you by what authority I do these things" (Matthew 21:24–27; cf. Mark 11:29–33; Luke 20:3–8).

Setting: The temple in Jerusalem. The Sadducees question Jesus about Levirate marriage (marriage to a brother-in-law), in order to test Him as He teaches.

But Jesus answered and said to them, "You are mistaken, not understanding the Scriptures nor the power of God. For in the resurrection they neither marry nor are given in marriage, but are like angels in heaven. But regarding the resurrection of the dead, have you not read what was spoken to you by God: 'I AM THE GOD OF ABRAHAM, AND THE GOD OF ISAAC, AND THE GOD OF JACOB'? He is not the God of the dead but of the living" (Matthew 22:29–32, Jesus quotes from Exodus 3:6; cf. Mark 12:18–27; Luke 20:27–38; see Deuteronomy 25:5; John 20:9).

Setting: The temple in Jerusalem. Jesus exposes the truth about Pharisaism to the crowds and His disciples after the Jewish religious leaders test Him with questions.

Then Jesus spoke to the crowds and to His disciples, saying: "The scribes and the Pharisees have seated themselves in the chair of Moses; therefore all that they tell you, do and observe, but do not do according to their deeds; for they say *things* and do not do *them.* They tie up heavy burdens and lay them on men's shoulders, but they themselves are unwilling to move them with *so much as* a finger. But they do all their deeds to be noticed by men; for they broaden their phylacteries and lengthen their tassels *of their garments.* They love the place of honor at banquets and the chief seats in the synagogues, and respectful greetings in the market places, and being called Rabbi by men. But do not be called Rabbi; for One is your Teacher, and you are all brothers. Do not call *anyone* on earth your father; for One is your Father, He who is in heaven. Do not be called leaders; for One is your Leader, *that is,* Christ. But the greatest among you shall be your servant. Whoever exalts himself shall be humbled; and whoever humbles himself shall be exalted" (Matthew 23:1–12; cf. Matthew 20:26; Mark 12:38–40; Luke 20:46, 47; see Exodus 13:9; Deuteronomy 33:3; Matthew 6:1, 5, 6, 9, 16; Mark 14:11; Luke 11:43; 14:11).

Setting: The temple in Jerusalem. After the Jewish religious leaders test Him with questions, Jesus pronounces the fourth of eight woes on them in front of the crowds and His disciples.

"Woe to you, blind guides, who say, "Whoever swears by the temple, *that* is nothing; but whoever swears by the gold of the temple is obligated.' You fools and blind men! Which is more important, the gold or the temple that sanctified the gold? And, 'Whoever swears by the altar, *that* is nothing, but whoever swears by the offering on it, he is obligated.' You blind men, which is more important, the offering, or the altar that sanctifies the offering? Therefore, whoever swears by the altar, swears *both* by the altar and by everything on it. And whoever swears by the temple, swears *both* by the temple and by Him who dwells within it. And whoever swears by heaven, swears *both* by the throne of God and by Him who sits upon it" (Matthew 23:16–22; see Exodus 29:37; 1 Kings 8:13; Isaiah 66:1; Matthew 15:14).

Setting: The Mount of Olives, just east of Jerusalem. During His discourse, after answering His disciples' questions as to when the temple will be destroyed and Jerusalem overrun, along with the signs of His coming and the end of the age, Jesus teaches them the Parable of the Fig Tree.

"Now learn the Parable from the Fig Tree: when its branch has already become tender and puts forth its leaves, you know that summer is near; so, you too, when you see all these things, recognize that He is near, *right* at the door. Truly, I say to you, this generation will not pass away until all these things take place. Heaven and earth will pass away, but My words will not pass away. But of that day and hour no one knows, not even the angels of heaven, nor the Son, but the Father alone. For the coming of the Son of Man will be just like the days of Noah. For as in those days before the flood they were eating and drinking, marrying and giving in marriage, until the day that Noah entered the ark, and they did not understand until the flood came and took them all away; so will the coming of the Son of Man be. Then there will be two men in the field; one will be taken and one will be left. Two women *will be* grinding at the mill; one will be taken and one will be left" (Matthew 24:32–41; cf. Mark 13:28–32; Luke 17:34–36; 21:28–33; see Genesis 6:5; 7:7; Matthew 5:18; 10:23; James 5:9).

Setting: On a mountain in Galilee. Following His resurrection from the dead in Jerusalem, Jesus conveys the Great Commission to His eleven remaining disciples.

And Jesus came up and spoke to them, saying, "All authority has been given to Me in heaven and on earth. Go therefore and make disciples of all the nations, baptizing them in the name of the Father and the Son and the Holy Spirit, teaching them to observe all that I commanded you; and lo, I am with you always, even to the end of the age" (Matthew 28:18–20; cf. Mark 16:15; see Daniel 7:13).

Setting: On the road to Bethany. After Jesus instructs the money changers while cleansing the temple, Peter draws the Lord's and His disciples' attention to an earlier-cursed fig tree.

And Jesus answered saying to them, "Have faith in God. Truly, I say to you, whoever says to this mountain, 'Be taken up and cast into the sea,' and does not doubt in his heart, but believes that what he says is going to happen, it will be *granted* him. Therefore I say to you, all things for which you pray and ask, believe that you have received them, and they will be *granted* you. Whenever you stand praying, forgive, if you have anything against anyone, so that your Father who is in heaven will also forgive you your transgressions. [But if you do not forgive, neither will your Father who is in heaven forgive your transgressions'] (Mark 11:22–26; cf. Matthew 21:19–22; see Matthew 6:14, 15; Matthew 7:7; 17:20).

Setting: The temple in Jerusalem. After Jesus teaches about faith and forgiveness, utilizing a cursed fig tree as an object lesson, His authority is questioned by the chief priests, scribes, and elders.

And Jesus said to them, "I will ask you one question, and you answer Me, and *then* I will tell you by what authority I do these things. Was the baptism of John from heaven, or from men? Answer Me." They *began* reasoning among themselves, saying, "If we say 'From heaven,' He will say, 'Then why did you not believe him?' "But shall we say 'From men'?"—they were afraid of the people, for everyone considered John to have been a real prophet. Answering Jesus, they said, "We do not know." And Jesus said to them, "Nor will I tell you by what authority I do these things" (Mark 11:29–33; cf. Matthew 21:23–27; Luke 20:1–8).

Setting: The temple in Jerusalem. After some of the Pharisees and Herodians attempt to trap Jesus in a statement, some Sadducees question Him about the status of marriage after death.

Jesus said to them, "Is this not the reason you are mistaken, that you do not understand the Scriptures or the power of God? For when they rise from the dead, they neither marry nor are given in marriage, but are like angels in heaven. But regarding the fact that the dead rise again, have you not read in the book of Moses, in the *passage* about *the burning* bush, how God spoke to him, saying, 'I AM THE GOD OF ABRAHAM, AND THE GOD OF ISAAC, and the God of Jacob?' He is not the God of the dead, but of the living; you are greatly mistaken" (Mark 12:24–27, Jesus quotes from Exodus 3:6; cf. Matthew 22:29–33; Luke 20:34–40).

Setting: The Mount of Olives, east of the temple in Jerusalem. After giving His disciples more details about the temple's coming destruction, Jesus elaborates during His Olivet Discourse about other future events.

"But in those days, after that tribulation, THE SUN WILL BE DARKENED AND THE MOON WILL NOT GIVE ITS LIGHT, AND THE STARS WILL BE FALLING from heaven, and the powers that are in the heavens will be shaken. Then they will see THE SON OF MAN COMING IN CLOUDS with great power and glory. And then He will send forth the angels, and will gather together His elect from the four winds, from the farthest end of the earth to the farthest end of heaven" (Mark 13:24–27. Jesus quotes from Isaiah 13:10; 34:4; Daniel 7:13; cf. Matthew 24:29–31; Luke 21:25–27).

Setting: On the Mount of Olives, east of the temple in Jerusalem. After predicting the temple's destruction, Jesus responds during His Olivet Discourse to questions from Peter, James, John, and Andrew about other future events.

"Now learn the parable from the fig tree: when its branch has already become tender and puts forth its leaves, you know that summer is near. Even so, you too, when you see these things happening, recognize that He is near, *right* at the door. Truly I say to you, this generation will not pass away until all these things take place. Heaven and earth will pass away, but My words will not pass away. But of the day or hour no one knows, not even the angels in heaven, nor the Son, but the Father *alone*" (Mark 13:28–32; cf. Matthew 24:32–36; Luke 21:28–33).

Setting: Galilee. After selecting His twelve disciples, Jesus teaches the Beatitudes (part of the Sermon on the Mount) to those disciples and a great throng of people from Judea, Jerusalem, and the central coastal region of Tyre and Sidon.

"Blessed are you when men hate you, and ostracize you, and insult you, and scorn your name as evil, for the sake of the Son of Man. Be glad in that day and leap *for joy*, for behold, your reward is great in heaven. For in the same way their fathers used to treat the prophets" (Luke 6:22, 23; cf. Matthew 5:10–12; see 2 Chronicles 36:16).

Setting: On the way from Galilee to Jerusalem. The Lord pronounces woes on cities who reject the gospel as He appoints seventy followers and sends them out in pairs to every place He Himself will soon visit.

"Woe to you, Chorazin! Woe to you, Bethsaida! For if the miracles had been performed in Tyre and Sidon which occurred in you, they would have repented long ago, sitting in sackcloth and ashes. But it will be more tolerable for Tyre and Sidon in the judgment than for you. And you, Capernaum, will not be exalted to heaven, will you? You will be brought down to Hades! The one who listens to you listens to Me, and the one who rejects you rejects Me; and he who rejects Me rejects the One who sent Me" (Luke 10:13–16; cf. Matthew 11:21–23; see Matthew 10:40; Luke 10:1).

Setting: On the way from Galilee to Jerusalem. The Lord responds to a report from the seventy sent out in pairs to every place He Himself will soon visit.

And He said to them, "I was watching Satan fall from heaven like lightning. Behold, I have given you authority to tread on serpents and scorpions, and over all the power of the enemy, and nothing will injure you. Nevertheless do not rejoice in this, that the spirits are subject to you, but rejoice that your names are recorded in heaven" (Luke 10:18–20; see Psalm 91:13; Isaiah 14:12–14; Luke 9:1).

Setting: On the way from Galilee to Jerusalem. The Lord responds to a report from the seventy sent out in pairs to every place where He Himself would soon visit.

At that very time He rejoiced greatly in the Holy Spirit, and said, "I praise You, O Father, Lord of heaven and earth, that You have hidden these things from *the* wise and intelligent and have revealed them to infants. Yes, Father, for this way was well-pleasing in Your sight. All things have been handed over to Me by My Father, and no one knows who the Son is except the Father, and who the Father is except the Son, and anyone to whom the Son wills to reveal *Him*" (Luke 10:21, 22; cf. Matthew 11:25–27; see Luke 10:1, 17; John 3:35; 10:15).

Setting: On the way from Galilee to Jerusalem. After Jesus presents to large crowds the demands of discipleship, the Pharisees and scribes complain He associates with tax collectors and sinners.

So He told them this parable, saying, "What man among you, if he has a hundred sheep and has lost one of them, does not leave the ninety-nine in the open pasture and go after the one which is lost until he finds it? When he has found it, he lays it on his shoulders, rejoicing. And when he comes home, he calls together his friends and his neighbors, saying to them, 'Rejoice with me, for I have found my sheep which was lost!' I tell you that in the same way, there will be *more* joy in heaven over one sinner who repents than over ninety-nine righteous persons who need no repentance" (Luke 15:3–7; cf. Matthew 18:12–14; see Matthew 9:11–13; Luke 5:29–32).

Setting: On the way from Galilee to Jerusalem. Jesus conveys the illustration of the prodigal son because the Pharisees and scribes complain He associates with tax collectors and sinners.

And He said, "A man had two sons. The younger of them said to his father, 'Father, give me the share of the estate that falls to me.' So he divided his wealth between them. And not many days later, the younger son gathered everything together and went on a journey into a distant country, and there he squandered his estate with loose living. Now when he had spent everything, a severe famine occurred in that country, and he began to be impoverished. So he went and hired himself out to one of the citizens of that country, and he sent him into his fields to feed swine. And he would have gladly filled his stomach with the pods that the swine were eating, and no one was giving *anything* to him. But when he came to his senses, he said, 'How many of my father's hired men have more than enough bread, but I am dying here with hunger! I will get up and go to my father, and will say to him, "Father, I have sinned against heaven, and in your sight; I am no longer worthy to be called your son; make me as one of your hired men."' So he got up and came to his father. But while he was still a long way off, his father saw him and felt compassion *for him,* and ran and embraced him and kissed him. And the son said to him, "Father, I have sinned against heaven and in your sight; I am no longer worthy to be called your son.' But the father said to his slaves, 'Quickly bring out the best robe and put it on him, and put a ring on his hand and sandals on his feet; and bring the fattened calf, kill it, and let us eat and celebrate; for this son of mine was dead and has come to life again; he was lost and has been found.' And they began to celebrate. Now his older son was in the field, when he came and approached the house, he heard music and dancing. And he summoned one of the servants and *began* inquiring what these things could be. And he said to him, 'Your brother has come, and your father has killed the fattened calf because he has received him back safe and sound.' But he became angry and was not willing to go in; and his father came out and *began* pleading with him. But he answered and said to his father, 'Look! For so many years I have been serving you and I have never neglected a command of yours; and *yet* you have never given me a young goat, so that I might celebrate with my friends; but when this son of yours came, who has devoured your wealth with prostitutes, you killed the fattened calf for him.' And he said to him, 'Son, you have always been with me, and all that is mine is yours. But we had to celebrate and rejoice, for this brother of yours was dead and *has begun* to live, and was lost and has been found' " (Luke 15:11–32; see Proverbs 29:2; Luke 15:1, 2).

Setting: On the way from Galilee to Jerusalem. The Lord responds to the Pharisees' scoffing at His teaching His disciples about stewardship.

And He said to them, "You are those who justify yourselves in the sight of men, but God knows your hearts; for that which is highly esteemed among men is detestable in the sight of God. The Law and the Prophets *were proclaimed* until John; since that time the gospel of the kingdom of God has been preached, and everyone is forcing his way into it. But is it easier for heaven and earth to pass away than for one stroke of a letter of the Law to fail" (Luke 16:15–17; cf. Matthew 5:18; see 1 Samuel 16:7; Matthew 4:23; 11:11–14).

Setting: Samaria, on the way from Galilee to Jerusalem. After the Pharisees question Him about the coming of the kingdom of God, Jesus tells His disciples of His second coming.

And He said to the disciples, "The days will come when you will long to see one of the days of the Son of Man, and you will not see it. They will say to you, 'Look there! Look here!' Do not go away, and do not run after *them.* For just like the lightning, when it flashes out of one part of the sky, shines to the other part of the sky, so will the Son of Man be in His day. But first He must suffer many things and be rejected by this generation. And just as it happened in the days of Noah, so it will be also in the days of the Son of Man: they were eating, they were drinking, they were marrying, they were being given in marriage, until the day that Noah entered the ark, and the flood came and destroyed them all. It was the same as happened in the days of Lot: they were eating, they were drinking, they were buying, they were selling, they were planting, they were building; but on the day that Lot went out from Sodom it rained fire and brimstone from heaven and destroyed them all. It will be just the same on the day that the Son of Man is revealed. On that day, the one who is on the housetop and whose goods are in the house must not go down to take them out; and likewise the one who is in the field must not turn back. Remember Lot's wife. Whoever seeks to keep his life will lose it, and whoever loses *his life* will preserve it. I tell you, on that night there will be two in one bed; one will be taken and the other will be left. There will be two women grinding at the same place; one will be taken and the other will be left. [Two men will be in the field; one will be taken and the other will be left."] And answering they said to Him, "Where, Lord?" And He said to them, "Where the body *is*, there also the vultures will be gathered" (Luke 17:22–37; see Genesis 19; Matthew 10:39; 16:21, 27; 24:17–28, 37–41).

Setting: On the way from Galilee to Jerusalem. After instructing His disciples about persistence in prayer, Jesus conveys a parable about self-righteousness.

And He also told this parable to some people who trusted in themselves that they were righteous, and viewed others with contempt: "Two men went up into the temple to pray, one a Pharisee and the other a tax collector. The Pharisee stood and was praying this to himself: 'God, I thank You that I am not like other people: swindlers, unjust, adulterers, or even like this tax collector. I fast twice a week; I pay tithes of all that I get.' But the tax collector, standing some distance away, was even unwilling to lift up his eyes to heaven, but was beating his breast, saying, 'God, be merciful to me, the sinner!' I tell you, this man went to his house justified rather than the other; for everyone who exalts himself will be humbled, but he who humbles himself will be exalted" (Luke 18:9–14; see Ezra 9:6; Matthew 6:5, 23:12; Luke 11:42, 16:15; Romans 14:3, 10).

Setting: The temple in Jerusalem. A few days before Jesus' crucifixion, with His conflict with the religious leaders of Israel escalating, the chief priests and the scribes question His authority to teach and preach.

Jesus answered and said to them, "I will also ask you a question, and you tell Me: Was the baptism of John from heaven or from men?" They reasoned among themselves, saying, "If we say, 'From heaven,' He will say, 'Why did you not believe him?' But if we say, 'From men,' all the people will stone us to death, for they are convinced that John was a prophet." So they answered that they did not know where *it came* from. And Jesus said to them, "Nor will I tell you by what authority I do these things" (Luke 20:3–8; cf. Matthew 21:23–27; Mark 11:27–33).

Setting: The Mount of Olives, east of the temple in Jerusalem. After ministering in the temple a few days before His crucifixion, and giving His disciples more details regarding the temple's future destruction, Jesus elaborates during His Olivet Discourse about things to come.

Then He continued by saying to them, "Nation will rise against nation and kingdom against kingdom, and there will be great earthquakes, and in various places plagues and famines; and there will be terrors and great signs from heaven. But before all these things, they will lay their hands on you and will persecute you, delivering you to the synagogues and prisons, bringing you before kings and governors for My name's sake. It will lead to an opportunity for your testimony. So make up your minds not to prepare beforehand to defend yourselves; for I will give you utterance and wisdom which none of your opponents will be able to resist or refute. But you will be betrayed even by parents and brothers and relatives and friends, and they will put *some* of you to death, and you will be hated by all because of My name. Yet not a hair of your head will perish. By your endurance you will gain your lives" (Luke 21:10–19; cf. Matthew 10:19–22; 24:7–14; Mark 13:8–13).

Setting: The Mount of Olives, just east of Jerusalem. After ministering in the temple a few days before His crucifixion, and giving His disciples more details regarding His return, Jesus conveys the Parable of the Fig Tree during His Olivet Discourse.

Then He told them a parable: "Behold the fig tree and all the trees; as soon as they put forth *leaves,* you see it and know for yourselves that summer is now near. So you also, when you see these things happening, recognize that the kingdom of God is near. Truly, I say to you, this generation will not pass away until all things take place. Heaven and earth will pass away, but My words will not pass away" (Luke 21:29–33; cf. Matthew 24:32–35; Mark 13:28–31; see Matthew 5:18).

Setting: Jerusalem. At the time for the Passover of the Jews, after the Lord cleanses the temple, a Pharisee, Nicodemus, asks Him by night the meaning of "born of the Spirit."

Jesus answered and said to him, "Are you the teacher of Israel and do not understand these things? Truly, truly, I say to you, we speak of what we know and testify of what we have seen, and you do not accept our testimony. If I told you earthly things and you do not believe, how will you believe if I tell you heavenly things? No one has ascended into heaven, but He who descended from heaven: the Son of Man. As Moses lifted up the serpent in the wilderness, even so must the Son of Man be lifted up; so that whoever believes will in Him have eternal life" (John 3:10–15; see Numbers 21:9; Proverbs 30:4; John 12:34; 20:30, 31).

Setting: Capernaum. The day after Jesus walks on the Sea of Galilee to join His disciples in a boat, the people He miraculously fed with a lad's five loaves and two fish quiz Him about the signs and works He performs so they may believe in Him.

Jesus then said to them, "Truly, truly, I say to you, it is not Moses who has given you the bread out of heaven, but it is My Father who gives you the true bread out of heaven. For the bread of God is that which comes down out of heaven, and gives life to the world" (John 6:32, 33; see John 6:50).

Setting: Capernaum. The day after Jesus walks on the Sea of Galilee to join His disciples in a boat, the people He miraculously fed with a lad's five loaves and two fish ask Him to always give them this bread out of heaven.

Jesus said to them, "I am the bread of life; he who comes to Me will not hunger, and he who believes in Me will never thirst. But I said to you that you have seen Me, and yet do not believe. All that the Father gives Me will come to Me, and the one who comes to Me I will certainly not cast out. For I have come down from heaven, not to do My own will, but the will of Him who sent Me. This is the will of Him who sent Me, that of all that He has given Me I lose nothing, but raise it up on the last day. For this is the will of My Father, that everyone who beholds the Son and believes in Him will have eternal life, and I Myself will raise him up on the last day" (John 6:35–40; see John 3:13, 16; 4:13, 14; 6:51).

Setting: Capernaum of Galilee. After Jesus informs the people whom He miraculously fed with a lad's five loaves and two fish how they might receive the bread out of heaven, the Jewish religious leaders grumble because He claims that He came down out of heaven.

Therefore the Jews were grumbling about Him, because He said, "I am the bread that came down out of heaven." They were saying, "Is not this Jesus, the son of Joseph, whose father and mother we know? How does He now say, 'I have come down out of heaven'?" Jesus answered and said to them, "Do not grumble among yourselves. No one can come to Me unless the Father who sent Me draws him; and I will raise him up on the last day. It is written in the prophets, 'AND THEY SHALL ALL BE TAUGHT OF GOD.' Everyone who has heard and learned from the Father, comes to Me. Not that anyone has seen the Father, except the One who is from God; He has seen the Father. Truly, truly, I say to you, he who believes has eternal life. I am the bread of life. Your fathers ate the manna in the wilderness, and they died. This is the bread which comes down out of heaven, so that one may eat of it and not die. I am the living bread that came down out of heaven; if anyone eats of this bread, he will live forever; and the bread also which I will give for the life of the world is My flesh" (John 6:41–51, Jesus quotes from Isaiah 54:13; see John 1:18, 29; 3:36; 6:58; 7:27).

Setting: Capernaum of Galilee. After Jesus informs the people whom He miraculously fed with a lad's five loaves and two fish how they might receive the bread out of heaven, the Jewish religious leaders argue with one another when He says He will give His flesh to the world to eat.

So Jesus said to them, "Truly, truly, I say to you, unless you eat the flesh of the Son of Man and drink His blood, you have no life in yourselves. He who eats My flesh and drinks My blood has eternal life, and I will raise him up on the last day. For My flesh is true food, and My blood is true drink. He who eats My flesh and drinks My blood abides in Me, and I in him. As the living Father sent Me, and I live because of the Father, so he who eats Me, he also will live because of Me. This is the bread which came down out of heaven; not as the fathers ate and died; he who eats this bread will live forever" (John 6:53–58; see Matthew 16:16; Luke 4:22; John 3:36; John 6:26–40 9:16; 15:4).

[HEAVEN from ascending to where He was before]
Setting: The synagogue at Capernaum of Galilee. After the Jewish religious leaders argue with one another when Jesus says He will give His flesh to the world to eat, some of His disciples also express difficulty with His statements.

But Jesus, conscious that His disciples grumbled at this, said to them, "Does this cause you to stumble? *What* then if you see the Son of Man ascending to where He was before? It is the Spirit who gives life; the flesh profits nothing; the words that I have spoken to you are spirit and are life. But there are some of you who do not believe." For Jesus knew from the beginning who they were who did not believe, and who it was that would betray Him. And He was saying, "For this reason I have said to you, that no one can come to Me unless it has been granted him from the Father" (John 6:61–65; see Matthew 11:6; 13:11; John 3:13).

[HEAVEN from where I am from]
Setting: The temple in Jerusalem. After receiving encouragement from His blood brothers in Galilee to attend the upcoming Feast of Booths in order to demonstrate His works to His disciples and the world, Jesus goes and teaches, causing discussion whether He is the Christ.

Then Jesus cried out in the temple, teaching and saying, "You both know Me and know where I am from; and I have not come of Myself, but He who sent Me is true, whom you do not know. I know Him, because I am from Him, and He sent Me" (John 7:28, 29; see John 3:17; 6:46; 7:10–15; 8:42).

[HEAVEN from I go to Him who sent Me and where I am, you cannot come]
Setting: The temple in Jerusalem. During the Feast of Booths, Jesus causes discussion whether He is the Christ. Many believe in Him, while the chief priests and Pharisees plan to seize Him.

Therefore Jesus said, "For a little while longer I am with you, then I go to Him who sent Me. You will seek Me, and will not find Me; and where I am, you cannot come" (John 7:33, 34; see John 7:10–15; 12:35).

[HEAVEN from where I am, you cannot come]
Setting: The temple in Jerusalem. During the Feast of Booths, Jesus causes discussion whether He is the Christ. Many believe in Him, while the chief priests and Pharisees attempt to understand where Jesus intends to go that they cannot find Him.

What is this statement that He said, 'You will seek Me, and will not find Me; and where I am, you cannot come'? (John 7:36; see John 7:10–15)

[HEAVEN from where I came from; where I am going; and where I come from]
Setting: The temple in Jerusalem. Following the Feast of Booths and the scribes' and Pharisees' failed attempt to stone a woman for adultery, Jesus returns the next day to teach. His enemies question His testimony about Himself.

Jesus answered and said to them, "Even if I testify about Myself, My testimony is true, for I know where I came from and where I am going; but you do not know where I come from or where I am going. You judge according to the flesh; I am not judging anyone. But even if I do judge, My judgment is true; for I am not alone *in it,* but I and the Father who sent Me. Even in your law it has been written that the testimony of two men is true. I am He who testifies about Myself, and the Father who sent Me testifies about Me." So they were saying to Him, "Where is Your Father?" Jesus answered, "You know neither Me nor My Father; if you knew Me, you would know My Father also" (John 8:14–19; see Deuteronomy 17:6; 19:15; Matthew 18:16; John 3:17; 5:30, 37;

7:28; 8:42).

[HEAVEN from where I am going and from above]
Setting: The temple treasury in Jerusalem. Following the Feast of Booths and the scribes' and Pharisees' failed attempt to stone a woman for adultery, Jesus returns the next day to teach. His enemies question His testimony about Himself.

Then He said again to them, "I go away, and you will seek Me, and will die in your sin; where I am going, you cannot come." So the Jews were saying, "Surely He will not kill Himself, will He, since He says, "Where I am going, you cannot come'?" And He was saying to them, "You are from below, I am from above; you are of this world, I am not of this world. Therefore I said to you that you will die in your sins; for unless you believe that I am *He,* you will die in your sins." So they were saying to Him, "Who are You?" Jesus said to them, "What have I been saying to you *from* the beginning? I have many things to speak and to judge concerning you, but He who sent Me is true; and the things which I heard from Him, these I speak to the world" (John 8:21–26; see John 3:31–33; 5:34, 35; 17:14, 16).

[HEAVEN from Where I am going]
Setting: Jerusalem. Before the Passover, after revealing to His disciples Judas will betray Him to the chief priests and Pharisees, Jesus conveys how He will soon be glorified in His death, and commands them to love one another.

Therefore when he had gone out, Jesus said, "Now is the Son of Man glorified, and God is glorified in Him; if God is glorified in Him, God will also glorify Him in Himself, and will glorify Him immediately. Little children, I am with you a little while longer. You will seek Me; and as I said to the Jews, now I also say to you, 'Where I am going, you cannot come.' A new commandment I give to you, that you love one another, even as I have loved you, that you also love one another. By this all men will know that you are My disciples, if you have love for one another" (John 13:31–35; see Leviticus 19:18; John 7:33, 34; 17:1; 1 John 3:14).

[HEAVEN from Where I go]
Setting: Jerusalem. Before the Passover, after revealing to His disciples they cannot follow Him back to heaven, Jesus takes issue with Peter's assertion he would lay down his life for the Lord.

Simon Peter said to Him, "Lord, where are You going?" Jesus answered, "Where I go, you cannot follow Me now; but you will follow later." Peter said to Him, "Lord, why can I not follow You right now? I will lay down my life for You." Jesus answered, "Will you lay down your life for Me? Truly, truly, I say to you, a rooster will not crow until you deny Me three times" (John 13:36–38; see Matthew 26:34; Mark 14:30, 72; Luke 22:33, 34).

[HEAVEN from My Father's House and where I am going]
Setting: Jerusalem. Before the Passover, after taking issue with Peter's assertion he would lay down his life for Him, Jesus comforts and gives hope to His disciples regarding their future after He returns to heaven.

"Do not let your heart be troubled; believe in God, believe also in Me. In My Father's house are many dwelling places; if it were not so, I would have told you; for I go to prepare a place for you. If I go and prepare a place for you, I will come again and receive you to Myself, that where I am, *there* you may be also. And you know the way where I am going" (John 14:1–4; see John 13:35; 14:27, 28).

[HEAVEN from I am going to Him who sent Me]
Setting: Jerusalem. Before the Passover, after warning His disciples of the persecution they will face after His departure to heaven, Jesus elaborates about the coming ministry of the Holy Spirit.

"But now I am going to Him who sent Me; and none of you asks Me, 'Where are You going?' But because I have said these things to you, sorrow has filled your heart. But I tell you the truth, it is to your advantage that I go away; for if I do not go away, the Helper will not come to you; but if I go, I will send Him to you. And He, when He comes, will convict the world concerning sin and righteousness and judgment; concerning sin, because they do not believe in Me; and concerning righteousness, because I go to the Father and you no longer see Me; and concerning judgment, because the ruler of this world has been judged" (John 16:5–11; see John 7:33; 12:31; 14:1, 16; 15:22, 24).

[HEAVEN from I am leaving the world again and going to the Father]
Setting: Jerusalem. Before the Passover, after empathizing with His disciples' sadness over His prophecies and giving them the hope for the future, Jesus conveys promises about praying in His name.

"In that day you will not question Me about anything. Truly, truly, I say to you, if you ask the Father for anything in My name, He will give it to you. Until now you have asked for nothing in My name; ask and you will receive, so that your joy may be made full. These things I have spoken to you in figurative language; an hour is coming when I will no longer speak to you in figurative language, but will tell you plainly of the Father. In that day you will ask in My name, and I do not say to you that I will request of the Father on your behalf; for the Father Himself loves you, because you have loved Me and have believed that I came forth from the Father. I came forth from the Father and have come into the world; I am leaving the world again and going to the Father" (John 16:23–28; see Matthew 13:34; John 8:42; 13:1, 3; 14:14, 21, 23; 15:16).

[HEAVEN from from above]
Setting: Jerusalem. Pilate (Roman governor of Judea) continues to find no guilt in Jesus, but has Him scourged in an attempt to appease the hostile Jewish religious leaders, then seeks more information as to where the King of the Jews is from.

Jesus answered, "You would have no authority over Me, unless it had been given you from above; for this reason he who delivered Me to you has *the* greater sin" (John 19:11; see Romans 13:1).

Setting: On the island of Patmos (in the Aegean Sea about fifty miles southwest of Ephesus in modern Turkey). On the Lord's Day (Sunday), about fifty years after Jesus' resurrection, the disciple John encounters the Lord Jesus Christ, who communicates a new revelation for the apostle to record for the church in Philadelphia and to six other churches in Asia.

"And to the angel of the church in Philadelphia write: He who is holy, who is true, who has the key of David, who opens and no one will shut, and who shuts and no one opens, says this: 'I know your deeds. Behold, I have put before you an open door which no one can shut, because you have a little power, and have kept My word, and have not denied My name. Behold, I will cause *those* of the synagogue of Satan, who say that they are Jews and are not, but lie—I will make them come and bow down at your feet, and *make them* know that I have loved you. Because you have kept the word of My perseverance, I also will keep you from the hour of testing, that *hour* which is about to come upon the whole world, to test those who dwell on the earth. I am coming quickly; hold fast what you have, so that no one will take your crown. He who overcomes, I will make him a pillar in the temple of My God, and he will not go out from it anymore; and I will write on him the name of My God, and the name of the city of My God, the new Jerusalem, which comes down out of heaven from My God, and My new name. He who has an ear, let him hear what the Spirit says to the churches' " (Revelation 3:7–13; see Isaiah 22:22; Galatians 2:9; Revelation 2:9–10, 13, 25; 14:1).

HEAVEN, BREAD OUT OF (Also see BREAD)
Setting: Capernaum. The day after Jesus walks on the Sea of Galilee to join His disciples in a boat, the people He miraculously fed with a lad's five loaves and two fish quiz Him about the signs and works He performs so they may believe in Him.

Jesus then said to them, "Truly, truly, I say to you, it is not Moses who has given you the bread out of heaven, but it is My Father who gives you the true bread out of heaven. For the bread of God is that which comes down out of heaven, and gives life to the world" (John 6:32, 33; see John 6:50).

HEAVEN, CLOUDS OF

Setting: Jerusalem. After being betrayed by Judas and arrested, Jesus appears before Caiaphas the high priest and the Council, who interrogate and try to entrap Him.

Jesus said to him, "You have said it *yourself;* nevertheless I tell you, hereafter you will see THE SON OF MAN SITTING AT THE RIGHT HAND OF POWER, AND COMING ON THE CLOUDS OF HEAVEN" (Matthew 26:64, Jesus quotes from Daniel 7:13; cf. Mark 14:62).

Setting: Jerusalem. Following His betrayal by Judas and arrest, Jesus confirms He is the Christ to the high priest and all the chief priests, as they seek justification for putting Him to death.

And Jesus said, "I am; and you shall see THE SON OF MAN SITTING AT THE RIGHT HAND OF POWER, and COMING WITH THE CLOUDS OF HEAVEN" (Mark 14:62, Jesus quotes from Psalm 110:1; Daniel 7:13; cf. Matthew 26:57–68; see Luke 22:54).

HEAVEN, FARTHEST END OF

Setting: On the Mount of Olives, east of the temple in Jerusalem. After predicting the temple's destruction, Jesus responds during His Olivet Discourse to questions from Peter, James, John, and Andrew about other future events.

"But in those days, after that tribulation, THE SUN WILL BE DARKENED AND THE MOON WILL NOT GIVE ITS LIGHT, AND THE STARS WILL BE FALLING from heaven, and the powers that are in the heavens will be shaken. Then they will see THE SON OF MAN COMING IN CLOUDS with great power and glory. And then He will send forth the angels, and will gather together His elect from the four winds, from the farthest end of the earth to the farthest end of heaven" (Mark 13:24–27. Jesus quotes from Isaiah 13:10; 34:4 and Daniel 7:13; cf. Matthew 24:29–31 and Luke 21:25–27).

HEAVEN, KINGDOM OF (Listed as KINGDOM OF HEAVEN)

HEAVEN, MESSENGERS FROM (Also see ANGEL; and ANGELS)

HEAVEN, RICHES IN (See TREASURE; and TREASURES)

HEAVEN, TREASURE(S) IN (Also see REWARDS; TREASURE; and TREASURES)

Setting: Galilee. During the early part of His ministry, Jesus preaches the Sermon on the Mount to His disciples and the multitudes.

"Do not store up for yourselves treasures on earth, where moth and rust destroy, and where thieves break in and steal. But store up for yourselves treasures in heaven, where neither moth nor rust destroys, and where thieves do not break in or steal; for where your treasure is, there your heart will be also" (Matthew 6:19–21; cf. Luke 12:34; see Proverbs 23:4; Matthew 19:21).

Setting: Judea beyond the Jordan (Perea). Jesus shares with a rich, young ruler how he can obtain eternal life.

And He said to him, "Why are you asking Me about what is good? There is *only* One who is good; but if you wish to enter into life, keep the commandments." *Then* he said to Him, 'Which ones?' And Jesus said, "YOU SHALL NOT COMMIT MURDER; YOU SHALL NOT COMMIT ADULTERY; YOU SHALL NOT STEAL; YOU SHALL NOT BEAR FALSE WITNESS; HONOR YOUR FATHER AND MOTHER; and YOU SHALL LOVE YOUR NEIGHBOR AS YOURSELF." The young man said to Him, "All these things I have kept; what am I still lacking?" Jesus said to him, "If you wish to complete go *and* sell your possessions and give to *the* poor, and you will have treasure in heaven; and come, follow Me" (Matthew 19:16–22, Jesus quotes from Exodus 20:13–15; Leviticus 19:18; cf. Leviticus 18:5; Mark 10:17–21; Luke 10:25–28; 12:33; 18:18–24).

Setting: Judea beyond the Jordan (Perea). After demonstrating to His disciples the importance of little children, Jesus encounters a rich man seeking eternal life.

And Jesus said to him, "Why do you call Me good? No one is good except God alone. You know the commandments, 'DO NOT MURDER, DO NOT COMMIT ADULTERY, DO NOT STEAL, DO NOT BEAR FALSE WITNESS, Do not defraud, HONOR YOUR FATHER AND MOTHER.'" And he said to Him, "Teacher, I have kept all these things from my youth up." Looking at him, Jesus felt a love for him and said to him, "One thing you lack: go and sell all you possess and give to the poor, and you will have treasure in heaven; and come, follow Me" (Mark 10:18–21; Jesus quotes from Exodus 20:12–16; cf. Matthew 19:16–22; Luke 18:18–24; see Matthew 6:20).

Setting: On the way from Galilee to Jerusalem. After giving a parable about riches and greed, Jesus challenges the crowd and His disciples concerning godly living.

"Sell your possessions and give to charity; make yourselves money belts which do not wear out, an unfailing treasure in heaven, where no thief comes near nor moth destroys. For where your treasure is, there your heart will be also" (Luke 12:33, 34; cf. Matthew 6:19–21; 19:21).

Setting: On the way from Galilee to Jerusalem. After speaking of the importance of children, Jesus responds to a ruler's question about inheriting eternal life.

A ruler questioned Him, saying, "Good Teacher, what shall I do to inherit eternal life?" And Jesus said to him, "Why do you call Me good? No one is good except God alone. You know the commandments, 'DO NOT COMMIT ADULTERY, DO NOT MURDER, DO NOT STEAL, DO NOT BEAR FALSE WITNESS, HONOR YOUR FATHER AND MOTHER.'" And he said, "All these things I have kept from *my* youth." When Jesus heard *this,* He said to him, "One thing you still lack; sell all that you possess and distribute it to the poor, and you shall have treasure in heaven; and come, follow Me" (Luke 18:18–22, Jesus quotes from Exodus 20:12–16; cf. Matthew 19:16–22; Mark 10:17–22; see Luke 10:25–28).

HEAVEN AND EARTH (Listed under EARTH, HEAVEN and)

HEAVENLY FATHER (Listed under FATHER, HEAVENLY)

HEAVENLY THINGS (Listed under THINGS, HEAVENLY)

HEAVENLY TREASURE (Listed under TREASURE, HEAVENLY)

HEAVENS (HEAVENS, POWERS OF THE; and HEAVENS, POWERS THAT ARE IN THE are separate entries; also see MOON; STARS; and SUN)

Setting: After beginning His public ministry and choosing His first disciples, Andrew and Simon (Peter) near Bethany beyond the Jordan, and Philip in Galilee, Jesus calls Philip's friend, Nathanael (some believe he may have been also called Bartholomew) as His next follower.

Jesus saw Nathanael coming to Him, and said of him, "Behold, an Israelite indeed, in whom there is no deceit!" Nathanael said to Him, "How do you know me?" Jesus answered and said to him, "Before Philip called you, when you were under the fig tree, I saw you." Nathanael answered Him, "Rabbi, You are the Son of God; You are the King of Israel." Jesus answered and said to him, "Because I said to you that I saw you under the fig tree, do you believe? You will see greater things than these." And He said to him, "Truly, truly, I say to you, you will see the heavens opened and the angels of God ascending and descending on the Son of Man" (John 1:47–51).

HEAVENS, POWERS OF THE (Also see HEAVENS, POWERS THAT ARE IN THE)

Setting: The Mount of Olives, just east of Jerusalem. During His discourse, Jesus answers His disciples' questions as to when the temple will be destroyed and Jerusalem overrun, along with the signs of His coming and the end of the age.

"But immediately after the tribulation of those days THE SUN WILL BE DARKENED, AND THE MOON WILL NOT GIVE ITS LIGHT, AND THE STARS WILL FALL from the sky, and the powers of the heavens will be shaken. And then the sign of the Son of Man will appear in the sky, and then all the tribes of the earth will mourn, and they will see the SON OF MAN COMING ON THE CLOUDS OF THE SKY with power and great glory. And He will send forth His angels with A GREAT TRUMPET and THEY WILL GATHER TOGETHER His elect from the four winds, from one end of the sky to the other" (Matthew 24:29–31, Jesus quotes from Isaiah 13:10, Daniel 7:13; Exodus 19:16; cf. Mark 13:24–27; Luke 21:25–27).

Setting: The Mount of Olives, east of the temple in Jerusalem. After ministering in the temple a few days before His crucifixion, and giving His disciples more details regarding future events, Jesus speaks during His Olivet Discourse of His return.

"There will be signs in sun and moon and stars, and on the earth dismay among the nations, in perplexity at the roaring of the sea and the waves, men fainting from fear and the expectation of the things which are coming upon the world; for the powers of the heavens will be shaken. Then they will see THE SON OF MAN COMING IN A CLOUD with power and great glory. But when these things begin to take place, straighten up and lift up your heads, because your redemption is drawing near" (Luke 21:25–28, Jesus quotes from Daniel 7:13; cf. Matthew 24:29–31; Mark 13:24–27).

HEAVENS, POWERS THAT ARE IN THE (Also see HEAVENS, POWERS OF THE)

Setting: On the Mount of Olives, east of the temple in Jerusalem. After prophesying the temple's destruction, Jesus responds during His Olivet Discourse to questions from Peter, James, John, and Andrew about other future events.

"But in those days, after that tribulation, THE SUN WILL BE DARKENED AND THE MOON WILL NOT GIVE ITS LIGHT, AND THE STARS WILL BE FALLING from heaven, and the powers that are in the heavens will be shaken. Then they will see THE SON OF MAN COMING IN CLOUDS with great power and glory. And then He will send forth the angels, and will gather together His elect from the four winds, from the farthest end of the earth to the farthest end of heaven" (Mark 13:24–27. Jesus quotes from Isaiah 13:10; 34:4; Daniel 7:13; cf. Matthew 24:29–31; Luke 21:25–27).

HEAVY BURDENS (Listed under BURDENS, HEAVY)

HEAVY-LADEN (Also see BURDEN)

Setting: Throughout Galilee. After rendering a thanksgiving prayer to His Father in heaven, Jesus offers rest to all who are weary and heavy-laden as He preaches and teaches.

"Come to Me, all who are weary and heavy-laden, and I will give you rest. Take My yoke upon you and learn from Me, for I am gentle and humble in heart, and YOU WILL FIND REST FOR YOUR SOULS. For My yoke is easy and My burden is light" (Matthew 11:28–30, Jesus quotes from Jeremiah 6:16; see Jeremiah 31:35; 1 John 5:3).

HEBREWS (See JEWS)

HEDGES

Setting: On the way from Galilee to Jerusalem. After speaking a parable to the invited guests and the host at a banquet, Jesus responds to a guest's proclamation about the blessings of eating bread in the kingdom of God.

But He said to him, "A man was giving a big dinner, and he invited many; and at the dinner hour he sent his slave to say to those who had been invited, 'Come; for everything is ready now.' But they all alike began to make excuses. The first one said to him, 'I have bought a piece of land and I need to go out and look at it; please consider me excused.' Another one said, 'I have bought five yoke of oxen, and I am going to try them out; please consider me excused.' Another one said, I have married a wife, and for that reason I cannot come.' And the slave came *back* and reported this to his master. Then the head of the household became angry and said to his slave, 'Go out at once into the streets and lanes of the city and bring in here the poor and crippled and blind and lame.' And the slave said, 'Master, what you commanded has been done, and still there is room.' And the master said to the slave, 'Go out into the highways and along the hedges, and compel *them* to come in, so that my house may be filled. For I tell you, none of those men who were invited shall taste of my dinner'" (Luke 14:16–24; see Deuteronomy 24:5; Matthew 22:2–14; Luke 14:1–2).

HEEL (Also see FEET; and FOOT)

Setting: **Jerusalem. Before the Passover, with His death on the cross nearing, Jesus explains the reason for His vivid example of servanthood in washing His disciples' feet.**

So when He had washed their feet, and taken His garments and reclined *at the table* again, He said to them, "Do you know what I have done to you? You call Me Teacher and Lord; and you are right, for *so* I am. If I then, the Lord and the Teacher, washed your feet, you also ought to wash one another's feet. For I gave you an example that you also should do as I did to you. Truly, truly I say to you, a slave is not greater than his master, nor *is* one who is sent greater than the one who sent him. If you know these things, you are blessed if you do them. I do not speak of all of you. I know the ones I have chosen; but *it is* that the Scripture may be fulfilled, 'HE WHO EATS MY BREAD HAS LIFTED UP HIS HEEL AGAINST ME.' From now on I am telling you before *it* comes to pass, so that when it does occur, you may believe that I am *He*. Truly, truly, I say to you, he who receives whomever I send receives Me; and he who receives Me receives Him who sent Me" (John 13:12–20; Jesus quotes from Psalm 41:9; see Matthew 7:24; 10:24, 40; John 8:24; 14:29; 1 Peter 5:3).

HEIR (Also see INHERITANCE)

Setting: **The temple in Jerusalem. Jesus delivers another parable to the chief priests and elders after they question His authority.**

"Listen to another parable. There was a landowner who PLANTED A VINEYARD AND PUT A WALL AROUND IT AND DUG A WINE PRESS IN IT, AND BUILT A TOWER, and rented it out to vine-growers and went on a journey. When the harvest time approached, he sent his slaves to the vine-growers to receive his produce. The vine-growers took his slaves and beat one, and killed another, and stoned a third. Again he sent another group of slaves larger than the first; and they did the same thing to them. But afterward he sent his son to them, saying, 'They will respect my son.' But when the vine-growers saw the son, they said among themselves, 'This is the heir; come, let us kill him and seize his inheritance.' They took him, and threw him out of the vineyard and killed him. Therefore when the owner of the vineyard comes, what will he do to those vine-growers?" (Matthew 21:33–40; Jesus quotes from Isaiah 5:1, 2; cf. Mark 12:1–9; Luke 20:9–15).

Setting: **The temple in Jerusalem. Having His authority questioned by the chief priests, scribes, and elders, Jesus begins to teach them in parables.**

And He began to speak to them in parables: "A man PLANTED A VINEYARD AND PUT A WALL AROUND IT, AND DUG A VAT UNDER THE WINE PRESS AND BUILT A TOWER, and rented it out to vine-growers and went on a journey. At the *harvest* time he sent a slave to the vine-growers, in order to receive *some* of the produce of the vineyard from the vine-growers. They took him, and beat him and sent him away empty-handed. Again he sent them another slave, and they wounded him in the head, and treated him shamefully. And he sent another, and that one they killed; and *so with* many others, beating some and killing others. He had one more to *send*, a beloved son; he sent him last *of all* to them, saying, 'They will respect my son.' But those vine-growers said to one another, 'This is the heir; come, let us kill him, and the inheritance will be ours!' They took him, and killed him and threw him out of the vineyard. What will the owner of the vineyard do? He will come and destroy the vine-growers, and will give the vineyard to others. Have you not even read this Scripture: 'THE STONE WHICH THE BUILDERS REJECTED, THIS BECAME THE CHIEF CORNER *stone;* THIS CAME ABOUT FROM THE LORD, AND IT IS MARVELOUS IN OUR EYES'?" (Mark 12:1–11, Jesus quotes from Psalm 118:22, 23; Isaiah 5:1, 2; cf. Matthew 21:33–46; Luke 20:9–19).

Setting: **The temple in Jerusalem. A few days before His crucifixion, after the chief priests and scribes question His authority to teach and preach, Jesus conveys the Parable of the Vine-Growers to the people.**

And He began to tell the people this parable: "A man planted a vineyard and rented it out to vine-growers, and went on a journey for a long time. At the *harvest* time he sent a slave to the vine-growers, so that they would give him *some* of the produce of the vineyard; but the vine-growers beat him and sent him away empty-handed. And he proceeded to send another slave; and they beat him also and treated him shamefully and sent him away empty-handed. And he proceeded to send a third; and this one also they wounded and cast out. The owner of the vineyard said, 'What shall I do? I will send my beloved son; perhaps they will respect him.' But when the vine-growers saw him, they reasoned with one another, saying, 'This is the heir; let us kill him so that the inheritance will be ours.' So they threw him out of the vineyard and killed him. What, then, will the owner of the vineyard do to them? He will come and destroy these vine-growers and will give the vineyard to others." When they heard it, they said, "May it never be!" But Jesus looked at them and said, "What then is this that is written: 'THE STONE WHICH THE BUILDERS REJECTED, THIS BECAME THE CHIEF CORNER *stone*'? Everyone who falls on that stone will be broken to pieces; but on whomever it falls, it will scatter him like dust" (Luke 20:9–18, Jesus quotes from Psalm 118:22; cf. Matthew 21:33–44; Mark 12:1–11; see Ephesians 2:20).

HELL (Specifics such as HELL, SENTENCE OF are separate entries; also see FIRE, ETERNAL; FIRE, FURNACE OF; and HADES)

Setting: Galilee. During the early part of His ministry, Jesus preaches the Sermon on the Mount to His disciples and the multitudes.

"If your right eye makes you stumble, tear it out and throw it from you; for it is better for you to lose one of the parts of your body, than for your whole body to be thrown into hell. If your right hand makes you stumble, cut it off and throw it from you; for it is better for you to lose one of the parts of your body, than for your whole body to go into hell" (Matthew 5:29, 30; cf. Matthew 18:8, 9).

Setting: Galilee. After His disciples observe His ministry, Jesus summons and specifically instructs them about their ministry ahead involving true discipleship.

"Therefore do not fear them, for there is nothing concealed that will not be revealed, or hidden that will not be known. What I tell you in the darkness, speak in the light; and what you hear *whispered* in your ear, proclaim upon the housetops. Do not fear those who kill the body but are unable to kill the soul; but rather fear Him who is able to destroy both soul and body in hell" (Matthew 10:26–28; cf. Mark 4:22; Luke 12:3; see Hebrews 10:31).

Setting: Capernaum of Galilee. As Jesus teaches His disciples in private, they ask Him about greatness.

But Jesus said, "Do not hinder him, for there is no one who will perform a miracle in My name, and be able soon afterward to speak evil of Me. For he who is not against us is for us. For whoever gives you a cup of water to drink because of your name as *followers* of Christ, truly I say to you, he will not lose his reward. Whoever causes one of these little ones who believe to stumble, it would be better for him if, with a heavy millstone hung around his neck, he had been cast into the sea. If your hand causes you to stumble, cut it off; it is better for you to enter life crippled, than, having your two hands, to go into hell, into the unquenchable fire, [where THEIR WORM DOES NOT DIE, AND THE FIRE IS NOT QUENCHED.] If your foot causes you to stumble, cut it off; it is better for you to enter life lame, than, having your two feet, to be cast into hell, [where THEIR WORM DOES NOT DIE, AND THE FIRE IS NOT QUENCHED.] If your eye causes you to stumble, throw it out; it is better for you to enter the kingdom of God with one eye, than, having two eyes, to be cast into hell, where THEIR WORM DOES NOT DIE, AND THE FIRE IS NOT QUENCHED. For everyone will be salted with fire. Salt is good; but if the salt becomes unsalty, with what will you make it salty *again?* Have salt in yourselves, and be at peace with one another" (Mark 9:39–50; Jesus quotes from Isaiah 66:24; cf. Matthew 18:6–9; Luke 9:49, 50; see Matthew 5:13, 29, 30; 10:42; 12:30; 18:5, 6).

Setting: On the way from Galilee to Jerusalem. Jesus warns His disciples of future events as the scribes and Pharisees turn hostile and question Him repeatedly in an attempt to catch Him in something He might say.

Under these circumstances, after so many thousands of people had gathered together that they were stepping on one another, He began saying to His disciples first *of all,* "Beware of the leaven of the Pharisees, which is hypocrisy. But there is nothing covered up that will not be revealed, and hidden that will not be known. Accordingly, whatever you have said in the dark will be heard in the light, and what you have whispered in the inner rooms will be proclaimed upon the housetops. I say to you, My friends, do not be afraid of those who kill the body and after that have no more that they can do. But I will warn you whom to fear: fear

the One who, after He has killed, has authority to cast into hell; yes, I tell you, fear Him! Are not five sparrows sold for two cents? *Yet* not one of them is forgotten before God. Indeed, the very hairs of your head are all numbered. Do not fear; you are more valuable than many sparrows" (Luke 12:1–7; cf. Matthew 10:26–31; see Matthew 16:6; Hebrews 10:31).

HELL, FIERY

Setting: Galilee. During the early part of His ministry, Jesus preaches the Sermon on the Mount to His disciples and the multitudes.

"But I say to you that everyone who is angry with his brother shall be guilty before the court; and whoever says to his brother, 'You good-for-nothing,' shall be guilty before the supreme court; and whoever says, 'You fool,' shall be guilty *enough to go* into the fiery hell" (Matthew 5:22).

Setting: Capernaum of Galilee. Jesus elaborates about stumbling blocks after His disciples ask about greatness in the kingdom of heaven.

"Woe to the world because of *its* stumbling blocks! For it is inevitable that stumbling blocks come; but woe to that man through whom the stumbling block comes! If your hand or your foot causes you to stumble, cut if off and throw it from you; it is better for you to enter life crippled or lame, than to have two hands or two feet and be cast into the eternal fire. If your eye causes you to stumble, pluck it out and throw it from you. It is better for you to enter life with one eye, than to have two eyes and be cast into the fiery hell" (Matthew 18:7–9; cf. Matthew 5:29, 30; Mark 9:43–48; Luke 17:1).

HELL, SENTENCE OF (Also see JUDGMENT)

Setting: The temple in Jerusalem. After the Jewish religious leaders test Him with questions, Jesus pronounces the eighth of eight woes on them in front of the crowds and His disciples.

"Woe to you, scribes and Pharisees, hypocrites! For you build the tombs of the prophets and adorn the monuments of the righteous, and say, 'If we had been *living* in the days of our fathers, we would not have been partners with them in *shedding* the blood of the prophets.' So you testify against yourselves, that you are sons of those who murdered the prophets. Fill up, then, the measure *of the guilt* of you fathers. You serpents, you brood of vipers, how will you escape the sentence of hell? Therefore, behold, I am sending you prophets and wise men and scribes; some of them you will kill and crucify, and some of them you will scourge in your synagogues, and persecute from city to city, so that upon you may fall *the guilt of* all the righteous blood shed on earth, from the blood of righteous Abel to the blood of Zechariah, the son of Berechiah, whom you murdered between the temple and the altar. Truly I say to you, all these things will come upon this generation" (Matthew 23:29–36; cf. 2 Chronicles 24:21; Zechariah 1:1; Matthew 3:7; Luke 11:47–52; see Matthew 10:23).

HELL, SON OF

Setting: The temple in Jerusalem. After the Jewish religious leaders test Him with questions, Jesus pronounces the third of eight woes on them in front of the crowds and His disciples.

"Woe to you, scribes and Pharisees, hypocrites, because you travel around on sea and land to make one proselyte; and when he becomes one, you make him twice as much a son of hell as yourselves" (Matthew 23:15).

HELPER (Holy Spirit; also see HOLY SPIRIT; and SPIRIT OF GOD)

Setting: Jerusalem. Before the Passover, after responding to Philip's request for Him to show His disciples the Father, Jesus conveys the upcoming role of the Holy Spirit in their lives.

"If you love Me, you will keep My commandments. I will ask the Father, and He will give you another Helper, that He may be with you forever; *that* is the Spirit of truth, whom the world cannot receive, because it does not see Him or know Him, *but* you know Him because He abides with you and will be in you" (John 14:15–17; see John 7:39; 14:1–14, 21, 23; 15:26; 1 John 5:3).

Setting: Jerusalem. Before the Passover, after responding to Philip's request for Him to show His disciples the

Father, Jesus conveys the upcoming ministry of the Holy Spirit in their lives.

"These things I have spoken to you while abiding with you. But the Helper, the Holy Spirit, whom the Father will send in My name, He will teach you all things, and bring to your remembrance all that I said to you" (John 14:25, 26; see John 16:13).

Setting: Jerusalem. Before the Passover, with His departure in mind, after explaining He is the vine and His disciples are the branches, Jesus elaborates more about the future ministry of the Holy Spirit.

"When the Helper comes, whom I will send to you from the Father, *that is* the Spirit of truth who proceeds from the Father, He will testify about Me, and you *will* testify also, because you have been with Me from the beginning" (John 15:26, 27; see Luke 24:48; John 14:16).

Setting: Jerusalem. Before the Passover, after warning His disciples of the persecution they will face after His departure to heaven, Jesus elaborates about the coming ministry of the Holy Spirit.

"But now I am going to Him who sent Me; and none of you asks Me, 'Where are You going?' But because I have said these things to you, sorrow has filled your heart. But I tell you the truth, it is to your advantage that I go away; for if I do not go away, the Helper will not come to you; but if I go, I will send Him to you. And He, when He comes, will convict the world concerning sin and righteousness and judgment; concerning sin, because they do not believe in Me; and concerning righteousness, because I go to the Father and you no longer see Me; and concerning judgment, because the ruler of this world has been judged" (John 16:5–11; see John 7:33; 12:31; 14:1, 16; 15:22, 24).

HEN (Also see CHICKS; and ROOSTER)

Setting: The temple in Jerusalem. With His death on the cross just days away, Jesus laments over Jerusalem's hardheartedness and lack of repentance.

"Jerusalem, Jerusalem, who kills the prophets and stones those who are sent to her! How often I wanted to gather your children together, the way a hen gathers her chicks under her wings, and you were unwilling. Behold, your house is being left to you desolate! For I say to you, from now on you will not see Me until you say, 'BLESSED IS HE WHO COMES IN THE NAME OF THE LORD!'" (Matthew 23:37–39, Jesus quotes from Psalm 118:26; cf. 1 Kings 9:7; Luke 13:34, 35).

Setting: On the way from Galilee to Jerusalem. While teaching in the cities and villages, after Jesus responds to a question about who is saved, some Pharisees ask Him to leave, claiming Herod Antipas (tetrarch of Galilee and Perea) seeks to kill Him.

And He said to them, "Go and tell that fox, 'Behold, I cast out demons and perform cures today and tomorrow, and the third *day* I reach My goal.' Nevertheless I must journey on today and tomorrow and the next *day*; for it cannot be that a prophet would perish outside of Jerusalem. O Jerusalem, Jerusalem, *the city* that kills the prophets and stones those sent to her! How often I wanted to gather your children together, just as a hen *gathers* her brood under her wings, and you would not *have it*! Behold, your house is left to you *desolate*; and I say to you, you will not see Me until *the time* comes when you say, 'BLESSED IS HE WHO COMES IN THE NAME OF THE LORD!'" (Luke 13:32–35, Jesus quotes from Psalm 118:26; cf. Matthew 23:37).

HERB, GARDEN (Also see GARDEN; PLANT; PLANTS, GARDEN; and check spices such as CUMMIN; DILL; and MINT)

Setting: On the way from Galilee to Jerusalem. After speaking of how a lamp illuminates, the Lord has lunch with a Pharisee who is surprised He doesn't wash before eating.

But the Lord said to him, "Now you Pharisees clean the outside of the cup and of the platter; but inside of you, you are full of robbery and wickedness. You foolish ones, did not He who made the outside make the inside also? But give that which is within as charity, and then all things are clean for you. But woe to you Pharisees! You pay tithe of mint and rue and every *kind of* garden herb, and *yet* disregard justice and the love of God; but these are the things you should have done without neglecting the others. Woe to you Pharisees! For you love the chief seats in the synagogues and the respectful greetings in the market places. Woe to you! For you are like concealed tombs, and the people who walk over *them* are unaware *of it*" (Luke 11:39–44; cf. Matthew 23:6–7, 23–27; see Matthew 15:2; Titus 1:15).

HERESY (See APOSTLES, FALSE; CHRISTS, FALSE; DECEPTION; MESSIAHS, FALSE; and TEACHERS, FALSE)

HEROD (Antipas; HEROD, LEAVEN OF is a separate entry)

[HEROD from that fox]

Setting: On the way from Galilee to Jerusalem. While teaching in the cities and villages, after Jesus responds to a question about who is saved. some Pharisees ask Him to leave, claiming Herod Antipas (tetrarch of Galilee and Perea) seeks to kill Him.

And He said to them, "Go and tell that fox, 'Behold, I cast out demons and perform cures today and tomorrow, and the third *day* I reach My goal.' Nevertheless I must journey on today and tomorrow and the next *day*; for it cannot be that a prophet would perish outside of Jerusalem. O Jerusalem, Jerusalem, *the city* that kills the prophets and stones those sent to her! How often I wanted to gather your children together, just as a hen *gathers* her brood under her wings, and you would not *have it*! Behold, your house is left to you *desolate*; and I say to you, you will not see Me until *the time* comes when you say, 'BLESSED IS HE WHO COMES IN THE NAME OF THE LORD!'" (Luke 13:32–35, Jesus quotes from Psalm 118:26; cf. Matthew 23:37).

HEROD, LEAVEN OF (Also see HEROD)

Setting: The district of Dalmanutha. The Pharisees argue with Jesus, seeking a sign from heaven to test Him. The Lord warns His disciples about them.

And He was giving orders to them, saying, "Watch out! Beware of the leaven of the Pharisees and the leaven of Herod" (Mark 8:15; cf. Matthew 16:5–7).

HIDDEN MANNA (Listed under MANNA, HIDDEN)

HIDDEN THINGS (Listed under THINGS, HIDDEN)

HIGH, ON (Also see HEAVEN)

Setting: Jerusalem. After rising from the grave on the third day following being crucified, and appearing to two of His followers on the road to Emmaus, Jesus gives instruction to some of the disciples about His mission on earth and the promise of power from God.

Now He said to them, "These are My words which I spoke to you while I was still with you, that all things which are written about Me in the Law of Moses and the Prophets and the Psalms must be fulfilled." Then He opened their minds to understand the Scriptures, and He said to them, "Thus it is written, that the Christ would suffer and rise again from the dead the third day, and that repentance for forgiveness of sins would be proclaimed in His name to all the nations, beginning from Jerusalem. You are witnesses of these things. And behold, I am sending forth the promise of My Father upon you; but you are to stay in the city until you are clothed with power from on high" (Luke 24:44–49; see Matthew 28:18, 19; Acts 1:8).

HIGH PRIEST (Also see CAIAPHAS)

Setting: Galilee. Early in His ministry, the Pharisees question why Jesus allows His disciples to harvest grain on the Sabbath.

And He said to them, "Have you never read what David did when he was in need and he and his companions became hungry; how he entered the house of God in the time of Abiathar *the* high priest, and ate the consecrated bread, which is not lawful for *anyone* to eat except the priests, and he also gave it to those who were with him?" Jesus said to them, "The Sabbath was made for man, and not man for the Sabbath. So the Son of Man is Lord even of the Sabbath" (Mark 2:25–28; cf. Matthew 12:1–8; Luke 6:1–5; see Exodus 23:12).

HIGH-PRIESTLY PRAYER (Listed under PRAYER, HIGH-PRIESTLY)

HIGHER (Also see PRIVILEGE)

Setting: On the way from Galilee to Jerusalem. As He observes the guests selecting places of honor at the table, Jesus speaks a parable to the guests of a Pharisee leader on the Sabbath.

And He *began* speaking a parable to the invited guests when He noticed how they had been picking out the places of honor *at the table,* saying to them, "When you are invited by someone to a wedding feast, do not take the place of honor, for someone more distinguished than you may have been invited by him, and he who invited you both will come and say to you, 'Give *your* place to this man, and then in disgrace you proceed to occupy the last place. But when you are invited, go and recline at the last place, so that when the one who has invited you comes, he may say to you, 'Friend, move up higher'; then you will have honor in the sight of all who are at the table with you. For everyone who exalts himself will be humbled, and he who humbles himself will be exalted" (Luke 14:7–11; see 2 Samuel 22:28; Proverbs 25:6, 7; Matthew 23:6).

HIGHWAYS (HIGHWAYS, MAIN is a separate entry; also see ROAD; and STREETS)

Setting: On the way from Galilee to Jerusalem. After He speaks a parable to the invited guests and the host at a banquet, Jesus responds to a guest's proclamation about the blessings of eating bread in the kingdom of God.

But He said to him, "A man was giving a big dinner, and he invited many; and at the dinner hour he sent his slave to say to those who had been invited, 'Come; for everything is ready now.' But they all alike began to make excuses. The first one said to him, 'I have bought a piece of land and I need to go out and look at it; please consider me excused.' Another one said, 'I have bought five yoke of oxen, and I am going to try them out; please consider me excused.' Another one said, I have married a wife, and for that reason I cannot come.' And the slave came *back* and reported this to his master. Then the head of the household became angry and said to his slave, 'Go out at once into the streets and lanes of the city and bring in here the poor and crippled and blind and lame.' And the slave said, 'Master, what you commanded has been done, and still there is room.' And the master said to the slave, 'Go out into the highways and along the hedges, and compel *them* to come in, so that my house may be filled. For I tell you, none of those men who were invited shall taste of my dinner'" (Luke 14:16–24; see Deuteronomy 24:5; Matthew 22:2–14).

HIGHWAYS, MAIN (Also see HIGHWAYS; ROAD; and STREETS)

Setting: The temple in Jerusalem. Jesus speaks another parable to the chief priests and elders after they question His authority.

Jesus spoke to them again in parables, saying, "The kingdom of heaven may be compared to a king who gave a wedding feast for his son. And he sent out his slaves to call those who had been invited to the wedding feast, and they were unwilling to come. Again he sent out other slaves saying, 'Tell those who have been invited, "Behold, I have prepared my dinner; my oxen and my fattened livestock are *all* butchered and everything is ready; come to the wedding feast." But they paid no attention and went their way, one to his own farm, another to his business, and the rest seized his slaves and mistreated them and killed them. But the king was enraged, and he sent his armies and destroyed those murderers and set their city on fire. Then he said to his slaves, 'The wedding is ready, but those who were invited were not worthy. 'Go therefore to the main highways, and as many as you find *there,* invite to the wedding feast.' Those slaves went out into the streets and gathered together all they found, both evil and good; and the wedding hall was filled with dinner guests. But when the king came in to look over the dinner guests, he saw a man there who was not dressed in wedding clothes, and he said to him, 'Friend, how did you come in here without wedding clothes?' And the man was speechless. Then the king said to the servants, 'Bind him hand and foot, and throw him into the outer darkness; in that place there will be weeping and gnashing of teeth.' For many are called, but few *are* chosen" (Matthew 22:1–14; cf. Matthew 8:11, 12).

HILL (Also see HILLS; MOUNTAIN: and MOUNTAINS)

Setting: Galilee. During the early part of His ministry, Jesus preaches the Sermon on the Mount to His disciples and the multitudes.

"You are the light of the world. A city set on a hill cannot be hidden; nor does *anyone* light a lamp and put it under a basket, but on the lampstand, and it gives light to all who are in the house. Let your light shine before men in such a way that they may see your good works, and glorify your Father who is in heaven" (Matthew 5:14–16; cf. Mark 4:21; 1 Peter 2:12).

HILLS (Also see HILL; and MOUNTAINS)

Setting: Jerusalem. After being arrested and appearing before the Council of Elders (Sanhedrin), Pontius Pilate (Roman governor of Judea), Herod Antipas (tetrarch of Galilee and Perea), and Pilate a second time (when Pilate bows to the crowd's pressure and grants that Jesus be crucified), the Lord prophesies to the women mourning Him regarding the coming judgment of Jerusalem.

But Jesus turning to them said, "Daughters of Jerusalem, stop weeping for Me, but weep for yourselves and for your children. For behold, the days are coming when they will say, 'Blessed are the barren, and the wombs that never bore, and the breasts that never nursed.' Then they will begin TO SAY TO THE MOUNTAINS, 'FALL ON US,' AND TO THE HILLS, 'COVER US.' For if they do these things when the tree is green, what will happen when it is dry?" (Luke 23:28–31, Jesus quotes from Hosea 10:8; see Matthew 24:19).

HIRED HAND (Listed under HAND, HIRED)

HIRED MEN (Listed under MEN, HIRED)

HIRELING (See HAND, HIRED)

HITS (Also see STRIKE; and VIOLENCE)

Setting: Galilee. After selecting His twelve disciples, Jesus teaches the Sermon on the Mount to those disciples and a great throng of people from Judea, Jerusalem, and the central coastal region of Tyre and Sidon.

"But I say to you who hear, love your enemies, do good to those who hate you, bless those who curse you, pray for those who mistreat you. Whoever hits you on the cheek, offer him the other also; and whoever takes away your coat, do not withhold your shirt from him either. Give to everyone who asks of you, and whoever takes away what is yours, do not demand it back. Treat others the same way you want them to treat you. If you love those who love you, what credit is *that* to you? For even sinners love those who love them. If you do good to those who do good to you, what credit is *that* to you? For even sinners do the same. If you lend to those from whom you expect to receive, what credit is *that* to you? Even sinners lend to sinners in order to receive back the same *amount*. But love your enemies, and do good, and lend, expecting nothing in return; and your reward will be great, and you will be sons of the Most High; for He Himself is kind to ungrateful and evil *men*. Be merciful, just as your Father is merciful" (Luke 6:27–36; cf. Matthew 5:9, 39–48; Matthew 7:12).

HOLES

Setting: By the Sea of Galilee. Following a time of casting out evil spirits from the demon-possessed and healing the ill (in fulfillment of Isaiah 53:4), Jesus lays out to an inquiring scribe the demands of discipleship.

Then a scribe came and said to Him, "Teacher, I will follow You wherever you go." Jesus said to him, "The foxes have holes and the birds of the air *have* nests, but the Son of Man has nowhere to lay His head." Another of the disciples said to Him, "Lord, permit me first to go and bury my father." But Jesus said to him, "Follow Me, and allow the dead to bury their own dead" (Matthew 8:19–22; cf. Luke 9:57–60).

Setting: On the way from Galilee to Jerusalem. The Lord responds to someone seeking to follow Him.

And Jesus said to him, "The foxes have holes and the birds of the air *have* nests, but the Son of Man has nowhere to lay His head" (Luke 9:58; cf. Matthew 8:19–22).

HOLINESS (See RIGHTEOUSNESS)

HOLY FATHER (Listed under FATHER, HOLY)

HOLY PLACE (Listed under PLACE, HOLY; also see TEMPLE)

HOLY SPIRIT (Also see SPIRIT (Holy); SPIRIT OF GOD; SPIRIT OF THE LORD; and TRUTH, SPIRIT OF; also see HOLY SPIRIT, BAPTISM OF THE; and HOLY SPIRIT, BLASPHEMY AGAINST THE)

[HOLY SPIRIT from Spirit of your Father]

Setting: Galilee. After His disciples observe His ministry, Jesus summons and specifically instructs them about the upcoming hardships of their ministry to the people of Israel.

"Behold, I send you out as sheep in the midst of wolves; so be shrewd as serpents and innocent as doves. But beware of men, for they will hand you over to *the* courts and scourge you in their synagogues; and you will even be brought before governors and kings for My sake, as a testimony to them and to the Gentiles. But when they hand you over, do not worry about how or what you are to say; for it will be given you in that hour what you are to say. For it is not you who speak, but *it* is the Spirit of your Father who speaks in you" (Matthew 10:16–20; cf. Luke 10:3).

[HOLY SPIRIT from Spirit of God]

Setting: Galilee. After Jesus heals a blind, mute, demon-possessed man, the Pharisees accuse Him in front of crowds of being a worker of Beelzebul (Satan).

And knowing their thoughts Jesus said to them, "Any kingdom divided against itself is laid waste; and any city or house divided against itself will not stand. If Satan casts out Satan, he is divided against himself; how then will his kingdom stand? If I by Beelzebul cast out demons, by whom do your sons cast *them* out? For this reason they will be your judges. But if I cast out demons by the Spirit of God, then the kingdom of God has come upon you. Or how can anyone enter the strong man's house and carry off his property, unless he first binds the strong *man?* And then he will plunder his house" (Matthew 12:25–29; cf. Matthew 9:34; Mark 3:23–27; Luke 11:17–20).

Setting: Galilee. After Jesus heals a blind, mute, demon-possessed man, the Pharisees accuse Him in front of crowds of being a worker of Satan. The Lord warns them about the unpardonable sin.

"He who is not with Me is against Me; and he who does not gather with Me scatters. Therefore I say to you, any sin and blasphemy shall be forgiven people, but blasphemy against the Spirit shall not be forgiven. Whoever speaks a word against the Son of Man, it shall be forgiven him; but whoever speaks against the Holy Spirit, it shall not be forgiven him, either in this age or in the *age* to come" (Matthew 12:30–32; cf. Luke 12:10; see Mark 9:40).

Setting: On a mountain in Galilee. Following His resurrection from the dead in Jerusalem, Jesus conveys the Great Commission to His eleven remaining disciples.

And Jesus came up and spoke to them, saying, "All authority has been given to Me in heaven and on earth. Go therefore and make disciples of all the nations, baptizing them in the name of the Father and the Son and the Holy Spirit, teaching them to observe all that I commanded you; and lo, I am with you always, even to the end of the age" (Matthew 28:18–20; cf. Mark 16:15; see Daniel 7:13).

Setting: Galilee. After Jesus selects His twelve disciples, scribes from Jerusalem attribute His miraculous powers to Beelzebul (Satan).

And He called them to Himself and began speaking to them in parables, "How can Satan cast out Satan? If a kingdom is divided against itself, that kingdom cannot stand. If a house is divided against itself, that house will not be able to stand. If Satan has risen up against himself and is divided, he cannot stand, but he is finished! But no one can enter the strong man's house and plunder his property unless he first binds the strong man, and then he will plunder his house. Truly I say to you, all sins shall be forgiven the sons of men, and whatever blasphemies they utter; but whoever blasphemes against the Holy Spirit never has forgiveness, but is guilty of an eternal sin"—because they were saying, "He has an unclean spirit" (Mark 3:23–30; cf. Matthew 12:25–32; Luke 12:10).

Setting: The temple in Jerusalem. After commending a scribe for his nearness to the kingdom of God, Jesus teaches the crowd.

And Jesus *began* to say, as He taught in the temple, "How *is it that* the scribes say that the Christ is the son of David? David himself said in the Holy Spirit, 'THE LORD SAID TO MY LORD, SIT AT MY RIGHT HAND, UNTIL I PUT YOUR ENEMIES BENEATH YOUR FEET.'" David himself calls Him 'Lord'; so in what sense is He his son?" And the large crowd enjoyed listening to Him (Mark 12:35–37, Jesus quotes from Psalm 110:1; cf. Matthew 22:41–46; Luke 20:41–44).

Setting: On the Mount of Olives, east of the temple in Jerusalem. After prophesying the temple's destruction, Jesus responds during His Olivet Discourse to questions from Peter, James, John, and Andrew about other future events.

And Jesus began to say to them, "See to it that no one misleads you. Many will come in My name, saying, 'I am *He!*' and will mislead many. When you hear of wars and rumors of wars, do not be frightened; *those things* must take place; but *that is* not yet the end. For nation will rise up against nation, and kingdom against kingdom; there will be earthquakes in various places; there will *also be* famines. These things are *merely* the beginning of birth pangs. But be on your guard; for they will deliver you to *the* courts, and you will be flogged in *the* synagogues, and you will stand before governors and kings for My sake, as a testimony to them. The gospel must first be preached to all the nations. When they arrest you and hand you over, do not worry beforehand about what you are to say, but say whatever is given you in that hour; for it is not you who speak, but *it is* the Holy Spirit. Brother will betray brother to death, and a father *his* child; and children will rise up against parents and have them put to death. You will be hated by all because of My name, but the one who endures to the end, he will be saved" (Mark 13:5–13; cf. Matthew 24:4–14; Luke 21:7–19; see Matthew 10:17–22).

Setting: On the way from Galilee to Jerusalem. After revealing to His disciples how to pray, Jesus illustrates God's benevolence in answering prayer and giving the Holy Spirit.

"Now suppose one of you fathers is asked by his son for a fish; he will not give him a snake instead of a fish, will he? Or *if* he is asked for an egg, he will not give him a scorpion, will he? If you then, being evil, know how to give good gifts to your children, how much more will *your* heavenly Father give the Holy Spirit to those who ask Him?"
(Luke 11:11–13; cf. Matthew 7:9–11).

Setting: On the way from Galilee to Jerusalem. Jesus warns His disciples of future events, as the scribes and Pharisees turn hostile and question Him repeatedly in an attempt to catch Him in something He might say.

"And I say to you, everyone who confesses Me before men, the Son of Man will confess him also before the angels of God; but he who denies Me before men will be denied before the angels of God. And everyone who speaks a word against the Son of Man, it will be forgiven him; but he who blasphemes against the Holy Spirit, it will not be forgiven him. When they bring you before the synagogues and the rulers and the authorities, do not worry about how or what you are to speak in your defense, or what you are to say; for the Holy Spirit will teach you in that very hour what you ought to say" (Luke 12:8–12; cf. Matthew 10:32, 33; 12:31, 32; see Matthew 10:20).

[HOLY SPIRIT from power from on high]
Setting: Jerusalem. After rising from the tomb on the third day after being crucified, and appearing to two of His followers on the road to Emmaus, Jesus gives instruction to His disciples (except Thomas) about His mission on earth and the promise of future power from God.

Now He said to them, "These are My words which I spoke to you while I was still with you, that all things which are written about Me in the Law of Moses and the Prophets and the Psalms must be fulfilled." Then He opened their minds to understand the Scriptures, and He said to them, "Thus it is written, that the Christ would suffer and rise again from the dead the third day, and that repentance for forgiveness of sins would be proclaimed in His name to all the nations, beginning from Jerusalem. You are witnesses of these things. And behold, I am sending forth the promise of My Father upon you; but you are to stay in the city until you are clothed with power from on high" (Luke 24:44–49; see Matthew 28:19, 20; Acts 1:8).

[HOLY SPIRIT from Helper and Spirit of truth]
Setting: Jerusalem. Before the Passover, after responding to Philip's request for Him to show His disciples the Father, Jesus conveys the upcoming role of the Holy Spirit in their lives.

"If you love Me, you will keep My commandments. I will ask the Father, and He will give you another Helper, that He may be with you forever; *that* is the Spirit of truth, whom the world cannot receive, because it does not see Him or know Him, *but* you know Him because He abides with you and will be in you" (John 14:15–17; see John 7:39; 15:26; 1 John 5:3).

[HOLY SPIRIT from the Helper, the Holy Spirit]
Setting: Jerusalem. Before the Passover, after responding to Philip's request for Him to show His disciples the Father, Jesus conveys the upcoming ministry of the Holy Spirit in their lives.

"These things I have spoken to you while abiding with you. But the Helper, the Holy Spirit, whom the Father will send in My name, He will teach you all things, and bring to your remembrance all that I said to you" (John 14:25, 26; see John 16:13).

[HOLY SPIRIT from Helper and Spirit of truth]
Setting: Jerusalem. Before the Passover, with His departure in mind, after explaining He is the vine and His disciples are the branches, Jesus elaborates more about the future ministry of the Holy Spirit.

"When the Helper comes, whom I will send to you from the Father, *that is* the Spirit of truth who proceeds from the Father, He will testify about Me, and you *will* testify also, because you have been with Me from the beginning" (John 15:26, 27; see Luke 24:48; John 14:16).

[HOLY SPIRIT from Helper]
Setting: Jerusalem. Before the Passover, after warning His disciples of the persecution they will face after His departure to heaven, Jesus elaborates about the coming ministry of the Holy Spirit.

"But now I am going to Him who sent Me; and none of you asks Me, 'Where are You going?' But because I have said these things to you, sorrow has filled your heart. But I tell you the truth, it is to your advantage that I do away; for if I do not go away, the Helper will not come to you; but if I go, I will send Him to you. And He, when He comes, will convict the world concerning sin and righteousness and judgment; concerning sin, because they do not believe in Me; and concerning righteousness, because I go to the Father and you no longer see Me; and concerning judgment, because the ruler of this world has been judged" (John 16:5–11; see John 7:33; 12:31; 14:1, 16; 15:22, 24).

[HOLY SPIRIT from Spirit of truth]
Setting: Jerusalem. Before the Passover, after warning His disciples of the persecution they will face after His departure to heaven, Jesus elaborates about the coming ministry of the Holy Spirit.

"I have many more things to say to you, but you cannot bear *them* now. But when He, the Spirit of truth, comes, He will guide you into all the truth; for He will not speak on His own initiative, but whatever He hears, He will speak; and He will disclose to you what is to come. He will glorify Me, for He will take of Mine and will disclose *it* to you. All things that the Father has are Mine; therefore I said that He takes of Mine and will disclose *it* to you (John 16:12–15; see John 7:39; 14:17, 26; 17:10).

Setting: Jerusalem. After Mary Magdalene encounters the risen Jesus in the morning, He appears that evening in the midst of His disciples (except Thomas), who are in hiding behind closed doors due to fear of the Jewish religious leaders.

So when it was evening on that day, the first *day* of the week, and when the doors were shut where the disciples were, for fear of the Jews, Jesus came and stood in their midst and said to them, "Peace *be* with you." And when He had said this, He showed them both His hands and His side. The disciples then rejoiced when they saw the Lord. So Jesus said to them again, "Peace *be* with you; as the Father has sent Me, I also send you." And when He had said this, He breathed on them and said to them, "Receive the Holy Spirit. If you forgive the sins of any, *their sins* have been forgiven them; if you retain the *sins* of any, they have been retained" (John 20:19–23; cf. Luke 24:36–43; see Matthew 16:19; Mark 16:14).

Setting: Jerusalem. Luke, writing in Acts, presents quotes from Jesus' post-resurrection appearances, in which He informs and instructs His disciples of their imminent baptism with the Holy Spirit.

Gathering them together, He commanded them not to leave Jerusalem, but to wait for what the Father had promised, "Which," *He said,* "you heard of from Me; for John baptized with water, but you will be baptized with the Holy Spirit not many days from now" (Acts 1:4, 5; see Luke 24:49; John 14:16, 26; Acts 2:1–4).

Setting: Jerusalem. Luke, writing in Acts, presents quotes from Jesus' post-resurrection appearances, in which He responds to His disciples' question of whether He is about to restore the kingdom to Israel.

He said to them, "It is not for you to know times or epochs which the Father has fixed by His own authority; but you will receive power when the Holy Spirit has come upon you; and you shall be My witnesses both in Jerusalem, and in all Judea and Samaria, and even to the remotest part of the earth" (Acts 1:7, 8; see Luke 24:48, 49; Acts 2:1–4).

HOLY SPIRIT, BAPTISM OF THE

[BAPTISM OF THE HOLY SPIRIT from baptized with the Holy Spirit]
Setting: Jerusalem. Luke, writing in Acts, presents quotes from Jesus' post-resurrection appearances, in which He informs and instructs His disciples of their imminent baptism with the Holy Spirit.

Gathering them together, He commanded them not to leave Jerusalem, but to wait for what the Father had promised, "Which," *He said,* "you heard of from Me; for John baptized with water, but you will be baptized with the Holy Spirit not many days from now" (Acts 1:4, 5; see Luke 24:49; John 14:16, 26; Acts 2:1–4).

[BAPTISM OF THE HOLY SPIRIT from you will receive power when the Holy Spirit has come upon you]
Setting: Jerusalem. Luke, writing in Acts, presents quotes from Jesus' post-resurrection appearances, in which He responds to His disciples' question of whether He is about to restore the kingdom to Israel.

He said to them, "It is not for you to know times or epochs which the Father has fixed by His own authority; but you will receive power when the Holy Spirit has come upon you; and you shall be My witnesses both in Jerusalem, and in all Judea and Samaria, and even to the remotest part of the earth" (Acts 1:7, 8; see Luke 24:48, 49; Acts 2:1–4).

[BAPTISM OF THE HOLY SPIRIT from baptized with the Holy Spirit]
Setting: Jerusalem. Luke, writing in Acts, records Peter (following a time of ministry to the Gentiles and returning to Jerusalem) recalling the words of Jesus regarding the baptism of the Holy Spirit.

And I remembered the word of the Lord, how He used to say, "John baptized with water, but you will be baptized with the Holy Spirit" (Acts 11:16; cf. Acts 1:5).

HOLY SPIRIT, BLASPHEMY AGAINST THE (Also see SIN, UNFORGIVABLE)

[BLASPHEMY AGAINST THE HOLY SPIRIT from blasphemy against the Spirit]
Setting: Galilee. After Jesus heals a blind, mute, demon-possessed man, the Pharisees accuse Him in front of crowds of being a worker of Satan. The Lord warns them about the unpardonable sin.

"He who is not with Me is against Me; and he who does not gather with Me scatters. Therefore I say to you, any sin and blasphemy shall be forgiven people, but blasphemy against the Spirit shall not be forgiven. Whoever speaks a word against the Son of Man, it shall be forgiven him; but whoever speaks against the Holy Spirit, it shall not be forgiven him, either in this age or in the *age* to come" (Matthew 12:30–32; cf. Luke 12:10; see Mark 9:40).

[BLASPHEMY AGAINST THE HOLY SPIRIT from blasphemes against the Holy Spirit]
Setting: Galilee. After Jesus selects His twelve disciples, scribes from Jerusalem attribute His miraculous powers to Beelzebul (Satan).

And He called them to Himself and began speaking to them in parables, "How can Satan cast out Satan? If a kingdom is divided against itself, that kingdom cannot stand. If a house is divided against itself, that house will not be able to stand. If Satan has risen up against himself and is divided, he cannot stand, but he is finished! But no one can enter the strong man's house and plunder his property unless he first binds the strong man, and then he will plunder his house. Truly I say to you, all sins shall be forgiven the sons of men, and whatever blasphemies they utter; but whoever blasphemes against the Holy Spirit never has forgiveness, but is guilty of an eternal sin"—because they were saying, "He has an unclean spirit" (Mark 3:23–30; cf. Matthew 12:25–32; Luke 12:10).

[BLASPHEMY AGAINST THE HOLY SPIRIT from blasphemes against the Holy Spirit]
Setting: On the way from Galilee to Jerusalem. Jesus warns His disciples of future events, as the scribes and Pharisees turn hostile and question Him repeatedly in an attempt to catch Him in something He might say.

"And I say to you, everyone who confesses Me before men, the Son of Man will confess him also before the angels of God; but he who denies Me before men will be denied before the angels of God. And everyone who speaks a word against the Son of Man, it will be forgiven him; but he who blasphemes against the Holy Spirit, it will not be forgiven him. When they bring you before the synagogues and the rulers and the authorities, do not worry about how or what you are to speak in your defense, or what you are to say; for the Holy Spirit will teach you in that very hour what you ought to say" (Luke 12:8–12; cf. Matthew 10:32, 33; 12:31, 32; see Matthew 10:20).

HOLY SPIRIT, NAME OF THE FATHER AND THE SON AND THE
Setting: On a mountain in Galilee. Following His resurrection from the dead in Jerusalem, Jesus conveys the Great Commission to His eleven remaining disciples.

And Jesus came up and spoke to them, saying, "All authority has been given to Me in heaven and on earth. Go therefore and make disciples of all the nations, baptizing them in the name of the Father and the Son and the Holy Spirit, teaching them to observe all that I commanded you; and lo, I am with you always, even to the end of the age" (Matthew 28:18–20; cf. Mark 16:15; see Daniel 7:13).

HOME (Also see HOMES; HOUSE; and HOUSES)
Setting: Capernaum near the Sea of Galilee. After Jesus heals and forgives the sins of a paralytic in front of crowds, some scribes accuse the Lord of blasphemy.

And they brought to Him a paralytic lying on a bed. Seeing their faith, Jesus said to the paralytic, "Take courage, son; your sins are forgiven." And some scribes said to themselves. "This *fellow* blasphemes." And Jesus knowing their thoughts said, "Why are you thinking evil in your hearts? Which is easier to say, 'Your sins are forgiven,' or to say, 'Get up, and walk'? But so that you may know that the Son of Man has authority on earth to forgive sins"—then He said to the paralytic, "Get up, pick up your bed and go home" (Matthew 9:2–6; cf. Mark 2:3–12; Luke 5:17–26).

Setting: Capernaum. After Jesus heals and forgives the sins of a paralytic man, some scribes believe Jesus commits blasphemy.

Immediately Jesus, aware in His spirit that they were reasoning that way within themselves, said to them, "Why are you reasoning about these things in your hearts? Which is easier, to say to the paralytic, 'Your sins are forgiven'; or to say, 'Get up, and pick up your pallet and walk'? "But so that you may know that the Son of Man has authority on earth to forgive sins"—He said to the paralytic, "I say to you, get up, pick up your pallet and go home" (Mark 2:8–11; cf. Matthew 9:4–7; Luke 5:21–24).

Setting: The country of the Gerasenes, on the east side of the Sea of Galilee. Jesus encounters and heals a man possessed by a legion of demons.

And He did not let him, but He said to him, "Go home to your people and report to them what great things the Lord has done for you, and *how* He had mercy on you" (Mark 5:19; cf. Luke 8:39; see Matthew 8:33, 34; Luke 8:36–38).

Setting: Capernaum of Galilee. After Jesus heals and forgives the sins of a paralytic man, some Pharisees and teachers of the law from Galilee and Judea accuse Him of blasphemy.

But Jesus, aware of their reasonings, answered and said to them, "Why are you reasoning in your hearts? Which is easier, to say, 'Your sins have been forgiven you,' or to say, 'Get up and walk'? But, so that you may know that the Son of Man has authority on earth to forgive sins,"—He said to the paralytic—"I say to you, get up, and pick up your stretcher and go home" (Luke 5:22–24; cf. Matthew 9:4–8; Mark 2:8–12; see Matthew 4:24).

Setting: On the way from Galilee to Jerusalem. After Jesus presents to large crowds the demands of discipleship, the Pharisees and scribes complain He associates with tax collectors and sinners.

So He told them this parable, saying, "What man among you, if he has a hundred sheep and has lost one of them, does not leave the ninety-nine in the open pasture and go after the one which is lost until he finds it? When he has found it, he lays it on his shoulders, rejoicing. And when he comes home, he calls together his friends and his neighbors, saying to them, 'Rejoice with me, for I have found my sheep which was lost!' I tell you that in the same way, there will be *more* joy in heaven over one sinner who repents than over ninety-nine righteous persons who need no repentance" (Luke 15:3–7; cf. Matthew 18:12–14; see Matthew 9:11–13; Luke 5:29–32).

Setting: Jerusalem. Before the Passover, after conveying promises about praying in His name, Jesus prophesies His disciples' scattering and assures them that in the midst of tribulation they will have His peace.

"Jesus answered them, "Do you now believe? Behold, an hour is coming, and has *already* come, for you to be scattered, each to his own *home,* and to leave Me alone; and *yet* I am not alone, because the Father is with Me. These things I have spoken to you, so that in Me you may have peace. In the world you have tribulation, but take courage, I have overcome the world" (John 16:31–33; see Zechariah 13:7; John 8:29; 14:27; Romans 8:37).

HOMES (Also see HOME; HOUSE; HOUSES; and DWELLING PLACES)

Setting: Decapolis near the Sea of Galilee. Jesus miraculously feeds more than 4,000 primarily Gentile people.

In those days, when there was again a large crowd and they had nothing to eat, Jesus called His disciples and said to them, "I feel compassion for the people because they have remained with Me now three days and have nothing to eat. If I send them away hungry to their homes, they will faint on their way; and some of them have come a great distance" (Mark 8:1–3; cf. Matthew 15:32–38; see Matthew 9:36).

Setting: On the way from Galilee to Jerusalem. The Lord teaches His disciples about stewardship after giving them the story of the prodigal son.

Now He was also saying to the disciples, "There was a rich man who had a manager, and this *manager* was reported to him as squandering his possessions. And he called him and said to him, 'What is this I hear about you? Give an accounting of your management, for you can no longer be a manager.' The manager said to himself, 'What shall I do, since my master is taking the management away from me? I am not strong enough to dig; I am ashamed to beg. I know what I shall do, so that when I am removed from the management people will welcome me into their homes.' And he summoned each one of his master's debtors, and he

began saying to the first, 'How much do you owe my master?' And he said, 'A hundred measures of oil.' And he said to him, 'Take your bill, and sit down quickly and write fifty.' Then he said to another, 'And how much do you owe?' And he said, 'A hundred measures of wheat.' He said to him, 'Take your bill, and write eighty.' And his master praised the unrighteous manager because he had acted shrewdly; for the sons of this age are more shrewd in relation to their own kind than the sons of light. And I say to you, make friends for yourselves by means of the wealth of unrighteousness, so that when it fails, they will receive you into the eternal dwellings. He who is faithful in a very little thing is faithful also in much; and he who is unrighteous in a very little thing is unrighteous also in much. Therefore if you have not been faithful in the *use of* unrighteous wealth, who will entrust the *true riches* to you? And if you have not been faithful in *the use of* that which is another's, who will give you that which is your own? No servant can serve two masters; for either he will hate the one and love the other, or else he will be devoted to one and despise the other. You cannot serve God and wealth" (Luke 16:1–13; cf. Matthew 6:24; see Matthew 25:14–30).

HOMETOWN

Setting: The synagogue in Jesus' hometown of Nazareth. The townspeople take offense at Jesus' teaching.

And they took offense at Him. But Jesus said to them, "A prophet is not without honor except in his hometown and in his *own* household" (Matthew 13:57; cf. Mark 6:4; see Matthew 11:6).

Setting: The synagogue in Jesus' hometown of Nazareth. While ministering throughout the villages of Galilee, the townspeople become offended and question Jesus' teaching, wisdom, and ability to perform miracles.

Jesus said to them, "A prophet is not without honor except in his hometown and among his *own* relatives and in his *own* household" (Mark 6:4; cf. Matthew 13:54–58).

Setting: The synagogue in Jesus' hometown of Nazareth in Galilee. At the beginning of Jesus' public ministry, He comments to the congregation after reading on the Sabbath from the book of the prophet Isaiah.

And He said to them, "No doubt you will quote this proverb to Me, 'Physician, heal yourself! Whatever we heard was done at Capernaum, do here in your hometown as well.'" And He said, "Truly I say to you, no prophet is welcome in his hometown. But I say to you in truth, there were many widows in Israel in the days of Elijah, when the sky was shut up for three years and six months, when a great famine came over all the land; and yet Elijah was sent to none of them, but only to Zarephath, *in the land* of Sidon, to a woman who was a widow. And there were many lepers in Israel in the time of Elisha the prophet; and none of them was cleansed, but only Naaman the Syrian" (Luke 4:23–27; Jesus refers to 1 Kings 17:1, 9; 2 Kings 5:1–14; see Matthew 13:53–58).

HONOR (HONOR, PLACE OF; and HONOR, PLACES OF are separate entries; also see RESPECT)

[HONOR from honored]

Setting: Galilee. During the early part of His ministry, Jesus preaches the Sermon on the Mount to His disciples and the multitudes.

"So when you give to the poor, do not sound a trumpet before you, as the hypocrites do in the synagogues and in the streets, so that they may be honored by men. Truly I say to you, they have their reward in full. But when you give to the poor, do not let your left hand know what your right hand is doing, so that your giving will be in secret; and your Father who sees *what is done* in secret will reward you" (Matthew 6:2–4; see Jeremiah 17:10; Matthew 6:16).

Setting: The synagogue in Jesus' hometown of Nazareth. The townspeople take offense at Jesus' teaching.

And they took offense at Him. But Jesus said to them, "A prophet is not without honor except in his hometown and in his *own* household" (Matthew 13:57; cf. Mark 6:4; see Matthew 11:6; John 4:44).

Setting: Galilee. Pharisees and scribes from Jerusalem question Jesus about His disciples' lack of obedience to tradition and the commandments.

And He answered and said to them, "Why do you yourselves transgress the commandment of God for the sake of tradition? For God said, 'HONOR YOUR FATHER AND MOTHER,' and, 'HE WHO SPEAKS EVIL OF FATHER OR MOTHER IS TO BE PUT TO DEATH.' But you say, 'Whoever says to *his* father or mother, "Whatever I have that would help you has been given *to God*," he is not to honor his father or mother.' And *by this* you invalidated the word of God for the sake of your tradition. You hypocrites, rightly did Isaiah prophesy of you: 'THIS PEOPLE HONORS ME WITH THEIR LIPS, BUT THEIR HEART IS FAR AWAY FROM ME. BUT IN VAIN DO THEY WORSHIP ME, TEACHING AS DOCTRINES THE PRECEPTS OF MEN' "(Matthew 15:3–9, Jesus quotes from Exodus 20:12, 21:17, Leviticus 20:9; Isaiah 29:13; cf. Mark 7:5–7; see Colossians 2:22).

Setting: Judea beyond the Jordan (Perea). A young man asks Jesus how he can inherit eternal life.

And He said to him, "Why are you asking Me about what is good? There is *only* One who is good; but if you wish to enter into life, keep the commandments." *Then* he said to Him, 'Which ones?' And Jesus said, "YOU SHALL NOT COMMIT MURDER; YOU SHALL NOT COMMIT ADULTERY; YOU SHALL NOT STEAL; YOU SHALL NOT BEAR FALSE WITNESS; HONOR YOUR FATHER AND MOTHER; and YOU SHALL LOVE YOUR NEIGHBOR AS YOURSELF." The young man said to Him, "All these things I have kept; what am I still lacking?" Jesus said to him, "If you wish to complete go *and* sell your possessions and give to *the* poor, and you will have treasure in heaven; and come, follow Me" (Matthew 19:16–22, Jesus quotes from Exodus 20:13–15; Leviticus 19:18; cf. Leviticus 18:5; Mark 10:17–21; Luke 10:25–28; 12:33; 18:18–24).

Setting: The synagogue in Jesus' hometown of Nazareth. While ministering throughout the villages of Galilee, the townspeople become offended and question Jesus' teaching, wisdom, and ability to perform miracles.

Jesus said to them, "A prophet is not without honor except in his hometown and among his *own* relatives and in his *own* household" (Mark 6:4; cf. Matthew 13:54–58; see John 4:44).

Setting: Galilee. The Pharisees and some of the scribes from Jerusalem question why Jesus' disciples do not follow the tradition of ceremonial hand cleansing before eating bread.

And He said to them, "Rightly did Isaiah prophesy of you hypocrites, as it is written: 'THIS PEOPLE HONORS ME WITH THEIR LIPS, BUT THEIR HEART IS FAR AWAY FROM ME. BUT IN VAIN DO THEY WORSHIP ME, TEACHING AS DOCTRINES THE PRECEPTS OF MEN.' Neglecting the commandment of God, you hold to the tradition of men." He was also saying to them, "You are experts at setting aside the commandment of God in order to keep tradition. For Moses said, 'HONOR YOUR FATHER AND YOUR MOTHER'; and, 'HE WHO SPEAKS EVIL OF FATHER OR MOTHER, IS TO BE PUT TO DEATH'; but you say, 'If a man says to *his* father or *his* mother, whatever I have that would help you is Corban (that is to say, given *to God*),' you no longer permit him to do anything for *his* father or *his* mother; *thus* invalidating the word of God by your tradition which you have handed down; and you do many things such as that" (Mark 7:6–13, Jesus quotes from Exodus 20:12; 21:17; Isaiah 29:13; cf. Matthew 15:1–6).

Setting: Judea beyond the Jordan (Perea). After demonstrating to His disciples the importance of little children, Jesus encounters a rich man seeking eternal life.

And Jesus said to him, "Why do you call Me good? No one is good except God alone. You know the commandments, 'DO NOT MURDER, DO NOT COMMIT ADULTERY, DO NOT STEAL, DO NOT BEAR FALSE WITNESS, Do not defraud, HONOR YOUR FATHER AND MOTHER.'" And he said to Him, "Teacher, I have kept all these things from my youth up." Looking at him, Jesus felt a love for him and said to him, "One thing you lack: go and sell all you possess and give to the poor, and you will have treasure in heaven; and come, follow Me" (Mark 10:18–21; Jesus quotes from Exodus 20:12–16; cf. Matthew 19:16–22; Luke 18:18–24; see Matthew 6:20).

Setting: On the way from Galilee to Jerusalem. As He observes the guests selecting places of honor at the table, Jesus speaks a parable to the guests of a Pharisee leader on the Sabbath.

And He *began* speaking a parable to the invited guests when He noticed how they had been picking out the places of honor *at the table,* saying to them, "When you are invited by someone to a wedding feast, do not take the place of honor, for someone more distinguished than you may have been invited by him, and he who invited you both will come and say to you, 'Give *your* place to this man, and then in disgrace you proceed to occupy the last place. But when you are invited, go and recline at the last place, so that when the one who has invited you comes, he may say to you, 'Friend, move up higher'; then you will have honor in the sight of all who are at the table with you. For everyone who exalts himself will be humbled, and he who humbles himself will be exalted" (Luke 14:7–11; see 2 Samuel 22:28; Proverbs 25:6, 7; Matthew 23:6).

Setting: On the way from Galilee to Jerusalem. After speaking of the importance of children, Jesus responds to a ruler's question about inheriting eternal life.

A ruler questioned Him, saying, "Good Teacher, what shall I do to inherit eternal life?" And Jesus said to him, "Why do you call Me good? No one is good except God alone. You know the commandments, 'DO NOT COMMIT ADULTERY, DO NOT MURDER, DO NOT STEAL, DO NOT BEAR FALSE WITNESS, HONOR YOUR FATHER AND MOTHER.'" And he said, "All these things I have kept from *my* youth." When Jesus heard *this,* He said to him, "One thing you still lack; sell all that you possess and distribute it to the poor, and you shall have treasure in heaven; and come, follow Me" (Luke 18:18–22, Jesus quotes from Exodus 20:12–16; cf. Matthew 19:16–22; Mark 10:17–22; see Luke 10:25–28).

Setting: Jerusalem, by the pool of Bethesda. During the Feast of the Jews in Jerusalem, Jesus responds to criticism from the Jewish religious leaders for healing a lame man on the Sabbath and for referring to God as His Father (thereby making Himself equal with God).

Therefore Jesus answered and was saying to them, "Truly, truly, I say to you, the Son can do nothing of Himself, unless *it is* something He sees the Father doing; for whatever the Father does, these things the Son also does in like manner. For the Father loves the Son, and shows Him all things that He Himself is doing; and *the Father* will show Him greater works than these, so that you will marvel. For just as the Father raises the dead and gives them life, even so the Son also gives life to whom He wishes. For not even the Father judges anyone, but He has given all judgment to the Son, so that all will honor the Son even as they honor the Father. He who does not honor the Son does not honor the Father who sent Him" (John 5:19–23; see Luke 10:16; John 3:35; 11:25; 14:12).

Setting: The temple treasury in Jerusalem. While Jesus is interacting with the scribes and Pharisees about His testimony, their ancestry, and their motives, they state their belief Jesus is a demon-possessed Samaritan.

Jesus answered, "I do not have a demon; but I honor My Father, and you dishonor Me. But I do not seek My glory; there is One who seeks and judges. Truly, truly, I say to you, if anyone keeps My word he will never see death" (John 8:49–51; see Matthew 16:28; John 5:41; 7:20).

Setting: Jerusalem. Just days before the Passover, with the chief priests and Pharisees plotting to seize Him, crowds welcome Jesus with palm branches and praise, and some Greeks ask to meet Him.

And Jesus answered them, saying, "The hour has come for the Son of Man to be glorified. Truly, truly, I say to you, unless a grain of wheat falls into the earth and dies, it remains alone; but if it dies, it bears much fruit. He who loves his life loses it, and he who hates his life in this world will keep it to life eternal. If anyone serves Me, he must follow Me; and where I am, there My servant will be also; if anyone serves Me, the Father will honor him" (John 12:23–26; see Matthew 10:39).

HONOR, PLACE OF (Also see HONOR, PLACES OF)

[PLACE OF HONOR from to sit on My right and on *My* left, this is not Mine to give]

Setting: On the way to Jerusalem. The mother of disciples James and John asks Jesus to make her sons exalted rulers with Him in His coming kingdom.

And He said to her, "What do you wish?" She said to Him, 'Command that in Your kingdom these two sons of mine may sit one on Your right and one on Your left.' But Jesus answered, "You do not know what you are asking. Are you able to drink the cup that I am about to drink?" They said to Him, 'We are able.' He said to them, "My cup you shall drink; but to sit on My right and on *My* left, this is not Mine to give, but it is for those for whom it has been prepared by My Father" (Matthew 20:21–23; cf. Mark 10:35–40; see Matthew 19:28; Acts 12:2).

Setting: The temple in Jerusalem. Jesus exposes the truth about Pharisaism to the crowds and His disciples after the Jewish religious leaders test Him with questions.

Then Jesus spoke to the crowds and to His disciples, saying: "The scribes and the Pharisees have seated themselves in the chair of Moses; therefore all that they tell you, do and observe, but do not do according to their deeds; for they say *things* and do not do *them.* They tie up heavy burdens and lay them on men's shoulders, but they themselves are unwilling to move them with *so much as* a finger. But they do all their deeds to be noticed by men; for they broaden their phylacteries and lengthen their tassels *of their garments.* They love the place of honor at banquets and the chief seats in the synagogues, and respectful greetings in the market places, and being called Rabbi by men. But do not be called Rabbi; for One is your Teacher, and you are all brothers. Do not call *anyone* on earth your father; for One is your Father, He who is in heaven. Do not be called leaders; for One is your Leader, *that is,* Christ. But the greatest among you shall be your servant. Whoever exalts himself shall be humbled; and whoever humbles himself shall be exalted" (Matthew 23:1–12; cf. Matthew 20:26; Mark 12:38–40; Luke 20:46, 47; see Exodus 13:9; Deuteronomy 33:3; Matthew 6:1, 5, 6, 9, 16; Mark 14:11; Luke 11:43; 14:11).

[PLACE OF HONOR from to sit on My right or on *My* left, this is not Mine to give]
Setting: On the way to Jerusalem. After Jesus prophesies His persecution, death, and resurrection, James and John ask for special honor and privileges in His coming kingdom.

And He said to them, "What do you want Me to do for you?" They said to Him, "Grant that we may sit, one on Your right and one on *Your* left, in Your glory." But Jesus said to them, "You do not know what you are asking. Are you able to drink the cup that I drink, or to be baptized with the baptism with which I am baptized?" They said to Him, "We are able." And Jesus said to them, "The cup that I drink you shall drink; and you shall be baptized with the baptism with which I am baptized. But to sit on My right or on *My* left, this is not Mine to give; but it is for those for whom it has been prepared" (Mark 10:36–40; cf. Matthew 20:20–23; see Matthew 19:28; Acts 12:2).

Setting: On the way from Galilee to Jerusalem. When He observes the guests selecting places of honor at the table, Jesus speaks a parable to the guests of a Pharisee leader on the Sabbath.

And He *began* speaking a parable to the invited guests when He noticed how they had been picking out the places of honor *at the table,* saying to them, "When you are invited by someone to a wedding feast, do not take the place of honor, for someone more distinguished than you may have been invited by him, and he who invited you both will come and say to you, 'Give *your* place to this man,' and then in disgrace you proceed to occupy the last place. But when you are invited, go and recline at the last place, so that when the one who has invited you comes, he may say to you, 'Friend, move up higher'; then you will have honor in the sight of all who are at the table with you. For everyone who exalts himself will be humbled, and he who humbles himself will be exalted" (Luke 14:7–11; see 2 Samuel 22:28; Proverbs 25:6, 7; Matthew 23:6; Luke 14:1, 2).

HONOR, PLACES OF (Also see HONOR, PLACE OF)
Setting: The temple in Jerusalem. Jesus warns the crowd about the scribes after commending one scribe for his nearness to the kingdom of God.

In His teaching He was saying: "Beware of the scribes who like to walk around in long robes, and *like* respectful greetings in the market places, and chief seats in the synagogues and places of honor at banquets, who devour widows' houses, and for appearance's sake offer long prayers; these will receive greater condemnation" (Mark 12:38–40; cf. Matthew 23:1–7; Luke 20:45–47).

Setting: The temple in Jerusalem. A few days before His crucifixion, after posing a question to the scribes, who do not answer, Jesus warns His disciples about the lifestyle of the scribes.

"Beware of the scribes, who like to walk around in long robes, and love respectful greetings in the market places, and chief seats in the synagogues and places of honor at banquets, who devour widows' houses, and for appearance's sake offer long prayers. These will receive greater condemnation" (Luke 20:46, 47; cf. Matthew 23:1–7; Mark 12:38–40; see Luke 11:43).

HONORING FATHER AND MOTHER

[HONORING FATHER AND MOTHER from HONOR YOUR FATHER AND MOTHER]
Setting: Galilee. Pharisees and scribes from Jerusalem accuse Jesus' disciples of disobedience to tradition and the commandments.

And He answered and said to them, "Why do you yourselves transgress the commandment of God for the sake of tradition? For God said, 'HONOR YOUR FATHER AND MOTHER,' and, 'HE WHO SPEAKS EVIL OF FATHER OR MOTHER IS TO BE PUT TO DEATH.' But you say, 'Whoever says to *his* father or mother, "Whatever I have that would help you has been given *to God*," he is not to honor his father or mother.' And *by this* you invalidated the word of God for the sake of your tradition. You hypocrites, rightly did Isaiah prophesy of you: 'THIS PEOPLE HONORS ME WITH THEIR LIPS, BUT THEIR HEART IS FAR AWAY FROM ME. BUT IN VAIN DO THEY WORSHIP ME, TEACHING AS DOCTRINES THE PRECEPTS OF MEN'" (Matthew 15:3–9, Jesus quotes from Exodus 20:12, 21:17, Leviticus 20:9; Isaiah 29:13; cf. Mark 7:5–7; see Colossians 2:22).

[HONORING FATHER AND MOTHER from HONOR YOUR FATHER AND MOTHER]
Setting: Judea beyond the Jordan (Perea). Jesus shares with a rich, young ruler how to obtain eternal life.

And He said to him, "Why are you asking Me about what is good? There is *only* One who is good; but if you wish to enter into life, keep the commandments." *Then* he said to Him, 'Which ones?' And Jesus said, "YOU SHALL NOT COMMIT MURDER; YOU SHALL NOT COMMIT ADULTERY; YOU SHALL NOT STEAL; YOU SHALL NOT BEAR FALSE WITNESS; HONOR YOUR FATHER AND MOTHER; and YOU SHALL LOVE YOUR NEIGHBOR AS YOURSELF." The young man said to Him, "All these things I have kept; what am I still lacking?" Jesus said to him, "If you wish to complete go *and* sell your possessions and give to *the* poor, and you will have treasure in heaven; and come, follow Me" (Matthew 19:16–22, Jesus quotes from Exodus 20:13–15; Leviticus 19:18; cf. Leviticus 18:5; Mark 10:17–21; Luke 10:25–28; 12:33; 18:18–24).

[HONORING FATHER AND MOTHER from HONOR YOUR FATHER AND YOUR MOTHER]
Setting: Galilee. The Pharisees and some of the scribes from Jerusalem question why Jesus' disciples do not follow the tradition of ceremonial hand cleansing before eating bread.

And He said to them, "Rightly did Isaiah prophesy of you hypocrites, as it is written: 'THIS PEOPLE HONORS ME WITH THEIR LIPS, BUT THEIR HEART IS FAR AWAY FROM ME. BUT IN VAIN DO THEY WORSHIP ME, TEACHING AS DOCTRINES THE PRECEPTS OF MEN.' Neglecting the commandment of God, you hold to the tradition of men." He was also saying to them, "You are experts at setting aside the commandment of God in order to keep tradition. For Moses said, 'HONOR YOUR FATHER AND YOUR MOTHER'; and, 'HE WHO SPEAKS EVIL OF FATHER OR MOTHER, IS TO BE PUT TO DEATH'; but you say, 'If a man says to *his* father or *his* mother, whatever I have that would help you is Corban (that is to say, given *to God*),' you no longer permit him to do anything for *his* father or *his* mother; *thus* invalidating the word of God by your tradition which you have handed down; and you do many things such as that" (Mark 7:6–13, Jesus quotes from Exodus 20:12; 21:17; Isaiah 29:13; cf. Matthew 15:1–6).

[HONORING FATHER AND MOTHER from HONOR YOUR FATHER AND MOTHER]
Setting: Judea beyond the Jordan (Perea). After demonstrating to His disciples the importance of little children, Jesus encounters a rich man seeking eternal life.

And Jesus said to him, "Why do you call Me good? No one is good except God alone. You know the commandments, 'DO NOT MURDER, DO NOT COMMIT ADULTERY, DO NOT STEAL, DO NOT BEAR FALSE WITNESS, Do not defraud, HONOR YOUR FATHER AND MOTHER.'" And he said to Him, "Teacher, I have kept all these things from my youth up." Looking at him, Jesus felt a love for him and said to him, "One thing you lack: go and sell all you possess and give to the poor, and you will have treasure in heaven; and come, follow Me" (Mark 10:18–21; Jesus quotes from Exodus 20:12–16; cf. Matthew 19:16–22; Luke 18:18–24; see Matthew 6:20).

[HONORING FATHER AND MOTHER from HONOR YOUR FATHER AND MOTHER]
Setting: Judea beyond the Jordan (Perea). After speaking of the importance of children, Jesus responds to a ruler's question about obtaining eternal life.

A ruler questioned Him, saying, "Good Teacher, what shall I do to inherit eternal life?" And Jesus said to him, "Why do you call Me good? No one is good except God alone. You know the commandments, 'DO NOT COMMIT ADULTERY, DO NOT MURDER, DO NOT STEAL, DO NOT BEAR FALSE WITNESS, HONOR YOUR FATHER AND MOTHER.'" And he said, "All these things I have kept from *my* youth." When Jesus heard *this,* He said to him, "One thing you still lack; sell all that you possess and distribute it to the poor, and you shall have treasure in heaven; and come, follow Me" (Luke 18:18–22, Jesus quotes from Exodus 20:12–16; cf. Matthew 19:16–22; Mark 10:17–22; see Luke 10:25–28).

HOOK (Also see FISH)

Setting: Capernaum of Galilee. Jesus pays the two-drachma temple tax for Peter and Himself in a miraculous manner.

He said, "Yes." And when he came into the house, Jesus spoke to him first, saying, "What do you think, Simon? From whom do the kings of the earth collect customs or poll-tax, from their sons or from strangers?" When Peter said, "From strangers," Jesus said to him, "Then the sons are exempt. However, so that we do not offend them, go to the sea and throw in a hook, and take the first fish that comes up; and when you open its mouth, you will find a shekel. Take that and give it to them for you and Me" (Matthew 17:25–27; see Exodus 30:11–16; 22:17–19; Romans 13:7).

HOPE

Setting: Jerusalem. During the Feast of the Jews, Jesus responds to criticism from the Jewish religious leaders by referring to God as His Father and informing them that God, John the Baptist, His works, and the Scriptures all testify to His mission.

"You search the Scriptures because you think that in them you have eternal life; it is these that testify about Me; and you are unwilling to come to Me so that you may have life. I do not receive glory from men; but I know you, that you do not have the love of God in yourselves. I have come in My Father's name, and you do not receive Me; if another comes in his own name, you will receive him. How can you believe, when you receive glory from one another and you do not seek the glory that is from the *one and* only God? Do not think that I will accuse you before the Father; the one who accuses you is Moses, in whom you have set your hope. For if you believed Moses, you would believe Me, for he wrote about Me. But if you do not believe his writings, how will you believe My words?" (John 5:39–47; see Matthew 24:5; Luke 16:29, 31; 24:27; John 5:18–38; 9:28; 17:3).

HOSANNA (See GLORIFYING GOD; and PRAISE)

HOSPITALITY (Also see DINNER; LUNCHEON; RECEPTION; and WELCOME)

[HOSPITALITY from stay at his house]

Setting: Galilee. After His twelve disciples observe His ministry, Jesus summons and specifically instructs them about their ministry to the people of Israel.

These twelve Jesus sent out after instructing them: "Do not go in *the* way of *the* Gentiles, and do not enter *any* city of the Samaritans; but rather go to the lost sheep of the house of Israel. And as you go, preach, saying, 'The kingdom of heaven is at hand.' Heal *the* sick, raise *the* dead, cleanse *the* lepers, cast out demons. Freely you received, freely give. Do not acquire gold, or silver, or copper for your money belts, or a bag for *your* journey, or even two coats, or sandals, or a staff; for the worker is worthy of his support. And whatever city or village you enter, inquire who is worthy in it, and stay at his house until you leave *that city*. As you enter the house, give it your greeting. If the house is worthy, give it your *blessing of* peace. But if it is not worthy, take back your *blessing of* peace. Whoever does not receive you, nor heed your words, as you go out of that house or that city, shake the dust off your feet. Truly I say to you, it will be more tolerable for *the* land of Sodom and Gomorrah in the day of judgment than for that city" (Matthew 10:5–15; cf. Mark 6:7–11; Luke 9:1–5; see Matthew 3:2; 11:22, 24; 15:24; Luke 22:35; 1 Corinthians 9:14).

[HOSPITALITY from And whoever in the name of a disciple gives to one of these little ones even a cup of cold water to drink]

Setting: Galilee. After His twelve disciples observe His ministry, Jesus summons and specifically instructs them about their ministry ahead, which will include rewards.

"He who receives you receives Me, and he who receives Me receives Him who sent me. He who receives a prophet in the name of a prophet shall receive a prophet's reward; and he who receives a righteous man in the name of a righteous man shall receive a righteous man's reward. And whoever in the name of a disciple gives to one of these little ones even a cup of cold water to drink, truly I say to you, he shall not lose his reward" (Matthew 10:40–42; cf. Matthew 25:40, 44, 45; see Mark 9:37).

[HOSPITALITY from For I was hungry, and you gave Me *something* to eat; I was thirsty, and you gave Me *something* to drink]
Setting: The Mount of Olives, just east of Jerusalem. During His discourse, after answering His disciples' questions as to when the temple will be destroyed and Jerusalem overrun, along with the signs of His coming and the end of the age, Jesus reveals the future judgments following His return.

"But when the Son of Man comes in His glory, and all the angels with Him, then He will sit on His glorious throne. All the nations will be gathered before Him; and He will separate them from one another, as the shepherd separates the sheep from the goats; and He will put the sheep on His right, and the goats on the left. Then the King will say to those on His right, 'Come, you who are blessed of My Father, inherit the kingdom prepared for you from the foundation of the world. 'For I was hungry, and you gave Me *something* to eat; I was thirsty, and you gave Me *something* to drink; I was a stranger, and you invited Me in; naked, and you clothed Me; I was sick, and you visited Me; I was in prison, and you came to Me.' Then the righteous will answer Him, 'Lord, when did we see You hungry and feed You, or thirsty, and give you *something* to drink? And when did we see You a stranger, and invite You in, or naked, and clothe You? When did we see You sick, or in prison, and come to You?' The King will answer and say to them, 'Truly I say to you, to the extent that you did it to one of these brothers of Mine, *even* the least *of them,* you did it to Me.' Then He will also say to those on His left, 'Depart from Me, accursed ones, into the eternal fire which has been prepared for the devil and his angels; for I was hungry, and you gave Me *nothing* to eat; I was thirsty, and you gave Me nothing to drink; I was a stranger, and you did not invite Me in; naked, and you did not clothe Me; sick, and in prison, and you did not visit Me.' Then they themselves also will answer, 'Lord, when did we see You hungry, or thirsty, or a stranger, or naked, or sick, or in prison, and did not take care of You?' Then He will answer them, 'Truly I say to you, to the extent that you did not do it to one of the least of these, you did not do it to Me.' These will go away into eternal punishment, but the righteous into eternal life" (Matthew 25:31–46; see Matthew 7:23; 16:27; 19:29).

[HOSPITALITY from I entered your house; you gave Me no water for My feet]
Setting: Galilee. After Jesus praises John the Baptist to the crowds, Simon, a Pharisee, invites the Lord to dinner. A sinful woman anoints His feet with perfume, prompting Him to instruct His host about forgiveness.

Turning toward the woman, He said to Simon, "Do you see this woman? I entered your house; you gave Me no water for My feet, but she has wet My feet with her tears and wiped them with her hair. You gave Me no kiss; but she, since the time I came in, has not ceased to kiss My feet. You did not anoint My head with oil, but she anointed My feet with perfume. For this reason I say to you, her sins, which are many, have been forgiven, for she loved much; but he who is forgiven little, loves little." Then He said to her, "Your sins have been forgiven." Those who were reclining *at the table* with Him began to say to themselves, "Who is this *man* who even forgives sins?" And He said to the woman, "Your faith has saved you; go in peace" (Luke 7:44–50; see Matthew 9:2; Mark 5:34; Luke 5:21).

[HOSPITALITY from they receive you, eat what is set before you]
Setting: On the way from Galilee to Jerusalem. The Lord appoints seventy followers and sends them out in pairs to every place He Himself will soon visit.

And He was saying to them, "The harvest is plentiful, but the laborers are few; therefore beseech the Lord of the harvest to send out laborers into His harvest. Go; behold, I send you out as lambs in the midst of wolves. Carry no money belt, no bag, no shoes; and greet no one on the way. Whatever house you enter, first say, 'Peace be to this house.' If a man of peace is there, your peace will rest on him; but if not, it will return to you. Stay in that house, eating and drinking what they give you; for the laborer is worthy of his wages. Do not keep moving from house to house. Whatever city you enter and they receive you, eat what is set before you; and heal those in it who are sick, and say to them, 'The kingdom of God has come near to you.' But whatever city you enter and they do not receive you, go out into its streets and say, 'Even the dust of your city which clings to our feet we wipe off *in protest* against you; yet be sure of this, that the kingdom of God has come near.' I say to you, it will be more tolerable in that day for Sodom than for that city" (Luke 10:2–12; see Genesis 19:24–28; Matthew 9:37, 38, 10:9–14, 16; 1 Corinthians 10:27).

[HOSPITALITY from welcome me into their homes]
Setting: On the way from Galilee to Jerusalem. The Lord teaches His disciples about stewardship after giving them the story of the prodigal son.

Now He was also saying to the disciples, "There was a rich man who had a manager, and this *manager* was reported to him as squandering his possessions. And he called him and said to him, 'What is this I hear about you? Give an accounting of your management, for you can no longer be a manager.' The manager said to himself, 'What shall I do, since my master is taking the management away from me? I am not strong enough to dig; I am ashamed to beg. I know what I shall do, so that when I am removed from the management people will welcome me into their homes.' And he summoned each one of his master's debtors, and he *began* saying to the first, 'How much do you owe my master?' And he said, 'A hundred measures of oil.' And he said to him, 'Take your bill, and sit down quickly and write fifty.' Then he said to another, 'And how much do you owe?' And he said, 'A hundred measures of wheat.' He said to him, 'Take your bill, and write eighty.' And his master praised the unrighteous manager because he had acted shrewdly; for the sons of this age are more shrewd in relation to their own kind than the sons of light. And I say to you, make friends for yourselves by means of the wealth of unrighteousness, so that when it fails, they will receive you into the eternal dwellings. He who is faithful in a very little thing is faithful also in much; and he who is unrighteous in a very little thing is unrighteous also in much. Therefore if you have not been faithful in the *use of* unrighteous wealth, who will entrust the *true riches* to you? And if you have not been faithful in *the use of* that which is another's, who will give you that which is your own? No servant can serve two masters; for either he will hate the one and love the other, or else he will be devoted to one and despise the other. You cannot serve God and wealth" (Luke 16:1–13; cf. Matthew 6:24; see Matthew 25:14–30).

[HOSPITALITY from stay at your house]
Setting: Jericho, on the way to Jerusalem for the crucifixion. After taking time to heal a blind man, Jesus informs a curious, short tax collector observing them from a sycamore tree that He will stay at his house that night.

When Jesus came to the place, He looked up and said to him, "Zaccheus, hurry and come down, for today I must stay at your house" (Luke 19:5).

HOT

Setting: On the island of Patmos (in the Aegean Sea about fifty miles southwest of Ephesus in modern Turkey). On the Lord's Day (Sunday), about fifty years after Jesus' resurrection, the disciple John encounters the Lord Jesus Christ, who communicates a new revelation for the apostle to record for the church in Laodicea and to six other churches in Asia.

"To the angel of the church in Laodicea write: The Amen, the faithful and true Witness, the Beginning of the creation of God, says this: 'I know your deeds, that you are neither cold nor hot; I wish that you were cold or hot. So because you are lukewarm, and neither hot nor cold, I will spit you out of My mouth. Because you say, "I am rich, and have become wealthy, and have need of nothing," and you do not know that you are wretched and miserable and poor and blind and naked, I advise you to buy from Me gold refined by fire so that you may become rich, and white garments so that you may clothe yourself, and *that* the shame of your nakedness will not be revealed; and eye salve to anoint your eyes so that you may see. Those whom I love, I reprove and discipline; therefore be zealous and repent. Behold, I stand at the door and knock; if anyone hears My voice and opens the door, I will come in to him and will dine with him, and he with Me. He who overcomes, I will grant to him to sit down with Me on My throne, as I also overcame and sat down with My Father on His throne. He who has an ear, let him hear what the Spirit says to the churches'" (Revelation 3:14–22; see Proverbs 3:12; Hosea 12:8; John 14:23; 16:33).

HOUR **(HOUR, DAY AND; and HOUR, DINNER are separate entries; also see HOURS; and TIME)**

Setting: Galilee. During the early part of His ministry, Jesus preaches the Sermon on the Mount to His disciples and the multitudes.

"For this reason I say to you, do not be worried about your life, *as to* what you will eat or what you will drink; nor for your body, *as to* what you will put on. Is not life more than food, and the body more than clothing? Look at the birds of the air, that they do not sow, nor reap nor gather into barns, and *yet* your heavenly Father feeds them. Are you not worth much more than they? And who of you by being worried can add a *single* hour to his life? And why are you worried about clothing? Observe how the lilies of the field grow; they do not toil nor do they spin, yet I say to you that not even Solomon in all his glory clothed himself like one of these. But if God so clothes the grass of the field, which is *alive* today and tomorrow is thrown into the furnace, *will He* not much more *clothe* you? You of little faith! Do not worry then, saying 'What will we eat?' or 'What will we drink?' or 'What will be wear for clothing?" For the Gentiles eagerly seek all these things; for your heavenly Father knows that you need all these things. But seek first His kingdom and His righteousness, and all these things will be added to you. So do not worry about tomorrow; for tomorrow will care for itself. Each day has enough trouble of its own" (Matthew 6:25–34; cf. Luke 12:22–31; see 1 Kings 10:4–7; Job 35:11; Matthew 8:26).

Setting: Galilee. After His disciples observe His ministry, Jesus summons and specifically instructs them about the upcoming hardships of *their* ministry to the people of Israel.

"Behold, I send you out as sheep in the midst of wolves; so be shrewd as serpents and innocent as doves. But beware of men, for they will hand you over to *the* courts and scourge you in their synagogues; and you will even be brought before governors and kings for My sake, as a testimony to them and to the Gentiles. But when they hand you over, do not worry about how or what you are to say; for it will be given you in that hour what you are to say. For it is not you who speak, but *it* is the Spirit of your Father who speaks in you" (Matthew 10:16–20; cf. Luke 10:3).

Setting: Judea beyond the Jordan (Perea). Jesus illustrates the kingdom of heaven to His disciples through the story of laborers in the vineyard.

"For the kingdom of heaven is like a landowner who went out early in the morning to hire laborers for his vineyard. When he had agreed with the laborers for a denarius for the day, he sent them into his vineyard. And he went out about the third hour and saw others standing idle in the market place; and to those he said, 'You also go into the vineyard, and whatever is right I will give you.' And *so* they went. Again he went out about the sixth and the ninth hour, and did the same thing. And about the eleventh *hour* he went out and found others standing *around;* and he said to them, 'Why have you been standing idle here all day long?' They said to him, 'Because no one hired us.' He said to them, 'You go into the vineyard too.' When evening came, the owner of the vineyard said to his foreman, 'Call the laborers and pay them their wages, beginning with the last *group* to the first.' When those *hired* about the eleventh hour came, each one received a denarius. When those *hired* first came, they thought that they would receive more; but each of them also received a denarius. When they received it, they grumbled at the landowner, saying, 'These last men have worked *only* one hour, and you have made them equal to us who have borne the burden and the scorching heat of the day.' But he answered and said to one of them, 'Friend, I am doing you no wrong; did you not agree with me for a denarius? Take what is yours and go, but I wish to give to this last man the same as to you. It is not lawful for me to do what I wish with what is my own? Or is your eye envious because I am generous?' So the last shall be first, and the first last" (Matthew 20:1–16; cf. Matthew 19:30).

Setting: The Mount of Olives, just east of Jerusalem. During His discourse, after answering His disciples' questions as to when the temple will be destroyed and Jerusalem overrun, along with the signs of His coming and the end of the age, Jesus reemphasizes to His disciples that they should be on the alert for His return.

"Therefore be on the alert, for you do not know which day your Lord is coming. But be sure of this, that if the head of the house had known at what time of the night the thief was coming, he would have been on the alert and would not have allowed his house to be broken into. For this reason you also must be ready; for the Son of Man is coming at an hour when you do not think *He will.* Who then is the faithful and sensible slave whom his master put in charge of his household to give their food at the proper time?

Blessed is that slave whom his master finds so doing when he comes. Truly I say to you that he will put him in charge of all his possessions. But if that evil slave says in his heart, 'My master is not coming for a long time,' and begins to beat his fellow slaves and eat and drink with drunkards; the master of that slave will come on a day when he does not expect *him* and at an hour which he does not know, and will cut him in pieces and assign him a place with the hypocrites; in that place there will be weeping and gnashing of teeth" (Matthew 24:42–51; cf. Mark 13:33–37; Luke 12:39–46; 21:34–36; see Matthew 8:11, 12; 25:21–23).

Setting: Jerusalem. After celebrating the Passover meal with His disciples, Jesus retreats to the Garden of Gethsemane on the Mount of Olives to pray prior to His betrayal by Judas.

Then Jesus came with them to a place called Gethsemane, and said to His disciples, "Sit here while I go over there and pray." And He took with Him Peter and the two sons of Zebedee, and began to be grieved and distressed. Then He said to them, "My soul is deeply grieved, to the point of death; remain here and keep watch with Me." And He went a little beyond *them,* and fell on His face and prayed, saying, "My Father, if it is possible, let this cup pass from Me; yet not as I will, but as You will." And He came to the disciples and found them sleeping, and said to Peter, "So, you *men* could not keep watch with Me for one hour? Keep watching and praying that you may not enter into temptation; the spirit is willing, but the flesh is weak." He went away again a second time and prayed, saying, "My Father, if this cannot pass away unless I drink it, Your will be done." Again He came and found them sleeping, for their eyes were heavy. And He left them again, and went away and prayed a third time, saying the same thing once more. Then He came to the disciples and said to them, "Are you still sleeping and resting? Behold the hour is at hand and the Son of Man is being betrayed into the hands of sinners. Get up, let us be going; behold the one who betrays Me is at hand!" (Matthew 26:36–46; cf. Mark 14:32–42; Luke 22:40–46; see Matthew 20:22; John 12:27).

Setting: On the Mount of Olives, east of the temple in Jerusalem. After predicting the temple's destruction, Jesus responds during His Olivet Discourse to questions from Peter, James, John, and Andrew about other future events.

And Jesus began to say to them, "See to it that no one misleads you. Many will come in My name, saying, 'I am *He!'* and will mislead many. When you hear of wars and rumors of wars, do not be frightened; *those things* must take place; but *that is* not yet the end. For nation will rise up against nation, and kingdom against kingdom; there will be earthquakes in various places; there will *also be* famines. These things are *merely* the beginning of birth pangs. But be on your guard; for they will deliver you to *the* courts, and you will be flogged in *the* synagogues, and you will stand before governors and kings for My sake, as a testimony to them. The gospel must first be preached to all the nations. When they arrest you and hand you over, do not worry beforehand about what you are to say, but say whatever is given you in that hour; for it is not you who speak, but *it is* the Holy Spirit. Brother will betray brother to death, and a father *his* child; and children will rise up against parents and have them put to death. You will be hated by all because of My name, but the one who endures to the end, he will be saved" (Mark 13:5–13; cf. Matthew 24:4–14; Luke 21:7–19; see Matthew 10:17–22).

Setting: Gethsemane on the Mount of Olives, east of the temple in Jerusalem. Jesus agonizes over His impending death, disappointed that His disciples keep falling asleep instead of watching and praying with Him.

They came to a place named Gethsemane; and He said to the disciples, "Sit here until I have prayed." And He took with Him Peter and James and John, and began to be very distressed and troubled. And He said to them, "My soul is deeply grieved to the point of death; remain here and keep watch." And He went a little beyond *them,* and fell to the ground and *began* to pray that if it were possible, the hour might pass Him by. And He was saying, "Abba! Father! All things are possible for You; remove this cup from Me; yet not what I will, but what You will." And He came and found them sleeping, and said to Peter, "Simon, are you asleep? Could you not keep watch for one hour? Keep watching and praying that you may not come into temptation; the spirit is willing, but the flesh is weak" (Mark 14:32–38; cf. Matthew 26:36–41; Luke 22:41–46; see Romans 8:15; Galatians 4:6).

Setting: Gethsemane on the Mount of Olives, east of the temple in Jerusalem. Jesus prepares to meet Judas the betrayer, while His other disciples keep falling asleep instead of watching and praying with Him.

And He came the third time, and said to them, "Are you still sleeping and resting? It is enough; the hour has come; behold, the

Son of Man is being betrayed into the hands of sinners. Get up, let us be going; behold, the one who betrays Me is at hand!" (Mark 14:41, 42; cf. Matthew 26:45, 46).

Setting: On the way from Galilee to Jerusalem. Jesus warns His disciples of future events as the scribes and Pharisees turn hostile and question Him repeatedly in an attempt to catch Him in something He might say.

"And I say to you, everyone who confesses Me before men, the Son of Man will confess him also before the angels of God; but he who denies Me before men will be denied before the angels of God. And everyone who speaks a word against the Son of Man, it will be forgiven him; but he who blasphemes against the Holy Spirit, it will not be forgiven him. When they bring you before the synagogues and the rulers and the authorities, do not worry about how or what you are to speak in your defense, or what you are to say; for the Holy Spirit will teach you in that very hour what you ought to say" (Luke 12:8–12; cf. Matthew 10:32, 33; 12:31, 32; see Matthew 10:20).

Setting: On the way from Galilee to Jerusalem. Jesus comforts the crowd and His disciples after giving a parable about riches and greed. The scribes and Pharisees turn hostile and question Him repeatedly in an attempt to catch Him in something He might say.

And He said to His disciples, "For this reason I say to you, do not worry about *your* life, *as to* what you will eat; nor for your body, *as to* what you will put on. For life is more than food, and the body more than clothing. Consider the ravens, for they neither sow nor reap; they have no storeroom nor barn, and *yet* God feeds them; how much more valuable you are than the birds! And which of you by worrying can add a *single* hour to his life's span? If then you cannot do even a very little thing, why do you worry about other matters? Consider the lilies, how they grow: they neither toil nor spin; but I tell you, not even Solomon in all his glory clothed himself like one of these. But if God so clothes the grass in the field, which is *alive* today and tomorrow is thrown into the furnace, how much more *will He clothe* you? You men of little faith! And do not seek what you will eat and what you will drink, and do not keep worrying. For all these things the nations of the world eagerly seek; but your Father knows that you need these things. But seek His kingdom, and these things will be added to you. Do not be afraid, little flock, for your Father has chosen gladly to give you the kingdom" (Luke 12:22–32; cf. Matthew 6:25–33; see 1 Kings 10:4–7; Job 38:41).

Setting: On the way from Galilee to Jerusalem. After giving a parable about riches and greed, Jesus uses a parable to challenge the crowd and His disciples to be ready for His return.

"Be dressed in readiness, and *keep* your lamps lit. Be like men who are waiting for their master when he returns from the wedding feast, so that they may immediately open *the door* to him when he comes and knocks. Blessed are those slaves whom the master will find on the alert when he comes; truly I say to you, that he will gird himself *to serve,* and have them recline *at the table,* and will come up and wait on them. Whether he comes in the second watch, or even in the third and finds *them* so, blessed are those *slaves.* But be sure of this, that if the head of the house had known at what hour the thief was coming, he would not have allowed his house to be broken into. You too, be ready; for the Son of Man is coming at an hour that you do not expect" (Luke 12:35–40; cf. Matthew 24:42–44; see Mark 13:33; Ephesians 6:14).

Setting: On the way from Galilee to Jerusalem. When Jesus uses a parable to challenge the crowd and His disciples to be ready for His return, Peter asks Him whom He is addressing.

And the Lord said, "Who then is the faithful and sensible steward, whom his master will put in charge of his servants, to give them their rations at the proper time? Blessed is that slave whom his master finds so doing when he comes. Truly I say to you that he will put him in charge of all his possessions. But if that slave says in his heart, 'My master will be a long time in coming,' and begins to beat the slaves, *both* men and women, and to eat and drink and get drunk; the master of that slave will come on a day when he does not expect *him* and at an hour he does not know, and will cut him in pieces, and assign him a place with the unbelievers. And that slave who knew his master's will and did not get ready or act in accord with his will, will receive many lashes, but the one who did know *it,* and committed deeds worthy of flogging, will receive but few. From everyone who has been given much, much will be required; and to whom they entrusted much, of him they will ask all the more" (Luke 12:42–48; cf. Matthew 24:45–51; see Leviticus 5:17).

Setting: Gethsemane on the Mount of Olives, east of the temple in Jerusalem. After praying for deliverance, with His crucifixion imminent, Jesus chastises the religious leaders after Judas betrays Him and the hostile crowd surround Him.

Then Jesus said to the chief priests and officers of the temple and elders who had come against Him, "Have you come out with swords and clubs as you would against a robber? While I was with you daily in the temple, you did not lay hands on Me; but this hour and the power of darkness are yours" (Luke 22:52, 53; cf. Matthew 26:47–56; Mark 14:43–50; see Luke 22:1–4).

Setting: Cana of Galilee. On the third day of His public ministry, after choosing Andrew, Peter, Philip, and Nathanael to be His disciples, Jesus attends a wedding. His mother prompts Him to perform His first miracle, turning water into wine.

And Jesus said to her, "Woman, what does that have to do with us? My hour has not yet come" (John 2:4; see John 7:6, 8, 30).

Setting: Sychar in Samaria, on the way to Galilee. Jesus interacts with a Samaritan woman at Jacob's well, while His disciples shop for food.

Jesus said to her, "Woman, believe Me, an hour is coming when neither in this mountain nor in Jerusalem will you worship the Father. You worship what you do not know; we worship what we know, for salvation is from the Jews. But an hour is coming, and now is, when the true worshipers will worship the Father in spirit and truth; for such people the Father seeks to be His worshipers. God is spirit, and those who worship Him must worship in spirit and truth" (John 4:21–24; see Isaiah 2:3; Philippians 3:3).

Setting: Jerusalem. During the Feast of the Jews, Jesus responds to criticism from the Jewish religious leaders by referring to God as His Father (thereby making Himself equal with God) and stating He will someday participate in the resurrection and judgment of men.

"Truly, truly, I say to you, an hour is coming and now is, when the dead will hear the voice of the Son of God, and those who hear will live. For just as the Father has life in Himself, even so He gave to the Son also to have life in Himself; and He gave Him authority to execute judgment, because He is *the* Son of Man. Do not marvel at this; for an hour is coming, in which all who are in the tombs will hear His voice, and will come forth; those who did the good *deeds* to a resurrection of life, those who committed the evil *deeds* to a resurrection of judgment" (John 5:25–29; see Daniel 12:2; John 1:4; 11:24).

Setting: Jerusalem. Just days before the Passover, with the chief priests and Pharisees plotting to seize Him, crowds welcome Jesus with palm branches and praise, and some Greeks ask to meet Him.

And Jesus answered them, saying, "The hour has come for the Son of Man to be glorified. Truly, truly, I say to you, unless a grain of wheat falls into the earth and dies, it remains alone; but if it dies, it bears much fruit. He who loves his life loses it, and he who hates his life in this world will keep it to life eternal. If anyone serves Me, he must follow Me; and where I am, there My servant will be also; if anyone serves Me, the Father will honor him" (John 12:23–26; see Matthew 10:39).

Setting: Jerusalem. Just days before the Passover, with the chief priests and Pharisees plotting to seize Him and crowds welcoming Him with palm branches and praise, Jesus expresses anxiety about His upcoming death by crucifixion.

"Now My soul has become troubled; and what shall I say, 'Father, save Me from this hour'? But for this purpose I came to this hour. Father glorify Your name." Then a voice came out of heaven: "I have glorified it, and will glorify it again." So the crowd *of people* who stood by and heard it were saying that it had thundered; others were saying, "An angel has spoken to Him." Jesus answered and said, "This voice has not come for My sake, but for your sakes. Now judgment is upon this world; now the ruler of this world will be cast out. And I, if I am lifted up from the earth, will draw all men to Myself" (John 12:27–32; see Matthew 3:17; 26:38; John 3:14; 6:44; 11:42; 14:30).

Setting: Jerusalem. Before the Passover, after explaining He is the vine and His disciples are the branches, Jesus warns His disciples of the persecution they will face after His departure to heaven.

"These things I have spoken to you so that you may be kept from stumbling. They will make you outcasts from the synagogue, but an hour is coming for everyone who kills you to think that he is offering service to God. These things they will do because they have not known the Father or Me. But these things I have spoken to you, so that when their hour comes, you may remember that I told you of them. These things I did not say to you at the beginning, because I was with you" (John 16:1–4; see John 8:19, 55; 9:22; 13:19; 15:18–27).

Setting: Jerusalem. Before the Passover, after warning His disciples of the persecution they will face after His departure to heaven, empathizing with their sadness over His prophecies, Jesus gives them hope for the future.

"A little while, and you will no longer see Me; and again a little while, and you will see Me." *Some* of His disciples then said to one another, "What is this thing He is telling us, 'A little while, and you will not see Me; and again a little while, and you will see Me'; and, 'because I go to the Father'?" So they were saying, "What is this that He says, 'A little while'? We do not know what He is talking about." Jesus knew that they wished to question Him, and He said to them, "Are you deliberating together about this, that I said, 'A little while, and you will not see Me, and again a little while, and you will see Me'? Truly, truly, I say to you, that you will weep and lament, but the world will rejoice; you will grieve, but your grief will be turned into joy. Whenever a woman is in labor she has pain, because her hour has come; but when she gives birth to the child, she no longer remembers the anguish because of the joy that a child has been born into the world. Therefore you too have grief now; but I will see you again, and your heart will rejoice, and no one *will* take your joy away from you" (John 16:16–22; see Mark 9:32; Luke 23:27; John 14:18–24; 16:5, 6; 20:20).

Setting: Jerusalem. Before the Passover, after empathizing with His disciples' sadness over His prophecies and giving them hope for the future, Jesus conveys promises about praying in His name.

"In that day you will not question Me about anything. Truly, truly, I say to you, if you ask the Father for anything in My name, He will give it to you. Until now you have asked for nothing in My name; ask and you will receive, so that your joy may be made full. These things I have spoken to you in figurative language; an hour is coming when I will no longer speak to you in figurative language, but will tell you plainly of the Father. In that day you will ask in My name, and I do not say to you that I will request of the Father on your behalf; for the Father Himself loves you, because you have loved Me and have believed that I came forth from the Father. I came forth from the Father and have come into the world; I am leaving the world again and going to the Father" (John 16:23–28; see Matthew 13:34; John 8:42; 13:1, 3; 14:14, 21, 23; 15:16).

Setting: Jerusalem. Before the Passover, after conveying promises about praying in His name, Jesus prophesies His disciples' scattering and gives them assurance that in the midst of tribulation they will have His peace.

"Jesus answered them, "Do you now believe? Behold, an hour is coming, and has *already* come, for you to be scattered, each to his own *home,* and to leave Me alone; and *yet* I am not alone, because the Father is with Me. These things I have spoken to you, so that in Me you may have peace. In the world you have tribulation, but take courage, I have overcome the world" (John 16:31–33; see Zechariah 13:7; John 8:29; 14:27; Romans 8:37).

Setting: Jerusalem. Before the Passover, after giving His disciples assurance that in the midst of tribulation they will have His peace, Jesus prays His high-priestly prayer.

Jesus spoke these things; and lifting up His eyes to heaven, He said, "Father, the hour has come; glorify Your Son, that the Son may glorify You, even as You gave Him authority over all flesh, that to all whom You have given Him, He may give eternal life. This is eternal life, that they may know You, the only true God, and Jesus Christ whom You have sent. I glorified You on the earth, having accomplished the work which You have given Me to do. Now, Father, glorify Me together with Yourself, with the glory which I had with You before the world was. I have manifested Your name to the men whom You gave Me out of the world; they were Yours and You gave them to Me, and they have kept Your word. Now they have come to know that everything You have given

Me is from You; for the words which You gave Me I have given to them; and they received *them* and truly understood that I came forth from You, and they believed You sent Me. I ask on their behalf; I do not ask on behalf of the world, but of those whom You have given Me; for they are Yours; and all things that are Mine are Yours, and Yours are Mine; and have been glorified in them. I am no longer in the world; and *yet* they themselves are in the world, and I come to You. Holy Father, keep them in Your name, *the name* which You have given Me, that they may be even as We *are.* While I was with them, I was keeping them in Your name which You have given Me; and I guarded them and not one of them perished but the son of perdition, so that the Scripture would be fulfilled" (John 17:1–12; see Luke 22:32; John 1:1; 3:35; 4:34; 5:44; 6:37–39, 70; 8:42; 11:41; 12:49; 13:18, 31; 16:15; 17:20; Philippians 2:9).

Setting: On the island of Patmos (in the Aegean Sea about fifty miles southwest of Ephesus in modern Turkey). On the Lord's Day (Sunday), about fifty years after Jesus' resurrection, the disciple John encounters the Lord Jesus Christ, who communicates a new revelation for the apostle to record for the church in Sardis and to six other churches in Asia.

"To the angel of the church in Sardis write: He who has the seven Spirits of God and the seven stars, says this: 'I know your deeds, that you have a name that you are alive, but you are dead. Wake up, and strengthen the things that remain, which were about to die; for I have not found your deeds completed in the sight of My God. So remember what you have received and heard; and keep *it,* and repent. Therefore if you do not wake up, I will come like a thief, and you will not know at what hour I will come to you. But you have a few people in Sardis who have not soiled their garments; and they will walk with Me in white, for they are worthy. He who overcomes will thus be clothed in white garments; and I will not erase his name from the book of life, and I will confess his name before My Father and before His angels. He who has an ear, let him hear what the Spirit says to the churches' " (Revelation 3:1–6; see Matthew 10:32; Revelation 1:16).

Setting: On the island of Patmos (in the Aegean Sea about fifty miles southwest of Ephesus in modern Turkey). On the Lord's Day (Sunday), about fifty years after Jesus' resurrection, the disciple John encounters the Lord Jesus Christ, who communicates a new revelation for the apostle to record for the church in Philadelphia and to six other churches in Asia.

"And to the angel of the church in Philadelphia write: He who is holy, who is true, who has the key of David, who opens and no one will shut, and who shuts and no one opens, says this: 'I know your deeds. Behold, I have put before you an open door which no one can shut, because you have a little power, and have kept My word, and have not denied My name. Behold, I will cause *those* of the synagogue of Satan, who say that they are Jews and are not, but lie—I will make them come and bow down at your feet, and *make them* know that I have loved you. Because you have kept the word of My perseverance, I also will keep you from the hour of testing, that *hour* which is about to come upon the whole world, to test those who dwell on the earth. I am coming quickly; hold fast what you have, so that no one will take your crown. He who overcomes, I will make him a pillar in the temple of My God, and he will not go out from it anymore; and I will write on him the name of My God, and the name of the city of My God, the new Jerusalem, which comes down out of heaven from My God, and My new name. He who has an ear, let him hear what the Spirit says to the churches' " (Revelation 3:7–13; see Isaiah 22:22; Galatians 2:9; Revelation 2:9, 10, 13, 25; 14:1).

HOUR, DAY AND

Setting: The Mount of Olives, just east of Jerusalem. During His discourse, after answering His disciples' questions as to when the temple will be destroyed and Jerusalem overrun, along with the signs of His coming and the end of the age, Jesus teaches them the Parable of the Fig Tree.

"Now learn the parable from the fig tree: when its branch has already become tender and puts forth its leaves, you know that summer is near; so, you too, when you see all these things, recognize that He is near, *right* at the door. Truly, I say to you, this generation will not pass away until all these things take place. Heaven and earth will pass away, but My words will not pass away. But of that day and hour no one knows, not even the angels of heaven, nor the Son, but the Father alone. For the coming of the Son of Man will be just like the days of Noah. For as in those days before the flood they were eating and drinking, marrying and giving in marriage, until the day that Noah entered the ark, and they did not understand until the flood came and took them all away; so will the coming of the Son of Man be. Then there will be two men in the field; one will be taken and one will be left. Two women *will be* grinding at the mill; one will be taken and one will be left" (Matthew 24:32–41; cf. Mark 13:28–32; Luke 17:34–36;

21:28–33; see Genesis 6:5; 7:7; Matthew 5:18; 10:23; James 5:9).

[DAY AND HOUR from on a day when he does not expect *him* and at an hour which he does not know]
Setting: The Mount of Olives, just east of Jerusalem. During His discourse, after answering His disciples' questions as to when the temple will be destroyed and Jerusalem overrun, along with the signs of His coming and the end of the age, Jesus reemphasizes to His disciples that they should be on the alert for His return.

"Therefore be on the alert, for you do not know which day your Lord is coming. But be sure of this, that if the head of the house had known at what time of the night the thief was coming, he would have been on the alert and would not have allowed his house to be broken into. For this reason you also must be ready; for the Son of Man is coming at an hour when you do not think *He will.* Who then is the faithful and sensible slave whom his master put in charge of his household to give their food at the proper time? Blessed is that slave whom his master finds so doing when he comes. Truly I say to you that he will put him in charge of all his possessions. But if that evil slave says in his heart, 'My master is not coming for a long time,' and begins to beat his fellow slaves and eat and drink with drunkards; the master of that slave will come on a day when he does not expect *him* and at an hour which he does not know, and will cut him in pieces and assign him a place with the hypocrites; in that place there will be weeping and gnashing of teeth" (Matthew 24:42–51; cf. Mark 13:33–37; Luke 12:39–46; 21:34–36; see Matthew 8:11, 12; 25:21–23).

[DAY AND HOUR from the day nor the hour]
Setting: The Mount of Olives, just east of Jerusalem. During His discourse, after answering His disciples' questions as to when the temple will be destroyed and Jerusalem overrun, along with the signs of His coming and the end of the age, Jesus reemphasizes to His disciples that they should be on the alert for His return.

"Then the kingdom of heaven will be comparable to ten virgins, who took their lamps and went out to meet the bridegroom. Five of them were foolish, and five were prudent. For when the foolish took their lamps, they took no oil with them, but the prudent took oil in flasks along with their lamps. Now while the bridegroom was delaying, they all got drowsy and *began* to sleep. But at midnight there was a shout, 'Behold, the bridegroom! Come out to meet *him*.' Then all those virgins rose and trimmed their lamps. The foolish said to the prudent, 'Give us some of your oil, for our lamps are going out.' But the prudent answered, 'No, there will not be enough for us and you *too;* go instead to the dealers and buy *some* for yourselves.' And while they were going away to make the purchase, the bridegroom came, and those who were ready went in with him to the wedding feast; and the door was shut. Later the other virgins also came, saying, 'Lord, lord, open up for us.' But he answered, 'Truly I say to you, I do not know you.' Be on the alert then, for you do not know the day nor the hour" (Matthew 25:1–13; cf. Matthew 24:42; Luke 12:35; see Matthew 7:21, 24).

[DAY AND HOUR from day or hour]
Setting: On the Mount of Olives, east of the temple in Jerusalem. After predicting the temple's destruction, Jesus responds during His Olivet Discourse to questions from Peter, James, John, and Andrew about other future events.

"Now learn the parable from the fig tree: when its branch has already become tender and puts forth its leaves, you know that summer is near. Even so, you too, when you see these things happening, recognize that He is near, *right* at the door. Truly I say to you, this generation will not pass away until all these things take place. Heaven and earth will pass away, but My words will not pass away. But of the day or hour no one knows, not even the angels in heaven, nor the Son, but the Father *alone*" (Mark 13:28–32; cf. Matthew 24:32–36; Luke 21:28–33).

[DAY AND HOUR from on a day when he does not expect *him* and at an hour he does not know]
Setting: On the way from Galilee to Jerusalem. When Jesus uses a parable to challenge the crowd and His disciples to be ready for His return, Peter asks Him whom He is addressing.

And the Lord said, "Who then is the faithful and sensible steward, whom his master will put in charge of his servants, to give them their rations at the proper time? Blessed is that slave whom his master finds so doing when he comes. Truly I say to you that he will put him in charge of all his possessions. But if that slave says in his heart, 'My master will be a long time in coming,' and begins to beat the slaves, *both* men and women, and to eat and drink and get drunk; the master of that slave will come on a day when he does not expect *him* and at an hour he does not know, and will cut him in pieces, and assign him a place with the unbelievers. And that slave who knew his master's will and did not get ready or act in accord with his will, will receive many lashes, but the one who did know *it,* and committed deeds worthy of flogging, will receive but few. From everyone who has been given much, much will be required; and to whom they entrusted much, of him they will ask all the more" (Luke 12:42–48; cf. Matthew 24:45–51; see Leviticus 5:17).

HOUR, DINNER (Also see DINNER; GUESTS, DINNER; and HOSPITALITY)

Setting: On the way from Galilee to Jerusalem. After He speaks a parable to the invited guests and the host at a banquet, Jesus responds to a guest's proclamation about the blessings of eating bread in the kingdom of God.

But He said to him, "A man was giving a big dinner, and he invited many; and at the dinner hour he sent his slave to say to those who had been invited, 'Come; for everything is ready now.' But they all alike began to make excuses. The first one said to him, 'I have bought a piece of land and I need to go out and look at it; please consider me excused.' Another one said, 'I have bought five yoke of oxen, and I am going to try them out; please consider me excused.' Another one said, I have married a wife, and for that reason I cannot come.' And the slave came *back* and reported this to his master. Then the head of the household became angry and said to his slave, 'Go out at once into the streets and lanes of the city and bring in here the poor and crippled and blind and lame.' And the slave said, 'Master, what you commanded has been done, and still there is room.' And the master said to the slave, 'Go out into the highways and along the hedges, and compel *them* to come in, so that my house may be filled. For I tell you, none of those men who were invited shall taste of my dinner'" (Luke 14:16–24; see Deuteronomy 24:5; Matthew 22:2–14; Luke 14:1–2).

HOURS (Also see HOUR)

Setting: Beyond the Jordan. While avoiding the Jerusalem Pharisees, Jesus receives word from Lazarus's sisters in Bethany of His friend's sickness and decides to go there.

Then after this He said to the disciples, "Let us go to Judea again." The disciples said to Him, "Rabbi, the Jews were just now seeking to stone You, and are You going there again?" Jesus answered, "Are there not twelve hours in the day? If anyone walks in the day, he does not stumble, because he sees the light of this world. But if anyone walks in the night, he stumbles, because the light is not in him." This He said, and after that He said to them, "Our friend Lazarus has fallen asleep; but I go, so that I may awaken him out of sleep" (John 11:7–11; see John 8:59; 10:39).

HOUSE (Specifics such as HOUSE, FATHER'S; HOUSE, HEAD OF THE; and HOUSE OF GOD are separate entries; also see HOME; and HOUSES)

Setting: Galilee. During the early part of His ministry, Jesus preaches the Sermon on the Mount to His disciples and the multitudes.

"You are the light of the world. A city set on a hill cannot be hidden; nor does *anyone* light a lamp and put it under a basket, but on the lampstand, and it gives light to all who are in the house. Let your light shine before men in such a way that they may see your good works, and glorify your Father who is in heaven" (Matthew 5:14–16; cf. Mark 4:21; 1 Peter 2:12).

Setting: Galilee. During the early part of His ministry, Jesus preaches the Sermon on the Mount to His disciples and the multitudes.

"Therefore everyone who hears these words of Mine and acts on them, may be compared to a wise man who built his house on the rock. And the rain fell, and the floods came, and the winds blew and slammed against that house; and *yet* it did not fall, for it had been founded on the rock. Everyone who hears these words of Mine and does not act on them, will be like a foolish man who built his house on the sand. The rain fell, and the floods came, and the winds blew and slammed against that house; and it fell—and great was its fall" (Matthew 7:24–28; cf. Luke 6:47–49 and see Matthew 7:29).

Setting: Galilee. After His twelve disciples observe His ministry, Jesus summons and specifically instructs them about their ministry to the people of Israel.

These twelve Jesus sent out after instructing them: "Do not go in *the* way of *the* Gentiles, and do not enter *any* city of the Samaritans; but rather go to the lost sheep of the house of Israel. And as you go, preach, saying, 'The kingdom of heaven is at hand.' Heal *the* sick, raise *the* dead, cleanse *the* lepers, cast out demons. Freely you received, freely give. Do not acquire gold, or silver, or copper for your money belts, or a bag for *your* journey, or even two coats, or sandals, or a staff; for the worker is worthy of his support. And whatever city or village you enter, inquire who is worthy in it, and stay at his house until you leave *that city*. As you enter the house, give it your greeting. If the house is worthy, give it your *blessing of* peace. But if it is not worthy, take back your *blessing of* peace. Whoever does not receive you, nor heed your words, as you go out of that house or that city, shake the dust off your feet. Truly I say to you, it will be more tolerable for *the* land of Sodom and Gomorrah in the day of judgment than for that city" (Matthew 10:5–15; cf. Mark 6:7–11; Luke 9:1–5; see Matthew 3:2; 11:22, 24; 15:24; Luke 22:35; 1 Corinthians 9:14).

Setting: Galilee. After He heals a blind, mute, demon-possessed man, the Pharisees accuse Jesus in front of crowds of being a worker of Satan.

And knowing their thoughts Jesus said to them, "Any kingdom divided against itself is laid waste; and any city or house divided against itself will not stand. If Satan casts out Satan, he is divided against himself; how then will his kingdom stand? If I by Beelzebul cast out demons, by whom do your sons cast *them* out? For this reason they will be your judges. But if I cast out demons by the Spirit of God, then the kingdom of God has come upon you. Or how can anyone enter the strong man's house and carry off his property, unless he first binds the strong *man?* And then he will plunder his house" (Matthew 12:25–29; cf. Matthew 9:34; Mark 3:23–27; Luke 11:17–20).

Setting: Galilee. Jesus responds to some Pharisees and scribes who ask Him for a miraculous sign.

"Now when the unclean spirit goes out of a man, it passes through waterless places seeking rest, and does not find *it.* Then it says, 'I will return to my house from which I came'; and when it comes, it finds *it* unoccupied, swept, and put in order. Then it goes and takes along with it seven other spirits more wicked than itself, and they go in and live there; and the last state of that man becomes worse than the first. That is the way it will also be for this evil generation" (Matthew 12:43–45; cf. Luke 11:24–26; see Matthew 12:38; Mark 5:9).

Setting: The district of Tyre and Sidon. A Canaanite woman appeals to Jesus to heal her demon-possessed daughter.

But He answered and said, "I was sent only to the lost sheep of the house of Israel." But she came and *began* to bow down before Him, saying, "Lord, help me!" And He answered and said, "It is not good to take the children's bread and throw it to the dogs." But she said, "Yes, Lord; but even the dogs feed from the crumbs which fall from their masters' table." Then Jesus said to her, "O woman, your faith is great; it shall be done for you as you wish." And her daughter was healed at once (Matthew 15:24–28; cf. Mark 7: 24–30; see Matthew 9:22; 10:5–6).

Setting: The temple in Jerusalem. After being welcomed with blessings from the crowds, Jesus cleanses the temple by driving out the money changers and merchants.

And He said to them, "It is written, 'MY HOUSE SHALL BE CALLED A HOUSE OF PRAYER'; but you are making it a ROBBERS' DEN" (Matthew 21:13; Jesus quotes from Isaiah 56:7; Jeremiah 7:11; cf. Mark 11:15–18; Luke 19:46).

Setting: The temple in Jerusalem. With His death on the cross just days away, Jesus laments over Jerusalem's hard-heartedness and lack of repentance.

"Jerusalem, Jerusalem, who kills the prophets and stones those who are sent to her! How often I wanted to gather your children together, the way a hen gathers her chicks under her wings, and you were unwilling. Behold, your house is being left to you desolate! For I say to you, from now on you will not see Me until you say, 'BLESSED IS HE WHO COMES IN THE NAME OF THE LORD!'" (Matthew 23:37–39, Jesus quotes from Psalm 118:26; cf. 1 Kings 9:7; Luke 13:34, 35).

Setting: The Mount of Olives, just east of Jerusalem. During His discourse, Jesus answers His disciples' questions as to when the temple will be destroyed and Jerusalem overrun, along with the signs of His coming and the end of the age.

"Therefore when you see the ABOMINATION OF DESOLATION which was spoken of through Daniel the prophet, standing in the holy place (let the reader understand), then those who are in Judea must flee to the mountains. Whoever is on the housetop must not go down to get the things that are in his house. Whoever is in the field must not turn back to get his cloak. But woe to those who are pregnant and to those who are nursing babies in those days! But pray that your flight will not be in the winter, or on a Sabbath. For then there will be a great tribulation, such as has not occurred since the beginning of the world until now, nor ever will. Unless those days had been cut short, no life would have been saved; but for the sake of the elect those days will be cut short. Then if anyone says to you, 'Behold, here is the Christ,' or "There *He is,*' do not believe *him.* For false Christs and false prophets will arise and will show great signs and wonders, so as to mislead, if possible, even the elect. Behold, I have told you in advance. So if they say to you, 'Behold, He is in the wilderness,' do not go out, *or,* 'Behold, He is in the inner rooms,' do not believe *them.* For just as the lightning comes from the east and flashes even to the west, so will the coming of the Son of Man be. Wherever a corpse is, there the vultures will gather" (Matthew 24:15–28, Jesus quotes from Daniel 9:27; cf. Daniel 12:1; Mark 13:14–23; Luke 17:22–31; 21:20–24; 23:29; see John 4:48).

Setting: The Mount of Olives, just east of Jerusalem. During His discourse, after answering His disciples' questions as to when the temple will be destroyed and Jerusalem overrun, along with the signs of His coming and the end of the age, Jesus reemphasizes to His disciples that they should be on the alert for His return.

"Therefore be on the alert, for you do not know which day your Lord is coming. But be sure of this, that if the head of the house had known at what time of the night the thief was coming, he would have been on the alert and would not have allowed his house to be broken into. For this reason you also must be ready; for the Son of Man is coming at an hour when you do not think *He will.* Who then is the faithful and sensible slave whom his master put in charge of his household to give their food at the proper time? Blessed is that slave whom his master finds so doing when he comes. Truly I say to you that he will put him in charge of all his possessions. But if that evil slave says in his heart, 'My master is not coming for a long time,' and begins to beat his fellow slaves and eat and drink with drunkards; the master of that slave will come on a day when he does not expect *him* and at an hour which he does not know, and will cut him in pieces and assign him a place with the hypocrites; in that place there will be weeping and gnashing of teeth" (Matthew 24:42–51; cf. Mark 13:33–37; Luke 12:39–46; 21:34–36; see Matthew 8:11, 12; 25:21–23).

Setting: Jerusalem. On the first day of the Feast of Unleavened Bread, just after Judas makes arrangements to betray Him to the chief priests, Jesus informs His disciples where they will celebrate the Passover.

And He said, "Go into the city to a certain man, and say to him, 'The Teacher says, "My time is near; I *am to* keep the Passover at your house with My disciples" ' " (Matthew 26:18; cf. Mark 14:13–15; Luke 22:7–13).

Setting: Galilee. Early in His ministry, the Pharisees question Jesus why He allows His disciples to harvest grain on the Sabbath.

And He said to them, "Have you never read what David did when he was in need and he and his companions became hungry; how he entered the house of God in the time of Abiathar *the* high priest, and ate the consecrated bread, which is not lawful for *anyone* to eat except the priests, and he also gave it to those who were with him?" Jesus said to them, "The Sabbath was made for man, and not man for the Sabbath. So the Son of Man is Lord even of the Sabbath" (Mark 2:25–28; cf. Matthew 12:1–8; Luke 6:1–5; see Exodus 23:12).

Setting: Galilee. After Jesus selects His twelve disciples, scribes from Jerusalem attribute His miraculous powers to Beelzebul, or Satan.

And He called them to Himself and began speaking to them in parables, "How can Satan cast out Satan? If a kingdom is divided against itself, that kingdom cannot stand. If a house is divided against itself, that house will not be able to stand. If Satan has risen up against himself and is divided, he cannot stand, but he is finished! But no one can enter the strong man's house and plunder his property unless he first binds the strong man, and then he will plunder his house. Truly I say to you, all sins shall be forgiven the sons of men, and whatever blasphemies they utter; but whoever blasphemes against the Holy Spirit never has forgiveness, but is guilty of an eternal sin"—because they were saying, "He has an unclean spirit" (Mark 3:23–30; cf. Matthew 12:25–32; Luke 12:10).

Setting: Jesus' hometown of Nazareth. After encountering unbelief, Jesus sends the Twelve out in pairs with authority and instructions about ministry.

And He summoned the twelve and began to send them out in pairs, and gave them authority over the unclean spirits; and He instructed them that they should take nothing for *their* journey, except a mere staff—no bread, no bag, no money in their belt—but to wear sandals; and *He added,* "Do not put on two tunics." And He said to them, "Wherever you enter a house, stay there until you leave town. Any place that does not receive you or listen to you, as you go out from there, shake the dust off the soles of your feet for a testimony against them" (Mark 6:7–11; cf. Matthew 10:1–14; Luke 9:1–5).

Setting: Judea beyond the Jordan (Perea). After informing a rich man how righteous believers may have treasure in heaven, Jesus conveys to His disciples the reward of those who sacrifice in this life to follow Him.

Jesus said, "Truly I say to you, there is no one who has left house or brothers or sisters or mother or father or children or farms, for My sake and for the gospel's sake, but that he will receive a hundred times as much now in the present age, houses and brothers and sisters and mothers and children and farms, along with persecutions; and in the age to come, eternal life. But many *who are* first will be last, and the last, first" (Mark 10:29–31; cf. Matthew 19:27–30; Luke 18:28–30; see Matthew 6:33).

Setting: Jerusalem. Following His triumphal entry, cursing of a fig tree, and cleansing the temple of the money changers, Jesus rebukes the corrupt practices the Jewish religious leaders permit in His house.

And He *began* to teach and say to them, "Is it not written, 'MY HOUSE SHALL BE CALLED A HOUSE OF PRAYER FOR ALL THE NATIONS'? But you have made it a ROBBERS' DEN" (Mark 11:17, Jesus quotes from Isaiah 56:7; Jeremiah 7:11; cf. Matthew 21:12, 13; Luke 19:45–48).

Setting: On the Mount of Olives, east of the temple in Jerusalem. After predicting the temple's destruction, Jesus responds during His Olivet Discourse to questions from Peter, James, John, and Andrew about other future events.

"But when you see the ABOMINATION OF DESOLATION standing where it should not be (let the reader understand), then those who are in Judea must flee to the mountains. The one who is on the housetop must not go down, or go in to get anything out of his house; and the one who is in the field must not turn back to get his coat. But woe to those who are pregnant and to those who are nursing babies in those days! But pray that it may not happen in winter. For those days will be a *time of* tribulation such as has not occurred since the beginning of the creation which God created until now, and never will. Unless the Lord had shortened *those* days, no life would have been saved; but for the sake of the elect, whom He chose, He shortened the days. And then if anyone says to you, 'Behold, here is the Christ'; or, 'Behold, *He is* there'; do not believe *him*; for false Christs and false prophets will arise, and will show signs and wonders, in order to lead astray, if possible, the elect. But take heed; behold, I have told you everything in advance" (Mark 13:14–23; cf. Matthew 24:15–28; Luke 21:20–24; see Daniel 9:27; 12:1; Luke 17:31).

Setting: On the Mount of Olives, east of the temple in Jerusalem. After predicting the temple's destruction, Jesus responds during His Olivet Discourse to questions from Peter, James, John, and Andrew about other future events.

"Take heed, keep on the alert; for you do not know when the *appointed* time will come. *It is* like a man away on a journey, *who* upon leaving his house and putting his slaves in charge, *assigning* to each one his task, also commanded the doorkeeper to stay on the alert. Therefore, be on the alert—for you do not know when the master of the house is coming, whether in the evening, at midnight, or when the rooster crows, or in the morning—in case he should come suddenly and find you asleep. What I say to you I say to all, 'Be on the alert!'" (Mark 13:33–37; cf. Matthew 24:42, 43; Luke 21:34–36; see Luke 12:36–38; Ephesians 6:18).

Setting: Probably Galilee. As Jesus and His disciples pass through some grain fields, some of the Pharisees question why His followers harvest grain on the Sabbath.

And Jesus answering them said, "Have you not even read what David did when he was hungry, he and those who were with him, how he entered the house of God, and took and ate the consecrated bread which is not lawful for any to eat except the priests alone, and gave it to his companions?" And He was saying to them, "The Son of Man is Lord of the Sabbath" (Luke 6:3–5; cf. Matthew 12:1–8; Mark 2:23–28; see Exodus 20:8; Leviticus 24:1–9; Deuteronomy 5:12; 1 Samuel 21:1–6).

Setting: Galilee. After selecting His twelve disciples, Jesus teaches the Sermon on the Mount to those disciples and a great throng of people from Judea, Jerusalem, and the central coastal region of Tyre and Sidon.

"Why do you call Me, 'Lord, Lord,' and do not do what I say? Everyone who comes to Me and hears My words and acts on them, I will show you whom he is like; he is like a man building a house, who dug deep and laid a foundation on the rock; and when a flood occurred, the torrent burst against that house and could not shake it, because it had been well built. But the one who has heard and has not acted *accordingly,* is like a man who built a house on the ground without any foundation; and the torrent burst against it and immediately it collapsed, and the ruin of that house was great" (Luke 6:46–49; cf. Matthew 7:24–27; see Luke 6:12–19; James 1:22).

Setting: Galilee. After Jesus praises John the Baptist to the crowds, Simon, a Pharisee, invites the Lord to dinner, where a sinful woman anoints His feet with perfume, prompting Him to instruct His host about forgiveness.

Turning toward the woman, He said to Simon, "Do you see this woman? I entered your house; you gave Me no water for My feet, but she has wet My feet with her tears and wiped them with her hair. You gave Me no kiss; but she, since the time I came in, has not ceased to kiss My feet. You did not anoint My head with oil, but she anointed My feet with perfume. For this reason I say to you, her sins, which are many, have been forgiven, for she loved much; but he who is forgiven little, loves little." Then He said to her, "Your sins have been forgiven." Those who were reclining *at the table* with Him began to say to themselves, "Who is this *man* who even forgives sins?" And He said to the woman, "Your faith has saved you; go in peace" (Luke 7:44–50; see Matthew 9:2; Mark 5:34; Luke 5:21).

Setting: The country of the Gerasenes, opposite Galilee. Jesus heals a demon-possessed man who then desires to join His ministry, but the Lord sends him home.

"Return to your house and describe what great things God has done for you." So he went away, proclaiming throughout the whole city what great things Jesus had done for him (Luke 8:39; cf. Matthew 8:28–34; Mark 5:1–20).

Setting: Galilee. After raising Jairus's daughter from the dead, Jesus calls the Twelve together and gives them power and authority over demons, along with the ability to cure diseases.

And He said to them, "Take nothing for *your* journey, neither a staff, nor a bag, nor bread, nor money; and do not *even* have two tunics apiece. Whatever house you enter, stay there until you leave that city. And as for those who do not receive you, go out from that city, shake the dust off your feet as a testimony against them" (Luke 9:3–5; cf. Matthew 10:1–15; Mark 6:7–11; see Luke 10:4–12).

Setting: On the way from Galilee to Jerusalem. The Lord appoints seventy followers and sends them out in pairs to every place He Himself will soon visit.

And He was saying to them, "The harvest is plentiful, but the laborers are few; therefore beseech the Lord of the harvest to send out laborers into His harvest. Go; behold, I send you out as lambs in the midst of wolves. Carry no money belt, no bag, no shoes; and greet no one on the way. Whatever house you enter, first say, 'Peace be to this house.' If a man of peace is there, your peace will rest on him; but if not, it will return to you. Stay in that house, eating and drinking what they give you; for the laborer is worthy of his wages. Do not keep moving from house to house. Whatever city you enter and they receive you, eat what is set before you; and heal those in it who are sick, and say to them, 'The kingdom of God has come near to you.' But whatever city you enter and they do not receive you, go out into its streets and say, 'Even the dust of your city which clings to our feet we wipe off *in protest* against you; yet be sure of this, that the kingdom of God has come near.' I say to you, it will be more tolerable in that day for Sodom than for that city" (Luke 10:2–12; see Genesis 19:24–28; Matthew 9:37, 38, 10:9–14, 16; 1 Corinthians 10:27).

Setting: On the way from Galilee to Jerusalem. After some in the crowd test Him, demanding a sign from heaven, Jesus illustrates His power over Satan.

"When a strong *man*, fully armed, guards his own house, his possessions are undisturbed. But when someone stronger than he attacks him and overpowers him, he takes away from him all his armor on which he had relied and distributes his plunder. He who is not with Me is against Me; and he who does not gather with Me, scatters" (Luke 11:21–23; cf. Matthew 12:29, 30).

Setting: On the way from Galilee to Jerusalem. After some in the crowd test Him, demanding a sign from heaven, Jesus illustrates His power over Satan.

"When the unclean spirit goes out of a man, it passes through waterless places seeking rest, and not finding any, it says, 'I will return to my house from which I came.' And when it comes, it finds it swept clean and put in order. Then it goes and takes *along* seven other spirits more evil than itself, and they go in and live there; and the last state of that man becomes worse than the first" (Luke 11:24–26; cf. Matthew 12:43–45; see Luke 11:14–16).

Setting: On the way from Galilee to Jerusalem. After giving a parable about riches and greed, Jesus uses another to challenge the crowd and His disciples to be ready for His return.

"Be dressed in readiness, and *keep* your lamps lit. Be like men who are waiting for their master when he returns from the wedding feast, so that they may immediately open *the door* to him when he comes and knocks. Blessed are those slaves whom the master will find on the alert when he comes; truly I say to you, that he will gird himself *to serve,* and have them recline *at the table,* and will come up and wait on them. Whether he comes in the second watch, or even in the third and finds *them* so, blessed are those *slaves*. But be sure of this, that if the head of the house had known at what hour the thief was coming, he would not have allowed his house to be broken into. You too, be ready; for the Son of Man is coming at an hour that you do not expect" (Luke 12:35–40; cf. Matthew 24:42–44; see Mark 13:33; Ephesians 6:14).

Setting: On the way from Galilee to Jerusalem. After Jesus responds to a question about who is saved, some Pharisees ask Him to leave, claiming Herod Antipas (tetrarch of Galilee and Perea) seeks to kill Him.

And He said to them, "Go and tell that fox, 'Behold, I cast out demons and perform cures today and tomorrow, and the third *day* I reach My goal.' Nevertheless I must journey on today and tomorrow and the next *day*; for it cannot be that a prophet would perish outside of Jerusalem. O Jerusalem, Jerusalem, *the city* that kills the prophets and stones those sent to her! How often I wanted to gather your children together, just as a hen *gathers* her brood under her wings, and you would not *have it*! Behold, your house is left to you *desolate*; and I say to you, you will not see Me until *the time* comes when you say, 'BLESSED IS HE WHO COMES IN THE NAME OF THE LORD!'" (Luke 13:32–35, Jesus quotes from Psalm 118:26; cf. Matthew 23:37).

Setting: On the way from Galilee to Jerusalem. After He speaks a parable to the invited guests and the host at a banquet, Jesus responds to a guest's proclamation about the blessings of eating bread in the kingdom of God.

But He said to him, "A man was giving a big dinner, and he invited many; and at the dinner hour he sent his slave to say to those who had been invited, 'Come; for everything is ready now.' But they all alike began to make excuses. The first one said to him, 'I have bought a piece of land and I need to go out and look at it; please consider me excused.' Another one said, 'I have bought five yoke of oxen, and I am going to try them out; please consider me excused.' Another one said, I have married a wife, and for that reason I cannot come.' And the slave came *back* and reported this to his master. Then the head of the household became angry and said to his slave, 'Go out at once into the streets and lanes of the city and bring in here the poor and crippled and blind and lame.' And the slave said, 'Master, what you commanded has been done, and still there is room.' And the master said to the slave, 'Go out into the highways and along the hedges, and compel *them* to come in, so that my house may be filled. For I tell you, none of those men who were invited shall taste of my dinner'" (Luke 14:16–24; see Deuteronomy 24:5; Matthew 22:2–14; Luke 14:1, 2).

Setting: On the way from Galilee to Jerusalem. Jesus conveys the principles of the lost sheep and the lost coin because the Pharisees and scribes complain He associates with tax collectors and sinners.

"So He told them this parable, saying, "What man among you, if he has a hundred sheep and has lost one of them, does not leave the ninety-nine in the open pasture and go after the one which is lost until he finds it? When he has found it, he lays it on his shoulders, rejoicing. And when he comes home, he calls together his friends and his neighbors, saying to them, 'Rejoice with me, for I have found my sheep which was lost!' I tell you that in the same way, there will be more joy in heaven over one sinner who repents than over ninety-nine righteous persons who need no repentance. Or what woman, if she has ten silver coins and loses one coin, does not light a lamp and sweep the house and search carefully until she finds it? When she has found it, she calls together her friends and neighbors, saying, 'Rejoice with me, for I have found the coin which I had lost!' In the same way, I tell you, there is joy in the presence of the angels of God over one sinner who repents" (Luke 15:3–10; cf. Matthew 18:12-14; see Matthew 9:11-13).

Setting: On the way from Galilee to Jerusalem. Jesus conveys the illustration of the prodigal son because the Pharisees and scribes complain He associates with tax collectors and sinners.

And He said, "A man had two sons. The younger of them said to his father, 'Father, give me the share of the estate that falls to me.' So he divided his wealth between them. And not many days later, the younger son gathered everything together and went on a journey into a distant country, and there he squandered his estate with loose living. Now when he had spent everything, a severe famine occurred in that country, and he began to be impoverished. So he went and hired himself out to one of the citizens of that country, and he sent him into his fields to feed swine. And he would have gladly filled his stomach with the pods that the swine were eating, and no one was giving *anything* to him. But when he came to his senses, he said, 'How many of my father's hired men have more than enough bread, but I am dying here with hunger! I will get up and go to my father, and will say to him, "Father, I have sinned against heaven, and in your sight; I am no longer worthy to be called your son; make me as one of your hired men."' So he got up and came to his father. But while he was still a long way off, his father saw him and felt compassion *for him,* and ran and embraced him and kissed him. And the son said to him, "Father, I have sinned against heaven and in your sight; I am no longer worthy to be called your son.' But the father said to his slaves, 'Quickly bring out the best robe and put it on him, and put a ring on his hand and sandals on his feet; and bring the fattened calf, kill it, and let us eat and celebrate; for this son of mine was dead and has come to life again; he was lost and has been found.' And they began to celebrate. Now his older son was in the field, when he came and approached the house, he heard music and dancing. And he summoned one of the servants and *began* inquiring what these things could be. And he said to him, 'Your brother has come, and your father has killed the fattened calf because he has received him back safe and sound.' But he became angry and was not willing to go in; and his father came out and *began* pleading with him. But he answered and said to his father, 'Look! For so many years I have been serving you and I have never neglected a command of yours; and *yet* you have never given me a young goat, so that I might celebrate with my friends; but when this son of yours came, who has devoured your wealth with prostitutes, you killed the fattened calf for him.' And he said to him, 'Son, you have always been with me, and all that is mine is yours. But we had to celebrate and rejoice, for this brother of yours was dead and *has begun* to live, and was lost and has been found'" (Luke 15:11–32; see Proverbs 29:2; Luke 15:1, 2).

Setting: Samaria, on the way from Galilee to Jerusalem. After the Pharisees question Him about the coming of the kingdom of God, Jesus tells His disciples of His second coming.

And He said to the disciples, "The days will come when you will long to see one of the days of the Son of Man, and you will not see it. They will say to you, 'Look there! Look here!' Do not go away, and do not run after *them*. For just like the lightning, when it flashes out of one part of the sky, shines to the other part of the sky, so will the Son of Man be in His day. But first He must suffer many things and be rejected by this generation. And just as it happened in the days of Noah, so it will be also in the days of the Son of Man: they were eating, they were drinking, they were marrying, they were being given in marriage, until the day that Noah entered the ark, and the flood came and destroyed them all. It was the same as happened in the days of Lot: they were eating, they were drinking, they were buying, they were selling, they were planting, they were building; but on the day that Lot went out from Sodom it rained fire and brimstone from heaven and destroyed them all. It will be just the same on the day that the Son of Man is revealed. On that day, the one who is on the housetop and whose goods are in the house must not go down to take them out; and likewise the one who is in the field must not turn back. Remember Lot's wife. Whoever seeks to keep his life will lose it, and whoever loses *his life* will preserve it. I tell you, on that night there will be two in one bed; one will be taken and the other will be left. There will be two women grinding at the same place; one will be taken and the other will be left. [Two men will be in the field; one will be taken and the other will be left.]" And answering they said to Him, "Where, Lord?" And He said to them, "Where the body *is*, there also the vultures will be gathered" (Luke 17:22–37; see Genesis 19; Matthew 10:39; 16:21, 27; 24:17–28, 37–41).

Setting: On the way from Galilee to Jerusalem. After instructing His disciples about persistence in prayer, Jesus conveys a parable about self-righteousness.

And He also told this parable to some people who trusted in themselves that they were righteous, and viewed others with contempt: "Two men went up into the temple to pray, one a Pharisee and the other a tax collector. The Pharisee stood and was praying this to himself: 'God, I thank You that I am not like other people: swindlers, unjust, adulterers, or even like this tax collector. I fast twice a week; I pay tithes of all that I get.' But the tax collector, standing some distance away, was even unwilling to lift up his eyes to heaven, but was beating his breast, saying, 'God, be merciful to me, the sinner!' I tell you, this man went to his house justified rather than the other; for everyone who exalts himself will be humbled, but he who humbles himself will be exalted" (Luke 18:9–14; see Ezra 9:6; Matthew 6:5, 23:12; Luke 11:42, 16:15; Romans 14:3, 10).

Setting: On the way from Galilee to Jerusalem. After responding to His disciples' question about salvation, Jesus replies to Peter's statement about the disciples' personal sacrifice.

Peter said, "Behold, we have left our own *homes* and followed You." And He said to them, "Truly I say to you, there is no one who has left house or wife or brothers or parents or children, for the sake of the kingdom of God, who will not receive many times as much at this time and in the age to come, eternal life" (Luke 18:28–30; cf. Matthew 19:27–29; Mark 10:28–30; see Matthew 6:33; Luke 5:11).

Setting: Jericho, on the way to Jerusalem for the crucifixion. After taking time to heal a blind man, Jesus informs a curious, short tax collector observing Him from a sycamore tree that He will stay at his house that night.

When Jesus came to the place, He looked up and said to him, "Zaccheus, hurry and come down, for today I must stay at your house" (Luke 19:5).

Setting: Jericho, on the way to Jerusalem. After taking time to heal a blind man, Jesus comments on Zaccheus's response to Him.

And Jesus said to him, "Today salvation has come to this house, because he, too, is a son of Abraham. For the Son of Man has come to seek and to save that which was lost" (Luke 19:9, 10; cf. Matthew 18:11).

Setting: Approaching Jerusalem. After weeping as He sees the city ahead of Him, the Lord enters the temple and drives out the money changers and the merchants.

Jesus entered the temple and began to drive out those who were selling, saying to them, "It is written, 'AND MY HOUSE SHALL BE A HOUSE OF PRAYER,' but you have made it a ROBBERS' DEN" (Luke 19:45, 46, Jesus quotes from Isaiah 56:7; Jeremiah 7:11; cf. Matthew 21:12, 13; Mark 11:15–17; Luke 19:47, 48; John 2:13–17).

Setting: Jerusalem. With the Passover (Feast of Unleavened Bread) approaching, Jesus informs His disciples where they will celebrate the feast. The chief priests and scribes seek to kill Him, and Satan enters Judas Iscariot in order to betray the Lord.

And Jesus sent Peter and John, saying, "Go and prepare the Passover for us, so that we may eat it." They said to Him, "Where do You want us to prepare it?" And He said to them, "When you have entered the city, a man will meet you carrying a pitcher of water; follow him into the house that he enters. And you shall say to the owner of the house, 'The Teacher says to you, "Where is the guest room in which I may eat the Passover with My disciples?"' And he will show you a large, furnished upper room; prepare it there" (Luke 22:8–12; cf. Matthew 26:17–19; Mark 14:12–16).

Setting: The temple treasury in Jerusalem. After the scribes and Pharisees question His testimony about Himself, Jesus reveals to those Jews who believe in Him how He will make them free.

So Jesus was saying to those Jews who had believed Him, "If you continue in My word, *then* you are truly disciples of Mine; and you will know the truth, and the truth will make you free." They answered Him, "We are Abraham's descendants and have never yet been enslaved to anyone; how is it that You say, 'You will become free'?" Jesus answered them, "Truly, truly, I say to you, everyone who commits sin is the slave of sin. The slave does not remain in the house forever; the son does remain forever. So if the Son makes you free, you will be free indeed. I know that you are Abraham's descendants; yet you seek to kill Me, because My word has no place in you. I speak the things which I have seen with *My* Father; therefore you also do the things which you heard from *your* father" (John 8:31–38; see Romans 6:16).

Setting: Damascus. Luke, writing in Acts, conveys how the Lord Jesus instructs one of His disciples, Ananias, to locate Saul of Tarsus to touch him in order to restore his vision.

Now there was a disciple at Damascus named Ananias; and the Lord said to him in a vision, "Ananias." And he said, "Here I am, Lord." And the Lord *said* to him, "Get up and go to the street called Straight, and inquire at the house of Judas for a man from Tarsus named Saul, for he is praying, and he was seen in a vision a man named Ananias come in and lay his hands on him, so that he might regain his sight" (Acts 9:10–12; see Acts 22:12–14).

HOUSE, DIVIDED (Also see DIVISION)

[DIVIDED HOUSE from house divided]

Setting: Galilee. After He heals a blind, mute, demon-possessed man, the Pharisees accuse Jesus in front of crowds of being a worker of Satan.

And knowing their thoughts Jesus said to them, "Any kingdom divided against itself is laid waste; and any city or house divided against itself will not stand. If Satan casts out Satan, he is divided against himself; how then will his kingdom stand? If I by Beelzebul cast out demons, by whom do your sons cast *them* out? For this reason they will be your judges. But if I cast out demons by the Spirit of God, then the kingdom of God has come upon you. Or how can anyone enter the strong man's house and carry off his property, unless he first binds the strong *man?* And then he will plunder his house" (Matthew 12:25–29; cf. Matthew 9:34; Mark 3:23–27; Luke 11:17–20).

[DIVIDED HOUSE from house is divided]

Setting: Galilee. After Jesus selects His twelve disciples, scribes from Jerusalem attribute His miraculous powers to Beelzebul, or Satan.

And He called them to Himself and began speaking to them in parables, "How can Satan cast out Satan? If a kingdom is divided against itself, that kingdom cannot stand. If a house is divided against itself, that house will not be able to stand. If Satan has risen up against himself and is divided, he cannot stand, but he is finished! But no one can enter the strong man's house and plunder his property unless he first binds the strong man, and then he will plunder his house. Truly I say to you, all sins shall be forgiven the sons of men, and whatever blasphemies they utter; but whoever blasphemes against the Holy Spirit never has forgiveness, but is guilty of an eternal sin"—because they were saying, "He has an unclean spirit" (Mark 3:23–30; cf. Matthew 12:25–32; Luke 12:10).

[DIVIDED HOUSE from house *divided*]

Setting: On the way from Galilee to Jerusalem. After Jesus casts out a demon, some in the crowd test Him, demanding a sign from heaven.

But He knew their thoughts and said to them, "Any kingdom divided against itself is laid waste; and a house *divided* against itself falls. If Satan also is divided against himself, how will his kingdom stand? For you say that I cast out demons by Beelzebul. And if I by Beelzebul cast out demons, by whom do your sons cast them out? So they will be your judges. But if I cast out demons by the finger of God, then the kingdom of God has come upon you" (Luke 11:17–20; cf. Matthew 12:25–28; Mark 3:23–27; see Exodus 8:19; Matthew 3:2, 10:25).

HOUSE, FATHER'S (God's)

Setting: The temple in Jerusalem. After attending His first Passover, the twelve-year-old Jesus remains in Jerusalem interacting with the teachers. His parents, headed back to Nazareth, return to Jerusalem looking for Him.

And He said to them, "Why is it that you were looking for Me? Did you not know that I had to be in My Father's *house?"* (Luke 2:49).

Setting: Jerusalem. After beginning His ministry in Galilee by selecting His disciples and performing a miracle at a wedding in Cana, Jesus attends the Passover of the Jews, where He confronts those perverting the temple for business.

And He made a scourge of cords, and drove *them* all out of the temple, with the sheep and the oxen; and He poured out the coins of the money changers and overturned their tables; and to those who were selling the doves He said, "Take these things away; stop making My Father's house a place of business" (John 2:15, 16; cf. Matthew 21:12, 13; see Deuteronomy 16:1–6; John 1:11–14, 17).

Setting: Jerusalem. Before the Passover, after taking issue with Peter's assertion he would lay down his life for Him, Jesus comforts and gives hope to His disciples regarding their future after His return to heaven.

"Do not let your heart be troubled; believe in God, believe also in Me. In My Father's house are many dwelling places; if it were not so, I would have told you; for I go to prepare a place for you. If I go and prepare a place for you, I will come again and receive you to Myself, that where I am, *there* you may be also. And you know the way where I am going" (John 14:1–4; see John 13:35; 14:27, 28).

HOUSE, FATHER'S (human)

Setting: On the way from Galilee to Jerusalem. After He responds to the Pharisees' scoffing at His teaching His disciples about stewardship and the permanence of the Law, Jesus conveys the story of the rich man and Lazarus.

"Now there was a rich man, and he habitually dressed in purple and fine linen, joyously living in splendor every day. And a poor man named Lazarus was laid at his gate, covered with sores, and longing to be fed with the *crumbs* which were falling from the rich man's table; besides, even the dogs were coming and licking his sores. Now the poor man died and was carried away by the angels to Abraham's bosom; and the rich man also died and was buried. In Hades he lifted up his eyes, being in torment, and saw Abraham far away and Lazarus in his bosom. And he cried out and said, 'Father Abraham, have mercy on me, and send Lazarus so that he may dip the tip of his finger in water and cool off my tongue, for I am in agony in this flame.' But Abraham said, 'Child, remember that during your life you received your good things, and likewise Lazarus bad things; but now he is being comforted here, and you are in agony. And besides all this, between us and you there is a great chasm fixed, so that those who wish to come over from here to you will not be able, and *that* none may cross over from there to us.' And he said, 'Then I beg you, father, that you send him to my father's house—for I have five brothers—in order that he may warn them, so that they will not also come to this place of torment.' But Abraham said, 'They have Moses and the Prophets; let them hear them.' But he said, 'No, father Abraham, but if someone goes to them from the dead, they will repent!' But he said to him, 'If they do not listen to Moses and the Prophets, they will not be persuaded even if someone rises from the dead' " (Luke 16:19–31; see Luke 3:8; 6:24; 16:1, 14).

HOUSE, HEAD OF THE (Also see HOUSE, OWNER OF THE; HOUSEHOLD, HEAD OF A; and HOUSEHOLD, HEAD OF THE)

Setting: Galilee. After His twelve disciples observe His ministry, Jesus summons and specifically instructs them about the difficulties ahead involving true discipleship.

"A disciple is not above his teacher, nor a slave above his master. It is enough for the disciple that he become like his teacher, and the slave like his master. If they have called the head of the house Beelzebul, how much more *will they malign* the members of his household!" (Matthew 10:24, 25; cf. Luke 6:40; see 2 Kings 1:2).

Setting: The Mount of Olives, just east of Jerusalem. During His discourse, after answering His disciples' questions as to when the temple will be destroyed and Jerusalem overrun, along with the signs of His coming and the end of the age, Jesus reemphasizes to His disciples that they should be on the alert for His return.

"Therefore be on the alert, for you do not know which day your Lord is coming. But be sure of this, that if the head of the house had known at what time of the night the thief was coming, he would have been on the alert and would not have allowed his house to be broken into. For this reason you also must be ready; for the Son of Man is coming at an hour when you do not think *He will.* Who then is the faithful and sensible slave whom his master put in charge of his household to give their food at the proper time? Blessed is that slave whom his master finds so doing when he comes. Truly I say to you that he will put him in charge of all his possessions. But if that evil slave says in his heart, 'My master is not coming for a long time,' and begins to beat his fellow slaves and eat and drink with drunkards; the master of that slave will come on a day when he does not expect *him* and at an hour which he does not know, and will cut him in pieces and assign him a place with the hypocrites; in that place there will be weeping and gnashing of teeth" (Matthew 24:42–51; cf. Mark 13:33–37; Luke 12:39–46; 21:34–36; see Matthew 8:11, 12; 25:21–23).

Setting: On the way from Galilee to Jerusalem. After giving a parable about riches and greed, Jesus uses another to challenge the crowd and His disciples to be ready for His return.

"Be dressed in readiness, and *keep* your lamps lit. Be like men who are waiting for their master when he returns from the wedding feast, so that they may immediately open *the door* to him when he comes and knocks. Blessed are those slaves whom the master will find on the alert when he comes; truly I say to you, that he will gird himself *to serve,* and have them recline *at the table,* and will come up and wait on them. Whether he comes in the second watch, or even in the third and finds *them* so, blessed are those *slaves.* But be sure of this, that if the head of the house had known at what hour the thief was coming, he would not have allowed his house to be broken into. You too, be ready; for the Son of Man is coming at an hour that you do not expect" (Luke 12:35–40; cf. Matthew 24:42–44; see Mark 13:33; Ephesians 6:14).

Setting: On the way from Galilee to Jerusalem. While teaching in the cities and villages, Jesus responds to a question about who is saved.

And someone said to Him, "Lord, are there *just* a few who are being saved?" And He said to them, "Strive to enter through the narrow door; for many, I tell you, will seek to enter and will not be able. Once the head of the house gets up and shuts the door, and you begin to stand outside and knock on the door, saying, 'Lord, open up to us!' then He will answer and say to you, 'I do not know where you are from.' Then you will begin to say, 'We ate and drank in Your presence, and You taught in our streets'; and He will say, 'I tell you, I do not know where you are from; DEPART FROM ME, ALL YOU EVILDOERS.' In that place there will be weeping and gnashing of teeth when you see Abraham and Isaac and Jacob and all the prophets in the kingdom of God, but you yourselves being thrown out. And they will come from east and west and from north and south, and will recline *at the table* in the kingdom of God. And behold, *some* are last who will be first and *some* are first who will be last" (Luke 13:23–30, Jesus quotes from Psalm 6:8; cf. Matthew 7:13, 23; 8:11, 12; see Matthew 19:30; Luke 3:8).

HOUSE, MY (Also see TEMPLE)

Setting: Jerusalem. After being welcomed with blessings from the crowds, Jesus cleanses the temple by driving out the money changers and the merchants.

And He said to them, "It is written, 'MY HOUSE SHALL BE CALLED A HOUSE OF PRAYER'; but you are making it a ROBBERS' DEN" (Matthew 21:13; Jesus quotes from Isaiah 56:7; Jeremiah 7:11; cf. Mark 11:15–18; Luke 19:46).

Setting: Jerusalem. Following His triumphal entry, cursing of a fig tree, and cleansing the temple of the money changers, Jesus rebukes the corrupt practices the Jewish religious leaders permit in His house.

And He *began* to teach and say to them, "Is it not written, 'MY HOUSE SHALL BE CALLED A HOUSE OF PRAYER FOR ALL THE NATIONS'? But you have made it a ROBBERS' DEN" (Mark 11:17, Jesus quotes from Isaiah 56:7; Jeremiah 7:11; cf. Matthew 21:12, 13; Luke 19:45–48).

Setting: Approaching Jerusalem. After weeping as He sees the city ahead of Him, the Lord enters the temple and drives out the money changers and merchants.

Jesus entered the temple and began to drive out those who were selling, saying to them, "It is written, 'AND MY HOUSE SHALL BE A HOUSE OF PRAYER,' but you have made it a ROBBERS' DEN" (Luke 19:45, 46, Jesus quotes from Isaiah 56:7; Jeremiah 7:11; cf. Matthew 21:12, 13; Mark 11:15–17; see John 2:13–17).

HOUSE, OWNER OF THE (Also see HOUSE, HEAD OF THE)

Setting: Jerusalem. On the first day of the Feast of Unleavened Bread, when the Passover lamb is to be sacrificed, Jesus responds to His disciples' question about His plans for the Passover meal.

And He sent two of His disciples and said to them, "Go into the city, and a man will meet you carrying a pitcher of water; follow him; and wherever he enters, say to the owner of the house, 'The Teacher says, "Where is My guest room in which I may eat the Passover with My disciples?"' And he himself will show you a large upper room furnished *and* ready; prepare for us there" (Mark 14:13–15; cf. Matthew 26:17–19; Luke 22:7–13).

Setting: Jerusalem. With the Passover (Feast of Unleavened Bread) approaching, Jesus informs His disciples where they will celebrate the feast. The chief priests and scribes seek to kill Him, and Satan enters Judas Iscariot in order to betray the Lord.

And Jesus sent Peter and John, saying, "Go and prepare the Passover for us, so that we may eat it." They said to Him, "Where do You want us to prepare it?" And He said to them, "When you have entered the city, a man will meet you carrying a pitcher of water; follow him into the house that he enters. And you shall say to the owner of the house, 'The Teacher says to you, "Where is the guest room in which I may eat the Passover with My disciples?"' And he will show you a large, furnished upper room; prepare it there" (Luke 22:8–12; cf. Matthew 26:17–19; Mark 14:12–16).

HOUSE, PARABLE OF THE OWNER OF THE (See HOUSEHOLD, PARABLE OF THE HEAD OF A)

HOUSE, STRONG MAN'S

Setting: Galilee. After He heals a blind, mute, demon-possessed man, the Pharisees accuse Jesus in front of crowds of being a worker of Satan.

And knowing their thoughts Jesus said to them, "Any kingdom divided against itself is laid waste; and any city or house divided against itself will not stand. If Satan casts out Satan, he is divided against himself; how then will his kingdom stand? If I by Beelzebul cast out demons, by whom do your sons cast *them* out? For this reason they will be your judges. But if I cast out demons by the Spirit of God, then the kingdom of God has come upon you. Or how can anyone enter the strong man's house and carry off his property, unless he first binds the strong *man?* And then he will plunder his house" (Matthew 12:25–29; cf. Matthew 9:34; Mark 3:23–27; Luke 11:17–20).

Setting: Galilee. After Jesus selects His twelve disciples, scribes from Jerusalem attribute His miraculous powers to Beelzebul, or Satan.

And He called them to Himself and began speaking to them in parables, "How can Satan cast out Satan? If a kingdom is divided against itself, that kingdom cannot stand. If a house is divided against itself, that house will not be able to stand. If Satan has risen up against himself and is divided, he cannot stand, but he is finished! But no one can enter the strong man's house and plunder his property unless he first binds the strong man, and then he will plunder his house. Truly I say to you, all sins shall be forgiven the sons of men, and whatever blasphemies they utter; but whoever blasphemes against the Holy Spirit never has forgiveness, but is guilty of an eternal sin"—because they were saying, "He has an unclean spirit" (Mark 3:23–30; cf. Matthew 12:25–32; Luke 12:10).

[STRONG MAN'S HOUSE from When a strong *man*, fully armed, guards his own house]
Setting: On the way from Galilee to Jerusalem. After some in the crowd test Him, demanding a sign from heaven, Jesus illustrates His power over Satan.

"When a strong *man*, fully armed, guards his own house, his possessions are undisturbed. But when someone stronger than he attacks him and overpowers him, he takes away from him all his armor on which he had relied and distributes his plunder. He who is not with Me is against Me; and he who does not gather with Me, scatters" (Luke 11:21–23; cf. Matthew 12:29, 30).

HOUSE OF GOD (Also see HOUSE, MY; and TEMPLE)

Setting: Galilee. Jesus responds to the Pharisees' objection to His disciples' picking grain from the fields on the Sabbath.

But He said to them, "Have you not read what David did when he became hungry, he and his companions, how they entered the house of God, and ate the consecrated bread, which was not lawful for him to eat nor for those with him, but for the priests alone? Or, have you not read in the Law, that on the Sabbath the priests in the temple break the Sabbath and are innocent? But I say to you that something greater than the temple is here. But if you had known what this means, 'I DESIRE COMPASSION, AND NOT A SACRIFICE,' you would not have condemned the innocent. For the Son of Man is Lord of the Sabbath" (Matthew 12:3–8, Jesus quotes from Hosea 6:6; cf. Mark 2:25–28; Luke 6:3–5; see 1 Samuel 21:6).

Setting: Galilee. Early in His ministry, the Pharisees question Jesus as to why He allows His disciples to harvest grain on the Sabbath.

And He said to them, "Have you never read what David did when he was in need and he and his companions became hungry; how he entered the house of God in the time of Abiathar *the* high priest, and ate the consecrated bread, which is not lawful for *anyone* to eat except the priests, and he also gave it to those who were with him?" Jesus said to them, "The Sabbath was made for man, and not man for the Sabbath. So the Son of Man is Lord even of the Sabbath" (Mark 2:25–28; cf. Matthew 12:1–8; Luke 6:1–5; see Exodus 23:12).

Setting: Probably Galilee. As Jesus and His disciples pass through some grain fields, some of the Pharisees question why His followers harvest grain on the Sabbath.

And Jesus answering them said, "Have you not even read what David did when he was hungry, he and those who were with him, how he entered the house of God, and took and ate the consecrated bread which is not lawful for any to eat except the priests alone, and gave it to his companions?" And He was saying to them, "The Son of Man is Lord of the Sabbath" (Luke 6:3–5; cf. Matthew 12:1–8; Mark 2:23–28; see Exodus 20:8; Leviticus 24:1–9; Deuteronomy 5:12; 1 Samuel 21:1–6).

Setting: On the way from Galilee to Jerusalem. After Jesus pronounces woes upon the Pharisees, a lawyer replies that His remarks are an insult to lawyers, too.

But He said, "Woe to you lawyers as well! For you weigh men down with burdens hard to bear, while you yourselves will not even touch the burdens with one of your fingers. Woe to you! For you build the tombs of the prophets, and *it was* your fathers *who* killed them. So you are witnesses and approve the deeds of your fathers; because it was they who killed them, and you build *their tombs*. For this reason also the wisdom of God said, 'I will send them prophets and apostles, and *some* of them they will kill and *some* they will persecute, so that the blood of all the prophets, shed since the foundation of the world, may be charged against this generation, from the blood of Abel to the blood of Zechariah, who was killed between the altar and the house *of God*; yes, I tell you, it shall be charged against this generation.' Woe to you lawyers! For you have taken away the key of knowledge; you yourselves did not enter, and you hindered those who were entering" (Luke 11:46–52; cf. Matthew 23:29–32; see 2 Chronicles 24:20, 21; Matthew 23:4, 13).

HOUSE OF JUDAS (See JUDAS [OF DAMASCUS]), HOUSE OF

HOUSE OF ISRAEL (Listed under ISRAEL, HOUSE OF)

HOUSE OF PRAYER (Listed under PRAYER, HOUSE OF)

HOUSEHOLD (HOUSEHOLD, HEAD OF A is a separate entry)

Setting: Galilee. After His disciples observe His ministry, Jesus summons and specifically instructs them about the difficulties ahead involving true discipleship.

"A disciple is not above his teacher, nor a slave above his master. It is enough for the disciple that he become like his teacher, and the slave like his master. If they have called the head of the house Beelzebul, how much more *will they malign* the members of his household!" (Matthew 10:24, 25; cf. Luke 6:40; see 2 Kings 1:2).

Setting: Galilee. After His disciples observe His ministry, Jesus summons and specifically instructs them about their ministry hardships ahead involving true discipleship.

"Do not think that I came to bring peace on the earth; I did not come to bring peace, but a sword. For I came to SET A MAN AGAINST HIS FATHER, AND A DAUGHTER AGAINST HER MOTHER, AND A DAUGHTER-IN-LAW AGAINST HER MOTHER-IN-LAW; and A MAN'S ENEMIES WILL BE THE MEMBERS OF HIS HOUSEHOLD" (Matthew 10:34–36; Jesus quotes from Micah 7:6; cf. Luke 12:51–53).

Setting: The synagogue in Jesus' hometown of Nazareth. The townspeople take offense at Jesus' teaching.

And they took offense at Him. But Jesus said to them, "A prophet is not without honor except in his hometown and in his *own* household" (Matthew 13:57; cf. Mark 6:4; see Matthew 11:6).

Setting: The Mount of Olives, just east of Jerusalem. During His discourse, after answering His disciples' questions as to when the temple will be destroyed and Jerusalem overrun, along with the signs of His coming and the end of the age, Jesus reemphasizes to His disciples that they should be on the alert for His return.

"Therefore be on the alert, for you do not know which day your Lord is coming. But be sure of this, that if the head of the house had known at what time of the night the thief was coming, he would have been on the alert and would not have allowed his house to be broken into. For this reason you also must be ready; for the Son of Man is coming at an hour when you do not think *He will*. Who then is the faithful and sensible slave whom his master put in charge of his household to give their food at the proper time? Blessed is that slave whom his master finds so doing when he comes. Truly I say to you that he will put him in charge of all his possessions. But if that evil slave says in his heart, 'My master is not coming for a long time,' and begins to beat his fellow slaves and eat and drink with drunkards; the master of that slave will come on a day when he does not expect *him* and at an hour which he does not know, and will cut him in pieces and assign him a place with the hypocrites; in that place there will be weeping and gnashing of teeth" (Matthew 24:42–51; cf. Mark 13:33–37; Luke 12:39–46; 21:34–36; see Matthew 8:11, 12; 25:21–23).

Setting: The synagogue in Jesus' hometown of Nazareth. The townspeople become offended and question Jesus' teaching, wisdom, and ability to perform miracles.

Jesus said to them, "A prophet is not without honor except in his hometown and among his *own* relatives and in his *own* household" (Mark 6:4; cf. Matthew 13:54–58).

Setting: On the way from Galilee to Jerusalem. After clarifying a parable for Peter and the crowd, Jesus conveys how a relationship with Him divides families.

"I have come to cast fire upon the earth; and how I wish it were already kindled! But I have a baptism to undergo, and how distressed I am until it is accomplished! Do you suppose that I came to grant peace on earth? I tell you, no, but rather division; for from now on five *members* in one household will be divided, three against two and two against three. They will be divided, father against son and son against father, mother against daughter, and daughter against mother, mother-in-law against daughter-in-law and daughter-in-law against mother-in-law" (Luke 12:49–53; cf. Matthew 10:34–36; see Micah 7:6; Mark 10:38).

HOUSEHOLD, HEAD OF A (Also see HOUSE, HEAD OF THE)

Setting: By the Sea of Galilee. Jesus teaches the Parable of the Head of a Household to His disciples.

And Jesus said to them, "Therefore every scribe who has become a disciple of the kingdom of heaven is like a head of a household, who brings out of his treasure things new and old" (Matthew 13:52).

HOUSEHOLD, HEAD OF THE (Also see HOUSE, HEAD OF A)

Setting: On the way from Galilee to Jerusalem. After He speaks a parable to the invited guests and the host at a banquet, Jesus responds to a guest's proclamation about the blessings of eating bread in the kingdom of God.

But He said to him, "A man was giving a big dinner, and he invited many; and at the dinner hour he sent his slave to say to those who had been invited, 'Come; for everything is ready now.' But they all alike began to make excuses. The first one said to him, 'I have bought a piece of land and I need to go out and look at it; please consider me excused.' Another one said, 'I have bought five yoke of oxen, and I am going to try them out; please consider me excused.' Another one said, I have married a wife, and for that reason I cannot come.' And the slave came *back* and reported this to his master. Then the head of the household became angry and said to his slave, 'Go out at once into the streets and lanes of the city and bring in here the poor and crippled and blind and lame.' And the slave said, 'Master, what you commanded has been done, and still there is room.' And the master said to the slave, 'Go out into the highways and along the hedges, and compel *them* to come in, so that my house may be filled. For I tell you, none of those men who were invited shall taste of my dinner'" (Luke 14:16–24; see Deuteronomy 24:5; Matthew 22:2–14; Luke 14:1–2).

HOUSEHOLD, PARABLE OF THE HEAD OF A

[PARABLE OF THE HEAD OF A HOUSEHOLD from a head of a household]

Setting: By the Sea of Galilee. Jesus teaches the Parable of the Head of a Household to His disciples.

And Jesus said to them, "Therefore every scribe who has become a disciple of the kingdom of heaven is like a head of a household, who brings out of his treasure things new and old" (Matthew 13:52).

HOUSES (HOUSES, WIDOWS' is a separate entry; also see HOME; HOMES; and HOUSE)

Setting: Judea beyond the Jordan (Perea). Jesus promises rewards to His disciples for their personal sacrifice and commitment to following Him.

And Jesus said to them, "Truly I say to you, that you who have followed Me, in the regeneration when the Son of Man will sit on His glorious throne, you also shall sit upon twelve thrones, judging the twelve tribes of Israel. And everyone who has left houses or brothers or sisters or father or mother or children or farms for My name's sake, will receive many times as much, and will inherit eternal life. But many *who* are first will be last; and *the* last, first" (Matthew 19:28–30; cf. Matthew 6:33; 20:15; Mark 10:29, 30; Luke 18:29, 30; 22:30).

Setting: Judea beyond the Jordan (Perea). After informing a rich man how righteous believers may have treasure in heaven, Jesus conveys to His disciples the reward of those who sacrifice in this life to follow Him.

Jesus said, "Truly I say to you, there is no one who has left house or brothers or sisters or mother or father or children or farms, for My sake and for the gospel's sake, but that he will receive a hundred times as much now in the present age, houses and brothers and sisters and mothers and children and farms, along with persecutions; and in the age to come, eternal life. But many *who are* first will be last, and the last, first" (Mark 10:29–31; cf. Matthew 19:27–30; Luke 18:28–30; see Matthew 6:33).

HOUSES, WIDOWS'

Setting: The temple in Jerusalem. After the Jewish religious leaders test Him with questions, Jesus pronounces the second of eight woes on them in front of the crowds and His disciples.

["Woe to you, scribes and Pharisees, hypocrites, because you devour widows' houses, and for a pretense you make long prayers; therefore you will receive greater condemnation] (Matthew 23:14; cf. Mark 12:40; Luke 20:47).

Setting: The temple in Jerusalem. Jesus warns the crowd about the scribes, after commending one scribe for his nearness to the kingdom of God.

In His teaching He was saying: "Beware of the scribes who like to walk around in long robes, and *like* respectful greetings in the market places, and chief seats in the synagogues and places of honor at banquets, who devour widows' houses, and for appearance's sake offer long prayers; these will receive greater condemnation" (Mark 12:38–40; cf. Matthew 23:1–7; Luke 20:45–47).

Setting: The temple in Jerusalem. A few days before His crucifixion, after posing a question to the scribes, who do not answer, He warns His disciples about the lifestyle of the scribes.

"Beware of the scribes, who like to walk around in long robes, and love respectful greetings in the market places, and chief seats in the synagogues and places of honor at banquets, who devour widows' houses, and for appearance's sake offer long prayers. These will receive greater condemnation" (Luke 20:46, 47; cf. Matthew 23:1–7; Mark 12:38–40; see Luke 11:43).

HOUSETOP (Also see HOUSETOPS)

Setting: The Mount of Olives, just east of Jerusalem. During His discourse, Jesus answers His disciples' questions as to when the temple will be destroyed and Jerusalem overrun, along with the signs of His coming and the end of the age.

"Therefore when you see the ABOMINATION OF DESOLATION which was spoken of through Daniel the prophet, standing in the holy place (let the reader understand), then those who are in Judea must flee to the mountains. Whoever is on the housetop must not go down to get the things that are in his house. Whoever is in the field must not turn back to get his cloak. But woe to those who are pregnant and to those who are nursing babies in those days! But pray that your flight will not be in the winter, or on a Sabbath. For then there will be a great tribulation, such as has not occurred since the beginning of the world until now, nor ever will. Unless those days had been cut short, no life would have been saved; but for the sake of the elect those days will be cut short. Then if anyone says to you, 'Behold, here is the Christ,' or "There *He is,*' do not believe *him.* For false Christs and false prophets will arise and will show great signs and wonders, so as to mislead, if possible, even the elect. Behold, I have told you in advance. So if they say to you, 'Behold, He is in the wilderness,' do not go out, *or,* 'Behold, He is in the inner rooms,' do not believe *them.* For just as the lightning comes from the east and flashes even to the west, so will the coming of the Son of Man be. Wherever a corpse is, there the vultures will gather" (Matthew 24:15–28, Jesus quotes from Daniel 9:27; cf. Daniel 12:1; Mark 13:14–23; Luke 17:22–31; 21:20–24; 23:29; see John 4:48).

Setting: On the Mount of Olives, east of the temple in Jerusalem. After predicting the temple's destruction, Jesus responds during His Olivet Discourse to questions from Peter, James, John, and Andrew about other future events.

"But when you see the ABOMINATION OF DESOLATION standing where it should not be (let the reader understand), then those who are in Judea must flee to the mountains. The one who is on the housetop must not go down, or go in to get anything out of his house; and the one who is in the field must not turn back to get his coat. But woe to those who are pregnant and to those who are nursing babies in those days! But pray that it may not happen in winter. For those days will be a *time of* tribulation such as has not occurred since the beginning of the creation which God created until now, and never will. Unless the Lord had shortened *those* days, no life would have been saved; but for the sake of the elect, whom He chose, He shortened the days. And then if anyone says to you, 'Behold, here is the Christ'; or, 'Behold, *He is* there'; do not believe *him*; for false Christs and false prophets will arise, and will show signs and wonders, in order to lead astray, if possible, the elect. But take heed; behold, I have told you everything in advance" (Mark 13:14–23; cf. Matthew 24:15–28; Luke 21:20–24; see Daniel 9:27; 12:1; Luke 17:31).

Setting: Samaria, on the way from Galilee to Jerusalem. After the Pharisees question Him about the coming of the kingdom of God, Jesus tells His disciples of His second coming.

And He said to the disciples, "The days will come when you will long to see one of the days of the Son of Man, and you will not see it. They will say to you, 'Look there! Look here!' Do not go away, and do not run after *them*. For just like the lightning, when it flashes out of one part of the sky, shines to the other part of the sky, so will the Son of Man be in His day. But first He must suffer many things and be rejected by this generation. And just as it happened in the days of Noah, so it will be also in the days of the Son of Man: they were eating, they were drinking, they were marrying, they were being given in marriage, until the day that Noah entered the ark, and the flood came and destroyed them all. It was the same as happened in the days of Lot: they were eating, they were drinking, they were buying, they were selling, they were planting, they were building; but on the day that Lot went out from Sodom it rained fire and brimstone from heaven and destroyed them all. It will be just the same on the day that the Son of Man is revealed. On that day, the one who is on the housetop and whose goods are in the house must not go down to take them out; and likewise the one who is in the field must not turn back. Remember Lot's wife. Whoever seeks to keep his life will lose it, and whoever loses *his life* will preserve it. I tell you, on that night there will be two in one bed; one will be taken and the other will be left. There will be two women grinding at the same place; one will be taken and the other will be left. [Two men will be in the field; one will be taken and the other will be left."] And answering they said to Him, "Where, Lord?" And He said to them, "Where the body *is*, there also the vultures will be gathered" (Luke 17:22–37; see Genesis 19; Matthew 10:39; 16:21, 27; 24:17–28, 37–41).

HOUSETOPS (Also see HOUSETOP)

Setting: Galilee. After His disciples observe His ministry, Jesus summons and specifically instructs them about their ministry ahead involving true discipleship.

"Therefore do not fear them, for there is nothing concealed that will not be revealed, or hidden that will not be known. What I tell you in the darkness, speak in the light; and what you hear *whispered* in your ear, proclaim upon the housetops. Do not fear those who kill the body but are unable to kill the soul; but rather fear Him who is able to destroy both soul and body in hell" (Matthew 10:26–28; cf. Mark 4:22; Luke 12:3; see Hebrews 10:31).

Setting: On the way from Galilee to Jerusalem. Jesus warns His disciples of future events as the scribes and Pharisees turn hostile and question Him repeatedly in an attempt to catch Him in something He might say.

Under these circumstances, after so many thousands of people had gathered together that they were stepping on one another, He began saying to His disciples first *of all*, "Beware of the leaven of the Pharisees, which is hypocrisy. But there is nothing covered up that will not be revealed, and hidden that will not be known. Accordingly, whatever you have said in the dark will be heard in the light, and what you have whispered in the inner rooms will be proclaimed upon the housetops. I say to you, My friends, do not be afraid of those who kill the body and after that have no more that they can do. But I will warn you whom to fear: fear the One who, after He has killed, has authority to cast into hell; yes, I tell you, fear Him! Are not five sparrows sold for two cents? *Yet* not one of them is forgotten before God. Indeed, the very hairs of your head are all numbered. Do not fear; you are more valuable than many sparrows" (Luke 12:1–7; cf. Matthew 10:26–31; see Matthew 16:6; Hebrews 10:31).

HUMAN JUDGMENT (See JUDGMENT, HUMAN)

HUMAN SPIRIT (See SPIRIT [human])

HUMAN VALUE

[HUMAN VALUE from you are more valuable than many sparrows]

Setting: Galilee. After His disciples observe His ministry, Jesus summons and specifically instructs them about their ministry ahead involving true discipleship.

"Are not two sparrows sold for a cent? And *yet* not one of them will fall to the ground apart from your Father. But the very hairs of your head are all numbered. So do not fear; you are more valuable than many sparrows" (Matthew 10:29–31; cf. Luke 12:6; see Matthew 12:12).

[HUMAN VALUE from How much more valuable then is a man than a sheep]

Setting: A synagogue in Galilee. Jesus answers questions posed by the Pharisees about the Sabbath.

And He said to them, "What man is there among you who has a sheep, and if it falls into a pit on the Sabbath, will he not take hold of it and lift it out? How much more valuable then is a man than a sheep! So then, it is lawful to do good on the Sabbath." Then He said to the man, "Stretch out your hand!" He stretched it out, and it was restored to normal, like the other (Matthew 12:11–13; cf. Matthew 10:31; Mark 3:4–5; Luke 6:9, 10; Luke 14:5; see Matthew 8:3).

[HUMAN VALUE from you are more valuable than many sparrows]

Setting: On the way from Galilee to Jerusalem. Jesus warns His disciples of future events, as the scribes and Pharisees turn hostile and question Him repeatedly in an attempt to catch Him in something He might say.

Under these circumstances, after so many thousands of people had gathered together that they were stepping on one another, He began saying to His disciples first *of all,* "Beware of the leaven of the Pharisees, which is hypocrisy. But there is nothing covered up that will not be revealed, and hidden that will not be known. Accordingly, whatever you have said in the dark will be heard in the light, and what you have whispered in the inner rooms will be proclaimed upon the housetops. I say to you, My friends, do not be afraid of those who kill the body and after that have no more that they can do. But I will warn you whom to fear: fear the One who, after He has killed, has authority to cast into hell; yes, I tell you, fear Him! Are not five sparrows sold for two cents? *Yet* not one of them is forgotten before God. Indeed, the very hairs of your head are all numbered. Do not fear; you are more valuable than many sparrows" (Luke 12:1–7; cf. Matthew 10:26–31; see Matthew 16:6; Hebrews 10:31).

[HUMAN VALUE from how much more valuable you are than the birds]

Setting: On the way from Galilee to Jerusalem. After giving a parable about riches and greed, Jesus comforts the crowd and His disciples. The scribes and Pharisees turn hostile and question Him repeatedly in an attempt to catch Him in something He might say.

And He said to His disciples, "For this reason I say to you, do not worry about *your* life, *as to* what you will eat; nor for your body, *as to* what you will put on. For life is more than food, and the body more than clothing. Consider the ravens, for they neither sow nor reap; they have no storeroom nor barn, and *yet* God feeds them; how much more valuable you are than the birds! And which of you by worrying can add a *single* hour to his life's span? If then you cannot do even a very little thing, why do you worry about other matters? Consider the lilies, how they grow: they neither toil nor spin; but I tell you, not even Solomon in all his glory clothed himself like one of these. But if God so clothes the grass in the field, which is *alive* today and tomorrow is thrown into the furnace, how much more *will He clothe* you? You men of little faith! And do not seek what you will eat and what you will drink, and do not keep worrying. For all these things the nations of the world eagerly seek; but your Father knows that you need these things. But seek His kingdom, and these things will be added to you. Do not be afraid, little flock, for your Father has chosen gladly to give you the kingdom" (Luke 12:22–32; cf. Matthew 6:25–33; see 1 Kings 10:4–7; Job 38:41).

HUMAN WORTH (See HUMAN VALUE)

HUMBLE IN HEART (Listed as HEART, HUMBLE IN; also see HUMILITY)

HUMILIATION (See DISGRACE)

HUMILITY (HEART, HUMBLE IN listed as a separate entry; also see EXALTATION; FOOTWASHING; GREATNESS; SERVANT; SERVANTS; and SERVICE)

[HUMILITY from humbles]

Setting: Capernaum of Galilee. Jesus answers His disciples' question about greatness, or rank, in the kingdom of heaven.

And He called a child to Himself and set him before them, and said, "Truly I say to you, unless you are converted and become like children, you will not enter the kingdom of heaven. Whoever then humbles himself as this child, he is the greatest in the kingdom of heaven. And whoever receives one such child in My name receives Me; but whoever causes one of these little ones who believe in Me to stumble, it would be better for him to have a heavy millstone hung around his neck, and to be drowned in the depth of the sea" (Matthew 18:2–6; cf. Matthew 19:14; Mark 9:33–37, 42; Luke 9:47, 48; 17:1, 2).

[HUMILITY from whoever wishes to become great among you shall be your servant]

Setting: On the way to Jerusalem, where Jesus will die on the cross. Jesus teaches His disciples about true greatness after the mother of disciples James and John asks Him to make her sons exalted rulers with Him in His coming kingdom.

But Jesus called them to Himself and said, "You know that the rulers of the Gentiles lord it over them, and *their* great men exercise authority over them. It is not this way among you, but whoever wishes to become great among you shall be your servant, and whoever wishes to be first among you shall be your slave; just as the Son of Man did not come to be served, but to serve, and to give His life a ransom for many" (Matthew 20:25–28; cf. Matthew 23:11; 26:28; Mark 10:42–45).

[HUMILITY from humbled and humbles]

Setting: The temple in Jerusalem. Jesus exposes the truth about Pharisaism to the crowds and His disciples after the Jewish religious leaders test Him with questions.

Then Jesus spoke to the crowds and to His disciples, saying: "The scribes and the Pharisees have seated themselves in the chair of Moses; therefore all that they tell you, do and observe, but do not do according to their deeds; for they say *things* and do not do *them.* They tie up heavy burdens and lay them on men's shoulders, but they themselves are unwilling to move them with *so much as* a finger. But they do all their deeds to be noticed by men; for they broaden their phylacteries and lengthen their tassels *of their garments.* They love the place of honor at banquets and the chief seats in the synagogues, and respectful greetings in the market places, and being called Rabbi by men. But do not be called Rabbi; for One is your Teacher, and you are all brothers. Do not call *anyone* on earth your father; for One is your Father, He who is in heaven. Do not be called leaders; for One is your Leader, *that is,* Christ. But the greatest among you shall be your servant. Whoever exalts himself shall be humbled; and whoever humbles himself shall be exalted" (Matthew 23:1–12; cf. Matthew 20:26; Mark 12:38–40; Luke 20:46, 47; see Exodus 13:9; Deuteronomy 33:3; Matthew 6:1, 5, 6, 9, 16; Mark 14:11; Luke 11:43; 14:11).

[HUMILITY from whoever wishes to become great among you shall be your servant]

Setting: On the road to Jerusalem. James and John ask Jesus for special honor and privileges in His kingdom. The other disciples become angry, so the Lord uses this moment to teach them about servanthood.

Calling them to Himself, Jesus said to them, "You know that those who are recognized as rulers of the Gentiles lord it over them; and their great men exercise authority over them. But it is not this way among you, but whoever wishes to become great among you shall be your servant; and whoever wishes to be first among you shall be slave of all. For even the Son of Man did not come to be served, but to serve, and to give His life a ransom for many" (Mark 10:42–45; cf. Matthew 20:25–28).

[HUMILITY from humbled and humbles]

Setting: On the way from Galilee to Jerusalem. As He observes the guests selecting places of honor at the table, Jesus speaks a parable to the guests of a Pharisee leader on the Sabbath.

And He *began* speaking a parable to the invited guests when He noticed how they had been picking out the places of honor *at the table,* saying to them, "When you are invited by someone to a wedding feast, do not take the place of honor, for someone more distinguished than you may have been invited by him, and he who invited you both will come and say to you, 'Give *your* place to this man, and then in disgrace you proceed to occupy the last place. But when you are invited, go and recline at the last place, so that when the one who has invited you comes, he may say to you, 'Friend, move up higher'; then you will have honor in the sight of all who are at the table with you. For everyone who exalts himself will be humbled, and he who humbles himself will be exalted" (Luke 14:7–11; see 2 Samuel 22:28; Proverbs 25:6, 7; Matthew 23:6; Luke 14:1, 2).

[HUMILITY from unwilling to lift up his eyes to heaven]
Setting: On the way from Galilee to Jerusalem. After instructing His disciples about persistence in prayer, Jesus conveys a parable about self-righteousness.

And He also told this parable to some people who trusted in themselves that they were righteous, and viewed others with contempt: "Two men went up into the temple to pray, one a Pharisee and the other a tax collector. The Pharisee stood and was praying this to himself: 'God, I thank You that I am not like other people: swindlers, unjust, adulterers, or even like this tax collector. I fast twice a week; I pay tithes of all that I get.' But the tax collector, standing some distance away, was even unwilling to lift up his eyes to heaven, but was beating his breast, saying, 'God, be merciful to me, the sinner!' I tell you, this man went to his house justified rather than the other; for everyone who exalts himself will be humbled, but he who humbles himself will be exalted" (Luke 18:9–14; see Ezra 9:6; Matthew 6:5, 23:12; Luke 11:42; 16:15; Romans 14:3, 10).

[HUMILITY from you also ought to wash one another's feet]
Setting: Jerusalem. Before the Passover, with His death on the cross nearing, Jesus explains the reason for His vivid example of servanthood in washing His disciples' feet.

So when He had washed their feet, and taken His garments and reclined *at the table* again, He said to them, "Do you know what I have done to you? You call Me Teacher and Lord; and you are right, for *so* I am. If I then, the Lord and the Teacher, washed your feet, you also ought to wash one another's feet. For I gave you an example that you also should do as I did to you. Truly, truly I say to you, a slave is not greater than his master, nor *is* one who is sent greater than the one who sent him. If you know these things, you are blessed if you do them. I do not speak of all of you. I know the ones I have chosen; but *it is* that the Scripture may be fulfilled, 'HE WHO EATS MY BREAD HAS LIFTED UP HIS HEEL AGAINST ME.' From now on I am telling you before *it* comes to pass, so that when it does occur, you may believe that I am *He*. Truly, truly, I say to you, he who receives whomever I send receives Me; and he who receives Me receives Him who sent Me" (John 13:12–20; Jesus quotes from Psalm 41:9; see Matthew 7:24; 10:24, 40; John 8:24; 14:29; 1 Peter 5:3).

HUNDRED

Setting: Capernaum of Galilee. Jesus illustrates to His disciples the value of little ones.

"What do you think? If any man has a hundred sheep, and one of them has gone astray, does he not leave the ninety-nine on the mountains and go and search for the one that is straying? If it turns out that he finds it, truly I say to you, he rejoices over it more than the ninety-nine which have not gone astray. So it is not *the* will of your Father who is in heaven that one of these little ones perish" (Matthew 18:12–14; cf. Luke 15:4–7).

Setting: Capernaum of Galilee. Jesus illustrates forgiveness after Peter asks Him if forgiving someone seven times who has sinned against him is adequate.

"For this reason the kingdom of heaven may be compared to a king who wished to settle accounts with his slaves. When he had begun to settle *them,* one who owed him ten thousand talents was brought to him. But since he did not have *the means* to repay, his lord commanded him to be sold, along with his wife and children and all that he had, and repayment to be made. So the slave fell *to the ground* and prostrated himself before him, saying, 'Have patience with me and I will repay you everything.' And the lord of that slave felt compassion and released him and forgave him the debt. But that slave went out and found one of his fellow slaves who owed him a hundred denarii; and he seized him and *began* to choke *him,* saying, 'Pay back what you owe.' So his fellow slave fell *to the ground* and *began* to plead with him, saying, 'Have patience with me and I will repay you.' But he was unwilling and went and threw him in prison until he should pay back what was owed. So when his fellow slaves saw what had happened, they were deeply grieved and came and reported to their lord all that had happened. Then summoning him, his lord said to him, 'You wicked slave, I forgave you all that debt because you pleaded with me. Should you not also have had mercy on your fellow slave, in the same way that I had mercy on you?' And his lord, moved with anger, handed him over to the torturers until he should repay all that was owed him. My heavenly Father will also do the same to you, if each of you does not forgive his brother from your heart" (Matthew 18:23–35; cf. Matthew 6:12, 14, 15; Luke 7:42; see Matthew 25:19–28).

Setting: Judea beyond the Jordan (Perea). After informing a rich man how righteous believers may have treasure in heaven, Jesus conveys to His disciples the reward of those who sacrifice in this life to follow Him.

Jesus said, "Truly I say to you, there is no one who has left house or brothers or sisters or mother or father or children or farms, for My sake and for the gospel's sake, but that he will receive a hundred times as much now in the present age, houses and brothers and sisters and mothers and children and farms, along with persecutions; and in the age to come, eternal life. But many *who are* first will be last, and the last, first" (Mark 10:29–31; cf. Matthew 19:27–30; Luke 18:28–30; see Matthew 6:33).

Setting: Galilee. After Jesus praises John the Baptist to the crowds, Simon, a Pharisee, invites the Lord to dinner. A sinful woman anoints His feet with perfume, prompting Him to convey a parable.

And Jesus answered him, "Simon, I have something to say to you." And he replied, "Say it, Teacher." "A moneylender had two debtors: one owed five hundred denarii, and the other fifty. When they were unable to repay, he graciously forgave them both. So which of them will love him more?" Simon answered and said, "I suppose the one whom he forgave more." And He said to him, "You have judged correctly" (Luke 7:40–43; see Matthew 18:23–35).

Setting: Galilee. After His visit in the home of Simon the Pharisee, Jesus goes into the villages and cities, proclaiming and preaching the kingdom of God.

When a large crowd was coming together, and those from various cities were journeying to Him, He spoke by way of a parable: "The sower went out to sow his seed; and as he sowed, some fell beside the road, and it was trampled under foot and the birds of the air ate it up. Other *seed* fell on rocky *soil,* and as soon as it grew up, it was withered away, because it had no moisture. Other *seed* fell among the thorns; and the thorns grew up with it and choked it out. Other *seed* fell into the good soil, and grew up, and produced a crop a hundred times as great." As He said these things, He would call out, "He who has ears to hear, let him hear" (Luke 8:4–8; cf. Matthew 13:2–9; Mark 4:3–9).

Setting: On the way from Galilee to Jerusalem. After Jesus presents to large crowds the demands of discipleship, the Pharisees and scribes complain He associates with tax collectors and sinners.

So He told them this parable, saying, "What man among you, if he has a hundred sheep and has lost one of them, does not leave the ninety-nine in the open pasture and go after the one which is lost until he finds it? When he has found it, he lays it on his shoulders, rejoicing. And when he comes home, he calls together his friends and his neighbors, saying to them, 'Rejoice with me, for I have found my sheep which was lost!' I tell you that in the same way, there will be *more* joy in heaven over one sinner who repents than over ninety-nine righteous persons who need no repentance" (Luke 15:3–7; cf. Matthew 18:12–14; see Matthew 9:11–13; Luke 5:29–32).

Setting: On the way from Galilee to Jerusalem. The Lord teaches His disciples about stewardship after giving them the story of the prodigal son.

Now He was also saying to the disciples, "There was a rich man who had a manager, and this *manager* was reported to him as squandering his possessions. And he called him and said to him, 'What is this I hear about you? Give an accounting of your management, for you can no longer be a manager.' The manager said to himself, 'What shall I do, since my master is taking the management away from me? I am not strong enough to dig; I am ashamed to beg. I know what I shall do, so that when I am removed from the management people will welcome me into their homes.' And he summoned each one of his master's debtors, and he

began saying to the first, 'How much do you owe my master?' And he said, 'A hundred measures of oil.' And he said to him, 'Take your bill, and sit down quickly and write fifty.' Then he said to another, 'And how much do you owe?' And he said, 'A hundred measures of wheat.' He said to him, 'Take your bill, and write eighty.' And his master praised the unrighteous manager because he had acted shrewdly; for the sons of this age are more shrewd in relation to their own kind than the sons of light. And I say to you, make friends for yourselves by means of the wealth of unrighteousness, so that when it fails, they will receive you into the eternal dwellings. He who is faithful in a very little thing is faithful also in much; and he who is unrighteous in a very little thing is unrighteous also in much. Therefore if you have not been faithful in the *use of* unrighteous wealth, who will entrust the *true riches* to you? And if you have not been faithful in *the use of* that which is another's, who will give you that which is your own? No servant can serve two masters; for either he will hate the one and love the other, or else he will be devoted to one and despise the other. You cannot serve God and wealth" (Luke 16:1–13; cf. Matthew 6:24; see Matthew 25:14–30).

HUNDRED, FIVE (Listed under HUNDRED)

HUNDREDFOLD

Setting: By the Sea of Galilee. While teaching and preaching to the crowds from a boat, Jesus conveys the Parable of the Sower.

And He spoke many things to them in parables, saying, "Behold, the sower went out to sow; and as he sowed, some *seeds* fell beside the road, and the birds came and ate them up. Others fell on the rocky places, where they did not have much soil; and immediately they sprang up, because they had no depth of soil. But when the sun had risen, they were scorched; and because they had no root, they withered away. Others fell among the thorns, and the thorns came up and choked them out. And others fell on the good soil and yielded a crop, some a hundredfold, some sixty, and some thirty. He who has ears, let him hear" (Matthew 13:3–9; cf. Mark 4:3–9; Luke 8:4–8; see Matthew 13:1, 2, 18–23).

Setting: By the Sea of Galilee. With the religious leadership rejecting His message, Jesus begins to teach in parables and explains the meaning of the Parable of the Sower to His disciples.

"Hear then the parable of the sower. When anyone hears the word of the kingdom and does not understand it, the evil *one* comes and snatches away what has been sown in his heart. This is the one on whom seed was sown beside the road. The one on whom seed was sown on the rocky places, this is the man who hears the word and immediately receives it with joy; yet he has no *firm* root in himself, but is *only* temporary, and when affliction or persecution arises because of the word, immediately he falls away. And the one on whom seed was sown among the thorns, this is the man who hears the word, and the worry of the world and the deceitfulness of wealth choke the word, and it becomes unfruitful. And the one on whom seed was sown on the good soil, this is the man who hears the word and understands it; who indeed bears fruit and brings forth, some a hundredfold, some sixty, and some thirty" (Matthew 13:18–23; cf. Mark 4:13–20; Luke 8:11–15; see Matthew 13:8).

Setting: By the Sea of Galilee. During the early part of His ministry, just after a visit from his mother and brothers, Jesus instructs a very large crowd with the Parable of the Sower from a boat.

"Listen *to this!* Behold, the sower went out to sow; as he was sowing, some *seed* fell beside the road, and the birds came and ate it up. Other *seed* fell on the rocky *ground* where it did not have much soil; and immediately it sprang up because it had no depth of soil. And after the sun had risen, it was scorched; and because it had no root, it withered away. Other *seed* fell among the thorns, and the thorns came up and choked it, and it yielded no crop. Other *seeds* fell into the good soil, and as the grew up and increased, they yielded a crop and produced thirty, sixty, and a hundredfold." And He was saying, "He who has ears to hear, let him hear" (Mark 4:3–9; cf. Matthew 13:3–9; Luke 8:5–8).

Setting: By the Sea of Galilee. During the early part of His ministry, after presenting the Parable of the Sower to a very large crowd from a boat, Jesus explains the meaning of the parable to His disciples and followers.

And He said to them, "Do you not understand this parable? How will you understand all the parables? The sower sows the word. These are the ones who are beside the road where the word is sown; and when they hear, immediately Satan comes and takes away the word which has been sown in them. In a similar way these are the ones on whom seed was sown on the rocky places, who, when they hear the word, immediately receive it with joy; and they have no *firm* root in themselves, but are *only* temporary; then, when affliction or persecution arises because of the word, immediately they fall away. And others are the ones on whom seed was sown among the thorns; these are the ones who have heard the word, but the worries of the world and the deceitfulness of riches, and the desires for other things enter in and choke the word, and it becomes unfruitful. And those are the ones on whom seed was sown on the good soil; and they hear the word and accept it and bear fruit, thirty, sixty, and a hundredfold" (Mark 4:13–20; cf. Matthew 13:18–23; Luke 8:11–15).

HUNGER (Also see FASTING; and FOOD)

Setting: Galilee. Early in His ministry, Jesus presents the Beatitudes (part of the Sermon on the Mount) to His disciples and the gathered crowds from Galilee, Decapolis, Jerusalem, Judea, and beyond the Jordan.

"Blessed are those who hunger and thirst for righteousness, for they shall be satisfied" (Matthew 5:6; see Matthew 5:1; 13:35).

[HUNGER from hungry]

Setting: Galilee. Jesus responds to the Pharisees' objection to His disciples' picking grain from the fields on the Sabbath.

But He said to them, "Have you not read what David did when he became hungry, he and his companions, how they entered the house of God, and ate the consecrated bread, which was not lawful for him to eat nor for those with him, but for the priests alone? Or, have you not read in the Law, that on the Sabbath the priests in the temple break the Sabbath and are innocent? But I say to you that something greater than the temple is here. But if you had known what this means, 'I DESIRE COMPASSION, AND NOT A SACRIFICE,' you would not have condemned the innocent. For the Son of Man is Lord of the Sabbath" (Matthew 12:3–8, Jesus quotes from Hosea 6:6; cf. Mark 2:25–28; Luke 6:3–5; see 1 Samuel 21:6).

[HUNGER from hungry]

Setting: Near the Sea of Galilee. After being impressed by a Canaanite woman's faith, Jesus restores her daughter of demon possession, then feeds more than 4,000 primarily Gentile people following Him.

And Jesus called His disciples to Him, and said, "I feel compassion for the people, because they have remained with Me now three days and have nothing to eat; and I do not want to send them away hungry, for they might faint on the way." The disciples said to Him, "Where would we get so many loaves in *this* desolate place to satisfy a large crowd?" And Jesus said to them, "How many loaves do you have?" And they said, "Seven and a few small fish" (Matthew 15:32–34; cf. Mark 8:1–9).

[HUNGER from hungry]

Setting: The Mount of Olives, just east of Jerusalem. During His discourse, after answering His disciples' questions as to when the temple will be destroyed and Jerusalem overrun, along with the signs of His coming and the end of the age, Jesus reveals the future judgments following His return.

"But when the Son of Man comes in His glory, and all the angels with Him, then He will sit on His glorious throne. All the nations will be gathered before Him; and He will separate them from one another, as the shepherd separates the sheep from the goats; and He will put the sheep on His right, and the goats on the left. Then the King will say to those on His right, 'Come, you who are blessed of My Father, inherit the kingdom prepared for you from the foundation of the world. 'For I was hungry, and you gave Me *something* to eat; I was thirsty, and you gave Me *something* to drink; I was a stranger, and you invited Me in; naked, and you clothed Me; I was sick, and you visited Me; I was in prison, and you came to Me.' Then the righteous will answer Him, 'Lord, when did we see You hungry and feed You, or thirsty, and give you *something* to drink? And when did we see You a stranger, and invite You in, or naked, and clothe You? When did we see You sick, or in prison, and come to You?' The King will answer and say to them, 'Truly I say to you, to the extent that you did it to one of these brothers of Mine, *even* the least *of them,* you did it to Me.' Then He will also say to those on His left, 'Depart from Me, accursed ones, into the eternal fire which has been prepared for the devil and his angels; for I was hungry, and you gave Me *nothing* to eat; I was thirsty, and you gave Me nothing to drink; I was a stranger, and you did not invite Me in; naked, and you did not clothe Me; sick, and in prison, and you did not visit Me.' Then they themselves also will answer, 'Lord, when did we see You hungry, or thirsty, or a stranger, or naked, or sick, or in prison, and did not take care of You?' Then He will answer them, 'Truly I say to you, to the extent that you did not do it to one of the least of these, you did not do it to Me.' These will go away into eternal punishment, but the righteous into eternal life" (Matthew 25:31–46; see Matthew 7:23; 16:27; 19:29).

[HUNGER from hungry]
Setting: Galilee. Early in His ministry, the Pharisees ask Jesus why He allows His disciples to harvest grain on the Sabbath.

And He said to them, "Have you never read what David did when he was in need and he and his companions became hungry; how he entered the house of God in the time of Abiathar *the* high priest, and ate the consecrated bread, which is not lawful for *anyone* to eat except the priests, and he also gave it to those who were with him?" Jesus said to them, "The Sabbath was made for man, and not man for the Sabbath. So the Son of Man is Lord even of the Sabbath" (Mark 2:25–28; cf. Matthew 12:1–8; Luke 6:1–5; see Exodus 23:12).

[HUNGER from hungry]
Setting: Decapolis, near the Sea of Galilee. Jesus miraculously feeds more than 4,000 people, primarily Gentiles.

In those days, when there was again a large crowd and they had nothing to eat, Jesus called His disciples and said to them, "I feel compassion for the people because they have remained with Me now three days and have nothing to eat. If I send them away hungry to their homes, they will faint on their way; and some of them have come a great distance" (Mark 8:1–3; cf. Matthew 15:32–38; see Matthew 9:36).

[HUNGER from hungry]
Setting: Probably in Galilee. As Jesus and His disciples pass through some grain fields, some of the Pharisees ask why His followers harvest grain on the Sabbath.

And Jesus answering them said, "Have you not even read what David did when he was hungry, he and those who were with him, how he entered the house of God, and took and ate the consecrated bread which is not lawful for any to eat except the priests alone, and gave it to his companions?" And He was saying to them, "The Son of Man is Lord of the Sabbath" (Luke 6:3–5; cf. Matthew 12:1–8; Mark 2:23–28; see Exodus 20:8; Leviticus 24:1–9; Deuteronomy 5:12; 1 Samuel 21:1–6).

Setting: Galilee. After selecting His twelve disciples, Jesus teaches the Beatitudes (part of the Sermon on the Mount) to those disciples and a great throng of people from Judea, Jerusalem, and the central coastal region of Tyre and Sidon.

"Blessed *are* you who hunger now, for you shall be satisfied. Blessed *are* you who weep now, for you shall laugh" (Luke 6:21; cf. Matthew 5:4, 6).

[HUNGER from hungry]
Setting: Galilee. After selecting His twelve disciples, Jesus teaches the Beatitudes (part of the Sermon on the Mount) to those disciples and a great throng of people from Judea, Jerusalem, and the central coastal region of Tyre and Sidon.

"Woe to you who are well-fed now, for you shall be hungry. Woe *to you* who laugh now, for you shall mourn and weep" (Luke 6:25; cf. Matthew 5:4).

Setting: On the way from Galilee to Jerusalem. Jesus conveys the illustration of the prodigal son because the Pharisees and scribes complain He associates with tax collectors and sinners.

And He said, "A man had two sons. The younger of them said to his father, 'Father, give me the share of the estate that falls to me.' So he divided his wealth between them. And not many days later, the younger son gathered everything together and went on a journey into a distant country, and there he squandered his estate with loose living. Now when he had spent everything, a severe famine occurred in that country, and he began to be impoverished. So he went and hired himself out to one of the citizens of that country, and he sent him into his fields to feed swine. And he would have gladly filled his stomach with the pods that the swine were eating, and no one was giving *anything* to him. But when he came to his senses, he said, 'How many of my father's hired men have more than enough bread, but I am dying here with hunger! I will get up and go to my father, and will say to him, "Father, I have sinned against heaven, and in your sight; I am no longer worthy to be called your son; make me as one of your hired men."' So he got up and came to his father. But while he was still a long way off, his father saw him and felt compassion *for him,* and ran and embraced him and kissed him. And the son said to him, "Father, I have sinned against heaven and in your sight; I am no longer worthy to be called your son.' But the father said to his slaves, 'Quickly bring out the best robe and put it on him, and put a ring on his hand and sandals on his feet; and bring the fattened calf, kill it, and let us eat and celebrate; for this son of mine was dead and has come to life again; he was lost and has been found.' And they began to celebrate. Now his older son was in the field, when he came and approached the house, he heard music and dancing. And he summoned one of the servants and *began* inquiring what these things could be. And he said to him, 'Your brother has come, and your father has killed the fattened calf because he has received him back safe and sound.' But he became angry and was not willing to go in; and his father came out and *began* pleading with him. But he answered and said to his father, 'Look! For so many years I have been serving you and I have never neglected a command of yours; and *yet* you have never given me a young goat, so that I might celebrate with my friends; but when this son of yours came, who has devoured your wealth with prostitutes, you killed the fattened calf for him.' And he said to him, 'Son, you have always been with me, and all that is mine is yours. But we had to celebrate and rejoice, for this brother of yours was dead and *has begun* to live, and was lost and has been found'" (Luke 15:11–32; see Proverbs 29:2; Luke 15:1, 2).

Setting: Capernaum. The day after walking on the Sea of Galilee to join His disciples in a boat, the people Jesus miraculously fed with a lad's five loaves and two fish ask Him to always give them this bread out of heaven.

Jesus said to them, "I am the bread of life; he who comes to Me will not hunger, and he who believes in Me will never thirst. But I said to you that you have seen Me, and yet do not believe. All that the Father gives Me will come to Me, and the one who comes to Me I will certainly not cast out. For I have come down from heaven, not to do My own will, but the will of Him who sent Me. This is the will of Him who sent Me, that of all that He has given Me I lose nothing, but raise it up on the last day. For this is the will of My Father, that everyone who beholds the Son and believes in Him will have eternal life, and I Myself will raise him up on the last day" (John 6:35–40; see John 3:13, 16; 4:13, 14).

HUSBAND (Also see HUSBANDS; MARRIAGE; and WIFE)

Setting: Judea beyond the Jordan (Perea). Jesus teaches the crowds gathered around Him about divorce after the Pharisees test and question Him on the subject.

And He answered and said to them, "What did Moses command you?" They said, "Moses permitted a *man* TO WRITE A CERTIFICATE OF DIVORCE AND SEND *her* AWAY." But Jesus said to them, "Because of your hardness of heart he wrote you this commandment. But from the beginning of creation, *God* MADE THEM MALE AND FEMALE. FOR THIS REASON A MAN SHALL LEAVE HIS FATHER AND MOTHER, AND THE TWO SHALL BECOME ONE FLESH; so they are no longer two, but one flesh. What therefore God has joined together, let no man separate. In the house the disciples *began* questioning Him about this again. And He said to them, "Whoever divorces his wife and marries another woman commits adultery against her; and if she herself divorces her husband and marries another man, she is committing adultery" (Mark 10:3–12, Jesus quotes from Genesis 1:27; 2:24; cf. Matthew 19:1–9; see Deuteronomy 24:1–3; Matthew 5:32; see Romans 7:2, 3; 1 Corinthians 7:10, 11, 13, 39; 1 Timothy 2:14).

Setting: On the way from Galilee to Jerusalem. The Lord responds to the Pharisees' scoffing at His teaching His disciples about stewardship with an illustration of the earthly commitment of marriage.

"Everyone who divorces his wife and marries another commits adultery, and he who marries one who is divorced from a husband commits adultery" (Luke 16:18; cf. Matthew 5:31, 32; 19:9; Mark 10:11, 12; see Romans 7:2, 3; 1 Corinthians 7:10, 39).

Setting: Sychar in Samaria, on the way to Galilee. Jesus interacts with a Samaritan woman at Jacob's well, while His disciples shop for food.

He said to her, "Go, call your husband and come here." The woman answered and said, "I have no husband." Jesus said to her, "You have correctly said, 'I have no husband'; for you have had five husbands, and the one whom you now have is not your husband; this you have said truly" (John 4:16–18; see John 6:35).

HUSBANDS (Also see HUSBAND)

Setting: Sychar in Samaria, on the way to Galilee. Jesus interacts with a Samaritan woman at Jacob's well, while His disciples shop for food.

He said to her, "Go, call your husband and come here." The woman answered and said, "I have no husband." Jesus said to her, "You have correctly said, 'I have no husband'; for you have had five husbands, and the one whom you now have is not your husband; this you have said truly" (John 4:16–18; see John 6:35).

HYMN, FUNERAL (See DIRGE)

HYPOCRISY (Also see HYPOCRITE; HYPOCRITES; and PRETENSE)

[HYPOCRISY from Beware of practicing your righteousness before men to be noticed by them]
Setting: Galilee. During the early part of His ministry, Jesus preaches the Sermon on the Mount to His disciples and the multitudes.

"Beware of practicing your righteousness before men to be noticed by them; otherwise you have no reward with your Father who is in heaven" (Matthew 6:1; cf. Matthew 6:5, 16).

[HYPOCRISY from Why do you look at the speck that is in your brother's eye, but do not notice the log that is in your own eye]
Setting: Galilee. During the early part of His ministry, Jesus preaches the Sermon on the Mount to His disciples and the multitudes.

"Do not judge so that you will not be judged. For in the way you judge, you will be judged; and by your standard of measure, it will be measured to you. Why do you look at the speck that is in your brother's eye, but do not notice the log that is in your own eye? Or how can you say to your brother, 'Let me take the speck out of your eye, and behold, the log is in your own eye? You hypocrite, first take the log out of your own eye, and then you will see clearly to take the speck out of your brother's eye" (Matthew 7:1–5; cf. Mark 4:24; Luke 6:37–42; Romans 2:1; Romans 14:10, 13).

[HYPOCRISY from they say *things* and do not do *them*]
Setting: The temple in Jerusalem. Jesus exposes the truth about Pharisaism to the crowds and His disciples after the Jewish religious leaders test Him with questions.

Then Jesus spoke to the crowds and to His disciples, saying: "The scribes and the Pharisees have seated themselves in the chair of Moses; therefore all that they tell you, do and observe, but do not do according to their deeds; for they say *things* and do not do *them.* They tie up heavy burdens and lay them on men's shoulders, but they themselves are unwilling to move them with *so much as* a finger. But they do all their deeds to be noticed by men; for they broaden their phylacteries and lengthen their tassels *of their garments.* They love the place of honor at banquets and the chief seats in the synagogues, and respectful greetings in the market places, and being called Rabbi by men. But do not be called Rabbi; for One is your Teacher, and you are all brothers. Do not call *anyone* on earth your father; for One is your Father, He who is in heaven. Do not be called leaders; for One is your Leader, *that is,* Christ. But the greatest among you shall be your servant. Whoever exalts himself shall be humbled; and whoever humbles himself shall be exalted" (Matthew 23:1–12; cf. Matthew 20:26; Mark 12:38–40; Luke 20:46, 47; see Exodus 13:9; Deuteronomy 33:3; Matthew 6:1, 5, 6, 9, 16; Mark 14:11; Luke 11:43; 14:11).

Setting: The temple in Jerusalem. After the Jewish religious leaders test Him with questions, Jesus pronounces the seventh of eight woes on them in front of the crowds and His disciples.

"Woe to you, scribes and Pharisees, hypocrites! For you are like whitewashed tombs which on the outside appear beautiful, but inside they are full of dead men's bones and all uncleanness. So you, too, outwardly appear righteous to men, but inwardly you are full of hypocrisy and lawlessness" (Matthew 23:27, 28; cf. Luke 11:44).

[HYPOCRISY from for appearance's sake offer long prayers]
Setting: The temple in Jerusalem. Jesus warns the crowd about the scribes after commending one scribe for his nearness to the kingdom of God.

In His teaching He was saying: "Beware of the scribes who like to walk around in long robes, and *like* respectful greetings in the market places, and chief seats in the synagogues and places of honor at banquets, who devour widows' houses, and for appearance's sake offer long prayers; these will receive greater condemnation" (Mark 12:38–40; cf. Matthew 23:1–7; Luke 20:45–47).

[HYPOCRISY from Why do you look at the speck that is in your brother's eye, but do not notice the log that is in your own eye]
Setting: On a mountain in Galilee. After selecting His twelve disciples, Jesus teaches the Sermon on the Mount to His disciples and a great throng of people from Judea, Jerusalem, and the central coastal region of Tyre and Sidon.

And He also spoke a parable to them: "A blind man cannot guide a blind man, can he? Will they not both fall into a pit? A pupil is not above his teacher; but everyone, after he has been fully trained, will be like his teacher. Why do you look at the speck that is in your brother's eye, but do not notice the log that is in your own eye? Or how can you say to your brother, 'Brother, let me take out the speck that is in your eye,' when you yourself do not see the log that is in your own eye? You hypocrite, first take the log out of your own eye, and then you will see clearly to take out the speck that is in your brother's eye. For there is no good tree which produces bad fruit, nor, on the other hand, a bad tree which produces good fruit. For each tree is known by its own fruit. For men do not gather figs from thorns, nor do they pick grapes from a briar bush. The good man out of the good treasure of his heart brings forth what is good; and the evil *man* out of the evil *treasure* brings forth what is evil; for his mouth speaks from that which fills his heart" (Luke 6:39–45; cf. Matthew 7:3–6. 16, 18, 20; 12:35; see Matthew 10:24; 15:14; Luke 6:12–19).

Setting: On the way from Galilee to Jerusalem. Jesus warns His disciples of future events, as the scribes and Pharisees turn hostile and question Him repeatedly in an attempt to catch Him in something He might say.

Under these circumstances, after so many thousands of people had gathered together that they were stepping on one another, He began saying to His disciples first *of all*, "Beware of the leaven of the Pharisees, which is hypocrisy. But there is nothing covered up that will not be revealed, and hidden that will not be known. Accordingly, whatever you have said in the dark will be heard in the light, and what you have whispered in the inner rooms will be proclaimed upon the housetops. I say to you, My friends, do not be afraid of those who kill the body and after that have no more that they can do. But I will warn you whom to fear: fear the One who, after He has killed, has authority to cast into hell; yes, I tell you, fear Him! Are not five sparrows sold for two cents? *Yet* not one of them is forgotten before God. Indeed, the very hairs of your head are all numbered. Do not fear; you are more valuable than many sparrows" (Luke 12:1–7; cf. Matthew 10:26–31; see Matthew 16:6; Hebrews 10:31).

[HYPOCRISY from for appearance's sake offer long prayers]
Setting: The temple in Jerusalem. A few days before His crucifixion, after posing a question to the scribes, who do not answer, Jesus warns His disciples about the lifestyle of the scribes.

"Beware of the scribes, who like to walk around in long robes, and love respectful greetings in the market places, and chief seats in the synagogues and places of honor at banquets, who devour widows' houses, and for appearance's sake offer long prayers. These will receive greater condemnation" (Luke 20:46, 47; cf. Matthew 23:1–7; Mark 12:38–40; see Luke 11:43).

HYPOCRITE (Also see HYPOCRISY; HYPOCRITES; and PRETENSE)

Setting: Galilee. During the early part of His ministry, Jesus preaches the Sermon on the Mount to His disciples

and the multitudes.

"Do not judge so that you will not be judged. For in the way you judge, you will be judged; and by your standard of measure, it will be measured to you. Why do you look at the speck that is in your brother's eye, but do not notice the log that is in your own eye? Or how can you say to your brother, 'Let me take the speck out of your eye, and behold, the log is in your own eye? You hypocrite, first take the log out of your own eye, and then you will see clearly to take the speck out of your brother's eye" (Matthew 7:1–5; cf. Mark 4:24; Luke 6:37–42; Romans 2:1; Romans 14:10, 13).

Setting: Galilee. After selecting His twelve disciples, Jesus teaches the Sermon on the Mount to those disciples and a great throng of people from Judea, Jerusalem, and the central coastal region of Tyre and Sidon.

And He also spoke a parable to them: "A blind man cannot guide a blind man, can he? Will they not both fall into a pit? A pupil is not above his teacher; but everyone, after he has been fully trained, will be like his teacher. Why do you look at the speck that is in your brother's eye, but do not notice the log that is in your own eye? Or how can you say to your brother, 'Brother, let me take out the speck that is in your eye,' when you yourself do not see the log that is in your own eye? You hypocrite, first take the log out of your own eye, and then you will see clearly to take out the speck that is in your brother's eye. For there is no good tree which produces bad fruit, nor, on the other hand, a bad tree which produces good fruit. For each tree is known by its own fruit. For men do not gather figs from thorns, nor do they pick grapes from a briar bush. The good man out of the good treasure of his heart brings forth what is good; and the evil *man* out of the evil *treasure* brings forth what is evil; for his mouth speaks from that which fills his heart" (Luke 6:39–45; cf. Matthew 7:3–6. 16, 18, 20; 12:35; see Matthew 10:24; 15:14; Luke 6:12–19).

HYPOCRITES (Also see HYPOCRISY; HYPOCRITE; and PRETENSE)

Setting: Galilee. During the early part of His ministry, Jesus preaches the Sermon on the Mount to His disciples and the multitudes.

"So when you give to the poor, do not sound a trumpet before you, as the hypocrites do in the synagogues and in the streets, so that they may be honored by men. Truly I say to you, they have their reward in full. But when you give to the poor, do not let your left hand know what your right hand is doing, so that your giving will be in secret; and your Father who sees *what is done* in secret will reward you" (Matthew 6:2–4; see Jeremiah 17:10; Matthew 6:16).

Setting: Galilee. During the early part of His ministry, Jesus preaches the Sermon on the Mount to His disciples and the multitudes.

"When you pray, you are not to be like the hypocrites; for they love to stand and pray in the synagogues and on the street corners so that they may be seen by men. Truly I say to you, they have their reward in full. But you, when you pray, go into your inner room, close your door and pray to your Father who is in secret, and your Father who sees *what is done* in secret will reward you" (Matthew 6:5, 6; see Mark 11:25).

Setting: Galilee. During the early part of His ministry, Jesus preaches the Sermon on the Mount to His disciples and the multitudes.

"Whenever you fast, do not put on a gloomy face as the hypocrites *do,* for they neglect their appearance so that they will be noticed by men when they are fasting. Truly I say to you, they have their reward in full. But you, when you fast, anoint your head and wash your face so that your fasting will not be noticed by men, but by your Father who is in secret; and your Father who sees *what is done* in secret will reward you" (Matthew 6:16–18; see Matthew 6:4, 6).

Setting: Galilee. Pharisees and scribes from Jerusalem question Jesus about His disciples' lack of obedience to tradition and the commandments.

And He answered and said to them, "Why do you yourselves transgress the commandment of God for the sake of tradition? For God said, 'HONOR YOUR FATHER AND MOTHER,' and, 'HE WHO SPEAKS EVIL OF FATHER OR MOTHER IS TO BE PUT TO DEATH.' But you say, 'Whoever says to *his* father or mother, "Whatever I have that would help you has been given *to God*," he is not to honor his father or mother.' And *by this* you invalidated the word of God for the sake of your tradition. You hypocrites, rightly did Isaiah prophesy of you: 'THIS PEOPLE HONORS ME WITH THEIR LIPS, BUT THEIR HEART IS FAR AWAY FROM ME. BUT IN VAIN DO THEY WORSHIP ME, TEACHING AS DOCTRINES THE PRECEPTS OF MEN' "(Matthew 15:3–9, Jesus quotes from Exodus 20:12, 21:17, Leviticus 20:9; Isaiah 29:13; cf. Mark 7:5–7; see Colossians 2:22).

Setting: The temple in Jerusalem. The Pharisees send their disciples and the Herodians to test Jesus about the poll-tax, in order to trap Him.

But Jesus perceived their malice, and said, "Why are you testing Me, you hypocrites? Show Me the coin *used* for the poll-tax." And they brought Him a denarius. And He said to them, "Whose likeness and inscription is this?" They said to Him, "Caesar's." Then He said to them, "Then render to Caesar the things that are Caesar's; and to God the things that are God's" (Matthew 22:18–21; cf. Matthew 17:25; Mark 12:15–17; Luke 20:22–25).

Setting: The temple in Jerusalem. After the Jewish religious leaders test Him with questions, Jesus pronounces the first of eight woes on them in front of the crowds and His disciples.

"But woe to you, scribes and Pharisees, hypocrites, because you shut off the kingdom of heaven from people; for you do not enter in yourselves, nor do you allow those who are entering to go in (Matthew 23:13; cf. Luke 11:52).

Setting: The temple in Jerusalem. After the Jewish religious leaders test Him with questions, Jesus pronounces the second of eight woes on them in front of the crowds and His disciples.

["Woe to you, scribes and Pharisees, hypocrites, because you devour widows' houses, and for a pretense you make long prayers; therefore you will receive greater condemnation] (Matthew 23:14; cf. Mark 12:40; Luke 20:47).

Setting: The temple in Jerusalem. After the Jewish religious leaders test Him with questions, Jesus pronounces the third of eight woes on them in front of the crowds and His disciples.

"Woe to you, scribes and Pharisees, hypocrites, because you travel around on sea and land to make one proselyte; and when he becomes one, you make him twice as much a son of hell as yourselves" (Matthew 23:15).

Setting: The temple in Jerusalem. After the Jewish religious leaders test Him with questions, Jesus pronounces the fifth of eight woes on them in front of the crowds and His disciples.

"Woe to you, scribes and Pharisees, hypocrites! For you tithe the mint and dill and cummin, and have neglected the weightier provisions of the law: justice and mercy and faithfulness; but these are things you should have done without neglecting the others. You blind guides, who strain out a gnat and swallow a camel!" (Matthew 23:23, 24).

Setting: The temple in Jerusalem. After the Jewish religious leaders test Him with questions, Jesus pronounces the sixth of eight woes on them in front of the crowds and His disciples.

"Woe to you, scribes and Pharisees, hypocrites! For you clean the outside of the cup and of the dish, but inside they are full of robbery and self-indulgence. You blind Pharisee, first clean the inside of the cup and of the dish, so that the outside of it may become clean also" (Matthew 23:25, 26; see Mark 7:4).

Setting: The temple in Jerusalem. After the Jewish religious leaders test Him with questions, Jesus pronounces the seventh of eight woes on them in front of the crowds and His disciples.

"Woe to you, scribes and Pharisees, hypocrites! For you are like whitewashed tombs which on the outside appear beautiful, but inside they are full of dead men's bones and all uncleanness. So you, too, outwardly appear righteous to men, but inwardly you are full of hypocrisy and lawlessness" (Matthew 23:27, 28; cf. Luke 11:44).

Setting: The temple in Jerusalem. After the Jewish religious leaders test Him with questions, Jesus pronounces the eighth of eight woes on them in front of the crowds and His disciples.

"Woe to you, scribes and Pharisees, hypocrites! For you build the tombs of the prophets and adorn the monuments of the righteous, and say, 'If we had been *living* in the days of our fathers, we would not have been partners with them in *shedding* the blood of the prophets.' So you testify against yourselves, that you are sons of those who murdered the prophets. Fill up, then, the measure *of the guilt* of you fathers. You serpents, you brood of vipers, how will you escape the sentence of hell? Therefore, behold, I am sending you prophets and wise men and scribes; some of them you will kill and crucify, and some of them you will scourge in your synagogues, and persecute from city to city, so that upon you may fall *the guilt of* all the righteous blood shed on earth, from the blood of righteous Abel to the blood of Zechariah, the son of Berechiah, whom you murdered between the temple and the altar. Truly I say to you, all these things will come upon this generation" (Matthew 23:29–36; cf. 2 Chronicles 24:21; Zechariah 1:1; Matthew 3:7; Luke 11:47–52; see Matthew 10:23).

Setting: The Mount of Olives, just east of Jerusalem. During His discourse, after answering His disciples' questions as to when the temple will be destroyed and Jerusalem overrun, along with the signs of His coming and the end of the age, Jesus reemphasizes to His disciples that they should be on the alert for His return.

"Therefore be on the alert, for you do not know which day your Lord is coming. But be sure of this, that if the head of the house had known at what time of the night the thief was coming, he would have been on the alert and would not have allowed his house to be broken into. For this reason you also must be ready; for the Son of Man is coming at an hour when you do not think *He will.* Who then is the faithful and sensible slave whom his master put in charge of his household to give their food at the proper time? Blessed is that slave whom his master finds so doing when he comes. Truly I say to you that he will put him in charge of all his possessions. But if that evil slave says in his heart, 'My master is not coming for a long time,' and begins to beat his fellow slaves and eat and drink with drunkards; the master of that slave will come on a day when he does not expect *him* and at an hour which he does not know, and will cut him in pieces and assign him a place with the hypocrites; in that place there will be weeping and gnashing of teeth" (Matthew 24:42–51; cf. Mark 13:33–37; Luke 12:39–46; 21:34–36; see Matthew 8:11, 12; 25:21–23).

Setting: Galilee. The Pharisees and some of the scribes from Jerusalem ask Jesus why His disciples do not follow the tradition of ceremonial hand cleansing before eating bread.

And He said to them, "Rightly did Isaiah prophesy of you hypocrites, as it is written: 'THIS PEOPLE HONORS ME WITH THEIR LIPS, BUT THEIR HEART IS FAR AWAY FROM ME. BUT IN VAIN DO THEY WORSHIP ME, TEACHING AS DOCTRINES THE PRECEPTS OF MEN.' Neglecting the commandment of God, you hold to the tradition of men." He was also saying to them, "You are experts at setting aside the commandment of God in order to keep tradition. For Moses said, 'HONOR YOUR FATHER AND YOUR MOTHER'; and, 'HE WHO SPEAKS EVIL OF FATHER OR MOTHER, IS TO BE PUT TO DEATH'; but you say, 'If a man says to *his* father or *his* mother, whatever I have that would help you is Corban (that is to say, given *to God*),' you no longer permit him to do anything for *his* father or *his* mother; *thus* invalidating the word of God by your tradition which you have handed down; and you do many things such as that" (Mark 7:6–13, Jesus quotes from Exodus 20:12; 21:17; Isaiah 29:13; cf. Matthew 15:1–6).

Setting: On the way from Galilee to Jerusalem. After telling how a relationship with Him will divide families, Jesus chastises the crowds for being able to discern the weather but not the present age.

And He was also saying to the crowds, "When you see a cloud rising in the west, immediately you say, 'A shower is coming,' and so it turns out. And when *you see* a south wind blowing, you say, 'It will be a hot day,' and it turns out *that way*. You hypocrites! You know how to analyze the appearance of the earth and the sky, but why do you not analyze this present time?" (Luke 12:54–56; cf. Matthew 16:2, 3).

Setting: On the way from Galilee to Jerusalem. Jesus responds to a synagogue official's anger when He heals a woman, sick for eighteen years, in the synagogue on the Sabbath.

But the Lord answered him and said, "You hypocrites, does not each of you on the Sabbath untie his ox or his donkey from the stall and lead him away to water *him?* And this woman, a daughter of Abraham as she is, whom Satan has bound for eighteen long years, should she not have been released from this bond on the Sabbath day?" (Luke 13:15, 16; see Luke 13:10–14, 17; 14:5).

I

IDENTIFICATION WITH JESUS (See BAPTISM; and JESUS, CONFESSING)

IDENTITY, JESUS' (See CHRIST, THE; DAVID, SON OF; GOD, JESUS AS; JESUS CHRIST; JESUS' "I AM" STATEMENTS; JESUS' NAME; LORD; MESSIAH; NAME, MY; SON OF GOD; and SON OF MAN)

IDOLS

Setting: On the island of Patmos (in the Aegean Sea about fifty miles southwest of Ephesus in modern Turkey). On the Lord's Day (Sunday), about fifty years after Jesus' resurrection, the disciple John encounters the Lord Jesus Christ, who communicates a new revelation for the apostle to record for the church in Pergamum and to six other churches in Asia.

"And to the angel of the church in Pergamum write: The One who has the sharp two-edged sword says this: 'I know where you dwell, where Satan's throne is; and you hold fast My name, and did not deny My faith even in the days of Antipas, My witness, My faithful one, who was killed among you, where Satan dwells. But I have a few things against you, because you have there some who hold the teaching of Balaam, who kept teaching Balak to put a stumbling block before the sons of Israel, to eat things sacrificed to idols and to commit *acts of* immorality. So you also have some who in the same way hold the teaching of the Nicolaitans. Therefore repent; or else I am coming to you quickly, and I will make war against them with the sword of My mouth. He who has an ear, let him hear what the Spirit says to the churches. To him who overcomes, to him I will give *some* of the hidden manna, and I will give him a white stone, and a new name written on the stone which no one knows but he who receives it' (Revelation 2:12–17; see Numbers 25:1–3; Isaiah 62:2; Revelation 1:16; 2:5, 6, 16).

Setting: On the island of Patmos (in the Aegean Sea about fifty miles southwest of Ephesus in modern Turkey). On the Lord's Day (Sunday), about fifty years after Jesus' resurrection, the disciple John encounters the Lord Jesus Christ, who communicates a new revelation for the apostle to record for the church in Thyatira and to six other churches in Asia.

"And to the angel of the church in Thyatira write: The Son of God, who has eyes like a flame of fire, and His feet are like burnished bronze, says this: 'I know your deeds, and your love and faith and service and perseverance, and that your deeds of late are greater than at first. But I have *this* against you, that you tolerate the woman Jezebel, who calls herself a prophetess, and she teaches and leads My bond-servants astray so that they commit *acts of* immorality and eat things sacrificed to idols. I gave her time to repent, and she does not want to repent of her immorality. Behold, I will throw her on a bed *of sickness,* and those who commit adultery with her into great tribulation, unless they repent of her deeds. And I will kill her children with pestilence, and all the churches will know that I am He who searches the minds and hearts; and I will give to each one of you according to your deeds. But I say to you, the rest who are in Thyatira, who do not hold this teaching, who have not known the deep things of Satan, as they call them—I place no other burden on you. Nevertheless what you have, hold fast until I come. He who overcomes, and he who keeps My deeds until the end, TO HIM I WILL GIVE AUTHORITY OVER THE NATIONS; AND HE SHALL RULE THEM WITH A ROD OF IRON, AS THE VESSELS OF THE POTTER ARE BROKEN TO PIECES, as I also have received *authority* from My Father; and I will give him the morning star. He who has an ear, let him hear what the Spirit says to the churches' (Revelation 2:18–29; Jesus quotes from Psalm 2:8, 9; Isaiah 30:14; see 1 Kings 16:31; Psalm 7:9; Romans 2:5; 1 Corinthians 2:10; 2 Peter 3:9; Revelation 1:14; 2:7; 3:11; 17:1–20).

IGNORANCE

[IGNORANCE from they do not know what they are doing]

Setting: Golgotha (Calvary), just outside Jerusalem. After being arrested, tried, and sentenced to crucifixion by Pilate (Roman governor of Judea), the Lord, while hanging between two criminals, requests from His Father forgiveness for the crucifiers.

But Jesus was saying, "Father, forgive them; for they do not know what they are doing." And they cast lots, dividing up His garments among themselves (Luke 23:34; see Psalm 22:18; Matthew 27:33–36; Mark 15:22–24; John 19:23–25).

IMMINENCY (See JESUS' RETURN)

IMMORALITY (Also see specific sins such as ADULTERIES; and FORNICATIONS)

Setting: Judea beyond the Jordan (Perea). Jesus responds to the Pharisees' follow-up question in front of a large crowd about Moses' command regarding a certificate of divorce.

He said to them, "Because of your hardness of heart Moses permitted you to divorce your wives; but from the beginning it has not been this way. And I say to you, whoever divorces his wife, except for immorality, and marries another woman commits adultery" (Matthew 19:8, 9; cf. Deuteronomy 24:1–4; Matthew 5:32; 19:7; Mark 10:1–12; see Romans 7:2, 3; 1 Corinthians 7:10, 39).

[IMMORALITY from loose living and prostitutes]

Setting: On the way from Galilee to Jerusalem. Jesus conveys the illustration of the prodigal son because the Pharisees and scribes complain He associates with tax collectors and sinners.

And He said, "A man had two sons. The younger of them said to his father, 'Father, give me the share of the estate that falls to me.' So he divided his wealth between them. And not many days later, the younger son gathered everything together and went on a journey into a distant country, and there he squandered his estate with loose living. Now when he had spent everything, a severe famine occurred in that country, and he began to be impoverished. So he went and hired himself out to one of the citizens of that country, and he sent him into his fields to feed swine. And he would have gladly filled his stomach with the pods that the swine were eating, and no one was giving *anything* to him. But when he came to his senses, he said, 'How many of my father's hired men have more than enough bread, but I am dying here with hunger! I will get up and go to my father, and will say to him, "Father, I have sinned against heaven, and in your sight; I am no longer worthy to be called your son; make me as one of your hired men."' So he got up and came to his father. But while he was still a long way off, his father saw him and felt compassion *for him,* and ran and embraced him and kissed him. And the son said to him, "Father, I have sinned against heaven and in your sight; I am no longer worthy to be called your son.' But the father said to his slaves, 'Quickly bring out the best robe and put it on him, and put a ring on his hand and sandals on his feet; and bring the fattened calf, kill it, and let us eat and celebrate; for this son of mine was dead and has come to life again; he was lost and has been found.' And they began to celebrate. Now his older son was in the field, when he came and approached the house, he heard music and dancing. And he summoned one of the servants and *began* inquiring what these things could be. And he said to him, 'Your brother has come, and your father has killed the fattened calf because he has received him back safe and sound.' But he became angry and was not willing to go in; and his father came out and *began* pleading with him. But he answered and said to his father, 'Look! For so many years I have been serving you and I have never neglected a command of yours; and *yet* you have never given me a young goat, so that I might celebrate with my friends; but when this son of yours came, who has devoured your wealth with prostitutes, you killed the fattened calf for him.' And he said to him, 'Son, you have always been with me, and all that is mine is yours. But we had to celebrate and rejoice, for this brother of yours was dead and *has begun* to live, and was lost and has been found'" (Luke 15:11–32; see Proverbs 29:2).

Setting: On the island of Patmos (in the Aegean Sea about fifty miles southwest of Ephesus in modern Turkey). On the Lord's Day (Sunday), about fifty years after Jesus' resurrection, the disciple John encounters the Lord Jesus Christ, who communicates a new revelation for the apostle to record for the church in Pergamum and to six other churches in Asia.

"And to the angel of the church in Pergamum write: The One who has the sharp two-edged sword says this: 'I know where you dwell, where Satan's throne is; and you hold fast My name, and did not deny My faith even in the days of Antipas, My witness, My faithful one, who was killed among you, where Satan dwells. But I have a few things against you, because you have there some who hold the teaching of Balaam, who kept teaching Balak to put a stumbling block before the sons of Israel, to eat things sacrificed to idols and to commit *acts of* immorality. So you also have some who in the same way hold the teaching of the Nicolaitans. Therefore repent; or else I am coming to you quickly, and I will make war against them with the sword of My mouth. He who has an ear, let him hear what the Spirit says to the churches. To him who overcomes, to him I will give *some* of the hidden manna, and I will give him a white stone, and a new name written on the stone which no one knows but he who receives it' (Revelation 2:12–17; see Numbers 25:1–3; Isaiah 62:2; Revelation 1:16; 2:5, 6, 16).

Setting: On the island of Patmos (in the Aegean Sea about fifty miles southwest of Ephesus in modern Turkey). On the Lord's Day (Sunday), about fifty years after Jesus' resurrection, the disciple John encounters the Lord Jesus Christ, who communicates a new revelation for the apostle to record for the church in Thyatira and to six other churches in Asia.

"And to the angel of the church in Thyatira write: The Son of God, who has eyes like a flame of fire, and His feet are like burnished bronze, says this: 'I know your deeds, and your love and faith and service and perseverance, and that your deeds of late are greater than at first. But I have *this* against you, that you tolerate the woman Jezebel, who calls herself a prophetess, and she teaches and leads My bond-servants astray so that they commit *acts of* immorality and eat things sacrificed to idols. I gave her time to repent, and she does not want to repent of her immorality. Behold, I will throw her on a bed *of sickness*, and those who commit adultery with her into great tribulation, unless they repent of her deeds. And I will kill her children with pestilence, and all the churches will know that I am He who searches the minds and hearts; and I will give to each one of you according to your deeds. But I say to you, the rest who are in Thyatira, who do not hold this teaching, who have not known the deep things of Satan, as they call them—I place no other burden on you. Nevertheless what you have, hold fast until I come. He who overcomes, and he who keeps My deeds until the end, TO HIM I WILL GIVE AUTHORITY OVER THE NATIONS; AND HE SHALL RULE THEM WITH A ROD OF IRON, AS THE VESSELS OF THE POTTER ARE BROKEN TO PIECES, as I also have received *authority* from My Father; and I will give him the morning star. He who has an ear, let him hear what the Spirit says to the churches' (Revelation 2:18–29; Jesus quotes from Psalm 2:8, 9; Isaiah 30:14; see 1 Kings 16:31; Psalm 7:9; Romans 2:5; 1 Corinthians 2:10; 2 Peter 3:9; Revelation 1:14; 2:7; 3:11; 17:1–20).

IMPACT, PERSONAL (See TESTIMONY)

INDEBTEDNESS (Also see DEBT; DEBTORS; DEBTS; and LOANS)

Setting: On the way from Galilee to Jerusalem via Bethany. After Jesus visits the home of Martha and Mary, one of the disciples asks Him to teach them to pray.

And He said to them, "When you pray, say: 'Father, hallowed be Your name. Your kingdom come. Give us each day our daily bread. And forgive us our sins, for we ourselves also forgive everyone who is indebted to us. And lead us not into temptation'" (Luke 11:2–4; cf. Matthew 6:9–13).

INDULGENCE IN PLEASURE (See DISSIPATION)

INDWELLING (See ABODE)

INFANTS (Also see BABIES, NURSING; CHILD; and CHILDREN)

Setting: Galilee. After pronouncing woes against unrepentant cities as He teaches and preaches, Jesus prays a thanksgiving prayer to His Father in heaven.

At that time Jesus said, "I praise You, Father, Lord of heaven and earth, that you have hidden these things from *the* wise and intelligent and have revealed them to infants. Yes, Father, for this way was well-pleasing in Your sight. All things have been handed over to Me by My Father; and no one knows the Son except the Father; nor does anyone know the Father except the Son, and anyone to whom the Son wills to reveal *Him*" (Matthew 11:25–27; cf. Luke 10:21, 22).

Setting: The temple in Jerusalem. After driving out the money changers and merchants, Jesus comments to the indignant chief priests and scribes about the praises the children render to Him.

But when the chief priests and the scribes saw the wonderful things that He had done, and the children who were shouting in the temple, "Hosanna to the Son of David," they became indignant and said to Him, "Do You hear what these *children* are saying?" And Jesus said to them, "Yes, have you never read, 'OUT OF THE MOUTH OF INFANTS AND NURSING BABIES YOU HAVE PREPARED PRAISE FOR YOURSELF'?" (Matthew 21:15, 16, Jesus quotes from Psalm 8:2; see Matthew 9:27).

Setting: On the way from Galilee to Jerusalem. The Lord responds to a report from the seventy sent out in pairs to every place He Himself will soon visit.

At that very time He rejoiced greatly in the Holy Spirit, and said, "I praise You, O Father, Lord of heaven and earth, that You have hidden these things from *the* wise and intelligent and have revealed them to infants. Yes, Father, for this way was well-pleasing in Your sight. All things have been handed over to Me by My Father, and no one knows who the Son is except the Father, and who the Father is except the Son, and anyone to whom the Son wills to reveal *Him*" (Luke 10:21, 22; cf. Matthew 11:25–27; see Luke 10:1, 17; John 3:35; 10:15).

INFANTS, MOUTH OF (See INFANTS)

INFERTILITY (See BARRENNESS)

INFLUENCE, BAD (See APOSTLES, FALSE; CHRISTS, FALSE; PROPHETS, FALSE; and TEACHERS, FALSE)

[BAD INFLUENCE from Whoever then annuls one of the least of these commandments, and teaches others *to do* the same]
Setting: Galilee. During the early part of His ministry, Jesus preaches the Sermon on the Mount to His disciples and the multitudes.

"Whoever then annuls one of the least of these commandments, and teaches others *to do* the same, shall be called least in the kingdom of heaven; but whoever keeps and teaches *them*, he shall be called great in the kingdom of heaven" (Matthew 5:19; cf. Matthew 11:11).

INFLUENCE, PERSONAL (See TESTIMONY)

INFLUENCE, SPHERE OF (See TESTIMONY)

INGRATITUDE

[INGRATITUDE from ungrateful]
Setting: Galilee. After selecting His twelve disciples, Jesus teaches the Sermon on the Mount to those disciples and a great throng of people from Judea, Jerusalem, and the central coastal region of Tyre and Sidon.

"But I say to you who hear, love your enemies, do good to those who hate you, bless those who curse you, pray for those who mistreat you. Whoever hits you on the cheek, offer him the other also; and whoever takes away your coat, do not withhold your shirt from him either. Give to everyone who asks of you, and whoever takes away what is yours, do not demand it back. Treat others the same way you want them to treat you. If you love those who love you, what credit is *that* to you? For even sinners love those who love them. If you do good to those who do good to you, what credit is *that* to you? For even sinners do the same. If you lend to those from whom you expect to receive, what credit is *that* to you? Even sinners lend to sinners in order to receive back the same *amount.* But love your enemies, and do good, and lend, expecting nothing in return; and your reward will be great, and you will be sons of the Most High; for He Himself is kind to ungrateful and evil *men*. Be merciful, just as your Father is merciful" (Luke 6:27–36; cf. Matthew 5:9, 39–48; 7:12; see Luke 6:12–19).

[INGRATITUDE from But the nine—where are they? Was no one found who returned to give glory to God, except this foreigner]

Setting: Samaria, on the way from Galilee to Jerusalem. The Lord stops to heal ten lepers who ask for cleansing.

When He saw them, He said to them, "Go and show yourselves to the priests." And as they were going, they were cleansed. Now one of them, when he saw that he had been healed, turned back, glorifying God with a loud voice, and he fell on his face at His feet, giving thanks to Him. And he was a Samaritan. Then Jesus answered and said, "Were there not ten cleansed? But the nine—where are they? Was no one found who returned to give glory to God, except this foreigner? "And He said to him, "Stand up and go; your faith has made you well" (Luke 17:14–19; see Leviticus 14:1–32).

INHERITANCE (Also see ESTATE; and HEIR)

[INHERITANCE from inherit]

Setting: Galilee. Early in His ministry, Jesus presents the Beatitudes (part of the Sermon on the Mount) to His disciples and the gathered crowds from Galilee, Decapolis, Jerusalem, Judea, and beyond the Jordan.

"Blessed are the gentle, for they shall inherit the earth" (Matthew 5:5; cf. Psalm 37:11; see Matthew 5:1; 13:35).

[INHERITANCE from inherit]

Setting: Judea beyond the Jordan (Perea). Jesus promises rewards to His disciples for their personal sacrifice and commitment to following Him.

And Jesus said to them, "Truly I say to you, that you who have followed Me, in the regeneration when the Son of Man will sit on His glorious throne, you also shall sit upon twelve thrones, judging the twelve tribes of Israel. And everyone who has left houses or brothers or sisters or father or mother or children or farms for My name's sake, will receive many times as much, and will inherit eternal life. But many *who* are first will be last; and *the* last, first" (Matthew 19:28–30; cf. Matthew 6:33; 20:15; Mark 10:29, 30; Luke 18:29, 30; 22:30).

Setting: The temple in Jerusalem. Jesus delivers another parable to the chief priests and elders after they question His authority.

"Listen to another parable. There was a landowner who PLANTED A VINEYARD AND PUT A WALL AROUND IT AND DUG A WINE PRESS IN IT, AND BUILT A TOWER, and rented it out to vine-growers and went on a journey. When the harvest time approached, he sent his slaves to the vine-growers to receive his produce. The vine-growers took his slaves and beat one, and killed another, and stoned a third. Again he sent another group of slaves larger than the first; and they did the same thing to them. But afterward he sent his son to them, saying, 'They will respect my son.' But when the vine-growers saw the son, they said among themselves, 'This is the heir; come, let us kill him and seize his inheritance.' They took him, and threw him out of the vineyard and killed him. Therefore when the owner of the vineyard comes, what will he do to those vine-growers?" (Matthew 21:33–40; Jesus quotes from Isaiah 5:1, 2; cf. Mark 12:1–9; Luke 20:9–15; see Matthew 21:45, 46).

[INHERITANCE from inherit]

Setting: The Mount of Olives, just east of Jerusalem. During His discourse, after answering His disciples' questions as to when the temple will be destroyed and Jerusalem overrun, along with the signs of His coming and the end of the age, Jesus reveals the future judgments following His return.

"But when the Son of Man comes in His glory, and all the angels with Him, then He will sit on His glorious throne. All the nations will be gathered before Him; and He will separate them from one another, as the shepherd separates the sheep from the goats; and He will put the sheep on His right, and the goats on the left. Then the King will say to those on His right, 'Come, you who are blessed of My Father, inherit the kingdom prepared for you from the foundation of the world. 'For I was hungry, and you gave Me *something* to eat; I was thirsty, and you gave Me *something* to drink; I was a stranger, and you invited Me in; naked, and you clothed Me; I was sick, and you visited Me; I was in prison, and you came to Me.' Then the righteous will answer Him, 'Lord, when did we see You hungry and feed You, or thirsty, and give you *something* to drink? And when did we see You a stranger, and invite You in, or naked, and clothe You? When did we see You sick, or in prison, and come to You?' The King will answer and say to them,

'Truly I say to you, to the extent that you did it to one of these brothers of Mine, *even* the least *of them,* you did it to Me.' Then He will also say to those on His left, 'Depart from Me, accursed ones, into the eternal fire which has been prepared for the devil and his angels; for I was hungry, and you gave Me *nothing* to eat; I was thirsty, and you gave Me nothing to drink; I was a stranger, and you did not invite Me in; naked, and you did not clothe Me; sick, and in prison, and you did not visit Me.' Then they themselves also will answer, 'Lord, when did we see You hungry, or thirsty, or a stranger, or naked, or sick, or in prison, and did not take care of You?' Then He will answer them, 'Truly I say to you, to the extent that you did not do it to one of the least of these, you did not do it to Me.' These will go away into eternal punishment, but the righteous into eternal life" (Matthew 25:31–46; see Matthew 7:23; 16:27; 19:29).

Setting: The temple in Jerusalem. Having His authority questioned by the chief priests, scribes, and elders, Jesus begins to teach them in parables.

And He began to speak to them in parables: "A man PLANTED A VINEYARD AND PUT A WALL AROUND IT, AND DUG A VAT UNDER THE WINE PRESS AND BUILT A TOWER, and rented it out to vine-growers and went on a journey. At the *harvest* time he sent a slave to the vine-growers, in order to receive *some* of the produce of the vineyard from the vine-growers. They took him, and beat him and sent him away empty-handed. Again he sent them another slave, and they wounded him in the head, and treated him shamefully. And he sent another, and that one they killed; and *so with* many others, beating some and killing others. He had one more to *send,* a beloved son; he sent him last *of all* to them, saying, 'They will respect my son.' But those vine-growers said to one another, 'This is the heir; come, let us kill him, and the inheritance will be ours!' They took him, and killed him and threw him out of the vineyard. What will the owner of the vineyard do? He will come and destroy the vine-growers, and will give the vineyard to others. Have you not even read this Scripture: 'THE STONE WHICH THE BUILDERS REJECTED, THIS BECAME THE CHIEF CORNER *stone;* THIS CAME ABOUT FROM THE LORD, AND IT IS MARVELOUS IN OUR EYES'?" (Mark 12:1–11, Jesus quotes from Psalm 118:22, 23; Isaiah 5:1, 2; cf. Matthew 21:33–46; Luke 20:9–19).

Setting: The temple in Jerusalem. A few days before His crucifixion, after the chief priests and the scribes question His authority to teach and preach, Jesus conveys the Parable of the Vine-Growers to the people.

And He began to tell the people this parable: "A man planted a vineyard and rented it out to vine-growers, and went on a journey for a long time. At the *harvest* time he sent a slave to the vine-growers, so that they would give him *some* of the produce of the vineyard; but the vine-growers beat him and sent him away empty-handed. And he proceeded to send another slave; and they beat him also and treated him shamefully and sent him away empty-handed. And he proceeded to send a third; and this one also they wounded and cast out. The owner of the vineyard said, 'What shall I do? I will send my beloved son; perhaps they will respect him.' But when the vine-growers saw him, they reasoned with one another, saying, 'This is the heir; let us kill him so that the inheritance will be ours.' So they threw him out of the vineyard and killed him. What, then, will the owner of the vineyard do to them? He will come and destroy these vine-growers and will give the vineyard to others." When they heard it, they said, "May it never be!" But Jesus looked at them and said, "What then is this that is written: 'THE STONE WHICH THE BUILDERS REJECTED, THIS BECAME THE CHIEF CORNER *stone*'? Everyone who falls on that stone will be broken to pieces; but on whomever it falls, it will scatter him like dust" (Luke 20:9–18, Jesus quotes from Psalm 118:22; cf. Matthew 21:33–44; Mark 12:1–11; see Ephesians 2:20).

Setting: Caesarea. Luke, writing in Acts, gives Paul's retelling of his conversion to Christ as he appears before King Agrippa following his hearing before the Jewish Council in Jerusalem and arrest by the Roman commander (on his way to Rome after the apostle's third missionary journey).

"And when we had fallen to the ground, I heard a voice saying to me in the Hebrew dialect, 'Saul, Saul, why are you persecuting Me? It is hard for you to kick against the goads.' And I said, 'Who are You, Lord?' And the Lord said, 'I am Jesus whom you are persecuting. But get up and stand on your feet; for this purpose I have appeared to you, to appoint you a minister and a witness not only to the things which you have seen, but also to the things in which I will appear to you; rescuing you from the *Jewish* people and from the Gentiles, to whom I am sending you, to open their eyes so that they may turn from darkness to light and from the dominion of Satan to God, that they may receive forgiveness of sins and an inheritance among those who have been sanctified by faith in Me' (Acts 26:14–18; see Isaiah 35:5; Acts 21:40; 22:14).

INITIATIVE

Setting: On the way from Galilee to Jerusalem. After chastising the crowds for being able to discern the weather but not the present age, Jesus exhorts them to settle any financial disputes outside of court.

"And why do you not even on your own initiative judge what is right? For while you are going with your opponent to appear before the magistrate, on *your* way *there* make an effort to settle with him, so that he may not drag you before the judge, and the judge turn you over to the officer, and the officer throw you into prison. I say to you, you will not get out of there until you have paid the very last cent" (Luke 12:57–59; cf. Matthew 5:25, 26).

Setting: Jerusalem. During the Feast of the Jews, Jesus responds to criticism from the Jewish religious leaders by referring to God as His Father (thereby making Himself equal with God) and informing them that God, John the Baptist, and His works all testify to His mission.

"I can do nothing on My own initiative. As I hear, I judge; and My judgment is just, because I do not seek My own will, but the will of Him who sent Me. If I *alone* testify about Myself, My testimony is not true. There is another who testifies of Me, and I know that the testimony which He gives about Me is true. You have sent to John, and he has testified to the truth. But the testimony which I receive is not from man, but I say these things so that you may be saved. He was the lamp that was burning and was shining and you were willing to rejoice for a while in his light. But the testimony which I have is greater than the *testimony of* John; for the works which the Father has given Me to accomplish—the very works that I do—testify about Me, that the Father has sent Me. And the Father who sent Me, He has testified of Me. You have neither heard His voice at any time nor seen His form. You do not have His word abiding in you, for you do not believe Him whom He sent" (John 5:30–38; see Matthew 3:17; Mark 1:4, 5; John 1:7, 15, 32; 4:34; 8:14–16; 10:25, 37, 38).

Setting: The temple treasury in Jerusalem. Following the Feast of Booths and the scribes' and Pharisees' failed attempt to stone a woman for adultery, Jesus returns to teach. His enemies question His testimony about Himself.

So Jesus said, "When you lift up the Son of Man, then you will know that I am *He,* and I do nothing on my own initiative, but I speak these things as the Father taught Me. And He who sent Me is with Me; He has not left Me alone, for I always do the things that are pleasing to Him" (John 8:28, 29; see John 3:14).

Setting: The temple treasury in Jerusalem. After the scribes and Pharisees question His testimony about Himself, Jesus interacts with them regarding their ancestry and motives.

Jesus said to them, "If God were your Father, you would love Me, for I proceeded forth and have come from God, for I have not even come on My own initiative, but He sent Me. Why do you not understand what I am saying? *It is* because you cannot hear My word. You are of *your* father the devil, and you want to do the desires of your father. He was a murderer from the beginning, and does not stand in the truth because there is no truth in him. Whenever he speaks a lie, he speaks from his own *nature,* for he is a liar and the father of lies. But because I speak the truth, you do not believe Me. Which one of you convicts Me of sin? If I speak truth, why do not believe Me? He who is of God hears the words of God; for this reason you do not hear *them,* because you are not of God" (John 8:42–47; see John 18:37; 1 John 3:8; 4:6, 5:1).

Setting: Jerusalem. Following the Pharisees' interrogation and dismissal of the formerly blind man Jesus healed on the Sabbath, the Lord conveys the Parable of the Good Shepherd to the Pharisees, using figures of speech they do not understand.

So Jesus said to them again, "Truly, truly, I say to you, I am the door of the sheep. All who came before Me are thieves and robbers, but the sheep did not hear them. I am the door; if anyone enters through Me, he will be saved, and will go in and out and find pasture. The thief comes only to steal and kill and destroy; I came that they may have life, and have *it* abundantly. I am the good shepherd; the good shepherd lays down His life for the sheep. He who is a hired hand, and not a shepherd, who is not the owner of the sheep, sees the wolf coming, and leaves the sheep and flees, and the wolf snatches them and scatters *them. He*

flees because he is a hired hand and is not concerned about the sheep. I am the good shepherd, and I know My own and My own know Me, even as the Father knows Me and I know the Father; and I lay down My life for the sheep. I have other sheep, which are not of this fold; I must bring them also, and they will hear My voice; and they will become one flock *with* one shepherd. For this reason the Father loves Me, because I lay down My life so that I may take it again. No one has taken it away from Me, but I lay it down on My own initiative. I have authority to take it up again. This commandment I received from My Father" (John 10:7–18; see Isaiah 40:11; 56:8; Jeremiah 23:1; Matthew 11:27).

Setting: Jerusalem. Just days before the Passover, with the chief priests and Pharisees plotting to seize Jesus, who is expressing anxiety about His upcoming death by crucifixion, some of the people believe in Him, while others are rejecting His message.

And Jesus cried out and said, "He who believes in Me, does not believe in Me but in Him who sent Me. He who sees Me sees the One who sent Me. I have come *as* Light into the world, so that everyone who believes in Me will not remain in darkness. If anyone hears My sayings and does not keep them, I do not judge him; for I did not come to judge the world, but to save the world. He who rejects Me and does not receive My sayings, has one who judges him; the word I spoke is what will judge him at the last day. For I did not speak on My own initiative, but the Father Himself who sent Me has given Me a commandment *as to* what to say and what to speak. I know that His commandment is eternal life; therefore the things I speak, I speak just as the Father as told Me" (John 12:44–50; see Matthew 10:40; Luke 10:16; John 1:4; 3:17; 5:19; 6:68; 14:9).

Setting: Jerusalem. Before the Passover, after answering Thomas' question about where He is going and how they will know the way, Jesus responds to Philip's request for Him to show His disciples the Father.

Jesus said to him, "Have I been so long with you, and *yet* you have not come to know Me, Philip? He who has seen Me has seen the Father; how *can* you say, 'Show us the Father'? Do you not believe that I am in the Father, and the Father is in Me? The words that I say to you I do not speak on My own initiative, but the Father abiding in Me does His works. Believe Me that I am in the Father and the Father is in Me; otherwise believe because of the works themselves. Truly, truly, I say to you, he who believes in Me, the works that I do, he will do also; and greater *works* than these he will do; because I go to the Father. Whatever you ask in My name, that will I do, so that the Father may be glorified in the Son. If you ask Me anything in My name, I will do *it*" (John 14:9–14; see Matthew 7:7; John 1:14; 5:19, 20, 36; 10:37, 38; 15:16).

Setting: Jerusalem. Before the Passover, after warning His disciples of the persecution they will face after His departure to heaven, Jesus elaborates about the coming ministry of the Holy Spirit.

"I have many more things to say to you, but you cannot bear *them* now. But when He, the Spirit of truth, comes, He will guide you into all the truth; for He will not speak on His own initiative, but whatever He hears, He will speak; and He will disclose to you what is to come. He will glorify Me, for He will take of Mine and will disclose *it* to you. All things that the Father has are Mine; therefore I said that He takes of Mine and will disclose *it* to you (John 16:12–15; see John 7:39; 14:17, 26; 17:10).

Setting: Jerusalem. After the previous and current high priest (Annas and Caiaphas) question Jesus, and Peter denies the second and third times being His disciple, the Lord is brought before Pilate (Roman governor of Judea).

Jesus answered, "Are you saying this on your own initiative, or did others tell you about Me?" (John 18:34).

INN

Setting: On the way from Galilee to Jerusalem. While being tested by a lawyer, Jesus tells him the story of the good Samaritan.

Jesus replied and said, "A man was going down from Jerusalem to Jericho, and fell among robbers, and they stripped him and beat him, and went away leaving him half dead. And by chance a priest was going down on that road, and when he saw him, he passed by on the other side. Likewise a Levite also, when he came to the place and saw him, passed by on the other side. But a

Samaritan, who was on a journey, came upon him; and when he saw him, he felt compassion, and came to him and bandaged up his wounds, pouring oil and wine on *them;* and he put him on his own beast, and brought him to an inn and took care of him. On the next day he took out two denarii and gave them to the innkeeper and said, 'Take care of him; and whatever more you spend, when I return I will repay you.' Which of these three do you think proved to be a neighbor to the man who fell into the robbers' *hands?*" And he said, "The one who showed mercy toward him." Then Jesus said to him, "Go and do the same" (Luke 10:30–37).

INNER ROOM (Listed under ROOM, INNER; also see ROOMS, INNER)

INNER ROOMS (Listed under ROOMS, INNER; also see ROOM, INNER)

INNERMOST BEING (Listed under BEING, INNERMOST)

INNKEEPER

Setting: On the way from Galilee to Jerusalem. While being tested by a lawyer, Jesus tells him the story of the good Samaritan.

Jesus replied and said, "A man was going down from Jerusalem to Jericho, and fell among robbers, and they stripped him and beat him, and went away leaving him half dead. And by chance a priest was going down on that road, and when he saw him, he passed by on the other side. Likewise a Levite also, when he came to the place and saw him, passed by on the other side. But a Samaritan, who was on a journey, came upon him; and when he saw him, he felt compassion, and came to him and bandaged up his wounds, pouring oil and wine on *them;* and he put him on his own beast, and brought him to an inn and took care of him. On the next day he took out two denarii and gave them to the innkeeper and said, 'Take care of him; and whatever more you spend, when I return I will repay you.' Which of these three do you think proved to be a neighbor to the man who fell into the robbers' *hands?*" And he said, "The one who showed mercy toward him." Then Jesus said to him, "Go and do the same" (Luke 10:30–37).

INNOCENT

Setting: Galilee. After His disciples observe His ministry, Jesus summons and specifically instructs them about the upcoming hardships of their ministry to the people of Israel.

"Behold, I send you out as sheep in the midst of wolves; so be shrewd as serpents and innocent as doves. But beware of men, for they will hand you over to *the* courts and scourge you in their synagogues; and you will even be brought before governors and kings for My sake, as a testimony to them and to the Gentiles. But when they hand you over, do not worry about how or what you are to say; for it will be given you in that hour what you are to say. For it is not you who speak, but *it* is the Spirit of your Father who speaks in you" (Matthew 10:16–20; cf. Luke 10:3).

Setting: Galilee. Jesus responds to the Pharisees' objection to His disciples' picking grain from the fields on the Sabbath.

But He said to them, "Have you not read what David did when he became hungry, he and his companions, how they entered the house of God, and ate the consecrated bread, which was not lawful for him to eat nor for those with him, but for the priests alone? Or, have you not read in the Law, that on the Sabbath the priests in the temple break the Sabbath and are innocent? But I say to you that something greater than the temple is here. But if you had known what this means, 'I DESIRE COMPASSION, AND NOT A SACRIFICE,' you would not have condemned the innocent. For the Son of Man is Lord of the Sabbath" (Matthew 12:3–8, Jesus quotes from Hosea 6:6; cf. Mark 2:25–28; Luke 6:3–5; see 1 Samuel 21:6).

INSCRIPTION

Setting: The temple in Jerusalem. The Pharisees send their disciples and the Herodians to test Jesus about the poll-tax, in order to trap Him while He teaches.

But Jesus perceived their malice, and said, "Why are you testing Me, you hypocrites? Show Me the coin *used* for the poll-tax." And they brought Him a denarius. And He said to them, "Whose likeness and inscription is this?" They said to Him, "Caesar's."

Then He said to them, "Then render to Caesar the things that are Caesar's; and to God the things that are God's" (Matthew 22:18–21; cf. Matthew 17:25; Mark 12:15–17; Luke 20:22–25).

Setting: The temple in Jerusalem. After Jesus teaches the chief priests, scribes, and elders in parables, they send some of the Pharisees and Herodians in an attempt to trap Him in a statement.

"Shall we pay or shall we not pay?" But He, knowing their hypocrisy, said to them, "Why are you testing Me? Bring Me a denarius to look at." They brought *one.* And He said to them, "Whose likeness and inscription is this?" And they said to Him, "Caesar's." And Jesus said to them, "Render to Caesar the things that are Caesar's, and to God the things that are God's." And they were amazed at Him (Mark 12:15–17; cf. Matthew 22:15–22; Luke 20:20–26).

Setting: The temple in Jerusalem. A few days before His crucifixion, after Jesus conveys the Parable of the Vine-Growers to the people, the scribes and Pharisees seek to trap Him by questioning Him about paying taxes to Caesar.

But He detected their trickery and said to them, "Show Me a denarius. Whose likeness and inscription does it have?" They said "Caesar's." And He said to them, "Then render to Caesar the things that are Caesar's, and to God the things that are God's" (Luke 20:23–25; cf. Matthew 22:15–21; Mark 12:13–17).

INSECTS (See specific kinds like MOTHS)

INSTRUCTION (See TEACHING)

INSTRUMENT

Setting: Damascus. Luke, writing in Acts, tells of the reluctance of Ananias, one of Jesus' followers, to locate Saul of Tarsus (a known enemy of the church) in order to restore his vision.

But the Lord said to him, "Go, for he is a chosen instrument of Mine, to bear My name before the Gentiles and kings and the sons of Israel; for I will show him how much he must suffer for My name's sake" (Acts 9:15, 16; see Acts 13:2; 20:22–24).

INSULT (Also see OFFENSE)

Setting: Galilee. Early in His ministry, Jesus presents the Beatitudes (part of the Sermon on the Mount) to His disciples and the gathered crowds from Galilee, Decapolis, Jerusalem, Judea, and beyond the Jordan.

"Blessed are you when *people* insult you and persecute you, and falsely say all kinds of evil against you because of Me. Rejoice and be glad, for your reward in heaven is great; for in the same way they persecuted the prophets who were before you" (Matthew 5:11, 12; cf. 2 Chronicles 36:16; Luke 6:22, 23; 1 Peter 4:14; see Matthew 5:1; 13:35).

Setting: Galilee. After selecting His twelve disciples, Jesus teaches the Beatitudes (part of the Sermon on the Mount) to those disciples and a great throng of people from Judea, Jerusalem, and the central coastal region of Tyre and Sidon.

"Blessed are you when men hate you, and ostracize you, and insult you, and scorn your name as evil, for the sake of the Son of Man. Be glad in that day and leap *for joy*, for behold, your reward is great in heaven. For in the same way their fathers used to treat the prophets" (Luke 6:22, 23; cf. Matthew 5:10–12; see 2 Chronicles 36:16).

INTELLIGENT

Setting: Galilee. After pronouncing woes against unrepentant cities as He teaches and preaches, Jesus prays a thanksgiving prayer to His Father in heaven.

At that time Jesus said, "I praise You, Father, Lord of heaven and earth, that you have hidden these things from *the* wise and intelligent and have revealed them to infants. Yes, Father, for this way was well-pleasing in Your sight. All things have been handed over to Me by My Father; and no one knows the Son except the Father; nor does anyone know the Father except the Son, and anyone to whom the Son wills to reveal *Him*" (Matthew 11:25–27; cf. Luke 10:21, 22).

Setting: On the way from Galilee to Jerusalem. The Lord responds to a report from the seventy sent out in pairs to every place He Himself will soon visit.

At that very time He rejoiced greatly in the Holy Spirit, and said, "I praise You, O Father, Lord of heaven and earth, that You have hidden these things from *the* wise and intelligent and have revealed them to infants. Yes, Father, for this way was well-pleasing in Your sight. All things have been handed over to Me by My Father, and no one knows who the Son is except the Father, and who the Father is except the Son, and anyone to whom the Son wills to reveal *Him*" (Luke 10:21, 22; cf. Matthew 11:25–27; see Luke 10:1, 17; John 3:35; 10:15).

INTEREST (Also see BANK; and LOANS)

Setting: The Mount of Olives, just east of Jerusalem. During His discourse, after answering His disciples' questions as to when the temple will be destroyed and Jerusalem overrun, along with the signs of His coming and the end of the age, Jesus reemphasizes to the disciples that they should be on the alert for His return.

"For *it is* just like a man *about* to go on a journey, who called his own slaves and entrusted his possessions to them. To one he gave five talents, to another, two, and to another, one, each according to his own ability; and he went on his journey. Immediately the one who had received the five talents went and traded with them, and gained five more talents. In the same manner the one who *had received* the two *talents* gained two more. But he who received the one *talent* went away, and dug a *hole* in the ground and hid his master's money. Now after a long time the master of those slaves came and settled accounts with them. The one who had received the five talents came up and brought five more talents, saying, 'Master, you entrusted five talents to me. See, I have gained five more talents.' His master said to him, 'Well done, good and faithful slave. You were faithful with a few things, I will put you in charge of many things; enter into the joy of your master.' Also the one who *had received* the two talents came up and said, 'Master, you entrusted two talents to me. See, I have gained two more talents.' His master said to him, 'Well done, good and faithful slave. You were faithful with a few things, I will put you in charge of many things; enter into the joy of your master.' And the one also who had received the one talent came up and said, 'Master, I knew you to be a hard man, reaping where you did not sow and gathering where you scattered no *seed.* And I was afraid, and went away and hid your talent in the ground. See, you have what is yours.' But his master answered and said to him, 'You wicked, lazy slave, you knew that I reap where I did not sow and gather where I scattered no *seed.* Then you ought to have put my money in the bank, and on my arrival I would have received my *money* back with interest. 'Therefore take away the talent from him, and give it to the one who has ten talents.' For to everyone who has, *more* shall be given, and he will have an abundance; but from the one who does not have, even what he does have shall be taken away. Throw out the worthless slave into the outer darkness; in that place there will be weeping and gnashing of teeth" (Matthew 25:14–30; cf. Matthew 8:12; 13:12; 24:45–47; see Matthew 18:23, 24; Luke 12:44).

Setting: Jericho, on the way to Jerusalem. After commending Zaccheus's faith in Him, Jesus provides a parable about stewardship.

So He said, "A nobleman went to a distant country to receive a kingdom for himself, and *then* return. And he called ten of his slaves, and gave them ten minas and said to them, 'Do business *with this* until I come *back.*' But his citizens hated him and sent a delegation after him, saying, 'We do not want this man to reign over us.' When he returned, after receiving the kingdom, he ordered that these slaves, to whom he had given the money, be called to him so that he might know what business they had done. The first appeared, saying, 'Master, your mina has made ten minas more.' And he said to him, 'Well done, good slave, because you have been faithful in a very little thing, you are to be in authority over ten cities.' The second came, saying, 'Your mina, master, has made five minas.' And he said to him, also, 'And you are to be over five cities.' Another came, saying, 'Master, here is your mina, which I kept put away in a handkerchief; for I was afraid of you, because you are an exacting man; you take up what you did not lay down and reap what you did not sow.' He said to him, 'By your own words I will judge you, you worthless slave. Did you know that I am an exacting man, taking up what I did not lay down and reaping what I did not sow? Then why did you not put my money in the bank, and having come, I would have collected it with interest?' Then he said to the bystanders, 'Take the mina away from him and give it to the one who has the ten minas.' And they said to him, 'Master, he has ten minas *already*.' I tell you that to everyone who has, more shall be given, but from the one who does not have, even what he does have shall be taken away. But these enemies of mine, who did not want me to reign over them, bring them here and slay them in my presence" (Luke 19:12–27; cf. Matthew 25:14–30; see Matthew 13:12; Luke 16:10).

INTERESTS, GOD'S

Setting: Near Caesarea Philippi. Jesus responds to Peter for rebuking Him when He prophesies His death and resurrection.

But He turned and said to Peter, "Get behind Me, Satan! You are a stumbling block to Me; for you are not setting your mind on God's interests, but man's" (Matthew 16:23; cf. Mark 8:33).

Setting: Caesarea Philippi. After Peter proclaims that Jesus is the Christ (Messiah), he rebukes Jesus when He prophesies His suffering and death at the hands of the elders, chief priests, and scribes.

But turning around and seeing His disciples, He rebuked Peter and said, "Get behind Me, Satan; for you are not setting your mind on God's interests, but man's" (Mark 8:33; cf. Matthew 16:21–23; Luke 9:22).

INTERESTS, MAN'S

[MAN'S INTERESTS inferred from context]

Setting: Near Caesarea Philippi. Jesus responds to Peter for rebuking Him when He prophesies His death and resurrection.

But He turned and said to Peter, "Get behind Me, Satan! You are a stumbling block to Me; for you are not setting your mind on God's interests, but man's" (Matthew 16:23; cf. Mark 8:33).

[MAN'S INTERESTS inferred from context]

Setting: Caesarea Philippi. After Peter proclaims that Jesus is the Christ (Messiah), he rebukes Jesus when He prophesies His suffering and death at the hands of the elders, chief priests, and scribes.

But turning around and seeing His disciples, He rebuked Peter and said, "Get behind Me, Satan; for you are not setting your mind on God's interests, but man's" (Mark 8:33; cf. Matthew 16:21–23; Luke 9:22).

INTIMACY (See FELLOWSHIP)

INVISIBILITY, GOD'S

[GOD'S INVISIBILITY from You have neither heard His voice at any time nor seen His form]

Setting: Jerusalem. During the Feast of the Jews, Jesus responds to criticism from the Jewish religious leaders by referring to God as His Father (thereby making Himself equal with God) and informing them that God, John the Baptist, and His works all testify to His mission.

"I can do nothing on My own initiative. As I hear, I judge; and My judgment is just, because I do not seek My own will, but the will of Him who sent Me. If I *alone* testify about Myself, My testimony is not true. There is another who testifies of Me, and I know that the testimony which He gives about Me is true. You have sent to John, and he has testified to the truth. But the testimony which I receive is not from man, but I say these things so that you may be saved. He was the lamp that was burning and was shining and you were willing to rejoice for a while in his light. But the testimony which I have is greater than the *testimony of* John; for the works which the Father has given Me to accomplish—the very works that I do—testify about Me, that the Father has sent Me. And the Father who sent Me, He has testified of Me. You have neither heard His voice at any time nor seen His form. You do not have His word abiding in you, for you do not believe Him whom He sent" (John 5:30–38; see Matthew 3:17; Mark 1:4, 5; John 1:7, 15, 32; 4:34; 8:14–16; 10:25, 37, 38).

INVITATION (Also see GUESTS, DINNER)

[INVITATION from invited and invite]

Setting: The temple in Jerusalem. Jesus speaks another parable to the chief priests and elders after they question His authority.

Jesus spoke to them again in parables, saying, "The kingdom of heaven may be compared to a king who gave a wedding feast for his son. And he sent out his slaves to call those who had been invited to the wedding feast, and they were unwilling to come. Again he sent out other slaves saying, 'Tell those who have been invited, "Behold, I have prepared my dinner; my oxen and my fattened livestock are *all* butchered and everything is ready; come to the wedding feast." But they paid no attention and went their way, one to his own farm, another to his business, and the rest seized his slaves and mistreated them and killed them. But the king was enraged, and he sent his armies and destroyed those murderers and set their city on fire. Then he said to his slaves, 'The wedding is ready, but those who were invited were not worthy. 'Go therefore to the main highways, and as many as you find *there,* invite to the wedding feast.' Those slaves went out into the streets and gathered together all they found, both evil and good; and the wedding hall was filled with dinner guests. But when the king came in to look over the dinner guests, he saw a man there who was not dressed in wedding clothes, and he said to him, 'Friend, how did you come in here without wedding clothes?' And the man was speechless. Then the king said to the servants, 'Bind him hand and foot, and throw him into the outer darkness; in that place there will be weeping and gnashing of teeth' For many are called, but few *are* chosen" (Matthew 22:1–14; cf. Matthew 8:11, 12).

[INVITATION from invited and invite]

Setting: The Mount of Olives, just east of Jerusalem. During His discourse, after answering His disciples' questions as to when the temple will be destroyed and Jerusalem overrun, along with the signs of His coming and the end of the age, Jesus reveals the future judgments following His return.

"But when the Son of Man comes in His glory, and all the angels with Him, then He will sit on His glorious throne. All the nations will be gathered before Him; and He will separate them from one another, as the shepherd separates the sheep from the goats; and He will put the sheep on His right, and the goats on the left. Then the King will say to those on His right, 'Come, you who are blessed of My Father, inherit the kingdom prepared for you from the foundation of the world. 'For I was hungry, and you gave Me *something* to eat; I was thirsty, and you gave Me *something* to drink; I was a stranger, and you invited Me in; naked, and you clothed Me; I was sick, and you visited Me; I was in prison, and you came to Me.' Then the righteous will answer Him, 'Lord, when did we see You hungry and feed You, or thirsty, and give you *something* to drink? And when did we see You a stranger, and invite You in, or naked, and clothe You? When did we see You sick, or in prison, and come to You?' The King will answer and say to them, 'Truly I say to you, to the extent that you did it to one of these brothers of Mine, *even* the least *of them,* you did it to Me.' Then He will also say to those on His left, 'Depart from Me, accursed ones, into the eternal fire which has been prepared for the devil and his angels; for I was hungry, and you gave Me *nothing* to eat; I was thirsty, and you gave Me nothing to drink; I was a stranger, and you did not invite Me in; naked, and you did not clothe Me; sick, and in prison, and you did not visit Me.' Then they themselves also will answer, 'Lord, when did we see You hungry, or thirsty, or a stranger, or naked, or sick, or in prison, and did not take care of You?' Then He will answer them, 'Truly I say to you, to the extent that you did not do it to one of the least of these, you did not do it to Me.' These will go away into eternal punishment, but the righteous into eternal life" (Matthew 25:31–46; see Matthew 7:23; 16:27, 19:29).

[INVITATION from invited]

Setting: On the way from Galilee to Jerusalem. As He observes the guests selecting places of honor at the table, Jesus speaks a parable to the guests of a Pharisee leader on the Sabbath.

And He *began* speaking a parable to the invited guests when He noticed how they had been picking out the places of honor *at the table,* saying to them, "When you are invited by someone to a wedding feast, do not take the place of honor, for someone more distinguished than you may have been invited by him, and he who invited you both will come and say to you, 'Give *your* place to this man, and then in disgrace you proceed to occupy the last place. But when you are invited, go and recline at the last place, so that when the one who has invited you comes, he may say to you, 'Friend, move up higher'; then you will have honor in the sight of all who are at the table with you. For everyone who exalts himself will be humbled, and he who humbles himself will be exalted" (Luke 14:7–11; see 2 Samuel 22:28; Proverbs 25:6, 7; Matthew 23:6).

[INVITATION from invite]
Setting: On the way from Galilee to Jerusalem. After Jesus speaks a parable to the guests of a Pharisee leader on the Sabbath, He comments to the host about the people to invite in the future.

And He also went on to say to the one who had invited Him, "When you give a luncheon or a dinner, do not invite your friends or your brothers or your relatives or rich neighbors, otherwise they may also invite you in return and *that* will be your repayment. But when you give a reception, invite *the* poor, *the* crippled, *the* lame, *the* blind, and you will be blessed, since they do not have *the means* to repay you; for you will be repaid at the resurrection of the righteous" (Luke 14:12–14; see John 5:28, 29).

[INVITATION from invited]
Setting: On the way from Galilee to Jerusalem. After Jesus speaks a parable to the invited guests and the host at a banquet, He responds to a guest's proclamation about the blessings of eating bread in the kingdom of God.

But He said to him, "A man was giving a big dinner, and he invited many; and at the dinner hour he sent his slave to say to those who had been invited, 'Come; for everything is ready now.' But they all alike began to make excuses. The first one said to him, 'I have bought a piece of land and I need to go out and look at it; please consider me excused.' Another one said, 'I have bought five yoke of oxen, and I am going to try them out; please consider me excused.' Another one said, I have married a wife, and for that reason I cannot come.' And the slave came *back* and reported this to his master. Then the head of the household became angry and said to his slave, 'Go out at once into the streets and lanes of the city and bring in here the poor and crippled and blind and lame.' And the slave said, 'Master, what you commanded has been done, and still there is room.' And the master said to the slave, 'Go out into the highways and along the hedges, and compel *them* to come in, so that my house may be filled. For I tell you, none of those men who were invited shall taste of my dinner'" (Luke 14:16–24; see Deuteronomy 24:5; Matthew 22:2–14).

IRON
Setting: On the island of Patmos (in the Aegean Sea about fifty miles southwest of Ephesus in modern Turkey). On the Lord's Day (Sunday), about fifty years after Jesus' resurrection, the disciple John encounters the Lord Jesus Christ, who communicates a new revelation for the apostle to record for the church in Thyatira and to six other churches in Asia.

"And to the angel of the church in Thyatira write: The Son of God, who has eyes like a flame of fire, and His feet are like burnished bronze, says this: 'I know your deeds, and your love and faith and service and perseverance, and that your deeds of late are greater than at first. But I have *this* against you, that you tolerate the woman Jezebel, who calls herself a prophetess, and she teaches and leads My bond-servants astray so that they commit *acts of* immorality and eat things sacrificed to idols. I gave her time to repent, and she does not want to repent of her immorality. Behold, I will throw her on a bed *of sickness,* and those who commit adultery with her into great tribulation, unless they repent of her deeds. And I will kill her children with pestilence, and all the churches will know that I am He who searches the minds and hearts; and I will give to each one of you according to your deeds. But I say to you, the rest who are in Thyatira, who do not hold this teaching, who have not known the deep things of Satan, as they call them—I place no other burden on you. Nevertheless what you have, hold fast until I come. He who overcomes, and he who keeps My deeds until the end, TO HIM I WILL GIVE AUTHORITY OVER THE NATIONS; AND HE SHALL RULE THEM WITH A ROD OF IRON, AS THE VESSELS OF THE POTTER ARE BROKEN TO PIECES, as I also have received *authority* from My Father; and I will give him the morning star. He who has an ear, let him hear what the Spirit says to the churches' (Revelation 2:18–29; Jesus quotes from Psalm 2:8, 9; Isaiah 30:14; see 1 Kings 16:31; Psalm 7:9; Romans 2:5; 1 Corinthians 2:10; 2 Peter 3:9; Revelation 1:14; 2:7; 3:11; 17:1–20).

ISAAC
Setting: Entering Capernaum. After the Lord gives the Sermon on the Mount and cleanses a leper, a Roman centurion implores Him to heal his servant.

Now when Jesus heard *this,* He marveled, and said to those who were following, "Truly I say to you, I have not found such great faith with anyone in Israel. I say to you that many will come from east and west, and recline *at the table* with Abraham, Isaac and Jacob in the kingdom of heaven; but the sons of the kingdom will be cast out into the outer darkness; in that place there will be weeping and gnashing of teeth." And Jesus said to the centurion, "Go; it shall be done for you as you have believed." And the servant was healed that *very* moment (Matthew 8:10–13; cf. Luke 7:9, 10).

Setting: The temple in Jerusalem. The Sadducees question Jesus about Levirate marriage (marriage to a brother-in-law) in order to test Him as He teaches.

But Jesus answered and said to them, "You are mistaken, not understanding the Scriptures nor the power of God. For in the resurrection they neither marry nor are given in marriage, but are like angels in heaven. But regarding the resurrection of the dead, have you not read what was spoken to you by God: 'I AM THE GOD OF ABRAHAM, AND THE GOD OF ISAAC, AND THE GOD OF JACOB'? He is not the God of the dead but of the living" (Matthew 22:29–32, Jesus quotes from Exodus 3:6; cf. Mark 12:18–27; Luke 20:27–38; see Deuteronomy 25:5; John 20:9).

Setting: The temple in Jerusalem. After some of the Pharisees and Herodians attempt to trap Jesus in a statement, some Sadducees question Him about the status of marriage after death.

Jesus said to them, "Is this not the reason you are mistaken, that you do not understand the Scriptures or the power of God? For when they rise from the dead, they neither marry nor are given in marriage, but are like angels in heaven. But regarding the fact that the dead rise again, have you not read in the book of Moses, in the *passage* about *the burning* bush, how God spoke to him, saying, 'I AM THE GOD OF ABRAHAM, AND THE GOD OF ISAAC, and the God of Jacob'? He is not the God of the dead, but of the living; you are greatly mistaken" (Mark 12:24–27, Jesus quotes from Exodus 3:6; cf. Matthew 22:29–33; Luke 20:34–40).

Setting: On the way from Galilee to Jerusalem. While teaching in the cities and villages, Jesus responds to a question about who is saved.

And someone said to Him, "Lord, are here *just* a few who are being saved?" And He said to them, "Strive to enter through the narrow door; for many, I tell you, will seek to enter and will not be able. Once the head of the house gets up and shuts the door, and you begin to stand outside and knock on the door, saying, 'Lord, open up to us!' then He will answer and say to you, 'I do not know where you are from.' Then you will begin to say, 'We ate and drank in Your presence, and You taught in our streets'; and He will say, 'I tell you, I do not know where you are from; DEPART FROM ME, ALL YOU EVILDOERS.' In that place there will be weeping and gnashing of teeth when you see Abraham and Isaac and Jacob and all the prophets in the kingdom of God, but you yourselves being thrown out. And they will come from east and west and from north and south, and will recline *at the table* in the kingdom of God. And behold, *some* are last who will be first and *some* are first who will be last" (Luke 13:23–30, Jesus quotes from Psalm 6:8; cf. Matthew 7:13, 23; 8:11, 12; see Matthew 19:30; Luke 3:8).

Setting: The temple in Jerusalem. A few days before His crucifixion, after the scribes and Pharisees seek to trap Jesus by questioning Him about paying taxes to Caesar, some Sadducees (who say there is no resurrection) ask Him a question about the resurrection.

Jesus said to them, "The sons of this age marry and are given in marriage, but those who are considered worthy to attain to that age and the resurrection from the dead, neither marry nor are given in marriage; for they cannot even die anymore, because they are like angels, and are sons of God, being sons of the resurrection. But that the dead are raised, even Moses showed, in the *passage about the burning* bush, where he calls the Lord THE GOD OF ABRAHAM, AND THE GOD OF ISAAC, AND THE GOD OF JACOB. Now He is not the God of the dead but of the living; for all live to Him" (Luke 20:34–38, Jesus quotes from Exodus 3:6; cf. Matthew 22:23–32; Mark 12:18–27).

ISAIAH (Old Testament Prophet; also see PROPHET; and PROPHETS)

Setting: By the Sea of Galilee. Jesus responds to His disciples' questions about the Parable of the Sower, which He has just taught from a boat.

Jesus answered them, "To you it has been granted to know the mysteries of the kingdom of heaven, but to them it has not been granted. For whoever has, to him *more* shall be given, and he will have an abundance; but whoever does not have, even what he has shall be taken away from him. Therefore, I speak to them in parables; because while seeing they do not see, and while hearing they do not hear, nor do they understand. In their case the prophecy of Isaiah is being fulfilled, which says, 'YOU WILL KEEP ON HEARING, BUT WILL NOT UNDERSTAND; YOU WILL KEEP ON SEEING, BUT WILL NOT PERCEIVE; FOR THE HEART OF THIS PEOPLE HAS BECOME DULL, WITH THEIR EARS THEY SCARCELY HEAR, AND THEY HAVE CLOSED THEIR EYES, OTHERWISE THEYWOULD SEE WITH THEIR EYES, HEAR WITH THEIR EARS, AND UNDERSTAND WITH THEIR HEART AND RETURN, AND I WOULD HEAL THEM.' But blessed are your eyes, because they see; and your ears, because they hear. For truly I say to you that many prophets and righteous men desired to see what you see, and did not see *it*, and to hear what you hear, and did not hear *it*" (Matthew 13:11–17, Jesus quotes from Isaiah 6:9, 10; cf. Matthew 25:29; Mark 4:11–13; Luke 8:10; see Deuteronomy 29:4; John 8:56).

Setting: Galilee. Pharisees and scribes from Jerusalem question Jesus about His disciples' lack of obedience to tradition and the commandments.

And He answered and said to them, "Why do you yourselves transgress the commandment of God for the sake of tradition? For God said, 'HONOR YOUR FATHER AND MOTHER,' and, 'HE WHO SPEAKS EVIL OF FATHER OR MOTHER IS TO BE PUT TO DEATH.' But you say, 'Whoever says to *his* father or mother, "Whatever I have that would help you has been given *to God*," he is not to honor his father or mother.' And *by this* you invalidated the word of God for the sake of your tradition. You hypocrites, rightly did Isaiah prophesy of you: 'THIS PEOPLE HONORS ME WITH THEIR LIPS, BUT THEIR HEART IS FAR AWAY FROM ME. BUT IN VAIN DO THEY WORSHIP ME, TEACHING AS DOCTRINES THE PRECEPTS OF MEN'" (Matthew 15:3–9, Jesus quotes from Exodus 20:12, 21:17, Leviticus 20:9; Isaiah 29:13; cf. Mark 7:5–7; see Colossians 2:22).

Setting: Galilee. The Pharisees and some of the scribes from Jerusalem ask Jesus why His disciples do not follow the tradition of ceremonial hand cleansing before eating bread.

And He said to them, "Rightly did Isaiah prophesy of you hypocrites, as it is written: 'THIS PEOPLE HONORS ME WITH THEIR LIPS, BUT THEIR HEART IS FAR AWAY FROM ME. BUT IN VAIN DO THEY WORSHIP ME, TEACHING AS DOCTRINES THE PRECEPTS OF MEN.' Neglecting the commandment of God, you hold to the tradition of men." He was also saying to them, "You are experts at setting aside the commandment of God in order to keep tradition. For Moses said, 'HONOR YOUR FATHER AND YOUR MOTHER'; and, 'HE WHO SPEAKS EVIL OF FATHER OR MOTHER, IS TO BE PUT TO DEATH'; but you say, 'If a man says to *his* father or *his* mother, whatever I have that would help you is Corban (that is to say, given *to God*),' you no longer permit him to do anything for *his* father or *his* mother; *thus* invalidating the word of God by your tradition which you have handed down; and you do many things such as that" (Mark 7:6–13, Jesus quotes from Exodus 20:12; 21:17; Isaiah 29:13; cf. Matthew 15:1–6).

ISRAEL (ISRAEL, CITIES OF; ISRAEL, HOUSE OF; ISRAEL, SONS OF; ISRAEL, TEACHER OF; and ISRAEL, TWELVE TRIBES OF are separate entries)

Setting: Entering Capernaum. After the Lord Jesus gives the Sermon on the Mount and cleanses a leper, a Roman centurion implores Him to heal his servant.

Now when Jesus heard *this,* He marveled, and said to those who were following, "Truly I say to you, I have not found such great faith with anyone in Israel. I say to you that many will come from east and west, and recline *at the table* with Abraham, Isaac and Jacob in the kingdom of heaven; but the sons of the kingdom will be cast out into the outer darkness; in that place there will be weeping and gnashing of teeth." And Jesus said to the centurion, "Go; it shall be done for you as you have believed." And the servant was healed that *very* moment (Matthew 8:10–13; cf. Luke 7:9, 10).

Setting: The temple in Jerusalem. With the Pharisees and Herodians failing to trap Jesus in a statement, one of the scribes asks Him which commandment is foremost.

Jesus answered, "The foremost is, 'HEAR, O ISRAEL! THE LORD OUR GOD IS ONE LORD; AND YOU SHALL LOVE THE LORD YOUR GOD WITH ALL YOUR HEART, AND WITH ALL YOUR SOUL, AND WITH ALL YOUR MIND AND WITH ALL YOUR STRENGTH.' The second is this, 'YOU

SHALL LOVE YOUR NEIGHBOR AS YOURSELF.' There is no other commandment greater than these" (Mark 12:29–31, Jesus quotes from Deuteronomy 6:4, 5; Leviticus 19:18; cf. Matthew 22:34–40).

Setting: The synagogue in Jesus' hometown of Nazareth in Galilee. At the beginning of His public ministry, Jesus comments to the congregation after reading on the Sabbath from the book of the prophet Isaiah.

And He said to them, "No doubt you will quote this proverb to Me, 'Physician, heal yourself! Whatever we heard was done at Capernaum, do here in your hometown as well.'" And He said, "Truly I say to you, no prophet is welcome in his hometown. But I say to you in truth, there were many widows in Israel in the days of Elijah, when the sky was shut up for three years and six months, when a great famine came over all the land; and yet Elijah was sent to none of them, but only to Zarephath, *in the land* of Sidon, to a woman who was a widow. And there were many lepers in Israel in the time of Elisha the prophet; and none of them was cleansed, but only Naaman the Syrian" (Luke 4:23–27; Jesus refers to 1 Kings 17:1, 9; 2 Kings 5:1–14; see Matthew 13:53–58).

Setting: Capernaum in Galilee. After Jesus completes His Sermon on the Mount, a Roman centurion asks Him to heal his gravely ill slave.

Now when Jesus heard this, He marveled at him, and turned and said to the crowd that was following Him, "I say to you, not even in Israel have I found such great faith" (Luke 7:9; cf. Matthew 8:1–10).

ISRAEL, CITIES, TOWNS, AND VILLAGES OF (Also see ISRAEL, CITIES OF) Jesus does not make reference to every city, town, or village in Israel and the surrounding areas. The New Testament text contains locations not indexed in this book. The following are listed by name:

BETHSAIDA
CAPERNAUM
CHORAZIN
JERICHO
JERUSALEM
NAZARETH
SIDON
TYRE

ISRAEL, CITIES OF (Also see individual cities such as JERUSALEM)
Setting: Galilee. After His disciples observe His ministry, Jesus summons and specifically instructs them about the upcoming difficulties of their ministry to the people of Israel.

"Brother will betray brother to death, and a father *his* child; and children will rise up against parents and cause them to be put to death. You will be hated by all because of My name, but it is the one who has endured to the end who will be saved. But whenever they persecute you in one city, flee to the next; for truly I say to you, you will not finish *going through* the cities of Israel until the Son of Man comes" (Matthew 10:21–23; cf. Matthew 10:35, 36; 16:27, 28; 24:9).

ISRAEL, HOUSE OF
Setting: Galilee. After His twelve disciples observe His ministry, Jesus summons and specifically instructs them about their ministry to the people of Israel.

These twelve Jesus sent out after instructing them: "Do not go in *the* way of *the* Gentiles, and do not enter *any* city of the Samaritans; but rather go to the lost sheep of the house of Israel. And as you go, preach, saying, 'The kingdom of heaven is at hand.' Heal *the* sick, raise *the* dead, cleanse *the* lepers, cast out demons. Freely you received, freely give. Do not acquire gold, or silver, or copper for your money belts, or a bag for *your* journey, or even two coats, or sandals, or a staff; for the worker is worthy of his support. And whatever city or village you enter, inquire who is worthy in it, and stay at his house until you leave *that city*.

As you enter the house, give it your greeting. If the house is worthy, give it your *blessing of* peace. But if it is not worthy, take back your *blessing of* peace. Whoever does not receive you, nor heed your words, as you go out of that house or that city, shake the dust off your feet. Truly I say to you, it will be more tolerable for *the* land of Sodom and Gomorrah in the day of judgment than for that city" (Matthew 10:5–15; cf. Mark 6:7–11; Luke 9:1–5; see Matthew 3:2; 10:1–4; 11:22, 24; 15:24; Luke 22:35; 1 Corinthians 9:14).

Setting: The district of Tyre and Sidon. A Canaanite woman appeals to Jesus to heal her demon-possessed daughter.

But He answered and said, "I was sent only to the lost sheep of the house of Israel." But she came and *began* to bow down before Him, saying, "Lord, help me!" And He answered and said, "It is not good to take the children's bread and throw it to the dogs." But she said, "Yes, Lord; but even the dogs feed from the crumbs which fall from their masters' table." Then Jesus said to her, "O woman, your faith is great; it shall be done for you as you wish." And her daughter was healed at once (Matthew 15:24–28; cf. Mark 7: 24–30; see Matthew 9:22; 10:5, 6).

ISRAEL, JUDGMENT OF (Also see TRIBULATION)

[JUDGMENT OF ISRAEL from you also shall sit upon twelve thrones, judging the twelve tribes of Israel]
Setting: Judea beyond the Jordan (Perea). Jesus promises rewards to His disciples for their personal sacrifice and commitment to following Him.

And Jesus said to them, "Truly I say to you, that you who have followed Me, in the regeneration when the Son of Man will sit on His glorious throne, you also shall sit upon twelve thrones, judging the twelve tribes of Israel. And everyone who has left houses or brothers or sisters or father or mother or children or farms for My name's sake, will receive many times as much, and will inherit eternal life. But many *who* are first will be last; and *the* last, first" (Matthew 19:28–30; cf. Matthew 6:33; 20:15; Mark 10:29, 30; Luke 18:29, 30; 22:30).

[JUDGMENT OF ISRAEL from you will sit on thrones judging the twelve tribes of Israel]
Setting: An upper room in Jerusalem. During the Feast of Unleavened Bread (Passover), Jesus celebrates the Passover meal and institutes the Lord's Supper. After His disciples argue over who is the greatest among them, He details the kingdom benefits they will experience.

"You are those who have stood by Me in My trials; for just as My Father has granted Me a kingdom, I grant you that you may eat and drink at My table in My kingdom, and you will sit on thrones judging the twelve tribes of Israel" (Luke 22:28–30; cf. Matthew 19:28).

[JUDGMENT OF ISRAEL from Then they will begin TO SAY TO THE MOUNTAINS, 'FALL ON US,' AND TO THE HILLS, 'COVER US]
Setting: Jerusalem. After being arrested and appearing before the Council of Elders (Sanhedrin), Pontius Pilate (Roman governor of Judea), Herod Antipas (tetrarch of Galilee and Perea), and Pilate a second time (when Pilate bows to the crowd's pressure and grants that Jesus be crucified), the Lord prophesies to the women mourning Him regarding the coming judgment of Jerusalem.

But Jesus turning to them said, "Daughters of Jerusalem, stop weeping for Me, but weep for yourselves and for your children. For behold, the days are coming when they will say, 'Blessed are the barren, and the wombs that never bore, and the breasts that never nursed.' Then they will begin TO SAY TO THE MOUNTAINS, 'FALL ON US,' AND TO THE HILLS, 'COVER US.' For it they do these things when the tree is green, what will happen when it is dry?" (Luke 23:28–31, Jesus quotes from Hosea 10:8; see Matthew 24:19).

ISRAEL, SONS OF

Setting: Damascus. Luke, writing in Acts, describes the reluctance of Ananias, one of Jesus' followers, to locate Saul of Tarsus (a known enemy of the church) in order to restore his vision.

But the Lord said to him, "Go, for he is a chosen instrument of Mine, to bear My name before the Gentiles and kings and the sons of Israel; for I will show him how much he must suffer for My name's sake" (Acts 9:15, 16; see Acts 13:2; 20:22–24).

Setting: On the island of Patmos (in the Aegean Sea about fifty miles southwest of Ephesus in modern Turkey). On the Lord's Day (Sunday), about fifty years after Jesus' resurrection, the disciple John encounters the Lord Jesus Christ, who communicates a new revelation for the apostle to record for the church in Pergamum and to six other churches in Asia.

"And to the angel of the church in Pergamum write: The One who has the sharp two-edged sword says this: 'I know where you dwell, where Satan's throne is; and you hold fast My name, and did not deny My faith even in the days of Antipas, My witness, My faithful one, who was killed among you, where Satan dwells. But I have a few things against you, because you have there some who hold the teaching of Balaam, who kept teaching Balak to put a stumbling block before the sons of Israel, to eat things sacrificed to idols and to commit *acts of* immorality. So you also have some who in the same way hold the teaching of the Nicolaitans. Therefore repent; or else I am coming to you quickly, and I will make war against them with the sword of My mouth. He who has an ear, let him hear what the Spirit says to the churches. To him who overcomes, to him I will give *some* of the hidden manna, and I will give him a white stone, and a new name written on the stone which no one knows but he who receives it' (Revelation 2:12–17; see Numbers 25:1–3; Isaiah 62:2; Revelation 1:16; 2:5, 6, 16).

ISRAEL, TEACHER OF

Setting: Jerusalem. At the time for the Passover of the Jews, after the Lord cleanses the temple, a Pharisee, Nicodemus, asks Him by night the meaning of "born of the Spirit."

Jesus answered and said to him, "Are you the teacher of Israel and do not understand these things? Truly, truly, I say to you, we speak of what we know and testify of what we have seen, and you do not accept our testimony. If I told you earthly things and you do not believe, how will you believe if I tell you heavenly things? No one has ascended into heaven, but He who descended from heaven: the Son of Man. As Moses lifted up the serpent in the wilderness, even so must the Son of Man be lifted up; so that whoever believes will in Him have eternal life" (John 3:10–15; see Numbers 21:9; Proverb 30:4; John 12:34; 20:30, 31).

ISRAEL, TRIBES OF (See ISRAEL, TWELVE TRIBES OF)

ISRAEL, TWELVE TRIBES OF

Setting: Judea beyond the Jordan (Perea). Jesus promises rewards to His disciples for their personal sacrifice and commitment to following Him.

And Jesus said to them, "Truly I say to you, that you who have followed Me, in the regeneration when the Son of Man will sit on His glorious throne, you also shall sit upon twelve thrones, judging the twelve tribes of Israel. And everyone who has left houses or brothers or sisters or father or mother or children or farms for My name's sake, will receive many times as much, and will inherit eternal life. But many *who* are first will be last; and *the* last, first" (Matthew 19:28–30; cf. Matthew 6:33; 20:15; Mark 10:29, 30; Luke 18:29, 30; 22:30)

Setting: An upper room in Jerusalem. During the Feast of Unleavened Bread (Passover), Jesus celebrates the Passover meal and institutes the Lord's Supper. His disciples argue over who is the greatest among them, and the Lord details the kingdom benefits they will experience.

"You are those who have stood by Me in My trials; for just as My Father has granted Me a kingdom, I grant you that you may eat and drink at My table in My kingdom, and you will sit on thrones judging the twelve tribes of Israel" (Luke 22:28–30; cf. Matthew 19:28).

ISRAELITE

Setting: Galilee. After beginning His public ministry and choosing His first disciples, Andrew and Simon (Peter) near Bethany beyond the Jordan, and Philip in Galilee, Jesus calls Philip's friend, Nathanael, (some believe he may have been also called Bartholomew) as His next follower.

Jesus saw Nathanael coming to Him, and said of him, "Behold, an Israelite indeed, in whom there is no deceit!" Nathanael said to Him, "How do you know me?" Jesus answered and said to him, "Before Philip called you, when you were under the fig tree, I saw you." Nathanael answered Him, "Rabbi, You are the Son of God; You are the King of Israel." Jesus answered and said to him, "Because I said to you that I saw you under the fig tree, do you believe? You will see greater things than these." And He said to him, "Truly, truly, I say to you, you will see the heavens opened and the angels of God ascending and descending on the Son of Man" (John 1:47–51).

ITSELF

Setting: Galilee. During the early part of His ministry, Jesus preaches the Sermon on the Mount to His disciples and the multitudes.

"For this reason I say to you, do not be worried about your life, *as to* what you will eat or what you will drink; nor for your body, *as to* what you will put on. Is not life more than food, and the body more than clothing? Look at the birds of the air, that they do not sow, nor reap nor gather into barns, and *yet* your heavenly Father feeds them. Are you not worth much more than they? And who of you by being worried can add a *single* hour to his life? And why are you worried about clothing? Observe how the lilies of the field grow; they do not toil nor do they spin, yet I say to you that not even Solomon in all his glory clothed himself like one of these. But if God so clothes the grass of the field, which is *alive* today and tomorrow is thrown into the furnace, *will He* not much more *clothe* you? You of little faith! Do not worry then, saying 'What will we eat?' or 'What will we drink?' or 'What will be wear for clothing?" For the Gentiles eagerly seek all these things; for your heavenly Father knows that you need all these things. But seek first His kingdom and His righteousness, and all these things will be added to you. So do not worry about tomorrow; for tomorrow will care for itself. Each day has enough trouble of its own" (Matthew 6:25–34; cf. Luke 12:22–31; see 1 Kings 10:4–7; Job 35:11; Matthew 8:26).

Setting: Galilee. After He heals a blind, mute, demon-possessed man, the Pharisees accuse Jesus in front of crowds of being a worker of Beelzebul (Satan).

And knowing their thoughts Jesus said to them, "Any kingdom divided against itself is laid waste; and any city or house divided against itself will not stand. If Satan casts out Satan, he is divided against himself; how then will his kingdom stand? If I by Beelzebul cast out demons, by whom do your sons cast *them* out? For this reason they will be your judges. But if I cast out demons by the Spirit of God, then the kingdom of God has come upon you. Or how can anyone enter the strong man's house and carry off his property, unless he first binds the strong *man?* And then he will plunder his house" (Matthew 12:25–29; cf. Matthew 9:34; Mark 3:23–27, Luke 11:17–20).

Setting: Galilee. Jesus responds to some Pharisees and scribes who ask Him for a miraculous sign.

"Now when the unclean spirit goes out of a man, it passes through waterless places seeking rest, and does not find *it.* Then it says, 'I will return to my house from which I came'; and when it comes, it finds *it* unoccupied, swept, and put in order. Then it goes and takes along with it seven other spirits more wicked than itself, and they go in and live there; and the last state of that man becomes worse than the first. That is the way it will also be for this evil generation" (Matthew 12:43–45; cf. Luke 11:24–26; see Matthew 12:38; Mark 5:9).

Setting: Galilee. After Jesus selects His twelve disciples, scribes from Jerusalem attribute His miraculous powers to Satan.

And He called them to Himself and began speaking to them in parables, "How can Satan cast out Satan? If a kingdom is divided against itself, that kingdom cannot stand. If a house is divided against itself, that house will not be able to stand. If Satan has risen up against himself and is divided, he cannot stand, but he is finished! But no one can enter the strong man's house and plunder his property unless he first binds the strong man, and then he will plunder his house. Truly I say to you, all sins shall be forgiven the sons of men, and whatever blasphemies they utter; but whoever blasphemes against the Holy Spirit never has forgiveness, but is guilty of an eternal sin"—because they were saying, "He has an unclean spirit" (Mark 3:23–30; cf. Matthew 12:25–32; Luke 12:10).

Setting: Galilee. Following His explanation of the Parable of the Sower to His disciples, Jesus conveys the Parable of the Seed.

And He was saying, "The kingdom of God is like a man who casts seed upon the soil; and he goes to bed at night and gets up by day, and the seed sprouts and grows—how, he himself does not know. The soil produces crops by itself; first the blade, then the head, then the mature grain in the head. But when the crop permits, he immediately puts in the sickle, because the harvest has come" (Mark 4:26–29; see Joel 3:13).

Setting: On the way from Galilee to Jerusalem. After Jesus casts out a demon, some in the crowd test Him, demanding a sign from heaven.

But He knew their thoughts and said to them, "Any kingdom divided against itself is laid waste; and a house *divided* against itself falls. If Satan also is divided against himself, how will his kingdom stand? For you say that I cast out demons by Beelzebul. And if I by Beelzebul cast out demons, by whom do your sons cast them out? So they will be your judges. But if I cast out demons by the finger of God, then the kingdom of God has come upon you" (Luke 11:17–20; cf. Matthew 12:25–28; Mark 3:23–27; see Exodus 8:19; Matthew 3:2, 10:25).

Setting: On the way from Galilee to Jerusalem. After some in the crowd test Him, demanding a sign from heaven, Jesus illustrates His power over Satan.

"When the unclean spirit goes out of a man, it passes through waterless places seeking rest, and not finding any, it says, 'I will return to my house from which I came.' And when it comes, it finds it swept clean and put in order. Then it goes and takes *along* seven other spirits more evil than itself, and they go in and live there; and the last state of that man becomes worse than the first" (Luke 11:24–26; cf. Matthew 12:43–45; see Luke 11:14–16).

Setting: Jerusalem. Before the Passover, after He conveys the upcoming ministry of the Holy Spirit in His disciples' lives with His imminent departure from them, Jesus explains He is the vine and His disciples are the branches.

"I am the true vine, and My Father is the vinedresser. Every branch in Me that does not bear fruit, He takes away; and every *branch* that bears fruit, He prunes it so that it may bear more fruit. You are already clean because of the word which I have spoken to you. Abide in Me, and I in you. As the branch cannot bear fruit of itself unless it abides in the vine, so neither *can* you unless you abide in Me. I am the vine, you are the branches; he who abides in Me and I in him, he bears much fruit, for apart from Me you can do nothing. If anyone does not abide in Me, he is thrown away as a branch and dries up; and they gather them, and cast them into the fire and they are burned. If you abide in Me, and My words abide in you, ask whatever you wish, and it will be done for you. My Father is glorified by this, that you bear much fruit, and *so* prove to be My disciples. Just as the Father has loved Me, I have also loved you; abide in My love. If you keep My commandments, you will abide in My love; just as I have kept My Father's commandments and abide in His love. These things I have spoken to you so that My joy may be in you, and *that* your joy may be made full" (John 15:1–11; see Matthew 5:16; 7:7; John 3:29, 35; 6:56; 8:29, 31; 13:10; 15:16).

J

JACOB

Setting: Entering Capernaum. After the Lord gives the Sermon on the Mount and cleanse a leper, a Roman centurion implores Jesus to heal his servant.

Now when Jesus heard *this,* He marveled, and said to those who were following, "Truly I say to you, I have not found such great faith with anyone in Israel. I say to you that many will come from east and west, and recline *at the table* with Abraham, Isaac and Jacob in the kingdom of heaven; but the sons of the kingdom will be cast out into the outer darkness; in that place there will be weeping and gnashing of teeth." And Jesus said to the centurion, "Go; it shall be done for you as you have believed." And the servant was healed that *very* moment (Matthew 8:10–13; cf. Luke 7:9, 10).

Setting: The temple in Jerusalem. The Sadducees question Jesus about Levirate marriage (marriage to a brother-in-law) in order to test Him as He teaches.

But Jesus answered and said to them, "You are mistaken, not understanding the Scriptures nor the power of God. For in the resurrection they neither marry nor are given in marriage, but are like angels in heaven. But regarding the resurrection of the dead, have you not read what was spoken to you by God: 'I AM THE GOD OF ABRAHAM, AND THE GOD OF ISAAC, AND THE GOD OF JACOB'? He is not the God of the dead but of the living" (Matthew 22:29–32, Jesus quotes from Exodus 3:6; cf. Mark 12:18–27; Luke 20:27–38; see Deuteronomy 25:5; John 20:9).

Setting: The temple in Jerusalem. After some of the Pharisees and Herodians attempt to trap Jesus in a statement, some Sadducees question Him about the status of marriage after death.

Jesus said to them, "Is this not the reason you are mistaken, that you do not understand the Scriptures or the power of God? For when they rise from the dead, they neither marry nor are given in marriage, but are like angels in heaven. But regarding the fact that the dead rise again, have you not read in the book of Moses, in the *passage* about *the burning* bush, how God spoke to him, saying, 'I AM THE GOD OF ABRAHAM, AND THE GOD OF ISAAC, and the God of Jacob?' He is not the God of the dead, but of the living; you are greatly mistaken" (Mark 12:24–27, Jesus quotes from Exodus 3:6; cf. Matthew 22:29–33; Luke 20:34–40).

Setting: On the way from Galilee to Jerusalem. While teaching in the cities and villages, Jesus responds to a question about who is saved.

And someone said to Him, "Lord, are here *just* a few who are being saved?" And He said to them, "Strive to enter through the narrow door; for many, I tell you, will seek to enter and will not be able. Once the head of the house gets up and shuts the door, and you begin to stand outside and knock on the door, saying, 'Lord, open up to us!' then He will answer and say to you, 'I do not know where you are from.' Then you will begin to say, 'We ate and drank in Your presence, and You taught in our streets'; and He will say, 'I tell you, I do not know where you are from; DEPART FROM ME, ALL YOU EVILDOERS.' In that place there will be weeping and gnashing of teeth when you see Abraham and Isaac and Jacob and all the prophets in the kingdom of God, but you yourselves being thrown out. And they will come from east and west and from north and south, and will recline *at the table* in the kingdom of God. And behold, *some* are last who will be first and *some* are first who will be last" (Luke 13:23–30, Jesus quotes from Psalm 6:8; cf. Matthew 7:13, 23; 8:11, 12; see Matthew 19:30; Luke 3:8).

Setting: The temple in Jerusalem. A few days before His crucifixion, after the scribes and Pharisees seek to trap Jesus by questioning Him about paying taxes to Caesar, some Sadducees (who say there is no resurrection) ask Him a question about the resurrection.

Jesus said to them, "The sons of this age marry and are given in marriage, but those who are considered worthy to attain to that age and the resurrection from the dead, neither marry nor are given in marriage; for they cannot even die anymore, because they are like angels, and are sons of God, being sons of the resurrection. But that the dead are raised, even Moses showed, in the *passage about the burning* bush, where he calls the Lord THE GOD OF ABRAHAM, AND THE GOD OF ISAAC, AND THE GOD OF JACOB. Now He is not the God of the dead but of the living; for all live to Him" (Luke 20:34–38, Jesus quotes from Exodus 3:6; cf. Matthew 22:23–32; Mark 12:18–27).

JEALOUSY (See other emotions, such as ANGER; ENVY; HATE; and HATRED)

JERICHO

Setting: On the way from Galilee to Jerusalem. While being tested by a lawyer, Jesus tells him the story of the good Samaritan.

Jesus replied and said, "A man was going down from Jerusalem to Jericho, and fell among robbers, and they stripped him and beat him, and went away leaving him half dead. And by chance a priest was going down on that road, and when he saw him, he passed by on the other side. Likewise a Levite also, when he came to the place and saw him, passed by on the other side. But a Samaritan, who was on a journey, came upon him; and when he saw him, he felt compassion, and came to him and bandaged up his wounds, pouring oil and wine on *them;* and he put him on his own beast, and brought him to an inn and took care of him. On the next day he took out two denarii and gave them to the innkeeper and said, 'Take care of him; and whatever more you spend, when I return I will repay you.' Which of these three do you think proved to be a neighbor to the man who fell into the robbers' *hands?*" And he said, "The one who showed mercy toward him." Then Jesus said to him, "Go and do the same" (Luke 10:30–37).

JERUSALEM (JERUSALEM, DAUGHTERS OF; and JERUSALEM, NEW are separate entries; also see PROPHECY OF THE DESTRUCTION OF JERUSALEM)

Setting: Galilee. During the early part of His ministry, Jesus preaches the Sermon on the Mount to His disciples and the multitudes.

"Again, you have heard that the ancients were told, 'YOU SHALL NOT MAKE FALSE VOWS, BUT SHALL FULFILL YOUR VOWS TO THE LORD.' But I say to you, make no oath at all, either by heaven, for it is the throne of God, or by the earth, for it is the footstool of His feet, or by Jerusalem, for it is THE CITY OF THE GREAT KING. Nor shall you make an oath by your head, for you cannot make one hair white or black. But let your statement be 'Yes, yes' *or* 'No, no'; anything beyond these is of evil" (Matthew 5:33–37, Jesus quotes from Leviticus 19:12, Psalm 48:2; Isaiah 66:1; cf. James 5:12).

Setting: Judea beyond the Jordan (Perea). Before going to Jerusalem, Jesus again tells His disciples of His impending death and resurrection.

As Jesus was about to go up to Jerusalem, He took the twelve *disciples* aside by themselves, and on the way He said to them, "Behold, we are going up to Jerusalem; and the Son of Man will be delivered to the chief priests and scribes, and they will condemn Him to death, and will hand Him over to the Gentiles to mock and scourge and crucify *Him,* and on the third day, He will be raised up" (Matthew 20:17–19; cf. Matthew 16:21; Mark 10:32–34; Luke 18:31–33).

Setting: The temple in Jerusalem. With His death on the cross just days away, Jesus laments over the city's hard-heartedness and lack of repentance.

"Jerusalem, Jerusalem, who kills the prophets and stones those who are sent to her! How often I wanted to gather your children together, the way a hen gathers her chicks under her wings, and you were unwilling. Behold, your house is being left to you desolate! For I say to you, from now on you will not see Me until you say, 'BLESSED IS HE WHO COMES IN THE NAME OF THE LORD!'" (Matthew 23:37–39, Jesus quotes from Psalm 118:26; cf. 1 Kings 9:7; Luke 13:34, 35)

[JERUSALEM from city]

Setting: Just outside Jerusalem. On the first day of the Feast of the Unleavened Bread, just after Judas makes arrangements to betray Him to the chief priests, Jesus informs His disciples where they will celebrate the Passover.

And He said, "Go into the city to a certain man, and say to him, 'The Teacher says, "My time is near; I *am to* keep the Passover at your house with My disciples"'" (Matthew 26:18; cf. Mark 14:13–15; Luke 22:7–13).

Setting: On the road to Jerusalem. After encouraging His disciples with a revelation of their future reward, Jesus prophesies His persecution, death, and resurrection.

They were on the road going up to Jerusalem, and Jesus was walking on ahead of them; and they were amazed, and those who followed were fearful. And again He took the twelve aside and began to tell them what was going to happen to Him, *saying*, "Behold, we are going up to Jerusalem, and the Son of Man will be delivered to the chief priests and the scribes; and they will condemn Him to death and will hand Him over to the Gentiles. They will mock Him and spit on Him, and scourge Him and kill *Him*, and three days later He will rise again" (Mark 10:32–34; cf. Matthew 20:17–19; Luke 18:31–34; see Matthew 16:21; Mark 8:31).

[JERUSALEM from city]

Setting: Just outside Jerusalem. On the first day of the Feast of Unleavened Bread, when the Passover lamb is to be sacrificed, Jesus responds to His disciples' question about His plans for the Passover meal.

And He sent two of His disciples and said to them, "Go into the city, and a man will meet you carrying a pitcher of water; follow him; and wherever he enters, say to the owner of the house, 'The Teacher says, "Where is My guest room in which I may eat the Passover with My disciples?"' And he himself will show you a large upper room furnished *and* ready; prepare for us there" (Mark 14:13–15; cf. Matthew 26:17–19; Luke 22:7–13).

Setting: On the way from Galilee to Jerusalem. While being tested by a lawyer, Jesus tells him the story of the good Samaritan.

Jesus replied and said, "A man was going down from Jerusalem to Jericho, and fell among robbers, and they stripped him and beat him, and went away leaving him half dead. And by chance a priest was going down on that road, and when he saw him, he passed by on the other side. Likewise a Levite also, when he came to the place and saw him, passed by on the other side. But a Samaritan, who was on a journey, came upon him; and when he saw him, he felt compassion, and came to him and bandaged up his wounds, pouring oil and wine on *them;* and he put him on his own beast, and brought him to an inn and took care of him. On the next day he took out two denarii and gave them to the innkeeper and said, 'Take care of him; and whatever more you spend, when I return I will repay you.' Which of these three do you think proved to be a neighbor to the man who fell into the robbers' *hands?*" And he said, "The one who showed mercy toward him." Then Jesus said to him, "Go and do the same" (Luke 10:30–37).

Setting: On the way from Galilee to Jerusalem. After some present report to Him about the Galileans whose blood Pilate (Roman governor of Judea) had mixed with their sacrifices, Jesus responds to their concern by calling them to repentance.

And Jesus said to them, "Do you suppose that these Galileans were *greater* sinners than all *other* Galileans because they suffered this *fate*? I tell you, no, but unless you repent, you will all likewise perish. Or do you suppose that those eighteen on whom the tower in Siloam fell and killed them were *worse* culprits than all the men who live in Jerusalem? I tell you, no, but unless you repent, you will all likewise perish" (Luke 13:2–5; see John 9:2, 3).

Setting: On the way from Galilee to Jerusalem. While teaching in the cities and villages, after Jesus responds to a question about who is saved, some Pharisees ask Him to leave, claiming Herod Antipas (tetrarch of Galilee and Perea) seeks to kill Him.

And He said to them, "Go and tell that fox, 'Behold, I cast out demons and perform cures today and tomorrow, and the third *day* I reach My goal.' Nevertheless I must journey on today and tomorrow and the next *day*; for it cannot be that a prophet would perish outside of Jerusalem. O Jerusalem, Jerusalem, *the city* that kills the prophets and stones those sent to her! How often I wanted to gather your children together, just as a hen *gathers* her brood under her wings, and you would not *have it*! Behold, your house is left to you *desolate*; and I say to you, you will not see Me until *the time* comes when you say, 'BLESSED IS HE WHO COMES IN THE NAME OF THE LORD!'" (Luke 13:32–35, Jesus quotes from Psalm 118:26; cf. Matthew 23:37).

Setting: On the way from Galilee to Jerusalem. After responding to Peter's statement about His disciples' personal sacrifice in following Him, Jesus tells them of the sacrifice He will make in Jerusalem.

Then He took the twelve aside and said to them, "Behold, we are going up to Jerusalem, and all things which are written through the prophets about the Son of Man will be accomplished. For He will be handed over to the Gentiles, and will be mocked and mistreated and spit upon, and after they have scourged Him, they will kill Him; and the third day He will rise again" (Luke 18:31–33; cf. Matthew 20:17–19; Mark 10:32–34).

Setting: On the Mount of Olives, east of the temple in Jerusalem. After ministering in the temple a few days before His crucifixion, and giving the disciples more details regarding future events, Jesus elaborates more during His Olivet Discourse about things to come.

"But when you see Jerusalem surrounded by armies, then recognize that her desolation is near. Then those who are in Judea must flee to the mountains, and those who are in the midst of the city must leave, and those who are in the country must not enter the city; because these are days of vengeance, so that all things which are written will be fulfilled. Woe to those who are pregnant and to those who are nursing babies in those days; for there will be a great distress upon the land and wrath to this people; and they will fall by the edge of the sword, and will be led captive into all the nations; and Jerusalem will be trampled under foot by the Gentiles until the times of the Gentiles are fulfilled" (Luke 21:20–24; see Matthew 24:15–18; Mark 13:14–16; Luke 19:43).

[JERUSALEM from city]

Setting: Just outside Jerusalem. With the Passover (Feast of Unleavened Bread) approaching, Jesus informs His disciples where they will celebrate the feast, as the chief priests and scribes seek to kill Him, and Satan enters Judas Iscariot in order to betray the Lord.

And Jesus sent Peter and John, saying, "Go and prepare the Passover for us, so that we may eat it." They said to Him, "Where do You want us to prepare it?" And He said to them, "When you have entered the city, a man will meet you carrying a pitcher of water; follow him into the house that he enters. And you shall say to the owner of the house, 'The Teacher says to you, "Where is the guest room in which I may eat the Passover with My disciples?"' And he will show you a large, furnished upper room; prepare it there" (Luke 22:8–12; cf. Matthew 26:17–19; Mark 14:12–16).

Setting: Jerusalem. After rising from the grave on the third day following being crucified, and appearing to two of His followers on the road to Emmaus, Jesus gives instruction to His disciples (except Thomas) about His mission on earth and the promise of power from God.

Now He said to them, "These are My words which I spoke to you while I was still with you, that all things which are written about Me in the Law of Moses and the Prophets and the Psalms must be fulfilled." Then He opened their minds to understand the Scriptures, and He said to them, "Thus it is written, that the Christ would suffer and rise again from the dead the third day, and that repentance for forgiveness of sins would be proclaimed in His name to all the nations, beginning from Jerusalem. You are witnesses of these things. And behold, I am sending forth the promise of My Father upon you; but you are to stay in the city until you are clothed with power from on high" (Luke 24:44–49; see Matthew 28:19, 20; Acts 1:8).

Setting: Sychar in Samaria, on the way to Galilee. Jesus interacts with a woman at Jacob's well, while His disciples are buying food.

Jesus said to her, "Woman, believe Me, an hour is coming when neither in this mountain nor in Jerusalem will you worship the Father. You worship what you do not know; we worship what we know, for salvation is from the Jews. But an hour is coming, and now is, when the true worshipers will worship the Father in spirit and truth; for such people the Father seeks to be His worshipers. God is spirit, and those who worship Him must worship in spirit and truth" (John 4:21–24; see Isaiah 2:3; Philippians 3:3).

Setting: Jerusalem. Luke, writing in Acts, presents quotes from Jesus' post-resurrection appearances, in which He responds to their question if He is about to restore the kingdom to Israel.

He said to them, "It is not for you to know times or epochs which the Father has fixed by His own authority; but you will receive power when the Holy Spirit has come upon you; and you shall be My witnesses both in Jerusalem, and in all Judea and Samaria, and even to the remotest part of the earth" (Acts 1:7, 8; see Luke 24:48, 49; Acts 2:1–4).

Setting: Jerusalem. Luke, writing in Acts, recounts Paul's speech to a hostile Jewish crowd (after his third missionary journey), during which he recounts his instructions from the Lord following his conversion on the road to Damascus.

It happened when I returned to Jerusalem and was praying in the temple, that I fell into a trance, and I saw Him saying to me, 'Make haste, and get out of Jerusalem quickly, because they will not accept your testimony about Me' (Acts 22:17, 18; see Acts 9:29).

Setting: Jerusalem. Luke, writing in Acts, presents Jesus' encouraging words in an appearance to Paul in the Roman barracks following his hearing before the Jewish Council in Jerusalem and arrest by the Roman commander (after his third missionary journey).

But on the night *immediately* following, the Lord stood at his side and said, "Take courage; for as you have solemnly witnessed to My cause at Jerusalem, so you must witness at Rome also" (Acts 23:11; see Acts 19:21).

JERUSALEM, DAUGHTERS OF

Setting: Jerusalem. After being arrested and appearing before the Council of Elders (Sanhedrin), Pontius Pilate (Roman governor of Judea), Herod Antipas (tetrarch of Galilee and Perea), and Pilate a second time (when Pilate bows to the crowd's pressure and grants that Jesus be crucified), the Lord prophesies to the women mourning Him regarding the coming judgment of Jerusalem.

But Jesus turning to them said, "Daughters of Jerusalem, stop weeping for Me, but weep for yourselves and for your children. For behold, the days are coming when they will say, 'Blessed are the barren, and the wombs that never bore, and the breasts that never nursed.' Then they will begin TO SAY TO THE MOUNTAINS, 'FALL ON US,' AND TO THE HILLS, 'COVER US.' For it they do these things when the tree is green, what will happen when it is dry?" (Luke 23:28–31, Jesus quotes from Hosea 10:8; see Matthew 24:19).

JERUSALEM, NEW

Setting: On the island of Patmos (in the Aegean Sea about fifty miles southwest of Ephesus in modern Turkey). On the Lord's Day (Sunday), about fifty years after Jesus' resurrection, the disciple John encounters the Lord Jesus Christ, who communicates a new revelation for the apostle to record for the church in Philadelphia and to six other churches in Asia.

"And to the angel of the church in Philadelphia write: He who is holy, who is true, who has the key of David, who opens and no one will shut, and who shuts and no one opens, says this: 'I know your deeds. Behold, I have put before you an open door which no one can shut, because you have a little power, and have kept My word, and have not denied My name. Behold, I will cause *those* of the synagogue of Satan, who say that they are Jews and are not, but lie—I will make them come and bow down at your feet, and *make them* know that I have loved you. Because you have kept the word of My perseverance, I also will keep you from the hour of testing, that *hour* which is about to come upon the whole world, to test those who dwell on the earth. I am coming quickly; hold fast what you have, so that no one will take your crown. He who overcomes, I will make him a pillar in the temple of My God, and he will not go out from it anymore; and I will write on him the name of My God, and the name of the city of My God, the new Jerusalem, which comes down out of heaven from My God, and My new name. He who has an ear, let him hear what the Spirit says to the churches' " (Revelation 3:7–13; see Isaiah 22:22; Galatians 2:9; Revelation 2:9, 10, 13, 25; 14:1).

JERUSALEM, PROPHECY OF THE DESTRUCTION OF (See PROPHECY OF THE DESTRUCTION OF JERUSALEM)

JESUS (Also see CHRIST, THE; DAVID, SON OF; GOD, JESUS AS; JESUS CHRIST; JESUS' NAME; KING OF THE JEWS; LORD; MESSIAH; NAME, MY; SON OF GOD; and SON OF MAN)

Setting: On the road to Damascus. Luke, writing in Acts, reveals how Saul of Tarsus (who will later have the name Paul), a persecutor of the disciples of Jesus, receives the Lord's calling and is temporarily blind.

As he was traveling, it happened that he was approaching Damascus, and suddenly a light from heaven flashed around him; and he fell to the ground and heard a voice saying to him. "Saul, Saul, why are you persecuting Me?" And he said, "Who are You, Lord?" And He *said,* "I am Jesus whom you are persecuting, but get up and enter the city, and it will be told you what you must do" (Acts 9:3–6; see Acts 22:7, 8).

Setting: Jerusalem. Luke, writing in Acts, presents Paul's speech (following his third missionary journey) to a hostile Jewish crowd about His divine encounter with Jesus on the road to Damascus.

"But it happened that as I was on my way, approaching Damascus about noontime, a very bright light suddenly flashed from heaven all around me, and I fell to the ground, and heard a voice saying to me, 'Saul, Saul, why are you persecuting Me?' And I answered, 'Who are You, Lord?' And He said to me, 'I am Jesus the Nazarene, whom you are persecuting.' And those who were with me saw the light, to be sure, but did not understand the voice of the One who was speaking to me. And I said, 'What shall I do, Lord?' And the Lord said to me, 'Get up and go on into Damascus, and there you will be told of all that has been appointed for you to do' (Acts 22:6–10; see Acts 9:7; 26:9).

Setting: Caesarea. Luke, writing in Acts, gives Paul's retelling of his conversion to Christ as he appears before King Agrippa following his hearing before the Jewish Council in Jerusalem and arrest by the Roman commander (on his way to Rome after the apostle's third missionary journey).

"And when we had fallen to the ground, I heard a voice saying to me in the Hebrew dialect, 'Saul, Saul, why are you persecuting Me? It is hard for you to kick against the goads.' And I said, 'Who are You, Lord?' And the Lord said, 'I am Jesus whom you are persecuting. But get up and stand on your feet; for this purpose I have appeared to you, to appoint you a minister and a witness not only to the things which you have seen, but also to the things in which I will appear to you; rescuing you from the *Jewish* people and from the Gentiles, to whom I am sending you, to open their eyes so that they may turn from darkness to light and from the dominion of Satan to God, that they may receive forgiveness of sins and an inheritance among those who have been sanctified by faith in Me' (Acts 26:14–18; see Isaiah 35:5; Acts 21:40; 22:14).

Setting: On the island of Patmos (in the Aegean Sea about fifty miles southwest of Ephesus in modern Turkey). In the final chapter of the Lord Jesus Christ's Revelation via the disciple John, approximately fifty years after His resurrection, the Lord authenticates the truthfulness of His message, along with His earthly lineage through King David.

"I, Jesus, have sent My angel to testify to you these things for the churches. I am the root and the descendant of David, the bright morning star" (Revelation 22:16).

JESUS, ASHAMED OF

[ASHAMED OF JESUS from ashamed of Me and My words]

Setting: Caesarea Philippi. After rebuking Peter for desiring to thwart His mission to the cross, Jesus summons a crowd, along with His disciples, and informs them of the high costs of following Him.

And He summoned the crowd with His disciples, and said to them, "If anyone wishes to come after Me, he must deny himself, and take up his cross and follow Me. For whoever wishes to save his life will lose it, but whoever loses his life for My sake and the gospel's will save it. For what does it profit a man to gain the whole world, and forfeit his soul? For what will a man give in exchange for his soul? For whoever is ashamed of Me and My words in this adulterous and sinful generation, the Son of Man will also be ashamed of him when He comes in the glory of His Father with the holy angels" (Mark 8:34–38; cf. Matthew 16:24–28; Luke 9:23–27; see Matthew 10:33, 38, 39).

[ASHAMED OF JESUS from ashamed of Me and My words]

Setting: Galilee. Following Peter's pronouncement Jesus is the Christ of God, the Lord conveys the demands of discipleship and the hope regarding the kingdom of God.

And He was saying to *them* all, "If anyone wishes to come after Me, he must deny himself, and take up his cross daily and follow Me. For whoever wishes to save his life will lose it, but whoever loses his life for My sake, he is the one who will save it. For what is a man profited if he gains the whole world, and loses or forfeits himself? For whoever is ashamed of Me and My words, the Son of Man will be ashamed of him when He comes in His glory, and *the glory* of the Father and of the holy angels. But I say to you truthfully, there are some of those standing here who will not taste death until they see the kingdom of God" (Luke 9:23–27; cf. Matthew 16:24–26, 28; Mark 8:34–37; see Matthew 10:33, 38, 39).

JESUS, BAPTISM OF

[BAPTISM OF JESUS from Permit *it* at this time]

Setting: Bethany beyond the Jordan. Before being tempted by the devil and commencing His public ministry, Jesus arrives from Galilee to be baptized by John the Baptist. John questions his worthiness to baptize the Lord.

But Jesus answering said to him, "Permit *it* at this time; for in this way it is fitting for us to fulfill all righteousness." Then he permitted Him (Matthew 3:15).

JESUS, BETRAYAL OF (See JUDAS, BETRAYAL OF JESUS BY; also see BETRAYAL, PROPHECY OF JESUS')

JESUS, CONFESSING (Also see BAPTISM; and TESTIMONY)

[CONFESSING JESUS from confesses Me]

Setting: Galilee. Jesus explains the meaning of discipleship as He commissions His twelve disciples for ministry.

"Therefore everyone who confesses Me before men, I will also confess him before My Father who is in heaven. But whoever denies Me before men, I will also deny him before My Father who is in heaven" (Matthew 10:32, 33; cf. Mark 8:38; Luke 12:8).

[CONFESSING JESUS from confesses Me]

Setting: On the way from Galilee to Jerusalem. Jesus warns His disciples of future events as the scribes and Pharisees turn hostile and question Him repeatedly in an attempt to catch Him in something He might say.

"And I say to you, everyone who confesses Me before men, the Son of Man will confess him also before the angels of God; but he who denies Me before men will be denied before the angels of God. And everyone who speaks a word against the Son of Man, it will be forgiven him; but he who blasphemes against the Holy Spirit, it will not be forgiven him. When they bring you before the synagogues and the rulers and the authorities, do not worry about how or what you are to speak in your defense, or what you are to say; for the Holy Spirit will teach you in that very hour what you ought to say" (Luke 12:8–12; cf. Matthew 10:32, 33; 12:31, 32; see Matthew 10:20).

JESUS, DENYING (Also see PETER'S DENIAL)

[DENYING JESUS from But whoever denies Me before men, I will also deny him before My Father who is in heaven]

Setting: Galilee. Jesus explains the meaning of discipleship as He commissions His twelve disciples for ministry.

"Therefore everyone who confesses Me before men, I will also confess him before My Father who is in heaven. But whoever denies Me before men, I will also deny him before My Father who is in heaven" (Matthew 10:32, 33; cf. Mark 8:38; Luke 12:8).

[DENYING JESUS from denies Me]

Setting: On the way from Galilee to Jerusalem. Jesus warns His disciples of future events as the scribes and Pharisees turn hostile and question Him repeatedly in an attempt to catch Him in something He might say.

"And I say to you, everyone who confesses Me before men, the Son of Man will confess him also before the angels of God; but he who denies Me before men will be denied before the angels of God. And everyone who speaks a word against the Son of Man, it will be forgiven him; but he who blasphemes against the Holy Spirit, it will not be forgiven him. When they bring you before the synagogues and the rulers and the authorities, do not worry about how or what you are to speak in your defense, or what you are to say; for the Holy Spirit will teach you in that very hour what you ought to say" (Luke 12:8–12; cf. Matthew 10:32, 33; 12:31, 32; see Matthew 10:20).

JESUS, DEPENDENCE ON (Also see GOD, DEPENDENCE ON)

[DEPENDENCE ON JESUS from apart from Me you can do nothing]

Setting: Jerusalem. Before the Passover, after He conveys the upcoming ministry of the Holy Spirit in His disciples' lives with His imminent departure from them, Jesus explains He is the vine and they are the branches.

"I am the true vine, and My Father is the vinedresser. Every branch in Me that does not bear fruit, He takes away; and every *branch* that bears fruit, He prunes it so that it may bear more fruit. You are already clean because of the word which I have spoken to you. Abide in Me, and I in you. As the branch cannot bear fruit of itself unless it abides in the vine, so neither *can* you unless you abide in Me. I am the vine, you are the branches; he who abides in Me and I in him, he bears much fruit, for apart from Me you can do nothing. If anyone does not abide in Me, he is thrown away as a branch and dries up; and they gather them, and cast them into the fire and they are burned. If you abide in Me, and My words abide in you, ask whatever you wish, and it will be done for you. My Father is glorified by this, that you bear much fruit, and *so* prove to be My disciples. Just as the Father has loved Me, I have also loved you; abide in My love. If you keep My commandments, you will abide in My love; just as I have kept My Father's commandments and abide in His love. These things I have spoken to you so that My joy may be in you, and *that* your joy may be made full" (John 15:1–11; see Matthew 5:16; 7:7; John 3:29, 35; 6:56; 8:29, 31; 13:10; 15:16).

JESUS, FOLLOWING (See FOLLOWING JESUS CHRIST)

JESUS, HATRED OF (Also see PERSECUTION; and SUFFERING)

[HATRED OF JESUS from hates me]

Setting: Capernaum of Galilee. Jesus' blood brothers, who do not yet believe in Him, encourage Him to attend the upcoming Feast of Booths in Jerusalem in order to demonstrate His works to His disciples and the world.

So Jesus said to them, "My time is not yet here, but your time is always opportune. The world cannot hate you, but it hates Me because I testify of it, that its deeds are evil. Go up to the feast yourselves; I do not go up to this feast because My time has not yet fully come" (John 7:6–8; see John 3:19, 20; 15:18–20).

[HATRED OF JESUS from it has hated Me before *it hated* you]

Setting: Jerusalem. Before the Passover, with His impending departure in mind, after explaining He is the vine and His disciples are the branches, Jesus prepares them for persecution from the world.

"If the world hates you, you know that it has hated Me before *it hated* you. If you were of the world, the world would love its own; but because you are not of the world, but I chose you out of the world, because of this the world hates you. Remember the word that I said to you, 'A slave is not greater than his master.' If they persecuted Me, they will also persecute you; if they kept My word, they will keep yours also. But all these things they will do to you for My name's sake, because they do not know the One who sent Me. If I had not come and spoken to them, they would not have sin, but now they have no excuse for their sin" (John 15:18–22; see Matthew 10:22; John 7:7; 8:19, 55; 9:41; 1 Corinthians 4:12).

[HATRED OF JESUS from hates me and hated me]
Setting: Jerusalem. Before the Passover, with His impending departure in mind, after explaining He is the vine and His disciples are the branches, Jesus prepares them for hatred by the world.

"He who hates Me hates My Father also. If I had not done among them the works which no one else did, they would not have sin; but now they have both seen and hated Me and My Father as well. But *they have done this* to fulfill the word that is written in their Law, 'THEY HATED ME WITHOUT A CAUSE'" (John 15:23–25, Jesus quotes from Psalm 35:19; see John 9:41).

JESUS, IDENTIFICATION WITH (See BAPTISM; and JESUS, CONFESSING)

JESUS, KNOWING (Also see GOD, KNOWING)

[KNOWING JESUS from My own know Me]
Setting: Jerusalem. Following the Pharisees' interrogation and dismissal of the formerly blind man Jesus healed on the Sabbath, the Lord conveys the Parable of the Good Shepherd to the Pharisees, using figures of speech they do not understand.

So Jesus said to them again, "Truly, truly, I say to you, I am the door of the sheep. All who came before Me are thieves and robbers, but the sheep did not hear them. I am the door; if anyone enters through Me, he will be saved, and will go in and out and find pasture. The thief comes only to steal and kill and destroy; I came that they may have life, and have *it* abundantly. I am the good shepherd; the good shepherd lays down His life for the sheep. He who is a hired hand, and not a shepherd, who is not the owner of the sheep, sees the wolf coming, and leaves the sheep and flees, and the wolf snatches them and scatters *them. He flees* because he is a hired hand and is not concerned about the sheep. I am the good shepherd, and I know My own and My own know Me, even as the Father knows Me and I know the Father; and I lay down My life for the sheep. I have other sheep, which are not of this fold; I must bring them also, and they will hear My voice, and they will become one flock *with* one shepherd. For this reason the Father loves Me, because I lay down My life so that I may take it again. No one has taken it away from Me, but I lay it down on My own initiative. I have authority to take it up again. This commandment I received from My Father" (John 10:7–18; see Isaiah 40:11; 56:8; Jeremiah 23:1; Matthew 11:27).

JESUS, OPPOSITION TO

[OPPOSITION TO JESUS from He who is not with Me is against Me; and he who does not gather with Me scatters]
Setting: Galilee. After He heals a blind, mute, demon-possessed man, Jesus warns the Pharisees about the unpardonable sin, as they accuse Him in front of crowds of being a worker of Satan.

"He who is not with Me is against Me; and he who does not gather with Me scatters. Therefore I say to you, any sin and blasphemy shall be forgiven people, but blasphemy against the Spirit shall not be forgiven. Whoever speaks a word against the Son of Man, it shall be forgiven him; but whoever speaks against the Holy Spirit, it shall not be forgiven him, either in this age or in the *age* to come" (Matthew 12:30–32; cf. Luke 12:10; see Mark 9:40).

[OPPOSITION TO JESUS from He who is not with Me is against Me; and he who does not gather with Me, scatters]
Setting: On the way from Galilee to Jerusalem. After some in the crowd test Him, demanding a sign from heaven, Jesus illustrates His power over Satan.

"When a strong *man*, fully armed, guards his own house, his possessions are undisturbed. But when someone stronger than he attacks him and overpowers him, he takes away from him all his armor on which he had relied and distributes his plunder. He who is not with Me is against Me; and he who does not gather with Me, scatters" (Luke 11:21–23; cf. Matthew 12:29, 30).

JESUS, POWER OF (Also see MIRACLE; MIRACLES; POWER OF GOD; POWER, RIGHT HAND OF; SIGNS AND WONDERS; and WORKS, JESUS')

[POWER OF JESUS from no one will snatch them out of My hand]

Setting: Jerusalem. At the Feast of Dedication, just after Jesus conveys the Parable of the Good Shepherd to the Pharisees (who do not understand it), they ask Him plainly if He is the Christ.

Jesus answered them, "I told you, and you do not believe; the works that I do in My Father's name, these testify of Me. But you do not believe because you are not of My sheep. My sheep hear My voice, and I know them, and they follow Me; and I give eternal life to them, and they will never perish; and no one will snatch them out of My hand. My Father, who has given *them* to Me, is greater than all; and no one is able to snatch *them* out of the Father's hand. I and the Father are one" (John 10:25–30; see John 8:47; 17:1, 2, 20, 21).

JESUS PRAISING HIS FATHER (Listed under FATHER, JESUS PRAISING HIS)

JESUS, REJECTING (Also see REJECTION)

[REJECTING JESUS from everyone who hears these words of Mine and does not act on them]

Setting: Galilee. During the early part of His ministry, Jesus preaches the Sermon on the Mount to His disciples and the multitudes.

"Therefore everyone who hears these words of Mine and acts on them, may be compared to a wise man who built his house on the rock. And the rain fell, and the floods came, and the winds blew and slammed against that house; and *yet* it did not fall, for it had been founded on the rock. Everyone who hears these words of Mine and does not act on them, will be like a foolish man who built his house on the sand. The rain fell, and the floods came, and the winds blew and slammed against that house; and it fell—and great was its fall" (Matthew 7:24–28; cf. Luke 6:47–49).

[REJECTING JESUS from the one who rejects you rejects Me]

Setting: On the way from Galilee to Jerusalem. The Lord pronounces woes on cities who reject the gospel, as He appoints seventy followers and sends them out in pairs to every place He Himself will soon visit.

"Woe to you, Chorazin! Woe to you, Bethsaida! For if the miracles had been performed in Tyre and Sidon which occurred in you, they would have repented long ago, sitting in sackcloth and ashes. But it will be more tolerable for Tyre and Sidon in the judgment than for you. And you, Capernaum, will not be exalted to heaven, will you? You will be brought down to Hades! The one who listens to you listens to Me, and the one who rejects you rejects Me; and he who rejects Me rejects the One who sent Me" (Luke 10:13–16; cf. Matthew 11:21–23; see Matthew 10:40; Luke 10:1).

[REJECTING JESUS from you are unwilling to come to Me and you do not receive Me]

Setting: Jerusalem. During the Feast of the Jews, Jesus responds to criticism from the Jewish religious leaders by referring to God as His Father (thereby making Himself equal with God) and informing them that God, John the Baptist, His works, and the Scriptures all testify to His mission.

"You search the Scriptures because you think that in them you have eternal life; it is these that testify about Me; and you are unwilling to come to Me so that you may have life. I do not receive glory from men; but I know you, that you do not have the love of God in yourselves. I have come in My Father's name, and you do not receive Me; if another comes in his own name, you will receive him. How can you believe, when you receive glory from one another and you do not seek the glory that is from the *one and* only God? Do not think that I will accuse you before the Father; the one who accuses you is Moses, in whom you have set your hope. For if you believed Moses, you would believe Me, for he wrote about Me. But if you do not believe his writings, how will you believe My words?" (John 5:39–47; see Matthew 24:5; Luke 16:29, 31; 24:27; John 9:28; 17:3).

[REJECTING JESUS from He who rejects Me]
Setting: Jerusalem. Just days before the Passover, with the chief priests and Pharisees plotting to seize Jesus, who is expressing anxiety about His upcoming death by crucifixion, some of the Jews believe in Jesus, while others are rejecting His message.

And Jesus cried out and said, "He who believes in Me, does not believe in Me but in Him who sent Me. He who sees Me sees the One who sent Me. I have come *as* Light into the world, so that everyone who believes in Me will not remain in darkness. If anyone hears My sayings and does not keep them, I do not judge him; for I did not come to judge the world, but to save the world. He who rejects Me and does not receive My sayings, has one who judges him; the word I spoke is what will judge him at the last day. For I did not speak on My own initiative, but the Father Himself who sent Me has given Me a commandment *as to* what to say and what to speak. I know that His commandment is eternal life; therefore the things I speak, I speak just as the Father as told Me" (John 12:44–50; see Matthew 10:40; Luke 10:16; John 1:4; 3:17; 5:19; 6:68; 14:9).

JESUS, TEMPTATION OF (See TEMPTATION OF JESUS)

JESUS, TESTING

[TESTING JESUS from Why are you testing Me]
Setting: The temple in Jerusalem. The Pharisees send their disciples and the Herodians to test Jesus about the poll-tax, in order to trap Him while He teaches.

But Jesus perceived their malice, and said, "Why are you testing Me, you hypocrites? Show Me the coin *used* for the poll-tax." And they brought Him a denarius. And He said to them, "Whose likeness and inscription is this?" They said to Him, "Caesar's." Then He said to them, "Then render to Caesar the things that are Caesar's; and to God the things that are God's" (Matthew 22:18–21; cf. Matthew 17:25; Mark 12:15–17; Luke 20:22–25).

[TESTING JESUS from Why are you testing Me]
Setting: The temple in Jerusalem. After Jesus teaches the chief priests, scribes, and elders in parables, they send some of the Pharisees and Herodians in an attempt to trap Him in a statement.

"Shall we pay or shall we not pay?" But He, knowing their hypocrisy, said to them, "Why are you testing Me? Bring Me a denarius to look at." They brought *one.* And He said to them, "Whose likeness and inscription is this?" And they said to Him, "Caesar's." And Jesus said to them, "Render to Caesar the things that are Caesar's, and to God the things that are God's." And they were amazed at Him (Mark 12:15–17; cf. Matthew 22:15–22; Luke 20:20–26).

JESUS AS A BOY

[JESUS AS A BOY from context]
Setting: After attending His first Passover in Jerusalem, the twelve-year-old Jesus remains in the temple interacting with the teachers, while His parents return to Jerusalem when they realize He is not in the caravan heading back to Nazareth.

And He said to them, "Why is it that you were looking for Me? Did you not know that I had to be in My Father's *house?"* (Luke 2:49).

JESUS AS GOD (Listed under GOD, JESUS AS)

JESUS AS JUDGE (Listed under JUDGE, JESUS AS)

JESUS AS KING (Listed under KING, JESUS AS)

JESUS AS SHEPHERD (Listed under SHEPHERD, JESUS AS)

JESUS CHRIST (Also see CHRIST, THE; DAVID, SON OF; GOD, JESUS AS; JESUS; JESUS' NAME; KING OF THE JEWS; LORD; MESSIAH; NAME, MY; SON OF GOD; and SON OF MAN)

Setting: Jerusalem. Before the Passover, after giving His disciples assurance that in the midst of tribulation they will have His peace, Jesus prays His high-priestly prayer. Jesus spoke these things; and lifting up His eyes to heaven, He said, "Father, the hour has come; glorify Your Son, that the Son may glorify You, even as You gave Him authority over all flesh, that to all whom You have given Him, He may give eternal life. This is eternal life, that they may know You, the only true God, and Jesus Christ whom You have sent. I glorified You on the earth, having accomplished the work which You have given Me to do. Now, Father, glorify Me together with Yourself, with the glory which I had with You before the world was. I have manifested Your name to the men whom You gave Me out of the world; they were Yours and You gave them to Me, and they have kept Your word. Now they have come to know that everything You have given Me is from You; for the words which You gave Me I have given to them; and they received *them* and truly understood that I came forth from You, and they believed You sent Me. I ask on their behalf; I do not ask on behalf of the world, but of those whom You have given Me; for they are Yours; and all things that are Mine are Yours, and Yours are Mine; and have been glorified in them. I am no longer in the world; and *yet* they themselves are in the world, and I come to You. Holy Father, keep them in Your name, *the name* which You have given Me, that they may be even as We *are.* While I was with them, I was keeping them in Your name which You have given Me; and I guarded them and not one of them perished but the son of perdition, so that the Scripture would be fulfilled" (John 17:1–12; see Luke 22:32; John 1:1; 3:35; 4:34; 5:44; 6:37–39, 70; 8:42; 11:41; 12:49; 13:18, 31; 16:15; 17:20; Philippians 2:9).

JESUS' ARREST

[JESUS' ARREST from arrest Me]

Setting: Gethsemane on the Mount of Olives, just outside Jerusalem. As He submits to His Father's will and allows Judas to betray Him, Jesus reveals that this incident is a fulfillment of prophecy.

At that time Jesus said to the crowds, "Have you come out with swords and clubs to arrest Me as *you would* against a robber? Every day I used to sit in the temple teaching and you did not seize Me. But all this has taken place to fulfill the Scriptures of the prophets" (Matthew 26:55, 56; cf. Mark 14:48, 49; Luke 22:52, 53; see Matthew 26:24).

[JESUS' ARREST from arrest Me]

Setting: Gethsemane on the Mount of Olives, east of the temple in Jerusalem. Judas betrays Jesus with a kiss in front of the crowd of the chief priests, scribes, and elders seeking to seize Him with swords and clubs.

And Jesus said to them, "Have you come out with swords and clubs to arrest Me, as *you would* against a robber? Every day I was with you in the temple teaching, and you did not seize Me; but *this has taken place* to fulfill the Scriptures" (Mark 14:48, 49; cf. Matthew 26:55, 56; Luke 22:52, 53; see Mark 14: 26–47).

[JESUS' ARREST from come out with swords and clubs as you would against a robber]

Setting: Gethsemane on the Mount of Olives, east of the temple in Jerusalem. After praying for deliverance, with His crucifixion imminent, Jesus chastises the religious leaders after Judas betrays Him and the hostile crowd surround Him.

Then Jesus said to the chief priests and officers of the temple and elders who had come against Him, "Have you come out with swords and clubs as you would against a robber? While I was with you daily in the temple, you did not lay hands on Me; but this hour and the power of darkness are yours" (Luke 22:52 53; cf. Matthew 26:47–56; Mark 14:43–50; see Luke 22:1–4; 47–51).

JESUS' ASCENSION

[JESUS' ASCENSION from I have not yet ascended to the Father and I ascend to My Father and your Father, and My God and Your God]

Setting: Jerusalem. On the day after the Sabbath, the risen Jesus first appears to Mary Magdalene after she shows Simon Peter and John the empty tomb where He had been buried after dying on the cross for the sins of the world.

Jesus said to her, "Woman, why are you weeping? Whom are you seeking?" Supposing Him to be the gardener, she said to Him, "Sir, if you have carried Him away, tell me where you have laid Him, and I will take Him away." Jesus said to her, "Mary!" She turned and said to Him in Hebrew "Rabboni!" (which means, Teacher). Jesus said to her, "Stop clinging to Me, for I have not yet ascended to the Father; but go to My brethren and say to them, 'I ascend to My Father and your Father, and My God and Your God'" (John 20:15–17; see Mark 16:9–11; John 7:33; 19:31–42; 20:1–14, 18).

JESUS' BETRAYAL (See JUDAS, BETRAYAL OF JESUS BY)

JESUS' BLOOD (See BLOOD, HIS; BLOOD, MY; BLOOD, NEW COVENANT IN MY; and COVENANT, BLOOD OF THE)

JESUS' BODY (See BODY, MY)

JESUS' DEATH (See CROSS; CRUCIFIXION; JESUS' WORDS WHILE ON THE CROSS; and SALVATION)

JESUS' DYING WORDS (See JESUS' LAST WORDS)

JESUS' EXCLUSIVITY

[JESUS' EXCLUSIVITY from I am the door; if anyone enters through Me, he will be saved]

Setting: Jerusalem. Following the Pharisees' interrogation and dismissal of the formerly blind man Jesus healed on the Sabbath, the Lord conveys the Parable of the Good Shepherd to the Pharisees using figures of speech they do not understand.

So Jesus said to them again, "Truly, truly, I say to you, I am the door of the sheep. All who came before Me are thieves and robbers, but the sheep did not hear them. I am the door; if anyone enters through Me, he will be saved, and will go in and out and find pasture. The thief comes only to steal and kill and destroy; I came that they may have life, and have *it* abundantly. I am the good shepherd; the good shepherd lays down His life for the sheep. He who is a hired hand, and not a shepherd, who is not the owner of the sheep, sees the wolf coming, and leaves the sheep and flees, and the wolf snatches them and scatters *them. He flees* because he is a hired hand and is not concerned about the sheep. I am the good shepherd, and I know My own and My own know Me, even as the Father knows Me and I know the Father; and I lay down My life for the sheep. I have other sheep, which are not of this fold; I must bring them also, and they will hear My voice; and they will become one flock *with* one shepherd. For this reason the Father loves Me, because I lay down My life so that I may take it again. No one has taken it away from Me, but I lay it down on My own initiative. I have authority to take it up again. This commandment I received from My Father" (John 10:7–18; see Isaiah 40:11; 56:8; Jeremiah 23:1; Matthew 11:27).

[JESUS' EXCLUSIVITY from I am the way, and the truth, and the life; no one comes to the Father but through Me]

Setting: Jerusalem. Before the Passover, as Jesus comforts and gives hope to His disciples regarding their future after He returns to heaven, Thomas asks where He is going and how they will know the way.

Jesus said to him, "I am the way, and the truth, and the life; no one comes to the Father but through Me. If you had known Me, you would have known My Father also; from now on you know Him, and have seen Him" (John 14:6, 7; see John 8:19; 10:9; 11:25).

JESUS' GLORIFICATION (Also see GLORIFICATON, GOD'S; GLORIFYING GOD; RESURRECTION; and TRANSFIGURATION)

[JESUS' GLORIFICATION from it is My Father who glorifies Me]

Setting: The temple treasury in Jerusalem. While Jesus is interacting with the scribes and Pharisees, they state their belief that He is a demon-possessed Samaritan because of His statement that anyone who keeps His word will never taste death.

Jesus answered, "If I glorify Myself, My glory is nothing; it is My Father who glorifies Me, of whom you say, 'He is our God'; and you have not come to know Him, but I know Him; and if I say that I do not know Him, I will be a liar like you, but I do know Him and keep His word. Your father Abraham rejoiced to see My day, and he saw *it* and was glad" (John 8:54–56; see Matthew 13:17; John 7:29).

[JESUS' GLORIFICATION from the Son of God may be glorified by it]

Setting: Jerusalem. Following the Feast of Dedication and the Pharisees' desire to stone Him, Jesus goes beyond the Jordan, where He hears of the sickness of Lazarus of Bethany.

But when Jesus heard *this,* He said, "This sickness is not to end in death, but for the glory of God, so that the Son of God may be glorified by it" (John 11:4).

[JESUS' GLORIFICATION from the Son of Man to be glorified]

Setting: Jerusalem. Just days before the Passover, with the chief priests and Pharisees plotting to seize Him, crowds welcome Jesus to Jerusalem with palm branches and praise, and some Greeks ask to meet Him.

And Jesus answered them, saying, "The hour has come for the Son of Man to be glorified. Truly, truly, I say to you, unless a grain of wheat falls into the earth and dies, it remains alone; but if it dies, it bears much fruit. He who loves his life loses it, and he who hates his life in this world will keep it to life eternal. If anyone serves Me, he must follow Me; and where I am, there My servant will be also; if anyone serves Me, the Father will honor him" (John 12:23–26; see Matthew 10:39).

[JESUS' GLORIFICATION from the Son of Man glorified]

Setting: Jerusalem. Before the Passover, after revealing to His disciples that Judas will betray Him to the chief priests and Pharisees, Jesus conveys how He will soon be glorified in His death, and commands the disciples to love one another.

Therefore when he had gone out, Jesus said, "Now is the Son of Man glorified, and God is glorified in Him; if God is glorified in Him, God will also glorify Him in Himself, and will glorify Him immediately. Little children, I am with you a little while longer. You will seek Me; and as I said to the Jews, now I also say to you, 'Where I am going, you cannot come.' A new commandment I give to you, that you love one another, even as I have loved you, that you also love one another. By this all men will know that you are My disciples, if you have love for one another" (John 13:31–35; see Leviticus 19:18; John 7:33, 34; 13:1–30; 17:1; 1 John 3:14).

[JESUS' GLORIFICATION from He will glorify Me]

Setting: Jerusalem. Before the Passover, after warning His disciples of the persecution they will face after His departure to heaven, Jesus elaborates about the coming ministry of the Holy Spirit.

"I have many more things to say to you, but you cannot bear *them* now. But when He, the Spirit of truth, comes, He will guide you into all the truth; for He will not speak on His own initiative, but whatever He hears, He will speak; and He will disclose to you what is to come. He will glorify Me, for He will take of Mine and will disclose *it* to you. All things that the Father has are Mine; therefore I said that He takes of Mine and will disclose *it* to you (John 16:12–15; see John 7:39; 14:17, 26; 17:10).

[JESUS' GLORIFICATION from glorify Your Son and glorify Me together with Yourself]

Setting: Jerusalem. Before the Passover, after giving His disciples assurance that in the midst of tribulation they will have His peace, Jesus prays His high-priestly prayer.

Jesus spoke these things; and lifting up His eyes to heaven, He said, "Father, the hour has come; glorify Your Son, that the Son may glorify You, even as You gave Him authority over all flesh, that to all whom You have given Him, He may give eternal life. This is eternal life, that they may know You, the only true God, and Jesus Christ whom You have sent. I glorified You on the earth, having accomplished the work which you have given Me to do. Now, Father, glorify Me together with Yourself, with the glory which I had with You before the world was. I have manifested Your name to the men whom You gave Me out of the world; they were Yours and You gave them to Me, and they have kept Your word. Now they have come to know that everything You have given Me is from You; for the words which You gave Me I have given to them; and they received *them* and truly understood that I came forth from You, and they believed You sent Me. I ask on their behalf; I do not ask on behalf of the world, but of those whom You have given Me; for they are Yours; and all things that are Mine are Yours, and Yours are Mine; and I have been glorified in them. I am no longer in the world; and yet they themselves are in the world, and I come to You. Holy Father, keep them in Your name, *the name* which You have given Me, that they may be even as We *are*. While I was with them, I was keeping them in Your name which You have given Me; and I guarded them and not one of them perished but the son of perdition, so that the Scripture would be fulfilled" (John 17:1–12; see Luke 22:32; John 1:1; 3:35; 4:34; 5:44; 6:37–39, 70; 8:42; 11:41; 12:49; 13:18, 31; 16:15; 17:20; Philippians 2:9).

JESUS' HEAD

[JESUS' HEAD from His head]
Setting: By the Sea of Galilee. Following a time of casting out evil spirits from the demon-possessed and healing the ill (in fulfillment of Isaiah 53:4), Jesus lays out to an inquiring scribe the demands of discipleship.

Then a scribe came and said to Him, "Teacher, I will follow You wherever you go." Jesus said to him, "The foxes have holes and the birds of the air *have* nests, but the Son of Man has nowhere to lay His head." Another of the disciples said to Him, "Lord, permit me first to go and bury my father." But Jesus said to him, "Follow Me, and allow the dead to bury their own dead" (Matthew 8:19–22; cf. Luke 9:57–60).

[JESUS' HEAD from My head]
Setting: Galilee. After Jesus praises John the Baptist to the crowds, Simon, a Pharisee, invites the Lord to dinner. A sinful woman anoints His feet with perfume, prompting Him to instruct His host about forgiveness.

Turning toward the woman, He said to Simon, "Do you see this woman? I entered your house; you gave Me no water for My feet, but she has wet My feet with her tears and wiped them with her hair. You gave Me no kiss; but she, since the time I came in, has not ceased to kiss My feet. You did not anoint My head with oil, but she anointed My feet with perfume. For this reason I say to you, her sins, which are many, have been forgiven, for she loved much; but he who is forgiven little, loves little." Then He said to her, "Your sins have been forgiven." Those who were reclining *at the table* with Him began to say to themselves, "Who is this *man* who even forgives sins?" And He said to the woman, "Your faith has saved you; go in peace" (Luke 7:44–50; see Matthew 9:2; Mark 5:34; Luke 5:21).

[JESUS' HEAD from His head]
Setting: On the way from Galilee to Jerusalem. The Lord responds to someone seeking to follow Him.

And Jesus said to him, "The foxes have holes and the birds of the air *have* nests, but the Son of Man has nowhere to lay His head" (Luke 9:58; cf. Matthew 8:19–22).

JESUS' "I AM" STATEMENTS (Jesus; statements about Himself; also see CHRIST, THE; DAVID, SON OF; GOD, JESUS AS; SON OF GOD; JESUS CHRIST; JESUS' NAME; LORD; MESSIAH; NAME, MY; and SON OF MAN)

Setting: Capernaum. The day after Jesus walks on the Sea of Galilee to join His disciples in a boat, the people He miraculously fed with a lad's five loaves and two fish ask Jesus to always give them this bread out of heaven.

Jesus said to them, "I am the bread of life; he who comes to Me will not hunger, and he who believes in Me will never thirst. But I said to you that you have seen Me, and yet do not believe. All that the Father gives Me will come to Me, and the one who comes to Me I will certainly not cast out. For I have come down from heaven, not to do My own will, but the will of Him who sent Me. This

is the will of Him who sent Me, that of all that He has given Me I lose nothing, but raise it up on the last day. For this is the will of My Father, that everyone who beholds the Son and believes in Him will have eternal life, and I Myself will raise him up on the last day" (John 6:35–40; see John 3:13, 16; 4:13, 14; 6:25–34, 48, 51).

Setting: Capernaum of Galilee. After Jesus informs the people whom He miraculously fed with a lad's five loaves and two fish how they might receive the bread out of heaven, the Jewish religious leaders grumble because Jesus claims that He came down out of heaven.

Therefore the Jews were grumbling about Him, because He said, "I am the bread that came down out of heaven." They were saying, "Is not this Jesus, the son of Joseph, whose father and mother we know? How does He now say, 'I have come down out of heaven'?" Jesus answered and said to them, "Do not grumble among yourselves. No one can come to Me unless the Father who sent Me draws him; and I will raise him up on the last day. It is written in the prophets, 'AND THEY SHALL ALL BE TAUGHT OF GOD.' Everyone who has heard and learned from the Father, comes to Me. Not that anyone has seen the Father, except the One who is from God; He has seen the Father. Truly, truly, I say to you, he who believes has eternal life. I am the bread of life. Your fathers ate the manna in the wilderness, and they died. This is the bread which comes down out of heaven, so that one may eat of it and not die. I am the living bread that came down out of heaven; if anyone eats of this bread, he will live forever; and the bread also which I will give for the life of the world is My flesh" (John 6:41–51, Jesus quotes from Isaiah 54:13; see John 1:18, 29; 3:36; 6:26–40, 58; 7:27).

Setting: The temple in Jerusalem. Following the Feast of Booths, Jesus retires to the Mount of Olives, and returns the next day to teach. He addresses the scribes and Pharisees after their failed attempt to stone a woman caught in adultery.

Then Jesus again spoke to them, saying, "I am the Light of the world; he who follows Me will not walk in the darkness, but will have the Light of life" (John 8:12; see John 1:4; 8:1–11).

Setting: The temple treasury in Jerusalem. After Jesus avoids being stoned by the scribes and Pharisees, His disciples wonder whose sin had caused the blindness of a man He has just healed.

Jesus answered, "*It was* neither *that* this man sinned, nor his parents; but *it was* so that the works of God might be displayed in him. We must work the works of Him who sent Me as long as it is day; night is coming when no one can work. While I am in the world, I am the Light of the world." When He had said this, He spat on the ground, and made clay of the spittle, and applied the clay to his eyes, and said to him, "Go, wash in the pool of Siloam" (which is translated, Sent). So he went away and washed, and came *back* seeing (John 9:3–7; see John 8:12; 9:1, 2; 11:4; 12:46).

Setting: Jerusalem. Following the Pharisees' interrogation and dismissal of the formerly blind man Jesus healed on the Sabbath, the Lord conveys the Parable of the Good Shepherd to the Pharisees using figures of speech they do not understand.

So Jesus said to them again, "Truly, truly, I say to you, I am the door of the sheep. All who came before Me are thieves and robbers, but the sheep did not hear them. I am the door; if anyone enters through Me, he will be saved, and will go in and out and find pasture. The thief comes only to steal and kill and destroy; I came that they may have life, and have *it* abundantly. I am the good shepherd; the good shepherd lays down His life for the sheep. He who is a hired hand, and not a shepherd, who is not the owner of the sheep, sees the wolf coming, and leaves the sheep and flees, and the wolf snatches them and scatters *them. He flees* because he is a hired hand and is not concerned about the sheep. I am the good shepherd, and I know My own and My own know Me, even as the Father knows Me and I know the Father; and I lay down My life for the sheep. I have other sheep, which are not of this fold; I must bring them also, and they will hear My voice; and they will become one flock *with* one shepherd. For this reason the Father loves Me, because I lay down My life so that I may take it again. No one has taken it away from Me, but I lay it down on My own initiative. I have authority to take it up again. This commandment I received from My Father" (John 10:7–18; see Isaiah 40:11; 56:8; Jeremiah 23:1; Matthew 11:27; John 10:1–5, 19–21, 27).

Setting: Jerusalem. At the Feast of Dedication, the Pharisees desire to stone Jesus when He claims to be equal with God when they ask Him plainly whether He is the Christ.

Jesus answered them, "Has it not been written in your Law, 'I SAID, YOU ARE GODS'? If he called them gods, to whom the word of God came (and the Scripture cannot be broken), do you say of Him, whom the Father sanctified and sent into the world, 'You are blaspheming,' because I said, 'I am the Son of God'? If I do not do the works of My Father, do not believe Me; but if I do them, though you do not believe Me, believe the works, so that you may know and understand that the Father is in Me, and I in the Father" (John 10:34–38, Jesus quotes from Psalm 82:6; see John 10:22–33, 39; 14:10, 20).

Setting: Beyond the Jordan. Jesus travels with His disciples to Bethany in Judea to see Lazarus's sisters, Martha and Mary, after the death of His friend.

Jesus said to her, "Your brother will rise again." Martha said to Him, "I know that he will rise again in the resurrection on the last day." Jesus said to her, "I am the resurrection and the life; he who believes in Me will live even if he dies, and everyone who lives and believes in Me will never die. Do you believe this?" (John 11:23–26; see Daniel 12:2; John 1:4; 6:47–51; 11:1–22).

Setting: Jerusalem. Before the Passover, as Jesus comforts and gives hope to His disciples regarding their future with Him returning to heaven, Thomas asks where He is going and how they will know the way.

Jesus said to him, "I am the way, and the truth, and the life; no one comes to the Father but through Me. If you had known Me, you would have known My Father also; from now on you know Him, and have seen Him" (John 14:6, 7; see John 8:19; 10:9; 11:25; 14:1–5).

Setting: Jerusalem. Before the Passover, after He conveys the upcoming ministry of the Holy Spirit in His disciples' lives, with His imminent departure from them, Jesus explains He is the vine and they are the branches.

"I am the true vine, and My Father is the vinedresser. Every branch in Me that does not bear fruit, He takes away; and every *branch* that bears fruit, He prunes it so that it may bear more fruit. You are already clean because of the word which I have spoken to you. Abide in Me, and I in you. As the branch cannot bear fruit of itself unless it abides in the vine, so neither *can* you unless you abide in Me. I am the vine, you are the branches; he who abides in Me and I in him, he bears much fruit, for apart from Me you can do nothing. If anyone does not abide in Me, he is thrown away as a branch and dries up; and they gather them, and cast them into the fire and they are burned. If you abide in Me, and My words abide in you, ask whatever you wish, and it will be done for you. My Father is glorified by this, that you bear much fruit, and *so* prove to be My disciples. Just as the Father has loved Me, I have also loved you; abide in My love. If you keep My commandments, you will abide in My love; just as I have kept My Father's commandments and abide in His love. These things I have spoken to you so that My joy may be in you, and *that* your joy may be made full" (John 15:1–11; see Matthew 5:16; 7:7; John 3:29, 35; 6:56; 8:29, 31; 13:10; 15:16).

Setting: Jerusalem. After the previous and current high priests (Annas and Caiaphas) question Jesus, and Peter denies the second and third times being the Lord's disciple, Pontius Pilate (Roman governor of Judea), asks Jesus if He is a king.

Therefore Pilate said to Him, "So You are a king?" Jesus answered, "You say *correctly* that I am a king. For this I have been born, and for this I have come into the world, to testify to the truth. Everyone who is of the truth hears my voice" (John 18:37; cf. Matthew 27:11; Mark 15:2; Luke 23:3 see John 18:28–36).

Setting: On the small island of Patmos (in the Aegean Sea about fifty miles southwest of Ephesus in modern Turkey). An angel speaks the first words of the revelation of Jesus Christ, approximately fifty years after His resurrection, to His bond-servant, the apostle John.

"I am the Alpha and the Omega," says the Lord God, "who is and who was and who is to come, the Almighty" (Revelation 1:8; see Revelation 1:1–7; 21:6).

Setting: On the island of Patmos (in the Aegean Sea about fifty miles southwest of Ephesus in modern Turkey). On the Lord's Day (Sunday), about fifty years after Jesus' resurrection, the disciple John encounters the Lord Jesus Christ, who communicates a new revelation for the apostle to record for the church in Thyatira and to six other churches in Asia.

When I saw Him, I fell at His feet like a dead man. And He placed His right hand on me, saying, "Do not be afraid; I am the first and the last, and the living One; and I was dead, and behold, I am alive forevermore, and I have the keys of death and of Hades. Therefore write the things which you have seen, and the things which are, and the things which will take place after these things. As for the mystery of the seven stars which you saw in My right hand, and the seven golden lampstands: the seven stars are the angels of the seven churches, and the seven lampstands are the seven churches" (Revelation 1:17–20; see Isaiah 44:6; Luke 24:5; Revelation 1:1–16; 2:8).

Setting: On the island of Patmos (in the Aegean Sea about fifty miles southwest of Ephesus in modern Turkey). In the final chapter of the Lord Jesus Christ's Revelation via the disciple John, approximately fifty years after His resurrection, the Lord reveals His coming return, reward, and eternality.

"Behold, I am coming quickly, and My reward *is* with Me, to render to every man according to what he has done. I am the Alpha and the Omega, the first and the last, the beginning and the end" (Revelation 22:12, 13; see Isaiah 40:10; 44:6; Revelation 22:11).

Setting: On the island of Patmos (in the Aegean Sea about fifty miles southwest of Ephesus in modern Turkey). In the final chapter of the Lord Jesus Christ's Revelation via the disciple John, approximately fifty years after His resurrection, the Lord authenticates the truthfulness of His message, along with His earthly lineage through King David.

"I, Jesus, have sent My angel to testify to you these things for the churches. I am the root and the descendant of David, the bright morning star" (Revelation 22:16; see Revelation 22:17–19).

JESUS' IDENTITY (See CHRIST, THE; DAVID, SON OF; GOD, JESUS AS; JESUS CHRIST; JESUS "I AM" STATEMENTS; JESUS' NAME; LORD; MESSIAH; NAME, MY; SON OF GOD; and SON OF MAN)

JESUS' LAST WORDS (Also see JESUS' WORDS WHILE ON THE CROSS)

[JESUS' LAST WORDS from Father, INTO YOUR HANDS I COMMIT MY SPIRIT]

Setting: On Golgotha (Calvary), just outside Jerusalem. While being mocked and ridiculed while hanging nailed to a cross, after granting forgiveness to one of the criminals being crucified with Him who asks to be remembered in Christ's kingdom, Jesus dies.

And Jesus, crying out with a loud voice, said, "Father, INTO YOUR HANDS I COMMIT MY SPIRIT." Having said this, He breathed His last (Luke 23:46, Jesus quotes from Psalm 31:5; cf. Matthew 27:45–50; Mark 15:33–37; John 19:28–30).

[JESUS' LAST WORDS from" It is finished!"]

Setting: On Golgotha (Calvary), just outside Jerusalem. After receiving some sour wine to quench His thirst on the cross, Jesus accomplishes with a statement of completion His work of dying for the sins of the world.

Therefore when Jesus had received the sour wine, He said, "It is finished!" And He bowed His head and gave up His spirit (John 19:30; see Matthew 27:50; Mark 15:37; Luke 23:46).

JESUS' LIFE

[JESUS' LIFE from Son of Man and His life]

Setting: On the way to Jerusalem, where Jesus will die on the cross. Jesus teaches His disciples about true greatness after the mother of James and John, the sons of Zebedee, asks Him to make her sons exalted rulers with Him in His coming kingdom.

But Jesus called them to Himself and said, "You know that the rulers of the Gentiles lord it over them, and *their* great men exercise authority over them. It is not this way among you, but whoever wishes to become great among you shall be your servant, and whoever wishes to be first among you shall be your slave; just as the Son of Man did not come to be served, but to serve, and to give His life a ransom for many" (Matthew 20:25–28; cf. Matthew 23:11; 26:28; Mark 10:42–45).

[JESUS' LIFE from Son of Man and His life]
Setting: On the road to Jerusalem. Disciples James and John ask Jesus for special honor and privileges in His kingdom. The other disciples become angry, so He uses this moment to teach them about servanthood.

Calling them to Himself, Jesus said to them, "You know that those who are recognized as rulers of the Gentiles lord it over them; and their great men exercise authority over them. But it is not this way among you, but whoever wishes to become great among you shall be your servant; and whoever wishes to be first among you shall be slave of all. For even the Son of Man did not come to be served, but to serve, and to give His life a ransom for many" (Mark 10:42–45; cf. Matthew 20:25–28).

[JESUS' LIFE from My life]
Setting: In Jerusalem, following the Pharisees' interrogation and dismissal of the formerly blind man Jesus healed on the Sabbath, the Lord conveys the Parable of the Good Shepherd to the Pharisees, using figures of speech they do not understand.

So Jesus said to them again, "Truly, truly, I say to you, I am the door of the sheep. All who came before Me are thieves and robbers, but the sheep did not hear them. I am the door; if anyone enters through Me, he will be saved, and will go in and out and find pasture. The thief comes only to steal and kill and destroy; I came that they may have life, and have *it* abundantly. I am the good shepherd; the good shepherd lays down His life for the sheep. He who is a hired hand, and not a shepherd, who is not the owner of the sheep, sees the wolf coming, and leaves the sheep and flees, and the wolf snatches them and scatters *them. He flees* because he is a hired hand and is not concerned about the sheep. I am the good shepherd, and I know My own and My own know Me, even as the Father knows Me and I know the Father; and I lay down My life for the sheep. I have other sheep, which are not of this fold; I must bring them also, and they will hear My voice; and they will become one flock *with* one shepherd. For this reason the Father loves Me, because I lay down My life so that I may take it again. No one has taken it away from Me, but I lay it down on My own initiative. I have authority to take it up again. This commandment I received from My Father" (John 10:7–18; see Isaiah 40:11; 56:8; Jeremiah 23:1; Matthew 11:27).

JESUS' MISSION (Also see JESUS' PURPOSE; and JESUS' WORK)

[JESUS' MISSION from the Law or the Prophets; I did not come to abolish but to fulfill]
Setting: Galilee. During the early part of His ministry, Jesus preaches the Sermon on the Mount to His disciples and the multitudes.

"Do not think that I came to abolish the Law or the Prophets; I did not come to abolish but to fulfill" (Matthew 5:17).

[JESUS' MISSION from Do not think that I came to bring peace on the earth; I did not come to bring peace, but a sword]
Setting: Galilee. After His disciples observe His ministry, Jesus summons and specifically instructs them about their ministry hardships ahead involving true discipleship.

"Do not think that I came to bring peace on the earth; I did not come to bring peace, but a sword. For I came to SET A MAN AGAINST HIS FATHER, AND A DAUGHTER AGAINST HER MOTHER, AND A DAUGHTER-IN-LAW AGAINST HER MOTHER-IN-LAW; and A MAN'S ENEMIES WILL BE THE MEMBERS OF HIS HOUSEHOLD" (Matthew 10:34–36; Jesus quotes from Micah 7:6; cf. Luke 12:51–53).

[JESUS' MISSION from "I was sent only to the lost sheep of the house of Israel."]
Setting: The district of Tyre and Sidon. A Canaanite woman appeals to Jesus to heal her demon-possessed daughter.

But He answered and said, "I was sent only to the lost sheep of the house of Israel." But she came and *began* to bow down before Him, saying, "Lord, help me!" And He answered and said, "It is not good to take the children's bread and throw it to the dogs." But she said, "Yes, Lord; but even the dogs feed from the crumbs which fall from their masters' table." Then Jesus said to her, "O woman, your faith is great; it shall be done for you as you wish." And her daughter was healed at once (Matthew 15:24–28; cf. Mark 7: 24–30; see Matthew 9:22; 10:5, 6).

[JESUS' MISSION from the Son of Man did not come to be served, but to serve, and to give His life a ransom for many]
Setting: On the way to Jerusalem, where Jesus will die on the cross. Jesus teaches His disciples about true greatness after the mother of disciples James and John asks Him to make her sons exalted rulers with Him in His coming kingdom.

But Jesus called them to Himself and said, "You know that the rulers of the Gentiles lord it over them, and *their* great men exercise authority over them. It is not this way among you, but whoever wishes to become great among you shall be your servant, and whoever wishes to be first among you shall be your slave; just as the Son of Man did not come to be served, but to serve, and to give His life a ransom for many" (Matthew 20:25–28; cf. Matthew 23:11; 26:28; Mark 10:42–45).

[JESUS' MISSION from preach and for that is what I came for]
Setting: Capernaum in Galilee. Early in His ministry, after healing people and casting out demons, Jesus decides to take His disciples to a nearby town and preach.

He said to them, "Let us go somewhere else to the towns nearby; so that I may preach there also; for that is what I came for" (Mark 1:38; cf. Luke 4:43).

[JESUS' MISSION from the Son of Man did not come to be served, but to serve, and to give His life a ransom for many]
Setting: On the road to Jerusalem. James and John ask Jesus for special honor and privileges in His kingdom. The other disciples become angry, so the Lord uses this moment to teach all of them about servanthood.

Calling them to Himself, Jesus said to them, "You know that those who are recognized as rulers of the Gentiles lord it over them; and their great men exercise authority over them. But it is not this way among you, but whoever wishes to become great among you shall be your servant; and whoever wishes to be first among you shall be slave of all. For even the Son of Man did not come to be served, but to serve, and to give His life a ransom for many" (Mark 10:42–45; cf. Matthew 20:25–28).

[JESUS' MISSION from I have not come to call the righteous but sinners to repentance]
Setting: Levi's (Matthew) house in Capernaum. At a reception following Jesus' call of Levi to become His disciple, the Pharisees and their scribes question why the Lord associates with tax collectors and sinners.

And Jesus answered and said to them, "*It is* not those who are well who need a physician, but those who are sick. I have not come to call the righteous but sinners to repentance" (Luke 5:31, 32; cf. Matthew 9:10–13; Mark 2:15–17).

[JESUS' MISSION from Do you suppose that I came to grant peace on earth? I tell you, no, but rather division]
Setting: On the way from Galilee to Jerusalem. After clarifying a parable for Peter and the crowd, Jesus conveys how a relationship with Him divides families.

"I have come to cast fire upon the earth; and how I wish it were already kindled! But I have a baptism to undergo, and how distressed I am until it is accomplished! Do you suppose that I came to grant peace on earth? I tell you, no, but rather division; for from now on five *members* in one household will be divided, three against two and two against three. They will be divided, father against son and son against father, mother against daughter, and daughter against mother, mother-in-law against daughter-in-law and daughter-in-law against mother-in-law" (Luke 12:49–53; cf. Matthew 10:34–36; see Micah 7:6; Mark 10:38).

[JESUS' MISSION from the Son of Man has come to seek and save that which was lost]
Setting: Jericho, on the way to Jerusalem. After taking time to heal a blind man, Jesus comments on Zaccheus's response to Him.

And Jesus said to him, "Today salvation has come to this house, because he, too, is a son of Abraham. For the Son of Man has come to seek and to save that which was lost" (Luke 19:9, 10; cf. Matthew 18:11).

[JESUS' MISSION from For I have come down from heaven, not to do My own will, but the will of Him who sent Me]
Setting: Capernaum. The day after Jesus walks on the Sea of Galilee to join His disciples in a boat, the people He miraculously fed with a lad's five loaves and two fish ask the Lord to always give them this bread out of heaven.

Jesus said to them, "I am the bread of life; he who comes to Me will not hunger, and he who believes in Me will never thirst. But I said to you that you have seen Me, and yet do not believe. All that the Father gives Me will come to Me, and the one who comes to Me I will certainly not cast out. For I have come down from heaven, not to do My own will, but the will of Him who sent Me. This is the will of Him who sent Me, that of all that He has given Me I lose nothing, but raise it up on the last day. For this is the will of My Father, that everyone who beholds the Son and believes in Him will have eternal life, and I Myself will raise him up on the last day" (John 6:35–40; see John 3:13, 16; 4:13, 14).

[JESUS' MISSION from For judgment I came into this world]
Setting: Jerusalem. Following the Pharisees' interrogation and dismissal of the formerly blind man Jesus restored his sight on the Sabbath, the Lord addresses the Pharisees about His mission in this world.

And Jesus said, "For judgment I came into this world, so that those who do not see may see, and that those who see may become blind" (John 9:39; see Luke 4:18; John 5:22, 27).

[JESUS' MISSION from I have come *as* Light into the world, so that everyone who believes in Me will not remain in darkness]
Setting: Jerusalem. Just days before the Passover, with the chief priests and Pharisees plotting to seize Jesus, who is expressing anxiety about His upcoming crucifixion, some of the Jews believe in Jesus, while others are rejecting His message.

And Jesus cried out and said, "He who believes in Me, does not believe in Me but in Him who sent Me. He who sees Me sees the One who sent Me. I have come *as* Light into the world, so that everyone who believes in Me will not remain in darkness. If anyone hears My sayings and does not keep them, I do not judge him; for I did not come to judge the world, but to save the world. He who rejects Me and does not receive My sayings, has one who judges him; the word I spoke is what will judge him at the last day. For I did not speak on My own initiative, but the Father Himself who sent Me has given Me a commandment *as to* what to say and what to speak. I know that His commandment is eternal life; therefore the things I speak, I speak just as the Father as told Me" (John 12:44–50; see Matthew 10:40; Luke 10:16; John 1:4; 3:17; 5:19; 6:68; 14:9).

[JESUS' MISSION from As You sent Me into the world]
Setting: Jerusalem. Before the Passover, after giving His disciples hope that in the midst of tribulation they will have His peace, Jesus continues praying His high-priestly prayer.

"But now I come to You; and these things I speak in the world so that they may have My joy made full in themselves. I have given them Your word; and the world has hated them, because they are not of the world, even as I am not of the world. I do not ask You to take them out of the world, but to keep them from the evil *one.* They are not of the world, even as I am not of the world. Sanctify them in the truth; Your word is truth. As You sent Me into the world, I also have sent them into the world. For their sakes I sanctify Myself, that they themselves also may be sanctified in truth. I do not ask on behalf of these alone, but for those also who believe in Me through their word; that they may all be one; even as You, Father, *are* in Me and I in You, that they also maybe in Us, so that the world may believe that You sent Me" (John 17:13–21; see Matthew 10:5, 38; John 7:33; 15:3, 11, 19).

[JESUS' MISSION from for this I have come into the world, to testify to the truth]
Setting: Jerusalem. After the previous and current high priests (Annas and Caiaphas) question Jesus, and Peter denies the second and third times being His disciple, Pilate (Roman governor of Judea) questions the Lord in an attempt to determine if He is a king.

Therefore Pilate said to Him, "So You are a king?" Jesus answered, "You say *correctly* that I am a king. For this I have been born, and for this I have come into the world, to testify to the truth. Everyone who is of the truth hears my voice" (John 18:37; cf. Matthew 27:11; Mark 15:2; Luke 23:3).

JESUS' NAME (Also see JESUS; LORD (God); LORD, NAME OF THE; and NAME, MY)

[JESUS' NAME from Your name]
Setting: Galilee. During the early part of His ministry, Jesus preaches the Sermon on the Mount to His disciples and the multitudes.

"Not everyone who says to Me, 'Lord, Lord,' will enter the kingdom of heaven, but he who does the will of My Father who is in heaven *will enter.* Many will say to Me on that day, 'Lord, Lord, did we not prophesy in Your name, and in Your name cast out demons, and in Your name perform many miracles?' And then I will declare to them, 'I never knew you, DEPART FROM ME, YOU WHO PRACTICE LAWLESSNESS'"(Matthew 7:21–23, Jesus quotes from Psalm 6:8; cf. Matthew 25:11–13; see Luke 6:46).

[JESUS' NAME from His name]
Setting: Jerusalem. After rising from the grave on the third day following being crucified, and appearing to two of His followers on the road to Emmaus, Jesus gives instruction to His disciples (except Thomas) about His mission on earth and the promise of future power from God.

Now He said to them, "These are My words which I spoke to you while I was still with you, that all things which are written about Me in the Law of Moses and the Prophets and the Psalms must be fulfilled." Then He opened their minds to understand the Scriptures, and He said to them, "Thus it is written, that the Christ would suffer and rise again from the dead the third day, and that repentance for forgiveness of sins would be proclaimed in His name to all the nations, beginning from Jerusalem. You are witnesses of these things. And behold, I am sending forth the promise of My Father upon you; but you are to stay in the city until you are clothed with power from on high" (Luke 24:44–49; see Matthew 28:19, 20; Acts 1:8).

[JESUS' NAME from the name of the only begotten Son of God]
Setting: Jerusalem. At the time for the Passover of the Jews, after the Lord cleanses the temple, a Pharisee, Nicodemus, asks Him by night the meaning of "born again."

"For God so loved the world, that He gave His only begotten Son, that whoever believes in Him shall not perish, but have eternal life. For God did not send the Son into the world to judge the world, but that the world might be saved through Him. He who believes in Him is not judged; he who does not believe has been judged already, because he has not believed in the name of the only begotten Son of God. This is the judgment, that the Light has come into the world, and men loved darkness rather than the Light, for their deeds were evil. For everyone who does evil hates the Light, and does not come to the Light for fear that his deeds will be exposed. But he who practices the truth comes to the Light, so that his deeds may be manifested as having been wrought in God" (John 3:16–21; see Luke 19:10; John 1:4; 1:18; Romans 5:8; 1 John 1:6, 7).

JESUS' NAME'S SAKE (Listed under SAKE, JESUS' NAME'S)

JESUS' OBEDIENCE (Listed under OBEDIENCE, JESUS')

JESUS' OMNISCIENCE (Listed under OMNISCIENCE, JESUS')

JESUS' POST-RESURRECTION APPEARANCES

Setting: Jerusalem. The day after the Sabbath, after rising from the dead, Jesus appears to Mary Magdalene and the other Mary with instructions for His disciples.

Then Jesus said to them, "Do not be afraid; go and take word to My brethren to leave for Galilee, and there they will see Me" (Matthew 28:10; see Matthew 28:1–9; John 20:17).

Setting: On a mountain in Galilee. Forty days after His resurrection from the dead after having been crucified in Jerusalem, Jesus conveys the Great Commission to the eleven remaining disciples.

And Jesus came up and spoke to them, saying, "All authority has been given to Me in heaven and on earth. Go therefore and make disciples of all the nations, baptizing them in the name of the Father and the Son and the Holy Spirit, teaching them to observe all that I commanded you; and lo, I am with you always, even to the end of the age" (Matthew 28:18–20; cf. Mark 16:15; see Daniel 7:13; Matthew 28:16, 17).

Setting: On a mountain in Galilee. Forty days after His resurrection from the dead after having been crucified in Jerusalem, Jesus commissions His disciples to preach His gospel to the world.

And He said to them, "Go into all the world and preach the gospel to all creation. He who has believed and has been baptized shall be saved; but he who has disbelieved shall be condemned. These signs will accompany those who have believed: in My name they will cast out demons, they will speak with new tongues; they will pick up serpents, and if they drink any deadly *poison,* it will not hurt them; they will lay hands on the sick, and they will recover" (Mark 16:15–18; cf. Matthew 28:16–20; see Mark 9:38; John 3:18, 36; 1 Corinthians 15:6).

Note: Some scholars question the authenticity of Mark 16:19-20 as these verses do not appear in some early New Testament manuscripts.

Setting: On the way from Jerusalem. After dying on the cross the day before the Sabbath, being buried in a tomb by Joseph of Arimathea, Jesus rises from the grave on the day after the Sabbath and appears to two of His followers on the road to Emmaus.

And He said to them, "What are these words that you are exchanging with one another as you are walking?" And they stood still, looking sad (Luke 24:17; see Mark 16:12, 13; Luke 24:1–16).

Setting: On the way from Jerusalem. After rising from the grave on the third day, following His crucifixion, Jesus appears to two of His followers on the road to Emmaus and asks them a question.

And He said to them, "What things?" And they said to Him, "The things about Jesus the Nazarene, who was a prophet mighty in deed and word in the sight of God and all the people, and how the chief priests and our rulers delivered Him to the sentence of death, and crucified Him (Luke 24:19, 20; see Matthew 21:11; Luke 24:1–18).

Setting: On the way from Jerusalem. After rising from the grave on the third day, following His crucifixion, Jesus appears to two of His followers on the road to Emmaus, elaborating on the purpose of His coming to earth. They had heard reports the tomb was empty.

And He said to them, "O foolish men and slow of heart to believe in all that the prophets have spoken! Was it not necessary for the Christ to suffer these things and to enter into His glory?" (Luke 24:25, 26; see Luke 24:1–24, 44).

Setting: Jerusalem. After rising from the grave on the third day, after having been crucified, and appearing to two of His followers on the road to Emmaus, Jesus appears to others.

While they were telling these things, He Himself stood in their midst and said to them, "Peace be to you." But they were startled and frightened and thought they were seeing a spirit. And He said to them, "Why are you troubled, and why do doubts arise in your hearts? See My hands and My feet, that it is I Myself; touch Me and see, for a spirit does not have flesh and bones as you see that I have." And when He had said this, He showed them His hands and His feet. While they still could not believe *it* because of their joy and amazement. He said to them, "Have you anything to eat?" They gave Him a piece of a broiled fish; and He took it and ate *it* before them (Luke 24:36–43; see Mark 16:14; Luke 24:1–24, 44; John 20:27; Acts 10:40, 41).

Setting: Jerusalem. After rising from the grave on the third day, following being crucified, and appearing to two of His followers on the road to Emmaus, Jesus gives instruction to some of the Twelve about His mission on earth and the promise of future power from God.

Now He said to them, "These are My words which I spoke to you while I was still with you, that all things which are written about Me in the Law of Moses and the Prophets and the Psalms must be fulfilled." Then He opened their minds to understand the Scriptures, and He said to them, "Thus it is written, that the Christ would suffer and rise again from the dead the third day, and that repentance for forgiveness of sins would be proclaimed in His name to all the nations, beginning from Jerusalem. You are witnesses of these things. And behold, I am sending forth the promise of My Father upon you; but you are to stay in the city until you are clothed with power from on high" (Luke 24:44–49; see Matthew 28:19, 20; Luke 24:1–43; Acts 1:8).

Setting: Jerusalem. The risen Jesus first appears to Mary Magdalene after she tells Simon Peter and John about the empty tomb where Jesus had been the day before the Sabbath after dying on the cross for the sins of the world.

Jesus said to her, "Woman, why are you weeping? Whom are you seeking?" Supposing Him to be the gardener, she said to Him, "Sir, if you have carried Him away, tell me where you have laid Him, and I will take Him away." Jesus said to her, "Mary!" She turned and said to Him in Hebrew "Rabboni!" (which means, Teacher). Jesus said to her, "Stop clinging to Me, for I have not yet ascended to the Father; but go to My brethren and say to them, 'I ascend to My Father and your Father, and My God and Your God'" (John 20:15–17; see Mark 16:9–11; John 7:33; 19:31–42; 20:1–14, 18).

Setting: Jerusalem. After Mary Magdalene encounters the risen Jesus in the morning, in the evening He stands in the midst of His disciples (with the exception of Thomas) in hiding behind closed doors due to fear of the Jewish religious leaders.

So when it was evening on that day, the first *day* of the week, and when the doors were shut where the disciples were, for fear of the Jews, Jesus came and stood in their midst and said to them, "Peace *be* with you." And when He had said this, He showed them both His hands and His side. The disciples then rejoiced when they saw the Lord. So Jesus said to them again, "Peace *be* with you; as the Father has sent Me, I also send you." And when He had said this, He breathed on them and said to them, "Receive the Holy Spirit. If you forgive the sins of any, *their sins* have been forgiven them; if you retain the *sins* of any, they have been retained" (John 20:19–23; cf. Luke 24:36–43; see Matthew 16:19; Mark 16:14; John 20:1–18).

Setting: Jerusalem. The risen Jesus meets with His disciple Thomas (Didymus), who had doubts about the testimony of the other disciples claiming to have seen and spoken with the Lord eight days earlier.

After eight days His disciples were again inside, and Thomas with them. Jesus came, the doors having been shut, and stood in their midst and said, "Peace *be* with you." Then He said to Thomas, "Reach here with your finger, and see My hands; and reach here your hand and put it into My side; and do not be unbelieving, but believing." Thomas answered and said to Him, "My Lord and my God!" Jesus said to him, "Because you have seen Me, have you believed? Blessed *are* they who did not see, and *yet* believed" (John 20:26–29; see Luke 24:36, 40; John 20:1–25, 30, 31; 1 Peter 1:8).

Setting: By the Sea of Galilee (Tiberias). During His third post-resurrection appearance to His disciples, Jesus directs them to a great catch of fish following their unsuccessful night of fishing.

So Jesus said to them, "Children, you do not have any fish, do you?" They answered Him, "No." And He said to them, "Cast the net on the right-hand side of the boat and you will find a *catch*." So they cast, and then they were not able to haul it in because of the great number of fish (John 21:5, 6; see Luke 5:4; John 21:1–4).

Setting: By the Sea of Galilee (Tiberias). In His third post-resurrection appearance to His disciples, after providing them a great catch of fish following their unsuccessful night of fishing, Jesus asks them to bring Him some of the fish.

Jesus said to them, "Bring some of the fish which you have now caught" (John 21:10; see John 21:1–9, 11).

Setting: By the Sea of Galilee (Tiberias). In His third post-resurrection appearance to His disciples, after providing them a great catch of fish following their unsuccessful night of fishing, Jesus invites them to have breakfast with Him.

Jesus said to them, "Come *and* have breakfast." None of the disciples ventured to question Him, "Who are You?" knowing that it was the Lord (John 21:12; see John 21:1–11).

Setting: By the Sea of Galilee (Tiberias). During His third appearance to His disciples after His resurrection from the dead in Jerusalem, Jesus quizzes Peter three times regarding his love for Him.

So when they had finished breakfast, Jesus said to Simon Peter, "Simon, *son* of John, do you love Me more than these?" He said to Him, "Yes, Lord; You know that I love You." He said to him, "Tend My lambs." He said to him again a second time, "Simon, *son* of John, do you love Me?" He said to Him, "Yes, Lord; You know that I love You." He said to him, "Shepherd My sheep." He said to him the third time, "Simon, *son* of John, do you love Me?" Peter was grieved because He said to him the third time, "Do you love Me?" And he said to Him, "Lord, You know all things; You know that I love You." Jesus said to him, "Tend My sheep" (John 21:15–17; see Matthew 26:33; Mark 14:29; John 21:1–14).

Setting: By the Sea of Galilee (Tiberias). During the Lord's third post-resurrection appearance to the disciples, after quizzing Peter regarding his love for Him, Jesus gives this disciple details about his aging and his eventual death.

"Truly, truly, I say to you, when you were younger, you used to gird yourself and walk wherever you wished; but when you grow old, you will stretch out your hands and someone else will gird you, and bring you where you do not wish to *go*." Now this He said, signifying by what kind of death he would glorify God. And when He had spoken this, He said to him, "Follow Me!" (John 21:18, 19; see John 21:1–17).

Setting: By the Sea of Galilee (Tiberias). During His third post-resurrection appearance to the disciples, after quizzing Peter regarding his love for Him, Jesus responds to Peter's inquiry about the future of the disciple John.

Jesus said to him, "If I want him to remain until I come, what *is that* to you? You follow Me!" Therefore this saying went out among the brethren that that disciple would not die; yet Jesus did not say to him that he would not die, but *only*, "If I want him to remain until I come, what *is that* to you?" (John 21:22, 23; see Matthew 8:22; 16:27; John 21:1–21).

Setting: Jerusalem. Luke, writing in Acts, presents quotations from Jesus' post-resurrection appearances prior to returning to heaven, during which He informs and instructs His disciples of their imminent baptism with the Holy Spirit as they remain in Jerusalem.

Gathering them together, He commanded them not to leave Jerusalem, but to wait for what the Father had promised, "Which," *He said,* "you heard of from Me; for John baptized with water, but you will be baptized with the Holy Spirit not many days from now" (Acts 1:4, 5; see Luke 24:49; John 14:16, 26; Acts 1:1–3; 2:1–4).

Setting: Jerusalem. Luke, writing in Acts, presents quotations from Jesus' post-resurrection appearances, during which He responds to His disciples' question if He is about to restore the kingdom to Israel as they remain in Jerusalem.

He said to them, "It is not for you to know times or epochs which the Father has fixed by His own authority; but you will receive power when the Holy Spirit has come upon you; and you shall be My witnesses both in Jerusalem, and in all Judea and Samaria, and even to the remotest part of the earth" (Acts 1:7, 8; see Luke 24:48, 49; Acts 1:1–6; 2:1–4).

JESUS' POWER (See POWER, JESUS'; also see DEMONS, CASTING OUT; DOMINION; HEALING; MIRACLE; MIRACLES; POWER OF GOD; RESUSCITATION; and SIGNS AND WONDERS)

JESUS' PREEXISTENCE

[JESUS' PREEXISTENCE from Your father Abraham rejoiced to see My day]
Setting: The temple treasury in Jerusalem. While Jesus is interacting with the scribes and Pharisees, they state their belief Jesus is a demon-possessed Samaritan because of His statement that anyone who keeps His word will never taste death.

Jesus answered, "If I glorify Myself, My glory is nothing; it is My Father who glorifies Me, of whom you say, 'He is our God'; and you have not come to know Him, but I know Him; and if I say that I do not know Him, I will be a liar like you, but I do know Him and keep His word. Your father Abraham rejoiced to see My day, and he saw *it* and was glad" (John 8:54–56; see Matthew 13:17; John 7:29).

[JESUS' PREEXISTENCE from before Abraham was born, I am]
Setting: The temple treasury in Jerusalem. While Jesus is interacting with the scribes and Pharisees, they question how He, not yet fifty years old in their eyes, could claim to have seen Abraham.

Jesus said to them, "Truly, truly, I say to you, before Abraham was born, I am" (John 8:58; see Exodus 3:14).

[JESUS' PREEXISTENCE from I had with You before the world was]
Setting: Jerusalem. Before the Passover, after giving His disciples hope that in the midst of tribulation they will have His peace, Jesus prays His high-priestly prayer.

Jesus spoke these things; and lifting up His eyes to heaven, He said, "Father, the hour has come; glorify Your Son, that the Son may glorify You, even as You gave Him authority over all flesh, that to all whom You have given Him, He may give eternal life. This is eternal life, that they may know You, the only true God, and Jesus Christ whom You have sent. I glorified You on the earth, having accomplished the work which You have given Me to do. Now, Father, glorify Me together with Yourself, with the glory which I had with You before the world was. I have manifested Your name to the men whom You gave Me out of the world; they were Yours and You gave them to Me, and they have kept Your word. Now they have come to know that everything You have given Me is from You; for the words which You gave Me I have given to them; and they received *them* and truly understood that I came forth from You, and they believed You sent Me. I ask on their behalf; I do not ask on behalf of the world, but of those whom You have given Me; for they are Yours; and all things that are Mine are Yours, and Yours are Mine; and I have been glorified in them. I am no longer in the world; and *yet* they themselves are in the world, and I come to You. Holy Father, keep them in Your name, *the name* which You have given Me, that they may be even as We *are.* While I was with them, I was keeping them in Your name which You have given Me; and I guarded them and not one of them perished but the son of perdition, so that the Scripture would be fulfilled" (John 17:1–12; see Luke 22:32; John 1:1; 3:35; 4:34; 5:44; 6:37–39, 70; 8:42; 11:41; 12:49; 13:18, 31; 16:15; Philippians 2:9).

[JESUS' PREEXISTENCE from who is and who was and who is to come, the Almighty]
Setting: On the small island of Patmos (in the Aegean Sea about fifty miles southwest of Ephesus in modern Turkey). Approximately fifty years after Jesus' resurrection, His angel speaks the first words of His revelation to His bond-servant, the apostle John.

"I am the Alpha and the Omega," says the Lord God, "who is and who was and who is to come, the Almighty" (Revelation 1:8; see Revelation 21:6).

JESUS' PRESENCE (Listed under PRESENCE, JESUS')

JESUS' PURPOSE (Also see ETERNAL LIFE; JESUS' MISSION; JESUS' WORK; and SALVATION)

[JESUS' PURPOSE from the Son of Man has come to save that which was lost]
Setting: Capernaum of Galilee. After conveying the value of little ones when His disciples ask Him about greatness in the kingdom of heaven, Jesus states His earthly mission.

["For the Son of Man has come to save that which was lost] (Matthew 18:11; cf. Luke 19:10).

[JESUS' PURPOSE from the Son of Man did not come to be served, but to serve, and to give His life a ransom for many]
Setting: On the way to Jerusalem, where Jesus will die on the cross. Jesus teaches His disciples about true greatness after the mother of disciples James and John asks Him to make her sons exalted rulers with Him in His coming kingdom.

But Jesus called them to Himself and said, "You know that the rulers of the Gentiles lord it over them, and *their* great men exercise authority over them. It is not this way among you, but whoever wishes to become great among you shall be your servant, and whoever wishes to be first among you shall be your slave; just as the Son of Man did not come to be served, but to serve, and to give His life a ransom for many" (Matthew 20:25–28; cf. Matthew 23:11; 26:28; Mark 10:42–45).

[JESUS' PURPOSE from For even the Son of Man did not come to be served, but to serve, and to give His life a ransom for many]
Setting: On the road to Jerusalem. James and John ask Jesus for special honor and privileges in His kingdom. The other disciples become angry, so the Lord uses this moment to teach all of them about servanthood.

Calling them to Himself, Jesus said to them, "You know that those who are recognized as rulers of the Gentiles lord it over them; and their great men exercise authority over them. But it is not this way among you, but whoever wishes to become great among you shall be your servant; and whoever wishes to be first among you shall be slave of all. For even the Son of Man did not come to be served, but to serve, and to give His life a ransom for many" (Mark 10:42–45; cf. Matthew 20:25–28).

[JESUS' PURPOSE from I must preach the kingdom of God to the other cities also, for I was sent for this purpose]
Setting: Capernaum. After healing Simon Peter's mother-in-law from a high fever, Jesus tries to retreat to a secluded place in Galilee, but when the crowds locate Him, He proclaims His mission.

But He said to them, "I must preach the kingdom of God to the other cities also, for I was sent for this purpose" (Luke 4:43; cf. Matthew 4:23, 24; Mark 1:35–39).

[JESUS' PURPOSE from the Son of Man did not come to destroy men's lives, but to save them]
Setting: Galilee. After clarifying who the disciples' co-laborers are, Jesus prepares to go to Jerusalem by sending messengers ahead to Samaria, where they experience rejection and seek retribution.

But He turned and rebuked them, [and said, "You do not know what kind of spirit you are of; for the Son of Man did not come to destroy men's lives, but to save them."] And they went on to another village. (Luke 9:55, 56; see 2 Kings 1:9–14; Luke 13:22).

[JESUS' PURPOSE from the Son of Man has come to seek and to save that which was lost]
Setting: Jericho, on the way to Jerusalem. After taking time to heal a blind man, Jesus comments on Zaccheus's response to Him.

And Jesus said to him, "Today salvation has come to this house, because he, too, is a son of Abraham. For the Son of Man has come to seek and to save that which was lost" (Luke 19:9, 10; cf. Matthew 18:11).

[JESUS' PURPOSE from For God did not send the Son into the world to judge the world, but that the world might be saved through Him]
Setting: Jerusalem. At the time for the Passover of the Jews, after the Lord cleanses the temple, a Pharisee, Nicodemus, asks Him by night the meaning of "born again."

"For God so loved the world, that He gave His only begotten Son, that whoever believes in Him shall not perish, but have eternal life. For God did not send the Son into the world to judge the world, but that the world might be saved through Him. He who believes in Him is not judged; he who does not believe has been judged already, because he has not believed in the name of the only begotten Son of God. This is the judgment, that the Light has come into the world, and men loved darkness rather than the Light, for their deeds were evil. For everyone who does evil hates the Light, and does not come to the Light for fear that his deeds will be exposed. But he who practices the truth comes to the Light, so that his deeds may be manifested as having been wrought in God" (John 3:16–21; see Luke 19:10; John 1:4; 1:18; 3:1–15; Romans 5:8; 1 John 1:6, 7).

[JESUS' PURPOSE from I came that they may have life, and have *it* abundantly]
Setting: Jerusalem. Following the Pharisees' interrogation and dismissal of the formerly blind man Jesus healed on the Sabbath, the Lord conveys the Parable of the Good Shepherd to the Pharisees, using figures of speech they do not understand.

So Jesus said to them again, "Truly, truly, I say to you, I am the door of the sheep. All who came before Me are thieves and robbers, but the sheep did not hear them. I am the door; if anyone enters through Me, he will be saved, and will go in and out and find pasture. The thief comes only to steal and kill and destroy; I came that they may have life, and have *it* abundantly. I am the good shepherd; the good shepherd lays down His life for the sheep. He who is a hired hand, and not a shepherd, who is not the owner of the sheep, sees the wolf coming, and leaves the sheep and flees, and the wolf snatches them and scatters *them. He flees* because he is a hired hand and is not concerned about the sheep. I am the good shepherd, and I know My own and My own know Me, even as the Father knows Me and I know the Father; and I lay down My life for the sheep. I have other sheep, which are not of this fold; I must bring them also, and they will hear My voice; and they will become one flock *with* one shepherd. For this reason the Father loves Me, because I lay down My life so that I may take it again. No one has taken it away from Me, but I lay it down on My own initiative. I have authority to take it up again. This commandment I received from My Father" (John 10:7–18; see Isaiah 40:11; 56:8; Jeremiah 23:1; Matthew 11:27).

[JESUS' PURPOSE from for this purpose I came to this hour]
Setting: Jerusalem. Just days before the Passover, with the chief priests and Pharisees plotting to seize Him and crowds welcoming Him with palm branches and praise, Jesus expresses anxiety about His upcoming crucifixion.

"Now My soul has become troubled; and what shall I say, 'Father, save Me from this hour'? But for this purpose I came to this hour. Father glorify Your name." Then a voice came out of heaven: "I have glorified it, and will glorify it again." So the crowd *of people* who stood by and heard it were saying that it had thundered; others were saying, "An angel has spoken to Him." Jesus answered and said, "This voice has not come for My sake, but for your sakes. Now judgment is upon this world; now the ruler of this world will be cast out. And I, if I am lifted up from the earth, will draw all men to Myself" (John 12:27–32; see Matthew 3:17; 26:38; John 3:14; 6:44; 11:42; 14:30).

JESUS' RESPONSES AT HIS OFFICIAL TRIALS (Listed under TRIALS, JESUS' RESPONSES AT HIS OFFICIAL)

JESUS' RETURN (Also see LORD, COMING OF THE; and SON OF MAN, COMING OF THE)

[JESUS' RETURN from the end will come]

Setting: The Mount of Olives, just east of Jerusalem. During His Olivet Discourse, Jesus answers His disciples' questions as to when the temple will be destroyed and Jerusalem overrun, along with the signs of His coming and the end of the age.

And Jesus answered and said to them, "See to it that no one misleads you. For many will come in My name, saying, 'I am the Christ,' and will mislead many. You will be hearing of wars and rumors of wars. See that you are not frightened, for *those things* must take place, but *that* is not yet the end. For nation will rise against nation, and kingdom against kingdom, and in various places there will be famines and earthquakes. But all these things are *merely* the beginning of birth pangs. Then they will deliver you to tribulation, and will kill you, and you will be hated by all nations because of My name. At that time many will fall away and will betray one another and hate one another. Many false prophets will arise and will mislead many. Because lawlessness is increased, most people's love will grow cold. But the one who endures to the end, he will be saved. This gospel of the kingdom shall be preached in the whole world as a testimony to all the nations, and then the end will come" (Matthew 24:4–14; cf. Jeremiah 29:8; Matthew 7:15; 10:17, 22; Mark 13:3–13; Luke 21:7–19; Revelation 6:4).

[JESUS' RETURN from He is near, *right* at the door]

Setting: On the Mount of Olives, just east of Jerusalem. During His Olivet Discourse, after answering His disciples' questions as to when the temple will be destroyed and Jerusalem overrun, along with the signs of His coming and the end of the age, Jesus teaches them the Parable of the Fig Tree.

"Now learn the parable from the fig tree: when its branch has already become tender and puts forth its leaves, you know that summer is near; so, you too, when you see all these things, recognize that He is near, *right* at the door. Truly, I say to you, this generation will not pass away until all these things take place. Heaven and earth will pass away, but My words will not pass away. But of that day and hour no one knows, not even the angels of heaven, nor the Son, but the Father alone. For the coming of the Son of Man will be just like the days of Noah. For as in those days before the flood they were eating and drinking, marrying and giving in marriage, until the day that Noah entered the ark, and they did not understand until the flood came and took them all away; so will the coming of the Son of Man be. Then there will be two men in the field; one will be taken and one will be left. Two women *will be* grinding at the mill; one will be taken and one will be left" (Matthew 24:32–41; cf. Mark 13:28–32; Luke 17:34–36; 21:28–33; see Genesis 6:5; 7:7; Matthew 5:18; 10:23; James 5:9).

[JESUS' RETURN from the bridegroom came]

Setting: On the Mount of Olives, just east of Jerusalem. During His Olivet Discourse, after answering His disciples' questions as to when the temple will be destroyed and Jerusalem overrun, along with the signs of His coming and the end of the age, Jesus reemphasizes to His disciples that they should be on the alert for His return.

"Then the kingdom of heaven will be comparable to ten virgins, who took their lamps and went out to meet the bridegroom. Five of them were foolish, and five were prudent. For when the foolish took their lamps, they took no oil with them, but the prudent took oil in flasks along with their lamps. Now while the bridegroom was delaying, they all got drowsy and *began* to sleep. But at midnight there was a shout, 'Behold, the bridegroom! Come out to meet *him.*' Then all those virgins rose and trimmed their lamps. The foolish said to the prudent, 'Give us some of your oil, for our lamps are going out.' But the prudent answered, 'No, there will not be enough for us and you *too;* go instead to the dealers and buy *some* for yourselves.' And while they were going away to make the purchase, the bridegroom came, and those who were ready went in with him to the wedding feast; and the door was shut. Later the other virgins also came, saying, 'Lord, lord, open up for us.' But he answered, 'Truly I say to you, I do not know you.' Be on the alert then, for you do not know the day nor the hour" (Matthew 25:1–13; cf. Matthew 24:42; Luke 12:35; see Matthew 7:21, 24).

[JESUS' RETURN from He is near, *right* at the door]
Setting: On the Mount of Olives, east of the temple in Jerusalem. After prophesying the temple's destruction, Jesus responds during His Olivet Discourse to questions from Peter, James, John, and Andrew about other future events.

"Now learn the parable from the fig tree: when its branch has already become tender and puts forth its leaves, you know that summer is near. Even so, you too, when you see these things happening, recognize that He is near, *right* at the door. Truly I say to you, this generation will not pass away until all these things take place. Heaven and earth will pass away, but My words will not pass away. But of the day or hour no one knows, not even the angels in heaven, nor the Son, but the Father *alone*" (Mark 13:28–32; cf. Matthew 24:32–36; Luke 21:28–33).

[JESUS' RETURN from for you do not know when the master of the house is coming]
Setting: On the Mount of Olives, east of the temple in Jerusalem. After prophesying the temple's destruction, Jesus responds during His Olivet Discourse to questions from Peter, James, John, and Andrew about other future events.

"Take heed, keep on the alert; for you do not know when the *appointed* time will come. *It is* like a man away on a journey, *who* upon leaving his house and putting his slaves in charge, *assigning* to each one his task, also commanded the doorkeeper to stay on the alert. Therefore, be on the alert—for you do not know when the master of the house is coming, whether in the evening, at midnight, or when the rooster crows, or in the morning—in case he should come suddenly and find you asleep. What I say to you I say to all, 'Be on the alert!' " (Mark 13:33–37; cf. Matthew 24:42, 43; Luke 21:34–36; see Luke 12:36–38; Ephesians 6:18).

[JESUS' RETURN from on the day that the Son of Man is revealed]
Setting: Samaria, on the way from Galilee to Jerusalem. After the Pharisees question Him about the coming of the kingdom of God, Jesus tells His disciples of His second coming.

And He said to the disciples, "The days will come when you will long to see one of the days of the Son of Man, and you will not see it. They will say to you, 'Look there! Look here!' Do not go away, and do not run after *them*. For just like the lightning, when it flashes out of one part of the sky, shines to the other part of the sky, so will the Son of Man be in His day. But first He must suffer many things and be rejected by this generation. And just as it happened in the days of Noah, so it will be also in the days of the Son of Man: they were eating, they were drinking, they were marrying, they were being given in marriage, until the day that Noah entered the ark, and the flood came and destroyed them all. It was the same as happened in the days of Lot: they were eating, they were drinking, they were buying, they were selling, they were planting, they were building; but on the day that Lot went out from Sodom it rained fire and brimstone from heaven and destroyed them all. It will be just the same on the day that the Son of Man is revealed. On that day, the one who is on the housetop and whose goods are in the house must not go down to take them out; and likewise the one who is in the field must not turn back. Remember Lot's wife. Whoever seeks to keep his life will lose it, and whoever loses *his life* will preserve it. I tell you, on that night there will be two in one bed; one will be taken and the other will be left. There will be two women grinding at the same place; one will be taken and the other will be left. [Two men will be in the field; one will be taken and the other will be left."] And answering they said to Him, "Where, Lord?" And He said to them, "Where the body *is*, there also the vultures will be gathered" (Luke 17:22–37; see Genesis 19; Matthew 10:39; 16:21, 27; 24:17–28, 37–41).

[JESUS' RETURN from I will come to you]
Setting: Jerusalem. Before the Passover, after responding to Philip's request for Him to show His disciples the Father, Jesus conveys the upcoming role of the Holy Spirit in their lives.

"I will not leave you as orphans; I will come to you. After a little while the world will no longer see Me, but you *will* see Me; because I live, you will live also. In that day you will know that I am in the Father, and you in Me, and I in you. He who has My commandments and keeps them is the one who loves Me; and he who loves Me will be loved by My Father, and I will love him and will disclose Myself to him" (John 14:18–21; see John 6:57; 10:37, 38; 16:16, 22).

[JESUS' RETURN from I go away, and I will come to you]
Setting: Jerusalem. Before the Passover, after He conveys the upcoming ministry of the Holy Spirit in His disciples' lives, Jesus again relates peace, hope, and comfort to them regarding His return to the Father.

"Peace I leave with you; My peace I give to you; not as the world gives do I give to you. Do not let your heart be troubled, nor let it be fearful. You heard that I said to you, 'I go away, and I will come to you,' If you loved Me, you would have rejoiced because I go to the Father, for the Father is greater than I. Now I have told you before it happens, so that when it happens, you may believe. I will not speak much more with you, for the ruler of the world is coming, and he has nothing in Me; but so that the world may know that I love the Father, I do exactly as the Father commanded Me. Get up, let us go from here" (John 14:27–31; see John 10:18, 29; 12:31; 13:19; 16:33).

[JESUS' RETURN from until I come]
Setting: By the Sea of Galilee. During His third post-resurrection appearance to the disciples, after quizzing Peter three times regarding the disciple's love for Him, Jesus responds to his inquiry about the future of John the disciple.

Jesus said to him, "If I want him to remain until I come, what *is that* to you? You follow Me!" Therefore this saying went out among the brethren that that disciple would not die; yet Jesus did not say to him that he would not die, but *only*, "If I want him to remain until I come, what *is that* to you?" (John 21:22, 23; see Matthew 8:22; 16:27).

[JESUS' RETURN from hold fast until I come]
Setting: On the island of Patmos (in the Aegean Sea about fifty miles southwest of Ephesus in modern Turkey). On the Lord's Day (Sunday), approximately fifty years after the Resurrection, the disciple John encounters the Lord Jesus Christ, who communicates a new revelation for the apostle to record for the church in Thyatira and to six other churches in Asia.

"And to the angel of the church in Thyatira write: The Son of God, who has eyes like a flame of fire, and His feet are like burnished bronze, says this: 'I know your deeds, and your love and faith and service and perseverance, and that your deeds of late are greater than at first. But I have *this* against you, that you tolerate the woman Jezebel, who calls herself a prophetess, and she teaches and leads My bond-servants astray so that they commit *acts of* immorality and eat things sacrificed to idols. I gave her time to repent, and she does not want to repent of her immorality. Behold, I will throw her on a bed *of sickness,* and those who commit adultery with her into great tribulation, unless they repent of her deeds. And I will kill her children with pestilence, and all the churches will know that I am He who searches the minds and hearts; and I will give to each one of you according to your deeds. But I say to you, the rest who are in Thyatira, who do not hold this teaching, who have not known the deep things of Satan, as they call them—I place no other burden on you. Nevertheless what you have, hold fast until I come. He who overcomes, and he who keeps My deeds until the end, TO HIM I WILL GIVE AUTHORITY OVER THE NATIONS; AND HE SHALL RULE THEM WITH A ROD OF IRON, AS THE VESSELS OF THE POTTER ARE BROKEN TO PIECES, as I also have received *authority* from My Father; and I will give him the morning star. He who has an ear, let him hear what the Spirit says to the churches' (Revelation 2:18–29; Jesus quotes from Psalm 2:8, 9; Isaiah 30:14; see 1 Kings 16:31; Psalm 7:9; Romans 2:5; 1 Corinthians 2:10; 2 Peter 3:9; Revelation 1:14; 2:7; 3:11; 17:1–20).

[JESUS' RETURN from I am coming quickly]
Setting: On the island of Patmos (in the Aegean Sea about fifty miles southwest of Ephesus in modern Turkey). On the Lord's Day (Sunday), approximately fifty years after the Resurrection, the disciple John encounters the Lord Jesus Christ, who communicates a new revelation for the apostle to record for the church in Philadelphia and to six other churches in Asia.

"And to the angel of the church in Philadelphia write: He who is holy, who is true, who has the key of David, who opens and no one will shut, and who shuts and no one opens, says this: 'I know your deeds. Behold, I have put before you an open door which no one can shut, because you have a little power, and have kept My word, and have not denied My name. Behold, I will cause *those* of the synagogue of Satan, who say that they are Jews and are not, but lie—I will make them come and bow down at your feet, and *make them* know that I have loved you. Because you have kept the word of My perseverance, I also will keep you from the hour of testing, that *hour* which is about to come upon the whole world, to test those who dwell on the earth. I am coming quickly; hold fast what you have, so that no one will take your crown. He who overcomes, I will make him a pillar in the temple of My God, and he will not go out from it anymore; and I will write on him the name of My God, and the name of the city of My

God, the new Jerusalem, which comes down out of heaven from My God, and My new name. He who has an ear, let him hear what the Spirit says to the churches' " (Revelation 3:7–13; see Isaiah 22:22; Galatians 2:9; Revelation 2:9, 10, 13, 25; 14:1).

[JESUS' RETURN from I am coming quickly]
Setting: On the island of Patmos (in the Aegean Sea about fifty miles southwest of Ephesus in modern Turkey). In the final chapter of the Lord Jesus Christ's revelation via the disciple John, approximately fifty years after the Resurrection, the Lord reveals His upcoming return and the blessing to those who heed the words of the prophecy of this book.

"And behold, I am coming quickly. Blessed is he who heeds the words of the prophecy of this book" (Revelation 22:7; see Revelation 1:3).

[JESUS' RETURN from I am coming quickly]
Setting: On the island of Patmos (in the Aegean Sea about fifty miles southwest of Ephesus in modern Turkey). In the final chapter of the Lord Jesus Christ's revelation via the disciple John, approximately fifty years after the Resurrection, the Lord reveals His upcoming return, reward, and eternality.

"Behold, I am coming quickly, and My reward *is* with Me, to render to every man according to what he has done. I am the Alpha and the Omega, the first and the last, the beginning and the end" (Revelation 22:12, 13; see Isaiah 40:10; 44:6).

[JESUS' RETURN from I am coming quickly and Come, Lord Jesus]
Setting: On the island of Patmos (in the Aegean Sea about fifty miles southwest of Ephesus in modern Turkey). In the final chapter of the Lord Jesus Christ's revelation via the disciple John, approximately fifty years after the Resurrection, the Lord reveals His upcoming return to the earth.

He who testifies to these things says, "Yes, I am coming quickly." Amen. Come, Lord Jesus (Revelation 22:20).

JESUS' SAKE (See SAKE, MY)

JESUS' TEACHING

[JESUS' TEACHING from My teaching]
Setting: The temple in Jerusalem. After receiving encouragement from His blood brothers in Galilee to attend the upcoming Feast of Booths in order to demonstrate His works to His disciples and the world, Jesus goes and teaches, astonishing the Jewish religious leaders.

So Jesus answered them and said, "My teaching is not Mine, but His who sent Me. If anyone is willing to do His will, he will know of the teaching, whether it is of God or *whether* I speak of Myself. He who speaks from himself seeks his own glory; but He who is seeking the glory of the One who sent Him, He is true, and there is no unrighteousness in Him" (John 7:16–18; see John 5:41).

[JESUS' TEACHING from I always taught]
Setting: Jerusalem. After Jesus is betrayed by Judas, and Peter denies he is the Lord's disciple, Annas, former high priest and father-in-law of the current high priest (Caiaphas), questions Jesus about His disciples and His teaching.

Jesus answered him, "I have spoken openly to the world; I always taught in synagogues and in the temple, where all the Jews come together; and I spoke nothing in secret. Why do you question Me? Question those who have heard what I spoke to them; they know what I said" (John 18:20, 21; see John 7:26).

JESUS' WORDS (See WORD, MY; and WORDS, MY)

JESUS' WORDS DURING HIS CRUCIFIXION (See JESUS' WORDS WHILE ON THE CROSS)

JESUS' WORDS WHILE ON THE CROSS (Also, see JESUS' LAST WORDS)

Setting: Golgotha, just outside Jerusalem. Jesus speaks words of despair while dying on the cross for the sins of the world.

About the ninth hour Jesus cried out with a loud voice, saying, "ELI, ELI, LAMA SABACHTHANI?" that is, "MY GOD, MY GOD, WHY HAVE YOU FORSAKEN ME?" (Matthew 27:46, Jesus quotes from Psalm 22:1; cf. Mark 15:34).

Setting: Golgotha, just outside Jerusalem. After being arrested, tried, and sentenced to crucifixion by Pontius Pilate (Roman governor of Judea), the Lord, while hanging between two criminals, requests from His Father forgiveness for His crucifiers.

But Jesus was saying, "Father, forgive them; for they do not know what they are doing." And they cast lots, dividing up His garments among themselves (Luke 23:34; see Psalm 22:18; Matthew 27:33–36; Mark 15:22–24; John 19:23–25).

Setting: Golgotha, just outside Jerusalem. While Jesus is being mocked and ridiculed on the cross, one of the criminals being crucified with Him asks to be remembered in His kingdom, which Jesus grants with forgiveness and entrance into Paradise.

And He said to him, "Truly I say to you, today you shall be with Me in Paradise" (Luke 23:43; see Matthew 27:39–44; Mark 15:29–32).

Setting: Golgotha, just outside Jerusalem. While being mocked and ridiculed on the cross, after granting forgiveness to one of the criminals being crucified with Him who asks to be remembered in His kingdom, Jesus dies.

And Jesus, crying out with a loud voice, said, "Father, INTO YOUR HANDS I COMMIT MY SPIRIT." Having said this, He breathed His last (Luke 23:46, Jesus quotes from Psalm 31:5; cf. Matthew 27:45–50; Mark 15:33–37; John 19:28–30).

Setting: The Place of the Skull (Golgotha), just outside Jerusalem. While being crucified, Jesus unselfishly asks His disciple, John, to care for His mother.

When Jesus saw His mother, and the disciple whom He loved standing nearby, He said to His mother, "Woman, behold, your son!" Then He said to the disciple, "Behold, your mother!" From that hour the disciple took her into his own *household* (John 19:26, 27).

Setting: Golgotha (the Place of the Skull), just outside Jerusalem. After asking His disciple John to care for His mother, in the midst of fulfilling Scripture as He dies on the cross for the sins of the world, Jesus expresses His thirst.

After this, Jesus, knowing that all things had already been accomplished, to fulfill the Scripture, said, *"I am thirsty"* (John 19:28; see Psalm 69:21; Matthew 27:48; Mark 15:36).

Setting: Golgotha, just outside Jerusalem. After receiving some sour wine to quench His thirst while on the cross, Jesus accomplishes His work of dying for the sins of the world with a statement of completion.

Therefore when Jesus had received the sour wine, He said, "It is finished!" And He bowed His head and gave up His spirit (John 19:30; see Matthew 27:50; Mark 15:37; Luke 23:46).

JESUS' WORK (Also see FATHER, WORKS OF MY; JESUS' MISSION; and JESUS' PURPOSE)

[JESUS' WORK from I did not come to abolish but to fulfill]

Setting: Galilee. During the early part of His ministry, Jesus preaches the Sermon on the Mount to His disciples and the multitudes.

"Do not think that I came to abolish the Law or the Prophets; I did not come to abolish but to fulfill" (Matthew 5:17).

[JESUS' WORK from I did not come to call the righteous, but sinners]

Setting: Capernaum, near the Sea of Galilee. Jesus calls Matthew from his tax-collection booth to be His disciple.

But when Jesus heard *this,* He said, "*It is* not those who are healthy who need a physician, but those who are sick. But go and learn what this means: 'I DESIRE COMPASSION, AND NOT SACRIFICE,' for I did not come to call the righteous, but sinners" (Matthew 9:12, 13, Jesus quotes from Hosea 6:6; cf. Mark 2:17; Luke 5:31, 32; see Mark 2:15, 16).

[JESUS' WORK from the Son of Man did not come to be served, but to serve, and to give His life a ransom for many]

Setting: On the way to Jerusalem, where Jesus will die on the cross. Jesus teaches His disciples about true greatness after the mother of disciples James and John asks Him to make her sons exalted rulers with Him in His coming kingdom.

But Jesus called them to Himself and said, "You know that the rulers of the Gentiles lord it over them, and *their* great men exercise authority over them. It is not this way among you, but whoever wishes to become great among you shall be your servant, and whoever wishes to be first among you shall be your slave; just as the Son of Man did not come to be served, but to serve, and to give His life a ransom for many" (Matthew 20:25–28; cf. Matthew 23:11; 26:28; Mark 10:42–45).

[JESUS' WORK from I did not come to call the righteous, but sinners]

Setting: The home of Levi (Matthew) the tax collector in Capernaum, near the Sea of Galilee. The scribes of the Pharisees take issue with Jesus' association with sinners and tax collectors after He calls Levi (Matthew) the tax collector to be His disciple.

And hearing *this,* Jesus said to them, "*It is* not those who are healthy who need a physician, but those who are sick; I did not come to call the righteous, but sinners" (Mark 2:17; cf. Matthew 9:12, 13; Luke 5:29–32).

[JESUS' WORK from the Son of Man did not come to be served, but to serve, and to give His life a ransom for many]

Setting: On the road to Jerusalem. James and John ask Jesus for special honor and privileges in His kingdom. The other disciples become angry, so the Lord uses this moment to teach all of them about servanthood.

Calling them to Himself, Jesus said to them, "You know that those who are recognized as rulers of the Gentiles lord it over them; and their great men exercise authority over them. But it is not this way among you, but whoever wishes to become great among you shall be your servant; and whoever wishes to be first among you shall be slave of all. For even the Son of Man did not come to be served, but to serve, and to give His life a ransom for many" (Mark 10:42–45; cf. Matthew 20:25–28).

[JESUS' WORK from I was sent for this purpose]

Setting: Galilee. After healing Simon Peter's mother-in-law of a high fever, Jesus tries to retreat to a secluded place, but when the crowds locate Him, He proclaims His mission.

But He said to them, "I must preach the kingdom of God to the other cities also, for I was sent for this purpose" (Luke 4:43; cf. Matthew 4:23, 24; Mark 1:35–39).

[JESUS' WORK from I have not come to call the righteous but sinners to repentance]
Setting: The house of Levi (Matthew) in Capernaum. At a reception for Jesus, after He calls Levi to become His disciple, the Pharisees and their scribes question why the Lord associates with tax collectors and sinners.

And Jesus answered and said to them, "*It is* not those who are well who need a physician, but those who are sick. I have not come to call the righteous but sinners to repentance" (Luke 5:31, 32; cf. Matthew 9:10–13; Mark 2:15–17).

[JESUS' WORK from the Son of Man did not come to destroy men's lives, but to save them]
Setting: Galilee. After clarifying who the disciples' co-laborers are, Jesus prepares to go to Jerusalem by sending messengers ahead to Samaria, where they experience rejection and seek retribution.

But He turned and rebuked them, [and said, "You do not know what kind of spirit you are of; for the Son of Man did not come to destroy men's lives, but to save them."] And they went on to another village (Luke 9:55, 56; see 2 Kings 1:9–14; Luke 13:22).

[JESUS' WORK from the Son of Man has come to seek and to save that which was lost]
Setting: Jericho, on the way to Jerusalem. After taking time to heal a blind man, Jesus comments on Zaccheus's response to Him.

And Jesus said to him, "Today salvation has come to this house, because he, too, is a son of Abraham. For the Son of Man has come to seek and to save that which was lost" (Luke 19:9, 10; cf. Matthew 18:11).

[JESUS' WORK from My food is to do the will of Him who sent Me]
Setting: Sychar in Samaria, on the way to Galilee. After Jesus converses with a Samaritan woman at Jacob's well, the disciples return with food. They try to get Jesus to eat, but are surprised when He speaks of other food.

Jesus said to them, "My food is to do the will of Him who sent Me and to accomplish His work. Do you not say, 'There are yet four months, and *then* comes the harvest'? Behold, I say to you, lift up your eyes and look on the fields, that they are white for harvest. Already he who reaps is receiving wages and is gathering fruit for life eternal; so that he who sows and he who reaps may rejoice together. For in this *case* the saying is true, 'One sows and another reaps.' I sent you to reap that for which you have not labored; others have labored and you have entered into their labor" (John 4:34–38; see Matthew 9:37, 38; John 5:36).

[JESUS' WORK from I Myself am working]
Setting: By the pool of Bethesda in Jerusalem. During a feast of the Jews, Jesus responds to criticism from the Jewish religious leaders for healing a lame man on the Sabbath.

But He answered them, "My Father is working until now, and I Myself am working" (John 5:17).

[JESUS' WORK from these things the Son also does in like manner]
Setting: By the pool of Bethesda in Jerusalem. During a feast of the Jews, Jesus responds to criticism from the Jewish religious leaders for healing a lame man on the Sabbath and for referring to God as His Father (thereby making Himself equal with God).

Therefore Jesus answered and was saying to them, "Truly, truly, I say to you, the Son can do nothing of Himself, unless *it is* something He sees the Father doing; for whatever the Father does, these things the Son also does in like manner. For the Father loves the Son, and shows Him all things that He Himself is doing; and *the Father* will show Him greater works than these, so that you will marvel. For just as the Father raises the dead and gives them life, even so the Son also gives life to whom He wishes. For not even the Father judges anyone, but He has given all judgment to the Son, so that all will honor the Son even as they honor the Father. He who does not honor the Son does not honor the Father who sent Him" (John 5:19–23; see Luke 10:16; John 3:35; 11:25; 14:12).

[JESUS' WORK from the very works that I do]
Setting: Jerusalem. During a feast of the Jews, Jesus responds to criticism from the Jewish religious leaders by referring to God as His Father (thereby making Himself equal with God) and informing them that God, John the Baptist, and His works all testify to His mission.

"I can do nothing on My own initiative. As I hear, I judge; and My judgment is just, because I do not seek My own will, but the will of Him who sent Me. If I *alone* testify about Myself, My testimony is not true. There is another who testifies of Me, and I know that the testimony which He gives about Me is true. You have sent to John, and he has testified to the truth. But the testimony which I receive is not from man, but I say these things so that you may be saved. He was the lamp that was burning and was shining and you were willing to rejoice for a while in his light. But the testimony which I have is greater than the *testimony of* John; for the works which the Father has given Me to accomplish—the very works that I do—testify about Me, that the Father has sent Me. And the Father who sent Me, He has testified of Me. You have neither heard His voice at any time nor seen His form. You do not have His word abiding in you, for you do not believe Him whom He sent" (John 5:30–38; see Matthew 3:17; Mark 1:4, 5; John 1:7, 15, 32; 4:34; 8:14–16; 10:25, 37, 38).

[JESUS' WORK from works that I do in My Father's name]
Setting: Jerusalem. At the Feast of Dedication, just after Jesus conveys the Parable of the Good Shepherd to the Pharisees (who do not understand it), they ask Him plainly if He is the Christ.

Jesus answered them, "I told you, and you do not believe; the works that I do in My Father's name, these testify of Me. But you do not believe because you are not of My sheep. My sheep hear My voice, and I know them, and they follow Me; and I give eternal life to them, and they will never perish; and no one will snatch them out of My hand. My Father, who has given *them* to Me, is greater than all; and no one is able to snatch *them* out of the Father's hand. I and the Father are one" (John 10:25–30; see John 8:47; 10:4; 17:1, 2, 20, 21).

[JESUS' WORK from works that I do]
Setting: Jerusalem. Before the Passover, after answering Thomas' question where the Lord is going and how His disciples will know the way, Jesus responds to Philip's request for Him to show them the Father.

Jesus said to him, "Have I been so long with you, and *yet* you have not come to know Me, Philip? He who has seen Me has seen the Father; how *can* you say, 'Show us the Father'? Do you not believe that I am in the Father, and the Father is in Me? The words that I say to you I do not speak on My own initiative, but the Father abiding in Me does His works. Believe Me that I am in the Father and the Father is in Me; otherwise believe because of the works themselves. Truly, truly, I say to you, he who believes in Me, the works that I do, he will do also; and greater *works* than these he will do; because I go to the Father. Whatever you ask in My name, that will I do, so that the Father may be glorified in the Son. If you ask Me anything in My name, I will do *it*" (John 14:9–14; see Matthew 7:7; John 1:14; 5:19, 20, 36; 10:37, 38; 15:16).

[JESUS' WORK from having accomplished the work which You have given Me to do]
Setting: Jerusalem. Before the Passover, after giving His disciples assurance that in the midst of tribulation they will have His peace, Jesus prays His high-priestly prayer.

Jesus spoke these things; and lifting up His eyes to heaven, He said, "Father, the hour has come; glorify Your Son, that the Son may glorify You, even as You gave Him authority over all flesh, that to all whom You have given Him, He may give eternal life. This is eternal life, that they may know You, the only true God, and Jesus Christ whom You have sent. I glorified You on the earth, having accomplished the work which You have given Me to do. Now, Father, glorify Me together with Yourself, with the glory which I had with You before the world was. I have manifested Your name to the men whom You gave Me out of the world; they were Yours and You gave them to Me, and they have kept Your word. Now they have come to know that everything You have given Me is from You; for the words which You gave Me I have given to them; and they received *them* and truly understood that I came forth from You, and they believed You sent Me. I ask on their behalf; I do not ask on behalf of the world, but of those whom You have given Me; for they are Yours; and all things that are Mine are Yours, and Yours are Mine; and I have been glorified in them. I am no longer in the world; and *yet* they themselves are in the world, and I come to You. Holy Father, keep them in Your name, *the name* which You have given Me, that they may be even as We *are.* While I was with them, I was keeping them in Your name which You have given Me; and I guarded them and not one of them perished but the son of perdition, so that the Scripture would be fulfilled" (John 17:1–12; see Luke 22:32; John 1:1; 3:35; 4:34; 5:44; 6:37–39, 70; 8:42; 11:41; 12:49; 13:18, 31; 16:15; Philippians 2:9).

[JESUS' WORK from It is finished]

Setting: On a hill called Golgotha (Calvary), just outside Jerusalem. After receiving some sour wine to quench His thirst on the cross, Jesus accomplishes with a statement of completion His work of dying for the sins of the world.

Therefore when Jesus had received the sour wine, He said, "It is finished!" And He bowed His head and gave up His spirit (John 19:30; see Matthew 27:50; Mark 15:37; Luke 23:46).

JEWISH PEOPLE

Setting: Caesarea. Luke, writing in Acts, gives Paul's retelling of his conversion to Christ as he appears before King Agrippa following his hearing before the Jewish Council in Jerusalem and arrest by the Roman commander (on his way to Rome after the apostle's third missionary journey).

"And when we had fallen to the ground, I heard a voice saying to me in the Hebrew dialect, 'Saul, Saul, why are you persecuting Me? It is hard for you to kick against the goads.' And I said, 'Who are You, Lord?' And the Lord said, 'I am Jesus whom you are persecuting. But get up and stand on your feet; for this purpose I have appeared to you, to appoint you a minister and a witness not only to the things which you have seen, but also to the things in which I will appear to you; rescuing you from the *Jewish* people and from the Gentiles, to whom I am sending you, to open their eyes so that they may turn from darkness to light and from the dominion of Satan to God, that they may receive forgiveness of sins and an inheritance among those who have been sanctified by faith in Me' (Acts 26:14–18; see Isaiah 35:5 Acts 21:40; 22:14).

JEWS (KING OF THE JEWS is a separate entry; also see JEWISH PEOPLE)

Setting: Sychar in Samaria, on the way to Galilee. Jesus interacts with a woman at Jacob's well, while His disciples are buying food.

Jesus said to her, "Woman, believe Me, an hour is coming when neither in this mountain nor in Jerusalem will you worship the Father. You worship what you do not know; we worship what we know, for salvation is from the Jews. But an hour is coming, and now is, when the true worshipers will worship the Father in spirit and truth; for such people the Father seeks to be His worshipers. God is spirit, and those who worship Him must worship in spirit and truth" (John 4:21–24; see Isaiah 2:3; Philippians 3:3).

Setting: Jerusalem. Before the Passover, after revealing to His disciples that Judas will betray Him to the chief priests and Pharisees, Jesus conveys how He will soon be glorified in His death, and commands them to love one another.

Therefore when he had gone out, Jesus said, "Now is the Son of Man glorified, and God is glorified in Him; if God is glorified in Him, God will also glorify Him in Himself, and will glorify Him immediately. Little children, I am with you a little while longer. You will seek Me; and as I said to the Jews, now I also say to you, 'Where I am going, you cannot come.' A new commandment I give to you, that you love one another, even as I have loved you, that you also love one another. By this all men will know that you are My disciples, if you have love for one another" (John 13:31–35; see Leviticus 19:18; John 7:33, 34; 17:1; 1 John 3:14).

Setting: Jerusalem. After Jesus is betrayed by Judas and Peter denies he is Jesus' disciple, former high priest Annas and high priest Caiaphas (his son-in-law) question the Lord about His disciples and His teaching.

Jesus answered him, "I have spoken openly to the world; I always taught in synagogues and in the temple, where all the Jews come together; and I spoke nothing in secret. Why do you question Me? Question those who have heard what I spoke to them; they know what I said" (John 18:20, 21; see John 7:26).

Setting: Jerusalem. After the previous and current high priests (Annas and Caiaphas) question Jesus, and Peter denies for the second and third times being the Lord's disciple, Pilate (Roman governor of Judea), asks Jesus what He has done.

Jesus answered, "My kingdom is not of this world. If My kingdom were of this world, then My servants would be fighting so that I would not be handed over to the Jews; but as it is, My kingdom is not of this realm" (John 18:36; see Matthew 26:53).

Setting: On the island of Patmos (in the Aegean Sea about fifty miles southwest of Ephesus in modern Turkey). On the Lord's Day (Sunday), about fifty years after Jesus' resurrection, the disciple John encounters the Lord Jesus Christ, who communicates a new revelation for the apostle to record for the church in Smyrna and to six other churches in Asia.

"And to the angel of the church in Smyrna write: The first and the last, who was dead, and has come to life, says this: 'I know your tribulation and your poverty (but you are rich), and the blasphemy by those who say they are Jews and are not, but are a synagogue of Satan. Do not fear what you are about to suffer. Behold, the devil is about to cast some of you into prison, so that you will be tested, and you will have tribulation for ten days. Be faithful until death, and I will give you the crown of life. He who has an ear, let him hear what the Spirit says to the churches. He who overcomes will not be hurt by the second death' (Revelation 2:8–11; see Isaiah 44:6; Revelation 1:9, 18; 2:13; 20:6, 14).

Setting: On the island of Patmos (in the Aegean Sea about fifty miles southwest of Ephesus in modern Turkey). On the Lord's Day (Sunday), about fifty years after Jesus' resurrection, the disciple John encounters the Lord Jesus Christ, who communicates a new revelation for the apostle to record for the church in Philadelphia and to six other churches in Asia.

"And to the angel of the church in Philadelphia write: He who is holy, who is true, who has the key of David, who opens and no one will shut, and who shuts and no one opens, says this: 'I know your deeds. Behold, I have put before you an open door which no one can shut, because you have a little power, and have kept My word, and have not denied My name. Behold, I will cause *those* of the synagogue of Satan, who say that they are Jews and are not, but lie—I will make them come and bow down at your feet, and *make them* know that I have loved you. Because you have kept the word of My perseverance, I also will keep you from the hour of testing, that *hour* which is about to come upon the whole world, to test those who dwell on the earth. I am coming quickly; hold fast what you have, so that no one will take your crown. He who overcomes, I will make him a pillar in the temple of My God, and he will not go out from it anymore; and I will write on him the name of My God, and the name of the city of My God, the new Jerusalem, which comes down out of heaven from My God, and My new name. He who has an ear, let him hear what the Spirit says to the churches' " (Revelation 3:7–13; see Isaiah 22:22; Galatians 2:9; Revelation 2:9, 10, 13, 25; 14:1).

JEWS, KING OF THE (See KING OF THE JEWS)

JEZEBEL

Setting: On the island of Patmos (in the Aegean Sea about fifty miles southwest of Ephesus in modern Turkey). On the Lord's Day (Sunday), about fifty years after Jesus' resurrection, the disciple John encounters the Lord Jesus Christ, who communicates a new revelation for the apostle to record for the church in Thyatira and to six other churches in Asia.

"And to the angel of the church in Thyatira write: The Son of God, who has eyes like a flame of fire, and His feet are like burnished bronze, says this: 'I know your deeds, and your love and faith and service and perseverance, and that your deeds of late are greater than at first. But I have *this* against you, that you tolerate the woman Jezebel, who calls herself a prophetess, and she teaches and leads My bond-servants astray so that they commit *acts of* immorality and eat things sacrificed to idols. I gave her time to repent, and she does not want to repent of her immorality. Behold, I will throw her on a bed *of sickness,* and those who commit adultery with her into great tribulation, unless they repent of her deeds. And I will kill her children with pestilence, and all the churches will know that I am He who searches the minds and hearts; and I will give to each one of you according to your deeds.

But I say to you, the rest who are in Thyatira, who do not hold this teaching, who have not known the deep things of Satan, as they call them—I place no other burden on you. Nevertheless what you have, hold fast until I come. He who overcomes, and he who keeps My deeds until the end, TO HIM I WILL GIVE AUTHORITY OVER THE NATIONS; AND HE SHALL RULE THEM WITH A ROD OF IRON, AS THE VESSELS OF THE POTTER ARE BROKEN TO PIECES, as I also have received *authority* from My Father; and I will give him the morning star. He who has an ear, let him hear what the Spirit says to the churches' (Revelation 2:18–29; Jesus quotes from Psalm 2:8, 9; Isaiah 30:14; see 1 Kings 16:31; Psalm 7:9; Romans 2:5; 1 Corinthians 2:10; 2 Peter 3:9; Revelation 1:14; 2:7; 3:11; 17:1–20).

JOHN (the Baptist; JOHN, BAPTISM OF; and JOHN THE BAPTIST are separate entries)

Setting: Galilee. As He teaches and preaches, Jesus responds to John the Baptist's question (asked by John's disciples) whether He is Israel's promised Messiah.

Jesus answered and said to them, "Go and report to John what you hear and see: *the* BLIND RECEIVE SIGHT and *the* lame walk, *the* lepers are cleansed and *the* deaf hear, *the* dead are raised up, and *the* POOR HAVE THE GOSPEL PREACHED TO THEM. And blessed is he who does not take offense at Me" (Matthew 11:4–6, Jesus quotes from Isaiah 35:5f; cf. Luke 7:22, 23).

Setting: Galilee. While speaking to the crowds, Jesus pays tribute to the ministry of John the Baptist, but emphasizes that the one who is least in the kingdom of heaven is greater than John.

As these men were going *away,* Jesus began to speak to the crowds about John, "What did you go out into the wilderness to see? A reed shaken by the wind? But what did you go out to see? A man dressed in soft *clothing?* Those who wear soft *clothing* are in kings' palaces! But what did you go out to see? A prophet? Yes, I tell you, and the one who is more than a prophet. This is the one about whom it is written, 'BEHOLD, I SEND MY MESSENGER AHEAD OF YOU, WHO WILL PREPARE YOUR WAY BEFORE YOU.' Truly, I say to you, among those born of women there has not arisen *anyone* greater than John the Baptist! Yet the one who is least in the kingdom of heaven is greater than he. From the days of John the Baptist until now the kingdom of heaven suffers violence, and violent men take it by force. For all the prophets and the Law prophesied until John. And, if you are willing to accept *it,* John himself is Elijah who was to come. He who has ears to hear, let him hear" (Matthew 11:7–15, Jesus quotes from Malachi 3:1; cf. Malachi 4:5; Luke 7:24–28; Luke 16:16; see Matthew 14:5).

Setting: Galilee. After praising John the Baptist as His forerunner, Jesus demonstrates the foolish thinking of the current generation of Jewish religious leaders by repeating what they say about John's ascetic lifestyle and ministry along with His own.

"But to what shall I compare this generation? It is like children sitting in the market places, who call out to the other *children,* and say, 'We played the flute for you, and you did not dance; we sang a dirge, and you did not mourn.' For John came neither eating nor drinking, and they say, 'He has a demon!' The Son of Man came eating and drinking, and they say, 'Behold, a gluttonous man and a drunkard, a friend of tax collectors and sinners! Yet wisdom is vindicated by her deeds" (Matthew 11:16–19; cf. Luke 7:31–35; see Matthew 9:11, 34; Luke 1:15).

Setting: The temple in Jerusalem. Jesus delivers a parable to the chief priests and elders after they question His authority.

"But what do you think? A man had two sons, and he came to the first and said, 'Son, go work today in the vineyard.' And he answered, 'I will not'; but afterward he regretted it and went. The man came to the second and said the same thing; and he answered, 'I *will,* sir'; but he did not go. Which of the two sons did the will of his father?" They said, "The first." Jesus said to them, "Truly, I say to you that the tax collectors and prostitutes will get into the kingdom of God before you. For John came to you in the way of righteousness and you did not believe him; but the tax collectors and prostitutes did believe him; and you, seeing *this,* did not even feel remorse afterward so as to believe him" (Matthew 21:28–32; cf. Luke 7:29, 30, 37–50).

Setting: The temple in Jerusalem. After Jesus teaches about faith and forgiveness utilizing a cursed fig tree as an object lesson, His authority is questioned by the chief priests, scribes, and elders.

And Jesus said to them, "I will ask you one question, and you answer Me, and *then* I will tell you by what authority I do these things. Was the baptism of John from heaven, or from men? Answer Me." They *began* reasoning among themselves, saying, "If we say 'From heaven,' He will say, 'Then why did you not believe him?' "But shall we say 'From men'?"—they were afraid of the people, for everyone considered John to have been a real prophet. Answering Jesus, they said, "We do not know." And Jesus said to them, "Nor will I tell you by what authority I do these things" (Mark 11:29–33; cf. Matthew 21:23–27; Luke 20:1–8).

Setting: Galilee. After Jesus raises a woman's son from the dead in Nain, the disciples of John the Baptist inquire whether He is the promised Messiah.

And He answered and said to them, "Go and report to John what you have seen and heard: *the* BLIND RECEIVE SIGHT, *the* lame walk, *the* lepers are cleansed, and *the* deaf hear, *the* dead are raised up, *the* POOR HAVE THE GOSPEL PREACHED TO THEM. Blessed is he who does not take offense at Me" (Luke 7:22, 23, Jesus quotes from Isaiah 35:5; 61:1; cf. Matthew 11:2–6).

Setting: Galilee. After He responds to the disciples of John the Baptist whether He is the promised Messiah, Jesus speaks to the crowds about John.

When the messengers of John had left, He began to speak to the crowds about John, "What did you go out into the wilderness to see? A reed shaken by the wind? But what did you go out to see? A man dressed in soft clothing? Those who are splendidly clothed and live in luxury are *found* in royal palaces! But what did you go out to see? A prophet? Yes, I say to you, and one who is more than a prophet. This is the one about whom it is written, 'BEHOLD, I SEND MY MESSENGER AHEAD OF YOU, WHO WILL PREPARE YOUR WAY BEFORE YOU.' I say to you, among those born of women there is no one greater than John; yet he who is least in the kingdom of God is greater than he" (Luke 7:24–28, Jesus quotes from Malachi 3:1; cf. Matthew 11:7–11).

Setting: On the way from Galilee to Jerusalem. The Lord responds to the Pharisees' scoffing at His teaching His disciples about stewardship.

And He said to them, "You are those who justify yourselves in the sight of men, but God knows your hearts; for that which is highly esteemed among men is detestable in the sight of God. The Law and the Prophets *were proclaimed* until John; since that time the gospel of the kingdom of God has been preached, and everyone is forcing his way into it. But is it easier for heaven and earth to pass away than for one stroke of a letter of the Law to fail" (Luke 16:15–17; cf. Matthew 5:18; see 1 Samuel 16:7; Matthew 4:23; 11:11–14).

Setting: Jerusalem. During the Feast of the Jews, Jesus responds to criticism from the Jewish religious leaders by referring to God as His Father (thereby making Himself equal with God) and informing them that God, John the Baptist, and His works all testify to His mission.

"I can do nothing on My own initiative. As I hear, I judge; and My judgment is just, because I do not seek My own will, but the will of Him who sent Me. If I *alone* testify about Myself, My testimony is not true. There is another who testifies of Me, and I know that the testimony which He gives about Me is true. You have sent to John, and he has testified to the truth. But the testimony which I receive is not from man, but I say these things so that you may be saved. He was the lamp that was burning and was shining and you were willing to rejoice for a while in his light. But the testimony which I have is greater than the *testimony of* John, for the works which the Father has given Me to accomplish—the very works that I do—testify about Me, that the Father has sent Me. And the Father who sent Me, He has testified of Me. You have neither heard His voice at any time nor seen His form. You do not have His word abiding in you, for you do not believe Him whom He sent" (John 5:30–38; see Matthew 3:17; Mark 1:4, 5; John 1:7, 15, 32; 4:34; 8:14–16; 10:25, 37, 38).

Setting: Jerusalem. Luke, writing in Acts, presents quotes from Jesus' post-resurrection appearances, in which He informs and instructs His disciples of their imminent baptism with the Holy Spirit.

Gathering them together, He commanded them not to leave Jerusalem, but to wait for what the Father had promised, "Which," *He said,* "you heard of from Me; for John baptized with water, but you will be baptized with the Holy Spirit not many days from now" (Acts 1:4, 5; see Luke 24:49; John 14:16, 26; Acts 2:1–4).

Setting: Jerusalem. Luke, writing in Acts, records Peter (following a time of ministry to the Gentiles) recalling the words of Jesus regarding the baptism of the Holy Spirit.

And I remembered the word of the Lord, how He used to say, "John baptized with water, but you will be baptized with the Holy Spirit" (Acts 11:16; cf. Acts 1:5).

JOHN (Peter's father)

Setting: Bethany beyond the Jordan. After being baptized, Jesus begins His public ministry and chooses His first disciples, Andrew and Simon (Peter), who believe He is the Messiah.

He brought him to Jesus. Jesus looked at him and said, "You are Simon the son of John; you shall be called Cephas" (which is translated Peter) (John 1:42).

Setting: By the Sea of Galilee. During His third manifestation to His disciples after His resurrection from the dead in Jerusalem, Jesus quizzes Peter three times regarding his love for Him.

So when they had finished breakfast, Jesus said to Simon Peter, "Simon, *son* of John, do you love Me more than these?" He said to Him, "Yes, Lord; You know that I love You." He said to him, "Tend My lambs." He said to him again a second time, "Simon, *son* of John, do you love Me?" He said to Him, "Yes, Lord; You know that I love You." He said to him, "Shepherd My sheep." He said to him the third time, "Simon, *son* of John, do you love Me?" Peter was grieved because He said to him the third time, "Do you love Me?" And he said to Him, "Lord, You know all things; You know that I love You." Jesus said to him, "Tend My sheep" (John 21:15–17; see Matthew 26:33; Mark 14:29).

JOHN, BAPTISM OF (Also see BAPTISM; JOHN; and JOHN THE BAPTIST)

Setting: The temple in Jerusalem. Jesus returns after having spent the night in Bethany. The chief priests and elders question His authority in an effort to challenge His teaching to the nation.

Jesus said to them, "I will also ask you one thing, which if you tell Me, I will also tell you by what authority I do these things. The baptism of John was from what *source,* from heaven or from men?" And they *began* reasoning among themselves, saying "If we say 'From heaven,' He will say to us, 'Then why did you not believe him?' But if we say, 'From men,' we fear the people; for they all regard John as a prophet." And answering Jesus, they said, "We do not know." He also said to them, "Neither will I tell you by what authority I do these things" (Matthew 21:24–27; cf. Mark 11:29–33; Luke 20:3–8).

Setting: The temple in Jerusalem. After Jesus teaches about faith and forgiveness, utilizing a cursed fig tree as an object lesson, His authority is questioned by the chief priests, scribes, and elders.

And Jesus said to them, "I will ask you one question, and you answer Me, and *then* I will tell you by what authority I do these things. Was the baptism of John from heaven, or from men? Answer Me." They *began* reasoning among themselves, saying, "If we say 'From heaven,' He will say, 'Then why did you not believe him?' "But shall we say 'From men'?"—they were afraid of the people, for everyone considered John to have been a real prophet. Answering Jesus, they said, "We do not know." And Jesus said to them, "Nor will I tell you by what authority I do these things" (Mark 11:29–33; cf. Matthew 21:23–27; Luke 20:1–8).

Setting: The temple in Jerusalem. A few days before Jesus' crucifixion, with His conflict with the religious leaders of Israel escalating, the chief priests and the scribes question His authority to teach and preach.

Jesus answered and said to them, "I will also ask you a question, and you tell Me: Was the baptism of John from heaven or from men?" They reasoned among themselves, saying, "If we say, 'From heaven,' He will say, 'Why did you not believe him?' But if we say, 'From men,' all the people will stone us to death, for they are convinced that John was a prophet." So they answered that they did not know where *it came* from. And Jesus said to them, "Nor will I tell you by what authority I do these things" (Luke 20:3–8; cf. Matthew 21:23–27; Mark 11:27–33).

[JOHN, BAPTISM OF from John baptized with water]
Setting: Jerusalem. Luke, writing in Acts, presents quotes from Jesus' post-resurrection appearances, in which He informs and instructs His disciples about their imminent baptism with the Holy Spirit.

Gathering them together, He commanded them not to leave Jerusalem, but to wait for what the Father had promised, "Which," *He said,* "you heard of from Me; for John baptized with water, but you will be baptized with the Holy Spirit not many days from now" (Acts 1:4, 5; see Luke 24:49; John 14:16, 26; Acts 2:1–4).

[JOHN, BAPTISM OF from John baptized with water]
Setting: Jerusalem. Luke, writing in Acts, records Peter (following a time of ministry to the Gentiles) recalling the words of Jesus regarding the baptism of the Holy Spirit.

And I remembered the word of the Lord, how He used to say, "John baptized with water, but you will be baptized with the Holy Spirit" (Acts 11:16; cf. Acts 1:5).

JOHN THE BAPTIST (Also see JOHN)

Setting: Galilee. While speaking to the crowds, Jesus pays tribute to the ministry of John the Baptist, but emphasizes that the one who is least in the kingdom of heaven is greater than John.

As these men were going *away,* Jesus began to speak to the crowds about John, "What did you go out into the wilderness to see? A reed shaken by the wind? But what did you go out to see? A man dressed in soft *clothing?* Those who wear soft *clothing* are in kings' palaces! But what did you go out to see? A prophet? Yes, I tell you, and the one who is more than a prophet. This is the one about whom it is written, 'BEHOLD, I SEND MY MESSENGER AHEAD OF YOU, WHO WILL PREPARE YOUR WAY BEFORE YOU.' Truly, I say to you, among those born of women there has not arisen *anyone* greater than John the Baptist! Yet the one who is least in the kingdom of heaven is greater than he. From the days of John the Baptist until now the kingdom of heaven suffers violence, and violent men take it by force. For all the prophets and the Law prophesied until John. And, if you are willing to accept *it,* John himself is Elijah who was to come. He who has ears to hear, let him hear" (Matthew 11:7–15, Jesus quotes from Malachi 3:1; cf. Malachi 4:5; Luke 7:24–28; Luke 16:16; see Matthew 14:5).

Setting: Galilee. After Jesus praises John the Baptist to the crowds, He criticizes the Pharisees and lawyers, who reject God's purpose and John's message.

"To what then shall I compare the men of this generation, and what are they like? They are like children who sit in the market place and call to one another, and they say, 'We played the flute for you, and you did not dance; we sang a dirge, and you did not weep.' For John the Baptist has come eating no bread and drinking no wine, and you say, 'He has a demon!' The Son of Man has come eating and drinking, and you say, 'Behold, a gluttonous man and a drunkard, a friend of tax collectors and sinners!' Yet wisdom is vindicated by all her children" (Luke 7:31–35; cf. Matthew 11:16–19; see Luke 1:15, 7:29, 30).

[JOHN THE BAPTIST from John baptized]
Setting: Jerusalem. Luke, writing in Acts, presents quotes from Jesus' post-resurrection appearances, in which He informs and instructs His disciples about their imminent baptism with the Holy Spirit.

Gathering them together, He commanded them not to leave Jerusalem, but to wait for what the Father had promised, "Which," *He said,* "you heard of from Me; for John baptized with water, but you will be baptized with the Holy Spirit not many days from now" (Acts 1:4, 5; see Luke 24:49; John 14:16, 26; Acts 2:1–4).

[JOHN THE BAPTIST from John baptized]
Setting: Jerusalem. Luke, writing in Acts, records Peter (following a time of ministry to the Gentiles) recalling the words of Jesus regarding the baptism of the Holy Spirit.

And I remembered the word of the Lord, how He used to say, "John baptized with water, but you will be baptized with the Holy Spirit" (Acts 11:16; cf. Acts 1:5).

JONAH (JONAH, SIGN OF is a separate entry; also see NINEVEH)

Setting: Galilee. After Jesus warns the Pharisees about the unpardonable sin and their future judgment, some Pharisees and scribes ask Him to perform a miraculous sign for them in front of the crowds.

But He answered and said to them, "An evil and adulterous generation craves for a sign; and *yet* no sign will be given to it but the sign of Jonah the prophet; for just as JONAH WAS THREE DAYS AND THREE NIGHTS IN THE BELLY OF THE SEA MONSTER, so will the Son of Man be three days and three nights in the heart of the earth. The men of Nineveh will stand up with this generation at the judgment, and will condemn it because they repented at the preaching of Jonah; and behold, something greater than Jonah is here. *The* Queen of *the* South will rise up with this generation at the judgment and will condemn it, because she came from the ends of the earth to hear the wisdom of Solomon; and behold, something greater than Solomon is here" (Matthew 12:39–42; Jesus quotes from Jonah 1:17; cf. 1 Kings 10:1; Jonah 3:5; Matthew 16:1, 4; 12:38; Luke 11:29).

Setting: On the way from Galilee to Jerusalem. After revealing a problem with exorcism and responding to a blessing from a woman in the crowd, Jesus tells the increasing crowds about the sign of Jonah.

As the crowds were increasing, He began to say, "This generation is a wicked generation; it seeks for a sign, and *yet* no sign will be given to it but the sign of Jonah. For just as Jonah became a sign to the Ninevites, so will the Son of Man be to this generation. The Queen of the South will rise up with the men of this generation at the judgment and condemn them, because she came from the ends of the earth to hear the wisdom of Solomon; and behold, something greater than Solomon is here. The men of Nineveh will stand up with this generation at the judgment and condemn it, because they repented at the preaching of Jonah; and behold, something greater than Jonah is here" (Luke 11:29–32; cf. Matthew 16:4; see 1 Kings 10:1–10; Jonah 3:4, 5).

JONAH, SIGN OF (Also see JONAH; and RESURRECTION)

Setting: Galilee. After Jesus warns the Pharisees about the unpardonable sin and their future judgment, some Pharisees and scribes ask Him to perform a miraculous sign for them in front of the crowds.

But He answered and said to them, "An evil and adulterous generation craves for a sign; and *yet* no sign will be given to it but the sign of Jonah the prophet; for just as JONAH WAS THREE DAYS AND THREE NIGHTS IN THE BELLY OF THE SEA MONSTER, so will the Son of Man be three days and three nights in the heart of the earth. The men of Nineveh will stand up with this generation at the judgment, and will condemn it because they repented at the preaching of Jonah; and behold, something greater than Jonah is here. *The* Queen of *the* South will rise up with this generation at the judgment and will condemn it, because she came from the ends of the earth to hear the wisdom of Solomon; and behold, something greater than Solomon is here" (Matthew 12:39–42; Jesus quotes from Jonah 1:17; cf. 1 Kings 10:1; Jonah 3:5; Matthew 16:1, 4; 12:38; Luke 11:29).

Setting: Magadan of Galilee. The Pharisees and Sadducees, rejecting Jesus' message, continue to test Jesus by asking Him for a sign from heaven.

But He replied to them, "When it is evening, you say, '*It will be* fair weather, for the sky is red.' And in the morning, '*There will* be a storm today, for the sky is red and threatening.' Do you know how to discern the appearance of the sky, but cannot *discern* the signs of the times? An evil and adulterous generation seeks after a sign; and a sign will not be given it, except the sign of Jonah" And He left them and went away (Matthew 16:2–4; cf. Matthew 12:39; Mark 8:12; Luke 12:54–56).

Setting: On the way from Galilee to Jerusalem. After revealing a problem with exorcism and responding to a blessing from a woman in the crowd, Jesus tells the increasing crowds about the sign of Jonah.

As the crowds were increasing, He began to say, "This generation is a wicked generation; it seeks for a sign, and *yet* no sign will be given to it but the sign of Jonah. For just as Jonah became a sign to the Ninevites, so will the Son of Man be to this generation.

The Queen of the South will rise up with the men of this generation at the judgment and condemn them, because she came from the ends of the earth to hear the wisdom of Solomon; and behold, something greater than Solomon is here. The men of Nineveh will stand up with this generation at the judgment and condemn it, because they repented at the preaching of Jonah; and behold, something greater than Jonah is here" (Luke 11:29–32; cf. Matthew 16:4; see 1 Kings 10:1–10; Jonah 3:4, 5).

JOURNEY (Also see TRAVEL)

Setting: Galilee. After His twelve disciples observe His ministry, Jesus summons and specifically instructs them about their ministry to the people of Israel.

These twelve Jesus sent out after instructing them: "Do not go in *the* way of *the* Gentiles, and do not enter *any* city of the Samaritans; but rather go to the lost sheep of the house of Israel. And as you go, preach, saying, 'The kingdom of heaven is at hand.' Heal *the* sick, raise *the* dead, cleanse *the* lepers, cast out demons. Freely you received, freely give. Do not acquire gold, or silver, or copper for your money belts, or a bag for *your* journey, or even two coats, or sandals, or a staff; for the worker is worthy of his support. And whatever city or village you enter, inquire who is worthy in it, and stay at his house until you leave *that city*. As you enter the house, give it your greeting. If the house is worthy, give it your *blessing of* peace. But if it is not worthy, take back your *blessing of* peace. Whoever does not receive you, nor heed your words, as you go out of that house or that city, shake the dust off your feet. Truly I say to you, it will be more tolerable for *the* land of Sodom and Gomorrah in the day of judgment than for that city" (Matthew 10:5–15; cf. Mark 6:7–11; Luke 9:1–5; see Matthew 3:2; 11:22, 24; 15:24; Luke 22:35; 1 Corinthians 9:14).

Setting: The temple in Jerusalem. Jesus delivers another parable to the chief priests and elders after they question His authority.

"Listen to another parable. There was a landowner who PLANTED A VINEYARD AND PUT A WALL AROUND IT AND DUG A WINE PRESS IN IT, AND BUILT A TOWER, and rented it out to vine-growers and went on a journey. When the harvest time approached, he sent his slaves to the vine-growers to receive his produce. The vine-growers took his slaves and beat one, and killed another, and stoned a third. Again he sent another group of slaves larger than the first; and they did the same thing to them. But afterward he sent his son to them, saying, 'They will respect my son.' But when the vine-growers saw the son, they said among themselves, 'This is the heir; come, let us kill him and seize his inheritance.' They took him, and threw him out of the vineyard and killed him. Therefore when the owner of the vineyard comes, what will he do to those vine-growers?" (Matthew 21:33–40; Jesus quotes from Isaiah 5:1, 2; cf. Mark 12:1–9; Luke 20:9–15; see Matthew 21:45, 46).

Setting: The Mount of Olives, just east of Jerusalem. During His discourse, after answering His disciples' questions as to when the temple will be destroyed and Jerusalem overrun, along with the signs of His coming and the end of the age, Jesus reemphasizes to His disciples that they should be on the alert for His return.

"For *it is* just like a man *about* to go on a journey, who called his own slaves and entrusted his possessions to them. To one he gave five talents, to another, two, and to another, one, each according to his own ability; and he went on his journey. Immediately the one who had received the five talents went and traded with them, and gained five more talents. In the same manner the one who *had received* the two *talents* gained two more. But he who received the one *talent* went away, and dug a *hole* in the ground and hid his master's money. Now after a long time the master of those slaves came and settled accounts with them. The one who had received the five talents came up and brought five more talents, saying, 'Master, you entrusted five talents to me. See, I have gained five more talents.' His master said to him, 'Well done, good and faithful slave. You were faithful with a few things, I will put you in charge of many things; enter into the joy of your master.' Also the one who *had received* the two talents came up and said, 'Master, you entrusted two talents to me. See, I have gained two more talents.' His master said to him, 'Well done, good and faithful slave. You were faithful with a few things, I will put you in charge of many things; enter into the joy of your master.' And the one also who had received the one talent came up and said, 'Master, I knew you to be a hard man, reaping where you did not sow and gathering where you scattered no *seed*. And I was afraid, and went away and hid your talent in the ground. See, you have what is yours.' But his master answered and said to him, 'You wicked, lazy slave, you knew that I reap where I did not sow and gather where I scattered no *seed*. Then you ought to have put my money in the bank, and on my arrival I would have received my *money* back with interest. 'Therefore take away the talent from him, and give it to the one who has ten talents.' For to everyone who has, *more* shall be given, and he will have an abundance; but from the one who does not have, even what he does have shall be taken away. Throw out the worthless slave into the outer darkness; in that place there will be weeping and gnashing of teeth" (Matthew 25:14–30; cf. Matthew 8:12; 13:12; 24:45–47; see Matthew 18:23, 24; Luke 12:44).

Setting: The temple in Jerusalem. Having His authority questioned by the chief priests, scribes, and elders, Jesus begins to teach them in parables.

And He began to speak to them in parables: "A man PLANTED A VINEYARD AND PUT A WALL AROUND IT, AND DUG A VAT UNDER THE WINE PRESS AND BUILT A TOWER, and rented it out to vine-growers and went on a journey. At the *harvest* time he sent a slave to the vine-growers, in order to receive *some* of the produce of the vineyard from the vine-growers. They took him, and beat him and sent him away empty-handed. Again he sent them another slave, and they wounded him in the head, and treated him shamefully. And he sent another, and that one they killed; and *so with* many others, beating some and killing others. He had one more to *send*, a beloved son; he sent him last *of all* to them, saying, 'They will respect my son.' But those vine-growers said to one another, 'This is the heir; come, let us kill him, and the inheritance will be ours!' They took him, and killed him and threw him out of the vineyard. What will the owner of the vineyard do? He will come and destroy the vine-growers, and will give the vineyard to others. Have you not even read this Scripture: 'THE STONE WHICH THE BUILDERS REJECTED, THIS BECAME THE CHIEF CORNER *stone;* THIS CAME ABOUT FROM THE LORD, AND IT IS MARVELOUS IN OUR EYES'?" (Mark 12:1–11, Jesus quotes from Psalm 118:22, 23; Isaiah 5:1, 2; cf. Matthew 21:33–46; Luke 20:9–19).

Setting: On the Mount of Olives, east of the temple in Jerusalem. After prophesying the temple's destruction, Jesus responds during His Olivet Discourse to questions from Peter, James, John, and Andrew about other future events.

"Take heed, keep on the alert; for you do not know when the *appointed* time will come. *It is* like a man away on a journey, *who* upon leaving his house and putting his slaves in charge, *assigning* to each one his task, also commanded the doorkeeper to stay on the alert. Therefore, be on the alert—for you do not know when the master of the house is coming, whether in the evening, at midnight, or when the rooster crows, or in the morning—in case he should come suddenly and find you asleep. What I say to you I say to all, 'Be on the alert!' " (Mark 13:33–37; cf. Matthew 24:42, 43; Luke 21:34–36; see Luke 12:36–38; Ephesians 6:18).

Setting: Galilee. After raising Jairus's daughter from the dead, Jesus calls the twelve disciples together and gives them power and authority over demons, along with the ability to cure diseases.

And He said to them, "Take nothing for *your* journey, neither a staff, nor a bag, nor bread, nor money; and do not *even* have two tunics apiece. Whatever house you enter, stay there until you leave that city. And as for those who do not receive you, go out from that city, shake the dust off your feet as a testimony against them" (Luke 9:3–5; cf. Matthew 10:1–15; Mark 6:7–11; see Luke 10:4–12).

Setting: On the way from Galilee to Jerusalem. While being tested by a lawyer, Jesus tells him the story of the good Samaritan.

Jesus replied and said, "A man was going down from Jerusalem to Jericho, and fell among robbers, and they stripped him and beat him, and went away leaving him half dead. And by chance a priest was going down on that road, and when he saw him, he passed by on the other side. Likewise a Levite also, when he came to the place and saw him, passed by on the other side. But a Samaritan, who was on a journey, came upon him; and when he saw him, he felt compassion, and came to him and bandaged up his wounds, pouring oil and wine on *them;* and he put him on his own beast, and brought him to an inn and took care of him. On the next day he took out two denarii and gave them to the innkeeper and said, 'Take care of him; and whatever more you spend, when I return I will repay you.' Which of these three do you think proved to be a neighbor to the man who fell into the robbers' *hands?"* And he said, "The one who showed mercy toward him." Then Jesus said to him, "Go and do the same" (Luke 10:30–37).

Setting: On the way from Galilee to Jerusalem. After revealing to His disciples how to pray, Jesus illustrates persistence in prayer.

Then He said to them, "Suppose one of you has a friend, and goes to him at midnight and says to him, 'Friend, lend me three loaves; for a friend of mine has come to me from a journey, and I have nothing to set before him'; and from inside he answers and says, 'Do not bother me; the door has already been shut and my children and I are in bed; I cannot get up and give you *anything.*' I tell you, even though he will not get up and give him *anything* because he is his friend, yet because of his persistence he will get up and give him as much as he needs. So I say to you, ask, and it will be given to you; seek, and you will find; knock, and it will be opened to you. For everyone who asks, receives; and he who seeks, finds; and to him who knocks, it will be opened" (Luke 11:5–10; cf. Matthew 7:7, 8; see Luke 18:1–5).

Setting: On the way from Galilee to Jerusalem. Jesus conveys the illustration of the prodigal son because the Pharisees and scribes complain He associates with tax collectors and sinners.

And He said, "A man had two sons. The younger of them said to his father, 'Father, give me the share of the estate that falls to me.' So he divided his wealth between them. And not many days later, the younger son gathered everything together and went on a journey into a distant country, and there he squandered his estate with loose living. Now when he had spent everything, a severe famine occurred in that country, and he began to be impoverished. So he went and hired himself out to one of the citizens of that country, and he sent him into his fields to feed swine. And he would have gladly filled his stomach with the pods that the swine were eating, and no one was giving *anything* to him. But when he came to his senses, he said, 'How many of my father's hired men have more than enough bread, but I am dying here with hunger! I will get up and go to my father, and will say to him, "Father, I have sinned against heaven, and in your sight; I am no longer worthy to be called your son; make me as one of your hired men."' So he got up and came to his father. But while he was still a long way off, his father saw him and felt compassion *for him,* and ran and embraced him and kissed him. And the son said to him, "Father, I have sinned against heaven and in your sight; I am no longer worthy to be called your son.' But the father said to his slaves, 'Quickly bring out the best robe and put it on him, and put a ring on his hand and sandals on his feet; and bring the fattened calf, kill it, and let us eat and celebrate; for this son of mine was dead and has come to life again; he was lost and has been found.' And they began to celebrate. Now his older son was in the field, when he came and approached the house, he heard music and dancing. And he summoned one of the servants and *began* inquiring what these things could be. And he said to him, 'Your brother has come, and your father has killed the fattened calf because he has received him back safe and sound.' But he became angry and was not willing to go in; and his father came out and *began* pleading with him. But he answered and said to his father, 'Look! For so many years I have been serving you and I have never neglected a command of yours; and *yet* you have never given me a young goat, so that I might celebrate with my friends; but when this son of yours came, who has devoured your wealth with prostitutes, you killed the fattened calf for him.' And he said to him, 'Son, you have always been with me, and all that is mine is yours. But we had to celebrate and rejoice, for this brother of yours was dead and *has begun* to live, and was lost and has been found'" (Luke 15:11–32; see Proverbs 29:2).

Setting: The temple in Jerusalem. A few days before His crucifixion, after the chief priests and scribes question His authority to teach and preach, Jesus conveys the Parable of the Vine-Growers to the people.

And He began to tell the people this parable: "A man planted a vineyard and rented it out to vine-growers, and went on a journey for a long time. At the *harvest* time he sent a slave to the vine-growers, so that they would give him *some* of the produce of the vineyard; but the vine-growers beat him and sent him away empty-handed. And he proceeded to send another slave; and they beat him also and treated him shamefully and sent him away empty-handed. And he proceeded to send a third; and this one also they wounded and cast out. The owner of the vineyard said, 'What shall I do? I will send my beloved son; perhaps they will respect him.' But when the vine-growers saw him, they reasoned with one another, saying, 'This is the heir; let us kill him so that the inheritance will be ours.' So they threw him out of the vineyard and killed him. What, then, will the owner of the vineyard do to them? He will come and destroy these vine-growers and will give the vineyard to others." When they heard it, they said, "May it never be!" But Jesus looked at them and said, "What then is this that is written: 'THE STONE WHICH THE BUILDERS REJECTED, THIS BECAME THE CHIEF CORNER *stone*'? Everyone who falls on that stone will be broken to pieces; but on whomever it falls, it will scatter him like dust" (Luke 20:9–18, Jesus quotes from Psalm 118:22; cf. Matthew 21:33–44; Mark 12:1–11; see Ephesians 2:20).

JOY (Also see FULFILLMENT; GLADNESS; HAPPINESS; REJOICING; and SATISFACTION)

Setting: By the Sea of Galilee. With the religious leaders rejecting His message, Jesus begins to teach in parables, and explains the meaning of the Parable of the Sower to His disciples.

"Hear then the parable of the sower. When anyone hears the word of the kingdom and does not understand it, the evil *one* comes and snatches away what has been sown in his heart. This is the one on whom seed was sown beside the road. The one on whom seed was sown on the rocky places, this is the man who hears the word and immediately receives it with joy; yet he has no *firm* root in himself, but is *only* temporary, and when affliction or persecution arises because of the word, immediately he falls away. And the one on whom seed was sown among the thorns, this is the man who hears the word, and the worry of the world and the deceitfulness of wealth choke the word, and it becomes unfruitful. And the one on whom seed was sown on the good soil, this is the man who hears the word and understands it; who indeed bears fruit and brings forth, some a hundredfold, some sixty, and some thirty" (Matthew 13:18–23; cf. Mark 4:13–20; Luke 8:11–15).

Setting: By the Sea of Galilee. Since the religious leaders are rejecting His message, Jesus continues teaching the crowds with the Parable of the Hidden Treasure.

"The kingdom of heaven is like a treasure hidden in the field, which a man found and hid *again;* and from joy over it he goes and sells all that he has and buys that field" (Matthew 13:44).

Setting: The Mount of Olives, just east of Jerusalem. During His discourse, after answering His disciples' questions as to when the temple will be destroyed and Jerusalem overrun, along with the signs of His coming and the end of the age, Jesus reemphasizes to His disciples that they should be on the alert for His return.

"For *it is* just like a man *about* to go on a journey, who called his own slaves and entrusted his possessions to them. To one he gave five talents, to another, two, and to another, one, each according to his own ability; and he went on his journey. Immediately the one who had received the five talents went and traded with them, and gained five more talents. In the same manner the one who *had received* the two *talents* gained two more. But he who received the one *talent* went away, and dug a *hole* in the ground and hid his master's money. Now after a long time the master of those slaves came and settled accounts with them. The one who had received the five talents came up and brought five more talents, saying, 'Master, you entrusted five talents to me. See, I have gained five more talents.' His master said to him, 'Well done, good and faithful slave. You were faithful with a few things, I will put you in charge of many things; enter into the joy of your master.' Also the one who *had received* the two talents came up and said, 'Master, you entrusted two talents to me. See, I have gained two more talents.' His master said to him, 'Well done, good and faithful slave. You were faithful with a few things, I will put you in charge of many things; enter into the joy of your master.' And the one also who had received the one talent came up and said, 'Master, I knew you to be a hard man, reaping where you did not sow and gathering where you scattered no *seed.* And I was afraid, and went away and hid your talent in the ground. See, you have what is yours.' But his master answered and said to him, 'You wicked, lazy slave, you knew that I reap where I did not sow and gather where I scattered no *seed.* Then you ought to have put my money in the bank, and on my arrival I would have received my *money* back with interest. 'Therefore take away the talent from him, and give it to the one who has ten talents.' For to everyone who has, *more* shall be given, and he will have an abundance; but from the one who does not have, even what he does have shall be taken away. Throw out the worthless slave into the outer darkness; in that place there will be weeping and gnashing of teeth" (Matthew 25:14–30; cf. Matthew 8:12; 13:12; 24:45–47; see Matthew 18:23, 24; Luke 12:44).

Setting: By the Sea of Galilee. During the early part of His ministry, after presenting the Parable of the Sower from a boat to a very large crowd, Jesus explains the meaning of the parable to His disciples and other followers.

And He said to them, "Do you not understand this parable? How will you understand all the parables? The sower sows the word. These are the ones who are beside the road where the word is sown; and when they hear, immediately Satan comes and takes away the word which has been sown in them. In a similar way these are the ones on whom seed was sown on the rocky places, who, when they hear the word, immediately receive it with joy; and they have no *firm* root in themselves, but are *only* temporary; then, when affliction or persecution arises because of the word, immediately they fall away. And others are the ones on whom seed was sown among the thorns; these are the ones who have heard the word, but the worries of the world and the deceitfulness of riches, and the desires for other things enter in and choke the word, and it becomes unfruitful. And those are the ones on whom seed was sown on the good soil; and they hear the word and accept it and bear fruit, thirty, sixty, and a hundredfold" (Mark 4:13–20; cf. Matthew 13:18–23; Luke 8:11–15).

Setting: Galilee. After selecting His twelve disciples, Jesus teaches the Beatitudes (part of the Sermon on the Mount) to those disciples and a great throng of people from Judea, Jerusalem, and the central coastal region of Tyre and Sidon.

"Blessed are you when men hate you, and ostracize you, and insult you, and scorn your name as evil, for the sake of the Son of Man. Be glad in that day and leap *for joy*, for behold, your reward is great in heaven. For in the same way their fathers used to treat the prophets" (Luke 6:22, 23; cf. Matthew 5:10–12; see 2 Chronicles 36:16).

Setting: Galilee. After Jesus presents the Parable of the Sower to the crowds, His disciples ask Him to give them the parable's meaning.

And He said, "To you it has been granted to know the mysteries of the kingdom of God, but to the rest *it is* in parables, so that SEEING THEY MAY NOT SEE, AND HEARING THEY MAY NOT UNDERSTAND. Now the parable is this: the seed is the word of God. Those beside the road are those who have heard; then the devil comes and takes away the word from their heart, so that they will not believe and be saved. Those on the rocky *soil* are those who, when they hear, receive the word with joy; and these have no *firm* root; they believe for a while, and in time of temptation fall away. The *seed* which fell among the thorns, these are the ones who have heard, and as they go on their way they are choked with worries and riches and pleasures of *this* life, and bring no fruit to maturity. But the *seed* in the good soil, these are the ones who have heard the word in an honest and good heart, and hold it fast, and bear fruit with perseverance" (Luke 8:10–15, Jesus quotes from Isaiah 6:9; cf. Matthew 13:10–23; Mark 4:10–20).

Setting: On the way from Galilee to Jerusalem. After Jesus presents to large crowds the demands of discipleship, the Pharisees and scribes complain He associates with tax collectors and sinners.

So He told them this parable, saying, "What man among you, if he has a hundred sheep and has lost one of them, does not leave the ninety-nine in the open pasture and go after the one which is lost until he finds it? When he has found it, he lays it on his shoulders, rejoicing. And when he comes home, he calls together his friends and his neighbors, saying to them, 'Rejoice with me, for I have found my sheep which was lost!' I tell you that in the same way, there will be *more* joy in heaven over one sinner who repents than over ninety-nine righteous persons who need no repentance" (Luke 15:3–7; cf. Matthew 18:12–14; see Matthew 9:11–13; Luke 5:29–32).

Setting: On the way from Galilee to Jerusalem. Jesus conveys the principles of the lost sheep and the lost coin because the Pharisees and scribes complain He associates with tax collectors and sinners.

"So He told them this parable, saying, "What man among you, if he has a hundred sheep and has lost one of them, does not leave the ninety-nine in the open pasture and go after the one which is lost until he finds it? When he has found it, he lays it on his shoulders, rejoicing. And when he comes home, he calls together his friends and his neighbors, saying to them, 'Rejoice with me, for I have found my sheep which was lost!' I tell you that in the same way, there will be more joy in heaven over one sinner who repents than over ninety-nine righteous persons who need no repentance. Or what woman, if she has ten silver coins and loses one coin, does not light a lamp and sweep the house and search carefully until she finds it? When she has found it, she calls together her friends and neighbors, saying, 'Rejoice with me, for I have found the coin which I had lost!' In the same way, I tell you, there is joy in the presence of the angels of God over one sinner who repents" (Luke 15:3–10).

Setting: Jerusalem. Before the Passover, after He conveys the upcoming ministry of the Holy Spirit in His disciples' lives with His imminent departure from them, Jesus explains He is the vine and they are the branches.

"I am the true vine, and My Father is the vinedresser. Every branch in Me that does not bear fruit, He takes away; and every *branch* that bears fruit, He prunes it so that it may bear more fruit. You are already clean because of the word which I have spoken to you. Abide in Me, and I in you. As the branch cannot bear fruit of itself unless it abides in the vine, so neither *can* you unless you abide in Me. I am the vine, you are the branches; he who abides in Me and I in him, he bears much fruit, for apart from Me you can do nothing. If anyone does not abide in Me, he is thrown away as a branch and dries up; and they gather them, and cast them into the fire and they are burned. If you abide in Me, and My words abide in you, ask whatever you wish, and it will be done for you. My Father is glorified by this, that you bear much fruit, and *so* prove to be My disciples. Just as the Father has loved Me, I have also loved you; abide in My love. If you keep My commandments, you will abide in My love; just as I have kept My Father's commandments and abide in His love. These things I have spoken to you so that My joy may be in you, and *that* your joy may be made full" (John 15:1–11; see Matthew 5:16; 7:7; John 3:29, 35; 6:56; 8:29, 31; 13:10; 15:16).

Setting: Jerusalem. Before the Passover, after warning His disciples of the persecution they will face after His departure to heaven, empathizing with their sadness over His prophecies, Jesus gives them hope for the future.

"A little while, and you will no longer see Me; and again a little while, and you will see Me." *Some* of His disciples then said to one another, "What is this thing He is telling us, 'A little while, and you will not see Me; and again a little while, and you will see Me'; and, 'because I go to the Father'?" So they were saying, "What is this that He says, 'A little while'? We do not know what He is talking about." Jesus knew that they wished to question Him, and He said to them, "Are you deliberating together about this, that I said, 'A little while, and you will not see Me, and again a little while, and you will see Me'? Truly, truly, I say to you, that you will weep and lament, but the world will rejoice; you will grieve, but your grief will be turned into joy. Whenever a woman is in labor she has pain, because her hour has come; but when she gives birth to the child, she no longer remembers the anguish because of the joy that a child has been born into the world. Therefore you too have grief now; but I will see you again, and your heart will rejoice, and no one *will* take your joy away from you" (John 16:16–22; see Mark 9:32; Luke 23:27; John 14:18–24; 16:5, 6; 20:20).

Setting: Jerusalem. Before the Passover, after empathizing with His disciples' sadness over His prophecies and giving them hope for the future, Jesus conveys promises about praying in His name.

"In that day you will not question Me about anything. Truly, truly, I say to you, if you ask the Father for anything in My name, He will give it to you. Until now you have asked for nothing in My name; ask and you will receive, so that your joy may be made full. These things I have spoken to you in figurative language; an hour is coming when I will no longer speak to you in figurative language, but will tell you plainly of the Father. In that day you will ask in My name, and I do not say to you that I will request of the Father on your behalf; for the Father Himself loves you, because you have loved Me and have believed that I came forth from the Father. I came forth from the Father and have come into the world; I am leaving the world again and going to the Father" (John 16:23–28; see Matthew 13:34; John 8:42; 13:1, 3; 14:14, 21, 23; 15:16).

Setting: Jerusalem. Before the Passover, after giving His disciples assurance that in the midst of tribulation they will have His peace, Jesus continues praying His high-priestly prayer.

"But now I come to You; and these things I speak in the world so that they may have My joy made full in themselves. I have given them Your word; and the world has hated them, because they are not of the world, even as I am not of the world. I do not ask You to take them out of the world, but to keep them from the evil *one.* They are not of the world, even as I am not of the world. Sanctify them in the truth; Your word is truth. As You sent Me into the world, I also have sent them into the world. For their sakes I sanctify Myself, that they themselves also may be sanctified in truth. I do not ask on behalf of these alone, but for those also who believe in Me through their word; that they may all be one; even as You, Father, *are* in Me and I in You, that they also maybe in Us, so that the world may believe that You sent Me" (John 17:13–21; see Matthew 10:5, 38; John 7:33; 15:3, 11, 19).

JOY OF YOUR MASTER (Listed under MASTER, JOY OF YOUR)

JUDAS (Iscariot; JUDAS, BETRAYAL OF JESUS BY is a separate entry; also see BETRAYAL)

[JUDAS from that man by whom the Son of Man is betrayed]
Setting: An upper room in Jerusalem. While celebrating the Passover meal, Jesus shocks His disciples with the revelation one of them will soon betray Him to His enemies.

As they were eating, He said, "Truly I say to you that one of you will betray Me." Being deeply grieved, they each one began to say to Him, 'Surely not I, Lord?' And He answered, "He who dipped his hand with Me in the bowl is the one who will betray Me. The

Son of Man *is to* go, just as it is written of Him; but woe to that man by whom the Son of Man is betrayed! It would have been good for that man if he had not been born." And Judas, who was betraying Him, said, 'Surely it is not I, Rabbi?' Jesus said to him, "You have said *it* yourself" (Matthew 26:21–25; cf. Mark 14:18–21; Luke 22:21–23; John 13:21–30; see Psalm 41:9).

[JUDAS from the one who betrays Me]
Setting: Jerusalem. After celebrating the Passover meal with His disciples, Jesus retreats to the Garden of Gethsemane on the Mount of Olives to pray prior to His betrayal by Judas.

Then Jesus came with them to a place called Gethsemane, and said to His disciples, "Sit here while I go over there and pray." And He took with Him Peter and the two sons of Zebedee, and began to be grieved and distressed. Then He said to them, "My soul is deeply grieved, to the point of death; remain here and keep watch with Me." And He went a little beyond *them,* and fell on His face and prayed, saying, "My Father, if it is possible, let this cup pass from Me; yet not as I will, but as You will." And He came to the disciples and found them sleeping, and said to Peter, "So, you *men* could not keep watch with Me for one hour? Keep watching and praying that you may not enter into temptation; the spirit is willing, but the flesh is weak." He went away again a second time and prayed, saying, "My Father, if this cannot pass away unless I drink it, Your will be done." Again He came and found them sleeping, for their eyes were heavy. And He left them again, and went away and prayed a third time, saying the same thing once more. Then He came to the disciples and said to them, "Are you still sleeping and resting? Behold the hour is at hand and the Son of Man is being betrayed into the hands of sinners. Get up, let us be going; behold the one who betrays Me is at hand!" (Matthew 26:36–46; cf. Mark 14:32–42; Luke 22:40–46; see Matthew 20:22; John 12:27).

[JUDAS from that man by whom the Son of Man is betrayed]
Setting: A borrowed upper room in Jerusalem. While Jesus and His twelve disciples are eating the Passover meal, the Lord states that one of His disciples will betray Him.

As they were reclining *at the table* and eating, Jesus said, "Truly I say to you that one of you will betray Me—one who is eating with Me." They began to be grieved and to say to Him one by one, "Surely not I?" And He said to them, "*It is* one of the twelve, one who dips with Me in the bowl. For the Son of Man *is to* go just as it is written of Him; but woe to that man by whom the Son of Man is betrayed! *It would have been* good for that man if he had not been born" (Mark 14:18–21; cf. Matthew 26:21–24; Luke 22:21–23; John 13:21, 22).

[JUDAS from the one who betrays Me]
Setting: Gethsemane on the Mount of Olives, east of the temple in Jerusalem. Jesus prepares to meet Judas the betrayer, while His other disciples keep falling asleep instead of watching and praying with Him.

And He came the third time, and said to them, "Are you still sleeping and resting? It is enough; the hour has come; behold, the Son of Man is being betrayed into the hands of sinners. Get up, let us be going; behold, the one who betrays Me is at hand!" (Mark 14:41, 42; cf. Matthew 26:45, 46).

[JUDAS from that man by whom He is betrayed]
Setting: An upper room in Jerusalem. During the Feast of Unleavened Bread (Passover) just before His crucifixion, while celebrating the Passover meal with His disciples, Jesus institutes the Lord's Supper.

And when He had taken a cup *and* given thanks, He said, "Take this and share it among yourselves; for I say to you, I will not drink of the fruit of the vine from now on until the kingdom of God comes." And when he had taken *some* bread and given thanks, He broke it and gave it to them, saying, "This is My body which is given for you; do this in remembrance of Me." And in the same way *He took* the cup after they had eaten, saying, "This cup which is poured out for you is the new covenant in My blood. But behold, the hand of the one betraying Me is with Mine on the table. For indeed, the Son of Man is going as it has been determined; but woe to that man by whom He is betrayed!" (Luke 22:17–22; cf. Matthew 26:26–29; Mark 14:22–25; 1 Corinthians 11:23–26; see Psalm 41:9; Luke 14:15; 1 Corinthians 10:16).

Setting: Gethsemane on the Mount of Olives, east of the temple in Jerusalem. With His crucifixion imminent, after Jesus prays with His disciples nearby, Judas betrays Him to a crowd of His enemies with a kiss.

But Jesus said to him, "Judas, are you betraying the Son of Man with a kiss?" (Luke 22:48; see Matthew 26:48, 49; Mark 14:44, 45; Luke 12:47, 49–53; John 18:2–8).

[JUDAS from a devil]
Setting: The synagogue at Capernaum of Galilee. After some of His disciples express difficulty with Jesus' statements about eating His flesh, Simon Peter responds that the Lord proclaims words of eternal life.

Jesus answered them, "Did I Myself not choose you, the twelve, and *yet* one of you is a devil?" (John 6:70; see John 15:16, 19).

[JUDAS from HE WHO EATS MY BREAD HAS LIFTED UP HIS HEEL AGAINST ME]
Setting: Jerusalem. Before the Passover, with His death on the cross nearing, Jesus explains the reason for His vivid example of servanthood in washing His disciples' feet.

So when He had washed their feet, and taken His garments and reclined *at the table* again, He said to them, "Do you know what I have done to you? You call Me Teacher and Lord; and you are right, for *so* I am. If I then, the Lord and the Teacher, washed your feet, you also ought to wash one another's feet. For I gave you an example that you also should do as I did to you. Truly, truly I say to you, a slave is not greater than his master, nor *is* one who is sent greater than the one who sent him. If you know these things, you are blessed if you do them. I do not speak of all of you. I know the ones I have chosen; but *it is* that the Scripture may be fulfilled, 'HE WHO EATS MY BREAD HAS LIFTED UP HIS HEEL AGAINST ME.' From now on I am telling you before *it* comes to pass, so that when it does occur, you may believe that I am *He*. Truly, truly, I say to you, he who receives whomever I send receives Me; and he who receives Me receives Him who sent Me" (John 13:12–20; Jesus quotes from Psalm 41:9; see Matthew 7:24; 10:24, 40; John 8:24; 14:29; 1 Peter 5:3).

[JUDAS from That is the one for whom I shall dip the morsel and give it to him]
Setting: Jerusalem. Before the Passover, while troubled in spirit due to His upcoming death on the cross, Jesus reveals to His disciples that Judas will betray Him to the chief priests and Pharisees.

Jesus then answered, "That is the one for whom I shall dip the morsel and give it to him." So when He had dipped the morsel, He took and gave it to Judas, *the son* of Simon Iscariot. After the morsel, Satan then entered into him. Therefore Jesus said to him, "What you do, do quickly" (John 13:26, 27; cf. Matthew 26:23; Mark 14:20; see Luke 22:3, 21; John 6:71).

[JUDAS from son of perdition]
Setting: Jerusalem. Before the Passover, after giving His disciples assurance that in the midst of tribulation they will have His peace, Jesus prays His high-priestly prayer.

Jesus spoke these things; and lifting up His eyes to heaven, He said, "Father, the hour has come; glorify Your Son, that the Son may glorify You, even as You gave Him authority over all flesh, that to all whom You have given Him, He may give eternal life. This is eternal life, that they may know You, the only true God, and Jesus Christ whom You have sent. I glorified You on the earth, having accomplished the work which You have given Me to do. Now, Father, glorify Me together with Yourself, with the glory which I had with You before the world was. I have manifested Your name to the men whom You gave Me out of the world; they were Yours and You gave them to Me, and they have kept Your word. Now they have come to know that everything You have given Me is from You; for the words which You gave Me I have given to them; and they received *them* and truly understood that I came forth from You, and they believed You sent Me. I ask on their behalf; I do not ask on behalf of the world, but of those whom You have given Me; for they are Yours; and all things that are Mine are Yours, and Yours are Mine; and I have been glorified in them. I am no longer in the world; and *yet* they themselves are in the world, and I come to You. Holy Father, keep them in Your name, *the name* which You have given Me, that they may be even as We *are*. While I was with them, I was keeping them in Your name which You have given Me; and I guarded them and not one of them perished but the son of perdition, so that the Scripture would be fulfilled" (John 17:1–12; see Luke 22:32; John 1:1; 3:35; 4:34; 5:44; 6:37–39, 70; 8:42; 11:41; 12:49; 13:18, 31; 16:15; 17:20; Philippians 2:9).

JUDAS, BETRAYAL OF JESUS BY (Also see BETRAYAL, PROPHECY OF JESUS')

[BETRAYAL OF JESUS BY JUDAS from the one who betrays Me is at hand]

Setting: Jerusalem. After celebrating the Passover meal with His disciples, Jesus retreats to the Garden of Gethsemane on the Mount of Olives to pray prior to His betrayal by Judas.

Then Jesus came with them to a place called Gethsemane, and said to His disciples, "Sit here while I go over there and pray." And He took with Him Peter and the two sons of Zebedee, and began to be grieved and distressed. Then He said to them, "My soul is deeply grieved, to the point of death; remain here and keep watch with Me." And He went a little beyond *them,* and fell on His face and prayed, saying, "My Father, if it is possible, let this cup pass from Me; yet not as I will, but as You will." And He came to the disciples and found them sleeping, and said to Peter, "So, you *men* could not keep watch with Me for one hour? Keep watching and praying that you may not enter into temptation; the spirit is willing, but the flesh is weak." He went away again a second time and prayed, saying, "My Father, if this cannot pass away unless I drink it, Your will be done." Again He came and found them sleeping, for their eyes were heavy. And He left them again, and went away and prayed a third time, saying the same thing once more. Then He came to the disciples and said to them, "Are you still sleeping and resting? Behold the hour is at hand and the Son of Man is being betrayed into the hands of sinners. Get up, let us be going; behold the one who betrays Me is at hand!" (Matthew 26:36–46; cf. Mark 14:32–42; Luke 22:40–46; see Matthew 20:22; John 12:27).

[BETRAYAL OF JESUS BY JUDAS from Friend, *do* what you have come for]

Setting: The Garden of Gethsemane. After praying for God's will to be done, Jesus submits to His Father's will and allows Judas to betray Him.

And Jesus said to him, "Friend, *do* what you have come for." Then they came and laid hands on Jesus and seized Him (Matthew 26:50; cf. Mark 14:43–46; Luke 22:47, 48; John 18:2–9).

[BETRAYAL OF JESUS BY JUDAS from it must happen this way]

Setting: The Garden of Gethsemane. As Jesus submits to His Father's will and allows Judas to betray Him, Peter attempts to defend Him, but Jesus does not permit it.

Then Jesus said to him, "Put your sword back into its place; for all those who take up the sword shall perish by the sword. Or do you think that I cannot appeal to My Father, and He will at once put at My disposal more than twelve legions of angels? How then will the Scriptures be fulfilled, *which say* that it must happen this way?" (Matthew 26:52–54; cf. Mark 14:47; Luke 22:50, 51; John 18:10, 11; see Matthew 26:24).

[BETRAYAL OF JESUS BY JUDAS from all this has taken place to fulfill the Scriptures]

Setting: The Garden of Gethsemane. As He submits to His Father's will and allows Judas to betray Him, Jesus reveals that this incident is a fulfillment of prophecy.

At that time Jesus said to the crowds, "Have you come out with swords and clubs to arrest Me as *you would* against a robber? Every day I used to sit in the temple teaching and you did not seize Me. But all this has taken place to fulfill the Scriptures of the prophets" (Matthew 26:55, 56; cf. Mark 14:48, 49; Luke 22:52, 53; see Matthew 26:24).

[BETRAYAL OF JESUS BY JUDAS from the one who betrays Me]

Setting: Gethsemane on the Mount of Olives, east of the temple in Jerusalem. Jesus prepares to meet Judas the betrayer, while His other disciples keep falling asleep instead of watching and praying with Him.

And He came the third time, and said to them, "Are you still sleeping and resting? It is enough; the hour has come; behold, the Son of Man is being betrayed into the hands of sinners. Get up, let us be going; behold, the one who betrays Me is at hand!" (Mark 14:41, 42; cf. Matthew 26:45, 46).

[BETRAYAL OF JESUS BY JUDAS from the one betraying Me]
Setting: An upper room in Jerusalem. During the Feast of Unleavened Bread (Passover) just before Jesus' crucifixion, while celebrating the Passover meal with His disciples, Jesus institutes the Lord's Supper.

And when He had taken a cup *and* given thanks, He said, "Take this and share it among yourselves; for I say to you, I will not drink of the fruit of the vine from now on until the kingdom of God comes." And when he had taken *some* bread and given thanks, He broke it and gave it to them, saying, "This is My body which is given for you; do this in remembrance of Me." And in the same way *He took* the cup after they had eaten, saying, "This cup which is poured out for you is the new covenant in My blood. But behold, the hand of the one betraying Me is with Mine on the table. For indeed, the Son of Man is going as it has been determined; but woe to that man by whom He is betrayed!" (Luke 22:17–22; cf. Matthew 26:26–29; Mark 14:22–25; 1 Corinthians 11:23–26; see Psalm 41:9; Luke 14:15; 1 Corinthians 10:16).

[BETRAYAL OF JESUS BY JUDAS from Judas, are you betraying the Son of Man with a kiss]
Setting: On the Mount of Olives. With His crucifixion imminent, after Jesus prays, with His disciples nearby, Judas betrays Him to a crowd of His enemies with a kiss.

But Jesus said to him, "Judas, are you betraying the Son of Man with a kiss?" (Luke 22:48; see Matthew 26:48, 49; Mark 14:44, 45; Luke 12:47, 49–53; John 18:2–8).

[BETRAYAL OF JESUS BY JUDAS from What you do, do quickly]
Setting: Jerusalem. Before the Passover, while troubled in spirit due to His upcoming death on the cross, Jesus reveals to His disciples that Judas will betray Him to the chief priests and Pharisees.

Jesus then answered, "That is the one for whom I shall dip the morsel and give it to him." So when He had dipped the morsel, He took and gave it to Judas, *the son* of Simon Iscariot. After the morsel, Satan then entered into him. Therefore Jesus said to him, "What you do, do quickly" (John 13:26, 27; cf. Matthew 26:23; Mark 14:20; see Luke 22:3, 21; John 6:71).

JUDAS, HOUSE OF (of Damascus)

Setting: Damascus. Luke, writing in Acts, conveys how the Lord Jesus instructs one of His disciples, Ananias, to locate Saul of Tarsus to touch him in order to restore his vision.

Now there was a disciple at Damascus named Ananias; and the Lord said to him in a vision, "Ananias." And he said, "Here I am, Lord." And the Lord *said* to him, "Get up and go to the street called Straight, and inquire at the house of Judas for a man from Tarsus named Saul, for he is praying, and he was seen in a vision a man named Ananias come in and lay his hands on him, so that he might regain his sight" (Acts 9:10–12; see Acts 22:12–14).

JUDEA

Setting: The Mount of Olives, just east of Jerusalem. During His discourse, Jesus answers His disciples' questions as to when the temple will be destroyed and Jerusalem overrun, along with the signs of His coming and the end of the age.

"Therefore when you see the ABOMINATION OF DESOLATION which was spoken of through Daniel the prophet, standing in the holy place (let the reader understand), then those who are in Judea must flee to the mountains. Whoever is on the housetop must not go down to get the things that are in his house. Whoever is in the field must not turn back to get his cloak. But woe to those who are pregnant and to those who are nursing babies in those days! But pray that your flight will not be in the winter, or on a Sabbath. For then there will be a great tribulation, such as has not occurred since the beginning of the world until now, nor ever will. Unless those days had been cut short, no life would have been saved; but for the sake of the elect those days will be cut short. Then if anyone says to you, 'Behold, here is the Christ,' or "There *He is,*' do not believe *him.* For false Christs and false prophets will arise and will show great signs and wonders, so as to mislead, if possible, even the elect. Behold, I have told you in advance. So if they say to you, 'Behold, He is in the wilderness,' do not go out, *or,* 'Behold, He is in the inner rooms,' do not

believe *them.* For just as the lightning comes from the east and flashes even to the west, so will the coming of the Son of Man be. Wherever the corpse is, there the vultures will gather" (Matthew 24:15–28, Jesus quotes from Daniel 9:27; cf. Daniel 12:1; Mark 13:14–23; Luke 17:22–31; 21:20–24; 23:29; see John 4:48).

Setting: On the Mount of Olives, east of the temple in Jerusalem. After prophesying the temple's destruction, Jesus responds during His Olivet Discourse to questions from Peter, James, John, and Andrew about other future events.

"But when you see the ABOMINATION OF DESOLATION standing where it should not be (let the reader understand), then those who are in Judea must flee to the mountains. The one who is on the housetop must not go down, or go in to get anything out of his house; and the one who is in the field must not turn back to get his coat. But woe to those who are pregnant and to those who are nursing babies in those days! But pray that it may not happen in winter. For those days will be a *time of* tribulation such as has not occurred since the beginning of the creation which God created until now, and never will. Unless the Lord had shortened *those* days, no life would have been saved; but for the sake of the elect, whom He chose, He shortened the days. And then if anyone says to you, 'Behold, here is the Christ'; or, 'Behold, *He is* there'; do not believe *him*; for false Christs and false prophets will arise, and will show signs and wonders, in order to lead astray, if possible, the elect. But take heed; behold, I have told you everything in advance" (Mark 13:14–23; cf. Matthew 24:15–28; Luke 21:20–24; see Daniel 9:27; 12:1; Luke 17:31).

Setting: The Mount of Olives, east of the temple in Jerusalem. After ministering in the temple a few days before His crucifixion, and giving His disciples more details regarding the temple's future destruction, Jesus elaborates during His Olivet Discourse about things to come.

"But when you see Jerusalem surrounded by armies, then recognize that her desolation is near. Then those who are in Judea must flee to the mountains, and those who are in the midst of the city must leave, and those who are in the country must not enter the city; because these are days of vengeance, so that all things which are written will be fulfilled. Woe to those who are pregnant and to those who are nursing babies in those days; for there will be a great distress upon the land and wrath to this people; and they will fall by the edge of the sword, and will be led captive into all the nations; and Jerusalem will be trampled under foot by the Gentiles until the times of the Gentiles are fulfilled" (Luke 21:20–24; see Matthew 24:15–18; Mark 13:14–16; Luke 19:43).

Setting: Beyond the Jordan. While Jesus and His disciples are avoiding the Jerusalem Pharisees, He receives word from Lazarus's sisters in Bethany of His friend's sickness, and decides to go there.

Then after this He said to the disciples, "Let us go to Judea again." The disciples said to Him, "Rabbi, the Jews were just now seeking to stone You, and are You going there again?" Jesus answered, "Are there not twelve hours in the day? If anyone walks in the day, he does not stumble, because he sees the light of this world. But if anyone walks in the night, he stumbles, because the light is not in him." This He said, and after that He said to them, "Our friend Lazarus has fallen asleep; but I go, so that I may awaken him out of sleep" (John 11:7–11; see John 8:59; 10:39).

Setting: Jerusalem. Luke, writing in Acts, presents quotes from Jesus' post-resurrection appearances, in which He responds to their question if He is about to restore the kingdom to Israel.

He said to them, "It is not for you to know times or epochs which the Father has fixed by His own authority; but you will receive power when the Holy Spirit has come upon you; and you shall be My witnesses both in Jerusalem, and in all Judea and Samaria, and even to the remotest part of the earth" (Acts 1:7, 8; see Luke 24:48, 49; Acts 2:1–4).

JUDGE (Also see JUDGES; JUDGMENT; and MAGISTRATE)

Setting: Galilee. During the early part of His ministry, Jesus preaches the Sermon on the Mount to His disciples and the multitudes.

"Make friends quickly with your opponent at law while you are with him on the way, so that your opponent may not hand you over to the judge, and the judge to the officer, and you be thrown into prison. Truly I say to you, you will not come out of there until you have paid up the last cent'" (Matthew 5:25, 26; cf. Luke 12:58, 59).

Setting: On the way from Galilee to Jerusalem. After the scribes and Pharisees turn hostile and question Him repeatedly in an attempt to catch Him in something He might say, Jesus teaches the crowds and His disciples about greed and possessions.

But He said to him, "Man, who appointed Me a judge or arbitrator over you?" Then He said to them, "Beware, and be on your guard against every form of greed; for not *even* when one has an abundance does his life consist of his possessions" (Luke 12:14, 15; see 1 Timothy 6:6–10).

Setting: On the way from Galilee to Jerusalem. After chastising the crowds for being able to discern the weather but not the present age, Jesus exhorts them to settle any financial disputes outside of court.

"And why do you not even on your own initiative judge what is right? For while you are going with your opponent to appear before the magistrate, on *your* way *there* make an effort to settle with him, so that he may not drag you before the judge, and the judge turn you over to the officer, and the officer throw you into prison. I say to you, you will not get out of there until you have paid the very last cent" (Luke 12:57–59; cf. Matthew 5:25, 26).

Setting: On the way from Galilee to Jerusalem. After telling His disciples of His second coming, Jesus instructs them about persistence in prayer.

Now He was telling them a parable to show that at all times they ought to pray and not to lose heart, saying, "In a certain city there was a judge who did not fear God and did not respect man. There was a widow in that city, and she kept coming to him, saying, 'Give me legal protection from my opponent.' For a while he was unwilling; but afterward he said to himself, 'Even though I do not fear God nor respect man, yet because this woman bothers me, I will give her legal protection, otherwise by continually coming she will wear me out.'" And the Lord said, "Hear what the unrighteous judge said; now, will not God bring about justice for His elect who cry to Him day and night, and will He delay long over them? I tell you that He will bring about justice for them quickly. However, when the Son of Man comes, will He find faith on the earth?" (Luke 18:1–8; see Luke 11:5–10).

JUDGE, JESUS AS (Also see JUDGMENT)

[JESUS AS JUDGE from Many will say to Me on that day, 'Lord, Lord]
Setting: Galilee. During the early part of His ministry, Jesus preaches the Sermon on the Mount to His disciples and the multitudes.

"Not everyone who says to Me, 'Lord, Lord,' will enter the kingdom of heaven, but he who does the will of My Father who is in heaven *will enter.* Many will say to Me on that day, 'Lord, Lord, did we not prophesy in Your name, and in Your name cast out demons, and in Your name perform many miracles?' And then I will declare to them, 'I never knew you, DEPART FROM ME, YOU WHO PRACTICE LAWLESSNESS'" (Matthew 7:21–23, Jesus quotes from Psalm 6:8; cf. Matthew 25:11–13; see Luke 6:46).

[JESUS AS JUDGE from But whoever denies Me before men, I will also deny him before My Father who is in heaven]
Setting: Galilee. Jesus explains the meaning of discipleship as He commissions His twelve disciples for ministry.

"Therefore everyone who confesses Me before men, I will also confess him before My Father who is in heaven. But whoever denies Me before men, I will also deny him before My Father who is in heaven" (Matthew 10:32, 33; cf. Mark 8:38; Luke 12:8).

[JESUS AS JUDGE from the Son of Man will sit on His glorious throne]
Setting: Judea beyond the Jordan (Perea). Jesus promises rewards to His disciples for their personal sacrifice and commitment to following Him.

And Jesus said to them, "Truly I say to you, that you who have followed Me, in the regeneration when the Son of Man will sit on His glorious throne, you also shall sit upon twelve thrones, judging the twelve tribes of Israel. And everyone who has left houses or brothers or sisters or father or mother or children or farms for My name's sake, will receive many times as much, and will inherit eternal life. But many *who* are first will be last; and *the* last, first" (Matthew 19:28–30; cf. Matthew 6:33; 20:15; Mark 10:29, 30; Luke 18:29, 30; 22:30).

[JESUS AS JUDGE from He will sit on His glorious throne]
Setting: The Mount of Olives, just east of Jerusalem. During His discourse, after answering His disciples' questions as to when the temple will be destroyed and Jerusalem overrun, along with the signs of His coming and the end of the age, Jesus reveals the future judgments following His return.

"But when the Son of Man comes in His glory, and all the angels with Him, then He will sit on His glorious throne. All the nations will be gathered before Him; and He will separate them from one another, as the shepherd separates the sheep from the goats; and He will put the sheep on His right, and the goats on the left. Then the King will say to those on His right, 'Come, you who are blessed of My Father, inherit the kingdom prepared for you from the foundation of the world. 'For I was hungry, and you gave Me *something* to eat; I was thirsty, and you gave Me *something* to drink; I was a stranger, and you invited Me in; naked, and you clothed Me; I was sick, and you visited Me; I was in prison, and you came to Me.' Then the righteous will answer Him, 'Lord, when did we see You hungry and feed You, or thirsty, and give you *something* to drink? And when did we see You a stranger, and invite You in, or naked, and clothe You? When did we see You sick, or in prison, and come to You?' The King will answer and say to them, 'Truly I say to you, to the extent that you did it to one of these brothers of Mine, *even* the least *of them,* you did it to Me.' Then He will also say to those on His left, 'Depart from Me, accursed ones, into the eternal fire which has been prepared for the devil and his angels; for I was hungry, and you gave Me *nothing* to eat; I was thirsty, and you gave Me nothing to drink; I was a stranger, and you did not invite Me in; naked, and you did not clothe Me; sick, and in prison, and you did not visit Me.' Then they themselves also will answer, 'Lord, when did we see You hungry, or thirsty, or a stranger, or naked, or sick, or in prison, and did not take care of You?' Then He will answer them, 'Truly I say to you, to the extent that you did not do it to one of the least of these, you did not do it to Me.' These will go away into eternal punishment, but the righteous into eternal life" (Matthew 25:31–46; see Matthew 7:23; 16:27; 19:29).

[JESUS AS JUDGE from THE SON OF MAN SITTING AT THE RIGHT HAND OF POWER]
Setting: Jerusalem. After being betrayed by Judas and arrested, Jesus appears before Caiaphas the high priest and the Council, who interrogate and try to trap Him.

Jesus said to him, "You have said it *yourself;* nevertheless I tell you, hereafter you will see THE SON OF MAN SITTING AT THE RIGHT HAND OF POWER, AND COMING ON THE CLOUDS OF HEAVEN" (Matthew 26:64, Jesus quotes from Daniel 7:13; cf. Mark 14:62).

[JESUS AS JUDGE from the Son of Man will also be ashamed of him when He comes in the glory of His Father with the holy angels]
Setting: Caesarea Philippi. Following His rebuke of Peter for desiring to thwart His mission to the cross, Jesus summons a crowd along with His disciples and informs them of the high costs of following Him.

And He summoned the crowd with His disciples, and said to them, "If anyone wishes to come after Me, he must deny himself, and take up his cross and follow Me. For whoever wishes to save his life will lose it, but whoever loses his life for My sake and the gospel's will save it. For what does it profit a man to gain the whole world, and forfeit his soul? For what will a man give in exchange for his soul? For whoever is ashamed of Me and My words in this adulterous and sinful generation, the Son of Man will also be ashamed of him when He comes in the glory of His Father with the holy angels" (Mark 8:34–38; cf. Matthew 16:24–28; Luke 9:23–27; see Matthew 10:33, 38, 39).

[JESUS AS JUDGE from THE SON OF MAN SITTING AT THE RIGHT HAND OF POWER]
Setting: Jerusalem. Following His betrayal by Judas and His arrest, Jesus confirms to the high priest and all the chief priests that He is the Christ as they seek justification to put Him to death.

And Jesus said, "I am; and you shall see THE SON OF MAN SITTING AT THE RIGHT HAND OF POWER, and COMING WITH THE CLOUDS OF HEAVEN" (Mark 14:62, Jesus quotes from Psalm 110:1; Daniel 7:13; cf. Matthew 26:57–68; see Luke 22:54).

[JESUS AS JUDGE from the Son of Man will confess him also before the angels of God]
Setting: On the way from Galilee to Jerusalem. Jesus warns His disciples of future events as the scribes and Pharisees turn hostile and question Him repeatedly in an attempt to catch Him in something He might say.

"And I say to you, everyone who confesses Me before men, the Son of Man will confess him also before the angels of God; but he who denies Me before men will be denied before the angels of God. And everyone who speaks a word against the Son of Man, it will be forgiven him; but he who blasphemes against the Holy Spirit, it will not be forgiven him. When they bring you before the synagogues and the rulers and the authorities, do not worry about how or what you are to speak in your defense, or what you are to say; for the Holy Spirit will teach you in that very hour what you ought to say" (Luke 12:8–12; cf. Matthew 10:32, 33; 12:31, 32; see Matthew 10:20).

[JESUS AS JUDGE from Man, who appointed Me a judge or arbitrator over you]
Setting: On the way from Galilee to Jerusalem. After the scribes and Pharisees turn hostile and question Him repeatedly in an attempt to catch Him in something He might say, Jesus teaches the crowds and His disciples about greed and possessions.

But He said to him, "Man, who appointed Me a judge or arbitrator over you?" Then He said to them, "Beware, and be on your guard against every form of greed; for not *even* when one has an abundance does his life consist of his possessions" (Luke 12:14, 15; see 1 Timothy 6:6–10).

[JESUS AS JUDGE from to stand before the Son of Man]
Setting: Jerusalem. A few days before His crucifixion, after conveying the Parable of the Fig Tree, Jesus warns His disciples to keep alert regarding future events.

"Be on guard, so that your hearts will not be weighted down with dissipation and drunkenness and the worries of life, and that day will not come upon you suddenly like a trap; for it will come upon all those who dwell on the face of all the earth. But keep on the alert at all times, praying that you may have strength to escape all these things that are about to take place, and to stand before the Son of Man" (Luke 21:34–36; cf. Mark 13:33; see Matthew 24:42–44).

[JESUS AS JUDGE from He has given all judgment to the Son]
Setting: By the pool of Bethesda in Jerusalem. During the Feast of the Jews, Jesus responds to criticism from the Jewish religious leaders for healing a lame man on the Sabbath and for referring to God as His Father (thereby making Himself equal with God).

Therefore Jesus answered and was saying to them, "Truly, truly, I say to you, the Son can do nothing of Himself, unless *it is* something He sees the Father doing; for whatever the Father does, these things the Son also does in like manner. For the Father loves the Son, and shows Him all things that He Himself is doing; and *the Father* will show Him greater works than these, so that you will marvel. For just as the Father raises the dead and gives them life, even so the Son also gives life to whom He wishes. For not even the Father judges anyone, but He has given all judgment to the Son, so that all will honor the Son even as they honor the Father. He who does not honor the Son does not honor the Father who sent Him" (John 5:19–23; see Luke 10:16; John 3:35; 11:25; 14:12).

[JESUS AS JUDGE from He gave Him authority to execute judgment]
Setting: Jerusalem. During the Feast of the Jews, Jesus responds to criticism from the Jewish religious leaders by referring to God as His Father (thereby making Himself equal with God) and prophesying His participation in the resurrection and judgment of men.

"Truly, truly, I say to you, an hour is coming and now is, when the dead will hear the voice of the Son of God, and those who hear will live. For just as the Father has life in Himself, even so He gave to the Son also to have life in Himself; and He gave Him authority to execute judgment, because He is *the* Son of Man. Do not marvel at this; for an hour is coming, in which all who are in the tombs will hear His voice, and will come forth; those who did the good *deeds* to a resurrection of life, those who committed the evil *deeds* to a resurrection of judgment" (John 5:25–29; see Daniel 12:2; John 1:4; 11:24).

[JESUS AS JUDGE from My judgment is just]
Setting: Jerusalem. During the Feast of the Jews, Jesus responds to criticism from the Jewish religious leaders by referring to God as His Father (thereby making Himself equal with God) and informing them that God, John the Baptist, and His works all testify to His mission.

"I can do nothing on My own initiative. As I hear, I judge; and My judgment is just, because I do not seek My own will, but the will of Him who sent Me. If I *alone* testify about Myself, My testimony is not true. There is another who testifies of Me, and I know that the testimony which He gives about Me is true. You have sent to John, and he has testified to the truth. But the testimony which I receive is not from man, but I say these things so that you may be saved. He was the lamp that was burning and was shining and you were willing to rejoice for a while in his light. But the testimony which I have is greater than the *testimony of* John; for the works which the Father has given Me to accomplish—the very works that I do—testify about Me, that the Father has sent Me. And the Father who sent Me, He has testified of Me. You have neither heard His voice at any time nor seen His form. You do not have His word abiding in you, for you do not believe Him whom He sent" (John 5:30–38; see Matthew 3:17; Mark 1:4, 5; John 1:7, 15, 32; 4:34; 8:14–16; 10:25, 37, 38).

[JESUS AS JUDGE from My judgment is true]
Setting: The temple in Jerusalem. Following the Feast of Booths and the scribes' and Pharisees' failed attempt to stone a woman for adultery, Jesus returns the next day to teach. His enemies question His testimony about Himself.

Jesus answered and said to them, "Even if I testify about Myself, My testimony is true, for I know where I came from and where I am going; but you do not know where I come from or where I am going. You judge according to the flesh; I am not judging anyone. But even if I do judge, My judgment is true; for I am not alone *in it*, but I and the Father who sent Me. Even in your law it has been written that the testimony of two men is true. I am He who testifies about Myself, and the Father who sent Me testifies about Me." So they were saying to Him, "Where is Your Father?" Jesus answered, "You know neither Me nor My Father; if you knew Me, you would know My Father also" (John 8:14–19; see Deuteronomy 17:6; 19:15; Matthew 18:16; John 3:17; 5:30, 37; 7:28; 8:42).

[JESUS AS JUDGE from I have many things to speak and to judge concerning you]
Setting: The temple treasury in Jerusalem. Following the Feast of Booths and the scribes' and Pharisees' failed attempt to stone a woman for adultery, Jesus returns the next day to teach. His enemies question His testimony about Himself.

Then He said again to them, "I go away, and you will seek Me, and will die in your sin; where I am going, you cannot come." So the Jews were saying, "Surely He will not kill Himself, will He, since He says, "Where I am going, you cannot come'?" And He was saying to them, "You are from below, I am from above; you are of this world, I am not of this world. Therefore I said to you that you will die in your sins; for unless you believe that I am *He*, you will die in your sins." So they were saying to Him, "Who are You?" Jesus said to them, "What have I been saying to you *from* the beginning? I have many things to speak and to judge concerning you, but He who sent Me is true; and the things which I heard from Him, these I speak to the world" (John 8:21–26; see John 3:31–33; 5:34, 35; 17:14, 16).

[JESUS AS JUDGE from the word I spoke is what will judge him at the last day]
Setting: Jerusalem. Just days before the Passover, with the chief priests and Pharisees plotting to seize Jesus, who is expressing anxiety about His upcoming death by crucifixion, some people believe in Jesus, while others are rejecting His message.

And Jesus cried out and said, "He who believes in Me, does not believe in Me but in Him who sent Me. He who sees Me sees the One who sent Me. I have come *as* Light into the world, so that everyone who believes in Me will not remain in darkness. If anyone hears My sayings and does not keep them, I do not judge him; for I did not come to judge the world, but to save the world. He who rejects Me and does not receive My sayings, has one who judges him; the word I spoke is what will judge him at the last day. For I did not speak on My own initiative, but the Father Himself who sent Me has given Me a commandment *as to* what to say and what to speak. I know that His commandment is eternal life; therefore the things I speak, I speak just as the Father as told Me" (John 12:44–50; see Matthew 10:40; Luke 10:16; John 1:4; 3:17; 5:19; 6:68; 14:9).

JUDGE, PARABLE OF THE UNRIGHTEOUS

[PARABLE OF THE UNRIGHTEOUS JUDGE from parable and unrighteous judge]

Setting: On the way from Galilee to Jerusalem. After telling His disciples of His second coming, Jesus instructs them about persistence in prayer.

Now He was telling them a parable to show that at all times they ought to pray and not to lose heart, saying, "In a certain city there was a judge who did not fear God and did not respect man. There was a widow in that city, and she kept coming to him, saying, 'Give me legal protection from my opponent.' For a while he was unwilling; but afterward he said to himself, 'Even though I do not fear God nor respect man, yet because this woman bothers me, I will give her legal protection, otherwise by continually coming she will wear me out.'" And the Lord said, "Hear what the unrighteous judge said; now, will not God bring about justice for His elect who cry to Him day and night, and will He delay long over them? I tell you that He will bring about justice for them quickly. However, when the Son of Man comes, will He find faith on the earth?" (Luke 18:1–8; see Luke 11:5–10).

JUDGE, UNRIGHTEOUS

Setting: On the way from Galilee to Jerusalem. After telling His disciples of His second coming, Jesus instructs them about persistence in prayer.

Now He was telling them a parable to show that at all times they ought to pray and not to lose heart, saying, "In a certain city there was a judge who did not fear God and did not respect man. There was a widow in that city, and she kept coming to him, saying, 'Give me legal protection from my opponent.' For a while he was unwilling; but afterward he said to himself, 'Even though I do not fear God nor respect man, yet because this woman bothers me, I will give her legal protection, otherwise by continually coming she will wear me out.'" And the Lord said, "Hear what the unrighteous judge said; now, will not God bring about justice for His elect who cry to Him day and night, and will He delay long over them? I tell you that He will bring about justice for them quickly. However, when the Son of Man comes, will He find faith on the earth?" (Luke 18:1–8; see Luke 11:5–10).

JUDGES (Also see JUDGE; and JUDGMENT)

Setting: Galilee. After He heals a blind, mute, demon-possessed man, the Pharisees accuse Jesus in front of crowds of being a worker of Beelzebul (Satan).

And knowing their thoughts Jesus said to them, "Any kingdom divided against itself is laid waste; and any city or house divided against itself will not stand. If Satan casts out Satan, he is divided against himself; how then will his kingdom stand? If I by Beelzebul cast out demons, by whom do your sons cast *them* out? For this reason they will be your judges. But if I cast out demons by the Spirit of God, then the kingdom of God has come upon you. Or how can anyone enter the strong man's house and carry off his property, unless he first binds the strong *man?* And then he will plunder his house" (Matthew 12:25–29; cf. Matthew 9:34; Mark 3:23–27; Luke 11:17–20).

[JUDGES from you also shall sit upon twelve thrones, judging the twelve tribes of Israel]

Setting: Judea beyond the Jordan (Perea). Jesus promises rewards to His disciples for their personal sacrifice and commitment to following Him.

And Jesus said to them, "Truly I say to you, that you who have followed Me, in the regeneration when the Son of Man will sit on His glorious throne, you also shall sit upon twelve thrones, judging the twelve tribes of Israel. And everyone who has left houses or brothers or sisters or father or mother or children or farms for My name's sake, will receive many times as much, and will inherit eternal life. But many *who* are first will be last; and *the* last, first" (Matthew 19:28–30; cf. Matthew 6:33; 20:15; Mark 10:29, 30; Luke 18:29, 30; 22:30).

Setting: On the way from Galilee to Jerusalem. After Jesus casts out a demon, some in the crowd test Him, demanding a sign from heaven.

But He knew their thoughts and said to them, "Any kingdom divided against itself is laid waste; and a house *divided* against itself falls. If Satan also is divided against himself, how will his kingdom stand? For you say that I cast out demons by Beelzebul. And if I by Beelzebul cast out demons, by whom do your sons cast them out? So they will be your judges. But if I cast out demons by the finger of God, then the kingdom of God has come upon you". (Luke 11:17–20; cf. Matthew 12:25–28; Mark 3:23–27; see Exodus 8:19; Matthew 3:2, 10:25).

[JUDGES from you will sit on thrones judging the twelve tribes of Israel]
Setting: An upper room in Jerusalem. During the Feast of Unleavened Bread (Passover) just before His crucifixion, Jesus celebrates the Passover meal and institutes the Lord's Supper. After His disciples argue over who is the greatest among them, He details the kingdom benefits they will experience.

"You are those who have stood by Me in My trials; for just as My Father has granted Me a kingdom, I grant you that you may eat and drink at My table in My kingdom, and you will sit on thrones judging the twelve tribes of Israel" (Luke 22:28–30; cf. Matthew 19:28).

Setting: By the pool of Bethesda in Jerusalem. During the Feast of the Jews, Jesus responds to criticism from the Jewish religious leaders for healing a lame man on the Sabbath and for referring to God as His Father (thereby making Himself equal with God).

Therefore Jesus answered and was saying to them, "Truly, truly, I say to you, the Son can do nothing of Himself, unless *it is* something He sees the Father doing; for whatever the Father does, these things the Son also does in like manner. For the Father loves the Son, and shows Him all things that He Himself is doing; and *the Father* will show Him greater works than these, so that you will marvel. For just as the Father raises the dead and gives them life, even so the Son also gives life to whom He wishes. For not even the Father judges anyone, but He has given all judgment to the Son, so that all will honor the Son even as they honor the Father. He who does not honor the Son does not honor the Father who sent Him" (John 5:19–23; see Luke 10:16; John 3:35; 11:25; 14:12).

JUDGING OTHERS (Also see JUDGMENT, HUMAN)

[JUDGING OTHERS from For in the way you judge, you will be judged; and by your standard of measure, it will be measured to you]
Setting: Galilee. During the early part of His ministry, Jesus preaches the Sermon on the Mount to His disciples and the multitudes.

"Do not judge so that you will not be judged. For in the way you judge, you will be judged; and by your standard of measure, it will be measured to you. Why do you look at the speck that is in your brother's eye, but do not notice the log that is in your own eye? Or how can you say to your brother, 'Let me take the speck out of your eye, and behold, the log is in your own eye? You hypocrite, first take the log out of your own eye, and then you will see clearly to take the speck out of your brother's eye" (Matthew 7:1–5; cf. Mark 4:24; Luke 6:37–42; Romans 2:1; Romans 14:10, 13).

[JUDGING OTHERS from do not judge, and you will not be judged]
Setting: Galilee. After selecting His twelve disciples, Jesus teaches the Sermon on the Mount to those disciples and a great throng of people from Judea, Jerusalem, and the central coastal region of Tyre and Sidon.

"Do not judge, and you will not be judged; and do not condemn, and you will not be condemned; pardon, and you will be pardoned. Give and it will be given to you. They will pour into your lap a good measure—pressed down, shaken together, *and* running over. For by your standard of measure it will be measured to you in return" (Luke 6:37, 38; cf. Matthew 7:1–5; Mark 4:24; see Luke 6:12–19).

[JUDGING OTHERS from Do not judge according to appearance]
Setting: The temple in Jerusalem. After receiving encouragement from His blood brothers in Galilee to attend the upcoming Feast of Booths in order to demonstrate His works to His disciples and the world, Jesus goes and teaches, astonishing the Jewish religious leaders.

Jesus answered them, "I did one deed, and you all marvel. For this reason Moses has given you circumcision (not because it is from Moses, but from the fathers), and on *the* Sabbath you circumcise a man. If a man receives circumcision on *the* Sabbath so that the Law of Moses will not be broken, are you angry with Me because I made an entire man well on *the* Sabbath? Do not judge according to appearance, but judge with righteous judgment" (John 7:21–24; see Genesis 17:10–14; Leviticus 12:3; 19:15; Matthew 12:2; John 5:2–16; 7–20; 7:10–15).

[JUDGING OTHERS from You judge according to the flesh]
Setting: The temple in Jerusalem. Following the Feast of Booths and the scribes' and Pharisees' failed attempt to stone a woman for adultery, Jesus returns the next day to teach. His enemies question His testimony about Himself.

Jesus answered and said to them, "Even if I testify about Myself, My testimony is true, for I know where I came from and where I am going; but you do not know where I come from or where I am going. You judge according to the flesh; I am not judging anyone. But even if I do judge, My judgment is true; for I am not alone *in it,* but I and the Father who sent Me. Even in your law it has been written that the testimony of two men is true. I am He who testifies about Myself, and the Father who sent Me testifies about Me." So they were saying to Him, "Where is Your Father?" Jesus answered, "You know neither Me nor My Father; if you knew Me, you would know My Father also" (John 8:14–19; see Deuteronomy 17:6; 19:15; Matthew 18:16; John 3:17; 5:30, 37; 7:28).

JUDGMENT, DAY OF (Also see CONDEMNATION; JUDGE, JESUS AS; and JUDGMENT, DIVINE)

[DAY OF JUDGMENT from Not everyone who says to Me, 'Lord, Lord and on that day]
Setting: Galilee. During the early part of His ministry, Jesus preaches the Sermon on the Mount to His disciples and the multitudes.

"Not everyone who says to Me, 'Lord, Lord' will enter the kingdom of heaven, but he who does the will of My Father who is in heaven *will enter.* Many will say to Me on that day, 'Lord, Lord, did we not prophesy in Your name, and in Your name cast out demons, and in Your name perform many miracles?' And then I will declare to them, 'I never knew you, DEPART FROM ME, YOU WHO PRACTICE LAWLESSNESS'"(Matthew 7:21–23, Jesus quotes from Psalm 6:8; cf. Matthew 25:11–13; see Luke 6:46).

Setting: Galilee. After His twelve disciples observe His ministry, Jesus summons and specifically instructs them about their ministry to the people of Israel.

These twelve Jesus sent out after instructing them: "Do not go in *the* way of *the* Gentiles, and do not enter *any* city of the Samaritans; but rather go to the lost sheep of the house of Israel. And as you go, preach, saying, 'The kingdom of heaven is at hand.' Heal *the* sick, raise *the* dead, cleanse *the* lepers, cast out demons. Freely you received, freely give. Do not acquire gold, or silver, or copper for your money belts, or a bag for *your* journey, or even two coats, or sandals, or a staff; for the worker is worthy of his support. And whatever city or village you enter, inquire who is worthy in it, and stay at his house until you leave *that city*. As you enter the house, give it your greeting. If the house is worthy, give it your *blessing of* peace. But if it is not worthy, take back your *blessing of* peace. Whoever does not receive you, nor heed your words, as you go out of that house or that city, shake the dust off your feet. Truly I say to you, it will be more tolerable for *the* land of Sodom and Gomorrah in the day of judgment than for that city" (Matthew 10:5–15; cf. Mark 6:7–11; Luke 9:1–5; see Matthew 3:2; 11:22, 24; 15:24; Luke 22:35; 1 Corinthians 9:14).

[DAY OF JUDGMENT from Therefore everyone who confesses Me before men, I will also confess him before My Father who is in heaven. But whoever denies Me before men, I will also deny him before My Father who is in heaven]
Setting: Galilee. Jesus explains the meaning of discipleship as He commissions His twelve disciples for ministry.

"Therefore everyone who confesses Me before men, I will also confess him before My Father who is in heaven. But whoever denies Me before men, I will also deny him before My Father who is in heaven" (Matthew 10:32, 33; cf. Mark 8:38; Luke 12:8).

Setting: Galilee. After performing miracles throughout the region, Jesus pronounces woes against those cities who did not repent.

"Woe to you, Chorazin! Woe to you, Bethsaida! For if the miracles had occurred in Tyre and Sidon which occurred in you, they would have repented long ago in sackcloth and ashes. Nevertheless I say to you, it will be more tolerable for Tyre and Sidon in *the* day of judgment than for you. And you, Capernaum, will not be exalted to heaven, will you? You will descend to Hades; for if the miracles had occurred in Sodom which occurred in you, it would have remained to this day. Nevertheless, I say to you that it will be more tolerable for the land of Sodom in *the* day of judgment, than for you" (Matthew 11:21–24; cf. Matthew 10:15; Luke 10:13–15).

Setting: Galilee. After He heals a blind, mute, demon-possessed man, the Pharisees accuse Jesus in front of crowds of being a worker of Satan.

"Either make the tree good and its fruit good, or make the tree bad and its fruit bad; for the tree is known by its fruit. You brood of vipers, how can you, being evil, speak what is good? For the mouth speaks out of that which fills the heart. The good man brings out of *his* good treasure what is good; and the evil man brings out of *his* evil treasure what is evil. But I tell you that every careless word that people speak, they shall give an accounting for it in the day of judgment. For by your words you will be justified, and by your words you will be condemned" (Matthew 12:33–37; cf. Matthew 3:7; Matthew 7:16–18).

[DAY OF JUDGMENT from So it will be at the end of the age; the angels will come forth and take out the wicked from among the righteous, and will throw them into the furnace of fire; in that place there will be weeping and gnashing of teeth]

Setting: By the Sea of Galilee. Because the religious leaders are rejecting His message, Jesus continues teaching His disciples with the Parable of the Dragnet.

"Again, the kingdom of heaven is like a dragnet cast into the sea, and gathering *fish* of every kind; and when it was filled, they drew it up on the beach; and they sat down and gathered the good *fish* into containers, but the bad they threw away. So it will be at the end of the age; the angels will come forth and take out the wicked from among the righteous, and will throw them into the furnace of fire; in that place there will be weeping and gnashing of teeth. Have you understood all these things?" They said to Him, "Yes" (Matthew 13:47–51).

[DAY OF JUDGMENT from Come, you who are blessed of My Father, inherit the kingdom prepared for you from the foundation of the world and Depart from Me, accursed ones, into the eternal fire which has been prepared for the devil and his angels]

Setting: The Mount of Olives, just east of Jerusalem. During His discourse, after answering His disciples' questions as to when the temple will be destroyed and Jerusalem overrun, along with the signs of His coming and the end of the age, Jesus reveals the future judgments following His return.

"But when the Son of Man comes in His glory, and all the angels with Him, then He will sit on His glorious throne. All the nations will be gathered before Him; and He will separate them from one another, as the shepherd separates the sheep from the goats; and He will put the sheep on His right, and the goats on the left. Then the King will say to those on His right, 'Come, you who are blessed of My Father, inherit the kingdom prepared for you from the foundation of the world. 'For I was hungry, and you gave Me *something* to eat; I was thirsty, and you gave Me *something* to drink; I was a stranger, and you invited Me in; naked, and you clothed Me; I was sick, and you visited Me; I was in prison, and you came to Me.' Then the righteous will answer Him, 'Lord, when did we see You hungry and feed You, or thirsty, and give you *something* to drink? And when did we see You a stranger, and invite You in, or naked, and clothe You? When did we see You sick, or in prison, and come to You?' The King will answer and say to them, 'Truly I say to you, to the extent that you did it to one of these brothers of Mine, *even* the least *of them,* you did it to Me.' Then

He will also say to those on His left, 'Depart from Me, accursed ones, into the eternal fire which has been prepared for the devil and his angels; for I was hungry, and you gave Me *nothing* to eat; I was thirsty, and you gave Me nothing to drink; I was a stranger, and you did not invite Me in; naked, and you did not clothe Me; sick, and in prison, and you did not visit Me.' Then they themselves also will answer, 'Lord, when did we see You hungry, or thirsty, or a stranger, or naked, or sick, or in prison, and did not take care of You?' Then He will answer them, 'Truly I say to you, to the extent that you did not do it to one of the least of these, you did not do it to Me.' These will go away into eternal punishment, but the righteous into eternal life" (Matthew 25:31–46; see Matthew 7:23; 16:27; 19:29).

JUDGMENT, DIVINE (JUDGMENT, DAY OF is a separate entry; also see CONDEMNATION; PUNISHMENT, ETERNAL; and JUDGE, JESUS AS)

[DIVINE JUDGMENT from guilty before the court and guilty before the supreme court]
Setting: Galilee. During the early part of His ministry, Jesus preaches the Sermon on the Mount to His disciples and the multitudes.

"But I say to you that everyone who is angry with his brother shall be guilty before the court; and whoever says to his brother, 'You good-for-nothing,' shall be guilty before the supreme court; and whoever says, 'You fool,' shall be guilty *enough to go* into the fiery hell" (Matthew 5:22).

[DIVINE JUDGMENT from For in the way you judge, you will be judged; and by your standard of measure, it will be measured to you]
Setting: Galilee. During the early part of His ministry, Jesus preaches the Sermon on the Mount to His disciples and the multitudes.

"Do not judge so that you will not be judged. For in the way you judge, you will be judged; and by your standard of measure, it will be measured to you. Why do you look at the speck that is in your brother's eye, but do not notice the log that is in your own eye? Or how can you say to your brother, 'Let me take the speck out of your eye, and behold, the log is in your own eye? You hypocrite, first take the log out of your own eye, and then you will see clearly to take the speck out of your brother's eye" (Matthew 7:1–5; cf. Mark 4:24; Luke 6:37–42; Romans 2:1; 14:10, 13).

Setting: Galilee. After Jesus warns the Pharisees about the unpardonable sin and their future judgment, some Pharisees and scribes ask Him to perform a miraculous sign for them in front of the crowds.

[DIVINE JUDGMENT from judgment]

But He answered and said to them, "An evil and adulterous generation craves for a sign; and *yet* no sign will be given to it but the sign of Jonah the prophet; for just as JONAH WAS THREE DAYS AND THREE NIGHTS IN THE BELLY OF THE SEA MONSTER, so will the Son of Man be three days and three nights in the heart of the earth. The men of Nineveh will stand up with this generation at the judgment, and will condemn it because they repented at the preaching of Jonah; and behold, something greater than Jonah is here. *The* Queen of *the* South will rise up with this generation at the judgment and will condemn it, because she came from the ends of the earth to hear the wisdom of Solomon; and behold, something greater than Solomon is here" (Matthew 12:39–42; Jesus quotes from Jonah 1:17; cf. 1 Kings 10:1; Jonah 3:5; Matthew 16:1, 4; 12:38; Luke 11:29).

[DIVINE JUDGMENT from will throw them into the furnace of fire]
Setting: A house near the Sea of Galilee. Jesus explains the meaning of the Parable of the Wheat and the Tares to His disciples.

And He said, "The one who sows the good seed is the Son of Man, and the field is the world; and as *for* the good seed, these are the sons of the kingdom; and the tares are the sons of the evil *one;* and the enemy who sowed them is the devil, and the harvest is the end of the age; and the reapers are angels. So just as the tares are gathered up and burned with fire, so shall it be at the end of the age. The Son of Man will send forth His angels, and they will gather out of His kingdom all stumbling blocks, and those who commit lawlessness, and will throw them into the furnace of fire; in that place there will be weeping and gnashing of teeth. Then THE RIGHTEOUS WILL SHINE FORTH AS THE SUN in the kingdom of their Father. He who has ears, let him hear" (Matthew 13:37–43, Jesus quotes from Daniel 12:3; cf. Matthew 8:12; 13:50).

[DIVINE JUDGMENT from So it will be at the end of the age; the angels will come forth and take out the wicked from among the righteous, and will throw them into the furnace of fire; in that place there will be weeping and gnashing of teeth]
Setting: By the Sea of Galilee. Because the religious leaders are rejecting His message, Jesus continues teaching His disciples with the Parable of the Dragnet.

"Again, the kingdom of heaven is like a dragnet cast into the sea, and gathering *fish* of every kind; and when it was filled, they drew it up on the beach; and they sat down and gathered the good *fish* into containers, but the bad they threw away. So it will be at the end of the age; the angels will come forth and take out the wicked from among the righteous, and will throw them into the furnace of fire; in that place there will be weeping and gnashing of teeth. Have you understood all these things?" They said to Him, "Yes" (Matthew 13:47–51).

[DIVINE JUDGMENT from My heavenly Father will also do the same to you, if each of you does not forgive his brother from your heart]
Setting: Capernaum of Galilee. Jesus illustrates forgiveness after Peter asks Him if forgiving someone seven times who has sinned against him is adequate.

"For this reason the kingdom of heaven may be compared to a king who wished to settle accounts with his slaves. When he had begun to settle *them,* one who owed him ten thousand talents was brought to him. But since he did not have *the means* to repay, his lord commanded him to be sold, along with his wife and children and all that he had, and repayment to be made. So the slave fell *to the ground* and prostrated himself before him, saying, 'Have patience with me and I will repay you everything.' And the lord of that slave felt compassion and released him and forgave him the debt. But that slave went out and found one of his fellow slaves who owed him a hundred denarii; and he seized him and *began* to choke *him,* saying, 'Pay back what you owe.' So his fellow slave fell *to the ground* and *began* to plead with him, saying, 'Have patience with me and I will repay you.' But he was unwilling and went and threw him in prison until he should pay back what was owed. So when his fellow slaves saw what had happened, they were deeply grieved and came and reported to their lord all that had happened. Then summoning him, his lord said to him, 'You wicked slave, I forgave you all that debt because you pleaded with me. Should you not also have had mercy on your fellow slave, in the same way that I had mercy on you?' And his lord, moved with anger, handed him over to the torturers until he should repay all that was owed him. My heavenly Father will also do the same to you, if each of you does not forgive his brother from your heart" (Matthew 18:23–35; cf. Matthew 6:12, 14, 15; Luke 7:42; see Matthew 25:19–28).

[DIVINE JUDGMENT from Then there will be two men in the field; one will be taken and one will be left. Two women *will be* grinding at the mill; one will be taken and one will be left]
Setting: The Mount of Olives, just east of Jerusalem. During His discourse, after answering His disciples' questions as to when the temple will be destroyed and Jerusalem overrun, along with the signs of His coming and the end of the age, Jesus teaches them the Parable of the Fig Tree.

"Now learn the parable from the fig tree: when its branch has already become tender and puts forth its leaves, you know that summer is near; so, you too, when you see all these things, recognize that He is near, *right* at the door. Truly, I say to you, this generation will not pass away until all these things take place. Heaven and earth will pass away, but My words will not pass away. But of that day and hour no one knows, not even the angels of heaven, nor the Son, but the Father alone. For the coming of the Son of Man will be just like the days of Noah. For as in those days before the flood they were eating and drinking, marrying and giving in marriage, until the day that Noah entered the ark, and they did not understand until the flood came and took them all away; so will the coming of the Son of Man be. Then there will be two men in the field; one will be taken and one will be left. Two women *will be* grinding at the mill; one will be taken and one will be left" (Matthew 24:32–41; cf. Mark 13:28–32; Luke 17:34–36; 21:28–33; see Genesis 6:5; 7:7; Matthew 5:18; 10:23; James 5:9).

[DIVINE JUDGMENT from will cut him in pieces and assign him a place with the hypocrites; in that place there will be weeping and gnashing of teeth]
Setting: The Mount of Olives, just east of Jerusalem. During His discourse, after answering His disciples' questions as to when the temple will be destroyed and Jerusalem overrun, along with the signs of His coming and the end of the age, Jesus reemphasizes to the disciples that they should be on the alert for His return.

"Therefore be on the alert, for you do not know which day your Lord is coming. But be sure of this, that if the head of the house had known at what time of the night the thief was coming, he would have been on the alert and would not have allowed his house to be broken into. For this reason you also must be ready; for the Son of Man is coming at an hour when you do not think *He will.* Who then is the faithful and sensible slave whom his master put in charge of his household to give their food at the proper time? Blessed is that slave whom his master finds so doing when he comes. Truly I say to you that he will put him in charge of all his possessions. But if that evil slave says in his heart, 'My master is not coming for a long time,' and begins to beat his fellow slaves and eat and drink with drunkards; the master of that slave will come on a day when he does not expect *him* and at an hour which he does not know, and will cut him in pieces and assign him a place with the hypocrites; in that place there will be weeping and gnashing of teeth" (Matthew 24:42–51; cf. Mark 13:33–37; Luke 12:39–46; 21:34–36; see Matthew 8:11, 12; 25:21–23).

[DIVINE JUDGMENT from By your standard of measure it will be measured to you; and more will be given you besides]
Setting: Galilee. Following His explanation of the Parable of the Sower to His disciples, Jesus informs them about personal accountability and responsibility.

And He was saying to them, "Take care what you listen to. By your standard of measure it will be measured to you; and more will be given you besides. For whoever has, to him *more* shall be given; and whoever does not have, even what he has shall be taken away from him" (Mark 4:24, 25; cf. Matthew 13:12; Luke 8:18; see Matthew 7:2).

[DIVINE JUDGMENT from For by your standard of measure it will be measured to you in return]
Setting: On a mountain in Galilee. After selecting His twelve disciples, Jesus teaches the Sermon on the Mount to those disciples and a great throng of people from Judea, Jerusalem, and the central coastal region of Tyre and Sidon.

"Do not judge, and you will not be judged; and do not condemn, and you will not be condemned; pardon, and you will be pardoned. Give and it will be given to you. They will pour into your lap a good measure—pressed down, shaken together, *and* running over. For by your standard of measure it will be measured to you in return" (Luke 6:37, 38; cf. Matthew 7:1–5; Mark 4:24; see Luke 6:12–19).

[DIVINE JUDGMENT from I say to you, it will be more tolerable in that day for Sodom than for that city]
Setting: On the way from Galilee to Jerusalem. The Lord appoints seventy followers and sends them out in pairs to every place He Himself will soon visit.

And He was saying to them, "The harvest is plentiful, but the laborers are few; therefore beseech the Lord of the harvest to send out laborers into His harvest. Go; behold, I send you out as lambs in the midst of wolves. Carry no money belt, no bag, no shoes; and greet no one on the way. Whatever house you enter, first say, 'Peace be to this house.' If a man of peace is there, your peace will rest on him; but if not, it will return to you. Stay in that house, eating and drinking what they give you; for the laborer is worthy of his wages. Do not keep moving from house to house. Whatever city you enter and they receive you, eat what is set before you; and heal those in it who are sick, and say to them, 'The kingdom of God has come near to you.' But whatever city you enter and they do not receive you, go out into its streets and say, 'Even the dust of your city which clings to our feet we wipe off *in protest* against you; yet be sure of this, that the kingdom of God has come near.' I say to you, it will be more tolerable in that day for Sodom than for that city" (Luke 10:2–12; see Genesis 19:24–28; Matthew 9:37–38, 10:9–14, 16; 1 Corinthians 10:27).

[DIVINE JUDGMENT from judgment]
Setting: On the way from Galilee to Jerusalem. The Lord pronounces woes on cities who reject the gospel, as He appoints seventy followers and sends them out in pairs to every place He Himself will soon visit.

"Woe to you, Chorazin! Woe to you, Bethsaida! For if the miracles had been performed in Tyre and Sidon which occurred in you, they would have repented long ago, sitting in sackcloth and ashes. But it will be more tolerable for Tyre and Sidon in the judgment than for you. And you, Capernaum, will not be exalted to heaven, will you? You will be brought down to Hades! The one who listens to you listens to Me, and the one who rejects you rejects Me; and he who rejects Me rejects the One who sent Me" (Luke 10:13–16; cf. Matthew 11:21–23; see Matthew 10:40; Luke 10:1).

[DIVINE JUDGMENT from judgment]
Setting: On the way from Galilee to Jerusalem. After revealing a problem with exorcism and responding to a blessing from a woman in the crowd, Jesus tells the increasing crowds about the sign of Jonah.

As the crowds were increasing, He began to say, "This generation is a wicked generation; it seeks for a sign, and *yet* no sign will be given to it but the sign of Jonah. For just as Jonah became a sign to the Ninevites, so will the Son of Man be to this generation. The Queen of the South will rise up with the men of this generation at the judgment and condemn them, because she came from the ends of the earth to hear the wisdom of Solomon; and behold, something greater than Solomon is here. The men of Nineveh will stand up with this generation at the judgment and condemn it, because they repented at the preaching of Jonah; and behold, something greater than Jonah is here" (Luke 11:29–32; cf. Matthew 16:4; see 1 Kings 10:1–10; Jonah 3:4, 5).

[DIVINE JUDGMENT from From everyone who has been given much, much will be required; and to whom they entrusted much, of him they will ask all the more]
Setting: On the way from Galilee to Jerusalem. When Jesus uses a parable to challenge the crowd and His disciples to be ready for His return, Peter asks Him whom He is addressing.

And the Lord said, "Who then is the faithful and sensible steward, whom his master will put in charge of his servants, to give them their rations at the proper time? Blessed is that slave whom his master finds so doing when he comes. Truly I say to you that he will put him in charge of all his possessions. But if that slave says in his heart, 'My master will be a long time in coming,' and begins to beat the slaves, *both* men and women, and to eat and drink and get drunk; the master of that slave will come on a day when he does not expect *him* and at an hour he does not know, and will cut him in pieces, and assign him a place with the unbelievers. And that slave who knew his master's will and did not get ready or act in accord with his will, will receive many lashes, but the one who did know *it,* and committed deeds worthy of flogging, will receive but few. From everyone who has been given much, much will be required; and to whom they entrusted much, of him they will ask all the more" (Luke 12:42–48; cf. Matthew 24:45–51; see Leviticus 5:17).

[DIVINE JUDGMENT from There will be two women grinding at the same place; one will be taken and the other will be left. [Two men will be in the field; one will be taken and the other will be left."]]
Setting: Samaria, on the way from Galilee to Jerusalem. After the Pharisees question Him about the coming of the kingdom of God, Jesus tells His disciples of His second coming.

And He said to the disciples, "The days will come when you will long to see one of the days of the Son of Man, and you will not see it. They will say to you, 'Look there! Look here!' Do not go away, and do not run after *them.* For just like the lightning, when it flashes out of one part of the sky, shines to the other part of the sky, so will the Son of Man be in His day. But first He must suffer many things and be rejected by this generation. And just as it happened in the days of Noah, so it will be also in the days of the Son of Man: they were eating, they were drinking, they were marrying, they were being given in marriage, until the day that Noah entered the ark, and the flood came and destroyed them all. It was the same as happened in the days of Lot: they were eating, they were drinking, they were buying, they were selling, they were planting, they were building; but on the day that Lot went out from Sodom it rained fire and brimstone from heaven and destroyed them all. It will be just the same on the day that the Son of Man is revealed. On that day, the one who is on the housetop and whose goods are in the house must not go down to take them out; and likewise the one who is in the field must not turn back. Remember Lot's wife. Whoever seeks to keep his life will lose it, and whoever loses *his life* will preserve it. I tell you, on that night there will be two in one bed; one will be taken and the other will be left. There will be two women grinding at the same place; one will be taken and the other will be left. [Two men will be in the field; one will be taken and the other will be left."] And answering they said to Him, "Where, Lord?" And He said to them, "Where the body *is*, there also the vultures will be gathered" (Luke 17:22–37; see Genesis 19; Matthew 10:39; 16:21, 27; 24:17–28, 37–41).

[DIVINE JUDGMENT from By your own words I will judge you]
Setting: Jericho, on the way to Jerusalem. After commending Zaccheus's faith in Him, Jesus provides a parable about stewardship.

So He said, "A nobleman went to a distant country to receive a kingdom for himself, and *then* return. And he called ten of his slaves, and gave them ten minas and said to them, 'Do business *with this* until I come *back*.' But his citizens hated him and sent a delegation after him, saying, 'We do not want this man to reign over us.' When he returned, after receiving the kingdom, he ordered that these slaves, to whom he had given the money, be called to him so that he might know what business they had done. The first appeared, saying, 'Master, your mina has made ten minas more.' And he said to him, 'Well done, good slave, because you have been faithful in a very little thing, you are to be in authority over ten cities.' The second came, saying, 'Your mina, master, has made five minas.' And he said to him, also, 'And you are to be over five cities.' Another came, saying, 'Master, here is your mina, which I kept put away in a handkerchief; for I was afraid of you, because you are an exacting man; you take up what you did not lay down and reap what you did not sow.' He said to him, 'By your own words I will judge you, you worthless slave. Did you know that I am an exacting man, taking up what I did not lay down and reaping what I did not sow? Then why did you not put my money in the bank, and having come, I would have collected it with interest?' Then he said to the bystanders, 'Take the mina away from him and give it to the one who has the ten minas.' And they said to him, 'Master, he has ten minas *already*.' I tell you that to everyone who has, more shall be given, but from the one who does not have, even what he does have shall be taken away. But these enemies of mine, who did not want me to reign over them, bring them here and slay them in my presence" (Luke 19:12–27; cf. Matthew 25:14–30; see Matthew 13:12; Luke 16:10).

[DIVINE JUDGMENT from He who believes in Him is not judged; he who does not believe has been judged already, because he has not believed in the name of the only begotten Son of God and judgment]
Setting: Jerusalem. At the time of the Passover of the Jews, after the Lord cleanses the temple, a Pharisee, Nicodemus, asks Him by night the meaning of "born again."

"For God so loved the world, that He gave His only begotten Son, that whoever believes in Him shall not perish, but have eternal life. For God did not send the Son into the world to judge the world, but that the world might be saved through Him. He who believes in Him is not judged; he who does not believe has been judged already, because he has not believed in the name of the only begotten Son of God. This is the judgment, that the Light has come into the world, and men loved darkness rather than the Light, for their deeds were evil. For everyone who does evil hates the Light, and does not come to the Light for fear that his deeds will be exposed. But he who practices the truth comes to the Light, so that his deeds may be manifested as having been wrought in God" (John 3:16–21; see Luke 19:10; John 1:4; 1:18; Romans 5:8; 1 John 1:6, 7).

Setting: By the pool of Bethesda in Jerusalem. During the Feast of the Jews, Jesus responds to criticism from the Jewish religious leaders for healing a lame man on the Sabbath and for referring to God as His Father (thereby making Himself equal with God).

Therefore Jesus answered and was saying to them, "Truly, truly, I say to you, the Son can do nothing of Himself, unless *it is* something He sees the Father doing; for whatever the Father does, these things the Son also does in like manner. For the Father loves the Son, and shows Him all things that He Himself is doing; and *the Father* will show Him greater works than these, so that you will marvel. For just as the Father raises the dead and gives them life, even so the Son also gives life to whom He wishes. For not even the Father judges anyone, but He has given all judgment to the Son, so that all will honor the Son even as they honor the Father. He who does not honor the Son does not honor the Father who sent Him" (John 5:19–23; see Luke 10:16; John 3:35; 11:25; 14:12).

Setting: By the pool of Bethesda in Jerusalem. During the Feast of the Jews, Jesus responds to criticism from the Jewish religious leaders for healing a lame man on the Sabbath and for referring to God as His Father (thereby making Himself equal with God).

"Truly, truly, I say to you, he who hears My word, and believes Him who sent Me, has eternal life, and does not come into judgment, but has passed out of death into life" (John 5:24; see John 3:18; 12:44).

Setting: Jerusalem. During the Feast of the Jews, Jesus responds to criticism from the Jewish religious leaders by referring to God as His Father (thereby making Himself equal with God) and prophesying His participation in the resurrection and judgment of men.

"Truly, truly, I say to you, an hour is coming and now is, when the dead will hear the voice of the Son of God, and those who hear will live. For just as the Father has life in Himself, even so He gave to the Son also to have life in Himself; and He gave Him authority to execute judgment, because He is *the* Son of Man. Do not marvel at this; for an hour is coming, in which all who are in the tombs will hear His voice, and will come forth; those who did the good *deeds* to a resurrection of life, those who committed the evil *deeds* to a resurrection of judgment" (John 5:25–29; see Daniel 12:2; John 1:4; 11:24).

Setting: The temple in Jerusalem. After receiving encouragement from His blood brothers in Galilee to attend the upcoming Feast of Booths in order to demonstrate His works to His disciples and the world, Jesus goes and teaches, astonishing the Jewish religious leaders.

Jesus answered them, "I did one deed, and you all marvel. For this reason Moses has given you circumcision (not because it is from Moses, but from the fathers), and on *the* Sabbath you circumcise a man. If a man receives circumcision on *the* Sabbath so that the Law of Moses will not be broken, are you angry with Me because I made an entire man well on *the* Sabbath? Do not judge according to appearance, but judge with righteous judgment" (John 7:21–24; see Genesis 17:10–14; Leviticus 12:3; 19:15; Matthew 12:2; John 5:2–16; 7–20).

[DIVINE JUDGMENT from One who seeks and judges]
Setting: The temple treasury in Jerusalem. While Jesus is interacting with the scribes and Pharisees about His testimony, their ancestry, and their motives, they state their belief Jesus is a demon-possessed Samaritan.

Jesus answered, "I do not have a demon; but I honor My Father, and you dishonor Me. But I do not seek My glory; there is One who seeks and judges. Truly, truly, I say to you, if anyone keeps My word he will never see death" (John 8:49–51; see Matthew 16:28; John 5:41; 7:20).

Setting: Jerusalem. Following the Pharisees' interrogation and dismissal of the formerly blind man Jesus healed on the Sabbath, the Lord Jesus addresses the Pharisees about His mission in this world.

And Jesus said, "For judgment I came into this world, so that those who do not see may see, and that those who see may become blind" (John 9:39; see Luke 4:18; John 5:22, 27).

Setting: Approaching Jerusalem. Just days before the Passover, with the chief priests and Pharisees plotting to seize Him and crowds welcoming Him with palm branches and praise, Jesus expresses anxiety about His upcoming death by crucifixion.

"Now My soul has become troubled; and what shall I say, 'Father, save Me from this hour'? But for this purpose I came to this hour. Father glorify Your name." Then a voice came out of heaven: "I have glorified it, and will glorify it again." So the crowd *of people* who stood by and heard it were saying that it had thundered; others were saying, "An angel has spoken to Him." Jesus answered and said, "This voice has not come for My sake, but for your sakes. Now judgment is upon this world; now the ruler of this world will be cast out. And I, if I am lifted up from the earth, will draw all men to Myself" (John 12:27–32; see Matthew 3:17; 26:38; John 3:14; 6:44; 11:42; 14:30).

[DIVINE JUDGMENT from judgment and the ruler of this world has been judged]
Setting: Jerusalem. Before the Passover, after warning His disciples of the persecution they will face after His departure to heaven, Jesus elaborates about the coming ministry of the Holy Spirit.

"But now I am going to Him who sent Me; and none of you asks Me, 'Where are You going?' But because I have said these things to you, sorrow has filled your heart. But I tell you the truth, it is to your advantage that I go away; for if I do not go away, the Helper will not come to you; but if I go, I will send Him to you. And He, when He comes, will convict the world concerning sin and righteousness and judgment; concerning sin, because they do not believe in Me; and concerning righteousness, because I go to the Father and you no longer see Me; and concerning judgment, because the ruler of this world has been judged" (John 16:5–11; see John 7:33; 12:31; 14:1, 16; 15:22, 24).

JUDGMENT, HUMAN (Also see JUDGING OTHERS)

[HUMAN JUDGMENT from Truly I say to you, you will not come out of there until you have paid up the last cent]
Setting: Galilee. During the early part of His ministry, Jesus preaches the Sermon on the Mount to His disciples and the multitudes.

"Make friends quickly with your opponent at law while you are with him on the way, so that your opponent may not hand you over to the judge, and the judge to the officer, and you be thrown into prison. Truly I say to you, you will not come out of there until you have paid up the last cent" (Matthew 5:25, 26; cf. Luke 12:58, 59).

[HUMAN JUDGMENT from judging the twelve tribes of Israel]
Setting: Judea beyond the Jordan (Perea). Jesus promises rewards to His disciples for their personal sacrifice and commitment to following Him.

And Jesus said to them, "Truly I say to you, that you who have followed Me, in the regeneration when the Son of Man will sit on His glorious throne, you also shall sit upon twelve thrones, judging the twelve tribes of Israel. And everyone who has left houses or brothers or sisters or father or mother or children or farms for My name's sake, will receive many times as much, and will inherit eternal life. But many *who* are first will be last; and *the* last, first" (Matthew 19:28–30; cf. Matthew 6:33; 20:15; Mark 10:29, 30; Luke 18:29, 30; 22:30).

[HUMAN JUDGMENT from judged]
Setting: Galilee. After Jesus praises John the Baptist to the crowds, Simon, a Pharisee, invites the Lord to dinner. A sinful woman anoints His feet with perfume, prompting Him to convey a parable.

And Jesus answered him, "Simon, I have something to say to you." And he replied, "Say it, Teacher." "A moneylender had two debtors: one owed five hundred denarii, and the other fifty. When they were unable to repay, he graciously forgave them both. So which of them will love him more?" Simon answered and said, "I suppose the one whom he forgave more." And He said to him, "You have judged correctly" (Luke 7:40–43; see Matthew 18:23–35).

[HUMAN JUDGMENT from I say to you, you will not get out of there until you have paid the very last cent]
Setting: On the way from Galilee to Jerusalem. After chastising the crowds for being able to discern the weather but not the present age, Jesus exhorts them to settle any financial disputes outside of court.

"And why do you not even on your own initiative judge what is right? For while you are going with your opponent to appear before the magistrate, on *your* way *there* make an effort to settle with him, so that he may not drag you before the judge, and the judge turn you over to the officer, and the officer throw you into prison. I say to you, you will not get out of there until you have paid the very last cent" (Luke 12:57–59; cf. Matthew 5:25, 26).

[HUMAN JUDGMENT from judging the twelve tribes of Israel]
Setting: An upper room in Jerusalem. During the Feast of Unleavened Bread (Passover) just before His crucifixion, Jesus celebrates the Passover meal and institutes the Lord's Supper. After His disciples argue over who is the greatest among them, He details the kingdom benefits they will experience.

"You are those who have stood by Me in My trials; for just as My Father has granted Me a kingdom, I grant you that you may eat and drink at My table in My kingdom, and you will sit on thrones judging the twelve tribes of Israel" (Luke 22:28–30; cf. Matthew 19:28).

[HUMAN JUDGMENT from Do not judge according to appearance, but judge with righteous judgment]
Setting: The temple in Jerusalem. After receiving encouragement from His blood brothers in Galilee to attend the upcoming Feast of Booths in order to demonstrate His works to His disciples and the world, Jesus goes and teaches, astonishing the Jewish religious leaders.

Jesus answered them, "I did one deed, and you all marvel. For this reason Moses has given you circumcision (not because it is from Moses, but from the fathers), and on *the* Sabbath you circumcise a man. If a man receives circumcision on *the* Sabbath so that the Law of Moses will not be broken, are you angry with Me because I made an entire man well on *the* Sabbath? Do not judge according to appearance, but judge with righteous judgment" (John 7:21–24; see Genesis 17:10–14; Leviticus 12:3; 19:15; Matthew 12:2; John 5:2–16; 7–20).

JUDGMENT, RIGHTEOUS

Setting: The temple in Jerusalem. After receiving encouragement from His blood brothers in Galilee to attend the upcoming Feast of Booths in order to demonstrate His works to His disciples and the world, Jesus goes and teaches, astonishing the Jewish religious leaders.

Jesus answered them, "I did one deed, and you all marvel. For this reason Moses has given you circumcision (not because it is from Moses, but from the fathers), and on *the* Sabbath you circumcise a man. If a man receives circumcision on *the* Sabbath so that the Law of Moses will not be broken, are you angry with Me because I made an entire man well on *the* Sabbath? Do not judge according to appearance, but judge with righteous judgment" (John 7:21–24; see Genesis 17:10–14; Leviticus 12:3; 19:15; Matthew 12:2; John 5:2–16; 7–20).

JUDGMENT DAY (See JUDGMENT, DAY OF)

JUDGMENT OF ISRAEL (Listed under ISRAEL, JUDGMENT OF)

JUMP (See LEAP)

JUSTICE (Also see JUDGMENT)

Setting: The temple in Jerusalem. After the Jewish religious leaders test Him with questions, Jesus pronounces the fifth of eight woes on them in front of the crowds and His disciples.

"Woe to you, scribes and Pharisees, hypocrites! For you tithe the mint and dill and cummin, and have neglected the weightier provisions of the law: justice and mercy and faithfulness; but these are things you should have done without neglecting the others. You blind guides, who strain out a gnat and swallow a camel!" (Matthew 23:23, 24).

Setting: On the way from Galilee to Jerusalem. After speaking of how a lamp illuminates, the Lord has lunch with a Pharisee who is surprised He doesn't wash before eating.

But the Lord said to him, "Now you Pharisees clean the outside of the cup and of the platter; but inside of you, you are full of robbery and wickedness. You foolish ones, did not He who made the outside make the inside also? But give that which is within as charity, and then all things are clean for you. But woe to you Pharisees! You pay tithe of mint and rue and every *kind of* garden herb, and *yet* disregard justice and the love of God; but these are the things you should have done without neglecting the others. Woe to you Pharisees! For you love the chief seats in the synagogues and the respectful greetings in the market places. Woe to you! For you are like concealed tombs, and the people who walk over *them* are unaware *of it*" (Luke 11:39–44; cf. Matthew 23:6, 7, 23–27; see Matthew 15:2; Titus 1:15).

Setting: On the way from Galilee to Jerusalem. After telling His disciples about His second coming, Jesus instructs them about persistence in prayer.

Now He was telling them a parable to show that at all times they ought to pray and not to lose heart, saying, "In a certain city there was a judge who did not fear God and did not respect man. There was a widow in that city, and she kept coming to him, saying, 'Give me legal protection from my opponent.' For a while he was unwilling; but afterward he said to himself, 'Even though I do not fear God nor respect man, yet because this woman bothers me, I will give her legal protection, otherwise by continually coming she will wear me out.'" And the Lord said, "Hear what the unrighteous judge said; now, will not God bring about justice for His elect who cry to Him day and night, and will He delay long over them? I tell you that He will bring about justice for them quickly. However, when the Son of Man comes, will He find faith on the earth?" (Luke 18:1–8; see Luke 11:5–10).

JUSTIFICATION

[JUSTIFICATION from justified]

Setting: Galilee. After He heals a blind, mute, demon-possessed man, the Pharisees accuse Jesus in front of crowds of being a worker of Satan.

"Either make the tree good and its fruit good, or make the tree bad and its fruit bad; for the tree is known by its fruit. You brood of vipers, how can you, being evil, speak what is good? For the mouth speaks out of that which fills the heart. The good man brings out of *his* good treasure what is good; and the evil man brings out of *his* evil treasure what is evil. But I tell you that every careless word that people speak, they shall give an accounting for it in the day of judgment. For by your words you will be justified, and by your words you will be condemned" (Matthew 12:33–37; cf. Matthew 3:7; 7:16–18).

[JUSTIFICATION from justify]

Setting: On the way from Galilee to Jerusalem. The Lord responds to the Pharisees' scoffing at His teaching His disciples about stewardship.

And He said to them, "You are those who justify yourselves in the sight of men, but God knows your hearts; for that which is highly esteemed among men is detestable in the sight of God. The Law and the Prophets *were proclaimed* until John; since that time the gospel of the kingdom of God has been preached, and everyone is forcing his way into it. But is it easier for heaven and earth to pass away than for one stroke of a letter of the Law to fail" (Luke 16:15–17; cf. Matthew 5:18; see 1 Samuel 16:7; Matthew 4:23; 11:11–14).

[JUSTIFICATION from justified]

Setting: On the way from Galilee to Jerusalem. After instructing His disciples about persistence in prayer, Jesus conveys a parable about self-righteousness.

And He also told this parable to some people who trusted in themselves that they were righteous, and viewed others with contempt: "Two men went up into the temple to pray, one a Pharisee and the other a tax collector. The Pharisee stood and was praying this to himself: 'God, I thank You that I am not like other people: swindlers, unjust, adulterers, or even like this tax collector. I fast twice a week; I pay tithes of all that I get.' But the tax collector, standing some distance away, was even unwilling to lift up his eyes to heaven, but was beating his breast, saying, 'God, be merciful to me, the sinner!' I tell you, this man went to his house justified rather than the other; for everyone who exalts himself will be humbled, but he who humbles himself will be exalted" (Luke 18:9–14; see Ezra 9:6; Matthew 6:5, 23:12; Luke 11:42, 16:15; Romans 14:3, 10).

K

KEY (Also see KEYS)

Setting: On the way from Galilee to Jerusalem. After Jesus pronounces woes upon the Pharisees, a lawyer replies that His remarks are an insult to lawyers, too.

But He said, "Woe to you lawyers as well! For you weigh men down with burdens hard to bear, while you yourselves will not even touch the burdens with one of your fingers. Woe to you! For you build the tombs of the prophets, and *it was* your fathers *who* killed them. So you are witnesses and approve the deeds of your fathers; because it was they who killed them, and you build *their tombs*. For this reason also the wisdom of God said, 'I will send them prophets and apostles, and *some* of them they will kill and *some* they will persecute, so that the blood of all the prophets, shed since the foundation of the world, may be charged against this generation, from the blood of Abel to the blood of Zechariah, who was killed between the altar and the house *of God*; yes, I tell you, it shall be charged against this generation.' Woe to you lawyers! For you have taken away the key of knowledge; you yourselves did not enter, and you hindered those who were entering" (Luke 11:46–52; cf. Matthew 23:29–32; see 2 Chronicles 24:20, 21; Matthew 23:4, 13).

Setting: On the island of Patmos (in the Aegean Sea about fifty miles southwest of Ephesus in modern Turkey). On the Lord's Day (Sunday), about fifty years after Jesus' resurrection, the disciple John encounters the Lord Jesus Christ, who communicates a new revelation for the apostle to record for the church in Philadelphia and to six other churches in Asia.

"And to the angel of the church in Philadelphia write: He who is holy, who is true, who has the key of David, who opens and no one will shut, and who shuts and no one opens, says this: 'I know your deeds. Behold, I have put before you an open door which no one can shut, because you have a little power, and have kept My word, and have not denied My name. Behold, I will cause *those* of the synagogue of Satan, who say that they are Jews and are not, but lie—I will make them come and bow down at your feet, and *make them* know that I have loved you. Because you have kept the word of My perseverance, I also will keep you from the hour of testing, that *hour* which is about to come upon the whole world, to test those who dwell on the earth. I am coming quickly; hold fast what you have, so that no one will take your crown. He who overcomes, I will make him a pillar in the temple of My God, and he will not go out from it anymore; and I will write on him the name of My God, and the name of the city of My God, the new Jerusalem, which comes down out of heaven from My God, and My new name. He who has an ear, let him hear what the Spirit says to the churches' " (Revelation 3:7–13; see Isaiah 22:22; Galatians 2:9; Revelation 2:9, 10, 13, 25; 14:1).

KEY OF DAVID (See KEY)

KEYS (Also see AUTHORITY; and KEY)

Setting: Caesarea Philippi. Jesus responds to Simon Peter's declaration that He is the Christ, the Son of the living God.

And Jesus said to him, "Blessed are you, Simon Barjona, because flesh and blood did not reveal *this* to you, but My Father who is in heaven. I also say to you that you are Peter, and upon this rock I will build My church; and the gates of Hades will not overpower it. I will give you the keys of the kingdom of heaven; and whatever you bind on earth shall have been bound in heaven, and whatever you loose on earth shall have been loosed in heaven" (Matthew 16:17–19; cf. Matthew 18:18; Mark 8:29; Luke 9:20).

Setting: On the island of Patmos (in the Aegean Sea about fifty miles southwest of Ephesus in modern Turkey). On the Lord's Day (Sunday), approximately fifty years after His resurrection, the disciple John encounters the Lord Jesus Christ, who communicates new revelations for the apostle to record for the seven churches in Asia.

When I saw Him, I fell at His feet like a dead man. And He placed His right hand on me, saying, "Do not be afraid; I am the first and the last, and the living One; and I was dead, and behold, I am alive forevermore, and I have the keys of death and of Hades. Therefore write the things which you have seen, and the things which are, and the things which will take place after these things. As for the mystery of the seven stars which you saw in My right hand, and the seven golden lampstands: the seven stars are the angels of the seven churches, and the seven lampstands are the seven churches" (Revelation 1:17–20; see Isaiah 44:6; Luke 24:5; Revelation 2:8).

KILLING (See MURDER)

KIN (See RELATIVES)

KIND (genre)

Setting: By the Sea of Galilee. Because the religious leaders are rejecting His message, Jesus continues teaching His disciples with the Parable of the Dragnet.

"Again, the kingdom of heaven is like a dragnet cast into the sea, and gathering *fish* of every kind; and when it was filled, they drew it up on the beach; and they sat down and gathered the good *fish* into containers, but the bad they threw away. So it will be at the end of the age; the angels will come forth and take out the wicked from among the righteous, and will throw them into the furnace of fire; in that place there will be weeping and gnashing of teeth. Have you understood all these things?" They said to Him, "Yes" (Matthew 13:47–51).

Setting: Near the mountain where the Transfiguration occurred. Jesus reveals to His disciples why they cannot restore a demon-possessed boy.

And He said to them, "Because of the littleness of your faith; for truly I say to you, if you have faith the size of a mustard seed, you will say to this mountain, 'Move from here to there,' and it will move; and nothing will be impossible to you. ["But this kind does not go out except by prayer and fasting"] (Matthew 17:20, 21; cf. Matthew 21:21, 22; Mark 9:28, 29).

Setting: Galilee. After Jesus is transfigured before Peter, James, and John on a high mountain (perhaps Mount Hermon), the four discover the remaining disciples arguing with some scribes.

And He asked them, "What are you discussing with them?" And one of the crowd answered Him, "Teacher, I brought You my son, possessed with a spirit which makes him mute; and whenever it seizes him, it slams him *to the ground* and he foams *at the mouth,* and grinds his teeth and stiffens out. I told Your disciples to cast it out, and they could not *do it.* And He answered them, and said, "O unbelieving generation, how long shall I be with you? How long shall I put up with you? Bring him to Me!" They brought the boy to Him. When he saw Him, immediately the spirit threw him into a convulsion, and falling to the ground, be *began* rolling around and foaming *at the mouth.* And He asked his father, "How long has this been happening to him?" And he said, "From childhood. It has often thrown him both into the fire and into the water to destroy him. But if You can do anything, take pity on us and help us!" And Jesus said to him, "'If You can?' All things are possible to him who believes." Immediately the boy's father cried out and said, "I do believe; help my unbelief." When Jesus saw that a crowd was rapidly gathering, He rebuked the unclean spirit, saying to it, "You deaf and mute spirit, I command you, come out of him and do not enter him again." After crying out and throwing him into terrible convulsions, it came out; and *the boy* became so much like a corpse that most *of them,* said, "He is dead!" But Jesus took him by the hand and raised him; and he got up. When He came into *the* house, His disciples *began* questioning Him privately, "Why could we not drive it out?" And He said to them, "This kind cannot come out by anything but prayer" (Mark 9:16–29; cf. Matthew 17:14–21; Luke 9:37–43; see Matthew 17:20).

Setting: Galilee. After He clarifies who His disciples' co-laborers are, Jesus prepares to go to Jerusalem by sending messengers ahead to Samaria, where they experience rejection and seek retribution.

But He turned and rebuked them, [and said, "You do not know what kind of spirit you are of; for the Son of Man did not come to destroy men's lives, but to save them."] And they went on to another village (Luke 9:55, 56; see 2 Kings 1:9–14; Luke 13:22).

Setting: On the way from Galilee to Jerusalem. After speaking of how a lamp illuminates, the Lord has lunch with a Pharisee who is surprised He doesn't wash before eating.

But the Lord said to him, "Now you Pharisees clean the outside of the cup and of the platter; but inside of you, you are full of robbery and wickedness. You foolish ones, did not He who made the outside make the inside also? But give that which is within as charity, and then all things are clean for you. But woe to you Pharisees! You pay tithe of mint and rue and every *kind of* garden herb, and *yet* disregard justice and the love of God; but these are the things you should have done without neglecting the others. Woe to you Pharisees! For you love the chief seats in the synagogues and the respectful greetings in the market places. Woe to you! For you are like concealed tombs, and the people who walk over *them* are unaware *of it*" (Luke 11:39–44; cf. Matthew 23:6, 7, 23–27; see Matthew 15:2; Titus 1:15).

Setting: On the way from Galilee to Jerusalem. After giving the story of the prodigal son, the Lord teaches His disciples about stewardship.

Now He was also saying to the disciples, "There was a rich man who had a manager, and this *manager* was reported to him as squandering his possessions. And he called him and said to him, 'What is this I hear about you? Give an accounting of your management, for you can no longer be a manager.' The manager said to himself, 'What shall I do, since my master is taking the management away from me? I am not strong enough to dig; I am ashamed to beg. I know what I shall do, so that when I am removed from the management people will welcome me into their homes.' And he summoned each one of his master's debtors, and he *began* saying to the first, 'How much do you owe my master?' And he said, 'A hundred measures of oil.' And he said to him, 'Take your bill, and sit down quickly and write fifty.' Then he said to another, 'And how much do you owe?' And he said, 'A hundred measures of wheat.' He said to him, 'Take your bill, and write eighty.' And his master praised the unrighteous manager because he had acted shrewdly; for the sons of this age are more shrewd in relation to their own kind than the sons of light. And I say to you, make friends for yourselves by means of the wealth of unrighteousness, so that when it fails, they will receive you into the eternal dwellings. He who is faithful in a very little thing is faithful also in much; and he who is unrighteous in a very little thing is unrighteous also in much. Therefore if you have not been faithful in the *use of* unrighteous wealth, who will entrust the *true riches* to you? And if you have not been faithful in *the use of* that which is another's, who will give you that which is your own? No servant can serve two masters; for either he will hate the one and love the other, or else he will be devoted to one and despise the other. You cannot serve God and wealth" (Luke 16:1–13; cf. Matthew 6:24; see Matthew 25:14–30).

KINDNESS (Also see GIVING; and GRACIOUSNESS)

[KINDNESS from kind]

Setting: Galilee. After selecting His twelve disciples, Jesus teaches the Sermon on the Mount to those disciples and a great throng of people from Judea, Jerusalem, and the central coastal region of Tyre and Sidon.

"But I say to you who hear, love your enemies, do good to those who hate you, bless those who curse you, pray for those who mistreat you. Whoever hits you on the cheek, offer him the other also; and whoever takes away your coat, do not withhold your shirt from him either. Give to everyone who asks of you, and whoever takes away what is yours, do not demand it back. Treat others the same way you want them to treat you. If you love those who love you, what credit is *that* to you? For even sinners love those who love them. If you do good to those who do good to you, what credit is *that* to you? For even sinners do the same. If you lend to those from whom you expect to receive, what credit is *that* to you? Even sinners lend to sinners in order to receive back the same *amount.* But love your enemies, and do good, and lend, expecting nothing in return; and your reward will be great, and you will be sons of the Most High; for He Himself is kind to ungrateful and evil *men*. Be merciful, just as your Father is merciful" (Luke 6:27–36; cf. Matthew 5:9, 39–48; 7:12; see Luke 6:12–19).

KING (KING OF THE JEWS is a separate entry; also see KING, JESUS AS; and KINGS)

Setting: Galilee. During the early part of His ministry, Jesus preaches the Sermon on the Mount to His disciples and the multitudes.

"Again, you have heard that the ancients were told, 'YOU SHALL NOT MAKE FALSE VOWS, BUT SHALL FULFILL YOUR VOWS TO THE LORD.' But I say to you, make no oath at all, either by heaven, for it is the throne of God, or by the earth, for it is the footstool of His feet, or by Jerusalem, for it is THE CITY OF THE GREAT KING. Nor shall you make an oath by your head, for you cannot make one hair white or black. But let your statement be 'Yes, yes' *or* 'No, no'; anything beyond these is of evil" (Matthew 5:33–37, Jesus quotes from Leviticus 19:12, Psalm 48:2; Isaiah 66:1; cf. James 5:12).

Setting: Capernaum of Galilee. Jesus illustrates forgiveness after Peter asks Him if forgiving someone seven times who has sinned against him is adequate.

"For this reason the kingdom of heaven may be compared to a king who wished to settle accounts with his slaves. When he had begun to settle *them,* one who owed him ten thousand talents was brought to him. But since he did not have *the means* to repay, his lord commanded him to be sold, along with his wife and children and all that he had, and repayment to be made. So the slave fell *to the ground* and prostrated himself before him, saying, 'Have patience with me and I will repay you everything.' And the lord of that slave felt compassion and released him and forgave him the debt. But that slave went out and found one of his fellow slaves who owed him a hundred denarii; and he seized him and *began* to choke *him,* saying, 'Pay back what you owe.' So his fellow slave fell *to the ground* and *began* to plead with him, saying, 'Have patience with me and I will repay you.' But he was unwilling and went and threw him in prison until he should pay back what was owed. So when his fellow slaves saw what had happened, they were deeply grieved and came and reported to their lord all that had happened. Then summoning him, his lord said to him, 'You wicked slave, I forgave you all that debt because you pleaded with me. Should you not also have had mercy on your fellow slave, in the same way that I had mercy on you?' And his lord, moved with anger, handed him over to the torturers until he should repay all that was owed him. My heavenly Father will also do the same to you, if each of you does not forgive his brother from your heart" (Matthew 18:23–35; cf. Matthew 6:12, 14, 15; Luke 7:42; see Matthew 25:19–28).

Setting: The temple in Jerusalem. Jesus speaks another parable to the chief priests and elders after they question His authority.

Jesus spoke to them again in parables, saying, "The kingdom of heaven may be compared to a king who gave a wedding feast for his son. And he sent out his slaves to call those who had been invited to the wedding feast, and they were unwilling to come. Again he sent out other slaves saying, 'Tell those who have been invited, "Behold, I have prepared my dinner; my oxen and my fattened livestock are *all* butchered and everything is ready; come to the wedding feast." But they paid no attention and went their way, one to his own farm, another to his business, and the rest seized his slaves and mistreated them and killed them. But the king was enraged, and he sent his armies and destroyed those murderers and set their city on fire. Then he said to his slaves, 'The wedding is ready, but those who were invited were not worthy. 'Go therefore to the main highways, and as many as you find *there,* invite to the wedding feast.' Those slaves went out into the streets and gathered together all they found, both evil and good; and the wedding hall was filled with dinner guests. But when the king came in to look over the dinner guests, he saw a man there who was not dressed in wedding clothes, and he said to him, 'Friend, how did you come in here without wedding clothes?' And the man was speechless. Then the king said to the servants, 'Bind him hand and foot, and throw him into the outer darkness; in that place there will be weeping and gnashing of teeth.' For many are called, but few *are* chosen" (Matthew 22:1–14; cf. Matthew 8:11, 12).

Setting: On the way from Galilee to Jerusalem. After responding to a guest's proclamation about the blessings of eating bread in the kingdom of God, Jesus presents to large crowds the demands of discipleship.

Now large crowds were going along with Him; and He turned and said to them, "If anyone comes to Me, and does not hate his own father and mother and wife and children and brothers and sisters, yes, and even his own life, he cannot be My disciple. Whoever does not carry his own cross and come after Me cannot be My disciple. For which one of you, when he wants to build a tower, does not first sit down and calculate the cost to see if he has enough to complete it? Otherwise, when he has laid a foundation and is not able to finish, all who observe it begin to ridicule him, saying, 'This man began to build and was not able to finish.' Or what king, when he sets out to meet another king in battle, will not first sit down and consider whether he is strong enough with ten thousand *men* to encounter the one coming against him with twenty thousand? Or else, while the other is still far away, he sends a delegation and asks for terms of peace. So then, none of you can be My disciple who does not give up all his possessions. Therefore, salt is good; but if even salt has become tasteless, with what will it be seasoned? It is useless either for the soil or for the manure pile; it is thrown out. He who has ears to hear, let him hear" (Luke 14:25–35; cf. Matthew 5:13; 10:37–39; see Proverbs

20:18; Luke 14:1, 2; Philippians 3:7).

KING, JESUS AS (Also see JUDGE, JESUS AS; and KING OF THE JEWS)

[JESUS AS KING from the Son of Man will sit on His glorious throne]
Setting: Judea beyond the Jordan (Perea). Jesus promises rewards to His disciples for their personal sacrifice and commitment to following Him.

And Jesus said to them, "Truly I say to you, that you who have followed Me, in the regeneration when the Son of Man will sit on His glorious throne, you also shall sit upon twelve thrones, judging the twelve tribes of Israel. And everyone who has left houses or brothers or sisters or father or mother or children or farms for My name's sake, will receive many times as much, and will inherit eternal life. But many *who* are first will be last; and *the* last, first" (Matthew 19:28–30; cf. Matthew 6:33; 20:15; Mark 10:29, 30; Luke 18:29, 30; 22:30).

[JESUS AS KING from He will sit on His glorious throne]
Setting: The Mount of Olives, just east of Jerusalem. During His discourse, after answering His disciples' questions as to when the temple will be destroyed and Jerusalem overrun, along with the signs of His coming and the end of the age, Jesus reveals the future judgments following His return.

"But when the Son of Man comes in His glory, and all the angels with Him, then He will sit on His glorious throne. All the nations will be gathered before Him; and He will separate them from one another, as the shepherd separates the sheep from the goats; and He will put the sheep on His right, and the goats on the left. Then the King will say to those on His right, 'Come, you who are blessed of My Father, inherit the kingdom prepared for you from the foundation of the world. 'For I was hungry, and you gave Me *something* to eat; I was thirsty, and you gave Me *something* to drink; I was a stranger, and you invited Me in; naked, and you clothed Me; I was sick, and you visited Me; I was in prison, and you came to Me.' Then the righteous will answer Him, 'Lord, when did we see You hungry and feed You, or thirsty, and give you *something* to drink? And when did we see You a stranger, and invite You in, or naked, and clothe You? When did we see You sick, or in prison, and come to You?' The King will answer and say to them, 'Truly I say to you, to the extent that you did it to one of these brothers of Mine, *even* the least *of them,* you did it to Me.' Then He will also say to those on His left, 'Depart from Me, accursed ones, into the eternal fire which has been prepared for the devil and his angels; for I was hungry, and you gave Me *nothing* to eat; I was thirsty, and you gave Me nothing to drink; I was a stranger, and you did not invite Me in; naked, and you did not clothe Me; sick, and in prison, and you did not visit Me.' Then they themselves also will answer, 'Lord, when did we see You hungry, or thirsty, or a stranger, or naked, or sick, or in prison, and did not take care of You?' Then He will answer them, 'Truly I say to you, to the extent that you did not do it to one of the least of these, you did not do it to Me.' These will go away into eternal punishment, but the righteous into eternal life" (Matthew 25:31–46; see Matthew 7:23; 16:27; 19:29).

[JESUS AS KING from *It is as* you say]
Setting: Jerusalem. Prior to the crucifixion, Jesus verifies His true identity in front of the Roman governor of Judea, Pontius Pilate.

Now Jesus stood before the governor, and the governor questioned Him, saying, "Are You the King of the Jews?" And Jesus said to him, "*It is as* you say" (Matthew 27:11; cf. Mark 15:2, Luke 23:3; John 18:33, 34).

[JESUS AS KING from *It is as* you say]
Setting: Jerusalem. After interrogating Jesus subsequent to His betrayal by Judas and His arrest, the chief priests, elders, and scribes deliver Him to Pilate (Roman governor of Judea) for further questioning.

Pilate questioned Him, "Are You the King of the Jews?" And He answered him, "*It is as* you say" (Mark 15:2; cf. Matthew 27:2, 11–14; Luke 23:1–5; John 18:28–38).

[JESUS AS KING from *It is as you say*]
Setting: Jerusalem. After being arrested, mocked, and beaten, and appearing before the Council of Elders (Sanhedrin), with His crucifixion imminent, Jesus is brought before Pilate (Roman governor of Judea).

So Pilate asked Him, saying, "Are You the King of the Jews?" And He answered him and said, "*It is as* you say" (Luke 23:3; cf. Matthew 27:11–14; Mark 15:2–5; John 18:33–38; see Luke 22:70).

[JESUS AS KING from You say *correctly* that I am a king]
Setting: Jerusalem. After the previous and current high priests (Annas and Caiaphas) question Jesus, and Peter denies for the second and third times being the Lord's disciple, Pilate (Roman governor of Judea) questions Jesus in an attempt to determine if He is a king.

Therefore Pilate said to Him, "So You are a king?" Jesus answered, "You say *correctly* that I am a king. For this I have been born, and for this I have come into the world, to testify to the truth. Everyone who is of the truth hears my voice" (John 18:37; cf. Matthew 27:11; Mark 15:2; Luke 23:3 see John 18:28–36).

KING JESUS (See KING, JESUS AS)

KING OF THE JEWS (Also see CHRIST, THE; DAVID, SON OF; JESUS; KING, JESUS AS; MESSIAH; and SON OF MAN)

Setting: Jerusalem. Prior to the crucifixion, Jesus verifies His true identity before Pontius Pilate (Roman governor of Judea).

Now Jesus stood before the governor, and the governor questioned Him, saying, "Are You the King of the Jews?" And Jesus said to him, "*It is as* you say" (Matthew 27:11; cf. Mark 15:2, Luke 23:3; John 18:33, 34).

Setting: Jerusalem. After Jesus is betrayed by Judas and arrested in Jerusalem, the chief priests, elders, and scribes question Him, then deliver Him to Pilate (Roman governor of Judea) for further questioning.

Pilate questioned Him, "Are You the King of the Jews?" And He answered him, "*It is as* you say" (Mark 15:2; cf. Matthew 27:2, 11–14; Luke 23:1–5; John 18:28–38).

Setting: Jerusalem. After being arrested, mocked, and beaten, and appearing before the Council of Elders (Sanhedrin), with His crucifixion imminent, Jesus is brought before Pilate (Roman governor of Judea).

So Pilate asked Him, saying, "Are You the King of the Jews?" And He answered him and said, "*It is as* you say" (Luke 23:3; cf. Matthew 27:11–14; Mark 15:2–5; John 18:33–38; see Luke 22:70).

KING'S PALACES (Listed under PALACES, KING'S)

KINGDOM (Specifics such as KINGDOM OF GOD; and KINGDOM OF HEAVEN are separate entries)

Setting: Galilee. During the early part of His ministry, Jesus gives a model prayer to His disciples and the multitudes while conveying The Sermon on the Mount.

"Pray, then, in this way: 'Our Father who is in heaven, hallowed be Your name. Your kingdom come. Your will be done, on earth as it is in heaven. Give us this day our daily bread. And forgive us our debts, as we also have forgiven our debtors. And do not lead us into temptation, but deliver us from evil. [For Yours is the kingdom and the power and the glory forever. Amen]'" (Matthew 6:9–13; cf. Luke 11:2–4; see John 17:15).

Setting: Galilee. During the early part of His ministry, Jesus preaches the Sermon on the Mount to His disciples and the multitudes.

"For this reason I say to you, do not be worried about your life, *as to* what you will eat or what you will drink; nor for your body, *as to* what you will put on. Is not life more than food, and the body more than clothing? Look at the birds of the air, that they do not sow, nor reap nor gather into barns, and *yet* your heavenly Father feeds them. Are you not worth much more than they? And who of you by being worried can add a *single* hour to his life? And why are you worried about clothing? Observe how the lilies of the field grow; they do not toil nor do they spin, yet I say to you that not even Solomon in all his glory clothed himself like one of these. But if God so clothes the grass of the field, which is *alive* today and tomorrow is thrown into the furnace, *will He* not much more *clothe* you? You of little faith! Do not worry then, saying 'What will we eat?' or 'What will we drink?' or 'What will be wear for clothing?" For the Gentiles eagerly seek all these things; for your heavenly Father knows that you need all these things. But seek first His kingdom and His righteousness, and all these things will be added to you. So do not worry about tomorrow; for tomorrow will care for itself. Each day has enough trouble of its own" (Matthew 6:25–34; cf. Luke 12:22–31; see 1 Kings 10:4–7; Job 35:11; Matthew 8:26).

Setting: Galilee. After He heals a blind, mute, demon-possessed man, the Pharisees accuse Jesus in front of crowds of being a worker of Beelzebul (Satan).

And knowing their thoughts Jesus said to them, "Any kingdom divided against itself is laid waste; and any city or house divided against itself will not stand. If Satan casts out Satan, he is divided against himself; how then will his kingdom stand? If I by Beelzebul cast out demons, by whom do your sons cast *them* out? For this reason they will be your judges. But if I cast out demons by the Spirit of God, then the kingdom of God has come upon you. Or how can anyone enter the strong man's house and carry off his property, unless he first binds the strong *man?* And then he will plunder his house" (Matthew 12:25–29; cf. Matthew 9:34; Mark 3:23–27; Luke 11:17–20).

Setting: A house near the Sea of Galilee. Jesus explains the meaning of the Parable of the Wheat and the Tares to His disciples.

And He said, "The one who sows the good seed is the Son of Man, and the field is the world; and as *for* the good seed, these are the sons of the kingdom; and the tares are the sons of the evil *one;* and the enemy who sowed them is the devil, and the harvest is the end of the age; and the reapers are angels. So just as the tares are gathered up and burned with fire, so shall it be at the end of the age. The Son of Man will send forth His angels, and they will gather out of His kingdom all stumbling blocks, and those who commit lawlessness, and will throw them into the furnace of fire; in that place there will be weeping and gnashing of teeth. Then THE RIGHTEOUS WILL SHINE FORTH AS THE SUN in the kingdom of their Father. He who has ears, let him hear" (Matthew 13:37–43, Jesus quotes from Daniel 12:3; cf. Matthew 8:12; 13:50).

Setting: Near Caesarea Philippi. After rebuking Peter for trying to forbid Him to accomplish His earthly mission of dying and being resurrected, Jesus teaches His disciples about the costs of discipleship.

Then Jesus said to His disciples, "If anyone wishes to come after Me, he must deny himself, and take up his cross and follow Me. For whoever wishes to save his life will lose it; but whoever loses his life for My sake will find it. For what will it profit a man if he gains the whole world and forfeits his soul? Or what will a man give in exchange for his soul? For the Son of Man is going to come in the glory of His Father with His angels, and WILL THEN REPAY EVERY MAN ACCORDING TO HIS DEEDS. Truly, I say to you, there are some of you who are standing here who will not taste death until they see the Son of Man coming in His kingdom" (Matthew 16:24–28, Jesus quotes from Psalm 62:12; cf. Mark 8:34–37; Luke 9:23–27; see Matthew 10:38, 39).

Setting: The Mount of Olives, just east of Jerusalem. During His discourse, Jesus answers His disciples' questions as to when the temple will be destroyed and Jerusalem overrun, along with the signs of His coming and the end of the age.

And Jesus answered and said to them, "See to it that no one misleads you. For many will come in My name, saying, 'I am the Christ,' and will mislead many. You will be hearing of wars and rumors of wars. See that you are not frightened, for *those things* must take place, but *that* is not yet the end. For nation will rise against nation, and kingdom against kingdom, and in various places there will be famines and earthquakes. But all these things are *merely* the beginning of birth pangs. Then they will deliver you to tribulation, and will kill you, and you will be hated by all nations because of My name. At that time many will fall away and will betray one another and hate one another. Many false prophets will arise and will mislead many. Because lawlessness is increased, most people's love will grow cold. But the one who endures to the end, he will be saved. This gospel of the kingdom shall be preached in the whole world as a testimony to all the nations, and then the end will come" (Matthew 24:4–14; cf. Jeremiah 29:8; Matthew 7:15; 10:17, 22; Mark 13:3–13; Luke 21:7–19; Revelation 6:4).

Setting: The Mount of Olives, just east of Jerusalem. During His discourse, after answering His disciples' questions as to when the temple will be destroyed and Jerusalem overrun, along with the signs of His coming and the end of the age, Jesus reveals the future judgments following His return.

"But when the Son of Man comes in His glory, and all the angels with Him, then He will sit on His glorious throne. All the nations will be gathered before Him; and He will separate them from one another, as the shepherd separates the sheep from the goats; and He will put the sheep on His right, and the goats on the left. Then the King will say to those on His right, 'Come, you who are blessed of My Father, inherit the kingdom prepared for you from the foundation of the world. 'For I was hungry, and you gave Me *something* to eat; I was thirsty, and you gave Me *something* to drink; I was a stranger, and you invited Me in; naked, and you clothed Me; I was sick, and you visited Me; I was in prison, and you came to Me.' Then the righteous will answer Him, 'Lord, when did we see You hungry and feed You, or thirsty, and give you *something* to drink? And when did we see You a stranger, and invite You in, or naked, and clothe You? When did we see You sick, or in prison, and come to You?' The King will answer and say to them, 'Truly I say to you, to the extent that you did it to one of these brothers of Mine, *even* the least *of them,* you did it to Me.' Then He will also say to those on His left, 'Depart from Me, accursed ones, into the eternal fire which has been prepared for the devil and his angels; for I was hungry, and you gave Me *nothing* to eat; I was thirsty, and you gave Me nothing to drink; I was a stranger, and you did not invite Me in; naked, and you did not clothe Me; sick, and in prison, and you did not visit Me.' Then they themselves also will answer, 'Lord, when did we see You hungry, or thirsty, or a stranger, or naked, or sick, or in prison, and did not take care of You?' Then He will answer them, 'Truly I say to you, to the extent that you did not do it to one of the least of these, you did not do it to Me.' These will go away into eternal punishment, but the righteous into eternal life" (Matthew 25:31–46; see Matthew 7:23; 16:27; 19:29).

Setting: Galilee. After Jesus selects His twelve disciples, scribes from Jerusalem attribute His miraculous powers to Satan.

And He called them to Himself and began speaking to them in parables, "How can Satan cast out Satan? If a kingdom is divided against itself, that kingdom cannot stand. If a house is divided against itself, that house will not be able to stand. If Satan has risen up against himself and is divided, he cannot stand, but he is finished! But no one can enter the strong man's house and plunder his property unless he first binds the strong man, and then he will plunder his house. Truly I say to you, all sins shall be forgiven the sons of men, and whatever blasphemies they utter; but whoever blasphemes against the Holy Spirit never has forgiveness, but is guilty of an eternal sin"—because they were saying, "He has an unclean spirit" (Mark 3:23–30; cf. Matthew 12:25–32; Luke 12:10).

Setting: On the Mount of Olives, east of the temple in Jerusalem. After predicting the temple's destruction, Jesus responds during His Olivet Discourse to questions from Peter, James, John, and Andrew about other future events.

And Jesus began to say to them, "See to it that no one misleads you. Many will come in My name, saying, 'I am *He!*' and will mislead many. When you hear of wars and rumors of wars, do not be frightened; *those things* must take place; but *that is* not yet the end. For nation will rise up against nation, and kingdom against kingdom; there will be earthquakes in various places; there will *also be* famines. These things are *merely* the beginning of birth pangs. But be on your guard; for they will deliver you to *the* courts, and you will be flogged in *the* synagogues, and you will stand before governors and kings for My sake, as a testimony to them. The gospel must first be preached to all the nations. When they arrest you and hand you over, do not worry beforehand about what you are to say, but say whatever is given you in that hour; for it is not you who speak, but *it is* the Holy Spirit. Brother will betray brother to death, and a father *his* child; and children will rise up against parents and have them put to death. You will be hated by all because of My name, but the one who endures to the end, he will be saved" (Mark 13:5–13; cf. Matthew 24:4–14; Luke 21:7–19; see Matthew 10:17–22).

Setting: On the way from Galilee to Jerusalem via Bethany. After Jesus visits the home of Martha and Mary, one of His disciples asks Him to teach them to pray.

And He said to them, "When you pray, say: 'Father, hallowed be Your name. Your kingdom come. Give us each day our daily bread. And forgive us our sins, for we ourselves also forgive everyone who is indebted to us. And lead us not into temptation'" (Luke 11:2–4; cf. Matthew 6:9–13).

Setting: On the way from Galilee to Jerusalem. After Jesus casts out a demon, some in the crowd test Him, demanding a sign from heaven.

But He knew their thoughts and said to them, "Any kingdom divided against itself is laid waste; and a house *divided* against itself falls. If Satan also is divided against himself, how will his kingdom stand? For you say that I cast out demons by Beelzebul. And if I by Beelzebul cast out demons, by whom do your sons cast them out? So they will be your judges. But if I cast out demons by the finger of God, then the kingdom of God has come upon you" (Luke 11:17–20; cf. Matthew 12:25–28; Mark 3:23–27; see Exodus 8:19; Matthew 3:2, 10:25).

Setting: On the way from Galilee to Jerusalem. Jesus comforts the crowd and His disciples after giving a parable about riches and greed. The scribes and Pharisees turn hostile and question Him repeatedly in an attempt to catch Him in something He might say.

And He said to His disciples, "For this reason I say to you, do not worry about *your* life, *as to* what you will eat; nor for your body, *as to* what you will put on. For life is more than food, and the body more than clothing. Consider the ravens, for they neither sow nor reap; they have no storeroom nor barn, and *yet* God feeds them; how much more valuable you are than the birds! And which of you by worrying can add a *single* hour to his life's span? If then you cannot do even a very little thing, why do you worry about other matters? Consider the lilies, how they grow: they neither toil nor spin; but I tell you, not even Solomon in all his glory clothed himself like one of these. But if God so clothes the grass in the field, which is *alive* today and tomorrow is thrown into the furnace, how much more *will He clothe* you? You men of little faith! And do not seek what you will eat and what you will drink, and do not keep worrying. For all these things the nations of the world eagerly seek; but your Father knows that you need these things. But seek His kingdom, and these things will be added to you. Do not be afraid, little flock, for your Father has chosen gladly to give you the kingdom" (Luke 12:22–32; cf. Matthew 6:25–33; see 1 Kings 10:4–7; Job 38:41).

Setting: Jericho, en route to Jerusalem. After commending Zaccheus's faith in Him, Jesus provides a parable about stewardship.

So He said, "A nobleman went to a distant country to receive a kingdom for himself, and *then* return. And he called ten of his slaves, and gave them ten minas and said to them, 'Do business *with this* until I come *back*.' But his citizens hated him and sent a delegation after him, saying, 'We do not want this man to reign over us.' When he returned, after receiving the kingdom, he ordered that these slaves, to whom he had given the money, be called to him so that he might know what business they had done. The first appeared, saying, 'Master, your mina has made ten minas more.' And he said to him, 'Well done, good slave, because you have been faithful in a very little thing, you are to be in authority over ten cities.' The second came, saying, 'Your mina, master, has made five minas.' And he said to him, also, 'And you are to be over five cities.' Another came, saying, 'Master, here is your mina, which I kept put away in a handkerchief; for I was afraid of you, because you are an exacting man; you take up what you did not lay down and reap what you did not sow.' He said to him, 'By your own words I will judge you, you worthless slave. Did you know that I am an exacting man, taking up what I did not lay down and reaping what I did not sow? Then why did you not put my money in the bank, and having come, I would have collected it with interest?' Then he said to the bystanders, 'Take the mina away from him and give it to the one who has the ten minas.' And they said to him, 'Master, he has ten minas *already.*' I tell you that to everyone who has, more shall be given, but from the one who does not have, even what he does have shall be taken away. But these enemies of mine, who did not want me to reign over them, bring them here and slay them in my presence" (Luke 19:12–27; cf. Matthew 25:14–30; see Matthew 13:12; Luke 16:10).

Setting: On the Mount of Olives, east of the temple in Jerusalem. After ministering in the temple a few days before His crucifixion, and giving His disciples more details regarding the temple's future destruction, Jesus elaborates during His Olivet Discourse about things to come.

Then He continued by saying to them, "Nation will rise against nation and kingdom against kingdom, and there will be great earthquakes, and in various places plagues and famines; and there will be terrors and great signs from heaven. But before all these things, they will lay their hands on you and will persecute you, delivering you to the synagogues and prisons, bringing you before kings and governors for My name's sake. It will lead to an opportunity for your testimony. So make up your minds not to prepare beforehand to defend yourselves; for I will give you utterance and wisdom which none of your opponents will be able to resist or refute. But you will be betrayed even by parents and brothers and relatives and friends, and they will put *some* of you to death, and you will be hated by all because of My name. Yet not a hair of your head will perish. By your endurance you will gain your lives" (Luke 21:10–19; cf. Matthew 10:19–22; 24:7–14; Mark 13:8–13).

Setting: Jerusalem. During the Feast of Unleavened Bread (Passover) just before Jesus' crucifixion, Jesus celebrates the Passover meal and institutes the Lord's Supper. After His disciples argue over who is the greatest among them, He details the kingdom benefits they will experience.

"You are those who have stood by Me in My trials; for just as My Father has granted Me a kingdom, I grant you that you may eat and drink at My table in My kingdom, and you will sit on thrones judging the twelve tribes of Israel" (Luke 22:28–30; cf. Matthew 19:28).

Setting: Jerusalem. After the previous and current high priests (Annas and Caiaphas) question Jesus, and Peter denies the second and third times being the Lord's disciple, Pilate (Roman governor of Judea), asks Jesus what He has done.

Jesus answered, "My kingdom is not of this world. If My kingdom were of this world, then My servants would be fighting so that I would not be handed over to the Jews; but as it is, My kingdom is not of this realm" (John 18:36; see Matthew 26:53).

KINGDOM, DIVIDED

[DIVIDED KINGDOM from kingdom divided]

Setting: Galilee. After He heals a blind, mute, demon-possessed man, the Pharisees accuse Jesus in front of crowds of being a worker of Beelzebul (Satan).

And knowing their thoughts Jesus said to them, "Any kingdom divided against itself is laid waste; and any city or house divided against itself will not stand. If Satan casts out Satan, he is divided against himself; how then will his kingdom stand? If I by Beelzebul cast out demons, by whom do your sons cast *them* out? For this reason they will be your judges. But if I cast out demons by the Spirit of God, then the kingdom of God has come upon you. Or how can anyone enter the strong man's house and carry off his property, unless he first binds the strong *man?* And then he will plunder his house" (Matthew 12:25–29; cf. Matthew 9:34; Mark 3:23–27; Luke 11:17–20).

[DIVIDED KINGDOM from kingdom is divided]

Setting: Galilee. After Jesus selects His twelve disciples, scribes from Jerusalem attribute His miraculous powers to Satan.

And He called them to Himself and began speaking to them in parables, "How can Satan cast out Satan? If a kingdom is divided against itself, that kingdom cannot stand. If a house is divided against itself, that house will not be able to stand. If Satan has risen up against himself and is divided, he cannot stand, but he is finished! But no one can enter the strong man's house and plunder his property unless he first binds the strong man, and then he will plunder his house. Truly I say to you, all sins shall be forgiven the sons of men, and whatever blasphemies they utter; but whoever blasphemes against the Holy Spirit never has forgiveness, but is guilty of an eternal sin"—because they were saying, "He has an unclean spirit" (Mark 3:23–30; cf. Matthew 12:25–32; Luke 12:10).

[DIVIDED KINGDOM from kingdom divided]

Setting: On the way from Galilee to Jerusalem. After Jesus casts out a demon, some in the crowd test Him, demanding a sign from heaven.

But He knew their thoughts and said to them, "Any kingdom divided against itself is laid waste; and a house *divided* against itself falls. If Satan also is divided against himself, how will his kingdom stand? For you say that I cast out demons by Beelzebul. And if I by Beelzebul cast out demons, by whom do your sons cast them out? So they will be your judges. But if I cast out demons by the finger of God, then the kingdom of God has come upon you" (Luke 11:17–20; cf. Matthew 12:25–28; Mark 3:23–27; see Exodus 8:19; Matthew 3:2, 10:25).

KINGDOM, FATHER'S

Setting: An upper room in Jerusalem. While celebrating the Passover meal with His disciples, Jesus institutes the Lord's Supper ordinance before being arrested by His enemies.

While they were eating, Jesus took *some* bread, and after a blessing, He broke *it* and gave *it* to the disciples, and said, "Take, eat; this is My body." And when He had taken a cup and given thanks, He gave *it* to them saying, "Drink from it, all of you; for this is My blood of the covenant, which is poured out for many for forgiveness of sins. But I say to you, I will not drink of this fruit of the vine from now on until that day when I drink it new with you in My Father's kingdom" (Matthew 26:26–29; cf. Mark 14:22–25; Luke 22:17–20; 1 Corinthians 11:23–26; see 1 Corinthians 10:16).

KINGDOM, GOSPEL OF THE (Also see GOSPEL; and KINGDOM, WORD OF THE)

Setting: The Mount of Olives, just east of Jerusalem. During His discourse, Jesus answers His disciples' questions as to when the temple will be destroyed and Jerusalem overrun, along with the signs of His coming and the end of the age.

And Jesus answered and said to them, "See to it that no one misleads you. For many will come in My name, saying, 'I am the Christ,' and will mislead many. You will be hearing of wars and rumors of wars. See that you are not frightened, for *those things* must take place, but *that* is not yet the end. For nation will rise against nation, and kingdom against kingdom, and in various places there will be famines and earthquakes. But all these things are *merely* the beginning of birth pangs. Then they will deliver you to tribulation, and will kill you, and you will be hated by all nations because of My name. At that time many will fall away and will betray one another and hate one another. Many false prophets will arise and will mislead many. Because lawlessness is increased, most people's love will grow cold. But the one who endures to the end, he will be saved. This gospel of the kingdom shall be preached in the whole world as a testimony to all the nations, and then the end will come" (Matthew 24:4–14; cf. Jeremiah 29:8; Matthew 7:15; 10:17, 22; Mark 13:3–13; Luke 21:7–19; Revelation 6:4).

Setting: On the way from Galilee to Jerusalem. The Lord responds to the Pharisees' scoffing at His teaching His disciples about stewardship.

And He said to them, "You are those who justify yourselves in the sight of men, but God knows your hearts; for that which is highly esteemed among men is detestable in the sight of God. The Law and the Prophets *were proclaimed* until John; since that time the gospel of the kingdom of God has been preached, and everyone is forcing his way into it. But is it easier for heaven and earth to pass away than for one stroke of a letter of the Law to fail" (Luke 16:15–17; cf. Matthew 5:18; see 1 Samuel 16:7; Matthew 4:23; 11:11–14).

KINGDOM, SONS OF THE

Setting: Capernaum in Galilee. After the Lord gives the Sermon on the Mount and cleanses a leper, a Roman centurion implores Jesus to heal his servant.

Now when Jesus heard *this,* He marveled, and said to those who were following, "Truly I say to you, I have not found such great faith with anyone in Israel. I say to you that many will come from east and west, and recline *at the table* with Abraham, Isaac and Jacob in the kingdom of heaven; but the sons of the kingdom will be cast out into the outer darkness; in that place there will be weeping and gnashing of teeth." And Jesus said to the centurion, "Go; it shall be done for you as you have believed." And the servant was healed that *very* moment (Matthew 8:10–13; cf. Luke 7:9, 10).

Setting: A house near the Sea of Galilee. Jesus gives His disciples the meaning of the Parable of the Wheat and the Tares.

And He said, "The one who sows the good seed is the Son of Man, and the field is the world; and as *for* the good seed, these are the sons of the kingdom; and the tares are the sons of the evil *one;* and the enemy who sowed them is the devil, and the harvest is the end of the age; and the reapers are angels. So just as the tares are gathered up and burned with fire, so shall it be at the end of the age. The Son of Man will send forth His angels, and they will gather out of His kingdom all stumbling blocks, and those who commit lawlessness, and will throw them into the furnace of fire; in that place there will be weeping and gnashing of teeth. Then THE RIGHTEOUS WILL SHINE FORTH AS THE SUN in the kingdom of their Father. He who has ears, let him hear" (Matthew 13:37–43, Jesus quotes from Daniel 12:3; cf. Matthew 8:12; 13:50).

KINGDOM, WORD OF THE (Also see KINGDOM, GOSPEL OF THE)

Setting: By the Sea of Galilee. With the religious leaders rejecting His message, Jesus begins to teach in parables and gives His disciples the meaning of the Parable of the Sower.

"Hear then the parable of the sower. When anyone hears the word of the kingdom and does not understand it, the evil *one* comes and snatches away what has been sown in his heart. This is the one on whom seed was sown beside the road. The one on whom seed was sown on the rocky places, this is the man who hears the word and immediately receives it with joy; yet he has no *firm* root in himself, but is *only* temporary, and when affliction or persecution arises because of the word, immediately he falls away. And the one on whom seed was sown among the thorns, this is the man who hears the word, and the worry of the world and the deceitfulness of wealth choke the word, and it becomes unfruitful. And the one on whom seed was sown on the good soil, this is the man who hears the word and understands it; who indeed bears fruit and brings forth, some a hundredfold, some sixty, and some thirty" (Matthew 13:18–23; cf. Mark 4:13–20; Luke 8:11–15; see Matthew 13:8).

KINGDOM OF GOD (Also see ETERNAL LIFE; KINGDOM; and KINGDOM OF HEAVEN)

Setting: Galilee. After Jesus heals a blind, mute, demon-possessed man, the Pharisees accuse the Lord in front of crowds of being a worker of Satan.

And knowing their thoughts Jesus said to them, "Any kingdom divided against itself is laid waste; and any city or house divided against itself will not stand. If Satan casts out Satan, he is divided against himself; how then will his kingdom stand? If I by Beelzebul cast out demons, by whom do your sons cast *them* out? For this reason they will be your judges. But if I cast out demons by the Spirit of God, then the kingdom of God has come upon you. Or how can anyone enter the strong man's house and carry off his property, unless he first binds the strong *man?* And then he will plunder his house" (Matthew 12:25–29; cf. Matthew 9:34; Mark 3:23–27; Luke 11:17–20).

Setting: Judea beyond the Jordan (Perea). Jesus comments to His disciples about the rich, young ruler who asks how he might obtain eternal life, but rejects Jesus' instruction to sell his possessions and give the proceeds to the poor.

And Jesus said to His disciples, "Truly I say to you, it is hard for a rich man to enter the kingdom of heaven. Again, I say to you, it is easier for a camel to go through the eye of a needle, than for a rich man to enter the kingdom of God" (Matthew 19:23, 24; cf. Matthew 13:22; Mark 10:23–25; Luke 18:24).

Setting: The temple in Jerusalem. Jesus delivers a parable to the chief priests and elders after they question His authority.

"But what do you think? A man had two sons, and he came to the first and said, 'Son, go work today in the vineyard.' And he answered, 'I will not'; but afterward he regretted it and went. The man came to the second and said the same thing; and he answered, 'I *will,* sir'; but he did not go. Which of the two sons did the will of his father?" They said, "The first." Jesus said to them, "Truly, I say to you that the tax collectors and prostitutes will get into the kingdom of God before you. For John came to you in the way of righteousness and you did not believe him; but the tax collectors and prostitutes did believe him; and you, seeing *this,* did not even feel remorse afterward so as to believe him" (Matthew 21:28–32; cf. Luke 7:29, 30, 37–50).

Setting: The temple in Jerusalem. Jesus delivers a prophecy to the chief priests and elders after they question His authority.

Jesus said to them, "Did you never read in the Scriptures, 'THE STONE WHICH THE BUILDERS REJECTED, THIS BECAME THE CHIEF CORNER *stone;* THIS CAME ABOUT FROM THE LORD, AND IT IS MARVELOUS IN OUR EYES'? Therefore I say to you, the kingdom of God will be taken away from you and given to a people, producing the fruit of it. And he who falls on this stone will be broken to pieces; but on whomever it falls, it will scatter him like dust" (Matthew 21:42–44, Jesus quotes from Psalm 118:22; cf. Isaiah 8:14, 15; Mark 12:10, 11; Luke 20:17, 18).

Setting: Galilee. After being baptized by John in the Jordan River, Jesus commences His gospel-preaching ministry shortly after John is taken into custody by Herod Antipas.

Now after John had been taken into custody, Jesus came into Galilee, preaching the gospel of God, and saying, "The time is fulfilled, and the kingdom of God is at hand; repent and believe in the gospel" (Mark 1:14, 15, cf. Matthew 4:17; Galatians 4:4).

Setting: By the Sea of Galilee. After Jesus conveys the Parable of the Sower from a boat to a crowd, His disciples ask Him about it.

And He was saying to them, "To you has been given the mystery of the kingdom of God, but those who are outside get everything in parables, so that WHILE SEEING, THEY MAY SEE AND NOT PERCEIVE, AND WHILE HEARING, THEY MAY HEAR AND NOT UNDERSTAND, OTHERWISE THEY MIGHT RETURN AND BE FORGIVEN" (Mark 4:11, 12, Jesus quotes from Isaiah 6:9, 10; cf. Matthew 13:10–17).

Setting: Galilee. Following His explanation of the Parable of the Sower to His disciples, Jesus conveys the Parable of the Seed.

And He was saying, "The kingdom of God is like a man who casts seed upon the soil; and he goes to bed at night and gets up by day, and the seed sprouts and grows—how, he himself does not know. The soil produces crops by itself; first the blade, then the head, then the mature grain in the head. But when the crop permits, he immediately puts in the sickle, because the harvest has come" (Mark 4:26–29; see Joel 3:13).

Setting: Galilee. After giving the Parable of the Sower and the Parable of the Seed, Jesus continues teaching His disciples by presenting the Parable of the Mustard Seed.

And He said, "How shall we picture the kingdom of God, or by what parable shall we present it? *It is* like a mustard seed, which, when sown upon the soil, though it is smaller than all the seeds that are upon the soil, yet when it is sown, it grows up and becomes larger than all the garden plants and forms large branches; so that THE BIRDS OF THE AIR can NEST UNDER ITS SHADE" (Mark 4:30–32, Jesus quotes from Ezekiel 17:23; cf. Matthew 13:31, 32; Luke 13:18, 19).

Setting: Caesarea Philippi. After rebuking Peter for desiring to thwart His mission to the cross, Jesus summons a crowd, along with His disciples, and informs them of the hope involving the coming kingdom of God.

And Jesus was saying to them, "Truly I say to you, there are some of those who are standing here who will not taste death until they see the kingdom of God after it has come with power" (Mark 9:1; cf. Matthew 16:28; Luke 9:27).

Setting: Capernaum of Galilee. As Jesus teaches His disciples in private, they ask Him about greatness.

But Jesus said, "Do not hinder him, for there is no one who will perform a miracle in My name, and be able soon afterward to speak evil of Me. For he who is not against us is for us. For whoever gives you a cup of water to drink because of your name as *followers* of Christ, truly I say to you, he will not lose his reward. Whoever causes one of these little ones who believe to stumble, it would be better for him if, with a heavy millstone hung around his neck, he had been cast into the sea. If your hand causes you to stumble, cut it off; it is better for you to enter life crippled, than, having your two hands, to go into hell, into the unquenchable fire, [where THEIR WORM DOES NOT DIE, AND THE FIRE IS NOT QUENCHED.] If your foot causes you to stumble, cut it off; it is better for you to enter life lame, than, having your two feet, to be cast into hell, [where THEIR WORM DOES NOT DIE, AND THE FIRE IS NOT QUENCHED.] If your eye causes you to stumble, throw it out; it is better for you to enter the kingdom of God with one eye, than, having two eyes, to be cast into hell, where THEIR WORM DOES NOT DIE, AND THE FIRE IS NOT QUENCHED. For everyone will be salted with fire. Salt is good; but if the salt becomes unsalty, with what will you make it salty *again?* Have salt in yourselves, and be at peace with one another" (Mark 9:39–50; Jesus quotes from Isaiah 66:24; cf. Matthew 18:6–9; Luke 9:49, 50; see Matthew 5:13, 29, 30; 10:42; 12:30; 18:5, 6).

Setting: Judea beyond the Jordan (Perea). After the Pharisees test Him with questions about divorce, Jesus demonstrates to His disciples the importance of little children.

But when Jesus saw this, He was indignant and said to them, "Permit the children to come to Me; do not hinder them; for the kingdom of God belongs to such as these. Truly I say to you, whoever does not receive the kingdom of God like a child will not enter it *at all*" (Mark 10:14, 15; cf. Matthew 19:13–15; Luke 18:15–17; see Matthew 18:3).

Setting: Judea beyond the Jordan (Perea). After informing a rich man how righteous believers may have treasure in heaven, Jesus conveys to His disciples the difficulty the wealthy have entering the kingdom of God.

And Jesus, looking around, said to His disciples, "How hard it will be for those who are wealthy to enter the kingdom of God!" The disciples were amazed at His words. But Jesus answered again and said to them, "Children, how hard it is to enter the kingdom of God! It is easier for a camel to go through the eye of a needle than for a rich man to enter the kingdom of God." They were even more astonished and said to Him, "Then who can be saved?" Looking at them, Jesus said, "With people it is impossible, but not with God; for all things are possible with God" (Mark 10:23–27; cf. Matthew 19:23–26; Luke 18:24, 25).

Setting: The temple in Jerusalem. Jesus encourages one of the scribes, who agrees with His answer about which commandment is foremost.

When Jesus saw that he had answered intelligently, He said to him, "You are not far from the kingdom of God." After that, no one would venture to ask Him any more questions (Mark 12:34; see Matthew 22:26).

Setting: An upper room in Jerusalem. While celebrating the Feast of Unleavened Bread (Passover) with His disciples, Jesus institutes the ordinance of the Lord's Supper.

While they were eating, He took *some* bread, and after a blessing He broke *it*, and gave *it* to them, and said, "Take *it;* this is My body." And when He had taken a cup *and* given thanks, He gave *it* to them, and they all drank from it. And He said to them, "This is My blood of the covenant, which is poured out for many. Truly I say to you, I will never again drink of the fruit of the vine until that day when I drink it new in the kingdom of God" (Mark 14:22–25; cf. Matthew 26:26–29; Luke 22:17–20; 1 Corinthians 11:23–26; see Exodus 24:8).

Setting: Galilee. After healing Simon Peter's mother-in-law of a high fever, Jesus tries to retreat to a secluded place, but the crowds locate Him, and He proclaims His mission.

But He said to them, "I must preach the kingdom of God to the other cities also, for I was sent for this purpose" (Luke 4:43; cf. Matthew 4:23, 24; Mark 1:35–39).

Setting: On a mountain in Galilee. After selecting His twelve disciples, Jesus teaches the Beatitudes (part of the Sermon on the Mount) to His disciples and a great throng from Judea, Jerusalem, and the central coastal region of Tyre and Sidon.

And turning His gaze toward His disciples, He *began* to say, "Blessed *are* you *who are* poor, for yours is the kingdom of God" (Luke 6:20; cf. Matthew 5:3).

Setting: Galilee. After He responds to the disciples of John the Baptist whether He is the promised Messiah, Jesus speaks to the crowds about John.

When the messengers of John had left, He began to speak to the crowds about John, "What did you go out into the wilderness to see? A reed shaken by the wind? But what did you go out to see? A man dressed in soft clothing? Those who are splendidly clothed and live in luxury are *found* in royal palaces! But what did you go out to see? A prophet? Yes, I say to you, and one who is more than a prophet. This is the one about whom it is written, 'BEHOLD, I SEND MY MESSENGER AHEAD OF YOU, WHO WILL PREPARE YOUR WAY BEFORE YOU.' I say to you, among those born of women there is no one greater than John; yet he who is least in the kingdom of God is greater than he" (Luke 7:24–28, Jesus quotes from Malachi 3:1; cf. Matthew 11:7–11).

Setting: Galilee. After Jesus presents the Parable of the Sower to the crowds, His disciples ask Him to give them its meaning.

And He said, "To you it has been granted to know the mysteries of the kingdom of God, but to the rest *it is* in parables, so that SEEING THEY MAY NOT SEE, AND HEARING THEY MAY NOT UNDERSTAND. Now the parable is this: the seed is the word of God. Those beside the road are those who have heard; then the devil comes and takes away the word from their heart, so that they will not believe and be saved. Those on the rocky *soil* are those who, when they hear, receive the word with joy; and these have no *firm* root; they believe for a while, and in time of temptation fall away. The *seed* which fell among the thorns, these are the ones who have heard, and as they go on their way they are choked with worries and riches and pleasures of *this* life, and bring no fruit to maturity. But the *seed* in the good soil, these are the ones who have heard the word in an honest and good heart, and hold it fast, and bear fruit with perseverance" (Luke 8:10–15, Jesus quotes from Isaiah 6:9; cf. Matthew 13:10–23; Mark 4:10–20; see Luke 8:4–8).

Setting: Galilee. Following Peter's pronouncement Jesus is the Christ of God, the Lord conveys the demands of discipleship and the hope regarding the kingdom of God.

And He was saying to *them* all, "If anyone wishes to come after Me, he must deny himself, and take up his cross daily and follow Me. For whoever wishes to save his life will lose it, but whoever loses his life for My sake, he is the one who will save it. For what is a man profited if he gains the whole world, and loses or forfeits himself? For whoever is ashamed of Me and My words, the Son of Man will be ashamed of him when He comes in His glory, and *the glory* of the Father and of the holy angels. But I say to you truthfully, there are some of those standing here who will not taste death until they see the kingdom of God" (Luke 9:23–27; cf. Matthew 16:24–26, 28; Mark 8:34–37; see Matthew 10:33, 38, 39).

Setting: On the way from Galilee to Jerusalem. The Lord responds to several men seeking to follow Him.

And He said to another, "Follow Me." But he said, "Lord, permit me first to go and bury my father," But He said to him, "Allow the dead to bury their own dead; but as for you, go and proclaim everywhere the kingdom of God" (Luke 9:59, 60; cf. Matthew 8:19–22).

Setting: On the way from Galilee to Jerusalem. The Lord responds to several men seeking to follow Him.

But Jesus said to him, "No one, after putting his hand to the plow and looking back, is fit for the kingdom of God" (Luke 9:62; cf. Matthew 8:19–22; see Philippians 3:13).

Setting: On the way from Galilee to Jerusalem. The Lord appoints seventy followers and sends them out in pairs to every place He Himself will soon visit.

And He was saying to them, "The harvest is plentiful, but the laborers are few; therefore beseech the Lord of the harvest to send out laborers into His harvest. Go; behold, I send you out as lambs in the midst of wolves. Carry no money belt, no bag, no shoes; and greet no one on the way. Whatever house you enter, first say, 'Peace be to this house.' If a man of peace is there, your peace will rest on him; but if not, it will return to you. Stay in that house, eating and drinking what they give you; for the laborer is worthy of his wages. Do not keep moving from house to house. Whatever city you enter and they receive you, eat what is set before you; and heal those in it who are sick, and say to them, 'The kingdom of God has come near to you.' But whatever city you enter and they do not receive you, go out into its streets and say, 'Even the dust of your city which clings to our feet we wipe off *in protest* against you; yet be sure of this, that the kingdom of God has come near.' I say to you, it will be more tolerable in that day for Sodom than for that city" (Luke 10:2–12; see Genesis 19:24–28; Matthew 9:37, 38, 10:9–14, 16; 1 Corinthians 10:27).

Setting: On the way from Galilee to Jerusalem. After Jesus casts out a demon, some in the crowd test Him, demanding a sign from heaven.

But He knew their thoughts and said to them, "Any kingdom divided against itself is laid waste; and a house *divided* against itself falls. If Satan also is divided against himself, how will his kingdom stand? For you say that I cast out demons by Beelzebul. And if I by Beelzebul cast out demons, by whom do your sons cast them out? So they will be your judges. But if I cast out demons by the finger of God, then the kingdom of God has come upon you" (Luke 11:17–20; cf. Matthew 12:25–28; Mark 3:23–27; see Exodus 8:19; Matthew 3:2, 10:25).

Setting: On the way from Galilee to Jerusalem. After responding to a synagogue official's anger for healing a woman, sick eighteen years, in the synagogue on the Sabbath, Jesus conveys the Parable of the Mustard Seed and the Parable of the Leaven.

So He was saying, "What is the kingdom of God like, and to what shall I compare it? It is like a mustard seed which a man took and threw into his own garden; and it grew and became a tree, and THE BIRDS OF THE AIR NESTED IN ITS BRANCHES." And again He said, "To what shall I compare the kingdom of God? It is like leaven, which a woman took and hid in three pecks of flour until it was all leavened" (Luke 13:18–21, Jesus quotes from Ezekiel 17:23; cf. Matthew 13:31–34; Mark 4:30–32).

Setting: On the way from Galilee to Jerusalem. While teaching in the cities and villages, Jesus responds to a question about who is saved.

And someone said to Him, "Lord, are here *just* a few who are being saved?" And He said to them, "Strive to enter through the narrow door; for many, I tell you, will seek to enter and will not be able. Once the head of the house gets up and shuts the door, and you begin to stand outside and knock on the door, saying, 'Lord, open up to us!' then He will answer and say to you, 'I do not know where you are from.' Then you will begin to say, 'We ate and drank in Your presence, and You taught in our streets'; and He will say, 'I tell you, I do not know where you are from; DEPART FROM ME, ALL YOU EVILDOERS.' In that place there will be weeping and gnashing of teeth when you see Abraham and Isaac and Jacob and all the prophets in the kingdom of God, but you yourselves being thrown out. And they will come from east and west and from north and south, and will recline *at the table* in the kingdom of God. And behold, *some* are last who will be first and *some* are first who will be last" (Luke 13:23–30, Jesus quotes from Psalm 6:8; cf. Matthew 7:13, 23; 8:11, 12; see Matthew 19:30; Luke 3:8).

Setting: On the way from Galilee to Jerusalem. The Lord responds to the Pharisees' scoffing at His teaching His disciples about stewardship.

And He said to them, "You are those who justify yourselves in the sight of men, but God knows your hearts; for that which is highly esteemed among men is detestable in the sight of God. The Law and the Prophets *were proclaimed* until John; since that time the gospel of the kingdom of God has been preached, and everyone is forcing his way into it. But is it easier for heaven and earth to pass away than for one stroke of a letter of the Law to fail" (Luke 16:15–17; cf. Matthew 5:18; see 1 Samuel 16:7; Matthew 4:23; 11:11–14; Luke 16:1).

Setting: On the way from Galilee to Jerusalem. The Pharisees question Jesus about the coming of the kingdom of God.

Now having been questioned by the Pharisees as to when the kingdom of God was coming, He answered them and said, "The kingdom of God is not coming with signs to be observed; nor will they say, 'Look, here it is!' Or, 'There it is!' For behold, the kingdom of God is in your midst" (Luke 17:20, 21; see Luke 19:11).

Setting: On the way from Galilee to Jerusalem. After giving a parable about self-righteousness, Jesus speaks of the importance of children.

But Jesus called for them, saying, "Permit the children to come to Me, and do not hinder them, for the kingdom of God belongs to such as these. Truly I say to you, whoever does not receive the kingdom of God like a child will not enter it *at all*" (Luke 18:16, 17; cf. Matthew 19:13–15; Mark 10:13–16; see Matthew 18:3).

Setting: Judea beyond the Jordan (Perea). After responding to a ruler's question about inheriting eternal life, Jesus comments to him about the challenge of being wealthy and saved.

And Jesus looked at him and said, "How hard it is for those who are wealthy to enter the kingdom of God! For it is easier for a camel to go through the eye of a needle than for a rich man to enter the kingdom of God" (Luke 18:24, 25; cf. Matthew 19:23, 24; Mark 10:25).

Setting: Perea, en route from Galilee to Jerusalem. After responding to His disciples' question about salvation, Jesus replies to Peter's statement about their personal sacrifice.

Peter said, "Behold, we have left our own *homes* and followed You." And He said to them, "Truly I say to you, there is no one who has left house or wife or brothers or parents or children, for the sake of the kingdom of God, who will not receive many times as much at this time and in the age to come, eternal life" (Luke 18:28–30; cf. Matthew 19:27–29; Mark 10:28–30; see Matthew 6:33; Luke 5:11).

Setting: On the Mount of Olives, east of the temple in Jerusalem. After ministering in the temple a few days before His crucifixion, and giving His disciples more details regarding His return, Jesus conveys the Parable of the Fig Tree.

Then He told them a parable: "Behold the fig tree and all the trees; as soon as they put forth *leaves,* you see it and know for yourselves that summer is now near. So you also, when you see these things happening, recognize that the kingdom of God is near. Truly, I say to you, this generation will not pass away until all things take place. Heaven and earth will pass away, but My words will not pass away" (Luke 21:29–33; cf. Matthew 24:32–35; Mark 13:28–31; see Matthew 5:18).

Setting: An upper room in Jerusalem. During the Feast of Unleavened Bread (Passover) just before His crucifixion, after Judas consents to betray Him to the chief priests and officers, Jesus mentions His upcoming death during the Passover meal with His disciples.

And He said to them, "I have earnestly desired to eat this Passover with you before I suffer; for I say to you, I shall never again eat it until it is fulfilled in the kingdom of God" (Luke 22:15, 16; see Matthew 26:20; Luke 14:15).

Setting: An upper room in Jerusalem. During the Feast of Unleavened Bread (Passover) just before His crucifixion, while celebrating the Passover meal with His disciples, Jesus institutes the Lord's Supper.

And when He had taken a cup *and* given thanks, He said, "Take this and share it among yourselves; for I say to you, I will not drink of the fruit of the vine from now on until the kingdom of God comes." And when he had taken *some* bread and given thanks, He broke it and gave it to them, saying, "This is My body which is given for you; do this in remembrance of Me." And in the same way *He took* the cup after they had eaten, saying, "This cup which is poured out for you is the new covenant in My blood. But behold, the hand of the one betraying Me is with Mine on the table. For indeed, the Son of Man is going as it has been determined; but woe to that man by whom He is betrayed!" (Luke 22:17–22; cf. Matthew 26:26–29; Mark 14:22–25; 1 Corinthians 11:23–26; see Psalm 41:9; Luke 14:15; 1 Corinthians 10:16).

Setting: Jerusalem. At the time for the Passover of the Jews, after the Lord cleanses the temple, a Pharisee, Nicodemus, comes to Him by night to converse with Him.

Jesus answered and said to him, "Truly, truly, I say to you, unless one is born again he cannot see the kingdom of God" (John 3:3; see 2 Corinthians 5:17).

Setting: Jerusalem. At the time for the Passover of the Jews, after the Lord cleanses the temple, a Pharisee, Nicodemus, asks Him by night the meaning of "born again."

Jesus answered, "Truly, truly, I say to you, unless one is born of water and the Spirit he cannot enter into the kingdom of God. That which is born of the flesh is flesh, and that which is born of the Spirit is spirit. Do not be amazed that I said to you, 'You must be born again.' The wind blows where it wishes and you hear the sound of it, but do not know where it comes from and where it is going; so is everyone who is born of the Spirit" (John 3:5–8; see Psalm 135:7; John 1:13; 3:1–4).

KINGDOM OF HEAVEN (Also see ETERNAL LIFE; HEAVEN; KINGDOM; and KINGDOM OF GOD)

Setting: Galilee. After hearing that John the Baptist has been taken into custody, Jesus begins His ministry, settling in Capernaum in fulfillment of Isaiah 9:1, 2.

From that time Jesus began to preach and say, "Repent, for the kingdom of heaven is at hand" (Matthew 4:17; cf. Mark 1:15; see Matthew 4:12–16, Isaiah 9:1, 2).

Setting: Galilee. Early in His ministry, Jesus presents the Beatitudes (part of the Sermon on the Mount) to His disciples and the gathered crowds from Galilee, Decapolis, Jerusalem, Judea, and beyond the Jordan.

He opened His mouth and *began* to teach them, saying, "Blessed are the poor in spirit, for theirs is the kingdom of heaven" (Matthew 5:2, 3; see Matthew 13:35).

Setting: Galilee. Early in His ministry, Jesus presents the Beatitudes (part of the Sermon on the Mount) to His disciples and the gathered crowds from Galilee, Decapolis, Jerusalem, Judea, and beyond the Jordan.

"Blessed are those who have been persecuted for the sake of righteousness, for theirs is the kingdom of heaven" (Matthew 5:10; cf. Luke 6:22; 1 Peter 3:14; see Matthew 13:35).

Setting: Galilee. During the early part of His ministry, Jesus preaches the Sermon on the Mount to His disciples and the multitudes.

"Whoever then annuls one of the least of these commandments, and teaches others *to do* the same, shall be called least in the kingdom of heaven; but whoever keeps and teaches *them*, he shall be called great in the kingdom of heaven" (Matthew 5:19; cf. Matthew 11:11).

Setting: Galilee. During the early part of His ministry, Jesus preaches the Sermon on the Mount to His disciples and the multitudes.

"For I say to you that unless your righteousness surpasses *that* of the scribes and Pharisees, you will not enter the kingdom of heaven" (Matthew 5:20; cf. Luke 18:11, 12).

Setting: Galilee. During the early part of His ministry, Jesus preaches the Sermon on the Mount to His disciples and the multitudes.

"Not everyone who says to Me, 'Lord, Lord,' will enter the kingdom of heaven, but he who does the will of My Father who is in heaven *will enter.* Many will say to Me on that day, 'Lord, Lord, did we not prophesy in Your name, and in Your name cast out demons, and in Your name perform many miracles?' And then I will declare to them, 'I never knew you, DEPART FROM ME, YOU WHO PRACTICE LAWLESSNESS'"(Matthew 7:21–23, Jesus quotes from Psalm 6:8; cf. Matthew 25:11–13; see Luke 6:46).

Setting: Entering Capernaum. After the Lord gives the Sermon on the Mount and cleanses a leper, a Roman centurion implores Him to heal his servant.

Now when Jesus heard *this,* He marveled, and said to those who were following, "Truly I say to you, I have not found such great faith with anyone in Israel. I say to you that many will come from east and west, and recline *at the table* with Abraham, Isaac and Jacob in the kingdom of heaven; but the sons of the kingdom will be cast out into the outer darkness; in that place there will be weeping and gnashing of teeth." And Jesus said to the centurion, "Go; it shall be done for you as you have believed." And the servant was healed that *very* moment (Matthew 8:10–13; cf. Luke 7:9–10).

Setting: Galilee. After His twelve disciples observe His ministry, Jesus summons and specifically instructs them about their ministry to the people of Israel.

These twelve Jesus sent out after instructing them: "Do not go in *the* way of *the* Gentiles, and do not enter *any* city of the Samaritans; but rather go to the lost sheep of the house of Israel. And as you go, preach, saying, 'The kingdom of heaven is at hand.' Heal *the* sick, raise *the* dead, cleanse *the* lepers, cast out demons. Freely you received, freely give. Do not acquire gold, or silver, or copper for your money belts, or a bag for *your* journey, or even two coats, or sandals, or a staff; for the worker is worthy of his support. And whatever city or village you enter, inquire who is worthy in it, and stay at his house until you leave *that city.* As you enter the house, give it your greeting. If the house is worthy, give it your *blessing of* peace. But if it is not worthy, take back your *blessing of* peace. Whoever does not receive you, nor heed your words, as you go out of that house or that city, shake the dust off your feet. Truly I say to you, it will be more tolerable for *the* land of Sodom and Gomorrah in the day of judgment than for that city" (Matthew 10:5–15; cf. Mark 6:7–11; Luke 9:1–5; see Matthew 3:2; 11:22, 24; 15:24; Luke 22:35; 1 Corinthians 9:14).

Setting: Galilee. Jesus pays tribute to the ministry of John the Baptist, but emphasizes that the one who is least in the kingdom of heaven is greater than John.

As these men were going *away,* Jesus began to speak to the crowds about John, "What did you go out into the wilderness to see? A reed shaken by the wind? But what did you go out to see? A man dressed in soft *clothing?* Those who wear soft *clothing* are in kings' palaces! But what did you go out to see? A prophet? Yes, I tell you, and the one who is more than a prophet. This is the one about whom it is written, 'BEHOLD, I SEND MY MESSENGER AHEAD OF YOU, WHO WILL PREPARE YOUR WAY BEFORE YOU.' Truly, I say to you, among those born of women there has not arisen *anyone* greater than John the Baptist! Yet the one who is least in the kingdom of heaven is greater than he. From the days of John the Baptist until now the kingdom of heaven suffers violence, and violent men take it by force. For all the prophets and the Law prophesied until John. And, if you are willing to accept *it,* John himself is Elijah who was to come. He who has ears to hear, let him hear" (Matthew 11:7–15, Jesus quotes from Malachi 3:1; cf. Malachi 4:5; Luke 7:24–28; 16:16; see Matthew 14:5).

Setting: Galilee. After His twelve disciples observe His ministry, Jesus summons and specifically instructs them about their ministry to the people of Israel.

These twelve Jesus sent out after instructing them: "Do not go in *the* way of *the* Gentiles, and do not enter *any* city of the Samaritans; but rather go to the lost sheep of the house of Israel. And as you go, preach, saying, 'The kingdom of heaven is at hand.' Heal *the* sick, raise *the* dead, cleanse *the* lepers, cast out demons. Freely you received, freely give. Do not acquire gold, or silver, or copper for your money belts, or a bag for *your* journey, or even two coats, or sandals, or a staff; for the worker is worthy of his support. And whatever city or village you enter, inquire who is worthy in it, and stay at his house until you leave *that city*. As you enter the house, give it your greeting. If the house is worthy, give it your *blessing of* peace. But if it is not worthy, take back your *blessing of* peace. Whoever does not receive you, nor heed your words, as you go out of that house or that city, shake the dust off your feet. Truly I say to you, it will be more tolerable for *the* land of Sodom and Gomorrah in the day of judgment than for that city" (Matthew 10:5–15; cf. Mark 6:7–11; Luke 9:1–5; see Matthew 3:2; 11:22, 24; 15:24; Luke 22:35; 1 Corinthians 9:14).

Setting: Galilee. Jesus pays tribute to the ministry of John the Baptist, but emphasizes that the one who is least in the kingdom of heaven is greater than John.

As these men were going *away,* Jesus began to speak to the crowds about John, "What did you go out into the wilderness to see? A reed shaken by the wind? But what did you go out to see? A man dressed in soft *clothing?* Those who wear soft *clothing* are in kings' palaces! But what did you go out to see? A prophet? Yes, I tell you, and the one who is more than a prophet. This is the one about whom it is written, 'BEHOLD, I SEND MY MESSENGER AHEAD OF YOU, WHO WILL PREPARE YOUR WAY BEFORE YOU.' Truly, I say to you, among those born of women there has not arisen *anyone* greater than John the Baptist! Yet the one who is least in the kingdom of heaven is greater than he. From the days of John the Baptist until now the kingdom of heaven suffers violence, and violent men take it by force. For all the prophets and the Law prophesied until John. And, if you are willing to accept *it,* John himself is Elijah who was to come. He who has ears to hear, let him hear" (Matthew 11:7–15, Jesus quotes from Malachi 3:1; cf. Malachi 4:5; Luke 7:24–28; 16:16; see Matthew 14:5).

Setting: By the Sea of Galilee. Jesus responds to His disciples' questions about the Parable of the Sower, which He has just taught from a boat.

Jesus answered them, "To you it has been granted to know the mysteries of the kingdom of heaven, but to them it has not been granted. For whoever has, to him *more* shall be given, and he will have an abundance; but whoever does not have, even what he has shall be taken away from him. Therefore, I speak to them in parables; because while seeing they do not see, and while hearing they do not hear, nor do they understand. In their case the prophecy of Isaiah is being fulfilled, which says, 'YOU WILL KEEP ON HEARING, BUT WILL NOT UNDERSTAND; YOU WILL KEEP ON SEEING, BUT WILL NOT PERCEIVE; FOR THE HEART OF THIS PEOPLE HAS BECOME DULL, WITH THEIR EARS THEY SCARCELY HEAR, AND THEY HAVE CLOSED THEIR EYES, OTHERWISE THEYWOULD SEE WITH THEIR EYES, HEAR WITH THEIR EARS, AND UNDERSTAND WITH THEIR HEART AND RETURN, AND I WOULD HEAL THEM.' But blessed are your eyes, because they see; and your ears, because they hear. For truly I say to you that many prophets and righteous men desired to see what you see, and did not see *it,* and to hear what you hear, and did not hear *it*" (Matthew 13:11–17, Jesus quotes from Isaiah 6:9–10; cf. Matthew 25:29; Mark 4:11–13; Luke 8:10; see Deuteronomy 29:4; John 8:56).

Setting: By the Sea of Galilee. Because the religious leaders are rejecting His message, Jesus continues teaching the crowds with the Parable of the Wheat and the Tares.

Jesus presented another parable to them, saying, "The kingdom of heaven may be compared to a man who sowed good seed in his field. But while his men were sleeping, his enemy came and sowed tares among the wheat, and went away. But when the wheat sprouted and bore grain, then the tares became evident also. The slaves of the landowner came and said to him, 'Sir, did you not sow good seed in your field? How then does it have tares?' And he said to them, 'An enemy has done this!' The slaves said to him, 'Do you want us, then, to go and gather them up?' But he said, 'No; for while you are gathering up the tares, you may uproot the wheat with them. Allow both to grow together until the harvest; and in the time of the harvest I will say to the reapers, "First gather up the tares and bind them in bundles to burn them up; but gather the wheat into my barn" '" (Matthew 13:24–30; cf. Matthew 3:12).

Setting: By the Sea of Galilee. Because the religious leaders are rejecting His message, Jesus continues teaching the crowds with the Parable of the Mustard Seed.

He presented another parable to them, saying, "The kingdom of heaven is like a mustard seed, which a man took and sowed in his field; and this is smaller than all *other* seeds, but when it is full grown, it is larger than the garden plants and becomes a tree, so that THE BIRDS OF THE AIR come and NEST IN ITS BRANCHES." (Matthew 13:31, 32, Jesus quotes from Ezekiel 17:23; cf. Mark 4:30–32; Luke 13:18, 19).

Setting: By the Sea of Galilee. Because the religious leaders are rejecting His message, Jesus continues teaching the crowds with the Parable of the Leaven.

He spoke another parable to them, "The kingdom of heaven is like leaven, which a woman took and hid in three pecks of flour until it was all leavened" (Matthew 13:33).

Setting: By the Sea of Galilee. Because the religious leaders are rejecting His message, Jesus continues teaching the crowds with the Parable of the Hidden Treasure.

"The kingdom of heaven is like a treasure hidden in the field, which a man found and hid *again;* and from joy over it he goes and sells all that he has and buys that field" (Matthew 13:44).

Setting: By the Sea of Galilee. Jesus declares the Parable of the Pearl to the crowds.

"Again, the kingdom of heaven is like a merchant seeking fine pearls, and upon finding one pearl of great value, he went and sold all that he had and bought it" (Matthew 13:45, 46).

Setting: By the Sea of Galilee. Because the religious leaders are rejecting His message, Jesus continues teaching His disciples with the Parable of the Dragnet.

"Again, the kingdom of heaven is like a dragnet cast into the sea, and gathering *fish* of every kind; and when it was filled, they drew it up on the beach; and they sat down and gathered the good *fish* into containers, but the bad they threw away. So it will be at the end of the age; the angels will come forth and take out the wicked from among the righteous, and will throw them into the furnace of fire; in that place there will be weeping and gnashing of teeth. Have you understood all these things?" They said to Him, "Yes" (Matthew 13:47–51).

Setting: By the Sea of Galilee. Jesus teaches the Parable of the Head of a Household to His disciples.

And Jesus said to them, "Therefore every scribe who has become a disciple of the kingdom of heaven is like a head of a household, who brings out of his treasure things new and old" (Matthew 13:52).

Setting: Caesarea Philippi. Jesus responds to Simon Peter's declaration that He is the Christ, the Son of the living God.

And Jesus said to him, "Blessed are you, Simon Barjona, because flesh and blood did not reveal *this* to you, but My Father who is in heaven. I also say to you that you are Peter, and upon this rock I will build My church; and the gates of Hades will not overpower it. I will give you the keys of the kingdom of heaven; and whatever you bind on earth shall have been bound in heaven, and whatever you loose on earth shall have been loosed in heaven" (Matthew 16:17–19; cf. Matthew 18:18; Mark 8:29; Luke 9:20).

Setting: Capernaum of Galilee. Jesus answers His disciples' question about greatness, or rank, in the kingdom of heaven.

And He called a child to Himself and set him before them, and said, "Truly I say to you, unless you are converted and become like children, you will not enter the kingdom of heaven. Whoever then humbles himself as this child, he is the greatest in the kingdom of heaven. And whoever receives one such child in My name receives Me; but whoever causes one of these little ones who believe in Me to stumble, it would be better for him to have a heavy millstone hung around his neck, and to be drowned in the depth of the sea." (Matthew 18:2–6; cf. Matthew 19:14; Mark 9:33–37, 42; Luke 9:47, 48; Luke 17:1, 2).

Setting: Capernaum of Galilee. Jesus illustrates forgiveness after Peter asks Him if forgiving someone seven times who has sinned against him is adequate.

"For this reason the kingdom of heaven may be compared to a king who wished to settle accounts with his slaves. When he had begun to settle *them,* one who owed him ten thousand talents was brought to him. But since he did not have *the means* to repay, his lord commanded him to be sold, along with his wife and children and all that he had, and repayment to be made. So the slave fell *to the ground* and prostrated himself before him, saying, 'Have patience with me and I will repay you everything.' And the lord of that slave felt compassion and released him and forgave him the debt. But that slave went out and found one of his fellow slaves who owed him a hundred denarii; and he seized him and *began* to choke *him,* saying, 'Pay back what you owe.' So his fellow slave fell *to the ground* and *began* to plead with him, saying, 'Have patience with me and I will repay you.' But he was unwilling and went and threw him in prison until he should pay back what was owed. So when his fellow slaves saw what had happened, they were deeply grieved and came and reported to their lord all that had happened. Then summoning him, his lord said to him, 'You wicked slave, I forgave you all that debt because you pleaded with me. Should you not also have had mercy on your fellow slave, in the same way that I had mercy on you?' And his lord, moved with anger, handed him over to the torturers until he should repay all that was owed him. My heavenly Father will also do the same to you, if each of you does not forgive his brother from your heart" (Matthew 18:23–35; cf. Matthew 6:12, 14, 15; Luke 7:42; see Matthew 25:19–28).

Setting: Judea beyond the Jordan (Perea). After responding to the Pharisees' question about Moses' command regarding a certificate of divorce, Jesus answers a private question from His disciples.

But He said to them, "Not all men *can* accept this statement, but *only* those to whom it has been given. For there are eunuchs who were born that way from their mother's womb; and there are eunuchs who were made eunuchs by men; and there are *also* eunuchs who made themselves eunuchs for the sake of the kingdom of heaven. He who is able to accept *this,* let him accept *it*" (Matthew 19:11, 12; cf. 1 Corinthians 7:7).

Setting: Judea beyond the Jordan (Perea). Jesus shows His love for children after His disciples rebuke some children who want Jesus' blessing.

But Jesus said, "Let the children alone, and do not hinder them from coming to Me; for the kingdom of heaven belongs to such as these" (Matthew 19:14; cf. Mark 10:13–16; Luke 18:15–17; see Matthew 18:3; 19:13, 15).

Setting: Judea beyond the Jordan (Perea). Jesus comments to His disciples about the rich, young ruler who asks how he might obtain eternal life but rejects Jesus' instruction to sell his possessions and give the proceeds to the poor.

And Jesus said to His disciples, "Truly I say to you, it is hard for a rich man to enter the kingdom of heaven. Again, I say to you, it is easier for a camel to go through the eye of a needle, than for a rich man to enter the kingdom of God" (Matthew 19:23, 24; cf. Matthew 13:22; Mark 10:23–25; Luke 18:24).

Setting: Judea beyond the Jordan (Perea). Jesus illustrates the kingdom of heaven to His disciples through the story of laborers in the vineyard.

"For the kingdom of heaven is like a landowner who went out early in the morning to hire laborers for his vineyard. When he had agreed with the laborers for a denarius for the day, he sent them into his vineyard. And he went out about the third hour and saw others standing idle in the market place; and to those he said,' You also go into the vineyard, and whatever is right I will give you.' And *so* they went. Again he went out about the sixth and the ninth hour, and did the same thing. And about the eleventh *hour* he went out and found others standing *around;* and he said to them, 'Why have you been standing idle here all day long?' They said to him, 'Because no one hired us.' He said to them, 'You go into the vineyard too.' When evening came, the owner of the vineyard said to his foreman, 'Call the laborers and pay them their wages, beginning with the last *group* to the first.' When those *hired* about the eleventh hour came, each one received a denarius. When those *hired* first came, they thought that they would receive more; but each of them also received a denarius. When they received it, they grumbled at the landowner, saying, 'These last men have worked *only* one hour, and you have made them equal to us who have borne the burden and the scorching heat of the day.' But he answered and said to one of them, 'Friend, I am doing you no wrong; did you not agree with me for a denarius? Take what is yours and go, but I wish to give to this last man the same as to you. It is not lawful for me to do what I wish with what is my own? Or is your eye envious because I am generous?' So the last shall be first, and the first last" (Matthew 20:1–16; cf. Matthew 19:30).

Setting: The temple in Jerusalem. Jesus speaks another parable to the chief priests and elders after they question His authority.

Jesus spoke to them again in parables, saying, "The kingdom of heaven may be compared to a king who gave a wedding feast for his son. And he sent out his slaves to call those who had been invited to the wedding feast, and they were unwilling to come. Again he sent out other slaves saying, 'Tell those who have been invited, "Behold, I have prepared my dinner; my oxen and my fattened livestock are *all* butchered and everything is ready; come to the wedding feast." But they paid no attention and went their way, one to his own farm, another to his business, and the rest seized his slaves and mistreated them and killed them. But the king was enraged, and he sent his armies and destroyed those murderers and set their city on fire. Then he said to his slaves, 'The wedding is ready, but those who were invited were not worthy. 'Go therefore to the main highways, and as many as you find *there,* invite to the wedding feast.' Those slaves went out into the streets and gathered together all they found, both evil and good; and the wedding hall was filled with dinner guests. But when the king came in to look over the dinner guests, he saw a man there who was not dressed in wedding clothes, and he said to him, 'Friend, how did you come in here without wedding clothes?' And the man was speechless. Then the king said to the servants, 'Bind him hand and foot, and throw him into the outer darkness; in that place there will be weeping and gnashing of teeth.' For many are called, but few *are* chosen" (Matthew 22:1–14; cf. Matthew 8:11, 12).

Setting: The temple in Jerusalem. After the Jewish religious leaders test Him with questions, Jesus pronounces the first of eight woes on them in front of the crowds and His disciples.

"But woe to you, scribes and Pharisees, hypocrites, because you shut off the kingdom of heaven from people; for you do not enter in yourselves, nor do you allow those who are entering to go in" (Matthew 23:13; cf. Luke 11:52).

Setting: The Mount of Olives, just east of Jerusalem. During His discourse, after answering His disciples' questions as to when the temple will be destroyed and Jerusalem overrun, along with the signs of His coming and the end of the age, Jesus reemphasizes to His disciples that they should be on the alert for His return.

"Then the kingdom of heaven will be comparable to ten virgins, who took their lamps and went out to meet the bridegroom. Five of them were foolish, and five were prudent. For when the foolish took their lamps, they took no oil with them, but the prudent took oil in flasks along with their lamps. Now while the bridegroom was delaying, they all got drowsy and *began* to sleep. But at midnight there was a shout, 'Behold, the bridegroom! Come out to meet *him.*' Then all those virgins rose and trimmed their lamps. The foolish said to the prudent, 'Give us some of your oil, for our lamps are going out.' But the prudent answered, 'No, there will not be enough for us and you *too;* go instead to the dealers and buy *some* for yourselves.' And while they were going away to make the purchase, the bridegroom came, and those who were ready went in with him to the wedding feast; and the door was shut. Later the other virgins also came, saying, 'Lord, lord, open up for us.' But he answered, 'Truly I say to you, I do not know you.' Be on the alert then, for you do not know the day nor the hour" (Matthew 25:1–13; cf. Matthew 24:42; Luke 12:35; see Matthew 7:21, 24).

KINGDOM OF THEIR FATHER (Listed under FATHER, KINGDOM OF THEIR)

KINGDOM PRIVILEGE (Listed under PRIVILEGE, KINGDOM)

KINGS (Also see KING; and KINGDOM)

Setting: Galilee. After His disciples observe His own ministry, Jesus summons and specifically instructs them about the upcoming hardships of their ministry to the people of Israel.

"Behold, I send you out as sheep in the midst of wolves; so be shrewd as serpents and innocent as doves. But beware of men, for they will hand you over to *the* courts and scourge you in their synagogues; and you will even be brought before governors and kings for My sake, as a testimony to them and to the Gentiles. But when they hand you over, do not worry about how or what you are to say; for it will be given you in that hour what you are to say. For it is not you who speak, but *it* is the Spirit of your Father who speaks in you" (Matthew 10:16–20; cf. Luke 10:3).

Setting: Capernaum of Galilee. Jesus pays the two-drachma temple tax for Peter and Himself in a miraculous manner.

He said, "Yes." And when he came into the house, Jesus spoke to him first, saying, "What do you think, Simon? From whom do the kings of the earth collect customs or poll-tax, from their sons or from strangers?" When Peter said, "From strangers," Jesus said to him, "Then the sons are exempt. However, so that we do not offend them, go to the sea and throw in a hook, and take the first fish that comes up; and when you open its mouth, you will find a shekel. Take that and give it to them for you and Me" (Matthew 17:25–27; see Exodus 30:11–16; Matthew 17:24; 22:17–19; Romans 13:7).

Setting: On the Mount of Olives, east of the temple in Jerusalem. After predicting the temple's destruction, Jesus responds during His Olivet Discourse to questions from Peter, James, John, and Andrew about other future events.

And Jesus began to say to them, "See to it that no one misleads you. Many will come in My name, saying, 'I am *He!*' and will mislead many. When you hear of wars and rumors of wars, do not be frightened; *those things* must take place; but *that is* not yet the end. For nation will rise up against nation, and kingdom against kingdom; there will be earthquakes in various places; there will *also be* famines. These things are *merely* the beginning of birth pangs. But be on your guard; for they will deliver you to *the* courts, and you will be flogged in *the* synagogues, and you will stand before governors and kings for My sake, as a testimony to them. The gospel must first be preached to all the nations. When they arrest you and hand you over, do not worry beforehand about what you are to say, but say whatever is given you in that hour; for it is not you who speak, but *it is* the Holy Spirit. Brother will betray brother to death, and a father *his* child; and children will rise up against parents and have them put to death. You will be hated by all because of My name, but the one who endures to the end, he will be saved" (Mark 13:5–13; cf. Matthew 24:4–14; Luke 21:7–19; see Matthew 10:17–22).

Setting: On the way from Galilee to Jerusalem. After responding to a report from the seventy sent out in pairs to every place He Himself will soon visit, the Lord addresses His disciples in private.

Turning to the disciples, He said privately, "Blessed *are* the eyes which see the things you see, for I say to you, that many prophets and kings wished to see the things you see, and did not see *them*, and to hear the things which you hear, and did not hear *them*" (Luke 10:23, 24; cf. Matthew 13:16, 17; see Luke 10:17).

Setting: On the Mount of Olives, east of the temple in Jerusalem. After ministering in the temple a few days before His crucifixion, and giving His disciples more details regarding the temple's future destruction, Jesus elaborates during His Olivet Discourse about things to come.

Then He continued by saying to them, "Nation will rise against nation and kingdom against kingdom, and there will be great earthquakes, and in various places plagues and famines; and there will be terrors and great signs from heaven. But before all these things, they will lay their hands on you and will persecute you, delivering you to the synagogues and prisons, bringing you before kings and governors for My name's sake. It will lead to an opportunity for your testimony. So make up your minds not to prepare beforehand to defend yourselves; for I will give you utterance and wisdom which none of your opponents will be able to resist or refute. But you will be betrayed even by parents and brothers and relatives and friends, and they will put *some* of you to death, and you will be hated by all because of My name. Yet not a hair of your head will perish. By your endurance you will gain your lives" (Luke 21:10–19; cf. Matthew 10:19–22; 24:7–14; Mark 13:8–13).

Setting: An upper room in Jerusalem. During the Feast of Unleavened Bread (Passover) just before Jesus' crucifixion, while Jesus celebrates the Passover meal with His disciples and institutes the Lord's Supper, the disciples argue over who is the greatest among them.

And He said to them, "The kings of the Gentiles lord it over them; and those who have authority over them are called 'Benefactors.' But *it is* not this way with you, but the one who is the greatest among you must become like the youngest, and the leader like a servant. For who is greater, the one who reclines *at the table* or the one who serves? Is it not the one who reclines *at the table?* But I am among you as the one who serves" (Luke 22:25–27; cf. Matthew 20:25–28; 23:11; Mark 10:42–45).

Setting: Damascus. Luke, writing in Acts, describes the reluctance of Ananias, one of Jesus' disciples, to locate Saul of Tarsus (a known enemy of the church) in order to restore Saul's vision.

But the Lord said to him, "Go, for he is a chosen instrument of Mine, to bear My name before the Gentiles and kings and the sons of Israel; for I will show him how much he must suffer for My name's sake" (Acts 9:15, 16; see Acts 13:2; 20:22–24).

KINGS OF THE EARTH (Listed under EARTH, KINGS OF THE; also see KING and KINGS)

KINSHIP (See RELATIVES)

KISS

Setting: Galilee. After Jesus praises John the Baptist to the crowds, Simon, a Pharisee, invites Him to dinner. A sinful woman anoints His feet with perfume, prompting the Lord to instruct His host about forgiveness.

Turning toward the woman, He said to Simon, "Do you see this woman? I entered your house; you gave Me no water for My feet, but she has wet My feet with her tears and wiped them with her hair. You gave Me no kiss; but she, since the time I came in, has not ceased to kiss My feet. You did not anoint My head with oil, but she anointed My feet with perfume. For this reason I say to you, her sins, which are many, have been forgiven, for she loved much; but he who is forgiven little, loves little." Then He said to her, "Your sins have been forgiven." Those who were reclining *at the table* with Him began to say to themselves, "Who is this *man* who even forgives sins?" And He said to the woman, "Your faith has saved you; go in peace" (Luke 7:44–50; see Matthew 9:2; Mark 5:34; Luke 5:21).

[KISS from kissed]
Setting: On the way from Galilee to Jerusalem. Jesus conveys the illustration of the prodigal son because the Pharisees and scribes complain He associates with tax collectors and sinners.

And He said, "A man had two sons. The younger of them said to his father, 'Father, give me the share of the estate that falls to me.' So he divided his wealth between them. And not many days later, the younger son gathered everything together and went on a journey into a distant country, and there he squandered his estate with loose living. Now when he had spent everything, a severe famine occurred in that country, and he began to be impoverished. So he went and hired himself out to one of the citizens of that country, and he sent him into his fields to feed swine. And he would have gladly filled his stomach with the pods that the swine were eating, and no one was giving *anything* to him. But when he came to his senses, he said, 'How many of my father's hired men have more than enough bread, but I am dying here with hunger! I will get up and go to my father, and will say to him, "Father, I have sinned against heaven, and in your sight; I am no longer worthy to be called your son; make me as one of your hired men."'

So he got up and came to his father. But while he was still a long way off, his father saw him and felt compassion *for him,* and ran and embraced him and kissed him. And the son said to him, "Father, I have sinned against heaven and in your sight; I am no longer worthy to be called your son.' But the father said to his slaves, 'Quickly bring out the best robe and put it on him, and put a ring on his hand and sandals on his feet; and bring the fattened calf, kill it, and let us eat and celebrate; for this son of mine was dead and has come to life again; he was lost and has been found.' And they began to celebrate. Now his older son was in the field, when he came and approached the house, he heard music and dancing. And he summoned one of the servants and *began* inquiring what these things could be. And he said to him, 'Your brother has come, and your father has killed the fattened calf because he has received him back safe and sound.' But he became angry and was not willing to go in; and his father came out and *began* pleading with him. But he answered and said to his father, 'Look! For so many years I have been serving you and I have never neglected a command of yours; and *yet* you have never given me a young goat, so that I might celebrate with my friends; but when this son of yours came, who has devoured your wealth with prostitutes, you killed the fattened calf for him.' And he said to him, 'Son, you have always been with me, and all that is mine is yours. But we had to celebrate and rejoice, for this brother of yours was dead and *has begun* to live, and was lost and has been found'" (Luke 15:11–32; see Proverbs 29:2; Luke 15:1, 2).

Setting: On the Mount of Olives, east of the temple in Jerusalem. With His crucifixion imminent, after Jesus prays, with His disciples nearby, Judas betrays the Lord to a crowd of His enemies with a kiss.

But Jesus said to him, "Judas, are you betraying the Son of Man with a kiss?" (Luke 22:48; see Matthew 26:48, 49; Mark 14:44, 45; John 18:2–8).

KNOCK/KNOCKS (Also see DOOR)

Setting: Galilee. During the early part of His ministry, Jesus preaches the Sermon on the Mount to His disciples and the multitudes.

"Ask, and it will be given to you; seek, and you will find; knock, and it will be opened to you. For everyone who asks receives, and he who seeks finds, and to him who knocks it will be opened. Or what man is there among you who, when his son asks for a loaf, will give him a stone? Or if he asks for a fish, he will not give him a snake, will he? If you then, being evil, know how to give good gifts to your children, how much more will your Father who is in heaven give what is good to those who ask Him! In everything, therefore, treat people the same way you want them to treat you, for this is the Law and the Prophets" (Matthew 7:7–12; cf. Matthew 22:40; Luke 6:31; 11:9–13; see Psalm 84:11).

Setting: On the way from Galilee to Jerusalem. After revealing to His disciples how to pray, Jesus illustrates persistence in prayer.

Then He said to them, "Suppose one of you has a friend, and goes to him at midnight and says to him, 'Friend, lend me three loaves; for a friend of mine has come to me from a journey, and I have nothing to set before him'; and from inside he answers and says, 'Do not bother me; the door has already been shut and my children and I are in bed; I cannot get up and give you *anything.*' I tell you, even though he will not get up and give him *anything* because he is his friend, yet because of his persistence he will get up and give him as much as he needs. So I say to you, ask, and it will be given to you; seek, and you will find; knock, and it will be opened to you. For everyone who asks, receives; and he who seeks, finds; and to him who knocks, it will be opened" (Luke 11:5–10; cf. Matthew 7: 7, 8; see Luke 18:1–5).

Setting: On the way from Galilee to Jerusalem. After giving a parable about riches and greed, Jesus uses another to challenge the crowd and His disciples to be ready for His return.

"Be dressed in readiness, and *keep* your lamps lit. Be like men who are waiting for their master when he returns from the wedding feast, so that they may immediately open *the door* to him when he comes and knocks. Blessed are those slaves whom the master will find on the alert when he comes; truly I say to you, that he will gird himself *to serve,* and have them recline *at the table,* and will come up and wait on them. Whether he comes in the second watch, or even in the third and finds *them* so, blessed are those *slaves.* But be sure of this, that if the head of the house had known at what hour the thief was coming, he would not have allowed his house to be broken into. You too, be ready; for the Son of Man is coming at an hour that you do not expect"

(Luke 12:35–40; cf. Matthew 24:42–44; see Mark 13:33; Ephesians 6:14).

Setting: On the way from Galilee to Jerusalem. While teaching in the cities and villages, Jesus responds to a question about who is saved.

And someone said to Him, "Lord, are here *just* a few who are being saved?" And He said to them, "Strive to enter through the narrow door; for many, I tell you, will seek to enter and will not be able. Once the head of the house gets up and shuts the door, and you begin to stand outside and knock on the door, saying, 'Lord, open up to us!' then He will answer and say to you, 'I do not know where you are from.' Then you will begin to say, 'We ate and drank in Your presence, and You taught in our streets'; and He will say, 'I tell you, I do not know where you are from; DEPART FROM ME, ALL YOU EVILDOERS.' In that place there will be weeping and gnashing of teeth when you see Abraham and Isaac and Jacob and all the prophets in the kingdom of God, but you yourselves being thrown out. And they will come from east and west and from north and south, and will recline *at the table* in the kingdom of God. And behold, *some* are last who will be first and *some* are first who will be last" (Luke 13:23–30, Jesus quotes from Psalm 6:8; cf. Matthew 7:13, 23; 8:11, 12; see Matthew 19:30; Luke 3:8).

Setting: On the island of Patmos (in the Aegean Sea about fifty miles southwest of Ephesus in modern Turkey). On the Lord's Day (Sunday), about fifty years after Jesus' resurrection, the disciple John encounters the Lord Jesus Christ, who communicates a new revelation for the apostle to record for the church in Laodicea and to six other churches in Asia.

"To the angel of the church in Laodicea write: The Amen, the faithful and true Witness, the Beginning of the creation of God, says this: 'I know your deeds, that you are neither cold nor hot; I wish that you were cold or hot. So because you are lukewarm, and neither hot nor cold, I will spit you out of My mouth. Because you say, "I am rich, and have become wealthy, and have need of nothing," and you do not know that you are wretched and miserable and poor and blind and naked, I advise you to buy from Me gold refined by fire so that you may become rich, and white garments so that you may clothe yourself, and *that* the shame of your nakedness will not be revealed; and eye salve to anoint your eyes so that you may see. Those whom I love, I reprove and discipline; therefore be zealous and repent. Behold, I stand at the door and knock; if anyone hears My voice and opens the door, I will come in to him and will dine with him, and he with Me. He who overcomes, I will grant to him to sit down with Me on My throne, as I also overcame and sat down with My Father on His throne. He who has an ear, let him hear what the Spirit says to the churches'" (Revelation 3:14–22; see Proverbs 3:12; Hosea 12:8; John 14:23; 16:33).

KNOCKS (See KNOCK)

KNOWING GOD (Listed under GOD, KNOWING)

KNOWLEDGE (Specifics pertaining to God are listed under OMNISCIENCE, GOD'S; and OMNISCIENCE, JESUS'; also see MIND READING)

[KNOWLEDGE from know]
Setting: Galilee. During the early part of His ministry, Jesus preaches the Sermon on the Mount to His disciples and the multitudes.

"So when you give to the poor, do not sound a trumpet before you, as the hypocrites do in the synagogues and in the streets, so that they may be honored by men. Truly I say to you, they have their reward in full. But when you give to the poor, do not let your left hand know what your right hand is doing, so that your giving will be in secret; and your Father who sees *what is done* in secret will reward you" (Matthew 6:2–4; see Jeremiah 17:10; Matthew 6:16).

[KNOWLEDGE from know]
Setting: Galilee. During the early part of His ministry, Jesus preaches the Sermon on the Mount to His disciples and the multitudes.

"Ask, and it will be given to you; seek, and you will find; knock, and it will be opened to you. For everyone who asks receives, and he who seeks finds, and to him who knocks it will be opened. Or what man is there among you who, when his son asks for a loaf, will give him a stone? Or if he asks for a fish, he will not give him a snake, will he? If you then, being evil, know how to give good gifts to your children, how much more will your Father who is in heaven give what is good to those who ask Him! In everything, therefore, treat people the same way you want them to treat you, for this is the Law and the Prophets" (Matthew 7:7–12; cf. Matthew 22:40; Luke 6:31; 11:9–13; see Psalm 84:11).

[KNOWLEDGE from know]
Setting: Galilee. During the early part of His ministry, Jesus preaches the Sermon on the Mount to His disciples and the multitudes.

"Beware of the false prophets, who come to you in sheep's clothing, but inwardly are ravenous wolves. You will know them by their fruits. Grapes are not gathered from *bushes* nor figs from thistles, are they? So every good tree bears good fruit, but the bad tree bears bad fruit. A good tree cannot produce bad fruit, nor can a bad tree produce good fruit. Every tree that does not bear good fruit is cut down and thrown into the fire. So then, you will know them by their fruits" (Matthew 7:15–20; cf. Matthew 3:10; 12:33, 35; 24:11, 24; Luke 6:43–44).

[KNOWLEDGE from knew]
Setting: Galilee. During the early part of His ministry, Jesus preaches the Sermon on the Mount to His disciples and the multitudes.

"Not everyone who says to Me, 'Lord, Lord,' will enter the kingdom of heaven, but he who does the will of My Father who is in heaven *will enter.* Many will say to Me on that day, 'Lord, Lord, did we not prophesy in Your name, and in Your name cast out demons, and in Your name perform many miracles?' And then I will declare to them, 'I never knew you, DEPART FROM ME, YOU WHO PRACTICE LAWLESSNESS'" (Matthew 7:21–23, Jesus quotes from Psalm 6:8; cf. Matthew 25:11–13; see Luke 6:46).

[KNOWLEDGE from know]
Setting: Capernaum near the Sea of Galilee. After Jesus heals a paralytic and forgives him of his sins in front of crowds, some scribes accuse the Lord of blasphemy.

And they brought to Him a paralytic lying on a bed. Seeing their faith, Jesus said to the paralytic, "Take courage, son; your sins are forgiven." And some scribes said to themselves. "This *fellow* blasphemes." And Jesus knowing their thoughts said, "Why are you thinking evil in your hearts? Which is easier to say, 'Your sins are forgiven,' or to say, 'Get up, and walk'? But so that you may know that the Son of Man has authority on earth to forgive sins"—then He said to the paralytic, "Get up, pick up your bed and go home" (Matthew 9:2–6; cf. Mark 2:3–12; Luke 5:17–26).

[KNOWLEDGE from knows]
Setting: Somewhere in Galilee. After healing a woman with internal bleeding and resuscitating a synagogue official's daughter from the dead, Jesus gives sight to two blind men.

When He entered the house, the blind men came up to Him, and Jesus said to them, "Do you believe that I am able to do this?" They said to Him, "Yes, Lord." Then He touched their eyes saying, "It shall be done for you according to your faith." And their eyes were opened. And Jesus sternly warned them: "See that no one knows *about this!*" (Matthew 9:28–30).

[KNOWLEDGE from known]
Setting: Galilee. After His disciples observe His ministry, Jesus summons and specifically instructs them about their ministry ahead involving true discipleship.

"Therefore do not fear them, for there is nothing concealed that will not be revealed, or hidden that will not be known. What I tell you in the darkness, speak in the light; and what you hear *whispered* in your ear, proclaim upon the housetops. Do not fear those who kill the body but are unable to kill the soul; but rather fear Him who is able to destroy both soul and body in hell"

(Matthew 10:26–28; cf. Mark 4:22; Luke 12:3; see Hebrews 10:31).

[KNOWLEDGE from knows and know]
Setting: Galilee. After pronouncing woes against unrepentant cities as He teaches and preaches, Jesus prays a thanksgiving prayer to His Father in heaven.

At that time Jesus said, "I praise You, Father, Lord of heaven and earth, that you have hidden these things from *the* wise and intelligent and have revealed them to infants. Yes, Father, for this way was well-pleasing in Your sight. All things have been handed over to Me by My Father; and no one knows the Son except the Father; nor does anyone know the Father except the Son, and anyone to whom the Son wills to reveal *Him*" (Matthew 11:25–27; cf. Luke 10:21, 22).

[KNOWLEDGE from known]
Setting: Galilee. Jesus responds to the Pharisees' objection to His disciples' picking grain from the fields on the Sabbath.

But He said to them, "Have you not read what David did when he became hungry, he and his companions, how they entered the house of God, and ate the consecrated bread, which was not lawful for him to eat nor for those with him, but for the priests alone? Or, have you not read in the Law, that on the Sabbath the priests in the temple break the Sabbath and are innocent? But I say to you that something greater than the temple is here. But if you had known what this means, 'I DESIRE COMPASSION, AND NOT A SACRIFICE,' you would not have condemned the innocent. For the Son of Man is Lord of the Sabbath" (Matthew 12:3–8, Jesus quotes from Hosea 6:6; cf. Mark 2:25–28; Luke 6:3–5; see 1 Samuel 21:6).

[KNOWLEDGE from known]
Setting: Galilee. After He heals a blind, mute, demon-possessed man, the Pharisees accuse Jesus in front of crowds of being a worker of Satan.

"Either make the tree good and its fruit good, or make the tree bad and its fruit bad; for the tree is known by its fruit. You brood of vipers, how can you, being evil, speak what is good? For the mouth speaks out of that which fills the heart. The good man brings out of *his* good treasure what is good; and the evil man brings out of *his* evil treasure what is evil. But I tell you that every careless word that people speak, they shall give an accounting for it in the day of judgment. For by your words you will be justified, and by your words you will be condemned" (Matthew 12:33–37; cf. Matthew 3:7; 7:16–18).

[KNOWLEDGE from know]
Setting: By the Sea of Galilee. Jesus responds to His disciples' questions about the Parable of the Sower, which He has just taught from a boat.

Jesus answered them, "To you it has been granted to know the mysteries of the kingdom of heaven, but to them it has not been granted. For whoever has, to him *more* shall be given, and he will have an abundance; but whoever does not have, even what he has shall be taken away from him. Therefore, I speak to them in parables; because while seeing they do not see, and while hearing they do not hear, nor do they understand. In their case the prophecy of Isaiah is being fulfilled, which says, 'YOU WILL KEEP ON HEARING, BUT WILL NOT UNDERSTAND; YOU WILL KEEP ON SEEING, BUT WILL NOT PERCEIVE; FOR THE HEART OF THIS PEOPLE HAS BECOME DULL, WITH THEIR EARS THEY SCARCELY HEAR, AND THEY HAVE CLOSED THEIR EYES, OTHERWISE THEYWOULD SEE WITH THEIR EYES, HEAR WITH THEIR EARS, AND UNDERSTAND WITH THEIR HEART AND RETURN, AND I WOULD HEAL THEM.' But blessed are your eyes, because they see; and your ears, because they hear. For truly I say to you that many prophets and righteous men desired to see what you see, and did not see *it,* and to hear what you hear, and did not hear *it*" (Matthew 13:11–17, Jesus quotes from Isaiah 6:9–10; cf. Matthew 25:29; Mark 4:11–13; Luke 8:10; see Deuteronomy 29:4; John 8:56).

[KNOWLEDGE from know]
Setting: Magadan of Galilee. The Pharisees and Sadducees reject Jesus' message, then continue to test Him by asking for a sign from heaven.

But He replied to them, "When it is evening, you say, '*It will be* fair weather, for the sky is red.' And in the morning, '*There will* be a storm today, for the sky is red and threatening.' Do you know how to discern the appearance of the sky, but cannot *discern* the signs of the times? An evil and adulterous generation seeks after a sign; and a sign will not be given it, except the sign of Jonah." And He left them and went away (Matthew 16:2–4; cf. Matthew 12:39; Mark 8:12; Luke 12:54–56).

[KNOWLEDGE from know]
Setting: On the way to Jerusalem. The mother of disciples James and John asks Jesus to make her sons exalted rulers with Him in His coming kingdom.

And He said to her, "What do you wish?" She said to Him, 'Command that in Your kingdom these two sons of mine may sit one on Your right and one on Your left.' But Jesus answered, "You do not know what you are asking. Are you able to drink the cup that I am about to drink?" They said to Him, 'We are able.' He said to them, "My cup you shall drink; but to sit on My right and on *My* left, this is not Mine to give, but it is for those for whom it has been prepared by My Father" (Matthew 20:21–23; cf. Mark 10:35–40; see Matthew 19:28; Acts 12:2).

[KNOWLEDGE from know]
Setting: On the way to Jerusalem, where Jesus will die on the cross. Jesus teaches His disciples about true greatness after the mother of James and John, the sons of Zebedee, asks Him to make her sons exalted rulers with Him in His coming kingdom.

But Jesus called them to Himself and said, "You know that the rulers of the Gentiles lord it over them, and *their* great men exercise authority over them. It is not this way among you, but whoever wishes to become great among you shall be your servant, and whoever wishes to be first among you shall be your slave; just as the Son of Man did not come to be served, but to serve, and to give His life a ransom for many" (Matthew 20:25–28; cf. Matthew 23:11; 26:28; Mark 10:42–45).

[KNOWLEDGE from know and knows]
Setting: The Mount of Olives, just east of Jerusalem. During His discourse, after answering His disciples' questions as to when the temple will be destroyed and Jerusalem overrun, along with the signs of His coming and the end of the age, Jesus teaches them the Parable of the Fig Tree.

"Now learn the parable from the fig tree: when its branch has already become tender and puts forth its leaves, you know that summer is near; so, you too, when you see all these things, recognize that He is near, *right* at the door. Truly, I say to you, this generation will not pass away until all these things take place. Heaven and earth will pass away, but My words will not pass away. But of that day and hour no one knows, not even the angels of heaven, nor the Son, but the Father alone. For the coming of the Son of Man will be just like the days of Noah. For as in those days before the flood they were eating and drinking, marrying and giving in marriage, until the day that Noah entered the ark, and they did not understand until the flood came and took them all away; so will the coming of the Son of Man be. Then there will be two men in the field; one will be taken and one will be left. Two women *will be* grinding at the mill; one will be taken and one will be left" (Matthew 24:32–41; cf. Mark 13:28–32; Luke 17:34–36; 21:28–33; see Genesis 6:5; 7:7; Matthew 5:18; 10:23; James 5:9).

[KNOWLEDGE from know and known]
Setting: The Mount of Olives, just east of Jerusalem. During His discourse, after answering His disciples' questions as to when the temple will be destroyed and Jerusalem overrun, along with the signs of His coming and the end of the age, Jesus reemphasizes to the disciples that they should be on the alert for His return.

"Therefore be on the alert, for you do not know which day your Lord is coming. But be sure of this, that if the head of the house had known at what time of the night the thief was coming, he would have been on the alert and would not have allowed his house to be broken into. For this reason you also must be ready; for the Son of Man is coming at an hour when you do not think *He will*. Who then is the faithful and sensible slave whom his master put in charge of his household to give their food at the proper time? Blessed is that slave whom his master finds so doing when he comes. Truly I say to you that he will put him in charge of all his possessions. But if that evil slave says in his heart, 'My master is not coming for a long time,' and begins to beat his fellow slaves and eat and drink with drunkards; the master of that slave will come on a day when he does not expect *him* and at an hour which he does not know, and will cut him in pieces and assign him a place with the hypocrites; in that place there will be weeping and gnashing of teeth" (Matthew 24:42–51; cf. Mark 13:33–37; Luke 12:39–46; 21:34–36; see Matthew 8:11, 12; 25:21–23).

[KNOWLEDGE from know]
Setting: The Mount of Olives, just east of Jerusalem. During His discourse, after answering His disciples' questions as to when the temple will be destroyed and Jerusalem overrun, along with the signs of His coming and the end of the age, Jesus reemphasizes to the disciples that they should be on the alert for His return.

"Then the kingdom of heaven will be comparable to ten virgins, who took their lamps and went out to meet the bridegroom. Five of them were foolish, and five were prudent. For when the foolish took their lamps, they took no oil with them, but the prudent took oil in flasks along with their lamps. Now while the bridegroom was delaying, they all got drowsy and *began* to sleep. But at midnight there was a shout, 'Behold, the bridegroom! Come out to meet *him*.' Then all those virgins rose and trimmed their lamps. The foolish said to the prudent, 'Give us some of your oil, for our lamps are going out.' But the prudent answered, 'No, there will not be enough for us and you *too;* go instead to the dealers and buy *some* for yourselves.' And while they were going away to make the purchase, the bridegroom came, and those who were ready went in with him to the wedding feast; and the door was shut. Later the other virgins also came, saying, 'Lord, lord, open up for us.' But he answered, 'Truly I say to you, I do not know you.' Be on the alert then, for you do not know the day nor the hour" (Matthew 25:1–13; cf. Matthew 24:42; Luke 12:35; see Matthew 7:21, 24).

[KNOWLEDGE from knew]
Setting: The Mount of Olives, just east of Jerusalem. During His discourse, after answering His disciples' questions as to when the temple will be destroyed and Jerusalem overrun, along with the signs of His coming and the end of the age, Jesus reemphasizes to the disciples that they should be on the alert for His return.

"For *it is* just like a man *about* to go on a journey, who called his own slaves and entrusted his possessions to them. To one he gave five talents, to another, two, and to another, one, each according to his own ability; and he went on his journey. Immediately the one who had received the five talents went and traded with them, and gained five more talents. In the same manner the one who *had received* the two *talents* gained two more. But he who received the one *talent* went away, and dug a *hole* in the ground and hid his master's money. Now after a long time the master of those slaves came and settled accounts with them. The one who had received the five talents came up and brought five more talents, saying, 'Master, you entrusted five talents to me. See, I have gained five more talents.' His master said to him, 'Well done, good and faithful slave. You were faithful with a few things, I will put you in charge of many things; enter into the joy of your master.' Also the one who *had received* the two talents came up and said, 'Master, you entrusted two talents to me. See, I have gained two more talents.' His master said to him, 'Well done, good and faithful slave. You were faithful with a few things, I will put you in charge of many things; enter into the joy of your master.' And the one also who had received the one talent came up and said, 'Master, I knew you to be a hard man, reaping where you did not sow and gathering where you scattered no *seed.* And I was afraid, and went away and hid your talent in the ground. See, you have what is yours.' But his master answered and said to him, 'You wicked, lazy slave, you knew that I reap where I did not sow and gather where I scattered no *seed.* Then you ought to have put my money in the bank, and on my arrival I would have received my *money* back with interest. 'Therefore take away the talent from him, and give it to the one who has ten talents.' For to everyone who has, *more* shall be given, and he will have an abundance; but from the one who does not have, even what he does have shall be taken away. Throw out the worthless slave into the outer darkness; in that place there will be weeping and gnashing of teeth" (Matthew 25:14–30; cf. Matthew 8:12; 13:12; 24:45–47; see Matthew 18:23, 24; Luke 12:44).

[KNOWLEDGE from know]
Setting: On the Mount of Olives, just east of Jerusalem. During His discourse, after answering His disciples' questions as to when the temple will be destroyed and Jerusalem overrun, along with the signs of His coming and the end of the age, Jesus prophesies His crucifixion to His disciples.

When Jesus had finished all these words, He said to His disciples, "You know that after two days the Passover is coming, and the Son of Man is *to be* handed over for crucifixion" (Matthew 26:1, 2; see Mark 14:1, 2; Luke 22:1, 2).

[KNOWLEDGE from know]
Setting: Capernaum. When Jesus heals a paralytic man and forgives his sins, some scribes believe He commits blasphemy.

Immediately Jesus, aware in His spirit that they were reasoning that way within themselves, said to them, "Why are you reasoning about these things in your hearts? Which is easier, to say to the paralytic, 'Your sins are forgiven'; or to say, 'Get up, and pick up your pallet and walk'? "But so that you may know that the Son of Man has authority on earth to forgive sins"—He said to the paralytic, "I say to you, get up, pick up your pallet and go home" (Mark 2:8–11; cf. Matthew 9:4–7; Luke 5:21–24).

[KNOWLEDGE from know]
Setting: Galilee. Following His explanation of the Parable of the Sower to His disciples, Jesus conveys the Parable of the Seed.

And He was saying, "The kingdom of God is like a man who casts seed upon the soil; and he goes to bed at night and gets up by day, and the seed sprouts and grows—how, he himself does not know. The soil produces crops by itself; first the blade, then the head, then the mature grain in the head. But when the crop permits, he immediately puts in the sickle, because the harvest has come" (Mark 4:26–29; see Joel 3:13).

[KNOWLEDGE from know]
Setting: Judea beyond the Jordan (Perea). After demonstrating to His disciples the importance of little children, Jesus encounters a rich man seeking eternal life.

And Jesus said to him, "Why do you call Me good? No one is good except God alone. You know the commandments, 'DO NOT MURDER, DO NOT COMMIT ADULTERY, DO NOT STEAL, DO NOT BEAR FALSE WITNESS, Do not defraud, HONOR YOUR FATHER AND MOTHER.'" And he said to Him, "Teacher, I have kept all these things from my youth up." Looking at him, Jesus felt a love for him and said to him, "One thing you lack: go and sell all you possess and give to the poor, and you will have treasure in heaven; and come, follow Me" (Mark 10:18–21; Jesus quotes from Exodus 20:12–16; cf. Matthew 19:16–22; Luke 18:18–24; see Matthew 6:20).

[KNOWLEDGE from know]
Setting: On the road to Jerusalem. After Jesus prophesies His persecution, death, and resurrection, James and John ask Him for special honor and privileges in His coming kingdom.

And He said to them, "What do you want Me to do for you?" They said to Him, "Grant that we may sit, one on Your right and one on *Your* left, in Your glory." But Jesus said to them, "You do not know what you are asking. Are you able to drink the cup that I drink, or to be baptized with the baptism with which I am baptized?" They said to Him, "We are able." And Jesus said to them, "The cup that I drink you shall drink; and you shall be baptized with the baptism with which I am baptized. But to sit on My right or on *My* left, this is not Mine to give; but it is for those for whom it has been prepared" (Mark 10:36–40; cf. Matthew 20:20–23; see Matthew 19:28; Acts 12:2).

[KNOWLEDGE from know]
Setting: On the road to Jerusalem. When James and John ask Jesus for special honor and privileges in His kingdom, His other disciples become angry. Jesus uses this moment to teach them about servanthood.

Calling them to Himself, Jesus said to them, "You know that those who are recognized as rulers of the Gentiles lord it over them; and their great men exercise authority over them. But it is not this way among you, but whoever wishes to become great among you shall be your servant; and whoever wishes to be first among you shall be slave of all. For even the Son of Man did not come to be served, but to serve, and to give His life a ransom for many" (Mark 10:42–45; cf. Matthew 20:25–28).

[KNOWLEDGE from know and knows]
Setting: On the Mount of Olives, east of the temple in Jerusalem. After prophesying the temple's destruction, Jesus responds during His Olivet Discourse to questions from Peter, James, John, and Andrew about other future events.

"Now learn the parable from the fig tree: when its branch has already become tender and puts forth its leaves, you know that summer is near. Even so, you too, when you see these things happening, recognize that He is near, *right* at the door. Truly I say to you, this generation will not pass away until all these things take place. Heaven and earth will pass away, but My words will not pass away. But of the day or hour no one knows, not even the angels in heaven, nor the Son, but the Father *alone*" (Mark 13:28–32; cf. Matthew 24:32–36; Luke 21:28–33).

[KNOWLEDGE from know]
Setting: On the Mount of Olives, east of the temple in Jerusalem. After prophesying the temple's destruction, Jesus responds during His Olivet Discourse to questions from Peter, James, John, and Andrew about other future events.

"Take heed, keep on the alert; for you do not know when the *appointed* time will come. *It is* like a man away on a journey, *who* upon leaving his house and putting his slaves in charge, *assigning* to each one his task, also commanded the doorkeeper to stay on the alert. Therefore, be on the alert—for you do not know when the master of the house is coming, whether in the evening, at midnight, or when the rooster crows, or in the morning—in case he should come suddenly and find you asleep. What I say to you I say to all, 'Be on the alert!' " (Mark 13:33–37; cf. Matthew 24:42–43; Luke 21:34–36; see Luke 12:36–38; Ephesians 6:18).

[KNOWLEDGE from know]
Setting: The temple in Jerusalem. After attending His first Passover, twelve-year-old Jesus interacts with the teachers. Mary and Joseph return to Jerusalem after looking for Him in the caravan heading back to Nazareth.

And He said to them, "Why is it that you were looking for Me? Did you not know that I had to be in My Father's *house?*" (Luke 2:49).

[KNOWLEDGE from know]
Setting: Capernaum of Galilee. After Jesus heals a paralytic man and forgives his sins, some Pharisees and teachers of the law from Galilee and Judea accuse the Lord of blasphemy.

But Jesus, aware of their reasonings, answered and said to them, "Why are you reasoning in your hearts? Which is easier, to say, 'Your sins have been forgiven you,' or to say, 'Get up and walk'? But, so that you may know that the Son of Man has authority on earth to forgive sins,"—He said to the paralytic—"I say to you, get up, and pick up your stretcher and go home" (Luke 5:22–24; cf. Matthew 9:4–8; Mark 2:8–12; see Matthew 4:24).

[KNOWLEDGE from known]
Setting: Galilee. After selecting His twelve disciples, Jesus teaches the Sermon on the Mount to those disciples and a great throng of people from Judea, Jerusalem, and the central coastal region of Tyre and Sidon.

And He also spoke a parable to them: "A blind man cannot guide a blind man, can he? Will they not both fall into a pit? A pupil is not above his teacher; but everyone, after he has been fully trained, will be like his teacher. Why do you look at the speck that is in your brother's eye, but do not notice the log that is in your own eye? Or how can you say to your brother, 'Brother, let me take out the speck that is in your eye,' when you yourself do not see the log that is in your own eye? You hypocrite, first take the log out of your own eye, and then you will see clearly to take out the speck that is in your brother's eye. For there is no good tree which produces bad fruit, nor, on the other hand, a bad tree which produces good fruit. For each tree is known by its own fruit. For men do not gather figs from thorns, nor do they pick grapes from a briar bush. The good man out of the good treasure of his heart brings forth what is good; and the evil *man* out of the evil *treasure* brings forth what is evil; for his mouth speaks from that which fills his heart" (Luke 6:39–45; cf. Matthew 7:3–6. 16, 18, 20; 12:35; see Matthew 10:24; 15:14; Luke 6:12–19).

[KNOWLEDGE from know]
Setting: Galilee. After Jesus presents the Parable of the Sower to the crowds, His disciples ask Him to give them

the parable's meaning.

And He said, "To you it has been granted to know the mysteries of the kingdom of God, but to the rest *it is* in parables, so that SEEING THEY MAY NOT SEE, AND HEARING THEY MAY NOT UNDERSTAND. Now the parable is this: the seed is the word of God. Those beside the road are those who have heard; then the devil comes and takes away the word from their heart, so that they will not believe and be saved. Those on the rocky *soil* are those who, when they hear, receive the word with joy; and these have no *firm* root; they believe for a while, and in time of temptation fall away. The *seed* which fell among the thorns, these are the ones who have heard, and as they go on their way they are choked with worries and riches and pleasures of *this* life, and bring no fruit to maturity. But the *seed* in the good soil, these are the ones who have heard the word in an honest and good heart, and hold it fast, and bear fruit with perseverance" (Luke 8:10–15, Jesus quotes from Isaiah 6:9; cf. Matthew 13:10–23; Mark 4:10–20).

[KNOWLEDGE from known]
Setting: Galilee. After explaining the Parable of the Sower to His disciples, Jesus gives the Parable of the Lamp.

"Now no one after lighting a lamp covers it over with a container, or puts it under a bed; but he puts it on a lampstand, so that those who come in may see the light. For nothing is hidden that will not become evident, nor *anything* secret that will not be known and come to light. So take care how you listen; for whoever has, to him *more* shall be given; and whoever does not have, even what he thinks he has shall be taken away from him" (Luke 8:16–18; cf. Mark 4:21–23; see Matthew 5:14, 15; 10:26; 13:12).

[KNOWLEDGE from know]
Setting: Galilee. After He clarifies who His disciples' co-laborers are, Jesus prepares to go to Jerusalem by sending messengers ahead to Samaria, where they experience rejection and seek retribution.

But He turned and rebuked them, [and said, "You do not know what kind of spirit you are of; for the Son of Man did not come to destroy men's lives, but to save them."] And they went on to another village (Luke 9:55, 56; see 2 Kings 1:9–14; Luke 13:22).

[KNOWLEDGE from knows]
Setting: On the way from Galilee to Jerusalem. The Lord responds to a report from the seventy sent out in pairs to every place He Himself will soon visit.

At that very time He rejoiced greatly in the Holy Spirit, and said, "I praise You, O Father, Lord of heaven and earth, that You have hidden these things from *the* wise and intelligent and have revealed them to infants. Yes, Father, for this way was well-pleasing in Your sight. All things have been handed over to Me by My Father, and no one knows who the Son is except the Father, and who the Father is except the Son, and anyone to whom the Son wills to reveal *Him*" (Luke 10:21, 22; cf. Matthew 11:25–27; see Luke 10:1, 17; John 3:35; 10:15).

[KNOWLEDGE from know]
Setting: On the way from Galilee to Jerusalem. After revealing to His disciples how to pray, Jesus illustrates God's benevolence in answering prayer and giving the Holy Spirit.

"Now suppose one of you fathers is asked by his son for a fish; he will not give him a snake instead of a fish, will he? Or *if* he is asked for an egg, he will not give him a scorpion, will he? If you then, being evil, know how to give good gifts to your children, how much more will *your* heavenly Father give the Holy Spirit to those who ask Him?" (Luke 11:11–13; cf. Matthew 7:9–11).

Setting: On the way from Galilee to Jerusalem. After Jesus pronounces woes upon the Pharisees, a lawyer replies that His remarks are an insult to lawyers, too.

But He said, "Woe to you lawyers as well! For you weigh men down with burdens hard to bear, while you yourselves will not even touch the burdens with one of your fingers. Woe to you! For you build the tombs of the prophets, and *it was* your fathers *who* killed them. So you are witnesses and approve the deeds of your fathers; because it was they who killed them, and you build *their tombs*. For this reason also the wisdom of God said, 'I will send them prophets and apostles, and *some* of them they will kill and *some* they will persecute, so that the blood of all the prophets, shed since the foundation of the world, may be charged against this generation, from the blood of Abel to the blood of Zechariah, who was killed between the altar and the house *of God*; yes, I tell you, it shall be charged against this generation.' Woe to you lawyers! For you have taken away the key of knowledge; you yourselves did not enter, and you hindered those who were entering" (Luke 11:46–52; cf. Matthew 23:29–32; see 2 Chronicles 24:20, 21; Matthew 23:4, 13).

[KNOWLEDGE from known]
Setting: On the way from Galilee to Jerusalem. Jesus warns His disciples of future events as the scribes and Pharisees turn hostile and question Him repeatedly in an attempt to catch Him in something He might say.

Under these circumstances, after so many thousands of people had gathered together that they were stepping on one another, He began saying to His disciples first *of all,* "Beware of the leaven of the Pharisees, which is hypocrisy. But there is nothing covered up that will not be revealed, and hidden that will not be known. Accordingly, whatever you have said in the dark will be heard in the light, and what you have whispered in the inner rooms will be proclaimed upon the housetops. I say to you, My friends, do not be afraid of those who kill the body and after that have no more that they can do. But I will warn you whom to fear: fear the One who, after He has killed, has authority to cast into hell; yes, I tell you, fear Him! Are not five sparrows sold for two cents? *Yet* not one of them is forgotten before God. Indeed, the very hairs of your head are all numbered. Do not fear; you are more valuable than many sparrows" (Luke 12:1–7; cf. Matthew 10:26–31; see Matthew 16:6; Hebrews 10:31).

[KNOWLEDGE from known]
Setting: On the way from Galilee to Jerusalem. After giving a parable about riches and greed, Jesus uses another to challenge the crowd and His disciples to be ready for His return.

"Be dressed in readiness, and *keep* your lamps lit. Be like men who are waiting for their master when he returns from the wedding feast, so that they may immediately open *the door* to him when he comes and knocks. Blessed are those slaves whom the master will find on the alert when he comes; truly I say to you, that he will gird himself *to serve,* and have them recline *at the table,* and will come up and wait on them. Whether he comes in the second watch, or even in the third and finds *them* so, blessed are those *slaves*. But be sure of this, that if the head of the house had known at what hour the thief was coming, he would not have allowed his house to be broken into. You too, be ready; for the Son of Man is coming at an hour that you do not expect" (Luke 12:35–40; cf. Matthew 24:42–44; see Mark 13:33; Ephesians 6:14).

[KNOWLEDGE from know and knew]
Setting: On the way from Galilee to Jerusalem. When Jesus uses a parable to challenge the crowd and His disciples to be ready for His return, Peter asks Him whom He is addressing.

And the Lord said, "Who then is the faithful and sensible steward, whom his master will put in charge of his servants, to give them their rations at the proper time? Blessed is that slave whom his master finds so doing when he comes. Truly I say to you that he will put him in charge of all his possessions. But if that slave says in his heart, 'My master will be a long time in coming,' and begins to beat the slaves, *both* men and women, and to eat and drink and get drunk; the master of that slave will come on a day when he does not expect *him* and at an hour he does not know, and will cut him in pieces, and assign him a place with the unbelievers. And that slave who knew his master's will and did not get ready or act in accord with his will, will receive many lashes, but the one who did know *it,* and committed deeds worthy of flogging, will receive but few. From everyone who has been given much, much will be required; and to whom they entrusted much, of him they will ask all the more" (Luke 12:42–48; cf. Matthew 24:45–51; see Leviticus 5:17).

[KNOWLEDGE from know]
Setting: On the way from Galilee to Jerusalem. After telling how a relationship with Him will divide families, Jesus chastises the crowds for being able to discern the weather but not the present age.

And He was also saying to the crowds, "When you see a cloud rising in the west, immediately you say, 'A shower is coming,' and so it turns out. And when *you see* a south wind blowing, you say, 'It will be a hot day,' and it turns out *that way*. You hypocrites! You know how to analyze the appearance of the earth and the sky, but why do you not analyze this present time?" (Luke 12:54–56; cf. Matthew 16:2, 3).

[KNOWLEDGE from know]
Setting: On the way from Galilee to Jerusalem. While teaching in the cities and villages, Jesus responds to a question about who is saved.

And someone said to Him, "Lord, are here *just* a few who are being saved?" And He said to them, "Strive to enter through the narrow door; for many, I tell you, will seek to enter and will not be able. Once the head of the house gets up and shuts the door, and you begin to stand outside and knock on the door, saying, 'Lord, open up to us!' then He will answer and say to you, 'I do not know where you are from.' Then you will begin to say, 'We ate and drank in Your presence, and You taught in our streets'; and He will say, 'I tell you, I do not know where you are from; DEPART FROM ME, ALL YOU EVILDOERS.' In that place there will be weeping and gnashing of teeth when you see Abraham and Isaac and Jacob and all the prophets in the kingdom of God, but you yourselves being thrown out. And they will come from east and west and from north and south, and will recline *at the table* in the kingdom of God. And behold, *some* are last who will be first and *some* are first who will be last" (Luke 13:23–30, Jesus quotes from Psalm 6:8; cf. Matthew 7:13, 23; 8:11, 12; see Matthew 19:30; Luke 3:8).

[KNOWLEDGE from know]
Setting: On the way from Galilee to Jerusalem. After giving His disciples the story of the prodigal son, the Lord teaches them about stewardship.

Now He was also saying to the disciples, "There was a rich man who had a manager, and this *manager* was reported to him as squandering his possessions. And he called him and said to him, 'What is this I hear about you? Give an accounting of your management, for you can no longer be a manager.' The manager said to himself, 'What shall I do, since my master is taking the management away from me? I am not strong enough to dig; I am ashamed to beg. I know what I shall do, so that when I am removed from the management people will welcome me into their homes.' And he summoned each one of his master's debtors, and he *began* saying to the first, 'How much do you owe my master?' And he said, 'A hundred measures of oil.' And he said to him, 'Take your bill, and sit down quickly and write fifty.' Then he said to another, 'And how much do you owe?' And he said, 'A hundred measures of wheat.' He said to him, 'Take your bill, and write eighty.' And his master praised the unrighteous manager because he had acted shrewdly; for the sons of this age are more shrewd in relation to their own kind than the sons of light. And I say to you, make friends for yourselves by means of the wealth of unrighteousness, so that when it fails, they will receive you into the eternal dwellings. He who is faithful in a very little thing is faithful also in much; and he who is unrighteous in a very little thing is unrighteous also in much. Therefore if you have not been faithful in the *use of* unrighteous wealth, who will entrust the *true riches* to you? And if you have not been faithful in *the use of* that which is another's, who will give you that which is your own? No servant can serve two masters; for either he will hate the one and love the other, or else he will be devoted to one and despise the other. You cannot serve God and wealth" (Luke 16:1–13; cf. Matthew 6:24; see Matthew 25:14–30).

[KNOWLEDGE from know]
Setting: On the way from Galilee to Jerusalem. After speaking of the importance of children, Jesus responds to a ruler's question about inheriting eternal life.

A ruler questioned Him, saying, "Good Teacher, what shall I do to inherit eternal life?" And Jesus said to him, "Why do you call Me good? No one is good except God alone. You know the commandments, 'DO NOT COMMIT ADULTERY, DO NOT MURDER, DO NOT STEAL, DO NOT BEAR FALSE WITNESS, HONOR YOUR FATHER AND MOTHER.' " And he said "All these things I have kept from *my* youth." When Jesus heard *this*, He said to him, "One thing you still lack; sell all that you possess and distribute it to the poor, and you shall have treasure in heaven; and come, follow Me" (Luke 18:18–22, Jesus quotes from Exodus 20:12–16; cf. Matthew 19:16–22; Mark 10:17–22; see Luke 10:25–28).

[KNOWLEDGE from know]
Setting: Jericho, en route to Jerusalem. After commending Zaccheus's faith in Him, Jesus provides a parable about stewardship.

So He said, "A nobleman went to a distant country to receive a kingdom for himself, and *then* return. And he called ten of his slaves, and gave them ten minas and said to them, 'Do business *with this* until I come *back.*' But his citizens hated him and sent a delegation after him, saying, 'We do not want this man to reign over us.' When he returned, after receiving the kingdom, he ordered that these slaves, to whom he had given the money, be called to him so that he might know what business they had done. The first appeared, saying, 'Master, your mina has made ten minas more.' And he said to him, 'Well done, good slave, because you have been faithful in a very little thing, you are to be in authority over ten cities.' The second came, saying, 'Your mina, master, has made five minas.' And he said to him, also, 'And you are to be over five cities.' Another came, saying, 'Master, here is your mina, which I kept put away in a handkerchief; for I was afraid of you, because you are an exacting man; you take up what you did not lay down and reap what you did not sow.' He said to him, 'By your own words I will judge you, you worthless slave. Did you know that I am an exacting man, taking up what I did not lay down and reaping what I did not sow? Then why did you not put my money in the bank, and having come, I would have collected it with interest?' Then he said to the bystanders, 'Take the mina away from him and give it to the one who has the ten minas.' And they said to him, 'Master, he has ten minas *already.*' I tell you that to everyone who has, more shall be given, but from the one who does not have, even what he does have shall be taken away. But these enemies of mine, who did not want me to reign over them, bring them here and slay them in my presence" (Luke 19:12–27; cf. Matthew 25:14–30; see Matthew 13:12; Luke 16:10).

[KNOWLEDGE from known]

Setting: Approaching Jerusalem. After being praised by the people in a triumphal welcome, the Lord weeps as He sees the city ahead of Him.

When He approached *Jerusalem,* He saw the city and wept over it, saying, "If you had known in this day, even you, the things which make for peace! But now they have been hidden from your eyes. For the days will come upon you when your enemies will throw up a barricade against you, and surround you and hem you in on every side, and they will level you to the ground and your children within you, and they will not leave in you one stone upon another, because you did not recognize the time of your visitation" (Luke 19:41–44; see Matthew 24:1–2; Luke 13:34, 35).

[KNOWLEDGE from know]

Setting: The Mount of Olives, east of the temple in Jerusalem. After ministering in the temple a few days before His crucifixion, and giving the disciples more details regarding His return, Jesus conveys the Parable of the Fig Tree during His Olivet Discourse.

Then He told them a parable: "Behold the fig tree and all the trees; as soon as they put forth *leaves,* you see it and know for yourselves that summer is now near. So you also, when you see these things happening, recognize that the kingdom of God is near. Truly, I say to you, this generation will not pass away until all things take place. Heaven and earth will pass away, but My words will not pass away" (Luke 21:29–33; cf. Matthew 24:32–35; Mark 13:28–31; see Matthew 5:18).

[KNOWLEDGE from know]

Setting: An upper room in Jerusalem. During the Feast of Unleavened Bread (Passover) just before His crucifixion, Jesus celebrates the Passover meal with His disciples and institutes the Lord's Supper. When the disciples argue over who is the greatest among them, Jesus prophesies Peter's denial of Him.

"Simon, Simon, behold, Satan has demanded *permission* to sift you like wheat; but I have prayed for you, that your faith may not fail; and you, when once you have turned again, strengthen your brothers." But he said to Him, "Lord, with You I am ready to go both to prison and to death!" And He said, "I say to you, Peter, the rooster will not crow today until you have denied three times that you know Me" (Luke 22:31–34; cf. Matthew 26:33–35; John 13:36–38; see Job 1:6–12; John 17:15).

[KNOWLEDGE from know]

Setting: Golgotha (Calvary), just outside Jerusalem. After being arrested, tried, and sentenced to crucifixion by Pontius Pilate (Roman governor of Judea), the Lord Jesus, while hanging between two criminals, requests His Father's forgiveness for the crucifiers.

But Jesus was saying, "Father, forgive them; for they do not know what they are doing." And they cast lots, dividing up His garments among themselves (Luke 23:34; see Psalm 22:18; Matthew 27:33–36; Mark 15:22–24; John 19:23–25).

[KNOWLEDGE from know]
Setting: Jerusalem. At the time for the Passover of the Jews, after the Lord cleanses the temple, a Pharisee, Nicodemus, asks Him by night the meaning of "born again."

Jesus answered, "Truly, truly, I say to you, unless one is born of water and the Spirit he cannot enter into the kingdom of God. That which is born of the flesh is flesh, and that which is born of the Spirit is spirit. Do not be amazed that I said to you, 'You must be born again.' The wind blows where it wishes and you hear the sound of it, but do not know where it comes from and where it is going; so is everyone who is born of the Spirit" (John 3:5–8; see Psalm 135:7; John 1:13).

[KNOWLEDGE from know]
Setting: Jerusalem. At the time for the Passover of the Jews, after the Lord cleanses the temple, a Pharisee, Nicodemus, asks Him by night the meaning of "born of the Spirit."

Jesus answered and said to him, "Are you the teacher of Israel and do not understand these things? Truly, truly, I say to you, we speak of what we know and testify of what we have seen, and you do not accept our testimony. If I told you earthly things and you do not believe, how will you believe if I tell you heavenly things? No one has ascended into heaven, but He who descended from heaven: the Son of Man. As Moses lifted up the serpent in the wilderness, even so must the Son of Man be lifted up; so that whoever believes will in Him have eternal life" (John 3:10–15; see Numbers 21:9; Proverbs 30:4; John 12:34; 20:30, 31).

[KNOWLEDGE from knew]
Setting: Sychar in Samaria, on the way to Galilee. Jesus interacts with a woman at Jacob's well, while His disciples are buying food.

Jesus answered and said to her, "If you knew the gift of God, and who it is who says to you, 'Give Me a drink,' you would have asked Him, and He would have given you living water" (John 4:10).

[KNOWLEDGE from know]
Setting: Sychar in Samaria, on the way to Galilee. Jesus interacts with a woman at Jacob's well, while His disciples are buying food.

Jesus said to her, "Woman, believe Me, an hour is coming when neither in this mountain nor in Jerusalem will you worship the Father. You worship what you do not know; we worship what we know, for salvation is from the Jews. But an hour is coming, and now is, when the true worshipers will worship the Father in spirit and truth; for such people the Father seeks to be His worshipers. God is spirit, and those who worship Him must worship in spirit and truth" (John 4:21–24; see Isaiah 2:3; Philippians 3:3).

[KNOWLEDGE from know]
Setting: Sychar in Samaria, on the way Galilee. After Jesus converses with a Samaritan woman at Jacob's well, His disciples return with food and try to get Jesus to eat.

But He said to them, "I have food to eat that you do not know about" (John 4:32; see John 4:1–31).

[KNOWLEDGE from know]
Setting: Jerusalem. During the Feast of the Jews, Jesus responds to criticism from the Jewish religious leaders by referring to God as His Father (thereby making Himself equal with God) and informing them that God, John the Baptist, and His works all testify to His mission.

"I can do nothing on My own initiative. As I hear, I judge; and My judgment is just, because I do not seek My own will, but the will of Him who sent Me. If I *alone* testify about Myself, My testimony is not true. There is another who testifies of Me, and I know that the testimony which He gives about Me is true. You have sent to John, and he has testified to the truth. But the testimony which I receive is not from man, but I say these things so that you may be saved. He was the lamp that was burning and was shining and you were willing to rejoice for a while in his light. But the testimony which I have is greater than the *testimony of* John; for the works which the Father has given Me to accomplish—the very works that I do—testify about Me, that the Father has sent Me. And the Father who sent Me, He has testified of Me. You have neither heard His voice at any time nor seen His form. You do not have His word abiding in you, for you do not believe Him whom He sent" (John 5:30–38; see Matthew 3:17; Mark 1:4–5; John 1:7, 15, 32; 4:34; 8:14–16; 10:25, 37–38).

[KNOWLEDGE from know]
Setting: Jerusalem. During the Feast of the Jews, Jesus responds to criticism from the Jewish religious leaders by referring to God as His Father (thereby making Himself equal with God) and informing them that God, John the Baptist, and His works all testify to His mission.

"You search the Scriptures because you think that in them you have eternal life; it is these that testify about Me; and you are unwilling to come to Me so that you may have life. I do not receive glory from men; but I know you, that you do not have the love of God in yourselves. I have come in My Father's name, and you do not receive Me; if another comes in his own name, you will receive him. How can you believe, when you receive glory from one another and you do not seek the glory that is from the *one and* only God? Do not think that I will accuse you before the Father; the one who accuses you is Moses, in whom you have set your hope. For if you believed Moses, you would believe Me, for he wrote about Me. But if you do not believe his writings, how will you believe My words?" (John 5:39–47; see Matthew 24:5; Luke 16:29, 31; 24:27; John 9:28; 17:3).

[KNOWLEDGE from know]
Setting: The temple in Jerusalem. After receiving encouragement from His blood brothers in Galilee to attend the upcoming Feast of Booths in order to demonstrate His works to His disciples and the world, Jesus goes and teaches, astonishing the Jewish religious leaders.

So Jesus answered them and said, "My teaching is not Mine, but His who sent Me. If anyone is willing to do His will, he will know of the teaching, whether it is of God or *whether* I speak of Myself. He who speaks from himself seeks his own glory; but He who is seeking the glory of the One who sent Him, He is true, and there is no unrighteousness in Him" (John 7:16–18; see John 5:41).

[KNOWLEDGE from know]
Setting: The temple in Jerusalem. After receiving encouragement from His blood brothers in Galilee to attend the upcoming Feast of Booths in order to demonstrate His works to His disciples and the world, Jesus goes and teaches, causing discussion whether He is the Christ.

Then Jesus cried out in the temple, teaching and saying, "You both know Me and know where I am from; and I have not come of Myself, but He who sent Me is true, whom you do not know. I know Him, because I am from Him, and He sent Me" (John 7:28, 29; see John 3:17; 6:46; 8:42).

[KNOWLEDGE from know and knew]
Setting: The temple in Jerusalem. Following the Feast of Booths and the scribes' and Pharisees' failed attempt to stone a woman for adultery, Jesus returns the next day to teach. His enemies question His testimony about Himself.

Jesus answered and said to them, "Even if I testify about Myself, My testimony is true, for I know where I came from and where I am going; but you do not know where I come from or where I am going. You judge according to the flesh; I am not judging anyone. But even if I do judge, My judgment is true; for I am not alone *in it,* but I and the Father who sent Me. Even in your law it has been written that the testimony of two men is true. I am He who testifies about Myself, and the Father who sent Me testifies about Me." So they were saying to Him, "Where is Your Father?" Jesus answered, "You know neither Me nor My Father; if you knew Me, you would know My Father also" (John 8:14–19; see Deuteronomy 17:6; 19:15; Matthew 18:16; John 3:17; 5:30, 37; 7:28; 8:42).

[KNOWLEDGE from know]
Setting: The temple treasury in Jerusalem. Following the Feast of Booths and the scribes' and Pharisees' failed attempt

to stone a woman for adultery, Jesus returns the next day to teach. They question His testimony about Himself.

So Jesus said, "When you lift up the Son of Man, then you will know that I am *He,* and I do nothing on my own initiative, but I speak these things as the Father taught Me. And He who sent Me is with Me; He has not left Me alone, for I always do the things that are pleasing to Him" (John 8:28, 29; see John 3:14).

[KNOWLEDGE from know]
Setting: The temple treasury in Jerusalem. After the scribes and Pharisees question His testimony about Himself, Jesus reveals to those Jews who believe in Him how He will make them free.

So Jesus was saying to those Jews who had believed Him, "If you continue in My word, *then* you are truly disciples of Mine; and you will know the truth, and the truth will make you free." They answered Him, "We are Abraham's descendants and have never yet been enslaved to anyone; how is it that You say, 'You will become free'?" Jesus answered them, "Truly, truly, I say to you, everyone who commits sin is the slave of sin. The slave does not remain in the house forever; the son does remain forever. So if the Son makes you free, you will be free indeed. I know that you are Abraham's descendants; yet you seek to kill Me, because My word has no place in you. I speak the things which I have seen with *My* Father; therefore you also do the things which you heard from *your* father" (John 8:31–38; see Romans 6:16).

[KNOWLEDGE from know]
Setting: The temple treasury in Jerusalem. While Jesus is interacting with the scribes and Pharisees, they state their belief He is a demon-possessed Samaritan because of His statement that anyone who keeps His word will never taste death.

Jesus answered, "If I glorify Myself, My glory is nothing; it is My Father who glorifies Me, of whom you say, 'He is our God'; and you have not come to know Him, but I know Him; and if I say that I do not know Him, I will be a liar like you, but I do know Him and keep His word. Your father Abraham rejoiced to see My day, and he saw *it* and was glad" (John 8:54–56; see Matthew 13:17; John 7:29).

[KNOWLEDGE from know]
Setting: Jerusalem. Following the Pharisees' interrogation and dismissal of the formerly blind man Jesus healed on the Sabbath, the Lord speaks to the Pharisees, using parabolic language they do not understand.

"Truly, truly, I say to you, he who does not enter by the door into the fold of the sheep, but climbs up some other way, he is a thief and a robber. But he who enters by the door is a shepherd of the sheep. To him the doorkeeper opens, and the sheep hear his voice, and he calls his own sheep by name and leads them out. When he puts forth all his own, he goes ahead of them, and the sheep follow him because they know his voice. A stranger they simply will not follow, but will flee from him, because they do not know the voice of strangers" (John 10:1–5).

[KNOWLEDGE from know and knows]
Setting: Jerusalem. Following the Pharisees' interrogation and dismissal of the formerly blind man Jesus healed on the Sabbath, the Lord conveys the Parable of the Good Shepherd to the Pharisees, using figures of speech they do not understand.

So Jesus said to them again, "Truly, truly, I say to you, I am the door of the sheep. All who came before Me are thieves and robbers, but the sheep did not hear them. I am the door; if anyone enters through Me, he will be saved, and will go in and out and find pasture. The thief comes only to steal and kill and destroy; I came that they may have life, and have *it* abundantly. I am the good shepherd; the good shepherd lays down His life for the sheep. He who is a hired hand, and not a shepherd, who is not the owner of the sheep, sees the wolf coming, and leaves the sheep and flees, and the wolf snatches them and scatters *them. He flees* because he is a hired hand and is not concerned about the sheep. I am the good shepherd, and I know My own and My own know Me, even as the Father knows Me and I know the Father; and I lay down My life for the sheep. I have other sheep, which are not of this fold; I must bring them also, and they will hear My voice; and they will become one flock *with* one shepherd. For this reason the Father loves Me, because I lay down My life so that I may take it again. No one has taken it away from Me, but I lay it down on My own initiative. I have authority to take it up again. This commandment I received from My Father" (John 10:7–18; see Isaiah 40:11; 56:8; Jeremiah 23:1; Matthew 11:27).

[KNOWLEDGE from know]
Setting: Jerusalem. At the Feast of Dedication, just after Jesus conveys the Parable of the Good Shepherd to the Pharisees (who do not understand it), they ask Him plainly if He is the Christ.

Jesus answered them, "I told you, and you do not believe; the works that I do in My Father's name, these testify of Me. But you do not believe because you are not of My sheep. My sheep hear My voice, and I know them, and they follow Me; and I give eternal life to them, and they will never perish; and no one will snatch them out of My hand. My Father, who has given *them* to Me, is greater than all; and no one is able to snatch *them* out of the Father's hand. I and the Father are one" (John 10:25–30; see John 8:47; 17:1, 2, 20, 21).

[KNOWLEDGE from know]
Setting: Jerusalem. At the Feast of Dedication, the Jewish religious leaders seek to kill Him when Jesus claims to be equal with God after the Pharisees ask Him plainly whether He is the Christ.

Jesus answered them, "Has it not been written in your Law, 'I SAID, YOU ARE GODS'? If he called them gods, to whom the word of God came (and the Scripture cannot be broken), do you say of Him, whom the Father sanctified and sent into the world, 'You are blaspheming,' because I said, 'I am the Son of God'? If I do not do the works of My Father, do not believe Me; but if I do them, though you do not believe Me, believe the works, so that you may know and understand that the Father is in Me, and I in the Father" (John 10:34–38, Jesus quotes from Psalm 82:6; see John 14:10, 20).

[KNOWLEDGE from knew]
Setting: Bethany near Jerusalem. After the death of Lazarus, Jesus travels with His disciples from beyond the Jordan to visit his friend's sisters, Martha and Mary, and raises Lazarus from the dead.

Jesus said, "Remove the stone." Martha, the sister of the deceased, said to Him, "Lord, by this time there will be a stench, for he has been *dead* four days." Jesus said to her, "Did I not say to you that if you believe, you will see the glory of God?" So they removed the stone. Then Jesus raised His eyes, and said, "Father, I thank You that You have heard Me. I knew that You always hear Me; but because of the people standing around I said it, so that they may believe that you sent Me." When He had said these things, He cried out with a loud voice, "Lazarus, come forth." The man who had died came forth, bound hand and foot with wrappings, and his face was wrapped around with a cloth. Jesus said to them, "Unbind him, and let him go" (John 11:39–44; see Matthew 11:25).

[KNOWLEDGE from know]
Setting: Jerusalem. Just days before the Passover, with the chief priests and Pharisees plotting to seize Jesus, who is expressing anxiety about His upcoming death by crucifixion, the crowds ask the Lord about the identity of the Son of Man.

The crowd then answered Him, "We have heard out of the Law that the Christ is to remain forever; and how can You say, 'The Son of Man must be lifted up'? Who is this Son of Man?" So Jesus said to them, "For a little while longer the Light is among you. Walk while you have the Light, so that darkness will not overtake you; he who walks in the darkness does not know where he goes. While you have the Light, believe in the Light, so that you may become sons of Light." These things Jesus spoke, and He went away and hid Himself from them (John 12:34–36; see 1 John 1:6).

[KNOWLEDGE from know]
Setting: Jerusalem. Just days before the Passover, with the chief priests and Pharisees plotting to seize Jesus, who is expressing anxiety about His upcoming death by crucifixion, some of the Jews believe in Jesus, while others are

rejecting His message.

And Jesus cried out and said, "He who believes in Me, does not believe in Me but in Him who sent Me. He who sees Me sees the One who sent Me. I have come *as* Light into the world, so that everyone who believes in Me will not remain in darkness. If anyone hears My sayings and does not keep them, I do not judge him; for I did not come to judge the world, but to save the world. He who rejects Me and does not receive My sayings, has one who judges him; the word I spoke is what will judge him at the last day. For I did not speak on My own initiative, but the Father Himself who sent Me has given Me a commandment *as to* what to say and what to speak. I know that His commandment is eternal life; therefore the things I speak, I speak just as the Father as told Me" (John 12:44–50; see Matthew 10:40; Luke 10:16; John 1:4; 3:17; 5:19; 6:68; 14:9).

[KNOWLEDGE from know]
Setting: Jerusalem. Before the Passover, with His death on the cross nearing, Jesus explains the reason for His vivid example of servanthood in washing His disciples' feet.

So when He had washed their feet, and taken His garments and reclined *at the table* again, He said to them, "Do you know what I have done to you? You call Me Teacher and Lord; and you are right, for *so* I am. If I then, the Lord and the Teacher, washed your feet, you also ought to wash one another's feet. For I gave you an example that you also should do as I did to you. Truly, truly I say to you, a slave is not greater than his master, nor *is* one who is sent greater than the one who sent him. If you know these things, you are blessed if you do them. I do not speak of all of you. I know the ones I have chosen; but *it is* that the Scripture may be fulfilled, 'HE WHO EATS MY BREAD HAS LIFTED UP HIS HEEL AGAINST ME.' From now on I am telling you before *it* comes to pass, so that when it does occur, you may believe that I am *He*. Truly, truly, I say to you, he who receives whomever I send receives Me; and he who receives Me receives Him who sent Me" (John 13:12–20; Jesus quotes from Psalm 41:9; see Matthew 7:24; 10:24, 40; John 8:24; 14:29; 1 Peter 5:3).

[KNOWLEDGE from know]
Setting: Jerusalem. Before the Passover, after revealing to His disciples that Judas will betray Him to the chief priests and Pharisees, Jesus conveys how He will soon be glorified in His death, and commands the disciples to love one another.

Therefore when he had gone out, Jesus said, "Now is the Son of Man glorified, and God is glorified in Him; if God is glorified in Him, God will also glorify Him in Himself, and will glorify Him immediately. Little children, I am with you a little while longer. You will seek Me; and as I said to the Jews, now I also say to you, 'Where I am going, you cannot come.' A new commandment I give to you, that you love one another, even as I have loved you, that you also love one another. By this all men will know that you are My disciples, if you have love for one another" (John 13:31–35; see Leviticus 19:18; John 7:33, 34; 17:1; 1 John 3:14).

[KNOWLEDGE from know]
Setting: Jerusalem. Before the Passover, after taking issue with Peter's assertion that he would lay down his life for Him, Jesus comforts and gives hope to His disciples regarding their future after He returns to heaven.

"Do not let your heart be troubled; believe in God, believe also in Me. In My Father's house are many dwelling places; if it were not so, I would have told you; for I go to prepare a place for you. If I go and prepare a place for you, I will come again and receive you to Myself, that where I am, *there* you may be also. And you know the way where I am going" (John 14:1–4; see John 13:35; 14:27, 28).

[KNOWLEDGE from known and know]
Setting: Jerusalem. Before the Passover, as Jesus comforts and gives hope to His disciples regarding their future after He returns to heaven, Thomas asks where He is going and how they will know the way.

Jesus said to him, "I am the way, and the truth, and the life; no one comes to the Father but through Me. If you had known Me, you would have known My Father also; from now on you know Him, and have seen Him" (John 14:6, 7; see John 8:19; 10:9; 11:25).

[KNOWLEDGE from know]
Setting: Jerusalem. Before the Passover, after answering Thomas' question where He is going and how His disci-

ples will know the way, Jesus responds to Philip's request for Him to show them the Father.

Jesus said to him, "Have I been so long with you, and *yet* you have not come to know Me, Philip? He who has seen Me has seen the Father; how *can* you say, 'Show us the Father'? Do you not believe that I am in the Father, and the Father is in Me? The words that I say to you I do not speak on My own initiative, but the Father abiding in Me does His works. Believe Me that I am in the Father and the Father is in Me; otherwise believe because of the works themselves. Truly, truly, I say to you, he who believes in Me, the works that I do, he will do also; and greater *works* than these he will do; because I go to the Father. Whatever you ask in My name, that will I do, so that the Father may be glorified in the Son. If you ask Me anything in My name, I will do *it*" (John 14:9–14; see Matthew 7:7; John 1:14; 5:19, 20, 36; 10:37, 38; 15:16).

[KNOWLEDGE from know]
Setting: Jerusalem. Before the Passover, after responding to Philip's request for Him to show His disciples the Father, Jesus conveys the upcoming role of the Holy Spirit in their lives.

"If you love Me, you will keep My commandments. I will ask the Father, and He will give you another Helper, that He may be with you forever; *that* is the Spirit of truth, whom the world cannot receive, because it does not see Him or know Him, *but* you know Him because He abides with you and will be in you" (John 14:15–17; see John 7:39; 15:26; 1 John 5:3).

[KNOWLEDGE from know]
Setting: Jerusalem. Before the Passover, after responding to Philip's request for Him to show His disciples the Father, Jesus conveys the upcoming role of the Holy Spirit in their lives.

"I will not leave you as orphans; I will come to you. After a little while the world will no longer see Me, but you *will* see Me; because I live, you will live also. In that day you will know that I am in the Father, and you in Me, and I in you. He who has My commandments and keeps them is the one who loves Me; and he who loves Me will be loved by My Father, and I will love him and will disclose Myself to him" (John 14:18–21; see John 6:57; 10:37, 38; 16:16, 22).

[KNOWLEDGE from know]
Setting: Jerusalem. Before the Passover, after He conveys the upcoming ministry of the Holy Spirit in His disciples' lives, Jesus again relates peace, hope, and comfort to them regarding His return to the Father.

"Peace I leave with you; My peace I give to you; not as the world gives do I give to you. Do not let your heart be troubled, nor let it be fearful. You heard that I said to you, 'I go away, and I will come to you,' If you loved Me, you would have rejoiced because I go to the Father, for the Father is greater than I. Now I have told you before it happens, so that when it happens, you may believe. I will not speak much more with you, for the ruler of the world is coming, and he has nothing in Me; but so that the world may know that I love the Father, I do exactly as the Father commanded Me. Get up, let us go from here" (John 14:27–31; see John 10:18, 29; 12:31; 13:19; 16:33).

[KNOWLEDGE from know and known]
Setting: Jerusalem. Before the Passover, with His departure in mind, after explaining He is the vine and His disciples are the branches, Jesus instructs them to love one another.

"This is My commandment, that you love one another, just as I have loved you. Greater love has no one than this, that one lay down his life for his friends. You are My friends if you do what I command you. No longer do I call you slaves, for the slave does not know what his master is doing; but I have called you friends, for all things that I have heard from My Father I have made known to you. You did not choose Me but I chose you, and appointed you that you would go and bear fruit, and *that* your fruit would remain, so that whatever you ask of the Father in My name He may give to you. This I command you, that you love one another" (John 15:12–17; see Matthew 12:50; John 6:70; 8:26; 10:11; 13:34; 15:1–11).

[KNOWLEDGE from know]
Setting: Jerusalem. Before the Passover, with His departure in mind, after explaining He is the vine and His dis-

ciples are the branches, Jesus prepares them for persecution from the world.

"If the world hates you, you know that it has hated Me before *it hated* you. If you were of the world, the world would love its own; but because you are not of the world, but I chose you out of the world, because of this the world hates you. Remember the word that I said to you, 'A slave is not greater than his master.' If they persecuted Me, they will also persecute you; if they kept My word, they will keep yours also. But all these things they will do to you for My name's sake, because they do not know the One who sent Me. If I had not come and spoken to them, they would not have sin, but now they have no excuse for their sin" (John 15:18–22; see Matthew 10:22; John 7:7; 8:19, 55; 9:41; 1 Corinthians 4:12).

[KNOWLEDGE from known]
Setting: Jerusalem. Before the Passover, after explaining He is the vine and His disciples are the branches, Jesus warns them of the persecution they will face after His departure to heaven.

"These things I have spoken to you so that you may be kept from stumbling. They will make you outcasts from the synagogue, but an hour is coming for everyone who kills you to think that he is offering service to God. These things they will do because they have not known the Father or Me. But these things I have spoken to you, so that when their hour comes, you may remember that I told you of them. These things I did not say to you at the beginning, because I was with you" (John 16:1–4; see John 8:19, 55; 9:22; 13:19; 15:18–27).

[KNOWLEDGE from know]
Setting: Jerusalem. Before the Passover, after giving His disciples assurance that in the midst of tribulation they will have His peace, Jesus prays His high-priestly prayer.

Jesus spoke these things; and lifting up His eyes to heaven, He said, "Father, the hour has come; glorify Your Son, that the Son may glorify You, even as You gave Him authority over all flesh, that to all whom You have given Him, He may give eternal life. This is eternal life, that they may know You, the only true God, and Jesus Christ whom You have sent. I glorified You on the earth, having accomplished the work which You have given Me to do. Now, Father, glorify Me together with Yourself, with the glory which I had with You before the world was. I have manifested Your name to the men whom You gave Me out of the world; they were Yours and You gave them to Me, and they have kept Your word. Now they have come to know that everything You have given Me is from You; for the words which You gave Me I have given to them; and they received *them* and truly understood that I came forth from You, and they believed You sent Me. I ask on their behalf; I do not ask on behalf of the world, but of those whom You have given Me; for they are Yours; and all things that are Mine are Yours, and Yours are Mine; and I have been glorified in them. I am no longer in the world; and *yet* they themselves are in the world, and I come to You. Holy Father, keep them in Your name, *the name* which You have given Me, that they may be even as We *are.* While I was with them, I was keeping them in Your name which You have given Me; and I guarded them and not one of them perished but the son of perdition, so that the Scripture would be fulfilled" (John 17:1–12; see Luke 22:32; John 1:1; 3:35; 4:34; 5:44; 6:37–39, 70; 8:42; 11:41; 12:49; 13:18, 31; 16:15; 17:20; Philippians 2:9).

[KNOWLEDGE from know and known]
Setting: Jerusalem. Before the Passover, after giving His disciples assurance that in the midst of tribulation they will have His peace, Jesus continues praying His high-priestly prayer.

"The glory which You have given Me I have given to them, that they may be one, just as We are one; I in them and You in Me, that they may be perfected in unity, so that the world may know that you sent Me, and loved them, even as You have loved Me. Father, I desire that they also, whom You have given Me, be with Me where I am, so that they may see My glory which You have given Me, for You loved Me before the foundation of the world. O righteous Father, although the world has not known You, yet I have known You; and these have known that You sent Me; and I have made Your name known to them, and will make it known, so that the love with which You loved Me may be in them, and I in them" (John 17:22–26; see Matthew 25:34; John 1:14; 10:38; 15:9; 16:27).

[KNOWLEDGE from know]
Setting: Jerusalem. After being betrayed by Judas and having Peter deny Him, Jesus is questioned about His dis-

ciples and His teaching by Annas, former high priest and father-in-law of the current high priest (Caiaphas).

Jesus answered him, "I have spoken openly to the world; I always taught in synagogues and in the temple, where all the Jews come together; and I spoke nothing in secret. Why do you question Me? Question those who have heard what I spoke to them; they know what I said" (John 18:20, 21; see John 7:26).

[KNOWLEDGE from know]
Setting: Jerusalem. Luke, writing in Acts, presents quotes from Jesus' post-resurrection appearances, in which He responds to their question if He is about to restore the kingdom to Israel.

He said to them, "It is not for you to know times or epochs which the Father has fixed by His own authority; but you will receive power when the Holy Spirit has come upon you; and you shall be My witnesses both in Jerusalem, and in all Judea and Samaria, and even to the remotest part of the earth" (Acts 1:7, 8; see Luke 24:48, 49; Acts 2:1–4).

[KNOWLEDGE from knows]
Setting: On the island of Patmos (in the Aegean Sea about fifty miles southwest of Ephesus in modern Turkey). On the Lord's Day (Sunday), about fifty years after Jesus' resurrection, the disciple John encounters the Lord Jesus Christ, who communicates a new revelation for the apostle to record for the church in Pergamum and to six other churches in Asia.

"And to the angel of the church in Pergamum write: The One who has the sharp two-edged sword says this: 'I know where you dwell, where Satan's throne is; and you hold fast My name, and did not deny My faith even in the days of Antipas, My witness, My faithful one, who was killed among you, where Satan dwells. But I have a few things against you, because you have there some who hold the teaching of Balaam, who kept teaching Balak to put a stumbling block before the sons of Israel, to eat things sacrificed to idols and to commit *acts of* immorality. So you also have some who in the same way hold the teaching of the Nicolaitans. Therefore repent; or else I am coming to you quickly, and I will make war against them with the sword of My mouth. He who has an ear, let him hear what the Spirit says to the churches. To him who overcomes, to him I will give *some* of the hidden manna, and I will give him a white stone, and a new name written on the stone which no one knows but he who receives it' (Revelation 2:12–17; see Numbers 25:1–3; Isaiah 62:2; Revelation 1:16; 2:5, 6, 16).

[KNOWLEDGE from known]
Setting: On the island of Patmos (in the Aegean Sea about fifty miles southwest of Ephesus in modern Turkey). On the Lord's Day (Sunday), about fifty years after Jesus' resurrection, the disciple John encounters the Lord Jesus Christ, who communicates a new revelation for the apostle to record for the church in Thyatira and to six other churches in Asia.

"And to the angel of the church in Thyatira write: The Son of God, who has eyes like a flame of fire, and His feet are like burnished bronze, says this: 'I know your deeds, and your love and faith and service and perseverance, and that your deeds of late are greater than at first. But I have *this* against you, that you tolerate the woman Jezebel, who calls herself a prophetess, and she teaches and leads My bond-servants astray so that they commit *acts of* immorality and eat things sacrificed to idols. I gave her time to repent, and she does not want to repent of her immorality. Behold, I will throw her on a bed *of sickness,* and those who commit adultery with her into great tribulation, unless they repent of her deeds. And I will kill her children with pestilence, and all the churches will know that I am He who searches the minds and hearts; and I will give to each one of you according to your deeds. But I say to you, the rest who are in Thyatira, who do not hold this teaching, who have not known the deep things of Satan, as they call them—I place no other burden on you. Nevertheless what you have, hold fast until I come. He who overcomes, and he who keeps My deeds until the end, TO HIM I WILL GIVE AUTHORITY OVER THE NATIONS; AND HE SHALL RULE THEM WITH A ROD OF IRON, AS THE VESSELS OF THE POTTER ARE BROKEN TO PIECES, as I also have received *authority* from My Father; and I will give him the morning star. He who has an ear, let him hear what the Spirit says to the churches' (Revelation 2:18–29; Jesus quotes from Psalm 2:8, 9; Isaiah 30:14; see 1 Kings 16:31; Psalm 7:9; Romans 2:5; 1 Corinthians 2:10; 2 Peter 3:9; Revelation 1:14; 2:7; 3:11; 17:1–20).

[KNOWLEDGE from know]

Setting: On the island of Patmos (in the Aegean Sea about fifty miles southwest of Ephesus in modern Turkey). On the Lord's Day (Sunday), about fifty years after Jesus' resurrection, the disciple John encounters the Lord Jesus Christ, who communicates a new revelation for the apostle to record for the church in Sardis and to six other churches in Asia.

"To the angel of the church in Sardis write: He who has the seven Spirits of God and the seven stars, says this: 'I know your deeds, that you have a name that you are alive, but you are dead. Wake up, and strengthen the things that remain, which were about to die; for I have not found your deeds completed in the sight of My God. So remember what you have received and heard; and keep *it,* and repent. Therefore if you do not wake up, I will come like a thief, and you will not know at what hour I will come to you. But you have a few people in Sardis who have not soiled their garments; and they will walk with Me in white, for they are worthy. He who overcomes will thus be clothed in white garments; and I will not erase his name from the book of life, and I will confess his name before My Father and before His angels. He who has an ear, let him hear what the Spirit says to the churches' " (Revelation 3:1–6; see Matthew 10:32; Revelation 1:16).

[KNOWLEDGE from know]
Setting: On the island of Patmos (in the Aegean Sea about fifty miles southwest of Ephesus in modern Turkey). On the Lord's Day (Sunday), about fifty years after Jesus' resurrection, the disciple John encounters the Lord Jesus Christ, who communicates a new revelation for the apostle to record for the church in Philadelphia and to six other churches in Asia.

"And to the angel of the church in Philadelphia write: He who is holy, who is true, who has the key of David, who opens and no one will shut, and who shuts and no one opens, says this: 'I know your deeds. Behold, I have put before you an open door which no one can shut, because you have a little power, and have kept My word, and have not denied My name. Behold, I will cause *those* of the synagogue of Satan, who say that they are Jews and are not, but lie—I will make them come and bow down at your feet, and *make them* know that I have loved you. Because you have kept the word of My perseverance, I also will keep you from the hour of testing, that *hour* which is about to come upon the whole world, to test those who dwell on the earth. I am coming quickly; hold fast what you have, so that no one will take your crown. He who overcomes, I will make him a pillar in the temple of My God, and he will not go out from it anymore; and I will write on him the name of My God, and the name of the city of My God, the new Jerusalem, which comes down out of heaven from My God, and My new name. He who has an ear, let him hear what the Spirit says to the churches' " (Revelation 3:7–13; see Isaiah 22:22; Galatians 2:9; Revelation 2:9, 10, 13, 25; 14:1)

[KNOWLEDGE from know]
Setting: On the island of Patmos (in the Aegean Sea about fifty miles southwest of Ephesus in modern Turkey). On the Lord's Day (Sunday), about fifty years after Jesus' resurrection, the disciple John encounters the Lord Jesus Christ, who communicates a new revelation for the apostle to record for the church in Laodicea and to six other churches in Asia.

"To the angel of the church in Laodicea write: The Amen, the faithful and true Witness, the Beginning of the creation of God, says this: 'I know your deeds, that you are neither cold nor hot; I wish that you were cold or hot. So because you are lukewarm, and neither hot nor cold, I will spit you out of My mouth. Because you say, "I am rich, and have become wealthy, and have need of nothing," and you do not know that you are wretched and miserable and poor and blind and naked, I advise you to buy from Me gold refined by fire so that you may become rich, and white garments so that you may clothe yourself, and *that* the shame of your nakedness will not be revealed; and eye salve to anoint your eyes so that you may see. Those whom I love, I reprove and discipline; therefore be zealous and repent. Behold, I stand at the door and knock; if anyone hears My voice and opens the door, I will come in to him and will dine with him, and he with Me. He who overcomes, I will grant to him to sit down with Me on My throne, as I also overcame and sat down with My Father on His throne. He who has an ear, let him hear what the Spirit says to the churches' " (Revelation 3:14–22; see Proverbs 3:12; Hosea 12:8; John 14:23; 16:33).

KNOWLEDGE, KEY OF (See KEY)

L

LABOR (Also see WORK)

Setting: Sychar in Samaria. After Jesus converses with a Samaritan woman at Jacob's well, His disciples return with food. They try to get Jesus to eat, but are surprised when He speaks of other food.

Jesus said to them, "My food is to do the will of Him who sent Me and to accomplish His work. Do you not say, 'There are yet four months, and *then* comes the harvest'? Behold, I say to you, lift up your eyes and look on the fields, that they are white for harvest. Already he who reaps is receiving wages and is gathering fruit for life eternal; so that he who sows and he who reaps may rejoice together. For in this *case* the saying is true, 'One sows and another reaps.' I sent you to reap that for which you have not labored; others have labored and you have entered into their labor" (John 4:34–38; see Matthew 9:37, 38; John 5:36).

Setting: Jerusalem. Before the Passover, after warning His disciples of the persecution they will face after His departure to heaven, empathizing with their sadness over His prophecies, Jesus gives them hope for the future.

"A little while, and you will no longer see Me; and again a little while, and you will see Me." *Some* of His disciples then said to one another, "What is this thing He is telling us, 'A little while, and you will not see Me; and again a little while, and you will see Me'; and, 'because I go to the Father'?" So they were saying, "What is this that He says, 'A little while'? We do not know what He is talking about." Jesus knew that they wished to question Him, and He said to them, "Are you deliberating together about this, that I said, 'A little while, and you will not see Me, and again a little while, and you will see Me'? Truly, truly, I say to you, that you will weep and lament, but the world will rejoice; you will grieve, but your grief will be turned into joy. Whenever a woman is in labor she has pain, because her hour has come; but when she gives birth to the child, she no longer remembers the anguish because of the joy that a child has been born into the world. Therefore you too have grief now; but I will see you again, and your heart will rejoice, and no one *will* take your joy away from you" (John 16:16–22; see Mark 9:32; Luke 23:27; John 14:18–24; 16:5, 6; 20:20).

LABOR, MANUAL (Also see BUILDERS; and CONSTRUCTION)

[MANUAL LABOR from dig]

Setting: On the way from Galilee to Jerusalem. After some present report to Him about the Galileans whose blood Pilate (Roman governor of Judea) mixed with their sacrifices, Jesus responds to their concern by calling them to repentance and illustrating His point with a parable.

And He *began* telling this parable: "A man had a fig tree which had been planted in his vineyard; and he came looking for fruit on it and did not find any. And he said to the vineyard-keeper, 'Behold, for three years I have come looking for fruit on this fig tree without finding any. Cut it down! Why does it even use up the ground?' And he answered and said to him, 'Let it alone, sir, for this year too, until I dig around it and put fertilizer, and if it bears fruit next year, *fine*; but if not, cut it down'" (Luke 13:6–9; see Matthew 3:10).

[MANUAL LABOR from dig]

Setting: On the way from Galilee to Jerusalem. After giving His disciples the story of the prodigal son, the Lord teaches His disciples about stewardship.

Now He was also saying to the disciples, "There was a rich man who had a manager, and this *manager* was reported to him as squandering his possessions. And he called him and said to him, 'What is this I hear about you? Give an accounting of your management, for you can no longer be a manager.' The manager said to himself, 'What shall I do, since my master is taking the management away from me? I am not strong enough to dig; I am ashamed to beg. I know what I shall do, so that when I am removed from the management people will welcome me into their homes.' And he summoned each one of his master's debtors, and he *began* saying to the first, 'How much do you owe my master?' And he said, 'A hundred measures of oil.' And he said to him, 'Take your bill, and sit down quickly and write fifty.' Then he said to another, 'And how much do you owe?' And he said, 'A hundred measures of wheat.' He said to him, 'Take your bill, and write eighty.' And his master praised the unrighteous manager because he had acted shrewdly; for the sons of this age are more shrewd in relation to their own kind than the sons of light. And I say to you, make friends for yourselves by means of the wealth of unrighteousness, so that when it fails, they will receive you into the eternal dwellings. He who is faithful in a very little thing is faithful also in much; and he who is unrighteous in a very little thing is unrighteous also in much. Therefore if you have not been faithful in the *use of* unrighteous wealth, who will entrust the *true riches* to you? And if you have not been faithful in *the use of* that which is another's, who will give you that which is your own? No servant can serve two masters; for either he will hate the one and love the other, or else he will be devoted to one and despise the other. You cannot serve God and wealth" (Luke 16:1–13; cf. Matthew 6:24; see Matthew 25:14–30).

LABORER

Setting: On the way from Galilee to Jerusalem. The Lord appoints seventy followers and sends them out in pairs to every place He Himself will soon visit.

And He was saying to them, "The harvest is plentiful, but the laborers are few; therefore beseech the Lord of the harvest to send out laborers into His harvest. Go; behold, I send you out as lambs in the midst of wolves. Carry no money belt, no bag, no shoes; and greet no one on the way. Whatever house you enter, first say, 'Peace be to this house.' If a man of peace is there, your peace will rest on him; but if not, it will return to you. Stay in that house, eating and drinking what they give you; for the laborer is worthy of his wages. Do not keep moving from house to house. Whatever city you enter and they receive you, eat what is set before you; and heal those in it who are sick, and say to them, 'The kingdom of God has come near to you.' But whatever city you enter and they do not receive you, go out into its streets and say, 'Even the dust of your city which clings to our feet we wipe off *in protest* against you; yet be sure of this, that the kingdom of God has come near.' I say to you, it will be more tolerable in that day for Sodom than for that city" (Luke 10:2–12; see Genesis 19:24–28; Matthew 9:37, 38, 10:9–14, 16; 1 Corinthians 10:27).

LABORERS (Also see FOREMAN; LANDOWNER; and WORKERS)

Setting: Judea beyond the Jordan (Perea). Jesus illustrates the kingdom of heaven to His disciples through the story of laborers in the vineyard.

"For the kingdom of heaven is like a landowner who went out early in the morning to hire laborers for his vineyard. When he had agreed with the laborers for a denarius for the day, he sent them into his vineyard. And he went out about the third hour and saw others standing idle in the market place; and to those he said, 'You also go into the vineyard, and whatever is right I will give you.' And *so* they went. Again he went out about the sixth and the ninth hour, and did the same thing. And about the eleventh *hour* he went out and found others standing *around;* and he said to them, 'Why have you been standing idle here all day long?' They said to him, 'Because no one hired us.' He said to them, 'You go into the vineyard too.' When evening came, the owner of the vineyard said to his foreman, 'Call the laborers and pay them their wages, beginning with the last *group* to the first.' When those *hired* about the eleventh hour came, each one received a denarius. When those *hired* first came, they thought that they would receive more; but each of them also received a denarius. When they received it, they grumbled at the landowner, saying, 'These last men have worked *only* one hour, and you have made them equal to us who have borne the burden and the scorching heat of the day.' But he answered and said to one of them, 'Friend, I am doing you no wrong; did you not agree with me for a denarius? Take what is yours and go, but I wish to give to this last man the same as to you. It is not lawful for me to do what I wish with what is my own? Or is your eye envious because I am generous?' So the last shall be first, and the first last" (Matthew 20:1–16; cf. Matthew 19:30).

Setting: On the way from Galilee to Jerusalem. The Lord appoints seventy followers and sends them out in pairs to every place He Himself will soon visit.

And He was saying to them, "The harvest is plentiful, but the laborers are few; therefore beseech the Lord of the harvest to send out laborers into His harvest. Go; behold, I send you out as lambs in the midst of wolves. Carry no money belt, no bag, no shoes;

and greet no one on the way. Whatever house you enter, first say, 'Peace be to this house.' If a man of peace is there, your peace will rest on him; but if not, it will return to you. Stay in that house, eating and drinking what they give you; for the laborer is worthy of his wages. Do not keep moving from house to house. Whatever city you enter and they receive you, eat what is set before you; and heal those in it who are sick, and say to them, 'The kingdom of God has come near to you.' But whatever city you enter and they do not receive you, go out into its streets and say, 'Even the dust of your city which clings to our feet we wipe off *in protest* against you; yet be sure of this, that the kingdom of God has come near.' I say to you, it will be more tolerable in that day for Sodom than for that city" (Luke 10:2–12; see Genesis 19:24–28; Matthew 9:37, 38, 10:9–14, 16; 1 Corinthians 10:27).

LACK OF REMORSE (Listed under REMORSE, LACK OF)

LAKE

Setting: Galilee. After Jesus conveys who His true relatives are, He and His disciples set sail on the Sea of Galilee, where He will calm a storm.

Now on one of *those* days Jesus and His disciples got into a boat, and He said to them, "Let us go over to the other side of the lake." So they launched out (Luke 8:22; cf. Mark 4:35; see Matthew 8:18).

LAKE OF GALILEE (See GALILEE, SEA OF)

LAKE OF GENNESARET (See GALILEE, SEA OF)

LAKE OF TIBERIAS (See GALILEE, SEA OF)

LAMA SABACHTHANI (Listed under SABACHTHANI, LAMA)

LAMBS (Also see SHEEP)

Setting: On the way from Galilee to Jerusalem. The Lord appoints seventy followers and sends them out in pairs to every place He Himself will soon visit.

And He was saying to them, "The harvest is plentiful, but the laborers are few; therefore beseech the Lord of the harvest to send out laborers into His harvest. Go; behold, I send you out as lambs in the midst of wolves. Carry no money belt, no bag, no shoes; and greet no one on the way. Whatever house you enter, first say, 'Peace be to this house.' If a man of peace is there, your peace will rest on him; but if not, it will return to you. Stay in that house, eating and drinking what they give you; for the laborer is worthy of his wages. Do not keep moving from house to house. Whatever city you enter and they receive you, eat what is set before you; and heal those in it who are sick, and say to them, 'The kingdom of God has come near to you.' But whatever city you enter and they do not receive you, go out into its streets and say, 'Even the dust of your city which clings to our feet we wipe off *in protest* against you; yet be sure of this, that the kingdom of God has come near.' I say to you, it will be more tolerable in that day for Sodom than for that city" (Luke 10:2–12; see Genesis 19:24–28; Matthew 9:37, 38, 10:9–14, 16; 1 Corinthians 10:27).

Setting: By the Sea of Galilee. During His third appearance to His disciples after His resurrection from the dead in Jerusalem, Jesus quizzes Peter three times regarding his love for Him.

So when they had finished breakfast, Jesus said to Simon Peter, "Simon, *son* of John, do you love Me more than these?" He said to Him, "Yes, Lord; You know that I love You." He said to him, "Tend My lambs." He said to him again a second time, "Simon, *son* of John, do you love Me?" He said to Him, "Yes, Lord; You know that I love You." He said to him, "Shepherd My sheep." He said to him the third time, "Simon, *son* of John, do you love Me?" Peter was grieved because He said to him the third time, "Do you love Me?" And he said to Him, "Lord, You know all things; You know that I love You." Jesus said to him, "Tend My sheep" (John 21:15–17; see Matthew 26:33; Mark 14:29).

LAME (Also see CRIPPLED)

Setting: Galilee. While teaching and preaching, Jesus responds to John the Baptist's question (asked by John's disciples) whether He is Israel's promised Messiah.

Jesus answered and said to them, "Go and report to John what you hear and see: *the* BLIND RECEIVE SIGHT and *the* lame walk, *the* lepers are cleansed and *the* deaf hear, *the* dead are raised up, and *the* POOR HAVE THE GOSPEL PREACHED TO THEM. And blessed is he who does not take offense at Me" (Matthew 11:4–6, Jesus quotes from Isaiah 35:5f; cf. Luke 7:22, 23).

Setting: Capernaum of Galilee. Jesus elaborates about stumbling blocks after His disciples ask about greatness in the kingdom of heaven.

"Woe to the world because of *its* stumbling blocks! For it is inevitable that stumbling blocks come; but woe to that man through whom the stumbling block comes! If your hand or your foot causes you to stumble, cut if off and throw it from you; it is better for you to enter life crippled or lame, than to have two hands or two feet and be cast into the eternal fire. If your eye causes you to stumble, pluck it out and throw it from you. It is better for you to enter life with one eye, than to have two eyes and be cast into the fiery hell" (Matthew 18:7–9; cf. Matthew 5:29, 30; Mark 9:43–48; Luke 17:1).

Setting: Capernaum of Galilee. As Jesus teaches His disciples in private, they ask Him about greatness.

But Jesus said, "Do not hinder him, for there is no one who will perform a miracle in My name, and be able soon afterward to speak evil of Me. For he who is not against us is for us. For whoever gives you a cup of water to drink because of your name as *followers* of Christ, truly I say to you, he will not lose his reward. Whoever causes one of these little ones who believe to stumble, it would be better for him if, with a heavy millstone hung around his neck, he had been cast into the sea. If your hand causes you to stumble, cut it off; it is better for you to enter life crippled, than, having your two hands, to go into hell, into the unquenchable fire, [where THEIR WORM DOES NOT DIE, AND THE FIRE IS NOT QUENCHED.] If your foot causes you to stumble, cut it off; it is better for you to enter life lame, than, having your two feet, to be cast into hell, [where THEIR WORM DOES NOT DIE, AND THE FIRE IS NOT QUENCHED.] If your eye causes you to stumble, throw it out; it is better for you to enter the kingdom of God with one eye, than, having two eyes, to be cast into hell, where THEIR WORM DOES NOT DIE, AND THE FIRE IS NOT QUENCHED. For everyone will be salted with fire. Salt is good; but if the salt becomes unsalty, with what will you make it salty *again?* Have salt in yourselves, and be at peace with one another" (Mark 9:39–50; Jesus quotes from Isaiah 66:24; cf. Matthew 18:6–9; Luke 9:49, 50; see Matthew 5:13, 29, 30; 10:42; 12:30; 18:5, 6).

Setting: Galilee. After Jesus raises a woman's son from the dead in Nain, the disciples of John the Baptist inquire whether He is the promised Messiah.

And He answered and said to them, "Go and report to John what you have seen and heard: *the* BLIND RECEIVE SIGHT, *the* lame walk, *the* lepers are cleansed, and *the* deaf hear, *the* dead are raised up, *the* POOR HAVE THE GOSPEL PREACHED TO THEM. Blessed is he who does not take offense at Me" (Luke 7:22, 23, Jesus quotes from Isaiah 35:5; 61:1; cf. Matthew 11:2–6).

Setting: On the way from Galilee to Jerusalem. As He observes the guests selecting places of honor at the table, Jesus speaks a parable to the guests of a Pharisee leader on the Sabbath., The lord then comments to the host about the people to invite in the future.

And He also went on to say to the one who had invited Him, "When you give a luncheon or a dinner, do not invite your friends or your brothers or your relatives or rich neighbors, otherwise they may also invite you in return and *that* will be your repayment. But when you give a reception, invite *the* poor, *the* crippled, *the* lame, *the* blind, and you will be blessed, since they do not have *the means* to repay you; for you will be repaid at the resurrection of the righteous" (Luke 14:12–14; see John 5:28, 29).

Setting: On the way from Galilee to Jerusalem. After He speaks a parable to the invited guests and the host at a banquet, Jesus responds to a guest's proclamation about the blessings of eating bread in the kingdom of God.

But He said to him, "A man was giving a big dinner, and he invited many; and at the dinner hour he sent his slave to say to those who had been invited, 'Come; for everything is ready now.' But they all alike began to make excuses. The first one said to him, 'I have bought a piece of land and I need to go out and look at it; please consider me excused.' Another one said, 'I have bought five yoke of oxen, and I am going to try them out; please consider me excused.' Another one said, I have married a wife, and for that reason I cannot come.' And the slave came *back* and reported this to his master. Then the head of the household became angry and said to his slave, 'Go out at once into the streets and lanes of the city and bring in here the poor and crippled and blind and lame.' And the slave said, 'Master, what you commanded has been done, and still there is room.' And the master said to the slave, 'Go out into the highways and along the hedges, and compel *them* to come in, so that my house may be filled. For I tell you, none of those men who were invited shall taste of my dinner'" (Luke 14:16–24; see Deuteronomy 24:5; Matthew 22:2–14).

LAMENT (Also see GRIEF; MOURNING; SORROW; and WEEPING)

Setting: Jerusalem. Before the Passover, after warning His disciples of the persecution they will face after His departure to heaven, empathizing with their sadness over His prophecies, Jesus gives them hope for the future.

"A little while, and you will no longer see Me; and again a little while, and you will see Me." *Some* of His disciples then said to one another, "What is this thing He is telling us, 'A little while, and you will not see Me; and again a little while, and you will see Me'; and, 'because I go to the Father'?" So they were saying, "What is this that He says, 'A little while'? We do not know what He is talking about." Jesus knew that they wished to question Him, and He said to them, "Are you deliberating together about this, that I said, 'A little while, and you will not see Me, and again a little while, and you will see Me'? Truly, truly, I say to you, that you will weep and lament, but the world will rejoice; you will grieve, but your grief will be turned into joy. Whenever a woman is in labor she has pain, because her hour has come; but when she gives birth to the child, she no longer remembers the anguish because of the joy that a child has been born into the world. Therefore you too have grief now; but I will see you again, and your heart will rejoice, and no one *will* take your joy away from you" (John 16:16–22; see Mark 9:32; Luke 23:27; John 14:18–24; 20:20).

LAMP (Also see LAMPS; LAMPSTAND; and LIGHT)

Setting: Galilee. During the early part of His ministry, Jesus preaches the Sermon on the Mount to His disciples and the multitudes.

"You are the light of the world. A city set on a hill cannot be hidden; nor does *anyone* light a lamp and put it under a basket, but on the lampstand, and it gives light to all who are in the house. Let your light shine before men in such a way that they may see your good works, and glorify your Father who is in heaven" (Matthew 5:14–16; cf. Mark 4:21; 1 Peter 2:12).

Setting: Galilee. During the early part of His ministry, Jesus preaches the Sermon on the Mount to His disciples and the multitudes.

"The eye is the lamp of the body; so then if your eye is clear, your whole body will be full of light. But if your eye is bad, your whole body will be full of darkness. If then the light that is in you is darkness, how great is the darkness!" (Matthew 6:22, 23; cf. Luke 11:34, 35).

Setting: Galilee. Following His explanation of the Parable of the Sower to His disciples, Jesus illustrates what they should do with this truth.

And He was saying to them, "A lamp is not brought to be put under a basket, is it, or under a bed? Is it not *brought* to be put on the lampstand? For nothing is hidden, except to be revealed; nor has *anything* been secret, but that it would come to light. If anyone has ears to hear, let him hear" (Mark 4:21–23; cf. Luke 8:16, 17; see Matthew 5:14–16; Matthew 10:26).

Setting: Galilee. Following the explanation of the Parable of the Sower to His disciples, Jesus gives the Parable of the Lamp.

"Now no one after lighting a lamp covers it over with a container, or puts it under a bed; but he puts it on a lampstand, so that those who come in may see the light. For nothing is hidden that will not become evident, nor *anything* secret that will not be known and come to light. So take care how you listen; for whoever has, to him *more* shall be given; and whoever does not have, even what he thinks he has shall be taken away from him" (Luke 8:16–18; cf. Mark 4:21–23; see Matthew 5:14, 15; 10:26; 13:12).

Setting: On the way from Galilee to Jerusalem. After telling the increasing crowds of the sign of Jonah, Jesus illustrates His point by speaking of a lamp.

"No one, after lighting a lamp, puts it away in a cellar nor under a basket, but on the lampstand, so that those who enter may see the light. The eye is the lamp of your body; when your eye is clear, your whole body also is full of light; but when it is bad, your body also is full of darkness. Then watch out that the light in you is not darkness. If therefore your whole body is full of light, with no dark part in it, it will be wholly illumined, as when the lamp illumines you with its rays" (Luke 11:33–36; cf. Matthew 5:15, 6:22, 23).

Setting: On the way from Galilee to Jerusalem. Jesus conveys the principles of the lost sheep and the lost coin because the Pharisees and scribes complain He associates with tax collectors and sinners.

"So He told them this parable, saying, "What man among you, if he has a hundred sheep and has lost one of them, does not leave the ninety-nine in the open pasture and go after the one which is lost until he finds it? When he has found it, he lays it on his shoulders, rejoicing. And when he comes home, he calls together his friends and his neighbors, saying to them, 'Rejoice with me, for I have found my sheep which was lost!' I tell you that in the same way, there will be more joy in heaven over one sinner who repents than over ninety-nine righteous persons who need no repentance. Or what woman, if she has ten silver coins and loses one coin, does not light a lamp and sweep the house and search carefully until she finds it? When she has found it, she calls together her friends and neighbors, saying, 'Rejoice with me, for I have found the coin which I had lost!' In the same way, I tell you, there is joy in the presence of the angels of God over one sinner who repents" (Luke 15:3–10; cf. Matthew 18:12-14; see Matthew 9:11-13).

Setting: Jerusalem. During the Feast of the Jews, Jesus responds to criticism from the Jewish religious leaders by referring to God as His Father, thereby making Himself equal with God, and informing them God, John the Baptist, and His works testify to His mission.

"I can do nothing on My own initiative. As I hear, I judge; and My judgment is just, because I do not seek My own will, but the will of Him who sent Me. If I *alone* testify about Myself, My testimony is not true. There is another who testifies of Me, and I know that the testimony which He gives about Me is true. You have sent to John, and he has testified to the truth. But the testimony which I receive is not from man, but I say these things so that you may be saved. He was the lamp that was burning and was shining and you were willing to rejoice for a while in his light. But the testimony which I have is greater than the *testimony of* John; for the works which the Father has given Me to accomplish—the very works that I do—testify about Me, that the Father has sent Me. And the Father who sent Me, He has testified of Me. You have neither heard His voice at any time nor seen His form. You do not have His word abiding in you, for you do not believe Him whom He sent" (John 5:30–38; see Matthew 3:17; Mark 1:4, 5; John 1:7, 15, 32; 4:34; 8:14–16; 10:25, 37, 38).

LAMP, PARABLE OF THE

[PARABLE OF THE LAMP from lamp and lampstand]

Setting: Galilee. Following His explanation of the Parable of the Sower to His disciples, Jesus illustrates what they should do with this truth.

And He was saying to them, "A lamp is not brought to be put under a basket, is it, or under a bed? Is it not *brought* to be put on the lampstand? For nothing is hidden, except to be revealed; nor has *anything* been secret, but that it would come to light. If anyone has ears to hear, let him hear" (Mark 4:21–23; cf. Luke 8:16, 17; see Matthew 5:14–16; Matthew 10:26).

[PARABLE OF THE LAMP from lamp and lampstand]
Setting: Galilee. Following the explanation of the Parable of the Sower to His disciples, Jesus gives the Parable of the Lamp.

"Now no one after lighting a lamp covers it over with a container, or puts it under a bed; but he puts it on a lampstand, so that those who come in may see the light. For nothing is hidden that will not become evident, nor *anything* secret that will not be known and come to light. So take care how you listen; for whoever has, to him *more* shall be given; and whoever does not have, even what he thinks he has shall be taken away from him" (Luke 8:16–18; cf. Mark 4:21–23; see Matthew 5:14, 15; 10:26; 13:12).

LAMPS (Also see LAMP)

Setting: The Mount of Olives, just east of Jerusalem. During His discourse, after answering His disciples' questions as to when the temple will be destroyed and Jerusalem overrun, along with the signs of His coming and the end of the age, Jesus reemphasizes to His disciples that they should be on the alert for His return.

"Then the kingdom of heaven will be comparable to ten virgins, who took their lamps and went out to meet the bridegroom. Five of them were foolish, and five were prudent. For when the foolish took their lamps, they took no oil with them, but the prudent took oil in flasks along with their lamps. Now while the bridegroom was delaying, they all got drowsy and *began* to sleep. But at midnight there was a shout, 'Behold, the bridegroom! Come out to meet *him*.' Then all those virgins rose and trimmed their lamps. The foolish said to the prudent, 'Give us some of your oil, for our lamps are going out.' But the prudent answered, 'No, there will not be enough for us and you *too;* go instead to the dealers and buy *some* for yourselves.' And while they were going away to make the purchase, the bridegroom came, and those who were ready went in with him to the wedding feast; and the door was shut. Later the other virgins also came, saying, 'Lord, lord, open up for us.' But he answered, 'Truly I say to you, I do not know you.' Be on the alert then, for you do not know the day nor the hour" (Matthew 25:1–13; cf. Matthew 24:42; Luke 12:35; see Matthew 7:21, 24).

Setting: On the way from Galilee to Jerusalem. After giving a parable about riches and greed, Jesus uses another parable to challenge the crowd and His disciples to be ready for His return.

"Be dressed in readiness, and *keep* your lamps lit. Be like men who are waiting for their master when he returns from the wedding feast, so that they may immediately open *the door* to him when he comes and knocks. Blessed are those slaves whom the master will find on the alert when he comes; truly I say to you, that he will gird himself *to serve,* and have them recline *at the table,* and will come up and wait on them. Whether he comes in the second watch, or even in the third and finds *them* so, blessed are those *slaves*. But be sure of this, that if the head of the house had known at what hour the thief was coming, he would not have allowed his house to be broken into. You too, be ready; for the Son of Man is coming at an hour that you do not expect" (Luke 12:35–40; cf. Matthew 24:42–44; see Mark 13:33; Ephesians 6:14).

LAMPSTAND (Also see LAMP; and LAMPSTANDS)

Setting: Galilee. During the early part of His ministry, Jesus preaches the Sermon on the Mount to His disciples and the multitudes.

"You are the light of the world. A city set on a hill cannot be hidden; nor does *anyone* light a lamp and put it under a basket, but on the lampstand, and it gives light to all who are in the house. Let your light shine before men in such a way that they may see your good works, and glorify your Father who is in heaven" (Matthew 5:14–16; cf. Mark 4:21; 1 Peter 2:12).

Setting: Galilee. Following His explanation of the Parable of the Sower to His disciples, Jesus illustrates what they should do with this truth.

And He was saying to them, "A lamp is not brought to be put under a basket, is it, or under a bed? Is it not *brought* to be put on the lampstand? For nothing is hidden, except to be revealed; nor has *anything* been secret, but that it would come to light. If anyone has ears to hear, let him hear" (Mark 4:21–23; cf. Luke 8:16, 17; see Matthew 5:14–16; 10:26).

Setting: Galilee. Following the explanation of the Parable of the Sower to His disciples, Jesus gives the Parable of the Lamp.

"Now no one after lighting a lamp covers it over with a container, or puts it under a bed; but he puts it on a lampstand, so that those who come in may see the light. For nothing is hidden that will not become evident, nor *anything* secret that will not be known and come to light. So take care how you listen; for whoever has, to him *more* shall be given; and whoever does not have, even what he thinks he has shall be taken away from him" (Luke 8:16–18; cf. Mark 4:21–23; see Matthew 5:14, 15; 10:26; 13:12).

Setting: On the way from Galilee to Jerusalem. After telling the increasing crowds about the sign of Jonah, Jesus illustrates His point by speaking of a lamp.

"No one, after lighting a lamp, puts it away in a cellar nor under a basket, but on the lampstand, so that those who enter may see the light. The eye is the lamp of your body; when your eye is clear, your whole body also is full of light; but when it is bad, your body also is full of darkness. Then watch out that the light in you is not darkness. If therefore your whole body is full of light, with no dark part in it, it will be wholly illumined, as when the lamp illumines you with its rays" (Luke 11:33–36; cf. Matthew 5:15, 6:22, 23).

Setting: On the island of Patmos (in the Aegean Sea about fifty miles southwest of Ephesus in modern Turkey). On the Lord's Day (Sunday), about fifty years after Jesus' resurrection, the disciple John encounters the Lord Jesus Christ, who communicates a new revelation for the apostle to record for the church in Ephesus and to six other churches in Asia.

"To the angel of the church in Ephesus write: The One who holds the seven stars in His right hand, the One who walks among the seven golden lampstands, says this: 'I know your deeds and your toil and perseverance, and that you cannot tolerate evil men, and you put to the test those who call themselves apostles, and they are not, and you found them *to be* false; and you have perseverance and have endured for My name's sake, and have not grown weary. But I have *this* against you, that you have left your first love. Therefore remember from where you have fallen, and repent and do the deeds you did at first; or else I am coming to you and will remove your lampstand out of its place—unless you repent. Yet this you do have, that you hate the deeds of the Nicolaitans, which I also hate. He who has an ear, let him hear what the Spirit says to the churches. To him who overcomes, I will grant to eat of the tree of life which is in the Paradise of God' " (Revelation 2:1–7; see Genesis 2:9; Ezekiel 28:13; 1 John 4:1; Revelation 1:10, 11, 19, 20; 2:15, 16).

LAMPSTANDS (Also see LAMPSTAND)

Setting: On the island of Patmos (in the Aegean Sea about fifty miles southwest of Ephesus in modern Turkey). On the Lord's Day (Sunday), approximately fifty years after His resurrection, the disciple John encounters the Lord Jesus Christ, who communicates new revelations for the apostle to record for the seven churches in Asia.

When I saw Him, I fell at His feet like a dead man. And He placed His right hand on me, saying, "Do not be afraid; I am the first and the last, and the living One; and I was dead, and behold, I am alive forevermore, and I have the keys of death and of Hades. Therefore write the things which you have seen, and the things which are, and the things which will take place after these things. As for the mystery of the seven stars which you saw in My right hand, and the seven golden lampstands: the seven stars are the angels of the seven churches, and the seven lampstands are the seven churches" (Revelation 1:17–20; see Isaiah 44:6; Luke 24:5; Revelation 2:8).

Setting: On the island of Patmos (in the Aegean Sea about fifty miles southwest of Ephesus in modern Turkey). On the Lord's Day (Sunday), about fifty years after Jesus' resurrection, the disciple John encounters the Lord Jesus

Christ, who communicates a new revelation for the apostle to record for the church in Ephesus and to six other churches in Asia.

"To the angel of the church in Ephesus write: The One who holds the seven stars in His right hand, the One who walks among the seven golden lampstands, says this: 'I know your deeds and your toil and perseverance, and that you cannot tolerate evil men, and you put to the test those who call themselves apostles, and they are not, and you found them *to be* false; and you have perseverance and have endured for My name's sake, and have not grown weary. But I have *this* against you, that you have left your first love. Therefore remember from where you have fallen, and repent and do the deeds you did at first; or else I am coming to you and will remove your lampstand out of its place—unless you repent. Yet this you do have, that you hate the deeds of the Nicolaitans, which I also hate. He who has an ear, let him hear what the Spirit says to the churches. To him who overcomes, I will grant to eat of the tree of life which is in the Paradise of God' " (Revelation 2:1–7; see Genesis 2:9; Ezekiel 28:13; 1 John 4:1; Revelation 1:10, 11, 19, 20).

LAMPSTANDS, SEVEN (See LAMPSTANDS)

LAMPSTANDS, SEVEN GOLDEN (See LAMPSTANDS)

LAND (Also see LANDOWNER)

Setting: Galilee. After His twelve disciples observe His ministry, Jesus summons and specifically instructs them about their ministry to the people of Israel.

These twelve Jesus sent out after instructing them: "Do not go in *the* way of *the* Gentiles, and do not enter *any* city of the Samaritans; but rather go to the lost sheep of the house of Israel. And as you go, preach, saying, 'The kingdom of heaven is at hand.' Heal *the* sick, raise *the* dead, cleanse *the* lepers, cast out demons. Freely you received, freely give. Do not acquire gold, or silver, or copper for your money belts, or a bag for *your* journey, or even two coats, or sandals, or a staff; for the worker is worthy of his support. And whatever city or village you enter, inquire who is worthy in it, and stay at his house until you leave *that city*. As you enter the house, give it your greeting. If the house is worthy, give it your *blessing of* peace. But if it is not worthy, take back your *blessing of* peace. Whoever does not receive you, nor heed your words, as you go out of that house or that city, shake the dust off your feet. Truly I say to you, it will be more tolerable for *the* land of Sodom and Gomorrah in the day of judgment than for that city" (Matthew 10:5–15; cf. Mark 6:7–11; Luke 9:1–5; see Matthew 3:2; 11:22, 24; 15:24; Luke 22:35; 1 Corinthians 9:14).

Setting: Galilee. After performing miracles throughout the region, Jesus pronounces woes against those cities who did not repent.

"Woe to you, Chorazin! Woe to you, Bethsaida! For if the miracles had occurred in Tyre and Sidon which occurred in you, they would have repented long ago in sackcloth and ashes. Nevertheless I say to you, it will be more tolerable for Tyre and Sidon in *the* day of judgment than for you. And you, Capernaum, will not be exalted to heaven, will you? You will descend to Hades; for if the miracles had occurred in Sodom which occurred in you, it would have remained to this day. Nevertheless, I say to you that it will be more tolerable for the land of Sodom in *the* day of judgment, than for you" (Matthew 11:21–24; cf. Matthew 10:15; Luke 10:13–15).

Setting: The temple in Jerusalem. After the Jewish religious leaders test Him with questions, Jesus pronounces the third of eight woes on them in front of the crowds and His disciples.

"Woe to you, scribes and Pharisees, hypocrites, because you travel around on sea and land to make one proselyte; and when he becomes one, you make him twice as much a son of hell as yourselves" (Matthew 23:15).

Setting: The synagogue in Jesus' hometown of Nazareth. At the beginning of Jesus' public ministry, He comments to the congregation after reading on the Sabbath from the book of the prophet Isaiah.

And He said to them, "No doubt you will quote this proverb to Me, 'Physician, heal yourself! Whatever we heard was done at Capernaum, do here in your hometown as well.'" And He said, "Truly I say to you, no prophet is welcome in his hometown. But I say to you in truth, there were many widows in Israel in the days of Elijah, when the sky was shut up for three years and six months, when a great famine came over all the land; and yet Elijah was sent to none of them, but only to Zarephath, *in the land* of Sidon, to a woman who was a widow. And there were many lepers in Israel in the time of Elisha the prophet; and none of them was cleansed, but only Naaman the Syrian" (Luke 4:23–27; Jesus refers to 1 Kings 17:1, 9; 2 Kings 5:1–14; see Matthew 13:53–58).

Setting: On the way from Galilee to Jerusalem. After the scribes and Pharisees turn hostile and question Him repeatedly in an attempt to catch Him in something He might say, Jesus responds to a question from the crowd and gives a parable about riches and greed.

And He told them a parable, saying, "The land of a rich man was very productive. And he began reasoning to himself, saying, 'What shall I do, since I have no place to store my crops?' Then he said, 'This is what I will do: I will tear down my barns and build larger ones, and here I will store all my grain and my goods. And I will say to my soul, "Soul, you have many goods laid up for many years *to come;* take your ease, eat, drink *and* be merry."' "But God said to him, 'You fool! This *very* night your soul is required of you; and *now* who will own what you have prepared?' So is the man who stores up treasure for himself, and is not rich toward God" (Luke 12:16–21; see Job 27:8; Psalm 39:6; Ecclesiastes 12:9; Philippians 2:3).

Setting: On the way from Galilee to Jerusalem. After He speaks a parable to the invited guests and the host at a banquet, Jesus responds to a guest's proclamation about the blessings of eating bread in the kingdom of God.

But He said to him, "A man was giving a big dinner, and he invited many; and at the dinner hour he sent his slave to say to those who had been invited, 'Come; for everything is ready now.' But they all alike began to make excuses. The first one said to him, 'I have bought a piece of land and I need to go out and look at it; please consider me excused.' Another one said, 'I have bought five yoke of oxen, and I am going to try them out; please consider me excused.' Another one said, I have married a wife, and for that reason I cannot come.' And the slave came *back* and reported this to his master. Then the head of the household became angry and said to his slave, 'Go out at once into the streets and lanes of the city and bring in here the poor and crippled and blind and lame.' And the slave said, 'Master, what you commanded has been done, and still there is room.' And the master said to the slave, 'Go out into the highways and along the hedges, and compel *them* to come in, so that my house may be filled. For I tell you, none of those men who were invited shall taste of my dinner'" (Luke 14:16–24; see Deuteronomy 24:5; Matthew 22:2–14; Luke 14:1, 2).

Setting: On the Mount of Olives, east of the temple in Jerusalem. After ministering in the temple a few days before His crucifixion, and giving the disciples more details regarding future events, Jesus elaborates more during His Olivet Discourse about things to come.

"But when you see Jerusalem surrounded by armies, then recognize that her desolation is near. Then those who are in Judea must flee to the mountains, and those who are in the midst of the city must leave, and those who are in the country must not enter the city; because these are days of vengeance, so that all things which are written will be fulfilled. Woe to those who are pregnant and to those who are nursing babies in those days; for there will be a great distress upon the land and wrath to this people; and they will fall by the edge of the sword, and will be led captive into all the nations; and Jerusalem will be trampled under foot by the Gentiles until the times of the Gentiles are fulfilled" (Luke 21:20–24; see Matthew 24:15–18; Mark 13:14–16; Luke 19:43).

LANDOWNER (Also see FOREMAN; LABORERS; and WORKERS)

Setting: By the Sea of Galilee. Because the religious leaders are rejecting His message, Jesus continues teaching the crowds with the Parable of the Wheat and the Tares.

Jesus presented another parable to them, saying, "The kingdom of heaven may be compared to a man who sowed good seed in his field. But while his men were sleeping, his enemy came and sowed tares among the wheat, and went away. But when the wheat

sprouted and bore grain, then the tares became evident also. The slaves of the landowner came and said to him, 'Sir, did you not sow good seed in your field? How then does it have tares?' And he said to them, 'An enemy has done this!' The slaves said to him, 'Do you want us, then, to go and gather them up?' But he said, 'No; for while you are gathering up the tares, you may uproot the wheat with them. Allow both to grow together until the harvest; and in the time of the harvest I will say to the reapers, "First gather up the tares and bind them in bundles to burn them up; but gather the wheat into my barn"'" (Matthew 13:24–30; cf. Matthew 3:12).

Setting: Judea beyond the Jordan (Perea). Jesus illustrates the kingdom of heaven to His disciples through the story of laborers in the vineyard.

"For the kingdom of heaven is like a landowner who went out early in the morning to hire laborers for his vineyard. When he had agreed with the laborers for a denarius for the day, he sent them into his vineyard. And he went out about the third hour and saw others standing idle in the market place; and to those he said, 'You also go into the vineyard, and whatever is right I will give you.' And *so* they went. Again he went out about the sixth and the ninth hour, and did the same thing. And about the eleventh *hour* he went out and found others standing *around;* and he said to them, 'Why have you been standing idle here all day long?' They said to him, 'Because no one hired us.' He said to them, 'You go into the vineyard too.' When evening came, the owner of the vineyard said to his foreman, 'Call the laborers and pay them their wages, beginning with the last *group* to the first.' When those *hired* about the eleventh hour came, each one received a denarius. When those *hired* first came, they thought that they would receive more; but each of them also received a denarius. When they received it, they grumbled at the landowner, saying, 'These last men have worked *only* one hour, and you have made them equal to us who have borne the burden and the scorching heat of the day.' But he answered and said to one of them, 'Friend, I am doing you no wrong; did you not agree with me for a denarius? Take what is yours and go, but I wish to give to this last man the same as to you. It is not lawful for me to do what I wish with what is my own? Or is your eye envious because I am generous?' So the last shall be first, and the first last" (Matthew 20:1–16; cf. Matthew 19:30).

Setting: The temple in Jerusalem. Jesus delivers another parable to the chief priests and elders after they question His authority.

"Listen to another parable. There was a landowner who PLANTED A VINEYARD AND PUT A WALL AROUND IT AND DUG A WINE PRESS IN IT, AND BUILT A TOWER, and rented it out to vine-growers and went on a journey. When the harvest time approached, he sent his slaves to the vine-growers to receive his produce. The vine-growers took his slaves and beat one, and killed another, and stoned a third. Again he sent another group of slaves larger than the first; and they did the same thing to them. But afterward he sent his son to them, saying, 'They will respect my son.' But when the vine-growers saw the son, they said among themselves, 'This is the heir; come, let us kill him and seize his inheritance.' They took him, and threw him out of the vineyard and killed him. Therefore when the owner of the vineyard comes, what will he do to those vine-growers?" (Matthew 21:33–40; Jesus quotes from Isaiah 5:1, 2; cf. Mark 12:1–9; Luke 20:9–15).

LANDOWNER, PARABLE OF THE (See VINE-GROWERS, PARABLE OF THE)

LANES

Setting: On the way from Galilee to Jerusalem. After Jesus speaks a parable to the invited guests and host at a banquet, He responds to a guest's proclamation about the blessings of eating bread in the kingdom of God.

But He said to him, "A man was giving a big dinner, and he invited many; and at the dinner hour he sent his slave to say to those who had been invited, 'Come; for everything is ready now.' But they all alike began to make excuses. The first one said to him, 'I have bought a piece of land and I need to go out and look at it; please consider me excused.' Another one said, 'I have bought five yoke of oxen, and I am going to try them out; please consider me excused.' Another one said, I have married a wife, and for that reason I cannot come.' And the slave came *back* and reported this to his master. Then the head of the household became angry and said to his slave, 'Go out at once into the streets and lanes of the city and bring in here the poor and crippled and blind and lame.' And the slave said, 'Master, what you commanded has been done, and still there is room.' And the master said to the slave, 'Go out into the highways and along the hedges, and compel *them* to come in, so that my house may be filled. For I tell you, none of those men who were invited shall taste of my dinner'" (Luke 14:16–24; see Deuteronomy 24:5; Matthew 22:2–14; Luke 14:1, 2).

LANGUAGE (See LANGUAGE, FIGURATIVE; and SPEECH)

LANGUAGE, FIGURATIVE (Also see PARABLE; and PARABLES)

Setting: Jerusalem. Before the Passover, after empathizing with His disciples' sadness over His prophecies and giving them hope for the future, Jesus conveys promises about praying in His name.

"In that day you will not question Me about anything. Truly, truly, I say to you, if you ask the Father for anything in My name, He will give it to you. Until now you have asked for nothing in My name; ask and you will receive, so that your joy may be made full. These things I have spoken to you in figurative language; an hour is coming when I will no longer speak to you in figurative language, but will tell you plainly of the Father. In that day you will ask in My name, and I do not say to you that I will request of the Father on your behalf; for the Father Himself loves you, because you have loved Me and have believed that I came forth from the Father. I came forth from the Father and have come into the world; I am leaving the world again and going to the Father" (John 16:23–28; see Matthew 13:34; John 8:42; 13:1, 3; 14:14, 21, 23; 15:16).

LAODICEA

Setting: On the island of Patmos (in the Aegean Sea about fifty miles southwest of Ephesus in modern Turkey). On the Lord's Day (Sunday), approximately fifty years after His resurrection, the disciple John encounters the Lord Jesus Christ, who communicates new revelations for the apostle to record for the seven churches in Asia.

I was in the Spirit on the Lord's day, and I heard behind me a loud voice like *the sound* of a trumpet, saying, "Write in a book what you see, and send *it* to the seven churches: to Ephesus and to Smyrna and to Pergamum and to Thyatira and to Sardis and to Philadelphia and to Laodicea" (Revelation 1:10, 11; see Revelation 1:1–9; 19: 4:1).

Setting: On the island of Patmos (in the Aegean Sea about fifty miles southwest of Ephesus in modern Turkey). On the Lord's Day (Sunday), about fifty years after Jesus' resurrection, the disciple John encounters the Lord Jesus Christ, who communicates a new revelation for the apostle to record for the church in Laodicea and to six other churches in Asia.

"To the angel of the church in Laodicea write: The Amen, the faithful and true Witness, the Beginning of the creation of God, says this: 'I know your deeds, that you are neither cold nor hot; I wish that you were cold or hot. So because you are lukewarm, and neither hot nor cold, I will spit you out of My mouth. Because you say, "I am rich, and have become wealthy, and have need of nothing," and you do not know that you are wretched and miserable and poor and blind and naked, I advise you to buy from Me gold refined by fire so that you may become rich, and white garments so that you may clothe yourself, and *that* the shame of your nakedness will not be revealed; and eye salve to anoint your eyes so that you may see. Those whom I love, I reprove and discipline; therefore be zealous and repent. Behold, I stand at the door and knock; if anyone hears My voice and opens the door, I will come in to him and will dine with him, and he with Me. He who overcomes, I will grant to him to sit down with Me on My throne, as I also overcame and sat down with My Father on His throne. He who has an ear, let him hear what the Spirit says to the churches'" (Revelation 3:14–22; see Proverbs 3:12; Hosea 12:8; John 14:23; 16:33).

LAP

Setting: Galilee. After selecting His twelve disciples, Jesus teaches the Sermon on the Mount to those disciples and a great throng of people from Judea, Jerusalem, and the central coastal region of Tyre and Sidon.

"Do not judge, and you will not be judged; and do not condemn, and you will not be condemned; pardon, and you will be pardoned. Give and it will be given to you. They will pour into your lap a good measure—pressed down, shaken together, *and* running over. For by your standard of measure it will be measured to you in return" (Luke 6:37, 38; cf. Matthew 7:1–5; Mark 4:24; see Luke 6:12–19).

LASHES (Also see PUNISHMENT)

Setting: On the way from Galilee to Jerusalem. When Jesus uses a parable to challenge the crowd and His disciples to be ready for His return, Peter asks Him whom He is addressing.

And the Lord said, "Who then is the faithful and sensible steward, whom his master will put in charge of his servants, to give them their rations at the proper time? Blessed is that slave whom his master finds so doing when he comes. Truly I say to you that he will put him in charge of all his possessions. But if that slave says in his heart, 'My master will be a long time in coming,' and begins to beat the slaves, *both* men and women, and to eat and drink and get drunk; the master of that slave will come on a day when he does not expect *him* and at an hour he does not know, and will cut him in pieces, and assign him a place with the unbelievers. And that slave who knew his master's will and did not get ready or act in accord with his will, will receive many lashes, but the one who did know *it,* and committed deeds worthy of flogging, will receive but few. From everyone who has been given much, much will be required; and to whom they entrusted much, of him they will ask all the more" (Luke 12:42–48; cf. Matthew 24:45–51; see Leviticus 5:17).

LAST (Also see END; and OMEGA)

Setting: Galilee. During the early part of His ministry, Jesus preaches the Sermon on the Mount to His disciples and the multitudes.

"Make friends quickly with your opponent at law while you are with him on the way, so that your opponent may not hand you over to the judge, and the judge to the officer, and you be thrown into prison. Truly I say to you, you will not come out of there until you have paid up the last cent" (Matthew 5:25, 26; cf. Luke 12:58, 59).

Setting: Galilee. Jesus responds to some Pharisees and scribes who ask Him for a miraculous sign.

"Now when the unclean spirit goes out of a man, it passes through waterless places seeking rest, and does not find *it.* Then it says, 'I will return to my house from which I came'; and when it comes, it finds *it* unoccupied, swept, and put in order. Then it goes and takes along with it seven other spirits more wicked than itself, and they go in and live there; and the last state of that man becomes worse than the first. That is the way it will also be for this evil generation" (Matthew 12:43–45; cf. Luke 11:24–26; see Mark 5:9).

Setting: Judea beyond the Jordan (Perea). Jesus promises rewards to His disciples for their personal sacrifice and commitment to following Him.

And Jesus said to them, "Truly I say to you, that you who have followed Me, in the regeneration when the Son of Man will sit on His glorious throne, you also shall sit upon twelve thrones, judging the twelve tribes of Israel. And everyone who has left houses or brothers or sisters or father or mother or children or farms for My name's sake, will receive many times as much, and will inherit eternal life. But many *who* are first will be last; and *the* last, first" (Matthew 19:28–30; cf. Matthew 6:33; 20:15; Mark 10:29, 30; Luke 18:29, 30; 22:30).

Setting: Judea beyond the Jordan (Perea). Jesus illustrates the kingdom of heaven to His disciples through the story of laborers in the vineyard.

"For the kingdom of heaven is like a landowner who went out early in the morning to hire laborers for his vineyard. When he had agreed with the laborers for a denarius for the day, he sent them into his vineyard. And he went out about the third hour and saw others standing idle in the market place; and to those he said, 'You also go into the vineyard, and whatever is right I will give you.' And *so* they went. Again he went out about the sixth and the ninth hour, and did the same thing. And about the eleventh *hour* he went out and found others standing *around;* and he said to them, 'Why have you been standing idle here all day long?' They said to him, 'Because no one hired us.' He said to them, 'You go into the vineyard too.' When evening came, the owner of the vineyard said to his foreman, 'Call the laborers and pay them their wages, beginning with the last *group* to the first.' When those *hired* about the eleventh hour came, each one received a denarius. When those *hired* first came, they thought that they would receive more; but each of them also received a denarius. When they received it, they grumbled at the landowner, saying, 'These last men have worked *only* one hour, and you have made them equal to us who have borne the burden and the scorching heat of the day.' But he answered and said to one of them, 'Friend, I am doing you no wrong; did you not agree with me for a denarius? Take what is yours and go, but I wish to give to this last man the same as to you. It is not lawful for me to do what I wish with what is my own? Or is your eye envious because I am generous?' So the last shall be first, and the first last" (Matthew 20:1–16; cf. Matthew 19:30).

Setting: Capernaum of Galilee. As Jesus teaches His disciples in private, they ask Him about greatness.

They came to Capernaum; and when He was in the house, He *began* to question them, "What were you discussing on the way?" But they kept silent, for on the way they had discussed with one another which *of them* was the greatest. Sitting down, He called the twelve and said to them, "If anyone wants to be first, he shall be last of all and servant of all." Taking a child, He set him before them, and taking him in His arms, He said to them, "Whoever receives one child like this in My name receives Me; and whoever receives Me does not receive Me, but Him who sent Me" (Mark 9:33–37; cf. Matthew 18:1–5; Luke 9:46–48; see Matthew 20:26; 10:40).

Setting: Judea beyond the Jordan (Perea). After informing a rich man how righteous believers may have treasure in heaven, Jesus conveys to His disciples the reward of those who sacrifice in this life to follow Him.

Jesus said, "Truly I say to you, there is no one who has left house or brothers or sisters or mother or father or children or farms, for My sake and for the gospel's sake, but that he will receive a hundred times as much now in the present age, houses and brothers and sisters and mothers and children and farms, along with persecutions; and in the age to come, eternal life. But many *who are* first will be last, and the last, first" (Mark 10:29–31; cf. Matthew 19:27–30; Luke 18:28–30; see Matthew 6:33).

Setting: The temple in Jerusalem. Having His authority questioned by the chief priests, scribes, and elders, Jesus begins to teach them in parables.

And He began to speak to them in parables: "A man PLANTED A VINEYARD AND PUT A WALL AROUND IT, AND DUG A VAT UNDER THE WINE PRESS AND BUILT A TOWER, and rented it out to vine-growers and went on a journey. At the *harvest* time he sent a slave to the vine-growers, in order to receive *some* of the produce of the vineyard from the vine-growers. They took him, and beat him and sent him away empty-handed. Again he sent them another slave, and they wounded him in the head, and treated him shamefully. And he sent another, and that one they killed; and *so with* many others, beating some and killing others. He had one more to *send*, a beloved son; he sent him last *of all* to them, saying, 'They will respect my son.' But those vine-growers said to one another, 'This is the heir; come, let us kill him, and the inheritance will be ours!' They took him, and killed him and threw him out of the vineyard. What will the owner of the vineyard do? He will come and destroy the vine-growers, and will give the vineyard to others. Have you not even read this Scripture: 'THE STONE WHICH THE BUILDERS REJECTED, THIS BECAME THE CHIEF CORNER *stone;* THIS CAME ABOUT FROM THE LORD, AND IT IS MARVELOUS IN OUR EYES'?" (Mark 12:1–11, Jesus quotes from Psalm 118:22, 23; Isaiah 5:1, 2; cf. Matthew 21:33–46; Luke 20:9–19).

Setting: On the way from Galilee to Jerusalem. After some in the crowd test Him, demanding a sign from heaven, Jesus illustrates His power over Satan.

"When the unclean spirit goes out of a man, it passes through waterless places seeking rest, and not finding any, it says, 'I will return to my house from which I came.' And when it comes, it finds it swept clean and put in order. Then it goes and takes *along* seven other spirits more evil than itself, and they go in and live there; and the last state of that man becomes worse than the first" (Luke 11:24–26; cf. Matthew 12:43–45; see Luke 11:14–16).

Setting: On the way from Galilee to Jerusalem. After chastising the crowds for being able to discern the weather but not the present age, Jesus exhorts them to settle any financial disputes outside of court.

"And why do you not even on your own initiative judge what is right? For while you are going with your opponent to appear before the magistrate, on *your* way *there* make an effort to settle with him, so that he may not drag you before the judge, and the judge turn you over to the officer, and the officer throw you into prison. I say to you, you will not get out of there until you have paid the very last cent" (Luke 12:57–59; cf. Matthew 5:25, 26).

Setting: On the way from Galilee to Jerusalem. While teaching in the cities and villages, Jesus responds to a question about who is saved.

And someone said to Him, "Lord, are here *just* a few who are being saved?" And He said to them, "Strive to enter through the narrow door; for many, I tell you, will seek to enter and will not be able. Once the head of the house gets up and shuts the door, and you begin to stand outside and knock on the door, saying, 'Lord, open up to us!' then He will answer and say to you, 'I do not know where you are from.' Then you will begin to say, 'We ate and drank in Your presence, and You taught in our streets'; and He will say, 'I tell you, I do not know where you are from; DEPART FROM ME, ALL YOU EVILDOERS.' In that place there will be weeping and gnashing of teeth when you see Abraham and Isaac and Jacob and all the prophets in the kingdom of God, but you yourselves being thrown out. And they will come from east and west and from north and south, and will recline *at the table* in the kingdom of God. And behold, *some* are last who will be first and *some* are first who will be last" (Luke 13:23–30, Jesus quotes from Psalm 6:8; cf. Matthew 7:13, 23; 8:11, 12; see Matthew 19:30; Luke 3:8).

Setting: On the way from Galilee to Jerusalem. As He observes the guests selecting places of honor at the table, Jesus speaks a parable to the guests of a Pharisee leader on the Sabbath.

And He *began* speaking a parable to the invited guests when He noticed how they had been picking out the places of honor *at the table,* saying to them, "When you are invited by someone to a wedding feast, do not take the place of honor, for someone more distinguished than you may have been invited by him, and he who invited you both will come and say to you, 'Give *your* place to this man, and then in disgrace you proceed to occupy the last place. But when you are invited, go and recline at the last place, so that when the one who has invited you comes, he may say to you, 'Friend, move up higher'; then you will have honor in the sight of all who are at the table with you. For everyone who exalts himself will be humbled, and he who humbles himself will be exalted" (Luke 14:7–11; see 2 Samuel 22:28; Proverbs 25:6, 7; Matthew 23:6).

Setting: Capernaum. The day after Jesus walks on the Sea of Galilee to join His disciples in a boat, the people He miraculously fed with a lad's five loaves and two fish ask Him to always give them this bread out of heaven.

Jesus said to them, "I am the bread of life; he who comes to Me will not hunger, and he who believes in Me will never thirst. But I said to you that you have seen Me, and yet do not believe. All that the Father gives Me will come to Me, and the one who comes to Me I will certainly not cast out. For I have come down from heaven, not to do My own will, but the will of Him who sent Me. This is the will of Him who sent Me, that of all that He has given Me I lose nothing, but raise it up on the last day. For this is the will of My Father, that everyone who beholds the Son and believes in Him will have eternal life, and I Myself will raise him up on the last day" (John 6:35–40; see John 3:13, 16; 4:13, 14).

Setting: Capernaum of Galilee. After Jesus informs the people whom He miraculously fed with a lad's five loaves and two fish how they might receive the bread out of heaven, the Jewish religious leaders grumble because Jesus claims that He came down out of heaven.

Therefore the Jews were grumbling about Him, because He said, "I am the bread that came down out of heaven." They were saying, "Is not this Jesus, the son of Joseph, whose father and mother we know? How does He now say, 'I have come down out of heaven'?" Jesus answered and said to them, "Do not grumble among yourselves. No one can come to Me unless the Father who sent Me draws him; and I will raise him up on the last day. It is written in the prophets, 'AND THEY SHALL ALL BE TAUGHT OF GOD.' Everyone who has heard and learned from the Father, comes to Me. Not that anyone has seen the Father, except the One who is from God; He has seen the Father. Truly, truly, I say to you, he who believes has eternal life. I am the bread of life. Your fathers ate the manna in the wilderness, and they died. This is the bread which comes down out of heaven, so that one may eat of it and not die. I am the living bread that came down out of heaven; if anyone eats of this bread, he will live forever; and the bread also which I will give for the life of the world is My flesh" (John 6:41–51, Jesus quotes from Isaiah 54:13; see John 1:18, 29; 3:36; 7:27).

Setting: Capernaum of Galilee. After Jesus informs the people whom He miraculously fed how they might receive the bread out of heaven, the Jewish religious leaders argue with one another when Jesus says He will give His flesh to the world to eat.

So Jesus said to them, "Truly, truly, I say to you, unless you eat the flesh of the Son of Man and drink His blood, you have no life in yourselves. He who eats My flesh and drinks My blood has eternal life, and I will raise him up on the last day. For My flesh is true food, and My blood is true drink. He who eats My flesh and drinks My blood abides in Me, and I in him. As the living Father sent Me, and I live because of the Father, so he who eats Me, he also will live because of Me. This is the bread which came down out of heaven; not as the fathers ate and died; he who eats this bread will live forever" (John 6:53–58; see Matthew 16:16; Luke 4:22; John 3:36; 9:16; 15:4).

Setting: Jerusalem. Just days before the Passover, with the chief priests and Pharisees plotting to seize Jesus, who is expressing anxiety about His upcoming death by crucifixion, some of the Jews believe in Jesus, while others are rejecting His message.

And Jesus cried out and said, "He who believes in Me, does not believe in Me but in Him who sent Me. He who sees Me sees the One who sent Me. I have come *as* Light into the world, so that everyone who believes in Me will not remain in darkness. If anyone hears My sayings and does not keep them, I do not judge him; for I did not come to judge the world, but to save the world. He who rejects Me and does not receive My sayings, has one who judges him; the word I spoke is what will judge him at the last day. For I did not speak on My own initiative, but the Father Himself who sent Me has given Me a commandment *as to* what to say and what to speak. I know that His commandment is eternal life; therefore the things I speak, I speak just as the Father as told Me" (John 12:44–50; see Matthew 10:40; Luke 10:16; John 1:4; 3:17; 5:19; 6:68; 14:9).

Setting: On the island of Patmos (in the Aegean Sea about fifty miles southwest of Ephesus in modern Turkey). On the Lord's Day (Sunday), approximately fifty years after His resurrection, the disciple John encounters the Lord Jesus Christ, who communicates new revelations for the apostle to record for the seven churches in Asia.

When I saw Him, I fell at His feet like a dead man. And He placed His right hand on me, saying, "Do not be afraid; I am the first and the last, and the living One; and I was dead, and behold, I am alive forevermore, and I have the keys of death and of Hades. Therefore write the things which you have seen, and the things which are, and the things which will take place after these things. As for the mystery of the seven stars which you saw in My right hand, and the seven golden lampstands: the seven stars are the angels of the seven churches, and the seven lampstands are the seven churches" (Revelation 1:17–20; see Isaiah 44:6; Luke 24:5; Revelation 1:1–16; 2:8).

Setting: On the island of Patmos (in the Aegean Sea about fifty miles southwest of Ephesus in modern Turkey). On the Lord's Day (Sunday), about fifty years after Jesus' resurrection, the disciple John encounters the Lord Jesus Christ, who communicates a new revelation for the apostle to record for the church in Smyrna and to six other churches in Asia.

"And to the angel of the church in Smyrna write: The first and the last, who was dead, and has come to life, says this: 'I know your tribulation and your poverty (but you are rich), and the blasphemy by those who say they are Jews and are not, but are a synagogue of Satan. Do not fear what you are about to suffer. Behold, the devil is about to cast some of you into prison, so that you will be tested, and you will have tribulation for ten days. Be faithful until death, and I will give you the crown of life. He who has an ear, let him hear what the Spirit says to the churches. He who overcomes will not be hurt by the second death' (Revelation 2:8–11; see Isaiah 44:6; Revelation 1:9, 18; 20:6, 14).

Setting: On the island of Patmos (in the Aegean Sea about fifty miles southwest of Ephesus in modern Turkey). In the final chapter of the Lord Jesus Christ's Revelation via the disciple John, approximately fifty years after His resurrection, the Lord reveals His impending return, reward, and eternality.

"Behold, I am coming quickly, and My reward *is* with Me, to render to every man according to what he has done. I am the Alpha and the Omega, the first and the last, the beginning and the end" (Revelation 22:12, 13; see Isaiah 40:10; 44:6).

LAST DAY (Listed under DAY, LAST)

LAST SUPPER (See LORD'S SUPPER)

LAUGHTER (Also see GLADNESS; HAPPINESS; JOY; and SATISFACTION)

[LAUGHTER from laugh]

Setting: Galilee. After selecting His twelve disciples, Jesus teaches the Beatitudes (part of the Sermon on the Mount) to those disciples and a great throng of people from Judea, Jerusalem, and the central coastal region of Tyre and Sidon.

"Blessed *are* you who hunger now, for you shall be satisfied. Blessed *are* you who weep now, for you shall laugh" (Luke 6:21; cf. Matthew 5:4, 6).

[LAUGHTER from laugh]

Setting: Galilee. After selecting His twelve disciples, Jesus teaches the Beatitudes (part of the Sermon on the Mount) to those disciples and a great throng of people from Judea, Jerusalem, and the central coastal region of Tyre and Sidon.

"Woe to you who are well-fed now, for you shall be hungry. Woe *to you* who laugh now, for you shall mourn and weep" (Luke 6:25; cf. Matthew 5:4).

LAW (Also see MOSES, CHAIR OF; and MOSES, LAW OF)

Setting: Galilee. During the early part of His ministry, Jesus preaches the Sermon on the Mount to His disciples and the multitudes.

"Do not think that I came to abolish the Law or the Prophets; I did not come to abolish but to fulfill. For truly I say to you, until heaven and earth pass away, not the smallest letter or stroke shall pass from the Law until all is accomplished" (Matthew 5:17, 18; cf. Matthew 24:35).

Setting: Galilee. During the early part of His ministry, Jesus preaches the Sermon on the Mount to His disciples and the multitudes.

"Make friends quickly with your opponent at law while you are with him on the way, so that your opponent may not hand you over to the judge, and the judge to the officer, and you be thrown into prison. Truly I say to you, you will not come out of there until you have paid up the last cent" (Matthew 5:25, 26; cf. Luke 12:58, 59).

Setting: Galilee. During the early part of His ministry, Jesus preaches the Sermon on the Mount to His disciples and the multitudes.

"Ask, and it will be given to you; seek, and you will find; knock, and it will be opened to you. For everyone who asks receives, and he who seeks finds, and to him who knocks it will be opened. Or what man is there among you who, when his son asks for a loaf, will give him a stone? Or if he asks for a fish, he will not give him a snake, will he? If you then, being evil, know how to give good gifts to your children, how much more will your Father who is in heaven give what is good to those who ask Him! In everything, therefore, treat people the same way you want them to treat you, for this is the Law and the Prophets" (Matthew 7:7–12; cf. Matthew 22:40; Luke 6:31; 11:9–13; see Psalm 84:11).

Setting: Galilee. While speaking to the crowds, Jesus pays tribute to the ministry of John the Baptist, but emphasizes that the one who is least in the kingdom of heaven is greater than John.

As these men were going *away,* Jesus began to speak to the crowds about John, "What did you go out into the wilderness to see? A reed shaken by the wind? But what did you go out to see? A man dressed in soft *clothing?* Those who wear soft *clothing* are in kings' palaces! But what did you go out to see? A prophet? Yes, I tell you, and the one who is more than a prophet. This is the one about whom it is written, 'BEHOLD, I SEND MY MESSENGER AHEAD OF YOU, WHO WILL PREPARE YOUR WAY BEFORE YOU.' Truly, I say to you, among those born of women there has not arisen *anyone* greater than John the Baptist! Yet the one who is least in the kingdom of heaven is greater than he. From the days of John the Baptist until now the kingdom of heaven suffers violence, and violent men take it by force. For all the prophets and the Law prophesied until John. And, if you are willing to accept *it,* John himself is Elijah who was to come. He who has ears to hear, let him hear" (Matthew 11:7–15, Jesus quotes from Malachi 3:1; cf. Malachi 4:5; Luke 7:24–28; 16:16; see Matthew 14:5).

Setting: Galilee. While ministering, Jesus responds to the Pharisees' objection to His disciples' picking grain from the fields on the Sabbath.

But He said to them, "Have you not read what David did when he became hungry, he and his companions, how they entered the house of God, and ate the consecrated bread, which was not lawful for him to eat nor for those with him, but for the priests alone? Or, have you not read in the Law, that on the Sabbath the priests in the temple break the Sabbath and are innocent? But I say to you that something greater than the temple is here. But if you had known what this means, 'I DESIRE COMPASSION, AND NOT A SACRIFICE,' you would not have condemned the innocent. For the Son of Man is Lord of the Sabbath" (Matthew 12:3–8, Jesus quotes from Hosea 6:6; cf. Mark 2:25–28; Luke 6:3–5; see 1 Samuel 21:6).

Setting: The temple in Jerusalem. In order to test Jesus, a Pharisee lawyer asks Him as He teaches which is the great commandment of the Law.

And He said to him, " 'YOU SHALL LOVE THE LORD YOUR GOD WITH ALL YOUR HEART, AND WITH ALL YOUR SOUL, AND WITH ALL YOUR MIND.' This is the great and foremost commandment. The second is like it, 'YOU SHALL LOVE YOUR NEIGHBOR AS YOURSELF.' On these two commandments depend the whole Law and the Prophets" (Matthew 22:37–40; Jesus quotes from Leviticus 19:18; Deuteronomy 6:5; cf. Mark 12:28–34; see Matthew 7:12).

Setting: The temple in Jerusalem. After the Jewish religious leaders test Him with questions, Jesus pronounces the fifth of eight woes on them in front of the crowds and His disciples.

"Woe to you, scribes and Pharisees, hypocrites! For you tithe the mint and dill and cummin, and have neglected the weightier provisions of the law: justice and mercy and faithfulness; but these are things you should have done without neglecting the others. You blind guides, who strain out a gnat and swallow a camel!" (Matthew 23:23, 24).

Setting: On the way from Galilee to Jerusalem. After Jesus tells His disciples in private the privilege they are experiencing by living in the time of the Messiah, a lawyer tests Him.

And a lawyer stood up and put Him to the test, saying, "Teacher, what shall I do to inherit eternal life?" And He said to him, "What is written in the Law? How does it read to you?" And he answered, "YOU SHALL LOVE THE LORD YOUR GOD WITH ALL YOUR HEART, AND WITH ALL YOUR SOUL, AND WITH ALL YOUR STRENGTH, AND WITH ALL YOUR MIND; AND YOUR NEIGHBOR AS YOURSELF." And He said to him, "You have answered correctly; DO THIS AND YOU WILL LIVE" (Luke 10:25–28, Jesus quotes from Leviticus 18:5; see Deuteronomy 6:5; Matthew 19:16–19).

Setting: On the way from Galilee to Jerusalem. The Lord responds to the Pharisees' scoffing at His teaching His disciples about stewardship.

And He said to them, "You are those who justify yourselves in the sight of men, but God knows your hearts; for that which is highly esteemed among men is detestable in the sight of God. The Law and the Prophets *were proclaimed* until John; since that time the gospel of the kingdom of God has been preached, and everyone is forcing his way into it. But is it easier for heaven and earth to pass away than for one stroke of a letter of the Law to fail" (Luke 16:15–17; cf. Matthew 5:18; see 1 Samuel 16:7; Matthew 4:23; 11:11–14).

Setting: The temple in Jerusalem. After receiving encouragement from His blood brothers in Galilee to attend the upcoming Feast of Booths in order to demonstrate His works to His disciples and the world, Jesus goes and teaches, astonishing the Jewish religious leaders.

"Did not Moses give you the Law, and *yet* none of you carries out the Law? Why do you seek to kill Me?" (John 7:19; see Mark 11:18; John 1:17).

Setting: The temple in Jerusalem. Following the Feast of Booths and the scribes' and Pharisees' failed attempt to stone a woman for adultery, Jesus returns the next day to teach. His enemies question His testimony about Himself.

Jesus answered and said to them, "Even if I testify about Myself, My testimony is true, for I know where I came from and where I am going; but you do not know where I come from or where I am going. You judge according to the flesh; I am not judging anyone. But even if I do judge, My judgment is true; for I am not alone *in it,* but I and the Father who sent Me. Even in your law it has been written that the testimony of two men is true. I am He who testifies about Myself, and the Father who sent Me testifies about Me." So they were saying to Him, "Where is Your Father?" Jesus answered, "You know neither Me nor My Father; if you knew Me, you would know My Father also" (John 8:14–19; see Deuteronomy 17:6; 19:15; Matthew 18:16; John 3:17; 5:30, 37; 7:28; 8:42).

Setting: Jerusalem. At the Feast of Dedication, the Pharisees desire to stone Jesus because He claims to be equal with God when they ask Him plainly whether He is the Christ.

Jesus answered them, "Has it not been written in your Law, 'I SAID, YOU ARE GODS'? If he called them gods, to whom the word of God came (and the Scripture cannot be broken), do you say of Him, whom the Father sanctified and sent into the world, 'You are blaspheming,' because I said, 'I am the Son of God'? If I do not do the works of My Father, do not believe Me; but if I do them, though you do not believe Me, believe the works, so that you may know and understand that the Father is in Me, and I in the Father" (John 10:34–38, Jesus quotes from Psalm 82:6; see John 14:10, 20).

Setting: Jerusalem. Before the Passover in Jerusalem, with His departure in mind, after explaining He is the vine and His disciples are the branches, Jesus prepares them for hatred by the world.

"He who hates Me hates My Father also. If I had not done among them the works which no one else did, they would not have sin; but now they have both seen and hated Me and My Father as well. But *they have done this* to fulfill the word that is written in their Law, 'THEY HATED ME WITHOUT A CAUSE'" (John 15:23–25, Jesus quotes from Psalm 35:19; see John 9:41).

LAW, FULFILLMENT OF THE (Also see JESUS' MISSION; JESUS' PURPOSE; and SCRIPTURE, FULFILLMENT OF)

[FULFILLMENT OF THE LAW from Do not think that I came to abolish the Law or the Prophets; I did not come to abolish but to fulfill]

Setting: Galilee. During the early part of His ministry, Jesus preaches the Sermon on the Mount to His disciples and the multitudes.

"Do not think that I came to abolish the Law or the Prophets; I did not come to abolish but to fulfill" (Matthew 5:17).

LAW AND THE PROPHETS (Listed under PROPHETS, LAW AND THE)

LAW OF MOSES (Listed under MOSES, LAW OF)

LAWFULNESS

[LAWFULNESS from lawful]
Setting: Galilee. While ministering, Jesus responds to the Pharisees' objection to His disciples' picking grain from the fields on the Sabbath.

But He said to them, "Have you not read what David did when he became hungry, he and his companions, how they entered the house of God, and ate the consecrated bread, which was not lawful for him to eat nor for those with him, but for the priests alone? Or, have you not read in the Law, that on the Sabbath the priests in the temple break the Sabbath and are innocent? But I say to you that something greater than the temple is here. But if you had known what this means, 'I DESIRE COMPASSION, AND NOT A SACRIFICE,' you would not have condemned the innocent. For the Son of Man is Lord of the Sabbath" (Matthew 12:3–8, Jesus quotes from Hosea 6:6; cf. Mark 2:25–28; Luke 6:3–5; see 1 Samuel 21:6).

[LAWFULNESS from lawful]
Setting: A synagogue in Galilee. Jesus answers questions posed by the Pharisees about the Sabbath.

And He said to them, "What man is there among you who has a sheep, and if it falls into a pit on the Sabbath, will he not take hold of it and lift it out? How much more valuable then is a man than a sheep! So then, it is lawful to do good on the Sabbath." Then He said to the man, "Stretch out your hand!" He stretched it out, and it was restored to normal, like the other (Matthew 12:11–13; cf. Matthew 10:31; Mark 3:4, 5; Luke 6:9, 10; Luke 14:5; see Matthew 8:3).

[LAWFULNESS from lawful]
Setting: Judea beyond the Jordan (Perea). Jesus illustrates the kingdom of heaven to His disciples through the story of laborers in the vineyard.

"For the kingdom of heaven is like a landowner who went out early in the morning to hire laborers for his vineyard. When he had agreed with the laborers for a denarius for the day, he sent them into his vineyard. And he went out about the third hour and saw others standing idle in the market place; and to those he said, 'You also go into the vineyard, and whatever is right I will give you.' And *so* they went. Again he went out about the sixth and the ninth hour, and did the same thing. And about the eleventh *hour* he went out and found others standing *around;* and he said to them, 'Why have you been standing idle here all day long?' They said to him, 'Because no one hired us.' He said to them, 'You go into the vineyard too.' When evening came, the owner of the vineyard said to his foreman, 'Call the laborers and pay them their wages, beginning with the last *group* to the first.' When those *hired* about the eleventh hour came, each one received a denarius. When those *hired* first came, they thought that they would receive more; but each of them also received a denarius. When they received it, they grumbled at the landowner, saying, 'These last men have worked *only* one hour, and you have made them equal to us who have borne the burden and the scorching heat of the day.' But he answered and said to one of them, 'Friend, I am doing you no wrong; did you not agree with me for a denarius? Take what is yours and go, but I wish to give to this last man the same as to you. It is not lawful for me to do what I wish with what is my own? Or is your eye envious because I am generous?' So the last shall be first, and the first last" (Matthew 20:1–16; cf. Matthew 19:30).

[LAWFULNESS from lawful]
Setting: Galilee. Early in Jesus' ministry, the Pharisees ask Him why He allows His disciples to harvest grain on the Sabbath.

And He said to them, "Have you never read what David did when he was in need and he and his companions became hungry; how he entered the house of God in the time of Abiathar *the* high priest, and ate the consecrated bread, which is not lawful for *anyone* to eat except the priests, and he also gave it to those who were with him?" Jesus said to them, "The Sabbath was made for man, and not man for the Sabbath. So the Son of Man is Lord even of the Sabbath" (Mark 2:25–28; cf. Matthew 12:1–8; Luke 6:1–5; see Exodus 23:12).

[LAWFULNESS from lawful]
Setting: A synagogue in Galilee. Early in His ministry, Jesus heals a man's withered hand on the Sabbath, while the Pharisees observe.

He said to the man with the withered hand, "Get up and come forward!" And He said to them, "Is it lawful to do good or do harm on the Sabbath, to save a life or to kill?" But they kept silent. After looking around at them with anger, grieved at their hardness of heart, He said to the man, "Stretch out your hand." And he stretched it out, and his hand was restored (Mark 3:3–5; cf. Matthew 12:9–14; Luke 6:6–11).

[LAWFULNESS from lawful]
Setting: Probably in Galilee. As Jesus and His disciples pass through some grain fields, some of the Pharisees question why His followers harvest grain on the Sabbath.

And Jesus answering them said, "Have you not even read what David did when he was hungry, he and those who were with him, how he entered the house of God, and took and ate the consecrated bread which is not lawful for any to eat except the priests alone, and gave it to his companions?" And He was saying to them, "The Son of Man is Lord of the Sabbath" (Luke 6:3–5; cf. Matthew 12:1–8; Mark 2:23–28; see Exodus 20:8; Leviticus 24:1–9; Deuteronomy 5:12; 1 Samuel 21:1–6).

[LAWFULNESS from lawful]
Setting: A synagogue in Galilee. On the Sabbath, as Jesus teaches, the scribes and Pharisees watch to see if He heals a man's withered hand.

But He knew what they were thinking, and He said to the man with the withered hand, "Get up and come forward!" And he got up and came forward. And Jesus said to them, "I ask you, is it lawful to do good or to do harm on the Sabbath, to save a life or destroy it?" And looking around at them all, He said to him, "Stretch out your hand!" And he did *so;* and his hand was restored (Luke 6:8–10; cf. Matthew 12:9–13; Mark 3:1–5).

[LAWFULNESS from lawful]
Setting: On the way from Galilee to Jerusalem. Jesus goes into the house of a Pharisee leader, where a man suffering from dropsy sits, to eat bread on the Sabbath.

And Jesus answered and spoke to the lawyers and Pharisees, saying, "Is it lawful to heal on the Sabbath, or not?" But they kept silent. And He took hold of him and healed him, and sent him away. And He said to them, "Which one of you will have a son or an ox fall into a well, and will not immediately pull him out on a Sabbath day?" And they could make no reply to this (Luke 14:3–6, cf. Matthew 12:11–13).

LAWLESSNESS

Setting: Galilee. During the early part of His ministry, Jesus preaches the Sermon on the Mount to His disciples and the multitudes.

"Not everyone who says to Me, 'Lord, Lord,' will enter the kingdom of heaven, but he who does the will of My Father who is in heaven *will enter.* Many will say to Me on that day, 'Lord, Lord, did we not prophesy in Your name, and in Your name cast out demons, and in Your name perform many miracles?' And then I will declare to them, 'I never knew you, DEPART FROM ME, YOU WHO PRACTICE LAWLESSNESS'" (Matthew 7:21–23, Jesus quotes from Psalm 6:8; cf. Matthew 25:11–13; see Luke 6:46).

Setting: A house near the Sea of Galilee. Jesus explains the meaning of the Parable of the Wheat and the Tares to His disciples.

And He said, "The one who sows the good seed is the Son of Man, and the field is the world; and as *for* the good seed, these are the sons of the kingdom; and the tares are the sons of the evil *one;* and the enemy who sowed them is the devil, and the harvest is the end of the age; and the reapers are angels. So just as the tares are gathered up and burned with fire, so shall it be at the end of the age. The Son of Man will send forth His angels, and they will gather out of His kingdom all stumbling blocks, and those who commit lawlessness, and will throw them into the furnace of fire; in that place there will be weeping and gnashing of teeth. Then THE RIGHTEOUS WILL SHINE FORTH AS THE SUN in the kingdom of their Father. He who has ears, let him hear" (Matthew 13:37–43, Jesus quotes from Daniel 12:3; cf. Matthew 8:12; 13:50).

Setting: The temple in Jerusalem. After the Jewish religious leaders test Him with questions, Jesus pronounces the seventh of eight woes on them in front of the crowds and His disciples.

"Woe to you, scribes and Pharisees, hypocrites! For you are like whitewashed tombs which on the outside appear beautiful, but inside they are full of dead men's bones and all uncleanness. So you, too, outwardly appear righteous to men, but inwardly you are full of hypocrisy and lawlessness" (Matthew 23:27, 28; cf. Luke 11:44).

Setting: The Mount of Olives, just east of Jerusalem. During His discourse, Jesus answers His disciples' questions as to when the temple will be destroyed and Jerusalem overrun, along with the signs of His coming and the end of the age.

And Jesus answered and said to them, "See to it that no one misleads you. For many will come in My name, saying, 'I am the Christ,' and will mislead many. You will be hearing of wars and rumors of wars. See that you are not frightened, for *those things* must take place, but *that* is not yet the end. For nation will rise against nation, and kingdom against kingdom, and in various places there will be famines and earthquakes. But all these things are *merely* the beginning of birth pangs. Then they will deliver you to tribulation, and will kill you, and you will be hated by all nations because of My name. At that time many will fall away and will betray one another and hate one another. Many false prophets will arise and will mislead many. Because lawlessness is increased, most people's love will grow cold. But the one who endures to the end, he will be saved. This gospel of the kingdom shall be preached in the whole world as a testimony to all the nations, and then the end will come" (Matthew 24:4–14; cf. Jeremiah 29:8; Matthew 7:15; 10:17, 22; Mark 13:3–13; Luke 21:7–19; Revelation 6:4).

LAWSUIT (Also see COURT; and LAWYER)

[LAWSUIT from sue you]

Setting: Galilee. During the early part of His ministry, Jesus preaches the Sermon on the Mount to His disciples and the multitudes.

"If anyone wants to sue you and take your shirt, let him have your coat also" (Matthew 5:40).

LAWYER (See COURT; LAWSUIT; LAWYERS; and SCRIBES)

LAWYERS (Also see COURT; LAWSUIT; and SCRIBES)

Setting: On the way from Galilee to Jerusalem. After Jesus pronounces woes upon the Pharisees, a lawyer replies that His remarks are an insult to lawyers, too.

But He said, "Woe to you lawyers as well! For you weigh men down with burdens hard to bear, while you yourselves will not even touch the burdens with one of your fingers. Woe to you! For you build the tombs of the prophets, and *it was* your fathers *who* killed them. So you are witnesses and approve the deeds of your fathers; because it was they who killed them, and you build *their tombs*. For this reason also the wisdom of God said, 'I will send them prophets and apostles, and *some* of them they will kill and *some* they will persecute, so that the blood of all the prophets, shed since the foundation of the world, may be charged against this generation, from the blood of Abel to the blood of Zechariah, who was killed between the altar and the house *of God*; yes, I tell you, it shall be charged against this generation.' Woe to you lawyers! For you have taken away the key of knowledge; you yourselves did not enter, and you hindered those who were entering." (Luke 11:46–52; cf. Matthew 23:29–32; see 2 Chronicles 24:20, 21; Matthew 23:4, 13).

LAYING HANDS ON (Listed as HANDS, LAYING ON)

LAZARUS (of Bethany)

Setting: Beyond the Jordan. While Jesus and His disciples are avoiding the Jerusalem Pharisees, Jesus receives word from Lazarus's sisters in Bethany of His friend's sickness, and decides to go there.

Then after this He said to the disciples, "Let us go to Judea again." The disciples said to Him, "Rabbi, the Jews were just now seeking to stone You, and are You going there again?" Jesus answered, "Are there not twelve hours in the day? If anyone walks in the day, he does not stumble, because he sees the light of this world. But if anyone walks in the night, he stumbles, because the light is not in him." This He said, and after that He said to them, "Our friend Lazarus has fallen asleep; but I go, so that I may awaken him out of sleep" (John 11:7–11; see John 8:59; 10:39).

Setting: Beyond the Jordan. While Jesus and His disciples are avoiding the Jerusalem Pharisees, Jesus communicates Lazarus's death to His disciples, deciding to go there.

So Jesus then said to them plainly, "Lazarus is dead, and I am glad for your sakes that I was not there, so that you may believe; but let us go to him" (John 11:14, 15)

Setting: Bethany near Jerusalem. After the death of His friend, Lazarus, Jesus travels with His disciples from beyond the Jordan to visit Lazarus's sisters, Martha and Mary, and raises Lazarus from the dead.

Jesus said, "Remove the stone." Martha, the sister of the deceased, said to Him, "Lord, by this time there will be a stench, for he has been *dead* four days." Jesus said to her, "Did I not say to you that if you believe, you will see the glory of God?" So they removed the stone. Then Jesus raised His eyes, and said, "Father, I thank You that You have heard Me. I knew that You always hear Me; but because of the people standing around I said it, so that they may believe that you sent Me." When He had said these things, He cried out with a loud voice, "Lazarus, come forth." The man who had died came forth, bound hand and foot with wrappings, and his face was wrapped around with a cloth. Jesus said to them, "Unbind him, and let him go" (John 11:39–44; see Matthew 11:25).

LAZARUS (the poor man)

Setting: On the way from Galilee to Jerusalem. After He responds to the Pharisees' scoffing at His teaching His disciples about stewardship and the permanence of the Law, Jesus conveys the story of the rich man and Lazarus.

"Now there was a rich man, and he habitually dressed in purple and fine linen, joyously living in splendor every day. And a poor man named Lazarus was laid at his gate, covered with sores, and longing to be fed with the *crumbs* which were falling from the rich man's table; besides, even the dogs were coming and licking his sores. Now the poor man died and was carried away by the angels to Abraham's bosom; and the rich man also died and was buried. In Hades he lifted up his eyes, being in torment, and saw Abraham far away and Lazarus in his bosom. And he cried out and said, 'Father Abraham, have mercy on me, and send Lazarus so that he may dip the tip of his finger in water and cool off my tongue, for I am in agony in this flame.' But Abraham said, 'Child, remember that during your life you received your good things, and likewise Lazarus bad things; but now he is being comforted here, and you are in agony. And besides all this, between us and you there is a great chasm fixed, so that those who wish to come over from here to you will not be able, and *that* none may cross over from there to us.' And he said, 'Then I beg you, father, that you send him to my father's house—for I have five brothers—in order that he may warn them, so that they will not also come to this place of torment.' But Abraham said, 'They have Moses and the Prophets; let them hear them.' But he said, 'No, father Abraham, but if someone goes to them from the dead, they will repent!' But he said to him, 'If they do not listen to Moses and the Prophets, they will not be persuaded even if someone rises from the dead' " (Luke 16:19–31; see Luke 3:8; 6:24; 16:1, 14).

LEADER (Also see LEADERS)

Setting: The temple in Jerusalem. Jesus exposes the truth about Pharisaism to the crowds and His disciples after the Jewish religious leaders test Him with questions.

Then Jesus spoke to the crowds and to His disciples, saying: "The scribes and the Pharisees have seated themselves in the chair of Moses; therefore all that they tell you, do and observe, but do not do according to their deeds; for they say *things* and do not do *them.* They tie up heavy burdens and lay them on men's shoulders, but they themselves are unwilling to move them with *so much as* a finger. But they do all their deeds to be noticed by men; for they broaden their phylacteries and lengthen their tassels *of their garments.* They love the place of honor at banquets and the chief seats in the synagogues, and respectful greetings in the market places, and being called Rabbi by men. But do not be called Rabbi; for One is your Teacher, and you are all brothers. Do not call *anyone* on earth your father; for One is your Father, He who is in heaven. Do not be called leaders; for One is your Leader, *that is,* Christ. But the greatest among you shall be your servant. Whoever exalts himself shall be humbled; and whoever humbles himself shall be exalted" (Matthew 23:1–12; cf. Matthew 20:26; Mark 12:38–40; Luke 20:46, 47; see Exodus 13:9; Deuteronomy 33:3; Matthew 6:1, 5, 6, 9, 16; Mark 14:11; Luke 11:43; 14:11).

Setting: An upper room in Jerusalem. During the Feast of Unleavened Bread (Passover) just before Jesus' crucifixion, while Jesus celebrates the Passover meal with His disciples and institutes the Lord's Supper, the disciples argue over who is the greatest among them.

And He said to them, "The kings of the Gentiles lord it over them; and those who have authority over them are called 'Benefactors.' But *it is* not this way with you, but the one who is the greatest among you must become like the youngest, and the leader like a servant. For who is greater, the one who reclines *at the table* or the one who serves? Is it not the one who reclines *at the table?* But I am among you as the one who serves" (Luke 22:25–27; cf. Matthew 20:25–28; 23:11; Mark 10:42–45; Luke 22:1–24).

[LEADER from leads]
Setting: Jerusalem. Following the Pharisees' interrogation and dismissal of the formerly blind man Jesus healed on the Sabbath, the Lord speaks to the Pharisees, using parabolic language they do not understand.

"Truly, truly, I say to you, he who does not enter by the door into the fold of the sheep, but climbs up some other way, he is a thief and a robber. But he who enters by the door is a shepherd of the sheep. To him the doorkeeper opens, and the sheep hear his voice, and he calls his own sheep by name and leads them out. When he puts forth all his own, he goes ahead of them, and the sheep follow him because they know his voice. A stranger they simply will not follow, but will flee from him, because they do not know the voice of strangers" (John 10:1–5).

[LEADER from leads]
Setting: On the island of Patmos (in the Aegean Sea about fifty miles southwest of Ephesus in modern Turkey). On the Lord's Day (Sunday), about fifty years after Jesus' resurrection, the disciple John encounters the Lord Jesus Christ, who communicates a new revelation for the apostle to record for the church in Thyatira and to six other churches in Asia.

"And to the angel of the church in Thyatira write: The Son of God, who has eyes like a flame of fire, and His feet are like burnished bronze, says this: 'I know your deeds, and your love and faith and service and perseverance, and that your deeds of late are greater than at first. But I have *this* against you, that you tolerate the woman Jezebel, who calls herself a prophetess, and she teaches and leads My bond-servants astray so that they commit *acts of* immorality and eat things sacrificed to idols. I gave her time to repent, and she does not want to repent of her immorality. Behold, I will throw her on a bed *of sickness,* and those who commit adultery with her into great tribulation, unless they repent of her deeds. And I will kill her children with pestilence, and all the churches will know that I am He who searches the minds and hearts; and I will give to each one of you according to your deeds. But I say to you, the rest who are in Thyatira, who do not hold this teaching, who have not known the deep things of Satan, as they call them—I place no other burden on you. Nevertheless what you have, hold fast until I come. He who overcomes, and he who keeps My deeds until the end, TO HIM I WILL GIVE AUTHORITY OVER THE NATIONS; AND HE SHALL RULE THEM WITH A ROD OF IRON, AS THE VESSELS OF THE POTTER ARE BROKEN TO PIECES, as I also have received *authority* from My Father; and I will give him the morning star. He who has an ear, let him hear what the Spirit says to the churches' (Revelation 2:18–29; Jesus quotes from Psalm 2:8, 9; Isaiah 30:14; see 1 Kings 16:31; Psalm 7:9; Romans 2:5; 1 Corinthians 2:10; 2 Peter 3:9; Revelation 1:14; 2:7; 3:11; 17:1–20).

LEADERS (Also see LEADER)

Setting: The temple in Jerusalem. Jesus exposes the truth about Pharisaism to the crowds and His disciples after the Jewish religious leaders test Him with questions.

Then Jesus spoke to the crowds and to His disciples, saying: "The scribes and the Pharisees have seated themselves in the chair of Moses; therefore all that they tell you, do and observe, but do not do according to their deeds; for they say *things* and do not do *them.* They tie up heavy burdens and lay them on men's shoulders, but they themselves are unwilling to move them with *so much as* a finger. But they do all their deeds to be noticed by men; for they broaden their phylacteries and lengthen their tassels *of their garments.* They love the place of honor at banquets and the chief seats in the synagogues, and respectful greetings in the market places, and being called Rabbi by men. But do not be called Rabbi; for One is your Teacher, and you are all brothers. Do not call *anyone* on earth your father; for One is your Father, He who is in heaven. Do not be called leaders; for One is your Leader, *that is,* Christ. But the greatest among you shall be your servant. Whoever exalts himself shall be humbled; and whoever humbles himself shall be exalted" (Matthew 23:1–12; cf. Matthew 20:26; Mark 12:38–40; Luke 20:46, 47; see Exodus 13:9; Deuteronomy 33:3; Matthew 6:1, 5, 6, 9, 16; Mark 14:11; Luke 11:43; 14:11).

LEADERS, WOES TO THE RELIGIOUS (Also see CONDEMNATION)

[WOES TO THE RELIGIOUS LEADERS from woe to you, scribes and Pharisees] ***Setting:*** The temple in Jerusalem. After the Jewish religious leaders test Him with questions, Jesus pronounces the first of eight woes on them in front of the crowds and His disciples.

"But woe to you, scribes and Pharisees, hypocrites, because you shut off the kingdom of heaven from people; for you do not enter in yourselves, nor do you allow those who are entering to go in (Matthew 23:13; cf. Luke 11:52).

[WOES TO THE RELIGIOUS LEADERS from Woe to you, scribes and Pharisees]
Setting: The temple in Jerusalem. After the Jewish religious leaders test Him with questions, Jesus pronounces the second of eight woes on them in front of the crowds and His disciples.

["Woe to you, scribes and Pharisees, hypocrites, because you devour widows' houses, and for a pretense you make long prayers; therefore you will receive greater condemnation] (Matthew 23:14; cf. Mark 12:40; Luke 20:47).

[WOES TO THE RELIGIOUS LEADERS from Woe to you, scribes and Pharisees]
Setting: The temple in Jerusalem. After the Jewish religious leaders test Him with questions, Jesus pronounces the third of eight woes on them in front of the crowds and His disciples.

"Woe to you, scribes and Pharisees, hypocrites, because you travel around on sea and land to make one proselyte; and when he becomes one, you make him twice as much a son of hell as yourselves" (Matthew 23:15).

[WOES TO THE RELIGIOUS LEADERS from Woe to you, blind guides]
Setting: The temple in Jerusalem. After the Jewish religious leaders test Him with questions, Jesus pronounces the fourth of eight woes on them in front of the crowds and His disciples.

"Woe to you, blind guides, who say, "Whoever swears by the temple, *that* is nothing; but whoever swears by the gold of the temple is obligated.' You fools and blind men! Which is more important, the gold or the temple that sanctified the gold? And, 'Whoever swears by the altar, *that* is nothing, but whoever swears by the offering on it, he is obligated.' You blind men, which is more important, the offering, or the altar that sanctifies the offering? Therefore, whoever swears by the altar, swears *both* by the altar and by everything on it. And whoever swears by the temple, swears *both* by the temple and by Him who dwells within it. And whoever swears by heaven, swears *both* by the throne of God and by Him who sits upon it" (Matthew 23:16–22; see Exodus 29:37; 1 Kings 8:13; Isaiah 66:1; Matthew 15:14).

[WOES TO THE RELIGIOUS LEADERS from Woe to you, scribes and Pharisees]
Setting: The temple in Jerusalem. After the Jewish religious leaders test Him with questions, Jesus pronounces the fifth of eight woes on them in front of the crowds and His disciples.

"Woe to you, scribes and Pharisees, hypocrites! For you tithe the mint and dill and cummin, and have neglected the weightier provisions of the law: justice and mercy and faithfulness; but these are things you should have done without neglecting the others. You blind guides, who strain out a gnat and swallow a camel!" (Matthew 23:23, 24).

[WOES TO THE RELIGIOUS LEADERS from Woe to you, scribes and Pharisees]
Setting: The temple in Jerusalem. After the Jewish religious leaders test Him with questions, Jesus pronounces the sixth of eight woes on them in front of the crowds and His disciples.

"Woe to you, scribes and Pharisees, hypocrites! For you clean the outside of the cup and of the dish, but inside they are full of robbery and self-indulgence. You blind Pharisee, first clean the inside of the cup and of the dish, so that the outside of it may become clean also" (Matthew 23:25, 26; see Mark 7:4).

[WOES TO THE RELIGIOUS LEADERS from Woe to you, scribes and Pharisees]
Setting: The temple in Jerusalem. After the Jewish religious leaders test Him with questions, Jesus pronounces the seventh of eight woes on them in front of the crowds and His disciples.

"Woe to you, scribes and Pharisees, hypocrites! For you are like whitewashed tombs which on the outside appear beautiful, but inside they are full of dead men's bones and all uncleanness. So you, too, outwardly appear righteous to men, but inwardly you are full of hypocrisy and lawlessness" (Matthew 23:27, 28; cf. Luke 11:44).

[WOES TO THE RELIGIOUS LEADERS from Woe to you, scribes and Pharisees]
Setting: The temple in Jerusalem. After the Jewish religious leaders test Him with questions, Jesus pronounces the eighth of eight woes on them in front of the crowds and His disciples.

"Woe to you, scribes and Pharisees, hypocrites! For you build the tombs of the prophets and adorn the monuments of the righteous, and say, 'If we had been *living* in the days of our fathers, we would not have been partners with them in *shedding* the blood of the prophets.' So you testify against yourselves, that you are sons of those who murdered the prophets. Fill up, then, the measure *of the guilt* of you fathers. You serpents, you brood of vipers, how will you escape the sentence of hell? Therefore, behold, I am sending you prophets and wise men and scribes; some of them you will kill and crucify, and some of them you will scourge in your synagogues, and persecute from city to city, so that upon you may fall *the guilt of* all the righteous blood shed on earth, from the blood of righteous Abel to the blood of Zechariah, the son of Berechiah, whom you murdered between the temple and the altar. Truly I say to you, all these things will come upon this generation" (Matthew 23:29–36; cf. 2 Chronicles 24:21; Zechariah 1:1; Matthew 3:7; Luke 11:47–52; see Matthew 10:23).

[WOES TO THE RELIGIOUS LEADERS from woe to you Pharisees]
Setting: On the way from Galilee to Jerusalem. After speaking of how a lamp illuminates, the Lord has lunch with a Pharisee who is surprised He doesn't wash before eating.

But the Lord said to him, "Now you Pharisees clean the outside of the cup and of the platter; but inside of you, you are full of robbery and wickedness. You foolish ones, did not He who made the outside make the inside also? But give that which is within as charity, and then all things are clean for you. But woe to you Pharisees! You pay tithe of mint and rue and every *kind of* garden herb, and *yet* disregard justice and the love of God; but these are the things you should have done without neglecting the others. Woe to you Pharisees! For you love the chief seats in the synagogues and the respectful greetings in the market places. Woe to you! For you are like concealed tombs, and the people who walk over *them* are unaware *of it*" (Luke 11:39–44; cf. Matthew 23:6, 7, 23–27; see Matthew 15:2; Titus 1:15).

[WOES TO THE RELIGIOUS LEADERS from Woe to you lawyers]
Setting: On the way from Galilee to Jerusalem. After Jesus pronounces woes upon the Pharisees, a lawyer replies that His remarks are an insult to lawyers, too.

But He said, "Woe to you lawyers as well! For you weigh men down with burdens hard to bear, while you yourselves will not even touch the burdens with one of your fingers. Woe to you! For you build the tombs of the prophets, and *it was* your fathers *who* killed them. So you are witnesses and approve the deeds of your fathers; because it was they who killed them, and you build *their tombs*. For this reason also the wisdom of God said, 'I will send them prophets and apostles, and *some* of them they will kill and *some* they will persecute, so that the blood of all the prophets, shed since the foundation of the world, may be charged against this generation, from the blood of Abel to the blood of Zechariah, who was killed between the altar and the house *of God*; yes, I tell you, it shall be charged against this generation.' Woe to you lawyers! For you have taken away the key of knowledge; you yourselves did not enter, and you hindered those who were entering" (Luke 11:46–52; cf. Matthew 23:29–32; see 2 Chronicles 24:20, 21; Matthew 23:4, 13).

LEAPING

[LEAPING from leap]
Setting: Galilee. After selecting His twelve disciples, Jesus teaches the Beatitudes (part of the Sermon on the Mount) to those disciples and a great throng of people from Judea, Jerusalem, and the central coastal region of Tyre and Sidon.

"Blessed are you when men hate you, and ostracize you, and insult you, and scorn your name as evil, for the sake of the Son of Man. Be glad in that day and leap *for joy*, for behold, your reward is great in heaven. For in the same way their fathers used to treat the prophets" (Luke 6:22, 23; cf. Matthew 5:10–12; see 2 Chronicles 36:16; Luke 6:12–19).

LEARNER (See DISCIPLE)

LEAST (THESE, LEAST OF is a separate entry)

Setting: Galilee. While speaking to the crowds, Jesus pays tribute to the ministry of John the Baptist, but emphasizes that the one who is least in the kingdom of heaven is greater than John.

As these men were going *away*, Jesus began to speak to the crowds about John, "What did you go out into the wilderness to see? A reed shaken by the wind? But what did you go out to see? A man dressed in soft *clothing?* Those who wear soft *clothing* are in kings' palaces! But what did you go out to see? A prophet? Yes, I tell you, and the one who is more than a prophet. This is the one about whom it is written, 'BEHOLD, I SEND MY MESSENGER AHEAD OF YOU, WHO WILL PREPARE YOUR WAY BEFORE YOU.' Truly, I say to you, among those born of women there has not arisen *anyone* greater than John the Baptist! Yet the one who is least in the kingdom of heaven is greater than he. From the days of John the Baptist until now the kingdom of heaven suffers violence, and violent men take it by force. For all the prophets and the Law prophesied until John. And, if you are willing to accept *it,* John himself is Elijah who was to come. He who has ears to hear, let him hear" (Matthew 11:7–15, Jesus quotes from Malachi 3:1; cf. Malachi 4:5; Luke 7:24–28; 16:16; see Matthew 14:5).

Setting: The Mount of Olives, just east of Jerusalem. During His discourse, after answering His disciples' questions as to when the temple will be destroyed and Jerusalem overrun, along with the signs of His coming and the end of the age, Jesus reveals the future judgments following His return.

"But when the Son of Man comes in His glory, and all the angels with Him, then He will sit on His glorious throne. All the nations will be gathered before Him; and He will separate them from one another, as the shepherd separates the sheep from the goats; and He will put the sheep on His right, and the goats on the left. Then the King will say to those on His right, 'Come, you who are blessed of My Father, inherit the kingdom prepared for you from the foundation of the world. 'For I was hungry, and you gave Me *something* to eat; I was thirsty, and you gave Me *something* to drink; I was a stranger, and you invited Me in; naked, and you clothed Me; I was sick, and you visited Me; I was in prison, and you came to Me.' Then the righteous will answer Him, 'Lord, when did we see You hungry and feed You, or thirsty, and give you *something* to drink? And when did we see You a stranger, and invite You in, or naked, and clothe You? When did we see You sick, or in prison, and come to You?' The King will answer and say to them, 'Truly I say to you, to the extent that you did it to one of these brothers of Mine, *even* the least *of them,* you did it to Me.' Then He will also say to those on His left, 'Depart from Me, accursed ones, into the eternal fire which has been prepared for the devil and his angels; for I was hungry, and you gave Me *nothing* to eat; I was thirsty, and you gave Me nothing to drink; I was a stranger, and you did not invite Me in; naked, and you did not clothe Me; sick, and in prison, and you did not visit Me.' Then they themselves also will answer, 'Lord, when did we see You hungry, or thirsty, or a stranger, or naked, or sick, or in prison, and did not take care of You?' Then He will answer them, 'Truly I say to you, to the extent that you did not do it to one of the least of these, you did not do it to Me.' These will go away into eternal punishment, but the righteous into eternal life" (Matthew 25:31–46; see Matthew 7:23; 16:27; 19:29).

Setting: Galilee. After He responds to the disciples of John the Baptist when they ask whether He is the promised Messiah, Jesus speaks to the crowds about John.

When the messengers of John had left, He began to speak to the crowds about John, "What did you go out into the wilderness to see? A reed shaken by the wind? But what did you go out to see? A man dressed in soft clothing? Those who are splendidly clothed and live in luxury are *found* in royal palaces! But what did you go out to see? A prophet? Yes, I say to you, and one who is more than a prophet. This is the one about whom it is written, 'BEHOLD, I SEND MY MESSENGER AHEAD OF YOU, WHO WILL PREPARE YOUR WAY BEFORE YOU.' I say to you, among those born of women there is no one greater than John; yet he who is least in the kingdom of God is greater than he" (Luke 7:24–28, Jesus quotes from Malachi 3:1; cf. Matthew 11:7–11).

Setting: Galilee. After Jesus prophesies His death, an argument arises among His disciples as to who is the greatest. The Lord solves the matter by using a child as a teaching illustration.

But Jesus, knowing what they were thinking in their heart, took a child and stood him by His side, and said to them, "Whoever receives this child in My name receives Me, and whoever receives Me receives Him who sent Me; for the one who is least among all of you, this is the one who is great" (Luke 9:47, 48; cf. Matthew 18:1–5; Mark 9:33–47; see Matthew 10:40; Luke 22:24).

LEAST OF THESE (Listed under THESE, LEAST OF)

LEAVEN (PHARISEES, LEAVEN OF THE is a separate entry; also see BREAD; and TEACHING)

Setting: By the Sea of Galilee. Because the religious leaders are rejecting His message, Jesus continues teaching the crowds with the Parable of the Leaven.

He spoke another parable to them, "The kingdom of heaven is like leaven, which a woman took and hid in three pecks of flour until it was all leavened" (Matthew 13:33).

Setting: On the way from Galilee to Jerusalem. After responding to a synagogue official's anger for healing a woman, sick eighteen years, in the synagogue on the Sabbath, Jesus conveys the Parable of the Mustard Seed and the Parable of the Leaven.

So He was saying, "What is the kingdom of God like, and to what shall I compare it? It is like a mustard seed which a man took and threw into his own garden; and it grew and became a tree, and THE BIRDS OF THE AIR NESTED IN ITS BRANCHES." And again He said, "To what shall I compare the kingdom of God? It is like leaven, which a woman took and hid in three pecks of flour until it was all leavened" (Luke 13:18–21, Jesus quotes from Ezekiel 17:23; cf. Matthew 13:31–34; Mark 4:30–32).

LEAVEN, PARABLE OF THE

[PARABLE OF THE LEAVEN from parable and leaven]

Setting: By the Sea of Galilee. Because the religious leaders are rejecting His message, Jesus continues teaching the crowds with the Parable of the Leaven.

He spoke another parable to them, "The kingdom of heaven is like leaven, which a woman took and hid in three pecks of flour until it was all leavened" (Matthew 13:33).

LEAVEN OF HEROD (Listed under HEROD, LEAVEN OF)

LEAVEN OF THE PHARISEES (Listed under PHARISEES, LEAVEN OF THE)

LEAVEN OF THE PHARISEES AND SADDUCEES (Listed under SADDUCEES, LEAVEN OF THE PHARISEES AND LEAVES (foliage; also see BRANCH; BRANCHES; ROOT; and TREE)

Setting: On the Mount of Olives, just east of Jerusalem. After answering His disciples' questions as to when the temple will be destroyed and Jerusalem overrun, along with the signs of His coming and the end of the age, Jesus teaches them the Parable of the Fig Tree during His Olivet Discourse.

"Now learn the parable from the fig tree: when its branch has already become tender and puts forth its leaves, you know that summer is near; so, you too, when you see all these things, recognize that He is near, *right* at the door. Truly, I say to you, this generation will not pass away until all these things take place. Heaven and earth will pass away, but My words will not pass away. But of that day and hour no one knows, not even the angels of heaven, nor the Son, but the Father alone. For the coming of the Son of Man will be just like the days of Noah. For as in those days before the flood they were eating and drinking, marrying and giving in marriage, until the day that Noah entered the ark, and they did not understand until the flood came and took them all away; so will the coming of the Son of Man be. Then there will be two men in the field; one will be taken and one will be left. Two women *will be* grinding at the mill; one will be taken and one will be left" (Matthew 24:32–41; cf. Mark 13:28–32; Luke 17:34–36; 21:28–33; see Genesis 6:5; 7:7; Matthew 5:18; 10:23; James 5:9).

Setting: On the Mount of Olives, east of the temple in Jerusalem. After predicting the temple's destruction, Jesus responds during His Olivet Discourse to questions from Peter, James, John, and Andrew about other future events.

"Now learn the parable from the fig tree: when its branch has already become tender and puts forth its leaves, you know that summer is near. Even so, you too, when you see these things happening, recognize that He is near, *right* at the door. Truly I say to you, this generation will not pass away until all these things take place. Heaven and earth will pass away, but My words will not pass away. But of the day or hour no one knows, not even the angels in heaven, nor the Son, but the Father *alone*" (Mark 13:28–32; cf. Matthew 24:32–36; Luke 21:28–33).

Setting: On the Mount of Olives, east of the temple in Jerusalem. After ministering in the temple a few days before His crucifixion, and giving the disciples more details regarding His return, Jesus conveys the Parable of the Fig Tree during His Olivet Discourse.

Then He told them a parable: "Behold the fig tree and all the trees; as soon as they put forth *leaves,* you see it and know for yourselves that summer is now near. So you also, when you see these things happening, recognize that the kingdom of God is near. Truly, I say to you, this generation will not pass away until all things take place. Heaven and earth will pass away, but My words will not pass away" (Luke 21:29–33; cf. Matthew 24:32–35; Mark 13:28–31; see Matthew 5:18).

LEFT (position)

Setting: Galilee. During the early part of His ministry, Jesus preaches the Sermon on the Mount to His disciples and the multitudes.

"So when you give to the poor, do not sound a trumpet before you, as the hypocrites do in the synagogues and in the streets, so that they may be honored by men. Truly I say to you, they have their reward in full. But when you give to the poor, do not let your left hand know what your right hand is doing, so that your giving will be in secret; and your Father who sees *what is done* in secret will reward you" (Matthew 6:2–4; see Jeremiah 17:10; Matthew 6:16).

Setting: On the way to Jerusalem. The mother of James and John, the sons of Zebedee, asks Jesus to make her sons exalted rulers with Him in His coming kingdom.

And He said to her, "What do you wish?" She said to Him, 'Command that in Your kingdom these two sons of mine may sit one on Your right and one on Your left.' But Jesus answered, "You do not know what you are asking. Are you able to drink the cup that I am about to drink?" They said to Him, 'We are able.' He said to them, "My cup you shall drink; but to sit on My right and on *My* left, this is not Mine to give, but it is for those for whom it has been prepared by My Father" (Matthew 20:21–23; cf. Mark 10:35–40; see Matthew 19:28; Acts 12:2).

Setting: The Mount of Olives, just east of Jerusalem. During His discourse, after answering His disciples' questions as to when the temple will be destroyed and Jerusalem overrun, along with the signs of His coming and the end of the age, Jesus reveals the future judgments following His return.

"But when the Son of Man comes in His glory, and all the angels with Him, then He will sit on His glorious throne. All the nations will be gathered before Him; and He will separate them from one another, as the shepherd separates the sheep from the goats; and He will put the sheep on His right, and the goats on the left. Then the King will say to those on His right, 'Come, you who are blessed of My Father, inherit the kingdom prepared for you from the foundation of the world. 'For I was hungry, and you gave Me *something* to eat; I was thirsty, and you gave Me *something* to drink; I was a stranger, and you invited Me in; naked, and you clothed Me; I was sick, and you visited Me; I was in prison, and you came to Me.' Then the righteous will answer Him, 'Lord, when did we see You hungry and feed You, or thirsty, and give you *something* to drink? And when did we see You a stranger, and invite You in, or naked, and clothe You? When did we see You sick, or in prison, and come to You?' The King will answer and say to them, 'Truly I say to you, to the extent that you did it to one of these brothers of Mine, *even* the least *of them,* you did it to Me.' Then He will also say to those on His left, 'Depart from Me, accursed ones, into the eternal fire which has been prepared for the devil and his angels; for I was hungry, and you gave Me *nothing* to eat; I was thirsty, and you gave Me nothing to drink; I was a stranger, and you did not invite Me in; naked, and you did not clothe Me; sick, and in prison, and you did not visit Me.' Then they themselves also will answer, 'Lord, when did we see You hungry, or thirsty, or a stranger, or naked, or sick, or in prison, and did not take care of You?' Then He will answer them, 'Truly I say to you, to the extent that you did not do it to one of the least of these, you did not do it to Me.' These will go away into eternal punishment, but the righteous into eternal life" (Matthew 25:31–46; see Matthew 7:23; 16:27; 19:29).

Setting: On the road to Jerusalem. After Jesus prophesies His persecution, death, and resurrection, James and John ask for special honor and privileges in His coming kingdom.

And He said to them, "What do you want Me to do for you?" They said to Him, "Grant that we may sit, one on Your right and one on *Your* left, in Your glory." But Jesus said to them, "You do not know what you are asking. Are you able to drink the cup that I drink, or to be baptized with the baptism with which I am baptized?" They said to Him, "We are able." And Jesus said to them, "The cup that I drink you shall drink; and you shall be baptized with the baptism with which I am baptized. But to sit on My right or on *My* left, this is not Mine to give; but it is for those for whom it has been prepared" (Mark 10:36–40; cf. Matthew 20:20–23; see Matthew 19:28; Acts 12:2).

LEFTOVERS

[LEFTOVERS from leftover fragments]

Setting: By the Sea of Galilee. After revealing to the Jewish religious leaders during the Feast of the Jews in Jerusalem that God, John the Baptist, His works, and the Scriptures testify to His mission, Jesus returns and miraculously feeds more than 5,000 people with a lad's five barley loaves and two fish.

Jesus said, "Have the people sit down." Now there was much grass in the place. So the men sat down, in number about five thousand. Jesus took the loaves, and having given thanks, He distributed to those who were seated; likewise also of the fish as much as they wanted. When they were filled, He said to the disciples, "Gather up the leftover fragments so that nothing will be lost" (John 6:10–12; cf. Matthew 14:17–21; Mark 6:38–44; Luke 9:14–17; see Matthew 15:32–38; John 6:1–9).

LEGAL PROTECTION **(Listed under PROTECTION, LEGAL)**

LEGALISM **(See PHARISEES, LEAVEN OF THE)**

LEGALISTIC TEACHING **(See, PHARISEES, LEAVEN OF THE)**

LEGIONS OF ANGELS **(Listed under ANGELS, LEGIONS OF; also see ANGELS)**

LENDER **(See LOANS; and MONEYLENDER)**

LEPER **(See LEPERS and LEPROSY, CLEANSING FROM)**

LEPER, CLEANSING A **(See LEPROSY, CLEANSING FROM and LEPERS)**

LEPERS **(See LEPROSY, CLEANSING FROM; also see UNCLEANNESS)**

Setting: Galilee. After His twelve disciples observe His ministry, Jesus summons and specifically instructs them about their ministry to the people of Israel.

These twelve Jesus sent out after instructing them: "Do not go in *the* way of *the* Gentiles, and do not enter *any* city of the Samaritans; but rather go to the lost sheep of the house of Israel. And as you go, preach, saying, 'The kingdom of heaven is at hand.' Heal *the* sick, raise *the* dead, cleanse *the* lepers, cast out demons. Freely you received, freely give. Do not acquire gold, or silver, or copper for your money belts, or a bag for *your* journey, or even two coats, or sandals, or a staff; for the worker is worthy of his support. And whatever city or village you enter, inquire who is worthy in it, and stay at his house until you leave *that city*. As you enter the house, give it your greeting. If the house is worthy, give it your *blessing of* peace. But if it is not worthy, take back your *blessing of* peace. Whoever does not receive you, nor heed your words, as you go out of that house or that city, shake the dust off your feet. Truly I say to you, it will be more tolerable for *the* land of Sodom and Gomorrah in the day of judgment than for that city" (Matthew 10:5–15; cf. Mark 6:7–11; Luke 9:1–5; see Matthew 3:2; 11:22, 24; 15:24; Luke 22:35; 1 Corinthians 9:14).

Setting: Galilee. As Jesus teaches and preaches, He responds to John the Baptist's question (asked by John's disciples) whether He is Israel's promised Messiah.

Jesus answered and said to them, "Go and report to John what you hear and see: *the* BLIND RECEIVE SIGHT and *the* lame walk, *the* lepers are cleansed and *the* deaf hear, *the* dead are raised up, and *the* POOR HAVE THE GOSPEL PREACHED TO THEM. And blessed is he who does not take offense at Me" (Matthew 11:4–6, Jesus quotes from Isaiah 35:5f; cf. Luke 7:22, 23).

Setting: The synagogue in Jesus' hometown of Nazareth in Galilee. At the beginning of His public ministry, Jesus comments to the congregation after reading on the Sabbath from the book of the prophet Isaiah.

And He said to them, "No doubt you will quote this proverb to Me, 'Physician, heal yourself! Whatever we heard was done at Capernaum, do here in your hometown as well.'" And He said, "Truly I say to you, no prophet is welcome in his hometown. But I say to you in truth, there were many widows in Israel in the days of Elijah, when the sky was shut up for three years and six months, when a great famine came over all the land; and yet Elijah was sent to none of them, but only to Zarephath, *in the land* of Sidon, to a woman who was a widow. And there were many lepers in Israel in the time of Elisha the prophet; and none of them was cleansed, but only Naaman the Syrian" (Luke 4:23–27; Jesus refers to 1 Kings 17:1, 9; 2 Kings 5:1–14; see Matthew 13:53–58).

Setting: Galilee. After He raises a woman's son from the dead in Nain, the disciples of John the Baptist inquire whether Jesus is the promised Messiah.

And He answered and said to them, "Go and report to John what you have seen and heard: *the* BLIND RECEIVE SIGHT, *the* lame walk, *the* lepers are cleansed, and *the* deaf hear, *the* dead are raised up, *the* POOR HAVE THE GOSPEL PREACHED TO THEM. Blessed is he who does not take offense at Me" (Luke 7:22, 23, Jesus quotes from Isaiah 35:5; 61:1; cf. Matthew 11:2–6).

[LEPERS from Go and show yourselves to the priests]
Setting: Samaria, on the way from Galilee to Jerusalem. The Lord stops to heal ten lepers who ask for cleansing.

When He saw them, He said to them, "Go and show yourselves to the priests." And as they were going, they were cleansed. Now one of them, when he saw that he had been healed, turned back, glorifying God with a loud voice, and he fell on his face at His feet, giving thanks to Him. And he was a Samaritan. Then Jesus answered and said, "Were there not ten cleansed? But the nine—where are they? Was no one found who returned to give glory to God, except this foreigner? "And He said to him, "Stand up and go; your faith has made you well" (Luke 17:14–19; see Leviticus 14:1–32).

LEPROSY (See LEPROSY, CLEANSING FROM; LEPERS; and UNCLEANNESS)

LEPROSY, CLEANSING FROM (Also see LEPERS)

[CLEANSING FROM LEPROSY from I am willing; be cleansed]
Setting: Galilee. When Jesus comes down after preaching The Sermon on the Mount, large crowds follow Him as a leper approaches Him asking for cleansing.

Jesus stretched out His hand and touched him, saying, "I am willing; be cleansed." And immediately his leprosy was cleansed. And Jesus said to him, "See that you tell no one; but go, show yourself to the priest and present the offering that Moses commanded, as a testimony to them" (Matthew 8:3, 4; cf. Mark 1:40–44; Luke 5:12–14).

[CLEANSING FROM LEPROSY from *the* lepers are cleansed]
Setting: Galilee. As He teaches and preaches in Galilee, Jesus responds to John the Baptist's question (asked by John's disciples) whether He is Israel's promised Messiah.

Jesus answered and said to them, "Go and report to John what you hear and see: *the* BLIND RECEIVE SIGHT and *the* lame walk, *the* lepers are cleansed and *the* deaf hear, *the* dead are raised up, and *the* POOR HAVE THE GOSPEL PREACHED TO THEM. And blessed is he who does not take offense at Me" (Matthew 11:4–6, Jesus quotes from Isaiah 35:5f; cf. Luke 7:22, 23).

[CLEANSING FROM LEPROSY from I am willing; be cleansed]
Setting: The synagogues of Galilee. Early in His ministry, as Jesus preaches and casts out demons, a leper beseeches Him for healing.

Moved with compassion, Jesus stretched out His hand and touched him, and said to him, "I am willing; be cleansed." Immediately the leprosy left him and he was cleansed. And He sternly warned him and immediately sent him away, and He said to him, "See that you say nothing to anyone; but go, show yourself to the priest and offer for your cleansing what Moses commanded, as a testimony to them" (Mark 1:41–44; cf. Luke 5:12–14; see Leviticus 14:1–32; Matthew 8:3).

[CLEANSING FROM LEPROSY from And there were many lepers in Israel in the time of Elisha the prophet; and none of them was cleansed, but only Naaman the Syrian]
Setting: The synagogue in Jesus' hometown of Nazareth in Galilee. At the beginning of Jesus' public ministry, He comments to the congregation after reading on the Sabbath from the book of the prophet Isaiah.

And He said to them, "No doubt you will quote this proverb to Me, 'Physician, heal yourself! Whatever we heard was done at Capernaum, do here in your hometown as well.'" And He said, "Truly I say to you, no prophet is welcome in his hometown. But I say to you in truth, there were many widows in Israel in the days of Elijah, when the sky was shut up for three years and six months, when a great famine came over all the land; and yet Elijah was sent to none of them, but only to Zarephath, *in the land* of Sidon, to a woman who was a widow. And there were many lepers in Israel in the time of Elisha the prophet; and none of them was cleansed, but only Naaman the Syrian" (Luke 4:23–27; Jesus refers to 1 Kings 17:1, 9; 2 Kings 5:1–14; see Matthew 13:53–58).

[CLEANSING FROM LEPROSY from I am willing; be cleansed]
Setting: Galilee. Early in His ministry, after calling Simon (Peter), James, and John to follow Him, Jesus heals a leper.

And He stretched out His hand and touched Him, saying, "I am willing; be cleansed." And immediately the leprosy left him. And He ordered him to tell no one, "But go and show yourself to the priest and make an offering for your cleansing, just as Moses commanded, as a testimony to them" (Luke 5:13, 14; cf. Matthew 8:2–4; Mark 1:40, 45; see Leviticus 13:49).

[CLEANSING FROM LEPROSY from *the* lepers are cleansed]
Setting: Galilee. After He raises a woman's son from the dead in Nain, the disciples of John the Baptist ask Jesus whether He is the promised Messiah.

And He answered and said to them, "Go and report to John what you have seen and heard: *the* BLIND RECEIVE SIGHT, *the* lame walk, *the* lepers are cleansed, and *the* deaf hear, *the* dead are raised up, *the* POOR HAVE THE GOSPEL PREACHED TO THEM. Blessed is he who does not take offense at Me" (Luke 7:22, 23, Jesus quotes from Isaiah 35:5; 61:1; cf. Matthew 11:2–6).

[CLEANSING FROM LEPROSY from they were cleansed]
Setting: Samaria, on the way from Galilee to Jerusalem. The Lord stops to heal ten lepers who ask for cleansing.

When He saw them, He said to them, "Go and show yourselves to the priests." And as they were going, they were cleansed. Now one of them, when he saw that he had been healed, turned back, glorifying God with a loud voice, and he fell on his face at His feet, giving thanks to Him. And he was a Samaritan. Then Jesus answered and said, "Were there not ten cleansed? But the nine—where are they? Was no one found who returned to give glory to God, except this foreigner? "And He said to him, "Stand up and go; your faith has made you well" (Luke 17:14–19; see Leviticus 14:1–32).

LETTER
Setting: Galilee. During the early part of His ministry, Jesus preaches the Sermon on the Mount to His disciples and the multitudes.

"Do not think that I came to abolish the Law or the Prophets; I did not come to abolish but to fulfill. For truly I say to you, until heaven and earth pass away, not the smallest letter or stroke shall pass from the Law until all is accomplished" (Matthew 5:17, 18; cf. Matthew 24:35).

Setting: On the way from Galilee to Jerusalem. The Lord responds to the Pharisees' scoffing at His teaching His disciples about stewardship.

And He said to them, "You are those who justify yourselves in the sight of men, but God knows your hearts; for that which is highly esteemed among men is detestable in the sight of God. The Law and the Prophets *were proclaimed* until John; since that time the gospel of the kingdom of God has been preached, and everyone is forcing his way into it. But is it easier for heaven and earth to pass away than for one stroke of a letter of the Law to fail" (Luke 16:15–17; cf. Matthew 5:18; see 1 Samuel 16:7; Matthew 4:23; 11:11–14).

LEVIRATE MARRIAGE (Listed under MARRIAGE, LEVIRATE)

LEVITE
Setting: On the way from Galilee to Jerusalem. While being tested by a lawyer, Jesus tells him the story of the good Samaritan.

Jesus replied and said, "A man was going down from Jerusalem to Jericho, and fell among robbers, and they stripped him and beat him, and went away leaving him half dead. And by chance a priest was going down on that road, and when he saw him, he passed by on the other side. Likewise a Levite also, when he came to the place and saw him, passed by on the other side. But a Samaritan, who was on a journey, came upon him; and when he saw him, he felt compassion, and came to him and bandaged up his wounds, pouring oil and wine on *them;* and he put him on his own beast, and brought him to an inn and took care of him. On the next day he took out two denarii and gave them to the innkeeper and said, 'Take care of him; and whatever more you spend, when I return I will repay you.' Which of these three do you think proved to be a neighbor to the man who fell into the robbers' *hands?*" And he said, "The one who showed mercy toward him." Then Jesus said to him, "Go and do the same" (Luke 10:30–37).

LIAR (Also see LIE; LIES; and WITNESS, FALSE)

Setting: The temple treasury in Jerusalem. After the scribes and Pharisees question His testimony about Himself, Jesus interacts with them regarding their ancestry and motives.

Jesus said to them, "If God were your Father, you would love Me, for I proceeded forth and have come from God, for I have not even come on My own initiative, but He sent Me. Why do you not understand what I am saying? *It is* because you cannot hear My word. You are of *your* father the devil, and you want to do the desires of your father. He was a murderer from the beginning, and does not stand in the truth because there is no truth in him. Whenever he speaks a lie, he speaks from his own *nature,* for he is a liar and the father of lies. But because I speak the truth, you do not believe Me. Which one of you convicts Me of sin? If I speak truth, why do not believe Me? He who is of God hears the words of God; for this reason you do not hear *them,* because you are not of God" (John 8:42–47; see John 8:1–41; 18:37; 1 John 3:8; 4:6; 5:1).

Setting: The temple treasury in Jerusalem. While Jesus is interacting with the scribes and Pharisees, they state their belief Jesus is a demon-possessed Samaritan because of His statement that anyone who keeps His word will never taste death.

Jesus answered, "If I glorify Myself, My glory is nothing; it is My Father who glorifies Me, of whom you say, 'He is our God'; and you have not come to know Him, but I know Him; and if I say that I do not know Him, I will be a liar like you, but I do know Him and keep His word. Your father Abraham rejoiced to see My day, and he saw *it* and was glad" (John 8:54–56; see Matthew 13:17; John 7:29).

LIE (Also see LIAR; LIES; and WITNESS, FALSE)

Setting: The temple treasury in Jerusalem. After the scribes and Pharisees question His testimony about Himself, Jesus interacts with them regarding their ancestry and motives.

Jesus said to them, "If God were your Father, you would love Me, for I proceeded forth and have come from God, for I have not even come on My own initiative, but He sent Me. Why do you not understand what I am saying? *It is* because you cannot hear My word. You are of *your* father the devil, and you want to do the desires of your father. He was a murderer from the beginning, and does not stand in the truth because there is no truth in him. Whenever he speaks a lie, he speaks from his own *nature,* for he is a liar and the father of lies. But because I speak the truth, you do not believe Me. Which one of you convicts Me of sin? If I speak truth, why do not believe Me? He who is of God hears the words of God; for this reason you do not hear *them,* because you are not of God" (John 8:42–47; see John 18:37; 1 John 3:8; 4:6; 5:1).

Setting: On the island of Patmos (in the Aegean Sea about fifty miles southwest of Ephesus in modern Turkey). On the Lord's Day (Sunday), about fifty years after Jesus' resurrection, the disciple John encounters the Lord Jesus Christ, who communicates a new revelation for the apostle to record for the church in Philadelphia and to six other churches in Asia.

"And to the angel of the church in Philadelphia write: He who is holy, who is true, who has the key of David, who opens and no one will shut, and who shuts and no one opens, says this: 'I know your deeds. Behold, I have put before you an open door which no one can shut, because you have a little power, and have kept My word, and have not denied My name. Behold, I will cause *those* of the synagogue of Satan, who say that they are Jews and are not, but lie—I will make them come and bow down at your feet, and *make them* know that I have loved you. Because you have kept the word of My perseverance, I also will keep you from the hour of testing, that *hour* which is about to come upon the whole world, to test those who dwell on the earth. I am coming quickly; hold fast what you have, so that no one will take your crown. He who overcomes, I will make him a pillar in the temple of My God, and he will not go out from it anymore; and I will write on him the name of My God, and the name of the city of My God, the new Jerusalem, which comes down out of heaven from My God, and My new name. He who has an ear, let him hear what the Spirit says to the churches' " (Revelation 3:7–13; see Isaiah 22:22; Galatians 2:9; Revelation 2:9, 10, 13, 25; 14:1).

LIES (Also see LIAR; LIE; and WITNESS, FALSE)

Setting: **The temple treasury in Jerusalem. After the scribes and Pharisees question His testimony about Himself, Jesus interacts with them regarding their ancestry and motives.**

Jesus said to them, "If God were your Father, you would love Me, for I proceeded forth and have come from God, for I have not even come on My own initiative, but He sent Me. Why do you not understand what I am saying? *It is* because you cannot hear My word. You are of *your* father the devil, and you want to do the desires of your father. He was a murderer from the beginning, and does not stand in the truth because there is no truth in him. Whenever he speaks a lie, he speaks from his own *nature,* for he is a liar and the father of lies. But because I speak the truth, you do not believe Me. Which one of you convicts Me of sin? If I speak truth, why do not believe Me? He who is of God hears the words of God; for this reason you do not hear *them,* because you are not of God" (John 8:42–47; see John 18:37; 1 John 3:8; 4:6; 5:1).

LIFE (Specifics such as ABUNDANT LIFE; ETERNAL LIFE; LIFE, BREAD OF; and TREE OF LIFE are separate entries; also see ALIVE; LIFE'S SPAN; and LIVES)

Setting: **Galilee. During the early part of His ministry, Jesus preaches the Sermon on the Mount to His disciples and the multitudes.**

"For this reason I say to you, do not be worried about your life, *as to* what you will eat or what you will drink; nor for your body, *as to* what you will put on. Is not life more than food, and the body more than clothing? Look at the birds of the air, that they do not sow, nor reap nor gather into barns, and *yet* your heavenly Father feeds them. Are you not worth much more than they? And who of you by being worried can add a *single* hour to his life? And why are you worried about clothing? Observe how the lilies of the field grow; they do not toil nor do they spin, yet I say to you that not even Solomon in all his glory clothed himself like one of these. But if God so clothes the grass of the field, which is *alive* today and tomorrow is thrown into the furnace, *will He* not much more *clothe* you? You of little faith! Do not worry then, saying 'What will we eat?' or 'What will we drink?' or 'What will be wear for clothing?" For the Gentiles eagerly seek all these things; for your heavenly Father knows that you need all these things. But seek first His kingdom and His righteousness, and all these things will be added to you. So do not worry about tomorrow; for tomorrow will care for itself. Each day has enough trouble of its own" (Matthew 6:25–34; cf. Luke 12:22–31; see 1 Kings 10:4–7; Job 35:11; Matthew 8:26).

Setting: **Galilee. After His twelve disciples observe His ministry, Jesus summons and specifically instructs them about their ministry ahead involving true discipleship.**

"He who loves father or mother more than Me is not worthy of Me; and he who loves son or daughter more than Me is not worthy of Me. And he who does not take his cross and follow after Me is not worthy of Me. He who has found his life will lose it, and he who has lost his life for My sake will find it" (Matthew 10:37–39; cf. Matthew 16:24, 25).

Setting: **Near Caesarea Philippi. After rebuking Peter for trying to forbid Him to accomplish His earthly mission of dying and being resurrected, Jesus teaches His disciples about the costs of discipleship.**

Then Jesus said to His disciples, "If anyone wishes to come after Me, he must deny himself, and take up his cross and follow Me. For whoever wishes to save his life will lose it; but whoever loses his life for My sake will find it. For what will it profit a man if he gains the whole world and forfeits his soul? Or what will a man give in exchange for his soul? For the Son of Man is going to come in the glory of His Father with His angels, and WILL THEN REPAY EVERY MAN ACCORDING TO HIS DEEDS. Truly, I say to you, there are some of you who are standing here who will not taste death until they see the Son of Man coming in His kingdom" (Matthew 16:24–28, Jesus quotes from Psalm 62:12; cf. Mark 8:34–37; Luke 9:23–27; see Matthew 10:38, 39).

Setting: On the Mount of Olives, just east of Jerusalem. During His discourse, Jesus answers His disciples' questions as to when the temple will be destroyed and Jerusalem overrun, along with the signs of His coming and the end of the age.

"Therefore when you see the ABOMINATION OF DESOLATION which was spoken of through Daniel the prophet, standing in the holy place (let the reader understand), then those who are in Judea must flee to the mountains. Whoever is on the housetop must not go down to get the things that are in his house. Whoever is in the field must not turn back to get his cloak. But woe to those who are pregnant and to those who are nursing babies in those days! But pray that your flight will not be in the winter, or on a Sabbath. For then there will be a great tribulation, such as has not occurred since the beginning of the world until now, nor ever will. Unless those days had been cut short, no life would have been saved; but for the sake of the elect those days will be cut short. Then if anyone says to you, 'Behold, here is the Christ,' or 'There *He is,*' do not believe *him.* For false Christs and false prophets will arise and will show great signs and wonders, so as to mislead, if possible, even the elect. Behold, I have told you in advance. So if they say to you, 'Behold, He is in the wilderness,' do not go out, *or,* 'Behold, He is in the inner rooms,' do not believe *them.* For just as the lightning comes from the east and flashes even to the west, so will the coming of the Son of Man be. Wherever the corpse is, there the vultures will gather" (Matthew 24:15–28, Jesus quotes from Daniel 9:27; cf. Daniel 12:1; Mark 13:14–23; Luke 17:22–31; 21:20–24; 23:29; see John 4:48).

Setting: A synagogue in Galilee. Early in His ministry, Jesus heals a man's withered hand on the Sabbath, while the Pharisees observe.

He said to the man with the withered hand, "Get up and come forward!" And He said to them, "Is it lawful to do good or do harm on the Sabbath, to save a life or to kill?" But they kept silent. After looking around at them with anger, grieved at their hardness of heart, He said to the man, "Stretch out your hand." And he stretched it out, and his hand was restored (Mark 3:3–5; cf. Matthew 12:9–14; Luke 6:6–11).

Setting: Caesarea Philippi. After rebuking Peter for desiring to thwart His mission to the cross, Jesus summons a crowd, along with His disciples, and informs them of the high costs of following Him.

And He summoned the crowd with His disciples, and said to them, "If anyone wishes to come after Me, he must deny himself, and take up his cross and follow Me. For whoever wishes to save his life will lose it, but whoever loses his life for My sake and the gospel's will save it. For what does it profit a man to gain the whole world, and forfeit his soul? For what will a man give in exchange for his soul? For whoever is ashamed of Me and My words in this adulterous and sinful generation, the Son of Man will also be ashamed of him when He comes in the glory of His Father with the holy angels" (Mark 8:34–38; cf. Matthew 16:24–28; Luke 9:23–27; see Matthew 10:33, 38, 39).

Setting: On the Mount of Olives, east of the temple in Jerusalem. After predicting the temple's destruction, Jesus responds during His Olivet Discourse to questions from Peter, James, John, and Andrew about other future events.

"But when you see the ABOMINATION OF DESOLATION standing where it should not be (let the reader understand), then those who are in Judea must flee to the mountains. The one who is on the housetop must not go down, or go in to get anything out of his house; and the one who is in the field must not turn back to get his coat. But woe to those who are pregnant and to those who are nursing babies in those days! But pray that it may not happen in winter. For those days will be a *time of* tribulation such as has not occurred since the beginning of the creation which God created until now, and never will. Unless the Lord had shortened *those* days, no life would have been saved; but for the sake of the elect, whom He chose, He shortened the days. And then if anyone says to you, 'Behold, here is the Christ'; or, 'Behold, *He is* there'; do not believe *him*; for false Christs and false prophets will arise, and will show signs and wonders, in order to lead astray, if possible, the elect. But take heed; behold, I have told you everything in advance" (Mark 13:14–23; cf. Matthew 24:15–28; Luke 21:20–24; see Daniel 9:27; 12:1; Luke 17:31).

Setting: A synagogue in Galilee. As Jesus teaches on the Sabbath, the scribes and Pharisees watch to see if He heals a man's withered hand.

But He knew what they were thinking, and He said to the man with the withered hand, "Get up and come forward!" And he got up and came forward. And Jesus said to them, "I ask you, is it lawful to do good or to do harm on the Sabbath, to save a life or destroy it?" And looking around at them all, He said to him, "Stretch out your hand!" And he did *so;* and his hand was restored (Luke 6:8–10; cf. Matthew 12:9–13; Mark 3:1–5).

Setting: Galilee. After Jesus presents the Parable of the Sower to the crowds, His disciples ask Him to give them the parable's meaning.

And He said, "To you it has been granted to know the mysteries of the kingdom of God, but to the rest *it is* in parables, so that SEEING THEY MAY NOT SEE, AND HEARING THEY MAY NOT UNDERSTAND. Now the parable is this: the seed is the word of God. Those beside the road are those who have heard; then the devil comes and takes away the word from their heart, so that they will not believe and be saved. Those on the rocky *soil* are those who, when they hear, receive the word with joy; and these have no *firm* root; they believe for a while, and in time of temptation fall away. The *seed* which fell among the thorns, these are the ones who have heard, and as they go on their way they are choked with worries and riches and pleasures of *this* life, and bring no fruit to maturity. But the *seed* in the good soil, these are the ones who have heard the word in an honest and good heart, and hold it fast, and bear fruit with perseverance" (Luke 8:10–15, Jesus quotes from Isaiah 6:9; cf. Matthew 13:10–23; Mark 4:10–20).

Setting: Galilee. Following Peter's pronouncement Jesus is the Christ of God, the Lord conveys the demands of discipleship and the hope regarding the kingdom of God.

And He was saying to *them* all, "If anyone wishes to come after Me, he must deny himself, and take up his cross daily and follow Me. For whoever wishes to save his life will lose it, but whoever loses his life for My sake, he is the one who will save it. For what is a man profited if he gains the whole world, and loses or forfeits himself? For whoever is ashamed of Me and My words, the Son of Man will be ashamed of him when He comes in His glory, and *the glory* of the Father and of the holy angels. But I say to you truthfully, there are some of those standing here who will not taste death until they see the kingdom of God" (Luke 9:23–27; cf. Matthew 16:24–26, 28; Mark 8:34–37; see Matthew 10:33, 38, 39).

Setting: On the way from Galilee to Jerusalem. After the scribes and Pharisees turn hostile and question Him repeatedly in an attempt to catch Him in something He might say, Jesus teaches the crowds and His disciples about greed and possessions.

But He said to him, "Man, who appointed Me a judge or arbitrator over you?" Then He said to them, "Beware, and be on your guard against every form of greed; for not *even* when one has an abundance does his life consist of his possessions" (Luke 12:14, 15; see 1 Timothy 6:6–10).

Setting: On the way from Galilee to Jerusalem. After giving a parable about riches and greed, Jesus comforts the crowd and His disciples. The scribes and Pharisees turn hostile and question Him repeatedly in an attempt to catch Him in something He might say.

And He said to His disciples, "For this reason I say to you, do not worry about *your* life, *as to* what you will eat; nor for your body, *as to* what you will put on. For life is more than food, and the body more than clothing. Consider the ravens, for they neither sow nor reap; they have no storeroom nor barn, and *yet* God feeds them; how much more valuable you are than the birds! And which of you by worrying can add a *single* hour to his life's span? If then you cannot do even a very little thing, why do you worry about other matters? Consider the lilies, how they grow: they neither toil nor spin; but I tell you, not even Solomon in all his glory clothed himself like one of these. But if God so clothes the grass in the field, which is *alive* today and tomorrow is thrown into the furnace, how much more *will He clothe* you? You men of little faith! And do not seek what you will eat and what you will drink, and do not keep worrying. For all these things the nations of the world eagerly seek; but your Father knows that you need these things. But seek His kingdom, and these things will be added to you. Do not be afraid, little flock, for your Father has chosen gladly to give you the kingdom" (Luke 12:22–32; cf. Matthew 6:25–33; see 1 Kings 10:4–7; Job 38:41).

Setting: On the way from Galilee to Jerusalem. After He responds to a guest's proclamation about the blessings of eating bread in the kingdom of God, Jesus presents to large crowds the demands of discipleship.

Now large crowds were going along with Him; and He turned and said to them, "If anyone comes to Me, and does not hate his own father and mother and wife and children and brothers and sisters, yes, and even his own life, he cannot be My disciple. Whoever does not carry his own cross and come after Me cannot be My disciple. For which one of you, when he wants to build a tower, does not first sit down and calculate the cost to see if he has enough to complete it? Otherwise, when he has laid a foundation and is not able to finish, all who observe it begin to ridicule him, saying, 'This man began to build and was not able to finish.' Or what king, when he sets out to meet another king in battle, will not first sit down and consider whether he is strong enough with ten thousand *men* to encounter the one coming against him with twenty thousand? Or else, while the other is still far away, he sends a delegation and asks for terms of peace. So then, none of you can be My disciple who does not give up all his possessions. Therefore, salt is good; but if even salt has become tasteless, with what will it be seasoned? It is useless either for the soil or for the manure pile; it is thrown out. He who has ears to hear, let him hear" (Luke 14:25–35; cf. Matthew 5:13; 10:37–39; see Proverbs 20:18; Philippians 3:7).

Setting: On the way from Galilee to Jerusalem. Jesus conveys the illustration of the prodigal son because the Pharisees and scribes complain He associates with tax collectors and sinners.

And He said, "A man had two sons. The younger of them said to his father, 'Father, give me the share of the estate that falls to me.' So he divided his wealth between them. And not many days later, the younger son gathered everything together and went on a journey into a distant country, and there he squandered his estate with loose living. Now when he had spent everything, a severe famine occurred in that country, and he began to be impoverished. So he went and hired himself out to one of the citizens of that country, and he sent him into his fields to feed swine. And he would have gladly filled his stomach with the pods that the swine were eating, and no one was giving *anything* to him. But when he came to his senses, he said, 'How many of my father's hired men have more than enough bread, but I am dying here with hunger! I will get up and go to my father, and will say to him, "Father, I have sinned against heaven, and in your sight; I am no longer worthy to be called your son; make me as one of your hired men."' So he got up and came to his father. But while he was still a long way off, his father saw him and felt compassion *for him,* and ran and embraced him and kissed him. And the son said to him, "Father, I have sinned against heaven and in your sight; I am no longer worthy to be called your son.' But the father said to his slaves, 'Quickly bring out the best robe and put it on him, and put a ring on his hand and sandals on his feet; and bring the fattened calf, kill it, and let us eat and celebrate; for this son of mine was dead and has come to life again; he was lost and has been found.' And they began to celebrate. Now his older son was in the field, when he came and approached the house, he heard music and dancing. And he summoned one of the servants and *began* inquiring what these things could be. And he said to him, 'Your brother has come, and your father has killed the fattened calf because he has received him back safe and sound.' But he became angry and was not willing to go in; and his father came out and *began* pleading with him. But he answered and said to his father, 'Look! For so many years I have been serving you and I have never neglected a command of yours; and *yet* you have never given me a young goat, so that I might celebrate with my friends; but when this son of yours came, who has devoured your wealth with prostitutes, you killed the fattened calf for him.' And he said to him, 'Son, you have always been with me, and all that is mine is yours. But we had to celebrate and rejoice, for this brother of yours was dead and *has begun* to live, and was lost and has been found'" (Luke 15:11–32; see Proverbs 29:2; Luke 15:1, 2).

Setting: On the way from Galilee to Jerusalem. After He responds to the Pharisees' scoffing at His teaching His disciples about stewardship and the permanence of the Law, Jesus conveys the story of the rich man and Lazarus.

"Now there was a rich man, and he habitually dressed in purple and fine linen, joyously living in splendor every day. And a poor man named Lazarus was laid at his gate, covered with sores, and longing to be fed with the *crumbs* which were falling from the rich man's table; besides, even the dogs were coming and licking his sores. Now the poor man died and was carried away by the angels to Abraham's bosom; and the rich man also died and was buried. In Hades he lifted up his eyes, being in torment, and saw Abraham far away and Lazarus in his bosom. And he cried out and said, 'Father Abraham, have mercy on me, and send Lazarus so that he may dip the tip of his finger in water and cool off my tongue, for I am in agony in this flame.' But Abraham said, 'Child, remember that during your life you received your good things, and likewise Lazarus bad things; but now he is being comforted here, and you are in agony. And besides all this, between us and you there is a great chasm fixed, so that those who wish to come over from here to you will not be able, and *that* none may cross over from there to us.' And he said, 'Then I beg you, father, that you send him to my father's house—for I have five brothers—in order that he may warn them, so that they will not also come to this place of torment.' But Abraham said, 'They have Moses and the Prophets; let them hear them.' But he said, 'No, father Abraham, but if someone goes to them from the dead, they will repent!' But he said to him, 'If they do not listen to Moses and the Prophets, they will not be persuaded even if someone rises from the dead' " (Luke 16:19–31; see Luke 3:8; 6:24; 16:1, 14).

Setting: On the way from Galilee to Jerusalem. After the Pharisees question Him about the coming of the kingdom of God, Jesus tells His disciples of His second coming.

And He said to the disciples, "The days will come when you will long to see one of the days of the Son of Man, and you will not see it. They will say to you, 'Look there! Look here!' Do not go away, and do not run after *them*. For just like the lightning, when it flashes out of one part of the sky, shines to the other part of the sky, so will the Son of Man be in His day. But first He must suffer many things and be rejected by this generation. And just as it happened in the days of Noah, so it will be also in the days of the Son of Man: they were eating, they were drinking, they were marrying, they were being given in marriage, until the day that Noah entered the ark, and the flood came and destroyed them all. It was the same as happened in the days of Lot: they were eating, they were drinking, they were buying, they were selling, they were planting, they were building; but on the day that Lot went out from Sodom it rained fire and brimstone from heaven and destroyed them all. It will be just the same on the day that the Son of Man is revealed. On that day, the one who is on the housetop and whose goods are in the house must not go down to take them out; and likewise the one who is in the field must not turn back. Remember Lot's wife. Whoever seeks to keep his life will lose it, and whoever loses *his life* will preserve it. I tell you, on that night there will be two in one bed; one will be taken and the other will be left. There will be two women grinding at the same place; one will be taken and the other will be left. [Two men will be in the field; one will be taken and the other will be left."] And answering they said to Him, "Where, Lord?" And He said to them, "Where the body *is*, there also the vultures will be gathered" (Luke 17:22–37; see Genesis 19; Matthew 10:39; 16:21, 27; 24:17–28, 37–41).

Setting: On the Mount of Olives, just east of Jerusalem. During His discourse, following a time of ministry in the temple a few days before His crucifixion, after conveying the Parable of the Fig Tree, Jesus warns His disciples to keep alert regarding future events.

"Be on guard, so that your hearts will not be weighted down with dissipation and drunkenness and the worries of life, and that day will not come upon you suddenly like a trap; for it will come upon all those who dwell on the face of all the earth. But keep on the alert at all times, praying that you may have strength to escape all these things that are about to take place, and to stand before the Son of Man" (Luke 21:34–36; cf. Mark 13:33; see Matthew 24:42–44).

Setting: By the pool of Bethesda in Jerusalem. During the Feast of the Jews, Jesus responds to criticism from the Jewish religious leaders for healing a lame man on the Sabbath and for referring to God as His Father, thereby making Himself equal with God.

Therefore Jesus answered and was saying to them, "Truly, truly, I say to you, the Son can do nothing of Himself, unless *it is* something He sees the Father doing; for whatever the Father does, these things the Son also does in like manner. For the Father loves the Son, and shows Him all things that He Himself is doing; and *the Father* will show Him greater works than these, so that you will marvel. For just as the Father raises the dead and gives them life, even so the Son also gives life to whom He wishes. For not even the Father judges anyone, but He has given all judgment to the Son, so that all will honor the Son even as they honor the Father. He who does not honor the Son does not honor the Father who sent Him" (John 5:19–23; see Luke 10:16; John 3:35; 11:25; 14:12).

Setting: Jerusalem. During the Feast of the Jews, Jesus responds to criticism from the Jewish religious leaders by referring to God as His Father (thereby making Himself equal with God) and prophesying His participation in the resurrection and judgment of men.

"Truly, truly, I say to you, an hour is coming and now is, when the dead will hear the voice of the Son of God, and those who hear will live. For just as the Father has life in Himself, even so He gave to the Son also to have life in Himself; and He gave Him authority to execute judgment, because He is *the* Son of Man. Do not marvel at this; for an hour is coming, in which all who are in the tombs will hear His voice, and will come forth; those who did the good *deeds* to a resurrection of life, those who committed the evil *deeds* to a resurrection of judgment" (John 5:25–29; see Daniel 12:2; John 1:4; 11:24).

Setting: Capernaum. The day after Jesus walks on the Sea of Galilee to join His disciples in a boat, the people He miraculously fed with a lad's five loaves and two fish quiz the Lord about the signs and works He performs so they may believe in Him.

Jesus then said to them, "Truly, truly, I say to you, it is not Moses who has given you the bread out of heaven, but it is My Father who gives you the true bread out of heaven. For the bread of God is that which comes down out of heaven, and gives life to the world" (John 6:32, 33; see John 6:50).

Setting: Capernaum. The day after Jesus walks on the Sea of Galilee to join His disciples in a boat, the people He miraculously fed with a lad's five loaves and two fish ask the Lord to always give them this bread out of heaven.

Jesus said to them, "I am the bread of life; he who comes to Me will not hunger, and he who believes in Me will never thirst. But I said to you that you have seen Me, and yet do not believe. All that the Father gives Me will come to Me, and the one who comes to Me I will certainly not cast out. For I have come down from heaven, not to do My own will, but the will of Him who sent Me. This is the will of Him who sent Me, that of all that He has given Me I lose nothing, but raise it up on the last day. For this is the will of My Father, that everyone who beholds the Son and believes in Him will have eternal life, and I Myself will raise him up on the last day" (John 6:35–40; see John 3:13, 16; 4:13, 14).

Setting: Capernaum of Galilee. After Jesus informs the people whom He miraculously fed with a lad's five loaves and two fish how they might receive the bread out of heaven, the Jewish religious leaders grumble because Jesus claims that He came down out of heaven.

Therefore the Jews were grumbling about Him, because He said, "I am the bread that came down out of heaven." They were saying, "Is not this Jesus, the son of Joseph, whose father and mother we know? How does He now say, 'I have come down out of heaven'?" Jesus answered and said to them, "Do not grumble among yourselves. No one can come to Me unless the Father who sent Me draws him; and I will raise him up on the last day. It is written in the prophets, 'AND THEY SHALL ALL BE TAUGHT OF GOD.' Everyone who has heard and learned from the Father, comes to Me. Not that anyone has seen the Father, except the One who is from God; He has seen the Father. Truly, truly, I say to you, he who believes has eternal life. I am the bread of life. Your fathers ate the manna in the wilderness, and they died. This is the bread which comes down out of heaven, so that one may eat of it and not die. I am the living bread that came down out of heaven; if anyone eats of this bread, he will live forever; and the bread also which I will give for the life of the world is My flesh" (John 6:41–51, Jesus quotes from Isaiah 54:13; see John 1:18, 29; 3:36; 7:27).

Setting: Capernaum of Galilee. After Jesus informs the people whom He miraculously fed with a lad's five loaves and two fish how they might receive the bread out of heaven, the Jewish religious leaders argue with one another when Jesus says He will give His flesh to the world to eat.

So Jesus said to them, "Truly, truly, I say to you, unless you eat the flesh of the Son of Man and drink His blood, you have no life in yourselves. He who eats My flesh and drinks My blood has eternal life, and I will raise him up on the last day. For My flesh is true food, and My blood is true drink. He who eats My flesh and drinks My blood abides in Me, and I in him. As the living Father sent Me, and I live because of the Father, so he who eats Me, he also will live because of Me. This is the bread which came down out of heaven; not as the fathers ate and died; he who eats this bread will live forever" (John 6:53–58; see Matthew 16:16; Luke 4:22; John 3:36; John 9:16; 15:4).

Setting: The synagogue at Capernaum of Galilee. After the Jewish religious leaders argue with one another when Jesus says He will give His flesh to the world to eat, some of His disciples also express difficulty with His statements.

But, Jesus, conscious that His disciples grumbled at this, said to them, "Does this cause you to stumble? *What* then if you see the Son of Man ascending to where He was before? It is the Spirit who gives life; the flesh profits nothing; the words that I have spoken to you are spirit and are life. But there are some of you who do not believe." For Jesus knew from the beginning who they were who did not believe, and who it was that would betray Him. And He was saying, "For this reason I have said to you, that no one can come to Me unless it has been granted him from the Father" (John 6:61–65; see Matthew 11:6; 13:11; John 3:13).

Setting: Jerusalem. Following the Pharisees' interrogation and dismissal of the formerly blind man Jesus healed on the Sabbath, the Lord conveys the Parable of the Good Shepherd to the Pharisees, using figures of speech they do not understand.

So Jesus said to them again, "Truly, truly, I say to you, I am the door of the sheep. All who came before Me are thieves and robbers, but the sheep did not hear them. I am the door; if anyone enters through Me, he will be saved, and will go in and out and find pasture. The thief comes only to steal and kill and destroy; I came that they may have life, and have *it* abundantly. I am the good shepherd; the good shepherd lays down His life for the sheep. He who is a hired hand, and not a shepherd, who is not the owner of the sheep, sees the wolf coming, and leaves the sheep and flees, and the wolf snatches them and scatters *them. He flees* because he is a hired hand and is not concerned about the sheep. I am the good shepherd, and I know My own and My own know Me, even as the Father knows Me and I know the Father; and I lay down My life for the sheep. I have other sheep, which are not of this fold; I must bring them also, and they will hear My voice; and they will become one flock *with* one shepherd. For this reason the Father loves Me, because I lay down My life so that I may take it again. No one has taken it away from Me, but I lay it down on My own initiative. I have authority to take it up again. This commandment I received from My Father" (John 10:7–18; see Isaiah 40:11; 56:8; Jeremiah 23:1; Matthew 11:27).

Setting: Bethany near Jerusalem. Jesus travels with His disciples to Bethany in Judea to see Lazarus's sisters, Martha and Mary, after the death of His friend.

Jesus said to her, "Your brother will rise again." Martha said to Him, "I know that he will rise again in the resurrection on the last day." Jesus said to her, "I am the resurrection and the life; he who believes in Me will live even if he dies, and everyone who lives and believes in Me will never die. Do you believe this?" (John 11:23–26; see Daniel 12:2; John 1:4; 6:47–51).

Setting: Jerusalem. Just days before the Passover, with the chief priests and Pharisees plotting to seize Jesus, crowds welcome Him to Jerusalem with palm branches and praise, and some Greeks ask to meet Him.

And Jesus answered them, saying, "The hour has come for the Son of Man to be glorified. Truly, truly, I say to you, unless a grain of wheat falls into the earth and dies, it remains alone; but if it dies, it bears much fruit. He who loves his life loses it, and he who hates his life in this world will keep it to life eternal. If anyone serves Me, he must follow Me; and where I am, there My servant will be also; if anyone serves Me, the Father will honor him" (John 12:23–26; see Matthew 10:39).

Setting: Jerusalem. Before the Passover, after revealing to His disciples they cannot follow Him back to heaven, Jesus takes issue with Peter's assertion he would lay down his life for Him.

Simon Peter said to Him, "Lord, where are You going?" Jesus answered, "Where I go, you cannot follow Me now; but you will follow later." Peter said to Him, "Lord, why can I not follow You right now? I will lay down my life for You." Jesus answered, "Will you lay down your life for Me? Truly, truly, I say to you, a rooster will not crow until you deny Me three times" (John 13:36–38; see Matthew 26:34; Mark 14:30, 72; Luke 22:33, 34).

Setting: Jerusalem. Before the Passover, with His departure in mind, after explaining He is the vine and His disciples are the branches, Jesus instructs them to love one another.

"This is My commandment, that you love one another, just as I have loved you. Greater love has no one than this, that one lay down his life for his friends. You are My friends if you do what I command you. No longer do I call you slaves, for the slave does not know what his master is doing; but I have called you friends, for all things that I have heard from My Father I have made known to you. You did not choose Me but I chose you, and appointed you that you would go and bear fruit, and *that* your fruit would remain, so that whatever you ask of the Father in My name He may give to you. This I command you, that you love one another" (John 15:12–17; see Matthew 12:50; John 6:70; 8:26; 10:11; 13:34).

Setting: On the island of Patmos (in the Aegean Sea about fifty miles southwest of Ephesus in modern Turkey). On the Lord's Day (Sunday), about fifty years after Jesus' resurrection, the disciple John encounters the Lord Jesus Christ, who communicates a new revelation for the apostle to record for the church in Smyrna and to six other churches in Asia.

"And to the angel of the church in Smyrna write: The first and the last, who was dead, and has come to life, says this: 'I know your tribulation and your poverty (but you are rich), and the blasphemy by those who say they are Jews and are not, but are a synagogue of Satan. Do not fear what you are about to suffer. Behold, the devil is about to cast some of you into prison, so that you will be tested, and you will have tribulation for ten days. Be faithful until death, and I will give you the crown of life. He who has an ear, let him hear what the Spirit says to the churches. He who overcomes will not be hurt by the second death' (Revelation 2:8–11; see Isaiah 44:6; Revelation 1:9, 18; 2:13; 20:6, 14).

LIFE, BOOK OF

[BOOK OF LIFE from your names are recorded in heaven]

Setting: On the way from Galilee to Jerusalem. The Lord responds to a report from the seventy sent out in pairs to every place He Himself will soon visit.

And He said to them, "I was watching Satan fall from heaven like lightning. Behold, I have given you authority to tread on serpents and scorpions, and over all the power of the enemy, and nothing will injure you. Nevertheless do not rejoice in this, that the spirits are subject to you, but rejoice that your names are recorded in heaven" (Luke 10:18–20; see Psalm 91:13; Isaiah 14:12–14; Luke 9:1).

Setting: On the island of Patmos (in the Aegean Sea about fifty miles southwest of Ephesus in modern Turkey). On the Lord's Day (Sunday), about fifty years after Jesus' resurrection, the disciple John encounters the Lord Jesus Christ, who communicates a new revelation for the apostle to record for the church in Sardis and to six other churches in Asia.

"To the angel of the church in Sardis write: He who has the seven Spirits of God and the seven stars, says this: 'I know your deeds, that you have a name that you are alive, but you are dead. Wake up, and strengthen the things that remain, which were about to die; for I have not found your deeds completed in the sight of My God. So remember what you have received and heard; and keep *it,* and repent. Therefore if you do not wake up, I will come like a thief, and you will not know at what hour I will come to you. But you have a few people in Sardis who have not soiled their garments; and they will walk with Me in white, for they are worthy. He who overcomes will thus be clothed in white garments; and I will not erase his name from the book of life, and I will confess his name before My Father and before His angels. He who has an ear, let him hear what the Spirit says to the churches' " (Revelation 3:1–6; see Matthew 10:32; Revelation 1:16).

LIFE, BREAD OF

Setting: Capernaum. The day after Jesus walks on the Sea of Galilee to join His disciples in a boat, the people He miraculously fed with a lad's five loaves and two fish ask the Lord to always give them this bread out of heaven.

Jesus said to them, "I am the bread of life; he who comes to Me will not hunger, and he who believes in Me will never thirst. But I said to you that you have seen Me, and yet do not believe. All that the Father gives Me will come to Me, and the one who comes to Me I will certainly not cast out. For I have come down from heaven, not to do My own will, but the will of Him who sent Me. This

is the will of Him who sent Me, that of all that He has given Me I lose nothing, but raise it up on the last day. For this is the will of My Father, that everyone who beholds the Son and believes in Him will have eternal life, and I Myself will raise him up on the last day" (John 6:35–40; see John 3:13, 16; 4:13, 14).

Setting: Capernaum of Galilee. After informing the people whom He miraculously fed with a lad's five loaves and two fish how they might receive the bread out of heaven, the Jewish religious leaders grumble because Jesus claims that He came down out of heaven.

Therefore the Jews were grumbling about Him, because He said, "I am the bread that came down out of heaven." They were saying, "Is not this Jesus, the son of Joseph, whose father and mother we know? How does He now say, 'I have come down out of heaven'?" Jesus answered and said to them, "Do not grumble among yourselves. No one can come to Me unless the Father who sent Me draws him; and I will raise him up on the last day. It is written in the prophets, 'AND THEY SHALL ALL BE TAUGHT OF GOD.' Everyone who has heard and learned from the Father, comes to Me. Not that anyone has seen the Father, except the One who is from God; He has seen the Father. Truly, truly, I say to you, he who believes has eternal life. I am the bread of life. Your fathers ate the manna in the wilderness, and they died. This is the bread which comes down out of heaven, so that one may eat of it and not die. I am the living bread that came down out of heaven; if anyone eats of this bread, he will live forever; and the bread also which I will give for the life of the world is My flesh" (John 6:41–51, Jesus quotes from Isaiah 54:13; see John 1:18, 29; 3:36; 7:27).

LIFE, CROWN OF

Setting: On the island of Patmos (in the Aegean Sea about fifty miles southwest of Ephesus in modern Turkey). On the Lord's Day (Sunday), about fifty years after Jesus' resurrection, the disciple John encounters the Lord Jesus Christ, who communicates a new revelation for the apostle to record for the church in Smyrna and to six other churches in Asia.

"And to the angel of the church in Smyrna write: The first and the last, who was dead, and has come to life, says this: 'I know your tribulation and your poverty (but you are rich), and the blasphemy by those who say they are Jews and are not, but are a synagogue of Satan. Do not fear what you are about to suffer. Behold, the devil is about to cast some of you into prison, so that you will be tested, and you will have tribulation for ten days. Be faithful until death, and I will give you the crown of life. He who has an ear, let him hear what the Spirit says to the churches. He who overcomes will not be hurt by the second death' (Revelation 2:8–11; see Isaiah 44:6; Revelation 1:9, 18; 20:6, 14).

LIFE, DIFFICULTIES IN (See PERSECUTION; SUFFERING; TRIBULATION; and TROUBLE)

LIFE, ETERNAL (See ETERNAL LIFE)

LIFE, JESUS' (See JESUS' LIFE)

LIFE, LIGHT OF

Setting: The temple in Jerusalem. Following the Feast of Booths, Jesus retires to the Mount of Olives, and returns the next day to teach. He addresses the scribes and Pharisees after their failed attempt to stone a woman caught in adultery.

Then Jesus again spoke to them, saying, "I am the Light of the world; he who follows Me will not walk in the darkness, but will have the Light of life" (John 8:12; see John 1:4).

LIFE, PURPOSE IN (See FOLLOWING JESUS CHRIST)

LIFE, TREE OF (See TREE OF LIFE)

LIFE'S DIFFICULTIES (See PERSECUTION; SUFFERING; TRIBULATION; and TROUBLE)

LIFE'S SPAN (Also see LIFE)
[LIFE'S SPAN from a *single* hour to his life]
Setting: Galilee. During the early part of His ministry, Jesus preaches the Sermon on the Mount to His disciples and the multitudes.

"For this reason I say to you, do not be worried about your life, *as to* what you will eat or what you will drink; nor for your body, *as to* what you will put on. Is not life more than food, and the body more than clothing? Look at the birds of the air, that they do not sow, nor reap nor gather into barns, and *yet* your heavenly Father feeds them. Are you not worth much more than they? And who of you by being worried can add a *single* hour to his life? And why are you worried about clothing? Observe how the lilies of the field grow; they do not toil nor do they spin, yet I say to you that not even Solomon in all his glory clothed himself like one of these. But if God so clothes the grass of the field, which is *alive* today and tomorrow is thrown into the furnace, *will He* not much more *clothe* you? You of little faith! Do not worry then, saying 'What will we eat?' or 'What will we drink?' or 'What will be wear for clothing?" For the Gentiles eagerly seek all these things; for your heavenly Father knows that you need all these things. But seek first His kingdom and His righteousness, and all these things will be added to you. So do not worry about tomorrow; for tomorrow will care for itself. Each day has enough trouble of its own" (Matthew 6:25–34; cf. Luke 12:22–31; see 1 Kings 10:4–7; Job 35:11; Matthew 8:26).

Setting: On the way from Galilee to Jerusalem. After giving a parable about riches and greed, Jesus comforts the crowd and His disciples. The scribes and Pharisees turn hostile and question Him repeatedly in an attempt to catch Him in something He might say.

And He said to His disciples, "For this reason I say to you, do not worry about *your* life, *as to* what you will eat; nor for your body, *as to* what you will put on. For life is more than food, and the body more than clothing. Consider the ravens, for they neither sow nor reap; they have no storeroom nor barn, and *yet* God feeds them; how much more valuable you are than the birds! And which of you by worrying can add a *single* hour to his life's span? If then you cannot do even a very little thing, why do you worry about other matters? Consider the lilies, how they grow: they neither toil nor spin; but I tell you, not even Solomon in all his glory clothed himself like one of these. But if God so clothes the grass in the field, which is *alive* today and tomorrow is thrown into the furnace, how much more *will He clothe* you? You men of little faith! And do not seek what you will eat and what you will drink, and do not keep worrying. For all these things the nations of the world eagerly seek; but your Father knows that you need these things. But seek His kingdom, and these things will be added to you. Do not be afraid, little flock, for your Father has chosen gladly to give you the kingdom" (Luke 12:22–32; cf. Matthew 6:25–33; see 1 Kings 10:4–7; Job 38:41).

LIGHT (illumination; LIGHT, SONS OF is a separate entry)
Setting: Galilee. During the early part of His ministry, Jesus preaches the Sermon on the Mount to His disciples and the multitudes.

"You are the light of the world. A city set on a hill cannot be hidden; nor does *anyone* light a lamp and put it under a basket, but on the lampstand, and it gives light to all who are in the house. Let your light shine before men in such a way that they may see your good works, and glorify your Father who is in heaven" (Matthew 5:14–16; cf. Mark 4:21; 1 Peter 2:12).

Setting: Galilee. During the early part of His ministry, Jesus preaches the Sermon on the Mount to His disciples and the multitudes.

"The eye is the lamp of the body; so then if your eye is clear, your whole body will be full of light. But if your eye is bad, your whole body will be full of darkness. If then the light that is in you is darkness, how great is the darkness!" (Matthew 6:22, 23; cf. Luke 11:34, 35).

Setting: Galilee. After His disciples observe His ministry, Jesus summons and specifically instructs them about their ministry ahead involving true discipleship.

"Therefore do not fear them, for there is nothing concealed that will not be revealed, or hidden that will not be known. What I tell you in the darkness, speak in the light; and what you hear *whispered* in your ear, proclaim upon the housetops. Do not fear those who kill the body but are unable to kill the soul; but rather fear Him who is able to destroy both soul and body in hell" (Matthew 10:26–28; cf. Mark 4:22; Luke 12:3; see Hebrews 10:31).

Setting: The Mount of Olives, just east of Jerusalem. During His discourse, Jesus answers His disciples' questions as to when the temple will be destroyed and Jerusalem overrun, along with the signs of His coming and the end of the age.

"But immediately after the tribulation of those days THE SUN WILL BE DARKENED, AND THE MOON WILL NOT GIVE ITS LIGHT, AND THE STARS WILL FALL from the sky, and the powers of the heavens will be shaken. And then the sign of the Son of Man will appear in the sky, and then all the tribes of the earth will mourn, and they will see the SON OF MAN COMING ON THE CLOUDS OF THE SKY with power and great glory. And He will send forth His angels with A GREAT TRUMPET and THEY WILL GATHER TOGETHER His elect from the four winds, from one end of the sky to the other" (Matthew 24:29–31, Jesus quotes from Isaiah 13:10, Daniel 7:13; Exodus 19:16; cf. Mark 13:24–27; Luke 21:25–27).

Setting: Galilee. Following His explanation of the Parable of the Sower to His disciples, Jesus illustrates what they should do with this truth.

And He was saying to them, "A lamp is not brought to be put under a basket, is it, or under a bed? Is it not *brought* to be put on the lampstand? For nothing is hidden, except to be revealed; nor has *anything* been secret, but that it would come to light. If anyone has ears to hear, let him hear" (Mark 4:21–23; cf. Luke 8:16, 17; see Matthew 5:14–16; Matthew 10:26).

Setting: On the Mount of Olives, east of the temple in Jerusalem. After predicting the temple's destruction, Jesus responds during His Olivet Discourse to questions from Peter, James, John, and Andrew about other future events.

"But in those days, after that tribulation, THE SUN WILL BE DARKENED AND THE MOON WILL NOT GIVE ITS LIGHT, AND THE STARS WILL BE FALLING from heaven, and the powers that are in the heavens will be shaken. Then they will see THE SON OF MAN COMING IN CLOUDS with great power and glory. And then He will send forth the angels, and will gather together His elect from the four winds, from the farthest end of the earth to the farthest end of heaven" (Mark 13:24–27. Jesus quotes from Isaiah 13:10; 34:4; Daniel 7:13; cf. Matthew 24:29–31; Luke 21:25–27).

Setting: Galilee. Following the explanation of the Parable of the Sower to His disciples, Jesus gives the Parable of the Lamp.

"Now no one after lighting a lamp covers it over with a container, or puts it under a bed; but he puts it on a lampstand, so that those who come in may see the light. For nothing is hidden that will not become evident, nor *anything* secret that will not be known and come to light. So take care how you listen; for whoever has, to him *more* shall be given; and whoever does not have, even what he thinks he has shall be taken away from him" (Luke 8:16–18; cf. Mark 4:21–23; see Matthew 5:14, 15; 10:26; 13:12).

Setting: On the way from Galilee to Jerusalem. After telling the increasing crowds about the sign of Jonah, Jesus illustrates His point by speaking about a lamp.

"No one, after lighting a lamp, puts it away in a cellar nor under a basket, but on the lampstand, so that those who enter may see the light. The eye is the lamp of your body; when your eye is clear, your whole body also is full of light; but when it is bad, your body also is full of darkness. Then watch out that the light in you is not darkness. If therefore your whole body is full of light, with no dark part in it, it will be wholly illumined, as when the lamp illumines you with its rays" (Luke 11:33–36; cf. Matthew 5:15, 6:22, 23).

Setting: On the way from Galilee to Jerusalem. Jesus warns His disciples of future events, as the scribes and Pharisees turn hostile and question Him repeatedly in an attempt to catch Him in something He might say.

Under these circumstances, after so many thousands of people had gathered together that they were stepping on one another, He began saying to His disciples first *of all,* "Beware of the leaven of the Pharisees, which is hypocrisy. But there is nothing covered up that will not be revealed, and hidden that will not be known. Accordingly, whatever you have said in the dark will be heard in the light, and what you have whispered in the inner rooms will be proclaimed upon the housetops. I say to you, My friends, do not be afraid of those who kill the body and after that have no more that they can do. But I will warn you whom to fear: fear the One who, after He has killed, has authority to cast into hell; yes, I tell you, fear Him! Are not five sparrows sold for two cents? *Yet* not one of them is forgotten before God. Indeed, the very hairs of your head are all numbered. Do not fear; you are more valuable than many sparrows". (Luke 12:1–7; cf. Matthew 10:26–31; see Matthew 16:6; Hebrews 10:31).

Setting: Jerusalem. At the time for the Passover of the Jews, after the Lord cleanses the temple, a Pharisee, Nicodemus, asks Him by night the meaning of "born again."

"For God so loved the world, that He gave His only begotten Son, that whoever believes in Him shall not perish, but have eternal life. For God did not send the Son into the world to judge the world, but that the world might be saved through Him. He who believes in Him is not judged; he who does not believe has been judged already, because he has not believed in the name of the only begotten Son of God. This is the judgment, that the Light has come into the world, and men loved darkness rather than the Light, for their deeds were evil. For everyone who does evil hates the Light, and does not come to the Light for fear that his deeds will be exposed. But he who practices the truth comes to the Light, so that his deeds may be manifested as having been wrought in God" (John 3:16–21; see Luke 19:10; John 1:4; 1:18; Romans 5:8; 1 John 1:6, 7).

Setting: Jerusalem. During the feast of the Jews, Jesus responds to criticism from the Jewish religious leaders by referring to God as His Father (thereby making Himself equal with God) and informing them that God, John the Baptist, and His works all testify to His mission.

"I can do nothing on My own initiative. As I hear, I judge; and My judgment is just, because I do not seek My own will, but the will of Him who sent Me. If I *alone* testify about Myself, My testimony is not true. There is another who testifies of Me, and I know that the testimony which He gives about Me is true. You have sent to John, and he has testified to the truth. But the testimony which I receive is not from man, but I say these things so that you may be saved. He was the lamp that was burning and was shining and you were willing to rejoice for a while in his light. But the testimony which I have is greater than the *testimony of* John; for the works which the Father has given Me to accomplish—the very works that I do—testify about Me, that the Father has sent Me. And the Father who sent Me, He has testified of Me. You have neither heard His voice at any time nor seen His form. You do not have His word abiding in you, for you do not believe Him whom He sent" (John 5:30–38; see Matthew 3:17; Mark 1:4, 5; John 1:7, 15, 32; 4:34; 8:14–16; 10:25, 37, 38).

Setting: The temple in Jerusalem. Following the Feast of Booths, Jesus retires to the Mount of Olives, and returns the next day to teach. He addresses the scribes and Pharisees after their failed attempt to stone a woman caught in adultery.

Then Jesus again spoke to them, saying, "I am the Light of the world; he who follows Me will not walk in the darkness, but will have the Light of life" (John 8:12; see John 1:4).

Setting: The temple treasury in Jerusalem. After Jesus avoids being stoned by the scribes and Pharisees, His disciples wonder if blindness is caused by sin, as the Lord heals a man born blind.

Jesus answered, "*It was* neither *that* this man sinned, nor his parents; but *it was* so that the works of God might be displayed in him. We must work the works of Him who sent Me as long as it is day; night is coming when no one can work. While I am in the world, I am the Light of the world." When He had said this, He spat on the ground, and made clay of the spittle, and applied the clay to his eyes, and said to him, "Go, wash in the pool of Siloam" (which is translated, Sent). So he went away and washed, and came *back* seeing (John 9:3–7; see John 8:12; 11:4; 12:46).

Setting: Beyond the Jordan. While Jesus and His disciples are avoiding the Jerusalem Pharisees, Jesus receives word from Lazarus's sisters in Bethany of His friend's sickness and decides to go there.

Then after this He said to the disciples, "Let us go to Judea again." The disciples said to Him, "Rabbi, the Jews were just now seeking to stone You, and are You going there again?" Jesus answered, "Are there not twelve hours in the day? If anyone walks in the day, he does not stumble, because he sees the light of this world. But if anyone walks in the night, he stumbles, because the light is not in him." This He said, and after that He said to them, "Our friend Lazarus has fallen asleep; but I go, so that I may awaken him out of sleep" (John 11:7–11; see John 8:59; 10:39).

Setting: Jerusalem. Just days before the Passover, with the chief priests and Pharisees plotting to seize Jesus, who is expressing anxiety about His upcoming death by crucifixion, the crowds ask Him about the identity of the Son of Man.

The crowd then answered Him, "We have heard out of the Law that the Christ is to remain forever; and how can You say, 'The Son of Man must be lifted up'? Who is this Son of Man?" So Jesus said to them, "For a little while longer the Light is among you. Walk while you have the Light, so that darkness will not overtake you; he who walks in the darkness does not know where he goes. While you have the Light, believe in the Light, so that you may become sons of Light." These things Jesus spoke, and He went away and hid Himself from them (John 12:34–36; see 1 John 1:6).

Setting: Jerusalem. Just days before the Passover, with the chief priests and Pharisees plotting to seize Jesus, who is expressing anxiety about His upcoming death by crucifixion, some of the Jews believe in Him, while others are rejecting His message.

And Jesus cried out and said, "He who believes in Me, does not believe in Me but in Him who sent Me. He who sees Me sees the One who sent Me. I have come *as* Light into the world, so that everyone who believes in Me will not remain in darkness. If anyone hears My sayings and does not keep them, I do not judge him; for I did not come to judge the world, but to save the world. He who rejects Me and does not receive My sayings, has one who judges him; the word I spoke is what will judge him at the last day. For I did not speak on My own initiative, but the Father Himself who sent Me has given Me a commandment *as to* what to say and what to speak. I know that His commandment is eternal life; therefore the things I speak, I speak just as the Father as told Me" (John 12:44–50; see Matthew 10:40; Luke 10:16; John 1:4; 3:17; 5:19; 6:68; 14:9).

Setting: Caesarea. Luke, writing in Acts, gives Paul's retelling of his conversion to Christ as he appears before King Agrippa following his hearing before the Jewish Council in Jerusalem and arrest by the Roman commander (on his way to Rome after the apostle's third missionary journey).

"And when we had fallen to the ground, I heard a voice saying to me in the Hebrew dialect, 'Saul, Saul, why are you persecuting Me? It is hard for you to kick against the goads.' And I said, 'Who are You, Lord?' And the Lord said, 'I am Jesus whom you are persecuting. But get up and stand on your feet; for this purpose I have appeared to you, to appoint you a minister and a witness not only to the things which you have seen, but also to the things in which I will appear to you; rescuing you from the *Jewish* people and from the Gentiles, to whom I am sending you, to open their eyes so that they may turn from darkness to light and from the dominion of Satan to God, that they may receive forgiveness of sins and an inheritance among those who have been sanctified by faith in Me' (Acts 26:14–18; see Isaiah 35:5; Acts 21:40; 22:14).

LIGHT, SONS OF

Setting: On the way from Galilee to Jerusalem. After giving the story of the prodigal son, the Lord teaches His disciples about stewardship.

Now He was also saying to the disciples, "There was a rich man who had a manager, and this *manager* was reported to him as squandering his possessions. And he called him and said to him, 'What is this I hear about you? Give an accounting of your management, for you can no longer be a manager.' The manager said to himself, 'What shall I do, since my master is taking the management away from me? I am not strong enough to dig; I am ashamed to beg. I know what I shall do, so that when I am removed from the management people will welcome me into their homes.' And he summoned each one of his master's debtors, and he *began* saying to the first, 'How much do you owe my master?' And he said, 'A hundred measures of oil.' And he said to him, 'Take your bill, and sit down quickly and write fifty.' Then he said to another, 'And how much do you owe?' And he said, 'A hundred measures of wheat.' He said to him, 'Take your bill, and write eighty.' And his master praised the unrighteous manager because he had acted shrewdly; for the sons of this age are more shrewd in relation to their own kind than the sons of light. And I say to you, make friends for yourselves by means of the wealth of unrighteousness, so that when it fails, they will receive you into the eternal dwellings. He who is faithful in a very little thing is faithful also in much; and he who is unrighteous in a very little thing is unrighteous also in much. Therefore if you have not been faithful in the *use of* unrighteous wealth, who will entrust the *true riches* to you? And if you have not been faithful in *the use of* that which is another's, who will give you that which is your own? No servant can serve two masters; for either he will hate the one and love the other, or else he will be devoted to one and despise the other. You cannot serve God and wealth" (Luke 16:1–13; cf. Matthew 6:24; see Matthew 25:14–30).

Setting: Jerusalem. Just days before the Passover, with the chief priests and Pharisees plotting to seize Jesus, who is expressing anxiety about His upcoming death by crucifixion, the crowds ask Him about the identity of the Son of Man.

The crowd then answered Him, "We have heard out of the Law that the Christ is to remain forever; and how can You say, 'The Son of Man must be lifted up'? Who is this Son of Man?" So Jesus said to them, "For a little while longer the Light is among you. Walk while you have the Light, so that darkness will not overtake you; he who walks in the darkness does not know where he goes. While you have the Light, believe in the Light, so that you may become sons of Light." These things Jesus spoke, and He went away and hid Himself from them (John 12:34–36; see 1 John 1:6).

LIGHT OF LIFE (Listed under LIFE, LIGHT OF)

LIGHT OF THE WORLD (Listed under WORLD, LIGHT OF THE)

LIGHTNING (Also see RAIN; STORM; and WEATHER)

Setting: On the Mount of Olives, just east of Jerusalem. During His discourse, Jesus answers His disciples' questions as to when the temple will be destroyed and Jerusalem overrun, along with the signs of His coming and the end of the age.

"Therefore when you see the ABOMINATION OF DESOLATION which was spoken of through Daniel the prophet, standing in the holy place (let the reader understand), then those who are in Judea must flee to the mountains. Whoever is on the housetop must not go down to get the things that are in his house. Whoever is in the field must not turn back to get his cloak. But woe to those who are pregnant and to those who are nursing babies in those days! But pray that your flight will not be in the winter, or on a Sabbath. For then there will be a great tribulation, such as has not occurred since the beginning of the world until now, nor ever will. Unless those days had been cut short, no life would have been saved; but for the sake of the elect those days will be cut short. Then if anyone says to you, 'Behold, here is the Christ,' or "There *He is,*' do not believe *him.* For false Christs and false prophets will arise and will show great signs and wonders, so as to mislead, if possible, even the elect. Behold, I have told you in advance. So if they say to you, 'Behold, He is in the wilderness,' do not go out, *or,* 'Behold, He is in the inner rooms,' do not believe *them.* For just as the lightning comes from the east and flashes even to the west, so will the coming of the Son of Man be. Wherever the corpse is, there the vultures will gather" (Matthew 24:15–28, Jesus quotes from Daniel 9:27; cf. Daniel 12:1; Mark 13:14–23; Luke 17:22–31; 21:20–24; 23:29; see John 4:48).

Setting: On the way from Galilee to Jerusalem. The Lord responds to a report from the seventy sent out in pairs to every place He Himself will soon visit.

And He said to them, "I was watching Satan fall from heaven like lightning. Behold, I have given you authority to tread on serpents and scorpions, and over all the power of the enemy, and nothing will injure you. Nevertheless do not rejoice in this, that the spirits are subject to you, but rejoice that your names are recorded in heaven" (Luke 10:18–20; see Psalm 91:13; Isaiah 14:12–14; Luke 9:1).

Setting: On the way from Galilee to Jerusalem. After the Pharisees question Him about the coming of the kingdom of God, Jesus tells His disciples of His second coming.

And He said to the disciples, "The days will come when you will long to see one of the days of the Son of Man, and you will not see it. They will say to you, 'Look there! Look here!' Do not go away, and do not run after *them*. For just like the lightning, when it flashes out of one part of the sky, shines to the other part of the sky, so will the Son of Man be in His day. But first He must suffer many things and be rejected by this generation. And just as it happened in the days of Noah, so it will be also in the days of the Son of Man: they were eating, they were drinking, they were marrying, they were being given in marriage, until the day that Noah entered the ark, and the flood came and destroyed them all. It was the same as happened in the days of Lot: they were eating, they were drinking, they were buying, they were selling, they were planting, they were building; but on the day that Lot went out from Sodom it rained fire and brimstone from heaven and destroyed them all. It will be just the same on the day that the Son of Man is revealed. On that day, the one who is on the housetop and whose goods are in the house must not go down to take them out; and likewise the one who is in the field must not turn back. Remember Lot's wife. Whoever seeks to keep his life will lose it, and whoever loses *his life* will preserve it. I tell you, on that night there will be two in one bed; one will be taken and the other will be left. There will be two women grinding at the same place; one will be taken and the other will be left. [Two men will be in the field; one will be taken and the other will be left."] And answering they said to Him, "Where, Lord?" And He said to them, "Where the body *is*, there also the vultures will be gathered" (Luke 17:22–37; see Genesis 19; Matthew 10:39; 16:21, 27; 24:17–28, 37–41).

LIKENESS

Setting: The temple in Jerusalem. The Pharisees send their disciples and the Herodians to test Jesus about the poll-tax, in order to trap Him while He teaches.

But Jesus perceived their malice, and said, "Why are you testing Me, you hypocrites? Show Me the coin *used* for the poll-tax." And they brought Him a denarius. And He said to them, "Whose likeness and inscription is this?" They said to Him, "Caesar's." Then He said to them, "Then render to Caesar the things that are Caesar's; and to God the things that are God's" (Matthew 22:18–21; cf. Matthew 17:25; Mark 12:15–17; Luke 20:22–25).

Setting: The temple in Jerusalem. After Jesus teaches the chief priests, scribes, and elders in parables, they send some of the Pharisees and Herodians in an attempt to trap Him in a statement.

"Shall we pay or shall we not pay?" But He, knowing their hypocrisy, said to them, "Why are you testing Me? Bring Me a denarius to look at." They brought *one.* And He said to them, "Whose likeness and inscription is this?" And they said to Him, "Caesar's." And Jesus said to them, "Render to Caesar the things that are Caesar's, and to God the things that are God's." And they were amazed at Him (Mark 12:15–17; cf. Matthew 22:15–22; Luke 20:20–26).

Setting: The temple in Jerusalem. A few days before His crucifixion, after Jesus conveys the Parable of the Vine-Growers to the people, the scribes and Pharisees seek to trap Him by questioning Him about paying taxes to Caesar.

But He detected their trickery and said to them, "Show Me a denarius. Whose likeness and inscription does it have?" They said "Caesar's." And He said to them, "Then render to Caesar the things that are Caesar's, and to God the things that are God's" (Luke 20:23–25; cf. Matthew 22:15–21; Mark 12:13–17).

LILIES (Also see FLOWERS)

Setting: Galilee. During the early part of His ministry, Jesus preaches the Sermon on the Mount to His disciples and the multitudes.

"For this reason I say to you, do not be worried about your life, *as to* what you will eat or what you will drink; nor for your body, *as to* what you will put on. Is not life more than food, and the body more than clothing? Look at the birds of the air, that they do not sow, nor reap nor gather into barns, and *yet* your heavenly Father feeds them. Are you not worth much more than they? And who of you by being worried can add a *single* hour to his life? And why are you worried about clothing? Observe how the lilies of the field grow; they do not toil nor do they spin, yet I say to you that not even Solomon in all his glory clothed himself like one of these. But if God so clothes the grass of the field, which is *alive* today and tomorrow is thrown into the furnace, *will He* not much more *clothe* you? You of little faith! Do not worry then, saying 'What will we eat?' or 'What will we drink?' or 'What will be wear for clothing?" For the Gentiles eagerly seek all these things; for your heavenly Father knows that you need all these things. But seek first His kingdom and His righteousness, and all these things will be added to you. So do not worry about tomorrow; for tomorrow will care for itself. Each day has enough trouble of its own" (Matthew 6:25–34; cf. Luke 12:22–31; see 1 Kings 10:4–7; Job 35:11; Matthew 8:26).

Setting: On the way from Galilee to Jerusalem. Jesus comforts the crowd and His disciples after giving a parable about riches and greed. The scribes and Pharisees turn hostile and question Him repeatedly in an attempt to catch Him in something He might say.

And He said to His disciples, "For this reason I say to you, do not worry about *your* life, *as to* what you will eat; nor for your body, *as to* what you will put on. For life is more than food, and the body more than clothing. Consider the ravens, for they neither sow nor reap; they have no storeroom nor barn, and *yet* God feeds them; how much more valuable you are than the birds! And which of you by worrying can add a *single* hour to his life's span? If then you cannot do even a very little thing, why do you worry about other matters? Consider the lilies, how they grow: they neither toil nor spin; but I tell you, not even Solomon in all his glory clothed himself like one of these. But if God so clothes the grass in the field, which is *alive* today and tomorrow is thrown into the furnace, how much more *will He clothe* you? You men of little faith! And do not seek what you will eat and what you will drink, and do not keep worrying. For all these things the nations of the world eagerly seek; but your Father knows that you need these things. But seek His kingdom, and these things will be added to you. Do not be afraid, little flock, for your Father has chosen gladly to give you the kingdom" (Luke 12:22–32; cf. Matthew 6:25–33; see 1 Kings 10:4–7; Job 38:41).

LINEN, FINE

Setting: On the way from Galilee to Jerusalem. After He responds to the Pharisees' scoffing at His teaching His disciples about stewardship and the permanence of the Law, Jesus conveys the story of the rich man and Lazarus.

"Now there was a rich man, and he habitually dressed in purple and fine linen, joyously living in splendor every day. And a poor man named Lazarus was laid at his gate, covered with sores, and longing to be fed with the *crumbs* which were falling from the rich man's table; besides, even the dogs were coming and licking his sores. Now the poor man died and was carried away by the angels to Abraham's bosom; and the rich man also died and was buried. In Hades he lifted up his eyes, being in torment, and saw Abraham far away and Lazarus in his bosom. And he cried out and said, 'Father Abraham, have mercy on me, and send Lazarus so that he may dip the tip of his finger in water and cool off my tongue, for I am in agony in this flame.' But Abraham said, 'Child, remember that during your life you received your good things, and likewise Lazarus bad things; but now he is being comforted here, and you are in agony. And besides all this, between us and you there is a great chasm fixed, so that those who wish to come over from here to you will not be able, and *that* none may cross over from there to us.' And he said, 'Then I beg you, father, that you send him to my father's house—for I have five brothers—in order that he may warn them, so that they will not also come to this place of torment.' But Abraham said, 'They have Moses and the Prophets; let them hear them.' But he said, 'No, father Abraham, but if someone goes to them from the dead, they will repent!' But he said to him, 'If they do not listen to Moses and the Prophets, they will not be persuaded even if someone rises from the dead' " (Luke 16:19–31; see Luke 3:8; 6:24; 16:1, 14).

LIPS (Also see MOUTH)

Setting: Galilee. Pharisees and scribes from Jerusalem question Jesus about His disciples' lack of obedience to tradition and the commandments.

And He answered and said to them, "Why do you yourselves transgress the commandment of God for the sake of tradition? For God said, 'HONOR YOUR FATHER AND MOTHER,' and, 'HE WHO SPEAKS EVIL OF FATHER OR MOTHER IS TO BE PUT TO DEATH.' But you say, 'Whoever says to *his* father or mother, "Whatever I have that would help you has been given *to God*," he is not to honor his father or mother.' And *by this* you invalidated the word of God for the sake of your tradition. You hypocrites, rightly did Isaiah prophesy of you: 'THIS PEOPLE HONORS ME WITH THEIR LIPS, BUT THEIR HEART IS FAR AWAY FROM ME. BUT IN VAIN DO THEY WORSHIP ME, TEACHING AS DOCTRINES THE PRECEPTS OF MEN'" (Matthew 15:3–9, Jesus quotes from Exodus 20:12, 21:17, Leviticus 20:9; Isaiah 29:13; cf. Mark 7:5–7; see Colossians 2:22).

Setting: Galilee. The Pharisees and some of the scribes from Jerusalem question why Jesus' disciples do not follow the tradition of ceremonial hand cleansing before eating bread.

And He said to them, "Rightly did Isaiah prophesy of you hypocrites, as it is written: 'THIS PEOPLE HONORS ME WITH THEIR LIPS, BUT THEIR HEART IS FAR AWAY FROM ME. BUT IN VAIN DO THEY WORSHIP ME, TEACHING AS DOCTRINES THE PRECEPTS OF MEN.' Neglecting the commandment of God, you hold to the tradition of men." He was also saying to them, "You are experts at setting aside the commandment of God in order to keep tradition. For Moses said, 'HONOR YOUR FATHER AND YOUR MOTHER'; and, 'HE WHO SPEAKS EVIL OF FATHER OR MOTHER, IS TO BE PUT TO DEATH'; but you say, 'If a man says to *his* father or *his* mother, whatever I have that would help you is Corban (that is to say, given *to God*),' you no longer permit him to do anything for *his* father or *his* mother; *thus* invalidating the word of God by your tradition which you have handed down; and you do many things such as that" (Mark 7:6–13, Jesus quotes from Exodus 20:12; 21:17; Isaiah 29:13; cf. Matthew 15:1–6).

LISTENING (Also see EAR; EARS; and HEARING)

[LISTENING from listen]

Setting: Capernaum of Galilee. After conveying to His disciples the value of little ones, Jesus gives instruction about church discipline.

"If your brother sins, go and show him his fault in private; if he listens to you, you have won your brother. But if he does not listen *to you,* take one or two more with you, so that BY THE MOUTH OF TWO OR THREE WITNESSES EVERY FACT MAY BE CONFIRMED. If he refuses to listen to them, tell it to the church; and if he refuses to listen even to the church, let him be to you as a Gentile and a tax collector. Truly I say to you, whatever you bind of earth shall have been bound in heaven; and whatever you loose on earth shall have been loosed in heaven. Again, I say to you, that if two of you agree on earth about anything that they may ask, it shall be done for them by My Father who is in heaven. For there two or three have gathered together in My name, I am there in their midst" (Matthew 18:15–20. Jesus quotes from Deuteronomy 19:15; cf. Matthew 7:7; 16:19; see Leviticus 19:17; Matthew 28:20; 2 Thessalonians 3:6, 14).

[LISTENING from listen]

Setting: The temple in Jerusalem. Jesus delivers another parable to the chief priests and elders after they question His authority.

"Listen to another parable. There was a landowner who PLANTED A VINEYARD AND PUT A WALL AROUND IT AND DUG A WINE PRESS IN IT, AND BUILT A TOWER, and rented it out to vine-growers and went on a journey. When the harvest time approached, he sent his slaves to the vine-growers to receive his produce. The vine-growers took his slaves and beat one, and killed another, and stoned a third. Again he sent another group of slaves larger than the first; and they did the same thing to them. But afterward he sent his son to them, saying, 'They will respect my son.' But when the vine-growers saw the son, they said among themselves, 'This is the heir; come, let us kill him and seize his inheritance.' They took him, and threw him out of the vineyard and killed him. Therefore when the owner of the vineyard comes, what will he do to those vine-growers?" (Matthew 21:33–40; Jesus quotes from Isaiah 5:1, 2; cf. Mark 12:1–9; Luke 20:9–15; see Matthew 21:45, 46).

[LISTENING from listen]

Setting: By the Sea of Galilee. During the early part of His ministry, just after a visit from his mother and brothers, Jesus instructs a very large crowd with the Parable of the Sower from a boat.

"Listen *to this!* Behold, the sower went out to sow; as he was sowing, some *seed* fell beside the road, and the birds came and ate it up. Other *seed* fell on the rocky *ground* where it did not have much soil; and immediately it sprang up because it had no depth of soil. And after the sun had risen, it was scorched; and because it had no root, it withered away. Other *seed* fell among the thorns, and the thorns came up and choked it, and it yielded no crop. Other *seeds* fell into the good soil, and as the grew up and increased, they yielded a crop and produced thirty, sixty, and a hundredfold." And He was saying, "He who has ears to hear, let him hear" (Mark 4:3–9; cf. Matthew 13:3–9; Luke 8:5–8).

[LISTENING from listen]
Setting: Galilee. After explaining the Parable of the Sower to His disciples, Jesus informs them about personal accountability and responsibility.

And He was saying to them, "Take care what you listen to. By your standard of measure it will be measured to you; and more will be given you besides. For whoever has, to him *more* shall be given; and whoever does not have, even what he has shall be taken away from him" (Mark 4:24, 25; cf. Matthew 13:12; Luke 8:18; see Matthew 7:2).

[LISTENING from listen]
Setting: Jesus' hometown of Nazareth. After encountering unbelief, Jesus sends the Twelve out in pairs with authority and instructions about ministry.

And He summoned the twelve and began to send them out in pairs, and gave them authority over the unclean spirits; and He instructed them that they should take nothing for *their* journey, except a mere staff—no bread, no bag, no money in their belt—but to wear sandals; and *He added,* "Do not put on two tunics." And He said to them, "Wherever you enter a house, stay there until you leave town. Any place that does not receive you or listen to you, as you go out from there, shake the dust off the soles of your feet for a testimony against them" (Mark 6:7–11; cf. Matthew 10:1–14; Luke 9:1–5).

[LISTENING from listen]
Setting: Galilee. After the Pharisees and scribes from Jerusalem question His disciples' lack of obedience to tradition, Jesus speaks to a crowd and explains His teaching to His disciples.

After He called the crowd to Him again, He *began* saying to them, "Listen to Me, all of you, and understand: there is nothing outside the man which can defile him if it goes into him; but the things which proceed out of the man are what defile the man. [If anyone has ears to hear, let him hear."] When he had left the crowd *and* entered the house, His disciples questioned Him about the parable. And He said to them, "Are you so lacking in understanding also? Do you not understand that whatever goes into the man from outside cannot defile him, because it does not go into his heart, but into his stomach, and is eliminated?" (*Thus He* declared all foods clean.) And He was saying, "That which proceeds out of the man, that is what defiles the man. For from within, out of the heart of men, proceed the evil thoughts, fornications, thefts, murders, adulteries, deeds of coveting *and* wickedness, *as well* as deceit, sensuality, envy, slander, pride *and* foolishness. All these evil things proceed from within and defile the man" (Mark 7:14–23; cf. Matthew 15:10–20).

[LISTENING from listen]
Setting: Galilee. After explaining the Parable of the Sower to His disciples, Jesus gives the Parable of the Lamp.

"Now no one after lighting a lamp covers it over with a container, or puts it under a bed; but he puts it on a lampstand, so that those who come in may see the light. For nothing is hidden that will not become evident, nor *anything* secret that will not be known and come to light. So take care how you listen; for whoever has, to him *more* shall be given; and whoever does not have, even what he thinks he has shall be taken away from him" (Luke 8:16–18; cf. Mark 4:21–23; see Matthew 5:14, 15; 10:26; 13:12).

[LISTENING from listens]
Setting: On the way from Galilee to Jerusalem. The Lord pronounces woes on cities who reject the gospel as He appoints seventy followers and sends them out in pairs to every place He Himself will soon visit.

"Woe to you, Chorazin! Woe to you, Bethsaida! For if the miracles had been performed in Tyre and Sidon which occurred in you, they would have repented long ago, sitting in sackcloth and ashes. But it will be more tolerable for Tyre and Sidon in the judgment than for you. And you, Capernaum, will not be exalted to heaven, will you? You will be brought down to Hades! The one who listens to you listens to Me, and the one who rejects you rejects Me; and he who rejects Me rejects the One who sent Me" (Luke 10:13–16; cf. Matthew 11:21–23; see Matthew 10:40).

[LISTENING from listen]
Setting: On the way from Galilee to Jerusalem. After He responds to the Pharisees' scoffing at His teaching His disciples about stewardship and the permanence of the Law, Jesus conveys the story of the rich man and Lazarus.

"Now there was a rich man, and he habitually dressed in purple and fine linen, joyously living in splendor every day. And a poor man named Lazarus was laid at his gate, covered with sores, and longing to be fed with the *crumbs* which were falling from the rich man's table; besides, even the dogs were coming and licking his sores. Now the poor man died and was carried away by the angels to Abraham's bosom; and the rich man also died and was buried. In Hades he lifted up his eyes, being in torment, and saw Abraham far away and Lazarus in his bosom. And he cried out and said, 'Father Abraham, have mercy on me, and send Lazarus so that he may dip the tip of his finger in water and cool off my tongue, for I am in agony in this flame.' But Abraham said, 'Child, remember that during your life you received your good things, and likewise Lazarus bad things; but now he is being comforted here, and you are in agony. And besides all this, between us and you there is a great chasm fixed, so that those who wish to come over from here to you will not be able, and *that* none may cross over from there to us.' And he said, 'Then I beg you, father, that you send him to my father's house—for I have five brothers—in order that he may warn them, so that they will not also come to this place of torment.' But Abraham said, 'They have Moses and the Prophets; let them hear them.' But he said, 'No, father Abraham, but if someone goes to them from the dead, they will repent!' But he said to him, 'If they do not listen to Moses and the Prophets, they will not be persuaded even if someone rises from the dead' " (Luke 16:19–31; see Luke 3:8; 6:24; 16:1, 14).

LITTLE FAITH (Listed under FAITH, LITTLE)

LITTLE ONES (Also see BABIES, NURSING; CHILD; CHILDREN; and INFANTS)
Setting: Galilee. After His twelve disciples observe His ministry, Jesus summons and specifically instructs them about their ministry ahead that will include rewards.

"He who receives you receives Me, and he who receives Me receives Him who sent me. He who receives a prophet in the name of a prophet shall receive a prophet's reward; and he who receives a righteous man in the name of a righteous man shall receive a righteous man's reward. And whoever in the name of a disciple gives to one of these little ones even a cup of cold water to drink, truly I say to you, he shall not lose his reward" (Matthew 10:40–42; cf. Matthew 25:40, 44, 45; see Mark 9:37).

Setting: Capernaum of Galilee. Jesus answers His disciples' question about greatness, or rank, in the kingdom of heaven.

And He called a child to Himself and set him before them, and said, "Truly I say to you, unless you are converted and become like children, you will not enter the kingdom of heaven. Whoever then humbles himself as this child, he is the greatest in the kingdom of heaven. And whoever receives one such child in My name receives Me; but whoever causes one of these little ones who believe in Me to stumble, it would be better for him to have a heavy millstone hung around his neck, and to be drowned in the depth of the sea"
(Matthew 18:2–6; cf. Matthew 19:14; Mark 9:33–37, 42; Luke 9:47, 48; Luke 17:1, 2).

Setting: Capernaum of Galilee. After His disciples ask Him about greatness in the kingdom of heaven, Jesus elaborates about the value of little ones.

"See that you do not despise one of these little ones, for I say to you that their angels in heaven continually see the face of My Father who is in heaven" (Matthew 18:10; see Luke 1:19).

Setting: Capernaum of Galilee. Jesus illustrates to His disciples the value of little ones.

"What do you think? If any man has a hundred sheep, and one of them has gone astray, does he not leave the ninety-nine on the mountains and go and search for the one that is straying? If it turns out that he finds it, truly I say to you, he rejoices over it more than the ninety-nine which have not gone astray. So it is not *the* will of your Father who is in heaven that one of these little ones perish" (Matthew 18:12–14; cf. Luke 15:4–7).

Setting: Capernaum of Galilee. As Jesus teaches His disciples in private, they ask Him about greatness.

But Jesus said, "Do not hinder him, for there is no one who will perform a miracle in My name, and be able soon afterward to speak evil of Me. For he who is not against us is for us. For whoever gives you a cup of water to drink because of your name as *followers* of Christ, truly I say to you, he will not lose his reward. Whoever causes one of these little ones who believe to stumble, it would be better for him if, with a heavy millstone hung around his neck, he had been cast into the sea. If your hand causes you to stumble, cut it off; it is better for you to enter life crippled, than, having your two hands, to go into hell, into the unquenchable fire, [where THEIR WORM DOES NOT DIE, AND THE FIRE IS NOT QUENCHED.] If your foot causes you to stumble, cut it off; it is better for you to enter life lame, than, having your two feet, to be cast into hell, [where THEIR WORM DOES NOT DIE, AND THE FIRE IS NOT QUENCHED.] If your eye causes you to stumble, throw it out; it is better for you to enter the kingdom of God with one eye, than, having two eyes, to be cast into hell, where THEIR WORM DOES NOT DIE, AND THE FIRE IS NOT QUENCHED. For everyone will be salted with fire. Salt is good; but if the salt becomes unsalty, with what will you make it salty *again?* Have salt in yourselves, and be at peace with one another" (Mark 9:39–50; Jesus quotes from Isaiah 66:24; cf. Matthew 18:6–9; Luke 9:49, 50; see Matthew 5:13, 29, 30; 10:42; 12:30; 18:5, 6).

Setting: On the way from Galilee to Jerusalem. After conveying the story of the rich man and Lazarus, the Lord gives His disciples instruction on forgiveness.

He said to His disciples, "It is inevitable that stumbling blocks come, but woe to him through whom they come! It would be better for him if a millstone were hung around his neck and he were thrown into the sea, than that he would cause one of these little ones to stumble. Be on your guard! If your brother sins, rebuke him; and if he repents, forgive him. And if he sins against you seven times a day, and returns to you seven times, saying, 'I repent,' forgive him" (Luke 17:1–4; see Matthew 18:5–7, 15, 21, 22).

LIVES (Also see LIFE)

Setting: Galilee. After He clarifies who His disciples' co-laborers are, Jesus prepares to go to Jerusalem by sending messengers ahead to Samaria, where they experience rejection and seek retribution.

But He turned and rebuked them, [and said, "You do not know what kind of spirit you are of; for the Son of Man did not come to destroy men's lives, but to save them."] And they went on to another village (Luke 9:55, 56; see 2 Kings 1:9–14; Luke 13:22).

Setting: On the Mount of Olives, east of the temple in Jerusalem. After ministering in the temple a few days before His crucifixion, and giving His disciples more details regarding the temple's future destruction, Jesus elaborates during His Olivet Discourse about things to come.

Then He continued by saying to them, "Nation will rise against nation and kingdom against kingdom, and there will be great earthquakes, and in various places plagues and famines; and there will be terrors and great signs from heaven. But before all these things, they will lay their hands on you and will persecute you, delivering you to the synagogues and prisons, bringing you before kings and governors for My name's sake. It will lead to an opportunity for your testimony. So make up your minds not to prepare beforehand to defend yourselves; for I will give you utterance and wisdom which none of your opponents will be able to resist or refute. But you will be betrayed even by parents and brothers and relatives and friends, and they will put *some* of you to death, and you will be hated by all because of My name. Yet not a hair of your head will perish. By your endurance you will gain your lives" (Luke 21:10–19; cf. Matthew 10:19–22; 24:7–14; Mark 13:8–13).

LIVES, MEN'S (See LIVES)

LIVESTOCK, FATTENED (Also see OXEN)

Setting: The temple in Jerusalem. Jesus speaks another parable to the chief priests and elders after they question His authority.

Jesus spoke to them again in parables, saying, "The kingdom of heaven may be compared to a king who gave a wedding feast for his son. And he sent out his slaves to call those who had been invited to the wedding feast, and they were unwilling to come. Again he sent out other slaves saying, 'Tell those who have been invited, "Behold, I have prepared my dinner; my oxen and my fattened livestock are *all* butchered and everything is ready; come to the wedding feast." But they paid no attention and went their way, one to his own farm, another to his business, and the rest seized his slaves and mistreated them and killed them. But the king was enraged, and he sent his armies and destroyed those murderers and set their city on fire. Then he said to his slaves, 'The wedding is ready, but those who were invited were not worthy. 'Go therefore to the main highways, and as many as you find *there,* invite to the wedding feast.' Those slaves went out into the streets and gathered together all they found, both evil and good; and the wedding hall was filled with dinner guests. But when the king came in to look over the dinner guests, he saw a man there who was not dressed in wedding clothes, and he said to him, 'Friend, how did you come in here without wedding clothes?' And the man was speechless. Then the king said to the servants, 'Bind him hand and foot, and throw him into the outer darkness; in that place there will be weeping and gnashing of teeth.' For many are called, but few *are* chosen" (Matthew 22:1–14; cf. Matthew 8:11, 12).

LIVING (LIVING, GOD OF THE is a separate entry; also see ALIVE; and LIFE]

Setting: The temple in Jerusalem. After the Jewish religious leaders test Him with questions, Jesus pronounces the eighth of eight woes on them in front of the crowds and His disciples.

"Woe to you, scribes and Pharisees, hypocrites! For you build the tombs of the prophets and adorn the monuments of the righteous, and say, 'If we had been *living* in the days of our fathers, we would not have been partners with them in *shedding* the blood of the prophets.' So you testify against yourselves, that you are sons of those who murdered the prophets. Fill up, then, the measure *of the guilt* of you fathers. You serpents, you brood of vipers, how will you escape the sentence of hell? Therefore, behold, I am sending you prophets and wise men and scribes; some of them you will kill and crucify, and some of them you will scourge in your synagogues, and persecute from city to city, so that upon you may fall *the guilt of* all the righteous blood shed on earth, from the blood of righteous Abel to the blood of Zechariah, the son of Berechiah, whom you murdered between the temple and the altar. Truly I say to you, all these things will come upon this generation" (Matthew 23:29–36; cf. 2 Chronicles 24:21; Zechariah 1:1; Matthew 3:7; Luke 11:47–52; see Matthew 10:23).

Setting: On the way from Galilee to Jerusalem. After He responds to the Pharisees' scoffing at His teaching His disciples about stewardship and the permanence of the Law, Jesus conveys the story of the rich man and Lazarus.

"Now there was a rich man, and he habitually dressed in purple and fine linen, joyously living in splendor every day. And a poor man named Lazarus was laid at his gate, covered with sores, and longing to be fed with the *crumbs* which were falling from the rich man's table; besides, even the dogs were coming and licking his sores. Now the poor man died and was carried away by the angels to Abraham's bosom; and the rich man also died and was buried. In Hades he lifted up his eyes, being in torment, and saw Abraham far away and Lazarus in his bosom. And he cried out and said, 'Father Abraham, have mercy on me, and send Lazarus so that he may dip the tip of his finger in water and cool off my tongue, for I am in agony in this flame.' But Abraham said, 'Child, remember that during your life you received your good things, and likewise Lazarus bad things; but now he is being comforted here, and you are in agony. And besides all this, between us and you there is a great chasm fixed, so that those who wish to come over from here to you will not be able, and *that* none may cross over from there to us.' And he said, 'Then I beg you, father, that you send him to my father's house—for I have five brothers—in order that he may warn them, so that they will not also come to this place of torment.' But Abraham said, 'They have Moses and the Prophets; let them hear them.' But he said, 'No, father Abraham, but if someone goes to them from the dead, they will repent!' But he said to him, 'If they do not listen to Moses and the Prophets, they will not be persuaded even if someone rises from the dead' " (Luke 16:19–31; see Luke 3:8; 6:24; 16:1, 14).

Setting: Sychar in Samaria, on the way to Galilee. Jesus interacts with a Samaritan woman at Jacob's well, while His disciples are buying food.

Jesus answered and said to her, "If you knew the gift of God, and who it is who says to you, 'Give Me a drink,' you would have asked Him, and He would have given you living water" (John 4:10).

Setting: Capernaum of Galilee. After Jesus informs the people whom He miraculously fed how they might receive the bread out of heaven, the Jewish religious leaders grumble because He claims that He came down out of heaven.

Therefore the Jews were grumbling about Him, because He said, "I am the bread that came down out of heaven." They were saying, "Is not this Jesus, the son of Joseph, whose father and mother we know? How does He now say, 'I have come down out of heaven'?" Jesus answered and said to them, "Do not grumble among yourselves. No one can come to Me unless the Father who sent Me draws him; and I will raise him up on the last day. It is written in the prophets, 'AND THEY SHALL ALL BE TAUGHT OF GOD.' Everyone who has heard and learned from the Father, comes to Me. Not that anyone has seen the Father, except the One who is from God; He has seen the Father. Truly, truly, I say to you, he who believes has eternal life. I am the bread of life. Your fathers ate the manna in the wilderness, and they died. This is the bread which comes down out of heaven, so that one may eat of it and not die. I am the living bread that came down out of heaven; if anyone eats of this bread, he will live forever; and the bread also which I will give for the life of the world is My flesh" (John 6:41–51, Jesus quotes from Isaiah 54:13; see John 1:18, 29; 3:36; 7:27).

Setting: Capernaum of Galilee. After Jesus informs the people whom He miraculously fed how they might receive the bread out of heaven, the Jewish religious leaders argue with one another when Jesus says He will give His flesh to the world to eat.

So Jesus said to them, "Truly, truly, I say to you, unless you eat the flesh of the Son of Man and drink His blood, you have no life in yourselves. He who eats My flesh and drinks My blood has eternal life, and I will raise him up on the last day. For My flesh is true food, and My blood is true drink. He who eats My flesh and drinks My blood abides in Me, and I in him. As the living Father sent Me, and I live because of the Father, so he who eats Me, he also will live because of Me. This is the bread which came down out of heaven; not as the fathers ate and died; he who eats this bread will live forever" (John 6:53–58; see Matthew 16:16; Luke 4:22; John 3:36; John 9:16; 15:4).

Setting: Jerusalem. On the last day of the Feast of Booths, after causing discussion whether He is the Christ, Jesus offers salvation and the abundant life to His hearers. The chief priests and Pharisees attempt to understand where He says He will be going soon.

Now on the last day, the great *day* of the feast, Jesus stood and cried out, saying, "If anyone is thirsty, let him come to Me and drink. He who believes in Me, as the Scripture said, 'From his innermost being will flow rivers of living water'" (John 7:37, 38; see John 7:10–15, 39–44).

Setting: On the island of Patmos (in the Aegean Sea about fifty miles southwest of Ephesus in modern Turkey). On the Lord's Day (Sunday), approximately fifty years after His resurrection, the disciple John encounters the Lord Jesus Christ, who communicates new revelations for the apostle to record for the seven churches in Asia.

When I saw Him, I fell at His feet like a dead man. And He placed His right hand on me, saying, "Do not be afraid; I am the first and the last, and the living One; and I was dead, and behold, I am alive forevermore, and I have the keys of death and of Hades. Therefore write the things which you have seen, and the things which are, and the things which will take place after these things. As for the mystery of the seven stars which you saw in My right hand, and the seven golden lampstands: the seven stars are the angels of the seven churches, and the seven lampstands are the seven churches" (Revelation 1:17–20; see Isaiah 44:6; Luke 24:5; Revelation 1:1–16; 2:8).

LIVING, GOD OF THE

[GOD OF THE LIVING from He is not the God of the dead but of the living]
Setting: The temple in Jerusalem. As He teaches, the Sadducees question Jesus about Levirate marriage (marriage to a brother-in-law) in order to test Him.

But Jesus answered and said to them, "You are mistaken, not understanding the Scriptures nor the power of God. For in the resurrection they neither marry nor are given in marriage, but are like angels in heaven. But regarding the resurrection of the dead, have you not read what was spoken to you by God: 'I AM THE GOD OF ABRAHAM, AND THE GOD OF ISAAC, AND THE GOD OF JACOB'? He is not the God of the dead but of the living" (Matthew 22:29–32, Jesus quotes from Exodus 3:6; cf. Mark 12:18–27; Luke 20:27–38; see Deuteronomy 25:5; John 20:9).

[GOD OF THE LIVING from He is not the God of the dead, but of the living]
Setting: The temple in Jerusalem. After some of the Pharisees and Herodians attempt to trap Jesus in a statement, some Sadducees question Him about the status of marriage after death.

Jesus said to them, "Is this not the reason you are mistaken, that you do not understand the Scriptures or the power of God? For when they rise from the dead, they neither marry nor are given in marriage, but are like angels in heaven. But regarding the fact that the dead rise again, have you not read in the book of Moses, in the *passage* about *the burning* bush, how God spoke to him, saying, 'I AM THE GOD OF ABRAHAM, AND THE GOD OF ISAAC, and the God of Jacob?' He is not the God of the dead, but of the living; you are greatly mistaken" (Mark 12:24–27, Jesus quotes from Exodus 3:6; cf. Matthew 22:29–33; Luke 20:34–40).

[GOD OF THE LIVING from He is not the God of the dead but of the living]
Setting: The temple in Jerusalem. After the scribes and Pharisees seek to trap Jesus by questioning Him about paying taxes to Caesar, some Sadducees (who say there is no resurrection) ask Him a question about the resurrection.

Jesus said to them, "The sons of this age marry and are given in marriage, but those who are considered worthy to attain to that age and the resurrection from the dead, neither marry nor are given in marriage; for they cannot even die anymore, because they are like angels, and are sons of God, being sons of the resurrection. But that the dead are raised, even Moses showed, in the *passage about the burning* bush, where he calls the Lord THE GOD OF ABRAHAM, AND THE GOD OF ISAAC, AND THE GOD OF JACOB. Now He is not the God of the dead but of the living; for all live to Him" (Luke 20:34–38, Jesus quotes from Exodus 3:6; cf. Matthew 22:23–32; Mark 12:18–27).

LIVING, GODLY (Also see OBEDIENCE; RIGHTEOUSNESS; and TESTIMONY)

[GODLY LIVING from Let your light shine before men in such a way that they may see your good works]
Setting: Galilee. During the early part of His ministry, Jesus preaches the Sermon on the Mount to His disciples and the multitudes.

"You are the light of the world. A city set on a hill cannot be hidden; nor does *anyone* light a lamp and put it under a basket, but on the lampstand, and it gives light to all who are in the house. Let your light shine before men in such a way that they may see your good works, and glorify your Father who is in heaven" (Matthew 5:14–16; cf. Mark 4:21; 1 Peter 2:12).

[GODLY LIVING from he who practices the truth]
Setting: Jerusalem. At the time for the Passover of the Jews, after the Lord cleanses the temple, a Pharisee, Nicodemus, asks Him by night the meaning of "born again."

"For God so loved the world, that He gave His only begotten Son, that whoever believes in Him shall not perish, but have eternal life. For God did not send the Son into the world to judge the world, but that the world might be saved through Him. He who believes in Him is not judged; he who does not believe has been judged already, because he has not believed in the name of the only begotten Son of God. This is the judgment, that the Light has come into the world, and men loved darkness rather than the Light, for their deeds were evil. For everyone who does evil hates the Light, and does not come to the Light for fear that his deeds will be exposed. But he who practices the truth comes to the Light, so that his deeds may be manifested as having been wrought in God" (John 3:16–21; see Luke 19:10; John 1:4; 1:18; Romans 5:8; 1 John 1:6, 7).

LIVING, LOOSE

Setting: On the way from Galilee to Jerusalem. Jesus conveys the illustration of the prodigal son because the Pharisees and scribes complain He associates with tax collectors and sinners.

And He said, "A man had two sons. The younger of them said to his father, 'Father, give me the share of the estate that falls to me.' So he divided his wealth between them. And not many days later, the younger son gathered everything together and went on a journey into a distant country, and there he squandered his estate with loose living. Now when he had spent everything, a severe famine occurred in that country, and he began to be impoverished. So he went and hired himself out to one of the citizens of that country, and he sent him into his fields to feed swine. And he would have gladly filled his stomach with the pods that the swine were eating, and no one was giving *anything* to him. But when he came to his senses, he said, 'How many of my father's hired men have more than enough bread, but I am dying here with hunger! I will get up and go to my father, and will say to him, "Father, I have sinned against heaven, and in your sight; I am no longer worthy to be called your son; make me as one of your hired men."' So he got up and came to his father. But while he was still a long way off, his father saw him and felt compassion *for him,* and ran and embraced him and kissed him. And the son said to him, "Father, I have sinned against heaven and in your sight; I am no longer worthy to be called your son.' But the father said to his slaves, 'Quickly bring out the best robe and put it on him, and put a ring on his hand and sandals on his feet; and bring the fattened calf, kill it, and let us eat and celebrate; for this son of mine was dead and has come to life again; he was lost and has been found.' And they began to celebrate. Now his older son was in the field, when he came and approached the house, he heard music and dancing. And he summoned one of the servants and *began* inquiring what these things could be. And he said to him, 'Your brother has come, and your father has killed the fattened calf because he has received him back safe and sound.' But he became angry and was not willing to go in; and his father came out and *began* pleading with him. But he answered and said to his father, 'Look! For so many years I have been serving you and I have never neglected a command of yours; and *yet* you have never given me a young goat, so that I might celebrate with my friends; but when this son of yours came, who has devoured your wealth with prostitutes, you killed the fattened calf for him.' And he said to him, 'Son, you have always been with me, and all that is mine is yours. But we had to celebrate and rejoice, for this brother of yours was dead and *has begun* to live, and was lost and has been found'" (Luke 15:11–32; see Proverbs 29:2; Luke 15:1, 2).

LIVING BREAD (Listed under BREAD, LIVING)

LIVING ONE

Setting: On the island of Patmos (in the Aegean Sea about fifty miles southwest of Ephesus in modern Turkey). On the Lord's Day (Sunday), approximately fifty years after His resurrection, the disciple John encounters the Lord Jesus Christ, who communicates new revelations for the apostle to record for the seven churches in Asia.

When I saw Him, I fell at His feet like a dead man. And He placed His right hand on me, saying, "Do not be afraid; I am the first and the last, and the living One; and I was dead, and behold, I am alive forevermore, and I have the keys of death and of Hades. Therefore write the things which you have seen, and the things which are, and the things which will take place after these things. As for the mystery of the seven stars which you saw in My right hand, and the seven golden lampstands: the seven stars are the angels of the seven churches, and the seven lampstands are the seven churches" (Revelation 1:17–20; see Isaiah 44:6; Luke 24:5; Revelation 1:1–16; 2:8).

LIVING TOGETHER (Also see SEXUAL SIN)

[LIVING TOGETHER from the one whom you now have is not your husband]

Setting: Sychar in Samaria, on the way to Galilee. Jesus interacts with a Samaritan woman at Jacob's well, while the disciples are buying food.

He said to her, "Go, call your husband and come here." The woman answered and said, "I have no husband." Jesus said to her, "You have correctly said, 'I have no husband'; for you have had five husbands, and the one whom you now have is not your husband; this you have said truly" (John 4:16–18; see John 6:35).

LIVING WATER (Listed as WATER, LIVING)

LOAF (Specifics such as LOAVES, FIVE are separate entries; also see BREAD; LOAVES; and WHEAT)

Setting: Galilee. During the early part of His ministry, Jesus preaches the Sermon on the Mount to His disciples and the multitudes.

"Ask, and it will be given to you; seek, and you will find; knock, and it will be opened to you. For everyone who asks receives, and he who seeks finds, and to him who knocks it will be opened. Or what man is there among you who, when his son asks for a loaf, will give him a stone? Or if he asks for a fish, he will not give him a snake, will he? If you then, being evil, know how to give good gifts to your children, how much more will your Father who is in heaven give what is good to those who ask Him! In everything, therefore, treat people the same way you want them to treat you, for this is the Law and the Prophets" (Matthew 7:7–12; cf. Matthew 22:40; Luke 6:31; 11:9–13; see Psalm 84:11).

[LOAF from loaves]

Setting: Capernaum. The day after Jesus walks on the Sea of Galilee to join His disciples in a boat, the people He miraculously fed ask Him how He crossed the water, because He had not entered the boat from land with His disciples.

Jesus answered them and said, "Truly, truly, I say to you, you seek Me, not because you saw signs, but because you ate of the loaves and were filled. Do not work for the food which perishes, but for the food which endures to eternal life, which the Son of Man will give to you, for on Him the Father, God, has set His seal" (John 6:26, 27; see John 3:33).

LOANS (Also see BANK; DEBT; INTEREST; and MONEYLENDER)

[LOANS from borrow from you]

Setting: Galilee. During the early part of His ministry, Jesus preaches the Sermon on the Mount to His disciples and the multitudes.

"Give to him who asks of you, and do not turn away from him who wants to borrow from you" (Matthew 5:42; see Deuteronomy 15:7–11).

[LOANS from If you lend and lend, expecting nothing in return]

Setting: Galilee. After selecting His twelve disciples, Jesus teaches the Sermon on the Mount to those disciples and a great throng of people from Judea, Jerusalem, and the central coastal region of Tyre and Sidon.

"But I say to you who hear, love your enemies, do good to those who hate you, bless those who curse you, pray for those who mistreat you. Whoever hits you on the cheek, offer him the other also; and whoever takes away your coat, do not withhold your shirt from him either. Give to everyone who asks of you, and whoever takes away what is yours, do not demand it back. Treat others the same way you want them to treat you. If you love those who love you, what credit is *that* to you? For even sinners love those who love them. If you do good to those who do good to you, what credit is *that* to you? For even sinners do the same. If you lend to those from whom you expect to receive, what credit is *that* to you? Even sinners lend to sinners in order to receive back the same *amount.* But love your enemies, and do good, and lend, expecting nothing in return; and your reward will be great, and you will be sons of the Most High; for He Himself is kind to ungrateful and evil *men*. Be merciful, just as your Father is merciful" (Luke 6:27–36; cf. Matthew 5:9, 39–48; Matthew 7:12).

[LOANS from lend me]

Setting: On the way from Galilee to Jerusalem. After revealing to His disciples how to pray, Jesus illustrates persistence in prayer.

Then He said to them, "Suppose one of you has a friend, and goes to him at midnight and says to him, 'Friend, lend me three loaves; for a friend of mine has come to me from a journey, and I have nothing to set before him'; and from inside he answers and says, 'Do not bother me; the door has already been shut and my children and I are in bed; I cannot get up and give you *anything.*' I tell you, even though he will not get up and give him *anything* because he is his friend, yet because of his persistence he will get up and give him as much as he needs. So I say to you, ask, and it will be given to you; seek, and you will find; knock, and it will be opened to you. For everyone who asks, receives; and he who seeks, finds; and to him who knocks, it will be opened" (Luke 11:5–10; cf. Matthew 7:7, 8; see Luke 18:1–5).

LOAVES, FIVE

Setting: By the Sea of Galilee. Jesus repeats the warning to His disciples about the teaching of the religious leaders of the day, the Pharisees and Sadducees.

But Jesus aware of this, said, "You men of little faith, why do you discuss among yourselves that you have no bread? Do you not yet understand or remember the five loaves of the five thousand and how many baskets *full* you picked up? Or the seven loaves of the four thousand, and how many large baskets *full* you picked up? How is it that you do not understand that I did not speak to you concerning bread? But beware of the leaven of the Pharisees and Sadducees" (Matthew 16:8–11; cf. Matthew 14:17–21; 15:34–38; Mark 8:17–21).

[FIVE LOAVES from loaves and Five]

Setting: By the Sea of Galilee. After a long day of ministry, Jesus prepares to demonstrate the power of God to His disciples by feeding more than 5,000 people.

But He answered them, "You give them *something* to eat!" And they said to Him, "Shall we go and spend two hundred denarii on bread and give them *something* to eat? And He said to them, "How many loaves do you have? Go look!" And when they found out, they said, "Five, and two fish" (Mark 6:37, 38; cf. Matthew 14:16, 17; Luke 9:13, 14; John 6:5–9; see Mark 3:20).

Setting: The district of Dalmanutha. After the Pharisees argue with Jesus, seeking a sign from heaven to test Him, He and His disciples cross to the other side of the Sea of Galilee. The disciples discuss with one another that they have no bread.

And Jesus, aware of this, said to them, "Why do you discuss *the fact* that you have no bread? Do you not yet see or understand? Do you have a hardened heart? HAVING EYES, DO YOU NOT SEE? AND HAVING EARS, DO YOU NOT HEAR? And do you not remember, when I broke the five loaves for the five thousand, how many baskets full of broken pieces you picked you? They said to Him, "Twelve." When *I broke* the seven for the four thousand, how many large baskets full of broken pieces did you pick up?" They said to Him, "Seven." And He was saying to them, "Do you not yet understand?" (Mark 8:17–21, Jesus quotes from Jeremiah 5:21; cf. Matthew 16:5–12; see Matthew 14:19, 20; Mark 6:41–44, 52; 8:6–9).

LOAVES, SEVEN

[SEVEN LOAVES from loaves and Seven]

Setting: Near the Sea of Galilee. After being impressed by the faith of a Canaanite woman, Jesus cures her daughter of demonic possession, then feeds more than 4,000 people, primarily Gentiles.

And Jesus called His disciples to Him, and said, "I feel compassion for the people, because they have remained with Me now three days and have nothing to eat; and I do not want to send them away hungry, for they might faint on the way." The disciples said to Him, "Where would we get so many loaves in *this* desolate place to satisfy a large crowd?" And Jesus said to them, "How many loaves do you have?" And they said, "Seven and a few small fish" (Matthew 15:32–34; cf. Mark 8:1–9).

Setting: By the Sea of Galilee. Jesus repeats the warning to His disciples about the teaching of the religious leaders of the day (the Pharisees and Sadducees).

But Jesus aware of this, said, "You men of little faith, why do you discuss among yourselves that you have no bread? Do you not yet understand or remember the five loaves of the five thousand and how many baskets *full* you picked up? Or the seven loaves of the four thousand, and how many large baskets *full* you picked up? How is it that you do not understand that I did not speak to you concerning bread? But beware of the leaven of the Pharisees and Sadducees" (Matthew 16:8–11; cf. Matthew 14:17–21; 15:34–38; Mark 8:17–21).

[SEVEN LOAVES from loaves and Seven]
Setting: Decapolis, near the Sea of Galilee. Jesus miraculously feeds more than 4,000 people, primarily Gentiles.

And He was asking them, "How many loaves do you have?" And they said, "Seven" (Mark 8:5; cf. Matthew 15:34; see Matthew 15:32, 33, 35–38; Mark 8:6–9).

[SEVEN LOAVES from loaves and Seven]
Setting: The district of Dalmanutha. After the Pharisees argue with Him, seeking a sign from heaven to test Him, Jesus and His disciples cross to the other side of the Sea of Galilee. The disciples discuss with one another that they have no bread.

And Jesus, aware of this, said to them, "Why do you discuss *the fact* that you have no bread? Do you not yet see or understand? Do you have a hardened heart? HAVING EYES, DO YOU NOT SEE? AND HAVING EARS, DO YOU NOT HEAR? And do you not remember, when I broke the five loaves for the five thousand, how many baskets full of broken pieces you picked you? They said to Him, "Twelve." When *I broke* the seven for the four thousand, how many large baskets full of broken pieces did you pick up?" They said to Him, "Seven." And He was saying to them, "Do you not yet understand?" (Mark 8:17–21, Jesus quotes from Jeremiah 5:21; cf. Matthew 16:5–12; see Matthew 14:18, 19; Mark 6:41–44, 52; 8:6–9).

LOAVES, THREE

Setting: On the way from Galilee to Jerusalem. After revealing to His disciples how to pray, Jesus illustrates persistence in prayer.

Then He said to them, "Suppose one of you has a friend, and goes to him at midnight and says to him, 'Friend, lend me three loaves; for a friend of mine has come to me from a journey, and I have nothing to set before him'; and from inside he answers and says, 'Do not bother me; the door has already been shut and my children and I are in bed; I cannot get up and give you *anything.*' I tell you, even though he will not get up and give him *anything* because he is his friend, yet because of his persistence he will get up and give him as much as he needs. So I say to you, ask, and it will be given to you; seek, and you will find; knock, and it will be opened to you. For everyone who asks, receives; and he who seeks, finds; and to him who knocks, it will be opened" (Luke 11:5–10; cf. Matthew 7:7, 8).

LOG

Setting: Galilee. During the early part of His ministry, Jesus preaches the Sermon on the Mount to His disciples and the multitudes.

"Do not judge so that you will not be judged. For in the way you judge, you will be judged; and by your standard of measure, it will be measured to you. Why do you look at the speck that is in your brother's eye, but do not notice the log that is in your own eye? Or how can you say to your brother, 'Let me take the speck out of your eye, and behold, the log is in your own eye? You hypocrite, first take the log out of your own eye, and then you will see clearly to take the speck out of your brother's eye" (Matthew 7:1–5; cf. Mark 4:24; Luke 6:37–42; Romans 2:1; 14:10, 13).

Setting: Galilee. After selecting His twelve disciples, Jesus teaches the Sermon on the Mount to those disciples and a great throng of people from Judea, Jerusalem, and the central coastal region of Tyre and Sidon.

And He also spoke a parable to them: "A blind man cannot guide a blind man, can he? Will they not both fall into a pit? A pupil is not above his teacher; but everyone, after he has been fully trained, will be like his teacher. Why do you look at the speck that is in your brother's eye, but do not notice the log that is in your own eye? Or how can you say to your brother, 'Brother, let me take out the speck that is in your eye,' when you yourself do not see the log that is in your own eye? You hypocrite, first take the log out of your own eye, and then you will see clearly to take out the speck that is in your brother's eye. For there is no good tree which produces bad fruit, nor, on the other hand, a bad tree which produces good fruit. For each tree is known by its own fruit. For men do not gather figs from thorns, nor do they pick grapes from a briar bush. The good man out of the good treasure of his heart brings forth what is good; and the evil *man* out of the evil *treasure* brings forth what is evil; for his mouth speaks from that which fills his heart" (Luke 6:39–45; cf. Matthew 7:3–6. 16, 18, 20; 12:35; see Matthew 10:24; 15:14; Luke 6:12–19).

LONELINESS (See FELLOWSHIP)

LONG PRAYERS (Listed under PRAYERS, LONG; also see HYPOCRITES and PRETENSE)

LONG ROBES (Listed under ROBES, LONG)

LORD (God)

Setting: Judea near the Jordan River. Following Jesus' baptism, before He begins His public ministry, the Spirit leads Him into the wilderness for forty days of temptation by Satan.

Jesus said to him, "On the other hand, it is written, 'YOU SHALL NOT PUT THE LORD YOUR GOD TO THE TEST'" (Matthew 4:7, Jesus quotes from Deuteronomy 6:16; cf. Luke 4:12).

Setting: Judea near the Jordan River. Following Jesus' baptism, before He begins His public ministry, the Spirit leads Him into the wilderness for forty days of temptation by Satan.

Then Jesus said to him, "Go, Satan! For it is written, 'YOU SHALL WORSHIP THE LORD YOUR GOD, AND SERVE HIM ONLY' (Matthew 4:10, Jesus quotes from Deuteronomy 6:13; cf. Luke 4:8).

Setting: Galilee. During the early part of His ministry, Jesus preaches the Sermon on the Mount to His disciples and the multitudes.

"Again, you have heard that the ancients were told, 'YOU SHALL NOT MAKE FALSE VOWS, BUT SHALL FULFILL YOUR VOWS TO THE LORD.' But I say to you, make no oath at all, either by heaven, for it is the throne of God, or by the earth, for it is the footstool of His feet, or by Jerusalem, for it is THE CITY OF THE GREAT KING. Nor shall you make an oath by your head, for you cannot make one hair white or black. But let your statement be 'Yes, yes' *or* 'No, no'; anything beyond these is of evil" (Matthew 5:33–37, Jesus quotes from Leviticus 19:12, Psalm 48:2; Isaiah 66:1; cf. James 5:12).

Setting: Galilee. During the early part of His ministry, Jesus preaches the Sermon on the Mount to His disciples and the multitudes.

"Not everyone who says to Me, 'Lord, Lord,' will enter the kingdom of heaven, but he who does the will of My Father who is in heaven *will enter.* Many will say to Me on that day, 'Lord, Lord, did we not prophesy in Your name, and in Your name cast out demons, and in Your name perform many miracles?' And then I will declare to them, 'I never knew you, DEPART FROM ME, YOU WHO PRACTICE LAWLESSNESS'"(Matthew 7:21–23, Jesus quotes from Psalm 6:8; cf. Matthew 25:11–13; see Luke 6:46).

Setting: Galilee. While healing the sick, raising the dead, and casting out demons in the villages and cities, Jesus comments on the enormity of the task and the need to ask the Lord of the harvest for additional workers.

Then He said to His disciples, "The harvest is plentiful, but the workers are few. Therefore beseech the Lord of the harvest to send out workers into His harvest" (Matthew 9:37, 38; cf. Luke 10:2).

Setting: Galilee. After pronouncing woes against unrepentant cities as He teaches and preaches, Jesus prays a thanksgiving prayer to His Father in heaven.

At that time Jesus said, "I praise You, Father, Lord of heaven and earth, that you have hidden these things from *the* wise and intelligent and have revealed them to infants. Yes, Father, for this way was well-pleasing in Your sight. All things have been handed over to Me by My Father; and no one knows the Son except the Father; nor does anyone know the Father except the Son, and anyone to whom the Son wills to reveal *Him*" (Matthew 11:25–27; cf. Luke 10:21, 22).

Setting: Galilee. Jesus responds to the Pharisees' objection to His disciples' picking grain from the fields on the Sabbath.

But He said to them, "Have you not read what David did when he became hungry, he and his companions, how they entered the house of God, and ate the consecrated bread, which was not lawful for him to eat nor for those with him, but for the priests alone? Or, have you not read in the Law, that on the Sabbath the priests in the temple break the Sabbath and are innocent? But I say to you that something greater than the temple is here. But if you had known what this means, 'I DESIRE COMPASSION, AND NOT A SACRIFICE,' you would not have condemned the innocent. For the Son of Man is Lord of the Sabbath" (Matthew 12:3–8, Jesus quotes from Hosea 6:6; cf. Mark 2:25–28; Luke 6:3–5; see 1 Samuel 21:6).

Setting: Entering Bethphage, on the way to Jerusalem for Jesus' crucifixion. Just after healing some blind men in Jericho, Jesus instructs two disciples to acquire a donkey and colt to be used in His triumphal entry into Jerusalem.

When they had approached Jerusalem and had come to Bethphage, at the Mount of Olives, then Jesus sent two disciples, saying to them, "Go into the village opposite you, and immediately you will find a donkey tied *there* and a colt with her; untie them and bring them to Me. If anyone says anything to you, you shall say, 'The Lord has need of them,' and immediately he will send them" (Matthew 21:1–3; cf. Mark 11:1–3; Luke 19:29–31).

Setting: The temple in Jerusalem. Jesus delivers a prophecy to the chief priests and elders after they question His authority.

Jesus said to them, "Did you never read in the Scriptures, 'THE STONE WHICH THE BUILDERS REJECTED, THIS BECAME THE CHIEF CORNER *stone;* THIS CAME ABOUT FROM THE LORD, AND IT IS MARVELOUS IN OUR EYES'? Therefore I say to you, the kingdom of God will be taken away from you and given to a people, producing the fruit of it. And he who falls on this stone will be broken to pieces; but on whomever it falls, it will scatter him like dust" (Matthew 21:42–44, Jesus quotes from Psalm 118:22; cf. Isaiah 8:14, 15; Mark 12:10, 11; Luke 20:17, 18).

Setting: The temple in Jerusalem. A Pharisee lawyer asks Jesus which is the great commandment of the Law, in order to test Him as He teaches.

And He said to him, " 'YOU SHALL LOVE THE LORD YOUR GOD WITH ALL YOUR HEART, AND WITH ALL YOUR SOUL, AND WITH ALL YOUR MIND.' This is the great and foremost commandment. The second is like it, 'YOU SHALL LOVE YOUR NEIGHBOR AS YOURSELF.' On these two commandments depend the whole Law and the Prophets" (Matthew 22:37–40; Jesus quotes from Leviticus 19:18; Deuteronomy 6:5; cf. Mark 12:28–34; see Matthew 7:12).

Setting: The temple in Jerusalem. Following the Sadducees' and Pharisees' unsuccessful attempts to test Him with questions, with the crowds listening, Jesus poses a question to some of the Pharisees.

"What do you think about the Christ, whose son is He?" They said to Him, "The *son* of David." He said to them, "Then how does David in the Spirit call Him 'Lord,' saying, 'THE LORD SAID TO MY LORD, SIT AT MY RIGHT HAND, UNTIL I PUT YOUR ENEMIES BENEATH YOUR FEET"'? "If David then calls Him 'Lord," how is He his son?" (Matthew 22:42–45; Jesus quotes from Psalm 110:1; cf. Mark 12:35–37; Luke 20:41–44; see 2 Samuel 23:2).

Setting: The temple in Jerusalem. With His death on the cross just days away, Jesus laments over Jerusalem's hard-heartedness and lack of repentance.

"Jerusalem, Jerusalem, who kills the prophets and stones those who are sent to her! How often I wanted to gather your children together, the way a hen gathers her chicks under her wings, and you were unwilling. Behold, your house is being left to you desolate! For I say to you, from now on you will not see Me until you say, 'BLESSED IS HE WHO COMES IN THE NAME OF THE LORD!'" (Matthew 23:37–39, Jesus quotes from Psalm 118:26; cf. 1 Kings 9:7; Luke 13:34, 35)

Setting: On the Mount of Olives, just east of Jerusalem. During His discourse, after answering His disciples' questions as to when the temple will be destroyed and Jerusalem overrun, along with the signs of His coming and the end of the age, Jesus reemphasizes to His disciples that they should be on the alert for His return.

"Therefore be on the alert, for you do not know which day your Lord is coming. But be sure of this, that if the head of the house had known at what time of the night the thief was coming, he would have been on the alert and would not have allowed his house to be broken into. For this reason you also must be ready; for the Son of Man is coming at an hour when you do not think *He will.* Who then is the faithful and sensible slave whom his master put in charge of his household to give their food at the proper time? Blessed is that slave whom his master finds so doing when he comes. Truly I say to you that he will put him in charge of all his possessions. But if that evil slave says in his heart, 'My master is not coming for a long time,' and begins to beat his fellow slaves and eat and drink with drunkards; the master of that slave will come on a day when he does not expect *him* and at an hour which he does not know, and will cut him in pieces and assign him a place with the hypocrites; in that place there will be weeping and gnashing of teeth" (Matthew 24:42–51; cf. Mark 13:33–37; Luke 12:39–46; 21:34–36; see Matthew 8:11, 12; 25:21–23).

Setting: The Mount of Olives, just east of Jerusalem. During His discourse, after answering His disciples' questions as to when the temple will be destroyed and Jerusalem overrun, along with the signs of His coming and the end of the age, Jesus reveals the future judgments following His return.

"But when the Son of Man comes in His glory, and all the angels with Him, then He will sit on His glorious throne. All the nations will be gathered before Him; and He will separate them from one another, as the shepherd separates the sheep from the goats; and He will put the sheep on His right, and the goats on the left. Then the King will say to those on His right, 'Come, you who are blessed of My Father, inherit the kingdom prepared for you from the foundation of the world. 'For I was hungry, and you gave Me *something* to eat; I was thirsty, and you gave Me *something* to drink; I was a stranger, and you invited Me in; naked, and you clothed Me; I was sick, and you visited Me; I was in prison, and you came to Me.' Then the righteous will answer Him, 'Lord, when did we see You hungry and feed You, or thirsty, and give you *something* to drink? And when did we see You a stranger, and invite You in, or naked, and clothe You? When did we see You sick, or in prison, and come to You?' The King will answer and say to them, 'Truly I say to you, to the extent that you did it to one of these brothers of Mine, *even* the least *of them,* you did it to Me.' Then He will also say to those on His left, 'Depart from Me, accursed ones, into the eternal fire which has been prepared for the devil and his angels; for I was hungry, and you gave Me *nothing* to eat; I was thirsty, and you gave Me nothing to drink; I was a stranger, and you did not invite Me in; naked, and you did not clothe Me; sick, and in prison, and you did not visit Me.' Then they themselves also will answer, 'Lord, when did we see You hungry, or thirsty, or a stranger, or naked, or sick, or in prison, and did not take care of You?' Then He will answer them, 'Truly I say to you, to the extent that you did not do it to one of the least of these, you did not do it to Me.' These will go away into eternal punishment, but the righteous into eternal life" (Matthew 25:31–46; see Matthew 7:23; 16:27; 19:29).

Setting: Galilee. Early in His ministry, the Pharisees ask Jesus why He allows His disciples to harvest grain on the Sabbath.

And He said to them, "Have you never read what David did when he was in need and he and his companions became hungry; how he entered the house of God in the time of Abiathar *the* high priest, and ate the consecrated bread, which is not lawful for *anyone* to eat except the priests, and he also gave it to those who were with him?" Jesus said to them, "The Sabbath was made for man, and not man for the Sabbath. So the Son of Man is Lord even of the Sabbath" (Mark 2:25–28; cf. Matthew 12:1–8; Luke 6:1–5; see Exodus 23:12).

Setting: The country of the Gerasenes, across the Sea of Galilee from Capernaum. Jesus encounters and heals a man possessed by a legion of demons.

And He did not let him, but He said to him, "Go home to your people and report to them what great things the Lord has done for you, and *how* He had mercy on you" (Mark 5:19; cf. Luke 8:39; see Matthew 8:33, 34; Luke 8:36–38).

Setting: Approaching Jerusalem for the Lord's impending death on the cross. Jesus instructs two of His disciples to obtain a colt for His triumphal entry into the city.

As they approached Jerusalem, at Bethphage and Bethany, near the Mount of Olives, He sent two of His disciples, and said to them, "Go into the village opposite you, and immediately as you enter it, you will find a colt tied *there,* on which no one yet has ever sat; untie it and bring it *here.* If anyone says to you, 'Why are you doing this?' you say, 'The Lord has need of it'; and immediately he will send it back here" (Mark 11:1–3; cf. Matthew 21:1–3; Luke 19:29–31; see Matthew 21:4–7; Luke 19:32–35; John 12:12–15).

Setting: The temple in Jerusalem. Having His authority questioned by the chief priests, scribes, and elders, Jesus begins to teach them in parables.

And He began to speak to them in parables: "A man PLANTED A VINEYARD AND PUT A WALL AROUND IT, AND DUG A VAT UNDER THE WINE PRESS AND BUILT A TOWER, and rented it out to vine-growers and went on a journey. At the *harvest* time he sent a slave to the vine-growers, in order to receive *some* of the produce of the vineyard from the vine-growers. They took him, and beat him and sent him away empty-handed. Again he sent them another slave, and they wounded him in the head, and treated him shamefully. And he sent another, and that one they killed; and *so with* many others, beating some and killing others. He had one more to *send,* a beloved son; he sent him last *of all* to them, saying, 'They will respect my son.' But those vine-growers said to one another, 'This is the heir; come, let us kill him, and the inheritance will be ours!' They took him, and killed him and threw him out of the vineyard. What will the owner of the vineyard do? He will come and destroy the vine-growers, and will give the vineyard to others. Have you not even read this Scripture: 'THE STONE WHICH THE BUILDERS REJECTED, THIS BECAME THE CHIEF CORNER *stone;* THIS CAME ABOUT FROM THE LORD, AND IT IS MARVELOUS IN OUR EYES'?" (Mark 12:1–11, Jesus quotes from Psalm 118:22, 23; Isaiah 5:1, 2; cf. Matthew 21:33–46; Luke 20:9–19).

Setting: The temple in Jerusalem. With the Pharisees and Herodians failing to trap Jesus in a statement, one of the scribes asks Him which commandment is foremost.

Jesus answered, "The foremost is, 'HEAR, O ISRAEL! THE LORD OUR GOD IS ONE LORD; AND YOU SHALL LOVE THE LORD YOUR GOD WITH ALL YOUR HEART, AND WITH ALL YOUR SOUL, AND WITH ALL YOUR MIND AND WITH ALL YOUR STRENGTH.' The second is this, 'YOU SHALL LOVE YOUR NEIGHBOR AS YOURSELF.' There is no other commandment greater than these" (Mark 12:29–31, Jesus quotes from Deuteronomy 6:4, 5; Leviticus 19:18; cf. Matthew 22:34–40).

Setting: The temple in Jerusalem. Jesus teaches the crowd after commending a scribe for his nearness to the kingdom of God.

And Jesus *began* to say, as He taught in the temple, "How *is it that* the scribes say that the Christ is the son of David? David himself said in the Holy Spirit, 'THE LORD SAID TO MY LORD, SIT AT MY RIGHT HAND, UNTIL I PUT YOUR ENEMIES BENEATH YOUR FEET.'" David himself calls Him 'Lord'; so in what sense is He his son?" And the large crowd enjoyed listening to Him (Mark 12:35–37, Jesus quotes from Psalm 110:1; cf. Matthew 22:41–46; Luke 20:41–44).

Setting: On the Mount of Olives, east of the temple in Jerusalem. After predicting the temple's destruction, Jesus responds during His Olivet Discourse to questions from Peter, James, John, and Andrew about other future events.

"But when you see the ABOMINATION OF DESOLATION standing where it should not be (let the reader understand), then those who are in Judea must flee to the mountains. The one who is on the housetop must not go down, or go in to get anything out of his house; and the one who is in the field must not turn back to get his coat. But woe to those who are pregnant and to those who are nursing babies in those days! But pray that it may not happen in winter. For those days will be a *time of* tribulation such as has not occurred since the beginning of the creation which God created until now, and never will. Unless the Lord had shortened *those* days, no life would have been saved; but for the sake of the elect, whom He chose, He shortened the days. And then if anyone says to you, 'Behold, here is the Christ'; or, 'Behold, *He is* there'; do not believe *him*; for false Christs and false prophets will arise, and will show signs and wonders, in order to lead astray, if possible, the elect. But take heed; behold, I have told you everything in advance" (Mark 13:14–23; cf. Matthew 24:15–28; Luke 21:20–24; see Daniel 9:27; 12:1; Luke 17:31).

Setting: Judea, near the Jordan River. Following Jesus' baptism, and before He begins His public ministry, the Spirit leads Him into the wilderness for forty days of temptation by Satan.

Jesus answered him, "It is written, 'YOU SHALL WORSHIP THE LORD YOUR GOD AND SERVE HIM ONLY'" (Luke 4:8, Jesus quotes from Deuteronomy 6:13; cf. Matthew 4:10).

Setting: Judea, near the Jordan River. Following Jesus' baptism, and before He begins His public ministry, the Spirit leads Him into the wilderness for forty days of temptation by Satan.

And Jesus answered and said to him, "It is said, 'YOU SHALL NOT PUT THE LORD YOUR GOD TO THE TEST'" (Luke 4:12, Jesus quotes from Deuteronomy 6:16; cf. Matthew 4:7).

Setting: The synagogue in Jesus' hometown of Nazareth in Galilee. At the beginning of His public ministry, Jesus reads on the Sabbath from the book of the prophet Isaiah.

And the book of the prophet Isaiah was handed to Him. And He opened the book and found the place where it was written, "THE SPIRIT OF THE LORD IS UPON ME, BECAUSE HE ANOINTED ME TO PREACH THE GOSPEL TO THE POOR. HE HAS SENT ME TO PROCLAIM RELEASE TO THE CAPTIVES, AND RECOVERY OF SIGHT TO THE BLIND, TO SET FREE THOSE WHO ARE OPPRESSED, TO PROCLAIM THE FAVORABLE YEAR OF THE LORD." And He closed the book, gave it back to the attendant and sat down; and the eyes of all in the synagogue were fixed on Him. And He began to say to them, "Today this Scripture has been fulfilled in your hearing" (Luke 4:17–21, Jesus quotes from Isaiah 61:1, 2).

Setting: Probably Galilee. As Jesus and His disciples pass through some grain fields, some of the Pharisees ask Jesus why His followers harvest grain on the Sabbath.

And Jesus answering them said, "Have you not even read what David did when he was hungry, he and those who were with him, how he entered the house of God, and took and ate the consecrated bread which is not lawful for any to eat except the priests alone, and gave it to his companions?" And He was saying to them, "The Son of Man is Lord of the Sabbath" (Luke 6:3–5; cf. Matthew 12:1–8; Mark 2:23–28; see Exodus 20:8; Leviticus 24:1–9; Deuteronomy 5:12; 1 Samuel 21:1–6).

Setting: Galilee. After selecting His twelve disciples, Jesus teaches the Sermon on the Mount to those disciples and a great throng of people from Judea, Jerusalem, and the central coastal region of Tyre and Sidon.

"Why do you call Me, 'Lord, Lord,' and do not do what I say? Everyone who comes to Me and hears My words and acts on them, I will show you whom he is like; he is like a man building a house, who dug deep and laid a foundation on the rock; and when a flood occurred, the torrent burst against that house and could not shake it, because it had been well built. But the one who has heard and has not acted *accordingly,* is like a man who built a house on the ground without any foundation; and the torrent burst against it and immediately it collapsed, and the ruin of that house was great" (Luke 6:46–49; cf. Matthew 7:24–27; see Luke 6:12–19; James 1:22).

Setting: On the way from Galilee to Jerusalem. The Lord appoints seventy followers and sends them out in pairs to every place He Himself will soon visit.

And He was saying to them, "The harvest is plentiful, but the laborers are few; therefore beseech the Lord of the harvest to send out laborers into His harvest. Go; behold, I send you out as lambs in the midst of wolves. Carry no money belt, no bag, no shoes; and greet no one on the way. Whatever house you enter, first say, 'Peace be to this house.' If a man of peace is there, your peace will rest on him; but if not, it will return to you. Stay in that house, eating and drinking what they give you; for the laborer is worthy of his wages. Do not keep moving from house to house. Whatever city you enter and they receive you, eat what is set before you; and heal those in it who are sick, and say to them, 'The kingdom of God has come near to you.' But whatever city you enter and they do not receive you, go out into its streets and say, 'Even the dust of your city which clings to our feet we wipe off *in protest* against you; yet be sure of this, that the kingdom of God has come near.' I say to you, it will be more tolerable in that day for Sodom than for that city" (Luke 10:2–12; see Genesis 19:24–28; Matthew 9:37, 38, 10:9–14, 16; 1 Corinthians 10:27).

Setting: On the way from Galilee to Jerusalem. The Lord responds to a report from the seventy sent out in pairs to every place He Himself will soon visit.

At that very time He rejoiced greatly in the Holy Spirit, and said, "I praise You, O Father, Lord of heaven and earth, that You have hidden these things from *the* wise and intelligent and have revealed them to infants. Yes, Father, for this way was well-pleasing in Your sight. All things have been handed over to Me by My Father, and no one knows who the Son is except the Father, and who the Father is except the Son, and anyone to whom the Son wills to reveal *Him*" (Luke 10:21, 22; cf. Matthew 11:25–27; see Luke 10:1, 17; John 3:35; 10:15).

Setting: On the way from Galilee to Jerusalem. While teaching in the cities and villages, Jesus responds to a question about who is saved.

And someone said to Him, "Lord, are here *just* a few who are being saved?" And He said to them, "Strive to enter through the narrow door; for many, I tell you, will seek to enter and will not be able. Once the head of the house gets up and shuts the door, and you begin to stand outside and knock on the door, saying, 'Lord, open up to us!' then He will answer and say to you, 'I do not know where you are from.' Then you will begin to say, 'We ate and drank in Your presence, and You taught in our streets'; and He will say, 'I tell you, I do not know where you are from; DEPART FROM ME, ALL YOU EVILDOERS.' In that place there will be weeping and gnashing of teeth when you see Abraham and Isaac and Jacob and all the prophets in the kingdom of God, but you yourselves being thrown out. And they will come from east and west and from north and south, and will recline *at the table* in the kingdom of God. And behold, *some* are last who will be first and *some* are first who will be last" (Luke 13:23–30, Jesus quotes from Psalm 6:8; cf. Matthew 7:13, 23; 8:11, 12; see Matthew 19:30; Luke 3:8).

Setting: On the way from Galilee to Jerusalem. After Jesus responds to a question about who is saved, some Pharisees ask Him to leave, claiming Herod Antipas (tetrarch of Galilee and Perea) seeks to kill Him.

And He said to them, "Go and tell that fox, 'Behold, I cast out demons and perform cures today and tomorrow, and the third *day* I reach My goal.' Nevertheless I must journey on today and tomorrow and the next *day*; for it cannot be that a prophet would perish outside of Jerusalem. O Jerusalem, Jerusalem, *the city* that kills the prophets and stones those sent to her! How often I wanted to gather your children together, just as a hen *gathers* her brood under her wings, and you would not *have it*! Behold, your house is left to you *desolate*; and I say to you, you will not see Me until *the time* comes when you say, 'BLESSED IS HE WHO COMES IN THE NAME OF THE LORD!'" (Luke 13:32–35, Jesus quotes from Psalm 118:26; cf. Matthew 23:37).

Setting: Jericho. After providing a parable about stewardship, Jesus and His disciples head to the outskirts of Jerusalem to prepare for His triumphal entry into the city and His upcoming crucifixion.

When He approached Bethphage and Bethany, near the mount that is called Olivet, He sent two of the disciples, saying, "Go into the village ahead of *you;* there, as you enter, you will find a colt tied on which no one yet has ever sat; untie it and bring it *here.* If anyone asks you, 'Why are you untying it?' you shall say, 'The Lord has need of it'" (Luke 19:29–31; cf. Matthew 21:1–3; Mark 11:1–3).

Setting: The temple in Jerusalem. A few days before His crucifixion, after the scribes and Pharisees seek to trap Jesus by questioning Him about paying taxes to Caesar, some Sadducees (who say there is no resurrection) ask Him a question about the resurrection.

Jesus said to them, "The sons of this age marry and are given in marriage, but those who are considered worthy to attain to that age and the resurrection from the dead, neither marry nor are given in marriage; for they cannot even die anymore, because they are like angels, and are sons of God, being sons of the resurrection. But that the dead are raised, even Moses showed, in the *passage about the burning* bush, where he calls the Lord THE GOD OF ABRAHAM, AND THE GOD OF ISAAC, AND THE GOD OF JACOB. Now He is not the God of the dead but of the living; for all live to Him" (Luke 20:34–38, Jesus quotes from Exodus 3:6; cf. Matthew 22:23–32; Mark 12:18–27).

Setting: The temple in Jerusalem. A few days before His crucifixion, after some of the Sadducees question Him about the resurrection, Jesus poses a question to the scribes, who say He answered well.

Then He said to them, "How *is it that* they say the Christ is David's son? For David himself says in the book of Psalms, 'THE LORD SAID TO MY LORD, SIT AT MY RIGHT HAND, UNTIL I MAKE YOUR ENEMIES A FOOTSTOOL FOR YOUR FEET.' Therefore David calls Him 'Lord,' and how is He his son?" (Luke 20:41–44, Jesus quotes from Psalm 110:1; cf. Matthew 22:41–46; Mark 12:35–37).

Setting: Jerusalem. Before the Passover, with His death on the cross nearing, Jesus explains the reason for His vivid example of servanthood in washing His disciples' feet.

So when He had washed their feet, and taken His garments and reclined *at the table* again, He said to them, "Do you know what I have done to you? You call Me Teacher and Lord; and you are right, for *so* I am. If I then, the Lord and the Teacher, washed your feet, you also ought to wash one another's feet. For I gave you an example that you also should do as I did to you. Truly, truly I say to you, a slave is not greater than his master, nor *is* one who is sent greater than the one who sent him. If you know these things, you are blessed if you do them. I do not speak of all of you. I know the ones I have chosen; but *it is* that the Scripture may be fulfilled, 'HE WHO EATS MY BREAD HAS LIFTED UP HIS HEEL AGAINST ME.' From now on I am telling you before *it* comes to pass, so that when it does occur, you may believe that I am *He*. Truly, truly, I say to you, he who receives whomever I send receives Me; and he who receives Me receives Him who sent Me" (John 13:12–20; Jesus quotes from Psalm 41:9; see Matthew 7:24; 10:24, 40; John 8:24; 14:29; 1 Peter 5:3).

LORD (human)

Setting: Capernaum of Galilee. Jesus illustrates forgiveness after Peter asks Him if forgiving someone seven times who has sinned against him is adequate.

"For this reason the kingdom of heaven may be compared to a king who wished to settle accounts with his slaves. When he had begun to settle *them,* one who owed him ten thousand talents was brought to him. But since he did not have *the means* to repay, his lord commanded him to be sold, along with his wife and children and all that he had, and repayment to be made. So the slave fell *to the ground* and prostrated himself before him, saying, 'Have patience with me and I will repay you everything.' And the lord of that slave felt compassion and released him and forgave him the debt. But that slave went out and found one of his fellow slaves who owed him a hundred denarii; and he seized him and *began* to choke *him,* saying, 'Pay back what you owe.' So his fellow slave fell *to the ground* and *began* to plead with him, saying, 'Have patience with me and I will repay you.' But he was unwilling and went and threw him in prison until he should pay back what was owed. So when his fellow slaves saw what had happened, they were deeply grieved and came and reported to their lord all that had happened. Then summoning him, his lord said to him, 'You wicked slave, I forgave you all that debt because you pleaded with me. Should you not also have had mercy on your fellow slave, in the same way that I had mercy on you?' And his lord, moved with anger, handed him over to the torturers until he should repay all that was owed him. My heavenly Father will also do the same to you, if each of you does not forgive his brother from your heart" (Matthew 18:23–35; cf. Matthew 6:12, 14, 15; Luke 7:42; see Matthew 25:19–28).

Setting: The temple in Jerusalem. Following the Sadducees' and Pharisees' unsuccessful attempts to test Him with questions, with the crowds listening, Jesus poses a question to some of the Pharisees.

"What do you think about the Christ, whose son is He?" They said to Him, "The *son* of David." He said to them, "Then how does David in the Spirit call Him 'Lord,' saying, 'THE LORD SAID TO MY LORD, SIT AT MY RIGHT HAND, UNTIL I PUT YOUR ENEMIES BENEATH YOUR FEET'"? "If David then calls Him 'Lord," how is He his son?" (Matthew 22:42–45; Jesus quotes from Psalm 110:1; cf. Mark 12:35–37; Luke 20:41–44; see 2 Samuel 23:2).

Setting: The Mount of Olives, just east of Jerusalem. During His discourse, after answering His disciples' questions as to when the temple will be destroyed and Jerusalem overrun, along with the signs of His coming and the end of the age, Jesus reemphasizes to the disciples that they should be on the alert for His return.

"Then the kingdom of heaven will be comparable to ten virgins, who took their lamps and went out to meet the bridegroom. Five of them were foolish, and five were prudent. For when the foolish took their lamps, they took no oil with them, but the prudent took oil in flasks along with their lamps. Now while the bridegroom was delaying, they all got drowsy and *began* to sleep. But at midnight there was a shout, 'Behold, the bridegroom! Come out to meet *him*.' Then all those virgins rose and trimmed their lamps. The foolish said to the prudent, 'Give us some of your oil, for our lamps are going out.' But the prudent answered, 'No, there will not be enough for us and you *too;* go instead to the dealers and buy *some* for yourselves.' And while they were going away to make the purchase, the bridegroom came, and those who were ready went in with him to the wedding feast; and the door was shut. Later the other virgins also came, saying, 'Lord, lord, open up for us.' But he answered, 'Truly I say to you, I do not know you.' Be on the alert then, for you do not know the day nor the hour" (Matthew 25:1–13; cf. Matthew 24:42; Luke 12:35; see Matthew 7:21, 24).

LORD, COMING OF THE (Also see JESUS' RETURN; and SON OF MAN, COMING OF THE)

[COMING OF THE LORD from HE WHO COMES IN THE NAME OF THE LORD]
Setting: The temple in Jerusalem. With His death on the cross just days away, Jesus laments over Jerusalem's hard-heartedness and lack of repentance.

"Jerusalem, Jerusalem, who kills the prophets and stones those who are sent to her! How often I wanted to gather your children together, the way a hen gathers her chicks under her wings, and you were unwilling. Behold, your house is being left to you desolate! For I say to you, from now on you will not see Me until you say, 'BLESSED IS HE WHO COMES IN THE NAME OF THE LORD!'" (Matthew 23:37–39, Jesus quotes from Psalm 118:26; cf. 1 Kings 9:7; Luke 13:34, 35).

[COMING OF THE LORD from recognize that He is near, *right* at the door]
Setting: The Mount of Olives, just east of Jerusalem. During His discourse, after answering His disciples' questions as to when the temple will be destroyed and Jerusalem overrun, along with the signs of His coming and the end of the age, Jesus teaches them the Parable of the Fig Tree.

"Now learn the parable from the fig tree: when its branch has already become tender and puts forth its leaves, you know that summer is near; so, you too, when you see all these things, recognize that He is near, *right* at the door. Truly, I say to you, this generation will not pass away until all these things take place. Heaven and earth will pass away, but My words will not pass away. But of that day and hour no one knows, not even the angels of heaven, nor the Son, but the Father alone. For the coming of the Son of Man will be just like the days of Noah. For as in those days before the flood they were eating and drinking, marrying and giving in marriage, until the day that Noah entered the ark, and they did not understand until the flood came and took them all away; so will the coming of the Son of Man be. Then there will be two men in the field; one will be taken and one will be left. Two women *will be* grinding at the mill; one will be taken and one will be left" (Matthew 24:32–41; cf. Mark 13:28–32; Luke 17:34–36; 21:28–33; see Genesis 6:5; 7:7; Matthew 5:18; 10:23; James 5:9).

[COMING OF THE LORD from your Lord is coming]
Setting: The Mount of Olives, just east of Jerusalem. During His discourse, after answering His disciples' questions as to when the temple will be destroyed and Jerusalem overrun, along with the signs of His coming and the end of the age, Jesus reemphasizes to His disciples that they should be on the alert for His return.

"Therefore be on the alert, for you do not know which day your Lord is coming. But be sure of this, that if the head of the house had known at what time of the night the thief was coming, he would have been on the alert and would not have allowed his house to be broken into. For this reason you also must be ready; for the Son of Man is coming at an hour when you do not think *He will.* Who then is the faithful and sensible slave whom his master put in charge of his household to give their food at the proper time? Blessed is that slave whom his master finds so doing when he comes. Truly I say to you that he will put him in charge of all his possessions. But if that evil slave says in his heart, 'My master is not coming for a long time,' and begins to beat his fellow slaves and eat and drink with drunkards; the master of that slave will come on a day when he does not expect *him* and at an hour which he does not know, and will cut him in pieces and assign him a place with the hypocrites; in that place there will be weeping and gnashing of teeth" (Matthew 24:42–51; cf. Mark 13:33–37; Luke 12:39–46; 21:34–36; see Matthew 8:11, 12; 25:21–23).

[COMING OF THE LORD from He is near, *right* at the door]
Setting: On the Mount of Olives, east of the temple in Jerusalem. After predicting the temple's destruction, Jesus responds during His Olivet Discourse to questions from Peter, James, John, and Andrew about other future events.

"Now learn the parable from the fig tree: when its branch has already become tender and puts forth its leaves, you know that summer is near. Even so, you too, when you see these things happening, recognize that He is near, *right* at the door. Truly I say to you, this generation will not pass away until all these things take place. Heaven and earth will pass away, but My words will not pass away. But of the day or hour no one knows, not even the angels in heaven, nor the Son, but the Father *alone*" (Mark 13:28–32; cf. Matthew 24:32–36; Luke 21:28–33).

[COMING OF THE LORD from when the master of the house is coming]
Setting: On the Mount of Olives, east of the temple in Jerusalem. After predicting the temple's destruction, Jesus responds during His Olivet Discourse to questions from Peter, James, John, and Andrew about other future events.

"Take heed, keep on the alert; for you do not know when the *appointed* time will come. *It is* like a man away on a journey, *who* upon leaving his house and putting his slaves in charge, *assigning* to each one his task, also commanded the doorkeeper to stay on the alert. Therefore, be on the alert—for you do not know when the master of the house is coming, whether in the evening, at midnight, or when the rooster crows, or in the morning—in case he should come suddenly and find you asleep. What I say to you I say to all, 'Be on the alert!' " (Mark 13:33–37; cf. Matthew 24:42–43; Luke 21:34–36; see Luke 12:36–38; Ephesians 6:18).

[COMING OF THE LORD from HE WHO COMES IN THE NAME OF THE LORD]
Setting: On the way from Galilee to Jerusalem. After Jesus responds to a question about who is saved, some Pharisees ask Him to leave, claiming Herod Antipas (tetrarch of Galilee and Perea) seeks to kill Him.

And He said to them, "Go and tell that fox, 'Behold, I cast out demons and perform cures today and tomorrow, and the third *day* I reach My goal.' Nevertheless I must journey on today and tomorrow and the next *day*; for it cannot be that a prophet would perish outside of Jerusalem. O Jerusalem, Jerusalem, *the city* that kills the prophets and stones those sent to her! How often I wanted to gather your children together, just as a hen *gathers* her brood under her wings, and you would not *have it*! Behold, your house is left to you *desolate*; and I say to you, you will not see Me until *the time* comes when you say, 'BLESSED IS HE WHO COMES IN THE NAME OF THE LORD!'" (Luke 13:32–35, Jesus quotes from Psalm 118:26; cf. Matthew 23:37).

LORD, LOVING THE (See GOD, LOVING)

LORD, NAME OF THE

Setting: The temple in Jerusalem. With His death on the cross just days away, Jesus laments over Jerusalem's hard-heartedness and lack of repentance.

"Jerusalem, Jerusalem, who kills the prophets and stones those who are sent to her! How often I wanted to gather your children together, the way a hen gathers her chicks under her wings, and you were unwilling. Behold, your house is being left to you desolate! For I say to you, from now on you will not see Me until you say, 'BLESSED IS HE WHO COMES IN THE NAME OF THE LORD!'" (Matthew 23:37–39, Jesus quotes from Psalm 118:26; cf. 1 Kings 9:7; Luke 13:34, 35).

Setting: On the way from Galilee to Jerusalem. After Jesus responds to a question about who is saved, some Pharisees ask Him to leave, claiming Herod Antipas (tetrarch of Galilee and Perea) seeks to kill Him.

And He said to them, "Go and tell that fox, 'Behold, I cast out demons and perform cures today and tomorrow, and the third *day* I reach My goal.' Nevertheless I must journey on today and tomorrow and the next *day*; for it cannot be that a prophet would perish outside of Jerusalem. O Jerusalem, Jerusalem, *the city* that kills the prophets and stones those sent to her! How often I wanted to gather your children together, just as a hen *gathers* her brood under her wings, and you would not *have it*! Behold, your house is left to you *desolate*; and I say to you, you will not see Me until *the time* comes when you say, 'BLESSED IS HE WHO COMES IN THE NAME OF THE LORD!'" (Luke 13:32–35, Jesus quotes from Psalm 118:26; cf. Matthew 23:37).

LORD, SPIRIT OF THE (See SPIRIT OF THE LORD)

LORD, YEAR OF THE (See YEAR OF THE LORD)

LORD'S PRAYER

[LORD'S PRAYER inferred from context]

Setting: Galilee. During the early part of His ministry, Jesus gives a model prayer to His disciples and the multitudes while conveying the Sermon on the Mount.

"Pray, then, in this way: 'Our Father who is in heaven, hallowed be Your name. Your kingdom come. Your will be done, on earth as it is in heaven. Give us this day our daily bread. And forgive us our debts, as we also have forgiven our debtors. And do not lead us into temptation, but deliver us from evil. [For Yours is the kingdom and the power and the glory forever. Amen]'" (Matthew 6:9–13; cf. Luke 11:2–4; see John 17:15).

[LORD'S PRAYER inferred from context]

Setting: On the way from Galilee to Jerusalem. After Jesus visits in the home of Martha and Mary in Bethany, one of His disciples asks Him to teach them to pray.

And He said to them, "When you pray, say: 'Father, hallowed be Your name. Your kingdom come. Give us each day our daily bread. And forgive us our sins, for we ourselves also forgive everyone who is indebted to us. And lead us not into temptation'" (Luke 11:2–4; cf. Matthew 6:9–13).

LORD'S SUPPER (Also see BLOOD, NEW COVENANT IN MY)

[LORD'S SUPPER inferred from context]

Setting: An upper room in Jerusalem. While celebrating the Passover meal with His disciples, Jesus institutes the Lord's Supper ordinance before being arrested by His enemies.

While they were eating, Jesus took *some* bread, and after a blessing, He broke *it* and gave *it* to the disciples, and said, "Take, eat; this is My body." And when He had taken a cup and given thanks, He gave *it* to them saying, "Drink from it, all of you; for this is My blood of the covenant, which is poured out for many for forgiveness of sins. But I say to you, I will not drink of this fruit of the vine from now on until that day when I drink it new with you in My Father's kingdom" (Matthew 26:26–29; cf. Mark 14:22–25; Luke 22:17–20; 1 Corinthians 11:23–26; see 1 Corinthians 10:16).

[LORD'S SUPPER inferred from context]

Setting: An upper room in Jerusalem. While celebrating the Feast of Unleavened Bread (Passover) with His disciples, Jesus institutes the ordinance of the Lord's Supper.

While they were eating, He took *some* bread, and after a blessing He broke *it*, and gave *it* to them, and said, "Take *it;* this is My body." And when He had taken a cup *and* given thanks, He gave *it* to them, and they all drank from it. And He said to them, "This is My blood of the covenant, which is poured out for many. Truly I say to you, I will never again drink of the fruit of the vine until that day when I drink it new in the kingdom of God" (Mark 14:22–25; cf. Matthew 26:26–29; Luke 22:17–20; 1 Corinthians 11:23–26; see Exodus 24:8).

[LORD'S SUPPER inferred from context]
Setting: An upper room in Jerusalem. During the Feast of Unleavened Bread (Passover) just before His crucifixion, while celebrating the Passover meal with His disciples, Jesus institutes the Lord's Supper.

And when He had taken a cup *and* given thanks, He said, "Take this and share it among yourselves; for I say to you, I will not drink of the fruit of the vine from now on until the kingdom of God comes." And when he had taken *some* bread and given thanks, He broke it and gave it to them, saying, "This is My body which is given for you; do this in remembrance of Me." And in the same way *He took* the cup after they had eaten, saying, "This cup which is poured out for you is the new covenant in My blood. But behold, the hand of the one betraying Me is with Mine on the table. For indeed, the Son of Man is going as it has been determined; but woe to that man by whom He is betrayed!" (Luke 22:17–22; cf. Matthew 26:26–29; Mark 14:22–25; 1 Corinthians 11:23–26; see Psalm 41:9; Luke 14:15; 1 Corinthians 10:16).

[LORD'S SUPPER inferred from context]
Setting: An upper room in Jerusalem. During his third missionary journey, writing from Ephesus to the church at Corinth, the apostle Paul recounts the Lord Jesus' words as He institutes the Lord's Supper.

For I received from the Lord that which I also delivered to you, that the Lord Jesus in the night in which He was betrayed took bread; and when He had given thanks, He broke it and said, "This is My body, which is for you; do this in remembrance of Me." In the same way *He took* the cup also after supper, saying, "This cup is the new covenant in My blood; do this, as often as you drink *it,* in remembrance of Me" (1 Corinthians 11:23–25; cf. Matthew 26:26–28; Mark 14:22–24; Luke 22:17–20).

LORD'S TABLE (See LORD'S SUPPER)

LORD OF HEAVEN AND EARTH (Listed under EARTH, LORD OF HEAVEN AND)

LORD OF THE HARVEST (Listed under HARVEST, LORD OF THE; also see GREAT COMMISSION; and HARVEST)

LORD OF THE SABBATH (Listed under SABBATH, LORD OF THE)

LOSS (See GRIEF; MOURNING; SORROW; and WEEPING)

LOST (LOST, CONCERN FOR THE is a separate entry)

[LOST from gone astray]
***Setting:* Capernaum of Galilee. Jesus illustrates to His disciples the value of little ones.**

"What do you think? If any man has a hundred sheep, and one of them has gone astray, does he not leave the ninety-nine on the mountains and go and search for the one that is straying? If it turns out that he finds it, truly I say to you, he rejoices over it more than the ninety-nine which have not gone astray. So it is not *the* will of your Father who is in heaven that one of these little ones perish" (Matthew 18:12–14; cf. Luke 15:4–7).

Setting: On the way from Galilee to Jerusalem. After Jesus presents to large crowds the demands of discipleship, the Pharisees and scribes complain He associates with tax collectors and sinners.

So He told them this parable, saying, "What man among you, if he has a hundred sheep and has lost one of them, does not leave the ninety-nine in the open pasture and go after the one which is lost until he finds it? When he has found it, he lays it on his shoulders, rejoicing. And when he comes home, he calls together his friends and his neighbors, saying to them, 'Rejoice with me, for I have found my sheep which was lost!' I tell you that in the same way, there will be *more* joy in heaven over one sinner who repents than over ninety-nine righteous persons who need no repentance" (Luke 15:3–7; cf. Matthew 18:12–14; see Matthew 9:11–13; Luke 5:29–32).

Setting: On the way from Galilee to Jerusalem. Jesus conveys the principles of the lost sheep and the lost coin because the Pharisees and scribes complain He associates with tax collectors and sinners.

"So He told them this parable, saying, "What man among you, if he has a hundred sheep and has lost one of them, does not leave the ninety-nine in the open pasture and go after the one which is lost until he finds it? When he has found it, he lays it on his shoulders, rejoicing. And when he comes home, he calls together his friends and his neighbors, saying to them, 'Rejoice with me, for I have found my sheep which was lost!' I tell you that in the same way, there will be more joy in heaven over one sinner who repents than over ninety-nine righteous persons who need no repentance. Or what woman, if she has ten silver coins and loses one coin, does not light a lamp and sweep the house and search carefully until she finds it? When she has found it, she calls together her friends and neighbors, saying, 'Rejoice with me, for I have found the coin which I had lost!' In the same way, I tell you, there is joy in the presence of the angels of God over one sinner who repents" (Luke 15:3–10).

Setting: On the way from Galilee to Jerusalem. Jesus conveys the illustration of the prodigal son because the Pharisees and scribes complain He associates with tax collectors and sinners.

And He said, "A man had two sons. The younger of them said to his father, 'Father, give me the share of the estate that falls to me.' So he divided his wealth between them. And not many days later, the younger son gathered everything together and went on a journey into a distant country, and there he squandered his estate with loose living. Now when he had spent everything, a severe famine occurred in that country, and he began to be impoverished. So he went and hired himself out to one of the citizens of that country, and he sent him into his fields to feed swine. And he would have gladly filled his stomach with the pods that the swine were eating, and no one was giving *anything* to him. But when he came to his senses, he said, 'How many of my father's hired men have more than enough bread, but I am dying here with hunger! I will get up and go to my father, and will say to him, "Father, I have sinned against heaven, and in your sight; I am no longer worthy to be called your son; make me as one of your hired men."' So he got up and came to his father. But while he was still a long way off, his father saw him and felt compassion *for him,* and ran and embraced him and kissed him. And the son said to him, "Father, I have sinned against heaven and in your sight; I am no longer worthy to be called your son.' But the father said to his slaves, 'Quickly bring out the best robe and put it on him, and put a ring on his hand and sandals on his feet; and bring the fattened calf, kill it, and let us eat and celebrate; for this son of mine was dead and has come to life again; he was lost and has been found.' And they began to celebrate. Now his older son was in the field, when he came and approached the house, he heard music and dancing. And he summoned one of the servants and *began* inquiring what these things could be. And he said to him, 'Your brother has come, and your father has killed the fattened calf because he has received him back safe and sound.' But he became angry and was not willing to go in; and his father came out and *began* pleading with him. But he answered and said to his father, 'Look! For so many years I have been serving you and I have never neglected a command of yours; and *yet* you have never given me a young goat, so that I might celebrate with my friends; but when this son of yours came, who has devoured your wealth with prostitutes, you killed the fattened calf for him.' And he said to him, 'Son, you have always been with me, and all that is mine is yours. But we had to celebrate and rejoice, for this brother of yours was dead and *has begun* to live, and was lost and has been found'" (Luke 15:11–32; see Proverbs 29:2; Luke 15:1, 2).

Setting: Jericho, on the way from Galilee to Jerusalem. After taking time to heal a blind man, Jesus comments on Zaccheus's response to Him.

And Jesus said to him, "Today salvation has come to this house, because he, too, is a son of Abraham. For the Son of Man has come to seek and to save that which was lost" (Luke 19:9, 10; cf. Matthew 18:11).

Setting: Near the Sea of Galilee. After revealing to the Jewish religious leaders during the Feast of the Jews in

Jerusalem that God, John the Baptist, His works, and the Scriptures all testify to His mission, Jesus returns to Galilee. He miraculously feeds more than 5,000 people with a lad's five barley loaves and two fish.

Jesus said, "Have the people sit down." Now there was much grass in the place. So the men sat down, in number about five thousand. Jesus took the loaves, and having given thanks, He distributed to those who were seated; likewise also of the fish as much as they wanted. When they were filled, He said to the disciples, "Gather up the leftover fragments so that nothing will be lost" (John 6:10–12; cf. Matthew 14:17–21; Mark 6:38–44; Luke 9:14–17; see Matthew 15:32–38).

Setting: Jerusalem. After Jesus prays His high-priestly prayer on behalf of His disciples, they go over the ravine of the Kidron to a garden. There Judas awaits to seize Him with a Roman cohort, officers from the chief priests, and the Pharisees.

So Jesus, knowing all the things that were coming upon Him, went forth and said to them, "Whom do you seek?" They answered Him, "Jesus the Nazarene." He said to them, "I am *He*." And Judas also, who was betraying Him, was standing with them. So when He said to them, "I am *He*," they drew back and fell to the ground. Therefore He again asked them, "Whom do you seek?" And they said, "Jesus the Nazarene." Jesus answered, "I told you that I am *He*; so if you seek Me, let these go their way," to fulfill the word which He spoke, "Of those whom You have given Me I lost not one" (John 18:4–9; see John 6:64; 17:12).

LOST, CONCERN FOR THE

[CONCERN FOR THE LOST from go to the lost sheep of the house of Israel]
Setting: Galilee. After His twelve disciples observe His ministry, Jesus summons and specifically instructs them about their ministry to the people of Israel.

These twelve Jesus sent out after instructing them: "Do not go in *the* way of *the* Gentiles, and do not enter *any* city of the Samaritans; but rather go to the lost sheep of the house of Israel. And as you go, preach, saying, 'The kingdom of heaven is at hand.' Heal *the* sick, raise *the* dead, cleanse *the* lepers, cast out demons. Freely you received, freely give. Do not acquire gold, or silver, or copper for your money belts, or a bag for *your* journey, or even two coats, or sandals, or a staff; for the worker is worthy of his support. And whatever city or village you enter, inquire who is worthy in it, and stay at his house until you leave *that city*. As you enter the house, give it your greeting. If the house is worthy, give it your *blessing of* peace. But if it is not worthy, take back your *blessing of* peace. Whoever does not receive you, nor heed your words, as you go out of that house or that city, shake the dust off your feet. Truly I say to you, it will be more tolerable for *the* land of Sodom and Gomorrah in the day of judgment than for that city" (Matthew 10:5–15; cf. Mark 6:7–11; Luke 9:1–5; see Matthew 3:2; 11:22, 24; 15:24; Luke 22:35; 1 Corinthians 9:14).

[CONCERN FOR THE LOST from I was sent only to the lost sheep of the house of Israel]
Setting: The district of Tyre and Sidon. A Canaanite woman appeals to Jesus to heal her demon-possessed daughter.

But He answered and said, "I was sent only to the lost sheep of the house of Israel." But she came and *began* to bow down before Him, saying, "Lord, help me!" And He answered and said, "It is not good to take the children's bread and throw it to the dogs." But she said, "Yes, Lord; but even the dogs feed from the crumbs which fall from their masters' table." Then Jesus said to her, "O woman, your faith is great; it shall be done for you as you wish" And her daughter was healed at once (Matthew 15:24–28; cf. Mark 7: 24–30; see Matthew 9:22; 10:5, 6).

[CONCERN FOR THE LOST from For the Son of Man has come to save that which was lost]
Setting: Capernaum of Galilee. After conveying to His disciples the value of little ones (in answer to their question about greatness in the kingdom of heaven), Jesus states His earthly mission.

["For the Son of Man has come to save that which was lost"] (Matthew 18:11; cf. Luke 19:10).

[CONCERN FOR THE LOST from one of them has gone astray and So it is not *the* will of your Father who is in

heaven that one of these little ones perish]
Setting: Capernaum of Galilee. Jesus illustrates to His disciples the value of little ones.

"What do you think? If any man has a hundred sheep, and one of them has gone astray, does he not leave the ninety-nine on the mountains and go and search for the one that is straying? If it turns out that he finds it, truly I say to you, he rejoices over it more than the ninety-nine which have not gone astray. So it is not *the* will of your Father who is in heaven that one of these little ones perish" (Matthew 18:12–14; cf. Luke 15:4–7).

[CONCERN FOR THE LOST from the Son of Man has come to seek and to save that which was lost]
Setting: Jericho, on the way from Galilee to Jerusalem. After taking time to heal a blind man, Jesus comments on Zaccheus's response to Him.

And Jesus said to him, "Today salvation has come to this house, because he, too, is a son of Abraham. For the Son of Man has come to seek and to save that which was lost" (Luke 19:9, 10; cf. Matthew 18:11).

LOST, THE (See LOST, CONCERN FOR THE)

LOT

Setting: On the way from Galilee to Jerusalem. After the Pharisees question Him about the coming of the kingdom of God, Jesus tells His disciples of His second coming.

And He said to the disciples, "The days will come when you will long to see one of the days of the Son of Man, and you will not see it. They will say to you, 'Look there! Look here!' Do not go away, and do not run after *them*. For just like the lightning, when it flashes out of one part of the sky, shines to the other part of the sky, so will the Son of Man be in His day. But first He must suffer many things and be rejected by this generation. And just as it happened in the days of Noah, so it will be also in the days of the Son of Man: they were eating, they were drinking, they were marrying, they were being given in marriage, until the day that Noah entered the ark, and the flood came and destroyed them all. It was the same as happened in the days of Lot: they were eating, they were drinking, they were buying, they were selling, they were planting, they were building; but on the day that Lot went out from Sodom it rained fire and brimstone from heaven and destroyed them all. It will be just the same on the day that the Son of Man is revealed. On that day, the one who is on the housetop and whose goods are in the house must not go down to take them out; and likewise the one who is in the field must not turn back. Remember Lot's wife. Whoever seeks to keep his life will lose it, and whoever loses *his life* will preserve it. I tell you, on that night there will be two in one bed; one will be taken and the other will be left. There will be two women grinding at the same place; one will be taken and the other will be left. [Two men will be in the field; one will be taken and the other will be left."] And answering they said to Him, "Where, Lord?" And He said to them, "Where the body *is*, there also the vultures will be gathered" (Luke 17:22–37; see Genesis 19; Matthew 10:39; 16:21, 27; 24:17–28, 37–41).

LOT'S WIFE (Listed under WIFE, LOT'S)

LOVE (Specifics such as LOVE, FIRST are separate entries; also see GRACIOUSNESS)

Setting: Galilee. During the early part of His ministry, Jesus preaches the Sermon on the Mount to His disciples and the multitudes.

"You have heard that it was said, 'YOU SHALL LOVE YOUR NEIGHBOR and hate your enemy.' But I say to you, love your enemies and pray for those who persecute you, so that you may be sons of your Father who is in heaven; for He causes His sun to rise on *the* evil and *the* good, and sends rain on *the* righteous and *the* unrighteous. For if you love those who love you, what reward do you have? Do not even the tax collectors do the same? If you greet only your brothers, what more are you doing *than others?* Do not even the Gentiles do the same? Therefore, you are to be perfect, as your heavenly Father is perfect" (Matthew 5:43–48, Jesus quotes from Leviticus 19:18; cf. Leviticus 19:2; Luke 6:27–36).

Setting: Galilee. During the early part of His ministry, Jesus preaches the Sermon on the Mount to His disciples

and the multitudes.

"When you pray, you are not to be like the hypocrites; for they love to stand and pray in the synagogues and on the street corners so that they may be seen by men. Truly I say to you, they have their reward in full. But you, when you pray, go into your inner room, close your door and pray to your Father who is in secret, and your Father who sees *what is done* in secret will reward you" (Matthew 6:5, 6; see Mark 11:25).

Setting: Galilee. During the early part of His ministry, Jesus preaches the Sermon on the Mount to His disciples and the multitudes.

"No one can serve two masters; for either he will hate the one and love the other, or he will be devoted to one and despise the other. You cannot serve God and wealth (Matthew 6:24).

[LOVE from treat people the same way you want them to treat you]
Setting: Galilee. During the early part of His ministry, Jesus preaches the Sermon on the Mount to His disciples and the multitudes.

"In everything, therefore, treat people the same way you want them to treat you, for this is the Law and the Prophets" (Matthew 7:12; cf. Matthew 22:20; Luke 6:3).

Setting: Judea beyond the Jordan (Perea). Jesus shares with a rich, young ruler how he can obtain eternal life.

And He said to him, "Why are you asking Me about what is good? There is *only* One who is good; but if you wish to enter into life, keep the commandments." *Then* he said to Him, 'Which ones?' And Jesus said, "YOU SHALL NOT COMMIT MURDER; YOU SHALL NOT COMMIT ADULTERY; YOU SHALL NOT STEAL; YOU SHALL NOT BEAR FALSE WITNESS; HONOR YOUR FATHER AND MOTHER; and YOU SHALL LOVE YOUR NEIGHBOR AS YOURSELF." The young man said to Him, "All these things I have kept; what am I still lacking?" Jesus said to him, "If you wish to complete go *and* sell your possessions and give to *the* poor, and you will have treasure in heaven; and come, follow Me" (Matthew 19:16–22, Jesus quotes from Exodus 20:13–15; Leviticus 19:18; cf. Leviticus 18:5; Mark 10:17–21; Luke 10:25–28; 12:33; 18:18–24).

Setting: The temple in Jerusalem. A Pharisee lawyer asks Jesus which is the great commandment of the Law, in order to test Him as He teaches.

And He said to him, " 'YOU SHALL LOVE THE LORD YOUR GOD WITH ALL YOUR HEART, AND WITH ALL YOUR SOUL, AND WITH ALL YOUR MIND.' This is the great and foremost commandment. The second is like it, 'YOU SHALL LOVE YOUR NEIGHBOR AS YOURSELF.' On these two commandments depend the whole Law and the Prophets" (Matthew 22:37–40; Jesus quotes from Leviticus 19:18; Deuteronomy 6:5; cf. Mark 12:28–34; see Matthew 7:12).

Setting: The temple in Jerusalem. Jesus exposes the truth about Pharisaism to the crowds and His disciples after the Jewish religious leaders test Him with questions.

Then Jesus spoke to the crowds and to His disciples, saying: "The scribes and the Pharisees have seated themselves in the chair of Moses; therefore all that they tell you, do and observe, but do not do according to their deeds; for they say *things* and do not do *them.* They tie up heavy burdens and lay them on men's shoulders, but they themselves are unwilling to move them with *so much as* a finger. But they do all their deeds to be noticed by men; for they broaden their phylacteries and lengthen their tassels *of their garments.* They love the place of honor at banquets and the chief seats in the synagogues, and respectful greetings in the market places, and being called Rabbi by men. But do not be called Rabbi; for One is your Teacher, and you are all brothers. Do not call *anyone* on earth your father; for One is your Father, He who is in heaven. Do not be called leaders; for One is your Leader, *that is,* Christ. But the greatest among you shall be your servant. Whoever exalts himself shall be humbled; and whoever humbles himself shall be exalted" (Matthew 23:1–12; cf. Matthew 20:26; Mark 12:38–40; Luke 20:46, 47; see Exodus 13:9;

Deuteronomy 33:3; Matthew 6:1, 5, 6, 9, 16; Mark 14:11; Luke 11:43; 14:11).

[LOVE from Truly I say to you, to the extent that you did it to one of these brothers of Mine, *even* the least *of them,* you did it to Me]

Setting: The Mount of Olives, just east of Jerusalem. During His discourse, after answering His disciples' questions as to when the temple will be destroyed and Jerusalem overrun, along with the signs of His coming and the end of the age, Jesus reveals the future judgments following His return.

"But when the Son of Man comes in His glory, and all the angels with Him, then He will sit on His glorious throne. All the nations will be gathered before Him; and He will separate them from one another, as the shepherd separates the sheep from the goats; and He will put the sheep on His right, and the goats on the left. Then the King will say to those on His right, 'Come, you who are blessed of My Father, inherit the kingdom prepared for you from the foundation of the world. 'For I was hungry, and you gave Me *something* to eat; I was thirsty, and you gave Me *something* to drink; I was a stranger, and you invited Me in; naked, and you clothed Me; I was sick, and you visited Me; I was in prison, and you came to Me.' Then the righteous will answer Him, 'Lord, when did we see You hungry and feed You, or thirsty, and give you *something* to drink? And when did we see You a stranger, and invite You in, or naked, and clothe You? When did we see You sick, or in prison, and come to You?' The King will answer and say to them, 'Truly I say to you, to the extent that you did it to one of these brothers of Mine, *even* the least *of them,* you did it to Me.' Then He will also say to those on His left, 'Depart from Me, accursed ones, into the eternal fire which has been prepared for the devil and his angels; for I was hungry, and you gave Me *nothing* to eat; I was thirsty, and you gave Me nothing to drink; I was a stranger, and you did not invite Me in; naked, and you did not clothe Me; sick, and in prison, and you did not visit Me.' Then they themselves also will answer, 'Lord, when did we see You hungry, or thirsty, or a stranger, or naked, or sick, or in prison, and did not take care of You?' Then He will answer them, 'Truly I say to you, to the extent that you did not do it to one of the least of these, you did not do it to Me.' These will go away into eternal punishment, but the righteous into eternal life" (Matthew 25:31–46; see Matthew 7:23; 16:27; 19:29).

Setting: The temple in Jerusalem. With the Pharisees and Herodians failing to trap Jesus in a statement, one of the scribes asks Him which commandment is foremost.

Jesus answered, "The foremost is, 'HEAR, O ISRAEL! THE LORD OUR GOD IS ONE LORD; AND YOU SHALL LOVE THE LORD YOUR GOD WITH ALL YOUR HEART, AND WITH ALL YOUR SOUL, AND WITH ALL YOUR MIND AND WITH ALL YOUR STRENGTH.' The second is this, 'YOU SHALL LOVE YOUR NEIGHBOR AS YOURSELF.' There is no other commandment greater than these" (Mark 12:29–31, Jesus quotes from Deuteronomy 6:4, 5; Leviticus 19:18; cf. Matthew 22:34–40; see Mark 12:28).

Setting: Galilee. After selecting His twelve disciples, Jesus teaches the Sermon on the Mount to those disciples and a great throng of people from Judea, Jerusalem, and the central coastal region of Tyre and Sidon.

"But I say to you who hear, love your enemies, do good to those who hate you, bless those who curse you, pray for those who mistreat you. Whoever hits you on the cheek, offer him the other also; and whoever takes away your coat, do not withhold your shirt from him either. Give to everyone who asks of you, and whoever takes away what is yours, do not demand it back. Treat others the same way you want them to treat you. If you love those who love you, what credit is *that* to you? For even sinners love those who love them. If you do good to those who do good to you, what credit is *that* to you? For even sinners do the same. If you lend to those from whom you expect to receive, what credit is *that* to you? Even sinners lend to sinners in order to receive back the same *amount.* But love your enemies, and do good, and lend, expecting nothing in return; and your reward will be great, and you will be sons of the Most High; for He Himself is kind to ungrateful and evil *men.* Be merciful, just as your Father is merciful" (Luke 6:27–36; cf. Matthew 5:9, 39–48; 7:12).

Setting: Galilee. After Jesus praises John the Baptist to the crowds, Simon, a Pharisee, invites the Lord to dinner. A sinful woman anoints His feet with perfume, prompting Him to convey a parable.

And Jesus answered him, "Simon, I have something to say to you." And he replied, "Say it, Teacher." "A moneylender had two debtors: one owed five hundred denarii, and the other fifty. When they were unable to repay, he graciously forgave them both. So which of them will love him more?" Simon answered and said, "I suppose the one whom he forgave more." And He said to him, "You have judged correctly" (Luke 7:40–43; see Matthew 18:23–35).

[LOVE from loved and loves]

Setting: Galilee. After Jesus praises John the Baptist to the crowds, Simon, a Pharisee, invites the Lord to dinner. A sinful woman anoints His feet with perfume, prompting Him to instruct His host about forgiveness.

Turning toward the woman, He said to Simon, "Do you see this woman? I entered your house; you gave Me no water for My feet, but she has wet My feet with her tears and wiped them with her hair. You gave Me no kiss; but she, since the time I came in, has not ceased to kiss My feet. You did not anoint My head with oil, but she anointed My feet with perfume. For this reason I say to you, her sins, which are many, have been forgiven, for she loved much; but he who is forgiven little, loves little." Then He said to her, "Your sins have been forgiven." Those who were reclining *at the table* with Him began to say to themselves, "Who is this *man* who even forgives sins?" And He said to the woman, "Your faith has saved you; go in peace" (Luke 7:44–50; see Matthew 9:2; Mark 5:34; Luke 5:21).

Setting: On the way from Galilee to Jerusalem. After speaking of how a lamp illuminates, the Lord has lunch with a Pharisee, who is surprised He doesn't wash before eating.

But the Lord said to him, "Now you Pharisees clean the outside of the cup and of the platter; but inside of you, you are full of robbery and wickedness. You foolish ones, did not He who made the outside make the inside also? But give that which is within as charity, and then all things are clean for you. But woe to you Pharisees! You pay tithe of mint and rue and every *kind of* garden herb, and *yet* disregard justice and the love of God; but these are the things you should have done without neglecting the others. Woe to you Pharisees! For you love the chief seats in the synagogues and the respectful greetings in the market places. Woe to you! For you are like concealed tombs, and the people who walk over *them* are unaware *of it*" (Luke 11:39–44; cf. Matthew 23:6, 7, 23–27; see Matthew 15:2; Titus 1:15).

Setting: On the way from Galilee to Jerusalem. After giving the story of the prodigal son, the Lord teaches His disciples about stewardship.

Now He was also saying to the disciples, "There was a rich man who had a manager, and this *manager* was reported to him as squandering his possessions. And he called him and said to him, 'What is this I hear about you? Give an accounting of your management, for you can no longer be a manager.' The manager said to himself, 'What shall I do, since my master is taking the management away from me? I am not strong enough to dig; I am ashamed to beg. I know what I shall do, so that when I am removed from the management people will welcome me into their homes.' And he summoned each one of his master's debtors, and he *began* saying to the first, 'How much do you owe my master?' And he said, 'A hundred measures of oil.' And he said to him, 'Take your bill, and sit down quickly and write fifty.' Then he said to another, 'And how much do you owe?' And he said, 'A hundred measures of wheat.' He said to him, 'Take your bill, and write eighty.' And his master praised the unrighteous manager because he had acted shrewdly; for the sons of this age are more shrewd in relation to their own kind than the sons of light. And I say to you, make friends for yourselves by means of the wealth of unrighteousness, so that when it fails, they will receive you into the eternal dwellings. He who is faithful in a very little thing is faithful also in much; and he who is unrighteous in a very little thing is unrighteous also in much. Therefore if you have not been faithful in the *use of* unrighteous wealth, who will entrust the *true riches* to you? And if you have not been faithful in *the use of* that which is another's, who will give you that which is your own? No servant can serve two masters; for either he will hate the one and love the other, or else he will be devoted to one and despise the other. You cannot serve God and wealth" (Luke 16:1–13; cf. Matthew 6:24; see Matthew 25:14–30).

Setting: The temple in Jerusalem. While ministering a few days before His crucifixion, after posing a question to the scribes, who do not answer, Jesus warns His disciples about the lifestyle of the scribes.

"Beware of the scribes, who like to walk around in long robes, and love respectful greetings in the market places, and chief seats in the synagogues and places of honor at banquets, who devour widows' houses, and for appearance's sake offer long prayers. These will receive greater condemnation" (Luke 20:46, 47; cf. Matthew 23:1–7; Mark 12:38–40; see Luke 11:43).

[LOVE from loved]

Setting: Jerusalem. At the time for the Passover of the Jews, after the Lord cleanses the temple, a Pharisee, Nicodemus, asks Him by night the meaning of "born again."

"For God so loved the world, that He gave His only begotten Son, that whoever believes in Him shall not perish, but have eternal life. For God did not send the Son into the world to judge the world, but that the world might be saved through Him. He who believes in Him is not judged; he who does not believe has been judged already, because he has not believed in the name of the only begotten Son of God. This is the judgment, that the Light has come into the world, and men loved darkness rather than the Light, for their deeds were evil. For everyone who does evil hates the Light, and does not come to the Light for fear that his deeds will be exposed. But he who practices the truth comes to the Light, so that his deeds may be manifested as having been wrought in God" (John 3:16–21; see Luke 19:10; John 1:4; 1:18; Romans 5:8; 1 John 1:6, 7).

Setting: Jerusalem. During the feast of the Jews, Jesus responds to criticism from the Jewish religious leaders by referring to God as His Father (thereby making Himself equal with God) and informing them that God, John the Baptist, the Scriptures, and His works all testify to His mission.

"You search the Scriptures because you think that in them you have eternal life; it is these that testify about Me; and you are unwilling to come to Me so that you may have life. I do not receive glory from men; but I know you, that you do not have the love of God in yourselves. I have come in My Father's name, and you do not receive Me; if another comes in his own name, you will receive him. How can you believe, when you receive glory from one another and you do not seek the glory that is from the *one and* only God? Do not think that I will accuse you before the Father; the one who accuses you is Moses, in whom you have set your hope. For if you believed Moses, you would believe Me, for he wrote about Me. But if you do not believe his writings, how will you believe My words?" (John 5:39–47; see Matthew 24:5; Luke 16:29, 31; 24:27; John 9:28; 17:3).

Setting: The temple treasury in Jerusalem. After the scribes and Pharisees question His testimony about Himself, Jesus interacts with them regarding their ancestry and motives.

Jesus said to them, "If God were your Father, you would love Me, for I proceeded forth and have come from God, for I have not even come on My own initiative, but He sent Me. Why do you not understand what I am saying? *It is* because you cannot hear My word. You are of *your* father the devil, and you want to do the desires of your father. He was a murderer from the beginning, and does not stand in the truth because there is no truth in him. Whenever he speaks a lie, he speaks from his own *nature,* for he is a liar and the father of lies. But because I speak the truth, you do not believe Me. Which one of you convicts Me of sin? If I speak truth, why do not believe Me? He who is of God hears the words of God; for this reason you do not hear *them,* because you are not of God" (John 8:42–47; see John 18:37; 1 John 3:8; 4:6; 5:1).

Setting: Jerusalem. After revealing to His disciples that Judas will betray Him to the chief priests and Pharisees, Jesus conveys how He will soon be glorified in His death, and commands them to love one another.

Therefore when he had gone out, Jesus said, "Now is the Son of Man glorified, and God is glorified in Him; if God is glorified in Him, God will also glorify Him in Himself, and will glorify Him immediately. Little children, I am with you a little while longer. You will seek Me; and as I said to the Jews, now I also say to you, 'Where I am going, you cannot come.' A new commandment I give to you, that you love one another, even as I have loved you, that you also love one another. By this all men will know that you are My disciples, if you have love for one another" (John 13:31–35; see Leviticus 19:18; John 7:33, 34; 17:1; 1 John 3:14).

Setting: Jerusalem. Before the Passover, after responding to Philip's request for Him to show His disciples the Father, Jesus conveys the upcoming role of the Holy Spirit in their lives.

"If you love Me, you will keep My commandments. I will ask the Father, and He will give you another Helper, that He may be with you forever; *that* is the Spirit of truth, whom the world cannot receive, because it does not see Him or know Him, *but* you know Him because He abides with you and will be in you" (John 14:15–17; see John 7:39; 15:26; 1 John 5:3).

Setting: Jerusalem. Before the Passover, after responding to Philip's request for Him to show His disciples the Father, Jesus conveys the upcoming role of the Holy Spirit in their lives.

"I will not leave you as orphans; I will come to you. After a little while the world will no longer see Me, but you *will* see Me; because I live, you will live also. In that day you will know that I am in the Father, and you in Me, and I in you. He who has My commandments and keeps them is the one who loves Me; and he who loves Me will be loved by My Father, and I will love him and will disclose Myself to him" (John 14:18–21; see John 6:57; 10:37, 38; 16:16, 22).

Setting: Jerusalem. Before the Passover, after conveying the upcoming ministry of the Holy Spirit in His disciples' lives, Jesus answers Judas' (not Iscariot) question why He discloses Himself to His disciples but not the whole world.

Jesus answered and said to him, "If anyone loves Me, he will keep My word; and My Father will love him, and We will come to him and make Our abode with him. He who does not love Me does not keep My words; and the word which you hear is not Mine, but the Father's who sent Me" (John 14:23, 24; see John 7:16; 8:51).

Setting: Jerusalem. Before the Passover, after He conveys the upcoming ministry of the Holy Spirit in His disciples' lives, Jesus again relates peace, hope, and comfort to them regarding His return to the Father.

"Peace I leave with you; My peace I give to you; not as the world gives do I give to you. Do not let your heart be troubled, nor let it be fearful. You heard that I said to you, 'I go away, and I will come to you.' If you loved Me, you would have rejoiced because I go to the Father, for the Father is greater than I. Now I have told you before it happens, so that when it happens, you may believe. I will not speak much more with you, for the ruler of the world is coming, and he has nothing in Me; but so that the world may know that I love the Father, I do exactly as the Father commanded Me. Get up, let us go from here" (John 14:27–31; see John 10:18, 29; 12:31; 13:19; 16:33).

Setting: Jerusalem. Before the Passover, after He conveys the upcoming ministry of the Holy Spirit in His disciples' lives, with His imminent departure from them, Jesus explains He is the vine and they are the branches.

"I am the true vine, and My Father is the vinedresser. Every branch in Me that does not bear fruit, He takes away; and every *branch* that bears fruit, He prunes it so that it may bear more fruit. You are already clean because of the word which I have spoken to you. Abide in Me, and I in you. As the branch cannot bear fruit of itself unless it abides in the vine, so neither *can* you unless you abide in Me. I am the vine, you are the branches; he who abides in Me and I in him, he bears much fruit, for apart from Me you can do nothing. If anyone does not abide in Me, he is thrown away as a branch and dries up; and they gather them, and cast them into the fire and they are burned. If you abide in Me, and My words abide in you, ask whatever you wish, and it will be done for you. My Father is glorified by this, that you bear much fruit, and *so* prove to be My disciples. Just as the Father has loved Me, I have also loved you; abide in My love. If you keep My commandments, you will abide in My love; just as I have kept My Father's commandments and abide in His love. These things I have spoken to you so that My joy may be in you, and *that* your joy may be made full" (John 15:1–11; see Matthew 5:16; 7:7; John 3:29, 35; 6:56; 8:29, 31; 13:10; 15:16).

Setting: Jerusalem. Before the Passover, with His imminent departure in mind, after explaining He is the vine and His disciples are the branches, Jesus instructs them to love one another.

"This is My commandment, that you love one another, just as I have loved you. Greater love has no one than this, that one lay down his life for his friends. You are My friends if you do what I command you. No longer do I call you slaves, for the slave does not know what his master is doing; but I have called you friends, for all things that I have heard from My Father I have made known to you. You did not choose Me but I chose you, and appointed you that you would go and bear fruit, and *that* your fruit would remain, so that whatever you ask of the Father in My name He may give to you. This I command you, that you love one another" (John 15:12–17; see Matthew 12:50; John 6:70; 8:26; 10:11; 13:34).

Setting: Jerusalem. Before the Passover, with His imminent departure in mind, after explaining He is the vine and His disciples are the branches, Jesus prepares them for persecution from the world.

"If the world hates you, you know that it has hated Me before *it hated* you. If you were of the world, the world would love its own; but because you are not of the world, but I chose you out of the world, because of this the world hates you. Remember the word that I said to you, 'A slave is not greater than his master.' If they persecuted Me, they will also persecute you; if they kept My word, they will keep yours also. But all these things they will do to you for My name's sake, because they do not know the One who sent Me. If I had not come and spoken to them, they would not have sin, but now they have no excuse for their sin" (John 15:18–22; see Matthew 10:22; John 7:7; 8:19, 55; 9:41; 1 Corinthians 4:12).

[LOVE from loves and loved]

Setting: Jerusalem. Before the Passover, after empathizing with His disciples' sadness over His prophecies and giving them hope for the future, Jesus conveys promises about praying in His name.

"In that day you will not question Me about anything. Truly, truly, I say to you, if you ask the Father for anything in My name, He will give it to you. Until now you have asked for nothing in My name; ask and you will receive, so that your joy may be made full. These things I have spoken to you in figurative language; an hour is coming when I will no longer speak to you in figurative language, but will tell you plainly of the Father. In that day you will ask in My name, and I do not say to you that I will request of the Father on your behalf; for the Father Himself loves you, because you have loved Me and have believed that I came forth from the Father. I came forth from the Father and have come into the world; I am leaving the world again and going to the Father" (John 16:23–28; see Matthew 13:34; John 8:42; 13:1, 3; 14:14, 21, 23; 15:16).

Setting: Jerusalem. Before the Passover, after giving His disciples assurance that in the midst of tribulation they will have His peace, Jesus continues praying His high-priestly prayer.

"The glory which You have given Me I have given to them, that they may be one, just as We are one; I in them and You in Me, that they may be perfected in unity, so that the world may know that you sent Me, and loved them, even as You have loved Me. Father, I desire that they also, whom You have given Me, be with Me where I am, so that they may see My glory which You have given Me, for You loved Me before the foundation of the world. O righteous Father, although the world has not known You, yet I have known You; and these have known that You sent Me; and I have made Your name known to them, and will make it known, so that the love with which You loved Me may be in them, and I in them" (John 17:22–26; see Matthew 25:34; John 1:14; 10:38; 15:9; 16:27).

Setting: By the Sea of Galilee. During His third appearance to His disciples after His resurrection from the dead in Jerusalem, Jesus quizzes Peter three times regarding his love for Him.

So when they had finished breakfast, Jesus said to Simon Peter, "Simon, *son* of John, do you love Me more than these?" He said to Him, "Yes, Lord; You know that I love You." He said to him, "Tend My lambs." He said to him again a second time, "Simon, *son* of John, do you love Me?" He said to Him, "Yes, Lord; You know that I love You." He said to him, "Shepherd My sheep." He said to him the third time, "Simon, *son* of John, do you love Me?" Peter was grieved because He said to him the third time, "Do you love Me?" And he said to Him, "Lord, You know all things; You know that I love You." Jesus said to him, "Tend My sheep" (John 21:15–17; see Matthew 26:33; Mark 14:29).

Setting: On the island of Patmos (in the Aegean Sea about fifty miles southwest of Ephesus in modern Turkey). On the Lord's Day (Sunday), about fifty years after Jesus' resurrection, the disciple John encounters the Lord Jesus Christ, who communicates a new revelation for the apostle to record for the church in Thyatira and to six other churches in Asia.

"And to the angel of the church in Thyatira write: The Son of God, who has eyes like a flame of fire, and His feet are like burnished bronze, says this: 'I know your deeds, and your love and faith and service and perseverance, and that your deeds of late are greater than at first. But I have *this* against you, that you tolerate the woman Jezebel, who calls herself a prophetess, and she teaches and leads My bond-servants astray so that they commit *acts of* immorality and eat things sacrificed to idols. I gave her time to repent, and she does not want to repent of her immorality. Behold, I will throw her on a bed *of sickness,* and those who commit adultery with her into great tribulation, unless they repent of her deeds. And I will kill her children with pestilence, and all the churches will know that I am He who searches the minds and hearts; and I will give to each one of you according to your deeds. But I say to you, the rest who are in Thyatira, who do not hold this teaching, who have not known the deep things of Satan, as they call them—I place no other burden on you. Nevertheless what you have, hold fast until I come. He who overcomes, and he who keeps My deeds until the end, TO HIM I WILL GIVE AUTHORITY OVER THE NATIONS; AND HE SHALL RULE THEM WITH A ROD OF IRON, AS THE VESSELS OF THE POTTER ARE BROKEN TO PIECES, as I also have received *authority* from My Father; and I will give him the morning star. He who has an ear, let him hear what the Spirit says to the churches' (Revelation 2:18–29; Jesus quotes from Psalm 2:8, 9; Isaiah 30:14; see 1 Kings 16:31; Psalm 7:9; Romans 2:5; 1 Corinthians 2:10; 2 Peter 3:9; Revelation 1:14; 2:7; 3:11; 17:1–20).

[LOVE from loved]

Setting: On the island of Patmos (in the Aegean Sea about fifty miles southwest of Ephesus in modern Turkey). On the Lord's Day (Sunday), about fifty years after Jesus' resurrection, the disciple John encounters the Lord Jesus Christ, who communicates a new revelation for the apostle to record for the church in Philadelphia and to six other churches in Asia.

"And to the angel of the church in Philadelphia write: He who is holy, who is true, who has the key of David, who opens and no one will shut, and who shuts and no one opens, says this: 'I know your deeds. Behold, I have put before you an open door which no one can shut, because you have a little power, and have kept My word, and have not denied My name. Behold, I will cause *those* of the synagogue of Satan, who say that they are Jews and are not, but lie—I will make them come and bow down at your feet, and *make them* know that I have loved you. Because you have kept the word of My perseverance, I also will keep you from the hour of testing, that *hour* which is about to come upon the whole world, to test those who dwell on the earth. I am coming quickly; hold fast what you have, so that no one will take your crown. He who overcomes, I will make him a pillar in the temple of My God, and he will not go out from it anymore; and I will write on him the name of My God, and the name of the city of My God, the new Jerusalem, which comes down out of heaven from My God, and My new name. He who has an ear, let him hear what the Spirit says to the churches' " (Revelation 3:7–13; see Isaiah 22:22; Galatians 2:9; Revelation 2:9, 10, 13, 25; 14:1).

Setting: On the island of Patmos (in the Aegean Sea about fifty miles southwest of Ephesus in modern Turkey). On the Lord's Day (Sunday), about fifty years after Jesus' resurrection, the disciple John encounters the Lord Jesus Christ, who communicates a new revelation for the apostle to record for the church in Laodicea and to six other churches in Asia.

"To the angel of the church in Laodicea write: The Amen, the faithful and true Witness, the Beginning of the creation of God, says this: 'I know your deeds, that you are neither cold nor hot; I wish that you were cold or hot. So because you are lukewarm, and neither hot nor cold, I will spit you out of My mouth. Because you say, "I am rich, and have become wealthy, and have need of nothing," and you do not know that you are wretched and miserable and poor and blind and naked, I advise you to buy from Me gold refined by fire so that you may become rich, and white garments so that you may clothe yourself, and *that* the shame of your nakedness will not be revealed; and eye salve to anoint your eyes so that you may see. Those whom I love, I reprove and discipline; therefore be zealous and repent. Behold, I stand at the door and knock; if anyone hears My voice and opens the door, I will come in to him and will dine with him, and he with Me. He who overcomes, I will grant to him to sit down with Me on My throne, as I also overcame and sat down with My Father on His throne. He who has an ear, let him hear what the Spirit says to the churches'" (Revelation 3:14–22; see Proverbs 3:12; Hosea 12:8; John 14:23; 16:33).

LOVE, FIRST

Setting: On the island of Patmos (in the Aegean Sea about fifty miles southwest of Ephesus in modern Turkey). On the Lord's Day (Sunday), about fifty years after Jesus' resurrection, the disciple John encounters the Lord Jesus Christ, who communicates a new revelation for the apostle to record for the church in Ephesus and to six other churches in Asia.

"To the angel of the church in Ephesus write: The One who holds the seven stars in His right hand, the One who walks among the seven golden lampstands, says this: 'I know your deeds and your toil and perseverance, and that you cannot tolerate evil men, and you put to the test those who call themselves apostles, and they are not, and you found them *to be* false; and you have perseverance and have endured for My name's sake, and have not grown weary. But I have *this* against you, that you have left your first love. Therefore remember from where you have fallen, and repent and do the deeds you did at first; or else I am coming to you and will remove your lampstand out of its place—unless you repent. Yet this you do have, that you hate the deeds of the Nicolaitans, which I also hate. He who has an ear, let him hear what the Spirit says to the churches. To him who overcomes, I will grant to eat of the tree of life which is in the Paradise of God' " (Revelation 2:1–7; see Genesis 2:9; Ezekiel 28:13; 1 John 4:1; Revelation 1:10, 11, 19, 20; 2:15, 16).

LOVE, GOD'S (See LOVE OF GOD)

LOVE, GREATER

Setting: Jerusalem. Before the Passover, with His upcoming departure in mind, after explaining He is the vine and His disciples are the branches, Jesus instructs them to love one another.

"This is My commandment, that you love one another, just as I have loved you. Greater love has no one than this, that one lay down his life for his friends. You are My friends if you do what I command you. No longer do I call you slaves, for the slave does not know what his master is doing; but I have called you friends, for all things that I have heard from My Father I have made known to you. You did not choose Me but I chose you, and appointed you that you would go and bear fruit, and *that* your fruit would remain, so that whatever you ask of the Father in My name He may give to you. This I command you, that you love one another" (John 15:12–17; see Matthew 12:50; John 6:70; 8:26; 10:11; 13:34).

LOVE, PEOPLE'S

Setting: On the Mount of Olives, just east of Jerusalem. During His discourse, Jesus answers His disciples' questions as to when the temple will be destroyed and Jerusalem overrun, along with the signs of His coming and the end of the age.

And Jesus answered and said to them, "See to it that no one misleads you. For many will come in My name, saying, 'I am the Christ,' and will mislead many. You will be hearing of wars and rumors of wars. See that you are not frightened, for *those things* must take place, but *that* is not yet the end. For nation will rise against nation, and kingdom against kingdom, and in various places there will be famines and earthquakes. But all these things are *merely* the beginning of birth pangs. Then they will deliver you to tribulation, and will kill you, and you will be hated by all nations because of My name. At that time many will fall away and will betray one another and hate one another. Many false prophets will arise and will mislead many. Because lawlessness is increased, most people's love will grow cold. But the one who endures to the end, he will be saved. This gospel of the kingdom shall be preached in the whole world as a testimony to all the nations, and then the end will come" (Matthew 24:4–14; cf. Jeremiah 29:8; Matthew 7:15; 10:17, 22; Mark 13:3–13; Luke 21:7–19; Revelation 6:4).

LOVE, SACRIFICIAL (See COMMITMENT; and DEVOTION)

LOVE, UNCONDITIONAL (Also see LOVE; LOVE, GREATER; and NEIGHBOR)

[UNCONDITIONAL LOVE from For if you love those who love you, what reward do you have]

Setting: Galilee. During the early part of His ministry, Jesus preaches the Sermon on the Mount to His disciples and the multitudes.

"You have heard that it was said, 'YOU SHALL LOVE YOUR NEIGHBOR and hate your enemy.' But I say to you, love your enemies and pray for those who persecute you, so that you may be sons of your Father who is in heaven; for He causes His sun to rise on *the* evil and *the* good, and sends rain on *the* righteous and *the* unrighteous. For if you love those who love you, what reward do you have? Do not even the tax collectors do the same? If you greet only your brothers, what more are you doing *than others?* Do not even the Gentiles do the same? Therefore, you are to be perfect, as your heavenly Father is perfect" (Matthew 5:43–48, Jesus quotes from Leviticus 19:18; cf. Leviticus 19:2; Luke 6:27–36).

[UNCONDITIONAL LOVE from treat people the same way you want them to treat you]
Setting: Galilee. During the early part of His ministry, Jesus preaches the Sermon on the Mount to His disciples and the multitudes.

"In everything, therefore, treat people the same way you want them to treat you, for this is the Law and the Prophets" (Matthew 7:12; cf. Matthew 22:20; Luke 6:3).

[UNCONDITIONAL LOVE from Treat others the same way you want them to treat you]
Setting: Galilee. After selecting His twelve disciples, Jesus teaches the Sermon on the Mount to those disciples and a great throng of people from Judea, Jerusalem, and the central coastal region of Tyre and Sidon.

"But I say to you who hear, love your enemies, do good to those who hate you, bless those who curse you, pray for those who mistreat you. Whoever hits you on the cheek, offer him the other also; and whoever takes away your coat, do not withhold your shirt from him either. Give to everyone who asks of you, and whoever takes away what is yours, do not demand it back. Treat others the same way you want them to treat you. If you love those who love you, what credit is *that* to you? For even sinners love those who love them. If you do good to those who do good to you, what credit is *that* to you? For even sinners do the same. If you lend to those from whom you expect to receive, what credit is *that* to you? Even sinners lend to sinners in order to receive back the same *amount*. But love your enemies, and do good, and lend, expecting nothing in return; and your reward will be great, and you will be sons of the Most High; for He Himself is kind to ungrateful and evil *men*. Be merciful, just as your Father is merciful" (Luke 6:27–36; cf. Matthew 5:9, 39–48; Matthew 7:12).

[UNCONDITIONAL LOVE from For God so loved the world, that He gave His only begotten Son]
Setting: Jerusalem. At the time for the Passover of the Jews, after the Lord cleanses the temple, a Pharisee, Nicodemus, asks Him by night the meaning of "born again."

"For God so loved the world, that He gave His only begotten Son, that whoever believes in Him shall not perish, but have eternal life. For God did not send the Son into the world to judge the world, but that the world might be saved through Him. He who believes in Him is not judged; he who does not believe has been judged already, because he has not believed in the name of the only begotten Son of God. This is the judgment, that the Light has come into the world, and men loved darkness rather than the Light, for their deeds were evil. For everyone who does evil hates the Light, and does not come to the Light for fear that his deeds will be exposed. But he who practices the truth comes to the Light, so that his deeds may be manifested as having been wrought in God" (John 3:16–21; see Luke 19:10; John 1:4; 1:18; Romans 5:8; 1 John 1:6, 7).

LOVE OF GOD (Also see GIFTS, GOOD)

Setting: On the way from Galilee to Jerusalem. After speaking of how a lamp illuminates, the Lord has lunch with a Pharisee who is surprised He doesn't wash before eating.

But the Lord said to him, "Now you Pharisees clean the outside of the cup and of the platter; but inside of you, you are full of robbery and wickedness. You foolish ones, did not He who made the outside make the inside also? But give that which is within as charity, and then all things are clean for you. But woe to you Pharisees! You pay tithe of mint and rue and every *kind of* garden herb, and *yet* disregard justice and the love of God; but these are the things you should have done without neglecting the others. Woe to you Pharisees! For you love the chief seats in the synagogues and the respectful greetings in the market places. Woe to you! For you are like concealed tombs, and the people who walk over *them* are unaware *of it*" (Luke 11:39–44; cf. Matthew 23:6, 7, 23–27; see Matthew 15:2; Titus 1:15).

[LOVE OF GOD from For God so loved the world]
Setting: Jerusalem. At the time of the Passover of the Jews, after the Lord cleanses the temple, a Pharisee, Nicodemus, asks Him by night the meaning of "born again."

"For God so loved the world, that He gave His only begotten Son, that whoever believes in Him shall not perish, but have eternal life. For God did not send the Son into the world to judge the world, but that the world might be saved through Him. He who believes in Him is not judged; he who does not believe has been judged already, because he has not believed in the name of the only begotten Son of God. This is the judgment, that the Light has come into the world, and men loved darkness rather than the Light, for their deeds were evil. For everyone who does evil hates the Light, and does not come to the Light for fear that his deeds will be exposed. But he who practices the truth comes to the Light, so that his deeds may be manifested as having been wrought in God" (John 3:16–21; see Luke 19:10; John 1:4; 1:18; Romans 5:8; 1 John 1:6, 7).

Setting: Jerusalem. During the Feast of the Jews, Jesus responds to criticism and persecution from the Jewish religious leaders by referring to God as His Father (thereby making Himself equal with God) and informing them that God, John the Baptist, His works, and the Scriptures all testify to His mission.

"You search the Scriptures because you think that in them you have eternal life; it is these that testify about Me; and you are unwilling to come to Me so that you may have life. I do not receive glory from men; but I know you, that you do not have the love of God in yourselves. I have come in My Father's name, and you do not receive Me; if another comes in his own name, you will receive him. How can you believe, when you receive glory from one another and you do not seek the glory that is from the *one and* only God? Do not think that I will accuse you before the Father; the one who accuses you is Moses, in whom you have set your hope. For if you believed Moses, you would believe Me, for he wrote about Me. But if you do not believe his writings, how will you believe My words?" (John 5:39–47; see Matthew 24:5; Luke 16:29, 31; 24:27; John 9:28; 17:3)

LOVES (Also see LOVE)

Setting: Galilee. After His twelve disciples observe His ministry, Jesus summons and specifically instructs them about their ministry ahead involving true discipleship.

"He who loves father or mother more than Me is not worthy of Me; and he who loves son or daughter more than Me is not worthy of Me. And he who does not take his cross and follow after Me is not worthy of Me. He who has found his life will lose it, and he who has lost his life for My sake will find it" (Matthew 10:37–39; cf. Matthew 16:24, 25).

Setting: Galilee. After Jesus praises John the Baptist to the crowds, Simon, a Pharisee, invites the Lord to dinner. A sinful woman anoints His feet with perfume, prompting Him to instruct His host about forgiveness.

Turning toward the woman, He said to Simon, "Do you see this woman? I entered your house; you gave Me no water for My feet, but she has wet My feet with her tears and wiped them with her hair. You gave Me no kiss; but she, since the time I came in, has not ceased to kiss My feet. You did not anoint My head with oil, but she anointed My feet with perfume. For this reason I say to you, her sins, which are many, have been forgiven, for she loved much; but he who is forgiven little, loves little." Then He said to her, "Your sins have been forgiven." Those who were reclining *at the table* with Him began to say to themselves, "Who is this *man* who even forgives sins?" And He said to the woman, "Your faith has saved you; go in peace" (Luke 7:44–50; see Matthew 9:2; Mark 5:34; Luke 5:21).

Setting: By the pool of Bethesda in Jerusalem. During the Feast of the Jews, Jesus responds to criticism from the Jewish religious leaders for healing a lame man on the Sabbath and for referring to God as His Father (thereby making Himself equal with God).

Therefore Jesus answered and was saying to them, "Truly, truly, I say to you, the Son can do nothing of Himself, unless *it is* something He sees the Father doing; for whatever the Father does, these things the Son also does in like manner. For the Father loves the Son, and shows Him all things that He Himself is doing; and *the Father* will show Him greater works than these, so that you will marvel. For just as the Father raises the dead and gives them life, even so the Son also gives life to whom He wishes. For not even the Father judges anyone, but He has given all judgment to the Son, so that all will honor the Son even as they honor the Father. He who does not honor the Son does not honor the Father who sent Him" (John 5:19–23; see Luke 10:16; John 3:35; 11:25; 14:12).

Setting: Jerusalem. Following the Pharisees' interrogation and dismissal of the formerly blind man Jesus healed on the Sabbath, the Lord conveys the Parable of the Good Shepherd to the Pharisees, using figures of speech they do not understand.

So Jesus said to them again, "Truly, truly, I say to you, I am the door of the sheep. All who came before Me are thieves and robbers, but the sheep did not hear them. I am the door; if anyone enters through Me, he will be saved, and will go in and out and find pasture. The thief comes only to steal and kill and destroy; I came that they may have life, and have *it* abundantly. I am the good shepherd; the good shepherd lays down His life for the sheep. He who is a hired hand, and not a shepherd, who is not the owner of the sheep, sees the wolf coming, and leaves the sheep and flees, and the wolf snatches them and scatters *them. He flees* because he is a hired hand and is not concerned about the sheep. I am the good shepherd, and I know My own and My own know Me, even as the Father knows Me and I know the Father; and I lay down My life for the sheep. I have other sheep, which are not of this fold; I must bring them also, and they will hear My voice; and they will become one flock *with* one shepherd. For this reason the Father loves Me, because I lay down My life so that I may take it again. No one has taken it away from Me, but I lay it down on My own initiative. I have authority to take it up again. This commandment I received from My Father" (John 10:7–18; see Isaiah 40:11; 56:8; Jeremiah 23:1; Matthew 11:27).

Setting: Jerusalem. Just days before the Passover, with the chief priests and Pharisees plotting to seize Jesus, crowds welcome Him to Jerusalem with palm branches and praise, and some Greeks ask to meet Him.

And Jesus answered them, saying, "The hour has come for the Son of Man to be glorified. Truly, truly, I say to you, unless a grain of wheat falls into the earth and dies, it remains alone; but if it dies, it bears much fruit. He who loves his life loses it, and he who hates his life in this world will keep it to life eternal. If anyone serves Me, he must follow Me; and where I am, there My servant will be also; if anyone serves Me, the Father will honor him" (John 12:23–26; see Matthew 10:39).

Setting: Jerusalem. Before the Passover, after responding to Philip's request for Him to show His disciples the Father, Jesus conveys the upcoming role of the Holy Spirit in their lives.

"I will not leave you as orphans; I will come to you. After a little while the world will no longer see Me, but you *will* see Me, because I live, you will live also. In that day you will know that I am in the Father, and you in Me, and I in you. He who has My commandments and keeps them is the one who loves Me; and he who loves Me will be loved by My Father, and I will love him and will disclose Myself to him" (John 14:18–21; see John 6:57; 10:37, 38; 16:16, 22).

Setting: Jerusalem. Before the Passover, after conveying the upcoming ministry of the Holy Spirit in His disciples' lives, Jesus answers Judas' (not Iscariot) question why He discloses Himself to His disciples but not the whole world.

Jesus answered and said to him, "If anyone loves Me, he will keep My word; and My Father will love him, and We will come to him and make Our abode with him. He who does not love Me does not keep My words; and the word which you hear is not Mine, but the Father's who sent Me" (John 14:23, 24; see John 7:16; 8:51).

Setting: Jerusalem. Before the Passover, after empathizing with His disciples' sadness over His prophecies and giving them hope for the future, Jesus conveys promises about praying in His name.

"In that day you will not question Me about anything. Truly, truly, I say to you, if you ask the Father for anything in My name, He will give it to you. Until now you have asked for nothing in My name; ask and you will receive, so that your joy may be made full. These things I have spoken to you in figurative language; an hour is coming when I will no longer speak to you in figurative language, but will tell you plainly of the Father. In that day you will ask in My name, and I do not say to you that I will request of the Father on your behalf; for the Father Himself loves you, because you have loved Me and have believed that I came forth from the Father. I came forth from the Father and have come into the world; I am leaving the world again and going to the Father" (John 16:23–28; see Matthew 13:34; John 8:42; 13:1, 3; 14:14, 21, 23; 15:16).

LOVING GOD (Also see OBEDIENCE)

[LOVING GOD from LOVE THE LORD YOUR GOD]
Setting: The temple in Jerusalem. As Jesus teaches, a Pharisee lawyer asks Him which is the great commandment of the Law, in order to test Him.

And He said to him, " 'YOU SHALL LOVE THE LORD YOUR GOD WITH ALL YOUR HEART, AND WITH ALL YOUR SOUL, AND WITH ALL YOUR MIND.' This is the great and foremost commandment. The second is like it, 'YOU SHALL LOVE YOUR NEIGHBOR AS YOURSELF.' On these two commandments depend the whole Law and the Prophets" (Matthew 22:37–40; Jesus quotes from Leviticus 19:18; Deuteronomy 6:5; cf. Mark 12:28–34; see Matthew 7:12).

[LOVING GOD from LOVE THE LORD YOUR GOD]
Setting: The temple in Jerusalem. With the Pharisees and Herodians failing to trap Jesus in a statement, one of the scribes asks Him which commandment is foremost.

Jesus answered, "The foremost is, 'HEAR, O ISRAEL! THE LORD OUR GOD IS ONE LORD; AND YOU SHALL LOVE THE LORD YOUR GOD WITH ALL YOUR HEART, AND WITH ALL YOUR SOUL, AND WITH ALL YOUR MIND AND WITH ALL YOUR STRENGTH.' The second is this, 'YOU SHALL LOVE YOUR NEIGHBOR AS YOURSELF.' There is no other commandment greater than these" (Mark 12:29–31, Jesus quotes from Deuteronomy 6:4–5; Leviticus 19:18; cf. Matthew 22:34–40).

[LOVING GOD from DO THIS (referring to LOVE THE LORD YOUR GOD)]
Setting: On the way from Galilee to Jerusalem. After Jesus conveys to His disciples in private the privilege of living in the time of the Messiah, a lawyer tests Him.

And a lawyer stood up and put Him to the test, saying, "Teacher, what shall I do to inherit eternal life?" And He said to him, "What is written in the Law? How does it read to you?" And he answered, "YOU SHALL LOVE THE LORD YOUR GOD WITH ALL YOUR HEART, AND WITH ALL YOUR SOUL, AND WITH ALL YOUR STRENGTH, AND WITH ALL YOUR MIND; AND YOUR NEIGHBOR AS YOURSELF." And He said to him, "You have answered correctly; DO THIS AND YOU WILL LIVE" (Luke 10:25–28, Jesus quotes from Leviticus 18:5; see Deuteronomy 6:5; Matthew 19:16–19).

LOVING YOUR NEIGHBOR (See NEIGHBOR)

LUCIFER (See BEELZEBUL; DEVIL; EVIL ONE; and SATAN)

LUGGAGE (See BAG)

LUKEWARM

Setting: On the island of Patmos (in the Aegean Sea about fifty miles southwest of Ephesus in modern Turkey). On the Lord's Day (Sunday), about fifty years after Jesus' resurrection, the disciple John encounters the Lord Jesus Christ, who communicates a new revelation for the apostle to record for the church in Laodicea and to six other churches in Asia.

"To the angel of the church in Laodicea write: The Amen, the faithful and true Witness, the Beginning of the creation of God, says this: 'I know your deeds, that you are neither cold nor hot; I wish that you were cold or hot. So because you are lukewarm, and neither hot nor cold, I will spit you out of My mouth. Because you say, "I am rich, and have become wealthy, and have need of nothing," and you do not know that you are wretched and miserable and poor and blind and naked, I advise you to buy from Me gold refined by fire so that you may become rich, and white garments so that you may clothe yourself, and *that* the shame of your nakedness will not be revealed; and eye salve to anoint your eyes so that you may see. Those whom I love, I reprove and discipline; therefore be zealous and repent. Behold, I stand at the door and knock; if anyone hears My voice and opens the door, I will come in to him and will dine with him, and he with Me. He who overcomes, I will grant to him to sit down with Me on My throne, as I also overcame and sat down with My Father on His throne. He who has an ear, let him hear what the Spirit says to the churches'" (Revelation 3:14–22; see Proverbs 3:12; Hosea 12:8; John 14:23; 16:33).

LUNCHEON (Also see BANQUETS; DINNER; and HOSPITALITY)

Setting: On the way from Galilee to Jerusalem. As He observes the guests selecting places of honor at the table, Jesus speaks a parable to the guests of a Pharisee leader on the Sabbath. The Lord then comments to the host about the people to invite in the future.

And He also went on to say to the one who had invited Him, "When you give a luncheon or a dinner, do not invite your friends or your brothers or your relatives or rich neighbors, otherwise they may also invite you in return and *that* will be your repayment. But when you give a reception, invite *the* poor, *the* crippled, *the* lame, *the* blind, and you will be blessed, since they do not have *the means* to repay you; for you will be repaid at the resurrection of the righteous" (Luke 14:12–14; see Luke 14:1, 2, 15; John 5:28, 29).

LUST

Setting: Galilee. During the early part of His ministry, Jesus preaches the Sermon on the Mount to His disciples and the multitudes.

"You have heard that it was said, 'YOU SHALL NOT COMMIT ADULTERY'; but I say to you that everyone who looks at a woman with lust for her has already committed adultery with her in his heart" (Matthew 5:27, 28, Jesus quotes from Exodus 20:14; see 2 Samuel 11:2–5).

LUXURY

Setting: Galilee. After He responds to the disciples of John the Baptist whether He is the promised Messiah, Jesus speaks to the crowds about John.

When the messengers of John had left, He began to speak to the crowds about John, "What did you go out into the wilderness to see? A reed shaken by the wind? But what did you go out to see? A man dressed in soft clothing? Those who are splendidly clothed and live in luxury are *found* in royal palaces! But what did you go out to see? A prophet? Yes, I say to you, and one who is more than a prophet. This is the one about whom it is written, 'BEHOLD, I SEND MY MESSENGER AHEAD OF YOU, WHO WILL PREPARE YOUR WAY BEFORE YOU.' I say to you, among those born of women there is no one greater than John; yet he who is least in the kingdom of God is greater than he" (Luke 7:24–28, Jesus quotes from Malachi 3:1; cf. Matthew 11:7–11).

LYING (See DECEPTION; LIAR; LIE; LIES; VOWS; and WITNESS, FALSE)

M

MAGISTRATE (Also see JUDGE)

Setting: On the way from Galilee to Jerusalem. After chastising the crowds for being able to discern the weather but not the present age, Jesus exhorts them to settle any financial disputes outside of court.

"And why do you not even on your own initiative judge what is right? For while you are going with your opponent to appear before the magistrate, on *your* way *there* make an effort to settle with him, so that he may not drag you before the judge, and the judge turn you over to the officer, and the officer throw you into prison. I say to you, you will not get out of there until you have paid the very last cent" (Luke 12:57–59; cf. Matthew 5:25, 26).

MAIN HIGHWAYS (Listed under HIGHWAYS, MAIN; also see ROAD; and STREETS)

MALE (Also see MAN; and MEN)

Setting: Judea beyond the Jordan (Perea). After replying to Peter's question about forgiveness, the Pharisees test Jesus in front of a large crowd with a question about divorce.

And He answered and said, "Have you not read that He who created *them* from the beginning MADE THEM MALE AND FEMALE, and said, 'FOR THIS REASON A MAN SHALL LEAVE HIS FATHER AND MOTHER AND BE JOINED TO HIS WIFE, AND THE TWO SHALL BECOME ONE FLESH'? So they are no longer two, but one flesh. What therefore God has joined together, let no man separate" (Matthew 19:4–6, Jesus quotes from Genesis 1:27; 2:24; cf. Mark 10:5–9; see 1 Timothy 2:14).

Setting: Judea beyond the Jordan (Perea). Jesus teaches the crowds gathered around Him about divorce after the Pharisees test and question Him on the subject.

And He answered and said to them, "What did Moses command you?" They said, "Moses permitted a *man* TO WRITE A CERTIFICATE OF DIVORCE AND SEND *her* AWAY." But Jesus said to them, "Because of your hardness of heart he wrote you this commandment. But from the beginning of creation, *God* MADE THEM MALE AND FEMALE. FOR THIS REASON A MAN SHALL LEAVE HIS FATHER AND MOTHER, AND THE TWO SHALL BECOME ONE FLESH; so they are no longer two, but one flesh. What therefore God has joined together, let no man separate. In the house the disciples *began* questioning Him about this again. And He said to them, "Whoever divorces his wife and marries another woman commits adultery against her; and if she herself divorces her husband and marries another man, she is committing adultery" (Mark 10:3–12, Jesus quotes from Genesis 1:27; 2:24; cf. Matthew 19:1–9; see Deuteronomy 24:1–3; Matthew 5:32; see Romans 7:2, 3; 1 Corinthians 7:10, 11, 13, 39; 1 Timothy 2:14).

MAMMON (See MONEY; and WEALTH)

MAN (Specifics such as MAN, GOOD; and SON OF MAN are separate entries; also see MALE; and MEN)

Setting: Judea, near the Jordan River. Following His baptism, and before He begins His public ministry, Jesus is led by the Spirit into the wilderness to be tempted for forty days by Satan.

But He answered and said, "It is written, 'MAN SHALL NOT LIVE ON BREAD ALONE, BUT ON EVERY WORD THAT PROCEEDS OUT OF THE MOUTH OF GOD'" (Matthew 4:4, Jesus quotes from Deuteronomy 8:3; cf. Luke 4:4).

Setting: Galilee. During the early part of His ministry, Jesus preaches the Sermon on the Mount to His disciples and the multitudes.

"Ask, and it will be given to you; seek, and you will find; knock, and it will be opened to you. For everyone who asks receives, and he who seeks finds, and to him who knocks it will be opened. Or what man is there among you who, when his son asks for a loaf, will give him a stone? Or if he asks for a fish, he will not give him a snake, will he? If you then, being evil, know how to give good gifts to your children, how much more will your Father who is in heaven give what is good to those who ask Him! In everything, therefore, treat people the same way you want them to treat you, for this is the Law and the Prophets" (Matthew 7:7–12; cf. Matthew 22:40; Luke 6:31; 11:9–13; see Psalm 84:11).

Setting: Galilee. After His disciples observe His ministry, Jesus summons and specifically instructs them about the hardships of their ministry ahead involving true discipleship.

"Do not think that I came to bring peace on the earth; I did not come to bring peace, but a sword. For I came to SET A MAN AGAINST HIS FATHER, AND A DAUGHTER AGAINST HER MOTHER, AND A DAUGHTER-IN-LAW AGAINST HER MOTHER-IN-LAW; and A MAN'S ENEMIES WILL BE THE MEMBERS OF HIS HOUSEHOLD" (Matthew 10:34–36; Jesus quotes from Micah 7:6; cf. Luke 12:51–53).

Setting: Galilee. While speaking to the crowds, Jesus pays tribute to the ministry of John the Baptist, but emphasizes that the one who is least in the kingdom of heaven is greater than John.

As these men were going *away,* Jesus began to speak to the crowds about John, "What did you go out into the wilderness to see? A reed shaken by the wind? But what did you go out to see? A man dressed in soft *clothing?* Those who wear soft *clothing* are in kings' palaces! But what did you go out to see? A prophet? Yes, I tell you, and the one who is more than a prophet. This is the one about whom it is written, 'BEHOLD, I SEND MY MESSENGER AHEAD OF YOU, WHO WILL PREPARE YOUR WAY BEFORE YOU.' Truly, I say to you, among those born of women there has not arisen *anyone* greater than John the Baptist! Yet the one who is least in the kingdom of heaven is greater than he. From the days of John the Baptist until now the kingdom of heaven suffers violence, and violent men take it by force. For all the prophets and the Law prophesied until John. And, if you are willing to accept *it,* John himself is Elijah who was to come. He who has ears to hear, let him hear" (Matthew 11:7–15, Jesus quotes from Malachi 3:1; cf. Malachi 4:5; Luke 7:24–28; Luke 16:16; see Matthew 14:5).

Setting: A synagogue in Galilee. Jesus answers questions about the Sabbath posed by the Pharisees.

And He said to them, "What man is there among you who has a sheep, and if it falls into a pit on the Sabbath, will he not take hold of it and lift it out? How much more valuable then is a man than a sheep! So then, it is lawful to do good on the Sabbath." Then He said to the man, "Stretch out your hand!" He stretched it out, and it was restored to normal, like the other (Matthew 12:11–13; cf. Matthew 10:31; Mark 3:4, 5; Luke 6:9, 10; 14:5; see Matthew 8:3).

Setting: Galilee. Jesus responds to some Pharisees and scribes who ask Him for a miraculous sign.

"Now when the unclean spirit goes out of a man, it passes through waterless places seeking rest, and does not find *it.* Then it says, 'I will return to my house from which I came'; and when it comes, it finds *it* unoccupied, swept, and put in order. Then it goes and takes along with it seven other spirits more wicked than itself, and they go in and live there; and the last state of that man becomes worse than the first. That is the way it will also be for this evil generation" (Matthew 12:43–45; cf. Luke 11:24–26; see Mark 5:9).

Setting: By the Sea of Galilee. With the religious leaders rejecting His message, Jesus begins to teach in parables and gives His disciples the meaning of the Parable of the Sower.

"Hear then the parable of the sower. When anyone hears the word of the kingdom and does not understand it, the evil *one* comes and snatches away what has been sown in his heart. This is the one on whom seed was sown beside the road. The one on whom seed was sown on the rocky places, this is the man who hears the word and immediately receives it with joy; yet he has no *firm* root in himself, but is *only* temporary, and when affliction or persecution arises because of the word, immediately he falls away. And the one on whom seed was sown among the thorns, this is the man who hears the word, and the worry of the world and the deceitfulness of wealth choke the word, and it becomes unfruitful. And the one on whom seed was sown on the good soil, this is the man who hears the word and understands it; who indeed bears fruit and brings forth, some a hundredfold, some sixty, and some thirty" (Matthew 13:18–23; cf. Mark 4:13–20; Luke 8:11–15; see Matthew 13:8).

Setting: By the Sea of Galilee. Because the religious leaders are rejecting His message, Jesus continues teaching the crowds with the Parable of the Wheat and the Tares.

Jesus presented another parable to them, saying, "The kingdom of heaven may be compared to a man who sowed good seed in his field. But while his men were sleeping, his enemy came and sowed tares among the wheat, and went away. But when the wheat sprouted and bore grain, then the tares became evident also. The slaves of the landowner came and said to him, 'Sir, did you not sow good seed in your field? How then does it have tares?' And he said to them, 'An enemy has done this!' The slaves said to him, 'Do you want us, then, to go and gather them up?' But he said, 'No; for while you are gathering up the tares, you may uproot the wheat with them. Allow both to grow together until the harvest; and in the time of the harvest I will say to the reapers, "First gather up the tares and bind them in bundles to burn them up; but gather the wheat into my barn"'" (Matthew 13:24–30; cf. Matthew 3:12).

Setting: By the Sea of Galilee. Because the religious leaders are rejecting His message, Jesus continues teaching the crowds with the Parable of the Mustard Seed.

He presented another parable to them, saying, "The kingdom of heaven is like a mustard seed, which a man took and sowed in his field; and this is smaller than all other seeds, but when it is full grown, it is larger than the garden plants and becomes a tree, so that THE BIRDS OF THE AIR come and NEST IN ITS BRANCHES" (Matthew 13:31, 32, Jesus quotes from Ezekiel 17:23; cf. Mark 4:30–32; Luke 13:18, 19).

Setting: By the Sea of Galilee. Because the religious leaders are rejecting His message, Jesus continues teaching the crowds with the Parable of the Hidden Treasure.

"The kingdom of heaven is like a treasure hidden in the field, which a man found and hid *again;* and from joy over it he goes and sells all that he has and buys that field" (Matthew 13:44).

Setting: Galilee. After the Pharisees and scribes question Him about His disciples' lack of obedience to tradition and the commandments, Jesus instructs the crowd.

After Jesus called the crowd to Him, He said to them, "Hear and understand. *It is* not what enters into the mouth *that* defiles the man, but what proceeds out of the mouth, this defiles the man" (Matthew 15:10, 11; cf. Matthew 15:18).

Setting: Galilee. Jesus gives the crowd the meaning of His instruction about what defiles a man.

Peter said to Him, "Explain the parable to us." Jesus said, "Are you still lacking in understanding also? Do you not understand that everything that goes into the mouth passes into the stomach and is eliminated? But the things that proceed out of the mouth come from the heart, and those defile the man. For out of the heart come evil thoughts, murders, adulteries, fornications, thefts, false witness, slanders. These are the things which defile a man; but to eat with unwashed hands does not defile the man" (Matthew 15:15–20; cf. Mark 7:18–23; see Galatians 5:19–21).

Setting: Near Caesarea Philippi. After rebuking Peter for trying to forbid Him to accomplish His earthly mission of dying and being resurrected, Jesus teaches His disciples about the costs of discipleship.

Then Jesus said to His disciples, "If anyone wishes to come after Me, he must deny himself, and take up his cross and follow Me. For whoever wishes to save his life will lose it; but whoever loses his life for My sake will find it. For what will it profit a man if he gains the whole world and forfeits his soul? Or what will a man give in exchange for his soul? For the Son of Man is going to come in the glory of His Father with His angels, and WILL THEN REPAY EVERY MAN ACCORDING TO HIS DEEDS. Truly, I say to you, there are some of you who are standing here who will not taste death until they see the Son of Man coming in His kingdom" (Matthew 16:24–28, Jesus quotes from Psalm 62:12; cf. Mark 8:34–37; Luke 9:23–27; see Matthew 10:38, 39).

Setting: Capernaum of Galilee. Jesus elaborates about stumbling blocks after His disciples ask Him about greatness in the kingdom of heaven.

"Woe to the world because of *its* stumbling blocks! For it is inevitable that stumbling blocks come; but woe to that man through whom the stumbling block comes! If your hand or your foot causes you to stumble, cut if off and throw it from you; it is better for you to enter life crippled or lame, than to have two hands or two feet and be cast into the eternal fire. If your eye causes you to stumble, pluck it out and throw it from you. It is better for you to enter life with one eye, than to have two eyes and be cast into the fiery hell" (Matthew 18:7–9; cf. Matthew 5:29, 30; Mark 9:43–48; Luke 17:1).

Setting: Capernaum of Galilee. Jesus illustrates to His disciples the value of little ones.

"What do you think? If any man has a hundred sheep, and one of them has gone astray, does he not leave the ninety-nine on the mountains and go and search for the one that is straying? If it turns out that he finds it, truly I say to you, he rejoices over it more than the ninety-nine which have not gone astray. So it is not *the* will of your Father who is in heaven that one of these little ones perish" (Matthew 18:12–14; cf. Luke 15:4–7).

Setting: Judea beyond the Jordan (Perea) After Jesus replies to Peter's question about forgiveness, the Pharisees test the Lord in front of a large crowd with a question about divorce.

And He answered and said, "Have you not read that He who created *them* from the beginning MADE THEM MALE AND FEMALE, and said, 'FOR THIS REASON A MAN SHALL LEAVE HIS FATHER AND MOTHER AND BE JOINED TO HIS WIFE, AND THE TWO SHALL BECOME ONE FLESH'? So they are no longer two, but one flesh. What therefore God has joined together, let no man separate" (Matthew 19:4–6, Jesus quotes from Genesis 1:27; 2:24; cf. Mark 10:5–9; see 1 Timothy 2:14).

Setting: Judea beyond the Jordan (Perea). Jesus illustrates the kingdom of heaven to His disciples through the story of laborers in the vineyard.

"For the kingdom of heaven is like a landowner who went out early in the morning to hire laborers for his vineyard. When he had agreed with the laborers for a denarius for the day, he sent them into his vineyard. And he went out about the third hour and saw others standing idle in the market place; and to those he said, 'You also go into the vineyard, and whatever is right I will give you.' And *so* they went. Again he went out about the sixth and the ninth hour, and did the same thing. And about the eleventh *hour* he went out and found others standing *around;* and he said to them, 'Why have you been standing idle here all day long?' They said to him, 'Because no one hired us.' He said to them, 'You go into the vineyard too.' When evening came, the owner of the vineyard said to his foreman, 'Call the laborers and pay them their wages, beginning with the last *group* to the first.' When those *hired* about the eleventh hour came, each one received a denarius. When those *hired* first came, they thought that they would receive more; but each of them also received a denarius. When they received it, they grumbled at the landowner, saying, 'These last men have worked *only* one hour, and you have made them equal to us who have borne the burden and the scorching heat of the day.' But he answered and said to one of them, 'Friend, I am doing you no wrong; did you not agree with me for a denarius? Take what is yours and go, but I wish to give to this last man the same as to you. It is not lawful for me to do what I wish with what is my own? Or is your eye envious because I am generous?' So the last shall be first, and the first last" (Matthew 20:1–16; cf. Matthew 19:30).

Setting: The temple in Jerusalem. Jesus delivers a parable to the chief priests and elders after they question His authority.

"But what do you think? A man had two sons, and he came to the first and said, 'Son, go work today in the vineyard.' And he answered, 'I will not'; but afterward he regretted it and went. The man came to the second and said the same thing; and he answered, 'I *will,* sir'; but he did not go. Which of the two sons did the will of his father?" They said, "The first." Jesus said to them, "Truly, I say to you that the tax collectors and prostitutes will get into the kingdom of God before you. For John came to you in the way of righteousness and you did not believe him; but the tax collectors and prostitutes did believe him; and you, seeing *this,* did not even feel remorse afterward so as to believe him" (Matthew 21:28–32; cf. Luke 7:29, 30, 37–50).

Setting: The temple in Jerusalem. Jesus speaks another parable to the chief priests and elders after they question His authority.

Jesus spoke to them again in parables, saying, "The kingdom of heaven may be compared to a king who gave a wedding feast for his son. And he sent out his slaves to call those who had been invited to the wedding feast, and they were unwilling to come. Again he sent out other slaves saying, 'Tell those who have been invited, "Behold, I have prepared my dinner; my oxen and my fattened livestock are *all* butchered and everything is ready; come to the wedding feast." But they paid no attention and went their way, one to his own farm, another to his business, and the rest seized his slaves and mistreated them and killed them. But the king was enraged, and he sent his armies and destroyed those murderers and set their city on fire. Then he said to his slaves, 'The wedding is ready, but those who were invited were not worthy. 'Go therefore to the main highways, and as many as you find *there,* invite to the wedding feast.' Those slaves went out into the streets and gathered together all they found, both evil and good; and the wedding hall was filled with dinner guests. But when the king came in to look over the dinner guests, he saw a man there who was not dressed in wedding clothes, and he said to him, 'Friend, how did you come in here without wedding clothes?' And the man was speechless. Then the king said to the servants, 'Bind him hand and foot, and throw him into the outer darkness; in that place there will be weeping and gnashing of teeth.' For many are called, but few *are* chosen" (Matthew 22:1–14; cf. Matthew 8:11, 12).

Setting: The Mount of Olives, just east of Jerusalem. During His discourse, after answering His disciples' questions as to when the temple will be destroyed and Jerusalem overrun, along with the signs of His coming and the end of the age, Jesus reemphasizes to His disciples that they should be on the alert for His return.

"For *it is* just like a man *about* to go on a journey, who called his own slaves and entrusted his possessions to them. To one he gave five talents, to another, two, and to another, one, each according to his own ability; and he went on his journey. Immediately the one who had received the five talents went and traded with them, and gained five more talents. In the same manner the one who *had received* the two *talents* gained two more. But he who received the one *talent* went away, and dug a *hole* in the ground and hid his master's money. Now after a long time the master of those slaves came and settled accounts with them. The one who had received the five talents came up and brought five more talents, saying, 'Master, you entrusted five talents to me. See, I have gained five more talents.' "Histalents.' His master said to him, 'Well done, good and faithful slave. You were faithful with a few things, I will put you in charge of many things; enter into the joy of your master.' Also the one who *had received* the two talents came up and said, 'Master, you entrusted two talents to me. See, I have gained two more talents.' His master said to him, 'Well done, good and faithful slave. You were faithful with a few things, I will put you in charge of many things; enter into the joy of your master.' And the one also who had received the one talent came up and said, 'Master, I knew you to be a hard man, reaping where you did not sow and gathering where you scattered no *seed.* And IAnd I was afraid, and went away and hid your talent in the ground. See, you have what is yours.' But his master answered and said to him, 'You wicked, lazy slave, you knew that I reap where I did not sow and gather where I scattered no *seed.* Then you ought to have put my money in the bank, and on my arrival I would have received my *money* back with interest. 'Therefore take away the talent from him, and give it to the one who has ten talents.' For to everyone who has, *more* shall be given, and he will have an abundance; but from the one who does not have, even what he does have shall be taken away. Throw out the worthless slave into the outer darkness; in that place there will be weeping and gnashing of teeth" (Matthew 25:14–30; cf. Matthew 8:12; 3:12; 24:45–47; see Matthew 18:23, 24; Luke 12:44).

Setting: Just outside Jerusalem. On the first day of the Feast of Unleavened Bread, Jesus informs His disciples where they will celebrate the Passover, just after Judas makes arrangements with the chief priests to betray Him.

And He said, "Go into the city to a certain man, and say to him, 'The Teacher says, "My time is near; I *am to* keep the Passover at your house with My disciples"'" (Matthew 26:18; cf. Mark 14:13–15; Luke 22:7–13).

Setting: Galilee. Early in His ministry, the Pharisees question Jesus why He allows His disciples to harvest grain on the Sabbath.

And He said to them, "Have you never read what David did when he was in need and he and his companions became hungry; how he entered the house of God in the time of Abiathar *the* high priest, and ate the consecrated bread, which is not lawful for *anyone* to eat except the priests, and he also gave it to those who were with him?" Jesus said to them, "The Sabbath was made for man, and not man for the Sabbath. So the Son of Man is Lord even of the Sabbath" (Mark 2:25–28; cf. Matthew 12:1–8; Luke 6:1–5; see Exodus 23:12).

Setting: Galilee. After explaining the Parable of the Sower to His disciples, Jesus conveys the Parable of the Seed.

And He was saying, "The kingdom of God is like a man who casts seed upon the soil; and he goes to bed at night and gets up by day, and the seed sprouts and grows—how, he himself does not know. The soil produces crops by itself; first the blade, then the head, then the mature grain in the head. But when the crop permits, he immediately puts in the sickle, because the harvest has come" (Mark 4:26–29; see Joel 3:13).

Setting: The country of the Gerasenes, across the Sea of Galilee from Capernaum. Jesus encounters and heals a demon-possessed man.

For He had been saying to him, "Come out of the man, you unclean spirit!" And He was asking him, "What is your name?" And he said to Him, "My name is Legion; for we are many" (Mark 5:8, 9; cf. Luke 8:30; see Matthew 8:28–32; Luke 8:26–33).

Setting: Galilee. The Pharisees and some of the scribes from Jerusalem question why Jesus' disciples do not follow the tradition of ceremonial hand cleansing before eating bread.

And He said to them, "Rightly did Isaiah prophesy of you hypocrites, as it is written: 'THIS PEOPLE HONORS ME WITH THEIR LIPS, BUT THEIR HEART IS FAR AWAY FROM ME. BUT IN VAIN DO THEY WORSHIP ME, TEACHING AS DOCTRINES THE PRECEPTS OF MEN.' Neglecting the commandment of God, you hold to the tradition of men." He was also saying to them, "You are experts at setting aside the commandment of God in order to keep tradition. For Moses said, 'HONOR YOUR FATHER AND YOUR MOTHER'; and, 'HE WHO SPEAKS EVIL OF FATHER OR MOTHER, IS TO BE PUT TO DEATH'; but you say, 'If a man says to *his* father or *his* mother, whatever I have that would help you is Corban (that is to say, given *to God*),' you no longer permit him to do anything for *his* father or *his* mother; *thus* invalidating the word of God by your tradition which you have handed down; and you do many things such as that" (Mark 7:6–13, Jesus quotes from Exodus 20:12; 21:17; Isaiah 29:13; cf. Matthew 15:1–6).

Setting: Galilee. After the Pharisees and scribes from Jerusalem object to His disciples' lack of obedience to tradition, Jesus speaks to a crowd and explains His teaching to His disciples.

After He called the crowd to Him again, He *began* saying to them, "Listen to Me, all of you, and understand: there is nothing outside the man which can defile him if it goes into him; but the things which proceed out of the man are what defile the man. [If anyone has ears to hear, let him hear."] When he had left the crowd *and* entered the house, His disciples questioned Him about the parable. And He said to them, "Are you so lacking in understanding also? Do you not understand that whatever goes into the man from outside cannot defile him, because it does not go into his heart, but into his stomach, and is eliminated?" (*Thus He* declared all foods clean.) And He was saying, "That which proceeds out of the man, that is what defiles the man. For from within, out of the heart of men, proceed the evil thoughts, fornications, thefts, murders, adulteries, deeds of coveting *and* wickedness, *as well* as deceit, sensuality, envy, slander, pride *and* foolishness. All these evil things proceed from within and defile the man" (Mark 7:14–23; cf. Matthew 15:10–20).

Setting: Caesarea Philippi. After He rebukes Peter for desiring to thwart His mission to the cross, Jesus summons a crowd, along with His disciples, and informs them of the high costs of following Him.

And He summoned the crowd with His disciples, and said to them, "If anyone wishes to come after Me, he must deny himself, and take up his cross and follow Me. For whoever wishes to save his life will lose it, but whoever loses his life for My sake and the gospel's will save it. For what does it profit a man to gain the whole world, and forfeit his soul? For what will a man give in exchange for his soul? For whoever is ashamed of Me and My words in this adulterous and sinful generation, the Son of Man will also be ashamed of him when He comes in the glory of His Father with the holy angels" (Mark 8:34–38; cf. Matthew 16:24–28; Luke 9:23–27; see Matthew 10:33, 38, 39).

Setting: Judea beyond the Jordan (Perea). Jesus teaches the crowds gathered around Him about divorce after the Pharisees test and question Him on the subject.

And He answered and said to them, "What did Moses command you?" They said, "Moses permitted a *man* TO WRITE A CERTIFICATE OF DIVORCE AND SEND *her* AWAY." But Jesus said to them, "Because of your hardness of heart he wrote you this commandment. But from the beginning of creation, *God* MADE THEM MALE AND FEMALE. FOR THIS REASON A MAN SHALL LEAVE HIS FATHER AND MOTHER, AND THE TWO SHALL BECOME ONE FLESH; so they are no longer two, but one flesh. What therefore God has joined together, let no man separate. In the house the disciples *began* questioning Him about this again. And He said to them, "Whoever divorces his wife and marries another woman commits adultery against her; and if she herself divorces her husband and marries another man, she is committing adultery" (Mark 10:3–12, Jesus quotes from Genesis 1:27; 2:24; cf. Matthew 19:1–9; see Deuteronomy 24:1–3; Matthew 5:32; see Romans 7:2, 3; 1 Corinthians 7:10, 11, 13, 39; 1 Timothy 2:14).

Setting: The temple in Jerusalem. Having His authority questioned by the chief priests, scribes, and elders, Jesus begins to teach them in parables.

And He began to speak to them in parables: "A man PLANTED A VINEYARD AND PUT A WALL AROUND IT, AND DUG A VAT UNDER THE WINE PRESS AND BUILT A TOWER, and rented it out to vine-growers and went on a journey. At the *harvest* time he sent a slave to the vine-growers, in order to receive *some* of the produce of the vineyard from the vine-growers. They took him, and beat him and sent him away empty-handed. Again he sent them another slave, and they wounded him in the head, and treated him shamefully. And he sent another, and that one they killed; and *so with* many others, beating some and killing others. He had one more to *send*, a beloved son; he sent him last *of all* to them, saying, 'They will respect my son.' But those vine-growers said to one another, 'This is the heir; come, let us kill him, and the inheritance will be ours!' They took him, and killed him and threw him out of the vineyard. What will the owner of the vineyard do? He will come and destroy the vine-growers, and will give the vineyard to others. Have you not even read this Scripture: 'THE STONE WHICH THE BUILDERS REJECTED, THIS BECAME THE CHIEF CORNER *stone;* THIS CAME ABOUT FROM THE LORD, AND IT IS MARVELOUS IN OUR EYES'?" (Mark 12:1–11, Jesus quotes from Psalm 118:22, 23; Isaiah 5:1, 2; cf. Matthew 21:33–46; Luke 20:9–19).

Setting: On the Mount of Olives, east of the temple in Jerusalem. After predicting the temple's destruction, Jesus responds during His Olivet Discourse to questions from Peter, James, John, and Andrew about other future events.

"Take heed, keep on the alert; for you do not know when the *appointed* time will come. *It is* like a man away on a journey, *who* upon leaving his house and putting his slaves in charge, *assigning* to each one his task, also commanded the doorkeeper to stay on the alert. Therefore, be on the alert—for you do not know when the master of the house is coming, whether in the evening, at midnight, or when the rooster crows, or in the morning—in case he should come suddenly and find you asleep. What I say to you I say to all, 'Be on the alert!'" (Mark 13:33–37; cf. Matthew 24:42, 43; Luke 21:34–36; see Luke 12:36–38; Ephesians 6:18).

Setting: Just outside Jerusalem. On the first day of the Feast of Unleavened Bread, when the Passover lamb is sacrificed, Jesus responds to His disciples' question about His plans for the Passover meal.

And He sent two of His disciples and said to them, "Go into the city, and a man will meet you carrying a pitcher of water; follow him; and wherever he enters, say to the owner of the house, 'The Teacher says, "Where is My guest room in which I may eat the Passover with My disciples?"' And he himself will show you a large upper room furnished *and* ready; prepare for us there" (Mark 14:13–15; cf. Matthew 26:17–19; Luke 22:7–13).

Setting: A borrowed upper room in Jerusalem. While Jesus and His twelve disciples are eating the Passover meal, the Lord states that one of His disciples will betray Him.

As they were reclining *at the table* and eating, Jesus said, "Truly I say to you that one of you will betray Me—one who is eating with Me." They began to be grieved and to say to Him one by one, "Surely not I?" And He said to them, "*It is* one of the twelve, one who dips with Me in the bowl. For the Son of Man *is to* go just as it is written of Him; but woe to that man by whom the Son of Man is betrayed! *It would have been* good for that man if he had not been born" (Mark 14:18–21; cf. Matthew 26:21–24; Luke 22:22, 23; John 13:21, 22).

Setting: Judea, near the Jordan River. Following His baptism, and before He begins His public ministry, Jesus is led by the Spirit into the wilderness for forty days of temptation by Satan.

And Jesus answered him, "It is written, 'MAN SHALL NOT LIVE ON BREAD ALONE'" (Luke 4:4, Jesus quotes from Deuteronomy 8:3; cf. Matthew 4:1–4; see Mark 1:12, 13).

Setting: Galilee. After selecting His twelve disciples, Jesus teaches the Sermon on the Mount to those disciples and a great throng of people from Judea, Jerusalem, and the central coastal region of Tyre and Sidon.

"Why do you call Me, 'Lord, Lord,' and do not do what I say? Everyone who comes to Me and hears My words and acts on them, I will show you whom he is like; he is like a man building a house, who dug deep and laid a foundation on the rock; and when a flood occurred, the torrent burst against that house and could not shake it, because it had been well built. But the one who has heard and has not acted *accordingly,* is like a man who built a house on the ground without any foundation; and the torrent burst against it and immediately it collapsed, and the ruin of that house was great" (Luke 6:46–49; cf. Matthew 7:24–27; see Luke 6:12–19; James 1:22).

Setting: Galilee. After He responds to the disciples of John the Baptist whether He is the promised Messiah, Jesus speaks to the crowds about John.

When the messengers of John had left, He began to speak to the crowds about John, "What did you go out into the wilderness to see? A reed shaken by the wind? But what did you go out to see? A man dressed in soft clothing? Those who are splendidly clothed and live in luxury are *found* in royal palaces! But what did you go out to see? A prophet? Yes, I say to you, and one who is more than a prophet. This is the one about whom it is written, 'BEHOLD, I SEND MY MESSENGER AHEAD OF YOU, WHO WILL PREPARE YOUR WAY BEFORE YOU.' I say to you, among those born of women there is no one greater than John; yet he who is least in the kingdom of God is greater than he" (Luke 7:24–28, Jesus quotes from Malachi 3:1; cf. Matthew 11:7–11).

Setting: Galilee. Following Peter's pronouncement that Jesus is the Christ of God, the Lord conveys the demands of discipleship and the hope regarding the kingdom of God.

And He was saying to *them* all, "If anyone wishes to come after Me, he must deny himself, and take up his cross daily and follow Me. For whoever wishes to save his life will lose it, but whoever loses his life for My sake, he is the one who will save it. For what is a man profited if he gains the whole world, and loses or forfeits himself? For whoever is ashamed of Me and My words, the Son of Man will be ashamed of him when He comes in His glory, and *the glory* of the Father and of the holy angels. But I say to you truthfully, there are some of those standing here who will not taste death until they see the kingdom of God" (Luke 9:23–27; cf. Matthew 16:24–26, 28; Mark 8:34–37; see Matthew 10:33, 38, 39).

Setting: On the way from Galilee to Jerusalem. The Lord appoints seventy followers and sends them out in pairs to every place He Himself will soon visit.

And He was saying to them, "The harvest is plentiful, but the laborers are few; therefore beseech the Lord of the harvest to send out laborers into His harvest. Go; behold, I send you out as lambs in the midst of wolves. Carry no money belt, no bag, no shoes;

and greet no one on the way. Whatever house you enter, first say, 'Peace be to this house.' If a man of peace is there, your peace will rest on him; but if not, it will return to you. Stay in that house, eating and drinking what they give you; for the laborer is worthy of his wages. Do not keep moving from house to house. Whatever city you enter and they receive you, eat what is set before you; and heal those in it who are sick, and say to them, 'The kingdom of God has come near to you.' But whatever city you enter and they do not receive you, go out into its streets and say, 'Even the dust of your city which clings to our feet we wipe off *in protest* against you; yet be sure of this, that the kingdom of God has come near.' I say to you, it will be more tolerable in that day for Sodom than for that city" (Luke 10:2–12; see Genesis 19:24–28; Matthew 9:37, 38, 10:9–14, 16; 1 Corinthians 10:27).

Setting: On the way from Galilee to Jerusalem. While being tested by a lawyer, Jesus tells him the story of the good Samaritan.

Jesus replied and said, "A man was going down from Jerusalem to Jericho, and fell among robbers, and they stripped him and beat him, and went away leaving him half dead. And by chance a priest was going down on that road, and when he saw him, he passed by on the other side. Likewise a Levite also, when he came to the place and saw him, passed by on the other side. But a Samaritan, who was on a journey, came upon him; and when he saw him, he felt compassion, and came to him and bandaged up his wounds, pouring oil and wine on *them;* and he put him on his own beast, and brought him to an inn and took care of him. On the next day he took out two denarii and gave them to the innkeeper and said, 'Take care of him; and whatever more you spend, when I return I will repay you.' Which of these three do you think proved to be a neighbor to the man who fell into the robbers' *hands?"* And he said, "The one who showed mercy toward him." Then Jesus said to him, "Go and do the same" (Luke 10:30–37).

Setting: On the way from Galilee to Jerusalem. After some in the crowd test Him by demanding a sign from heaven, Jesus illustrates His power over Satan.

"When the unclean spirit goes out of a man, it passes through waterless places seeking rest, and not finding any, it says, 'I will return to my house from which I came.' And when it comes, it finds it swept clean and put in order. Then it goes and takes *along* seven other spirits more evil than itself, and they go in and live there; and the last state of that man becomes worse than the first" (Luke 11:24–26; cf. Matthew 12:43–45; see Luke 11:14–16).

Setting: On the way from Galilee to Jerusalem. After the scribes and Pharisees turn hostile and question Him repeatedly in an attempt to catch Him in something He might say, Jesus teaches the crowds and His disciples about greed and possessions.

But He said to him, "Man, who appointed Me a judge or arbitrator over you?" Then He said to them, "Beware, and be on your guard against every form of greed; for not *even* when one has an abundance does his life consist of his possessions" (Luke 12:14, 15; see 1 Timothy 6:6–10).

Setting: On the way from Galilee to Jerusalem. After the scribes and Pharisees turn hostile and question Him repeatedly in an attempt to catch Him in something He might say, Jesus responds to a question from the crowd and gives a parable about riches and greed.

And He told them a parable, saying, "The land of a rich man was very productive. And he began reasoning to himself, saying, 'What shall I do, since I have no place to store my crops?' Then he said, 'This is what I will do: I will tear down my barns and build larger ones, and here I will store all my grain and my goods. And I will say to my soul, "Soul, you have many goods laid up for many years *to come;* take your ease, eat, drink *and* be merry."' "But God said to him, 'You fool! This *very* night your soul is required of you; and *now* who will own what you have prepared?' So is the man who stores up treasure for himself, and is not rich toward God" (Luke 12:16–21; see Job 27:8; Psalm 39:6; Ecclesiastes 12:9; Philippians 2:3).

Setting: On the way from Galilee to Jerusalem. After some present report to Him about the Galileans whose blood Pilate (Roman governor of Judea) had mixed with their sacrifices, Jesus responds to their concern by calling them to repentance and illustrating His point with a parable.

And He *began* telling this parable: "A man had a fig tree which had been planted in his vineyard; and he came looking for fruit on it and did not find any. And he said to the vineyard-keeper, 'Behold, for three years I have come looking for fruit on this fig tree without finding any. Cut it down! Why does it even use up the ground?' And he answered and said to him, 'Let it alone, sir, for this year too, until I dig around it and put fertilizer; and if it bears fruit next year, *fine*; but if not, cut it down'" (Luke 13:6–9; see Matthew 3:10).

Setting: On the way from Galilee to Jerusalem. After responding to a synagogue official's anger when He heals a woman, sick eighteen years, in the synagogue on the Sabbath, Jesus conveys the Parable of the Mustard Seed and the Parable of the Leaven.

So He was saying, "What is the kingdom of God like, and to what shall I compare it? It is like a mustard seed which a man took and threw into his own garden; and it grew and became a tree, and THE BIRDS OF THE AIR NESTED IN ITS BRANCHES." And again He said, "To what shall I compare the kingdom of God? It is like leaven, which a woman took and hid in three pecks of flour until it was all leavened" (Luke 13:18–21, Jesus quotes from Ezekiel 17:23; cf. Matthew 13:31–34; Mark 4:30–32).

Setting: On the way from Galilee to Jerusalem. As He observes them selecting places of honor at the table, Jesus speaks a parable to the invited guests of a Pharisee leader on the Sabbath.

And He *began* speaking a parable to the invited guests when He noticed how they had been picking out the places of honor *at the table,* saying to them, "When you are invited by someone to a wedding feast, do not take the place of honor, for someone more distinguished than you may have been invited by him, and he who invited you both will come and say to you, 'Give *your* place to this man, and then in disgrace you proceed to occupy the last place. But when you are invited, go and recline at the last place, so that when the one who has invited you comes, he may say to you, 'Friend, move up higher'; then you will have honor in the sight of all who are at the table with you. For everyone who exalts himself will be humbled, and he who humbles himself will be exalted" (Luke 14:7–11; see 2 Samuel 22:28; Proverb 25:6, 7; Matthew 23:6).

Setting: On the way from Galilee to Jerusalem. After He speaks a parable to the invited guests and the host at a banquet, Jesus responds to a guest's proclamation about the blessings of eating bread in the kingdom of God.

But He said to him, "A man was giving a big dinner, and he invited many; and at the dinner hour he sent his slave to say to those who had been invited, 'Come; for everything is ready now.' But they all alike began to make excuses. The first one said to him, 'I have bought a piece of land and I need to go out and look at it; please consider me excused.' Another one said, 'I have bought five yoke of oxen, and I am going to try them out; please consider me excused.' Another one said, I have married a wife, and for that reason I cannot come.' And the slave came *back* and reported this to his master. Then the head of the household became angry and said to his slave, 'Go out at once into the streets and lanes of the city and bring in here the poor and crippled and blind and lame.' And the slave said, 'Master, what you commanded has been done, and still there is room.' And the master said to the slave, 'Go out into the highways and along the hedges, and compel *them* to come in, so that my house may be filled. For I tell you, none of those men who were invited shall taste of my dinner'" (Luke 14:16–24; see Deuteronomy 24:5; Matthew 22:2–14).

Setting: On the way from Galilee to Jerusalem. After He responds to a guest's proclamation about the blessings of eating bread in the kingdom of God, Jesus presents to large crowds the demands of discipleship.

Now large crowds were going along with Him; and He turned and said to them, "If anyone comes to Me, and does not hate his own father and mother and wife and children and brothers and sisters, yes, and even his own life, he cannot be My disciple. Whoever does not carry his own cross and come after Me cannot be My disciple. For which one of you, when he wants to build a tower, does not first sit down and calculate the cost to see if he has enough to complete it? Otherwise, when he has laid a foundation and is not able to finish, all who observe it begin to ridicule him, saying, 'This man began to build and was not able to finish.' Or what king, when he sets out to meet another king in battle, will not first sit down and consider whether he is strong enough with ten thousand *men* to encounter the one coming against him with twenty thousand? Or else, while the other is still far away, he

sends a delegation and asks for terms of peace. So then, none of you can be My disciple who does not give up all his possessions. Therefore, salt is good; but if even salt has become tasteless, with what will it be seasoned? It is useless either for the soil or for the manure pile; it is thrown out. He who has ears to hear, let him hear" (Luke 14:25–35; cf. Matthew 5:13; 10:37–39; see Proverb 20:18; Philippians 3:7).

Setting: On the way from Galilee to Jerusalem. After Jesus presents to large crowds the demands of discipleship, the Pharisees and scribes complain He associates with tax collectors and sinners.

So He told them this parable, saying, "What man among you, if he has a hundred sheep and has lost one of them, does not leave the ninety-nine in the open pasture and go after the one which is lost until he finds it? When he has found it, he lays it on his shoulders, rejoicing. And when he comes home, he calls together his friends and his neighbors, saying to them, 'Rejoice with me, for I have found my sheep which was lost!' I tell you that in the same way, there will be *more* joy in heaven over one sinner who repents than over ninety-nine righteous persons who need no repentance" (Luke 15:3–7; cf. Matthew 18:12–14; see Matthew 9:11–13; Luke 5:29–32; 15:1, 2).

Setting: On the way from Galilee to Jerusalem. Jesus conveys the illustration of the prodigal son because the Pharisees and scribes complain He associates with tax collectors and sinners.

And He said, "A man had two sons. The younger of them said to his father, 'Father, give me the share of the estate that falls to me.' So he divided his wealth between them. And not many days later, the younger son gathered everything together and went on a journey into a distant country, and there he squandered his estate with loose living. Now when he had spent everything, a severe famine occurred in that country, and he began to be impoverished. So he went and hired himself out to one of the citizens of that country, and he sent him into his fields to feed swine. And he would have gladly filled his stomach with the pods that the swine were eating, and no one was giving *anything* to him. But when he came to his senses, he said, 'How many of my father's hired men have more than enough bread, but I am dying here with hunger! I will get up and go to my father, and will say to him, "Father, I have sinned against heaven, and in your sight; I am no longer worthy to be called your son; make me as one of your hired men."' So he got up and came to his father. But while he was still a long way off, his father saw him and felt compassion *for him,* and ran and embraced him and kissed him. And the son said to him, "Father, I have sinned against heaven and in your sight; I am no longer worthy to be called your son.' But the father said to his slaves, 'Quickly bring out the best robe and put it on him, and put a ring on his hand and sandals on his feet; and bring the fattened calf, kill it, and let us eat and celebrate; for this son of mine was dead and has come to life again; he was lost and has been found.' And they began to celebrate. Now his older son was in the field, when he came and approached the house, he heard music and dancing. And he summoned one of the servants and *began* inquiring what these things could be. And he said to him, 'Your brother has come, and your father has killed the fattened calf because he has received him back safe and sound. 'But he became angry and was not willing to go in; and his father came out and *began* pleading with him. But he answered and said to his father, 'Look! For so many years I have been serving you and I have never neglected a command of yours; and *yet* you have never given me a young goat, so that I might celebrate with my friends; but when this son of yours came, who has devoured your wealth with prostitutes, you killed the fattened calf for him. 'And he said to him, 'Son, you have always been with me, and all that is mine is yours. But we had to celebrate and rejoice, for this brother of yours was dead and *has begun* to live, and was lost and has been found'" (Luke 15:11–32; see Proverb 29:2; Luke 15:1, 2).

Setting: On the way from Galilee to Jerusalem. After telling His disciples of His second coming, Jesus instructs them about persistence in prayer.

Now He was telling them a parable to show that at all times they ought to pray and not to lose heart, saying, "In a certain city there was a judge who did not fear God and did not respect man. There was a widow in that city, and she kept coming to him, saying, 'Give me legal protection from my opponent.' For a while he was unwilling; but afterward he said to himself, 'Even though I do not fear God nor respect man, yet because this woman bothers me, I will give her legal protection, otherwise by continually coming she will wear me out.'" And the Lord said, "Hear what the unrighteous judge said; now, will not God bring about justice for His elect who cry to Him day and night, and will He delay long over them? I tell you that He will bring about justice for them quickly. However, when the Son of Man comes, will He find faith on the earth?" (Luke 18:1–8; see Luke 11:5–10).

Setting: On the way from Galilee to Jerusalem. After instructing His disciples about persistence in prayer, Jesus conveys a parable about self-righteousness.

And He also told this parable to some people who trusted in themselves that they were righteous, and viewed others with contempt: "Two men went up into the temple to pray, one a Pharisee and the other a tax collector. The Pharisee stood and was praying this to himself: 'God, I thank You that I am not like other people: swindlers, unjust, adulterers, or even like this tax collector. I fast twice a week; I pay tithes of all that I get.' But the tax collector, standing some distance away, was even unwilling to lift up his eyes to heaven, but was beating his breast, saying, 'God, be merciful to me, the sinner!' I tell you, this man went to his house justified rather than the other; for everyone who exalts himself will be humbled, but he who humbles himself will be exalted" (Luke 18:9–14; see Ezra 9:6; Matthew 6:5, 23:12; Luke 11:42, 16:15; Romans 14:3, 10).

Setting: Jericho, on the way to Jerusalem. After commending Zaccheus's faith in Him, Jesus provides a parable about stewardship.

So He said, "A nobleman went to a distant country to receive a kingdom for himself, and *then* return. And he called ten of his slaves, and gave them ten minas and said to them, 'Do business *with this* until I come *back.*' But his citizens hated him and sent a delegation after him, saying, 'We do not want this man to reign over us.' When he returned, after receiving the kingdom, he ordered that these slaves, to whom he had given the money, be called to him so that he might know what business they had done. The first appeared, saying, 'Master, your mina has made ten minas more.' And he said to him, 'Well done, good slave, because you have been faithful in a very little thing, you are to be in authority over ten cities.' The second came, saying, 'Your mina, master, has made five minas.' And he said to him, also, 'And you are to be over five cities.' Another came, saying, 'Master, here is your mina, which I kept put away in a handkerchief; for I was afraid of you, because you are an exacting man; you take up what you did not lay down and reap what you did not sow.' He said to him, 'By your own words I will judge you, you worthless slave. Did you know that I am an exacting man, taking up what I did not lay down and reaping what I did not sow? Then why did you not put my money in the bank, and having come, I would have collected it with interest?' Then he said to the bystanders, 'Take the mina away from him and give it to the one who has the ten minas.' And they said to him, 'Master, he has ten minas *already.*' I tell you that to everyone who has, more shall be given, but from the one who does not have, even what he does have shall be taken away. But these enemies of mine, who did not want me to reign over them, bring them here and slay them in my presence" (Luke 19:12–27; cf. Matthew 25:14–30; see Matthew 13:12; Luke 16:10).

Setting: The temple in Jerusalem. While ministering a few days before His crucifixion, after the chief priests and the scribes question His authority to teach and preach, Jesus conveys the Parable of the Vine-Growers to the people.

And He began to tell the people this parable: "A man planted a vineyard and rented it out to vine-growers, and went on a journey for a long time. At the *harvest* time he sent a slave to the vine-growers, so that they would give him *some* of the produce of the vineyard; but the vine-growers beat him and sent him away empty-handed. And he proceeded to send another slave; and they beat him also and treated him shamefully and sent him away empty-handed. And he proceeded to send a third; and this one also they wounded and cast out. The owner of the vineyard said, 'What shall I do? I will send my beloved son; perhaps they will respect him.' But when the vine-growers saw him, they reasoned with one another, saying, 'This is the heir; let us kill him so that the inheritance will be ours.' So they threw him out of the vineyard and killed him. What, then, will the owner of the vineyard do to them? He will come and destroy these vine-growers and will give the vineyard to others." When they heard it, they said, "May it never be!" But Jesus looked at them and said, "What then is this that is written: 'THE STONE WHICH THE BUILDERS REJECTED, THIS BECAME THE CHIEF CORNER *stone*'? Everyone who falls on that stone will be broken to pieces; but on whomever it falls, it will scatter him like dust" (Luke 20:9–18, Jesus quotes from Psalm 118:22; cf. Matthew 21:33–44; Mark 12:1–11; see Ephesians 2:20).

Setting: Jerusalem. With the Passover (Feast of Unleavened Bread) approaching, Jesus informs His disciples where they will celebrate the feast, as the chief priests and scribes seek to kill Him, and Satan enters Judas Iscariot in order to betray the Lord.

And Jesus sent Peter and John, saying, "Go and prepare the Passover for us, so that we may eat it." They said to Him, "Where do You want us to prepare it?" And He said to them, "When you have entered the city, a man will meet you carrying a pitcher of water; follow him into the house that he enters. And you shall say to the owner of the house, 'The Teacher says to you, "Where is the guest room in which I may eat the Passover with My disciples?"' And he will show you a large, furnished upper room; prepare it there" (Luke 22:8–12; cf. Matthew 26:17–19; Mark 14:12–16).

Setting: An upper room in Jerusalem. During the Feast of Unleavened Bread (Passover) just before His crucifixion, while celebrating the Passover meal with His disciples, Jesus institutes the Lord's Supper.

And when He had taken a cup *and* given thanks, He said, "Take this and share it among yourselves; for I say to you, I will not drink of the fruit of the vine from now on until the kingdom of God comes." And when he had taken *some* bread and given thanks, He broke it and gave it to them, saying, "This is My body which is given for you; do this in remembrance of Me." And in the same way *He took* the cup after they had eaten, saying, "This cup which is poured out for you is the new covenant in My blood. But behold, the hand of the one betraying Me is with Mine on the table. For indeed, the Son of Man is going as it has been determined; but woe to that man by whom He is betrayed!" (Luke 22:17–22; cf. Matthew 26:26–29; Mark 14:22–25; 1 Corinthians 11:23–26; see Psalm 41:9; Luke 14:15; 1 Corinthians 10:16).

Setting: Jerusalem. During a feast of the Jews, Jesus responds to criticism from the religious leaders by referring to God as His Father (thereby making Himself equal with God) and informing them that God, John the Baptist, and His works all testify to His mission.

"I can do nothing on My own initiative. As I hear, I judge; and My judgment is just, because I do not seek My own will, but the will of Him who sent Me. If I *alone* testify about Myself, My testimony is not true. There is another who testifies of Me, and I know that the testimony which He gives about Me is true. You have sent to John, and he has testified to the truth. But the testimony which I receive is not from man, but I say these things so that you may be saved. He was the lamp that was burning and was shining and you were willing to rejoice for a while in his light. But the testimony which I have is greater than the *testimony of* John; for the works which the Father has given Me to accomplish—the very works that I do—testify about Me, that the Father has sent Me. And the Father who sent Me, He has testified of Me. You have neither heard His voice at any time nor seen His form. You do not have His word abiding in you, for you do not believe Him whom He sent" (John 5:30–38; see Matthew 3:17; Mark 1:4, 5; John 1:7, 15, 32; 4:34; 8:14–16; 10:25, 37, 38).

Setting: The temple in Jerusalem. After receiving encouragement from His blood brothers in Galilee to attend the upcoming Feast of Booths in order to demonstrate His works to His disciples and the world, Jesus goes and teaches, astonishing the Jewish religious leaders.

Jesus answered them, "I did one deed, and you all marvel. For this reason Moses has given you circumcision (not because it is from Moses, but from the fathers), and on *the* Sabbath you circumcise a man. If a man receives circumcision on *the* Sabbath so that the Law of Moses will not be broken, are you angry with Me because I made an entire man well on *the* Sabbath? Do not judge according to appearance, but judge with righteous judgment" (John 7:21–24; see Genesis 17:10–14; Leviticus 12:3; 19:15; Matthew 12:2; John 5:2–16; 7–20; 7:10–15).

Setting: The temple treasury in Jerusalem. After the scribes and Pharisees question His testimony about Himself, Jesus interacts with them regarding their ancestry and motives.

They answered and said to Him, "Abraham is our father." Jesus said to them, "If you are Abraham's children, do the deeds of Abraham. But as it is, you are seeking to kill Me, a man who has told you the truth, which I heard from God; this Abraham did not do. You are doing the deeds of your father." They said to Him, "We were not born of fornication; we have one Father: God" (John 8:39–41; see Romans 9:6, 7).

Setting: The temple treasury in Jerusalem. After Jesus avoids being stoned by the scribes and Pharisees, His disciples wonder if blindness is caused by sin as the Lord heals a man born blind.

Jesus answered, "*It was* neither *that* this man sinned, nor his parents; but *it was* so that the works of God might be displayed in him. We must work the works of Him who sent Me as long as it is day; night is coming when no one can work. While I am in the world, I am the Light of the world." When He had said this, He spat on the ground, and made clay of the spittle, and applied the clay to his eyes, and said to him, "Go, wash in the pool of Siloam" (which is translated, Sent). So he went away and washed, and came *back* seeing (John 9:3–7; see John 8:12; 11:4; 12:46).

Setting: Damascus. Luke, writing in Acts, conveys how the Lord instructs one of His disciples, Ananias, to locate Saul of Tarsus to touch him in order to restore Saul's vision.

Now there was a disciple at Damascus named Ananias; and the Lord said to him in a vision, "Ananias." And he said, "Here I am, Lord." And the Lord *said* to him, "Get up and go to the street called Straight, and inquire at the house of Judas for a man from Tarsus named Saul, for he is praying, and he was seen in a vision a man named Ananias come in and lay his hands on him, so that he might regain his sight" (Acts 9:10–12; see 22:12–14).

Setting: Corinth. Luke, writing in Acts, records the Lord's comforting revelation through a vision to Paul as he works among the Jews and Gentiles during his second missionary journey, testifying that Jesus is the Christ (Messiah).

And the Lord said to Paul in the night by a vision, "Do not be afraid *any longer,* but go on speaking and do not be silent; for I am with you, and no man will attack you in order to harm you, for I have many people in this city" (Acts 18:9, 10).

Setting: On the island of Patmos (in the Aegean Sea about fifty miles southwest of Ephesus in modern Turkey). In the final chapter of the Lord Jesus Christ's revelation via the disciple John, approximately fifty years after His resurrection, the Lord reveals His upcoming return, reward, and eternality.

"Behold, I am coming quickly, and My reward *is* with Me, to render to every man according to what he has done. I am the Alpha and the Omega, the first and the last, the beginning and the end" (Revelation 22:12, 13; see Isaiah 40:10; 44:6).

MAN, BLIND (Also see BLINDNESS; and MEN, SPIRITUALLY BLIND)

Setting: Galilee. After rebuking the Pharisees and scribes for questioning His disciples' obedience to tradition and the commandments, Jesus instructs His disciples.

But He answered and said, "Every plant which My heavenly Father did not plant shall be uprooted. Let them alone; they are blind guides of the blind. And if a blind man guides a blind man, both will fall into a pit" (Matthew 15:13, 14; cf. Matthew 23:16; Luke 6:39).

Setting: Galilee. After selecting His twelve disciples, Jesus teaches the Sermon on the Mount to those disciples and a great throng of people from Judea, Jerusalem, and the central coastal region of Tyre and Sidon.

And He also spoke a parable to them: "A blind man cannot guide a blind man, can he? Will they not both fall into a pit? A pupil is not above his teacher; but everyone, after he has been fully trained, will be like his teacher. Why do you look at the speck that is in your brother's eye, but do not notice the log that is in your own eye? Or how can you say to your brother, 'Brother, let me take out the speck that is in your eye,' when you yourself do not see the log that is in your own eye? You hypocrite, first take the log out of your own eye, and then you will see clearly to take out the speck that is in your brother's eye. For there is no good tree which produces bad fruit, nor, on the other hand, a bad tree which produces good fruit. For each tree is known by its own fruit. For men do not gather figs from thorns, nor do they pick grapes from a briar bush. The good man out of the good treasure of his heart brings forth what is good; and the evil *man* out of the evil *treasure* brings forth what is evil; for his mouth speaks from that which fills his heart" (Luke 6:39–45; cf. Matthew 7:3–6. 16, 18, 20; 12:35; see Matthew 10:24; 15:14; Luke 6:12–19).

MAN, CASTRATED (See EUNUCH)

MAN, EVIL (Also see EVIL; MEN, EVIL; and PERSON, EVIL)

Setting: Galilee. After Jesus heals a blind, mute, demon-possessed man, the Pharisees accuse Him in front of crowds of being a worker of Satan.

"Either make the tree good and its fruit good, or make the tree bad and its fruit bad; for the tree is known by its fruit. You brood of vipers, how can you, being evil, speak what is good? For the mouth speaks out of that which fills the heart. The good man brings out of *his* good treasure what is good; and the evil man brings out of *his* evil treasure what is evil. But I tell you that every careless word that people speak, they shall give an accounting for it in the day of judgment. For by your words you will be justified, and by your words you will be condemned" (Matthew 12:33–37; cf. Matthew 3:7; 7:16–18).

Setting: Galilee. After selecting His twelve disciples, Jesus teaches the Sermon on the Mount to those disciples and a great throng of people from Judea, Jerusalem, and the central coastal region of Tyre and Sidon.

And He also spoke a parable to them: "A blind man cannot guide a blind man, can he? Will they not both fall into a pit? A pupil is not above his teacher; but everyone, after he has been fully trained, will be like his teacher. Why do you look at the speck that is in your brother's eye, but do not notice the log that is in your own eye? Or how can you say to your brother, 'Brother, let me take out the speck that is in your eye,' when you yourself do not see the log that is in your own eye? You hypocrite, first take the log out of your own eye, and then you will see clearly to take out the speck that is in your brother's eye. For there is no good tree which produces bad fruit, nor, on the other hand, a bad tree which produces good fruit. For each tree is known by its own fruit. For men do not gather figs from thorns, nor do they pick grapes from a briar bush. The good man out of the good treasure of his heart brings forth what is good; and the evil *man* out of the evil *treasure* brings forth what is evil; for his mouth speaks from that which fills his heart" (Luke 6:39–45; cf. Matthew 7:3–6. 16, 18, 20; 12:35; see Matthew 10:24; 15:14; Luke 6:12–19).

MAN, EXACTING (Also see MAN, HARD)

Setting: Jericho, on the way to Jerusalem. After commending Zaccheus's faith in Him, Jesus provides a parable about stewardship.

So He said, "A nobleman went to a distant country to receive a kingdom for himself, and *then* return. And he called ten of his slaves, and gave them ten minas and said to them, 'Do business *with this* until I come *back.*' But his citizens hated him and sent a delegation after him, saying, 'We do not want this man to reign over us.' When he returned, after receiving the kingdom, he ordered that these slaves, to whom he had given the money, be called to him so that he might know what business they had done. The first appeared, saying, 'Master, your mina has made ten minas more.' And he said to him, 'Well done, good slave, because you have been faithful in a very little thing, you are to be in authority over ten cities.' The second came, saying, 'Your mina, master, has made five minas.' And he said to him, also, 'And you are to be over five cities.' Another came, saying, 'Master, here is your mina, which I kept put away in a handkerchief; for I was afraid of you, because you are an exacting man; you take up what you did not lay down and reap what you did not sow.' He said to him, 'By your own words I will judge you, you worthless slave. Did you know that I am an exacting man, taking up what I did not lay down and reaping what I did not sow? Then why did you not put my money in the bank, and having come, I would have collected it with interest?' Then he said to the bystanders, 'Take the mina away from him and give it to the one who has the ten minas.' And they said to him, 'Master, he has ten minas *already.*' I tell you that to everyone who has, more shall be given, but from the one who does not have, even what he does have shall be taken away. But these enemies of mine, who did not want me to reign over them, bring them here and slay them in my presence" (Luke 19:12–27; cf. Matthew 25:14–30; see Matthew 13:12; Luke 16:10).

MAN, FOOLISH (Also see FOOL; FOOLS; FOOLISHNESS; and MEN, FOOLISH)

Setting: Galilee. During the early part of His ministry, Jesus preaches the Sermon on the Mount to His disciples and the multitudes.

"Therefore everyone who hears these words of Mine and acts on them, may be compared to a wise man who built his house on the rock. And the rain fell, and the floods came, and the winds blew and slammed against that house; and *yet* it did not fall, for it had been founded on the rock. Everyone who hears these words of Mine and does not act on them, will be like a foolish man who built his house on the sand. The rain fell, and the floods came, and the winds blew and slammed against that house; and it fell—and great was its fall" (Matthew 7:24–28; cf. Luke 6:47–49).

MAN, GLUTTONOUS

Setting: Galilee. After praising John the Baptist as His forerunner, Jesus demonstrates the foolish thinking of the Jewish religious leaders by repeating what they say about John's ascetic lifestyle and ministry along with His own.

"But to what shall I compare this generation? It is like children sitting in the market places, who call out to the other *children,* and say, 'We played the flute for you, and you did not dance; we sang a dirge, and you did not mourn.' For John came neither eating nor drinking, and they say, 'He has a demon!' The Son of Man came eating and drinking, and they say, 'Behold, a gluttonous man and a drunkard, a friend of tax collectors and sinners! Yet wisdom is vindicated by her deeds" (Matthew 11:16–19; cf. Luke 7:31–35; see Matthew 9:11, 34; Luke 1:15).

Setting: Galilee. After praising John the Baptist to the crowds, Jesus criticizes the Pharisees and lawyers who reject God's purpose and John's message.

"To what then shall I compare the men of this generation, and what are they like? They are like children who sit in the market place and call to one another, and they say, 'We played the flute for you, and you did not dance; we sang a dirge, and you did not weep.' For John the Baptist has come eating no bread and drinking no wine, and you say, 'He has a demon!' The Son of Man has come eating and drinking, and you say, 'Behold, a gluttonous man and a drunkard, a friend of tax collectors and sinners!' Yet wisdom is vindicated by all her children" (Luke 7:31–35; cf. Matthew 11:16–19; see Luke 1:15).

MAN, GOOD

Setting: Galilee. After Jesus heals a blind, mute, demon-possessed man, the Pharisees accuse Him in front of crowds of being a worker of Satan.

"Either make the tree good and its fruit good, or make the tree bad and its fruit bad; for the tree is known by its fruit. You brood of vipers, how can you, being evil, speak what is good? For the mouth speaks out of that which fills the heart. The good man brings out of *his* good treasure what is good; and the evil man brings out of *his* evil treasure what is evil. But I tell you that every careless word that people speak, they shall give an accounting for it in the day of judgment. For by your words you will be justified, and by your words you will be condemned" (Matthew 12:33–37; cf. Matthew 3:7; 7:16–18).

Setting: Galilee. After selecting His twelve disciples, Jesus teaches the Sermon on the Mount to those disciples and a great throng of people from Judea, Jerusalem, and the central coastal region of Tyre and Sidon.

And He also spoke a parable to them: "A blind man cannot guide a blind man, can he? Will they not both fall into a pit? A pupil is not above his teacher; but everyone, after he has been fully trained, will be like his teacher. Why do you look at the speck that is in your brother's eye, but do not notice the log that is in your own eye? Or how can you say to your brother, 'Brother, let me take out the speck that is in your eye,' when you yourself do not see the log that is in your own eye? You hypocrite, first take the log out of your own eye, and then you will see clearly to take out the speck that is in your brother's eye. For there is no good tree which produces bad fruit, nor, on the other hand, a bad tree which produces good fruit. For each tree is known by its own fruit. For men do not gather figs from thorns, nor do they pick grapes from a briar bush. The good man out of the good treasure of his heart brings forth what is good; and the evil *man* out of the evil *treasure* brings forth what is evil; for his mouth speaks from that which fills his heart" (Luke 6:39–45; cf. Matthew 7:3–6. 16, 18, 20; 12:35; see Matthew 10:24; 15:14; Luke 6:12–19).

MAN, HARD (Also see MAN, EXACTING)

Setting: The Mount of Olives, just east of Jerusalem. During His Olivet Discourse, after answering His disciples' questions as to when the temple will be destroyed and Jerusalem overrun, along with the signs of His coming and the end of the age, Jesus reemphasizes to His disciples that they should be on the alert for His return.

"For *it is* just like a man *about* to go on a journey, who called his own slaves and entrusted his possessions to them. To one he gave five talents, to another, two, and to another, one, each according to his own ability; and he went on his journey. Immediately the one who had received the five talents went and traded with them, and gained five more talents. In the same manner the one who *had received* the two *talents* gained two more. But he who received the one *talent* went away, and dug a *hole* in the ground and hid his master's money. Now after a long time the master of those slaves came and settled accounts with them. The one who had received the five talents came up and brought five more talents, saying, 'Master, you entrusted five talents to me. See, I have gained five more talents.' His master said to him, 'Well done, good and faithful slave. You were faithful with a few things, I will put you in charge of many things; enter into the joy of your master.' Also the one who *had received* the two talents came up and said, 'Master, you entrusted two talents to me. See, I have gained two more talents.' His master said to him, 'Well done, good and faithful slave. You were faithful with a few things, I will put you in charge of many things; enter into the joy of your master.' And the one also who had received the one talent came up and said, 'Master, I knew you to be a hard man, reaping where you did not sow and gathering where you scattered no *seed.* And I was afraid, and went away and hid your talent in the ground. See, you have what is yours.' But his master answered and said to him, 'You wicked, lazy slave, you knew that I reap where I did not sow and gather where I scattered no *seed.* Then you ought to have put my money in the bank, and on my arrival I would have received my *money* back with interest. 'Therefore take away the talent from him, and give it to the one who has ten talents.' For to everyone who has, *more* shall be given, and he will have an abundance; but from the one who does not have, even what he does have shall be taken away. Throw out the worthless slave into the outer darkness; in that place there will be weeping and gnashing of teeth" (Matthew 25:14–30; cf. Matthew 8:12; 13:12; 24:45–47; see Matthew 18:23, 24; Luke 12:44).

MAN, PARABLE OF THE RICH MAN

[PARABLE OF THE RICH MAN from parable and rich man]

Setting: On the way from Galilee to Jerusalem. After the scribes and Pharisees turn hostile and question Him repeatedly in an attempt to catch Him in something He might say, Jesus responds to a question from the crowd and gives a parable about riches and greed.

And He told them a parable, saying, "The land of a rich man was very productive. And he began reasoning to himself, saying, 'What shall I do, since I have no place to store my crops?' Then he said, 'This is what I will do: I will tear down my barns and build larger ones, and here I will store all my grain and my goods. And I will say to my soul, "Soul, you have many goods laid up for many years *to come;* take your ease, eat, drink *and* be merry."' "But God said to him, 'You fool! This *very* night your soul is required of you; and *now* who will own what you have prepared?' So is the man who stores up treasure for himself, and is not rich toward God" (Luke 12:16–21; see Job 27:8; Psalm 39:6; Ecclesiastes 12:9; Philippians 2:3).

MAN, PARALYZED (See CRIPPLED; and LAME)

MAN, PHYSICALLY BLIND (See MAN, BLIND; and BLINDNESS)

MAN, POOR

Setting: On the way from Galilee to Jerusalem. After responding to the Pharisees' scoffing at His teaching the disciples about stewardship and the permanence of the Law, Jesus conveys the story of the rich man and Lazarus.

"Now there was a rich man, and he habitually dressed in purple and fine linen, joyously living in splendor every day. And a poor man named Lazarus was laid at his gate, covered with sores, and longing to be fed with the *crumbs* which were falling from the rich man's table; besides, even the dogs were coming and licking his sores. Now the poor man died and was carried away by the angels to Abraham's bosom; and the rich man also died and was buried. In Hades he lifted up his eyes, being in torment, and saw Abraham far away and Lazarus in his bosom. And he cried out and said, 'Father Abraham, have mercy on me, and send Lazarus so that he may dip the tip of his finger in water and cool off my tongue, for I am in agony in this flame.' But Abraham said, 'Child, remember that during your life you received your good things, and likewise Lazarus bad things; but now he is being comforted here, and you are in agony. And besides all this, between us and you there is a great chasm fixed, so that those who wish to come over from here to you will not be able, and *that* none may cross over from there to us.' And he said, 'Then I beg you, father, that you send him to my father's house—for I have five brothers—in order that he may warn them, so that they will not also come to this place of torment.' But Abraham said, 'They have Moses and the Prophets; let them hear them.' But he said, 'No, father Abraham, but if someone goes to them from the dead, they will repent!' But he said to him, 'If they do not listen to Moses and the Prophets, they will not be persuaded even if someone rises from the dead' " (Luke 16:19–31; see Luke 3:8; 6:24; 16:1, 14).

MAN, RICH (Also see WEALTH)

Setting: Judea beyond the Jordan (Perea). Jesus comments to His disciples about the rich, young ruler who asks how he can obtain eternal life but rejects Jesus' instruction to sell his possessions and give the proceeds to the poor.

And Jesus said to His disciples, "Truly I say to you, it is hard for a rich man to enter the kingdom of heaven. Again, I say to you, it is easier for a camel to go through the eye of a needle, than for a rich man to enter the kingdom of God" (Matthew 19:23, 24; cf. Matthew 13:22; Mark 10:23–25; Luke 18:24).

Setting: Judea beyond the Jordan (Perea). After informing a rich man how righteous believers may have treasure in heaven, Jesus conveys to His disciples the difficulty the wealthy have entering the kingdom of God.

And Jesus, looking around, said to His disciples, "How hard it will be for those who are wealthy to enter the kingdom of God!" The disciples were amazed at His words. But Jesus answered again and said to them, "Children, how hard it is to enter the kingdom of God! It is easier for a camel to go through the eye of a needle than for a rich man to enter the kingdom of God." They were even more astonished and said to Him, "Then who can be saved?" Looking at them, Jesus said, "With people it is impossible, but not with God; for all things are possible with God" (Mark 10:23–27; cf. Matthew 19:23–26; Luke 18:24, 25).

Setting: On the way from Galilee to Jerusalem. After the scribes and Pharisees turn hostile and question Him repeatedly in an attempt to catch Him in something He might say, Jesus responds to a question from the crowd and gives a parable about riches and greed.

And He told them a parable, saying, "The land of a rich man was very productive. And he began reasoning to himself, saying, 'What shall I do, since I have no place to store my crops?' Then he said, 'This is what I will do: I will tear down my barns and build larger ones, and there I will store all my grain and my goods. And I will say to my soul, "Soul, you have many goods laid up for many years *to come;* take your ease, eat, drink *and* be merry."' "But God said to him, 'You fool! This *very* night your soul is required of you; and *now* who will own what you have prepared?' So is the man who stores up treasure for himself, and is not rich toward God" (Luke 12:16–21; see Job 27:8; Psalm 39:6; Ecclesiastes 12:9; Philippians 2:3).

Setting: On the way from Galilee to Jerusalem. After giving the story of the prodigal son, the Lord teaches His disciples about stewardship.

Now He was also saying to the disciples, "There was a rich man who had a manager, and this *manager* was reported to him as squandering his possessions. And he called him and said to him, 'What is this I hear about you? Give an accounting of your management, for you can no longer be a manager.' The manager said to himself, 'What shall I do, since my master is taking the management away from me? I am not strong enough to dig; I am ashamed to beg. I know what I shall do, so that when I am removed from the management people will welcome me into their homes.' And he summoned each one of his master's debtors, and he *began* saying to the first, 'How much do you owe my master?' And he said, 'A hundred measures of oil.' And he said to him, 'Take your bill, and sit down quickly and write fifty.' Then he said to another, 'And how much do you owe?' And he said, 'A hundred measures of wheat.' He said to him, 'Take your bill, and write eighty.' And his master praised the unrighteous manager because he had acted shrewdly; for the sons of this age are more shrewd in relation to their own kind than the sons of light. And I say to you, make friends for yourselves by means of the wealth of unrighteousness, so that when it fails, they will receive you into the eternal dwellings. He who is faithful in a very little thing is faithful also in much; and he who is unrighteous in a very little thing is unrighteous also in much. Therefore if you have not been faithful in the *use of* unrighteous wealth, who will entrust the true *riches* to you? And if you have not been faithful in *the use of* that which is another's, who will give you that which is your own? No servant can serve two masters; for either he will hate the one and love the other, or else he will be devoted to one and despise the other. You cannot serve God and wealth" (Luke 16:1–13; cf. Matthew 6:24; see Matthew 25:14–30).

Setting: On the way from Galilee to Jerusalem. After responding to the Pharisees' scoffing at His teaching the disciples about stewardship and the permanence of the Law, Jesus conveys the story of the rich man and Lazarus.

"Now there was a rich man, and he habitually dressed in purple and fine linen, joyously living in splendor every day. And a poor man named Lazarus was laid at his gate, covered with sores, and longing to be fed with the *crumbs* which were falling from the rich man's table; besides, even the dogs were coming and licking his sores. Now the poor man died and was carried away by the angels to Abraham's bosom; and the rich man also died and was buried. In Hades he lifted up his eyes, being in torment, and saw Abraham far away and Lazarus in his bosom. And he cried out and said, 'Father Abraham, have mercy on me, and send Lazarus so that he may dip the tip of his finger in water and cool off my tongue, for I am in agony in this flame.' But Abraham said, 'Child, remember that during your life you received your good things, and likewise Lazarus bad things; but now he is being comforted here, and you are in agony. And besides all this, between us and you there is a great chasm fixed, so that those who wish to come over from here to you will not be able, and *that* none may cross over from there to us.' And he said, 'Then I beg you, father, that you send him to my father's house—for I have five brothers—in order that he may warn them, so that they will not also come to this place of torment.' But Abraham said, 'They have Moses and the Prophets; let them hear them.' But he said, 'No, father Abraham, but if someone goes to them from the dead, they will repent!' But he said to him, 'If they do not listen to Moses and the Prophets, they will not be persuaded even if someone rises from the dead'" (Luke 16:19–31; see Luke 3:8; 6:24; 16:1, 14).

Setting: On the way from Galilee to Jerusalem. After responding to a ruler's question about obtaining eternal life, Jesus comments to him about the challenge of being wealthy and saved.

And Jesus looked at him and said, "How hard it is for those who are wealthy to enter the kingdom of God! For it is easier for a camel to go through the eye of a needle than for a rich man to enter the kingdom of God" (Luke 18:24, 25; cf. Matthew 19:23, 24; Mark 10:25).

MAN, RIGHTEOUS

Setting: Galilee. After His twelve disciples observe His ministry, Jesus summons and specifically instructs them about their ministry ahead that will include rewards.

"He who receives you receives Me, and he who receives Me receives Him who sent me. He who receives a prophet in the name of a prophet shall receive a prophet's reward; and he who receives a righteous man in the name of a righteous man shall receive a righteous man's reward. And whoever in the name of a disciple gives to one of these little ones even a cup of cold water to drink, truly I say to you, he shall not lose his reward" (Matthew 10:40–42; cf. Matthew 25:40, 44, 45; see Mark 9:37).

MAN, SON OF (See SON OF MAN)

MAN, STERILE (See CELIBACY; and EUNUCH)

MAN, STRONG

Setting: Galilee. After Jesus heals a blind, mute, demon-possessed man, the Pharisees accuse the Lord in front of crowds of being a worker of Beelzebul (Satan).

And knowing their thoughts Jesus said to them, "Any kingdom divided against itself is laid waste; and any city or house divided against itself will not stand. If Satan casts out Satan, he is divided against himself; how then will his kingdom stand? If I by Beelzebul cast out demons, by whom do your sons cast *them* out? For this reason they will be your judges. But if I cast out demons by the Spirit of God, then the kingdom of God has come upon you. Or how can anyone enter the strong man's house and carry off his property, unless he first binds the strong *man?* And then he will plunder his house" (Matthew 12:25–29; cf. Matthew 9:34; Mark 3:23–27; Luke 11:17–20).

Setting: Galilee. After Jesus selects His twelve disciples, scribes from Jerusalem attribute His miraculous powers to Satan.

And He called them to Himself and began speaking to them in parables, "How can Satan cast out Satan? If a kingdom is divided against itself, that kingdom cannot stand. If a house is divided against itself, that house will not be able to stand. If Satan has risen up against himself and is divided, he cannot stand, but he is finished! But no one can enter the strong man's house and plunder his property unless he first binds the strong man, and then he will plunder his house. Truly I say to you, all sins shall be forgiven the sons of men, and whatever blasphemies they utter; but whoever blasphemes against the Holy Spirit never has forgiveness, but is guilty of an eternal sin"—because they were saying, "He has an unclean spirit" (Mark 3:23–30; cf. Matthew 12:25–32; Luke 12:10).

Setting: On the way from Galilee to Jerusalem. After some in the crowd test Him, demanding a sign from heaven, Jesus illustrates His power over Satan.

"When a strong *man*, fully armed, guards his own house, his possessions are undisturbed. But when someone stronger than he attacks him and overpowers him, he takes away from him all his armor on which he had relied and distributes his plunder. He who is not with Me is against Me; and he who does not gather with Me, scatters" (Luke 11:21–23; cf. Matthew 12:29, 30).

MAN, VALUE OF (See HUMAN VALUE)

MAN, WISE (Also see MEN, WISE)

Setting: Galilee. During the early part of His ministry, Jesus preaches the Sermon on the Mount to His disciples and the multitudes.

"Therefore everyone who hears these words of Mine and acts on them, may be compared to a wise man who built his house on the rock. And the rain fell, and the floods came, and the winds blew and slammed against that house; and *yet* it did not fall, for it had been founded on the rock. Everyone who hears these words of Mine and does not act on them, will be like a foolish man who built his house on the sand. The rain fell, and the floods came, and the winds blew and slammed against that house; and it fell—and great was its fall" (Matthew 7:24–28; cf. Luke 6:47–49).

MAN, YOUNG

Setting: Galilee. After healing a Roman centurion's slave in Capernaum from a distance, Jesus travels to Nain, where He raises a young man from the dead.

When the Lord saw her, He felt compassion for her and said to her, "Do not weep." And He came up and touched the coffin; and the bearers came to a halt. And He said, "Young man, I say to you, arise!" (Luke 7:13, 14).

MAN'S APPROVAL (Listed under APPROVAL, MAN'S)

MAN'S INTERESTS (Listed under INTERESTS, MAN'S)

MAN OF PEACE (Listed under PEACE, MAN OF)

MANAGER

Setting: On the way from Galilee to Jerusalem. After giving the story of the prodigal son, the Lord teaches His disciples about stewardship.

Now He was also saying to the disciples, "There was a rich man who had a manager, and this *manager* was reported to him as squandering his possessions. And he called him and said to him, 'What is this I hear about you? Give an accounting of your management, for you can no longer be a manager.' The manager said to himself, 'What shall I do, since my master is taking the management away from me? I am not strong enough to dig; I am ashamed to beg. I know what I shall do, so that when I am removed from the management people will welcome me into their homes.' And he summoned each one of his master's debtors, and he *began* saying to the first, 'How much do you owe my master?' And he said, 'A hundred measures of oil.' And he said to him, 'Take your bill, and sit down quickly and write fifty.' Then he said to another, 'And how much do you owe?' And he said, 'A hundred measures of wheat.' He said to him, 'Take your bill, and write eighty.' And his master praised the unrighteous manager because he had acted shrewdly; for the sons of this age are more shrewd in relation to their own kind than the sons of light. And I say to you, make friends for yourselves by means of the wealth of unrighteousness, so that when it fails, they will receive you into the eternal dwellings. He who is faithful in a very little thing is faithful also in much; and he who is unrighteous in a very little thing is unrighteous also in much. Therefore if you have not been faithful in the *use of* unrighteous wealth, who will entrust the true *riches* to you? And if you have not been faithful in *the use of* that which is another's, who will give you that which is your own? No servant can serve two masters; for either he will hate the one and love the other, or else he will be devoted to one and despise the other. You cannot serve God and wealth" (Luke 16:1–13; cf. Matthew 6:24; see Matthew 25:14–30).

MANAGER, DISHONEST (See MANAGER)

MANAGER, SHREWD (See MANAGER)

MANAGER, UNRIGHTEOUS (See MANAGER)

MANAGEMENT (Also see STEWARDSHIP)

Setting: On the way from Galilee to Jerusalem. After giving the story of the prodigal son, the Lord teaches His disciples about stewardship.

Now He was also saying to the disciples, "There was a rich man who had a manager, and this *manager* was reported to him as squandering his possessions. And he called him and said to him, 'What is this I hear about you? Give an accounting of your management, for you can no longer be a manager.' The manager said to himself, 'What shall I do, since my master is taking the management away from me? I am not strong enough to dig; I am ashamed to beg. I know what I shall do, so that when I am removed from the management people will welcome me into their homes.' And he summoned each one of his master's debtors, and he *began* saying to the first, 'How much do you owe my master?' And he said, 'A hundred measures of oil.' And he said to him, 'Take your bill, and sit down quickly and write fifty.' Then he said to another, 'And how much do you owe?' And he said, 'A hundred measures of wheat.' He said to him, 'Take your bill, and write eighty.' And his master praised the unrighteous manager because he had acted shrewdly; for the sons of this age are more shrewd in relation to their own kind than the sons of light. And I say to you, make friends for yourselves by means of the wealth of unrighteousness, so that when it fails, they will receive you into the eternal dwellings. He who is faithful in a very little thing is faithful also in much; and he who is unrighteous in a very little thing is unrighteous also in much. Therefore if you have not been faithful in the *use of* unrighteous wealth, who will entrust the true *riches* to you? And if you have not been faithful in *the use of* that which is another's, who will give you that which is your own? No servant can serve two masters; for either he will hate the one and love the other, or else he will be devoted to one and despise the other. You cannot serve God and wealth" (Luke 16:1–13; cf. Matthew 6:24; see Matthew 25:14–30).

MANDATE, CHRISTIAN (See GREAT COMMISSION)

MANNA

Setting: Capernaum of Galilee. After Jesus informs the people whom He miraculously fed with a lad's five loaves and two fish how they might receive the bread out of heaven, the Jewish religious leaders grumble when the Lord claims He came down out of heaven.

Therefore the Jews were grumbling about Him, because He said, "I am the bread that came down out of heaven." They were saying, "Is not this Jesus, the son of Joseph, whose father and mother we know? How does He now say, 'I have come down out of heaven'?" Jesus answered and said to them, "Do not grumble among yourselves. No one can come to Me unless the Father who sent Me draws him; and I will raise him up on the last day. It is written in the prophets, 'AND THEY SHALL ALL BE TAUGHT OF GOD.' Everyone who has heard and learned from the Father, comes to Me. Not that anyone has seen the Father, except the One who is from God; He has seen the Father. Truly, truly, I say to you, he who believes has eternal life. I am the bread of life. Your fathers ate the manna in the wilderness, and they died. This is the bread which comes down out of heaven, so that one may eat of it and not die. I am the living bread that came down out of heaven; if anyone eats of this bread, he will live forever; and the bread also which I will give for the life of the world is My flesh" (John 6:41–51, Jesus quotes from Isaiah 54:13; see John 1:18, 29; 3:36; 7:27).

Setting: On the island of Patmos (in the Aegean Sea about fifty miles southwest of Ephesus in modern Turkey). On the Lord's Day (Sunday), approximately fifty years after Jesus' resurrection, the disciple John encounters the Lord Jesus Christ, who communicates a new revelation for the apostle to record for the church in Pergamum and to six other churches in Asia.

"And to the angel of the church in Pergamum write: The One who has the sharp two-edged sword says this: 'I know where you dwell, where Satan's throne is; and you hold fast My name, and did not deny My faith even in the days of Antipas, My witness, My faithful one, who was killed among you, where Satan dwells. But I have a few things against you, because you have there some who hold the teaching of Balaam, who kept teaching Balak to put a stumbling block before the sons of Israel, to eat things sacrificed to idols and to commit *acts of* immorality. So you also have some who in the same way hold the teaching of the Nicolaitans. Therefore repent; or else I am coming to you quickly, and I will make war against them with the sword of My mouth. He who has an ear, let him hear what the Spirit says to the churches. To him who overcomes, to him I will give *some* of the hidden manna, and I will give him a white stone, and a new name written on the stone which no one knows but he who receives it' (Revelation 2:12–17; see Numbers 25:1–3; Isaiah 62:2; Revelation 1:16; 2:5, 6, 16).

MANNA, HIDDEN (See MANNA)

MANNER

Setting: On the Mount of Olives, just east of Jerusalem. During His Olivet Discourse, after answering His disciples' questions as to when the temple will be destroyed and Jerusalem overrun, along with the signs of His coming and the end of the age, Jesus reemphasizes to His disciples that they should be on the alert for His return.

"For *it is* just like a man *about* to go on a journey, who called his own slaves and entrusted his possessions to them. To one he gave five talents, to another, two, and to another, one, each according to his own ability; and he went on his journey. Immediately the one who had received the five talents went and traded with them, and gained five more talents. In the same manner the one who *had received* the two *talents* gained two more. But he who received the one *talent* went away, and dug a *hole* in the ground and hid his master's money. Now after a long time the master of those slaves came and settled accounts with them. The one who had received the five talents came up and brought five more talents, saying, 'Master, you entrusted five talents to me. See, I have gained five more talents.' His master said to him, 'Well done, good and faithful slave. You were faithful with a few things, I will put you in charge of many things; enter into the joy of your master.' Also the one who *had received* the two talents came up and said, 'Master, you entrusted two talents to me. See, I have gained two more talents.' His master said to him, 'Well done, good and faithful slave. You were faithful with a few things, I will put you in charge of many things; enter into the joy of your master.' And the one also who had received the one talent came up and said, 'Master, I knew you to be a hard man, reaping where you did not sow and gathering where you scattered no *seed.* And I was afraid, and went away and hid your talent in the ground. See, you have what is yours.' But his master answered and said to him, 'You wicked, lazy slave, you knew that I reap where

I did not sow and gather where I scattered no *seed.* Then you ought to have put my money in the bank, and on my arrival I would have received my *money* back with interest. 'Therefore take away the talent from him, and give it to the one who has ten talents.' For to everyone who has, *more* shall be given, and he will have an abundance; but from the one who does not have, even what he does have shall be taken away. Throw out the worthless slave into the outer darkness; in that place there will be weeping and gnashing of teeth" (Matthew 25:14–30; cf. Matthew 8:12; 13:12; 24:45–47; see Matthew 18:23, 24; Luke 12:44).

Setting: By the pool of Bethesda in Jerusalem. During a feast of the Jews, Jesus responds to criticism from the Jewish religious leaders for healing a lame man on the Sabbath and for referring to God as His Father (thereby making Himself equal with God).

Therefore Jesus answered and was saying to them, "Truly, truly, I say to you, the Son can do nothing of Himself, unless *it is* something He sees the Father doing; for whatever the Father does, these things the Son also does in like manner. For the Father loves the Son, and shows Him all things that He Himself is doing; and *the Father* will show Him greater works than these, so that you will marvel. For just as the Father raises the dead and gives them life, even so the Son also gives life to whom He wishes. For not even the Father judges anyone, but He has given all judgment to the Son, so that all will honor the Son even as they honor the Father. He who does not honor the Son does not honor the Father who sent Him" (John 5:19–23; see Luke 10:16; John 3:35; 11:25; 14:12).

MANUAL LABOR (Listed under LABOR, MANUAL)

MANURE PILE (Listed under PILE, MANURE)

MARANATHA (See JESUS' RETURN; and LORD, COMING OF THE)

MARKET PLACE (Listed under PLACE, MARKET; also see PLACES, MARKET)

MARKET PLACES (Listed under PLACES, MARKET; also see PLACE, MARKET)

MARRIAGE (MARRIAGE, LEVIRATE is a separate entry; also see DIVORCE; FLESH, ONE; HUSBAND; REMARRIAGE; WEDDING; and WIFE)

[MARRIAGE from marries]

Setting: Galilee. During the early part of His ministry, Jesus preaches the Sermon on the Mount to His disciples and the multitudes.

"It was said, 'WHOEVER SENDS HIS WIFE AWAY, LET HIM GIVE HER A CERTIFICATE OF DIVORCE'; but I say to you that everyone who divorces his wife, except for *the* reason of unchastity, makes her commit adultery; and whoever marries a divorced woman commits adultery" (Matthew 5:31, 32, Jesus quotes from Deuteronomy 24: 1, 3; cf. Matthew 19:9; see Romans 7:2, 3; 1 Corinthians 7:10, 39).

[MARRIAGE from BE JOINED and joined together]

Setting: Judea beyond the Jordan (Perea). After Jesus replies to Peter's question about forgiveness, in front of a large crowd, the Pharisees test the Lord with a question about divorce.

And He answered and said, "Have you not read that He who created *them* from the beginning MADE THEM MALE AND FEMALE, and said, 'FOR THIS REASON A MAN SHALL LEAVE HIS FATHER AND MOTHER AND BE JOINED TO HIS WIFE, AND THE TWO SHALL BECOME ONE FLESH'? So they are no longer two, but one flesh. What therefore God has joined together, let no man separate" (Matthew 19:4–6, Jesus quotes from Genesis 1:27; 2:24; cf. Mark 10:5–9; see 1 Timothy 2:14).

[MARRIAGE from marries]

Setting: Judea beyond the Jordan (Perea). In front of a large crowd, Jesus responds to the Pharisees' follow-up question about Moses' command regarding a certificate of divorce.

He said to them. "Because of your hardness of heart Moses permitted you to divorce your wives; but from the beginning it has not been this way. And I say to you, whoever divorces his wife, except for immorality, and marries another woman commits adultery" (Matthew 19:8, 9; cf. Deuteronomy 24:1–4; Matthew 5:32; 19:7; Mark 10:1–12; see Romans 7:2, 3; 1 Corinthians 7:10, 39).

Setting: On the Mount of Olives, just east of Jerusalem. During His Olivet Discourse, after answering His disciples' questions as to when the temple will be destroyed and Jerusalem overrun, along with the signs of His coming and the end of the age, Jesus teaches them the Parable of the Fig Tree.

"Now learn the parable from the fig tree: when its branch has already become tender and puts forth its leaves, you know that summer is near; so, you too, when you see all these things, recognize that He is near, *right* at the door. Truly, I say to you, this generation will not pass away until all these things take place. Heaven and earth will pass away, but My words will not pass away. But of that day and hour no one knows, not even the angels of heaven, nor the Son, but the Father alone. For the coming of the Son of Man will be just like the days of Noah. For as in those days before the flood they were eating and drinking, marrying and giving in marriage, until the day that Noah entered the ark, and they did not understand until the flood came and took them all away; so will the coming of the Son of Man be. Then there will be two men in the field; one will be taken and one will be left. Two women *will be* grinding at the mill; one will be taken and one will be left" (Matthew 24:32–41; cf. Mark 13:28–32; Luke 17:34–36; 21:28–33; see Genesis 6:5; 7:7; Matthew 5:18; 10:23; James 5:9).

[MARRIAGE from marries and joined together]
Setting: Judea beyond the Jordan (Perea). Jesus teaches the crowds gathered around Him about divorce after the Pharisees test and question Him on the subject.

And He answered and said to them, "What did Moses command you?" They said, "Moses permitted a *man* TO WRITE A CERTIFICATE OF DIVORCE AND SEND *her* AWAY." But Jesus said to them, "Because of your hardness of heart he wrote you this commandment. But from the beginning of creation, *God* MADE THEM MALE AND FEMALE. FOR THIS REASON A MAN SHALL LEAVE HIS FATHER AND MOTHER, AND THE TWO SHALL BECOME ONE FLESH; so they are no longer two, but one flesh. What therefore God has joined together, let no man separate. In the house the disciples *began* questioning Him about this again. And He said to them, "Whoever divorces his wife and marries another woman commits adultery against her; and if she herself divorces her husband and marries another man, she is committing adultery" (Mark 10:3–12, Jesus quotes from Genesis 1:27; 2:24; cf. Matthew 19:1–9; see Deuteronomy 24:1–3; Matthew 5:32; see Romans 7:2, 3; 1 Corinthians 7:10, 11, 13, 39; 1 Timothy 2:14).

[MARRIAGE from married]
Setting: On the way from Galilee to Jerusalem. After speaking a parable to the invited guests and the host at a banquet, Jesus responds to a guest's proclamation about the blessings of eating bread in the kingdom of God.

But He said to him, "A man was giving a big dinner, and he invited many; and at the dinner hour he sent his slave to say to those who had been invited, 'Come; for everything is ready now.' But they all alike began to make excuses. The first one said to him, 'I have bought a piece of land and I need to go out and look at it; please consider me excused.' Another one said, 'I have bought five yoke of oxen, and I am going to try them out; please consider me excused.' Another one said, I have married a wife, and for that reason I cannot come.' And the slave came *back* and reported this to his master. Then the head of the household became angry and said to his slave, 'Go out at once into the streets and lanes of the city and bring in here the poor and crippled and blind and lame.' And the slave said, 'Master, what you commanded has been done, and still there is room.' And the master said to the slave, 'Go out into the highways and along the hedges, and compel *them* to come in, so that my house may be filled. For I tell you, none of those men who were invited shall taste of my dinner'" (Luke 14:16–24; see Deuteronomy 24:5; Matthew 22:2–14).

[MARRIAGE from marries]
Setting: On the way from Galilee to Jerusalem. The Lord responds to the Pharisees' scoffing at His teaching His disciples about stewardship with an illustration of the earthly commitment of marriage.

"Everyone who divorces his wife and marries another commits adultery, and he who marries one who is divorced from a husband commits adultery" (Luke 16:18; cf. Matthew 5:31, 32; 19:9; Mark 10:11, 12; see Romans 7:2, 3; 1 Corinthians 7:10, 39).

Setting: On the way from Galilee to Jerusalem. After the Pharisees question Him about the coming of the kingdom of God, Jesus tells His disciples of His second coming.

And He said to the disciples, "The days will come when you will long to see one of the days of the Son of Man, and you will not see it. They will say to you, 'Look there! Look here!' Do not go away, and do not run after *them.* For just like the lightning, when it flashes out of one part of the sky, shines to the other part of the sky, so will the Son of Man be in His day. But first He must suffer many things and be rejected by this generation. And just as it happened in the days of Noah, so it will be also in the days of the Son of Man: they were eating, they were drinking, they were marrying, they were being given in marriage, until the day that Noah entered the ark, and the flood came and destroyed them all. It was the same as happened in the days of Lot: they were eating, they were drinking, they were buying, they were selling, they were planting, they were building; but on the day that Lot went out from Sodom it rained fire and brimstone from heaven and destroyed them all. It will be just the same on the day that the Son of Man is revealed. On that day, the one who is on the housetop and whose goods are in the house must not go down to take them out; and likewise the one who is in the field must not turn back. Remember Lot's wife. Whoever seeks to keep his life will lose it, and whoever loses *his life* will preserve it. I tell you, on that night there will be two in one bed; one will be taken and the other will be left. There will be two women grinding at the same place; one will be taken and the other will be left. [Two men will be in the field; one will be taken and the other will be left."] And answering they said to Him, "Where, Lord?" And He said to them, "Where the body *is,* there also the vultures will be gathered" (" (Luke 17:22–37; see Genesis 19; Matthew 10:39; 16:21, 27; 24:17–28, 37–41).

MARRIAGE, LEVIRATE (Also see MARRIAGE)

[LEVIRATE MARRIAGE inferred from context]
Setting: The temple in Jerusalem. The Sadducees question Jesus about Levirate marriage (marriage to a brother-in-law), in order to test Him.

But Jesus answered and said to them, "You are mistaken, not understanding the Scriptures nor the power of God. For in the resurrection they neither marry nor are given in marriage, but are like angels in heaven. But regarding the resurrection of the dead, have you not read what was spoken to you by God: 'I AM THE GOD OF ABRAHAM, AND THE GOD OF ISAAC, AND THE GOD OF JACOB'? He is not the God of the dead but of the living" (Matthew 22:29–32, Jesus quotes from Exodus 3:6; cf. Mark 12:18–27; Luke 20:27–38; see Deuteronomy 25:5; John 20:9).

[LEVIRATE MARRIAGE inferred from context]
Setting: The temple in Jerusalem. After some of the Pharisees and Herodians attempt to trap Jesus in a statement, some Sadducees question Him about the status of marriage after death.

Jesus said to them, "Is this not the reason you are mistaken, that you do not understand the Scriptures or the power of God? For when they rise from the dead, they neither marry nor are given in marriage, but are like angels in heaven. But regarding the fact that the dead rise again, have you not read in the book of Moses, in the *passage* about *the burning* bush, how God spoke to him, saying, 'I AM THE GOD OF ABRAHAM, AND THE GOD OF ISAAC, and the God of Jacob?' He is not the God of the dead, but of the living; you are greatly mistaken" (Mark 12:24–27, Jesus quotes from Exodus 3:6; cf. Matthew 22:29–33; Luke 20:34–40).

[LEVIRATE MARRIAGE inferred from context]
Setting: The temple in Jerusalem. While ministering a few days before His crucifixion, after the scribes and Pharisees seek to trap Jesus by questioning Him about paying taxes to Caesar, some Sadducees (who say that there is no resurrection) ask Him a question about the resurrection.

Jesus said to them, "The sons of this age marry and are given in marriage, but those who are considered worthy to attain to that age and the resurrection from the dead, neither marry nor are given in marriage; for they cannot even die anymore, because they are like angels, and are sons of God, being sons of the resurrection. But that the dead are raised, even Moses showed, in the *passage about the burning* bush, where he calls the Lord THE GOD OF ABRAHAM, AND THE GOD OF ISAAC, AND THE GOD OF JACOB. Now He is not the God of the dead but of the living; for all live to Him" (Luke 20:34–38, Jesus quotes from Exodus 3:6; cf. Matthew 22:23–32; Mark 12:18–27).

MARRIES (See MARRIAGE; and REMARRIAGE)

MARTHA

Setting: On the way from Galilee to Jerusalem. After being tested by a lawyer, the Lord and His disciples are welcomed into the home of Martha and Mary in Bethany.

But the Lord answered and said to her, "Martha, Martha, you are worried and bothered about so many things; but *only* one thing is necessary, for Mary has chosen the good part, which shall not be taken away from her" (Luke 10:41, 42; see Matthew 6:25).

MARTYRDOM (See MARTYRS; and PROPHETS, BLOOD OF THE)

MARTYRS (Also see MARTYRDOM; and PROPHETS, BLOOD OF THE)

[MARTYRS from will kill you]

Setting: The Mount of Olives, just east of Jerusalem. During His Olivet Discourse, Jesus answers His disciples' questions as to when the temple will be destroyed and Jerusalem overrun, along with the signs of His coming and the end of the age.

And Jesus answered and said to them, "See to it that no one misleads you. For many will come in My name, saying, 'I am the Christ,' and will mislead many. You will be hearing of wars and rumors of wars. See that you are not frightened, for *those things* must take place, but *that* is not yet the end. For nation will rise against nation, and kingdom against kingdom, and in various places there will be famines and earthquakes. But all these things are *merely* the beginning of birth pangs. Then they will deliver you to tribulation, and will kill you, and you will be hated by all nations because of My name. At that time many will fall away and will betray one another and hate one another. Many false prophets will arise and will mislead many. Because lawlessness is increased, most people's love will grow cold. But the one who endures to the end, he will be saved. This gospel of the kingdom shall be preached in the whole world as a testimony to all the nations, and then the end will come" (Matthew 24:4–14; cf. Jeremiah 29:8; Matthew 7:15; 10:17, 22; Mark 13:3–13; Luke 21:7–19; Revelation 6:4).

MARY (Jesus' mother; see MOTHER, JESUS')

MARY (Magdalene)

Setting: Jerusalem. The risen Jesus first appears to Mary Magdalene after she tells Simon Peter and John about the empty tomb where Jesus' body had been laid the day before the Sabbath. He had died on the cross for the sins of the world.

Jesus said to her, "Woman, why are you weeping? Whom are you seeking?" Supposing Him to be the gardener, she said to Him, "Sir, if you have carried Him away, tell me where you have laid Him, and I will take Him away." Jesus said to her, "Mary!" She turned and said to Him in Hebrew "Rabboni!" (which means, Teacher). Jesus said to her, "Stop clinging to Me, for I have not yet ascended to the Father; but go to My brethren and say to them, 'I ascend to My Father and your Father, and My God and Your God'" (John 20:15–17; see Mark 16:9–11; John 7:33; 19:31–42).

MARY (of Bethany)

Setting: On the way from Galilee to Jerusalem. After being tested by a lawyer, the Lord and His disciples are welcomed into the home of Martha and Mary in Bethany.

But the Lord answered and said to her, "Martha, Martha, you are worried and bothered about so many things; but *only* one thing is necessary, for Mary has chosen the good part, which shall not be taken away from her" (Luke 10:41, 42; see Matthew 6:25).

MASTER (Also see MASTERS)

Setting: Galilee. After His disciples observe His ministry, Jesus summons and specifically instructs them about the difficulties ahead involving true discipleship.

"A disciple is not above his teacher, nor a slave above his master. It is enough for the disciple that he become like his teacher, and the slave like his master. If they have called the head of the house Beelzebul, how much more *will they malign* the members of his household!" (Matthew 10:24, 25; cf. Luke 6:40; see 2 Kings 1:2).

Setting: On the Mount of Olives, just east of Jerusalem. During His Olivet Discourse, after answering His disciples' questions as to when the temple will be destroyed and Jerusalem overrun, along with the signs of His coming and the end of the age, Jesus reemphasizes to His disciples that they should be on the alert for His return.

"Therefore be on the alert, for you do not know which day your Lord is coming. But be sure of this, that if the head of the house had known at what time of the night the thief was coming, he would have been on the alert and would not have allowed his house to be broken into. For this reason you also must be ready; for the Son of Man is coming at an hour when you do not think *He will.* Who then is the faithful and sensible slave whom his master put in charge of his household to give their food at the proper time? Blessed is that slave whom his master finds so doing when he comes. Truly I say to you that he will put him in charge of all his possessions. But if that evil slave says in his heart, 'My master is not coming for a long time,' and begins to beat his fellow slaves and eat and drink with drunkards; the master of that slave will come on a day when he does not expect *him* and at an hour which he does not know, and will cut him in pieces and assign him a place with the hypocrites; in that place there will be weeping and gnashing of teeth" (Matthew 24:42–51; cf. Mark 13:33–37; Luke 12:39–46; 21:34–36; see Matthew 8:11, 12; Matthew 25:21–23).

Setting: On the Mount of Olives, just east of Jerusalem. During His Olivet Discourse, after answering His disciples' questions as to when the temple will be destroyed and Jerusalem overrun, along with the signs of His coming and the end of the age, Jesus reemphasizes to His disciples that they should be on the alert for His return.

"For *it is* just like a man *about* to go on a journey, who called his own slaves and entrusted his possessions to them. To one he gave five talents, to another, two, and to another, one, each according to his own ability; and he went on his journey. Immediately the one who had received the five talents went and traded with them, and gained five more talents. In the same manner the one who *had received* the two *talents* gained two more. But he who received the one *talent* went away, and dug a *hole* in the ground and hid his master's money. Now after a long time the master of those slaves came and settled accounts with them. The one who had received the five talents came up and brought five more talents, saying, 'Master, you entrusted five talents to me. See, I have gained five more talents.' His master said to him, 'Well done, good and faithful slave. You were faithful with a few things, I will put you in charge of many things; enter into the joy of your master.' Also the one who *had received* the two talents came up and said, 'Master, you entrusted two talents to me. See, I have gained two more talents.' His master said to him, 'Well done, good and faithful slave. You were faithful with a few things, I will put you in charge of many things; enter into the joy of your master.' And the one also who had received the one talent came up and said, 'Master, I knew you to be a hard man, reaping where you did not sow and gathering where you scattered no *seed.* And I was afraid, and went away and hid your talent in the ground. See, you have what is yours.' But his master answered and said to him, 'You wicked, lazy slave, you knew that I reap where I did not sow and gather where I scattered no *seed.* Then you ought to have put my money in the bank, and on my arrival I would have received my *money* back with interest. 'Therefore take away the talent from him, and give it to the one who has ten talents.' For to everyone who has, *more* shall be given, and he will have an abundance; but from the one who does not have, even what he does have shall be taken away. Throw out the worthless slave into the outer darkness; in that place there will be weeping and gnashing of teeth" (Matthew 25:14–30; cf. Matthew 8:12; 13:12; 24:45–47; see Matthew 18:23, 24; Luke 12:44).

Setting: On the Mount of Olives, east of the temple in Jerusalem. After predicting the temple's destruction, Jesus responds during His Olivet Discourse to questions from Peter, James, John, and Andrew about other future events.

"Take heed, keep on the alert; for you do not know when the *appointed* time will come. *It is* like a man away on a journey, *who* upon leaving his house and putting his slaves in charge, *assigning* to each one his task, also commanded the doorkeeper to stay on the alert. Therefore, be on the alert—for you do not know when the master of the house is coming, whether in the evening, at midnight, or when the rooster crows, or in the morning—in case he should come suddenly and find you asleep. What I say to you I say to all, 'Be on the alert!' " (Mark 13:33–37; cf. Matthew 24:42–43; Luke 21:34–36; see Luke 12:36–38; Ephesians 6:18).

Setting: On the way from Galilee to Jerusalem. After giving a parable about riches and greed, Jesus uses another parable to challenge the crowd and His disciples to be ready for His return.

"Be dressed in readiness, and *keep* your lamps lit. Be like men who are waiting for their master when he returns from the wedding feast, so that they may immediately open *the door* to him when he comes and knocks. Blessed are those slaves whom the master will find on the alert when he comes; truly I say to you, that he will gird himself *to serve,* and have them recline *at the table,* and will come up and wait on them. Whether he comes in the second watch, or even in the third and finds *them* so, blessed are those *slaves*. But be sure of this, that if the head of the house had known at what hour the thief was coming, he would not have allowed his house to be broken into. You too, be ready; for the Son of Man is coming at an hour that you do not expect" (Luke 12:35–40; cf. Matthew 24:42–44; see Mark 13:33; Ephesians 6:14).

Setting: On the way from Galilee to Jerusalem. When Jesus uses a parable to challenge the crowd and His disciples to be ready for His return, Peter asks Him whom He is addressing.

And the Lord said, "Who then is the faithful and sensible steward, whom his master will put in charge of his servants, to give them their rations at the proper time? Blessed is that slave whom his master finds so doing when he comes. Truly I say to you that he will put him in charge of all his possessions. But if that slave says in his heart, 'My master will be a long time in coming,' and begins to beat the slaves, *both* men and women, and to eat and drink and get drunk; the master of that slave will come on a day when he does not expect *him* and at an hour he does not know, and will cut him in pieces, and assign him a place with the unbelievers. And that slave who knew his master's will and did not get ready or act in accord with his will, will receive many lashes, but the one who did know *it,* and committed deeds worthy of flogging, will receive but few. From everyone who has been given much, much will be required; and to whom they entrusted much, of him they will ask all the more" (Luke 12:42–48; cf. Matthew 24:45–51; see Leviticus 5:17).

Setting: On the way from Galilee to Jerusalem. After speaking a parable to the invited guests and the host at a banquet, Jesus responds to a guest's proclamation about the blessings of eating bread in the kingdom of God.

But He said to him, "A man was giving a big dinner, and he invited many; and at the dinner hour he sent his slave to say to those who had been invited, 'Come; for everything is ready now.' But they all alike began to make excuses. The first one said to him, 'I have bought a piece of land and I need to go out and look at it; please consider me excused.' Another one said, 'I have bought five yoke of oxen, and I am going to try them out; please consider me excused.' Another one said, I have married a wife, and for that reason I cannot come.' And the slave came *back* and reported this to his master. Then the head of the household became angry and said to his slave, 'Go out at once into the streets and lanes of the city and bring in here the poor and crippled and blind and lame.' And the slave said, 'Master, what you commanded has been done, and still there is room.' And the master said to the slave, 'Go out into the highways and along the hedges, and compel *them* to come in, so that my house may be filled. For I tell you, none of those men who were invited shall taste of my dinner'" (Luke 14:16–24; see Deuteronomy 24:5; Matthew 22:2–14).

Setting: On the way from Galilee to Jerusalem. After giving the story of the prodigal son, the Lord teaches His disciples about stewardship.

Now He was also saying to the disciples, "There was a rich man who had a manager, and this *manager* was reported to him as squandering his possessions. And he called him and said to him, 'What is this I hear about you? Give an accounting of your management, for you can no longer be a manager.' The manager said to himself, 'What shall I do, since my master is taking the management away from me? I am not strong enough to dig; I am ashamed to beg. I know what I shall do, so that when I am removed from the management people will welcome me into their homes.' And he summoned each one of his master's debtors, and he *began* saying to the first, 'How much do you owe my master?' And he said, 'A hundred measures of oil.' And he said to him, 'Take your bill, and sit down quickly and write fifty.' Then he said to another, 'And how much do you owe?' And he said, 'A hundred measures of wheat.' He said to him, 'Take your bill, and write eighty.' And his master praised the unrighteous manager because he had acted shrewdly; for the sons of this age are more shrewd in relation to their own kind than the sons of light. And I say to you, make friends for yourselves by means of the wealth of unrighteousness, so that when it fails, they will receive you into the eternal dwellings. He who is faithful in a very little thing is faithful also in much; and he who is unrighteous in a very little thing is unrighteous also in much. Therefore if you have not been faithful in the *use of* unrighteous wealth, who will entrust the true *riches* to you? And if you have not been faithful in *the use of* that which is another's, who will give you that which is your own? No servant can serve two masters; for either he will hate the one and love the other, or else he will be devoted to one and despise the other. You cannot serve God and wealth" (Luke 16:1–13; cf. Matthew 6:24; see Matthew 25:14–30).

Setting: Jericho, on the way to Jerusalem. After commending Zaccheus's faith in Him, Jesus provides a parable about stewardship.

So He said, "A nobleman went to a distant country to receive a kingdom for himself, and *then* return. And he called ten of his slaves, and gave them ten minas and said to them, 'Do business *with this* until I come *back*.' But his citizens hated him and sent a delegation after him, saying, 'We do not want this man to reign over us.' When he returned, after receiving the kingdom, he ordered that these slaves, to whom he had given the money, be called to him so that he might know what business they had done. The first appeared, saying, 'Master, your mina has made ten minas more.' And he said to him, 'Well done, good slave, because you have been faithful in a very little thing, you are to be in authority over ten cities.' The second came, saying, 'Your mina, master, has made five minas.' And he said to him, also, 'And you are to be over five cities.' Another came, saying, 'Master, here is your mina, which I kept put away in a handkerchief; for I was afraid of you, because you are an exacting man; you take up what you did not lay down and reap what you did not sow.' He said to him, 'By your own words I will judge you, you worthless slave. Did you know that I am an exacting man, taking up what I did not lay down and reaping what I did not sow? Then why did you not put my money in the bank, and having come, I would have collected it with interest?' Then he said to the bystanders, 'Take the mina away from him and give it to the one who has the ten minas.' And they said to him, 'Master, he has ten minas *already*.' I tell you that to everyone who has, more shall be given, but from the one who does not have, even what he does have shall be taken away. But these enemies of mine, who did not want me to reign over them, bring them here and slay them in my presence" (Luke 19:12–27; cf. Matthew 25:14–30; see Matthew 13:12; Luke 16:10).

Setting: Jerusalem. Before the Passover, with His death on the cross nearing, Jesus explains the reason for His vivid example of servanthood in washing His disciples' feet.

So when He had washed their feet, and taken His garments and reclined *at the table* again, He said to them, "Do you know what I have done to you? You call Me Teacher and Lord; and you are right, for *so* I am. If I then, the Lord and the Teacher, washed your feet, you also ought to wash one another's feet. For I gave you an example that you also should do as I did to you. Truly, truly I say to you, a slave is not greater than his master, nor *is* one who is sent greater than the one who sent him. If you know these things, you are blessed if you do them. I do not speak of all of you. I know the ones I have chosen; but *it is* that the Scripture may be fulfilled, 'HE WHO EATS MY BREAD HAS LIFTED UP HIS HEEL AGAINST ME.' From now on I am telling you before *it* comes to pass, so that when it does occur, you may believe that I am *He*. Truly, truly, I say to you, he who receives whomever I send receives Me; and he who receives Me receives Him who sent Me" (John 13:12–20; Jesus quotes from Psalm 41:9; see Matthew 7:24; 10:24, 40; John 8:24; 14:29; 1 Peter 5:3).

Setting: Jerusalem. Before the Passover, with His departure in mind, after explaining He is the vine and His disciples are the branches, Jesus commands them to love one another.

"This is My commandment, that you love one another, just as I have loved you. Greater love has no one than this, that one lay down his life for his friends. You are My friends if you do what I command you. No longer do I call you slaves, for the slave does not know what his master is doing; but I have called you friends, for all things that I have heard from My Father I have made known to you. You did not choose Me but I chose you, and appointed you that you would go and bear fruit, and *that* your fruit would remain, so that whatever you ask of the Father in My name He may give to you. This I command you, that you love one another" (John 15:12–17; see Matthew 12:50; John 6:70; 8:26; 10:11; 13:34).

Setting: Jerusalem. Before the Passover, with His departure in mind, after explaining He is the vine and His disciples are the branches, Jesus prepares them for persecution from the world.

"If the world hates you, you know that it has hated Me before *it hated* you. If you were of the world, the world would love its own; but because you are not of the world, but I chose you out of the world, because of this the world hates you. Remember the word that I said to you, 'A slave is not greater than his master.' If they persecuted Me, they will also persecute you; if they kept My word, they will keep yours also. But all these things they will do to you for My name's sake, because they do not know the One who sent Me. If I had not come and spoken to them, they would not have sin, but now they have no excuse for their sin" (John 15:18–22; see Matthew 10:22; John 7:7; 8:19, 55; 9:41; 1 Corinthians 4:12).

MASTER, JOY OF YOUR

Setting: On the Mount of Olives, just east of Jerusalem. During His Olivet Discourse, after answering His disciples' questions as to when the temple will be destroyed and Jerusalem overrun, along with the signs of His coming and the end of the age, Jesus reemphasizes to His disciples that they should be on the alert for His return.

"For *it is* just like a man *about* to go on a journey, who called his own slaves and entrusted his possessions to them. To one he gave five talents, to another, two, and to another, one, each according to his own ability; and he went on his journey. Immediately the one who had received the five talents went and traded with them, and gained five more talents. In the same manner the one who *had received* the two *talents* gained two more. But he who received the one *talent* went away, and dug a *hole* in the ground and hid his master's money. Now after a long time the master of those slaves came and settled accounts with them. The one who had received the five talents came up and brought five more talents, saying, 'Master, you entrusted five talents to me. See, I have gained five more talents.' His master said to him, 'Well done, good and faithful slave. You were faithful with a few things, I will put you in charge of many things; enter into the joy of your master.' Also the one who *had received* the two talents came up and said, 'Master, you entrusted two talents to me. See, I have gained two more talents.' His master said to him, 'Well done, good and faithful slave. You were faithful with a few things, I will put you in charge of many things; enter into the joy of your master.' And the one also who had received the one talent came up and said, 'Master, I knew you to be a hard man, reaping where you did not sow and gathering where you scattered no *seed.* And I was afraid, and went away and hid your talent in the ground. See, you have what is yours.' But his master answered and said to him, 'You wicked, lazy slave, you knew that I reap where I did not sow and gather where I scattered no *seed.* Then you ought to have put my money in the bank, and on my arrival I would have received my *money* back with interest. 'Therefore take away the talent from him, and give it to the one who has ten talents.' For to everyone who has, *more* shall be given, and he will have an abundance; but from the one who does not have, even what he does have shall be taken away. Throw out the worthless slave into the outer darkness; in that place there will be weeping and gnashing of teeth" (Matthew 25:14–30; cf. Matthew 8:12; 13:12; 24:45–47; see Matthew 18:23, 24; Luke 12:44).

MASTER'S MONEY (Listed under MONEY, MASTER'S)

MASTERS (Also see MASTER)

Setting: Galilee. During the early part of His ministry, Jesus preaches the Sermon on the Mount to His disciples and the multitudes.

"No one can serve two masters; for either he will hate the one and love the other, or he will be devoted to one and despise the other. You cannot serve God and wealth (Matthew 6:24).

Setting: On the way from Galilee to Jerusalem. After giving the story of the prodigal son, the Lord teaches His disciples about stewardship.

Now He was also saying to the disciples, "There was a rich man who had a manager, and this *manager* was reported to him as squandering his possessions. And he called him and said to him, 'What is this I hear about you? Give an accounting of your management, for you can no longer be a manager.' The manager said to himself, 'What shall I do, since my master is taking the management away from me? I am not strong enough to dig; I am ashamed to beg. I know what I shall do, so that when I am removed from the management people will welcome me into their homes.' And he summoned each one of his master's debtors, and he *began* saying to the first, 'How much do you owe my master?' And he said, 'A hundred measures of oil.' And he said to him, 'Take your bill, and sit down quickly and write fifty.' Then he said to another, 'And how much do you owe?' And he said, 'A hundred measures of wheat.' He said to him, 'Take your bill, and write eighty.' And his master praised the unrighteous manager because he had acted shrewdly; for the sons of this age are more shrewd in relation to their own kind than the sons of light. And I say to you, make friends for yourselves by means of the wealth of unrighteousness, so that when it fails, they will receive you into the eternal dwellings. He who is faithful in a very little thing is faithful also in much; and he who is unrighteous in a very little thing is unrighteous also in much. Therefore if you have not been faithful in the *use of* unrighteous wealth, who will entrust the true *riches* to you? And if you have not been faithful in *the use of* that which is another's, who will give you that which is your own? No servant can serve two masters; for either he will hate the one and love the other, or else he will be devoted to one and despise the other. You cannot serve God and wealth" (Luke 16:1–13; cf. Matthew 6:24; see Matthew 25:14–30).

MAT (See PALLET)

MATERIALISM (See MONEY; POSSESSIONS; TREASURE; and WEALTH)

MATTERS

Setting: On the way from Galilee to Jerusalem. After giving a parable about riches and greed, Jesus comforts the crowd and His disciples. The scribes and Pharisees turn hostile and question Him repeatedly in an attempt to catch Him in something He might say.

And He said to His disciples, "For this reason I say to you, do not worry about *your* life, *as to* what you will eat; nor for your body, *as to* what you will put on. For life is more than food, and the body more than clothing. Consider the ravens, for they neither sow nor reap; they have no storeroom nor barn, and *yet* God feeds them; how much more valuable you are than the birds! And which of you by worrying can add a *single* hour to his life's span? If then you cannot do even a very little thing, why do you worry about other matters? Consider the lilies, how they grow: they neither toil nor spin; but I tell you, not even Solomon in all his glory clothed himself like one of these. But if God so clothes the grass in the field, which is *alive* today and tomorrow is thrown into the furnace, how much more *will He clothe* you? You men of little faith! And do not seek what you will eat and what you will drink, and do not keep worrying. For all these things the nations of the world eagerly seek; but your Father knows that you need these things. But seek His kingdom, and these things will be added to you. Do not be afraid, little flock, for your Father has chosen gladly to give you the kingdom" (Luke 12:22–32; cf. Matthew 6:25–33; see 1 Kings 10:4–7; Job 38:41).

MATURITY

[MATURITY from mature]

Setting: Galilee. Following His explanation of the Parable of the Sower to His disciples, Jesus conveys the Parable of the Seed.

And He was saying, "The kingdom of God is like a man who casts seed upon the soil; and he goes to bed at night and gets up by day, and the seed sprouts and grows—how, he himself does not know. The soil produces crops by itself; first the blade, then the head, then the mature grain in the head. But when the crop permits, he immediately puts in the sickle, because the harvest has come" (Mark 4:26–29; see Joel 3:13).

Setting: Galilee. After Jesus presents the Parable of the Sower to the crowds, His disciples ask Him to give them the parable's meaning.

And He said, "To you it has been granted to know the mysteries of the kingdom of God, but to the rest *it is* in parables, so that SEEING THEY MAY NOT SEE, AND HEARING THEY MAY NOT UNDERSTAND. Now the parable is this: the seed is the word of God. Those beside the road are those who have heard; then the devil comes and takes away the word from their heart, so that they will not believe and be saved. Those on the rocky *soil* are those who, when they hear, receive the word with joy; and these have no *firm* root; they believe for a while, and in time of temptation fall away. The *seed* which fell among the thorns, these are the ones who have heard, and as they go on their way they are choked with worries and riches and pleasures of *this* life, and bring no fruit to maturity. But the *seed* in the good soil, these are the ones who have heard the word in an honest and good heart, and hold it fast, and bear fruit with perseverance" (Luke 8:10–15, Jesus quotes from Isaiah 6:9; cf. Matthew 13:10–23; Mark 4:10–20).

MEAL (See DINNER; FLOUR; FOOD; HOSPITALITY; LUNCHEON; and RECEPTION)

MEANINGLESS REPETITION (Listed under REPETITION, MEANINGLESS; also see PRAYER)

MEASURE (Specifics such as MEASURE, GOOD; and MEASURE, STANDARD OF are separate entries; also see MEASURES)

Setting: The temple in Jerusalem. After the Jewish religious leaders test Him with questions, Jesus pronounces the eighth of eight woes on them in front of the crowds and His disciples.

"Woe to you, scribes and Pharisees, hypocrites! For you build the tombs of the prophets and adorn the monuments of the righteous, and say, 'If we had been *living* in the days of our fathers, we would not have been partners with them in *shedding* the blood of the prophets.' So you testify against yourselves, that you are sons of those who murdered the prophets. Fill up, then, the measure *of the guilt* of you fathers. You serpents, you brood of vipers, how will you escape the sentence of hell? Therefore, behold, I am sending you prophets and wise men and scribes; some of them you will kill and crucify, and some of them you will scourge in your synagogues, and persecute from city to city, so that upon you may fall *the guilt of* all the righteous blood shed on earth, from the blood of righteous Abel to the blood of Zechariah, the son of Berechiah, whom you murdered between the temple and the altar. Truly I say to you, all these things will come upon this generation" (Matthew 23:29–36; cf. 2 Chronicles 24:21; Zechariah 1:1; Matthew 3:7; Luke 11:47–52; see Matthew 10:23).

MEASURE, GOOD

Setting: Galilee. After selecting His twelve disciples, Jesus teaches the Sermon on the Mount to those disciples and a great throng of people from Judea, Jerusalem, and the central coastal region of Tyre and Sidon.

"Do not judge, and you will not be judged; and do not condemn, and you will not be condemned; pardon, and you will be pardoned. Give and it will be given to you. They will pour into your lap a good measure—pressed down, shaken together, *and* running over. For by your standard of measure it will be measured to you in return" (Luke 6:37, 38; cf. Matthew 7:1–5; Mark 4:24; see Luke 6:12–19).

MEASURE, STANDARD OF

Setting: Galilee. During the early part of His ministry, Jesus preaches the Sermon on the Mount to His disciples and the multitudes.

"Do not judge so that you will not be judged. For in the way you judge, you will be judged; and by your standard of measure, it will be measured to you. Why do you look at the speck that is in your brother's eye, but do not notice the log that is in your own eye? Or how can you say to your brother, 'Let me take the speck out of your eye, and behold, the log is in your own eye? You hypocrite, first take the log out of your own eye, and then you will see clearly to take the speck out of your brother's eye" (Matthew 7:1–5; cf. Mark 4:24; Luke 6:37–42; Romans 2:1; Romans 14:10, 13).

Setting: Galilee. Following His explanation of the Parable of the Sower to His disciples, Jesus informs them about personal accountability and responsibility.

And He was saying to them, "Take care what you listen to. By your standard of measure it will be measured to you; and more will be given you besides. For whoever has, to him *more* shall be given; and whoever does not have, even what he has shall be taken away from him" (Mark 4:24, 25; cf. Matthew 13:12; Luke 8:18; see Matthew 7:2).

Setting: Galilee. After selecting His twelve disciples, Jesus teaches the Sermon on the Mount to those disciples and a great throng of people from Judea, Jerusalem, and the central coastal region of Tyre and Sidon.

"Do not judge, and you will not be judged; and do not condemn, and you will not be condemned; pardon, and you will be pardoned. Give and it will be given to you. They will pour into your lap a good measure—pressed down, shaken together, *and* running over. For by your standard of measure it will be measured to you in return" (Luke 6:37, 38; cf. Matthew 7:1–5; Mark 4:24; see Luke 6:12–19).

MEASURES (Also see MEASURE)

Setting: On the way from Galilee to Jerusalem. After giving the story of the prodigal son, the Lord teaches His disciples about stewardship.

Now He was also saying to the disciples, "There was a rich man who had a manager, and this *manager* was reported to him as squandering his possessions. And he called him and said to him, 'What is this I hear about you? Give an accounting of your management, for you can no longer be a manager.' The manager said to himself, 'What shall I do, since my master is taking the management away from me? I am not strong enough to dig; I am ashamed to beg. I know what I shall do, so that when I am removed from the management people will welcome me into their homes.' And he summoned each one of his master's debtors, and he *began* saying to the first, 'How much do you owe my master?' And he said, 'A hundred measures of oil.' And he said to him, 'Take your bill, and sit down quickly and write fifty.' Then he said to another, 'And how much do you owe?' And he said, 'A hundred measures of wheat.' He said to him, 'Take your bill, and write eighty.' And his master praised the unrighteous manager because he had acted shrewdly; for the sons of this age are more shrewd in relation to their own kind than the sons of light. And I say to you, make friends for yourselves by means of the wealth of unrighteousness, so that when it fails, they will receive you into the eternal dwellings. He who is faithful in a very little thing is faithful also in much; and he who is unrighteous in a very little thing is unrighteous also in much. Therefore if you have not been faithful in the *use of* unrighteous wealth, who will entrust the true *riches* to you? And if you have not been faithful in *the use of* that which is another's, who will give you that which is your own? No servant can serve two masters; for either he will hate the one and love the other, or else he will be devoted to one and despise the other. You cannot serve God and wealth" (Luke 16:1–13; cf. Matthew 6:24; see Matthew 25:14–30).

MEMBERS

Setting: Galilee. After His disciples observe His ministry, Jesus summons and specifically instructs them about the difficulties ahead involving true discipleship.

"A disciple is not above his teacher, nor a slave above his master. It is enough for the disciple that he become like his teacher, and the slave like his master. If they have called the head of the house Beelzebul, how much more *will they malign* the members of his household!" (Matthew 10:24, 25; cf. Luke 6:40; see 2 Kings 1:2).

Setting: Galilee. After His disciples observe His ministry, Jesus summons and specifically instructs them about their ministry hardships ahead involving true discipleship.

"Do not think that I came to bring peace on the earth; I did not come to bring peace, but a sword. For I came to SET A MAN AGAINST HIS FATHER, AND A DAUGHTER AGAINST HER MOTHER, AND A DAUGHTER-IN-LAW AGAINST HER MOTHER-IN-LAW; and A MAN'S ENEMIES WILL BE THE MEMBERS OF HIS HOUSEHOLD" (Matthew 10:34–36; Jesus quotes from Micah 7:6; cf. Luke 12:51–53).

Setting: On the way from Galilee to Jerusalem. After clarifying a parable for Peter and the crowd, Jesus conveys how a relationship with Him divides families.

"I have come to cast fire upon the earth; and how I wish it were already kindled! But I have a baptism to undergo, and how distressed I am until it is accomplished! Do you suppose that I came to grant peace on earth? I tell you, no, but rather division; for from now on five *members* in one household will be divided, three against two and two against three. They will be divided, father against son and son against father, mother against daughter, and daughter against mother, mother-in-law against daughter-in-law and daughter-in-law against mother-in-law" (Luke 12:49–53; cf. Matthew 10:34–36; see Micah 7:6; Mark 10:38).

MEMORY (Also see MIND; REMEMBER; REMEMBRANCE; and THOUGHTS)

Setting: The home of Simon the leper in Bethany. Jesus rebukes His disciples after they criticize a woman for pouring a costly vial of perfume on His head in preparation for His burial.

But Jesus, aware of this, said to them, "Why do you bother the woman? For she has done a good deed to Me. For you always have the poor with you; but you do not always have Me. For when she poured this perfume on My body, she did it to prepare Me for burial. Truly I say to you, wherever this gospel is preached in the whole world, what this woman has done will also be spoken of in memory of her" (Matthew 26:10–13; cf. Mark 14:3–9; Luke 7:37–39; John 12:2–8; see Deuteronomy 15:11).

Setting: The home of Simon the leper in Bethany. Two days before the Feast of Unleavened Bread (Passover), Jesus commends a woman who anoints His head with costly perfume. Some there think it should have been sold and the proceeds given to the poor.

But Jesus said, "Let her alone; why do you bother her? She has done a good deed to Me. For you always have the poor with you, and whenever you wish you can do good to them; but you do not always have Me. She has done what she could; she has anointed My body beforehand for the burial. Truly I say to you, wherever the gospel is preached in the whole world, what this woman has done will also be spoken of in memory of her" (Mark 14:6–9; cf. Matthew 26:6–13; John 12:2–8; see Deuteronomy 15:11).

MEN (Specifics such as MEN, BLIND and MEN, EVIL are separate entries; also see MALE; MAN; and PEOPLE)

Setting: Galilee. During the early part of His ministry, Jesus preaches the Sermon on the Mount to His disciples and the multitudes.

"You are the salt of the earth; but if the salt has become tasteless, how can it be made salty *again*? It is not longer good for anything, except to be thrown out and trampled under foot by men" (Matthew 5:13; cf. Mark 9:50).

Setting: Galilee. During the early part of His ministry, Jesus preaches the Sermon on the Mount to His disciples and the multitudes.

"You are the light of the world. A city set on a hill cannot be hidden; nor does *anyone* light a lamp and put it under a basket, but on the lampstand, and it gives light to all who are in the house. Let your light shine before men in such a way that they may see your good works, and glorify your Father who is in heaven" (Matthew 5:14–16; cf. Mark 4:21; 1 Peter 2:12).

Setting: Galilee. During the early part of His ministry, Jesus preaches the Sermon on the Mount to His disciples and the multitudes.

"Beware of practicing your righteousness before men to be noticed by them; otherwise you have no reward with your Father who is in heaven" (Matthew 6:1; cf. Matthew 6:5, 16).

Setting: Galilee. During the early part of His ministry, Jesus preaches the Sermon on the Mount to His disciples and the multitudes.

"So when you give to the poor, do not sound a trumpet before you, as the hypocrites do in the synagogues and in the streets, so that they may be honored by men. Truly I say to you, they have their reward in full. But when you give to the poor, do not let your left hand know what your right hand is doing, so that your giving will be in secret; and your Father who sees *what is done* in secret will reward you" (Matthew 6:2–4; see Jeremiah 17:10; Matthew 6:16).

Setting: Galilee. During the early part of His ministry, Jesus preaches the Sermon on the Mount to His disciples and the multitudes.

"When you pray, you are not to be like the hypocrites; for they love to stand and pray in the synagogues and on the street corners so that they may be seen by men. Truly I say to you, they have their reward in full. But you, when you pray, go into your inner room, close your door and pray to your Father who is in secret, and your Father who sees *what is done* in secret will reward you" (Matthew 6:5, 6; see Mark 11:25).

Setting: Galilee. During the early part of His ministry, Jesus preaches the Sermon on the Mount to His disciples and the multitudes.

"Whenever you fast, do not put on a gloomy face as the hypocrites *do,* for they neglect their appearance so that they will be noticed by men when they are fasting. Truly I say to you, they have their reward in full. But you, when you fast, anoint your head and wash your face so that your fasting will not be noticed by men, but by your Father who is in secret; and your Father who sees *what is done* in secret will reward you" (Matthew 6:16–18).

Setting: On the Sea of Galilee. After giving one of His disciples and a scribe the demands of discipleship, Jesus calms a great storm when His disciples fear for their lives.

He said to them, "Why are you afraid, you men of little faith?" Then He got up and rebuked the winds and the sea, and it became perfectly calm (Matthew 8:26; see Mark 4:35–41; Luke 8:22–25).

Setting: Galilee. After His disciples observe His ministry, Jesus summons and specifically instructs them about the upcoming hardships of their ministry to the people of Israel.

"Behold, I send you out as sheep in the midst of wolves; so be shrewd as serpents and innocent as doves. But beware of men, for they will hand you over to *the* courts and scourge you in their synagogues; and you will even be brought before governors and kings for My sake, as a testimony to them and to the Gentiles. But when they hand you over, do not worry about how or what you are to say; for it will be given you in that hour what you are to say. For it is not you who speak, but *it* is the Spirit of your Father who speaks in you" (Matthew 10:16–20; cf. Luke 10:3).

Setting: Galilee. Jesus gives the meaning of discipleship as He commissions His twelve disciples for ministry.

"Therefore everyone who confesses Me before men, I will also confess him before My Father who is in heaven. But whoever denies Me before men, I will also deny him before My Father who is in heaven" (Matthew 10:32, 33; cf. Mark 8:38; Luke 12:8).

Setting: Galilee. After Jesus warns the Pharisees about the unpardonable sin and their future judgment, some Pharisees and scribes ask Him to perform a miraculous sign for them in front of the crowds.

But He answered and said to them, "An evil and adulterous generation craves for a sign; and *yet* no sign will be given to it but the sign of Jonah the prophet; for just as JONAH WAS THREE DAYS AND THREE NIGHTS IN THE BELLY OF THE SEA MONSTER, so will the Son of Man be three days and three nights in the heart of the earth. The men of Nineveh will stand up with this generation at the judgment, and will condemn it because they repented at the preaching of Jonah; and behold, something greater than Jonah is here. *The* Queen of *the* South will rise up with this generation at the judgment and will condemn it, because she came from the ends of the earth to hear the wisdom of Solomon; and behold, something greater than Solomon is here" (Matthew 12:39–42; Jesus quotes from Jonah 1:17; cf. 1 Kings 10:1; Jonah 3:5; Matthew 16:1, 4; 12:38; Luke 11:29).

Setting: By the Sea of Galilee. Because the Jewish religious leaders are rejecting His message, Jesus continues teaching the crowds with the Parable of the Wheat and the Tares.

Jesus presented another parable to them, saying, "The kingdom of heaven may be compared to a man who sowed good seed in his field. But while his men were sleeping, his enemy came and sowed tares among the wheat, and went away. But when the wheat sprouted and bore grain, then the tares became evident also. The slaves of the landowner came and said to him, 'Sir, did you not sow good seed in your field? How then does it have tares?' And he said to them, 'An enemy has done this!' The slaves said to him, 'Do you want us, then, to go and gather them up?' But he said, 'No; for while you are gathering up the tares, you may uproot the wheat with them. Allow both to grow together until the harvest; and in the time of the harvest I will say to the reapers, "First gather up the tares and bind them in bundles to burn them up; but gather the wheat into my barn"'" (Matthew 13:24–30; cf. Matthew 3:12).

Setting: By the Sea of Galilee. Jesus repeats a warning to His disciples about the teaching of the Jewish religious leaders of the day, the Pharisees and the Sadducees.

But Jesus aware of this, said, "You men of little faith, why do you discuss among yourselves that you have no bread? Do you not yet understand or remember the five loaves of the five thousand and how many baskets *full* you picked up? Or the seven loaves of the four thousand, and how many large baskets *full* you picked up? How is it that you do not understand that I did not speak to you concerning bread? But beware of the leaven of the Pharisees and Sadducees" (Matthew 16:8–11; cf. Matthew 14:17–21; 15:34–38; Mark 8:17–21).

Setting: Judea beyond the Jordan (Perea). After responding to the Pharisees' question about Moses' command regarding a certificate of divorce, Jesus answers the disciples' private question.

But He said to them, "Not all men *can* accept this statement, but *only* those to whom it has been given. For there are eunuchs who were born that way from their mother's womb; and there are eunuchs who were made eunuchs by men; and there are *also* eunuchs who made themselves eunuchs for the sake of the kingdom of heaven. He who is able to accept *this,* let him accept *it*" (Matthew 19:11, 12; cf. 1 Corinthians 7:7).

Setting: The temple in Jerusalem. Jesus returns after spending the night in Bethany. The chief priests and elders question His authority to teach to the nation.

Jesus said to them, "I will also ask you one thing, which if you tell Me, I will also tell you by what authority I do these things. The baptism of John was from what *source,* from heaven or from men?" And they *began* reasoning among themselves, saying "If we say 'From heaven,' He will say to us, 'Then why did you not believe him?' But if we say, 'From men,' we fear the people; for they all regard John as a prophet." And answering Jesus, they said, "We do not know." He also said to them, "Neither will I tell you by what authority I do these things" (Matthew 21:24–27; cf. Mark 11:29–33; Luke 20:3–8).

Setting: The temple in Jerusalem. Jesus exposes the truth about Pharisaism to the crowds and His disciples after the Jewish religious leaders test Him with questions.

Then Jesus spoke to the crowds and to His disciples, saying: "The scribes and the Pharisees have seated themselves in the chair of Moses; therefore all that they tell you, do and observe, but do not do according to their deeds; for they say *things* and do not do *them.* They tie up heavy burdens and lay them on men's shoulders, but they themselves are unwilling to move them with *so much as* a finger. But they do all their deeds to be noticed by men; for they broaden their phylacteries and lengthen their tassels *of their garments.* They love the place of honor at banquets and the chief seats in the synagogues, and respectful greetings in the market places, and being called Rabbi by men. But do not be called Rabbi; for One is your Teacher, and you are all brothers. Do not call *anyone* on earth your father; for One is your Father, He who is in heaven. Do not be called leaders; for One is your Leader, *that is,* Christ. But the greatest among you shall be your servant. Whoever exalts himself shall be humbled; and whoever humbles himself shall be exalted" (Matthew 23:1–12; cf. Matthew 20:26; Mark 12:38–40; Luke 20:46, 47; see Exodus 13:9; Deuteronomy 33:3; Matthew 6:1, 5, 6, 9, 16; Mark 14:11; Luke 11:43; 14:11).

Setting: The temple in Jerusalem. After the Jewish religious leaders test Him with questions, Jesus pronounces the seventh of eight woes on them in front of the crowds and His disciples.

"Woe to you, scribes and Pharisees, hypocrites! For you are like whitewashed tombs which on the outside appear beautiful, but inside they are full of dead men's bones and all uncleanness. So you, too, outwardly appear righteous to men, but inwardly you are full of hypocrisy and lawlessness" (Matthew 23:27, 28; cf. Luke 11:44).

Setting: An upper room in Jerusalem. After celebrating the Passover meal with His disciples, Jesus retreats to the Garden of Gethsemane on the Mount of Olives to pray prior to His betrayal by Judas.

Then Jesus came with them to a place called Gethsemane, and said to His disciples, "Sit here while I go over there and pray." And He took with Him Peter and the two sons of Zebedee, and began to be grieved and distressed. Then He said to them, "My soul is deeply grieved, to the point of death; remain here and keep watch with Me." And He went a little beyond *them,* and fell on His face and prayed, saying, "My Father, if it is possible, let this cup pass from Me; yet not as I will, but as You will." And He came to the disciples and found them sleeping, and said to Peter, "So, you *men* could not keep watch with Me for one hour? Keep watching and praying that you may not enter into temptation; the spirit is willing, but the flesh is weak." He went away again a second time and prayed, saying, "My Father, if this cannot pass away unless I drink it, Your will be done." Again He came and found them sleeping, for their eyes were heavy. And He left them again, and went away and prayed a third time, saying the same thing once more. Then He came to the disciples and said to them, "Are you still sleeping and resting? Behold the hour is at hand and the Son of Man is being betrayed into the hands of sinners. Get up, let us be going; behold the one who betrays Me is at hand!" (Matthew 26:36–46; cf. Mark 14:32–42; Luke 22:40–46; see Matthew 20:22; John 12:27).

Setting: Galilee. After the Pharisees and scribes from Jerusalem object to His disciples' lack of obedience to the tradition regarding ceremonial cleansing, Jesus speaks to a crowd and explains His teaching to the disciples.

After He called the crowd to Him again, He *began* saying to them, "Listen to Me, all of you, and understand: there is nothing outside the man which can defile him if it goes into him; but the things which proceed out of the man are what defile the man. [If anyone has ears to hear, let him hear."] When he had left the crowd *and* entered the house, His disciples questioned Him about the parable. And He said to them, "Are you so lacking in understanding also? Do you not understand that whatever goes into the man from outside cannot defile him, because it does not go into his heart, but into his stomach, and is eliminated?" (*Thus He* declared all foods clean.) And He was saying, "That which proceeds out of the man, that is what defiles the man. For from within, out of the heart of men, proceed the evil thoughts, fornications, thefts, murders, adulteries, deeds of coveting *and* wickedness, *as well* as deceit, sensuality, envy, slander, pride *and* foolishness. All these evil things proceed from within and defile the man" (Mark 7:14–23; cf. Matthew 15:10–20).

Setting: The temple in Jerusalem. After Jesus teaches about faith and forgiveness, utilizing a cursed fig tree as an object lesson, His authority is questioned by the chief priests, scribes, and elders.

And Jesus said to them, "I will ask you one question, and you answer Me, and *then* I will tell you by what authority I do these things. Was the baptism of John from heaven, or from men? Answer Me." They *began* reasoning among themselves, saying, "If we say 'From heaven,' He will say, 'Then why did you not believe him?' "But shall we say 'From men'?"—they were afraid of the people, for everyone considered John to have been a real prophet. Answering Jesus, they said, "We do not know." And Jesus said to them, "Nor will I tell you by what authority I do these things" (Mark 11:29–33; cf. Matthew 21:23–27; Luke 20:1–8).

Setting: By the Sea of Galilee. After teaching the people from Simon Peter's boat, Jesus calls Simon, James, and John to follow Him. (This appears to be a permanent call, as Simon and other companions are with Him earlier in Mark 1:35–39 and Luke 4:38, 39).

When He had finished speaking, He said to Simon, "Put out into the deep water and let down your nets for a catch." ". . . and so also *were* James and John, sons of Zebedee, who were partners with Simon. And Jesus said to Simon, "Do not fear, from now on you will be catching men" (Luke 5:4, 10; see John 21:6).

Setting: Galilee. After selecting His twelve disciples, Jesus teaches the Beatitudes (part of the Sermon on the Mount) to those disciples and a great throng of people from Judea, Jerusalem, and the central coastal region of Tyre and Sidon.

"Blessed are you when men hate you, and ostracize you, and insult you, and scorn your name as evil, for the sake of the Son of Man. Be glad in that day and leap *for joy,* for behold, your reward is great in heaven. For in the same way their fathers used to treat the prophets" (Luke 6:22, 23; cf. Matthew 5:10–12; see 2 Chronicles 36:16).

Setting: Galilee. After selecting His twelve disciples, Jesus teaches the Beatitudes (part of the Sermon on the Mount) to those disciples and a great throng of people from Judea, Jerusalem, and the central coastal region of Tyre and Sidon.

"Woe *to you* when all men speak well of you, for their fathers used to treat the false prophets in the same way" (Luke 6:26; see Matthew 7:15; 24:11, 24; Luke 6:12–19).

Setting: Galilee. After selecting His twelve disciples, Jesus teaches the Sermon on the Mount to those disciples and a great throng of people from Judea, Jerusalem, and the central coastal region of Tyre and Sidon.

And He also spoke a parable to them: "A blind man cannot guide a blind man, can he? Will they not both fall into a pit? A pupil is not above his teacher; but everyone, after he has been fully trained, will be like his teacher. Why do you look at the speck that is in your brother's eye, but do not notice the log that is in your own eye? Or how can you say to your brother, 'Brother, let me take out the speck that is in your eye,' when you yourself do not see the log that is in your own eye? You hypocrite, first take the log out of your own eye, and then you will see clearly to take out the speck that is in your brother's eye. For there is no good tree which produces bad fruit, nor, on the other hand, a bad tree which produces good fruit. For each tree is known by its own fruit. For men do not gather figs from thorns, nor do they pick grapes from a briar bush. The good man out of the good treasure of his heart brings forth what is good; and the evil *man* out of the evil *treasure* brings forth what is evil; for his mouth speaks from that which fills his heart" (Luke 6:39–45; cf. Matthew 7:3–6. 16, 18, 20; 12:35; see Matthew 10:24; 15:14; Luke 6:12–19).

Setting: Galilee. After praising John the Baptist to the crowds, Jesus criticizes the Pharisees and lawyers who reject God's purpose and John's message.

"To what then shall I compare the men of this generation, and what are they like? They are like children who sit in the market place and call to one another, and they say, 'We played the flute for you, and you did not dance; we sang a dirge, and you did not weep.' For John the Baptist has come eating no bread and drinking no wine, and you say, 'He has a demon!' The Son of Man has come eating and drinking, and you say, 'Behold, a gluttonous man and a drunkard, a friend of tax collectors and sinners!' Yet wisdom is vindicated by all her children" (Luke 7:31–35; cf. Matthew 11:16–19; see Luke 1:15).

Setting: On the way from Galilee to Jerusalem. After revealing a problem with exorcism and responding to a blessing from a woman in the crowd, Jesus tells the increasing crowds of the sign of Jonah.

As the crowds were increasing, He began to say, "This generation is a wicked generation; it seeks for a sign, and *yet* no sign will be given to it but the sign of Jonah. For just as Jonah became a sign to the Ninevites, so will the Son of Man be to this generation. The Queen of the South will rise up with the men of this generation at the judgment and condemn them, because she came from the ends of the earth to hear the wisdom of Solomon; and behold, something greater than Solomon is here. The men of Nineveh will stand up with this generation at the judgment and condemn it, because they repented at the preaching of Jonah; and behold, something greater than Jonah is here" (Luke 11:29–32; cf. Matthew 16:4; see 1 Kings 10:1–10; Jonah 3:4, 5).

Setting: On the way from Galilee to Jerusalem. After Jesus pronounces woes upon the Pharisees, a lawyer replies that His remarks are an insult to lawyers, too.

But He said, "Woe to you lawyers as well! For you weigh men down with burdens hard to bear, while you yourselves will not even touch the burdens with one of your fingers. Woe to you! For you build the tombs of the prophets, and *it was* your fathers *who* killed them. So you are witnesses and approve the deeds of your fathers; because it was they who killed them, and you build *their tombs*. For this reason also the wisdom of God said, 'I will send them prophets and apostles, and *some* of them they will kill and *some* they will persecute, so that the blood of all the prophets, shed since the foundation of the world, may be charged against this generation, from the blood of Abel to the blood of Zechariah, who was killed between the altar and the house *of God*; yes, I tell you, it shall be charged against this generation.' Woe to you lawyers! For you have taken away the key of knowledge; you yourselves did not enter, and you hindered those who were entering" (Luke 11:46–52; cf. Matthew 23:29–32; see 2 Chronicles 24:20, 21; Matthew 23:4, 13).

Setting: On the way from Galilee to Jerusalem. Jesus warns His disciples of future events as the scribes and Pharisees turn hostile and question Him repeatedly in an attempt to catch Him in something He might say.

"And I say to you, everyone who confesses Me before men, the Son of Man will confess him also before the angels of God; but he who denies Me before men will be denied before the angels of God. And everyone who speaks a word against the Son of Man, it will be forgiven him; but he who blasphemes against the Holy Spirit, it will not be forgiven him. When they bring you before the synagogues and the rulers and the authorities, do not worry about how or what you are to speak in your defense, or what you are to say; for the Holy Spirit will teach you in that very hour what you ought to say" (Luke 12:8–12; cf. Matthew 10:32, 33; 12:31, 32; see Matthew 10:20).

Setting: On the way from Galilee to Jerusalem. After giving a parable about riches and greed, Jesus comforts the crowd and His disciples. The scribes and Pharisees turn hostile and question Him repeatedly in an attempt to catch Him in something He might say.

And He said to His disciples, "For this reason I say to you, do not worry about *your* life, *as to* what you will eat; nor for your body, *as to* what you will put on. For life is more than food, and the body more than clothing. Consider the ravens, for they neither sow nor reap; they have no storeroom nor barn, and *yet* God feeds them; how much more valuable you are than the birds! And which of you by worrying can add a *single* hour to his life's span? If then you cannot do even a very little thing, why do you worry about other matters? Consider the lilies, how they grow: they neither toil nor spin; but I tell you, not even Solomon in all his glory clothed himself like one of these. But if God so clothes the grass in the field, which is *alive* today and tomorrow is thrown into the furnace, how much more *will He clothe* you? You men of little faith! And do not seek what you will eat and what you will drink, and do not keep worrying. For all these things the nations of the world eagerly seek; but your Father knows that you need these things. But seek His kingdom, and these things will be added to you. Do not be afraid, little flock, for your Father has chosen gladly to give you the kingdom" (Luke 12:22–32; cf. Matthew 6:25–33; see 1 Kings 10:4–7; Job 38:41).

Setting: On the way from Galilee to Jerusalem. After giving a parable about riches and greed, Jesus uses another parable to challenge the crowd and His disciples to be ready for His return.

"Be dressed in readiness, and *keep* your lamps lit. Be like men who are waiting for their master when he returns from the wedding feast, so that they may immediately open *the door* to him when he comes and knocks. Blessed are those slaves whom the master will find on the alert when he comes; truly I say to you, that he will gird himself *to serve,* and have them recline *at the table,* and will come up and wait on them. Whether he comes in the second watch, or even in the third and finds *them* so, blessed are those *slaves*. But be sure of this, that if the head of the house had known at what hour the thief was coming, he would not have allowed his house to be broken into. You too, be ready; for the Son of Man is coming at an hour that you do not expect" (Luke 12:35–40; cf. Matthew 24:42–44; see Mark 13:33; Ephesians 6:14).

Setting: On the way from Galilee to Jerusalem. When Jesus uses a parable to challenge the crowd and His disciples to be ready for His return, Peter asks Him whom He is addressing.

And the Lord said, "Who then is the faithful and sensible steward, whom his master will put in charge of his servants, to give them their rations at the proper time? Blessed is that slave whom his master finds so doing when he comes. Truly I say to you that he will put him in charge of all his possessions. But if that slave says in his heart, 'My master will be a long time in coming,' and begins to beat the slaves, *both* men and women, and to eat and drink and get drunk; the master of that slave will come on a day when he does not expect *him* and at an hour he does not know, and will cut him in pieces, and assign him a place with the unbelievers. And that slave who knew his master's will and did not get ready or act in accord with his will, will receive many lashes, but the one who did know *it,* and committed deeds worthy of flogging, will receive but few. From everyone who has been given much, much will be required; and to whom they entrusted much, of him they will ask all the more" (Luke 12:42–48; cf. Matthew 24:45–51; see Leviticus 5:17).

Setting: On the way from Galilee to Jerusalem. After some present report to Him about the Galileans whose blood Pilate (Roman governor of Judea) had mixed with their sacrifices, Jesus responds to their concern by calling them to repentance.

And Jesus said to them, "Do you suppose that these Galileans were *greater* sinners than all *other* Galileans because they suffered this *fate*? I tell you, no, but unless you repent, you will all likewise perish. Or do you suppose that those eighteen on whom the tower in Siloam fell and killed them were *worse* culprits than all the men who live in Jerusalem? I tell you, no, but unless you repent, you will all likewise perish" (Luke 13:2–5; see John 9:2, 3).

Setting: On the way from Galilee to Jerusalem. After speaking a parable to the invited guests and the host at a banquet, Jesus responds to a guest's proclamation about the blessings of eating bread in the kingdom of God.

But He said to him, "A man was giving a big dinner, and he invited many; and at the dinner hour he sent his slave to say to those who had been invited, 'Come; for everything is ready now.' But they all alike began to make excuses. The first one said to him, 'I have bought a piece of land and I need to go out and look at it; please consider me excused.' Another one said, 'I have bought five yoke of oxen, and I am going to try them out; please consider me excused.' Another one said, I have married a wife, and for that reason I cannot come.' And the slave came *back* and reported this to his master. Then the head of the household became angry and said to his slave, 'Go out at once into the streets and lanes of the city and bring in here the poor and crippled and blind and lame.' And the slave said, 'Master, what you commanded has been done, and still there is room.' And the master said to the slave, 'Go out into the highways and along the hedges, and compel *them* to come in, so that my house may be filled. For I tell you, none of those men who were invited shall taste of my dinner'" (Luke 14:16–24; see Deuteronomy 24:5; Matthew 22:2–14).

Setting: On the way from Galilee to Jerusalem. After He responds to a guest's proclamation about the blessings of eating bread in the kingdom of God, Jesus presents to large crowds the demands of discipleship.

Now large crowds were going along with Him; and He turned and said to them, "If anyone comes to Me, and does not hate his own father and mother and wife and children and brothers and sisters, yes, and even his own life, he cannot be My disciple. Whoever does not carry his own cross and come after Me cannot be My disciple. For which one of you, when he wants to build a tower, does not first sit down and calculate the cost to see if he has enough to complete it? Otherwise, when he has laid a foundation and is not able to finish, all who observe it begin to ridicule him, saying, 'This man began to build and was not able to finish.' Or what king, when he sets out to meet another king in battle, will not first sit down and consider whether he is strong enough with ten thousand *men* to encounter the one coming against him with twenty thousand? Or else, while the other is still far away, he sends a delegation and asks for terms of peace. So then, none of you can be My disciple who does not give up all his possessions. Therefore, salt is good; but if even salt has become tasteless, with what will it be seasoned? It is useless either for the soil or for the manure pile; it is thrown out. He who has ears to hear, let him hear" (Luke 14:25–35; cf. Matthew 5:13; 10:37–39; see Proverb 20:18; Philippians 3:7).

Setting: On the way from Galilee to Jerusalem. The Lord responds to the Pharisees' scoffing at His teaching His disciples about stewardship.

And He said to them, "You are those who justify yourselves in the sight of men, but God knows your hearts; for that which is highly esteemed among men is detestable in the sight of God. The Law and the Prophets *were proclaimed* until John; since that time the gospel of the kingdom of God has been preached, and everyone is forcing his way into it. But is it easier for heaven and earth to pass away than for one stroke of a letter of the Law to fail" (Luke 16:15–17; cf. Matthew 5:18; see 1 Samuel 16:7; Matthew 4:23; 11:11–14).

Setting: The temple in Jerusalem. While Jesus ministers a few days before His crucifixion, with His conflict with the religious leaders of Israel escalating, the chief priests and the scribes question His authority to teach and preach.

Jesus answered and said to them, "I will also ask you a question, and you tell Me: Was the baptism of John from heaven or from men?" They reasoned among themselves, saying, "If we say, 'From heaven,' He will say, 'Why did you not believe him?' But if we say, 'From men,' all the people will stone us to death, for they are convinced that John was a prophet." So they answered that they did not know where *it came* from. And Jesus said to them, "Nor will I tell you by what authority I do these things" (Luke 20:3–8; cf. Matthew 21:23–27; Mark 11:27–33).

Setting: The Mount of Olives, just east of Jerusalem. After ministering in the temple a few days before His crucifixion, and giving His disciples more details regarding future events, Jesus speaks during His Olivet Discourse of His return.

"There will be signs in sun and moon and stars, and on the earth dismay among the nations, in perplexity at the roaring of the sea and the waves, men fainting from fear and the expectation of the things which are coming upon the world; for the powers of the heavens will be shaken. Then they will see THE SON OF MAN COMING IN A CLOUD with power and great glory. But when these things begin to take place, straighten up and lift up your heads, because your redemption is drawing near" (Luke 21:25–28, Jesus quotes from Daniel 7:13; cf. Matthew 24:29–31; Mark 13:24–27).

Setting: Jerusalem. At the time for the Passover of the Jews, after the Lord cleanses the temple, a Pharisee, Nicodemus, asks Him by night the meaning of "born again."

"For God so loved the world, that He gave His only begotten Son, that whoever believes in Him shall not perish, but have eternal life. For God did not send the Son into the world to judge the world, but that the world might be saved through Him. He who believes in Him is not judged; he who does not believe has been judged already, because he has not believed in the name of the only begotten Son of God. This is the judgment, that the Light has come into the world, and men loved darkness rather than the Light, for their deeds were evil. For everyone who does evil hates the Light, and does not come to the Light for fear that his deeds will be exposed. But he who practices the truth comes to the Light, so that his deeds may be manifested as having been wrought in God" (John 3:16–21; see Luke 19:10; John 1:4; 1:18; Romans 5:8; 1 John 1:6, 7).

Setting: Jerusalem. During a feast of the Jews, Jesus responds to criticism from the Jewish religious leaders by referring to God as His Father (thereby making Himself equal with God) and informing them that God, John the Baptist, the Scriptures, and His works all testify to His mission.

"You search the Scriptures because you think that in them you have eternal life; it is these that testify about Me; and you are unwilling to come to Me so that you may have life. I do not receive glory from men; but I know you, that you do not have the love of God in yourselves. I have come in My Father's name, and you do not receive Me; if another comes in his own name, you will receive him. How can you believe, when you receive glory from one another and you do not seek the glory that is from the *one and* only God? Do not think that I will accuse you before the Father; the one who accuses you is Moses, in whom you have set your hope. For if you believed Moses, you would believe Me, for he wrote about Me. But if you do not believe his writings, how will you believe My words?" (John 5:39–47; see Matthew 24:5; Luke 16:29, 31; 24:27; 9:28; 17:3).

Setting: Jerusalem. Just days before the Passover, with the chief priests and Pharisees plotting to seize Him and crowds welcoming Him with palm branches and praise, Jesus expresses anxiety about His upcoming crucifixion.

"Now My soul has become troubled; and what shall I say, 'Father, save Me from this hour'? But for this purpose I came to this hour. Father glorify Your name." Then a voice came out of heaven: "I have glorified it, and will glorify it again." So the crowd *of people* who stood by and heard it were saying that it had thundered; others were saying, "An angel has spoken to Him." Jesus answered and said, "This voice has not come for My sake, but for your sakes. Now judgment is upon this world; now the ruler of this world will be cast out. And I, if I am lifted up from the earth, will draw all men to Myself" (John 12:27–32; see Matthew 3:17; 26:38; John 3:14; 6:44; 11:42; 14:30).

Setting: Jerusalem. Before the Passover, after revealing to His disciples that Judas will betray Him to the chief priests and Pharisees, Jesus conveys how He will soon be glorified in His death, and commands the disciples to love one another.

Therefore when he had gone out, Jesus said, "Now is the Son of Man glorified, and God is glorified in Him; if God is glorified in Him, God will also glorify Him in Himself, and will glorify Him immediately. Little children, I am with you a little while longer. You will seek Me; and as I said to the Jews, now I also say to you, 'Where I am going, you cannot come.' A new commandment I give to you, that you love one another, even as I have loved you, that you also love one another. By this all men will know that you are My disciples, if you have love for one another" (John 13:31–35; see Leviticus 19:18; John 7:33, 34; 17:1; 1 John 3:14).

Setting: Jerusalem. Before the Passover, after giving His disciples hope that in the midst of tribulation they will have His peace, Jesus prays His high-priestly prayer.

Jesus spoke these things; and lifting up His eyes to heaven, He said, "Father, the hour has come; glorify Your Son, that the Son may glorify You, even as You gave Him authority over all flesh, that to all whom You have given Him, He may give eternal life. This is eternal life, that they may know You, the only true God, and Jesus Christ whom You have sent. I glorified You on the earth, having accomplished the work which You have given Me to do. Now, Father, glorify Me together with Yourself, with the glory which I had with You before the world was. I have manifested Your name to the men whom You gave Me out of the world; they were Yours and You gave them to Me, and they have kept Your word. Now they have come to know that everything You have given Me is from You; for the words which You gave Me I have given to them; and they received *them* and truly understood that I came forth from You, and they believed You sent Me. I ask on their behalf; I do not ask on behalf of the world, but of those whom You have given Me; for they are Yours; and all things that are Mine are Yours, and Yours are Mine; and I have been glorified in them. I am no longer in the world; and *yet* they themselves are in the world, and I come to You. Holy Father, keep them in Your name, *the name* which You have given Me, that they may be even as We *are.* While I was with them, I was keeping them in Your name which You have given Me; and I guarded them and not one of them perished but the son of perdition, so that the Scripture would be fulfilled" (John 17:1–12; see Luke 22:32; John 1:1; 3:35; 4:34; 5:44; 6:37–39, 70; 8:42; 11:41; 12:49; 13:18, 31; 16:15; 17:20; Philippians 2:9).

MEN, BLIND (See MAN, BLIND; and MEN, SPIRITUALLY BLIND)

MEN, EVIL (Also see MAN, EVIL)

Setting: Galilee. After selecting His twelve disciples, Jesus teaches the Sermon on the Mount to those disciples and a great throng of people from Judea, Jerusalem, and the central coastal region of Tyre and Sidon.

"But I say to you who hear, love your enemies, do good to those who hate you, bless those who curse you, pray for those who mistreat you. Whoever hits you on the cheek, offer him the other also; and whoever takes away your coat, do not withhold your shirt from him either. Give to everyone who asks of you, and whoever takes away what is yours, do not demand it back. Treat others the same way you want them to treat you. If you love those who love you, what credit is *that* to you? For even sinners love those who love them. If you do good to those who do good to you, what credit is *that* to you? For even sinners do the same. If you lend to those from whom you expect to receive, what credit is *that* to you? Even sinners lend to sinners in order to receive back the same *amount.* But love your enemies, and do good, and lend, expecting nothing in return; and your reward will be great, and you will be sons of the Most High; for He Himself is kind to ungrateful and evil *men.* Be merciful, just as your Father is merciful" (Luke 6:27–36; cf. Matthew 5:9, 39–48; Matthew 7:12).

Setting: On the island of Patmos (in the Aegean Sea about fifty miles southwest of Ephesus in modern Turkey). On the Lord's Day (Sunday), approximately fifty years after Jesus' resurrection, the disciple John encounters the Lord Jesus Christ, who communicates a new revelation for the apostle to record for the church in Ephesus and to six other churches in Asia.

"To the angel of the church in Ephesus write: The One who holds the seven stars in His right hand, the One who walks among the seven golden lampstands, says this: 'I know your deeds and your toil and perseverance, and that you cannot tolerate evil men, and you put to the test those who call themselves apostles, and they are not, and you found them *to be* false; and you have perseverance and have endured for My name's sake, and have not grown weary. But I have *this* against you, that you have left your first love. Therefore remember from where you have fallen, and repent and do the deeds you did at first; or else I am coming to you and will remove your lampstand out of its place—unless you repent. Yet this you do have, that you hate the deeds of the

Nicolaitans, which I also hate. He who has an ear, let him hear what the Spirit says to the churches. To him who overcomes, I will grant to eat of the tree of life which is in the Paradise of God' " (Revelation 2:1–7; see Genesis 2:9; Ezekiel 28:13; 1 John 4:1; Revelation 1:10, 11, 19).

MEN, FISHERS OF (Also see EVANGELISM)

Setting: By the Sea of Galilee. As He commences His public ministry, Jesus calls two brothers who are fishermen, Simon (Peter) and Andrew, to be His disciples.

And He said to them, "Follow Me, and I will make you fishers of men" (Matthew 4:19; cf. Mark 4:17).

Setting: Along the Sea of Galilee. Jesus calls Simon (Peter) and his brother, Andrew, to be His disciples.

And Jesus said to them, "Follow Me, and I will make you become fishers of men" (Mark 1:17; cf. Matthew 4:19).

[FISHERS OF MEN from you will be catching men]
Setting: By the Sea of Galilee. After teaching the people from Simon Peter's boat, Jesus calls Simon, James, and John to follow Him. (This appears to be a permanent call, as Simon and other companions are with Him earlier in Mark 1:35–39 and Luke 4:38, 39.)

When He had finished speaking, He said to Simon, "Put out into the deep water and let down your nets for a catch." ". . . and so also *were* James and John, sons of Zebedee, who were partners with Simon. And Jesus said to Simon, "Do not fear, from now on you will be catching men" (Luke 5:4, 10; see John 21:6).

MEN, FOOLISH (Also see MAN, FOOLISH)

Setting: On the road to Emmaus. After rising from the grave on the third day after being crucified, Jesus appears to two of His followers (who had heard reports the tomb was empty), elaborating on the purpose of His coming to earth.

And He said to them, "O foolish men and slow of heart to believe in all that the prophets have spoken! Was it not necessary for the Christ to suffer these things and to enter into His glory?" (Luke 24:25, 26).

MEN, GREAT (Also see GREATNESS)

Setting: On the way to Jerusalem, where Jesus will die on the cross. Jesus teaches His disciples about true greatness after the mother of disciples James and John asks Him to make her sons exalted rulers with Him in His coming kingdom.

But Jesus called them to Himself and said, "You know that the rulers of the Gentiles lord it over them, and *their* great men exercise authority over them. It is not this way among you, but whoever wishes to become great among you shall be your servant, and whoever wishes to be first among you shall be your slave; just as the Son of Man did not come to be served, but to serve, and to give His life a ransom for many" (Matthew 20:25–28; cf. Matthew 23:11; 26:28; Mark 10:42–45).

Setting: On the road to Jerusalem. James and John ask Jesus for special honor and privileges in His kingdom. The other disciples become angry, so the Lord uses this moment to teach all of them about servanthood.

Calling them to Himself, Jesus said to them, "You know that those who are recognized as rulers of the Gentiles lord it over them; and their great men exercise authority over them. But it is not this way among you, but whoever wishes to become great among you shall be your servant; and whoever wishes to be first among you shall be slave of all. For even the Son of Man did not come to be served, but to serve, and to give His life a ransom for many" (Mark 10:42–45; cf. Matthew 20:25–28).

MEN, HANDS OF

Setting: Galilee. Following the Transfiguration, Jesus repeats to His disciples that He must suffer, die, and be raised.

And while they were gathering together in Galilee, Jesus said to them, "The Son of Man is going to be delivered into the hands of men; and they will kill Him, and He will be raised on the third day." And they were deeply grieved (Matthew 17:22, 23; cf. Matthew 16:21; Mark 9:30–32; Luke 9:44, 45).

Setting: Galilee. After casting out an unclean spirit from a young boy, Jesus teaches His disciples in secret about His coming death and resurrection.

From there they went out and *began* to go through Galilee, and He did not want anyone to know *about it.* For He was teaching His disciples and telling them, "The Son of Man is to be delivered into the hands of men, and they will kill Him; and when He has been killed, He will rise three days later." But they did not understand *this* statement, and they were afraid to ask Him (Mark 9:30–32; cf. Matthew 17:22, 23; Luke 9:43–45; see Matthew 16:21).

Setting: Galilee. After healing the demon-possessed son of a man in the crowd, Jesus prophesies His upcoming death.

"Let these words sink into your ears; for the Son of Man is going to be delivered into the hands of men" (Luke 9:44; cf. Matthew 17:22, 23; Mark 9:31, 32).

MEN, HIRED

Setting: On the way from Galilee to Jerusalem. Jesus conveys the illustration of the prodigal son because the Pharisees and scribes complain He associates with tax collectors and sinners.

And He said, "A man had two sons. The younger of them said to his father, 'Father, give me the share of the estate that falls to me.' So he divided his wealth between them. And not many days later, the younger son gathered everything together and went on a journey into a distant country, and there he squandered his estate with loose living. Now when he had spent everything, a severe famine occurred in that country, and he began to be impoverished. So he went and hired himself out to one of the citizens of that country, and he sent him into his fields to feed swine. And he would have gladly filled his stomach with the pods that the swine were eating, and no one was giving *anything* to him. But when he came to his senses, he said, 'How many of my father's hired men have more than enough bread, but I am dying here with hunger! I will get up and go to my father, and will say to him, "Father, I have sinned against heaven, and in your sight; I am no longer worthy to be called your son; make me as one of your hired men."' So he got up and came to his father. But while he was still a long way off, his father saw him and felt compassion *for him,* and ran and embraced him and kissed him. And the son said to him, "Father, I have sinned against heaven and in your sight; I am no longer worthy to be called your son.' But the father said to his slaves, 'Quickly bring out the best robe and put it on him, and put a ring on his hand and sandals on his feet; and bring the fattened calf, kill it, and let us eat and celebrate; for this son of mine was dead and has come to life again; he was lost and has been found.' And they began to celebrate. Now his older son was in the field, when he came and approached the house, he heard music and dancing. And he summoned one of the servants and *began* inquiring what these things could be. And he said to him, 'Your brother has come, and your father has killed the fattened calf because he has received him back safe and sound. 'But he became angry and was not willing to go in; and his father came out and *began* pleading with him. But he answered and said to his father, 'Look! For so many years I have been serving you and I have never neglected a command of yours; and *yet* you have never given me a young goat, so that I might celebrate with my friends; but when this son of yours came, who has devoured your wealth with prostitutes, you killed the fattened calf for him. 'And he said to him, 'Son, you have always been with me, and all that is mine is yours. But we had to celebrate and rejoice, for this brother of yours was dead and *has begun* to live, and was lost and has been found'" (Luke 15:11–32; see Proverb 29:2).

MEN, LAST

Setting: Judea beyond the Jordan (Perea). Jesus illustrates the kingdom of heaven to His disciples through the story of laborers in the vineyard.

"For the kingdom of heaven is like a landowner who went out early in the morning to hire laborers for his vineyard. When he had agreed with the laborers for a denarius for the day, he sent them into his vineyard. And he went out about the third hour and saw others standing idle in the market place; and to those he said, 'You also go into the vineyard, and whatever is right I will give you.' And *so* they went. Again he went out about the sixth and the ninth hour, and did the same thing. And about the eleventh *hour* he went out and found others standing *around;* and he said to them, 'Why have you been standing idle here all day long?' They said to him, 'Because no one hired us.' He said to them, 'You go into the vineyard too.' When evening came, the owner of the vineyard said to his foreman, 'Call the laborers and pay them their wages, beginning with the last *group* to the first.' When those *hired* about the eleventh hour came, each one received a denarius. When those *hired* first came, they thought that they would receive more; but each of them also received a denarius. When they received it, they grumbled at the landowner, saying, 'These last men have worked *only* one hour, and you have made them equal to us who have borne the burden and the scorching heat of the day.' But he answered and said to one of them, 'Friend, I am doing you no wrong; did you not agree with me for a denarius? Take what is yours and go, but I wish to give to this last man the same as to you. It is not lawful for me to do what I wish with what is my own? Or is your eye envious because I am generous?' So the last shall be first, and the first last." (Matthew 20:1–16; cf. Matthew 19:30)

MEN, PLEASING (See APPROVAL, MAN'S)

MEN, PRECEPTS OF (Also see TRADITION)

Setting: Galilee. Pharisees and scribes from Jerusalem accuse Jesus' disciples of disobedience to tradition and the commandments.

And He answered and said to them, "Why do you yourselves transgress the commandment of God for the sake of tradition? For God said, 'HONOR YOUR FATHER AND MOTHER,' and, 'HE WHO SPEAKS EVIL OF FATHER OR MOTHER IS TO BE PUT TO DEATH.' But you say, 'Whoever says to *his* father or mother, "Whatever I have that would help you has been given *to God,*" he is not to honor his father or mother.' And *by this* you invalidated the word of God for the sake of your tradition. You hypocrites, rightly did Isaiah prophesy of you: 'THIS PEOPLE HONORS ME WITH THEIR LIPS, BUT THEIR HEART IS FAR AWAY FROM ME. BUT IN VAIN DO THEY WORSHIP ME, TEACHING AS DOCTRINES THE PRECEPTS OF MEN'" (Matthew 15:3–9, Jesus quotes from Exodus 20:12, 21:17, Leviticus 20:9; Isaiah 29:13; cf. Mark 7:5–7; see Colossians 2:22).

Setting: Galilee. The Pharisees and some of the scribes from Jerusalem question why Jesus' disciples do not follow the tradition of ceremonial hand cleansing before eating bread.

And He said to them, "Rightly did Isaiah prophesy of you hypocrites, as it is written: 'THIS PEOPLE HONORS ME WITH THEIR LIPS, BUT THEIR HEART IS FAR AWAY FROM ME. BUT IN VAIN DO THEY WORSHIP ME, TEACHING AS DOCTRINES THE PRECEPTS OF MEN.' Neglecting the commandment of God, you hold to the tradition of men." He was also saying to them, "You are experts at setting aside the commandment of God in order to keep tradition. For Moses said, 'HONOR YOUR FATHER AND YOUR MOTHER'; and, 'HE WHO SPEAKS EVIL OF FATHER OR MOTHER, IS TO BE PUT TO DEATH'; but you say, 'If a man says to *his* father or *his* mother, whatever I have that would help you is Corban (that is to say, given *to God*),' you no longer permit him to do anything for *his* father or *his* mother; *thus* invalidating the word of God by your tradition which you have handed down; and you do many things such as that" (Mark 7:6–13, Jesus quotes from Exodus 20:12; 21:17; Isaiah 29:13; cf. Matthew 15:1–6).

MEN, RIGHTEOUS (Also see RIGHTEOUSNESS)

Setting: By the Sea of Galilee. Jesus responds to the disciples' questions about the Parable of the Sower, which He has just taught from a boat.

Jesus answered them, "To you it has been granted to know the mysteries of the kingdom of heaven, but to them it has not been granted. For whoever has, to him *more* shall be given, and he will have an abundance; but whoever does not have, even what he has shall be taken away from him. Therefore, I speak to them in parables; because while seeing they do not see, and while hearing they do not hear, nor do they understand. In their case the prophecy of Isaiah is being fulfilled, which says, 'YOU WILL KEEP ON HEARING, BUT WILL NOT UNDERSTAND; YOU WILL KEEP ON SEEING, BUT WILL NOT PERCEIVE; FOR THE HEART OF THIS PEOPLE HAS BECOME DULL, WITH THEIR EARS THEY SCARCELY HEAR, AND THEY HAVE CLOSED THEIR EYES, OTHERWISE THEYWOULD SEE WITH THEIR

EYES, HEAR WITH THEIR EARS, AND UNDERSTAND WITH THEIR HEART AND RETURN, AND I WOULD HEAL THEM.' But blessed are your eyes, because they see; and your ears, because they hear. For truly I say to you that many prophets and righteous men desired to see what you see, and did not see *it,* and to hear what you hear, and did not hear *it*" (Matthew 13:11–17, Jesus quotes from Isaiah 6:9, 10; cf. Matthew 25:29; Mark 4:11–13; Luke 8:10; see Deuteronomy 29:4; John 8:56).

MEN, SIGHT OF

Setting: On the way from Galilee to Jerusalem. The Lord responds to the Pharisees' scoffing at His teaching His disciples about stewardship.

And He said to them, "You are those who justify yourselves in the sight of men, but God knows your hearts; for that which is highly esteemed among men is detestable in the sight of God. The Law and the Prophets *were proclaimed* until John; since that time the gospel of the kingdom of God has been preached, and everyone is forcing his way into it. But is it easier for heaven and earth to pass away than for one stroke of a letter of the Law to fail" (Luke 16:15–17; cf. Matthew 5:18; see 1 Samuel 16:7; Matthew 4:23; 11:11–14).

MEN, SONS OF

Setting: Galilee. After Jesus selects His twelve disciples, scribes from Jerusalem attribute His miraculous powers to Satan.

And He called them to Himself and began speaking to them in parables, "How can Satan cast out Satan? If a kingdom is divided against itself, that kingdom cannot stand. If a house is divided against itself, that house will not be able to stand. If Satan has risen up against himself and is divided, he cannot stand, but he is finished! But no one can enter the strong man's house and plunder his property unless he first binds the strong man, and then he will plunder his house. Truly I say to you, all sins shall be forgiven the sons of men, and whatever blasphemies they utter; but whoever blasphemes against the Holy Spirit never has forgiveness, but is guilty of an eternal sin"—because they were saying, "He has an unclean spirit" (Mark 3:23–30; cf. Matthew 12:25–32; Luke 12:10).

MEN, SPIRITUALLY BLIND (Also see GUIDES, BLIND)

[SPIRITUALLY BLIND MEN from blind guides of the blind]

Setting: Galilee. After rebuking the Pharisees and scribes for questioning His disciples' obedience to tradition and the commandments, Jesus instructs the disciples.

But He answered and said, "Every plant which My heavenly Father did not plant shall be uprooted. Let them alone; they are blind guides of the blind. And if a blind man guides a blind man, both will fall into a pit" (Matthew 15:13, 14; cf. Matthew 23:16; Luke 6:39).

[SPIRITUALLY BLIND MEN from blind guides and blind men]

Setting: The temple in Jerusalem. After the Jewish religious leaders test Him with questions, Jesus pronounces the fourth of eight woes on them in front of the crowds and His disciples.

"Woe to you, blind guides, who say, 'Whoever swears by the temple, *that* is nothing; but whoever swears by the gold of the temple is obligated.' You fools and blind men! Which is more important, the gold or the temple that sanctified the gold? And, 'Whoever swears by the altar, *that* is nothing, but whoever swears by the offering on it, he is obligated.' You blind men, which is more important, the offering, or the altar that sanctifies the offering? Therefore, whoever swears by the altar, swears *both* by the altar and by everything on it. And whoever swears by the temple, swears *both* by the temple and by Him who dwells within it. And whoever swears by heaven, swears *both* by the throne of God and by Him who sits upon it" (Matthew 23:16–22; see Exodus 29:37; 1 Kings 8:13; Isaiah 66:1; Matthew 15:14).

[SPIRITUALLY BLIND MEN from blind guides]

Setting: The temple in Jerusalem. After the Jewish religious leaders test Him with questions, Jesus pronounces the fifth of eight woes on them in front of the crowds and His disciples.

"Woe to you, scribes and Pharisees, hypocrites! For you tithe mint and dill and cummin, and have neglected the weightier provisions of the law: justice and mercy and faithfulness; but these are things you should have done without neglecting the others. You blind guides, who strain out a gnat and swallow a camel!" (Matthew 23:23, 24).

[SPIRITUALLY BLIND MEN from blind Pharisee]
Setting: The temple in Jerusalem. After the Jewish religious leaders test Him with questions, Jesus pronounces the sixth of eight woes on them in front of the crowds and His disciples.

"Woe to you, scribes and Pharisees, hypocrites! For you clean the outside of the cup and of the dish, but inside they are full of robbery and self-indulgence. You blind Pharisee, first clean the inside of the cup and of the dish, so that the outside of it may become clean also" (Matthew 23:25, 26; see Mark 7:4).

[SPIRITUALLY BLIND MEN from those who do not see]
Setting: Jerusalem. Following the Pharisees' interrogation and dismissal of the formerly blind man Jesus healed on the Sabbath, the Lord addresses the Pharisees about His mission in this world.

And Jesus said, "For judgment I came into this world, so that those who do not see may see, and that those who see may become blind" (John 9:39; see Luke 4:18; John 5:22, 27).

[SPIRITUALLY BLIND MEN inferred from context]
Setting: Jerusalem. Following the Pharisees' interrogation and dismissal of the formerly blind man Jesus healed on the Sabbath, the Lord responds to the Pharisees' question whether they are spiritually blind.

Jesus said to them, "If you were blind, you would have no sin; but since you say, 'We see,' your sin remains" (John 9:41; see John 15:22–24).

MEN, TRADITION OF (See TRADITION OF MEN)

MEN, TWO

Setting: On the Mount of Olives, just east of Jerusalem. During His Olivet Discourse, after answering His disciples' questions as to when the temple will be destroyed and Jerusalem overrun, along with the signs of His coming and the end of the age, Jesus teaches them the Parable of the Fig Tree.

"Now learn the parable from the fig tree: when its branch has already become tender and puts forth its leaves, you know that summer is near; so, you too, when you see all these things, recognize that He is near, *right* at the door. Truly, I say to you, this generation will not pass away until all these things take place. Heaven and earth will pass away, but My words will not pass away. But of that day and hour no one knows, not even the angels of heaven, nor the Son, but the Father alone. For the coming of the Son of Man will be just like the days of Noah. For as in those days before the flood they were eating and drinking, marrying and giving in marriage, until the day that Noah entered the ark, and they did not understand until the flood came and took them all away; so will the coming of the Son of Man be. Then there will be two men in the field; one will be taken and one will be left. Two women *will be* grinding at the mill; one will be taken and one will be left" (Matthew 24:32–41; cf. Mark 13:28–32; Luke 17:34–36; 21:28–33; see Genesis 6:5; 7:7; Matthew 5:18; 10:23; James 5:9).

Setting: On the way from Galilee to Jerusalem. After the Pharisees question Him about the coming of the kingdom of God, Jesus tells His disciples of His second coming.

And He said to the disciples, "The days will come when you will long to see one of the days of the Son of Man, and you will not see it. They will say to you, 'Look there! Look here!' Do not go away, and do not run after *them*. For just like the lightning, when it flashes out of one part of the sky, shines to the other part of the sky, so will the Son of Man be in His day. But first He must suffer many things and be rejected by this generation. And just as it happened in the days of Noah, so it will be also in the days of the

Son of Man: they were eating, they were drinking, they were marrying, they were being given in marriage, until the day that Noah entered the ark, and the flood came and destroyed them all. It was the same as happened in the days of Lot: they were eating, they were drinking, they were buying, they were selling, they were planting, they were building; but on the day that Lot went out from Sodom it rained fire and brimstone from heaven and destroyed them all. It will be just the same on the day that the Son of Man is revealed. On that day, the one who is on the housetop and whose goods are in the house must not go down to take them out; and likewise the one who is in the field must not turn back. Remember Lot's wife. Whoever seeks to keep his life will lose it, and whoever loses *his life* will preserve it. I tell you, on that night there will be two in one bed; one will be taken and the other will be left. There will be two women grinding at the same place; one will be taken and the other will be left. [Two men will be in the field; one will be taken and the other will be left."] And answering they said to Him, "Where, Lord?" And He said to them, "Where the body *is*, there also the vultures will be gathered" (Luke 17:22–37; see Genesis 19; Matthew 10:39; 16:21, 27; 24:17–28, 37–41).

Setting: On the way from Galilee to Jerusalem. After instructing His disciples about persistence in prayer, Jesus conveys a parable about self-righteousness.

And He also told this parable to some people who trusted in themselves that they were righteous, and viewed others with contempt: "Two men went up into the temple to pray, one a Pharisee and the other a tax collector. The Pharisee stood and was praying this to himself: 'God, I thank You that I am not like other people: swindlers, unjust, adulterers, or even like this tax collector. I fast twice a week; I pay tithes of all that I get.' But the tax collector, standing some distance away, was even unwilling to lift up his eyes to heaven, but was beating his breast, saying, 'God, be merciful to me, the sinner!' I tell you, this man went to his house justified rather than the other; for everyone who exalts himself will be humbled, but he who humbles himself will be exalted" (Luke 18:9–14; see Ezra 9:6; Matthew 6:5, 23:12; Luke 11:42, 16:15; Romans 14:3, 10).

Setting: The temple in Jerusalem. Following the Feast of Booths and the scribes' and Pharisees' failed attempt to stone a woman for committing adultery, Jesus returns the next day to teach. His enemies question His testimony about Himself.

Jesus answered and said to them, "Even if I testify about Myself, My testimony is true, for I know where I came from and where I am going; but you do not know where I come from or where I am going. You judge according to the flesh; I am not judging anyone. But even if I do judge, My judgment is true; for I am not alone *in it,* but I and the Father who sent Me. Even in your law it has been written that the testimony of two men is true. I am He who testifies about Myself, and the Father who sent Me testifies about Me." So they were saying to Him, "Where is Your Father?" Jesus answered, "You know neither Me nor My Father; if you knew Me, you would know My Father also" (John 8:14–19; see Deuteronomy 17:6; 19:15; Matthew 18:16; John 3:17; 5:30, 37; 7:28).

MEN, VIOLENT

Setting: Galilee. While speaking to the crowds, Jesus pays tribute to the ministry of John the Baptist, but emphasizes that the one who is least in the kingdom of heaven is greater than John.

As these men were going *away,* Jesus began to speak to the crowds about John, "What did you go out into the wilderness to see? A reed shaken by the wind? But what did you go out to see? A man dressed in soft *clothing?* Those who wear soft *clothing* are in kings' palaces! But what did you go out to see? A prophet? Yes, I tell you, and the one who is more than a prophet. This is the one about whom it is written, 'BEHOLD, I SEND MY MESSENGER AHEAD OF YOU, WHO WILL PREPARE YOUR WAY BEFORE YOU.' Truly, I say to you, among those born of women there has not arisen *anyone* greater than John the Baptist! Yet the one who is least in the kingdom of heaven is greater than he. From the days of John the Baptist until now the kingdom of heaven suffers violence, and violent men take it by force. For all the prophets and the Law prophesied until John. And, if you are willing to accept *it,* John himself is Elijah who was to come. He who has ears to hear, let him hear" (Matthew 11:7–15, Jesus quotes from Malachi 3:1; cf. Malachi 4:5; Luke 7:24–28; Luke 16:16; see Matthew 14:5).

MEN, WISE (Also see MAN, WISE)

Setting: The temple in Jerusalem. After the Jewish religious leaders test Him with questions, Jesus pronounces the eighth of eight woes on them in front of the crowds and His disciples.

"Woe to you, scribes and Pharisees, hypocrites! For you build the tombs of the prophets and adorn the monuments of the righteous, and say, 'If we had been *living* in the days of our fathers, we would not have been partners with them in *shedding* the blood of the prophets.' So you testify against yourselves, that you are sons of those who murdered the prophets. Fill up, then, the measure *of the guilt* of you fathers. You serpents, you brood of vipers, how will you escape the sentence of hell? Therefore, behold, I am sending you prophets and wise men and scribes; some of them you will kill and crucify, and some of them you will scourge in your synagogues, and persecute from city to city, so that upon you may fall *the guilt of* all the righteous blood shed on earth, from the blood of righteous Abel to the blood of Zechariah, the son of Berechiah, whom you murdered between the temple and the altar. Truly I say to you, all these things will come upon this generation" (Matthew 23:29–36; cf. 2 Chronicles 24:21; Zechariah 1:1; Matthew 3:7; Luke 11:47–52; see Matthew 10:23).

MEN IN THE FIELD (Listed under FIELD, MEN IN THE)

MEN'S APPROVAL (See APPROVAL, MAN'S)

MEN'S LIVES (Listed as LIVES, MEN'S)

MERCHANT (Also see COMMERCE; and DEALERS)

Setting: By the Sea of Galilee. Jesus declares the Parable of the Pearl to the crowds.

"Again, the kingdom of heaven is like a merchant seeking fine pearls, and upon finding one pearl of great value, he went and sold all that he had and bought it" (Matthew 13:45, 46).

MERCHANTS (See COMMERCE; DEALERS; MERCHANT)

MERCIFUL (Also see COMPASSION; and MERCY)

Setting: Galilee. Early in His ministry, Jesus presents the Beatitudes (part of the Sermon on the Mount) to His disciples and the gathered crowds from Galilee, Decapolis, Jerusalem, Judea, and beyond the Jordan.

"Blessed are the merciful, for they shall receive mercy" (Matthew 5:7; cf. Proverb 11:17; see 13:35).

Setting: Galilee. After selecting His twelve disciples, Jesus teaches the Sermon on the Mount to those disciples and a great throng of people from Judea, Jerusalem, and the central coastal region of Tyre and Sidon.

"But I say to you who hear, love your enemies, do good to those who hate you, bless those who curse you, pray for those who mistreat you. Whoever hits you on the cheek, offer him the other also; and whoever takes away your coat, do not withhold your shirt from him either. Give to everyone who asks of you, and whoever takes away what is yours, do not demand it back. Treat others the same way you want them to treat you. If you love those who love you, what credit is *that* to you? For even sinners love those who love them. If you do good to those who do good to you, what credit is *that* to you? For even sinners do the same. If you lend to those from whom you expect to receive, what credit is *that* to you? Even sinners lend to sinners in order to receive back the same *amount*. But love your enemies, and do good, and lend, expecting nothing in return; and your reward will be great, and you will be sons of the Most High; for He Himself is kind to ungrateful and evil *men*. Be merciful, just as your Father is merciful" (Luke 6:27–36; cf. Matthew 5:9, 39–48; Matthew 7:12).

Setting: On the way from Galilee to Jerusalem. After instructing His disciples about persistence in prayer, Jesus conveys a parable about self-righteousness.

And He also told this parable to some people who trusted in themselves that they were righteous, and viewed others with contempt: "Two men went up into the temple to pray, one a Pharisee and the other a tax collector. The Pharisee stood and was praying this to himself: 'God, I thank You that I am not like other people: swindlers, unjust, adulterers, or even like this tax collector. I fast twice a week; I pay tithes of all that I get.' But the tax collector, standing some distance away, was even unwilling to lift up his eyes to heaven, but was beating his breast, saying, 'God, be merciful to me, the sinner!' I tell you, this man went to his house justified rather than the other; for everyone who exalts himself will be humbled, but he who humbles himself will be exalted" (Luke 18:9–14; see Ezra 9:6; Matthew 6:5, 23:12; Luke 11:42; 16:15; Romans 14:3, 10).

MERCY (Also see COMPASSION; and MERCIFUL)

Setting: Galilee. Early in His ministry, Jesus presents the Beatitudes (part of the Sermon on the Mount) to His disciples and the gathered crowds from Galilee, Decapolis, Jerusalem, Judea, and beyond the Jordan.

"Blessed are the merciful, for they shall receive mercy" (Matthew 5:7; cf. Proverb 11:17; see Matthew 13:35).

Setting: Capernaum of Galilee. Jesus illustrates the matter of forgiveness after Peter asks Him if forgiving someone up to seven times who has sinned against him is adequate.

"For this reason the kingdom of heaven may be compared to a king who wished to settle accounts with his slaves. When he had begun to settle *them,* one who owed him ten thousand talents was brought to him. But since he did not have *the means* to repay, his lord commanded him to be sold, along with his wife and children and all that he had, and repayment to be made. So the slave fell *to the ground* and prostrated himself before him, saying, 'Have patience with me and I will repay you everything.' And the lord of that slave felt compassion and released him and forgave him the debt. But that slave went out and found one of his fellow slaves who owed him a hundred denarii; and he seized him and *began* to choke *him,* saying, 'Pay back what you owe.' So his fellow slave fell *to the ground* and *began* to plead with him, saying, 'Have patience with me and I will repay you.' But he was unwilling and went and threw him in prison until he should pay back what was owed. So when his fellow slaves saw what had happened, they were deeply grieved and came and reported to their lord all that had happened. Then summoning him, his lord said to him, 'You wicked slave, I forgave you all that debt because you pleaded with me. Should you not also have had mercy on your fellow slave, in the same way that I had mercy on you?' And his lord, moved with anger, handed him over to the torturers until he should repay all that was owed him. My heavenly Father will also do the same to you, if each of you does not forgive his brother from your heart" (Matthew 18:23–35; cf. Matthew 6:12, 14, 15; Luke 7:42; see Matthew 25:19–28).

Setting: The temple in Jerusalem. After the Jewish religious leaders test Him with questions, Jesus pronounces the fifth of eight woes on them in front of the crowds and His disciples.

"Woe to you, scribes and Pharisees, hypocrites! For you tithe the mint and dill and cummin, and have neglected the weightier provisions of the law: justice and mercy and faithfulness; but these are things you should have done without neglecting the others. You blind guides, who strain out a gnat and swallow a camel!" (Matthew 23:23, 24).

Setting: The country of the Gerasenes, on the east side of the Sea of Galilee. Jesus encounters and heals a man possessed by a legion of demons.

And He did not let him, but He said to him, "Go home to your people and report to them what great things the Lord has done for you, and *how* He had mercy on you" (Mark 5:19; cf. Luke 8:39; see Matthew 8:33, 34; Luke 8:36–38).

Setting: On the way from Galilee to Jerusalem. While being tested by a lawyer, Jesus tells him the story of the good Samaritan.

Jesus replied and said, "A man was going down from Jerusalem to Jericho, and fell among robbers, and they stripped him and beat him, and went away leaving him half dead. And by chance a priest was going down on that road, and when he saw him, he passed by on the other side. Likewise a Levite also, when he came to the place and saw him, passed by on the other side. But a Samaritan, who was on a journey, came upon him; and when he saw him, he felt compassion, and came to him and bandaged up his wounds, pouring oil and wine on *them;* and he put him on his own beast, and brought him to an inn and took care of him. On the next day he took out two denarii and gave them to the innkeeper and said, 'Take care of him; and whatever more you spend, when I return I will repay you.' Which of these three do you think proved to be a neighbor to the man who fell into the robbers' *hands?"* And he said, "The one who showed mercy toward him." Then Jesus said to him, "Go and do the same" (Luke 10:30–37).

Setting: On the way from Galilee to Jerusalem. After responding to the Pharisees' scoffing at His teaching the disciples about stewardship and the permanence of the Law, Jesus conveys the story of the rich man and Lazarus.

"Now there was a rich man, and he habitually dressed in purple and fine linen, joyously living in splendor every day. And a poor man named Lazarus was laid at his gate, covered with sores, and longing to be fed with the *crumbs* which were falling from the rich man's table; besides, even the dogs were coming and licking his sores. Now the poor man died and was carried away by the angels to Abraham's bosom; and the rich man also died and was buried. In Hades he lifted up his eyes, being in torment, and saw Abraham far away and Lazarus in his bosom. And he cried out and said, 'Father Abraham, have mercy on me, and send Lazarus so that he may dip the tip of his finger in water and cool off my tongue, for I am in agony in this flame.' But Abraham said, 'Child, remember that during your life you received your good things, and likewise Lazarus bad things; but now he is being comforted here, and you are in agony. And besides all this, between us and you there is a great chasm fixed, so that those who wish to come over from here to you will not be able, and *that* none may cross over from there to us.' And he said, 'Then I beg you, father, that you send him to my father's house—for I have five brothers—in order that he may warn them, so that they will not also come to this place of torment.' But Abraham said, 'They have Moses and the Prophets; let them hear them.' But he said, 'No, father Abraham, but if someone goes to them from the dead, they will repent!' But he said to him, 'If they do not listen to Moses and the Prophets, they will not be persuaded even if someone rises from the dead' " (Luke 16:19–31; see Luke 3:8; 6:24).

MESSENGER (Also see ANGEL)

Setting: Galilee. While speaking to the crowds, Jesus pays tribute to the ministry of John the Baptist, but emphasizes that the one who is least in the kingdom of heaven is greater than John.

As these men were going *away,* Jesus began to speak to the crowds about John, "What did you go out into the wilderness to see? A reed shaken by the wind? But what did you go out to see? A man dressed in soft *clothing?* Those who wear soft *clothing* are in kings' palaces! But what did you go out to see? A prophet? Yes, I tell you, and the one who is more than a prophet. This is the one about whom it is written, 'BEHOLD, I SEND MY MESSENGER AHEAD OF YOU, WHO WILL PREPARE YOUR WAY BEFORE YOU.' Truly, I say to you, among those born of women there has not arisen *anyone* greater than John the Baptist! Yet the one who is least in the kingdom of heaven is greater than he. From the days of John the Baptist until now the kingdom of heaven suffers violence, and violent men take it by force. For all the prophets and the Law prophesied until John. And, if you are willing to accept *it,* John himself is Elijah who was to come. He who has ears to hear, let him hear" (Matthew 11:7–15, Jesus quotes from Malachi 3:1; cf. Malachi 4:5; Luke 7:24–28; 16:16; see Matthew 14:5).

Setting: Galilee. After Jesus responds to the disciples of John the Baptist whether He is the promised Messiah, the Lord speaks to the crowds about John.

When the messengers of John had left, He began to speak to the crowds about John, "What did you go out into the wilderness to see? A reed shaken by the wind? But what did you go out to see? A man dressed in soft clothing? Those who are splendidly clothed and live in luxury are *found* in royal palaces! But what did you go out to see? A prophet? Yes, I say to you, and one who is more than a prophet. This is the one about whom it is written, 'BEHOLD, I SEND MY MESSENGER AHEAD OF YOU, WHO WILL PREPARE YOUR WAY BEFORE YOU.' I say to you, among those born of women there is no one greater than John; yet he who is least in the kingdom of God is greater than he" (Luke 7:24–28, Jesus quotes from Malachi 3:1; cf. Matthew 11:7–11).

MESSENGERS FROM HEAVEN (See ANGEL; and ANGELS)

MESSIAH (Also see CHRIST, THE; DAVID, SON OF; KING, JESUS AS; KING OF THE JEWS; SON OF GOD; and SON OF MAN)

[MESSIAH from *the* BLIND RECEIVE SIGHT and *the* lame walk, *the* lepers are cleansed and *the* deaf hear, *the* dead are raised up]

Setting: Galilee. As He teaches and preaches, Jesus responds to John the Baptist's question (posed by some of John's disciples) whether He is Israel's promised Messiah.

Jesus answered and said to them, "Go and report to John what you hear and see: *the* BLIND RECEIVE SIGHT and *the* lame walk, *the* lepers are cleansed and *the* deaf hear, *the* dead are raised up, and *the* POOR HAVE THE GOSPEL PREACHED TO THEM. And blessed is he who does not take offense at Me" (Matthew 11:4–6, Jesus quotes from Isaiah 35:5f; cf. Luke 7:22, 23).

[MESSIAH from I am]
Setting: Jerusalem. Following His betrayal by Judas and His arrest, Jesus confirms He is the Christ to the high priest and all the chief priests, as they seek justification for putting Him to death.

And Jesus said, "I am; and you shall see THE SON OF MAN SITTING AT THE RIGHT HAND OF POWER, and COMING WITH THE CLOUDS OF HEAVEN" (Mark 14:62, Jesus quotes from Psalm 110:1; Daniel 7:13; cf. Matthew 26:57–68; see Luke 22:54).

[MESSIAH from THE SPIRIT OF THE LORD IS UPON ME, BECAUSE HE ANOINTED ME TO PREACH THE GOSPEL TO THE POOR. HE HAS SENT ME TO PROCLAIM RELEASE TO THE CAPTIVES, AND RECOVERY OF SIGHT TO THE BLIND, TO SET FREE THOSE WHO ARE OPPRESSED, TO PROCLAIM THE FAVORABLE YEAR OF THE LORD]
Setting: The synagogue in Jesus' hometown of Nazareth in Galilee. At the beginning of His public ministry, Jesus fulfills prophecy by reading on the Sabbath from the book of the prophet Isaiah.

And the book of the prophet Isaiah was handed to Him. And He opened the book and found the place where it was written, "THE SPIRIT OF THE LORD IS UPON ME, BECAUSE HE ANOINTED ME TO PREACH THE GOSPEL TO THE POOR. HE HAS SENT ME TO PROCLAIM RELEASE TO THE CAPTIVES, AND RECOVERY OF SIGHT TO THE BLIND, TO SET FREE THOSE WHO ARE OPPRESSED, TO PROCLAIM THE FAVORABLE YEAR OF THE LORD." And He closed the book, gave it back to the attendant and sat down; and the eyes of all in the synagogue were fixed on Him. And He began to say to them, "Today this Scripture has been fulfilled in your hearing" (Luke 4:17–21, Jesus quotes from Isaiah 61:1, 2).

[MESSIAH from *the* BLIND RECEIVE SIGHT, *the* lame walk, *the* lepers are cleansed, and *the* deaf hear, *the* dead are raised up, *the* POOR HAVE THE GOSPEL PREACHED TO THEM]
Setting: Galilee. After Jesus raises a woman's son from the dead in Nain, the disciples of John the Baptist inquire whether He is the promised Messiah.

And He answered and said to them, "Go and report to John what you have seen and heard: *the* BLIND RECEIVE SIGHT, *the* lame walk, *the* lepers are cleansed, and *the* deaf hear, *the* dead are raised up, *the* POOR HAVE THE GOSPEL PREACHED TO THEM. Blessed is he who does not take offense at Me" (Luke 7:22, 23, Jesus quotes from Isaiah 35:5; 61:1; cf. Matthew 11:2–6).

[MESSIAH from many prophets and kings wished to see the things you see, and did not see *them*, and to hear the things which you hear, and did not hear *them*]
Setting: On the way from Galilee to Jerusalem. After responding to a report from the seventy sent out in pairs to every place He Himself will soon visit, the Lord addresses His disciples in private.

Turning to the disciples, He said privately, "Blessed *are* the eyes which see the things you see, for I say to you, that many prophets and kings wished to see the things you see, and did not see *them*, and to hear the things which you hear, and did not hear *them*" (Luke 10:23, 24; cf. Matthew 13:16, 17; see Luke 10:17).

[MESSIAH from I who speak to you am *He*]
Setting: Sychar in Samaria, on the way to Galilee. Jesus interacts with a Samaritan woman at Jacob's well, while His disciples are buying food.

The woman said to Him, "I know that Messiah is coming (He who is called Christ); when that One comes, He will declare all things to us." Jesus said to her, "I who speak to you am *He*" (John 4:25, 26; see Matthew 1:16; John 8:28, 58).

[MESSIAH from I am *He*]
Setting: The temple treasury in Jerusalem. Following the Feast of Booths and the scribes' and Pharisees' failed attempt to stone a woman for adultery, Jesus returns the next day to teach. They question His testimony about Himself.

Then He said again to them, "I go away, and you will seek Me, and will die in your sin; where I am going, you cannot come." So the Jews were saying, "Surely He will not kill Himself, will He, since He says, "Where I am going, you cannot come'?" And He was saying to them, "You are from below, I am from above; you are of this world, I am not of this world. Therefore I said to you that you will die in your sins; for unless you believe that I am *He*, you will die in your sins." So they were saying to Him, "Who are You?" Jesus said to them, "What have I been saying to you *from* the beginning? I have many things to speak and to judge concerning you, but He who sent Me is true; and the things which I heard from Him, these I speak to the world" (John 8:21–26; see John 3:31–33; 5:34, 35; 17:14, 16).

[MESSIAH from I am *He*]
Setting: The temple treasury in Jerusalem. Following the Feast of Booths and the scribes' and Pharisees' failed attempt to stone a woman for committing adultery, Jesus returns the next day to teach. They question His testimony about Himself.

So Jesus said, "When you lift up the Son of Man, then you will know that I am *He*, and I do nothing on my own initiative, but I speak these things as the Father taught Me. And He who sent Me is with Me; He has not left Me alone, for I always do the things that are pleasing to Him" (John 8:28, 29; see John 3:14).

[MESSIAH from I am *He*]
Setting: Jerusalem. Before the Passover, with His death on the cross nearing, Jesus explains the reason for His vivid example of servanthood in washing His disciples' feet.

So when He had washed their feet, and taken His garments and reclined *at the table* again, He said to them, "Do you know what I have done to you? You call Me Teacher and Lord; and you are right, for *so* I am. If I then, the Lord and the Teacher, washed your feet, you also ought to wash one another's feet. For I gave you an example that you also should do as I did to you. Truly, truly I say to you, a slave is not greater than his master, nor *is* one who is sent greater than the one who sent him. If you know these things, you are blessed if you do them. I do not speak of all of you. I know the ones I have chosen; but *it is* that the Scripture may be fulfilled, 'HE WHO EATS MY BREAD HAS LIFTED UP HIS HEEL AGAINST ME.' From now on I am telling you before *it* comes to pass, so that when it does occur, you may believe that I am *He*. Truly, truly, I say to you, he who receives whomever I send receives Me; and he who receives Me receives Him who sent Me" (John 13:12–20; Jesus quotes from Psalm 41:9; see Matthew 7:24; 10:24, 40; John 8:24; 14:29; 1 Peter 5:3).

MESSIAH, PRAISING JESUS AS THE

[PRAISING JESUS AS THE MESSIAH from OUT OF THE MOUTH OF INFANTS AND NURSING BABIES YOU HAVE PREPARED PRAISE FOR YOURSELF]
Setting: The temple in Jerusalem. After cleansing the temple by driving out the money changers and merchants, Jesus comments to the indignant chief priests and scribes about the praises the children render unto Him.

But when the chief priests and the scribes saw the wonderful things that He had done, and the children who were shouting in the temple, "Hosanna to the Son of David," they became indignant and said to Him, "Do You hear what these *children* are saying?" And Jesus said to them, "Yes, have you never read, 'OUT OF THE MOUTH OF INFANTS AND NURSING BABIES YOU HAVE PREPARED PRAISE FOR YOURSELF'?" (Matthew 21:15, 16, Jesus quotes from Psalm 8:2; see Matthew 9:27).

MESSIAHS, FALSE (See CHRISTS, FALSE)

MIDNIGHT (Also see EVENING; and NIGHT)

Setting: On the Mount of Olives, just east of Jerusalem. During His Olivet Discourse, after answering His disciples' questions as to when the temple will be destroyed and Jerusalem overrun, along with the signs of His coming and the end of the age, Jesus reemphasizes to His disciples that they should be on the alert for His return.

"Then the kingdom of heaven will be comparable to ten virgins, who took their lamps and went out to meet the bridegroom. Five of them were foolish, and five were prudent. For when the foolish took their lamps, they took no oil with them, but the prudent took oil in flasks along with their lamps. Now while the bridegroom was delaying, they all got drowsy and *began* to sleep. But at midnight there was a shout, 'Behold, the bridegroom! Come out to meet *him.*' Then all those virgins rose and trimmed their lamps. The foolish said to the prudent, 'Give us some of your oil, for our lamps are going out.' But the prudent answered, 'No, there will not be enough for us and you *too;* go instead to the dealers and buy *some* for yourselves.' And while they were going away to make the purchase, the bridegroom came, and those who were ready went in with him to the wedding feast; and the door was shut. Later the other virgins also came, saying, 'Lord, lord, open up for us.' But he answered, 'Truly I say to you, I do not know you.' Be on the alert then, for you do not know the day nor the hour" (Matthew 25:1–13; cf. Matthew 24:42; Luke 12:35; see Matthew 7:21, 24).

Setting: On the Mount of Olives, east of the temple in Jerusalem. After predicting the temple's destruction, Jesus responds during His Olivet Discourse to questions from Peter, James, John, and Andrew about other future events.

"Take heed, keep on the alert; for you do not know when the *appointed* time will come. *It is* like a man away on a journey, *who* upon leaving his house and putting his slaves in charge, *assigning* to each one his task, also commanded the doorkeeper to stay on the alert. Therefore, be on the alert—for you do not know when the master of the house is coming, whether in the evening, at midnight, or when the rooster crows, or in the morning—in case he should come suddenly and find you asleep. What I say to you I say to all, 'Be on the alert!' " (Mark 13:33–37; cf. Matthew 24:42–43; Luke 21:34–36; see Luke 12:36–38; Ephesians 6:18).

Setting: On the way from Galilee to Jerusalem. After revealing to His disciples how to pray, Jesus illustrates persistence in prayer.

Then He said to them, "Suppose one of you has a friend, and goes to him at midnight and says to him, 'Friend, lend me three loaves; for a friend of mine has come to me from a journey, and I have nothing to set before him'; and from inside he answers and says, 'Do not bother me; the door has already been shut and my children and I are in bed; I cannot get up and give you *anything.*' I tell you, even though he will not get up and give him *anything* because he is his friend, yet because of his persistence he will get up and give him as much as he needs. So I say to you, ask, and it will be given to you; seek, and you will find; knock, and it will be opened to you. For everyone who asks, receives; and he who seeks, finds; and to him who knocks, it will be opened" (Luke 11:5–10; cf. Matthew 7:7, 8; see Luke 18:1–5).

MILE

Setting: Galilee. During the early part of His ministry, Jesus preaches the Sermon on the Mount to His disciples and the multitudes.

"Whoever forces you to go one mile, go with him two" (Matthew 5:41).

MILL (Also see MILLSTONE)

Setting: On the Mount of Olives, just east of Jerusalem. During His Olivet Discourse, after answering His disciples' questions as to when the temple will be destroyed and Jerusalem overrun, along with the signs of His coming and the end of the age, Jesus teaches them the Parable of the Fig Tree.

"Now learn the parable from the fig tree: when its branch has already become tender and puts forth its leaves, you know that summer is near; so, you too, when you see all these things, recognize that He is near, *right* at the door. Truly, I say to you, this generation will not pass away until all these things take place. Heaven and earth will pass away, but My words will not pass away. But of that day and hour no one knows, not even the angels of heaven, nor the Son, but the Father alone. For the coming of the Son of Man will be just like the days of Noah. For as in those days before the flood they were eating and drinking, marrying and giving in marriage, until the day that Noah entered the ark, and they did not understand until the flood came and took them all away; so will the coming of the Son of Man be. Then there will be two men in the field; one will be taken and one will be left. Two women *will be* grinding at the mill; one will be taken and one will be left" (Matthew 24:32–41; cf. Mark 13:28–32; Luke 17:34–36; 21:28–33; see Genesis 6:5; 7:7; Matthew 5:18; 10:23; James 5:9).

MILLSTONE (Also see MILL)

Setting: Capernaum of Galilee. Jesus answers His disciples' question about greatness, or rank, in the kingdom of heaven.

And He called a child to Himself and set him before them, and said, "Truly I say to you, unless you are converted and become like children, you will not enter the kingdom of heaven. Whoever then humbles himself as this child, he is the greatest in the kingdom of heaven. And whoever receives one such child in My name receives Me; but whoever causes one of these little ones who believe in Me to stumble, it would be better for him to have a heavy millstone hung around his neck, and to be drowned in the depth of the sea"(Matthew 18:2–6; cf. Matthew 19:14; Mark 9:33–37, 42; Luke 9:47, 48; Luke 17:1, 2).

Setting: Capernaum of Galilee. As Jesus teaches His disciples in private, they ask Him about greatness.

But Jesus said, "Do not hinder him, for there is no one who will perform a miracle in My name, and be able soon afterward to speak evil of Me. For he who is not against us is for us. For whoever gives you a cup of water to drink because of your name as *followers* of Christ, truly I say to you, he will not lose his reward. Whoever causes one of these little ones who believe to stumble, it would be better for him if, with a heavy millstone hung around his neck, he had been cast into the sea. If your hand causes you to stumble, cut it off; it is better for you to enter life crippled, than, having your two hands, to go into hell, into the unquenchable fire, [where THEIR WORM DOES NOT DIE, AND THE FIRE IS NOT QUENCHED.] If your foot causes you to stumble, cut it off; it is better for you to enter life lame, than, having your two feet, to be cast into hell, [where THEIR WORM DOES NOT DIE, AND THE FIRE IS NOT QUENCHED.] If your eye causes you to stumble, throw it out; it is better for you to enter the kingdom of God with one eye, than, having two eyes, to be cast into hell, where THEIR WORM DOES NOT DIE, AND THE FIRE IS NOT QUENCHED. For everyone will be salted with fire. Salt is good; but if the salt becomes unsalty, with what will you make it salty *again?* Have salt in yourselves, and be at peace with one another" (Mark 9:39–50; Jesus quotes from Isaiah 66:24; cf. Matthew 18:6–9; Luke 9:49, 50; see Matthew 5:13, 29, 30; 10:42; 12:30; 18:5, 6).

Setting: On the way from Galilee to Jerusalem. After conveying the story of the rich man and Lazarus, the Lord gives His disciples instruction on forgiveness.

He said to His disciples, "It is inevitable that stumbling blocks come, but woe to him through whom they come! It would be better for him if a millstone were hung around his neck and he were thrown into the sea, than that he would cause one of these little ones to stumble. Be on your guard! If your brother sins, rebuke him; and if he repents, forgive him. And if he sins against you seven times a day, and returns to you seven times, saying, 'I repent,' forgive him" (Luke 17:1–4; see Matthew 18:5–7, 15, 21, 22).

MINA (Also see MINAS; MONEY; and TALENTS, PARABLE OF THE)

Setting: Jericho, on the way to Jerusalem. After commending Zaccheus's faith in Him, Jesus provides a parable about stewardship.

So He said, "A nobleman went to a distant country to receive a kingdom for himself, and *then* return. And he called ten of his slaves, and gave them ten minas and said to them, 'Do business *with this* until I come *back.*' But his citizens hated him and sent a delegation after him, saying, 'We do not want this man to reign over us.' When he returned, after receiving the kingdom, he ordered that these slaves, to whom he had given the money, be called to him so that he might know what business they had done. The first appeared, saying, 'Master, your mina has made ten minas more.' And he said to him, 'Well done, good slave, because you have been faithful in a very little thing, you are to be in authority over ten cities.' The second came, saying, 'Your mina, master, has made five minas.' And he said to him, also, 'And you are to be over five cities.' Another came, saying, 'Master, here is your mina, which I kept put away in a handkerchief; for I was afraid of you, because you are an exacting man; you take up what you did not lay down and reap what you did not sow.' He said to him, 'By your own words I will judge you, you worthless slave. Did you know that I am an exacting man, taking up what I did not lay down and reaping what I did not sow? Then why did you not put my money in the bank, and having come, I would have collected it with interest?' Then he said to the bystanders, 'Take the mina away from him and give it to the one who has the ten minas.' And they said to him, 'Master, he has ten minas *already.*' I tell you that to everyone who has, more shall be given, but from the one who does not have, even what he does have shall be taken away. But these enemies of mine, who did not want me to reign over them, bring them here and slay them in my presence" (Luke 19:12–27; cf. Matthew 25:14–30; see Matthew 13:12; Luke 16:10).

MINAS (Also see MINA; and MONEY)

Setting: Jericho, on the way to Jerusalem. After commending Zaccheus's faith in Him, Jesus provides a parable about stewardship.

So He said, "A nobleman went to a distant country to receive a kingdom for himself, and *then* return. And he called ten of his slaves, and gave them ten minas and said to them, 'Do business *with this* until I come *back.*' But his citizens hated him and sent a delegation after him, saying, 'We do not want this man to reign over us.' When he returned, after receiving the kingdom, he ordered that these slaves, to whom he had given the money, be called to him so that he might know what business they had done. The first appeared, saying, 'Master, your mina has made ten minas more.' And he said to him, 'Well done, good slave, because you have been faithful in a very little thing, you are to be in authority over ten cities.' The second came, saying, 'Your mina, master, has made five minas.' And he said to him, also, 'And you are to be over five cities.' Another came, saying, 'Master, here is your mina, which I kept put away in a handkerchief; for I was afraid of you, because you are an exacting man; you take up what you did not lay down and reap what you did not sow.' He said to him, 'By your own words I will judge you, you worthless slave. Did you know that I am an exacting man, taking up what I did not lay down and reaping what I did not sow? Then why did you not put my money in the bank, and having come, I would have collected it with interest?' Then he said to the bystanders, 'Take the mina away from him and give it to the one who has the ten minas.' And they said to him, 'Master, he has ten minas *already.*' I tell you that to everyone who has, more shall be given, but from the one who does not have, even what he does have shall be taken away. But these enemies of mine, who did not want me to reign over them, bring them here and slay them in my presence" (Luke 19:12–27; cf. Matthew 25:14–30; see Matthew 13:12; Luke 16:10).

MINAS, PARABLE OF THE (See TALENTS, PARABLE OF THE)

MIND (MIND READING is a separate entry; also see HEART; MEMORY; MINDS; REASONING; and THOUGHTS)

Setting: Near Caesarea Philippi. When Jesus prophesies His death and resurrection, Peter rebukes Him, and He responds.

But He turned and said to Peter, "Get behind Me, Satan! You are a stumbling block to Me; for you are not setting your mind on God's interests, but man's" (Matthew 16:23; cf. Mark 8:33).

Setting: The temple in Jerusalem. A Pharisee lawyer asks Jesus which is the great commandment of the Law, in order to test Him as He teaches.

And He said to him, " 'YOU SHALL LOVE THE LORD YOUR GOD WITH ALL YOUR HEART, AND WITH ALL YOUR SOUL, AND WITH ALL YOUR MIND.' This is the great and foremost commandment. The second is like it, 'YOU SHALL LOVE YOUR NEIGHBOR AS YOURSELF.' On these two commandments depend the whole Law and the Prophets" (Matthew 22:37–40; Jesus quotes from Leviticus 19:18; Deuteronomy 6:5; cf. Mark 12:28–34; see Matthew 7:12).

Setting: Caesarea Philippi. After Peter proclaims that Jesus is the Christ (Messiah), he rebukes Jesus when He prophesies His suffering and death at the hands of the elders, chief priests, and scribes.

But turning around and seeing His disciples, He rebuked Peter and said, "Get behind Me, Satan; for you are not setting your mind on God's interests, but man's" (Mark 8:33; cf. Matthew 16:21–23; Luke 9:22).

Setting: The temple in Jerusalem. With the Pharisees and Herodians failing to trap Jesus in a statement, one of the scribes asks Him which commandment is foremost.

Jesus answered, "The foremost is, 'HEAR, O ISRAEL! THE LORD OUR GOD IS ONE LORD; AND YOU SHALL LOVE THE LORD YOUR GOD WITH ALL YOUR HEART, AND WITH ALL YOUR SOUL, AND WITH ALL YOUR MIND AND WITH ALL YOUR STRENGTH.' The second is this, 'YOU SHALL LOVE YOUR NEIGHBOR AS YOURSELF.' There is no other commandment greater than these" (Mark 12:29–31, Jesus quotes from Deuteronomy 6:4, 5; Leviticus 19:18; cf. Matthew 22:34–40).

MIND READING (Also see OMNISCIENCE, JESUS')

[MIND READING from Jesus knowing their thoughts and Why are you thinking evil in your hearts]

Setting: Capernaum, near the Sea of Galilee. After Jesus heals a paralytic and forgives his sins in front of crowds, some scribes accuse the Lord of blasphemy.

And they brought to Him a paralytic lying on a bed. Seeing their faith, Jesus said to the paralytic, "Take courage, son; your sins are forgiven." And some scribes said to themselves. "This *fellow* blasphemes." And Jesus knowing their thoughts said, "Why are you thinking evil in your hearts? Which is easier to say, 'Your sins are forgiven,' or to say, 'Get up, and walk'? But so that you may know that the Son of Man has authority on earth to forgive sins"—then He said to the paralytic, "Get up, pick up your bed and go home" (Matthew 9:2–6; cf. Mark 2:3–12; Luke 5:17–26).

[MIND READING from knowing their thoughts Jesus said]

Setting: Galilee. After Jesus heals a blind, mute, demon-possessed man, the Pharisees accuse the Lord in front of crowds of being a worker of Beelzebul (Satan).

And knowing their thoughts Jesus said to them, "Any kingdom divided against itself is laid waste; and any city or house divided against itself will not stand. If Satan casts out Satan, he is divided against himself; how then will his kingdom stand? If I by Beelzebul cast out demons, by whom do your sons cast *them* out? For this reason they will be your judges. But if I cast out demons by the Spirit of God, then the kingdom of God has come upon you. Or how can anyone enter the strong man's house and carry off his property, unless he first binds the strong *man?* And then he will plunder his house" (Matthew 12:25–29; cf. Matthew 9:34; Mark 3:23–27; Luke 11:17–20).

[MIND READING from aware in His spirit that they were reasoning that way within themselves and Why are you reasoning about these things in your hearts]

Setting: Capernaum. When Jesus heals a paralytic man and forgives his sins, some scribes believe the Lord commits blasphemy.

Immediately Jesus, aware in His spirit that they were reasoning that way within themselves, said to them, "Why are you reasoning about these things in your hearts? Which is easier, to say to the paralytic, 'Your sins are forgiven'; or to say, 'Get up, and pick up your pallet and walk'? "But so that you may know that the Son of Man has authority on earth to forgive sins"—He said to the paralytic, "I say to you, get up, pick up your pallet and go home" (Mark 2:8–11; cf. Matthew 9:4–7; Luke 5:21–24).

[MIND READING from But Jesus, aware of their reasonings]

Setting: Capernaum of Galilee. When Jesus heals a paralytic man and forgives his sins, some Pharisees and teachers of the law from Galilee and Judea accuse the Lord of committing blasphemy.

But Jesus, aware of their reasonings, answered and said to them, "Why are you reasoning in your hearts? Which is easier, to say,

'Your sins have been forgiven you,' or to say, 'Get up and walk'? But, so that you may know that the Son of Man has authority on earth to forgive sins,"—He said to the paralytic—"I say to you, get up, and pick up your stretcher and go home" (Luke 5:22–24; cf. Matthew 9:4–8; Mark 2:8–12; see Matthew 4:24).

[MIND READING from He knew what they were thinking]
Setting: A synagogue in Galilee. As Jesus teaches on a Sabbath, the scribes and Pharisees watch to see if He heals a man's withered hand.

But He knew what they were thinking, and He said to the man with the withered hand, "Get up and come forward!" And he got up and came forward. And Jesus said to them, "I ask you, is it lawful to do good or to do harm on the Sabbath, to save a life or destroy it?" And looking around at them all, He said to him, "Stretch out your hand!" And he did *so;* and his hand was restored (Luke 6:8–10; cf. Matthew 12:9–13; Mark 3:1–5).

[MIND READING from Jesus, knowing what they were thinking in their heart]
Setting: Galilee. After Jesus prophesies His death, an argument arises among His disciples about which of them is the greatest. The Lord resolves the matter by using a child as a teaching illustration.

But Jesus, knowing what they were thinking in their heart, took a child and stood him by His side, and said to them, "Whoever receives this child in My name receives Me, and whoever receives Me receives Him who sent Me; for the one who is least among all of you, this is the one who is great" (Luke 9:47, 48; cf. Matthew 18:1–5; Mark 9:33–47; see Matthew 10:40; Luke 22:24).

[MIND READING from He knew their thoughts]
Setting: On the way from Galilee to Jerusalem. After Jesus casts out a demon, some in the crowd test Him, demanding a sign from heaven.

But He knew their thoughts and said to them, "Any kingdom divided against itself is laid waste; and a house *divided* against itself falls. If Satan also is divided against himself, how will his kingdom stand? For you say that I cast out demons by Beelzebul. And if I by Beelzebul cast out demons, by whom do your sons cast them out? So they will be your judges. But if I cast out demons by the finger of God, then the kingdom of God has come upon you" (Luke 11:17–20; cf. Matthew 12:25–28; Mark 3:23–27; see Exodus 8:19; Matthew 3:2, 10:25).

[MIND READING from For Jesus knew from the beginning who they were who did not believe, and who it was that would betray Him]
Setting: The synagogue at Capernaum of Galilee. After the Jewish religious leaders argue with one another when Jesus says He will give His flesh to the world to eat, some of His disciples also express difficulty with His statements.

But, Jesus, conscious that His disciples grumbled at this, said to them, "Does this cause you to stumble? *What* then if you see the Son of Man ascending to where He was before? It is the Spirit who gives life; the flesh profits nothing; the words that I have spoken to you are spirit and are life. But there are some of you who do not believe." For Jesus knew from the beginning who they were who did not believe, and who it was that would betray Him. And He was saying, "For this reason I have said to you, that no one can come to Me unless it has been granted him from the Father" (John 6:61–65; see Matthew 11:6; 13:11; John 3:13).

[MIND READING from Jesus knew that they wished to question Him]
Setting: Jerusalem. Before the Passover, after warning His disciples of the persecution they will face after His departure to heaven, empathizing with their sadness over His prophecies, Jesus gives them the hope for the future.

"A little while, and you will no longer see Me; and again a little while, and you will see Me." *Some* of His disciples then said to one another, "What is this thing He is telling us, 'A little while, and you will not see Me; and again a little while, and you will see Me'; and, 'because I go to the Father'?" So they were saying, "What is this that He says, 'A little while'? We do not know what He is talking about." Jesus knew that they wished to question Him, and He said to them, "Are you deliberating together about this, that I said, 'A little while, and you will not see Me, and again a little while, and you will see Me'? Truly, truly, I say to you, that you will weep and lament, but the world will rejoice; you will grieve, but your grief will be turned into joy. Whenever a woman is in labor she has pain, because her hour has come; but when she gives birth to the child, she no longer remembers the anguish because of the joy that a child has been born into the world. Therefore you too have grief now; but I will see you again, and your heart will rejoice, and no one *will* take your joy away from you" (John 16:16–22; see Mark 9:32; Luke 23:27; John 14:18–24; 16:5, 6; 20:20).

[MIND READING from Jesus, knowing all the things]
Setting: Jerusalem. After Jesus prays His high-priestly prayer on behalf of His disciples, they all go over the ravine of the Kidron to a garden where Judas waits to seize the Lord with a Roman cohort and officers from the chief priests and the Pharisees.

So Jesus, knowing all the things that were coming upon Him, went forth and said to them, "Whom do you seek?" They answered Him, "Jesus the Nazarene." He said to them, "I am *He*." And Judas also, who was betraying Him, was standing with them. So when He said to them, "I am *He*," they drew back and fell to the ground. Therefore He again asked them, "Whom do you seek?" And they said, "Jesus the Nazarene." Jesus answered, "I told you that I am *He*; so if you seek Me, let these go their way," to fulfill the word which He spoke, "Of those whom You have given Me I lost not one" (John 18:4–9; see John 6:64; 17:12).

MIND YOUR OWN BUSINESS (Listed under BUSINESS, MIND YOUR OWN)

MINDS (Also see MIND)

Setting: On the Mount of Olives, east of the temple in Jerusalem. After ministering in the temple a few days before His crucifixion, and giving His disciples more details regarding the temple's future destruction, Jesus elaborates during His Olivet Discourse about things to come.

Then He continued by saying to them, "Nation will rise against nation and kingdom against kingdom, and there will be great earthquakes, and in various places plagues and famines; and there will be terrors and great signs from heaven. But before all these things, they will lay their hands on you and will persecute you, delivering you to the synagogues and prisons, bringing you before kings and governors for My name's sake. It will lead to an opportunity for your testimony. So make up your minds not to prepare beforehand to defend yourselves; for I will give you utterance and wisdom which none of your opponents will be able to resist or refute. But you will be betrayed even by parents and brothers and relatives and friends, and they will put *some* of you to death, and you will be hated by all because of My name. Yet not a hair of your head will perish. By your endurance you will gain your lives" (Luke 21:10–19; cf. Matthew 10:19–22; 24:7–14; Mark 13:8–13).

Setting: On the island of Patmos (in the Aegean Sea about fifty miles southwest of Ephesus in modern Turkey). On the Lord's Day (Sunday), approximately fifty years after Jesus' resurrection, the disciple John encounters the Lord Jesus Christ, who communicates a new revelation for the apostle to record for the church in Thyatira and to six other churches in Asia.

"And to the angel of the church in Thyatira write: The Son of God, who has eyes like a flame of fire, and His feet are like burnished bronze, says this: 'I know your deeds, and your love and faith and service and perseverance, and that your deeds of late are greater than at first. But I have *this* against you, that you tolerate the woman Jezebel, who calls herself a prophetess, and she teaches and leads My bond-servants astray so that they commit *acts of* immorality and eat things sacrificed to idols. I gave her time to repent, and she does not want to repent of her immorality. Behold, I will throw her on a bed *of sickness*, and those who commit adultery with her into great tribulation, unless they repent of her deeds. And I will kill her children with pestilence, and all the churches will know that I am He who searches the minds and hearts; and I will give to each one of you according to your deeds. But I say to you, the rest who are in Thyatira, who do not hold this teaching, who have not known the deep things of Satan, as they call them—I place no other burden on you. Nevertheless what you have, hold fast until I come. He who overcomes, and he who keeps My deeds until the end, TO HIM I WILL GIVE AUTHORITY OVER THE NATIONS; AND HE SHALL RULE THEM WITH A ROD OF IRON, AS THE VESSELS OF THE POTTER ARE BROKEN TO PIECES, as I also have received *authority* from My Father; and I will give him the morning star. He who has an ear, let him hear what the Spirit says to the churches' (Revelation 2:18–29; Jesus quotes from Psalm 2:8, 9; Isaiah 30:14; see 1 Kings 16:31; Psalm 7:9; Romans 2:5; 1 Corinthians 2:10; 2 Peter 3:9; Revelation 1:14; 2:7; 3:11; 17:1–20).

MINISTER

Setting: Caesarea. Luke, writing in Acts, gives Paul's retelling of his conversion to Christ as he appears before King Agrippa following his hearing before the Jewish Council in Jerusalem and arrest by the Roman commander (on his way to Rome after the apostle's third missionary journey).

"And when we had fallen to the ground, I heard a voice saying to me in the Hebrew dialect, 'Saul, Saul, why are you persecuting Me? It is hard for you to kick against the goads.' And I said, 'Who are You, Lord?' And the Lord said, 'I am Jesus whom you are persecuting. But get up and stand on your feet; for this purpose I have appeared to you, to appoint you a minister and a witness not only to the things which you have seen, but also to the things in which I will appear to you; rescuing you from the *Jewish* people and from the Gentiles, to whom I am sending you, to open their eyes so that they may turn from darkness to light and from the dominion of Satan to God, that they may receive forgiveness of sins and an inheritance among those who have been sanctified by faith in Me' (Acts 26:14–18; see Isaiah 35:5; Acts 21:40; 22:14).

MINISTRY

[MINISTRY from harvest]

Setting: The villages and cities of Galilee. While healing the sick, raising the dead, and casting out demons, Jesus comments on the enormity of the task and the need to ask the Lord of the harvest for additional workers.

Then He said to His disciples, "The harvest is plentiful, but the workers are few. Therefore beseech the Lord of the harvest to send out workers into His harvest" (Matthew 9:37, 38; cf. Luke 10:2).

[MINISTRY from whoever wishes to become great among you shall be your servant]

Setting: On the way to Jerusalem, where Jesus will die on the cross. Jesus teaches His disciples about true greatness after the mother of disciples James and John asks Him to make her sons exalted rulers with Him in His coming kingdom.

But Jesus called them to Himself and said, "You know that the rulers of the Gentiles lord it over them, and *their* great men exercise authority over them. It is not this way among you, but whoever wishes to become great among you shall be your servant, and whoever wishes to be first among you shall be your slave; just as the Son of Man did not come to be served, but to serve, and to give His life a ransom for many" (Matthew 20:25–28; cf. Matthew 23:11; Matthew 26:28; Mark 10:42–45).

[MINISTRY from to the extent that you did it to one of these brothers of Mine, *even* the least *of them*, you did it to Me]

Setting: On the Mount of Olives, just east of Jerusalem. During His Olivet Discourse, after answering His disciples' questions as to when the temple will be destroyed and Jerusalem overrun, along with the signs of His coming and the end of the age, Jesus reveals the future judgments following His return.

"But when the Son of Man comes in His glory, and all the angels with Him, then He will sit on His glorious throne. All the nations will be gathered before Him; and He will separate them from one another, as the shepherd separates the sheep from the goats; and He will put the sheep on His right, and the goats on the left. Then the King will say to those on His right, 'Come, you who are blessed of My Father, inherit the kingdom prepared for you from the foundation of the world. 'For I was hungry, and you gave Me *something* to eat; I was thirsty, and you gave Me *something* to drink; I was a stranger, and you invited Me in; naked, and you clothed Me; I was sick, and you visited Me; I was in prison, and you came to Me.' Then the righteous will answer Him, 'Lord, when did we see You hungry and feed You, or thirsty, and give you *something* to drink? And when did we see You a stranger, and invite You in, or naked, and clothe You? When did we see You sick, or in prison, and come to You?' The King will answer and say to them, 'Truly I say to you, to the extent that you did it to one of these brothers of Mine, *even* the least *of them*, you did it to Me.' Then He will also say to those on His left, 'Depart from Me, accursed ones, into the eternal fire which has been prepared for the devil

and his angels; for I was hungry, and you gave Me *nothing* to eat; I was thirsty, and you gave Me nothing to drink; I was a stranger, and you did not invite Me in; naked, and you did not clothe Me; sick, and in prison, and you did not visit Me.' Then they themselves also will answer, 'Lord, when did we see You hungry, or thirsty, or a stranger, or naked, or sick, or in prison, and did not take care of You?' Then He will answer them, 'Truly I say to you, to the extent that you did not do it to one of the least of these, you did not do it to Me.' These will go away into eternal punishment, but the righteous into eternal life" (Matthew 25:31–46; see Matthew 7:23; 16:27; 19:29).

[MINISTRY from whoever gives you a cup of water]
Setting: Capernaum of Galilee. As Jesus teaches His disciples in private, they ask Him about greatness.

But Jesus said, "Do not hinder him, for there is no one who will perform a miracle in My name, and be able soon afterward to speak evil of Me. For he who is not against us is for us. For whoever gives you a cup of water to drink because of your name as *followers* of Christ, truly I say to you, he will not lose his reward. Whoever causes one of these little ones who believe to stumble, it would be better for him if, with a heavy millstone hung around his neck, he had been cast into the sea. If your hand causes you to stumble, cut it off; it is better for you to enter life crippled, than, having your two hands, to go into hell, into the unquenchable fire, [where THEIR WORM DOES NOT DIE, AND THE FIRE IS NOT QUENCHED.] If your foot causes you to stumble, cut it off; it is better for you to enter life lame, than, having your two feet, to be cast into hell, [where THEIR WORM DOES NOT DIE, AND THE FIRE IS NOT QUENCHED.] If your eye causes you to stumble, throw it out; it is better for you to enter the kingdom of God with one eye, than, having two eyes, to be cast into hell, where THEIR WORM DOES NOT DIE, AND THE FIRE IS NOT QUENCHED. For everyone will be salted with fire. Salt is good; but if the salt becomes unsalty, with what will you make it salty *again?* Have salt in yourselves, and be at peace with one another" (Mark 9:39–50; Jesus quotes from Isaiah 66:24; cf. Matthew 18:6–9; Luke 9:49, 50; see Matthew 5:13, 29, 30; 10:42; 12:30; 18:5, 6).

[MINISTRY from whoever wishes to become great among you shall be your servant]
Setting: On the road to Jerusalem. James and John ask Jesus for special honor and privileges in His kingdom. The other disciples become angry, so the Lord uses this moment to teach all of them about servanthood.

Calling them to Himself, Jesus said to them, "You know that those who are recognized as rulers of the Gentiles lord it over them; and their great men exercise authority over them. But it is not this way among you, but whoever wishes to become great among you shall be your servant; and whoever wishes to be first among you shall be slave of all. For even the Son of Man did not come to be served, but to serve, and to give His life a ransom for many" (Mark 10:42–45; cf. Matthew 20:25–28).

[MINISTRY from he who is not against you is for you]
Setting: Galilee. Following His illustration about true greatness, with a child as an object lesson, Jesus gives His disciples insights about who their co-laborers in ministry are.

But Jesus said to him, "Do not hinder *him;* for he who is not against you is for you" (Luke 9:50; cf. Matthew 12:30; Mark 9:38–40; see Luke 9:49).

[MINISTRY from harvest]
Setting: On the way from Galilee to Jerusalem. The Lord appoints seventy followers and sends them out in pairs to every place He Himself will soon visit.

And He was saying to them, "The harvest is plentiful, but the laborers are few; therefore beseech the Lord of the harvest to send out laborers into His harvest. Go; behold, I send you out as lambs in the midst of wolves. Carry no money belt, no bag, no shoes; and greet no one on the way. Whatever house you enter, first say, 'Peace be to this house.' If a man of peace is there, your peace will rest on him; but if not, it will return to you. Stay in that house, eating and drinking what they give you; for the laborer is worthy of his wages. Do not keep moving from house to house. Whatever city you enter and they receive you, eat what is set before you; and heal those in it who are sick, and say to them, 'The kingdom of God has come near to you.' But whatever city you enter and they do not receive you, go out into its streets and say, 'Even the dust of your city which clings to our feet we wipe off *in protest* against you; yet be sure of this, that the kingdom of God has come near.' I say to you, it will be more tolerable in that day for Sodom than for that city" (Luke 10:2–12; see Genesis 19:24–28; Matthew 9:37, 38, 10:9–14, 16; 1 Corinthians 10:27).

MINISTRY, CHALLENGES OF (See MINISTRY, DIFFICULTIES IN)

MINISTRY, DIFFICULTIES IN (See ADVERSITY; PERSECUTION; and TROUBLE)

MINISTRY, DISCERNMENT IN

[DISCERNMENT IN MINISTRY from do not throw your pearls before swine]
Setting: Galilee. During the early part of His ministry, Jesus preaches the Sermon on the Mount to His disciples and the multitudes.

"Do not give what is holy to dogs, and do not throw your pearls before swine, or they will trample them under their feet, and turn and tear you to pieces" (Matthew 7:6; see Matthew 15:26).

MINISTRY, OPPOSITION IN (Also see PERSECUTION)

[OPPOSITION IN MINISTRY from I send you out as sheep in the midst of wolves and But beware of men, for they will hand you over to *the* courts and scourge you in their synagogues; and you will even be brought before governors and kings for My sake, as a testimony to them and to the Gentiles]
Setting: Galilee. After His disciples observe His ministry, Jesus summons and specifically instructs them about the upcoming hardships of their ministry to the people of Israel.

"Behold, I send you out as sheep in the midst of wolves; so be shrewd as serpents and innocent as doves. But beware of men, for they will hand you over to *the* courts and scourge you in their synagogues; and you will even be brought before governors and kings for My sake, as a testimony to them and to the Gentiles. But when they hand you over, do not worry about how or what you are to say; for it will be given you in that hour what you are to say. For it is not you who speak, but *it* is the Spirit of your Father who speaks in you" (Matthew 10:16–20; cf. Luke 10:3).

[OPPOSITION IN MINISTRY from What I tell you in the darkness, speak in the light; and what you hear *whispered* in your ear, proclaim upon the housetops]
Setting: Galilee. After His disciples observe His ministry, Jesus summons and specifically instructs them about their ministry ahead involving true discipleship.

"Therefore do not fear them, for there is nothing concealed that will not be revealed, or hidden that will not be known. What I tell you in the darkness, speak in the light; and what you hear *whispered* in your ear, proclaim upon the housetops. Do not fear those who kill the body but are unable to kill the soul; but rather fear Him who is able to destroy both soul and body in hell" (Matthew 10:26–28; cf. Mark 4:22; Luke 12:3; see Hebrews 10:31).

[OPPOSITION IN MINISTRY from I send you out as lambs in the midst of wolves]
Setting: On the way from Galilee to Jerusalem. The Lord appoints seventy followers and sends them out in pairs to every place He Himself will soon visit.

And He was saying to them, "The harvest is plentiful, but the laborers are few; therefore beseech the Lord of the harvest to send out laborers into His harvest. Go; behold, I send you out as lambs in the midst of wolves. Carry no money belt, no bag, no shoes; and greet no one on the way. Whatever house you enter, first say, 'Peace be to this house.' If a man of peace is there, your peace will rest on him; but if not, it will return to you. Stay in that house, eating and drinking what they give you; for the laborer is worthy of his wages. Do not keep moving from house to house. Whatever city you enter and they receive you, eat what is set before you; and heal those in it who are sick, and say to them, 'The kingdom of God has come near to you.' But whatever city you enter and they do not receive you, go out into its streets and say, 'Even the dust of your city which clings to our feet we wipe off *in protest* against you; yet be sure of this, that the kingdom of God has come near.' I say to you, it will be more tolerable in that day for Sodom than for that city" (Luke 10:2–12; see Genesis 19:24–28; Matthew 9:37, 38, 10:9–14, 16; 1 Corinthians 10:27).

MINT (Also see other spices such as CUMMIN; and DILL)

Setting: The temple in Jerusalem. After the Jewish religious leaders test Him with questions, Jesus pronounces the fifth of eight woes on them in front of the crowds and His disciples.

"Woe to you, scribes and Pharisees, hypocrites! For you tithe mint and dill and cummin, and have neglected the weightier provisions of the law: justice and mercy and faithfulness; but these are things you should have done without neglecting the others. You blind guides, who strain out a gnat and swallow a camel!" (Matthew 23:23, 24).

Setting: On the way from Galilee to Jerusalem. After speaking of how a lamp illuminates, the Lord has lunch with a Pharisee who is surprised He doesn't wash before eating.

But the Lord said to him, "Now you Pharisees clean the outside of the cup and of the platter; but inside of you, you are full of robbery and wickedness. You foolish ones, did not He who made the outside make the inside also? But give that which is within as charity, and then all things are clean for you. But woe to you Pharisees! You pay tithe of mint and rue and every *kind of* garden herb, and *yet* disregard justice and the love of God; but these are the things you should have done without neglecting the others. Woe to you Pharisees! For you love the chief seats in the synagogues and the respectful greetings in the market places. Woe to you! For you are like concealed tombs, and the people who walk over *them* are unaware *of it*" (Luke 11:39–44; cf. Matthew 23:6, 7, 23–27; see Matthew 15:2; Titus 1:15).

MIRACLE (A miracle happening to one person. For miracles involving more than one person, see MIRACLES; Also see DEMONS, CASTING OUT; HEALING; LEPROSY, CLEANSING FROM; RESURRECTION; RESUSCITATION; SIGNS AND WONDERS; and WORKS)

[MIRACLE from immediately his leprosy was cleansed]

Setting: Galilee. When Jesus comes down after preaching The Sermon on the Mount, large crowds follow Him, as a leper approaches Him asking for cleansing.

Jesus stretched out His hand and touched him, saying, "I am willing, be cleansed." And immediately his leprosy was cleansed. And Jesus said to him, "See that you tell no one; but go, show yourself to the priest and present the offering that Moses commanded, as a testimony to them" (Matthew 8:3, 4; cf. Mark 1:40–44; Luke 5:12–14).

[MIRACLE from heal]

Setting: Entering Capernaum of Galilee. After cleansing a leper, the Lord marvels at the faith of a Roman centurion who implores Him to heal his servant.

Jesus said to him, "I will come and heal him" (Matthew 8:7; see Luke 7:1–10).

[MIRACLE from And the servant was healed that *very* moment]

Setting: Entering Capernaum. After the Lord gives the Sermon on the Mount and cleanses a leper, a Roman centurion implores Jesus to heal his servant.

Now when Jesus heard *this,* He marveled, and said to those who were following, "Truly I say to you, I have not found such great faith with anyone in Israel. I say to you that many will come from east and west, and recline *at the table* with Abraham, Isaac and Jacob in the kingdom of heaven; but the sons of the kingdom will be cast out into the outer darkness; in that place there will be weeping and gnashing of teeth." And Jesus said to the centurion, "Go; it shall be done for you as you have believed." And the servant was healed that *very* moment (Matthew 8:10–13; cf. Luke 7:9, 10).

[MIRACLE from Then He got up and rebuked the winds and the sea, and it became perfectly calm]

Setting: On the Sea of Galilee. After giving one of His disciples and a scribe the demands of discipleship, Jesus calms a great storm when His disciples fear for their lives.

He said to them, "Why are you afraid, you men of little faith?" Then He got up and rebuked the winds and the sea, and it became perfectly calm (Matthew 8:26; see Mark 4:35–41; Luke 8:22–25).

[MIRACLE from they came out and went into the swine]
Setting: The country of the Gadarenes. After calming a great storm on the Sea of Galilee with His voice, Jesus casts demons out of two men into a herd of swine.

And He said to them, "Go!" And they came out and went into the swine, and the whole herd rushed down the steep bank into the sea and perished in the waters (Matthew 8:32; see Mark 5:1–14; Luke 8:26–35).

[MIRACLE from He said to the paralytic, "Get up, pick up your bed and go home"]
Setting: Capernaum, near the Sea of Galilee. After Jesus heals a paralytic and forgives his sins in front of crowds, some scribes accuse the Lord of blasphemy.

And they brought to Him a paralytic lying on a bed. Seeing their faith, Jesus said to the paralytic, "Take courage, son; your sins are forgiven." And some scribes said to themselves. "This *fellow* blasphemes." And Jesus knowing their thoughts said, "Why are you thinking evil in your hearts? Which is easier to say, 'Your sins are forgiven,' or to say, 'Get up, and walk'? But so that you may know that the Son of Man has authority on earth to forgive sins"—then He said to the paralytic, "Get up, pick up your bed and go home" (Matthew 9:2–6; cf. Mark 2:3–12; Luke 5:17–26).

[MIRACLE from At once the woman was made well]
Setting: Capernaum, near the Sea of Galilee. Jesus heals a woman who has been suffering with internal bleeding for twelve years.

But Jesus turning and seeing her said, "Daughter, take courage; your faith has made you well." At once the woman was made well (Matthew 9:22; cf. Mark 5:34; Luke 8:48).

[MIRACLE from He entered and took her by the hand, and the girl got up]
Setting: Capernaum, near the Sea of Galilee. After healing a woman who has been suffering with internal bleeding for twelve years, Jesus brings a synagogue official's daughter back from death.

When Jesus came into the official's house, and saw the flute-players and the crowd in noisy disorder, He said, "Leave; for the girl has not died, but is asleep." And they *began* laughing at Him. But when the crowd had been sent out, He entered and took her by the hand, and the girl got up (Matthew 9:23–25; cf. Mark 5:21–24, 35–43; Luke 8:41, 42, 49–56).

[MIRACLE from "Stretch out your hand!" and it was restored to normal, like the other]
Setting: A synagogue in Galilee. Jesus answers questions posed by the Pharisees about the Sabbath.

And He said to them, "What man is there among you who has a sheep, and if it falls into a pit on the Sabbath, will he not take hold of it and lift it out? How much more valuable then is a man than a sheep! So then, it is lawful to do good on the Sabbath." Then He said to the man, "Stretch out your hand!" He stretched it out, and it was restored to normal, like the other (Matthew 12:11–13; cf. Matthew 10:31; Mark 3:4, 5; Luke 6:9, 10; 14:5; see Matthew 8:3).

[MIRACLE from walked on the water]
Setting: On the Sea of Galilee. Following the miraculous feeding of more than 5,000 of His countrymen, in order to take an opportunity to pray, Jesus makes His disciples get into a boat. He joins them later by walking on the water during a storm.

But immediately Jesus spoke to them, saying, "Take courage, it is I; do not be afraid." Peter said to Him, "Lord, if it is You, command me to come to You on the water." And He said, "Come!" And Peter got out of the boat, and walked on the water and came toward Jesus. But seeing the wind, he became frightened, and beginning to sink, he cried out, "Lord, save me!" Immediately Jesus stretched out His hand and took hold of him, and said to him, "You of little faith, why did you doubt?" (Matthew 14:27–31; cf. Mark 6:47–52; John 6:16–21).

[MIRACLE from And her daughter was healed at once]
Setting: district of Tyre and Sidon. A Canaanite woman appeals to Jesus to heal her demon-possessed daughter.

But He answered and said, "I was sent only to the lost sheep of the house of Israel." But she came and *began* to bow down before Him, saying, "Lord, help me!" And He answered and said, "It is not good to take the children's bread and throw it to the dogs." But she said, "Yes, Lord; but even the dogs feed from the crumbs which fall from their masters' table." Then Jesus said to her, "O woman, your faith is great; it shall be done for you as you wish." And her daughter was healed at once (Matthew 15:24–28; cf. Mark 7: 24–30; see Matthew 9:22; 10:5, 6).

[MIRACLE from the demon came out of him, and the boy was cured at once]
Setting: Descending the mountain after Jesus' transfiguration with Moses and Elijah. After responding to Peter, James, and John's question about Elijah's future coming, Jesus expresses dismay over His disciples' inability to heal a man's demon-possessed son.

And Jesus answered and said, "You unbelieving and perverted generation, how long shall I be with you? How long shall I put up with you? Bring him here to Me." And Jesus rebuked him, and the demon came out of him, and the boy was cured at once (Matthew 17:17, 18; cf. Mark 9:19–29; Luke 9:41–43).

[MIRACLE from take the first fish that comes up; and when you open its mouth, you will find a shekel]
Setting: Capernaum of Galilee. Jesus pays the two-drachma temple tax for Peter and Himself in a miraculous manner.

He said, "Yes." And when he came into the house, Jesus spoke to him first, saying, "What do you think, Simon? From whom do the kings of the earth collect customs or poll-tax, from their sons or from strangers?" When Peter said, "From strangers," Jesus said to him, "Then the sons are exempt. However, so that we do not offend them, go to the sea and throw in a hook, and take the first fish that comes up; and when you open its mouth, you will find a shekel. Take that and give it to them for you and Me" (Matthew 17:25–27; see Exodus 30:11–16; Matthew 22:17–19; Romans 13:7).

[MIRACLE from "No longer shall there ever be *any* fruit from you." And at once the fig tree withered]
Setting: The road from Bethany to Jerusalem. The day after cleansing the temple in Jerusalem by driving out the money changers and merchants, having spent the night in Bethany, Jesus becomes hungry and notices a barren fig tree.

Seeing a lone fig tree by the road, He came to it and found nothing on it except leaves only; and He said to it, "No longer shall there ever be *any* fruit from you." And at once the fig tree withered (Matthew 21:19; cf. Mark 11:12–14; see Luke 13:6–9).

[MIRACLE from "Be quiet, and come out of him!"]
Setting: The synagogue at Capernaum in Galilee. Early in His ministry, after calling some of His disciples, Jesus removes a demon from a man.

And Jesus rebuked him, saying, "Be quiet, and come out of him!" (Mark 1:25; cf. Luke 4:33–35).

[MIRACLE from "I am willing; be cleansed." and leprosy]
Setting: Galilee. Early in His ministry, as Jesus preaches and casts out demons in the synagogues, a leper beseeches Him for healing.

Moved with compassion, Jesus stretched out His hand and touched him, and said to him, "I am willing; be cleansed." Immediately the leprosy left him and he was cleansed. And He sternly warned him and immediately sent him away, and He said to him, "See that you say nothing to anyone, but go, show yourself to the priest and offer for your cleansing what Moses commanded, as a testimony to them" (Mark 1:41–44; cf. Luke 5:12–14; see Leviticus 14:1–32; Matthew 8:3).

[MIRACLE from your sins are forgiven]
Setting: Galilee. Early in Jesus' gospel-preaching ministry, word spreads of His healing abilities, so some friends of a paralytic man bring him to the Lord.

And Jesus seeing their faith said to the paralytic, "Son, your sins are forgiven" (Mark 2:5; cf. Matthew 9:1–3; Luke 5:17–20).

[MIRACLE from "I say to you, get up, pick up your pallet and go home"]
Setting: Capernaum. When Jesus heals a paralytic man and forgives his sins, some scribes believe the Lord commits blasphemy.

Immediately Jesus, aware in His spirit that they were reasoning that way within themselves, said to them, "Why are you reasoning about these things in your hearts? Which is easier, to say to the paralytic, 'Your sins are forgiven'; or to say, 'Get up, and pick up your pallet and walk'? "But so that you may know that the Son of Man has authority on earth to forgive sins"—He said to the paralytic, "I say to you, get up, pick up your pallet and go home" (Mark 2:8–11; cf. Matthew 9:4–7; Luke 5:21–24).

[MIRACLE from "Stretch out your hand"]
Setting: A synagogue in Galilee. Early in His ministry, in front of the Pharisees, Jesus heals a man's withered hand on the Sabbath.

He said to the man with the withered hand, "Get up and come forward!" And He said to them, "Is it lawful to do good or do harm on the Sabbath, to save a life or to kill?" But they kept silent. After looking around at them with anger, grieved at their hardness of heart, He said to the man, "Stretch out your hand." And he stretched it out, and his hand was restored (Mark 3:3–5; cf. Matthew 12:9–14; Luke 6:6–11).

[MIRACLE from "Hush, be still." And the wind died down and it became perfectly calm]
Setting: On the Sea of Galilee. Jesus, in a boat with His disciples, calms the sea in the midst of a storm.

And He got up and rebuked the wind and said to the sea, "Hush, be still." And the wind died down and it became perfectly calm. And He said to them, "Why are you afraid? Do you still have no faith?" (Mark 4:39, 40: cf. Matthew 13:26; Luke 8:25; see Psalm 65:7; Matthew 14:31).

[MIRACLE from "Come out of the man, you unclean spirit!"]
Setting: The country of the Gerasenes, across the Sea of Galilee. Jesus encounters and heals a demon-possessed man.

For He had been saying to him, "Come out of the man, you unclean spirit!" And He was asking him, "What is your name?" And he said to Him, "My name is Legion; for we are many" (Mark 5:8, 9; cf. Luke 8:30; see Matthew 8:28–32; Luke 8:26–33).

[MIRACLE from "Who touched My garments?"]
Setting: By the Sea of Galilee. After Jesus returns from ministry to the Gerasenes, a woman who has had a hemorrhage for twelve years touches Jesus in order to be healed.

Immediately Jesus, perceiving in Himself that the power *proceeding* from Him had gone forth, turned around in the crowd and said, "Who touched My garments?" (Mark 5:30; see Matthew 9:20, 21; Luke 8:43–48).

[MIRACLE from Daughter, your faith has made you well]

Setting: By the Sea of Galilee. After Jesus returns from ministry to the Gerasenes, a woman who has had a hemorrhage for twelve years touches His garment in order to be healed.

And He said to her, "Daughter, your faith has made you well; go in peace and be healed of your affliction" (Mark 5:34; cf. Matthew 9:22; Luke 8:48; see Luke 7:50).

[MIRACLE from "Little girl, I say to you, get up!"]
Setting: The home of Jairus, a synagogue official in Capernaum, by the Sea of Galilee. Jesus revives Jairus's daughter, who had died.

Taking the child by the hand, He said to her, "Talitha kum!" (which translated means, "Little girl, I say to you, get up!") (Mark 5:41; cf. Matthew 9:25; Luke 8:54; see Luke 7:14; 8:55, 56).

[MIRACLE from they saw Him walking on the sea]
Setting: On the Sea of Galilee. After feeding more than 5,000 people through God's miraculous provision, and returning from a time of prayer on a mountain, Jesus startles His disciples by walking on the water as they sail toward Bethsaida.

But when they saw Him walking on the sea, they supposed that it was a ghost, and cried out; for they all saw Him and were terrified. But immediately He spoke with them and said to them, "Take courage; it is I, do not be afraid" (Mark 6:49, 50; cf. Matthew 14:26, 27; John 6:19, 20).

[MIRACLE from the demon has gone out of your daughter]
Setting: The region of Tyre. After the Pharisees and scribes from Jerusalem question His disciples' obedience to tradition, Jesus casts out a demon from the daughter of a Gentile (Syrophoenician) woman.

And He was saying to her, "Let the children be satisfied first, for it is not good to take the children's bread and throw it to the dogs." But she answered and said to Him, "Yes, Lord *but* even the dogs under the table feed on the children's crumbs. And He said to her, "Because of this answer go; the demon has gone out of your daughter" (Mark 7:27–29; cf. Matthew 15:21–28).

[MIRACLE from "Be opened!"]
Setting: Decapolis, near the Sea of Galilee. After casting out a demon from a Gentile woman's daughter in Tyre, Jesus restores a man's hearing and speech.

Jesus took him aside from the crowd, by himself, and put His fingers into his ears, and after spitting, He touched his tongue *with the saliva*; and looking up to heaven with a deep sigh, He said to him, "Ephphatha!" that is, "Be opened!" (Mark 7:33, 34; see Matthew 15:29–31; Mark 8:23).

[MIRACLE from "Do you see anything?"]
Setting: Bethsaida of Galilee. After Jesus' disciples discuss with one another that they have no bread, Jesus gives sight to a blind man.

Taking the blind man by the hand, He brought him out of the village; and after spitting on his eyes and laying His hands on him, He asked him, "Do you see anything?" (Mark 8:23).

[MIRACLE from "You deaf and mute spirit, I command you, come out of him and do not enter him again."]
Setting: Galilee. After returning from a high mountain (perhaps Mount Hermon) where Jesus was transfigured before Peter, James, and John, the four discover the remaining disciples arguing with some scribes.

And He asked them, "What are you discussing with them?" And one of the crowd answered Him, "Teacher, I brought You my son, possessed with a spirit which makes him mute; and whenever it seizes him, it slams him *to the ground* and he foams *at the mouth,* and grinds his teeth and stiffens out. I told Your disciples to cast it out, and they could not *do it.* And He answered them, and said, "O unbelieving generation, how long shall I be with you? How long shall I put up with you? Bring him to Me!" They brought the boy to Him. When he saw Him, immediately the spirit threw him into a convulsion, and falling to the ground, be *began* rolling around and foaming *at the mouth.* And He asked his father, "How long has this been happening to him?" And he said, "From childhood. It has often thrown him both into the fire and into the water to destroy him. But if You can do anything, take pity on us and help us!" And Jesus said to him, "'If You can?' All things are possible to him who believes." Immediately the boy's father cried out and said, "I do believe; help my unbelief." When Jesus saw that a crowd was rapidly gathering, He rebuked the unclean spirit, saying to it, "You deaf and mute spirit, I command you, come out of him and do not enter him again." After crying out and throwing him into terrible convulsions, it came out; and *the boy* became so much like a corpse that most *of them,* said, "He is dead!" But Jesus took him by the hand and raised him; and he got up. When He came into *the* house, His disciples *began* questioning Him privately, "Why could we not drive it out?" And He said to them, "This kind cannot come out by anything but prayer" (Mark 9:16–29; cf. Matthew 17:14–21; Luke 9:37–43; see Matthew 17:20).

Setting: Capernaum of Galilee. As Jesus teaches His disciples in private, they ask Him about greatness.

But Jesus said, "Do not hinder him, for there is no one who will perform a miracle in My name, and be able soon afterward to speak evil of Me. For he who is not against us is for us. For whoever gives you a cup of water to drink because of your name as *followers* of Christ, truly I say to you, he will not lose his reward. Whoever causes one of these little ones who believe to stumble, it would be better for him if, with a heavy millstone hung around his neck, he had been cast into the sea. If your hand causes you to stumble, cut it off; it is better for you to enter life crippled, than, having your two hands, to go into hell, into the unquenchable fire, [where THEIR WORM DOES NOT DIE, AND THE FIRE IS NOT QUENCHED.] If your foot causes you to stumble, cut it off; it is better for you to enter life lame, than, having your two feet, to be cast into hell, [where THEIR WORM DOES NOT DIE, AND THE FIRE IS NOT QUENCHED.] If your eye causes you to stumble, throw it out; it is better for you to enter the kingdom of God with one eye, than, having two eyes, to be cast into hell, where THEIR WORM DOES NOT DIE, AND THE FIRE IS NOT QUENCHED. For everyone will be salted with fire. Salt is good; but if the salt becomes unsalty, with what will you make it salty *again?* Have salt in yourselves, and be at peace with one another" (Mark 9:39–50; Jesus quotes from Isaiah 66:24; cf. Matthew 18:6–9; Luke 9:49, 50; see Matthew 5:13, 29, 30; 10:42; 12:30; 18:5, 6.

[MIRACLE from "Go; your faith has made you well."]
Setting: Jericho, on the road to Jerusalem. A blind beggar named Bartimaeus cries out to Jesus for healing.

And Jesus stopped and said, "Call him *here.*" So they called the blind man, saying to him, "Take courage, stand up! He is calling for you." Throwing aside his cloak, he jumped up and came to Jesus. And answering him, Jesus said, "What do you want Me to do for you?" And the blind man said to him, "Rabboni, *I want* to regain my sight!" And Jesus said to him, "Go; your faith has made you well." Immediately he regained his sight and *began* following Him on the road (Mark 10:49–52; cf. Matthew 20:29–34; Luke 18:35–43; see Matthew 9:2, 22).

[MIRACLE from: "May no one ever eat fruit from you again!"]
Setting: Between Bethany and Jerusalem. The day after His triumphal entry into Jerusalem, just days before His impending death on the cross, Jesus curses a fig tree that has no fruit on it.

He said to it, "May no one ever eat fruit from you again!" And His disciples were listening (Mark 11:14; cf. Matthew 21:18, 19).

[MIRACLE from "Be quiet and come out of him!"]
Setting: The synagogue in Capernaum of Galilee. While teaching, Jesus heals a demon-possessed man.

But Jesus rebuked him, saying, "Be quiet and come out of him!" And when the demon had thrown him down in the midst *of the people,* he came out of him without doing him any harm (Luke 4:35; cf. Mark 1:21–28).

[MIRACLE from Luke 5:6: large catch of fish]

Setting: By the Sea of Galilee. After teaching the people from Simon's (Peter) boat, Jesus calls Simon, James, and John to follow Him. (This appears to be a permanent call as Simon and other companions are with Him earlier in Mark 1:35–39; Luke 4:38, 39).

When He had finished speaking, He said to Simon, "Put out into the deep water and let down your nets for a catch." ". . . and so also *were* James and John, sons of Zebedee, who were partners with Simon. And Jesus said to Simon, "Do not fear, from now on you will be catching men" (Luke 5:4, 10; see John 21:6).

[MIRACLE from "I am willing; be cleansed." And immediately the leprosy left him]
Setting: Galilee. Early in His ministry, after calling Andrew, Simon (Peter), James, and John to follow Him, Jesus heals a leper.

And He stretched out His hand and touched Him, saying, "I am willing; be cleansed." And immediately the leprosy left him. And He ordered him to tell no one, "But go and show yourself to the priest and make an offering for your cleansing, just as Moses commanded, as a testimony to them" (Luke 5:13, 14; cf. Matthew 8:2–4; Mark 1:40–45; see Leviticus 13:49).

[MIRACLE from "Friend, your sins are forgiven you"]
Setting: Galilee. While Jesus is teaching, with some Pharisees and teachers of the law from Galilee and Judea observing, several men lower a paralyzed man through the roof in front of the Lord.

Seeing their faith, He said, "Friend, your sins are forgiven you" (Luke 5:20; cf. Mark 2:2–12; see Matthew 9:1–8).

[MIRACLE from "I say to you, get up, and pick up your stretcher and go home"]
Setting: Capernaum of Galilee. When Jesus heals a paralytic man and forgives his sins, some Pharisees and teachers of the law from Galilee and Judea accuse the Lord of committing blasphemy.

But Jesus, aware of their reasonings, answered and said to them, "Why are you reasoning in your hearts? Which is easier, to say, 'Your sins have been forgiven you,' or to say, 'Get up and walk'? But, so that you may know that the Son of Man has authority on earth to forgive sins,"—He said to the paralytic—"I say to you, get up, and pick up your stretcher and go home" (Luke 5:22–24; cf. Matthew 9:4–8; Mark 2:8–12; see Matthew 4:24).

[MIRACLE from "Stretch out your hand!"]
Setting: A synagogue in Galilee. On the Sabbath, as Jesus teaches, the scribes and Pharisees watch to see if He heals a man's withered hand.

But He knew what they were thinking, and He said to the man with the withered hand, "Get up and come forward!" And he got up and came forward. And Jesus said to them, "I ask you, is it lawful to do good or to do harm on the Sabbath, to save a life or destroy it?" And looking around at them all, He said to him, "Stretch out your hand!" And he did *so;* and his hand was restored (Luke 6:8–10; cf. Matthew 12:9–13; Mark 3:1–5).

[MIRACLE from "Young man, I say to you, arise!"]
Setting: Galilee. After healing a Roman centurion's slave from a distance in Capernaum, Jesus travels to Nain, where He raises a young man from the dead.

When the Lord saw her, He felt compassion for her and said to her, "Do not weep." And He came up and touched the coffin; and the bearers came to a halt. And He said, "Young man, I say to you, arise!" (Luke 7:13, 14).

[MIRACLE from He commands even the winds and the water, and they obey Him]
Setting: Galilee. After Jesus conveys who His true relatives are, He and His disciples set sail on the Sea of Galilee, where He calms a storm.

And He said to them, "Where is your faith?" They were fearful and amazed, saying to one another, "Who then is this, that He commands even the winds and the water, and they obey Him?" (Luke 8:25; cf. Matthew 8:23 27; Mark 4:35 41).

[MIRACLE from Luke 8:38: the man whom the demons had gone out of was begging Him]
Setting: The country of the Gerasenes, east of the Sea of Galilee. Jesus heals a demon-possessed man who then desires to join His ministry, but the Lord sends him home.

"Return to your house and describe what great things God has done for you." So he went away, proclaiming throughout the whole city what great things Jesus had done for him (Luke 8:39; cf. Matthew 8:28–34; Mark 5:1–20).

[MIRACLE from "Daughter, your faith has made you well; go in peace"]
Setting: Galilee. After ministering in the country of the Gerasenes, east of the Sea of Galilee, Jesus returns. A woman, ill for twelve years, receives healing by touching His garment.

And Jesus said, "Who is the one who touched Me?" And while they were all denying it, Peter said, "Master, the people are crowding and pressing in on You." But Jesus said, "Someone did touch Me, for I was aware, that power had gone out of Me." When the woman saw that she had not escaped notice, she came trembling and fell down before Him, and declared in the presence of all the people the reason why she had touched Him, and how she had been immediately healed. And He said to her, "Daughter, your faith has made you well; go in peace" (Luke 8:45–48; cf. Matthew 9:20; Mark 5:25–34).

[MIRACLE from "Child, arise!"]
Setting: Capernaum in Galilee. After healing a woman ill for twelve years, Jesus receives word that the daughter of a synagogue official has died.

But when Jesus heard *this,* He answered him, "Do not be afraid *any longer;* only believe and she will be made well." When He came to the house, He did not allow anyone to enter with Him except Peter and John and James and the girl's father and mother. Now they were all weeping and lamenting for her; but He said, "Stop weeping; for she has not died, but is asleep." And they *began* laughing at Him, knowing that she had died. He, however, took her by the hand and called, saying, "Child, arise!" And her spirit returned, and she got up immediately; and He gave orders for *something* to be given her to eat (Luke 8:50–55; cf. Matthew 9:18, 19, 23–26; Mark 5:21–24, 35–43).

[MIRACLE from "Woman, you are freed from your sickness"]
Setting: On the way from Galilee to Jerusalem. Jesus teaches on the Sabbath in a synagogue, where a woman who has been sick eighteen years seeks healing.

When Jesus saw her, He called her over and said to her, "Woman, you are freed from your sickness" (Luke 13:12)

[MIRACLE from released from this bond]
Setting: On the way from Galilee to Jerusalem. Jesus responds to an official's anger for healing a woman, sick eighteen years, in one of the synagogues on the Sabbath.

But the Lord answered him and said, "You hypocrites, does not each of you on the Sabbath untie his ox or his donkey from the stall and lead him away to water *him?* And this woman, a daughter of Abraham as she is, whom Satan has bound for eighteen long years, should she not have been released from this bond on the Sabbath day?" (Luke 13:15, 16, 17; see Luke 14:5).

[MIRACLE from "Receive your sight; your faith has made you well"]
Setting: On the way from Galilee to Jerusalem. After telling the disciples of the sacrifice He will make in Jerusalem, while approaching Jericho, He takes time to heal a blind man.

And Jesus stopped and commanded that he be brought to Him; and when he came near, He questioned him, "What do you want

Me to do for you?" And he said, "Lord, *I want* to regain my sight!" And Jesus said to him, "Receive your sight; your faith has made you well" (Luke 18:40–42; cf. Matthew 20:29–34; Mark 10:46–52).

[MIRACLE from He touched his ear and healed him]
Setting: Gethsemane on the Mount of Olives, east of the temple in Jerusalem. In the midst of His betrayal by Judas, Jesus commands His disciples not to resist His arrest with violence after one of them (Peter, according to John 18:10) cuts off the right ear of a slave of the high priest.

But Jesus answered and said, "Stop! No more of this." And He touched his ear and healed him (Luke 22:51; see Matthew 26:51–53; Mark 14:46, 47; John 18:10, 11).

[MIRACLE inferred from context]
Setting: Cana of Galilee. On the third day of His public ministry, after choosing Andrew, Peter, and Nathanael to be His disciples, Jesus attends a wedding. His mother prompts Him to perform His first miracle, that of turning water into wine.

Jesus said to them, "Fill the waterpots with water." So they filled them up to the brim. And He said to them, "Draw *some* out now and take it to the headwaiter." So they took it *to him* (John 2:7, 8).

[MIRACLE from "Go, your son lives"]
Setting: Cana of Galilee. After conversing with a Samaritan woman at Jacob's well, and ministering to the Samaritan people for two days, Jesus encounters a royal official pleading for healing for his son, sick at the point of death in Capernaum.

Jesus said to him, "Go; your son lives." The man believed the word that Jesus spoke to him and started off (John 4:50; see Matthew 8:5–13).

[MIRACLE from Get up, pick up your pallet and walk]
Setting: By the pool of Bethesda in Jerusalem. After performing His second miracle by healing the royal official's son from Capernaum, during the Feast of the Jews, Jesus heals a man on the Sabbath who has been ill for thirty-eight years.

Jesus said to him, "Get up, pick up your pallet and walk" (John 5:8; see Matthew 9:6).

[MIRACLE from John 6:9: five loaves and two fish feeding 5,000]
Setting: By the Sea of Galilee. After revealing to the Jewish religious leaders during a feast of the Jews in Jerusalem how God, John the Baptist, His works, and the Scriptures all testify to His mission, Jesus miraculously feeds more than 5,000 people with a lad's five barley loaves and two fish.

Jesus said, "Have the people sit down." Now there was much grass in the place. So the men sat down, in number about five thousand. Jesus took the loaves, and having given thanks, He distributed to those who were seated; likewise also of the fish as much as they wanted. When they were filled, He said to the disciples, "Gather up the leftover fragments so that nothing will be lost" (John 6:10–12; cf. Matthew 14:17–21; Mark 6:38–44; Luke 9:14–17; see Matthew 15:32–38).

[MIRACLE from John 6:19: walking on the sea]
Setting: Galilee. Perceiving that the people want to make Him king after He miraculously feeds more than 5,000 of them, Jesus withdraws to a mountain. His disciples board a boat and start across the Sea of Galilee, where He will join them by walking on water during a storm.

But He said to them, "It is I; do not be afraid" (John 6:20; cf. Matthew 14:27; Mark 6:50).

[MIRACLE from "Go, wash in the pool of Siloam" and and came *back* seeing]
Setting: The temple treasury in Jerusalem. After Jesus avoids being stoned by the scribes and Pharisees, His disciples wonder if blindness is caused by sin as the Lord heals a man born blind.

Jesus answered, "*It was* neither *that* this man sinned, nor his parents; but *it was* so that the works of God might be displayed in him. We must work the works of Him who sent Me as long as it is day; night is coming when no one can work. While I am in the world, I am the Light of the world." When He had said this, He spat on the ground, and made clay of the spittle, and applied the clay to his eyes, and said to him, "Go, wash in the pool of Siloam" (which is translated, Sent). So he went away and washed, and came *back* seeing
(John 9:3–7; see John 8:12; 11:4; 12:46).

[MIRACLE from "Lazarus, come forth"]
Setting: From beyond the Jordan. After the death of His friend Lazarus, Jesus travels with His disciples to Bethany in Judea to visit Lazarus's sisters, Martha and Mary. The Lord raises Lazarus from the dead.

Jesus said, "Remove the stone." Martha, the sister of the deceased, said to Him, "Lord, by this time there will be a stench, for he has been *dead* four days." Jesus said to her, "Did I not say to you that if you believe, you will see the glory of God?" So they removed the stone. Then Jesus raised His eyes, and said, "Father, I thank You that You have heard Me. I knew that You always hear Me; but because of the people standing around I said it, so that they may believe that you sent Me." When He had said these things, He cried out with a loud voice, "Lazarus, come forth." The man who had died came forth, bound hand and foot with wrappings, and his face was wrapped around with a cloth. Jesus said to them, "Unbind him, and let him go" (John 11:39–44; see Matthew 11:25).

[MIRACLE (the Resurrection) from Stop clinging to Me, for I have not yet ascended to the Father]
Setting: Jerusalem. The risen Jesus first appears to Mary Magdalene after she tells Simon Peter and John about the empty tomb where the Lord's body had been laid the day before the Sabbath. He had died on the cross for the sins of the world.

Jesus said to her, "Woman, why are you weeping? Whom are you seeking?" Supposing Him to be the gardener, she said to Him, "Sir, if you have carried Him away, tell me where you have laid Him, and I will take Him away." Jesus said to her, "Mary!" She turned and said to Him in Hebrew "Rabboni!" (which means, Teacher). Jesus said to her, "Stop clinging to Me, for I have not yet ascended to the Father; but go to My brethren and say to them, 'I ascend to My Father and your Father, and My God and your God'" (John 20:15–17; see Mark 16:9–11; John 7:33; 19:31–42).

[MIRACLE from the doors were shut and Jesus came and stood in their midst]
Setting: Jerusalem. After Mary Magdalene encounters the risen Jesus in the morning, He appears that evening in the midst of His disciples (except Thomas), who are in hiding behind closed doors due to fear of the Jewish religious leaders.

So when it was evening on that day, the first *day* of the week, and when the doors were shut where the disciples were, for fear of the Jews, Jesus came and stood in their midst and said to them, "Peace *be* with you." And when He had said this, He showed them both His hands and His side. The disciples then rejoiced when they saw the Lord. So Jesus said to them again, "Peace *be* with you; as the Father has sent Me, I also send you." And when He had said this, He breathed on them and said to them, "Receive the Holy Spirit. If you forgive the sins of any, *their sins* have been forgiven them; if you retain the *sins* of any, they have been retained" (John 20:19–23; cf. Luke 24:36–43; see Matthew 16:19; Mark 16:14).

[MIRACLE from "Cast the net on the right-hand side of the boat and you will find a *catch*." So they cast, and then they were not able to haul it in because of the great number of fish]
Setting: By the Sea of Galilee (Tiberias). During His third post-resurrection appearance to His disciples, Jesus directs them to a great catch of fish following their unsuccessful night of fishing.

So Jesus said to them, "Children, you do not have any fish, do you?" They answered Him, "No." And He said to them, "Cast the net on the right-hand side of the boat and you will find a *catch*." So they cast, and then they were not able to haul it in because of the great number of fish (John 21:5, 6; see Luke 5:4).

[MIRACLE from a light from heaven flashed around him]
Setting: On the road to Damascus. Luke, writing in Acts, reveals how Saul of Tarsus (who will later have the name Paul), a persecutor of the disciples of Jesus, receives the Lord's calling and is temporarily blinded.

As he was traveling, it happened that he was approaching Damascus, and suddenly a light from heaven flashed around him; and he fell to the ground and heard a voice saying to him. "Saul, Saul, why are you persecuting Me?" And he said, "Who are You, Lord?" And He *said,* "I am Jesus whom you are persecuting, but get up and enter the city, and it will be told you what you must do" (Acts 9:3–6; see Acts 22:7, 8).

MIRACLE, FIRST

[FIRST MIRACLE from John 2:9: the headwaiter tasted the water which had become wine]
Setting: Cana of Galilee. On the third day of His public ministry, after choosing Andrew, Peter, and Nathanael to be His disciples, Jesus attends a wedding. His mother prompts Him to perform His first miracle, that of turning water into wine.

Jesus said to them, "Fill the waterpots with water." So they filled them up to the brim. And He said to them, "Draw *some* out now and take it to the headwaiter" So they took it *to him* (John 2:7, 8).

MIRACLES **(Miracles involving more than one person. For a specific miracle, see MIRACLE. Also see DEMONS, CASTING OUT; HEALING; LEPROSY, CLEANSING FROM: MIRACLE; RESURRECTION; SIGNS AND WONDERS; and WORKS)**

Setting: Galilee. During the early part of His ministry, Jesus preaches the Sermon on the Mount to His disciples and the multitudes.

"Not everyone who says to Me, 'Lord, Lord,' will enter the kingdom of heaven, but he who does the will of My Father who is in heaven *will enter.* Many will say to Me on that day, 'Lord, Lord, did we not prophesy in Your name, and in Your name cast out demons, and in Your name perform many miracles?' And then I will declare to them, 'I never knew you, DEPART FROM ME, YOU WHO PRACTICE LAWLESSNESS'"(Matthew 7:21–23, Jesus quotes from Psalm 6:8; cf. Matthew 25:11–13; see Luke 6:46).

[MIRACLES from And their eyes were opened]
Setting: The region of Galilee. After bringing a young girl back to life, the Lord heals some blind men.

When He entered the house, the blind men came up to Him, and Jesus said to them, "Do you believe that I am able to do this?" They said to Him, "Yes, Lord." Then He touched their eyes saying, "It shall be done for you according to your faith." And their eyes were opened. And Jesus sternly warned them: "See that no one knows *about this!"* (Matthew 9:28–30).

[MIRACLES from *the* BLIND RECEIVE SIGHT and *the* lame walk, *the* lepers are cleansed and *the* deaf hear, *the* dead are raised up]
Setting: Galilee. As He teaches and preaches, Jesus responds to John the Baptist's question (posed by some of John's disciples) whether He is Israel's promised Messiah.

Jesus answered and said to them, "Go and report to John what you hear and see: *the* BLIND RECEIVE SIGHT and *the* lame walk, *the* lepers are cleansed and *the* deaf hear, *the* dead are raised up, and *the* POOR HAVE THE GOSPEL PREACHED TO THEM. And blessed is he who does not take offense at Me" (Matthew 11:4–6, Jesus quotes from Isaiah 35:5f; cf. Luke 7:22, 23).

Setting: Galilee. After performing miracles throughout the region, Jesus pronounces woes against those cities who did not repent.

"Woe to you, Chorazin! Woe to you, Bethsaida! For if the miracles had occurred in Tyre and Sidon which occurred in you, they would have repented long ago in sackcloth and ashes. Nevertheless I say to you, it will be more tolerable for Tyre and Sidon in *the* day of judgment than for you. And you, Capernaum, will not be exalted to heaven, will you? You will descend to Hades; for if the miracles had occurred in Sodom which occurred in you, it would have remained to this day. Nevertheless, I say to you that it will be more tolerable for the land of Sodom in *the* day of judgment, than for you" (Matthew 11:21–24; cf. Matthew 10:15; Luke 10:13–15).

[MIRACLES from Matthew 15:38: And those who ate were four thousand men, besides women and children.]
Setting: Near the Sea of Galilee. After being impressed by the faith of a Canaanite woman, Jesus restores her demon-possessed daughter, then feeds more than 4,000 people, primarily Gentiles.

And Jesus called His disciples to Him, and said, "I feel compassion for the people, because they have remained with Me now three days and have nothing to eat; and I do not want to send them away hungry, for they might faint on the way." The disciples said to Him, "Where would we get so many loaves in *this* desolate place to satisfy a large crowd?" And Jesus said to them, "How many loaves do you have?" And they said, "Seven and a few small fish" (Matthew 15:32–34; cf. Mark 8:1–9).

[MIRACLES from immediately they regained their sight]
Setting: Departing Jericho on the way to Jerusalem, where the crucifixion will take place. Two blind men sitting by the road loudly cry out for the Lord to restore their sight.

And Jesus stopped and called them, and said, "What do you want Me to do for you?" They said to Him, "Lord, *we want* our eyes to be opened." Moved with compassion, Jesus touched their eyes; and immediately they regained their sight and followed Him (Matthew 20:32–34; cf. Mark 10:49–52; Luke 18:40–43).

[MIRACLES from Mark 6:44: There were five thousand men who ate the loaves.]
Setting: By the Sea of Galilee. After a long day of ministry, Jesus prepares to demonstrate to His disciples the power of God by feeding more than 5,000 people.

But He answered them, "You give them *something* to eat!" And they said to Him, "Shall we go and spend two hundred denarii on bread and give them *something* to eat? And He said to them, "How many loaves do you have? Go look!" And when they found out, they said, "Five, and two fish" (Mark 6:37, 38; cf. Matthew 14:16, 17; Luke 9:13, 14; John 6:5–9; see Mark 3:20).

[MIRACLES from Mark 8:8, 9: And they ate and were satisfied; and About four thousand were *there;*]
Setting: Decapolis, near the Sea of Galilee. Jesus miraculously feeds more than 4,000 people, primarily Gentiles.

In those days, when there was again a large crowd and they had nothing to eat, Jesus called His disciples and said to them, "I feel compassion for the people because they have remained with Me now three days and have nothing to eat. If I send them away hungry to their homes, they will faint on their way; and some of them have come a great distance" (Mark 8:1–3; cf. Matthew 15:32–38; see Matthew 9:36).

[MIRACLES from in My name they will cast out demons, they will speak with new tongues; they will pick up serpents, and if they drink any deadly *poison,* it will not hurt them; they will lay hands on the sick, and they will recover]
Setting: Following His resurrection from the dead after being crucified, Jesus commissions His disciples to preach His gospel to the world.

And He said to them, "Go into all the world and preach the gospel to all creation. He who has believed and has been baptized shall be saved; but he who has disbelieved shall be condemned. These signs will accompany those who have believed: in My name they will cast out demons, they will speak with new tongues; they will pick up serpents, and if they drink any deadly *poison,* it

will not hurt them; they will lay hands on the sick, and they will recover" (Mark 16:15–18; cf. Matthew 28:16–20; see Mark 9:38; John 3:18, 36; 1 Corinthians 15:6).

[Note: Some scholars question the authenticity of Mark 16:9–20 as these verses do not appear in some early New Testament manuscripts]

[MIRACLES from *the* BLIND RECEIVE SIGHT, *the* lame walk, *the* lepers are cleansed, and *the* deaf hear, *the* dead are raised up]

Setting: Galilee. After Jesus raises a woman's son from the dead in Nain, the disciples of John the Baptist inquire whether He is the promised Messiah.

And He answered and said to them, "Go and report to John what you have seen and heard: *the* BLIND RECEIVE SIGHT, *the* lame walk, *the* lepers are cleansed, and *the* deaf hear, *the* dead are raised up, *the* POOR HAVE THE GOSPEL PREACHED TO THEM. Blessed is he who does not take offense at Me" (Luke 7:22, 23, Jesus quotes from Isaiah 35:5; 61:1; cf. Matthew 11:2–6).

Setting: On the way from Galilee to Jerusalem. The Lord pronounces woes on cities who reject the gospel, as He appoints seventy followers and sends them out in pairs to every place He Himself will soon visit.

"Woe to you, Chorazin! Woe to you, Bethsaida! For if the miracles had been performed in Tyre and Sidon which occurred in you, they would have repented long ago, sitting in sackcloth and ashes. But it will be more tolerable for Tyre and Sidon in the judgment than for you. And you, Capernaum, will not be exalted to heaven, will you? You will be brought down to Hades! The one who listens to you listens to Me, and the one who rejects you rejects Me; and he who rejects Me rejects the One who sent Me" (Luke 10:13–16; cf. Matthew 11:21–23; see Matthew 10:40).

[MIRACLES from I cast out demons and perform cures]

Setting: On the way from Galilee to Jerusalem. While Jesus is teaching in the cities and villages, after He responds to a question about who is saved, some Pharisees ask Him to leave, claiming Herod Antipas (tetrarch of Galilee and Perea) seeks to kill Him.

And He said to them, "Go and tell that fox, 'Behold, I cast out demons and perform cures today and tomorrow, and the third *day* I reach My goal.' Nevertheless I must journey on today and tomorrow and the next *day*; for it cannot be that a prophet would perish outside of Jerusalem. O Jerusalem, Jerusalem, *the city* that kills the prophets and stones those sent to her! How often I wanted to gather your children together, just as a hen *gathers* her brood under her wings, and you would not *have it*! Behold, your house is left to you *desolate*; and I say to you, you will not see Me until *the time* comes when you say, 'BLESSED IS HE WHO COMES IN THE NAME OF THE LORD!'" (Luke 13:32–35, Jesus quotes from Psalm 118:26; cf. Matthew 23:37).

[MIRACLES from Were there not ten cleansed?]

Setting: On the way from Galilee to Jerusalem. The Lord pauses to heal ten lepers who ask for cleansing.

When He saw them, He said to them, "Go and show yourselves to the priests." And as they were going, they were cleansed. Now one of them, when he saw that he had been healed, turned back, glorifying God with a loud voice, and he fell on his face at His feet, giving thanks to Him. And he was a Samaritan. Then Jesus answered and said, "Were there not ten cleansed? But the nine—where are they? Was no one found who returned to give glory to God, except this foreigner?" And He said to him, "Stand up and go; your faith has made you well" (Luke 17:14–19; see Leviticus 14:1–32).

[MIRACLES from John 6:9 – five loaves and two fish feed 5,000 and the men sat down, in number about five thousand. Jesus took the loaves, and having given thanks, He distributed to those who were seated; likewise also of the fish as much as they wanted.]

Setting: By the Sea of Galilee. After revealing to the Jewish religious leaders during a feast of the Jews in Jerusalem that God, John the Baptist, His works, and the Scriptures all testify to His mission, Jesus miraculously feeds more than 5,000 people with a lad's five barley loaves and two fish.

Jesus said, "Have the people sit down." Now there was much grass in the place. So the men sat down, in number about five thousand. Jesus took the loaves, and having given thanks, He distributed to those who were seated; likewise also of the fish as much as they wanted. When they were filled, He said to the disciples, "Gather up the leftover fragments so that nothing will be lost" (John 6:10–12; cf. Matthew 14:17–21; Mark 6:38–44; Luke 9:14–17; see Matthew 15:32–38).

MIRACULOUS POWERS (See MIRACLE; MIRACLES; and SIGNS AND WONDERS)

MISERABLE

Setting: On the island of Patmos (in the Aegean Sea about fifty miles southwest of Ephesus in modern Turkey). On the Lord's Day (Sunday), approximately fifty years after Jesus' resurrection, the disciple John encounters the Lord Jesus Christ, who communicates a new revelation for the apostle to record for the church in Laodicea and to six other churches in Asia.

"To the angel of the church in Laodicea write: The Amen, the faithful and true Witness, the Beginning of the creation of God, says this: 'I know your deeds, that you are neither cold nor hot; I wish that you were cold or hot. So because you are lukewarm, and neither hot nor cold, I will spit you out of My mouth. Because you say, "I am rich, and have become wealthy, and have need of nothing," and you do not know that you are wretched and miserable and poor and blind and naked, I advise you to buy from Me gold refined by fire so that you may become rich, and white garments so that you may clothe yourself, and *that* the shame of your nakedness will not be revealed; and eye salve to anoint your eyes so that you may see. Those whom I love, I reprove and discipline; therefore be zealous and repent. Behold, I stand at the door and knock; if anyone hears My voice and opens the door, I will come in to him and will dine with him, and he with Me. He who overcomes, I will grant to him to sit down with Me on My throne, as I also overcame and sat down with My Father on His throne. He who has an ear, let him hear what the Spirit says to the churches'" (Revelation 3:14–22; see Proverb 3:12; Hosea 12:8; John 14:23; 16:33).

MISSION, JESUS' (See JESUS' MISSION)

MISSION, PAUL'S (See PAUL'S MISSION)

MISTAKEN

Setting: The temple in Jerusalem. The Sadducees question Jesus about Levirate marriage (marriage to a brother-in-law), in order to test Him.

But Jesus answered and said to them, "You are mistaken, not understanding the Scriptures nor the power of God. For in the resurrection they neither marry nor are given in marriage, but are like angels in heaven. But regarding the resurrection of the dead, have you not read what was spoken to you by God: 'I AM THE GOD OF ABRAHAM, AND THE GOD OF ISAAC, AND THE GOD OF JACOB'? He is not the God of the dead but of the living" (Matthew 22:29–32, Jesus quotes from Exodus 3:6; cf. Mark 12:18–27; Luke 20:27–38; see Deuteronomy 25:5; Matthew 22:23–28; John 20:9).

Setting: The temple in Jerusalem. After some of the Pharisees and Herodians attempt to trap Jesus in a statement, some Sadducees question Him about the status of marriage after death.

Jesus said to them, "Is this not the reason you are mistaken, that you do not understand the Scriptures or the power of God? For when they rise from the dead, they neither marry nor are given in marriage, but are like angels in heaven. But regarding the fact that the dead rise again, have you not read in the book of Moses, in the *passage* about *the burning* bush, how God spoke to him, saying, 'I AM THE GOD OF ABRAHAM, AND THE GOD OF ISAAC, and the God of Jacob?' He is not the God of the dead, but of the living; you are greatly mistaken" (Mark 12:24–27, Jesus quotes from Exodus 3:6; cf. Matthew 22:29–33; Luke 20:34–40).

MISTREATMENT (Also see PERSECUTION; and SUFFERING)

[MISTREATMENT from mistreated]

Setting: The temple in Jerusalem. Jesus speaks another parable to the chief priests and elders after they question His authority.

Jesus spoke to them again in parables, saying, "The kingdom of heaven may be compared to a king who gave a wedding feast for his son. And he sent out his slaves to call those who had been invited to the wedding feast, and they were unwilling to come. Again he sent out other slaves saying, 'Tell those who have been invited, "Behold, I have prepared my dinner; my oxen and my fattened livestock are *all* butchered and everything is ready; come to the wedding feast." But they paid no attention and went their way, one to his own farm, another to his business, and the rest seized his slaves and mistreated them and killed them. But the king was enraged, and he sent his armies and destroyed those murderers and set their city on fire. Then he said to his slaves, 'The wedding is ready, but those who were invited were not worthy. 'Go therefore to the main highways, and as many as you find *there,* invite to the wedding feast.' Those slaves went out into the streets and gathered together all they found, both evil and good; and the wedding hall was filled with dinner guests. But when the king came in to look over the dinner guests, he saw a man there who was not dressed in wedding clothes, and he said to him, 'Friend, how did you come in here without wedding clothes?' And the man was speechless. Then the king said to the servants, 'Bind him hand and foot, and throw him into the outer darkness; in that place there will be weeping and gnashing of teeth.' For many are called, but few *are* chosen" (Matthew 22:1–14; cf. Matthew 8:11, 12).

[MISTREATMENT from mistreat]
Setting: Galilee. After selecting His twelve disciples, Jesus teaches the Sermon on the Mount to those disciples and a great throng of people from Judea, Jerusalem, and the central coastal region of Tyre and Sidon.

"But I say to you who hear, love your enemies, do good to those who hate you, bless those who curse you, pray for those who mistreat you. Whoever hits you on the cheek, offer him the other also; and whoever takes away your coat, do not withhold your shirt from him either. Give to everyone who asks of you, and whoever takes away what is yours, do not demand it back. Treat others the same way you want them to treat you. If you love those who love you, what credit is *that* to you? For even sinners love those who love them. If you do good to those who do good to you, what credit is *that* to you? For even sinners do the same. If you lend to those from whom you expect to receive, what credit is *that* to you? Even sinners lend to sinners in order to receive back the same *amount.* But love your enemies, and do good, and lend, expecting nothing in return; and your reward will be great, and you will be sons of the Most High; for He Himself is kind to ungrateful and evil *men*. Be merciful, just as your Father is merciful" (Luke 6:27–36; cf. Matthew 5:9, 39–48; Matthew 7:12).

[MISTREATMENT from mistreated]
Setting: On the way from Galilee to Jerusalem. After responding to Peter's statement about the disciples' personal sacrifice in following Him, Jesus tells them of the sacrifice He will make in Jerusalem.

Then He took the twelve aside and said to them, "Behold, we are going up to Jerusalem, and all things which are written through the prophets about the Son of Man will be accomplished. For He will be handed over to the Gentiles, and will be mocked and mistreated and spit upon, and after they have scourged Him, they will kill Him; and the third day He will rise again" (Luke 18:31–33; cf. Matthew 20:17–19; Mark 10:32–34).

MITE, WIDOW'S

[WIDOW'S MITE from this poor widow put in more than all the contributors to the treasury]
Setting: Opposite the temple treasury in Jerusalem. Jesus focuses His disciples' attention on a widow's monetary sacrifice.

Calling His disciples to Him, He said to them, "Truly I say to you, this poor widow put in more than all the contributors to the treasury; for they all put in out of their surplus, but she, out of her poverty, put in all she owned, all she had to live on" (Mark 12:43, 44; cf. Luke 21:1–4).

[WIDOW'S MITE from this poor widow put in more than all *of them*]
Setting: The temple in Jerusalem. A few days before His crucifixion, after warning the disciples about the lifestyle of the scribes, Jesus points out a poor widow's sacrificial giving to the temple treasury.

And He said, "Truly I say to you, this poor widow put in more than all *of them;* for they all out of their surplus put into the offering; but she out of her poverty put in all that she had to live on" (Luke 21:3, 4; cf. Mark 12:41–44).

MOCKERY

[MOCKERY from mock]

Setting: On the road to Jerusalem. Before going to Jerusalem, Jesus again tells His disciples of His impending death and resurrection.

As Jesus was about to go up to Jerusalem, He took the twelve *disciples* aside by themselves, and on the way He said to them, "Behold, we are going up to Jerusalem; and the Son of Man will be delivered to the chief priests and scribes, and they will condemn Him to death, and will hand Him over to the Gentiles to mock and scourge and crucify *Him,* and on the third day, He will be raised up" (Matthew 20:17–19; cf. Matthew 16:21; Mark 10:32–34; Luke 18:31–33).

[MOCKERY from mock]

Setting: On the road to Jerusalem. After encouraging His disciples with a revelation of their future reward, Jesus prophesies His persecution, death, and resurrection.

They were on the road going up to Jerusalem, and Jesus was walking on ahead of them; and they were amazed, and those who followed were fearful. And again He took the twelve aside and began to tell them what was going to happen to Him, *saying,* "Behold, we are going up to Jerusalem, and the Son of Man will be delivered to the chief priests and the scribes; and they will condemn Him to death and will hand Him over to the Gentiles. They will mock Him and spit on Him, and scourge Him and kill *Him,* and three days later He will rise again" (Mark 10:32–34; cf. Matthew 20:17–19; Luke 18:31–34; see Matthew 16:21; Mark 8:31).

[MOCKERY from mocked]

Setting: On the way from Galilee to Jerusalem. After responding to Peter's statement about the disciples' personal sacrifice in following Him, Jesus tells them of the sacrifice He will make in Jerusalem.

Then He took the twelve aside and said to them, "Behold, we are going up to Jerusalem, and all things which are written through the prophets about the Son of Man will be accomplished. For He will be handed over to the Gentiles, and will be mocked and mistreated and spit upon, and after they have scourged Him, they will kill Him; and the third day He will rise again" (Luke 18:31–33; cf. Matthew 20:17–19; Mark 10:32–34).

MODEL PRAYER (See LORD'S PRAYER)

MOISTURE (Also see RAIN; and WATER)

Setting: Galilee. After His visit in the home of Simon the Pharisee, Jesus goes into the villages and cities proclaiming and preaching the kingdom of God.

When a large crowd was coming together, and those from various cities were journeying to Him, He spoke by way of a parable: "The sower went out to sow his seed; and as he sowed, some fell beside the road, and it was trampled under foot and the birds of the air ate it up. Other *seed* fell on rocky *soil,* and as soon as it grew up, it was withered away, because it had no moisture. Other *seed* fell among the thorns; and the thorns grew up with it and choked it out. Other *seed* fell into the good soil, and grew up, and produced a crop a hundred times as great." As He said these things, He would call out, "He who has ears to hear, let him hear" (Luke 8:4–8; cf. Matthew 13:2–9; Mark 4:3–9).

MONEY (BELT, MONEY is a separate entry; also see COIN; GIVING; MATERIALISM; MONEY, MASTER'S; POOR, GIVING TO THE; POSSESSIONS; TREASURE; TREASURES; and WEALTH)

[MONEY from him who wants to borrow from you]

Setting: Galilee. During the early part of His ministry, Jesus preaches the Sermon on the Mount to His disciples and the multitudes.

"Give to him who asks of you, and do not turn away from him who wants to borrow from you" (Matthew 5:42; see Deuteronomy 15:7–11).

Setting: Galilee. After raising Jairus's daughter from the dead, Jesus calls the twelve disciples together and gives them power and authority over demons, along with the ability to cure diseases.

And He said to them, "Take nothing for *your* journey, neither a staff, nor a bag, nor bread, nor money; and do not *even* have two tunics apiece. Whatever house you enter, stay there until you leave that city. And as for those who do not receive you, go out from that city, shake the dust off your feet as a testimony against them" (Luke 9:3–5; cf. Matthew 10:1–15; Mark 6:7–11; see Luke 10:4–12).

Setting: Jericho, on the way to Jerusalem. After commending Zaccheus's faith in Him, Jesus provides a parable about stewardship.

So He said, "A nobleman went to a distant country to receive a kingdom for himself, and *then* return. And he called ten of his slaves, and gave them ten minas and said to them, 'Do business *with this* until I come *back*.' But his citizens hated him and sent a delegation after him, saying, 'We do not want this man to reign over us.' When he returned, after receiving the kingdom, he ordered that these slaves, to whom he had given the money, be called to him so that he might know what business they had done. The first appeared, saying, 'Master, your mina has made ten minas more.' And he said to him, 'Well done, good slave, because you have been faithful in a very little thing, you are to be in authority over ten cities.' The second came, saying, 'Your mina, master, has made five minas.' And he said to him, also, 'And you are to be over five cities.' Another came, saying, 'Master, here is your mina, which I kept put away in a handkerchief; for I was afraid of you, because you are an exacting man; you take up what you did not lay down and reap what you did not sow.' He said to him, 'By your own words I will judge you, you worthless slave. Did you know that I am an exacting man, taking up what I did not lay down and reaping what I did not sow? Then why did you not put my money in the bank, and having come, I would have collected it with interest?' Then he said to the bystanders, 'Take the mina away from him and give it to the one who has the ten minas.' And they said to him, 'Master, he has ten minas *already*.' I tell you that to everyone who has, more shall be given, but from the one who does not have, even what he does have shall be taken away. But these enemies of mine, who did not want me to reign over them, bring them here and slay them in my presence" (Luke 19:12–27; cf. Matthew 25:14–30; see Matthew 13:12; Luke 16:10).

MONEY BELT (Listed under BELT, MONEY)

MONEY BELTS (Listed under BELTS, MONEY)

MONEY CHANGERS (See ROBBERS' DEN)

MONEY, MASTER'S (Also see STEWARDSHIP)

Setting: On the Mount of Olives, just east of Jerusalem. During His Olivet Discourse, after answering His disciples' questions as to when the temple will be destroyed and Jerusalem overrun, along with the signs of His coming and the end of the age, Jesus reemphasizes to His disciples that they should be on the alert for His return.

"For *it is* just like a man *about* to go on a journey, who called his own slaves and entrusted his possessions to them. To one he gave five talents, to another, two, and to another, one, each according to his own ability; and he went on his journey. Immediately the one who had received the five talents went and traded with them, and gained five more talents. In the same manner the one who *had received* the two *talents* gained two more. But he who received the one *talent* went away, and dug a *hole* in the ground and hid his master's money. Now after a long time the master of those slaves came and settled accounts with them. The one who had received the five talents came up and brought five more talents, saying, 'Master, you entrusted five talents to me. See, I have gained five more talents.' His master said to him, 'Well done, good and faithful slave. You were faithful with a few things, I will put you in charge of many things; enter into the joy of your master.' Also the one who *had received* the two talents came up and said, 'Master, you entrusted two talents to me. See, I have gained two more talents.' His master said to him, 'Well done, good and faithful slave. You were faithful with a few things, I will put you in charge of many things; enter into the joy of your master.' And the one also who had received the one talent came up and said, 'Master, I knew you to be a hard man, reaping where you did not sow and gathering where you scattered no *seed.* And I was afraid, and went away and hid your talent in the ground. See, you have what is yours.' But his master answered and said to him, 'You wicked, lazy slave, you knew that I reap where I did not sow and gather where I scattered no *seed.* Then you ought to have put my money in the bank, and on my arrival I would have received my *money* back with interest. 'Therefore take away the talent from him, and give it to the one who has ten talents.' For to everyone who has, *more* shall be given, and he will have an abundance; but from the one who does not have, even what he does have shall be taken away. Throw out the worthless slave into the outer darkness; in that place there will be weeping and gnashing of teeth" (Matthew 25:14–30; cf. Matthew 8:12; 13:12; 24:45–47; see Matthew 18:23, 24; Luke 12:44).

MONEYLENDER, PARABLE OF THE (See DEBTORS, PARABLE OF TWO)

MONSTER, SEA

Setting: Galilee. After Jesus warns the Pharisees about the unpardonable sin and their future judgment, some Pharisees and scribes ask Him to perform a miraculous sign for them in front of the crowds.

But He answered and said to them, "An evil and adulterous generation craves for a sign; and *yet* no sign will be given to it but the sign of Jonah the prophet; for just as JONAH WAS THREE DAYS AND THREE NIGHTS IN THE BELLY OF THE SEA MONSTER, so will the Son of Man be three days and three nights in the heart of the earth. The men of Nineveh will stand up with this generation at the judgment, and will condemn it because they repented at the preaching of Jonah; and behold, something greater than Jonah is here. *The* Queen of *the* South will rise up with this generation at the judgment and will condemn it, because she came from the ends of the earth to hear the wisdom of Solomon; and behold, something greater than Solomon is here" (Matthew 12:39–42; Jesus quotes from Jonah 1:17; cf. 1 Kings 10:1; Jonah 3:5; Matthew 16:1, 4; 12:38; Luke 11:29).

MONTHS

Setting: The synagogue in Jesus' hometown of Nazareth in Galilee. At the beginning of His public ministry, Jesus comments to the congregation after reading on the Sabbath from the book of the prophet Isaiah.

And He said to them, "No doubt you will quote this proverb to Me, 'Physician, heal yourself! Whatever we heard was done at Capernaum, do here in your hometown as well.'" And He said, "Truly I say to you, no prophet is welcome in his hometown. But I say to you in truth, there were many widows in Israel in the days of Elijah, when the sky was shut up for three years and six months, when a great famine came over all the land; and yet Elijah was sent to none of them, but only to Zarephath, *in the land* of Sidon, to a woman who was a widow. And there were many lepers in Israel in the time of Elisha the prophet; and none of them was cleansed, but only Naaman the Syrian" (Luke 4:23–27; Jesus refers to 1 Kings 17:1, 9; 2 Kings 5:1–14; see Matthew 13:53–58).

Setting: Sychar in Samaria. After Jesus converses with a Samaritan woman at Jacob's well, the disciples return with food. They try to get Jesus to eat, but are surprised when He speaks of other food.

Jesus said to them, "My food is to do the will of Him who sent Me and to accomplish His work. Do you not say, 'There are yet four months, and *then* comes the harvest'? Behold, I say to you, lift up your eyes and look on the fields, that they are white for harvest. Already he who reaps is receiving wages and is gathering fruit for life eternal; so that he who sows and he who reaps may rejoice together. For in this *case* the saying is true, 'One sows and another reaps.' I sent you to reap that for which you have not labored; others have labored and you have entered into their labor" (John 4:34–38; see Matthew 9:37, 38; John 5:36).

MONUMENTS OF THE RIGHTEOUS (Listed under RIGHTEOUS, MONUMENTS OF THE)

MOON (Also see HEAVENS; STAR; and STARS)

Setting: The Mount of Olives, just east of Jerusalem. During His Olivet Discourse, Jesus answers His disciples' questions as to when the temple will be destroyed and Jerusalem overrun, along with the signs of His coming and the end of the age.

"But immediately after the tribulation of those days THE SUN WILL BE DARKENED, AND THE MOON WILL NOT GIVE ITS LIGHT, AND THE STARS WILL FALL from the sky, and the powers of the heavens will be shaken. And then the sign of the Son of Man will appear in the sky, and then all the tribes of the earth will mourn, and they will see the SON OF MAN COMING ON THE CLOUDS OF THE SKY with power and great glory. And He will send forth His angels with A GREAT TRUMPET and THEY WILL GATHER TOGETHER His elect from the four winds, from one end of the sky to the other" (Matthew 24:29–31, Jesus quotes from Isaiah 13:10, Daniel 7:13; Exodus 19:16; cf. Mark 13:24–27; Luke 21:25–27).

Setting: On the Mount of Olives, east of the temple in Jerusalem. After predicting the temple's destruction, Jesus responds during His Olivet Discourse to questions from Peter, James, John, and Andrew about other future events.

"But in those days, after that tribulation, THE SUN WILL BE DARKENED AND THE MOON WILL NOT GIVE ITS LIGHT, AND THE STARS WILL BE FALLING from heaven, and the powers that are in the heavens will be shaken. Then they will see THE SON OF MAN COMING IN CLOUDS with great power and glory. And then He will send forth the angels, and will gather together His elect from the four winds, from the farthest end of the earth to the farthest end of heaven" (Mark 13:24–27. Jesus quotes from Isaiah 13:10; 34:4; Daniel 7:13; cf. Matthew 24:29–31; Luke 21:25–27).

Setting: The Mount of Olives, just east of Jerusalem. After ministering in the temple a few days before His crucifixion, and giving His disciples more details regarding future events, Jesus speaks during His Olivet Discourse of His return.

"There will be signs in sun and moon and stars, and on the earth dismay among the nations, in perplexity at the roaring of the sea and the waves, men fainting from fear and the expectation of the things which are coming upon the world; for the powers of the heavens will be shaken. Then they will see THE SON OF MAN COMING IN A CLOUD with power and great glory. But when these things begin to take place, straighten up and lift up your heads, because your redemption is drawing near" (Luke 21:25–28, Jesus quotes from Daniel 7:13; cf. Matthew 24:29–31; Mark 13:24–27).

MORNING (MORNING STAR is listed under STAR)

Setting: Magadan of Galilee. Jesus' enemies, the Pharisees and Sadducees, rejecting His message, continue to test Him by asking for a sign from heaven.

But He replied to them, "When it is evening, you say, '*It will be* fair weather, for the sky is red.' And in the morning, '*There will* be a storm today, for the sky is red and threatening.' Do you know how to discern the appearance of the sky, but cannot *discern* the signs of the times? An evil and adulterous generation seeks after a sign; and a sign will not be given it, except the sign of Jonah." And He left them and went away (Matthew 16:2–4; cf. Matthew 12:39; Mark 8:12; Luke 12:54–56).

Setting: Judea beyond the Jordan (Perea). Jesus illustrates the kingdom of heaven to His disciples through the story of laborers in the vineyard.

"For the kingdom of heaven is like a landowner who went out early in the morning to hire laborers for his vineyard. When he had agreed with the laborers for a denarius for the day, he sent them into his vineyard. And he went out about the third hour and saw others standing idle in the market place; and to those he said, 'You also go into the vineyard, and whatever is right I will give you.' And *so* they went. Again he went out about the sixth and the ninth hour, and did the same thing. And about the eleventh *hour* he went out and found others standing *around;* and he said to them, 'Why have you been standing idle here all day long?' They said to him, 'Because no one hired us.' He said to them, 'You go into the vineyard too.' When evening came, the owner of the vineyard said to his foreman, 'Call the laborers and pay them their wages, beginning with the last *group* to the first.' When those *hired* about the eleventh hour came, each one received a denarius. When those *hired* first came, they thought that they would receive more; but each of them also received a denarius. When they received it, they grumbled at the landowner, saying, 'These last men have worked *only* one hour, and you have made them equal to us who have borne the burden and the scorching heat of the day.' But he answered and said to one of them, 'Friend, I am doing you no wrong; did you not agree with me for a denarius? Take what is yours and go, but I wish to give to this last man the same as to you. It is not lawful for me to do what I wish with

what is my own? Or is your eye envious because I am generous?' So the last shall be first, and the first last" (Matthew 20:1 16, cf. Matthew 19:30).

Setting: On the Mount of Olives, east of the temple in Jerusalem. After predicting the temple's destruction, Jesus responds during His Olivet Discourse to questions from Peter, James, John, and Andrew about other future events.

"Take heed, keep on the alert; for you do not know when the *appointed* time will come. *It is* like a man away on a journey, *who* upon leaving his house and putting his slaves in charge, *assigning* to each one his task, also commanded the doorkeeper to stay on the alert. Therefore, be on the alert—for you do not know when the master of the house is coming, whether in the evening, at midnight, or when the rooster crows, or in the morning—in case he should come suddenly and find you asleep. What I say to you I say to all, 'Be on the alert!' " (Mark 13:33–37; cf. Matthew 24:42, 43; Luke 21:34–36; see Luke 12:36–38; Ephesians 6:18).

MORNING STAR (See STAR)

MORSEL (Also see BREAD; and CRUMBS)

Setting: Jerusalem. Before the Passover, troubled in spirit due to His upcoming death on the cross, Jesus reveals to His disciples that Judas will betray Him to the chief priests and Pharisees.

Jesus then answered, "That is the one for whom I shall dip the morsel and give it to him." So when He had dipped the morsel, He took and gave it to Judas, *the son* of Simon Iscariot. After the morsel, Satan then entered into him. Therefore Jesus said to him, "What you do, do quickly" (John 13:26, 27; cf. Matthew 26:23; Mark 14:20; see Luke 22:3, 21; John 6:71).

MOSES (MOSES, BOOK OF; MOSES, CHAIR OF; and MOSES, LAW OF are separate entries)

Setting: Galilee. When Jesus comes down after preaching The Sermon on the Mount, large crowds follow Him as a leper approaches Him asking for cleansing.

Jesus stretched out His hand and touched him, saying, "I am willing, be cleansed." And immediately his leprosy was cleansed. And Jesus said to him, "See that you tell no one; but go, show yourself to the priest and present the offering that Moses commanded, as a testimony to them" (Matthew 8:3, 4; cf. Mark 1:40–44; Luke 5:12–14).

Setting: Judea beyond the Jordan (Perea). Jesus responds to the Pharisees' follow up question in front of a large crowd about Moses' command regarding a certificate of divorce.

He said to them. "Because of your hardness of heart Moses permitted you to divorce your wives; but from the beginning it has not been this way. And I say to you, whoever divorces his wife, except for immorality, and marries another woman commits adultery" (Matthew 19:8, 9; cf. Deuteronomy 24:1–4; Matthew 5:32; 19:7; Mark 10:1–12; see Romans 7:2, 3; 1 Corinthians 7:10, 39).

Setting: Galilee. Early in His ministry, as Jesus preaches and casts out demons in the synagogues, a leper beseeches Him for healing.

Moved with compassion, Jesus stretched out His hand and touched him, and said to him, "I am willing; be cleansed." Immediately the leprosy left him and he was cleansed. And He sternly warned him and immediately sent him away, and He said to him, "See that you say nothing to anyone; but go, show yourself to the priest and offer for your cleansing what Moses commanded, as a testimony to them" (Mark 1:41–44; cf. Luke 5:12–14; see Leviticus 14:1–32; Matthew 8:3).

Setting: Galilee. The Pharisees and some of the scribes from Jerusalem question why Jesus' disciples do not follow the tradition of ceremonial hand cleansing before eating bread.

And He said to them, "Rightly did Isaiah prophesy of you hypocrites, as it is written: 'THIS PEOPLE HONORS ME WITH THEIR LIPS, BUT THEIR HEART IS FAR AWAY FROM ME. BUT IN VAIN DO THEY WORSHIP ME, TEACHING AS DOCTRINES THE PRECEPTS OF MEN.' Neglecting the commandment of God, you hold to the tradition of men." He was also saying to them, "You are experts at setting aside the commandment of God in order to keep tradition. For Moses said, 'HONOR YOUR FATHER AND YOUR MOTHER'; and, 'HE WHO SPEAKS EVIL OF FATHER OR MOTHER, IS TO BE PUT TO DEATH'; but you say, 'If a man says to *his* father or *his* mother, whatever I have that would help you is Corban (that is to say, given *to God*),' you no longer permit him to do anything for *his* father or *his* mother; *thus* invalidating the word of God by your tradition which you have handed down; and you do many things such as that" (Mark 7:6–13, Jesus quotes from Exodus 20:12; 21:17; Isaiah 29:13; cf. Matthew 15:1–6).

Setting: Judea beyond the Jordan (Perea). Jesus teaches the crowds gathered around Him about divorce after the Pharisees test and question Him on the subject.

And He answered and said to them, "What did Moses command you?" They said, "Moses permitted a *man* TO WRITE A CERTIFICATE OF DIVORCE AND SEND *her* AWAY." But Jesus said to them, "Because of your hardness of heart he wrote you this commandment. But from the beginning of creation, *God* MADE THEM MALE AND FEMALE. FOR THIS REASON A MAN SHALL LEAVE HIS FATHER AND MOTHER, AND THE TWO SHALL BECOME ONE FLESH; so they are no longer two, but one flesh. What therefore God has joined together, let no man separate. In the house the disciples *began* questioning Him about this again. And He said to them, "Whoever divorces his wife and marries another woman commits adultery against her; and if she herself divorces her husband and marries another man, she is committing adultery" (Mark 10:3–12, Jesus quotes from Genesis 1:27; 2:24; cf. Matthew 19:1–9; see Deuteronomy 24:1–3; Matthew 5:32; see Romans 7:2, 3; 1 Corinthians 7:10, 11, 13, 39; 1 Timothy 2:14).

Setting: Galilee. Early in His ministry, after calling Andrew, Simon (Peter), James, and John to follow Him, Jesus heals a leper.

And He stretched out His hand and touched Him, saying, "I am willing; be cleansed." And immediately the leprosy left him. And He ordered him to tell no one, "But go and show yourself to the priest and make an offering for your cleansing, just as Moses commanded, as a testimony to them" (Luke 5:13, 14; cf. Matthew 8:2–4; Mark 1:40–45; see Leviticus 13:49).

Setting: On the way from Galilee to Jerusalem. After responding to the Pharisees' scoffing at His teaching the disciples about stewardship and the permanence of the Law, Jesus conveys the story of the rich man and Lazarus.

"Now there was a rich man, and he habitually dressed in purple and fine linen, joyously living in splendor every day. And a poor man named Lazarus was laid at his gate, covered with sores, and longing to be fed with the *crumbs* which were falling from the rich man's table; besides, even the dogs were coming and licking his sores. Now the poor man died and was carried away by the angels to Abraham's bosom; and the rich man also died and was buried. In Hades he lifted up his eyes, being in torment, and saw Abraham far away and Lazarus in his bosom. And he cried out and said, 'Father Abraham, have mercy on me, and send Lazarus so that he may dip the tip of his finger in water and cool off my tongue, for I am in agony in this flame.' But Abraham said, 'Child, remember that during your life you received your good things, and likewise Lazarus bad things; but now he is being comforted here, and you are in agony. And besides all this, between us and you there is a great chasm fixed, so that those who wish to come over from here to you will not be able, and *that* none may cross over from there to us.' And he said, 'Then I beg you, father, that you send him to my father's house—for I have five brothers—in order that he may warn them, so that they will not also come to this place of torment.' But Abraham said, 'They have Moses and the Prophets; let them hear them.' But he said, 'No, father Abraham, but if someone goes to them from the dead, they will repent!' But he said to him, 'If they do not listen to Moses and the Prophets, they will not be persuaded even if someone rises from the dead' " (Luke 16:19–31; see Luke 3:8; 6:24; 16:1, 14).

Setting: The temple in Jerusalem. While ministering a few days before His crucifixion, after the scribes and Pharisees seek to trap Jesus by questioning Him about paying taxes to Caesar, some Sadducees (who say that there is no resurrection) ask Him a question about the resurrection.

Jesus said to them, "The sons of this age marry and are given in marriage, but those who are considered worthy to attain to that age and the resurrection from the dead, neither marry nor are given in marriage; for they cannot even die anymore, because they are like angels, and are sons of God, being sons of the resurrection. But that the dead are raised, even Moses showed, in the *passage about the burning* bush, where he calls the Lord THE GOD OF ABRAHAM, AND THE GOD OF ISAAC, AND THE GOD OF JACOB. Now

He is not the God of the dead but of the living; for all live to Him" (Luke 20:34–38, Jesus quotes from Exodus 3:6; cf. Matthew 22:23–32; Mark 12:18–27).

Setting: Jerusalem. At the time for the Passover of the Jews, after the Lord cleanses the temple, a Pharisee, Nicodemus, asks Him by night the meaning of "born of the Spirit."

Jesus answered and said to him, "Are you the teacher of Israel and do not understand these things? Truly, truly, I say to you, we speak of what we know and testify of what we have seen, and you do not accept our testimony. If I told you earthly things and you do not believe, how will you believe if I tell you heavenly things? No one has ascended into heaven, but He who descended from heaven: the Son of Man. As Moses lifted up the serpent in the wilderness, even so must the Son of Man be lifted up; so that whoever believes will in Him have eternal life" (John 3:10–15; see Numbers 21:9; Proverb 30:4; John 12:34; 20:30, 31).

Setting: Jerusalem. During a feast of the Jews, Jesus responds to criticism from the Jewish religious leaders by referring to God as His Father (thereby making Himself equal with God) and informing them that God, John the Baptist, the Scriptures, and His works all testify to His mission.

"You search the Scriptures because you think that in them you have eternal life; it is these that testify about Me; and you are unwilling to come to Me so that you may have life. I do not receive glory from men; but I know you, that you do not have the love of God in yourselves. I have come in My Father's name, and you do not receive Me; if another comes in his own name, you will receive him. How can you believe, when you receive glory from one another and you do not seek the glory that is from the *one and* only God? Do not think that I will accuse you before the Father; the one who accuses you is Moses, in whom you have set your hope. For if you believed Moses, you would believe Me, for he wrote about Me. But if you do not believe his writings, how will you believe My words?" (John 5:39–47; see Matthew 24:5; Luke 16:29, 31; 24:27; 9:28; 17:3).

Setting: Capernaum. The day after Jesus walks on the Sea of Galilee to join His disciples in a boat, the people He miraculously fed with a lad's five loaves and two fish quiz Jesus about the signs and works He performs so they may believe in Him.

Jesus then said to them, "Truly, truly, I say to you, it is not Moses who has given you the bread out of heaven, but it is My Father who gives you the true bread out of heaven. For the bread of God is that which comes down out of heaven, and gives life to the world" (John 6:32, 33; see John 6:50).

Setting: The temple in Jerusalem. After receiving encouragement from His blood brothers in Galilee to attend the upcoming Feast of Booths in order to demonstrate His works to His disciples and the world, Jesus goes and teaches, astonishing the Jewish religious leaders.

"Did not Moses give you the Law, and *yet* none of you carries out the Law? Why do you seek to kill Me?" (John 7:19; see Mark 11:18; John 1:17).

Setting: The temple in Jerusalem. After receiving encouragement from His blood brothers in Galilee to attend the upcoming Feast of Booths in order to demonstrate His works to His disciples and the world, Jesus goes and teaches, astonishing the Jewish religious leaders.

Jesus answered them, "I did one deed, and you all marvel. For this reason Moses has given you circumcision (not because it is from Moses, but from the fathers), and on the Sabbath you circumcise a man. If a man receives circumcision on the Sabbath so that the Law of Moses will not be broken, are you angry with Me because I made an entire man well on the Sabbath? Do not judge according to appearance, but judge with righteous judgment" (John 7:21–24; see Genesis 17:10–14; Leviticus 12:3; 19:15; Matthew 12:2; John 5:2–16; 7–20).

MOSES, BOOK OF (Also see MOSES, LAW OF)

Setting: The temple in Jerusalem. After some of the Pharisees and Herodians attempt to trap Jesus in a statement, some Sadducees question Him about the status of marriage after death.

Jesus said to them, "Is this not the reason you are mistaken, that you do not understand the Scriptures or the power of God? For when they rise from the dead, they neither marry nor are given in marriage, but are like angels in heaven. But regarding the fact that the dead rise again, have you not read in the book of Moses, in the *passage* about *the burning* bush, how God spoke to him, saying, 'I AM THE GOD OF ABRAHAM, AND THE GOD OF ISAAC, and the God of Jacob?' He is not the God of the dead, but of the living; you are greatly mistaken" (Mark 12:24–27, Jesus quotes from Exodus 3:6; cf. Matthew 22:29–33; Luke 20:34–40).

MOSES, CHAIR OF (Also see MOSES)

Setting: The temple in Jerusalem. Jesus exposes the truth about Pharisaism to the crowds and His disciples after the Jewish religious leaders test Him with questions.

Then Jesus spoke to the crowds and to His disciples, saying: "The scribes and the Pharisees have seated themselves in the chair of Moses; therefore all that they tell you, do and observe, but do not do according to their deeds; for they say *things* and do not do *them.* They tie up heavy burdens and lay them on men's shoulders, but they themselves are unwilling to move them with *so much as* a finger. But they do all their deeds to be noticed by men; for they broaden their phylacteries and lengthen their tassels *of their garments.* They love the place of honor at banquets and the chief seats in the synagogues, and respectful greetings in the market places, and being called Rabbi by men. But do not be called Rabbi; for One is your Teacher, and you are all brothers. Do not call *anyone* on earth your father; for One is your Father, He who is in heaven. Do not be called leaders; for One is your Leader, *that is,* Christ. But the greatest among you shall be your servant. Whoever exalts himself shall be humbled; and whoever humbles himself shall be exalted" (Matthew 23:1–12; cf. Matthew 20:26; Mark 12:38–40; Luke 20:46, 47; see Exodus 13:9; Deuteronomy 33:3; Matthew 6:1, 5, 6, 9, 16; Mark 14:11; Luke 11:43; 14:11).

MOSES, LAW OF (Also see MOSES, BOOK OF)

Setting: Jerusalem. After rising from the grave on the third day after being crucified, and appearing to two of His followers on the road to Emmaus, Jesus gives instruction to His disciples (except Thomas) about His mission on earth and the promise of future power from God.

Now He said to them, "These are My words which I spoke to you while I was still with you, that all things which are written about Me in the Law of Moses and the Prophets and the Psalms must be fulfilled." Then He opened their minds to understand the Scriptures, and He said to them, "Thus it is written, that the Christ would suffer and rise again from the dead the third day, and that repentance for forgiveness of sins would be proclaimed in His name to all the nations, beginning from Jerusalem. You are witnesses of these things. And behold, I am sending forth the promise of My Father upon you; but you are to stay in the city until you are clothed with power from on high" (Luke 24:44–49; see Matthew 28:19, 20; Acts 1:8).

Setting: The temple in Jerusalem. After receiving encouragement from His blood brothers in Galilee to attend the upcoming Feast of Booths in order to demonstrate His works to His disciples and the world, Jesus goes and teaches, astonishing the Jewish religious leaders.

Jesus answered them, "I did one deed, and you all marvel. For this reason Moses has given you circumcision (not because it is from Moses, but from the fathers), and on *the* Sabbath you circumcise a man. If a man receives circumcision on *the* Sabbath so that the Law of Moses will not be broken, are you angry with Me because I made an entire man well on *the* Sabbath? Do not judge according to appearance, but judge with righteous judgment" (John 7:21–24; see Genesis 17:10–14; Leviticus 12:3; 19:15; Matthew 12:2; John 5:2–16; 7–20).

MOST HIGH, SONS OF THE

Setting: Galilee. After selecting His twelve disciples, Jesus teaches the Sermon on the Mount to those disciples and a great throng of people from Judea, Jerusalem, and the central coastal region of Tyre and Sidon.

"But I say to you who hear, love your enemies, do good to those who hate you, bless those who curse you, pray for those who mistreat you. Whoever hits you on the cheek, offer him the other also; and whoever takes away your coat, do not withhold your shirt from him either. Give to everyone who asks of you, and whoever takes away what is yours, do not demand it back. Treat others the same way you want them to treat you. If you love those who love you, what credit is *that* to you? For even sinners love those who love them. If you do good to those who do good to you, what credit is *that* to you? For even sinners do the same. If you lend to those from whom you expect to receive, what credit is *that* to you? Even sinners lend to sinners in order to receive back the same *amount*. But love your enemies, and do good, and lend, expecting nothing in return; and your reward will be great, and you will be sons of the Most High; for He Himself is kind to ungrateful and evil *men*. Be merciful, just as your Father is merciful" (Luke 6:27–36; cf. Matthew 5:9, 39–48; Matthew 7:12).

MOTH

Setting: Galilee. During the early part of His ministry, Jesus preaches the Sermon on the Mount to His disciples and the multitudes.

"Do not store up for yourselves treasures on earth, where moth and rust destroy, and where thieves break in and steal. But store up for yourselves treasures in heaven, where neither moth nor rust destroys, and where thieves do not break in or steal; for where your treasure is, there your heart will be also" (Matthew 6:19–21; cf. Luke 12:34; see Proverb 23:4; Matthew 19:21).

Setting: On the way from Galilee to Jerusalem. After giving a parable about riches and greed, Jesus challenges the crowd and His disciples concerning godly living.

"Sell your possessions and give to charity; make yourselves money belts which do not wear out, an unfailing treasure in heaven, where no thief comes near nor moth destroys. For where your treasure is, there your heart will be also" (Luke 12:33, 34; cf. Matthew 6:19–21; 19:21).

MOTHER (FATHER AND/OR MOTHER; and HONORING FATHER AND MOTHER are separate entries; also see MOTHERS)

Setting: Galilee. After His disciples observe His ministry, Jesus summons and specifically instructs them about their ministry hardships ahead involving true discipleship.

"Do not think that I came to bring peace on the earth; I did not come to bring peace, but a sword. For I came to SET A MAN AGAINST HIS FATHER, AND A DAUGHTER AGAINST HER MOTHER, AND A DAUGHTER-IN-LAW AGAINST HER MOTHER-IN-LAW; and A MAN'S ENEMIES WILL BE THE MEMBERS OF HIS HOUSEHOLD" (Matthew 10:34–36; Jesus quotes from Micah 7:6; cf. Luke 12:51–53).

Setting: Galilee. Jesus' mother, Mary, and His brothers wait to see Him as He teaches and preaches.

But Jesus answered the one who was telling Him and said, "Who is My mother and who are My brothers?" And stretching out His hand toward His disciples, He said, "Behold, My mother and My brothers! For whoever does the will of My Father who is in heaven, he is My brother and sister and mother" (Matthew 12:48–50; cf. Mark 3:31–35; Luke 8:19–21).

Setting: Galilee. During the early part of His ministry, just after selecting His twelve disciples, when informed that His mother and brothers are waiting to see Him, Jesus explains to the crowd who His true relatives are.

Answering them, He said, "Who are My mother and My brothers?" Looking about at those who were sitting around Him, He said, "Behold My mother and My brothers! For whoever does the will of God, he is My brother and sister and mother" (Mark 3:33–35; cf. Matthew 12:46–50; Luke 8:19, 21).

Setting: Galilee. After giving the Parable of the Lamp to His disciples, when informed that His mother and brothers are seeking Him, Jesus conveys who His true relatives are.

But He answered and said to them, "My mother and My brothers are these who hear the word of God and do it" (Luke 8:21; cf. Matthew 12:26–50; Mark 3:31–35.

Setting: On the way from Galilee to Jerusalem. After clarifying a parable for Peter and the crowd, Jesus conveys how a relationship with Him divides families.

"I have come to cast fire upon the earth; and how I wish it were already kindled! But I have a baptism to undergo, and how distressed I am until it is accomplished! Do you suppose that I came to grant peace on earth? I tell you, no, but rather division; for from now on five *members* in one household will be divided, three against two and two against three. They will be divided, father against son and son against father, mother against daughter, and daughter against mother, mother-in-law against daughter-in-law and daughter-in-law against mother-in-law" (Luke 12:49–53; cf. Matthew 10:34–36; see Micah 7:6; Mark 10:38).

Setting: The Place of the Skull (Golgotha), just outside Jerusalem. While hanging nailed to a cross, Jesus unselfishly asks His disciple, John, to care for His mother.

When Jesus saw His mother, and the disciple whom He loved standing nearby, He said to His mother, "Woman, behold, your son!" Then He said to the disciple, "Behold, your mother!" From that hour the disciple took her into his own *household* (John 19:26, 27).

MOTHER, HONORING FATHER AND (See HONORING FATHER AND MOTHER)

MOTHER, JESUS'

[JESUS' MOTHER from Woman]

Setting: Cana of Galilee. On the third day of His public ministry, after choosing Andrew, Peter, and Nathanael to be His disciples, Jesus attends a wedding. His mother prompts Him to perform His first miracle, that of turning water into wine.

And Jesus said to her, "Woman, what does that have to do with us? My hour has not yet come" (John 2:4; see John 7:6, 8, 30).

[JESUS' MOTHER from Jesus saw His mother and Woman]

Setting: On the Place of the Skull (Golgotha), just outside Jerusalem. While being crucified, Jesus unselfishly asks His disciple, John, to care for His mother.

When Jesus saw His mother, and the disciple whom He loved standing nearby, He said to His mother, "Woman, behold, your son!" Then He said to the disciple, "Behold, your mother!" From that hour the disciple took her into his own *household* (John 19:26, 27).

MOTHER'S WOMB (Listed under WOMB, MOTHER'S)

MOTHER-IN-LAW

Setting: Galilee. After His disciples observe His ministry, Jesus summons and specifically instructs them about their ministry hardships ahead involving true discipleship.

"Do not think that I came to bring peace on the earth; I did not come to bring peace, but a sword. For I came to SET A MAN AGAINST HIS FATHER, AND A DAUGHTER AGAINST HER MOTHER, AND A DAUGHTER-IN-LAW AGAINST HER MOTHER-IN-LAW; and A MAN'S ENEMIES WILL BE THE MEMBERS OF HIS HOUSEHOLD" (Matthew 10:34–36; Jesus quotes from Micah 7:6; cf. Luke 12:51–53).

Setting: On the way from Galilee to Jerusalem. After clarifying a parable for Peter and the crowd, Jesus conveys how a relationship with Him divides families.

"I have come to cast fire upon the earth; and how I wish it were already kindled! But I have a baptism to undergo, and how distressed I am until it is accomplished! Do you suppose that I came to grant peace on earth? I tell you, no, but rather division; for from now on five *members* in one household will be divided, three against two and two against three. They will be divided, father

against son and son against father, mother against daughter, and daughter against mother, mother-in-law against daughter-in-law and daughter-in-law against mother-in-law" (Luke 12:49–53; cf. Matthew 10:34–36; see Micah 7:6; Mark 10:38).

MOTHERS (Also see MOTHER)

Setting: Judea beyond the Jordan (Perea). After informing a rich man how righteous believers may have treasure in heaven, Jesus tells His disciples about the reward of those who sacrifice in this life to follow Him.

Jesus said, "Truly I say to you, there is no one who has left house or brothers or sisters or mother or father or children or farms, for My sake and for the gospel's sake, but that he will receive a hundred times as much now in the present age, houses and brothers and sisters and mothers and children and farms, along with persecutions; and in the age to come, eternal life. But many *who are* first will be last, and the last, first" (Mark 10:29–31; cf. Matthew 19:27–30; Luke 18:28–30; see Matthew 6:33).

MOTIVES (Also see HYPOCRITES)

[MOTIVES inferred from context]

Setting: Galilee. During the early part of His ministry, Jesus preaches the Sermon on the Mount to His disciples and the multitudes.

"Beware of practicing your righteousness before men to be noticed by them; otherwise you have no reward with your Father who is in heaven" (Matthew 6:1; cf. Matthew 6:5, 16).

[MOTIVES inferred from context]

Setting: Galilee. During the early part of His ministry, Jesus preaches the Sermon on the Mount to His disciples and the multitudes.

"When you pray, you are not to be like the hypocrites; for they love to stand and pray in the synagogues and on the street corners so that they may be seen by men. Truly I say to you, they have their reward in full. But you, when you pray, go into your inner room, close your door and pray to your Father who is in secret, and your Father who sees *what is done* in secret will reward you" (Matthew 6:5, 6; see Mark 11:25).

[MOTIVES inferred from context]

Setting: Galilee. During the early part of His ministry, Jesus preaches the Sermon on the Mount to His disciples and the multitudes.

"Whenever you fast, do not put on a gloomy face as the hypocrites *do,* for they neglect their appearance so that they will be noticed by men when they are fasting. Truly I say to you, they have their reward in full. But you, when you fast, anoint your head and wash your face so that your fasting will not be noticed by men, but by your Father who is in secret; and your Father who sees *what is done* in secret will reward you" (Matthew 6:16–18; see Matthew 6:4, 6).

MOUNT, SERMON ON THE (See specific verses in Matthew 5–7 and Luke 6)

MOUNTAIN (Also see MOUNTAINS)

Setting: Near the mountain where the Transfiguration has just taken place. Jesus reveals to His disciples why they could not cure a demon-possessed boy.

And He said to them, "Because of the littleness of your faith; for truly I say to you, if you have faith the size of a mustard seed, you will say to this mountain, 'Move from here to there,' and it will move; and nothing will be impossible to you. ["But this kind does not go out except by prayer and fasting"] (Matthew 17:20, 21; cf. Matthew 21:21, 22; Mark 9:28, 29).

Setting: On the way from Bethany to Jerusalem. The day after Jesus curses a fig tree (an illustration of the nation Israel), the disciples ask Him how it has so quickly withered.

And Jesus answered and said to them, "Truly I say to you, if you have faith and do not doubt, you will not only do what was done to the fig tree, but even if you say to this mountain, 'Be taken up and cast into the sea,' it will happen. And all things you ask in prayer, believing, you will receive" (Matthew 21:21, 22; cf. Matthew 7:7; 17:20; Mark 11:20–24).

Setting: Just outside Jerusalem. The day after Jesus instructs the money changers while He cleanses the temple, Peter draws the Lord's and His disciples' attention to an earlier-cursed fig tree.

And Jesus answered saying to them, "Have faith in God. Truly, I say to you, whoever says to this mountain, 'Be taken up and cast into the sea,' and does not doubt in his heart, but believes that what he says is going to happen, it will be *granted* him. Therefore I say to you, all things for which you pray and ask, believe that you have received them, and they will be *granted* you. Whenever you stand praying, forgive, if you have anything against anyone, so that your Father who is in heaven will also forgive you your transgressions. [But if you do not forgive, neither will your Father who is in heaven forgive your transgressions'] (Mark 11:22–26; cf. Matthew 21:19–22; see Matthew 6:14, 15; 7:7; 17:20).

Setting: Sychar in Samaria, on the way to Galilee. Jesus interacts with a Samaritan woman at Jacob's well, while the disciples are buying food.

Jesus said to her, "Woman, believe Me, an hour is coming when neither in this mountain nor in Jerusalem will you worship the Father. You worship what you do not know; we worship what we know, for salvation is from the Jews. But an hour is coming, and now is, when the true worshipers will worship the Father in spirit and truth; for such people the Father seeks to be His worshipers. God is spirit, and those who worship Him must worship in spirit and truth" (John 4:21–24; see Isaiah 2:3; Philippians 3:3).

MOUNTAINS (Also see MOUNTAIN)

Setting: Capernaum of Galilee. Jesus illustrates to His disciples the value of little ones.

"What do you think? If any man has a hundred sheep, and one of them has gone astray, does he not leave the ninety-nine on the mountains and go and search for the one that is straying? If it turns out that he finds it, truly I say to you, he rejoices over it more than the ninety-nine which have not gone astray. So it is not *the* will of your Father who is in heaven that one of these little ones perish" (Matthew 18:12–14; cf. Luke 15:4–7).

Setting: The Mount of Olives, just east of Jerusalem. During His Olivet Discourse, Jesus answers His disciples' questions as to when the temple will be destroyed and Jerusalem overrun, along with the signs of His coming and the end of the age.

"Therefore when you see the ABOMINATION OF DESOLATION which was spoken of through Daniel the prophet, standing in the holy place (let the reader understand), then those who are in Judea must flee to the mountains. Whoever is on the housetop must not go down to get the things that are in his house. Whoever is in the field must not turn back to get his cloak. But woe to those who are pregnant and to those who are nursing babies in those days! But pray that your flight will not be in the winter, or on a Sabbath. For then there will be a great tribulation, such as has not occurred since the beginning of the world until now, nor ever will. Unless those days had been cut short, no life would have been saved; but for the sake of the elect those days will be cut short. Then if anyone says to you, 'Behold, here is the Christ,' or "There *He is,*' do not believe *him.* For false Christs and false prophets will arise and will show great signs and wonders, so as to mislead, if possible, even the elect. Behold, I have told you in advance. So if they say to you, 'Behold, He is in the wilderness,' do not go out, *or,* 'Behold, He is in the inner rooms,' do not believe *them.* For just as the lightning comes from the east and flashes even to the west, so will the coming of the Son of Man be. Wherever the corpse is, there the vultures will gather" (Matthew 24:15–28, Jesus quotes from Daniel 9:27; cf. Daniel 12:1; Mark 13:14–23; Luke 17:22–31; 21:20–24; 23:29; see John 4:48).

Setting: On the Mount of Olives, east of the temple in Jerusalem. After predicting the temple's destruction, Jesus responds during His Olivet Discourse to questions from Peter, James, John, and Andrew about other future events.

"But when you see the ABOMINATION OF DESOLATION standing where it should not be (let the reader understand), then those who are in Judea must flee to the mountains. The one who is on the housetop must not go down, or go in to get anything out of his house; and the one who is in the field must not turn back to get his coat. But woe to those who are pregnant and to those who are nursing babies in those days! But pray that it may not happen in winter. For those days will be a *time of* tribulation such as has not occurred since the beginning of the creation which God created until now, and never will. Unless the Lord had shortened *those* days, no life would have been saved; but for the sake of the elect, whom He chose, He shortened the days. And then if anyone says to you, 'Behold, here is the Christ'; or, 'Behold, *He is* there'; do not believe *him*; for false Christs and false prophets will arise, and will show signs and wonders, in order to lead astray, if possible, the elect. But take heed; behold, I have told you everything in advance" (Mark 13:14–23; cf. Matthew 24:15–28; Luke 21:20–24; see Daniel 9:27; 12:1; Luke 17:31).

Setting: On the Mount of Olives, east of the temple in Jerusalem. After ministering in the temple a few days before His crucifixion, and giving the disciples more details regarding future events, Jesus elaborates more during His Olivet Discourse about things to come.

"But when you see Jerusalem surrounded by armies, then recognize that her desolation is near. Then those who are in Judea must flee to the mountains, and those who are in the midst of the city must leave, and those who are in the country must not enter the city; because these are days of vengeance, so that all things which are written will be fulfilled. Woe to those who are pregnant and to those who are nursing babies in those days; for there will be a great distress upon the land and wrath to this people; and they will fall by the edge of the sword, and will be led captive into all the nations; and Jerusalem will be trampled under foot by the Gentiles until the times of the Gentiles are fulfilled" (Luke 21:20–24; see Matthew 24:15–18; Mark 13:14–16; Luke 19:43).

Setting: Jerusalem. After being arrested and appearing before the Council of Elders (Sanhedrin), Pontius Pilate (Roman governor of Judea), Herod Antipas (tetrarch of Galilee and Perea), and Pilate a second time (when Pilate bows to the crowd's pressure and grants that Jesus be crucified), the Lord prophesies to the women mourning Him regarding the coming judgment of Jerusalem.

But Jesus turning to them said, "Daughters of Jerusalem, stop weeping for Me, but weep for yourselves and for your children. For behold, the days are coming when they will say, 'Blessed are the barren, and the wombs that never bore, and the breasts that never nursed.' Then they will begin TO SAY TO THE MOUNTAINS, 'FALL ON US,' AND TO THE HILLS, 'COVER US. 'For it they do these things when the tree is green, what will happen when it is dry?" (Luke 23:28–31, Jesus quotes from Hosea 10:8; see Matthew 24:19).

MOURNERS (See GRIEF; and MOURNING)

MOURNING (Also see GRIEF; LAMENT; SORROW; and WEEPING)

[MOURNING from mourn]
Setting: Galilee. Early in His ministry, Jesus presents the Beatitudes (part of the Sermon on the Mount) to His disciples and the gathered crowds from Galilee, Decapolis, Jerusalem, Judea, and beyond the Jordan.

"Blessed are those who mourn, for they shall be comforted" (Matthew 5:4; see Isaiah 61:2; Matthew 13:35).

[MOURNING from mourn]
Setting: Capernaum, near the Sea of Galilee. John the Baptist's disciples ask Jesus why His disciples do not participate in fasting, while they and the Pharisees do.

And Jesus said to them, "The attendants of the bridegroom cannot mourn as long as the bridegroom is with them, can they? But the days will come when the bridegroom is taken away from them, and then they will fast. But no one puts a patch of unshrunk cloth on an old garment; for the patch pulls away from the garment, and a worse tear results. Nor do *people* put new wine into old wineskins; otherwise the wineskins burst, and the wine pours out and the wineskins are ruined; but they put new wine into fresh wineskins, and both are preserved" (Matthew 9:15–17; cf. Mark 2:18–22; Luke 5:33–39).

[MOURNING from mourn]

Setting: Galilee. After praising John the Baptist as His forerunner, Jesus demonstrates the foolish thinking of the current generation of Jewish religious leaders by repeating what they say about John's ascetic lifestyle and ministry along with His own.

"But to what shall I compare this generation? It is like children sitting in the market places, who call out to the other *children,* and say, 'We played the flute for you, and you did not dance; we sang a dirge, and you did not mourn.' For John came neither eating nor drinking, and they say, 'He has a demon!' The Son of Man came eating and drinking, and they say, 'Behold, a gluttonous man and a drunkard, a friend of tax collectors and sinners! Yet wisdom is vindicated by her deeds" (Matthew 11:16–19; cf. Luke 7:31–35; see Matthew 9:11, 34; Luke 1:15).

[MOURNING from mourn]
Setting: The Mount of Olives, just east of Jerusalem. During His Olivet Discourse, Jesus answers His disciples' questions as to when the temple will be destroyed and Jerusalem overrun, along with the signs of His coming and the end of the age.

"But immediately after the tribulation of those days THE SUN WILL BE DARKENED, AND THE MOON WILL NOT GIVE ITS LIGHT, AND THE STARS WILL FALL from the sky, and the powers of the heavens will be shaken. And then the sign of the Son of Man will appear in the sky, and then all the tribes of the earth will mourn, and they will see the SON OF MAN COMING ON THE CLOUDS OF THE SKY with power and great glory. And He will send forth His angels with A GREAT TRUMPET and THEY WILL GATHER TOGETHER His elect from the four winds, from one end of the sky to the other" (Matthew 24:29–31, Jesus quotes from Isaiah 13:10, Daniel 7:13; Exodus 19:16; cf. Mark 13:24–27; Luke 21:25–27).

[MOURNING from mourn]
Setting: Galilee. After selecting His twelve disciples, Jesus teaches the Beatitudes (part of the Sermon on the Mount) to those disciples and a great throng of people from Judea, Jerusalem, and the central coastal region of Tyre and Sidon.

"Woe to you who are well-fed now, for you shall be hungry. Woe *to you* who laugh now, for you shall mourn and weep" (Luke 6:25; cf. Matthew 5:4).

MOUTH (MOUTH OF INFANTS is a separate entry; also see LIPS; TEETH; and TONGUE)
Setting: Judea, near the Jordan River. Following His baptism, and before He begins His public ministry, Jesus is led by the Spirit into the Judean wilderness to be tempted by Satan.

But He answered and said, "It is written, 'MAN SHALL NOT LIVE ON BREAD ALONE, BUT ON EVERY WORD THAT PROCEEDS OUT OF THE MOUTH OF GOD'" (Matthew 4:4, Jesus quotes from Deuteronomy 8:3; cf. Luke 4:4).

Setting: Galilee. After Jesus heals a blind, mute, demon-possessed man, the Pharisees accuse the Lord in front of crowds of being a worker of Satan.

"Either make the tree good and its fruit good, or make the tree bad and its fruit bad; for the tree is known by its fruit. You brood of vipers, how can you, being evil, speak what is good? For the mouth speaks out of that which fills the heart. The good man brings out of *his* good treasure what is good; and the evil man brings out of *his* evil treasure what is evil. But I tell you that every careless word that people speak, they shall give an accounting for it in the day of judgment. For by your words you will be justified, and by your words you will be condemned" (Matthew 12:33–37; cf. Matthew 3:7; 7:16–18).

Setting: Galilee. After the Pharisees and scribes question His disciples' obedience to tradition and the commandments, Jesus instructs the crowd.

After Jesus called the crowd to Him, He said to them, "Hear and understand. *It is* not what enters into the mouth *that* defiles the man, but what proceeds out of the mouth, this defiles the man" (Matthew 15:10, 11; cf. Matthew 15:18).

Setting: Galilee. Jesus explains to the crowd the meaning of His instruction about what defiles a man.

Peter said to Him, "Explain the parable to us." Jesus said, "Are you still lacking in understanding also? Do you not understand that everything that goes into the mouth passes into the stomach and is eliminated? But the things that proceed out of the mouth come from the heart, and those defile the man. For out of the heart come evil thoughts, murders, adulteries, fornications, thefts, false witness, slanders. These are the things which defile a man; but to eat with unwashed hands does not defile the man" (Matthew 15:15–20; cf. Mark 7:18–23; see Galatians 5:19–21).

Setting: Capernaum of Galilee. Jesus pays the two-drachma temple tax for Peter and Himself in a miraculous manner.

He said, "Yes." And when he came into the house, Jesus spoke to him first, saying, "What do you think, Simon? From whom do the kings of the earth collect customs or poll-tax, from their sons or from strangers?" When Peter said, "From strangers," Jesus said to him, "Then the sons are exempt. However, so that we do not offend them, go to the sea and throw in a hook, and take the first fish that comes up; and when you open its mouth, you will find a shekel. Take that and give it to them for you and Me" (Matthew 17:25–27; see Exodus 30:11–16; Matthew 22:17–19; Romans 13:7).

Setting: Capernaum of Galilee. After conveying to His disciples the value of little ones, Jesus gives instruction about church discipline.

"If your brother sins, go and show him his fault in private; if he listens to you, you have won your brother. But if he does not listen *to you,* take one or two more with you, so that BY THE MOUTH OF TWO OR THREE WITNESSES EVERY FACT MAY BE CONFIRMED. If he refuses to listen to them, tell it to the church; and if he refuses to listen even to the church, let him be to you as a Gentile and a tax collector. Truly I say to you, whatever you bind of earth shall have been bound in heaven; and whatever you loose on earth shall have been loosed in heaven. Again, I say to you, that if two of you agree on earth about anything that they may ask, it shall be done for them by My Father who is in heaven. For there two or three have gathered together in My name, I am there in their midst" (Matthew 18:15–20. Jesus quotes from Deuteronomy 19:15; cf. Matthew 7:7; 16:19; see Leviticus 19:17; Matthew 28:20; 2 Thessalonians 3:6, 14).

Setting: Jerusalem. After cleansing the temple by driving out the money changers and merchants, Jesus comments to the indignant chief priests and scribes about the praises the children render unto Him.

But when the chief priests and the scribes saw the wonderful things that He had done, and the children who were shouting in the temple, "Hosanna to the Son of David," they became indignant and said to Him, "Do You hear what these *children* are saying?" And Jesus said to them, "Yes, have you never read, 'OUT OF THE MOUTH OF INFANTS AND NURSING BABIES YOU HAVE PREPARED PRAISE FOR YOURSELF'?" (Matthew 21:15, 16, Jesus quotes from Psalm 8:2; see Matthew 9:27).

Setting: Galilee. After selecting His twelve disciples, Jesus teaches the Sermon on the Mount to those disciples and a great throng of people from Judea, Jerusalem, and the central coastal region of Tyre and Sidon.

And He also spoke a parable to them: "A blind man cannot guide a blind man, can he? Will they not both fall into a pit? A pupil is not above his teacher; but everyone, after he has been fully trained, will be like his teacher. Why do you look at the speck that is in your brother's eye, but do not notice the log that is in your own eye? Or how can you say to your brother, 'Brother, let me take out the speck that is in your eye,' when you yourself do not see the log that is in your own eye? You hypocrite, first take the log out of your own eye, and then you will see clearly to take out the speck that is in your brother's eye. For there is no good tree which produces bad fruit, nor, on the other hand, a bad tree which produces good fruit. For each tree is known by its own fruit. For men do not gather figs from thorns, nor do they pick grapes from a briar bush. The good man out of the good treasure of his heart brings forth what is good; and the evil *man* out of the evil *treasure* brings forth what is evil; for his mouth speaks from that which fills his heart" (Luke 6:39–45; cf. Matthew 7:3–6. 16, 18, 20; 12:35; see Matthew 10:24; 15:14; Luke 6:12–19).

Setting: On the island of Patmos (in the Aegean Sea about fifty miles southwest of Ephesus in modern Turkey). On the Lord's Day (Sunday), approximately fifty years after Jesus' resurrection, the disciple John encounters the Lord Jesus Christ, who communicates a new revelation for the apostle to record for the church in Pergamum and to six other churches in Asia.

"And to the angel of the church in Pergamum write: The One who has the sharp two-edged sword says this: 'I know where you dwell, where Satan's throne is; and you hold fast My name, and did not deny My faith even in the days of Antipas, My witness, My faithful one, who was killed among you, where Satan dwells. But I have a few things against you, because you have there some who hold the teaching of Balaam, who kept teaching Balak to put a stumbling block before the sons of Israel, to eat things sacrificed to idols and to commit *acts of* immorality. So you also have some who in the same way hold the teaching of the Nicolaitans. Therefore repent; or else I am coming to you quickly, and I will make war against them with the sword of My mouth. He who has an ear, let him hear what the Spirit says to the churches. To him who overcomes, to him I will give *some* of the hidden manna, and I will give him a white stone, and a new name written on the stone which no one knows but he who receives it' (Revelation 2:12–17; see Numbers 25:1–3; Isaiah 62:2; Revelation 1:16; 2:5, 6, 16).

Setting: On the island of Patmos (in the Aegean Sea about fifty miles southwest of Ephesus in modern Turkey). On the Lord's Day (Sunday), approximately fifty years after Jesus' resurrection, the disciple John encounters the Lord Jesus Christ, who communicates a new revelation for the apostle to record for the church in Laodicea and to six other churches in Asia.

"To the angel of the church in Laodicea write: The Amen, the faithful and true Witness, the Beginning of the creation of God, says this: 'I know your deeds, that you are neither cold nor hot; I wish that you were cold or hot. So because you are lukewarm, and neither hot nor cold, I will spit you out of My mouth. Because you say, "I am rich, and have become wealthy, and have need of nothing," and you do not know that you are wretched and miserable and poor and blind and naked, I advise you to buy from Me gold refined by fire so that you may become rich, and white garments so that you may clothe yourself, and *that* the shame of your nakedness will not be revealed; and eye salve to anoint your eyes so that you may see. Those whom I love, I reprove and discipline; therefore be zealous and repent. Behold, I stand at the door and knock; if anyone hears My voice and opens the door, I will come in to him and will dine with him, and he with Me. He who overcomes, I will grant to him to sit down with Me on My throne, as I also overcame and sat down with My Father on His throne. He who has an ear, let him hear what the Spirit says to the churches'" (Revelation 3:14–22; see Proverb 3:12; Hosea 12:8; John 14:23; 16:33).

MOUTH OF INFANTS (See INFANTS)

MULBERRY TREE (Listed under TREE, MULBERRY)

MULTITUDE/MULTITUDES (See PEOPLE)

MURDER (Also see MURDERS; MURDERER; and MURDERERS)

Setting: Galilee. During the early part of His ministry, Jesus preaches the Sermon on the Mount to His disciples and the multitudes.

"You have heard that the ancients were told, 'YOU SHALL NOT COMMIT MURDER' and 'whoever commits murder shall be liable to the court' (Matthew 5:21, Jesus quotes from Exodus 20:13).

[MURDER from kill Him]

Setting: Galilee. Following the Transfiguration, Jesus repeats to His disciples that He must suffer, die, and be raised.

And while they were gathering together in Galilee, Jesus said to them, "The Son of Man is going to be delivered into the hands of men; and they will kill Him, and He will be raised on the third day." And they were deeply grieved (Matthew 17:22, 23; cf. Matthew 16:21; Mark 9:30–32; Luke 9:44, 45).

Setting: Judea beyond the Jordan (Perea). Jesus shares with a rich, young ruler how to obtain eternal life.

And He said to him, "Why are you asking Me about what is good? There is *only* One who is good; but if you wish to enter into life, keep the commandments." *Then* he said to Him, 'Which ones?' And Jesus said, "YOU SHALL NOT COMMIT MURDER; YOU SHALL NOT COMMIT ADULTERY; YOU SHALL NOT STEAL; YOU SHALL NOT BEAR FALSE WITNESS; HONOR YOUR FATHER AND MOTHER; and YOU SHALL LOVE YOUR NEIGHBOR AS YOURSELF." The young man said to Him, "All these things I have kept; what am I still lacking?" Jesus said to him, "If you wish to complete go *and* sell your possessions and give to *the* poor, and you will have treasure in heaven; and come, follow Me" (Matthew 19:16–22, Jesus quotes from Exodus 20:13–15; Leviticus 19:18; cf. Leviticus 18:5; Mark 10:17–21; Luke 10:25–28; 12:33; 18:18–24).

[MURDER from kill him and killed him]

Setting: The temple in Jerusalem. Jesus delivers another parable to the chief priests and elders after they question His authority.

"Listen to another parable. There was a landowner who PLANTED A VINEYARD AND PUT A WALL AROUND IT AND DUG A WINE PRESS IN IT, AND BUILT A TOWER, and rented it out to vine-growers and went on a journey. When the harvest time approached, he sent his slaves to the vine-growers to receive his produce. The vine-growers took his slaves and beat one, and killed another, and stoned a third. Again he sent another group of slaves larger than the first; and they did the same thing to them. But afterward he sent his son to them, saying, 'They will respect my son.' But when the vine-growers saw the son, they said among themselves, 'This is the heir; come, let us kill him and seize his inheritance.' They took him, and threw him out of the vineyard and killed him. Therefore when the owner of the vineyard comes, what will he do to those vine-growers?" (Matthew 21:33–40; Jesus quotes from Isaiah 5:1, 2; cf. Mark 12:1–9; Luke 20:9–15).

[MURDER from murdered]

Setting: The temple in Jerusalem. After the Jewish religious leaders test Him with questions, Jesus pronounces the eighth of eight woes on them in front of the crowds and His disciples.

"Woe to you, scribes and Pharisees, hypocrites! For you build the tombs of the prophets and adorn the monuments of the righteous, and say, 'If we had been *living* in the days of our fathers, we would not have been partners with them in *shedding* the blood of the prophets.' So you testify against yourselves, that you are sons of those who murdered the prophets. Fill up, then, the measure *of the guilt* of you fathers. You serpents, you brood of vipers, how will you escape the sentence of hell? Therefore, behold, I am sending you prophets and wise men and scribes; some of them you will kill and crucify, and some of them you will scourge in your synagogues, and persecute from city to city, so that upon you may fall *the guilt of* all the righteous blood shed on earth, from the blood of righteous Abel to the blood of Zechariah, the son of Berechiah, whom you murdered between the temple and the altar. Truly I say to you, all these things will come upon this generation" (Matthew 23:29–36; cf. 2 Chronicles 24:21; Zechariah 1:1; Matthew 3:7; Luke 11:47–52; see Matthew 10:23).

[MURDER from kill Him]

Setting: Galilee. After casting out an unclean spirit from a young boy, Jesus teaches His disciples in secret about His coming death and resurrection.

From there they went out and *began* to go through Galilee, and He did not want anyone to know *about it.* For He was teaching His disciples and telling them, "The Son of Man is to be delivered into the hands of men, and they will kill Him; and when He has been killed, He will rise three days later." But they did not understand *this* statement, and they were afraid to ask Him (Mark 9:30–32; cf. Matthew 17:22, 23; Luke 9:43–45; see Matthew 16:21).

Setting: Judea beyond the Jordan (Perea). After demonstrating to His disciples the importance of little children, Jesus encounters a rich man seeking eternal life.

And Jesus said to him, "Why do you call Me good? No one is good except God alone. You know the commandments, 'DO NOT MURDER, DO NOT COMMIT ADULTERY, DO NOT STEAL, DO NOT BEAR FALSE WITNESS, Do not defraud, HONOR YOUR FATHER AND MOTHER.'"

And he said to Him, "Teacher, I have kept all these things from my youth up." Looking at him, Jesus felt a love for him and said to him, "One thing you lack: go and sell all you possess and give to the poor, and you will have treasure in heaven; and come, follow Me" (Mark 10:18–21; Jesus quotes from Exodus 20:12–16; cf. Matthew 19:16–22; Luke 18:18–24; see Matthew 6:20).

[MURDER from kill *Him*]

Setting: On the road to Jerusalem. After encouraging His disciples with a revelation of their future reward, Jesus prophesies His persecution, death, and resurrection.

They were on the road going up to Jerusalem, and Jesus was walking on ahead of them; and they were amazed, and those who followed were fearful. And again He took the twelve aside and began to tell them what was going to happen to Him, *saying*, "Behold, we are going up to Jerusalem, and the Son of Man will be delivered to the chief priests and the scribes; and they will condemn Him to death and will hand Him over to the Gentiles. They will mock Him and spit on Him, and scourge Him and kill *Him*, and three days later He will rise again" (Mark 10:32–34; cf. Matthew 20:17–19; Luke 18:31–34; see Matthew 16:21; Mark 8:31).

[MURDER from killed; killing; and kill him]

Setting: The temple in Jerusalem. Having His authority questioned by the chief priests, scribes, and elders, Jesus begins to teach them in parables.

And He began to speak to them in parables: "A man PLANTED A VINEYARD AND PUT A WALL AROUND IT, AND DUG A VAT UNDER THE WINE PRESS AND BUILT A TOWER, and rented it out to vine-growers and went on a journey. At the *harvest* time he sent a slave to the vine-growers, in order to receive *some* of the produce of the vineyard from the vine-growers. They took him, and beat him and sent him away empty-handed. Again he sent them another slave, and they wounded him in the head, and treated him shamefully. And he sent another, and that one they killed; and *so with* many others, beating some and killing others. He had one more to *send*, a beloved son; he sent him last *of all* to them, saying, 'They will respect my son.' But those vine-growers said to one another, 'This is the heir; come, let us kill him, and the inheritance will be ours!' They took him, and killed him and threw him out of the vineyard. What will the owner of the vineyard do? He will come and destroy the vine-growers, and will give the vineyard to others. Have you not even read this Scripture: 'THE STONE WHICH THE BUILDERS REJECTED, THIS BECAME THE CHIEF CORNER *stone;* THIS CAME ABOUT FROM THE LORD, AND IT IS MARVELOUS IN OUR EYES'?" (Mark 12:1–11, Jesus quotes from Psalm 118:22, 23; Isaiah 5:1, 2; cf. Matthew 21:33–46; Luke 20:9–19).

[MURDER from the blood of Abel to the blood of Zechariah, who was killed]

Setting: On the way from Galilee to Jerusalem. After Jesus pronounces woes upon the Pharisees, a lawyer replies that His remarks are an insult to lawyers, too.

But He said, "Woe to you lawyers as well! For you weigh men down with burdens hard to bear, while you yourselves will not even touch the burdens with one of your fingers. Woe to you! For you build the tombs of the prophets, and *it was* your fathers *who* killed them. So you are witnesses and approve the deeds of your fathers; because it was they who killed them, and you build *their tombs*. For this reason also the wisdom of God said, 'I will send them prophets and apostles, and *some* of them they will kill and *some* they will persecute, so that the blood of all the prophets, shed since the foundation of the world, may be charged against this generation, from the blood of Abel to the blood of Zechariah, who was killed between the altar and the house *of God*; yes, I tell you, it shall be charged against this generation.' Woe to you lawyers! For you have taken away the key of knowledge; you yourselves did not enter, and you hindered those who were entering" (Luke 11:46–52; cf. Matthew 23:29–32; see 2 Chronicles 24:20, 21; Matthew 23:4, 13).

Setting: Judea beyond the Jordan (Perea). After speaking of the importance of children, Jesus responds to a ruler's question about obtaining eternal life.

A ruler questioned Him, saying, "Good Teacher, what shall I do to inherit eternal life?" And Jesus said to him, "Why do you call Me good? No one is good except God alone. You know the commandments, 'DO NOT COMMIT ADULTERY, DO NOT MURDER, DO NOT STEAL, DO NOT BEAR FALSE WITNESS, HONOR YOUR FATHER AND MOTHER.'" And he said, "All these things I have kept from *my* youth." When Jesus heard *this,* He said to him, "One thing you still lack; sell all that you possess and distribute it to the poor, and you shall have treasure in heaven; and come, follow Me" (Luke 18:18–22, Jesus quotes from Exodus 20:12–16; cf. Matthew 19:16–22; Mark 10:17–22; see Luke 10:25–28).

[MURDER from kill Him]

Setting: On the way from Galilee to Jerusalem. After responding to Peter's statement about the disciples' personal sacrifice in following Him, Jesus tells them of the sacrifice He will make in Jerusalem.

Then He took the twelve aside and said to them, "Behold, we are going up to Jerusalem, and all things which are written through the prophets about the Son of Man will be accomplished. For He will be handed over to the Gentiles, and will be mocked and mistreated and spit upon, and after they have scourged Him, they will kill Him; and the third day He will rise again" (Luke 18:31–33; cf. Matthew 20:17–19; Mark 10:32–34).

[MURDER from kill him and killed him]

Setting: The temple in Jerusalem. While ministering a few days before His crucifixion, after the chief priests and the scribes question His authority to teach and preach, Jesus conveys the Parable of the Vine-Growers to the people.

And He began to tell the people this parable: "A man planted a vineyard and rented it out to vine-growers, and went on a journey for a long time. At the *harvest* time he sent a slave to the vine-growers, so that they would give him *some* of the produce of the vineyard; but the vine-growers beat him and sent him away empty-handed. And he proceeded to send another slave; and they beat him also and treated him shamefully and sent him away empty-handed. And he proceeded to send a third; and this one also they wounded and cast out. The owner of the vineyard said, 'What shall I do? I will send my beloved son; perhaps they will respect him.' But when the vine-growers saw him, they reasoned with one another, saying, 'This is the heir; let us kill him so that the inheritance will be ours.' So they threw him out of the vineyard and killed him. What, then, will the owner of the vineyard do to them? He will come and destroy these vine-growers and will give the vineyard to others." When they heard it, they said, "May it never be!" But Jesus looked at them and said, "What then is this that is written: 'THE STONE WHICH THE BUILDERS REJECTED, THIS BECAME THE CHIEF CORNER *stone*'? Everyone who falls on that stone will be broken to pieces; but on whomever it falls, it will scatter him like dust" (Luke 20:9–18, Jesus quotes from Psalm 118:22; cf. Matthew 21:33–44; Mark 12:1–11; see Ephesians 2:20).

[MURDER from kill Me]

Setting: The temple in Jerusalem. After receiving encouragement from His blood brothers in Galilee to attend the upcoming Feast of Booths in order to demonstrate His works to His disciples and the world, Jesus goes and teaches, astonishing the Jewish religious leaders.

"Did not Moses give you the Law, and *yet* none of you carries out the Law? Why do you seek to kill Me?" (John 7:19; see Mark 11:18; John 1:17).

[MURDER from kill Me]

Setting: The temple treasury in Jerusalem. After the scribes and Pharisees question His testimony about Himself, Jesus reveals to those Jews who believe in Him how He will make them free.

So Jesus was saying to those Jews who had believed Him, "If you continue in My word, *then* you are truly disciples of Mine; and you will know the truth, and the truth will make you free." They answered Him, "We are Abraham's descendants and have never yet been enslaved to anyone; how is it that You say, 'You will become free'?" Jesus answered them, "Truly, truly, I say to you, everyone who commits sin is the slave of sin. The slave does not remain in the house forever; the son does remain forever. So if the Son makes you free, you will be free indeed. I know that you are Abraham's descendants; yet you seek to kill Me, because My word has no place in you. I speak the things which I have seen with *My* Father; therefore you also do the things which you heard from *your* father" (John 8:31–38; see Romans 6:16).

[MURDER from kill Me]

Setting: The temple treasury in Jerusalem. After the scribes and Pharisees question His testimony about Himself, Jesus interacts with them regarding their ancestry and motives.

They answered and said to Him, "Abraham is our father." Jesus said to them, "If you are Abraham's children, do the deeds of Abraham. But as it is, you are seeking to kill Me, a man who has told you the truth, which I heard from God; this Abraham did not do. You are doing the deeds of your father." They said to Him, "We were not born of fornication; we have one Father: God" (John 8:39–41; see Romans 9:6, 7).

MURDERER (Also see MURDER; and MURDERERS)

Setting: The temple treasury in Jerusalem. After the scribes and Pharisees question His testimony about Himself, Jesus interacts with them regarding their ancestry and motives.

Jesus said to them, "If God were your Father, you would love Me, for I proceeded forth and have come from God, for I have not even come on My own initiative, but He sent Me. Why do you not understand what I am saying? *It is* because you cannot hear My word. You are of *your* father the devil, and you want to do the desires of your father. He was a murderer from the beginning, and does not stand in the truth because there is no truth in him. Whenever he speaks a lie, he speaks from his own *nature,* for he is a liar and the father of lies. But because I speak the truth, you do not believe Me. Which one of you convicts Me of sin? If I speak truth, why do not believe Me? He who is of God hears the words of God; for this reason you do not hear *them,* because you are not of God" (John 8:42–47; see John 18:37; 1 John 3:8; 4:6; 5:1).

MURDERERS (Also see MURDER; and MURDERS)

Setting: The temple in Jerusalem. Jesus speaks another parable to the chief priests and elders after they question His authority.

Jesus spoke to them again in parables, saying, "The kingdom of heaven may be compared to a king who gave a wedding feast for his son. And he sent out his slaves to call those who had been invited to the wedding feast, and they were unwilling to come. Again he sent out other slaves saying, 'Tell those who have been invited, "Behold, I have prepared my dinner; my oxen and my fattened livestock are *all* butchered and everything is ready; come to the wedding feast." But they paid no attention and went their way, one to his own farm, another to his business, and the rest seized his slaves and mistreated them and killed them. But the king was enraged, and he sent his armies and destroyed those murderers and set their city on fire. Then he said to his slaves, 'The wedding is ready, but those who were invited were not worthy. 'Go therefore to the main highways, and as many as you find *there,* invite to the wedding feast.' Those slaves went out into the streets and gathered together all they found, both evil and good; and the wedding hall was filled with dinner guests. But when the king came in to look over the dinner guests, he saw a man there who was not dressed in wedding clothes, and he said to him, 'Friend, how did you come in here without wedding clothes?' And the man was speechless. Then the king said to the servants, 'Bind him hand and foot, and throw him into the outer darkness; in that place there will be weeping and gnashing of teeth.' For many are called, but few *are* chosen" (Matthew 22:1–14; cf. Matthew 8:11, 12).

MURDERS (Also see MURDER; and MURDERERS)

Setting: Galilee. Jesus gives the crowd the meaning of His instruction about what defiles a man.

Peter said to Him, "Explain the parable to us." Jesus said, "Are you still lacking in understanding also? Do you not understand that everything that goes into the mouth passes into the stomach and is eliminated? But the things that proceed out of the mouth come from the heart, and those defile the man. For out of the heart come evil thoughts, murders, adulteries, fornications, thefts, false witness, slanders. These are the things which defile a man; but to eat with unwashed hands does not defile the man" (Matthew 15:15–20; cf. Mark 7:18–23; see Galatians 5:19–21).

Setting: Galilee. After the Pharisees and scribes from Jerusalem object to His disciples' lack of obedience to the tradition regarding ceremonial cleansing, Jesus speaks to a crowd and explains His teaching to the disciples.

After He called the crowd to Him again, He *began* saying to them, "Listen to Me, all of you, and understand: there is nothing outside the man which can defile him if it goes into him; but the things which proceed out of the man are what defile the man. [If anyone has ears to hear, let him hear."] When he had left the crowd *and* entered the house, His disciples questioned Him about the parable. And He said to them, "Are you so lacking in understanding also? Do you not understand that whatever goes into the man from outside cannot defile him, because it does not go into his heart, but into his stomach, and is eliminated?" (*Thus He* declared all foods clean.) And He was saying, "That which proceeds out of the man, that is what defiles the man. For from within, out of the heart of men, proceed the evil thoughts, fornications, thefts, murders, adulteries, deeds of coveting *and* wickedness, *as well* as deceit, sensuality, envy, slander, pride *and* foolishness. All these evil things proceed from within and defile the man" (Mark 7:14–23; cf. Matthew 15:10–20).

MUSIC (Also see DANCE; and DANCING)

Setting: On the way from Galilee to Jerusalem. Jesus conveys the illustration of the prodigal son because the Pharisees and scribes complain He associates with tax collectors and sinners.

And He said, "A man had two sons. The younger of them said to his father, 'Father, give me the share of the estate that falls to me.' So he divided his wealth between them. And not many days later, the younger son gathered everything together and went on a journey into a distant country, and there he squandered his estate with loose living. Now when he had spent everything, a severe famine occurred in that country, and he began to be impoverished. So he went and hired himself out to one of the citizens of that country, and he sent him into his fields to feed swine. And he would have gladly filled his stomach with the pods that the swine were eating, and no one was giving *anything* to him. But when he came to his senses, he said, 'How many of my father's hired men have more than enough bread, but I am dying here with hunger! I will get up and go to my father, and will say to him, "Father, I have sinned against heaven, and in your sight; I am no longer worthy to be called your son; make me as one of your hired men."' So he got up and came to his father. But while he was still a long way off, his father saw him and felt compassion *for him,* and ran and embraced him and kissed him. And the son said to him, "Father, I have sinned against heaven and in your sight; I am no longer worthy to be called your son.' But the father said to his slaves, 'Quickly bring out the best robe and put it on him, and put a ring on his hand and sandals on his feet; and bring the fattened calf, kill it, and let us eat and celebrate; for this son of mine was dead and has come to life again; he was lost and has been found.' And they began to celebrate. Now his older son was in the field, when he came and approached the house, he heard music and dancing. And he summoned one of the servants and *began* inquiring what these things could be. And he said to him, 'Your brother has come, and your father has killed the fattened calf because he has received him back safe and sound. 'But he became angry and was not willing to go in; and his father came out and *began* pleading with him. But he answered and said to his father, 'Look! For so many years I have been serving you and I have never neglected a command of yours; and *yet* you have never given me a young goat, so that I might celebrate with my friends; but when this son of yours came, who has devoured your wealth with prostitutes, you killed the fattened calf for him. 'And he said to him, 'Son, you have always been with me, and all that is mine is yours. But we had to celebrate and rejoice, for this brother of yours was dead and *has begun* to live, and was lost and has been found'" (Luke 15:11–32; see Proverb 29:2).

MUSIC – FLUTE (See FLUTE)

MUSICAL INSTRUMENTS – FLUTE (See FLUTE)

MUSTARD SEED (Listed under SEED, MUSTARD)

MUTE (deaf and)

Setting: Galilee. After returning from a high mountain (perhaps Mount Hermon) where Jesus was transfigured in front of Peter, James, and John, the four discover the remaining disciples arguing with some scribes.

And He asked them, "What are you discussing with them?" And one of the crowd answered Him, "Teacher, I brought You my son, possessed with a spirit which makes him mute; and whenever it seizes him, it slams him *to the ground* and he foams *at the mouth,* and grinds his teeth and stiffens out. I told Your disciples to cast it out, and they could not *do it.* And He answered them, and said, "O unbelieving generation, how long shall I be with you? How long shall I put up with you? Bring him to Me!" They brought the boy to Him. When he saw Him, immediately the spirit threw him into a convulsion, and falling to the ground, be *began* rolling around and foaming *at the mouth.* And He asked his father, "How long has this been happening to him?" And he said, "From childhood. It has often thrown him both into the fire and into the water to destroy him. But if You can do anything, take pity on us and help us!" And Jesus said to him, "'If You can?' All things are possible to him who believes." Immediately the boy's father cried out and said, "I do believe; help my unbelief." When Jesus saw that a crowd was rapidly gathering, He rebuked the unclean spirit, saying to it, "You deaf and mute spirit, I command you, come out of him and do not enter him again." After crying out and throwing him into terrible convulsions, it came out; and *the boy* became so much like a corpse that most *of them,* said, "He is dead!" But Jesus took him by the hand and raised him; and he got up. When He came into *the* house, His disciples *began* questioning Him privately, "Why could we not drive it out?" And He said to them, "This kind cannot come out by anything but prayer" (Mark 9:16–29; cf. Matthew 17:14–21; Luke 9:37–43; see Matthew 17:20).

MY WORD (Listed under WORD, MY)

MYSTERIES (Also see MYSTERY; SECRET; and SECRETS)

Setting: By the Sea of Galilee. Jesus responds to the disciples' questions about the Parable of the Sower, which He has just taught from a boat to a crowd.

Jesus answered them, "To you it has been granted to know the mysteries of the kingdom of heaven, but to them it has not been granted. For whoever has, to him *more* shall be given, and he will have an abundance; but whoever does not have, even what he has shall be taken away from him. Therefore, I speak to them in parables; because while seeing they do not see, and while hearing they do not hear, nor do they understand. In their case the prophecy of Isaiah is being fulfilled, which says, 'YOU WILL KEEP ON HEARING, BUT WILL NOT UNDERSTAND; YOU WILL KEEP ON SEEING, BUT WILL NOT PERCEIVE; FOR THE HEART OF THIS PEOPLE HAS BECOME DULL, WITH THEIR EARS THEY SCARCELY HEAR, AND THEY HAVE CLOSED THEIR EYES, OTHERWISE THEY WOULD SEE WITH THEIR EYES, HEAR WITH THEIR EARS, AND UNDERSTAND WITH THEIR HEART AND RETURN, AND I WOULD HEAL THEM.' But blessed are your eyes, because they see; and your ears, because they hear. For truly I say to you that many prophets and righteous men desired to see what you see, and did not see *it,* and to hear what you hear, and did not hear *it*" (Matthew 13:11–17, Jesus quotes from Isaiah 6:9, 10; cf. Matthew 25:29; Mark 4:11–13; Luke 8:10; see Deuteronomy 29:4; John 8:56).

Setting: Galilee. After Jesus presents the Parable of the Sower to the crowds, His disciples ask Him to give them the parable's meaning.

And He said, "To you it has been granted to know the mysteries of the kingdom of God, but to the rest *it is* in parables, so that SEEING THEY MAY NOT SEE, AND HEARING THEY MAY NOT UNDERSTAND. Now the parable is this: the seed is the word of God. Those beside the road are those who have heard; then the devil comes and takes away the word from their heart, so that they will not believe and be saved. Those on the rocky *soil* are those who, when they hear, receive the word with joy; and these have no *firm* root; they believe for a while, and in time of temptation fall away. The *seed* which fell among the thorns, these are the ones who have heard, and as they go on their way they are choked with worries and riches and pleasures of *this* life, and bring no fruit to maturity. But the *seed* in the good soil, these are the ones who have heard the word in an honest and good heart, and hold it fast, and bear fruit with perseverance" (Luke 8:10–15, Jesus quotes from Isaiah 6:9; cf. Matthew 13:10–23; Mark 4:10–20).

MYSTERY (Also see MYSTERIES; SECRET; and SECRETS)

Setting: By the Sea of Galilee. After Jesus conveys the Parable of the Sower from a boat to a crowd, His disciples ask Him questions about it.

And He was saying to them, "To you has been given the mystery of the kingdom of God, but those who are outside get everything in parables, so that WHILE SEEING, THEY MAY SEE AND NOT PERCEIVE, AND WHILE HEARING, THEY MAY HEAR AND NOT UNDERSTAND, OTHERWISE THEY MIGHT RETURN AND BE FORGIVEN" (Mark 4:11, 12, Jesus quotes from Isaiah 6:9, 10; cf. Matthew 13:10–17).

Setting: On the island of Patmos (in the Aegean Sea about fifty miles southwest of Ephesus in modern Turkey). On the Lord's Day (Sunday), approximately fifty years after His resurrection, the disciple John encounters the Lord Jesus Christ, who communicates new revelations for the apostle to record for the seven churches in Asia.

When I saw Him, I fell at His feet like a dead man. And He placed His right hand on me, saying, "Do not be afraid; I am the first and the last, and the living One; and I was dead, and behold, I am alive forevermore, and I have the keys of death and of Hades. Therefore write the things which you have seen, and the things which are, and the things which will take place after these things. As for the mystery of the seven stars which you saw in My right hand, and the seven golden lampstands: the seven stars are the angels of the seven churches, and the seven lampstands are the seven churches" (Revelation 1:17–20; see Isaiah 44:6; Luke 24:5; Revelation 2:8).

N

NAAMAN

Setting: The synagogue in Jesus' hometown of Nazareth in Galilee. At the beginning of His public ministry, Jesus comments to the congregation after reading on the Sabbath from the book of the prophet Isaiah.

And He said to them, "No doubt you will quote this proverb to Me, 'Physician, heal yourself! Whatever we heard was done at Capernaum, do here in your hometown as well.'" And He said, "Truly I say to you, no prophet is welcome in his hometown. But I say to you in truth, there were many widows in Israel in the days of Elijah, when the sky was shut up for three years and six months, when a great famine came over all the land; and yet Elijah was sent to none of them, but only to Zarephath, *in the land* of Sidon, to a woman who was a widow. And there were many lepers in Israel in the time of Elisha the prophet; and none of them was cleansed, but only Naaman the Syrian" (Luke 4:23–27; Jesus refers to 1 Kings 17:1, 9; 2 Kings 5:1–14; see Matthew 13:53–58).

NAKED (Also see NAKEDNESS)

Setting: On the Mount of Olives, just east of Jerusalem. During His Olivet Discourse, after answering His disciples' questions as to when the temple will be destroyed and Jerusalem overrun, along with the signs of His coming and the end of the age, Jesus reveals the future judgments following His return.

"But when the Son of Man comes in His glory, and all the angels with Him, then He will sit on His glorious throne. All the nations will be gathered before Him; and He will separate them from one another, as the shepherd separates the sheep from the goats; and He will put the sheep on His right, and the goats on the left. Then the King will say to those on His right, 'Come, you who are blessed of My Father, inherit the kingdom prepared for you from the foundation of the world. 'For I was hungry, and you gave Me *something* to eat; I was thirsty, and you gave Me *something* to drink; I was a stranger, and you invited Me in; naked, and you clothed Me; I was sick, and you visited Me; I was in prison, and you came to Me.' Then the righteous will answer Him, 'Lord, when did we see You hungry and feed You, or thirsty, and give you *something* to drink? And when did we see You a stranger, and invite You in, or naked, and clothe You? When did we see You sick, or in prison, and come to You?' The King will answer and say to them, 'Truly I say to you, to the extent that you did it to one of these brothers of Mine, *even* the least *of them,* you did it to Me.' Then He will also say to those on His left, 'Depart from Me, accursed ones, into the eternal fire which has been prepared for the devil and his angels; for I was hungry, and you gave Me *nothing* to eat; I was thirsty, and you gave Me nothing to drink; I was a stranger, and you did not invite Me in; naked, and you did not clothe Me; sick, and in prison, and you did not visit Me.' Then they themselves also will answer, 'Lord, when did we see You hungry, or thirsty, or a stranger, or naked, or sick, or in prison, and did not take care of You?' Then He will answer them, 'Truly I say to you, to the extent that you did not do it to one of the least of these, you did not do it to Me.' These will go away into eternal punishment, but the righteous into eternal life" (Matthew 25:31–46; see Matthew 7:23; 16:27; 19:29).

NAKEDNESS (Also see NAKED)

Setting: On the island of Patmos (in the Aegean Sea about fifty miles southwest of Ephesus in modern Turkey). On the Lord's Day (Sunday), approximately fifty years after Jesus' resurrection, the disciple John encounters the Lord Jesus Christ, who communicates a new revelation for the apostle to record for the church in Laodicea and to six other churches in Asia.

"To the angel of the church in Laodicea write: The Amen, the faithful and true Witness, the Beginning of the creation of God, says this: 'I know your deeds, that you are neither cold nor hot; I wish that you were cold or hot. So because you are lukewarm, and neither hot nor cold, I will spit you out of My mouth. Because you say, "I am rich, and have become wealthy, and have need of nothing," and you do not know that you are wretched and miserable and poor and blind and naked, I advise you to buy from Me gold refined by fire so that you may become rich, and white garments so that you may clothe yourself, and *that* the shame of

your nakedness will not be revealed; and eye salve to anoint your eyes so that you may see. Those whom I love, I reprove and discipline; therefore be zealous and repent. Behold, I stand at the door and knock; if anyone hears My voice and opens the door, I will come in to him and will dine with him, and he with Me. He who overcomes, I will grant to him to sit down with Me on My throne, as I also overcame and sat down with My Father on His throne. He who has an ear, let him hear what the Spirit says to the churches'" (Revelation 3:14–22; see Proverb 3:12; Hosea 12:8; John 14:23; 16:33).

NAME (Specifics such as JESUS' NAME; NAME, FATHER'S; and NAME, MY are separate entries; also see NAMES)

Setting: Galilee. After His twelve disciples observe His ministry, Jesus summons and specifically instructs them about their ministry ahead that will include rewards.

"He who receives you receives Me, and he who receives Me receives Him who sent me. He who receives a prophet in the name of a prophet shall receive a prophet's reward; and he who receives a righteous man in the name of a righteous man shall receive a righteous man's reward. And whoever in the name of a disciple gives to one of these little ones even a cup of cold water to drink, truly I say to you, he shall not lose his reward" (Matthew 10:40–42; cf. Matthew 25:40, 44, 45; see Mark 9:37).

Setting: The temple in Jerusalem. With His death on the cross just days away, Jesus laments over Jerusalem's hardheartedness and lack of repentance.

"Jerusalem, Jerusalem, who kills the prophets and stones those who are sent to her! How often I wanted to gather your children together, the way a hen gathers her chicks under her wings, and you were unwilling. Behold, your house is being left to you desolate! For I say to you, from now on you will not see Me until you say, 'BLESSED IS HE WHO COMES IN THE NAME OF THE LORD!'" (Matthew 23:37–39, Jesus quotes from Psalm 118:26; cf. 1 Kings 9:7; Luke 13:34, 35).

Setting: On a mountain in Galilee. Following His resurrection from the dead in Jerusalem, Jesus conveys the Great Commission to His eleven remaining disciples.

And Jesus came up and spoke to them, saying, "All authority has been given to Me in heaven and on earth. Go therefore and make disciples of all the nations, baptizing them in the name of the Father and the Son and the Holy Spirit, teaching them to observe all that I commanded you; and lo, I am with you always, even to the end of the age" (Matthew 28:18–20; cf. Mark 16:15; see Daniel 7:13).

Setting: The country of the Gerasenes, across from the Sea of Galilee. Jesus encounters and heals a demon-possessed man.

For He had been saying to him, "Come out of the man, you unclean spirit!" And He was asking Him, "What is your name?" And he said to Him, "My name is Legion; for we are many" (Mark 5:8, 9; cf. Luke 8:30; see Matthew 8:28–32; Luke 8:26–33).

Setting: Capernaum of Galilee. As Jesus teaches His disciples in private, they ask Him about greatness.

But Jesus said, "Do not hinder him, for there is no one who will perform a miracle in My name, and be able soon afterward to speak evil of Me. For he who is not against us is for us. For whoever gives you a cup of water to drink because of your name as *followers* of Christ, truly I say to you, he will not lose his reward. Whoever causes one of these little ones who believe to stumble, it would be better for him if, with a heavy millstone hung around his neck, he had been cast into the sea. If your hand causes you to stumble, cut it off; it is better for you to enter life crippled, than, having your two hands, to go into hell, into the unquenchable fire, [where THEIR WORM DOES NOT DIE, AND THE FIRE IS NOT QUENCHED.] If your foot causes you to stumble, cut it off; it is better for you to enter life lame, than, having your two feet, to be cast into hell, [where THEIR WORM DOES NOT DIE, AND THE FIRE IS NOT QUENCHED.] If your eye causes you to stumble, throw it out; it is better for you to enter the kingdom of God with one eye, than, having two eyes, to be cast into hell, where THEIR WORM DOES NOT DIE, AND THE FIRE IS NOT QUENCHED. For everyone will be salted with fire. Salt is good; but if the salt becomes unsalty, with what will you make it salty *again?* Have salt in yourselves, and be at peace with one another" (Mark 9:39–50; Jesus quotes from Isaiah 66:24; cf. Matthew 18:6–9; Luke 9:49, 50; see Matthew 5:13, 29, 30; 10:42; 12:30; 18:5, 6).

Setting: Galilee. After selecting His twelve disciples, Jesus teaches the Beatitudes (part of the Sermon on the Mount) to those disciples and a great throng of people from Judea, Jerusalem, and the central coastal region of Tyre and Sidon.

"Blessed are you when men hate you, and ostracize you, and insult you, and scorn your name as evil, for the sake of the Son of Man. Be glad in that day and leap *for joy*, for behold, your reward is great in heaven. For in the same way their fathers used to treat the prophets" (Luke 6:22, 23; cf. Matthew 5:10–12; see 2 Chronicles 36:16).

Setting: The country of the Gerasenes, east of the Sea of Galilee. After Jesus calms a storm on the Sea of Galilee, He and His disciples land and encounter a demon-possessed man.

And Jesus asked him, "What is your name?" And he said. "Legion"; for many demons had entered him (Luke 8:30; cf. Matthew 8:28, 29; Mark 5:1–9).

Setting: On the way from Galilee to Jerusalem. While teaching in the cities and villages, Jesus responds to a question about who is saved. Some Pharisees ask Him to leave, claiming Herod Antipas (tetrarch of Galilee and Perea) seeks to kill Him.

And He said to them, "Go and tell that fox, 'Behold, I cast out demons and perform cures today and tomorrow, and the third *day* I reach My goal.' Nevertheless I must journey on today and tomorrow and the next *day*; for it cannot be that a prophet would perish outside of Jerusalem. O Jerusalem, Jerusalem, *the city* that kills the prophets and stones those sent to her! How often I wanted to gather your children together, just as a hen *gathers* her brood under her wings, and you would not *have it*! Behold, your house is left to you *desolate*; and I say to you, you will not see Me until *the time* comes when you say, 'BLESSED IS HE WHO COMES IN THE NAME OF THE LORD!'" (Luke 13:32–35, Jesus quotes from Psalm 118:26; cf. Matthew 23:37).

Setting: Jerusalem. During a feast of the Jews, Jesus responds to criticism from the religious leaders by referring to God as His Father (thereby making Himself equal with God) and informing them that God, John the Baptist, the Scriptures, and His works all testify to His mission.

"You search the Scriptures because you think that in them you have eternal life; it is these that testify about Me; and you are unwilling to come to Me so that you may have life. I do not receive glory from men; but I know you, that you do not have the love of God in yourselves. I have come in My Father's name, and you do not receive Me; if another comes in his own name, you will receive him. How can you believe, when you receive glory from one another and you do not seek the glory that is from the *one and* only God? Do not think that I will accuse you before the Father; the one who accuses you is Moses, in whom you have set your hope. For if you believed Moses, you would believe Me, for he wrote about Me. But if you do not believe his writings, how will you believe My words?" (John 5:39–47; see Matthew 24:5; Luke 16:29, 31; 24:27; John 9:28; 17:3).

Setting: Jerusalem. Following the Pharisees' interrogation and dismissal of the formerly blind man Jesus healed on the Sabbath, the Lord speaks to the Pharisees, using parabolic language they do not understand.

"Truly, truly, I say to you, he who does not enter by the door into the fold of the sheep, but climbs up some other way, he is a thief and a robber. But he who enters by the door is a shepherd of the sheep. To him the doorkeeper opens, and the sheep hear his voice, and he calls his own sheep by name and leads them out. When he puts forth all his own, he goes ahead of them, and the sheep follow him because they know his voice. A stranger they simply will not follow, but will flee from him, because they do not know the voice of strangers" (John 10:1–5; see John 10:27).

Setting: Jerusalem. Before the Passover, after giving His disciples hope that in the midst of tribulation they will have His peace, Jesus prays His high-priestly prayer.

Jesus spoke these things; and lifting up His eyes to heaven, He said, "Father, the hour has come; glorify Your Son, that the Son may glorify You, even as You gave Him authority over all flesh, that to all whom You have given Him, He may give eternal life. This is eternal life, that they may know You, the only true God, and Jesus Christ whom You have sent. I glorified You on the earth, having accomplished the work which You have given Me to do. Now, Father, glorify Me together with Yourself, with the glory which I had with You before the world was. I have manifested Your name to the men whom You gave Me out of the world; they were Yours and You gave them to Me, and they have kept Your word. Now they have come to know that everything You have given Me is from You; for the words which You gave Me I have given to them; and they received *them* and truly understood that I came forth from You, and they believed You sent Me. I ask on their behalf; I do not ask on behalf of the world, but of those whom You have given Me; for they are Yours; and all things that are Mine are Yours, and Yours are Mine; and I have been glorified in them. I am no longer in the world; and *yet* they themselves are in the world, and I come to You. Holy Father, keep them in Your name, *the name* which You have given Me, that they may be even as We *are*. While I was with them, I was keeping them in Your name which You have given Me; and I guarded them and not one of them perished but the son of perdition, so that the Scripture would be fulfilled" (John 17:1–12; see Luke 22:32; John 1:1; 3:35; 4:34; 5:44; 6:37–39, 70; 8:42; 11:41; 12:49; 13:18, 31; 16:15; Philippians 2:9).

Setting: On the island of Patmos (in the Aegean Sea about fifty miles southwest of Ephesus in modern Turkey). On the Lord's Day (Sunday), approximately fifty years after Jesus' resurrection, the disciple John encounters the Lord Jesus Christ, who communicates a new revelation for the apostle to record for the church in Sardis and to six other churches in Asia.

"To the angel of the church in Sardis write: He who has the seven Spirits of God and the seven stars, says this: 'I know your deeds, that you have a name that you are alive, but you are dead. Wake up, and strengthen the things that remain, which were about to die; for I have not found your deeds completed in the sight of My God. So remember what you have received and heard; and keep *it*, and repent. Therefore if you do not wake up, I will come like a thief, and you will not know at what hour I will come to you. But you have a few people in Sardis who have not soiled their garments; and they will walk with Me in white, for they are worthy. He who overcomes will thus be clothed in white garments; and I will not erase his name from the book of life, and I will confess his name before My Father and before His angels. He who has an ear, let him hear what the Spirit says to the churches' " (Revelation 3:1–6; see Matthew 10:32; Revelation 1:16).

Setting: On the island of Patmos (in the Aegean Sea about fifty miles southwest of Ephesus in modern Turkey). On the Lord's Day (Sunday), approximately fifty years after Jesus' resurrection, the disciple John encounters the Lord Jesus Christ, who communicates a new revelation for the apostle to record for the church in Philadelphia and to six other churches in Asia.

"And to the angel of the church in Philadelphia write: He who is holy, who is true, who has the key of David, who opens and no one will shut, and who shuts and no one opens, says this: 'I know your deeds. Behold, I have put before you an open door which no one can shut, because you have a little power, and have kept My word, and have not denied My name. Behold, I will cause *those* of the synagogue of Satan, who say that they are Jews and are not, but lie—I will make them come and bow down at your feet, and *make them* know that I have loved you. Because you have kept the word of My perseverance, I also will keep you from the hour of testing, that *hour* which is about to come upon the whole world, to test those who dwell on the earth. I am coming quickly; hold fast what you have, so that no one will take your crown. He who overcomes, I will make him a pillar in the temple of My God, and he will not go out from it anymore; and I will write on him the name of My God, and the name of the city of My God, the new Jerusalem, which comes down out of heaven from My God, and My new name. He who has an ear, let him hear what the Spirit says to the churches' " (Revelation 3:7–13; see Isaiah 22:22; Galatians 2:9; Revelation 2:9, 10, 13, 25; 14:1).

NAME, FATHER'S

[FATHER'S NAME from Your name]

Setting: Galilee. During the early part of His ministry, while conveying The Sermon on the Mount, Jesus gives a model prayer to His disciples and the multitudes.

"Pray, then, in this way: 'Our Father who is in heaven, hallowed be Your name. Your kingdom come. Your will be done, on earth as it is in heaven. Give us this day our daily bread. And forgive us our debts, as we also have forgiven our debtors. And do not lead us into temptation, but deliver us from evil. [For Yours is the kingdom and the power and the glory forever. Amen]'" (Matthew 6:9–13; cf. Luke 11:2–4; see John 17:15).

[FATHER'S NAME from Your name]
Setting: On the way from Galilee to Jerusalem. After Jesus visits in the home of Martha and Mary of Bethany, one of His disciples asks Him to teach them to pray.

And He said to them, "When you pray, say: 'Father, hallowed be Your name. Your kingdom come. Give us each day our daily bread. And forgive us our sins, for we ourselves also forgive everyone who is indebted to us. And lead us not into temptation'" (Luke 11:2–4; cf. Matthew 6:9–13).

Setting: Jerusalem. During a feast of the Jews, Jesus responds to criticism from the religious leaders by referring to God as His Father (thereby making Himself equal with God) and informing them that God, John the Baptist, the Scriptures, and His works all testify to His mission.

"You search the Scriptures because you think that in them you have eternal life; it is these that testify about Me; and you are unwilling to come to Me so that you may have life. I do not receive glory from men; but I know you, that you do not have the love of God in yourselves. I have come in My Father's name, and you do not receive Me; if another comes in his own name, you will receive him. How can you believe, when you receive glory from one another and you do not seek the glory that is from the *one and* only God? Do not think that I will accuse you before the Father; the one who accuses you is Moses, in whom you have set your hope. For if you believed Moses, you would believe Me, for he wrote about Me. But if you do not believe his writings, how will you believe My words?" (John 5:39–47; see Matthew 24:5; Luke 16:29, 31; 24:27; John 9:28; 17:3).

Setting: Jerusalem. At the Feast of Dedication, just after Jesus conveys the Parable of the Good Shepherd to the Pharisees (who do not understand it), they ask Him plainly if He is the Christ.

Jesus answered them, "I told you, and you do not believe; the works that I do in My Father's name, these testify of Me. But you do not believe because you are not of My sheep. My sheep hear My voice, and I know them, and they follow Me; and I give eternal life to them, and they will never perish; and no one will snatch them out of My hand. My Father, who has given *them* to Me, is greater than all; and no one is able to snatch *them* out of the Father's hand. I and the Father are one" (John 10:25–30; see John 8:47; 10:4; 17:1, 2, 20, 21).

[FATHER'S NAME from Your name]
Setting: Jerusalem. Just days before the Passover, with the chief priests and Pharisees plotting to seize Him and crowds welcoming Him with palm branches and praise, Jesus expresses anxiety about His upcoming crucifixion.

"Now My soul has become troubled; and what shall I say, 'Father, save Me from this hour'? But for this purpose I came to this hour. Father glorify Your name." Then a voice came out of heaven: "I have glorified it, and will glorify it again." So the crowd *of people* who stood by and heard it were saying that it had thundered; others were saying, "An angel has spoken to Him." Jesus answered and said, "This voice has not come for My sake, but for your sakes. Now judgment is upon this world; now the ruler of this world will be cast out. And I, if I am lifted up from the earth, will draw all men to Myself" (John 12:27–32; see Matthew 3:17; 26:38; John 3:14; 6:44; 11:42; 14:30).

[FATHER'S NAME from Your name]
Setting: Jerusalem. Before the Passover, after giving His disciples hope that in the midst of tribulation they will have His peace, Jesus prays His high-priestly prayer.

Jesus spoke these things; and lifting up His eyes to heaven, He said, "Father, the hour has come; glorify Your Son, that the Son may glorify You, even as You gave Him authority over all flesh, that to all whom You have given Him, He may give eternal life. This is eternal life, that they may know You, the only true God, and Jesus Christ whom You have sent. I glorified You on the earth, having accomplished the work which You have given Me to do. Now, Father, glorify Me together with Yourself, with the glory which I had with You before the world was. I have manifested Your name to the men whom You gave Me out of the world; they were Yours and You gave them to Me, and they have kept Your word. Now they have come to know that everything You have given Me is from You; for the words which You gave Me I have given to them; and they received *them* and truly understood that I came forth from You, and they believed You sent Me. I ask on their behalf; I do not ask on behalf of the world, but of those whom You have given Me; for they are Yours; and all things that are Mine are Yours, and Yours are Mine; and I have been glorified in them. I am no longer in the world; and *yet* they themselves are in the world, and I come to You. Holy Father, keep them in Your name, *the name* which You have given Me, that they may be even as We *are.* While I was with them, I was keeping them in Your name which You have given Me; and I guarded them and not one of them perished but the son of perdition, so that the Scripture would be fulfilled" (John 17:1–12; see Luke 22:32; John 1:1; 3:35; 4:34; 5:44; 6:37–39, 70; 8:42; 11:41; 12:49; 13:18, 31; 16:15; Philippians 2:9).

[FATHER'S NAME from Your name]

Setting: Jerusalem. Before the Passover, after giving His disciples hope that in the midst of tribulation they will have His peace, Jesus continues praying His high-priestly prayer.

"The glory which You have given Me I have given to them, that they may be one, just as We are one; I in them and You in Me, that they may be perfected in unity, so that the world may know that you sent Me, and loved them, even as You have loved Me. Father, I desire that they also, whom You have given Me, be with Me where I am, so that they may see My glory which You have given Me, for You loved Me before the foundation of the world. O righteous Father, although the world has not known You, yet I have known You; and these have known that You sent Me; and I have made Your name known to them, and will make it known, so that the love with which You loved Me may be in them, and I in them" (John 17:22–26; see Matthew 25:34; John 1:14; 10:38; 15:9; 16:27).

NAME, JESUS' (See JESUS' NAME)

NAME, MY (Jesus'; also see JESUS; JESUS' NAME; and LORD, NAME OF THE)

Setting: Galilee. After His disciples observe His ministry, Jesus summons and specifically instructs them about the upcoming difficulties of their ministry to the people of Israel.

"Brother will betray brother to death, and a father *his* child; and children will rise up against parents and cause them to be put to death. You will be hated by all because of My name, but it is the one who has endured to the end who will be saved. But whenever they persecute you in one city, flee to the next; for truly I say to you, you will not finish *going through* the cities of Israel until the Son of Man comes" (Matthew 10:21–23; cf. Matthew 16:27, 28; 24:9).

Setting: Capernaum of Galilee. Jesus answers His disciples' question about greatness, or rank, in the kingdom of heaven.

And He called a child to Himself and set him before them, and said, "Truly I say to you, unless you are converted and become like children, you will not enter the kingdom of heaven. Whoever then humbles himself as this child, he is the greatest in the kingdom of heaven. And whoever receives one such child in My name receives Me; but whoever causes one of these little ones who believe in Me to stumble, it would be better for him to have a heavy millstone hung around his neck, and to be drowned in the depth of the sea"
(Matthew 18:2–6; cf. Matthew 19:14; Mark 9:33–37, 42; Luke 9:47, 48; Luke 17:1, 2).

Setting: Capernaum of Galilee. After conveying to His disciples the value of little ones, Jesus gives instruction about church discipline.

"If your brother sins, go and show him his fault in private; if he listens to you, you have won your brother. But if he does not listen *to you,* take one or two more with you, so that BY THE MOUTH OF TWO OR THREE WITNESSES EVERY FACT MAY BE CONFIRMED. If he refuses to listen to them, tell it to the church; and if he refuses to listen even to the church, let him be to you as a Gentile and a tax collector. Truly I say to you, whatever you bind of earth shall have been bound in heaven; and whatever you loose on earth shall have been loosed in heaven. Again, I say to you, that if two of you agree on earth about anything that they may ask, it shall be done for them by My Father who is in heaven. For there two or three have gathered together in My name, I am there in their midst" (Matthew 18:15–20. Jesus quotes from Deuteronomy 19:15; cf. Matthew 7:7; 16:19; see Leviticus 19:17; Matthew 28:20; 2 Thessalonians 3:6, 14).

Setting: On the Mount of Olives, just east of Jerusalem. During His Olivet Discourse, Jesus answers His disciples' questions as to when the temple will be destroyed and Jerusalem overrun, along with the signs of His coming and the end of the age.

And Jesus answered and said to them, "See to it that no one misleads you. For many will come in My name, saying, 'I am the Christ,' and will mislead many. You will be hearing of wars and rumors of wars. See that you are not frightened, for *those things* must take place, but *that* is not yet the end. For nation will rise against nation, and kingdom against kingdom, and in various places there will be famines and earthquakes. But all these things are *merely* the beginning of birth pangs. Then they will deliver you to tribulation, and will kill you, and you will be hated by all nations because of My name. At that time many will fall away and will betray one another and hate one another. Many false prophets will arise and will mislead many. Because lawlessness is increased, most people's love will grow cold. But the one who endures to the end, he will be saved. This gospel of the kingdom shall be preached in the whole world as a testimony to all the nations, and then the end will come" (Matthew 24:4–14; cf. Jeremiah 29:8; Matthew 7:15; 10:17, 22; Mark 13:3–13; Luke 21:7–19; Revelation 6:4).

Setting: Capernaum of Galilee. As Jesus teaches His disciples in private, they ask Him about greatness.

They came to Capernaum; and when He was in the house, He *began* to question them, "What were you discussing on the way?" But they kept silent, for on the way they had discussed with one another which *of them* was the greatest. Sitting down, He called the twelve and said to them, "If anyone wants to be first, he shall be last of all and servant of all." Taking a child, He set him before them, and taking him in His arms, He said to them, "Whoever receives one child like this in My name receives Me; and whoever receives Me does not receive Me, but Him who sent Me" (Mark 9:33–37; cf. Matthew 18:1–5; Luke 9:46–48; see Matthew 20:26; 10:40).

Setting: Capernaum of Galilee. As Jesus teaches His disciples in private, they ask Him about greatness.

But Jesus said, "Do not hinder him, for there is no one who will perform a miracle in My name, and be able soon afterward to speak evil of Me. For he who is not against us is for us. For whoever gives you a cup of water to drink because of your name as *followers* of Christ, truly I say to you, he will not lose his reward. Whoever causes one of these little ones who believe to stumble, it would be better for him if, with a heavy millstone hung around his neck, he had been cast into the sea. If your hand causes you to stumble, cut it off; it is better for you to enter life crippled, than, having your two hands, to go into hell, into the unquenchable fire, [where THEIR WORM DOES NOT DIE, AND THE FIRE IS NOT QUENCHED.] If your foot causes you to stumble, cut it off; it is better for you to enter life lame, than, having your two feet, to be cast into hell, [where THEIR WORM DOES NOT DIE, AND THE FIRE IS NOT QUENCHED.] If your eye causes you to stumble, throw it out; it is better for you to enter the kingdom of God with one eye, than, having two eyes, to be cast into hell, where THEIR WORM DOES NOT DIE, AND THE FIRE IS NOT QUENCHED. For everyone will be salted with fire. Salt is good; but if the salt becomes unsalty, with what will you make it salty *again?* Have salt in yourselves, and be at peace with one another" (Mark 9:39–50; Jesus quotes from Isaiah 66:24; cf. Matthew 18:6–9; Luke 9:49, 50; see Matthew 5:13, 29, 30; 10:42; 12:30; 18:5, 6.

Setting: On the Mount of Olives, east of the temple in Jerusalem. After predicting the temple's destruction, Jesus responds during His Olivet Discourse to questions from Peter, James, John, and Andrew about other future events.

And Jesus began to say to them, "See to it that no one misleads you. Many will come in My name, saying, 'I am *He!*' and will mislead many. When you hear of wars and rumors of wars, do not be frightened; *those things* must take place; but *that is* not yet the end. For nation will rise up against nation, and kingdom against kingdom; there will be earthquakes in various places; there will *also be* famines. These things are *merely* the beginning of birth pangs. But be on your guard; for they will deliver you to *the* courts, and you will be flogged in *the* synagogues, and you will stand before governors and kings for My sake, as a testimony to them. The gospel must first be preached to all the nations. When they arrest you and hand you over, do not worry beforehand about what you are to say, but say whatever is given you in that hour; for it is not you who speak, but *it is* the Holy Spirit. Brother will betray brother to death, and a father *his* child; and children will rise up against parents and have them put to death. You will be hated by all because of My name, but the one who endures to the end, he will be saved" (Mark 13:5–13; cf. Matthew 24:4–14; Luke 21:7–19; see Matthew 10:17–22).

Setting: Following His resurrection from the dead after being crucified, Jesus commissions His disciples to preach His gospel to the world.

And He said to them, "Go into all the world and preach the gospel to all creation. He who has believed and has been baptized shall be saved; but he who has disbelieved shall be condemned. These signs will accompany those who have believed: in My name they will cast out demons, they will speak with new tongues; they will pick up serpents, and if they drink any deadly *poison,* it will not hurt them; they will lay hands on the sick, and they will recover" (Mark 16:15–18; cf. Matthew 28:16–20; see Mark 9:38; John 3:18, 36; 1 Corinthians 15:6).

[Note: Some scholars question the authenticity of Mark 16:9–20 as these verses do not appear in some early New Testament manuscripts.]

Setting: Galilee. After Jesus prophesies His death, an argument arises among His disciples as to who is the greatest among them. The Lord resolves the matter by using a child as a teaching illustration.

But Jesus, knowing what they were thinking in their heart, took a child and stood him by His side, and said to them, "Whoever receives this child in My name receives Me, and whoever receives Me receives Him who sent Me; for the one who is least among all of you, this is the one who is great" (Luke 9:47, 48; cf. Matthew 18:1–5; Mark 9:33–47; see Matthew 10:40; Luke 22:24).

Setting: The temple in Jerusalem. While ministering a few days before His crucifixion, after Jesus prophesies the destruction of the temple during His Olivet Discourse, His disciples ask Him when this will happen.

And He said, "See to it that you are not misled; for many will come in My name, saying, 'I am *He*,' and, 'The time is near.' Do not go after them. When you hear of wars and disturbances, do not be terrified; for these things must take place first, but the end *does* not *follow* immediately" (Luke 21:8, 9; cf. Matthew 24:4–8; Mark 13:5–8).

Setting: On the Mount of Olives, east of the temple in Jerusalem. After ministering in the temple a few days before His crucifixion, and giving His disciples more details regarding the temple's future destruction, Jesus elaborates during His Olivet Discourse about things to come.

Then He continued by saying to them, "Nation will rise against nation and kingdom against kingdom, and there will be great earthquakes, and in various places plagues and famines; and there will be terrors and great signs from heaven. But before all these things, they will lay their hands on you and will persecute you, delivering you to the synagogues and prisons, bringing you before kings and governors for My name's sake. It will lead to an opportunity for your testimony. So make up your minds not to prepare beforehand to defend yourselves; for I will give you utterance and wisdom which none of your opponents will be able to resist or refute. But you will be betrayed even by parents and brothers and relatives and friends, and they will put *some* of you to death, and you will be hated by all because of My name. Yet not a hair of your head will perish. By your endurance you will gain your lives" (Luke 21:10–19; cf. Matthew 10:19–22; 24:7–14; Mark 13:8–13).

Setting: Jerusalem. Before the Passover, after answering Thomas' question where Jesus is going and how His disciples will know the way, the Lord responds to Philip's request for Him to show them the Father.

Jesus said to him, "Have I been so long with you, and *yet* you have not come to know Me, Philip? He who has seen Me has seen the Father; how *can* you say, 'Show us the Father'? Do you not believe that I am in the Father, and the Father is in Me? The words that I say to you I do not speak on My own initiative, but the Father abiding in Me does His works. Believe Me that I am in the Father and the Father is in Me; otherwise believe because of the works themselves. Truly, truly, I say to you, he who believes in Me, the works that I do, he will do also; and greater *works* than these he will do; because I go to the Father. Whatever you ask in My name, that will I do, so that the Father may be glorified in the Son. If you ask Me anything in My name, I will do *it*" (John 14:9–14; see Matthew 7:7; John 1:14; 5:19, 20, 36; 10:37, 38; 15:16).

Setting: Jerusalem. Before the Passover, after responding to Philip's request for Jesus to show His disciples the Father, the Lord conveys the upcoming ministry of the Holy Spirit in their lives.

"These things I have spoken to you while abiding with you. But the Helper, the Holy Spirit, whom the Father will send in My name, He will teach you all things, and bring to your remembrance all that I said to you" (John 14:25, 26; see John 16:13).

Setting: Jerusalem. Before the Passover, with His departure in mind, after explaining He is the vine and His disciples are the branches, Jesus commands them to love one another.

"This is My commandment, that you love one another, just as I have loved you. Greater love has no one than this, that one lay down his life for his friends. You are My friends if you do what I command you. No longer do I call you slaves, for the slave does not know what his master is doing; but I have called you friends, for all things that I have heard from My Father I have made known to you. You did not choose Me but I chose you, and appointed you that you would go and bear fruit, and *that* your fruit would remain, so that whatever you ask of the Father in My name He may give to you. This I command you, that you love one another" (John 15:12–17; see Matthew 12:50; John 6:70; 8:26; 10:11; 13:34).

Setting: Jerusalem. Before the Passover, after empathizing with His disciples' sadness over His prophecies and giving them the hope for the future, Jesus conveys promises about praying in His name.

"In that day you will not question Me about anything. Truly, truly, I say to you, if you ask the Father for anything in My name, He will give it to you. Until now you have asked for nothing in My name; ask and you will receive, so that your joy may be made full. These things I have spoken to you in figurative language; an hour is coming when I will no longer speak to you in figurative language, but will tell you plainly of the Father. In that day you will ask in My name, and I do not say to you that I will request of the Father on your behalf; for the Father Himself loves you, because you have loved Me and have believed that I came forth from the Father. I came forth from the Father and have come into the world; I am leaving the world again and going to the Father" (John 16:23–28; see Matthew 13:34; John 8:42; 13:1, 3; 14:14, 21, 23; 15:16).

Setting: Damascus. Luke, writing in Acts, details the reluctance of Ananias, one of Jesus' followers, to locate Saul of Tarsus (a known enemy of the church), in order to restore Saul's vision.

But the Lord said to him, "Go, for he is a chosen instrument of Mine, to bear My name before the Gentiles and kings and the sons of Israel; for I will show him how much he must suffer for My name's sake" (Acts 9:15, 16; see Acts 13:2; 20:22 24).

Setting: On the island of Patmos (in the Aegean Sea about fifty miles southwest of Ephesus in modern Turkey). On the Lord's Day (Sunday), approximately fifty years after Jesus' resurrection, the disciple John encounters the Lord Jesus Christ, who communicates a new revelation for the apostle to record for the church in Pergamum and to six other churches in Asia.

"And to the angel of the church in Pergamum write: The One who has the sharp two-edged sword says this: 'I know where you dwell, where Satan's throne is; and you hold fast My name, and did not deny My faith even in the days of Antipas, My witness, My faithful one, who was killed among you, where Satan dwells. But I have a few things against you, because you have there some who hold the teaching of Balaam, who kept teaching Balak to put a stumbling block before the sons of Israel, to eat things sacrificed to idols and to commit *acts of* immorality. So you also have some who in the same way hold the teaching of the Nicolaitans. Therefore repent; or else I am coming to you quickly, and I will make war against them with the sword of My mouth. He who has an ear, let him hear what the Spirit says to the churches. To him who overcomes, to him I will give *some* of the hidden manna, and I will give him a white stone, and a new name written on the stone which no one knows but he who receives it' (Revelation 2:12–17; see Numbers 25:1–3; Isaiah 62:2; Revelation 1:16; 2:5, 6, 16).

Setting: On the island of Patmos (in the Aegean Sea about fifty miles southwest of Ephesus in modern Turkey). On the Lord's Day (Sunday), approximately fifty years after Jesus' resurrection, the disciple John encounters the Lord Jesus Christ, who communicates a new revelation for the apostle to record for the church in Philadelphia and to six other churches in Asia.

"And to the angel of the church in Philadelphia write: He who is holy, who is true, who has the key of David, who opens and no one will shut, and who shuts and no one opens, says this: 'I know your deeds. Behold, I have put before you an open door which no one can shut, because you have a little power, and have kept My word, and have not denied My name. Behold, I will cause *those* of the synagogue of Satan, who say that they are Jews and are not, but lie—I will make them come and bow down at your feet, and *make them* know that I have loved you. Because you have kept the word of My perseverance, I also will keep you from the hour of testing, that *hour* which is about to come upon the whole world, to test those who dwell on the earth. I am coming quickly; hold fast what you have, so that no one will take your crown. He who overcomes, I will make him a pillar in the temple of My God, and he will not go out from it anymore; and I will write on him the name of My God, and the name of the city of My God, the new Jerusalem, which comes down out of heaven from My God, and My new name. He who has an ear, let him hear what the Spirit says to the churches' " (Revelation 3:7–13; see Isaiah 22:22; Galatians 2:9; Revelation 2:9, 10, 13, 25; 14:1).

NAME, NEW

Setting: On the island of Patmos (in the Aegean Sea about fifty miles southwest of Ephesus in modern Turkey). On the Lord's Day (Sunday), approximately fifty years after Jesus' resurrection, the disciple John encounters the Lord Jesus Christ, who communicates a new revelation for the apostle to record for the church in Pergamum and to six other churches in Asia.

"And to the angel of the church in Pergamum write: The One who has the sharp two-edged sword says this: 'I know where you dwell, where Satan's throne is; and you hold fast My name, and did not deny My faith even in the days of Antipas, My witness, My faithful one, who was killed among you, where Satan dwells. But I have a few things against you, because you have there some who hold the teaching of Balaam, who kept teaching Balak to put a stumbling block before the sons of Israel, to eat things sacrificed to idols and to commit *acts of* immorality. So you also have some who in the same way hold the teaching of the Nicolaitans. Therefore repent; or else I am coming to you quickly, and I will make war against them with the sword of My mouth. He who has an ear, let him hear what the Spirit says to the churches. To him who overcomes, to him I will give *some* of the hidden manna, and I will give him a white stone, and a new name written on the stone which no one knows but he who receives it' (Revelation 2:12–17; see Numbers 25:1–3; Isaiah 62:2; Revelation 1:16).

Setting: On the island of Patmos (in the Aegean Sea about fifty miles southwest of Ephesus in modern Turkey). On the Lord's Day (Sunday), approximately fifty years after Jesus' resurrection, the disciple John encounters the Lord Jesus Christ, who communicates a new revelation for the apostle to record for the church in Philadelphia and to six other churches in Asia.

"And to the angel of the church in Philadelphia write: He who is holy, who is true, who has the key of David, who opens and no one will shut, and who shuts and no one opens, says this: 'I know your deeds. Behold, I have put before you an open door which no one can shut, because you have a little power, and have kept My word, and have not denied My name. Behold, I will cause *those* of the synagogue of Satan, who say that they are Jews and are not, but lie—I will make them come and bow down at your feet, and *make them* know that I have loved you. Because you have kept the word of My perseverance, I also will keep you from the hour of testing, that *hour* which is about to come upon the whole world, to test those who dwell on the earth. I am coming quickly; hold fast what you have, so that no one will take your crown. He who overcomes, I will make him a pillar in the temple of My God, and he will not go out from it anymore; and I will write on him the name of My God, and the name of the city of My God, the new Jerusalem, which comes down out of heaven from My God, and My new name. He who has an ear, let him hear what the Spirit says to the churches' " (Revelation 3:7–13; see Isaiah 22:22; Galatians 2:9; Revelation 2:9, 10, 13, 25; 14:1).

NAME OF JESUS (See JESUS; JESUS' NAME; and NAME, MY)

NAME OF THE FATHER AND THE SON AND THE HOLY SPIRIT (Listed under HOLY SPIRIT, NAME OF THE FATHER AND THE SON AND THE)

NAME OF THE LORD (Listed under LORD, NAME OF THE)

NAMES (Also see NAME)

Setting: On the way from Galilee to Jerusalem. The Lord responds to a report from the seventy sent out in pairs to every place He Himself will soon visit.

And He said to them, "I was watching Satan fall from heaven like lightning. Behold, I have given you authority to tread on serpents and scorpions, and over all the power of the enemy, and nothing will injure you. Nevertheless do not rejoice in this, that the spirits are subject to you, but rejoice that your names are recorded in heaven" (Luke 10:18–20; see Psalm 91:13; Isaiah 14:12–14; Luke 9:1).

NARROW GATE (Listed under GATE, NARROW)

NATHANAEL

[NATHANAEL from an Israelite indeed, in whom there is no deceit!]

Setting: Galilee. After beginning His public ministry and choosing His first disciples, Andrew and Simon (Peter) near Bethany beyond the Jordan, and Philip in Galilee, Jesus calls Philip's friend, Nathanael, (some believe he may have been also called Bartholomew) as His next follower.

Jesus saw Nathanael coming to Him, and said of him, "Behold, an Israelite indeed, in whom there is no deceit!" Nathanael said to Him, "How do you know me?" Jesus answered and said to him, "Before Philip called you, when you were under the fig tree, I saw you." Nathanael answered Him, "Rabbi, You are the Son of God; You are the King of Israel." Jesus answered and said to him, "Because I said to you that I saw you under the fig tree, do you believe? You will see greater things than these." And He said to him, "Truly, truly, I say to you, you will see the heavens opened and the angels of God ascending and descending on the Son of Man" (John 1:47–51).

NATION (Also see NATIONS; and PEOPLE)

Setting: The Mount of Olives, just east of Jerusalem. During His Olivet Discourse, Jesus answers His disciples' questions as to when the temple will be destroyed and Jerusalem overrun, along with the signs of His coming and the end of the age.

And Jesus answered and said to them, "See to it that no one misleads you. For many will come in My name, saying, 'I am the Christ,' and will mislead many. You will be hearing of wars and rumors of wars. See that you are not frightened, for *those things* must take place, but *that* is not yet the end. For nation will rise against nation, and kingdom against kingdom, and in various places there will be famines and earthquakes. But all these things are *merely* the beginning of birth pangs. Then they will deliver you to tribulation, and will kill you, and you will be hated by all nations because of My name. At that time many will fall away and will betray one another and hate one another. Many false prophets will arise and will mislead many. Because lawlessness is increased, most people's love will grow cold. But the one who endures to the end, he will be saved. This gospel of the kingdom shall be preached in the whole world as a testimony to all the nations, and then the end will come" (Matthew 24:4–14; cf. Jeremiah 29:8; Matthew 7:15; 10:17, 22; Mark 13:3–13; Luke 21:7–19; Revelation 6:4).

Setting: On the Mount of Olives, east of the temple in Jerusalem. After predicting the temple's destruction, Jesus responds during His Olivet Discourse to questions from Peter, James, John, and Andrew about other future events.

And Jesus began to say to them, "See to it that no one misleads you. Many will come in My name, saying, 'I am *He!*' and will mislead many. When you hear of wars and rumors of wars, do not be frightened; *those things* must take place; but *that is* not yet the end. For nation will rise up against nation, and kingdom against kingdom; there will be earthquakes in various places; there will *also be* famines. These things are *merely* the beginning of birth pangs. But be on your guard; for they will deliver you to *the* courts, and you will be flogged in *the* synagogues, and you will stand before governors and kings for My sake, as a testimony to them. The gospel must first be preached to all the nations. When they arrest you and hand you over, do not worry beforehand about what you are to say, but say whatever is given you in that hour; for it is not you who speak, but *it is* the Holy Spirit. Brother will betray brother to death, and a father *his* child; and children will rise up against parents and have them put to death. You will be hated by all because of My name, but the one who endures to the end, he will be saved" (Mark 13:5–13; cf. Matthew 24:4–14; Luke 21:7–19; see Matthew 10:17–22).

Setting: On the Mount of Olives, east of the temple in Jerusalem. After ministering in the temple a few days before His crucifixion, and giving His disciples more details regarding the temple's future destruction, Jesus elaborates during His Olivet Discourse about things to come.

Then He continued by saying to them, "Nation will rise against nation and kingdom against kingdom, and there will be great earthquakes, and in various places plagues and famines; and there will be terrors and great signs from heaven. But before all these things, they will lay their hands on you and will persecute you, delivering you to the synagogues and prisons, bringing you before kings and governors for My name's sake. It will lead to an opportunity for your testimony. So make up your minds not to prepare beforehand to defend yourselves; for I will give you utterance and wisdom which none of your opponents will be able to resist or refute. But you will be betrayed even by parents and brothers and relatives and friends, and they will put *some* of you to death, and you will be hated by all because of My name. Yet not a hair of your head will perish. By your endurance you will gain your lives" (Luke 21:10–19; cf. Matthew 10:19–22; 24:7–14; Mark 13:8–13).

NATIONS (Also see NATION)

Setting: The Mount of Olives, just east of Jerusalem. During His Olivet Discourse, Jesus answers His disciples' questions as to when the temple will be destroyed and Jerusalem overrun, along with the signs of His coming and the end of the age.

And Jesus answered and said to them, "See to it that no one misleads you. For many will come in My name, saying, 'I am the Christ,' and will mislead many. You will be hearing of wars and rumors of wars. See that you are not frightened, for *those things* must take place, but *that* is not yet the end. For nation will rise against nation, and kingdom against kingdom, and in various places there will be famines and earthquakes. But all these things are *merely* the beginning of birth pangs. Then they will deliver you to tribulation, and will kill you, and you will be hated by all nations because of My name. At that time many will fall away and will betray one another and hate one another. Many false prophets will arise and will mislead many. Because lawlessness is increased, most people's love will grow cold. But the one who endures to the end, he will be saved. This gospel of the kingdom shall be preached in the whole world as a testimony to all the nations, and then the end will come" (Matthew 24:4–14; cf. Jeremiah 29:8; Matthew 7:15; 10:17, 22; Mark 13:3–13; Luke 21:7–19; Revelation 6:4).

Setting: On the Mount of Olives, just east of Jerusalem. During His Olivet Discourse, after answering His disciples' questions as to when the temple will be destroyed and Jerusalem overrun, along with the signs of His coming and the end of the age, Jesus reveals the future judgments following His return.

"But when the Son of Man comes in His glory, and all the angels with Him, then He will sit on His glorious throne. All the nations will be gathered before Him; and He will separate them from one another, as the shepherd separates the sheep from the goats; and He will put the sheep on His right, and the goats on the left. Then the King will say to those on His right, 'Come, you who are blessed of My Father, inherit the kingdom prepared for you from the foundation of the world. 'For I was hungry, and you gave Me *something* to eat; I was thirsty, and you gave Me *something* to drink; I was a stranger, and you invited Me in; naked, and you clothed Me; I was sick, and you visited Me; I was in prison, and you came to Me.' Then the righteous will answer Him, 'Lord, when did we see You hungry and feed You, or thirsty, and give you *something* to drink? And when did we see You a stranger, and invite You in, or naked, and clothe You? When did we see You sick, or in prison, and come to You?' The King will answer and say to them, 'Truly I say to you, to the extent that you did it to one of these brothers of Mine, *even* the least *of them,* you did it to Me.' Then He will also say to those on His left, 'Depart from Me, accursed ones, into the eternal fire which has been prepared for the devil and his angels; for I was hungry, and you gave Me *nothing* to eat; I was thirsty, and you gave Me nothing to drink; I was a stranger, and you did not invite Me in; naked, and you did not clothe Me; sick, and in prison, and you did not visit Me.' Then they themselves also will answer, 'Lord, when did we see You hungry, or thirsty, or a stranger, or naked, or sick, or in prison, and did not take care of You?' Then He will answer them, 'Truly I say to you, to the extent that you did not do it to one of the least of these, you did not do it to Me.' These will go away into eternal punishment, but the righteous into eternal life" (Matthew 25:31–46; see Matthew 7:23; 16:27; 19:29).

Setting: On a mountain in Galilee. Following His resurrection from the dead in Jerusalem, Jesus conveys the Great Commission to His eleven remaining disciples.

And Jesus came up and spoke to them, saying, "All authority has been given to Me in heaven and on earth. Go therefore and make disciples of all the nations, baptizing them in the name of the Father and the Son and the Holy Spirit, teaching them to observe all that I commanded you; and lo, I am with you always, even to the end of the age" (Matthew 28:18–20; cf. Mark 16:15; see Daniel 7:13).

Setting: Jerusalem. Following His triumphal entry, cursing of a fig tree, and cleansing of the temple of the money changers, Jesus rebukes the Jewish religious leaders for the corrupt practices they permit in His house.

And He *began* to teach and say to them, "Is it not written, 'MY HOUSE SHALL BE CALLED A HOUSE OF PRAYER FOR ALL THE NATIONS'? But you have made it a ROBBERS' DEN" (Mark 11:17, Jesus quotes from Isaiah 56:7; Jeremiah 7:11; cf. Matthew 21:12, 13; Luke 19:45–48).

Setting: On the Mount of Olives, east of the temple in Jerusalem. After predicting the temple's destruction, Jesus responds during His Olivet Discourse to questions from Peter, James, John, and Andrew about other future events.

And Jesus began to say to them, "See to it that no one misleads you. Many will come in My name, saying, 'I am *He!*' and will mislead many. When you hear of wars and rumors of wars, do not be frightened; *those things* must take place; but *that is* not yet the end. For nation will rise up against nation, and kingdom against kingdom; there will be earthquakes in various places; there will *also be* famines. These things are *merely* the beginning of birth pangs. But be on your guard; for they will deliver you to *the* courts, and you will be flogged in *the* synagogues, and you will stand before governors and kings for My sake, as a testimony to them. The gospel must first be preached to all the nations. When they arrest you and hand you over, do not worry beforehand about what you are to say, but say whatever is given you in that hour; for it is not you who speak, but *it is* the Holy Spirit. Brother will betray brother to death, and a father *his* child; and children will rise up against parents and have them put to death. You will be hated by all because of My name, but the one who endures to the end, he will be saved" (Mark 13:5–13; cf. Matthew 24:4–14; Luke 21:7–19; see Matthew 10:17–22).

Setting: On the way from Galilee to Jerusalem. After giving a parable about riches and greed, Jesus comforts the crowd and His disciples. The scribes and Pharisees turn hostile and question Him repeatedly in an attempt to catch Him in something He might say.

And He said to His disciples, "For this reason I say to you, do not worry about *your* life, *as to* what you will eat; nor for your body, *as to* what you will put on. For life is more than food, and the body more than clothing. Consider the ravens, for they neither sow nor reap; they have no storeroom nor barn, and *yet* God feeds them; how much more valuable you are than the birds! And which of you by worrying can add a *single* hour to his life's span? If then you cannot do even a very little thing, why do you worry about other matters? Consider the lilies, how they grow: they neither toil nor spin; but I tell you, not even Solomon in all his glory clothed himself like one of these. But if God so clothes the grass in the field, which is *alive* today and tomorrow is thrown into the furnace, how much more *will He clothe* you? You men of little faith! And do not seek what you will eat and what you will drink, and do not keep worrying. For all these things the nations of the world eagerly seek; but your Father knows that you need these things. But seek His kingdom, and these things will be added to you. Do not be afraid, little flock, for your Father has chosen gladly to give you the kingdom" (Luke 12:22–32; cf. Matthew 6:25–33; see 1 Kings 10:4–7; Job 38:41).

Setting: On the Mount of Olives, east of the temple in Jerusalem. After ministering in the temple a few days before His crucifixion, and giving the disciples more details regarding future events, Jesus elaborates more during His Olivet Discourse about things to come.

"But when you see Jerusalem surrounded by armies, then recognize that her desolation is near. Then those who are in Judea must flee to the mountains, and those who are in the midst of the city must leave, and those who are in the country must not enter the city; because these are days of vengeance, so that all things which are written will be fulfilled. Woe to those who are pregnant and to those who are nursing babies in those days; for there will be a great distress upon the land and wrath to this people; and they will fall by the edge of the sword, and will be led captive into all the nations; and Jerusalem will be trampled under foot by the Gentiles until the times of the Gentiles are fulfilled"(Luke 21:20–24; see Matthew 24:15–18; Mark 13:14–16; Luke 19:43).

Setting: The Mount of Olives, just east of Jerusalem. After ministering in the temple a few days before His crucifixion, and giving His disciples more details regarding future events, Jesus speaks during His Olivet Discourse of His return.

"There will be signs in sun and moon and stars, and on the earth dismay among the nations, in perplexity at the roaring of the sea and the waves, men fainting from fear and the expectation of the things which are coming upon the world; for the powers of the heavens will be shaken. Then they will see THE SON OF MAN COMING IN A CLOUD with power and great glory. But when these things begin to take place, straighten up and lift up your heads, because your redemption is drawing near" (Luke 21:25–28, Jesus quotes from Daniel 7:13; cf. Matthew 24:29–31; Mark 13:24–27).

Setting: Jerusalem. After rising from the grave on the third day after being crucified, and appearing to two of His followers on the road to Emmaus, Jesus gives instruction to His disciples (except Thomas) about His mission on earth and the promise of future power from God.

Now He said to them, "These are My words which I spoke to you while I was still with you, that all things which are written about Me in the Law of Moses and the Prophets and the Psalms must be fulfilled." Then He opened their minds to understand the Scriptures, and He said to them, "Thus it is written, that the Christ would suffer and rise again from the dead the third day, and that repentance for forgiveness of sins would be proclaimed in His name to all the nations, beginning from Jerusalem. You are witnesses of these things. And behold, I am sending forth the promise of My Father upon you; but you are to stay in the city until you are clothed with power from on high" (Luke 24:44–49; see Matthew 28:19, 20; Acts 1:8).

Setting: On the island of Patmos (in the Aegean Sea about fifty miles southwest of Ephesus in modern Turkey). On the Lord's Day (Sunday), approximately fifty years after Jesus' resurrection, the disciple John encounters the Lord Jesus Christ, who communicates a new revelation for the apostle to record for the church in Thyatira and to six other churches in Asia.

"And to the angel of the church in Thyatira write: The Son of God, who has eyes like a flame of fire, and His feet are like burnished bronze, says this: 'I know your deeds, and your love and faith and service and perseverance, and that your deeds of late are greater than at first. But I have *this* against you, that you tolerate the woman Jezebel, who calls herself a prophetess, and she teaches and leads My bond-servants astray so that they commit *acts of* immorality and eat things sacrificed to idols. I gave her time to repent, and she does not want to repent of her immorality. Behold, I will throw her on a bed *of sickness,* and those who commit adultery with her into great tribulation, unless they repent of her deeds. And I will kill her children with pestilence, and all the churches will know that I am He who searches the minds and hearts; and I will give to each one of you according to your deeds. But I say to you, the rest who are in Thyatira, who do not hold this teaching, who have not known the deep things of Satan, as they call them—I place no other burden on you. Nevertheless what you have, hold fast until I come. He who overcomes, and he who keeps My deeds until the end, TO HIM I WILL GIVE AUTHORITY OVER THE NATIONS; AND HE SHALL RULE THEM WITH A ROD OF IRON, AS THE VESSELS OF THE POTTER ARE BROKEN TO PIECES, as I also have received *authority* from My Father; and I will give him the morning star. He who has an ear, let him hear what the Spirit says to the churches' (Revelation 2:18–29; Jesus quotes from Psalm 2:8, 9; Isaiah 30:14; see 1 Kings 16:31; Psalm 7:9; Romans 2:5; 1 Corinthians 2:10; 2 Peter 3:9; Revelation 1:14; 2:7; 3:11; 17:1–20).

NATURAL DISASTERS (See specifics such as EARTHQUAKES; FAMINES; PESTILENCE; and PLAGUES)

NATURE

Setting: The temple treasury in Jerusalem. After the scribes and Pharisees question His testimony about Himself, Jesus interacts with them regarding their ancestry and motives.

Jesus said to them, "If God were your Father, you would love Me, for I proceeded forth and have come from God, for I have not even come on My own initiative, but He sent Me. Why do you not understand what I am saying? *It is* because you cannot hear My word. You are of *your* father the devil, and you want to do the desires of your father. He was a murderer from the beginning, and does not stand in the truth because there is no truth in him. Whenever he speaks a lie, he speaks from his own *nature,* for he is a liar and the father of lies. But because I speak the truth, you do not believe Me. Which one of you convicts Me of sin? If I speak truth, why do not believe Me? He who is of God hears the words of God; for this reason you do not hear *them,* because you are not of God" (John 8:42–47; see John 8:1–41; 18:37; 1 John 3:8; 4:6; 5:1).

NAZARENE, JESUS THE

Setting: Jerusalem. After Jesus prays His high-priestly prayer on behalf of His disciples, He and they go over the ravine of the Kidron to a garden where Judas awaits to seize the Lord with a Roman cohort and officers from the chief priests and the Pharisees.

So Jesus, knowing all the things that were coming upon Him, went forth and said to them, "Whom do you seek?" They answered Him, "Jesus the Nazarene." He said to them, "I am *He.*" And Judas also, who was betraying Him, was standing with them. So when He said to them, "I am *He,*" they drew back and fell to the ground. Therefore He again asked them, "Whom do you seek?" And they said, "Jesus the Nazarene." Jesus answered, "I told you that I am *He*; so if you seek Me, let these go their way," to fulfill the word which He spoke, "Of those whom You have given Me I lost not one" (John 18:4–9; see John 6:64; 17:12).

Setting: Jerusalem. Luke, writing in Acts, presents the account of Paul's speech (following his third missionary journey) to a hostile Jewish crowd about His divine encounter with Jesus on the road to Damascus.

"But it happened that as I was on my way, approaching Damascus about noontime, a very bright light suddenly flashed from heaven all around me, and I fell to the ground, and heard a voice saying to me, 'Saul, Saul, why are you persecuting Me?' And I answered, 'Who are You, Lord?' And He said to me, 'I am Jesus the Nazarene, whom you are persecuting.' And those who were with me saw the light, to be sure, but did not understand the voice of the One who was speaking to me. And I said, 'What shall I do, Lord?' And the Lord said to me, 'Get up and go on into Damascus, and there you will be told of all that has been appointed for you to do' (Acts 22:6–10; see Acts 9:7; 26:9).

NAZARETH

[NAZARETH from hometown]

Setting: The synagogue in Jesus' hometown of Nazareth. The congregation takes offense following Jesus' teaching.

And they took offense at Him. But Jesus said to them, "A prophet is not without honor except in his hometown and in his *own* household" (Matthew 13:57; cf. Mark 6:4; see Matthew 11:6).

[NAZARETH from hometown]

Setting: The synagogue in Jesus' hometown of Nazareth. While ministering throughout the villages of Galilee, Jesus teaches in His hometown. The townspeople become offended and question His teaching, wisdom, and ability to perform miracles.

Jesus said to them, "A prophet is not without honor except in his hometown and among his *own* relatives and in his *own* household" (Mark 6:4; cf. Matthew 13:54–58).

NECK

Setting: Capernaum of Galilee. Jesus answers His disciples' question about greatness, or rank, in the kingdom of heaven.

And He called a child to Himself and set him before them, and said, "Truly I say to you, unless you are converted and become like children, you will not enter the kingdom of heaven. Whoever then humbles himself as this child, he is the greatest in the kingdom of heaven. And whoever receives one such child in My name receives Me; but whoever causes one of these little ones who believe in Me to stumble, it would be better for him to have a heavy millstone hung around his neck, and to be drowned in the depth of the sea" (Matthew 18:2–6; cf. Matthew 19:14; Mark 9:33–37, 42; Luke 9:47, 48; 17:1, 2).

Setting: Capernaum of Galilee. As Jesus teaches His disciples in private, they ask Him about greatness.

But Jesus said, "Do not hinder him, for there is no one who will perform a miracle in My name, and be able soon afterward to speak evil of Me. For he who is not against us is for us. For whoever gives you a cup of water to drink because of your name as *followers* of Christ, truly I say to you, he will not lose his reward. Whoever causes one of these little ones who believe to stumble, it would be better for him if, with a heavy millstone hung around his neck, he had been cast into the sea. If your hand causes you to stumble, cut it off; it is better for you to enter life crippled, than, having your two hands, to go into hell, into the unquenchable fire, [where THEIR WORM DOES NOT DIE, AND THE FIRE IS NOT QUENCHED.] If your foot causes you to stumble, cut it off; it is better for you to enter life lame, than, having your two feet, to be cast into hell, [where THEIR WORM DOES NOT DIE, AND THE FIRE IS NOT QUENCHED.] If your eye causes you to stumble, throw it out; it is better for you to enter the kingdom of God with one eye, than, having two eyes, to be cast into hell, where THEIR WORM DOES NOT DIE, AND THE FIRE IS NOT QUENCHED. For everyone will be salted with fire. Salt is good; but if the salt becomes unsalty, with what will you make it salty *again?* Have salt in yourselves, and be at peace with one another" (Mark 9:39–50; Jesus quotes from Isaiah 66:24; cf. Matthew 18:6–9; Luke 9:49, 50; see Matthew 5:13, 29, 30; 10:42; 12:30, 18:5, 6).

Setting: On the way from Galilee to Jerusalem. After conveying the story of the rich man and Lazarus, the Lord gives His disciples instruction on forgiveness.

He said to His disciples, "It is inevitable that stumbling blocks come, but woe to him through whom they come! It would be better for him if a millstone were hung around his neck and he were thrown into the sea, than that he would cause one of these little ones to stumble. Be on your guard! If your brother sins, rebuke him; and if he repents, forgive him. And if he sins against you seven times a day, and returns to you seven times, saying, 'I repent,' forgive him" (Luke 17:1–4; see Matthew 18:5–7, 15, 21, 22).

NEED/NEEDS (Also see BREAD, DAILY; GOD, DEPENDENCE ON; PROVISION, GOD'S; and WORRY)

Setting: Galilee. During the early part of His ministry, Jesus preaches the Sermon on the Mount to His disciples and the multitudes.

"And when you are praying, do not use meaningless repetition as the Gentiles do, for they suppose that they will be heard for their many words. So do not be like them; for your Father knows what you need before you ask Him" (Matthew 6:7, 8; see 1 Kings 18:26–29).

Setting: Galilee. During the early part of His ministry, Jesus preaches the Sermon on the Mount to His disciples and the multitudes.

"For this reason I say to you, do not be worried about your life, *as to* what you will eat or what you will drink; nor for your body, *as to* what you will put on. Is not life more than food, and the body more than clothing? Look at the birds of the air, that they do not sow, nor reap nor gather into barns, and *yet* your heavenly Father feeds them. Are you not worth much more than they? And who of you by being worried can add a *single* hour to his life? And why are you worried about clothing? Observe how the lilies of the field grow; they do not toil nor do they spin, yet I say to you that not even Solomon in all his glory clothed himself like one of these. But if God so clothes the grass of the field, which is *alive* today and tomorrow is thrown into the furnace, *will He* not much more *clothe* you? You of little faith! Do not worry then, saying 'What will we eat?' or 'What will we drink?' or 'What will be wear for clothing?" For the Gentiles eagerly seek all these things; for your heavenly Father knows that you need all these things. But seek first His kingdom and His righteousness, and all these things will be added to you. So do not worry about tomorrow; for tomorrow will care for itself. Each day has enough trouble of its own" (Matthew 6:25–34; cf. Luke 12:22–31; see 1 Kings 10:4–7; Job 35:11; Matthew 8:26).

Setting: Capernaum, near the Sea of Galilee. Jesus calls Levi (Matthew) the tax collector to be His disciple.

But when Jesus heard *this,* He said, "*It is* not those who are healthy who need a physician, but those who are sick. But go and learn what this means: 'I DESIRE COMPASSION, AND NOT SACRIFICE,' for I did not come to call the righteous, but sinners" (Matthew 9:12, 13, Jesus quotes from Hosea 6:6; cf. Mark 2:17; Luke 5:31, 32; see Mark 2:15, 16).

Setting: By the Sea of Galilee. Late in the day, after He hears the news of John the Baptist's beheading and heals the sick from the crowd following Him, Jesus miraculously feeds more than 5,000 of His countrymen.

But Jesus said to them, "They do not need to go away; you give them *something* to eat!" They said to Him, "We have here only five loaves and two fish." And He said, "Bring them here to Me" (Matthew 14:16–18; cf. Mark 6:35–44; Luke 9:12–17; John 6:4–13; see Matthew 16:9).

Setting: Entering Bethphage, just outside Jerusalem. Days before His crucifixion, after healing some blind men in Jericho, Jesus instructs two of His disciples to acquire a donkey and colt to be used in His triumphal entry into the city.

When they had approached Jerusalem and had come to Bethphage, at the Mount of Olives, then Jesus sent two disciples, saying to them, "Go into the village opposite you, and immediately you will find a donkey tied *there* and a colt with her; untie them and bring them to Me. If anyone says anything to you, you shall say, 'The Lord has need of them,' and immediately he will send them" (Matthew 21:1–3; cf. Mark 11:1–3; Luke 19:29–31).

Setting: The home of Levi in Capernaum, near the Sea of Galilee. The scribes of the Pharisees question Jesus' associating with sinners and tax collectors after He calls Levi (Matthew) the tax collector to be His disciple.

And hearing *this,* Jesus said to them, "*It is* not those who are healthy who need a physician, but those who are sick; I did not come to call the righteous, but sinners" (Mark 2:17; cf. Matthew 9:12, 13; Luke 5:29–32).

Setting: Galilee. Early in His ministry, the Pharisees question Jesus why He allows His disciples to harvest grain on the Sabbath.

And He said to them, "Have you never read what David did when he was in need and he and his companions became hungry; how he entered the house of God in the time of Abiathar *the* high priest, and ate the consecrated bread, which is not lawful for *anyone* to eat except the priests, and he also gave it to those who were with him?" Jesus said to them, "The Sabbath was made for man, and not man for the Sabbath. So the Son of Man is Lord even of the Sabbath" (Mark 2:25–28; cf. Matthew 12:1–8; Luke 6:1–5; see Exodus 23:12).

Setting: Approaching Jerusalem. As Jesus and His disciples approach the city for the Lord's impending death on the cross, He instructs two of them to obtain a colt for His triumphal entry.

As they approached Jerusalem, at Bethphage and Bethany, near the Mount of Olives, He sent two of His disciples, and said to them, "Go into the village opposite you, and immediately as you enter it, you will find a colt tied *there*, on which no one yet has ever sat; untie it and bring it *here*. If anyone says to you, 'Why are you doing this?' you say, 'The Lord has need of it'; and immediately he will send it back here" (Mark 11:1–3; cf. Matthew 21:1–3; Luke 19:29–31; see Matthew 21:4–7; Luke 19:32–35; John 12:12–15).

Setting: The home of Levi in Capernaum. At a reception for Jesus following His call of Levi (Matthew) to be His disciple, the Pharisees and their scribes question why Jesus associates with tax collectors and sinners.

And Jesus answered and said to them, "*It is* not those who are well who need a physician, but those who are sick. I have not come to call the righteous but sinners to repentance" (Luke 5:31, 32; cf. Matthew 9:10–13; Mark 2:15–17).

Setting: On the way from Galilee to Jerusalem. After revealing to His disciples how to pray, Jesus illustrates persistence in prayer.

Then He said to them, "Suppose one of you has a friend, and goes to him at midnight and says to him, 'Friend, lend me three loaves; for a friend of mine has come to me from a journey, and I have nothing to set before him'; and from inside he answers and says, 'Do not bother me; the door has already been shut and my children and I are in bed; I cannot get up and give you *anything*.' I tell you, even though he will not get up and give him *anything* because he is his friend, yet because of his persistence he will get up and give him as much as he needs. So I say to you, ask, and it will be given to you; seek, and you will find; knock, and it will be opened to you. For everyone who asks, receives; and he who seeks, finds; and to him who knocks, it will be opened" (Luke 11:5–10; cf. Matthew 7:7, 8; see Luke 18:1–5).

Setting: On the way from Galilee to Jerusalem. After giving a parable about riches and greed, Jesus comforts the crowd and His disciples. The scribes and Pharisees turn hostile and question Him repeatedly in an attempt to catch Him in something He might say.

And He said to His disciples, "For this reason I say to you, do not worry about *your* life, *as to* what you will eat; nor for your body, *as to* what you will put on. For life is more than food, and the body more than clothing. Consider the ravens, for they neither sow nor reap; they have no storeroom nor barn, and *yet* God feeds them; how much more valuable you are than the birds! And which of you by worrying can add a *single* hour to his life's span? If then you cannot do even a very little thing, why do you worry about other matters? Consider the lilies, how they grow: they neither toil nor spin; but I tell you, not even Solomon in all his glory clothed himself like one of these. But if God so clothes the grass in the field, which is *alive* today and tomorrow is thrown into the furnace, how much more *will He clothe* you? You men of little faith! And do not seek what you will eat and what you will drink, and do not keep worrying. For all these things the nations of the world eagerly seek; but your Father knows that you need these things. But seek His kingdom, and these things will be added to you. Do not be afraid, little flock, for your Father has chosen gladly to give you the kingdom" (Luke 12:22–32; cf. Matthew 6:25–33; see 1 Kings 10:4–7; Job 38:41).

Setting: On the way from Galilee to Jerusalem. After speaking a parable to the invited guests and the host at a banquet, Jesus responds to a guest's proclamation about the blessings of eating bread in the kingdom of God.

But He said to him, "A man was giving a big dinner, and he invited many; and at the dinner hour he sent his slave to say to those who had been invited, 'Come; for everything is ready now.' But they all alike began to make excuses. The first one said to him, 'I have bought a piece of land and I need to go out and look at it; please consider me excused.' Another one said, 'I have bought five yoke of oxen, and I am going to try them out; please consider me excused.' Another one said, I have married a wife, and for that reason I cannot come.' And the slave came *back* and reported this to his master. Then the head of the household became angry and said to his slave, 'Go out at once into the streets and lanes of the city and bring in here the poor and crippled and blind and lame.' And the slave said, 'Master, what you commanded has been done, and still there is room.' And the master said to the slave, 'Go out into the highways and along the hedges, and compel *them* to come in, so that my house may be filled. For I tell you, none of those men who were invited shall taste of my dinner'" (Luke 14:16–24; see Deuteronomy 24:5; Matthew 22:2–14).

Setting: On the way from Galilee to Jerusalem. After Jesus presents to large crowds the demands of discipleship, the Pharisees and scribes complain He associates with tax collectors and sinners.

So He told them this parable, saying, "What man among you, if he has a hundred sheep and has lost one of them, does not leave the ninety-nine in the open pasture and go after the one which is lost until he finds it? When he has found it, he lays it on his shoulders, rejoicing. And when he comes home, he calls together his friends and his neighbors, saying to them, 'Rejoice with me, for I have found my sheep which was lost!' I tell you that in the same way, there will be *more* joy in heaven over one sinner who repents than over ninety-nine righteous persons who need no repentance" (Luke 15:3–7; cf. Matthew 18:12–14; see Matthew 9:11–13; Luke 5:29–32).

Setting: Approaching Jerusalem. After providing a parable about stewardship in Jericho, Jesus and His disciples head to the outskirts of Jerusalem to prepare for His triumphal entry into the city and His upcoming crucifixion.

When He approached Bethphage and Bethany, near the mount that is called Olivet, He sent two of the disciples, saying, "Go into the village ahead of *you;* there, as you enter, you will find a colt tied on which no one yet has ever sat; untie it and bring it *here.* If anyone asks you, 'Why are you untying it?' you shall say, 'The Lord has need of it'" (Luke 19:29–31; cf. Matthew 21:1–3; Mark 11:1–3).

Setting: Jerusalem. Before the Passover, with His crucifixion nearing, Jesus eats supper with His disciples and assumes the role of a servant by washing their feet.

Jesus answered and said to him, "What I do you do not realize now, but you will understand hereafter." Peter said to Him, "Never shall You wash my feet!" Jesus answered him, "If I do not wash you, you have no part with Me." Simon Peter said to Him, "Lord, *then wash* not only my feet, but also my hand and my head." Jesus said to him, "He who has bathed needs only to wash his feet, but is completely clean; and you are clean, but not all *of you*. For He knew the one who was betraying Him; for this reason He said, "Not all of you are clean" (John 13:7–11; see John 6:64: 15:3).

Setting: On the island of Patmos (in the Aegean Sea about fifty miles southwest of Ephesus in modern Turkey). On the Lord's Day (Sunday), approximately fifty years after Jesus' resurrection, the disciple John encounters the Lord Jesus Christ, who communicates a new revelation for the apostle to record for the church in Laodicea and to six other churches in Asia.

"To the angel of the church in Laodicea write: The Amen, the faithful and true Witness, the Beginning of the creation of God, says this: 'I know your deeds, that you are neither cold nor hot; I wish that you were cold or hot. So because you are lukewarm, and neither hot nor cold, I will spit you out of My mouth. Because you say, "I am rich, and have become wealthy, and have need of nothing," and you do not know that you are wretched and miserable and poor and blind and naked, I advise you to buy from Me gold refined by fire so that you may become rich, and white garments so that you may clothe yourself, and *that* the shame of your nakedness will not be revealed; and eye salve to anoint your eyes so that you may see. Those whom I love, I reprove and discipline; therefore be zealous and repent. Behold, I stand at the door and knock; if anyone hears My voice and opens the door, I will come in to him and will dine with him, and he with Me. He who overcomes, I will grant to him to sit down with Me on My throne, as I also overcame and sat down with My Father on His throne. He who has an ear, let him hear what the Spirit says to the churches'" (Revelation 3:14–22; see Proverb 3:12; Hosea 12:8; John 14:23; 16:33).

NEEDLE, EYE OF A

Setting: Judea beyond the Jordan (Perea). Jesus comments to His disciples about the rich, young ruler who asks how to obtain eternal life but rejects Jesus' instruction to sell his possessions and give the proceeds to the poor.

And Jesus said to His disciples, "Truly I say to you, it is hard for a rich man to enter the kingdom of heaven. Again, I say to you, it is easier for a camel to go through the eye of a needle, than for a rich man to enter the kingdom of God" (Matthew 19:23, 24; cf. Matthew 13:22; Mark 10:23–25; Luke 18:24).

Setting: Judea beyond the Jordan (Perea). After informing a rich man how righteous believers may have treasure in heaven, Jesus conveys to His disciples the difficulty the wealthy have entering the kingdom of God.

And Jesus, looking around, said to His disciples, "How hard it will be for those who are wealthy to enter the kingdom of God!" The disciples were amazed at His words. But Jesus answered again and said to them, "Children, how hard it is to enter the kingdom of God! It is easier for a camel to go through the eye of a needle than for a rich man to enter the kingdom of God." They were even more astonished and said to Him, "Then who can be saved?" Looking at them, Jesus said, "With people it is impossible, but not with God; for all things are possible with God" (Mark 10:23–27; cf. Matthew 19:23–26; Luke 18:24, 25).

Setting: On the way from Galilee to Jerusalem. After responding to a ruler's question about obtaining eternal life, Jesus comments to him about the challenge of being wealthy and saved.

And Jesus looked at him and said, "How hard it is for those who are wealthy to enter the kingdom of God! For it is easier for a camel to go through the eye of a needle than for a rich man to enter the kingdom of God" (Luke 18:24, 25; cf. Matthew 19:23, 24; Mark 10:25).

NEEDY (See POOR)

NEGLECT

Setting: Galilee. During the early part of His ministry, Jesus preaches the Sermon on the Mount to His disciples and the multitudes.

"Whenever you fast, do not put on a gloomy face as the hypocrites *do,* for they neglect their appearance so that they will be noticed by men when they are fasting. Truly I say to you, they have their reward in full. But you, when you fast, anoint your head and wash your face so that your fasting will not be noticed by men, but by your Father who is in secret; and your Father who sees *what is done* in secret will reward you" (Matthew 6:16–18; see Matthew 6:4, 6).

[NEGLECT from neglecting]
Setting: The temple in Jerusalem. After the Jewish religious leaders test Him with questions, Jesus pronounces the fifth of eight woes on them in front of the crowds and His disciples.

"Woe to you, scribes and Pharisees, hypocrites! For you tithe the mint and dill and cummin, and have neglected the weightier provisions of the law: justice and mercy and faithfulness; but these are things you should have done without neglecting the others. You blind guides, who strain out a gnat and swallow a camel!" (Matthew 23:23, 24).

[NEGLECT from neglecting]
Setting: Galilee. The Pharisees and some of the scribes from Jerusalem question why Jesus' disciples do not follow the tradition of ceremonial hand cleansing before eating bread.

And He said to them, "Rightly did Isaiah prophesy of you hypocrites, as it is written: 'THIS PEOPLE HONORS ME WITH THEIR LIPS, BUT THEIR HEART IS FAR AWAY FROM ME. BUT IN VAIN DO THEY WORSHIP ME, TEACHING AS DOCTRINES THE PRECEPTS OF MEN.' Neglecting the commandment of God, you hold to the tradition of men." He was also saying to them, "You are experts at setting aside the commandment of God in order to keep tradition. For Moses said, 'HONOR YOUR FATHER AND YOUR MOTHER'; and, 'HE WHO SPEAKS EVIL OF FATHER OR MOTHER, IS TO BE PUT TO DEATH'; but you say, 'If a man says to *his* father or *his* mother, whatever I have that would help you is Corban (that is to say, given *to God*),' you no longer permit him to do anything for *his* father or *his* mother; *thus* invalidating the word of God by your tradition which you have handed down; and you do many things such as that" (Mark 7:6–13, Jesus quotes from Exodus 20:12; 21:17; Isaiah 29:13; cf. Matthew 15:1–6).

[NEGLECT from neglecting]
Setting: On the way from Galilee to Jerusalem. After speaking of how a lamp illuminates, the Lord has lunch with a Pharisee who is surprised He doesn't wash before eating.

But the Lord said to him, "Now you Pharisees clean the outside of the cup and of the platter; but inside of you, you are full of robbery and wickedness. You foolish ones, did not He who made the outside make the inside also? But give that which is within as charity, and then all things are clean for you. But woe to you Pharisees! You pay tithe of mint and rue and every *kind of* garden herb, and *yet* disregard justice and the love of God; but these are the things you should have done without neglecting the others. Woe to you Pharisees! For you love the chief seats in the synagogues and the respectful greetings in the market places. Woe to you! For you are like concealed tombs, and the people who walk over *them* are unaware *of it*" (Luke 11:39–44; cf. Matthew 23:6, 7, 23–27; see Matthew 15:2; Titus 1:15).

[NEGLECT from neglected]
Setting: On the way from Galilee to Jerusalem. Jesus conveys the illustration of the prodigal son because the Pharisees and scribes complain He associates with tax collectors and sinners.

And He said, "A man had two sons. The younger of them said to his father, 'Father, give me the share of the estate that falls to me.' So he divided his wealth between them. And not many days later, the younger son gathered everything together and went on a journey into a distant country, and there he squandered his estate with loose living. Now when he had spent everything, a severe famine occurred in that country, and he began to be impoverished. So he went and hired himself out to one of the citizens of that country, and he sent him into his fields to feed swine. And he would have gladly filled his stomach with the pods that the swine were eating, and no one was giving *anything* to him. But when he came to his senses, he said, 'How many of my father's hired men have more than enough bread, but I am dying here with hunger! I will get up and go to my father, and will say to him, "Father, I have sinned against heaven, and in your sight; I am no longer worthy to be called your son; make me as one of your hired men."' So he got up and came to his father. But while he was still a long way off, his father saw him and felt compassion *for him,* and ran and embraced him and kissed him. And the son said to him, "Father, I have sinned against heaven and in your sight; I am no longer worthy to be called your son.' But the father said to his slaves, 'Quickly bring out the best robe and put it on him, and put a ring on his hand and sandals on his feet; and bring the fattened calf, kill it, and let us eat and celebrate; for this son of mine was dead and has come to life again; he was lost and has been found.' And they began to celebrate. Now his older son was in the field, when he came and approached the house, he heard music and dancing. And he summoned one of the servants and *began* inquiring what these things could be. And he said to him, 'Your brother has come, and your father has killed the fattened calf because he has received him back safe and sound. 'But he became angry and was not willing to go in; and his father came out and *began* pleading with him. But he answered and said to his father, 'Look! For so many years I have been serving you and I have never neglected a command of yours; and *yet* you have never given me a young goat, so that I might celebrate with my friends; but when this son of yours came, who has devoured your wealth with prostitutes, you killed the fattened calf for him. 'And he said to him, 'Son, you have always been with me, and all that is mine is yours. But we had to celebrate and rejoice, for this brother of yours was dead and *has begun* to live, and was lost and has been found'" (Luke 15:11–32; see Proverb 29:2; Luke 15:1, 2).

NEIGHBOR (Also see GOLDEN RULE; and NEIGHBORS)

Setting: Galilee. During the early part of His ministry, Jesus preaches the Sermon on the Mount to His disciples and the multitudes.

"You have heard that it was said, 'YOU SHALL LOVE YOUR NEIGHBOR and hate your enemy.' But I say to you, love your enemies and pray for those who persecute you, so that you may be sons of your Father who is in heaven; for He causes His sun to rise on *the* evil and *the* good, and sends rain on *the* righteous and *the* unrighteous. For if you love those who love you, what reward do you have? Do not even the tax collectors do the same? If you greet only your brothers, what more are you doing *than others?* Do not even the Gentiles do the same? Therefore, you are to be perfect, as your heavenly Father is perfect" (Matthew 5:43–48, Jesus quotes from Leviticus 19:18; cf. Leviticus 19:2; Luke 6:27–36).

Setting: Judea beyond the Jordan (Perea). Jesus shares with a rich, young ruler how to obtain eternal life.

And He said to him, "Why are you asking Me about what is good? There is *only* One who is good; but if you wish to enter into life, keep the commandments." *Then* he said to Him, 'Which ones?' And Jesus said, "YOU SHALL NOT COMMIT MURDER; YOU SHALL NOT COMMIT ADULTERY; YOU SHALL NOT STEAL; YOU SHALL NOT BEAR FALSE WITNESS; HONOR YOUR FATHER AND MOTHER; and YOU SHALL

LOVE YOUR NEIGHBOR AS YOURSELF." The young man said to Him, "All these things I have kept; what am I still lacking?" Jesus said to him, "If you wish to complete go *and* sell your possessions and give to *the* poor, and you will have treasure in heaven; and come, follow Me" (Matthew 19:16–22, Jesus quotes from Exodus 20:13–15; Leviticus 19:18; cf. Leviticus 18:5; Mark 10:17–21; Luke 10:25–28; 12:33; 18:18–24).

Setting: he temple in Jerusalem. A Pharisee lawyer asks Jesus which is the great commandment of the Law, in order to test Him as He teaches.

And He said to him, " 'YOU SHALL LOVE THE LORD YOUR GOD WITH ALL YOUR HEART, AND WITH ALL YOUR SOUL, AND WITH ALL YOUR MIND.' This is the great and foremost commandment. The second is like it, 'YOU SHALL LOVE YOUR NEIGHBOR AS YOURSELF.' On these two commandments depend the whole Law and the Prophets" (Matthew 22:37–40; Jesus quotes from Leviticus 19:18; Deuteronomy 6:5; cf. Mark 12:28–34; see Matthew 7:12).

Setting: The temple in Jerusalem. With the Pharisees and Herodians failing to trap Jesus in a statement, one of the scribes asks Him which commandment is foremost.

Jesus answered, "The foremost is, 'HEAR, O ISRAEL! THE LORD OUR GOD IS ONE LORD; AND YOU SHALL LOVE THE LORD YOUR GOD WITH ALL YOUR HEART, AND WITH ALL YOUR SOUL, AND WITH ALL YOUR MIND AND WITH ALL YOUR STRENGTH.' The second is this, 'YOU SHALL LOVE YOUR NEIGHBOR AS YOURSELF.' There is no other commandment greater than these" (Mark 12:29–31, Jesus quotes from Deuteronomy 6:4, 5; Leviticus 19:18; cf. Matthew 22:34–40).

Setting: On the way from Galilee to Jerusalem. After Jesus tells His disciples in private the privilege they are experiencing by living in the time of the Messiah, a lawyer tests Him.

And a lawyer stood up and put Him to the test, saying, "Teacher, what shall I do to inherit eternal life?" And He said to him, "What is written in the Law? How does it read to you?" And he answered, "YOU SHALL LOVE THE LORD YOUR GOD WITH ALL YOUR HEART, AND WITH ALL YOUR SOUL, AND WITH ALL YOUR STRENGTH, AND WITH ALL YOUR MIND; AND YOUR NEIGHBOR AS YOURSELF." And He said to him, "You have answered correctly; DO THIS AND YOU WILL LIVE" (Luke 10:25–28, Jesus quotes from Leviticus 18:5; see Deuteronomy 6:5; Matthew 19:16–19).

Setting: On the way from Galilee to Jerusalem. While being tested by a lawyer, Jesus tells him the story of the good Samaritan.

Jesus replied and said, "A man was going down from Jerusalem to Jericho, and fell among robbers, and they stripped him and beat him, and went away leaving him half dead. And by chance a priest was going down on that road, and when he saw him, he passed by on the other side. Likewise a Levite also, when he came to the place and saw him, passed by on the other side. But a Samaritan, who was on a journey, came upon him; and when he saw him, he felt compassion, and came to him and bandaged up his wounds, pouring oil and wine on *them;* and he put him on his own beast, and brought him to an inn and took care of him. On the next day he took out two denarii and gave them to the innkeeper and said, 'Take care of him; and whatever more you spend, when I return I will repay you.' Which of these three do you think proved to be a neighbor to the man who fell into the robbers' *hands?*" And he said, "The one who showed mercy toward him." Then Jesus said to him, "Go and do the same" (Luke 10:30–37).

NEIGHBORS (Also see NEIGHBOR)

[NEIGHBORS from people]

Setting: Galilee. During the early part of His ministry, Jesus preaches the Sermon on the Mount to His disciples and the multitudes.

"In everything, therefore, treat people the same way you want them to treat you, for this is the Law and the Prophets" (Matthew 7:12; cf. Matthew 22:20; Luke 6:3).

[NEIGHBORS from these brothers of Mine]

Setting: On the Mount of Olives, just east of Jerusalem. During His Olivet Discourse, after answering His disciples' questions as to when the temple will be destroyed and Jerusalem overrun, along with the signs of His coming and the end of the age, Jesus reveals the future judgments following His return.

"But when the Son of Man comes in His glory, and all the angels with Him, then He will sit on His glorious throne. All the nations will be gathered before Him; and He will separate them from one another, as the shepherd separates the sheep from the goats; and He will put the sheep on His right, and the goats on the left. Then the King will say to those on His right, 'Come, you who are blessed of My Father, inherit the kingdom prepared for you from the foundation of the world. 'For I was hungry, and you gave Me *something* to eat; I was thirsty, and you gave Me *something* to drink; I was a stranger, and you invited Me in; naked, and you clothed Me; I was sick, and you visited Me; I was in prison, and you came to Me.' Then the righteous will answer Him, 'Lord, when did we see You hungry and feed You, or thirsty, and give you *something* to drink? And when did we see You a stranger, and invite You in, or naked, and clothe You? When did we see You sick, or in prison, and come to You?' The King will answer and say to them, 'Truly I say to you, to the extent that you did it to one of these brothers of Mine, *even* the least *of them,* you did it to Me.' Then He will also say to those on His left, 'Depart from Me, accursed ones, into the eternal fire which has been prepared for the devil and his angels; for I was hungry, and you gave Me *nothing* to eat; I was thirsty, and you gave Me nothing to drink; I was a stranger, and you did not invite Me in; naked, and you did not clothe Me; sick, and in prison, and you did not visit Me.' Then they themselves also will answer, 'Lord, when did we see You hungry, or thirsty, or a stranger, or naked, or sick, or in prison, and did not take care of You?' Then He will answer them, 'Truly I say to you, to the extent that you did not do it to one of the least of these, you did not do it to Me.' These will go away into eternal punishment, but the righteous into eternal life" (Matthew 25:31–46; see Matthew 7:23; 16:27; 19:29).

Setting: On the way from Galilee to Jerusalem. After Jesus, observing the invited guests of a Pharisee leader selecting places of honor at the table, speaks a parable to them, He comments to the host about the people to invite in the future.

And He also went on to say to the one who had invited Him, "When you give a luncheon or a dinner, do not invite your friends or your brothers or your relatives or rich neighbors, otherwise they may also invite you in return and *that* will be your repayment. But when you give a reception, invite *the* poor, *the* crippled, *the* lame, *the* blind, and you will be blessed, since they do not have *the means* to repay you; for you will be repaid at the resurrection of the righteous" (Luke 14:12–14; see Luke 14:1, 2; John 5:28, 29).

Setting: On the way from Galilee to Jerusalem. After Jesus presents to large crowds the demands of discipleship, the Pharisees and scribes complain He associates with tax collectors and sinners.

So He told them this parable, saying, "What man among you, if he has a hundred sheep and has lost one of them, does not leave the ninety-nine in the open pasture and go after the one which is lost until he finds it? When he has found it, he lays it on his shoulders, rejoicing. And when he comes home, he calls together his friends and his neighbors, saying to them, 'Rejoice with me, for I have found my sheep which was lost!' I tell you that in the same way, there will be *more* joy in heaven over one sinner who repents than over ninety-nine righteous persons who need no repentance" (Luke 15:3–7; cf. Matthew 18:12–14; see Matthew 9:11–13; Luke 5:29–32).

Setting: On the way from Galilee to Jerusalem. Jesus conveys the principles of the lost sheep and the lost coin because the Pharisees and scribes complain He associates with tax collectors and sinners.

"So He told them this parable, saying, "What man among you, if he has a hundred sheep and has lost one of them, does not leave the ninety-nine in the open pasture and go after the one which is lost until he finds it? When he has found it, he lays it on his shoulders, rejoicing. And when he comes home, he calls together his friends and his neighbors, saying to them, 'Rejoice with me, for I have found my sheep which was lost!' I tell you that in the same way, there will be more joy in heaven over one sinner who repents than over ninety-nine righteous persons who need no repentance. Or what woman, if she has ten silver coins and loses one coin, does not light a lamp and sweep the house and search carefully until she finds it? When she has found it, she calls together her friends and neighbors, saying, 'Rejoice with me, for I have found the coin which I had lost!' In the same way, I tell you, there is joy in the presence of the angels of God over one sinner who repents" (Luke 15:3–10).

NEIGHBORS, RICH (See NEIGHBORS)

NEST (Also see BIRDS; and NESTS)

Setting: By the Sea of Galilee. Because the Jewish religious leaders are rejecting His message, Jesus continues teaching the crowds with the Parable of the Mustard Seed.

He presented another parable to them, saying, "The kingdom of heaven is like a mustard seed, which a man took and sowed in his field; and this is smaller than all other seeds, but when it is full grown, it is larger than the garden plants and becomes a tree, so that THE BIRDS OF THE AIR come and NEST IN ITS BRANCHES" (Matthew 13:31, 32, Jesus quotes from Ezekiel 17:23; cf. Mark 4:30–32; Luke 13:18, 19).

Setting: Galilee. After giving the Parable of the Sower and the Parable of the Seed, Jesus continues teaching His disciples by presenting the Parable of the Mustard Seed.

And He said, "How shall we picture the kingdom of God, or by what parable shall we present it? *It is* like a mustard seed, which, when sown upon the soil, though it is smaller than all the seeds that are upon the soil, yet when it is sown, it grows up and becomes larger than all the garden plants and forms large branches; so that THE BIRDS OF THE AIR can NEST UNDER ITS SHADE" (Mark 4:30–32, Jesus quotes from Ezekiel 17:23; cf. Matthew 13:31, 32; Luke 13:18, 19).

[NEST from nested]

Setting: On the way from Galilee to Jerusalem. Jesus conveys the Parable of the Mustard Seed and the Parable of the Leaven after responding to a synagogue official's anger when the Lord heals a woman, sick eighteen years, in the synagogue on the Sabbath.

So He was saying, "What is the kingdom of God like, and to what shall I compare it? It is like a mustard seed which a man took and threw into his own garden; and it grew and became a tree, and THE BIRDS OF THE AIR NESTED IN ITS BRANCHES." And again He said, "To what shall I compare the kingdom of God? It is like leaven, which a woman took and hid in three pecks of flour until it was all leavened" (Luke 13:18–21, Jesus quotes from Ezekiel 17:23; cf. Matthew 13:31–34; Mark 4:30–32).

NESTS (Also see BIRDS; and NEST)

Setting: By the Sea of Galilee. Following a time of casting out evil spirits from the demon-possessed and healing the ill in fulfillment of Isaiah 53:4, Jesus lays out to an inquiring scribe the demands of discipleship.

Then a scribe came and said to Him, "Teacher, I will follow You wherever you go." Jesus said to him, "The foxes have holes and the birds of the air *have* nests, but the Son of Man has nowhere to lay His head." Another of the disciples said to Him, "Lord, permit me first to go and bury my father." But Jesus said to him, "Follow Me, and allow the dead to bury their own dead" (Matthew 8:19–22; cf. Luke 9:57–60).

Setting: On the way from Galilee to Jerusalem. The Lord responds to someone seeking to follow Him.

And Jesus said to him, "The foxes have holes and the birds of the air *have* nests, but the Son of Man has nowhere to lay His head" (Luke 9:58; cf. Matthew 8:19–22).

NET (Also see DRAGNET; and NETS)

Setting: By the Sea of Galilee (Tiberias). During His third post-resurrection appearance to His disciples, Jesus directs them to a great catch of fish following their unsuccessful night of fishing.

So Jesus said to them, "Children, you do not have any fish, do you?" They answered Him, "No." And He said to them, "Cast the net on the right-hand side of the boat and you will find a *catch*." So they cast, and then they were not able to haul it in because of the great number of fish (John 21:5, 6; see Luke 5:4).

NETS (Also see NET)

Setting: By the Sea of Galilee. After teaching the people from Simon's (Peter) boat, Jesus calls Simon, James, and John to follow Him. (This appears to be a permanent call as Simon and other companions are with Him earlier in Mark 1:35–39 and Luke 4:38, 39.)

When He had finished speaking, He said to Simon, "Put out into the deep water and let down your nets for a catch." ". . . and so also *were* James and John, sons of Zebedee, who were partners with Simon. And Jesus said to Simon, "Do not fear, from now on you will be catching men" (Luke 5:4, 10; see John 21:6).

NEW COMMANDMENT (Listed under COMMANDMENT, NEW)

NEW COVENANT (Listed under COVENANT, NEW)

NEW COVENANT IN MY BLOOD (Listed under BLOOD, NEW COVENANT IN MY)

NEW NAME (Listed under NAME, NEW)

NEW TONGUES (Listed under TONGUES, NEW)

NEWS, GOOD (See GOSPEL)

NICOLAITANS

Setting: On the island of Patmos (in the Aegean Sea about fifty miles southwest of Ephesus in modern Turkey). On the Lord's Day (Sunday), approximately fifty years after Jesus' resurrection, the disciple John encounters the Lord Jesus Christ, who communicates a new revelation for the apostle to record for the church in Ephesus and to six other churches in Asia.

"To the angel of the church in Ephesus write: The One who holds the seven stars in His right hand, the One who walks among the seven golden lampstands, says this: 'I know your deeds and your toil and perseverance, and that you cannot tolerate evil men, and you put to the test those who call themselves apostles, and they are not, and you found them *to be* false; and you have perseverance and have endured for My name's sake, and have not grown weary. But I have *this* against you, that you have left your first love. Therefore remember from where you have fallen, and repent and do the deeds you did at first; or else I am coming to you and will remove your lampstand out of its place—unless you repent. Yet this you do have, that you hate the deeds of the Nicolaitans, which I also hate. He who has an ear, let him hear what the Spirit says to the churches. To him who overcomes, I will grant to eat of the tree of life which is in the Paradise of God' " (Revelation 2:1–7; see Genesis 2:9; Ezekiel 28:13; 1 John 4:1; Revelation 1:10, 11, 19, 20; 2:15, 16).

Setting: On the island of Patmos (in the Aegean Sea about fifty miles southwest of Ephesus in modern Turkey). On the Lord's Day (Sunday), approximately fifty years after Jesus' resurrection, the disciple John encounters the Lord Jesus Christ, who communicates a new revelation for the apostle to record for the church in Pergamum and to six other churches in Asia.

"And to the angel of the church in Pergamum write: The One who has the sharp two-edged sword says this: 'I know where you dwell, where Satan's throne is; and you hold fast My name, and did not deny My faith even in the days of Antipas, My witness, My faithful one, who was killed among you, where Satan dwells. But I have a few things against you, because you have there some who hold the teaching of Balaam, who kept teaching Balak to put a stumbling block before the sons of Israel, to eat things sacrificed to idols and to commit *acts of* immorality. So you also have some who in the same way hold the teaching of the Nicolaitans. Therefore repent; or else I am coming to you quickly, and I will make war against them with the sword of My mouth. He who has an ear, let him hear what the Spirit says to the churches. To him who overcomes, to him I will give *some* of the hidden manna, and I will give him a white stone, and a new name written on the stone which no one knows but he who receives it' (Revelation 2:12–17; see Numbers 25:1–3; Isaiah 62:2; Revelation 1:16; 2:5, 6, 16).

NIGHT (NIGHT, TIME OF THE is a separate entry; also see EVENING; and MIDNIGHT)

Setting: On the way to the Mount of Olives. After celebrating the Passover meal in Jerusalem, prior to His betrayal by Judas, Jesus states that all His disciples will deny Him that very day.

Then Jesus said to them, "You will all fall away because of Me this night, for it is written, 'I WILL STRIKE DOWN THE SHEPHERD, AND THE SHEEP OF THE FLOCK SHALL BE SCATTERED.' But after I have been raised, I will go ahead of you to Galilee." But Peter said to Him, '*Even* though all may fall away because of You, I will never fall away.' Jesus said to him, "Truly I say to you that this *very* night, before a rooster crows, you will deny Me three times" (Matthew 26:31–34, Jesus quotes from Zechariah 13:7; cf. Mark 14:26–31; see Matthew 28:7, 10, 16; John 13:37).

Setting: Galilee. Following His explanation of the Parable of the Sower to His disciples, Jesus conveys the Parable of the Seed.

And He was saying, "The kingdom of God is like a man who casts seed upon the soil; and he goes to bed at night and gets up by day, and the seed sprouts and grows—how, he himself does not know. The soil produces crops by itself; first the blade, then the head, then the mature grain in the head. But when the crop permits, he immediately puts in the sickle, because the harvest has come" (Mark 4:26–29; see Joel 3:13).

Setting: A borrowed upper room in Jerusalem. After Jesus and His twelve disciples celebrate the Passover and He institutes the Lord's Supper, they go to the Mount of Olives.

And Jesus said to them, "You will all fall away, because it is written, 'I WILL STRIKE DOWN THE SHEPHERD, AND THE SHEEP SHALL BE SCATTERED.' But after I have been raised, I will go ahead of you to Galilee." But Peter said to Him, "*Even* though all may fall away, yet I will not." And Jesus said to him, "Truly I say to you, that this very night, before a rooster crows twice, you yourself will deny Me three times" (Mark 14:27–30, Jesus quotes from Zechariah 13:7; cf. Matthew 26:30–34; see Mark 14:72).

Setting: On the way from Galilee to Jerusalem. After the scribes and Pharisees turn hostile and question Him repeatedly in an attempt to catch Him in something He might say, Jesus responds to a question from the crowd and gives a parable about riches and greed

And He told them a parable, saying, "The land of a rich man was very productive. And he began reasoning to himself, saying, 'What shall I do, since I have no place to store my crops?' Then he said, 'This is what I will do: I will tear down my barns and build larger ones, and here I will store all my grain and my goods. And I will say to my soul, "Soul, you have many goods laid up for many years *to come;* take your ease, eat, drink *and* be merry."' "But God said to him, 'You fool! This *very* night your soul is required of you; and *now* who will own what you have prepared?' So is the man who stores up treasure for himself, and is not rich toward God" (Luke 12:16–21; see Job 27:8; Psalm 39:6; Ecclesiastes 12:9; Philippians 2:3).

Setting: On the way from Galilee to Jerusalem. After the Pharisees question Him about the coming of the kingdom of God, Jesus tells His disciples of His second coming.

And He said to the disciples, "The days will come when you will long to see one of the days of the Son of Man, and you will not see it. They will say to you, 'Look there! Look here!' Do not go away, and do not run after *them.* For just like the lightning, when it flashes out of one part of the sky, shines to the other part of the sky, so will the Son of Man be in His day. But first He must suffer many things and be rejected by this generation. And just as it happened in the days of Noah, so it will be also in the days of the Son of Man: they were eating, they were drinking, they were marrying, they were being given in marriage, until the day that Noah entered the ark, and the flood came and destroyed them all. It was the same as happened in the days of Lot: they were eating, they were drinking, they were buying, they were selling, they were planting, they were building; but on the day that Lot went out from Sodom it rained fire and brimstone from heaven and destroyed them all. It will be just the same on the day that the Son of Man is revealed. On that day, the one who is on the housetop and whose goods are in the house must not go down to take them out; and likewise the one who is in the field must not turn back. Remember Lot's wife. Whoever seeks to keep his life will lose it, and whoever loses *his life* will preserve it. I tell you, on that night there will be two in one bed; one will be taken and the other will be left. There will be two women grinding at the same place; one will be taken and the other will be left. [Two men will be in the field; one will be taken and the other will be left."] And answering they said to Him, "Where, Lord?" And He said to them, "Where the body *is*, there also the vultures will be gathered" (Luke 17:22–37; see Genesis 19; Matthew 10:39; 16:21, 27; 24:17–28, 37–41).

Setting: On the way from Galilee to Jerusalem. After telling His disciples of His second coming, Jesus instructs them about persistence in prayer.

Now He was telling them a parable to show that at all times they ought to pray and not to lose heart, saying, "In a certain city there was a judge who did not fear God and did not respect man. There was a widow in that city, and she kept coming to him, saying, 'Give me legal protection from my opponent.' For a while he was unwilling; but afterward he said to himself, 'Even though I do not fear God nor respect man, yet because this woman bothers me, I will give her legal protection, otherwise by continually coming she will wear me out.'" And the Lord said, "Hear what the unrighteous judge said; now, will not God bring about justice for His elect who cry to Him day and night, and will He delay long over them? I tell you that He will bring about justice for them quickly. However, when the Son of Man comes, will He find faith on the earth?" (Luke 18:1–8; see Luke 11:5–10).

Setting: The temple treasury in Jerusalem. After Jesus avoids being stoned by the scribes and Pharisees, His disciples wonder if blindness is caused by sin as the Lord heals a man born blind.

Jesus answered, "*It was* neither *that* this man sinned, nor his parents; but *it was* so that the works of God might be displayed in him. We must work the works of Him who sent Me as long as it is day; night is coming when no one can work. While I am in the world, I am the Light of the world." When He had said this, He spat on the ground, and made clay of the spittle, and applied the clay to his eyes, and said to him, "Go, wash in the pool of Siloam" (which is translated, Sent). So he went away and washed, and came *back* seeing (John 9:3–7; see John 8:12; 11:4; 12:46).

Setting: Beyond the Jordan. While He and His disciples are avoiding the Jerusalem Pharisees, Jesus receives word from Lazarus's sisters in Bethany of His friend's sickness and decides to go there.

Then after this He said to the disciples, "Let us go to Judea again." The disciples said to Him, "Rabbi, the Jews were just now seeking to stone You, and are You going there again?" Jesus answered, "Are there not twelve hours in the day? If anyone walks in the day, he does not stumble, because he sees the light of this world. But if anyone walks in the night, he stumbles, because the light is not in him." This He said, and after that He said to them, "Our friend Lazarus has fallen asleep; but I go, so that I may awaken him out of sleep" (John 11:7–11; see John 8:59; 10:39).

NIGHT, TIME OF THE

Setting: On the Mount of Olives, just east of Jerusalem. During His Olivet Discourse, after answering His disciples' questions as to when the temple will be destroyed and Jerusalem overrun, along with the signs of His coming and the end of the age, Jesus reemphasizes to His disciples that they should be on the alert for His return.

"Therefore be on the alert, for you do not know which day your Lord is coming. But be sure of this, that if the head of the house had known at what time of the night the thief was coming, he would have been on the alert and would not have allowed his house to be broken into. For this reason you also must be ready; for the Son of Man is coming at an hour when you do not think *He will*. Who then is the faithful and sensible slave whom his master put in charge of his household to give their food at the proper time?

Blessed is that slave whom his master finds so doing when he comes. Truly I say to you that he will put him in charge of all his possessions. But if that evil slave says in his heart, 'My master is not coming for a long time,' and begins to beat his fellow slaves and eat and drink with drunkards; the master of that slave will come on a day when he does not expect *him* and at an hour which he does not know, and will cut him in pieces and assign him a place with the hypocrites; in that place there will be weeping and gnashing of teeth" (Matthew 24:42–51; cf. Mark 13:33–37; Luke 12:39–46; Luke 21:34–36; see Matthew 8:11, 12; 25:21–23).

NIGHTS, THREE

Setting: Galilee. After Jesus warns the Pharisees about the unpardonable sin and their future judgment, some Pharisees and scribes ask Him to perform a miraculous sign for them in front of the crowds.

But He answered and said to them, "An evil and adulterous generation craves for a sign; and *yet* no sign will be given to it but the sign of Jonah the prophet; for just as JONAH WAS THREE DAYS AND THREE NIGHTS IN THE BELLY OF THE SEA MONSTER, so will the Son of Man be three days and three nights in the heart of the earth. The men of Nineveh will stand up with this generation at the judgment, and will condemn it because they repented at the preaching of Jonah; and behold, something greater than Jonah is here. *The* Queen of *the* South will rise up with this generation at the judgment and will condemn it, because she came from the ends of the earth to hear the wisdom of Solomon; and behold, something greater than Solomon is here" (Matthew 12:39–42; Jesus quotes from Jonah 1:17; cf. 1 Kings 10:1; Jonah 3:5; Matthew 16:1, 4; 12:38; Luke 11:29).

NINE

Setting: On the way from Galilee to Jerusalem. The Lord stops to heal ten lepers who ask for cleansing.

When He saw them, He said to them, "Go and show yourselves to the priests." And as they were going, they were cleansed. Now one of them, when he saw that he had been healed, turned back, glorifying God with a loud voice, and he fell on his face at His feet, giving thanks to Him. And he was a Samaritan. Then Jesus answered and said, "Were there not ten cleansed? But the nine—where are they? Was no one found who returned to give glory to God, except this foreigner?" And He said to him, "Stand up and go; your faith has made you well" (Luke 17:14–19; see Leviticus 14:1–32).

NINETY-NINE

Setting: Capernaum of Galilee. Jesus illustrates to His disciples the value of little ones.

"What do you think? If any man has a hundred sheep, and one of them has gone astray, does he not leave the ninety-nine on the mountains and go and search for the one that is straying? If it turns out that he finds it, truly I say to you, he rejoices over it more than the ninety-nine which have not gone astray. So it is not *the* will of your Father who is in heaven that one of these little ones perish" (Matthew 18:12–14; cf. Luke 15:4–7).

Setting: On the way from Galilee to Jerusalem. After Jesus presents to large crowds the demands of discipleship, the Pharisees and scribes complain He associates with tax collectors and sinners.

So He told them this parable, saying, "What man among you, if he has a hundred sheep and has lost one of them, does not leave the ninety-nine in the open pasture and go after the one which is lost until he finds it? When he has found it, he lays it on his shoulders, rejoicing. And when he comes home, he calls together his friends and his neighbors, saying to them, 'Rejoice with me, for I have found my sheep which was lost!' I tell you that in the same way, there will be *more* joy in heaven over one sinner who repents than over ninety-nine righteous persons who need no repentance" (Luke 15:3–7; cf. Matthew 18:12–14; see Matthew 9:11–13; Luke 5:29–32).

NINEVEH (Also see JONAH)

Setting: Galilee. After Jesus warns the Pharisees about the unpardonable sin and their future judgment, some Pharisees and scribes ask Him to perform a miraculous sign for them in front of the crowds.

But He answered and said to them, "An evil and adulterous generation craves for a sign; and *yet* no sign will be given to it but the sign of Jonah the prophet; for just as JONAH WAS THREE DAYS AND THREE NIGHTS IN THE BELLY OF THE SEA MONSTER, so will the Son of Man be three days and three nights in the heart of the earth. The men of Nineveh will stand up with this generation at the judgment, and will condemn it because they repented at the preaching of Jonah; and behold, something greater than Jonah is here. *The* Queen of *the* South will rise up with this generation at the judgment and will condemn it, because she came from the ends of the earth to hear the wisdom of Solomon; and behold, something greater than Solomon is here" (Matthew 12:39–42; Jesus quotes from Jonah 1:17; cf. 1 Kings 10:1; Jonah 3:5; Matthew 16:1, 4; Luke 11:29).

Setting: On the way from Galilee to Jerusalem. After revealing a problem with exorcism and responding to a blessing from a woman in the crowd, Jesus tells the increasing crowds of the sign of Jonah.

As the crowds were increasing, He began to say, "This generation is a wicked generation; it seeks for a sign, and *yet* no sign will be given to it but the sign of Jonah. For just as Jonah became a sign to the Ninevites, so will the Son of Man be to this generation. The Queen of the South will rise up with the men of this generation at the judgment and condemn them, because she came from the ends of the earth to hear the wisdom of Solomon; and behold, something greater than Solomon is here. The men of Nineveh will stand up with this generation at the judgment and condemn it, because they repented at the preaching of Jonah; and behold, something greater than Jonah is here" (Luke 11:29–32; cf. Matthew 16:4; see 1 Kings 10:1–10; Jonah 3:4, 5).

NINEVITES

Setting: On the way from Galilee to Jerusalem. After revealing a problem with exorcism and responding to a blessing from a woman in the crowd, Jesus tells the increasing crowds of the sign of Jonah.

As the crowds were increasing, He began to say, "This generation is a wicked generation; it seeks for a sign, and *yet* no sign will be given to it but the sign of Jonah. For just as Jonah became a sign to the Ninevites, so will the Son of Man be to this generation. The Queen of the South will rise up with the men of this generation at the judgment and condemn them, because she came from the ends of the earth to hear the wisdom of Solomon; and behold, something greater than Solomon is here. The men of Nineveh will stand up with this generation at the judgment and condemn it, because they repented at the preaching of Jonah; and behold, something greater than Jonah is here" (Luke 11:29–32; cf. Matthew 16:4; see 1 Kings 10:1–10; Jonah 3:4, 5).

NOAH (Also see ARK)

Setting: On the Mount of Olives, just east of Jerusalem. During His Olivet Discourse, after answering His disciples' questions as to when the temple will be destroyed and Jerusalem overrun, along with the signs of His coming and the end of the age, Jesus teaches them the Parable of the Fig Tree.

"Now learn the parable from the fig tree: when its branch has already become tender and puts forth its leaves, you know that summer is near; so, you too, when you see all these things, recognize that He is near, *right* at the door. Truly, I say to you, this generation will not pass away until all these things take place. Heaven and earth will pass away, but My words will not pass away. But of that day and hour no one knows, not even the angels of heaven, nor the Son, but the Father alone. For the coming of the Son of Man will be just like the days of Noah. For as in those days before the flood they were eating and drinking, marrying and giving in marriage, until the day that Noah entered the ark, and they did not understand until the flood came and took them all away; so will the coming of the Son of Man be. Then there will be two men in the field; one will be taken and one will be left. Two women *will be* grinding at the mill; one will be taken and one will be left" (Matthew 24:32–41; cf. Mark 13:28–32; Luke 17:34–36; 21:28–33; see Genesis 6:5; 7:7; Matthew 5:18; 10:23; James 5:9).

Setting: On the way from Galilee to Jerusalem. After the Pharisees question Him about the coming of the kingdom of God, Jesus tells His disciples of His second coming.

And He said to the disciples, "The days will come when you will long to see one of the days of the Son of Man, and you will not see it. They will say to you, 'Look there! Look here!' Do not go away, and do not run after *them*. For just like the lightning, when it flashes out of one part of the sky, shines to the other part of the sky, so will the Son of Man be in His day. But first He must suffer many things and be rejected by this generation. And just as it happened in the days of Noah, so it will be also in the days of the Son of Man: they were eating, they were drinking, they were marrying, they were being given in marriage, until the day that Noah entered the ark, and the flood came and destroyed them all. It was the same as happened in the days of Lot: they were eating, they were drinking, they were buying, they were selling, they were planting, they were building; but on the day that Lot went out from Sodom it rained fire and brimstone from heaven and destroyed them all. It will be just the same on the day that the Son of Man is revealed. On that day, the one who is on the housetop and whose goods are in the house must not go down to take them out; and likewise the one who is in the field must not turn back. Remember Lot's wife. Whoever seeks to keep his life will lose it, and whoever loses *his life* will preserve it. I tell you, on that night there will be two in one bed; one will be taken and the other will be left. There will be two women grinding at the same place; one will be taken and the other will be left. [Two men will be in the field; one will be taken and the other will be left."] And answering they said to Him, "Where, Lord?" And He said to them, "Where the body *is*, there also the vultures will be gathered" (Luke 17:22–37; see Genesis 19; Matthew 10:39; 16:21, 27; 24:17–28, 37–41).

NOBLEMAN

Setting: Jericho, on the way to Jerusalem. After commending Zaccheus's faith in Him, Jesus provides a parable about stewardship.

So He said, "A nobleman went to a distant country to receive a kingdom for himself, and *then* return. And he called ten of his slaves, and gave them ten minas and said to them, 'Do business *with this* until I come *back*.' But his citizens hated him and sent a delegation after him, saying, 'We do not want this man to reign over us.' When he returned, after receiving the kingdom, he ordered that these slaves, to whom he had given the money, be called to him so that he might know what business they had done. The first appeared, saying, 'Master, your mina has made ten minas more.' And he said to him, 'Well done, good slave, because you have been faithful in a very little thing, you are to be in authority over ten cities.' The second came, saying, 'Your mina, master, has made five minas.' And he said to him, also, 'And you are to be over five cities.' Another came, saying, 'Master, here is your mina, which I kept put away in a handkerchief; for I was afraid of you, because you are an exacting man; you take up what you did not lay down and reap what you did not sow.' He said to him, 'By your own words I will judge you, you worthless slave. Did you know that I am an exacting man, taking up what I did not lay down and reaping what I did not sow? Then why did you not put my money in the bank, and having come, I would have collected it with interest?' Then he said to the bystanders, 'Take the mina away from him and give it to the one who has the ten minas.' And they said to him, 'Master, he has ten minas *already*.' I tell you that to everyone who has, more shall be given, but from the one who does not have, even what he does have shall be taken away. But these enemies of mine, who did not want me to reign over them, bring them here and slay them in my presence" (Luke 19:12–27; cf. Matthew 25:14–30; see Matthew 13:12; Luke 16:10).

NOBLEMAN, PARABLE OF THE (See NOBLEMAN; also see TALENTS, PARABLE OF THE)

NO FRUIT (Listed under FRUIT, NO)

NONE

Setting: The synagogue in Jesus' hometown of Nazareth in Galilee. At the beginning of His public ministry, Jesus comments to the congregation after reading on the Sabbath from the book of the prophet Isaiah.

And He said to them, "No doubt you will quote this proverb to Me, 'Physician, heal yourself! Whatever we heard was done at Capernaum, do here in your hometown as well.'" And He said, "Truly I say to you, no prophet is welcome in his hometown. But I say to you in truth, there were many widows in Israel in the days of Elijah, when the sky was shut up for three years and six months, when a great famine came over all the land; and yet Elijah was sent to none of them, but only to Zarephath, *in the land* of Sidon, to a woman who was a widow. And there were many lepers in Israel in the time of Elisha the prophet; and none of them was cleansed, but only Naaman the Syrian" (Luke 4:23–27; Jesus refers to 1 Kings 17:1, 9; 2 Kings 5:1–14; see Matthew 13:53–58).

Setting: On the way from Galilee to Jerusalem. After speaking a parable to the invited guests and the host at a banquet, Jesus responds to a guest's proclamation about the blessings of eating bread in the kingdom of God.

But He said to him, "A man was giving a big dinner, and he invited many; and at the dinner hour he sent his slave to say to those who had been invited, 'Come; for everything is ready now.' But they all alike began to make excuses. The first one said to him, 'I have bought a piece of land and I need to go out and look at it; please consider me excused.' Another one said, 'I have bought five yoke of oxen, and I am going to try them out; please consider me excused.' Another one said, I have married a wife, and for that reason I cannot come.' And the slave came *back* and reported this to his master. Then the head of the household became angry and said to his slave, 'Go out at once into the streets and lanes of the city and bring in here the poor and crippled and blind and lame.' And the slave said, 'Master, what you commanded has been done, and still there is room.' And the master said to the slave, 'Go out into the highways and along the hedges, and compel *them* to come in, so that my house may be filled. For I tell you, none of those men who were invited shall taste of my dinner'" (Luke 14:16–24; see Deuteronomy 24:5; Matthew 22:2–14; Luke 14:1, 2).

Setting: On the way from Galilee to Jerusalem. After He responds to a guest's proclamation about the blessings of eating bread in the kingdom of God, Jesus presents to large crowds the demands of discipleship.

Now large crowds were going along with Him; and He turned and said to them, "If anyone comes to Me, and does not hate his own father and mother and wife and children and brothers and sisters, yes, and even his own life, he cannot be My disciple. Whoever does not carry his own cross and come after Me cannot be My disciple. For which one of you, when he wants to build a tower, does not first sit down and calculate the cost to see if he has enough to complete it? Otherwise, when he has laid a foundation and is not able to finish, all who observe it begin to ridicule him, saying, 'This man began to build and was not able to finish.' Or what king, when he sets out to meet another king in battle, will not first sit down and consider whether he is strong enough with ten thousand *men* to encounter the one coming against him with twenty thousand? Or else, while the other is still far away, he sends a delegation and asks for terms of peace. So then, none of you can be My disciple who does not give up all his possessions. Therefore, salt is good; but if even salt has become tasteless, with what will it be seasoned? It is useless either for the soil or for the manure pile; it is thrown out. He who has ears to hear, let him hear" (Luke 14:25–35; cf. Matthew 5:13; 10:37–39; see Proverb 20:18; Luke 14:1, 2; Philippians 3:7)

Setting: On the way from Galilee to Jerusalem. After responding to the Pharisees' scoffing at His teaching the disciples about stewardship and the permanence of the Law, Jesus conveys the story of the rich man and Lazarus.

"Now there was a rich man, and he habitually dressed in purple and fine linen, joyously living in splendor every day. And a poor man named Lazarus was laid at his gate, covered with sores, and longing to be fed with the *crumbs* which were falling from the rich man's table; besides, even the dogs were coming and licking his sores. Now the poor man died and was carried away by the angels to Abraham's bosom; and the rich man also died and was buried. In Hades he lifted up his eyes, being in torment, and saw Abraham far away and Lazarus in his bosom. And he cried out and said, 'Father Abraham, have mercy on me, and send Lazarus so that he may dip the tip of his finger in water and cool off my tongue, for I am in agony in this flame.' But Abraham said, 'Child, remember that during your life you received your good things, and likewise Lazarus bad things; but now he is being comforted here, and you are in agony. And besides all this, between us and you there is a great chasm fixed, so that those who wish to come over from here to you will not be able, and *that* none may cross over from there to us.' And he said, 'Then I beg you, father, that you send him to my father's house—for I have five brothers—in order that he may warn them, so that they will not also come to this place of torment.' But Abraham said, 'They have Moses and the Prophets; let them hear them.' But he said, 'No, father Abraham, but if someone goes to them from the dead, they will repent!' But he said to him, 'If they do not listen to Moses and the Prophets, they will not be persuaded even if someone rises from the dead' " (Luke 16:19–31; see Luke 6:8; 6:24; 16:1).

Setting: On the Mount of Olives, east of the temple in Jerusalem. After ministering in the temple a few days before His crucifixion, and giving His disciples more details regarding the temple's future destruction, Jesus elaborates during His Olivet Discourse about things to come.

Then He continued by saying to them, "Nation will rise against nation and kingdom against kingdom, and there will be great earthquakes, and in various places plagues and famines; and there will be terrors and great signs from heaven. But before all these things, they will lay their hands on you and will persecute you, delivering you to the synagogues and prisons, bringing you before kings and governors for My name's sake. It will lead to an opportunity for your testimony. So make up your minds not to

prepare beforehand to defend yourselves; for I will give you utterance and wisdom which none of your opponents will be able to resist or refute. But you will be betrayed even by parents and brothers and relatives and friends, and they will put *some* of you to death, and you will be hated by all because of My name. Yet not a hair of your head will perish. By your endurance you will gain your lives" (Luke 21:10–19; cf. Matthew 10:19–22; 24:7–14; Mark 13:8–13).

Setting: The temple in Jerusalem. After receiving encouragement from His blood brothers in Galilee to attend the upcoming Feast of Booths in order to demonstrate His works to His disciples and the world, Jesus goes and teaches, astonishing the Jewish religious leaders.

"Did not Moses give you the Law, and *yet* none of you carries out the Law? Why do you seek to kill Me?" (John 7:19; see Mark 11:18; John 1:17).

Setting: Jerusalem. Before the Passover, after warning His disciples of the persecution they will face after His departure to heaven, Jesus elaborates about the coming ministry of the Holy Spirit.

"But now I am going to Him who sent Me; and none of you asks Me, 'Where are You going?' But because I have said these things to you, sorrow has filled your heart. But I tell you the truth, it is to your advantage that I go away; for if I do not go away, the Helper will not come to you; but if I go, I will send Him to you. And He, when He comes, will convict the world concerning sin and righteousness and judgment; concerning sin, because they do not believe in Me; and concerning righteousness, because I go to the Father and you no longer see Me; and concerning judgment, because the ruler of this world has been judged" (John 16:5–11; see John 7:33; 12:31; 14:1, 16; 15:22, 24).

NORTH (Also see EAST; SOUTH; and WEST)

Setting: On the way from Galilee to Jerusalem. While teaching in the cities and villages, Jesus responds to a question about who is saved.

And someone said to Him, "Lord, are there *just* a few who are being saved?" And He said to them, "Strive to enter through the narrow door; for many, I tell you, will seek to enter and will not be able. Once the head of the house gets up and shuts the door, and you begin to stand outside and knock on the door, saying, 'Lord, open up to us!' then He will answer and say to you, 'I do not know where you are from.' Then you will begin to say, 'We ate and drank in Your presence, and You taught in our streets'; and He will say, 'I tell you, I do not know where you are from; DEPART FROM ME, ALL YOU EVILDOERS.' In that place there will be weeping and gnashing of teeth when you see Abraham and Isaac and Jacob and all the prophets in the kingdom of God, but you yourselves being thrown out. And they will come from east and west and from north and south, and will recline *at the table* in the kingdom of God. And behold, *some* are last who will be first and *some* are first who will be last" (Luke 13:23–30, Jesus quotes from Psalm 6:8; cf. Matthew 7:13, 23; 8:11, 12; see Matthew 19:30; Luke 3:8).

NOTHING

Setting: Galilee. After His disciples observe His ministry, Jesus summons and specifically instructs them about their ministry ahead involving true discipleship.

"Therefore do not fear them, for there is nothing concealed that will not be revealed, or hidden that will not be known. What I tell you in the darkness, speak in the light; and what you hear *whispered* in your ear, proclaim upon the housetops. Do not fear those who kill the body but are unable to kill the soul; but rather fear Him who is able to destroy both soul and body in hell" (Matthew 10:26–28; cf. Mark 4:22; Luke 12:3; see Hebrews 10:31).

Setting: Near the Sea of Galilee. After being impressed by a Canaanite woman's faith, Jesus restores her daughter from demon possession, then feeds more than 4,000 people, primarily Gentiles, who are following Him.

And Jesus called His disciples to Him, and said, "I feel compassion for the people, because they have remained with Me now three days and have nothing to eat; and I do not want to send them away hungry, for they might faint on the way." The disciples said to Him, "Where would we get so many loaves in *this* desolate place to satisfy a large crowd?" And Jesus said to them, "How many loaves do you have?" And they said, "Seven and a few small fish" (Matthew 15:32–34; cf. Mark 8:1–9).

Setting: Galilee, near the mountain where the Transfiguration took place. Jesus reveals to His disciples why they could not heal a demon-possessed boy.

And He said to them, "Because of the littleness of your faith; for truly I say to you, if you have faith the size of a mustard seed, you will say to this mountain, 'Move from here to there,' and it will move; and nothing will be impossible to you. ["But this kind does not go out except by prayer and fasting"] (Matthew 17:20, 21; cf. Matthew 21:21, 22; Mark 9:28, 29).

Setting: The temple in Jerusalem. After the Jewish religious leaders test Him with questions, Jesus pronounces the fourth of eight woes on them in front of the crowds and His disciples.

"Woe to you, blind guides, who say, "Whoever swears by the temple, *that* is nothing; but whoever swears by the gold of the temple is obligated.' You fools and blind men! Which is more important, the gold or the temple that sanctified the gold? And, 'Whoever swears by the altar, *that* is nothing, but whoever swears by the offering on it, he is obligated.' You blind men, which is more important, the offering, or the altar that sanctifies the offering? Therefore, whoever swears by the altar, swears *both* by the altar and by everything on it. And whoever swears by the temple, swears *both* by the temple and by Him who dwells within it. And whoever swears by heaven, swears *both* by the throne of God and by Him who sits upon it" (Matthew 23:16–22; see Exodus 29:37; 1 Kings 8:13; Isaiah 66:1; Matthew 15:14).

Setting: On the Mount of Olives, just east of Jerusalem. During His Olivet Discourse, after answering His disciples' questions as to when the temple will be destroyed and Jerusalem overrun, along with the signs of His coming and the end of the age, Jesus reveals the future judgments following His return.

"But when the Son of Man comes in His glory, and all the angels with Him, then He will sit on His glorious throne. All the nations will be gathered before Him; and He will separate them from one another, as the shepherd separates the sheep from the goats; and He will put the sheep on His right, and the goats on the left. Then the King will say to those on His right, 'Come, you who are blessed of My Father, inherit the kingdom prepared for you from the foundation of the world. 'For I was hungry, and you gave Me *something* to eat; I was thirsty, and you gave Me *something* to drink; I was a stranger, and you invited Me in; naked, and you clothed Me; I was sick, and you visited Me; I was in prison, and you came to Me.' Then the righteous will answer Him, 'Lord, when did we see You hungry and feed You, or thirsty, and give you *something* to drink? And when did we see You a stranger, and invite You in, or naked, and clothe You? When did we see You sick, or in prison, and come to You?' The King will answer and say to them, 'Truly I say to you, to the extent that you did it to one of these brothers of Mine, *even* the least *of them,* you did it to Me.' Then He will also say to those on His left, 'Depart from Me, accursed ones, into the eternal fire which has been prepared for the devil and his angels; for I was hungry, and you gave Me *nothing* to eat; I was thirsty, and you gave Me nothing to drink; I was a stranger, and you did not invite Me in; naked, and you did not clothe Me; sick, and in prison, and you did not visit Me.' Then they themselves also will answer, 'Lord, when did we see You hungry, or thirsty, or a stranger, or naked, or sick, or in prison, and did not take care of You?' Then He will answer them, 'Truly I say to you, to the extent that you did not do it to one of the least of these, you did not do it to Me.' These will go away into eternal punishment, but the righteous into eternal life" (Matthew 25:31–46; see Matthew 7:23; 16:27; 19:29).

Setting: Galilee. As Jesus preaches and casts out demons in the synagogues, a leper beseeches Him for healing.

Moved with compassion, Jesus stretched out His hand and touched him, and said to him, "I am willing; be cleansed." Immediately the leprosy left him and he was cleansed. And He sternly warned him and immediately sent him away, and He said to him, "See that you say nothing to anyone; but go, show yourself to the priest and offer for your cleansing what Moses commanded, as a testimony to them" (Mark 1:41–44; cf. Luke 5:12–14; see Leviticus 14:1–32; Matthew 8:3).

Setting: Galilee. Following His explanation of the Parable of the Sower to His disciples, Jesus illustrates what they should do with this truth.

And He was saying to them, "A lamp is not brought to be put under a basket, is it, or under a bed? Is it not *brought* to be put on the lampstand? For nothing is hidden, except to be revealed; nor has *anything* been secret, but that it would come to light. If anyone has ears to hear, let him hear" (Mark 4:21–23; cf. Luke 8:16, 17; see Matthew 5:14–16; Matthew 10:26).

Setting: Galilee. After the Pharisees and scribes from Jerusalem object to His disciples' lack of obedience to the tradition regarding ceremonial cleansing, Jesus speaks to a crowd and explains His teaching to the disciples.

After He called the crowd to Him again, He *began* saying to them, "Listen to Me, all of you, and understand: there is nothing outside the man which can defile him if it goes into him; but the things which proceed out of the man are what defile the man. [If anyone has ears to hear, let him hear."] When he had left the crowd *and* entered the house, His disciples questioned Him about the parable. And He said to them, "Are you so lacking in understanding also? Do you not understand that whatever goes into the man from outside cannot defile him, because it does not go into his heart, but into his stomach, and is eliminated?" (*Thus He* declared all foods clean.) And He was saying, "That which proceeds out of the man, that is what defiles the man. For from within, out of the heart of men, proceed the evil thoughts, fornications, thefts, murders, adulteries, deeds of coveting *and* wickedness, *as well* as deceit, sensuality, envy, slander, pride *and* foolishness. All these evil things proceed from within and defile the man" (Mark 7:14–23; cf. Matthew 15:10–20).

Setting: Decapolis, near the Sea of Galilee. Jesus miraculously feeds more than 4,000 people, primarily Gentiles.

In those days, when there was again a large crowd and they had nothing to eat, Jesus called His disciples and said to them, "I feel compassion for the people because they have remained with Me now three days and have nothing to eat. If I send them away hungry to their homes, they will faint on their way; and some of them have come a great distance" (Mark 8:1–3; cf. Matthew 15:32–38; see Matthew 9:36).

Setting: Galilee. After selecting His twelve disciples, Jesus teaches the Sermon on the Mount to those disciples and a great throng of people from Judea, Jerusalem, and the central coastal region of Tyre and Sidon.

"But I say to you who hear, love your enemies, do good to those who hate you, bless those who curse you, pray for those who mistreat you. Whoever hits you on the cheek, offer him the other also; and whoever takes away your coat, do not withhold your shirt from him either. Give to everyone who asks of you, and whoever takes away what is yours, do not demand it back. Treat others the same way you want them to treat you. If you love those who love you, what credit is that to you? For even sinners love those who love them. If you do good to those who do good to you, what credit is that to you? For even sinners do the same. If you lend to those from whom you expect to receive, what credit is that to you? Even sinners lend to sinners in order to receive back the same amount. But love your enemies, and do good, and lend, expecting nothing in return; and your reward will be great, and you will be sons of the Most High; for He Himself is kind to ungrateful and evil men. Be merciful, just as your Father is merciful" (Luke 6:27–36; cf. Matthew 5:9, 39–48; Matthew 7:12).

Setting: Galilee. After explaining the Parable of the Sower to His disciples, Jesus gives the Parable of the Lamp.

"Now no one after lighting a lamp covers it over with a container, or puts it under a bed; but he puts it on a lampstand, so that those who come in may see the light. For nothing is hidden that will not become evident, nor *anything* secret that will not be known and come to light. So take care how you listen; for whoever has, to him *more* shall be given; and whoever does not have, even what he thinks he has shall be taken away from him" (Luke 8:16–18; cf. Mark 4:21–23; see Matthew 5:14, 15; 10:26; 13:12).

Setting: Galilee. After raising Jairus's daughter from the dead, Jesus calls the twelve disciples together and gives them power and authority over demons, along with the ability to cure diseases.

And He said to them, "Take nothing for *your* journey, neither a staff, nor a bag, nor bread, nor money; and do not *even* have two tunics apiece. Whatever house you enter, stay there until you leave that city. And as for those who do not receive you, go out from that city, shake the dust off your feet as a testimony against them" (Luke 9:3–5; cf. Matthew 10:1–15; Mark 6:7–11; see Luke 10:4–12).

Setting: On the way from Galilee to Jerusalem. The Lord responds to a report from the seventy sent out in pairs to every place He Himself will soon visit.

And He said to them, "I was watching Satan fall from heaven like lightning. Behold, I have given you authority to tread on serpents and scorpions, and over all the power of the enemy, and nothing will injure you. Nevertheless do not rejoice in this, that the spirits are subject to you, but rejoice that your names are recorded in heaven" (Luke 10:18–20; see Psalm 91:13; Isaiah 14:12–14; Luke 9:1).

Setting: On the way from Galilee to Jerusalem. After revealing to His disciples how to pray, Jesus illustrates persistence in prayer.

Then He said to them, "Suppose one of you has a friend, and goes to him at midnight and says to him, 'Friend, lend me three loaves; for a friend of mine has come to me from a journey, and I have nothing to set before him'; and from inside he answers and says, 'Do not bother me; the door has already been shut and my children and I are in bed; I cannot get up and give you *anything.*' I tell you, even though he will not get up and give him *anything* because he is his friend, yet because of his persistence he will get up and give him as much as he needs. So I say to you, ask, and it will be given to you; seek, and you will find; knock, and it will be opened to you. For everyone who asks, receives; and he who seeks, finds; and to him who knocks, it will be opened" (Luke 11:5–10; cf. Matthew 7:7, 8; see Luke 18:1–5).

Setting: On the way from Galilee to Jerusalem. Jesus warns His disciples of future events as the scribes and Pharisees turn hostile and question Him repeatedly in an attempt to catch Him in something He might say.

Under these circumstances, after so many thousands of people had gathered together that they were stepping on one another, He began saying to His disciples first *of all,* "Beware of the leaven of the Pharisees, which is hypocrisy. But there is nothing covered up that will not be revealed, and hidden that will not be known. Accordingly, whatever you have said in the dark will be heard in the light, and what you have whispered in the inner rooms will be proclaimed upon the housetops. I say to you, My friends, do not be afraid of those who kill the body and after that have no more that they can do. But I will warn you whom to fear: fear the One who, after He has killed, has authority to cast into hell; yes, I tell you, fear Him! Are not five sparrows sold for two cents? *Yet* not one of them is forgotten before God. Indeed, the very hairs of your head are all numbered. Do not fear; you are more valuable than many sparrows" (Luke 12:1–7; cf. Matthew 10:26–31; see Matthew 16:6; Hebrews 10:31).

Setting: The temple in Jerusalem. During a feast of the Jews, Jesus addresses the formerly lame man He healed earlier on the Sabbath at the pool of Bethesda.

Afterward Jesus found him in the temple and tells him, "Behold, you have become well; do not sin anymore, so that nothing worse happens to you" (John 5:14).

Setting: By the pool of Bethesda in Jerusalem. During a feast of the Jews, Jesus responds to criticism from the Jewish religious leaders for healing a lame man on the Sabbath and for referring to God as His Father (thereby making Himself equal with God).

Therefore Jesus answered and was saying to them, "Truly, truly, I say to you, the Son can do nothing of Himself, unless *it is* something He sees the Father doing; for whatever the Father does, these things the Son also does in like manner. For the Father loves the Son, and shows Him all things that He Himself is doing; and *the Father* will show Him greater works than these, so that you will marvel. For just as the Father raises the dead and gives them life, even so the Son also gives life to whom He wishes. For not even the Father judges anyone, but He has given all judgment to the Son, so that all will honor the Son even as they honor the Father. He who does not honor the Son does not honor the Father who sent Him" (John 5:19–23; see Luke 10:16; John 3:35; 11:25; 14:12).

Setting: Jerusalem. During a feast of the Jews, Jesus responds to criticism from the religious leaders by referring to God as His Father (thereby making Himself equal with God) and informing them that God, John the Baptist, and His works all testify to His mission.

"I can do nothing on My own initiative. As I hear, I judge; and My judgment is just, because I do not seek My own will, but the will of Him who sent Me. If I *alone* testify about Myself, My testimony is not true. There is another who testifies of Me, and I know that the testimony which He gives about Me is true. You have sent to John, and he has testified to the truth. But the testimony which I receive is not from man, but I say these things so that you may be saved. He was the lamp that was burning and was shining and you were willing to rejoice for a while in his light. But the testimony which I have is greater than the *testimony of* John; for the works which the Father has given Me to accomplish—the very works that I do—testify about Me, that the Father has sent Me. And the Father who sent Me, He has testified of Me. You have neither heard His voice at any time nor seen His form. You do not have His word abiding in you, for you do not believe Him whom He sent" (John 5:30–38; see Matthew 3:17; Mark 1:4, 5; John 1:7, 15, 32; 4:34; 8:14–16; 10:25, 37, 38).

Setting: By the Sea of Galilee. After revealing to the Jewish religious leaders during a feast of the Jews in Jerusalem that God, John the Baptist, the Scriptures, and His works testify to His mission, Jesus returns to Galilee and miraculously feeds more than 5,000 people with a lad's five barley loaves and two fish.

Jesus said, "Have the people sit down." Now there was much grass in the place. So the men sat down, in number about five thousand. Jesus took the loaves, and having given thanks, He distributed to those who were seated; likewise also of the fish as much as they wanted. When they were filled, He said to the disciples, "Gather up the leftover fragments so that nothing will be lost" (John 6:10–12; cf. Matthew 14:17–21; Mark 6:38–44; Luke 9:14–17; see Matthew 15:32–38).

Setting: Capernaum. The day after Jesus walks on the Sea of Galilee to join His disciples in a boat, the people He miraculously fed with a lad's five loaves and two fish ask the Lord to always give them this bread out of heaven.

Jesus said to them, "I am the bread of life; he who comes to Me will not hunger, and he who believes in Me will never thirst. But I said to you that you have seen Me, and yet do not believe. All that the Father gives Me will come to Me, and the one who comes to Me I will certainly not cast out. For I have come down from heaven, not to do My own will, but the will of Him who sent Me. This is the will of Him who sent Me, that of all that He has given Me I lose nothing, but raise it up on the last day. For this is the will of My Father, that everyone who beholds the Son and believes in Him will have eternal life, and I Myself will raise him up on the last day" (John 6:35–40; see John 3:13, 16; 4:13, 14).

Setting: The synagogue at Capernaum of Galilee. After the Jewish religious leaders argue with one another when Jesus says He will give His flesh to the world to eat, some of His disciples also express difficulty with His statements.

But, Jesus, conscious that His disciples grumbled at this, said to them, "Does this cause you to stumble? *What* then if you see the Son of Man ascending to where He was before? It is the Spirit who gives life; the flesh profits nothing; the words that I have spoken to you are spirit and are life. But there are some of you who do not believe." For Jesus knew from the beginning who they were who did not believe, and who it was that would betray Him. And He was saying, "For this reason I have said to you, that no one can come to Me unless it has been granted him from the Father" (John 6:61–65; see Matthew 11:6; 13:11; John 3:13).

Setting: The temple treasury in Jerusalem. Following the Feast of Booths and the scribes' and Pharisees' failed attempt to stone a woman for committing adultery, Jesus returns the next day to teach. They question His testimony about Himself.

So Jesus said, "When you lift up the Son of Man, then you will know that I am *He,* and I do nothing on my own initiative, but I speak these things as the Father taught Me. And He who sent Me is with Me; He has not left Me alone, for I always do the things that are pleasing to Him" (John 8:28, 29; see John 3:14).

Setting: The temple treasury in Jerusalem. While Jesus is interacting with the scribes and Pharisees, they state their belief that Jesus is a demon-possessed Samaritan because of His statement that anyone who keeps His word will never taste death.

Jesus answered, "If I glorify Myself, My glory is nothing; it is My Father who glorifies Me, of whom you say, 'He is our God'; and you have not come to know Him, but I know Him; and if I say that I do not know Him, I will be a liar like you, but I do know Him and keep His word. Your father Abraham rejoiced to see My day, and he saw *it* and was glad" (John 8:54–56; see Matthew 13:17; John 7:29).

Setting: Jerusalem. Before the Passover, after He conveys the upcoming ministry of the Holy Spirit in His disciples' lives, Jesus again relates peace, hope, and comfort to them regarding His return to the Father.

"Peace I leave with you; My peace I give to you; not as the world gives do I give to you. Do not let your heart be troubled, nor let it be fearful. You heard that I said to you, 'I go away, and I will come to you,' If you loved Me, you would have rejoiced because I go to the Father, for the Father is greater than I. Now I have told you before it happens, so that when it happens, you may believe. I will not speak much more with you, for the ruler of the world is coming, and he has nothing in Me; but so that the world may know that I love the Father, I do exactly as the Father commanded Me. Get up, let us go from here" (John 14:27–31; see John 10:18, 29; 12:31; 13:19; 16:33).

Setting: Jerusalem. Before the Passover, after He conveys the upcoming ministry of the Holy Spirit in His disciples' lives with His imminent departure from them, Jesus explains He is the vine and His disciples are the branches.

"I am the true vine, and My Father is the vinedresser. Every branch in Me that does not bear fruit, He takes away; and every *branch* that bears fruit, He prunes it so that it may bear more fruit. You are already clean because of the word which I have spoken to you. Abide in Me, and I in you. As the branch cannot bear fruit of itself unless it abides in the vine, so neither *can* you unless you abide in Me. I am the vine, you are the branches; he who abides in Me and I in him, he bears much fruit, for apart from Me you can do nothing. If anyone does not abide in Me, he is thrown away as a branch and dries up; and they gather them, and cast them into the fire and they are burned. If you abide in Me, and My words abide in you, ask whatever you wish, and it will be done for you. My Father is glorified by this, that you bear much fruit, and *so* prove to be My disciples. Just as the Father has loved Me, I have also loved you; abide in My love. If you keep My commandments, you will abide in My love; just as I have kept My Father's commandments and abide in His love. These things I have spoken to you so that My joy may be in you, and *that* your joy may be made full" (John 15:1–11; see Matthew 5:16; 7:7; John 3:29, 35; 6:56; 8:29, 31; 13:10).

Setting: Jerusalem. Before the Passover, after empathizing with His disciples' sadness over His prophecies and giving them the hope for the future, Jesus conveys promises about praying in His name.

"In that day you will not question Me about anything. Truly, truly, I say to you, if you ask the Father for anything in My name, He will give it to you. Until now you have asked for nothing in My name; ask and you will receive, so that your joy may be made full. These things I have spoken to you in figurative language; an hour is coming when I will no longer speak to you in figurative language, but will tell you plainly of the Father. In that day you will ask in My name, and I do not say to you that I will request of the Father on your behalf; for the Father Himself loves you, because you have loved Me and have believed that I came forth from the Father. I came forth from the Father and have come into the world; I am leaving the world again and going to the Father" (John 16:23–28; see Matthew 13:34; John 8:42; 13:1, 3; 14:14, 21, 23; 15:16).

Setting: Jerusalem. After Jesus is betrayed by Judas and has Peter deny he was Jesus' disciple, Annas, former high priest and the current high priest's (Caiaphas) father-in-law, questions Jesus about His disciples and His teaching.

Jesus answered him, "I have spoken openly to the world; I always taught in synagogues and in the temple, where all the Jews come together; and I spoke nothing in secret. Why do you question Me? Question those who have heard what I spoke to them; they know what I said" (John 18:20, 21; see John 7:26).

Setting: On the island of Patmos (in the Aegean Sea about fifty miles southwest of Ephesus in modern Turkey). On the Lord's Day (Sunday), approximately fifty years after Jesus' resurrection, the disciple John encounters the Lord

Jesus Christ, who communicates a new revelation for the apostle to record for the church in Laodicea and to six other churches in Asia.

"To the angel of the church in Laodicea write: The Amen, the faithful and true Witness, the Beginning of the creation of God, says this: 'I know your deeds, that you are neither cold nor hot; I wish that you were cold or hot. So because you are lukewarm, and neither hot nor cold, I will spit you out of My mouth. Because you say, "I am rich, and have become wealthy, and have need of nothing," and you do not know that you are wretched and miserable and poor and blind and naked, I advise you to buy from Me gold refined by fire so that you may become rich, and white garments so that you may clothe yourself, and *that* the shame of your nakedness will not be revealed; and eye salve to anoint your eyes so that you may see. Those whom I love, I reprove and discipline; therefore be zealous and repent. Behold, I stand at the door and knock; if anyone hears My voice and opens the door, I will come in to him and will dine with him, and he with Me. He who overcomes, I will grant to him to sit down with Me on My throne, as I also overcame and sat down with My Father on His throne. He who has an ear, let him hear what the Spirit says to the churches'" (Revelation 3:14–22; see Proverb 3:12; Hosea 12:8; John 14:23; 16:33).

NOURISHMENT (See FOOD)

NOWHERE

Setting: By the Sea of Galilee. Following a time of casting out evil spirits from the demon-possessed and healing the ill in fulfillment of Isaiah 53:4, Jesus lays out to an inquiring scribe the demands of discipleship.

Then a scribe came and said to Him, "Teacher, I will follow You wherever you go." Jesus said to him, "The foxes have holes and the birds of the air *have* nests, but the Son of Man has nowhere to lay His head." Another of the disciples said to Him, "Lord, permit me first to go and bury my father." But Jesus said to him, "Follow Me, and allow the dead to bury their own dead" (Matthew 8:19–22; cf. Luke 9:57–60).

Setting: On the way from Galilee to Jerusalem. The Lord responds to someone seeking to follow Him.

And Jesus said to him, "The foxes have holes and the birds of the air *have* nests, but the Son of Man has nowhere to lay His head" (Luke 9:58; cf. Matthew 8:19–22).

NUMBERED

Setting: Galilee. After His disciples observe His ministry, Jesus summons and specifically instructs them about their ministry ahead involving true discipleship.

"Are not two sparrows sold for a cent? And *yet* not one of them will fall to the ground apart from your Father. But the very hairs of your head are all numbered. So do not fear; you are more valuable than many sparrows" (Matthew 10:29–31; cf. Luke 12:6; see Matthew 12:12).

Setting: On the way from Galilee to Jerusalem. Jesus warns His disciples of future events as the scribes and Pharisees turn hostile and question Him repeatedly in an attempt to catch Him in something He might say.

Under these circumstances, after so many thousands of people had gathered together that they were stepping on one another, He began saying to His disciples first *of all*, "Beware of the leaven of the Pharisees, which is hypocrisy. But there is nothing covered up that will not be revealed, and hidden that will not be known. Accordingly, whatever you have said in the dark will be heard in the light, and what you have whispered in the inner rooms will be proclaimed upon the housetops. I say to you, My friends, do not be afraid of those who kill the body and after that have no more that they can do. But I will warn you whom to fear: fear the One who, after He has killed, has authority to cast into hell; yes, I tell you, fear Him! Are not five sparrows sold for two cents? *Yet* not one of them is forgotten before God. Indeed, the very hairs of your head are all numbered. Do not fear; you are more valuable than many sparrows" (Luke 12:1–7; cf. Matthew 10:26–31; see Matthew 16:6; Hebrews 10:31).

Setting: Jerusalem. During the Feast of Unleavened Bread (Passover) just before Jesus' crucifixion, while celebrating the Passover meal, instituting the Lord's Supper, and prophesying Peter's denial of Him, the Lord instructs

His disciples to prepare to persevere without Him.

And He said to them, "When I sent you out without money belt and bag and sandals, you did not lack anything, did you?" They said, "*No*, nothing." And He said to them, "But now, whoever has a money belt is to take it along, likewise also a bag, and whoever has no sword is to sell his coat and buy one. For I tell you that this which is written must be fulfilled in Me, 'AND HE WAS NUMBERED WITH TRANSGRESSORS'; for that which refers to Me has *its* fulfillment." They said, "Lord, look, here are two swords." And He said to them, "It is enough" (Luke 22:35–38, Jesus quotes from Isaiah 53:12; see Matthew 10:5–15; Mark 6:7–11; Luke 9:1–5; 10:1–12; 22:49; John 17:4).

NURSING BABIES (Listed under BABIES, NURSING; also see CHILDREN; INFANTS; and LITTLE ONES)

O

OATH **(Also see SWEARING; and VOWS)**

Setting: Galilee. During the early part of His ministry, Jesus preaches the Sermon on the Mount to His disciples and the multitudes.

"Again, you have heard that the ancients were told, 'YOU SHALL NOT MAKE FALSE VOWS, BUT SHALL FULFILL YOUR VOWS TO THE LORD.' But I say to you, make no oath at all, either by heaven, for it is the throne of God, or by the earth, for it is the footstool of His feet, or by Jerusalem, for it is THE CITY OF THE GREAT KING. Nor shall you make an oath by your head, for you cannot make one hair white or black. But let your statement be 'Yes, yes' *or* 'No, no'; anything beyond these is of evil" (Matthew 5:33–37, Jesus quotes from Leviticus 19:12, Psalm 48:2; Isaiah 66:1; cf. James 5:12).

OBEDIENCE **(Also see BAPTISM; COMMENDATION; COMMITMENT; DEVOTION; DISCIPLE; DISCIPLESHIP; FAITHFULNESS; FOLLOWING JESUS CHRIST; GOD, LOVING; LIVING, GODLY; OBEDIENCE, JESUS'; REWARDS; and WILL OF GOD)**

[OBEDIENCE from does the will of My Father]

Setting: Galilee. During the early part of His ministry, Jesus preaches the Sermon on the Mount to His disciples and the multitudes.

"Not everyone who says to Me, 'Lord, Lord,' will enter the kingdom of heaven, but he who does the will of My Father who is in heaven *will enter.* Many will say to Me on that day, 'Lord, Lord, did we not prophesy in Your name, and in Your name cast out demons, and in Your name perform many miracles?' And then I will declare to them, 'I never knew you, DEPART FROM ME, YOU WHO PRACTICE LAWLESSNESS'"(Matthew 7:21–23, Jesus quotes from Psalm 6:8; cf. Matthew 25:11–13; see Luke 6:46).

[OBEDIENCE from everyone who hears these words of Mine and acts of them]

Setting: Galilee. During the early part of His ministry, Jesus preaches the Sermon on the Mount to His disciples and the multitudes.

"Therefore everyone who hears these words of Mine and acts on them, may be compared to a wise man who built his house on the rock. And the rain fell, and the floods came, and the winds blew and slammed against that house; and *yet* it did not fall, for it had been founded on the rock. Everyone who hears these words of Mine and does not act on them, will be like a foolish man who built his house on the sand. The rain fell, and the floods came, and the winds blew and slammed against that house; and it fell—and great was its fall" (Matthew 7:24–28; cf. Luke 6:47–49).

[OBEDIENCE from whoever does the will of My Father]

Setting: Galilee. Jesus' mother, Mary, and His brothers wait to see Him as He teaches and preaches.

But Jesus answered the one who was telling Him and said, "Who is My mother and who are My brothers?" And stretching out His hand toward His disciples, He said, "Behold, My mother and My brothers! For whoever does the will of My Father who is in heaven, he is My brother and sister and mother" (Matthew 12:48–50; cf. Mark 3:31–35; Luke 8:19–21).

[OBEDIENCE from keep the commandments]

Setting: Judea beyond the Jordan (Perea). Jesus shares with a rich, young ruler how to obtain eternal life.

And He said to him, "Why are you asking Me about what is good? There is *only* One who is good; but if you wish to enter into life, keep the commandments." *Then* he said to Him, 'Which ones?' And Jesus said, "YOU SHALL NOT COMMIT MURDER; YOU SHALL NOT

COMMIT ADULTERY; YOU SHALL NOT STEAL; YOU SHALL NOT BEAR FALSE WITNESS; HONOR YOUR FATHER AND MOTHER; and YOU SHALL LOVE YOUR NEIGHBOR AS YOURSELF." The young man said to Him, "All these things I have kept; what am I still lacking?" Jesus said to him, "If you wish to complete go *and* sell your possessions and give to *the* poor, and you will have treasure in heaven; and come, follow Me" (Matthew 19:16–22, Jesus quotes from Exodus 20:13–15; Leviticus 19:18; cf. Leviticus 18:5; Mark 10:17–21; Luke 10:25–28; 12:33; 18:18–24).

[OBEDIENCE from but afterward he regretted it and went]
Setting: The temple in Jerusalem. Jesus delivers a parable to the chief priests and elders after they question His authority.

"But what do you think? A man had two sons, and he came to the first and said, 'Son, go work today in the vineyard.' And he answered, 'I will not'; but afterward he regretted it and went. The man came to the second and said the same thing; and he answered, 'I *will,* sir'; but he did not go. Which of the two sons did the will of his father?" They said, "The first." Jesus said to them, "Truly, I say to you that the tax collectors and prostitutes will get into the kingdom of God before you. For John came to you in the way of righteousness and you did not believe him; but the tax collectors and prostitutes did believe him; and you, seeing *this,* did not even feel remorse afterward so as to believe him" (Matthew 21:28–32; cf. Luke 7:29, 30, 37–50).

[OBEDIENCE from do and observe]
Setting: The temple in Jerusalem. Jesus exposes the truth about Pharisaism to the crowds and His disciples after the Jewish religious leaders test Him with questions.

Then Jesus spoke to the crowds and to His disciples, saying: "The scribes and the Pharisees have seated themselves in the chair of Moses; therefore all that they tell you, do and observe, but do not do according to their deeds; for they say *things* and do not do *them.* They tie up heavy burdens and lay them on men's shoulders, but they themselves are unwilling to move them with *so much as* a finger. But they do all their deeds to be noticed by men; for they broaden their phylacteries and lengthen their tassels *of their garments.* They love the place of honor at banquets and the chief seats in the synagogues, and respectful greetings in the market places, and being called Rabbi by men. But do not be called Rabbi; for One is your Teacher, and you are all brothers. Do not call *anyone* on earth your father; for One is your Father, He who is in heaven. Do not be called leaders; for One is your Leader, *that is,* Christ. But the greatest among you shall be your servant. Whoever exalts himself shall be humbled; and whoever humbles himself shall be exalted" (Matthew 23:1–12; cf. Matthew 20:26; Mark 12:38–40; Luke 20:46, 47; see Exodus 13:9; Deuteronomy 33:3; Matthew 6:1, 5, 6, 9, 16; Mark 14:11; Luke 11:43; 14:11).

[OBEDIENCE from teaching them to observe all that I commanded]
Setting: On a mountain in Galilee. Following His resurrection from the dead in Jerusalem, Jesus conveys the Great Commission to His eleven remaining disciples.

And Jesus came up and spoke to them, saying, "All authority has been given to Me in heaven and on earth. Go therefore and make disciples of all the nations, baptizing them in the name of the Father and the Son and the Holy Spirit, teaching them to observe all that I commanded you; and lo, I am with you always, even to the end of the age" (Matthew 28:18–20; cf. Mark 16:15; see Daniel 7:13).

[OBEDIENCE from whoever does the will of God]
Setting: Galilee. During the early part of His ministry, just after selecting His twelve disciples, when informed that His mother and brothers are waiting to see Him, Jesus explains to the crowd who His true relatives are.

Answering them, He said, "Who are My mother and My brothers?" Looking about at those who were sitting around Him, He said, "Behold My mother and My brothers! For whoever does the will of God, he is My brother and sister and mother" (Mark 3:33–35; cf. Matthew 12:46–50; Luke 8:19–21).

[OBEDIENCE from acts on them]
Setting: Galilee. After selecting His twelve disciples, Jesus teaches the Sermon on the Mount to those disciples and a great throng of people from Judea, Jerusalem, and the central coastal region of Tyre and Sidon.

"Why do you call Me, 'Lord, Lord,' and do not do what I say? Everyone who comes to Me and hears My words and acts on them, I will show you whom he is like; he is like a man building a house, who dug deep and laid a foundation on the rock; and when a flood occurred, the torrent burst against that house and could not shake it, because it had been well built. But the one who has heard and has not acted *accordingly,* is like a man who built a house on the ground without any foundation; and the torrent burst against it and immediately it collapsed, and the ruin of that house was great" (Luke 6:46–49; cf. Matthew 7:24–27; see Luke 6:12–19; James 1:22).

[OBEDIENCE from do it]
Setting: Galilee. After giving the Parable of the Lamp to His disciples, when informed that His mother and brothers are seeking Him, Jesus conveys who His true relatives are.

But He answered and said to them, "My mother and My brothers are these who hear the word of God and do it" (Luke 8:21; cf. Matthew 12:26–50; Mark 3:31–35).

[OBEDIENCE from observe it]
Setting: On the way from Galilee to Jerusalem. After revealing a problem with exorcism, Jesus responds to a blessing from a woman in the crowd.

But He said, "On the contrary, blessed are those who hear the word of God and observe it" (Luke 11:28).

Setting: On the way from Galilee to Jerusalem. After His disciples ask that their faith be increased following His instruction to them on forgiveness, the Lord illustrates with the mustard seed and an obedient slave.

And the Lord said, "If you had faith like a mustard seed, you would say to this mulberry tree, 'Be uprooted and be planted in the sea'; and it would obey you. Which of you, having a slave plowing or tending sheep, will say to him when he has come from the field, 'Come immediately and sit down to eat'? But will he not say to him, "Prepare something for me to eat, and *properly* clothe yourself and serve me while I eat and drink; and afterward you may eat and drink'? He does not thank the slave because he did the things which were commanded, does he? So you too, when you do all the things which are commanded you, say, 'We are unworthy slaves; we have done *only* that which we ought to have done'" (Luke 17:6–10; see Matthew 13:31; Luke 12:37).

[OBEDIENCE from if anyone keeps My word]
Setting: The temple treasury in Jerusalem. While Jesus is interacting with the scribes and Pharisees about His testimony, their ancestry, and their motives, they state their belief that Jesus is a demon-possessed Samaritan.

Jesus answered, "I do not have a demon; but I honor My Father, and you dishonor Me. But I do not seek My glory; there is One who seeks and judges. Truly, truly, I say to you, if anyone keeps My word he will never see death" (John 8:49–51; see Matthew 16:28; John 5:41; 7:20).

[OBEDIENCE from If anyone keeps My word]
Setting: The temple treasury in Jerusalem. While Jesus is interacting with the scribes and Pharisees, they state their belief that Jesus is a demon-possessed Samaritan because of His statement that anyone who keeps His word will never taste death.

The Jews said to Him, "Now we know that You have a demon. Abraham died, and the prophets *also;* and You say, 'If anyone keeps My word, he will never taste of death'" (John 8:52).

[OBEDIENCE from keep My commandments]
Setting: Jerusalem. Before the Passover, after responding to Philip's request for Him to show His disciples the Father, Jesus conveys the upcoming role of the Holy Spirit in their lives.

"If you love Me, you will keep My commandments. I will ask the Father, and He will give you another Helper, that He may be with you forever; *that* is the Spirit of truth, whom the world cannot receive, because it does not see Him or know Him, *but* you know Him because He abides with you and will be in you" (John 14:15–17; see John 7:39; 15:26; 1 John 5:3).

[OBEDIENCE from He who has My commandments and keeps them]
Setting: Jerusalem. Before the Passover, after responding to Philip's request for Him to show His disciples the Father, Jesus conveys the upcoming role of the Holy Spirit in their lives.

"I will not leave you as orphans; I will come to you. After a little while the world will no longer see Me, but you *will* see Me; because I live, you will live also. In that day you will know that I am in the Father, and you in Me, and I in you. He who has My commandments and keeps them is the one who loves Me; and he who loves Me will be loved by My Father, and I will love him and will disclose Myself to him" (John 14:18–21; see John 6:57; 10:37, 38; 16:16, 22).

[OBEDIENCE from keep My word]
Setting: Jerusalem. Before the Passover, after conveying the upcoming ministry of the Holy Spirit in His disciples' lives, Jesus answers Judas' (not Iscariot) question why He discloses Himself to the disciples and not to the whole world.

Jesus answered and said to him, "If anyone loves Me, he will keep My word; and My Father will love him, and We will come to him and make Our abode with him. He who does not love Me does not keep My words; and the word which you hear is not Mine, but the Father's who sent Me" (John 14:23, 24; see John 7:16; 8:51).

[OBEDIENCE from keep My commandments and kept My Father's commandments]
Setting: Jerusalem. Before the Passover, after He conveys the upcoming ministry of the Holy Spirit in His disciples' lives with His imminent departure from them, Jesus explains He is the vine and His disciples are the branches.

"I am the true vine, and My Father is the vinedresser. Every branch in Me that does not bear fruit, He takes away; and every *branch* that bears fruit, He prunes it so that it may bear more fruit. You are already clean because of the word which I have spoken to you. Abide in Me, and I in you. As the branch cannot bear fruit of itself unless it abides in the vine, so neither *can* you unless you abide in Me. I am the vine, you are the branches; he who abides in Me and I in him, he bears much fruit, for apart from Me you can do nothing. If anyone does not abide in Me, he is thrown away as a branch and dries up; and they gather them, and cast them into the fire and they are burned. If you abide in Me, and My words abide in you, ask whatever you wish, and it will be done for you. My Father is glorified by this, that you bear much fruit, and *so* prove to be My disciples. Just as the Father has loved Me, I have also loved you; abide in My love. If you keep My commandments, you will abide in My love; just as I have kept My Father's commandments and abide in His love. These things I have spoken to you so that My joy may be in you, and *that* your joy may be made full" (John 15:1–11; see Matthew 5:16; 7:7; John 3:29, 35; 6:56; 8:29, 31; 13:10).

[OBEDIENCE from what I command you]
Setting: Jerusalem. Before the Passover, with His departure in mind, after explaining He is the vine and His disciples are the branches, Jesus commands them to love one another.

"This is My commandment, that you love one another, just as I have loved you. Greater love has no one than this, that one lay down his life for his friends. You are My friends if you do what I command you. No longer do I call you slaves, for the slave does not know what his master is doing; but I have called you friends, for all things that I have heard from My Father I have made known to you. You did not choose Me but I chose you, and appointed you that you would go and bear fruit, and *that* your fruit would remain, so that whatever you ask of the Father in My name He may give to you. This I command you, that you love one another" (John 15:12–17; see Matthew 12:50; John 6:70; 8:26; 10:11; 13:34).

[OBEDIENCE from kept Your word]
Setting: Jerusalem. Before the Passover, after giving His disciples assurance that in the midst of tribulation they will have His peace, Jesus prays His high-priestly prayer.

Jesus spoke these things; and lifting up His eyes to heaven, He said, "Father, the hour has come; glorify Your Son, that the Son may glorify You, even as You gave Him authority over all flesh, that to all whom You have given Him, He may give eternal life. This is eternal life, that they may know You, the only true God, and Jesus Christ whom You have sent. I glorified You on the earth, having accomplished the work which You have given Me to do. Now, Father, glorify Me together with Yourself, with the glory which I had with You before the world was. I have manifested Your name to the men whom You gave Me out of the world; they were Yours and You gave them to Me, and they have kept Your word. Now they have come to know that everything You have given Me is from You; for the words which You gave Me I have given to them; and they received *them* and truly understood that I came forth from You, and they believed You sent Me. I ask on their behalf; I do not ask on behalf of the world, but of those whom You have given Me; for they are Yours; and all things that are Mine are Yours, and Yours are Mine; and I have been glorified in them. I am no longer in the world; and *yet* they themselves are in the world, and I come to You. Holy Father, keep them in Your name, *the name* which You have given Me, that they may be even as We *are.* While I was with them, I was keeping them in Your name which You have given Me; and I guarded them and not one of them perished but the son of perdition, so that the Scripture would be fulfilled" (John 17:1–12; see Luke 22:32; John 1:1; 3:35; 4:34; 5:44; 6:37–39, 70; 8:42; 11:41; 12:49; 13:18, 31; 16:15; Philippians 2:9).

[OBEDIENCE from keeps My deeds]
Setting: On the island of Patmos (in the Aegean Sea about fifty miles southwest of Ephesus in modern Turkey). On the Lord's Day (Sunday), approximately fifty years after Jesus' resurrection, the disciple John encounters the Lord Jesus Christ, who communicates a new revelation for the apostle to record for the church in Thyatira and to six other churches in Asia.

"And to the angel of the church in Thyatira write: The Son of God, who has eyes like a flame of fire, and His feet are like burnished bronze, says this: 'I know your deeds, and your love and faith and service and perseverance, and that your deeds of late are greater than at first. But I have *this* against you, that you tolerate the woman Jezebel, who calls herself a prophetess, and she teaches and leads My bond-servants astray so that they commit *acts of* immorality and eat things sacrificed to idols. I gave her time to repent, and she does not want to repent of her immorality. Behold, I will throw her on a bed *of sickness,* and those who commit adultery with her into great tribulation, unless they repent of her deeds. And I will kill her children with pestilence, and all the churches will know that I am He who searches the minds and hearts; and I will give to each one of you according to your deeds. But I say to you, the rest who are in Thyatira, who do not hold this teaching, who have not known the deep things of Satan, as they call them—I place no other burden on you. Nevertheless what you have, hold fast until I come. He who overcomes, and he who keeps My deeds until the end, TO HIM I WILL GIVE AUTHORITY OVER THE NATIONS; AND HE SHALL RULE THEM WITH A ROD OF IRON, AS THE VESSELS OF THE POTTER ARE BROKEN TO PIECES, as I also have received *authority* from My Father; and I will give him the morning star. He who has an ear, let him hear what the Spirit says to the churches' (Revelation 2:18–29; Jesus quotes from Psalm 2:8, 9; Isaiah 30:14; see 1 Kings 16:31; Psalm 7:9; Romans 2:5; 1 Corinthians 2:10; 2 Peter 3:9; Revelation 1:14; 2:7; 3:11; 17:1–20).

OBEDIENCE, JESUS'

[JESUS' OBEDIENCE from not as I will, but as You will and Your will be done]
Setting: An upper room in Jerusalem. After celebrating the Passover meal with His disciples, Jesus retreats to the Garden of Gethsemane on the Mount of Olives to pray prior to His betrayal by Judas.

Then Jesus came with them to a place called Gethsemane, and said to His disciples, "Sit here while I go over there and pray." And He took with Him Peter and the two sons of Zebedee, and began to be grieved and distressed. Then He said to them, "My soul is deeply grieved, to the point of death; remain here and keep watch with Me." And He went a little beyond *them,* and fell on His face and prayed, saying, "My Father, if it is possible, let this cup pass from Me; yet not as I will, but as You will." And He came to the disciples and found them sleeping, and said to Peter, "So, you *men* could not keep watch with Me for one hour? Keep watching and praying that you may not enter into temptation; the spirit is willing, but the flesh is weak." He went away again a second time and prayed, saying, "My Father, if this cannot pass away unless I drink it, Your will be done." Again He came and found them sleeping, for their eyes were heavy. And He left them again, and went away and prayed a third time, saying the same thing once more. Then He came to the disciples and said to them, "Are you still sleeping and resting? Behold the hour is at hand and the Son of Man is being betrayed into the hands of sinners. Get up, let us be going; behold the one who betrays Me is at hand!" (Matthew 26:36–46; cf. Mark 14:32–42; Luke 22:40–46; see Matthew 20:22; John 12:27).

[JESUS' OBEDIENCE from yet not what I will, but what You will]
Setting: Gethsemane on the Mount of Olives, east of the temple in Jerusalem. Jesus agonizes over His impending death, disappointed His disciples keep falling asleep instead of watching and praying with Him.

They came to a place named Gethsemane; and He said to the disciples, "Sit here until I have prayed." And He took with Him Peter and James and John, and began to be very distressed and troubled. And He said to them, "My soul is deeply grieved to the point of death; remain here and keep watch." And He went a little beyond *them,* and fell to the ground and *began* to pray that if it were possible, the hour might pass Him by. And He was saying, "Abba! Father! All things are possible for You; remove this cup from Me; yet not what I will, but what You will." And He came and found them sleeping, and said to Peter, "Simon, are you asleep? Could you not keep watch for one hour? Keep watching and praying that you may not come into temptation; the spirit is willing, but the flesh is weak" (Mark 14:32–38; cf. Matthew 26:36–41; Luke 22:41–46; see Romans 8:15; Galatians 4:6).

[JESUS' OBEDIENCE from yet not My will, but Yours be done]
Setting: Jerusalem. After celebrating the Passover meal and instructing His disciples to prepare to persevere without Him, with His crucifixion imminent, Jesus proceeds to the Mount of Olives to pray.

And He came out and proceeded as was His custom to the Mount of Olives; and the disciples also followed Him. When He arrived at the place, He said to them, "Pray that you may not enter into temptation." And He withdrew from them about a stone's throw, and He knelt down and *began* to pray, saying, "Father, if You are willing, remove this cup from Me; yet not My will, but Yours be done" (Luke 22:39–42; cf. Matthew 26:36–42; Mark 14:32–49; see Luke 21:37).

[JESUS' OBEDIENCE from I do exactly as the Father commanded Me]
Setting: Jerusalem. Before the Passover, after He conveys the upcoming ministry of the Holy Spirit in His disciples' lives, Jesus again relates peace, hope, and comfort to them regarding His return to the Father.

"Peace I leave with you; My peace I give to you; not as the world gives do I give to you. Do not let your heart be troubled, nor let it be fearful. You heard that I said to you, 'I go away, and I will come to you,' If you loved Me, you would have rejoiced because I go to the Father, for the Father is greater than I. Now I have told you before it happens, so that when it happens, you may believe. I will not speak much more with you, for the ruler of the world is coming, and he has nothing in Me; but so that the world may know that I love the Father, I do exactly as the Father commanded Me. Get up, let us go from here" (John 14:27–31; see John 10:18, 29; 12:31; 13:19; 16:33).

OBLIGATIONS

[OBLIGATIONS from allow the dead to bury their own dead]
Setting: By the Sea of Galilee. Following a time of casting out evil spirits from the demon-possessed and healing the ill in fulfillment of Isaiah 53:4, Jesus lays out to an inquiring scribe the demands of discipleship.

Then a scribe came and said to Him, "Teacher, I will follow You wherever you go." Jesus said to him, "The foxes have holes and the birds of the air *have* nests, but the Son of Man has nowhere to lay His head." Another of the disciples said to Him, "Lord, permit me first to go and bury my father." But Jesus said to him, "Follow Me, and allow the dead to bury their own dead" (Matthew 8:19–22; cf. Luke 9:57–60).

[OBLIGATIONS from Allow the dead to bury their own dead]
Setting: On the way from Galilee to Jerusalem. The Lord responds to several men seeking to follow Him.

And He said to another, "Follow Me." But he said, "Lord, permit me first to go and bury my father," But He said to him, "Allow the dead to bury their own dead; but as for you, go and proclaim everywhere the kingdom of God" (Luke 9:59, 60; cf. Matthew 8:19–22).

OFFENSE (Also see FORGIVENESS; INSULTS; RECONCILIATION; and STUMBLE)

Setting: Galilee. As He teaches and preaches, Jesus responds to John the Baptist's question (posed by some of John's disciples) whether He is Israel's promised Messiah.

Jesus answered and said to them, "Go and report to John what you hear and see: *the* BLIND RECEIVE SIGHT and *the* lame walk, *the* lepers are cleansed and *the* deaf hear, *the* dead are raised up, and *the* POOR HAVE THE GOSPEL PREACHED TO THEM. And blessed is he who does not take offense at Me" (Matthew 11:4–6, Jesus quotes from Isaiah 35:5f; cf. Luke 7:22, 23).

[OFFENSE from offend]
Setting: Capernaum of Galilee. Jesus pays the two-drachma temple tax for Peter and Himself in a miraculous manner.

He said, "Yes." And when he came into the house, Jesus spoke to him first, saying, "What do you think, Simon? From whom do the kings of the earth collect customs or poll-tax, from their sons or from strangers?" When Peter said, "From strangers," Jesus said to him, "Then the sons are exempt. However, so that we do not offend them, go to the sea and throw in a hook, and take the first fish that comes up; and when you open its mouth, you will find a shekel. Take that and give it to them for you and Me" (Matthew 17:25–27; see Exodus 30:11–16; Matthew 17:24; 22:17–19; Romans 13:7).

Setting: Galilee. After Jesus raises a woman's son from the dead in Nain, the disciples of John the Baptist inquire whether He is the promised Messiah.

And He answered and said to them, "Go and report to John what you have seen and heard: *the* BLIND RECEIVE SIGHT, *the* lame walk, *the* lepers are cleansed, and *the* deaf hear, *the* dead are raised up, *the* POOR HAVE THE GOSPEL PREACHED TO THEM. Blessed is he who does not take offense at Me" (Luke 7:22, 23, Jesus quotes from Isaiah 35:5; 61:1; cf. Matthew 11:2–6).

OFFER OF HEALING (Listed under HEALING, OFFER OF)

OFFERING (Also see GIFTS; GIVING; STEWARDSHIP; TITHE; and WORSHIP)

Setting: Galilee. During the early part of His ministry, Jesus preaches the Sermon on the Mount to His disciples and the multitudes.

"Therefore if you are presenting your offering at the altar, and there remember that your brother has something against you, leave your offering there before the altar and go; first be reconciled to your brother, and then come and present your offering" (Matthew 5:23, 24; see Romans 12:17, 18).

Setting: Galilee. When Jesus comes down after preaching The Sermon on the Mount, large crowds follow Him, as a leper approaches Him asking for cleansing.

Jesus stretched out His hand and touched him, saying, "I am willing, be cleansed." And immediately his leprosy was cleansed. And Jesus said to him, "See that you tell no one; but go, show yourself to the priest and present the offering that Moses commanded, as a testimony to them" (Matthew 8:3, 4; cf. Mark 1:40–44; Luke 5:12–14).

Setting: The temple in Jerusalem. After the Jewish religious leaders test Him with questions, Jesus pronounces the fourth of eight woes on them in front of the crowds and His disciples.

"Woe to you, blind guides, who say, 'Whoever swears by the temple, *that* is nothing; but whoever swears by the gold of the temple is obligated.' You fools and blind men! Which is more important, the gold or the temple that sanctified the gold? And, 'Whoever swears by the altar, *that* is nothing, but whoever swears by the offering on it, he is obligated.' You blind men, which is more important, the offering, or the altar that sanctifies the offering? Therefore, whoever swears by the altar, swears *both* by the altar and by everything on it. And whoever swears by the temple, swears *both* by the temple and by Him who dwells within it. And whoever swears by heaven, swears *both* by the throne of God and by Him who sits upon it" (Matthew 23:16–22; see Exodus 29:37; 1 Kings 8:13; Isaiah 66:1; Matthew 15:14).

[OFFERING inferred]
Setting: Opposite the temple treasury in Jerusalem. Jesus focuses His disciples' attention on a widow's monetary sacrifice.

Calling His disciples to Him, He said to them, "Truly I say to you, this poor widow put in more than all the contributors to the treasury; for they all put in out of their surplus, but she, out of her poverty, put in all she owned, all she had to live on" (Mark 12:43, 44; cf. Luke 21:1–4).

Setting: Galilee. Early in His ministry, after calling Andrew, Simon (Peter), James, and John to follow Him, Jesus heals a leper.

And He stretched out His hand and touched Him, saying, "I am willing; be cleansed." And immediately the leprosy left him. And He ordered him to tell no one, "But go and show yourself to the priest and make an offering for your cleansing, just as Moses commanded, as a testimony to them" (Luke 5:13, 14; cf. Matthew 8:2–4; Mark 1:40–45; see Leviticus 13:49).

Setting: The temple in Jerusalem. While ministering a few days before His crucifixion, after warning His disciples about the lifestyle of the scribes, Jesus points out a poor widow's sacrificial giving to the temple treasury.

And He said, "Truly I say to you, this poor widow put in more than all *of them;* for they all out of their surplus put into the offering; but she out of her poverty put in all that she had to live on" (Luke 21:3, 4; cf. Mark 12:41–44).

OFFERING, WIDOW'S (See MITE, WIDOW'S)

OFFICER

Setting: Galilee. During the early part of His ministry, Jesus preaches the Sermon on the Mount to His disciples and the multitudes.

"Make friends quickly with your opponent at law while you are with him on the way, so that your opponent may not hand you over to the judge, and the judge to the officer, and you be thrown into prison. Truly I say to you, you will not come out of there until you have paid up the last cent'" (Matthew 5:25, 26; cf. Luke 12:58, 59).

Setting: On the way from Galilee to Jerusalem. After chastising the crowds for being able to discern the weather but not the present age, Jesus exhorts them to settle any financial disputes outside of court.

"And why do you not even on your own initiative judge what is right? For while you are going with your opponent to appear before the magistrate, on *your* way *there* make an effort to settle with him, so that he may not drag you before the judge, and the judge turn you over to the officer, and the officer throw you into prison. I say to you, you will not get out of there until you have paid the very last cent" (Luke 12:57–59; cf. Matthew 5:25, 26).

OIL

Setting: On the Mount of Olives, just east of Jerusalem. During His Olivet Discourse, after answering His disciples' questions as to when the temple will be destroyed and Jerusalem overrun, along with the signs of His coming and the end of the age, Jesus reemphasizes to His disciples that they should be on the alert for His return.

"Then the kingdom of heaven will be comparable to ten virgins, who took their lamps and went out to meet the bridegroom. Five of them were foolish, and five were prudent. For when the foolish took their lamps, they took no oil with them, but the prudent took oil in flasks along with their lamps. Now while the bridegroom was delaying, they all got drowsy and *began* to sleep. But at midnight there was a shout, 'Behold, the bridegroom! Come out to meet *him.'* Then all those virgins rose and trimmed their lamps. The foolish said to the prudent, 'Give us some of your oil, for our lamps are going out.' But the prudent answered, 'No, there will not be enough for us and you *too;* go instead to the dealers and buy *some* for yourselves.' And while they were going away to make the purchase, the bridegroom came, and those who were ready went in with him to the wedding feast; and the door was shut. Later the other virgins also came, saying, 'Lord, lord, open up for us.' But he answered, 'Truly I say to you, I do not know you.' Be on the alert then, for you do not know the day nor the hour" (Matthew 25:1–13; cf. Matthew 24:42; Luke 12:35; see Matthew 7:21, 24).

Setting: Galilee. After Jesus praises John the Baptist to the crowds, Simon, a Pharisee, invites the Lord to dinner. A sinful woman anoints His feet with perfume, prompting Him to instruct His host about forgiveness.

Turning toward the woman, He said to Simon, "Do you see this woman? I entered your house; you gave Me no water for My feet, but she has wet My feet with her tears and wiped them with her hair. You gave Me no kiss; but she, since the time I came in, has not ceased to kiss My feet. You did not anoint My head with oil, but she anointed My feet with perfume. For this reason I say to you, her sins, which are many, have been forgiven, for she loved much; but he who is forgiven little, loves little." Then He said to her, "Your sins have been forgiven." Those who were reclining *at the table* with Him began to say to themselves, "Who is this *man* who even forgives sins?" And He said to the woman, "Your faith has saved you; go in peace" (Luke 7:44–50; see Matthew 9:2; Mark 5:34; Luke 5:21).

Setting: On the way from Galilee to Jerusalem. While being tested by a lawyer, Jesus tells him the story of the good Samaritan.

Jesus replied and said, "A man was going down from Jerusalem to Jericho, and fell among robbers, and they stripped him and beat him, and went away leaving him half dead. And by chance a priest was going down on that road, and when he saw him, he passed by on the other side. Likewise a Levite also, when he came to the place and saw him, passed by on the other side. But a Samaritan, who was on a journey, came upon him; and when he saw him, he felt compassion, and came to him and bandaged up his wounds, pouring oil and wine on *them;* and he put him on his own beast, and brought him to an inn and took care of him. On the next day he took out two denarii and gave them to the innkeeper and said, 'Take care of him; and whatever more you spend, when I return I will repay you.' Which of these three do you think proved to be a neighbor to the man who fell into the robbers' *hands?*" And he said, "The one who showed mercy toward him." Then Jesus said to him, "Go and do the same" (Luke 10:30–37).

Setting: On the way from Galilee to Jerusalem. After giving the story of the prodigal son, the Lord teaches His disciples about stewardship.

Now He was also saying to the disciples, "There was a rich man who had a manager, and this *manager* was reported to him as squandering his possessions. And he called him and said to him, 'What is this I hear about you? Give an accounting of your management, for you can no longer be a manager.' The manager said to himself, 'What shall I do, since my master is taking the management away from me? I am not strong enough to dig; I am ashamed to beg. I know what I shall do, so that when I am removed from the management people will welcome me into their homes.' And he summoned each one of his master's debtors, and he *began* saying to the first, 'How much do you owe my master?' And he said, 'A hundred measures of oil.' And he said to him, 'Take your bill, and sit down quickly and write fifty.' Then he said to another, 'And how much do you owe?' And he said, 'A hundred measures of wheat.' He said to him, 'Take your bill, and write eighty.' And his master praised the unrighteous manager because he had acted shrewdly; for the sons of this age are more shrewd in relation to their own kind than the sons of light. And I say to you, make friends for yourselves by means of the wealth of unrighteousness, so that when it fails, they will receive you into the eternal dwellings. He who is faithful in a very little thing is faithful also in much; and he who is unrighteous in a very little thing is unrighteous also in much. Therefore if you have not been faithful in the *use of* unrighteous wealth, who will entrust the true *riches* to you? And if you have not been faithful in *the use of* that which is another's, who will give you that which is your own? No servant can serve two masters; for either he will hate the one and love the other, or else he will be devoted to one and despise the other. You cannot serve God and wealth" (Luke 16:1–13; cf. Matthew 6:24; see Matthew 25:14–30).

OIL IN FLASKS (See OIL)

OLD (Also see specifics such as GARMENT, OLD)

Setting: By the Sea of Galilee. Jesus teaches the Parable of the Head of a Household to His disciples.

And Jesus said to them, "Therefore every scribe who has become a disciple of the kingdom of heaven is like a head of a household, who brings out of his treasure things new and old" (Matthew 13:52).

Setting: Capernaum near the Sea of Galilee. John the Baptist's disciples and the Pharisees question why Jesus' disciples do not fast, while they do.

And Jesus said to them, "While the bridegroom is with them, the attendants of the bridegroom cannot fast, can they? So long as they have the bridegroom with them, they cannot fast. But the days will come when the bridegroom is taken away from them, and then they will fast in that day. No one sews a patch of unshrunk cloth on an old garment; otherwise the patch pulls away from it, the new from the old, and a worse tear results. No one puts new wine into old wineskins; otherwise the wine will burst the skins, and the wine is lost and the skins as *well;* but *one puts* new wine into fresh wineskins" (Mark 2:19–22; cf. Matthew 9:14–17; Luke 5:33–38).

Setting: The home of Levi (Matthew) in Capernaum. At a reception for Jesus following Levi's call to be a disciple, the Lord tells a parable to the Pharisees and their scribes, who question His association with tax collectors and sinners.

And He was also telling them a parable: "No one tears a piece of cloth from a new garment and puts it on an old garment; otherwise he will both tear the new, and the piece from the new will not match the old. And no one puts new wine into old wineskins; otherwise the new wine will burst the skins and it will be spilled out, and the skins will be ruined. But new wine must be put into fresh wineskins. And no one, after drinking old *wine* wishes for new; for he says, 'The old is good *enough*'" (Luke 5:36–39; cf. Matthew 9:16, 17; Mark 2:21, 22).

Setting: By the Sea of Galilee. During the Lord's third post-resurrection appearance to His disciples, after quizzing Peter regarding the disciple's love for Him, Jesus gives him details about his aging and his eventual death.

"Truly, truly, I say to you, when you were younger, you used to gird yourself and walk wherever you wished; but when you grow old, you will stretch out your hands and someone else will gird you, and bring you where you do not wish to *go*." Now this He said, signifying by what kind of death he would glorify God. And when He had spoken this, He said to him, "Follow Me!" (John 21:18, 19).

OLD GARMENT (Listed under GARMENT, OLD)

OLD TESTAMENT (Also see BIBLE; SCRIPTURE; SCRIPTURES; WORD, GOD'S; WORD OF GOD; and WRITINGS)

[OLD TESTAMENT from the Law or the Prophets and the Law]

Setting: Galilee. During the early part of His ministry, Jesus preaches the Sermon on the Mount to His disciples and the multitudes.

"Do not think that I came to abolish the Law or the Prophets; I did not come to abolish but to fulfill. For truly I say to you, until heaven and earth pass away, not the smallest letter or stroke shall pass from the Law until all is accomplished" (Matthew 5:17, 18; cf. Matthew 24:35).

[OLD TESTAMENT from the Law and the Prophets]

Setting: Galilee. During the early part of His ministry, Jesus preaches the Sermon on the Mount to His disciples and the multitudes.

"Ask, and it will be given to you; seek, and you will find; knock, and it will be opened to you. For everyone who asks receives, and he who seeks finds, and to him who knocks it will be opened. Or what man is there among you who, when his son asks for a loaf, will give him a stone? Or if he asks for a fish, he will not give him a snake, will he? If you then, being evil, know how to give good gifts to your children, how much more will your Father who is in heaven give what is good to those who ask Him! In everything, therefore, treat people the same way you want them to treat you, for this is the Law and the Prophets" (Matthew 7:7–12; cf. Matthew 22:40; Luke 6:31; 11:9–13; see Psalm 84:11).

[OLD TESTAMENT from the prophets and the Law]
Setting: Galilee. While speaking to the crowds, Jesus pays tribute to the ministry of John the Baptist, but emphasizes that the one who is least in the kingdom of heaven is greater than John.

As these men were going *away,* Jesus began to speak to the crowds about John, "What did you go out into the wilderness to see? A reed shaken by the wind? But what did you go out to see? A man dressed in soft *clothing?* Those who wear soft *clothing* are in kings' palaces! But what did you go out to see? A prophet? Yes, I tell you, and the one who is more than a prophet. This is the one about whom it is written, 'BEHOLD, I SEND MY MESSENGER AHEAD OF YOU, WHO WILL PREPARE YOUR WAY BEFORE YOU.' Truly, I say to you, among those born of women there has not arisen *anyone* greater than John the Baptist! Yet the one who is least in the kingdom of heaven is greater than he. From the days of John the Baptist until now the kingdom of heaven suffers violence, and violent men take it by force. For all the prophets and the Law prophesied until John. And, if you are willing to accept *it,* John himself is Elijah who was to come. He who has ears to hear, let him hear" (Matthew 11:7–15, Jesus quotes from Malachi 3:1; cf. Malachi 4:5; Luke 7:24–28; 16:16; see Matthew 14:5).

[OLD TESTAMENT from the Law]
Setting: Galilee. Jesus responds to the Pharisees' objection to His disciples' picking grain from the fields on the Sabbath.

But He said to them, "Have you not read what David did when he became hungry, he and his companions, how they entered the house of God, and ate the consecrated bread, which was not lawful for him to eat nor for those with him, but for the priests alone? Or, have you not read in the Law, that on the Sabbath the priests in the temple break the Sabbath and are innocent? But I say to you that something greater than the temple is here. But if you had known what this means, 'I DESIRE COMPASSION, AND NOT A SACRIFICE,' you would not have condemned the innocent. For the Son of Man is Lord of the Sabbath" (Matthew 12:3–8, Jesus quotes from Hosea 6:6; cf. Mark 2:25–28; Luke 6:3–5; see 1 Samuel 21:6).

[OLD TESTAMENT from the Scriptures]
Setting: The temple in Jerusalem. Jesus delivers a prophecy to the chief priests and elders after they question His authority.

Jesus said to them, "Did you never read in the Scriptures, 'THE STONE WHICH THE BUILDERS REJECTED, THIS BECAME THE CHIEF CORNER *stone;* THIS CAME ABOUT FROM THE LORD, AND IT IS MARVELOUS IN OUR EYES'? Therefore I say to you, the kingdom of God will be taken away from you and given to a people, producing the fruit of it. And he who falls on this stone will be broken to pieces; but on whomever it falls, it will scatter him like dust" (Matthew 21:42–44, Jesus quotes from Psalm 118:22; cf. Isaiah 8:14, 15; Mark 12:10, 11; Luke 20:17, 18).

[OLD TESTAMENT from the Scriptures]
Setting: The temple in Jerusalem. The Sadducees question Jesus about Levirate marriage (marriage to a brother-in-law), in order to test Him.

But Jesus answered and said to them, "You are mistaken, not understanding the Scriptures nor the power of God. For in the resurrection they neither marry nor are given in marriage, but are like angels in heaven. But regarding the resurrection of the dead, have you not read what was spoken to you by God: 'I AM THE GOD OF ABRAHAM, AND THE GOD OF ISAAC, AND THE GOD OF JACOB'? He is not the God of the dead but of the living" (Matthew 22:29–32, Jesus quotes from Exodus 3:6; cf. Mark 12:18–27; Luke 20:27–38; see Deuteronomy 25:5; John 20:9).

[OLD TESTAMENT from Law and the Prophets]
Setting: The temple in Jerusalem. As Jesus teaches, a Pharisee lawyer asks Him which is the great commandment of the Law in order to test Him.

And He said to him, " 'YOU SHALL LOVE THE LORD YOUR GOD WITH ALL YOUR HEART, AND WITH ALL YOUR SOUL, AND WITH ALL YOUR MIND.' This is the great and foremost commandment. The second is like it, 'YOU SHALL LOVE YOUR NEIGHBOR AS YOURSELF.' On these two commandments depend the whole Law and the Prophets" (Matthew 22:37–40; Jesus quotes from Leviticus 19:18; Deuteronomy 6:5; cf. Mark 12:28–34; see Matthew 7:12).

[OLD TESTAMENT from the Scriptures be fulfilled]
Setting: Gethsemane on the Mount of Olives, east of the temple in Jerusalem. As Jesus submits to His Father's will and allows Judas to betray Him, Peter attempts to defend Him by force, but the Lord does not permit it.

Then Jesus said to him, "Put your sword back into its place; for all those who take up the sword shall perish by the sword. Or do you think that I cannot appeal to My Father, and He will at once put at My disposal more than twelve legions of angels? How then will the Scriptures be fulfilled, *which say* that it must happen this way?" (Matthew 26:52–54; cf. Mark 14:47; Luke 22:50, 51; John 18:10, 11; see Matthew 26:24).

[OLD TESTAMENT from the Scriptures of the prophets]
Setting: Gethsemane on the Mount of Olives, east of the temple in Jerusalem. As He submits to His Father's will and allows Judas to betray Him, Jesus reveals that this is a fulfillment of prophecy.

At that time Jesus said to the crowds, "Have you come out with swords and clubs to arrest Me as *you would* against a robber? Every day I used to sit in the temple teaching and you did not seize Me. But all this has taken place to fulfill the Scriptures of the prophets" (Matthew 26:55, 56; cf. Mark 14:48, 49; Luke 22:52, 53; see Matthew 26:24).

[OLD TESTAMENT from the Scriptures]
Setting: The temple in Jerusalem. After some of the Pharisees and Herodians attempt to trap Jesus in a statement, some Sadducees question Him about the status of marriage after death.

Jesus said to them, "Is this not the reason you are mistaken, that you do not understand the Scriptures or the power of God? For when they rise from the dead, they neither marry nor are given in marriage, but are like angels in heaven. But regarding the fact that the dead rise again, have you not read in the book of Moses, in the *passage* about *the burning* bush, how God spoke to him, saying, 'I AM THE GOD OF ABRAHAM, AND THE GOD OF ISAAC, and the God of Jacob?' He is not the God of the dead, but of the living; you are greatly mistaken" (Mark 12:24–27, Jesus quotes from Exodus 3:6; cf. Matthew 22:29–33; Luke 20:34–40).

[OLD TESTAMENT from to fulfill the Scriptures]
Setting: Gethsemane on the Mount of Olives, east of the temple in Jerusalem. Judas betrays Jesus with a kiss in front of a crowd from the chief priests, scribes, and elders seeking to seize the Lord with swords and clubs.

And Jesus said to them, "Have you come out with swords and clubs to arrest Me, as *you would* against a robber? Every day I was with you in the temple teaching, and you did not seize Me; but *this has taken place* to fulfill the Scriptures" (Mark 14:48, 49; cf. Matthew 26:55, 56; Luke 22:52, 53).

[OLD TESTAMENT from the Law]
Setting: On the way from Galilee to Jerusalem. After Jesus tells His disciples in private the privilege they are experiencing by living in the time of the Messiah, a lawyer tests Him.

And a lawyer stood up and put Him to the test, saying, "Teacher, what shall I do to inherit eternal life?" And He said to him, "What is written in the Law? How does it read to you?" And he answered, "YOU SHALL LOVE THE LORD YOUR GOD WITH ALL YOUR HEART, AND WITH ALL YOUR SOUL, AND WITH ALL YOUR STRENGTH, AND WITH ALL YOUR MIND; AND YOUR NEIGHBOR AS YOURSELF." And He said to him, "You have answered correctly; DO THIS AND YOU WILL LIVE" (Luke 10:25–28, Jesus quotes from Leviticus 18:5; see Deuteronomy 6:5; Matthew 19:16–19).

[OLD TESTAMENT from The Law and the Prophets]
Setting: On the way from Galilee to Jerusalem. The Lord responds to the Pharisees' scoffing at His teaching His disciples about stewardship.

And He said to them, "You are those who justify yourselves in the sight of men, but God knows your hearts; for that which is highly esteemed among men is detestable in the sight of God. The Law and the Prophets *were proclaimed* until John; since that time the gospel of the kingdom of God has been preached, and everyone is forcing his way into it. But is it easier for heaven and earth to pass away than for one stroke of a letter of the Law to fail" (Luke 16:15–17; cf. Matthew 5:18; see 1 Samuel 16:7; Matthew 4:23; 11:11–14).

[OLD TESTAMENT from the Law of Moses and the Prophets and the Psalms]
Setting: Jerusalem. After rising from the tomb on the third day after being crucified, and appearing to two of His followers on the road to Emmaus, Jesus gives instruction to His disciples (except Thomas) about His mission on earth and the promise of future power from God.

Now He said to them, "These are My words which I spoke to you while I was still with you, that all things which are written about Me in the Law of Moses and the Prophets and the Psalms must be fulfilled." Then He opened their minds to understand the Scriptures, and He said to them, "Thus it is written, that the Christ would suffer and rise again from the dead the third day, and that repentance for forgiveness of sins would be proclaimed in His name to all the nations, beginning from Jerusalem. You are witnesses of these things. And behold, I am sending forth the promise of My Father upon you; but you are to stay in the city until you are clothed with power from on high" (Luke 24:44–49; see Matthew 28:19, 20; Acts 1:8).

[OLD TESTAMENT from the Scriptures]
Setting: Jerusalem. During a feast of the Jews, Jesus responds to criticism from the Jewish religious leaders by referring to God as His Father (thereby making Himself equal with God) and informing them that God, John the Baptist, the Scriptures, and His works all testify to His mission.

"You search the Scriptures because you think that in them you have eternal life; it is these that testify about Me; and you are unwilling to come to Me so that you may have life. I do not receive glory from men; but I know you, that you do not have the love of God in yourselves. I have come in My Father's name, and you do not receive Me; if another comes in his own name, you will receive him. How can you believe, when you receive glory from one another and you do not seek the glory that is from the *one and* only God? Do not think that I will accuse you before the Father; the one who accuses you is Moses, in whom you have set your hope. For if you believed Moses, you would believe Me, for he wrote about Me. But if you do not believe his writings, how will you believe My words?" (John 5:39–47; see Matthew 24:5; Luke 16:29, 31; 24:27; John 9:28; 17:3).

[OLD TESTAMENT from the Law]
Setting: The temple in Jerusalem. After receiving encouragement from His blood brothers in Galilee to attend the upcoming Feast of Booths in order to demonstrate His works to His disciples and the world, Jesus goes and teaches, astonishing the Jewish religious leaders.

"Did not Moses give you the Law, and *yet* none of you carries out the Law? Why do you seek to kill Me?" (John 7:19; see Mark 11:18; John 1:17).

[OLD TESTAMENT from the Law of Moses]
Setting: The temple in Jerusalem. After receiving encouragement from His blood brothers in Galilee to attend the upcoming Feast of Booths in order to demonstrate His works to His disciples and the world, Jesus goes and teaches, astonishing the Jewish religious leaders.

Jesus answered them, "I did one deed, and you all marvel. For this reason Moses has given you circumcision (not because it is from Moses, but from the fathers), and on *the* Sabbath you circumcise a man. If a man receives circumcision on *the* Sabbath so that the Law of Moses will not be broken, are you angry with Me because I made an entire man well on *the* Sabbath? Do not judge according to appearance, but judge with righteous judgment" (John 7:21–24; see Genesis 17:10–14; Leviticus 12:3; 19:15; Matthew 12:2; John 5:2–16; 7–20).

[OLD TESTAMENT from your Law]
Setting: Jerusalem. At the Feast of Dedication, the Pharisees desire to stone Jesus because He claims to be equal with God when they ask Him plainly whether He is the Christ.

Jesus answered them, "Has it not been written in your Law, 'I SAID, YOU ARE GODS'? If he called them gods, to whom the word of God came (and the Scripture cannot be broken), do you say of Him, whom the Father sanctified and sent into the world, 'You are blaspheming,' because I said, 'I am the Son of God'? If I do not do the works of My Father, do not believe Me; but if I do them, though you do not believe Me, believe the works, so that you may know and understand that the Father is in Me, and I in the Father" (John 10:34–38, Jesus quotes from Psalm 82:6; see John 14:10, 20).

OLD WINESKINS (See WINESKINS, PARABLE OF THE NEW WINE IN OLD)

OLDER SON (Listed under SON, OLDER)

OMEGA (Also see END; and LAST)
Setting: On the island of Patmos (in the Aegean Sea about fifty miles southwest of Ephesus in modern Turkey). On the Lord's Day (Sunday), approximately fifty years after His resurrection, the disciple John encounters the Lord Jesus Christ, who communicates new revelations for the apostle to record for the seven churches in Asia.

"I am the Alpha and the Omega," says the Lord God, "who is and who was and who is to come, the Almighty" (Revelation 1:8; see Revelation 21:6).

Setting: On the island of Patmos (in the Aegean Sea about fifty miles southwest of Ephesus in modern Turkey). In the final chapter of the Lord Jesus Christ's revelation via the disciple John, approximately fifty years after His resurrection, the Lord reveals His coming return, reward, and eternality.

"Behold, I am coming quickly, and My reward *is* with Me, to render to every man according to what he has done. I am the Alpha and the Omega, the first and the last, the beginning and the end" (Revelation 22:12, 13; see Isaiah 40:10; 44:6; Revelation 22:11).

OMNIPOTENCE (See POWER OF GOD)

OMNISCIENCE, GOD'S (Also see KNOWLEDGE; and OMNISCIENCE, JESUS')
[GOD'S OMNISCIENCE from your Father knows what you need before you ask Him]
Setting: Galilee. During the early part of His ministry, Jesus preaches the Sermon on the Mount to His disciples and the multitudes.

"And when you are praying, do not use meaningless repetition as the Gentiles do, for they suppose that they will be heard for their many words. So do not be like them; for your Father knows what you need before you ask Him" (Matthew 6:7, 8; see 1 Kings 18:26–29).

[GOD'S OMNISCIENCE from your heavenly Father knows that you need all these things]
Setting: Galilee. During the early part of His ministry, Jesus preaches the Sermon on the Mount to His disciples and the multitudes.

"For this reason I say to you, do not be worried about your life, *as to* what you will eat or what you will drink; nor for your body, *as to* what you will put on. Is not life more than food, and the body more than clothing? Look at the birds of the air, that they do not sow, nor reap nor gather into barns, and *yet* your heavenly Father feeds them. Are you not worth much more than they? And who of you by being worried can add a *single* hour to his life? And why are you worried about clothing? Observe how the lilies of the field grow; they do not toil nor do they spin, yet I say to you that not even Solomon in all his glory clothed himself like one of these. But if God so clothes the grass of the field, which is *alive* today and tomorrow is thrown into the furnace, *will He* not much more *clothe* you? You of little faith! Do not worry then, saying 'What will we eat?' or 'What will we drink?' or 'What will be wear for clothing?" For the Gentiles eagerly seek all these things; for your heavenly Father knows that you need all these things. But seek first His kingdom and His righteousness, and all these things will be added to you. So do not worry about tomorrow; for tomorrow will care for itself. Each day has enough trouble of its own" (Matthew 6:25–34; cf. Luke 12:22–31; see 1 Kings 10:4–7; Job 35:11; Matthew 8:26).

[GOD'S OMNISCIENCE from not one of them will fall to the ground apart from your Father. But the very hairs of your head are all numbered.]
Setting: Galilee. After His disciples observe His ministry, Jesus summons and specifically instructs them about their ministry ahead involving true discipleship.

"Are not two sparrows sold for a cent? And *yet* not one of them will fall to the ground apart from your Father. But the very hairs of your head are all numbered. So do not fear; you are more valuable than many sparrows" (Matthew 10:29–31; cf. Luke 12:6; see Matthew 12:12).

[GOD'S OMNISCIENCE from But of that day and hour no one knows, not even the angels of heaven, nor the Son, but the Father alone]
Setting: On the Mount of Olives, just east of Jerusalem. During His Olivet Discourse, after answering His disciples' questions as to when the temple will be destroyed and Jerusalem overrun, along with the signs of His coming and the end of the age, Jesus teaches them the Parable of the Fig Tree.

"Now learn the parable from the fig tree: when its branch has already become tender and puts forth its leaves, you know that summer is near; so, you too, when you see all these things, recognize that He is near, *right* at the door. Truly, I say to you, this generation will not pass away until all these things take place. Heaven and earth will pass away, but My words will not pass away. But of that day and hour no one knows, not even the angels of heaven, nor the Son, but the Father alone. For the coming of the Son of Man will be just like the days of Noah. For as in those days before the flood they were eating and drinking, marrying and giving in marriage, until the day that Noah entered the ark, and they did not understand until the flood came and took them all away; so will the coming of the Son of Man be. Then there will be two men in the field; one will be taken and one will be left. Two women *will be* grinding at the mill; one will be taken and one will be left" (Matthew 24:32–41; cf. Mark 13:28–32; Luke 17:34–36; 21:28–33; see Genesis 6:5; 7:7; Matthew 5:18; 10:23; James 5:9).

[GOD'S OMNISCIENCE from But of the day or hour no one knows, not even the angels in heaven, nor the Son, but the Father *alone]*
Setting: On the Mount of Olives, east of the temple in Jerusalem. After predicting the temple's destruction, Jesus responds during His Olivet Discourse to questions from Peter, James, John, and Andrew about other future events.

"Now learn the parable from the fig tree: when its branch has already become tender and puts forth its leaves, you know that summer is near. Even so, you too, when you see these things happening, recognize that He is near, *right* at the door. Truly I say to you, this generation will not pass away until all these things take place. Heaven and earth will pass away, but My words will not pass away. But of the day or hour no one knows, not even the angels in heaven, nor the Son, but the Father *alone*" (Mark 13:28–32; cf. Matthew 24:32–36; Luke 21:28–33).

[GOD'S OMNISCIENCE from Indeed, the very hairs of your head are all numbered]
Setting: On the way from Galilee to Jerusalem. Jesus warns His disciples of future events as the scribes and Pharisees turn hostile and question Him repeatedly in an attempt to catch Him in something He might say.

Under these circumstances, after so many thousands of people had gathered together that they were stepping on one another,

He began saying to His disciples first *of all,* "Beware of the leaven of the Pharisees, which is hypocrisy. But there is nothing covered up that will not be revealed, and hidden that will not be known. Accordingly, whatever you have said in the dark will be heard in the light, and what you have whispered in the inner rooms will be proclaimed upon the housetops. I say to you, My friends, do not be afraid of those who kill the body and after that have no more that they can do. But I will warn you whom to fear: fear the One who, after He has killed, has authority to cast into hell; yes, I tell you, fear Him! Are not five sparrows sold for two cents? *Yet* not one of them is forgotten before God. Indeed, the very hairs of your head are all numbered. Do not fear; you are more valuable than many sparrows" (Luke 12:1–7; cf. Matthew 10:26–31; see Matthew 16:6; Hebrews 10:31).

[GOD'S OMNISCIENCE from your Father knows that you need these things]
Setting: On the way from Galilee to Jerusalem. After giving a parable about riches and greed, Jesus comforts the crowd and His disciples. The scribes and Pharisees turn hostile and question Him repeatedly in an attempt to catch Him in something He might say.

And He said to His disciples, "For this reason I say to you, do not worry about *your* life, *as to* what you will eat; nor for your body, *as to* what you will put on. For life is more than food, and the body more than clothing. Consider the ravens, for they neither sow nor reap; they have no storeroom nor barn, and *yet* God feeds them; how much more valuable you are than the birds! And which of you by worrying can add a *single* hour to his life's span? If then you cannot do even a very little thing, why do you worry about other matters? Consider the lilies, how they grow: they neither toil nor spin; but I tell you, not even Solomon in all his glory clothed himself like one of these. But if God so clothes the grass in the field, which is *alive* today and tomorrow is thrown into the furnace, how much more *will He clothe* you? You men of little faith! And do not seek what you will eat and what you will drink, and do not keep worrying. For all these things the nations of the world eagerly seek; but your Father knows that you need these things. But seek His kingdom, and these things will be added to you. Do not be afraid, little flock, for your Father has chosen gladly to give you the kingdom" (Luke 12:22–32; cf. Matthew 6:25–33; see 1 Kings 10:4–7; Job 38:41).

[GOD'S OMNISCIENCE from God knows your hearts]
Setting: On the way from Galilee to Jerusalem. The Lord responds to the Pharisees' scoffing at His teaching His disciples about stewardship.

And He said to them, "You are those who justify yourselves in the sight of men, but God knows your hearts; for that which is highly esteemed among men is detestable in the sight of God. The Law and the Prophets *were proclaimed* until John; since that time the gospel of the kingdom of God has been preached, and everyone is forcing his way into it. But is it easier for heaven and earth to pass away than for one stroke of a letter of the Law to fail" (Luke 16:15–17; cf. Matthew 5:18; see 1 Samuel 16:7; Matthew 4:23; 11:11–14).

OMNISCIENCE, JESUS' (Also see MIND READING; and OMNISCIENCE, GOD'S)

[JESUS' OMNISCIENCE from you will find a donkey tied *there* and a colt with her; untie them and bring them to Me]
Setting: On the way to Jerusalem for the crucifixion. After healing some blind men in Jericho, Jesus instructs two of His disciples as they enter Bethphage to acquire a donkey and colt to be used in His triumphal entry into the city.

When they had approached Jerusalem and had come to Bethphage, at the Mount of Olives, then Jesus sent two disciples, saying to them, "Go into the village opposite you, and immediately you will find a donkey tied *there* and a colt with her; untie them and bring them to Me. If anyone says anything to you, you shall say, 'The Lord has need of them,' and immediately he will send them" (Matthew 21:1–3; cf. Mark 11:1–3; Luke 19:29–31).

[JESUS' OMNISCIENCE from you will find a colt tied *there,* on which no one yet has ever sat; untie it and bring it *here*]
Setting: Bethphage, just outside Jerusalem. As He and His disciples approach Jerusalem for His impending death on the cross, the Lord instructs two of the disciples to obtain a colt for His triumphal entry into the city.

As they approached Jerusalem, at Bethphage and Bethany, near the Mount of Olives, He sent two of His disciples, and said to them, "Go into the village opposite you, and immediately as you enter it, you will find a colt tied *there,* on which no one yet has ever sat; untie it and bring it *here.* If anyone says to you, 'Why are you doing this?' you say, 'The Lord has need of it'; and immediately he will send it back here" (Mark 11:1–3; cf. Matthew 21:1–3; Luke 19:29–31; see Matthew 21:4–7; Luke 19:32–35; John 12:12–15).

[JESUS' OMNISCIENCE from you will find a colt tied on which no one yet has ever sat; untie it and bring it *here*]
Setting: Approaching Jerusalem. After Jesus provides a parable about stewardship in Jericho, He and His disciples head to the outskirts of Jerusalem to prepare for His triumphal entry into the city and His crucifixion.

When He approached Bethphage and Bethany, near the mount that is called Olivet, He sent two of the disciples, saying, "Go into the village ahead of *you;* there, as you enter, you will find a colt tied on which no one yet has ever sat; untie it and bring it *here.* If anyone asks you, 'Why are you untying it?' you shall say, 'The Lord has need of it'" (Luke 19:29–31; cf. Matthew 21:1–3; Mark 11:1–3).

[JESUS' OMNISCIENCE from Before Philip called you, when you were under the fig tree, I saw you]
Setting: Galilee. After beginning His public ministry and choosing His first disciples, Andrew and Simon (Peter) near Bethany beyond the Jordan, and Philip in Galilee, Jesus calls Philip's friend, Nathanael, (some believe he may have been also called Bartholomew) as His next follower.

Jesus saw Nathanael coming to Him, and said of him, "Behold, an Israelite indeed, in whom there is no deceit!" Nathanael said to Him, "How do you know me?" Jesus answered and said to him, "Before Philip called you, when you were under the fig tree, I saw you." Nathanael answered Him, "Rabbi, You are the Son of God; You are the King of Israel." Jesus answered and said to him, "Because I said to you that I saw you under the fig tree, do you believe? You will see greater things than these." And He said to him, "Truly, truly, I say to you, you will see the heavens opened and the angels of God ascending and descending on the Son of Man" (John 1:47–51).

[JESUS' OMNISCIENCE from you have had five husbands, and the one whom you now have is not your husband]
Setting: Sychar in Samaria, on the way to Galilee. Jesus interacts with a Samaritan woman at Jacob's well, while the disciples are buying food.

He said to her, "Go, call your husband and come here." The woman answered and said, "I have no husband." Jesus said to her, "You have correctly said, 'I have no husband'; for you have had five husbands, and the one whom you now have is not your husband; this you have said truly" (John 4:16–18; see John 6:35).

[JESUS' OMNISCIENCE from knew that he had already been a long time *in that condition*]
Setting: Jerusalem. After performing His second Galilean miracle by healing the son of a royal official from Capernaum (the first miracle: turning water into wine at the wedding in Cana), Jesus returns to Jerusalem for a feast of the Jews. He offers healing to a man who has been ill for thirty-eight years.

When Jesus saw him lying *there,* and knew that he had already been a long time *in that condition,* He said to him, "Do you wish to get well?" (John 5:6).

[JESUS' OMNISCIENCE from For Jesus knew from the beginning who they were who did not believe, and who it was that would betray Him]
Setting: The synagogue at Capernaum of Galilee. After the Jewish religious leaders argue with one another when Jesus says He will give His flesh to the world to eat, some of His disciples also express difficulty with His statements.

But, Jesus, conscious that His disciples grumbled at this, said to them, "Does this cause you to stumble? *What* then if you see the Son of Man ascending to where He was before? It is the Spirit who gives life; the flesh profits nothing; the words that I have spoken to you are spirit and are life. But there are some of you who do not believe." For Jesus knew from the beginning who they were who did not believe, and who it was that would betray Him. And He was saying, "For this reason I have said to you, that no one can come to Me unless it has been granted him from the Father" (John 6:61–65; see Matthew 11:6; 13:11; John 3:13).

[JESUS' OMNISCIENCE from This sickness is not to end in death]
Setting: Beyond the Jordan. Following the Feast of Dedication and the Pharisees' desire to stone Him while in Jerusalem, Jesus hears of the sickness of his friend Lazarus of Bethany.

But when Jesus heard *this,* He said, "This sickness is not to end in death, but for the glory of God, so that the Son of God may be glorified by it" (John 11:4).

[JESUS' OMNISCIENCE from Lazarus is dead]
Setting: Beyond the Jordan. While He and His disciples are avoiding the Jerusalem Pharisees, Jesus communicates Lazarus's death in Bethany to His disciples and decides to go there.

So Jesus then said to them plainly, "Lazarus is dead, and I am glad for your sakes that I was not there, so that you may believe; but let us go to him" (John 11:14, 15).

[JESUS' OMNISCIENCE from He knew the one who was betraying Him]
Setting: Jerusalem. Before the Passover, with His crucifixion nearing, Jesus eats supper with His disciples and assumes the role of a servant, washing their feet.

Jesus answered and said to him, "What I do you do not realize now, but you will understand hereafter." Peter said to Him, "Never shall You wash my feet!" Jesus answered him, "If I do not wash you, you have no part with Me." Simon Peter said to Him, "Lord, *then wash* not only my feet, but also my hand and my head." Jesus said to him, "He who has bathed needs only to wash his feet, but is completely clean; and you are clean, but not all *of you.* For He knew the one who was betraying Him; for this reason He said, "Not all of you are clean" (John 13:7–11; see John 6:64; 15:3).

[JESUS' OMNISCIENCE from Jesus knew that they wished to question Him]
Setting: Jerusalem. Before the Passover, after warning His disciples of the persecution they will face after His departure to heaven, empathizing with their sadness over His prophecies, Jesus gives them the hope for the future.

"A little while, and you will no longer see Me; and again a little while, and you will see Me." *Some* of His disciples then said to one another, "What is this thing He is telling us, 'A little while, and you will not see Me; and again a little while, and you will see Me'; and, 'because I go to the Father'?" So they were saying, "What is this that He says, 'A little while'? We do not know what He is talking about." Jesus knew that they wished to question Him, and He said to them, "Are you deliberating together about this, that I said, 'A little while, and you will not see Me, and again a little while, and you will see Me'? Truly, truly, I say to you, that you will weep and lament, but the world will rejoice; you will grieve, but your grief will be turned into joy. Whenever a woman is in labor she has pain, because her hour has come; but when she gives birth to the child, she no longer remembers the anguish because of the joy that a child has been born into the world. Therefore you too have grief now; but I will see you again, and your heart will rejoice, and no one *will* take your joy away from you" (John 16:16–22; see Mark 9:32; Luke 23:27; John 14:18–24; 16:5, 6; 20:20).

[JESUS' OMNISCIENCE from Jesus, knowing all the things that were coming upon Him]
Setting: Jerusalem. After Jesus prays His high-priestly prayer on behalf of His disciples, He and they go over the ravine of the Kidron to a garden where Judas awaits to seize the Lord with a Roman cohort and officers from the chief priests and the Pharisees.

So Jesus, knowing all the things that were coming upon Him, went forth and said to them, "Whom do you seek?" They answered

Him, "Jesus the Nazarene." He said to them, "I am *He*." And Judas also, who was betraying Him, was standing with them. So when He said to them, "I am *He*," they drew back and fell to the ground. Therefore He again asked them, "Whom do you seek?" And they said, "Jesus the Nazarene." Jesus answered, "I told you that I am *He*; so if you seek Me, let these go their way," to fulfill the word which He spoke, "Of those whom You have given Me I lost not one" (John 18:4–9; see John 6:64; 17:12).

[JESUS' OMNISCIENCE from Jesus, knowing that all things had already been accomplished]
Setting: Golgotha (the Place of the Skull), just outside Jerusalem. After asking His disciple John to care for His mother, in the midst of fulfilling Scripture as He dies on the cross for the sins of the world, Jesus expresses His thirst.

[JESUS' OMNISCIENCE from I know your deeds]
After this, Jesus, knowing that all things had already been accomplished, to fulfill the Scripture, said, "I am thirsty" (John 19:28; see Psalm 69:21; Matthew 27:48; Mark 15:36).

[JESUS' OMNISCIENCE from I know your deeds]
Setting: On the island of Patmos (in the Aegean Sea about fifty miles southwest of Ephesus in modern Turkey). On the Lord's Day (Sunday), approximately fifty years after Jesus' resurrection, the disciple John encounters the Lord Jesus Christ, who communicates a new revelation for the apostle to record for the church in Ephesus and to six other churches in Asia.

"To the angel of the church in Ephesus write: The One who holds the seven stars in His right hand, the One who walks among the seven golden lampstands, says this: 'I know your deeds and your toil and perseverance, and that you cannot tolerate evil men, and you put to the test those who call themselves apostles, and they are not, and you found them *to be* false; and you have perseverance and have endured for My name's sake, and have not grown weary. But I have *this* against you, that you have left your first love. Therefore remember from where you have fallen, and repent and do the deeds you did at first; or else I am coming to you and will remove your lampstand out of its place—unless you repent. Yet this you do have, that you hate the deeds of the Nicolaitans, which I also hate. He who has an ear, let him hear what the Spirit says to the churches. To him who overcomes, I will grant to eat of the tree of life which is in the Paradise of God' " (Revelation 2:1–7; see Genesis 2:9; Ezekiel 28:13; 1 John 4:1; Revelation 1:10, 11, 19, 20; 2:15, 16).

[JESUS' OMNISCIENCE from I know your tribulation]
Setting: On the island of Patmos (in the Aegean Sea about fifty miles southwest of Ephesus in modern Turkey). On the Lord's Day (Sunday), approximately fifty years after Jesus' resurrection, the disciple John encounters the Lord Jesus Christ, who communicates a new revelation for the apostle to record for the church in Smyrna and to six other churches in Asia.

"And to the angel of the church in Smyrna write: The first and the last, who was dead, and has come to life, says this: 'I know your tribulation and your poverty (but you are rich), and the blasphemy by those who say they are Jews and are not, but are a synagogue of Satan. Do not fear what you are about to suffer. Behold, the devil is about to cast some of you into prison, so that you will be tested, and you will have tribulation for ten days. Be faithful until death, and I will give you the crown of life. He who has an ear, let him hear what the Spirit says to the churches. He who overcomes will not be hurt by the second death' (Revelation 2:8–11; see Isaiah 44:6; Revelation 1:9, 18; 2:13; 20:6, 14).

[JESUS' OMNISCIENCE from I know where you dwell]
Setting: On the island of Patmos (in the Aegean Sea about fifty miles southwest of Ephesus in modern Turkey). On the Lord's Day (Sunday), approximately fifty years after Jesus' resurrection, the disciple John encounters the Lord Jesus Christ, who communicates a new revelation for the apostle to record for the church in Pergamum and to six other churches in Asia.

"And to the angel of the church in Pergamum write: The One who has the sharp two-edged sword says this: 'I know where you dwell, where Satan's throne is; and you hold fast My name, and did not deny My faith even in the days of Antipas, My witness, My faithful one, who was killed among you, where Satan dwells. But I have a few things against you, because you have there some who hold the teaching of Balaam, who kept teaching Balak to put a stumbling block before the sons of Israel, to eat things sacrificed to idols and to commit *acts of* immorality. So you also have some who in the same way hold the teaching of the Nicolaitans. Therefore repent; or else I am coming to you quickly, and I will make war against them with the sword of My mouth. He who has an ear, let him hear what the Spirit says to the churches. To him who overcomes, to him I will give *some* of the hidden manna, and I will give him a white stone, and a new name written on the stone which no one knows but he who receives it' (Revelation 2:12–17; see Numbers 25:1–3; Isaiah 62:2; Revelation 1:16; 2:5, 6, 16).

[JESUS' OMNISCIENCE from I know your deeds]
Setting: On the island of Patmos (in the Aegean Sea about fifty miles southwest of Ephesus in modern Turkey). On the Lord's Day (Sunday), approximately fifty years after Jesus' resurrection, the disciple John encounters the Lord Jesus Christ, who communicates a new revelation for the apostle to record for the church in Thyatira and to six other churches in Asia.

"And to the angel of the church in Thyatira write: The Son of God, who has eyes like a flame of fire, and His feet are like burnished bronze, says this: 'I know your deeds, and your love and faith and service and perseverance, and that your deeds of late are greater than at first. But I have *this* against you, that you tolerate the woman Jezebel, who calls herself a prophetess, and she teaches and leads My bond-servants astray so that they commit *acts of* immorality and eat things sacrificed to idols. I gave her time to repent, and she does not want to repent of her immorality. Behold, I will throw her on a bed *of sickness,* and those who commit adultery with her into great tribulation, unless they repent of her deeds. And I will kill her children with pestilence, and all the churches will know that I am He who searches the minds and hearts; and I will give to each one of you according to your deeds. But I say to you, the rest who are in Thyatira, who do not hold this teaching, who have not known the deep things of Satan, as they call them—I place no other burden on you. Nevertheless what you have, hold fast until I come. He who overcomes, and he who keeps My deeds until the end, TO HIM I WILL GIVE AUTHORITY OVER THE NATIONS; AND HE SHALL RULE THEM WITH A ROD OF IRON, AS THE VESSELS OF THE POTTER ARE BROKEN TO PIECES, as I also have received *authority* from My Father; and I will give him the morning star. He who has an ear, let him hear what the Spirit says to the churches' (Revelation 2:18–29; Jesus quotes from Psalm 2:8, 9; Isaiah 30:14; see 1 Kings 16:31; Psalm 7:9; Romans 2:5; 1 Corinthians 2:10; 2 Peter 3:9; Revelation 1:14; 2:7; 3:11; 17:1–20).

[JESUS' OMNISCIENCE from I know your deeds]
Setting: On the island of Patmos (in the Aegean Sea about fifty miles southwest of Ephesus in modern Turkey). On the Lord's Day (Sunday), approximately fifty years after Jesus' resurrection, the disciple John encounters the Lord Jesus Christ, who communicates a new revelation for the apostle to record for the church in Sardis and to six other churches in Asia.

"To the angel of the church in Sardis write: He who has the seven Spirits of God and the seven stars, says this: 'I know your deeds, that you have a name that you are alive, but you are dead. Wake up, and strengthen the things that remain, which were about to die; for I have not found your deeds completed in the sight of My God. So remember what you have received and heard; and keep *it,* and repent. Therefore if you do not wake up, I will come like a thief, and you will not know at what hour I will come to you. But you have a few people in Sardis who have not soiled their garments; and they will walk with Me in white, for they are worthy. He who overcomes will thus be clothed in white garments; and I will not erase his name from the book of life, and I will confess his name before My Father and before His angels. He who has an ear, let him hear what the Spirit says to the churches' " (Revelation 3:1–6; see Matthew 10:32; Revelation 1:16).

[JESUS' OMNISCIENCE from I know your deeds]
Setting: On the island of Patmos (in the Aegean Sea about fifty miles southwest of Ephesus in modern Turkey). On the Lord's Day (Sunday), approximately fifty years after Jesus' resurrection, the disciple John encounters the Lord Jesus Christ, who communicates a new revelation for the apostle to record for the church in Philadelphia and to six other churches in Asia.

"And to the angel of the church in Philadelphia write: He who is holy, who is true, who has the key of David, who opens and no one will shut, and who shuts and no one opens, says this: 'I know your deeds. Behold, I have put before you an open door which no one can shut, because you have a little power, and have kept My word, and have not denied My name. Behold, I will cause *those* of the synagogue of Satan, who say that they are Jews and are not, but lie—I will make them come and bow down at your feet, and *make them* know that I have loved you. Because you have kept the word of My perseverance, I also will keep you from the hour of testing, that *hour* which is about to come upon the whole world, to test those who dwell on the earth. I am coming quickly; hold fast what you have, so that no one will take your crown. He who overcomes, I will make him a pillar in the temple of My God, and he will not go out from it anymore; and I will write on him the name of My God, and the name of the city of My God, the new Jerusalem, which comes down out of heaven from My God, and My new name. He who has an ear, let him hear what the Spirit says to the churches' " (Revelation 3:7–13; see Isaiah 22:22; Galatians 2:9; Revelation 2:9, 10, 13, 25; 14:1).

[JESUS' OMNISCIENCE from I know your deeds]

Setting: On the island of Patmos (in the Aegean Sea about fifty miles southwest of Ephesus in modern Turkey). On the Lord's Day (Sunday), approximately fifty years after Jesus' resurrection, the disciple John encounters the Lord Jesus Christ, who communicates a new revelation for the apostle to record for the church in Laodicea and to six other churches in Asia.

"To the angel of the church in Laodicea write: The Amen, the faithful and true Witness, the Beginning of the creation of God, says this: 'I know your deeds, that you are neither cold nor hot; I wish that you were cold or hot. So because you are lukewarm, and neither hot nor cold, I will spit you out of My mouth. Because you say, "I am rich, and have become wealthy, and have need of nothing," and you do not know that you are wretched and miserable and poor and blind and naked, I advise you to buy from Me gold refined by fire so that you may become rich, and white garments so that you may clothe yourself, and *that* the shame of your nakedness will not be revealed; and eye salve to anoint your eyes so that you may see. Those whom I love, I reprove and discipline; therefore be zealous and repent. Behold, I stand at the door and knock; if anyone hears My voice and opens the door, I will come in to him and will dine with him, and he with Me. He who overcomes, I will grant to him to sit down with Me on My throne, as I also overcame and sat down with My Father on His throne. He who has an ear, let him hear what the Spirit says to the churches'" (Revelation 3:14–22; see Proverb 3:12; Hosea 12:8; John 14:23; 16:33).

ONE (See specific entries such as FLESH, ONE)

ONE ANOTHER

Setting: The Mount of Olives, just east of Jerusalem. During His discourse, Jesus answers His disciples' question as to when the temple will be destroyed and Jerusalem overrun, along with the signs of His coming and the end of the age.

And Jesus answered and said to them, "See to it that no one misleads you. For many will come in My name, saying, 'I am the Christ,' and will mislead many. You will be hearing of wars and rumors of wars. See that you are not frightened, for *those things* must take place, but *that* is not yet the end. For nation will rise against nation, and kingdom against kingdom, and in various places there will be famines and earthquakes. But all these things are *merely* the beginning of birth pangs. Then they will deliver you to tribulation, and will kill you, and you will be hated by all nations because of My name. At that time many will fall away and will betray one another and hate one another. Many false prophets will arise and will mislead many. Because lawlessness is increased, most people's love will grow cold. But the one who endures to the end, he will be saved. This gospel of the kingdom shall be preached in the whole world as a testimony to all the nations, and then the end will come" (Matthew 24:4–14; cf. Jeremiah 29:8; Matthew 7:15; 10:17, 22; Mark 13:3–13; Luke 21:7–19; Revelation 6:4; see Matthew 24:3).

Setting: The Mount of Olives, just east of Jerusalem. During His discourse, after answering His disciples' questions as to when the temple will be destroyed and Jerusalem overrun, along with the signs of His coming and the end of the age, Jesus reveals the future judgments following His return.

"But when the Son of Man comes in His glory, and all the angels with Him, then He will sit on His glorious throne. All the nations will be gathered before Him; and He will separate them from one another, as the shepherd separates the sheep from the goats; and He will put the sheep on His right, and the goats on the left. Then the King will say to those on His right, 'Come, you who are blessed of My Father, inherit the kingdom prepared for you from the foundation of the world. 'For I was hungry, and you gave Me *something* to eat; I was thirsty, and you gave Me *something* to drink; I was a stranger, and you invited Me in; naked, and you clothed Me; I was sick, and you visited Me; I was in prison, and you came to Me.' Then the righteous will answer Him, 'Lord, when did we see You hungry and feed You, or thirsty, and give you *something* to drink? And when did we see You a stranger, and invite You in, or naked, and clothe You? When did we see You sick, or in prison, and come to You?' The King will answer and say to them, 'Truly I say to you, to the extent that you did it to one of these brothers of Mine, *even* the least *of them,* you did it to Me.' Then He will also say to those on His left, 'Depart from Me, accursed ones, into the eternal fire which has been prepared for the devil and his angels; for I was hungry, and you gave Me *nothing* to eat; I was thirsty, and you gave Me nothing to drink; I was a stranger, and you did not invite Me in; naked, and you did not clothe Me; sick, and in prison, and you did not visit Me.' Then they themselves also will answer, 'Lord, when did we see You hungry, or thirsty, or a stranger, or naked, or sick, or in prison, and did not take care of You?' Then He will answer them, 'Truly I say to you, to the extent that you did not do it to one of the least of these, you did not do it to Me.' These will go away into eternal punishment, but the righteous into eternal life" (Matthew 25:31–46; see Matthew 7:23; 16:27; 19:29).

Setting: Capernaum of Galilee. As Jesus teaches His disciples in private, they ask Him about greatness.

But Jesus said, "Do not hinder him, for there is no one who will perform a miracle in My name, and be able soon afterward to speak evil of Me. For he who is not against us is for us. For whoever gives you a cup of water to drink because of your name as *followers* of Christ, truly I say to you, he will not lose his reward. Whoever causes one of these little ones who believe to stumble, it would be better for him if, with a heavy millstone hung around his neck, he had been cast into the sea. If your hand causes you to stumble, cut it off; it is better for you to enter life crippled, than, having your two hands, to go into hell, into the unquenchable fire, [where THEIR WORM DOES NOT DIE, AND THE FIRE IS NOT QUENCHED.] If your foot causes you to stumble, cut it off; it is better for you to enter life lame, than, having your two feet, to be cast into hell, [where THEIR WORM DOES NOT DIE, AND THE FIRE IS NOT QUENCHED.] If your eye causes you to stumble, throw it out; it is better for you to enter the kingdom of God with one eye, than, having two eyes, to be cast into hell, where THEIR WORM DOES NOT DIE, AND THE FIRE IS NOT QUENCHED. For everyone will be salted with fire. Salt is good; but if the salt becomes unsalty, with what will you make it salty *again?* Have salt in yourselves, and be at peace with one another" (Mark 9:39–50; Jesus quotes from Isaiah 66:24; cf. Matthew 18:6–9; Luke 9:49, 50; see Matthew 5:13, 29, 30; 10:42; 12:30; 18:5, 6; Mark 9:38).

Setting: The temple in Jerusalem. Having His authority questioned by the chief priests, scribes, and elders, Jesus begins to teach them in parables.

And He began to speak to them in parables: "A man PLANTED A VINEYARD AND PUT A WALL AROUND IT, AND DUG A VAT UNDER THE WINE PRESS AND BUILT A TOWER, and rented it out to vine-growers and went on a journey. At the *harvest* time he sent a slave to the vine-growers, in order to receive *some* of the produce of the vineyard from the vine-growers. They took him, and beat him and sent him away empty-handed. Again he sent them another slave, and they wounded him in the head, and treated him shamefully. And he sent another, and that one they killed; and *so with* many others, beating some and killing others. He had one more to *send,* a beloved son; he sent him last *of all* to them, saying, 'They will respect my son.' But those vine-growers said to one another, 'This is the heir; come, let us kill him, and the inheritance will be ours!' They took him, and killed him and threw him out of the vineyard. What will the owner of the vineyard do? He will come and destroy the vine-growers, and will give the vineyard to others. Have you not even read this Scripture: 'THE STONE WHICH THE BUILDERS REJECTED, THIS BECAME THE CHIEF CORNER *stone;* THIS CAME ABOUT FROM THE LORD, AND IT IS MARVELOUS IN OUR EYES'?" (Mark 12:1–11, Jesus quotes from Psalm 118:22, 23; Isaiah 5:1, 2; cf. Matthew 21:33–46; Luke 20:9–19; see Mark 12:12).

Setting: Galilee. After He praises John the Baptist to the crowds, Jesus criticizes the Pharisees and lawyers who reject God's purpose and John's message.

"To what then shall I compare the men of this generation, and what are they like? They are like children who sit in the market place and call to one another, and they say, 'We played the flute for you, and you did not dance; we sang a dirge, and you did not weep.' For John the Baptist has come eating no bread and drinking no wine, and you say, 'He has a demon!' The Son of Man has come eating and drinking, and you say, 'Behold, a gluttonous man and a drunkard, a friend of tax collectors and sinners!'

Yet wisdom is vindicated by all her children" (Luke 7:31–35; cf. Matthew 11:16–19; see Luke 1:15, 7:29, 30).

Setting: The temple in Jerusalem. While ministering a few days before His crucifixion, after the chief priests and the scribes question His authority to teach and preach, Jesus conveys the Parable of the Vine-Growers to the people.

And He began to tell the people this parable: "A man planted a vineyard and rented it out to vine-growers, and went on a journey for a long time. At the *harvest* time he sent a slave to the vine-growers, so that they would give him *some* of the produce of the vineyard; but the vine-growers beat him and sent him away empty-handed. And he proceeded to send another slave; and they beat him also and treated him shamefully and sent him away empty-handed. And he proceeded to send a third; and this one also they wounded and cast out. The owner of the vineyard said, 'What shall I do? I will send my beloved son; perhaps they will respect him.' But when the vine-growers saw him, they reasoned with one another, saying, 'This is the heir; let us kill him so that the inheritance will be ours.' So they threw him out of the vineyard and killed him. What, then, will the owner of the vineyard do to them? He will come and destroy these vine-growers and will give the vineyard to others." When they heard it, they said, "May it never be!" But Jesus looked at them and said, "What then is this that is written: 'THE STONE WHICH THE BUILDERS REJECTED, THIS BECAME THE CHIEF CORNER *stone*'? Everyone who falls on that stone will be broken to pieces; but on whomever it falls, it will scatter him like dust" (Luke 20:9–18, Jesus quotes from Psalm 118:22; cf. Matthew 21:33–44; Mark 12:1–11; see Luke 20:1–8; Ephesians 2:20).

Setting: On the way from Jerusalem. After dying on the cross the day before the Sabbath, being buried in a tomb by Joseph of Arimathea, Jesus rises from the grave on the day after the Sabbath and appears to two of His followers on the road to Emmaus.

And He said to them, "What are these words that you are exchanging with one another as you are walking?" And they stood still, looking sad (Luke 24:17, see Mark 16:12, 13; Luke 24:1–16).

Setting: Jerusalem. During the Feast of the Jews, Jesus responds to criticism from the Jewish religious leaders by referring to God as His own Father (thereby making Himself equal with God) and informing them that God, John the Baptist, and His works all testify to His mission.

"You search the Scriptures because you think that in them you have eternal life; it is these that testify about Me; and you are unwilling to come to Me so that you may have life. I do not receive glory from men; but I know you, that you do not have the love of God in yourselves. I have come in My Father's name, and you do not receive Me; if another comes in his own name, you will receive him. How can you believe, when you receive glory from one another and you do not seek the glory that is from the *one and* only God? Do not think that I will accuse you before the Father; the one who accuses you is Moses, in whom you have set your hope. For if you believed Moses, you would believe Me, for he wrote about Me. But if you do not believe his writings, how will you believe My words?" (John 5:39–47; see Matthew 24:5; Luke 16:29, 31; 24:27; John 5:18–38; 9:28; 17:3).

Setting: Jerusalem. Before the Passover, after revealing to His disciples that Judas will betray Him to the chief priests and Pharisees, Jesus conveys how He will soon be glorified in His death, and commands them to love one another.

Therefore when he had gone out, Jesus said, "Now is the Son of Man glorified, and God is glorified in Him; if God is glorified in Him, God will also glorify Him in Himself, and will glorify Him immediately. Little children, I am with you a little while longer. You will seek Me; and as I said to the Jews, now I also say to you, 'Where I am going, you cannot come.' A new commandment I give to you, that you love one another, even as I have loved you, that you also love one another. By this all men will know that you are My disciples, if you have love for one another" (John 13:31–35; see Leviticus 19:18; John 7:33, 34; 13:1–30; 17:1; 1 John 3:14).

Setting: Jerusalem. Before the Passover, with His imminent departure in mind, after explaining He is the vine and His disciples are the branches, Jesus commands them to love one another.

"This is My commandment, that you love one another, just as I have loved you. Greater love has no one than this, that one lay down his life for his friends. You are My friends if you do what I command you. No longer do I call you slaves, for the slave does not know what his master is doing; but I have called you friends, for all things that I have heard from My Father I have made known to you. You did not choose Me but I chose you, and appointed you that you would go and bear fruit, and *that* your fruit would remain, so that whatever you ask of the Father in My name He may give to you. This I command you, that you love one another" (John 15:12–17; see Matthew 12:50; John 6:70; 8:26; 10:11; 13:34; 15:1–11).

ONE, EVIL (See EVIL ONE)

ONE FLESH (Listed under FLESH, ONE; also see MARRIAGE)

ONES, ACCURSED

Setting: On the Mount of Olives, just east of Jerusalem. During His Olivet Discourse, after answering His disciples' questions as to when the temple will be destroyed and Jerusalem overrun, along with the signs of His coming and the end of the age, Jesus reveals the future judgments following His return.

"But when the Son of Man comes in His glory, and all the angels with Him, then He will sit on His glorious throne. All the nations will be gathered before Him; and He will separate them from one another, as the shepherd separates the sheep from the goats; and He will put the sheep on His right, and the goats on the left. Then the King will say to those on His right, 'Come, you who are blessed of My Father, inherit the kingdom prepared for you from the foundation of the world. 'For I was hungry, and you gave Me *something* to eat; I was thirsty, and you gave Me *something* to drink; I was a stranger, and you invited Me in; naked, and you clothed Me; I was sick, and you visited Me; I was in prison, and you came to Me.' Then the righteous will answer Him, 'Lord, when did we see You hungry and feed You, or thirsty, and give you *something* to drink? And when did we see You a stranger, and invite You in, or naked, and clothe You? When did we see You sick, or in prison, and come to You?' The King will answer and say to them, 'Truly I say to you, to the extent that you did it to one of these brothers of Mine, *even* the least *of them,* you did it to Me.' Then He will also say to those on His left, 'Depart from Me, accursed ones, into the eternal fire which has been prepared for the devil and his angels; for I was hungry, and you gave Me *nothing* to eat; I was thirsty, and you gave Me nothing to drink; I was a stranger, and you did not invite Me in; naked, and you did not clothe Me; sick, and in prison, and you did not visit Me.' Then they themselves also will answer, 'Lord, when did we see You hungry, or thirsty, or a stranger, or naked, or sick, or in prison, and did not take care of You?' Then He will answer them, 'Truly I say to you, to the extent that you did not do it to one of the least of these, you did not do it to Me.' These will go away into eternal punishment, but the righteous into eternal life" (Matthew 25:31–46; see Matthew 7:23; 16:27; 19:29).

ONES, FOOLISH (Also see FOOLS)

Setting: On the way from Galilee to Jerusalem. After speaking of how a lamp illuminates, the Lord has lunch with a Pharisee who is surprised He doesn't wash before eating.

But the Lord said to him, "Now you Pharisees clean the outside of the cup and of the platter; but inside of you, you are full of robbery and wickedness. You foolish ones, did not He who made the outside make the inside also? But give that which is within as charity, and then all things are clean for you. But woe to you Pharisees! You pay tithe of mint and rue and every *kind of* garden herb, and *yet* disregard justice and the love of God; but these are the things you should have done without neglecting the others. Woe to you Pharisees! For you love the chief seats in the synagogues and the respectful greetings in the market places. Woe to you! For you are like concealed tombs, and the people who walk over *them* are unaware *of it*" (Luke 11:39–44; cf. Matthew 23:6, 7, 23–27; see Matthew 15:2; Titus 1:15).

ONES, LITTLE (See LITTLE ONES)

OPEN DOOR (Listed under DOOR, OPEN)

OPPONENT (Also see ENEMIES; ENEMY; and OPPONENTS)

Setting: Galilee. During the early part of His ministry, Jesus preaches the Sermon on the Mount to His disciples and the multitudes.

"Make friends quickly with your opponent at law while you are with him on the way, so that your opponent may not hand you over to the judge, and the judge to the officer, and you be thrown into prison. Truly I say to you, you will not come out of there until you have paid up the last cent.'" (Matthew 5:25, 26; cf. Luke 12:58, 59)

Setting: On the way from Galilee to Jerusalem. After chastising the crowds for being able to discern the weather but not the present age, Jesus exhorts them to settle any financial disputes outside of court.

"And why do you not even on your own initiative judge what is right? For while you are going with your opponent to appear before the magistrate, on *your* way *there* make an effort to settle with him, so that he may not drag you before the judge, and the judge turn you over to the officer, and the officer throw you into prison. I say to you, you will not get out of there until you have paid the very last cent" (Luke 12:57–59; cf. Matthew 5:25, 26).

Setting: On the way from Galilee to Jerusalem. After telling His disciples of His second coming, Jesus instructs them about persistence in prayer.

Now He was telling them a parable to show that at all times they ought to pray and not to lose heart, saying, "In a certain city there was a judge who did not fear God and did not respect man. There was a widow in that city, and she kept coming to him, saying, 'Give me legal protection from my opponent.' For a while he was unwilling; but afterward he said to himself, 'Even though I do not fear God nor respect man, yet because this woman bothers me, I will give her legal protection, otherwise by continually coming she will wear me out.'" And the Lord said, "Hear what the unrighteous judge said; now, will not God bring about justice for His elect who cry to Him day and night, and will He delay long over them? I tell you that He will bring about justice for them quickly. However, when the Son of Man comes, will He find faith on the earth?" (Luke 18:1–8; see Luke 11:5–10).

OPPONENTS (Also see ENEMIES; ENEMY; and OPPONENT)

Setting: On the Mount of Olives, east of the temple in Jerusalem. After ministering in the temple a few days before His crucifixion, and giving His disciples more details regarding the temple's future destruction, Jesus elaborates during His Olivet Discourse about things to come.

Then He continued by saying to them, "Nation will rise against nation and kingdom against kingdom, and there will be great earthquakes, and in various places plagues and famines; and there will be terrors and great signs from heaven. But before all these things, they will lay their hands on you and will persecute you, delivering you to the synagogues and prisons, bringing you before kings and governors for My name's sake. It will lead to an opportunity for your testimony. So make up your minds not to prepare beforehand to defend yourselves; for I will give you utterance and wisdom which none of your opponents will be able to resist or refute. But you will be betrayed even by parents and brothers and relatives and friends, and they will put *some* of you to death, and you will be hated by all because of My name. Yet not a hair of your head will perish. By your endurance you will gain your lives" (Luke 21:10–19; cf. Matthew 10:19–22; 24:7–14; Mark 13:8–13).

OPPORTUNITY

Setting: On the Mount of Olives, east of the temple in Jerusalem. After ministering in the temple a few days before His crucifixion, and giving His disciples more details regarding the temple's future destruction, Jesus elaborates during His Olivet Discourse about things to come.

Then He continued by saying to them, "Nation will rise against nation and kingdom against kingdom, and there will be great earthquakes, and in various places plagues and famines; and there will be terrors and great signs from heaven. But before all these things, they will lay their hands on you and will persecute you, delivering you to the synagogues and prisons, bringing you before kings and governors for My name's sake. It will lead to an opportunity for your testimony. So make up your minds not to prepare beforehand to defend yourselves; for I will give you utterance and wisdom which none of your opponents will be able to resist or refute. But you will be betrayed even by parents and brothers and relatives and friends, and they will put *some* of you to death, and you will be hated by all because of My name. Yet not a hair of your head will perish. By your endurance you will gain your lives" (Luke 21:10–19; cf. Matthew 10:19–22; 24:7–14; Mark 13:8–13).

[OPPORTUNITY from opportune]

Setting: Capernaum of Galilee. Jesus' blood brothers, who do not yet believe in Him, encourage Him to attend the upcoming Feast of Booths in Jerusalem in order to demonstrate His works to His disciples and the world.

So Jesus said to them, "My time is not yet here, but your time is always opportune. The world cannot hate you, but it hates Me because I testify of it, that its deeds are evil. Go up to the feast yourselves; I do not go up to this feast because My time has not yet fully come" (John 7:6–8; see John 3:19, 20; 15:18–20).

OPPOSITION IN MINISTRY (Listed under MINISTRY, OPPOSITION IN)

OPPOSITION TO JESUS (Listed under JESUS, OPPOSITION TO)

OPPRESSED

Setting: The synagogue in Jesus' hometown of Nazareth in Galilee. At the beginning of His public ministry, Jesus reads on the Sabbath from the book of the prophet Isaiah.

And the book of the prophet Isaiah was handed to Him. And He opened the book and found the place where it was written, "THE SPIRIT OF THE LORD IS UPON ME, BECAUSE HE ANOINTED ME TO PREACH THE GOSPEL TO THE POOR. HE HAS SENT ME TO PROCLAIM RELEASE TO THE CAPTIVES, AND RECOVERY OF SIGHT TO THE BLIND, TO SET FREE THOSE WHO ARE OPPRESSED, TO PROCLAIM THE FAVORABLE YEAR OF THE LORD." And He closed the book, gave it back to the attendant and sat down; and the eyes of all in the synagogue were fixed on Him. And He began to say to them, "Today this Scripture has been fulfilled in your hearing" (Luke 4:17–21, Jesus quotes from Isaiah 61:1, 2).

ORDINANCES (See BAPTISM; and LORD'S SUPPER)

ORPHANS

Setting: Jerusalem. Before the Passover, after responding to Philip's request for Him to show His disciples the Father, Jesus conveys the upcoming role of the Holy Spirit in their lives.

"I will not leave you as orphans; I will come to you. After a little while the world will no longer see Me, but you *will* see Me; because I live, you will live also. In that day you will know that I am in the Father, and you in Me, and I in you. He who has My commandments and keeps them is the one who loves Me; and he who loves Me will be loved by My Father, and I will love him and will disclose Myself to him" (John 14:18–21; see John 6:57; 10:37, 38; 16:16, 22).

OTHER SIDE (Listed under SIDE, OTHER)

OTHERS

Setting: Galilee. During the early part of His ministry, Jesus preaches the Sermon on the Mount to His disciples and the multitudes.

"Whoever then annuls one of the least of these commandments, and teaches others *to do* the same, shall be called least in the kingdom of heaven; but whoever keeps and teaches *them*, he shall be called great in the kingdom of heaven" (Matthew 5:19; cf. Matthew 11:11).

Setting: Galilee. During the early part of His ministry, Jesus preaches the Sermon on the Mount to His disciples and the multitudes.

"You have heard that it was said, 'YOU SHALL LOVE YOUR NEIGHBOR and hate your enemy.' But I say to you, love your enemies and pray for those who persecute you, so that you may be sons of your Father who is in heaven; for He causes His sun to rise on *the* evil and *the* good, and sends rain on *the* righteous and *the* unrighteous. For if you love those who love you, what reward do you have? Do not even the tax collectors do the same? If you greet only your brothers, what more are you doing *than others?* Do not even the Gentiles do the same? Therefore, you are to be perfect, as your heavenly Father is perfect" (Matthew 5:43–48, Jesus quotes from Leviticus 19:18; cf. Leviticus 19:2; Luke 6:27–36).

Setting: Galilee. During the early part of His ministry, Jesus preaches the Sermon on the Mount to His disciples and the multitudes.

"For if you forgive others for their transgressions, your heavenly Father will also forgive you. But if you do not forgive others, then your Father will not forgive your transgressions" (Matthew 6:14, 15; cf. Matthew 18:15; see Mark 7:2).

Setting: By the Sea of Galilee. While teaching and preaching to the crowds from a boat, Jesus conveys the Parable of the Sower.

And He spoke many things to them in parables, saying, "Behold, the sower went out to sow; and as he sowed, some *seeds* fell beside the road, and the birds came and ate them up. Others fell on the rocky places, where they did not have much soil; and immediately they sprang up, because they had no depth of soil. But when the sun had risen, they were scorched; and because they had no root, they withered away. Others fell among the thorns, and the thorns came up and choked them out. And others fell on the good soil and yielded a crop, some a hundredfold, some sixty, and some thirty. He who has ears, let him hear" (Matthew 13:3–9; cf. Mark 4:3–9; Luke 8:4–8).

Setting: Judea beyond the Jordan (Perea). Jesus illustrates the kingdom of heaven to His disciples through the story of laborers in the vineyard.

"For the kingdom of heaven is like a landowner who went out early in the morning to hire laborers for his vineyard. When he had agreed with the laborers for a denarius for the day, he sent them into his vineyard. And he went out about the third hour and saw others standing idle in the market place; and to those he said, 'You also go into the vineyard, and whatever is right I will give you.' And *so* they went. Again he went out about the sixth and the ninth hour, and did the same thing. And about the eleventh *hour* he went out and found others standing *around;* and he said to them, 'Why have you been standing idle here all day long?' They said to him, 'Because no one hired us.' He said to them, 'You go into the vineyard too.' When evening came, the owner of the vineyard said to his foreman, 'Call the laborers and pay them their wages, beginning with the last *group* to the first.' When those *hired* about the eleventh hour came, each one received a denarius. When those *hired* first came, they thought that they would receive more; but each of them also received a denarius. When they received it, they grumbled at the landowner, saying, 'These last men have worked *only* one hour, and you have made them equal to us who have borne the burden and the scorching heat of the day.' But he answered and said to one of them, 'Friend, I am doing you no wrong; did you not agree with me for a denarius? Take what is yours and go, but I wish to give to this last man the same as to you. It is not lawful for me to do what I wish with what is my own? Or is your eye envious because I am generous?' So the last shall be first, and the first last" (Matthew 20:1–16; cf. Matthew 19:30).

Setting: The temple in Jerusalem. After the Jewish religious leaders test Him with questions, Jesus pronounces the fifth of eight woes on them in front of the crowds and His disciples.

"Woe to you, scribes and Pharisees, hypocrites! For you tithe the mint and dill and cummin, and have neglected the weightier provisions of the law: justice and mercy and faithfulness; but these are things you should have done without neglecting the others. You blind guides, who strain out a gnat and swallow a camel!" (Matthew 23:23, 24).

Setting: By the Sea of Galilee. During the early part of His ministry, after presenting the Parable of the Sower from a boat to a very large crowd, Jesus gives the meaning of the parable to His disciples and other followers.

And He said to them, "Do you not understand this parable? How will you understand all the parables? The sower sows the word. These are the ones who are beside the road where the word is sown; and when they hear, immediately Satan comes and takes away the word which has been sown in them. In a similar way these are the ones on whom seed was sown on the rocky places, who, when they hear the word, immediately receive it with joy; and they have no *firm* root in themselves, but are *only* temporary; then, when affliction or persecution arises because of the word, immediately they fall away. And others are the ones on whom seed was sown among the thorns; these are the ones who have heard the word, but the worries of the world and the deceitfulness of riches, and the desires for other things enter in and choke the word, and it becomes unfruitful. And those are the ones on whom seed was sown on the good soil; and they hear the word and accept it and bear fruit, thirty, sixty, and a hundredfold" (Mark 4:13–20; cf. Matthew 13:18–23; Luke 8:11–15).

Setting: The temple in Jerusalem. Having His authority questioned by the chief priests, scribes, and elders, Jesus begins to teach them in parables.

And He began to speak to them in parables: "A man PLANTED A VINEYARD AND PUT A WALL AROUND IT, AND DUG A VAT UNDER THE WINE PRESS AND BUILT A TOWER, and rented it out to vine-growers and went on a journey. At the *harvest* time he sent a slave to the vine-growers, in order to receive *some* of the produce of the vineyard from the vine-growers. They took him, and beat him and sent him away empty-handed. Again he sent them another slave, and they wounded him in the head, and treated him shamefully. And he sent another, and that one they killed; and *so with* many others, beating some and killing others. He had one more to *send*, a beloved son; he sent him last *of all* to them, saying, 'They will respect my son.' But those vine-growers said to one another, 'This is the heir; come, let us kill him, and the inheritance will be ours!' They took him, and killed him and threw him out of the vineyard. What will the owner of the vineyard do? He will come and destroy the vine-growers, and will give the vineyard to others. Have you not even read this Scripture: 'THE STONE WHICH THE BUILDERS REJECTED, THIS BECAME THE CHIEF CORNER *stone;* THIS CAME ABOUT FROM THE LORD, AND IT IS MARVELOUS IN OUR EYES'?" (Mark 12:1–11, Jesus quotes from Psalm 118:22, 23; Isaiah 5:1, 2; cf. Matthew 21:33–46; Luke 20:9–19).

Setting: Galilee. After selecting His twelve disciples, Jesus teaches the Sermon on the Mount to His disciples and a great throng from Judea, Jerusalem, and the central coastal region of Tyre and Sidon.

"But I say to you who hear, love your enemies, do good to those who hate you, bless those who curse you, pray for those who mistreat you. Whoever hits you on the cheek, offer him the other also; and whoever takes away your coat, do not withhold your shirt from him either. Give to everyone who asks of you, and whoever takes away what is yours, do not demand it back. Treat others the same way you want them to treat you. If you love those who love you, what credit is *that* to you? For even sinners love those who love them. If you do good to those who do good to you, what credit is *that* to you? For even sinners do the same. If you lend to those from whom you expect to receive, what credit is *that* to you? Even sinners lend to sinners in order to receive back the same *amount.* But love your enemies, and do good, and lend, expecting nothing in return; and your reward will be great, and you will be sons of the Most High; for He Himself is kind to ungrateful and evil *men*. Be merciful, just as your Father is merciful" (Luke 6:27–36; cf. Matthew 5:9, 39–48; Matthew 7:12).

Setting: On the way from Galilee to Jerusalem. After speaking of how a lamp illuminates, the Lord has lunch with a Pharisee who is surprised He doesn't wash before eating.

But the Lord said to him, "Now you Pharisees clean the outside of the cup and of the platter; but inside of you, you are full of robbery and wickedness. You foolish ones, did not He who made the outside make the inside also? But give that which is within as charity, and then all things are clean for you. But woe to you Pharisees! You pay tithe of mint and rue and every *kind of* garden herb, and *yet* disregard justice and the love of God; but these are the things you should have done without neglecting the others. Woe to you Pharisees! For you love the chief seats in the synagogues and the respectful greetings in the market places. Woe to you! For you are like concealed tombs, and the people who walk over *them* are unaware *of it*" (Luke 11:39–44; cf. Matthew 23:6, 7, 23–27; see Matthew 15:2; Titus 1:15).

Setting: The temple in Jerusalem. While ministering a few days before His crucifixion, after the chief priests and the scribes question His authority to teach and preach, Jesus conveys the Parable of the Vine-Growers to the people.

And He began to tell the people this parable: "A man planted a vineyard and rented it out to vine-growers, and went on a journey for a long time. At the *harvest* time he sent a slave to the vine-growers, so that they would give him *some* of the produce of the vineyard; but the vine-growers beat him and sent him away empty-handed. And he proceeded to send another slave; and they beat him also and treated him shamefully and sent him away empty-handed. And he proceeded to send a third; and this one also they wounded and cast out. The owner of the vineyard said, 'What shall I do? I will send my beloved son; perhaps they will respect him.' But when the vine-growers saw him, they reasoned with one another, saying, 'This is the heir; let us kill him so that the inheritance will be ours.' So they threw him out of the vineyard and killed him. What, then, will the owner of the vineyard do to them? He will come and destroy these vine-growers and will give the vineyard to others." When they heard it, they said, "May it never be!" But Jesus looked at them and said, "What then is this that is written: 'THE STONE WHICH THE BUILDERS REJECTED, THIS BECAME THE CHIEF CORNER *stone*'? Everyone who falls on that stone will be broken to pieces; but on whomever it falls, it will scatter him like dust" (Luke 20:9–18, Jesus quotes from Psalm 118:22; cf. Matthew 21:33–44; Mark 12:1–11; see Ephesians 2:20).

Setting: Sychar in Samaria. After Jesus converses with a Samaritan woman at Jacob's well, the disciples return with food. They try to get Jesus to eat, but are surprised when He speaks of other food.

Jesus said to them, "My food is to do the will of Him who sent Me and to accomplish His work. Do you not say, 'There are yet four months, and *then* comes the harvest'? Behold, I say to you, lift up your eyes and look on the fields, that they are white for harvest. Already he who reaps is receiving wages and is gathering fruit for life eternal; so that he who sows and he who reaps may rejoice together. For in this *case* the saying is true, 'One sows and another reaps.' I sent you to reap that for which you have not labored; others have labored and you have entered into their labor" (John 4:34–38; see Matthew 9:37, 38; John 5:36).

Setting: Jerusalem. After the previous and current high priests (Annas and Caiaphas) question Jesus, and Peter denies for the second and third times being His disciple, the Lord is brought before Pilate (Roman governor of Judea).

Jesus answered, "Are you saying this on your own initiative, or did others tell you about Me?" (John 18:34).

OTHERS, GIFTS TO (See GIFTS TO OTHER PEOPLE)

OURS

Setting: The temple in Jerusalem. Having His authority questioned by the chief priests, scribes, and elders, Jesus begins to teach them in parables.

And He began to speak to them in parables: "A man PLANTED A VINEYARD AND PUT A WALL AROUND IT, AND DUG A VAT UNDER THE WINE PRESS AND BUILT A TOWER, and rented it out to vine-growers and went on a journey. At the *harvest* time he sent a slave to the vine-growers, in order to receive *some* of the produce of the vineyard from the vine-growers. They took him, and beat him and sent him away empty-handed. Again he sent them another slave, and they wounded him in the head, and treated him shamefully. And he sent another, and that one they killed; and *so with* many others, beating some and killing others. He had one more to *send*, a beloved son; he sent him last *of all* to them, saying, 'They will respect my son.' But those vine-growers said to one another, 'This is the heir; come, let us kill him, and the inheritance will be ours!' They took him, and killed him and threw him out of the vineyard. What will the owner of the vineyard do? He will come and destroy the vine-growers, and will give the vineyard to others. Have you not even read this Scripture: 'THE STONE WHICH THE BUILDERS REJECTED, THIS BECAME THE CHIEF CORNER *stone;* THIS CAME ABOUT FROM THE LORD, AND IT IS MARVELOUS IN OUR EYES'?" (Mark 12:1–11, Jesus quotes from Psalm 118:22, 23; Isaiah 5:1, 2; cf. Matthew 21:33–46; Luke 20:9–19).

Setting: The temple in Jerusalem. While ministering a few days before His crucifixion, after the chief priests and the scribes question His authority to teach and preach, Jesus conveys the Parable of the Vine-Growers to the people.

And He began to tell the people this parable: "A man planted a vineyard and rented it out to vine-growers, and went on a journey for a long time. At the *harvest* time he sent a slave to the vine-growers, so that they would give him *some* of the produce of the vineyard; but the vine-growers beat him and sent him away empty-handed. And he proceeded to send another slave; and they beat him also and treated him shamefully and sent him away empty-handed. And he proceeded to send a third; and this one also they wounded and cast out. The owner of the vineyard said, 'What shall I do? I will send my beloved son; perhaps they will respect him.' But when the vine-growers saw him, they reasoned with one another, saying, 'This is the heir; let us kill him so that the inheritance will be ours.' So they threw him out of the vineyard and killed him. What, then, will the owner of the vineyard do to them? He will come and destroy these vine-growers and will give the vineyard to others." When they heard it, they said, "May it never be!" But Jesus looked at them and said, "What then is this that is written: 'THE STONE WHICH THE BUILDERS REJECTED, THIS BECAME THE CHIEF CORNER *stone*'? Everyone who falls on that stone will be broken to pieces; but on whomever it falls, it will scatter him like dust" (Luke 20:9–18, Jesus quotes from Psalm 118:22; cf. Matthew 21:33–44; Mark 12:1–11; see Ephesians 2:20).

OUTCASTS

[OUTCASTS from *the* poor, *the* crippled, *the* lame, *the* blind]

Setting: On the way from Galilee to Jerusalem. After Jesus, observing the invited guests of a Pharisee leader selecting places of honor at the table, speaks a parable to them, He comments to the host about the people to invite in the future.

And He also went on to say to the one who had invited Him, "When you give a luncheon or a dinner, do not invite your friends or your brothers or your relatives or rich neighbors, otherwise they may also invite you in return and *that* will be your repayment. But when you give a reception, invite *the* poor, *the* crippled, *the* lame, *the* blind, and you will be blessed, since they do not have *the means* to repay you; for you will be repaid at the resurrection of the righteous" (Luke 14:12–14; see John 5:28, 29).

Setting: Jerusalem. Before the Passover, after explaining He is the vine and His disciples are the branches, Jesus warns the disciples of the persecution they will face after His departure to heaven.

"These things I have spoken to you so that you may be kept from stumbling. They will make you outcasts from the synagogue, but an hour is coming for everyone who kills you to think that he is offering service to God. These things they will do because they have not known the Father or Me. But these things I have spoken to you, so that when their hour comes, you may remember that I told you of them. These things I did not say to you at the beginning, because I was with you" (John 16:1–4; see John 8:19, 55; 9:22; 13:19; 15:18–27).

OUTER DARKNESS (Listed under DARKNESS, OUTER)

OUTSIDE

Setting: The temple in Jerusalem. After the Jewish religious leaders test Him with questions, Jesus pronounces the sixth of eight woes on them in front of the crowds and His disciples.

"Woe to you, scribes and Pharisees, hypocrites! For you clean the outside of the cup and of the dish, but inside they are full of robbery and self-indulgence. You blind Pharisee, first clean the inside of the cup and of the dish, so that the outside of it may become clean also" (Matthew 23:25, 26; see Mark 7:4).

Setting: The temple in Jerusalem. After the Jewish religious leaders test Him with questions, Jesus pronounces the seventh of eight woes on them in front of the crowds and His disciples.

"Woe to you, scribes and Pharisees, hypocrites! For you are like whitewashed tombs which on the outside appear beautiful, but inside they are full of dead men's bones and all uncleanness. So you, too, outwardly appear righteous to men, but inwardly you are full of hypocrisy and lawlessness" (Matthew 23:27, 28; cf. Luke 11:44).

Setting: By the Sea of Galilee. After Jesus conveys the Parable of the Sower from a boat to a crowd, His disciples ask Him questions about it.

And He was saying to them, "To you has been given the mystery of the kingdom of God, but those who are outside get everything in parables, so that WHILE SEEING, THEY MAY SEE AND NOT PERCEIVE, AND WHILE HEARING, THEY MAY HEAR AND NOT UNDERSTAND, OTHERWISE THEY MIGHT RETURN AND BE FORGIVEN" (Mark 4:11, 12, Jesus quotes from Isaiah 6:9, 10; cf. Matthew 13:10–17).

Setting: Galilee. After the Pharisees and scribes from Jerusalem object to His disciples' lack of obedience to the tradition regarding ceremonial cleansing, Jesus speaks to a crowd and explains His teaching to the disciples.

After He called the crowd to Him again, He *began* saying to them, "Listen to Me, all of you, and understand: there is nothing outside the man which can defile him if it goes into him; but the things which proceed out of the man are what defile the man. [If anyone has ears to hear, let him hear."] When he had left the crowd *and* entered the house, His disciples questioned Him about the parable. And He said to them, "Are you so lacking in understanding also? Do you not understand that whatever goes into the man from outside cannot defile him, because it does not go into his heart, but into his stomach, and is eliminated?" (*Thus He* declared all foods clean.) And He was saying, "That which proceeds out of the man, that is what defiles the man. For from within, out of the heart of men, proceed the evil thoughts, fornications, thefts, murders, adulteries, deeds of coveting *and* wickedness, *as well* as deceit, sensuality, envy, slander, pride *and* foolishness. All these evil things proceed from within and defile the man" (Mark 7:14–23; cf. Matthew 15:10–20).

Setting: On the way from Galilee to Jerusalem. After speaking of how a lamp illuminates, the Lord has lunch with a Pharisee who is surprised He doesn't wash before eating.

But the Lord said to him, "Now you Pharisees clean the outside of the cup and of the platter; but inside of you, you are full of robbery and wickedness. You foolish ones, did not He who made the outside make the inside also? But give that which is within as charity, and then all things are clean for you. But woe to you Pharisees! You pay tithe of mint and rue and every *kind of* garden herb, and *yet* disregard justice and the love of God; but these are the things you should have done without neglecting the others. Woe to you Pharisees! For you love the chief seats in the synagogues and the respectful greetings in the market places. Woe to you! For you are like concealed tombs, and the people who walk over *them* are unaware *of it*" (Luke 11:39–44; cf. Matthew 23:6, 7, 23–27; see Matthew 15:2; Titus 1:15).

Setting: On the way from Galilee to Jerusalem. While teaching in the cities and villages, Jesus responds to a question about who is saved.

And someone said to Him, "Lord, are here *just* a few who are being saved?" And He said to them, "Strive to enter through the narrow door; for many, I tell you, will seek to enter and will not be able. Once the head of the house gets up and shuts the door, and you begin to stand outside and knock on the door, saying, 'Lord, open up to us!' then He will answer and say to you, 'I do not know where you are from.' Then you will begin to say, 'We ate and drank in Your presence, and You taught in our streets'; and He will say, 'I tell you, I do not know where you are from; DEPART FROM ME, ALL YOU EVILDOERS.' In that place there will be weeping and gnashing of teeth when you see Abraham and Isaac and Jacob and all the prophets in the kingdom of God, but you yourselves being thrown out. And they will come from east and west and from north and south, and will recline *at the table* in the kingdom of God. And behold, *some* are last who will be first and *some* are first who will be last" (Luke 13:23–30, Jesus quotes from Psalm 6:8; cf. Matthew 7:13, 23; 8:11, 12; see Matthew 19:30; Luke 3:8).

Setting: On the way from Galilee to Jerusalem. While teaching in the cities and villages, Jesus responds to a question about who is saved. Some Pharisees ask Him to leave, claiming Herod Antipas (tetrarch of Galilee and Perea) seeks to kill Him.

And He said to them, "Go and tell that fox, 'Behold, I cast out demons and perform cures today and tomorrow, and the third *day* I reach My goal.' Nevertheless I must journey on today and tomorrow and the next *day*; for it cannot be that a prophet would perish outside of Jerusalem. O Jerusalem, Jerusalem, *the city* that kills the prophets and stones those sent to her! How often I wanted to gather your children together, just as a hen *gathers* her brood under her wings, and you would not *have it*! Behold, your house is left to you *desolate*; and I say to you, you will not see Me until *the time* comes when you say, 'BLESSED IS HE WHO COMES IN THE NAME OF THE LORD!'" (Luke 13:32–35, Jesus quotes from Psalm 118:26; cf. Matthew 23:37).

OVERCOMER (See VICTORY)

OVERCOMING THE WORLD (See VICTORY)

OWN (See OWNER; STEWARD; and STEWARDSHIP)

OWNER (Also see STEWARD; and STEWARDSHIP)

Setting: Judea beyond the Jordan (Perea). Jesus illustrates the kingdom of heaven to His disciples through the story of laborers in the vineyard.

"For the kingdom of heaven is like a landowner who went out early in the morning to hire laborers for his vineyard. When he had agreed with the laborers for a denarius for the day, he sent them into his vineyard. And he went out about the third hour and saw others standing idle in the market place; and to those he said,' You also go into the vineyard, and whatever is right I will give you.' And so they went. Again he went out about the sixth and the ninth hour, and did the same thing. And about the eleventh hour he went out and found others standing around; and he said to them, 'Why have you been standing idle here all day long?' They said to him, 'Because no one hired us.' He said to them, 'You go into the vineyard too.' When evening came, the owner of the vineyard said to his foreman, 'Call the laborers and pay them their wages, beginning with the last group to the first.' When those hired about the eleventh hour came, each one received a denarius. When those hired first came, they thought that they would receive more; but each of them also received a denarius. When they received it, they grumbled at the landowner, saying, 'These last men have worked only one hour, and you have made them equal to us who have borne the burden and the scorching heat of the day.' But he answered and said to one of them, 'Friend, I am doing you no wrong; did you not agree with me for a denarius? Take what is yours and go, but I wish to give to this last man the same as to you. It is not lawful for me to do what I wish with what is my own? Or is your eye envious because I am generous?' So the last shall be first, and the first last" (Matthew 20:1–16; cf. Matthew 19:30).

Setting: The temple in Jerusalem. Jesus delivers another parable to the chief priests and elders after they question His authority.

"Listen to another parable. There was a landowner who PLANTED A VINEYARD AND PUT A WALL AROUND IT AND DUG A WINE PRESS IN IT, AND BUILT A TOWER, and rented it out to vine-growers and went on a journey. When the harvest time approached, he sent his slaves to the vine-growers to receive his produce. The vine-growers took his slaves and beat one, and killed another, and stoned a third. Again he sent another group of slaves larger than the first; and they did the same thing to them. But afterward he sent his son to them, saying, 'They will respect my son.' But when the vine-growers saw the son, they said among themselves, 'This is the heir; come, let us kill him and seize his inheritance.' They took him, and threw him out of the vineyard and killed him. Therefore when the owner of the vineyard comes, what will he do to those vine-growers?" (Matthew 21:33–40; Jesus quotes from Isaiah 5:1, 2; cf. Mark 12:1–9; Luke 20:9–15).

Setting: The temple in Jerusalem. Having His authority questioned by the chief priests, scribes, and elders, Jesus begins to teach them in parables.

And He began to speak to them in parables: "A man PLANTED A VINEYARD AND PUT A WALL AROUND IT, AND DUG A VAT UNDER THE WINE PRESS AND BUILT A TOWER, and rented it out to vine-growers and went on a journey. At the *harvest* time he sent a slave to the vine-growers, in order to receive *some* of the produce of the vineyard from the vine-growers. They took him, and beat him and sent him away empty-handed. Again he sent them another slave, and they wounded him in the head, and treated him shamefully. And he sent another, and that one they killed; and *so with* many others, beating some and killing others. He had one more to *send*, a beloved son; he sent him last *of all* to them, saying, 'They will respect my son.' But those vine-growers said to one another, 'This is the heir; come, let us kill him, and the inheritance will be ours!' They took him, and killed him and threw him out of the vineyard. What will the owner of the vineyard do? He will come and destroy the vine-growers, and will give the vineyard to others. Have you not even read this Scripture: 'THE STONE WHICH THE BUILDERS REJECTED, THIS BECAME THE CHIEF CORNER *stone;* THIS CAME ABOUT FROM THE LORD, AND IT IS MARVELOUS IN OUR EYES'?" (Mark 12:1–11, Jesus quotes from Psalm 118:22, 23; Isaiah 5:1, 2; cf. Matthew 21:33–46; Luke 20:9–19).

Setting: Jerusalem. On the first day of the Feast of Unleavened Bread, when the Passover lamb is sacrificed, Jesus responds to His disciples' question about His plans for the Passover meal.

And He sent two of His disciples and said to them, "Go into the city, and a man will meet you carrying a pitcher of water; follow him; and wherever he enters, say to the owner of the house, 'The Teacher says, "Where is My guest room in which I may eat the Passover with My disciples?"' And he himself will show you a large upper room furnished *and* ready; prepare for us there" (Mark 14:13–15; cf. Matthew 26:17–19; Luke 22:7–13).

Setting: The temple in Jerusalem. While ministering a few days before His crucifixion, after the chief priests and the scribes question His authority to teach and preach, Jesus conveys the Parable of the Vine-Growers to the people.

And He began to tell the people this parable: "A man planted a vineyard and rented it out to vine-growers, and went on a journey for a long time. At the *harvest* time he sent a slave to the vine-growers, so that they would give him *some* of the produce of the vineyard; but the vine-growers beat him and sent him away empty-handed. And he proceeded to send another slave; and they beat him also and treated him shamefully and sent him away empty-handed. And he proceeded to send a third; and this one also they wounded and cast out. The owner of the vineyard said, 'What shall I do? I will send my beloved son; perhaps they will respect him.' But when the vine-growers saw him, they reasoned with one another, saying, 'This is the heir; let us kill him so that the inheritance will be ours.' So they threw him out of the vineyard and killed him. What, then, will the owner of the vineyard do to them? He will come and destroy these vine-growers and will give the vineyard to others." When they heard it, they said, "May it never be!" But Jesus looked at them and said, "What then is this that is written: 'THE STONE WHICH THE BUILDERS REJECTED, THIS BECAME THE CHIEF CORNER *stone*'? Everyone who falls on that stone will be broken to pieces; but on whomever it falls, it will scatter him like dust" (Luke 20:9–18, Jesus quotes from Psalm 118:22; cf. Matthew 21:33–44; Mark 12:1–11; see Ephesians 2:20).

Setting: Jerusalem. With the Passover (Feast of Unleavened Bread) approaching, Jesus informs His disciples where they will celebrate the feast. The chief priests and scribes seek to kill Him, and Satan enters Judas Iscariot in order to betray the Lord.

And Jesus sent Peter and John, saying, "Go and prepare the Passover for us, so that we may eat it." They said to Him, "Where do You want us to prepare it?" And He said to them, "When you have entered the city, a man will meet you carrying a pitcher of water; follow him into the house that he enters. And you shall say to the owner of the house, 'The Teacher says to you, "Where is the guest room in which I may eat the Passover with My disciples?"' And he will show you a large, furnished upper room; prepare it there" (Luke 22:8–12; cf. Matthew 26:17–19; Mark 14:12–16).

Setting: Jerusalem. Following the Pharisees' interrogation and dismissal of the formerly blind man Jesus healed on the Sabbath, the Lord conveys the Parable of the Good Shepherd to the Pharisees, using figures of speech they do not understand.

So Jesus said to them again, "Truly, truly, I say to you, I am the door of the sheep. All who came before Me are thieves and robbers, but the sheep did not hear them. I am the door; if anyone enters through Me, he will be saved, and will go in and out and find pasture. The thief comes only to steal and kill and destroy; I came that they may have life, and have *it* abundantly. I am the good shepherd; the good shepherd lays down His life for the sheep. He who is a hired hand, and not a shepherd, who is not the owner of the sheep, sees the wolf coming, and leaves the sheep and flees, and the wolf snatches them and scatters *them. He flees* because he is a hired hand and is not concerned about the sheep. I am the good shepherd, and I know My own and My own know Me, even as the Father knows Me and I know the Father; and I lay down My life for the sheep. I have other sheep, which are not of this fold; I must bring them also, and they will hear My voice; and they will become one flock *with* one shepherd. For this reason the Father loves Me, because I lay down My life so that I may take it again. No one has taken it away from Me, but I lay it down on My own initiative. I have authority to take it up again. This commandment I received from My Father" (John 10:7–18; see Isaiah 40:11; 56:8; Jeremiah 23:1; Matthew 11:27).

OWNER OF THE HOUSE (Listed under HOUSE, OWNER OF THE)

OWNER OF THE VINEYARD (Listed under VINEYARD, OWNER OF THE)

OX (Also see OXEN)

Setting: On the way from Galilee to Jerusalem. Jesus responds to a synagogue official's anger after He heals a woman, sick eighteen years, in the synagogue on the Sabbath.

But the Lord answered him and said, "You hypocrites, does not each of you on the Sabbath untie his ox or his donkey from the stall and lead him away to water *him?* And this woman, a daughter of Abraham as she is, whom Satan has bound for eighteen long years, should she not have been released from this bond on the Sabbath day?" (Luke 13:15, 16; see Luke 14:5).

Setting: On the way from Galilee to Jerusalem. Jesus goes into the house of a Pharisee leader on the Sabbath to eat bread. A man suffering from dropsy is sitting there.

And Jesus answered and spoke to the lawyers and Pharisees, saying, "Is it lawful to heal on the Sabbath, or not?" But they kept silent. And He took hold of him and healed him, and sent him away. And He said to them, "Which one of you will have a son or an ox fall into a well, and will not immediately pull him out on a Sabbath day?" And they could make no reply to this (Luke 14:3–6, cf. Matthew 12:11–13).

OXEN (Also see LIVESTOCK, FATTENED; and OX)

Setting: The temple in Jerusalem. Jesus speaks another parable to the chief priests and elders after they question His authority.

Jesus spoke to them again in parables, saying, "The kingdom of heaven may be compared to a king who gave a wedding feast for his son. And he sent out his slaves to call those who had been invited to the wedding feast, and they were unwilling to come. Again he sent out other slaves saying, 'Tell those who have been invited, "Behold, I have prepared my dinner; my oxen and my fattened livestock are *all* butchered and everything is ready; come to the wedding feast." But they paid no attention and went their way, one to his own farm, another to his business, and the rest seized his slaves and mistreated them and killed them. But the king was enraged, and he sent his armies and destroyed those murderers and set their city on fire. Then he said to his slaves, 'The wedding is ready, but those who were invited were not worthy. 'Go therefore to the main highways, and as many as you find *there,* invite to the wedding feast.' Those slaves went out into the streets and gathered together all they found, both evil and good; and the wedding hall was filled with dinner guests. But when the king came in to look over the dinner guests, he saw a man there who was not dressed in wedding clothes, and he said to him, 'Friend, how did you come in here without wedding clothes?' And the man was speechless. Then the king said to the servants, 'Bind him hand and foot, and throw him into the outer darkness; in that place there will be weeping and gnashing of teeth.' For many are called, but few *are* chosen" (Matthew 22:1–14; cf. Matthew 8:11, 12).

Setting: On the way from Galilee to Jerusalem. After speaking a parable to the invited guests and the host at a banquet, Jesus responds to a guest's proclamation about the blessings of eating bread in the kingdom of God.

But He said to him, "A man was giving a big dinner, and he invited many; and at the dinner hour he sent his slave to say to those who had been invited, 'Come; for everything is ready now.' But they all alike began to make excuses. The first one said to him, 'I have bought a piece of land and I need to go out and look at it; please consider me excused.' Another one said, 'I have bought five yoke of oxen, and I am going to try them out; please consider me excused.' Another one said, I have married a wife, and for that reason I cannot come.' And the slave came *back* and reported this to his master. Then the head of the household became angry and said to his slave, 'Go out at once into the streets and lanes of the city and bring in here the poor and crippled and blind and lame.' And the slave said, 'Master, what you commanded has been done, and still there is room.' And the master said to the slave, 'Go out into the highways and along the hedges, and compel *them* to come in, so that my house may be filled. For I tell you, none of those men who were invited shall taste of my dinner'" (Luke 14:16–24; see Deuteronomy 24:5; Matthew 22:2–14; Luke 14:1, 2).

P

PAIN (Also see AGONY; and TORMENT)

Setting: Jerusalem. Before the Passover, after warning His disciples of the persecution they will face after His departure to heaven, empathizing with their sadness over His prophecies, Jesus gives them the hope for the future.

"A little while, and you will no longer see Me; and again a little while, and you will see Me." *Some* of His disciples then said to one another, "What is this thing He is telling us, 'A little while, and you will not see Me; and again a little while, and you will see Me'; and, 'because I go to the Father'?" So they were saying, "What is this that He says, 'A little while'? We do not know what He is talking about." Jesus knew that they wished to question Him, and He said to them, "Are you deliberating together about this, that I said, 'A little while, and you will not see Me, and again a little while, and you will see Me'? Truly, truly, I say to you, that you will weep and lament, but the world will rejoice; you will grieve, but your grief will be turned into joy. Whenever a woman is in labor she has pain, because her hour has come; but when she gives birth to the child, she no longer remembers the anguish because of the joy that a child has been born into the world. Therefore you too have grief now; but I will see you again, and your heart will rejoice, and no one *will* take your joy away from you" (John 16:16–22; see Mark 9:32; Luke 23:27; John 14:18–24; 16:5, 6; 20:20).

PAINS, BIRTH (See PANGS, BIRTH)

PALACES, KINGS'

Setting: Galilee. While speaking to the crowds, Jesus pays tribute to the ministry of John the Baptist, but emphasizes that the one who is least in the kingdom of heaven is greater than John.

As these men were going *away,* Jesus began to speak to the crowds about John, "What did you go out into the wilderness to see? A reed shaken by the wind? But what did you go out to see? A man dressed in soft *clothing?* Those who wear soft *clothing* are in kings' palaces! But what did you go out to see? A prophet? Yes, I tell you, and the one who is more than a prophet. This is the one about whom it is written, 'BEHOLD, I SEND MY MESSENGER AHEAD OF YOU, WHO WILL PREPARE YOUR WAY BEFORE YOU.' Truly, I say to you, among those born of women there has not arisen *anyone* greater than John the Baptist! Yet the one who is least in the kingdom of heaven is greater than he. From the days of John the Baptist until now the kingdom of heaven suffers violence, and violent men take it by force. For all the prophets and the Law prophesied until John. And, if you are willing to accept *it,* John himself is Elijah who was to come. He who has ears to hear, let him hear" (Matthew 11:7–15, Jesus quotes from Malachi 3:1; cf. Malachi 4:5; Luke 7:24–28; 16:16; see Matthew 14:5).

PALACES, ROYAL

Setting: Galilee. After Jesus answers the disciples of John the Baptist whether He is the promised Messiah, the Lord speaks to the crowds about John.

When the messengers of John had left, He began to speak to the crowds about John, "What did you go out into the wilderness to see? A reed shaken by the wind? But what did you go out to see? A man dressed in soft clothing? Those who are splendidly clothed and live in luxury are *found* in royal palaces! But what did you go out to see? A prophet? Yes, I say to you, and one who is more than a prophet. This is the one about whom it is written, 'BEHOLD, I SEND MY MESSENGER AHEAD OF YOU, WHO WILL PREPARE YOUR WAY BEFORE YOU.' I say to you, among those born of women there is no one greater than John; yet he who is least in the kingdom of God is greater than he" (Luke 7:24–28, Jesus quotes from Malachi 3:1; cf. Matthew 11:7–11).

PALLET (Also see BED; and STRETCHER)

Setting: Capernaum. When Jesus heals a paralytic man and forgives his sins, some scribes believe the Lord commits blasphemy.

Immediately Jesus, aware in His spirit that they were reasoning that way within themselves, said to them, "Why are you reasoning about these things in your hearts? Which is easier, to say to the paralytic, 'Your sins are forgiven'; or to say, 'Get up, and pick up your pallet and walk'? "But so that you may know that the Son of Man has authority on earth to forgive sins"—He said to the paralytic, "I say to you, get up, pick up your pallet and go home" (Mark 2:8–11; cf. Matthew 9:4–7; Luke 5:21–24).

Setting: Galilee. After performing His second Galilean miracle by healing the son of a royal official from Capernaum (the first miracle: turning water into wine at a wedding in Cana), Jesus returns to Jerusalem for a feast of the Jews. There He heals a man by the pool of Bethesda on the Sabbath who has been ill for thirty-eight years.

Jesus said to him, "Get up, pick up your pallet and walk" (John 5:8; see Matthew 9:6).

Setting: Jerusalem. The lame man healed by Jesus at the pool of Bethesda quotes Jesus' command upon being questioned by the Jewish religious leaders why he is carrying his pallet on the Sabbath.

But he answered them, He who made me well was the one who said to me, 'Pick up your pallet and walk.' They asked him, "Who is the man who said to you, 'Pick up *your pallet* and walk'? (John 5:11, 12).

PANGS, BIRTH (Also see BIRTH; and BORN)

Setting: The Mount of Olives, just east of Jerusalem. During His Olivet Discourse, Jesus answers His disciples' questions as to when the temple will be destroyed and Jerusalem overrun, along with the signs of His coming and the end of the age.

And Jesus answered and said to them, "See to it that no one misleads you. For many will come in My name, saying, 'I am the Christ,' and will mislead many. You will be hearing of wars and rumors of wars. See that you are not frightened, for *those things* must take place, but *that* is not yet the end. For nation will rise against nation, and kingdom against kingdom, and in various places there will be famines and earthquakes. But all these things are *merely* the beginning of birth pangs. Then they will deliver you to tribulation, and will kill you, and you will be hated by all nations because of My name. At that time many will fall away and will betray one another and hate one another. Many false prophets will arise and will mislead many. Because lawlessness is increased, most people's love will grow cold. But the one who endures to the end, he will be saved. This gospel of the kingdom shall be preached in the whole world as a testimony to all the nations, and then the end will come" (Matthew 24:4–14; cf. Jeremiah 29:8; Matthew 7:15; 10:17, 22; Mark 13:3–13; Luke 21:7–19; Revelation 6:4).

Setting: On the Mount of Olives, east of the temple in Jerusalem. After predicting the temple's destruction, Jesus responds during His Olivet Discourse to questions from Peter, James, John, and Andrew about other future events.

And Jesus began to say to them, "See to it that no one misleads you. Many will come in My name, saying, 'I am *He!*' and will mislead many. When you hear of wars and rumors of wars, do not be frightened; *those things* must take place; but *that is* not yet the end. For nation will rise up against nation, and kingdom against kingdom; there will be earthquakes in various places; there will *also be* famines. These things are *merely* the beginning of birth pangs. But be on your guard; for they will deliver you to *the* courts, and you will be flogged in *the* synagogues, and you will stand before governors and kings for My sake, as a testimony to them. The gospel must first be preached to all the nations. When they arrest you and hand you over, do not worry beforehand about what you are to say, but say whatever is given you in that hour; for it is not you who speak, but *it is* the Holy Spirit. Brother will betray brother to death, and a father *his* child; and children will rise up against parents and have them put to death. You will be hated by all because of My name, but the one who endures to the end, he will be saved" (Mark 13:5–13; cf. Matthew 24:4–14; Luke 21:7–19; see Matthew 10:17–22).

PARABLE (See LANGUAGE, FIGURATIVE; PARABLES; and specific parables such as DINNER, PARABLE OF THE)

Setting: By the Sea of Galilee. With the religious leaders rejecting His message, Jesus begins to teach in parables, and gives His disciples the meaning of the Parable of the Sower.

"Hear then the parable of the sower. When anyone hears the word of the kingdom and does not understand it, the evil *one* comes and snatches away what has been sown in his heart. This is the one on whom seed was sown beside the road. The one on whom seed was sown on the rocky places, this is the man who hears the word and immediately receives it with joy; yet he has no *firm* root in himself, but is *only* temporary, and when affliction or persecution arises because of the word, immediately he falls away. And the one on whom seed was sown among the thorns, this is the man who hears the word, and the worry of the world and the deceitfulness of wealth choke the word, and it becomes unfruitful. And the one on whom seed was sown on the good soil, this is the man who hears the word and understands it; who indeed bears fruit and brings forth, some a hundredfold, some sixty, and some thirty" (Matthew 13:18–23; cf. Mark 4:13–20; Luke 8:11–15).

Setting: The temple in Jerusalem. Jesus delivers another parable to the chief priests and elders after they question His authority.

"Listen to another parable. There was a landowner who PLANTED A VINEYARD AND PUT A WALL AROUND IT AND DUG A WINE PRESS IN IT, AND BUILT A TOWER, and rented it out to vine-growers and went on a journey. When the harvest time approached, he sent his slaves to the vine-growers to receive his produce. The vine-growers took his slaves and beat one, and killed another, and stoned a third. Again he sent another group of slaves larger than the first; and they did the same thing to them. But afterward he sent his son to them, saying, 'They will respect my son.' But when the vine-growers saw the son, they said among themselves, 'This is the heir; come, let us kill him and seize his inheritance.' They took him, and threw him out of the vineyard and killed him. Therefore when the owner of the vineyard comes, what will he do to those vine-growers?" (Matthew 21:33–40; Jesus quotes from Isaiah 5:1, 2; cf. Mark 12:1–9; Luke 20:9–15; see Matthew 21:45, 46).

Setting: On the Mount of Olives, just east of Jerusalem. During His Olivet Discourse, after answering His disciples' questions as to when the temple will be destroyed and Jerusalem overrun, along with the signs of His coming and the end of the age, Jesus teaches them the Parable of the Fig Tree.

"Now learn the parable from the fig tree: when its branch has already become tender and puts forth its leaves, you know that summer is near; so, you too, when you see all these things, recognize that He is near, *right* at the door. Truly, I say to you, this generation will not pass away until all these things take place. Heaven and earth will pass away, but My words will not pass away. But of that day and hour no one knows, not even the angels of heaven, nor the Son, but the Father alone. For the coming of the Son of Man will be just like the days of Noah. For as in those days before the flood they were eating and drinking, marrying and giving in marriage, until the day that Noah entered the ark, and they did not understand until the flood came and took them all away; so will the coming of the Son of Man be. Then there will be two men in the field; one will be taken and one will be left. Two women *will be* grinding at the mill; one will be taken and one will be left" (Matthew 24:32–41; cf. Mark 13:28–32; Luke 17:34–36; 21:28–33; see Genesis 6:5; 7:7; Matthew 5:18; 10:23; James 5:9).

Setting: By the Sea of Galilee. During the early part of His ministry, after presenting the Parable of the Sower from a boat to a very large crowd, Jesus gives the meaning of the parable to His disciples and other followers.

And He said to them, "Do you not understand this parable? How will you understand all the parables? The sower sows the word. These are the ones who are beside the road where the word is sown; and when they hear, immediately Satan comes and takes away the word which has been sown in them. In a similar way these are the ones on whom seed was sown on the rocky places, who, when they hear the word, immediately receive it with joy; and they have no *firm* root in themselves, but are *only* temporary; then, when affliction or persecution arises because of the word, immediately they fall away. And others are the ones on whom seed was sown among the thorns; these are the ones who have heard the word, but the worries of the world and the deceitfulness of riches, and the desires for other things enter in and choke the word, and it becomes unfruitful. And those are the ones on whom seed was sown on the good soil; and they hear the word and accept it and bear fruit, thirty, sixty, and a hundredfold" (Mark 4:13–20; cf. Matthew 13:18–23; Luke 8:11–15).

Setting: Galilee. After giving the Parable of the Sower and the Parable of the Seed, Jesus continues teaching His disciples by presenting the Parable of the Mustard Seed.

And He said, "How shall we picture the kingdom of God, or by what parable shall we present it? *It is* like a mustard seed, which, when sown upon the soil, though it is smaller than all the seeds that are upon the soil, yet when it is sown, it grows up and becomes larger than all the garden plants and forms large branches; so that THE BIRDS OF THE AIR can NEST UNDER ITS SHADE" (Mark 4:30–32, Jesus quotes from Ezekiel 17:23; cf. Matthew 13:31, 32; Luke 13:18, 19).

Setting: On the Mount of Olives, east of the temple in Jerusalem. After predicting the temple's destruction, Jesus responds during His Olivet Discourse to questions from Peter, James, John, and Andrew about other future events.

"Now learn the parable from the fig tree: when its branch has already become tender and puts forth its leaves, you know that summer is near. Even so, you too, when you see these things happening, recognize that He is near, *right* at the door. Truly I say to you, this generation will not pass away until all these things take place. Heaven and earth will pass away, but My words will not pass away. But of the day or hour no one knows, not even the angels in heaven, nor the Son, but the Father *alone*" (Mark 13:28–32; cf. Matthew 24:32–36; Luke 21:28–33).

Setting: Galilee. After Jesus presents the Parable of the Sower to the crowds, His disciples ask Him to give them the parable's meaning.

And He said, "To you it has been granted to know the mysteries of the kingdom of God, but to the rest *it is* in parables, so that SEEING THEY MAY NOT SEE, AND HEARING THEY MAY NOT UNDERSTAND. Now the parable is this: the seed is the word of God. Those beside the road are those who have heard; then the devil comes and takes away the word from their heart, so that they will not believe and be saved. Those on the rocky *soil* are those who, when they hear, receive the word with joy; and these have no *firm* root; they believe for a while, and in time of temptation fall away. The *seed* which fell among the thorns, these are the ones who have heard, and as they go on their way they are choked with worries and riches and pleasures of *this* life, and bring no fruit to maturity. But the *seed* in the good soil, these are the ones who have heard the word in an honest and good heart, and hold it fast, and bear fruit with perseverance" (Luke 8:10–15, Jesus quotes from Isaiah 6:9; cf. Matthew 13:10–23; Mark 4:10–20).

PARABLE OF THE BARREN FIG TREE (See TREE, PARABLE OF THE UNFRUITFUL FIG)

PARABLE OF THE COSTLY PEARL (See PEARL, PARABLE OF THE)

PARABLE OF THE DEBTORS (See DEBTORS, PARABLE OF TWO)

PARABLE OF THE DINNER (See DINNER, PARABLE OF THE)

PARABLE OF THE DRAGNET (See DRAGNET, PARABLE OF THE)

PARABLE OF THE FAITHFUL AND SENSIBLE STEWARD (See STEWARD, PARABLE OF THE FAITHFUL AND SENSIBLE)

PARABLE OF THE FAITHFUL AND WISE SERVANT (See STEWARD, PARABLE OF THE FAITHFUL AND SENSIBLE)

PARABLE OF THE FIG TREE (See TREE, PARABLE OF THE FIG)

PARABLE OF THE GOOD SAMARITAN (See SAMARITAN, PARABLE OF THE GOOD)

PARABLE OF THE GOOD SHEPHERD (See SHEPHERD, PARABLE OF THE GOOD)

PARABLE OF THE GREAT BANQUET (See DINNER, PARABLE OF THE)

PARABLE OF THE GREAT FEAST (See DINNER, PARABLE OF THE)

PARABLE OF THE GROWING SEED (See SEED, PARABLE OF THE)

PARABLE OF THE GUESTS (See GUESTS, PARABLE OF THE)

PARABLE OF THE GUESTS OF THE BANQUET (See GUESTS, PARABLE OF THE)

PARABLE OF THE HEAD OF A HOUSEHOLD (See HOUSEHOLD, PARABLE OF THE HEAD OF A)

PARABLE OF THE HIDDEN TREASURE (See TREASURE, PARABLE OF THE HIDDEN)

PARABLE OF THE LABORERS IN THE VINEYARD (See VINEYARD, PARABLE OF THE LABORERS IN THE)

PARABLE OF THE LAMP (See LAMP, PARABLE OF THE)

PARABLE OF THE LANDOWNER (See VINE-GROWERS, PARABLE OF THE)

PARABLE OF THE LEAVEN (See LEAVEN, PARABLE OF THE)

PARABLE OF THE LOST COIN (See COIN, PARABLE OF THE LOST)

PARABLE OF THE LOST SHEEP (See SHEEP, PARABLE OF THE LOST)

PARABLE OF THE LOST SON (See SON, PARABLE OF THE PRODIGAL)

PARABLE OF THE LOVING FATHER (See SON, PARABLE OF THE PRODIGAL)

PARABLE OF THE LOWEST SEAT AT THE FEAST (See GUESTS, PARABLE OF THE)

PARABLE OF THE MARRIAGE FEAST (See FEAST, PARABLE OF THE WEDDING)

PARABLE OF THE MINAS (See TALENTS, PARABLE OF THE)

PARABLE OF THE MONEYLENDER (See DEBTORS, PARABLE OF TWO)

PARABLE OF THE MUSTARD SEED (See SEED, PARABLE OF THE MUSTARD)

PARABLE OF THE NET (See DRAGNET, PARABLE OF THE)

PARABLE OF THE NEW CLOTH (See CLOTH, PARABLE OF THE NEW)

PARABLE OF THE NEW WINE IN OLD WINESKINS (See WINESKINS, PARABLE OF THE NEW WINE IN OLD)

PARABLE OF THE NOBLEMAN (See TALENTS, PARABLE OF THE)

PARABLE OF THE OWNER OF A HOUSE (See HOUSEHOLD, PARABLE OF THE HEAD OF A)

PARABLE OF THE PATCHED GARMENT (See CLOTH, PARABLE OF THE NEW)

PARABLE OF THE PEARL (See PEARL, PARABLE OF THE)

PARABLE OF THE PERSISTENT WIDOW (See JUDGE, PARABLE OF THE UNRIGHTEOUS)

PARABLE OF THE PHARISEE AND THE TAX COLLECTOR (See COLLECTOR, PARABLE OF THE PHARISEE AND THE TAX)

PARABLE OF THE PRICELESS PEARL (See PEARL, PARABLE OF THE)

PARABLE OF THE PRODIGAL SON (See SON, PARABLE OF THE PRODIGAL)

PARABLE OF THE RICH FOOL (See MAN, PARABLE OF THE RICH)

PARABLE OF THE RICH MAN (See MAN, PARABLE OF THE RICH)

PARABLE OF THE SEED (See SEED, PARABLE OF THE)

PARABLE OF THE SOILS (See SOWER, PARABLE OF THE)

PARABLE OF THE SOWER (See SOWER, PARABLE OF THE)

PARABLE OF THE TALENTS (See TALENTS, PARABLE OF THE)

PARABLE OF THE TEN MAIDENS (See VIRGINS, PARABLE OF THE TEN)

PARABLE OF THE TEN VIRGINS (See VIRGINS, PARABLE OF THE TEN)

PARABLE OF THE TENANTS (See VINE-GROWERS, PARABLE OF THE)

PARABLE OF TWO DEBTORS (See DEBTORS, PARABLE OF TWO)

PARABLE OF THE TWO SONS (See SONS, PARABLE OF THE TWO)

PARABLE OF THE UNFORGIVING SERVANT or SLAVE (See SLAVE, PARABLE OF THE UNMERCIFUL)

PARABLE OF THE UNFRUITFUL FIG TREE (See TREE, PARABLE OF THE UNFRUITFUL FIG)

PARABLE OF THE UNJUST JUDGE (See JUDGE, PARABLE OF THE UNRIGHTEOUS)

PARABLE OF THE UNMERCIFUL SLAVE (See SLAVE, PARABLE OF THE UNMERCIFUL)

PARABLE OF THE UNRIGHTEOUS JUDGE (See JUDGE, PARABLE OF THE UNRIGHTEOUS)

PARABLE OF THE UNSHRUNK CLOTH (See CLOTH, PARABLE OF THE NEW)

PARABLE OF THE VALUABLE PEARL (See PEARL, PARABLE OF THE)

PARABLE OF THE VINE-GROWERS (See VINE-GROWERS, PARABLE OF THE)

PARABLE OF THE VINEYARD (See VINEYARD, PARABLE OF THE)

PARABLE OF THE WATCHFUL SLAVES (See SLAVES, PARABLE OF THE WATCHFUL)

PARABLE OF THE WEDDING BANQUET (See FEAST, PARABLE OF THE WEDDING)

PARABLE OF THE WEDDING FEAST (See FEAST, PARABLE OF THE WEDDING)

PARABLE OF THE WEEDS AMONG THE WHEAT (See TARES, PARABLE OF THE WHEAT AND THE)

PARABLE OF THE WEEDS AND THE WHEAT (See TARES, PARABLE OF THE WHEAT AND THE)

PARABLE OF THE WHEAT AMONG THE TARES (See TARES, PARABLE OF THE WHEAT AND THE)

PARABLE OF THE WHEAT AND THE TARES (See TARES, PARABLE OF THE WHEAT AND THE)

PARABLE OF THE WHEAT AND THE WEEDS (See TARES, PARABLE OF THE WHEAT AND THE)

PARABLE OF THE WICKED TENANTS (See VINE-GROWERS, PARABLE OF THE)

PARABLE OF THE WORKERS IN THE VINEYARD (See VINEYARD, PARABLE OF THE LABORERS IN THE)

PARABLE OF THE YEAST (See LEAVEN, PARABLE OF THE)

PARABLE OF TWO DEBTORS (See DEBTORS, PARABLE OF TWO)

PARABLES (See LANGUAGE, FIGURATIVE and PARABLE; also see specific parables such as SOWER, PARABLE OF THE)

Setting: By the Sea of Galilee. Jesus responds to His disciples' questions about the Parable of the Sower, which He has just taught from a boat to a crowd.

Jesus answered them, "To you it has been granted to know the mysteries of the kingdom of heaven, but to them it has not been granted. For whoever has, to him *more* shall be given, and he will have an abundance; but whoever does not have, even what he has shall be taken away from him. Therefore, I speak to them in parables; because while seeing they do not see, and while hearing they do not hear, nor do they understand. In their case the prophecy of Isaiah is being fulfilled, which says, 'YOU WILL KEEP ON HEARING, BUT WILL NOT UNDERSTAND; YOU WILL KEEP ON SEEING, BUT WILL NOT PERCEIVE; FOR THE HEART OF THIS PEOPLE HAS BECOME DULL, WITH THEIR EARS THEY SCARCELY HEAR, AND THEY HAVE CLOSED THEIR EYES, OTHERWISE THEYWOULD SEE WITH THEIR EYES, HEAR WITH THEIR EARS, AND UNDERSTAND WITH THEIR HEART AND RETURN, AND I WOULD HEAL THEM.' But blessed are your eyes, because they see; and your ears, because they hear. For truly I say to you that many prophets and righteous men desired to see what you see, and did not see *it*, and to hear what you hear, and did not hear *it*" (Matthew 13:11–17, Jesus quotes from Isaiah 6:9, 10; cf. Matthew 25:29; Mark 4:11–13; Luke 8:10; see Deuteronomy 29:4; John 8:56).

Setting: By the Sea of Galilee. After Jesus conveys the Parable of the Sower from a boat to a crowd, His disciples ask Him questions about it.

And He was saying to them, "To you has been given the mystery of the kingdom of God, but those who are outside get everything in parables, so that WHILE SEEING, THEY MAY SEE AND NOT PERCEIVE, AND WHILE HEARING, THEY MAY HEAR AND NOT UNDERSTAND, OTHERWISE THEY MIGHT RETURN AND BE FORGIVEN" (Mark 4:11, 12, Jesus quotes from Isaiah 6:9, 10; cf. Matthew 13:10–17).

Setting: By the Sea of Galilee. During the early part of His ministry, after presenting the Parable of the Sower from a boat to a very large crowd, Jesus gives the meaning of the parable to His disciples and other followers.

And He said to them, "Do you not understand this parable? How will you understand all the parables? The sower sows the word. These are the ones who are beside the road where the word is sown; and when they hear, immediately Satan comes and takes away the word which has been sown in them. In a similar way these are the ones on whom seed was sown on the rocky places, who, when they hear the word, immediately receive it with joy; and they have no *firm* root in themselves, but are *only* temporary; then, when affliction or persecution arises because of the word, immediately they fall away. And others are the ones on whom seed was sown among the thorns; these are the ones who have heard the word, but the worries of the world and the deceitfulness of riches, and the desires for other things enter in and choke the word, and it becomes unfruitful. And those are the ones on whom seed was sown on the good soil; and they hear the word and accept it and bear fruit, thirty, sixty, and a hundredfold" (Mark 4:13–20; cf. Matthew 13:18–23; Luke 8:11–15).

Setting: Galilee. After Jesus presents the Parable of the Sower to the crowds, His disciples ask Him to give them the parable's meaning.

And He said, "To you it has been granted to know the mysteries of the kingdom of God, but to the rest *it is* in parables, so that SEEING THEY MAY NOT SEE, AND HEARING THEY MAY NOT UNDERSTAND. Now the parable is this: the seed is the word of God. Those beside the road are those who have heard; then the devil comes and takes away the word from their heart, so that they will not believe and be saved. Those on the rocky *soil* are those who, when they hear, receive the word with joy; and these have no *firm* root; they believe for a while, and in time of temptation fall away. The *seed* which fell among the thorns, these are the ones who have heard, and as they go on their way they are choked with worries and riches and pleasures of *this* life, and bring no fruit to maturity. But the *seed* in the good soil, these are the ones who have heard the word in an honest and good heart, and hold it fast, and bear fruit with perseverance" (Luke 8:10–15, Jesus quotes from Isaiah 6:9; cf. Matthew 13:10–23; Mark 4:10–20).

PARACLETE (See HELPER; and HOLY SPIRIT)

PARADISE (PARADISE OF GOD is a separate entry; also see HEAVEN)

Setting: Jerusalem. While Jesus is being mocked and ridiculed while hanging nailed to a cross, one of the criminals being crucified with Him asks to be remembered in His kingdom, which Christ grants with forgiveness and entrance into Paradise.

And He said to him, "Truly I say to you, today you shall be with Me in Paradise" (Luke 23:43; see Matthew 27:39–44; Mark 15:29–32).

PARADISE OF GOD (Also see HEAVEN)

Setting: On the island of Patmos (in the Aegean Sea about fifty miles southwest of Ephesus in modern Turkey). On the Lord's Day (Sunday), about fifty years after Jesus' resurrection, the disciple John encounters the Lord Jesus Christ, who communicates a new revelation for the apostle to record for the church in Ephesus and to six other churches in Asia.

"To the angel of the church in Ephesus write: The One who holds the seven stars in His right hand, the One who walks among the seven golden lampstands, says this: 'I know your deeds and your toil and perseverance, and that you cannot tolerate evil men, and you put to the test those who call themselves apostles, and they are not, and you found them *to be* false; and you have perseverance and have endured for My name's sake, and have not grown weary. But I have *this* against you, that you have left your first love. Therefore remember from where you have fallen, and repent and do the deeds you did at first; or else I am coming to you and will remove your lampstand out of its place—unless you repent. Yet this you do have, that you hate the deeds of the Nicolaitans, which I also hate. He who has an ear, let him hear what the Spirit says to the churches. To him who overcomes, I will grant to eat of the tree of life which is in the Paradise of God' " (Revelation 2:1–7; see Genesis 2:9; Ezekiel 28:13; 1 John 4:1; Revelation 1:10, 11, 19, 20; 2:15, 16).

PARALYTIC (See CRIPPLED; and LAME)

PARALYZED MAN (See CRIPPLED; and LAME)

PARDON (Also see FORGIVENESS)

Setting: Galilee. After selecting His twelve disciples, Jesus teaches the Sermon on the Mount to those disciples and a great throng of people from Judea, Jerusalem, and the central coastal region of Tyre and Sidon.

"Do not judge, and you will not be judged; and do not condemn, and you will not be condemned; pardon, and you will be pardoned. Give and it will be given to you. They will pour into your lap a good measure—pressed down, shaken together, *and* running over. For by your standard of measure it will be measured to you in return" (Luke 6:37, 38; cf. Matthew 7:1–5; Mark 4:24; see Luke 6:12–19).

PARENTS (Also see FAMILY; and FATHER AND MOTHER)

Setting: Galilee. After His disciples observe His ministry, Jesus summons and specifically instructs them about the upcoming difficulties of their ministry to the people of Israel.

"Brother will betray brother to death, and a father *his* child; and children will rise up against parents and cause them to be put to death. You will be hated by all because of My name, but it is the one who has endured to the end who will be saved. But whenever they persecute you in one city, flee to the next; for truly I say to you, you will not finish *going through* the cities of Israel until the Son of Man comes" (Matthew 10:21–23; cf. Matthew 10:35, 36; 16:27, 28; 24:9).

Setting: On the Mount of Olives, east of the temple in Jerusalem. After predicting the temple's destruction, Jesus responds during His Olivet Discourse to questions from Peter, James, John, and Andrew about other future events.

And Jesus began to say to them, "See to it that no one misleads you. Many will come in My name, saying, 'I am *He!*' and will mislead many. When you hear of wars and rumors of wars, do not be frightened; *those things* must take place; but *that is* not yet the end. For nation will rise up against nation, and kingdom against kingdom; there will be earthquakes in various places; there will *also be* famines. These things are *merely* the beginning of birth pangs. But be on your guard; for they will deliver you to *the* courts, and you will be flogged in *the* synagogues, and you will stand before governors and kings for My sake, as a testimony to them. The gospel must first be preached to all the nations. When they arrest you and hand you over, do not worry beforehand about what you are to say, but say whatever is given you in that hour; for it is not you who speak, but *it is* the Holy Spirit. Brother will betray brother to death, and a father *his* child; and children will rise up against parents and have them put to death. You will be hated by all because of My name, but the one who endures to the end, he will be saved" (Mark 13:5–13, cf. Matthew 24:4–14; Luke 21:7–19; see Matthew 10:17–22).

Setting: Perea, en route from Galilee to Jerusalem. After responding to His disciples' question about salvation, Jesus replies to Peter's statement about the disciples' personal sacrifice.

Peter said, "Behold, we have left our own *homes* and followed You." And He said to them, "Truly I say to you, there is no one who has left house or wife or brothers or parents or children, for the sake of the kingdom of God, who will not receive many times as much at this time and in the age to come, eternal life" (Luke 18:28–30; cf. Matthew 19:27–29; Mark 10:28–30; see Matthew 6:33; Luke 5:11).

Setting: On the Mount of Olives, east of the temple in Jerusalem. After ministering in the temple a few days before His crucifixion, and giving His disciples more details regarding the temple's future destruction, Jesus elaborates during His Olivet Discourse about things to come.

Then He continued by saying to them, "Nation will rise against nation and kingdom against kingdom, and there will be great earthquakes, and in various places plagues and famines; and there will be terrors and great signs from heaven. But before all these things, they will lay their hands on you and will persecute you, delivering you to the synagogues and prisons, bringing you before kings and governors for My name's sake. It will lead to an opportunity for your testimony. So make up your minds not to

prepare beforehand to defend yourselves; for I will give you utterance and wisdom which none of your opponents will be able to resist or refute. But you will be betrayed even by parents and brothers and relatives and friends, and they will put *some* of you to death, and you will be hated by all because of My name. Yet not a hair of your head will perish. By your endurance you will gain your lives" (Luke 21:10–19; cf. Matthew 10:19–22; 24:7–14; Mark 13:8–13).

Setting: The temple treasury in Jerusalem. After Jesus avoids being stoned by the scribes and Pharisees, His disciples wonder if blindness is caused by sin as the Lord heals a man born blind.

Jesus answered, "*It was* neither *that* this man sinned, nor his parents; but *it was* so that the works of God might be displayed in him. We must work the works of Him who sent Me as long as it is day; night is coming when no one can work. While I am in the world, I am the Light of the world." When He had said this, He spat on the ground, and made clay of the spittle, and applied the clay to his eyes, and said to him, "Go, wash in the pool of Siloam" (which is translated, Sent). So he went away and washed, and came *back* seeing (John 9:3–7; see John 8:12; 11:4; 12:46).

PART

Setting: On the way from Galilee to Jerusalem. After Jesus is tested by a lawyer, the Lord and His disciples are welcomed into the home of Martha and Mary in Bethany.

But the Lord answered and said to her, "Martha, Martha, you are worried and bothered about so many things; but *only* one thing is necessary, for Mary has chosen the good part, which shall not be taken away from her" (Luke 10:41, 42; see Matthew 6:25).

Setting: On the way from Galilee to Jerusalem. After telling the increasing crowds of the sign of Jonah, Jesus illustrates His point by speaking about a lamp.

"No one, after lighting a lamp, puts it away in a cellar nor under a basket, but on the lampstand, so that those who enter may see the light. The eye is the lamp of your body; when your eye is clear, your whole body also is full of light; but when it is bad, your body also is full of darkness. Then watch out that the light in you is not darkness. If therefore your whole body is full of light, with no dark part in it, it will be wholly illumined, as when the lamp illumines you with its rays" (Luke 11:33–36; cf. Matthew 5:15, 6:22, 23).

Setting: On the way from Galilee to Jerusalem. After the Pharisees question Him about the coming of the kingdom of God, Jesus tells His disciples of His second coming.

And He said to the disciples, "The days will come when you will long to see one of the days of the Son of Man, and you will not see it. They will say to you, 'Look there! Look here!' Do not go away, and do not run after *them*. For just like the lightning, when it flashes out of one part of the sky, shines to the other part of the sky, so will the Son of Man be in His day. But first He must suffer many things and be rejected by this generation. And just as it happened in the days of Noah, so it will be also in the days of the Son of Man: they were eating, they were drinking, they were marrying, they were being given in marriage, until the day that Noah entered the ark, and the flood came and destroyed them all. It was the same as happened in the days of Lot: they were eating, they were drinking, they were buying, they were selling, they were planting, they were building; but on the day that Lot went out from Sodom it rained fire and brimstone from heaven and destroyed them all. It will be just the same on the day that the Son of Man is revealed. On that day, the one who is on the housetop and whose goods are in the house must not go down to take them out; and likewise the one who is in the field must not turn back. Remember Lot's wife. Whoever seeks to keep his life will lose it, and whoever loses *his life* will preserve it. I tell you, on that night there will be two in one bed; one will be taken and the other will be left. There will be two women grinding at the same place; one will be taken and the other will be left. [Two men will be in the field; one will be taken and the other will be left."] And answering they said to Him, "Where, Lord?" And He said to them, "Where the body *is*, there also the vultures will be gathered" (Luke 17:22–37; see Genesis 19; Matthew 10:39; 16:21, 27; 24:17–28, 37–41).

Setting: **Jerusalem. Before the Passover, with His crucifixion nearing, Jesus eats supper with His disciples and assumes the role of a servant, washing their feet.**

Jesus answered and said to him, "What I do you do not realize now, but you will understand hereafter." Peter said to Him, "Never shall You wash my feet!" Jesus answered him, "If I do not wash you, you have no part with Me." Simon Peter said to Him, "Lord, *then wash* not only my feet, but also my hand and my head." Jesus said to him, "He who has bathed needs only to wash his feet, but is completely clean; and you are clean, but not all *of you*. For He knew the one who was betraying Him; for this reason He said, "Not all of you are clean" (John 13:7–11; see John 6:64; 15:3).

Setting: **Jerusalem. Luke, writing in Acts, presents quotes from Jesus' post-resurrection appearances, in which He responds to His disciples' question if He is about to restore the kingdom to Israel.**

He said to them, "It is not for you to know times or epochs which the Father has fixed by His own authority; but you will receive power when the Holy Spirit has come upon you; and you shall be My witnesses both in Jerusalem, and in all Judea and Samaria, and even to the remotest part of the earth" (Acts 1:7, 8; see Luke 24:48, 49; Acts 2:1–4).

PART, GOOD (See PART)

PARTNERS

Setting: **The temple in Jerusalem. After the Jewish religious leaders test Him with questions, Jesus pronounces the eighth of eight woes upon them in front of the crowds and His disciples.**

"Woe to you, scribes and Pharisees, hypocrites! For you build the tombs of the prophets and adorn the monuments of the righteous, and say, 'If we had been *living* in the days of our fathers, we would not have been partners with them in *shedding* the blood of the prophets.' So you testify against yourselves, that you are sons of those who murdered the prophets. Fill up, then, the measure *of the guilt* of you fathers. You serpents, you brood of vipers, how will you escape the sentence of hell? Therefore, behold, I am sending you prophets and wise men and scribes; some of them you will kill and crucify, and some of them you will scourge in your synagogues, and persecute from city to city, so that upon you may fall *the guilt of* all the righteous blood shed on earth, from the blood of righteous Abel to the blood of Zechariah, the son of Berechiah, whom you murdered between the temple and the altar. Truly I say to you, all these things will come upon this generation" (Matthew 23:29–36; cf. 2 Chronicles 24:21; Zechariah 1:1; Matthew 3:7; Luke 11:47–52; see Matthew 10:23).

Setting: **Galilee. During the early part of His ministry, Jesus preaches the Sermon on the Mount to His disciples and the multitudes.**

"If your right eye makes you stumble, tear it out and throw it from you; for it is better for you to lose one of the parts of your body, than for your whole body to be thrown into hell. If your right hand makes you stumble, cut it off and throw it from you; for it is better for you to lose one of the parts of your body, than for your whole body to go into hell" (Matthew 5:29, 30; cf. Matthew 18:8, 9).

PARTY (See BANQUETS; and DINNER)

PASS AWAY (Listed under AWAY, PASS)

PASSOVER (Also see LORD'S SUPPER)

Setting: **On the Mount of Olives, just east of Jerusalem. During His Olivet Discourse, after answering His disciples' questions as to when the temple will be destroyed and Jerusalem overrun, along with the signs of His coming and the end of the age, Jesus prophesies His crucifixion.**

When Jesus had finished all these words, He said to His disciples, "You know that after two days the Passover is coming, and the Son of Man is *to be* handed over for crucifixion" (Matthew 26:1, 2; see Mark 14:1, 2; Luke 22:1, 2).

Setting: **Jerusalem. On the first day of the Feast of Unleavened Bread, just after Judas makes arrangements with the chief priests to betray Him, Jesus informs His disciples where they will celebrate the Passover.**

And He said, "Go into the city to a certain man, and say to him, 'The Teacher says, "My time is near; I *am to* keep the Passover at your house with My disciples"'" (Matthew 26:18; cf. Mark 14:13–15; Luke 22:7–13).

Setting: **Jerusalem. On the first day of the Feast of Unleavened Bread, when the Passover lamb is being sacrificed, Jesus responds to His disciples' question about His plans for the Passover meal.**

And He sent two of His disciples and said to them, "Go into the city, and a man will meet you carrying a pitcher of water; follow him; and wherever he enters, say to the owner of the house, 'The Teacher says, "Where is My guest room in which I may eat the Passover with My disciples?"' And he himself will show you a large upper room furnished *and* ready; prepare for us there" (Mark 14:13–15; cf. Matthew 26:17–19; Luke 22:7–13).

Setting: **Jerusalem. With the Passover (Feast of Unleavened Bread) approaching, Jesus informs His disciples where they will celebrate the feast, as the chief priests and scribes seek to kill Him, and Satan enters Judas Iscariot in order to betray the Lord.**

And Jesus sent Peter and John, saying, "Go and prepare the Passover for us, so that we may eat it." They said to Him, "Where do You want us to prepare it?" And He said to them, "When you have entered the city, a man will meet you carrying a pitcher of water; follow him into the house that he enters. And you shall say to the owner of the house, 'The Teacher says to you, "Where is the guest room in which I may eat the Passover with My disciples?"' And he will show you a large, furnished upper room; prepare it there" (Luke 22:8–12; cf. Matthew 26:17–19; Mark 14:12–16).

Setting: **Jerusalem. During the Feast of Unleavened Bread (Passover) just before Jesus' crucifixion, after Judas consents to betray Him to the chief priests and officers, during the Passover meal with His disciples, the Lord mentions His upcoming death.**

And He said to them, "I have earnestly desired to eat this Passover with you before I suffer; for I say to you, I shall never again eat it until it is fulfilled in the kingdom of God" (Luke 22:15, 16; see Matthew 26:20; Luke 14:15).

PASTURE

Setting: **On the way from Galilee to Jerusalem. After Jesus presents to large crowds the demands of discipleship, the Pharisees and scribes complain He associates with tax collectors and sinners.**

So He told them this parable, saying, "What man among you, if he has a hundred sheep and has lost one of them, does not leave the ninety-nine in the open pasture and go after the one which is lost until he finds it? When he has found it, he lays it on his shoulders, rejoicing. And when he comes home, he calls together his friends and his neighbors, saying to them, 'Rejoice with me, for I have found my sheep which was lost!' I tell you that in the same way, there will be *more* joy in heaven over one sinner who repents than over ninety-nine righteous persons who need no repentance" (Luke 15:3–7; cf. Matthew 18:12–14; see Matthew 9:11–13; Luke 5:29–32).

Setting: **Jerusalem. Following the Pharisees' interrogation and dismissal of the formerly blind man Jesus healed on the Sabbath, the Lord conveys the Parable of the Good Shepherd to the Pharisees, using figures of speech they do not understand.**

So Jesus said to them again, "Truly, truly, I say to you, I am the door of the sheep. All who came before Me are thieves and robbers, but the sheep did not hear them. I am the door; if anyone enters through Me, he will be saved, and will go in and out and find pasture. The thief comes only to steal and kill and destroy; I came that they may have life, and have *it* abundantly. I am the good shepherd; the good shepherd lays down His life for the sheep. He who is a hired hand, and not a shepherd, who is not the owner of the sheep, sees the wolf coming, and leaves the sheep and flees, and the wolf snatches them and scatters *them. He flees* because he is a hired hand and is not concerned about the sheep. I am the good shepherd, and I know My own and My own know Me, even as the Father knows Me and I know the Father; and I lay down My life for the sheep. I have other sheep, which are not of this fold; I must bring them also, and they will hear My voice; and they will become one flock *with* one shepherd. For this reason the Father loves Me, because I lay down My life so that I may take it again. No one has taken it away from Me, but I lay it down on My own initiative. I have authority to take it up again. This commandment I received from My Father" (John 10:7–18; see Isaiah 40:11; 56:8; Jeremiah 23:1; Matthew 11:27).

PATCH (Also see CLOTH)

Setting: Capernaum, near the Sea of Galilee. John the Baptist's disciples ask Jesus why His disciples do not participate in fasting, while they and the Pharisees do.

And Jesus said to them, "The attendants of the bridegroom cannot mourn as long as the bridegroom is with them, can they? But the days will come when the bridegroom is taken away from them, and then they will fast. But no one puts a patch of unshrunk cloth on an old garment; for the patch pulls away from the garment, and a worse tear results. Nor do *people* put new wine into old wineskins; otherwise the wineskins burst, and the wine pours out and the wineskins are ruined; but they put new wine into fresh wineskins, and both are preserved" (Matthew 9:15–17; cf. Mark 2:18–22; Luke 5:33–39).

Setting: Capernaum. John the Baptist's disciples and the Pharisees question why Jesus' disciples do not fast when they do.

And Jesus said to them, "While the bridegroom is with them, the attendants of the bridegroom cannot fast, can they? So long as they have the bridegroom with them, they cannot fast. But the days will come when the bridegroom is taken away from them, and then they will fast in that day. No one sews a patch of unshrunk cloth on an old garment; otherwise the patch pulls away from it, the new from the old, and a worse tear results. No one puts new wine into old wineskins; otherwise the wine will burst the skins, and the wine is lost and the skins as *well;* but *one puts* new wine into fresh wineskins" (Mark 2:19–22; cf. Matthew 9:14–17; Luke 5:33–38).

PATIENCE

Setting: Capernaum of Galilee. Jesus illustrates the matter of forgiveness after Peter asks Him if forgiving someone seven times who has sinned against him is adequate.

"For this reason the kingdom of heaven may be compared to a king who wished to settle accounts with his slaves. When he had begun to settle *them,* one who owed him ten thousand talents was brought to him. But since he did not have *the means* to repay, his lord commanded him to be sold, along with his wife and children and all that he had, and repayment to be made. So the slave fell *to the ground* and prostrated himself before him, saying, 'Have patience with me and I will repay you everything.' And the lord of that slave felt compassion and released him and forgave him the debt. But that slave went out and found one of his fellow slaves who owed him a hundred denarii; and he seized him and *began* to choke *him,* saying, 'Pay back what you owe.' So his fellow slave fell *to the ground* and *began* to plead with him, saying, 'Have patience with me and I will repay you.' But he was unwilling and went and threw him in prison until he should pay back what was owed. So when his fellow slaves saw what had happened, they were deeply grieved and came and reported to their lord all that had happened. Then summoning him, his lord said to him, 'You wicked slave, I forgave you all that debt because you pleaded with me. Should you not also have had mercy on your fellow slave, in the same way that I had mercy on you?' And his lord, moved with anger, handed him over to the torturers until he should repay all that was owed him. My heavenly Father will also do the same to you, if each of you does not forgive his brother from your heart" (Matthew 18:23–35; cf. Matthew 6:12, 14, 15; Luke 7:42; see Matthew 25:19–28).

PAUL (See SAUL)

PAUL'S CONVERSION (Saul)

[PAUL'S CONVERSION inferred from context]

Setting: On the way from Jerusalem to Damascus. Luke, writing in Acts, reveals how Saul of Tarsus (later named Paul), a persecutor of the disciples of Jesus, receives the Lord's calling, and is temporarily blinded.

As he was traveling, it happened that he was approaching Damascus, and suddenly a light from heaven flashed around him; and he fell to the ground and heard a voice saying to him. "Saul, Saul, why are you persecuting Me?" And he said, "Who are You, Lord?" And He *said,* "I am Jesus whom you are persecuting, but get up and enter the city, and it will be told you what you must do" (Acts 9:3–6; see Acts 22:7, 8).

[PAUL'S CONVERSION inferred from context]
Setting: Jerusalem. Luke, writing in Acts, presents the account of Paul's speech (following his third missionary journey) to a hostile Jewish crowd about His divine encounter with Jesus on the road to Damascus.

"But it happened that as I was on my way, approaching Damascus about noontime, a very bright light suddenly flashed from heaven all around me, and I fell to the ground, and heard a voice saying to me, 'Saul, Saul, why are you persecuting Me?' And I answered, 'Who are You, Lord?' And He said to me, 'I am Jesus the Nazarene, whom you are persecuting.' And those who were with me saw the light, to be sure, but did not understand the voice of the One who was speaking to me. And I said, 'What shall I do, Lord?' And the Lord said to me, 'Get up and go on into Damascus, and there you will be told of all that has been appointed for you to do' (Acts 22:6–10; see Acts 9:7; 26:9).

[PAUL'S CONVERSION inferred from context]
Setting: Caesarea. Luke, writing in Acts, gives Paul's retelling of his conversion to Christ as he appears before King Agrippa following his hearing before the Jewish Council in Jerusalem and arrest by the Roman commander (on his way to Rome after the apostle's third missionary journey).

"And when we had fallen to the ground, I heard a voice saying to me in the Hebrew dialect, 'Saul, Saul, why are you persecuting Me? It is hard for you to kick against the goads.' And I said, 'Who are You, Lord?' And the Lord said, 'I am Jesus whom you are persecuting. But get up and stand on your feet; for this purpose I have appeared to you, to appoint you a minister and a witness not only to the things which you have seen, but also to the things in which I will appear to you; rescuing you from the *Jewish* people and from the Gentiles, to whom I am sending you, to open their eyes so that they may turn from darkness to light and from the dominion of Satan to God, that they may receive forgiveness of sins and an inheritance among those who have been sanctified by faith in Me' (Acts 26:14–18; see Isaiah 35:5; Acts 21:40; 22:14).

PAUL'S MISSION (Saul's)

[PAUL'S MISSION from Saul and it will be told you what you must do]
Setting: On the road to Damascus. Luke, writing in Acts, describes how Saul of Tarsus (who will later have the name Paul), a persecutor of the followers of Jesus, receives the Lord's calling and is temporarily blinded.

As he was traveling, it happened that he was approaching Damascus, and suddenly a light from heaven flashed around him; and he fell to the ground and heard a voice saying to him. "Saul, Saul, why are you persecuting Me?" And he said, "Who are You, Lord?" And He *said,* "I am Jesus whom you are persecuting, but get up and enter the city, and it will be told you what you must do" (Acts 9:3–6; see Acts 22:7, 8).

[PAUL'S MISSION from all that has been appointed for you to do]
Setting: Jerusalem. Luke, writing in Acts, presents the account of Paul's speech (following his third missionary journey) to a hostile Jewish crowd about His divine encounter with Jesus on the road to Damascus.

"But it happened that as I was on my way, approaching Damascus about noontime, a very bright light suddenly flashed from heaven all around me, and I fell to the ground, and heard a voice saying to me, 'Saul, Saul, why are you persecuting Me?' And I answered, 'Who are You, Lord?' And He said to me, 'I am Jesus the Nazarene, whom you are persecuting.' And those who were with me saw the light, to be sure, but did not understand the voice of the One who was speaking to me. And I said, 'What shall I do, Lord?' And the Lord said to me, 'Get up and go on into Damascus, and there you will be told of all that has been appointed for you to do' (Acts 22:6–10; see Acts 9:7; 26:9).

[PAUL'S MISSION from I will send you far away to the Gentiles]
Setting: Jerusalem. Luke, writing in Acts, recounts Paul's speech to a hostile Jewish crowd (after his third missionary journey), in which Paul recounts his instructions from the Lord Jesus following his conversion on the road to Damascus.

"And He said to me, 'Go! For I will send you far away to the Gentiles'" (Acts 22:21; see Acts 9:15).

[PAUL'S MISSION from to appoint you a minister and a witness]
Setting: Caesarea. Luke, writing in Acts, gives Paul's retelling of his conversion to Christ as he appears before King Agrippa following his hearing before the Jewish Council in Jerusalem and arrest by the Roman commander (on his way to Rome after the apostle's third missionary journey).

"And when we had fallen to the ground, I heard a voice saying to me in the Hebrew dialect, 'Saul, Saul, why are you persecuting Me? It is hard for you to kick against the goads.' And I said, 'Who are You, Lord?' And the Lord said, 'I am Jesus whom you are persecuting. But get up and stand on your feet; for this purpose I have appeared to you, to appoint you a minister and a witness not only to the things which you have seen, but also to the things in which I will appear to you; rescuing you from the *Jewish* people and from the Gentiles, to whom I am sending you, to open their eyes so that they may turn from darkness to light and from the dominion of Satan to God, that they may receive forgiveness of sins and an inheritance among those who have been sanctified by faith in Me' (Acts 26:14–18; see Isaiah 35:5; Acts 21:40; 22:14).

PAY (Also see COMPENSATION; and WAGES)

Setting: Capernaum of Galilee. Jesus illustrates the matter of forgiveness after Peter asks Him if forgiving someone seven times who has sinned against him is adequate.

"For this reason the kingdom of heaven may be compared to a king who wished to settle accounts with his slaves. When he had begun to settle *them,* one who owed him ten thousand talents was brought to him. But since he did not have *the means* to repay, his lord commanded him to be sold, along with his wife and children and all that he had, and repayment to be made. So the slave fell *to the ground* and prostrated himself before him, saying, 'Have patience with me and I will repay you everything.' And the lord of that slave felt compassion and released him and forgave him the debt. But that slave went out and found one of his fellow slaves who owed him a hundred denarii; and he seized him and *began* to choke *him,* saying, 'Pay back what you owe.' So his fellow slave fell *to the ground* and *began* to plead with him, saying, 'Have patience with me and I will repay you.' But he was unwilling and went and threw him in prison until he should pay back what was owed. So when his fellow slaves saw what had happened, they were deeply grieved and came and reported to their lord all that had happened. Then summoning him, his lord said to him, 'You wicked slave, I forgave you all that debt because you pleaded with me. Should you not also have had mercy on your fellow slave, in the same way that I had mercy on you?' And his lord, moved with anger, handed him over to the torturers until he should repay all that was owed him. My heavenly Father will also do the same to you, if each of you does not forgive his brother from your heart" (Matthew 18:23–35; cf. Matthew 6:12, 14, 15; Luke 7:42; see Matthew 25:19–28).

Setting: Perea. Jesus illustrates the kingdom of heaven to His disciples through the story of laborers in the vineyard.

"For the kingdom of heaven is like a landowner who went out early in the morning to hire laborers for his vineyard. When he had agreed with the laborers for a denarius for the day, he sent them into his vineyard. And he went out about the third hour and saw others standing idle in the market place; and to those he said, 'You also go into the vineyard, and whatever is right I will give you.' And *so* they went. Again he went out about the sixth and the ninth hour, and did the same thing. And about the eleventh *hour* he went out and found others standing *around;* and he said to them, 'Why have you been standing idle here all day long?' They said to him, 'Because no one hired us.' He said to them, 'You go into the vineyard too.' When evening came, the owner of the vineyard said to his foreman, 'Call the laborers and pay them their wages, beginning with the last *group* to the first.' When those *hired* about the eleventh hour came, each one received a denarius. When those *hired* first came, they thought that they would receive more; but each of them also received a denarius. When they received it, they grumbled at the landowner, saying, 'These

last men have worked *only* one hour, and you have made them equal to us who have borne the burden and the scorching heat of the day.' But he answered and said to one of them, 'Friend, I am doing you no wrong; did you not agree with me for a denarius? Take what is yours and go, but I wish to give to this last man the same as to you. It is not lawful for me to do what I wish with what is my own? Or is your eye envious because I am generous?' So the last shall be first, and the first last" (Matthew 20:1–16; cf. Matthew 19:30).

Setting: On the way from Galilee to Jerusalem. After speaking of how a lamp illuminates, the Lord has lunch with a Pharisee who is surprised He doesn't wash before eating.

But the Lord said to him, "Now you Pharisees clean the outside of the cup and of the platter; but inside of you, you are full of robbery and wickedness. You foolish ones, did not He who made the outside make the inside also? But give that which is within as charity, and then all things are clean for you. But woe to you Pharisees! You pay tithe of mint and rue and every *kind of* garden herb, and *yet* disregard justice and the love of God; but these are the things you should have done without neglecting the others. Woe to you Pharisees! For you love the chief seats in the synagogues and the respectful greetings in the market places. Woe to you! For you are like concealed tombs, and the people who walk over *them* are unaware *of it*" (Luke 11:39–44; cf. Matthew 23:6, 7, 23–27; see Matthew 15:2; Titus 1:15).

Setting: On the way from Galilee to Jerusalem. After instructing His disciples about persistence in prayer, Jesus conveys a parable about self-righteousness.

And He also told this parable to some people who trusted in themselves that they were righteous, and viewed others with contempt: "Two men went up into the temple to pray, one a Pharisee and the other a tax collector. The Pharisee stood and was praying this to himself: 'God, I thank You that I am not like other people: swindlers, unjust, adulterers, or even like this tax collector. I fast twice a week; I pay tithes of all that I get.' But the tax collector, standing some distance away, was even unwilling to lift up his eyes to heaven, but was beating his breast, saying, 'God, be merciful to me, the sinner!' I tell you, this man went to his house justified rather than the other; for everyone who exalts himself will be humbled, but he who humbles himself will be exalted" (Luke 18:9–14; see Ezra 9:6; Matthew 6:5, 23:12; Luke 11:42; 16:15; Romans 14:3, 10).

PEACE **(Specifics such as PEACE, BLESSING OF; PEACE, MAN OF; and PEACE, TERMS OF are separate entries; also see PEACEMAKERS)**

Setting: Galilee. After His disciples observe His ministry, Jesus summons and specifically instructs them about their ministry hardships ahead involving true discipleship.

"Do not think that I came to bring peace on the earth; I did not come to bring peace, but a sword. For I came to SET A MAN AGAINST HIS FATHER, AND A DAUGHTER AGAINST HER MOTHER, AND A DAUGHTER-IN-LAW AGAINST HER MOTHER-IN-LAW; and A MAN'S ENEMIES WILL BE THE MEMBERS OF HIS HOUSEHOLD" (Matthew 10:34–36; Jesus quotes from Micah 7:6; cf. Luke 12:51–53).

Setting: By the Sea of Galilee. After Jesus returns from ministry to the Gerasenes, a woman who has had a hemorrhage for twelve years touches Jesus in order to be healed.

And He said to her, "Daughter, your faith has made you well; go in peace and be healed of your affliction" (Mark 5:34; cf. Matthew 9:22; Luke 8:48; see Luke 7:50).

Setting: Capernaum of Galilee. As Jesus teaches His disciples in private, they ask Him about greatness.

But Jesus said, "Do not hinder him, for there is no one who will perform a miracle in My name, and be able soon afterward to speak evil of Me. For he who is not against us is for us. For whoever gives you a cup of water to drink because of your name as *followers* of Christ, truly I say to you, he will not lose his reward. Whoever causes one of these little ones who believe to stumble, it would be better for him if, with a heavy millstone hung around his neck, he had been cast into the sea. If your hand causes you to stumble, cut it off; it is better for you to enter life crippled, than, having your two hands, to go into hell, into the unquenchable fire, [where THEIR WORM DOES NOT DIE, AND THE FIRE IS NOT QUENCHED.] If your foot causes you to stumble, cut it off; it is better for you to enter life lame, than, having your two feet, to be cast into hell, [where THEIR WORM DOES NOT DIE, AND THE FIRE IS NOT QUENCHED.] If your eye causes you to stumble, throw it out; it is better for you to enter the kingdom of God with one eye, than, having two eyes, to be cast into hell, where THEIR WORM DOES NOT DIE, AND THE FIRE IS NOT QUENCHED. For everyone will be salted with fire. Salt is good; but if the salt becomes unsalty, with what will you make it salty *again?* Have salt in yourselves, and be at peace with one another" (Mark 9:39–50; Jesus quotes from Isaiah 66:24; cf. Matthew 18:6–9; Luke 9:49, 50; see Matthew 5:13, 29, 30; 10:42; 12:30; 18:5, 6).

Setting: Galilee. After Jesus praises John the Baptist to the crowds, Simon, a Pharisee, invites the Lord to dinner. A sinful woman anoints His feet with perfume, prompting Him to instruct His host about forgiveness.

Turning toward the woman, He said to Simon, "Do you see this woman? I entered your house; you gave Me no water for My feet, but she has wet My feet with her tears and wiped them with her hair. You gave Me no kiss; but she, since the time I came in, has not ceased to kiss My feet. You did not anoint My head with oil, but she anointed My feet with perfume. For this reason I say to you, her sins, which are many, have been forgiven, for she loved much; but he who is forgiven little, loves little." Then He said to her, "Your sins have been forgiven." Those who were reclining *at the table* with Him began to say to themselves, "Who is this *man* who even forgives sins?" And He said to the woman, "Your faith has saved you; go in peace" (Luke 7:44–50; see Matthew 9:2; Mark 5:34; Luke 5:21).

Setting: Galilee. After Jesus returns from ministering in the country of the Gerasenes east of the Sea of Galilee, a woman, ill for twelve years, receives healing by touching His garment.

And Jesus said, "Who is the one who touched Me?" And while they were all denying it, Peter said, "Master, the people are crowding and pressing in on You." But Jesus said, "Someone did touch Me, for I was aware, that power had gone out of Me." When the woman saw that she had not escaped notice, she came trembling and fell down before Him, and declared in the presence of all the people the reason why she had touched Him, and how she had been immediately healed. And He said to her, "Daughter, your faith has made you well; go in peace" (Luke 8:45–48; cf. Matthew 9:20; Mark 5:25–34).

Setting: On the way from Galilee to Jerusalem. The Lord appoints seventy followers and sends them out in pairs to every place He Himself will soon visit.

And He was saying to them, "The harvest is plentiful, but the laborers are few; therefore beseech the Lord of the harvest to send out laborers into His harvest. Go; behold, I send you out as lambs in the midst of wolves. Carry no money belt, no bag, no shoes; and greet no one on the way. Whatever house you enter, first say, 'Peace be to this house.' If a man of peace is there, your peace will rest on him; but if not, it will return to you. Stay in that house, eating and drinking what they give you; for the laborer is worthy of his wages. Do not keep moving from house to house. Whatever city you enter and they receive you, eat what is set before you; and heal those in it who are sick, and say to them, 'The kingdom of God has come near to you.' But whatever city you enter and they do not receive you, go out into its streets and say, 'Even the dust of your city which clings to our feet we wipe off *in protest* against you; yet be sure of this, that the kingdom of God has come near.' I say to you, it will be more tolerable in that day for Sodom than for that city" (Luke 10:2–12; see Genesis 19:24–28; Matthew 9:37, 38, 10:9–14, 16; 1 Corinthians 10:27).

Setting: On the way from Galilee to Jerusalem. After clarifying a parable for Peter and the crowd, Jesus conveys how a relationship with Him divides families.

"I have come to cast fire upon the earth; and how I wish it were already kindled! But I have a baptism to undergo, and how distressed I am until it is accomplished! Do you suppose that I came to grant peace on earth? I tell you, no, but rather division; for from now on five *members* in one household will be divided, three against two and two against three. They will be divided, father against son and son against father, mother against daughter, and daughter against mother, mother-in-law against daughter-in-law and daughter-in-law against mother-in-law" (Luke 12:49–53; cf. Matthew 10:34–36; see Micah 7:6; Mark 10:38).

Setting: Approaching Jerusalem. After being praised by the people in a triumphal entry, the Lord weeps as He sees the city ahead of Him.

When He approached *Jerusalem,* He saw the city and wept over it, saying, "If you had known in this day, even you, the things which make for peace! But now they have been hidden from your eyes. For the days will come upon you when your enemies will throw up a barricade against you, and surround you and hem you in on every side, and they will level you to the ground and your children within you, and they will not leave in you one stone upon another, because you did not recognize the time of your visitation" (Luke 19:41–44; see Matthew 24:1, 2; Luke 13:34, 35).

Setting: Jerusalem. After rising from the tomb on the third day after being crucified, and appearing to two of His followers on the road to Emmaus, Jesus appears to His disciples (except Thomas).

While they were telling these things, He Himself stood in their midst and said to them, "Peace be to you." But they were startled and frightened and thought they were seeing a spirit. And He said to them, "Why are you troubled, and why do doubts arise in your hearts? See My hands and My feet, that it is I Myself; touch Me and see, for a spirit does not have flesh and bones as you see that I have." And when He had said this, He showed them His hands and His feet. While they still could not believe *it* because of their joy and amazement. He said to them, "Have you anything to eat?" They gave Him a piece of a broiled fish; and He took it and ate *it* before them (Luke 24:36–43; see Mark 16:14; John 20:27; Acts 10:40, 41).

Setting: Jerusalem. Before the Passover, after He conveys the upcoming ministry of the Holy Spirit in His disciples' lives, Jesus again relates peace, hope, and comfort to them regarding His return to the Father.

"Peace I leave with you; My peace I give to you; not as the world gives do I give to you. Do not let your heart be troubled, nor let it be fearful. You heard that I said to you, 'I go away, and I will come to you.' If you loved Me, you would have rejoiced because I go to the Father, for the Father is greater than I. Now I have told you before it happens, so that when it happens, you may believe. I will not speak much more with you, for the ruler of the world is coming, and he has nothing in Me; but so that the world may know that I love the Father, I do exactly as the Father commanded Me. Get up, let us go from here" (John 14:27–31; see John 10:18, 29; 12:31; 13:19; 16:33).

Setting: Jerusalem. Before the Passover, after conveying promises about praying in His name, Jesus prophesies the disciples' scattering and gives them hope that in the midst of tribulation they will have His peace.

"Jesus answered them, "Do you now believe? Behold, an hour is coming, and has *already* come, for you to be scattered, each to his own *home,* and to leave Me alone; and *yet* I am not alone, because the Father is with Me. These things I have spoken to you, so that in Me you may have peace. In the world you have tribulation, but take courage, I have overcome the world" (John 16:31–33; see Zechariah 13:7; John 8:29; 14:27; Romans 8:37).

Setting: Jerusalem. After Mary Magdalene encounters the risen Jesus in the morning, He appears that evening in the midst of His disciples (except Thomas), who are in hiding behind closed doors due to fear of the Jewish religious leaders.

So when it was evening on that day, the first *day* of the week, and when the doors were shut where the disciples were, for fear of the Jews, Jesus came and stood in their midst and said to them, "Peace *be* with you." And when He had said this, He showed them both His hands and His side. The disciples then rejoiced when they saw the Lord. So Jesus said to them again, "Peace *be* with you; as the Father has sent Me, I also send you." And when He had said this, He breathed on them and said to them, "Receive the Holy Spirit. If you forgive the sins of any, *their sins* have been forgiven them; if you retain the *sins* of any, they have been retained" (John 20:19–23; cf. Luke 24:36–43; see Matthew 16:19; Mark 16:14).

Setting: Jerusalem. The risen Jesus meets with His disciple Thomas (Didymus), who has had doubts about the testimony of the other disciples claiming to have seen and spoken with the Lord eight days earlier.

After eight days His disciples were again inside, and Thomas with them. Jesus came, the doors having been shut, and stood in their midst and said, "Peace *be* with you." Then He said to Thomas, "Reach here with your finger, and see My hands; and reach here your hand and put it into My side; and do not be unbelieving, but believing." Thomas answered and said to Him, "My Lord and my God!" Jesus said to him, "Because you have seen Me, have you believed? Blessed *are* they who did not see, and *yet* believed" (John 20:26–29; see Luke 24:36, 40; 1 Peter 1:8).

PEACE, BLESSING OF

Setting: Galilee. After His twelve disciples observe His ministry, Jesus summons and specifically instructs them about their ministry to the people of Israel.

These twelve Jesus sent out after instructing them: "Do not go in *the* way of *the* Gentiles, and do not enter *any* city of the Samaritans; but rather go to the lost sheep of the house of Israel. And as you go, preach, saying, 'The kingdom of heaven is at hand.' Heal *the* sick, raise *the* dead, cleanse *the* lepers, cast out demons. Freely you received, freely give. Do not acquire gold, or silver, or copper for your money belts, or a bag for *your* journey, or even two coats, or sandals, or a staff; for the worker is worthy of his support. And whatever city or village you enter, inquire who is worthy in it, and stay at his house until you leave *that city*. As you enter the house, give it your greeting. If the house is worthy, give it your *blessing of* peace. But if it is not worthy, take back your *blessing of* peace. Whoever does not receive you, nor heed your words, as you go out of that house or that city, shake the dust off your feet. Truly I say to you, it will be more tolerable for *the* land of Sodom and Gomorrah in the day of judgment than for that city" (Matthew 10:5–15; cf. Mark 6:7–11; Luke 9:1–5; see Matthew 3:2; 11:22, 24; 15:24; Luke 22:35; 1 Corinthians 9:14).

PEACE, MAN OF

Setting: On the way from Galilee to Jerusalem. The Lord appoints seventy followers and sends them out in pairs to every place He Himself will soon visit.

And He was saying to them, "The harvest is plentiful, but the laborers are few; therefore beseech the Lord of the harvest to send out laborers into His harvest. Go; behold, I send you out as lambs in the midst of wolves. Carry no money belt, no bag, no shoes; and greet no one on the way. Whatever house you enter, first say, 'Peace be to this house.' If a man of peace is there, your peace will rest on him; but if not, it will return to you. Stay in that house, eating and drinking what they give you; for the laborer is worthy of his wages. Do not keep moving from house to house. Whatever city you enter and they receive you, eat what is set before you; and heal those in it who are sick, and say to them, 'The kingdom of God has come near to you.' But whatever city you enter and they do not receive you, go out into its streets and say, 'Even the dust of your city which clings to our feet we wipe off *in protest* against you; yet be sure of this, that the kingdom of God has come near.' I say to you, it will be more tolerable in that day for Sodom than for that city" (Luke 10:2–12; see Genesis 19:24–28; Matthew 9:37, 38, 10:9–14, 16; 1 Corinthians 10:27).

PEACE, TERMS OF

Setting: On the way from Galilee to Jerusalem. After He responds to a guest's proclamation about the blessings of eating bread in the kingdom of God, Jesus presents to large crowds the demands of discipleship.

Now large crowds were going along with Him; and He turned and said to them, "If anyone comes to Me, and does not hate his own father and mother and wife and children and brothers and sisters, yes, and even his own life, he cannot be My disciple. Whoever does not carry his own cross and come after Me cannot be My disciple. For which one of you, when he wants to build a tower, does not first sit down and calculate the cost to see if he has enough to complete it? Otherwise, when he has laid a foundation and is not able to finish, all who observe it begin to ridicule him, saying, 'This man began to build and was not able to finish.' Or what king, when he sets out to meet another king in battle, will not first sit down and consider whether he is strong enough with ten thousand *men* to encounter the one coming against him with twenty thousand? Or else, while the other is still far away, he sends a delegation and asks for terms of peace. So then, none of you can be My disciple who does not give up all his possessions. Therefore, salt is good; but if even salt has become tasteless, with what will it be seasoned? It is useless either for the soil or for the manure pile; it is thrown out. He who has ears to hear, let him hear" (Luke 14:25–35; cf. Matthew 5:13; 10:37–39; see Proverb 20:18; Philippians 3:7).

PEACEMAKERS (Also see FORGIVENESS; PEACE; and RECONCILIATION)

Setting: Galilee. Early in His ministry, Jesus presents the Beatitudes (part of the Sermon on the Mount) to His disciples and the gathered crowds from Galilee, Decapolis, Jerusalem, Judea, and beyond the Jordan.

"Blessed are the peacemakers, for they shall be called sons of God" (Matthew 5:9; see Matthew 5:1; 13:35).

PEARL (Also see PEARLS)

Setting: By the Sea of Galilee. Jesus declares the Parable of the Pearl to the crowds.

"Again, the kingdom of heaven is like a merchant seeking fine pearls, and upon finding one pearl of great value, he went and sold all that he had and bought it" (Matthew 13:45, 46).

PEARL, PARABLE OF THE

Setting: By the Sea of Galilee. Jesus declares the Parable of the Pearl to the crowds.

"Again, the kingdom of heaven is like a merchant seeking fine pearls, and upon finding one pearl of great value, he went and sold all that he had and bought it" (Matthew 13:45, 46).

PEARL OF GREAT PRICE (See PEARL, PARABLE OF THE)

PEARL OF GREAT VALUE (See PEARL, PARABLE OF THE)

PEARLS (Also see PEARL)

Setting: Galilee. During the early part of His ministry, Jesus preaches the Sermon on the Mount to His disciples and the multitudes.

"Do not give what is holy to dogs, and do not throw your pearls before swine, or they will trample them under their feet, and turn and tear you to pieces" (Matthew 7:6; see Matthew 15:26).

Setting: By the Sea of Galilee. Jesus declares the Parable of the Pearl to the crowds.

"Again, the kingdom of heaven is like a merchant seeking fine pearls, and upon finding one pearl of great value, he went and sold all that he had and bought it" (Matthew 13:45, 46).

PECKS, THREE

Setting: By the Sea of Galilee. Because the religious leaders are rejecting His message, Jesus continues teaching the crowds with the Parable of the Leaven.

He spoke another parable to them, "The kingdom of heaven is like leaven, which a woman took and hid in three pecks of flour until it was all leavened" (Matthew 13:33).

Setting: On the way from Galilee to Jerusalem. Jesus conveys the Parable of the Mustard Seed and the Parable of the Leaven after responding to a synagogue official's anger over the Lord's healing a woman, sick eighteen years, in the synagogue on the Sabbath.

So He was saying, "What is the kingdom of God like, and to what shall I compare it? It is like a mustard seed which a man took and threw into his own garden; and it grew and became a tree, and THE BIRDS OF THE AIR NESTED IN ITS BRANCHES." And again He said, "To what shall I compare the kingdom of God? It is like leaven, which a woman took and hid in three pecks of flour until it was all leavened" (Luke 13:18–21, Jesus quotes from Ezekiel 17:23; cf. Matthew 13:31–34; Mark 4:30–32).

PENALTY OF DEATH (See DEATH, PUT TO)

PENNY (See CENT; COIN; and MONEY)

PENTATEUCH (See MOSES, LAW OF)

PENTECOST, PROPHECY OF

[PROPHECY OF PENTECOST from you are to stay in the city until you are clothed with power from on high]
Setting: Jerusalem. After rising from the tomb on the third day after being crucified, and appearing to two of His followers on the road to Emmaus, Jesus gives instruction to His disciples (except Thomas) about His mission on earth and the promise of future power from God.

Now He said to them, "These are My words which I spoke to you while I was still with you, that all things which are written about Me in the Law of Moses and the Prophets and the Psalms must be fulfilled." Then He opened their minds to understand the Scriptures, and He said to them, "Thus it is written, that the Christ would suffer and rise again from the dead the third day, and that repentance for forgiveness of sins would be proclaimed in His name to all the nations, beginning from Jerusalem. You are witnesses of these things. And behold, I am sending forth the promise of My Father upon you; but you are to stay in the city until you are clothed with power from on high" (Luke 24:44–49; see Matthew 28:19, 20; Acts 1:8).

PEOPLE (Also see MEN; OTHERS; PERSONS; and WOMEN)

Setting: Galilee. Early in His ministry, Jesus presents the Beatitudes (part of the Sermon on the Mount) to His disciples and the gathered crowds from Galilee, Decapolis, Jerusalem, Judea, and beyond the Jordan.

"Blessed are you when *people* insult you and persecute you, and falsely say all kinds of evil against you because of Me. Rejoice and be glad, for your reward in heaven is great; for in the same way they persecuted the prophets who were before you" (Matthew 5:11, 12; cf. 2 Chronicles 36:16; Luke 6:22, 23; 1 Peter 4:14; see Matthew 5:1; 13:35).

Setting: Galilee. During the early part of His ministry, Jesus preaches the Sermon on the Mount to His disciples and the multitudes.

"In everything, therefore, treat people the same way you want them to treat you, for this is the Law and the Prophets" (Matthew 7:12; cf. Matthew 22:20; Luke 6:3).

Setting: Capernaum near the Sea of Galilee. John the Baptist's disciples ask Jesus why His own disciples do not participate in fasting, while they and the Pharisees do.

And Jesus said to them, "The attendants of the bridegroom cannot mourn as long as the bridegroom is with them, can they? But the days will come when the bridegroom is taken away from them, and then they will fast. But no one puts a patch of unshrunk cloth on an old garment; for the patch pulls away from the garment, and a worse tear results. Nor do *people* put new wine into old wineskins; otherwise the wineskins burst, and the wine pours out and the wineskins are ruined; but they put new wine into fresh wineskins, and both are preserved" (Matthew 9:15–17; cf. Mark 2:18–22; Luke 5:33–39).

Setting: Galilee. After He heals a blind, mute, demon-possessed man, the Pharisees accuse Jesus of being a worker of Satan. Jesus warns them about the unpardonable sin.

"He who is not with Me is against Me; and he who does not gather with Me scatters. Therefore I say to you, any sin and blasphemy shall be forgiven people, but blasphemy against the Spirit shall not be forgiven. Whoever speaks a word against the Son of Man, it shall be forgiven him; but whoever speaks against the Holy Spirit, it shall not be forgiven him, either in this age or in the *age* to come" (Matthew 12:30–32; cf. Luke 12:10; see Mark 9:40).

Setting: Galilee. After Jesus heals a blind, mute, demon-possessed man, the Pharisees accuse the Lord in front of crowds of being a worker of Satan.

"Either make the tree good and its fruit good, or make the tree bad and its fruit bad; for the tree is known by its fruit. You brood of vipers, how can you, being evil, speak what is good? For the mouth speaks out of that which fills the heart. The good man brings out of *his* good treasure what is good; and the evil man brings out of *his* evil treasure what is evil. But I tell you that every careless word that people speak, they shall give an accounting for it in the day of judgment. For by your words you will be justified, and by your words you will be condemned" (Matthew 12:33–37; cf. Matthew 3:7; 7:16–18).

Setting: By the Sea of Galilee. Jesus responds to His disciples' questions about the Parable of the Sower, which He has just taught from a boat to a crowd.

Jesus answered them, "To you it has been granted to know the mysteries of the kingdom of heaven, but to them it has not been granted. For whoever has, to him *more* shall be given, and he will have an abundance; but whoever does not have, even what he has shall be taken away from him. Therefore, I speak to them in parables; because while seeing they do not see, and while hearing they do not hear, nor do they understand. In their case the prophecy of Isaiah is being fulfilled, which says, 'YOU WILL KEEP ON HEARING, BUT WILL NOT UNDERSTAND; YOU WILL KEEP ON SEEING, BUT WILL NOT PERCEIVE; FOR THE HEART OF THIS PEOPLE HAS BECOME DULL, WITH THEIR EARS THEY SCARCELY HEAR, AND THEY HAVE CLOSED THEIR EYES, OTHERWISE THEY WOULD SEE WITH THEIR EYES, HEAR WITH THEIR EARS, AND UNDERSTAND WITH THEIR HEART AND RETURN, AND I WOULD HEAL THEM.' But blessed are your eyes, because they see; and your ears, because they hear. For truly I say to you that many prophets and righteous men desired to see what you see, and did not see *it*, and to hear what you hear, and did not hear *it*" (Matthew 13:11–17, Jesus quotes from Isaiah 6:9, 10; cf. Matthew 25:29; Mark 4:11–13; Luke 8:10; see Deuteronomy 29:4; John 8:56).

Setting: Galilee. Pharisees and scribes from Jerusalem accuse Jesus' disciples of disobeying tradition and the commandments.

And He answered and said to them, "Why do you yourselves transgress the commandment of God for the sake of tradition? For God said, 'HONOR YOUR FATHER AND MOTHER,' and, 'HE WHO SPEAKS EVIL OF FATHER OR MOTHER IS TO BE PUT TO DEATH.' But you say, 'Whoever says to *his* father or mother, "Whatever I have that would help you has been given *to God*," he is not to honor his father or mother.' And *by this* you invalidated the word of God for the sake of your tradition. You hypocrites, rightly did Isaiah prophesy of you: 'THIS PEOPLE HONORS ME WITH THEIR LIPS, BUT THEIR HEART IS FAR AWAY FROM ME. BUT IN VAIN DO THEY WORSHIP ME, TEACHING AS DOCTRINES THE PRECEPTS OF MEN'" (Matthew 15:3–9, Jesus quotes from Exodus 20:12, 21:17, Leviticus 20:9; Isaiah 29:13; cf. Mark 7:5–7; see Colossians 2:22).

Setting: Near the Sea of Galilee. Impressed by a Canaanite woman's faith, Jesus restores her daughter of demon possession, then feeds more than 4,000 people, primarily Gentiles, following Him.

And Jesus called His disciples to Him, and said, "I feel compassion for the people, because they have remained with Me now three days and have nothing to eat; and I do not want to send them away hungry, for they might faint on the way." The disciples said to Him, "Where would we get so many loaves in *this* desolate place to satisfy a large crowd?" And Jesus said to them, "How many loaves do you have?" And they said, "Seven and a few small fish" (Matthew 15:32–34; cf. Mark 8:1–9).

Setting: The district of Caesarea Philippi. After repeating the warning to His disciples about the teaching of the religious leaders of the day (the Pharisees and Sadducees) by the Sea of Galilee, Jesus quizzes them on who people think He is.

Now when Jesus came into the district of Caesarea Philippi, He was asking His disciples. "Who do people say that the Son of Man is?" And they said, "Some *say* John the Baptist; and others, Elijah; but still others, Jeremiah, or one of the prophets." He said to them, "But who do you say that I am?" Simon Peter answered, "You are the Christ, the Son of the living God" (Matthew 16:13–16; cf. Mark 8:27–29; Luke 9:18–21; see Matthew 14:1, 2).

Setting: Judea beyond the Jordan (Perea). When His disciples are astonished over His statement about the difficulty of a rich man obtaining eternal life, Jesus makes a pronouncement.

And looking at them, Jesus said to them, "With people this is impossible, but with God all things are possible" (Matthew 19:26; cf. Genesis 18:14; Mark 10:27; Luke 18:27).

Setting: The temple in Jerusalem. Jesus delivers a prophecy to the chief priests and elders after they question His authority.

Jesus said to them, "Did you never read in the Scriptures, 'THE STONE WHICH THE BUILDERS REJECTED, THIS BECAME THE CHIEF CORNER *stone;* THIS CAME ABOUT FROM THE LORD, AND IT IS MARVELOUS IN OUR EYES'? Therefore I say to you, the kingdom of God will be taken away from you and given to a people, producing the fruit of it. And he who falls on this stone will be broken to pieces; but on whomever it falls, it will scatter him like dust" (Matthew 21:42–44, Jesus quotes from Psalm 118:22; cf. Isaiah 8:14, 15; Mark 12:10, 11; Luke 20:17, 18).

Setting: The temple in Jerusalem. After the Jewish religious leaders test Him with questions, Jesus pronounces the first of eight woes upon them in front of the crowds and His disciples.

"But woe to you, scribes and Pharisees, hypocrites, because you shut off the kingdom of heaven from people; for you do not enter in yourselves, nor do you allow those who are entering to go in (Matthew 23:13; cf. Luke 11:52).

Setting: The country of the Gerasenes, on the east side of the Sea of Galilee. Jesus encounters and heals a man possessed by a legion of demons.

And He did not let him, but He said to him, "Go home to your people and report to them what great things the Lord has done for you, and *how* He had mercy on you" (Mark 5:19; cf. Luke 8:39; see Matthew 8:33, 34; Luke 8:36–38).

Setting: Galilee. The Pharisees and some of the scribes from Jerusalem question why Jesus' disciples do not follow the tradition of ceremonial hand cleansing before eating bread.

And He said to them, "Rightly did Isaiah prophesy of you hypocrites, as it is written: 'THIS PEOPLE HONORS ME WITH THEIR LIPS, BUT THEIR HEART IS FAR AWAY FROM ME. BUT IN VAIN DO THEY WORSHIP ME, TEACHING AS DOCTRINES THE PRECEPTS OF MEN.' Neglecting the commandment of God, you hold to the tradition of men." He was also saying to them, "You are experts at setting aside the commandment of God in order to keep tradition. For Moses said, 'HONOR YOUR FATHER AND YOUR MOTHER'; and, 'HE WHO SPEAKS EVIL OF FATHER OR MOTHER, IS TO BE PUT TO DEATH'; but you say, 'If a man says to *his* father or *his* mother, whatever I have that would help you is Corban (that is to say, given *to God*),' you no longer permit him to do anything for *his* father or *his* mother; *thus* invalidating the word of God by your tradition which you have handed down; and you do many things such as that" (Mark 7:6–13, Jesus quotes from Exodus 20:12; 21:17; Isaiah 29:13; cf. Matthew 15:1–6).

Setting: Decapolis, near the Sea of Galilee. Jesus miraculously feeds more than 4,000 people, primarily Gentiles.

In those days, when there was again a large crowd and they had nothing to eat, Jesus called His disciples and said to them, "I feel compassion for the people because they have remained with Me now three days and have nothing to eat. If I send them away hungry to their homes, they will faint on their way; and some of them have come a great distance" (Mark 8:1–3; cf. Matthew 15:32–38; see Matthew 9:36).

Setting: Caesarea Philippi. After giving sight to a blind man in Bethsaida, Jesus asks His disciples who they think He is.

Jesus went out, along with His disciples, to the villages of Caesarea Philippi; and on the way He questioned His disciples, saying to them, "Who do people say that I am?" They told Him, saying, "John the Baptist; and others *say* Elijah; but others, one of the prophets." And He *continued* by questioning them, "But who do you say that I am?" Peter answered and said to Him, "You are the Christ." And He warned them to tell no one about Him (Mark 8:27–30; cf. Matthew 16:13–20; Luke 9:18–21; see John 6:68, 69).

Setting: Judea beyond the Jordan (Perea). After informing a rich man how righteous believers may have treasure in heaven, Jesus conveys to His disciples the difficulty the wealthy have entering the kingdom of God.

And Jesus, looking around, said to His disciples, "How hard it will be for those who are wealthy to enter the kingdom of God!" The disciples were amazed at His words. But Jesus answered again and said to them, "Children, how hard it is to enter the kingdom of God! It is easier for a camel to go through the eye of a needle than for a rich man to enter the kingdom of God." They were even more astonished and said to Him, "Then who can be saved?" Looking at them, Jesus said, "With people it is impossible, but not with God; for all things are possible with God" (Mark 10:23–27; cf. Matthew 19:23–26; Luke 18:24, 25).

Setting: Galilee. After feeding a crowd of 5,000 near Bethsaida, and praying alone, Jesus questions the disciples about the concept of His identity.

And it happened that while He was praying alone, the disciples were with Him, and He questioned them, saying, "Who do the people say that I am?" They answered and said, "John the Baptist, and others *say* Elijah; but others, that one of the prophets of old has risen again." And He said to them, "But who do you say that I am?" And Peter answered and said, "The Christ of God" (Luke 9:18–20; cf. Matthew 16:13–20; Mark 8:27–30).

Setting: On the way from Galilee to Jerusalem. After speaking of how a lamp illuminates, the Lord has lunch with a Pharisee who is surprised He doesn't wash before eating.

But the Lord said to him, "Now you Pharisees clean the outside of the cup and of the platter; but inside of you, you are full of robbery and wickedness. You foolish ones, did not He who made the outside make the inside also? But give that which is within as charity, and then all things are clean for you. But woe to you Pharisees! You pay tithe of mint and rue and every *kind of* garden herb, and *yet* disregard justice and the love of God; but these are the things you should have done without neglecting the others. Woe to you Pharisees! For you love the chief seats in the synagogues and the respectful greetings in the market places. Woe to you! For you are like concealed tombs, and the people who walk over *them* are unaware *of it*" (Luke 11:39–44; cf. Matthew 23:6, 7, 23–27; see Matthew 15:2; Titus 1:15).

Setting: On the way from Galilee to Jerusalem. After giving the story of the prodigal son, the Lord teaches His disciples about stewardship.

Now He was also saying to the disciples, "There was a rich man who had a manager, and this *manager* was reported to him as squandering his possessions. And he called him and said to him, 'What is this I hear about you? Give an accounting of your management, for you can no longer be a manager.' The manager said to himself, 'What shall I do, since my master is taking the management away from me? I am not strong enough to dig; I am ashamed to beg. I know what I shall do, so that when I am removed from the management people will welcome me into their homes.' And he summoned each one of his master's debtors, and he *began* saying to the first, 'How much do you owe my master?' And he said, 'A hundred measures of oil.' And he said to him, 'Take your bill, and sit down quickly and write fifty.' Then he said to another, 'And how much do you owe?' And he said, 'A hundred measures of wheat.' He said to him, 'Take your bill, and write eighty.' And his master praised the unrighteous manager because he had acted shrewdly; for the sons of this age are more shrewd in relation to their own kind than the sons of light. And I say to you, make friends for yourselves by means of the wealth of unrighteousness, so that when it fails, they will receive you into the eternal dwellings. He who is faithful in a very little thing is faithful also in much; and he who is unrighteous in a very little thing is unrighteous also in much. Therefore if you have not been faithful in the *use of* unrighteous wealth, who will entrust the true *riches* to you? And if you have not been faithful in *the use of* that which is another's, who will give you that which is your own? No servant can serve two masters; for either he will hate the one and love the other, or else he will be devoted to one and despise the other. You cannot serve God and wealth" (Luke 16:1–13; cf. Matthew 6:24; see Matthew 25:14–30).

Setting: On the way from Galilee to Jerusalem. After instructing His disciples about persistence in prayer, Jesus conveys a parable about self-righteousness.

And He also told this parable to some people who trusted in themselves that they were righteous, and viewed others with contempt: "Two men went up into the temple to pray, one a Pharisee and the other a tax collector. The Pharisee stood and was praying this to himself: 'God, I thank You that I am not like other people: swindlers, unjust, adulterers, or even like this tax collector. I fast twice a week; I pay tithes of all that I get.' But the tax collector, standing some distance away, was even unwilling to lift up his eyes to heaven, but was beating his breast, saying, 'God, be merciful to me, the sinner!' I tell you, this man went to his house justified rather than the other; for everyone who exalts himself will be humbled, but he who humbles himself will be exalted" (Luke 18:9–14; see Ezra 9:6; Matthew 6:5, 23:12; Luke 11:42, 16:15; Romans 14:3, 10).

Setting: Perea, en route from Galilee to Jerusalem. After responding to a ruler's question about obtaining eternal life, Jesus replies to His disciples' conclusion about being saved.

But He said, "The things that are impossible with people are possible with God" (Luke 18:27; cf. Matthew 19:26).

Setting: On the Mount of Olives, east of the temple in Jerusalem. After ministering in the temple a few days before His crucifixion, and giving the disciples more details regarding future events, Jesus elaborates more during His Olivet Discourse about things to come.

"But when you see Jerusalem surrounded by armies, then recognize that her desolation is near. Then those who are in Judea must flee to the mountains, and those who are in the midst of the city must leave, and those who are in the country must not enter the city; because these are days of vengeance, so that all things which are written will be fulfilled. Woe to those who are pregnant and to those who are nursing babies in those days; for there will be a great distress upon the land and wrath to this people; and they will fall by the edge of the sword, and will be led captive into all the nations; and Jerusalem will be trampled under foot by the Gentiles until the times of the Gentiles are fulfilled" (Luke 21:20–24; see Matthew 24:15–18; Mark 13:14–16; Luke 19:43).

Setting: Sychar in Samaria, on the way to Galilee. Jesus interacts with a Samaritan woman at Jacob's well, while the disciples are buying food.

Jesus said to her, "Woman, believe Me, an hour is coming when neither in this mountain nor in Jerusalem will you worship the Father. You worship what you do not know; we worship what we know, for salvation is from the Jews. But an hour is coming, and now is, when the true worshipers will worship the Father in spirit and truth; for such people the Father seeks to be His worshipers. God is spirit, and those who worship Him must worship in spirit and truth" (John 4:21–24; see Isaiah 2:3; Philippians 3:3).

Setting: Cana of Galilee. After conversing with a Samaritan woman at Jacob's well, and ministering to the Samaritans for two days, Jesus encounters a royal official seeking healing for his son, sick at the point of death in Capernaum.

So Jesus said to him, "Unless you *people* see signs and wonders, you *simply* will not believe" (John 4:48).

Setting: By the Sea of Galilee. After revealing to the Jewish religious leaders during a feast of the Jews in Jerusalem that God, John the Baptist, His works, and the Scriptures all testify to His mission, Jesus miraculously feeds more than 5,000 people with a lad's five barley loaves and two fish.

Jesus said, "Have the people sit down." Now there was much grass in the place. So the men sat down, in number about five thousand. Jesus took the loaves, and having given thanks, He distributed to those who were seated; likewise also of the fish as much as they wanted. When they were filled, He said to the disciples, "Gather up the leftover fragments so that nothing will be lost" (John 6:10–12; cf. Matthew 14:17–21; Mark 6:38–44; Luke 9:14–17; see Matthew 15:32–38).

Setting: From beyond the Jordan. After the death of His friend Lazarus, Jesus travels with His disciples to Bethany in Judea to visit the dead man's sisters, Martha and Mary. The Lord raises Lazarus from the dead.

Jesus said, "Remove the stone." Martha, the sister of the deceased, said to Him, "Lord, by this time there will be a stench, for he has been *dead* four days." Jesus said to her, "Did I not say to you that if you believe, you will see the glory of God?" So they removed the stone. Then Jesus raised His eyes, and said, "Father, I thank You that You have heard Me. I knew that You always hear Me; but because of the people standing around I said it, so that they may believe that you sent Me." When He had said these things, He cried out with a loud voice, "Lazarus, come forth." The man who had died came forth, bound hand and foot with wrappings, and his face was wrapped around with a cloth. Jesus said to them, "Unbind him, and let him go" (John 11:39–44; see Matthew 11:25).

Setting: Corinth. Luke, writing in Acts, records the Lord's comforting revelation through a vision to Paul, who is working among the Jews and Gentiles at Corinth during his second missionary journey, testifying that Jesus is the Christ (Messiah).

And the Lord said to Paul in the night by a vision, "Do not be afraid *any longer,* but go on speaking and do not be silent; for I am with you, and no man will attack you in order to harm you, for I have many people in this city" (Acts 18:9, 10).

Setting: Caesarea. Luke, writing in Acts, gives Paul's retelling of his conversion to Christ as he appears before King Agrippa following his hearing before the Jewish Council in Jerusalem and arrest by the Roman commander (on his way to Rome after the apostle's third missionary journey).

"And when we had fallen to the ground, I heard a voice saying to me in the Hebrew dialect, 'Saul, Saul, why are you persecuting Me? It is hard for you to kick against the goads.' And I said, 'Who are You, Lord?' And the Lord said, 'I am Jesus whom you are persecuting. But get up and stand on your feet; for this purpose I have appeared to you, to appoint you a minister and a witness not only to the things which you have seen, but also to the things in which I will appear to you; rescuing you from the *Jewish* people and from the Gentiles, to whom I am sending you, to open their eyes so that they may turn from darkness to light and from the dominion of Satan to God, that they may receive forgiveness of sins and an inheritance among those who have been sanctified by faith in Me' (Acts 26:14–18; see Isaiah 35:5; Acts 21:40; 22:14).

Setting: On the island of Patmos (in the Aegean Sea about fifty miles southwest of Ephesus in modern Turkey). On the Lord's Day (Sunday), approximately fifty years after the Resurrection, the disciple John encounters the Lord Jesus Christ, who communicates a new revelation for the apostle to record for the church in Sardis and to six other churches in Asia.

"To the angel of the church in Sardis write: He who has the seven Spirits of God and the seven stars, says this: 'I know your deeds, that you have a name that you are alive, but you are dead. Wake up, and strengthen the things that remain, which were about to die; for I have not found your deeds completed in the sight of My God. So remember what you have received and heard; and keep *it,* and repent. Therefore if you do not wake up, I will come like a thief, and you will not know at what hour I will come to you. But you have a few people in Sardis who have not soiled their garments; and they will walk with Me in white, for they are worthy. He who overcomes will thus be clothed in white garments; and I will not erase his name from the book of life, and I will confess his name before My Father and before His angels. He who has an ear, let him hear what the Spirit says to the churches' " (Revelation 3:1–6; see Matthew 10:32; Revelation 1:16).

PEOPLE, GIFTS TO OTHER (See GIFTS TO OTHER PEOPLE)

PEOPLE, JEWISH (See JEWISH PEOPLE)

PEOPLE, PLEASING (See APPROVAL, MAN'S)

PEOPLE'S LOVE (Listed under LOVE, PEOPLE'S)

PERDITION, SON OF (Also see JUDAS)

Setting: Jerusalem. Before the Passover, after giving His disciples hope that in the midst of tribulation they will have His peace, Jesus prays His high-priestly prayer.

Jesus spoke these things; and lifting up His eyes to heaven, He said, "Father, the hour has come; glorify Your Son, that the Son may glorify You, even as You gave Him authority over all flesh, that to all whom You have given Him, He may give eternal life. This is eternal life, that they may know You, the only true God, and Jesus Christ whom You have sent. I glorified You on the earth, having accomplished the work which You have given Me to do. Now, Father, glorify Me together with Yourself, with the glory which I had with You before the world was. I have manifested Your name to the men whom You gave Me out of the world; they were Yours and You gave them to Me, and they have kept Your word. Now they have come to know that everything You have given Me is from You; for the words which You gave Me I have given to them; and they received *them* and truly understood that I came forth from You, and they believed You sent Me. I ask on their behalf; I do not ask on behalf of the world, but of those whom You have given Me; for they are Yours; and all things that are Mine are Yours, and Yours are Mine; and I have been glorified in them. I am no longer in the world; and *yet* they themselves are in the world, and I come to You. Holy Father, keep them in Your name, *the name* which You have given Me, that they may be even as We *are.* While I was with them, I was keeping them in Your name which You have given Me; and I guarded them and not one of them perished but the son of perdition, so that the Scripture would be fulfilled" (John 17:1–12; see Luke 22:32; John 1:1; 3:35; 4:34; 5:44; 6:37–39, 70; 8:42; 11:41; 12:49; 13:18, 31; 16:15; Philippians 2:9).

PERFECT

Setting: Galilee. During the early part of His ministry, Jesus preaches the Sermon on the Mount to His disciples and the multitudes.

"You have heard that it was said, 'YOU SHALL LOVE YOUR NEIGHBOR and hate your enemy.' But I say to you, love your enemies and pray for those who persecute you, so that you may be sons of your Father who is in heaven; for He causes His sun to rise on *the* evil and *the* good, and sends rain on *the* righteous and *the* unrighteous. For if you love those who love you, what reward do you have? Do not even the tax collectors do the same? If you greet only your brothers, what more are you doing *than others?* Do not even the Gentiles do the same? Therefore, you are to be perfect, as your heavenly Father is perfect" (Matthew 5:43–48, Jesus quotes from Leviticus 19:18; cf. Leviticus 19:2; Luke 6:27–36).

PERFUME

Setting: The home of Simon the leper in Bethany. Jesus rebukes His disciples after they criticize a woman for pouring a costly vial of perfume on His head in preparation for His burial.

But Jesus, aware of this, said to them, "Why do you bother the woman? For she has done a good deed to Me. For you always have the poor with you; but you do not always have Me. For when she poured this perfume on My body, she did it to prepare Me for burial. Truly I say to you, wherever this gospel is preached in the whole world, what this woman has done will also be spoken of in memory of her" (Matthew 26:10–13; cf. Mark 14:3–9; Luke 7:37–39; John 12:2–8; see Deuteronomy 15:11).

Setting: Galilee. After Jesus praises John the Baptist to the crowds, Simon, a Pharisee, invites the Lord to dinner. A sinful woman anoints His feet with perfume, prompting Him to instruct His host about forgiveness.

Turning toward the woman, He said to Simon, "Do you see this woman? I entered your house; you gave Me no water for My feet, but she has wet My feet with her tears and wiped them with her hair. You gave Me no kiss; but she, since the time I came in, has not ceased to kiss My feet. You did not anoint My head with oil, but she anointed My feet with perfume. For this reason I say to you, her sins, which are many, have been forgiven, for she loved much; but he who is forgiven little, loves little." Then He said to her, "Your sins have been forgiven." Those who were reclining *at the table* with Him began to say to themselves, "Who is this *man* who even forgives sins?" And He said to the woman, "Your faith has saved you; go in peace" (Luke 7:44–50; see Matthew 9:2; Mark 5:34; Luke 5:21).

PERGAMUM

Setting: On the island of Patmos (in the Aegean Sea about fifty miles southwest of Ephesus in modern Turkey). On the Lord's Day (Sunday), approximately fifty years after the Resurrection, the disciple John encounters the Lord Jesus Christ, who communicates new revelations for the apostle to record for the seven churches in Asia.

I was in the Spirit on the Lord's day, and I heard behind me a loud voice like *the sound* of a trumpet, saying, "Write in a book what you see, and send *it* to the seven churches: to Ephesus and to Smyrna and to Pergamum and to Thyatira and to Sardis and to Philadelphia and to Laodicea" (Revelation 1:10, 11; see Revelation 4:1).

Setting: On the island of Patmos (in the Aegean Sea about fifty miles southwest of Ephesus in modern Turkey). On the Lord's Day (Sunday), approximately fifty years after the Resurrection, the disciple John encounters the Lord Jesus Christ, who communicates a new revelation for the apostle to record for the church in Pergamum and to six other churches in Asia.

"And to the angel of the church in Pergamum write: The One who has the sharp two-edged sword says this: 'I know where you dwell, where Satan's throne is; and you hold fast My name, and did not deny My faith even in the days of Antipas, My witness, My faithful one, who was killed among you, where Satan dwells. But I have a few things against you, because you have there some who hold the teaching of Balaam, who kept teaching Balak to put a stumbling block before the sons of Israel, to eat things sacrificed to idols and to commit *acts of* immorality. So you also have some who in the same way hold the teaching of the Nicolaitans. Therefore repent; or else I am coming to you quickly, and I will make war against them with the sword of My mouth. He who has an ear, let him hear what the Spirit says to the churches. To him who overcomes, to him I will give *some* of the hidden manna, and I will give him a white stone, and a new name written on the stone which no one knows but he who receives it' (Revelation 2:12–17; see Numbers 25:1–3; Isaiah 62:2; Revelation 1:16; 2:5, 6, 16).

PERISH (Also see DEATH)

Setting: Capernaum of Galilee. Jesus illustrates to His disciples the value of little ones.

"What do you think? If any man has a hundred sheep, and one of them has gone astray, does he not leave the ninety-nine on the mountains and go and search for the one that is straying? If it turns out that he finds it, truly I say to you, he rejoices over it more than the ninety-nine which have not gone astray. So it is not *the* will of your Father who is in heaven that one of these little ones perish" (Matthew 18:12–14; cf. Luke 15:4–7).

Setting: Gethsemane on the Mount of Olives, east of the temple in Jerusalem. As Jesus submits to His Father's will and allows Judas to betray Him, Peter attempts to defend Him by force, but Jesus does not permit it.

Then Jesus said to him, "Put your sword back into its place; for all those who take up the sword shall perish by the sword. Or do you think that I cannot appeal to My Father, and He will at once put at My disposal more than twelve legions of angels? How then will the Scriptures be fulfilled, *which say* that it must happen this way?" (Matthew 26:52–54; cf. Mark 14:47; Luke 22:50, 51; John 18:10, 11).

Setting: On the way from Galilee to Jerusalem. After some present report to Him about the Galileans whose blood Pilate (Roman governor of Judea) mixed with their sacrifices, Jesus responds to their concern by calling them to repentance.

And Jesus said to them, "Do you suppose that these Galileans were *greater* sinners than all *other* Galileans because they suffered this *fate*? I tell you, no, but unless you repent, you will all likewise perish. Or do you suppose that those eighteen on whom the tower in Siloam fell and killed them were *worse* culprits than all the men who live in Jerusalem? I tell you, no, but unless you repent, you will all likewise perish" (Luke 13:2–5; see John 9:2, 3).

Setting: On the way from Galilee to Jerusalem. After Jesus responds to a question while teaching in the cities and villages about who is saved, some Pharisees ask Him to leave, claiming Herod Antipas (tetrarch of Galilee and Perea) seeks to end His life.

And He said to them, "Go and tell that fox, 'Behold, I cast out demons and perform cures today and tomorrow, and the third *day* I reach My goal.' Nevertheless I must journey on today and tomorrow and the next *day*; for it cannot be that a prophet would perish outside of Jerusalem. O Jerusalem, Jerusalem, *the city* that kills the prophets and stones those sent to her! How often I wanted to gather your children together, just as a hen *gathers* her brood under her wings, and you would not *have it*! Behold, your house is left to you *desolate*; and I say to you, you will not see Me until *the time* comes when you say, 'BLESSED IS HE WHO COMES IN THE NAME OF THE LORD!'" (Luke 13:32–35, Jesus quotes from Psalm 118:26; cf. Matthew 23:37).

Setting: On the Mount of Olives, east of the temple in Jerusalem. After ministering in the temple a few days before His crucifixion, and giving His disciples more details regarding the temple's future destruction, Jesus elaborates during His Olivet Discourse about things to come.

Then He continued by saying to them, "Nation will rise against nation and kingdom against kingdom, and there will be great earthquakes, and in various places plagues and famines; and there will be terrors and great signs from heaven. But before all these things, they will lay their hands on you and will persecute you, delivering you to the synagogues and prisons, bringing you before kings and governors for My name's sake. It will lead to an opportunity for your testimony. So make up your minds not to prepare beforehand to defend yourselves; for I will give you utterance and wisdom which none of your opponents will be able to resist or refute. But you will be betrayed even by parents and brothers and relatives and friends, and they will put *some* of you to death, and you will be hated by all because of My name. Yet not a hair of your head will perish. By your endurance you will gain your lives" (Luke 21:10–19; cf. Matthew 10:19–22; 24:7–14; Mark 13:8–13).

Setting: Jerusalem. At the time for the Passover of the Jews, after the Lord cleanses the temple, a Pharisee, Nicodemus, asks Him by night the meaning of "born again."

"For God so loved the world, that He gave His only begotten Son, that whoever believes in Him shall not perish, but have eternal life. For God did not send the Son into the world to judge the world, but that the world might be saved through Him. He who believes in Him is not judged; he who does not believe has been judged already, because he has not believed in the name of the only begotten Son of God. This is the judgment, that the Light has come into the world, and men loved darkness rather than the Light, for their deeds were evil. For everyone who does evil hates the Light, and does not come to the Light for fear that his deeds will be exposed. But he who practices the truth comes to the Light, so that his deeds may be manifested as having been wrought in God" (John 3:16–21; see Luke 19:10; John 1:4; 1:18; Romans 5:8; 1 John 1:6, 7).

Setting: Jerusalem. At the Feast of Dedication, just after Jesus conveys the Parable of the Good Shepherd to the Pharisees (who do not understand it), they ask Him plainly if He is the Christ.

Jesus answered them, "I told you, and you do not believe; the works that I do in My Father's name, these testify of Me. But you do not believe because you are not of My sheep. My sheep hear My voice, and I know them, and they follow Me; and I give eternal life to them, and they will never perish; and no one will snatch them out of My hand. My Father, who has given *them* to Me, is greater than all; and no one is able to snatch *them* out of the Father's hand. I and the Father are one" (John 10:25–30; see John 8:47; 17:1, 2, 20, 21).

[PERISH from perished]

Setting: Jerusalem. Before the Passover, after giving His disciples hope that in the midst of tribulation they will have His peace, Jesus prays His high-priestly prayer.

Jesus spoke these things; and lifting up His eyes to heaven, He said, "Father, the hour has come; glorify Your Son, that the Son may glorify You, even as You gave Him authority over all flesh, that to all whom You have given Him, He may give eternal life. This is eternal life, that they may know You, the only true God, and Jesus Christ whom You have sent. I glorified You on the earth, having accomplished the work which You have given Me to do. Now, Father, glorify Me together with Yourself, with the glory which

I had with You before the world was. I have manifested Your name to the men whom You gave Me out of the world; they were Yours and You gave them to Me, and they have kept Your word. Now they have come to know that everything You have given Me is from You; for the words which You gave Me I have given to them; and they received *them* and truly understood that I came forth from You, and they believed You sent Me. I ask on their behalf; I do not ask on behalf of the world, but of those whom You have given Me; for they are Yours; and all things that are Mine are Yours, and Yours are Mine; and I have been glorified in them. I am no longer in the world; and *yet* they themselves are in the world, and I come to You. Holy Father, keep them in Your name, *the name* which You have given Me, that they may be even as We *are.* While I was with them, I was keeping them in Your name which You have given Me; and I guarded them and not one of them perished but the son of perdition, so that the Scripture would be fulfilled" (John 17:1–12; see Luke 22:32; John 1:1; 3:35; 4:34; 5:44; 6:37–39, 70; 8:42; 11:41; 12:49; 13:18, 31; 16:15; Philippians 2:9).

PERMISSION

Setting: Jerusalem. During the Feast of Unleavened Bread (Passover) just before His crucifixion, Jesus celebrates the Passover meal with His disciples and institutes the Lord's Supper. The disciples later argue over who is the greatest among them, and Jesus prophesies Peter's three denials of Him.

"Simon, Simon, behold, Satan has demanded *permission* to sift you like wheat; but I have prayed for you, that your faith may not fail; and you, when once you have turned again, strengthen your brothers." But he said to Him, "Lord, with You I am ready to go both to prison and to death!" And He said, "I say to you, Peter, the rooster will not crow today until you have denied three times that you know Me" (Luke 22:31–34; cf. Matthew 26:33, 35; John 13:36–38; see Job 1:6–12; John 17:15).

PERPLEXITY

Setting: On the Mount of Olives, just east of Jerusalem. After ministering in the temple a few days before His crucifixion, and giving His disciples more details regarding future events, Jesus speaks during His Olivet Discourse of His return.

"There will be signs in sun and moon and stars, and on the earth dismay among the nations, in perplexity at the roaring of the sea and the waves, men fainting from fear and the expectation of the things which are coming upon the world; for the powers of the heavens will be shaken. Then they will see THE SON OF MAN COMING IN A CLOUD with power and great glory. But when these things begin to take place, straighten up and lift up your heads, because your redemption is drawing near" (Luke 21:25–28, Jesus quotes from Daniel 7:13; cf. Matthew 24:29–31; Mark 13:24–27).

PERSECUTE/PERSECUTED (Also see AFFLICTION; MISTREATMENT; PERSECUTION; SUFFERING; and TRIBULATION)

Setting: Galilee. Early in His ministry, Jesus presents the Beatitudes (part of the Sermon on the Mount) to His disciples and the gathered crowds from Galilee, Decapolis, Jerusalem, Judea, and beyond the Jordan.

"Blessed are those who have been persecuted for the sake of righteousness, for theirs is the kingdom of heaven" (Matthew 5:10; cf. Luke 6:22; 1 Peter 3:14; see Matthew 13:35).

Setting: Galilee. Early in His ministry, Jesus presents the Beatitudes (part of the Sermon on the Mount) to His disciples and the gathered crowds from Galilee, Decapolis, Jerusalem, Judea, and beyond the Jordan.

"Blessed are you when *people* insult you and persecute you, and falsely say all kinds of evil against you because of Me. Rejoice and be glad, for your reward in heaven is great; for in the same way they persecuted the prophets who were before you" (Matthew 5:11, 12; cf. 2 Chronicles 36:16; Luke 6:22, 23; 1 Peter 4:14; see Matthew 13:35).

Setting: Galilee. During the early part of His ministry, Jesus preaches the Sermon on the Mount to His disciples and the multitudes.

"You have heard that it was said, 'YOU SHALL LOVE YOUR NEIGHBOR and hate your enemy.' But I say to you, love your enemies and pray for those who persecute you, so that you may be sons of your Father who is in heaven; for He causes His sun to rise on *the* evil and *the* good, and sends rain on *the* righteous and *the* unrighteous. For if you love those who love you, what reward do you have? Do not even the tax collectors do the same? If you greet only your brothers, what more are you doing *than others?* Do not even the Gentiles do the same? Therefore, you are to be perfect, as your heavenly Father is perfect" (Matthew 5:43–48, Jesus quotes from Leviticus 19:18; cf. Leviticus 19:2; Luke 6:27–36).

Setting: Galilee. After His disciples observe His ministry, Jesus summons and specifically instructs them about the upcoming difficulties of their ministry to the people of Israel.

"Brother will betray brother to death, and a father *his* child; and children will rise up against parents and cause them to be put to death. You will be hated by all because of My name, but it is the one who has endured to the end who will be saved. But whenever they persecute you in one city, flee to the next; for truly I say to you, you will not finish *going through* the cities of Israel until the Son of Man comes" (Matthew 10:21–23; cf. Matthew 10:35, 36; 16:27, 28; 24:9).

Setting: The temple in Jerusalem. After the Jewish religious leaders test Him with questions, Jesus pronounces the eighth of eight woes upon them in front of the crowds and His disciples.

"Woe to you, scribes and Pharisees, hypocrites! For you build the tombs of the prophets and adorn the monuments of the righteous, and say, 'If we had been *living* in the days of our fathers, we would not have been partners with them in *shedding* the blood of the prophets.' So you testify against yourselves, that you are sons of those who murdered the prophets. Fill up, then, the measure *of the guilt* of you fathers. You serpents, you brood of vipers, how will you escape the sentence of hell? Therefore, behold, I am sending you prophets and wise men and scribes; some of them you will kill and crucify, and some of them you will scourge in your synagogues, and persecute from city to city, so that upon you may fall *the guilt of* all the righteous blood shed on earth, from the blood of righteous Abel to the blood of Zechariah, the son of Berechiah, whom you murdered between the temple and the altar. Truly I say to you, all these things will come upon this generation" (Matthew 23:29–36; cf. 2 Chronicles 24:21; Zechariah 1:1; Matthew 3:7; Luke 11:47–52; see Matthew 10:23).

Setting: On the way from Galilee to Jerusalem. After Jesus pronounces woes upon the Pharisees, a lawyer replies that His remarks are an insult to lawyers, too.

But He said, "Woe to you lawyers as well! For you weigh men down with burdens hard to bear, while you yourselves will not even touch the burdens with one of your fingers. Woe to you! For you build the tombs of the prophets, and *it was* your fathers *who* killed them. So you are witnesses and approve the deeds of your fathers; because it was they who killed them, and you build *their tombs*. For this reason also the wisdom of God said, 'I will send them prophets and apostles, and *some* of them they will kill and *some* they will persecute, so that the blood of all the prophets, shed since the foundation of the world, may be charged against this generation, from the blood of Abel to the blood of Zechariah, who was killed between the altar and the house *of God*; yes, I tell you, it shall be charged against this generation.' Woe to you lawyers! For you have taken away the key of knowledge; you yourselves did not enter, and you hindered those who were entering" (Luke 11:46–52; cf. Matthew 23:29–32; see 2 Chronicles 24:20, 21; Matthew 23:4, 13).

Setting: On the Mount of Olives, east of the temple in Jerusalem. After ministering in the temple a few days before His crucifixion, and giving His disciples more details regarding the temple's future destruction, Jesus elaborates during His Olivet Discourse about things to come.

Then He continued by saying to them, "Nation will rise against nation and kingdom against kingdom, and there will be great earthquakes, and in various places plagues and famines; and there will be terrors and great signs from heaven. But before all these things, they will lay their hands on you and will persecute you, delivering you to the synagogues and prisons, bringing you before kings and governors for My name's sake. It will lead to an opportunity for your testimony. So make up your minds not to prepare beforehand to defend yourselves; for I will give you utterance and wisdom which none of your opponents will be able to resist or refute. But you will be betrayed even by parents and brothers and relatives and friends, and they will put *some* of you to death, and you will be hated by all because of My name. Yet not a hair of your head will perish. By your endurance you will gain your lives" (Luke 21:10–19; cf. Matthew 10:19–22; 24:7–14; Mark 13:8–13).

Setting: Jerusalem. Before the Passover, with His departure in mind, after explaining He is the vine and His disciples are the branches, Jesus prepares them for persecution from the world.

"If the world hates you, you know that it has hated Me before *it hated* you. If you were of the world, the world would love its own; but because you are not of the world, but I chose you out of the world, because of this the world hates you. Remember the word that I said to you, 'A slave is not greater than his master.' If they persecuted Me, they will also persecute you; if they kept My word, they will keep yours also. But all these things they will do to you for My name's sake, because they do not know the One who sent Me. If I had not come and spoken to them, they would not have sin, but now they have no excuse for their sin" (John 15:18–22; see Matthew 10:22; John 7:7; 8:19, 55; 9:41; 1 Corinthians 4:12).

PERSECUTION (Also see AFFLICTION; MISTREATMENT; PERSECUTED; PERSECUTIONS; SUFFERING; and TRIBULATION)

[PERSECUTION from they will hand you over to *the* courts and scourge you in their synagogues]

Setting: Galilee. After His disciples observe His ministry, Jesus summons and specifically instructs them about the upcoming hardships of their ministry to the people of Israel.

"Behold, I send you out as sheep in the midst of wolves; so be shrewd as serpents and innocent as doves. But beware of men, for they will hand you over to *the* courts and scourge you in their synagogues; and you will even be brought before governors and kings for My sake, as a testimony to them and to the Gentiles. But when they hand you over, do not worry about how or what you are to say; for it will be given you in that hour what you are to say. For it is not you who speak, but *it* is the Spirit of your Father who speaks in you" (Matthew 10:16–20; cf. Luke 10:3).

Setting: By the Sea of Galilee. With the religious leaders rejecting His message, Jesus begins to teach in parables and gives His disciples the meaning of the Parable of the Sower.

"Hear then the parable of the sower. When anyone hears the word of the kingdom and does not understand it, the evil *one* comes and snatches away what has been sown in his heart. This is the one on whom seed was sown beside the road. The one on whom seed was sown on the rocky places, this is the man who hears the word and immediately receives it with joy; yet he has no *firm* root in himself, but is *only* temporary, and when affliction or persecution arises because of the word, immediately he falls away. And the one on whom seed was sown among the thorns, this is the man who hears the word, and the worry of the world and the deceitfulness of wealth choke the word, and it becomes unfruitful. And the one on whom seed was sown on the good soil, this is the man who hears the word and understands it; who indeed bears fruit and brings forth, some a hundredfold, some sixty, and some thirty" (Matthew 13:18–23; cf. Mark 4:13–20; Luke 8:11–15).

[PERSECUTION from who kills the prophets and stones those who are sent to her]

Setting: The temple in Jerusalem. With His death on the cross just days away, Jesus laments over Jerusalem's hardheartedness and lack of repentance.

"Jerusalem, Jerusalem, who kills the prophets and stones those who are sent to her! How often I wanted to gather your children together, the way a hen gathers her chicks under her wings, and you were unwilling. Behold, your house is being left to you desolate! For I say to you, from now on you will not see Me until you say, 'BLESSED IS HE WHO COMES IN THE NAME OF THE LORD!'" (Matthew 23:37–39, Jesus quotes from Psalm 118:26; cf. 1 Kings 9:7; Luke 13:34, 35).

[PERSECUTION from they will deliver you to tribulation]

Setting: The Mount of Olives, just east of Jerusalem. During His Olivet Discourse, Jesus answers His disciples' questions as to when the temple will be destroyed and Jerusalem overrun, along with the signs of His coming and the end of the age.

And Jesus answered and said to them, "See to it that no one misleads you. For many will come in My name, saying, 'I am the Christ,' and will mislead many. You will be hearing of wars and rumors of wars. See that you are not frightened, for *those things* must take place, but *that* is not yet the end. For nation will rise against nation, and kingdom against kingdom, and in various places there will be famines and earthquakes. But all these things are *merely* the beginning of birth pangs. Then they will deliver you to tribulation, and will kill you, and you will be hated by all nations because of My name. At that time many will fall away and will betray one another and hate one another. Many false prophets will arise and will mislead many. Because lawlessness is increased, most people's love will grow cold. But the one who endures to the end, he will be saved. This gospel of the kingdom shall be preached in the whole world as a testimony to all the nations, and then the end will come" (Matthew 24:4–14; cf. Jeremiah 29:8; Matthew 7:15; 10:17, 22; Mark 13:3–13; Luke 21:7–19; Revelation 6:4).

Setting: By the Sea of Galilee. During the early part of His ministry, after presenting the Parable of the Sower from a boat to a very large crowd, Jesus gives the meaning of the parable to His disciples and other followers.

And He said to them, "Do you not understand this parable? How will you understand all the parables? The sower sows the word. These are the ones who are beside the road where the word is sown; and when they hear, immediately Satan comes and takes away the word which has been sown in them. In a similar way these are the ones on whom seed was sown on the rocky places, who, when they hear the word, immediately receive it with joy; and they have no *firm* root in themselves, but are *only* temporary; then, when affliction or persecution arises because of the word, immediately they fall away. And others are the ones on whom seed was sown among the thorns; these are the ones who have heard the word, but the worries of the world and the deceitfulness of riches, and the desires for other things enter in and choke the word, and it becomes unfruitful. And those are the ones on whom seed was sown on the good soil; and they hear the word and accept it and bear fruit, thirty, sixty, and a hundredfold" (Mark 4:13–20; cf. Matthew 13:18–23; Luke 8:11–15).

[PERSECUTION from baptized with the baptism with which I am baptized]
Setting: On the road to Jerusalem. After Jesus prophesies His persecution, death, and resurrection, James and John ask for special honor and privileges in His coming kingdom.

And He said to them, "What do you want Me to do for you?" They said to Him, "Grant that we may sit, one on Your right and one on *Your* left, in Your glory." But Jesus said to them, "You do not know what you are asking. Are you able to drink the cup that I drink, or to be baptized with the baptism with which I am baptized?" They said to Him, "We are able." And Jesus said to them, "The cup that I drink you shall drink; and you shall be baptized with the baptism with which I am baptized. But to sit on My right or on *My* left, this is not Mine to give; but it is for those for whom it has been prepared" (Mark 10:36–40; cf. Matthew 20:20–23; see Matthew 19:28; Acts 12:2).

[PERSECUTION from for they will deliver you to *the* courts, and you will be flogged in *the* synagogues]
Setting: On the Mount of Olives, east of the temple in Jerusalem. After predicting the temple's destruction, Jesus responds during His Olivet Discourse to questions from Peter, James, John, and Andrew about other future events.

And Jesus began to say to them, "See to it that no one misleads you. Many will come in My name, saying, 'I am *He!*' and will mislead many. When you hear of wars and rumors of wars, do not be frightened; *those things* must take place; but *that is* not yet the end. For nation will rise up against nation, and kingdom against kingdom; there will be earthquakes in various places; there will *also be* famines. These things are *merely* the beginning of birth pangs. But be on your guard; for they will deliver you to *the* courts, and you will be flogged in *the* synagogues, and you will stand before governors and kings for My sake, as a testimony to them. The gospel must first be preached to all the nations. When they arrest you and hand you over, do not worry beforehand about what you are to say, but say whatever is given you in that hour; for it is not you who speak, but *it is* the Holy Spirit. Brother will betray brother to death, and a father *his* child; and children will rise up against parents and have them put to death. You will be hated by all because of My name, but the one who endures to the end, he will be saved" (Mark 13:5–13; cf. Matthew 24:4–14; Luke 21:7–19; see Matthew 10:17–22).

[PERSECUTION from scorn your name as evil, for the sake of the Son of Man]
Setting: Galilee. After selecting His twelve disciples, Jesus teaches the Beatitudes (part of the Sermon on the Mount) to those disciples and a great throng of people from Judea, Jerusalem, and the central coastal region of Tyre and Sidon.

"Blessed are you when men hate you, and ostracize you, and insult you, and scorn your name as evil, for the sake of the Son of Man. Be glad in that day and leap *for joy*, for behold, your reward is great in heaven. For in the same way their fathers used to treat the prophets" (Luke 6:22, 23; cf. Matthew 5:10–12; see 2 Chronicles 36:16).

[PERSECUTION from they bring you before the synagogues and the rulers and the authorities]
Setting: On the way from Galilee to Jerusalem. Jesus warns His disciples of future events, as the scribes and Pharisees turn hostile and question Him repeatedly in an attempt to catch Him in something He might say.

"And I say to you, everyone who confesses Me before men, the Son of Man will confess him also before the angels of God; but he who denies Me before men will be denied before the angels of God. And everyone who speaks a word against the Son of Man, it will be forgiven him; but he who blasphemes against the Holy Spirit, it will not be forgiven him. When they bring you before the synagogues and the rulers and the authorities, do not worry about how or what you are to speak in your defense, or what you are to say; for the Holy Spirit will teach you in that very hour what you ought to say" (Luke 12:8–12; cf. Matthew 10:32, 33; 12:31, 32; see Matthew 10:20).

[PERSECUTION from kills the prophets and stones those sent to her]
Setting: On the way from Galilee to Jerusalem. While teaching in the cities and villages, Jesus responds to a question about who is saved. Some Pharisees ask Him to leave, claiming Herod Antipas (tetrarch of Galilee and Perea) seeks to kill Him.

And He said to them, "Go and tell that fox, 'Behold, I cast out demons and perform cures today and tomorrow, and the third *day* I reach My goal.' Nevertheless I must journey on today and tomorrow and the next *day*; for it cannot be that a prophet would perish outside of Jerusalem. O Jerusalem, Jerusalem, *the city* that kills the prophets and stones those sent to her! How often I wanted to gather your children together, just as a hen *gathers* her brood under her wings, and you would not *have it*! Behold, your house is left to you *desolate*; and I say to you, you will not see Me until *the time* comes when you say, 'BLESSED IS HE WHO COMES IN THE NAME OF THE LORD!'" (Luke 13:32–35, Jesus quotes from Psalm 118:26; cf. Matthew 23:37).

[PERSECUTION from mocked; mistreated; spit upon; scourged; and they will kill him]
Setting: On the way from Galilee to Jerusalem. After responding to Peter's statement about the disciples' personal sacrifice in following Him, Jesus tells them of the sacrifice He will make in Jerusalem.

Then He took the twelve aside and said to them, "Behold, we are going up to Jerusalem, and all things which are written through the prophets about the Son of Man will be accomplished. For He will be handed over to the Gentiles, and will be mocked and mistreated and spit upon, and after they have scourged Him, they will kill Him; and the third day He will rise again" (Luke 18:31–33; cf. Matthew 20:17–19; Mark 10:32–34).

[PERSECUTION from persecuting]
Setting: On the road to Damascus. Luke, writing in Acts, describes how Saul of Tarsus (who will later have the name Paul), a persecutor of the disciples of Jesus, receives the Lord's calling and is temporarily blinded.

As he was traveling, it happened that he was approaching Damascus, and suddenly a light from heaven flashed around him; and he fell to the ground and heard a voice saying to him. "Saul, Saul, why are you persecuting Me?" And he said, "Who are You, Lord?" And He *said*, "I am Jesus whom you are persecuting, but get up and enter the city, and it will be told you what you must do" (Acts 9:3–6; see Acts 22:7, 8).

[PERSECUTION from persecuting]

Setting: Jerusalem. Luke, writing in Acts, presents the account of Paul's speech (following his third missionary journey) to a hostile Jewish crowd about His divine encounter with Jesus on the road to Damascus.

"But it happened that as I was on my way, approaching Damascus about noontime, a very bright light suddenly flashed from heaven all around me, and I fell to the ground, and heard a voice saying to me, 'Saul, Saul, why are you persecuting Me?' And I answered, 'Who are You, Lord?' And He said to me, 'I am Jesus the Nazarene, whom you are persecuting.' And those who were with me saw the light, to be sure, but did not understand the voice of the One who was speaking to me. And I said, 'What shall I do, Lord?' And the Lord said to me, 'Get up and go on into Damascus, and there you will be told of all that has been appointed for you to do' (Acts 22: [PERSECUTION from persecuting]

Setting: Caesarea. Luke, writing in Acts, gives Paul's retelling of his conversion to Christ as he appears before King Agrippa following his hearing before the Jewish Council in Jerusalem and arrest by the Roman commander (on his way to Rome after the apostle's third missionary journey).

"And when we had fallen to the ground, I heard a voice saying to me in the Hebrew dialect, 'Saul, Saul, why are you persecuting Me? It is hard for you to kick against the goads.' And I said, 'Who are You, Lord?' And the Lord said, 'I am Jesus whom you are persecuting. But get up and stand on your feet; for this purpose I have appeared to you, to appoint you a minister and a witness not only to the things which you have seen, but also to the things in which I will appear to you; rescuing you from the *Jewish* people and from the Gentiles, to whom I am sending you, to open their eyes so that they may turn from darkness to light and from the dominion of Satan to God, that they may receive forgiveness of sins and an inheritance among those who have been sanctified by faith in Me' (Acts 26:14–18; see Isaiah 35:5; Acts 21:40; 22:14).

PERSECUTIONS (Also see PERSECUTE/PERSECUTED; and PERSECUTION)

Setting: Judea beyond the Jordan (Perea). After informing a rich man how righteous believers may have treasure in heaven, Jesus tells His disciples about the reward of those who sacrifice in this life to follow Him.

Jesus said, "Truly I say to you, there is no one who has left house or brothers or sisters or mother or father or children or farms, for My sake and for the gospel's sake, but that he will receive a hundred times as much now in the present age, houses and brothers and sisters and mothers and children and farms, along with persecutions; and in the age to come, eternal life. But many *who are* first will be last, and the last, first" (Mark 10:29–31; cf. Matthew 19:27–30; Luke 18:28–30; see Matthew 6:33).

PERSEVERANCE (Also see ENDURANCE)

Setting: Galilee. After Jesus presents the Parable of the Sower to the crowds, His disciples ask Him to give them the parable's meaning.

And He said, "To you it has been granted to know the mysteries of the kingdom of God, but to the rest *it is* in parables, so that SEEING THEY MAY NOT SEE, AND HEARING THEY MAY NOT UNDERSTAND. Now the parable is this: the seed is the word of God. Those beside the road are those who have heard; then the devil comes and takes away the word from their heart, so that they will not believe and be saved. Those on the rocky *soil* are those who, when they hear, receive the word with joy; and these have no *firm* root; they believe for a while, and in time of temptation fall away. The *seed* which fell among the thorns, these are the ones who have heard, and as they go on their way they are choked with worries and riches and pleasures of *this* life, and bring no fruit to maturity. But the *seed* in the good soil, these are the ones who have heard the word in an honest and good heart, and hold it fast, and bear fruit with perseverance" (Luke 8:10–15, Jesus quotes from Isaiah 6:9; cf. Matthew 13:10–23; Mark 4:10–20).

Setting: On the island of Patmos (in the Aegean Sea about fifty miles southwest of Ephesus in modern Turkey). On the Lord's Day (Sunday), approximately fifty years after the Resurrection, the disciple John encounters the Lord Jesus Christ, who communicates a new revelation for the apostle to record for the church in Ephesus and to six other churches in Asia.

"To the angel of the church in Ephesus write: The One who holds the seven stars in His right hand, the One who walks among the seven golden lampstands, says this: 'I know your deeds and your toil and perseverance, and that you cannot tolerate evil men, and you put to the test those who call themselves apostles, and they are not, and you found them *to be* false; and you have perseverance and have endured for My name's sake, and have not grown weary. But I have *this* against you, that you have left your first love. Therefore remember from where you have fallen, and repent and do the deeds you did at first; or else I am coming to you and will remove your lampstand out of its place—unless you repent. Yet this you do have, that you hate the deeds of the Nicolaitans, which I also hate. He who has an ear, let him hear what the Spirit says to the churches. To him who overcomes, I will grant to eat of the tree of life which is in the Paradise of God' " (Revelation 2:1–7; see Genesis 2:9; Ezekiel 28:13; 1 John 4:1; Revelation 1:10, 11, 19, 20).

Setting: On the island of Patmos (in the Aegean Sea about fifty miles southwest of Ephesus in modern Turkey). On the Lord's Day (Sunday), approximately fifty years after the Resurrection, the disciple John encounters the Lord Jesus Christ, who communicates a new revelation for the apostle to record for the church in Thyatira and to six other churches in Asia.

"And to the angel of the church in Thyatira write: The Son of God, who has eyes like a flame of fire, and His feet are like burnished bronze, says this: 'I know your deeds, and your love and faith and service and perseverance, and that your deeds of late are greater than at first. But I have *this* against you, that you tolerate the woman Jezebel, who calls herself a prophetess, and she teaches and leads My bond-servants astray so that they commit *acts of* immorality and eat things sacrificed to idols. I gave her time to repent, and she does not want to repent of her immorality. Behold, I will throw her on a bed *of sickness,* and those who commit adultery with her into great tribulation, unless they repent of her deeds. And I will kill her children with pestilence, and all the churches will know that I am He who searches the minds and hearts; and I will give to each one of you according to your deeds. But I say to you, the rest who are in Thyatira, who do not hold this teaching, who have not known the deep things of Satan, as they call them—I place no other burden on you. Nevertheless what you have, hold fast until I come. He who overcomes, and he who keeps My deeds until the end, TO HIM I WILL GIVE AUTHORITY OVER THE NATIONS; AND HE SHALL RULE THEM WITH A ROD OF IRON, AS THE VESSELS OF THE POTTER ARE BROKEN TO PIECES, as I also have received *authority* from My Father; and I will give him the morning star. He who has an ear, let him hear what the Spirit says to the churches' (Revelation 2:18–29; Jesus quotes from Psalm 2:8, 9; Isaiah 30:14; see 1 Kings 16:31; Psalm 7:9; Romans 2:5; 1 Corinthians 2:10; 2 Peter 3:9; Revelation 1:14; 2:7; 3:11; 17:1–20).

Setting: On the island of Patmos (in the Aegean Sea about fifty miles southwest of Ephesus in modern Turkey). On the Lord's Day (Sunday), approximately fifty years after the Resurrection, the disciple John encounters the Lord Jesus Christ, who communicates a new revelation for the apostle to record for the church in Philadelphia and to six other churches in Asia.

"And to the angel of the church in Philadelphia write: He who is holy, who is true, who has the key of David, who opens and no one will shut, and who shuts and no one opens, says this: 'I know your deeds. Behold, I have put before you an open door which no one can shut, because you have a little power, and have kept My word, and have not denied My name. Behold, I will cause *those* of the synagogue of Satan, who say that they are Jews and are not, but lie—I will make them come and bow down at your feet, and *make them* know that I have loved you. Because you have kept the word of My perseverance, I also will keep you from the hour of testing, that *hour* which is about to come upon the whole world, to test those who dwell on the earth. I am coming quickly; hold fast what you have, so that no one will take your crown. He who overcomes, I will make him a pillar in the temple of My God, and he will not go out from it anymore; and I will write on him the name of My God, and the name of the city of My God, the new Jerusalem, which comes down out of heaven from My God, and My new name. He who has an ear, let him hear what the Spirit says to the churches' " (Revelation 3:7–13; see Isaiah 22:22; Galatians 2:9; Revelation 2:9, 10, 13, 25; 14:1).

PERSISTENCE

Setting: On the way from Galilee to Jerusalem. After revealing to His disciples how to pray, Jesus illustrates persistence in prayer.

Then He said to them, "Suppose one of you has a friend, and goes to him at midnight and says to him, 'Friend, lend me three loaves; for a friend of mine has come to me from a journey, and I have nothing to set before him'; and from inside he answers and says, 'Do not bother me; the door has already been shut and my children and I are in bed; I cannot get up and give you *anything.*' I tell you, even though he will not get up and give him *anything* because he is his friend, yet because of his persistence he will get up and give him as much as he needs. So I say to you, ask, and it will be given to you; seek, and you will find; knock, and it will be opened to you. For everyone who asks, receives; and he who seeks, finds; and to him who knocks, it will be opened" (Luke 11:5–10; cf. Matthew 7:7, 8; see Luke 18:1–5).

PERSON, EVIL (Also see EVIL; and MAN, EVIL)

Setting: Galilee. During the early part of His ministry, Jesus preaches the Sermon on the Mount to His disciples and the multitudes.

"You have heard that it was said, 'AN EYE FOR AN EYE, AND A TOOTH FOR A TOOTH.' But I say to you, do not resist an evil person; but whoever slaps you on your right cheek, turn the other to him also" (Matthew 5:38, 39, Jesus quotes from Exodus 21:24; cf. Leviticus 24:20).

PERSONAL IMPACT (See TESTIMONY)

PERSONAL INFLUENCE (See TESTIMONY)

PERSONAL RESPONSIBILITY (See ACCOUNTABILITY; and STEWARDSHIP)

PERSONAL SACRIFICE (Listed under SACRIFICE, PERSONAL)

PERSONS, RIGHTEOUS (Also see RIGHTEOUS)

Setting: On the way from Galilee to Jerusalem. After Jesus presents to large crowds the demands of discipleship, the Pharisees and scribes complain He associates with tax collectors and sinners.

So He told them this parable, saying, "What man among you, if he has a hundred sheep and has lost one of them, does not leave the ninety-nine in the open pasture and go after the one which is lost until he finds it? When he has found it, he lays it on his shoulders, rejoicing. And when he comes home, he calls together his friends and his neighbors, saying to them, 'Rejoice with me, for I have found my sheep which was lost!' I tell you that in the same way, there will be *more* joy in heaven over one sinner who repents than over ninety-nine righteous persons who need no repentance" (Luke 15:3–7; cf. Matthew 18:12–14; see Matthew 9:11–13; Luke 5:29–32).

PERSUASION

[PERSUASION from persuaded]

Setting: On the way from Galilee to Jerusalem. After responding to the Pharisees' scoffing at His teaching the disciples about stewardship and the permanence of the Law, Jesus conveys the story of the rich man and Lazarus.

"Now there was a rich man, and he habitually dressed in purple and fine linen, joyously living in splendor every day. And a poor man named Lazarus was laid at his gate, covered with sores, and longing to be fed with the *crumbs* which were falling from the rich man's table; besides, even the dogs were coming and licking his sores. Now the poor man died and was carried away by the angels to Abraham's bosom; and the rich man also died and was buried. In Hades he lifted up his eyes, being in torment, and saw Abraham far away and Lazarus in his bosom. And he cried out and said, 'Father Abraham, have mercy on me, and send Lazarus so that he may dip the tip of his finger in water and cool off my tongue, for I am in agony in this flame.' But Abraham said, 'Child, remember that during your life you received your good things, and likewise Lazarus bad things; but now he is being comforted here, and you are in agony. And besides all this, between us and you there is a great chasm fixed, so that those who wish to come over from here to you will not be able, and *that* none may cross over from there to us.' And he said, 'Then I beg you, father, that you send him to my father's house—for I have five brothers—in order that he may warn them, so that they will not also come to this place of torment.' But Abraham said, 'They have Moses and the Prophets; let them hear them.' But he said, 'No, father Abraham, but if someone goes to them from the dead, they will repent!' But he said to him, 'If they do not listen to Moses and the Prophets, they will not be persuaded even if someone rises from the dead.'" (Luke 16:19–31; see Luke 3:8; 6:24; 16:1, 14)

PESTILENCE

Setting: On the island of Patmos (in the Aegean Sea about fifty miles southwest of Ephesus in modern Turkey). On the Lord's Day (Sunday), approximately fifty years after the Resurrection, the disciple John encounters the Lord Jesus Christ, who communicates a new revelation for the apostle to record for the church in Thyatira and to six other churches in Asia.

"And to the angel of the church in Thyatira write: The Son of God, who has eyes like a flame of fire, and His feet are like burnished bronze, says this: 'I know your deeds, and your love and faith and service and perseverance, and that your deeds of late are greater than at first. But I have *this* against you, that you tolerate the woman Jezebel, who calls herself a prophetess, and she teaches and leads My bond-servants astray so that they commit *acts of* immorality and eat things sacrificed to idols. I gave her time to repent, and she does not want to repent of her immorality. Behold, I will throw her on a bed *of sickness,* and those who commit adultery with her into great tribulation, unless they repent of her deeds. And I will kill her children with pestilence, and all the churches will know that I am He who searches the minds and hearts; and I will give to each one of you according to your deeds. But I say to you, the rest who are in Thyatira, who do not hold this teaching, who have not known the deep things of Satan, as they call them—I place no other burden on you. Nevertheless what you have, hold fast until I come. He who overcomes, and he who keeps My deeds until the end, TO HIM I WILL GIVE AUTHORITY OVER THE NATIONS; AND HE SHALL RULE THEM WITH A ROD OF IRON, AS THE VESSELS OF THE POTTER ARE BROKEN TO PIECES, as I also have received *authority* from My Father; and I will give him the morning star. He who has an ear, let him hear what the Spirit says to the churches' (Revelation 2:18–29; Jesus quotes from Psalm 2:8, 9; Isaiah 30:14; see 1 Kings 16:31; Psalm 7:9; Romans 2:5; 1 Corinthians 2:10; 2 Peter 3:9; Revelation 1:14; 2:7; 3:11; 17:1–20).

PETER (Also see CEPHAS; SIMON; and SIMON BARJONA)

Setting: Caesarea Philippi. Jesus responds to Simon Peter's declaration that He is the Christ, the Son of the living God.

And Jesus said to him, "Blessed are you, Simon Barjona, because flesh and blood did not reveal *this* to you, but My Father who is in heaven. I also say to you that you are Peter, and upon this rock I will build My church; and the gates of Hades will not overpower it. I will give you the keys of the kingdom of heaven; and whatever you bind on earth shall have been bound in heaven, and whatever you loose on earth shall have been loosed in heaven" (Matthew 16:17–19; cf. Matthew 18:18; Mark 8:29; Luke 9:20).

Setting: Jerusalem. During the Feast of Unleavened Bread (Passover) just before His crucifixion, Jesus celebrates the Passover meal with His disciples and institutes the Lord's Supper. The disciples argue over who is the greatest among them, and Jesus prophesies Peter's three denials of Him.

"Simon, Simon, behold, Satan has demanded *permission* to sift you like wheat; but I have prayed for you, that your faith may not fail; and you, when once you have turned again, strengthen your brothers." But he said to Him, "Lord, with You I am ready to go both to prison and to death!" And He said, "I say to you, Peter, the rooster will not crow today until you have denied three times that you know Me" (Luke 22:31–34; cf. Matthew 26:33–35; John 13:36–38; see Job 1:6–12; John 17:15).

PETER'S DECLARATION OF JESUS AS THE CHRIST

[PETER'S DECLARATION OF JESUS AS THE CHRIST from Blessed are you, Simon Barjona, because flesh and blood did not reveal *this* to you, but My Father who is in heaven]

Setting: Caesarea Philippi. Jesus responds to Simon Peter's declaration that He is the Christ, the Son of the living God.

And Jesus said to him, "Blessed are you, Simon Barjona, because flesh and blood did not reveal *this* to you, but My Father who is in heaven. I also say to you that you are Peter, and upon this rock I will build My church; and the gates of Hades will not overpower it. I will give you the keys of the kingdom of heaven; and whatever you bind on earth shall have been bound in heaven, and whatever you loose on earth shall have been loosed in heaven" (Matthew 16:17–19; cf. Matthew 18:18; Mark 8:29 and Luke 9:20; see Matthew 16:13–16).

PETER'S DENIAL (Also see PROPHECY OF PETER'S DENIAL)

[PETER'S DENIAL from Before a rooster crows, you will deny Me three times]

Setting: Jerusalem. As Jesus appears before Caiaphas the high priest and the Council for interrogation for the purpose of entrapping Him, Peter, while sitting outside in the courtyard, denies knowing Jesus, fulfilling Jesus' earlier prophecy.

And Peter remembered the word which Jesus had said, "Before a rooster crows, you will deny Me three times." And he went out and wept bitterly (Matthew 26:75; cf. Matthew 26:34; Mark 14:72; Luke 22:61; John 18:25–27).

[PETER'S DENIAL from Before a rooster crows twice, you will deny Me three times]

Setting: The courtyard of Caiaphas the high priest in Jerusalem. While Jesus is being falsely accused before the chief priests and the whole Council, Peter denies he knows Jesus, then remembers his Lord's statement that he would deny him three times before a rooster crowed twice.

Immediately a rooster crowed a second time. And Peter remembered how Jesus had made the remark to him, "Before a rooster crows twice, you will deny Me three times." And he began to weep (Mark 14:72; cf. Matthew 26:75; Luke 22:61; John 18:26, 27; see Mark 14:30, 68).

[PETER'S DENIAL from Before a rooster crows today, you will deny Me three times]

Setting: Jerusalem, in the courtyard of the high priest. After Jesus' arrest by His enemies, Peter recalls Jesus' prophecy when the Lord turns and looks at him following his third denial and the crowing of a rooster.

The Lord turned and looked at Peter. And Peter remembered the word of the Lord, how He had told him, "Before a rooster crows today, you will deny Me three times" (Luke 22:61; cf. Matthew 26:75; Luke 14:72; John 18:26, 27; see Luke 22:34).

PETER'S RESTORATION

[PETER'S RESTORATION from context]

Setting: By the Sea of Galilee. During His third appearance to His disciples after His resurrection from the dead in Jerusalem, Jesus quizzes Peter three times regarding the disciple's love for Him.

So when they had finished breakfast, Jesus said to Simon Peter, "Simon, *son* of John, do you love Me more than these?" He said to Him, "Yes, Lord; You know that I love You." He said to him, "Tend My lambs." He said to him again a second time, "Simon, *son* of John, do you love Me?" He said to Him, "Yes, Lord; You know that I love You." He said to him, Shepherd My sheep." He said to him the third time, "Simon, *son* of John, do you love Me?" Peter was grieved because He said to him the third time, "Do you love Me?" And he said to Him, "Lord, You know all things; You know that I love You." Jesus said to him, "Tend My sheep" (John 21:15–17; see Matthew 26:33; Mark 14:29).

PHARISEE (PHARISEE, BLIND is a separate entry; also see ELDERS; PHARISEES; SADDUCEES; and SCRIBES)

Setting: On the way from Galilee to Jerusalem. After instructing His disciples about persistence in prayer, Jesus conveys a parable about self-righteousness.

And He also told this parable to some people who trusted in themselves that they were righteous, and viewed others with contempt: "Two men went up into the temple to pray, one a Pharisee and the other a tax collector. The Pharisee stood and was praying this to himself: 'God, I thank You that I am not like other people: swindlers, unjust, adulterers, or even like this tax collector. I fast twice a week; I pay tithes of all that I get.' But the tax collector, standing some distance away, was even unwilling to lift up his eyes to heaven, but was beating his breast, saying, 'God, be merciful to me, the sinner!' I tell you, this man went to his house justified rather than the other; for everyone who exalts himself will be humbled, but he who humbles himself will be exalted" (Luke 18:9–14; see Ezra 9:6; Matthew 6:5, 23:12; Luke 11:42, 16:15; Romans 14:3, 10).

PHARISEE, BLIND

Setting: The temple in Jerusalem. After the Jewish religious leaders test Him with questions, Jesus pronounces the sixth of eight woes upon them in front of the crowds and His disciples.

"Woe to you, scribes and Pharisees, hypocrites! For you clean the outside of the cup and of the dish, but inside they are full of robbery and self-indulgence. You blind Pharisee, first clean the inside of the cup and of the dish, so that the outside of it may become clean also" (Matthew 23:25, 26; see Mark 7:4).

PHARISEES (PHARISEES, LEAVEN OF THE is a separate entry; also, see CHIEF PRIESTS; ELDERS; HYPOCRITES; PHARISEE; SADDUCEES; and SCRIBES)

Setting: Galilee. During the early part of His ministry, Jesus preaches the Sermon on the Mount to His disciples and the multitudes.

"For I say to you that unless your righteousness surpasses *that* of the scribes and Pharisees, you will not enter the kingdom of heaven." (Matthew 5:20; cf. Luke 18:11, 12).

Setting: The temple in Jerusalem. Jesus exposes the truth about Pharisaism to the crowds and His disciples after the Jewish religious leaders test Him with questions.

Then Jesus spoke to the crowds and to His disciples, saying: "The scribes and the Pharisees have seated themselves in the chair of Moses; therefore all that they tell you, do and observe, but do not do according to their deeds; for they say *things* and do not do *them.* They tie up heavy burdens and lay them on men's shoulders, but they themselves are unwilling to move them with *so much as* a finger. But they do all their deeds to be noticed by men; for they broaden their phylacteries and lengthen their tassels *of their garments.* They love the place of honor at banquets and the chief seats in the synagogues, and respectful greetings in the market places, and being called Rabbi by men. But do not be called Rabbi; for One is your Teacher, and you are all brothers. Do not call *anyone* on earth your father; for One is your Father, He who is in heaven. Do not be called leaders; for One is your Leader, *that is,* Christ. But the greatest among you shall be your servant. Whoever exalts himself shall be humbled; and whoever humbles himself shall be exalted" (Matthew 23:1–12; cf. Matthew 20:26; Mark 12:38–40; Luke 20:46, 47; see Exodus 13:9; Deuteronomy 33:3; Matthew 6:1, 5, 6, 9, 16; Mark 14:11; Luke 11:43; 14:11).

Setting: The temple in Jerusalem. After the Jewish religious leaders test Him with questions, Jesus pronounces the first of eight woes upon them in front of the crowds and His disciples.

"But woe to you, scribes and Pharisees, hypocrites, because you shut off the kingdom of heaven from people; for you do not enter in yourselves, nor do you allow those who are entering to go in (Matthew 23:13; cf. Luke 11:52).

Setting: The temple in Jerusalem. After the Jewish religious leaders test Him with questions, Jesus pronounces the second of eight woes upon them in front of the crowds and His disciples.

["Woe to you, scribes and Pharisees, hypocrites, because you devour widows' houses, and for a pretense you make long prayers; therefore you will receive greater condemnation] (Matthew 23:14; cf. Mark 12:40; Luke 20:47).

Setting: The temple in Jerusalem. After the Jewish religious leaders test Him with questions, Jesus pronounces the third of eight woes upon them in front of the crowds and His disciples.

"Woe to you, scribes and Pharisees, hypocrites, because you travel around on sea and land to make one proselyte; and when he becomes one, you make him twice as much a son of hell as yourselves" (Matthew 23:15).

Setting: The temple in Jerusalem. After the Jewish religious leaders test Him with questions, Jesus pronounces the fifth of eight woes upon them in front of the crowds and His disciples.

"Woe to you, scribes and Pharisees, hypocrites! For you tithe mint and dill and cummin, and have neglected the weightier provisions of the law: justice and mercy and faithfulness; but these are things you should have done without neglecting the others. You blind guides, who strain out a gnat and swallow a camel!" (Matthew 23:23, 24).

Setting: The temple in Jerusalem. After the Jewish religious leaders test Him with questions, Jesus pronounces the sixth of eight woes upon them in front of the crowds and His disciples.

"Woe to you, scribes and Pharisees, hypocrites! For you clean the outside of the cup and of the dish, but inside they are full of robbery and self-indulgence. You blind Pharisee, first clean the inside of the cup and of the dish, so that the outside of it may become clean also" (Matthew 23:25, 26; see Mark 7:4).

Setting: The temple in Jerusalem. After the Jewish religious leaders test Him with questions, Jesus pronounces the seventh of eight woes upon them in front of the crowds and His disciples.

"Woe to you, scribes and Pharisees, hypocrites! For you are like whitewashed tombs which on the outside appear beautiful, but inside they are full of dead men's bones and all uncleanness. So you, too, outwardly appear righteous to men, but inwardly you are full of hypocrisy and lawlessness" (Matthew 23:27, 28; cf. Luke 11:44).

Setting: The temple in Jerusalem. After the Jewish religious leaders test Him with questions, Jesus pronounces the eighth of eight woes upon them in front of the crowds and His disciples.

"Woe to you, scribes and Pharisees, hypocrites! For you build the tombs of the prophets and adorn the monuments of the righteous, and say, 'If we had been *living* in the days of our fathers, we would not have been partners with them in *shedding* the blood of the prophets.' So you testify against yourselves, that you are sons of those who murdered the prophets. Fill up, then, the measure *of the guilt* of you fathers. You serpents, you brood of vipers, how will you escape the sentence of hell? Therefore, behold, I am sending you prophets and wise men and scribes; some of them you will kill and crucify, and some of them you will scourge in your synagogues, and persecute from city to city, so that upon you may fall *the guilt of* all the righteous blood shed on earth, from the blood of righteous Abel to the blood of Zechariah, the son of Berechiah, whom you murdered between the temple and the altar. Truly I say to you, all these things will come upon this generation" (Matthew 23:29–36; cf. 2 Chronicles 24:21; Zechariah 1:1; Matthew 3:7; Luke 11:47–52; see Matthew 10:23).

Setting: On the way from Galilee to Jerusalem. After speaking of how a lamp illuminates, the Lord has lunch with a Pharisee who is surprised He doesn't wash before eating.

But the Lord said to him, "Now you Pharisees clean the outside of the cup and of the platter; but inside of you, you are full of robbery and wickedness. You foolish ones, did not He who made the outside make the inside also? But give that which is within as charity, and then all things are clean for you. But woe to you Pharisees! You pay tithe of mint and rue and every *kind of* garden herb, and *yet* disregard justice and the love of God; but these are the things you should have done without neglecting the others. Woe to you Pharisees! For you love the chief seats in the synagogues and the respectful greetings in the market places. Woe to you! For you are like concealed tombs, and the people who walk over *them* are unaware *of it*" (Luke 11:39–44; cf. Matthew 23:6, 7, 23–27; see Matthew 15:2; Titus 1:15).

PHARISEES, LEAVEN OF THE

Setting: Across the Sea of Galilee from Magadan. Jesus warns His disciples about the teaching of some of the religious leaders of His time—the Pharisees and the Sadducees.

And Jesus said to them, "Watch out and beware of the leaven of the Pharisees and Sadducees" (Matthew 16:6; cf. Matthew 16:12; Mark 8:15).

Setting: By the Sea of Galilee. Jesus repeats a warning to His disciples about the teaching of the religious leaders of His time—the Pharisees and the Sadducees.

But Jesus aware of this, said, "You men of little faith, why do you discuss among yourselves that you have no bread? Do you not yet understand or remember the five loaves of the five thousand and how many baskets *full* you picked up? Or the seven loaves of the four thousand, and how many large baskets *full* you picked up? How is it that you do not understand that I did not speak to you concerning bread? But beware of the leaven of the Pharisees and Sadducees" (Matthew 16:8–11; cf. Matthew 14:17–21; 15:34–38; Mark 8:17–21).

Setting: The district of Dalmanutha. After the Pharisees argue with Him, seeking a sign from heaven to test Him, Jesus warns His disciples about them.

And He was giving orders to them, saying, "Watch out! Beware of the leaven of the Pharisees and the leaven of Herod" (Mark 8:15; cf. Matthew 16:5–7).

Setting: On the way from Galilee to Jerusalem. Jesus warns His disciples of future events, as the scribes and Pharisees turn hostile and question Him repeatedly in an attempt to catch Him in something He might say.

Under these circumstances, after so many thousands of people had gathered together that they were stepping on one another, He began saying to His disciples first *of all,* "Beware of the leaven of the Pharisees, which is hypocrisy. But there is nothing covered up that will not be revealed, and hidden that will not be known. Accordingly, whatever you have said in the dark will be heard in the light, and what you have whispered in the inner rooms will be proclaimed upon the housetops. I say to you, My friends, do not be afraid of those who kill the body and after that have no more that they can do. But I will warn you whom to fear: fear the One who, after He has killed, has authority to cast into hell; yes, I tell you, fear Him! Are not five sparrows sold for two cents? *Yet* not one of them is forgotten before God. Indeed, the very hairs of your head are all numbered. Do not fear; you are more valuable than many sparrows" (Luke 12:1–7; cf. Matthew 10:26–31; see Matthew 16:6; Hebrews 10:31).

PHILADELPHIA

Setting: On the island of Patmos (in the Aegean Sea about fifty miles southwest of Ephesus in modern Turkey). On the Lord's Day (Sunday), approximately fifty years after the Resurrection, the disciple John encounters the Lord Jesus Christ, who communicates new revelations for the apostle to record for the seven churches in Asia.

I was in the Spirit on the Lord's day, and I heard behind me a loud voice like *the sound* of a trumpet, saying, "Write in a book what you see, and send *it* to the seven churches: to Ephesus and to Smyrna and to Pergamum and to Thyatira and to Sardis and to Philadelphia and to Laodicea" (Revelation 1:10, 11).

Setting: On the island of Patmos (in the Aegean Sea about fifty miles southwest of Ephesus in modern Turkey). On the Lord's Day (Sunday), approximately fifty years after the Resurrection, the disciple John encounters the Lord Jesus Christ, who communicates a new revelation for the apostle to record for the church in Philadelphia and to six other churches in Asia.

"And to the angel of the church in Philadelphia write: He who is holy, who is true, who has the key of David, who opens and no one will shut, and who shuts and no one opens, says this: 'I know your deeds. Behold, I have put before you an open door which no one can shut, because you have a little power, and have kept My word, and have not denied My name. Behold, I will cause *those* of the synagogue of Satan, who say that they are Jews and are not, but lie—I will make them come and bow down at your feet, and *make them* know that I have loved you. Because you have kept the word of My perseverance, I also will keep you from the hour of testing, that *hour* which is about to come upon the whole world, to test those who dwell on the earth. I am coming quickly; hold fast what you have, so that no one will take your crown. He who overcomes, I will make him a pillar in the temple of My God, and he will not go out from it anymore; and I will write on him the name of My God, and the name of the city of My God, the new Jerusalem, which comes down out of heaven from My God, and My new name. He who has an ear, let him hear what the Spirit says to the churches' " (Revelation 3:7–13; see Isaiah 22:22; Galatians 2:9; Revelation 2:9, 10, 13, 25; 14:1).

PHILIP

Setting: Galilee. After beginning His public ministry and choosing His first disciples, Andrew and Simon (Peter) near Bethany beyond the Jordan, and Philip in Galilee, Jesus calls Philip's friend, Nathanael, (some believe he may have been also called Bartholomew) as His next follower.

Jesus saw Nathanael coming to Him, and said of him, "Behold, an Israelite indeed, in whom there is no deceit!" Nathanael said to Him, "How do you know me?" Jesus answered and said to him, "Before Philip called you, when you were under the fig tree, I saw you." Nathanael answered Him, "Rabbi, You are the Son of God; You are the King of Israel." Jesus answered and said to him, "Because I said to you that I saw you under the fig tree, do you believe? You will see greater things than these." And He said to him, "Truly, truly, I say to you, you will see the heavens opened and the angels of God ascending and descending on the Son of Man" (John 1:47–51).

Setting: Jerusalem. Before the Passover, after answering Thomas' question about where He is going and how His disciples will know the way, Jesus responds to Philip's request for Him to show them the Father.

Jesus said to him, "Have I been so long with you, and *yet* you have not come to know Me, Philip? He who has seen Me has seen the Father; how *can* you say, 'Show us the Father'? Do you not believe that I am in the Father, and the Father is in Me? The words that I say to you I do not speak on My own initiative, but the Father abiding in Me does His works. Believe Me that I am in the Father and the Father is in Me; otherwise believe because of the works themselves. Truly, truly, I say to you, he who believes in Me, the works that I do, he will do also; and greater *works* than these he will do; because I go to the Father. Whatever you ask in My name, that will I do, so that the Father may be glorified in the Son. If you ask Me anything in My name, I will do *it*" (John 14:9–14; see Matthew 7:7; John 1:14; 5:19, 20, 36; 10:37, 38; 15:16).

PHYLACTERIES

Setting: The temple in Jerusalem. Jesus exposes the truth about Pharisaism to the crowds and His disciples after the Jewish religious leaders test Him with questions.

Then Jesus spoke to the crowds and to His disciples, saying: "The scribes and the Pharisees have seated themselves in the chair of Moses; therefore all that they tell you, do and observe, but do not do according to their deeds; for they say *things* and do not do *them.* They tie up heavy burdens and lay them on men's shoulders, but they themselves are unwilling to move them with *so much as* a finger. But they do all their deeds to be noticed by men; for they broaden their phylacteries and lengthen their tassels *of their garments.* They love the place of honor at banquets and the chief seats in the synagogues, and respectful greetings in the market places, and being called Rabbi by men. But do not be called Rabbi; for One is your Teacher, and you are all brothers. Do not call *anyone* on earth your father; for One is your Father, He who is in heaven. Do not be called leaders; for One is your Leader, *that is,* Christ. But the greatest among you shall be your servant. Whoever exalts himself shall be humbled; and whoever humbles himself shall be exalted" (Matthew 23:1–12; cf. Matthew 20:26; Mark 12:38–40; Luke 20:46, 47; see Exodus 13:9; Deuteronomy 33:3; Matthew 6:1, 5, 6, 9, 16; Mark 14:11; Luke 11:43; 14:11).

PHYSICIAN

Setting: Capernaum, near the Sea of Galilee. Jesus calls Matthew from his tax-collection booth to be His disciple.

But when Jesus heard *this,* He said, "*It is* not those who are healthy who need a physician, but those who are sick. But go and learn what this means: 'I DESIRE COMPASSION, AND NOT SACRIFICE,' for I did not come to call the righteous, but sinners" (Matthew 9:12, 13, Jesus quotes from Hosea 6:6; cf. Mark 2:17; Luke 5:31, 32; see Mark 2:15, 16).

Setting: The home of Levi (Matthew) the tax collector in Capernaum, near the Sea of Galilee. The scribes of the Pharisees take issue with Jesus' association with sinners and tax collectors after He calls Levi (Matthew) the tax collector to be His disciple.

And hearing *this,* Jesus said to them, "*It is* not those who are healthy who need a physician, but those who are sick; I did not come to call the righteous, but sinners" (Mark 2:17; cf. Matthew 9:12, 13; Luke 5:29–32).

Setting: The synagogue in Jesus' hometown of Nazareth in Galilee. At the beginning of His public ministry, Jesus comments to the congregation after reading on the Sabbath from the book of the prophet Isaiah.

And He said to them, "No doubt you will quote this proverb to Me, 'Physician, heal yourself! Whatever we heard was done at Capernaum, do here in your hometown as well.'" And He said, "Truly I say to you, no prophet is welcome in his hometown. But I say to you in truth, there were many widows in Israel in the days of Elijah, when the sky was shut up for three years and six months, when a great famine came over all the land; and yet Elijah was sent to none of them, but only to Zarephath, *in the land* of Sidon, to a woman who was a widow. And there were many lepers in Israel in the time of Elisha the prophet; and none of them was cleansed, but only Naaman the Syrian" (Luke 4:23–27; Jesus refers to 1 Kings 17:1, 9; 2 Kings 5:1–14; see Matthew 13:53–58).

Setting: The house of Levi (Matthew) in Capernaum. At a reception after Jesus calls Matthew to be His disciple, the Pharisees and their scribes question why the Lord associates with tax collectors and sinners.

And Jesus answered and said to them, "*It is* not those who are well who need a physician, but those who are sick. I have not come to call the righteous but sinners to repentance" (Luke 5:31, 32; cf. Matthew 9:10–13; Mark 2:15–17).

PIECE (Also see PIECES)

Setting: The home of Levi (Matthew) in Capernaum. At a reception for Jesus following Levi's call to be a disciple, the Lord tells a parable to the Pharisees and their scribes, who question His association with tax collectors and sinners.

And He was also telling them a parable: "No one tears a piece of cloth from a new garment and puts it on an old garment; otherwise he will both tear the new, and the piece from the new will not match the old. And no one puts new wine into old wineskins; otherwise the new wine will burst the skins and it will be spilled out, and the skins will be ruined. But new wine must be put into fresh wineskins. And no one, after drinking old *wine* wishes for new; for he says, 'The old is good *enough*'" (Luke 5:36–39; cf. Matthew 9:16, 17; Mark 2:21, 22).

Setting: On the way from Galilee to Jerusalem. After speaking a parable to the invited guests and the host at a banquet, Jesus responds to a guest's proclamation about the blessings of eating bread in the kingdom of God.

But He said to him, "A man was giving a big dinner, and he invited many; and at the dinner hour he sent his slave to say to those who had been invited, 'Come; for everything is ready now.' But they all alike began to make excuses. The first one said to him, 'I have bought a piece of land and I need to go out and look at it; please consider me excused.' Another one said, 'I have bought five yoke of oxen, and I am going to try them out; please consider me excused.' Another one said, I have married a wife, and for that reason I cannot come.' And the slave came *back* and reported this to his master. Then the head of the household became angry and said to his slave, 'Go out at once into the streets and lanes of the city and bring in here the poor and crippled and blind and lame.' And the slave said, 'Master, what you commanded has been done, and still there is room.' And the master said to the slave, 'Go out into the highways and along the hedges, and compel *them* to come in, so that my house may be filled. For I tell you, none of those men who were invited shall taste of my dinner'" (Luke 14:16–24; see Deuteronomy 24:5; Matthew 22:2–14).

PIECES (PIECES, BROKEN; and PIECES, BROKEN TO are separate entries; also see PIECE)

Setting: Galilee. During the early part of His ministry, Jesus preaches the Sermon on the Mount to His disciples and the multitudes.

"Do not give what is holy to dogs, and do not throw your pearls before swine, or they will trample them under their feet, and turn and tear you to pieces" (Matthew 7:6; see Matthew 15:26).

Setting: On the Mount of Olives, just east of Jerusalem. During His Olivet Discourse, after answering His disciples' questions as to when the temple will be destroyed and Jerusalem overrun, along with the signs of His coming and the end of the age, Jesus reemphasizes to His disciples that they should be on the alert for His return.

"Therefore be on the alert, for you do not know which day your Lord is coming. But be sure of this, that if the head of the house had known at what time of the night the thief was coming, he would have been on the alert and would not have allowed his house to be broken into. For this reason you also must be ready; for the Son of Man is coming at an hour when you do not think *He will.* Who then is the faithful and sensible slave whom his master put in charge of his household to give their food at the proper time? Blessed is that slave whom his master finds so doing when he comes. Truly I say to you that he will put him in charge of all his possessions. But if that evil slave says in his heart, 'My master is not coming for a long time,' and begins to beat his fellow slaves and eat and drink with drunkards; the master of that slave will come on a day when he does not expect *him* and at an hour which he does not know, and will cut him in pieces and assign him a place with the hypocrites; in that place there will be weeping and gnashing of teeth" (Matthew 24:42–51; cf. Mark 13:33–37; Luke 12:39–46; 21:34–36; see Matthew 8:11, 12; 25:21–23).

Setting: On the way from Galilee to Jerusalem. When Jesus uses a parable to challenge the crowd and His disciples to be ready for His return, Peter asks Him whom He is addressing.

And the Lord said, "Who then is the faithful and sensible steward, whom his master will put in charge of his servants, to give them their rations at the proper time? Blessed is that slave whom his master finds so doing when he comes. Truly I say to you that he will put him in charge of all his possessions. But if that slave says in his heart, 'My master will be a long time in coming,' and begins to beat the slaves, *both* men and women, and to eat and drink and get drunk; the master of that slave will come on a day when he does not expect *him* and at an hour he does not know, and will cut him in pieces, and assign him a place with the unbelievers. And that slave who knew his master's will and did not get ready or act in accord with his will, will receive many lashes, but the one who did know *it,* and committed deeds worthy of flogging, will receive but few. From everyone who has been given much, much will be required; and to whom they entrusted much, of him they will ask all the more" (Luke 12:42–48; cf. Matthew 24:45–51; see Leviticus 5:17).

PIECES, BROKEN (Also see PIECES, BROKEN TO)

Setting: The district of Dalmanutha. After the Pharisees argue with Jesus, seeking a sign from heaven to test Him, the Lord and His disciples cross to the other side of the Sea of Galilee, where the disciples discuss with one another that they have no bread.

And Jesus, aware of this, said to them, "Why do you discuss *the fact* that you have no bread? Do you not yet see or understand? Do you have a hardened heart? HAVING EYES, DO YOU NOT SEE? AND HAVING EARS, DO YOU NOT HEAR? And do you not remember, when I broke the five loaves for the five thousand, how many baskets full of broken pieces you picked you? They said to Him, "Twelve." When *I broke* the seven for the four thousand, how many large baskets full of broken pieces did you pick up?" They said to Him, "Seven." And He was saying to them, "Do you not yet understand?" (Mark 8:17–21, Jesus quotes from Jeremiah 5:21; cf. Matthew 16:5–12; see Matthew 14:19, 20; Mark 6:41–44, 52; 8:6–9).

PIECES, BROKEN TO (Also see PIECES, BROKEN)

Setting: The temple in Jerusalem. Jesus delivers a prophecy to the chief priests and elders after they question His authority.

Jesus said to them, "Did you never read in the Scriptures, 'THE STONE WHICH THE BUILDERS REJECTED, THIS BECAME THE CHIEF CORNER *stone;* THIS CAME ABOUT FROM THE LORD, AND IT IS MARVELOUS IN OUR EYES'? Therefore I say to you, the kingdom of God will be taken away from you and given to a people, producing the fruit of it. And he who falls on this stone will be broken to pieces; but on whomever it falls, it will scatter him like dust" (Matthew 21:42–44, Jesus quotes from Psalm 118:22; cf. Isaiah 8:14, 15; Mark 12:10, 11; Luke 20:17, 18).

Setting: The temple in Jerusalem. While ministering a few days before His crucifixion, after the chief priests and scribes question His authority to teach and preach, Jesus conveys the Parable of the Vine-Growers to the people.

And He began to tell the people this parable: "A man planted a vineyard and rented it out to vine-growers, and went on a journey for a long time. At the *harvest* time he sent a slave to the vine-growers, so that they would give him *some* of the produce of the vineyard; but the vine-growers beat him and sent him away empty-handed. And he proceeded to send another slave; and they beat him also and treated him shamefully and sent him away empty-handed. And he proceeded to send a third; and this one also they wounded and cast out. The owner of the vineyard said, 'What shall I do? I will send my beloved son; perhaps they will respect him.' But when the vine-growers saw him, they reasoned with one another, saying, 'This is the heir; let us kill him so that the inheritance will be ours.' So they threw him out of the vineyard and killed him. What, then, will the owner of the vineyard do to them? He will come and destroy these vine-growers and will give the vineyard to others." When they heard it, they said, "May it never be!" But Jesus looked at them and said, "What then is this that is written: 'THE STONE WHICH THE BUILDERS REJECTED, THIS BECAME THE CHIEF CORNER *stone*'? Everyone who falls on that stone will be broken to pieces; but on whomever it falls, it will scatter him like dust" (Luke 20:9–18, Jesus quotes from Psalm 118:22; cf. Matthew 21:33–44; Mark 12:1–11; see Ephesians 2:20).

Setting: On the island of Patmos (in the Aegean Sea about fifty miles southwest of Ephesus in modern Turkey). On the Lord's Day (Sunday), approximately fifty years after the Resurrection, the disciple John encounters the Lord Jesus Christ, who communicates a new revelation for the apostle to record for the church in Thyatira and to six other churches in Asia.

"And to the angel of the church in Thyatira write: The Son of God, who has eyes like a flame of fire, and His feet are like burnished bronze, says this: 'I know your deeds, and your love and faith and service and perseverance, and that your deeds of late are greater than at first. But I have *this* against you, that you tolerate the woman Jezebel, who calls herself a prophetess, and she teaches and leads My bond-servants astray so that they commit *acts of* immorality and eat things sacrificed to idols. I gave her time to repent, and she does not want to repent of her immorality. Behold, I will throw her on a bed *of sickness,* and those who commit adultery with her into great tribulation, unless they repent of her deeds. And I will kill her children with pestilence, and all the churches will know that I am He who searches the minds and hearts; and I will give to each one of you according to your deeds. But I say to you, the rest who are in Thyatira, who do not hold this teaching, who have not known the deep things of Satan, as they call them—I place no other burden on you. Nevertheless what you have, hold fast until I come. He who overcomes, and he who keeps My deeds until the end, TO HIM I WILL GIVE AUTHORITY OVER THE NATIONS; AND HE SHALL RULE THEM WITH A ROD OF IRON, AS THE VESSELS OF THE POTTER ARE BROKEN TO PIECES, as I also have received *authority* from My Father; and I will give him the morning star. He who has an ear, let him hear what the Spirit says to the churches' (Revelation 2:18–29; Jesus quotes from Psalm 2:8, 9; Isaiah 30:14; see 1 Kings 16:31; Psalm 7:9; Romans 2:5; 1 Corinthians 2:10; 2 Peter 3:9; Revelation 1:14; 2:7; 3:11; 17:1–20).

PIGS (See SWINE)

PILATE (See GOVERNORS)

PILE, MANURE (Also see FERTILIZER)

Setting: On the way from Galilee to Jerusalem. After He responds to a guest's proclamation about the blessings of eating bread in the kingdom of God, Jesus presents to large crowds the demands of discipleship.

Now large crowds were going along with Him; and He turned and said to them, "If anyone comes to Me, and does not hate his own father and mother and wife and children and brothers and sisters, yes, and even his own life, he cannot be My disciple. Whoever does not carry his own cross and come after Me cannot be My disciple. For which one of you, when he wants to build a tower, does not first sit down and calculate the cost to see if he has enough to complete it? Otherwise, when he has laid a foundation and is not able to finish, all who observe it begin to ridicule him, saying, 'This man began to build and was not able to finish.' Or what king, when he sets out to meet another king in battle, will not first sit down and consider whether he is strong enough with ten thousand *men* to encounter the one coming against him with twenty thousand? Or else, while the other is still far away, he sends a delegation and asks for terms of peace. So then, none of you can be My disciple who does not give up all his possessions.

Therefore, salt is good; but if even salt has become tasteless, with what will it be seasoned? It is useless either for the soil or for the manure pile; it is thrown out. He who has ears to hear, let him hear" (Luke 14:25–35; cf. Matthew 5:13; 10:37–39; see Proverb 20:18; Philippians 3:7).

PILLAR

Setting: On the island of Patmos (in the Aegean Sea about fifty miles southwest of Ephesus in modern Turkey). On the Lord's Day (Sunday), approximately fifty years after the Resurrection, the disciple John encounters the Lord Jesus Christ, who communicates a new revelation for the apostle to record for the church in Philadelphia and to six other churches in Asia.

"And to the angel of the church in Philadelphia write: He who is holy, who is true, who has the key of David, who opens and no one will shut, and who shuts and no one opens, says this: 'I know your deeds. Behold, I have put before you an open door which no one can shut, because you have a little power, and have kept My word, and have not denied My name. Behold, I will cause *those* of the synagogue of Satan, who say that they are Jews and are not, but lie—I will make them come and bow down at your feet, and *make them* know that I have loved you. Because you have kept the word of My perseverance, I also will keep you from the hour of testing, that *hour* which is about to come upon the whole world, to test those who dwell on the earth. I am coming quickly; hold fast what you have, so that no one will take your crown. He who overcomes, I will make him a pillar in the temple of My God, and he will not go out from it anymore; and I will write on him the name of My God, and the name of the city of My God, the new Jerusalem, which comes down out of heaven from My God, and My new name. He who has an ear, let him hear what the Spirit says to the churches' " (Revelation 3:7–13; see Isaiah 22:22; Galatians 2:9; Revelation 2:9, 10, 13, 25; 14:1).

PIT

Setting: A synagogue in Galilee. Jesus answers questions posed by the Pharisees about the Sabbath.

And He said to them, "What man is there among you who has a sheep, and if it falls into a pit on the Sabbath, will he not take hold of it and lift it out? How much more valuable then is a man than a sheep! So then, it is lawful to do good on the Sabbath." Then He said to the man, "Stretch out your hand!" He stretched it out, and it was restored to normal, like the other (Matthew 12:11–13; cf. Matthew 10:31; Mark 3:4, 5; Luke 6:9, 10; Luke 14:5; see Matthew 8:3).

Setting: Galilee. After rebuking the Pharisees and scribes for questioning His disciples' obedience to tradition and the commandments, Jesus instructs the disciples.

But He answered and said, "Every plant which My heavenly Father did not plant shall be uprooted. Let them alone; they are blind guides of the blind. And if a blind man guides a blind man, both will fall into a pit" (Matthew 15:13, 14; cf. Matthew 23:16; Luke 6:39).

Setting: Galilee. After selecting His twelve disciples, Jesus teaches the Sermon on the Mount to those disciples and a great throng of people from Judea, Jerusalem, and the central coastal region of Tyre and Sidon.

And He also spoke a parable to them: "A blind man cannot guide a blind man, can he? Will they not both fall into a pit? A pupil is not above his teacher; but everyone, after he has been fully trained, will be like his teacher. Why do you look at the speck that is in your brother's eye, but do not notice the log that is in your own eye? Or how can you say to your brother, 'Brother, let me take out the speck that is in your eye,' when you yourself do not see the log that is in your own eye? You hypocrite, first take the log out of your own eye, and then you will see clearly to take out the speck that is in your brother's eye. For there is no good tree which produces bad fruit, nor, on the other hand, a bad tree which produces good fruit. For each tree is known by its own fruit. For men do not gather figs from thorns, nor do they pick grapes from a briar bush. The good man out of the good treasure of his heart brings forth what is good; and the evil *man* out of the evil *treasure* brings forth what is evil; for his mouth speaks from that which fills his heart" (Luke 6:39–45; cf. Matthew 7:3–6. 16, 18, 20; 12:35; see Matthew 10:24; 15:14; Luke 6:12–19).

PITCHER

Setting: Jerusalem. On the first day of the Feast of Unleavened Bread, when the Passover lamb is being sacrificed, Jesus responds to His disciples' question about His plans for the Passover meal.

And He sent two of His disciples and said to them, "Go into the city, and a man will meet you carrying a pitcher of water; follow him; and wherever he enters, say to the owner of the house, 'The Teacher says, "Where is My guest room in which I may eat the Passover with My disciples?"' And he himself will show you a large upper room furnished *and* ready; prepare for us there" (Mark 14:13–15; cf. Matthew 26:17–19; Luke 22:7–13).

Setting: Jerusalem. With the Passover (Feast of Unleavened Bread) approaching, Jesus informs His disciples where they will celebrate the feast. The chief priests and scribes seek to kill Him, and Satan enters Judas Iscariot in order to betray the Lord.

And Jesus sent Peter and John, saying, "Go and prepare the Passover for us, so that we may eat it." They said to Him, "Where do You want us to prepare it?" And He said to them, "When you have entered the city, a man will meet you carrying a pitcher of water; follow him into the house that he enters. And you shall say to the owner of the house, 'The Teacher says to you, "Where is the guest room in which I may eat the Passover with My disciples?"' And he will show you a large, furnished upper room; prepare it there" (Luke 22:8–12; cf. Matthew 26:17–19; Mark 14:12–16).

PLACE (Specifics such as PLACE, HOLY; and PLACE, MARKET are separate entries; also see PLACES)

Setting: Entering Capernaum. After Jesus gives the Sermon on the Mount and cleanses a leper, a Roman centurion implores the Lord to heal his servant.

Now when Jesus heard *this,* He marveled, and said to those who were following, "Truly I say to you, I have not found such great faith with anyone in Israel. I say to you that many will come from east and west, and recline *at the table* with Abraham, Isaac and Jacob in the kingdom of heaven; but the sons of the kingdom will be cast out into the outer darkness; in that place there will be weeping and gnashing of teeth." And Jesus said to the centurion, "Go; it shall be done for you as you have believed." And the servant was healed that *very* moment (Matthew 8:10–13; cf. Luke 7:9, 10).

Setting: A house near the Sea of Galilee. Jesus gives the meaning of the Parable of the Wheat and the Tares to His disciples.

And He said, "The one who sows the good seed is the Son of Man, and the field is the world; and as *for* the good seed, these are the sons of the kingdom; and the tares are the sons of the evil *one;* and the enemy who sowed them is the devil, and the harvest is the end of the age; and the reapers are angels. So just as the tares are gathered up and burned with fire, so shall it be at the end of the age. The Son of Man will send forth His angels, and they will gather out of His kingdom all stumbling blocks, and those who commit lawlessness, and will throw them into the furnace of fire; in that place there will be weeping and gnashing of teeth. Then THE RIGHTEOUS WILL SHINE FORTH AS THE SUN in the kingdom of their Father. He who has ears, let him hear" (Matthew 13:37–43, Jesus quotes from Daniel 12:3; cf. Matthew 8:12; 13:50).

Setting: By the Sea of Galilee. Because the religious leaders are rejecting His message, Jesus continues teaching His disciples with the Parable of the Dragnet.

"Again, the kingdom of heaven is like a dragnet cast into the sea, and gathering *fish* of every kind; and when it was filled, they drew it up on the beach; and they sat down and gathered the good *fish* into containers, but the bad they threw away. So it will be at the end of the age; the angels will come forth and take out the wicked from among the righteous, and will throw them into the furnace of fire; in that place there will be weeping and gnashing of teeth. Have you understood all these things?" They said to Him, "Yes" (Matthew 13:47–51).

Setting: The temple in Jerusalem. Jesus speaks another parable to the chief priests and elders after they question His authority.

Jesus spoke to them again in parables, saying, "The kingdom of heaven may be compared to a king who gave a wedding feast for his son. And he sent out his slaves to call those who had been invited to the wedding feast, and they were unwilling to come. Again he sent out other slaves saying, 'Tell those who have been invited, "Behold, I have prepared my dinner; my oxen and my fattened livestock are *all* butchered and everything is ready; come to the wedding feast." But they paid no attention and went their way, one to his own farm, another to his business, and the rest seized his slaves and mistreated them and killed them. But the king was enraged, and he sent his armies and destroyed those murderers and set their city on fire. Then he said to his slaves, 'The wedding is ready, but those who were invited were not worthy. 'Go therefore to the main highways, and as many as you find *there,* invite to the wedding feast.' Those slaves went out into the streets and gathered together all they found, both evil and good; and the wedding hall was filled with dinner guests. But when the king came in to look over the dinner guests, he saw a man there who was not dressed in wedding clothes, and he said to him, 'Friend, how did you come in here without wedding clothes?' And the man was speechless. Then the king said to the servants, 'Bind him hand and foot, and throw him into the outer darkness; in that place there will be weeping and gnashing of teeth.' For many are called, but few *are* chosen" (Matthew 22:1–14; cf. Matthew 8:11, 12).

Setting: The temple in Jerusalem. Jesus exposes the truth about Pharisaism to the crowds and His disciples after the Jewish religious leaders test Him with questions.

Then Jesus spoke to the crowds and to His disciples, saying: "The scribes and the Pharisees have seated themselves in the chair of Moses; therefore all that they tell you, do and observe, but do not do according to their deeds; for they say *things* and do not do *them.* They tie up heavy burdens and lay them on men's shoulders, but they themselves are unwilling to move them with *so much as* a finger. But they do all their deeds to be noticed by men; for they broaden their phylacteries and lengthen their tassels *of their garments.* They love the place of honor at banquets and the chief seats in the synagogues, and respectful greetings in the market places, and being called Rabbi by men. But do not be called Rabbi; for One is your Teacher, and you are all brothers. Do not call *anyone* on earth your father; for One is your Father, He who is in heaven. Do not be called leaders; for One is your Leader, *that is,* Christ. But the greatest among you shall be your servant. Whoever exalts himself shall be humbled; and whoever humbles himself shall be exalted" (Matthew 23:1–12; cf. Matthew 20:26; Mark 12:38–40; Luke 20:46, 47; see Exodus 13:9; Deuteronomy 33:3; Matthew 6:1, 5, 6, 9, 16; Mark 14:11; Luke 11:43; 14:11).

Setting: On the Mount of Olives, just east of Jerusalem. During His Olivet Discourse, after answering His disciples' questions as to when the temple will be destroyed and Jerusalem overrun, along with the signs of His coming and the end of the age, Jesus reemphasizes to His disciples that they should be on the alert for His return.

"Therefore be on the alert, for you do not know which day your Lord is coming. But be sure of this, that if the head of the house had known at what time of the night the thief was coming, he would have been on the alert and would not have allowed his house to be broken into. For this reason you also must be ready; for the Son of Man is coming at an hour when you do not think *He will.* Who then is the faithful and sensible slave whom his master put in charge of his household to give their food at the proper time? Blessed is that slave whom his master finds so doing when he comes. Truly I say to you that he will put him in charge of all his possessions. But if that evil slave says in his heart, 'My master is not coming for a long time,' and begins to beat his fellow slaves and eat and drink with drunkards; the master of that slave will come on a day when he does not expect *him* and at an hour which he does not know, and will cut him in pieces and assign him a place with the hypocrites; in that place there will be weeping and gnashing of teeth" (Matthew 24:42–51; cf. Mark 13:33–37; Luke 12:39–46; 21:34–36; see Matthew 8:11, 12; 25:21–23).

Setting: On the Mount of Olives, just east of Jerusalem. During His Olivet Discourse, after answering His disciples' questions as to when the temple will be destroyed and Jerusalem overrun, along with the signs of His coming and the end of the age, Jesus reemphasizes to His disciples that they should be on the alert for His return.

"For *it is* just like a man *about* to go on a journey, who called his own slaves and entrusted his possessions to them. To one he gave five talents, to another, two, and to another, one, each according to his own ability; and he went on his journey. Immediately the one who had received the five talents went and traded with them, and gained five more talents. In the same manner the one who *had received* the two *talents* gained two more. But he who received the one *talent* went away, and dug a *hole* in the ground and hid his master's money. Now after a long time the master of those slaves came and settled accounts with them. The one who had received the five talents came up and brought five more talents, saying, 'Master, you entrusted five talents to me. See, I have gained five more talents.' His master said to him, 'Well done, good and faithful slave. You were faithful with a few things, I will put you in charge of many things; enter into the joy of your master.' Also the one who *had received* the two talents came up and said, 'Master, you entrusted two talents to me. See, I have gained two more talents.' His master said to him, 'Well done, good and faithful slave. You were faithful with a few things, I will put you in charge of many things; enter into the joy of your master.' And the one also who had received the one talent came up and said, 'Master, I knew you to be a hard man, reaping where you did not sow and gathering where you scattered no *seed.* And I was afraid, and went away and hid your talent in the ground. See, you have what is yours.' But his master answered and said to him, 'You wicked, lazy slave, you knew that I reap where I did not sow and gather where I scattered no *seed.* Then you ought to have put my money in the bank, and on my arrival I would have received my *money* back with interest. 'Therefore take away the talent from him, and give it to the one who has ten talents.' For to everyone who has, *more* shall be given, and he will have an abundance; but from the one who does not have, even what he does have shall be taken away. Throw out the worthless slave into the outer darkness; in that place there will be weeping and gnashing of teeth" (Matthew 25:14–30; cf. Matthew 8:12; 3:12; 24:45–47; see Matthew 18:23, 24; Luke 12:44).

Setting: Gethsemane on the Mount of Olives, east of the temple in Jerusalem. As Jesus submits to His Father's will and allows Judas to betray Him, Peter attempts to defend the Lord by force, but He does not permit it.

Then Jesus said to him, "Put your sword back into its place; for all those who take up the sword shall perish by the sword. Or do you think that I cannot appeal to My Father, and He will at once put at My disposal more than twelve legions of angels? How then will the Scriptures be fulfilled, *which say* that it must happen this way?" (Matthew 26:52–54; cf. Mark 14:47; Luke 22:50, 51; John 18:10, 11).

Setting: Jesus' hometown of Nazareth in Galilee. After encountering unbelief, Jesus sends the Twelve out in pairs with authority and instructions about ministry.

And He summoned the twelve and began to send them out in pairs, and gave them authority over the unclean spirits; and He instructed them that they should take nothing for *their* journey, except a mere staff—no bread, no bag, no money in their belt—but to wear sandals; and *He added,* "Do not put on two tunics." And He said to them, "Wherever you enter a house, stay there until you leave town. Any place that does not receive you or listen to you, as you go out from there, shake the dust off the soles of your feet for a testimony against them" (Mark 6:7–11; cf. Matthew 10:1–14; Luke 9:1–5).

Setting: On the way from Galilee to Jerusalem. While being tested by a lawyer, Jesus tells him the story of the good Samaritan.

Jesus replied and said, "A man was going down from Jerusalem to Jericho, and fell among robbers, and they stripped him and beat him, and went away leaving him half dead. And by chance a priest was going down on that road, and when he saw him, he passed by on the other side. Likewise a Levite also, when he came to the place and saw him, passed by on the other side. But a Samaritan, who was on a journey, came upon him; and when he saw him, he felt compassion, and came to him and bandaged up his wounds, pouring oil and wine on *them;* and he put him on his own beast, and brought him to an inn and took care of him. On the next day he took out two denarii and gave them to the innkeeper and said, 'Take care of him; and whatever more you spend, when I return I will repay you.' Which of these three do you think proved to be a neighbor to the man who fell into the robbers' *hands?*" And he said, "The one who showed mercy toward him." Then Jesus said to him, "Go and do the same" (Luke 10:30–37).

Setting: On the way from Galilee to Jerusalem. After the scribes and Pharisees turn hostile and question Him repeatedly in an attempt to catch Him in something He might say, Jesus responds to a question from the crowd and gives a parable about riches and greed.

And He told them a parable, saying, "The land of a rich man was very productive. And he began reasoning to himself, saying, 'What shall I do, since I have no place to store my crops?' Then he said, 'This is what I will do: I will tear down my barns and build larger ones, and here I will store all my grain and my goods. And I will say to my soul, "Soul, you have many goods laid up for many years *to come;* take your ease, eat, drink *and* be merry."' "But God said to him, 'You fool! This *very* night your soul is required of you; and *now* who will own what you have prepared?' So is the man who stores up treasure for himself, and is not rich toward God" (Luke 12:16–21; see Job 27:8; Psalm 39:6; Ecclesiastes 12:9; Philippians 2:3).

Setting: On the way from Galilee to Jerusalem. When Jesus uses a parable to challenge the crowd and His disciples to be ready for His return, Peter asks Him whom He is addressing.

And the Lord said, "Who then is the faithful and sensible steward, whom his master will put in charge of his servants, to give them their rations at the proper time? Blessed is that slave whom his master finds so doing when he comes. Truly I say to you that he will put him in charge of all his possessions. But if that slave says in his heart, 'My master will be a long time in coming,' and begins to beat the slaves, *both* men and women, and to eat and drink and get drunk; the master of that slave will come on a day when he does not expect *him* and at an hour he does not know, and will cut him in pieces, and assign him a place with the unbelievers. And that slave who knew his master's will and did not get ready or act in accord with his will, will receive many lashes, but the one who did know *it,* and committed deeds worthy of flogging, will receive but few. From everyone who has been given much, much will be required; and to whom they entrusted much, of him they will ask all the more" (Luke 12:42–48; cf. Matthew 24:45–51; see Leviticus 5:17).

Setting: On the way from Galilee to Jerusalem. Jesus, after observing the guests selecting places of honor at the table in the house of a Pharisee leader on the Sabbath, speaks a parable to them.

And He *began* speaking a parable to the invited guests when He noticed how they had been picking out the places of honor *at the table,* saying to them, "When you are invited by someone to a wedding feast, do not take the place of honor, for someone more distinguished than you may have been invited by him, and he who invited you both will come and say to you, 'Give *your* place to this man,' and then in disgrace you proceed to occupy the last place. But when you are invited, go and recline at the last place, so that when the one who has invited you comes, he may say to you, 'Friend, move up higher'; then you will have honor in the sight of all who are at the table with you. For everyone who exalts himself will be humbled, and he who humbles himself will be exalted" (Luke 14:7–11; see 2 Samuel 22:28; Proverb 25:6, 7; Matthew 23:6).

Setting: On the way from Galilee to Jerusalem. After responding to the Pharisees' scoffing at His teaching the disciples about stewardship and the permanence of the Law, Jesus conveys the story of the rich man and Lazarus.

"Now there was a rich man, and he habitually dressed in purple and fine linen, joyously living in splendor every day. And a poor man named Lazarus was laid at his gate, covered with sores, and longing to be fed with the *crumbs* which were falling from the rich man's table; besides, even the dogs were coming and licking his sores. Now the poor man died and was carried away by the angels to Abraham's bosom; and the rich man also died and was buried. In Hades he lifted up his eyes, being in torment, and saw Abraham far away and Lazarus in his bosom. And he cried out and said, 'Father Abraham, have mercy on me, and send Lazarus so that he may dip the tip of his finger in water and cool off my tongue, for I am in agony in this flame.' But Abraham said, 'Child, remember that during your life you received your good things, and likewise Lazarus bad things; but now he is being comforted here, and you are in agony. And besides all this, between us and you there is a great chasm fixed, so that those who wish to come over from here to you will not be able, and *that* none may cross over from there to us.' And he said, 'Then I beg you, father, that you send him to my father's house—for I have five brothers—in order that he may warn them, so that they will not also come to this place of torment.' But Abraham said, 'They have Moses and the Prophets; let them hear them.' But he said, 'No, father Abraham, but if someone goes to them from the dead, they will repent!' But he said to him, 'If they do not listen to Moses and the Prophets, they will not be persuaded even if someone rises from the dead' " (Luke 16:19–31; see Luke 3:8; 6:24).

Setting: On the way from Galilee to Jerusalem. After the Pharisees question Him about the coming of the kingdom of God, Jesus tells His disciples of His second coming.

And He said to the disciples, "The days will come when you will long to see one of the days of the Son of Man, and you will not see it. They will say to you, 'Look there! Look here!' Do not go away, and do not run after *them.* For just like the lightning, when it flashes out of one part of the sky, shines to the other part of the sky, so will the Son of Man be in His day. But first He must suffer many things and be rejected by this generation. And just as it happened in the days of Noah, so it will be also in the days of the Son of Man: they were eating, they were drinking, they were marrying, they were being given in marriage, until the day that Noah entered the ark, and the flood came and destroyed them all. It was the same as happened in the days of Lot: they were eating, they were drinking, they were buying, they were selling, they were planting, they were building; but on the day that Lot went out from Sodom it rained fire and brimstone from heaven and destroyed them all. It will be just the same on the day that the Son of Man is revealed. On that day, the one who is on the housetop and whose goods are in the house must not go down to take them out; and likewise the one who is in the field must not turn back. Remember Lot's wife. Whoever seeks to keep his life will lose it, and whoever loses *his life* will preserve it. I tell you, on that night there will be two in one bed; one will be taken and the other will be left. There will be two women grinding at the same place; one will be taken and the other will be left. [Two men will be in the field; one will be taken and the other will be left."] And answering they said to Him, "Where, Lord?" And He said to them, "Where the body *is*, there also the vultures will be gathered" (Luke 17:22–37; see Genesis 19; Matthew 10:39; 16:21, 27; 24:17–28, 37–41).

Setting: Jerusalem. After beginning His ministry in Galilee by selecting His disciples and performing a miracle at a wedding in Cana, Jesus attends the Passover of the Jews and confronts those perverting the temple for business.

And He made a scourge of cords, and drove *them* all out of the temple, with the sheep and the oxen; and He poured out the coins of the money changers and overturned their tables; and to those who were selling the doves He said, "Take these things away; stop making My Father's house a place of business" (John 2:15, 16; cf. Matthew 21:12, 13; see Deuteronomy 16:1–6; John 1:11–14, 17).

Setting: The temple treasury in Jerusalem. After the scribes and Pharisees question His testimony about Himself, Jesus reveals to those Jews who believe in Him how He will make them free.

So Jesus was saying to those Jews who had believed Him, "If you continue in My word, *then* you are truly disciples of Mine; and you will know the truth, and the truth will make you free." They answered Him, "We are Abraham's descendants and have never yet been enslaved to anyone; how is it that You say, 'You will become free'?" Jesus answered them, "Truly, truly, I say to you, everyone who commits sin is the slave of sin. The slave does not remain in the house forever; the son does remain forever. So if the Son makes you free, you will be free indeed. I know that you are Abraham's descendants; yet you seek to kill Me, because My word has no place in you. I speak the things which I have seen with *My* Father; therefore you also do the things which you heard from *your* father" (John 8:31–38; see Romans 6:16).

Setting: Jerusalem. Before the Passover, after taking issue with Peter's assertion that he would lay down his life for Him, Jesus comforts and gives hope to His disciples regarding their future after He returns to heaven.

"Do not let your heart be troubled; believe in God, believe also in Me. In My Father's house are many dwelling places; if it were not so, I would have told you; for I go to prepare a place for you. If I go and prepare a place for you, I will come again and receive you to Myself, that where I am, *there* you may be also. And you know the way where I am going" (John 14:1–4; see John 13:35; 14:27, 28).

Setting: On the island of Patmos (in the Aegean Sea about fifty miles southwest of Ephesus in modern Turkey). On the Lord's Day (Sunday), approximately fifty years after the Resurrection, the disciple John encounters the Lord Jesus Christ, who communicates a new revelation for the apostle to record for the church in Ephesus and to six other churches in Asia.

"To the angel of the church in Ephesus write: The One who holds the seven stars in His right hand, the One who walks among the seven golden lampstands, says this: 'I know your deeds and your toil and perseverance, and that you cannot tolerate evil men, and you put to the test those who call themselves apostles, and they are not, and you found them *to be* false; and you have perseverance and have endured for My name's sake, and have not grown weary. But I have *this* against you, that you have left your first love. Therefore remember from where you have fallen, and repent and do the deeds you did at first; or else I am coming to you and will remove your lampstand out of its place—unless you repent. Yet this you do have, that you hate the deeds of the Nicolaitans, which I also hate. He who has an ear, let him hear what the Spirit says to the churches. To him who overcomes, I will grant to eat of the tree of life which is in the Paradise of God' " (Revelation 2:1–7; see Genesis 2:9; Ezekiel 28:13; 1 John 4:1; Revelation 1:10, 11, 19, 20).

PLACE, HOLY (Also see TEMPLE)

Setting: The Mount of Olives, just east of Jerusalem. During His Olivet Discourse, Jesus answers His disciples' questions as to when the temple will be destroyed and Jerusalem overrun, along with the signs of His coming and the end of the age.

"Therefore when you see the ABOMINATION OF DESOLATION which was spoken of through Daniel the prophet, standing in the holy place (let the reader understand), then those who are in Judea must flee to the mountains. Whoever is on the housetop must not go down to get the things that are in his house. Whoever is in the field must not turn back to get his cloak. But woe to those who are pregnant and to those who are nursing babies in those days! But pray that your flight will not be in the winter, or on a Sabbath. For then there will be a great tribulation, such as has not occurred since the beginning of the world until now, nor ever will. Unless those days had been cut short, no life would have been saved; but for the sake of the elect those days will be cut short. Then if anyone says to you, 'Behold, here is the Christ,' or "There *He is,*' do not believe *him.* For false Christs and false prophets will arise and will show great signs and wonders, so as to mislead, if possible, even the elect. Behold, I have told you in advance. So if they say to you, 'Behold, He is in the wilderness,' do not go out, *or,* 'Behold, He is in the inner rooms,' do not believe *them.* For just as the lightning comes from the east and flashes even to the west, so will the coming of the Son of Man be. Wherever the corpse is, there the vultures will gather" (Matthew 24:15–28, Jesus quotes from Daniel 9:27; cf. Daniel 12:1; Mark 13:14–23; Luke 17:22–31; 21:20–24; 23:29; see John 4:48).

PLACE, LAST

Setting: On the way from Galilee to Jerusalem. Jesus, after observing the guests selecting places of honor at the table in the house of a Pharisee leader on the Sabbath, speaks a parable to them.

And He *began* speaking a parable to the invited guests when He noticed how they had been picking out the places of honor *at the table,* saying to them, "When you are invited by someone to a wedding feast, do not take the place of honor, for someone more distinguished than you may have been invited by him, and he who invited you both will come and say to you, 'Give *your* place to this man, and then in disgrace you proceed to occupy the last place. But when you are invited, go and recline at the last place, so that when the one who has invited you comes, he may say to you, 'Friend, move up higher'; then you will have honor in the sight of all who are at the table with you. For everyone who exalts himself will be humbled, and he who humbles himself will be exalted" (Luke 14:7–11; see 2 Samuel 22:28; Proverb 25:6, 7; Matthew 23:6).

PLACE, LONELY (See PLACE, SECLUDED)

PLACE, MARKET (Also see BUSINESS; and PLACES, MARKET)

Setting: Judea beyond the Jordan (Perea). Jesus illustrates the kingdom of heaven to His disciples through the story of laborers in the vineyard.

"For the kingdom of heaven is like a landowner who went out early in the morning to hire laborers for his vineyard. When he had agreed with the laborers for a denarius for the day, he sent them into his vineyard. And he went out about the third hour and saw others standing idle in the market place; and to those he said, 'You also go into the vineyard, and whatever is right I will give you.' And *so* they went. Again he went out about the sixth and the ninth hour, and did the same thing. And about the eleventh *hour* he went out and found others standing *around;* and he said to them, 'Why have you been standing idle here all day long?' They said to him, 'Because no one hired us.' He said to them, 'You go into the vineyard too.' When evening came, the owner of the vineyard said to his foreman, 'Call the laborers and pay them their wages, beginning with the last *group* to the first.' When those *hired* about the eleventh hour came, each one received a denarius. When those *hired* first came, they thought that they would receive more; but each of them also received a denarius. When they received it, they grumbled at the landowner, saying, 'These last men have worked *only* one hour, and you have made them equal to us who have borne the burden and the scorching heat of the day.' But he answered and said to one of them, 'Friend, I am doing you no wrong; did you not agree with me for a denarius? Take what is yours and go, but I wish to give to this last man the same as to you. It is not lawful for me to do what I wish with

what is my own? Or is your eye envious because I am generous?' So the last shall be first, and the first last" (Matthew 20:1–16; cf. Matthew 19:30).

Setting: Galilee. After praising John the Baptist to the crowds, Jesus criticizes the Pharisees and lawyers who reject God's purpose and John's message.

"To what then shall I compare the men of this generation, and what are they like? They are like children who sit in the market place and call to one another, and they say, 'We played the flute for you, and you did not dance; we sang a dirge, and you did not weep.' For John the Baptist has come eating no bread and drinking no wine, and you say, 'He has a demon!' The Son of Man has come eating and drinking, and you say, 'Behold, a gluttonous man and a drunkard, a friend of tax collectors and sinners!' Yet wisdom is vindicated by all her children" (Luke 7:31–35; cf. Matthew 11:16–19; see Luke 1:15).

PLACE, SECLUDED

Setting: Galilee. After Jesus' disciples report to Him about their ministry in the cities and villages, He instructs them to rest.

And He said to them, "Come away by yourselves to a secluded place and rest a while." (For there were many *people* coming and going, and they did not even have time to eat) (Mark 6:31; see Mark 3:20).

PLACE OF HONOR (Listed under HONOR, PLACE OF)

PLACE OF TORMENT (Listed under TORMENT, PLACE OF)

PLACES (Specifics such as PLACES, MARKET; and PLACES, ROCKY are separate entries; also see PLACE)

Setting: The temple in Jerusalem. After commending one scribe for his nearness to the kingdom of God, Jesus warns the crowd about the majority of the scribes.

In His teaching He was saying: "Beware of the scribes who like to walk around in long robes, and *like* respectful greetings in the market places, and chief seats in the synagogues and places of honor at banquets, who devour widows' houses, and for appearance's sake offer long prayers; these will receive greater condemnation" (Mark 12:38–40; cf. Matthew 23:1–7; Luke 20:45–47).

PLACES, DWELLING (See DWELLING PLACES)

PLACES, MARKET (Also see BUSINESS; and PLACE, MARKET)

Setting: Galilee. After praising John the Baptist as His forerunner, Jesus demonstrates the foolish thinking of the Jewish religious leaders by repeating what they say about John's ascetic lifestyle and ministry along with His own.

"But to what shall I compare this generation? It is like children sitting in the market places, who call out to the other *children,* and say, 'We played the flute for you, and you did not dance; we sang a dirge, and you did not mourn.' For John came neither eating nor drinking, and they say, 'He has a demon!' The Son of Man came eating and drinking, and they say, 'Behold, a gluttonous man and a drunkard, a friend of tax collectors and sinners! Yet wisdom is vindicated by her deeds" (Matthew 11:16–19; cf. Luke 7:31–35; see Matthew 9:11, 34; Luke 1:15).

Setting: The temple in Jerusalem. Jesus exposes the truth about Pharisaism to the crowds and His disciples after the Jewish religious leaders test Him with questions.

Then Jesus spoke to the crowds and to His disciples, saying: "The scribes and the Pharisees have seated themselves in the chair of Moses; therefore all that they tell you, do and observe, but do not do according to their deeds; for they say *things* and do not do *them.* They tie up heavy burdens and lay them on men's shoulders, but they themselves are unwilling to move them with *so much as* a finger. But they do all their deeds to be noticed by men; for they broaden their phylacteries and lengthen their tassels *of their garments.* They love the place of honor at banquets and the chief seats in the synagogues, and respectful greetings in the market places, and being called Rabbi by men. But do not be called Rabbi; for One is your Teacher, and you are all brothers. Do not call *anyone* on earth your father; for One is your Father, He who is in heaven. Do not be called leaders; for One is your Leader, *that is,* Christ. But the greatest among you shall be your servant. Whoever exalts himself shall be humbled; and whoever humbles himself shall be exalted" (Matthew 23:1–12; cf. Matthew 20:26; Mark 12:38–40; Luke 20:46, 47; see Exodus 13:9; Deuteronomy 33:3; Matthew 6:1, 5, 6, 9, 16; Mark 14:11; Luke 11:43; 14:11).

Setting: The temple in Jerusalem. After commending one scribe for his nearness to the kingdom of God, Jesus warns the crowd about the majority of the scribes.

In His teaching He was saying: "Beware of the scribes who like to walk around in long robes, and *like* respectful greetings in the market places, and chief seats in the synagogues and places of honor at banquets, who devour widows' houses, and for appearance's sake offer long prayers; these will receive greater condemnation" (Mark 12:38–40; cf. Matthew 23:1–7; Luke 20:45–47).

Setting: On the way from Galilee to Jerusalem. After speaking of how a lamp illuminates, the Lord has lunch with a Pharisee who is surprised He doesn't wash before eating.

But the Lord said to him, "Now you Pharisees clean the outside of the cup and of the platter; but inside of you, you are full of robbery and wickedness. You foolish ones, did not He who made the outside make the inside also? But give that which is within as charity, and then all things are clean for you. But woe to you Pharisees! You pay tithe of mint and rue and every *kind of* garden herb, and *yet* disregard justice and the love of God; but these are the things you should have done without neglecting the others. Woe to you Pharisees! For you love the chief seats in the synagogues and the respectful greetings in the market places. Woe to you! For you are like concealed tombs, and the people who walk over *them* are unaware *of it*" (Luke 11:39–44; cf. Matthew 23:6, 7, 23–27; see Matthew 15:2; Titus 1:15).

Setting: The temple in Jerusalem. While ministering a few days before His crucifixion, after posing a question to the scribes, who do not answer, Jesus warns His disciples about the lifestyle of the scribes.

"Beware of the scribes, who like to walk around in long robes, and love respectful greetings in the market places, and chief seats in the synagogues and places of honor at banquets, who devour widows' houses, and for appearance's sake offer long prayers. These will receive greater condemnation" (Luke 20:46, 47; cf. Matthew 23:1–7; Mark 12:38–40; see Luke 11:43).

PLACES, ROCKY

Setting: By the Sea of Galilee. While teaching and preaching to the crowds from a boat, Jesus conveys the Parable of the Sower.

And He spoke many things to them in parables, saying, "Behold, the sower went out to sow; and as he sowed, some *seeds* fell beside the road, and the birds came and ate them up. Others fell on the rocky places, where they did not have much soil; and immediately they sprang up, because they had no depth of soil. But when the sun had risen, they were scorched; and because they had no root, they withered away. Others fell among the thorns, and the thorns came up and choked them out. And others fell on the good soil and yielded a crop, some a hundredfold, some sixty, and some thirty. He who has ears, let him hear" (Matthew 13:3–9; cf. Mark 4:3–9; Luke 8:4–8).

Setting: By the Sea of Galilee. With the religious leaders rejecting His message, Jesus begins to teach in parables, and gives His disciples the meaning of the Parable of the Sower.

"Hear then the parable of the sower. When anyone hears the word of the kingdom and does not understand it, the evil *one* comes and snatches away what has been sown in his heart. This is the one on whom seed was sown beside the road. The one on whom seed was sown on the rocky places, this is the man who hears the word and immediately receives it with joy; yet he has no *firm* root in himself, but is *only* temporary, and when affliction or persecution arises because of the word, immediately he falls away. And the one on whom seed was sown among the thorns, this is the man who hears the word, and the worry of the world and the deceitfulness of wealth choke the word, and it becomes unfruitful. And the one on whom seed was sown on the good soil, this is the man who hears the word and understands it; who indeed bears fruit and brings forth, some a hundredfold, some sixty, and some thirty" (Matthew 13:18–23; cf. Mark 4:13–20; Luke 8:11–15).

Setting: By the Sea of Galilee. During the early part of His ministry, after presenting the Parable of the Sower from a boat to a very large crowd, Jesus gives the meaning of the parable to His disciples and other followers.

And He said to them, "Do you not understand this parable? How will you understand all the parables? The sower sows the word. These are the ones who are beside the road where the word is sown; and when they hear, immediately Satan comes and takes away the word which has been sown in them. In a similar way these are the ones on whom seed was sown on the rocky places, who, when they hear the word, immediately receive it with joy; and they have no *firm* root in themselves, but are *only* temporary; then, when affliction or persecution arises because of the word, immediately they fall away. And others are the ones on whom seed was sown among the thorns; these are the ones who have heard the word, but the worries of the world and the deceitfulness of riches, and the desires for other things enter in and choke the word, and it becomes unfruitful. And those are the ones on whom seed was sown on the good soil; and they hear the word and accept it and bear fruit, thirty, sixty, and a hundredfold" (Mark 4:13–20; cf. Matthew 13:18–23; Luke 8:11–15).

PLACES, VARIOUS

Setting: The Mount of Olives, just east of Jerusalem. During His Olivet Discourse, Jesus answers His disciples' questions as to when the temple will be destroyed and Jerusalem overrun, along with the signs of His coming and the end of the age.

And Jesus answered and said to them, "See to it that no one misleads you. For many will come in My name, saying, 'I am the Christ,' and will mislead many. You will be hearing of wars and rumors of wars. See that you are not frightened, for *those things* must take place, but *that* is not yet the end. For nation will rise against nation, and kingdom against kingdom, and in various places there will be famines and earthquakes. But all these things are *merely* the beginning of birth pangs. Then they will deliver you to tribulation, and will kill you, and you will be hated by all nations because of My name. At that time many will fall away and will betray one another and hate one another. Many false prophets will arise and will mislead many. Because lawlessness is increased, most people's love will grow cold. But the one who endures to the end, he will be saved. This gospel of the kingdom shall be preached in the whole world as a testimony to all the nations, and then the end will come" (Matthew 24:4–14; cf. Jeremiah 29:8; Matthew 7:15; 10:17, 22; Mark 13:3–13; Luke 21:7–19; Revelation 6:4).

Setting: On the Mount of Olives, east of the temple in Jerusalem. After predicting the temple's destruction, Jesus responds during His Olivet Discourse to questions from Peter, James, John, and Andrew about other future events.

And Jesus began to say to them, "See to it that no one misleads you. Many will come in My name, saying, 'I am *He!*' and will mislead many. When you hear of wars and rumors of wars, do not be frightened; *those things* must take place; but *that is* not yet the end. For nation will rise up against nation, and kingdom against kingdom; there will be earthquakes in various places; there will *also be* famines. These things are *merely* the beginning of birth pangs. But be on your guard; for they will deliver you to *the* courts, and you will be flogged in *the* synagogues, and you will stand before governors and kings for My sake, as a testimony to them. The gospel must first be preached to all the nations. When they arrest you and hand you over, do not worry beforehand about what you are to say, but say whatever is given you in that hour; for it is not you who speak, but *it is* the Holy Spirit. Brother will betray brother to death, and a father *his* child; and children will rise up against parents and have them put to death. You will be hated by all because of My name, but the one who endures to the end, he will be saved" (Mark 13:5–13; cf. Matthew 24:4–14; Luke 21:7–19; see Matthew 10:17–22).

Setting: On the Mount of Olives, east of the temple in Jerusalem. After ministering in the temple a few days before His crucifixion, and giving His disciples more details regarding the temple's future destruction, Jesus elaborates during His Olivet Discourse about things to come.

Then He continued by saying to them, "Nation will rise against nation and kingdom against kingdom, and there will be great earthquakes, and in various places plagues and famines; and there will be terrors and great signs from heaven. But before all these things, they will lay their hands on you and will persecute you, delivering you to the synagogues and prisons, bringing you before kings and governors for My name's sake. It will lead to an opportunity for your testimony. So make up your minds not to prepare beforehand to defend yourselves; for I will give you utterance and wisdom which none of your opponents will be able to resist or refute. But you will be betrayed even by parents and brothers and relatives and friends, and they will put *some* of you to death, and you will be hated by all because of My name. Yet not a hair of your head will perish. By your endurance you will gain your lives" (Luke 21:10–19; cf. Matthew 10:19–22; 24:7–14; Mark 13:8–13).

PLACES, WATERLESS

Setting: Galilee. Jesus responds to some Pharisees and scribes who ask Him for a miraculous sign as He ministers.

"Now when the unclean spirit goes out of a man, it passes through waterless places seeking rest, and does not find *it*. Then it says, 'I will return to my house from which I came'; and when it comes, it finds *it* unoccupied, swept, and put in order. Then it goes and takes along with it seven other spirits more wicked than itself, and they go in and live there; and the last state of that man becomes worse than the first. That is the way it will also be for this evil generation" (Matthew 12:43–45; cf. Luke 11:24–26; see Mark 5:9).

Setting: On the way from Galilee to Jerusalem. After some in the crowd test Him, demanding a sign from heaven, Jesus illustrates His power over Satan.

"When the unclean spirit goes out of a man, it passes through waterless places seeking rest, and not finding any, it says, 'I will return to my house from which I came.' And when it comes, it finds it swept clean and put in order. Then it goes and takes *along* seven other spirits more evil than itself, and they go in and live there; and the last state of that man becomes worse than the first" (Luke 11:24–26; cf. Matthew 12:43–45).

PLAGUES (Also see PESTILENCE)

Setting: On the Mount of Olives, east of the temple in Jerusalem. After ministering in the temple a few days before His crucifixion, and giving His disciples more details regarding the temple's future destruction, Jesus elaborates during His Olivet Discourse about things to come.

Then He continued by saying to them, "Nation will rise against nation and kingdom against kingdom, and there will be great earthquakes, and in various places plagues and famines, and there will be terrors and great signs from heaven. But before all these things, they will lay their hands on you and will persecute you, delivering you to the synagogues and prisons, bringing you before kings and governors for My name's sake. It will lead to an opportunity for your testimony. So make up your minds not to prepare beforehand to defend yourselves; for I will give you utterance and wisdom which none of your opponents will be able to resist or refute. But you will be betrayed even by parents and brothers and relatives and friends, and they will put *some* of you to death, and you will be hated by all because of My name. Yet not a hair of your head will perish. By your endurance you will gain your lives" (Luke 21:10–19; cf. Matthew 10:19–22; 24:7–14; Mark 13:8–13).

PLANT (Also see PLANTS, GARDEN)

Setting: Galilee. After rebuking the Pharisees and scribes for questioning His disciples' obedience to tradition and the commandments, Jesus instructs the disciples.

But He answered and said, "Every plant which My heavenly Father did not plant shall be uprooted. Let them alone; they are blind guides of the blind. And if a blind man guides a blind man, both will fall into a pit" (Matthew 15:13, 14; cf. Matthew 23:16; Luke 6:39).

PLANTING (Also see CROPS; and HARVEST)

Setting: On the way from Galilee to Jerusalem. After the Pharisees question Him about the coming of the kingdom of God, Jesus tells His disciples of His second coming.

And He said to the disciples, "The days will come when you will long to see one of the days of the Son of Man, and you will not see it. They will say to you, 'Look there! Look here!' Do not go away, and do not run after *them*. For just like the lightning, when it flashes out of one part of the sky, shines to the other part of the sky, so will the Son of Man be in His day. But first He must suffer many things and be rejected by this generation. And just as it happened in the days of Noah, so it will be also in the days of the Son of Man: they were eating, they were drinking, they were marrying, they were being given in marriage, until the day that Noah entered the ark, and the flood came and destroyed them all. It was the same as happened in the days of Lot: they were eating, they were drinking, they were buying, they were selling, they were planting, they were building; but on the day that Lot went out from Sodom it rained fire and brimstone from heaven and destroyed them all. It will be just the same on the day that the Son of Man is revealed. On that day, the one who is on the housetop and whose goods are in the house must not go down to take them out; and likewise the one who is in the field must not turn back. Remember Lot's wife. Whoever seeks to keep his life will lose it, and whoever loses *his life* will preserve it. I tell you, on that night there will be two in one bed; one will be taken and the other will be left. There will be two women grinding at the same place; one will be taken and the other will be left. [Two men will be in the field; one will be taken and the other will be left."] And answering they said to Him, "Where, Lord?" And He said to them, "Where the body *is*, there also the vultures will be gathered" (Luke 17:22–37; see Genesis 19; Matthew 10:39; 16:21, 27; 24:17–28, 37–41).

PLANTS, GARDEN (Also see GARDEN; HERB, GARDEN; and PLANT)

Setting: By the Sea of Galilee. Because the religious leaders are rejecting His message, Jesus continues teaching the crowds with the Parable of the Mustard Seed.

He presented another parable to them, saying, "The kingdom of heaven is like a mustard seed, which a man took and sowed in his field; and this is smaller than all *other* seeds, but when it is full grown, it is larger than the garden plants and becomes a tree, so that THE BIRDS OF THE AIR come and NEST IN ITS BRANCHES" (Matthew 13:31, 32, Jesus quotes from Ezekiel 17:23; cf. Mark 4:30–32; Luke 13:18, 19).

Setting: Galilee. After giving the Parable of the Sower and the Parable of the Seed, Jesus continues teaching His disciples by presenting the Parable of the Mustard Seed.

And He said, "How shall we picture the kingdom of God, or by what parable shall we present it? *It is* like a mustard seed, which, when sown upon the soil, though it is smaller than all the seeds that are upon the soil, yet when it is sown, it grows up and becomes larger than all the garden plants and forms large branches; so that THE BIRDS OF THE AIR can NEST UNDER ITS SHADE" (Mark 4:30–32, Jesus quotes from Ezekiel 17:23; cf. Matthew 13:31, 32; Luke 13:18, 19).

PLATTER

Setting: On the way from Galilee to Jerusalem. After speaking of how a lamp illuminates, the Lord has lunch with a Pharisee who is surprised He doesn't wash before eating.

But the Lord said to him, "Now you Pharisees clean the outside of the cup and of the platter; but inside of you, you are full of robbery and wickedness. You foolish ones, did not He who made the outside make the inside also? But give that which is within as charity, and then all things are clean for you. But woe to you Pharisees! You pay tithe of mint and rue and every *kind of* garden herb, and *yet* disregard justice and the love of God; but these are the things you should have done without neglecting the others. Woe to you Pharisees! For you love the chief seats in the synagogues and the respectful greetings in the market places. Woe to you! For you are like concealed tombs, and the people who walk over *them* are unaware *of it*" (Luke 11:39–44; cf. Matthew 23:6, 7, 23–27; see Matthew 15:2; Titus 1:15).

PLEASING MEN (See APPROVAL, MAN'S)

PLEASING PEOPLE (See APPROVAL, MAN'S)

PLEASURE, INDULGENCE IN (See DISSIPATION)

PLEASURES (Also see DISSIPATION)

Setting: Galilee. After Jesus presents the Parable of the Sower to the crowds, His disciples ask Him to give them the parable's meaning.

And He said, "To you it has been granted to know the mysteries of the kingdom of God, but to the rest *it is* in parables, so that SEEING THEY MAY NOT SEE, AND HEARING THEY MAY NOT UNDERSTAND. Now the parable is this: the seed is the word of God. Those beside the road are those who have heard; then the devil comes and takes away the word from their heart, so that they will not believe and be saved. Those on the rocky *soil* are those who, when they hear, receive the word with joy; and these have no *firm* root; they believe for a while, and in time of temptation fall away. The *seed* which fell among the thorns, these are the ones who have heard, and as they go on their way they are choked with worries and riches and pleasures of *this* life, and bring no fruit to maturity. But the *seed* in the good soil, these are the ones who have heard the word in an honest and good heart, and hold it fast, and bear fruit with perseverance" (Luke 8:10–15, Jesus quotes from Isaiah 6:9; cf. Matthew 13:10–23; Mark 4:10–20).

PLOW

Setting: On the way from Galilee to Jerusalem. The Lord responds to several men seeking to follow Him.

But Jesus said to him, "No one, after putting his hand to the plow and looking back, is fit for the kingdom of God" (Luke 9:62; cf. Matthew 8:19–22; see Philippians 3:13).

PLUNDER (Also see POSSESSIONS; PROPERTY; THEFT; and WEALTH)

Setting: Galilee. After Jesus heals a blind, mute, demon-possessed man, the Pharisees accuse the Lord in front of crowds of being a worker of Beelzebul (Satan).

And knowing their thoughts Jesus said to them, "Any kingdom divided against itself is laid waste; and any city or house divided against itself will not stand. If Satan casts out Satan, he is divided against himself; how then will his kingdom stand? If I by Beelzebul cast out demons, by whom do your sons cast *them* out? For this reason they will be your judges. But if I cast out demons by the Spirit of God, then the kingdom of God has come upon you. Or how can anyone enter the strong man's house and carry off his property, unless he first binds the strong *man?* And then he will plunder his house" (Matthew 12:25–29; cf. Matthew 9:34; Mark 3:23–27; Luke 11:17–20).

Setting: Galilee. After Jesus selects His twelve disciples, scribes from Jerusalem attribute His miraculous powers to Satan.

And He called them to Himself and began speaking to them in parables, "How can Satan cast out Satan? If a kingdom is divided against itself, that kingdom cannot stand. If a house is divided against itself, that house will not be able to stand. If Satan has risen up against himself and is divided, he cannot stand, but he is finished! But no one can enter the strong man's house and plunder his property unless he first binds the strong man, and then he will plunder his house. Truly I say to you, all sins shall be forgiven the sons of men, and whatever blasphemies they utter; but whoever blasphemes against the Holy Spirit never has forgiveness, but is guilty of an eternal sin"—because they were saying, "He has an unclean spirit" (Mark 3:23–30; cf. Matthew 12:25–32; Luke 12:10).

Setting: On the way from Galilee to Jerusalem. After some in the crowd test Him, demanding a sign from heaven, Jesus illustrates His power over Satan.

"When a strong *man*, fully armed, guards his own house, his possessions are undisturbed. But when someone stronger than he attacks him and overpowers him, he takes away from him all his armor on which he had relied and distributes his plunder. He who is not with Me is against Me; and he who does not gather with Me, scatters" (Luke 11:21–23; cf. Matthew 12:29, 30).

PODS

Setting: On the way from Galilee to Jerusalem. Jesus conveys the illustration of the prodigal son because the Pharisees and scribes complain He associates with tax collectors and sinners.

And He said, "A man had two sons. The younger of them said to his father, 'Father, give me the share of the estate that falls to me.' So he divided his wealth between them. And not many days later, the younger son gathered everything together and went on a journey into a distant country, and there he squandered his estate with loose living. Now when he had spent everything, a severe famine occurred in that country, and he began to be impoverished. So he went and hired himself out to one of the citizens of that country, and he sent him into his fields to feed swine. And he would have gladly filled his stomach with the pods that the swine were eating, and no one was giving *anything* to him. But when he came to his senses, he said, 'How many of my father's hired men have more than enough bread, but I am dying here with hunger! I will get up and go to my father, and will say to him, "Father, I have sinned against heaven, and in your sight; I am no longer worthy to be called your son; make me as one of your hired men."' So he got up and came to his father. But while he was still a long way off, his father saw him and felt compassion *for him,* and ran and embraced him and kissed him. And the son said to him, "Father, I have sinned against heaven and in your sight; I am no longer worthy to be called your son.' But the father said to his slaves, 'Quickly bring out the best robe and put it on him, and put a ring on his hand and sandals on his feet; and bring the fattened calf, kill it, and let us eat and celebrate; for this son of mine was dead and has come to life again; he was lost and has been found.' And they began to celebrate. Now his older son was in the field, when he came and approached the house, he heard music and dancing. And he summoned one of the servants and *began* inquiring what these things could be. And he said to him, 'Your brother has come, and your father has killed the fattened calf because he has received him back safe and sound.' But he became angry and was not willing to go in; and his father came out and *began* pleading with him. But he answered and said to his father, 'Look! For so many years I have been serving you and I have never neglected a command of yours; and *yet* you have never given me a young goat, so that I might celebrate with my friends; but when this son of yours came, who has devoured your wealth with prostitutes, you killed the fattened calf for him.' And he said to him, 'Son, you have always been with me, and all that is mine is yours. But we had to celebrate and rejoice, for this brother of yours was dead and *has begun* to live, and was lost and has been found'" (Luke 15:11–32; see Proverb 29:2).

POINT OF DEATH (Listed under DEATH, POINT OF)

POISON

Setting: Following His resurrection from the dead after being crucified, Jesus commissions His disciples to preach His gospel to the world.

And He said to them, "Go into all the world and preach the gospel to all creation. He who has believed and has been baptized shall be saved; but he who has disbelieved shall be condemned. These signs will accompany those who have believed: in My name they will cast out demons, they will speak with new tongues; they will pick up serpents, and if they drink any deadly *poison,* it will not hurt them; they will lay hands on the sick, and they will recover" (Mark 16:15–18; cf. Matthew 28:16–20; see Mark 9:38; John 3:18, 36; 1 Corinthians 15:6).

[Note: Some scholars question the authenticity of Mark 16:9–20 as these verses do not appear in some early New Testament manuscripts.]

POLL-TAX (Also see TAXES)

Setting: Capernaum of Galilee. Jesus pays the two-drachma temple tax for Peter and Himself in a miraculous manner.

He said, "Yes." And when he came into the house, Jesus spoke to him first, saying, "What do you think, Simon? From whom do the kings of the earth collect customs or poll-tax, from their sons or from strangers?" When Peter said, "From strangers," Jesus said to him, "Then the sons are exempt. However, so that we do not offend them, go to the sea and throw in a hook, and take the first fish that comes up; and when you open its mouth, you will find a shekel. Take that and give it to them for you and Me" (Matthew 17:25–27; see Exodus 30:11–16; Matthew 22:17–19; Romans 13:7).

Setting: The temple in Jerusalem. The Pharisees send their disciples and the Herodians to test Jesus about the poll-tax in order to trap Him.

But Jesus perceived their malice, and said, "Why are you testing Me, you hypocrites? Show Me the coin *used* for the poll-tax." And they brought Him a denarius. And He said to them, "Whose likeness and inscription is this?" They said to Him, "Caesar's." Then He said to them, "Then render to Caesar the things that are Caesar's; and to God the things that are God's" (Matthew 22:18–21; cf. Matthew 17:25; Mark 12:15–17; Luke 20:22–25).

POOL OF SILOAM (Listed under SILOAM, POOL OF)

POOR (POOR, GIVING TO THE is a separate entry; also see CHARITY and POVERTY)

Setting: Galilee. As He teaches and preaches, Jesus responds to John the Baptist's question (posed by some of John's disciples) whether He is Israel's promised Messiah.

Jesus answered and said to them, "Go and report to John what you hear and see: *the* BLIND RECEIVE SIGHT and *the* lame walk, *the* lepers are cleansed and *the* deaf hear, *the* dead are raised up, and *the* POOR HAVE THE GOSPEL PREACHED TO THEM. And blessed is he who does not take offense at Me" (Matthew 11:4–6, Jesus quotes from Isaiah 35:5f; cf. Luke 7:22, 23).

Setting: The home of Simon the leper in Bethany. Jesus rebukes His disciples after they criticize a woman for pouring a costly vial of perfume on His head in preparation for His burial.

But Jesus, aware of this, said to them, "Why do you bother the woman? For she has done a good deed to Me. For you always have the poor with you; but you do not always have Me. For when she poured this perfume on My body, she did it to prepare Me for burial. Truly I say to you, wherever this gospel is preached in the whole world, what this woman has done will also be spoken of in memory of her" (Matthew 26:10–13; cf. Mark 14:3–9; Luke 7:37–39; John 12:2–8; see Deuteronomy 15:11).

Setting: The home of Simon the leper in Bethany. Two days before the Feast of Unleavened Bread (Passover), Jesus commends a woman who anoints His head with costly perfume, which some there think should have been sold and the proceeds given to the poor.

But Jesus said, "Let her alone; why do you bother her? She has done a good deed to Me. For you always have the poor with you, and whenever you wish you can do good to them; but you do not always have Me. She has done what she could; she has anointed My body beforehand for the burial. Truly I say to you, wherever the gospel is preached in the whole world, what this woman has done will also be spoken of in memory of her" (Mark 14:6–9; cf. Matthew 26:6–13; John 12:2–8; see Deuteronomy 15:11).

Setting: The synagogue in Jesus' hometown of Nazareth in Galilee. At the beginning of His public ministry, Jesus reads on the Sabbath from the book of the prophet Isaiah.

And the book of the prophet Isaiah was handed to Him. And He opened the book and found the place where it was written, "THE SPIRIT OF THE LORD IS UPON ME, BECAUSE HE ANOINTED ME TO PREACH THE GOSPEL TO THE POOR. HE HAS SENT ME TO PROCLAIM RELEASE TO THE CAPTIVES, AND RECOVERY OF SIGHT TO THE BLIND, TO SET FREE THOSE WHO ARE OPPRESSED, TO PROCLAIM THE FAVORABLE YEAR OF THE LORD." And He closed the book, gave it back to the attendant and sat down; and the eyes of all in the synagogue were fixed on Him. And He began to say to them, "Today this Scripture has been fulfilled in your hearing" (Luke 4:17–21, Jesus quotes from Isaiah 61:1, 2).

Setting: Galilee. After selecting His twelve disciples, Jesus teaches the Beatitudes (part of the Sermon on the Mount) to those disciples and a great throng of people from Judea, Jerusalem, and the central coastal region of Tyre and Sidon.

And turning His gaze toward His disciples, He *began* to say, "Blessed *are* you *who are* poor, for yours is the kingdom of God" (Luke 6:20; cf. Matthew 5:3).

Setting: Galilee. After Jesus raises a woman's son from the dead in Nain, the disciples of John the Baptist inquire whether He is the promised Messiah.

And He answered and said to them, "Go and report to John what you have seen and heard: *the* BLIND RECEIVE SIGHT, *the* lame walk, *the* lepers are cleansed, and *the* deaf hear, *the* dead are raised up, *the* POOR HAVE THE GOSPEL PREACHED TO THEM. Blessed is he who does not take offense at Me" (Luke 7:22, 23, Jesus quotes from Isaiah 35:5; 61:1; cf. Matthew 11:2–6).

Setting: On the way from Galilee to Jerusalem. After Jesus, observing the invited guests of a Pharisee leader selecting places of honor at the table, speaks a parable to them, He comments to the host about the people to invite in the future.

And He also went on to say to the one who had invited Him, "When you give a luncheon or a dinner, do not invite your friends or your brothers or your relatives or rich neighbors, otherwise they may also invite you in return and *that* will be your repayment. But when you give a reception, invite *the* poor, *the* crippled, *the* lame, *the* blind, and you will be blessed, since they do not have *the means* to repay you; for you will be repaid at the resurrection of the righteous" (Luke 14:12–14; see John 5:28, 29).

Setting: On the way from Galilee to Jerusalem. After speaking a parable to the invited guests and the host at a banquet, Jesus responds to a guest's proclamation about the blessings of eating bread in the kingdom of God.

But He said to him, "A man was giving a big dinner, and he invited many; and at the dinner hour he sent his slave to say to those who had been invited, 'Come; for everything is ready now.' But they all alike began to make excuses. The first one said to him, 'I have bought a piece of land and I need to go out and look at it; please consider me excused.' Another one said, 'I have bought five yoke of oxen, and I am going to try them out; please consider me excused.' Another one said, I have married a wife, and for that reason I cannot come.' And the slave came *back* and reported this to his master. Then the head of the household became angry and said to his slave, 'Go out at once into the streets and lanes of the city and bring in here the poor and crippled and blind and lame.' And the slave said, 'Master, what you commanded has been done, and still there is room.' And the master said to the slave, 'Go out into the highways and along the hedges, and compel *them* to come in, so that my house may be filled. For I tell you, none of those men who were invited shall taste of my dinner'" (Luke 14:16–24; see Deuteronomy 24:5; Matthew 22:2–14).

[POOR from impoverished]
Setting: On the way from Galilee to Jerusalem. Jesus conveys the illustration of the prodigal son because the Pharisees and scribes complain He associates with tax collectors and sinners.

And He said, "A man had two sons. The younger of them said to his father, 'Father, give me the share of the estate that falls to me.' So he divided his wealth between them. And not many days later, the younger son gathered everything together and went on a journey into a distant country, and there he squandered his estate with loose living. Now when he had spent everything, a severe famine occurred in that country, and he began to be impoverished. So he went and hired himself out to one of the citizens of that country, and he sent him into his fields to feed swine. And he would have gladly filled his stomach with the pods that the swine were eating, and no one was giving *anything* to him. But when he came to his senses, he said, 'How many of my father's hired men have more than enough bread, but I am dying here with hunger! I will get up and go to my father, and will say to him, "Father, I have sinned against heaven, and in your sight; I am no longer worthy to be called your son; make me as one of your hired men."' So he got up and came to his father. But while he was still a long way off, his father saw him and felt compassion *for him,* and ran and embraced him and kissed him. And the son said to him, "Father, I have sinned against heaven and in your sight; I am no longer worthy to be called your son.' But the father said to his slaves, 'Quickly bring out the best robe and put it on him, and put a ring on his hand and sandals on his feet; and bring the fattened calf, kill it, and let us eat and celebrate; for this son of mine was dead and has come to life again; he was lost and has been found.' And they began to celebrate. Now his older son was in the field, when he came and approached the house, he heard music and dancing. And he summoned one of the servants and *began* inquiring what these things could be. And he said to him, 'Your brother has come, and your father has killed the fattened calf because he has received him back safe and sound.' But he became angry and was not willing to go in; and his father came out and *began* pleading with him. But he answered and said to his father, 'Look! For so many years I have been serving you and I have never neglected a command of yours; and *yet* you have never given me a young goat, so that I might celebrate with my friends; but when this son of yours came, who has devoured your wealth with prostitutes, you killed the fattened calf for him.' And he said to him, 'Son, you have always been with me, and all that is mine is yours. But we had to celebrate and rejoice, for this brother of yours was dead and *has begun* to live, and was lost and has been found' " (Luke 15:11–32; see Proverb 29:2).

Setting: Bethany near Jerusalem. Six days before the Passover in Jerusalem, as the chief priests and Pharisees plot to seize Him, Jesus visits Lazarus, Martha, and Mary. Mary anoints the Lord's feet with costly perfume, made of pure nard.

Therefore Jesus said, "Let her alone, so that she may keep it for the day of My burial. For you always have the poor with you, but you do not always have Me" (John 12:7, 8; cf. Matthew 26:6–13; Mark 14:3–9; see Deuteronomy 15:11).

Setting: On the island of Patmos (in the Aegean Sea about fifty miles southwest of Ephesus in modern Turkey). On the Lord's Day (Sunday), approximately fifty years after the Resurrection, the disciple John encounters the Lord Jesus Christ, who communicates a new revelation for the apostle to record for the church in Laodicea and to six other churches in Asia.

"To the angel of the church in Laodicea write: The Amen, the faithful and true Witness, the Beginning of the creation of God, says this: 'I know your deeds, that you are neither cold nor hot; I wish that you were cold or hot. So because you are lukewarm, and neither hot nor cold, I will spit you out of My mouth. Because you say, "I am rich, and have become wealthy, and have need of nothing," and you do not know that you are wretched and miserable and poor and blind and naked, I advise you to buy from Me gold refined by fire so that you may become rich, and white garments so that you may clothe yourself, and *that* the shame of your nakedness will not be revealed; and eye salve to anoint your eyes so that you may see. Those whom I love, I reprove and discipline; therefore be zealous and repent. Behold, I stand at the door and knock; if anyone hears My voice and opens the door, I will come in to him and will dine with him, and he with Me. He who overcomes, I will grant to him to sit down with Me on My throne, as I also overcame and sat down with My Father on His throne. He who has an ear, let him hear what the Spirit says to the churches'" (Revelation 3:14–22; see Proverb 3:12; Hosea 12:8; John 14:23; 16:33).

POOR, GIVING TO THE (Also see CHARITY; POOR; and WORKS, GOOD)

[GIVING TO THE POOR from give to the poor]

Setting: Galilee. During the early part of His ministry, Jesus preaches the Sermon on the Mount to His disciples and the multitudes.

"So when you give to the poor, do not sound a trumpet before you, as the hypocrites do in the synagogues and in the streets, so that they may be honored by men. Truly I say to you, they have their reward in full. But when you give to the poor, do not let your left hand know what your right hand is doing, so that your giving will be in secret; and your Father who sees *what is done* in secret will reward you" (Matthew 6:2–4; see Jeremiah 17:10).

[GIVING TO THE POOR from give to *the* poor]

Setting: Judea beyond the Jordan (Perea). Jesus shares with a rich, young ruler how to obtain eternal life.

And He said to him, "Why are you asking Me about what is good? There is *only* One who is good; but if you wish to enter into life, keep the commandments." *Then* he said to Him, 'Which ones?' And Jesus said, "YOU SHALL NOT COMMIT MURDER; YOU SHALL NOT COMMIT ADULTERY; YOU SHALL NOT STEAL; YOU SHALL NOT BEAR FALSE WITNESS; HONOR YOUR FATHER AND MOTHER; and YOU SHALL LOVE YOUR NEIGHBOR AS YOURSELF." The young man said to Him, "All these things I have kept; what am I still lacking?" Jesus said to him, "If you wish to complete go *and* sell your possessions and give to *the* poor, and you will have treasure in heaven; and come, follow Me" (Matthew 19:16–22, Jesus quotes from Exodus 20:13–15; Leviticus 19:18; cf. Leviticus 18:5; Mark 10:17–21;

Luke 10:25–28; 12:33; 18:18–24).

[GIVING TO THE POOR from give to the poor]
Setting: Judea beyond the Jordan (Perea). After demonstrating to His disciples the importance of little children, Jesus encounters a rich man seeking eternal life.

And Jesus said to him, "Why do you call Me good? No one is good except God alone. You know the commandments, 'DO NOT MURDER, DO NOT COMMIT ADULTERY, DO NOT STEAL, DO NOT BEAR FALSE WITNESS, Do not defraud, HONOR YOUR FATHER AND MOTHER.'" And he said to Him, "Teacher, I have kept all these things from my youth up." Looking at him, Jesus felt a love for him and said to him, "One thing you lack: go and sell all you possess and give to the poor, and you will have treasure in heaven; and come, follow Me" (Mark 10:18–21; Jesus quotes from Exodus 20:12–16; cf. Matthew 19:16–22; Luke 18:18–24; see Matthew 6:20).

[GIVING TO THE POOR from poor and you can do good to them]
Setting: The home of Simon the leper in Bethany. Two days before the Feast of Unleavened Bread (Passover), Jesus commends a woman who anoints His head with costly perfume, which some there think should have been sold and the proceeds given to the poor.

But Jesus said, "Let her alone; why do you bother her? She has done a good deed to Me. For you always have the poor with you, and whenever you wish you can do good to them; but you do not always have Me. She has done what she could; she has anointed My body beforehand for the burial. Truly I say to you, wherever the gospel is preached in the whole world, what this woman has done will also be spoken of in memory of her" (Mark 14:6–9; cf. Matthew 26:6–13; John 12:2–8; see Deuteronomy 15:11).

[GIVIING TO THE POOR from distribute it to the poor]
Setting: Judea beyond the Jordan (Perea). After speaking of the importance of children, Jesus responds to a ruler's question about obtaining eternal life.

A ruler questioned Him, saying, "Good Teacher, what shall I do to inherit eternal life?" And Jesus said to him, "Why do you call Me good? No one is good except God alone. You know the commandments, 'DO NOT COMMIT ADULTERY, DO NOT MURDER, DO NOT STEAL, DO NOT BEAR FALSE WITNESS, HONOR YOUR FATHER AND MOTHER.'" And he said, "All these things I have kept from *my* youth." When Jesus heard *this,* He said to him, "One thing you still lack; sell all that you possess and distribute it to the poor, and you shall have treasure in heaven; and come, follow Me" (Luke 18:18–22, Jesus quotes from Exodus 20:12–16; cf. Matthew 19:16–22; Mark 10:17–22; see Luke 10:25–28).

POOR IN SPIRIT (Listed under SPIRIT, POOR IN)

POPULARITY (See APPROVAL, MAN'S; and PRAISE RECEIVED FROM OTHERS)

PORNOGRAPHY (Also see LUST; and SEXUAL SIN)

[PORNOGRAPHY from everyone who looks at a woman with lust for her has already committed adultery]
Setting: Galilee. During the early part of His ministry, Jesus preaches the Sermon on the Mount to His disciples and the multitudes.

"You have heard that it was said, 'YOU SHALL NOT COMMIT ADULTERY'; but I say to you that everyone who looks at a woman with lust for her has already committed adultery with her in his heart" (Matthew 5:27, 28, Jesus quotes from Exodus 20:14; see 2 Samuel 11:2–5).

POSSESSION, DEMON (See DEMON POSSESSION)

POSSESSIONS (Also see GREED; MONEY; PROPERTY; TREASURE; TREASURES; and WEALTH)

[POSSESSIONS from For what will it profit a man if he gains the whole world and forfeits his soul]

Setting: Near Caesarea Philippi. After rebuking Peter for trying to forbid Him to accomplish His earthly mission of dying and being resurrected, Jesus teaches His disciples about the costs of following Him.

Then Jesus said to His disciples, "If anyone wishes to come after Me, he must deny himself, and take up his cross and follow Me. For whoever wishes to save his life will lose it; but whoever loses his life for My sake will find it. For what will it profit a man if he gains the whole world and forfeits his soul? Or what will a man give in exchange for his soul? For the Son of Man is going to come in the glory of His Father with His angels, and WILL THEN REPAY EVERY MAN ACCORDING TO HIS DEEDS. Truly, I say to you, there are some of you who are standing here who will not taste death until they see the Son of Man coming in His kingdom" (Matthew 16:24–28, Jesus quotes from Psalm 62:12; cf. Mark 8:34–37; Luke 9:23–27; see Matthew 10:38, 39).

Setting: Judea beyond the Jordan (Perea). Jesus shares with a rich, young ruler how to obtain eternal life.

And He said to him, "Why are you asking Me about what is good? There is *only* One who is good; but if you wish to enter into life, keep the commandments." *Then* he said to Him, 'Which ones?' And Jesus said, "YOU SHALL NOT COMMIT MURDER; YOU SHALL NOT COMMIT ADULTERY; YOU SHALL NOT STEAL; YOU SHALL NOT BEAR FALSE WITNESS; HONOR YOUR FATHER AND MOTHER; and YOU SHALL LOVE YOUR NEIGHBOR AS YOURSELF." The young man said to Him, "All these things I have kept; what am I still lacking?" Jesus said to him, "If you wish to complete go *and* sell your possessions and give to *the* poor, and you will have treasure in heaven; and come, follow Me" (Matthew 19:16–22, Jesus quotes from Exodus 20:13–15; Leviticus 19:18; cf. Leviticus 18:5; Mark 10:17–21; Luke 10:25–28; 12:33; 18:18–24).

Setting: On the Mount of Olives, just east of Jerusalem. During His Olivet Discourse, after answering His disciples' questions as to when the temple will be destroyed and Jerusalem overrun, along with the signs of His coming and the end of the age, Jesus reemphasizes to His disciples that they should be on the alert for His return.

"Therefore be on the alert, for you do not know which day your Lord is coming. But be sure of this, that if the head of the house had known at what time of the night the thief was coming, he would have been on the alert and would not have allowed his house to be broken into. For this reason you also must be ready; for the Son of Man is coming at an hour when you do not think *He will.* Who then is the faithful and sensible slave whom his master put in charge of his household to give their food at the proper time? Blessed is that slave whom his master finds so doing when he comes. Truly I say to you that he will put him in charge of all his possessions. But if that evil slave says in his heart, 'My master is not coming for a long time,' and begins to beat his fellow slaves and eat and drink with drunkards; the master of that slave will come on a day when he does not expect *him* and at an hour which he does not know, and will cut him in pieces and assign him a place with the hypocrites; in that place there will be weeping and gnashing of teeth" (Matthew 24:42–51; cf. Mark 13:33–37; Luke 12:39–46; 21:34–36; see Matthew 8:11, 12; 25:21–23).

Setting: On the Mount of Olives, just east of Jerusalem. During His Olivet Discourse, after answering His disciples' questions as to when the temple will be destroyed and Jerusalem overrun, along with the signs of His coming and the end of the age, Jesus reemphasizes to His disciples that they should be on the alert for His return.

"For *it is* just like a man *about* to go on a journey, who called his own slaves and entrusted his possessions to them. To one he gave five talents, to another, two, and to another, one, each according to his own ability; and he went on his journey. Immediately the one who had received the five talents went and traded with them, and gained five more talents. In the same manner the one who *had received* the two *talents* gained two more. But he who received the one *talent* went away, and dug a *hole* in the ground and hid his master's money. Now after a long time the master of those slaves came and settled accounts with them. The one who had received the five talents came up and brought five more talents, saying, 'Master, you entrusted five talents to me. See, I have gained five more talents.' His master said to him, 'Well done, good and faithful slave. You were faithful with a few things, I will put you in charge of many things; enter into the joy of your master.' Also the one who *had received* the two talents came up and said, 'Master, you entrusted two talents to me. See, I have gained two more talents.' His master said to him, 'Well done, good and faithful slave. You were faithful with a few things, I will put you in charge of many things; enter into the joy of your master.' And the one also who had received the one talent came up and said, 'Master, I knew you to be a hard man, reaping where you did not sow and gathering where you scattered no *seed.* And I was afraid, and went away and hid your talent in the ground. See, you have what is yours.' But his master answered and said to him, 'You wicked, lazy slave, you knew that I reap where I did not sow and gather where I scattered no *seed.* Then you ought to have put my money in the bank, and on my arrival I would have received my *money* back with interest. 'Therefore take away the talent from him, and give it to the one who has ten talents.' For to everyone who has, *more* shall be given, and he will have an abundance; but from the one who does not have, even what he does have shall be taken away. Throw out the worthless slave into the outer darkness; in that place there will be weeping and gnashing of teeth" (Matthew 25:14–30; cf. Matthew 8:12; 13:12; 24:45–47; see Matthew 18:23, 24; Luke 12:44).

[POSSESSIONS from For what does it profit a man to gain the whole world, and forfeit his soul]
Setting: Caesarea Philippi. After rebuking Peter for desiring to thwart His mission to the cross, Jesus summons a crowd, along with His disciples, and informs them of the high costs of following Him.

And He summoned the crowd with His disciples, and said to them, "If anyone wishes to come after Me, he must deny himself, and take up his cross and follow Me. For whoever wishes to save his life will lose it, but whoever loses his life for My sake and the gospel's will save it. For what does it profit a man to gain the whole world, and forfeit his soul? For what will a man give in exchange for his soul? For whoever is ashamed of Me and My words in this adulterous and sinful generation, the Son of Man will also be ashamed of him when He comes in the glory of His Father with the holy angels" (Mark 8:34–38; cf. Matthew 16:24–28; Luke 9:23–27; see Matthew 10:33, 38, 39).

[POSSESSIONS from all you possess]
Setting: Judea beyond the Jordan (Perea). After demonstrating to His disciples the importance of little children, Jesus encounters a rich man seeking eternal life.

And Jesus said to him, "Why do you call Me good? No one is good except God alone. You know the commandments, 'DO NOT MURDER, DO NOT COMMIT ADULTERY, DO NOT STEAL, DO NOT BEAR FALSE WITNESS, Do not defraud, HONOR YOUR FATHER AND MOTHER.'" And he said to Him, "Teacher, I have kept all these things from my youth up." Looking at him, Jesus felt a love for him and said to him, "One thing you lack: go and sell all you possess and give to the poor, and you will have treasure in heaven; and come, follow Me" (Mark 10:18–21; Jesus quotes from Exodus 20:12–16; cf. Matthew 19:16–22; Luke 18:18–24; see Matthew 6:20).

[POSSESSIONS from For what is a man profited if he gains the whole world, and loses or forfeits himself]
Setting: Galilee. Following Peter's pronouncement that Jesus is the Christ of God, the Lord conveys the demands of discipleship and the hope regarding the kingdom of God.

And He was saying to *them* all, "If anyone wishes to come after Me, he must deny himself, and take up his cross daily and follow Me. For whoever wishes to save his life will lose it, but whoever loses his life for My sake, he is the one who will save it. For what is a man profited if he gains the whole world, and loses or forfeits himself? For whoever is ashamed of Me and My words, the Son of Man will be ashamed of him when He comes in His glory, and *the glory* of the Father and of the holy angels. But I say to you truthfully, there are some of those standing here who will not taste death until they see the kingdom of God" (Luke 9:23–27; cf. Matthew 16:24–26, 28; Mark 8:34–37; see Matthew 10:33, 38, 39).

Setting: On the way from Galilee to Jerusalem. After some in the crowd test Him, demanding a sign from heaven, Jesus illustrates His power over Satan.

"When a strong *man*, fully armed, guards his own house, his possessions are undisturbed. But when someone stronger than he attacks him and overpowers him, he takes away from him all his armor on which he had relied and distributes his plunder. He who is not with Me is against Me; and he who does not gather with Me, scatters" (Luke 11:21–23; cf. Matthew 12:29, 30).

Setting: On the way from Galilee to Jerusalem. After the scribes and Pharisees turn hostile and question Him repeatedly in an attempt to catch Him in something He might say, Jesus teaches the crowds and His disciples about greed and possessions.

But He said to him, "Man, who appointed Me a judge or arbitrator over you?" Then He said to them, "Beware, and be on your guard against every form of greed; for not *even* when one has an abundance does his life consist of his possessions" (Luke 12:14, 15; see 1 Timothy 6:6–10).

Setting: On the way from Galilee to Jerusalem. After giving a parable about riches and greed, Jesus challenges the crowd and His disciples concerning godly living.

"Sell your possessions and give to charity; make yourselves money belts which do not wear out, an unfailing treasure in heaven, where no thief comes near nor moth destroys. For where your treasure is, there your heart will be also" (Luke 12:33, 34; cf. Matthew 6:19–21; 19:21).

Setting: On the way from Galilee to Jerusalem. When Jesus uses a parable to challenge the crowd and His disciples to be ready for His return, Peter asks Him whom He is addressing.

And the Lord said, "Who then is the faithful and sensible steward, whom his master will put in charge of his servants, to give them their rations at the proper time? Blessed is that slave whom his master finds so doing when he comes. Truly I say to you that he will put him in charge of all his possessions. But if that slave says in his heart, 'My master will be a long time in coming,' and begins to beat the slaves, *both* men and women, and to eat and drink and get drunk; the master of that slave will come on a day when he does not expect *him* and at an hour he does not know, and will cut him in pieces, and assign him a place with the unbelievers. And that slave who knew his master's will and did not get ready or act in accord with his will, will receive many lashes, but the one who did know *it,* and committed deeds worthy of flogging, will receive but few. From everyone who has been given much, much will be required; and to whom they entrusted much, of him they will ask all the more" (Luke 12:42–48; cf. Matthew 24:45–51; see Leviticus 5:17).

Setting: On the way from Galilee to Jerusalem. After He responds to a guest's proclamation about the blessings of eating bread in the kingdom of God, Jesus presents to large crowds the demands of discipleship.

Now large crowds were going along with Him; and He turned and said to them, "If anyone comes to Me, and does not hate his own father and mother and wife and children and brothers and sisters, yes, and even his own life, he cannot be My disciple. Whoever does not carry his own cross and come after Me cannot be My disciple. For which one of you, when he wants to build a tower, does not first sit down and calculate the cost to see if he has enough to complete it? Otherwise, when he has laid a foundation and is not able to finish, all who observe it begin to ridicule him, saying, 'This man began to build and was not able to finish.' Or what king, when he sets out to meet another king in battle, will not first sit down and consider whether he is strong enough with ten thousand *men* to encounter the one coming against him with twenty thousand? Or else, while the other is still far away, he sends a delegation and asks for terms of peace. So then, none of you can be My disciple who does not give up all his possessions. Therefore, salt is good; but if even salt has become tasteless, with what will it be seasoned? It is useless either for the soil or for the manure pile; it is thrown out. He who has ears to hear, let him hear" (Luke 14:25–35; cf. Matthew 5:13; 10:37–39; see Proverb 20:18; Philippians 3:7).

Setting: On the way from Galilee to Jerusalem. After giving the story of the prodigal son, the Lord teaches His disciples about stewardship.

Now He was also saying to the disciples, "There was a rich man who had a manager, and this *manager* was reported to him as squandering his possessions. And he called him and said to him, 'What is this I hear about you? Give an accounting of your management, for you can no longer be a manager.' The manager said to himself, 'What shall I do, since my master is taking the management away from me? I am not strong enough to dig; I am ashamed to beg. I know what I shall do, so that when I am removed from the management people will welcome me into their homes.' And he summoned each one of his master's debtors, and he *began* saying to the first, 'How much do you owe my master?' And he said, 'A hundred measures of oil.' And he said to him, 'Take your bill, and sit down quickly and write fifty.' Then he said to another, 'And how much do you owe?' And he said, 'A hundred measures of wheat.' He said to him, 'Take your bill, and write eighty.' And his master praised the unrighteous manager because he had acted shrewdly; for the sons of this age are more shrewd in relation to their own kind than the sons of light. And I say to you, make friends for yourselves by means of the wealth of unrighteousness, so that when it fails, they will receive you into the eternal dwellings. He who is faithful in a very little thing is faithful also in much; and he who is unrighteous in a very little thing is unrighteous also in much. Therefore if you have not been faithful in the *use of* unrighteous wealth, who will entrust the true *riches* to you? And if you have not been faithful in *the use of* that which is another's, who will give you that which is your own? No servant can serve two masters; for either he will hate the one and love the other, or else he will be devoted to one and despise the other. You cannot serve God and wealth" (Luke 16:1–13; cf. Matthew 6:24; see Matthew 25:14–30).

[POSSESSIONS from all that you possess]
Setting: Judea beyond the Jordan (Perea). After speaking of the importance of children, Jesus responds to a ruler's question about obtaining eternal life.

A ruler questioned Him, saying, "Good Teacher, what shall I do to inherit eternal life?" And Jesus said to him, "Why do you call Me good? No one is good except God alone. You know the commandments, 'DO NOT COMMIT ADULTERY, DO NOT MURDER, DO NOT STEAL, DO NOT BEAR FALSE WITNESS, HONOR YOUR FATHER AND MOTHER.'" And he said, "All these things I have kept from *my* youth." When Jesus heard *this,* He said to him, "One thing you still lack; sell all that you possess and distribute it to the poor, and you shall have treasure in heaven; and come, follow Me" (Luke 18:18–22, Jesus quotes from Exodus 20:12–16; cf. Matthew 19:16–22; Mark 10:17–22; see Luke 10:25–28).

POSSIBILITIES WITH GOD (Listed under GOD, POSSIBILITIES WITH)

POTTER

Setting: On the island of Patmos (in the Aegean Sea about fifty miles southwest of Ephesus in modern Turkey). On the Lord's Day (Sunday), approximately fifty years after the Resurrection, the disciple John encounters the Lord Jesus Christ, who communicates a new revelation for the apostle to record for the church in Thyatira and to six other churches in Asia.

"And to the angel of the church in Thyatira write: The Son of God, who has eyes like a flame of fire, and His feet are like burnished bronze, says this: 'I know your deeds, and your love and faith and service and perseverance, and that your deeds of late are greater than at first. But I have *this* against you, that you tolerate the woman Jezebel, who calls herself a prophetess, and she teaches and leads My bond-servants astray so that they commit *acts of* immorality and eat things sacrificed to idols. I gave her time to repent, and she does not want to repent of her immorality. Behold, I will throw her on a bed *of sickness,* and those who commit adultery with her into great tribulation, unless they repent of her deeds. And I will kill her children with pestilence, and all the churches will know that I am He who searches the minds and hearts; and I will give to each one of you according to your deeds. But I say to you, the rest who are in Thyatira, who do not hold this teaching, who have not known the deep things of Satan, as they call them—I place no other burden on you. Nevertheless what you have, hold fast until I come. He who overcomes, and he who keeps My deeds until the end, TO HIM I WILL GIVE AUTHORITY OVER THE NATIONS; AND HE SHALL RULE THEM WITH A ROD OF IRON, AS THE VESSELS OF THE POTTER ARE BROKEN TO PIECES, as I also have received *authority* from My Father; and I will give him the morning star. He who has an ear, let him hear what the Spirit says to the churches' (Revelation 2:18–29; Jesus quotes from Psalm 2:8, 9; Isaiah 30:14; see 1 Kings 16:31; Psalm 7:9; Romans 2:5; 1 Corinthians 2:10; 2 Peter 3:9; Revelation 1:14; 2:7; 3:11; 17:1–20).

POVERTY (Also see POOR)

Setting: Opposite the treasury, near the temple in Jerusalem. Jesus focuses His disciples' attention on a widow's monetary sacrifice.

Calling His disciples to Him, He said to them, "Truly I say to you, this poor widow put in more than all the contributors to the treasury; for they all put in out of their surplus, but she, out of her poverty, put in all she owned, all she had to live on" (Mark 12:43, 44; cf. Luke 21:1–4).

Setting: The temple in Jerusalem. While ministering a few days before His crucifixion, after warning His disciples about the lifestyle of the scribes, Jesus points out a poor widow's sacrificial giving to the temple treasury.

And He said, "Truly I say to you, this poor widow put in more than all *of them;* for they all out of their surplus put into the offering; but she out of her poverty put in all that she had to live on" (Luke 21:3, 4; cf. Mark 12:41–44).

Setting: On the island of Patmos (in the Aegean Sea about fifty miles southwest of Ephesus in modern Turkey). On the Lord's Day (Sunday), approximately fifty years after the Resurrection, the disciple John encounters the Lord Jesus Christ, who communicates a new revelation for the apostle to record for the church in Smyrna and to six other churches in Asia.

"And to the angel of the church in Smyrna write: The first and the last, who was dead, and has come to life, says this: 'I know your tribulation and your poverty (but you are rich), and the blasphemy by those who say they are Jews and are not, but are a synagogue of Satan. Do not fear what you are about to suffer. Behold, the devil is about to cast some of you into prison, so that you will be tested, and you will have tribulation for ten days. Be faithful until death, and I will give you the crown of life. He who has an ear, let him hear what the Spirit says to the churches. He who overcomes will not be hurt by the second death' (Revelation 2:8–11; see Isaiah 44:6; Revelation 1:9, 18; 20:6, 14).

POWER (POWER, GREAT; POWER, JESUS'; POWER, LITTLE; POWER OF GOD; and POWER, RIGHT HAND OF are separate entries; also see AUTHORITY; and POWERS)

Setting: Galilee. During the early part of His ministry, Jesus gives a model prayer to His disciples and the multitudes while conveying the Sermon on the Mount.

"Pray, then, in this way: 'Our Father who is in heaven, hallowed be Your name. Your kingdom come. Your will be done, on earth as it is in heaven. Give us this day our daily bread. And forgive us our debts, as we also have forgiven our debtors. And do not lead us into temptation, but deliver us from evil. [For Yours is the kingdom and the power and the glory forever. Amen]'" (Matthew 6:9–13; cf. Luke 11:2–4; see John 17:15).

Setting: The Mount of Olives, just east of Jerusalem. During His Olivet Discourse, Jesus answers His disciples' questions as to when the temple will be destroyed and Jerusalem overrun, along with the signs of His coming and the end of the age.

"But immediately after the tribulation of those days THE SUN WILL BE DARKENED, AND THE MOON WILL NOT GIVE ITS LIGHT, AND THE STARS WILL FALL from the sky, and the powers of the heavens will be shaken. And then the sign of the Son of Man will appear in the sky, and then all the tribes of the earth will mourn, and they will see the SON OF MAN COMING ON THE CLOUDS OF THE SKY with power and great glory. And He will send forth His angels with A GREAT TRUMPET and THEY WILL GATHER TOGETHER His elect from the four winds, from one end of the sky to the other" (Matthew 24:29–31, Jesus quotes from Isaiah 13:10, Daniel 7:13; Exodus 19:16; cf. Mark 13:24–27; Luke 21:25–27).

Setting: Caesarea Philippi. After He rebukes Peter for desiring to thwart His mission to the cross, Jesus summons a crowd, along with His disciples, and informs them of the hope involving the coming kingdom of God.

And Jesus was saying to them, "Truly I say to you, there are some of those who are standing here who will not taste death until they see the kingdom of God after it has come with power" (Mark 9:1; cf. Matthew 16:28; Luke 9:27).

Setting: Capernaum. After ministering in the country of the Gerasenes, east of the Sea of Galilee, Jesus returns, and a woman, ill for twelve years, receives healing by touching His garment.

And Jesus said, "Who is the one who touched Me?" And while they were all denying it, Peter said, "Master, the people are crowding and pressing in on You." But Jesus said, "Someone did touch Me, for I was aware, that power had gone out of Me." When the woman saw that she had not escaped notice, she came trembling and fell down before Him, and declared in the presence of all the people the reason why she had touched Him, and how she had been immediately healed. And He said to her, "Daughter, your faith has made you well; go in peace" (Luke 8:45–48; cf. Matthew 9:20; Mark 5:25–34).

Setting: On the way from Galilee to Jerusalem. The Lord responds to a report from the seventy sent out in pairs to every place He Himself will soon visit.

And He said to them, "I was watching Satan fall from heaven like lightning. Behold, I have given you authority to tread on serpents and scorpions, and over all the power of the enemy, and nothing will injure you. Nevertheless do not rejoice in this, that the spirits are subject to you, but rejoice that your names are recorded in heaven" (Luke 10:18–20; see Psalm 91:13; Isaiah 14:12–14; Luke 9:1).

Setting: On the Mount of Olives, just east of Jerusalem. After ministering in the temple a few days before His crucifixion, and giving His disciples more details regarding future events, Jesus speaks during His Olivet Discourse of His return.

"There will be signs in sun and moon and stars, and on the earth dismay among the nations, in perplexity at the roaring of the sea and the waves, men fainting from fear and the expectation of the things which are coming upon the world; for the powers of the heavens will be shaken. Then they will see THE SON OF MAN COMING IN A CLOUD with power and great glory. But when these things begin to take place, straighten up and lift up your heads, because your redemption is drawing near" (Luke 21:25–28, Jesus quotes from Daniel 7:13; cf. Matthew 24:29–31; Mark 13:24–27).

Setting: Gethsemane on the Mount of Olives, east of the temple in Jerusalem. After praying for deliverance, with His crucifixion imminent, Jesus chastises the religious leaders after Judas betrays Him and the hostile crowd surrounds Him.

Then Jesus said to the chief priests and officers of the temple and elders who had come against Him, "Have you come out with swords and clubs as you would against a robber? While I was with you daily in the temple, you did not lay hands on Me; but this hour and the power of darkness are yours" (Luke 22:52, 53; cf. Matthew 26:47–56; Mark 14:43–50).

Setting: Jerusalem. After rising from the tomb on the third day after being crucified, and appearing to two of His followers on the road to Emmaus, Jesus gives instruction to His disciples (except Thomas) about His mission on earth and the promise of future power from God.

Now He said to them, "These are My words which I spoke to you while I was still with you, that all things which are written about Me in the Law of Moses and the Prophets and the Psalms must be fulfilled." Then He opened their minds to understand the Scriptures, and He said to them, "Thus it is written, that the Christ would suffer and rise again from the dead the third day, and that repentance for forgiveness of sins would be proclaimed in His name to all the nations, beginning from Jerusalem. You are witnesses of these things. And behold, I am sending forth the promise of My Father upon you; but you are to stay in the city until you are clothed with power from on high" (Luke 24:44–49; see Matthew 28:19, 20; Acts 1:8).

Setting: Jerusalem. Luke, writing in Acts, presents quotes from Jesus' post-resurrection appearances, in which He responds to their question if He is about to restore the kingdom to Israel.

He said to them, "It is not for you to know times or epochs which the Father has fixed by His own authority; but you will receive power when the Holy Spirit has come upon you; and you shall be My witnesses both in Jerusalem, and in all Judea and Samaria, and even to the remotest part of the earth" (Acts 1:7, 8; see Luke 24:48, 49; Acts 2:1–4).

Setting: During his third missionary journey, writing (from Macedonia) a second letter to the church at Corinth, the apostle Paul recounts the Lord's response to his three petitions asking God to remove the affliction caused by the thorn in his flesh from Satan.

And He has said to me, "My grace is sufficient for you, for power is perfected in weakness." Most gladly, therefore, I will rather boast about my weaknesses, so that the power of Christ may dwell in me (2 Corinthians 12:9; see 1 Corinthians 2:1–5).

POWER, GOD'S (See POWER OF GOD; also see POWER)

POWER, GREAT

Setting: On the Mount of Olives, east of the temple in Jerusalem. After prophesying the temple's destruction, Jesus responds during His Olivet Discourse to questions from Peter, James, John, and Andrew about other future events.

"But in those days, after that tribulation, THE SUN WILL BE DARKENED AND THE MOON WILL NOT GIVE ITS LIGHT, AND THE STARS WILL BE FALLING from heaven, and the powers that are in the heavens will be shaken. Then they will see THE SON OF MAN COMING IN CLOUDS with great power and glory. And then He will send forth the angels, and will gather together His elect from the four winds, from the farthest end of the earth to the farthest end of heaven" (Mark 13:24–27. Jesus quotes from Isaiah 13:10; 34:4; Daniel 7:13; cf. Matthew 24:29–31; Luke 21:25–27).

POWER, JESUS' (Also see DEMONS, CASTING OUT; DOMINION; HEALING; MIRACLE; MIRACLES; POWER OF GOD; RESUSCITATION; and SIGNS AND WONDERS)

[JESUS' POWER from All things have been handed over to Me by My Father]
Setting: Galilee. As He teaches and preaches, after pronouncing woes upon unrepentant cities, Jesus prays a thanksgiving prayer to His Father in heaven.

At that time Jesus said, "I praise You, Father, Lord of heaven and earth, that you have hidden these things from *the* wise and intelligent and have revealed them to infants. Yes, Father, for this way was well-pleasing in Your sight. All things have been handed over to Me by My Father; and no one knows the Son except the Father; nor does anyone know the Father except the Son, and anyone to whom the Son wills to reveal *Him*" (Matthew 11:25–27; cf. Luke 10:21, 22).

[JESUS' POWER from All things have been handed over to Me by My Father]
Setting: On the way from Galilee to Jerusalem. The Lord responds to a report from the seventy sent out in pairs to every place He Himself will soon visit.

At that very time He rejoiced greatly in the Holy Spirit, and said, "I praise You, O Father, Lord of heaven and earth, that You have hidden these things from *the* wise and intelligent and have revealed them to infants. Yes, Father, for this way was well-pleasing in Your sight. All things have been handed over to Me by My Father, and no one knows who the Son is except the Father, and who the Father is except the Son, and anyone to whom the Son wills to reveal *Him*." (Luke 10:21, 22; cf. Matthew 11:25–27; see John 3:35; 10:15).

POWER, LITTLE

Setting: On the island of Patmos (in the Aegean Sea about fifty miles southwest of Ephesus in modern Turkey). On the Lord's Day (Sunday), approximately fifty years after the Resurrection, the disciple John encounters the Lord Jesus Christ, who communicates a new revelation for the apostle to record for the church in Philadelphia and to six other churches in Asia.

"And to the angel of the church in Philadelphia write: He who is holy, who is true, who has the key of David, who opens and no one will shut, and who shuts and no one opens, says this: 'I know your deeds. Behold, I have put before you an open door which no one can shut, because you have a little power, and have kept My word, and have not denied My name. Behold, I will cause *those* of the synagogue of Satan, who say that they are Jews and are not, but lie—I will make them come and bow down at your feet, and *make them* know that I have loved you. Because you have kept the word of My perseverance, I also will keep you from the hour of testing, that *hour* which is about to come upon the whole world, to test those who dwell on the earth. I am coming quickly; hold fast what you have, so that no one will take your crown. He who overcomes, I will make him a pillar in the temple of My God, and he will not go out from it anymore; and I will write on him the name of My God, and the name of the city of My God, the new Jerusalem, which comes down out of heaven from My God, and My new name. He who has an ear, let him hear what the Spirit says to the churches' " (Revelation 3:7–13; see Isaiah 22:22; Galatians 2:9; Revelation 2:9, 10, 13, 25; 14:1).

POWER, RIGHT HAND OF (Also see POWER, GOD'S; and THRONE OF GOD)

Setting: Jerusalem. After being betrayed by Judas and arrested, Jesus appears before Caiaphas the high priest and the Council for interrogation aimed at entrapping Him.

Jesus said to him, "You have said it *yourself;* nevertheless I tell you, hereafter you will see THE SON OF MAN SITTING AT THE RIGHT HAND OF POWER, AND COMING ON THE CLOUDS OF HEAVEN" (Matthew 26:64, Jesus quotes from Daniel 7:13; cf. Mark 14:62).

Setting: Jerusalem. Following His betrayal by Judas and His arrest, Jesus confirms for the high priest and all the chief priests that He is the Christ, as they seek justification for putting Him to death.

And Jesus said, "I am; and you shall see THE SON OF MAN SITTING AT THE RIGHT HAND OF POWER, and COMING WITH THE CLOUDS OF HEAVEN" (Mark 14:62, Jesus quotes from Psalm 110:1; Daniel 7:13; cf. Matthew 26:57–68; see Luke 22:54).

[RIGHT HAND OF POWER from RIGHT HAND of the power OF GOD]

Setting: Jerusalem. After being arrested, having Peter deny Him, and being mocked and beaten, with His crucifixion imminent, Jesus appears before the Sanhedrin (Council of Elders).

"If You are the Christ, tell us." But He said to them, "If I tell you, you will not believe; and if I ask you a question, you will not answer. But from now on THE SON OF MAN WILL BE SEATED AT THE RIGHT HAND of the power OF GOD." And they all said, "Are You the Son of God, then? And He said to them, "Yes, I am" (Luke 22:67–70, Jesus quotes from Psalm 110:1; cf. Matthew 26:57–65; Mark 14:55–65).

POWER OF DARKNESS (Listed under DARKNESS, POWER OF)

POWER OF GOD (Also see GOD, POSSIBILITIES WITH; MIRACLE; MIRACLES; POWER; POWER, JESUS'; and POWER, RIGHT HAND OF)

Setting: The temple in Jerusalem. As Jesus teaches, the Sadducees question Him about Levirate marriage (marriage to a brother-in-law), in order to test Him.

But Jesus answered and said to them, "You are mistaken, not understanding the Scriptures nor the power of God. For in the resurrection they neither marry nor are given in marriage, but are like angels in heaven. But regarding the resurrection of the dead, have you not read what was spoken to you by God: 'I AM THE GOD OF ABRAHAM, AND THE GOD OF ISAAC, AND THE GOD OF JACOB'? He is not the God of the dead but of the living" (Matthew 22:29–32, Jesus quotes from Exodus 3:6; cf. Mark 12:18–27; Luke 20:27–38; see Deuteronomy 25:5; John 20:9).

Setting: The temple in Jerusalem. After some of the Pharisees and Herodians attempt to trap Jesus in a statement, some Sadducees question Him about the status of marriage after death.

Jesus said to them, "Is this not the reason you are mistaken, that you do not understand the Scriptures or the power of God? For when they rise from the dead, they neither marry nor are given in marriage, but are like angels in heaven. But regarding the fact that the dead rise again, have you not read in the book of Moses, in the *passage* about *the burning* bush, how God spoke to him, saying, 'I AM THE GOD OF ABRAHAM, AND THE GOD OF ISAAC, and the God of Jacob?' He is not the God of the dead, but of the living; you are greatly mistaken" (Mark 12:24–27, Jesus quotes from Exodus 3:6; cf. Matthew 22:29–33; Luke 20:31–40).

Setting: Jerusalem. After being arrested, having Peter deny Him, and being mocked and beaten, with His crucifixion imminent, Jesus appears before the Sanhedrin (Council of Elders).

"If You are the Christ, tell us." But He said to them, "If I tell you, you will not believe; and if I ask you a question, you will not answer. But from now on THE SON OF MAN WILL BE SEATED AT THE RIGHT HAND of the power OF GOD." And they all said, "Are You the Son of God, then? And He said to them, "Yes, I am" (Luke 22:67–70, Jesus quotes from Psalm 110:1; cf. Matthew 26:57–65; Mark 14:55–65).

[POWER OF GOD from no one is able to snatch *them* out of the Father's hand]
Setting: Jerusalem. At the Feast of Dedication, just after Jesus conveys the Parable of the Good Shepherd to the Pharisees (who do not understand it), they ask Him plainly if He is the Christ (Messiah).

Jesus answered them, "I told you, and you do not believe; the works that I do in My Father's name, these testify of Me. But you do not believe because you are not of My sheep. My sheep hear My voice, and I know them, and they follow Me; and I give eternal life to them, and they will never perish; and no one will snatch them out of My hand. My Father, who has given *them* to Me, is greater than all; and no one is able to snatch *them* out of the Father's hand. I and the Father are one" (John 10:25–30; see John 8:47; 10:4, 22–24; 17:1, 2, 20, 21).

POWERS (Also see POWER)

Setting: The Mount of Olives, just east of Jerusalem. During His Olivet Discourse, Jesus answers His disciples' questions as to when the temple will be destroyed and Jerusalem overrun, along with the signs of His coming and the end of the age.

"But immediately after the tribulation of those days THE SUN WILL BE DARKENED, AND THE MOON WILL NOT GIVE ITS LIGHT, AND THE STARS WILL FALL from the sky, and the powers of the heavens will be shaken. And then the sign of the Son of Man will appear in the sky, and then all the tribes of the earth will mourn, and they will see the SON OF MAN COMING ON THE CLOUDS OF THE SKY with power and great glory. And He will send forth His angels with A GREAT TRUMPET and THEY WILL GATHER TOGETHER His elect from the four winds, from one end of the sky to the other" (Matthew 24:29–31, Jesus quotes from Isaiah 13:10, Daniel 7:13; Exodus 19:16; cf. Mark 13:24–27; Luke 21:25–27).

Setting: On the Mount of Olives, east of the temple in Jerusalem. After predicting the temple's destruction, Jesus responds during His Olivet Discourse to questions from Peter, James, John, and Andrew about other future events.

"But in those days, after that tribulation, THE SUN WILL BE DARKENED AND THE MOON WILL NOT GIVE ITS LIGHT, AND THE STARS WILL BE FALLING from heaven, and the powers that are in the heavens will be shaken. Then they will see THE SON OF MAN COMING IN CLOUDS with great power and glory. And then He will send forth the angels, and will gather together His elect from the four winds, from the farthest end of the earth to the farthest end of heaven" (Mark 13:24–27. Jesus quotes from Isaiah 13:10; 34:4; Daniel 7:13; cf. Matthew 24:29–31; Luke 21:25–27).

Setting: On the Mount of Olives, just east of Jerusalem. After ministering in the temple a few days before His crucifixion, and giving His disciples more details regarding future events, Jesus speaks during His Olivet Discourse of His return.

"There will be signs in sun and moon and stars, and on the earth dismay among the nations, in perplexity at the roaring of the sea and the waves, men fainting from fear and the expectation of the things which are coming upon the world; for the powers of the heavens will be shaken. Then they will see THE SON OF MAN COMING IN A CLOUD with power and great glory. But when these things begin to take place, straighten up and lift up your heads, because your redemption is drawing near" (Luke 21:25–28, Jesus quotes from Daniel 7:13; cf. Matthew 24:29–31; Mark 13:24–27).

POWERS, MIRACULOUS (See MIRACLE; MIRACLES; and SIGNS AND WONDERS)

POWERS OF THE HEAVENS (Listed under HEAVENS, POWERS OF THE)

POWERS THAT ARE IN THE HEAVENS (Listed under HEAVENS, POWERSTHAT ARE IN THE)

PRAISE (Also see GLORIFYING GOD; and WORSHIP)

Setting: Galilee. As He teaches and preaches, after pronouncing woes against unrepentant cities, Jesus prays a thanksgiving prayer to His Father in heaven.

At that time Jesus said, "I praise You, Father, Lord of heaven and earth, that you have hidden these things from *the* wise and intelligent and have revealed them to infants. Yes, Father, for this way was well-pleasing in Your sight. All things have been handed over to Me by My Father; and no one knows the Son except the Father; nor does anyone know the Father except the Son, and anyone to whom the Son wills to reveal *Him*" (Matthew 11:25–27; cf. Luke 10:21, 22).

Setting: Jerusalem. After cleansing the temple by driving out the money changers and merchants, Jesus comments to the indignant chief priests and scribes about the praises the children render unto Him.

But when the chief priests and the scribes saw the wonderful things that He had done, and the children who were shouting in the temple, "Hosanna to the Son of David," they became indignant and said to Him, "Do You hear what these *children* are saying?" And Jesus said to them, "Yes, have you never read, 'OUT OF THE MOUTH OF INFANTS AND NURSING BABIES YOU HAVE PREPARED PRAISE FOR YOURSELF'?" (Matthew 21:15, 16, Jesus quotes from Psalm 8:2; see Matthew 9:27).

Setting: On the way from Galilee to Jerusalem. The Lord responds to a report from the seventy sent out in pairs to every place He Himself will soon visit.

At that very time He rejoiced greatly in the Holy Spirit, and said, "I praise You, O Father, Lord of heaven and earth, that You have hidden these things from *the* wise and intelligent and have revealed them to infants. Yes, Father, for this way was well-pleasing in Your sight. All things have been handed over to Me by My Father, and no one knows who the Son is except the Father, and who the Father is except the Son, and anyone to whom the Son wills to reveal *Him*" (Luke 10:21, 22; cf. Matthew 11:25–27; see Luke 10:1, 17; John 3:35; John 10:15).

[PRAISE from praised]

Setting: On the way from Galilee to Jerusalem. After giving the story of the prodigal son, the Lord teaches His disciples about stewardship.

Now He was also saying to the disciples, "There was a rich man who had a manager, and this *manager* was reported to him as squandering his possessions. And he called him and said to him, 'What is this I hear about you? Give an accounting of your management, for you can no longer be a manager.' The manager said to himself, 'What shall I do, since my master is taking the management away from me? I am not strong enough to dig; I am ashamed to beg. I know what I shall do, so that when I am removed from the management people will welcome me into their homes.' And he summoned each one of his master's debtors, and he *began* saying to the first, 'How much do you owe my master?' And he said, 'A hundred measures of oil.' And he said to him, 'Take your bill, and sit down quickly and write fifty.' Then he said to another, 'And how much do you owe?' And he said, 'A hundred measures of wheat.' He said to him, 'Take your bill, and write eighty.' And his master praised the unrighteous manager because he had acted shrewdly; for the sons of this age are more shrewd in relation to their own kind than the sons of light. And I say to you, make friends for yourselves by means of the wealth of unrighteousness, so that when it fails, they will receive you into the eternal dwellings. He who is faithful in a very little thing is faithful also in much; and he who is unrighteous in a very little thing is unrighteous also in much. Therefore if you have not been faithful in the *use of* unrighteous wealth, who will entrust the true *riches* to you? And if you have not been faithful in *the use of* that which is another's, who will give you that which is your own? No servant can serve two masters; for either he will hate the one and love the other, or else he will be devoted to one and despise

No servant can serve two masters; for either he will hate the one and love the other, or else he will be devoted to one and despise the other. You cannot serve God and wealth" (Luke 16:1–13; cf. Matthew 6:24; see Matthew 25:14–30).

PRAISE RECEIVED FROM OTHERS (also see APPROVAL, MAN'S)
[PRAISE RECEIVED FROM OTHERS from all men speak well of you]
Setting: Galilee. After selecting His twelve disciples, Jesus teaches the Beatitudes (part of the Sermon on the Mount) to those disciples and a great throng of people from Judea, Jerusalem, and the central coastal region of Tyre and Sidon.

"Woe *to you* when all men speak well of you, for their fathers used to treat the false prophets in the same way" (Luke 6:26; see Matthew 7:15; 24:11, 24).

[PRAISE RECEIVED FROM OTHERS from you receive glory from one another]
Setting: Jerusalem. Jesus responds to criticism from the Jewish religious leaders during a feast of the Jews by referring to God as His Father (thereby making Himself equal with God) and informing them that God, John the Baptist, His works, and the Scriptures all testify to His mission.

"You search the Scriptures because you think that in them you have eternal life; it is these that testify about Me; and you are unwilling to come to Me so that you may have life. I do not receive glory from men; but I know you, that you do not have the love of God in yourselves. I have come in My Father's name, and you do not receive Me; if another comes in his own name, you will receive him. How can you believe, when you receive glory from one another and you do not seek the glory that is from the *one and* only God? Do not think that I will accuse you before the Father; the one who accuses you is Moses, in whom you have set your hope. For if you believed Moses, you would believe Me, for he wrote about Me. But if you do not believe his writings, how will you believe My words?" (John 5:39–47; see Matthew 24:5; Luke 16:29, 31; 24:27; John 9:28; 17:3).

PRAISING GOD (Also see FATHER, JESUS PRAISING HIS; GLORIFYING GOD; and WORSHIP)
[PRAISING GOD from OUT OF THE MOUTH OF INFANTS AND NURSING BABIES YOU HAVE PREPARED PRAISE FOR YOURSELF]
Setting: Jerusalem. After cleansing the temple by driving out the money changers and merchants, Jesus comments to the indignant chief priests and scribes about the praises the children render Him.

But when the chief priests and the scribes saw the wonderful things that He had done, and the children who were shouting in the temple, "Hosanna to the Son of David," they became indignant and said to Him, "Do You hear what these *children* are saying?" And Jesus said to them, "Yes, have you never read, 'OUT OF THE MOUTH OF INFANTS AND NURSING BABIES YOU HAVE PREPARED PRAISE FOR YOURSELF'?" (Matthew 21:15, 16, Jesus quotes from Psalm 8:2; see Matthew 9:27; 21:14).

PRAYER (Specifics such as LORD'S PRAYER; PRAYER, HIGH-PRIESTLY; and PRAYER, HOUSE OF are separate entries; also see ASKING; BESEECHING; PRAYERS; and REPETITION, MEANINGLESS)
PRAYER from pray]
Setting: Galilee. During the early part of His ministry, Jesus preaches the Sermon on the Mount to His disciples and the multitudes.

"You have heard that it was said, 'YOU SHALL LOVE YOUR NEIGHBOR and hate your enemy.' But I say to you, love your enemies and pray for those who persecute you, so that you may be sons of your Father who is in heaven; for He causes His sun to rise on *the* evil and *the* good, and sends rain on *the* righteous and *the* unrighteous. For if you love those who love you, what reward do you have? Do not even he tax collectors do the same? If you greet only your brothers, what more are you doing *than others?* Do not even the Gentiles do the same? Therefore, you are to be perfect, as your heavenly Father is perfect" (Matthew 5:43–48, Jesus quotes from Leviticus 19:18; cf. Leviticus 19:2; Luke 6:27–36).

[PRAYER from pray]

Setting: Galilee. During the early part of His ministry, Jesus preaches the Sermon on the Mount to His disciples and the multitudes.

"When you pray, you are not to be like the hypocrites; for they love to stand and pray in the synagogues and on the street corners so that they may be seen by men. Truly I say to you, they have their reward in full. But you, when you pray, go into your inner room, close your door and pray to your Father who is in secret, and your Father who sees *what is done* in secret will reward you" (Matthew 6:5, 6; see Mark 11:25).

[PRAYER from praying and ask Him]
Setting: Galilee. During the early part of His ministry, Jesus preaches the Sermon on the Mount to His disciples and the multitudes.

"And when you are praying, do not use meaningless repetition as the Gentiles do, for they suppose that they will be heard for their many words. So do not be like them; for your Father knows what you need before you ask Him" (Matthew 6:7, 8; see 1 Kings 18:26–29).

[PRAYER from pray]
Setting: Galilee. During the early part of His ministry, Jesus gives a model prayer to His disciples and the multitudes while conveying the Sermon on the Mount.

"Pray, then, in this way: 'Our Father who is in heaven, hallowed be Your name. Your kingdom come. Your will be done, on earth as it is in heaven. Give us this day our daily bread. And forgive us our debts, as we also have forgiven our debtors. And do not lead us into temptation, but deliver us from evil. [For Yours is the kingdom and the power and the glory forever. Amen]'" (Matthew 6:9–13; cf. Luke 11:2–4; see John 17:15).

Setting: Galilee, near the mountain where the Transfiguration took place. Jesus reveals to His disciples why they could not cure a demon-possessed boy.

And He said to them, "Because of the littleness of your faith; for truly I say to you, if you have faith the size of a mustard seed, you will say to this mountain, 'Move from here to there,' and it will move; and nothing will be impossible to you. ["But this kind does not go out except by prayer and fasting"] (Matthew 17:20, 21; cf. Matthew 21:21, 22; Mark 9:28, 29).

Setting: On the way from Bethany to Jerusalem. The day after Jesus curses a fig tree (an illustration of the nation Israel), His disciples ask Him how it has so quickly withered.

And Jesus answered and said to them, "Truly I say to you, if you have faith and do not doubt, you will not only do what was done to the fig tree, but even if you say to this mountain, 'Be taken up and cast into the sea,' it will happen. And all things you ask in prayer, believing, you will receive" (Matthew 21:21, 22; cf. Matthew 7:7; 17:20; Mark 11:20–24).

[PRAYER from pray]
Setting: The Mount of Olives, just east of Jerusalem. During His discourse, Jesus answers His disciples' questions as to when the temple will be destroyed and Jerusalem overrun, along with the signs of His coming and the end of the age.

"Therefore when you see the ABOMINATION OF DESOLATION which was spoken of through Daniel the prophet, standing in the holy place (let the reader understand), then those who are in Judea must flee to the mountains. Whoever is on the housetop must not go down to get the things that are in his house. Whoever is in the field must not turn back to get his cloak. But woe to those who are pregnant and to those who are nursing babies in those days! But pray that your flight will not be in the winter, or on a Sabbath. For then there will be a great tribulation, such as has not occurred since the beginning of the world until now, nor ever will. Unless those days had been cut short, no life would have been saved; but for the sake of the elect those days will be cut short. Then if anyone says to you, 'Behold, here is the Christ,' or "There *He is,*' do not believe *him.* For false Christs and false prophets will arise and will show great signs and wonders, so as to mislead, if possible, even the elect. Behold, I have told you in advance. So if they say to you, 'Behold, He is in the wilderness,' do not go out, *or,* 'Behold, He is in the inner rooms,' do not believe *them.* For just as the lightning comes from the east and flashes even to the west, so will the coming of the Son of Man be. Wherever the corpse is, there the vultures will gather" (Matthew 24:15–28, Jesus quotes from Daniel 9:27; cf. Daniel 12:1; Mark 13:14–23; Luke 17:22–31; 21:20–24; 23:29; see John 4:48).

[PRAYER from pray; praying; and prayed]
Setting: An upper room in Jerusalem. After celebrating the Passover meal with His disciples, Jesus retreats to the Garden of Gethsemane on the Mount of Olives to pray prior to His betrayal by Judas.

Then Jesus came with them to a place called Gethsemane, and said to His disciples, "Sit here while I go over there and pray." And He took with Him Peter and the two sons of Zebedee, and began to be grieved and distressed. Then He said to them, "My soul is deeply grieved, to the point of death; remain here and keep watch with Me." And He went a little beyond *them,* and fell on His face and prayed, saying, "My Father, if it is possible, let this cup pass from Me; yet not as I will, but as You will." And He came to the disciples and found them sleeping, and said to Peter, "So, you *men* could not keep watch with Me for one hour? Keep watching and praying that you may not enter into temptation; the spirit is willing, but the flesh is weak." He went away again a second time and prayed, saying, "My Father, if this cannot pass away unless I drink it, Your will be done." Again He came and found them sleeping, for their eyes were heavy. And He left them again, and went away and prayed a third time, saying the same thing once more. Then He came to the disciples and said to them, "Are you still sleeping and resting? Behold the hour is at hand and the Son of Man is being betrayed into the hands of sinners. Get up, let us be going; behold the one who betrays Me is at hand!" (Matthew 26:36–46; cf. Mark 14:32–42; Luke 22:40–46; see Matthew 20:22; John 12:27).

Setting: Galilee. Upon returning from a high mountain (perhaps Mount Hermon) where Jesus was transfigured in front of Peter, James, and John, the four discover the remaining disciples arguing with some scribes.

And He asked them, "What are you discussing with them?" And one of the crowd answered Him, "Teacher, I brought You my son, possessed with a spirit which makes him mute; and whenever it seizes him, it slams him *to the ground* and he foams *at the mouth,* and grinds his teeth and stiffens out. I told Your disciples to cast it out, and they could not *do it.* And He answered them, and said, "O unbelieving generation, how long shall I be with you? How long shall I put up with you? Bring him to Me!" They brought the boy to Him. When he saw Him, immediately the spirit threw him into a convulsion, and falling to the ground, be *began* rolling around and foaming *at the mouth.* And He asked his father, "How long has this been happening to him?" And he said, "From childhood. It has often thrown him both into the fire and into the water to destroy him. But if You can do anything, take pity on us and help us!" And Jesus said to him, "'If You can?' All things are possible to him who believes." Immediately the boy's father cried out and said, "I do believe; help my unbelief." When Jesus saw that a crowd was rapidly gathering, He rebuked the unclean spirit, saying to it, "You deaf and mute spirit, I command you, come out of him and do not enter him again." After crying out and throwing him into terrible convulsions, it came out; and *the boy* became so much like a corpse that most *of them,* said, "He is dead!" But Jesus took him by the hand and raised him; and he got up. When He came into *the* house, His disciples *began* questioning Him privately, "Why could we not drive it out?" And He said to them, "This kind cannot come out by anything but prayer" (Mark 9:16–29; cf. Matthew 17:14–21; Luke 9:37–43; see Matthew 17:20).

[PRAYER from pray and praying]
Setting: Just outside Jerusalem. The day after Jesus instructs the money changers while He cleanses the temple, Peter draws the Lord's and His disciples' attention to an earlier-cursed fig tree.

And Jesus answered saying to them, "Have faith in God. Truly, I say to you, whoever says to this mountain, 'Be taken up and cast into the sea,' and does not doubt in his heart, but believes that what he says is going to happen, it will be *granted* him. Therefore I say to you, all things for which you pray and ask, believe that you have received them, and they will be *granted* you. Whenever you stand praying, forgive, if you have anything against anyone, so that your Father who is in heaven will also forgive you your transgressions. [But if you do not forgive, neither will your Father who is in heaven forgive your transgressions'] (Mark

11:22–26; cf. Matthew 21:19–22; see Matthew 6:14, 15; 7:7; 17:20).

[PRAYER from pray]
Setting: On the Mount of Olives, east of the temple in Jerusalem. After predicting the temple's destruction, Jesus responds during His Olivet Discourse to questions from Peter, James, John, and Andrew about other future events.

"But when you see the ABOMINATION OF DESOLATION standing where it should not be (let the reader understand), then those who are in Judea must flee to the mountains. The one who is on the housetop must not go down, or go in to get anything out of his house; and the one who is in the field must not turn back to get his coat. But woe to those who are pregnant and to those who are nursing babies in those days! But pray that it may not happen in winter. For those days will be a *time of* tribulation such as has not occurred since the beginning of the creation which God created until now, and never will. Unless the Lord had shortened *those* days, no life would have been saved; but for the sake of the elect, whom He chose, He shortened the days. And then if anyone says to you, 'Behold, here is the Christ'; or, 'Behold, *He is* there'; do not believe *him*; for false Christs and false prophets will arise, and will show signs and wonders, in order to lead astray, if possible, the elect. But take heed; behold, I have told you everything in advance" (Mark 13:14–23; cf. Matthew 24:15–28; Luke 21:20–24; see Daniel 9:27; 12:1; Luke 17:31).

[PRAYER from prayed and praying]
Setting: Gethsemane on the Mount of Olives, east of the temple in Jerusalem. Jesus agonizes over His impending death, disappointed His disciples keep falling asleep instead of watching and praying with Him.

They came to a place named Gethsemane; and He said to the disciples, "Sit here until I have prayed." And He took with Him Peter and James and John, and began to be very distressed and troubled. And He said to them, "My soul is deeply grieved to the point of death; remain here and keep watch." And He went a little beyond *them,* and fell to the ground and *began* to pray that if it were possible, the hour might pass Him by. And He was saying, "Abba! Father! All things are possible for You; remove this cup from Me; yet not what I will, but what You will." And He came and found them sleeping, and said to Peter, "Simon, are you asleep? Could you not keep watch for one hour? Keep watching and praying that you may not come into temptation; the spirit is willing, but the flesh is weak" (Mark 14:32–38; cf. Matthew 26:36–41; Luke 22:41–46; see Romans 8:15; Galatians 4:6).

[PRAYER from pray]
Setting: Galilee. After selecting His twelve disciples, Jesus teaches the Sermon on the Mount to those disciples and a great throng of people from Judea, Jerusalem, and the central coastal region of Tyre and Sidon.

"But I say to you who hear, love your enemies, do good to those who hate you, bless those who curse you, pray for those who mistreat you. Whoever hits you on the cheek, offer him the other also; and whoever takes away your coat, do not withhold your shirt from him either. Give to everyone who asks of you, and whoever takes away what is yours, do not demand it back. Treat others the same way you want them to treat you. If you love those who love you, what credit is *that* to you? For even sinners love those who love them. If you do good to those who do good to you, what credit is *that* to you? For even sinners do the same. If you lend to those from whom you expect to receive, what credit is *that* to you? Even sinners lend to sinners in order to receive back the same *amount.* But love your enemies, and do good, and lend, expecting nothing in return; and your reward will be great, and you will be sons of the Most High; for He Himself is kind to ungrateful and evil *men.* Be merciful, just as your Father is merciful" (Luke 6:27–36; cf. Matthew 5:9, 39–48; 7:12).

[PRAYER from pray]
Setting: On the way from Galilee to Jerusalem. After Jesus visits in the home of Martha and Mary in Bethany, one of His disciples asks Him to teach them to pray.

And He said to them, "When you pray, say: 'Father, hallowed be Your name. Your kingdom come. Give us each day our daily bread. And forgive us our sins, for we ourselves also forgive everyone who is indebted to us. And lead us not into temptation'" (Luke 11:2–4; cf. Matthew 6:9–13).

[PRAYER from pray]

Setting: On the way route from Galilee to Jerusalem. After telling His disciples of His second coming, Jesus instructs them about persistence in prayer.

Now He was telling them a parable to show that at all times they ought to pray and not to lose heart, saying, "In a certain city there was a judge who did not fear God and did not respect man. There was a widow in that city, and she kept coming to him, saying, 'Give me legal protection from my opponent.' For a while he was unwilling; but afterward he said to himself, 'Even though I do not fear God nor respect man, yet because this woman bothers me, I will give her legal protection, otherwise by continually coming she will wear me out.' "And the Lord said, "Hear what the unrighteous judge said; now, will not God bring about justice for His elect who cry to Him day and night, and will He delay long over them? I tell you that He will bring about justice for them quickly. However, when the Son of Man comes, will He find faith on the earth?" (Luke 18:1–8).

[PRAYER from pray and praying]
Setting: On the way route from Galilee to Jerusalem. After instructing His disciples about persistence in prayer, Jesus conveys a parable about self-righteousness.

And He also told this parable to some people who trusted in themselves that they were righteous, and viewed others with contempt: "Two men went up into the temple to pray, one a Pharisee and the other a tax collector. The Pharisee stood and was praying this to himself: 'God, I thank You that I am not like other people: swindlers, unjust, adulterers, or even like this tax collector. I fast twice a week; I pay tithes of all that I get.' But the tax collector, standing some distance away, was even unwilling to lift up his eyes to heaven, but was beating his breast, saying, 'God, be merciful to me, the sinner!' I tell you, this man went to his house justified rather than the other; for everyone who exalts himself will be humbled, but he who humbles himself will be exalted" (Luke 18:9–14; see Ezra 9:6; Matthew 6:5, 23:12; Luke 11:42, 16:15; Romans 14:3, 10).

[PRAYER from praying]
Setting: The temple in Jerusalem. Following a time of ministry in the temple a few days before His crucifixion, after conveying the Parable of the Fig Tree, Jesus warns His disciples to keep alert regarding future events.

"Be on guard, so that your hearts will not be weighted down with dissipation and drunkenness and the worries of life, and that day will not come upon you suddenly like a trap; for it will come upon all those who dwell on the face of all the earth. But keep on the alert at all times, praying that you may have strength to escape all these things that are about to take place, and to stand before the Son of Man" (Luke 21:34–36; cf. Mark 13:33; see Matthew 24:42–44).

[PRAYER from prayed]
Setting: Jerusalem. During the Feast of Unleavened Bread (Passover) just before His crucifixion, Jesus celebrates the Passover meal with His disciples and institutes the Lord's Supper. The disciples later argue over who is the greatest among them, and the Lord predicts Peter's upcoming denial of Him.

"Simon, Simon, behold, Satan has demanded *permission* to sift you like wheat; but I have prayed for you, that your faith may not fail; and you, when once you have turned again, strengthen your brothers." But he said to Him, "Lord, with You I am ready to go both to prison and to death!" And He said, "I say to you, Peter, the rooster will not crow today until you have denied three times that you know Me" (Luke 22:31–34; cf. Matthew 26:33–35; John 13:36–38; see Job 1:6–12; John 17:15).

[PRAYER from pray]
Setting: Jerusalem. After celebrating the Passover meal and instructing His disciples to prepare to persevere without Him, with His crucifixion imminent, Jesus proceeds to the Mount of Olives to pray.

And He came out and proceeded as was His custom to the Mount of Olives; and the disciples also followed Him. When He arrived at the place, He said to them, "Pray that you may not enter into temptation." And He withdrew from them about a stone's throw, and He knelt down and *began* to pray, saying, "Father, if You are willing, remove this cup from Me; yet not My will, but Yours be done" (Luke 22:39–42; cf. Matthew 26:36–42; Mark 14:32–49; see Luke 21:37).

Setting: Jerusalem. After celebrating the Passover meal and instructing His disciples to prepare to persevere without Him, with His crucifixion imminent, Jesus proceeds to the Mount of Olives to pray.

When He rose from prayer, He came to the disciples and found them sleeping from sorrow, and said to them, "Why are you sleeping? Get up and pray that you may not enter into temptation" (Luke 22:45, 46; cf. Matthew 26:40–46; Mark 14:37–42; see Matthew 4:11; Hebrews 5:7).

[PRAYER from praying]
Setting: Damascus. Luke, writing in Acts, conveys how the Lord instructs one of His disciples, Ananias, to locate Saul of Tarsus to touch him in order to restore Saul's vision.

Now there was a disciple at Damascus named Ananias; and the Lord said to him in a vision, "Ananias." And he said, "Here I am, Lord." And the Lord *said* to him, "Get up and go to the street called Straight, and inquire at the house of Judas for a man from Tarsus named Saul, for he is praying, and he was seen in a vision a man named Ananias come in and lay his hands on him, so that he might regain his sight" (Acts 9:10–12; see Acts 22:12–14).

PRAYER, BOLDNESS IN (See PRAYER, PERSISTENCE IN)

PRAYER, DISCIPLES' (See LORD'S PRAYER)

PRAYER, FAITH IN

[FAITH IN PRAYER from And all things you ask in prayer, believing, you will receive] ***Setting:*** On the way from Bethany to Jerusalem. The day after Jesus curses a fig tree (an illustration of the nation Israel), His disciples ask Him how it has so quickly withered.

And Jesus answered and said to them, "Truly I say to you, if you have faith and do not doubt, you will not only do what was done to the fig tree, but even if you say to this mountain, 'Be taken up and cast into the sea,' it will happen. And all things you ask in prayer, believing, you will receive" (Matthew 21:21, 22; cf. Matthew 7:7; Matthew 17:20; Mark 11:20–24).

[FAITH IN PRAYER from pray and ask, believe that you have received them]
Setting: Just outside Jerusalem. The day after Jesus instructs the money changers while He cleanses the temple, Peter draws the Lord's and His disciples' attention to an earlier-cursed fig tree.

And Jesus answered saying to them, "Have faith in God. Truly, I say to you, whoever says to this mountain, 'Be taken up and cast into the sea,' and does not doubt in his heart, but believes that what he says is going to happen, it will be *granted* him. Therefore I say to you, all things for which you pray and ask, believe that you have received them, and they will be *granted* you. Whenever you stand praying, forgive, if you have anything against anyone, so that your Father who is in heaven will also forgive you your transgressions. [But if you do not forgive, neither will your Father who is in heaven forgive your transgressions'] (Mark 11:22–26; cf. Matthew 21:19–22; see Matthew 6:14, 15; 7:7; 17:20).

PRAYER, HIGH-PRIESTLY

[HIGH-PRIESTLY PRAYER inferred from context]
Setting: Jerusalem. Before the Passover, after giving His disciples hope that in the midst of tribulation they will have His peace, Jesus prays His high-priestly prayer.

Jesus spoke these things; and lifting up His eyes to heaven, He said, "Father, the hour has come; glorify Your Son, that the Son may glorify You, even as You gave Him authority over all flesh, that to all whom You have given Him, He may give eternal life. This is eternal life, that they may know You, the only true God, and Jesus Christ whom You have sent. I glorified You on the earth, having accomplished the work which You have given Me to do. Now, Father, glorify Me together with Yourself, with the glory which I had with You before the world was. I have manifested Your name to the men whom You gave Me out of the world; they were Yours and You gave them to Me, and they have kept Your word. Now they have come to know that everything You have given Me is from You; for the words which You gave Me I have given to them; and they received *them* and truly understood that I came forth from You, and they believed You sent Me. I ask on their behalf; I do not ask on behalf of the world, but of those whom You have given Me; for they are Yours; and all things that are Mine are Yours, and Yours are Mine; and I have been glorified in them. I am no longer in the world; and *yet* they themselves are in the world, and I come to You. Holy Father, keep them in Your name, *the name* which You have given Me, that they may be even as We *are*. While I was with them, I was keeping them in Your name which You have given Me; and I guarded them and not one of them perished but the son of perdition, so that the Scripture would be fulfilled" (John 17:1–12; see Luke 22:32; John 1:1; 3:35; 4:34; 5:44; 6:37–39, 70; 8:42; 11:41; 12:49; 13:18, 31; 16:15; Philippians 2:9).

[HIGH-PRIESTLY PRAYER inferred from context]
Setting: Jerusalem. Before the Passover, after giving His disciples hope that in the midst of tribulation they will have His peace, Jesus continues praying His high-priestly prayer.

"But now I come to You; and these things I speak in the world so that they may have My joy made full in themselves. I have given them Your word; and the world has hated them, because they are not of the world, even as I am not of the world. I do not ask You to take them out of the world, but to keep them from the evil *one*. They are not of the world, even as I am not of the world. Sanctify them in the truth; Your word is truth. As You sent Me into the world, I also have sent them into the world. For their sakes I sanctify Myself, that they themselves also may be sanctified in truth. I do not ask on behalf of these alone, but for those also who believe in Me through their word; that they may all be one; even as You, Father, *are* in Me and I in You, that they also maybe in Us, so that the world may believe that You sent Me" (John 17:13–21; see Matthew 10:5, 38; John 7:33; 15:3, 11, 19).

[HIGH-PRIESTLY PRAYER inferred from context]
Setting: Jerusalem. Before the Passover, after giving His disciples hope that in the midst of tribulation they will have His peace, Jesus continues praying His high-priestly prayer.

"The glory which You have given Me I have given to them, that they may be one, just as We are one; I in them and You in Me, that they may be perfected in unity, so that the world may know that you sent Me, and loved them, even as You have loved Me. Father I desire that they also, whom You have given Me, be with Me where I am, so that they may see My glory which You have given Me, for You loved Me before the foundation of the world. O righteous Father, although the world has not known You, yet I have known You; and these have known that You sent Me; and I have made Your name known to them, and will make it known, so that the love with which You loved Me may be in them, and I in them" (John 17:22–26; see Matthew 25:34; John 1:14; 10:38; 15:9; 16:27).

PRAYER, HOUSE OF

Setting: Jerusalem. After being welcomed with blessings from the crowds, Jesus cleanses the temple by driving out the money changers and merchants.

And He said to them, "It is written, 'MY HOUSE SHALL BE CALLED A HOUSE OF PRAYER'; but you are making it a ROBBERS' DEN" (Matthew 21:13; Jesus quotes from Isaiah 56:7; Jeremiah 7:11; cf. Mark 11:15–18; Luke 19:46).

Setting: Jerusalem. Following His triumphal entry, cursing of a fig tree, and cleansing of the temple of the money changers, Jesus rebukes the Jewish religious leaders for the corrupt practices they permit in His house.

And He *began* to teach and say to them, "Is it not written, 'MY HOUSE SHALL BE CALLED A HOUSE OF PRAYER FOR ALL THE NATIONS'? But you have made it a ROBBERS' DEN" (Mark 11:17, Jesus quotes from Isaiah 56:7; Jeremiah 7:11; cf. Matthew 21:12, 13; Luke 19:45–48).

Setting: Jerusalem. After weeping as He sees the city ahead of Him, the Lord enters the temple and drives out the money changers and merchants.

Jesus entered the temple and began to drive out those who were selling, saying to them, "It is written, 'AND MY HOUSE SHALL BE

A HOUSE OF PRAYER,' but you have made it a ROBBERS' DEN" (Luke 19:45, 46, Jesus quotes from Isaiah 56:7; Jeremiah 7:11; cf. Matthew 21:12, 13; Mark 11:15–17; Luke 19:47, 48; John 2:13–17).

PRAYER, LORD'S (See LORD'S PRAYER)

PRAYER, MODEL (See LORD'S PRAYER)

PRAYER, PERSISTENCE IN

[PERSISTENCE IN PRAYER from For everyone who asks receives, and he who seeks finds, and to him who knocks it will be opened]

Setting: Galilee. During the early part of His ministry, Jesus preaches the Sermon on the Mount to His disciples and the multitudes.

"Ask, and it will be given to you; seek, and you will find; knock, and it will be opened to you. For everyone who asks receives, and he who seeks finds, and to him who knocks it will be opened. Or what man is there among you who, when his son asks for a loaf, will give him a stone? Or if he asks for a fish, he will not give him a snake, will he? If you then, being evil, know how to give good gifts to your children, how much more will your Father who is in heaven give what is good to those who ask Him! In everything, therefore, treat people the same way you want them to treat you, for this is the Law and the Prophets" (Matthew 7:7–12; cf. Matthew 22:40; Luke 6:31; 11:9–13; see Psalm 84:11).

[PERSISTENCE IN PRAYER from because of his persistence he will get up and give him as much as he needs]
Setting: On the way from Galilee to Jerusalem. After revealing to His disciples how to pray, Jesus illustrates persistence in prayer.

Then He said to them, "Suppose one of you has a friend, and goes to him at midnight and says to him, 'Friend, lend me three loaves; for a friend of mine has come to me from a journey, and I have nothing to set before him'; and from inside he answers and says, 'Do not bother me; the door has already been shut and my children and I are in bed; I cannot get up and give you *anything.*' I tell you, even though he will not get up and give him *anything* because he is his friend, yet because of his persistence he will get up and give him as much as he needs. So I say to you, ask, and it will be given to you; seek, and you will find; knock, and it will be opened to you. For everyone who asks, receives; and he who seeks, finds; and to him who knocks, it will be opened" (Luke 11:5–10; cf. Matthew 7:7, 8; see Luke 18:1–5).

[PERSISTENCE IN PRAYER from will not God bring about justice for His elect who cry to Him day and night]
Setting: On the way from Galilee to Jerusalem. After telling His disciples of His second coming, Jesus instructs them about persistence in prayer.

Now He was telling them a parable to show that at all times they ought to pray and not to lose heart, saying, "In a certain city there was a judge who did not fear God and did not respect man. There was a widow in that city, and she kept coming to him, saying, 'Give me legal protection from my opponent.' For a while he was unwilling; but afterward he said to himself, 'Even though I do not fear God nor respect man, yet because this woman bothers me, I will give her legal protection, otherwise by continually coming she will wear me out.'" And the Lord said, "Hear what the unrighteous judge said; now, will not God bring about justice for His elect who cry to Him day and night, and will He delay long over them? I tell you that He will bring about justice for them quickly. However, when the Son of Man comes, will He find faith on the earth?" (Luke 18:1–8).

PRAYER AND FASTING (Listed under FASTING, PRAYER AND)

PRAYERS (See PRAYER and specifics such as PRAYERS, LONG)

PRAYERS, LONG (Also see HYPOCRISY; HYPOCRITES; and PRETENSE)

the second of eight woes upon them in front of the crowds and His disciples.

["Woe to you, scribes and Pharisees, hypocrites, because you devour widows' houses, and for a pretense you make long prayers; therefore you will receive greater condemnation] (Matthew 23:14; cf. Mark 12:40; Luke 20:47).

Setting: The temple in Jerusalem. After commending one scribe for his nearness to the kingdom of God, Jesus warns the crowd about the majority of the scribes.

In His teaching He was saying: "Beware of the scribes who like to walk around in long robes, and *like* respectful greetings in the market places, and chief seats in the synagogues and places of honor at banquets, who devour widows' houses, and for appearance's sake offer long prayers; these will receive greater condemnation" (Mark 12:38–40; cf. Matthew 23:1–7; Luke 20:45–47).

Setting: The temple in Jerusalem. While ministering a few days before His crucifixion, after posing a question to the scribes, who do not answer, Jesus warns His disciples about the lifestyle of the scribes.

"Beware of the scribes, who like to walk around in long robes, and love respectful greetings in the market places, and chief seats in the synagogues and places of honor at banquets, who devour widows' houses, and for appearance's sake offer long prayers. These will receive greater condemnation" (Luke 20:46, 47; cf. Matthew 23:1–7; Mark 12:38–40; see Luke 11:43).

PREACHING (Also see DOCTRINE; EVANGELISM; GOSPEL; PROCLAMATION; TEACHERS; and TEACHING)

[PREACHING from preach]

Setting: Galilee. After His twelve disciples observe His ministry, Jesus summons and specifically instructs them about their ministry to the people of Israel.

These twelve Jesus sent out after instructing them: "Do not go in *the* way of *the* Gentiles, and do not enter *any* city of the Samaritans; but rather go to the lost sheep of the house of Israel. And as you go, preach, saying, 'The kingdom of heaven is at hand.' Heal *the* sick, raise *the* dead, cleanse *the* lepers, cast out demons. Freely you received, freely give. Do not acquire gold, or silver, or copper for your money belts, or a bag for *your* journey, or even two coats, or sandals, or a staff; for the worker is worthy of his support. And whatever city or village you enter, inquire who is worthy in it, and stay at his house until you leave *that city*. As you enter the house, give it your greeting. If the house is worthy, give it your *blessing of* peace. But if it is not worthy, take back your *blessing of* peace. Whoever does not receive you, nor heed your words, as you go out of that house or that city, shake the dust off your feet. Truly I say to you, it will be more tolerable for *the* land of Sodom and Gomorrah in the day of judgment than for that city" (Matthew 10:5–15; cf. Mark 6:7–11; Luke 9:1–5; see Matthew 3:2; 11:22, 24; 15:24; Luke 22:35; 1 Corinthians 9:14).

[PREACHING from PREACHED]

Setting: Galilee. As He teaches and preaches, Jesus responds to John the Baptist's question (posed by some of John's disciples) whether He is Israel's promised Messiah.

Jesus answered and said to them, "Go and report to John what you hear and see: *the* BLIND RECEIVE SIGHT and *the* lame walk, *the* lepers are cleansed and *the* deaf hear, *the* dead are raised up, and *the* POOR HAVE THE GOSPEL PREACHED TO THEM. And blessed is he who does not take offense at Me" (Matthew 11:4–6, Jesus quotes from Isaiah 35:5f; cf. Luke 7:22, 23).

Setting: Galilee. After Jesus warns the Pharisees about the unpardonable sin and their future judgment, some Pharisees and scribes ask Him to perform a miraculous sign for them in front of the crowds.

But He answered and said to them, "An evil and adulterous generation craves for a sign; and *yet* no sign will be given to it but the sign of Jonah the prophet; for just as JONAH WAS THREE DAYS AND THREE NIGHTS IN THE BELLY OF THE SEA MONSTER, so will the Son of Man be three days and three nights in the heart of the earth. The men of Nineveh will stand up with this generation at the judgment, and will condemn it because they repented at the preaching of Jonah; and behold, something greater than Jonah is here. *The* Queen of *the* South will rise up with this generation at the judgment and will condemn it, because she came from the here. *The* Queen of *the* South will rise up with this generation at the judgment and will condemn it, because she came from the ends of the earth to hear the wisdom of Solomon; and behold, something greater than Solomon is here" (Matthew 12:39–42; Jesus quotes from Jonah 1:17; cf. 1 Kings 10:1; Jonah 3:5; Matthew 16:1, 4; Luke 11:29).

[PREACHING from preached]
Setting: The Mount of Olives, just east of Jerusalem. During His Olivet Discourse, Jesus answers His disciples' questions as to when the temple will be destroyed and Jerusalem overrun, along with the signs of His coming and the end of the age.

And Jesus answered and said to them, "See to it that no one misleads you. For many will come in My name, saying, 'I am the Christ,' and will mislead many. You will be hearing of wars and rumors of wars. See that you are not frightened, for *those things* must take place, but *that* is not yet the end. For nation will rise against nation, and kingdom against kingdom, and in various places there will be famines and earthquakes. But all these things are *merely* the beginning of birth pangs. Then they will deliver you to tribulation, and will kill you, and you will be hated by all nations because of My name. At that time many will fall away and will betray one another and hate one another. Many false prophets will arise and will mislead many. Because lawlessness is increased, most people's love will grow cold. But the one who endures to the end, he will be saved. This gospel of the kingdom shall be preached in the whole world as a testimony to all the nations, and then the end will come" (Matthew 24:4–14; cf. Jeremiah 29:8; Matthew 7:15; 10:17, 22; Mark 13:3–13; Luke 21:7–19; Revelation 6:4).

[PREACHING from preached]
Setting: The home of Simon the leper in Bethany. Jesus rebukes His disciples when they criticize a woman for pouring a costly vial of perfume on His head in preparation for His burial.

But Jesus, aware of this, said to them, "Why do you bother the woman? For she has done a good deed to Me. For you always have the poor with you; but you do not always have Me. For when she poured this perfume on My body, she did it to prepare Me for burial. Truly I say to you, wherever this gospel is preached in the whole world, what this woman has done will also be spoken of in memory of her" (Matthew 26:10–13; cf. Mark 14:3–9; Luke 7:37–39; John 12:2–8; see Deuteronomy 15:11).

[PREACHING from preach]
Setting: Capernaum in Galilee. Early in His ministry, after healing people and casting out demons, Jesus decides to take His disciples to a nearby town and preach.

He said to them, "Let us go somewhere else to the towns nearby, so that I may preach there also; for that is what I came for" (Mark 1:38; cf. Luke 4:43).

[PREACHING from preached]
Setting: On the Mount of Olives, east of the temple in Jerusalem. After predicting the temple's destruction, Jesus responds during His Olivet Discourse to questions from Peter, James, John, and Andrew about other future events.

And Jesus began to say to them, "See to it that no one misleads you. Many will come in My name, saying, 'I am *He!*' and will mislead many. When you hear of wars and rumors of wars, do not be frightened; *those things* must take place; but *that is* not yet the end. For nation will rise up against nation, and kingdom against kingdom; there will be earthquakes in various places; there will *also be* famines. These things are *merely* the beginning of birth pangs. But be on your guard; for they will deliver you to *the* courts, and you will be flogged in *the* synagogues, and you will stand before governors and kings for My sake, as a testimony to them. The gospel must first be preached to all the nations. When they arrest you and hand you over, do not worry beforehand about what you are to say, but say whatever is given you in that hour; for it is not you who speak, but *it is* the Holy Spirit. Brother will betray brother to death, and a father *his* child; and children will rise up against parents and have them put to death. You will be hated by all because of My name, but the one who endures to the end, he will be saved (Mark 13:5–13; cf. Matthew 24:4–14; Luke 21:7–19; see Matthew 10:17–22).

[PREACHING from preached]
Setting: The home of Simon the leper in Bethany. Two days before the Feast of Unleavened Bread (Passover), Jesus commends a woman who anoints His head with costly perfume, which some there think should have been sold and the proceeds given to the poor.

But Jesus said, "Let her alone; why do you bother her? She has done a good deed to Me. For you always have the poor with you, and whenever you wish you can do good to them; but you do not always have Me. She has done what she could; she has anointed My body beforehand for the burial. Truly I say to you, wherever the gospel is preached in the whole world, what this woman has done will also be spoken of in memory of her" (Mark 14:6–9; cf. Matthew 26:6–13; John 12:2–8; see Deuteronomy 15:11).

[PREACHING from preach]
Setting: Following His resurrection from the dead after being crucified, Jesus commissions His disciples to preach His gospel to the world.

And He said to them, "Go into all the world and preach the gospel to all creation. He who has believed and has been baptized shall be saved; but he who has disbelieved shall be condemned. These signs will accompany those who have believed: in My name they will cast out demons, they will speak with new tongues; they will pick up serpents, and if they drink any deadly *poison*, it will not hurt them; they will lay hands on the sick, and they will recover" (Mark 16:15–18; cf. Matthew 28:16–20; see Mark 9:38; John 3:18, 36; 1 Corinthians 15:6).

[Note: Some scholars question the authenticity of Mark 16:9–20 as these verses do not appear in some early New Testament manuscripts.]

[PREACHING from PREACH]
Setting: The synagogue in Jesus' hometown of Nazareth in Galilee. At the beginning of His public ministry, Jesus reads on the Sabbath from the book of the prophet Isaiah.

And the book of the prophet Isaiah was handed to Him. And He opened the book and found the place where it was written, "THE SPIRIT OF THE LORD IS UPON ME, BECAUSE HE ANOINTED ME TO PREACH THE GOSPEL TO THE POOR. HE HAS SENT ME TO PROCLAIM RELEASE TO THE CAPTIVES, AND RECOVERY OF SIGHT TO THE BLIND, TO SET FREE THOSE WHO ARE OPPRESSED, TO PROCLAIM THE FAVORABLE YEAR OF THE LORD." And He closed the book, gave it back to the attendant and sat down; and the eyes of all in the synagogue were fixed on Him. And He began to say to them, "Today this Scripture has been fulfilled in your hearing" (Luke 4:17–21, Jesus quotes from Isaiah 61:1, 2).

[PREACHING from preach]
Setting: Capernaum. After healing Simon Peter's mother-in-law from a high fever, Jesus tries to retreat to a secluded place in Galilee, but when the crowds locate Him, He proclaims His mission.

But He said to them, "I must preach the kingdom of God to the other cities also, for I was sent for this purpose" (Luke 4:43; cf. Matthew 4:23, 24; Mark 1:35–39).

[PREACHING from PREACHED]
Setting: Galilee. After Jesus raises a woman's son from the dead in Nain, the disciples of John the Baptist inquire whether He is the promised Messiah.

And He answered and said to them, "Go and report to John what you have seen and heard: *the* BLIND RECEIVE SIGHT, *the* lame walk, *the* lepers are cleansed, and *the* deaf hear, *the* dead are raised up, *the* POOR HAVE THE GOSPEL PREACHED TO THEM. Blessed is he who does not take offense at Me" (Luke 7:22, 23, Jesus quotes from Isaiah 35:5; 61:1; cf. Matthew 11:2–6).

[PREACHING from preaching]

Setting: On the way from Galilee to Jerusalem. After revealing a problem with exorcism and responding to a blessing from a woman in the crowd, Jesus tells the increasing crowds of the sign of Jonah.

As the crowds were increasing, He began to say, "This generation is a wicked generation; it seeks for a sign, and *yet* no sign will be given to it but the sign of Jonah. For just as Jonah became a sign to the Ninevites, so will the Son of Man be to this generation. The Queen of the South will rise up with the men of this generation at the judgment and condemn them, because she came from the ends of the earth to hear the wisdom of Solomon; and behold, something greater than Solomon is here. The men of Nineveh will stand up with this generation at the judgment and condemn it, because they repented at the preaching of Jonah; and behold, something greater than Jonah is here" (Luke 11:29–32; cf. Matthew 16:4; see 1 Kings 10:1–10; Jonah 3:4, 5).

[PREACHING from preached]
Setting: On the way from Galilee to Jerusalem. The Lord responds to the Pharisees' scoffing at His teaching His disciples about stewardship.

And He said to them, "You are those who justify yourselves in the sight of men, but God knows your hearts; for that which is highly esteemed among men is detestable in the sight of God. The Law and the Prophets *were proclaimed* until John; since that time the gospel of the kingdom of God has been preached, and everyone is forcing his way into it. But is it easier for heaven and earth to pass away than for one stroke of a letter of the Law to fail" (Luke 16:15–17; cf. Matthew 5:18; see 1 Samuel 16:7; Matthew 4:23; 11:11–14).

PRECEPTS OF MEN (Listed under MEN, PRECEPTS OF)

PREDETERMINED

[PREDETERMINED from it has been determined]
Setting: An upper room in Jerusalem. During the Feast of Unleavened Bread (Passover) just before His crucifixion, while celebrating the Passover meal with His disciples, Jesus institutes the Lord's Supper.

And when He had taken a cup *and* given thanks, He said, "Take this and share it among yourselves; for I say to you, I will not drink of the fruit of the vine from now on until the kingdom of God comes." And when he had taken *some* bread and given thanks, He broke it and gave it to them, saying, "This is My body which is given for you; do this in remembrance of Me." And in the same way *He took* the cup after they had eaten, saying, "This cup which is poured out for you is the new covenant in My blood. But behold, the hand of the one betraying Me is with Mine on the table. For indeed, the Son of Man is going as it has been determined; but woe to that man by whom He is betrayed!" (Luke 22:17–22; cf. Matthew 26:26–29; Mark 14:22–25; 1 Corinthians 11:23–26; see Psalm 41:9; Luke 14:15; 1 Corinthians 10:16).

PREDICTING THE FUTURE (See FUTURE, PREDICTING THE)

PREDICTION OF JESUS' BETRAYAL (See BETRAYAL, PROPHECY OF JESUS')

PREDICTION OF JESUS' DEATH (See PROPHECY OF JESUS' DEATH)

PREDICTION OF JESUS' RESURRECTION (See PROPHECY OF JESUS' RESURRECTION)

PREDICTION OF THE CHURCH (See CHURCH, PROPHECY OF THE)

PREDICTION OF THE TEMPLE'S DESTRUCTION (See TEMPLE, PROPHECY OF THD DESTRUCTION OF THE)

PREEMINENCE (See FIRST; and GREATNESS)

PREEXISTENCE, JESUS' (See JESUS' PREEXISTENCE)

PREGNANT

Setting: On the Mount of Olives, just east of Jerusalem. During His Olivet Discourse, Jesus answers His disciples' questions as to when the temple will be destroyed and Jerusalem overrun, along with the signs of His coming and the end of the age.

"Therefore when you see the ABOMINATION OF DESOLATION which was spoken of through Daniel the prophet, standing in the holy place (let the reader understand), then those who are in Judea must flee to the mountains. Whoever is on the housetop must not go down to get the things that are in his house. Whoever is in the field must not turn back to get his cloak. But woe to those who are pregnant and to those who are nursing babies in those days! But pray that your flight will not be in the winter, or on a Sabbath. For then there will be a great tribulation, such as has not occurred since the beginning of the world until now, nor ever will. Unless those days had been cut short, no life would have been saved; but for the sake of the elect those days will be cut short. Then if anyone says to you, 'Behold, here is the Christ,' or "There *He is,'* do not believe *him.* For false Christs and false prophets will arise and will show great signs and wonders, so as to mislead, if possible, even the elect. Behold, I have told you in advance. So if they say to you, 'Behold, He is in the wilderness,' do not go out, *or,* 'Behold, He is in the inner rooms,' do not believe *them.* For just as the lightning comes from the east and flashes even to the west, so will the coming of the Son of Man be. Wherever the corpse is, there the vultures will gather" (Matthew 24:15–28, Jesus quotes from Daniel 9:27; cf. Daniel 12:1; Mark 13:14–23; Luke 17:22–31; 21:20–24; 23:29; see John 4:48).

Setting: On the Mount of Olives, east of the temple in Jerusalem. After predicting the temple's destruction, Jesus responds during His Olivet Discourse to questions from Peter, James, John, and Andrew about other future events.

"But when you see the ABOMINATION OF DESOLATION standing where it should not be (let the reader understand), then those who are in Judea must flee to the mountains. The one who is on the housetop must not go down, or go in to get anything out of his house; and the one who is in the field must not turn back to get his coat. But woe to those who are pregnant and to those who are nursing babies in those days! But pray that it may not happen in winter. For those days will be a *time of* tribulation such as has not occurred since the beginning of the creation which God created until now, and never will. Unless the Lord had shortened *those* days, no life would have been saved; but for the sake of the elect, whom He chose, He shortened the days. And then if anyone says to you, 'Behold, here is the Christ'; or, 'Behold, *He is* there'; do not believe *him*; for false Christs and false prophets will arise, and will show signs and wonders, in order to lead astray, if possible, the elect. But take heed; behold, I have told you everything in advance" (Mark 13:14–23; cf. Matthew 24:15–28; Luke 21:20–24; see Daniel 9:27; 12:1; Luke 17:31).

Setting: On the Mount of Olives, east of the temple in Jerusalem. After ministering in the temple a few days before His crucifixion, and giving the disciples more details regarding future events, Jesus elaborates more during His Olivet Discourse about things to come.

"But when you see Jerusalem surrounded by armies, then recognize that her desolation is near. Then those who are in Judea must flee to the mountains, and those who are in the midst of the city must leave, and those who are in the country must not enter the city; because these are days of vengeance, so that all things which are written will be fulfilled. Woe to those who are pregnant and to those who are nursing babies in those days; for there will be a great distress upon the land and wrath to this people; and they will fall by the edge of the sword, and will be led captive into all the nations; and Jerusalem will be trampled under foot by the Gentiles until the times of the Gentiles are fulfilled" (Luke 21:20–24; see Matthew 24:15–18; Mark 13:14–16; Luke 19:43).

PREPARATION (See ALERTNESS; READINESS; and WATCHFULNESS)

[PREPARATION from PREPARE]

Setting: Galilee. While speaking to the crowds, Jesus pays tribute to the ministry of John the Baptist, but emphasizes that the one who is least in the kingdom of heaven is greater than John.

As these men were going *away,* Jesus began to speak to the crowds about John, "What did you go out into the wilderness to see? A reed shaken by the wind? But what did you go out to see? A man dressed in soft *clothing?* Those who wear soft *clothing* are in kings' palaces! But what did you go out to see? A prophet? Yes, I tell you, and the one who is more than a prophet. This is the one about whom it is written, 'BEHOLD, I SEND MY MESSENGER AHEAD OF YOU, WHO WILL PREPARE YOUR WAY BEFORE YOU.' Truly, I say to you, among those born of women there has not arisen *anyone* greater than John the Baptist! Yet the one who is least in the kingdom of heaven is greater than he. From the days of John the Baptist until now the kingdom of heaven suffers violence, and violent men take it by force. For all the prophets and the Law prophesied until John. And, if you are willing to accept *it,* John himself is Elijah who was to come. He who has ears to hear, let him hear" (Matthew 11:7–15, Jesus quotes from Malachi 3:1; cf. Malachi 4:5; Luke 7:24–28; 16:16; see Matthew 14:5).

[PREPARATION from prepared]
Setting: On the way to Jerusalem. The mother of James and John, the sons of Zebedee, asks Jesus to make her sons exalted rulers with Him in His coming kingdom.

And He said to her, "What do you wish?" She said to Him, 'Command that in Your kingdom these two sons of mine may sit one on Your right and one on Your left.' But Jesus answered, "You do not know what you are asking. Are you able to drink the cup that I am about to drink?" They said to Him, 'We are able.' He said to them, "My cup you shall drink; but to sit on My right and on *My* left, this is not Mine to give, but it is for those for whom it has been prepared by My Father" (Matthew 20:21–23; cf. Mark 10:35–40; see Matthew 19:28; Acts 12:2).

[PREPARATION from PREPARED]
Setting: Jerusalem. After cleansing the temple by driving out the money changers and merchants, Jesus comments to the indignant chief priests and scribes about the praises the children render unto Him.

But when the chief priests and the scribes saw the wonderful things that He had done, and the children who were shouting in the temple, "Hosanna to the Son of David," they became indignant and said to Him, "Do You hear what these *children* are saying?" And Jesus said to them, "Yes, have you never read, 'OUT OF THE MOUTH OF INFANTS AND NURSING BABIES YOU HAVE PREPARED PRAISE FOR YOURSELF'?" (Matthew 21:15, 16, Jesus quotes from Psalm 8:2; see Matthew 9:27).

[PREPARATION from prepared]
Setting: The temple in Jerusalem. Jesus speaks another parable to the chief priests and elders after they question His authority.

Jesus spoke to them again in parables, saying, "The kingdom of heaven may be compared to a king who gave a wedding feast for his son. And he sent out his slaves to call those who had been invited to the wedding feast, and they were unwilling to come. Again he sent out other slaves saying, 'Tell those who have been invited, "Behold, I have prepared my dinner; my oxen and my fattened livestock are *all* butchered and everything is ready; come to the wedding feast." But they paid no attention and went their way, one to his own farm, another to his business, and the rest seized his slaves and mistreated them and killed them. But the king was enraged, and he sent his armies and destroyed those murderers and set their city on fire. Then he said to his slaves, 'The wedding is ready, but those who were invited were not worthy. 'Go therefore to the main highways, and as many as you find *there,* invite to the wedding feast.' Those slaves went out into the streets and gathered together all they found, both evil and good; and the wedding hall was filled with dinner guests. But when the king came in to look over the dinner guests, he saw a man there who was not dressed in wedding clothes, and he said to him, 'Friend, how did you come in here without wedding clothes?' And the man was speechless. Then the king said to the servants, 'Bind him hand and foot, and throw him into the outer darkness; in that place there will be weeping and gnashing of teeth.' For many are called, but few *are* chosen" (Matthew 22:1–14; cf. Matthew 8:11, 12).

[PREPARATION from prepared]
Setting: On the Mount of Olives, just east of Jerusalem. During His Olivet Discourse, after answering His disciples' questions as to when the temple will be destroyed and Jerusalem overrun, along with the signs of His coming and the end of the age, Jesus reveals the future judgments following His return.

"But when the Son of Man comes in His glory, and all the angels with Him, then He will sit on His glorious throne. All the nations will be gathered before Him; and He will separate them from one another, as the shepherd separates the sheep from the goats; and He will put the sheep on His right, and the goats on the left. Then the King will say to those on His right, 'Come, you who are blessed of My Father, inherit the kingdom prepared for you from the foundation of the world. 'For I was hungry, and you gave Me *something* to eat; I was thirsty, and you gave Me *something* to drink; I was a stranger, and you invited Me in; naked, and you clothed Me; I was sick, and you visited Me; I was in prison, and you came to Me.' Then the righteous will answer Him, 'Lord, when did we see You hungry and feed You, or thirsty, and give you *something* to drink? And when did we see You a stranger, and invite You in, or naked, and clothe You? When did we see You sick, or in prison, and come to You?' The King will answer and say to them, 'Truly I say to you, to the extent that you did it to one of these brothers of Mine, *even* the least *of them,* you did it to Me.' Then He will also say to those on His left, 'Depart from Me, accursed ones, into the eternal fire which has been prepared for the devil and his angels; for I was hungry, and you gave Me *nothing* to eat; I was thirsty, and you gave Me nothing to drink; I was a stranger, and you did not invite Me in; naked, and you did not clothe Me; sick, and in prison, and you did not visit Me.' Then they themselves also will answer, 'Lord, when did we see You hungry, or thirsty, or a stranger, or naked, or sick, or in prison, and did not take care of You?' Then He will answer them, 'Truly I say to you, to the extent that you did not do it to one of the least of these, you did not do it to Me.' These will go away into eternal punishment, but the righteous into eternal life" (Matthew 25:31–46; see Matthew 7:23; 16:27; 19:29).

[PREPARATION from prepare]

Setting: The home of Simon the leper in Bethany. Jesus rebukes His disciples when they criticize a woman for pouring a costly vial of perfume on His head in preparation for His burial.

But Jesus, aware of this, said to them, "Why do you bother the woman? For she has done a good deed to Me. For you always have the poor with you; but you do not always have Me. For when she poured this perfume on My body, she did it to prepare Me for burial. Truly I say to you, wherever this gospel is preached in the whole world, what this woman has done will also be spoken of in memory of her" (Matthew 26:10–13; cf. Mark 14:3–9; Luke 7:37–39; John 12:2–8; see Deuteronomy 15:11).

[PREPARATION from prepared]

Setting: On the road to Jerusalem. After Jesus prophesies His persecution, death, and resurrection, James and John ask for special honor and privileges in His coming kingdom.

And He said to them, "What do you want Me to do for you?" They said to Him, "Grant that we may sit, one on Your right and one on *Your* left, in Your glory." But Jesus said to them, "You do not know what you are asking. Are you able to drink the cup that I drink, or to be baptized with the baptism with which I am baptized?" They said to Him, "We are able." And Jesus said to them, "The cup that I drink you shall drink; and you shall be baptized with the baptism with which I am baptized. But to sit on My right or on *My* left, this is not Mine to give; but it is for those for whom it has been prepared" (Mark 10:36–40; cf. Matthew 20:20–23; see Matthew 19:28; Acts 12:2).

[PREPARATION from prepare]

Setting: Jerusalem. On the first day of the Feast of Unleavened Bread, when the Passover lamb is being sacrificed, Jesus responds to His disciples' question about His plans for the Passover meal.

And He sent two of His disciples and said to them, "Go into the city, and a man will meet you carrying a pitcher of water; follow him; and wherever he enters, say to the owner of the house, 'The Teacher says, "Where is My guest room in which I may eat the Passover with My disciples?"' And he himself will show you a large upper room furnished *and* ready; prepare for us there" (Mark 14:13–15; cf. Matthew 26:17–19; Luke 22:7–13).

[PREPARATION from PREPARE]

Setting: Galilee. After responding to the disciples of John the Baptist whether He is the promised Messiah, the Lord speaks to the crowds about John.

When the messengers of John had left, He began to speak to the crowds about John, "What did you go out into the wilderness to see? A reed shaken by the wind? But what did you go out to see? A man dressed in soft clothing? Those who are splendidly clothed and live in luxury are *found* in royal palaces! But what did you go out to see? A prophet? Yes, I say to you, and one who is more than a prophet. This is the one about whom it is written, 'BEHOLD, I SEND MY MESSENGER AHEAD OF YOU, WHO WILL PREPARE YOUR WAY BEFORE YOU.' I say to you, among those born of women there is no one greater than John; yet he who is least in the kingdom of God is greater than he" (Luke 7:24–28, Jesus quotes from Malachi 3:1; cf. Matthew 11:7–11).

[PREPARATION from prepared]
Setting: **On the way from Galilee to Jerusalem. After the scribes and Pharisees turn hostile and question Him repeatedly in an attempt to catch Him in something He might say, Jesus responds to a question from the crowd and gives a parable about riches and greed.**

And He told them a parable, saying, "The land of a rich man was very productive. And he began reasoning to himself, saying, 'What shall I do, since I have no place to store my crops?' Then he said, 'This is what I will do: I will tear down my barns and build larger ones, and here I will store all my grain and my goods. And I will say to my soul, "Soul, you have many goods laid up for many years *to come;* take your ease, eat, drink *and* be merry."' "But God said to him, 'You fool! This *very* night your soul is required of you; and *now* who will own what you have prepared?' So is the man who stores up treasure for himself, and is not rich toward God" (Luke 12:16–21; see Job 27:8; Psalm 39:6; Ecclesiastes 12:9; Philippians 2:3).

[PREPARATION from prepare]
Setting: **On the way from Galilee to Jerusalem. After His disciples ask that their faith be increased following His instruction on forgiveness, the Lord illustrates with the mustard seed and an obedient slave.**

And the Lord said, "If you had faith like a mustard seed, you would say to this mulberry tree, 'Be uprooted and be planted in the sea'; and it would obey you. Which of you, having a slave plowing or tending sheep, will say to him when he has come from the field, 'Come immediately and sit down to eat'? But will he not say to him, "Prepare something for me to eat, and *properly* clothe yourself and serve me while I eat and drink; and afterward you may eat and drink'? He does not thank the slave because he did the things which were commanded, does he? So you too, when you do all the things which are commanded you, say, 'We are unworthy slaves; we have done *only* that which we ought to have done'" (Luke 17:6–10; see Matthew 13:31; Luke 12:37).

[PREPARATION from prepare]
Setting: **On the Mount of Olives, east of the temple in Jerusalem. After ministering in the temple a few days before His crucifixion, and giving His disciples more details regarding the temple's future destruction, Jesus elaborates during His Olivet Discourse about things to come.**

Then He continued by saying to them, "Nation will rise against nation and kingdom against kingdom, and there will be great earthquakes, and in various places plagues and famines; and there will be terrors and great signs from heaven. But before all these things, they will lay their hands on you and will persecute you, delivering you to the synagogues and prisons, bringing you before kings and governors for My name's sake. It will lead to an opportunity for your testimony. So make up your minds not to prepare beforehand to defend yourselves; for I will give you utterance and wisdom which none of your opponents will be able to resist or refute. But you will be betrayed even by parents and brothers and relatives and friends, and they will put *some* of you to death, and you will be hated by all because of My name. Yet not a hair of your head will perish. By your endurance you will gain your lives" (Luke 21:10–19; cf. Matthew 10:19–22; 24:7–14; Mark 13:8–13).

[PREPARATION from prepare]
Setting: **Jerusalem. With the Passover (Feast of Unleavened Bread) approaching, Jesus informs His disciples where they will celebrate the feast. The chief priests and scribes seek to kill Him, and Satan enters Judas Iscariot in order to betray the Lord.**

And Jesus sent Peter and John, saying, "Go and prepare the Passover for us, so that we may eat it." They said to Him, "Where do You want us to prepare it?" And He said to them, "When you have entered the city, a man will meet you carrying a pitcher of water; follow him into the house that he enters. And you shall say to the owner of the house, 'The Teacher says to you, "Where is the guest room in which I may eat the Passover with My disciples?"' And he will show you a large, furnished upper room; prepare it there" (Luke 22:8–12; cf. Matthew 26:17–19; Mark 14:12–16).

[PREPARATION from prepare]

Setting: Jerusalem. Before the Passover, after taking issue with Peter's assertion that he would lay down his life for Him, Jesus comforts and gives hope to His disciples regarding their future after He returns to heaven.

"Do not let your heart be troubled; believe in God, believe also in Me. In My Father's house are many dwelling places; if it were not so, I would have told you; for I go to prepare a place for you. If I go and prepare a place for you, I will come again and receive you to Myself, that where I am, *there* you may be also. And you know the way where I am going" (John 14:1–4; see John 13:35).

PRESENCE (Also see PRESENCE, JESUS')

Setting: On the way from Galilee to Jerusalem. Jesus conveys the principles of the lost sheep and the lost coin because the Pharisees and scribes complain He associates with tax collectors and sinners.

"So He told them this parable, saying, "What man among you, if he has a hundred sheep and has lost one of them, does not leave the ninety-nine in the open pasture and go after the one which is lost until he finds it? When he has found it, he lays it on his shoulders, rejoicing. And when he comes home, he calls together his friends and his neighbors, saying to them, 'Rejoice with me, for I have found my sheep which was lost!' I tell you that in the same way, there will be more joy in heaven over one sinner who repents than over ninety-nine righteous persons who need no repentance. Or what woman, if she has ten silver coins and loses one coin, does not light a lamp and sweep the house and search carefully until she finds it? When she has found it, she calls together her friends and neighbors, saying, 'Rejoice with me, for I have found the coin which I had lost!' In the same way, I tell you, there is joy in the presence of the angels of God over one sinner who repents" (Luke 15:3–10).

Setting: Jericho, on the way to Jerusalem. After commending Zaccheus's faith in Him, Jesus provides a parable about stewardship.

So He said, "A nobleman went to a distant country to receive a kingdom for himself, and *then* return. And he called ten of his slaves, and gave them ten minas and said to them, 'Do business *with this* until I come *back.*' But his citizens hated him and sent a delegation after him, saying, 'We do not want this man to reign over us.' When he returned, after receiving the kingdom, he ordered that these slaves, to whom he had given the money, be called to him so that he might know what business they had done. The first appeared, saying, 'Master, your mina has made ten minas more.' And he said to him, 'Well done, good slave, because you have been faithful in a very little thing, you are to be in authority over ten cities.' The second came, saying, 'Your mina, master, has made five minas.' And he said to him, also, 'And you are to be over five cities.' Another came, saying, 'Master, here is your mina, which I kept put away in a handkerchief; for I was afraid of you, because you are an exacting man; you take up what you did not lay down and reap what you did not sow.' He said to him, 'By your own words I will judge you, you worthless slave. Did you know that I am an exacting man, taking up what I did not lay down and reaping what I did not sow? Then why did you not put my money in the bank, and having come, I would have collected it with interest?' Then he said to the bystanders, 'Take the mina away from him and give it to the one who has the ten minas.' And they said to him, 'Master, he has ten minas *already.*' I tell you that to everyone who has, more shall be given, but from the one who does not have, even what he does have shall be taken away. But these enemies of mine, who did not want me to reign over them, bring them here and slay them in my presence" (Luke 19:12–27; cf. Matthew 25:14–30; see Matthew 13:12; Luke 16:10).

PRESENCE, JESUS' (Also see PRESENCE)

[JESUS' PRESENCE from I am there in their midst]

Setting: Capernaum of Galilee. After conveying to His disciples the value of little ones, Jesus gives instruction about church discipline.

"If your brother sins, go and show him his fault in private; if he listens to you, you have won your brother. But if he does not listen *to you,* take one or two more with you, so that BY THE MOUTH OF TWO OR THREE WITNESSES EVERY FACT MAY BE CONFIRMED. If he refuses to listen to them, tell it to the church; and if he refuses to listen even to the church, let him be to you as a Gentile and a tax collector. Truly I say to you, whatever you bind of earth shall have been bound in heaven; and whatever you loose on earth midst" (Matthew 18:15–20. Jesus quotes from Deuteronomy 19:15; cf. Matthew 7:7; 16:19; see Leviticus 19:17; Matthew 28:20; 2 Thessalonians 3:6, 14).

[JESUS' PRESENCE from I am with you always]
Setting: On a mountain in Galilee. Following His resurrection from the dead in Jerusalem, Jesus conveys the Great Commission to His eleven remaining disciples.

And Jesus came up and spoke to them, saying, "All authority has been given to Me in heaven and on earth. Go therefore and make disciples of all the nations, baptizing them in the name of the Father and the Son and the Holy Spirit, teaching them to observe all that I commanded you; and lo, I am with you always, even to the end of the age" (Matthew 28:18–20; cf. Mark 16:15; see Daniel 7:13).

[JESUS' PRESENCE from Your presence]
Setting: On the way from Galilee to Jerusalem. While teaching in the cities and villages, Jesus responds to a question about who is saved.

And someone said to Him, "Lord, are here *just* a few who are being saved?" And He said to them, "Strive to enter through the narrow door; for many, I tell you, will seek to enter and will not be able. Once the head of the house gets up and shuts the door, and you begin to stand outside and knock on the door, saying, 'Lord, open up to us!' then He will answer and say to you, 'I do not know where you are from.' Then you will begin to say, 'We ate and drank in Your presence, and You taught in our streets'; and He will say, 'I tell you, I do not know where you are from; DEPART FROM ME, ALL YOU EVILDOERS.' In that place there will be weeping and gnashing of teeth when you see Abraham and Isaac and Jacob and all the prophets in the kingdom of God, but you yourselves being thrown out. And they will come from east and west and from north and south, and will recline *at the table* in the kingdom of God. And behold, *some* are last who will be first and *some* are first who will be last" (Luke 13:23–30, Jesus quotes from Psalm 6:8; cf. Matthew 7:13, 23; 8:11, 12; see Matthew 19:30; Luke 3:8).

[JESUS' PRESENCE from I am with you]
Setting: The temple in Jerusalem. While teaching during the Feast of Booths, Jesus causes discussion about whether He is the Christ. Many believe in Him, while the chief priests and Pharisees plan to seize Him.

Therefore Jesus said, "For a little while longer I am with you, then I go to Him who sent Me. You will seek Me, and will not find Me; and where I am, you cannot come" (John 7:33, 34; see John 12:35).

[JESUS' PRESENCE from I am with you]
Setting: Jerusalem. Before the Passover, after revealing to His disciples that Judas will betray Him to the chief priests and Pharisees, Jesus conveys how He will soon be glorified in His death, and commands the disciples to love one another.

Therefore when he had gone out, Jesus said, "Now is the Son of Man glorified, and God is glorified in Him; if God is glorified in Him, God will also glorify Him in Himself, and will glorify Him immediately. Little children, I am with you a little while longer. You will seek Me; and as I said to the Jews, now I also say to you, 'Where I am going, you cannot come.' A new commandment I give to you, that you love one another, even as I have loved you, that you also love one another. By this all men will know that you are My disciples, if you have love for one another" (John 13:31–35; see Leviticus 19:18; John 7:33, 34; 17:1; 1 John 3:14).

PRESENCE OF GOD (Listed under GOD, PRESENCE OF)

PRESENT, THE (Also see AGE, THIS)
[THE PRESENT from the present age]
Setting: Judea beyond the Jordan (Perea). After informing a rich man how righteous believers may have treasure

in heaven, Jesus tells His disciples about the reward of those who sacrifice in this life to follow Him.

Jesus said, "Truly I say to you, there is no one who has left house or brothers or sisters or mother or father or children or farms, for My sake and for the gospel's sake, but that he will receive a hundred times as much now in the present age, houses and brothers and sisters and mothers and children and farms, along with persecutions; and in the age to come, eternal life. But many *who are* first will be last, and the last, first" (Mark 10:29–31; cf. Matthew 19:27–30; Luke 18:28–30; see Matthew 6:33).

[THE PRESENT from this present time]
Setting: On the way from Galilee to Jerusalem. After telling how a relationship with Him will divide families, Jesus chastises the crowds for being able to discern the weather but not the present age.

And He was also saying to the crowds, "When you see a cloud rising in the west, immediately you say, 'A shower is coming,' and so it turns out. And when *you see* a south wind blowing, you say, 'It will be a hot day,' and it turns out *that way*. You hypocrites! You know how to analyze the appearance of the earth and the sky, but why do you not analyze this present time?" (Luke 12:54–56; cf. Matthew 16:2, 3).

[THE PRESENT from the things which are]
Setting: On the island of Patmos (in the Aegean Sea about fifty miles southwest of Ephesus in modern Turkey). On the Lord's Day (Sunday), approximately fifty years after the Resurrection, the disciple John encounters the Lord Jesus Christ, who communicates new revelations for the apostle to record for the seven churches in Asia.

When I saw Him, I fell at His feet like a dead man. And He placed His right hand on me, saying, "Do not be afraid; I am the first and the last, and the living One; and I was dead, and behold, I am alive forevermore, and I have the keys of death and of Hades. Therefore write the things which you have seen, and the things which are, and the things which will take place after these things. As for the mystery of the seven stars which you saw in My right hand, and the seven golden lampstands: the seven stars are the angels of the seven churches, and the seven lampstands are the seven churches" (Revelation 1:17–20; see Isaiah 44:6; Luke 24:5; Revelation 2:8).

PRESS, WINE (See WINE PRESS)

PRESTIGE (See GREETINGS, RESPECTFUL)

PRETENSE (Also see HYPOCRITES; HYPOCRISY; PRAYERS, LONG; and SAKE, APPEARANCE'S)

[PRETENSE from practicing your righteousness before men to be noticed by them]
Setting: Galilee. During the early part of His ministry, Jesus preaches the Sermon on the Mount to His disciples and the multitudes.

"Beware of practicing your righteousness before men to be noticed by them; otherwise you have no reward with your Father who is in heaven" (Matthew 6:1; cf. Matthew 6:16).

[PRETENSE from when you give to the poor, do not sound a trumpet before you]
Setting: Galilee. During the early part of His ministry, Jesus preaches the Sermon on the Mount to His disciples and the multitudes.

"So when you give to the poor, do not sound a trumpet before you, as the hypocrites do in the synagogues and in the streets, so that they may be honored by men. Truly I say to you, they have their reward in full. But when you give to the poor, do not let your left hand know what your right hand is doing, so that your giving will be in secret; and your Father who sees *what is done* in secret will reward you" (Matthew 6:2–4; see Jeremiah 17:10; Matthew 6:16).

will reward you" (Matthew 6:2–4; see Jeremiah 17:10; Matthew 6:16).

[PRETENSE from they love to stand and pray in the synagogues and on the street corners so that they may be seen by men]
Setting: Galilee. During the early part of His ministry, Jesus preaches the Sermon on the Mount to His disciples and the multitudes.

"When you pray, you are not to be like the hypocrites; for they love to stand and pray in the synagogues and on the street corners so that they may be seen by men. Truly I say to you, they have their reward in full. But you, when you pray, go into your inner room, close your door and pray to your Father who is in secret, and your Father who sees *what is done* in secret will reward you" (Matthew 6:5, 6; see Mark 11:25).

[PRETENSE from THIS PEOPLE HONORS ME WITH THEIR LIPS, BUT THEIR HEART IS FAR AWAY]
Setting: Galilee. Pharisees and scribes from Jerusalem accuse Jesus' disciples of disobeying tradition and the commandments.

And He answered and said to them, "Why do you yourselves transgress the commandment of God for the sake of tradition? For God said, 'HONOR YOUR FATHER AND MOTHER,' and, 'HE WHO SPEAKS EVIL OF FATHER OR MOTHER IS TO BE PUT TO DEATH.' But you say, 'Whoever says to *his* father or mother, "Whatever I have that would help you has been given *to God*," he is not to honor his father or mother.' And *by this* you invalidated the word of God for the sake of your tradition. You hypocrites, rightly did Isaiah prophesy of you: 'THIS PEOPLE HONORS ME WITH THEIR LIPS, BUT THEIR HEART IS FAR AWAY FROM ME. BUT IN VAIN DO THEY WORSHIP ME, TEACHING AS DOCTRINES THE PRECEPTS OF MEN'" (Matthew 15:3–9, Jesus quotes from Exodus 20:12, 21:17, Leviticus 20:9; Isaiah 29:13; cf. Mark 7:5–7; see Colossians 2:22).

Setting: The temple in Jerusalem. After the Jewish religious leaders test Him with questions, Jesus pronounces the second of eight woes upon them in front of the crowds and His disciples.

["Woe to you, scribes and Pharisees, hypocrites, because you devour widows' houses, and for a pretense you make long prayers; therefore you will receive greater condemnation] (Matthew 23:14; cf. Mark 12:40; Luke 20:47).

[PRETENSE from For you clean the outside of the cup and of the dish]
Setting: The temple in Jerusalem. After the Jewish religious leaders test Him with questions, Jesus pronounces the sixth of eight woes upon them in front of the crowds and His disciples.

"Woe to you, scribes and Pharisees, hypocrites! For you clean the outside of the cup and of the dish, but inside they are full of robbery and self-indulgence. You blind Pharisee, first clean the inside of the cup and of the dish, so that the outside of it may become clean also" (Matthew 23:25, 26; see Mark 7:4).

[PRETENSE from THIS PEOPLE HONORS ME WITH THEIR LIPS, BUT THEIR HEART IS FAR AWAY FROM ME]
Setting: Galilee. The Pharisees and some of the scribes from Jerusalem question why Jesus' disciples do not follow the tradition of ceremonial hand cleansing before eating bread.

And He said to them, "Rightly did Isaiah prophesy of you hypocrites, as it is written: 'THIS PEOPLE HONORS ME WITH THEIR LIPS, BUT THEIR HEART IS FAR AWAY FROM ME. BUT IN VAIN DO THEY WORSHIP ME, TEACHING AS DOCTRINES THE PRECEPTS OF MEN.' Neglecting the commandment of God, you hold to the tradition of men." He was also saying to them, "You are experts at setting aside the commandment of God in order to keep tradition. For Moses said, 'HONOR YOUR FATHER AND YOUR MOTHER'; and, 'HE WHO SPEAKS EVIL OF FATHER OR MOTHER, IS TO BE PUT TO DEATH'; but you say, 'If a man says to *his* father or *his* mother, whatever I have that would help you is Corban (that is to say, given *to God*),' you no longer permit him to do anything for *his* father or *his* mother; *thus* invalidating the word of God by your tradition which you have handed down; and you do many things such as that" (Mark 7:6–13, Jesus quotes from Exodus 20:12; 21:17; Isaiah 29:13; cf. Matthew 15:1–6).

[PRETENSE from you Pharisees clean the outside of the cup and of the platter]
Setting: On the way from Galilee to Jerusalem. After speaking of how a lamp illuminates, the Lord has lunch with a Pharisee who is surprised He doesn't wash before eating.

But the Lord said to him, "Now you Pharisees clean the outside of the cup and of the platter; but inside of you, you are full of robbery and wickedness. You foolish ones, did not He who made the outside make the inside also? But give that which is within as charity, and then all things are clean for you. But woe to you Pharisees! You pay tithe of mint and rue and every *kind of* garden herb, and *yet* disregard justice and the love of God; but these are the things you should have done without neglecting the others. Woe to you Pharisees! For you love the chief seats in the synagogues and the respectful greetings in the market places. Woe to you! For you are like concealed tombs, and the people who walk over *them* are unaware *of it*" (Luke 11:39–44; cf. Matthew 23:6, 7, 23–27; see Matthew 15:2; Titus 1:15).

PRICE, PEARL OF GREAT (See PEARL, PARABLE OF THE)

PRIDE (Also see ARROGANCE; GREATNESS; and SELF-RIGHTEOUSNESS)

Setting: Galilee. After the Pharisees and scribes from Jerusalem object to His disciples' lack of obedience to the tradition regarding ceremonial cleansing, Jesus speaks to a crowd and explains His teaching to the disciples.

After He called the crowd to Him again, He *began* saying to them, "Listen to Me, all of you, and understand: there is nothing outside the man which can defile him if it goes into him; but the things which proceed out of the man are what defile the man. [If anyone has ears to hear, let him hear."] When he had left the crowd *and* entered the house, His disciples questioned Him about the parable. And He said to them, "Are you so lacking in understanding also? Do you not understand that whatever goes into the man from outside cannot defile him, because it does not go into his heart, but into his stomach, and is eliminated?" (*Thus He* declared all foods clean.) And He was saying, "That which proceeds out of the man, that is what defiles the man. For from within, out of the heart of men, proceed the evil thoughts, fornications, thefts, murders, adulteries, deeds of coveting *and* wickedness, *as well* as deceit, sensuality, envy, slander, pride *and* foolishness. All these evil things proceed from within and defile the man" (Mark 7:14–23; cf. Matthew 15:10–20).

[PRIDE from God, I thank You that I am not like other people]
Setting: On the way from Galilee to Jerusalem. After instructing His disciples about persistence in prayer, Jesus conveys a parable about self-righteousness.

And He also told this parable to some people who trusted in themselves that they were righteous, and viewed others with contempt: "Two men went up into the temple to pray, one a Pharisee and the other a tax collector. The Pharisee stood and was praying this to himself: 'God, I thank You that I am not like other people: swindlers, unjust, adulterers, or even like this tax collector. I fast twice a week; I pay tithes of all that I get.' But the tax collector, standing some distance away, was even unwilling to lift up his eyes to heaven, but was beating his breast, saying, 'God, be merciful to me, the sinner!' I tell you, this man went to his house justified rather than the other; for everyone who exalts himself will be humbled, but he who humbles himself will be exalted" (Luke 18:9–14; see Ezra 9:6; Matthew 6:5, 23:12; Luke 11:42; 16:15; Romans 14:3, 10).

PRIEST (Also see HIGH PRIEST)

Setting: Galilee. When Jesus comes down after preaching the Sermon on the Mount, large crowds follow Him, and a leper approaches Him asking for cleansing.

Jesus stretched out His hand and touched him, saying, "I am willing, be cleansed." And immediately his leprosy was cleansed. And Jesus said to him, "See that you tell no one; but go, show yourself to the priest and present the offering that Moses commanded, as a testimony to them" (Matthew 8:3, 4; cf. Mark 1:40–44; Luke 5:12–14).

Setting: Galilee. As Jesus preaches and casts out demons in the synagogues, a leper beseeches Him for healing.

Moved with compassion, Jesus stretched out His hand and touched him, and said to him, "I am willing; be cleansed." Immediately the leprosy left him and he was cleansed. And He sternly warned him and immediately sent him away, and He said to him,

"See that you say nothing to anyone; but go, show yourself to the priest and offer for your cleansing what Moses commanded, as a testimony to them" (Mark 1:41–44; cf. Luke 5:12–14; see Leviticus 14:1–32; Matthew 8:3).

Setting: Galilee. Early in His ministry, after calling Andrew, Simon (Peter), James, and John to follow Him, Jesus heals a leper.

And He stretched out His hand and touched Him, saying, "I am willing; be cleansed." And immediately the leprosy left him. And He ordered him to tell no one, "But go and show yourself to the priest and make an offering for your cleansing, just as Moses commanded, as a testimony to them" (Luke 5:13, 14; cf. Matthew 8:2–4; Mark 1:40–45; see Leviticus 13:49).

Setting: On the way from Galilee to Jerusalem. While being tested by a lawyer, Jesus tells him the story of the good Samaritan.

Jesus replied and said, "A man was going down from Jerusalem to Jericho, and fell among robbers, and they stripped him and beat him, and went away leaving him half dead. And by chance a priest was going down on that road, and when he saw him, he passed by on the other side. Likewise a Levite also, when he came to the place and saw him, passed by on the other side. But a Samaritan, who was on a journey, came upon him; and when he saw him, he felt compassion, and came to him and bandaged up his wounds, pouring oil and wine on *them;* and he put him on his own beast, and brought him to an inn and took care of him. On the next day he took out two denarii and gave them to the innkeeper and said, 'Take care of him; and whatever more you spend, when I return I will repay you.' Which of these three do you think proved to be a neighbor to the man who fell into the robbers' *hands?"* And he said, "The one who showed mercy toward him." Then Jesus said to him, "Go and do the same" (Luke 10:30–37).

PRIEST, HIGH (See HIGH PRIEST)

PRIESTS (CHIEF PRIESTS is a separate entry)

Setting: Galilee. Jesus responds to the Pharisees' objection to His disciples' picking grain from the fields on the Sabbath.

But He said to them, "Have you not read what David did when he became hungry, he and his companions, how they entered the house of God, and ate the consecrated bread, which was not lawful for him to eat nor for those with him, but for the priests alone? Or, have you not read in the Law, that on the Sabbath the priests in the temple break the Sabbath and are innocent? But I say to you that something greater than the temple is here. But if you had known what this means, 'I DESIRE COMPASSION, AND NOT A SACRIFICE,' you would not have condemned the innocent. For the Son of Man is Lord of the Sabbath" (Matthew 12:3–8, Jesus quotes from Hosea 6:6; cf. Mark 2:25–28; Luke 6:3–5; see 1 Samuel 21:6).

Setting: Galilee. Early in His ministry, the Pharisees question why Jesus allows His disciples to harvest grain on the Sabbath.

And He said to them, "Have you never read what David did when he was in need and he and his companions became hungry; how he entered the house of God in the time of Abiathar *the* high priest, and ate the consecrated bread, which is not lawful for *anyone* to eat except the priests, and he also gave it to those who were with him?" Jesus said to them, "The Sabbath was made for man, and not man for the Sabbath. So the Son of Man is Lord even of the Sabbath" (Mark 2:25–28; cf. Matthew 12:1–8; Luke 6:1–5; see Exodus 23:12).

Setting: Probably Galilee. As Jesus and His disciples pass through some grain fields, some of the Pharisees ask Him why His followers harvest grain on the Sabbath.

And Jesus answering them said, "Have you not even read what David did when he was hungry, he and those who were with him, how he entered the house of God, and took and ate the consecrated bread which is not lawful for any to eat except the priests alone, and gave it to his companions?" And He was saying to them, "The Son of Man is Lord of the Sabbath" (Luke 6:3–5; cf. Matthew 12:1–8; Mark 2:23–28; see Exodus 20:8; Leviticus 24:1–9; Deuteronomy 5:12; 1 Samuel 21:1–6).

Setting: On the way from Galilee to Jerusalem. The Lord stops to heal ten lepers who ask for cleansing.

When He saw them, He said to them, "Go and show yourselves to the priests." And as they were going, they were cleansed. Now one of them, when he saw that he had been healed, turned back, glorifying God with a loud voice, and he fell on his face at His feet, giving thanks to Him. And he was a Samaritan. Then Jesus answered and said, "Were there not ten cleansed? But the nine—where are they? Was no one found who returned to give glory to God, except this foreigner?" And He said to him, "Stand up and go; your faith has made you well" (Luke 17:14–19; see Leviticus 14:1–32).

PRIESTS, CHIEF (See CHIEF PRIESTS)

PRIORITIES (Also see FIRST; FOLLOWING JESUS CHRIST; and TREASURE)

[PRIORITIES from Do not store up for yourselves treasures on earth]
Setting: Galilee. During the early part of His ministry, Jesus preaches the Sermon on the Mount to His disciples and the multitudes.

"Do not store up for yourselves treasures on earth, where moth and rust destroy, and where thieves break in and steal. But store up for yourselves treasures in heaven, where neither moth nor rust destroys, and where thieves do not break in or steal; for where your treasure is, there your heart will be also" (Matthew 6:19–21; cf. Luke 12:34; see Proverb 23:4; Matthew 19:21).

[PRIORITIES from seek first His kingdom and His righteousness]
Setting: Galilee. During the early part of His ministry, Jesus preaches the Sermon on the Mount to His disciples and the multitudes.

"For this reason I say to you, do not be worried about your life, *as to* what you will eat or what you will drink; nor for your body, *as to* what you will put on. Is not life more than food, and the body more than clothing? Look at the birds of the air, that they do not sow, nor reap nor gather into barns, and *yet* your heavenly Father feeds them. Are you not worth much more than they? And who of you by being worried can add a *single* hour to his life? And why are you worried about clothing? Observe how the lilies of the field grow; they do not toil nor do they spin, yet I say to you that not even Solomon in all his glory clothed himself like one of these. But if God so clothes the grass of the field, which is *alive* today and tomorrow is thrown into the furnace, *will He* not much more *clothe* you? You of little faith! Do not worry then, saying 'What will we eat?' or 'What will we drink?' or 'What will be wear for clothing?" For the Gentiles eagerly seek all these things; for your heavenly Father knows that you need all these things. But seek first His kingdom and His righteousness, and all these things will be added to you. So do not worry about tomorrow; for tomorrow will care for itself. Each day has enough trouble of its own" (Matthew 6:25–34; cf. Luke 12:22–31; see 1 Kings 10:4–7; Job 35:11; Matthew 8:26).

[PRIORITIES from For what will it profit a man if he gains the whole world and forfeits his soul]
Setting: Near Caesarea Philippi. After rebuking Peter for trying to forbid Him to accomplish His earthly mission of dying and being resurrected, Jesus teaches His disciples about the costs of following Him.

Then Jesus said to His disciples, "If anyone wishes to come after Me, he must deny himself, and take up his cross and follow Me. For whoever wishes to save his life will lose it; but whoever loses his life for My sake will find it. For what will it profit a man if he gains the whole world and forfeits his soul? Or what will a man give in exchange for his soul? For the Son of Man is going to come in the glory of His Father with His angels, and WILL THEN REPAY EVERY MAN ACCORDING TO HIS DEEDS. Truly, I say to you, there are some of you who are standing here who will not taste death until they see the Son of Man coming in His kingdom" (Matthew 16:24–28, Jesus quotes from Psalm 62:12; cf. Mark 8:34–37; Luke 9:23–27; see Matthew 10:38, 39).

[PRIORITIES from YOU SHALL LOVE THE LORD YOUR GOD WITH ALL YOUR HEART, AND WITH ALL YOUR SOUL, AND WITH ALL YOUR MIND]
Setting: The temple in Jerusalem. A Pharisee lawyer asks Jesus which is the great commandment of the Law, in order to test Him as He teaches.

And He said to him, " 'YOU SHALL LOVE THE LORD YOUR GOD WITH ALL YOUR HEART, AND WITH ALL YOUR SOUL, AND WITH ALL YOUR MIND.' This is the great and foremost commandment. The second is like it, 'YOU SHALL LOVE YOUR NEIGHBOR AS YOURSELF.' On these two commandments depend the whole Law and the Prophets" (Matthew 22:37–40; Jesus quotes from Leviticus 19:18; Deuteronomy 6:5; cf. Mark 12:28–34; see Matthew 7:12).

[PRIORITIES from For what does it profit a man to gain the whole world, and forfeit his soul]
Setting: Caesarea Philippi. After rebuking Peter for desiring to thwart His mission to the cross, Jesus summons a crowd, along with His disciples, and informs them of the high costs of following Him.

And He summoned the crowd with His disciples, and said to them, "If anyone wishes to come after Me, he must deny himself, and take up his cross and follow Me. For whoever wishes to save his life will lose it, but whoever loses his life for My sake and the gospel's will save it. For what does it profit a man to gain the whole world, and forfeit his soul? For what will a man give in exchange for his soul? For whoever is ashamed of Me and My words in this adulterous and sinful generation, the Son of Man will also be ashamed of him when He comes in the glory of His Father with the holy angels" (Mark 8:34–38; cf. Matthew 16:24–28; Luke 9:23–27; see Matthew 10:33, 38, 39).

[PRIORITIES from YOU SHALL LOVE THE LORD YOUR GOD WITH ALL YOUR HEART, AND WITH ALL YOUR SOUL, AND WITH ALL YOUR MIND AND WITH ALL YOUR STRENGTH]
Setting: The temple in Jerusalem. With the Pharisees and Herodians failing to trap Jesus in a statement, one of the scribes asks Him which commandment is foremost.

Jesus answered, "The foremost is, 'HEAR, O ISRAEL! THE LORD OUR GOD IS ONE LORD; AND YOU SHALL LOVE THE LORD YOUR GOD WITH ALL YOUR HEART, AND WITH ALL YOUR SOUL, AND WITH ALL YOUR MIND AND WITH ALL YOUR STRENGTH.' The second is this, 'YOU SHALL LOVE YOUR NEIGHBOR AS YOURSELF.' There is no other commandment greater than these" (Mark 12:29–31, Jesus quotes from Deuteronomy 6:4, 5; Leviticus 19:18; cf. Matthew 22:34–40).

[PRIORITIES from For what is a man profited if he gains the whole world, and loses or forfeits himself]
Setting: Galilee. Following Peter's pronouncement that Jesus is the Christ of God, the Lord conveys the demands of discipleship and the hope regarding the kingdom of God.

And He was saying to *them* all, "If anyone wishes to come after Me, he must deny himself, and take up his cross daily and follow Me. For whoever wishes to save his life will lose it, but whoever loses his life for My sake, he is the one who will save it. For what is a man profited if he gains the whole world, and loses or forfeits himself? For whoever is ashamed of Me and My words, the Son of Man will be ashamed of him when He comes in His glory, and *the glory* of the Father and of the holy angels. But I say to you truthfully, there are some of those standing here who will not taste death until they see the kingdom of God" (Luke 9:23–27; cf. Matthew 16:24–26, 28; Mark 8:34–37; see Matthew 10:33, 38, 39).

[PRIORITIES from YOU SHALL LOVE THE LORD YOUR GOD WITH ALL YOUR HEART, AND WITH ALL YOUR SOUL, AND WITH ALL YOUR STRENGTH, AND WITH ALL YOUR MIND; AND YOUR NEIGHBOR AS YOURSELF]
Setting: On the way from Galilee to Jerusalem. After Jesus tells His disciples in private the privilege they are experiencing by living in the time of the Messiah, a lawyer tests Him.

And a lawyer stood up and put Him to the test, saying, "Teacher, what shall I do to inherit eternal life?" And He said to him, "What is written in the Law? How does it read to you?" And he answered, "YOU SHALL LOVE THE LORD YOUR GOD WITH ALL YOUR HEART, AND WITH ALL YOUR SOUL, AND WITH ALL YOUR STRENGTH, AND WITH ALL YOUR MIND; AND YOUR NEIGHBOR AS YOURSELF." And He said to him, "You have answered correctly; DO THIS AND YOU WILL LIVE" (Luke 10:25–28, Jesus quotes from Leviticus 18:5; see Deuteronomy 6:5; Matthew 19:16–19).

[PRIORITIES from Mary has chosen the good part]
Setting: On the way from Galilee to Jerusalem. After Jesus is tested by a lawyer, He and His disciples are welcomed

into the home of Martha and Mary in Bethany.

But the Lord answered and said to her, "Martha, Martha, you are worried and bothered about so many things; but *only* one thing is necessary, for Mary has chosen the good part, which shall not be taken away from her" (Luke 10:41, 42; see Matthew 6:25).

[PRIORITIES from seek His kingdom]

Setting: On the way from Galilee to Jerusalem. After giving a parable about riches and greed, Jesus comforts the crowd and His disciples. The scribes and Pharisees turn hostile and question Him repeatedly in an attempt to catch Him in something He might say.

And He said to His disciples, "For this reason I say to you, do not worry about *your* life, *as to* what you will eat; nor for your body, *as to* what you will put on. For life is more than food, and the body more than clothing. Consider the ravens, for they neither sow nor reap; they have no storeroom nor barn, and *yet* God feeds them; how much more valuable you are than the birds! And which of you by worrying can add a *single* hour to his life's span? If then you cannot do even a very little thing, why do you worry about other matters? Consider the lilies, how they grow: they neither toil nor spin; but I tell you, not even Solomon in all his glory clothed himself like one of these. But if God so clothes the grass in the field, which is *alive* today and tomorrow is thrown into the furnace, how much more *will He clothe* you? You men of little faith! And do not seek what you will eat and what you will drink, and do not keep worrying. For all these things the nations of the world eagerly seek; but your Father knows that you need these things. But seek His kingdom, and these things will be added to you. Do not be afraid, little flock, for your Father has chosen gladly to give you the kingdom" (Luke 12:22–32; cf. Matthew 6:25–33; see 1 Kings 10:4–7; Job 38:41).

PRISON (Also see PRISONS)

Setting: Galilee. During the early part of His ministry, Jesus preaches the Sermon on the Mount to His disciples and the multitudes.

"Make friends quickly with your opponent at law while you are with him on the way, so that your opponent may not hand you over to the judge, and the judge to the officer, and you be thrown into prison. Truly I say to you, you will not come out of there until you have paid up the last cent'" (Matthew 5:25, 26; cf. Luke 12:58, 59).

Setting: Capernaum of Galilee. Jesus illustrates the matter of forgiveness after Peter asks Him if forgiving someone seven times who has sinned against him is adequate.

"For this reason the kingdom of heaven may be compared to a king who wished to settle accounts with his slaves. When he had begun to settle *them,* one who owed him ten thousand talents was brought to him. But since he did not have *the means* to repay, his lord commanded him to be sold, along with his wife and children and all that he had, and repayment to be made. So the slave fell *to the ground* and prostrated himself before him, saying, 'Have patience with me and I will repay you everything.' And the lord of that slave felt compassion and released him and forgave him the debt. But that slave went out and found one of his fellow slaves who owed him a hundred denarii; and he seized him and *began* to choke *him,* saying, 'Pay back what you owe.' So his fellow slave fell *to the ground* and *began* to plead with him, saying, 'Have patience with me and I will repay you.' But he was unwilling and went and threw him in prison until he should pay back what was owed. So when his fellow slaves saw what had happened, they were deeply grieved and came and reported to their lord all that had happened. Then summoning him, his lord said to him, 'You wicked slave, I forgave you all that debt because you pleaded with me. Should you not also have had mercy on your fellow slave, in the same way that I had mercy on you?' And his lord, moved with anger, handed him over to the torturers until he should repay all that was owed him. My heavenly Father will also do the same to you, if each of you does not forgive his brother from your heart" (Matthew 18:23–35; cf. Matthew 6:12, 14, 15; Luke 7:42; see Matthew 25:19–28).

Setting: On the Mount of Olives, just east of Jerusalem. During His Olivet Discourse, after answering His disciples' questions as to when the temple will be destroyed and Jerusalem overrun, along with the signs of His coming and the end of the age, Jesus reveals the future judgments following His return.

"But when the Son of Man comes in His glory, and all the angels with Him, then He will sit on His glorious throne. All the nations will be gathered before Him; and He will separate them from one another, as the shepherd separates the sheep from the goats; and He will put the sheep on His right, and the goats on the left. Then the King will say to those on His right, 'Come, you who are blessed of My Father, inherit the kingdom prepared for you from the foundation of the world. 'For I was hungry, and you gave Me *something* to eat; I was thirsty, and you gave Me *something* to drink; I was a stranger, and you invited Me in; naked, and you clothed Me; I was sick, and you visited Me; I was in prison, and you came to Me.' Then the righteous will answer Him, 'Lord, when did we see You hungry and feed You, or thirsty, and give you *something* to drink? And when did we see You a stranger, and invite You in, or naked, and clothe You? When did we see You sick, or in prison, and come to You?' The King will answer and say to them, 'Truly I say to you, to the extent that you did it to one of these brothers of Mine, *even* the least *of them,* you did it to Me.' Then He will also say to those on His left, 'Depart from Me, accursed ones, into the eternal fire which has been prepared for the devil and his angels; for I was hungry, and you gave Me *nothing* to eat; I was thirsty, and you gave Me nothing to drink; I was a stranger, and you did not invite Me in; naked, and you did not clothe Me; sick, and in prison, and you did not visit Me.' Then they themselves also will answer, 'Lord, when did we see You hungry, or thirsty, or a stranger, or naked, or sick, or in prison, and did not take care of You?' Then He will answer them, 'Truly I say to you, to the extent that you did not do it to one of the least of these, you did not do it to Me.' These will go away into eternal punishment, but the righteous into eternal life" (Matthew 25:31–46; see Matthew 7:23; 16:27; 19:29).

Setting: On the way from Galilee to Jerusalem. After chastising the crowds for being able to discern the weather but not the present age, Jesus exhorts them to settle any financial disputes outside of court.

"And why do you not even on your own initiative judge what is right? For while you are going with your opponent to appear before the magistrate, on *your* way *there* make an effort to settle with him, so that he may not drag you before the judge, and the judge turn you over to the officer, and the officer throw you into prison. I say to you, you will not get out of there until you have paid the very last cent." (Luke 12:57–59; cf. Matthew 5:25, 26)

Setting: On the island of Patmos (in the Aegean Sea about fifty miles southwest of Ephesus in modern Turkey). On the Lord's Day (Sunday), approximately fifty years after the Resurrection, the disciple John encounters the Lord Jesus Christ, who communicates a new revelation for the apostle to record for the church in Smyrna and to six other churches in Asia.

"And to the angel of the church in Smyrna write: The first and the last, who was dead, and has come to life, says this: 'I know your tribulation and your poverty (but you are rich), and the blasphemy by those who say they are Jews and are not, but are a synagogue of Satan. Do not fear what you are about to suffer. Behold, the devil is about to cast some of you into prison, so that you will be tested, and you will have tribulation for ten days. Be faithful until death, and I will give you the crown of life. He who has an ear, let him hear what the Spirit says to the churches. He who overcomes will not be hurt by the second death' (Revelation 2:8–11; see Isaiah 44:6; Revelation 1:9, 18; 20:6, 14).

PRISONS (Also see PRISON)

Setting: On the Mount of Olives, east of the temple in Jerusalem. After ministering in the temple a few days before His crucifixion, and giving His disciples more details regarding the temple's future destruction, Jesus elaborates during His Olivet Discourse about things to come.

Then He continued by saying to them, "Nation will rise against nation and kingdom against kingdom, and there will be great earthquakes, and in various places plagues and famines; and there will be terrors and great signs from heaven. But before all these things, they will lay their hands on you and will persecute you, delivering you to the synagogues and prisons, bringing you before kings and governors for My name's sake. It will lead to an opportunity for your testimony. So make up your minds not to prepare beforehand to defend yourselves; for I will give you utterance and wisdom which none of your opponents will be able to resist or refute. But you will be betrayed even by parents and brothers and relatives and friends, and they will put *some* of you to death, and you will be hated by all because of My name. Yet not a hair of your head will perish. By your endurance you will gain your lives" (Luke 21:10–19; cf. Matthew 10:19–22; 24:7–14; Mark 13:8–13).

PRIVATE CONFRONTATION (Listed under CONFRONTATION, PRIVATE)

PRIVILEGE (Also see HIGHER; and HONOR, PLACE OF)
[PRIVILEGE from many prophets and righteous men desired to see what you see, and did not see *it,* and to hear what you hear, and did not hear *it*]
Setting: By the Sea of Galilee. Jesus responds to His disciples' questions about the Parable of the Sower, which He has just taught from a boat to a crowd.

Jesus answered them, "To you it has been granted to know the mysteries of the kingdom of heaven, but to them it has not been granted. For whoever has, to him *more* shall be given, and he will have an abundance; but whoever does not have, even what he has shall be taken away from him. Therefore, I speak to them in parables; because while seeing they do not see, and while hearing they do not hear, nor do they understand. In their case the prophecy of Isaiah is being fulfilled, which says, 'YOU WILL KEEP ON HEARING, BUT WILL NOT UNDERSTAND; YOU WILL KEEP ON SEEING, BUT WILL NOT PERCEIVE; FOR THE HEART OF THIS PEOPLE HAS BECOME DULL, WITH THEIR EARS THEY SCARCELY HEAR, AND THEY HAVE CLOSED THEIR EYES, OTHERWISE THEYWOULD SEE WITH THEIR EYES, HEAR WITH THEIR EARS, AND UNDERSTAND WITH THEIR HEART AND RETURN, AND I WOULD HEAL THEM.' But blessed are your eyes, because they see; and your ears, because they hear. For truly I say to you that many prophets and righteous men desired to see what you see, and did not see *it,* and to hear what you hear, and did not hear *it*" (Matthew 13:11–17, Jesus quotes from Isaiah 6:9, 10; cf. Matthew 25:29; Mark 4:11–13; Luke 8:10; see Deuteronomy 29:4; John 8:56).

[PRIVILEGE from to sit on My right and on *My* left, this is not Mine to give, but it is for those for whom it has been prepared by My Father]
Setting: On the way to Jerusalem. The mother of James and John, the sons of Zebedee, asks Jesus to make her sons exalted rulers with Him in His coming kingdom.

And He said to her, "What do you wish?" She said to Him, 'Command that in Your kingdom these two sons of mine may sit one on Your right and one on Your left.' But Jesus answered, "You do not know what you are asking. Are you able to drink the cup that I am about to drink?" They said to Him, 'We are able.' He said to them, "My cup you shall drink; but to sit on My right and on *My* left, this is not Mine to give, but it is for those for whom it has been prepared by My Father" (Matthew 20:21–23; cf. Mark 10:35–40; see Matthew 19:28; Acts 12:2).

[PRIVILEGE to sit on My right or on *My* left, this is not Mine to give; but it is for those for whom it has been prepared]
Setting: On the road to Jerusalem. After Jesus prophesies His persecution, death, and resurrection, James and John ask for special honor and privileges in His coming kingdom.

And He said to them, "What do you want Me to do for you?" They said to Him, "Grant that we may sit, one on Your right and one on *Your* left, in Your glory." But Jesus said to them, "You do not know what you are asking. Are you able to drink the cup that I drink, or to be baptized with the baptism with which I am baptized?" They said to Him, "We are able." And Jesus said to them, "The cup that I drink you shall drink; and you shall be baptized with the baptism with which I am baptized. But to sit on My right or on *My* left, this is not Mine to give; but it is for those for whom it has been prepared" (Mark 10:36–40; cf. Matthew 20:20–23; see Matthew 19:28; Acts 12:2).

[PRIVILEGE from many prophets and kings wished to see the things you see, and did not see *them*, and to hear the things which you hear, and did not hear *them*]
Setting: On the way from Galilee to Jerusalem. After responding to a report from the seventy sent out in pairs to every place He Himself will soon visit, the Lord addresses His disciples in private.

Turning to the disciples, He said privately, "Blessed *are* the eyes which see the things you see, for I say to you, that many prophets and kings wished to see the things you see, and did not see *them*, and to hear the things which you hear, and did not hear *them*" (Luke 10:23, 24; cf. Matthew 13:16, 17).

PROBLEMS (See TROUBLE)

PROCLAMATION (Also see EVANGELISM; GOSPEL; and PREACHING)

[PROCLAMATION from proclaim]

Setting: Galilee. After His disciples observe His ministry, Jesus summons and specifically instructs them about their ministry ahead involving true discipleship.

"Therefore do not fear them, for there is nothing concealed that will not be revealed, or hidden that will not be known. What I tell you in the darkness, speak in the light; and what you hear *whispered* in your ear, proclaim upon the housetops. Do not fear those who kill the body but are unable to kill the soul; but rather fear Him who is able to destroy both soul and body in hell" (Matthew 10:26–28; cf. Mark 4:22; Luke 12:3; see Hebrews 10:31).

[PROCLAMATION from PROCLAIM]

Setting: The synagogue in Jesus' hometown of Nazareth in Galilee. At the beginning of His public ministry, Jesus reads on the Sabbath from the book of the prophet Isaiah.

And the book of the prophet Isaiah was handed to Him. And He opened the book and found the place where it was written, "THE SPIRIT OF THE LORD IS UPON ME, BECAUSE HE ANOINTED ME TO PREACH THE GOSPEL TO THE POOR. HE HAS SENT ME TO PROCLAIM RELEASE TO THE CAPTIVES, AND RECOVERY OF SIGHT TO THE BLIND, TO SET FREE THOSE WHO ARE OPPRESSED, TO PROCLAIM THE FAVORABLE YEAR OF THE LORD." And He closed the book, gave it back to the attendant and sat down; and the eyes of all in the synagogue were fixed on Him. And He began to say to them, "Today this Scripture has been fulfilled in your hearing" (Luke 4:17–21, Jesus quotes from Isaiah 61:1, 2).

[PROCLAMATION from proclaim]

Setting: On the way from Galilee to Jerusalem. The Lord responds to several men seeking to follow Him.

And He said to another, "Follow Me." But he said, "Lord, permit me first to go and bury my father," But He said to him, "Allow the dead to bury their own dead; but as for you, go and proclaim everywhere the kingdom of God" (Luke 9:59, 60; cf. Matthew 8:19–22).

[PROCLAMATION from proclaimed]

Setting: On the way from Galilee to Jerusalem. Jesus warns His disciples of future events, as the scribes and Pharisees turn hostile and question Him repeatedly in an attempt to catch Him in something He might say.

Under these circumstances, after so many thousands of people had gathered together that they were stepping on one another, He began saying to His disciples first *of all,* "Beware of the leaven of the Pharisees, which is hypocrisy. But there is nothing covered up that will not be revealed, and hidden that will not be known. Accordingly, whatever you have said in the dark will be heard in the light, and what you have whispered in the inner rooms will be proclaimed upon the housetops. I say to you, My friends, do not be afraid of those who kill the body and after that have no more that they can do. But I will warn you whom to fear: fear the One who, after He has killed, has authority to cast into hell; yes, I tell you, fear Him! Are not five sparrows sold for two cents? *Yet* not one of them is forgotten before God. Indeed, the very hairs of your head are all numbered. Do not fear; you are more valuable than many sparrows" (Luke 12:1–7; cf. Matthew 10:26–31; see Matthew 16:6; Hebrews 10:31).

[PROCLAMATION from *proclaimed*]

Setting: On the way from Galilee to Jerusalem. The Lord responds to the Pharisees' scoffing at His teaching His disciples about stewardship.

And He said to them, "You are those who justify yourselves in the sight of men, but God knows your hearts; for that which is highly esteemed among men is detestable in the sight of God. The Law and the Prophets *were proclaimed* until John; since that time the gospel of the kingdom of God has been preached, and everyone is forcing his way into it. But is it easier for heaven and earth to pass away than for one stroke of a letter of the Law to fail" (Luke 16:15–17; cf. Matthew 5:18; see 1 Samuel 16:7; Matthew

4:23; 11:11–14).

[PROCLAMATION from proclaimed]
Setting: Jerusalem. After rising from the tomb on the third day after being crucified, and appearing to two of His followers on the road to Emmaus, Jesus gives instruction to His disciples (except Thomas) about His mission on earth and the promise of future power from God.

Now He said to them, "These are My words which I spoke to you while I was still with you, that all things which are written about Me in the Law of Moses and the Prophets and the Psalms must be fulfilled." Then He opened their minds to understand the Scriptures, and He said to them, "Thus it is written, that the Christ would suffer and rise again from the dead the third day, and that repentance for forgiveness of sins would be proclaimed in His name to all the nations, beginning from Jerusalem. You are witnesses of these things. And behold, I am sending forth the promise of My Father upon you; but you are to stay in the city until you are clothed with power from on high" (Luke 24:44–49; see Matthew 28:19, 20; Acts 1:8).

PROD (See GOADS)

PRODIGAL SON (See SON, PARABLE OF THE PRODIGAL)

PRODUCE (Also see HARVEST)

[PRODUCE from brings forth]
Setting: By the Sea of Galilee. With the religious leaders rejecting His message, Jesus begins to teach in parables, and gives His disciples the meaning of the Parable of the Sower.

"Hear then the parable of the sower. When anyone hears the word of the kingdom and does not understand it, the evil *one* comes and snatches away what has been sown in his heart. This is the one on whom seed was sown beside the road. The one on whom seed was sown on the rocky places, this is the man who hears the word and immediately receives it with joy; yet he has no *firm* root in himself, but is *only* temporary, and when affliction or persecution arises because of the word, immediately he falls away. And the one on whom seed was sown among the thorns, this is the man who hears the word, and the worry of the world and the deceitfulness of wealth choke the word, and it becomes unfruitful. And the one on whom seed was sown on the good soil, this is the man who hears the word and understands it; who indeed bears fruit and brings forth, some a hundredfold, some sixty, and some thirty" (Matthew 13:18–23; cf. Mark 4:13–20; Luke 8:11–15).

Setting: The temple in Jerusalem. Jesus delivers another parable to the chief priests and elders after they question His authority.

"Listen to another parable. There was a landowner who PLANTED A VINEYARD AND PUT A WALL AROUND IT AND DUG A WINE PRESS IN IT, AND BUILT A TOWER, and rented it out to vine-growers and went on a journey. When the harvest time approached, he sent his slaves to the vine-growers to receive his produce. The vine-growers took his slaves and beat one, and killed another, and stoned a third. Again he sent another group of slaves larger than the first; and they did the same thing to them. But afterward he sent his son to them, saying, 'They will respect my son.' But when the vine-growers saw the son, they said among themselves, 'This is the heir; come, let us kill him and seize his inheritance.' They took him, and threw him out of the vineyard and killed him. Therefore when the owner of the vineyard comes, what will he do to those vine-growers?" (Matthew 21:33–40; Jesus quotes from Isaiah 5:1, 2; cf. Mark 12:1–9; Luke 20:9–15).

Setting: The temple in Jerusalem. Having His authority questioned by the chief priests, scribes, and elders, Jesus begins to teach them in parables.

And He began to speak to them in parables: "A man PLANTED A VINEYARD AND PUT A WALL AROUND IT, AND DUG A VAT UNDER THE WINE PRESS AND BUILT A TOWER, and rented it out to vine-growers and went on a journey. At the *harvest* time he sent a slave to the vine-growers, in order to receive *some* of the produce of the vineyard from the vine-growers. They took him, and beat him and sent him away empty-handed. Again he sent them another slave, and they wounded him in the head, and treated him shamefully. And he sent another, and that one they killed; and *so with* many others, beating some and killing others. He had one more to *send*, a beloved son; he sent him last *of all* to them, saying, 'They will respect my son.' But those vine-growers said to one another, 'This is the heir; come, let us kill him, and the inheritance will be ours!' They took him, and killed him and threw him out of the vineyard. What will the owner of the vineyard do? He will come and destroy the vine-growers, and will give the vineyard to others. Have you not even read this Scripture: 'THE STONE WHICH THE BUILDERS REJECTED, THIS BECAME THE CHIEF CORNER *stone;* THIS CAME ABOUT FROM THE LORD, AND IT IS MARVELOUS IN OUR EYES'?" (Mark 12:1–11, Jesus quotes from Psalm 118:22, 23; Isaiah 5:1, 2; cf. Matthew 21:33–46; Luke 20:9–19).

Setting: The temple in Jerusalem. While ministering a few days before His crucifixion, after the chief priests and the scribes question His authority to teach and preach, Jesus conveys the Parable of the Vine-Growers to the people.

And He began to tell the people this parable: "A man planted a vineyard and rented it out to vine-growers, and went on a journey for a long time. At the *harvest* time he sent a slave to the vine-growers, so that they would give him *some* of the produce of the vineyard; but the vine-growers beat him and sent him away empty-handed. And he proceeded to send another slave; and they beat him also and treated him shamefully and sent him away empty-handed. And he proceeded to send a third; and this one also they wounded and cast out. The owner of the vineyard said, 'What shall I do? I will send my beloved son; perhaps they will respect him.' But when the vine-growers saw him, they reasoned with one another, saying, 'This is the heir; let us kill him so that the inheritance will be ours.' So they threw him out of the vineyard and killed him. What, then, will the owner of the vineyard do to them? He will come and destroy these vine-growers and will give the vineyard to others." When they heard it, they said, "May it never be!" But Jesus looked at them and said, "What then is this that is written: 'THE STONE WHICH THE BUILDERS REJECTED, THIS BECAME THE CHIEF CORNER *stone*'? Everyone who falls on that stone will be broken to pieces; but on whomever it falls, it will scatter him like dust" (Luke 20:9–18, Jesus quotes from Psalm 118:22; cf. Matthew 21:33–44; Mark 12:1–11; see Ephesians 2:20).

PROFANITY (See CURSE)

PROFIT

Setting: Near Caesarea Philippi. After rebuking Peter for trying to forbid Him to accomplish His earthly mission of dying and being resurrected, Jesus teaches His disciples about the costs of following Him.

Then Jesus said to His disciples, "If anyone wishes to come after Me, he must deny himself, and take up his cross and follow Me. For whoever wishes to save his life will lose it; but whoever loses his life for My sake will find it. For what will it profit a man if he gains the whole world and forfeits his soul? Or what will a man give in exchange for his soul? For the Son of Man is going to come in the glory of His Father with His angels, and WILL THEN REPAY EVERY MAN ACCORDING TO HIS DEEDS. Truly, I say to you, there are some of you who are standing here who will not taste death until they see the Son of Man coming in His kingdom" (Matthew 16:24–28, Jesus quotes from Psalm 62:12; cf. Mark 8:34–37; Luke 9:23–27; see Matthew 10:38, 39).

Setting: Caesarea Philippi. After rebuking Peter for desiring to thwart His mission to the cross, Jesus summons a crowd, along with His disciples, and informs them of the high costs of following Him.

And He summoned the crowd with His disciples, and said to them, "If anyone wishes to come after Me, he must deny himself, and take up his cross and follow Me. For whoever wishes to save his life will lose it, but whoever loses his life for My sake and the gospel's will save it. For what does it profit a man to gain the whole world, and forfeit his soul? For what will a man give in exchange for his soul? For whoever is ashamed of Me and My words in this adulterous and sinful generation, the Son of Man will also be ashamed of him when He comes in the glory of His Father with the holy angels" (Mark 8:34–38; cf. Matthew 16:24–28; Luke 9:23–27; see Matthew 10:33, 38, 39).

[PROFIT from profited]

Setting: Galilee. Following Peter's pronouncement that Jesus is the Christ of God, the Lord conveys the demands of discipleship and the hope regarding the kingdom of God.

And He was saying to *them* all, "If anyone wishes to come after Me, he must deny himself, and take up his cross daily and follow Me. For whoever wishes to save his life will lose it, but whoever loses his life for My sake, he is the one who will save it. For what is a man profited if he gains the whole world, and loses or forfeits himself? For whoever is ashamed of Me and My words, the Son of Man will be ashamed of him when He comes in His glory, and *the glory* of the Father and of the holy angels. But I say to you truthfully, there are some of those standing here who will not taste death until they see the kingdom of God" (Luke 9:23–27; cf. Matthew 16:24–26, 28; Mark 8:34–37; see Matthew 10:33, 38, 39).

PROMINENCE (See HIGHER; HONOR, PLACE OF; and PRIVILEGE)

PROMISCUITY (See IMMORALITY; and SEXUAL SIN)

PROMISE (Also see PROMISES)

Setting: Jerusalem. After rising from the tomb on the third day after being crucified, and appearing to two of His followers on the road to Emmaus, Jesus gives instruction to His disciples (except Thomas) about His mission on earth and the promise of future power from God.

Now He said to them, "These are My words which I spoke to you while I was still with you, that all things which are written about Me in the Law of Moses and the Prophets and the Psalms must be fulfilled." Then He opened their minds to understand the Scriptures, and He said to them, "Thus it is written, that the Christ would suffer and rise again from the dead the third day, and that repentance for forgiveness of sins would be proclaimed in His name to all the nations, beginning from Jerusalem. You are witnesses of these things. And behold, I am sending forth the promise of My Father upon you; but you are to stay in the city until you are clothed with power from on high" (Luke 24:44–49; see Matthew 28:19, 20; Acts 1:8).

PROMISES (See OATH; PROMISE; SWEARING; and VOWS)

PROPER TIME (Listed as TIME, PROPER)

PROPERTY (Also see LAND; and POSSESSIONS)

Setting: Galilee. After Jesus heals a blind, mute, demon-possessed man, the Pharisees accuse the Lord in front of crowds of being a worker of Beelzebul (Satan).

And knowing their thoughts Jesus said to them, "Any kingdom divided against itself is laid waste; and any city or house divided against itself will not stand. If Satan casts out Satan, he is divided against himself; how then will his kingdom stand? If I by Beelzebul cast out demons, by whom do your sons cast *them* out? For this reason they will be your judges. But if I cast out demons by the Spirit of God, then the kingdom of God has come upon you. Or how can anyone enter the strong man's house and carry off his property, unless he first binds the strong *man?* And then he will plunder his house" (Matthew 12:25–29; cf. Matthew 9:34; Mark 3:23–27; Luke 11:17–20).

Setting: Galilee. After Jesus selects His twelve disciples, scribes from Jerusalem attribute His miraculous powers to Satan.

And He called them to Himself and began speaking to them in parables, "How can Satan cast out Satan? If a kingdom is divided against itself, that kingdom cannot stand. If a house is divided against itself, that house will not be able to stand. If Satan has risen up against himself and is divided, he cannot stand, but he is finished! But no one can enter the strong man's house and plunder his property unless he first binds the strong man, and then he will plunder his house. Truly I say to you, all sins shall be forgiven the sons of men, and whatever blasphemies they utter; but whoever blasphemes against the Holy Spirit never has forgiveness, but is guilty of an eternal sin"—because they were saying, "He has an unclean spirit" (Mark 3:23–30; cf. Matthew 12:25–32; Luke 12:10).

PROPERTY TAX (Listed as TAX, PROPERTY; also see TAXES)

PROPHECY (Also see CHURCH, PROPHECY OF THE; FUTURE, PREDICTING THE; JESUS' RETURN; PETER'S DENIAL; PROPHECY, FULFILLMENT OF; PROPHECY OF JESUS' DEATH; PROPHECY OF JESUS' RESURRECTION; PROPHECY OF PETER'S DENIAL; PROPHECY OF THE DESTRUCTION OF JERUSALEM; PROPHESY; TEMPLE, PROPHECY OF THE DESTRUCTION OF THE; and WRITINGS)

Setting: By the Sea of Galilee. Jesus responds to His disciples' questions about the Parable of the Sower, which He has just taught from a boat to a crowd.

Jesus answered them, "To you it has been granted to know the mysteries of the kingdom of heaven, but to them it has not been granted. For whoever has, to him *more* shall be given, and he will have an abundance; but whoever does not have, even what he has shall be taken away from him. Therefore, I speak to them in parables; because while seeing they do not see, and while hearing they do not hear, nor do they understand. In their case the prophecy of Isaiah is being fulfilled, which says, 'YOU WILL KEEP ON HEARING, BUT WILL NOT UNDERSTAND; YOU WILL KEEP ON SEEING, BUT WILL NOT PERCEIVE; FOR THE HEART OF THIS PEOPLE HAS BECOME DULL, WITH THEIR EARS THEY SCARCELY HEAR, AND THEY HAVE CLOSED THEIR EYES, OTHERWISE THEYWOULD SEE WITH THEIR EYES, HEAR WITH THEIR EARS, AND UNDERSTAND WITH THEIR HEART AND RETURN, AND I WOULD HEAL THEM.' But blessed are your eyes, because they see; and your ears, because they hear. For truly I say to you that many prophets and righteous men desired to see what you see, and did not see *it,* and to hear what you hear, and did not hear *it*" (Matthew 13:11–17, Jesus quotes from Isaiah 6:9, 10; cf. Matthew 25:29; Mark 4:11–13; Luke 8:10; see Deuteronomy 29:4; John 8:56).

[PROPHECY from Behold, I have told you in advance.]

Setting: The Mount of Olives, just east of Jerusalem. During His Olivet Discourse, Jesus answers His disciples' questions as to when the temple will be destroyed and Jerusalem overrun, along with the signs of His coming and the end of the age.

"Therefore when you see the ABOMINATION OF DESOLATION which was spoken of through Daniel the prophet, standing in the holy place (let the reader understand), then those who are in Judea must flee to the mountains. Whoever is on the housetop must not go down to get the things that are in his house. Whoever is in the field must not turn back to get his cloak. But woe to those who are pregnant and to those who are nursing babies in those days! But pray that your flight will not be in the winter, or on a Sabbath. For then there will be a great tribulation, such as has not occurred since the beginning of the world until now, nor ever will. Unless those days had been cut short, no life would have been saved; but for the sake of the elect those days will be cut short. Then if anyone says to you, 'Behold, here is the Christ,' or "There *He is,*' do not believe *him.* For false Christs and false prophets will arise and will show great signs and wonders, so as to mislead, if possible, even the elect. Behold, I have told you in advance. So if they say to you, 'Behold, He is in the wilderness,' do not go out, *or,* 'Behold, He is in the inner rooms,' do not believe *them.* For just as the lightning comes from the east and flashes even to the west, so will the coming of the Son of Man be. Wherever the corpse is, there the vultures will gather" (Matthew 24:15–28, Jesus quotes from Daniel 9:27; cf. Daniel 12:1; Mark 13:14–23; Luke 17:22–31; 21:20–24; 23:29; see John 4:48).

[PROPHECY from behold, I have told you everything in advance]

Setting: On the Mount of Olives, east of the temple in Jerusalem. After predicting the temple's destruction, Jesus responds during His Olivet Discourse to questions from Peter, James, John, and Andrew about other future events.

"But when you see the ABOMINATION OF DESOLATION standing where it should not be (let the reader understand), then those who are in Judea must flee to the mountains. The one who is on the housetop must not go down, or go in to get anything out of his house; and the one who is in the field must not turn back to get his coat. But woe to those who are pregnant and to those who are nursing babies in those days! But pray that it may not happen in winter. For those days will be a *time of* tribulation such as has not occurred since the beginning of the creation which God created until now, and never will. Unless the Lord had shortened *those* days, no life would have been saved; but for the sake of the elect, whom He chose, He shortened the days. And then if anyone says to you, 'Behold, here is the Christ'; or, 'Behold, *He is* there'; do not believe *him*; for false Christs and false prophets will arise, and will show signs and wonders, in order to lead astray, if possible, the elect. But take heed; behold, I have told you everything in advance" (Mark 13:14–23; cf. Matthew 24:15–28; Luke 21:20–24; see Daniel 9:27; 12:1; Luke 17:31).

[PROPHECY from Now I have told you before it happens]
Setting: Jerusalem. Before the Passover, after He conveys the upcoming ministry of the Holy Spirit in His disciples' lives, Jesus again relates peace, hope, and comfort to them regarding His return to the Father.

"Peace I leave with you; My peace I give to you; not as the world gives do I give to you. Do not let your heart be troubled, nor let it be fearful. You heard that I said to you, 'I go away, and I will come to you,' If you loved Me, you would have rejoiced because I go to the Father, for the Father is greater than I. Now I have told you before it happens, so that when it happens, you may believe. I will not speak much more with you, for the ruler of the world is coming, and he has nothing in Me; but so that the world may know that I love the Father, I do exactly as the Father commanded Me. Get up, let us go from here" (John 14:27–31; see John 10:18, 29; 12:31; 13:19; 16:33).

[PROPHECY from these things I have spoken to you, so that when their hour comes, you may remember that I told you of them]
Setting: Jerusalem. Before the Passover, after explaining He is the vine and His disciples are the branches, Jesus warns the disciples of the persecution they will face after His departure to heaven.

"These things I have spoken to you so that you may be kept from stumbling. They will make you outcasts from the synagogue, but an hour is coming for everyone who kills you to think that he is offering service to God. These things they will do because they have not known the Father or Me. But these things I have spoken to you, so that when their hour comes, you may remember that I told you of them. These things I did not say to you at the beginning, because I was with you" (John 16:1–4; see John 8:19, 55; 9:22; 13:19; 15:18–27).

Setting: On the island of Patmos (in the Aegean Sea about fifty miles southwest of Ephesus in modern Turkey). In the final chapter of the Lord Jesus Christ's revelation via the disciple John, approximately fifty years after the Resurrection, the Lord reveals His upcoming return and the blessing to those who heed the words of the prophecy of this book.

"And behold, I am coming quickly. Blessed is he who heeds the words of the prophecy of this book" (Revelation 22:7; see Revelation 1:3).

PROPHECY, FULFILLMENT OF (Also see SCRIPTURE, FULFILLMENT OF; and SCRIPTURES, FULFILLMENT OF) [FULFILLMENT OF PROPHECY from BEHOLD, I SEND MY MESSENGER AHEAD OF YOU, WHO WILL PREPARE YOUR WAY BEFORE YOU]

Setting: Galilee. While speaking to the crowds, Jesus pays tribute to the ministry of John the Baptist, but emphasizes that the one who is least in the kingdom of heaven is greater than John.

As these men were going *away,* Jesus began to speak to the crowds about John, "What did you go out into the wilderness to see? A reed shaken by the wind? But what did you go out to see? A man dressed in soft *clothing?* Those who wear soft *clothing* are in kings' palaces! But what did you go out to see? A prophet? Yes, I tell you, and the one who is more than a prophet. This is the one about whom it is written, 'BEHOLD, I SEND MY MESSENGER AHEAD OF YOU, WHO WILL PREPARE YOUR WAY BEFORE YOU.' Truly, I say to you, among those born of women there has not arisen *anyone* greater than John the Baptist! Yet the one who is least in the kingdom of heaven is greater than he. From the days of John the Baptist until now the kingdom of heaven suffers violence, and violent men take it by force. For all the prophets and the Law prophesied until John. And, if you are willing to accept *it,* John himself is Elijah who was to come. He who has ears to hear, let him hear" (Matthew 11:7–15, Jesus quotes from Malachi 3:1; cf. Malachi 4:5; Luke 7:24–28; Luke 16:16; see Matthew 14:5).

[FULFILLMENT OF PROPHECY from all the things which are written through the prophets about the Son of Man will be accomplished]
Setting: On the way from Galilee to Jerusalem. After responding to Peter's statement about the disciples' personal sacrifice in following Him, Jesus tells them of the sacrifice He will make in Jerusalem.

Then He took the twelve aside and said to them, "Behold, we are going up to Jerusalem, and all things which are written through the prophets about the Son of Man will be accomplished. For He will be handed over to the Gentiles, and will be mocked and mistreated and spit upon, and after they have scourged Him, they will kill Him; and the third day He will rise again" (Luke 18:31–33; cf. Matthew 20:17–19; Mark 10:32–34).

[FUFILLMENT OF PROPHECY from all things which are written will be fulfilled]

Setting: On the Mount of Olives, east of the temple in Jerusalem. After ministering in the temple a few days before His crucifixion, and giving the disciples more details regarding future events, Jesus elaborates more during His Olivet Discourse about things to come.

"But when you see Jerusalem surrounded by armies, then recognize that her desolation is near. Then those who are in Judea must flee to the mountains, and those who are in the midst of the city must leave, and those who are in the country must not enter the city; because these are days of vengeance, so that all things which are written will be fulfilled. Woe to those who are pregnant and to those who are nursing babies in those days; for there will be a great distress upon the land and wrath to this people; and they will fall by the edge of the sword, and will be led captive into all the nations; and Jerusalem will be trampled under foot by the Gentiles until the times of the Gentiles are fulfilled" (Luke 21:20–24; see Matthew 24:15–18; Mark 13:14–16; Luke 19:43).

[FUFILLMENT OF PROPHECY from this which is written must be fulfilled in Me and fulfillment]

Setting: Jerusalem. During the Feast of Unleavened Bread (Passover) just before His crucifixion, Jesus celebrates the Passover meal with His disciples, institutes the Lord's Supper, and prophesies Peter's denial of Him. The Lord also instructs the disciples to prepare to persevere without Him.

And He said to them, "When I sent you out without money belt and bag and sandals, you did not lack anything, did you?" They said, "*No*, nothing." And He said to them, "But now, whoever has a money belt is to take it along, likewise also a bag, and whoever has no sword is to sell his coat and buy one. For I tell you that this which is written must be fulfilled in Me, 'AND HE WAS NUMBERED WITH TRANSGRESSORS'; for that which refers to Me has *its* fulfillment." They said, "Lord, look, here are two swords." And He said to them, "It is enough" (Luke 22:35–38, Jesus quotes from Isaiah 53:12; see Matthew 10:5–15; Mark 6:7–11; Luke 9:1–5; 10:1–12; 22:49; John 17:4).

[FULFILLMENT OF PROPHECY from all things which are written about Me in the Law of Moses and the Prophets and the Psalms must be fulfilled]

Setting: Jerusalem. After rising from the tomb on the third day after being crucified, and appearing to two of His followers on the road to Emmaus, Jesus gives instruction to His disciples (except Thomas) about His mission on earth and the promise of future power from God.

Now He said to them, "These are My words which I spoke to you while I was still with you, that all things which are written about Me in the Law of Moses and the Prophets and the Psalms must be fulfilled." Then He opened their minds to understand the Scriptures, and He said to them, "Thus it is written, that the Christ would suffer and rise again from the dead the third day, and that repentance for forgiveness of sins would be proclaimed in His name to all the nations, beginning from Jerusalem. You are witnesses of these things. And behold, I am sending forth the promise of My Father upon you; but you are to stay in the city until you are clothed with power from on high" (Luke 24:44–49; see Matthew 28:19, 20; Acts 1:8).

[FULFILLMENT OF PROPHECY from THEY HATED ME WITHOUT A CAUSE]

Setting: Jerusalem. Before the Passover, with His upcoming departure in mind, after explaining He is the vine and His disciples are the branches, Jesus prepares them for hatred by the world.

"He who hates Me hates My Father also. If I had not done among them the works which no one else did, they would not have sin; but now they have both seen and hated Me and My Father as well. But *they have done this* to fulfill the word that is written in their Law, 'THEY HATED ME WITHOUT A CAUSE'" (John 15:23–25, Jesus quotes from Psalm 35:19; see John 9:41).

[FULFILLMENT OF PROPHECY from Of those whom You have given Me I lost not one]

Setting: Jerusalem. After Jesus prays His high-priestly prayer on behalf of His disciples, they all go over the ravine of the Kidron to a garden where Judas waits to seize the Lord with a Roman cohort and officers from the chief priests and the Pharisees.

So Jesus, knowing all the things that were coming upon Him, went forth and said to them, "Whom do you seek?" They answered Him, "Jesus the Nazarene." He said to them, "I am *He*." And Judas also, who was betraying Him, was standing with them. So when He said to them, "I am *He*," they drew back and fell to the ground. Therefore He again asked them, "Whom do you seek?" And they said, "Jesus the Nazarene." Jesus answered, "I told you that I am *He*; so if you seek Me, let these go their way," to fulfill the word which He spoke, "Of those whom You have given Me I lost not one" (John 18:4–9; see John 6:64; 17:12).

PROPHECY OF JESUS' BETRAYAL (Listed under BETRAYAL, PROPHECY OF JESUS')

PROPHECY OF JESUS' DEATH

[PROPHECY OF JESUS' DEATH from the Son of Man be three days and three nights in the heart of the earth]

Setting: Galilee. As Jesus ministers, after warning the Pharisees about the unpardonable sin and their future judgment, some of the Pharisees and scribes ask Him to perform a miraculous sign for them in front of the crowds.

But He answered and said to them, "An evil and adulterous generation craves for a sign; and *yet* no sign will be given to it but the sign of Jonah the prophet; for just as JONAH WAS THREE DAYS AND THREE NIGHTS IN THE BELLY OF THE SEA MONSTER, so will the Son of Man be three days and three nights in the heart of the earth. The men of Nineveh will stand up with this generation at the judgment, and will condemn it because they repented at the preaching of Jonah; and behold, something greater than Jonah is here. *The* Queen of *the* South will rise up with this generation at the judgment and will condemn it, because she came from the ends of the earth to hear the wisdom of Solomon; and behold, something greater than Solomon is here" (Matthew 12:39–42; Jesus quotes from Jonah 1:17; cf. 1 Kings 10:1; Jonah 3:5; Matthew 16:1, 4; 12:38; Luke 11:29).

[PROPHECY OF JESUS' DEATH from the Son of Man is going to suffer at their hands]

Setting: Galilee, on the way down a mountain. Following the Transfiguration, Peter, James, and John ask Him why Elijah must come before the Messiah.

And He answered and said, "Elijah is coming and will restore all things; but I say to you that Elijah already came, and they did not recognize him, but did to him whatever they wished. So also the Son of Man is going to suffer at their hands" (Matthew 17:11, 12; cf. Mark 9:11–13; see Matthew 17:13).

[PROPHECY OF JESUS' DEATH from The Son of Man is going to be delivered into the hands of men; and they will kill him]

Setting: Galilee. Following the Transfiguration, Jesus repeats to His disciples that He must suffer, die, and be raised from the dead.

And while they were gathering together in Galilee, Jesus said to them, "The Son of Man is going to be delivered into the hands of men; and they will kill Him, and He will be raised on the third day." And they were deeply grieved. (Matthew 17:22, 23; cf. Matthew 16:21; Mark 9:30–32; Luke 9:44, 45).

[PROPHECY OF JESUS' DEATH from they will condemn Him to death and will hand Him over to the Gentiles]

Setting: Judea beyond the Jordan (Perea). Before going to Jerusalem, Jesus again tells His disciples of His impending death and resurrection.

As Jesus was about to go up to Jerusalem, He took the twelve *disciples* aside by themselves, and on the way He said to them, "Behold, we are going up to Jerusalem; and the Son of Man will be delivered to the chief priests and scribes, and they will condemn Him to death, and will hand Him over to the Gentiles to mock and scourge and crucify *Him,* and on the third day, He will be raised up" (Matthew 20:17–19; cf. Matthew 16:21; Mark 10:32–34; Luke 18:31–33).

[PROPHECY OF JESUS' DEATH from the Son of Man is *to be* handed over for crucifixion]

Setting: The Mount of Olives, just east of Jerusalem. After answering His disciples' questions as to when the temple will be destroyed and Jerusalem overrun, along with the signs of His coming and the end of the age, Jesus prophesies His crucifixion to them.

When Jesus had finished all these words, He said to His disciples, "You know that after two days the Passover is coming, and the Son of Man is to be handed over for crucifixion" (Matthew 26:1, 2; see Mark 14:1, 2; Luke 22:1, 2).

[PROPHECY OF JESUS' DEATH from she did it to prepare Me for burial]
Setting: The home of Simon the leper in Bethany. Jesus rebukes His disciples for criticizing a woman for pouring a costly vial of perfume on Jesus' head in preparation for His burial.

But Jesus, aware of this, said to them, "Why do you bother the woman? For she has done a good deed to Me. For you always have the poor with you; but you do not always have Me. For when she poured this perfume on My body, she did it to prepare Me for burial. Truly I say to you, wherever this gospel is preached in the whole world, what this woman has done will also be spoken of in memory of her" (Matthew 26:10–13; cf. Mark 14:3–9; Luke 7:37–39; John 12:2–8; see Deuteronomy 15:11; Matthew 26:6–9).

[PROPHECY OF JESUS' DEATH from The Son of Man *is to* go, just as it is written of Him]
Setting: An upper room in Jerusalem. While celebrating the Passover meal, Jesus surprises His disciples with the revelation that one of them will soon betray Him to His enemies.

As they were eating, He said, "Truly I say to you that one of you will betray Me." Being deeply grieved, they each one began to say to Him, 'Surely not I, Lord?' And He answered, "He who dipped his hand with Me in the bowl is the one who will betray Me. The Son of Man *is to* go, just as it is written of Him; but woe to that man by whom the Son of Man is betrayed! It would have been good for that man if he had not been born." And Judas, who was betraying Him, said, 'Surely it is not I, Rabbi?' Jesus said to him, "You have said *it* yourself" (Matthew 26:21–25; cf. Mark 14:18–21; Luke 22:21, 23; John 13:21–30; see Psalm 41:9; Matthew 26:20).

[PROPHECY OF JESUS' DEATH from I WILL STRIKE DOWN THE SHEPHERD]
Setting: Jerusalem. After celebrating the Passover meal, as Jesus and His disciples go out to the Mount of Olives prior to His betrayal by Judas, Jesus states that all His disciples will deny Him that very day.

Then Jesus said to them, "You will all fall away because of Me this night, for it is written, 'I WILL STRIKE DOWN THE SHEPHERD, AND THE SHEEP OF THE FLOCK SHALL BE SCATTERED.' But after I have been raised, I will go ahead of you to Galilee." But Peter said to Him, '*Even* though all may fall away because of You, I will never fall away.' Jesus said to him, "Truly I say to you that this *very* night, before a rooster crows, you will deny Me three times" (Matthew 26:31–34, Jesus quotes from Zechariah 13:7; cf. Mark 14:26–31; see Matthew 26:30, 35, 75; 28:7, 10, 16; John 13:37).

[PROPHECY OF JESUS' DEATH from the Son of Man that He will suffer many things and be treated with contempt]
Setting: A high mountain (some think Mount Hermon) in Galilee. After informing a crowd and His disciples of the hope involving the coming kingdom of God, Jesus takes Peter, James, and John and reveals His glory through the Transfiguration, and answers their question about Elijah.

And He said to them, "Elijah does first come and restore all things. And *yet* how is it written of the Son of Man that He will suffer many things and be treated with contempt? But I say to you that Elijah has indeed come, and they did to him whatever they wished, just as it is written of him" (Mark 9:12, 13; cf. Matthew 17:1–13; Luke 9:28–36; see Malachi 4:5, 6; Matthew 16:21; Mark 9:2–11).

[PROPHECY OF JESUS' DEATH from they will kill Him; and when He has been killed]
Setting: Galilee. After casting out an unclean spirit from a young boy, Jesus teaches His disciples in secret about His

coming death and resurrection.

From there they went out and *began* to go through Galilee, and He did not want anyone to know *about it.* For He was teaching His disciples and telling them, "The Son of Man is to be delivered into the hands of men, and they will kill Him; and when He has been killed, He will rise three days later." But they did not understand *this* statement, and they were afraid to ask Him (Mark 9:30–32; cf. Matthew 17:22, 23; Luke 9:43–45; see Matthew 16:21).

[PROPHECY OF JESUS' DEATH from they will condemn Him to death and will hand Him over to the Gentiles]
Setting: On the road to Jerusalem. Jesus prophesies His persecution, death, and resurrection after encouraging His disciples with a revelation of their future reward.

They were on the road going up to Jerusalem, and Jesus was walking on ahead of them; and they were amazed, and those who followed were fearful. And again He took the twelve aside and began to tell them what was going to happen to Him, *saying,* "Behold, we are going up to Jerusalem, and the Son of Man will be delivered to the chief priests and the scribes; and they will condemn Him to death and will hand Him over to the Gentiles. They will mock Him and spit on Him, and scourge Him and kill *Him,* and three days later He will rise again" (Mark 10:32–34; cf. Matthew 20:17–19; Luke 18:31–34; see Matthew 16:21; Mark 8:31).

[PROPHECY OF JESUS' DEATH from she has anointed My body beforehand for the burial]
Setting: The home of Simon the leper in Bethany. Two days before the Feast of Unleavened Bread (Passover), Jesus commends a woman who anoints His head with costly perfume, which some think should have been sold and the proceeds given to the poor.

But Jesus said, "Let her alone; why do you bother her? She has done a good deed to Me. For you always have the poor with you, and whenever you wish you can do good to them; but you do not always have Me. She has done what she could; she has anointed My body beforehand for the burial. Truly I say to you, wherever the gospel is preached in the whole world, what this woman has done will also be spoken of in memory of her" (Mark 14:6–9; cf. Matthew 26:6–13; John 12:2–8; see Deuteronomy 15:11).

[PROPHECY OF JESUS' DEATH from For the Son of Man *is to* go just as it is written of Him]
Setting: A borrowed upper room in Jerusalem. While Jesus and His twelve disciples are eating the Passover meal, the Lord prophesies that His betrayal by one of His disciples.

As they were reclining *at the table* and eating, Jesus said, "Truly I say to you that one of you will betray Me—one who is eating with Me." They began to be grieved and to say to Him one by one, "Surely not I?" And He said to them, "*It is* one of the twelve, one who dips with Me in the bowl. For the Son of Man *is to* go just as it is written of Him; but woe to that man by whom the Son of Man is betrayed! *It would have been* good for that man if he had not been born" (Mark 14:18–21; cf. Matthew 26:21–24; Luke 22:21–23; John 13:21, 22).

[PROPHECY OF JESUS' DEATH from I WILL STRIKE DOWN THE SHEPHERD, AND THE SHEEP SHALL BE SCATTERED]
Setting: A borrowed upper room in Jerusalem. After Jesus and His twelve disciples celebrate the Passover and the Lord's Supper, they go to the Mount of Olives.

And Jesus said to them, "You will all fall away, because it is written, 'I WILL STRIKE DOWN THE SHEPHERD, AND THE SHEEP SHALL BE SCATTERED.' But after I have been raised, I will go ahead of you to Galilee." But Peter said to Him, "*Even* though all may fall away, yet I will not." And Jesus said to him, "Truly I say to you, that this very night, before a rooster crows twice, you yourself will deny Me three times" (Mark 14:27–30, Jesus quotes from Zechariah 13:7; cf. Matthew 26:30–34; see Mark 14:72).

[PROPHECY OF JESUS' DEATH from The Son of Man must suffer many things and be rejected by the elders and chief priests and scribes, and be killed]
Setting: Galilee. Following Peter's pronouncement that Jesus is the Christ of God, the Lord warns His disciples

not to reveal His identity to anyone.

But He warned them and instructed *them* not to tell this to anyone, saying, "The Son of Man must suffer many things and be rejected by the elders and chief priests and scribes, and be killed and be raised up on the third day" (Luke 9:21, 22; cf. Matthew 16:21; Mark 8:31).

[PROPHECY OF JESUS' DEATH from the Son of Man is going to be delivered into the hands of men]
Setting: Galilee. After He heals the demon-possessed son of a man in the crowd, the Lord prophesies His own death.

"Let these words sink into your ears; for the Son of Man is going to be delivered into the hands of men" (Luke 9:44; cf. Matthew 17:22, 23; Mark 9:31, 32; see Luke 9:22, 37–43, 45).

[PROPHECY OF JESUS' DEATH from He must suffer many things]
Setting: On the way from Galilee to Jerusalem. Following the Pharisees' interrogation of Him about the coming of the kingdom of God, Jesus tells His disciples of His second coming.

And He said to the disciples, "The days will come when you will long to see one of the days of the Son of Man, and you will not see it. They will say to you, 'Look there! Look here!' Do not go away, and do not run after *them*. For just like the lightning, when it flashes out of one part of the sky, shines to the other part of the sky, so will the Son of Man be in His day. But first He must suffer many things and be rejected by this generation. And just as it happened in the days of Noah, so it will be also in the days of the Son of Man: they were eating, they were drinking, they were marrying, they were being given in marriage, until the day that Noah entered the ark, and the flood came and destroyed them all. It was the same as happened in the days of Lot: they were eating, they were drinking, they were buying, they were selling, they were planting, they were building; but on the day that Lot went out from Sodom it rained fire and brimstone from heaven and destroyed them all. It will be just the same on the day that the Son of Man is revealed. On that day, the one who is on the housetop and whose goods are in the house must not go down to take them out; and likewise the one who is in the field must not turn back. Remember Lot's wife. Whoever seeks to keep his life will lose it, and whoever loses *his life* will preserve it. I tell you, on that night there will be two in one bed; one will be taken and the other will be left. There will be two women grinding at the same place; one will be taken and the other will be left. [Two men will be in the field; one will be taken and the other will be left."] And answering they said to Him, "Where, Lord?" And He said to them, "Where the body *is*, there also the vultures will be gathered" (Luke 17:22–37; see Genesis 19; Matthew 10:39; 16:21, 27; 24:17–28, 37–41).

[PROPHECY OF JESUS' DEATH from they will kill Him]
Setting: On the way from Galilee to Jerusalem. After responding to Peter's statement about His disciples' personal sacrifice in following Him, Jesus tells them of the upcoming sacrifice He will make in Jerusalem.

Then He took the twelve aside and said to them, "Behold, we are going up to Jerusalem, and all things which are written through the prophets about the Son of Man will be accomplished. For He will be handed over to the Gentiles, and will be mocked and mistreated and spit upon, and after they have scourged Him, they will kill Him; and the third day He will rise again" (Luke 18:31–33; cf. Matthew 20:17–19; Mark 10:32–34; see Luke 18:34).

[PROPHECY OF JESUS' DEATH from this which is written must be fulfilled in Me, 'AND HE WAS NUMBERED WITH TRANSGRESSORS']
Setting: Jerusalem. During the Feast of Unleavened Bread (Passover) just before His crucifixion, while celebrating the Passover meal, instituting the Lord's Supper, and prophesying Peter's upcoming denial of Him, Jesus instructs His disciples to prepare to persevere without Him.

And He said to them, "When I sent you out without money belt and bag and sandals, you did not lack anything, did you?" They said, "*No*, nothing." And He said to them, "But now, whoever has a money belt is to take it along, likewise also a bag, and whoever has no sword is to sell his coat and buy one. For I tell you that this which is written must be fulfilled in Me, 'AND HE WAS NUMBERED WITH TRANSGRESSORS'; for that which refers to Me has *its* fulfillment." They said, "Lord, look, here are two swords." And He said to them, "It is enough" (Luke 22:35–38, Jesus quotes from Isaiah 53:12; see Matthew 10:5–15; Mark 6:7–11; Luke 9:1–5; 10:1–12; 22:49; John 17:4).

[PROPHECY OF JESUS' DEATH from Destroy this temple]
Setting: The temple in Jerusalem. After Jesus cleanses the temple during the Passover of the Jews, the Jewish religious leaders question His authority to do these things.

Jesus answered them, "Destroy this temple, and in three days I will raise it up" (John 2:19; cf. Matthew 26:61; see John 2:13–17).

[PROPHECY OF JESUS' DEATH from the Son of Man be lifted up]
Setting: Jerusalem. Before the Passover, after the Lord cleanses the temple, a man of the Pharisees, Nicodemus, asks Him by night the meaning of "born of the Spirit."

Jesus answered and said to him, "Are you the teacher of Israel and do not understand these things? Truly, truly, I say to you, we speak of what we know and testify of what we have seen, and you do not accept our testimony. If I told you earthly things and you do not believe, how will you believe if I tell you heavenly things? No one has ascended into heaven, but He who descended from heaven: the Son of Man. As Moses lifted up the serpent in the wilderness, even so must the Son of Man be lifted up; so that whoever believes will in Him have eternal life" (John 3:10–15; see Numbers 21:9; Proverbs 30:4; John 12:34; 20:30, 31).

[PROPHECY OF JESUS' DEATH from When you lift up the Son of Man]
Setting: The temple treasury in Jerusalem. Following the Feast of Booths and the scribes' and Pharisees' failed attempt to stone a woman for adultery, Jesus returns the next day to teach. They question His testimony about Himself.

So Jesus said, "When you lift up the Son of Man, then you will know that I am *He,* and I do nothing on my own initiative, but I speak these things as the Father taught Me. And He who sent Me is with Me; He has not left Me alone, for I always do the things that are pleasing to Him" (John 8:28, 29; see John 3:14; 8:1–27, 30).

[PROPHECY OF JESUS' DEATH from if I am lifted up from the earth]
Setting: Jerusalem. Just days before the Passover, with the chief priests and Pharisees plotting to seize Him and crowds welcoming Him to Jerusalem with palm branches and praise, Jesus expresses anxiety about His upcoming death by crucifixion.

"Now My soul has become troubled; and what shall I say, 'Father, save Me from this hour'? But for this purpose I came to this hour. Father glorify Your name." Then a voice came out of heaven: "I have glorified it, and will glorify it again." So the crowd *of people* who stood by and heard it were saying that it had thundered; others were saying, "An angel has spoken to Him." Jesus answered and said, "This voice has not come for My sake, but for your sakes. Now judgment is upon this world; now the ruler of this world will be cast out. And I, if I am lifted up from the earth, will draw all men to Myself" (John 12:27–32; see Matthew 3:17; 26:38; John 3:14; 6:44; 11:42; 12:9–22; 14:30).

[PROPHECY OF JESUS' DEATH from A little while, and you will no longer see Me]
Setting: Jerusalem. Before the Passover, after warning His disciples of the persecution they will face after His departure to heaven, empathizing with their sadness over His prophecies, Jesus gives them hope for the future.

"A little while, and you will no longer see Me; and again a little while, and you will see Me." *Some* of His disciples then said to one another, "What is this thing He is telling us, 'A little while, and you will not see Me; and again a little while, and you will see Me'; and, 'because I go to the Father'?" So they were saying, "What is this that He says, 'A little while'? We do not know what He is talking about." Jesus knew that they wished to question Him, and He said to them, "Are you deliberating together about this, that I said, 'A little while, and you will not see Me, and again a little while, and you will see Me'? Truly, truly, I say to you, that you will weep and lament, but the world will rejoice; you will grieve, but your grief will be turned into joy. Whenever a woman is in labor she has pain, because her hour has come; but when she gives birth to the child, she no longer remembers the anguish because of the joy that a child has been born into the world. Therefore you too have grief now; but I will see you again, and your heart will rejoice, and no one *will* take your joy away from you" (John 16:16–22; see Mark 9:32; Luke 23:27; John 14:18–24; 16:5, 6; 20:20).

PROPHECY OF JESUS' RESURRECTION (Also see RESURRECTION)

[PROPHECY OF JESUS' RESURRECTION from the sign of Jonah]

Setting: Galilee. After Jesus warns the Pharisees about the unpardonable sin and their future judgment, some Pharisees and scribes ask Him to perform a miraculous sign for them in front of the crowds.

But He answered and said to them, "An evil and adulterous generation craves for a sign; and *yet* no sign will be given to it but the sign of Jonah the prophet; for just as JONAH WAS THREE DAYS AND THREE NIGHTS IN THE BELLY OF THE SEA MONSTER, so will the Son of Man be three days and three nights in the heart of the earth. The men of Nineveh will stand up with this generation at the judgment, and will condemn it because they repented at the preaching of Jonah; and behold, something greater than Jonah is here. *The* Queen of *the* South will rise up with this generation at the judgment and will condemn it, because she came from the ends of the earth to hear the wisdom of Solomon; and behold, something greater than Solomon is here" (Matthew 12:39–42; Jesus quotes from Jonah 1:17; cf. 1 Kings 10:1; Jonah 3:5; Matthew 16:1, 4; Luke 11:29).

[PROPHECY OF JESUS' RESURRECTION from the sign of Jonah]

Setting: Magadan of Galilee. Jesus' enemies, the Pharisees and Sadducees, rejecting His message, continue to test Him by asking for a sign from heaven.

But He replied to them, "When it is evening, you say, '*It will be* fair weather, for the sky is red.' And in the morning, '*There will* be a storm today, for the sky is red and threatening.' Do you know how to discern the appearance of the sky, but cannot *discern* the signs of the times? An evil and adulterous generation seeks after a sign; and a sign will not be given it, except the sign of Jonah." And He left them and went away (Matthew 16:2–4; cf. Matthew 12:39; Mark 8:12; Luke 12:54–56).

[PROPHECY OF JESUS' RESURRECTION from until the Son of Man has risen from the dead]

Setting: Galilee. Jesus instructs Peter, James, and John to keep the Transfiguration, which has just occurred on a high mountain, secret until after His resurrection.

As they were coming down from the mountain, Jesus commanded them, saying, "Tell the vision to no one until the Son of Man has risen from the dead" (Matthew 17:9; cf. Mark 9:9–13; Luke 9:28–36).

[PROPHECY OF JESUS' RESURRECTION from He will be raised on the third day]

Setting: Galilee. Following the Transfiguration, Jesus repeats to His disciples that He must suffer, die, and be raised.

And while they were gathering together in Galilee, Jesus said to them, "The Son of Man is going to be delivered into the hands of men; and they will kill Him, and He will be raised on the third day." And they were deeply grieved (Matthew 17:22, 23; cf. Matthew 16:21; Mark 9:30–32; Luke 9:44, 45).

[PROPHECY OF JESUS' RESURRECTION from on the third day, He will be raised up]

Setting: Judea beyond the Jordan (Perea). Before going to Jerusalem, Jesus again tells His disciples of His impending death and resurrection.

As Jesus was about to go up to Jerusalem, He took the twelve *disciples* aside by themselves, and on the way He said to them, "Behold, we are going up to Jerusalem; and the Son of Man will be delivered to the chief priests and scribes, and they will condemn

Him to death, and will hand Him over to the Gentiles to mock and scourge and crucify *Him,* and on the third day, He will be raised up" (Matthew 20:17–19; cf. Matthew 16:21; Mark 10:32–34; Luke 18:31–33).

[PROPHECY OF JESUS' RESURRECTION from after I have been raised]

Setting: On the way to the Mount of Olives. After celebrating the Passover meal in Jerusalem with His disciples, prior to His betrayal by Judas, Jesus tells them they will all deny Him that very day.

Then Jesus said to them, "You will all fall away because of Me this night, for it is written, 'I WILL STRIKE DOWN THE SHEPHERD, AND THE SHEEP OF THE FLOCK SHALL BE SCATTERED.' But after I have been raised, I will go ahead of you to Galilee." But Peter said to Him, '*Even* though all may fall away because of You, I will never fall away.' Jesus said to him, "Truly I say to you that this *very* night, before a rooster crows, you will deny Me three times" (Matthew 26:31–34, Jesus quotes from Zechariah 13:7; cf. Mark 14:26–31; see Matthew 28:7, 10, 16; John 13:37).

[PROPHECY OF JESUS' RESURRECTION from He will rise three days later]

Setting: Galilee. After casting out an unclean spirit from a young boy, Jesus teaches His disciples in secret about His coming death and resurrection.

From there they went out and *began* to go through Galilee, and He did not want anyone to know *about it.* For He was teaching His disciples and telling them, "The Son of Man is to be delivered into the hands of men, and they will kill Him; and when He has been killed, He will rise three days later." But they did not understand *this* statement, and they were afraid to ask Him (Mark 9:30–32; cf. Matthew 17:22, 23; see Matthew 16:21).

[PROPHECY OF JESUS' RESURRECTION from three days later He will rise again]

Setting: On the road to Jerusalem. After encouraging His disciples with a revelation of their future reward, Jesus prophesies His persecution, death, and resurrection.

They were on the road going up to Jerusalem, and Jesus was walking on ahead of them; and they were amazed, and those who followed were fearful. And again He took the twelve aside and began to tell them what was going to happen to Him, *saying,* "Behold, we are going up to Jerusalem, and the Son of Man will be delivered to the chief priests and the scribes; and they will condemn Him to death and will hand Him over to the Gentiles. They will mock Him and spit on Him, and scourge Him and kill *Him,* and three days later He will rise again" (Mark 10:32–34; cf. Matthew 20:17–19; Luke 18:31–34; see Matthew 16:21; Mark 8:31).

[PROPHECY OF JESUS' RESURRECTION from after I have been raised]

Setting: A borrowed upper room in Jerusalem. Jesus and His twelve disciples celebrate the Passover and the Lord's Supper, then go to the Mount of Olives.

And Jesus said to them, "You will all fall away, because it is written, 'I WILL STRIKE DOWN THE SHEPHERD, AND THE SHEEP SHALL BE SCATTERED.' But after I have been raised, I will go ahead of you to Galilee." But Peter said to Him, "*Even* though all may fall away, yet I will not." And Jesus said to him, "Truly I say to you, that this very night, before a rooster crows twice, you yourself will deny Me three times" (Mark 14:27–30, Jesus quotes from Zechariah 13:7; cf. Matthew 26:30–34; see Mark 14:72).

[PROPHECY OF JESUS' RESURRECTION from be raised up on the third day]

Setting: Galilee. Following Peter's pronouncement that Jesus is the Christ of God, the Lord warns His disciples not to reveal His identity to anyone.

But He warned them and instructed *them* not to tell this to anyone, saying, "The Son of Man must suffer many things and be rejected by the elders and chief priests and scribes, and be killed and be raised up on the third day" (Luke 9:21, 22; cf. Matthew 16:21; Mark 8:31).

[PROPHECY OF JESUS' RESURRECTION from the sign of Jonah]

Setting: On the way from Galilee to Jerusalem. After revealing a problem with exorcism and responding to a blessing from a woman in the crowd, Jesus tells the increasing crowds of the sign of Jonah.

As the crowds were increasing, He began to say, "This generation is a wicked generation; it seeks for a sign, and *yet* no sign will be given to it but the sign of Jonah. For just as Jonah became a sign to the Ninevites, so will the Son of Man be to this generation. The Queen of the South will rise up with the men of this generation at the judgment and condemn them, because she came from the ends of the earth to hear the wisdom of Solomon; and behold, something greater than Solomon is here. The men of Nineveh will stand up with this generation at the judgment and condemn it, because they repented at the preaching of Jonah; and behold, something greater than Jonah is here" (Luke 11:29–32; cf. Matthew 16:4; see 1 Kings 10:1–10; Jonah 3:4, 5).

[PROPHECY OF JESUS' RESURRECTION from the third day He will rise again]

Setting: On the way from Galilee to Jerusalem. After responding to Peter's statement about the disciples' personal sacrifice in following Him, Jesus tells them of the sacrifice He will make in Jerusalem.

Then He took the twelve aside and said to them, "Behold, we are going up to Jerusalem, and all things which are written through the prophets about the Son of Man will be accomplished. For He will be handed over to the Gentiles, and will be mocked and mistreated and spit upon, and after they have scourged Him, they will kill Him; and the third day He will rise again" (Luke 18:31–33; cf. Matthew 20:17–19; Mark 10:32–34).

[PROPHECY OF JESUS' RESURRECTION from in three days I will raise it up]

Setting: Jerusalem. After Jesus cleanses the temple during the Passover of the Jews, the Jewish religious leaders question His authority to do such things.

Jesus answered them, "Destroy this temple, and in three days I will raise it up" (John 2:19; cf. Matthew 26:61).

[PROPHECY OF JESUS' RESURRECTION from you *will* see Me]

Setting: Jerusalem. Before the Passover, after responding to Philip's request for Him to show His disciples the Father, Jesus conveys the upcoming role of the Holy Spirit in their lives.

"I will not leave you as orphans; I will come to you. After a little while the world will no longer see Me, but you *will* see Me; because I live, you will live also. In that day you will know that I am in the Father, and you in Me, and I in you. He who has My commandments and keeps them is the one who loves Me; and he who loves Me will be loved by My Father, and I will love him and will disclose Myself to him" (John 14:18–21; see John 6:57; 10:37, 38; 16:16, 22).

[PROPHECY OF JESUS' RESURRECTION from you will see Me]

Setting: Jerusalem. Before the Passover, after warning His disciples of the persecution they will face after His departure to heaven, empathizing with their sadness over His prophecies, Jesus gives them the hope for the future.

"A little while, and you will no longer see Me; and again a little while, and you will see Me." *Some* of His disciples then said to one another, "What is this thing He is telling us, 'A little while, and you will not see Me; and again a little while, and you will see Me'; and, 'because I go to the Father'?" So they were saying, "What is this that He says, 'A little while'? We do not know what He is talking about." Jesus knew that they wished to question Him, and He said to them, "Are you deliberating together about this, that I said, 'A little while, and you will not see Me, and again a little while, and you will see Me'? Truly, truly, I say to you, that you will weep and lament, but the world will rejoice; you will grieve, but your grief will be turned into joy. Whenever a woman is in labor she has pain, because her hour has come; but when she gives birth to the child, she no longer remembers the anguish because of the joy that a child has been born into the world. Therefore you too have grief now; but I will see you again, and your heart will rejoice, and no one *will* take your joy away from you" (John 16:16–22; see Mark 9:32; Luke 23:27; John 14:18–24; 16:5, 6; 20:20).

PROPHECY OF JESUS' TRANSFIGURATION (Listed under TRANSFIGURATION, PROPHECY OF JESUS')

PROPHECY OF PETER'S DENIAL (Also see JESUS, DENYING; and PETER'S DENIAL)

[PROPHECY OF PETER'S DENIAL from Truly I say to you that this *very* night, before a rooster crows, you will deny Me three times]

Setting: On the way from an upper room in Jerusalem to the Mount of Olives. After celebrating the Passover meal, prior to His betrayal by Judas, Jesus states that all His disciples will deny Him that very day.

Then Jesus said to them, "You will all fall away because of Me this night, for it is written, 'I WILL STRIKE DOWN THE SHEPHERD, AND THE SHEEP OF THE FLOCK SHALL BE SCATTERED.' But after I have been raised, I will go ahead of you to Galilee." But Peter said to Him, '*Even* though all may fall away because of You, I will never fall away.' Jesus said to him, "Truly I say to you that this *very* night, before a rooster crows, you will deny Me three times" (Matthew 26:31–34, Jesus quotes from Zechariah 13:7; cf. Mark 14:26–31; see Matthew 26:30, 35, 75; 28:7, 10, 16; John 13:37).

[PROPHECY OF PETER'S DENIAL from before a rooster crows twice, you yourself will deny Me three times]

Setting: Jerusalem. After Jesus and His twelve disciples celebrate the Passover and the Lord's Supper in a borrowed upper room, they go to the Mount of Olives.

And Jesus said to them, "You will all fall away, because it is written, 'I WILL STRIKE DOWN THE SHEPHERD, AND THE SHEEP SHALL BE SCATTERED.' But after I have been raised, I will go ahead of you to Galilee." But Peter said to Him, "*Even* though all may fall away, yet I will not." And Jesus said to him, "Truly I say to you, that this very night, before a rooster crows twice, you yourself will deny Me three times" (Mark 14:27–30, Jesus quotes from Zechariah 13:7; cf. Matthew 26:30–34; see Mark 14:72).

[PROPHECY OF PETER'S DENIAL from I say to you, Peter, the rooster will not crow today until you have denied three times that you know Me]

Setting: Jerusalem. During the Feast of Unleavened Bread (Passover) just before His crucifixion, while celebrating the Passover meal and instituting the Lord's Supper, Jesus prophesies Peter's denials of Him.

"Simon, Simon, behold, Satan has demanded *permission* to sift you like wheat; but I have prayed for you, that your faith may not fail; and you, when once you have turned again, strengthen your brothers." But he said to Him, "Lord, with You I am ready to go both to prison and to death!" And He said, "I say to you, Peter, the rooster will not crow today until you have denied three times that you know Me" (Luke 22:31–34; cf. Matthew 26:33–35; John 13:36–38; see Job 1:6–12; Luke 22:28–30; John 17:15).

[PROPHECY OF PETER'S DENIAL from Truly, truly, I say to you, a rooster will not crow until you deny Me three times]

Setting: Jerusalem. Before the Passover, after revealing to His disciples they cannot follow Him back to heaven, Jesus takes issue with Peter's assertion he would lay down his life for Jesus.

Simon Peter said to Him, "Lord, where are You going?" Jesus answered, "Where I go, you cannot follow Me now; but you will follow later." Peter said to Him, "Lord, why can I not follow You right now? I will lay down my life for You." Jesus answered, "Will you lay down your life for Me? Truly, truly, I say to you, a rooster will not crow until you deny Me three times" (John 13:36–38; see Matthew 26:34; Mark 14:30, 72; Luke 22:33, 34; John 13:1–35).

PROPHECY OF PENTECOST (Listed under PENTECOST, PROPHECY OF)

PROPHECY OF THE CHURCH (Listed under CHURCH, PROPHECY OF THE)

PROPHECY OF THE DESTRUCTION OF JERUSALEM

[PROPHECY OF THE DESTRUCTION OF JERUSALEM from Behold, your house is being left to you desolate]

Setting: The temple in Jerusalem. With His death on the cross just days away, Jesus laments over the city's hard-heartedness and lack of repentance.

"Jerusalem, Jerusalem, who kills the prophets and stones those who are sent to her! How often I wanted to gather your children together, the way a hen gathers her chicks under her wings, and you were unwilling. Behold, your house is being left to you desolate! For I say to you, from now on you will not see Me until you say, 'BLESSED IS HE WHO COMES IN THE NAME OF THE LORD!'" (Matthew 23:37–39, Jesus quotes from Psalm 118:26; cf. 1 Kings 9:7; Luke 13:34, 35).

[PROPHECY OF THE DESTRUCTION OF JERUSALEM from Behold, your house is left to you *desolate*]
Setting: On the way from Galilee to Jerusalem. While teaching in the cities and villages, after Jesus responds to a question about who is saved, some Pharisees ask Him to leave, claiming Herod Antipas (tetrarch of Galilee and Perea) seeks to kill Him.

And He said to them, "Go and tell that fox, 'Behold, I cast out demons and perform cures today and tomorrow, and the third *day* I reach My goal.' Nevertheless I must journey on today and tomorrow and the next *day*; for it cannot be that a prophet would perish outside of Jerusalem. O Jerusalem, Jerusalem, *the city* that kills the prophets and stones those sent to her! How often I wanted to gather your children together, just as a hen *gathers* her brood under her wings, and you would not *have it*! Behold, your house is left to you *desolate*; and I say to you, you will not see Me until *the time* comes when you say, 'BLESSED IS HE WHO COMES IN THE NAME OF THE LORD!'" (Luke 13:32–35, Jesus quotes from Psalm 118:26; cf. Matthew 23:37).

[PROPHECY OF THE DESTRUCTION OF JERUSALEM from For the days will come upon you when your enemies will throw up a barricade against you, and surround you and hem you in on every side, and they will level you to the ground and your children within you, and they will not leave in you one stone upon another, because you did not recognize the time of your visitation]
Setting: Approaching Jerusalem. After being praised by the people in a triumphal welcome, the Lord weeps as He sees the city ahead of Him.

When He approached *Jerusalem,* He saw the city and wept over it, saying, "If you had known in this day, even you, the things which make for peace! But now they have been hidden from your eyes. For the days will come upon you when your enemies will throw up a barricade against you, and surround you and hem you in on every side, and they will level you to the ground and your children within you, and they will not leave in you one stone upon another, because you did not recognize the time of your visitation" (Luke 19:41–44; see Matthew 24:1, 2; Luke 13:34, 35).

[PROPHECY OF THE DESTRUCTION OF JERUSALEM from when you see Jerusalem surrounded by armies, then recognize that her desolation is near]
Setting: On the Mount of Olives, east of the temple in Jerusalem. After ministering in the temple a few days before His crucifixion, and giving the disciples more details regarding future events, Jesus elaborates more during His Olivet Discourse about things to come.

"But when you see Jerusalem surrounded by armies, then recognize that her desolation is near. Then those who are in Judea must flee to the mountains, and those who are in the midst of the city must leave, and those who are in the country must not enter the city; because these are days of vengeance, so that all things which are written will be fulfilled. Woe to those who are pregnant and to those who are nursing babies in those days; for there will be a great distress upon the land and wrath to this people; and they will fall by the edge of the sword, and will be led captive into all the nations; and Jerusalem will be trampled under foot by the Gentiles until the times of the Gentiles are fulfilled" (Luke 21:20–24; see Matthew 24:15–18; Mark 13:14–16; Luke 19:43).

[PROPHECY OF THE DESTRUCTION OF JERUSALEM from For behold, the days are coming when they will say, 'Blessed are the barren, and the wombs that never bore, and the breasts that never nursed]

Setting: Jerusalem. After being arrested and appearing before the Council of Elders (Sanhedrin), Pontius Pilate (Roman governor of Judea), Herod Antipas (tetrarch of Galilee and Perea), and Pilate a second time (when Pilate bows to the crowd's pressure and grants that Jesus be crucified), the Lord prophesies to the women mourning Him regarding the coming judgment of Jerusalem.

But Jesus turning to them said, "Daughters of Jerusalem, stop weeping for Me, but weep for yourselves and for your children. For behold, the days are coming when they will say, 'Blessed are the barren, and the wombs that never bore, and the breasts that never nursed.' Then they will begin TO SAY TO THE MOUNTAINS, 'FALL ON US,' AND TO THE HILLS, 'COVER US.' For if they do these things when the tree is green, what will happen when it is dry?" (Luke 23:28–31, Jesus quotes from Hosea 10:8; see Matthew 24:19).

PROPHECY OF THE TEMPLE'S DESTRUCTION (See TEMPLE, PROPHECY OF THE DESTRUCTION OF THE)

PROPHESY (Also see PROPHECY)

Setting: Galilee. During the early part of His ministry, Jesus preaches the Sermon on the Mount to His disciples and the multitudes.

"Not everyone who says to Me, 'Lord, Lord,' will enter the kingdom of heaven, but he who does the will of My Father who is in heaven *will enter.* Many will say to Me on that day, 'Lord, Lord, did we not prophesy in Your name, and in Your name cast out demons, and in Your name perform many miracles?' And then I will declare to them, 'I never knew you, DEPART FROM ME, YOU WHO PRACTICE LAWLESSNESS'" (Matthew 7:21–23, Jesus quotes from Psalm 6:8; cf. Matthew 25:11–13; see Luke 6:46).

[PROPHESY from prophesied]

Setting: Galilee. While speaking to the crowds, Jesus pays tribute to the ministry of John the Baptist, but emphasizes that the one who is least in the kingdom of heaven is greater than John.

As these men were going *away,* Jesus began to speak to the crowds about John, "What did you go out into the wilderness to see? A reed shaken by the wind? But what did you go out to see? A man dressed in soft *clothing?* Those who wear soft *clothing* are in kings' palaces! But what did you go out to see? A prophet? Yes, I tell you, and the one who is more than a prophet. This is the one about whom it is written, 'BEHOLD, I SEND MY MESSENGER AHEAD OF YOU, WHO WILL PREPARE YOUR WAY BEFORE YOU.' Truly, I say to you, among those born of women there has not arisen *anyone* greater than John the Baptist! Yet the one who is least in the kingdom of heaven is greater than he. From the days of John the Baptist until now the kingdom of heaven suffers violence, and violent men take it by force. For all the prophets and the Law prophesied until John. And, if you are willing to accept *it,* John himself is Elijah who was to come. He who has ears to hear, let him hear" (Matthew 11:7–15, Jesus quotes from Malachi 3:1; cf. Malachi 4:5; Luke 7:24–28; Luke 16:16; see Matthew 14:5).

Setting: Galilee. Pharisees and scribes from Jerusalem accuse Jesus' disciples of disobeying tradition and the commandments.

And He answered and said to them, "Why do you yourselves transgress the commandment of God for the sake of tradition? For God said, 'HONOR YOUR FATHER AND MOTHER,' and, 'HE WHO SPEAKS EVIL OF FATHER OR MOTHER IS TO BE PUT TO DEATH.' But you say, 'Whoever says to *his* father or mother, "Whatever I have that would help you has been given *to God,*" he is not to honor his father or mother.' And *by this* you invalidated the word of God for the sake of your tradition. You hypocrites, rightly did Isaiah prophesy of you: 'THIS PEOPLE HONORS ME WITH THEIR LIPS, BUT THEIR HEART IS FAR AWAY FROM ME. BUT IN VAIN DO THEY WORSHIP ME, TEACHING AS DOCTRINES THE PRECEPTS OF MEN'" (Matthew 15:3–9, Jesus quotes from Exodus 20:12, 21:17; Leviticus 20:9; Isaiah 29:13; cf. Mark 7:5–7; see Colossians 2:22).

Setting: Galilee. The Pharisees and some of the scribes from Jerusalem question why Jesus' disciples do not follow the tradition of ceremonial hand cleansing before eating bread.

And He said to them, "Rightly did Isaiah prophesy of you hypocrites, as it is written: 'THIS PEOPLE HONORS ME WITH THEIR LIPS, BUT THEIR HEART IS FAR AWAY FROM ME. BUT IN VAIN DO THEY WORSHIP ME, TEACHING AS DOCTRINES THE PRECEPTS OF MEN.' Neglecting the commandment of God, you hold to the tradition of men." He was also saying to them, "You are experts at setting aside the commandment of God in order to keep tradition. For Moses said, 'HONOR YOUR FATHER AND YOUR MOTHER'; and, 'HE WHO SPEAKS EVIL OF FATHER OR MOTHER, IS TO BE PUT TO DEATH'; but you say, 'If a man says to *his* father or *his* mother, whatever I have that would help you is Corban (that is to say, given *to God*),' you no longer permit him to do anything for *his* father or *his* mother; *thus* invalidating the word of God by your tradition which you have handed down; and you do many things such as that" (Mark 7:6–13, Jesus quotes from Exodus 20:12; 21:17; Isaiah 29:13; cf. Matthew 15:1–6).

PROPHET (See specific names such as ELIJAH; also see PROPHETESS; and PROPHETS)

Setting: Galilee. After His twelve disciples observe His ministry, Jesus summons and specifically instructs them about their ministry ahead that will include rewards.

"He who receives you receives Me, and he who receives Me receives Him who sent me. He who receives a prophet in the name of a prophet shall receive a prophet's reward; and he who receives a righteous man in the name of a righteous man shall receive a righteous man's reward. And whoever in the name of a disciple gives to one of these little ones even a cup of cold water to drink, truly I say to you, he shall not lose his reward" (Matthew 10:40–42; cf. Matthew 25:40, 44, 45; see Mark 9:37).

Setting: Galilee. While speaking to the crowds, Jesus pays tribute to the ministry of John the Baptist, but emphasizes that the one who is least in the kingdom of heaven is greater than John.

As these men were going *away,* Jesus began to speak to the crowds about John, "What did you go out into the wilderness to see? A reed shaken by the wind? But what did you go out to see? A man dressed in soft *clothing?* Those who wear soft *clothing* are in kings' palaces! But what did you go out to see? A prophet? Yes, I tell you, and the one who is more than a prophet. This is the one about whom it is written, 'BEHOLD, I SEND MY MESSENGER AHEAD OF YOU, WHO WILL PREPARE YOUR WAY BEFORE YOU.' Truly, I say to you, among those born of women there has not arisen *anyone* greater than John the Baptist! Yet the one who is least in the kingdom of heaven is greater than he. From the days of John the Baptist until now the kingdom of heaven suffers violence, and violent men take it by force. For all the prophets and the Law prophesied until John. And, if you are willing to accept *it,* John himself is Elijah who was to come. He who has ears to hear, let him hear" (Matthew 11:7–15, Jesus quotes from Malachi 3:1; cf. Malachi 4:5; Luke 7:24–28; Luke 16:16; see Matthew 14:5).

Setting: Galilee. After Jesus warns the Pharisees about the unpardonable sin and their future judgment, some Pharisees and scribes ask Him to perform a miraculous sign for them in front of the crowds.

But He answered and said to them, "An evil and adulterous generation craves for a sign; and *yet* no sign will be given to it but the sign of Jonah the prophet; for just as JONAH WAS THREE DAYS AND THREE NIGHTS IN THE BELLY OF THE SEA MONSTER, so will the Son of Man be three days and three nights in the heart of the earth. The men of Nineveh will stand up with this generation at the judgment, and will condemn it because they repented at the preaching of Jonah; and behold, something greater than Jonah is here. *The* Queen of *the* South will rise up with this generation at the judgment and will condemn it, because she came from the ends of the earth to hear the wisdom of Solomon; and behold, something greater than Solomon is here" (Matthew 12:39–42; Jesus quotes from Jonah 1:17; cf. 1 Kings 10:1; Jonah 3:5; Matthew 16:1, 4; Luke 11:29).

Setting: The synagogue in Jesus' hometown of Nazareth. The congregation take offense when Jesus tries to teach them.

And they took offense at Him. But Jesus said to them, "A prophet is not without honor except in his hometown and in his *own* household" (Matthew 13:57; cf. Mark 6:4; see Matthew 11:6).

Setting: The Mount of Olives, just east of Jerusalem. During His Olivet Discourse, Jesus answers His disciples' questions as to when the temple will be destroyed and Jerusalem overrun, along with the signs of His coming and the end of the age.

"Therefore when you see the ABOMINATION OF DESOLATION which was spoken of through Daniel the prophet, standing in the holy place (let the reader understand), then those who are in Judea must flee to the mountains. Whoever is on the housetop must not go down to get the things that are in his house. Whoever is in the field must not turn back to get his cloak. But woe to those who are pregnant and to those who are nursing babies in those days! But pray that your flight will not be in the winter, or on a

Sabbath. For then there will be a great tribulation, such as has not occurred since the beginning of the world until now, nor ever will. Unless those days had been cut short, no life would have been saved; but for the sake of the elect those days will be cut short. Then if anyone says to you, 'Behold, here is the Christ,' or "There *He is*,' do not believe *him*. For false Christs and false prophets will arise and will show great signs and wonders, so as to mislead, if possible, even the elect. Behold, I have told you in advance. So if they say to you, 'Behold, He is in the wilderness,' do not go out, *or*, 'Behold, He is in the inner rooms,' do not believe *them*. For just as the lightning comes from the east and flashes even to the west, so will the coming of the Son of Man be. Wherever the corpse is, there the vultures will gather" (Matthew 24:15–28, Jesus quotes from Daniel 9:27; cf. Daniel 12:1; Mark 13:14–23; Luke 17:22–31; 21:20–24; 23:29; see John 4:48).

Setting: The synagogue in Jesus' hometown of Nazareth. While ministering throughout the villages of Galilee, Jesus teaches in His hometown. The townspeople become offended and question His teaching, wisdom, and ability to perform miracles.

Jesus said to them, "A prophet is not without honor except in his hometown and among his *own* relatives and in his *own* household" (Mark 6:4; cf. Matthew 13:54–58).

[PROPHET from slave and *so with* many others]
Setting: The temple in Jerusalem. Having His authority questioned by the chief priests, scribes, and elders, Jesus begins to teach them in parables.

And He began to speak to them in parables: "A man PLANTED A VINEYARD AND PUT A WALL AROUND IT, AND DUG A VAT UNDER THE WINE PRESS AND BUILT A TOWER, and rented it out to vine-growers and went on a journey. At the *harvest* time he sent a slave to the vine-growers, in order to receive *some* of the produce of the vineyard from the vine-growers. They took him, and beat him and sent him away empty-handed. Again he sent them another slave, and they wounded him in the head, and treated him shamefully. And he sent another, and that one they killed; and *so with* many others, beating some and killing others. He had one more to *send*, a beloved son; he sent him last *of all* to them, saying, 'They will respect my son.' But those vine-growers said to one another, 'This is the heir; come, let us kill him, and the inheritance will be ours!' They took him, and killed him and threw him out of the vineyard. What will the owner of the vineyard do? He will come and destroy the vine-growers, and will give the vineyard to others. Have you not even read this Scripture: 'THE STONE WHICH THE BUILDERS REJECTED, THIS BECAME THE CHIEF CORNER *stone*; THIS CAME ABOUT FROM THE LORD, AND IT IS MARVELOUS IN OUR EYES'?" (Mark 12:1–11, Jesus quotes from Psalm 118:22, 23; Isaiah 5:1, 2; cf. Matthew 21:33–46; Luke 20:9–19).

Setting: The synagogue in Jesus' hometown of Nazareth in Galilee. At the beginning of His public ministry, Jesus comments to the congregation after reading on the Sabbath from the book of the prophet Isaiah.

And He said to them, "No doubt you will quote this proverb to Me, 'Physician, heal yourself! Whatever we heard was done at Capernaum, do here in your hometown as well.'" And He said, "Truly I say to you, no prophet is welcome in his hometown. But I say to you in truth, there were many widows in Israel in the days of Elijah, when the sky was shut up for three years and six months, when a great famine came over all the land; and yet Elijah was sent to none of them, but only to Zarephath, *in the land* of Sidon, to a woman who was a widow. And there were many lepers in Israel in the time of Elisha the prophet; and none of them was cleansed, but only Naaman the Syrian" (Luke 4:23–27; Jesus refers to 1 Kings 17:1, 9; 2 Kings 5:1–14; see Matthew 13:53–58).

Setting: Galilee. After Jesus responds to the disciples of John the Baptist whether He is the promised Messiah, the Lord speaks to the crowds about John.

When the messengers of John had left, He began to speak to the crowds about John, "What did you go out into the wilderness to see? A reed shaken by the wind? But what did you go out to see? A man dressed in soft clothing? Those who are splendidly clothed and live in luxury are *found* in royal palaces! But what did you go out to see? A prophet? Yes, I say to you, and one who is more than a prophet. This is the one about whom it is written, 'BEHOLD, I SEND MY MESSENGER AHEAD OF YOU, WHO WILL PREPARE YOUR WAY BEFORE YOU.' I say to you, among those born of women there is no one greater than John; yet he who is least in the kingdom of God is greater than he" (Luke 7:24–28, Jesus quotes from Malachi 3:1; cf. Matthew 11:7–11).

Setting: On the way from Galilee to Jerusalem. While teaching in the cities and villages, Jesus responds to a question about who is saved. Some Pharisees ask Him to leave, claiming Herod Antipas (tetrarch of Galilee and Perea) seeks to kill Him.

And He said to them, "Go and tell that fox, 'Behold, I cast out demons and perform cures today and tomorrow, and the third *day* I reach My goal.' Nevertheless I must journey on today and tomorrow and the next *day*; for it cannot be that a prophet would perish outside of Jerusalem. O Jerusalem, Jerusalem, *the city* that kills the prophets and stones those sent to her! How often I wanted to gather your children together, just as a hen *gathers* her brood under her wings, and you would not *have it*! Behold, your house is left to you *desolate*; and I say to you, you will not see Me until *the time* comes when you say, 'BLESSED IS HE WHO COMES IN THE NAME OF THE LORD!'" (Luke 13:32–35, Jesus quotes from Psalm 118:26; cf. Matthew 23:37).

[PROPHET from slave]

Setting: The temple in Jerusalem. While ministering a few days before His crucifixion, after the chief priests and the scribes question His authority to teach and preach, Jesus conveys the Parable of the Vine-Growers to the people.

And He began to tell the people this parable: "A man planted a vineyard and rented it out to vine-growers, and went on a journey for a long time. At the *harvest* time he sent a slave to the vine-growers, so that they would give him *some* of the produce of the vineyard; but the vine-growers beat him and sent him away empty-handed. And he proceeded to send another slave; and they beat him also and treated him shamefully and sent him away empty-handed. And he proceeded to send a third; and this one also they wounded and cast out. The owner of the vineyard said, 'What shall I do? I will send my beloved son; perhaps they will respect him.' But when the vine-growers saw him, they reasoned with one another, saying, 'This is the heir; let us kill him so that the inheritance will be ours.' So they threw him out of the vineyard and killed him. What, then, will the owner of the vineyard do to them? He will come and destroy these vine-growers and will give the vineyard to others." When they heard it, they said, "May it never be!" But Jesus looked at them and said, "What then is this that is written: 'THE STONE WHICH THE BUILDERS REJECTED, THIS BECAME THE CHIEF CORNER *stone*'? Everyone who falls on that stone will be broken to pieces; but on whomever it falls, it will scatter him like dust" (Luke 20:9–18, Jesus quotes from Psalm 118:22; cf. Matthew 21:33–44; Mark 12:1–11; see Ephesians 2:20).

PROPHET'S REWARD (Listed under REWARD, PROPHET'S; also see REWARD; and REWARDS)

PROPHETESS (Also see PROPHET)

Setting: On the island of Patmos (in the Aegean Sea about fifty miles southwest of Ephesus in modern Turkey). On the Lord's Day (Sunday), approximately fifty years after the Resurrection, the disciple John encounters the Lord Jesus Christ, who communicates a new revelation for the apostle to record for the church in Thyatira and to six other churches in Asia.

"And to the angel of the church in Thyatira write: The Son of God, who has eyes like a flame of fire, and His feet are like burnished bronze, says this: 'I know your deeds, and your love and faith and service and perseverance, and that your deeds of late are greater than at first. But I have *this* against you, that you tolerate the woman Jezebel, who calls herself a prophetess, and she teaches and leads My bond-servants astray so that they commit *acts of* immorality and eat things sacrificed to idols. I gave her time to repent, and she does not want to repent of her immorality. Behold, I will throw her on a bed *of sickness,* and those who commit adultery with her into great tribulation, unless they repent of her deeds. And I will kill her children with pestilence, and all the churches will know that I am He who searches the minds and hearts; and I will give to each one of you according to your deeds. But I say to you, the rest who are in Thyatira, who do not hold this teaching, who have not known the deep things of Satan, as they call them—I place no other burden on you. Nevertheless what you have, hold fast until I come. He who overcomes, and he who keeps My deeds until the end, TO HIM I WILL GIVE AUTHORITY OVER THE NATIONS; AND HE SHALL RULE THEM WITH A ROD OF IRON, AS THE VESSELS OF THE POTTER ARE BROKEN TO PIECES, as I also have received *authority* from My Father; and I will give him the morning star. He who has an ear, let him hear what the Spirit says to the churches' (Revelation 2:18–29; Jesus quotes from Psalm 2:8, 9; Isaiah 30:14; see 1 Kings 16:31; Psalm 7:9; Romans 2:5; 1 Corinthians 2:10; 2 Peter 3:9; Revelation 1:14; 2:7; 3:11; 17:1–20).

PROPHETS (Specifics such as PROPHETS, BLOOD OF THE; PROPHETS, LAW AND THE; and PROPHETS, FALSE are separate entries; also see specific names such as ELIJAH; also see PROPHET)
Setting: Galilee. Early in His ministry, Jesus presents the Beatitudes (part of the Sermon on the Mount) to His disciples and the gathered crowds from Galilee, Decapolis, Jerusalem, Judea, and beyond the Jordan.

"Blessed are you when *people* insult you and persecute you, and falsely say all kinds of evil against you because of Me. Rejoice and be glad, for your reward in heaven is great; for in the same way they persecuted the prophets who were before you" (Matthew 5:11, 12; cf. 2 Chronicles 36:16; Luke 6:22, 23; 1 Peter 4:14; see Matthew 13:35).

Setting: Galilee. During the early part of His ministry, Jesus preaches the Sermon on the Mount to His disciples and the multitudes.

"Do not think that I came to abolish the Law or the Prophets; I did not come to abolish but to fulfill" (Matthew 5:17).

Setting: Galilee. While speaking to the crowds, Jesus pays tribute to the ministry of John the Baptist, but emphasizes that the one who is least in the kingdom of heaven is greater than John.

As these men were going *away,* Jesus began to speak to the crowds about John, "What did you go out into the wilderness to see? A reed shaken by the wind? But what did you go out to see? A man dressed in soft *clothing?* Those who wear soft *clothing* are in kings' palaces! But what did you go out to see? A prophet? Yes, I tell you, and the one who is more than a prophet. This is the one about whom it is written, 'BEHOLD, I SEND MY MESSENGER AHEAD OF YOU, WHO WILL PREPARE YOUR WAY BEFORE YOU.' Truly, I say to you, among those born of women there has not arisen *anyone* greater than John the Baptist! Yet the one who is least in the kingdom of heaven is greater than he. From the days of John the Baptist until now the kingdom of heaven suffers violence, and violent men take it by force. For all the prophets and the Law prophesied until John. And, if you are willing to accept *it,* John himself is Elijah who was to come. He who has ears to hear, let him hear" (Matthew 11:7–15, Jesus quotes from Malachi 3:1; cf. Malachi 4:5; Luke 7:24–28; 16:16; see Matthew 14:5).

Setting: By the Sea of Galilee. Jesus responds to His disciples' questions about the Parable of the Sower, which He has just taught from a boat to a crowd.

Jesus answered them, "To you it has been granted to know the mysteries of the kingdom of heaven, but to them it has not been granted. For whoever has, to him *more* shall be given, and he will have an abundance; but whoever does not have, even what he has shall be taken away from him. Therefore, I speak to them in parables; because while seeing they do not see, and while hearing they do not hear, nor do they understand. In their case the prophecy of Isaiah is being fulfilled, which says, 'YOU WILL KEEP ON HEARING, BUT WILL NOT UNDERSTAND; YOU WILL KEEP ON SEEING, BUT WILL NOT PERCEIVE; FOR THE HEART OF THIS PEOPLE HAS BECOME DULL, WITH THEIR EARS THEY SCARCELY HEAR, AND THEY HAVE CLOSED THEIR EYES, OTHERWISE THEYWOULD SEE WITH THEIR EYES, HEAR WITH THEIR EARS, AND UNDERSTAND WITH THEIR HEART AND RETURN, AND I WOULD HEAL THEM.' But blessed are your eyes, because they see; and your ears, because they hear. For truly I say to you that many prophets and righteous men desired to see what you see, and did not see *it,* and to hear what you hear, and did not hear *it*" (Matthew 13:11–17, Jesus quotes from Isaiah 6:9, 10; cf. Matthew 25:29; Mark 4:11–13; Luke 8:10; see Deuteronomy 29:4; John 8:56).

[PROPHETS from slaves]
Setting: The temple in Jerusalem. Jesus delivers another parable to the chief priests and elders after they question His authority.

"Listen to another parable. There was a landowner who PLANTED A VINEYARD AND PUT A WALL AROUND IT AND DUG A WINE PRESS IN IT, AND BUILT A TOWER, and rented it out to vine-growers and went on a journey. When the harvest time approached, he sent his slaves to the vine-growers to receive his produce. The vine-growers took his slaves and beat one, and killed another, and stoned a third. Again he sent another group of slaves larger than the first; and they did the same thing to them. But afterward he sent his son to them, saying, 'They will respect my son.' But when the vine-growers saw the son, they said among themselves, 'This is the heir; come, let us kill him and seize his inheritance.' They took him, and threw him out of the vineyard and killed him. Therefore when the owner of the vineyard comes, what will he do to those vine-growers?" (Matthew 21:33–40; Jesus quotes from Isaiah 5:1, 2; cf. Mark 12:1–9; Luke 20:9–15).

[PROPHETS from slaves]

Setting: The temple in Jerusalem. Jesus speaks another parable to the chief priests and elders after they question His authority.

Jesus spoke to them again in parables, saying, "The kingdom of heaven may be compared to a king who gave a wedding feast for his son. And he sent out his slaves to call those who had been invited to the wedding feast, and they were unwilling to come. Again he sent out other slaves saying, 'Tell those who have been invited, "Behold, I have prepared my dinner; my oxen and my fattened livestock are *all* butchered and everything is ready; come to the wedding feast." But they paid no attention and went their way, one to his own farm, another to his business, and the rest seized his slaves and mistreated them and killed them. But the king was enraged, and he sent his armies and destroyed those murderers and set their city on fire. Then he said to his slaves, 'The wedding is ready, but those who were invited were not worthy. 'Go therefore to the main highways, and as many as you find *there,* invite to the wedding feast.' Those slaves went out into the streets and gathered together all they found, both evil and good; and the wedding hall was filled with dinner guests. But when the king came in to look over the dinner guests, he saw a man there who was not dressed in wedding clothes, and he said to him, 'Friend, how did you come in here without wedding clothes?' And the man was speechless. Then the king said to the servants, 'Bind him hand and foot, and throw him into the outer darkness; in that place there will be weeping and gnashing of teeth.' For many are called, but few *are* chosen" (Matthew 22:1–14; cf. Matthew 8:11, 12).

Setting: The temple in Jerusalem. After the Jewish religious leaders test Him with questions, Jesus pronounces the eighth of eight woes upon them in front of the crowds and His disciples.

"Woe to you, scribes and Pharisees, hypocrites! For you build the tombs of the prophets and adorn the monuments of the righteous, and say, 'If we had been *living* in the days of our fathers, we would not have been partners with them in *shedding* the blood of the prophets.' So you testify against yourselves, that you are sons of those who murdered the prophets. Fill up, then, the measure *of the guilt* of you fathers. You serpents, you brood of vipers, how will you escape the sentence of hell? Therefore, behold, I am sending you prophets and wise men and scribes; some of them you will kill and crucify, and some of them you will scourge in your synagogues, and persecute from city to city, so that upon you may fall *the guilt of* all the righteous blood shed on earth, from the blood of righteous Abel to the blood of Zechariah, the son of Berechiah, whom you murdered between the temple and the altar. Truly I say to you, all these things will come upon this generation" (Matthew 23:29–36; cf. 2 Chronicles 24:21; Zechariah 1:1; Matthew 3:7; Luke 11:47–52; see Matthew 10:23).

Setting: The temple in Jerusalem. With His death on the cross just days away, Jesus laments over Jerusalem's hardheartedness and lack of repentance.

"Jerusalem, Jerusalem, who kills the prophets and stones those who are sent to her! How often I wanted to gather your children together, the way a hen gathers her chicks under her wings, and you were unwilling. Behold, your house is being left to you desolate! For I say to you, from now on you will not see Me until you say, 'BLESSED IS HE WHO COMES IN THE NAME OF THE LORD!'" (Matthew 23:37–39, Jesus quotes from Psalm 118:26; cf. 1 Kings 9:7; Luke 13:34, 35).

[PROPHETS from slave and *so with* many others]

Setting: The temple in Jerusalem. Having His authority questioned by the chief priests, scribes, and elders, Jesus begins to teach them in parables.

And He began to speak to them in parables: "A man PLANTED A VINEYARD AND PUT A WALL AROUND IT, AND DUG A VAT UNDER THE WINE PRESS AND BUILT A TOWER, and rented it out to vine-growers and went on a journey. At the *harvest* time he sent a slave to the vine-growers, in order to receive *some* of the produce of the vineyard from the vine-growers. They took him, and beat him and sent him away empty-handed. Again he sent them another slave, and they wounded him in the head, and treated him shamefully. And he sent another, and that one they killed; and *so with* many others, beating some and killing others. He had one more to *send*, a beloved son; he sent him last *of all* to them, saying, 'They will respect my son.' But those vine-growers said to one another, 'This is the heir; come, let us kill him, and the inheritance will be ours!' They took him, and killed him and threw him out of the vineyard. What will the owner of the vineyard do? He will come and destroy the vine-growers, and will give the vineyard to others. Have you not even read this Scripture: 'THE STONE WHICH THE BUILDERS REJECTED, THIS BECAME THE CHIEF CORNER *stone;* THIS CAME ABOUT FROM THE LORD, AND IT IS MARVELOUS IN OUR EYES'?" (Mark 12:1–11, Jesus quotes from Psalm 118:22, 23; Isaiah 5:1, 2; cf. Matthew 21:33–46; Luke 20:9–19).

Setting: Galilee. After selecting His twelve disciples, Jesus teaches the Beatitudes (part of the Sermon on the Mount) to those disciples and a great throng of people from Judea, Jerusalem, and the central coastal region of Tyre and Sidon.

"Blessed are you when men hate you, and ostracize you, and insult you, and scorn your name as evil, for the sake of the Son of Man. Be glad in that day and leap *for joy*, for behold, your reward is great in heaven. For in the same way their fathers used to treat the prophets" (Luke 6:22, 23; cf. Matthew 5:10–12; see 2 Chronicles 36:16).

Setting: On the way from Galilee to Jerusalem. After responding to a report from the seventy sent out in pairs to every place He Himself will soon visit, the Lord addresses His disciples in private.

Turning to the disciples, He said privately, "Blessed *are* the eyes which see the things you see, for I say to you, that many prophets and kings wished to see the things you see, and did not see *them*, and to hear the things which you hear, and did not hear *them*" (Luke 10:23, 24; cf. Matthew 13:16, 17).

Setting: On the way from Galilee to Jerusalem. After Jesus pronounces woes upon the Pharisees, a lawyer replies that His remarks are an insult to lawyers, too.

But He said, "Woe to you lawyers as well! For you weigh men down with burdens hard to bear, while you yourselves will not even touch the burdens with one of your fingers. Woe to you! For you build the tombs of the prophets, and *it was* your fathers *who* killed them. So you are witnesses and approve the deeds of your fathers; because it was they who killed them, and you build *their tombs*. For this reason also the wisdom of God said, 'I will send them prophets and apostles, and *some* of them they will kill and *some* they will persecute, so that the blood of all the prophets, shed since the foundation of the world, may be charged against this generation, from the blood of Abel to the blood of Zechariah, who was killed between the altar and the house *of God*; yes, I tell you, it shall be charged against this generation.' Woe to you lawyers! For you have taken away the key of knowledge; you yourselves did not enter, and you hindered those who were entering" (Luke 11:46–52; cf. Matthew 23:29–32; see 2 Chronicles 24:20, 21; Matthew 23:4, 13).

Setting: On the way from Galilee to Jerusalem. While teaching in the cities and villages, Jesus responds to a question about who is saved.

And someone said to Him, "Lord, are there *just* a few who are being saved?" And He said to them, "Strive to enter through the narrow door; for many, I tell you, will seek to enter and will not be able. Once the head of the house gets up and shuts the door, and you begin to stand outside and knock on the door, saying, 'Lord, open up to us!' then He will answer and say to you, 'I do not know where you are from.' Then you will begin to say, 'We ate and drank in Your presence, and You taught in our streets'; and He will say, 'I tell you, I do not know where you are from; DEPART FROM ME, ALL YOU EVILDOERS.' In that place there will be weeping and gnashing of teeth when you see Abraham and Isaac and Jacob and all the prophets in the kingdom of God, but you yourselves being thrown out. And they will come from east and west and from north and south, and will recline *at the table* in the kingdom of God. And behold, *some* are last who will be first and *some* are first who will be last" (Luke 13:23–30, Jesus quotes from Psalm 6:8; cf. Matthew 7:13, 23; 8:11, 12; see Matthew 19:30; Luke 3:8).

Setting: On the way from Galilee to Jerusalem. While teaching in the cities and villages, Jesus responds to a question about who is saved. Some Pharisees ask Him to leave, claiming Herod Antipas (tetrarch of Galilee and Perea) seeks to kill Him.

And He said to them, "Go and tell that fox, 'Behold, I cast out demons and perform cures today and tomorrow, and the third *day* I reach My goal.' Nevertheless I must journey on today and tomorrow and the next *day*; for it cannot be that a prophet would perish outside of Jerusalem. O Jerusalem, Jerusalem, *the city* that kills the prophets and stones those sent to her! How often I wanted to gather your children together, just as a hen *gathers* her brood under her wings, and you would not *have it*! Behold, your house is left to you *desolate*; and I say to you, you will not see Me until *the time* comes when you say, 'BLESSED IS HE WHO COMES IN THE NAME OF THE LORD!'" (Luke 13:32–35, Jesus quotes from Psalm 118:26; cf. Matthew 23:37).

Setting: On the way from Galilee to Jerusalem. After responding to the Pharisees' scoffing at His teaching the disciples about stewardship and the permanence of the Law, Jesus conveys the story of the rich man and Lazarus.

"Now there was a rich man, and he habitually dressed in purple and fine linen, joyously living in splendor every day. And a poor man named Lazarus was laid at his gate, covered with sores, and longing to be fed with the *crumbs* which were falling from the rich man's table; besides, even the dogs were coming and licking his sores. Now the poor man died and was carried away by the angels to Abraham's bosom; and the rich man also died and was buried. In Hades he lifted up his eyes, being in torment, and saw Abraham far away and Lazarus in his bosom. And he cried out and said, 'Father Abraham, have mercy on me, and send Lazarus so that he may dip the tip of his finger in water and cool off my tongue, for I am in agony in this flame.' But Abraham said, 'Child, remember that during your life you received your good things, and likewise Lazarus bad things; but now he is being comforted here, and you are in agony. And besides all this, between us and you there is a great chasm fixed, so that those who wish to come over from here to you will not be able, and *that* none may cross over from there to us.' And he said, 'Then I beg you, father, that you send him to my father's house—for I have five brothers—in order that he may warn them, so that they will not also come to this place of torment.' But Abraham said, 'They have Moses and the Prophets; let them hear them.' But he said, 'No, father Abraham, but if someone goes to them from the dead, they will repent!' But he said to him, 'If they do not listen to Moses and the Prophets, they will not be persuaded even if someone rises from the dead' " (Luke 16:19–31; see Luke 3:8; 6:24; 16:1, 14).

Setting: On the way from Galilee to Jerusalem. After responding to Peter's statement about the disciples' personal sacrifice in following Him, Jesus tells them of the sacrifice He will make in Jerusalem.

Then He took the twelve aside and said to them, "Behold, we are going up to Jerusalem, and all things which are written through the prophets about the Son of Man will be accomplished. For He will be handed over to the Gentiles, and will be mocked and mistreated and spit upon, and after they have scourged Him, they will kill Him; and the third day He will rise again" (Luke 18:31–33; cf. Matthew 20:17–19; Mark 10:32–34).

Setting: On the road to Emmaus. After rising from the tomb on the third day after being crucified, Jesus appears to two of His followers (who have heard reports the tomb is empty) and elaborates on the purpose of His coming to earth.

And He said to them, "O foolish men and slow of heart to believe in all that the prophets have spoken! Was it not necessary for the Christ to suffer these things and to enter into His glory?" (Luke 24:25, 26).

Setting: Jerusalem. After rising from the tomb on the third day after being crucified, and appearing to two of His followers on the road to Emmaus, Jesus gives instruction to His disciples (except Thomas) about His mission on earth and the promise of future power from God.

Now He said to them, "These are My words which I spoke to you while I was still with you, that all things which are written about Me in the Law of Moses and the Prophets and the Psalms must be fulfilled." Then He opened their minds to understand the Scriptures, and He said to them, "Thus it is written, that the Christ would suffer and rise again from the dead the third day, and that repentance for forgiveness of sins would be proclaimed in His name to all the nations, beginning from Jerusalem. You are witnesses of these things. And behold, I am sending forth the promise of My Father upon you; but you are to stay in the city until you are clothed with power from on high" (Luke 24:44–49; see Matthew 28:19, 20; Acts 1:8).

Setting: Capernaum of Galilee. After Jesus informs the people whom He miraculously fed with a lad's five loaves and two fish how they might receive the bread out of heaven, the Jewish religious leaders grumble when the Lord claims that He came down out of heaven.

Therefore the Jews were grumbling about Him, because He said, "I am the bread that came down out of heaven." They were saying, "Is not this Jesus, the son of Joseph, whose father and mother we know? How does He now say, 'I have come down out of heaven'?" Jesus answered and said to them, "Do not grumble among yourselves. No one can come to Me unless the Father who sent Me draws him; and I will raise him up on the last day. It is written in the prophets, 'AND THEY SHALL ALL BE TAUGHT OF GOD.' Everyone who has heard and learned from the Father, comes to Me. Not that anyone has seen the Father, except the One who is from God; He has seen the Father. Truly, truly, I say to you, he who believes has eternal life. I am the bread of life. Your fathers ate the manna in the wilderness, and they died. This is the bread which comes down out of heaven, so that one may eat of it and not die. I am the living bread that came down out of heaven; if anyone eats of this bread, he will live forever; and the bread also which I will give for the life of the world is My flesh" (John 6:41–51, Jesus quotes from Isaiah 54:13; see John 1:18, 29; 3:36; 7:27).

PROPHETS, BLOOD OF THE (Also see MARTYRDOM; and MARTYRS)

Setting: The temple in Jerusalem. After the Jewish religious leaders test Him with questions, Jesus pronounces the eighth of eight woes upon them in front of the crowds and His disciples.

"Woe to you, scribes and Pharisees, hypocrites! For you build the tombs of the prophets and adorn the monuments of the righteous, and say, 'If we had been *living* in the days of our fathers, we would not have been partners with them in *shedding* the blood of the prophets.' So you testify against yourselves, that you are sons of those who murdered the prophets. Fill up, then, the measure *of the guilt* of you fathers. You serpents, you brood of vipers, how will you escape the sentence of hell? Therefore, behold, I am sending you prophets and wise men and scribes; some of them you will kill and crucify, and some of them you will scourge in your synagogues, and persecute from city to city, so that upon you may fall *the guilt of* all the righteous blood shed on earth, from the blood of righteous Abel to the blood of Zechariah, the son of Berechiah, whom you murdered between the temple and the altar. Truly I say to you, all these things will come upon this generation" (Matthew 23:29–36; cf. 2 Chronicles 24:21; Zechariah 1:1; Matthew 3:7; Luke 11:47–52; see Matthew 10:23).

PROPHETS, FALSE (Also see CHRISTS, FALSE; DECEPTION; and TEACHERS, FALSE)

Setting: Galilee. During the early part of His ministry, Jesus preaches the Sermon on the Mount to His disciples and the multitudes.

"Beware of the false prophets, who come to you in sheep's clothing, but inwardly are ravenous wolves. You will know them by their fruits. Grapes are not gathered from *bushes* nor figs from thistles, are they? So every good tree bears good fruit, but the bad tree bears bad fruit. A good tree cannot produce bad fruit, nor can a bad tree produce good fruit. Every tree that does not bear good fruit is cut down and thrown into the fire. So then, you will know them by their fruits" (Matthew 7:15–20; cf. Matthew 3:10; Matthew 12:33, 35; Matthew 24:11, 24; Luke 6:43, 44; see 2 Peter 2:1).

[FALSE PROPHETS from Lord, Lord, did we not prophesy in Your name, and in Your name cast out demons, and in Your name perform many miracles?' And then I will declare to them, 'I never knew you]

Setting: Galilee. During the early part of His ministry, Jesus preaches the Sermon on the Mount to His disciples and the multitudes.

"Not everyone who says to Me, 'Lord, Lord,' will enter the kingdom of heaven, but he who does the will of My Father who is in heaven *will enter.* Many will say to Me on that day, 'Lord, Lord, did we not prophesy in Your name, and in Your name cast out demons, and in Your name perform many miracles?' And then I will declare to them, 'I never knew you, DEPART FROM ME, YOU WHO PRACTICE LAWLESSNESS'" (Matthew 7:21–23, Jesus quotes from Psalm 6:8; cf. Matthew 25:11–13; see Luke 6:46; 2 Peter 2:1).

Setting: The Mount of Olives, just east of Jerusalem. During His Olivet Discourse, Jesus answers His disciples' questions as to when the temple will be destroyed and Jerusalem overrun, along with the signs of His coming and the end of the age.

And Jesus answered and said to them, "See to it that no one misleads you. For many will come in My name, saying, 'I am the Christ,' and will mislead many. You will be hearing of wars and rumors of wars. See that you are not frightened, for *those things* must take place, but *that* is not yet the end. For nation will rise against nation, and kingdom against kingdom, and in various places there will be famines and earthquakes. But all these things are *merely* the beginning of birth pangs. Then they will deliver you to tribulation, and will kill you, and you will be hated by all nations because of My name. At that time many will fall away and will betray one another and hate one another. Many false prophets will arise and will mislead many. Because lawlessness is increased, most people's love will grow cold. But the one who endures to the end, he will be saved. This gospel of the kingdom shall be preached in the whole world as a testimony to all the nations, and then the end will come" (Matthew 24:4–14; cf. Jeremiah 29:8; Matthew 7:15; 10:17, 22; Mark 13:3–13; Luke 21:7–19; Revelation 6:4; see 2 Peter 2:1).

Setting: The Mount of Olives, just east of Jerusalem. During His Olivet Discourse, Jesus answers His disciples' questions as to when the temple will be destroyed and Jerusalem overrun, along with the signs of His coming and the end of the age.

"Therefore when you see the ABOMINATION OF DESOLATION which was spoken of through Daniel the prophet, standing in the holy place (let the reader understand), then those who are in Judea must flee to the mountains. Whoever is on the housetop must not go down to get the things that are in his house. Whoever is in the field must not turn back to get his cloak. But woe to those who are pregnant and to those who are nursing babies in those days! But pray that your flight will not be in the winter, or on a Sabbath. For then there will be a great tribulation, such as has not occurred since the beginning of the world until now, nor ever will. Unless those days had been cut short, no life would have been saved; but for the sake of the elect those days will be cut short. Then if anyone says to you, 'Behold, here is the Christ,' or "There *He is,*' do not believe *him.* For false Christs and false prophets will arise and will show great signs and wonders, so as to mislead, if possible, even the elect. Behold, I have told you in advance. So if they say to you, 'Behold, He is in the wilderness,' do not go out, *or,* 'Behold, He is in the inner rooms,' do not believe *them.* For just as the lightning comes from the east and flashes even to the west, so will the coming of the Son of Man be. Wherever the corpse is, there the vultures will gather" (Matthew 24:15–28, Jesus quotes from Daniel 9:27; cf. Daniel 12:1; Mark 13:14–23; Luke 17:22–31; 21:20–24; Luke 23:29; see John 4:48; 2 Peter 2:1).

Setting: On the Mount of Olives, east of the temple in Jerusalem. After predicting the temple's destruction, Jesus responds during His Olivet Discourse to questions from Peter, James, John, and Andrew about other future events.

"But when you see the ABOMINATION OF DESOLATION standing where it should not be (let the reader understand), then those who are in Judea must flee to the mountains. The one who is on the housetop must not go down, or go in to get anything out of his house; and the one who is in the field must not turn back to get his coat. But woe to those who are pregnant and to those who are nursing babies in those days! But pray that it may not happen in winter. For those days will be a *time of* tribulation such as has not occurred since the beginning of the creation which God created until now, and never will. Unless the Lord had shortened *those* days, no life would have been saved; but for the sake of the elect, whom He chose, He shortened the days. And then if anyone says to you, 'Behold, here is the Christ'; or, 'Behold, *He is* there', do not believe *him*; for false Christs and false prophets will arise, and will show signs and wonders, in order to lead astray, if possible, the elect. But take heed; behold, I have told you everything in advance" (Mark 13:14–23; cf. Matthew 24:15–28; Luke 21:20–24; see Daniel 9:27; 12:1; Luke 17:31; 2 Peter 2:1).

Setting: Galilee. After selecting His twelve disciples, Jesus teaches the Beatitudes (part of the Sermon on the Mount) to those disciples and a great throng of people from Judea, Jerusalem, and the central coastal region of Tyre and Sidon.

"Woe *to you* when all men speak well of you, for their fathers used to treat the false prophets in the same way" (Luke 6:26; see Matthew 7:15; 24:11, 24; 2 Peter 2:1).

PROPHETS, LAW AND THE (Also see OLD TESTAMENT; PROPHETS, SCRIPTURES OF THE; SCRIPTURE; and SCRIPTURES)

Setting: Galilee. During the early part of His ministry, Jesus preaches the Sermon on the Mount to His disciples and the multitudes.

"Ask, and it will be given to you; seek, and you will find; knock, and it will be opened to you. For everyone who asks receives, and he who seeks finds, and to him who knocks it will be opened. Or what man is there among you who, when his son asks for a loaf, will give him a stone? Or if he asks for a fish, he will not give him a snake, will he? If you then, being evil, know how to give good gifts to your children, how much more will your Father who is in heaven give what is good to those who ask Him! In everything, therefore, treat people the same way you want them to treat you, for this is the Law and the Prophets" (Matthew 7:7–12; cf. Matthew 22:40; Luke 6:31; 11:9–13; see Psalm 84:11).

Setting: The temple in Jerusalem. A Pharisee lawyer asks Jesus which is the great commandment of the Law, in order to test Him as He teaches.

And He said to him, " 'YOU SHALL LOVE THE LORD YOUR GOD WITH ALL YOUR HEART, AND WITH ALL YOUR SOUL, AND WITH ALL YOUR MIND.' This is the great and foremost commandment. The second is like it, 'YOU SHALL LOVE YOUR NEIGHBOR AS YOURSELF.' On these two commandments depend the whole Law and the Prophets" (Matthew 22:37–40; Jesus quotes from Leviticus 19:18; Deuteronomy 6:5; cf. Mark 12:28–34).

Setting: On the way from Galilee to Jerusalem. The Lord responds to the Pharisees' scoffing at His teaching His disciples about stewardship.

And He said to them, "You are those who justify yourselves in the sight of men, but God knows your hearts; for that which is highly esteemed among men is detestable in the sight of God. The Law and the Prophets *were proclaimed* until John; since that time the gospel of the kingdom of God has been preached, and everyone is forcing his way into it. But is it easier for heaven and earth to pass away than for one stroke of a letter of the Law to fail" (Luke 16:15–17; cf. Matthew 5:18; see 1 Samuel 16:7; Matthew 4:23; 11:11–14).

PROPHETS, SCRIPTURES OF THE (Also see OLD TESTAMENT; PROPHETS, LAW AND THE; SCRIPTURE; and SCRIPTURES)

Setting: Gethsemane on the Mount of Olives, east of the temple in Jerusalem. As Jesus submits to His Father's will and allows Judas to betray Him, the Lord reveals that this incident is a fulfillment of prophecy.

At that time Jesus said to the crowds, "Have you come out with swords and clubs to arrest Me as *you would* against a robber? Every day I used to sit in the temple teaching and you did not seize Me. But all this has taken place to fulfill the Scriptures of the prophets" (Matthew 26:55, 56; cf. Mark 14:48, 49; Luke 22:52, 53).

PROPHETS, TOMBS OF THE

Setting: The temple in Jerusalem. After the Jewish religious leaders test Him with questions, Jesus pronounces the eighth of eight woes upon them in front of the crowds and His disciples.

"Woe to you, scribes and Pharisees, hypocrites! For you build the tombs of the prophets and adorn the monuments of the righteous, and say, 'If we had been *living* in the days of our fathers, we would not have been partners with them in *shedding* the blood of the prophets.' So you testify against yourselves, that you are sons of those who murdered the prophets. Fill up, then, the measure *of the guilt* of you fathers. You serpents, you brood of vipers, how will you escape the sentence of hell? Therefore, behold, I am sending you prophets and wise men and scribes; some of them you will kill and crucify, and some of them you will scourge in your synagogues, and persecute from city to city, so that upon you may fall *the guilt of* all the righteous blood shed on earth, from the blood of righteous Abel to the blood of Zechariah, the son of Berechiah, whom you murdered between the temple and the altar. Truly I say to you, all these things will come upon this generation" (Matthew 23:29–36; cf. 2 Chronicles 24:21; Zechariah

1:1; Matthew 3:7; Luke 11:47–52; see Matthew 10:23).

Setting: On the way from Galilee to Jerusalem. After Jesus pronounces woes upon the Pharisees, a lawyer replies that His remarks are an insult to lawyers, too.

But He said, "Woe to you lawyers as well! For you weigh men down with burdens hard to bear, while you yourselves will not even touch the burdens with one of your fingers. Woe to you! For you build the tombs of the prophets, and *it was* your fathers *who* killed them. So you are witnesses and approve the deeds of your fathers; because it was they who killed them, and you build *their tombs*. For this reason also the wisdom of God said, 'I will send them prophets and apostles, and *some* of them they will kill and *some* they will persecute, so that the blood of all the prophets, shed since the foundation of the world, may be charged against this generation, from the blood of Abel to the blood of Zechariah, who was killed between the altar and the house *of God*; yes, I tell you, it shall be charged against this generation.' Woe to you lawyers! For you have taken away the key of knowledge; you yourselves did not enter, and you hindered those who were entering" (Luke 11:46–52; cf. Matthew 23:29–32; see 2 Chronicles 24:20, 21; Matthew 23:4, 13).

PROSELYTE

Setting: The temple in Jerusalem. After the Jewish religious leaders test Him with questions, Jesus pronounces the third of eight woes upon them in front of the crowds and His disciples.

"Woe to you, scribes and Pharisees, hypocrites, because you travel around on sea and land to make one proselyte; and when he becomes one, you make him twice as much a son of hell as yourselves" (Matthew 23:15).

PROSTITUTES (Also see ADULTERY; FORNICATIONS; IMMORALITY; and SEXUAL SIN)

Setting: The temple in Jerusalem. Jesus delivers a parable to the chief priests and elders after they question His authority.

"But what do you think? A man had two sons, and he came to the first and said, 'Son, go work today in the vineyard.' And he answered, 'I will not'; but afterward he regretted it and went. The man came to the second and said the same thing; and he answered, 'I *will,* sir'; but he did not go. Which of the two sons did the will of his father?" They said, "The first." Jesus said to them, "Truly, I say to you that the tax collectors and prostitutes will get into the kingdom of God before you. For John came to you in the way of righteousness and you did not believe him; but the tax collectors and prostitutes did believe him; and you, seeing *this,* did not even feel remorse afterward so as to believe him" (Matthew 21:28–32; cf. Luke 7:29, 30, 37–50).

Setting: On the way from Galilee to Jerusalem. Jesus conveys the illustration of the prodigal son because the Pharisees and scribes complain He associates with tax collectors and sinners.

And He said, "A man had two sons. The younger of them said to his father, 'Father, give me the share of the estate that falls to me.' So he divided his wealth between them. And not many days later, the younger son gathered everything together and went on a journey into a distant country, and there he squandered his estate with loose living. Now when he had spent everything, a severe famine occurred in that country, and he began to be impoverished. So he went and hired himself out to one of the citizens of that country, and he sent him into his fields to feed swine. And he would have gladly filled his stomach with the pods that the swine were eating, and no one was giving *anything* to him. But when he came to his senses, he said, 'How many of my father's hired men have more than enough bread, but I am dying here with hunger! I will get up and go to my father, and will say to him, "Father, I have sinned against heaven, and in your sight; I am no longer worthy to be called your son; make me as one of your hired men."' So he got up and came to his father. But while he was still a long way off, his father saw him and felt compassion *for him,* and ran and embraced him and kissed him. And the son said to him, "Father, I have sinned against heaven and in your sight; I am no longer worthy to be called your son.' But the father said to his slaves, 'Quickly bring out the best robe and put it on him, and put a ring on his hand and sandals on his feet; and bring the fattened calf, kill it, and let us eat and celebrate; for this son of mine was dead and has come to life again; he was lost and has been found.' And they began to celebrate. Now his older son was in the field, when he came and approached the house, he heard music and dancing. And he summoned one of the servants and *began* inquiring what these things could be. And he said to him, 'Your brother has come, and your father has killed the fattened calf because he has received him back safe and sound.' But he became angry and was not willing to go in; and his father came out and *began* pleading with him. But he answered and said to his father, 'Look! For so many years I have been serving you and I have never neglected a command of yours; and *yet* you have never given me a young goat, so that I might celebrate with my friends; but when this son of yours came, who has devoured your wealth with prostitutes, you killed the fattened calf for him.' And he said to him, 'Son, you have always been with me, and all that is mine is yours. But we had to celebrate and rejoice, for this brother of yours was dead and *has begun* to live, and was lost and has been found'" (Luke 15:11–32; see Proverb 29:2).

PROTECTION

Setting: On the way from Galilee to Jerusalem. After telling His disciples of His second coming, Jesus instructs them about persistence in prayer.

Now He was telling them a parable to show that at all times they ought to pray and not to lose heart, saying, "In a certain city there was a judge who did not fear God and did not respect man. There was a widow in that city, and she kept coming to him, saying, 'Give me legal protection from my opponent.' For a while he was unwilling; but afterward he said to himself, 'Even though I do not fear God nor respect man, yet because this woman bothers me, I will give her legal protection, otherwise by continually coming she will wear me out.'" And the Lord said, "Hear what the unrighteous judge said; now, will not God bring about justice for His elect who cry to Him day and night, and will He delay long over them? I tell you that He will bring about justice for them quickly. However, when the Son of Man comes, will He find faith on the earth?" (Luke 18:1–8; see Luke 11:5–10).

[PROTECTION from keep them and guarded]

Setting: Jerusalem. Before the Passover, after giving His disciples hope that in the midst of tribulation they will have His peace, Jesus prays His high-priestly prayer.

Jesus spoke these things; and lifting up His eyes to heaven, He said, "Father, the hour has come; glorify Your Son, that the Son may glorify You, even as You gave Him authority over all flesh, that to all whom You have given Him, He may give eternal life. This is eternal life, that they may know You, the only true God, and Jesus Christ whom You have sent. I glorified You on the earth, having accomplished the work which You have given Me to do. Now, Father, glorify Me together with Yourself, with the glory which I had with You before the world was. I have manifested Your name to the men whom You gave Me out of the world; they were Yours and You gave them to Me, and they have kept Your word. Now they have come to know that everything You have given Me is from You; for the words which You gave Me I have given to them; and they received *them* and truly understood that I came forth from You, and they believed You sent Me. I ask on their behalf; I do not ask on behalf of the world, but of those whom You have given Me; for they are Yours; and all things that are Mine are Yours, and Yours are Mine; and I have been glorified in them. I am no longer in the world; and *yet* they themselves are in the world, and I come to You. Holy Father, keep them in Your name, *the name* which You have given Me, that they may be even as We *are*. While I was with them, I was keeping them in Your name which You have given Me; and I guarded them and not one of them perished but the son of perdition, so that the Scripture would be fulfilled" (John 17:1–12; see Luke 22:32; John 1:1; 3:35; 4:34; 5:44; 6:37–39, 70; 8:42; 11:41; 12:49; 13:18, 31; 16:15; Philippians 2:9).

[PROTECTION from I lost not one]

Setting: Jerusalem. After Jesus prays His high-priestly prayer on behalf of His disciples, they all go over the ravine of the Kidron to a garden where Judas waits to seize the Lord with a Roman cohort and officers from the chief priests and the Pharisees.

So Jesus, knowing all the things that were coming upon Him, went forth and said to them, "Whom do you seek?" They answered Him, "Jesus the Nazarene." He said to them, "I am *He*." And Judas also, who was betraying Him, was standing with them. So when He said to them, "I am *He*," they drew back and fell to the ground. Therefore He again asked them, "Whom do you seek?" And they said, "Jesus the Nazarene." Jesus answered, "I told you that I am *He*; so if you seek Me, let these go their way," to fulfill the word which He spoke, "Of those whom You have given Me I lost not one" (John 18:4–9; see John 6:64; 17:12).

PROTECTION, LEGAL (See PROTECTION)

PROTEST

Setting: On the way from Galilee to Jerusalem. The Lord appoints seventy followers and sends them out in pairs to every place He Himself will soon visit.

And He was saying to them, "The harvest is plentiful, but the laborers are few; therefore beseech the Lord of the harvest to send out laborers into His harvest. Go; behold, I send you out as lambs in the midst of wolves. Carry no money belt, no bag, no shoes; and greet no one on the way. Whatever house you enter, first say, 'Peace be to this house.' If a man of peace is there, your peace will rest on him; but if not, it will return to you. Stay in that house, eating and drinking what they give you; for the laborer is worthy of his wages. Do not keep moving from house to house. Whatever city you enter and they receive you, eat what is set before you; and heal those in it who are sick, and say to them, 'The kingdom of God has come near to you.' But whatever city you enter and they do not receive you, go out into its streets and say, 'Even the dust of your city which clings to our feet we wipe off *in protest* against you; yet be sure of this, that the kingdom of God has come near.' I say to you, it will be more tolerable in that day for Sodom than for that city" (Luke 10:2–12; see Genesis 19:24–28; Matthew 9:37, 38, 10:9–14, 16; 1 Corinthians 10:27).

PROVERB

Setting: The synagogue in Jesus' hometown of Nazareth in Galilee. At the beginning of His public ministry, Jesus comments to the congregation after reading on the Sabbath from the book of the prophet Isaiah.

And He said to them, "No doubt you will quote this proverb to Me, 'Physician, heal yourself! Whatever we heard was done at Capernaum, do here in your hometown as well.'" And He said, "Truly I say to you, no prophet is welcome in his hometown. But I say to you in truth, there were many widows in Israel in the days of Elijah, when the sky was shut up for three years and six months, when a great famine came over all the land; and yet Elijah was sent to none of them, but only to Zarephath, *in the land* of Sidon, to a woman who was a widow. And there were many lepers in Israel in the time of Elisha the prophet; and none of them was cleansed, but only Naaman the Syrian" (Luke 4:23–27; Jesus refers to 1 Kings 17:1, 9; 2 Kings 5:1–14; see Matthew 13:53–58).

PROVISION, GOD'S (Also see BREAD, DAILY; GOD, DEPENDENCE ON; and NEEDS)

[GOD'S PROVISION from your heavenly Father knows that you need all these things]

Setting: Galilee. During the early part of His ministry, Jesus preaches the Sermon on the Mount to His disciples and the multitudes.

"For this reason I say to you, do not be worried about your life, *as to* what you will eat or what you will drink; nor for your body, *as to* what you will put on. Is not life more than food, and the body more than clothing? Look at the birds of the air, that they do not sow, nor reap nor gather into barns, and *yet* your heavenly Father feeds them. Are you not worth much more than they? And who of you by being worried can add a *single* hour to his life? And why are you worried about clothing? Observe how the lilies of the field grow; they do not toil nor do they spin, yet I say to you that not even Solomon in all his glory clothed himself like one of these. But if God so clothes the grass of the field, which is *alive* today and tomorrow is thrown into the furnace, *will He* not much more *clothe* you? You of little faith! Do not worry then, saying 'What will we eat?' or 'What will we drink?' or 'What will be wear for clothing?" For the Gentiles eagerly seek all these things; for your heavenly Father knows that you need all these things. But seek first His kingdom and His righteousness, and all these things will be added to you. So do not worry about tomorrow; for tomorrow will care for itself. Each day has enough trouble of its own" (Matthew 6:25–34; cf. Luke 12:22–31; see 1 Kings 10:4–7; Job 35:11; Matthew 8:26).

[GOD'S PROVISION from how much more will your Father who is in heaven give what is good to those who ask Him]

Setting: Galilee. During the early part of His ministry, Jesus preaches the Sermon on the Mount to His disciples and the multitudes.

"Ask, and it will be given to you; seek, and you will find; knock, and it will be opened to you. For everyone who asks receives, and he who seeks finds, and to him who knocks it will be opened. Or what man is there among you who, when his son asks for a loaf, will give him a stone? Or if he asks for a fish, he will not give him a snake, will he? If you then, being evil, know how to give good gifts to your children, how much more will your Father who is in heaven give what is good to those who ask Him! In everything, therefore, treat people the same way you want them to treat you, for this is the Law and the Prophets" (Matthew 7:7–12; cf. Matthew 22:40; Luke 6:31; 11:9–13; see Psalm 84:11).

[GOD'S PROVISION from your Father knows that you need these things]
Setting: On the way from Galilee to Jerusalem. After giving a parable about riches and greed, Jesus comforts the crowd and His disciples. The scribes and Pharisees turn hostile and question Him repeatedly in an attempt to catch Him in something He might say.

And He said to His disciples, "For this reason I say to you, do not worry about *your* life, *as to* what you will eat; nor for your body, *as to* what you will put on. For life is more than food, and the body more than clothing. Consider the ravens, for they neither sow nor reap; they have no storeroom nor barn, and *yet* God feeds them; how much more valuable you are than the birds! And which of you by worrying can add a *single* hour to his life's span? If then you cannot do even a very little thing, why do you worry about other matters? Consider the lilies, how they grow: they neither toil nor spin; but I tell you, not even Solomon in all his glory clothed himself like one of these. But if God so clothes the grass in the field, which is *alive* today and tomorrow is thrown into the furnace, how much more *will He clothe* you? You men of little faith! And do not seek what you will eat and what you will drink, and do not keep worrying. For all these things the nations of the world eagerly seek; but your Father knows that you need these things. But seek His kingdom, and these things will be added to you. Do not be afraid, little flock, for your Father has chosen gladly to give you the kingdom" (Luke 12:22–32; cf. Matthew 6:25–33; see 1 Kings 10:4–7; Job 38:41).

[GOD'S PROVISION from if you ask the Father for anything in My name, He will give it to you]
Setting: Jerusalem. Before the Passover, after empathizing with His disciples' sadness over His prophecies and giving them the hope for the future, Jesus conveys promises about praying in His name.

"In that day you will not question Me about anything. Truly, truly, I say to you, if you ask the Father for anything in My name, He will give it to you. Until now you have asked for nothing in My name; ask and you will receive, so that your joy may be made full. These things I have spoken to you in figurative language; an hour is coming when I will no longer speak to you in figurative language, but will tell you plainly of the Father. In that day you will ask in My name, and I do not say to you that I will request of the Father on your behalf; for the Father Himself loves you, because you have loved Me and have believed that I came forth from the Father. I came forth from the Father and have come into the world; I am leaving the world again and going to the Father" (John 16:23–28; see Matthew 13:34; John 8:42; 13:1, 3; 14:14, 21, 23; 15:16).

PRUDENCE

[PRUDENCE from prudent]
Setting: On the Mount of Olives, just east of Jerusalem. During His Olivet Discourse, after answering His disciples' questions as to when the temple will be destroyed and Jerusalem overrun, along with the signs of His coming and the end of the age, Jesus reemphasizes to His disciples that they should be on the alert for His return.

"Then the kingdom of heaven will be comparable to ten virgins, who took their lamps and went out to meet the bridegroom. Five of them were foolish, and five were prudent. For when the foolish took their lamps, they took no oil with them, but the prudent took oil in flasks along with their lamps. Now while the bridegroom was delaying, they all got drowsy and *began* to sleep. But at midnight there was a shout, 'Behold, the bridegroom! Come out to meet *him*.' Then all those virgins rose and trimmed their lamps. The foolish said to the prudent, 'Give us some of your oil, for our lamps are going out.' But the prudent answered, 'No, there will not be enough for us and you *too;* go instead to the dealers and buy *some* for yourselves.' And while they were going away to make the purchase, the bridegroom came, and those who were ready went in with him to the wedding feast; and the door was shut. Later the other virgins also came, saying, 'Lord, lord, open up for us.' But he answered, 'Truly I say to you, I do not know you.' Be on the alert then, for you do not know the day nor the hour" (Matthew 25:1–13; cf. Matthew 24:42; Luke 12:35; see Matthew 7:21, 24).

PSALMS

Setting: The temple in Jerusalem. While ministering a few days before His crucifixion, after some of the Sadducees question Him about the resurrection, Jesus poses a question to the scribes, who say He answered well.

Then He said to them, "How *is it that* they say the Christ is David's son? For David himself says in the book of Psalms, 'THE LORD SAID TO MY LORD, SIT AT MY RIGHT HAND, UNTIL I MAKE YOUR ENEMIES A FOOTSTOOL FOR YOUR FEET.' Therefore David calls Him 'Lord,' and how is He his son?" (Luke 20:41–44, Jesus quotes from Psalm 110:1; cf. Matthew 22:41–46; Mark 12:35–37).

Setting: Jerusalem. After rising from the tomb on the third day after being crucified, and appearing to two of His followers on the road to Emmaus, Jesus gives instruction to His disciples (except Thomas) about His mission on earth and the promise of future power from God.

Now He said to them, "These are My words which I spoke to you while I was still with you, that all things which are written about Me in the Law of Moses and the Prophets and the Psalms must be fulfilled." Then He opened their minds to understand the Scriptures, and He said to them, "Thus it is written, that the Christ would suffer and rise again from the dead the third day, and that repentance for forgiveness of sins would be proclaimed in His name to all the nations, beginning from Jerusalem. You are witnesses of these things. And behold, I am sending forth the promise of My Father upon you; but you are to stay in the city until you are clothed with power from on high" (Luke 24:44–49; see Matthew 28:19, 20; Acts 1:8).

PUNISHMENT, DEGREES OF (Also see CONDEMNATION; JUDGMENT, DIVINE; and PUNISHMENT, ETERNAL)

[DEGREES OF PUNISHMENT from will receive many lashes]

Setting: On the way from Galilee to Jerusalem. When Jesus uses a parable to challenge the crowd and His disciples to be ready for His return, Peter asks Him whom He is addressing.

And the Lord said, "Who then is the faithful and sensible steward, whom his master will put in charge of his servants, to give them their rations at the proper time? Blessed is that slave whom his master finds so doing when he comes. Truly I say to you that he will put him in charge of all his possessions. But if that slave says in his heart, 'My master will be a long time in coming,' and begins to beat the slaves, *both* men and women, and to eat and drink and get drunk; the master of that slave will come on a day when he does not expect *him* and at an hour he does not know, and will cut him in pieces, and assign him a place with the unbelievers. And that slave who knew his master's will and did not get ready or act in accord with his will, will receive many lashes, but the one who did know *it,* and committed deeds worthy of flogging, will receive but few. From everyone who has been given much, much will be required; and to whom they entrusted much, of him they will ask all the more" (Luke 12:42–48; cf. Matthew 24:45–51; see Leviticus 5:17).

PUNISHMENT, ETERNAL (Also see FIRE, ETERNAL; FIRE, FURNACE OF; FIRE, UNQUENCHABLE; GOD, SEPARATION FROM; HELL; and JUDGMENT, DIVINE)

Setting: On the Mount of Olives, just east of Jerusalem. During His Olivet Discourse, after answering His disciples' questions as to when the temple will be destroyed and Jerusalem overrun, along with the signs of His coming and the end of the age, Jesus reveals the future judgments following His return.

"But when the Son of Man comes in His glory, and all the angels with Him, then He will sit on His glorious throne. All the nations will be gathered before Him; and He will separate them from one another, as the shepherd separates the sheep from the goats; and He will put the sheep on His right, and the goats on the left. Then the King will say to those on His right, 'Come, you who are blessed of My Father, inherit the kingdom prepared for you from the foundation of the world. 'For I was hungry, and you gave Me *something* to eat; I was thirsty, and you gave Me *something* to drink; I was a stranger, and you invited Me in; naked, and you clothed Me; I was sick, and you visited Me; I was in prison, and you came to Me.' Then the righteous will answer Him, 'Lord, when did we see You hungry and feed You, or thirsty, and give you *something* to drink? And when did we see You a stranger, and invite You in, or naked, and clothe You? When did we see You sick, or in prison, and come to You?' The King will answer and say to them, 'Truly I say to you, to the extent that you did it to one of these brothers of Mine, *even* the least *of them,* you did it to Me.' Then

He will also say to those on His left, 'Depart from Me, accursed ones, into the eternal fire which has been prepared for the devil and his angels; for I was hungry, and you gave Me *nothing* to eat; I was thirsty, and you gave Me nothing to drink; I was a stranger, and you did not invite Me in; naked, and you did not clothe Me; sick, and in prison, and you did not visit Me.' Then they themselves also will answer, 'Lord, when did we see You hungry, or thirsty, or a stranger, or naked, or sick, or in prison, and did not take care of You?' Then He will answer them, 'Truly I say to you, to the extent that you did not do it to one of the least of these, you did not do it to Me.' These will go away into eternal punishment, but the righteous into eternal life" (Matthew 25:31–46; see Matthew 7:23; 16:27; 19:29).

PUPIL (Also see DISCIPLE)

Setting: Galilee. After selecting His twelve disciples, Jesus teaches the Sermon on the Mount to those disciples and a great throng of people from Judea, Jerusalem, and the central coastal region of Tyre and Sidon.

And He also spoke a parable to them: "A blind man cannot guide a blind man, can he? Will they not both fall into a pit? A pupil is not above his teacher; but everyone, after he has been fully trained, will be like his teacher. Why do you look at the speck that is in your brother's eye, but do not notice the log that is in your own eye? Or how can you say to your brother, 'Brother, let me take out the speck that is in your eye,' when you yourself do not see the log that is in your own eye? You hypocrite, first take the log out of your own eye, and then you will see clearly to take out the speck that is in your brother's eye. For there is no good tree which produces bad fruit, nor, on the other hand, a bad tree which produces good fruit. For each tree is known by its own fruit. For men do not gather figs from thorns, nor do they pick grapes from a briar bush. The good man out of the good treasure of his heart brings forth what is good; and the evil *man* out of the evil *treasure* brings forth what is evil; for his mouth speaks from that which fills his heart" (Luke 6:39–45; cf. Matthew 7:3–6. 16, 18, 20; 12:35; see Matthew 10:24; 15:14; Luke 6:12–19).

PURE

Setting: Galilee. Early in His ministry, Jesus presents the Beatitudes (part of the Sermon on the Mount) to His disciples and the gathered crowds from Galilee, Decapolis, Jerusalem, Judea, and beyond the Jordan.

"Blessed are the pure in heart, for they shall see God" (Matthew 5:8; see Matthew 13:35).

PURPLE

Setting: On the way from Galilee to Jerusalem. After responding to the Pharisees' scoffing at His teaching the disciples about stewardship and the permanence of the Law, Jesus conveys the story of the rich man and Lazarus.

"Now there was a rich man, and he habitually dressed in purple and fine linen, joyously living in splendor every day. And a poor man named Lazarus was laid at his gate, covered with sores, and longing to be fed with the *crumbs* which were falling from the rich man's table; besides, even the dogs were coming and licking his sores. Now the poor man died and was carried away by the angels to Abraham's bosom; and the rich man also died and was buried. In Hades he lifted up his eyes, being in torment, and saw Abraham far away and Lazarus in his bosom. And he cried out and said, 'Father Abraham, have mercy on me, and send Lazarus so that he may dip the tip of his finger in water and cool off my tongue, for I am in agony in this flame.' But Abraham said, 'Child, remember that during your life you received your good things, and likewise Lazarus bad things; but now he is being comforted here, and you are in agony. And besides all this, between us and you there is a great chasm fixed, so that those who wish to come over from here to you will not be able, and *that* none may cross over from there to us.' And he said, 'Then I beg you, father, that you send him to my father's house—for I have five brothers—in order that he may warn them, so that they will not also come to this place of torment.' But Abraham said, 'They have Moses and the Prophets; let them hear them.' But he said, 'No, father Abraham, but if someone goes to them from the dead, they will repent!' But he said to him, 'If they do not listen to Moses and the Prophets, they will not be persuaded even if someone rises from the dead' " (Luke 16:19–31; see Luke 3:8; 6:24; 16:1, 14).

PURPOSE

Setting: Caesarea. Luke, writing in Acts, gives Paul's retelling of his conversion to Christ as he appears before King Agrippa following his hearing before the Jewish Council in Jerusalem and arrest by the Roman commander (on his way to Rome after the apostle's third missionary journey).

"And when we had fallen to the ground, I heard a voice saying to me in the Hebrew dialect, 'Saul, Saul, why are you persecuting Me? It is hard for you to kick against the goads.' And I said, 'Who are You, Lord?' And the Lord said, 'I am Jesus whom you are persecuting. But get up and stand on your feet; for this purpose I have appeared to you, to appoint you a minister and a witness not only to the things which you have seen, but also to the things in which I will appear to you; rescuing you from the *Jewish* people and from the Gentiles, to whom I am sending you, to open their eyes so that they may turn from darkness to light and from the dominion of Satan to God, that they may receive forgiveness of sins and an inheritance among those who have been sanctified by faith in Me' (Acts 26:14–18; see Isaiah 35:5; Acts 21:40; 22:14).

PURPOSE, JESUS' (See JESUS' PURPOSE)

PURPOSE IN LIFE (See FOLLOWING JESUS CHRIST; and TESTIMONY)

Q

QUEEN OF SHEBA (See SOUTH, QUEEN OF THE)

QUEEN OF THE SOUTH (Listed under SOUTH, QUEEN OF THE)

QUESTION

Setting: The temple in Jerusalem. After Jesus teaches about faith and forgiveness, utilizing a cursed fig tree as an object lesson, His authority is questioned by the chief priests, scribes, and elders.

And Jesus said to them, "I will ask you one question, and you answer Me, and *then* I will tell you by what authority I do these things. Was the baptism of John from heaven, or from men? Answer Me." They *began* reasoning among themselves, saying, "If we say 'From heaven,' He will say, 'Then why did you not believe him?' "But shall we say 'From men'?"—they were afraid of the people, for everyone considered John to have been a real prophet. Answering Jesus, they said, "We do not know." And Jesus said to them, "Nor will I tell you by what authority I do these things" (Mark 11:29–33; cf. Matthew 21:23–27; Luke 20:1–8).

Setting: The temple in Jerusalem. While Jesus ministers a few days before His crucifixion, with His conflict with the religious leaders of Israel escalating, the chief priests and the scribes question His authority to teach and preach.

Jesus answered and said to them, "I will also ask you a question, and you tell Me: Was the baptism of John from heaven or from men?" They reasoned among themselves, saying, "If we say, 'From heaven,' He will say, 'Why did you not believe him?' But if we say, 'From men,' all the people will stone us to death, for they are convinced that John was a prophet." So they answered that they did not know where *it came* from. And Jesus said to them, "Nor will I tell you by what authority I do these things" (Luke 20:3–8; cf. Matthew 21:23–27; Mark 11:27–33).

Setting: Jerusalem. After being arrested, having Peter deny Him, and being mocked and beaten, with His crucifixion imminent, Jesus appears before the Sanhedrin (Council of Elders).

"If You are the Christ, tell us." But He said to them, "If I tell you, you will not believe; and if I ask you a question, you will not answer. But from now on THE SON OF MAN WILL BE SEATED AT THE RIGHT HAND of the power OF GOD." And they all said, "Are You the Son of God, then? And He said to them, "Yes, I am" (Luke 22:67–70, Jesus quotes from Psalm 110:1; cf. Matthew 26:57–65; Mark 14:55–65).

Setting: Jerusalem. Before the Passover, after empathizing with His disciples' sadness over His prophecies and giving them the hope for the future, Jesus conveys promises about praying in His name.

"In that day you will not question Me about anything. Truly, truly, I say to you, if you ask the Father for anything in My name, He will give it to you. Until now you have asked for nothing in My name; ask and you will receive, so that your joy may be made full. These things I have spoken to you in figurative language; an hour is coming when I will no longer speak to you in figurative language, but will tell you plainly of the Father. In that day you will ask in My name, and I do not say to you that I will request of the Father on your behalf; for the Father Himself loves you, because you have loved Me and have believed that I came forth from the Father. I came forth from the Father and have come into the world; I am leaving the world again and going to the Father" (John 16:23–28; see Matthew 13:34; John 8:42; 13:1, 3; 14:14, 21, 23; 15:16).

Setting: Jerusalem. After Jesus is betrayed by Judas, and Peter denies he is the Lord's disciple, Annas, former high priest and father-in-law of the current high priest (Caiaphas), questions Jesus about His disciples and His teaching.

Jesus answered him, "I have spoken openly to the world; I always taught in synagogues and in the temple, where all the Jews come together; and I spoke nothing in secret. Why do you question Me? Question those who have heard what I spoke to them; they know what I said" (John 18:20, 21; see John 7:26).

QUOTATIONS (Also see WRITINGS)

Setting: The synagogue in Jesus' hometown of Nazareth in Galilee. At the beginning of His public ministry, Jesus comments to the congregation after reading on the Sabbath from the book of the prophet Isaiah.

[QUOTATIONS from quote]

And He said to them, "No doubt you will quote this proverb to Me, 'Physician, heal yourself! Whatever we heard was done at Capernaum, do here in your hometown as well.'" And He said, "Truly I say to you, no prophet is welcome in his hometown. But I say to you in truth, there were many widows in Israel in the days of Elijah, when the sky was shut up for three years and six months, when a great famine came over all the land; and yet Elijah was sent to none of them, but only to Zarephath, *in the land* of Sidon, to a woman who was a widow. And there were many lepers in Israel in the time of Elisha the prophet; and none of them was cleansed, but only Naaman the Syrian" (Luke 4:23–27; Jesus refers to 1 Kings 17:1, 9; 2 Kings 5:1–14; see Matthew 13:53–58).

QUOTATIONS FROM THE TEN COMMANDMENTS (See specific commandments such as ADULTERY; COVETING, DEEDS OF; GOD, LOVING; HONORING FATHER AND MOTHER; MURDER; NEIGHBOR; STEALING; and WITNESS, FALSE; also see COMMANDMENTS)

R

RABBI

Setting: The temple in Jerusalem. Jesus exposes the truth about Pharisaism to the crowds and His disciples after the Jewish religious leaders test Him with questions.

Then Jesus spoke to the crowds and to His disciples, saying: "The scribes and the Pharisees have seated themselves in the chair of Moses; therefore all that they tell you, do and observe, but do not do according to their deeds; for they say *things* and do not do *them.* They tie up heavy burdens and lay them on men's shoulders, but they themselves are unwilling to move them with *so much as* a finger. But they do all their deeds to be noticed by men; for they broaden their phylacteries and lengthen their tassels *of their garments.* They love the place of honor at banquets and the chief seats in the synagogues, and respectful greetings in the market places, and being called Rabbi by men. But do not be called Rabbi; for One is your Teacher, and you are all brothers. Do not call *anyone* on earth your father; for One is your Father, He who is in heaven. Do not be called leaders; for One is your Leader, *that is,* Christ. But the greatest among you shall be your servant. Whoever exalts himself shall be humbled; and whoever humbles himself shall be exalted" (Matthew 23:1–12; cf. Matthew 20:26; Mark 12:38–40; Luke 20:46, 47; see Exodus 13:9; Deuteronomy 33:3; Matthew 6:1, 5, 6, 9, 16; Mark 14:11; Luke 11:43; 14:11).

RAIN (Also see LIGHTNING; MOISTURE; SHOWER; STORM; WATER; and WEATHER)

Setting: Galilee. During the early part of His ministry, Jesus preaches the Sermon on the Mount to His disciples and the multitudes.

"You have heard that it was said, 'YOU SHALL LOVE YOUR NEIGHBOR and hate your enemy.' But I say to you, love your enemies and pray for those who persecute you, so that you may be sons of your Father who is in heaven; for He causes His sun to rise on *the* evil and *the* good, and sends rain on *the* righteous and *the* unrighteous. For if you love those who love you, what reward do you have? Do not even the tax collectors do the same? If you greet only your brothers, what more are you doing *than others?* Do not even the Gentiles do the same? Therefore, you are to be perfect, as your heavenly Father is perfect" (Matthew 5:43–48, Jesus quotes from Leviticus 19:18; cf. Leviticus 19:2; Luke 6:27–36).

Setting: Galilee. During the early part of His ministry, Jesus preaches the Sermon on the Mount to His disciples and the multitudes.

"Therefore everyone who hears these words of Mine and acts on them, may be compared to a wise man who built his house on the rock. And the rain fell, and the floods came, and the winds blew and slammed against that house; and *yet* it did not fall, for it had been founded on the rock. Everyone who hears these words of Mine and does not act on them, will be like a foolish man who built his house on the sand. The rain fell, and the floods came, and the winds blew and slammed against that house; and it fell—and great was its fall" (Matthew 7:24–28; cf. Luke 6:47–49).

RANSOM

Setting: On the way to Jerusalem, where Jesus will die on the cross. Jesus teaches His disciples about true greatness after the mother of disciples James and John asks Him to make her sons exalted rulers with Him in His coming kingdom.

But Jesus called them to Himself and said, "You know that the rulers of the Gentiles lord it over them, and *their* great men exercise authority over them. It is not this way among you, but whoever wishes to become great among you shall be your servant, and whoever wishes to be first among you shall be your slave; just as the Son of Man did not come to be served, but to serve, and to give His life a ransom for many" (Matthew 20:25–28; cf. Matthew 23:11; 26:28; Mark 10:42–45).

Setting: On the road to Jerusalem. James and John ask Jesus for special honor and privileges in His kingdom. The other disciples become angry, so the Lord uses this moment to teach all of them about servanthood.

Calling them to Himself, Jesus said to them, "You know that those who are recognized as rulers of the Gentiles lord it over them; and their great men exercise authority over them. But it is not this way among you, but whoever wishes to become great among you shall be your servant; and whoever wishes to be first among you shall be slave of all. For even the Son of Man did not come to be served, but to serve, and to give His life a ransom for many" (Mark 10:42–45; cf. Matthew 20:25–28).

RATIONS (Also see BREAD; BREAD, DAILY; and FOOD)

Setting: On the way from Galilee to Jerusalem. When Jesus uses a parable to challenge the crowd and His disciples to be ready for His return, Peter asks Him whom He is addressing.

And the Lord said, "Who then is the faithful and sensible steward, whom his master will put in charge of his servants, to give them their rations at the proper time? Blessed is that slave whom his master finds so doing when he comes. Truly I say to you that he will put him in charge of all his possessions. But if that slave says in his heart, 'My master will be a long time in coming,' and begins to beat the slaves, *both* men and women, and to eat and drink and get drunk; the master of that slave will come on a day when he does not expect *him* and at an hour he does not know, and will cut him in pieces, and assign him a place with the unbelievers. And that slave who knew his master's will and did not get ready or act in accord with his will, will receive many lashes, but the one who did know *it,* and committed deeds worthy of flogging, will receive but few. From everyone who has been given much, much will be required; and to whom they entrusted much, of him they will ask all the more" (Luke 12:42–48; cf. Matthew 24:45–51; see Leviticus 5:17).

RAVENS (Also see BIRDS; DOVES; and SPARROWS)

Setting: On the way from Galilee to Jerusalem. After giving a parable about riches and greed, Jesus comforts the crowd and His disciples. The scribes and Pharisees turn hostile and question Him repeatedly in an attempt to catch Him in something He might say.

And He said to His disciples, "For this reason I say to you, do not worry about *your* life, *as to* what you will eat; nor for your body, *as to* what you will put on. For life is more than food, and the body more than clothing. Consider the ravens, for they neither sow nor reap; they have no storeroom nor barn, and *yet* God feeds them; how much more valuable you are than the birds! And which of you by worrying can add a *single* hour to his life's span? If then you cannot do even a very little thing, why do you worry about other matters? Consider the lilies, how they grow: they neither toil nor spin; but I tell you, not even Solomon in all his glory clothed himself like one of these. But if God so clothes the grass in the field, which is *alive* today and tomorrow is thrown into the furnace, how much more *will He clothe* you? You men of little faith! And do not seek what you will eat and what you will drink, and do not keep worrying. For all these things the nations of the world eagerly seek; but your Father knows that you need these things. But seek His kingdom, and these things will be added to you. Do not be afraid, little flock, for your Father has chosen gladly to give you the kingdom" (Luke 12:22–32; cf. Matthew 6:25–33; see 1 Kings 10:4–7; Job 38:41).

RAYS (Also see LIGHT; and SUN)

Setting: On the way from Galilee to Jerusalem. After telling the increasing crowds of the sign of Jonah, Jesus illustrates His point by speaking about a lamp.

"No one, after lighting a lamp, puts it away in a cellar nor under a basket, but on the lampstand, so that those who enter may see the light. The eye is the lamp of your body; when your eye is clear, your whole body also is full of light; but when it is bad, your body also is full of darkness. Then watch out that the light in you is not darkness. If therefore your whole body is full of light, with no dark part in it, it will be wholly illumined, as when the lamp illumines you with its rays" (Luke 11:33–36; cf. Matthew 5:15, 6:22, 23).

READINESS (Also see ALERTNESS; PREPAREDNESS; and WATCHFULNESS)

[READINESS from ready]

Setting: The temple in Jerusalem. Jesus speaks another parable to the chief priests and elders after they question His authority.

Jesus spoke to them again in parables, saying, "The kingdom of heaven may be compared to a king who gave a wedding feast for his son. And he sent out his slaves to call those who had been invited to the wedding feast, and they were unwilling to come. Again he sent out other slaves saying, 'Tell those who have been invited, "Behold, I have prepared my dinner; my oxen and my fattened livestock are *all* butchered and everything is ready; come to the wedding feast." But they paid no attention and went their way, one to his own farm, another to his business, and the rest seized his slaves and mistreated them and killed them. But the king was enraged, and he sent his armies and destroyed those murderers and set their city on fire. Then he said to his slaves, 'The wedding is ready, but those who were invited were not worthy. 'Go therefore to the main highways, and as many as you find *there,* invite to the wedding feast.' Those slaves went out into the streets and gathered together all they found, both evil and good; and the wedding hall was filled with dinner guests. But when the king came in to look over the dinner guests, he saw a man there who was not dressed in wedding clothes, and he said to him, 'Friend, how did you come in here without wedding clothes?' And the man was speechless. Then the king said to the servants, 'Bind him hand and foot, and throw him into the outer darkness; in that place there will be weeping and gnashing of teeth.' For many are called, but few *are* chosen" (Matthew 22:1–14; cf. Matthew 8:11, 12).

[READINESS from on the alert and be ready]
Setting: On the Mount of Olives, just east of Jerusalem. During His Olivet Discourse, after answering His disciples' questions as to when the temple will be destroyed and Jerusalem overrun, along with the signs of His coming and the end of the age, Jesus reemphasizes to His disciples that they should be on the alert for His return.

"Therefore be on the alert, for you do not know which day your Lord is coming. But be sure of this, that if the head of the house had known at what time of the night the thief was coming, he would have been on the alert and would not have allowed his house to be broken into. For this reason you also must be ready; for the Son of Man is coming at an hour when you do not think *He will.* Who then is the faithful and sensible slave whom his master put in charge of his household to give their food at the proper time? Blessed is that slave whom his master finds so doing when he comes. Truly I say to you that he will put him in charge of all his possessions. But if that evil slave says in his heart, 'My master is not coming for a long time,' and begins to beat his fellow slaves and eat and drink with drunkards; the master of that slave will come on a day when he does not expect *him* and at an hour which he does not know, and will cut him in pieces and assign him a place with the hypocrites; in that place there will be weeping and gnashing of teeth" (Matthew 24:42–51; cf. Mark 13:33–37; Luke 12:39–46; 21:34–36; see Matthew 8:11, 12; 25:21–23).

[READINESS from ready]
Setting: On the Mount of Olives, just east of Jerusalem. During His Olivet Discourse, after answering His disciples' questions as to when the temple will be destroyed and Jerusalem overrun, along with the signs of His coming and the end of the age, Jesus reemphasizes to His disciples that they should be on the alert for His return.

"Then the kingdom of heaven will be comparable to ten virgins, who took their lamps and went out to meet the bridegroom. Five of them were foolish, and five were prudent. For when the foolish took their lamps, they took no oil with them, but the prudent took oil in flasks along with their lamps. Now while the bridegroom was delaying, they all got drowsy and *began* to sleep. But at midnight there was a shout, 'Behold, the bridegroom! Come out to meet *him.*' Then all those virgins rose and trimmed their lamps. The foolish said to the prudent, 'Give us some of your oil, for our lamps are going out.' But the prudent answered, 'No, there will not be enough for us and you *too;* go instead to the dealers and buy *some* for yourselves.' And while they were going away to make the purchase, the bridegroom came, and those who were ready went in with him to the wedding feast; and the door was shut. Later the other virgins also came, saying, 'Lord, lord, open up for us.' But he answered, 'Truly I say to you, I do not know you.' Be on the alert then, for you do not know the day nor the hour" (Matthew 25:1–13; cf. Matthew 24:42; Luke 12:35; see Matthew 7:21, 24).

[READINESS from ready]
Setting: Jerusalem. On the first day of the Feast of Unleavened Bread, when the Passover lamb is being sacrificed, Jesus responds to His disciples' question about His plans for the Passover meal.

And He sent two of His disciples and said to them, "Go into the city, and a man will meet you carrying a pitcher of water; follow him; and wherever he enters, say to the owner of the house, 'The Teacher says, "Where is My guest room in which I may eat the

Passover with My disciples?"' And he himself will show you a large upper room furnished *and* ready; prepare for us there" (Mark 14:13–15; cf. Matthew 26:17–19; Luke 22:7–13).

Setting: On the way from Galilee to Jerusalem. After giving a parable about riches and greed, Jesus uses another parable to challenge the crowd and His disciples to be ready for His return.

"Be dressed in readiness, and *keep* your lamps lit. Be like men who are waiting for their master when he returns from the wedding feast, so that they may immediately open *the door* to him when he comes and knocks. Blessed are those slaves whom the master will find on the alert when he comes; truly I say to you, that he will gird himself *to serve,* and have them recline *at the table,* and will come up and wait on them. Whether he comes in the second watch, or even in the third and finds *them* so, blessed are those *slaves*. But be sure of this, that if the head of the house had known at what hour the thief was coming, he would not have allowed his house to be broken into. You too, be ready; for the Son of Man is coming at an hour that you do not expect" (Luke 12:35–40; cf. Matthew 24:42–44; see Mark 13:33; Ephesians 6:14).

[READINESS from ready]
Setting: On the way from Galilee to Jerusalem. When Jesus uses a parable to challenge the crowd and His disciples to be ready for His return, Peter asks Him whom He is addressing.

And the Lord said, "Who then is the faithful and sensible steward, whom his master will put in charge of his servants, to give them their rations at the proper time? Blessed is that slave whom his master finds so doing when he comes. Truly I say to you that he will put him in charge of all his possessions. But if that slave says in his heart, 'My master will be a long time in coming,' and begins to beat the slaves, *both* men and women, and to eat and drink and get drunk; the master of that slave will come on a day when he does not expect *him* and at an hour he does not know, and will cut him in pieces, and assign him a place with the unbelievers. And that slave who knew his master's will and did not get ready or act in accord with his will, will receive many lashes, but the one who did know *it,* and committed deeds worthy of flogging, will receive but few. From everyone who has been given much, much will be required; and to whom they entrusted much, of him they will ask all the more" (Luke 12:42–48; cf. Matthew 24:45–51; see Leviticus 5:17).

[READINESS from ready]
Setting: On the way from Galilee to Jerusalem. After speaking a parable to the invited guests and the host at a banquet, Jesus responds to a guest's proclamation about the blessings of eating bread in the kingdom of God.

But He said to him, "A man was giving a big dinner, and he invited many; and at the dinner hour he sent his slave to say to those who had been invited, 'Come; for everything is ready now.' But they all alike began to make excuses. The first one said to him, 'I have bought a piece of land and I need to go out and look at it; please consider me excused.' Another one said, 'I have bought five yoke of oxen, and I am going to try them out; please consider me excused.' Another one said, I have married a wife, and for that reason I cannot come.' And the slave came *back* and reported this to his master. Then the head of the household became angry and said to his slave, 'Go out at once into the streets and lanes of the city and bring in here the poor and crippled and blind and lame.' And the slave said, 'Master, what you commanded has been done, and still there is room.' And the master said to the slave, 'Go out into the highways and along the hedges, and compel *them* to come in, so that my house may be filled. For I tell you, none of those men who were invited shall taste of my dinner'" (Luke 14:16–24; see Deuteronomy 24:5; Matthew 22:2–14).

READING, MIND (See MIND READING)

REALM

Setting: Jerusalem. After the previous and current high priests (Annas and Caiaphas) question Jesus, and Peter denies the second and third times being the Lord's disciple, Pilate (Roman governor of Judea) asks Jesus what He has done.

Jesus answered, "My kingdom is not of this world. If My kingdom were of this world, then My servants would be fighting so that I would not be handed over to the Jews; but as it is, My kingdom is not of this realm" (John 18:36; see Matthew 26:53).

REAPERS (Also see GATHERING; HARVEST; HARVEST TIME; and REAPING)

Setting: By the Sea of Galilee. Because the religious leaders are rejecting His message, Jesus continues teaching the crowds with the Parable of the Wheat and the Tares.

Jesus presented another parable to them, saying, "The kingdom of heaven may be compared to a man who sowed good seed in his field. But while his men were sleeping, his enemy came and sowed tares among the wheat, and went away. But when the wheat sprouted and bore grain, then the tares became evident also. The slaves of the landowner came and said to him, 'Sir, did you not sow good seed in your field? How then does it have tares?' And he said to them, 'An enemy has done this!' The slaves said to him, 'Do you want us, then, to go and gather them up?' But he said, 'No; for while you are gathering up the tares, you may uproot the wheat with them. Allow both to grow together until the harvest; and in the time of the harvest I will say to the reapers, "First gather up the tares and bind them in bundles to burn them up; but gather the wheat into my barn" '" (Matthew 13:24–30; cf. Matthew 3:12).

Setting: A house near the Sea of Galilee. Jesus gives His disciples the meaning of the Parable of the Wheat and the Tares.

And He said, "The one who sows the good seed is the Son of Man, and the field is the world; and as *for* the good seed, these are the sons of the kingdom; and the tares are the sons of the evil *one;* and the enemy who sowed them is the devil, and the harvest is the end of the age; and the reapers are angels. So just as the tares are gathered up and burned with fire, so shall it be at the end of the age. The Son of Man will send forth His angels, and they will gather out of His kingdom all stumbling blocks, and those who commit lawlessness, and will throw them into the furnace of fire; in that place there will be weeping and gnashing of teeth. Then THE RIGHTEOUS WILL SHINE FORTH AS THE SUN in the kingdom of their Father. He who has ears, let him hear" (Matthew 13:37–43, Jesus quotes from Daniel 12:3; cf. Matthew 8:12; 13:50).

REAPING (See CROP; CROPS; GATHERING; HARVEST; PRODUCE; REAPERS; and SOWING)

[REAPING from reap]

Setting: Galilee. During the early part of His ministry, Jesus preaches the Sermon on the Mount to His disciples and the multitudes.

"For this reason I say to you, do not be worried about your life, *as to* what you will eat or what you will drink; nor for your body, *as to* what you will put on. Is not life more than food, and the body more than clothing? Look at the birds of the air, that they do not sow, nor reap nor gather into barns, and *yet* your heavenly Father feeds them. Are you not worth much more than they? And who of you by being worried can add a *single* hour to his life? And why are you worried about clothing? Observe how the lilies of the field grow; they do not toil nor do they spin, yet I say to you that not even Solomon in all his glory clothed himself like one of these. But if God so clothes the grass of the field, which is *alive* today and tomorrow is thrown into the furnace, *will He* not much more *clothe* you? You of little faith! Do not worry then, saying 'What will we eat?' or 'What will we drink?' or 'What will be wear for clothing?" For the Gentiles eagerly seek all these things; for your heavenly Father knows that you need all these things. But seek first His kingdom and His righteousness, and all these things will be added to you. So do not worry about tomorrow; for tomorrow will care for itself. Each day has enough trouble of its own" (Matthew 6:25–34; cf. Luke 12:22–31; see 1 Kings 10:4–7; Job 35:11; Matthew 8:26).

Setting: On the Mount of Olives, just east of Jerusalem. During His Olivet Discourse, after answering His disciples' questions as to when the temple will be destroyed and Jerusalem overrun, along with the signs of His coming and the end of the age, Jesus reemphasizes to His disciples that they should be on the alert for His return.

"For *it is* just like a man *about* to go on a journey, who called his own slaves and entrusted his possessions to them. To one he gave five talents, to another, two, and to another, one, each according to his own ability; and he went on his journey. Immediately the one who had received the five talents went and traded with them, and gained five more talents. In the same manner the one who *had received* the two *talents* gained two more. But he who received the one *talent* went away, and dug a *hole* in the ground and hid his master's money. Now after a long time the master of those slaves came and settled accounts with them. The one who had received the five talents came up and brought five more talents, saying, 'Master, you entrusted five talents to me. See, I have gained five more talents.' His master said to him, 'Well done, good and faithful slave. You were faithful with a few things, I will put you in charge of many things; enter into the joy of your master.' Also the one who *had received* the two talents came up and said, 'Master, you entrusted two talents to me. See, I have gained two more talents.' His master said to him, 'Well done, good and faithful slave. You were faithful with a few things, I will put you in charge of many things; enter into the joy of your master.' And the one also who had received the one talent came up and said, 'Master, I knew you to be a hard man, reaping where you did not sow and gathering where you scattered no *seed*. And I was afraid, and went away and hid your talent in the ground. See, you have what is yours.' But his master answered and said to him, 'You wicked, lazy slave, you knew that I reap where I did not sow and gather where I scattered no *seed*. Then you ought to have put my money in the bank, and on my arrival I would have received my *money* back with interest. 'Therefore take away the talent from him, and give it to the one who has ten talents.' For to everyone who has, *more* shall be given, and he will have an abundance; but from the one who does not have, even what he does have shall be taken away. Throw out the worthless slave into the outer darkness; in that place there will be weeping and gnashing of teeth" (Matthew 25:14–30; cf. Matthew 8:12; 13:12; 24:45–47; see Matthew 18:23, 24; Luke 12:44).

[REAPING from reap]

Setting: On the way from Galilee to Jerusalem. After giving a parable about riches and greed, Jesus comforts the crowd and His disciples. The scribes and Pharisees turn hostile and question Him repeatedly in an attempt to catch Him in something He might say.

And He said to His disciples, "For this reason I say to you, do not worry about *your* life, *as to* what you will eat; nor for your body, *as to* what you will put on. For life is more than food, and the body more than clothing. Consider the ravens, for they neither sow nor reap; they have no storeroom nor barn, and *yet* God feeds them; how much more valuable you are than the birds! And which of you by worrying can add a *single* hour to his life's span? If then you cannot do even a very little thing, why do you worry about other matters? Consider the lilies, how they grow: they neither toil nor spin; but I tell you, not even Solomon in all his glory clothed himself like one of these. But if God so clothes the grass in the field, which is *alive* today and tomorrow is thrown into the furnace, how much more *will He clothe* you? You men of little faith! And do not seek what you will eat and what you will drink, and do not keep worrying. For all these things the nations of the world eagerly seek; but your Father knows that you need these things. But seek His kingdom, and these things will be added to you. Do not be afraid, little flock, for your Father has chosen gladly to give you the kingdom" (Luke 12:22–32; cf. Matthew 6:25–33; see 1 Kings 10:4–7; Job 38:41).

Setting: Jericho, on the way to Jerusalem. After commending Zaccheus's faith in Him, Jesus provides a parable about stewardship.

So He said, "A nobleman went to a distant country to receive a kingdom for himself, and *then* return. And he called ten of his slaves, and gave them ten minas and said to them, 'Do business *with this* until I come *back*.' But his citizens hated him and sent a delegation after him, saying, 'We do not want this man to reign over us.' When he returned, after receiving the kingdom, he ordered that these slaves, to whom he had given the money, be called to him so that he might know what business they had done. The first appeared, saying, 'Master, your mina has made ten minas more.' And he said to him, 'Well done, good slave, because you have been faithful in a very little thing, you are to be in authority over ten cities.' The second came, saying, 'Your mina, master, has made five minas.' And he said to him, also, 'And you are to be over five cities.' Another came, saying, 'Master, here is your mina, which I kept put away in a handkerchief; for I was afraid of you, because you are an exacting man; you take up what you did not lay down and reap what you did not sow.' He said to him, 'By your own words I will judge you, you worthless slave. Did you know that I am an exacting man, taking up what I did not lay down and reaping what I did not sow? Then why did you not put my money in the bank, and having come, I would have collected it with interest?' Then he said to the bystanders, 'Take the mina away from him and give it to the one who has the ten minas.' And they said to him, 'Master, he has ten minas *already*.' I tell you that to everyone who has, more shall be given, but from the one who does not have, even what he does have shall be taken away. But these enemies of mine, who did not want me to reign over them, bring them here and slay them in my presence" (Luke 19:12–27; cf. Matthew 25:14–30; see Matthew 13:12; Luke 16:10).

[REAPING from reaps and reap]

Setting: Sychar in Samaria, on the way to Galilee. After Jesus converses with a Samaritan woman at Jacob's well, the disciples return with food. They try to get Jesus to eat, but are surprised when He speaks of other food.

Jesus said to them, "My food is to do the will of Him who sent Me and to accomplish His work. Do you not say, 'There are yet four months, and *then* comes the harvest'? Behold, I say to you, lift up your eyes and look on the fields, that they are white for harvest. Already he who reaps is receiving wages and is gathering fruit for life eternal; so that he who sows and he who reaps may rejoice together. For in this *case* the saying is true, 'One sows and another reaps.' I sent you to reap that for which you have not labored; others have labored and you have entered into their labor" (John 4:34–38; see Matthew 9:37, 38; John 5:36).

REASON (Also see CAUSE)

Setting: Galilee. During the early part of His ministry, Jesus preaches the Sermon on the Mount to His disciples and the multitudes.

"It was said, 'WHOEVER SENDS HIS WIFE AWAY, LET HIM GIVE HER A CERTIFICATE OF DIVORCE'; but I say to you that everyone who divorces his wife, except for *the* reason of unchastity, makes her commit adultery; and whoever marries a divorced woman commits adultery" (Matthew 5:31, 32, Jesus quotes from Deuteronomy 24:1, 3; cf. Matthew 19:9; see Romans 7:2, 3; 1 Corinthians 7:10, 39).

Setting: Galilee. During the early part of His ministry, Jesus preaches the Sermon on the Mount to His disciples and the multitudes.

"For this reason I say to you, do not be worried about your life, *as to* what you will eat or what you will drink; nor for your body, *as to* what you will put on. Is not life more than food, and the body more than clothing? Look at the birds of the air, that they do not sow, nor reap nor gather into barns, and *yet* your heavenly Father feeds them. Are you not worth much more than they? And who of you by being worried can add a *single* hour to his life? And why are you worried about clothing? Observe how the lilies of the field grow; they do not toil nor do they spin, yet I say to you that not even Solomon in all his glory clothed himself like one of these. But if God so clothes the grass of the field, which is *alive* today and tomorrow is thrown into the furnace, *will He* not much more *clothe* you? You of little faith! Do not worry then, saying 'What will we eat?' or 'What will we drink?' or 'What will be wear for clothing?' For the Gentiles eagerly seek all these things; for your heavenly Father knows that you need all these things. But seek first His kingdom and His righteousness, and all these things will be added to you. So do not worry about tomorrow; for tomorrow will care for itself. Each day has enough trouble of its own" (Matthew 6:25–34; cf. Luke 12:22–31; see 1 Kings 10:4–7; Job 35:11; Matthew 8:26).

Setting: Galilee. After He heals a blind, mute, demon-possessed man, the Pharisees accuse Jesus in front of crowds of being a worker of Beelzebul (Satan).

And knowing their thoughts Jesus said to them, "Any kingdom divided against itself is laid waste; and any city or house divided against itself will not stand. If Satan casts out Satan, he is divided against himself; how then will his kingdom stand? If I by Beelzebul cast out demons, by whom do your sons cast *them* out? For this reason they will be your judges. But if I cast out demons by the Spirit of God, then the kingdom of God has come upon you. Or how can anyone enter the strong man's house and carry off his property, unless he first binds the strong *man?* And then he will plunder his house" (Matthew 12:25–29; cf. Matthew 9:34; Mark 3:23–27; Luke 11:17–20).

Setting: Capernaum of Galilee. Jesus illustrates the matter of forgiveness after Peter asks Him if forgiving someone seven times who has sinned against him is adequate.

"For this reason the kingdom of heaven may be compared to a king who wished to settle accounts with his slaves. When he had begun to settle *them,* one who owed him ten thousand talents was brought to him. But since he did not have *the means* to repay, his lord commanded him to be sold, along with his wife and children and all that he had, and repayment to be made. So the slave fell *to the ground* and prostrated himself before him, saying, 'Have patience with me and I will repay you everything.' And the lord of that slave felt compassion and released him and forgave him the debt. But that slave went out and found one of his fellow slaves who owed him a hundred denarii; and he seized him and *began* to choke *him,* saying, 'Pay back what you owe.' So his fellow slave fell *to the ground* and *began* to plead with him, saying, 'Have patience with me and I will repay you.' But he was unwilling and went and threw him in prison until he should pay back what was owed. So when his fellow slaves saw what had happened, they were deeply grieved and came and reported to their lord all that had happened. Then summoning him, his lord said to him, 'You wicked slave, I forgave you all that debt because you pleaded with me. Should you not also have had mercy on your fellow slave, in the same way that I had mercy on you?' And his lord, moved with anger, handed him over to the torturers until he should repay all that was owed him. My heavenly Father will also do the same to you, if each of you does not forgive his brother from your heart" (Matthew 18:23–35; cf. Matthew 6:12, 14, 15; Luke 7:42; see Matthew 25:19–28).

Setting: Judea beyond the Jordan (Perea). After Jesus replies to Peter's question about forgiveness, in front of a large crowd, the Pharisees test the Lord with a question about divorce.

And He answered and said, "Have you not read that He who created *them* from the beginning MADE THEM MALE AND FEMALE, and said, 'FOR THIS REASON A MAN SHALL LEAVE HIS FATHER AND MOTHER AND BE JOINED TO HIS WIFE, AND THE TWO SHALL BECOME ONE FLESH'? So they are no longer two, but one flesh. What therefore God has joined together, let no man separate" (Matthew 19:4–6, Jesus quotes from Genesis 1:27; 2:24; cf. Mark 10:5–9; see 1 Timothy 2:14).

Setting: On the Mount of Olives, just east of Jerusalem. During His Olivet Discourse, after answering His disciples' questions as to when the temple will be destroyed and Jerusalem overrun, along with the signs of His coming and the end of the age, Jesus reemphasizes to His disciples that they should be on the alert for His return.

"Therefore be on the alert, for you do not know which day your Lord is coming. But be sure of this, that if the head of the house had known at what time of the night the thief was coming, he would have been on the alert and would not have allowed his house to be broken into. For this reason you also must be ready; for the Son of Man is coming at an hour when you do not think *He will.* Who then is the faithful and sensible slave whom his master put in charge of his household to give their food at the proper time? Blessed is that slave whom his master finds so doing when he comes. Truly I say to you that he will put him in charge of all his possessions. But if that evil slave says in his heart, 'My master is not coming for a long time,' and begins to beat his fellow slaves and eat and drink with drunkards; the master of that slave will come on a day when he does not expect *him* and at an hour which he does not know, and will cut him in pieces and assign him a place with the hypocrites; in that place there will be weeping and gnashing of teeth" (Matthew 24:42–51; cf. Mark 13:33–37; Luke 12:39–46; 21:34–36; see Matthew 8:11, 12; 25:21–23).

Setting: Judea beyond the Jordan (Perea). Jesus teaches the crowds gathered around Him about divorce after the Pharisees test and question Him on the subject.

And He answered and said to them, "What did Moses command you?" They said, "Moses permitted a *man* TO WRITE A CERTIFICATE OF DIVORCE AND SEND *her* AWAY." But Jesus said to them, "Because of your hardness of heart he wrote you this commandment. But from the beginning of creation, *God* MADE THEM MALE AND FEMALE. FOR THIS REASON A MAN SHALL LEAVE HIS FATHER AND MOTHER, AND THE TWO SHALL BECOME ONE FLESH; so they are no longer two, but one flesh. What therefore God has joined together, let no man separate. In the house the disciples *began* questioning Him about this again. And He said to them, "Whoever divorces his wife and marries another woman commits adultery against her; and if she herself divorces her husband and marries another man, she is committing adultery" (Mark 10:3–12, Jesus quotes from Genesis 1:27; 2:24; cf. Matthew 19:1–9; see Deuteronomy 24:1–3; Matthew 5:32; see Romans 7:2, 3; 1 Corinthians 7:10, 11, 13, 39; 1 Timothy 2:14).

Setting: The temple in Jerusalem. After some of the Pharisees and Herodians attempt to trap Jesus in a statement, some Sadducees question Him about the status of marriage after death.

Jesus said to them, "Is this not the reason you are mistaken, that you do not understand the Scriptures or the power of God? For when they rise from the dead, they neither marry nor are given in marriage, but are like angels in heaven. But regarding the fact that the dead rise again, have you not read in the book of Moses, in the *passage* about *the burning* bush, how God spoke to him, saying, 'I AM THE GOD OF ABRAHAM, AND THE GOD OF ISAAC, and the God of Jacob?' He is not the God of the dead, but of the living; you are greatly mistaken" (Mark 12:24–27, Jesus quotes from Exodus 3:6; cf. Matthew 22:29–33; Luke 20:34–40).

Setting: Galilee. After Jesus praises John the Baptist to the crowds, Simon, a Pharisee, invites the Lord to dinner. A sinful woman anoints His feet with perfume, prompting Him to instruct His host about forgiveness.

Turning toward the woman, He said to Simon, "Do you see this woman? I entered your house; you gave Me no water for My feet, but she has wet My feet with her tears and wiped them with her hair. You gave Me no kiss; but she, since the time I came in, has not ceased to kiss My feet. You did not anoint My head with oil, but she anointed My feet with perfume. For this reason I say to you, her sins, which are many, have been forgiven, for she loved much; but he who is forgiven little, loves little." Then He said to her, "Your sins have been forgiven." Those who were reclining *at the table* with Him began to say to themselves, "Who is this *man* who even forgives sins?" And He said to the woman, "Your faith has saved you; go in peace" (Luke 7:44–50; see Matthew 9:2; Mark 5:34; Luke 5:21).

Setting: On the way from Galilee to Jerusalem. After Jesus pronounces woes upon the Pharisees, a lawyer replies that His remarks are an insult to lawyers, too.

But He said, "Woe to you lawyers as well! For you weigh men down with burdens hard to bear, while you yourselves will not even touch the burdens with one of your fingers. Woe to you! For you build the tombs of the prophets, and *it was* your fathers *who* killed them. So you are witnesses and approve the deeds of your fathers; because it was they who killed them, and you build *their tombs*. For this reason also the wisdom of God said, 'I will send them prophets and apostles, and *some* of them they will kill and *some* they will persecute, so that the blood of all the prophets, shed since the foundation of the world, may be charged against this generation, from the blood of Abel to the blood of Zechariah, who was killed between the altar and the house *of God*; yes, I tell you, it shall be charged against this generation.' Woe to you lawyers! For you have taken away the key of knowledge; you yourselves did not enter, and you hindered those who were entering" (Luke 11:46–52; cf. Matthew 23:29–32; see 2 Chronicles 24:20, 21; Matthew 23:4, 13).

Setting: On the way from Galilee to Jerusalem. After giving a parable about riches and greed, Jesus comforts the crowd and His disciples. The scribes and Pharisees turn hostile and question Him repeatedly in an attempt to catch Him in something He might say.

And He said to His disciples, "For this reason I say to you, do not worry about *your* life, *as to* what you will eat; nor for your body, *as to* what you will put on. For life is more than food, and the body more than clothing. Consider the ravens, for they neither sow nor reap; they have no storeroom nor barn, and *yet* God feeds them; how much more valuable you are than the birds! And which of you by worrying can add a *single* hour to his life's span? If then you cannot do even a very little thing, why do you worry about other matters? Consider the lilies, how they grow: they neither toil nor spin; but I tell you, not even Solomon in all his glory clothed himself like one of these. But if God so clothes the grass in the field, which is *alive* today and tomorrow is thrown into the furnace, how much more *will He clothe* you? You men of little faith! And do not seek what you will eat and what you will drink, and do not keep worrying. For all these things the nations of the world eagerly seek; but your Father knows that you need these things. But seek His kingdom, and these things will be added to you. Do not be afraid, little flock, for your Father has chosen gladly to give you the kingdom" (Luke 12:22–32; cf. Matthew 6:25–33; see 1 Kings 10:4–7; Job 38:41).

Setting: On the way from Galilee to Jerusalem. At a banquet, after Jesus speaks a parable to the invited guests and the host, He responds to a guest's proclamation about the blessings of eating bread in the kingdom of God.

But He said to him, "A man was giving a big dinner, and he invited many; and at the dinner hour he sent his slave to say to those who had been invited, 'Come; for everything is ready now.' But they all alike began to make excuses. The first one said to him, 'I have bought a piece of land and I need to go out and look at it; please consider me excused.' Another one said, 'I have bought five yoke of oxen, and I am going to try them out; please consider me excused.' Another one said, I have married a wife, and for that reason I cannot come.' And the slave came *back* and reported this to his master. Then the head of the household became angry and said to his slave, 'Go out at once into the streets and lanes of the city and bring in here the poor and crippled and blind and lame.' And the slave said, 'Master, what you commanded has been done, and still there is room.' And the master said to the slave, 'Go out into the highways and along the hedges, and compel *them* to come in, so that my house may be filled. For I tell you, none of those men who were invited shall taste of my dinner'" (Luke 14:16–24; see Deuteronomy 24:5; Matthew 22:2–14).

Setting: The synagogue at Capernaum of Galilee. After the Jewish religious leaders argue with one another when Jesus says He will give His flesh to the world to eat, some of His disciples also express difficulty with His statements.

But, Jesus, conscious that His disciples grumbled at this, said to them, "Does this cause you to stumble? *What* then if you see the Son of Man ascending to where He was before? It is the Spirit who gives life; the flesh profits nothing; the words that I have spoken to you are spirit and are life. But there are some of you who do not believe." For Jesus knew from the beginning who they were who did not believe, and who it was that would betray Him. And He was saying, "For this reason I have said to you, that no one can come to Me unless it has been granted him from the Father" (John 6:61–65; see Matthew 11:6; 13:11; John 3:13).

Setting: The temple in Jerusalem. After receiving encouragement from His blood brothers in Galilee to attend the upcoming Feast of Booths in order to demonstrate His works to His disciples and the world, Jesus goes and teaches, astonishing the Jewish religious leaders.

Jesus answered them, "I did one deed, and you all marvel. For this reason Moses has given you circumcision (not because it is from Moses, but from the fathers), and on *the* Sabbath you circumcise a man. If a man receives circumcision on *the* Sabbath so that the Law of Moses will not be broken, are you angry with Me because I made an entire man well on *the* Sabbath? Do not judge according to appearance, but judge with righteous judgment" (John 7:21–24; see Genesis 17:10–14; Leviticus 12:3; 19:15; Matthew 12:2; John 5:2–16; 7–20; 7:10–15).

Setting: The temple treasury in Jerusalem. After the scribes and Pharisees question His testimony about Himself, Jesus argues with them regarding their ancestry and motives.

Jesus said to them, "If God were your Father, you would love Me, for I proceeded forth and have come from God, for I have not even come on My own initiative, but He sent Me. Why do you not understand what I am saying? *It is* because you cannot hear My word. You are of *your* father the devil, and you want to do the desires of your father. He was a murderer from the beginning, and does not stand in the truth because there is no truth in him. Whenever he speaks a lie, he speaks from his own *nature,* for he is a liar and the father of lies. But because I speak the truth, you do not believe Me. Which one of you convicts Me of sin? If I speak truth, why do not believe Me? He who is of God hears the words of God; for this reason you do not hear *them,* because you are not of God" (John 8:42–47; see John 8:1–41; 18:37; 1 John 3:8; 4:6; 5:1).

Setting: Jerusalem. Following the Pharisees' interrogation and dismissal of the formerly blind man Jesus healed on the Sabbath, the Lord conveys the Parable of the Good Shepherd to the Pharisees, using figures of speech they do not understand.

So Jesus said to them again, "Truly, truly, I say to you, I am the door of the sheep. All who came before Me are thieves and robbers, but the sheep did not hear them. I am the door; if anyone enters through Me, he will be saved, and will go in and out and find pasture. The thief comes only to steal and kill and destroy; I came that they may have life, and have *it* abundantly. I am the good shepherd; the good shepherd lays down His life for the sheep. He who is a hired hand, and not a shepherd, who is not the owner of the sheep, sees the wolf coming, and leaves the sheep and flees, and the wolf snatches them and scatters *them. He flees* because he is a hired hand and is not concerned about the sheep. I am the good shepherd, and I know My own and My own know Me, even as the Father knows Me and I know the Father; and I lay down My life for the sheep. I have other sheep, which are not of this fold; I must bring them also, and they will hear My voice; and they will become one flock *with* one shepherd. For this reason the Father loves Me, because I lay down My life so that I may take it again. No one has taken it away from Me, but I lay it down on My own initiative. I have authority to take it up again. This commandment I received from My Father" (John 10:7–18; see Isaiah 40:11; 56:8; Jeremiah 23:1; Matthew 11:27).

Setting: Jerusalem. Pontius Pilate (Roman governor of Judea) continues to find no guilt in Jesus, but has Him scourged in an attempt to appease the hostile Jewish religious leaders. Pilate seeks more information about where the King of the Jews is from.

Jesus answered, "You would have no authority over Me, unless it had been given you from above; for this reason he who delivered Me to you has *the* greater sin" (John 19:11; see Romans 13:1).

REASONING (Also see MIND; and THOUGHTS)

Setting: Capernaum. When Jesus heals a paralytic man and forgives his sins, some scribes believe the Lord commits blasphemy.

Immediately Jesus, aware in His spirit that they were reasoning that way within themselves, said to them, "Why are you reasoning about these things in your hearts? Which is easier, to say to the paralytic, 'Your sins are forgiven'; or to say, 'Get up, and pick up your pallet and walk'? "But so that you may know that the Son of Man has authority on earth to forgive sins"—He said to the paralytic, "I say to you, get up, pick up your pallet and go home" (Mark 2:8–11; cf. Matthew 9:4–7; Luke 5:21–24).

Setting: Capernaum of Galilee. When Jesus heals a paralytic man and forgives his sins, some Pharisees and teachers of the law from Galilee and Judea accuse the Lord of committing blasphemy.

But Jesus, aware of their reasonings, answered and said to them, "Why are you reasoning in your hearts? Which is easier, to say, 'Your sins have been forgiven you,' or to say, 'Get up and walk'? But, so that you may know that the Son of Man has authority on earth to forgive sins,"—He said to the paralytic—"I say to you, get up, and pick up your stretcher and go home" (Luke 5:22–24; cf. Matthew 9:4–8; Mark 2:8–12; see Matthew 4:24).

REBIRTH (See BORN AGAIN)

REBUKE (Also see REPROOF)

Setting: On the way from Galilee to Jerusalem. After conveying the story of the rich man and Lazarus, the Lord gives His disciples instruction on forgiveness.

He said to His disciples, "It is inevitable that stumbling blocks come, but woe to him through whom they come! It would be better for him if a millstone were hung around his neck and he were thrown into the sea, than that he would cause one of these little ones to stumble. Be on your guard! If your brother sins, rebuke him; and if he repents, forgive him. And if he sins against you seven times a day, and returns to you seven times, saying, 'I repent,' forgive him" (Luke 17:1–4; see Matthew 18:5–7, 15, 21, 22).

RECEIVE/RECEIVED/RECEIVES/RECEIVING

Setting: Galilee. Early in His ministry, Jesus presents the Beatitudes (part of the Sermon on the Mount) to His disciples and the gathered crowds from Galilee, Decapolis, Jerusalem, Judea, and beyond the Jordan.

"Blessed are the merciful, for they shall receive mercy" (Matthew 5:7; cf. Proverb 11:17; see Matthew 13:35).

Setting: Galilee. During the early part of His ministry, Jesus preaches the Sermon on the Mount to His disciples and the multitudes.

"Ask, and it will be given to you; seek, and you will find; knock, and it will be opened to you. For everyone who asks receives, and he who seeks finds, and to him who knocks it will be opened. Or what man is there among you who, when his son asks for a loaf, will give him a stone? Or if he asks for a fish, he will not give him a snake, will he? If you then, being evil, know how to give good gifts to your children, how much more will your Father who is in heaven give what is good to those who ask Him! In everything, therefore, treat people the same way you want them to treat you, for this is the Law and the Prophets" (Matthew 7:7–12; cf. Matthew 22:40; Luke 6:31; 11:9–13; see Psalm 84:11).

Setting: Galilee. After His twelve disciples observe His ministry, Jesus summons and specifically instructs them about their ministry to the people of Israel.

These twelve Jesus sent out after instructing them: "Do not go in *the* way of *the* Gentiles, and do not enter *any* city of the Samaritans; but rather go to the lost sheep of the house of Israel. And as you go, preach, saying, 'The kingdom of heaven is at hand.' Heal *the* sick, raise *the* dead, cleanse *the* lepers, cast out demons. Freely you received, freely give. Do not acquire gold, or silver, or copper for your money belts, or a bag for *your* journey, or even two coats, or sandals, or a staff; for the worker is worthy of his support. And whatever city or village you enter, inquire who is worthy in it, and stay at his house until you leave *that city*. As you enter the house, give it your greeting. If the house is worthy, give it your *blessing of* peace. But if it is not worthy, take back your *blessing of* peace. Whoever does not receive you, nor heed your words, as you go out of that house or that city, shake the dust off your feet. Truly I say to you, it will be more tolerable for *the* land of Sodom and Gomorrah in the day of judgment than for that city" (Matthew 10:5–15; cf. Mark 6:7–11; Luke 9:1–5; see Matthew 3:2; 10:1–4; 11:22, 24; 15:24; Luke 22:35; 1 Corinthians 9:14).

Setting: Galilee. After His twelve disciples observe His ministry, Jesus summons and specifically instructs them about their ministry ahead that will include rewards.

"He who receives you receives Me, and he who receives Me receives Him who sent me. He who receives a prophet in the name of a prophet shall receive a prophet's reward; and he who receives a righteous man in the name of a righteous man shall receive a righteous man's reward. And whoever in the name of a disciple gives to one of these little ones even a cup of cold water to drink, truly I say to you, he shall not lose his reward" (Matthew 10:40–42; cf. Matthew 25:40, 44, 45; see Mark 9:37).

Setting: Galilee. As He teaches and preaches, Jesus responds to John the Baptist's question (posed by some of John's disciples) whether He is Israel's promised Messiah.

Jesus answered and said to them, "Go and report to John what you hear and see: *the* BLIND RECEIVE SIGHT and *the* lame walk, *the* lepers are cleansed and *the* deaf hear, *the* dead are raised up, and *the* POOR HAVE THE GOSPEL PREACHED TO THEM. And blessed is he who does not take offense at Me" (Matthew 11:4–6, Jesus quotes from Isaiah 35:5f; cf. Luke 7:22, 23).

Setting: By the Sea of Galilee. With the religious leaders rejecting His message, Jesus begins to teach in parables, and gives His disciples the meaning of the Parable of the Sower.

"Hear then the parable of the sower. When anyone hears the word of the kingdom and does not understand it, the evil *one* comes and snatches away what has been sown in his heart. This is the one on whom seed was sown beside the road. The one on whom seed was sown on the rocky places, this is the man who hears the word and immediately receives it with joy; yet he has no *firm* root in himself, but is *only* temporary, and when affliction or persecution arises because of the word, immediately he falls away. And the one on whom seed was sown among the thorns, this is the man who hears the word, and the worry of the world and the deceitfulness of wealth choke the word, and it becomes unfruitful. And the one on whom seed was sown on the good soil, this is the man who hears the word and understands it; who indeed bears fruit and brings forth, some a hundredfold, some sixty, and some thirty" (Matthew 13:18–23; cf. Mark 4:13–20; Luke 8:11–15).

Setting: Capernaum of Galilee. Jesus answers His disciples' question about greatness, or rank, in the kingdom of heaven.

And He called a child to Himself and set him before them, and said, "Truly I say to you, unless you are converted and become like children, you will not enter the kingdom of heaven. Whoever then humbles himself as this child, he is the greatest in the king-

dom of heaven. And whoever receives one such child in My name receives Me, but whoever causes one of these little ones who believe in Me to stumble, it would be better for him to have a heavy millstone hung around his neck, and to be drowned in the depth of the sea"
(Matthew 18:2–6; cf. Matthew 19:14; Mark 9:33–37, 42; Luke 9:47, 48; 17:1, 2).

Setting: Judea beyond the Jordan (Perea). Jesus promises rewards to His disciples for their personal sacrifice and commitment to following Him.

And Jesus said to them, "Truly I say to you, that you who have followed Me, in the regeneration when the Son of Man will sit on His glorious throne, you also shall sit upon twelve thrones, judging the twelve tribes of Israel. And everyone who has left houses or brothers or sisters or father or mother or children or farms for My name's sake, will receive many times as much, and will inherit eternal life. But many *who* are first will be last; and *the* last, first" (Matthew 19:28–30; cf. Matthew 6:33; 20:15; Mark 10:29, 30; Luke 18:29, 30; Luke 22:30).

Setting: Judea beyond the Jordan (Perea). Jesus illustrates the kingdom of heaven to His disciples through the story of laborers in the vineyard.

"For the kingdom of heaven is like a landowner who went out early in the morning to hire laborers for his vineyard. When he had agreed with the laborers for a denarius for the day, he sent them into his vineyard. And he went out about the third hour and saw others standing idle in the market place; and to those he said,' You also go into the vineyard, and whatever is right I will give you.' And *so* they went. Again he went out about the sixth and the ninth hour, and did the same thing. And about the eleventh *hour* he went out and found others standing *around;* and he said to them, 'Why have you been standing idle here all day long?' They said to him, 'Because no one hired us.' He said to them, 'You go into the vineyard too.' When evening came, the owner of the vineyard said to his foreman, 'Call the laborers and pay them their wages, beginning with the last *group* to the first.' When those *hired* about the eleventh hour came, each one received a denarius. When those *hired* first came, they thought that they would receive more; but each of them also received a denarius. When they received it, they grumbled at the landowner, saying, 'These last men have worked *only* one hour, and you have made them equal to us who have borne the burden and the scorching heat of the day.' But he answered and said to one of them, 'Friend, I am doing you no wrong; did you not agree with me for a denarius? Take what is yours and go, but I wish to give to this last man the same as to you. It is not lawful for me to do what I wish with what is my own? Or is your eye envious because I am generous?' So the last shall be first, and the first last" (Matthew 20:1–16; cf. Matthew 19:30).

Setting: On the way from Bethany to Jerusalem. The day after Jesus curses a fig tree (an illustration of the nation Israel), His disciples ask Him how it has so quickly withered.

And Jesus answered and said to them, "Truly I say to you, if you have faith and do not doubt, you will not only do what was done to the fig tree, but even if you say to this mountain, 'Be taken up and cast into the sea,' it will happen. And all things you ask in prayer, believing, you will receive" (Matthew 21:21, 22; cf. Matthew 7:7; 17:20; Mark 11:20–24).

Setting: The temple in Jerusalem. Jesus delivers another parable to the chief priests and elders after they question His authority.

"Listen to another parable. There was a landowner who PLANTED A VINEYARD AND PUT A WALL AROUND IT AND DUG A WINE PRESS IN IT, AND BUILT A TOWER, and rented it out to vine-growers and went on a journey. When the harvest time approached, he sent his slaves to the vine-growers to receive his produce. The vine-growers took his slaves and beat one, and killed another, and stoned a third. Again he sent another group of slaves larger than the first; and they did the same thing to them. But afterward he sent his son to them, saying, 'They will respect my son.' But when the vine-growers saw the son, they said among themselves, 'This is the heir; come, let us kill him and seize his inheritance.' They took him, and threw him out of the vineyard and killed him. Therefore when the owner of the vineyard comes, what will he do to those vine-growers?" (Matthew 21:33–40; Jesus quotes from Isaiah 5:1, 2; cf. Mark 12:1–9; Luke 20:9–15).

Setting: The temple in Jerusalem. After the Jewish religious leaders test Him with questions, Jesus pronounces the second of eight woes upon them in front of the crowds and His disciples.

["Woe to you, scribes and Pharisees, hypocrites, because you devour widows' houses, and for a pretense you make long prayers; therefore you will receive greater condemnation] (Matthew 23:14; cf. Mark 12:40; Luke 20:47).

Setting: On the Mount of Olives, just east of Jerusalem. During His Olivet Discourse, after answering His disciples' questions as to when the temple will be destroyed and Jerusalem overrun, along with the signs of His coming and the end of the age, Jesus reemphasizes to His disciples that they should be on the alert for His return.

"For *it is* just like a man *about* to go on a journey, who called his own slaves and entrusted his possessions to them. To one he gave five talents, to another, two, and to another, one, each according to his own ability; and he went on his journey. Immediately the one who had received the five talents went and traded with them, and gained five more talents. In the same manner the one who *had received* the two *talents* gained two more. But he who received the one *talent* went away, and dug a *hole* in the ground and hid his master's money. Now after a long time the master of those slaves came and settled accounts with them. The one who had received the five talents came up and brought five more talents, saying, 'Master, you entrusted five talents to me. See, I have gained five more talents.' His master said to him, 'Well done, good and faithful slave. You were faithful with a few things, I will put you in charge of many things; enter into the joy of your master.' Also the one who *had received* the two talents came up and said, 'Master, you entrusted two talents to me. See, I have gained two more talents.' His master said to him, 'Well done, good and faithful slave. You were faithful with a few things, I will put you in charge of many things; enter into the joy of your master.' And the one also who had received the one talent came up and said, 'Master, I knew you to be a hard man, reaping where you did not sow and gathering where you scattered no *seed.* And I was afraid, and went away and hid your talent in the ground. See, you have what is yours.' But his master answered and said to him, 'You wicked, lazy slave, you knew that I reap where I did not sow and gather where I scattered no *seed.* Then you ought to have put my money in the bank, and on my arrival I would have received my *money* back with interest. 'Therefore take away the talent from him, and give it to the one who has ten talents.' For to everyone who has, *more* shall be given, and he will have an abundance; but from the one who does not have, even what he does have shall be taken away. Throw out the worthless slave into the outer darkness; in that place there will be weeping and gnashing of teeth" (Matthew 25:14–30; cf. Matthew 8:12; 13:12; 24:45–47; see Matthew 18:23, 24; Luke 12:44).

Setting: By the Sea of Galilee. During the early part of His ministry, after presenting the Parable of the Sower from a boat to a very large crowd, Jesus gives the meaning of the parable to His disciples and other followers.

And He said to them, "Do you not understand this parable? How will you understand all the parables? The sower sows the word. These are the ones who are beside the road where the word is sown; and when they hear, immediately Satan comes and takes away the word which has been sown in them. In a similar way these are the ones on whom seed was sown on the rocky places, who, when they hear the word, immediately receive it with joy; and they have no *firm* root in themselves, but are *only* temporary; then, when affliction or persecution arises because of the word, immediately they fall away. And others are the ones on whom seed was sown among the thorns; these are the ones who have heard the word, but the worries of the world and the deceitfulness of riches, and the desires for other things enter in and choke the word, and it becomes unfruitful. And those are the ones on whom seed was sown on the good soil; and they hear the word and accept it and bear fruit, thirty, sixty, and a hundredfold" (Mark 4:13–20; cf. Matthew 13:18–23; Luke 8:11–15).

Setting: Jesus' hometown of Nazareth in Galilee. After encountering unbelief, Jesus sends the Twelve out in pairs with authority and instructions about ministry.

And He summoned the twelve and began to send them out in pairs, and gave them authority over the unclean spirits; and He instructed them that they should take nothing for *their* journey, except a mere staff—no bread, no bag, no money in their belt—but to wear sandals; and *He added,* "Do not put on two tunics." And He said to them, "Wherever you enter a house, stay there until you leave town. Any place that does not receive you or listen to you, as you go out from there, shake the dust off the soles of your feet for a testimony against them" (Mark 6:7–11; cf. Matthew 10:1–14; Luke 9:1–5).

Setting: Capernaum of Galilee. As Jesus teaches His disciples in private, they ask Him about greatness.

They came to Capernaum; and when He was in the house, He *began* to question them, "What were you discussing on the way?" But they kept silent, for on the way they had discussed with one another which *of them* was the greatest. Sitting down, He called the twelve and said to them, "If anyone wants to be first, he shall be last of all and servant of all." Taking a child, He set him before them, and taking him in His arms, He said to them, "Whoever receives one child like this in My name receives Me; and whoever receives Me does not receive Me, but Him who sent Me" (Mark 9:33–37; cf. Matthew 18:1–5; see Matthew 20:26; Matthew 10:40).

Setting: Judea beyond the Jordan (Perea). After the Pharisees test and question Him about divorce, Jesus demonstrates to His disciples the importance of little children.

But when Jesus saw this, He was indignant and said to them, "Permit the children to come to Me; do not hinder them; for the kingdom of God belongs to such as these. Truly I say to you, whoever does not receive the kingdom of God like a child will not enter it *at all*" (Mark 10:14, 15; cf. Matthew 19:13–15; Luke 18:15–17; see Matthew 18:3).

Setting: Judea beyond the Jordan (Perea). After informing a rich man how righteous believers may have treasure in heaven, Jesus tells His disciples about the reward of those who sacrifice in this life to follow Him.

Jesus said, "Truly I say to you, there is no one who has left house or brothers or sisters or mother or father or children or farms, for My sake and for the gospel's sake, but that he will receive a hundred times as much now in the present age, houses and brothers and sisters and mothers and children and farms, along with persecutions; and in the age to come, eternal life. But many *who are* first will be last, and the last, first" (Mark 10:29–31; cf. Matthew 19:27–30; Luke 18:28–30; see Matthew 6:33).

Setting: The temple in Jerusalem. Having His authority questioned by the chief priests, scribes, and elders, Jesus begins to teach them in parables.

And He began to speak to them in parables: "A man PLANTED A VINEYARD AND PUT A WALL AROUND IT, AND DUG A VAT UNDER THE WINE PRESS AND BUILT A TOWER, and rented it out to vine-growers and went on a journey. At the *harvest* time he sent a slave to the vine-growers, in order to receive *some* of the produce of the vineyard from the vine-growers. They took him, and beat him and sent him away empty-handed. Again he sent them another slave, and they wounded him in the head, and treated him shamefully. And he sent another, and that one they killed; and *so with* many others, beating some and killing others. He had one more to *send*, a beloved son; he sent him last *of all* to them, saying, 'They will respect my son.' But those vine-growers said to one another, 'This is the heir; come, let us kill him, and the inheritance will be ours!' They took him, and killed him and threw him out of the vineyard. What will the owner of the vineyard do? He will come and destroy the vine-growers, and will give the vineyard to others. Have you not even read this Scripture: 'THE STONE WHICH THE BUILDERS REJECTED, THIS BECAME THE CHIEF CORNER *stone;* THIS CAME ABOUT FROM THE LORD, AND IT IS MARVELOUS IN OUR EYES'?" (Mark 12:1–11, Jesus quotes from Psalm 118:22, 23; Isaiah 5:1, 2; cf. Matthew 21:33–46; Luke 20:9–19).

Setting: The temple in Jerusalem. After commending one scribe for his nearness to the kingdom of God, Jesus warns the crowd about the majority of the scribes.

In His teaching He was saying: "Beware of the scribes who like to walk around in long robes, and *like* respectful greetings in the market places, and chief seats in the synagogues and places of honor at banquets, who devour widows' houses, and for appearance's sake offer long prayers; these will receive greater condemnation" (Mark 12:38–40; cf. Matthew 23:1–7; Luke 20:45–47).

Setting: Just outside Jerusalem. The day after Jesus instructs the money changers while He cleanses the temple, Peter draws the Lord's and His disciples' attention to an earlier-cursed fig tree.

And Jesus answered saying to them, "Have faith in God. Truly, I say to you, whoever says to this mountain, 'Be taken up and cast into the sea,' and does not doubt in his heart, but believes that what he says is going to happen, it will be *granted* him. Therefore

I say to you, all things for which you pray and ask, believe that you have received them, and they will be *granted* you. Whenever you stand praying, forgive, if you have anything against anyone, so that your Father who is in heaven will also forgive you your transgressions. [But if you do not forgive, neither will your Father who is in heaven forgive your transgressions'] (Mark 11:22–26; cf. Matthew 21:19–22; see Matthew 6:14, 15; 7:7; 17:20).

Setting: Galilee. After selecting His twelve disciples, Jesus teaches the Beatitudes (part of the Sermon on the Mount) to those disciples and a great throng of people from Judea, Jerusalem, and the central coastal region of Tyre and Sidon.

"But woe to you who are rich, for you are receiving your comfort in full" (Luke 6:24).

Setting: Galilee. After selecting His twelve disciples, Jesus teaches the Sermon on the Mount to those disciples and a great throng of people from Judea, Jerusalem, and the central coastal region of Tyre and Sidon.

"But I say to you who hear, love your enemies, do good to those who hate you, bless those who curse you, pray for those who mistreat you. Whoever hits you on the cheek, offer him the other also; and whoever takes away your coat, do not withhold your shirt from him either. Give to everyone who asks of you, and whoever takes away what is yours, do not demand it back. Treat others the same way you want them to treat you. If you love those who love you, what credit is *that* to you? For even sinners love those who love them. If you do good to those who do good to you, what credit is *that* to you? For even sinners do the same. If you lend to those from whom you expect to receive, what credit is *that* to you? Even sinners lend to sinners in order to receive back the same *amount*. But love your enemies, and do good, and lend, expecting nothing in return; and your reward will be great, and you will be sons of the Most High; for He Himself is kind to ungrateful and evil *men*. Be merciful, just as your Father is merciful" (Luke 6:27–36; cf. Matthew 5:9, 39–48; Matthew 7:12).

Setting: Galilee. After Jesus raises a woman's son from the dead in Nain, the disciples of John the Baptist inquire whether the Lord is the promised Messiah.

And He answered and said to them, "Go and report to John what you have seen and heard: *the* BLIND RECEIVE SIGHT, *the* lame walk, *the* lepers are cleansed, and *the* deaf hear, *the* dead are raised up, *the* POOR HAVE THE GOSPEL PREACHED TO THEM. Blessed is he who does not take offense at Me" (Luke 7:22, 23, Jesus quotes from Isaiah 35:5; 61:1; cf. Matthew 11:2–6).

Setting: Galilee. After Jesus presents the Parable of the Sower to the crowds, His disciples ask Him to give them the parable's meaning.

And He said, "To you it has been granted to know the mysteries of the kingdom of God, but to the rest *it is* in parables, so that SEEING THEY MAY NOT SEE, AND HEARING THEY MAY NOT UNDERSTAND. Now the parable is this: the seed is the word of God. Those beside the road are those who have heard; then the devil comes and takes away the word from their heart, so that they will not believe and be saved. Those on the rocky *soil* are those who, when they hear, receive the word with joy; and these have no *firm* root; they believe for a while, and in time of temptation fall away. The *seed* which fell among the thorns, these are the ones who have heard, and as they go on their way they are choked with worries and riches and pleasures of *this* life, and bring no fruit to maturity. But the *seed* in the good soil, these are the ones who have heard the word in an honest and good heart, and hold it fast, and bear fruit with perseverance" (Luke 8:10–15, Jesus quotes from Isaiah 6:9; cf. Matthew 13:10–23; Mark 4:10–20).

Setting: Galilee. After raising Jairus's daughter from the dead, Jesus calls the twelve disciples together and gives them power and authority over demons, along with the ability to cure diseases.

And He said to them, "Take nothing for *your* journey, neither a staff, nor a bag, nor bread, nor money; and do not *even* have two tunics apiece. Whatever house you enter, stay there until you leave that city. And as for those who do not receive you, go out from that city, shake the dust off your feet as a testimony against them" (Luke 9:3–5; cf. Matthew 10:1–15; Mark 6:7–11; see Luke 10:4–12).

Setting: Galilee. After Jesus prophesies His death, an argument arises among His disciples as to who is the greatest. The Lord resolves the matter by using a child as a teaching illustration.

But Jesus, knowing what they were thinking in their heart, took a child and stood him by His side, and said to them, "Whoever receives this child in My name receives Me, and whoever receives Me receives Him who sent Me; for the one who is least among all of you, this is the one who is great" (Luke 9:47, 48; cf. Matthew 18:1–5; Mark 9:33–47; see Matthew 10:40; Luke 22:24).

Setting: On the way from Galilee to Jerusalem. The Lord appoints seventy followers and sends them out in pairs to every place He Himself will soon visit.

And He was saying to them, "The harvest is plentiful, but the laborers are few; therefore beseech the Lord of the harvest to send out laborers into His harvest. Go; behold, I send you out as lambs in the midst of wolves. Carry no money belt, no bag, no shoes; and greet no one on the way. Whatever house you enter, first say, 'Peace be to this house.' If a man of peace is there, your peace will rest on him; but if not, it will return to you. Stay in that house, eating and drinking what they give you; for the laborer is worthy of his wages. Do not keep moving from house to house. Whatever city you enter and they receive you, eat what is set before you; and heal those in it who are sick, and say to them, 'The kingdom of God has come near to you.' But whatever city you enter and they do not receive you, go out into its streets and say, 'Even the dust of your city which clings to our feet we wipe off *in protest* against you; yet be sure of this, that the kingdom of God has come near.' I say to you, it will be more tolerable in that day for Sodom than for that city" (Luke 10:2–12; see Genesis 19:24–28; Matthew 9:37, 38, 10:9–14, 16; 1 Corinthians 10:27).

Setting: On the way from Galilee to Jerusalem. After revealing to His disciples how to pray, Jesus illustrates persistence in prayer.

Then He said to them, "Suppose one of you has a friend, and goes to him at midnight and says to him, 'Friend, lend me three loaves; for a friend of mine has come to me from a journey, and I have nothing to set before him'; and from inside he answers and says, 'Do not bother me; the door has already been shut and my children and I are in bed; I cannot get up and give you *anything.*' I tell you, even though he will not get up and give him *anything* because he is his friend, yet because of his persistence he will get up and give him as much as he needs. So I say to you, ask, and it will be given to you; seek, and you will find; knock, and it will be opened to you. For everyone who asks, receives; and he who seeks, finds; and to him who knocks, it will be opened" (Luke 11:5–10; cf. Matthew 7:7, 8).

Setting: On the way from Galilee to Jerusalem. When Jesus uses a parable to challenge the crowd and His disciples to be ready for His return, Peter asks Him whom He is addressing.

And the Lord said, "Who then is the faithful and sensible steward, whom his master will put in charge of his servants, to give them their rations at the proper time? Blessed is that slave whom his master finds so doing when he comes. Truly I say to you that he will put him in charge of all his possessions. But if that slave says in his heart, 'My master will be a long time in coming,' and begins to beat the slaves, *both* men and women, and to eat and drink and get drunk; the master of that slave will come on a day when he does not expect *him* and at an hour he does not know, and will cut him in pieces, and assign him a place with the unbelievers. And that slave who knew his master's will and did not get ready or act in accord with his will, will receive many lashes, but the one who did know *it,* and committed deeds worthy of flogging, will receive but few. From everyone who has been given much, much will be required; and to whom they entrusted much, of him they will ask all the more" (Luke 12:42–48; cf. Matthew 24:45–51; see Leviticus 5:17).

Setting: On the way from Galilee to Jerusalem. Jesus conveys the illustration of the prodigal son because the Pharisees and scribes complain He associates with tax collectors and sinners.

And He said, "A man had two sons. The younger of them said to his father, 'Father, give me the share of the estate that falls to me.' So he divided his wealth between them. And not many days later, the younger son gathered everything together and went on a journey into a distant country, and there he squandered his estate with loose living. Now when he had spent everything, a severe famine occurred in that country, and he began to be impoverished. So he went and hired himself out to one of the citizens of that country, and he sent him into his fields to feed swine. And he would have gladly filled his stomach with the pods that the swine were eating, and no one was giving *anything* to him. But when he came to his senses, he said, 'How many of my father's hired men have more than enough bread, but I am dying here with hunger! I will get up and go to my father, and will say to him, "Father, I have sinned against heaven, and in your sight; I am no longer worthy to be called your son; make me as one of your hired men."' So he got up and came to his father. But while he was still a long way off, his father saw him and felt compassion *for him,* and ran and embraced him and kissed him. And the son said to him, "Father, I have sinned against heaven and in your sight; I am no longer worthy to be called your son.' But the father said to his slaves, 'Quickly bring out the best robe and put it on him, and put a ring on his hand and sandals on his feet; and bring the fattened calf, kill it, and let us eat and celebrate; for this son of mine was dead and has come to life again; he was lost and has been found.' And they began to celebrate. Now his older son was in the field, when he came and approached the house, he heard music and dancing. And he summoned one of the servants and *began* inquiring what these things could be. And he said to him, 'Your brother has come, and your father has killed the fattened calf because he has received him back safe and sound.' But he became angry and was not willing to go in; and his father came out and *began* pleading with him. But he answered and said to his father, 'Look! For so many years I have been serving you and I have never neglected a command of yours; and *yet* you have never given me a young goat, so that I might celebrate with my friends; but when this son of yours came, who has devoured your wealth with prostitutes, you killed the fattened calf for him.' And he said to him, 'Son, you have always been with me, and all that is mine is yours. But we had to celebrate and rejoice, for this brother of yours was dead and *has begun* to live, and was lost and has been found' " (Luke 15:11–32; see Proverb 29:2).

Setting: On the way from Galilee to Jerusalem. After giving the story of the prodigal son, the Lord teaches His disciples about stewardship.

Now He was also saying to the disciples, "There was a rich man who had a manager, and this *manager* was reported to him as squandering his possessions. And he called him and said to him, 'What is this I hear about you? Give an accounting of your management, for you can no longer be a manager.' The manager said to himself, 'What shall I do, since my master is taking the management away from me? I am not strong enough to dig; I am ashamed to beg. I know what I shall do, so that when I am removed from the management people will welcome me into their homes.' And he summoned each one of his master's debtors, and he *began* saying to the first, 'How much do you owe my master?' And he said, 'A hundred measures of oil.' And he said to him, 'Take your bill, and sit down quickly and write fifty.' Then he said to another, 'And how much do you owe?' And he said, 'A hundred measures of wheat.' He said to him, 'Take your bill, and write eighty.' And his master praised the unrighteous manager because he had acted shrewdly; for the sons of this age are more shrewd in relation to their own kind than the sons of light. And I say to you, make friends for yourselves by means of the wealth of unrighteousness, so that when it fails, they will receive you into the eternal dwellings. He who is faithful in a very little thing is faithful also in much; and he who is unrighteous in a very little thing is unrighteous also in much. Therefore if you have not been faithful in the *use of* unrighteous wealth, who will entrust the true *riches* to you? And if you have not been faithful in *the use of* that which is another's, who will give you that which is your own? No servant can serve two masters; for either he will hate the one and love the other, or else he will be devoted to one and despise the other. You cannot serve God and wealth" (Luke 16:1–13; cf. Matthew 6:24; see Matthew 25:14–30).

Setting: On the way from Galilee to Jerusalem. After responding to the Pharisees' scoffing at His teaching the disciples about stewardship and the permanence of the Law, Jesus conveys the story of the rich man and Lazarus.

"Now there was a rich man, and he habitually dressed in purple and fine linen, joyously living in splendor every day. And a poor man named Lazarus was laid at his gate, covered with sores, and longing to be fed with the *crumbs* which were falling from the rich man's table; besides, even the dogs were coming and licking his sores. Now the poor man died and was carried away by the angels to Abraham's bosom; and the rich man also died and was buried. In Hades he lifted up his eyes, being in torment, and saw Abraham far away and Lazarus in his bosom. And he cried out and said, 'Father Abraham, have mercy on me, and send Lazarus so that he may dip the tip of his finger in water and cool off my tongue, for I am in agony in this flame.' But Abraham said, 'Child, remember that during your life you received your good things, and likewise Lazarus bad things; but now he is being comforted here, and you are in agony. And besides all this, between us and you there is a great chasm fixed, so that those who wish to come over from here to you will not be able, and *that* none may cross over from there to us.' And he said, 'Then I beg you, father, that you send him to my father's house—for I have five brothers—in order that he may warn them, so that they will not also come to this place of torment.' But Abraham said, 'They have Moses and the Prophets; let them hear them.' But he said, 'No, father Abraham, but if someone goes to them from the dead, they will repent!' But he said to him, 'If they do not listen to Moses and the Prophets, they will not be persuaded even if someone rises from the dead' " (Luke 16:19–31; see Luke 3:8; 6:24; 16:1, 14).

Setting: Perea, en route from Galilee to Jerusalem. After giving a parable about self-righteousness, Jesus speaks of the importance of children.

But Jesus called for them, saying, "Permit the children to come to Me, and do not hinder them, for the kingdom of God belongs to such as these. Truly I say to you, whoever does not receive the kingdom of God like a child will not enter it *at all*" (Luke 18:16, 17; cf. Matthew 19:13–15; Mark 10:13–16; see Matthew 18:3).

Setting: Perea, en route from Galilee to Jerusalem. After responding to His disciples' question about salvation, Jesus replies to Peter's statement about the disciples' personal sacrifice.

Peter said, "Behold, we have left our own *homes* and followed You." And He said to them, "Truly I say to you, there is no one who has left house or wife or brothers or parents or children, for the sake of the kingdom of God, who will not receive many times as much at this time and in the age to come, eternal life" (Luke 18:28–30; cf. Matthew 19:27–29; Mark 10:28–30; see Matthew 6:33; Luke 5:11).

Setting: On the way from Galilee to Jerusalem. After telling the disciples of the upcoming sacrifice He will make in Jerusalem, while approaching Jericho, Jesus takes time to heal a blind man.

And Jesus stopped and commanded that he be brought to Him; and when he came near, He questioned him, "What do you want Me to do for you?" And he said, "Lord, *I want* to regain my sight!" And Jesus said to him, "Receive your sight; your faith has made you well" (Luke 18:40–42; cf. Matthew 20:29–34; Mark 10:46–52).

Setting: Jericho, on the way to Jerusalem. After commending Zaccheus's faith in Him, Jesus provides a parable about stewardship.

So He said, "A nobleman went to a distant country to receive a kingdom for himself, and *then* return. And he called ten of his slaves, and gave them ten minas and said to them, 'Do business *with this* until I come *back*.' But his citizens hated him and sent a delegation after him, saying, 'We do not want this man to reign over us.' When he returned, after receiving the kingdom, he ordered that these slaves, to whom he had given the money, be called to him so that he might know what business they had done. The first appeared, saying, 'Master, your mina has made ten minas more.' And he said to him, 'Well done, good slave, because you have been faithful in a very little thing, you are to be in authority over ten cities.' The second came, saying, 'Your mina, master, has made five minas.' And he said to him, also, 'And you are to be over five cities.' Another came, saying, 'Master, here is your mina, which I kept put away in a handkerchief; for I was afraid of you, because you are an exacting man; you take up what you did not lay down and reap what you did not sow.' He said to him, 'By your own words I will judge you, you worthless slave. Did you know that I am an exacting man, taking up what I did not lay down and reaping what I did not sow? Then why did you not put my money in the bank, and having come, I would have collected it with interest?' Then he said to the bystanders, 'Take the mina away from him and give it to the one who has the ten minas.' And they said to him, 'Master, he has ten minas *already*.' I tell you that to everyone who has, more shall be given, but from the one who does not have, even what he does have shall be taken away. But these enemies of mine, who did not want me to reign over them, bring them here and slay them in my presence" (Luke 19:12–27; cf. Matthew 25:14–30; see Matthew 13:12; Luke 16:10).

Setting: The temple in Jerusalem. While ministering a few days before His crucifixion, after posing a question to the scribes, who do not answer, Jesus warns His disciples about the lifestyle of the scribes.

"Beware of the scribes, who like to walk around in long robes, and love respectful greetings in the market places, and chief seats in the synagogues and places of honor at banquets, who devour widows' houses, and for appearance's sake offer long prayers. These will receive greater condemnation" (Luke 20:46, 47; cf. Matthew 23:1–7; Mark 12:38–40; see Luke 11:43).

Setting: Sychar in Samaria, on the way to Galilee. After Jesus converses with a Samaritan woman at Jacob's well, the disciples return with food. They try to get Jesus to eat, but are surprised when He speaks of other food.

Jesus said to them, "My food is to do the will of Him who sent Me and to accomplish His work. Do you not say, 'There are yet four months, and *then* comes the harvest'? Behold, I say to you, lift up your eyes and look on the fields, that they are white for harvest. Already he who reaps is receiving wages and is gathering fruit for life eternal; so that he who sows and he who reaps may rejoice together. For in this *case* the saying is true, 'One sows and another reaps.' I sent you to reap that for which you have not labored; others have labored and you have entered into their labor" (John 4:34–38; see Matthew 9:37, 38; John 5:36).

Setting: Jerusalem. During a feast of the Jews, Jesus responds to criticism from the Jewish religious leaders by referring to God as His Father (thereby making Himself equal with God) and informing them that God, John the Baptist, and His works all testify to His mission.

"I can do nothing on My own initiative. As I hear, I judge; and My judgment is just, because I do not seek My own will, but the will of Him who sent Me. If I *alone* testify about Myself, My testimony is not true. There is another who testifies of Me, and I know that the testimony which He gives about Me is true. You have sent to John, and he has testified to the truth. But the testimony which I receive is not from man, but I say these things so that you may be saved. He was the lamp that was burning and was shining and you were willing to rejoice for a while in his light. But the testimony which I have is greater than the *testimony of* John; for the works which the Father has given Me to accomplish—the very works that I do—testify about Me, that the Father has sent Me. And the Father who sent Me, He has testified of Me. You have neither heard His voice at any time nor seen His form. You do not have His word abiding in you, for you do not believe Him whom He sent" (John 5:30–38; see Matthew 3:17; Mark 1:4, 5; John 1:7, 15, 32; 4:34; 8:14–16; 10:25, 37, 38).

Setting: Jerusalem. During a feast of the Jews, Jesus responds to criticism from the Jewish religious leaders by referring to God as His Father (thereby making Himself equal with God) and informing them that God, John the Baptist, the Scriptures, and His works all testify to His mission.

"You search the Scriptures because you think that in them you have eternal life; it is these that testify about Me; and you are unwilling to come to Me so that you may have life. I do not receive glory from men; but I know you, that you do not have the love of God in yourselves. I have come in My Father's name, and you do not receive Me; if another comes in his own name, you will receive him. How can you believe, when you receive glory from one another and you do not seek the glory that is from the *one and* only God? Do not think that I will accuse you before the Father; the one who accuses you is Moses, in whom you have set your hope. For if you believed Moses, you would believe Me, for he wrote about Me. But if you do not believe his writings, how will you believe My words?" (John 5:39–47; see Matthew 24:5; Luke 16:29, 31; 24:27; John 9:28; 17:3).

Setting: The temple in Jerusalem. After receiving encouragement from His blood brothers in Galilee to attend the upcoming Feast of Booths in order to demonstrate His works to His disciples and the world, Jesus goes and teaches, astonishing the Jewish religious leaders.

Jesus answered them, "I did one deed, and you all marvel. For this reason Moses has given you circumcision (not because it is from Moses, but from the fathers), and on *the* Sabbath you circumcise a man. If a man receives circumcision on *the* Sabbath so that the Law of Moses will not be broken, are you angry with Me because I made an entire man well on *the* Sabbath? Do not judge according to appearance, but judge with righteous judgment" (John 7:21–24; see Genesis 17:10–14; Leviticus 12:3; 19:15; Matthew 12:2; John 5:2–16; 7–20; 7:10–15).

Setting: Jerusalem. Following the Pharisees' interrogation and dismissal of the formerly blind man Jesus healed on the Sabbath, the Lord conveys the Parable of the Good Shepherd to the Pharisees, using figures of speech they do not understand.

So Jesus said to them again, "Truly, truly, I say to you, I am the door of the sheep. All who came before Me are thieves and robbers, but the sheep did not hear them. I am the door; if anyone enters through Me, he will be saved, and will go in and out and find pasture. The thief comes only to steal and kill and destroy; I came that they may have life, and have *it* abundantly. I am the good shepherd; the good shepherd lays down His life for the sheep. He who is a hired hand, and not a shepherd, who is not the owner of the sheep, sees the wolf coming, and leaves the sheep and flees, and the wolf snatches them and scatters *them. He flees* because he is a hired hand and is not concerned about the sheep. I am the good shepherd, and I know My own and My own know Me, even as the Father knows Me and I know the Father; and I lay down My life for the sheep. I have other sheep, which are not of this fold; I must bring them also, and they will hear My voice; and they will become one flock *with* one shepherd. For this reason the Father loves Me, because I lay down My life so that I may take it again. No one has taken it away from Me, but I lay it down on My own initiative. I have authority to take it up again. This commandment I received from My Father" (John 10:7–18; see Isaiah 40:11; 56:8; Jeremiah 23:1; Matthew 11:27).

Setting: Jerusalem. Just days before the Passover, with the chief priests and Pharisees plotting to seize Jesus, who is expressing anxiety about His upcoming crucifixion, some of the Jews believe in the Lord, while others are rejecting His message.

And Jesus cried out and said, "He who believes in Me, does not believe in Me but in Him who sent Me. He who sees Me sees the One who sent Me. I have come *as* Light into the world, so that everyone who believes in Me will not remain in darkness. If anyone hears My sayings and does not keep them, I do not judge him; for I did not come to judge the world, but to save the world. He who rejects Me and does not receive My sayings, has one who judges him; the word I spoke is what will judge him at the last day. For I did not speak on My own initiative, but the Father Himself who sent Me has given Me a commandment *as to* what to say and what to speak. I know that His commandment is eternal life; therefore the things I speak, I speak just as the Father as told Me" (John 12:44–50; see Matthew 10:40; Luke 10:16; John 1:4; 3:17; 5:19; 6:68; 14:9).

Setting: Jerusalem. Before the Passover, with His death on the cross nearing, Jesus explains the reason for His vivid example of servanthood in washing His disciples' feet.

So when He had washed their feet, and taken His garments and reclined *at the table* again, He said to them, "Do you know what I have done to you? You call Me Teacher and Lord; and you are right, for *so* I am. If I then, the Lord and the Teacher, washed your feet, you also ought to wash one another's feet. For I gave you an example that you also should do as I did to you. Truly, truly I say to you, a slave is not greater than his master, nor *is* one who is sent greater than the one who sent him. If you know these things, you are blessed if you do them. I do not speak of all of you. I know the ones I have chosen; but *it is* that the Scripture may be fulfilled, 'HE WHO EATS MY BREAD HAS LIFTED UP HIS HEEL AGAINST ME.' From now on I am telling you before *it* comes to pass, so that when it does occur, you may believe that I am *He*. Truly, truly, I say to you, he who receives whomever I send receives Me; and he who receives Me receives Him who sent Me" (John 13:12–20; Jesus quotes from Psalm 41:9; see Matthew 7:24; 10:24, 40; John 8:24; 13:1–11; 14:29; 1 Peter 5:3).

Setting: Jerusalem. Before the Passover, after taking issue with Peter's assertion that he would lay down his life for Him, Jesus comforts and gives hope to His disciples regarding their future after He returns to heaven.

"Do not let your heart be troubled; believe in God, believe also in Me. In My Father's house are many dwelling places; if it were not so, I would have told you; for I go to prepare a place for you. If I go and prepare a place for you, I will come again and receive you to Myself, that where I am, *there* you may be also. And you know the way where I am going" (John 14:1–4; see John 13:35; 14:27, 28).

Setting: Jerusalem. Before the Passover, after responding to Philip's request for Him to show His disciples the Father, Jesus conveys the upcoming role of the Holy Spirit in their lives.

"If you love Me, you will keep My commandments. I will ask the Father, and He will give you another Helper, that He may be with you forever; *that* is the Spirit of truth, whom the world cannot receive, because it does not see Him or know Him, *but* you know Him because He abides with you and will be in you" (John 14:15–17; see John 7:39; 14:1–14, 21, 23; 15:26; 1 John 5:3).

Setting: Jerusalem. Before the Passover, after empathizing with His disciples' sadness over His prophecies and giving them the hope for the future, Jesus conveys promises about praying in His name.

"In that day you will not question Me about anything. Truly, truly, I say to you, if you ask the Father for anything in My name, He will give it to you. Until now you have asked for nothing in My name; ask and you will receive, so that your joy may be made full. These things I have spoken to you in figurative language; an hour is coming when I will no longer speak to you in figurative language, but will tell you plainly of the Father. In that day you will ask in My name, and I do not say to you that I will request of the Father on your behalf; for the Father Himself loves you, because you have loved Me and have believed that I came forth from the Father. I came forth from the Father and have come into the world; I am leaving the world again and going to the Father" (John 16:23–28; see Matthew 13:34; John 8:42; 13:1, 3; 14:14, 21, 23; 15:16).

Setting: Jerusalem. Before the Passover, after giving His disciples hope that in the midst of tribulation they will have His peace, Jesus prays His high-priestly prayer.

Jesus spoke these things; and lifting up His eyes to heaven, He said, "Father, the hour has come; glorify Your Son, that the Son may glorify You, even as You gave Him authority over all flesh, that to all whom You have given Him, He may give eternal life. This is eternal life, that they may know You, the only true God, and Jesus Christ whom You have sent. I glorified You on the earth, having accomplished the work which You have given Me to do. Now, Father, glorify Me together with Yourself, with the glory which I had with You before the world was. I have manifested Your name to the men whom You gave Me out of the world; they were Yours and You gave them to Me, and they have kept Your word. Now they have come to know that everything You have given Me is from You; for the words which You gave Me I have given to them; and they received *them* and truly understood that I came forth from You, and they believed You sent Me. I ask on their behalf; I do not ask on behalf of the world, but of those whom You have given Me; for they are Yours; and all things that are Mine are Yours, and Yours are Mine; and I have been glorified in them. I am no longer in the world; and *yet* they themselves are in the world, and I come to You. Holy Father, keep them in Your name, *the name* which You have given Me, that they may be even as We *are.* While I was with them, I was keeping them in Your name which You have given Me; and I guarded them and not one of them perished but the son of perdition, so that the Scripture would be fulfilled" (John 17:1–12; see Luke 22:32; John 1:1; 3:35; 4:34; 5:44; 6:37–39, 70; 8:42; 11:41; 12:49; 13:18, 31; 16:15; Philippians 2:9).

Setting: Jerusalem. After Mary Magdalene encounters the risen Jesus in the morning, that evening He stands in the midst of His disciples (with the exception of Thomas), in hiding behind closed doors due to fear of the Jewish religious leadership.

So when it was evening on that day, the first *day* of the week, and when the doors were shut where the disciples were, for fear of the Jews, Jesus came and stood in their midst and said to them, "Peace *be* with you." And when He had said this, He showed them both His hands and His side. The disciples then rejoiced when they saw the Lord. So Jesus said to them again, "Peace *be* with you; as the Father has sent Me, I also send you." And when He had said this, He breathed on them and said to them, "Receive the Holy Spirit. If you forgive the sins of any, *their sins* have been forgiven them; if you retain the *sins* of any, they have been retained" (John 20:19–23; cf. Luke 24:36–43; see Matthew 16:19; Mark 16:14).

Setting: Jerusalem. Luke, writing in Acts, presents quotes from Jesus' post-resurrection appearances, in which He responds to His disciples' question whether He is about to restore the kingdom to Israel.

He said to them, "It is not for you to know times or epochs which the Father has fixed by His own authority; but you will receive power when the Holy Spirit has come upon you; and you shall be My witnesses both in Jerusalem, and in all Judea and Samaria, and even to the remotest part of the earth" (Acts 1:7, 8; see Luke 24:48, 49; Acts 2:1–4).

Setting: Ephesus. Luke, writing in Acts, recounts Paul's recollection of Jesus' words regarding giving and receiving during the apostle's farewell address to the elders of the church at Ephesus during his third missionary journey, just before leaving for Jerusalem.

"In everything I showed you that working hard in this manner you must help the weak and remember the words of the Lord Jesus, that He Himself said, "It is more blessed to give than to receive'" (Acts 20:35; see Matthew 10:8).

Setting: On the island of Patmos (in the Aegean Sea about fifty miles southwest of Ephesus in modern Turkey). On the Lord's Day (Sunday), approximately fifty years after the Resurrection, the disciple John encounters the Lord Jesus Christ, who communicates a new revelation for the apostle to record for the church in Pergamum and to six other churches in Asia.

"And to the angel of the church in Pergamum write: The One who has the sharp two-edged sword says this: 'I know where you dwell, where Satan's throne is; and you hold fast My name, and did not deny My faith even in the days of Antipas, My witness, My faithful one, who was killed among you, where Satan dwells. But I have a few things against you, because you have there some who hold the teaching of Balaam, who kept teaching Balak to put a stumbling block before the sons of Israel, to eat things sacrificed to idols and to commit *acts of* immorality. So you also have some who in the same way hold the teaching of the Nicolaitans. Therefore repent; or else I am coming to you quickly, and I will make war against them with the sword of My mouth. He who has an ear, let him hear what the Spirit says to the churches. To him who overcomes, to him I will give *some* of the hidden manna, and I will give him a white stone, and a new name written on the stone which no one knows but he who receives it' (Revelation 2:12–17; see Numbers 25:1–3; Isaiah 62:2; Revelation 1:16; 2:5, 6, 16).

Setting: On the island of Patmos (in the Aegean Sea about fifty miles southwest of Ephesus in modern Turkey). On the Lord's Day (Sunday), approximately fifty years after the Resurrection, the disciple John encounters the Lord Jesus Christ, who communicates a new revelation for the apostle to record for the church in Thyatira and to six other churches in Asia.

"And to the angel of the church in Thyatira write: The Son of God, who has eyes like a flame of fire, and His feet are like burnished bronze, says this: 'I know your deeds, and your love and faith and service and perseverance, and that your deeds of late are greater than at first. But I have *this* against you, that you tolerate the woman Jezebel, who calls herself a prophetess, and she teaches and leads My bond-servants astray so that they commit *acts of* immorality and eat things sacrificed to idols. I gave her time to repent, and she does not want to repent of her immorality. Behold, I will throw her on a bed *of sickness,* and those who commit adultery with her into great tribulation, unless they repent of her deeds. And I will kill her children with pestilence, and all the churches will know that I am He who searches the minds and hearts; and I will give to each one of you according to your deeds. But I say to you, the rest who are in Thyatira, who do not hold this teaching, who have not known the deep things of Satan, as they call them—I place no other burden on you. Nevertheless what you have, hold fast until I come. He who overcomes, and he who keeps My deeds until the end, TO HIM I WILL GIVE AUTHORITY OVER THE NATIONS; AND HE SHALL RULE THEM WITH A ROD OF IRON, AS THE VESSELS OF THE POTTER ARE BROKEN TO PIECES, as I also have received *authority* from My Father; and I will give him the morning star. He who has an ear, let him hear what the Spirit says to the churches' (Revelation 2:18–29; Jesus quotes from Psalm 2:8, 9; Isaiah 30:14; see 1 Kings 16:31; Psalm 7:9; Romans 2:5; 1 Corinthians 2:10; 2 Peter 3:9; Revelation 1:14; 2:7; 3:11; 17:1–20).

Setting: On the island of Patmos (in the Aegean Sea about fifty miles southwest of Ephesus in modern Turkey). On the Lord's Day (Sunday), approximately fifty years after the Resurrection, the disciple John encounters the Lord Jesus Christ, who communicates a new revelation for the apostle to record for the church in Sardis and to six other churches in Asia.

"To the angel of the church in Sardis write: He who has the seven Spirits of God and the seven stars, says this: 'I know your deeds, that you have a name that you are alive, but you are dead. Wake up, and strengthen the things that remain, which were about to die; for I have not found your deeds completed in the sight of My God. So remember what you have received and heard; and keep *it,* and repent. Therefore if you do not wake up, I will come like a thief, and you will not know at what hour I will come to you. But you have a few people in Sardis who have not soiled their garments; and they will walk with Me in white, for they are worthy. He who overcomes will thus be clothed in white garments; and I will not erase his name from the book of life, and I will confess his name before My Father and before His angels. He who has an ear, let him hear what the Spirit says to the churches' " (Revelation 3:1–6; see Matthew 10:32; Revelation 1:16).

RECEPTION (Also see BANQUETS; DINNER; FEAST, WEDDING; HOSPITALITY; and LUNCHEON)

Setting: On the way from Galilee to Jerusalem. After Jesus, observing the invited guests of a Pharisee leader selecting places of honor at the table, speaks a parable to them, He comments to the host about the people to invite in the future.

And He also went on to say to the one who had invited Him, "When you give a luncheon or a dinner, do not invite your friends or your brothers or your relatives or rich neighbors, otherwise they may also invite you in return and *that* will be your repayment. But when you give a reception, invite *the* poor, *the* crippled, *the* lame, *the* blind, and you will be blessed, since they do not have *the means* to repay you; for you will be repaid at the resurrection of the righteous" (Luke 14:12–14; see John 5:28, 29).

RECOGNITION

[RECOGNITION from recognize]

Setting: Galilee. Coming down the mountain after the Transfiguration, Peter, James, and John ask the Lord why Elijah must come before the Messiah.

And He answered and said, "Elijah is coming and will restore all things; but I say to you that Elijah already came, and they did not recognize him, but did to him whatever they wished. So also the Son of Man is going to suffer at their hands" (Matthew 17:11, 12; cf. Mark 9:11–13).

[RECOGNITION from recognize]

Setting: On the Mount of Olives, just east of Jerusalem. During His Olivet Discourse, after answering His disciples' questions as to when the temple will be destroyed and Jerusalem overrun, along with the signs of His coming and the end of the age, Jesus teaches them the Parable of the Fig Tree.

"Now learn the parable from the fig tree: when its branch has already become tender and puts forth its leaves, you know that summer is near; so, you too, when you see all these things, recognize that He is near, *right* at the door. Truly, I say to you, this generation will not pass away until all these things take place. Heaven and earth will pass away, but My words will not pass away. But of that day and hour no one knows, not even the angels of heaven, nor the Son, but the Father alone. For the coming of the Son of Man will be just like the days of Noah. For as in those days before the flood they were eating and drinking, marrying and giving in marriage, until the day that Noah entered the ark, and they did not understand until the flood came and took them all away; so will the coming of the Son of Man be. Then there will be two men in the field; one will be taken and one will be left. Two women *will be* grinding at the mill; one will be taken and one will be left" (Matthew 24:32–41; cf. Mark 13:28–32; Luke 17:34–36; 21:28–33; see Genesis 6:5; 7:7; Matthew 5:18; 10:23; James 5:9).

[RECOGNITION from recognized]

Setting: On the road to Jerusalem. James and John ask Jesus for special honor and privileges in His kingdom. The other disciples become angry, so Jesus uses this moment to teach them about servanthood.

Calling them to Himself, Jesus said to them, "You know that those who are recognized as rulers of the Gentiles lord it over them; and their great men exercise authority over them. But it is not this way among you, but whoever wishes to become great among you shall be your servant; and whoever wishes to be first among you shall be slave of all. For even the Son of Man did not come to be served, but to serve, and to give His life a ransom for many" (Mark 10:42–45; cf. Matthew 20:25–28).

[RECOGNITION from recognize]

Setting: On the Mount of Olives, east of the temple in Jerusalem. After prophesying the temple's destruction, Jesus responds during His Olivet Discourse to questions from Peter, James, John, and Andrew about other future events.

"Now learn the parable from the fig tree: when its branch has already become tender and puts forth its leaves, you know that summer is near. Even so, you too, when you see these things happening, recognize that He is near, *right* at the door. Truly I say

to you, this generation will not pass away until all these things take place. Heaven and earth will pass away, but My words will not pass away. But of the day or hour no one knows, not even the angels in heaven, nor the Son, but the Father *alone*" (Mark 13:28–32; cf. Matthew 24:32–36; Luke 21:28–33).

[RECOGNITION from recognize]
Setting: Approaching Jerusalem. After being praised by the people in a triumphal entry, the Lord weeps as He sees the city ahead of Him.

When He approached *Jerusalem,* He saw the city and wept over it, saying, "If you had known in this day, even you, the things which make for peace! But now they have been hidden from your eyes. For the days will come upon you when your enemies will throw up a barricade against you, and surround you and hem you in on every side, and they will level you to the ground and your children within you, and they will not leave in you one stone upon another, because you did not recognize the time of your visitation" (Luke 19:41–44; see Matthew 24:1, 2; Luke 13:34, 35).

[RECOGNITION from recognize]
Setting: On the Mount of Olives, east of the temple in Jerusalem. After ministering in the temple a few days before His crucifixion, and giving the disciples more details regarding future events, Jesus elaborates more during His Olivet Discourse about things to come.

"But when you see Jerusalem surrounded by armies, then recognize that her desolation is near. Then those who are in Judea must flee to the mountains, and those who are in the midst of the city must leave, and those who are in the country must not enter the city; because these are days of vengeance, so that all things which are written will be fulfilled. Woe to those who are pregnant and to those who are nursing babies in those days; for there will be a great distress upon the land and wrath to this people; and they will fall by the edge of the sword, and will be led captive into all the nations; and Jerusalem will be trampled under foot by the Gentiles until the times of the Gentiles are fulfilled" (Luke 21:20–24; see Matthew 24:15–18; Mark 13:14–16; Luke 19:43).

[RECOGNITION from recognize]
Setting: On the Mount of Olives, east of the temple in Jerusalem. After ministering in the temple a few days before His crucifixion, and giving the disciples more details regarding His return, Jesus conveys the Parable of the Fig Tree during His Olivet Discourse.

Then He told them a parable: "Behold the fig tree and all the trees; as soon as they put forth *leaves,* you see it and know for yourselves that summer is now near. So you also, when you see these things happening, recognize that the kingdom of God is near. Truly, I say to you, this generation will not pass away until all things take place. Heaven and earth will pass away, but My words will not pass away" (Luke 21:29–33; cf. Matthew 24:32–35; Mark 13:28–31; see Matthew 5:18).

RECOMPENSE (See REPAYMENT)

RECONCILIATION (Also see FORGIVENESS; GRUDGES; and PEACEMAKERS)

[RECONCILIATION from reconciled]
Setting: Galilee. During the early part of His ministry, Jesus preaches the Sermon on the Mount to His disciples and the multitudes.

"Therefore if you are presenting your offering at the altar, and there remember that your brother has something against you, leave your offering there before the altar and go; first be reconciled to your brother, and then come and present your offering" (Matthew 5:23, 24; see Romans 12:17, 18).

[RECONCILIATION from If your brother sins, go and show him his fault in private; if he listens to you, you have won your brother]

Setting: Capernaum of Galilee. After conveying to His disciples the value of little ones, Jesus gives instruction about church discipline.

"If your brother sins, go and show him his fault in private; if he listens to you, you have won your brother. But if he does not listen *to you,* take one or two more with you, so that BY THE MOUTH OF TWO OR THREE WITNESSES EVERY FACT MAY BE CONFIRMED. If he refuses to listen to them, tell it to the church; and if he refuses to listen even to the church, let him be to you as a Gentile and a tax collector. Truly I say to you, whatever you bind of earth shall have been bound in heaven; and whatever you loose on earth shall have been loosed in heaven. Again, I say to you, that if two of you agree on earth about anything that they may ask, it shall be done for them by My Father who is in heaven. For there two or three have gathered together in My name, I am there in their midst" (Matthew 18:15–20. Jesus quotes from Deuteronomy 19:15; cf. Matthew 7:7; 16:19; see Leviticus 19:17; Matthew 28:20; 2 Thessalonians 3:6, 14).

REDEMPTION (Also see SALVATION)

Setting: On the Mount of Olives, just east of Jerusalem. After ministering in the temple a few days before His crucifixion, and giving His disciples more details regarding future events, Jesus speaks during His Olivet Discourse of His return.

"There will be signs in sun and moon and stars, and on the earth dismay among the nations, in perplexity at the roaring of the sea and the waves, men fainting from fear and the expectation of the things which are coming upon the world; for the powers of the heavens will be shaken. Then they will see THE SON OF MAN COMING IN A CLOUD with power and great glory. But when these things begin to take place, straighten up and lift up your heads, because your redemption is drawing near" (Luke 21:25–28, Jesus quotes from Daniel 7:13; cf. Matthew 24:29–31; Mark 13:24–27).

REED

Setting: Galilee. While speaking to the crowds, Jesus pays tribute to the ministry of John the Baptist, but emphasizes that the one who is least in the kingdom of heaven is greater than John.

As these men were going *away,* Jesus began to speak to the crowds about John, "What did you go out into the wilderness to see? A reed shaken by the wind? But what did you go out to see? A man dressed in soft *clothing?* Those who wear soft *clothing* are in kings' palaces! But what did you go out to see? A prophet? Yes, I tell you, and the one who is more than a prophet. This is the one about whom it is written, 'BEHOLD, I SEND MY MESSENGER AHEAD OF YOU, WHO WILL PREPARE YOUR WAY BEFORE YOU.' Truly, I say to you, among those born of women there has not arisen *anyone* greater than John the Baptist! Yet the one who is least in the kingdom of heaven is greater than he. From the days of John the Baptist until now the kingdom of heaven suffers violence, and violent men take it by force. For all the prophets and the Law prophesied until John. And, if you are willing to accept *it,* John himself is Elijah who was to come. He who has ears to hear, let him hear" (Matthew 11:7–15, Jesus quotes from Malachi 3:1; cf. Malachi 4:5; Luke 7:24–28; 16:16; see Matthew 14:5).

Setting: Galilee. After Jesus answers the disciples of John the Baptist whether He is the promised Messiah, the Lord speaks to the crowds about John.

When the messengers of John had left, He began to speak to the crowds about John, "What did you go out into the wilderness to see? A reed shaken by the wind? But what did you go out to see? A man dressed in soft clothing? Those who are splendidly clothed and live in luxury are *found* in royal palaces! But what did you go out to see? A prophet? Yes, I say to you, and one who is more than a prophet. This is the one about whom it is written, 'BEHOLD, I SEND MY MESSENGER AHEAD OF YOU, WHO WILL PREPARE YOUR WAY BEFORE YOU.' I say to you, among those born of women there is no one greater than John; yet he who is least in the kingdom of God is greater than he" (Luke 7:24–28, Jesus quotes from Malachi 3:1; cf. Matthew 11:7–11; see Luke 7:29, 30).

REGENERATION

Setting: Judea beyond the Jordan (Perea). Jesus promises rewards to His disciples for their personal sacrifice and commitment to following Him.

And Jesus said to them, "Truly I say to you, that you who have followed Me, in the regeneration when the Son of Man will sit on His glorious throne, you also shall sit upon twelve thrones, judging the twelve tribes of Israel. And everyone who has left houses or brothers or sisters or father or mother or children or farms for My name's sake, will receive many times as much, and will inherit eternal life. But many *who* are first will be last; and *the* last, first" (Matthew 19:28–30; cf. Matthew 6:33; 20:15; Mark 10:29, 30; Luke 18:29, 30; 22:30).

REJECTING GOD (See JESUS, REJECTING)

REJECTING JESUS (Listed under JESUS, REJECTING)

REJECTING THE GOSPEL (Listed under GOSPEL, REJECTING THE)

REJECTION (Also see JESUS, REJECTING; UNBELIEF; and UNWELCOME)

[REJECTION from REJECTED]
Setting: The temple in Jerusalem. Jesus delivers a prophecy to the chief priests and elders after they question His authority.

Jesus said to them, "Did you never read in the Scriptures, 'THE STONE WHICH THE BUILDERS REJECTED, THIS BECAME THE CHIEF CORNER *stone;* THIS CAME ABOUT FROM THE LORD, AND IT IS MARVELOUS IN OUR EYES'? Therefore I say to you, the kingdom of God will be taken away from you and given to a people, producing the fruit of it. And he who falls on this stone will be broken to pieces; but on whomever it falls, it will scatter him like dust" (Matthew 21:42–44, Jesus quotes from Psalm 118:22; cf. Isaiah 8:14, 15; Mark 12:10, 11; Luke 20:17, 18).

[REJECTION from REJECTED]
Setting: The temple in Jerusalem. Having His authority questioned by the chief priests, scribes, and elders, Jesus begins to teach them in parables.

And He began to speak to them in parables: "A man PLANTED A VINEYARD AND PUT A WALL AROUND IT, AND DUG A VAT UNDER THE WINE PRESS AND BUILT A TOWER, and rented it out to vine-growers and went on a journey. At the *harvest* time he sent a slave to the vine-growers, in order to receive *some* of the produce of the vineyard from the vine-growers. They took him, and beat him and sent him away empty-handed. Again he sent them another slave, and they wounded him in the head, and treated him shamefully. And he sent another, and that one they killed; and *so with* many others, beating some and killing others. He had one more to *send*, a beloved son; he sent him last *of all* to them, saying, 'They will respect my son.' But those vine-growers said to one another, 'This is the heir; come, let us kill him, and the inheritance will be ours!' They took him, and killed him and threw him out of the vineyard. What will the owner of the vineyard do? He will come and destroy the vine-growers, and will give the vineyard to others. Have you not even read this Scripture: 'THE STONE WHICH THE BUILDERS REJECTED, THIS BECAME THE CHIEF CORNER *stone;* THIS CAME ABOUT FROM THE LORD, AND IT IS MARVELOUS IN OUR EYES'?" (Mark 12:1–11, Jesus quotes from Psalm 118:22, 23; Isaiah 5:1, 2; cf. Matthew 21:33–46; Luke 20:9–19).

[REJECTION from who do not receive you]
Setting: Galilee. After raising Jairus's daughter from the dead, Jesus calls the twelve disciples together and gives them power and authority over demons, along with the ability to cure diseases.

And He said to them, "Take nothing for *your* journey, neither a staff, nor a bag, nor bread, nor money; and do not *even* have two tunics apiece. Whatever house you enter, stay there until you leave that city. And as for those who do not receive you, go out from that city, shake the dust off your feet as a testimony against them" (Luke 9:3–5; cf. Matthew 10:1–15; Mark 6:7–11; see Luke 10:4–12).

[REJECTION from rejected]
Setting: Galilee. Following Peter's pronouncement that Jesus is the Christ of God, the Lord warns His disciples not to reveal His identity to anyone.

But He warned them and instructed *them* not to tell this to anyone, saying, "The Son of Man must suffer many things and be rejected by the elders and chief priests and scribes, and be killed and be raised up on the third day" (Luke 9:21, 22; cf. Matthew 16:21; Mark 8:31).

[REJECTION from But whatever city you enter and they do not receive you]
Setting: On the way from Galilee to Jerusalem. The Lord appoints seventy followers and sends them out in pairs to every place He Himself will soon visit.

And He was saying to them, "The harvest is plentiful, but the laborers are few; therefore beseech the Lord of the harvest to send out laborers into His harvest. Go; behold, I send you out as lambs in the midst of wolves. Carry no money belt, no bag, no shoes; and greet no one on the way. Whatever house you enter, first say, 'Peace be to this house.' If a man of peace is there, your peace will rest on him; but if not, it will return to you. Stay in that house, eating and drinking what they give you; for the laborer is worthy of his wages. Do not keep moving from house to house. Whatever city you enter and they receive you, eat what is set before you; and heal those in it who are sick, and say to them, 'The kingdom of God has come near to you.' But whatever city you enter and they do not receive you, go out into its streets and say, 'Even the dust of your city which clings to our feet we wipe off *in protest* against you; yet be sure of this, that the kingdom of God has come near.' I say to you, it will be more tolerable in that day for Sodom than for that city" (Luke 10:2–12; see Genesis 19:24–28; Matthew 9:37, 38, 10:9–14, 16; 1 Corinthians 10:27).

[REJECTION from the one who rejects you rejects Me]
Setting: On the way from Galilee to Jerusalem. The Lord pronounces woes on cities who reject the gospel, as He appoints seventy followers and sends them out in pairs to every place He Himself will soon visit.

"Woe to you, Chorazin! Woe to you, Bethsaida! For if the miracles had been performed in Tyre and Sidon which occurred in you, they would have repented long ago, sitting in sackcloth and ashes. But it will be more tolerable for Tyre and Sidon in the judgment than for you. And you, Capernaum, will not be exalted to heaven, will you? You will be brought down to Hades! The one who listens to you listens to Me, and the one who rejects you rejects Me; and he who rejects Me rejects the One who sent Me" (Luke 10:13–16; cf. Matthew 11:21–23; see Matthew 10:40).

[REJECTION from rejected]
Setting: On the way from Galilee to Jerusalem. After the Pharisees question Him about the coming of the kingdom of God, Jesus tells His disciples of His second coming.

And He said to the disciples, "The days will come when you will long to see one of the days of the Son of Man, and you will not see it. They will say to you, 'Look there! Look here!' Do not go away, and do not run after *them*. For just like the lightning, when it flashes out of one part of the sky, shines to the other part of the sky, so will the Son of Man be in His day. But first He must suffer many things and be rejected by this generation. And just as it happened in the days of Noah, so it will be also in the days of the Son of Man: they were eating, they were drinking, they were marrying, they were being given in marriage, until the day that Noah entered the ark, and the flood came and destroyed them all. It was the same as happened in the days of Lot: they were eating, they were drinking, they were buying, they were selling, they were planting, they were building; but on the day that Lot went out from Sodom it rained fire and brimstone from heaven and destroyed them all. It will be just the same on the day that the Son of Man is revealed. On that day, the one who is on the housetop and whose goods are in the house must not go down to take them out; and likewise the one who is in the field must not turn back. Remember Lot's wife. Whoever seeks to keep his life will lose it, and whoever loses *his life* will preserve it. I tell you, on that night there will be two in one bed; one will be taken and the other will be left. There will be two women grinding at the same place; one will be taken and the other will be left. [Two men will be in the field; one will be taken and the other will be left."] And answering they said to Him, "Where, Lord?" And He said to them, "Where the body *is*, there also the vultures will be gathered" (Luke 17:22–37; see Genesis 19; Matthew 10:39; 16:21, 27; 24:17–28, 37–41).

[REJECTION from REJECTED]
Setting: The temple in Jerusalem. While ministering a few days before His crucifixion, after the chief priests and the scribes question His authority to teach and preach, Jesus conveys the Parable of the Vine-Growers to the people.

And He began to tell the people this parable: "A man planted a vineyard and rented it out to vine-growers, and went on a journey for a long time. At the *harvest* time he sent a slave to the vine-growers, so that they would give him *some* of the produce of the vineyard; but the vine-growers beat him and sent him away empty-handed. And he proceeded to send another slave; and they beat him also and treated him shamefully and sent him away empty-handed. And he proceeded to send a third; and this one also they wounded and cast out. The owner of the vineyard said, 'What shall I do? I will send my beloved son; perhaps they will respect him.' But when the vine-growers saw him, they reasoned with one another, saying, 'This is the heir; let us kill him so that the inheritance will be ours.' So they threw him out of the vineyard and killed him. What, then, will the owner of the vineyard do to them? He will come and destroy these vine-growers and will give the vineyard to others." When they heard it, they said, "May it never be!" But Jesus looked at them and said, "What then is this that is written: 'THE STONE WHICH THE BUILDERS REJECTED, THIS BECAME THE CHIEF CORNER *stone*'? Everyone who falls on that stone will be broken to pieces; but on whomever it falls, it will scatter him like dust" (Luke 20:9–18, Jesus quotes from Psalm 118:22; cf. Matthew 21:33–44; Mark 12:1–11; see Ephesians 2:20).

[REJECTION from rejects]
Setting: Jerusalem. Just days before the Passover, with the chief priests and Pharisees plotting to seize Jesus, who is expressing anxiety about His upcoming crucifixion, some of the Jews believe in Him, while others are rejecting His message.

And Jesus cried out and said, "He who believes in Me, does not believe in Me but in Him who sent Me. He who sees Me sees the One who sent Me. I have come *as* Light into the world, so that everyone who believes in Me will not remain in darkness. If anyone hears My sayings and does not keep them, I do not judge him; for I did not come to judge the world, but to save the world. He who rejects Me and does not receive My sayings, has one who judges him; the word I spoke is what will judge him at the last day. For I did not speak on My own initiative, but the Father Himself who sent Me has given Me a commandment *as to* what to say and what to speak. I know that His commandment is eternal life; therefore the things I speak, I speak just as the Father has told Me" (John 12:44–50; see Matthew 10:40; Luke 10:16; John 1:4; 3:17; 5:19; 6:68; 14:9).

REJECTION BY GOD

[REJECTION BY GOD from DEPART FROM ME]
Setting: Galilee. During the early part of His ministry, Jesus preaches the Sermon on the Mount to His disciples and the multitudes.

"Not everyone who says to Me, 'Lord, Lord,' will enter the kingdom of heaven, but he who does the will of My Father who is in heaven *will enter.* Many will say to Me on that day, 'Lord, Lord, did we not prophesy in Your name, and in Your name cast out demons, and in Your name perform many miracles?' And then I will declare to them, 'I never knew you, DEPART FROM ME, YOU WHO PRACTICE LAWLESSNESS'" (Matthew 7:21–23, Jesus quotes from Psalm 6:8; cf. Matthew 25:11–13; see Luke 6:46).

[REJECTION BY GOD from Depart from Me]
Setting: On the Mount of Olives, just east of Jerusalem. During His Olivet Discourse, after answering His disciples' questions as to when the temple will be destroyed and Jerusalem overrun, along with the signs of His coming and the end of the age, Jesus reveals the future judgments following His return.

"But when the Son of Man comes in His glory, and all the angels with Him, then He will sit on His glorious throne. All the nations will be gathered before Him; and He will separate them from one another, as the shepherd separates the sheep from the goats; and He will put the sheep on His right, and the goats on the left. Then the King will say to those on His right, 'Come, you who are blessed of My Father, inherit the kingdom prepared for you from the foundation of the world. 'For I was hungry, and you gave Me *something* to eat; I was thirsty, and you gave Me *something* to drink; I was a stranger, and you invited Me in; naked, and you clothed Me; I was sick, and you visited Me; I was in prison, and you came to Me.' Then the righteous will answer Him, 'Lord, when did we see You hungry and feed You, or thirsty, and give you *something* to drink? And when did we see You a stranger, and invite You in, or naked, and clothe You? When did we see You sick, or in prison, and come to You?' The King will answer and say to them, 'Truly I say to you, to the extent that you did it to one of these brothers of Mine, *even* the least *of them,* you did it to Me.' Then He will also say to those on His left, 'Depart from Me, accursed ones, into the eternal fire which has been prepared for the devil

and his angels; for I was hungry, and you gave Me *nothing* to eat; I was thirsty, and you gave Me nothing to drink; I was a stranger, and you did not invite Me in; naked, and you did not clothe Me; sick, and in prison, and you did not visit Me.' Then they themselves also will answer, 'Lord, when did we see You hungry, or thirsty, or a stranger, or naked, or sick, or in prison, and did not take care of You?' Then He will answer them, 'Truly I say to you, to the extent that you did not do it to one of the least of these, you did not do it to Me.' These will go away into eternal punishment, but the righteous into eternal life" (Matthew 25:31–46; see Matthew 7:23; 16:27; 19:29).

[REJECTION BY GOD from DEPART FROM ME]
Setting: On the way from Galilee to Jerusalem. While teaching in the cities and villages, Jesus responds to a question about who is saved.

And someone said to Him, "Lord, are here *just* a few who are being saved?" And He said to them, "Strive to enter through the narrow door; for many, I tell you, will seek to enter and will not be able. Once the head of the house gets up and shuts the door, and you begin to stand outside and knock on the door, saying, 'Lord, open up to us!' then He will answer and say to you, 'I do not know where you are from.' Then you will begin to say, 'We ate and drank in Your presence, and You taught in our streets'; and He will say, 'I tell you, I do not know where you are from; DEPART FROM ME, ALL YOU EVILDOERS.' In that place there will be weeping and gnashing of teeth when you see Abraham and Isaac and Jacob and all the prophets in the kingdom of God, but you yourselves being thrown out. And they will come from east and west and from north and south, and will recline *at the table* in the kingdom of God. And behold, *some* are last who will be first and *some* are first who will be last" (Luke 13:23–30, Jesus quotes from Psalm 6:8; cf. Matthew 7:13, 23; 8:11, 12; see Matthew 19:30; Luke 3:8).

REJOICING (Also see CELEBRATION; and JOY)

[REJOICING from rejoice]
Setting: Galilee. Early in His ministry, Jesus presents the Beatitudes (part of the Sermon on the Mount) to His disciples and the gathered crowds from Galilee, Decapolis, Jerusalem, Judea, and beyond the Jordan.

"Blessed are you when *people* insult you and persecute you, and falsely say all kinds of evil against you because of Me. Rejoice and be glad, for your reward in heaven is great; for in the same way they persecuted the prophets who were before you" (Matthew 5:11, 12; cf. 2 Chronicles 36:16; Luke 6:22, 23; 1 Peter 4:14; see Matthew 13:35).

[REJOICING from rejoices]
Setting: Capernaum of Galilee. Jesus illustrates to His disciples the value of little ones.

"What do you think? If any man has a hundred sheep, and one of them has gone astray, does he not leave the ninety-nine on the mountains and go and search for the one that is straying? If it turns out that he finds it, truly I say to you, he rejoices over it more than the ninety-nine which have not gone astray. So it is not *the* will of your Father who is in heaven that one of these little ones perish" (Matthew 18:12–14; cf. Luke 15:4–7).

[REJOICING from rejoice]
Setting: On the way from Galilee to Jerusalem. The Lord responds to a report from the seventy sent out in pairs to every place He Himself will soon visit.

And He said to them, "I was watching Satan fall from heaven like lightning. Behold, I have given you authority to tread on serpents and scorpions, and over all the power of the enemy, and nothing will injure you. Nevertheless do not rejoice in this, that the spirits are subject to you, but rejoice that your names are recorded in heaven" (Luke 10:18–20; see Psalm 91:13; Isaiah 14:12–14; Luke 9:1).

Setting: On the way from Galilee to Jerusalem. After Jesus presents to large crowds the demands of discipleship, the Pharisees and scribes complain He associates with tax collectors and sinners.

So He told them this parable, saying, "What man among you, if he has a hundred sheep and has lost one of them, does not leave the ninety-nine in the open pasture and go after the one which is lost until he finds it? When he has found it, he lays it on his shoulders, rejoicing. And when he comes home, he calls together his friends and his neighbors, saying to them, 'Rejoice with me, for I have found my sheep which was lost!' I tell you that in the same way, there will be *more* joy in heaven over one sinner who repents than over ninety-nine righteous persons who need no repentance" (Luke 15:3–7; cf. Matthew 18:12–14; see Matthew 9:11–13; Luke 5:29–32).

[REJOICING from rejoice]
Setting: On the way from Galilee to Jerusalem. Jesus conveys the principles of the lost sheep and the lost coin because the Pharisees and scribes complain He associates with tax collectors and sinners.

"So He told them this parable, saying, "What man among you, if he has a hundred sheep and has lost one of them, does not leave the ninety-nine in the open pasture and go after the one which is lost until he finds it? When he has found it, he lays it on his shoulders, rejoicing. And when he comes home, he calls together his friends and his neighbors, saying to them, 'Rejoice with me, for I have found my sheep which was lost!' I tell you that in the same way, there will be more joy in heaven over one sinner who repents than over ninety-nine righteous persons who need no repentance. Or what woman, if she has ten silver coins and loses one coin, does not light a lamp and sweep the house and search carefully until she finds it? When she has found it, she calls together her friends and neighbors, saying, 'Rejoice with me, for I have found the coin which I had lost!' In the same way, I tell you, there is joy in the presence of the angels of God over one sinner who repents" (Luke 15:3–10; cf. Matthew 18:12-14; see Matthew 9:11-13).

[REJOICING from rejoice]
Setting: On the way from Galilee to Jerusalem. Jesus conveys the illustration of the prodigal son because the Pharisees and scribes complain He associates with tax collectors and sinners.

And He said, "A man had two sons. The younger of them said to his father, 'Father, give me the share of the estate that falls to me.' So he divided his wealth between them. And not many days later, the younger son gathered everything together and went on a journey into a distant country, and there he squandered his estate with loose living. Now when he had spent everything, a severe famine occurred in that country, and he began to be impoverished. So he went and hired himself out to one of the citizens of that country, and he sent him into his fields to feed swine. And he would have gladly filled his stomach with the pods that the swine were eating, and no one was giving *anything* to him. But when he came to his senses, he said, 'How many of my father's hired men have more than enough bread, but I am dying here with hunger! I will get up and go to my father, and will say to him, "Father, I have sinned against heaven, and in your sight; I am no longer worthy to be called your son; make me as one of your hired men."' So he got up and came to his father. But while he was still a long way off, his father saw him and felt compassion *for him,* and ran and embraced him and kissed him. And the son said to him, "Father, I have sinned against heaven and in your sight; I am no longer worthy to be called your son.' But the father said to his slaves, 'Quickly bring out the best robe and put it on him, and put a ring on his hand and sandals on his feet; and bring the fattened calf, kill it, and let us eat and celebrate; for this son of mine was dead and has come to life again; he was lost and has been found.' And they began to celebrate. Now his older son was in the field, when he came and approached the house, he heard music and dancing. And he summoned one of the servants and *began* inquiring what these things could be. And he said to him, 'Your brother has come, and your father has killed the fattened calf because he has received him back safe and sound.' But he became angry and was not willing to go in; and his father came out and *began* pleading with him. But he answered and said to his father, 'Look! For so many years I have been serving you and I have never neglected a command of yours; and *yet* you have never given me a young goat, so that I might celebrate with my friends; but when this son of yours came, who has devoured your wealth with prostitutes, you killed the fattened calf for him.' And he said to him, 'Son, you have always been with me, and all that is mine is yours. But we had to celebrate and rejoice, for this brother of yours was dead and *has begun* to live, and was lost and has been found' " (Luke 15:11–32; see Proverb 29:2).

[REJOICING from rejoice]
Setting: Sychar in Samaria, on the way to Galilee. After Jesus converses with a Samaritan woman at Jacob's well, the disciples return with food. They try to get Jesus to eat, but are surprised when He speaks of other food.

Jesus said to them, "My food is to do the will of Him who sent Me and to accomplish His work. Do you not say, 'There are yet four months, and *then* comes the harvest'? Behold, I say to you, lift up your eyes and look on the fields, that they are white for harvest. Already he who reaps is receiving wages and is gathering fruit for life eternal; so that he who sows and he who reaps may rejoice together. For in this *case* the saying is true, 'One sows and another reaps.' I sent you to reap that for which you have not labored; others have labored and you have entered into their labor" (John 4:34–38; see Matthew 9:37, 38; John 5:36).

[REJOICING from rejoice]
Setting: Jerusalem. During a feast of the Jews, Jesus responds to criticism from the Jewish religious leaders by referring to God as His Father (thereby making Himself equal with God) and informing them that God, John the Baptist, and His works all testify to His mission.

"I can do nothing on My own initiative. As I hear, I judge; and My judgment is just, because I do not seek My own will, but the will of Him who sent Me. If I *alone* testify about Myself, My testimony is not true. There is another who testifies of Me, and I know that the testimony which He gives about Me is true. You have sent to John, and he has testified to the truth. But the testimony which I receive is not from man, but I say these things so that you may be saved. He was the lamp that was burning and was shining and you were willing to rejoice for a while in his light. But the testimony which I have is greater than the *testimony of* John; for the works which the Father has given Me to accomplish—the very works that I do—testify about Me, that the Father has sent Me. And the Father who sent Me, He has testified of Me. You have neither heard His voice at any time nor seen His form. You do not have His word abiding in you, for you do not believe Him whom He sent" (John 5:30–38; see Matthew 3:17; Mark 1:4, 5; John 1:7, 15, 32; 4:34; 8:14–16; 10:25, 37, 38).

[REJOICING from rejoiced]
Setting: The temple treasury in Jerusalem. While Jesus is interacting with the scribes and Pharisees, they state their belief Jesus is a demon-possessed Samaritan because of His statement that anyone who keeps His word will never taste death.

Jesus answered, "If I glorify Myself, My glory is nothing; it is My Father who glorifies Me, of whom you say, 'He is our God'; and you have not come to know Him, but I know Him; and if I say that I do not know Him, I will be a liar like you, but I do know Him and keep His word. Your father Abraham rejoiced to see My day, and he saw *it* and was glad" (John 8:54–56; see Matthew 13:17; John 7:29).

[REJOICING from rejoiced]
Setting: Jerusalem. Before the Passover, after He conveys the upcoming ministry of the Holy Spirit in His disciples' lives, Jesus again relates peace, hope, and comfort to them regarding His return to the Father.

"Peace I leave with you; My peace I give to you; not as the world gives do I give to you. Do not let your heart be troubled, nor let it be fearful. You heard that I said to you, 'I go away, and I will come to you.' If you loved Me, you would have rejoiced because I go to the Father, for the Father is greater than I. Now I have told you before it happens, so that when it happens, you may believe. I will not speak much more with you, for the ruler of the world is coming, and he has nothing in Me; but so that the world may know that I love the Father, I do exactly as the Father commanded Me. Get up, let us go from here" (John 14:27–31; see John 10:18, 29; 12:31; 13:19; 16:33).

[REJOICING from rejoice]
Setting: Jerusalem. Before the Passover, after warning His disciples of the persecution they will face after His departure to heaven, empathizing with their sadness over His prophecies, Jesus gives them the hope for the future.

"A little while, and you will no longer see Me; and again a little while, and you will see Me." *Some* of His disciples then said to one another, "What is this thing He is telling us, 'A little while, and you will not see Me; and again a little while, and you will see Me'; and, 'because I go to the Father'?" So they were saying, "What is this that He says, 'A little while'? We do not know what He is talking about." Jesus knew that they wished to question Him, and He said to them, "Are you deliberating together about this, that I said, 'A little while, and you will not see Me, and again a little while, and you will see Me'? Truly, truly, I say to you, that you will weep and lament, but the world will rejoice; you will grieve, but your grief will be turned into joy. Whenever a woman is in labor she has pain, because her hour has come; but when she gives birth to the child, she no longer remembers the anguish because of the joy that a child has been born into the world. Therefore you too have grief now; but I will see you again, and your heart will rejoice, and no one *will* take your joy away from you" (John 16:16–22; see Mark 9:32; Luke 23:27; John 14:18–24; 16:5, 6; 20:20).

RELATIONSHIP

[RELATIONSHIP from I know My own and My own know Me]

Setting: Jerusalem. Following the Pharisees' interrogation and dismissal of the formerly blind man Jesus healed on the Sabbath, the Lord conveys the Parable of the Good Shepherd to the Pharisees, using figures of speech they do not understand.

So Jesus said to them again, "Truly, truly, I say to you, I am the door of the sheep. All who came before Me are thieves and robbers, but the sheep did not hear them. I am the door; if anyone enters through Me, he will be saved, and will go in and out and find pasture. The thief comes only to steal and kill and destroy; I came that they may have life, and have *it* abundantly. I am the good shepherd; the good shepherd lays down His life for the sheep. He who is a hired hand, and not a shepherd, who is not the owner of the sheep, sees the wolf coming, and leaves the sheep and flees, and the wolf snatches them and scatters *them. He flees* because he is a hired hand and is not concerned about the sheep. I am the good shepherd, and I know My own and My own know Me, even as the Father knows Me and I know the Father; and I lay down My life for the sheep. I have other sheep, which are not of this fold; I must bring them also, and they will hear My voice; and they will become one flock *with* one shepherd. For this reason the Father loves Me, because I lay down My life so that I may take it again. No one has taken it away from Me, but I lay it down on My own initiative. I have authority to take it up again. This commandment I received from My Father" (John 10:7–18; see Isaiah 40:11; 56:8; Jeremiah 23:1; Matthew 11:27).

[RELATIONSHIP from I know them]

Setting: Jerusalem. At the Feast of Dedication, just after Jesus conveys the Parable of the Good Shepherd to the Pharisees (who do not understand it), they ask Him plainly if He is the Christ.

Jesus answered them, "I told you, and you do not believe; the works that I do in My Father's name, these testify of Me. But you do not believe because you are not of My sheep. My sheep hear My voice, and I know them, and they follow Me; and I give eternal life to them, and they will never perish; and no one will snatch them out of My hand. My Father, who has given *them* to Me, is greater than all; and no one is able to snatch *them* out of the Father's hand. I and the Father are one" (John 10:25–30; see John 8:47; 17:1, 2, 20, 21).

RELATIONSHIPS (See specifics such as BROTHER; CHILDREN; MOTHER; and WIFE; also see FAMILY; FORGIVENESS; FRIENDS; HOUSEHOLD; LOVE; NEIGHBOR; OTHERS; PEACE; PEOPLE; and RELATIVES)

RELATIVES (See specifics such as SON; and FATHER; also see FAMILY; and HOUSEHOLD)

Setting: The synagogue in Jesus' hometown of Nazareth. While ministering throughout the villages of Galilee, when Jesus teaches in His hometown, the townspeople become offended and question His teaching, wisdom, and ability to perform miracles.

Jesus said to them, "A prophet is not without honor except in his hometown and among his *own* relatives and in his *own* household" (Mark 6:4; cf. Matthew 13:54–58).

Setting: On the way from Galilee to Jerusalem. After Jesus, observing the invited guests of a Pharisee leader selecting places of honor at the table, speaks a parable to them, He comments to the host about the people to invite in the future.

And He also went on to say to the one who had invited Him, "When you give a luncheon or a dinner, do not invite your friends or your brothers or your relatives or rich neighbors, otherwise they may also invite you in return and *that* will be your repayment. But when you give a reception, invite *the* poor, *the* crippled, *the* lame, *the* blind, and you will be blessed, since they do not have *the means* to repay you; for you will be repaid at the resurrection of the righteous" (Luke 14:12–14; see John 5:28, 29).

Setting: On the Mount of Olives, east of the temple in Jerusalem. After ministering in the temple a few days before His crucifixion, and giving His disciples more details regarding the temple's future destruction, Jesus elaborates during His Olivet Discourse about things to come.

Then He continued by saying to them, "Nation will rise against nation and kingdom against kingdom, and there will be great earthquakes, and in various places plagues and famines; and there will be terrors and great signs from heaven. But before all these things, they will lay their hands on you and will persecute you, delivering you to the synagogues and prisons, bringing you before kings and governors for My name's sake. It will lead to an opportunity for your testimony. So make up your minds not to prepare beforehand to defend yourselves; for I will give you utterance and wisdom which none of your opponents will be able to resist or refute. But you will be betrayed even by parents and brothers and relatives and friends, and they will put *some* of you to death, and you will be hated by all because of My name. Yet not a hair of your head will perish. By your endurance you will gain your lives" (Luke 21:10–19; cf. Matthew 10:19–22; 24:7–14; Mark 13:8–13).

RELEASE (Also see FREEDOM)

[RELEASE from released]

Setting: Capernaum of Galilee. Jesus illustrates the matter of forgiveness after Peter asks Him if forgiving someone seven times who has sinned against him is adequate.

"For this reason the kingdom of heaven may be compared to a king who wished to settle accounts with his slaves. When he had begun to settle *them,* one who owed him ten thousand talents was brought to him. But since he did not have *the means* to repay, his lord commanded him to be sold, along with his wife and children and all that he had, and repayment to be made. So the slave fell *to the ground* and prostrated himself before him, saying, 'Have patience with me and I will repay you everything.' And the lord of that slave felt compassion and released him and forgave him the debt. But that slave went out and found one of his fellow slaves who owed him a hundred denarii; and he seized him and *began* to choke *him,* saying, 'Pay back what you owe.' So his fellow slave fell *to the ground* and *began* to plead with him, saying, 'Have patience with me and I will repay you.' But he was unwilling and went and threw him in prison until he should pay back what was owed. So when his fellow slaves saw what had happened, they were deeply grieved and came and reported to their lord all that had happened. Then summoning him, his lord said to him, 'You wicked slave, I forgave you all that debt because you pleaded with me. Should you not also have had mercy on your fellow slave, in the same way that I had mercy on you?' And his lord, moved with anger, handed him over to the torturers until he should repay all that was owed him. My heavenly Father will also do the same to you, if each of you does not forgive his brother from your heart" (Matthew 18:23–35; cf. Matthew 6:12, 14, 15; Luke 7:42; see Matthew 25:19–28).

Setting: The synagogue in Jesus' hometown of Nazareth in Galilee. At the beginning of His public ministry, Jesus reads on the Sabbath from the book of the prophet Isaiah.

And the book of the prophet Isaiah was handed to Him. And He opened the book and found the place where it was written, "THE SPIRIT OF THE LORD IS UPON ME, BECAUSE HE ANOINTED ME TO PREACH THE GOSPEL TO THE POOR. HE HAS SENT ME TO PROCLAIM RELEASE TO THE CAPTIVES, AND RECOVERY OF SIGHT TO THE BLIND, TO SET FREE THOSE WHO ARE OPPRESSED, TO PROCLAIM THE FAVORABLE YEAR OF THE LORD." And He closed the book, gave it back to the attendant and sat down; and the eyes of all in the synagogue were fixed on Him. And He began to say to them, "Today this Scripture has been fulfilled in your hearing" (Luke 4:17–21, Jesus quotes from Isaiah 61:1, 2).

[RELEASE from released]

Setting: On the way from Galilee to Jerusalem. Jesus responds to a synagogue official's anger after He heals a woman, sick for eighteen years, in the synagogue on the Sabbath.

But the Lord answered him and said, "You hypocrites, does not each of you on the Sabbath untie his ox or his donkey from the stall and lead him away to water *him?* And this woman, a daughter of Abraham as she is, whom Satan has bound for eighteen long years, should she not have been released from this bond on the Sabbath day?" (Luke 13:15, 16; see Luke 14:5).

REMAIN

[REMAIN from remained]

Setting: Galilee. After performing miracles throughout the region, Jesus pronounces woes against those cities who do not repent.

"Woe to you, Chorazin! Woe to you, Bethsaida! For if the miracles had occurred in Tyre and Sidon which occurred in you, they would have repented long ago in sackcloth and ashes. Nevertheless I say to you, it will be more tolerable for Tyre and Sidon in *the* day of judgment than for you. And you, Capernaum, will not be exalted to heaven, will you? You will descend to Hades; for if the miracles had occurred in Sodom which occurred in you, it would have remained to this day. Nevertheless, I say to you that it will be more tolerable for the land of Sodom in *the* day of judgment, than for you" (Matthew 11:21–24; cf. Matthew 10:15; Luke 10:13–15).

[REMAIN from remained]

Setting: Near the Sea of Galilee. Impressed by a Canaanite woman's faith, Jesus restores her daughter of demon possession, then feeds more than 4,000 people, primarily Gentiles, who are following Him.

And Jesus called His disciples to Him, and said, "I feel compassion for the people, because they have remained with Me now three days and have nothing to eat; and I do not want to send them away hungry, for they might faint on the way." The disciples said to Him, "Where would we get so many loaves in *this* desolate place to satisfy a large crowd?" And Jesus said to them, "How many loaves do you have?" And they said, "Seven and a few small fish" (Matthew 15:32–34; cf. Mark 8:1–9).

Setting: An upper room in Jerusalem. After celebrating the Passover meal with His disciples, Jesus retreats to the Garden of Gethsemane on the Mount of Olives to pray prior to His betrayal by Judas.

Then Jesus came with them to a place called Gethsemane, and said to His disciples, "Sit here while I go over there and pray." And He took with Him Peter and the two sons of Zebedee, and began to be grieved and distressed. Then He said to them, "My soul is deeply grieved, to the point of death; remain here and keep watch with Me." And He went a little beyond *them,* and fell on His face and prayed, saying, "My Father, if it is possible, let this cup pass from Me; yet not as I will, but as You will." And He came to the disciples and found them sleeping, and said to Peter, "So, you *men* could not keep watch with Me for one hour? Keep watching and praying that you may not enter into temptation; the spirit is willing, but the flesh is weak." He went away again a second time and prayed, saying, "My Father, if this cannot pass away unless I drink it, Your will be done." Again He came and found them sleeping, for their eyes were heavy. And He left them again, and went away and prayed a third time, saying the same thing once more. Then He came to the disciples and said to them, "Are you still sleeping and resting? Behold the hour is at hand and the Son of Man is being betrayed into the hands of sinners. Get up, let us be going; behold the one who betrays Me is at hand!" (Matthew 26:36–46; cf. Mark 14:32–42; Luke 22:40–46; see Matthew 20:22; John 12:27).

[REMAIN from remained]

Setting: Decapolis, near the Sea of Galilee. Jesus miraculously feeds more than 4,000 people, primarily Gentiles.

In those days, when there was again a large crowd and they had nothing to eat, Jesus called His disciples and said to them, "I feel compassion for the people because they have remained with Me now three days and have nothing to eat. If I send them away hungry to their homes, they will faint on their way; and some of them have come a great distance" (Mark 8:1–3; cf. Matthew 15:32–38; see Matthew 9:36).

Setting: Gethsemane on the Mount of Olives, east of the temple in Jerusalem. Jesus agonizes over His impending death, disappointed His disciples keep falling asleep instead of watching and praying with Him.

They came to a place named Gethsemane; and He said to the disciples, "Sit here until I have prayed." And He took with Him Peter and James and John, and began to be very distressed and troubled. And He said to them, "My soul is deeply grieved to the point of death; remain here and keep watch." And He went a little beyond *them,* and fell to the ground and *began* to pray that if it were possible, the hour might pass Him by. And He was saying, "Abba! Father! All things are possible for You; remove this cup from Me; yet not what I will, but what You will." And He came and found them sleeping, and said to Peter, "Simon, are you asleep? Could you not keep watch for one hour? Keep watching and praying that you may not come into temptation; the spirit is willing, but the flesh is weak" (Mark 14:32–38; cf. Matthew 26:36–41; Luke 22:41–46; see Romans 8:15; Galatians 4:6).

Setting: The temple treasury in Jerusalem. After the scribes and Pharisees question His testimony about Himself, Jesus reveals to those Jews who believe in Him how He will make them free.

So Jesus was saying to those Jews who had believed Him, "If you continue in My word, *then* you are truly disciples of Mine; and you will know the truth, and the truth will make you free." They answered Him, "We are Abraham's descendants and have never yet been enslaved to anyone; how is it that You say, 'You will become free'?" Jesus answered them, "Truly, truly, I say to you, everyone who commits sin is the slave of sin. The slave does not remain in the house forever; the son does remain forever. So if the Son makes you free, you will be free indeed. I know that you are Abraham's descendants; yet you seek to kill Me, because My word has no place in you. I speak the things which I have seen with *My* Father; therefore you also do the things which you heard from *your* father" (John 8:31–38; see Romans 6:16).

Setting: Jerusalem. Just days before the Passover, with the chief priests and Pharisees plotting to seize Jesus, who is expressing anxiety about His upcoming crucifixion, some of the Jews believe in the Lord, while others are rejecting His message.

And Jesus cried out and said, "He who believes in Me, does not believe in Me but in Him who sent Me. He who sees Me sees the One who sent Me. I have come *as* Light into the world, so that everyone who believes in Me will not remain in darkness. If anyone hears My sayings and does not keep them, I do not judge him; for I did not come to judge the world, but to save the world. He who rejects Me and does not receive My sayings, has one who judges him; the word I spoke is what will judge him at the last day. For I did not speak on My own initiative, but the Father Himself who sent Me has given Me a commandment *as to* what to say and what to speak. I know that His commandment is eternal life; therefore the things I speak, I speak just as the Father as told Me" (John 12:44–50; see Matthew 10:40; Luke 10:16; John 1:4; 3:17; 5:19; 6:68; 14:9).

Setting: Jerusalem. Before the Passover, with His departure in mind, after explaining He is the vine and His disciples are the branches, Jesus commands them to love one another.

"This is My commandment, that you love one another, just as I have loved you. Greater love has no one than this, that one lay down his life for his friends. You are My friends if you do what I command you. No longer do I call you slaves, for the slave does not know what his master is doing; but I have called you friends, for all things that I have heard from My Father I have made known to you. You did not choose Me but I chose you, and appointed you that you would go and bear fruit, and *that* your fruit would remain, so that whatever you ask of the Father in My name He may give to you. This I command you, that you love one another" (John 15:12–17; see Matthew 12:50; John 6:70; 8:26; 10:11; 13:34).

Setting: By the Sea of Galilee. During His third post-resurrection appearance to the disciples, after quizzing Peter three times regarding the disciple's love for Him, Jesus responds to Peter's inquiry about the future of John the disciple.

Jesus said to him, "If I want him to remain until I come, what *is that* to you? You follow Me!" Therefore this saying went out among the brethren that that disciple would not die; yet Jesus did not say to him that he would not die, but *only,* "If I want him to remain until I come, what *is that* to you?" (John 21:22, 23; see Matthew 8:22; 16:27).

Setting: On the island of Patmos (in the Aegean Sea about fifty miles southwest of Ephesus in modern Turkey). On the Lord's Day (Sunday), approximately fifty years after the Resurrection, the disciple John encounters the Lord Jesus Christ, who communicates a new revelation for the apostle to record for the church in Sardis and to six other churches in Asia.

"To the angel of the church in Sardis write: He who has the seven Spirits of God and the seven stars, says this: 'I know your deeds, that you have a name that you are alive, but you are dead. Wake up, and strengthen the things that remain, which were about to die; for I have not found your deeds completed in the sight of My God. So remember what you have received and heard; and keep *it,* and repent. Therefore if you do not wake up, I will come like a thief, and you will not know at what hour I will come to you. But you have a few people in Sardis who have not soiled their garments; and they will walk with Me in white, for they are worthy. He who overcomes will thus be clothed in white garments; and I will not erase his name from the book of life, and I will confess his name before My Father and before His angels. He who has an ear, let him hear what the Spirit says to the churches' " (Revelation 3:1–6; see Matthew 10:32; Revelation 1:16).

REMAINS (stays)

Setting: Jerusalem. Following the Pharisees' interrogation and dismissal of the formerly blind man Jesus healed on the Sabbath, the Lord responds to their question whether they are spiritually blind.

Jesus said to them, "If you were blind, you would have no sin; but since you say, 'We see,' your sin remains" (John 9:41; see John 15:22–24).

Setting: Jerusalem. Just days before the Passover, with the chief priests and Pharisees plotting to seize Jesus, crowds welcome Him to Jerusalem with palm branches and praise, and some Greeks ask to meet Him.

And Jesus answered them, saying, "The hour has come for the Son of Man to be glorified. Truly, truly, I say to you, unless a grain of wheat falls into the earth and dies, it remains alone; but if it dies, it bears much fruit. He who loves his life loses it, and he who hates his life in this world will keep it to life eternal. If anyone serves Me, he must follow Me; and where I am, there My servant will be also; if anyone serves Me, the Father will honor him" (John 12:23–26; see Matthew 10:39).

REMARRIAGE (Also see DIVORCE; and MARRIAGE)

[REMARRIAGE from marries a divorced woman]

Setting: Galilee. During the early part of His ministry, Jesus preaches the Sermon on the Mount to His disciples and the multitudes.

"It was said, 'WHOEVER SENDS HIS WIFE AWAY, LET HIM GIVE HER A CERTIFICATE OF DIVORCE'; but I say to you that everyone who divorces his wife, except for *the* reason of unchastity, makes her commit adultery; and whoever marries a divorced woman commits adultery" (Matthew 5:31, 32, Jesus quotes from Deuteronomy 24: 1, 3; cf. Matthew 19:9; see Romans 7:2, 3; 1 Corinthians 7:10, 39).

[REMARRIAGE from marries another woman]

Setting: Judea beyond the Jordan (Perea). Jesus responds to the Pharisees' follow-up question in front of a large crowd about Moses' command regarding a certificate of divorce.

He said to them. "Because of your hardness of heart Moses permitted you to divorce your wives; but from the beginning it has not been this way. And I say to you, whoever divorces his wife, except for immorality, and marries another woman commits adultery" (Matthew 19:8, 9; cf. Deuteronomy 24:1–4; Matthew 5:32; 19:7; Mark 10:1–12; see Romans 7:2, 3; 1 Corinthians 7:10, 39).

[REMARRIAGE from in the resurrection they neither marry nor are given in marriage]

Setting: The temple in Jerusalem. The Sadducees question Jesus about Levirate marriage (marriage to a brother-in-law), in order to test Him.

But Jesus answered and said to them, "You are mistaken, not understanding the Scriptures nor the power of God. For in the resurrection they neither marry nor are given in marriage, but are like angels in heaven. But regarding the resurrection of the dead, have you not read what was spoken to you by God: 'I AM THE GOD OF ABRAHAM, AND THE GOD OF ISAAC, AND THE GOD OF JACOB'? He is not the God of the dead but of the living" (Matthew 22:29–32, Jesus quotes from Exodus 3:6; cf. Mark 12:18–27; Luke 20:27–38; see Deuteronomy 25:5; John 20:9).

[REMARRIAGE from marries another woman]
Setting: Judea beyond the Jordan (Perea). Jesus teaches the crowds gathered around Him about divorce after the Pharisees test and question Him on the subject.

And He answered and said to them, "What did Moses command you?" They said, "Moses permitted a *man* TO WRITE A CERTIFICATE OF DIVORCE AND SEND *her* AWAY." But Jesus said to them, "Because of your hardness of heart he wrote you this commandment. But from the beginning of creation, *God* MADE THEM MALE AND FEMALE. FOR THIS REASON A MAN SHALL LEAVE HIS FATHER AND MOTHER, AND THE TWO SHALL BECOME ONE FLESH; so they are no longer two, but one flesh. What therefore God has joined together, let no man separate. In the house the disciples *began* questioning Him about this again. And He said to them, "Whoever divorces his wife and marries another woman commits adultery against her; and if she herself divorces her husband and marries another man, she is committing adultery" (Mark 10:3–12, Jesus quotes from Genesis 1:27; 2:24; cf. Matthew 19:1–9; see Deuteronomy 24:1–3; Matthew 5:32; see Romans 7:2, 3; 1 Corinthians 7:10, 11, 13, 39; 1 Timothy 2:14).

[REMARRIAGE from they neither marry nor are given in marriage]
Setting: The temple in Jerusalem. After some of the Pharisees and Herodians attempt to trap Jesus in a statement, some Sadducees question Him about the status of marriage after death.

Jesus said to them, "Is this not the reason you are mistaken, that you do not understand the Scriptures or the power of God? For when they rise from the dead, they neither marry nor are given in marriage, but are like angels in heaven. But regarding the fact that the dead rise again, have you not read in the book of Moses, in the *passage* about *the burning* bush, how God spoke to him, saying, 'I AM THE GOD OF ABRAHAM, AND THE GOD OF ISAAC, and the God of Jacob?' He is not the God of the dead, but of the living; you are greatly mistaken" (Mark 12:24–27, Jesus quotes from Exodus 3:6; cf. Matthew 22:29–33; Luke 20:34–40).

[REMARRIAGE from he who marries one who is divorced from a husband]
Setting: On the way from Galilee to Jerusalem. The Lord responds to the Pharisees' scoffing at His teaching His disciples about stewardship with an illustration of the earthly commitment of marriage.

"Everyone who divorces his wife and marries another commits adultery, and he who marries one who is divorced from a husband commits adultery" (Luke 16:18; cf. Matthew 5:31, 32; 19:9; Mark 10:11, 12; see Luke 16:1, 14; Romans 7:2, 3; 1 Corinthians 7:10, 39).

[REMARRIAGE from neither marry nor are given in marriage]
Setting: The temple in Jerusalem. While ministering a few days before His crucifixion, after the scribes and Pharisees seek to trap Jesus by questioning Him about paying taxes to Caesar, some Sadducees (who say that there is no resurrection) ask the Lord a question about the resurrection.

Jesus said to them, "The sons of this age marry and are given in marriage, but those who are considered worthy to attain to that age and the resurrection from the dead, neither marry nor are given in marriage; for they cannot even die anymore, because they are like angels, and are sons of God, being sons of the resurrection. But that the dead are raised, even Moses showed, in the *passage about the burning* bush, where he calls the Lord THE GOD OF ABRAHAM, AND THE GOD OF ISAAC, AND THE GOD OF JACOB. Now He is not the God of the dead but of the living; for all live to Him" (Luke 20:34–38, Jesus quotes from Exodus 3:6; cf. Matthew 22:23–32; Mark 12:18–27).

REMEMBER/REMEMBERS (Also see MEMORY; and REMEMBRANCE)
Setting: Galilee. During the early part of His ministry, Jesus preaches the Sermon on the Mount to His disciples and the multitudes.

"Therefore if you are presenting your offering at the altar, and there remember that your brother has something against you, leave your offering there before the altar and go; first be reconciled to your brother, and then come and present your offering" (Matthew 5:23, 24; see Romans 12:17, 18).

Setting: By the Sea of Galilee. Jesus repeats a warning to His disciples about the teaching of the religious leaders of His time—the Pharisees and the Sadducees.

But Jesus aware of this, said, "You men of little faith, why do you discuss among yourselves that you have no bread? Do you not yet understand or remember the five loaves of the five thousand and how many baskets *full* you picked up? Or the seven loaves of the four thousand, and how many large baskets *full* you picked up? How is it that you do not understand that I did not speak to you concerning bread? But beware of the leaven of the Pharisees and Sadducees" (Matthew 16:8–11; cf. Matthew 14:17–21; 15:34–38; Mark 8:17–21).

Setting: The district of Dalmanutha. After the Pharisees argue with Jesus, seeking a sign from heaven to test Him, the Lord and His disciples cross to the other side of the Sea of Galilee. The disciples discuss with one another that they have no bread.

And Jesus, aware of this, said to them, "Why do you discuss *the fact* that you have no bread? Do you not yet see or understand? Do you have a hardened heart? HAVING EYES, DO YOU NOT SEE? AND HAVING EARS, DO YOU NOT HEAR? And do you not remember, when I broke the five loaves for the five thousand, how many baskets full of broken pieces you picked you? They said to Him, "Twelve." When *I broke* the seven for the four thousand, how many large baskets full of broken pieces did you pick up?" They said to Him, "Seven." And He was saying to them, "Do you not yet understand?" (Mark 8:17–21, Jesus quotes from Jeremiah 5:21; cf. Matthew 16:5–12; see Matthew 14:19, 20; Mark 6:41–44, 52).

Setting: On the way from Galilee to Jerusalem. After responding to the Pharisees' scoffing at His teaching the disciples about stewardship and the permanence of the Law, Jesus conveys the story of the rich man and Lazarus.

"Now there was a rich man, and he habitually dressed in purple and fine linen, joyously living in splendor every day. And a poor man named Lazarus was laid at his gate, covered with sores, and longing to be fed with the *crumbs* which were falling from the rich man's table; besides, even the dogs were coming and licking his sores. Now the poor man died and was carried away by the angels to Abraham's bosom; and the rich man also died and was buried. In Hades he lifted up his eyes, being in torment, and saw Abraham far away and Lazarus in his bosom. And he cried out and said, 'Father Abraham, have mercy on me, and send Lazarus so that he may dip the tip of his finger in water and cool off my tongue, for I am in agony in this flame.' But Abraham said, 'Child, remember that during your life you received your good things, and likewise Lazarus bad things; but now he is being comforted here, and you are in agony. And besides all this, between us and you there is a great chasm fixed, so that those who wish to come over from here to you will not be able, and *that* none may cross over from there to us.' And he said, 'Then I beg you, father, that you send him to my father's house—for I have five brothers—in order that he may warn them, so that they will not also come to this place of torment.' But Abraham said, 'They have Moses and the Prophets; let them hear them.' But he said, 'No, father Abraham, but if someone goes to them from the dead, they will repent!' But he said to him, 'If they do not listen to Moses and the Prophets, they will not be persuaded even if someone rises from the dead' " (Luke 16:19–31; see Luke 3:8; 6:24; 16:1, 14).

Setting: On the way from Galilee to Jerusalem. After the Pharisees question Him about the coming of the kingdom of God, Jesus tells His disciples of His second coming.

And He said to the disciples, "The days will come when you will long to see one of the days of the Son of Man, and you will not see it. They will say to you, 'Look there! Look here!' Do not go away, and do not run after *them*. For just like the lightning, when it flashes out of one part of the sky, shines to the other part of the sky, so will the Son of Man be in His day. But first He must suffer many things and be rejected by this generation. And just as it happened in the days of Noah, so it will be also in the days of the Son of Man: they were eating, they were drinking, they were marrying, they were being given in marriage, until the day that Noah entered the ark, and the flood came and destroyed them all. It was the same as happened in the days of Lot: they were eating, they were drinking, they were buying, they were selling, they were planting, they were building; but on the day that Lot went out from Sodom it rained fire and brimstone from heaven and destroyed them all. It will be just the same on the day that the Son of Man is revealed. On that day, the one who is on the housetop and whose goods are in the house must not go down to take them out; and likewise the one who is in the field must not turn back. Remember Lot's wife. Whoever seeks to keep his life will lose it, and whoever loses *his life* will preserve it. I tell you, on that night there will be two in one bed; one will be taken and the other will be left. There will be two women grinding at the same place; one will be taken and the other will be left. [Two men will be in the field; one will be taken and the other will be left."] And answering they said to Him, "Where, Lord?" And He said to them, "Where the body *is*, there also the vultures will be gathered" (Luke 17:22–37; see Genesis 19; Matthew 10:39; 16:21, 27; 24:17–28, 37–41).

Setting: Jerusalem. Before the Passover, with His departure in mind, after explaining He is the vine and His disciples are the branches, Jesus prepares them for persecution from the world.

"If the world hates you, you know that it has hated Me before *it hated* you. If you were of the world, the world would love its own; but because you are not of the world, but I chose you out of the world, because of this the world hates you. Remember the word that I said to you, 'A slave is not greater than his master.' If they persecuted Me, they will also persecute you; if they kept My word, they will keep yours also. But all these things they will do to you for My name's sake, because they do not know the One who sent Me. If I had not come and spoken to them, they would not have sin, but now they have no excuse for their sin" (John 15:18–22; see Matthew 10:22; John 7:7; 8:19, 55; 9:41; 1 Corinthians 4:12).

Setting: Jerusalem. Before the Passover, after explaining He is the vine and His disciples are the branches, Jesus warns the disciples of the persecution they will face after His departure to heaven.

"These things I have spoken to you so that you may be kept from stumbling. They will make you outcasts from the synagogue, but an hour is coming for everyone who kills you to think that he is offering service to God. These things they will do because they have not known the Father or Me. But these things I have spoken to you, so that when their hour comes, you may remember that I told you of them. These things I did not say to you at the beginning, because I was with you" (John 16:1–4; see John 8:19, 55; 9:22; 13:19; 15:18–27).

Setting: Jerusalem. Before the Passover, after warning His disciples of the persecution they will face after His departure to heaven, empathizing with their sadness over His prophecies, Jesus gives them the hope for the future.

"A little while, and you will no longer see Me; and again a little while, and you will see Me." *Some* of His disciples then said to one another, "What is this thing He is telling us, 'A little while, and you will not see Me; and again a little while, and you will see Me'; and, 'because I go to the Father'?" So they were saying, "What is this that He says, 'A little while'? We do not know what He is talking about." Jesus knew that they wished to question Him, and He said to them, "Are you deliberating together about this, that I said, 'A little while, and you will not see Me, and again a little while, and you will see Me'? Truly, truly, I say to you, that you will weep and lament, but the world will rejoice; you will grieve, but your grief will be turned into joy. Whenever a woman is in labor she has pain, because her hour has come; but when she gives birth to the child, she no longer remembers the anguish because of the joy that a child has been born into the world. Therefore you too have grief now; but I will see you again, and your heart will rejoice, and no one *will* take your joy away from you" (John 16:16–22; see Mark 9:32; Luke 23:27; John 14:18–24; 16:5, 6; 20:20).

Setting: On the island of Patmos (in the Aegean Sea about fifty miles southwest of Ephesus in modern Turkey). On the Lord's Day (Sunday), approximately fifty years after the Resurrection, the disciple John encounters the Lord Jesus Christ, who communicates a new revelation for the apostle to record for the church in Ephesus and to six other churches in Asia.

"To the angel of the church in Ephesus write: The One who holds the seven stars in His right hand, the One who walks among the seven golden lampstands, says this: 'I know your deeds and your toil and perseverance, and that you cannot tolerate evil men, and you put to the test those who call themselves apostles, and they are not, and you found them *to be* false; and you have perseverance and have endured for My name's sake, and have not grown weary. But I have *this* against you, that you have left your first love. Therefore remember from where you have fallen, and repent and do the deeds you did at first; or else I am coming to you and will remove your lampstand out of its place—unless you repent. Yet this you do have, that you hate the deeds of the

Nicolaitans, which I also hate. He who has an ear, let him hear what the Spirit says to the churches. To him who overcomes, I will grant to eat of the tree of life which is in the Paradise of God' " (Revelation 2:1–7; see Genesis 2:9; Ezekiel 28:13; 1 John 4:1; Revelation 1:10, 11, 19, 20; 2:15, 16).

Setting: On the island of Patmos (in the Aegean Sea about fifty miles southwest of Ephesus in modern Turkey). On the Lord's Day (Sunday), approximately fifty years after the Resurrection, the disciple John encounters the Lord Jesus Christ, who communicates a new revelation for the apostle to record for the church in Sardis and to six other churches in Asia.

"To the angel of the church in Sardis write: He who has the seven Spirits of God and the seven stars, says this: 'I know your deeds, that you have a name that you are alive, but you are dead. Wake up, and strengthen the things that remain, which were about to die; for I have not found your deeds completed in the sight of My God. So remember what you have received and heard; and keep *it,* and repent. Therefore if you do not wake up, I will come like a thief, and you will not know at what hour I will come to you. But you have a few people in Sardis who have not soiled their garments; and they will walk with Me in white, for they are worthy. He who overcomes will thus be clothed in white garments; and I will not erase his name from the book of life, and I will confess his name before My Father and before His angels. He who has an ear, let him hear what the Spirit says to the churches' " (Revelation 3:1–6; see Matthew 10:32; Revelation 1:16).

REMEMBRANCE (Also see MEMORY; and REMEMBER)

Setting: An upper room in Jerusalem. During the Feast of Unleavened Bread (Passover) just before His crucifixion, while celebrating the Passover meal with His disciples, Jesus institutes the Lord's Supper.

And when He had taken a cup *and* given thanks, He said, "Take this and share it among yourselves; for I say to you, I will not drink of the fruit of the vine from now on until the kingdom of God comes." And when he had taken *some* bread and given thanks, He broke it and gave it to them, saying, "This is My body which is given for you; do this in remembrance of Me." And in the same way *He took* the cup after they had eaten, saying, "This cup which is poured out for you is the new covenant in My blood. But behold, the hand of the one betraying Me is with Mine on the table. For indeed, the Son of Man is going as it has been determined; but woe to that man by whom He is betrayed!" (Luke 22:17–22; cf. Matthew 26:26–29; Mark 14:22–25; 1 Corinthians 11:23–26; see Psalm 41:9; Luke 14:15; 1 Corinthians 10:16).

Setting: Jerusalem. Before the Passover, after responding to Philip's request for Him to show His disciples the Father, Jesus conveys the upcoming ministry of the Holy Spirit in their lives.

"These things I have spoken to you while abiding with you. But the Helper, the Holy Spirit, whom the Father will send in My name, He will teach you all things, and bring to your remembrance all that I said to you" (John 14:25, 26; see John 16:13).

Setting: An upper room in Jerusalem. During his third missionary journey, writing from Ephesus to the church at Corinth, the apostle Paul recounts the Lord Jesus' words as He institutes the Lord's Supper.

For I received from the Lord that which I also delivered to you, that the Lord Jesus in the night in which He was betrayed took bread; and when He had given thanks, He broke it and said, "This is My body, which is for you; do this in remembrance of Me." In the same way *He took* the cup also after supper, saying, "This cup is the new covenant in My blood; do this, as often as you drink *it,* in remembrance of Me" (1 Corinthians 11:23–25; cf. Matthew 26:26–28; Mark 14:22–24; Luke 22:17–20).

REMORSE (lack of)

Setting: The temple in Jerusalem. Jesus delivers a parable to the chief priests and elders after they question His authority.

"But what do you think? A man had two sons, and he came to the first and said, 'Son, go work today in the vineyard.' And he answered, 'I will not'; but afterward he regretted it and went. The man came to the second and said the same thing; and he answered, 'I *will,* sir'; but he did not go. Which of the two sons did the will of his father?" They said, "The first." Jesus said to them, "Truly, I say to you that the tax collectors and prostitutes will get into the kingdom of God before you. For John came to you in the way of righteousness and you did not believe him; but the tax collectors and prostitutes did believe him; and you, seeing *this,* did not even feel remorse afterward so as to believe him" (Matthew 21:28–32; cf. Luke 7:29, 30, 37–50).

REPAYMENT (Also see DEBT; INTEREST; LOANS; MONEY; and REWARD)

[REPAYMENT from REPAY EVERY MAN ACCORDING TO HIS DEEDS]

Setting: Near Caesarea Philippi. After rebuking Peter for trying to forbid Him to accomplish His earthly mission of dying and being resurrected, Jesus teaches His disciples about the costs of following Him.

Then Jesus said to His disciples, "If anyone wishes to come after Me, he must deny himself, and take up his cross and follow Me. For whoever wishes to save his life will lose it; but whoever loses his life for My sake will find it. For what will it profit a man if he gains the whole world and forfeits his soul? Or what will a man give in exchange for his soul? For the Son of Man is going to come in the glory of His Father with His angels, and WILL THEN REPAY EVERY MAN ACCORDING TO HIS DEEDS. Truly, I say to you, there are some of you who are standing here who will not taste death until they see the Son of Man coming in His kingdom" (Matthew 16:24–28, Jesus quotes from Psalm 62:12; cf. Mark 8:34–37; Luke 9:23–27; see Matthew 10:38, 39).

Setting: Capernaum of Galilee. Jesus illustrates the matter of forgiveness after Peter asks Him if forgiving someone seven times who has sinned against him is adequate.

"For this reason the kingdom of heaven may be compared to a king who wished to settle accounts with his slaves. When he had begun to settle *them,* one who owed him ten thousand talents was brought to him. But since he did not have *the means* to repay, his lord commanded him to be sold, along with his wife and children and all that he had, and repayment to be made. So the slave fell *to the ground* and prostrated himself before him, saying, 'Have patience with me and I will repay you everything.' And the lord of that slave felt compassion and released him and forgave him the debt. But that slave went out and found one of his fellow slaves who owed him a hundred denarii; and he seized him and *began* to choke *him,* saying, 'Pay back what you owe.' So his fellow slave fell *to the ground* and *began* to plead with him, saying, 'Have patience with me and I will repay you.' But he was unwilling and went and threw him in prison until he should pay back what was owed. So when his fellow slaves saw what had happened, they were deeply grieved and came and reported to their lord all that had happened. Then summoning him, his lord said to him, 'You wicked slave, I forgave you all that debt because you pleaded with me. Should you not also have had mercy on your fellow slave, in the same way that I had mercy on you?' And his lord, moved with anger, handed him over to the torturers until he should repay all that was owed him. My heavenly Father will also do the same to you, if each of you does not forgive his brother from your heart" (Matthew 18:23–35; cf. Matthew 6:12, 14, 15; Luke 7:42; see Matthew 25:19–28).

[REPAYMENT from receive back the same *amount*]

Setting: Galilee. After selecting His twelve disciples, Jesus teaches the Sermon on the Mount to those disciples and a great throng of people from Judea, Jerusalem, and the central coastal region of Tyre and Sidon.

"But I say to you who hear, love your enemies, do good to those who hate you, bless those who curse you, pray for those who mistreat you. Whoever hits you on the cheek, offer him the other also; and whoever takes away your coat, do not withhold your shirt from him either. Give to everyone who asks of you, and whoever takes away what is yours, do not demand it back. Treat others the same way you want them to treat you. If you love those who love you, what credit is *that* to you? For even sinners love those who love them. If you do good to those who do good to you, what credit is *that* to you? For even sinners do the same. If you lend to those from whom you expect to receive, what credit is *that* to you? Even sinners lend to sinners in order to receive back the same *amount.* But love your enemies, and do good, and lend, expecting nothing in return; and your reward will be great, and you will be sons of the Most High; for He Himself is kind to ungrateful and evil *men*. Be merciful, just as your Father is merciful" (Luke 6:27–36; cf. Matthew 5:9, 39–48; Matthew 7:12).

[REPAYMENT from repay]

Setting: Galilee. After Jesus praises John the Baptist to the crowds, Simon, a Pharisee, invites Jesus to dinner. A sinful woman anoints the Lord's feet with perfume, prompting Him to convey a parable.

And Jesus answered him, "Simon, I have something to say to you." And he replied, "Say it, Teacher." "A moneylender had two debtors: one owed five hundred denarii, and the other fifty. When they were unable to repay, he graciously forgave them both. So which of them will love him more?" Simon answered and said, "I suppose the one whom he forgave more." And He said to him, "You have judged correctly" (Luke 7:40–43; see Matthew 18:23–35).

[REPAYMENT from repay]
Setting: On the way from Galilee to Jerusalem. While being tested by a lawyer, Jesus tells him the story of the good Samaritan.

Jesus replied and said, "A man was going down from Jerusalem to Jericho, and fell among robbers, and they stripped him and beat him, and went away leaving him half dead. And by chance a priest was going down on that road, and when he saw him, he passed by on the other side. Likewise a Levite also, when he came to the place and saw him, passed by on the other side. But a Samaritan, who was on a journey, came upon him; and when he saw him, he felt compassion, and came to him and bandaged up his wounds, pouring oil and wine on *them;* and he put him on his own beast, and brought him to an inn and took care of him. On the next day he took out two denarii and gave them to the innkeeper and said, 'Take care of him; and whatever more you spend, when I return I will repay you.' Which of these three do you think proved to be a neighbor to the man who fell into the robbers' *hands?*" And he said, "The one who showed mercy toward him." Then Jesus said to him, "Go and do the same" (Luke 10:30–37).

Setting: On the way from Galilee to Jerusalem. After Jesus, observing the invited guests of a Pharisee leader selecting places of honor at the table, speaks a parable to them, He comments to the host about the people to invite in the future.

And He also went on to say to the one who had invited Him, "When you give a luncheon or a dinner, do not invite your friends or your brothers or your relatives or rich neighbors, otherwise they may also invite you in return and *that* will be your repayment. But when you give a reception, invite *the* poor, *the* crippled, *the* lame, *the* blind, and you will be blessed, since they do not have *the means* to repay you; for you will be repaid at the resurrection of the righteous" (Luke 14:12–14; see Luke 14:1, 2, 15; John 5:28, 29).

REPENTANCE (Also see FORGIVENESS; GOSPEL; and SALVATION)

[REPENTANCE from repent]
Setting: Galilee. After hearing that John the Baptist has been taken into custody, Jesus begins His ministry, settling in Capernaum by the Sea of Galilee in fulfillment of Isaiah 9:1, 2.

From that time Jesus began to preach and say, "Repent, for the kingdom of heaven is at hand" (Matthew 4:17; cf. Mark 1:15).

[REPENTANCE from repented]
Setting: Galilee. After performing miracles throughout the region, Jesus pronounces woes against those cities who do not repent.

"Woe to you, Chorazin! Woe to you, Bethsaida! For if the miracles had occurred in Tyre and Sidon which occurred in you, they would have repented long ago in sackcloth and ashes. Nevertheless I say to you, it will be more tolerable for Tyre and Sidon in *the* day of judgment than for you. And you, Capernaum, will not be exalted to heaven, will you? You will descend to Hades; for if the miracles had occurred in Sodom which occurred in you, it would have remained to this day. Nevertheless, I say to you that it will be more tolerable for the land of Sodom in *the* day of judgment, than for you" (Matthew 11:21–24; cf. Matthew 10:15; Luke 10:13–15).

[REPENTANCE from repented]
Setting: Galilee. After Jesus warns the Pharisees about the unpardonable sin and their future judgment, some Pharisees and scribes ask Him to perform a miraculous sign for them in front of the crowds.

But He answered and said to them, "An evil and adulterous generation craves for a sign; and *yet* no sign will be given to it but the sign of Jonah the prophet; for just as JONAH WAS THREE DAYS AND THREE NIGHTS IN THE BELLY OF THE SEA MONSTER, so will the Son of Man be three days and three nights in the heart of the earth. The men of Nineveh will stand up with this generation at the judgment, and will condemn it because they repented at the preaching of Jonah; and behold, something greater than Jonah is here. *The* Queen of *the* South will rise up with this generation at the judgment and will condemn it, because she came from the ends of the earth to hear the wisdom of Solomon; and behold, something greater than Solomon is here" (Matthew 12:39–42; Jesus quotes from Jonah 1:17; cf. 1 Kings 10:1; Jonah 3:5; Matthew 16:1, 4; Luke 11:29).

[REPENTANCE from repent]
Setting: Galilee. After being baptized by John the Baptist in the Jordan River, Jesus commences His gospel-preaching ministry shortly after John is taken into custody by Herod Antipas.

Now after John had been taken into custody, Jesus came into Galilee, preaching the gospel of God, and saying, "The time is fulfilled, and the kingdom of God is at hand; repent and believe in the gospel" (Mark 1:14, 15, cf. Matthew 4:17; Galatians 4:4).

Setting: The house of Levi (Matthew) in Capernaum. At a reception following Jesus' call of Levi to become His disciple, the Pharisees and their scribes question why the Lord associates with tax collectors and sinners.

And Jesus answered and said to them, "*It is* not those who are well who need a physician, but those who are sick. I have not come to call the righteous but sinners to repentance" (Luke 5:31, 32; cf. Matthew 9:10–13; Mark 2:15–17; see Luke 5:29, 30).

[REPENTANCE from repented]
Setting: On the way from Galilee to Jerusalem. The Lord pronounces woes on cities who reject the gospel, as He appoints seventy followers and sends them out in pairs to every place He Himself will soon visit.

"Woe to you, Chorazin! Woe to you, Bethsaida! For if the miracles had been performed in Tyre and Sidon which occurred in you, they would have repented long ago, sitting in sackcloth and ashes. But it will be more tolerable for Tyre and Sidon in the judgment than for you. And you, Capernaum, will not be exalted to heaven, will you? You will be brought down to Hades! The one who listens to you listens to Me, and the one who rejects you rejects Me; and he who rejects Me rejects the One who sent Me" (Luke 10:13–16; cf. Matthew 11:21–23; see Matthew 10:40; Luke 10:1).

[REPENTANCE from repented]
Setting: On the way from Galilee to Jerusalem. After revealing a problem with exorcism and responding to a blessing from a woman in the crowd, Jesus tells the increasing crowds of the sign of Jonah.

As the crowds were increasing, He began to say, "This generation is a wicked generation; it seeks for a sign, and *yet* no sign will be given to it but the sign of Jonah. For just as Jonah became a sign to the Ninevites, so will the Son of Man be to this generation. The Queen of the South will rise up with the men of this generation at the judgment and condemn them, because she came from the ends of the earth to hear the wisdom of Solomon; and behold, something greater than Solomon is here. The men of Nineveh will stand up with this generation at the judgment and condemn it, because they repented at the preaching of Jonah; and behold, something greater than Jonah is here" (Luke 11:29–32; cf. Matthew 16:4; see 1 Kings 10:1–10; Jonah 3:4, 5).

[REPENTANCE from repent]
Setting: On the way from Galilee to Jerusalem. After some present report to Him about the Galileans whose blood Pilate (Roman governor of Judea) has mixed with their sacrifices, Jesus responds to their concern by calling them to repentance.

And Jesus said to them, "Do you suppose that these Galileans were *greater* sinners than all *other* Galileans because they suffered this *fate*? I tell you, no, but unless you repent, you will all likewise perish. Or do you suppose that those eighteen on whom the tower in Siloam fell and killed them were *worse* culprits than all the men who live in Jerusalem? I tell you, no, but unless you repent, you will all likewise perish" (Luke 13:2–5; see Luke 13:1; John 9:2, 3).

Setting: On the way from Galilee to Jerusalem. After Jesus presents to large crowds the demands of discipleship, the Pharisees and scribes complain He associates with tax collectors and sinners.

So He told them this parable, saying, "What man among you, if he has a hundred sheep and has lost one of them, does not leave the ninety-nine in the open pasture and go after the one which is lost until he finds it? When he has found it, he lays it on his shoulders, rejoicing. And when he comes home, he calls together his friends and his neighbors, saying to them, 'Rejoice with me, for I have found my sheep which was lost!' I tell you that in the same way, there will be *more* joy in heaven over one sinner who repents than over ninety-nine righteous persons who need no repentance" (Luke 15:3–7; cf. Matthew 18:12–14; see Matthew 9:11–13; Luke 5:29–32).

[REPENTANCE from repents]
Setting: On the way from Galilee to Jerusalem. After Jesus, observing the invited guests of a Pharisee leader selecting places of honor at the table, speaks a parable to them, He comments to the host about the people to invite in the future.

"Or what woman, if she has ten silver coins and loses one coin, does not light a lamp and sweep the house and search carefully until she finds it? When she has found it, she calls together her friends and neighbors, saying, 'Rejoice with me, for I have found the coin which I had lost!' In the same way, I tell you, there is joy in the presence of the angels of God over one sinner who repents" (Luke 15:8–10).

[REPENTANCE from repent]
Setting: On the way from Galilee to Jerusalem. After responding to the Pharisees' scoffing at His teaching the disciples about stewardship and the permanence of the Law, Jesus conveys the story of the rich man and Lazarus.

"Now there was a rich man, and he habitually dressed in purple and fine linen, joyously living in splendor every day. And a poor man named Lazarus was laid at his gate, covered with sores, and longing to be fed with the *crumbs* which were falling from the rich man's table; besides, even the dogs were coming and licking his sores. Now the poor man died and was carried away by the angels to Abraham's bosom; and the rich man also died and was buried. In Hades he lifted up his eyes, being in torment, and saw Abraham far away and Lazarus in his bosom. And he cried out and said, 'Father Abraham, have mercy on me, and send Lazarus so that he may dip the tip of his finger in water and cool off my tongue, for I am in agony in this flame.' But Abraham said, 'Child, remember that during your life you received your good things, and likewise Lazarus bad things; but now he is being comforted here, and you are in agony. And besides all this, between us and you there is a great chasm fixed, so that those who wish to come over from here to you will not be able, and *that* none may cross over from there to us.' And he said, 'Then I beg you, father, that you send him to my father's house—for I have five brothers—in order that he may warn them, so that they will not also come to this place of torment.' But Abraham said, 'They have Moses and the Prophets; let them hear them.' But he said, 'No, father Abraham, but if someone goes to them from the dead, they will repent!' But he said to him, 'If they do not listen to Moses and the Prophets, they will not be persuaded even if someone rises from the dead' " (Luke 16:19–31; see Luke 3:8; 6:24; 16:1, 14).

[REPENTANCE from repents and repent]
Setting: On the way from Galilee to Jerusalem. After conveying the story of the rich man and Lazarus, the Lord gives His disciples instruction on forgiveness.

He said to His disciples, "It is inevitable that stumbling blocks come, but woe to him through whom they come! It would be better for him if a millstone were hung around his neck and he were thrown into the sea, than that he would cause one of these little ones to stumble. Be on your guard! If your brother sins, rebuke him; and if he repents, forgive him. And if he sins against you seven times a day, and returns to you seven times, saying, 'I repent,' forgive him" (Luke 17:1–4; see Matthew 18:5–7, 15, 21, 22).

Setting: Jerusalem. After rising from the tomb on the third day after being crucified, and appearing to two of His followers on the road to Emmaus, Jesus gives instruction to His disciples (except Thomas) about His mission on earth and the promise of future power from God.

Now He said to them, "These are My words which I spoke to you while I was still with you, that all things which are written about Me in the Law of Moses and the Prophets and the Psalms must be fulfilled." Then He opened their minds to understand the Scriptures, and He said to them, "Thus it is written, that the Christ would suffer and rise again from the dead the third day, and that repentance for forgiveness of sins would be proclaimed in His name to all the nations, beginning from Jerusalem. You are witnesses of these things. And behold, I am sending forth the promise of My Father upon you; but you are to stay in the city until you are clothed with power from on high" (Luke 24:44–49; see Matthew 28:19, 20; Acts 1:8).

[REPENTANCE from repent]
Setting: On the island of Patmos (in the Aegean Sea about fifty miles southwest of Ephesus in modern Turkey). On the Lord's Day (Sunday), approximately fifty years after the Resurrection, the disciple John encounters the Lord Jesus Christ, who communicates a new revelation for the apostle to record for the church in Ephesus and to six other churches in Asia.

"To the angel of the church in Ephesus write: The One who holds the seven stars in His right hand, the One who walks among the seven golden lampstands, says this: 'I know your deeds and your toil and perseverance, and that you cannot tolerate evil men, and you put to the test those who call themselves apostles, and they are not, and you found them *to be* false; and you have perseverance and have endured for My name's sake, and have not grown weary. But I have *this* against you, that you have left your first love. Therefore remember from where you have fallen, and repent and do the deeds you did at first; or else I am coming to you and will remove your lampstand out of its place—unless you repent. Yet this you do have, that you hate the deeds of the Nicolaitans, which I also hate. He who has an ear, let him hear what the Spirit says to the churches. To him who overcomes, I will grant to eat of the tree of life which is in the Paradise of God' " (Revelation 2:1–7; see Genesis 2:9; Ezekiel 28:13; 1 John 4:1; Revelation 1:10, 11, 19, 20; 2:15, 16).

[REPENTANCE from repent]
Setting: On the island of Patmos (in the Aegean Sea about fifty miles southwest of Ephesus in modern Turkey). On the Lord's Day (Sunday), approximately fifty years after the Resurrection, the disciple John encounters the Lord Jesus Christ, who communicates a new revelation for the apostle to record for the church in Pergamum and to six other churches in Asia.

"And to the angel of the church in Pergamum write: The One who has the sharp two-edged sword says this: 'I know where you dwell, where Satan's throne is; and you hold fast My name, and did not deny My faith even in the days of Antipas, My witness, My faithful one, who was killed among you, where Satan dwells. But I have a few things against you, because you have there some who hold the teaching of Balaam, who kept teaching Balak to put a stumbling block before the sons of Israel, to eat things sacrificed to idols and to commit *acts of* immorality. So you also have some who in the same way hold the teaching of the Nicolaitans. Therefore repent; or else I am coming to you quickly, and I will make war against them with the sword of My mouth. He who has an ear, let him hear what the Spirit says to the churches. To him who overcomes, to him I will give *some* of the hidden manna, and I will give him a white stone, and a new name written on the stone which no one knows but he who receives it' (Revelation 2:12–17; see Numbers 25:1–3; Isaiah 62:2; Revelation 1:16; 2:5, 6, 16).

[REPENTANCE from repent]
Setting: On the island of Patmos (in the Aegean Sea about fifty miles southwest of Ephesus in modern Turkey). On the Lord's Day (Sunday), approximately fifty years after the Resurrection, the disciple John encounters the Lord Jesus Christ, who communicates a new revelation for the apostle to record for the church in Thyatira and to six other churches in Asia.

"And to the angel of the church in Thyatira write: The Son of God, who has eyes like a flame of fire, and His feet are like burnished bronze, says this: 'I know your deeds, and your love and faith and service and perseverance, and that your deeds of late are greater than at first. But I have *this* against you, that you tolerate the woman Jezebel, who calls herself a prophetess, and she teaches and leads My bond-servants astray so that they commit *acts of* immorality and eat things sacrificed to idols. I gave her time to repent, and she does not want to repent of her immorality. Behold, I will throw her on a bed *of sickness,* and those who commit adultery with her into great tribulation, unless they repent of her deeds. And I will kill her children with pestilence, and all the churches will know that I am He who searches the minds and hearts; and I will give to each one of you according to your deeds. But I say to you, the rest who are in Thyatira, who do not hold this teaching, who have not known the deep things of Satan, as they call them—I place no other burden on you. Nevertheless what you have, hold fast until I come. He who overcomes, and he who keeps My deeds until the end, TO HIM I WILL GIVE AUTHORITY OVER THE NATIONS; AND HE SHALL RULE THEM WITH A ROD OF IRON, AS THE VESSELS OF THE POTTER ARE BROKEN TO PIECES, as I also have received *authority* from My Father; and I will give him the morning star. He who has an ear, let him hear what the Spirit says to the churches' (Revelation 2:18–29; Jesus quotes from Psalm 2:8, 9; Isaiah 30:14; see 1 Kings 16:31; Psalm 7:9; Romans 2:5; 1 Corinthians 2:10; 2 Peter 3:9; Revelation 1:14; 2:7; 3:11; 17:1–20).

[REPENTANCE from repent]
Setting: On the island of Patmos (in the Aegean Sea about fifty miles southwest of Ephesus in modern Turkey). On the Lord's Day (Sunday), approximately fifty years after the Resurrection, the disciple John encounters the Lord Jesus Christ, who communicates a new revelation for the apostle to record for the church in Sardis and to six other churches in Asia.

"To the angel of the church in Sardis write: He who has the seven Spirits of God and the seven stars, says this: 'I know your deeds, that you have a name that you are alive, but you are dead. Wake up, and strengthen the things that remain, which were about to die; for I have not found your deeds completed in the sight of My God. So remember what you have received and heard; and keep *it,* and repent. Therefore if you do not wake up, I will come like a thief, and you will not know at what hour I will come to you. But you have a few people in Sardis who have not soiled their garments; and they will walk with Me in white, for they are worthy. He who overcomes will thus be clothed in white garments; and I will not erase his name from the book of life, and I will confess his name before My Father and before His angels. He who has an ear, let him hear what the Spirit says to the churches' " (Revelation 3:1–6; see Matthew 10:32; Revelation 1:16).

[REPENTANCE from repent]
Setting: On the island of Patmos (in the Aegean Sea about fifty miles southwest of Ephesus in modern Turkey). On the Lord's Day (Sunday), approximately fifty years after the Resurrection, the disciple John encounters the Lord Jesus Christ, who communicates a new revelation for the apostle to record for the church in Laodicea and to six other churches in Asia.

"To the angel of the church in Laodicea write: The Amen, the faithful and true Witness, the Beginning of the creation of God, says this: 'I know your deeds, that you are neither cold nor hot; I wish that you were cold or hot. So because you are lukewarm, and neither hot nor cold, I will spit you out of My mouth. Because you say, "I am rich, and have become wealthy, and have need of nothing," and you do not know that you are wretched and miserable and poor and blind and naked, I advise you to buy from Me gold refined by fire so that you may become rich, and white garments so that you may clothe yourself, and *that* the shame of your nakedness will not be revealed; and eye salve to anoint your eyes so that you may see. Those whom I love, I reprove and discipline; therefore be zealous and repent. Behold, I stand at the door and knock; if anyone hears My voice and opens the door, I will come in to him and will dine with him, and he with Me. He who overcomes, I will grant to him to sit down with Me on My throne, as I also overcame and sat down with My Father on His throne. He who has an ear, let him hear what the Spirit says to the churches'" (Revelation 3:14–22; see Proverb 3:12; Hosea 12:8; John 14:23; 16:33).

REPENTANCE, LACK OF

[LACK OF REPENTANCE from would have repented]
Setting: Galilee. After performing miracles throughout the region, Jesus pronounces woes against those cities who do not repent.

"Woe to you, Chorazin! Woe to you, Bethsaida! For if the miracles had occurred in Tyre and Sidon which occurred in you, they would have repented long ago in sackcloth and ashes. Nevertheless I say to you, it will be more tolerable for Tyre and Sidon in *the* day of judgment than for you. And you, Capernaum, will not be exalted to heaven, will you? You will descend to Hades; for if the miracles had occurred in Sodom which occurred in you, it would have remained to this day. Nevertheless, I say to you that it will be more tolerable for the land of Sodom in *the* day of judgment, than for you" (Matthew 11:21–24; cf. Matthew 10:15; Luke 10:13–15).

[LACK OF REPENTANCE from would have repented]
Setting: On the way from Galilee to Jerusalem. The Lord pronounces woes on cities who reject the gospel, as He appoints seventy followers and sends them out in pairs to every place He Himself will soon visit.

"Woe to you, Chorazin! Woe to you, Bethsaida! For if the miracles had been performed in Tyre and Sidon which occurred in you, they would have repented long ago, sitting in sackcloth and ashes. But it will be more tolerable for Tyre and Sidon in the judgment than for you. And you, Capernaum, will not be exalted to heaven, will you? You will be brought down to Hades! The one who listens to you listens to Me, and the one who rejects you rejects Me; and he who rejects Me rejects the One who sent Me" (Luke 10:13–16; cf. Matthew 11:21–23; see Matthew 10:40; Luke 10:1).

[LACK OF REPENTANCE from does not want to repent]
Setting: On the island of Patmos (in the Aegean Sea about fifty miles southwest of Ephesus in modern Turkey). On the Lord's Day (Sunday), approximately fifty years after the Resurrection, the disciple John encounters the Lord Jesus Christ, who communicates a new revelation for the apostle to record for the church in Thyatira and to six other churches in Asia.

"And to the angel of the church in Thyatira write: The Son of God, who has eyes like a flame of fire, and His feet are like burnished bronze, says this: 'I know your deeds, and your love and faith and service and perseverance, and that your deeds of late are greater than at first. But I have *this* against you, that you tolerate the woman Jezebel, who calls herself a prophetess, and she teaches and leads My bond-servants astray so that they commit *acts of* immorality and eat things sacrificed to idols. I gave her time to repent, and she does not want to repent of her immorality. Behold, I will throw her on a bed *of sickness,* and those who commit adultery with her into great tribulation, unless they repent of her deeds. And I will kill her children with pestilence, and all the churches will know that I am He who searches the minds and hearts; and I will give to each one of you according to your deeds. But I say to you, the rest who are in Thyatira, who do not hold this teaching, who have not known the deep things of Satan, as they call them—I place no other burden on you. Nevertheless what you have, hold fast until I come. He who overcomes, and he who keeps My deeds until the end, TO HIM I WILL GIVE AUTHORITY OVER THE NATIONS; AND HE SHALL RULE THEM WITH A ROD OF IRON, AS THE VESSELS OF THE POTTER ARE BROKEN TO PIECES, as I also have received *authority* from My Father; and I will give him the morning star. He who has an ear, let him hear what the Spirit says to the churches' (Revelation 2:18–29; Jesus quotes from Psalm 2:8, 9; Isaiah 30:14; see 1 Kings 16:31; Psalm 7:9; Romans 2:5; 1 Corinthians 2:10; 2 Peter 3:9; Revelation 1:14; 2:7; 3:11; 17:1–20).

REPETITION, MEANINGLESS (Also see PRAYER)

Setting: Galilee. During the early part of His ministry, Jesus preaches the Sermon on the Mount to His disciples and the multitudes.

"And when you are praying, do not use meaningless repetition as the Gentiles do, for they suppose that they will be heard for their many words. So do not be like them; for your Father knows what you need before you ask Him" (Matthew 6:7, 8; see 1 Kings 18:26–29).

REPROOF (Also see REBUKE)

[REPROOF from show him his fault]
Setting: Capernaum of Galilee. After conveying to His disciples the value of little ones, Jesus gives instruction about church discipline.

"If your brother sins, go and show him his fault in private; if he listens to you, you have won your brother. But if he does not listen *to you,* take one or two more with you, so that BY THE MOUTH OF TWO OR THREE WITNESSES EVERY FACT MAY BE CONFIRMED. If he refuses to listen to them, tell it to the church; and if he refuses to listen even to the church, let him be to you as a Gentile and a tax collector. Truly I say to you, whatever you bind of earth shall have been bound in heaven; and whatever you loose on earth shall have been loosed in heaven. Again, I say to you, that if two of you agree on earth about anything that they may ask, it shall be done for them by My Father who is in heaven. For there two or three have gathered together in My name, I am there in their midst" (Matthew 18:15–20. Jesus quotes from Deuteronomy 19:15; cf. Matthew 7:7; 16:19; see Leviticus 19:17; Matthew 28:20; 2 Thessalonians 3:6, 14).

[REPROOF from reprove]
Setting: On the island of Patmos (in the Aegean Sea about fifty miles southwest of Ephesus in modern Turkey). On the Lord's Day (Sunday), approximately fifty years after the Resurrection, the disciple John encounters the Lord Jesus Christ, who communicates a new revelation for the apostle to record for the church in Laodicea and to six other churches in Asia.

"To the angel of the church in Laodicea write: The Amen, the faithful and true Witness, the Beginning of the creation of God, says this: 'I know your deeds, that you are neither cold nor hot; I wish that you were cold or hot. So because you are lukewarm, and neither hot nor cold, I will spit you out of My mouth. Because you say, "I am rich, and have become wealthy, and have need of nothing," and you do not know that you are wretched and miserable and poor and blind and naked, I advise you to buy from Me gold refined by fire so that you may become rich, and white garments so that you may clothe yourself, and *that* the shame of your nakedness will not be revealed; and eye salve to anoint your eyes so that you may see. Those whom I love, I reprove and discipline; therefore be zealous and repent. Behold, I stand at the door and knock; if anyone hears My voice and opens the door, I will come in to him and will dine with him, and he with Me. He who overcomes, I will grant to him to sit down with Me on My throne, as I also overcame and sat down with My Father on His throne. He who has an ear, let him hear what the Spirit says to the churches'" (Revelation 3:14–22; see Proverb 3:12; Hosea 12:8; John 14:23; 16:33).

REQUEST (Also see ASKING; BESEECH; and WISH)

Setting: Jerusalem. Before the Passover, after empathizing with His disciples' sadness over His prophecies and giving them the hope for the future, Jesus conveys promises about praying in His name.

"In that day you will not question Me about anything. Truly, truly, I say to you, if you ask the Father for anything in My name, He will give it to you. Until now you have asked for nothing in My name; ask and you will receive, so that your joy may be made full. These things I have spoken to you in figurative language; an hour is coming when I will no longer speak to you in figurative language, but will tell you plainly of the Father. In that day you will ask in My name, and I do not say to you that I will request of the Father on your behalf; for the Father Himself loves you, because you have loved Me and have believed that I came forth from the Father. I came forth from the Father and have come into the world; I am leaving the world again and going to the Father" (John 16:23–28; see Matthew 13:34; John 8:42; 13:1, 3; 14:14, 21, 23; 15:16).

REQUESTS, PRAYER (See PRAYER)

RESPECT (Also see HONOR)

Setting: The temple in Jerusalem. Jesus delivers another parable to the chief priests and elders after they question His authority.

"Listen to another parable. There was a landowner who PLANTED A VINEYARD AND PUT A WALL AROUND IT AND DUG A WINE PRESS IN IT, AND BUILT A TOWER, and rented it out to vine-growers and went on a journey. When the harvest time approached, he sent his slaves to the vine-growers to receive his produce. The vine-growers took his slaves and beat one, and killed another, and stoned a third. Again he sent another group of slaves larger than the first; and they did the same thing to them. But afterward he sent his son to them, saying, 'They will respect my son.' But when the vine-growers saw the son, they said among themselves, 'This is the heir; come, let us kill him and seize his inheritance.' They took him, and threw him out of the vineyard and killed him. Therefore when the owner of the vineyard comes, what will he do to those vine-growers?" (Matthew 21:33–40; Jesus quotes from Isaiah 5:1, 2; cf. Mark 12:1–9; Luke 20:9–15).

Setting: The temple in Jerusalem. Having His authority questioned by the chief priests, scribes, and elders, Jesus begins to teach them in parables.

And He began to speak to them in parables: "A man PLANTED A VINEYARD AND PUT A WALL AROUND IT, AND DUG A VAT UNDER THE WINE PRESS AND BUILT A TOWER, and rented it out to vine-growers and went on a journey. At the *harvest* time he sent a slave to the vine-growers, in order to receive *some* of the produce of the vineyard from the vine-growers. They took him, and beat him and sent him away empty-handed. Again he sent them another slave, and they wounded him in the head, and treated him shamefully. And he sent another, and that one they killed; and *so with* many others, beating some and killing others. He had one more to *send*, a beloved son; he sent him last *of all* to them, saying, 'They will respect my son.' But those vine-growers said to one another, 'This is the heir; come, let us kill him, and the inheritance will be ours!' They took him, and killed him and threw him out of the vineyard. What will the owner of the vineyard do? He will come and destroy the vine-growers, and will give the vineyard to others. Have you not even read this Scripture: 'THE STONE WHICH THE BUILDERS REJECTED, THIS BECAME THE CHIEF CORNER *stone;* THIS CAME ABOUT FROM THE LORD, AND IT IS MARVELOUS IN OUR EYES'?" (Mark 12:1–11, Jesus quotes from Psalm 118:22, 23; Isaiah 5:1, 2; cf. Matthew 21:33–46; Luke 20:9–19).

Setting: On the way from Galilee to Jerusalem. After telling His disciples of His second coming, Jesus instructs them about persistence in prayer.

Now He was telling them a parable to show that at all times they ought to pray and not to lose heart, saying, "In a certain city there was a judge who did not fear God and did not respect man. There was a widow in that city, and she kept coming to him, saying, 'Give me legal protection from my opponent.' For a while he was unwilling; but afterward he said to himself, 'Even though I do not fear God nor respect man, yet because this woman bothers me, I will give her legal protection, otherwise by continually coming she will wear me out.'" And the Lord said, "Hear what the unrighteous judge said; now, will not God bring about justice for His elect who cry to Him day and night, and will He delay long over them? I tell you that He will bring about justice for them quickly. However, when the Son of Man comes, will He find faith on the earth?" (Luke 18:1–8; see Luke 11:5–10).

Setting: The temple in Jerusalem. While ministering a few days before His crucifixion, after the chief priests and the scribes question His authority to teach and preach, Jesus conveys the Parable of the Vine-Growers to the people.

And He began to tell the people this parable: "A man planted a vineyard and rented it out to vine-growers, and went on a journey for a long time. At the *harvest* time he sent a slave to the vine-growers, so that they would give him *some* of the produce of the vineyard; but the vine-growers beat him and sent him away empty-handed. And he proceeded to send another slave; and they beat him also and treated him shamefully and sent him away empty-handed. And he proceeded to send a third; and this one also they wounded and cast out. The owner of the vineyard said, 'What shall I do? I will send my beloved son; perhaps they will respect him.' But when the vine-growers saw him, they reasoned with one another, saying, 'This is the heir; let us kill him so that the inheritance will be ours.' So they threw him out of the vineyard and killed him. What, then, will the owner of the vineyard do to them? He will come and destroy these vine-growers and will give the vineyard to others." When they heard it, they said, "May it never be!" But Jesus looked at them and said, "What then is this that is written: 'THE STONE WHICH THE BUILDERS REJECTED, THIS BECAME THE CHIEF CORNER *stone*'? Everyone who falls on that stone will be broken to pieces; but on whomever it falls, it will scatter him like dust" (Luke 20:9–18, Jesus quotes from Psalm 118:22; cf. Matthew 21:33–44; Mark 12:1–11; see Ephesians 2:20).

RESPECTFUL GREETINGS (Listed under GREETINGS, RESPECTFUL)

RESPONDING TO GOD (See DISOBEDIENCE; and OBEDIENCE)

RESPONSIBILITY, PERSONAL (See ACCOUNTABILITY; and STEWARDSHIP)

REST (Also see SLEEP)

Setting: Throughout Galilee. After rendering a thanksgiving prayer to His Father in heaven, as He preaches and teaches, Jesus offers rest to all who are weary and heavy-laden.

"Come to Me, all who are weary and heavy-laden, and I will give you rest. Take My yoke upon you and learn from Me, for I am gentle and humble in heart, and YOU WILL FIND REST FOR YOUR SOULS. For My yoke is easy and My burden is light" (Matthew 11:28–30, Jesus quotes from Jeremiah 6:16; see Jeremiah 31:35; 1 John 5:3).

Setting: Galilee. Jesus responds to some Pharisees and scribes who ask Him for a miraculous sign as He ministers.

"Now when the unclean spirit goes out of a man, it passes through waterless places seeking rest, and does not find *it.* Then it says, 'I will return to my house from which I came'; and when it comes, it finds *it* unoccupied, swept, and put in order. Then it goes and takes along with it seven other spirits more wicked than itself, and they go in and live there; and the last state of that man becomes worse than the first. That is the way it will also be for this evil generation" (Matthew 12:43–45; cf. Luke 11:24–26; see Mark 5:9).

Setting: Galilee. After Jesus' disciples report to Him about their ministry in the cities and villages, He instructs them to rest.

And He said to them, "Come away by yourselves to a secluded place and rest a while." (For there were many *people* coming and going, and they did not even have time to eat) (Mark 6:31; see Mark 3:20).

Setting: On the way from Galilee to Jerusalem. The Lord appoints seventy followers and sends them out in pairs to every place He Himself will soon visit.

And He was saying to them, "The harvest is plentiful, but the laborers are few; therefore beseech the Lord of the harvest to send out laborers into His harvest. Go; behold, I send you out as lambs in the midst of wolves. Carry no money belt, no bag, no shoes; and greet no one on the way. Whatever house you enter, first say, 'Peace be to this house.' If a man of peace is there, your peace will rest on him; but if not, it will return to you. Stay in that house, eating and drinking what they give you; for the laborer is worthy of his wages. Do not keep moving from house to house. Whatever city you enter and they receive you, eat what is set before you; and heal those in it who are sick, and say to them, 'The kingdom of God has come near to you.' But whatever city you enter and they do not receive you, go out into its streets and say, 'Even the dust of your city which clings to our feet we wipe off *in protest* against you; yet be sure of this, that the kingdom of God has come near.' I say to you, it will be more tolerable in that day for Sodom than for that city" (Luke 10:2–12; see Genesis 19:24–28; Matthew 9:37, 38, 10:9–14, 16; 1 Corinthians 10:27).

Setting: On the way from Galilee to Jerusalem. After some in the crowd test Him, demanding a sign from heaven, Jesus illustrates His power over Satan.

"When the unclean spirit goes out of a man, it passes through waterless places seeking rest, and not finding any, it says, 'I will return to my house from which I came.' And when it comes, it finds it swept clean and put in order. Then it goes and takes *along* seven other spirits more evil than itself, and they go in and live there; and the last state of that man becomes worse than the first" (Luke 11:24–26; cf. Matthew 12:43–45).

REST (others, remainder)

Setting: The temple in Jerusalem. Jesus speaks another parable to the chief priests and elders after they question His authority.

Jesus spoke to them again in parables, saying, "The kingdom of heaven may be compared to a king who gave a wedding feast for his son. And he sent out his slaves to call those who had been invited to the wedding feast, and they were unwilling to come. Again he sent out other slaves saying, 'Tell those who have been invited, "Behold, I have prepared my dinner; my oxen and my fattened livestock are *all* butchered and everything is ready; come to the wedding feast." But they paid no attention and went their way, one to his own farm, another to his business, and the rest seized his slaves and mistreated them and killed them. But the king was enraged, and he sent his armies and destroyed those murderers and set their city on fire. Then he said to his slaves, 'The wedding is ready, but those who were invited were not worthy. 'Go therefore to the main highways, and as many as you find *there,* invite to the wedding feast.' Those slaves went out into the streets and gathered together all they found, both evil and good; and the wedding hall was filled with dinner guests. But when the king came in to look over the dinner guests, he saw a man there who was not dressed in wedding clothes, and he said to him, 'Friend, how did you come in here without wedding clothes?' And the man was speechless. Then the king said to the servants, 'Bind him hand and foot, and throw him into the outer darkness; in that place there will be weeping and gnashing of teeth.' For many are called, but few *are* chosen" (Matthew 22:1–14; cf. Matthew 8:11, 12).

Setting: Galilee. After Jesus presents the Parable of the Sower to the crowds, His disciples ask Him to give them the parable's meaning.

And He said, "To you it has been granted to know the mysteries of the kingdom of God, but to the rest *it is* in parables, so that SEEING THEY MAY NOT SEE, AND HEARING THEY MAY NOT UNDERSTAND. Now the parable is this: the seed is the word of God. Those beside the road are those who have heard; then the devil comes and takes away the word from their heart, so that they will not believe and be saved. Those on the rocky *soil* are those who, when they hear, receive the word with joy; and these have no *firm* root; they believe for a while, and in time of temptation fall away. The *seed* which fell among the thorns, these are the ones who have heard, and as they go on their way they are choked with worries and riches and pleasures of *this* life, and bring no fruit to maturity. But the *seed* in the good soil, these are the ones who have heard the word in an honest and good heart, and hold it fast, and bear fruit with perseverance" (Luke 8:10–15, Jesus quotes from Isaiah 6:9; cf. Matthew 13:10–23; Mark 4:10–20).

Setting: On the island of Patmos (in the Aegean Sea about fifty miles southwest of Ephesus in modern Turkey). On the Lord's Day (Sunday), approximately fifty years after the Resurrection, the disciple John encounters the Lord Jesus Christ, who communicates a new revelation for the apostle to record for the church in Thyatira and to six other churches in Asia.

"And to the angel of the church in Thyatira write: The Son of God, who has eyes like a flame of fire, and His feet are like burnished bronze, says this: 'I know your deeds, and your love and faith and service and perseverance, and that your deeds of late are greater than at first. But I have *this* against you, that you tolerate the woman Jezebel, who calls herself a prophetess, and she teaches and leads My bond-servants astray so that they commit *acts of* immorality and eat things sacrificed to idols. I gave her time to repent, and she does not want to repent of her immorality. Behold, I will throw her on a bed *of sickness,* and those who commit adultery with her into great tribulation, unless they repent of her deeds. And I will kill her children with pestilence, and all the churches will know that I am He who searches the minds and hearts; and I will give to each one of you according to your deeds. But I say to you, the rest who are in Thyatira, who do not hold this teaching, who have not known the deep things of Satan, as they call them—I place no other burden on you. Nevertheless what you have, hold fast until I come. He who overcomes, and he who keeps My deeds until the end, TO HIM I WILL GIVE AUTHORITY OVER THE NATIONS; AND HE SHALL RULE THEM WITH A ROD OF IRON, AS THE VESSELS OF THE POTTER ARE BROKEN TO PIECES, as I also have received *authority* from My Father; and I will give him the morning star. He who has an ear, let him hear what the Spirit says to the churches' (Revelation 2:18–29; Jesus quotes from Psalm 2:8, 9; Isaiah 30:14; see 1 Kings 16:31; Psalm 7:9; Romans 2:5; 1 Corinthians 2:10; 2 Peter 3:9; Revelation 1:14; 2:7; 3:11; 17:1–20).

RESTING, SLEEPING AND (Also see SLEEP)

Setting: An upper room in Jerusalem. After celebrating the Passover meal with His disciples, Jesus retreats to the Garden of Gethsemane on the Mount of Olives to pray prior to His betrayal by Judas.

Then Jesus came with them to a place called Gethsemane, and said to His disciples, "Sit here while I go over there and pray." And He took with Him Peter and the two sons of Zebedee, and began to be grieved and distressed. Then He said to them, "My soul is deeply grieved, to the point of death; remain here and keep watch with Me." And He went a little beyond *them,* and fell on His face and prayed, saying, "My Father, if it is possible, let this cup pass from Me; yet not as I will, but as You will." And He came to the disciples and found them sleeping, and said to Peter, "So, you *men* could not keep watch with Me for one hour? Keep watching and praying that you may not enter into temptation; the spirit is willing, but the flesh is weak." He went away again a second time and prayed, saying, "My Father, if this cannot pass away unless I drink it, Your will be done." Again He came and found them sleeping, for their eyes were heavy. And He left them again, and went away and prayed a third time, saying the same thing once more. Then He came to the disciples and said to them, "Are you still sleeping and resting? Behold the hour is at hand and the Son of Man is being betrayed into the hands of sinners. Get up, let us be going; behold the one who betrays Me is at hand!" (Matthew 26:36–46; cf. Mark 14:32–42; Luke 22:40–46; see Matthew 20:22; John 12:27).

Setting: Gethsemane on the Mount of Olives, east of the temple in Jerusalem. Jesus prepares to meet Judas the betrayer, while His other disciples keep falling asleep instead of watching and praying with Him.

And He came the third time, and said to them, "Are you still sleeping and resting? It is enough; the hour has come; behold, the Son of Man is being betrayed into the hands of sinners. Get up, let us be going; behold, the one who betrays Me is at hand!" (Mark 14:41, 42; cf. Matthew 26:45, 46).

RESTORATION

[RESTORATION from restore]
Setting: Galilee, on the way down a mountain. Following the Transfiguration, Peter, James, and John ask Him why Elijah must come before the Messiah.

And He answered and said, "Elijah is coming and will restore all things; but I say to you that Elijah already came, and they did not recognize him, but did to him whatever they wished. So also the Son of Man is going to suffer at their hands" (Matthew 17:11, 12; cf. Mark 9:11–13).

[RESTORATION from restore]
Setting: A high mountain (some think Mount Hermon) in Galilee. After informing a crowd and His disciples of the hope involving the coming kingdom of God, Jesus takes Peter, James, and John and reveals His glory through the Transfiguration, and answers their question about Elijah.

And He said to them, "Elijah does first come and restore all things. And *yet* how is it written of the Son of Man that He will suffer many things and be treated with contempt? But I say to you that Elijah has indeed come, and they did to him whatever they wished, just as it is written of him" (Mark 9:12, 13; cf. Matthew 17:1–13; Luke 9:28–36; see Malachi 4:5, 6; Matthew 16:21).

RESTORATION, PETER'S (See PETER'S RESTORATION)

RESURRECTION (PROPHECY OF JESUS' RESURRECTION and RESURRECTION, SONS OF THE are separate entries; also see JESUS' GLORIFICATION; JESUS' POST-RESURRECTION APPEARANCES; JONAH, SIGN OF; RESURRECTION FROM THE DEAD; RESURRECTION OF THE DEAD; and RESUSCITATION)

Setting: The temple in Jerusalem. The Sadducees question Jesus about Levirate marriage (marriage to a brother-in-law), in order to test Him.

But Jesus answered and said to them, "You are mistaken, not understanding the Scriptures nor the power of God. For in the resurrection they neither marry nor are given in marriage, but are like angels in heaven. But regarding the resurrection of the dead, have you not read what was spoken to you by God: 'I AM THE GOD OF ABRAHAM, AND THE GOD OF ISAAC, AND THE GOD OF JACOB'? He is not the God of the dead but of the living" (Matthew 22:29–32, Jesus quotes from Exodus 3:6; cf. Mark 12:18–27; Luke 20:27–38; see Deuteronomy 25:5; John 20:9).

[RESURRECTION from rise from the dead and the dead rise again]
Setting: The temple in Jerusalem. After some of the Pharisees and Herodians attempt to trap Jesus in a statement, some Sadducees question Him about the status of marriage after death.

Jesus said to them, "Is this not the reason you are mistaken, that you do not understand the Scriptures or the power of God? For when they rise from the dead, they neither marry nor are given in marriage, but are like angels in heaven. But regarding the fact that the dead rise again, have you not read in the book of Moses, in the *passage* about *the burning* bush, how God spoke to him, saying, 'I AM THE GOD OF ABRAHAM, AND THE GOD OF ISAAC, and the God of Jacob?' He is not the God of the dead, but of the living; you are greatly mistaken" (Mark 12:24–27, Jesus quotes from Exodus 3:6; cf. Matthew 22:29–33; Luke 20:34–40).

Setting: The temple in Jerusalem. While ministering a few days before His crucifixion, after the scribes and Pharisees seek to trap Jesus by questioning Him about paying taxes to Caesar, some Sadducees (who say that there is no resurrection) ask the Lord a question about the resurrection.

Jesus said to them, "The sons of this age marry and are given in marriage, but those who are considered worthy to attain to that age and the resurrection from the dead, neither marry nor are given in marriage; for they cannot even die anymore, because they are like angels, and are sons of God, being sons of the resurrection. But that the dead are raised, even Moses showed, in the *passage about the burning* bush, where he calls the Lord THE GOD OF ABRAHAM, AND THE GOD OF ISAAC, AND THE GOD OF JACOB. Now He is not the God of the dead but of the living; for all live to Him" (Luke 20:34–38, Jesus quotes from Exodus 3:6; cf. Matthew 22:23–32; Mark 12:18–27).

[RESURRECTION from to enter into His glory]

Setting: On the road to Emmaus. After rising from the tomb on the third day after being crucified, Jesus appears to two of His followers (who have heard reports the tomb is empty) and elaborates on the purpose of His coming to earth.

And He said to them, "O foolish men and slow of heart to believe in all that the prophets have spoken! Was it not necessary for the Christ to suffer these things and to enter into His glory?" (Luke 24:25, 26; see Luke 24:44).

[RESURRECTION from a spirit does not have flesh and bones as you see that I have]

Setting: Jerusalem. After rising from the tomb on the third day after being crucified, and appearing to two of His followers on the road to Emmaus, Jesus appears to His other disciples (except Thomas).

While they were telling these things, He Himself stood in their midst and said to them, "Peace be to you." But they were startled and frightened and thought they were seeing a spirit. And He said to them, "Why are you troubled, and why do doubts arise in your hearts? See My hands and My feet, that it is I Myself; touch Me and see, for a spirit does not have flesh and bones as you see that I have." And when He had said this, He showed them His hands and His feet. While they still could not believe *it* because of their joy and amazement. He said to them, "Have you anything to eat?" They gave Him a piece of a broiled fish; and He took it and ate *it* before them (Luke 24:36–43; see Mark 16:14; Luke John 20:27; Acts 10:40, 41).

[RESURRECTION from rise again]

Setting: Jerusalem. After rising from the tomb on the third day after being crucified, and appearing to two of His followers on the road to Emmaus, Jesus gives instruction to His disciples (except Thomas) about His mission on earth and the promise of future power from God.

Now He said to them, "These are My words which I spoke to you while I was still with you, that all things which are written about Me in the Law of Moses and the Prophets and the Psalms must be fulfilled." Then He opened their minds to understand the Scriptures, and He said to them, "Thus it is written, that the Christ would suffer and rise again from the dead the third day, and that repentance for forgiveness of sins would be proclaimed in His name to all the nations, beginning from Jerusalem. You are witnesses of these things. And behold, I am sending forth the promise of My Father upon you; but you are to stay in the city until you are clothed with power from on high" (Luke 24:44–49; see Matthew 28:19, 20; Acts 1:8).

[RESURRECTION from raises the dead]

Setting: By the pool of Bethesda in Jerusalem. During a feast of the Jews, Jesus responds to criticism from the Jewish religious leaders for healing a lame man on the Sabbath and for referring to God as His Father (thereby making Himself equal with God).

Therefore Jesus answered and was saying to them, "Truly, truly, I say to you, the Son can do nothing of Himself, unless *it is* something He sees the Father doing; for whatever the Father does, these things the Son also does in like manner. For the Father loves the Son, and shows Him all things that He Himself is doing; and *the Father* will show Him greater works than these, so that you will marvel. For just as the Father raises the dead and gives them life, even so the Son also gives life to whom He wishes. For not even the Father judges anyone, but He has given all judgment to the Son, so that all will honor the Son even as they honor the Father. He who does not honor the Son does not honor the Father who sent Him" (John 5:19–23; see Luke 10:16; John 3:35; 11:25; 14:12).

Setting: Jerusalem. During a feast of the Jews, Jesus responds to criticism from the Jewish religious leaders by referring to God as His Father (thereby making Himself equal with God) and prophesying His participation someday in the resurrection and judgment of men.

"Truly, truly, I say to you, an hour is coming and now is, when the dead will hear the voice of the Son of God, and those who hear will live. For just as the Father has life in Himself, even so He gave to the Son also to have life in Himself; and He gave Him authority to execute judgment, because He is *the* Son of Man. Do not marvel at this; for an hour is coming, in which all who are in the tombs will hear His voice, and will come forth; those who did the good *deeds* to a resurrection of life, those who committed the evil *deeds* to a resurrection of judgment" (John 5:25–29; see Daniel 12:2; John 1:4; 11:24).

[RESURRECTION from raise it up on the last day and raise him up on the last day]
Setting: Capernaum. The day after Jesus walks on the Sea of Galilee to join His disciples in a boat, the people He miraculously fed with a lad's five loaves and two fish ask the Lord to always give them this bread out of heaven.

Jesus said to them, "I am the bread of life; he who comes to Me will not hunger, and he who believes in Me will never thirst. But I said to you that you have seen Me, and yet do not believe. All that the Father gives Me will come to Me, and the one who comes to Me I will certainly not cast out. For I have come down from heaven, not to do My own will, but the will of Him who sent Me. This is the will of Him who sent Me, that of all that He has given Me I lose nothing, but raise it up on the last day. For this is the will of My Father, that everyone who beholds the Son and believes in Him will have eternal life, and I Myself will raise him up on the last day" (John 6:35–40; see John 3:13, 16; 4:13, 14).

[RESURRECTION from raise him up]
Setting: Capernaum of Galilee. After Jesus informs the people whom He miraculously fed with a lad's five loaves and two fish how they might receive the bread out of heaven, the Jewish religious leaders grumble when the Lord claims that He came down out of heaven.

Therefore the Jews were grumbling about Him, because He said, "I am the bread that came down out of heaven." They were saying, "Is not this Jesus, the son of Joseph, whose father and mother we know? How does He now say, 'I have come down out of heaven'?" Jesus answered and said to them, "Do not grumble among yourselves. No one can come to Me unless the Father who sent Me draws him; and I will raise him up on the last day. It is written in the prophets, 'AND THEY SHALL ALL BE TAUGHT OF GOD.' Everyone who has heard and learned from the Father, comes to Me. Not that anyone has seen the Father, except the One who is from God; He has seen the Father. Truly, truly, I say to you, he who believes has eternal life. I am the bread of life. Your fathers ate the manna in the wilderness, and they died. This is the bread which comes down out of heaven, so that one may eat of it and not die. I am the living bread that came down out of heaven; if anyone eats of this bread, he will live forever; and the bread also which I will give for the life of the world is My flesh" (John 6:41–51, Jesus quotes from Isaiah 54:13; see John 1:18, 29; 3:36; 7:27).

[RESURRECTION from raise him up]
Setting: Capernaum of Galilee. After Jesus informs the people whom He miraculously fed with a lad's five loaves and two fish how they might receive the bread out of heaven, the Jewish religious leaders argue with one another when the Lord says He will give His flesh to the world to eat.

So Jesus said to them, "Truly, truly, I say to you, unless you eat the flesh of the Son of Man and drink His blood, you have no life in yourselves. He who eats My flesh and drinks My blood has eternal life, and I will raise him up on the last day. For My flesh is true food, and My blood is true drink. He who eats My flesh and drinks My blood abides in Me, and I in him. As the living Father sent Me, and I live because of the Father, so he who eats Me, he also will live because of Me. This is the bread which came down out of heaven; not as the fathers ate and died; he who eats this bread will live forever" (John 6:53–58; see Matthew 16:16; Luke 4:22; John 3:36; John 9:16; 15:4).

Setting: Bethany near Jerusalem. Jesus travels with His disciples to Bethany in Judea to see Lazarus's sisters, Martha and Mary, after the death of His friend.

Jesus said to her, "Your brother will rise again." Martha said to Him, "I know that he will rise again in the resurrection on the last day." Jesus said to her, "I am the resurrection and the life; he who believes in Me will live even if he dies, and everyone who lives and believes in Me will never die. Do you believe this?" (John 11:23–26; see Daniel 12:2; John 1:4; 6:47–51).

[RESURRECTION from Stop clinging to Me, for I have not yet ascended to the Father]
Setting: Jerusalem. The risen Jesus first appears to Mary Magdalene after she tells Simon Peter and John about the empty tomb where Jesus' body had been laid the day before the Sabbath. He had died on the cross for the sins of the world.

Jesus said to her, "Woman, why are you weeping? Whom are you seeking?" Supposing Him to be the gardener, she said to Him, "Sir, if you have carried Him away, tell me where you have laid Him, and I will take Him away." Jesus said to her, "Mary!" She turned and said to Him in Hebrew "Rabboni!" (which means, Teacher). Jesus said to her, "Stop clinging to Me, for I have not yet ascended to the Father; but go to My brethren and say to them, 'I ascend to My Father and your Father, and My God and Your God'" (John 20:15–17; see Mark 16:9–11; John 7:33; 19:31–42).

RESURRECTION, FORETELLING OF JESUS' (See PROPHECY OF JESUS' RESURRECTION)

RESURRECTION, PROPHECY OF JESUS' (See PROPHECY OF JESUS' RESURRECTION)

RESURRECTION, SONS OF THE

Setting: The temple in Jerusalem. While ministering a few days before His crucifixion, after the scribes and Pharisees seek to trap Jesus by questioning Him about paying taxes to Caesar, some Sadducees (who say that there is no resurrection) ask the Lord a question about the resurrection.

Jesus said to them, "The sons of this age marry and are given in marriage, but those who are considered worthy to attain to that age and the resurrection from the dead, neither marry nor are given in marriage; for they cannot even die anymore, because they are like angels, and are sons of God, being sons of the resurrection. But that the dead are raised, even Moses showed, in the *passage about the burning* bush, where he calls the Lord THE GOD OF ABRAHAM, AND THE GOD OF ISAAC, AND THE GOD OF JACOB. Now He is not the God of the dead but of the living; for all live to Him" (Luke 20:34–38, Jesus quotes from Exodus 3:6; cf. Matthew 22:23–32; Mark 12:18–27; see Luke 20:27–33).

RESURRECTION FROM THE DEAD (RESURRECTION OF THE DEAD is a separate entry; also see RESURRECTION)

Setting: The temple in Jerusalem. A few days before His crucifixion, after the scribes and Pharisees seek to trap Jesus by questioning Him about paying taxes to Caesar, some Sadducees (who say there is no resurrection) ask Him a question about the resurrection.

Jesus said to them, "The sons of this age marry and are given in marriage, but those who are considered worthy to attain to that age and the resurrection from the dead, neither marry nor are given in marriage; for they cannot even die anymore, because they are like angels, and are sons of God, being sons of the resurrection. But that the dead are raised, even Moses showed, in the *passage about the burning* bush, where he calls the Lord THE GOD OF ABRAHAM, AND THE GOD OF ISAAC, AND THE GOD OF JACOB. Now He is not the God of the dead but of the living; for all live to Him" (Luke 20:34–38, Jesus quotes from Exodus 3:6; cf. Matthew 22:23–32; Mark 12:18–27; see Luke 20:27–33).

RESURRECTION OF THE DEAD (RESURRECTION FROM THE DEAD is a separate entry; also see RESURRECTION)

Setting: The temple in Jerusalem. As Jesus teaches, the Sadducees question Him about levirate marriage (marriage to a brother-in-law) in order to test Him.

But Jesus answered and said to them, "You are mistaken, not understanding the Scriptures nor the power of God. For in the resurrection they neither marry nor are given in marriage, but are like angels in heaven. But regarding the resurrection of the dead, have you not read what was spoken to you by God: 'I AM THE GOD OF ABRAHAM, AND THE GOD OF ISAAC, AND THE GOD OF JACOB'? He is not the God of the dead but of the living" (Matthew 22:29–32, Jesus quotes from Exodus 3:6; cf. Mark 12:18–27; Luke 20:27–38; see Deuteronomy 25:5; Matthew 22:23–28; John 20:9).

RESURRECTION OF THE RIGHTEOUS (Listed under RIGHTEOUS, RESURRECTION OF THE)

RESUSCITATION (Also see MIRACLE; MIRACLES; and RESURRECTION)

[RESUSCITATION from He entered and took her by the hand, and the girl got up]

Setting: Capernaum, near the Sea of Galilee. After He heals a woman who has been suffering with internal bleeding for twelve years, Jesus brings a synagogue official's daughter back from death.

When Jesus came into the official's house, and saw the flute-players and the crowd in noisy disorder, He said, "Leave; for the girl has not died, but is asleep." And they *began* laughing at Him. But when the crowd had been sent out, He entered and took her by the hand, and the girl got up (Matthew 9:23–25; cf. Mark 5:21–24, 35–43; Luke 8:41, 42, 49–56).

[RESUSCITATION from raise *the* dead]

Setting: Galilee. After His twelve disciples observe His ministry, Jesus summons and specifically instructs them about their ministry to the people of Israel.

These twelve Jesus sent out after instructing them: "Do not go in *the* way of *the* Gentiles, and do not enter *any* city of the Samaritans; but rather go to the lost sheep of the house of Israel. And as you go, preach, saying, 'The kingdom of heaven is at hand.' Heal *the* sick, raise *the* dead, cleanse *the* lepers, cast out demons. Freely you received, freely give. Do not acquire gold, or silver, or copper for your money belts, or a bag for *your* journey, or even two coats, or sandals, or a staff; for the worker is worthy of his support. And whatever city or village you enter, inquire who is worthy in it, and stay at his house until you leave *that city*. As you enter the house, give it your greeting. If the house is worthy, give it your *blessing of* peace. But if it is not worthy, take back your *blessing of* peace. Whoever does not receive you, nor heed your words, as you go out of that house or that city, shake the dust off your feet. Truly I say to you, it will be more tolerable for *the* land of Sodom and Gomorrah in the day of judgment than for that city" (Matthew 10:5–15; cf. Mark 6:7–11; Luke 9:1–5; see Matthew 3:2; 11:22, 24; 15:24; Luke 22:35; 1 Corinthians 9:14).

[RESUSCITATION from *the* dead are raised up]

Setting: Galilee. As He teaches and preaches, Jesus responds to John the Baptist's question (posed by some of John's disciples) whether He is Israel's promised Messiah.

Jesus answered and said to them, "Go and report to John what you hear and see: *the* BLIND RECEIVE SIGHT and *the* lame walk, *the* lepers are cleansed and *the* deaf hear, *the* dead are raised up, and *the* POOR HAVE THE GOSPEL PREACHED TO THEM. And blessed is he who does not take offense at Me" (Matthew 11:4–6, Jesus quotes from Isaiah 35:5f; cf. Luke 7:22, 23).

[RESUSCITATION from Little girl, I say to you, get up]

Setting: The home of Jairus, a synagogue official in Capernaum, by the Sea of Galilee. Jesus revives Jairus's daughter, who had died.

Taking the child by the hand, He said to her, "Talitha kum!" (which translated means, "Little girl, I say to you, get up!") (Mark 5:41; cf. Matthew 9:25; Luke 8:54; see Luke 8:55, 56; Luke 7:14).

[RESUSCITATION from Young man, I say to you, arise]
Setting: Galilee. After He heals the Roman centurion's slave in Capernaum from a distance, Jesus travels to Nain, where He raises a young man from the dead.

When the Lord saw her, He felt compassion for her and said to her, "Do not weep." And He came up and touched the coffin; and the bearers came to a halt. And He said, "Young man, I say to you, arise!" (Luke 7:13, 14).

[RESUSCITATION from *the* dead are raised up]
Setting: Galilee. After Jesus raises a woman's son from the dead in Nain, the disciples of John the Baptist inquire whether He is the promised Messiah.

And He answered and said to them, "Go and report to John what you have seen and heard: *the* BLIND RECEIVE SIGHT, *the* lame walk, *the* lepers are cleansed, and *the* deaf hear, *the* dead are raised up, *the* POOR HAVE THE GOSPEL PREACHED TO THEM. Blessed is he who does not take offense at Me" (Luke 7:22, 23, Jesus quotes from Isaiah 35:5; 61:1; cf. Matthew 11:2–6).

[RESUSCITATION from Child, arise]
Setting: Capernaum. After healing a woman, ill for twelve years, Jesus receives word that the daughter of a synagogue official has died.

But when Jesus heard *this,* He answered him, "Do not be afraid *any longer;* only believe and she will be made well." When He came to the house, He did not allow anyone to enter with Him except Peter and John and James and the girl's father and mother. Now they were all weeping and lamenting for her; but He said, "Stop weeping; for she has not died, but is asleep." And they *began* laughing at Him, knowing that she had died. He, however, took her by the hand and called, saying, "Child, arise!" And her spirit returned, and she got up immediately; and He gave orders for *something* to be given her to eat (Luke 8:50–55; cf. Matthew 9:18, 19, 23–26; Mark 5:21–24, 35–43).

[RESUSCITATION from awaken him out of sleep]
Setting: Beyond the Jordan. While He and His disciples are avoiding the Jerusalem Pharisees, Jesus receives word from Lazarus's sisters in Bethany of His friend's sickness, and decides to go there.

Then after this He said to the disciples, "Let us go to Judea again." The disciples said to Him, "Rabbi, the Jews were just now seeking to stone You, and are You going there again?" Jesus answered, "Are there not twelve hours in the day? If anyone walks in the day, he does not stumble, because he sees the light of this world. But if anyone walks in the night, he stumbles, because the light is not in him." This He said, and after that He said to them, "Our friend Lazarus has fallen asleep; but I go, so that I may awaken him out of sleep" (John 11:7–11; see John 8:59; 10:39).

[RESUSCITATION from will rise again]
Setting: Bethany near Jerusalem. Jesus travels with His disciples to Bethany in Judea to see Lazarus's sisters, Martha and Mary, after the death of His friend.

Jesus said to her, "Your brother will rise again." Martha said to Him, "I know that he will rise again in the resurrection on the last day." Jesus said to her, "I am the resurrection and the life; he who believes in Me will live even if he dies, and everyone who lives and believes in Me will never die. Do you believe this?" (John 11:23–26; see Daniel 12:2; John 1:4; 6:47–51).

[RESUSCITATION from Lazarus, come forth]
Setting: Bethany near Jerusalem. After the death of His friend Lazarus, Jesus travels with His disciples to Bethany in Judea to visit the dead man's sisters, Martha and Mary. The Lord raises Lazarus from the dead.

Jesus said, "Remove the stone." Martha, the sister of the deceased, said to Him, "Lord, by this time there will be a stench, for he has been *dead* four days." Jesus said to her, "Did I not say to you that if you believe, you will see the glory of God?" So they removed the stone. Then Jesus raised His eyes, and said, "Father, I thank You that You have heard Me. I knew that You always hear Me; but because of the people standing around I said it, so that they may believe that you sent Me." When He had said these things, He cried out with a loud voice, "Lazarus, come forth." The man who had died came forth, bound hand and foot with wrappings, and his face was wrapped around with a cloth. Jesus said to them, "Unbind him, and let him go" (John 11:39–44; see Matthew 11:25).

RETALIATION (See REVENGE; and VENGEANCE)

RETURN, JESUS' (See JESUS' RETURN)

RETURN OF JESUS (See JESUS' RETURN)

REVELATION (Also see DISCLOSURE)

[REVELATION from revealed and reveal]

Setting: Galilee. As He teaches and preaches, after pronouncing woes against unrepentant cities, Jesus prays a thanksgiving prayer to His Father in heaven.

At that time Jesus said, "I praise You, Father, Lord of heaven and earth, that you have hidden these things from *the* wise and intelligent and have revealed them to infants. Yes, Father, for this way was well-pleasing in Your sight. All things have been handed over to Me by My Father; and no one knows the Son except the Father; nor does anyone know the Father except the Son, and anyone to whom the Son wills to reveal *Him*" (Matthew 11:25–27; cf. Luke 10:21, 22).

[REVELATION from flesh and blood did not reveal *this* to you, but My Father who is in heaven]

Setting: Caesarea Philippi. Jesus responds to Simon Peter's declaration that He is the Christ, the Son of the living God.

And Jesus said to him, "Blessed are you, Simon Barjona, because flesh and blood did not reveal *this* to you, but My Father who is in heaven. I also say to you that you are Peter, and upon this rock I will build My church; and the gates of Hades will not overpower it. I will give you the keys of the kingdom of heaven; and whatever you bind on earth shall have been bound in heaven, and whatever you loose on earth shall have been loosed in heaven" (Matthew 16:17–19; cf. Matthew 18:18; Mark 8:29; Luke 9:20).

[REVELATION from revealed and reveal]

Setting: On the way from Galilee to Jerusalem. The Lord responds to a report from the seventy sent out in pairs to every place He Himself will soon visit.

At that very time He rejoiced greatly in the Holy Spirit, and said, "I praise You, O Father, Lord of heaven and earth, that You have hidden these things from *the* wise and intelligent and have revealed them to infants. Yes, Father, for this way was well-pleasing in Your sight. All things have been handed over to Me by My Father, and no one knows who the Son is except the Father, and who the Father is except the Son, and anyone to whom the Son wills to reveal *Him*" (Luke 10:21, 22; cf. Matthew 11:25–27; see Luke 10:1, 17; John 3:35; John 10:15).

REVELATION, DIVINE (See REVELATION)

REVENGE (Also see VENGEANCE)

[REVENGE from AN EYE FOR AN EYE, AND A TOOTH FOR A TOOTH]

Setting: Galilee. During the early part of His ministry, Jesus preaches the Sermon on the Mount to His disciples and the multitudes.

"You have heard that it was said, 'AN EYE FOR AN EYE, AND A TOOTH FOR A TOOTH.' But I say to you, do not resist an evil person; but whoever slaps you on your right cheek, turn the other to him also" (Matthew 5:38, 39, Jesus quotes from Exodus 21:24; cf. Leviticus 24:20).

REVERENCE (See DEVOTION; and WORSHIP)

REWARD (Also see CROWN; DISCIPLE; DISCIPLESHIP; REWARD, DISCIPLES'; REWARD, PROPHET'S; REWARDS; REWARD, RIGHTEOUS MAN'S; and STEWARDSHIP)

Setting: Galilee. Early in His ministry, Jesus presents the Beatitudes (part of the Sermon on the Mount) to His disciples and the gathered crowds from Galilee, Decapolis, Jerusalem, Judea, and beyond the Jordan.

"Blessed are you when *people* insult you and persecute you, and falsely say all kinds of evil against you because of Me. Rejoice and be glad, for your reward in heaven is great; for in the same way they persecuted the prophets who were before you" (Matthew 5:11, 12; cf. 2 Chronicles 36:16; Luke 6:22, 23; 1 Peter 4:14; see Matthew 13:35).

Setting: Galilee. During the early part of His ministry, Jesus preaches the Sermon on the Mount to His disciples and the multitudes.

"You have heard that it was said, 'YOU SHALL LOVE YOUR NEIGHBOR and hate your enemy.' But I say to you, love your enemies and pray for those who persecute you, so that you may be sons of your Father who is in heaven; for He causes His sun to rise on *the* evil and *the* good, and sends rain on *the* righteous and *the* unrighteous. For if you love those who love you, what reward do you have? Do not even the tax collectors do the same? If you greet only your brothers, what more are you doing *than others?* Do not even the Gentiles do the same? Therefore, you are to be perfect, as your heavenly Father is perfect" (Matthew 5:43–48, Jesus quotes from Leviticus 19:18; cf. Leviticus 19:2; Luke 6:27–36).

Setting: Galilee. During the early part of His ministry, Jesus preaches the Sermon on the Mount to His disciples and the multitudes.

"Beware of practicing your righteousness before men to be noticed by them; otherwise you have no reward with your Father who is in heaven" (Matthew 6:1; cf. Matthew 6:16).

Setting: Galilee. During the early part of His ministry, Jesus preaches the Sermon on the Mount to His disciples and the multitudes.

"So when you give to the poor, do not sound a trumpet before you, as the hypocrites do in the synagogues and in the streets, so that they may be honored by men. Truly I say to you, they have their reward in full. But when you give to the poor, do not let your left hand know what your right hand is doing, so that your giving will be in secret; and your Father who sees *what is done* in secret will reward you" (Matthew 6:2–4; see Jeremiah 17:10; Matthew 6:16).

Setting: Galilee. During the early part of His ministry, Jesus preaches the Sermon on the Mount to His disciples and the multitudes.

"When you pray, you are not to be like the hypocrites; for they love to stand and pray in the synagogues and on the street corners so that they may be seen by men. Truly I say to you, they have their reward in full. But you, when you pray, go into your inner room, close your door and pray to your Father who is in secret, and your Father who sees *what is done* in secret will reward you" (Matthew 6:5, 6; see Mark 11:25).

Setting: Galilee. During the early part of His ministry, Jesus preaches the Sermon on the Mount to His disciples and the multitudes.

"Whenever you fast, do not put on a gloomy face as the hypocrites *do,* for they neglect their appearance so that they will be noticed by men when they are fasting. Truly I say to you, they have their reward in full. But you, when you fast, anoint your head and wash your face so that your fasting will not be noticed by men, but by your Father who is in secret; and your Father who sees *what is done* in secret will reward you" (Matthew 6:16–18).

[REWARD from REPAY EVERY MAN ACCORDING TO HIS DEEDS]
Setting: Near Caesarea Philippi. After rebuking Peter for trying to forbid Him to accomplish His earthly mission of dying and being resurrected, Jesus teaches His disciples about the costs of following Him.

Then Jesus said to His disciples, "If anyone wishes to come after Me, he must deny himself, and take up his cross and follow Me. For whoever wishes to save his life will lose it; but whoever loses his life for My sake will find it. For what will it profit a man if he gains the whole world and forfeits his soul? Or what will a man give in exchange for his soul? For the Son of Man is going to come in the glory of His Father with His angels, and WILL THEN REPAY EVERY MAN ACCORDING TO HIS DEEDS. Truly, I say to you, there are some of you who are standing here who will not taste death until they see the Son of Man coming in His kingdom" (Matthew 16:24–28, Jesus quotes from Psalm 62:12; cf. Mark 8:34–37; Luke 9:23–27; see Matthew 10:38, 39).

[REWARD from will receive many times as much]
Setting: Judea beyond the Jordan (Perea). Jesus promises rewards to His disciples for their personal sacrifice and commitment to following Him.

And Jesus said to them, "Truly I say to you, that you who have followed Me, in the regeneration when the Son of Man will sit on His glorious throne, you also shall sit upon twelve thrones, judging the twelve tribes of Israel. And everyone who has left houses or brothers or sisters or father or mother or children or farms for My name's sake, will receive many times as much, and will inherit eternal life. But many *who* are first will be last; and *the* last, first" (Matthew 19:28–30; cf. Matthew 6:33; 20:15; Mark 10:29, 30; Luke 18:29, 30; 22:30).

Setting: Capernaum of Galilee. As Jesus teaches His disciples in private, they ask Him about greatness.

But Jesus said, "Do not hinder him, for there is no one who will perform a miracle in My name, and be able soon afterward to speak evil of Me. For he who is not against us is for us. For whoever gives you a cup of water to drink because of your name as *followers* of Christ, truly I say to you, he will not lose his reward. Whoever causes one of these little ones who believe to stumble, it would be better for him if, with a heavy millstone hung around his neck, he had been cast into the sea. If your hand causes you to stumble, cut it off; it is better for you to enter life crippled, than, having your two hands, to go into hell, into the unquenchable fire, [where THEIR WORM DOES NOT DIE, AND THE FIRE IS NOT QUENCHED.] If your foot causes you to stumble, cut it off; it is better for you to enter life lame, than, having your two feet, to be cast into hell, [where THEIR WORM DOES NOT DIE, AND THE FIRE IS NOT QUENCHED.] If your eye causes you to stumble, throw it out; it is better for you to enter the kingdom of God with one eye, than, having two eyes, to be cast into hell, where THEIR WORM DOES NOT DIE, AND THE FIRE IS NOT QUENCHED. For everyone will be salted with fire. Salt is good; but if the salt becomes unsalty, with what will you make it salty *again?* Have salt in yourselves, and be at peace with one another" (Mark 9:39–50; Jesus quotes from Isaiah 66:24; cf. Matthew 18:6–9; Luke 9:49, 50; see Matthew 5:13, 29, 30; 10:42; 12:30; 18:5, 6).

[REWARD from will receive a hundred times as much]
Setting: Judea beyond the Jordan (Perea). After informing a rich man how righteous believers may have treasure in heaven, Jesus tells His disciples about the reward of those who sacrifice in this life to follow Him.

Jesus said, "Truly I say to you, there is no one who has left house or brothers or sisters or mother or father or children or farms, for My sake and for the gospel's sake, but that he will receive a hundred times as much now in the present age, houses and brothers and sisters and mothers and children and farms, along with persecutions; and in the age to come, eternal life. But many *who are* first will be last, and the last, first" (Mark 10:29–31; cf. Matthew 19:27–30; Luke 18:28–30; see Matthew 6:33).

Setting: Galilee. After selecting His twelve disciples, Jesus teaches the Beatitudes (part of the Sermon on the Mount) to those disciples and a great throng of people from Judea, Jerusalem, and the central coastal region of Tyre and Sidon.

"Blessed are you when men hate you, and ostracize you, and insult you, and scorn your name as evil, for the sake of the Son of Man. Be glad in that day and leap *for joy*, for behold, your reward is great in heaven. For in the same way their fathers used to treat the prophets" (Luke 6:22, 23; cf. Matthew 5:10–12; see 2 Chronicles 36:16).

Setting: Galilee. After selecting His twelve disciples, Jesus teaches the Sermon on the Mount to those disciples and a great throng of people from Judea, Jerusalem, and the central coastal region of Tyre and Sidon.

"But I say to you who hear, love your enemies, do good to those who hate you, bless those who curse you, pray for those who mistreat you. Whoever hits you on the cheek, offer him the other also; and whoever takes away your coat, do not withhold your shirt from him either. Give to everyone who asks of you, and whoever takes away what is yours, do not demand it back. Treat others the same way you want them to treat you. If you love those who love you, what credit is *that* to you? For even sinners love those who love them. If you do good to those who do good to you, what credit is *that* to you? For even sinners do the same. If you lend to those from whom you expect to receive, what credit is *that* to you? Even sinners lend to sinners in order to receive back the same *amount.* But love your enemies, and do good, and lend, expecting nothing in return; and your reward will be great, and you will be sons of the Most High; for He Himself is kind to ungrateful and evil *men*. Be merciful, just as your Father is merciful" (Luke 6:27–36; cf. Matthew 5:9, 39–48; Matthew 7:12).

[REWARD from you will be repaid at the resurrection of the righteous]
Setting: On the way from Galilee to Jerusalem. After Jesus, observing the invited guests of a Pharisee leader selecting places of honor at the table, speaks a parable to them, He comments to the host about the people to invite in the future.

And He also went on to say to the one who had invited Him, "When you give a luncheon or a dinner, do not invite your friends or your brothers or your relatives or rich neighbors, otherwise they may also invite you in return and *that* will be your repayment. But when you give a reception, invite *the* poor, *the* crippled, *the* lame, *the* blind, and you will be blessed, since they do not have *the means* to repay you; for you will be repaid at the resurrection of the righteous" (Luke 14:12–14; see Luke 14:1, 2, 15; John 5:28, 29).

[REWARD from to everyone who has, more shall be given]
Setting: Jericho, on the way to Jerusalem. After commending Zaccheus's faith in Him, Jesus provides a parable about stewardship.

So He said, "A nobleman went to a distant country to receive a kingdom for himself, and *then* return. And he called ten of his slaves, and gave them ten minas and said to them, 'Do business *with this* until I come *back.*' But his citizens hated him and sent a delegation after him, saying, 'We do not want this man to reign over us.' When he returned, after receiving the kingdom, he ordered that these slaves, to whom he had given the money, be called to him so that he might know what business they had done. The first appeared, saying, 'Master, your mina has made ten minas more.' And he said to him, 'Well done, good slave, because you have been faithful in a very little thing, you are to be in authority over ten cities.' The second came, saying, 'Your mina, master, has made five minas.' And he said to him, also, 'And you are to be over five cities.' Another came, saying, 'Master, here is your mina, which I kept put away in a handkerchief; for I was afraid of you, because you are an exacting man; you take up what you did not lay down and reap what you did not sow.' He said to him, 'By your own words I will judge you, you worthless slave. Did you know that I am an exacting man, taking up what I did not lay down and reaping what I did not sow? Then why did you not put my money in the bank, and having come, I would have collected it with interest?' Then he said to the bystanders, 'Take the mina away from him and give it to the one who has the ten minas.' And they said to him, 'Master, he has ten minas *already.*' I tell you that to everyone who has, more shall be given, but from the one who does not have, even what he does have shall be taken away. But these enemies of mine, who did not want me to reign over them, bring them here and slay them in my presence" (Luke 19:12–27; cf. Matthew 25:14–30; see Matthew 13:12; Luke 16:10).

Setting: On the island of Patmos (in the Aegean Sea about fifty miles southwest of Ephesus in modern Turkey). In the final chapter of the Lord Jesus Christ's revelation via the disciple John, approximately fifty years after the Resurrection, the Lord reveals His upcoming return, reward, and eternality.

"Behold, I am coming quickly, and My reward *is* with Me, to render to every man according to what he has done. I am the Alpha and the Omega, the first and the last, the beginning and the end" (Revelation 22:12, 13; see Isaiah 40:10; 44:6).

REWARD, DISCIPLES' (Also see REWARD; and REWARDS)

[DISCIPLES' REWARD from everyone who has left houses or brothers or sisters or father or mother or children or farms for My name's sake, will receive many times as much]

Setting: Judea beyond the Jordan (Perea). Jesus promises rewards to His disciples for their personal sacrifice and commitment to following Him.

And Jesus said to them, "Truly I say to you, that you who have followed Me, in the regeneration when the Son of Man will sit on His glorious throne, you also shall sit upon twelve thrones, judging the twelve tribes of Israel. And everyone who has left houses or brothers or sisters or father or mother or children or farms for My name's sake, will receive many times as much, and will inherit eternal life. But many *who* are first will be last; and *the* last, first" (Matthew 19:28–30; cf. Matthew 6:33; 20:15; Mark 10:29, 30; Luke 18:29, 30; 22:30).

[DISCIPLES' REWARD from blessed and your reward is great in heaven]

Setting: Galilee. After selecting His twelve disciples, Jesus teaches the Beatitudes (part of the Sermon on the Mount) to those disciples and a great throng of people from Judea, Jerusalem, and the central coastal region of Tyre and Sidon.

"Blessed are you when men hate you, and ostracize you, and insult you, and scorn your name as evil, for the sake of the Son of Man. Be glad in that day and leap *for joy*, for behold, your reward is great in heaven. For in the same way their fathers used to treat the prophets." (Luke 6:22, 23; cf. Matthew 5:10–12; see 2 Chronicles 36:16; Luke 6:12–19)

[DISCIPLES' REWARD from receive many times as much at this time]

Setting: Perea, en route from Galilee to Jerusalem. After responding to His disciples' question about salvation, Jesus replies to Peter's statement about the disciples' personal sacrifice.

Peter said, "Behold, we have left our own *homes* and followed You." And He said to them, "Truly I say to you, there is no one who has left house or wife or brothers or parents or children, for the sake of the kingdom of God, who receive many times as much at this time and in the age to come, eternal life" (Luke 18:28–30; cf. Matthew 19:27–29; Mark 10:28–30; see Matthew 6:33; Luke 5:11).

REWARD, PROPHET'S (Also see REWARD; and REWARDS)

Setting: Galilee. After His twelve disciples observe His ministry, Jesus summons and specifically instructs them about their ministry ahead that will include rewards.

"He who receives you receives Me, and he who receives Me receives Him who sent me. He who receives a prophet in the name of a prophet shall receive a prophet's reward; and he who receives a righteous man in the name of a righteous man shall receive a righteous man's reward. And whoever in the name of a disciple gives to one of these little ones even a cup of cold water to drink, truly I say to you, he shall not lose his reward" (Matthew 10:40–42; cf. Matthew 25:40, 44, 45; see Mark 9:37).

REWARD, RIGHTEOUS MAN'S (Also see REWARD; and REWARDS)

Setting: Galilee. After His twelve disciples observe His ministry, Jesus summons and specifically instructs them about their ministry ahead that will include rewards.

"He who receives you receives Me, and he who receives Me receives Him who sent me. He who receives a prophet in the name of a prophet shall receive a prophet's reward; and he who receives a righteous man in the name of a righteous man shall receive a righteous man's reward. And whoever in the name of a disciple gives to one of these little ones even a cup of cold water to drink, truly I say to you, he shall not lose his reward" (Matthew 10:40–42; cf. Matthew 25:40, 44, 45; see Mark 9:37).

REWARDS (Also see FOLLOWING JESUS CHRIST; OBEDIENCE; REWARD; REWARD, DISCIPLES'; REWARD, PROPHET'S; REWARD, RIGHTEOUS MAN'S; SAKE, GOSPEL'S; and SAKE, MY)

[REWARDS from repaid at the resurrection of the righteous]

Setting: On the way from Galilee to Jerusalem. After Jesus, observing the invited guests of a Pharisee leader selecting places of honor at the table, speaks a parable to them, He comments to the host about the people to invite in the future.

And He also went on to say to the one who had invited Him, "When you give a luncheon or a dinner, do not invite your friends or your brothers or your relatives or rich neighbors, otherwise they may also invite you in return and *that* will be your repayment. But when you give a reception, invite *the* poor, *the* crippled, *the* lame, *the* blind, and you will be blessed, since they do not have *the means* to repay you; for you will be repaid at the resurrection of the righteous" (Luke 14:12–14; see Luke 14:1, 2, 15; John 5:28, 29).

RICH (Also see MATERIALISM; MAN, RICH; POSSESSIONS; RICHES; WEALTH; and WEALTHY)

Setting: Galilee. After selecting His twelve disciples, Jesus teaches the Beatitudes (part of the Sermon on the Mount) to those disciples and a great throng of people from Judea, Jerusalem, and the central coastal region of Tyre and Sidon.

"But woe to you who are rich, for you are receiving your comfort in full" (Luke 6:24).

Setting: On the way from Galilee to Jerusalem. After the scribes and Pharisees turn hostile and question Him repeatedly in an attempt to catch Him in something He might say, Jesus responds to a question from the crowd and gives a parable about riches and greed.

And He told them a parable, saying, "The land of a rich man was very productive. And he began reasoning to himself, saying, 'What shall I do, since I have no place to store my crops?' Then he said, 'This is what I will do: I will tear down my barns and build larger ones, and here I will store all my grain and my goods. And I will say to my soul, "Soul, you have many goods laid up for many years *to come;* take your ease, eat, drink *and* be merry."' "But God said to him, 'You fool! This *very* night your soul is required of you; and *now* who will own what you have prepared?' So is the man who stores up treasure for himself, and is not rich toward God" (Luke 12:16–21; see Job 27:8; Psalm 39:6; Ecclesiastes 12:9; Philippians 2:3).

Setting: On the island of Patmos (in the Aegean Sea about fifty miles southwest of Ephesus in modern Turkey). On the Lord's Day (Sunday), approximately fifty years after the Resurrection, the disciple John encounters the Lord Jesus Christ, who communicates a new revelation for the apostle to record for the church in Smyrna and to six other churches in Asia.

"And to the angel of the church in Smyrna write: The first and the last, who was dead, and has come to life, says this: 'I know your tribulation and your poverty (but you are rich), and the blasphemy by those who say they are Jews and are not, but are a synagogue of Satan. Do not fear what you are about to suffer. Behold, the devil is about to cast some of you into prison, so that you will be tested, and you will have tribulation for ten days. Be faithful until death, and I will give you the crown of life. He who has an ear, let him hear what the Spirit says to the churches. He who overcomes will not be hurt by the second death' (Revelation 2:8–11; see Isaiah 44:6; Revelation 1:9, 18; 20:6, 14).

Setting: On the island of Patmos (in the Aegean Sea about fifty miles southwest of Ephesus in modern Turkey). On the Lord's Day (Sunday), approximately fifty years after the Resurrection, the disciple John encounters the Lord Jesus Christ, who communicates a new revelation for the apostle to record for the church in Laodicea and to six other churches in Asia.

"To the angel of the church in Laodicea write: The Amen, the faithful and true Witness, the Beginning of the creation of God, says this: 'I know your deeds, that you are neither cold nor hot; I wish that you were cold or hot. So because you are lukewarm, and neither hot nor cold, I will spit you out of My mouth. Because you say, "I am rich, and have become wealthy, and have need of nothing," and you do not know that you are wretched and miserable and poor and blind and naked, I advise you to buy from Me gold refined by fire so that you may become rich, and white garments so that you may clothe yourself, and *that* the shame of

your nakedness will not be revealed; and eye salve to anoint your eyes so that you may see. Those whom I love, I reprove and discipline; therefore be zealous and repent. Behold, I stand at the door and knock; if anyone hears My voice and opens the door, I will come in to him and will dine with him, and he with Me. He who overcomes, I will grant to him to sit down with Me on My throne, as I also overcame and sat down with My Father on His throne. He who has an ear, let him hear what the Spirit says to the churches'" (Revelation 3:14–22; see Proverb 3:12; Hosea 12:8; John 14:23; 16:33).

RICH MAN (Listed under MAN, RICH)

RICH NEIGHBORS (See NEIGHBORS)

RICHES (Also see RICH; TREASURE; TREASURES; and WEALTH)

Setting: By the Sea of Galilee. During the early part of His ministry, after presenting the Parable of the Sower from a boat to a very large crowd, Jesus gives the meaning of the parable to His disciples and other followers.

And He said to them, "Do you not understand this parable? How will you understand all the parables? The sower sows the word. These are the ones who are beside the road where the word is sown; and when they hear, immediately Satan comes and takes away the word which has been sown in them. In a similar way these are the ones on whom seed was sown on the rocky places, who, when they hear the word, immediately receive it with joy; and they have no *firm* root in themselves, but are *only* temporary; then, when affliction or persecution arises because of the word, immediately they fall away. And others are the ones on whom seed was sown among the thorns; these are the ones who have heard the word, but the worries of the world and the deceitfulness of riches, and the desires for other things enter in and choke the word, and it becomes unfruitful. And those are the ones on whom seed was sown on the good soil; and they hear the word and accept it and bear fruit, thirty, sixty, and a hundredfold" (Mark 4:13–20; cf. Matthew 13:18–23; Luke 8:11–15).

Setting: Galilee. After Jesus presents the Parable of the Sower to the crowds, His disciples ask Him to give them the parable's meaning.

And He said, "To you it has been granted to know the mysteries of the kingdom of God, but to the rest *it is* in parables, so that SEEING THEY MAY NOT SEE, AND HEARING THEY MAY NOT UNDERSTAND. Now the parable is this: the seed is the word of God. Those beside the road are those who have heard; then the devil comes and takes away the word from their heart, so that they will not believe and be saved. Those on the rocky *soil* are those who, when they hear, receive the word with joy; and these have no *firm* root; they believe for a while, and in time of temptation fall away. The *seed* which fell among the thorns, these are the ones who have heard, and as they go on their way they are choked with worries and riches and pleasures of *this* life, and bring no fruit to maturity. But the *seed* in the good soil, these are the ones who have heard the word in an honest and good heart, and hold it fast, and bear fruit with perseverance" (Luke 8:10–15, Jesus quotes from Isaiah 6:9; cf. Matthew 13:10–23; Mark 4:10–20).

Setting: On the way from Galilee to Jerusalem. After giving the story of the prodigal son, the Lord teaches His disciples about stewardship.

Now He was also saying to the disciples, "There was a rich man who had a manager, and this *manager* was reported to him as squandering his possessions. And he called him and said to him, 'What is this I hear about you? Give an accounting of your management, for you can no longer be a manager.' The manager said to himself, 'What shall I do, since my master is taking the management away from me? I am not strong enough to dig; I am ashamed to beg. I know what I shall do, so that when I am removed from the management people will welcome me into their homes.' And he summoned each one of his master's debtors, and he *began* saying to the first, 'How much do you owe my master?' And he said, 'A hundred measures of oil.' And he said to him, 'Take your bill, and sit down quickly and write fifty.' Then he said to another, 'And how much do you owe?' And he said, 'A hundred measures of wheat.' He said to him, 'Take your bill, and write eighty.' And his master praised the unrighteous manager because he had acted shrewdly; for the sons of this age are more shrewd in relation to their own kind than the sons of light. And I say to you, make friends for yourselves by means of the wealth of unrighteousness, so that when it fails, they will receive you into the eternal dwellings. He who is faithful in a very little thing is faithful also in much; and he who is unrighteous in a very little thing is unrighteous also in much. Therefore if you have not been faithful in the *use of* unrighteous wealth, who will entrust the true *riches* to you? And if you have not been faithful in *the use of* that which is another's, who will give you that which is your own? No servant can serve two masters; for either he will hate the one and love the other, or else he will be devoted to one and despise the other. You cannot serve God and wealth" (Luke 16:1–13; cf. Matthew 6:24; see Matthew 25:14–30).

RICHES, DECEITFULNESS OF (See RICHES)

RIGHT (direction)

Setting: On the way to Jerusalem. The mother of James and John, the sons of Zebedee, asks Jesus to make her sons exalted rulers with Him in His coming kingdom.

And He said to her, "What do you wish?" She said to Him, 'Command that in Your kingdom these two sons of mine may sit one on Your right and one on Your left.' But Jesus answered, "You do not know what you are asking. Are you able to drink the cup that I am about to drink?" They said to Him, 'We are able.' He said to them, "My cup you shall drink; but to sit on My right and on *My* left, this is not Mine to give, but it is for those for whom it has been prepared by My Father" (Matthew 20:21–23; cf. Mark 10:35–40; see Matthew 19:28; Acts 12:2).

Setting: On the Mount of Olives, just east of Jerusalem. During His Olivet Discourse, after answering His disciples' questions as to when the temple will be destroyed and Jerusalem overrun, along with the signs of His coming and the end of the age, Jesus reveals the future judgments following His return.

"But when the Son of Man comes in His glory, and all the angels with Him, then He will sit on His glorious throne. All the nations will be gathered before Him; and He will separate them from one another, as the shepherd separates the sheep from the goats; and He will put the sheep on His right, and the goats on the left. Then the King will say to those on His right, 'Come, you who are blessed of My Father, inherit the kingdom prepared for you from the foundation of the world. 'For I was hungry, and you gave Me *something* to eat; I was thirsty, and you gave Me *something* to drink; I was a stranger, and you invited Me in; naked, and you clothed Me; I was sick, and you visited Me; I was in prison, and you came to Me.' Then the righteous will answer Him, 'Lord, when did we see You hungry and feed You, or thirsty, and give you *something* to drink? And when did we see You a stranger, and invite You in, or naked, and clothe You? When did we see You sick, or in prison, and come to You?' The King will answer and say to them, 'Truly I say to you, to the extent that you did it to one of these brothers of Mine, *even* the least *of them,* you did it to Me.' Then He will also say to those on His left, 'Depart from Me, accursed ones, into the eternal fire which has been prepared for the devil and his angels; for I was hungry, and you gave Me *nothing* to eat; I was thirsty, and you gave Me nothing to drink; I was a stranger, and you did not invite Me in; naked, and you did not clothe Me; sick, and in prison, and you did not visit Me.' Then they themselves also will answer, 'Lord, when did we see You hungry, or thirsty, or a stranger, or naked, or sick, or in prison, and did not take care of You?' Then He will answer them, 'Truly I say to you, to the extent that you did not do it to one of the least of these, you did not do it to Me.' These will go away into eternal punishment, but the righteous into eternal life" (Matthew 25:31–46; see Matthew 7:23; 16:27; 19:29).

Setting: On the road to Jerusalem. After Jesus prophesies His persecution, death, and resurrection, His disciples James and John ask for special honor and privileges in His coming kingdom.

And He said to them, "What do you want Me to do for you?" They said to Him, "Grant that we may sit, one on Your right and one on *Your* left, in Your glory." But Jesus said to them, "You do not know what you are asking. Are you able to drink the cup that I drink, or to be baptized with the baptism with which I am baptized?" They said to Him, "We are able." And Jesus said to them, "The cup that I drink you shall drink; and you shall be baptized with the baptism with which I am baptized. But to sit on My right or on *My* left, this is not Mine to give; but it is for those for whom it has been prepared" (Mark 10:36–40; cf. Matthew 20:20–23; see Matthew 19:28; Acts 12:2).

RIGHT (proper)

[RIGHT from rightly]

Setting: Galilee. Pharisees and scribes from Jerusalem accuse Jesus' disciples of disobeying tradition and the commandments.

And He answered and said to them, "Why do you yourselves transgress the commandment of God for the sake of tradition? For God said, 'HONOR YOUR FATHER AND MOTHER,' and, 'HE WHO SPEAKS EVIL OF FATHER OR MOTHER IS TO BE PUT TO DEATH.' But you say, 'Whoever says to *his* father or mother, "Whatever I have that would help you has been given *to God*," he is not to honor his father or mother.' And *by this* you invalidated the word of God for the sake of your tradition. You hypocrites, rightly did Isaiah prophesy of you: 'THIS PEOPLE HONORS ME WITH THEIR LIPS, BUT THEIR HEART IS FAR AWAY FROM ME. BUT IN VAIN DO THEY WORSHIP ME, TEACHING AS DOCTRINES THE PRECEPTS OF MEN'" (Matthew 15:3–9, Jesus quotes from Exodus 20:12, 21:17, Leviticus 20:9; Isaiah 29:13; cf. Mark 7:5–7; see Colossians 2:22).

Setting: **Judea beyond the Jordan (Perea). Jesus illustrates the kingdom of heaven to His disciples through the story of laborers in the vineyard.**

"For the kingdom of heaven is like a landowner who went out early in the morning to hire laborers for his vineyard. When he had agreed with the laborers for a denarius for the day, he sent them into his vineyard. And he went out about the third hour and saw others standing idle in the market place; and to those he said,' You also go into the vineyard, and whatever is right I will give you.' And *so* they went. Again he went out about the sixth and the ninth hour, and did the same thing. And about the eleventh *hour* he went out and found others standing *around;* and he said to them, 'Why have you been standing idle here all day long?' They said to him, 'Because no one hired us.' He said to them, 'You go into the vineyard too.' When evening came, the owner of the vineyard said to his foreman, 'Call the laborers and pay them their wages, beginning with the last *group* to the first.' When those *hired* about the eleventh hour came, each one received a denarius. When those *hired* first came, they thought that they would receive more; but each of them also received a denarius. When they received it, they grumbled at the landowner, saying, 'These last men have worked *only* one hour, and you have made them equal to us who have borne the burden and the scorching heat of the day.' But he answered and said to one of them, 'Friend, I am doing you no wrong; did you not agree with me for a denarius? Take what is yours and go, but I wish to give to this last man the same as to you. It is not lawful for me to do what I wish with what is my own? Or is your eye envious because I am generous?' So the last shall be first, and the first last" (Matthew 20:1–16; cf. Matthew 19:30).

[RIGHT from Rightly]

Setting: **Galilee. The Pharisees and some of the scribes from Jerusalem question why Jesus' disciples do not follow the tradition of ceremonial hand cleansing before eating bread.**

And He said to them, "Rightly did Isaiah prophesy of you hypocrites, as it is written: 'THIS PEOPLE HONORS ME WITH THEIR LIPS, BUT THEIR HEART IS FAR AWAY FROM ME. BUT IN VAIN DO THEY WORSHIP ME, TEACHING AS DOCTRINES THE PRECEPTS OF MEN.' Neglecting the commandment of God, you hold to the tradition of men." He was also saying to them, "You are experts at setting aside the commandment of God in order to keep tradition. For Moses said, 'HONOR YOUR FATHER AND YOUR MOTHER'; and, 'HE WHO SPEAKS EVIL OF FATHER OR MOTHER, IS TO BE PUT TO DEATH'; but you say, 'If a man says to *his* father or *his* mother, whatever I have that would help you is Corban (that is to say, given *to God*),' you no longer permit him to do anything for *his* father or *his* mother; *thus* invalidating the word of God by your tradition which you have handed down; and you do many things such as that" (Mark 7:6–13, Jesus quotes from Exodus 20:12; 21:17; Isaiah 29:13; cf. Matthew 15:1–6).

Setting: **On the way from Galilee to Jerusalem. After chastising the crowds for being able to discern the weather but not the present age, Jesus exhorts them to settle any financial disputes outside of court.**

"And why do you not even on your own initiative judge what is right? For while you are going with your opponent to appear before the magistrate, on *your* way *there* make an effort to settle with him, so that he may not drag you before the judge, and the judge turn you over to the officer, and the officer throw you into prison. I say to you, you will not get out of there until you have paid the very last cent" (Luke 12:57–59; cf. Matthew 5:25, 26).

Setting: **Jerusalem. Before the Passover, with His death on the cross nearing, Jesus explains the reason for His vivid example of servanthood in washing His disciples' feet.**

So when He had washed their feet, and taken His garments and reclined *at the table* again, He said to them, "Do you know what I have done to you? You call Me Teacher and Lord; and you are right, for *so* I am. If I then, the Lord and the Teacher, washed your feet, you also ought to wash one another's feet. For I gave you an example that you also should do as I did to you. Truly, truly I say to you, a slave is not greater than his master, nor *is* one who is sent greater than the one who sent him. If you know these things, you are blessed if you do them. I do not speak of all of you. I know the ones I have chosen; but *it is* that the Scripture may be fulfilled, 'HE WHO EATS MY BREAD HAS LIFTED UP HIS HEEL AGAINST ME.' From now on I am telling you before *it* comes to pass, so that when it does occur, you may believe that I am *He*. Truly, truly, I say to you, he who receives whomever I send receives Me; and he who receives Me receives Him who sent Me" (John 13:12–20; Jesus quotes from Psalm 41:9; see Matthew 7:24; 10:24, 40; John 8:24; 14:29; 1 Peter 5:3).

[RIGHT from rightly]
Setting: Jerusalem. After Jesus is betrayed by Judas and arrested by the Roman cohort, one of the officers strikes Jesus. He believes that the Lord exhibits disrespect for the former high priest with His response to Annas's question about His disciples and teaching.

Jesus answered him, "If I have spoken wrongly, testify of the wrong; but if rightly, why do you strike Me?" (John 18:23; see Matthew 5:39).

RIGHT HAND (Listed under HAND, RIGHT)

RIGHTEOUS (RIGHTEOUS, RESURRECTION OF THE is a separate entry; also see MEN, RIGHTEOUS; PERSONS, RIGHTEOUS; and RIGHTEOUSNESS)

Setting: Galilee. During the early part of His ministry, Jesus preaches the Sermon on the Mount to His disciples and the multitudes.

"You have heard that it was said, 'YOU SHALL LOVE YOUR NEIGHBOR and hate your enemy.' But I say to you, love your enemies and pray for those who persecute you, so that you may be sons of your Father who is in heaven; for He causes His sun to rise on *the* evil and *the* good, and sends rain on *the* righteous and *the* unrighteous. For if you love those who love you, what reward do you have? Do not even the tax collectors do the same? If you greet only your brothers, what more are you doing *than others?* Do not even the Gentiles do the same? Therefore, you are to be perfect, as your heavenly Father is perfect" (Matthew 5:43–48, Jesus quotes from Leviticus 19:18; cf. Leviticus 19:2; Luke 6:27–36).

Setting: Capernaum, near the Sea of Galilee. Jesus calls Levi (Matthew) from his tax-collection booth to be His disciple.

But when Jesus heard *this,* He said, "*It is* not those who are healthy who need a physician, but those who are sick. But go and learn what this means: 'I DESIRE COMPASSION, AND NOT SACRIFICE,' for I did not come to call the righteous, but sinners" (Matthew 9:12, 13, Jesus quotes from Hosea 6:6; cf. Mark 2:17; Luke 5:31, 32; see Mark 2:15, 16).

Setting: A house near the Sea of Galilee. Jesus gives His disciples the meaning of the Parable of the Wheat and the Tares.

And He said, "The one who sows the good seed is the Son of Man, and the field is the world; and as *for* the good seed, these are the sons of the kingdom; and the tares are the sons of the evil *one;* and the enemy who sowed them is the devil, and the harvest is the end of the age; and the reapers are angels. So just as the tares are gathered up and burned with fire, so shall it be at the end of the age. The Son of Man will send forth His angels, and they will gather out of His kingdom all stumbling blocks, and those who commit lawlessness, and will throw them into the furnace of fire; in that place there will be weeping and gnashing of teeth. Then THE RIGHTEOUS WILL SHINE FORTH AS THE SUN in the kingdom of their Father. He who has ears, let him hear" (Matthew 13:37–43, Jesus quotes from Daniel 12:3; cf. Matthew 8:12).

Setting: By the Sea of Galilee. Because the religious leaders are rejecting His message, Jesus continues teaching His disciples with the Parable of the Dragnet.

"Again, the kingdom of heaven is like a dragnet cast into the sea, and gathering *fish* of every kind; and when it was filled, they drew it up on the beach; and they sat down and gathered the good *fish* into containers, but the bad they threw away. So it will be at the end of the age; the angels will come forth and take out the wicked from among the righteous, and will throw them into the furnace of fire; in that place there will be weeping and gnashing of teeth. Have you understood all these things?" They said to Him, "Yes" (Matthew 13:47–51).

Setting: The temple in Jerusalem. After the Jewish religious leaders test Him with questions, Jesus pronounces the seventh of eight woes upon them in front of the crowds and His disciples.

"Woe to you, scribes and Pharisees, hypocrites! For you are like whitewashed tombs which on the outside appear beautiful, but inside they are full of dead men's bones and all uncleanness. So you, too, outwardly appear righteous to men, but inwardly you are full of hypocrisy and lawlessness" (Matthew 23:27, 28; cf. Luke 11:44).

Setting: On the Mount of Olives, just east of Jerusalem. During His Olivet Discourse, after answering His disciples' questions as to when the temple will be destroyed and Jerusalem overrun, along with the signs of His coming and the end of the age, Jesus reveals the future judgments following His return.

"But when the Son of Man comes in His glory, and all the angels with Him, then He will sit on His glorious throne. All the nations will be gathered before Him; and He will separate them from one another, as the shepherd separates the sheep from the goats; and He will put the sheep on His right, and the goats on the left. Then the King will say to those on His right, 'Come, you who are blessed of My Father, inherit the kingdom prepared for you from the foundation of the world. 'For I was hungry, and you gave Me *something* to eat; I was thirsty, and you gave Me *something* to drink; I was a stranger, and you invited Me in; naked, and you clothed Me; I was sick, and you visited Me; I was in prison, and you came to Me.' Then the righteous will answer Him, 'Lord, when did we see You hungry and feed You, or thirsty, and give you *something* to drink? And when did we see You a stranger, and invite You in, or naked, and clothe You? When did we see You sick, or in prison, and come to You?' The King will answer and say to them, 'Truly I say to you, to the extent that you did it to one of these brothers of Mine, *even* the least *of them,* you did it to Me.' Then He will also say to those on His left, 'Depart from Me, accursed ones, into the eternal fire which has been prepared for the devil and his angels; for I was hungry, and you gave Me *nothing* to eat; I was thirsty, and you gave Me nothing to drink; I was a stranger, and you did not invite Me in; naked, and you did not clothe Me; sick, and in prison, and you did not visit Me.' Then they themselves also will answer, 'Lord, when did we see You hungry, or thirsty, or a stranger, or naked, or sick, or in prison, and did not take care of You?' Then He will answer them, 'Truly I say to you, to the extent that you did not do it to one of the least of these, you did not do it to Me.' These will go away into eternal punishment, but the righteous into eternal life" (Matthew 25:31–46; Matthew 7:23; 16:27; 19:29).

Setting: The home of Levi (Matthew) the tax collector in Capernaum, near the Sea of Galilee. The scribes of the Pharisees question Jesus' associating with sinners and tax collectors after He calls Levi to be His disciple.

And hearing *this,* Jesus said to them, "*It is* not those who are healthy who need a physician, but those who are sick; I did not come to call the righteous, but sinners" (Mark 2:17; cf. Matthew 9:12, 13; Luke 5:29–32).

Setting: The house of Levi (Matthew) in Capernaum. At a reception following Jesus' call of Levi to become His disciple, the Pharisees and their scribes question why the Lord associates with tax collectors and sinners.

And Jesus answered and said to them, "*It is* not those who are well who need a physician, but those who are sick. I have not come to call the righteous but sinners to repentance" (Luke 5:31, 32; cf. Matthew 9:10–13; Mark 2:15–17).

RIGHTEOUS, MONUMENTS OF THE

Setting: The temple in Jerusalem. After the Jewish religious leaders test Him with questions, Jesus pronounces the eighth of eight woes upon them in front of the crowds and His disciples.

"Woe to you, scribes and Pharisees, hypocrites! For you build the tombs of the prophets and adorn the monuments of the righteous, and say, 'If we had been *living* in the days of our fathers, we would not have been partners with them in *shedding* the blood of the prophets.' So you testify against yourselves, that you are sons of those who murdered the prophets. Fill up, then, the measure *of the guilt* of you fathers. You serpents, you brood of vipers, how will you escape the sentence of hell? Therefore, behold, I am sending you prophets and wise men and scribes; some of them you will kill and crucify, and some of them you will scourge in your synagogues, and persecute from city to city, so that upon you may fall *the guilt of* all the righteous blood shed on earth, from the blood of righteous Abel to the blood of Zechariah, the son of Berechiah, whom you murdered between the temple and the altar. Truly I say to you, all these things will come upon this generation" (Matthew 23:29–36; cf. 2 Chronicles 24:21; Zechariah 1:1; Matthew 3:7; Luke 11:47–52; see Matthew 10:23).

RIGHTEOUS, RESURRECTION OF THE (Also see RESURRECTION)

Setting: On the way from Galilee to Jerusalem. After Jesus, observing the invited guests of a Pharisee leader selecting places of honor at the table, speaks a parable to them, He comments to the host about the people to invite in the future.

And He also went on to say to the one who had invited Him, "When you give a luncheon or a dinner, do not invite your friends or your brothers or your relatives or rich neighbors, otherwise they may also invite you in return and *that* will be your repayment. But when you give a reception, invite *the* poor, *the* crippled, *the* lame, *the* blind, and you will be blessed, since they do not have *the means* to repay you; for you will be repaid at the resurrection of the righteous" (Luke 14:12–14; see John 5:28, 29).

RIGHTEOUS FATHER (Listed under FATHER, RIGHTEOUS)

RIGHTEOUS JUDGMENT (Listed under JUDGMENT, RIGHTEOUS)

RIGHTEOUS MAN (Listed under MAN, RIGHTEOUS)

RIGHTEOUS MAN'S REWARD (Listed under REWARD, RIGHTEOUS MAN'S; also see REWARD and REWARDS)

RIGHTEOUS MEN (Listed under MEN, RIGHTEOUS; also see RIGHTEOUS; and RIGHTEOUSNESS)

RIGHTEOUS PERSONS (Listed under PERSONS, RIGHTEOUS)

RIGHTEOUSNESS (RIGHTEOUSNESS, WAY OF is a separate entry; also see LIVING, GODLY; MEN, RIGHTEOUS; RIGHTEOUS; and WORKS, GOOD)

Setting: Bethany beyond the Jordan. Before being tempted by the devil and commencing His public ministry, Jesus arrives from Galilee to be baptized by John the Baptist, who questions his own worthiness to baptize the Lord.

But Jesus answering said to him, "Permit *it* at this time; for in this way it is fitting for us to fulfill all righteousness." Then he permitted Him (Matthew 3:15).

Setting: Galilee. Early in His ministry, Jesus presents the Beatitudes (part of the Sermon on the Mount) to His disciples and the gathered crowds from Galilee, Decapolis, Jerusalem, Judea, and beyond the Jordan.

"Blessed are those who hunger and thirst for righteousness, for they shall be satisfied" (Matthew 5:6; see Matthew 13:35).

Setting: Galilee. Early in His ministry, Jesus presents the Beatitudes (part of the Sermon on the Mount) to His disciples and the gathered crowds from Galilee, Decapolis, Jerusalem, Judea, and beyond the Jordan.

"Blessed are those who have been persecuted for the sake of righteousness, for theirs is the kingdom of heaven" (Matthew 5:10; cf. Luke 6:22; 1 Peter 3:14; see Matthew 13:35).

Setting: Galilee. During the early part of His ministry, Jesus preaches the Sermon on the Mount to His disciples and the multitudes.

"For I say to you that unless your righteousness surpasses *that* of the scribes and Pharisees, you will not enter the kingdom of heaven" (Matthew 5:20; cf. Luke 18:11, 12).

Setting: Galilee. During the early part of His ministry, Jesus preaches the Sermon on the Mount to His disciples and the multitudes.

"Beware of practicing your righteousness before men to be noticed by them; otherwise you have no reward with your Father who is in heaven" (Matthew 6:1; cf. Matthew 6:16).

Setting: Galilee. During the early part of His ministry, Jesus preaches the Sermon on the Mount to His disciples and the multitudes.

"For this reason I say to you, do not be worried about your life, *as to* what you will eat or what you will drink; nor for your body, *as to* what you will put on. Is not life more than food, and the body more than clothing? Look at the birds of the air, that they do not sow, nor reap nor gather into barns, and *yet* your heavenly Father feeds them. Are you not worth much more than they? And who of you by being worried can add a *single* hour to his life? And why are you worried about clothing? Observe how the lilies of the field grow; they do not toil nor do they spin, yet I say to you that not even Solomon in all his glory clothed himself like one of these. But if God so clothes the grass of the field, which is *alive* today and tomorrow is thrown into the furnace, *will He* not much more *clothe* you? You of little faith! Do not worry then, saying 'What will we eat?' or 'What will we drink?' or 'What will be wear for clothing?" For the Gentiles eagerly seek all these things; for your heavenly Father knows that you need all these things. But seek first His kingdom and His righteousness, and all these things will be added to you. So do not worry about tomorrow; for tomorrow will care for itself. Each day has enough trouble of its own" (Matthew 6:25–34; cf. Luke 12:22–31; see 1 Kings 10:4–7; Job 35:11; Matthew 8:26).

Setting: Jerusalem. Before the Passover, after warning His disciples of the persecution they will face after His departure to heaven, Jesus elaborates about the coming ministry of the Holy Spirit.

"But now I am going to Him who sent Me; and none of you asks Me, 'Where are You going?' But because I have said these things to you, sorrow has filled your heart. But I tell you the truth, it is to your advantage that I go away; for if I do not go away, the Helper will not come to you; but if I go, I will send Him to you. And He, when He comes, will convict the world concerning sin and righteousness and judgment; concerning sin, because they do not believe in Me; and concerning righteousness, because I go to the Father and you no longer see Me; and concerning judgment, because the ruler of this world has been judged" (John 16:5–11; see John 7:33; 12:31; 14:1, 16; 15:22, 24).

RIGHTEOUSNESS, WAY OF

Setting: The temple in Jerusalem. Jesus delivers a parable to the chief priests and elders after they question His authority.

"But what do you think? A man had two sons, and he came to the first and said, 'Son, go work today in the vineyard.' And he answered, 'I will not'; but afterward he regretted it and went. The man came to the second and said the same thing; and he answered, 'I *will,* sir'; but he did not go. Which of the two sons did the will of his father?" They said, "The first." Jesus said to them, "Truly, I say to you that the tax collectors and prostitutes will get into the kingdom of God before you. For John came to you in the way of righteousness and you did not believe him; but the tax collectors and prostitutes did believe him; and you, seeing *this,* did not even feel remorse afterward so as to believe him" (Matthew 21:28–32; cf. Luke 7:29, 30, 37–50).

RING

Setting: On the way from Galilee to Jerusalem. Jesus conveys the illustration of the prodigal son because the Pharisees and scribes complain He associates with tax collectors and sinners.

And He said, "A man had two sons. The younger of them said to his father, 'Father, give me the share of the estate that falls to me.' So he divided his wealth between them. And not many days later, the younger son gathered everything together and went on a journey into a distant country, and there he squandered his estate with loose living. Now when he had spent everything, a severe famine occurred in that country, and he began to be impoverished. So he went and hired himself out to one of the citizens of that country, and he sent him into his fields to feed swine. And he would have gladly filled his stomach with the pods that the swine were eating, and no one was giving *anything* to him. But when he came to his senses, he said, 'How many of my father's hired men have more than enough bread, but I am dying here with hunger! I will get up and go to my father, and will say to him, "Father, I have sinned against heaven, and in your sight; I am no longer worthy to be called your son; make me as one of your hired men."' So he got up and came to his father. But while he was still a long way off, his father saw him and felt compassion *for him,* and ran and embraced him and kissed him. And the son said to him, "Father, I have sinned against heaven and in your sight; I am no longer worthy to be called your son.' But the father said to his slaves, 'Quickly bring out the best robe and put it on him, and put a ring on his hand and sandals on his feet; and bring the fattened calf, kill it, and let us eat and celebrate; for this son of mine was dead and has come to life again; he was lost and has been found.' And they began to celebrate. Now his older son was in the field, when he came and approached the house, he heard music and dancing. And he summoned one of the servants and *began* inquiring what these things could be. And he said to him, 'Your brother has come, and your father has killed the fattened calf because he has received him back safe and sound.' But he became angry and was not willing to go in; and his father came out and *began* pleading with him. But he answered and said to his father, 'Look! For so many years I have been serving you and I have never neglected a command of yours; and *yet* you have never given me a young goat, so that I might celebrate with my friends; but when this son of yours came, who has devoured your wealth with prostitutes, you killed the fattened calf for him.' And he said to him, 'Son, you have always been with me, and all that is mine is yours. But we had to celebrate and rejoice, for this brother of yours was dead and *has begun* to live, and was lost and has been found' " (Luke 15:11–32; see Proverb 29:2; Luke 15:1, 2).

RIVERS

Setting: Jerusalem. On the last day of the Feast of Booths, after Jesus causes discussion about whether He is the Christ, the chief priests and Pharisees attempt to understand where it is He says He will be going soon. Jesus offers salvation and the abundant life to His hearers.

Now on the last day, the great *day* of the feast, Jesus stood and cried out, saying, "If anyone is thirsty, let him come to Me and drink. He who believes in Me, as the Scripture said, 'From his innermost being will flow rivers of living water'" (John 7:37, 38).

ROAD (Also see HIGHWAYS, MAIN; and STREETS)

Setting: By the Sea of Galilee. While teaching and preaching to the crowds from a boat, Jesus conveys the Parable of the Sower.

And He spoke many things to them in parables, saying, "Behold, the sower went out to sow; and as he sowed, some *seeds* fell beside the road, and the birds came and ate them up. Others fell on the rocky places, where they did not have much soil; and immediately they sprang up, because they had no depth of soil. But when the sun had risen, they were scorched; and because they had no root, they withered away. Others fell among the thorns, and the thorns came up and choked them out. And others fell on the good soil and yielded a crop, some a hundredfold, some sixty, and some thirty. He who has ears, let him hear" (Matthew 13:3–9; cf. Mark 4:3–9; Luke 8:4–8).

Setting: By the Sea of Galilee. With the religious leaders rejecting His message, Jesus begins to teach in parables, and explains the meaning of the Parable of the Sower to His disciples.

"Hear then the parable of the sower. When anyone hears the word of the kingdom and does not understand it, the evil *one* comes and snatches away what has been sown in his heart. This is the one on whom seed was sown beside the road. The one on whom seed was sown on the rocky places, this is the man who hears the word and immediately receives it with joy; yet he has no *firm* root in himself, but is *only* temporary, and when affliction or persecution arises because of the word, immediately he falls away. And the one on whom seed was sown among the thorns, this is the man who hears the word, and the worry of the world and the deceitfulness of wealth choke the word, and it becomes unfruitful. And the one on whom seed was sown on the good soil, this is the man who hears the word and understands it; who indeed bears fruit and brings forth, some a hundredfold, some sixty, and some thirty" (Matthew 13:18–23; cf. Mark 4:13–20; Luke 8:11–15).

Setting: By the Sea of Galilee. During the early part of His ministry, just after a visit from his mother and brothers, Jesus instructs a very large crowd with the Parable of the Sower while in a boat.

"Listen *to this!* Behold, the sower went out to sow; as he was sowing, some *seed* fell beside the road, and the birds came and ate it up. Other *seed* fell on the rocky *ground* where it did not have much soil; and immediately it sprang up because it had no depth of soil. And after the sun had risen, it was scorched; and because it had no root, it withered away. Other *seed* fell among the thorns, and the thorns came up and choked it, and it yielded no crop. Other *seeds* fell into the good soil, and as the grew up and increased, they yielded a crop and produced thirty, sixty, and a hundredfold." And He was saying, "He who has ears to hear, let him hear" (Mark 4:3–9; cf. Matthew 13:3–9; Luke 8:5–8).

Setting: By the Sea of Galilee. During the early part of His ministry, after presenting the Parable of the Sower from a boat to a very large crowd, Jesus gives the meaning of the parable to His disciples and other followers.

And He said to them, "Do you not understand this parable? How will you understand all the parables? The sower sows the word. These are the ones who are beside the road where the word is sown; and when they hear, immediately Satan comes and takes away the word which has been sown in them. In a similar way these are the ones on whom seed was sown on the rocky places, who, when they hear the word, immediately receive it with joy; and they have no *firm* root in themselves, but are *only* temporary; then, when affliction or persecution arises because of the word, immediately they fall away. And others are the ones on whom seed was sown among the thorns; these are the ones who have heard the word, but the worries of the world and the deceitfulness of riches, and the desires for other things enter in and choke the word, and it becomes unfruitful. And those are the ones on whom seed was sown on the good soil; and they hear the word and accept it and bear fruit, thirty, sixty, and a hundredfold" (Mark 4:13–20; cf. Matthew 13:18–23; Luke 8:11–15).

Setting: Galilee. After His visit in the home of Simon the Pharisee, Jesus goes into the villages and cities, proclaiming and preaching the kingdom of God.

When a large crowd was coming together, and those from various cities were journeying to Him, He spoke by way of a parable: "The sower went out to sow his seed; and as he sowed, some fell beside the road, and it was trampled under foot and the birds of the air ate it up. Other *seed* fell on rocky *soil,* and as soon as it grew up, it was withered away, because it had no moisture. Other *seed* fell among the thorns; and the thorns grew up with it and choked it out. Other *seed* fell into the good soil, and grew up, and produced a crop a hundred times as great." As He said these things, He would call out, "He who has ears to hear, let him hear" (Luke 8:4–8; cf. Matthew 13:2–9; Mark 4:3–9).

Setting: Galilee. After Jesus presents the Parable of the Sower to the crowds, His disciples ask Him to give them the parable's meaning.

And He said, "To you it has been granted to know the mysteries of the kingdom of God, but to the rest *it is* in parables, so that SEEING THEY MAY NOT SEE, AND HEARING THEY MAY NOT UNDERSTAND. Now the parable is this: the seed is the word of God. Those beside the road are those who have heard; then the devil comes and takes away the word from their heart, so that they will not believe and be saved. Those on the rocky *soil* are those who, when they hear, receive the word with joy; and these have no *firm* root; they believe for a while, and in time of temptation fall away. The *seed* which fell among the thorns, these are the ones who have heard, and as they go on their way they are choked with worries and riches and pleasures of *this* life, and bring no fruit to maturity. But the *seed* in the good soil, these are the ones who have heard the word in an honest and good heart, and hold it fast, and bear fruit with perseverance" (Luke 8:10–15, Jesus quotes from Isaiah 6:9; cf. Matthew 13:10–23; Mark 4:10–20).

Setting: On the way from Galilee to Jerusalem. While being tested by a lawyer, Jesus tells him the story of the good Samaritan.

Jesus replied and said, "A man was going down from Jerusalem to Jericho, and fell among robbers, and they stripped him and beat him, and went away leaving him half dead. And by chance a priest was going down on that road, and when he saw him, he passed by on the other side. Likewise a Levite also, when he came to the place and saw him, passed by on the other side. But a Samaritan, who was on a journey, came upon him; and when he saw him, he felt compassion, and came to him and bandaged up his wounds, pouring oil and wine on *them;* and he put him on his own beast, and brought him to an inn and took care of him. On the next day he took out two denarii and gave them to the innkeeper and said, 'Take care of him; and whatever more you spend, when I return I will repay you.' Which of these three do you think proved to be a neighbor to the man who fell into the robbers' *hands?*" And he said, "The one who showed mercy toward him." Then Jesus said to him, "Go and do the same" (Luke 10:30–37).

ROBBER (Also see BURGLARY; ROBBERS; ROBBERY; STEALING; THEFT; and THIEVES)

Setting: Gethsemane on the Mount of Olives, east of the temple in Jerusalem. As He submits to His Father's will and allows Judas to betray Him, Jesus reveals that this incident is a fulfillment of prophecy.

At that time Jesus said to the crowds, "Have you come out with swords and clubs to arrest Me as *you would* against a robber? Every day I used to sit in the temple teaching and you did not seize Me. But all this has taken place to fulfill the Scriptures of the prophets" (Matthew 26:55, 56; cf. Mark 14:48, 49; Luke 22:52, 53; see Matthew 26:24).

Setting: Gethsemane on the Mount of Olives, east of the temple in Jerusalem. Judas betrays Jesus with a kiss before a crowd from the chief priests, scribes, and elders, seeking to seize Him with swords and clubs.

And Jesus said to them, "Have you come out with swords and clubs to arrest Me, as *you would* against a robber? Every day I was with you in the temple teaching, and you did not seize Me; but *this has taken place* to fulfill the Scriptures" (Mark 14:48, 49; cf. Matthew 26:55, 56; Luke 22:52, 53).

Setting: Gethsemane on the Mount of Olives, east of the temple in Jerusalem. After praying for deliverance, with His crucifixion imminent, Jesus chastises the religious leaders after Judas betrays Him and the hostile crowd surrounds Him.

Then Jesus said to the chief priests and officers of the temple and elders who had come against Him, "Have you come out with swords and clubs as you would against a robber? While I was with you daily in the temple, you did not lay hands on Me; but this hour and the power of darkness are yours" (Luke 22:52, 53; cf. Matthew 26:47–56; Mark 14:43–50).

Setting: Jerusalem. Following the Pharisees' interrogation and dismissal of the formerly blind man Jesus healed on the Sabbath, the Lord speaks to the Pharisees, using parabolic language they do not understand.

"Truly, truly, I say to you, he who does not enter by the door into the fold of the sheep, but climbs up some other way, he is a thief and a robber. But he who enters by the door is a shepherd of the sheep. To him the doorkeeper opens, and the sheep hear his voice, and he calls his own sheep by name and leads them out. When he puts forth all his own, he goes ahead of them, and the sheep follow him because they know his voice. A stranger they simply will not follow, but will flee from him, because they do not know the voice of strangers" (John 10:1–5).

ROBBERS (Also see BURGLARY; ROBBER; ROBBERY; STEALING; THEFT; and THIEVES)

Setting: On the way from Galilee to Jerusalem. While being tested by a lawyer, Jesus tells him the story of the good Samaritan.

Jesus replied and said, "A man was going down from Jerusalem to Jericho, and fell among robbers, and they stripped him and beat him, and went away leaving him half dead. And by chance a priest was going down on that road, and when he saw him, he passed by on the other side. Likewise a Levite also, when he came to the place and saw him, passed by on the other side. But a Samaritan, who was on a journey, came upon him; and when he saw him, he felt compassion, and came to him and bandaged up his wounds, pouring oil and wine on *them;* and he put him on his own beast, and brought him to an inn and took care of him. On the next day he took out two denarii and gave them to the innkeeper and said, 'Take care of him; and whatever more you spend, when I return I will repay you.' Which of these three do you think proved to be a neighbor to the man who fell into the robbers' *hands?*" And he said, "The one who showed mercy toward him." Then Jesus said to him, "Go and do the same" (Luke 10:30–37).

Setting: Jerusalem. Following the Pharisees' interrogation and dismissal of the formerly blind man Jesus healed on the Sabbath, the Lord conveys the Parable of the Good Shepherd to the Pharisees, using figures of speech they do not understand.

So Jesus said to them again, "Truly, truly, I say to you, I am the door of the sheep. All who came before Me are thieves and robbers, but the sheep did not hear them. I am the door; if anyone enters through Me, he will be saved, and will go in and out and find pasture. The thief comes only to steal and kill and destroy; I came that they may have life, and have *it* abundantly. I am the good shepherd; the good shepherd lays down His life for the sheep. He who is a hired hand, and not a shepherd, who is not the owner of the sheep, sees the wolf coming, and leaves the sheep and flees, and the wolf snatches them and scatters *them. He flees* because he is a hired hand and is not concerned about the sheep. I am the good shepherd, and I know My own and My own know Me, even as the Father knows Me and I know the Father; and I lay down My life for the sheep. I have other sheep, which are not of this fold; I must bring them also, and they will hear My voice; and they will become one flock *with* one shepherd. For this reason the Father loves Me, because I lay down My life so that I may take it again. No one has taken it away from Me, but I lay it down on My own initiative. I have authority to take it up again. This commandment I received from My Father" (John 10:7–18; see Isaiah 40:11; 56:8; Jeremiah 23:1; Matthew 11:27).

ROBBERS' DEN (Also see TEMPLE, CLEANSING THE)

Setting: Jerusalem. After being welcomed with blessings from the crowds, Jesus cleanses the temple by driving out the money changers and merchants.

And He said to them, "It is written, 'MY HOUSE SHALL BE CALLED A HOUSE OF PRAYER'; but you are making it a ROBBERS' DEN" (Matthew 21:13; Jesus quotes from Isaiah 56:7; Jeremiah 7:11; cf. Mark 11:15–18; Luke 19:46; see Matthew 21:12).

Setting: Jerusalem. Following His triumphal entry and cleansing the temple of the money changers, Jesus rebukes the corrupt practices the Jewish religious leaders permit in His house.

And He *began* to teach and say to them, "Is it not written, 'MY HOUSE SHALL BE CALLED A HOUSE OF PRAYER FOR ALL THE NATIONS'? But you have made it a ROBBERS' DEN" (Mark 11:17, Jesus quotes from Isaiah 56:7; Jeremiah 7:11; cf. Matthew 21:12, 13; Luke 19:45–48; see Mark 11:15, 16, 18).

Setting: Jerusalem. After Jesus weeps as He sees the city ahead of Him, the Lord enters the temple and drives out the money changers and merchants.

Jesus entered the temple and began to drive out those who were selling, saying to them, "It is written, 'AND MY HOUSE SHALL BE A HOUSE OF PRAYER,' but you have made it a ROBBERS' DEN" (Luke 19:45, 46, Jesus quotes from Isaiah 56:7; Jeremiah 7:11; cf. Matthew 21:12, 13; Mark 11:15–17; Luke 19:47, 48; John 2:13–17).

ROBBERY (Also see BURGLARY; ROBBER; ROBBERS; STEALING; and THEFT)

Setting: The temple in Jerusalem. After the Jewish religious leaders test Him with questions, Jesus pronounces the sixth of eight woes upon them in front of the crowds and His disciples.

"Woe to you, scribes and Pharisees, hypocrites! For you clean the outside of the cup and of the dish, but inside they are full of robbery and self-indulgence. You blind Pharisee, first clean the inside of the cup and of the dish, so that the outside of it may become clean also" (Matthew 23:25, 26; see Mark 7:4).

Setting: On the way from Galilee to Jerusalem. After speaking of how a lamp illuminates, the Lord has lunch with a Pharisee who is surprised He doesn't wash before eating.

But the Lord said to him, "Now you Pharisees clean the outside of the cup and of the platter; but inside of you, you are full of robbery and wickedness. You foolish ones, did not He who made the outside make the inside also? But give that which is within as charity, and then all things are clean for you. But woe to you Pharisees! You pay tithe of mint and rue and every *kind of* garden herb, and *yet* disregard justice and the love of God; but these are the things you should have done without neglecting the others. Woe to you Pharisees! For you love the chief seats in the synagogues and the respectful greetings in the market places. Woe to you! For you are like concealed tombs, and the people who walk over *them* are unaware *of it*" (Luke 11:39–44; cf. Matthew 23:6, 7, 23–27; see Matthew 15:2; Titus 1:15).

ROBE (Also see COAT; and ROBES)

Setting: On the way from Galilee to Jerusalem. Jesus conveys the illustration of the prodigal son because the Pharisees and scribes complain He associates with tax collectors and sinners.

And He said, "A man had two sons. The younger of them said to his father, 'Father, give me the share of the estate that falls to me.' So he divided his wealth between them. And not many days later, the younger son gathered everything together and went on a journey into a distant country, and there he squandered his estate with loose living. Now when he had spent everything, a severe famine occurred in that country, and he began to be impoverished. So he went and hired himself out to one of the citizens of that country, and he sent him into his fields to feed swine. And he would have gladly filled his stomach with the pods that the swine were eating, and no one was giving *anything* to him. But when he came to his senses, he said, 'How many of my father's hired men have more than enough bread, but I am dying here with hunger! I will get up and go to my father, and will say to him, "Father, I have sinned against heaven, and in your sight; I am no longer worthy to be called your son; make me as one of your hired men."' So he got up and came to his father. But while he was still a long way off, his father saw him and felt compassion *for him,* and ran and embraced him and kissed him. And the son said to him, "Father, I have sinned against heaven and in your sight; I am no longer worthy to be called your son.' But the father said to his slaves, 'Quickly bring out the best robe and put it on him, and put a ring on his hand and sandals on his feet; and bring the fattened calf, kill it, and let us eat and celebrate; for this son of mine was dead and has come to life again; he was lost and has been found.' And they began to celebrate. Now his older son was in the field, when he came and approached the house, he heard music and dancing. And he summoned one of the servants and *began* inquiring what these things could be. And he said to him, 'Your brother has come, and your father has killed the fattened calf because he has received him back safe and sound.' But he became angry and was not willing to go in; and his father came out and *began* pleading with him. But he answered and said to his father, 'Look! For so many years I have been serving you and I have never neglected a command of yours; and *yet* you have never given me a young goat, so that I might celebrate with my friends; but when this son of yours came, who has devoured your wealth with prostitutes, you killed the fattened calf for him.' And he said to him, 'Son, you have always been with me, and all that is mine is yours. But we had to celebrate and rejoice, for this brother of yours was dead and *has begun* to live, and was lost and has been found' " (Luke 15:11–32; see Proverb 29:2; Luke 15:1, 2).

ROBES (Also see GARMENTS; and ROBE)

Setting: The temple in Jerusalem. After commending one scribe for his nearness to the kingdom of God, Jesus warns the crowd about the majority of the scribes.

In His teaching He was saying: "Beware of the scribes who like to walk around in long robes, and *like* respectful greetings in the market places, and chief seats in the synagogues and places of honor at banquets, who devour widows' houses, and for appearance's sake offer long prayers; these will receive greater condemnation" (Mark 12:38–40; cf. Matthew 23:1–7; Luke 20:45–47).

Setting: The temple in Jerusalem. While ministering a few days before His crucifixion, after posing a question to the scribes, who do not answer, Jesus warns His disciples about the lifestyle of the scribes.

"Beware of the scribes, who like to walk around in long robes, and love respectful greetings in the market places, and chief seats in the synagogues and places of honor at banquets, who devour widows' houses, and for appearance's sake offer long prayers.

These will receive greater condemnation" (Luke 20:46, 47; cf. Matthew 23:1–7; Mark 12:38–40; see Luke 11:43).

ROBES, LONG (See ROBES)

ROCK (Also see STONE)

Setting: Galilee. During the early part of His ministry, Jesus preaches the Sermon on the Mount to His disciples and the multitudes.

"Therefore everyone who hears these words of Mine and acts on them, may be compared to a wise man who built his house on the rock. And the rain fell, and the floods came, and the winds blew and slammed against that house; and *yet* it did not fall, for it had been founded on the rock. Everyone who hears these words of Mine and does not act on them, will be like a foolish man who built his house on the sand. The rain fell, and the floods came, and the winds blew and slammed against that house; and it fell—and great was its fall" (Matthew 7:24–28; cf. Luke 6:47–49).

Setting: Caesarea Philippi. Jesus responds to Simon Peter's declaration that He is the Christ, the Son of the living God.

And Jesus said to him, "Blessed are you, Simon Barjona, because flesh and blood did not reveal *this* to you, but My Father who is in heaven. I also say to you that you are Peter, and upon this rock I will build My church; and the gates of Hades will not overpower it. I will give you the keys of the kingdom of heaven; and whatever you bind on earth shall have been bound in heaven, and whatever you loose on earth shall have been loosed in heaven" (Matthew 16:17–19; cf. Matthew 18:18; Mark 8:29; Luke 9:20).

Setting: Galilee. After selecting His twelve disciples, Jesus teaches the Sermon on the Mount to those disciples and a great throng of people from Judea, Jerusalem, and the central coastal region of Tyre and Sidon.

"Why do you call Me, 'Lord, Lord,' and do not do what I say? Everyone who comes to Me and hears My words and acts on them, I will show you whom he is like; he is like a man building a house, who dug deep and laid a foundation on the rock; and when a flood occurred, the torrent burst against that house and could not shake it, because it had been well built. But the one who has heard and has not acted *accordingly,* is like a man who built a house on the ground without any foundation; and the torrent burst against it and immediately it collapsed, and the ruin of that house was great" (Luke 6:46–49; cf. Matthew 7:24–27; see Luke 6:12–19; James 1:22).

ROCKY PLACES (Listed under PLACES, ROCKY)

ROD (Also see STAFF)

Setting: On the island of Patmos (in the Aegean Sea about fifty miles southwest of Ephesus in modern Turkey). On the Lord's Day (Sunday), approximately fifty years after the Resurrection, the disciple John encounters the Lord Jesus Christ, who communicates a new revelation for the apostle to record for the church in Thyatira and to six other churches in Asia.

"And to the angel of the church in Thyatira write: The Son of God, who has eyes like a flame of fire, and His feet are like burnished bronze, says this: 'I know your deeds, and your love and faith and service and perseverance, and that your deeds of late are greater than at first. But I have *this* against you, that you tolerate the woman Jezebel, who calls herself a prophetess, and she teaches and leads My bond-servants astray so that they commit *acts of* immorality and eat things sacrificed to idols. I gave her time to repent, and she does not want to repent of her immorality. Behold, I will throw her on a bed *of sickness,* and those who commit adultery with her into great tribulation, unless they repent of her deeds. And I will kill her children with pestilence, and all the churches will know that I am He who searches the minds and hearts; and I will give to each one of you according to your deeds. But I say to you, the rest who are in Thyatira, who do not hold this teaching, who have not known the deep things of Satan, as they call them—I place no other burden on you. Nevertheless what you have, hold fast until I come. He who overcomes, and he who keeps My deeds until the end, TO HIM I WILL GIVE AUTHORITY OVER THE NATIONS; AND HE SHALL RULE THEM WITH A ROD OF IRON, AS

THE VESSELS OF THE POTTER ARE BROKEN TO PIECES, as I also have received *authority* from My Father; and I will give him the morning star. He who has an ear, let him hear what the Spirit says to the churches' (Revelation 2:18–29; Jesus quotes from Psalm 2:8, 9 and Isaiah 30:14; see 1 Kings 16:31; Psalm 7:9; Romans 2:5; 1 Corinthians 2:10; 2 Peter 3:9; Revelation 1:14; 2:7; 3:11; 17:1–20).

ROME

Setting: The Roman barracks in Jerusalem. Luke, writing in Acts, presents Jesus' encouraging words in an appearance to Paul following his hearing before the Jewish Council and arrest by the Roman commander (after his third missionary journey).

But on the night *immediately* following, the Lord stood at his side and said, "Take courage; for as you have solemnly witnessed to My cause at Jerusalem, so you must witness at Rome also" (Acts 23:11; see Acts 19:21).

ROOM (Specifics such as ROOM, GUEST; and ROOM, INNER are separate entries)

Setting: On the way from Galilee to Jerusalem. After speaking a parable to the invited guests and the host at a banquet, Jesus responds to a guest's proclamation about the blessings of eating bread in the kingdom of God.

But He said to him, "A man was giving a big dinner, and he invited many; and at the dinner hour he sent his slave to say to those who had been invited, 'Come; for everything is ready now.' But they all alike began to make excuses. The first one said to him, 'I have bought a piece of land and I need to go out and look at it; please consider me excused.' Another one said, 'I have bought five yoke of oxen, and I am going to try them out; please consider me excused.' Another one said, I have married a wife, and for that reason I cannot come.' And the slave came *back* and reported this to his master. Then the head of the household became angry and said to his slave, 'Go out at once into the streets and lanes of the city and bring in here the poor and crippled and blind and lame.' And the slave said, 'Master, what you commanded has been done, and still there is room.' And the master said to the slave, 'Go out into the highways and along the hedges, and compel *them* to come in, so that my house may be filled. For I tell you, none of those men who were invited shall taste of my dinner'" (Luke 14:16–24; see Deuteronomy 24:5; Matthew 22:2–14).

ROOM, GUEST

Setting: Jerusalem. On the first day of the Feast of Unleavened Bread, when the Passover lamb is being sacrificed, Jesus responds to His disciples' question about His plans for the Passover meal.

And He sent two of His disciples and said to them, "Go into the city, and a man will meet you carrying a pitcher of water; follow him; and wherever he enters, say to the owner of the house, 'The Teacher says, "Where is My guest room in which I may eat the Passover with My disciples?"' And he himself will show you a large upper room furnished *and* ready; prepare for us there" (Mark 14:13–15; cf. Matthew 26:17–19; Luke 22:7–13).

Setting: Jerusalem. With the Passover (Feast of Unleavened Bread) approaching, Jesus informs His disciples where they will celebrate the feast. The chief priests and scribes seek to kill Him, and Satan enters Judas Iscariot in order to betray the Lord.

And Jesus sent Peter and John, saying, "Go and prepare the Passover for us, so that we may eat it." They said to Him, "Where do You want us to prepare it?" And He said to them, "When you have entered the city, a man will meet you carrying a pitcher of water; follow him into the house that he enters. And you shall say to the owner of the house, 'The Teacher says to you, "Where is the guest room in which I may eat the Passover with My disciples?"' And he will show you a large, furnished upper room; prepare it there" (Luke 22:8–12; cf. Matthew 26:17–19; Mark 14:12–16).

ROOM, INNER (Also see ROOMS, INNER)

Setting: Galilee. During the early part of His ministry, Jesus preaches the Sermon on the Mount to His disciples and the multitudes.

"When you pray, you are not to be like the hypocrites; for they love to stand and pray in the synagogues and on the street corners so that they may be seen by men. Truly I say to you, they have their reward in full. But you, when you pray, go into your inner room, close your door and pray to your Father who is in secret, and your Father who *sees what is done* in secret will reward you" (Matthew 6:5, 6; see Mark 11:25).

ROOM, UPPER

Setting: Jerusalem. On the first day of the Feast of Unleavened Bread, when the Passover lamb is being sacrificed, Jesus responds to His disciples' question about His plans for the Passover meal.

And He sent two of His disciples and said to them, "Go into the city, and a man will meet you carrying a pitcher of water; follow him; and wherever he enters, say to the owner of the house, 'The Teacher says, "Where is My guest room in which I may eat the Passover with My disciples?"' And he himself will show you a large upper room furnished *and* ready; prepare for us there" (Mark 14:13–15; cf. Matthew 26:17–19; Luke 22:7–13).

Setting: Jerusalem. With the Passover (Feast of Unleavened Bread) approaching, Jesus informs His disciples where they will celebrate the feast. The chief priests and scribes seek to kill Him, and Satan enters Judas Iscariot in order to betray the Lord.

And Jesus sent Peter and John, saying, "Go and prepare the Passover for us, so that we may eat it." They said to Him, "Where do You want us to prepare it?" And He said to them, "When you have entered the city, a man will meet you carrying a pitcher of water; follow him into the house that he enters. And you shall say to the owner of the house, 'The Teacher says to you, "Where is the guest room in which I may eat the Passover with My disciples?"' And he will show you a large, furnished upper room; prepare it there" (Luke 22:8–12; cf. Matthew 26:17–19; Mark 14:12–16).

ROOMS (See specifics such as ROOMS, INNER)

ROOMS, INNER (Also see ROOM, INNER)

Setting: The Mount of Olives, just east of Jerusalem. During His Olivet Discourse, Jesus answers His disciples' questions as to when the temple will be destroyed and Jerusalem overrun, along with the signs of His coming and the end of the age.

"Therefore when you see the ABOMINATION OF DESOLATION which was spoken of through Daniel the prophet, standing in the holy place (let the reader understand), then those who are in Judea must flee to the mountains. Whoever is on the housetop must not go down to get the things that are in his house. Whoever is in the field must not turn back to get his cloak. But woe to those who are pregnant and to those who are nursing babies in those days! But pray that your flight will not be in the winter, or on a Sabbath. For then there will be a great tribulation, such as has not occurred since the beginning of the world until now, nor ever will. Unless those days had been cut short, no life would have been saved; but for the sake of the elect those days will be cut short. Then if anyone says to you, 'Behold, here is the Christ,' or 'There *He is,*' do not believe *him.* For false Christs and false prophets will arise and will show great signs and wonders, so as to mislead, if possible, even the elect. Behold, I have told you in advance. So if they say to you, 'Behold, He is in the wilderness,' do not go out, *or,* 'Behold, He is in the inner rooms,' do not believe *them.* For just as the lightning comes from the east and flashes even to the west, so will the coming of the Son of Man be. Wherever the corpse is, there the vultures will gather" (Matthew 24:15–28, Jesus quotes from Daniel 9:27; cf. Daniel 12:1; Mark 13:14–23; Luke 17:22–31; 21:20–24; 23:29; see John 4:48).

Setting: On the way from Galilee to Jerusalem. Jesus warns His disciples of future events, as the scribes and Pharisees turn hostile and question Him repeatedly in an attempt to catch Him in something He might say.

Under these circumstances, after so many thousands of people had gathered together that they were stepping on one another, He began saying to His disciples first *of all,* "Beware of the leaven of the Pharisees, which is hypocrisy. But there is nothing covered up that will not be revealed, and hidden that will not be known. Accordingly, whatever you have said in the dark will be heard in the light, and what you have whispered in the inner rooms will be proclaimed upon the housetops. I say to you, My friends, do not be afraid of those who kill the body and after that have no more that they can do. But I will warn you whom to fear: fear

the One who, after He has killed, has authority to cast into hell; yes, I tell you, fear Him! Are not five sparrows sold for two cents? *Yet* not one of them is forgotten before God. Indeed, the very hairs of your head are all numbered. Do not fear; you are more valuable than many sparrows" (Luke 12:1–7; cf. Matthew 10:26–31; see Matthew 16:6; Hebrews 10:31).

ROOSTER (Also see BIRDS; CHICKS; and HEN)

Setting: On the way to the Mount of Olives. After celebrating the Passover meal with His disciples in Jerusalem, prior to His betrayal by Judas, Jesus tells them they all will deny Him that very day.

Then Jesus said to them, "You will all fall away because of Me this night, for it is written, 'I WILL STRIKE DOWN THE SHEPHERD, AND THE SHEEP OF THE FLOCK SHALL BE SCATTERED.' But after I have been raised, I will go ahead of you to Galilee." But Peter said to Him, '*Even* though all may fall away because of You, I will never fall away.' Jesus said to him, "Truly I say to you that this *very* night, before a rooster crows, you will deny Me three times" (Matthew 26:31–34, Jesus quotes from Zechariah 13:7; cf. Mark 14:26–31; see Matthew 28:7, 10, 16; John 13:37).

Setting: Jerusalem. As Jesus appears before Caiaphas the high priest and the Council for interrogation aimed to entrap Him, Peter, sitting outside in the courtyard, denies knowing Jesus, fulfilling the Lord's earlier prophecy.

And Peter remembered the word which Jesus had said, "Before a rooster crows, you will deny Me three times." And he went out and wept bitterly (Matthew 26:75; cf. Matthew 26:34; Mark 14:72; Luke 22:61; John 18:25–27).

Setting: On the Mount of Olives, east of the temple in Jerusalem. After prophesying the temple's destruction, Jesus responds during His Olivet Discourse to questions from Peter, James, John, and Andrew about other future events.

"Take heed, keep on the alert; for you do not know when the *appointed* time will come. *It is* like a man away on a journey, *who* upon leaving his house and putting his slaves in charge, *assigning* to each one his task, also commanded the doorkeeper to stay on the alert. Therefore, be on the alert—for you do not know when the master of the house is coming, whether in the evening, at midnight, or when the rooster crows, or in the morning—in case he should come suddenly and find you asleep. What I say to you I say to all, 'Be on the alert!' " (Mark 13:33–37; cf. Matthew 24:42, 43; Luke 21:34–36; see Luke 12:36–38; Ephesians 6:18).

Setting: A borrowed upper room in Jerusalem. After Jesus and His twelve disciples celebrate the Passover and the Lord's Supper, they go to the Mount of Olives.

And Jesus said to them, "You will all fall away, because it is written, 'I WILL STRIKE DOWN THE SHEPHERD, AND THE SHEEP SHALL BE SCATTERED.' But after I have been raised, I will go ahead of you to Galilee." But Peter said to Him, "*Even* though all may fall away, yet I will not." And Jesus said to him, "Truly I say to you, that this very night, before a rooster crows twice, you yourself will deny Me three times" (Mark 14:27–30, Jesus quotes from Zechariah 13:7; cf. Matthew 26:30–34; see Mark 14:72).

Setting: Jerusalem. While Jesus is being falsely accused before the chief priests and the whole Council, Peter, in the courtyard of Caiaphas the high priest, denies knowing Jesus. He then remembers His Lord's prophecy that he would deny Him three times before a rooster crowed twice.

Immediately a rooster crowed a second time. And Peter remembered how Jesus had made the remark to him, "Before a rooster crows twice, you will deny Me three times." And he began to weep (Mark 14:72; cf. Matthew 26:75; Luke 22:61; John 18:26, 27; see Mark 14:30).

Setting: Jerusalem. During the Feast of Unleavened Bread (Passover) just before His crucifixion, Jesus celebrates the Passover meal with His disciples and institutes the Lord's Supper. The disciples later argue over who is the greatest among them, and the Lord prophesies Peter's denial of Him.

"Simon, Simon, behold, Satan has demanded *permission* to sift you like wheat; but I have prayed for you, that your faith may not fail; and you, when once you have turned again, strengthen your brothers." But he said to Him, "Lord, with You I am ready to go both to prison and to death!" And He said, "I say to you, Peter, the rooster will not crow today until you have denied three times that you know Me" (Luke 22:31–34; cf. Matthew 26:33–35; John 13:36–38; see Job 1:6–12; John 17:15).

Setting: The courtyard of the high priest in Jerusalem. After Jesus' arrest, Peter recalls the Lord's prophecy about denying Him three times when the Lord turns and looks at him following the third denial and the crowing of a rooster.

The Lord turned and looked at Peter. And Peter remembered the word of the Lord, how He had told him, "Before a rooster crows today, you will deny Me three times" (Luke 22:61; cf. Matthew 26:75; Luke 14:72; John 18:26, 27; see Luke 22:34).

Setting: Jerusalem. Before the Passover, after revealing to His disciples they cannot follow Him back to heaven, Jesus takes issue with Peter's assertion that he would lay down his life for the Lord.

Simon Peter said to Him, "Lord, where are You going?" Jesus answered, "Where I go, you cannot follow Me now; but you will follow later." Peter said to Him, "Lord, why can I not follow You right now? I will lay down my life for You." Jesus answered, "Will you lay down your life for Me? Truly, truly, I say to you, a rooster will not crow until you deny Me three times" (John 13:36–38; see Matthew 26:34; Mark 14:30, 72; Luke 22:33, 34).

ROOT (Also see BRANCHES; LEAVES; ROOT, FIRM; and TREE)

Setting: By the Sea of Galilee. While teaching and preaching to the crowds from a boat, Jesus conveys the Parable of the Sower.

And He spoke many things to them in parables, saying, "Behold, the sower went out to sow; and as he sowed, some *seeds* fell beside the road, and the birds came and ate them up. Others fell on the rocky places, where they did not have much soil; and immediately they sprang up, because they had no depth of soil. But when the sun had risen, they were scorched; and because they had no root, they withered away. Others fell among the thorns, and the thorns came up and choked them out. And others fell on the good soil and yielded a crop, some a hundredfold, some sixty, and some thirty. He who has ears, let him hear" (Matthew 13:3–9; cf. Mark 4:3–9; Luke 8:4–8).

Setting: By the Sea of Galilee. With the religious leaders rejecting His message, Jesus begins to teach in parables, and gives His disciples the meaning of the Parable of the Sower.

"Hear then the parable of the sower. When anyone hears the word of the kingdom and does not understand it, the evil *one* comes and snatches away what has been sown in his heart. This is the one on whom seed was sown beside the road. The one on whom seed was sown on the rocky places, this is the man who hears the word and immediately receives it with joy; yet he has no *firm* root in himself, but is *only* temporary, and when affliction or persecution arises because of the word, immediately he falls away. And the one on whom seed was sown among the thorns, this is the man who hears the word, and the worry of the world and the deceitfulness of wealth choke the word, and it becomes unfruitful. And the one on whom seed was sown on the good soil, this is the man who hears the word and understands it; who indeed bears fruit and brings forth, some a hundredfold, some sixty, and some thirty" (Matthew 13:18–23; cf. Mark 4:13–20; Luke 8:11–15).

Setting: By the Sea of Galilee. During the early part of His ministry, just after a visit from his mother and brothers, Jesus instructs a very large crowd with the Parable of the Sower from a boat.

"Listen *to this!* Behold, the sower went out to sow; as he was sowing, some *seed* fell beside the road, and the birds came and ate it up. Other *seed* fell on the rocky *ground* where it did not have much soil; and immediately it sprang up because it had no depth of soil. And after the sun had risen, it was scorched; and because it had no root, it withered away. Other *seed* fell among the thorns, and the thorns came up and choked it, and it yielded no crop. Other *seeds* fell into the good soil, and as the grew up and increased, they yielded a crop and produced thirty, sixty, and a hundredfold." And He was saying, "He who has ears to hear, let him hear" (Mark 4:3–9; cf. Matthew 13:3–9;

Luke 8:5–8).

Setting: By the Sea of Galilee. During the early part of His ministry, after presenting the Parable of the Sower from a boat to a very large crowd, Jesus gives the meaning of the parable to His disciples and other followers.

And He said to them, "Do you not understand this parable? How will you understand all the parables? The sower sows the word. These are the ones who are beside the road where the word is sown; and when they hear, immediately Satan comes and takes away the word which has been sown in them. In a similar way these are the ones on whom seed was sown on the rocky places, who, when they hear the word, immediately receive it with joy; and they have no *firm* root in themselves, but are *only* temporary; then, when affliction or persecution arises because of the word, immediately they fall away. And others are the ones on whom seed was sown among the thorns; these are the ones who have heard the word, but the worries of the world and the deceitfulness of riches, and the desires for other things enter in and choke the word, and it becomes unfruitful. And those are the ones on whom seed was sown on the good soil; and they hear the word and accept it and bear fruit, thirty, sixty, and a hundredfold" (Mark 4:13–20; cf. Matthew 13:18–23; Luke 8:11–15).

Setting: Galilee. After Jesus presents the Parable of the Sower to the crowds, His disciples ask Him to give them the parable's meaning.

And He said, "To you it has been granted to know the mysteries of the kingdom of God, but to the rest *it is* in parables, so that SEEING THEY MAY NOT SEE, AND HEARING THEY MAY NOT UNDERSTAND. Now the parable is this: the seed is the word of God. Those beside the road are those who have heard; then the devil comes and takes away the word from their heart, so that they will not believe and be saved. Those on the rocky *soil* are those who, when they hear, receive the word with joy; and these have no *firm* root; they believe for a while, and in time of temptation fall away. The *seed* which fell among the thorns, these are the ones who have heard, and as they go on their way they are choked with worries and riches and pleasures of *this* life, and bring no fruit to maturity. But the *seed* in the good soil, these are the ones who have heard the word in an honest and good heart, and hold it fast, and bear fruit with perseverance" (Luke 8:10–15, Jesus quotes from Isaiah 6:9; cf. Matthew 13:10–23; Mark 4:10–20).

Setting: On the island of Patmos (in the Aegean Sea about fifty miles southwest of Ephesus in modern Turkey). In the final chapter of the Lord Jesus Christ's revelation via the disciple John, approximately fifty years after the Resurrection, the Lord authenticates the truthfulness of His message, along with His earthly lineage through King David.

"I, Jesus, have sent My angel to testify to you these things for the churches. I am the root and the descendant of David, the bright morning star" (Revelation 22:16).

RUE (Also see other spices such as CUMMIN; DILL; HERB; and MINT)

Setting: On the way from Galilee to Jerusalem. After speaking of how a lamp illuminates, the Lord has lunch with a Pharisee who is surprised He doesn't wash before eating.

But the Lord said to him, "Now you Pharisees clean the outside of the cup and of the platter; but inside of you, you are full of robbery and wickedness. You foolish ones, did not He who made the outside make the inside also? But give that which is within as charity, and then all things are clean for you. But woe to you Pharisees! You pay tithe of mint and rue and every *kind of* garden herb, and *yet* disregard justice and the love of God; but these are the things you should have done without neglecting the others. Woe to you Pharisees! For you love the chief seats in the synagogues and the respectful greetings in the market places. Woe to you! For you are like concealed tombs, and the people who walk over *them* are unaware *of it*" (Luke 11:39–44; cf. Matthew 23:6, 7, 23–27; see Matthew 15:2; Titus 1:15).

RULE, GOLDEN (See GOLDEN RULE)

RULER (Also see RULERS)

Setting: Jerusalem. Just days before the Passover, with the chief priests and Pharisees plotting to seize Him and crowds welcoming Him with palm branches and praise, Jesus expresses anxiety about His upcoming crucifixion.

"Now My soul has become troubled; and what shall I say, 'Father, save Me from this hour'? But for this purpose I came to this hour. Father glorify Your name." Then a voice came out of heaven: "I have glorified it, and will glorify it again." So the crowd *of people* who stood by and heard it were saying that it had thundered; others were saying, "An angel has spoken to Him." Jesus answered and said, "This voice has not come for My sake, but for your sakes. Now judgment is upon this world; now the ruler of this world will be cast out. And I, if I am lifted up from the earth, will draw all men to Myself" (John 12:27–32; see Matthew 3:17; 26:38; John 3:14; 6:44; 11:42; 14:30).

Setting: Jerusalem. Before the Passover, after He conveys the upcoming ministry of the Holy Spirit in His disciples' lives, Jesus again relates peace, hope, and comfort to them regarding His return to the Father.

"Peace I leave with you; My peace I give to you; not as the world gives do I give to you. Do not let your heart be troubled, nor let it be fearful. You heard that I said to you, 'I go away, and I will come to you,' If you loved Me, you would have rejoiced because I go to the Father, for the Father is greater than I. Now I have told you before it happens, so that when it happens, you may believe. I will not speak much more with you, for the ruler of the world is coming, and he has nothing in Me; but so that the world may know that I love the Father, I do exactly as the Father commanded Me. Get up, let us go from here" (John 14:27–31; see John 10:18, 29; 12:31; 13:19; 16:33).

Setting: Jerusalem. Before the Passover, after warning His disciples of the persecution they will face after His departure to heaven, Jesus elaborates about the coming ministry of the Holy Spirit.

"But now I am going to Him who sent Me; and none of you asks Me, 'Where are You going?' But because I have said these things to you, sorrow has filled your heart. But I tell you the truth, it is to your advantage that I go away; for if I do not go away, the Helper will not come to you; but if I go, I will send Him to you. And He, when He comes, will convict the world concerning sin and righteousness and judgment; concerning sin, because they do not believe in Me; and concerning righteousness, because I go to the Father and you no longer see Me; and concerning judgment, because the ruler of this world has been judged" (John 16:5–11; see John 7:33; 12:31; 14:1, 16; 15:22, 24).

RULER OF THE WORLD (Listed under WORLD, RULER OF THE)

RULERS (Also see AUTHORITIES; and RULER)

Setting: On the way to Jerusalem, where Jesus will die on the cross. Jesus teaches His disciples about true greatness after the mother of James and John asks Him to make her sons exalted rulers with Him in His coming kingdom.

But Jesus called them to Himself and said, "You know that the rulers of the Gentiles lord it over them, and *their* great men exercise authority over them. It is not this way among you, but whoever wishes to become great among you shall be your servant, and whoever wishes to be first among you shall be your slave; just as the Son of Man did not come to be served, but to serve, and to give His life a ransom for many" (Matthew 20:25–28; cf. Matthew 23:11; 26:28; Mark 10:42–45).

Setting: On the road to Jerusalem. James and John ask Jesus for special honor and privileges in His kingdom. The other disciples become angry, so the Lord uses this moment to teach all of them about servanthood.

Calling them to Himself, Jesus said to them, "You know that those who are recognized as rulers of the Gentiles lord it over them; and their great men exercise authority over them. But it is not this way among you, but whoever wishes to become great among you shall be your servant; and whoever wishes to be first among you shall be slave of all. For even the Son of Man did not come to be served, but to serve, and to give His life a ransom for many" (Mark 10:42–45; cf. Matthew 20:25–28).

Setting: On the way from Galilee to Jerusalem. Jesus warns His disciples of future events, as the scribes and Pharisees turn hostile and question Him repeatedly in an attempt to catch Him in something He might say.

"And I say to you, everyone who confesses Me before men, the Son of Man will confess him also before the angels of God; but he who denies Me before men will be denied before the angels of God. And everyone who speaks a word against the Son of Man, it will be forgiven him; but he who blasphemes against the Holy Spirit, it will not be forgiven him. When they bring you before the synagogues and the rulers and the authorities, do not worry about how or what you are to speak in your defense, or what you are to say; for the Holy Spirit will teach you in that very hour what you ought to say" (Luke 12:8–12; cf. Matthew 10:32, 33; 12:31, 32; see Matthew 10:20).

RUMORS OF WARS (Listed under WARS, RUMORS OF)

RUST

Setting: Galilee. During the early part of His ministry, Jesus preaches the Sermon on the Mount to His disciples and the multitudes.

"Do not store up for yourselves treasures on earth, where moth and rust destroy, and where thieves break in and steal. But store up for yourselves treasures in heaven, where neither moth nor rust destroys, and where thieves do not break in or steal; for where your treasure is, there your heart will be also" (Matthew 6:19–21; cf. Luke 12:34; see Proverb 23:4; Matthew 19:21).

S

SABACHTHANI, LAMA

Setting: On a hill called Golgotha (Calvary), just outside Jerusalem. Jesus utters words of despair while dying on a cross for the sins of the world.

About the ninth hour Jesus cried out with a loud voice, saying, "ELI, ELI, LAMA SABACHTHANI?" that is, "MY GOD, MY GOD, WHY HAVE YOU FORSAKEN ME?" (Matthew 27:46, Jesus quotes from Psalm 22:1; cf. Mark 15:34).

Setting: On a hill called Golgotha (Calvary), just outside Jerusalem. While hanging nailed to a cross, Jesus cries out these words at the ninth hour (3 p.m.)

At the ninth hour Jesus cried out with a loud voice, "ELOI, ELOI, LAMA SABACHTHANI?" which is translated, "MY GOD, MY GOD, WHY HAVE YOU FORSAKEN ME?" (Mark 15:34, Jesus quotes from Psalm 22:1; cf. Matthew 27:46).

SABBATH (SABBATH, LORD OF THE is a separate entry)

Setting: Galilee. Jesus responds to the Pharisees' objection to His disciples' picking grain from the fields on the Sabbath.

But He said to them, "Have you not read what David did when he became hungry, he and his companions, how they entered the house of God, and ate the consecrated bread, which was not lawful for him to eat nor for those with him, but for the priests alone? Or, have you not read in the Law, that on the Sabbath the priests in the temple break the Sabbath and are innocent? But I say to you that something greater than the temple is here. But if you had known what this means, 'I DESIRE COMPASSION, AND NOT A SACRIFICE,' you would not have condemned the innocent. For the Son of Man is Lord of the Sabbath" (Matthew 12:3–8, Jesus quotes from Hosea 6:6; cf. Mark 2:25–28; Luke 6:3–5; see 1 Samuel 21:6).

Setting: A synagogue in Galilee. Jesus answers questions posed by the Pharisees about the Sabbath.

And He said to them, "What man is there among you who has a sheep, and if it falls into a pit on the Sabbath, will he not take hold of it and lift it out? How much more valuable then is a man than a sheep! So then, it is lawful to do good on the Sabbath." Then He said to the man, "Stretch out your hand!" He stretched it out, and it was restored to normal, like the other (Matthew 12:11–13; cf. Matthew 10:31; Mark 3:4, 5; Luke 6:9, 10; 14:5; see Matthew 8:3).

Setting: The Mount of Olives, just east of Jerusalem. During His Olivet Discourse, Jesus answers His disciples' questions as to when the temple will be destroyed and Jerusalem overrun, along with the signs of His coming and the end of the age.

"Therefore when you see the ABOMINATION OF DESOLATION which was spoken of through Daniel the prophet, standing in the holy place (let the reader understand), then those who are in Judea must flee to the mountains. Whoever is on the housetop must not go down to get the things that are in his house. Whoever is in the field must not turn back to get his cloak. But woe to those who are pregnant and to those who are nursing babies in those days! But pray that your flight will not be in the winter, or on a Sabbath. For then there will be a great tribulation, such as has not occurred since the beginning of the world until now, nor ever will. Unless those days had been cut short, no life would have been saved; but for the sake of the elect those days will be cut short. Then if anyone says to you, 'Behold, here is the Christ,' or "There *He is,*' do not believe *him.* For false Christs and false prophets will arise and will show great signs and wonders, so as to mislead, if possible, even the elect. Behold, I have told you in advance. So if they say to you, 'Behold, He is in the wilderness,' do not go out, *or,* 'Behold, He is in the inner rooms,' do not

believe *them.* For just as the lightning comes from the east and flashes even to the west, so will the coming of the Son of Man be. Wherever the corpse is, there the vultures will gather" (Matthew 24:15–28, Jesus quotes from Daniel 9:27; cf. Daniel 12:1; Mark 13:14–23; Luke 17:22–31; 21:20–24; 23:29; see John 4:48).

Setting: Galilee. Early in His ministry, the Pharisees question why Jesus allows His disciples to harvest grain on the Sabbath.

And He said to them, "Have you never read what David did when he was in need and he and his companions became hungry; how he entered the house of God in the time of Abiathar *the* high priest, and ate the consecrated bread, which is not lawful for *anyone* to eat except the priests, and he also gave it to those who were with him?" Jesus said to them, "The Sabbath was made for man, and not man for the Sabbath. So the Son of Man is Lord even of the Sabbath" (Mark 2:25–28; cf. Matthew 12:1–8; Luke 6:1–5; see Exodus 23:12).

Setting: A synagogue in Galilee. Early in His ministry, in front of the Pharisees, Jesus heals a man's withered hand on the Sabbath.

He said to the man with the withered hand, "Get up and come forward!" And He said to them, "Is it lawful to do good or do harm on the Sabbath, to save a life or to kill?" But they kept silent. After looking around at them with anger, grieved at their hardness of heart, He said to the man, "Stretch out your hand." And he stretched it out, and his hand was restored (Mark 3:3–5; cf. Matthew 12:9–14; Luke 6:6–11).

Setting: A synagogue in Galilee. As Jesus teaches on a Sabbath, the scribes and Pharisees watch to see if He heals a man's withered hand.

But He knew what they were thinking, and He said to the man with the withered hand, "Get up and come forward!" And he got up and came forward. And Jesus said to them, "I ask you, is it lawful to do good or to do harm on the Sabbath, to save a life or destroy it?" And looking around at them all, He said to him, "Stretch out your hand!" And he did *so;* and his hand was restored (Luke 6:8–10; cf. Matthew 12:9–13; Mark 3:1–5).

Setting: On the way from Galilee to Jerusalem. Jesus responds to a synagogue official's anger over the Lord's healing of a woman, sick eighteen years, in the synagogue on the Sabbath.

But the Lord answered him and said, "You hypocrites, does not each of you on the Sabbath untie his ox or his donkey from the stall and lead him away to water *him?* And this woman, a daughter of Abraham as she is, whom Satan has bound for eighteen long years, should she not have been released from this bond on the Sabbath day?" (Luke 13:15, 16; see Luke 14:5).

Setting: On the way from Galilee to Jerusalem. Jesus goes into the house of a Pharisee leader on the Sabbath to eat bread. A man suffering from dropsy is sitting there.

And Jesus answered and spoke to the lawyers and Pharisees, saying, "Is it lawful to heal on the Sabbath, or not?" But they kept silent. And He took hold of him and healed him, and sent him away. And He said to them, "Which one of you will have a son or an ox fall into a well, and will not immediately pull him out on a Sabbath day?" And they could make no reply to this (Luke 14:3–6, cf. Matthew 12:11–13).

Setting: The temple in Jerusalem. After receiving encouragement from His blood brothers in Galilee to attend the upcoming Feast of Booths in order to demonstrate His works to His disciples and the world, Jesus goes and teaches, astonishing the Jewish religious leaders.

Jesus answered them, "I did one deed, and you all marvel. For this reason Moses has given you circumcision (not because it is from Moses, but from the fathers), and on *the* Sabbath you circumcise a man. If a man receives circumcision on *the* Sabbath so that the Law of Moses will not be broken, are you angry with Me because I made an entire man well on *the* Sabbath? Do not judge according to appearance, but judge with righteous judgment" (John 7:21–24; see Genesis 17:10–14; Leviticus 12:3; 19:15; Matthew 12:2; John 5:2–16; 7–20).

SABBATH, LORD OF THE

Setting: Galilee. Jesus responds to the Pharisees' objection to His disciples' picking grain from the fields on the Sabbath.

But He said to them, "Have you not read what David did when he became hungry, he and his companions, how they entered the house of God, and ate the consecrated bread, which was not lawful for him to eat nor for those with him, but for the priests alone? Or, have you not read in the Law, that on the Sabbath the priests in the temple break the Sabbath and are innocent? But I say to you that something greater than the temple is here. But if you had known what this means, 'I DESIRE COMPASSION, AND NOT A SACRIFICE,' you would not have condemned the innocent. For the Son of Man is Lord of the Sabbath" (Matthew 12:3–8, Jesus quotes from Hosea 6:6; cf. Mark 2:25–28; Luke 6:3–5; see 1 Samuel 21:6).

Setting: Galilee. Early in His ministry, the Pharisees question why Jesus allows His disciples to harvest grain on the Sabbath.

And He said to them, "Have you never read what David did when he was in need and he and his companions became hungry; how he entered the house of God in the time of Abiathar *the* high priest, and ate the consecrated bread, which is not lawful for *anyone* to eat except the priests, and he also gave it to those who were with him?" Jesus said to them, "The Sabbath was made for man, and not man for the Sabbath. So the Son of Man is Lord even of the Sabbath" (Mark 2:25–28; cf. Matthew 12:1–8; Luke 6:1–5; see Exodus 23:12).

Setting: Probably Galilee. As Jesus and His disciples pass through some grain fields, some of the Pharisees ask the Lord why His followers harvest grain on the Sabbath.

And Jesus answering them said, "Have you not even read what David did when he was hungry, he and those who were with him, how he entered the house of God, and took and ate the consecrated bread which is not lawful for any to eat except the priests alone, and gave it to his companions?" And He was saying to them, "The Son of Man is Lord of the Sabbath" (Luke 6:3–5; cf. Matthew 12:1–8; Mark 2:23–28; see Exodus 20:8; Leviticus 24:1–9; Deuteronomy 5:12; 1 Samuel 21:1–6).

SABBATH DAY

Setting: On the way from Galilee to Jerusalem. After healing a woman, sick for eighteen years, in one of the synagogues on the Sabbath, Jesus responds to a synagogue official's anger.

But the Lord answered him and said, "You hypocrites, does not each of you on the Sabbath untie his ox or his donkey from the stall and lead him away to water *him?* And this woman, a daughter of Abraham as she is, whom Satan has bound for eighteen long years, should she not have been released from this bond on the Sabbath day?" (Luke 13:15, 16; see Luke 13:10–14, 17; 14:5).

Setting: On the way from Galilee to Jerusalem. On the Sabbath, Jesus goes to eat in the house of a Pharisee leader, where a man suffering from dropsy sits.

And Jesus answered and spoke to the lawyers and Pharisees, saying, "Is it lawful to heal on the Sabbath, or not?" But they kept silent. And He took hold of him and healed him, and sent him away. And He said to them, "Which one of you will have a son or an ox fall into a well, and will not immediately pull him out on a Sabbath day?" And they could make no reply to this (Luke 14:3–6, cf. Matthew 12:11–13; see Luke 14:1, 2).

SACKCLOTH (Also see ASHES)

Setting: Galilee. After performing miracles throughout the region, Jesus pronounces woes against those cities who do not repent.

"Woe to you, Chorazin! Woe to you, Bethsaida! For if the miracles had occurred in Tyre and Sidon which occurred in you, they would have repented long ago in sackcloth and ashes. Nevertheless I say to you, it will be more tolerable for Tyre and Sidon in *the* day of judgment than for you. And you, Capernaum, will not be exalted to heaven, will you? You will descend to Hades; for if the miracles had occurred in Sodom which occurred in you, it would have remained to this day. Nevertheless, I say to you that it will be more tolerable for the land of Sodom in *the* day of judgment, than for you" (Matthew 11:21–24; cf. Matthew 10:15; Luke 10:13–15).

Setting: On the way from Galilee to Jerusalem. The Lord pronounces woes on cities who reject the gospel, as He appoints seventy followers and sends them out in pairs to every place He Himself will soon visit.

"Woe to you, Chorazin! Woe to you, Bethsaida! For if the miracles had been performed in Tyre and Sidon which occurred in you, they would have repented long ago, sitting in sackcloth and ashes. But it will be more tolerable for Tyre and Sidon in the judgment than for you. And you, Capernaum, will not be exalted to heaven, will you? You will be brought down to Hades! The one who listens to you listens to Me, and the one who rejects you rejects Me; and he who rejects Me rejects the One who sent Me" (Luke 10:13–16; cf. Matthew 11:21–23; see Matthew 10:40).

SACRAMENTS (See BAPTISM; and LORD'S SUPPER)

SACRIFICE

Setting: Capernaum, near the Sea of Galilee. Jesus calls Matthew from his tax-collection booth to be His disciple.

But when Jesus heard *this,* He said, "*It is* not those who are healthy who need a physician, but those who are sick. But go and learn what this means: 'I DESIRE COMPASSION, AND NOT SACRIFICE,' for I did not come to call the righteous, but sinners" (Matthew 9:12, 13, Jesus quotes from Hosea 6:6; cf. Mark 2:17; Luke 5:31, 32; see Mark 2:15, 16).

Setting: Galilee. Jesus responds to the Pharisees' objection to His disciples' picking grain from the fields on the Sabbath.

But He said to them, "Have you not read what David did when he became hungry, he and his companions, how they entered the house of God, and ate the consecrated bread, which was not lawful for him to eat nor for those with him, but for the priests alone? Or, have you not read in the Law, that on the Sabbath the priests in the temple break the Sabbath and are innocent? But I say to you that something greater than the temple is here. But if you had known what this means, 'I DESIRE COMPASSION, AND NOT A SACRIFICE,' you would not have condemned the innocent. For the Son of Man is Lord of the Sabbath" (Matthew 12:3–8, Jesus quotes from Hosea 6:6; cf. Mark 2:25–28; Luke 6:3–5; see 1 Samuel 21:6).

[SACRIFICE from to give His life a ransom for many]
Setting: On the way to Jerusalem, where Jesus will die on the cross. Jesus teaches His disciples about true greatness after the mother of disciples James and John asks Him to make her sons exalted rulers with Him in His coming kingdom.

But Jesus called them to Himself and said, "You know that the rulers of the Gentiles lord it over them, and *their* great men exercise authority over them. It is not this way among you, but whoever wishes to become great among you shall be your servant, and whoever wishes to be first among you shall be your slave; just as the Son of Man did not come to be served, but to serve, and to give His life a ransom for many" (Matthew 20:25–28; cf. Matthew 23:11; Matthew 26:28; Mark 10:42–45).

[SACRIFICE from and to give His life a ransom for many]
Setting: On the road to Jerusalem. James and John ask Jesus for special honor and privileges in His kingdom. The other disciples become angry, so the Lord uses this moment to teach all of them about servanthood.

Calling them to Himself, Jesus said to them, "You know that those who are recognized as rulers of the Gentiles lord it over them, and their great men exercise authority over them. But it is not this way among you, but whoever wishes to become great among you shall be your servant; and whoever wishes to be first among you shall be slave of all. For even the Son of Man did not come to be served, but to serve, and to give His life a ransom for many" (Mark 10:42–45; cf. Matthew 20:25–28).

SACRIFICE, PERSONAL (Also see COMMITMENT; DEVOTION; DISCIPLESHIP; FOLLOWING JESUS CHRIST; MITE, WIDOW'S; OBEDIENCE; REWARDS; and SELF-DENIAL)

[PERSONAL SACRIFICE inferred]
Setting: Galilee. After His twelve disciples observe His ministry, Jesus summons and specifically instructs them about their ministry ahead involving true discipleship.

"He who loves father or mother more than Me is not worthy of Me; and he who loves son or daughter more than Me is not worthy of Me. And he who does not take his cross and follow after Me is not worthy of Me. He who has found his life will lose it, and he who has lost his life for My sake will find it" (Matthew 10:37–39; cf. Matthew 16:24, 25).

[PERSONAL SACRIFICE from sell your possessions and give to the poor]
Setting: Judea beyond the Jordan (Perea). Jesus shares with a rich, young ruler how to obtain eternal life.

And He said to him, "Why are you asking Me about what is good? There is *only* One who is good; but if you wish to enter into life, keep the commandments." *Then* he said to Him, 'Which ones?' And Jesus said, "YOU SHALL NOT COMMIT MURDER; YOU SHALL NOT COMMIT ADULTERY; YOU SHALL NOT STEAL; YOU SHALL NOT BEAR FALSE WITNESS; HONOR YOUR FATHER AND MOTHER; and YOU SHALL LOVE YOUR NEIGHBOR AS YOURSELF." The young man said to Him, "All these things I have kept; what am I still lacking?" Jesus said to him, "If you wish to complete go *and* sell your possessions and give to *the* poor, and you will have treasure in heaven; and come, follow Me" (Matthew 19:16–22, Jesus quotes from Exodus 20:13–15; Leviticus 19:18; cf. Leviticus 18:5; Mark 10:17–21; Luke 10:25–28; 12:33; 18:18–24).

[PERSONAL SACRIFICE from everyone who has left houses or brothers]
Setting: Judea beyond the Jordan (Perea). Jesus promises rewards to His disciples for their personal sacrifice and commitment to following Him.

And Jesus said to them, "Truly I say to you, that you who have followed Me, in the regeneration when the Son of Man will sit on His glorious throne, you also shall sit upon twelve thrones, judging the twelve tribes of Israel. And everyone who has left houses or brothers or sisters or father or mother or children or farms for My name's sake, will receive many times as much, and will inherit eternal life. But many *who* are first will be last; and *the* last, first" (Matthew 19:28–30; cf. Matthew 6:33; 20:15; Mark 10:29, 30; Luke 18:29, 30; 22:30).

[PERSONAL SACRIFICE from whoever wishes to become great among you shall be your servant]
Setting: On the way to Jerusalem, where Jesus will die on the cross. Jesus teaches His disciples about true greatness after the mother of disciples James and John asks Him to make her sons exalted rulers with Him in His coming kingdom.

But Jesus called them to Himself and said, "You know that the rulers of the Gentiles lord it over them, and *their* great men exercise authority over them. It is not this way among you, but whoever wishes to become great among you shall be your servant, and whoever wishes to be first among you shall be your slave; just as the Son of Man did not come to be served, but to serve, and to give His life a ransom for many" (Matthew 20:25–28; cf. Matthew 23:11; 26:28; Mark 10:42–45).

[PERSONAL SACRIFICE from no one who has left house or brothers]
Setting: Judea beyond the Jordan (Perea). After informing a rich man how righteous believers may have treasure in heaven, Jesus tells His disciples about the reward of those who sacrifice in this life to follow Him.

Jesus said, "Truly I say to you, there is no one who has left house or brothers or sisters or mother or father or children or farms, for My sake and for the gospel's sake, but that he will receive a hundred times as much now in the present age, houses and brothers and sisters and mothers and children and farms, along with persecutions; and in the age to come, eternal life. But many *who are* first will be last, and the last, first" (Mark 10:29–31; cf. Matthew 19:27–30; Luke 18:28–30; see Matthew 6:33).

[PERSONAL SACRIFICE from whoever wishes to become great among you shall be your servant]
Setting: On the road to Jerusalem. James and John ask Jesus for special honor and privileges in His kingdom. The other disciples become angry, so the Lord uses this moment to teach all of them about servanthood.

Calling them to Himself, Jesus said to them, "You know that those who are recognized as rulers of the Gentiles lord it over them; and their great men exercise authority over them. But it is not this way among you, but whoever wishes to become great among you shall be your servant; and whoever wishes to be first among you shall be slave of all. For even the Son of Man did not come to be served, but to serve, and to give His life a ransom for many" (Mark 10:42–45; cf. Matthew 20:25–28).

[PERSONAL SACRIFICE from out of her poverty, put in all she owned, all she had to live on]
Setting: Opposite the temple treasury in Jerusalem. Jesus focuses His disciples' attention on a widow's monetary sacrifice.

Calling His disciples to Him, He said to them, "Truly I say to you, this poor widow put in more than all the contributors to the treasury; for they all put in out of their surplus, but she, out of her poverty, put in all she owned, all she had to live on" (Mark 12:43, 44; cf. Luke 21:1–4).

[PERSONAL SACRIFICE from Sell your possessions and give to charity]
Setting: On the way from Galilee to Jerusalem. After giving a parable about riches and greed, Jesus challenges the crowd and His disciples concerning godly living.

"Sell your possessions and give to charity; make yourselves money belts which do not wear out, an unfailing treasure in heaven, where no thief comes near nor moth destroys. For where your treasure is, there your heart will be also" (Luke 12:33, 34; cf. Matthew 6:19–21; 19:21).

[PERSONAL SACRIFICE from none of you can be My disciple who does not give up all his possessions]
Setting: On the way from Galilee to Jerusalem. After responding to a guest's proclamation about the blessings of eating bread in the kingdom of God, Jesus presents to large crowds the demands of discipleship.

Now large crowds were going along with Him; and He turned and said to them, "If anyone comes to Me, and does not hate his own father and mother and wife and children and brothers and sisters, yes, and even his own life, he cannot be My disciple. Whoever does not carry his own cross and come after Me cannot be My disciple. For which one of you, when he wants to build a tower, does not first sit down and calculate the cost to see if he has enough to complete it? Otherwise, when he has laid a foundation and is not able to finish, all who observe it begin to ridicule him, saying, 'This man began to build and was not able to finish.' Or what king, when he sets out to meet another king in battle, will not first sit down and consider whether he is strong enough with ten thousand *men* to encounter the one coming against him with twenty thousand? Or else, while the other is still far away, he sends a delegation and asks for terms of peace. So then, none of you can be My disciple who does not give up all his possessions. Therefore, salt is good; but if even salt has become tasteless, with what will it be seasoned? It is useless either for the soil or for the manure pile; it is thrown out. He who has ears to hear, let him hear" (Luke 14:25–35; cf. Matthew 5:13; 10:37–39; see Proverb 20:18; Luke 14:1, 2; Philippians 3:7).

[PERSONAL SACRIFICE from no one who has left house or wife]
Setting: Perea, en route from Galilee to Jerusalem. After responding to His disciples' question about salvation, Jesus replies to Peter's statement about the disciples' personal sacrifice.

Peter said, "Behold, we have left our own *homes* and followed You." And He said to them, "Truly I say to you, there is no one who has left house or wife or brothers or parents or children, for the sake of the kingdom of God, who will not receive many times as much at this time and in the age to come, eternal life" (Luke 18:28–30; cf. Matthew 19:27–29; Mark 10:28–30; see Matthew 6:33; Luke 5:11).

[PERSONAL SACRIFICE from out of her poverty put in all that she had to live on]
Setting: The temple in Jerusalem. While ministering a few days before His crucifixion, after warning His disciples about the lifestyle of the scribes, Jesus points out a poor widow's sacrificial giving to the temple treasury.

And He said, "Truly I say to you, this poor widow put in more than all *of them;* for they all out of their surplus put into the offering; but she out of her poverty put in all that she had to live on" (Luke 21:3, 4; cf. Mark 12:41–44).

[PERSONAL SACRIFICE from Greater love has no one than this, that one lay down his life for his friends]
Setting: Jerusalem. Before the Passover, with His departure in mind, after explaining He is the vine and His disciples are the branches, Jesus commands the disciples to love one another.

"This is My commandment, that you love one another, just as I have loved you. Greater love has no one than this, that one lay down his life for his friends. You are My friends if you do what I command you. No longer do I call you slaves, for the slave does not know what his master is doing; but I have called you friends, for all things that I have heard from My Father I have made known to you. You did not choose Me but I chose you, and appointed you that you would go and bear fruit, and *that* your fruit would remain, so that whatever you ask of the Father in My name He may give to you. This I command you, that you love one another" (John 15:12–17; see Matthew 12:50; John 6:70; 8:26; 10:11; 13:34).

SADDUCEES (See ELDERS; PHARISEE; PHARISEES; SADDUCEES, LEAVEN OF THE PHARISEES AND THE; and SCRIBES)

SADDUCEES, LEAVEN OF THE PHARISEES AND THE
Setting: Across the Sea of Galilee from the district of Dalmanutha. Jesus warns His disciples about the teaching of some of the religious leaders of His time—the Pharisees and the Sadducees.

And Jesus said to them, "Watch out and beware of the leaven of the Pharisees and the Sadducees" (Matthew 16:6; cf. Matthew 16:12; Mark 8:15).

Setting: Across the Sea of Galilee from the district of Dalmanutha. Jesus repeats a warning to His disciples about the teaching of the religious leaders of His time—the Pharisees and the Sadducees.

But Jesus aware of this, said, "You men of little faith, why do you discuss among yourselves that you have no bread? Do you not yet understand or remember the five loaves of the five thousand and how many baskets full you picked up? Or the seven loaves of the four thousand, and how many large baskets full you picked up? How is it that you do not understand that I did not speak to you concerning bread? But beware of the leaven of the Pharisees and the Sadducees" (Matthew 16:8–11; cf. Matthew 14:17–21; Matthew 15:34–38; Mark 8:17–21).

SADNESS (See ANGUISH; DESPAIR; GRIEF; MOURNING; and WEEPING)

SAINTS, PERSEVERANCE OF THE (See ENDURANCE; PERSEVERANCE)

SAKE (Specifics such as SAKE, APPEARANCE'S; and SAKE, MY are separate entries; also see SAKES)
Setting: Galilee. Early in His ministry, Jesus presents the Beatitudes (part of the Sermon on the Mount) to His disciples and the gathered crowds from Galilee, Decapolis, Jerusalem, Judea, and beyond the Jordan.

"Blessed are those who have been persecuted for the sake of righteousness, for theirs is the kingdom of heaven" (Matthew 5:10; cf. Luke 6:22; 1 Peter 3:14; see Matthew 5:1; 13:35).

Setting: Galilee. Pharisees and scribes from Jerusalem accuse Jesus' disciples of disobeying tradition and the commandments.

And He answered and said to them, "Why do you yourselves transgress the commandment of God for the sake of tradition? For God said, 'HONOR YOUR FATHER AND MOTHER,' and, 'HE WHO SPEAKS EVIL OF FATHER OR MOTHER IS TO BE PUT TO DEATH.' But you say, 'Whoever says to *his* father or mother, "Whatever I have that would help you has been given *to God*," he is not to honor his father or mother.' And *by this* you invalidated the word of God for the sake of your tradition. You hypocrites, rightly did Isaiah prophesy of you: 'THIS PEOPLE HONORS ME WITH THEIR LIPS, BUT THEIR HEART IS FAR AWAY FROM ME. BUT IN VAIN DO THEY WORSHIP ME, TEACHING AS DOCTRINES THE PRECEPTS OF MEN'" (Matthew 15:3–9, Jesus quotes from Exodus 20:12, 21:17, Leviticus 20:9; Isaiah 29:13; cf. Mark 7:5–7; see Colossians 2:22).

Setting: Judea beyond the Jordan (Perea). After responding to the Pharisees' question about Moses' command regarding a certificate of divorce, Jesus answers the disciples' private question.

But He said to them, "Not all men *can* accept this statement, but *only* those to whom it has been given. For there are eunuchs who were born that way from their mother's womb; and there are eunuchs who were made eunuchs by men; and there are *also* eunuchs who made themselves eunuchs for the sake of the kingdom of heaven. He who is able to accept *this,* let him accept *it*" (Matthew 19:11, 12; cf. 1 Corinthians 7:7).

Setting: The Mount of Olives, just east of Jerusalem. During His Olivet Discourse, Jesus answers His disciples' questions as to when the temple will be destroyed and Jerusalem overrun, along with the signs of His coming and the end of the age.

"Therefore when you see the ABOMINATION OF DESOLATION which was spoken of through Daniel the prophet, standing in the holy place (let the reader understand), then those who are in Judea must flee to the mountains. Whoever is on the housetop must not go down to get the things that are in his house. Whoever is in the field must not turn back to get his cloak. But woe to those who are pregnant and to those who are nursing babies in those days! But pray that your flight will not be in the winter, or on a Sabbath. For then there will be a great tribulation, such as has not occurred since the beginning of the world until now, nor ever will. Unless those days had been cut short, no life would have been saved; but for the sake of the elect those days will be cut short. Then if anyone says to you, 'Behold, here is the Christ,' or "There *He is,*' do not believe *him.* For false Christs and false prophets will arise and will show great signs and wonders, so as to mislead, if possible, even the elect. Behold, I have told you in advance. So if they say to you, 'Behold, He is in the wilderness,' do not go out, *or,* 'Behold, He is in the inner rooms,' do not believe *them.* For just as the lightning comes from the east and flashes even to the west, so will the coming of the Son of Man be. Wherever the corpse is, there the vultures will gather" (Matthew 24:15–28, Jesus quotes from Daniel 9:27; cf. Daniel 12:1; Mark 13:14–23; Luke 17:22–31; 21:20–24; 23:29; see John 4:48).

Setting: On the Mount of Olives, east of the temple in Jerusalem. After prophesying the temple's destruction, Jesus responds during His Olivet Discourse to questions from Peter, James, John, and Andrew about other future events.

"But when you see the ABOMINATION OF DESOLATION standing where it should not be (let the reader understand), then those who are in Judea must flee to the mountains. The one who is on the housetop must not go down, or go in to get anything out of his house; and the one who is in the field must not turn back to get his coat. But woe to those who are pregnant and to those who are nursing babies in those days! But pray that it may not happen in winter. For those days will be a *time of* tribulation such as has not occurred since the beginning of the creation which God created until now, and never will. Unless the Lord had shortened *those* days, no life would have been saved; but for the sake of the elect, whom He chose, He shortened the days. And then if anyone says to you, 'Behold, here is the Christ'; or, 'Behold, *He is* there'; do not believe *him*; for false Christs and false prophets will arise, and will show signs and wonders, in order to lead astray, if possible, the elect. But take heed; behold, I have told you everything in advance" (Mark 13:14–23; cf. Matthew 24:15–28; Luke 21:20–24; see Daniel 9:27; 12:1; Luke 17:31).

Setting: Perea, en route from Galilee to Jerusalem. After responding to His disciples' question about salvation, Jesus replies to Peter's statement about the disciples' personal sacrifice.

Peter said, "Behold, we have left our own *homes* and followed You." And He said to them, "Truly I say to you, there is no one who has left house or wife or brothers or parents or children, for the sake of the kingdom of God, who will not receive many times as much at this time and in the age to come, eternal life" (Luke 18:28–30; cf. Matthew 19:27–29; Mark 10:28–30; see Matthew 6:33; Luke 5:11).

SAKE, APPEARANCE'S

Setting: The temple in Jerusalem. After commending one scribe for his nearness to the kingdom of God, Jesus warns the crowd about the rest of the scribes.

In His teaching He was saying: "Beware of the scribes who like to walk around in long robes, and *like* respectful greetings in the market places, and chief seats in the synagogues and places of honor at banquets, who devour widows' houses, and for appearance's sake offer long prayers; these will receive greater condemnation" (Mark 12:38–40; cf. Matthew 23:1–7; Luke 20:45–47).

Setting: The temple in Jerusalem. While ministering a few days before His crucifixion, after posing a question to the scribes, who do not answer, Jesus warns His disciples about the lifestyle of the scribes.

"Beware of the scribes, who like to walk around in long robes, and love respectful greetings in the market places, and chief seats in the synagogues and places of honor at banquets, who devour widows' houses, and for appearance's sake offer long prayers. These will receive greater condemnation" (Luke 20:46, 47; cf. Matthew 23:1–7; Mark 12:38–40; see Luke 11:43).

SAKE, CHRIST'S (See SAKE, MY)

SAKE, GOSPEL'S (Also see ALLEGIANCE; COMMITMENT; DEVOTION; FOLLOWING JESUS CHRIST; REWARDS; SACRIFICE, PERSONAL; and SAKE, MY)

[GOSPEL'S SAKE from My sake and the gospel's]

Setting: Caesarea Philippi. After rebuking Peter for desiring to thwart His mission to the cross, Jesus summons a crowd, along with His disciples, and informs them of the high costs of following Him.

And He summoned the crowd with His disciples, and said to them, "If anyone wishes to come after Me, he must deny himself, and take up his cross and follow Me. For whoever wishes to save his life will lose it, but whoever loses his life for My sake and the gospel's will save it. For what does it profit a man to gain the whole world, and forfeit his soul? For what will a man give in exchange for his soul? For whoever is ashamed of Me and My words in this adulterous and sinful generation, the Son of Man will also be ashamed of him when He comes in the glory of His Father with the holy angels" (Mark 8:34–38; cf. Matthew 16:24–28; Luke 9:23–27; see Matthew 10:33, 38, 39).

Setting: Judea beyond the Jordan (Perea). After informing a rich man how righteous believers may have treasure in heaven, Jesus tells His disciples about the reward of those who sacrifice in this life to follow Him.

Jesus said, "Truly I say to you, there is no one who has left house or brothers or sisters or mother or father or children or farms, for My sake and for the gospel's sake, but that he will receive a hundred times as much now in the present age, houses and brothers and sisters and mothers and children and farms, along with persecutions; and in the age to come, eternal life. But many *who are* first will be last, and the last, first" (Mark 10:29–31; cf. Matthew 19:27–30; Luke 18:28–30; see Matthew 6:33).

SAKE, JESUS' (See SAKE, MY)

SAKE, JESUS' NAME'S (See SAKE, MY NAME'S)

SAKE, MY (Also see COMMITMENT; DEVOTION; FOLLOWING JESUS CHRIST; REWARDS; SACRIFICE, PERSONAL; and SAKE, GOSPEL'S)

Setting: Galilee. After His disciples observe His ministry, Jesus summons and specifically instructs them about the upcoming hardships of their ministry to the people of Israel.

"Behold, I send you out as sheep in the midst of wolves; so be shrewd as serpents and innocent as doves. But beware of men, for they will hand you over to *the* courts and scourge you in their synagogues; and you will even be brought before governors and kings for My sake, as a testimony to them and to the Gentiles. But when they hand you over, do not worry about how or what you are to say; for it will be given you in that hour what you are to say. For it is not you who speak, but *it* is the Spirit of your Father who speaks in you" (Matthew 10:16–20; cf. Luke 10:3).

Setting: Galilee. After His twelve disciples observe His ministry, Jesus summons and specifically instructs them about their ministry ahead involving true discipleship.

"He who loves father or mother more than Me is not worthy of Me; and he who loves son or daughter more than Me is not worthy of Me. And he who does not take his cross and follow after Me is not worthy of Me. He who has found his life will lose it, and he who has lost his life for My sake will find it" (Matthew 10:37–39; cf. Matthew 16:24, 25).

Setting: Near Caesarea Philippi. After rebuking Peter for trying to forbid Him to accomplish His earthly mission of dying and being resurrected, Jesus teaches His disciples about the costs of following Him.

Then Jesus said to His disciples, "If anyone wishes to come after Me, he must deny himself, and take up his cross and follow Me. For whoever wishes to save his life will lose it; but whoever loses his life for My sake will find it. For what will it profit a man if he gains the whole world and forfeits his soul? Or what will a man give in exchange for his soul? For the Son of Man is going to come in the glory of His Father with His angels, and WILL THEN REPAY EVERY MAN ACCORDING TO HIS DEEDS. Truly, I say to you, there are some of you who are standing here who will not taste death until they see the Son of Man coming in His kingdom" (Matthew 16:24–28, Jesus quotes from Psalm 62:12; cf. Mark 8:34–37; Luke 9:23–27; see Matthew 10:38, 39).

Setting: Caesarea Philippi. After rebuking Peter for desiring to thwart His mission to the cross, Jesus summons a crowd, along with His disciples, and informs them of the high costs of following Him.

And He summoned the crowd with His disciples, and said to them, "If anyone wishes to come after Me, he must deny himself, and take up his cross and follow Me. For whoever wishes to save his life will lose it, but whoever loses his life for My sake and the gospel's will save it. For what does it profit a man to gain the whole world, and forfeit his soul? For what will a man give in exchange for his soul? For whoever is ashamed of Me and My words in this adulterous and sinful generation, the Son of Man will also be ashamed of him when He comes in the glory of His Father with the holy angels" (Mark 8:34–38; cf. Matthew 16:24–28; Luke 9:23–27; see Matthew 10:33, 38, 39).

Setting: Judea beyond the Jordan (Perea). After informing a rich man how righteous believers may have treasure in heaven, Jesus tells His disciples about the reward of those who sacrifice in this life to follow Him.

Jesus said, "Truly I say to you, there is no one who has left house or brothers or sisters or mother or father or children or farms, for My sake and for the gospel's sake, but that he will receive a hundred times as much now in the present age, houses and brothers and sisters and mothers and children and farms, along with persecutions; and in the age to come, eternal life. But many *who are* first will be last, and the last, first" (Mark 10:29–31; cf. Matthew 19:27–30; Luke 18:28–30; see Matthew 6:33).

Setting: On the Mount of Olives, east of the temple in Jerusalem. After prophesying the temple's destruction, Jesus responds during His Olivet Discourse to questions from Peter, James, John, and Andrew about other future events.

And Jesus began to say to them, "See to it that no one misleads you. Many will come in My name, saying, 'I am *He!*' and will mislead many. When you hear of wars and rumors of wars, do not be frightened; *those things* must take place; but *that is* not yet the end. For nation will rise up against nation, and kingdom against kingdom; there will be earthquakes in various places; there will *also be* famines. These things are *merely* the beginning of birth pangs. But be on your guard; for they will deliver you to *the* courts, and you will be flogged in *the* synagogues, and you will stand before governors and kings for My sake, as a testimony to them. The gospel must first be preached to all the nations. When they arrest you and hand you over, do not worry beforehand about what you are to say, but say whatever is given you in that hour; for it is not you who speak, but *it is* the Holy Spirit. Brother will betray brother to death, and a father *his* child; and children will rise up against parents and have them put to death. You will be hated by all because of My name, but the one who endures to the end, he will be saved" (Mark 13:5–13; cf. Matthew 24:4–14; Luke 21:7–19; see Matthew 10:17–22).

[MY SAKE from sake of the Son of Man]

Setting: Galilee. After selecting His twelve disciples, Jesus teaches the Beatitudes (part of the Sermon on the Mount) to those disciples and a great throng of people from Judea, Jerusalem, and the central coastal region of Tyre and Sidon.

"Blessed are you when men hate you, and ostracize you, and insult you, and scorn your name as evil, for the sake of the Son of Man. Be glad in that day and leap *for joy*, for behold, your reward is great in heaven. For in the same way their fathers used to treat the prophets" (Luke 6:22, 23; cf. Matthew 5:10–12; see 2 Chronicles 36:16; Luke 6:12–19).

Setting: Galilee. Following Peter's pronouncement that Jesus is the Christ of God, the Lord conveys the demands of discipleship and the hope regarding the kingdom of God.

And He was saying to *them* all, "If anyone wishes to come after Me, he must deny himself, and take up his cross daily and follow Me. For whoever wishes to save his life will lose it, but whoever loses his life for My sake, he is the one who will save it. For what is a man profited if he gains the whole world, and loses or forfeits himself? For whoever is ashamed of Me and My words, the Son of Man will be ashamed of him when He comes in His glory, and *the glory* of the Father and of the holy angels. But I say to you truthfully, there are some of those standing here who will not taste death until they see the kingdom of God" (Luke 9:23–27; cf. Matthew 16:24–26, 28; Mark 8:34–37; see Matthew 10:33, 38, 39).

Setting: Jerusalem. Just days before the Passover, with the chief priests and Pharisees plotting to seize Him and crowds welcoming Him with palm branches and praise, Jesus expresses anxiety about His upcoming crucifixion.

"Now My soul has become troubled; and what shall I say, 'Father, save Me from this hour'? But for this purpose I came to this hour. Father glorify Your name." Then a voice came out of heaven: "I have glorified it, and will glorify it again." So the crowd *of people* who stood by and heard it were saying that it had thundered; others were saying, "An angel has spoken to Him." Jesus answered and said, "This voice has not come for My sake, but for your sakes. Now judgment is upon this world; now the ruler of this world will be cast out. And I, if I am lifted up from the earth, will draw all men to Myself" (John 12:27–32; see Matthew 3:17; 26:38; John 3:14; 6:44; 11:42; 14:30).

SAKE, MY NAME'S

Setting: Judea beyond the Jordan (Perea). Jesus promises rewards to His disciples for their personal sacrifice and commitment to following Him.

And Jesus said to them, "Truly I say to you, that you who have followed Me, in the regeneration when the Son of Man will sit on His glorious throne, you also shall sit upon twelve thrones, judging the twelve tribes of Israel. And everyone who has left houses or brothers or sisters or father or mother or children or farms for My name's sake, will receive many times as much, and will inherit eternal life. But many *who* are first will be last; and *the* last, first" (Matthew 19:28–30; cf. Matthew 6:33; 20:15; Mark 10:29, 30; Luke 18:29, 30; 22:30).

Setting: On the Mount of Olives, east of the temple in Jerusalem. After ministering in the temple a few days before His crucifixion, and giving His disciples more details regarding the temple's future destruction, Jesus elaborates during His Olivet Discourse about things to come.

Then He continued by saying to them, "Nation will rise against nation and kingdom against kingdom, and there will be great earthquakes, and in various places plagues and famines; and there will be terrors and great signs from heaven. But before all these things, they will lay their hands on you and will persecute you, delivering you to the synagogues and prisons, bringing you before kings and governors for My name's sake. It will lead to an opportunity for your testimony. So make up your minds not to prepare beforehand to defend yourselves; for I will give you utterance and wisdom which none of your opponents will be able to resist or refute. But you will be betrayed even by parents and brothers and relatives and friends, and they will put *some* of you to death, and you will be hated by all because of My name. Yet not a hair of your head will perish. By your endurance you will gain your lives" (Luke 21:10–19; cf. Matthew 10:19–22; 24:7–14; Mark 13:8–13).

Setting: Jerusalem. Before the Passover, with His departure in mind, after explaining He is the vine and His disciples are the branches, Jesus prepares them for persecution from the world.

"If the world hates you, you know that it has hated Me before *it hated* you. If you were of the world, the world would love its own; but because you are not of the world, but I chose you out of the world, because of this the world hates you. Remember the word that I said to you, 'A slave is not greater than his master.' If they persecuted Me, they will also persecute you; if they kept My word, they will keep yours also. But all these things they will do to you for My name's sake, because they do not know the One who sent Me. If I had not come and spoken to them, they would not have sin, but now they have no excuse for their sin" (John 15:18–22; see Matthew 10:22; John 7:7; 8:19, 55; 9:41; 1 Corinthians 4:12).

Setting: Damascus. Luke, writing in Acts, details the reluctance of Ananias, one of Jesus' followers, to locate Saul of Tarsus (a known enemy of the church), in order to restore Saul's vision.

But the Lord said to him, "Go, for he is a chosen instrument of Mine, to bear My name before the Gentiles and kings and the sons of Israel; for I will show him how much he must suffer for My name's sake" (Acts 9:15, 16; see Acts 13:2; 20:22–24).

Setting: On the island of Patmos (in the Aegean Sea about fifty miles southwest of Ephesus in modern Turkey). On the Lord's Day (Sunday), approximately fifty years after the Resurrection, the disciple John encounters the Lord Jesus Christ, who communicates a new revelation for the apostle to record for the church in Ephesus and to six other churches in Asia.

"To the angel of the church in Ephesus write: The One who holds the seven stars in His right hand, the One who walks among the seven golden lampstands, says this: 'I know your deeds and your toil and perseverance, and that you cannot tolerate evil men, and you put to the test those who call themselves apostles, and they are not, and you found them *to be* false; and you have perseverance and have endured for My name's sake, and have not grown weary. But I have *this* against you, that you have left your first love. Therefore remember from where you have fallen, and repent and do the deeds you did at first; or else I am coming to you and will remove your lampstand out of its place—unless you repent. Yet this you do have, that you hate the deeds of the Nicolaitans, which I also hate. He who has an ear, let him hear what the Spirit says to the churches. To him who overcomes, I will grant to eat of the tree of life which is in the Paradise of God' (Revelation 2:1–7; see Genesis 2:9; Ezekiel 28:13; 1 John 4:1; Revelation 1:10, 11, 19, 20).

SAKE OF THE ELECT (See ELECT)

SAKES (Also see SAKE)

Setting: Beyond the Jordan. While He and His disciples are avoiding the Jerusalem Pharisees, Jesus communicates Lazarus's death in Bethany to His disciples and decides to go there.

So Jesus then said to them plainly, "Lazarus is dead, and I am glad for your sakes that I was not there, so that you may believe; but let us go to him" (John 11:14, 15).

Setting: Jerusalem. Just days before the Passover, with the chief priests and Pharisees plotting to seize Him and crowds welcoming Him with palm branches and praise, Jesus expresses anxiety about His upcoming crucifixion.

"Now My soul has become troubled; and what shall I say, 'Father, save Me from this hour'? But for this purpose I came to this hour. Father glorify Your name." Then a voice came out of heaven: "I have glorified it, and will glorify it again." So the crowd *of people* who stood by and heard it were saying that it had thundered; others were saying, "An angel has spoken to Him." Jesus answered and said, "This voice has not come for My sake, but for your sakes. Now judgment is upon this world; now the ruler of this world will be cast out. And I, if I am lifted up from the earth, will draw all men to Myself" (John 12:27–32; see Matthew 3:17; 26:38; John 3:14; 6:44; 11:42; 14:30).

Setting: Jerusalem. Before the Passover, after giving His disciples assurance that in the midst of tribulation they will have His peace, Jesus continues praying His high-priestly prayer.

"But now I come to You; and these things I speak in the world so that they may have My joy made full in themselves. I have given them Your word; and the world has hated them, because they are not of the world, even as I am not of the world. I do not ask You to take them out of the world, but to keep them from the evil *one.* They are not of the world, even as I am not of the world. Sanctify them in the truth; Your word is truth. As You sent Me into the world, I also have sent them into the world. For their sakes I sanctify Myself, that they themselves also may be sanctified in truth. I do not ask on behalf of these alone, but for those also who believe in Me through their word; that they may all be one; even as You, Father, *are* in Me and I in You, that they also maybe in Us, so that the world may believe that You sent Me" (John 17:13–21; see Matthew 10:5, 38; John 7:33; 15:3, 11, 19).

SALIVA (See SPIT)

SALT

Setting: Galilee. During the early part of His ministry, Jesus preaches the Sermon on the Mount to His disciples and the multitudes.

"You are the salt of the earth; but if the salt has become tasteless, how can it be made salty *again*? It is not longer good for anything, except to be thrown out and trampled under foot by men" (Matthew 5:13; cf. Mark 9:50).

Setting: Capernaum of Galilee. As Jesus teaches His disciples in private, they ask Him about greatness.

But Jesus said, "Do not hinder him, for there is no one who will perform a miracle in My name, and be able soon afterward to speak evil of Me. For he who is not against us is for us. For whoever gives you a cup of water to drink because of your name as *followers* of Christ, truly I say to you, he will not lose his reward. Whoever causes one of these little ones who believe to stumble, it would be better for him if, with a heavy millstone hung around his neck, he had been cast into the sea. If your hand causes you to stumble, cut it off; it is better for you to enter life crippled, than, having your two hands, to go into hell, into the unquenchable fire, [where THEIR WORM DOES NOT DIE, AND THE FIRE IS NOT QUENCHED.] If your foot causes you to stumble, cut it off; it is better for you to enter life lame, than, having your two feet, to be cast into hell, [where THEIR WORM DOES NOT DIE, AND THE FIRE IS NOT QUENCHED.] If your eye causes you to stumble, throw it out; it is better for you to enter the kingdom of God with one eye, than, having two eyes, to be cast into hell, where THEIR WORM DOES NOT DIE, AND THE FIRE IS NOT QUENCHED. For everyone will be salted with fire. Salt is good; but if the salt becomes unsalty, with what will you make it salty *again?* Have salt in yourselves, and be at peace with one another" (Mark 9:39–50; Jesus quotes from Isaiah 66:24; cf. Matthew 18:6–9; Luke 9:49, 50; see Matthew 5:13, 29, 30; 10:42; 12:30; 18:5, 6).

Setting: On the way from Galilee to Jerusalem. After responding to a guest's proclamation about the blessings of eating bread in the kingdom of God, Jesus presents to large crowds the demands of discipleship.

Now large crowds were going along with Him; and He turned and said to them, "If anyone comes to Me, and does not hate his own father and mother and wife and children and brothers and sisters, yes, and even his own life, he cannot be My disciple. Whoever does not carry his own cross and come after Me cannot be My disciple. For which one of you, when he wants to build a tower, does not first sit down and calculate the cost to see if he has enough to complete it? Otherwise, when he has laid a foundation and is not able to finish, all who observe it begin to ridicule him, saying, 'This man began to build and was not able to finish.' Or what king, when he sets out to meet another king in battle, will not first sit down and consider whether he is strong enough with ten thousand *men* to encounter the one coming against him with twenty thousand? Or else, while the other is still far away, he sends a delegation and asks for terms of peace. So then, none of you can be My disciple who does not give up all his possessions. Therefore, salt is good; but if even salt has become tasteless, with what will it be seasoned? It is useless either for the soil or for the manure pile; it is thrown out. He who has ears to hear, let him hear" (Luke 14:25–35; cf. Matthew 5:13; 10:37–39; see Proverb 20:18; Philippians 3:7).

SALVATION (Also see BELIEF; BORN AGAIN; ETERNAL LIFE; FAITH; GOSPEL; JESUS' PURPOSE; KINGDOM OF GOD; KINGDOM OF HEAVEN; REPENTANCE; and SAVE/SAVED)

[SALVATION from the way is narrow that leads to life, and there are few who find it]
Setting: Galilee. During the early part of His ministry, Jesus preaches the Sermon on the Mount to His disciples and the multitudes.

"Enter through the narrow gate; for the gate is wide and the way is broad that leads to destruction, and there are many who enter through it. For the gate is small and the way is narrow that leads to life, and there are few who find it" (Matthew 7:13, 14; cf. Luke 13:24).

[SALVATION from he who does the will of My Father who is in heaven *will enter*]
Setting: Galilee. During the early part of His ministry, Jesus preaches the Sermon on the Mount to His disciples and the multitudes.

"Not everyone who says to Me, 'Lord, Lord,' will enter the kingdom of heaven, but he who does the will of My Father who is in heaven *will enter.* Many will say to Me on that day, 'Lord, Lord, did we not prophesy in Your name, and in Your name cast out demons, and in Your name perform many miracles?' And then I will declare to them, 'I never knew you, DEPART FROM ME, YOU WHO PRACTICE LAWLESSNESS'" (Matthew 7:21–23, Jesus quotes from Psalm 6:8; cf. Matthew 25:11–13; see Luke 6:46).

[SALVATION from many will come from east and west, and recline *at the table* with Abraham, Isaac and Jacob in the kingdom of heaven]
Setting: Entering Capernaum. After the Lord gives the Sermon on the Mount and cleanses a leper, a Roman centurion implores Jesus to heal his servant.

Now when Jesus heard *this,* He marveled, and said to those who were following, "Truly I say to you, I have not found such great faith with anyone in Israel. I say to you that many will come from east and west, and recline *at the table* with Abraham, Isaac and Jacob in the kingdom of heaven; but the sons of the kingdom will be cast out into the outer darkness; in that place there will be weeping and gnashing of teeth." And Jesus said to the centurion, "Go; it shall be done for you as you have believed." And the servant was healed that *very* moment (Matthew 8:10–13; cf. Luke 7:9, 10).

[SALVATION from the Son of Man has come to save]
Setting: Capernaum of Galilee. After conveying the value of little ones after His disciples ask Him about greatness in the kingdom of heaven, Jesus states His earthly mission.

["For the Son of Man has come to save that which was lost"] (Matthew 18:11; cf. Luke 19:10).

[SALVATION from it is hard for a rich man to enter the kingdom of heaven]
Setting: Judea beyond the Jordan (Perea). Jesus comments to His disciples about the rich, young ruler who asks how to obtain eternal life but rejects Jesus' instruction to sell his possessions and give the proceeds to the poor.

And Jesus said to His disciples, "Truly I say to you, it is hard for a rich man to enter the kingdom of heaven. Again, I say to you, it is easier for a camel to go through the eye of a needle, than for a rich man to enter the kingdom of God" (Matthew 19:23, 24; cf. Matthew 13:22; Mark 10:23–25; Luke 18:24).

[SALVATION from It is easier for a camel to go through the eye of a needle than for a rich man to enter the kingdom of God]
Setting: Judea beyond the Jordan (Perea). After informing a rich man how righteous believers may have treasure in heaven, Jesus conveys to His disciples the difficulty the wealthy have entering the kingdom of God.

And Jesus, looking around, said to His disciples, "How hard it will be for those who are wealthy to enter the kingdom of God!" The disciples were amazed at His words. But Jesus answered again and said to them, "Children, how hard it is to enter the kingdom of God! It is easier for a camel to go through the eye of a needle than for a rich man to enter the kingdom of God." They were even more astonished and said to Him, "Then who can be saved?" Looking at them, Jesus said, "With people it is impossible, but not with God; for all things are possible with God" (Mark 10:23–27; cf. Matthew 19:23–26; Luke 18:24, 25).

[SALVATION from Your sins have been forgiven]
Setting: Galilee. After Jesus praises John the Baptist to the crowds, Simon, a Pharisee, invites the Lord to dinner. A sinful woman anoints His feet with perfume, prompting Him to instruct His host about forgiveness.

Turning toward the woman, He said to Simon, "Do you see this woman? I entered your house; you gave Me no water for My feet, but she has wet My feet with her tears and wiped them with her hair. You gave Me no kiss; but she, since the time I came in, has not ceased to kiss My feet. You did not anoint My head with oil, but she anointed My feet with perfume. For this reason I say to you, her sins, which are many, have been forgiven, for she loved much; but he who is forgiven little, loves little." Then He said to her, "Your sins have been forgiven." Those who were reclining *at the table* with Him began to say to themselves, "Who is this *man* who even forgives sins?" And He said to the woman, "Your faith has saved you; go in peace" (Luke 7:44–50; see Matthew 9:2; Mark 5:34; Luke 5:21).

[SALVATION from be saved]
Setting: Galilee. After Jesus presents the Parable of the Sower to the crowds, His disciples ask Him to give them the parable's meaning.

And He said, "To you it has been granted to know the mysteries of the kingdom of God, but to the rest *it is* in parables, so that SEEING THEY MAY NOT SEE, AND HEARING THEY MAY NOT UNDERSTAND. Now the parable is this: the seed is the word of God. Those beside the road are those who have heard; then the devil comes and takes away the word from their heart, so that they will not believe and be saved. Those on the rocky *soil* are those who, when they hear, receive the word with joy; and these have no *firm* root; they believe for a while, and in time of temptation fall away. The *seed* which fell among the thorns, these are the ones who have heard, and as they go on their way they are choked with worries and riches and pleasures of *this* life, and bring no fruit to maturity. But the *seed* in the good soil, these are the ones who have heard the word in an honest and good heart, and hold it fast, and bear fruit with perseverance" (Luke 8:10–15, Jesus quotes from Isaiah 6:9; cf. Matthew 13:10–23; Mark 4:10–20).

[SALVATION from the Son of Man did not come to destroy men's lives, but to save them]
Setting: Galilee. After clarifying who the disciples' co-laborers are, Jesus prepares to go to Jerusalem by sending messengers ahead to Samaria, where they experience rejection and seek retribution.

But He turned and rebuked them, [and said, "You do not know what kind of spirit you are of; for the Son of Man did not come to destroy men's lives, but to save them."] And they went on to another village (Luke 9:55, 56; see 2 Kings 1:9–14; Luke 13:22).

[SALVATION from And they will come from east and west and from north and south, and will recline *at the table* in the kingdom of God.]
Setting: On the way from Galilee to Jerusalem. While teaching in the cities and villages, Jesus responds to a question about who is saved.

And someone said to Him, "Lord, are here *just* a few who are being saved?" And He said to them, "Strive to enter through the narrow door; for many, I tell you, will seek to enter and will not be able. Once the head of the house gets up and shuts the door, and you begin to stand outside and knock on the door, saying, 'Lord, open up to us!' then He will answer and say to you, 'I do not know where you are from.' Then you will begin to say, 'We ate and drank in Your presence, and You taught in our streets'; and He will say, 'I tell you, I do not know where you are from; DEPART FROM ME, ALL YOU EVILDOERS.' In that place there will be weeping and gnashing of teeth when you see Abraham and Isaac and Jacob and all the prophets in the kingdom of God, but you yourselves being thrown out. And they will come from east and west and from north and south, and will recline *at the table* in the kingdom of God. And behold, *some* are last who will be first and *some* are first who will be last" (Luke 13:23–30, Jesus quotes from Psalm 6:8; cf. Matthew 7:13, 23; 8:11, 12; see Matthew 19:30; Luke 3:8).

[SALVATION from How hard it is for those who are wealthy to enter the kingdom of God]
Setting: Perea, en route from Galilee to Jerusalem. After responding to a ruler's question about inheriting eternal life, Jesus comments to him about the challenge of being wealthy and saved.

And Jesus looked at him and said, "How hard it is for those who are wealthy to enter the kingdom of God! For it is easier for a camel to go through the eye of a needle than for a rich man to enter the kingdom of God" (Luke 18:24, 25; cf. Matthew 19:23, 24; Mark 10:25).

Setting: Jericho, on the way to Jerusalem. After taking time to heal a blind man, Jesus comments on Zaccheus's response to Him.

And Jesus said to him, "Today salvation has come to this house, because he, too, is a son of Abraham. For the Son of Man has come to seek and to save that which was lost" (Luke 19:9, 10; cf. Matthew 18:11).

[SALVATION from born again]
Setting: Jerusalem. At the time for the Passover of the Jews, after the Lord cleanses the temple, a Pharisee, Nicodemus, comes to Jesus by night to converse with Him.

Jesus answered and said to him, "Truly, truly, I say to you, unless one is born again he cannot see the kingdom of God" (John 3:3; see John 3:1, 2; 2 Corinthians 5:17).

[SALVATION from You must be born again]
Setting: Jerusalem. At the time for the Passover of the Jews, after the Lord cleanses the temple, a Pharisee, Nicodemus, asks Him by night the meaning of "born again."

Jesus answered, "Truly, truly, I say to you, unless one is born of water and the Spirit he cannot enter into the kingdom of God. That which is born of the flesh is flesh, and that which is born of the Spirit is spirit. Do not be amazed that I said to you, 'You must be born again.' The wind blows where it wishes and you hear the sound of it, but do not know where it comes from and where it is going; so is everyone who is born of the Spirit" (John 3:5–8; see Psalm 135:7; John 1:13).

[SALVATION from whoever believes will in Him have eternal life]
Setting: Jerusalem. At the time for the Passover of the Jews, after the Lord cleanses the temple, a Pharisee, Nicodemus, asks Him by night the meaning of "born of the Spirit."

Jesus answered and said to him, "Are you the teacher of Israel and do not understand these things? Truly, truly, I say to you, we speak of what we know and testify of what we have seen, and you do not accept our testimony. If I told you earthly things and you do not believe, how will you believe if I tell you heavenly things? No one has ascended into heaven, but He who descended from heaven: the Son of Man. As Moses lifted up the serpent in the wilderness, even so must the Son of Man be lifted up; so that whoever believes will in Him have eternal life" (John 3:10–15; see Numbers 21:9; Proverb 30:4; John 12:34; 20:30, 31).

[SALVATION from whoever believes in Him shall not perish, but have eternal life]
Setting: Jerusalem. At the time for the Passover of the Jews, after the Lord cleanses the temple, a Pharisee, Nicodemus, asks Him by night the meaning of "born again."

"For God so loved the world, that He gave His only begotten Son, that whoever believes in Him shall not perish, but have eternal life. For God did not send the Son into the world to judge the world, but that the world might be saved through Him. He who believes in Him is not judged; he who does not believe has been judged already, because he has not believed in the name of the only begotten Son of God. This is the judgment, that the Light has come into the world, and men loved darkness rather than the Light, for their deeds were evil. For everyone who does evil hates the Light, and does not come to the Light for fear that his deeds will be exposed. But he who practices the truth comes to the Light, so that his deeds may be manifested as having been wrought in God" (John 3:16–21; see Luke 19:10; John 1:4; 1:18; Romans 5:8; 1 John 1:6, 7).

Setting: Sychar in Samaria, on the way to Galilee. Jesus interacts with a Samaritan woman at Jacob's well, while the disciples are buying food.

Jesus said to her, "Woman, believe Me, an hour is coming when neither in this mountain nor in Jerusalem will you worship the Father. You worship what you do not know; we worship what we know, for salvation is from the Jews. But an hour is coming, and now is, when the true worshipers will worship the Father in spirit and truth; for such people the Father seeks to be His worshipers. God is spirit, and those who worship Him must worship in spirit and truth" (John 4:21–24; see Isaiah 2:3; Philippians 3:3).

[SALVATION from everyone who beholds the Son and believes in Him will have eternal life]
Setting: Capernaum. The day after Jesus walks on the Sea of Galilee to join His disciples in a boat, the people He miraculously fed with a lad's five loaves and two fish ask the Lord to always give them this bread out of heaven.

Jesus said to them, "I am the bread of life; he who comes to Me will not hunger, and he who believes in Me will never thirst. But I said to you that you have seen Me, and yet do not believe. All that the Father gives Me will come to Me, and the one who comes to Me I will certainly not cast out. For I have come down from heaven, not to do My own will, but the will of Him who sent Me. This is the will of Him who sent Me, that of all that He has given Me I lose nothing, but raise it up on the last day. For this is the will of My Father, that everyone who beholds the Son and believes in Him will have eternal life, and I Myself will raise him up on the last day" (John 6:35–40; see John 3:13, 16; 4:13, 14).

[SALVATION from If anyone is thirsty, let him come to Me and drink]
Setting: Jerusalem. On the last day of the Feast of Booths, after causing discussion about whether He is the Christ, the chief priests and Pharisees attempt to understand where it is He says He will be going soon. Jesus offers salvation and the abundant life to His hearers.

Now on the last day, the great *day* of the feast, Jesus stood and cried out, saying, "If anyone is thirsty, let him come to Me and drink. He who believes in Me, as the Scripture said, 'From his innermost being will flow rivers of living water'" (John 7:37, 38).

[SALVATION from he who believes in Me will live even if he dies, and everyone who lives and believes in Me will never die]
Setting: Bethany near Jerusalem. Jesus travels with His disciples to Bethany in Judea to see Lazarus's sisters, Martha and Mary, after the death of His friend.

Jesus said to her, "Your brother will rise again." Martha said to Him, "I know that he will rise again in the resurrection on the last day." Jesus said to her, "I am the resurrection and the life; he who believes in Me will live even if he dies, and everyone who lives and believes in Me will never die. Do you believe this?" (John 11:23–26; see Daniel 12:2; John 1:4; 6:47–51).

[SALVATION from everyone who believes in Me will not remain in darkness]
Setting: Jerusalem. Just days before the Passover, with the chief priests and Pharisees plotting to seize Jesus, who is expressing anxiety about His upcoming crucifixion, some of the Jews believe in the Lord, while others are rejecting His message.

And Jesus cried out and said, "He who believes in Me, does not believe in Me but in Him who sent Me. He who sees Me sees the One who sent Me. I have come *as* Light into the world, so that everyone who believes in Me will not remain in darkness. If anyone hears My sayings and does not keep them, I do not judge him; for I did not come to judge the world, but to save the world. He who rejects Me and does not receive My sayings, has one who judges him; the word I spoke is what will judge him at the last day. For I did not speak on My own initiative, but the Father Himself who sent Me has given Me a commandment *as to* what to say and what to speak. I know that His commandment is eternal life; therefore the things I speak, I speak just as the Father as told Me" (John 12:44–50; see Matthew 10:40; Luke 10:16; John 1:4; 3:17; 5:19; 6:68; 14:9).

[SALVATION from no one comes to the Father but through Me]
Setting: Jerusalem. Before the Passover, as Jesus comforts and gives hope to His disciples regarding their future after He returns to heaven, Thomas asks where He is going and how they will know the way.

Jesus said to him, "I am the way, and the truth, and the life; no one comes to the Father but through Me. If you had known Me, you would have known My Father also; from now on you know Him, and have seen Him" (John 14:6, 7; see John 8:19; 10:9; 11:25).

SALVATION (deliverance)

[SALVATION from he will be saved]
Setting: The Mount of Olives, just east of Jerusalem. During His Olivet Discourse, Jesus answers His disciples' questions as to when the temple will be destroyed and Jerusalem overrun, along with the signs of His coming and the end of the age.

And Jesus answered and said to them, "See to it that no one misleads you. For many will come in My name, saying, 'I am the Christ,' and will mislead many. You will be hearing of wars and rumors of wars. See that you are not frightened, for *those things* must take place, but *that* is not yet the end. For nation will rise against nation, and kingdom against kingdom, and in various places there will be famines and earthquakes. But all these things are *merely* the beginning of birth pangs. Then they will deliver you to tribulation, and will kill you, and you will be hated by all nations because of My name. At that time many will fall away and will betray one another and hate one another. Many false prophets will arise and will mislead many. Because lawlessness is increased, most people's love will grow cold. But the one who endures to the end, he will be saved. This gospel of the kingdom shall be preached in the whole world as a testimony to all the nations, and then the end will come" (Matthew 24:4–14; cf. Jeremiah 29:8; Matthew 7:15; 0:17, 22; Mark 13:3–13; Luke 21:7–19; Revelation 6:4).

[SALVATION from he will be saved]
Setting: On the Mount of Olives, east of the temple in Jerusalem. After prophesying the temple's destruction, Jesus responds during His Olivet Discourse to questions from Peter, James, John, and Andrew about other future events.

And Jesus began to say to them, "See to it that no one misleads you. Many will come in My name, saying, 'I am *He!*' and will mislead many. When you hear of wars and rumors of wars, do not be frightened; *those things* must take place; but *that is* not yet the end. For nation will rise up against nation, and kingdom against kingdom; there will be earthquakes in various places; there will *also bc* famines. These things are *merely* the beginning of birth pangs. But be on your guard; for they will deliver you to *the* courts, and you will be flogged in *the* synagogues, and you will stand before governors and kings for My sake, as a testimony to them. The gospel must first be preached to all the nations. When they arrest you and hand you over, do not worry beforehand about what you are to say, but say whatever is given you in that hour; for it is not you who speak, but *it is* the Holy Spirit. Brother will betray brother to death, and a father *his* child; and children will rise up against parents and have them put to death. You will be hated by all because of My name, but the one who endures to the end, he will be saved" (Mark 13:5–13; cf. Matthew 24:4–14; Luke 21:7–19; see Matthew 10:17–22).

SALVATION, ILLUSTRATION OF

Setting: Judea beyond the Jordan (Perea). Jesus illustrates the kingdom of heaven to His disciples through the story of laborers in the vineyard.

"For the kingdom of heaven is like a landowner who went out early in the morning to hire laborers for his vineyard. When he had agreed with the laborers for a denarius for the day, he sent them into his vineyard. And he went out about the third hour and saw others standing idle in the market place; and to those he said, 'You also go into the vineyard, and whatever is right I will give you.' And *so* they went. Again he went out about the sixth and the ninth hour, and did the same thing. And about the eleventh *hour* he went out and found others standing *around;* and he said to them, 'Why have you been standing idle here all day long?' They said to him, 'Because no one hired us.' He said to them, 'You go into the vineyard too.' When evening came, the owner of the vineyard said to his foreman, 'Call the laborers and pay them their wages, beginning with the last *group* to the first.' When those *hired* about the eleventh hour came, each one received a denarius. When those *hired* first came, they thought that they would receive more; but each of them also received a denarius. When they received it, they grumbled at the landowner, saying, 'These last men have worked *only* one hour, and you have made them equal to us who have borne the burden and the scorching heat of the day.' But he answered and said to one of them, 'Friend, I am doing you no wrong; did you not agree with me for a denarius? Take what is yours and go, but I wish to give to this last man the same as to you. It is not lawful for me to do what I wish with what is my own? Or is your eye envious because I am generous?' So the last shall be first, and the first last" (Matthew 20:1–16; cf. Matthew 19:30).

SALVE, EYE

Setting: On the island of Patmos (in the Aegean Sea about fifty miles southwest of Ephesus in modern Turkey). On the Lord's Day (Sunday), approximately fifty years after the Resurrection, the disciple John encounters the Lord Jesus Christ, who communicates a new revelation for the apostle to record for the church in Laodicea and to six other churches in Asia.

"To the angel of the church in Laodicea write: The Amen, the faithful and true Witness, the Beginning of the creation of God, says this: 'I know your deeds, that you are neither cold nor hot; I wish that you were cold or hot. So because you are lukewarm, and neither hot nor cold, I will spit you out of My mouth. Because you say, "I am rich, and have become wealthy, and have need of nothing," and you do not know that you are wretched and miserable and poor and blind and naked, I advise you to buy from Me gold refined by fire so that you may become rich, and white garments so that you may clothe yourself, and *that* the shame of your nakedness will not be revealed; and eye salve to anoint your eyes so that you may see. Those whom I love, I reprove and discipline; therefore be zealous and repent. Behold, I stand at the door and knock; if anyone hears My voice and opens the door, I will come in to him and will dine with him, and he with Me. He who overcomes, I will grant to him to sit down with Me on My throne, as I also overcame and sat down with My Father on His throne. He who has an ear, let him hear what the Spirit says to the churches'" (Revelation 3:14–22; see Proverb 3:12; Hosea 12:8; John 14:23; 16:33).

SAMARIA (Also see SAMARITAN)

Setting: Jerusalem. Luke, writing in Acts, presents quotes from Jesus' post-resurrection appearances, in which He responds to His disciples' question of whether He is about to restore the kingdom to Israel.

He said to them, "It is not for you to know times or epochs which the Father has fixed by His own authority; but you will receive power when the Holy Spirit has come upon you; and you shall be My witnesses both in Jerusalem, and in all Judea and Samaria, and even to the remotest part of the earth" (Acts 1:7, 8; see Luke 24:48, 49; Acts 2:1–4).

SAMARITAN (Also see LOVE; NEIGHBOR; SAMARIA; and SAMARITANS)

Setting: On the way from Galilee to Jerusalem. While being tested by a lawyer, Jesus tells him the story of the good Samaritan.

Jesus replied and said, "A man was going down from Jerusalem to Jericho, and fell among robbers, and they stripped him and beat him, and went away leaving him half dead. And by chance a priest was going down on that road, and when he saw him, he passed by on the other side. Likewise a Levite also, when he came to the place and saw him, passed by on the other side. But a Samaritan, who was on a journey, came upon him; and when he saw him, he felt compassion, and came to him and bandaged up his wounds, pouring oil and wine on *them;* and he put him on his own beast, and brought him to an inn and took care of him. On the next day he took out two denarii and gave them to the innkeeper and said, 'Take care of him; and whatever more you spend, when I return I will repay you.' Which of these three do you think proved to be a neighbor to the man who fell into the robbers' *hands?*" And he said, "The one who showed mercy toward him." Then Jesus said to him, "Go and do the same" (Luke 10:30–37).

[SAMARITAN also from foreigner]
Setting: On the way from Galilee to Jerusalem. The Lord stops to heal ten lepers who ask for cleansing.

When He saw them, He said to them, "Go and show yourselves to the priests." And as they were going, they were cleansed. Now one of them, when he saw that he had been healed, turned back, glorifying God with a loud voice, and he fell on his face at His feet, giving thanks to Him. And he was a Samaritan. Then Jesus answered and said, "Were there not ten cleansed? But the nine—where are they? Was no one found who returned to give glory to God, except this foreigner?" And He said to him, "Stand up and go; your faith has made you well" (Luke 17:14–19; see Leviticus 14:1–32).

SAMARITAN, GOOD (See SAMARITAN, PARABLE OF THE GOOD)

SAMARITAN, PARABLE OF THE GOOD
[PARABLE OF THE GOOD SAMARITAN from Samaritan and he felt compassion]
Setting: On the way from Galilee to Jerusalem. While being tested by a lawyer, Jesus tells him the story of the good Samaritan.

Jesus replied and said, "A man was going down from Jerusalem to Jericho, and fell among robbers, and they stripped him and beat him, and went away leaving him half dead. And by chance a priest was going down on that road, and when he saw him, he passed by on the other side. Likewise a Levite also, when he came to the place and saw him, passed by on the other side. But a Samaritan, who was on a journey, came upon him; and when he saw him, he felt compassion, and came to him and bandaged up his wounds, pouring oil and wine on *them;* and he put him on his own beast, and brought him to an inn and took care of him. On the next day he took out two denarii and gave them to the innkeeper and said, 'Take care of him; and whatever more you spend, when I return I will repay you.' Which of these three do you think proved to be a neighbor to the man who fell into the robbers' *hands?*" And he said, "The one who showed mercy toward him." Then Jesus said to him, "Go and do the same" (Luke 10:30–37).

SAMARITANS (Also see SAMARITAN)
Setting: Galilee. After His twelve disciples observe His ministry, Jesus summons and specifically instructs them about their ministry to the people of Israel.

These twelve Jesus sent out after instructing them: "Do not go in *the* way of *the* Gentiles, and do not enter *any* city of the Samaritans; but rather go to the lost sheep of the house of Israel. And as you go, preach, saying, 'The kingdom of heaven is at hand.' Heal *the* sick, raise *the* dead, cleanse *the* lepers, cast out demons. Freely you received, freely give. Do not acquire gold, or silver, or copper for your money belts, or a bag for *your* journey, or even two coats, or sandals, or a staff; for the worker is worthy of his support. And whatever city or village you enter, inquire who is worthy in it, and stay at his house until you leave *that city.* As you enter the house, give it your greeting. If the house is worthy, give it your *blessing of* peace. But if it is not worthy, take back your *blessing of* peace. Whoever does not receive you, nor heed your words, as you go out of that house or that city, shake the dust off your feet. Truly I say to you, it will be more tolerable for *the* land of Sodom and Gomorrah in the day of judgment than for that city" (Matthew 10:5–15; cf. Mark 6:7–11; Luke 9:1–5; see Matthew 3:2; 11:22, 24; 15:24; Luke 22:35; 1 Corinthians 9:14).

SAME
Setting: Galilee. Early in His ministry, Jesus presents the Beatitudes (part of the Sermon on the Mount) to His disciples and the gathered crowds from Galilee, Decapolis, Jerusalem, Judea, and beyond the Jordan.

"Blessed are you when *people* insult you and persecute you, and falsely say all kinds of evil against you because of Me. Rejoice and be glad, for your reward in heaven is great; for in the same way they persecuted the prophets who were before you" (Matthew 5:11, 12; cf. 2 Chronicles 36:16; Luke 6:22, 23; 1 Peter 4:14; see Matthew 13:35).

Setting: Galilee. During the early part of His ministry, Jesus preaches the Sermon on the Mount to His disciples and the multitudes.

"Whoever then annuls one of the least of these commandments, and teaches others *to do* the same, shall be called least in the kingdom of heaven; but whoever keeps and teaches *them*, he shall be called great in the kingdom of heaven" (Matthew 5:19; cf. Matthew 11:11).

Setting: Galilee. During the early part of His ministry, Jesus preaches the Sermon on the Mount to His disciples and the multitudes.

"You have heard that it was said, 'YOU SHALL LOVE YOUR NEIGHBOR and hate your enemy.' But I say to you, love your enemies and pray for those who persecute you, so that you may be sons of your Father who is in heaven; for He causes His sun to rise on *the* evil and *the* good, and sends rain on *the* righteous and *the* unrighteous. For if you love those who love you, what reward do you have? Do not even the tax collectors do the same? If you greet only your brothers, what more are you doing *than others?* Do not even the Gentiles do the same? Therefore, you are to be perfect, as your heavenly Father is perfect" (Matthew 5:43–48, Jesus quotes from Leviticus 19:18; cf. Leviticus 19:2; Luke 6:27–36).

Setting: Galilee. During the early part of His ministry, Jesus preaches the Sermon on the Mount to His disciples and the multitudes.

"Ask, and it will be given to you; seek, and you will find; knock, and it will be opened to you. For everyone who asks receives, and he who seeks finds, and to him who knocks it will be opened. Or what man is there among you who, when his son asks for a loaf, will give him a stone? Or if he asks for a fish, he will not give him a snake, will he? If you then, being evil, know how to give good gifts to your children, how much more will your Father who is in heaven give what is good to those who ask Him! In everything, therefore, treat people the same way you want them to treat you, for this is the Law and the Prophets" (Matthew 7:7–12; cf. Matthew 22:40; Luke 6:31; Luke 11:9–13; see Psalm 84:11).

Setting: Capernaum of Galilee. Jesus illustrates forgiveness after Peter asks Him if forgiving someone seven times who has sinned against him is adequate.

"For this reason the kingdom of heaven may be compared to a king who wished to settle accounts with his slaves. When he had begun to settle *them,* one who owed him ten thousand talents was brought to him. But since he did not have *the means* to repay, his lord commanded him to be sold, along with his wife and children and all that he had, and repayment to be made. So the slave fell *to the ground* and prostrated himself before him, saying, 'Have patience with me and I will repay you everything.' And the lord of that slave felt compassion and released him and forgave him the debt. But that slave went out and found one of his fellow slaves who owed him a hundred denarii; and he seized him and *began* to choke *him,* saying, 'Pay back what you owe.' So his fellow slave fell *to the ground* and *began* to plead with him, saying, 'Have patience with me and I will repay you.' But he was unwilling and went and threw him in prison until he should pay back what was owed. So when his fellow slaves saw what had happened, they were deeply grieved and came and reported to their lord all that had happened. Then summoning him, his lord said to him, 'You wicked slave, I forgave you all that debt because you pleaded with me. Should you not also have had mercy on your fellow slave, in the same way that I had mercy on you?' And his lord, moved with anger, handed him over to the torturers until he should repay all that was owed him. My heavenly Father will also do the same to you, if each of you does not forgive his brother from your heart" (Matthew 18:23–35; cf. Matthew 6:12, 14, 15; Luke 7:42; see Matthew 25:19–28).

Setting: Judea beyond the Jordan (Perea). Jesus illustrates the kingdom of heaven to His disciples through the story of laborers in the vineyard.

"For the kingdom of heaven is like a landowner who went out early in the morning to hire laborers for his vineyard. When he had agreed with the laborers for a denarius for the day, he sent them into his vineyard. And he went out about the third hour and saw others standing idle in the market place; and to those he said,' You also go into the vineyard, and whatever is right I will give you.' And *so* they went. Again he went out about the sixth and the ninth hour, and did the same thing. And about the eleventh *hour* he went out and found others standing *around;* and he said to them, 'Why have you been standing idle here all day long?' They said to him, 'Because no one hired us.' He said to them, 'You go into the vineyard too.' When evening came, the owner of the vineyard said to his foreman, 'Call the laborers and pay them their wages, beginning with the last *group* to the first.' When those *hired* about the eleventh hour came, each one received a denarius. When those *hired* first came, they thought that they would receive more; but each of them also received a denarius. When they received it, they grumbled at the landowner, saying, 'These last men have worked *only* one hour, and you have made them equal to us who have borne the burden and the scorching heat of the day.' But he answered and said to one of them, 'Friend, I am doing you no wrong; did you not agree with me for a denarius? Take what is yours and go, but I wish to give to this last man the same as to you. It is not lawful for me to do what I wish with what is my own? Or is your eye envious because I am generous?' So the last shall be first, and the first last" (Matthew 20:1–16; cf. Matthew 19:30).

Setting: The temple in Jerusalem. Jesus delivers a parable to the chief priests and elders after they question His authority.

"But what do you think? A man had two sons, and he came to the first and said, 'Son, go work today in the vineyard.' And he answered, 'I will not'; but afterward he regretted it and went. The man came to the second and said the same thing; and he answered, 'I *will,* sir'; but he did not go. Which of the two sons did the will of his father?" They said, "The first." Jesus said to them, "Truly, I say to you that the tax collectors and prostitutes will get into the kingdom of God before you. For John came to you in the way of righteousness and you did not believe him; but the tax collectors and prostitutes did believe him; and you, seeing *this,* did not even feel remorse afterward so as to believe him" (Matthew 21:28–32; cf. Luke 7:29, 30, 37–50).

Setting: The temple in Jerusalem. Jesus delivers another parable to the chief priests and elders after they question His authority.

"Listen to another parable. There was a landowner who PLANTED A VINEYARD AND PUT A WALL AROUND IT AND DUG A WINE PRESS IN IT, AND BUILT A TOWER, and rented it out to vine-growers and went on a journey. When the harvest time approached, he sent his slaves to the vine-growers to receive his produce. The vine-growers took his slaves and beat one, and killed another, and stoned a third. Again he sent another group of slaves larger than the first; and they did the same thing to them. But afterward he sent his son to them, saying, 'They will respect my son.' But when the vine-growers saw the son, they said among themselves, 'This is the heir; come, let us kill him and seize his inheritance.' They took him, and threw him out of the vineyard and killed him. Therefore when the owner of the vineyard comes, what will he do to those vine-growers?" (Matthew 21:33–40; Jesus quotes from Isaiah 5:1, 2; cf. Mark 12:1–9; Luke 20:9–15).

Setting: On the Mount of Olives, just east of Jerusalem. During His Olivet Discourse, after answering His disciples' questions as to when the temple will be destroyed and Jerusalem overrun, along with the signs of His coming and the end of the age, Jesus reemphasizes to His disciples that they should be on the alert for His return.

"For *it is* just like a man *about* to go on a journey, who called his own slaves and entrusted his possessions to them. To one he gave five talents, to another, two, and to another, one, each according to his own ability; and he went on his journey. Immediately the one who had received the five talents went and traded with them, and gained five more talents. In the same manner the one who *had received* the two *talents* gained two more. But he who received the one *talent* went away, and dug a *hole* in the ground and hid his master's money. Now after a long time the master of those slaves came and settled accounts with them. The one who had received the five talents came up and brought five more talents, saying, 'Master, you entrusted five talents to me. See, I have gained five more talents.' His master said to him, 'Well done, good and faithful slave. You were faithful with a few things, I will put you in charge of many things; enter into the joy of your master.' Also the one who *had received* the two talents came up and said, 'Master, you entrusted two talents to me. See, I have gained two more talents.' His master said to him, 'Well done, good and faithful slave. You were faithful with a few things, I will put you in charge of many things; enter into the joy of your master.' And the one also who had received the one talent came up and said, 'Master, I knew you to be a hard man, reaping where you did not sow and gathering where you scattered no *seed.* And I was afraid, and went away and hid your talent in the ground. See, you have what is yours.' But his master answered and said to him, 'You wicked, lazy slave, you knew that I reap where I did not sow and gather where I scattered no *seed.* Then you ought to have put my money in the bank, and on my arrival I would have received my *money* back with interest. 'Therefore take away the talent from him, and give it to the one who has ten talents.' For to everyone who has, *more* shall be given, and he will have an abundance; but from the one who does not have, even what he does have shall be taken away. Throw out the worthless slave into the outer darkness; in that place there will be weeping and gnashing of teeth" (Matthew 25:14–30; cf. Matthew 8:12; 3:12; 24:45–47; see Matthew 18:23, 24; Luke 12:44).

Setting: Galilee. After selecting His twelve disciples, Jesus teaches the Beatitudes (part of the Sermon on the Mount) to those disciples and a great throng of people from Judea, Jerusalem, and the central coastal region of Tyre and Sidon.

"Blessed are you when men hate you, and ostracize you, and insult you, and scorn your name as evil, for the sake of the Son of Man. Be glad in that day and leap *for joy*, for behold, your reward is great in heaven. For in the same way their fathers used to treat the prophets" (Luke 6:22, 23; cf. Matthew 5:10–12; see 2 Chronicles 36:16).

Setting: Galilee. After selecting His twelve disciples, Jesus teaches the Beatitudes (part of the Sermon on the Mount) to those disciples and a great throng of people from Judea, Jerusalem, and the central coastal region of Tyre and Sidon.

"Woe *to you* when all men speak well of you, for their fathers used to treat the false prophets in the same way" (Luke 6:26; see Matthew 7:15; 24:11, 24).

Setting: Galilee. After selecting His twelve disciples, Jesus teaches the Sermon on the Mount to those disciples and a great throng of people from Judea, Jerusalem, and the central coastal region of Tyre and Sidon.

"But I say to you who hear, love your enemies, do good to those who hate you, bless those who curse you, pray for those who mistreat you. Whoever hits you on the cheek, offer him the other also; and whoever takes away your coat, do not withhold your shirt from him either. Give to everyone who asks of you, and whoever takes away what is yours, do not demand it back. Treat others the same way you want them to treat you. If you love those who love you, what credit is *that* to you? For even sinners love those who love them. If you do good to those who do good to you, what credit is *that* to you? For even sinners do the same. If you lend to those from whom you expect to receive, what credit is *that* to you? Even sinners lend to sinners in order to receive back the same *amount.* But love your enemies, and do good, and lend, expecting nothing in return; and your reward will be great, and you will be sons of the Most High; for He Himself is kind to ungrateful and evil *men.* Be merciful, just as your Father is merciful" (Luke 6:27–36; cf. Matthew 5:9, 39–48; 7:12).

Setting: On the way from Galilee to Jerusalem. While being tested by a lawyer, Jesus tells him the story of the good Samaritan.

Jesus replied and said, "A man was going down from Jerusalem to Jericho, and fell among robbers, and they stripped him and beat him, and went away leaving him half dead. And by chance a priest was going down on that road, and when he saw him, he passed by on the other side. Likewise a Levite also, when he came to the place and saw him, passed by on the other side. But a Samaritan, who was on a journey, came upon him; and when he saw him, he felt compassion, and came to him and bandaged up his wounds, pouring oil and wine on *them;* and he put him on his own beast, and brought him to an inn and took care of him. On the next day he took out two denarii and gave them to the innkeeper and said, 'Take care of him; and whatever more you spend, when I return I will repay you.' Which of these three do you think proved to be a neighbor to the man who fell into the robbers' *hands?"* And he said, "The one who showed mercy toward him." Then Jesus said to him, "Go and do the same" (Luke 10:30–37).

Setting: On the way from Galilee to Jerusalem. After Jesus presents to large crowds the demands of discipleship, the Pharisees and scribes complain He associates with tax collectors and sinners.

So He told them this parable, saying, "What man among you, if he has a hundred sheep and has lost one of them, does not leave the ninety-nine in the open pasture and go after the one which is lost until he finds it? When he has found it, he lays it on his shoulders, rejoicing. And when he comes home, he calls together his friends and his neighbors, saying to them, 'Rejoice with me, for I have found my sheep which was lost!' I tell you that in the same way, there will be *more* joy in heaven over one sinner who repents than over ninety-nine righteous persons who need no repentance" (Luke 15:3–7; cf. Matthew 18:12–14; see Matthew 9:11–13; Luke 5:29–32).

Setting: On the way from Galilee to Jerusalem. Jesus conveys the principles of the lost sheep and the lost coin because the Pharisees and scribes complain He associates with tax collectors and sinners.

"So He told them this parable, saying, "What man among you, if he has a hundred sheep and has lost one of them, does not leave the ninety-nine in the open pasture and go after the one which is lost until he finds it? When he has found it, he lays it on his shoulders, rejoicing. And when he comes home, he calls together his friends and his neighbors, saying to them, 'Rejoice with me, for I have found my sheep which was lost!' I tell you that in the same way, there will be more joy in heaven over one sinner who repents than over ninety-nine righteous persons who need no repentance. Or what woman, if she has ten silver coins and loses one coin, does not light a lamp and sweep the house and search carefully until she finds it? When she has found it, she calls together her friends and neighbors, saying, 'Rejoice with me, for I have found the coin which I had lost!' In the same way, I tell you, there is joy in the presence of the angels of God over one sinner who repents" (Luke 15:3–10).

Setting: On the way from Galilee to Jerusalem. After the Pharisees question Him about the coming of the kingdom of God, Jesus tells His disciples of His second coming.

And He said to the disciples, "The days will come when you will long to see one of the days of the Son of Man, and you will not see it. They will say to you, 'Look there! Look here!' Do not go away, and do not run after *them*. For just like the lightning, when it flashes out of one part of the sky, shines to the other part of the sky, so will the Son of Man be in His day. But first He must suffer many things and be rejected by this generation. And just as it happened in the days of Noah, so it will be also in the days of the Son of Man: they were eating, they were drinking, they were marrying, they were being given in marriage, until the day that Noah entered the ark, and the flood came and destroyed them all. It was the same as happened in the days of Lot: they were eating, they were drinking, they were buying, they were selling, they were planting, they were building; but on the day that Lot went out from Sodom it rained fire and brimstone from heaven and destroyed them all. It will be just the same on the day that the Son of Man is revealed. On that day, the one who is on the housetop and whose goods are in the house must not go down to take them out; and likewise the one who is in the field must not turn back. Remember Lot's wife. Whoever seeks to keep his life will lose it, and whoever loses *his life* will preserve it. I tell you, on that night there will be two in one bed; one will be taken and the other will be left. There will be two women grinding at the same place; one will be taken and the other will be left. [Two men will be in the field; one will be taken and the other will be left."] And answering they said to Him, "Where, Lord?" And He said to them, "Where the body *is*, there also the vultures will be gathered" (Luke 17:22–37; see Genesis 19; Matthew 10:39; 16:21, 27; 24:17–28, 37–41).

Setting: On the island of Patmos (in the Aegean Sea about fifty miles southwest of Ephesus in modern Turkey). On the Lord's Day (Sunday), approximately fifty years after the Resurrection, the disciple John encounters the Lord Jesus Christ, who communicates a new revelation for the apostle to record for the church in Pergamum and to six other churches in Asia.

"And to the angel of the church in Pergamum write: The One who has the sharp two-edged sword says this: 'I know where you dwell, where Satan's throne is; and you hold fast My name, and did not deny My faith even in the days of Antipas, My witness, My faithful one, who was killed among you, where Satan dwells. But I have a few things against you, because you have there some who hold the teaching of Balaam, who kept teaching Balak to put a stumbling block before the sons of Israel, to eat things sacrificed to idols and to commit *acts of* immorality. So you also have some who in the same way hold the teaching of the Nicolaitans. Therefore repent; or else I am coming to you quickly, and I will make war against them with the sword of My mouth. He who has an ear, let him hear what the Spirit says to the churches. To him who overcomes, to him I will give *some* of the hidden manna,

and I will give him a white stone, and a new name written on the stone which no one knows but he who receives it' (Revelation 2:12–17; see Numbers 25:1–3; Isaiah 62:2; Revelation 1:16).

SANCTIFICATION

[SANCTIFICATION from sanctified]

Setting: Jerusalem. At the Feast of Dedication, the Pharisees desire to stone Jesus because He claims to be equal with God when they ask him plainly whether He is the Christ.

Jesus answered them, "Has it not been written in your Law, 'I SAID, YOU ARE GODS'? If he called them gods, to whom the word of God came (and the Scripture cannot be broken), do you say of Him, whom the Father sanctified and sent into the world, 'You are blaspheming,' because I said, 'I am the Son of God'? If I do not do the works of My Father, do not believe Me; but if I do them, though you do not believe Me, believe the works, so that you may know and understand that the Father is in Me, and I in the Father" (John 10:34–38, Jesus quotes from Psalm 82:6; see John 14:10, 20).

[SANCTIFICATION from sanctify and sanctified]

Setting: Jerusalem. Before the Passover, after giving His disciples assurance that in the midst of tribulation they will have His peace, Jesus continues praying His high-priestly prayer.

"But now I come to You; and these things I speak in the world so that they may have My joy made full in themselves. I have given them Your word; and the world has hated them, because they are not of the world, even as I am not of the world. I do not ask You to take them out of the world, but to keep them from the evil *one.* They are not of the world, even as I am not of the world. Sanctify them in the truth; Your word is truth. As You sent Me into the world, I also have sent them into the world. For their sakes I sanctify Myself, that they themselves also may be sanctified in truth. I do not ask on behalf of these alone, but for those also who believe in Me through their word; that they may all be one; even as You, Father, *are* in Me and I in You, that they also maybe in Us, so that the world may believe that You sent Me" (John 17:13–21; see Matthew 10:5, 38; John 7:33; 15:3, 11, 19).

[SANCTIFICATION from sanctified]

Setting: Caesarea. Luke, writing in Acts, gives Paul's retelling of his conversion to Christ as he appears before King Agrippa following his hearing before the Jewish Council in Jerusalem and arrest by the Roman commander (on his way to Rome after the apostle's third missionary journey).

"And when we had fallen to the ground, I heard a voice saying to me in the Hebrew dialect, 'Saul, Saul, why are you persecuting Me? It is hard for you to kick against the goads.' And I said, 'Who are You, Lord?' And the Lord said, 'I am Jesus whom you are persecuting. But get up and stand on your feet; for this purpose I have appeared to you, to appoint you a minister and a witness not only to the things which you have seen, but also to the things in which I will appear to you; rescuing you from the *Jewish* people and from the Gentiles, to whom I am sending you, to open their eyes so that they may turn from darkness to light and from the dominion of Satan to God, that they may receive forgiveness of sins and an inheritance among those who have been sanctified by faith in Me' (Acts 26:14–18; see Isaiah 35:5; Acts 21:40; 22:14).

SAND

Setting: Galilee. During the early part of His ministry, Jesus preaches the Sermon on the Mount to His disciples and the multitudes.

"Therefore everyone who hears these words of Mine and acts on them, may be compared to a wise man who built his house on the rock. And the rain fell, and the floods came, and the winds blew and slammed against that house; and *yet* it did not fall, for it had been founded on the rock. Everyone who hears these words of Mine and does not act on them, will be like a foolish man who built his house on the sand. The rain fell, and the floods came, and the winds blew and slammed against that house; and it fell—and great was its fall" (Matthew 7:24–28; cf. Luke 6:47–49).

SANDALS (Also see SHOES)

Setting: Galilee. After His twelve disciples observe His ministry, Jesus summons and specifically instructs them about their ministry to the people of Israel.

These twelve Jesus sent out after instructing them: "Do not go in *the* way of *the* Gentiles, and do not enter *any* city of the Samaritans; but rather go to the lost sheep of the house of Israel. And as you go, preach, saying, 'The kingdom of heaven is at hand.' Heal *the* sick, raise *the* dead, cleanse *the* lepers, cast out demons. Freely you received, freely give. Do not acquire gold, or silver, or copper for your money belts, or a bag for *your* journey, or even two coats, or sandals, or a staff; for the worker is worthy of his support. And whatever city or village you enter, inquire who is worthy in it, and stay at his house until you leave *that city*. As you enter the house, give it your greeting. If the house is worthy, give it your *blessing of* peace. But if it is not worthy, take back your *blessing of* peace. Whoever does not receive you, nor heed your words, as you go out of that house or that city, shake the dust off your feet. Truly I say to you, it will be more tolerable for *the* land of Sodom and Gomorrah in the day of judgment than for that city" (Matthew 10:5–15; cf. Mark 6:7–11; Luke 9:1–5; see Matthew 3:2; 11:22, 24; 15:24; Luke 22:35; 1 Corinthians 9:14).

Setting: Jesus' hometown of Nazareth in Galilee. After encountering unbelief, Jesus sends the Twelve out in pairs with authority and instructions about ministry.

And He summoned the twelve and began to send them out in pairs, and gave them authority over the unclean spirits; and He instructed them that they should take nothing for *their* journey, except a mere staff—no bread, no bag, no money in their belt—but to wear sandals; and *He added,* "Do not put on two tunics." And He said to them, "Wherever you enter a house, stay there until you leave town. Any place that does not receive you or listen to you, as you go out from there, shake the dust off the soles of your feet for a testimony against them" (Mark 6:7–11; cf. Matthew 10:1–14; Luke 9:1–5).

Setting: On the way from Galilee to Jerusalem. Jesus conveys the illustration of the prodigal son because the Pharisees and scribes complain He associates with tax collectors and sinners.

And He said, "A man had two sons. The younger of them said to his father, 'Father, give me the share of the estate that falls to me.' So he divided his wealth between them. And not many days later, the younger son gathered everything together and went on a journey into a distant country, and there he squandered his estate with loose living. Now when he had spent everything, a severe famine occurred in that country, and he began to be impoverished. So he went and hired himself out to one of the citizens of that country, and he sent him into his fields to feed swine. And he would have gladly filled his stomach with the pods that the swine were eating, and no one was giving *anything* to him. But when he came to his senses, he said, 'How many of my father's hired men have more than enough bread, but I am dying here with hunger! I will get up and go to my father, and will say to him, "Father, I have sinned against heaven, and in your sight; I am no longer worthy to be called your son; make me as one of your hired men."' So he got up and came to his father. But while he was still a long way off, his father saw him and felt compassion *for him,* and ran and embraced him and kissed him. And the son said to him, "Father, I have sinned against heaven and in your sight; I am no longer worthy to be called your son.' But the father said to his slaves, 'Quickly bring out the best robe and put it on him, and put a ring on his hand and sandals on his feet; and bring the fattened calf, kill it, and let us eat and celebrate; for this son of mine was dead and has come to life again; he was lost and has been found.' And they began to celebrate. Now his older son was in the field, when he came and approached the house, he heard music and dancing. And he summoned one of the servants and *began* inquiring what these things could be. And he said to him, 'Your brother has come, and your father has killed the fattened calf because he has received him back safe and sound.' But he became angry and was not willing to go in; and his father came out and *began* pleading with him. But he answered and said to his father, 'Look! For so many years I have been serving you and I have never neglected a command of yours; and *yet* you have never given me a young goat, so that I might celebrate with my friends; but when this son of yours came, who has devoured your wealth with prostitutes, you killed the fattened calf for him.' And he said to him, 'Son, you have always been with me, and all that is mine is yours. But we had to celebrate and rejoice, for this brother of yours was dead and *has begun* to live, and was lost and has been found' " (Luke 15:11–32; see Proverb 29:2).

Setting: Jerusalem. During the Feast of Unleavened Bread (Passover) just before His crucifixion, while celebrating the Passover meal, instituting the Lord's Supper, and prophesying Peter's denial of Him, Jesus instructs His disciples to prepare to persevere without Him.

And He said to them, "When I sent you out without money belt and bag and sandals, you did not lack anything, did you?" They said, "*No*, nothing." And He said to them, "But now, whoever has a money belt is to take it along, likewise also a bag, and whoever has no sword is to sell his coat and buy one. For I tell you that this which is written must be fulfilled in Me, 'AND HE WAS NUMBERED WITH TRANSGRESSORS'; for that which refers to Me has *its* fulfillment." They said, "Lord, look, here are two swords." And He said to them, "It is enough" (Luke 22:35–38, Jesus quotes from Isaiah 53:12; see Matthew 10:5–15; Mark 6:7–11; Luke 9:1–5; 10:1–12; John 17:4).

SANHEDRIN (See ELDERS)

SARDIS

Setting: On the island of Patmos (in the Aegean Sea about fifty miles southwest of Ephesus in modern Turkey). On the Lord's Day (Sunday), approximately fifty years after the Resurrection, the disciple John hears the voice of the Lord Jesus Christ, who communicates new revelations for the apostle to record for the seven churches in Asia.

I was in the Spirit on the Lord's day, and I heard behind me a loud voice like *the sound* of a trumpet, saying, "Write in a book what you see, and send *it* to the seven churches: to Ephesus and to Smyrna and to Pergamum and to Thyatira and to Sardis and to Philadelphia and to Laodicea" (Revelation 1:10, 11).

Setting: On the island of Patmos (in the Aegean Sea about fifty miles southwest of Ephesus in modern Turkey). On the Lord's Day (Sunday), approximately fifty years after the Resurrection, the disciple John encounters the Lord Jesus Christ, who communicates a new revelation for the apostle to record for the church in Sardis and to six other churches in Asia.

"To the angel of the church in Sardis write: He who has the seven Spirits of God and the seven stars, says this: 'I know your deeds, that you have a name that you are alive, but you are dead. Wake up, and strengthen the things that remain, which were about to die; for I have not found your deeds completed in the sight of My God. So remember what you have received and heard; and keep *it*, and repent. Therefore if you do not wake up, I will come like a thief, and you will not know at what hour I will come to you. But you have a few people in Sardis who have not soiled their garments; and they will walk with Me in white, for they are worthy. He who overcomes will thus be clothed in white garments; and I will not erase his name from the book of life, and I will confess his name before My Father and before His angels. He who has an ear, let him hear what the Spirit says to the churches'" (Revelation 3:1–6; see Matthew 10:32; Revelation 1:16).

SATAN (Specifics such as SATAN, DOMINION OF and SATAN, SYNAGOGUE OF are separate entries; also see BEELZEBUL; DEVIL; EVIL ONE; and WORLD, RULER OF THIS)

Setting: Judea, near the Jordan River. Following His baptism, and before He begins His public ministry, Jesus is led by the Spirit into the wilderness for forty days of temptation by Satan.

Then Jesus said to him, "Go, Satan! For it is written, 'YOU SHALL WORSHIP THE LORD YOUR GOD, AND SERVE HIM ONLY'" (Matthew 4:10, Jesus quotes from Deuteronomy 6:13; cf. Luke 4:8).

Setting: Galilee. After Jesus heals a blind, mute, demon-possessed man, the Pharisees accuse Him in front of crowds of being a worker of Beelzebul (Satan).

And knowing their thoughts Jesus said to them, "Any kingdom divided against itself is laid waste; and any city or house divided against itself will not stand. If Satan casts out Satan, he is divided against himself; how then will his kingdom stand? If I by Beelzebul cast out demons, by whom do your sons cast *them* out? For this reason they will be your judges. But if I cast out demons by the Spirit of God, then the kingdom of God has come upon you. Or how can anyone enter the strong man's house and carry off his property, unless he first binds the strong *man*? And then he will plunder his house" (Matthew 12:25–29; cf. Matthew 9:34; Mark 3:23–27; Luke 11:17–20).

Setting: Galilee. After Jesus selects His twelve disciples, scribes from Jerusalem attribute His miraculous powers to Satan.

And He called them to Himself and began speaking to them in parables, "How can Satan cast out Satan? If a kingdom is divided against itself, that kingdom cannot stand. If a house is divided against itself, that house will not be able to stand. If Satan has risen up against himself and is divided, he cannot stand, but he is finished! But no one can enter the strong man's house and plunder his property unless he first binds the strong man, and then he will plunder his house. Truly I say to you, all sins shall be forgiven the sons of men, and whatever blasphemies they utter; but whoever blasphemes against the Holy Spirit never has forgiveness, but is guilty of an eternal sin"—because they were saying, "He has an unclean spirit" (Mark 3:23–30; cf. Matthew 12:25–32; Luke 12:10).

Setting: By the Sea of Galilee. During the early part of His ministry, after presenting the Parable of the Sower from a boat to a very large crowd, Jesus gives the meaning of the parable to His disciples and other followers.

And He said to them, "Do you not understand this parable? How will you understand all the parables? The sower sows the word. These are the ones who are beside the road where the word is sown; and when they hear, immediately Satan comes and takes away the word which has been sown in them. In a similar way these are the ones on whom seed was sown on the rocky places, who, when they hear the word, immediately receive it with joy; and they have no *firm* root in themselves, but are *only* temporary; then, when affliction or persecution arises because of the word, immediately they fall away. And others are the ones on whom seed was sown among the thorns; these are the ones who have heard the word, but the worries of the world and the deceitfulness of riches, and the desires for other things enter in and choke the word, and it becomes unfruitful. And those are the ones on whom seed was sown on the good soil; and they hear the word and accept it and bear fruit, thirty, sixty, and a hundredfold" (Mark 4:13–20; cf. Matthew 13:18–23; Luke 8:11–15).

Setting: On the way from Galilee to Jerusalem. The Lord responds to a report from the seventy sent out in pairs to every place He Himself will soon visit.

And He said to them, "I was watching Satan fall from heaven like lightning. Behold, I have given you authority to tread on serpents and scorpions, and over all the power of the enemy, and nothing will injure you. Nevertheless do not rejoice in this, that the spirits are subject to you, but rejoice that your names are recorded in heaven" (Luke 10:18–20; see Psalm 91:13; Isaiah 14:12–14; Luke 9:1).

Setting: On the way from Galilee to Jerusalem. After Jesus casts out a demon, some in the crowd test the Lord, demanding a sign from heaven.

But He knew their thoughts and said to them, "Any kingdom divided against itself is laid waste; and a house *divided* against itself falls. If Satan also is divided against himself, how will his kingdom stand? For you say that I cast out demons by Beelzebul. And if I by Beelzebul cast out demons, by whom do your sons cast them out? So they will be your judges. But if I cast out demons by the finger of God, then the kingdom of God has come upon you" (Luke 11:17–20; cf. Matthew 12:25–28; Mark 3:23–27; see Exodus 8:19; Matthew 3:2, 10:25).

Setting: On the way from Galilee to Jerusalem. After Jesus heals a woman, sick for eighteen years, in the synagogue on the Sabbath, He encounters and responds to a synagogue official's anger.

But the Lord answered him and said, "You hypocrites, does not each of you on the Sabbath untie his ox or his donkey from the stall and lead him away to water *him?* And this woman, a daughter of Abraham as she is, whom Satan has bound for eighteen long years, should she not have been released from this bond on the Sabbath day?" (Luke 13:15, 16; see Luke 14:5).

Setting: An upper room in Jerusalem. During the Feast of Unleavened Bread (Passover) just before His crucifixion, Jesus celebrates the Passover meal with His disciples and institutes the Lord's Supper. The disciples argue over who is the greatest among them, and the Lord prophesies Peter's denial of Him.

"Simon, Simon, behold, Satan has demanded *permission* to sift you like wheat; but I have prayed for you, that your faith may not fail; and you, when once you have turned again, strengthen your brothers." But he said to Him, "Lord, with You I am ready to go both to prison and to death!" And He said, "I say to you, Peter, the rooster will not crow today until you have denied three times that you know Me" (Luke 22:31–34; cf. Matthew 26:33–35; John 13:36–38; see Job 1:6–12; John 17:15).

[SATAN from *your* father]
Setting: The temple treasury in Jerusalem. After the scribes and Pharisees question His testimony about Himself, Jesus reveals to those Jews who believe in Him how He will make them free.

So Jesus was saying to those Jews who had believed Him, "If you continue in My word, *then* you are truly disciples of Mine; and you will know the truth, and the truth will make you free." They answered Him, "We are Abraham's descendants and have never yet been enslaved to anyone; how is it that You say, 'You will become free'?" Jesus answered them, "Truly, truly, I say to you, everyone who commits sin is the slave of sin. The slave does not remain in the house forever; the son does remain forever. So if the Son makes you free, you will be free indeed. I know that you are Abraham's descendants; yet you seek to kill Me, because My word has no place in you. I speak the things which I have seen with *My* Father; therefore you also do the things which you heard from *your* father" (John 8:31–38; see Romans 6:16).

[SATAN from your father]
Setting: The temple treasury in Jerusalem. After the scribes and Pharisees question His testimony about Himself, Jesus argues with them regarding their ancestry and motives.

They answered and said to Him, "Abraham is our father." Jesus said to them, "If you are Abraham's children, do the deeds of Abraham. But as it is, you are seeking to kill Me, a man who has told you the truth, which I heard from God; this Abraham did not do. You are doing the deeds of your father." They said to Him, "We were not born of fornication; we have one Father: God" (John 8:39–41; see Romans 9:6, 7).

[SATAN from *your* father the devil; your father; and the father of lies]
Setting: The temple treasury in Jerusalem. After the scribes and Pharisees question His testimony about Himself, Jesus argues with them regarding their ancestry and motives.

Jesus said to them, "If God were your Father, you would love Me, for I proceeded forth and have come from God, for I have not even come on My own initiative, but He sent Me. Why do you not understand what I am saying? *It is* because you cannot hear My word. You are of *your* father the devil, and you want to do the desires of your father. He was a murderer from the beginning, and does not stand in the truth because there is no truth in him. Whenever he speaks a lie, he speaks from his own *nature,* for he is a liar and the father of lies. But because I speak the truth, you do not believe Me. Which one of you convicts Me of sin? If I speak truth, why do not believe Me? He who is of God hears the words of God; for this reason you do not hear *them,* because you are not of God" (John 8:42–47; see John 18:37; 1 John 3:8; 4:6; 5:1).

Setting: On the island of Patmos (in the Aegean Sea about fifty miles southwest of Ephesus in modern Turkey). On the Lord's Day (Sunday), approximately fifty years after the Resurrection, the disciple John encounters the Lord Jesus Christ, who communicates a new revelation for the apostle to record for the church in Pergamum and to six other churches in Asia.

"And to the angel of the church in Pergamum write: The One who has the sharp two-edged sword says this: 'I know where you dwell, where Satan's throne is; and you hold fast My name, and did not deny My faith even in the days of Antipas, My witness, My faithful one, who was killed among you, where Satan dwells. But I have a few things against you, because you have there some who hold the teaching of Balaam, who kept teaching Balak to put a stumbling block before the sons of Israel, to eat things sacrificed to idols and to commit *acts of* immorality. So you also have some who in the same way hold the teaching of the Nicolaitans. Therefore repent; or else I am coming to you quickly, and I will make war against them with the sword of My mouth. He who has an ear, let him hear what the Spirit says to the churches. To him who overcomes, to him I will give *some* of the hidden manna,

and I will give him a white stone, and a new name written on the stone which no one knows but he who receives it' (Revelation 2:12–17; see Numbers 25:1–3; Isaiah 62:2; Revelation 1:16).

SATAN (figurative use)

Setting: Near Caesarea Philippi. Jesus responds to Peter's rebuke for predicting His own death and resurrection.

But He turned and said to Peter, "Get behind Me, Satan! You are a stumbling block to Me; for you are not setting your mind on God's interests, but man's" (Matthew 16:23; cf. Mark 8:33).

Setting: Caesarea Philippi. After Peter proclaims that Jesus is the Christ (Messiah), he rebukes Jesus for predicting His own suffering and death at the hands of the elders, chief priests, and scribes.

But turning around and seeing His disciples, He rebuked Peter and said, "Get behind Me, Satan; for you are not setting your mind on God's interests, but man's" (Mark 8:33; cf. Matthew 16:21–23; Luke 9:22).

SATAN, DEEP THINGS OF

Setting: On the island of Patmos (in the Aegean Sea about fifty miles southwest of Ephesus in modern Turkey). On the Lord's Day (Sunday), approximately fifty years after the Resurrection, the disciple John encounters the Lord Jesus Christ, who communicates a new revelation for the apostle to record for the church in Thyatira and to six other churches in Asia.

"And to the angel of the church in Thyatira write: The Son of God, who has eyes like a flame of fire, and His feet are like burnished bronze, says this: 'I know your deeds, and your love and faith and service and perseverance, and that your deeds of late are greater than at first. But I have *this* against you, that you tolerate the woman Jezebel, who calls herself a prophetess, and she teaches and leads My bond-servants astray so that they commit *acts of* immorality and eat things sacrificed to idols. I gave her time to repent, and she does not want to repent of her immorality. Behold, I will throw her on a bed *of sickness,* and those who commit adultery with her into great tribulation, unless they repent of her deeds. And I will kill her children with pestilence, and all the churches will know that I am He who searches the minds and hearts; and I will give to each one of you according to your deeds. But I say to you, the rest who are in Thyatira, who do not hold this teaching, who have not known the deep things of Satan, as they call them—I place no other burden on you. Nevertheless what you have, hold fast until I come. He who overcomes, and he who keeps My deeds until the end, TO HIM I WILL GIVE AUTHORITY OVER THE NATIONS; AND HE SHALL RULE THEM WITH A ROD OF IRON, AS THE VESSELS OF THE POTTER ARE BROKEN TO PIECES, as I also have received *authority* from My Father; and I will give him the morning star. He who has an ear, let him hear what the Spirit says to the churches' (Revelation 2:18–29; Jesus quotes from Psalm 2:8, 9; Isaiah 30:14; see 1 Kings 16:31; Psalm 7:9; Romans 2:5; 1 Corinthians 2:10; 2 Peter 3:9; Revelation 1:14; 2:7; 3:11; 17:1–20).

SATAN, DOMINION OF

Setting: Caesarea. Luke, writing in Acts, gives Paul's retelling of his conversion to Christ as he appears before King Agrippa following his hearing before the Jewish Council in Jerusalem and arrest by the Roman commander (on his way to Rome after the apostle's third missionary journey).

"And when we had fallen to the ground, I heard a voice saying to me in the Hebrew dialect, 'Saul, Saul, why are you persecuting Me? It is hard for you to kick against the goads.' And I said, 'Who are You, Lord?' And the Lord said, 'I am Jesus whom you are persecuting. But get up and stand on your feet; for this purpose I have appeared to you, to appoint you a minister and a witness not only to the things which you have seen, but also to the things in which I will appear to you; rescuing you from the *Jewish* people and from the Gentiles, to whom I am sending you, to open their eyes so that they may turn from darkness to light and from the dominion of Satan to God, that they may receive forgiveness of sins and an inheritance among those who have been sanctified by faith in Me' (Acts 26:14–18; see Isaiah 35:5; Acts 21:40; 22:14).

SATAN, SYNAGOGUE OF (Also see THRONE, SATAN'S)

Setting: On the island of Patmos (in the Aegean Sea about fifty miles southwest of Ephesus in modern Turkey). On the Lord's Day (Sunday), approximately fifty years after the Resurrection, the disciple John encounters the Lord

Jesus Christ, who communicates a new revelation for the apostle to record for the church in Smyrna and to six other churches in Asia.

"And to the angel of the church in Smyrna write: The first and the last, who was dead, and has come to life, says this: 'I know your tribulation and your poverty (but you are rich), and the blasphemy by those who say they are Jews and are not, but are a synagogue of Satan. Do not fear what you are about to suffer. Behold, the devil is about to cast some of you into prison, so that you will be tested, and you will have tribulation for ten days. Be faithful until death, and I will give you the crown of life. He who has an ear, let him hear what the Spirit says to the churches. He who overcomes will not be hurt by the second death' (Revelation 2:8–11; see Isaiah 44:6; Revelation 1:9, 18; 20:6, 14).

Setting: On the island of Patmos (in the Aegean Sea about fifty miles southwest of Ephesus in modern Turkey). On the Lord's Day (Sunday), approximately fifty years after the Resurrection, the disciple John encounters the Lord Jesus Christ, who communicates a new revelation for the apostle to record for the church in Philadelphia and to six other churches in Asia.

"And to the angel of the church in Philadelphia write: He who is holy, who is true, who has the key of David, who opens and no one will shut, and who shuts and no one opens, says this: 'I know your deeds. Behold, I have put before you an open door which no one can shut, because you have a little power, and have kept My word, and have not denied My name. Behold, I will cause *those* of the synagogue of Satan, who say that they are Jews and are not, but lie—I will make them come and bow down at your feet, and *make them* know that I have loved you. Because you have kept the word of My perseverance, I also will keep you from the hour of testing, that *hour* which is about to come upon the whole world, to test those who dwell on the earth. I am coming quickly; hold fast what you have, so that no one will take your crown. He who overcomes, I will make him a pillar in the temple of My God, and he will not go out from it anymore; and I will write on him the name of My God, and the name of the city of My God, the new Jerusalem, which comes down out of heaven from My God, and My new name. He who has an ear, let him hear what the Spirit says to the churches'" (Revelation 3:7–13; see Isaiah 22:22; Galatians 2:9; Revelation 2:9, 10, 13, 25; 14:1).

SATAN, TEMPTATION BY (See TEMPTATION OF JESUS)

SATAN AND HIS ANGELS (See ANGELS, THE DEVIL AND HIS)

SATAN TEMPTING JESUS (See TEMPTATION OF JESUS)

SATAN'S THRONE (Listed under THRONE, SATAN'S)

SATISFACTION (Also see FULFILLMENT; GLADNESS; HAPPINESS; and JOY)

[SATISFACTION from satisfied]

Setting: Galilee. Early in His ministry, Jesus presents the Beatitudes (part of the Sermon on the Mount) to His disciples and the gathered crowds from Galilee, Decapolis, Jerusalem, Judea, and beyond the Jordan.

"Blessed are those who hunger and thirst for righteousness, for they shall be satisfied" (Matthew 5:6; see Matthew 13:35).

[SATISFACTION from satisfied]

Setting: The region of Tyre. After the Pharisees and scribes from Jerusalem question Jesus' disciples' obedience to the tradition regarding ceremonial cleansing, Jesus casts a demon out from the daughter of a Gentile (Syrophoenician) woman.

And He was saying to her, "Let the children be satisfied first, for it is not good to take the children's bread and throw it to the dogs." But she answered and said to Him, "Yes, Lord *but* even the dogs under the table feed on the children's crumbs. And He said to her, "Because of this answer go; the demon has gone out of your daughter" (Mark 7:27–29; cf. Matthew 15:21–28).

[SATISFACTION from satisfied]

Setting: Galilee. After selecting His twelve disciples, Jesus teaches the Beatitudes (part of the Sermon on the Mount) to those disciples and a great throng of people from Judea, Jerusalem, and the central coastal region of Tyre and Sidon.

"Blessed *are* you who hunger now, for you shall be satisfied. Blessed *are* you who weep now, for you shall laugh" (Luke 6:21; cf. Matthew 5:4, 6).

SAUL (Also see PAUL)

Setting: On the road to Damascus. Luke, writing in Acts, describes how Saul of Tarsus (who will later have the name Paul), a persecutor of the disciples of Jesus, receives the Lord's calling and is temporarily blinded.

As he was traveling, it happened that he was approaching Damascus, and suddenly a light from heaven flashed around him; and he fell to the ground and heard a voice saying to him. "Saul, Saul, why are you persecuting Me?" And he said, "Who are You, Lord?" And He *said,* "I am Jesus whom you are persecuting, but get up and enter the city, and it will be told you what you must do" (Acts 9:3–6; see Acts 22:7, 8).

Setting: Damascus. Luke, writing in Acts, conveys how the Lord instructs one of His disciples, Ananias, to locate Saul of Tarsus to touch him in order to restore Saul's vision.

Now there was a disciple at Damascus named Ananias; and the Lord said to him in a vision, "Ananias." And he said, "Here I am, Lord." And the Lord *said* to him, "Get up and go to the street called Straight, and inquire at the house of Judas for a man from Tarsus named Saul, for he is praying, and he was seen in a vision a man named Ananias come in and lay his hands on him, so that he might regain his sight" (Acts 9:10–12; see Acts 22:12–14).

[SAUL from a chosen instrument of Mine]

Setting: Damascus. Luke, writing in Acts, details the reluctance of Ananias, one of Jesus' followers, to locate Saul of Tarsus (a known enemy of the church), in order to restore Saul's vision.

But the Lord said to him, "Go, for he is a chosen instrument of Mine, to bear My name before the Gentiles and kings and the sons of Israel; for I will show him how much he must suffer for My name's sake" (Acts 9:15, 16; see Acts 13:2; 20:22–24).

Setting: Jerusalem. Luke, writing in Acts, presents the account of Paul's speech (following his third missionary journey) to a hostile Jewish crowd about His divine encounter with Jesus on the road to Damascus.

"But it happened that as I was on my way, approaching Damascus about noontime, a very bright light suddenly flashed from heaven all around me, and I fell to the ground, and heard a voice saying to me, 'Saul, Saul, why are you persecuting Me?' And I answered, 'Who are You, Lord?' And He said to me, 'I am Jesus the Nazarene, whom you are persecuting.' And those who were with me saw the light, to be sure, but did not understand the voice of the One who was speaking to me. And I said, 'What shall I do, Lord?' And the Lord said to me, 'Get up and go on into Damascus, and there you will be told of all that has been appointed for you to do' (Acts 22:6–10; see Acts 9:7; 26:9).

Setting: Caesarea. Luke, writing in Acts, gives Paul's retelling of his conversion to Christ as he appears before King Agrippa following his hearing before the Jewish Council in Jerusalem and arrest by the Roman commander (on his way to Rome after the apostle's third missionary journey).

"And when we had fallen to the ground, I heard a voice saying to me in the Hebrew dialect, 'Saul, Saul, why are you persecuting Me? It is hard for you to kick against the goads.' And I said, 'Who are You, Lord?' And the Lord said, 'I am Jesus whom you are persecuting. But get up and stand on your feet; for this purpose I have appeared to you, to appoint you a minister and a witness not only to the things which you have seen, but also to the things in which I will appear to you; rescuing you from the *Jewish* people and from the Gentiles, to whom I am sending you, to open their eyes so that they may turn from darkness to light and from the dominion of Satan to God, that they may receive forgiveness of sins and an inheritance among those who have been sanctified by faith in Me' (Acts 26:14–18; see Isaiah 35:5; Acts 21:40; 22:14).

SAUL'S MISSION (See PAUL'S MISSION)

SAVE/SAVED (Also see ETERNAL LIFE; JESUS' PURPOSE; JESUS' WORK; and SALVATION)

Setting: Galilee. After His disciples observe His ministry, Jesus summons and specifically instructs them about the upcoming difficulties of their ministry to the people of Israel.

"Brother will betray brother to death, and a father *his* child; and children will rise up against parents and cause them to be put to death. You will be hated by all because of My name, but it is the one who has endured to the end who will be saved. But whenever they persecute you in one city, flee to the next; for truly I say to you, you will not finish *going through* the cities of Israel until the Son of Man comes" (Matthew 10:21–23; cf. Matthew 16:27, 28; 24:9).

Setting: The Mount of Olives, just east of Jerusalem. During His Olivet Discourse, Jesus answers His disciples' questions as to when the temple will be destroyed and Jerusalem overrun, along with the signs of His coming and the end of the age.

And Jesus answered and said to them, "See to it that no one misleads you. For many will come in My name, saying, 'I am the Christ,' and will mislead many. You will be hearing of wars and rumors of wars. See that you are not frightened, for *those things* must take place, but *that* is not yet the end. For nation will rise against nation, and kingdom against kingdom, and in various places there will be famines and earthquakes. But all these things are *merely* the beginning of birth pangs. Then they will deliver you to tribulation, and will kill you, and you will be hated by all nations because of My name. At that time many will fall away and will betray one another and hate one another. Many false prophets will arise and will mislead many. Because lawlessness is increased, most people's love will grow cold. But the one who endures to the end, he will be saved. This gospel of the kingdom shall be preached in the whole world as a testimony to all the nations, and then the end will come" (Matthew 24:4–14; cf. Jeremiah 29:8; Matthew 7:15; 10:17, 22; Mark 13:3–13; Luke 21:7–19; Revelation 6:4).

Setting: Near Caesarea Philippi. After rebuking Peter for trying to forbid Him to accomplish His earthly mission of dying and being resurrected, Jesus teaches His disciples about the costs of following Him.

Then Jesus said to His disciples, "If anyone wishes to come after Me, he must deny himself, and take up his cross and follow Me. For whoever wishes to save his life will lose it; but whoever loses his life for My sake will find it. For what will it profit a man if he gains the whole world and forfeits his soul? Or what will a man give in exchange for his soul? For the Son of Man is going to come in the glory of His Father with His angels, and WILL THEN REPAY EVERY MAN ACCORDING TO HIS DEEDS. Truly, I say to you, there are some of you who are standing here who will not taste death until they see the Son of Man coming in His kingdom" (Matthew 16:24–28, Jesus quotes from Psalm 62:12; cf. Mark 8:34–37; Luke 9:23–27; see Matthew 10:38, 39).

Setting: Capernaum of Galilee. After conveying the value of little ones after His disciples ask Him about greatness in the kingdom of heaven, Jesus states His earthly mission.

["For the Son of Man has come to save that which was lost"] (Matthew 18:11; cf. Luke 19:10).

Setting: The Mount of Olives, just east of Jerusalem. During His Olivet Discourse, Jesus answers His disciples' questions as to when the temple will be destroyed and Jerusalem overrun, along with the signs of His coming and the end of the age.

"Therefore when you see the ABOMINATION OF DESOLATION which was spoken of through Daniel the prophet, standing in the holy place (let the reader understand), then those who are in Judea must flee to the mountains. Whoever is on the housetop must not go down to get the things that are in his house. Whoever is in the field must not turn back to get his cloak. But woe to those who are pregnant and to those who are nursing babies in those days! But pray that your flight will not be in the winter, or on a Sabbath. For then there will be a great tribulation, such as has not occurred since the beginning of the world until now, nor ever will. Unless those days had been cut short, no life would have been saved; but for the sake of the elect those days will be cut short. Then if anyone says to you, 'Behold, here is the Christ,' or "There *He is,*' do not believe *him.* For false Christs and false prophets will arise and will show great signs and wonders, so as to mislead, if possible, even the elect. Behold, I have told you in advance. So if they say to you, 'Behold, He is in the wilderness,' do not go out, *or,* 'Behold, He is in the inner rooms,' do not believe *them.* For just as the lightning comes from the east and flashes even to the west, so will the coming of the Son of Man be. Wherever the corpse is, there the vultures will gather" (Matthew 24:15–28, Jesus quotes from Daniel 9:27; cf. Daniel 12:1; Mark 13:14–23; Luke 17:22–31; 21:20–24; 23:29; see John 4:48).

Setting: A synagogue in Galilee. Early in His ministry, in front of the Pharisees, Jesus heals a man's withered hand on the Sabbath.

He said to the man with the withered hand, "Get up and come forward!" And He said to them, "Is it lawful to do good or do harm on the Sabbath, to save a life or to kill?" But they kept silent. After looking around at them with anger, grieved at their hardness of heart, He said to the man, "Stretch out your hand." And he stretched it out, and his hand was restored (Mark 3:3–5; cf. Matthew 12:9–14; Luke 6:6–11).

Setting: Caesarea Philippi. After rebuking Peter for desiring to thwart His mission to the cross, Jesus summons a crowd, along with His disciples, and informs them of the high costs of following Him.

And He summoned the crowd with His disciples, and said to them, "If anyone wishes to come after Me, he must deny himself, and take up his cross and follow Me. For whoever wishes to save his life will lose it, but whoever loses his life for My sake and the gospel's will save it. For what does it profit a man to gain the whole world, and forfeit his soul? For what will a man give in exchange for his soul? For whoever is ashamed of Me and My words in this adulterous and sinful generation, the Son of Man will also be ashamed of him when He comes in the glory of His Father with the holy angels" (Mark 8:34–38; cf. Matthew 16:24–28; Luke 9:23–27; see Matthew 10:33, 38, 39).

Setting: On the Mount of Olives, east of the temple in Jerusalem. After prophesying the temple's destruction, Jesus responds during His Olivet Discourse to questions from Peter, James, John, and Andrew about other future events.

And Jesus began to say to them, "See to it that no one misleads you. Many will come in My name, saying, 'I am *He!*' and will mislead many. When you hear of wars and rumors of wars, do not be frightened; *those things* must take place; but *that is* not yet the end. For nation will rise up against nation, and kingdom against kingdom; there will be earthquakes in various places; there will *also be* famines. These things are *merely* the beginning of birth pangs. But be on your guard; for they will deliver you to *the* courts, and you will be flogged in *the* synagogues, and you will stand before governors and kings for My sake, as a testimony to them. The gospel must first be preached to all the nations. When they arrest you and hand you over, do not worry beforehand about what you are to say, but say whatever is given you in that hour; for it is not you who speak, but *it is* the Holy Spirit. Brother will betray brother to death, and a father *his* child; and children will rise up against parents and have them put to death. You will be hated by all because of My name, but the one who endures to the end, he will be saved" (Mark 13:5–13; cf. Matthew 24:4–14; Luke 21:7–19; see Matthew 10:17–22).

Setting: On the Mount of Olives, east of the temple in Jerusalem. After prophesying the temple's destruction, Jesus responds during His Olivet Discourse to questions from Peter, James, John, and Andrew about other future events.

"But when you see the ABOMINATION OF DESOLATION standing where it should not be (let the reader understand), then those who are in Judea must flee to the mountains. The one who is on the housetop must not go down, or go in to get anything out of his house; and the one who is in the field must not turn back to get his coat. But woe to those who are pregnant and to those who are nursing babies in those days! But pray that it may not happen in winter. For those days will be a *time of* tribulation such as has not occurred since the beginning of the creation which God created until now, and never will. Unless the Lord had shortened *those* days, no life would have been saved; but for the sake of the elect, whom He chose, He shortened the days. And then if anyone says to you, 'Behold, here is the Christ'; or, 'Behold, *He is* there'; do not believe *him*; for false Christs and false prophets will arise, and will show signs and wonders, in order to lead astray, if possible, the elect. But take heed; behold, I have told you everything in advance" (Mark 13:14–23; cf. Matthew 24:15–28; Luke 21:20–24; see Daniel 9:27; 12:1; Luke 17:31).

Setting: Following His resurrection from the dead after being crucified, Jesus commissions His disciples to preach His gospel to the world.

And He said to them, "Go into all the world and preach the gospel to all creation. He who has believed and has been baptized shall be saved; but he who has disbelieved shall be condemned. These signs will accompany those who have believed: in My name they will cast out demons, they will speak with new tongues; they will pick up serpents, and if they drink any deadly *poison*, it will not hurt them; they will lay hands on the sick, and they will recover" (Mark 16:15–18; cf. Matthew 28:16–20; see Mark 9:38; John 3:18, 36; 1 Corinthians 15:6).

[Note: Some scholars question the authenticity of Mark 16:9–20 as these verses do not appear in some early New Testament manuscripts.]

Setting: A synagogue in Galilee. As Jesus teaches on a Sabbath, the scribes and Pharisees watch to see if He heals a man's withered hand.

But He knew what they were thinking, and He said to the man with the withered hand, "Get up and come forward!" And he got up and came forward. And Jesus said to them, "I ask you, is it lawful to do good or to do harm on the Sabbath, to save a life or destroy it?" And looking around at them all, He said to him, "Stretch out your hand!" And he did *so;* and his hand was restored (Luke 6:8–10; cf. Matthew 12:9–13; Mark 3:1–5).

Setting: Galilee. After Jesus praises John the Baptist to the crowds, Simon, a Pharisee, invites the Lord to dinner. A sinful woman anoints His feet with perfume, prompting Him to instruct His host about forgiveness.

Turning toward the woman, He said to Simon, "Do you see this woman? I entered your house; you gave Me no water for My feet, but she has wet My feet with her tears and wiped them with her hair. You gave Me no kiss; but she, since the time I came in, has not ceased to kiss My feet. You did not anoint My head with oil, but she anointed My feet with perfume. For this reason I say to you, her sins, which are many, have been forgiven, for she loved much; but he who is forgiven little, loves little." Then He said to her, "Your sins have been forgiven." Those who were reclining *at the table* with Him began to say to themselves, "Who is this *man* who even forgives sins?" And He said to the woman, "Your faith has saved you; go in peace" (Luke 7:44–50; see Matthew 9:2; Mark 5:34; Luke 5:21).

Setting: Galilee. After Jesus presents the Parable of the Sower to the crowds, His disciples ask Him to give them the parable's meaning.

And He said, "To you it has been granted to know the mysteries of the kingdom of God, but to the rest *it is* in parables, so that SEEING THEY MAY NOT SEE, AND HEARING THEY MAY NOT UNDERSTAND. Now the parable is this: the seed is the word of God. Those beside the road are those who have heard; then the devil comes and takes away the word from their heart, so that they will not believe and be saved. Those on the rocky *soil* are those who, when they hear, receive the word with joy; and these have no *firm* root; they believe for a while, and in time of temptation fall away. The *seed* which fell among the thorns, these are the ones who have heard, and as they go on their way they are choked with worries and riches and pleasures of *this* life, and bring no fruit to maturity. But the *seed* in the good soil, these are the ones who have heard the word in an honest and good heart, and hold it fast, and bear fruit with perseverance" (Luke 8:10–15, Jesus quotes from Isaiah 6:9; cf. Matthew 13:10–23; Mark 4:10–20).

Setting: Galilee. Following Peter's pronouncement Jesus is the Christ of God, the Lord conveys the demands of discipleship and the hope regarding the kingdom of God.

And He was saying to *them* all, "If anyone wishes to come after Me, he must deny himself, and take up his cross daily and follow Me. For whoever wishes to save his life will lose it, but whoever loses his life for My sake, he is the one who will save it. For what is a man profited if he gains the whole world, and loses or forfeits himself? For whoever is ashamed of Me and My words, the Son of Man will be ashamed of him when He comes in His glory, and *the glory* of the Father and of the holy angels. But I say to you truthfully, there are some of those standing here who will not taste death until they see the kingdom of God" (Luke 9:23–27; cf. Matthew 16:24–26, 28; Mark 8:34–37; see Matthew 10:33, 38, 39).

Setting: Galilee. After clarifying who the disciples' co-laborers are, Jesus prepares to go to Jerusalem by sending messengers ahead to Samaria, where they experience rejection and seek retribution.

But He turned and rebuked them, [and said, "You do not know what kind of spirit you are of; for the Son of Man did not come to destroy men's lives, but to save them."] And they went on to another village (Luke 9:55, 56; see 2 Kings 1:9–14; Luke 13:22).

Setting: Jericho, on the way to Jerusalem. After taking time to heal a blind man, Jesus comments on Zaccheus's response to Him.

And Jesus said to him, "Today salvation has come to this house, because he, too, is a son of Abraham. For the Son of Man has come to seek and to save that which was lost" (Luke 19:9, 10; cf. Matthew 18:11).

Setting: Jerusalem. At the time for the Passover of the Jews, after the Lord cleanses the temple, a Pharisee, Nicodemus, asks Him by night the meaning of "born again."

"For God so loved the world, that He gave His only begotten Son, that whoever believes in Him shall not perish, but have eternal life. For God did not send the Son into the world to judge the world, but that the world might be saved through Him. He who believes in Him is not judged; he who does not believe has been judged already, because he has not believed in the name of the only begotten Son of God. This is the judgment, that the Light has come into the world, and men loved darkness rather than the Light, for their deeds were evil. For everyone who does evil hates the Light, and does not come to the Light for fear that his deeds will be exposed. But he who practices the truth comes to the Light, so that his deeds may be manifested as having been wrought in God" (John 3:16–21; see Luke 19:10; John 1:4; 1:18; Romans 5:8; 1 John 1:6, 7).

Setting: Jerusalem. During a feast of the Jews, Jesus responds to criticism from the Jewish religious leaders by referring to God as His Father (thereby making Himself equal with God) and informing them that God, John the Baptist, and His works all testify to His mission.

"I can do nothing on My own initiative. As I hear, I judge; and My judgment is just, because I do not seek My own will, but the will of Him who sent Me. If I *alone* testify about Myself, My testimony is not true. There is another who testifies of Me, and I know that the testimony which He gives about Me is true. You have sent to John, and he has testified to the truth. But the testimony which I receive is not from man, but I say these things so that you may be saved. He was the lamp that was burning and was shining and you were willing to rejoice for a while in his light. But the testimony which I have is greater than the *testimony of* John; for the works which the Father has given Me to accomplish—the very works that I do—testify about Me, that the Father has sent Me. And the Father who sent Me, He has testified of Me. You have neither heard His voice at any time nor seen His form. You do not have His word abiding in you, for you do not believe Him whom He sent" (John 5:30–38; see Matthew 3:17; Mark 1:4, 5; John 1:7, 15, 32; 4:34; 8:14–16; 10:25, 37, 38).

Setting: Jerusalem. Following the Pharisees' interrogation and dismissal of the formerly blind man Jesus healed on the Sabbath, the Lord conveys the Parable of the Good Shepherd to the Pharisees, using figures of speech they do not understand.

So Jesus said to them again, "Truly, truly, I say to you, I am the door of the sheep. All who came before Me are thieves and robbers, but the sheep did not hear them. I am the door; if anyone enters through Me, he will be saved, and will go in and out and find pasture. The thief comes only to steal and kill and destroy; I came that they may have life, and have *it* abundantly. I am the good shepherd; the good shepherd lays down His life for the sheep. He who is a hired hand, and not a shepherd, who is not the owner of the sheep, sees the wolf coming, and leaves the sheep and flees, and the wolf snatches them and scatters *them. He flees* because he is a hired hand and is not concerned about the sheep. I am the good shepherd, and I know My own and My own know Me, even as the Father knows Me and I know the Father; and I lay down My life for the sheep. I have other sheep, which are not of this fold; I must bring them also, and they will hear My voice; and they will become one flock *with* one shepherd. For this reason the Father loves Me, because I lay down My life so that I may take it again. No one has taken it away from Me, but I lay it down on My own initiative. I have authority to take it up again. This commandment I received from My Father" (John 10:7–18; see Isaiah 40:11; 56:8; Jeremiah 23:1; Matthew 11:27).

Setting: Jerusalem. Just days before the Passover, with the chief priests and Pharisees plotting to seize Him and crowds welcoming Him with palm branches and praise, Jesus expresses anxiety about His upcoming crucifixion.

"Now My soul has become troubled; and what shall I say, 'Father, save Me from this hour'? But for this purpose I came to this hour. Father glorify Your name." Then a voice came out of heaven: "I have glorified it, and will glorify it again." So the crowd *of people* who stood by and heard it were saying that it had thundered; others were saying, "An angel has spoken to Him." Jesus answered and said, "This voice has not come for My sake, but for your sakes. Now judgment is upon this world; now the ruler of this world will be cast out. And I, if I am lifted up from the earth, will draw all men to Myself" (John 12:27–32; see Matthew 3:17; 26:38; John 3:14; 6:44; 11:42; 14:30).

Setting: Jerusalem. Just days before the Passover, with the chief priests and Pharisees plotting to seize Jesus, who is expressing anxiety about His upcoming crucifixion, some of the Jews believe in the Lord, while others are rejecting His message.

And Jesus cried out and said, "He who believes in Me, does not believe in Me but in Him who sent Me. He who sees Me sees the One who sent Me. I have come *as* Light into the world, so that everyone who believes in Me will not remain in darkness. If anyone hears My sayings and does not keep them, I do not judge him; for I did not come to judge the world, but to save the world. He who rejects Me and does not receive My sayings, has one who judges him; the word I spoke is what will judge him at the last day. For I did not speak on My own initiative, but the Father Himself who sent Me has given Me a commandment *as to* what to say and what to speak. I know that His commandment is eternal life; therefore the things I speak, I speak just as the Father as told Me" (John 12:44–50; see Matthew 10:40; Luke 10:16; John 1:4; 3:17; 5:19; 6:68; 14:9).

SAVIOR, JESUS AS (See JESUS' PURPOSE; JESUS' WORK; SALVATION; and SAVE)

SAYINGS (Also see WORD, MY; and WORDS, MY)

Setting: Jerusalem. Just days before the Passover, with the chief priests and Pharisees plotting to seize Jesus, who is expressing anxiety about His upcoming crucifixion, some of the Jews believe in the Lord, while others are rejecting His message.

And Jesus cried out and said, "He who believes in Me, does not believe in Me but in Him who sent Me. He who sees Me sees the One who sent Me. I have come *as* Light into the world, so that everyone who believes in Me will not remain in darkness. If anyone hears My sayings and does not keep them, I do not judge him; for I did not come to judge the world, but to save the world. He who rejects Me and does not receive My sayings, has one who judges him; the word I spoke is what will judge him at the last day. For I did not speak on My own initiative, but the Father Himself who sent Me has given Me a commandment *as to* what to say and what to speak. I know that His commandment is eternal life; therefore the things I speak, I speak just as the Father as told Me" (John 12:44–50; see Matthew 10:40; Luke 10:16; John 1:4; 3:17; 5:19; 6:68; 14:9).

SCATTERING (Also see GATHERING; REAPING; and SOWING)

[SCATTERING from scatters]

Setting: Galilee. After Jesus heals a blind, mute, demon-possessed man, the Pharisees accuse Him in front of crowds of being a worker of Satan. The Lord warns them about the unpardonable sin.

"He who is not with Me is against Me; and he who does not gather with Me scatters. Therefore I say to you, any sin and blasphemy shall be forgiven people, but blasphemy against the Spirit shall not be forgiven. Whoever speaks a word against the Son of Man, it shall be forgiven him; but whoever speaks against the Holy Spirit, it shall not be forgiven him, either in this age or in the *age* to come" (Matthew 12:30–32; cf. Luke 12:10; see Mark 9:40).

[SCATTERING from scattered]

Setting: On the Mount of Olives, just east of Jerusalem. During His Olivet Discourse, after answering His disciples' questions as to when the temple will be destroyed and Jerusalem overrun, along with the signs of His coming and the end of the age, Jesus reemphasizes to His disciples that they should be on the alert for His return.

"For *it is* just like a man *about* to go on a journey, who called his own slaves and entrusted his possessions to them. To one he gave five talents, to another, two, and to another, one, each according to his own ability; and he went on his journey. Immediately the one who had received the five talents went and traded with them, and gained five more talents. In the same manner the one who *had received* the two *talents* gained two more. But he who received the one *talent* went away, and dug a *hole* in the ground and hid his master's money. Now after a long time the master of those slaves came and settled accounts with them. The one who had received the five talents came up and brought five more talents, saying, 'Master, you entrusted five talents to me. See, I have gained five more talents.' His master said to him, 'Well done, good and faithful slave. You were faithful with a few things, I will put you in charge of many things; enter into the joy of your master.' Also the one who *had received* the two talents came up and said, 'Master, you entrusted two talents to me. See, I have gained two more talents.' His master said to him, 'Well done, good and faithful slave. You were faithful with a few things, I will put you in charge of many things; enter into the joy of your master.' And the one also who had received the one talent came up and said, 'Master, I knew you to be a hard man, reaping where you did not sow and gathering where you scattered no *seed.* And I was afraid, and went away and hid your talent in the ground. See, you have what is yours.' But his master answered and said to him, 'You wicked, lazy slave, you knew that I reap where I did not sow and gather where I scattered no *seed.* Then you ought to have put my money in the bank, and on my arrival I would have received my *money* back with interest. 'Therefore take away the talent from him, and give it to the one who has ten talents.' For to everyone who has, *more* shall be given, and he will have an abundance; but from the one who does not have, even what he does have shall be taken away. Throw out the worthless slave into the outer darkness; in that place there will be weeping and gnashing of teeth" (Matthew 25:14–30; cf. Matthew 8:12; 13:12; 24:45–47; see Matthew 18:23, 24; Luke 12:44).

[SCATTERING from SCATTERED]

Setting: On the way to the Mount of Olives. After celebrating the Passover meal in Jerusalem, prior to His betrayal by Judas, Jesus states that all His disciples will deny Him that very day.

Then Jesus said to them, "You will all fall away because of Me this night, for it is written, 'I WILL STRIKE DOWN THE SHEPHERD, AND THE SHEEP OF THE FLOCK SHALL BE SCATTERED.' But after I have been raised, I will go ahead of you to Galilee." But Peter said to Him, '*Even* though all may fall away because of You, I will never fall away.' Jesus said to him, "Truly I say to you that this *very* night, before a rooster crows, you will deny Me three times" (Matthew 26:31–34, Jesus quotes from Zechariah 13:7; cf. Mark 14:26–31; see Matthew 28:7, 10, 16; John 13:37).

[SCATTERING from SCATTERED]

Setting: A borrowed upper room in Jerusalem. After Jesus and His twelve disciples celebrate the Passover and the Lord's Supper, they go out to the Mount of Olives.

And Jesus said to them, "You will all fall away, because it is written, 'I WILL STRIKE DOWN THE SHEPHERD, AND THE SHEEP SHALL BE SCATTERED.' But after I have been raised, I will go ahead of you to Galilee." But Peter said to Him, "*Even* though all may fall away, yet I will not." And Jesus said to him, "Truly I say to you, that this very night, before a rooster crows twice, you yourself will deny Me three times" (Mark 14:27–30, Jesus quotes from Zechariah 13:7; cf. Matthew 26:30–34; see Mark 14:72).

[SCATTERING from scatters]
Setting: On the way from Galilee to Jerusalem. After some in the crowd test Him, demanding a sign from heaven, Jesus illustrates His power over Satan.

"When a strong *man*, fully armed, guards his own house, his possessions are undisturbed. But when someone stronger than he attacks him and overpowers him, he takes away from him all his armor on which he had relied and distributes his plunder. He who is not with Me is against Me; and he who does not gather with Me, scatters" (Luke 11:21–23; cf. Matthew 12:29, 30).

[SCATTERING from scatters]
Setting: Jerusalem. Following the Pharisees' interrogation and dismissal of the formerly blind man Jesus healed on the Sabbath, the Lord conveys the Parable of the Good Shepherd to the Pharisees, using figures of speech they do not understand.

So Jesus said to them again, "Truly, truly, I say to you, I am the door of the sheep. All who came before Me are thieves and robbers, but the sheep did not hear them. I am the door; if anyone enters through Me, he will be saved, and will go in and out and find pasture. The thief comes only to steal and kill and destroy; I came that they may have life, and have *it* abundantly. I am the good shepherd; the good shepherd lays down His life for the sheep. He who is a hired hand, and not a shepherd, who is not the owner of the sheep, sees the wolf coming, and leaves the sheep and flees, and the wolf snatches them and scatters *them. He flees* because he is a hired hand and is not concerned about the sheep. I am the good shepherd, and I know My own and My own know Me, even as the Father knows Me and I know the Father; and I lay down My life for the sheep. I have other sheep, which are not of this fold; I must bring them also, and they will hear My voice; and they will become one flock *with* one shepherd. For this reason the Father loves Me, because I lay down My life so that I may take it again. No one has taken it away from Me, but I lay it down on My own initiative. I have authority to take it up again. This commandment I received from My Father" (John 10:7–18; see Isaiah 40:11; 56:8; Jeremiah 23:1; Matthew 11:27).

[SCATTERING from scattered]
Setting: Jerusalem. Before the Passover, after conveying promises about praying in His name, Jesus prophesies the disciples' scattering and gives them assurance that in the midst of tribulation they will have His peace.

"Jesus answered them, "Do you now believe? Behold, an hour is coming, and has *already* come, for you to be scattered, each to his own *home,* and to leave Me alone; and *yet* I am not alone, because the Father is with Me. These things I have spoken to you, so that in Me you may have peace. In the world you have tribulation, but take courage, I have overcome the world" (John 16:31–33; see Zechariah 13:7; John 8:29; 14:27; Romans 8:37).

SCORCHING HEAT (Listed under HEAT, SCORCHING; also see SUN)

SCORPION (Also see SCORPIONS)
Setting: On the way from Galilee to Jerusalem. After revealing to His disciples how to pray, Jesus illustrates God's benevolence in answering prayer and giving the Holy Spirit.

"Now suppose one of you fathers is asked by his son for a fish; he will not give him a snake instead of a fish, will he? Or *if* he is asked for an egg, he will not give him a scorpion, will he? If you then, being evil, know how to give good gifts to your children, how much more will *your* heavenly Father give the Holy Spirit to those who ask Him?"
(Luke 11:11–13; cf. Matthew 7:9–11).

SCORPIONS (Also see SCORPION)
Setting: On the way from Galilee to Jerusalem. The Lord responds to a report from the seventy sent out in pairs to every place He Himself will soon visit.

And He said to them, "I was watching Satan fall from heaven like lightning. Behold, I have given you authority to tread on serpents and scorpions, and over all the power of the enemy, and nothing will injure you. Nevertheless do not rejoice in this, that the spirits are subject to you, but rejoice that your names are recorded in heaven" (Luke 10:18–20; see Psalm 91:13; Isaiah 14:12–14; Luke 9:1).

SCRIBE (Also see CHIEF PRIESTS; LAWYER; LAWYERS; and SCRIBES)

Setting: By the Sea of Galilee. Jesus teaches the Parable of the Head of a Household to His disciples.

And Jesus said to them, "Therefore every scribe who has become a disciple of the kingdom of heaven is like a head of a household, who brings out of his treasure things new and old" (Matthew 13:52).

SCRIBES (Also see CHIEF PRIESTS; ELDERS; GUIDES, BLIND; HYPOCRITES; PHARISEES; SADDUCEES; and SCRIBE)

Setting: Galilee. During the early part of His ministry, Jesus preaches the Sermon on the Mount to His disciples and the multitudes.

"For I say to you that unless your righteousness surpasses *that* of the scribes and Pharisees, you will not enter the kingdom of heaven" (Matthew 5:20; cf. Luke 18:11, 12).

Setting: Judea beyond the Jordan (Perea). Before going to Jerusalem, Jesus again tells His disciples of His impending death and resurrection.

As Jesus was about to go up to Jerusalem, He took the twelve *disciples* aside by themselves, and on the way He said to them, "Behold, we are going up to Jerusalem; and the Son of Man will be delivered to the chief priests and scribes, and they will condemn Him to death, and will hand Him over to the Gentiles to mock and scourge and crucify *Him,* and on the third day, He will be raised up" (Matthew 20:17–19; cf. Matthew 16:21; Mark 10:32–34; Luke 18:31–33).

Setting: The temple in Jerusalem. Jesus exposes the truth about Pharisaism to the crowds and His disciples after the Jewish religious leaders test Him with questions.

Then Jesus spoke to the crowds and to His disciples, saying: "The scribes and the Pharisees have seated themselves in the chair of Moses; therefore all that they tell you, do and observe, but do not do according to their deeds; for they say *things* and do not do *them.* They tie up heavy burdens and lay them on men's shoulders, but they themselves are unwilling to move them with *so much as* a finger. But they do all their deeds to be noticed by men; for they broaden their phylacteries and lengthen their tassels *of their garments.* They love the place of honor at banquets and the chief seats in the synagogues, and respectful greetings in the market places, and being called Rabbi by men. But do not be called Rabbi; for One is your Teacher, and you are all brothers. Do not call *anyone* on earth your father; for One is your Father, He who is in heaven. Do not be called leaders; for One is your Leader, *that is,* Christ. But the greatest among you shall be your servant. Whoever exalts himself shall be humbled; and whoever humbles himself shall be exalted" (Matthew 23:1–12; cf. Matthew 20:26; Mark 12:38–40; Luke 20:46, 47; see Exodus 13:9; Deuteronomy 33:3; Matthew 6:1, 5, 6, 9, 16; Mark 14:11; Luke 11:43; 14:11).

Setting: The temple in Jerusalem. After the Jewish religious leaders test Him with questions, Jesus pronounces the first of eight woes upon them in front of the crowds and His disciples.

"But woe to you, scribes and Pharisees, hypocrites, because you shut off the kingdom of heaven from people; for you do not enter in yourselves, nor do you allow those who are entering to go in (Matthew 23:13; cf. Luke 11:52).

Setting: The temple in Jerusalem. After the Jewish religious leaders test Him with questions, Jesus pronounces the second of eight woes upon them in front of the crowds and His disciples.

["Woe to you, scribes and Pharisees, hypocrites, because you devour widows' houses, and for a pretense you make long prayers; therefore you will receive greater condemnation] (Matthew 23:14; cf. Mark 12:40; Luke 20:47).

Setting: The temple in Jerusalem. After the Jewish religious leaders test Him with questions, Jesus pronounces the third of eight woes upon them in front of the crowds and His disciples.

"Woe to you, scribes and Pharisees, hypocrites, because you travel around on sea and land to make one proselyte; and when he becomes one, you make him twice as much a son of hell as yourselves" (Matthew 23:15).

Setting: The temple in Jerusalem. After the Jewish religious leaders test Him with questions, Jesus pronounces the fifth of eight woes upon them in front of the crowds and His disciples.

"Woe to you, scribes and Pharisees, hypocrites! For you tithe mint and dill and cummin, and have neglected the weightier provisions of the law: justice and mercy and faithfulness; but these are things you should have done without neglecting the others. You blind guides, who strain out a gnat and swallow a camel!" (Matthew 23:23, 24).

Setting: The temple in Jerusalem. After the Jewish religious leaders test Him with questions, Jesus pronounces the sixth of eight woes upon them in front of the crowds and His disciples.

"Woe to you, scribes and Pharisees, hypocrites! For you clean the outside of the cup and of the dish, but inside they are full of robbery and self-indulgence. You blind Pharisee, first clean the inside of the cup and of the dish, so that the outside of it may become clean also" (Matthew 23:25, 26; see Mark 7:4).

Setting: The temple in Jerusalem. After the Jewish religious leaders test Him with questions, Jesus pronounces the seventh of eight woes upon them in front of the crowds and His disciples.

"Woe to you, scribes and Pharisees, hypocrites! For you are like whitewashed tombs which on the outside appear beautiful, but inside they are full of dead men's bones and all uncleanness. So you, too, outwardly appear righteous to men, but inwardly you are full of hypocrisy and lawlessness" (Matthew 23:27, 28; cf. Luke 11:44).

Setting: The temple in Jerusalem. After the Jewish religious leaders test Him with questions, Jesus pronounces the eighth of eight woes upon them in front of the crowds and His disciples.

"Woe to you, scribes and Pharisees, hypocrites! For you build the tombs of the prophets and adorn the monuments of the righteous, and say, 'If we had been *living* in the days of our fathers, we would not have been partners with them in *shedding* the blood of the prophets.' So you testify against yourselves, that you are sons of those who murdered the prophets. Fill up, then, the measure *of the guilt* of you fathers. You serpents, you brood of vipers, how will you escape the sentence of hell? Therefore, behold, I am sending you prophets and wise men and scribes; some of them you will kill and crucify, and some of them you will scourge in your synagogues, and persecute from city to city, so that upon you may fall *the guilt of* all the righteous blood shed on earth, from the blood of righteous Abel to the blood of Zechariah, the son of Berechiah, whom you murdered between the temple and the altar. Truly I say to you, all these things will come upon this generation" (Matthew 23:29–36; cf. 2 Chronicles 24:21; Zechariah 1:1; Matthew 3:7; Luke 11:47–52; see Matthew 10:23).

Setting: On the road to Jerusalem. After encouraging His disciples with a revelation of their future reward, Jesus prophesies His persecution, death, and resurrection.

They were on the road going up to Jerusalem, and Jesus was walking on ahead of them; and they were amazed, and those who followed were fearful. And again He took the twelve aside and began to tell them what was going to happen to Him, *saying*, "Behold, we are going up to Jerusalem, and the Son of Man will be delivered to the chief priests and the scribes; and they will condemn Him to death and will hand Him over to the Gentiles. They will mock Him and spit on Him, and scourge Him and kill *Him,* and three days later He will rise again" (Mark 10:32–34; cf. Matthew 20:17–19; Luke 18:31–34; see Matthew 16:21; Mark 8:31).

Setting: The temple in Jerusalem. After commending one of the scribes for his nearness to the kingdom of God, Jesus teaches the crowd.

And Jesus *began* to say, as He taught in the temple, "How *is it that* the scribes say that the Christ is the son of David? David himself said in the Holy Spirit, 'THE LORD SAID TO MY LORD, SIT AT MY RIGHT HAND, UNTIL I PUT YOUR ENEMIES BENEATH YOUR FEET.'" David himself calls Him 'Lord'; so in what sense is He his son?" And the large crowd enjoyed listening to Him (Mark 12:35–37, Jesus quotes from Psalm 110:1; cf. Matthew 22:41–46; Luke 20:41–44).

Setting: The temple in Jerusalem. After commending one scribe for his nearness to the kingdom of God, Jesus warns the crowd about the rest of the scribes.

In His teaching He was saying: "Beware of the scribes who like to walk around in long robes, and *like* respectful greetings in the market places, and chief seats in the synagogues and places of honor at banquets, who devour widows' houses, and for appearance's sake offer long prayers; these will receive greater condemnation" (Mark 12:38–40; cf. Matthew 23:1–7; Luke 20:45–47).

Setting: Galilee. Following Peter's pronouncement that Jesus is the Christ of God, the Lord warns His disciples not to reveal His identity to anyone.

But He warned them and instructed *them* not to tell this to anyone, saying, "The Son of Man must suffer many things and be rejected by the elders and chief priests and scribes, and be killed and be raised up on the third day" (Luke 9:21, 22; cf. Matthew 16:21; Mark 8:31).

Setting: The temple in Jerusalem. While ministering a few days before His crucifixion, after posing a question to the scribes, who do not answer, Jesus warns His disciples about the lifestyle of the scribes.

"Beware of the scribes, who like to walk around in long robes, and love respectful greetings in the market places, and chief seats in the synagogues and places of honor at banquets, who devour widows' houses, and for appearance's sake offer long prayers. These will receive greater condemnation" (Luke 20:46, 47; cf. Matthew 23:1–7; Mark 12:38–40; see Luke 11:43).

SCRIPTURE (SCRIPTURE, FULFILLMENT OF; SCRIPTURES and SCRIPTURES, FULFILLMENT OF are separate entries; also see BIBLE; OLD TESTAMENT; PROPHETS, LAW AND THE; WORD; WORD, GOD'S; WORD OF GOD; and WORD, YOUR)

[SCRIPTURE from EVERY WORD THAT PROCEEDS OUT OF THE MOUTH OF GOD]

Setting: Judea, near the Jordan River. Following His baptism, and before He begins His public ministry, Jesus is led by the Spirit into the wilderness to be tempted by Satan for forty days.

But He answered and said, "It is written, 'MAN SHALL NOT LIVE ON BREAD ALONE, BUT ON EVERY WORD THAT PROCEEDS OUT OF THE MOUTH OF GOD'" (Matthew 4:4, Jesus quotes from Deuteronomy 8:3; cf. Luke 4:4).

Setting: The temple in Jerusalem. Having His authority questioned by the chief priests, scribes, and elders, Jesus begins to teach them in parables.

And He began to speak to them in parables: "A man PLANTED A VINEYARD AND PUT A WALL AROUND IT, AND DUG A VAT UNDER THE WINE PRESS AND BUILT A TOWER, and rented it out to vine-growers and went on a journey. At the *harvest* time he sent a slave to the vine-growers, in order to receive *some* of the produce of the vineyard from the vine-growers. They took him, and beat him and sent him away empty-handed. Again he sent them another slave, and they wounded him in the head, and treated him shamefully. And he sent another, and that one they killed; and *so with* many others, beating some and killing others. He had one more to *send*, a beloved son; he sent him last *of all* to them, saying, 'They will respect my son.' But those vine-growers said to one another, 'This is the heir; come, let us kill him, and the inheritance will be ours!' They took him, and killed him and threw him out of the vineyard. What will the owner of the vineyard do? He will come and destroy the vine-growers, and will give the vineyard to others. Have you not even read this Scripture: 'THE STONE WHICH THE BUILDERS REJECTED, THIS BECAME THE CHIEF CORNER *stone;* THIS CAME ABOUT FROM THE LORD, AND IT IS MARVELOUS IN OUR EYES'?" (Mark 12:1–11, Jesus quotes from Psalm 118:22, 23; Isaiah 5:1, 2; cf. Matthew 21:33–46; Luke 20:9–19).

[SCRIPTURE from the Law of Moses and the Prophets and the Psalms]
Setting: Jerusalem. After rising from the tomb on the third day after being crucified, and appearing to two of His followers on the road to Emmaus, Jesus gives instruction to His disciples (except Thomas) about His mission on earth and the promise of future power from God.

Now He said to them, "These are My words which I spoke to you while I was still with you, that all things which are written about Me in the Law of Moses and the Prophets and the Psalms must be fulfilled." Then He opened their minds to understand the Scriptures, and He said to them, "Thus it is written, that the Christ would suffer and rise again from the dead the third day, and that repentance for forgiveness of sins would be proclaimed in His name to all the nations, beginning from Jerusalem. You are witnesses of these things. And behold, I am sending forth the promise of My Father upon you; but you are to stay in the city until you are clothed with power from on high" (Luke 24:44–49; see Matthew 28:19, 20; Acts 1:8).

Setting: Jerusalem. On the last day of the Feast of Booths, after Jesus causes discussion about whether He is the Christ, the chief priests and Pharisees attempt to understand where it is He says He will be going soon. The Lord offers salvation and the abundant life to His hearers.

Now on the last day, the great *day* of the feast, Jesus stood and cried out, saying, "If anyone is thirsty, let him come to Me and drink. He who believes in Me, as the Scripture said, 'From his innermost being will flow rivers of living water'" (John 7:37, 38).

Setting: Jerusalem. At the Feast of Dedication, the Pharisees desire to stone Jesus because He claims to be equal with God when they ask him plainly whether He is the Christ.

Jesus answered them, "Has it not been written in your Law, 'I SAID, YOU ARE GODS'? If he called them gods, to whom the word of God came (and the Scripture cannot be broken), do you say of Him, whom the Father sanctified and sent into the world, 'You are blaspheming,' because I said, 'I am the Son of God'? If I do not do the works of My Father, do not believe Me; but if I do them, though you do not believe Me, believe the works, so that you may know and understand that the Father is in Me, and I in the Father" (John 10:34–38, Jesus quotes from Psalm 82:6; see John 14:10, 20).

SCRIPTURE, FULFILLMENT OF (SCRIPTURES, FULFILLMENT OF is a separate entry)

[FULFILLMENT OF SCRIPTURE from Scripture has been fulfilled]
Setting: The synagogue in Jesus' hometown of Nazareth in Galilee. At the beginning of His public ministry, Jesus reads on the Sabbath from the book of the prophet Isaiah.

And the book of the prophet Isaiah was handed to Him. And He opened the book and found the place where it was written, "THE SPIRIT OF THE LORD IS UPON ME, BECAUSE HE ANOINTED ME TO PREACH THE GOSPEL TO THE POOR. HE HAS SENT ME TO PROCLAIM RELEASE TO THE CAPTIVES, AND RECOVERY OF SIGHT TO THE BLIND, TO SET FREE THOSE WHO ARE OPPRESSED, TO PROCLAIM THE FAVORABLE YEAR OF THE LORD." And He closed the book, gave it back to the attendant and sat down; and the eyes of all in the synagogue were fixed on Him. And He began to say to them, "Today this Scripture has been fulfilled in your hearing" (Luke 4:17–21, Jesus quotes from Isaiah 61:1, 2).

[FULFILLMENT OF SCRIPTURE from all the things which are written through the prophets about the Son of Man will be accomplished]

Setting: On the way from Galilee to Jerusalem. After responding to Peter's statement about the disciples' personal sacrifice in following Him, Jesus tells them of the sacrifice He will make in Jerusalem.

Then He took the twelve aside and said to them, "Behold, we are going up to Jerusalem, and all things which are written through the prophets about the Son of Man will be accomplished. For He will be handed over to the Gentiles, and will be mocked and mistreated and spit upon, and after they have scourged Him, they will kill Him; and the third day He will rise again" (Luke 18:31–33; cf. Matthew 20:17–19; Mark 10:32–34).

[FULFILLMENT OF SCRIPTURE from that this which is written must be fulfilled in Me]
Setting: Jerusalem. During the Feast of Unleavened Bread (Passover) just before His crucifixion, while celebrating the Passover meal, instituting the Lord's Supper, and prophesying Peter's denial of Him, Jesus instructs His disciples to prepare to persevere without Him.

And He said to them, "When I sent you out without money belt and bag and sandals, you did not lack anything, did you?" They said, "*No*, nothing." And He said to them, "But now, whoever has a money belt is to take it along, likewise also a bag, and whoever has no sword is to sell his coat and buy one. For I tell you that this which is written must be fulfilled in Me, 'AND HE WAS NUMBERED WITH TRANSGRESSORS'; for that which refers to Me has *its* fulfillment." They said, "Lord, look, here are two swords." And He said to them, "It is enough" (Luke 22:35–38, Jesus quotes from Isaiah 53:12; see Matthew 10:5–15; Mark 6:7–11; Luke 9:1–5; 10:1–12; John 17:4).

[FULFILLMENT OF SCRIPTURE from Scripture may be fulfilled]
Setting: Jerusalem. Before the Passover, with His death on the cross nearing, Jesus explains the reason for His vivid example of servanthood in washing His disciples' feet.

So when He had washed their feet, and taken His garments and reclined *at the table* again, He said to them, "Do you know what I have done to you? You call Me Teacher and Lord; and you are right, for *so* I am. If I then, the Lord and the Teacher, washed your feet, you also ought to wash one another's feet. For I gave you an example that you also should do as I did to you. Truly, truly I say to you, a slave is not greater than his master, nor *is* one who is sent greater than the one who sent him. If you know these things, you are blessed if you do them. I do not speak of all of you. I know the ones I have chosen; but *it is* that the Scripture may be fulfilled, 'HE WHO EATS MY BREAD HAS LIFTED UP HIS HEEL AGAINST ME.' From now on I am telling you before *it* comes to pass, so that when it does occur, you may believe that I am *He*. Truly, truly, I say to you, he who receives whomever I send receives Me; and he who receives Me receives Him who sent Me" (John 13:12–20; Jesus quotes from Psalm 41:9; see Matthew 7:24; 10:24, 40; John 8:24; 14:29; 1 Peter 5:3).

[FULFILLMENT OF SCRIPTURE from to fulfill the word that is written in their Law]
Setting: Jerusalem. Before the Passover, with His upcoming departure in mind, after explaining He is the vine and His disciples are the branches, Jesus prepares them for hatred by the world.

"He who hates Me hates My Father also. If I had not done among them the works which no one else did, they would not have sin; but now they have both seen and hated Me and My Father as well. But *they have done this* to fulfill the word that is written in their Law, 'THEY HATED ME WITHOUT A CAUSE'" (John 15:23–25, Jesus quotes from Psalm 35:19; see John 9:41).

[FULFILLMENT OF SCRIPTURE from the Scripture would be fulfilled]
Setting: Jerusalem. Before the Passover, after giving His disciples assurance that in the midst of tribulation they will have His peace, Jesus prays His high-priestly prayer.

Jesus spoke these things; and lifting up His eyes to heaven, He said, "Father, the hour has come; glorify Your Son, that the Son may glorify You, even as You gave Him authority over all flesh, that to all whom You have given Him, He may give eternal life. This is eternal life, that they may know You, the only true God, and Jesus Christ whom You have sent. I glorified You on the earth, having accomplished the work which You have given Me to do. Now, Father, glorify Me together with Yourself, with the glory which I had with You before the world was. I have manifested Your name to the men whom You gave Me out of the world; they were Yours and You gave them to Me, and they have kept Your word. Now they have come to know that everything You have given Me is from You; for the words which You gave Me I have given to them; and they received *them* and truly understood that I came forth from You, and they believed You sent Me. I ask on their behalf; I do not ask on behalf of the world, but of those whom You have given Me; for they are Yours; and all things that are Mine are Yours, and Yours are Mine; and I have been glorified in them. I am no longer in the world; and *yet* they themselves are in the world, and I come to You. Holy Father, keep them in Your name, *the name* which You have given Me, that they may be even as We *are.* While I was with them, I was keeping them in Your name which You have given Me; and I guarded them and not one of them perished but the son of perdition, so that the Scripture would be fulfilled" (John 17:1–12; see Luke 22:32; John 1:1; 3:35; 4:34; 5:44; 6:37–39, 70; 8:42; 11:41; 12:49; 13:18, 31; 16:15; Philippians 2:9).

[FULFILLMENT OF SCRIPTURE from to fulfill the Scripture]
Setting: On the hill called Golgotha (the Place of the Skull), just outside Jerusalem. After asking His disciple John to care for His mother, in the midst of fulfilling Scripture as He dies on the cross for the sins of the world, Jesus expresses His thirst.

After this, Jesus, knowing that all things had already been accomplished, to fulfill the Scripture, said, "I am thirsty" (John 19:28; see Psalm 69:21; Matthew 27:48; Mark 15:36).

SCRIPTURES (SCRIPTURE; SCRIPTURE, FULFILLMENT OF; and SCRIPTURES, FULFILLMENT OF are separate entries; also see BIBLE; OLD TESTAMENT; PROPHETS, LAW AND THE; WORD, GOD'S; WORD, YOUR; and WRITINGS)
[SCRIPTURES from the Law and the Prophets]
Setting: Galilee. During the early part of His ministry, Jesus preaches the Sermon on the Mount to His disciples and the multitudes.

"In everything, therefore, treat people the same way you want them to treat you, for this is the Law and the Prophets" (Matthew 7:12; cf. Matthew 22:20; Luke 6:3).

Setting: The temple in Jerusalem. Jesus delivers a prophecy to the chief priests and elders after they question His authority.

Jesus said to them, "Did you never read in the Scriptures, 'THE STONE WHICH THE BUILDERS REJECTED, THIS BECAME THE CHIEF CORNER *stone;* THIS CAME ABOUT FROM THE LORD, AND IT IS MARVELOUS IN OUR EYES'? Therefore I say to you, the kingdom of God will be taken away from you and given to a people, producing the fruit of it. And he who falls on this stone will be broken to pieces; but on whomever it falls, it will scatter him like dust" (Matthew 21:42–44, Jesus quotes from Psalm 118:22; cf. Isaiah 8:14, 15; Mark 12:10, 11; Luke 20:17, 18).

Setting: The temple in Jerusalem. The Sadducees question Jesus about Levirate marriage (marriage to a brother-in-law), in order to test Him.

But Jesus answered and said to them, "You are mistaken, not understanding the Scriptures nor the power of God. For in the resurrection they neither marry nor are given in marriage, but are like angels in heaven. But regarding the resurrection of the dead, have you not read what was spoken to you by God: 'I AM THE GOD OF ABRAHAM, AND THE GOD OF ISAAC, AND THE GOD OF JACOB'? He is not the God of the dead but of the living" (Matthew 22:29–32, Jesus quotes from Exodus 3:6; cf. Mark 12:18–27; Luke 20:27–38; see Deuteronomy 25:5; John 20:9).

[SCRIPTURES from the whole Law and the Prophets]
Setting: The temple in Jerusalem. A Pharisee lawyer asks Jesus which is the great commandment of the Law, in order to test Him as He teaches.

And He said to him, "'YOU SHALL LOVE THE LORD YOUR GOD WITH ALL YOUR HEART, AND WITH ALL YOUR SOUL, AND WITH ALL YOUR MIND.' This is the great and foremost commandment. The second is like it,' YOU SHALL LOVE YOUR NEIGHBOR AS YOURSELF.' On these two commandments depend the whole Law and the Prophets" (Matthew 22:37–40; Jesus quotes from Leviticus 19:18; Deuteronomy 6:5; cf. Mark 12:28–34; see Matthew 7:12).

Setting: Gethsemane on the Mount of Olives, just east of the temple in Jerusalem. As Jesus submits to His Father's will and allows Judas to betray Him, Peter attempts to defend Him by force, but Jesus does not permit it.

Then Jesus said to him, "Put your sword back into its place; for all those who take up the sword shall perish by the sword. Or do you think that I cannot appeal to My Father, and He will at once put at My disposal more than twelve legions of angels? How then will the Scriptures be fulfilled, *which say* that it must happen this way?" (Matthew 26:52–54; cf. Mark 14:47; Luke 22:50–51; John 18:10, 11).

Setting: Gethsemane on the Mount of Olives, just east of the temple in Jerusalem. As He submits to His Father's will and allows Judas to betray Him, Jesus reveals that this incident is a fulfillment of prophecy.

At that time Jesus said to the crowds, "Have you come out with swords and clubs to arrest Me as *you would* against a robber? Every day I used to sit in the temple teaching and you did not seize Me. But all this has taken place to fulfill the Scriptures of the prophets" (Matthew 26:55, 56; cf. Mark 14:48, 49; Luke 22:52, 53; see Matthew 26:24).

Setting: The temple in Jerusalem. After some of the Pharisees and Herodians attempt to trap Jesus in a statement, some Sadducees question Him about the status of marriage after death.

Jesus said to them, "Is this not the reason you are mistaken, that you do not understand the Scriptures or the power of God? For when they rise from the dead, they neither marry nor are given in marriage, but are like angels in heaven. But regarding the fact that the dead rise again, have you not read in the book of Moses, in the *passage* about *the burning* bush, how God spoke to him, saying, 'I AM THE GOD OF ABRAHAM, AND THE GOD OF ISAAC, and the God of Jacob?' He is not the God of the dead, but of the living; you are greatly mistaken" (Mark 12:24–27, Jesus quotes from Exodus 3:6; cf. Matthew 22:29–33; Luke 20:34–40).

Setting: Gethsemane on the Mount of Olives, just east of the temple in Jerusalem. Judas betrays Jesus with a kiss in front of a crowd from the chief priests, scribes, and elders seeking to seize the Lord with swords and clubs.

And Jesus said to them, "Have you come out with swords and clubs to arrest Me, as *you would* against a robber? Every day I was with you in the temple teaching, and you did not seize Me; but *this has taken place* to fulfill the Scriptures" (Mark 14:48, 49; cf. Matthew 26:55, 56; Luke 22:52, 53).

[SCRIPTURES from The Law and the Prophets]
Setting: On the way from Galilee to Jerusalem. The Lord responds to the Pharisees' scoffing at His teaching His disciples about stewardship.

And He said to them, "You are those who justify yourselves in the sight of men, but God knows your hearts; for that which is highly esteemed among men is detestable in the sight of God. The Law and the Prophets *were proclaimed* until John; since that time the gospel of the kingdom of God has been preached, and everyone is forcing his way into it. But is it easier for heaven and earth to pass away than for one stroke of a letter of the Law to fail" (Luke 16:15–17; cf. Matthew 5:18; see 1 Samuel 16:7; Matthew 4:23; 11:11–14).

[SCRIPTURES from Moses and the Prophets]
Setting: On the way from Galilee to Jerusalem. After responding to the Pharisees' scoffing at His teaching the disciples about stewardship and the permanence of the Law, Jesus conveys the story of the rich man and Lazarus.

"Now there was a rich man, and he habitually dressed in purple and fine linen, joyously living in splendor every day. And a poor man named Lazarus was laid at his gate, covered with sores, and longing to be fed with the *crumbs* which were falling from the rich man's table; besides, even the dogs were coming and licking his sores. Now the poor man died and was carried away by the angels to Abraham's bosom; and the rich man also died and was buried. In Hades he lifted up his eyes, being in torment, and saw Abraham far away and Lazarus in his bosom. And he cried out and said, 'Father Abraham, have mercy on me, and send Lazarus so that he may dip the tip of his finger in water and cool off my tongue, for I am in agony in this flame.' But Abraham said, 'Child, remember that during your life you received your good things, and likewise Lazarus bad things; but now he is being comforted here, and you are in agony. And besides all this, between us and you there is a great chasm fixed, so that those who wish to come over from here to you will not be able, and *that* none may cross over from there to us.' And he said, 'Then I beg you, father, that you send him to my father's house—for I have five brothers—in order that he may warn them, so that they will not also come to this place of torment.' But Abraham said, 'They have Moses and the Prophets; let them hear them.' But he said, 'No, father Abraham, but if someone goes to them from the dead, they will repent!' But he said to him, 'If they do not listen to Moses and the Prophets, they will not be persuaded even if someone rises from the dead'" (Luke 16:19–31; see Luke 3:8; 6:24).

[SCRIPTURES from the Law of Moses and the Prophets and the Psalms]
Setting: Jerusalem. After rising from the tomb on the third day after being crucified, and appearing to two of His followers on the road to Emmaus, Jesus gives instruction to His disciples (except Thomas) about His mission on earth and the promise of future power from God.

Now He said to them, "These are My words which I spoke to you while I was still with you, that all things which are written about Me in the Law of Moses and the Prophets and the Psalms must be fulfilled." Then He opened their minds to understand the Scriptures, and He said to them, "Thus it is written, that the Christ would suffer and rise again from the dead the third day, and that repentance for forgiveness of sins would be proclaimed in His name to all the nations, beginning from Jerusalem. You are witnesses of these things. And behold, I am sending forth the promise of My Father upon you; but you are to stay in the city until you are clothed with power from on high" (Luke 24:44–49; see Matthew 28:19, 20; Acts 1:8).

Setting: Jerusalem. During a feast of the Jews, Jesus responds to criticism from the Jewish religious leaders by referring to God as His Father (thereby making Himself equal with God) and informing them that God, John the Baptist, the Scriptures, and His works all testify to His mission.

"You search the Scriptures because you think that in them you have eternal life; it is these that testify about Me; and you are unwilling to come to Me so that you may have life. I do not receive glory from men; but I know you, that you do not have the love of God in yourselves. I have come in My Father's name, and you do not receive Me; if another comes in his own name, you will receive him. How can you believe, when you receive glory from one another and you do not seek the glory that is from the *one and* only God? Do not think that I will accuse you before the Father; the one who accuses you is Moses, in whom you have set your hope. For if you believed Moses, you would believe Me, for he wrote about Me. But if you do not believe his writings, how will you believe My words?" (John 5:39–47; see Matthew 24:5; Luke 16:29, 31; 24:27; John 9:28; 17:3).

SCRIPTURES, FULFILLMENT OF (SCRIPTURE, FULFILLMENT OF is a separate entry)

[FULFILLMENT OF SCRIPTURES from the Law or the Prophets; I did not come to abolish but to fulfill]
Setting: Galilee. During the early part of His ministry, Jesus preaches the Sermon on the Mount to His disciples and the multitudes.

"Do not think that I came to abolish the Law or the Prophets; I did not come to abolish but to fulfill. For truly I say to you, until heaven and earth pass away, not the smallest letter or stroke shall pass from the Law until all is accomplished" (Matthew 5:17, 18; cf. Matthew 24:35).

[FULFILLMENT OF SCRIPTURES from the Scriptures be fulfilled]
Setting: Gethsemane on the Mount of Olives, just east of the temple in Jerusalem. As Jesus submits to His Father's will and allows Judas to betray Him, Peter attempts to defend Him by force, but Jesus does not permit it.

Then Jesus said to him, "Put your sword back into its place; for all those who take up the sword shall perish by the sword. Or do you think that I cannot appeal to My Father, and He will at once put at My disposal more than twelve legions of angels? How then will the Scriptures be fulfilled, *which say* that it must happen this way?" (Matthew 26:52–54; cf. Mark 14:47; Luke 22:50, 51; John 18:10, 11; see Matthew 26:24).

[FULFILLMENT OF SCRIPTURES from to fulfill the Scriptures of the prophets]
Setting: Gethsemane on the Mount of Olives, just east of the temple in Jerusalem. As He submits to His Father's will and allows Judas to betray Him, Jesus reveals that this is a fulfillment of prophecy.

At that time Jesus said to the crowds, "Have you come out with swords and clubs to arrest Me as *you would* against a robber? Every day I used to sit in the temple teaching and you did not seize Me. But all this has taken place to fulfill the Scriptures of the prophets" (Matthew 26:55, 56; cf. Mark 14:48, 49; Luke 22:52, 53; see Matthew 26:24).

[FULFILLMENT OF SCRIPTURES from to fulfill the Scriptures]
Setting: Gethsemane on the Mount of Olives, just east of the temple in Jerusalem. Judas betrays Jesus with a kiss in front of a crowd from the chief priests, scribes, and elders seeking to seize the Lord with swords and clubs.

And Jesus said to them, "Have you come out with swords and clubs to arrest Me, as *you would* against a robber? Every day I was with you in the temple teaching, and you did not seize Me; but *this has taken place* to fulfill the Scriptures" (Mark 14:48, 49; cf. Matthew 26:55, 56; Luke 22:52, 53).

[FULFILLMENT OF SCRIPTURES from the Law of Moses and the Prophets and the Psalms must be fulfilled]
Setting: Jerusalem. After rising from the tomb on the third day after being crucified, and appearing to two of His followers on the road to Emmaus, Jesus gives instruction to His disciples (except Thomas, who is absent) about His mission on earth and the promise of future power from God.

Now He said to them, "These are My words which I spoke to you while I was still with you, that all things which are written about Me in the Law of Moses and the Prophets and the Psalms must be fulfilled." Then He opened their minds to understand the Scriptures, and He said to them, "Thus it is written, that the Christ would suffer and rise again from the dead the third day, and that repentance for forgiveness of sins would be proclaimed in His name to all the nations, beginning from Jerusalem. You are witnesses of these things. And behold, I am sending forth the promise of My Father upon you; but you are to stay in the city until you are clothed with power from on high" (Luke 24:44–49; see Matthew 28:19, 20; Acts 1:8).

SCRIPTURES OF THE PROPHETS (Listed under PROPHETS, SCRIPTURES OF THE)

SCRIPTURES SUMMARIZED (See COMMANDMENT, FOREMOST)

SEA (Also see WAVES)

Setting: By the Sea of Galilee. Because the religious leaders are rejecting His message, Jesus continues teaching His disciples with the Parable of the Dragnet.

"Again, the kingdom of heaven is like a dragnet cast into the sea, and gathering *fish* of every kind; and when it was filled, they drew it up on the beach; and they sat down and gathered the good *fish* into containers, but the bad they threw away. So it will be at the end of the age; the angels will come forth and take out the wicked from among the righteous, and will throw them into the furnace of fire; in that place there will be weeping and gnashing of teeth. Have you understood all these things?" They said to Him, "Yes" (Matthew 13:47–51).

Setting: Capernaum of Galilee. Jesus pays the two-drachma temple tax for Peter and Himself in a miraculous manner.

He said, "Yes." And when he came into the house, Jesus spoke to him first, saying, "What do you think, Simon? From whom do the kings of the earth collect customs or poll-tax, from their sons or from strangers?" When Peter said, "From strangers," Jesus said to him, "Then the sons are exempt. However, so that we do not offend them, go to the sea and throw in a hook, and take the first fish that comes up; and when you open its mouth, you will find a shekel. Take that and give it to them for you and Me" (Matthew 17:25–27; see Exodus 30:11–16; Matthew 22:17–19; Romans 13:7).

Setting: Capernaum of Galilee. Jesus answers His disciples' question about greatness, or rank, in the kingdom of heaven.

And He called a child to Himself and set him before them, and said, "Truly I say to you, unless you are converted and become like children, you will not enter the kingdom of heaven. Whoever then humbles himself as this child, he is the greatest in the kingdom of heaven. And whoever receives one such child in My name receives Me; but whoever causes one of these little ones who believe in Me to stumble, it would be better for him to have a heavy millstone hung around his neck, and to be drowned in the depth of the sea"
(Matthew 18:2–6; cf. Matthew 19:14; Mark 9:33–37, 42; Luke 9:47, 48; Luke 17:1, 2).

Setting: On the way from Bethany to Jerusalem. The day after Jesus curses a fig tree (an illustration of the nation Israel), His disciples ask Him how it has so quickly withered.

And Jesus answered and said to them, "Truly I say to you, if you have faith and do not doubt, you will not only do what was done to the fig tree, but even if you say to this mountain, 'Be taken up and cast into the sea,' it will happen. And all things you ask in prayer, believing, you will receive" (Matthew 21:21, 22; cf. Matthew 7:7; Matthew 17:20; Mark 11:20–24).

Setting: The temple in Jerusalem. After the Jewish religious leaders test Him with questions, Jesus pronounces the third of eight woes on them in front of the crowds and His disciples.

"Woe to you, scribes and Pharisees, hypocrites, because you travel around on sea and land to make one proselyte; and when he becomes one, you make him twice as much a son of hell as yourselves" (Matthew 23:15).

Setting: Capernaum of Galilee. As Jesus teaches His disciples in private, they ask Him about greatness.

But Jesus said, "Do not hinder him, for there is no one who will perform a miracle in My name, and be able soon afterward to speak evil of Me. For he who is not against us is for us. For whoever gives you a cup of water to drink because of your name as *followers* of Christ, truly I say to you, he will not lose his reward. Whoever causes one of these little ones who believe to stumble, it would be better for him if, with a heavy millstone hung around his neck, he had been cast into the sea. If your hand causes you to stumble, cut it off; it is better for you to enter life crippled, than, having your two hands, to go into hell, into the unquenchable fire, [where THEIR WORM DOES NOT DIE, AND THE FIRE IS NOT QUENCHED.] If your foot causes you to stumble, cut it off; it is better for you to enter life lame, than, having your two feet, to be cast into hell, [where THEIR WORM DOES NOT DIE, AND THE FIRE IS NOT QUENCHED.] If your eye causes you to stumble, throw it out; it is better for you to enter the kingdom of God with one eye, than, having two eyes, to be cast into hell, where THEIR WORM DOES NOT DIE, AND THE FIRE IS NOT QUENCHED. For everyone will be salted with fire. Salt is good; but if the salt becomes unsalty, with what will you make it salty *again?* Have salt in yourselves, and be at peace with one another" (Mark 9:39–50; Jesus quotes from Isaiah 66:24; cf. Matthew 18:6–9; Luke 9:49, 50; see Matthew 5:13, 29, 30; 10:42; 12:30; 18:5, 6).

Setting: Just outside Jerusalem. The day after Jesus instructs the money changers while He cleanses the temple, Peter draws the Lord's and His disciples' attention to an earlier-cursed fig tree.

And Jesus answered saying to them, "Have faith in God. Truly, I say to you, whoever says to this mountain, 'Be taken up and cast into the sea,' and does not doubt in his heart, but believes that what he says is going to happen, it will be *granted* him. Therefore I say to you, all things for which you pray and ask, believe that you have received them, and they will be *granted* you. Whenever you stand praying, forgive, if you have anything against anyone, so that your Father who is in heaven will also forgive you your transgressions. [But if you do not forgive, neither will your Father who is in heaven forgive your transgressions'] (Mark 11:22–26; cf. Matthew 21:19–22; see Matthew 6:14, 15; 7:7; 17:20).

Setting: On the way from Galilee to Jerusalem. After conveying the story of the rich man and Lazarus, the Lord gives His disciples instruction on forgiveness.

He said to His disciples, "It is inevitable that stumbling blocks come, but woe to him through whom they come! It would be better for him if a millstone were hung around his neck and he were thrown into the sea, than that he would cause one of these little ones to stumble. Be on your guard! If your brother sins, rebuke him; and if he repents, forgive him. And if he sins against you seven times a day, and returns to you seven times, saying, 'I repent,' forgive him" (Luke 17:1–4; see Matthew 18:5–7, 15, 21, 22).

Setting: On the way from Galilee to Jerusalem. After His disciples ask that their faith be increased following His instruction to them on forgiveness, the Lord illustrates with the mustard seed and an obedient slave.

And the Lord said, "If you had faith like a mustard seed, you would say to this mulberry tree, 'Be uprooted and be planted in the sea'; and it would obey you. Which of you, having a slave plowing or tending sheep, will say to him when he has come from the field, 'Come immediately and sit down to eat'? But will he not say to him, "Prepare something for me to eat, and *properly* clothe yourself and serve me while I eat and drink; and afterward you may eat and drink'? He does not thank the slave because he did the things which were commanded, does he? So you too, when you do all the things which are commanded you, say, 'We are unworthy slaves; we have done *only* that which we ought to have done' " (Luke 17:6–10; see Matthew 13:31; Luke 12:37; 17:5).

Setting: On the Mount of Olives, just east of Jerusalem. After ministering in the temple a few days before His crucifixion, and giving His disciples more details regarding future events, Jesus speaks during His Olivet Discourse of His return.

"There will be signs in sun and moon and stars, and on the earth dismay among the nations, in perplexity at the roaring of the sea and the waves, men fainting from fear and the expectation of the things which are coming upon the world; for the powers of the heavens will be shaken. Then they will see THE SON OF MAN COMING IN A CLOUD with power and great glory. But when these things begin to take place, straighten up and lift up your heads, because your redemption is drawing near" (Luke 21:25–28, Jesus quotes from Daniel 7:13; cf. Matthew 24:29–31; Mark 13:24–27).

SEA, CALMING THE

[CALMING THE SEA from Hush, be still]

***Setting:* By the Sea of Galilee. Jesus calms the sea in the midst of a storm while in a boat with His disciples.**

And He got up and rebuked the wind and said to the sea, "Hush, be still." And the wind died down and it became perfectly calm. And He said to them, "Why are you afraid? Do you still have no faith?" (Mark 4:39, 40: cf. Matthew 18:26; Luke 8:25; see Psalm 65:7; Mark 4:35–39; Matthew 14:31).

SEA MONSTER (Listed under MONSTER, SEA)

SEA OF GALILEE (Listed under GALILEE, SEA OF)

SEAL

Setting: Capernaum. The day after Jesus walks on the Sea of Galilee to join His disciples in a boat, the people He miraculously fed with a lad's five loaves and two fish ask the Lord how He crossed the water, since He had not entered the boat from land with His disciples.

Jesus answered them and said, "Truly, truly, I say to you, you seek Me, not because you saw signs, but because you ate of the loaves and were filled. Do not work for the food which perishes, but for the food which endures to eternal life, which the Son of Man will give to you, for on Him the Father, God, has set His seal" (John 6:26, 27; see John 3:33).

SEASONS (See SUMMER; and WINTER)

SEATS, CHIEF (Also see CHIEF PRIESTS)

Setting: The temple in Jerusalem. Jesus exposes the truth about Pharisaism to the crowds and His disciples after the Jewish religious leaders test Him with questions.

Then Jesus spoke to the crowds and to His disciples, saying: "The scribes and the Pharisees have seated themselves in the chair of Moses; therefore all that they tell you, do and observe, but do not do according to their deeds; for they say *things* and do not do *them.* They tie up heavy burdens and lay them on men's shoulders, but they themselves are unwilling to move them with *so much as* a finger. But they do all their deeds to be noticed by men; for they broaden their phylacteries and lengthen their tassels *of their garments.* They love the place of honor at banquets and the chief seats in the synagogues, and respectful greetings in the market places, and being called Rabbi by men. But do not be called Rabbi; for One is your Teacher, and you are all brothers. Do not call *anyone* on earth your father; for One is your Father, He who is in heaven. Do not be called leaders; for One is your Leader, *that is,* Christ. But the greatest among you shall be your servant. Whoever exalts himself shall be humbled; and whoever humbles himself shall be exalted" (Matthew 23:1–12; cf. Matthew 20:26; Mark 12:38–40; Luke 20:46, 47; see Exodus 13:9; Deuteronomy 33:3; Matthew 6:1, 5, 6, 9, 16; Mark 14:11; Luke 11:43; 14:11).

Setting: The temple in Jerusalem. After commending one scribe for his nearness to the kingdom of God, Jesus warns the crowd about the rest of the scribes.

In His teaching He was saying: "Beware of the scribes who like to walk around in long robes, and *like* respectful greetings in the market places, and chief seats in the synagogues and places of honor at banquets, who devour widows' houses, and for appearance's sake offer long prayers; these will receive greater condemnation" (Mark 12:38–40; cf. Matthew 23:1–7; Luke 20:45–47).

Setting: On the way from Galilee to Jerusalem. After speaking of how a lamp illuminates, the Lord has lunch with a Pharisee who is surprised He doesn't wash before eating.

But the Lord said to him, "Now you Pharisees clean the outside of the cup and of the platter; but inside of you, you are full of robbery and wickedness. You foolish ones, did not He who made the outside make the inside also? But give that which is within as charity, and then all things are clean for you. But woe to you Pharisees! You pay tithe of mint and rue and every *kind of* garden herb, and *yet* disregard justice and the love of God; but these are the things you should have done without neglecting the others. Woe to you Pharisees! For you love the chief seats in the synagogues and the respectful greetings in the market places. Woe to you! For you are like concealed tombs, and the people who walk over *them* are unaware *of it*" (Luke 11:39–44; cf. Matthew 23:6, 7, 23–27; see Matthew 15:2; Titus 1:15).

Setting: The temple in Jerusalem. While ministering a few days before His crucifixion, after posing a question to the scribes, who do not answer, Jesus warns His disciples about the lifestyle of the scribes.

"Beware of the scribes, who like to walk around in long robes, and love respectful greetings in the market places, and chief seats in the synagogues and places of honor at banquets, who devour widows' houses, and for appearance's sake offer long prayers. These will receive greater condemnation" (Luke 20:46, 47; cf. Matthew 23:1–7; Mark 12:38–40; see Luke 11:43).

SECLUDED PLACE (Listed under PLACE, SECLUDED)

SECOND

Setting: The temple in Jerusalem. Jesus delivers a parable to the chief priests and elders after they question His authority.

"But what do you think? A man had two sons, and he came to the first and said, 'Son, go work today in the vineyard.' And he answered, 'I will not'; but afterward he regretted it and went. The man came to the second and said the same thing; and he answered, 'I *will,* sir'; but he did not go. Which of the two sons did the will of his father?" They said, "The first." Jesus said to them, "Truly, I say to you that the tax collectors and prostitutes will get into the kingdom of God before you. For John came to you in the way of righteousness and you did not believe him; but the tax collectors and prostitutes did believe him; and you, seeing *this,* did not even feel remorse afterward so as to believe him" (Matthew 21:28–32; cf. Luke 7:29, 30, 37–50).

Setting: The temple in Jerusalem. A Pharisee lawyer asks Jesus which is the great commandment of the Law, in order to test Him as He teaches.

And He said to him, "'YOU SHALL LOVE THE LORD YOUR GOD WITH ALL YOUR HEART, AND WITH ALL YOUR SOUL, AND WITH ALL YOUR MIND.' This is the great and foremost commandment. The second is like it,' YOU SHALL LOVE YOUR NEIGHBOR AS YOURSELF.' On these two commandments depend the whole Law and the Prophets" (Matthew 22:37–40; Jesus quotes from Leviticus 19:18; Deuteronomy 6:5; cf. Mark 12:28–34; see Matthew 7:12).

Setting: The temple in Jerusalem. With the Pharisees and Herodians failing to trap Jesus in a statement, one of the scribes asks Him which commandment is foremost.

Jesus answered, "The foremost is, 'HEAR, O ISRAEL! THE LORD OUR GOD IS ONE LORD; AND YOU SHALL LOVE THE LORD YOUR GOD WITH ALL YOUR HEART, AND WITH ALL YOUR SOUL, AND WITH ALL YOUR MIND AND WITH ALL YOUR STRENGTH.' The second is this, 'YOU SHALL LOVE YOUR NEIGHBOR AS YOURSELF.' There is no other commandment greater than these" (Mark 12:29–31, Jesus quotes from Deuteronomy 6:4, 5; Leviticus 19:18; cf. Matthew 22:34–40).

Setting: On the way from Galilee to Jerusalem. After giving a parable about riches and greed, Jesus uses another parable to challenge the crowd and His disciples to be ready for His return.

"Be dressed in readiness, and *keep* your lamps lit. Be like men who are waiting for their master when he returns from the wedding feast, so that they may immediately open *the door* to him when he comes and knocks. Blessed are those slaves whom the master will find on the alert when he comes; truly I say to you, that he will gird himself *to serve,* and have them recline *at the table,* and will come up and wait on them. Whether he comes in the second watch, or even in the third and finds *them* so, blessed are those *slaves.* But be sure of this, that if the head of the house had known at what hour the thief was coming, he would not have allowed his house to be broken into. You too, be ready; for the Son of Man is coming at an hour that you do not expect" (Luke 12:35–40; cf. Matthew 24:42–44; see Mark 13:33; Ephesians 6:14).

Setting: Jericho, on the way to Jerusalem. After commending Zaccheus's faith in Him, Jesus provides a parable about stewardship.

So He said, "A nobleman went to a distant country to receive a kingdom for himself, and *then* return. And he called ten of his slaves, and gave them ten minas and said to them, 'Do business *with this* until I come *back.*' But his citizens hated him and sent a delegation after him, saying, 'We do not want this man to reign over us.' When he returned, after receiving the kingdom, he ordered that these slaves, to whom he had given the money, be called to him so that he might know what business they had done. The first appeared, saying, 'Master, your mina has made ten minas more.' And he said to him, 'Well done, good slave, because you have been faithful in a very little thing, you are to be in authority over ten cities.' The second came, saying, 'Your mina, master, has made five minas.' And he said to him, also, 'And you are to be over five cities.' Another came, saying, 'Master, here is your mina, which I kept put away in a handkerchief; for I was afraid of you, because you are an exacting man; you take up what you did not lay down and reap what you did not sow.' He said to him, 'By your own words I will judge you, you worthless slave. Did you know that I am an exacting man, taking up what I did not lay down and reaping what I did not sow? Then why did you not put my money in the bank, and having come, I would have collected it with interest?' Then he said to the bystanders, 'Take the mina away from him and give it to the one who has the ten minas.' And they said to him, 'Master, he has ten minas *already.*' I tell you that to everyone who has, more shall be given, but from the one who does not have, even what he does have shall be taken away.

But these enemies of mine, who did not want me to reign over them, bring them here and slay them in my presence" (Luke 19:12–27; cf. Matthew 25:14–30; see Matthew 13:12; Luke 16:10).

Setting: On the island of Patmos (in the Aegean Sea about fifty miles southwest of Ephesus in modern Turkey). On the Lord's Day (Sunday), approximately fifty years after the Resurrection, the disciple John encounters the Lord Jesus Christ, who communicates a new revelation for the apostle to record for the church in Smyrna and to six other churches in Asia.

"And to the angel of the church in Smyrna write: The first and the last, who was dead, and has come to life, says this: 'I know your tribulation and your poverty (but you are rich), and the blasphemy by those who say they are Jews and are not, but are a synagogue of Satan. Do not fear what you are about to suffer. Behold, the devil is about to cast some of you into prison, so that you will be tested, and you will have tribulation for ten days. Be faithful until death, and I will give you the crown of life. He who has an ear, let him hear what the Spirit says to the churches. He who overcomes will not be hurt by the second death' (Revelation 2:8–11; see Isaiah 44:6; Revelation 1:9, 18; 20:6, 14).

SECOND CHANCES (Listed under CHANCES, SECOND)

SECOND COMING (See JESUS' RETURN; LORD, COMING OF THE; SON OF MAN, COMING OF THE)

SECOND DEATH (Listed under DEATH, SECOND)

SECRET (Also see MYSTERY; and SECRETS)

Setting: Galilee. During the early part of His ministry, Jesus preaches the Sermon on the Mount to His disciples and the multitudes.

"So when you give to the poor, do not sound a trumpet before you, as the hypocrites do in the synagogues and in the streets, so that they may be honored by men. Truly I say to you, they have their reward in full. But when you give to the poor, do not let your left hand know what your right hand is doing, so that your giving will be in secret; and your Father who sees *what is done* in secret will reward you" (Matthew 6:2–4; see Jeremiah 17:10).

Setting: Galilee. During the early part of His ministry, Jesus preaches the Sermon on the Mount to His disciples and the multitudes.

"When you pray, you are not to be like the hypocrites; for they love to stand and pray in the synagogues and on the street corners so that they may be seen by men. Truly I say to you, they have their reward in full. But you, when you pray, go into your inner room, close your door and pray to your Father who is in secret, and your Father who sees *what is done* in secret will reward you" (Matthew 6:5, 6; see Mark 11:25).

Setting: Galilee. During the early part of His ministry, Jesus preaches the Sermon on the Mount to His disciples and the multitudes.

"Whenever you fast, do not put on a gloomy face as the hypocrites *do,* for they neglect their appearance so that they will be noticed by men when they are fasting. Truly I say to you, they have their reward in full. But you, when you fast, anoint your head and wash your face so that your fasting will not be noticed by men, but by your Father who is in secret; and your Father who sees *what is done* in secret will reward you" (Matthew 6:16–18).

Setting: Galilee. Following His explanation of the Parable of the Sower to His disciples, Jesus illustrates what they should do with this truth.

And He was saying to them, "A lamp is not brought to be put under a basket, is it, or under a bed? Is it not *brought* to be put on the lampstand? For nothing is hidden, except to be revealed; nor has *anything* been secret, but that it would come to light. If anyone has ears to hear, let him hear" (Mark 4:21–23; cf. Luke 8:16, 17; see Matthew 5:14–16; 10:26).

Setting: Galilee. Following His explanation of the Parable of the Sower to His disciples, Jesus gives the Parable of the Lamp.

"Now no one after lighting a lamp covers it over with a container, or puts it under a bed; but he puts it on a lampstand, so that those who come in may see the light. For nothing is hidden that will not become evident, nor *anything* secret that will not be known and come to light. So take care how you listen; for whoever has, to him *more* shall be given; and whoever does not have, even what he thinks he has shall be taken away from him" (Luke 8:16–18; cf. Mark 4:21–23; see Matthew 5:14, 15; 10:26; 13:12).

Setting: Jerusalem. After Jesus is betrayed by Judas, and Peter denies he was His disciple, Annas, former high priest and father-in-law of the current high priest (Caiaphas), questions the Lord about His disciples and His teaching.

Jesus answered him, "I have spoken openly to the world; I always taught in synagogues and in the temple, where all the Jews come together; and I spoke nothing in secret. Why do you question Me? Question those who have heard what I spoke to them; they know what I said" (John 18:20, 21; see John 7:26).

SECRETS (Also see MYSTERIES; MYSTERY; PARABLES; and SECRET)

[SECRETS from hidden these things]
Setting: Galilee. After pronouncing woes against unrepentant cities as He teaches and preaches, Jesus prays a thanksgiving prayer to His Father in heaven.

At that time Jesus said, "I praise You, Father, Lord of heaven and earth, that you have hidden these things from *the* wise and intelligent and have revealed them to infants. Yes, Father, for this way was well-pleasing in Your sight. All things have been handed over to Me by My Father; and no one knows the Son except the Father; nor does anyone know the Father except the Son, and anyone to whom the Son wills to reveal *Him*" (Matthew 11:25–27; cf. Luke 10:21, 22).

[SECRETS from You have hidden these things]
Setting: On the way from Galilee to Jerusalem. The Lord responds to a report from the seventy sent out in pairs to every place He Himself will soon visit.

At that very time He rejoiced greatly in the Holy Spirit, and said, "I praise You, O Father, Lord of heaven and earth, that You have hidden these things from *the* wise and intelligent and have revealed them to infants. Yes, Father, for this way was well-pleasing in Your sight. All things have been handed over to Me by My Father, and no one knows who the Son is except the Father, and who the Father is except the Son, and anyone to whom the Son wills to reveal *Him*" (Luke 10:21, 22; cf. Matthew 11:25–27; see Luke 10:1, 17; John 3:35).

[SECRETS from there is nothing covered up that will not be revealed and whispered in the inner rooms]
Setting: On the way from Galilee to Jerusalem. Jesus warns His disciples of future events, as the scribes and Pharisees turn hostile and question Him repeatedly in an attempt to catch Him in something He might say.

Under these circumstances, after so many thousands of people had gathered together that they were stepping on one another, He began saying to His disciples first *of all,* "Beware of the leaven of the Pharisees, which is hypocrisy. But there is nothing covered up that will not be revealed, and hidden that will not be known. Accordingly, whatever you have said in the dark will be heard in the light, and what you have whispered in the inner rooms will be proclaimed upon the housetops. I say to you, My friends, do not be afraid of those who kill the body and after that have no more that they can do. But I will warn you whom to fear: fear

the One who, after He has killed, has authority to cast into hell; yes, I tell you, fear Him! Are not five sparrows sold for two cents? *Yet* not one of them is forgotten before God. Indeed, the very hairs of your head are all numbered. Do not fear; you are more valuable than many sparrows" (Luke 12:1–7; cf. Matthew 10:26–31; see Matthew 16:6; Hebrews 10:31).

SECURITY, ETERNAL (See ETERNAL SECURITY)

SEED (SEED, GOOD; and SEED, MUSTARD are separate entries; also see SEEDS)

Setting: By the Sea of Galilee. With the religious leaders rejecting His message, Jesus begins to teach in parables, and gives His disciples the meaning of the Parable of the Sower.

"Hear then the parable of the sower. When anyone hears the word of the kingdom and does not understand it, the evil *one* comes and snatches away what has been sown in his heart. This is the one on whom seed was sown beside the road. The one on whom seed was sown on the rocky places, this is the man who hears the word and immediately receives it with joy; yet he has no *firm* root in himself, but is *only* temporary, and when affliction or persecution arises because of the word, immediately he falls away. And the one on whom seed was sown among the thorns, this is the man who hears the word, and the worry of the world and the deceitfulness of wealth choke the word, and it becomes unfruitful. And the one on whom seed was sown on the good soil, this is the man who hears the word and understands it; who indeed bears fruit and brings forth, some a hundredfold, some sixty, and some thirty" (Matthew 13:18–23; cf. Mark 4:13–20; Luke 8:11–15).

Setting: On the Mount of Olives, just east of Jerusalem. During His Olivet Discourse, after answering His disciples' questions as to when the temple will be destroyed and Jerusalem overrun, along with the signs of His coming and the end of the age, Jesus reemphasizes to His disciples that they should be on the alert for His return.

"For *it is* just like a man *about* to go on a journey, who called his own slaves and entrusted his possessions to them. To one he gave five talents, to another, two, and to another, one, each according to his own ability; and he went on his journey. Immediately the one who had received the five talents went and traded with them, and gained five more talents. In the same manner the one who *had received* the two *talents* gained two more. But he who received the one *talent* went away, and dug a *hole* in the ground and hid his master's money. Now after a long time the master of those slaves came and settled accounts with them. The one who had received the five talents came up and brought five more talents, saying, 'Master, you entrusted five talents to me. See, I have gained five more talents.' His master said to him, 'Well done, good and faithful slave. You were faithful with a few things, I will put you in charge of many things; enter into the joy of your master.' Also the one who *had received* the two talents came up and said, 'Master, you entrusted two talents to me. See, I have gained two more talents.' His master said to him, 'Well done, good and faithful slave. You were faithful with a few things, I will put you in charge of many things; enter into the joy of your master.' And the one also who had received the one talent came up and said, 'Master, I knew you to be a hard man, reaping where you did not sow and gathering where you scattered no *seed.* And I was afraid, and went away and hid your talent in the ground. See, you have what is yours.' But his master answered and said to him, 'You wicked, lazy slave, you knew that I reap where I did not sow and gather where I scattered no *seed.* Then you ought to have put my money in the bank, and on my arrival I would have received my *money* back with interest. 'Therefore take away the talent from him, and give it to the one who has ten talents.' For to everyone who has, *more* shall be given, and he will have an abundance; but from the one who does not have, even what he does have shall be taken away. Throw out the worthless slave into the outer darkness; in that place there will be weeping and gnashing of teeth" (Matthew 25:14–30; cf. Matthew 8:12; 13:12; 24:45–47; see Matthew 18:23, 24; Luke 12:44).

Setting: By the Sea of Galilee. During the early part of His ministry, just after a visit from his mother and brothers, Jesus instructs a very large crowd with the Parable of the Sower from a boat.

"Listen *to this!* Behold, the sower went out to sow; as he was sowing, some *seed* fell beside the road, and the birds came and ate it up. Other *seed* fell on the rocky *ground* where it did not have much soil; and immediately it sprang up because it had no depth of soil. And after the sun had risen, it was scorched; and because it had no root, it withered away. Other *seed* fell among the thorns, and the thorns came up and choked it, and it yielded no crop. Other *seeds* fell into the good soil, and as the grew up and increased, they yielded a crop and produced thirty, sixty, and a hundredfold." And He was saying, "He who has ears to hear, let him hear" (Mark 4:3–9; cf. Matthew 13:3–9; Luke 8:5–8).

Setting: By the Sea of Galilee. During the early part of His ministry, after presenting the Parable of the Sower from a boat to a very large crowd, Jesus gives the meaning of the parable to His disciples and other followers.

And He said to them, "Do you not understand this parable? How will you understand all the parables? The sower sows the word. These are the ones who are beside the road where the word is sown; and when they hear, immediately Satan comes and takes away the word which has been sown in them. In a similar way these are the ones on whom seed was sown on the rocky places, who, when they hear the word, immediately receive it with joy; and they have no *firm* root in themselves, but are *only* temporary; then, when affliction or persecution arises because of the word, immediately they fall away. And others are the ones on whom seed was sown among the thorns; these are the ones who have heard the word, but the worries of the world and the deceitfulness of riches, and the desires for other things enter in and choke the word, and it becomes unfruitful. And those are the ones on whom seed was sown on the good soil; and they hear the word and accept it and bear fruit, thirty, sixty, and a hundredfold" (Mark 4:13–20; cf. Matthew 13:18–23; Luke 8:11–15).

Setting: Galilee. Following His explanation of the Parable of the Sower to His disciples, Jesus conveys the Parable of the Seed.

And He was saying, "The kingdom of God is like a man who casts seed upon the soil; and he goes to bed at night and gets up by day, and the seed sprouts and grows—how, he himself does not know. The soil produces crops by itself; first the blade, then the head, then the mature grain in the head. But when the crop permits, he immediately puts in the sickle, because the harvest has come" (Mark 4:26–29; see Joel 3:13).

Setting: Galilee. After His visit in the home of Simon the Pharisee, Jesus goes into the villages and cities, proclaiming and preaching the kingdom of God.

When a large crowd was coming together, and those from various cities were journeying to Him, He spoke by way of a parable: "The sower went out to sow his seed; and as he sowed, some fell beside the road, and it was trampled under foot and the birds of the air ate it up. Other *seed* fell on rocky *soil,* and as soon as it grew up, it was withered away, because it had no moisture. Other *seed* fell among the thorns; and the thorns grew up with it and choked it out. Other *seed* fell into the good soil, and grew up, and produced a crop a hundred times as great" As He said these things, He would call out, "He who has ears to hear, let him hear" (Luke 8:4–8; cf. Matthew 13:2–9; Mark 4:3–9).

Setting: Galilee. After Jesus presents the Parable of the Sower to the crowds, His disciples ask Him to give them the parable's meaning.

And He said, "To you it has been granted to know the mysteries of the kingdom of God, but to the rest *it is* in parables, so that SEEING THEY MAY NOT SEE, AND HEARING THEY MAY NOT UNDERSTAND. Now the parable is this: the seed is the word of God. Those beside the road are those who have heard; then the devil comes and takes away the word from their heart, so that they will not believe and be saved. Those on the rocky *soil* are those who, when they hear, receive the word with joy; and these have no *firm* root; they believe for a while, and in time of temptation fall away. The *seed* which fell among the thorns, these are the ones who have heard, and as they go on their way they are choked with worries and riches and pleasures of *this* life, and bring no fruit to maturity. But the *seed* in the good soil, these are the ones who have heard the word in an honest and good heart, and hold it fast, and bear fruit with perseverance" (Luke 8:10–15, Jesus quotes from Isaiah 6:9; cf. Matthew 13:10–23; Mark 4:10–20).

SEED, GOOD

Setting: By the Sea of Galilee. Because the religious leaders are rejecting His message, Jesus continues teaching the crowds with the Parable of the Wheat and the Tares.

Jesus presented another parable to them, saying, "The kingdom of heaven may be compared to a man who sowed good seed in his field. But while his men were sleeping, his enemy came and sowed tares among the wheat, and went away. But when the wheat sprouted and bore grain, then the tares became evident also. The slaves of the landowner came and said to him, 'Sir, did you not sow good seed in your field? How then does it have tares?' And he said to them, 'An enemy has done this!' The slaves said to him, 'Do you want us, then, to go and gather them up?' But he said, 'No; for while you are gathering up the tares, you may uproot the wheat with them. Allow both to grow together until the harvest; and in the time of the harvest I will say to the reapers, "First gather up the tares and bind them in bundles to burn them up; but gather the wheat into my barn" '" (Matthew 13:24–30; cf. Matthew 3:12).

Setting: A house near the Sea of Galilee. Jesus gives His disciples the meaning of the Parable of the Wheat and the Tares.

And He said, "The one who sows the good seed is the Son of Man, and the field is the world; and as *for* the good seed, these are the sons of the kingdom; and the tares are the sons of the evil *one;* and the enemy who sowed them is the devil, and the harvest is the end of the age; and the reapers are angels. So just as the tares are gathered up and burned with fire, so shall it be at the end of the age. The Son of Man will send forth His angels, and they will gather out of His kingdom all stumbling blocks, and those who commit lawlessness, and will throw them into the furnace of fire; in that place there will be weeping and gnashing of teeth. Then THE RIGHTEOUS WILL SHINE FORTH AS THE SUN in the kingdom of their Father. He who has ears, let him hear" (Matthew 13:37–43, Jesus quotes from Daniel 12:3; cf. Matthew 8:12).

SEED, MUSTARD (Also see SEED; and SEEDS)

Setting: By the Sea of Galilee. Because the religious leaders are rejecting His message, Jesus continues teaching the crowds with the Parable of the Mustard Seed.

He presented another parable to them, saying, "The kingdom of heaven is like a mustard seed, which a man took and sowed in his field; and this is smaller than all *other* seeds, but when it is full grown, it is larger than the garden plants and becomes a tree, so that THE BIRDS OF THE AIR come and NEST IN ITS BRANCHES" (Matthew 13:31, 32, Jesus quotes from Ezekiel 17:23; cf. Mark 4:30–32; Luke 13:18, 19).

Setting: Galilee, near the mountain where the Transfiguration took place. Jesus reveals to His disciples why they could not restore a demon possessed boy.

And He said to them, "Because of the littleness of your faith; for truly I say to you, if you have faith the size of a mustard seed, you will say to this mountain, 'Move from here to there,' and it will move; and nothing will be impossible to you. ["But this kind does not go out except by prayer and fasting"] (Matthew 17:20, 21; cf. Matthew 21:21, 22; Mark 9:28, 29).

Setting: Galilee. After giving the Parable of the Sower and the Parable of the Seed, Jesus continues teaching His disciples by presenting the Parable of the Mustard Seed.

And He said, "How shall we picture the kingdom of God, or by what parable shall we present it? *It is* like a mustard seed, which, when sown upon the soil, though it is smaller than all the seeds that are upon the soil, yet when it is sown, it grows up and becomes larger than all the garden plants and forms large branches; so that THE BIRDS OF THE AIR can NEST UNDER ITS SHADE" (Mark 4:30–32, Jesus quotes from Ezekiel 17:23; cf. Matthew 13:31, 32; Luke 13:18, 19).

Setting: On the way from Galilee to Jerusalem. After responding to a synagogue official's anger over Jesus' healing of a woman, sick for eighteen years, in the synagogue on the Sabbath, the Lord conveys the Parable of the Mustard Seed and the Parable of the Leaven.

So He was saying, "What is the kingdom of God like, and to what shall I compare it? It is like a mustard seed which a man took and threw into his own garden; and it grew and became a tree, and THE BIRDS OF THE AIR NESTED IN ITS BRANCHES." And again

He said, "To what shall I compare the kingdom of God? It is like leaven, which a woman took and hid in three pecks of flour until it was all leavened" (Luke 13:18–21, Jesus quotes from Ezekiel 17:23; cf. Matthew 13:31–34; Mark 4:30–32).

Setting: On the way from Galilee to Jerusalem. After His disciples ask that their faith be increased following His instruction to them on forgiveness, the Lord illustrates with the mustard seed and an obedient slave.

And the Lord said, "If you had faith like a mustard seed, you would say to this mulberry tree, 'Be uprooted and be planted in the sea'; and it would obey you. Which of you, having a slave plowing or tending sheep, will say to him when he has come from the field, 'Come immediately and sit down to eat'? But will he not say to him, "Prepare something for me to eat, and *properly* clothe yourself and serve me while I eat and drink; and afterward you may eat and drink'? He does not thank the slave because he did the things which were commanded, does he? So you too, when you do all the things which are commanded you, say, 'We are unworthy slaves; we have done *only* that which we ought to have done' " (Luke 17:6–10; see Matthew 13:31; Luke 12:37).

SEED, PARABLE OF THE

[PARABLE OF THE SEED from like a man who casts seed upon the soil]

Setting: Galilee. Following His explanation of the Parable of the Sower to His disciples, Jesus conveys the Parable of the Seed.

And He was saying, "The kingdom of God is like a man who casts seed upon the soil; and he goes to bed at night and gets up by day, and the seed sprouts and grows—how, he himself does not know. The soil produces crops by itself; first the blade, then the head, then the mature grain in the head. But when the crop permits, he immediately puts in the sickle, because the harvest has come" (Mark 4:26–29; see Joel 3:13).

SEED, PARABLE OF THE GROWING (See SEED, PARABLE OF THE)

SEED, PARABLE OF THE MUSTARD

[PARABLE OF THE MUSTARD SEED from parable and mustard seed]

Setting: By the Sea of Galilee. Because the religious leaders are rejecting His message, Jesus continues teaching the crowds with the Parable of the Mustard Seed.

He presented another parable to them, saying, "The kingdom of heaven is like a mustard seed, which a man took and sowed in his field; and this is smaller than all *other* seeds, but when it is full grown, it is larger than the garden plants and becomes a tree, so that THE BIRDS OF THE AIR come and NEST IN ITS BRANCHES" (Matthew 13:31, 32, Jesus quotes from Ezekiel 17:23; cf. Mark 4:30–32; Luke 13:18, 19).

[PARABLE OF THE MUSTARD SEED from like a mustard seed]

Setting: Galilee. After giving the Parable of the Sower and the Parable of the Seed, Jesus continues teaching His disciples by presenting the Parable of the Mustard Seed.

And He said, "How shall we picture the kingdom of God, or by what parable shall we present it? *It is* like a mustard seed, which, when sown upon the soil, though it is smaller than all the seeds that are upon the soil, yet when it is sown, it grows up and becomes larger than all the garden plants and forms large branches; so that THE BIRDS OF THE AIR can NEST UNDER ITS SHADE" (Mark 4:30–32, Jesus quotes from Ezekiel 17:23; cf. Matthew 13:31, 32; Luke 13:18, 19).

[PARABLE OF THE MUSTARD SEED from like a mustard seed]

Setting: On the way from Galilee to Jerusalem. After responding to a synagogue official's anger over Jesus' healing of a woman, sick for eighteen years, in the synagogue on the Sabbath, the Lord conveys the Parable of the Mustard Seed and the Parable of the Leaven.

So He was saying, "What is the kingdom of God like, and to what shall I compare it? It is like a mustard seed which a man took and threw into his own garden; and it grew and became a tree, and THE BIRDS OF THE AIR NESTED IN ITS BRANCHES." And again He said, "To what shall I compare the kingdom of God? It is like leaven, which a woman took and hid in three pecks of flour until it was all leavened" (Luke 13:18–21, Jesus quotes from Ezekiel 17:23; cf. Matthew 13:31–34; Mark 4:30–32).

SEEDS (Also see SEED)

Setting: By the Sea of Galilee. While teaching and preaching to the crowds from a boat, Jesus conveys the Parable of the Sower.

And He spoke many things to them in parables, saying, "Behold, the sower went out to sow; and as he sowed, some *seeds* fell beside the road, and the birds came and ate them up. Others fell on the rocky places, where they did not have much soil; and immediately they sprang up, because they had no depth of soil. But when the sun had risen, they were scorched; and because they had no root, they withered away. Others fell among the thorns, and the thorns came up and choked them out. And others fell on the good soil and yielded a crop, some a hundredfold, some sixty, and some thirty. He who has ears, let him hear" (Matthew 13:3–9; cf. Mark 4:3–9; Luke 8:4–8).

Setting: By the Sea of Galilee. Because the religious leaders are rejecting His message, Jesus continues teaching the crowds with the Parable of the Mustard Seed.

He presented another parable to them, saying, "The kingdom of heaven is like a mustard seed, which a man took and sowed in his field; and this is smaller than all *other* seeds, but when it is full grown, it is larger than the garden plants and becomes a tree, so that THE BIRDS OF THE AIR come and NEST IN ITS BRANCHES" (Matthew 13:31, 32, Jesus quotes from Ezekiel 17:23; cf. Mark 4:30–32; Luke 13:18, 19).

Setting: By the Sea of Galilee. During the early part of His ministry, just after a visit from his mother and brothers, Jesus instructs a very large crowd with the Parable of the Sower from a boat.

"Listen *to this!* Behold, the sower went out to sow; as he was sowing, some *seed* fell beside the road, and the birds came and ate it up. Other *seed* fell on the rocky *ground* where it did not have much soil; and immediately it sprang up because it had no depth of soil. And after the sun had risen, it was scorched; and because it had no root, it withered away. Other *seed* fell among the thorns, and the thorns came up and choked it, and it yielded no crop. Other *seeds* fell into the good soil, and as the grew up and increased, they yielded a crop and produced thirty, sixty, and a hundredfold." And He was saying, "He who has ears to hear, let him hear" (Mark 4:3–9; cf. Matthew 13:3–9; Luke 8:5–8).

Setting: Galilee. After giving the Parable of the Sower and the Parable of the Seed, Jesus continues teaching His disciples by presenting the Parable of the Mustard Seed.

And He said, "How shall we picture the kingdom of God, or by what parable shall we present it? *It is* like a mustard seed, which, when sown upon the soil, though it is smaller than all the seeds that are upon the soil, yet when it is sown, it grows up and becomes larger than all the garden plants and forms large branches; so that THE BIRDS OF THE AIR can NEST UNDER ITS SHADE" (Mark 4:30–32, Jesus quotes from Ezekiel 17:23; cf. Matthew 13:31–32; Luke 13:18, 19).

SEEING GOD (Listed as GOD, SEEING)

SELF-DENIAL (Also see DEVOTION; DISCIPLESHIP; FOLLOWING JESUS CHRIST; and SACRIFICE, PERSONAL)

[SELF-DENIAL from he must deny himself]

Setting: Near Caesarea Philippi. After rebuking Peter for trying to forbid Him to accomplish His earthly mission of dying and being resurrected, Jesus teaches His disciples about the costs of following Him.

Then Jesus said to His disciples, "If anyone wishes to come after Me, he must deny himself, and take up his cross and follow Me. For whoever wishes to save his life will lose it; but whoever loses his life for My sake will find it. For what will it profit a man if he gains the whole world and forfeits his soul? Or what will a man give in exchange for his soul? For the Son of Man is going to come in the glory of His Father with His angels, and WILL THEN REPAY EVERY MAN ACCORDING TO HIS DEEDS. Truly, I say to you, there are some of you who are standing here who will not taste death until they see the Son of Man coming in His kingdom" (Matthew 16:24–28, Jesus quotes from Psalm 62:12; cf. Mark 8:34–37; Luke 9:23–27; see Matthew 10:38, 39).

[SELF-DENIAL from he must deny himself]
Setting: Caesarea Philippi. After rebuking Peter for desiring to thwart His mission to the cross, Jesus summons a crowd, along with His disciples, and informs them of the high costs of following Him.

And He summoned the crowd with His disciples, and said to them, "If anyone wishes to come after Me, he must deny himself, and take up his cross and follow Me. For whoever wishes to save his life will lose it, but whoever loses his life for My sake and the gospel's will save it. For what does it profit a man to gain the whole world, and forfeit his soul? For what will a man give in exchange for his soul? For whoever is ashamed of Me and My words in this adulterous and sinful generation, the Son of Man will also be ashamed of him when He comes in the glory of His Father with the holy angels" (Mark 8:34–38; cf. Matthew 16:24–28; Luke 9:23–27; see Matthew 10:33, 38, 39).

[SELF-DENIAL from he must deny himself]
Setting: Galilee. Following Peter's pronouncement that Jesus is the Christ of God, the Lord conveys the demands of discipleship and the hope regarding the kingdom of God.

And He was saying to *them* all, "If anyone wishes to come after Me, he must deny himself, and take up his cross daily and follow Me. For whoever wishes to save his life will lose it, but whoever loses his life for My sake, he is the one who will save it. For what is a man profited if he gains the whole world, and loses or forfeits himself? For whoever is ashamed of Me and My words, the Son of Man will be ashamed of him when He comes in His glory, and *the glory* of the Father and of the holy angels. But I say to you truthfully, there are some of those standing here who will not taste death until they see the kingdom of God" (Luke 9:23–27; cf. Matthew 16:24–26, 28; Mark 8:34–37; see Matthew 10:33, 38, 39).

SELFISHNESS

[SELFISHNESS from treasure for himself]
Setting: On the way from Galilee to Jerusalem. After the scribes and Pharisees turn hostile and question Him repeatedly in an attempt to catch Him in something He might say, Jesus responds to a question from the crowd and gives a parable about riches and greed.

And He told them a parable, saying, "The land of a rich man was very productive. And he began reasoning to himself, saying, 'What shall I do, since I have no place to store my crops?' Then he said, 'This is what I will do: I will tear down my barns and build larger ones, and here I will store all my grain and my goods. And I will say to my soul, "Soul, you have many goods laid up for many years *to come;* take your ease, eat, drink *and* be merry."' But God said to him, 'You fool! This *very* night your soul is required of you; and *now* who will own what you have prepared?' So is the man who stores up treasure for himself, and is not rich toward God" (Luke 12:16–21; see Job 27:8; Psalm 39:6; Ecclesiastes 12:9; Philippians 2:3).

SELFLESSNESS (See SELF-DENIAL)

SELF-INDULGENCE

Setting: The temple in Jerusalem. After the Jewish religious leaders test Him with questions, Jesus pronounces the sixth of eight woes upon them in front of the crowds and His disciples.

"Woe to you, scribes and Pharisees, hypocrites! For you clean the outside of the cup and of the dish, but inside they are full of robbery and self-indulgence. You blind Pharisee, first clean the inside of the cup and of the dish, so that the outside of it may become clean also" (Matthew 23:25, 26; see Mark 7:4).

SELF-RIGHTEOUSNESS (Also see ARROGANCE; PRIDE; RIGHTEOUSNESS; and UNRIGHTEOUSNESS)

[SELF-RIGHTEOUS from Whoever exalts himself shall be humbled]

Setting: The temple in Jerusalem. Jesus exposes the truth about Pharisaism to the crowds and His disciples after the Jewish religious leaders test Him with questions.

Then Jesus spoke to the crowds and to His disciples, saying: "The scribes and the Pharisees have seated themselves in the chair of Moses; therefore all that they tell you, do and observe, but do not do according to their deeds; for they say *things* and do not do *them.* They tie up heavy burdens and lay them on men's shoulders, but they themselves are unwilling to move them with *so much as* a finger. But they do all their deeds to be noticed by men; for they broaden their phylacteries and lengthen their tassels *of their garments.* They love the place of honor at banquets and the chief seats in the synagogues, and respectful greetings in the market places, and being called Rabbi by men. But do not be called Rabbi; for One is your Teacher, and you are all brothers. Do not call *anyone* on earth your father; for One is your Father, He who is in heaven. Do not be called leaders; for One is your Leader, *that is,* Christ. But the greatest among you shall be your servant. Whoever exalts himself shall be humbled; and whoever humbles himself shall be exalted" (Matthew 23:1–12; cf. Matthew 20:26; Mark 12:38–40; Luke 20:46, 47; see Exodus 13:9; Deuteronomy 33:3; Matthew 6:1, 5, 6, 9, 16; Mark 14:11; Luke 11:43; 14:11).

[SELF-RIGHTEOUSNESS from everyone who exalts himself will be humbled]

Setting: On the way from Galilee to Jerusalem. As He observes the invited guests selecting places of honor at table in the house of a Pharisee leader on the Sabbath, Jesus speaks a parable to them.

And He *began* speaking a parable to the invited guests when He noticed how they had been picking out the places of honor *at the table,* saying to them, "When you are invited by someone to a wedding feast, do not take the place of honor, for someone more distinguished than you may have been invited by him, and he who invited you both will come and say to you, 'Give *your* place to this man, and then in disgrace you proceed to occupy the last place. But when you are invited, go and recline at the last place, so that when the one who has invited you comes, he may say to you, 'Friend, move up higher'; then you will have honor in the sight of all who are at the table with you. For everyone who exalts himself will be humbled, and he who humbles himself will be exalted." (Luke 14:7–11; see 2 Samuel 22:28; Proverb 25:6, 7; Matthew 23:6).

[SELF-RIGHTEOUS from everyone who exalts himself will be humbled]

Setting: On the way from Galilee to Jerusalem. After instructing His disciples about persistence in prayer, Jesus conveys a parable about self-righteousness.

And He also told this parable to some people who trusted in themselves that they were righteous, and viewed others with contempt: "Two men went up into the temple to pray, one a Pharisee and the other a tax collector. The Pharisee stood and was praying this to himself: 'God, I thank You that I am not like other people: swindlers, unjust, adulterers, or even like this tax collector. I fast twice a week; I pay tithes of all that I get.' But the tax collector, standing some distance away, was even unwilling to lift up his eyes to heaven, but was beating his breast, saying, 'God, be merciful to me, the sinner!' I tell you, this man went to his house justified rather than the other; for everyone who exalts himself will be humbled, but he who humbles himself will be exalted" (Luke 18:9–14; see Ezra 9:6; Matthew 6:5, 23:12; Luke 11:42, 16:15; Romans 14:3, 10).

SENSE

Setting: The temple in Jerusalem. Jesus teaches the crowd after commending a scribe for his nearness to the kingdom of God.

And Jesus *began* to say, as He taught in the temple, "How *is it that* the scribes say that the Christ is the son of David? David himself said in the Holy Spirit, 'THE LORD SAID TO MY LORD, SIT AT MY RIGHT HAND, UNTIL I PUT YOUR ENEMIES BENEATH YOUR FEET.'" David himself calls Him 'Lord'; so in what sense is He his son?" And the large crowd enjoyed listening to Him (Mark 12:35–37, Jesus quotes from Psalm 110:1; cf. Matthew 22:41–46; Luke 20:41–44).

SENSES

Setting: On the way from Galilee to Jerusalem. Jesus conveys the illustration of the prodigal son because the Pharisees and scribes complain He associates with tax collectors and sinners.

And He said, "A man had two sons. The younger of them said to his father, 'Father, give me the share of the estate that falls to me.' So he divided his wealth between them. And not many days later, the younger son gathered everything together and went on a journey into a distant country, and there he squandered his estate with loose living. Now when he had spent everything, a severe famine occurred in that country, and he began to be impoverished. So he went and hired himself out to one of the citizens of that country, and he sent him into his fields to feed swine. And he would have gladly filled his stomach with the pods that the swine were eating, and no one was giving *anything* to him. But when he came to his senses, he said, 'How many of my father's hired men have more than enough bread, but I am dying here with hunger! I will get up and go to my father, and will say to him, "Father, I have sinned against heaven, and in your sight; I am no longer worthy to be called your son; make me as one of your hired men."' So he got up and came to his father. But while he was still a long way off, his father saw him and felt compassion *for him,* and ran and embraced him and kissed him. And the son said to him, "Father, I have sinned against heaven and in your sight; I am no longer worthy to be called your son.' But the father said to his slaves, 'Quickly bring out the best robe and put it on him, and put a ring on his hand and sandals on his feet; and bring the fattened calf, kill it, and let us eat and celebrate; for this son of mine was dead and has come to life again; he was lost and has been found.' And they began to celebrate. Now his older son was in the field, when he came and approached the house, he heard music and dancing. And he summoned one of the servants and *began* inquiring what these things could be. And he said to him, 'Your brother has come, and your father has killed the fattened calf because he has received him back safe and sound.' But he became angry and was not willing to go in; and his father came out and *began* pleading with him. But he answered and said to his father, 'Look! For so many years I have been serving you and I have never neglected a command of yours; and *yet* you have never given me a young goat, so that I might celebrate with my friends; but when this son of yours came, who has devoured your wealth with prostitutes, you killed the fattened calf for him.' And he said to him, 'Son, you have always been with me, and all that is mine is yours. But we had to celebrate and rejoice, for this brother of yours was dead and *has begun* to live, and was lost and has been found' " (Luke 15:11–32; see Proverb 29:2).

SENSIBLE STEWARD (Listed under STEWARD, SENSIBLE)

SENSUALITY (Also see other sexual terms such as ADULTERIES)

Setting: Galilee. After the Pharisees and scribes from Jerusalem object to His disciples' lack of obedience to the tradition regarding ceremonial cleansing, Jesus speaks to a crowd and explains His teaching to the disciples.

After He called the crowd to Him again, He *began* saying to them, "Listen to Me, all of you, and understand: there is nothing outside the man which can defile him if it goes into him; but the things which proceed out of the man are what defile the man. [If anyone has ears to hear, let him hear."] When he had left the crowd *and* entered the house, His disciples questioned Him about the parable. And He said to them, "Are you so lacking in understanding also? Do you not understand that whatever goes into the man from outside cannot defile him, because it does not go into his heart, but into his stomach, and is eliminated?" (*Thus He* declared all foods clean.) And He was saying, "That which proceeds out of the man, that is what defiles the man. For from within, out of the heart of men, proceed the evil thoughts, fornications, thefts, murders, adulteries, deeds of coveting *and* wickedness, *as well* as deceit, sensuality, envy, slander, pride *and* foolishness. All these evil things proceed from within and defile the man" (Mark 7:14–23; cf. Matthew 15:10–20).

SENTENCE OF HELL (Listed under HELL, SENTENCE OF; also see DAMNATION, ETERNAL; FIRE, ETERNAL; FIRE, FURNACE OF; HELL; and PUNISHMENT, ETERNAL)

SEPARATION (See DISASSOCIATION)

SEPARATION FROM GOD (See DAMNATION, ETERNAL; DEATH, ETERNAL; FIRE, ETERNAL; FIRE, FURNACE OF; PUNISHMENT, ETERNAL; HELL; and HELL, SENTENCE OF)

SERMON ON THE MOUNT (See specific verses in Matthew 5–7 and Luke 6)

SERPENT (Also see SNAKE; and SERPENTS)

Setting: Jerusalem. At the time for the Passover of the Jews, after the Lord cleanses the temple, a Pharisee, Nicodemus, asks Him by night the meaning of "born of the Spirit."

Jesus answered and said to him, "Are you the teacher of Israel and do not understand these things? Truly, truly, I say to you, we speak of what we know and testify of what we have seen, and you do not accept our testimony. If I told you earthly things and you do not believe, how will you believe if I tell you heavenly things? No one has ascended into heaven, but He who descended from heaven: the Son of Man. As Moses lifted up the serpent in the wilderness, even so must the Son of Man be lifted up; so that whoever believes will in Him have eternal life" (John 3:10–15; see Numbers 21:9; Proverb 30:4; John 12:34; 20:30, 31).

SERPENTS (Also see SNAKE; and VIPERS, BROOD OF)

Setting: Galilee. After His disciples observe His ministry, Jesus summons and specifically instructs them about the upcoming hardships of their ministry to the people of Israel.

"Behold, I send you out as sheep in the midst of wolves; so be shrewd as serpents and innocent as doves. But beware of men, for they will hand you over to *the* courts and scourge you in their synagogues; and you will even be brought before governors and kings for My sake, as a testimony to them and to the Gentiles. But when they hand you over, do not worry about how or what you are to say; for it will be given you in that hour what you are to say. For it is not you who speak, but *it* is the Spirit of your Father who speaks in you" (Matthew 10:16–20; cf. Luke 10:3).

Setting: The temple in Jerusalem. After the Jewish religious leaders test Him with questions, Jesus pronounces the eighth of eight woes upon them in front of the crowds and His disciples.

"Woe to you, scribes and Pharisees, hypocrites! For you build the tombs of the prophets and adorn the monuments of the righteous, and say, 'If we had been *living* in the days of our fathers, we would not have been partners with them in *shedding* the blood of the prophets.' So you testify against yourselves, that you are sons of those who murdered the prophets. Fill up, then, the measure *of the guilt* of you fathers. You serpents, you brood of vipers, how will you escape the sentence of hell? Therefore, behold, I am sending you prophets and wise men and scribes; some of them you will kill and crucify, and some of them you will scourge in your synagogues, and persecute from city to city, so that upon you may fall *the guilt of* all the righteous blood shed on earth, from the blood of righteous Abel to the blood of Zechariah, the son of Berechiah, whom you murdered between the temple and the altar. Truly I say to you, all these things will come upon this generation" (Matthew 23:29–36; cf. 2 Chronicles 24:21; Zechariah 1:1; Matthew 3:7; Luke 11:47–52; see Matthew 10:23).

Setting: Following His resurrection from the dead after being crucified, Jesus commissions His disciples to preach His gospel to the world.

And He said to them, "Go into all the world and preach the gospel to all creation. He who has believed and has been baptized shall be saved; but he who has disbelieved shall be condemned. These signs will accompany those who have believed: in My name they will cast out demons, they will speak with new tongues; they will pick up serpents, and if they drink any deadly *poison,* it will not hurt them; they will lay hands on the sick, and they will recover" (Mark 16:15–18; cf. Matthew 28:16–20; see Mark 9:38, John 3:18, 36; 1 Corinthians 15:6).

[Note: Some scholars question the authenticity of Mark 16:9–20 as these verses do not appear in some early New Testament manuscripts.]

Setting: On the way from Galilee to Jerusalem. The Lord responds to a report from the seventy sent out in pairs to every place He Himself will soon visit.

And He said to them, "I was watching Satan fall from heaven like lightning. Behold, I have given you authority to tread on serpents and scorpions, and over all the power of the enemy, and nothing will injure you. Nevertheless do not rejoice in this, that the spirits are subject to you, but rejoice that your names are recorded in heaven" (Luke 10:18–20; see Psalm 91:13; Isaiah 14:12–14; Luke 9:1).

SERVANT (Also see SERVANTS; SERVICE; SLAVE; and SLAVES)

Setting: On the way to Jerusalem, where Jesus will die on the cross. Jesus teaches His disciples about true greatness after the mother of disciples James and John asks Him to make her sons exalted rulers with Him in His coming kingdom.

But Jesus called them to Himself and said, "You know that the rulers of the Gentiles lord it over them, and *their* great men exercise authority over them. It is not this way among you, but whoever wishes to become great among you shall be your servant, and whoever wishes to be first among you shall be your slave; just as the Son of Man did not come to be served, but to serve, and to give His life a ransom for many" (Matthew 20:25–28; cf. Matthew 23:11; 26:28; Mark 10:42–45).

Setting: The temple in Jerusalem. Jesus exposes the truth about Pharisaism to the crowds and His disciples after the Jewish religious leaders test Him with questions.

Then Jesus spoke to the crowds and to His disciples, saying: "The scribes and the Pharisees have seated themselves in the chair of Moses; therefore all that they tell you, do and observe, but do not do according to their deeds; for they say *things* and do not do *them.* They tie up heavy burdens and lay them on men's shoulders, but they themselves are unwilling to move them with *so much as* a finger. But they do all their deeds to be noticed by men; for they broaden their phylacteries and lengthen their tassels *of their garments.* They love the place of honor at banquets and the chief seats in the synagogues, and respectful greetings in the market places, and being called Rabbi by men. But do not be called Rabbi; for One is your Teacher, and you are all brothers. Do not call *anyone* on earth your father; for One is your Father, He who is in heaven. Do not be called leaders; for One is your Leader, *that is,* Christ. But the greatest among you shall be your servant. Whoever exalts himself shall be humbled; and whoever humbles himself shall be exalted" (Matthew 23:1–12; cf. Matthew 20:26; Mark 12:38–40; Luke 20:46, 47; see Exodus 13:9; Deuteronomy 33:3; Matthew 6:1, 5, 6, 9, 16; Mark 14:11; Luke 11:43; 14:11).

Setting: Capernaum of Galilee. As Jesus teaches His disciples in private, they ask Him about greatness.

They came to Capernaum; and when He was in the house, He *began* to question them, "What were you discussing on the way?" But they kept silent, for on the way they had discussed with one another which *of them* was the greatest. Sitting down, He called the twelve and said to them, "If anyone wants to be first, he shall be last of all and servant of all." Taking a child, He set him before them, and taking him in His arms, He said to them, "Whoever receives one child like this in My name receives Me; and whoever receives Me does not receive Me, but Him who sent Me" (Mark 9:33–37; cf. Matthew 18:1–5; Luke 9:46–48; see Matthew 20:26; 10:40).

Setting: On the road to Jerusalem. James and John ask Jesus for special honor and privileges in His kingdom. The other disciples become angry, so the Lord uses this moment to teach all of them about servanthood.

Calling them to Himself, Jesus said to them, "You know that those who are recognized as rulers of the Gentiles lord it over them; and their great men exercise authority over them. But it is not this way among you, but whoever wishes to become great among you shall be your servant; and whoever wishes to be first among you shall be slave of all. For even the Son of Man did not come to be served, but to serve, and to give His life a ransom for many" (Mark 10:42–45; cf. Matthew 20:25–28).

Setting: On the way from Galilee to Jerusalem. After giving the story of the prodigal son, the Lord teaches His disciples about stewardship.

Now He was also saying to the disciples, "There was a rich man who had a manager, and this *manager* was reported to him as squandering his possessions. And he called him and said to him, 'What is this I hear about you? Give an accounting of your management, for you can no longer be a manager.' The manager said to himself, 'What shall I do, since my master is taking the management away from me? I am not strong enough to dig; I am ashamed to beg. I know what I shall do, so that when I am removed from the management people will welcome me into their homes.' And he summoned each one of his master's debtors, and he *began* saying to the first, 'How much do you owe my master?' And he said, 'A hundred measures of oil.' And he said to him, 'Take your bill, and sit down quickly and write fifty.' Then he said to another, 'And how much do you owe?' And he said, 'A hundred measures of wheat.' He said to him, 'Take your bill, and write eighty.' And his master praised the unrighteous manager because he had acted shrewdly; for the sons of this age are more shrewd in relation to their own kind than the sons of light. And I say to you, make friends for yourselves by means of the wealth of unrighteousness, so that when it fails, they will receive you into the eternal dwellings. He who is faithful in a very little thing is faithful also in much; and he who is unrighteous in a very little thing is unrighteous also in much. Therefore if you have not been faithful in the *use of* unrighteous wealth, who will entrust the true *riches* to you? And if you have not been faithful in *the use of* that which is another's, who will give you that which is your own? No servant can serve two masters; for either he will hate the one and love the other, or else he will be devoted to one and despise the other. You cannot serve God and wealth" (Luke 16:1–13; cf. Matthew 6:24; see Matthew 25:14–30).

Setting: An upper room in Jerusalem. During the Feast of Unleavened Bread (Passover) just before His crucifixion, Jesus celebrates the Passover meal with His disciples and institutes the Lord's Supper. The disciples later argue over who is the greatest among them.

And He said to them, "The kings of the Gentiles lord it over them; and those who have authority over them are called 'Benefactors.' But *it is* not this way with you, but the one who is the greatest among you must become like the youngest, and the leader like a servant. For who is greater, the one who reclines *at the table* or the one who serves? Is it not the one who reclines *at the table?* But I am among you as the one who serves" (Luke 22:25–27; cf. Matthew 20:25–28; 23:11; Mark 10:42–45).

Setting: Jerusalem. Just days before the Passover, with the chief priests and Pharisees plotting to seize Him, crowds welcome Jesus with palm branches and praise, and some Greeks ask to meet Him.

And Jesus answered them, saying, "The hour has come for the Son of Man to be glorified. Truly, truly, I say to you, unless a grain of wheat falls into the earth and dies, it remains alone; but if it dies, it bears much fruit. He who loves his life loses it, and he who hates his life in this world will keep it to life eternal. If anyone serves Me, he must follow Me; and where I am, there My servant will be also; if anyone serves Me, the Father will honor him" (John 12:23–26; see Matthew 10:39).

SERVANT, CENTURION'S (See CENTURION)

SERVANT, PARABLE OF THE FAITHFUL AND WISE (See STEWARD, PARABLE OF THE FAITHFUL AND SENSIBLE)

SERVANTS (Also see SERVANT; SERVICE; SLAVE; and SLAVES)

Setting: The temple in Jerusalem. Jesus speaks another parable to the chief priests and elders after they question His authority.

Jesus spoke to them again in parables, saying, "The kingdom of heaven may be compared to a king who gave a wedding feast for his son. And he sent out his slaves to call those who had been invited to the wedding feast, and they were unwilling to come. Again he sent out other slaves saying, 'Tell those who have been invited, "Behold, I have prepared my dinner; my oxen and my fattened livestock are *all* butchered and everything is ready; come to the wedding feast." But they paid no attention and went their way, one to his own farm, another to his business, and the rest seized his slaves and mistreated them and killed them. But the king was enraged, and he sent his armies and destroyed those murderers and set their city on fire. Then he said to his slaves, 'The wedding is ready, but those who were invited were not worthy. 'Go therefore to the main highways, and as many as you find *there,* invite to the wedding feast.' Those slaves went out into the streets and gathered together all they found, both evil and good; and the wedding hall was filled with dinner guests. But when the king came in to look over the dinner guests, he saw a man there who was not dressed in wedding clothes, and he said to him, 'Friend, how did you come in here without wedding clothes?' And the man was speechless. Then the king said to the servants, 'Bind him hand and foot, and throw him into the outer darkness; in that place there will be weeping and gnashing of teeth.' For many are called, but few *are* chosen" (Matthew 22:1–14; cf. Matthew 8:11, 12).

Setting: On the way from Galilee to Jerusalem. After Jesus uses a parable to challenge the crowd and His disciples to be ready for His return, Peter asks Him whom He is addressing.

And the Lord said, "Who then is the faithful and sensible steward, whom his master will put in charge of his servants, to give them their rations at the proper time? Blessed is that slave whom his master finds so doing when he comes. Truly I say to you that he will put him in charge of all his possessions. But if that slave says in his heart, 'My master will be a long time in coming,' and begins to beat the slaves, *both* men and women, and to eat and drink and get drunk; the master of that slave will come on a day when he does not expect *him* and at an hour he does not know, and will cut him in pieces, and assign him a place with the unbelievers. And that slave who knew his master's will and did not get ready or act in accord with his will, will receive many lashes, but the one who did know *it,* and committed deeds worthy of flogging, will receive but few. From everyone who has been given much, much will be required; and to whom they entrusted much, of him they will ask all the more" (Luke 12:42–48; cf. Matthew 24:45–51; see Leviticus 5:17).

Setting: On the way from Galilee to Jerusalem. Jesus conveys the illustration of the prodigal son because the Pharisees and scribes complain He associates with tax collectors and sinners.

And He said, "A man had two sons. The younger of them said to his father, 'Father, give me the share of the estate that falls to me.' So he divided his wealth between them. And not many days later, the younger son gathered everything together and went on a journey into a distant country, and there he squandered his estate with loose living. Now when he had spent everything, a severe famine occurred in that country, and he began to be impoverished. So he went and hired himself out to one of the citizens of that country, and he sent him into his fields to feed swine. And he would have gladly filled his stomach with the pods that the swine were eating, and no one was giving *anything* to him. But when he came to his senses, he said, 'How many of my father's hired men have more than enough bread, but I am dying here with hunger! I will get up and go to my father, and will say to him, "Father, I have sinned against heaven, and in your sight; I am no longer worthy to be called your son; make me as one of your hired men."' So he got up and came to his father. But while he was still a long way off, his father saw him and felt compassion *for him,* and ran and embraced him and kissed him. And the son said to him, "Father, I have sinned against heaven and in your sight; I am no longer worthy to be called your son.' But the father said to his slaves, 'Quickly bring out the best robe and put it on him, and put a ring on his hand and sandals on his feet; and bring the fattened calf, kill it, and let us eat and celebrate; for this son of mine was dead and has come to life again; he was lost and has been found.' And they began to celebrate. Now his older son was in the field, when he came and approached the house, he heard music and dancing. And he summoned one of the servants and *began* inquiring what these things could be. And he said to him, 'Your brother has come, and your father has killed the fattened calf because he has received him back safe and sound.' But he became angry and was not willing to go in; and his father came out and *began* pleading with him. But he answered and said to his father, 'Look! For so many years I have been serving you and I have never neglected a command of yours; and *yet* you have never given me a young goat, so that I might celebrate with my friends; but when this son of yours came, who has devoured your wealth with prostitutes, you killed the fattened calf for him.' And he said to him, 'Son, you have always been with me, and all that is mine is yours. But we had to celebrate and rejoice, for this brother of yours was dead and *has begun* to live, and was lost and has been found' " (Luke 15:11–32; see Proverb 29:2).

Setting: Jerusalem. After the previous and current high priests (Annas and Caiaphas) question Jesus, and Peter denies the second and third times being the Lord's disciple, Pilate (Roman governor of Judea) asks Jesus what He has done.

Jesus answered, "My kingdom is not of this world. If My kingdom were of this world, then My servants would be fighting so that I would not be handed over to the Jews; but as it is, My kingdom is not of this realm" (John 18:36; see Matthew 26:53).

SERVICE (Also see FOOTWASHING; SERVANT; SERVANTS; and WORSHIP)

[SERVICE from serve]
Setting: Judea, near the Jordan River. Following His baptism and before He begins His public ministry, Jesus is led by the Spirit into the wilderness for forty days of temptation by Satan.

Then Jesus said to him, "Go, Satan! For it is written, 'YOU SHALL WORSHIP THE LORD YOUR GOD, AND SERVE HIM ONLY'" (Matthew 4:10, Jesus quotes from Deuteronomy 6:13; cf. Luke 4:8).

[SERVICE from serve]
Setting: Galilee. During the early part of His ministry, Jesus preaches the Sermon on the Mount to His disciples and the multitudes.

"No one can serve two masters, for either he will hate the one and love the other, or he will be devoted to one and despise the other. You cannot serve God and wealth (Matthew 6:24)

[SERVICE from the Son of Man did not come to be served, but to serve]
Setting: On the way to Jerusalem, where Jesus will die on the cross. Jesus teaches His disciples about true greatness after the mother of disciples James and John asks Him to make her sons exalted rulers with Him in His coming kingdom.

But Jesus called them to Himself and said, "You know that the rulers of the Gentiles lord it over them, and *their* great men exercise authority over them. It is not this way among you, but whoever wishes to become great among you shall be your servant, and whoever wishes to be first among you shall be your slave; just as the Son of Man did not come to be served, but to serve, and to give His life a ransom for many" (Matthew 20:25–28; cf. Matthew 23:11; 26:28; Mark 10:42–45).

[SERVICE from the Son of Man did not come to be served, but to serve]
Setting: On the road to Jerusalem. James and John ask Jesus for special honor and privileges in His kingdom. The other disciples become angry, so the Lord uses this moment to teach all of them about servanthood.

Calling them to Himself, Jesus said to them, "You know that those who are recognized as rulers of the Gentiles lord it over them; and their great men exercise authority over them. But it is not this way among you, but whoever wishes to become great among you shall be your servant; and whoever wishes to be first among you shall be slave of all. For even the Son of Man did not come to be served, but to serve, and to give His life a ransom for many" (Mark 10:42–45; cf. Matthew 20:25–28).

[SERVICE from serve]
Setting: Judea, near the Jordan River. Following His baptism and before He begins His public ministry, Jesus is led by the Spirit into the wilderness for forty days of temptation by Satan.

Jesus answered him, "It is written, 'YOU SHALL WORSHIP THE LORD YOUR GOD AND SERVE HIM ONLY'" (Luke 4:8, Jesus quotes from Deuteronomy 6:13; cf. Matthew 4:10).

[SERVICE from to serve]
Setting: On the way from Galilee to Jerusalem. After giving a parable about riches and greed, Jesus uses another parable to challenge the crowd and His disciples to be ready for His return.

"Be dressed in readiness, and *keep* your lamps lit. Be like men who are waiting for their master when he returns from the wedding feast, so that they may immediately open *the door* to him when he comes and knocks. Blessed are those slaves whom the master will find on the alert when he comes; truly I say to you, that he will gird himself *to serve,* and have them recline *at the table,* and will come up and wait on them. Whether he comes in the second watch, or even in the third and finds *them* so, blessed are those *slaves*. But be sure of this, that if the head of the house had known at what hour the thief was coming, he would not have allowed his house to be broken into. You too, be ready; for the Son of Man is coming at an hour that you do not expect" (Luke 12:35–40; cf. Matthew 24:42–44; see Mark 13:33; Ephesians 6:14).

[SERVICE from serving]
Setting: On the way from Galilee to Jerusalem. Jesus conveys the illustration of the prodigal son because the Pharisees and scribes complain He associates with tax collectors and sinners.

And He said, "A man had two sons. The younger of them said to his father, 'Father, give me the share of the estate that falls to me.' So he divided his wealth between them. And not many days later, the younger son gathered everything together and went on a journey into a distant country, and there he squandered his estate with loose living. Now when he had spent everything, a severe famine occurred in that country, and he began to be impoverished. So he went and hired himself out to one of the citizens of that country, and he sent him into his fields to feed swine. And he would have gladly filled his stomach with the pods that the swine were eating, and no one was giving *anything* to him. But when he came to his senses, he said, 'How many of my father's hired men have more than enough bread, but I am dying here with hunger! I will get up and go to my father, and will say to him, "Father, I have sinned against heaven, and in your sight; I am no longer worthy to be called your son; make me as one of your hired men."' So he got up and came to his father. But while he was still a long way off, his father saw him and felt compassion *for him,* and ran and embraced him and kissed him. And the son said to him, "Father, I have sinned against heaven and in your sight; I am no longer worthy to be called your son.' But the father said to his slaves, 'Quickly bring out the best robe and put it on him, and put a ring on his hand and sandals on his feet; and bring the fattened calf, kill it, and let us eat and celebrate; for this son of mine was dead and has come to life again; he was lost and has been found.' And they began to celebrate. Now his older son was in the field, when he came and approached the house, he heard music and dancing. And he summoned one of the servants and *began* inquiring what these things could be. And he said to him, 'Your brother has come, and your father has killed the fattened calf because he has received him back safe and sound.' But he became angry and was not willing to go in; and his father came out and *began* pleading with him. But he answered and said to his father, 'Look! For so many years I have been serving you and I have never neglected a command of yours; and *yet* you have never given me a young goat, so that I might celebrate with my friends; but when this son of yours came, who has devoured your wealth with prostitutes, you killed the fattened calf for him.' And he said to him, 'Son, you have always been with me, and all that is mine is yours. But we had to celebrate and rejoice, for this brother of yours was dead and *has begun* to live, and was lost and has been found' " (Luke 15:11–32; see Proverbs 29:2).

[SERVICE from serve]
Setting: On the way from Galilee to Jerusalem. After giving the story of the prodigal son, the Lord teaches His disciples about stewardship.

Now He was also saying to the disciples, "There was a rich man who had a manager, and this *manager* was reported to him as squandering his possessions. And he called him and said to him, 'What is this I hear about you? Give an accounting of your management, for you can no longer be a manager.' The manager said to himself, 'What shall I do, since my master is taking the management away from me? I am not strong enough to dig; I am ashamed to beg. I know what I shall do, so that when I am removed from the management people will welcome me into their homes.' And he summoned each one of his master's debtors, and he *began* saying to the first, 'How much do you owe my master?' And he said, 'A hundred measures of oil.' And he said to him, 'Take your bill, and sit down quickly and write fifty.' Then he said to another, 'And how much do you owe?' And he said, 'A hundred measures of wheat.' He said to him, 'Take your bill, and write eighty.' And his master praised the unrighteous manager because he had acted shrewdly; for the sons of this age are more shrewd in relation to their own kind than the sons of light. And I say to you, make friends for yourselves by means of the wealth of unrighteousness, so that when it fails, they will receive you into the eternal dwellings. He who is faithful in a very little thing is faithful also in much; and he who is unrighteous in a very little thing is unrighteous also in much. Therefore if you have not been faithful in the *use of* unrighteous wealth, who will entrust the true *riches* to you? And if you have not been faithful in *the use of* that which is another's, who will give you that which is your own? No servant can serve two masters; for either he will hate the one and love the other, or else he will be devoted to one and despise the other. You cannot serve God and wealth" (Luke 16:1–13; cf. Matthew 6:24; see Matthew 25:14–30).

[SERVICE from serve me]
Setting: On the way from Galilee to Jerusalem. After His disciples ask that their faith be increased following His instruction to them on forgiveness, the Lord illustrates with the mustard seed and an obedient slave.

And the Lord said, "If you had faith like a mustard seed, you would say to this mulberry tree, 'Be uprooted and be planted in the sea'; and it would obey you. Which of you, having a slave plowing or tending sheep, will say to him when he has come from the field, 'Come immediately and sit down to eat'? But will he not say to him, "Prepare something for me to eat, and *properly* clothe yourself and serve me while I eat and drink; and afterward you may eat and drink'? He does not thank the slave because he did the things which were commanded, does he? So you too, when you do all the things which are commanded you, say, 'We are unworthy slaves; we have done *only* that which we ought to have done' " (Luke 17:6–10; see Matthew 13:31; Luke 12:37; 17:5).

[SERVICE from who serves]
Setting: An upper room in Jerusalem. During the Feast of Unleavened Bread (Passover) just before His crucifixion, Jesus celebrates the Passover meal with His disciples and institutes the Lord's Supper. The disciples later argue over who is the greatest among them.

And He said to them, "The kings of the Gentiles lord it over them; and those who have authority over them are called 'Benefactors.' But *it is* not this way with you, but the one who is the greatest among you must become like the youngest, and the leader like a servant. For who is greater, the one who reclines *at the table* or the one who serves? Is it not the one who reclines *at the table?* But I am among you as the one who serves" (Luke 22:25–27; cf. Matthew 20:25–28; 23:11; Mark 10:42–45).

[SERVICE from serves]
Setting: Jerusalem. Just days before the Passover, with the chief priests and Pharisees plotting to seize Jesus, crowds welcome Him with palm branches and praise, and some Greeks ask to meet Him.

And Jesus answered them, saying, "The hour has come for the Son of Man to be glorified. Truly, truly, I say to you, unless a grain of wheat falls into the earth and dies, it remains alone; but if it dies, it bears much fruit. He who loves his life loses it, and he who hates his life in this world will keep it to life eternal. If anyone serves Me, he must follow Me; and where I am, there My servant will be also; if anyone serves Me, the Father will honor him" (John 12:23–26; see Matthew 10:39).

Setting: Jerusalem. Before the Passover, after explaining He is the vine and His disciples are the branches, Jesus warns them of the persecution they will face after His departure to heaven.

"These things I have spoken to you so that you may be kept from stumbling. They will make you outcasts from the synagogue, but an hour is coming for everyone who kills you to think that he is offering service to God. These things they will do because they have not known the Father or Me. But these things I have spoken to you, so that when their hour comes, you may remember that I told you of them. These things I did not say to you at the beginning, because I was with you" (John 16:1–4; see John 8:19, 55; 9:22; 13:19; 15:18–27).

Setting: On the island of Patmos (in the Aegean Sea about fifty miles southwest of Ephesus in modern Turkey). On the Lord's Day (Sunday), approximately fifty years after the Resurrection, the disciple John encounters the Lord Jesus Christ, who communicates a new revelation for the apostle to record for the church in Thyatira and to six other churches in Asia.

"And to the angel of the church in Thyatira write: The Son of God, who has eyes like a flame of fire, and His feet are like burnished bronze, says this: 'I know your deeds, and your love and faith and service and perseverance, and that your deeds of late are greater than at first. But I have *this* against you, that you tolerate the woman Jezebel, who calls herself a prophetess, and she teaches and leads My bond-servants astray so that they commit *acts of* immorality and eat things sacrificed to idols. I gave her time to repent, and she does not want to repent of her immorality. Behold, I will throw her on a bed *of sickness,* and those who commit adultery with her into great tribulation, unless they repent of her deeds. And I will kill her children with pestilence, and all the churches will know that I am He who searches the minds and hearts; and I will give to each one of you according to your deeds. But I say to you, the rest who are in Thyatira, who do not hold this teaching, who have not known the deep things of Satan, as they call them—I place no other burden on you. Nevertheless what you have, hold fast until I come. He who overcomes, and he who keeps My deeds until the end, TO HIM I WILL GIVE AUTHORITY OVER THE NATIONS; AND HE SHALL RULE THEM WITH A ROD OF IRON, AS THE VESSELS OF THE POTTER ARE BROKEN TO PIECES, as I also have received *authority* from My Father; and I will give him the morning star. He who has an ear, let him hear what the Spirit says to the churches' (Revelation 2:18–29; Jesus quotes from Psalm 2:8, 9; Isaiah 30:14; see 1 Kings 16:31; Psalm 7:9; Romans 2:5; 1 Corinthians 2:10; 2 Peter 3:9; Revelation 1:14; 3:11; 17:1–20).

SERVICE, FAITHFUL (See FAITHFULNESS; REWARDS; and SERVICE)

SERVING GOD (Also see WORKS, GOOD; and WORSHIP)

[SERVING GOD from SERVE HIM ONLY]

Setting: Judea near the Jordan River. Following His baptism, and before He begins His public ministry, Jesus is led by the Spirit into the Judean wilderness for forty days of temptation by Satan.

Then Jesus said to him, "Go, Satan! For it is written, 'YOU SHALL WORSHIP THE LORD YOUR GOD, AND SERVE HIM ONLY'" (Matthew 4:10, Jesus quotes from Deuteronomy 6:13; cf. Luke 4:8).

[SERVING GOD from serve God]

Setting: Galilee. During the early part of His ministry, Jesus preaches the Sermon on the Mount to His disciples and the multitudes.

"No one can serve two masters; for either he will hate the one and love the other, or he will be devoted to one and despise the other. You cannot serve God and wealth (Matthew 6:24).

[SERVING GOD from SERVE HIM ONLY]

Setting: Judea near the Jordan River. Following His baptism in the Jordan river, and before He begins His public ministry, Jesus is led by the Spirit into the Judean wilderness for forty days of temptation by Satan.

Jesus answered him, "It is written, 'YOU SHALL WORSHIP THE LORD YOUR GOD AND SERVE HIM ONLY'" (Luke 4:8, Jesus quotes from Deuteronomy 6:13; cf. Matthew 4:10).

[SERVING GOD from serve God]

Setting: On the way from Galilee to Jerusalem. The Lord teaches His disciples about stewardship after giving them the story of the prodigal son.

Now He was also saying to the disciples, "There was a rich man who had a manager, and this *manager* was reported to him as squandering his possessions. And he called him and said to him, 'What is this I hear about you? Give an accounting of your management, for you can no longer be a manager.' The manager said to himself, 'What shall I do, since my master is taking the management away from me? I am not strong enough to dig; I am ashamed to beg. I know what I shall do, so that when I am removed from the management people will welcome me into their homes.' And he summoned each one of his master's debtors, and he *began* saying to the first, 'How much do you owe my master?' And he said, 'A hundred measures of oil.' And he said to him, 'Take your bill, and sit down quickly and write fifty.' Then he said to another, 'And how much do you owe?' And he said, 'A hundred measures of wheat.' He said to him, 'Take your bill, and write eighty.' And his master praised the unrighteous manager because he had acted shrewdly; for the sons of this age are more shrewd in relation to their own kind than the sons of light. And I say to you, make friends for yourselves by means of the wealth of unrighteousness, so that when it fails, they will receive you into the eternal dwellings. He who is faithful in a very little thing is faithful also in much; and he who is unrighteous in a very little thing is unrighteous also in much. Therefore if you have not been faithful in the *use of* unrighteous wealth, who will entrust the *true riches* to you? And if you have not been faithful in *the use of* that which is another's, who will give you that which is your own? No servant can serve two masters; for either he will hate the one and love the other, or else he will be devoted to one and despise the other. You cannot serve God and wealth" (Luke 16:1–13; cf. Matthew 6:24; see Matthew 25:14–30).

SET APART (See SANCTIFICATION)

SETTLEMENT

[SETTLEMENT from make an effort to settle with him]

Setting: On the way from Galilee to Jerusalem. After chastising the crowds for being able to discern the weather but not the present age, Jesus exhorts them to settle any financial disputes outside of court.

"And why do you not even on your own initiative judge what is right? For while you are going with your opponent to appear before the magistrate, on *your* way *there* make an effort to settle with him, so that he may not drag you before the judge, and the judge turn you over to the officer, and the officer throw you into prison. I say to you, you will not get out of there until you have paid the very last cent" (Luke 12:57–59; cf. Matthew 5:25, 26).

SEVEN

Setting: Galilee. Jesus responds to some Pharisees and scribes who ask Him for a miraculous sign as He ministers.

"Now when the unclean spirit goes out of a man, it passes through waterless places seeking rest, and does not find *it.* Then it says, 'I will return to my house from which I came'; and when it comes, it finds *it* unoccupied, swept, and put in order. Then it goes and takes along with it seven other spirits more wicked than itself, and they go in and live there; and the last state of that man becomes worse than the first. That is the way it will also be for this evil generation" (Matthew 12:43–45; cf. Luke 11:24–26; Mark 5:9).

Setting: By the Sea of Galilee. Jesus repeats a warning to His disciples about the teaching of the religious leaders of His time—the Pharisees and the Sadducees.

But Jesus aware of this, said, "You men of little faith, why do you discuss among yourselves that you have no bread? Do you not yet understand or remember the five loaves of the five thousand and how many baskets full you picked up? Or the seven loaves of the four thousand, and how many large baskets full you picked up? How is it that you do not understand that I did not speak to you concerning bread? But beware of the leaven of the Pharisees and the Sadducees" (Matthew 16:8–11; cf. Matthew 14:17–21; Matthew 15:34–38; Mark 8:17–21).

Setting: Capernaum of Galilee. Peter asks Jesus if forgiving someone seven times who has sinned against him is adequate.

Jesus said to him, "I do not say to you, up to seven times, but up to seventy times seven" (Matthew 18:22; see Matthew 18:21; Luke 17:3, 4).

Setting: The district of Dalmanutha. After the Pharisees argue with Jesus, seeking a sign from heaven to test Him, Jesus and His disciples cross to the other side of the Sea of Galilee, where His disciples discuss with one another that they have no bread.

And Jesus, aware of this, said to them, "Why do you discuss *the fact* that you have no bread? Do you not yet see or understand? Do you have a hardened heart? HAVING EYES, DO YOU NOT SEE? AND HAVING EARS, DO YOU NOT HEAR? And do you not remember, when I broke the five loaves for the five thousand, how many baskets full of broken pieces you picked you? They said to Him, "Twelve." When *I broke* the seven for the four thousand, how many large baskets full of broken pieces did you pick up?" They said to Him, "Seven." And He was saying to them, "Do you not yet understand?" (Mark 8:17–21, Jesus quotes from Jeremiah 5:21; cf. Matthew 16:5–12; see Matthew 14:19, 20; Mark 6:41–44, 52).

Setting: On the way from Galilee to Jerusalem. After some in the crowd test Him, demanding a sign from heaven, Jesus illustrates His power over Satan.

"When the unclean spirit goes out of a man, it passes through waterless places seeking rest, and not finding any, it says, 'I will return to my house from which I came.' And when it comes, it finds it swept clean and put in order. Then it goes and takes *along* seven other spirits more evil than itself, and they go in and live there; and the last state of that man becomes worse than the first" (Luke 11:24–26; cf. Matthew 12:43–45).

Setting: On the way from Galilee to Jerusalem. After conveying the story of the rich man and Lazarus, the Lord gives His disciples instruction on forgiveness.

He said to His disciples, "It is inevitable that stumbling blocks come, but woe to him through whom they come! It would be better for him if a millstone were hung around his neck and he were thrown into the sea, than that he would cause one of these little ones to stumble. Be on your guard! If your brother sins, rebuke him; and if he repents, forgive him. And if he sins against you seven times a day, and returns to you seven times, saying, 'I repent,' forgive him" (Luke 17:1–4; see Matthew 18:5–7, 15, 21, 22).

Setting: On the island of Patmos (in the Aegean Sea about fifty miles southwest of Ephesus in modern Turkey). On the Lord's Day (Sunday), approximately fifty years after the Resurrection, the disciple John hears the voice of the Lord Jesus Christ, who communicates new revelations for the apostle to record for the seven churches in Asia.

I was in the Spirit on the Lord's day, and I heard behind me a loud voice like *the sound* of a trumpet, saying, "Write in a book what you see, and send *it* to the seven churches: to Ephesus and to Smyrna and to Pergamum and to Thyatira and to Sardis and to Philadelphia and to Laodicea" (Revelation 1:10, 11).

Setting: On the island of Patmos (in the Aegean Sea about fifty miles southwest of Ephesus in modern Turkey). On the Lord's Day (Sunday), approximately fifty years after the Resurrection, the disciple John encounters the Lord Jesus Christ, who communicates new revelations for the apostle to record for the seven churches in Asia.

When I saw Him, I fell at His feet like a dead man. And He placed His right hand on me, saying, "Do not be afraid; I am the first and the last, and the living One; and I was dead, and behold, I am alive forevermore, and I have the keys of death and of Hades. Therefore write the things which you have seen, and the things which are, and the things which will take place after these things. As for the mystery of the seven stars which you saw in My right hand, and the seven golden lampstands: the seven stars are the angels of the seven churches, and the seven lampstands are the seven churches" (Revelation 1:17–20; see Isaiah 44:6; Luke 24:5; Revelation 2:8).

Setting: On the island of Patmos (in the Aegean Sea about fifty miles southwest of Ephesus in modern Turkey). On the Lord's Day (Sunday), about fifty years after Jesus' resurrection, the disciple John encounters the Lord Jesus Christ, who communicates a new revelation for the apostle to record for the church in Ephesus and to six other churches in Asia.

"To the angel of the church in Ephesus write: The One who holds the seven stars in His right hand, the One who walks among the seven golden lampstands, says this: 'I know your deeds and your toil and perseverance, and that you cannot tolerate evil men, and you put to the test those who call themselves apostles, and they are not, and you found them *to be* false; and you have perseverance and have endured for My name's sake, and have not grown weary. But I have *this* against you, that you have left your first love. Therefore remember from where you have fallen, and repent and do the deeds you did at first; or else I am coming to you and will remove your lampstand out of its place—unless you repent. Yet this you do have, that you hate the deeds of the Nicolaitans, which I also hate. He who has an ear, let him hear what the Spirit says to the churches. To him who overcomes, I will grant to eat of the tree of life which is in the Paradise of God' (Revelation 2:1–7; see Genesis 2:9; Ezekiel 28:13; 1 John 4:1; Revelation 1:10, 11, 19, 20).

Setting: On the island of Patmos (in the Aegean Sea about fifty miles southwest of Ephesus in modern Turkey). On the Lord's Day (Sunday), approximately fifty years after the Resurrection, the disciple John encounters the Lord Jesus Christ, who communicates a new revelation for the apostle to record for the church in Sardis and to six other churches in Asia.

"To the angel of the church in Sardis write: He who has the seven Spirits of God and the seven stars, says this: 'I know your deeds, that you have a name that you are alive, but you are dead. Wake up, and strengthen the things that remain, which were about to die; for I have not found your deeds completed in the sight of My God. So remember what you have received and heard; and keep *it*, and repent. Therefore if you do not wake up, I will come like a thief, and you will not know at what hour I will come to you. But you have a few people in Sardis who have not soiled their garments; and they will walk with Me in white, for they are worthy. He who overcomes will thus be clothed in white garments; and I will not erase his name from the book of life, and I will confess his name before My Father and before His angels. He who has an ear, let him hear what the Spirit says to the churches'" (Revelation 3:1–6; see Matthew 10:32; Revelation 1:16).

SEVEN CHURCHES (Listed under CHURCHES, SEVEN)

SEVEN LAMPSTANDS (Listed under LAMPSTANDS, SEVEN)

SEVEN SPIRITS (Listed under SPIRITS, SEVEN)

SEVEN SPIRITS OF GOD

Setting: On the island of Patmos (in the Aegean Sea about fifty miles southwest of Ephesus in modern Turkey). On the Lord's Day (Sunday), about fifty years after Jesus' resurrection, the disciple John encounters the Lord Jesus Christ, who communicates a new revelation for the apostle to record for the church in Sardis and to six other churches in Asia.

"To the angel of the church in Sardis write: He who has the seven Spirits of God and the seven stars, says this: 'I know your deeds, that you have a name that you are alive, but you are dead. Wake up, and strengthen the things that remain, which were about to die; for I have not found your deeds completed in the sight of My God. So remember what you have received and heard; and keep *it,* and repent. Therefore if you do not wake up, I will come like a thief, and you will not know at what hour I will come to you. But you have a few people in Sardis who have not soiled their garments; and they will walk with Me in white, for they are worthy. He who overcomes will thus be clothed in white garments; and I will not erase his name from the book of life, and I will confess his name before My Father and before His angels. He who has an ear, let him hear what the Spirit says to the churches' " (Revelation 3:1–6; see Matthew 10:32; Revelation 1:16).

SEVENTY

Setting: Capernaum of Galilee. Peter asks Jesus if forgiving someone seven times who has sinned against him is adequate.

Jesus said to him, "I do not say to you, up to seven times, but up to seventy times seven" (Matthew 18:22; see Matthew 18:21; Luke 17:3, 4).

SEXES (Also see FEMALE; MALE; MAN; and WOMAN)

[SEXES from MALE AND FEMALE]

Setting: Judea beyond the Jordan (Perea). After Jesus replies to Peter's question about forgiveness, in front of a large crowd the Pharisees test the Lord with a question about divorce.

And He answered and said, "Have you not read that He who created *them* from the beginning MADE THEM MALE AND FEMALE, and said, 'FOR THIS REASON A MAN SHALL LEAVE HIS FATHER AND MOTHER AND BE JOINED TO HIS WIFE, AND THE TWO SHALL BECOME ONE FLESH'? So they are no longer two, but one flesh. What therefore God has joined together, let no man separate" (Matthew 19:4–6, Jesus quotes from Genesis 1:27; 2:24; cf. Mark 10:5–9).

[SEXES from MALE AND FEMALE]

Setting: Judea beyond the Jordan (Perea). Jesus teaches the crowds gathered around Him about divorce after the Pharisees test and question Him on the subject.

And He answered and said to them, "What did Moses command you?" They said, "Moses permitted a *man* TO WRITE A CERTIFICATE OF DIVORCE AND SEND *her* AWAY." But Jesus said to them, "Because of your hardness of heart he wrote you this commandment. But from the beginning of creation, *God* MADE THEM MALE AND FEMALE. FOR THIS REASON A MAN SHALL LEAVE HIS FATHER AND MOTHER, AND THE TWO SHALL BECOME ONE FLESH; so they are no longer two, but one flesh. What therefore God has joined together, let no man separate. In the house the disciples *began* questioning Him about this again. And He said to them, "Whoever divorces his wife and marries another woman commits adultery against her; and if she herself divorces her husband and marries another man, she is committing adultery" (Mark 10:3–12, Jesus quotes from Genesis 1:27; 2:24; cf. Matthew 19:1–9; see Deuteronomy 24:1–3; Matthew 5:32; see Romans 7:2, 3; 1 Corinthians 7:11, 13; 1 Timothy 2:14).

SEXUAL DESIRE

SEXUAL DESIRE from everyone who looks at a woman with lust for her]

Setting: Galilee. During the early part of His ministry, Jesus preaches the Sermon on the Mount to His disciples and the multitudes.

"You have heard that it was said, 'YOU SHALL NOT COMMIT ADULTERY'; but I say to you that everyone who looks at a woman with lust for her has already committed adultery with her in his heart" (Matthew 5:27, 28, Jesus quotes from Exodus 20:14; see 2 Samuel 11:2–5).

SEXUAL SIN (Also see ADULTERIES; ADULTERY; FORNICATIONS; IMMORALITY; LUST; and PORNOGRAPHY)

[SEXUAL SIN from loose living and prostitutes]

Setting: On the way from Galilee to Jerusalem. Jesus conveys the illustration of the prodigal son because the Pharisees and scribes complain He associates with tax collectors and sinners.

And He said, "A man had two sons. The younger of them said to his father, 'Father, give me the share of the estate that falls to me.' So he divided his wealth between them. And not many days later, the younger son gathered everything together and went on a journey into a distant country, and there he squandered his estate with loose living. Now when he had spent everything, a severe famine occurred in that country, and he began to be impoverished. So he went and hired himself out to one of the citizens of that country, and he sent him into his fields to feed swine. And he would have gladly filled his stomach with the pods that the swine were eating, and no one was giving *anything* to him. But when he came to his senses, he said, 'How many of my father's hired men have more than enough bread, but I am dying here with hunger! I will get up and go to my father, and will say to him, "Father, I have sinned against heaven, and in your sight; I am no longer worthy to be called your son; make me as one of your hired men."' So he got up and came to his father. But while he was still a long way off, his father saw him and felt compassion *for him,* and ran and embraced him and kissed him. And the son said to him, "Father, I have sinned against heaven and in your sight; I am no longer worthy to be called your son.' But the father said to his slaves, 'Quickly bring out the best robe and put it on him, and put a ring on his hand and sandals on his feet; and bring the fattened calf, kill it, and let us eat and celebrate; for this son of mine was dead and has come to life again; he was lost and has been found.' And they began to celebrate. Now his older son was in the field, when he came and approached the house, he heard music and dancing. And he summoned one of the servants and *began* inquiring what these things could be. And he said to him, 'Your brother has come, and your father has killed the fattened calf because he has received him back safe and sound.' But he became angry and was not willing to go in; and his father came out and *began* pleading with him. But he answered and said to his father, 'Look! For so many years I have been serving you and I have never neglected a command of yours; and *yet* you have never given me a young goat, so that I might celebrate with my friends; but when this son of yours came, who has devoured your wealth with prostitutes, you killed the fattened calf for him.' And he said to him, 'Son, you have always been with me, and all that is mine is yours. But we had to celebrate and rejoice, for this brother of yours was dead and *has begun* to live, and was lost and has been found' " (Luke 15:11–32; see Proverb 29:2).

SHADE

Setting: Galilee. After giving the Parable of the Sower and the Parable of the Seed, Jesus continues teaching His disciples by presenting the Parable of the Mustard Seed.

And He said, "How shall we picture the kingdom of God, or by what parable shall we present it? *It is* like a mustard seed, which, when sown upon the soil, though it is smaller than all the seeds that are upon the soil, yet when it is sown, it grows up and becomes larger than all the garden plants and forms large branches; so that THE BIRDS OF THE AIR can NEST UNDER ITS SHADE" (Mark 4:30–32, Jesus quotes from Ezekiel 17:23; cf. Matthew 13:31, 32; Luke 13:18, 19).

SHAME (Also see ASHAMED)

Setting: On the island of Patmos (in the Aegean Sea about fifty miles southwest of Ephesus in modern Turkey). On the Lord's Day (Sunday), approximately fifty years after the Resurrection, the disciple John encounters the Lord Jesus Christ, who communicates a new revelation for the apostle to record for the church in Laodicea and to six other churches in Asia.

"To the angel of the church in Laodicea write: The Amen, the faithful and true Witness, the Beginning of the creation of God, says this: 'I know your deeds, that you are neither cold nor hot; I wish that you were cold or hot. So because you are lukewarm, and neither hot nor cold, I will spit you out of My mouth. Because you say, "I am rich, and have become wealthy, and have need of nothing," and you do not know that you are wretched and miserable and poor and blind and naked, I advise you to buy from Me gold refined by fire so that you may become rich, and white garments so that you may clothe yourself, and *that* the shame of your nakedness will not be revealed; and eye salve to anoint your eyes so that you may see. Those whom I love, I reprove and discipline; therefore be zealous and repent. Behold, I stand at the door and knock; if anyone hears My voice and opens the door, I will come in to him and will dine with him, and he with Me. He who overcomes, I will grant to him to sit down with Me on My throne, as I also overcame and sat down with My Father on His throne. He who has an ear, let him hear what the Spirit says to the churches'" (Revelation 3:14–22; see Proverb 3:12; Hosea 12:8; John 14:23; 16:33).

SHARE

Setting: On the way from Galilee to Jerusalem. Jesus conveys the illustration of the prodigal son because the Pharisees and scribes complain He associates with tax collectors and sinners.

And He said, "A man had two sons. The younger of them said to his father, 'Father, give me the share of the estate that falls to me.' So he divided his wealth between them. And not many days later, the younger son gathered everything together and went on a journey into a distant country, and there he squandered his estate with loose living. Now when he had spent everything, a severe famine occurred in that country, and he began to be impoverished. So he went and hired himself out to one of the citizens of that country, and he sent him into his fields to feed swine. And he would have gladly filled his stomach with the pods that the swine were eating, and no one was giving *anything* to him. But when he came to his senses, he said, 'How many of my father's hired men have more than enough bread, but I am dying here with hunger! I will get up and go to my father, and will say to him, "Father, I have sinned against heaven, and in your sight; I am no longer worthy to be called your son; make me as one of your hired men."' So he got up and came to his father. But while he was still a long way off, his father saw him and felt compassion *for him,* and ran and embraced him and kissed him. And the son said to him, "Father, I have sinned against heaven and in your sight; I am no longer worthy to be called your son.' But the father said to his slaves, 'Quickly bring out the best robe and put it on him, and put a ring on his hand and sandals on his feet; and bring the fattened calf, kill it, and let us eat and celebrate; for this son of mine was dead and has come to life again; he was lost and has been found.' And they began to celebrate. Now his older son was in the field, when he came and approached the house, he heard music and dancing. And he summoned one of the servants and *began* inquiring what these things could be. And he said to him, 'Your brother has come, and your father has killed the fattened calf because he has received him back safe and sound.' But he became angry and was not willing to go in; and his father came out and *began* pleading with him. But he answered and said to his father, 'Look! For so many years I have been serving you and I have never neglected a command of yours; and *yet* you have never given me a young goat, so that I might celebrate with my friends; but when this son of yours came, who has devoured your wealth with prostitutes, you killed the fattened calf for him.' And he said to him, 'Son, you have always been with me, and all that is mine is yours. But we had to celebrate and rejoice, for this brother of yours was dead and *has begun* to live, and was lost and has been found' " (Luke 15:11–32; see Proverb 29:2).

SHEATH

Setting: A garden across the ravine of the Kidron from Jerusalem. Simon Peter attempts to defend Jesus with a sword during Judas's betrayal with a Roman cohort and officers from the chief priests and the Pharisees.

So Jesus said to Peter, "Put the sword into the sheath; the cup which the Father has given Me, shall I not drink it?" (John 18:11; see Matthew 20:22; 26:52; Luke 22:51).

SHEBA, QUEEN OF (See SOUTH, QUEEN OF THE)

SHEEP (SHEEP, LOST is a separate entry; also see FLOCK; LAMBS; and SHEPHERD)

Setting: Galilee. After His disciples observe His ministry, Jesus summons and specifically instructs them about the upcoming hardships of their ministry to the people of Israel.

"Behold, I send you out as sheep in the midst of wolves; so be shrewd as serpents and innocent as doves. But beware of men, for they will hand you over to *the* courts and scourge you in their synagogues; and you will even be brought before governors and kings for My sake, as a testimony to them and to the Gentiles. But when they hand you over, do not worry about how or what you are to say; for it will be given you in that hour what you are to say. For it is not you who speak, but *it* is the Spirit of your Father who speaks in you" (Matthew 10:16–20; cf. Luke 10:3).

Setting: A synagogue in Galilee. Jesus answers questions posed by the Pharisees about the Sabbath.

And He said to them, "What man is there among you who has a sheep, and if it falls into a pit on the Sabbath, will he not take hold of it and lift it out? How much more valuable then is a man than a sheep! So then, it is lawful to do good on the Sabbath." Then He said to the man, "Stretch out your hand!" He stretched it out, and it was restored to normal, like the other (Matthew 12:11–13; cf. Matthew 10:31; Mark 3:4, 5; Luke 6:9, 10; 14:5; see Matthew 8:3; 12:9, 10).

Setting: Capernaum of Galilee. Jesus illustrates to His disciples the value of little ones.

"What do you think? If any man has a hundred sheep, and one of them has gone astray, does he not leave the ninety-nine on the mountains and go and search for the one that is straying? If it turns out that he finds it, truly I say to you, he rejoices over it more than the ninety-nine which have not gone astray. So it is not *the* will of your Father who is in heaven that one of these little ones perish" (Matthew 18:12–14; cf. Luke 15:4–7).

Setting: On the Mount of Olives, just east of Jerusalem. During His Olivet Discourse, after answering His disciples' questions as to when the temple will be destroyed and Jerusalem overrun, along with the signs of His coming and the end of the age, Jesus reveals the future judgments following His return.

"But when the Son of Man comes in His glory, and all the angels with Him, then He will sit on His glorious throne. All the nations will be gathered before Him; and He will separate them from one another, as the shepherd separates the sheep from the goats; and He will put the sheep on His right, and the goats on the left. Then the King will say to those on His right, 'Come, you who are blessed of My Father, inherit the kingdom prepared for you from the foundation of the world. 'For I was hungry, and you gave Me *something* to eat; I was thirsty, and you gave Me *something* to drink; I was a stranger, and you invited Me in; naked, and you clothed Me; I was sick, and you visited Me; I was in prison, and you came to Me.' Then the righteous will answer Him, 'Lord, when did we see You hungry and feed You, or thirsty, and give you *something* to drink? And when did we see You a stranger, and invite You in, or naked, and clothe You? When did we see You sick, or in prison, and come to You?' The King will answer and say to them, 'Truly I say to you, to the extent that you did it to one of these brothers of Mine, *even* the least *of them,* you did it to Me.' Then He will also say to those on His left, 'Depart from Me, accursed ones, into the eternal fire which has been prepared for the devil and his angels; for I was hungry, and you gave Me *nothing* to eat; I was thirsty, and you gave Me nothing to drink; I was a stranger, and you did not invite Me in; naked, and you did not clothe Me; sick, and in prison, and you did not visit Me.' Then they themselves also will answer, 'Lord, when did we see You hungry, or thirsty, or a stranger, or naked, or sick, or in prison, and did not take care of You?' Then He will answer them, 'Truly I say to you, to the extent that you did not do it to one of the least of these, you did not do it to Me.' These will go away into eternal punishment, but the righteous into eternal life" (Matthew 25:31–46; see Matthew 7:23; 16:27; 19:29).

Setting: On the way to the Mount of Olives. After celebrating the Passover meal in Jerusalem, prior to His betrayal by Judas, Jesus states that all His disciples will deny Him that very day.

Then Jesus said to them, "You will all fall away because of Me this night, for it is written, 'I WILL STRIKE DOWN THE SHEPHERD, AND THE SHEEP OF THE FLOCK SHALL BE SCATTERED.' But after I have been raised, I will go ahead of you to Galilee." But Peter said to Him, '*Even* though all may fall away because of You, I will never fall away.' Jesus said to him, "Truly I say to you that this *very* night, before a rooster crows, you will deny Me three times" (Matthew 26:31–34, Jesus quotes from Zechariah 13:7; cf. Mark 14:26–31; see Matthew 28:7, 10, 16; John 13:37).

Setting: A borrowed upper room in Jerusalem. After Jesus and His twelve disciples celebrate the Passover and the Lord's Supper, they go out to the Mount of Olives.

And Jesus said to them, "You will all fall away, because it is written, 'I WILL STRIKE DOWN THE SHEPHERD, AND THE SHEEP SHALL BE SCATTERED.' But after I have been raised, I will go ahead of you to Galilee." But Peter said to Him, "*Even* though all may fall away, yet I will not." And Jesus said to him, "Truly I say to you, that this very night, before a rooster crows twice, you yourself will deny Me three times" (Mark 14:27–30, Jesus quotes from Zechariah 13:7; cf. Matthew 26:30–34; see Mark 14:72).

Setting: On the way from Galilee to Jerusalem. After Jesus presents to large crowds the demands of discipleship, the Pharisees and scribes complain He associates with tax collectors and sinners.

So He told them this parable, saying, "What man among you, if he has a hundred sheep and has lost one of them, does not leave the ninety-nine in the open pasture and go after the one which is lost until he finds it? When he has found it, he lays it on his shoulders, rejoicing. And when he comes home, he calls together his friends and his neighbors, saying to them, 'Rejoice with me, for I have found my sheep which was lost!' I tell you that in the same way, there will be *more* joy in heaven over one sinner who repents than over ninety-nine righteous persons who need no repentance" (Luke 15:3–7; cf. Matthew 18:12–14; see Matthew 9:11–13; Luke 5:29–32).

Setting: On the way from Galilee to Jerusalem. After His disciples ask that their faith be increased following His instruction to them on forgiveness, the Lord illustrates with the mustard seed and an obedient slave.

And the Lord said, "If you had faith like a mustard seed, you would say to this mulberry tree, 'Be uprooted and be planted in the sea'; and it would obey you. Which of you, having a slave plowing or tending sheep, will say to him when he has come from the field, 'Come immediately and sit down to eat'? But will he not say to him, "Prepare something for me to eat, and *properly* clothe yourself and serve me while I eat and drink; and afterward you may eat and drink'? He does not thank the slave because he did the things which were commanded, does he? So you too, when you do all the things which are commanded you, say, 'We are unworthy slaves; we have done *only* that which we ought to have done' " (Luke 17:6–10; see Matthew 13:31; Luke 12:37).

Setting: Jerusalem. Following the Pharisees' interrogation and dismissal of the formerly blind man Jesus healed on the Sabbath, the Lord speaks to the Pharisees, using parabolic language they do not understand.

"Truly, truly, I say to you, he who does not enter by the door into the fold of the sheep, but climbs up some other way, he is a thief and a robber. But he who enters by the door is a shepherd of the sheep. To him the doorkeeper opens, and the sheep hear his voice, and he calls his own sheep by name and leads them out. When he puts forth all his own, he goes ahead of them, and the sheep follow him because they know his voice. A stranger they simply will not follow, but will flee from him, because they do not know the voice of strangers" (John 10:1–5).

Setting: Jerusalem. Following the Pharisees' interrogation and dismissal of the formerly blind man Jesus healed on the Sabbath, the Lord conveys the Parable of the Good Shepherd to the Pharisees, using figures of speech they do not understand.

So Jesus said to them again, "Truly, truly, I say to you, I am the door of the sheep. All who came before Me are thieves and robbers, but the sheep did not hear them. I am the door; if anyone enters through Me, he will be saved, and will go in and out and find pasture. The thief comes only to steal and kill and destroy; I came that they may have life, and have *it* abundantly. I am the good shepherd; the good shepherd lays down His life for the sheep. He who is a hired hand, and not a shepherd, who is not the owner of the sheep, sees the wolf coming, and leaves the sheep and flees, and the wolf snatches them and scatters *them. He flees* because he is a hired hand and is not concerned about the sheep. I am the good shepherd, and I know My own and My own know Me, even as the Father knows Me and I know the Father; and I lay down My life for the sheep. I have other sheep, which are not of this fold; I must bring them also, and they will hear My voice; and they will become one flock *with* one shepherd. For this reason the Father loves Me, because I lay down My life so that I may take it again. No one has taken it away from Me, but I lay it down on My own initiative. I have authority to take it up again. This commandment I received from My Father" (John 10:7–18; see Isaiah 40:11; 56:8; Jeremiah 23:1; Matthew 11:27).

Setting: Jerusalem. At the Feast of Dedication, just after Jesus conveys the Parable of the Good Shepherd to the Pharisees (who do not understand it), they ask Him plainly if He is the Christ.

Jesus answered them, "I told you, and you do not believe; the works that I do in My Father's name, these testify of Me. But you do not believe because you are not of My sheep. My sheep hear My voice, and I know them, and they follow Me; and I give eternal life to them, and they will never perish; and no one will snatch them out of My hand. My Father, who has given *them* to Me, is greater than all; and no one is able to snatch *them* out of the Father's hand. I and the Father are one" (John 10:25–30; see John 8:47; 17:1, 2, 20, 21).

Setting: By the Sea of Galilee. During His third manifestation to His disciples after His resurrection from the dead in Jerusalem, Jesus quizzes Peter three times regarding the disciple's love for Him.

So when they had finished breakfast, Jesus said to Simon Peter, "Simon, *son* of John, do you love Me more than these?" He said to Him, "Yes, Lord; You know that I love You." He said to him, "Tend My lambs." He said to him again a second time, "Simon, *son* of John, do you love Me?" He said to Him, "Yes, Lord; You know that I love You." He said to him, "Shepherd My sheep." He said to him the third time, "Simon, *son* of John, do you love Me?" Peter was grieved because He said to him the third time, "Do you love Me?" And he said to Him, "Lord, You know all things; You know that I love You." Jesus said to him, "Tend My sheep" (John 21:15–17; see Matthew 26:33; Mark 14:29).

SHEEP, LOST

Setting: Galilee. After His twelve disciples observe His ministry, Jesus summons and specifically instructs them about their ministry to the people of Israel.

These twelve Jesus sent out after instructing them: "Do not go in *the* way of *the* Gentiles, and do not enter *any* city of the Samaritans; but rather go to the lost sheep of the house of Israel. And as you go, preach, saying, 'The kingdom of heaven is at hand.' Heal *the* sick, raise *the* dead, cleanse *the* lepers, cast out demons. Freely you received, freely give. Do not acquire gold, or silver, or copper for your money belts, or a bag for *your* journey, or even two coats, or sandals, or a staff; for the worker is worthy of his support. And whatever city or village you enter, inquire who is worthy in it, and stay at his house until you leave *that city*. As you enter the house, give it your greeting. If the house is worthy, give it your *blessing of* peace. But if it is not worthy, take back your *blessing of* peace. Whoever does not receive you, nor heed your words, as you go out of that house or that city, shake the dust off your feet. Truly I say to you, it will be more tolerable for *the* land of Sodom and Gomorrah in the day of judgment than for that city" (Matthew 10:5–15; cf. Mark 6:7–11; Luke 9:1–5; see Matthew 3:2; 11:22, 24; 15:24; Luke 22:35; 1 Corinthians 9:14).

Setting: The district of Tyre and Sidon. A Canaanite woman appeals to Jesus to heal her demon-possessed daughter.

But He answered and said, "I was sent only to the lost sheep of the house of Israel." But she came and *began* to bow down before Him, saying, "Lord, help me!" And He answered and said, "It is not good to take the children's bread and throw it to the dogs." But she said, "Yes, Lord; but even the dogs feed from the crumbs which fall from their masters' table." Then Jesus said to her, "O woman, your faith is great; it shall be done for you as you wish." And her daughter was healed at once (Matthew 15:24–28; cf. Mark 7: 24–30; see Matthew 9:22; 10:5, 6).

SHEEP, PARABLE OF THE LOST

[SHEEP, PARABLE OF THE LOST from sheep and gone astray]
Setting: Capernaum of Galilee. Jesus illustrates to His disciples the value of little ones.

"What do you think? If any man has a hundred sheep, and one of them has gone astray, does he not leave the ninety-nine on the mountains and go and search for the one that is straying? If it turns out that he finds it, truly I say to you, he rejoices over it more than the ninety-nine which have not gone astray. So it is not *the* will of your Father who is in heaven that one of these little ones perish" (Matthew 18:12–14; cf. Luke 15:4–7).

[SHEEP, PARABLE OF THE LOST from sheep; has lost one of them; and my sheep which was lost]
Setting: On the way from Galilee to Jerusalem. After Jesus presents to large crowds the demands of discipleship, the Pharisees and scribes complain He associates with tax collectors and sinners.

So He told them this parable, saying, "What man among you, if he has a hundred sheep and has lost one of them, does not leave the ninety-nine in the open pasture and go after the one which is lost until he finds it? When he has found it, he lays it on his shoulders, rejoicing. And when he comes home, he calls together his friends and his neighbors, saying to them, 'Rejoice with me, for I have found my sheep which was lost!' I tell you that in the same way, there will be *more* joy in heaven over one sinner who repents than over ninety-nine righteous persons who need no repentance" (Luke 15:3–7; cf. Matthew 18:12–14; see Matthew 9:11–13; Luke 5:29–32).

SHEEP'S CLOTHING (Listed under CLOTHING, SHEEP'S)

SHEEPFOLD (See FOLD)

SHEKEL (Also see COIN; COINS; and MONEY)

Setting: Capernaum of Galilee. Jesus pays the two-drachma temple tax for Peter and Himself in a miraculous manner.

He said, "Yes." And when he came into the house, Jesus spoke to him first, saying, "What do you think, Simon? From whom do the kings of the earth collect customs or poll-tax, from their sons or from strangers?" When Peter said, "From strangers," Jesus said to him, "Then the sons are exempt. However, so that we do not offend them, go to the sea and throw in a hook, and take the first fish that comes up; and when you open its mouth, you will find a shekel. Take that and give it to them for you and Me" (Matthew 17:25–27; see Exodus 30:11–16; Matthew 17:24; 22:17–19; Romans 13:7).

SHEKINAH (See TRANSFIGURATION)

SHEOL (See HADES and HELL)

SHEPHERD

Setting: On the Mount of Olives, just east of Jerusalem. During His Olivet Discourse, after answering His disciples' questions as to when the temple will be destroyed and Jerusalem overrun, along with the signs of His coming and the end of the age, Jesus reveals the future judgments following His return.

"But when the Son of Man comes in His glory, and all the angels with Him, then He will sit on His glorious throne. All the nations will be gathered before Him; and He will separate them from one another, as the shepherd separates the sheep from the goats; and He will put the sheep on His right, and the goats on the left. Then the King will say to those on His right, 'Come, you who are blessed of My Father, inherit the kingdom prepared for you from the foundation of the world. 'For I was hungry, and you gave Me *something* to eat; I was thirsty, and you gave Me *something* to drink; I was a stranger, and you invited Me in; naked, and you clothed Me; I was sick, and you visited Me; I was in prison, and you came to Me.' Then the righteous will answer Him, 'Lord, when did we see You hungry and feed You, or thirsty, and give you *something* to drink? And when did we see You a stranger, and invite

You in, or naked, and clothe You? When did we see You sick, or in prison, and come to You?' The King will answer and say to them, 'Truly I say to you, to the extent that you did it to one of these brothers of Mine, *even* the least *of them,* you did it to Me.' Then He will also say to those on His left, 'Depart from Me, accursed ones, into the eternal fire which has been prepared for the devil and his angels; for I was hungry, and you gave Me *nothing* to eat; I was thirsty, and you gave Me nothing to drink; I was a stranger, and you did not invite Me in; naked, and you did not clothe Me; sick, and in prison, and you did not visit Me.' Then they themselves also will answer, 'Lord, when did we see You hungry, or thirsty, or a stranger, or naked, or sick, or in prison, and did not take care of You?' Then He will answer them, 'Truly I say to you, to the extent that you did not do it to one of the least of these, you did not do it to Me.' These will go away into eternal punishment, but the righteous into eternal life" (Matthew 25:31–46; see Matthew 7:23; 16:27; 19:29).

Setting: On the way to the Mount of Olives. After celebrating the Passover meal in Jerusalem, prior to His betrayal by Judas, Jesus states that all His disciples will deny Him that very day.

Then Jesus said to them, "You will all fall away because of Me this night, for it is written, 'I WILL STRIKE DOWN THE SHEPHERD, AND THE SHEEP OF THE FLOCK SHALL BE SCATTERED.' But after I have been raised, I will go ahead of you to Galilee." But Peter said to Him, '*Even* though all may fall away because of You, I will never fall away.' Jesus said to him, "Truly I say to you that this *very* night, before a rooster crows, you will deny Me three times" (Matthew 26:31–34, Jesus quotes from Zechariah 13:7; cf. Mark 14:26–31; see Matthew 28:7, 10, 16; John 13:37).

Setting: A borrowed upper room in Jerusalem. After Jesus and His twelve disciples celebrate the Passover and the Lord's Supper, they go out to the Mount of Olives.

And Jesus said to them, "You will all fall away, because it is written, 'I WILL STRIKE DOWN THE SHEPHERD, AND THE SHEEP SHALL BE SCATTERED.' But after I have been raised, I will go ahead of you to Galilee." But Peter said to Him, "*Even* though all may fall away, yet I will not." And Jesus said to him, "Truly I say to you, that this very night, before a rooster crows twice, you yourself will deny Me three times" (Mark 14:27–30, Jesus quotes from Zechariah 13:7; cf. Matthew 26:30–34; see Mark 14:72).

Setting: Jerusalem. Following the Pharisees' interrogation and dismissal of the formerly blind man Jesus healed on the Sabbath, the Lord speaks to the Pharisees, using parabolic language they do not understand.

"Truly, truly, I say to you, he who does not enter by the door into the fold of the sheep, but climbs up some other way, he is a thief and a robber. But he who enters by the door is a shepherd of the sheep. To him the doorkeeper opens, and the sheep hear his voice, and he calls his own sheep by name and leads them out. When he puts forth all his own, he goes ahead of them, and the sheep follow him because they know his voice. A stranger they simply will not follow, but will flee from him, because they do not know the voice of strangers" (John 10:1–5).

Setting: Jerusalem. Following the Pharisees' interrogation and dismissal of the formerly blind man Jesus healed on the Sabbath, the Lord conveys the Parable of the Good Shepherd to the Pharisees, using figures of speech they do not understand.

So Jesus said to them again, "Truly, truly, I say to you, I am the door of the sheep. All who came before Me are thieves and robbers, but the sheep did not hear them. I am the door; if anyone enters through Me, he will be saved, and will go in and out and find pasture. The thief comes only to steal and kill and destroy; I came that they may have life, and have *it* abundantly. I am the good shepherd; the good shepherd lays down His life for the sheep. He who is a hired hand, and not a shepherd, who is not the owner of the sheep, sees the wolf coming, and leaves the sheep and flees, and the wolf snatches them and scatters *them. He flees* because he is a hired hand and is not concerned about the sheep. I am the good shepherd, and I know My own and My own know Me, even as the Father knows Me and I know the Father; and I lay down My life for the sheep. I have other sheep, which are not of this fold; I must bring them also, and they will hear My voice; and they will become one flock *with* one shepherd. For this reason the Father loves Me, because I lay down My life so that I may take it again. No one has taken it away from Me, but I lay it down on My own initiative. I have authority to take it up again. This commandment I received from My Father" (John 10:7–18; see Isaiah 40:11; 56:8; Jeremiah 23:1; Matthew 11:27).

Setting: By the Sea of Galilee. During His third manifestation to His disciples after His resurrection from the dead in Jerusalem, Jesus quizzes Peter three times regarding the disciple's love for Him.

So when they had finished breakfast, Jesus said to Simon Peter, "Simon, *son* of John, do you love Me more than these?" He said to Him, "Yes, Lord; You know that I love You." He said to him, "Tend My lambs." He said to him again a second time, "Simon, *son* of John, do you love Me?" He said to Him, "Yes, Lord; You know that I love You." He said to him, Shepherd My sheep." He said to him the third time, "Simon, *son* of John, do you love Me?" Peter was grieved because He said to him the third time, "Do you love Me?" And he said to Him, "Lord, You know all things; You know that I love You." Jesus said to him, "Tend My sheep" (John 21:15–17; see Matthew 26:33; Mark 14:29).

SHEPHERD, GOOD (See SHEPHERD, PARABLE OF THE GOOD)

SHEPHERD, JESUS AS (See SHEPHERD, GOOD)

SHEPHERD, PARABLE OF THE GOOD

[SHEPHERD, PARABLE OF THE GOOD from I am the good shepherd]

Setting: Jerusalem. Following the Pharisees' interrogation and dismissal of the formerly blind man Jesus healed on the Sabbath, the Lord conveys the Parable of the Good Shepherd to the Pharisees, using figures of speech they do not understand.

So Jesus said to them again, "Truly, truly, I say to you, I am the door of the sheep. All who came before Me are thieves and robbers, but the sheep did not hear them. I am the door; if anyone enters through Me, he will be saved, and will go in and out and find pasture. The thief comes only to steal and kill and destroy; I came that they may have life, and have *it* abundantly. I am the good shepherd; the good shepherd lays down His life for the sheep. He who is a hired hand, and not a shepherd, who is not the owner of the sheep, sees the wolf coming, and leaves the sheep and flees, and the wolf snatches them and scatters *them. He flees* because he is a hired hand and is not concerned about the sheep. I am the good shepherd, and I know My own and My own know Me, even as the Father knows Me and I know the Father; and I lay down My life for the sheep. I have other sheep, which are not of this fold; I must bring them also, and they will hear My voice; and they will become one flock *with* one shepherd. For this reason the Father loves Me, because I lay down My life so that I may take it again. No one has taken it away from Me, but I lay it down on My own initiative. I have authority to take it up again. This commandment I received from My Father" (John 10:7–18; see Isaiah 40:11; 56:8; Jeremiah 23:1; Matthew 11:27).

SHIRT (Also see CLOTHING; and GARMENT)

Setting: Galilee. During the early part of His ministry, Jesus preaches the Sermon on the Mount to His disciples and the multitudes.

"If anyone wants to sue you and take your shirt, let him have your coat also" (Matthew 5:40).

Setting: Galilee. After selecting His twelve disciples, Jesus teaches the Sermon on the Mount to those disciples and a great throng of people from Judea, Jerusalem, and the central coastal region of Tyre and Sidon.

"But I say to you who hear, love your enemies, do good to those who hate you, bless those who curse you, pray for those who mistreat you. Whoever hits you on the cheek, offer him the other also; and whoever takes away your coat, do not withhold your shirt from him either. Give to everyone who asks of you, and whoever takes away what is yours, do not demand it back. Treat others the same way you want them to treat you. If you love those who love you, what credit is *that* to you? For even sinners love those who love them. If you do good to those who do good to you, what credit is *that* to you? For even sinners do the same. If you lend to those from whom you expect to receive, what credit is *that* to you? Even sinners lend to sinners in order to receive back the same *amount.* But love your enemies, and do good, and lend, expecting nothing in return; and your reward will be great, and you will be sons of the Most High; for He Himself is kind to ungrateful and evil *men.* Be merciful, just as your Father is merciful" (Luke 6:27–36; cf. Matthew 5:9, 39–48; Matthew 7:12).

SHOES (Also see SANDALS)

Setting: On the way from Galilee to Jerusalem. The Lord appoints seventy followers and sends them out in pairs to every place He Himself will soon visit.

And He was saying to them, "The harvest is plentiful, but the laborers are few; therefore beseech the Lord of the harvest to send out laborers into His harvest. Go; behold, I send you out as lambs in the midst of wolves. Carry no money belt, no bag, no shoes; and greet no one on the way. Whatever house you enter, first say, 'Peace be to this house.' If a man of peace is there, your peace will rest on him; but if not, it will return to you. Stay in that house, eating and drinking what they give you; for the laborer is worthy of his wages. Do not keep moving from house to house. Whatever city you enter and they receive you, eat what is set before you; and heal those in it who are sick, and say to them, 'The kingdom of God has come near to you.' But whatever city you enter and they do not receive you, go out into its streets and say, 'Even the dust of your city which clings to our feet we wipe off *in protest* against you; yet be sure of this, that the kingdom of God has come near.' I say to you, it will be more tolerable in that day for Sodom than for that city" (Luke 10:2–12; see Genesis 19:24–28; Matthew 9:37, 38, 10:9–14, 16; 1 Corinthians 10:27).

SHOULDERS

Setting: The temple in Jerusalem. Jesus exposes the truth about Pharisaism to the crowds and His disciples after the Jewish religious leaders test Him with questions.

Then Jesus spoke to the crowds and to His disciples, saying: "The scribes and the Pharisees have seated themselves in the chair of Moses; therefore all that they tell you, do and observe, but do not do according to their deeds; for they say *things* and do not do *them.* They tie up heavy burdens and lay them on men's shoulders, but they themselves are unwilling to move them with *so much as* a finger. But they do all their deeds to be noticed by men; for they broaden their phylacteries and lengthen their tassels *of their garments.* They love the place of honor at banquets and the chief seats in the synagogues, and respectful greetings in the market places, and being called Rabbi by men. But do not be called Rabbi; for One is your Teacher, and you are all brothers. Do not call *anyone* on earth your father; for One is your Father, He who is in heaven. Do not be called leaders; for One is your Leader, *that is,* Christ. But the greatest among you shall be your servant. Whoever exalts himself shall be humbled; and whoever humbles himself shall be exalted" (Matthew 23:1–12; cf. Matthew 20:26; Mark 12:38–40; Luke 20:46, 47; see Exodus 13:9; Deuteronomy 33:3; Matthew 6:1, 5, 6, 9, 16; Mark 14:11; Luke 11:43; 14:11).

Setting: On the way from Galilee to Jerusalem. After Jesus presents to large crowds the demands of discipleship, the Pharisees and scribes complain He associates with tax collectors and sinners.

So He told them this parable, saying, "What man among you, if he has a hundred sheep and has lost one of them, does not leave the ninety-nine in the open pasture and go after the one which is lost until he finds it? When he has found it, he lays it on his shoulders, rejoicing. And when he comes home, he calls together his friends and his neighbors, saying to them, 'Rejoice with me, for I have found my sheep which was lost!' I tell you that in the same way, there will be *more* joy in heaven over one sinner who repents than over ninety-nine righteous persons who need no repentance" (Luke 15:3–7; cf. Matthew 18:12–14; see Matthew 9:11–13; Luke 5:29–32).

SHOUT

Setting: On the Mount of Olives, just east of Jerusalem. During His Olivet Discourse, after answering His disciples' questions as to when the temple will be destroyed and Jerusalem overrun, along with the signs of His coming and the end of the age, Jesus reemphasizes to His disciples that they should be on the alert for His return.

"Then the kingdom of heaven will be comparable to ten virgins, who took their lamps and went out to meet the bridegroom. Five of them were foolish, and five were prudent. For when the foolish took their lamps, they took no oil with them, but the prudent took oil in flasks along with their lamps. Now while the bridegroom was delaying, they all got drowsy and *began* to sleep. But at midnight there was a shout, 'Behold, the bridegroom! Come out to meet *him.*' Then all those virgins rose and trimmed their lamps. The foolish said to the prudent, 'Give us some of your oil, for our lamps are going out.' But the prudent answered, 'No, there will not be enough for us and you *too;* go instead to the dealers and buy *some* for yourselves.' And while they were going away to make the purchase, the bridegroom came, and those who were ready went in with him to the wedding feast; and the door was shut. Later the other virgins also came, saying, 'Lord, lord, open up for us.' But he answered, 'Truly I say to you, I do not know you.' Be on the alert then, for you do not know the day nor the hour" (Matthew 25:1–13; cf. Matthew 24:42; Luke 12:35; see Matthew 7:21, 24).

SHOWER (Also see RAIN; STORM; and WEATHER)

Setting: On the way from Galilee to Jerusalem. After telling how a relationship with Him will divide families, Jesus chastises the crowds for being able to discern the weather but not the present age.

And He was also saying to the crowds, "When you see a cloud rising in the west, immediately you say, 'A shower is coming,' and so it turns out. And when *you see* a south wind blowing, you say, 'It will be a hot day,' and it turns out *that way*. You hypocrites! You know how to analyze the appearance of the earth and the sky, but why do you not analyze this present time?" (Luke 12:54–56; cf. Matthew 16:2, 3).

SHREWD MANAGER (See MANAGER)

SHREWDNESS

[SHREWDNESS from shrewd]

Setting: Galilee. After His disciples observe His ministry, Jesus summons and specifically instructs them about the upcoming hardships of their ministry to the people of Israel.

"Behold, I send you out as sheep in the midst of wolves; so be shrewd as serpents and innocent as doves. But beware of men, for they will hand you over to *the* courts and scourge you in their synagogues; and you will even be brought before governors and kings for My sake, as a testimony to them and to the Gentiles. But when they hand you over, do not worry about how or what you are to say; for it will be given you in that hour what you are to say. For it is not you who speak, but *it* is the Spirit of your Father who speaks in you" (Matthew 10:16–20; cf. Luke 10:3).

[SHREWDNESS from shrewdly and shrewd]

Setting: On the way from Galilee to Jerusalem. After giving the story of the prodigal son, the Lord teaches His disciples about stewardship.

Now He was also saying to the disciples, "There was a rich man who had a manager, and this *manager* was reported to him as squandering his possessions. And he called him and said to him, 'What is this I hear about you? Give an accounting of your management, for you can no longer be a manager.' The manager said to himself, 'What shall I do, since my master is taking the management away from me? I am not strong enough to dig; I am ashamed to beg. I know what I shall do, so that when I am removed from the management people will welcome me into their homes.' And he summoned each one of his master's debtors, and he *began* saying to the first, 'How much do you owe my master?' And he said, 'A hundred measures of oil.' And he said to him, 'Take your bill, and sit down quickly and write fifty.' Then he said to another, 'And how much do you owe?' And he said, 'A hundred measures of wheat.' He said to him, 'Take your bill, and write eighty.' And his master praised the unrighteous manager because he had acted shrewdly; for the sons of this age are more shrewd in relation to their own kind than the sons of light. And I say to you, make friends for yourselves by means of the wealth of unrighteousness, so that when it fails, they will receive you into the eternal dwellings. He who is faithful in a very little thing is faithful also in much; and he who is unrighteous in a very little thing is unrighteous also in much. Therefore if you have not been faithful in the *use of* unrighteous wealth, who will entrust the true *riches* to you? And if you have not been faithful in *the use of* that which is another's, who will give you that which is your own? No servant can serve two masters; for either he will hate the one and love the other, or else he will be devoted to one and despise the other. You cannot serve God and wealth" (Luke 16:1–13; cf. Matthew 6:24; see Matthew 25:14–30).

SICK (See SICKNESS)

SICKLE (Also see HARVEST)

Setting: Galilee. Following His explanation of the Parable of the Sower to His disciples, Jesus conveys the Parable of the Seed.

And He was saying, "The kingdom of God is like a man who casts seed upon the soil; and he goes to bed at night and gets up by day, and the seed sprouts and grows—how, he himself does not know. The soil produces crops by itself; first the blade, then the head, then the mature grain in the head. But when the crop permits, he immediately puts in the sickle, because the harvest has come" (Mark 4:26–29; see Joel 3:13)

SICKNESS

[SICKNESS from sick]

Setting: Capernaum near the Sea of Galilee. Jesus calls Matthew from his tax-collection booth to be His disciple.

But when Jesus heard *this,* He said, "*It is* not those who are healthy who need a physician, but those who are sick. But go and learn what this means: 'I DESIRE COMPASSION, AND NOT SACRIFICE,' for I did not come to call the righteous, but sinners" (Matthew 9:12, 13, Jesus quotes from Hosea 6:6; cf. Mark 2:17; Luke 5:31, 32; see Mark 2:15, 16).

[SICKNESS from sick]

Setting: Galilee. After His twelve disciples observe His ministry, Jesus summons and specifically instructs them about their ministry to the people of Israel.

These twelve Jesus sent out after instructing them: "Do not go in *the* way of *the* Gentiles, and do not enter *any* city of the Samaritans; but rather go to the lost sheep of the house of Israel. And as you go, preach, saying, 'The kingdom of heaven is at hand.' Heal *the* sick, raise *the* dead, cleanse *the* lepers, cast out demons. Freely you received, freely give. Do not acquire gold, or silver, or copper for your money belts, or a bag for *your* journey, or even two coats, or sandals, or a staff; for the worker is worthy of his support. And whatever city or village you enter, inquire who is worthy in it, and stay at his house until you leave *that city.* As you enter the house, give it your greeting. If the house is worthy, give it your *blessing of* peace. But if it is not worthy, take back your *blessing of* peace. Whoever does not receive you, nor heed your words, as you go out of that house or that city, shake the dust off your feet. Truly I say to you, it will be more tolerable for *the* land of Sodom and Gomorrah in the day of judgment than for that city" (Matthew 10:5–15; cf. Mark 6:7–11; Luke 9:1–5; see Matthew 3:2; 11:22, 24; 15:24; Luke 22:35; 1 Corinthians 9:14).

[SICKNESS from sick]

Setting: On the Mount of Olives, just east of Jerusalem. During His Olivet Discourse, after answering His disciples' questions as to when the temple will be destroyed and Jerusalem overrun, along with the signs of His coming and the end of the age, Jesus reveals the future judgments following His return.

"But when the Son of Man comes in His glory, and all the angels with Him, then He will sit on His glorious throne. All the nations will be gathered before Him; and He will separate them from one another, as the shepherd separates the sheep from the goats; and He will put the sheep on His right, and the goats on the left. Then the King will say to those on His right, 'Come, you who are blessed of My Father, inherit the kingdom prepared for you from the foundation of the world. 'For I was hungry, and you gave Me *something* to eat; I was thirsty, and you gave Me *something* to drink; I was a stranger, and you invited Me in; naked, and you clothed Me; I was sick, and you visited Me; I was in prison, and you came to Me.' Then the righteous will answer Him, 'Lord, when did we see You hungry and feed You, or thirsty, and give you *something* to drink? And when did we see You a stranger, and invite You in, or naked, and clothe You? When did we see You sick, or in prison, and come to You?' The King will answer and say to them, 'Truly I say to you, to the extent that you did it to one of these brothers of Mine, *even* the least *of them,* you did it to Me.' Then He will also say to those on His left, 'Depart from Me, accursed ones, into the eternal fire which has been prepared for the devil and his angels; for I was hungry, and you gave Me *nothing* to eat; I was thirsty, and you gave Me nothing to drink; I was a stranger, and you did not invite Me in; naked, and you did not clothe Me; sick, and in prison, and you did not visit Me.' Then they themselves also will answer, 'Lord, when did we see You hungry, or thirsty, or a stranger, or naked, or sick, or in prison, and did not take care of You?' Then He will answer them, 'Truly I say to you, to the extent that you did not do it to one of the least of these, you did not do it to Me.' These will go away into eternal punishment, but the righteous into eternal life" (Matthew 25:31–46; see Matthew 7:23; 16:27; 19:29).

[SICKNESS from sick]
Setting: The home of Levi (Matthew) the tax collector in Capernaum near the Sea of Galilee. The scribes of the Pharisees question Jesus' association with sinners and tax collectors after He calls Levi from the tax-collection booth to be His disciple.

And hearing *this,* Jesus said to them, "*It is* not those who are healthy who need a physician, but those who are sick; I did not come to call the righteous, but sinners" (Mark 2:17; cf. Matthew 9:12, 13; Luke 5:29–32).

[SICKNESS from sick]
Setting: Following His resurrection from the dead after being crucified, Jesus commissions His disciples to preach His gospel to the world.

And He said to them, "Go into all the world and preach the gospel to all creation. He who has believed and has been baptized shall be saved; but he who has disbelieved shall be condemned. These signs will accompany those who have believed: in My name they will cast out demons, they will speak with new tongues; they will pick up serpents, and if they drink any deadly *poison,* it will not hurt them; they will lay hands on the sick, and they will recover" (Mark 16:15–18; cf. Matthew 28:16–20; see Mark 9:38; John 3:18, 36; 1 Corinthians 15:6).

[Note: Some scholars question the authenticity of Mark 16:9–20 as these verses do not appear in some early New Testament manuscripts.]

[SICKNESS from sick]
Setting: Levi's (Matthew) house in Capernaum. At a reception following Jesus' call of Levi to become His disciple, the Pharisees and their scribes question why the Lord associates with tax collectors and sinners.

And Jesus answered and said to them, "*It is* not those who are well who need a physician, but those who are sick. I have not come to call the righteous but sinners to repentance" (Luke 5:31, 32; cf. Matthew 9:10–13; Mark 2:15–17).

[SICKNESS from sick]
Setting: On the way from Galilee to Jerusalem. The Lord appoints seventy followers and sends them out in pairs to every place He Himself will soon visit.

And He was saying to them, "The harvest is plentiful, but the laborers are few; therefore beseech the Lord of the harvest to send out laborers into His harvest. Go; behold, I send you out as lambs in the midst of wolves. Carry no money belt, no bag, no shoes; and greet no one on the way. Whatever house you enter, first say, 'Peace be to this house.' If a man of peace is there, your peace will rest on him; but if not, it will return to you. Stay in that house, eating and drinking what they give you; for the laborer is worthy of his wages. Do not keep moving from house to house. Whatever city you enter and they receive you, eat what is set before you; and heal those in it who are sick, and say to them, 'The kingdom of God has come near to you.' But whatever city you enter and they do not receive you, go out into its streets and say, 'Even the dust of your city which clings to our feet we wipe off *in protest* against you; yet be sure of this, that the kingdom of God has come near.' I say to you, it will be more tolerable in that day for Sodom than for that city" (Luke 10:2–12; see Genesis 19:24–28; Matthew 9:37, 38, 10:9–14, 16; 1 Corinthians 10:27).

Setting: On the way from Galilee to Jerusalem. Jesus teaches in the synagogue on the Sabbath, where a woman who has been sick eighteen years seeks healing.

When Jesus saw her, He called her over and said to her, "Woman, you are freed from your sickness" (Luke 13:12).

Setting: Beyond the Jordan. Following the Feast of Dedication and the Pharisees' desire to stone Him in Jerusalem, Jesus hears of the sickness of Lazarus of Bethany.

But when Jesus heard *this,* He said, "This sickness is not to end in death, but for the glory of God, so that the Son of God may be glorified by it" (John 11:4).

Setting: On the island of Patmos (in the Aegean Sea about fifty miles southwest of Ephesus in modern Turkey). On the Lord's Day (Sunday), approximately fifty years after the Resurrection, the disciple John encounters the Lord Jesus Christ, who communicates a new revelation for the apostle to record for the church in Thyatira and to six other churches in Asia.

"And to the angel of the church in Thyatira write: The Son of God, who has eyes like a flame of fire, and His feet are like burnished bronze, says this: 'I know your deeds, and your love and faith and service and perseverance, and that your deeds of late are greater than at first. But I have *this* against you, that you tolerate the woman Jezebel, who calls herself a prophetess, and she teaches and leads My bond-servants astray so that they commit *acts of* immorality and eat things sacrificed to idols. I gave her time to repent, and she does not want to repent of her immorality. Behold, I will throw her on a bed *of sickness,* and those who commit adultery with her into great tribulation, unless they repent of her deeds. And I will kill her children with pestilence, and all the churches will know that I am He who searches the minds and hearts; and I will give to each one of you according to your deeds. But I say to you, the rest who are in Thyatira, who do not hold this teaching, who have not known the deep things of Satan, as they call them—I place no other burden on you. Nevertheless what you have, hold fast until I come. He who overcomes, and he who keeps My deeds until the end, TO HIM I WILL GIVE AUTHORITY OVER THE NATIONS; AND HE SHALL RULE THEM WITH A ROD OF IRON, AS THE VESSELS OF THE POTTER ARE BROKEN TO PIECES, as I also have received *authority* from My Father; and I will give him the morning star. He who has an ear, let him hear what the Spirit says to the churches' (Revelation 2:18–29; Jesus quotes from Psalm 2:8, 9; Isaiah 30:14; see 1 Kings 16:31; Psalm 7:9; Romans 2:5; 1 Corinthians 2:10; 2 Peter 3:9; Revelation 1:14; 3:11; 17:1–20).

SIDE (SIDE, MY and SIDE, OTHER are separate entries)

Setting: Approaching Jerusalem. After being praised by the people in a triumphal entry, the Lord weeps as He sees the city ahead of Him.

When He approached *Jerusalem,* He saw the city and wept over it, saying, "If you had known in this day, even you, the things which make for peace! But now they have been hidden from your eyes. For the days will come upon you when your enemies will throw up a barricade against you, and surround you and hem you in on every side, and they will level you to the ground and your children within you, and they will not leave in you one stone upon another, because you did not recognize the time of your visitation" (Luke 19:41–44; see Matthew 24:1, 2; Luke 13:34, 35).

Setting: By the Sea of Galilee (Tiberias). During His third post-resurrection appearance to His disciples, Jesus directs them to a great catch of fish following their unsuccessful night of fishing.

So Jesus said to them, "Children, you do not have any fish, do you?" They answered Him, "No." And He said to them, "Cast the net on the right-hand side of the boat and you will find a *catch.*" So they cast, and then they were not able to haul it in because of the great number of fish (John 21:5, 6; see Luke 5:4).

SIDE, MY (Jesus')

Setting: Jerusalem. The risen Jesus meets with His disciple Thomas (Didymus), who has had doubts about the testimony of the other disciples claiming to have seen and spoken with the Lord eight days earlier.

After eight days His disciples were again inside, and Thomas with them. Jesus came, the doors having been shut, and stood in their midst and said, "Peace *be* with you." Then He said to Thomas, "Reach here with your finger, and see My hands; and reach here your hand and put it into My side; and do not be unbelieving, but believing." Thomas answered and said to Him, "My Lord and my God!" Jesus said to him, "Because you have seen Me, have you believed? Blessed *are* they who did not see, and *yet* believed" (John 20:26–29; see Luke 24:36, 40; 1 Peter 1:8).

SIDE, OTHER

Setting: Galilee. After presenting the Parable of the Seed and Parable of the Mustard Seed and explaining the meanings to His disciples, Jesus and the disciples set out to cross the Sea of Galilee, where the Lord will calm a storm while on the water.

On that day, when evening came, He said to them, "Let us go over to the other side" (Mark 4:35; cf. Matthew 8:18; Luke 8:22; see Matthew 8:23–27; Luke 8:23–25).

Setting: Galilee. After Jesus conveys who His true relatives are, He and His disciples set sail on the Sea of Galilee, where He will calm a storm.

Now on one of *those* days Jesus and His disciples got into a boat, and He said to them, "Let us go over to the other side of the lake." So they launched out (Luke 8:22; cf. Mark 4:35; see Matthew 8:18).

Setting: On the way from Galilee to Jerusalem. While being tested by a lawyer, Jesus tells him the story of the good Samaritan.

Jesus replied and said, "A man was going down from Jerusalem to Jericho, and fell among robbers, and they stripped him and beat him, and went away leaving him half dead. And by chance a priest was going down on that road, and when he saw him, he passed by on the other side. Likewise a Levite also, when he came to the place and saw him, passed by on the other side. But a Samaritan, who was on a journey, came upon him; and when he saw him, he felt compassion, and came to him and bandaged up his wounds, pouring oil and wine on *them;* and he put him on his own beast, and brought him to an inn and took care of him. On the next day he took out two denarii and gave them to the innkeeper and said, 'Take care of him; and whatever more you spend, when I return I will repay you.' Which of these three do you think proved to be a neighbor to the man who fell into the robbers' *hands?*" And he said, "The one who showed mercy toward him." Then Jesus said to him, "Go and do the same" (Luke 10:30–37).

SIDON

Setting: Galilee. After performing miracles throughout the region, Jesus pronounces woes against those cities who do not repent.

"Woe to you, Chorazin! Woe to you, Bethsaida! For if the miracles had occurred in Tyre and Sidon which occurred in you, they would have repented long ago in sackcloth and ashes. Nevertheless I say to you, it will be more tolerable for Tyre and Sidon in *the* day of judgment than for you. And you, Capernaum, will not be exalted to heaven, will you? You will descend to Hades; for if the miracles had occurred in Sodom which occurred in you, it would have remained to this day. Nevertheless, I say to you that it will be more tolerable for the land of Sodom in *the* day of judgment, than for you" (Matthew 11:21–24; cf. Matthew 10:15; Luke 10:13–15).

Setting: The synagogue in Jesus' hometown of Nazareth in Galilee. At the beginning of His public ministry, Jesus comments to the congregation after reading on the Sabbath from the book of the prophet Isaiah.

And He said to them, "No doubt you will quote this proverb to Me, 'Physician, heal yourself! Whatever we heard was done at Capernaum, do here in your hometown as well.'" And He said, "Truly I say to you, no prophet is welcome in his hometown. But I say to you in truth, there were many widows in Israel in the days of Elijah, when the sky was shut up for three years and six months, when a great famine came over all the land; and yet Elijah was sent to none of them, but only to Zarephath, *in the land* of Sidon, to a woman who was a widow. And there were many lepers in Israel in the time of Elisha the prophet; and none of them was cleansed, but only Naaman the Syrian" (Luke 4:23–27; Jesus refers to 1 Kings 17:1, 9; 2 Kings 5:1–14; see Matthew 13:53–58).

Setting: On the way from Galilee to Jerusalem. The Lord pronounces woes on cities who reject the gospel, as He appoints seventy followers and sends them out in pairs to every place He Himself will soon visit.

"Woe to you, Chorazin! Woe to you, Bethsaida! For if the miracles had been performed in Tyre and Sidon which occurred in you, they would have repented long ago, sitting in sackcloth and ashes. But it will be more tolerable for Tyre and Sidon in the judgment than for you. And you, Capernaum, will not be exalted to heaven, will you? You will be brought down to Hades! The one who listens to you listens to Me, and the one who rejects you rejects Me; and he who rejects Me rejects the One who sent Me" (Luke 10:13–16; cf. Matthew 11:21–23; see Matthew 10:40).

SIGHT (SIGHT, GOD'S is a separate entry; also see EYE; EYES; and VISION)

Setting: Galilee. As He teaches and preaches, Jesus responds to John the Baptist's question (posed by some of John's disciples) whether He is Israel's promised Messiah.

Jesus answered and said to them, "Go and report to John what you hear and see: *the* BLIND RECEIVE SIGHT and *the* lame walk, *the* lepers are cleansed and *the* deaf hear, *the* dead are raised up, and *the* POOR HAVE THE GOSPEL PREACHED TO THEM. And blessed is he who does not take offense at Me" (Matthew 11:4–6, Jesus quotes from Isaiah 35:5f; cf. Luke 7:22, 23).

Setting: Galilee. As He teaches and preaches, after pronouncing woes against unrepentant cities, Jesus prays a thanksgiving prayer to His Father in heaven.

At that time Jesus said, "I praise You, Father, Lord of heaven and earth, that you have hidden these things from *the* wise and intelligent and have revealed them to infants. Yes, Father, for this way was well-pleasing in Your sight. All things have been handed over to Me by My Father; and no one knows the Son except the Father; nor does anyone know the Father except the Son, and anyone to whom the Son wills to reveal *Him*" (Matthew 11:25–27; cf. Luke 10:21, 22).

Setting: The synagogue in Jesus' hometown of Nazareth in Galilee. At the beginning of His public ministry, Jesus reads on the Sabbath from the book of the prophet Isaiah.

And the book of the prophet Isaiah was handed to Him. And He opened the book and found the place where it was written, "THE SPIRIT OF THE LORD IS UPON ME, BECAUSE HE ANOINTED ME TO PREACH THE GOSPEL TO THE POOR. HE HAS SENT ME TO PROCLAIM RELEASE TO THE CAPTIVES, AND RECOVERY OF SIGHT TO THE BLIND, TO SET FREE THOSE WHO ARE OPPRESSED, TO PROCLAIM THE FAVORABLE YEAR OF THE LORD." And He closed the book, gave it back to the attendant and sat down; and the eyes of all in the synagogue were fixed on Him. And He began to say to them, "Today this Scripture has been fulfilled in your hearing" (Luke 4:17–21, Jesus quotes from Isaiah 61:1, 2).

Setting: Galilee. After Jesus raises a woman's son from the dead in Nain, the disciples of John the Baptist inquire whether the Lord is the promised Messiah.

And He answered and said to them, "Go and report to John what you have seen and heard: *the* BLIND RECEIVE SIGHT, *the* lame walk, *the* lepers are cleansed, and *the* deaf hear, *the* dead are raised up, *the* POOR HAVE THE GOSPEL PREACHED TO THEM. Blessed is he who does not take offense at Me" (Luke 7:22, 23, Jesus quotes from Isaiah 35:5; 61:1; cf. Matthew 11:2–6).

Setting: On the way from Galilee to Jerusalem. The Lord responds to a report from the seventy sent out in pairs to every place He Himself will soon visit.

At that very time He rejoiced greatly in the Holy Spirit, and said, "I praise You, O Father, Lord of heaven and earth, that You have hidden these things from *the* wise and intelligent and have revealed them to infants. Yes, Father, for this way was well-pleasing in Your sight. All things have been handed over to Me by My Father, and no one knows who the Son is except the Father, and who the Father is except the Son, and anyone to whom the Son wills to reveal *Him*" (Luke 10:21, 22; cf. Matthew 11:25–27; see John 3:35; 10:15).

Setting: On the way from Galilee to Jerusalem. As He observes the invited guests selecting places of honor at table in the house of a Pharisee leader on the Sabbath, Jesus speaks a parable to them.

And He *began* speaking a parable to the invited guests when He noticed how they had been picking out the places of honor *at the table,* saying to them, "When you are invited by someone to a wedding feast, do not take the place of honor, for someone more distinguished than you may have been invited by him, and he who invited you both will come and say to you, 'Give *your* place to this man, and then in disgrace you proceed to occupy the last place. But when you are invited, go and recline at the last place, so that when the one who has invited you comes, he may say to you, 'Friend, move up higher'; then you will have honor in the sight of all who are at the table with you. For everyone who exalts himself will be humbled, and he who humbles himself will be exalted" (Luke 14:7–11; see 2 Samuel 22:28; Proverb 25:6, 7; Matthew 23:6).

Setting: On the way from Galilee to Jerusalem. Jesus conveys the illustration of the prodigal son because the Pharisees and scribes complain He associates with tax collectors and sinners.

And He said, "A man had two sons. The younger of them said to his father, 'Father, give me the share of the estate that falls to me.' So he divided his wealth between them. And not many days later, the younger son gathered everything together and went on a journey into a distant country, and there he squandered his estate with loose living. Now when he had spent everything, a severe famine occurred in that country, and he began to be impoverished. So he went and hired himself out to one of the citizens of that country, and he sent him into his fields to feed swine. And he would have gladly filled his stomach with the pods that the swine were eating, and no one was giving *anything* to him. But when he came to his senses, he said, 'How many of my father's hired men have more than enough bread, but I am dying here with hunger! I will get up and go to my father, and will say to him, "Father, I have sinned against heaven, and in your sight; I am no longer worthy to be called your son; make me as one of your hired men."' So he got up and came to his father. But while he was still a long way off, his father saw him and felt compassion *for him,* and ran and embraced him and kissed him. And the son said to him, "Father, I have sinned against heaven and in your sight; I am no longer worthy to be called your son.' But the father said to his slaves, 'Quickly bring out the best robe and put it on him, and put a ring on his hand and sandals on his feet; and bring the fattened calf, kill it, and let us eat and celebrate; for this son of mine was dead and has come to life again; he was lost and has been found.' And they began to celebrate. Now his older son was in the field, when he came and approached the house, he heard music and dancing. And he summoned one of the servants and *began* inquiring what these things could be. And he said to him, 'Your brother has come, and your father has killed the fattened calf because he has received him back safe and sound.' But he became angry and was not willing to go in; and his father came out and *began* pleading with him. But he answered and said to his father, 'Look! For so many years I have been serving you and I have never neglected a command of yours, and *yet* you have never given me a young goat, so that I might celebrate with my friends; but when this son of yours came, who has devoured your wealth with prostitutes, you killed the fattened calf for him.' And he said to him, 'Son, you have always been with me, and all that is mine is yours. But we had to celebrate and rejoice, for this brother of yours was dead and *has begun* to live, and was lost and has been found' " (Luke 15:11–32; see Proverb 29:2).

Setting: On the way from Galilee to Jerusalem. The Lord responds to the Pharisees' scoffing at His teaching His disciples about stewardship.

And He said to them, "You are those who justify yourselves in the sight of men, but God knows your hearts; for that which is highly esteemed among men is detestable in the sight of God. The Law and the Prophets *were proclaimed* until John; since that time the gospel of the kingdom of God has been preached, and everyone is forcing his way into it. But is it easier for heaven and earth to pass away than for one stroke of a letter of the Law to fail" (Luke 16:15–17; cf. Matthew 5:18; see 1 Samuel 16:7; Matthew 4:23; 11:11–14).

Setting: On the way from Galilee to Jerusalem. After telling the disciples of the upcoming sacrifice He will make in Jerusalem, while approaching Jericho, Jesus takes time to heal a blind man.

And Jesus stopped and commanded that he be brought to Him; and when he came near, He questioned him, "What do you want Me to do for you?" And he said, "Lord, *I want* to regain my sight!" And Jesus said to him, "Receive your sight; your faith has made you well" (Luke 18:40–42; cf. Matthew 20:29–34; Mark 10:46–52).

[SIGHT from We see]
Setting: Jerusalem. Following the Pharisees' interrogation and dismissal of the formerly blind man Jesus healed on the Sabbath, the Lord responds to the Pharisees' question of whether they are spiritually blind.

Jesus said to them, "If you were blind, you would have not sin; but since you say, 'We see,' your sin remains" (John 9:41; see John 15:22–24).

Setting: Damascus. Luke, writing in Acts, conveys how the Lord instructs one of His disciples, Ananias, to locate Saul of Tarsus to touch him in order to restore Saul's vision.

Now there was a disciple at Damascus named Ananias; and the Lord said to him in a vision, "Ananias." And he said, "Here I am, Lord." And the Lord *said* to him, "Get up and go to the street called Straight, and inquire at the house of Judas for a man from Tarsus named Saul, for he is praying, and he was seen in a vision a man named Ananias come in and lay his hands on him, so that he might regain his sight" (Acts 9:10–12; see Acts 22:12–14).

SIGHT, GOD'S (Also see GOD, SIGHT OF)

[GOD'S SIGHT from Your sight]
Setting: Galilee. As He teaches and preaches, after pronouncing woes against unrepentant cities, Jesus prays a thanksgiving prayer to His Father in heaven.

At that time Jesus said, "I praise You, Father, Lord of heaven and earth, that you have hidden these things from *the* wise and intelligent and have revealed them to infants. Yes, Father, for this way was well-pleasing in Your sight. All things have been handed over to Me by My Father; and no one knows the Son except the Father; nor does anyone know the Father except the Son, and anyone to whom the Son wills to reveal *Him*" (Matthew 11:25–27; cf. Luke 10:21, 22).

[GOD'S SIGHT from Your sight]
Setting: On the way from Galilee to Jerusalem. The Lord responds to a report from the seventy sent out in pairs to every place He Himself will soon visit.

At that very time He rejoiced greatly in the Holy Spirit, and said, "I praise You, O Father, Lord of heaven and earth, that You have hidden these things from *the* wise and intelligent and have revealed them to infants. Yes, Father, for this way was well-pleasing in Your sight. All things have been handed over to Me by My Father, and no one knows who the Son is except the Father, and who the Father is except the Son, and anyone to whom the Son wills to reveal *Him*" (Luke 10:21, 22; cf. Matthew 11:25–27; see John 3:35; 10:15).

[GOD'S SIGHT from sight of My God]
Setting: On the island of Patmos (in the Aegean Sea about fifty miles southwest of Ephesus in modern Turkey). On the Lord's Day (Sunday), approximately fifty years after the Resurrection, the disciple John encounters the Lord Jesus Christ, who communicates a new revelation for the apostle to record for the church in Sardis and to six other churches in Asia.

"To the angel of the church in Sardis write: He who has the seven Spirits of God and the seven stars, says this: 'I know your deeds, that you have a name that you are alive, but you are dead. Wake up, and strengthen the things that remain, which were about to die; for I have not found your deeds completed in the sight of My God. So remember what you have received and heard; and keep *it,* and repent. Therefore if you do not wake up, I will come like a thief, and you will not know at what hour I will come to you. But you have a few people in Sardis who have not soiled their garments; and they will walk with Me in white, for they are worthy. He who overcomes will thus be clothed in white garments; and I will not erase his name from the book of life, and I will confess his name before My Father and before His angels. He who has an ear, let him hear what the Spirit says to the churches'" (Revelation 3:1–6; see Matthew 10:32; Revelation 1:16).

SIGHT OF MEN (Listed under MEN, SIGHT OF)

SIGN (JONAH, SIGN OF; and SON OF MAN, SIGN OF THE are separate entries; also see SIGNS)

Setting: Galilee. After Jesus warns the Pharisees about the unpardonable sin and their future judgment, some Pharisees and scribes ask Him to perform a miraculous sign for them in front of the crowds.

But He answered and said to them, "An evil and adulterous generation craves for a sign; and *yet* no sign will be given to it but the sign of Jonah the prophet; for just as JONAH WAS THREE DAYS AND THREE NIGHTS IN THE BELLY OF THE SEA MONSTER, so will the Son of Man be three days and three nights in the heart of the earth. The men of Nineveh will stand up with this generation at the judgment, and will condemn it because they repented at the preaching of Jonah; and behold, something greater than Jonah is here. *The* Queen of *the* South will rise up with this generation at the judgment and will condemn it, because she came from the ends of the earth to hear the wisdom of Solomon; and behold, something greater than Solomon is here" (Matthew 12:39–42; Jesus quotes from Jonah 1:17; cf. 1 Kings 10:1; Jonah 3:5; Matthew 16:1, 4; Luke 11:29).

Setting: Magadan of Galilee. Jesus' enemies, the Pharisees and the Sadducees, rejecting His message, continue to test Him by asking for a sign from heaven.

But He replied to them, "When it is evening, you say, '*It will be* fair weather, for the sky is red.' And in the morning, '*There will* be a storm today, for the sky is red and threatening.' Do you know how to discern the appearance of the sky, but cannot *discern* the signs of the times? An evil and adulterous generation seeks after a sign; and a sign will not be given it, except the sign of Jonah." And He left them and went away (Matthew 16:2–4; cf. Matthew 12:39; Mark 8:12; Luke 12:54–56).

Setting: The Mount of Olives, just east of Jerusalem. During His Olivet Discourse, Jesus answers His disciples' questions as to when the temple will be destroyed and Jerusalem overrun, along with the signs of His coming and the end of the age.

"But immediately after the tribulation of those days THE SUN WILL BE DARKENED, AND THE MOON WILL NOT GIVE ITS LIGHT, AND THE STARS WILL FALL from the sky, and the powers of the heavens will be shaken. And then the sign of the Son of Man will appear in the sky, and then all the tribes of the earth will mourn, and they will see the SON OF MAN COMING ON THE CLOUDS OF THE SKY with power and great glory. And He will send forth His angels with A GREAT TRUMPET and THEY WILL GATHER TOGETHER His elect from the four winds, from one end of the sky to the other" (Matthew 24:29–31, Jesus quotes from Isaiah 13:10, Daniel 7:13; Exodus 19:16; cf. Mark 13:24–27; Luke 21:25–27).

Setting: The district of Dalmanutha. After Jesus miraculously feeds 4,000 people, the Pharisees argue with Him, seeking a sign from heaven to test Him.

Sighing deeply in His spirit, He said, "Why does this generation seek for a sign? Truly I say to you, no sign will be given to this generation" (Mark 8:12; cf. Matthew 16:1–4; see Matthew 12:39, 40).

Setting: On the way from Galilee to Jerusalem. After revealing a problem with exorcism and responding to a blessing from a woman in the crowd, Jesus tells the increasing crowds of the sign of Jonah.

As the crowds were increasing, He began to say, "This generation is a wicked generation; it seeks for a sign, and *yet* no sign will be given to it but the sign of Jonah. For just as Jonah became a sign to the Ninevites, so will the Son of Man be to this generation. The Queen of the South will rise up with the men of this generation at the judgment and condemn them, because she came from the ends of the earth to hear the wisdom of Solomon; and behold, something greater than Solomon is here. The men of Nineveh will stand up with this generation at the judgment and condemn it, because they repented at the preaching of Jonah; and behold, something greater than Jonah is here" (Luke 11:29–32; cf. Matthew 16:4; see 1 Kings 10:1–10; Jonah 3:4, 5).

SIGN OF JONAH (Listed under JONAH, SIGN OF)

SIGN OF THE SON OF MAN (Listed under SON OF MAN, SIGN OF THE)

SIGNIFICANCE (Also see GREATNESS)

[SIGNIFICANCE from he who has lost his life for My sake will find it]

Setting: Galilee. After His twelve disciples observe His ministry, Jesus summons and specifically instructs them about their ministry ahead involving true discipleship.

"He who loves father or mother more than Me is not worthy of Me; and he who loves son or daughter more than Me is not worthy of Me. And he who does not take his cross and follow after Me is not worthy of Me. He who has found his life will lose it, and he who has lost his life for My sake will find it" (Matthew 10:37–39; cf. Matthew 16:24, 25).

[SIGNIFICANCE from whoever loses his life for My sake will find it]

Setting: Near Caesarea Philippi. After rebuking Peter for trying to forbid Him to accomplish His earthly mission of dying and being resurrected, Jesus teaches His disciples about the costs of following Him.

Then Jesus said to His disciples, "If anyone wishes to come after Me, he must deny himself, and take up his cross and follow Me. For whoever wishes to save his life will lose it; but whoever loses his life for My sake will find it. For what will it profit a man if he gains the whole world and forfeits his soul? Or what will a man give in exchange for his soul? For the Son of Man is going to come in the glory of His Father with His angels, and WILL THEN REPAY EVERY MAN ACCORDING TO HIS DEEDS. Truly, I say to you, there are some of you who are standing here who will not taste death until they see the Son of Man coming in His kingdom" (Matthew 16:24–28, Jesus quotes from Psalm 62:12; cf. Mark 8:34–37; Luke 9:23–27; see Matthew 10:38, 39).

[SIGNIFICANCE from whoever loses his life for My sake and the gospel's will save it]

Setting: Caesarea Philippi. After rebuking Peter for desiring to thwart His mission to the cross, Jesus summons a crowd, along with His disciples, and informs them of the high costs of following Him.

And He summoned the crowd with His disciples, and said to them, "If anyone wishes to come after Me, he must deny himself, and take up his cross and follow Me. For whoever wishes to save his life will lose it, but whoever loses his life for My sake and the gospel's will save it. For what does it profit a man to gain the whole world, and forfeit his soul? For what will a man give in exchange for his soul? For whoever is ashamed of Me and My words in this adulterous and sinful generation, the Son of Man will also be ashamed of him when He comes in the glory of His Father with the holy angels" (Mark 8:34–38; cf. Matthew 16:24–28; Luke 9:23–27; see Matthew 10:33, 38, 39).

[SIGNIFICANCE from whoever loses his life for My sake, he is the one who will save it]

Setting: Galilee. Following Peter's pronouncement that Jesus is the Christ of God, the Lord conveys the demands of discipleship and the hope regarding the kingdom of God.

And He was saying to *them* all, "If anyone wishes to come after Me, he must deny himself, and take up his cross daily and follow Me. For whoever wishes to save his life will lose it, but whoever loses his life for My sake, he is the one who will save it. For what is a man profited if he gains the whole world, and loses or forfeits himself? For whoever is ashamed of Me and My words, the Son of Man will be ashamed of him when He comes in His glory, and *the glory* of the Father and of the holy angels. But I say to you truthfully, there are some of those standing here who will not taste death until they see the kingdom of God" (Luke 9:23–27; cf. Matthew 16:24–26, 28; Mark 8:34–37; see Matthew 10:33, 38, 39).

SIGNS (SIGNS AND WONDERS; SIGNS, GREAT; and TIMES, SIGNS OF THE are separate entries; also see SIGN)

Setting: Following His resurrection from the dead after being crucified, Jesus commissions His disciples to preach His gospel to the world.

And He said to them, "Go into all the world and preach the gospel to all creation. He who has believed and has been baptized shall be saved; but he who has disbelieved shall be condemned. These signs will accompany those who have believed: in My name they will cast out demons, they will speak with new tongues; they will pick up serpents, and if they drink any deadly *poison,* it will not hurt them; they will lay hands on the sick, and they will recover" (Mark 16:15–18; cf. Matthew 28:16–20; see Mark 9:38; John 3:18, 36; 1 Corinthians 15:6).

[Note: Some scholars question the authenticity of Mark 16:9–20 as these verses do not appear in some early New Testament manuscripts.]

Setting: On the way from Galilee to Jerusalem. The Pharisees question Jesus about the coming of the kingdom of God.

Now having been questioned by the Pharisees as to when the kingdom of God was coming, He answered them and said, "The kingdom of God is not coming with signs to be observed; nor will they say, 'Look, here it is!' Or, 'There it is!' For behold, the kingdom of God is in your midst" (Luke 17:20, 21; see Luke 19:11).

Setting: On the Mount of Olives, just east of Jerusalem. After ministering in the temple a few days before His crucifixion, and giving His disciples more details regarding future events, Jesus speaks during His Olivet Discourse of His return.

"There will be signs in sun and moon and stars, and on the earth dismay among the nations, in perplexity at the roaring of the sea and the waves, men fainting from fear and the expectation of the things which are coming upon the world; for the powers of the heavens will be shaken. Then they will see THE SON OF MAN COMING IN A CLOUD with power and great glory. But when these things begin to take place, straighten up and lift up your heads, because your redemption is drawing near" (Luke 21:25–28, Jesus quotes from Daniel 7:13; cf. Matthew 24:29–31; Mark 13:24–27).

Setting: Capernaum. The day after Jesus walks on the Sea of Galilee to join His disciples in a boat, the people He miraculously fed with a lad's five loaves and two fish ask the Lord how He crossed the water, since He had not entered the boat from land with His disciples.

Jesus answered them and said, "Truly, truly, I say to you, you seek Me, not because you saw signs, but because you ate of the loaves and were filled. Do not work for the food which perishes, but for the food which endures to eternal life, which the Son of Man will give to you, for on Him the Father, God, has set His seal" (John 6:26, 27; see John 3:33).

SIGNS, GREAT

Setting: The Mount of Olives, just east of Jerusalem. During His Olivet Discourse, Jesus answers His disciples' questions as to when the temple will be destroyed and Jerusalem overrun, along with the signs of His coming and the end of the age.

"Therefore when you see the ABOMINATION OF DESOLATION which was spoken of through Daniel the prophet, standing in the holy place (let the reader understand), then those who are in Judea must flee to the mountains. Whoever is on the housetop must not go down to get the things that are in his house. Whoever is in the field must not turn back to get his cloak. But woe to those who are pregnant and to those who are nursing babies in those days! But pray that your flight will not be in the winter, or on a Sabbath. For then there will be a great tribulation, such as has not occurred since the beginning of the world until now, nor ever will. Unless those days had been cut short, no life would have been saved; but for the sake of the elect those days will be cut short. Then if anyone says to you, 'Behold, here is the Christ,' or "There *He is,'* do not believe *him.* For false Christs and false prophets will arise and will show great signs and wonders, so as to mislead, if possible, even the elect. Behold, I have told you in advance. So if they say to you, 'Behold, He is in the wilderness,' do not go out, *or,* 'Behold, He is in the inner rooms,' do not believe *them.* For just as the lightning comes from the east and flashes even to the west, so will the coming of the Son of Man be. Wherever the corpse is, there the vultures will gather" (Matthew 24:15–28, Jesus quotes from Daniel 9:27; cf. Daniel 12:1; Mark 13:14–23; Luke 17:22–31; 21:20–24; 23:29; see John 4:48).

Setting: On the Mount of Olives, east of the temple in Jerusalem. After ministering in the temple a few days before His crucifixion, and giving His disciples more details regarding the temple's future destruction, Jesus elaborates during His Olivet Discourse about things to come.

Then He continued by saying to them, "Nation will rise against nation and kingdom against kingdom, and there will be great earthquakes, and in various places plagues and famines; and there will be terrors and great signs from heaven. But before all these things, they will lay their hands on you and will persecute you, delivering you to the synagogues and prisons, bringing you before kings and governors for My name's sake. It will lead to an opportunity for your testimony. So make up your minds not to prepare beforehand to defend yourselves; for I will give you utterance and wisdom which none of your opponents will be able to resist or refute. But you will be betrayed even by parents and brothers and relatives and friends, and they will put *some* of you to death, and you will be hated by all because of My name. Yet not a hair of your head will perish. By your endurance you will gain your lives" (Luke 21:10–19; cf. Matthew 10:19–22; 24:7–14; Mark 13:8–13).

SIGNS AND WONDERS (Also see DEMONS, CASTING OUT; HEALING; LEPROSY, CLEANSING FROM; MIRACLE; MIRACLES; RESUSCITATION; and RESURRECTION)

Setting: The Mount of Olives, just east of Jerusalem. During His Olivet Discourse, Jesus answers His disciples' questions as to when the temple will be destroyed and Jerusalem overrun, along with the signs of His coming and the end of the age.

"Therefore when you see the ABOMINATION OF DESOLATION which was spoken of through Daniel the prophet, standing in the holy place (let the reader understand), then those who are in Judea must flee to the mountains. Whoever is on the housetop must not go down to get the things that are in his house. Whoever is in the field must not turn back to get his cloak. But woe to those who are pregnant and to those who are nursing babies in those days! But pray that your flight will not be in the winter, or on a Sabbath. For then there will be a great tribulation, such as has not occurred since the beginning of the world until now, nor ever will. Unless those days had been cut short, no life would have been saved; but for the sake of the elect those days will be cut short. Then if anyone says to you, 'Behold, here is the Christ,' or "There *He is,*' do not believe *him.* For false Christs and false prophets will arise and will show great signs and wonders, so as to mislead, if possible, even the elect. Behold, I have told you in advance. So if they say to you, 'Behold, He is in the wilderness,' do not go out, *or,* 'Behold, He is in the inner rooms,' do not believe *them.* For just as the lightning comes from the east and flashes even to the west, so will the coming of the Son of Man be. Wherever the corpse is, there the vultures will gather" (Matthew 24:15–28, Jesus quotes from Daniel 9:27; cf. Daniel 12:1; Mark 13:14–23; Luke 17:22–31; 21:20–24; 23:29; see John 4:48).

Setting: On the Mount of Olives, east of the temple in Jerusalem. After prophesying the temple's destruction, Jesus responds during His Olivet Discourse to questions from Peter, James, John, and Andrew about other future events.

"But when you see the ABOMINATION OF DESOLATION standing where it should not be (let the reader understand), then those who are in Judea must flee to the mountains. The one who is on the housetop must not go down, or go in to get anything out of his house; and the one who is in the field must not turn back to get his coat. But woe to those who are pregnant and to those who are nursing babies in those days! But pray that it may not happen in winter. For those days will be a *time of* tribulation such as has not occurred since the beginning of the creation which God created until now, and never will. Unless the Lord had shortened *those* days, no life would have been saved; but for the sake of the elect, whom He chose, He shortened the days. And then if anyone says to you, 'Behold, here is the Christ'; or, 'Behold, *He is* there'; do not believe *him*; for false Christs and false prophets will arise, and will show signs and wonders, in order to lead astray, if possible, the elect. But take heed; behold, I have told you everything in advance" (Mark 13:14–23; cf. Matthew 24:15–28; Luke 21:20–24; see Daniel 9:27; 12:1; Luke 17:31).

Setting: Cana of Galilee. After conversing with a Samaritan woman at Jacob's well, and ministering to the Samaritans for two days, Jesus encounters a royal official seeking healing for his son, sick at the point of death in Capernaum.

So Jesus said to him, "Unless you *people* see signs and wonders, you *simply* will not believe" (John 4:48).

SIGNS OF THE TIMES (Listed under TIMES, SIGNS OF THE)

SILENCE

[SILENCE from silent]

Setting: Approaching Jerusalem. As the Lord rides a colt, His disciples and the people praise God for all the miracles they have witnessed Him performing; the Pharisees demand He rebukes His followers for such comments.

But Jesus answered, "I tell you, if these become silent, the stones will cry out!" (Luke 19:40; see Habbakkuk 2:1; Matthew 21:1–11; Mark 11:1–11; John 12:12–19).

[SILENCE from silent]

Setting: Corinth. Luke, writing in Acts, records the Lord's comforting revelation to Paul in a vision, as the apostle works among the Jews and Gentiles during his second missionary journey, testifying that Jesus is the Christ (Messiah).

And the Lord said to Paul in the night by a vision, "Do not be afraid *any longer,* but go on speaking and do not be silent; for I am with you, and no man will attack you in order to harm you, for I have many people in this city" (Acts 18:9, 10).

SILOAM

Setting: On the way from Galilee to Jerusalem. After some present report to Him about the Galileans whose blood Pilate (Roman governor of Judea) had mixed with their sacrifices, Jesus responds to their concern by calling them to repentance.

And Jesus said to them, "Do you suppose that these Galileans were *greater* sinners than all *other* Galileans because they suffered this *fate*? I tell you, no, but unless you repent, you will all likewise perish. Or do you suppose that those eighteen on whom the tower in Siloam fell and killed them were *worse* culprits than all the men who live in Jerusalem? I tell you, no, but unless you repent, you will all likewise perish" (Luke 13:2–5; see John 9:2, 3).

Setting: The temple treasury in Jerusalem. After Jesus avoids being stoned by the scribes and Pharisees, His disciples wonder if blindness is caused by sin as the Lord heals a man born blind.

Jesus answered, "*It was* neither *that* this man sinned, nor his parents; but *it was* so that the works of God might be displayed in him. We must work the works of Him who sent Me as long as it is day; night is coming when no one can work. While I am in the world, I am the Light of the world." When He had said this, He spat on the ground, and made clay of the spittle, and applied the clay to his eyes, and said to him, "Go, wash in the pool of Siloam" (which is translated, Sent). So he went away and washed, and came *back* seeing (John 9:3–7; see John 8:12; 11:4; 12:46).

Setting: Jerusalem. A formerly blind man testifies to his neighbors how Jesus gave him sight.

He answered, "The man who is called Jesus made clay, and anointed my eyes, and said to me, 'Go to Siloam and wash'; so I went away and washed, and I received sight" (John 9:11).

SILOAM, POOL OF (See SILOAM)

SILVER

Setting: Galilee. After His twelve disciples observe His ministry, Jesus summons and specifically instructs them about their ministry to the people of Israel.

These twelve Jesus sent out after instructing them: "Do not go in *the* way of *the* Gentiles, and do not enter *any* city of the Samaritans; but rather go to the lost sheep of the house of Israel. And as you go, preach, saying, 'The kingdom of heaven is at hand.'

Heal *the* sick, raise *the* dead, cleanse *the* lepers, cast out demons. Freely you received, freely give. Do not acquire gold, or silver, or copper for your money belts, or a bag for *your* journey, or even two coats, or sandals, or a staff; for the worker is worthy of his support. And whatever city or village you enter, inquire who is worthy in it, and stay at his house until you leave *that city*. As you enter the house, give it your greeting. If the house is worthy, give it your *blessing of* peace. But if it is not worthy, take back your *blessing of* peace. Whoever does not receive you, nor heed your words, as you go out of that house or that city, shake the dust off your feet. Truly I say to you, it will be more tolerable for *the* land of Sodom and Gomorrah in the day of judgment than for that city" (Matthew 10:5–15; cf. Mark 6:7–11; Luke 9:1–5; see Matthew 3:2; 11:22, 24; 15:24; Luke 22:35; 1 Corinthians 9:14).

Setting: On the way from Galilee to Jerusalem. Jesus conveys the principles of the lost sheep and the lost coin because the Pharisees and scribes complain He associates with tax collectors and sinners.

"So He told them this parable, saying, "What man among you, if he has a hundred sheep and has lost one of them, does not leave the ninety-nine in the open pasture and go after the one which is lost until he finds it? When he has found it, he lays it on his shoulders, rejoicing. And when he comes home, he calls together his friends and his neighbors, saying to them, 'Rejoice with me, for I have found my sheep which was lost!' I tell you that in the same way, there will be more joy in heaven over one sinner who repents than over ninety-nine righteous persons who need no repentance. Or what woman, if she has ten silver coins and loses one coin, does not light a lamp and sweep the house and search carefully until she finds it? When she has found it, she calls together her friends and neighbors, saying, 'Rejoice with me, for I have found the coin which I had lost!' In the same way, I tell you, there is joy in the presence of the angels of God over one sinner who repents" (Luke 15:3–10).

SIMON (Also see CEPHAS; and PETER; and SIMON BARJONA)

Setting: Capernaum of Galilee. Jesus pays the two-drachma temple tax for Peter and Himself in a miraculous manner.

He said, "Yes." And when he came into the house, Jesus spoke to him first, saying, "What do you think, Simon? From whom do the kings of the earth collect customs or poll-tax, from their sons or from strangers?" When Peter said, "From strangers," Jesus said to him, "Then the sons are exempt. However, so that we do not offend them, go to the sea and throw in a hook, and take the first fish that comes up; and when you open its mouth, you will find a shekel. Take that and give it to them for you and Me" (Matthew 17:25–27; see Exodus 30:11–16; Matthew 22:17–19; Romans 13:7).

Setting: Gethsemane on the Mount of Olives, just east of the temple in Jerusalem. Jesus agonizes over His impending death, disappointed His disciples keep falling asleep instead of watching and praying with Him.

They came to a place named Gethsemane; and He said to the disciples, "Sit here until I have prayed." And He took with Him Peter and James and John, and began to be very distressed and troubled. And He said to them, "My soul is deeply grieved to the point of death; remain here and keep watch." And He went a little beyond *them,* and fell to the ground and *began* to pray that if it were possible, the hour might pass Him by. And He was saying, "Abba! Father! All things are possible for You; remove this cup from Me; yet not what I will, but what You will." And He came and found them sleeping, and said to Peter, "Simon, are you asleep? Could you not keep watch for one hour? Keep watching and praying that you may not come into temptation; the spirit is willing, but the flesh is weak" (Mark 14:32–38; cf. Matthew 26:36–41; Luke 22:41–46, see Romans 8:15; Galatians 4:6).

Setting: Jerusalem. During the Feast of Unleavened Bread (Passover) just before His crucifixion, Jesus celebrates the Passover meal with His disciples and institutes the Lord's Supper. The disciples later argue over who is the greatest among them, and the Lord prophesies Peter's denial of Him.

"Simon, Simon, behold, Satan has demanded *permission* to sift you like wheat; but I have prayed for you, that your faith may not fail; and you, when once you have turned again, strengthen your brothers." But he said to Him, "Lord, with You I am ready to go both to prison and to death!" And He said, "I say to you, Peter, the rooster will not crow today until you have denied three times that you know Me" (Luke 22:31–34; cf. Matthew 26:33–35; John 13:36–38; see Job 1:6–12; John 17:15).

Setting: Bethany beyond the Jordan River. After His baptism, Jesus begins His public ministry and chooses His first disciples, Andrew and Simon (Peter), who believe He is the Messiah.

He brought him to Jesus. Jesus looked at him and said, "You are Simon the son of John; you shall be called Cephas" (which is translated Peter). (John 1:42).

Setting: By the Sea of Galilee. During His third manifestation to the disciples after His resurrection from the dead in Jerusalem, Jesus quizzes Peter three times regarding the disciple's love for Him.

So when they had finished breakfast, Jesus said to Simon Peter, "Simon, *son* of John, do you love Me more than these?" He said to Him, "Yes, Lord; You know that I love You." He said to him, "Tend My lambs." He said to him again a second time, "Simon, *son* of John, do you love Me?" He said to Him, "Yes, Lord; You know that I love You." He said to him, Shepherd My sheep." He said to him the third time, "Simon, *son* of John, do you love Me?" Peter was grieved because He said to him the third time, "Do you love Me?" And he said to Him, "Lord, You know all things; You know that I love You." Jesus said to him, "Tend My sheep" (John 21:15–17; see Matthew 26:33; Mark 14:29).

SIMON (the Pharisee)

Setting: Galilee. After Jesus praises John the Baptist to the crowds, Simon, a Pharisee, invites Jesus to dinner. A sinful woman anoints the Lord's feet with perfume, prompting Him to convey a parable.

And Jesus answered him, "Simon, I have something to say to you." And he replied, "Say it, Teacher." "A moneylender had two debtors: one owed five hundred denarii, and the other fifty. When they were unable to repay, he graciously forgave them both. So which of them will love him more?" Simon answered and said, "I suppose the one whom he forgave more." And He said to him, "You have judged correctly" (Luke 7:40–43; see Matthew 18:23–35).

SIMON BARJONA (Also see CEPHAS; PETER; and SIMON)

Setting: Caesarea Philippi. Jesus responds to Simon Peter's declaration that He is the Christ, the Son of the living God.

And Jesus said to him, "Blessed are you, Simon Barjona, because flesh and blood did not reveal *this* to you, but My Father who is in heaven. I also say to you that you are Peter, and upon this rock I will build My church; and the gates of Hades will not overpower it. I will give you the keys of the kingdom of heaven; and whatever you bind on earth shall have been bound in heaven, and whatever you loose on earth shall have been loosed in heaven" (Matthew 16:17–19; cf. Matthew 18:18; Mark 8:29; Luke 9:20; see Matthew 16:13–16).

SIN (Specifics such as SEXUAL SIN; SIN, ETERNAL and SIN, GREATER are separate entries; also see SINNER and SINS)

Setting: Galilee. After Jesus heals a blind, mute, demon-possessed man, the Pharisees accuse Him in front of crowds of being a worker of Satan. The Lord warns them about the unpardonable sin.

"He who is not with Me is against Me; and he who does not gather with Me scatters. Therefore I say to you, any sin and blasphemy shall be forgiven people, but blasphemy against the Spirit shall not be forgiven. Whoever speaks a word against the Son of Man, it shall be forgiven him; but whoever speaks against the Holy Spirit, it shall not be forgiven him, either in this age or in the *age* to come" (Matthew 12:30–32; cf. Luke 12:10; see Mark 9:40).

[SIN from sinned]

Setting: On the way from Galilee to Jerusalem. Jesus conveys the illustration of the prodigal son because the Pharisees and scribes complain He associates with tax collectors and sinners.

And He said, "A man had two sons. The younger of them said to his father, 'Father, give me the share of the estate that falls to me.' So he divided his wealth between them. And not many days later, the younger son gathered everything together and went on a journey into a distant country, and there he squandered his estate with loose living. Now when he had spent everything, a severe famine occurred in that country, and he began to be impoverished. So he went and hired himself out to one of the citizens of that country, and he sent him into his fields to feed swine. And he would have gladly filled his stomach with the pods that the swine were eating, and no one was giving *anything* to him. But when he came to his senses, he said, 'How many of my father's hired men have more than enough bread, but I am dying here with hunger! I will get up and go to my father, and will say to him, "Father, I have sinned against heaven, and in your sight; I am no longer worthy to be called your son; make me as one of your hired men."' So he got up and came to his father. But while he was still a long way off, his father saw him and felt compassion *for him,* and ran and embraced him and kissed him. And the son said to him, "Father, I have sinned against heaven and in your sight; I am no longer worthy to be called your son.' But the father said to his slaves, 'Quickly bring out the best robe and put it on him, and put a ring on his hand and sandals on his feet; and bring the fattened calf, kill it, and let us eat and celebrate; for this son of mine was dead and has come to life again; he was lost and has been found.' And they began to celebrate. Now his older son was in the field, when he came and approached the house, he heard music and dancing. And he summoned one of the servants and *began* inquiring what these things could be. And he said to him, 'Your brother has come, and your father has killed the fattened calf because he has received him back safe and sound.' But he became angry and was not willing to go in; and his father came out and *began* pleading with him. But he answered and said to his father, 'Look! For so many years I have been serving you and I have never neglected a command of yours; and *yet* you have never given me a young goat, so that I might celebrate with my friends; but when this son of yours came, who has devoured your wealth with prostitutes, you killed the fattened calf for him.' And he said to him, 'Son, you have always been with me, and all that is mine is yours. But we had to celebrate and rejoice, for this brother of yours was dead and *has begun* to live, and was lost and has been found' " (Luke 15:11–32; see Proverb 29:2).

Setting: The temple in Jerusalem. During a feast of the Jews, Jesus addresses the former lame man He healed earlier on the Sabbath at the pool of Bethesda.

Afterward Jesus found him in the temple and tells him, "Behold, you have become well; do not sin anymore, so that nothing worse happens to you" (John 5:14).

Setting: The temple in Jerusalem. Following the Feast of Booths, Jesus retires to the Mount of Olives, and returns the next day to teach. The scribes and Pharisees set a woman caught in adultery before Him to test whether He will follow Moses' command to stone her.

But when they persisted in asking Him, He straightened up, and said to them, "He who is without sin among you, let him *be the* first to throw a stone at her" (John 8:7; see Deuteronomy 17:2–7).

Setting: The temple in Jerusalem. Following the Feast of Booths, Jesus retires to the Mount of Olives, and returns the next day to teach. The scribes and Pharisees set a woman caught in adultery before Him to test whether He will follow Moses' command to stone her.

Straightening up, Jesus said to her, "Woman, where are they? Did no one condemn you?" She said, "No one, Lord." And Jesus said, "I do not condemn you either. Go. From now on sin no more" (John 8:10, 11; see John 3:17).

Setting: The temple treasury in Jerusalem. Following the Feast of Booths and the scribes' and Pharisees' failed attempt to stone a woman for adultery, Jesus returns the next day to teach. They question His testimony about Himself.

Then He said again to them, "I go away, and you will seek Me, and will die in your sin; where I am going, you cannot come." So the Jews were saying, "Surely He will not kill Himself, will He, since He says, "Where I am going, you cannot come'?" And He was saying to them, "You are from below, I am from above; you are of this world, I am not of this world. Therefore I said to you that you will die in your sins; for unless you believe that I am *He,* you will die in your sins." So they were saying to Him, "Who are You?" Jesus said to them, "What have I been saying to you *from* the beginning? I have many things to speak and to judge concerning you, but He who sent Me is true; and the things which I heard from Him, these I speak to the world" (John 8:21–26; see John 3:31–33; 5:34, 35; 17:14, 16).

Setting: The temple treasury in Jerusalem. After the scribes and Pharisees question His testimony about Himself, Jesus reveals to those Jews who believe in Him how He will make them free.

So Jesus was saying to those Jews who had believed Him, "If you continue in My word, *then* you are truly disciples of Mine; and you will know the truth, and the truth will make you free." They answered Him, "We are Abraham's descendants and have never yet been enslaved to anyone; how is it that You say, 'You will become free'?" Jesus answered them, "Truly, truly, I say to you, everyone who commits sin is the slave of sin. The slave does not remain in the house forever; the son does remain forever. So if the Son makes you free, you will be free indeed. I know that you are Abraham's descendants; yet you seek to kill Me, because My word has no place in you. I speak the things which I have seen with *My* Father; therefore you also do the things which you heard from *your* father" (John 8:31–38; see Romans 6:16).

Setting: The temple treasury in Jerusalem. After the scribes and Pharisees question His testimony about Himself, Jesus argues with them regarding their ancestry and motives.

Jesus said to them, "If God were your Father, you would love Me, for I proceeded forth and have come from God, for I have not even come on My own initiative, but He sent Me. Why do you not understand what I am saying? *It is* because you cannot hear My word. You are of *your* father the devil, and you want to do the desires of your father. He was a murderer from the beginning, and does not stand in the truth because there is no truth in him. Whenever he speaks a lie, he speaks from his own *nature,* for he is a liar and the father of lies. But because I speak the truth, you do not believe Me. Which one of you convicts Me of sin? If I speak truth, why do not believe Me? He who is of God hears the words of God; for this reason you do not hear *them,* because you are not of God" (John 8:42–47; see 18:37; 1 John 3:8; 4:6; 5:1).

[SIN from sinned]
Setting: The temple treasury in Jerusalem. After Jesus avoids being stoned by the scribes and Pharisees, His disciples wonder if blindness is caused by sin as the Lord heals a man born blind.

Jesus answered, "*It was* neither *that* this man sinned, nor his parents; but *it was* so that the works of God might be displayed in him. We must work the works of Him who sent Me as long as it is day; night is coming when no one can work. While I am in the world, I am the Light of the world." When He had said this, He spat on the ground, and made clay of the spittle, and applied the clay to his eyes, and said to him, "Go, wash in the pool of Siloam" (which is translated, Sent). So he went away and washed, and came *back* seeing (John 9:3–7; see John 8:12; 11:4; 12:46).

Setting: Jerusalem. Following the Pharisees' interrogation and dismissal of the formerly blind man Jesus healed on the Sabbath, the Lord responds to the Pharisees' question whether they are spiritually blind.

Jesus said to them, "If you were blind, you would have not sin; but since you say, 'We see,' your sin remains" (John 9:41; see 15:22–24).

Setting: Jerusalem. Before the Passover, with His departure in mind, after explaining He is the vine and His disciples are the branches, Jesus prepares them for persecution from the world.

"If the world hates you, you know that it has hated Me before *it hated* you. If you were of the world, the world would love its own; but because you are not of the world, but I chose you out of the world, because of this the world hates you. Remember the word that I said to you, 'A slave is not greater than his master.' If they persecuted Me, they will also persecute you; if they kept My word, they will keep yours also. But all these things they will do to you for My name's sake, because they do not know the One who sent Me. If I had not come and spoken to them, they would not have sin, but now they have no excuse for their sin" (John 15:18–22; see Matthew 10:22; John 7:7; 8:19, 55; 9:41; 1 Corinthians 4:12).

Setting: Jerusalem. Before the Passover, with His upcoming departure in mind, after explaining He is the vine and His disciples are the branches, Jesus prepares them for hatred by the world.

"He who hates Me hates My Father also. If I had not done among them the works which no one else did, they would not have sin; but now they have both seen and hated Me and My Father as well. But *they have done this* to fulfill the word that is written in their Law, 'THEY HATED ME WITHOUT A CAUSE'" (John 15:23–25, Jesus quotes from Psalm 35:19; see John 9:41).

Setting: Jerusalem. Before the Passover, after warning His disciples of the persecution they will face after His departure to heaven, Jesus elaborates about the coming ministry of the Holy Spirit.

"But now I am going to Him who sent Me; and none of you asks Me, 'Where are You going?' But because I have said these things to you, sorrow has filled your heart. But I tell you the truth, it is to your advantage that I do away; for if I do not go away, the Helper will not come to you; but if I go, I will send Him to you. And He, when He comes, will convict the world concerning sin and righteousness and judgment; concerning sin, because they do not believe in Me; and concerning righteousness, because I go to the Father and you no longer see Me; and concerning judgment, because the ruler of this world has been judged" (John 16:5–11; see John 7:33; 12:31; 14:1, 16; 15:22, 24).

SIN, ETERNAL

Setting: Galilee. After Jesus selects His twelve disciples, scribes from Jerusalem attribute His miraculous powers to Satan.

And He called them to Himself and began speaking to them in parables, "How can Satan cast out Satan? If a kingdom is divided against itself, that kingdom cannot stand. If a house is divided against itself, that house will not be able to stand. If Satan has risen up against himself and is divided, he cannot stand, but he is finished! But no one can enter the strong man's house and plunder his property unless he first binds the strong man, and then he will plunder his house. Truly I say to you, all sins shall be forgiven the sons of men, and whatever blasphemies they utter; but whoever blasphemes against the Holy Spirit never has forgiveness, but is guilty of an eternal sin"—because they were saying, "He has an unclean spirit" (Mark 3:23–30; cf. Matthew 12:25–32; Luke 12:10).

SIN, GREATER (Also see CONDEMNATION, GREATER)

Setting: Jerusalem. Pontius Pilate (Roman governor of Judea) continues to find no guilt in Jesus, but has Him scourged in an attempt to appease the hostile Jews. Pilate then seeks more information as to where the King of the Jews is from.

Jesus answered, "You would have no authority over Me, unless it had been given you from above; for this reason he who delivered Me to you has *the* greater sin" (John 19:11; see Romans 13:1).

SIN, JESUS' FULL PAYMENT FOR THE WORLD'S

[JESUS' FULL PAYMENT FOR THE WORLD'S SIN from "It is finished!"]

Setting: On the hill called Golgotha (Calvary), just outside Jerusalem. After receiving some sour wine to quench His thirst while hanging nailed to a cross, Jesus accomplishes His work of dying for the sins of the world with a statement of completion.

Therefore when Jesus had received the sour wine, He said, "It is finished!" And He bowed His head and gave up His spirit (John 19:30; see Matthew 27:50; Mark 15:37; Luke 23:46).

SIN, SEXUAL (See SEXUAL SIN)

SIN, UNFORGIVABLE

[UNFORGIVABLE SIN from it shall not be forgiven him]
Setting: Galilee. After Jesus heals a blind, mute, demon-possessed man, the Pharisees accuse Him in front of crowds of being a worker of Satan. The Lord warns them about the unpardonable sin.

"He who is not with Me is against Me; and he who does not gather with Me scatters. Therefore I say to you, any sin and blasphemy shall be forgiven people, but blasphemy against the Spirit shall not be forgiven. Whoever speaks a word against the Son of Man, it shall be forgiven him; but whoever speaks against the Holy Spirit, it shall not be forgiven him, either in this age or in the *age* to come" (Matthew 12:30–32; cf. Luke 12:10; see Mark 9:40).

[UNFORGIVABLE SIN from guilty of an eternal sin]
Setting: Galilee. After Jesus selects His twelve disciples, scribes from Jerusalem attribute His miraculous powers to Satan.

And He called them to Himself and began speaking to them in parables, "How can Satan cast out Satan? If a kingdom is divided against itself, that kingdom cannot stand. If a house is divided against itself, that house will not be able to stand. If Satan has risen up against himself and is divided, he cannot stand, but he is finished! But no one can enter the strong man's house and plunder his property unless he first binds the strong man, and then he will plunder his house. Truly I say to you, all sins shall be forgiven the sons of men, and whatever blasphemies they utter; but whoever blasphemes against the Holy Spirit never has forgiveness, but is guilty of an eternal sin"—because they were saying, "He has an unclean spirit" (Mark 3:23–30; cf. Matthew 12:25–32; Luke 12:10).

[UNFORGIVABLE SIN from he who blasphemes against the Holy Spirit, it will not be forgiven him]
Setting: On the way from Galilee to Jerusalem. Jesus warns His disciples of future events, as the scribes and Pharisees turn hostile and question Him repeatedly in an attempt to catch Him in something He might say.

"And I say to you, everyone who confesses Me before men, the Son of Man will confess him also before the angels of God; but he who denies Me before men will be denied before the angels of God. And everyone who speaks a word against the Son of Man, it will be forgiven him; but he who blasphemes against the Holy Spirit, it will not be forgiven him. When they bring you before the synagogues and the rulers and the authorities, do not worry about how or what you are to speak in your defense, or what you are to say; for the Holy Spirit will teach you in that very hour what you ought to say" (Luke 12:8–12; cf. Matthew 10:32, 33; 12:31, 32; see Matthew 10:20).

SIN, UNPARDONABLE (See SIN, UNFORGIVABLE)

SINGLENESS

[SINGLENESS from eunuchs who made themselves eunuchs for the sake of the kingdom of heaven]
Setting: Judea beyond the Jordan (Perea). After responding to the Pharisees' question about Moses' command regarding a certificate of divorce, Jesus answers the disciples' private question.

But He said to them, "Not all men *can* accept this statement, but *only* those to whom it has been given. For there are eunuchs who were born that way from their mother's womb; and there are eunuchs who were made eunuchs by men; and there are *also* eunuchs who made themselves eunuchs for the sake of the kingdom of heaven. He who is able to accept *this*, let him accept *it*" (Matthew 19:11, 12; cf. 1 Corinthians 7:7).

SINNER (Also see SIN and SINNERS)

Setting: On the way from Galilee to Jerusalem. After Jesus presents to large crowds the demands of discipleship, the Pharisees and scribes complain He associates with tax collectors and sinners.

So He told them this parable, saying, "What man among you, if he has a hundred sheep and has lost one of them, does not leave the ninety-nine in the open pasture and go after the one which is lost until he finds it? When he has found it, he lays it on his shoulders, rejoicing. And when he comes home, he calls together his friends and his neighbors, saying to them, 'Rejoice with me, for I have found my sheep which was lost!' I tell you that in the same way, there will be *more* joy in heaven over one sinner who repents than over ninety-nine righteous persons who need no repentance" (Luke 15:3–7; cf. Matthew 18:12–14; see Matthew 9:11–13; Luke 5:29–32).

Setting: On the way from Galilee to Jerusalem. Jesus conveys the principles of the lost sheep and the lost coin because the Pharisees and scribes complain He associates with tax collectors and sinners.

"So He told them this parable, saying, "What man among you, if he has a hundred sheep and has lost one of them, does not leave the ninety-nine in the open pasture and go after the one which is lost until he finds it? When he has found it, he lays it on his shoulders, rejoicing. And when he comes home, he calls together his friends and his neighbors, saying to them, 'Rejoice with me, for I have found my sheep which was lost!' I tell you that in the same way, there will be more joy in heaven over one sinner who repents than over ninety-nine righteous persons who need no repentance. Or what woman, if she has ten silver coins and loses one coin, does not light a lamp and sweep the house and search carefully until she finds it? When she has found it, she calls together her friends and neighbors, saying, 'Rejoice with me, for I have found the coin which I had lost!' In the same way, I tell you, there is joy in the presence of the angels of God over one sinner who repents" (Luke 15:3–10).

Setting: On the way from Galilee to Jerusalem. After instructing His disciples about persistence in prayer, Jesus conveys a parable about self-righteousness.

And He also told this parable to some people who trusted in themselves that they were righteous, and viewed others with contempt: "Two men went up into the temple to pray, one a Pharisee and the other a tax collector. The Pharisee stood and was praying this to himself: 'God, I thank You that I am not like other people: swindlers, unjust, adulterers, or even like this tax collector. I fast twice a week; I pay tithes of all that I get.' But the tax collector, standing some distance away, was even unwilling to lift up his eyes to heaven, but was beating his breast, saying, 'God, be merciful to me, the sinner!' I tell you, this man went to his house justified rather than the other; for everyone who exalts himself will be humbled, but he who humbles himself will be exalted" (Luke 18:9–14; see Ezra 9:6; Matthew 6:5, 23:12; Luke 11:42; 16:15; Romans 14:3, 10).

SINNERS (SINNERS, GREATER and SINNERS, HANDS OF are separate entries; also see SIN and SINNER)

Setting: Capernaum, near the Sea of Galilee. Jesus calls Matthew from the tax-collection booth to be His disciple.

But when Jesus heard *this,* He said, "*It is* not those who are healthy who need a physician, but those who are sick. But go and learn what this means: 'I DESIRE COMPASSION, AND NOT SACRIFICE,' for I did not come to call the righteous, but sinners" (Matthew 9:12, 13, Jesus quotes from Hosea 6:6; cf. Mark 2:17; Luke 5:31, 32; see Mark 2:15, 16).

Setting: Galilee. After praising John the Baptist as His forerunner, Jesus demonstrates the foolish thinking of the Jewish religious leaders by repeating what they say about John's ascetic lifestyle and ministry along with His own.

"But to what shall I compare this generation? It is like children sitting in the market places, who call out to the other *children,* and say, 'We played the flute for you, and you did not dance; we sang a dirge, and you did not mourn.' For John came neither eating nor drinking, and they say, 'He has a demon!' The Son of Man came eating and drinking, and they say, 'Behold, a gluttonous man and a drunkard, a friend of tax collectors and sinners! Yet wisdom is vindicated by her deeds" (Matthew 11:16–19; cf. Luke 7:31–35; see Matthew 9:11, 34; Luke 1:15).

Setting: The home of Levi (Matthew) the tax collector in Capernaum, near the Sea of Galilee. The scribes of the Pharisees question Jesus' association with sinners and tax collectors after He calls Levi from the tax-collection booth to be His disciple.

And hearing *this,* Jesus said to them, "*It is* not those who are healthy who need a physician, but those who are sick; I did not come to call the righteous, but sinners" (Mark 2:17; cf. Matthew 9:12, 13; Luke 5:29–32).

Setting: The house of Levi (Matthew) the tax collector in Capernaum. At a reception for Jesus after He calls Matthew to become His disciple, the Pharisees and their scribes question why Jesus spends time with tax collectors and sinners.

And Jesus answered and said to them, "*It is* not those who are well who need a physician, but those who are sick. I have not come to call the righteous but sinners to repentance" (Luke 5:31, 32; cf. Matthew 9:10–13; Mark 2:15–17).

Setting: Galilee. After selecting His twelve disciples, Jesus teaches the Sermon on the Mount to those disciples and a great throng of people from Judea, Jerusalem, and the central coastal region of Tyre and Sidon.

"But I say to you who hear, love your enemies, do good to those who hate you, bless those who curse you, pray for those who mistreat you. Whoever hits you on the cheek, offer him the other also; and whoever takes away your coat, do not withhold your shirt from him either. Give to everyone who asks of you, and whoever takes away what is yours, do not demand it back. Treat others the same way you want them to treat you. If you love those who love you, what credit is *that* to you? For even sinners love those who love them. If you do good to those who do good to you, what credit is *that* to you? For even sinners do the same. If you lend to those from whom you expect to receive, what credit is *that* to you? Even sinners lend to sinners in order to receive back the same *amount.* But love your enemies, and do good, and lend, expecting nothing in return; and your reward will be great, and you will be sons of the Most High; for He Himself is kind to ungrateful and evil *men.* Be merciful, just as your Father is merciful" (Luke 6:27–36; cf. Matthew 5:9, 39–48; Matthew 7:12).

Setting: Galilee. After praising John the Baptist to the crowds, Jesus criticizes the Pharisees and lawyers who reject God's purpose and John's message.

"To what then shall I compare the men of this generation, and what are they like? They are like children who sit in the market place and call to one another, and they say, 'We played the flute for you, and you did not dance; we sang a dirge, and you did not weep.' For John the Baptist has come eating no bread and drinking no wine, and you say, 'He has a demon!' The Son of Man has come eating and drinking, and you say, 'Behold, a gluttonous man and a drunkard, a friend of tax collectors and sinners!' Yet wisdom is vindicated by all her children" (Luke 7:31–35; cf. Matthew 11:16–19; see Luke 1:15).

SINNERS, GREATER

Setting: On the way from Galilee to Jerusalem. After some present report to Him about the Galileans whose blood Pilate (Roman governor of Judea) had mixed with their sacrifices, Jesus responds to their concern by calling them to repentance.

And Jesus said to them, "Do you suppose that these Galileans were *greater* sinners than all *other* Galileans because they suffered this *fate*? I tell you, no, but unless you repent, you will all likewise perish. Or do you suppose that those eighteen on whom the tower in Siloam fell and killed them were *worse* culprits than all the men who live in Jerusalem? I tell you, no, but unless you repent, you will all likewise perish" (Luke 13:2–5; see John 9:2, 3).

SINNERS, HANDS OF

Setting: An upper room in Jerusalem. After celebrating the Passover meal with His disciples, Jesus retreats to the Garden of Gethsemane on the Mount of Olives to pray prior to His betrayal by Judas.

Then Jesus came with them to a place called Gethsemane, and said to His disciples, "Sit here while I go over there and pray." And He took with Him Peter and the two sons of Zebedee, and began to be grieved and distressed. Then He said to them, "My soul is deeply grieved, to the point of death; remain here and keep watch with Me." And He went a little beyond *them,* and fell on His face and prayed, saying, "My Father, if it is possible, let this cup pass from Me; yet not as I will, but as You will." And He came to the disciples and found them sleeping, and said to Peter, "So, you *men* could not keep watch with Me for one hour? Keep watching and praying that you may not enter into temptation; the spirit is willing, but the flesh is weak." He went away again a second time and prayed, saying, "My Father, if this cannot pass away unless I drink it, Your will be done." Again He came and found them sleeping, for their eyes were heavy. And He left them again, and went away and prayed a third time, saying the same thing once more. Then He came to the disciples and said to them, "Are you still sleeping and resting? Behold the hour is at hand and the Son of Man is being betrayed into the hands of sinners. Get up, let us be going; behold the one who betrays Me is at hand!" (Matthew 26:36–46; cf. Mark 14:32–42; Luke 22:40–46; see Matthew 20:22; John 12:27).

Setting: Gethsemane on the Mount of Olives, just east of the temple in Jerusalem. Jesus prepares to meet Judas the betrayer, while His other disciples keep falling asleep instead of watching and praying with Him.

And He came the third time, and said to them, "Are you still sleeping and resting? It is enough; the hour has come; behold, the Son of Man is being betrayed into the hands of sinners. Get up, let us be going; behold, the one who betrays Me is at hand!" (Mark 14:41, 42; cf. Matthew 26:45, 46).

SINS (FORGIVENESS OF SINS is a separate entry; also see DEPRAVITY; SIN; SINNERS; and TRANSGRESSIONS)

Setting: Capernaum of Galilee. After conveying to His disciples the value of little ones, Jesus gives instruction about church discipline.

"If your brother sins, go and show him his fault in private; if he listens to you, you have won your brother. But if he does not listen *to you,* take one or two more with you, so that BY THE MOUTH OF TWO OR THREE WITNESSES EVERY FACT MAY BE CONFIRMED. If he refuses to listen to them, tell it to the church; and if he refuses to listen even to the church, let him be to you as a Gentile and a tax collector. Truly I say to you, whatever you bind of earth shall have been bound in heaven; and whatever you loose on earth shall have been loosed in heaven. Again, I say to you, that if two of you agree on earth about anything that they may ask, it shall be done for them by My Father who is in heaven. For there two or three have gathered together in My name, I am there in their midst" (Matthew 18:15–20. Jesus quotes from Deuteronomy 19:15; cf. Matthew 7:7; 16:19; see Leviticus 19:17; Matthew 28:20; 2 Thessalonians 3:6, 14).

Setting: Galilee. Early in Jesus' gospel-preaching ministry, word of Jesus' healing abilities spreads, so some friends bring a paralytic man to Him for healing.

And Jesus seeing their faith said to the paralytic, "Son, your sins are forgiven" (Mark 2:5; cf. Matthew 9:1–3; Luke 5:17–20).

Setting: Galilee. After Jesus selects His twelve disciples, scribes from Jerusalem attribute His miraculous powers to Beelzebul (Satan).

And He called them to Himself and began speaking to them in parables, "How can Satan cast out Satan? If a kingdom is divided against itself, that kingdom cannot stand. If a house is divided against itself, that house will not be able to stand. If Satan has risen up against himself and is divided, he cannot stand, but he is finished! But no one can enter the strong man's house and plunder his property unless he first binds the strong man, and then he will plunder his house. Truly I say to you, all sins shall be forgiven the sons of men, and whatever blasphemies they utter; but whoever blasphemes against the Holy Spirit never has forgiveness, but is guilty of an eternal sin"—because they were saying, "He has an unclean spirit" (Mark 3:23–30; cf. Matthew 12:25–32; Luke 12:10).

Setting: Galilee. After Jesus praises John the Baptist to the crowds, Simon, a Pharisee, invites the Lord to dinner. A sinful woman anoints His feet with perfume, prompting Him to instruct His host about forgiveness.

Turning toward the woman, He said to Simon, "Do you see this woman? I entered your house; you gave Me no water for My feet, but she has wet My feet with her tears and wiped them with her hair. You gave Me no kiss; but she, since the time I came in, has not ceased to kiss My feet. You did not anoint My head with oil, but she anointed My feet with perfume. For this reason I say to you, her sins, which are many, have been forgiven, for she loved much; but he who is forgiven little, loves little." Then He said to her, "Your sins have been forgiven." Those who were reclining *at the table* with Him began to say to themselves, "Who is this *man* who even forgives sins?" And He said to the woman, "Your faith has saved you; go in peace" (Luke 7:44–50; see Matthew 9:2; Mark 5:34; Luke 5:21).

Setting: On the way from Galilee to Jerusalem. After Jesus visits in the home of Martha and Mary of Bethany, one of His disciples asks Him to teach them to pray.

And He said to them, "When you pray, say: 'Father, hallowed be Your name. Your kingdom come. Give us each day our daily bread. And forgive us our sins, for we ourselves also forgive everyone who is indebted to us. And lead us not into temptation.'" (Luke 11:2–4; cf. Matthew 6:9–13)

Setting: On the way from Galilee to Jerusalem. After conveying the story of the rich man and Lazarus, the Lord gives His disciples instruction on forgiveness.

He said to His disciples, "It is inevitable that stumbling blocks come, but woe to him through whom they come! It would be better for him if a millstone were hung around his neck and he were thrown into the sea, than that he would cause one of these little ones to stumble. Be on your guard! If your brother sins, rebuke him; and if he repents, forgive him. And if he sins against you seven times a day, and returns to you seven times, saying, 'I repent,' forgive him" (Luke 17:1–4; see Matthew 18:5–7, 15, 21, 22).

Setting: The temple treasury in Jerusalem. Following the Feast of Booths and the scribes' and Pharisees' failed attempt to stone a woman for adultery, Jesus returns the next day to teach. They question His testimony about Himself.

Then He said again to them, "I go away, and you will seek Me, and will die in your sin; where I am going, you cannot come." So the Jews were saying, "Surely He will not kill Himself, will He, since He says, "Where I am going, you cannot come'?" And He was saying to them, "You are from below, I am from above; you are of this world, I am not of this world. Therefore I said to you that you will die in your sins; for unless you believe that I am *He,* you will die in your sins." So they were saying to Him, "Who are You?" Jesus said to them, "What have I been saying to you *from* the beginning? I have many things to speak and to judge concerning you, but He who sent Me is true; and the things which I heard from Him, these I speak to the world" (John 8:21–26; see John 3:31–33; 5:34, 35; 17:14, 16).

Setting: Jerusalem. After Mary Magdalene encounters the risen Jesus in the morning, He appears that evening in the midst of His disciples (except Thomas), who are in hiding behind closed doors due to fear of the Jewish religious leaders.

So when it was evening on that day, the first *day* of the week, and when the doors were shut where the disciples were, for fear of the Jews, Jesus came and stood in their midst and said to them, "Peace *be* with you." And when He had said this, He showed them both His hands and His side. The disciples then rejoiced when they saw the Lord. So Jesus said to them again, "Peace *be* with you; as the Father has sent Me, I also send you." And when He had said this, He breathed on them and said to them, "Receive the Holy Spirit. If you forgive the sins of any, *their sins* have been forgiven them; if you retain the *sins* of any, they have been retained" (John 20:19–23; cf. Luke 24:36–43; see Matthew 16:19; Mark 16:14).

SINS, FORGIVENESS OF (See FORGIVENESS OF SINS)

SISTER (Also see SISTERS)

Setting: Galilee. Jesus' mother, Mary, and His brothers wait to see Him as He teaches and preaches.

But Jesus answered the one who was telling Him and said, "Who is My mother and who are My brothers?" And stretching out His hand toward His disciples, He said, "Behold, My mother and My brothers! For whoever does the will of My Father who is in heaven, he is My brother and sister and mother" (Matthew 12:48–50; cf. Mark 3:31–35; Luke 8:19–21).

Setting: Galilee. During the early part of His ministry, just after selecting His twelve disciples, when informed that His mother and brothers are waiting to see Him, Jesus explains to the crowd who His true relatives are.

Answering them, He said, "Who are My mother and My brothers?" Looking about at those who were sitting around Him, He said, "Behold My mother and My brothers! For whoever does the will of God, he is My brother and sister and mother" (Mark 3:33–35; cf. Matthew 12:46–50; Luke 8:19–21).

SISTERS (Also see SISTER)

Setting: Judea beyond the Jordan (Perea). Jesus promises rewards to His disciples for their personal sacrifice and commitment to following Him.

And Jesus said to them, "Truly I say to you, that you who have followed Me, in the regeneration when the Son of Man will sit on His glorious throne, you also shall sit upon twelve thrones, judging the twelve tribes of Israel. And everyone who has left houses or brothers or sisters or father or mother or children or farms for My name's sake, will receive many times as much, and will inherit eternal life. But many *who* are first will be last; and *the* last, first" (Matthew 19:28–30; cf. Matthew 6:33; 20:15; Mark 10:29, 30; Luke 18:29, 30; 22:30).

Setting: Judea beyond the Jordan (Perea). After informing a rich man how righteous believers may have treasure in heaven, Jesus tells His disciples about the reward of those who sacrifice in this life to follow Him.

Jesus said, "Truly I say to you, there is no one who has left house or brothers or sisters or mother or father or children or farms, for My sake and for the gospel's sake, but that he will receive a hundred times as much now in the present age, houses and brothers and sisters and mothers and children and farms, along with persecutions; and in the age to come, eternal life. But many *who are* first will be last, and the last, first" (Mark 10:29–31; cf. Matthew 19:27–30; Luke 18:28–30; see Matthew 6:33).

Setting: On the way from Galilee to Jerusalem. After He responds to a guest's proclamation about the blessings of eating bread in the kingdom of God, Jesus presents to large crowds the demands of discipleship.

Now large crowds were going along with Him; and He turned and said to them, "If anyone comes to Me, and does not hate his own father and mother and wife and children and brothers and sisters, yes, and even his own life, he cannot be My disciple. Whoever does not carry his own cross and come after Me cannot be My disciple. For which one of you, when he wants to build a tower, does not first sit down and calculate the cost to see if he has enough to complete it? Otherwise, when he has laid a foundation and is not able to finish, all who observe it begin to ridicule him, saying, 'This man began to build and was not able to finish.' Or what king, when he sets out to meet another king in battle, will not first sit down and consider whether he is strong enough with ten thousand *men* to encounter the one coming against him with twenty thousand? Or else, while the other is still far away, he sends a delegation and asks for terms of peace. So then, none of you can be My disciple who does not give up all his possessions. Therefore, salt is good; but if even salt has become tasteless, with what will it be seasoned? It is useless either for the soil or for the manure pile; it is thrown out. He who has ears to hear, let him hear" (Luke 14:25–35; cf. Matthew 5:13; 10:37–39; see Proverb 20:18; Philippians 3:7).

SKIN DISEASES (See LEPERS and LEPROSY, CLEANSING FROM)

SKINS, WINE (Listed under WINESKINS)

SKY (Also see CLOUDS; STORM; and WEATHER)

Setting: Magadan of Galilee. Jesus' enemies, the Pharisees and the Sadducees, rejecting His message, continue to test Him by asking for a sign from heaven.

But He replied to them, "When it is evening, you say, '*It will be* fair weather, for the sky is red.' And in the morning, '*There will* be a storm today, for the sky is red and threatening.' Do you know how to discern the appearance of the sky, but cannot *discern* the signs of the times? An evil and adulterous generation seeks after a sign; and a sign will not be given it, except the sign of Jonah." And He left them and went away (Matthew 16:2–4; cf. Matthew 12:39; Mark 8:12; Luke 12:54–56).

Setting: The Mount of Olives, just east of Jerusalem. During His Olivet Discourse, Jesus answers His disciples' questions as to when the temple will be destroyed and Jerusalem overrun, along with the signs of His coming and the end of the age.

"But immediately after the tribulation of those days THE SUN WILL BE DARKENED, AND THE MOON WILL NOT GIVE ITS LIGHT, AND THE STARS WILL FALL from the sky, and the powers of the heavens will be shaken. And then the sign of the Son of Man will appear in the sky, and then all the tribes of the earth will mourn, and they will see the SON OF MAN COMING ON THE CLOUDS OF THE SKY with power and great glory. And He will send forth His angels with A GREAT TRUMPET and THEY WILL GATHER TOGETHER His elect from the four winds, from one end of the sky to the other" (Matthew 24:29–31, Jesus quotes from Isaiah 13:10, Daniel 7:13; Exodus 19:16; cf. Mark 13:24–27; Luke 21:25–27).

Setting: The synagogue in Jesus' hometown of Nazareth in Galilee. At the beginning of His public ministry, Jesus comments to the congregation after reading on the Sabbath from the book of the prophet Isaiah.

And He said to them, "No doubt you will quote this proverb to Me, 'Physician, heal yourself! Whatever we heard was done at Capernaum, do here in your hometown as well.'" And He said, "Truly I say to you, no prophet is welcome in his hometown. But I say to you in truth, there were many widows in Israel in the days of Elijah, when the sky was shut up for three years and six months, when a great famine came over all the land; and yet Elijah was sent to none of them, but only to Zarephath, *in the land* of Sidon, to a woman who was a widow. And there were many lepers in Israel in the time of Elisha the prophet; and none of them was cleansed, but only Naaman the Syrian" (Luke 4:23–27; Jesus refers to 1 Kings 17:1, 9; 2 Kings 5:1–14; see Matthew 13:53–58).

Setting: On the way from Galilee to Jerusalem. After telling how a relationship with Him will divide families, Jesus chastises the crowds for being able to discern the weather but not the present age.

And He was also saying to the crowds, "When you see a cloud rising in the west, immediately you say, 'A shower is coming,' and so it turns out. And when *you see* a south wind blowing, you say, 'It will be a hot day,' and it turns out *that way*. You hypocrites! You know how to analyze the appearance of the earth and the sky, but why do you not analyze this present time?" (Luke 12:54–56; cf. Matthew 16:2, 3).

Setting: On the way from Galilee to Jerusalem. After the Pharisees question Him about the coming of the kingdom of God, Jesus tells His disciples of His second coming.

And He said to the disciples, "The days will come when you will long to see one of the days of the Son of Man, and you will not see it. They will say to you, 'Look there! Look here!' Do not go away, and do not run after *them*. For just like the lightning, when it flashes out of one part of the sky, shines to the other part of the sky, so will the Son of Man be in His day. But first He must suffer many things and be rejected by this generation. And just as it happened in the days of Noah, so it will be also in the days of the Son of Man: they were eating, they were drinking, they were marrying, they were being given in marriage, until the day that Noah entered the ark, and the flood came and destroyed them all. It was the same as happened in the days of Lot: they were eating, they were drinking, they were buying, they were selling, they were planting, they were building; but on the day that Lot went out from Sodom it rained fire and brimstone from heaven and destroyed them all. It will be just the same on the day that the Son of Man is revealed. On that day, the one who is on the housetop and whose goods are in the house must not go down to take them out; and likewise the one who is in the field must not turn back. Remember Lot's wife. Whoever seeks to keep his life will lose it, and whoever loses *his life* will preserve it. I tell you, on that night there will be two in one bed; one will be taken and the other will be left. There will be two women grinding at the same place; one will be taken and the other will be left. [Two men will be in the field; one will be taken and the other will be left."] And answering they said to Him, "Where, Lord?" And He said to them, "Where the body *is*, there also the vultures will be gathered" (Luke 17:22–37; see Genesis 19; Matthew 10:39; 16:21, 27; 24:17–28, 37–41).

SLANDER (Also see SPEECH) [SLANDER from when *people* insult you and falsely say all kinds of evil against you]
Setting: Galilee. Early in His ministry, Jesus presents the Beatitudes (part of the Sermon on the Mount) to His disciples and the gathered crowds from Galilee, Decapolis, Jerusalem, Judea, and beyond the Jordan.

"Blessed are you when *people* insult you and persecute you, and falsely say all kinds of evil against you because of Me. Rejoice and be glad, for your reward in heaven is great; for in the same way they persecuted the prophets who were before you" (Matthew 5:11, 12; cf. 2 Chronicles 36:16; Luke 6:22, 23; 1 Peter 4:14; see Matthew 13:35).

[SLANDER from slanders]
Setting: Galilee. Jesus gives the crowd the meaning of His instruction about what defiles a man.

Peter said to Him, "Explain the parable to us." Jesus said, "Are you still lacking in understanding also? Do you not understand that everything that goes into the mouth passes into the stomach and is eliminated? But the things that proceed out of the mouth come from the heart, and those defile the man. For out of the heart come evil thoughts, murders, adulteries, fornications, thefts, false witness, slanders. These are the things which defile a man; but to eat with unwashed hands does not defile the man" (Matthew 15:15–20; cf. Mark 7:18–23; see Galatians 5:19–21).

Setting: Galilee. After the Pharisees and scribes from Jerusalem object to His disciples' lack of obedience to the tradition regarding ceremonial cleansing, Jesus speaks to a crowd and explains His teaching to the disciples.

After He called the crowd to Him again, He *began* saying to them, "Listen to Me, all of you, and understand: there is nothing outside the man which can defile him if it goes into him; but the things which proceed out of the man are what defile the man. [If anyone has ears to hear, let him hear."] When he had left the crowd *and* entered the house, His disciples questioned Him about the parable. And He said to them, "Are you so lacking in understanding also? Do you not understand that whatever goes into the man from outside cannot defile him, because it does not go into his heart, but into his stomach, and is eliminated?" (*Thus He* declared all foods clean.) And He was saying, "That which proceeds out of the man, that is what defiles the man. For from within, out of the heart of men, proceed the evil thoughts, fornications, thefts, murders, adulteries, deeds of coveting *and* wickedness, *as well* as deceit, sensuality, envy, slander, pride *and* foolishness. All these evil things proceed from within and defile the man" (Mark 7:14–23; cf. Matthew 15:10–20).

[SLANDER from insult you, and scorn your name as evil]
Setting: Galilee. After selecting His twelve disciples, Jesus teaches the Beatitudes (part of the Sermon on the Mount) to those disciples and a great throng of people from Judea, Jerusalem, and the central coastal region of Tyre and Sidon.

"Blessed are you when men hate you, and ostracize you, and insult you, and scorn your name as evil, for the sake of the Son of Man. Be glad in that day and leap *for joy*, for behold, your reward is great in heaven. For in the same way their fathers used to treat the prophets" (Luke 6:22, 23; cf. Matthew 5:10–12; see 2 Chronicles 36:16).

SLAP
[SLAP from slaps]
Setting: Galilee. During the early part of His ministry, Jesus preaches the Sermon on the Mount to His disciples and the multitudes.

"You have heard that it was said, 'AN EYE FOR AN EYE, AND A TOOTH FOR A TOOTH.' But I say to you, do not resist an evil person; but whoever slaps you on your right cheek, turn the other to him also" (Matthew 5:38, 39, Jesus quotes from Exodus 21:24; cf. Leviticus 24:20).

SLAVE (Specifics such as SLAVE, FAITHFUL and SLAVE, GOOD are separate entries; also see SERVANT; and SERVANTS)

Setting: Galilee. After His disciples observe His ministry, Jesus summons and specifically instructs them about the difficulties ahead involving true discipleship.

"A disciple is not above his teacher, nor a slave above his master. It is enough for the disciple that he become like his teacher, and the slave like his master. If they have called the head of the house Beelzebul, how much more *will they malign* the members of his household!" (Matthew 10:24, 25; cf. Luke 6:40; see 2 Kings 1:2).

Setting: Capernaum of Galilee. Jesus illustrates the matter of forgiveness after Peter asks Him if forgiving someone seven times who has sinned against him is adequate.

"For this reason the kingdom of heaven may be compared to a king who wished to settle accounts with his slaves. When he had begun to settle *them,* one who owed him ten thousand talents was brought to him. But since he did not have *the means* to repay, his lord commanded him to be sold, along with his wife and children and all that he had, and repayment to be made. So the slave fell *to the ground* and prostrated himself before him, saying, 'Have patience with me and I will repay you everything.' And the lord of that slave felt compassion and released him and forgave him the debt. But that slave went out and found one of his fellow slaves who owed him a hundred denarii; and he seized him and *began* to choke *him,* saying, 'Pay back what you owe.' So his fellow slave fell *to the ground* and *began* to plead with him, saying, 'Have patience with me and I will repay you.' But he was unwilling and went and threw him in prison until he should pay back what was owed. So when his fellow slaves saw what had happened, they were deeply grieved and came and reported to their lord all that had happened. Then summoning him, his lord said to him, 'You wicked slave, I forgave you all that debt because you pleaded with me. Should you not also have had mercy on your fellow slave, in the same way that I had mercy on you?' And his lord, moved with anger, handed him over to the torturers until he should repay all that was owed him. My heavenly Father will also do the same to you, if each of you does not forgive his brother from your heart" (Matthew 18:23–35; cf. Matthew 6:12, 14, 15; Luke 7:42; see Matthew 25:19–28).

Setting: On the way to Jerusalem, where Jesus will die on the cross. Jesus teaches His disciples about true greatness after the mother of disciples James and John asks Him to make her sons exalted rulers with Him in His coming kingdom.

But Jesus called them to Himself and said, "You know that the rulers of the Gentiles lord it over them, and *their* great men exercise authority over them. It is not this way among you, but whoever wishes to become great among you shall be your servant, and whoever wishes to be first among you shall be your slave; just as the Son of Man did not come to be served, but to serve, and to give His life a ransom for many" (Matthew 20:25–28; cf. Matthew 23:11; 26:28; Mark 10:42–45).

Setting: On the Mount of Olives, just east of Jerusalem. During His Olivet Discourse, after answering His disciples' questions as to when the temple will be destroyed and Jerusalem overrun, along with the signs of His coming and the end of the age, Jesus reemphasizes to His disciples that they should be on the alert for His return.

"Therefore be on the alert, for you do not know which day your Lord is coming. But be sure of this, that if the head of the house had known at what time of the night the thief was coming, he would have been on the alert and would not have allowed his house to be broken into. For this reason you also must be ready; for the Son of Man is coming at an hour when you do not think *He will.* Who then is the faithful and sensible slave whom his master put in charge of his household to give their food at the proper time? Blessed is that slave whom his master finds so doing when he comes. Truly I say to you that he will put him in charge of all his possessions. But if that evil slave says in his heart, 'My master is not coming for a long time,' and begins to beat his fellow slaves and eat and drink with drunkards; the master of that slave will come on a day when he does not expect *him* and at an hour which he does not know, and will cut him in pieces and assign him a place with the hypocrites; in that place there will be weeping and gnashing of teeth" (Matthew 24:42–51; cf. Mark 13:33–37; Luke 12:39–46; 21:34–36; see Matthew 8:11, 12; 25:21–23).

Setting: On the road to Jerusalem. James and John ask Jesus for special honor and privileges in His kingdom. The other disciples become angry, so the Lord uses this moment to teach all of them about servanthood.

Calling them to Himself, Jesus said to them, "You know that those who are recognized as rulers of the Gentiles lord it over them; and their great men exercise authority over them. But it is not this way among you, but whoever wishes to become great among you shall be your servant; and whoever wishes to be first among you shall be slave of all. For even the Son of Man did not come to be served, but to serve, and to give His life a ransom for many" (Mark 10:42–45; cf. Matthew 20:25–28).

Setting: The temple in Jerusalem. Having His authority questioned by the chief priests, scribes, and elders, Jesus begins to teach them in parables.

And He began to speak to them in parables: "A man PLANTED A VINEYARD AND PUT A WALL AROUND IT, AND DUG A VAT UNDER THE WINE PRESS AND BUILT A TOWER, and rented it out to vine-growers and went on a journey. At the *harvest* time he sent a slave to the vine-growers, in order to receive *some* of the produce of the vineyard from the vine-growers. They took him, and beat him and sent him away empty-handed. Again he sent them another slave, and they wounded him in the head, and treated him shamefully. And he sent another, and that one they killed; and *so with* many others, beating some and killing others. He had one more to *send*, a beloved son; he sent him last *of all* to them, saying, 'They will respect my son.' But those vine-growers said to one another, 'This is the heir; come, let us kill him, and the inheritance will be ours!' They took him, and killed him and threw him out of the vineyard. What will the owner of the vineyard do? He will come and destroy the vine-growers, and will give the vineyard to others. Have you not even read this Scripture: 'THE STONE WHICH THE BUILDERS REJECTED, THIS BECAME THE CHIEF CORNER *stone;* THIS CAME ABOUT FROM THE LORD, AND IT IS MARVELOUS IN OUR EYES'?" (Mark 12:1–11, Jesus quotes from Psalm 118:22, 23; Isaiah 5:1, 2; cf. Matthew 21:33–46; Luke 20:9–19).

Setting: On the way from Galilee to Jerusalem. After Jesus uses a parable to challenge the crowd and His disciples to be ready for His return, Peter asks Him whom He is addressing.

And the Lord said, "Who then is the faithful and sensible steward, whom his master will put in charge of his servants, to give them their rations at the proper time? Blessed is that slave whom his master finds so doing when he comes. Truly I say to you that he will put him in charge of all his possessions. But if that slave says in his heart, 'My master will be a long time in coming,' and begins to beat the slaves, *both* men and women, and to eat and drink and get drunk; the master of that slave will come on a day when he does not expect *him* and at an hour he does not know, and will cut him in pieces, and assign him a place with the unbelievers. And that slave who knew his master's will and did not get ready or act in accord with his will, will receive many lashes, but the one who did know *it,* and committed deeds worthy of flogging, will receive but few. From everyone who has been given much, much will be required; and to whom they entrusted much, of him they will ask all the more" (Luke 12:42–48; cf. Matthew 24:45–51; see Leviticus 5:17).

Setting: On the way from Galilee to Jerusalem. After speaking a parable to the invited guests and the host at a banquet, Jesus responds to a guest's proclamation about the blessings of eating bread in the kingdom of God.

But He said to him, "A man was giving a big dinner, and he invited many; and at the dinner hour he sent his slave to say to those who had been invited, 'Come; for everything is ready now.' But they all alike began to make excuses. The first one said to him, 'I have bought a piece of land and I need to go out and look at it; please consider me excused.' Another one said, 'I have bought five yoke of oxen, and I am going to try them out; please consider me excused.' Another one said, I have married a wife, and for that reason I cannot come.' And the slave came *back* and reported this to his master. Then the head of the household became angry and said to his slave, 'Go out at once into the streets and lanes of the city and bring in here the poor and crippled and blind and lame.' And the slave said, 'Master, what you commanded has been done, and still there is room.' And the master said to the slave, 'Go out into the highways and along the hedges, and compel *them* to come in, so that my house may be filled. For I tell you, none of those men who were invited shall taste of my dinner'" (Luke 14:16–24; see Deuteronomy 24:5; Matthew 22:2–14).

Setting: On the way from Galilee to Jerusalem. After His disciples ask that their faith be increased following His instruction to them on forgiveness, the Lord illustrates with the mustard seed and an obedient slave.

And the Lord said, "If you had faith like a mustard seed, you would say to this mulberry tree, 'Be uprooted and be planted in the sea'; and it would obey you. Which of you, having a slave plowing or tending sheep, will say to him when he has come from the field, 'Come immediately and sit down to eat'? But will he not say to him, "Prepare something for me to eat, and *properly* clothe yourself and serve me while I eat and drink; and afterward you may eat and drink'? He does not thank the slave because he did the things which were commanded, does he? So you too, when you do all the things which are commanded you, say, 'We are unworthy slaves; we have done *only* that which we ought to have done' " (Luke 17:6–10; see Matthew 13:31; Luke 12:37).

Setting: The temple in Jerusalem. While ministering a few days before His crucifixion, after the chief priests and the scribes question His authority to teach and preach, Jesus conveys the Parable of the Vine-Growers to the people.

And He began to tell the people this parable: "A man planted a vineyard and rented it out to vine-growers, and went on a journey for a long time. At the *harvest* time he sent a slave to the vine-growers, so that they would give him *some* of the produce of the vineyard; but the vine-growers beat him and sent him away empty-handed. And he proceeded to send another slave; and they beat him also and treated him shamefully and sent him away empty-handed. And he proceeded to send a third; and this one also they wounded and cast out. The owner of the vineyard said, 'What shall I do? I will send my beloved son; perhaps they will respect him.' But when the vine-growers saw him, they reasoned with one another, saying, 'This is the heir; let us kill him so that the inheritance will be ours.' So they threw him out of the vineyard and killed him. What, then, will the owner of the vineyard do to them? He will come and destroy these vine-growers and will give the vineyard to others." When they heard it, they said, "May it never be!" But Jesus looked at them and said, "What then is this that is written: 'THE STONE WHICH THE BUILDERS REJECTED, THIS BECAME THE CHIEF CORNER *stone*'? Everyone who falls on that stone will be broken to pieces; but on whomever it falls, it will scatter him like dust" (Luke 20:9–18, Jesus quotes from Psalm 118:22; cf. Matthew 21:33–44; Mark 12:1–11; see Ephesians 2:20).

Setting: The temple treasury in Jerusalem. After the scribes and Pharisees question His testimony about Himself, Jesus reveals to those Jews who believe in Him how He will make them free.

So Jesus was saying to those Jews who had believed Him, "If you continue in My word, *then* you are truly disciples of Mine; and you will know the truth, and the truth will make you free." They answered Him, "We are Abraham's descendants and have never yet been enslaved to anyone; how is it that You say, 'You will become free'?" Jesus answered them, "Truly, truly, I say to you, everyone who commits sin is the slave of sin. The slave does not remain in the house forever; the son does remain forever. So if the Son makes you free, you will be free indeed. I know that you are Abraham's descendants; yet you seek to kill Me, because My word has no place in you. I speak the things which I have seen with *My* Father; therefore you also do the things which you heard from *your* father" (John 8:31–38; see Romans 6:16).

Setting: Jerusalem. Before the Passover, with His death on the cross nearing, Jesus explains the reason for His vivid example of servanthood in washing His disciples' feet.

So when He had washed their feet, and taken His garments and reclined *at the table* again, He said to them, "Do you know what I have done to you? You call Me Teacher and Lord; and you are right, for *so* I am. If I then, the Lord and the Teacher, washed your feet, you also ought to wash one another's feet. For I gave you an example that you also should do as I did to you. Truly, truly I say to you, a slave is not greater than his master, nor *is* one who is sent greater than the one who sent him. If you know these things, you are blessed if you do them. I do not speak of all of you. I know the ones I have chosen; but *it is* that the Scripture may be fulfilled, 'HE WHO EATS MY BREAD HAS LIFTED UP HIS HEEL AGAINST ME.' From now on I am telling you before *it* comes to pass, so that when it does occur, you may believe that I am *He*. Truly, truly, I say to you, he who receives whomever I send receives Me; and he who receives Me receives Him who sent Me" (John 13:12–20; Jesus quotes from Psalm 41:9; see Matthew 7:24; 10:24, 40; John 8:24; 14:29; 1 Peter 5:3).

Setting: Jerusalem. Before the Passover, with His departure in mind, after explaining He is the vine and His disciples are the branches, Jesus commands them to love one another.

"This is My commandment, that you love one another, just as I have loved you. Greater love has no one than this, that one lay down his life for his friends. You are My friends if you do what I command you. No longer do I call you slaves, for the slave does not know what his master is doing; but I have called you friends, for all things that I have heard from My Father I have made known to you. You did not choose Me but I chose you, and appointed you that you would go and bear fruit, and *that* your fruit would remain, so that whatever you ask of the Father in My name He may give to you. This I command you, that you love one another" (John 15:12–17; see Matthew 12:50; John 6:70; 8:26; 10:11; 13:34).

Setting: Jerusalem. Before the Passover, with His departure in mind, after explaining He is the vine and His disciples are the branches, Jesus prepares them for persecution from the world.

"If the world hates you, you know that it has hated Me before *it hated* you. If you were of the world, the world would love its own; but because you are not of the world, but I chose you out of the world, because of this the world hates you. Remember the word that I said to you, 'A slave is not greater than his master.' If they persecuted Me, they will also persecute you; if they kept My word, they will keep yours also. But all these things they will do to you for My name's sake, because they do not know the One who sent Me. If I had not come and spoken to them, they would not have sin, but now they have no excuse for their sin" (John 15:18–22; see Matthew 10:22; John 7:7; 8:19, 55; 9:41; 1 Corinthians 4:12).

SLAVE, EVIL (Also see SLAVE, WICKED)

Setting: On the Mount of Olives, just east of Jerusalem. During His Olivet Discourse, after answering His disciples' questions as to when the temple will be destroyed and Jerusalem overrun, along with the signs of His coming and the end of the age, Jesus reemphasizes to His disciples that they should be on the alert for His return.

"Therefore be on the alert, for you do not know which day your Lord is coming. But be sure of this, that if the head of the house had known at what time of the night the thief was coming, he would have been on the alert and would not have allowed his house to be broken into. For this reason you also must be ready; for the Son of Man is coming at an hour when you do not think *He will.* Who then is the faithful and sensible slave whom his master put in charge of his household to give their food at the proper time? Blessed is that slave whom his master finds so doing when he comes. Truly I say to you that he will put him in charge of all his possessions. But if that evil slave says in his heart, 'My master is not coming for a long time,' and begins to beat his fellow slaves and eat and drink with drunkards; the master of that slave will come on a day when he does not expect *him* and at an hour which he does not know, and will cut him in pieces and assign him a place with the hypocrites; in that place there will be weeping and gnashing of teeth" (Matthew 24:42–51; cf. Mark 13:33–37; Luke 12:39–46; 21:34–36; see Matthew 8:11, 12; 25:21–23).

SLAVE, FAITHFUL AND SENSIBLE (Also see STEWARD, SENSIBLE)

Setting: On the Mount of Olives, just east of Jerusalem. During His Olivet Discourse, after answering His disciples' questions as to when the temple will be destroyed and Jerusalem overrun, along with the signs of His coming and the end of the age, Jesus reemphasizes to His disciples that they should be on the alert for His return.

"Therefore be on the alert, for you do not know which day your Lord is coming. But be sure of this, that if the head of the house had known at what time of the night the thief was coming, he would have been on the alert and would not have allowed his house to be broken into. For this reason you also must be ready; for the Son of Man is coming at an hour when you do not think *He will.* Who then is the faithful and sensible slave whom his master put in charge of his household to give their food at the proper time? Blessed is that slave whom his master finds so doing when he comes. Truly I say to you that he will put him in charge of all his possessions. But if that evil slave says in his heart, 'My master is not coming for a long time,' and begins to beat his fellow slaves and eat and drink with drunkards; the master of that slave will come on a day when he does not expect *him* and at an hour which he does not know, and will cut him in pieces and assign him a place with the hypocrites; in that place there will be weeping and gnashing of teeth" (Matthew 24:42–51; cf. Mark 13:33–37; Luke 12:39–46; 21:34–36; see Matthew 8:11, 12; 25:21–23).

SLAVE, GOOD

Setting: Jericho, on the way to Jerusalem. After commending Zaccheus's faith in Him, Jesus provides a parable about stewardship.

So He said, "A nobleman went to a distant country to receive a kingdom for himself, and *then* return. And he called ten of his slaves, and gave them ten minas and said to them, 'Do business *with this* until I come *back.*' But his citizens hated him and sent a delegation after him, saying, 'We do not want this man to reign over us.' When he returned, after receiving the kingdom, he ordered that these slaves, to whom he had given the money, be called to him so that he might know what business they had done. The first appeared, saying, 'Master, your mina has made ten minas more.' And he said to him, 'Well done, good slave, because you have been faithful in a very little thing, you are to be in authority over ten cities.' The second came, saying, 'Your mina, master, has made five minas.' And he said to him, also, 'And you are to be over five cities.' Another came, saying, 'Master, here is your mina, which I kept put away in a handkerchief; for I was afraid of you, because you are an exacting man; you take up what you did not lay down and reap what you did not sow.' He said to him, 'By your own words I will judge you, you worthless slave. Did you know that I am an exacting man, taking up what I did not lay down and reaping what I did not sow? Then why did you not put my money in the bank, and having come, I would have collected it with interest?' Then he said to the bystanders, 'Take the mina away from him and give it to the one who has the ten minas.' And they said to him, 'Master, he has ten minas *already.*' I tell you that to everyone who has, more shall be given, but from the one who does not have, even what he does have shall be taken away. But these enemies of mine, who did not want me to reign over them, bring them here and slay them in my presence" (Luke 19:12–27; cf. Matthew 25:14–30; see Matthew 13:12; Luke 16:10).

SLAVE, GOOD AND FAITHFUL (Also see STEWARDSHIP)

Setting: On the Mount of Olives, just east of Jerusalem. During His Olivet Discourse, after answering His disciples' questions as to when the temple will be destroyed and Jerusalem overrun, along with the signs of His coming and the end of the age, Jesus reemphasizes to His disciples that they should be on the alert for His return.

"For *it is* just like a man *about* to go on a journey, who called his own slaves and entrusted his possessions to them. To one he gave five talents, to another, two, and to another, one, each according to his own ability; and he went on his journey. Immediately the one who had received the five talents went and traded with them, and gained five more talents. In the same manner the one who *had received* the two *talents* gained two more. But he who received the one *talent* went away, and dug a *hole* in the ground and hid his master's money. Now after a long time the master of those slaves came and settled accounts with them. The one who had received the five talents came up and brought five more talents, saying, 'Master, you entrusted five talents to me. See, I have gained five more talents.' His master said to him, 'Well done, good and faithful slave. You were faithful with a few things, I will put you in charge of many things; enter into the joy of your master.' Also the one who *had received* the two talents came up and said, 'Master, you entrusted two talents to me. See, I have gained two more talents.' His master said to him, 'Well done, good and faithful slave. You were faithful with a few things, I will put you in charge of many things; enter into the joy of your master.' And the one also who had received the one talent came up and said, 'Master, I knew you to be a hard man, reaping where you did not sow and gathering where you scattered no *seed.* And I was afraid, and went away and hid your talent in the ground. See, you have what is yours.' But his master answered and said to him, 'You wicked, lazy slave, you knew that I reap where I did not sow and gather where I scattered no *seed.* Then you ought to have put my money in the bank, and on my arrival I would have received my *money* back with interest. 'Therefore take away the talent from him, and give it to the one who has ten talents.' For to everyone who has, *more* shall be given, and he will have an abundance; but from the one who does not have, even what he does have shall be taken away. Throw out the worthless slave into the outer darkness; in that place there will be weeping and gnashing of teeth" (Matthew 25:14–30; cf. Matthew 8:12; 13:12; 24:45–47; see Matthew 18:23, 24; Luke 12:44).

SLAVE, LAZY

Setting: On the Mount of Olives, just east of Jerusalem. During His Olivet Discourse, after answering His disciples' questions as to when the temple will be destroyed and Jerusalem overrun, along with the signs of His coming and the end of the age, Jesus reemphasizes to His disciples that they should be on the alert for His return.

"For *it is* just like a man *about* to go on a journey, who called his own slaves and entrusted his possessions to them. To one he gave five talents, to another, two, and to another, one, each according to his own ability; and he went on his journey. Immediately the one who had received the five talents went and traded with them, and gained five more talents. In the same manner the one who *had received* the two *talents* gained two more. But he who received the one *talent* went away, and dug a *hole* in the ground and hid his master's money. Now after a long time the master of those slaves came and settled accounts with them. The one who had received the five talents came up and brought five more talents, saying, 'Master, you entrusted five talents to me. See, I have gained five more talents.' His master said to him, 'Well done, good and faithful slave. You were faithful with a few things, I will put you in charge of many things; enter into the joy of your master.' Also the one who *had received* the two talents came up and said, 'Master, you entrusted two talents to me. See, I have gained two more talents.' His master said to him, 'Well done, good and faithful slave. You were faithful with a few things, I will put you in charge of many things; enter into the joy of your master.' And the one also who had received the one talent came up and said, 'Master, I knew you to be a hard man, reaping where you did not sow and gathering where you scattered no *seed.* And I was afraid, and went away and hid your talent in the ground. See, you have what is yours.' But his master answered and said to him, 'You wicked, lazy slave, you knew that I reap where I did not sow and gather where I scattered no *seed.* Then you ought to have put my money in the bank, and on my arrival I would have received my *money* back with interest. 'Therefore take away the talent from him, and give it to the one who has ten talents.' For to everyone who has, *more* shall be given, and he will have an abundance; but from the one who does not have, even what he does have shall be taken away. Throw out the worthless slave into the outer darkness; in that place there will be weeping and gnashing of teeth" (Matthew 25:14–30; cf. Matthew 8:12; 13:12; 24:45–47; see Matthew 18:23, 24; Luke 12:44).

SLAVE, PARABLE OF THE UNMERCIFUL

[PARABLE OF THE UNMERCIFUL SLAVE from Should you not also have had mercy on your fellow slave]

Setting: Capernaum of Galilee. Jesus illustrates the matter of forgiveness after Peter asks Him if forgiving someone seven times who has sinned against him is adequate.

"For this reason the kingdom of heaven may be compared to a king who wished to settle accounts with his slaves. When he had begun to settle *them,* one who owed him ten thousand talents was brought to him. But since he did not have *the means* to repay, his lord commanded him to be sold, along with his wife and children and all that he had, and repayment to be made. So the slave fell *to the ground* and prostrated himself before him, saying, 'Have patience with me and I will repay you everything.' And the lord of that slave felt compassion and released him and forgave him the debt. But that slave went out and found one of his fellow slaves who owed him a hundred denarii; and he seized him and *began* to choke *him,* saying, 'Pay back what you owe.' So his fellow slave fell *to the ground* and *began* to plead with him, saying, 'Have patience with me and I will repay you.' But he was unwilling and went and threw him in prison until he should pay back what was owed. So when his fellow slaves saw what had happened, they were deeply grieved and came and reported to their lord all that had happened. Then summoning him, his lord said to him, 'You wicked slave, I forgave you all that debt because you pleaded with me. Should you not also have had mercy on your fellow slave, in the same way that I had mercy on you?' And his lord, moved with anger, handed him over to the torturers until he should repay all that was owed him. My heavenly Father will also do the same to you, if each of you does not forgive his brother from your heart" (Matthew 18:23–35; cf. Matthew 6:12, 14, 15; Luke 7:42; see Matthew 25:19–28).

SLAVE, WICKED (Also see SLAVE, EVIL)

Setting: Capernaum of Galilee. Jesus illustrates the matter of forgiveness after Peter asks Him if forgiving someone seven times who has sinned against him is adequate.

"For this reason the kingdom of heaven may be compared to a king who wished to settle accounts with his slaves. When he had begun to settle *them,* one who owed him ten thousand talents was brought to him. But since he did not have *the means* to repay, his lord commanded him to be sold, along with his wife and children and all that he had, and repayment to be made. So the slave fell *to the ground* and prostrated himself before him, saying, 'Have patience with me and I will repay you everything.' And the lord of that slave felt compassion and released him and forgave him the debt. But that slave went out and found one of his fellow slaves who owed him a hundred denarii; and he seized him and *began* to choke *him,* saying, 'Pay back what you owe.' So his fellow slave fell *to the ground* and *began* to plead with him, saying, 'Have patience with me and I will repay you.' But he was unwilling and went and threw him in prison until he should pay back what was owed. So when his fellow slaves saw what had happened, they were deeply grieved and came and reported to their lord all that had happened. Then summoning him, his lord said to him, 'You wicked slave, I forgave you all that debt because you pleaded with me. Should you not also have had mercy on your fellow slave, in the same way that I had mercy on you?' And his lord, moved with anger, handed him over to the torturers until he should repay all that was owed him. My heavenly Father will also do the same to you, if each of you does not forgive his brother from your heart" (Matthew 18:23–35; cf. Matthew 6:12, 14, 15; Luke 7:42; see Matthew 25:19–28).

SLAVE, WICKED AND LAZY

Setting: On the Mount of Olives, just east of Jerusalem. During His Olivet Discourse, after answering His disciples' questions as to when the temple will be destroyed and Jerusalem overrun, along with the signs of His coming and the end of the age, Jesus reemphasizes to His disciples that they should be on the alert for His return.

"For *it is* just like a man *about* to go on a journey, who called his own slaves and entrusted his possessions to them. To one he gave five talents, to another, two, and to another, one, each according to his own ability; and he went on his journey. Immediately the one who had received the five talents went and traded with them, and gained five more talents. In the same manner the one who *had received* the two *talents* gained two more. But he who received the one *talent* went away, and dug a *hole* in the ground and hid his master's money. Now after a long time the master of those slaves came and settled accounts with them. The one who had received the five talents came up and brought five more talents, saying, 'Master, you entrusted five talents to me. See, I have gained five more talents.' His master said to him, 'Well done, good and faithful slave. You were faithful with a few things, I will put you in charge of many things; enter into the joy of your master.' Also the one who *had received* the two talents came up and said, 'Master, you entrusted two talents to me. See, I have gained two more talents.' His master said to him, 'Well done, good and faithful slave. You were faithful with a few things, I will put you in charge of many things; enter into the joy of your master.' And the one also who had received the one talent came up and said, 'Master, I knew you to be a hard man, reaping where you did not sow and gathering where you scattered no *seed.* And I was afraid, and went away and hid your talent in the ground. See, you have what is yours.' But his master answered and said to him, 'You wicked, lazy slave, you knew that I reap where I did not sow and gather where I scattered no *seed.* Then you ought to have put my money in the bank, and on my arrival I would have received my *money* back with interest. 'Therefore take away the talent from him, and give it to the one who has ten talents.' For to everyone who has, *more* shall be given, and he will have an abundance; but from the one who does not have, even what he does have shall be taken away. Throw out the worthless slave into the outer darkness; in that place there will be weeping and gnashing of teeth" (Matthew 25:14–30; cf. Matthew 8:12; 13:12; 24:45–47; see Matthew 18:23, 24; Luke 12:44).

SLAVE, WORTHLESS

Setting: On the Mount of Olives, just east of Jerusalem. During His Olivet Discourse, after answering His disciples' questions as to when the temple will be destroyed and Jerusalem overrun, along with the signs of His coming and the end of the age, Jesus reemphasizes to His disciples that they should be on the alert for His return.

"For *it is* just like a man *about* to go on a journey, who called his own slaves and entrusted his possessions to them. To one he gave five talents, to another, two, and to another, one, each according to his own ability; and he went on his journey. Immediately the one who had received the five talents went and traded with them, and gained five more talents. In the same manner the one who *had received* the two *talents* gained two more. But he who received the one *talent* went away, and dug a *hole* in the ground and hid his master's money. Now after a long time the master of those slaves came and settled accounts with them. The one who had received the five talents came up and brought five more talents, saying, 'Master, you entrusted five talents to me. See, I have gained five more talents.' His master said to him, 'Well done, good and faithful slave. You were faithful with a few things, I will put you in charge of many things; enter into the joy of your master.' Also the one who *had received* the two talents came up and said, 'Master, you entrusted two talents to me. See, I have gained two more talents.' His master said to him, 'Well done, good and faithful slave. You were faithful with a few things, I will put you in charge of many things; enter into the joy of your master.' And the one also who had received the one talent came up and said, 'Master, I knew you to be a hard man, reaping where you did not sow and gathering where you scattered no *seed.* And I was afraid, and went away and hid your talent in the ground. See, you have what is yours.' But his master answered and said to him, 'You wicked, lazy slave, you knew that I reap where I did not sow and gather where I scattered no *seed.* Then you ought to have put my money in the bank, and on my arrival I would have received my *money* back with interest. 'Therefore take away the talent from him, and give it to the one who has ten talents.' For to everyone who has, *more* shall be given, and he will have an abundance; but from the one who does not have, even what he does have shall be taken away. Throw out the worthless slave into the outer darkness; in that place there will be weeping and gnashing of teeth" (Matthew 25:14–30; cf. Matthew 8:12; 13:12; 24:45–47; see Matthew 18:23, 24; Luke 12:44).

Setting: Jericho, on the way to Jerusalem. After commending Zaccheus's faith in Him, Jesus provides a parable about stewardship.

So He said, "A nobleman went to a distant country to receive a kingdom for himself, and *then* return. And he called ten of his slaves, and gave them ten minas and said to them, 'Do business *with this* until I come *back.*' But his citizens hated him and sent a delegation after him, saying, 'We do not want this man to reign over us.' When he returned, after receiving the kingdom, he ordered that these slaves, to whom he had given the money, be called to him so that he might know what business they had done. The first appeared, saying, 'Master, your mina has made ten minas more.' And he said to him, 'Well done, good slave, because you have been faithful in a very little thing, you are to be in authority over ten cities.' The second came, saying, 'Your mina, master, has made five minas.' And he said to him, also, 'And you are to be over five cities.' Another came, saying, 'Master, here is your mina, which I kept put away in a handkerchief; for I was afraid of you, because you are an exacting man; you take up what you did not lay down and reap what you did not sow.' He said to him, 'By your own words I will judge you, you worthless slave. Did you know that I am an exacting man, taking up what I did not lay down and reaping what I did not sow? Then why did you not put my money in the bank, and having come, I would have collected it with interest?' Then he said to the bystanders, 'Take the mina away from him and give it to the one who has the ten minas.' And they said to him, 'Master, he has ten minas *already.*' I tell you that to everyone who has, more shall be given, but from the one who does not have, even what he does have shall be taken away. But these enemies of mine, who did not want me to reign over them, bring them here and slay them in my presence" (Luke 19:12–27; cf. Matthew 25:14–30; see Matthew 13:12; Luke 16:10).

SLAVES (Also see SERVANT; SERVANTS; and SLAVE)

Setting: By the Sea of Galilee. Because the religious leaders are rejecting His message, Jesus continues teaching the crowds with the Parable of the Wheat and the Tares.

Jesus presented another parable to them, saying, "The kingdom of heaven may be compared to a man who sowed good seed in his field. But while his men were sleeping, his enemy came and sowed tares among the wheat, and went away. But when the wheat sprouted and bore grain, then the tares became evident also. The slaves of the landowner came and said to him, 'Sir, did you not sow good seed in your field? How then does it have tares?' And he said to them, 'An enemy has done this!' The slaves said to him, 'Do you want us, then, to go and gather them up?' But he said, 'No; for while you are gathering up the tares, you may uproot the wheat with them. Allow both to grow together until the harvest; and in the time of the harvest I will say to the reapers, "First gather up the tares and bind them in bundles to burn them up; but gather the wheat into my barn" '" (Matthew 13:24–30; cf. Matthew 3:12).

Setting: Capernaum of Galilee. Jesus illustrates the matter of forgiveness after Peter asks Him if forgiving someone seven times who has sinned against him is adequate.

"For this reason the kingdom of heaven may be compared to a king who wished to settle accounts with his slaves. When he had begun to settle *them,* one who owed him ten thousand talents was brought to him. But since he did not have *the means* to repay, his lord commanded him to be sold, along with his wife and children and all that he had, and repayment to be made. So the slave fell *to the ground* and prostrated himself before him, saying, 'Have patience with me and I will repay you everything.' And the lord of that slave felt compassion and released him and forgave him the debt. But that slave went out and found one of his fellow slaves who owed him a hundred denarii; and he seized him and *began* to choke *him,* saying, 'Pay back what you owe.' So his fellow slave fell *to the ground* and *began* to plead with him, saying, 'Have patience with me and I will repay you.' But he was unwilling and went and threw him in prison until he should pay back what was owed. So when his fellow slaves saw what had happened, they were deeply grieved and came and reported to their lord all that had happened. Then summoning him, his lord said to him, 'You wicked slave, I forgave you all that debt because you pleaded with me. Should you not also have had mercy on your fellow slave, in the same way that I had mercy on you?' And his lord, moved with anger, handed him over to the torturers until he should repay all that was owed him. My heavenly Father will also do the same to you, if each of you does not forgive his brother from your heart" (Matthew 18:23–35; cf. Matthew 6:12, 14, 15; Luke 7:42; see Matthew 25:19–28).

Setting: The temple in Jerusalem. Jesus delivers another parable to the chief priests and elders after they question His authority.

"Listen to another parable. There was a landowner who PLANTED A VINEYARD AND PUT A WALL AROUND IT AND DUG A WINE PRESS IN IT, AND BUILT A TOWER, and rented it out to vine-growers and went on a journey. When the harvest time approached, he sent his

slaves to the vine-growers to receive his produce. The vine-growers took his slaves and beat one, and killed another, and stoned a third. Again he sent another group of slaves larger than the first; and they did the same thing to them. But afterward he sent his son to them, saying, 'They will respect my son.' But when the vine-growers saw the son, they said among themselves, 'This is the heir; come, let us kill him and seize his inheritance.' They took him, and threw him out of the vineyard and killed him. Therefore when the owner of the vineyard comes, what will he do to those vine-growers?" (Matthew 21:33–40; Jesus quotes from Isaiah 5:1, 2; cf. Mark 12:1–9; Luke 20:9–15).

Setting: The temple in Jerusalem. Jesus speaks another parable to the chief priests and elders after they question His authority.

Jesus spoke to them again in parables, saying, "The kingdom of heaven may be compared to a king who gave a wedding feast for his son. And he sent out his slaves to call those who had been invited to the wedding feast, and they were unwilling to come. Again he sent out other slaves saying, 'Tell those who have been invited, "Behold, I have prepared my dinner; my oxen and my fattened livestock are *all* butchered and everything is ready; come to the wedding feast." But they paid no attention and went their way, one to his own farm, another to his business, and the rest seized his slaves and mistreated them and killed them. But the king was enraged, and he sent his armies and destroyed those murderers and set their city on fire. Then he said to his slaves, 'The wedding is ready, but those who were invited were not worthy. 'Go therefore to the main highways, and as many as you find *there,* invite to the wedding feast.' Those slaves went out into the streets and gathered together all they found, both evil and good; and the wedding hall was filled with dinner guests. But when the king came in to look over the dinner guests, he saw a man there who was not dressed in wedding clothes, and he said to him, 'Friend, how did you come in here without wedding clothes?' And the man was speechless. Then the king said to the servants, 'Bind him hand and foot, and throw him into the outer darkness; in that place there will be weeping and gnashing of teeth.' For many are called, but few *are* chosen" (Matthew 22:1–14; cf. Matthew 8:11, 12).

Setting: On the Mount of Olives, just east of Jerusalem. During His Olivet Discourse, after answering His disciples' questions as to when the temple will be destroyed and Jerusalem overrun, along with the signs of His coming and the end of the age, Jesus reemphasizes to His disciples that they should be on the alert for His return.

"Therefore be on the alert, for you do not know which day your Lord is coming. But be sure of this, that if the head of the house had known at what time of the night the thief was coming, he would have been on the alert and would not have allowed his house to be broken into. For this reason you also must be ready; for the Son of Man is coming at an hour when you do not think *He will.* Who then is the faithful and sensible slave whom his master put in charge of his household to give their food at the proper time? Blessed is that slave whom his master finds so doing when he comes. Truly I say to you that he will put him in charge of all his possessions. But if that evil slave says in his heart, 'My master is not coming for a long time,' and begins to beat his fellow slaves and eat and drink with drunkards; the master of that slave will come on a day when he does not expect *him* and at an hour which he does not know, and will cut him in pieces and assign him a place with the hypocrites; in that place there will be weeping and gnashing of teeth" (Matthew 24:42–51; cf. Mark 13:33–37; Luke 12:39–46; 21:34–36; see Matthew 8:11, 12; 25:21–23).

Setting: On the Mount of Olives, just east of Jerusalem. During His Olivet Discourse, after answering His disciples' questions as to when the temple will be destroyed and Jerusalem overrun, along with the signs of His coming and the end of the age, Jesus reemphasizes to His disciples that they should be on the alert for His return.

"For *it is* just like a man *about* to go on a journey, who called his own slaves and entrusted his possessions to them. To one he gave five talents, to another, two, and to another, one, each according to his own ability; and he went on his journey. Immediately the one who had received the five talents went and traded with them, and gained five more talents. In the same manner the one who *had received* the two *talents* gained two more. But he who received the one *talent* went away, and dug a *hole* in the ground and hid his master's money. Now after a long time the master of those slaves came and settled accounts with them. The one who had received the five talents came up and brought five more talents, saying, 'Master, you entrusted five talents to me. See, I have gained five more talents.' His master said to him, 'Well done, good and faithful slave. You were faithful with a few things, I will put you in charge of many things; enter into the joy of your master.' Also the one who *had received* the two talents came up and said, 'Master, you entrusted two talents to me. See, I have gained two more talents.' His master said to him, 'Well done, good and faithful slave. You were faithful with a few things, I will put you in charge of many things; enter into the joy of your master.' And the one also who had received the one talent came up and said, 'Master, I knew you to be a hard man, reaping where you did not sow and gathering where you scattered no *seed.* And I was afraid, and went away and hid your talent in the ground. See, you have what is yours.' But his master answered and said to him, 'You wicked, lazy slave, you knew that I reap where I did not sow and gather where I scattered no *seed.* Then you ought to have put my money in the bank, and on my arrival I would have received my *money* back with interest. 'Therefore take away the talent from him, and give it to the one who has ten talents.' For to everyone who has, *more* shall be given, and he will have an abundance; but from the one who does not have, even what he does have shall be taken away. Throw out the worthless slave into the outer darkness; in that place there will be weeping and gnashing of teeth" (Matthew 25:14–30; cf. Matthew 8:12; 13:12; 24:45–47; see Matthew 18:23, 24; Luke 12:44).

Setting: On the Mount of Olives, east of the temple in Jerusalem. After prophesying the temple's destruction, Jesus responds during His Olivet Discourse to questions from Peter, James, John, and Andrew about other future events.

"Take heed, keep on the alert; for you do not know when the *appointed* time will come. *It is* like a man away on a journey, *who* upon leaving his house and putting his slaves in charge, *assigning* to each one his task, also commanded the doorkeeper to stay on the alert. Therefore, be on the alert—for you do not know when the master of the house is coming, whether in the evening, at midnight, or when the rooster crows, or in the morning—in case he should come suddenly and find you asleep. What I say to you I say to all, 'Be on the alert!'" (Mark 13:33–37; cf. Matthew 24:42, 43; Luke 21:34–36; see Luke 12:36–38; Ephesians 6:18).

Setting: On the way from Galilee to Jerusalem. After giving a parable about riches and greed, Jesus uses another parable to challenge the crowd and His disciples to be ready for His return.

"Be dressed in readiness, and *keep* your lamps lit. Be like men who are waiting for their master when he returns from the wedding feast, so that they may immediately open *the door* to him when he comes and knocks. Blessed are those slaves whom the master will find on the alert when he comes; truly I say to you, that he will gird himself *to serve,* and have them recline *at the table,* and will come up and wait on them. Whether he comes in the second watch, or even in the third and finds *them* so, blessed are those *slaves.* But be sure of this, that if the head of the house had known at what hour the thief was coming, he would not have allowed his house to be broken into. You too, be ready; for the Son of Man is coming at an hour that you do not expect" (Luke 12:35–40; cf. Matthew 24:42–44; see Mark 13:33; Ephesians 6:14).

Setting: On the way from Galilee to Jerusalem. After Jesus uses a parable to challenge the crowd and His disciples to be ready for His return, Peter asks Him whom He is addressing.

And the Lord said, "Who then is the faithful and sensible steward, whom his master will put in charge of his servants, to give them their rations at the proper time? Blessed is that slave whom his master finds so doing when he comes. Truly I say to you that he will put him in charge of all his possessions. But if that slave says in his heart, 'My master will be a long time in coming,' and begins to beat the slaves, *both* men and women, and to eat and drink and get drunk; the master of that slave will come on a day when he does not expect *him* and at an hour he does not know, and will cut him in pieces, and assign him a place with the unbelievers. And that slave who knew his master's will and did not get ready or act in accord with his will, will receive many lashes, but the one who did know *it,* and committed deeds worthy of flogging, will receive but few. From everyone who has been given much, much will be required; and to whom they entrusted much, of him they will ask all the more" (Luke 12:42–48; cf. Matthew 24:45–51; see Leviticus 5:17).

Setting: On the way from Galilee to Jerusalem. Jesus conveys the illustration of the prodigal son because the Pharisees and scribes complain He associates with tax collectors and sinners.

And He said, "A man had two sons. The younger of them said to his father, 'Father, give me the share of the estate that falls to me.' So he divided his wealth between them. And not many days later, the younger son gathered everything together and went

on a journey into a distant country, and there he squandered his estate with loose living. Now when he had spent everything, a severe famine occurred in that country, and he began to be impoverished. So he went and hired himself out to one of the citizens of that country, and he sent him into his fields to feed swine. And he would have gladly filled his stomach with the pods that the swine were eating, and no one was giving *anything* to him. But when he came to his senses, he said, 'How many of my father's hired men have more than enough bread, but I am dying here with hunger! I will get up and go to my father, and will say to him, "Father, I have sinned against heaven, and in your sight; I am no longer worthy to be called your son; make me as one of your hired men."' So he got up and came to his father. But while he was still a long way off, his father saw him and felt compassion *for him,* and ran and embraced him and kissed him. And the son said to him, "Father, I have sinned against heaven and in your sight; I am no longer worthy to be called your son.' But the father said to his slaves, 'Quickly bring out the best robe and put it on him, and put a ring on his hand and sandals on his feet; and bring the fattened calf, kill it, and let us eat and celebrate; for this son of mine was dead and has come to life again; he was lost and has been found.' And they began to celebrate. Now his older son was in the field, when he came and approached the house, he heard music and dancing. And he summoned one of the servants and *began* inquiring what these things could be. And he said to him, 'Your brother has come, and your father has killed the fattened calf because he has received him back safe and sound.' But he became angry and was not willing to go in; and his father came out and *began* pleading with him. But he answered and said to his father, 'Look! For so many years I have been serving you and I have never neglected a command of yours; and *yet* you have never given me a young goat, so that I might celebrate with my friends; but when this son of yours came, who has devoured your wealth with prostitutes, you killed the fattened calf for him.' And he said to him, 'Son, you have always been with me, and all that is mine is yours. But we had to celebrate and rejoice, for this brother of yours was dead and *has begun* to live, and was lost and has been found' " (Luke 15:11–32; see Proverb 29:2).

Setting: On the way from Galilee to Jerusalem. After His disciples ask that their faith be increased following His instruction to them on forgiveness, the Lord illustrates with the mustard seed and an obedient slave.

And the Lord said, "If you had faith like a mustard seed, you would say to this mulberry tree, 'Be uprooted and be planted in the sea'; and it would obey you. Which of you, having a slave plowing or tending sheep, will say to him when he has come from the field, 'Come immediately and sit down to eat'? But will he not say to him, "Prepare something for me to eat, and *properly* clothe yourself and serve me while I eat and drink; and afterward you may eat and drink'? He does not thank the slave because he did the things which were commanded, does he? So you too, when you do all the things which are commanded you, say, 'We are unworthy slaves; we have done *only* that which we ought to have done' " (Luke 17:6–10; see Matthew 13:31; Luke 12:37; 17:5).

Setting: Jericho, on the way to Jerusalem. After commending Zaccheus's faith in Him, Jesus provides a parable about stewardship.

So He said, "A nobleman went to a distant country to receive a kingdom for himself, and *then* return. And he called ten of his slaves, and gave them ten minas and said to them, 'Do business *with this* until I come *back.*' But his citizens hated him and sent a delegation after him, saying, 'We do not want this man to reign over us.' When he returned, after receiving the kingdom, he ordered that these slaves, to whom he had given the money, be called to him so that he might know what business they had done. The first appeared, saying, 'Master, your mina has made ten minas more.' And he said to him, 'Well done, good slave, because you have been faithful in a very little thing, you are to be in authority over ten cities.' The second came, saying, 'Your mina, master, has made five minas.' And he said to him, also, 'And you are to be over five cities.' Another came, saying, 'Master, here is your mina, which I kept put away in a handkerchief; for I was afraid of you, because you are an exacting man; you take up what you did not lay down and reap what you did not sow.' He said to him, 'By your own words I will judge you, you worthless slave. Did you know that I am an exacting man, taking up what I did not lay down and reaping what I did not sow? Then why did you not put my money in the bank, and having come, I would have collected it with interest?' Then he said to the bystanders, 'Take the mina away from him and give it to the one who has the ten minas.' And they said to him, 'Master, he has ten minas *already.*' I tell you that to everyone who has, more shall be given, but from the one who does not have, even what he does have shall be taken away. But these enemies of mine, who did not want me to reign over them, bring them here and slay them in my presence" (Luke 19:12–27; cf. Matthew 25:14–30; see Matthew 13:12; Luke 16:10).

Setting: Jerusalem. Before the Passover, with His departure in mind, after explaining He is the vine and His disciples are the branches, Jesus commands the disciples to love one another.

"This is My commandment, that you love one another, just as I have loved you. Greater love has no one than this, that one lay down his life for his friends. You are My friends if you do what I command you. No longer do I call you slaves, for the slave does not know what his master is doing; but I have called you friends, for all things that I have heard from My Father I have made known to you. You did not choose Me but I chose you, and appointed you that you would go and bear fruit, and *that* your fruit would remain, so that whatever you ask of the Father in My name He may give to you. This I command you, that you love one another" (John 15:12–17; see Matthew 12:50; John 6:70; 8:26; 10:11; 13:34).

SLAVES, PARABLE OF THE WATCHFUL

PARABLE OF THE WATCHFUL SLAVES from putting his slaves in charge and be on the alert]

Setting: On the Mount of Olives, east of the temple in Jerusalem. After prophesying the temple's destruction, Jesus responds during His Olivet Discourse to questions from Peter, James, John, and Andrew about other future events.

"Take heed, keep on the alert; for you do not know when the *appointed* time will come. *It is* like a man away on a journey, *who* upon leaving his house and putting his slaves in charge, *assigning* to each one his task, also commanded the doorkeeper to stay on the alert. Therefore, be on the alert—for you do not know when the master of the house is coming, whether in the evening, at midnight, or when the rooster crows, or in the morning—in case he should come suddenly and find you asleep. What I say to you I say to all, 'Be on the alert!'" (Mark 13:33–37; cf. Matthew 24:42, 43; Luke 21:34–36; see Luke 12:36–38; Ephesians 6:18).

SLEEP (Also see REST)

[SLEEP from sleeping]

Setting: By the Sea of Galilee. Because the religious leaders are rejecting His message, Jesus continues teaching the crowds with the Parable of the Wheat and the Tares.

Jesus presented another parable to them, saying, "The kingdom of heaven may be compared to a man who sowed good seed in his field. But while his men were sleeping, his enemy came and sowed tares among the wheat, and went away. But when the wheat sprouted and bore grain, then the tares became evident also. The slaves of the landowner came and said to him, 'Sir, did you not sow good seed in your field? How then does it have tares?' And he said to them, 'An enemy has done this!' The slaves said to him, 'Do you want us, then, to go and gather them up?' But he said, 'No; for while you are gathering up the tares, you may uproot the wheat with them. Allow both to grow together until the harvest; and in the time of the harvest I will say to the reapers, "First gather up the tares and bind them in bundles to burn them up; but gather the wheat into my barn" '" (Matthew 13:24–30; cf. Matthew 3:12).

Setting: On the Mount of Olives, just east of Jerusalem. During His Olivet Discourse, after answering His disciples' questions as to when the temple will be destroyed and Jerusalem overrun, along with the signs of His coming and the end of the age, Jesus reemphasizes to His disciples that they should be on the alert for His return.

"Then the kingdom of heaven will be comparable to ten virgins, who took their lamps and went out to meet the bridegroom. Five of them were foolish, and five were prudent. For when the foolish took their lamps, they took no oil with them, but the prudent took oil in flasks along with their lamps. Now while the bridegroom was delaying, they all got drowsy and *began* to sleep. But at midnight there was a shout, 'Behold, the bridegroom! Come out to meet *him*.' Then all those virgins rose and trimmed their lamps. The foolish said to the prudent, 'Give us some of your oil, for our lamps are going out.' But the prudent answered, 'No, there will not be enough for us and you *too;* go instead to the dealers and buy *some* for yourselves.' And while they were going away to make the purchase, the bridegroom came, and those who were ready went in with him to the wedding feast; and the door was shut. Later the other virgins also came, saying, 'Lord, lord, open up for us.' But he answered, 'Truly I say to you, I do not know you.' Be on the alert then, for you do not know the day nor the hour" (Matthew 25:1–13; cf. Matthew 24:42; Luke 12:35; see Matthew 7:21, 24).

[SLEEP from sleeping]

Setting: An upper room in Jerusalem. After celebrating the Passover meal with His disciples, Jesus retreats to the Garden of Gethsemane on the Mount of Olives to pray prior to His betrayal by Judas.

Then Jesus came with them to a place called Gethsemane, and said to His disciples, "Sit here while I go over there and pray." And He took with Him Peter and the two sons of Zebedee, and began to be grieved and distressed. Then He said to them, "My soul is deeply grieved, to the point of death; remain here and keep watch with Me." And He went a little beyond *them,* and fell on His face and prayed, saying, "My Father, if it is possible, let this cup pass from Me; yet not as I will, but as You will." And He came to the disciples and found them sleeping, and said to Peter, "So, you *men* could not keep watch with Me for one hour? Keep watching and praying that you may not enter into temptation; the spirit is willing, but the flesh is weak." He went away again a second time and prayed, saying, "My Father, if this cannot pass away unless I drink it, Your will be done." Again He came and found them sleeping, for their eyes were heavy. And He left them again, and went away and prayed a third time, saying the same thing once more. Then He came to the disciples and said to them, "Are you still sleeping and resting? Behold the hour is at hand and the Son of Man is being betrayed into the hands of sinners. Get up, let us be going; behold the one who betrays Me is at hand!" (Matthew 26:36–46; cf. Mark 14:32–42; Luke 22:40–46; see Matthew 20:22; John 12:27).

[SLEEP from asleep]
Setting: On the Mount of Olives, east of the temple in Jerusalem. After prophesying the temple's destruction, Jesus responds during His Olivet Discourse to questions from Peter, James, John, and Andrew about other future events.

"Take heed, keep on the alert; for you do not know when the *appointed* time will come. *It is* like a man away on a journey, *who* upon leaving his house and putting his slaves in charge, *assigning* to each one his task, also commanded the doorkeeper to stay on the alert. Therefore, be on the alert—for you do not know when the master of the house is coming, whether in the evening, at midnight, or when the rooster crows, or in the morning—in case he should come suddenly and find you asleep. What I say to you I say to all, 'Be on the alert!'" (Mark 13:33–37; cf. Matthew 24:42, 43; Luke 21:34–36; see Luke 12:36–38; Ephesians 6:18).

[SLEEP from asleep]
Setting: Gethsemane on the Mount of Olives, just east of the temple in Jerusalem. Jesus agonizes over His impending death, disappointed His disciples keep falling asleep instead of watching and praying with Him.

They came to a place named Gethsemane; and He said to the disciples, "Sit here until I have prayed." And He took with Him Peter and James and John, and began to be very distressed and troubled. And He said to them, "My soul is deeply grieved to the point of death; remain here and keep watch." And He went a little beyond *them,* and fell to the ground and *began* to pray that if it were possible, the hour might pass Him by. And He was saying, "Abba! Father! All things are possible for You; remove this cup from Me; yet not what I will, but what You will." And He came and found them sleeping, and said to Peter, "Simon, are you asleep? Could you not keep watch for one hour? Keep watching and praying that you may not come into temptation; the spirit is willing, but the flesh is weak" (Mark 14:32–38; cf. Matthew 26:36–41; Luke 22:41–46; see Romans 8:15; Galatians 4:6).

[SLEEP from sleeping]
Setting: Gethsemane on the Mount of Olives, just east of the temple in Jerusalem. Jesus prepares to meet Judas the betrayer, while His other disciples keep falling asleep instead of watching and praying with Him.

And He came the third time, and said to them, "Are you still sleeping and resting? It is enough; the hour has come; behold, the Son of Man is being betrayed into the hands of sinners. Get up, let us be going; behold, the one who betrays Me is at hand!" (Mark 14:41, 42; cf. Matthew 26:45, 46).

[SLEEP from sleeping]
Setting: Jerusalem. After celebrating the Passover meal and instructing His disciples to prepare to persevere without Him, with His crucifixion imminent, Jesus proceeds to the Mount of Olives to pray.

When He rose from prayer, He came to the disciples and found them sleeping from sorrow, and said to them, "Why are you sleeping? Get up and pray that you may not enter into temptation" (Luke 22:45, 46; cf. Matthew 26:40–46; Mark 14:37–42; see Matthew 4:11; Hebrews 5:7).

SLEEP (death)

[SLEEP from asleep]

Setting: Capernaum, near the Sea of Galilee. After healing a woman suffering with internal bleeding for twelve years, Jesus brings a synagogue official's daughter back from death.

When Jesus came into the official's house, and saw the flute-players and the crowd in noisy disorder, He said, "Leave; for the girl has not died, but is asleep." And they *began* laughing at Him. But when the crowd had been sent out, He entered and took her by the hand, and the girl got up (Matthew 9:23–25; cf. Mark 5:21–24, 35–43; Luke 8:41, 42, 49–56).

[SLEEP from asleep]

Setting: The home of Jairus, a synagogue official in Capernaum, by the Sea of Galilee. Jesus assures those present that Jairus' daughter has not died, but is only asleep.

And entering in, He said to them, "Why make a commotion and weep? The child has not died, but is asleep" (Mark 5:39; cf. Matthew 9:24; Luke 8:52; see Mark 5:37, 38, 40).

[SLEEP from asleep]

Setting: Capernaum. After healing a woman ill for twelve years, Jesus receives word that the daughter of a Galilee synagogue official has died.

But when Jesus heard *this,* He answered him, "Do not be afraid *any longer;* only believe and she will be made well." When He came to the house, He did not allow anyone to enter with Him except Peter and John and James and the girl's father and mother. Now they were all weeping and lamenting for her; but He said, "Stop weeping; for she has not died, but is asleep." And they *began* laughing at Him, knowing that she had died. He, however, took her by the hand and called, saying, "Child, arise!" And her spirit returned, and she got up immediately; and He gave orders for *something* to be given her to eat (Luke 8:50–55; cf. Matthew 9:18, 19, 23–26; Mark 5:21–24, 35–43).

[SLEEP from asleep]

Setting: Beyond the Jordan. While He and His disciples are avoiding the Jerusalem Pharisees, Jesus receives word from Lazarus's sisters in Bethany of His friend's sickness, and decides to go there.

Then after this He said to the disciples, "Let us go to Judea again." The disciples said to Him, "Rabbi, the Jews were just now seeking to stone You, and are You going there again?" Jesus answered, "Are there not twelve hours in the day? If anyone walks in the day, he does not stumble, because he sees the light of this world. But if anyone walks in the night, he stumbles, because the light is not in him." This He said, and after that He said to them, "Our friend Lazarus has fallen asleep; but I go, so that I may awaken him out of sleep" (John 11:7–11; see John 8:59; 10:39).

SLEEPING AND RESTING (Listed under RESTING, SLEEPING AND)

SMYRNA

Setting: On the island of Patmos (in the Aegean Sea about fifty miles southwest of Ephesus in modern Turkey). On the Lord's Day (Sunday), approximately fifty years after the Resurrection, the apostle John hears the voice of the Lord Jesus Christ, who communicates new revelations for the apostle to record for the seven churches in Asia.

I was in the Spirit on the Lord's day, and I heard behind me a loud voice like *the sound* of a trumpet, saying, "Write in a book what you see, and send *it* to the seven churches: to Ephesus and to Smyrna and to Pergamum and to Thyatira and to Sardis and to Philadelphia and to Laodicea" (Revelation 1:10, 11).

Setting: On the island of Patmos (in the Aegean Sea about fifty miles southwest of Ephesus in modern Turkey). On the Lord's Day (Sunday), approximately fifty years after the Resurrection, the disciple John encounters the Lord

Jesus Christ, who communicates a new revelation for the apostle to record for the church in Smyrna and to six other churches in Asia.

"And to the angel of the church in Smyrna write: The first and the last, who was dead, and has come to life, says this: 'I know your tribulation and your poverty (but you are rich), and the blasphemy by those who say they are Jews and are not, but are a synagogue of Satan. Do not fear what you are about to suffer. Behold, the devil is about to cast some of you into prison, so that you will be tested, and you will have tribulation for ten days. Be faithful until death, and I will give you the crown of life. He who has an ear, let him hear what the Spirit says to the churches. He who overcomes will not be hurt by the second death' (Revelation 2:8–11; see Isaiah 44:6; Revelation 1:9, 18; 20:6, 14).

SNAKE (Also see SERPENTS; SNAKES; and VIPERS, BROOD OF)

Setting: Galilee. During the early part of His ministry, Jesus preaches the Sermon on the Mount to His disciples and the multitudes.

"Ask, and it will be given to you; seek, and you will find; knock, and it will be opened to you. For everyone who asks receives, and he who seeks finds, and to him who knocks it will be opened. Or what man is there among you who, when his son asks for a loaf, will give him a stone? Or if he asks for a fish, he will not give him a snake, will he? If you then, being evil, know how to give good gifts to your children, how much more will your Father who is in heaven give what is good to those who ask Him! In everything, therefore, treat people the same way you want them to treat you, for this is the Law and the Prophets" (Matthew 7:7–12; cf. Matthew 22:40; Luke 6:31; Luke 11:9–13; see Psalm 84:11).

Setting: On the way from Galilee to Jerusalem. After revealing to His disciples how to pray, Jesus illustrates God's benevolence in answering prayer and giving the Holy Spirit.

"Now suppose one of you fathers is asked by his son for a fish; he will not give him a snake instead of a fish, will he? Or *if* he is asked for an egg, he will not give him a scorpion, will he? If you then, being evil, know how to give good gifts to your children, how much more will *your* heavenly Father give the Holy Spirit to those who ask Him?"
(Luke 11:11–13; cf. Matthew 7:9–11).

SNAKES (See SERPENT; SERPENTS; SNAKE; and VIPERS, BROOD OF)

SODOM

Setting: Galilee. After His twelve disciples observe His ministry, Jesus summons and specifically instructs them about their ministry to the people of Israel.

These twelve Jesus sent out after instructing them: "Do not go in *the* way of *the* Gentiles, and do not enter *any* city of the Samaritans; but rather go to the lost sheep of the house of Israel. And as you go, preach, saying, 'The kingdom of heaven is at hand.' Heal *the* sick, raise *the* dead, cleanse *the* lepers, cast out demons. Freely you received, freely give. Do not acquire gold, or silver, or copper for your money belts, or a bag for *your* journey, or even two coats, or sandals, or a staff; for the worker is worthy of his support. And whatever city or village you enter, inquire who is worthy in it, and stay at his house until you leave *that city*. As you enter the house, give it your greeting. If the house is worthy, give it your *blessing of* peace. But if it is not worthy, take back your *blessing of* peace. Whoever does not receive you, nor heed your words, as you go out of that house or that city, shake the dust off your feet. Truly I say to you, it will be more tolerable for *the* land of Sodom and Gomorrah in the day of judgment than for that city" (Matthew 10:5–15; cf. Mark 6:7–11; Luke 9:1–5; see Matthew 3:2; 11:22, 24; 15:24; Luke 22:35; 1 Corinthians 9:14).

Setting: Galilee. After performing miracles throughout the region, Jesus pronounces woes against those cities who do not repent.

"Woe to you, Chorazin! Woe to you, Bethsaida! For if the miracles had occurred in Tyre and Sidon which occurred in you, they would have repented long ago in sackcloth and ashes. Nevertheless I say to you, it will be more tolerable for Tyre and Sidon in *the* day of judgment than for you. And you, Capernaum, will not be exalted to heaven, will you? You will descend to Hades; for if the miracles had occurred in Sodom which occurred in you, it would have remained to this day. Nevertheless, I say to you that it will be more tolerable for the land of Sodom in *the* day of judgment, than for you" (Matthew 11:21–24; cf. Matthew 10:15; Luke 10:13–15).

Setting: On the way from Galilee to Jerusalem. The Lord appoints seventy followers and sends them out in pairs to every place He Himself will soon visit.

And He was saying to them, "The harvest is plentiful, but the laborers are few; therefore beseech the Lord of the harvest to send out laborers into His harvest. Go; behold, I send you out as lambs in the midst of wolves. Carry no money belt, no bag, no shoes; and greet no one on the way. Whatever house you enter, first say, 'Peace be to this house.' If a man of peace is there, your peace will rest on him; but if not, it will return to you. Stay in that house, eating and drinking what they give you; for the laborer is worthy of his wages. Do not keep moving from house to house. Whatever city you enter and they receive you, eat what is set before you; and heal those in it who are sick, and say to them, 'The kingdom of God has come near to you.' But whatever city you enter and they do not receive you, go out into its streets and say, 'Even the dust of your city which clings to our feet we wipe off *in protest* against you; yet be sure of this, that the kingdom of God has come near.' I say to you, it will be more tolerable in that day for Sodom than for that city" (Luke 10:2–12; see Genesis 19:24–28; Matthew 9:37, 38, 10:9–14, 16; 1 Corinthians 10:27).

Setting: On the way from Galilee to Jerusalem. After the Pharisees question Him about the coming of the kingdom of God, Jesus tells His disciples of His second coming.

And He said to the disciples, "The days will come when you will long to see one of the days of the Son of Man, and you will not see it. They will say to you, 'Look there! Look here!' Do not go away, and do not run after *them*. For just like the lightning, when it flashes out of one part of the sky, shines to the other part of the sky, so will the Son of Man be in His day. But first He must suffer many things and be rejected by this generation. And just as it happened in the days of Noah, so it will be also in the days of the Son of Man: they were eating, they were drinking, they were marrying, they were being given in marriage, until the day that Noah entered the ark, and the flood came and destroyed them all. It was the same as happened in the days of Lot: they were eating, they were drinking, they were buying, they were selling, they were planting, they were building; but on the day that Lot went out from Sodom it rained fire and brimstone from heaven and destroyed them all. It will be just the same on the day that the Son of Man is revealed. On that day, the one who is on the housetop and whose goods are in the house must not go down to take them out; and likewise the one who is in the field must not turn back. Remember Lot's wife. Whoever seeks to keep his life will lose it, and whoever loses *his life* will preserve it. I tell you, on that night there will be two in one bed; one will be taken and the other will be left. There will be two women grinding at the same place; one will be taken and the other will be left. [Two men will be in the field; one will be taken and the other will be left."] And answering they said to Him, "Where, Lord?" And He said to them, "Where the body *is*, there also the vultures will be gathered" (Luke 17:22–37; see Genesis 19; Matthew 10:39; 16:21, 27; 24:17–28, 37–41).

SOIL (Specifics such as SOIL, GOOD and SOIL, ROCKY are separate entries; also see EARTH; and GROUND)

Setting: By the Sea of Galilee. While teaching and preaching to the crowds from a boat, Jesus conveys the Parable of the Sower.

And He spoke many things to them in parables, saying, "Behold, the sower went out to sow; and as he sowed, some *seeds* fell beside the road, and the birds came and ate them up. Others fell on the rocky places, where they did not have much soil; and immediately they sprang up, because they had no depth of soil. But when the sun had risen, they were scorched; and because they had no root, they withered away. Others fell among the thorns, and the thorns came up and choked them out. And others fell on the good soil and yielded a crop, some a hundredfold, some sixty, and some thirty. He who has ears, let him hear" (Matthew 13:3–9; cf. Mark 4:3–9; Luke 8:4–8).

Setting: By the Sea of Galilee. During the early part of His ministry, just after a visit from his mother and brothers, Jesus instructs a very large crowd with the Parable of the Sower from a boat.

"Listen *to this!* Behold, the sower went out to sow; as he was sowing, some *seed* fell beside the road, and the birds came and ate it up. Other *seed* fell on the rocky *ground* where it did not have much soil; and immediately it sprang up because it had no depth of soil. And after the sun had risen, it was scorched; and because it had no root, it withered away. Other *seed* fell among the thorns, and the thorns came up and choked it, and it yielded no crop. Other *seeds* fell into the good soil, and as the grew up and increased, they yielded a crop and produced thirty, sixty, and a hundredfold." And He was saying, "He who has ears to hear, let him hear" (Mark 4:3–9; cf. Matthew 13:3–9; Luke 8:5–8).

Setting: Galilee. Following His explanation of the Parable of the Sower to His disciples, Jesus conveys the Parable of the Seed.

And He was saying, "The kingdom of God is like a man who casts seed upon the soil; and he goes to bed at night and gets up by day, and the seed sprouts and grows—how, he himself does not know. The soil produces crops by itself; first the blade, then the head, then the mature grain in the head. But when the crop permits, he immediately puts in the sickle, because the harvest has come" (Mark 4:26–29; see Joel 3:13)

Setting: Galilee. After giving the Parable of the Sower and the Parable of the Seed, Jesus continues teaching His disciples by presenting the Parable of the Mustard Seed.

And He said, "How shall we picture the kingdom of God, or by what parable shall we present it? *It is* like a mustard seed, which, when sown upon the soil, though it is smaller than all the seeds that are upon the soil, yet when it is sown, it grows up and becomes larger than all the garden plants and forms large branches; so that THE BIRDS OF THE AIR can NEST UNDER ITS SHADE" (Mark 4:30–32, Jesus quotes from Ezekiel 17:23; cf. Matthew 13:31, 32; Luke 13:18, 19).

Setting: On the way from Galilee to Jerusalem. After He responds to a guest's proclamation about the blessings of eating bread in the kingdom of God, Jesus presents to large crowds the demands of discipleship.

Now large crowds were going along with Him; and He turned and said to them, "If anyone comes to Me, and does not hate his own father and mother and wife and children and brothers and sisters, yes, and even his own life, he cannot be My disciple. Whoever does not carry his own cross and come after Me cannot be My disciple. For which one of you, when he wants to build a tower, does not first sit down and calculate the cost to see if he has enough to complete it? Otherwise, when he has laid a foundation and is not able to finish, all who observe it begin to ridicule him, saying, 'This man began to build and was not able to finish.' Or what king, when he sets out to meet another king in battle, will not first sit down and consider whether he is strong enough with ten thousand *men* to encounter the one coming against him with twenty thousand? Or else, while the other is still far away, he sends a delegation and asks for terms of peace. So then, none of you can be My disciple who does not give up all his possessions. Therefore, salt is good; but if even salt has become tasteless, with what will it be seasoned? It is useless either for the soil or for the manure pile; it is thrown out. He who has ears to hear, let him hear" (Luke 14:25–35; cf. Matthew 5:13; 10:37–39; see Proverb 20:18; Philippians 3:7).

SOIL, GOOD

Setting: By the Sea of Galilee. While teaching and preaching to the crowds from a boat, Jesus conveys the Parable of the Sower.

And He spoke many things to them in parables, saying, "Behold, the sower went out to sow; and as he sowed, some *seeds* fell beside the road, and the birds came and ate them up. Others fell on the rocky places, where they did not have much soil; and immediately they sprang up, because they had no depth of soil. But when the sun had risen, they were scorched; and because they had no root, they withered away. Others fell among the thorns, and the thorns came up and choked them out. And others fell on the good soil and yielded a crop, some a hundredfold, some sixty, and some thirty. He who has ears, let him hear" (Matthew 13:3–9; cf. Mark 4:3–9; Luke 8:4–8).

Setting: By the Sea of Galilee. With the religious leaders rejecting His message, Jesus begins to teach in parables, and gives His disciples the meaning of the Parable of the Sower.

"Hear then the parable of the sower. When anyone hears the word of the kingdom and does not understand it, the evil *one* comes and snatches away what has been sown in his heart. This is the one on whom seed was sown beside the road. The one on whom seed was sown on the rocky places, this is the man who hears the word and immediately receives it with joy; yet he has no *firm* root in himself, but is *only* temporary, and when affliction or persecution arises because of the word, immediately he falls away. And the one on whom seed was sown among the thorns, this is the man who hears the word, and the worry of the world and the deceitfulness of wealth choke the word, and it becomes unfruitful. And the one on whom seed was sown on the good soil, this is the man who hears the word and understands it; who indeed bears fruit and brings forth, some a hundredfold, some sixty, and some thirty" (Matthew 13:18–23; cf. Mark 4:13–20; Luke 8:11–15).

Setting: By the Sea of Galilee. During the early part of His ministry, just after a visit from his mother and brothers, Jesus instructs a very large crowd with the Parable of the Sower from a boat.

"Listen *to this!* Behold, the sower went out to sow; as he was sowing, some *seed* fell beside the road, and the birds came and ate it up. Other *seed* fell on the rocky *ground* where it did not have much soil; and immediately it sprang up because it had no depth of soil. And after the sun had risen, it was scorched; and because it had no root, it withered away. Other *seed* fell among the thorns, and the thorns came up and choked it, and it yielded no crop. Other *seeds* fell into the good soil, and as the grew up and increased, they yielded a crop and produced thirty, sixty, and a hundredfold." And He was saying, "He who has ears to hear, let him hear" (Mark 4:3–9; cf. Matthew 13:3–9; Luke 8:5–8).

Setting: By the Sea of Galilee. During the early part of His ministry, after presenting the Parable of the Sower from a boat to a very large crowd, Jesus gives the meaning of the parable to His disciples and other followers.

And He said to them, "Do you not understand this parable? How will you understand all the parables? The sower sows the word. These are the ones who are beside the road where the word is sown; and when they hear, immediately Satan comes and takes away the word which has been sown in them. In a similar way these are the ones on whom seed was sown on the rocky places, who, when they hear the word, immediately receive it with joy; and they have no *firm* root in themselves, but are *only* temporary; then, when affliction or persecution arises because of the word, immediately they fall away. And others are the ones on whom seed was sown among the thorns; these are the ones who have heard the word, but the worries of the world and the deceitfulness of riches, and the desires for other things enter in and choke the word, and it becomes unfruitful. And those are the ones on whom seed was sown on the good soil; and they hear the word and accept it and bear fruit, thirty, sixty, and a hundredfold" (Mark 4:13–20; cf. Matthew 13:18–23; Luke 8:11–15).

Setting: Galilee. After His visit in the home of Simon the Pharisee, Jesus goes into the villages and cities, proclaiming and preaching the kingdom of God.

When a large crowd was coming together, and those from various cities were journeying to Him, He spoke by way of a parable: "The sower went out to sow his seed; and as he sowed, some fell beside the road, and it was trampled under foot and the birds of the air ate it up. Other *seed* fell on rocky *soil,* and as soon as it grew up, it was withered away, because it had no moisture. Other *seed* fell among the thorns; and the thorns grew up with it and choked it out. Other *seed* fell into the good soil, and grew up, and produced a crop a hundred times as great." As He said these things, He would call out, "He who has ears to hear, let him hear" (Luke 8:4–8; cf. Matthew 13:2–9; Mark 4:3–9).

Setting: Galilee. After Jesus presents the Parable of the Sower to the crowds, His disciples ask Him to give them the parable's meaning.

And He said, "To you it has been granted to know the mysteries of the kingdom of God, but to the rest *it is* in parables, so that SEEING THEY MAY NOT SEE, AND HEARING THEY MAY NOT UNDERSTAND. Now the parable is this: the seed is the word of God. Those beside the road are those who have heard; then the devil comes and takes away the word from their heart, so that they will not believe and be saved. Those on the rocky *soil* are those who, when they hear, receive the word with joy; and these have no *firm* root; they believe for a while, and in time of temptation fall away. The *seed* which fell among the thorns, these are the ones who have heard, and as they go on their way they are choked with worries and riches and pleasures of *this* life, and bring no fruit to maturity. But the *seed* in the good soil, these are the ones who have heard the word in an honest and good heart, and hold it fast, and bear fruit with perseverance" (Luke 8:10–15, Jesus quotes from Isaiah 6:9; cf. Matthew 13:10–23; Mark 4:10–20).

SOIL, ROCKY (Also see GROUND, ROCKY and PLACES, ROCKY)

Setting: Galilee. After His visit in the home of Simon the Pharisee, Jesus goes into the villages and cities, proclaiming and preaching the kingdom of God.

When a large crowd was coming together, and those from various cities were journeying to Him, He spoke by way of a parable: "The sower went out to sow his seed; and as he sowed, some fell beside the road, and it was trampled under foot and the birds of the air ate it up. Other *seed* fell on rocky *soil,* and as soon as it grew up, it was withered away, because it had no moisture. Other *seed* fell among the thorns; and the thorns grew up with it and choked it out. Other *seed* fell into the good soil, and grew up, and produced a crop a hundred times as great." As He said these things, He would call out, "He who has ears to hear, let him hear" (Luke 8:4–8; cf. Matthew 13:2–9; Mark 4:3–9).

Setting: Galilee. After Jesus presents the Parable of the Sower to the crowds, His disciples ask Him to give them the parable's meaning.

And He said, "To you it has been granted to know the mysteries of the kingdom of God, but to the rest *it is* in parables, so that SEEING THEY MAY NOT SEE, AND HEARING THEY MAY NOT UNDERSTAND. Now the parable is this: the seed is the word of God. Those beside the road are those who have heard; then the devil comes and takes away the word from their heart, so that they will not believe and be saved. Those on the rocky *soil* are those who, when they hear, receive the word with joy; and these have no *firm* root; they believe for a while, and in time of temptation fall away. The *seed* which fell among the thorns, these are the ones who have heard, and as they go on their way they are choked with worries and riches and pleasures of *this* life, and bring no fruit to maturity. But the *seed* in the good soil, these are the ones who have heard the word in an honest and good heart, and hold it fast, and bear fruit with perseverance" (Luke 8:10–15, Jesus quotes from Isaiah 6:9; cf. Matthew 13:10–23; Mark 4:10–20).

SOILS, PARABLE OF THE (See SOWER, PARABLE OF THE)

SOLES

Setting: Jesus' hometown of Nazareth in Galilee. After encountering unbelief, Jesus sends the Twelve out in pairs with authority and instructions about ministry.

And He summoned the twelve and began to send them out in pairs, and gave them authority over the unclean spirits; and He instructed them that they should take nothing for *their* journey, except a mere staff—no bread, no bag, no money in their belt—but to wear sandals; and *He added,* "Do not put on two tunics." And He said to them, "Wherever you enter a house, stay there until you leave town. Any place that does not receive you or listen to you, as you go out from there, shake the dust off the soles of your feet for a testimony against them" (Mark 6:7–11; cf. Matthew 10:1–14; Luke 9:1–5).

SOLID FOUNDATION (Listed under FOUNDATION, SOLID)

SOLOMON (Also see KING and KINGS)

Setting: Galilee. During the early part of His ministry, Jesus preaches the Sermon on the Mount to His disciples and the multitudes.

"For this reason I say to you, do not be worried about your life, *as to* what you will eat or what you will drink; nor for your body, *as to* what you will put on. Is not life more than food, and the body more than clothing? Look at the birds of the air, that they do not sow, nor reap nor gather into barns, and *yet* your heavenly Father feeds them. Are you not worth much more than they? And who of you by being worried can add a *single* hour to his life? And why are you worried about clothing? Observe how the lilies of the field grow; they do not toil nor do they spin, yet I say to you that not even Solomon in all his glory clothed himself like one of these. But if God so clothes the grass of the field, which is *alive* today and tomorrow is thrown into the furnace, *will He* not much more *clothe* you? You of little faith! Do not worry then, saying 'What will we eat?' or 'What will we drink?' or 'What will be wear for clothing?" For the Gentiles eagerly seek all these things; for your heavenly Father knows that you need all these things. But seek first His kingdom and His righteousness, and all these things will be added to you. So do not worry about tomorrow; for tomorrow will care for itself. Each day has enough trouble of its own" (Matthew 6:25–34; cf. Luke 12:22–31; see 1 Kings 10:4–7; Job 35:11; Matthew 8:26).

Setting: Galilee. After Jesus warns the Pharisees about the unpardonable sin and their future judgment, some Pharisees and scribes ask Him to perform a miraculous sign for them in front of the crowds.

But He answered and said to them, "An evil and adulterous generation craves for a sign; and *yet* no sign will be given to it but the sign of Jonah the prophet; for just as JONAH WAS THREE DAYS AND THREE NIGHTS IN THE BELLY OF THE SEA MONSTER, so will the Son of Man be three days and three nights in the heart of the earth. The men of Nineveh will stand up with this generation at the judgment, and will condemn it because they repented at the preaching of Jonah; and behold, something greater than Jonah is here. *The* Queen of *the* South will rise up with this generation at the judgment and will condemn it, because she came from the ends of the earth to hear the wisdom of Solomon; and behold, something greater than Solomon is here" (Matthew 12:39–42; Jesus quotes from Jonah 1:17; cf. 1 Kings 10:1; Jonah 3:5; Matthew 16:1, 4; Luke 11:29).

Setting: On the way from Galilee to Jerusalem. After revealing a problem with exorcism and responding to a blessing from a woman in the crowd, Jesus tells the increasing crowds of the sign of Jonah.

As the crowds were increasing, He began to say, "This generation is a wicked generation; it seeks for a sign, and *yet* no sign will be given to it but the sign of Jonah. For just as Jonah became a sign to the Ninevites, so will the Son of Man be to this generation. The Queen of the South will rise up with the men of this generation at the judgment and condemn them, because she came from the ends of the earth to hear the wisdom of Solomon; and behold, something greater than Solomon is here. The men of Nineveh will stand up with this generation at the judgment and condemn it, because they repented at the preaching of Jonah; and behold, something greater than Jonah is here" (Luke 11:29–32; cf. Matthew 16:4; see 1 Kings 10:1–10; Jonah 3:4, 5).

Setting: On the way from Galilee to Jerusalem. After giving a parable about riches and greed, Jesus comforts the crowd and His disciples. The scribes and Pharisees turn hostile and question Him repeatedly in an attempt to catch Him in something He might say.

And He said to His disciples, "For this reason I say to you, do not worry about *your* life, *as to* what you will eat; nor for your body, *as to* what you will put on. For life is more than food, and the body more than clothing. Consider the ravens, for they neither sow nor reap; they have no storeroom nor barn, and *yet* God feeds them; how much more valuable you are than the birds! And which of you by worrying can add a *single* hour to his life's span? If then you cannot do even a very little thing, why do you worry about other matters? Consider the lilies, how they grow: they neither toil nor spin; but I tell you, not even Solomon in all his glory clothed himself like one of these. But if God so clothes the grass in the field, which is *alive* today and tomorrow is thrown into the furnace, how much more *will He clothe* you? You men of little faith! And do not seek what you will eat and what you will drink, and do not keep worrying. For all these things the nations of the world eagerly seek; but your Father knows that you need these things. But seek His kingdom, and these things will be added to you. Do not be afraid, little flock, for your Father has chosen gladly to give you the kingdom" (Luke 12:22–32; cf. Matthew 6:25–33; see 1 Kings 10:4–7; Job 38:41).

SOLOMON, WISDOM OF (See SOLOMON)

SOMEONE

Setting: Galilee. After Jesus ministers in the country of the Gerasenes east of Galilee, a woman, ill for twelve years, receives healing by touching His garment.

And Jesus said, "Who is the one who touched Me?" And while they were all denying it, Peter said, "Master, the people are crowding and pressing in on You." But Jesus said, "Someone did touch Me, for I was aware, that power had gone out of Me." When the woman saw that she had not escaped notice, she came trembling and fell down before Him, and declared in the presence of all the people the reason why she had touched Him, and how she had been immediately healed. And He said to her, "Daughter, your faith has made you well; go in peace" (Luke 8:45–48; cf. Matthew 9:20; Mark 5:25–34).

Setting: On the way from Galilee to Jerusalem. After some in the crowd test Him, demanding a sign from heaven, Jesus illustrates His power over Satan.

"When a strong *man*, fully armed, guards his own house, his possessions are undisturbed. But when someone stronger than he attacks him and overpowers him, he takes away from him all his armor on which he had relied and distributes his plunder. He who is not with Me is against Me; and he who does not gather with Me, scatters" (Luke 11:21–23; cf. Matthew 12:29, 30).

Setting: On the way from Galilee to Jerusalem. As He observes the invited guests selecting places of honor at table in the house of a Pharisee leader on the Sabbath, Jesus speaks a parable to them.

And He *began* speaking a parable to the invited guests when He noticed how they had been picking out the places of honor *at the table,* saying to them, "When you are invited by someone to a wedding feast, do not take the place of honor, for someone more distinguished than you may have been invited by him, and he who invited you both will come and say to you, 'Give *your* place to this man, and then in disgrace you proceed to occupy the last place. But when you are invited, go and recline at the last place, so that when the one who has invited you comes, he may say to you, 'Friend, move up higher'; then you will have honor in the sight of all who are at the table with you. For everyone who exalts himself will be humbled, and he who humbles himself will be exalted" (Luke 14:7–11; see 2 Samuel 22:28; Proverb 25:6, 7; Matthew 23:6).

Setting: On the way from Galilee to Jerusalem. After responding to the Pharisees' scoffing at His teaching the disciples about stewardship and the permanence of the Law, Jesus conveys the story of the rich man and Lazarus.

"Now there was a rich man, and he habitually dressed in purple and fine linen, joyously living in splendor every day. And a poor man named Lazarus was laid at his gate, covered with sores, and longing to be fed with the *crumbs* which were falling from the rich man's table; besides, even the dogs were coming and licking his sores. Now the poor man died and was carried away by the angels to Abraham's bosom; and the rich man also died and was buried. In Hades he lifted up his eyes, being in torment, and saw Abraham far away and Lazarus in his bosom. And he cried out and said, 'Father Abraham, have mercy on me, and send Lazarus so that he may dip the tip of his finger in water and cool off my tongue, for I am in agony in this flame.' But Abraham said, 'Child, remember that during your life you received your good things, and likewise Lazarus bad things; but now he is being comforted here, and you are in agony. And besides all this, between us and you there is a great chasm fixed, so that those who wish to come over from here to you will not be able, and *that* none may cross over from there to us.' And he said, 'Then I beg you, father, that you send him to my father's house—for I have five brothers—in order that he may warn them, so that they will not also come to this place of torment.' But Abraham said, 'They have Moses and the Prophets; let them hear them.' But he said, 'No, father Abraham, but if someone goes to them from the dead, they will repent!' But he said to him, 'If they do not listen to Moses and the Prophets, they will not be persuaded even if someone rises from the dead'" (Luke 16:19–31; see Luke 3:8; 6:24).

Setting: By the Sea of Galilee. During the Lord's third post-resurrection appearance to His disciples, after quizzing Peter three times regarding the disciple's love for Him, Jesus gives him details about his aging and eventual death.

"Truly, truly, I say to you, when you were younger, you used to gird yourself and walk wherever you wished; but when you grow old, you will stretch out your hands and someone else will gird you, and bring you where you do not wish to *go*." Now this He said, signifying by what kind of death he would glorify God. And when He had spoken this, He said to him, "Follow Me!" (John 21:18, 19).

SOMETHING (Also see ANYTHING)

Setting: Galilee. During the early part of His ministry, Jesus preaches the Sermon on the Mount to His disciples and the multitudes.

"Therefore if you are presenting your offering at the altar, and there remember that your brother has something against you, leave your offering there before the altar and go; first be reconciled to your brother, and then come and present your offering" (Matthew 5:23, 24; see Romans 12:17, 18).

Setting: Galilee. Jesus responds to the Pharisees' objection to His disciples' picking grain from the fields on the Sabbath.

But He said to them, "Have you not read what David did when he became hungry, he and his companions, how they entered the house of God, and ate the consecrated bread, which was not lawful for him to eat nor for those with him, but for the priests alone? Or, have you not read in the Law, that on the Sabbath the priests in the temple break the Sabbath and are innocent? But I say to you that something greater than the temple is here. But if you had known what this means, 'I DESIRE COMPASSION, AND NOT A SACRIFICE,' you would not have condemned the innocent. For the Son of Man is Lord of the Sabbath" (Matthew 12:3–8, Jesus quotes from Hosea 6:6; cf. Mark 2:25–28; Luke 6:3–5; see 1 Samuel 21:6).

Setting: Galilee. After Jesus warns the Pharisees about the unpardonable sin and their future judgment, some Pharisees and scribes ask Him to perform a miraculous sign for them in front of the crowds.

But He answered and said to them, "An evil and adulterous generation craves for a sign; and *yet* no sign will be given to it but the sign of Jonah the prophet; for just as JONAH WAS THREE DAYS AND THREE NIGHTS IN THE BELLY OF THE SEA MONSTER, so will the Son of Man be three days and three nights in the heart of the earth. The men of Nineveh will stand up with this generation at the judgment, and will condemn it because they repented at the preaching of Jonah; and behold, something greater than Jonah is here. *The* Queen of *the* South will rise up with this generation at the judgment and will condemn it, because she came from the ends of the earth to hear the wisdom of Solomon; and behold, something greater than Solomon is here" (Matthew 12:39–42; Jesus quotes from Jonah 1:17; cf. 1 Kings 10:1; Jonah 3:5; Matthew 16:1, 4; Luke 11:29).

Setting: By the Sea of Galilee. Late in the day, after He hears the news of John the Baptist's beheading and heals the sick in the crowd following Him, Jesus miraculously feeds more than 5,000 of His countrymen.

But Jesus said to them, "They do not need to go away; you give them *something* to eat!" They said to Him, "We have here only five loaves and two fish." And He said, "Bring them here to Me" (Matthew 14:16–18; cf. Mark 6:35–44; Luke 9:12–17; John 6:4–13; see Matthew 16:9).

Setting: On the Mount of Olives, just east of Jerusalem. During His Olivet Discourse, after answering His disciples' questions as to when the temple will be destroyed and Jerusalem overrun, along with the signs of His coming and the end of the age, Jesus reveals the future judgments following His return.

"But when the Son of Man comes in His glory, and all the angels with Him, then He will sit on His glorious throne. All the nations will be gathered before Him; and He will separate them from one another, as the shepherd separates the sheep from the goats; and He will put the sheep on His right, and the goats on the left. Then the King will say to those on His right, 'Come, you who are blessed of My Father, inherit the kingdom prepared for you from the foundation of the world. 'For I was hungry, and you gave Me *something* to eat; I was thirsty, and you gave Me *something* to drink; I was a stranger, and you invited Me in; naked, and you clothed Me; I was sick, and you visited Me; I was in prison, and you came to Me.' Then the righteous will answer Him, 'Lord, when did we see You hungry and feed You, or thirsty, and give you *something* to drink? And when did we see You a stranger, and invite You in, or naked, and clothe You? When did we see You sick, or in prison, and come to You?' The King will answer and say to them, 'Truly I say to you, to the extent that you did it to one of these brothers of Mine, *even* the least *of them,* you did it to Me.' Then He will also say to those on His left, 'Depart from Me, accursed ones, into the eternal fire which has been prepared for the devil and his angels; for I was hungry, and you gave Me *nothing* to eat; I was thirsty, and you gave Me nothing to drink; I was a stranger, and you did not invite Me in; naked, and you did not clothe Me; sick, and in prison, and you did not visit Me.' Then they themselves also will answer, 'Lord, when did we see You hungry, or thirsty, or a stranger, or naked, or sick, or in prison, and did not take care of You?' Then He will answer them, 'Truly I say to you, to the extent that you did not do it to one of the least of these, you did not do it to Me.' These will go away into eternal punishment, but the righteous into eternal life" (Matthew 25:31–46; see Matthew 7:23; 16:27; 19:29).

Setting: By the Sea of Galilee. After a long day of ministry, Jesus prepares to demonstrate to His disciples the power of God by feeding more than 5,000 people.

But He answered them, "You give them *something* to eat!" And they said to Him, "Shall we go and spend two hundred denarii on bread and give them *something* to eat? And He said to them, "How many loaves do you have? Go look!" And when they found out, they said, "Five, and two fish" (Mark 6:37, 38; cf. Matthew 14:16, 17; Luke 9:13, 14; John 6:5–9; see Mark 3:20).

Setting: Galilee. After Jesus praises John the Baptist to the crowds, Simon, a Pharisee, invites the Lord to dinner. A sinful woman anoints His feet with perfume, prompting Him to convey a parable.

And Jesus answered him, "Simon, I have something to say to you." And he replied, "Say it, Teacher." "A moneylender had two debtors: one owed five hundred denarii, and the other fifty. When they were unable to repay, he graciously forgave them both. So which of them will love him more?" Simon answered and said, "I suppose the one whom he forgave more." And He said to him, "You have judged correctly" (Luke 7:40–43; see Matthew 18:23–35).

Setting: Galilee. Following a day of ministry, Jesus and His disciples try to withdraw to Bethsaida, but the large crowds have been relishing His teaching about the kingdom of God all day, so they must be fed physically, too.

But He said to them, "You give them *something* to eat!" And they said, "We have no more than five loaves and two fish, unless perhaps we go and buy food for all these people." (For there were about five thousand men.) And He said to His disciples, "Have them sit down *to eat* in groups of about fifty each" (Luke 9:13, 14; cf. Matthew 14:15–21; Mark 6:35–44; John 6:4–13).

Setting: On the way from Galilee to Jerusalem. After revealing a problem with exorcism and responding to a blessing from a woman in the crowd, Jesus tells the increasing crowds of the sign of Jonah.

As the crowds were increasing, He began to say, "This generation is a wicked generation; it seeks for a sign, and *yet* no sign will be given to it but the sign of Jonah. For just as Jonah became a sign to the Ninevites, so will the Son of Man be to this generation. The Queen of the South will rise up with the men of this generation at the judgment and condemn them, because she came from the ends of the earth to hear the wisdom of Solomon; and behold, something greater than Solomon is here. The men of Nineveh will stand up with this generation at the judgment and condemn it, because they repented at the preaching of Jonah; and behold, something greater than Jonah is here" (Luke 11:29–32; cf. Matthew 16:4; see 1 Kings 10:1–10; Jonah 3:4, 5).

Setting: On the way from Galilee to Jerusalem. After His disciples ask that their faith be increased following His instruction to them on forgiveness, the Lord illustrates with the mustard seed and an obedient slave.

And the Lord said, "If you had faith like a mustard seed, you would say to this mulberry tree, 'Be uprooted and be planted in the sea'; and it would obey you. Which of you, having a slave plowing or tending sheep, will say to him when he has come from the field, 'Come immediately and sit down to eat'? But will he not say to him, "Prepare something for me to eat, and *properly* clothe yourself and serve me while I eat and drink; and afterward you may eat and drink'? He does not thank the slave because he did the things which were commanded, does he? So you too, when you do all the things which are commanded you, say, 'We are unworthy slaves; we have done *only* that which we ought to have done' " (Luke 17:6–10; see Matthew 13:31; Luke 12:37).

Setting: By the pool of Bethesda in Jerusalem. During a feast of the Jews, Jesus responds to criticism from the Jewish religious leaders for healing a lame man on the Sabbath and for referring to God as His Father (thereby making Himself equal with God).

Therefore Jesus answered and was saying to them, "Truly, truly, I say to you, the Son can do nothing of Himself, unless *it is* something He sees the Father doing; for whatever the Father does, these things the Son also does in like manner. For the Father loves the Son, and shows Him all things that He Himself is doing; and *the Father* will show Him greater works than these, so that you will marvel. For just as the Father raises the dead and gives them life, even so the Son also gives life to whom He wishes. For not even the Father judges anyone, but He has given all judgment to the Son, so that all will honor the Son even as they honor the Father. He who does not honor the Son does not honor the Father who sent Him" (John 5:19–23; see Luke 10:16; John 3:35; 11:25; 14:12).

SON (human; also see SON [Jesus]; and SONS)

Setting: Galilee. During the early part of His ministry, Jesus preaches the Sermon on the Mount to His disciples and the multitudes.

"Ask, and it will be given to you; seek, and you will find; knock, and it will be opened to you. For everyone who asks receives, and he who seeks finds, and to him who knocks it will be opened. Or what man is there among you who, when his son asks for a loaf, will give him a stone? Or if he asks for a fish, he will not give him a snake, will he? If you then, being evil, know how to give good gifts to your children, how much more will your Father who is in heaven give what is good to those who ask Him! In everything, therefore, treat people the same way you want them to treat you, for this is the Law and the Prophets" (Matthew 7:7–12; cf. Matthew 22:40; Luke 6:31; 11:9–13; see Psalm 84:11).

Setting: Capernaum, near the Sea of Galilee. After Jesus heals a paralytic and forgives his sins in front of crowds, some scribes accuse the Lord of blasphemy.

And they brought to Him a paralytic lying on a bed. Seeing their faith, Jesus said to the paralytic, "Take courage, son; your sins are forgiven." And some scribes said to themselves. "This *fellow* blasphemes." And Jesus knowing their thoughts said, "Why are you thinking evil in your hearts? Which is easier to say, 'Your sins are forgiven,' or to say, 'Get up, and walk'? But so that you may know that the Son of Man has authority on earth to forgive sins"—then He said to the paralytic, "Get up, pick up your bed and go home" (Matthew 9:2–6; cf. Mark 2:3–12; Luke 5:17–26).

Setting: Galilee. After His twelve disciples observe His ministry, Jesus summons and specifically instructs them about their ministry ahead involving true discipleship.

"He who loves father or mother more than Me is not worthy of Me; and he who loves son or daughter more than Me is not worthy of Me. And he who does not take his cross and follow after Me is not worthy of Me. He who has found his life will lose it, and he who has lost his life for My sake will find it" (Matthew 10:37–39; cf. Matthew 16:24, 25).

Setting: The temple in Jerusalem. Jesus delivers a parable to the chief priests and elders after they question His authority.

"But what do you think? A man had two sons, and he came to the first and said, 'Son, go work today in the vineyard.' And he answered, 'I will not'; but afterward he regretted it and went. The man came to the second and said the same thing; and he answered, 'I *will,* sir'; but he did not go. Which of the two sons did the will of his father?" They said, "The first." Jesus said to them, "Truly, I say to you that the tax collectors and prostitutes will get into the kingdom of God before you. For John came to you in the way of righteousness and you did not believe him; but the tax collectors and prostitutes did believe him; and you, seeing *this,* did not even feel remorse afterward so as to believe him" (Matthew 21:28–32; cf. Luke 7:29, 30, 37–50).

Setting: The temple in Jerusalem. Jesus delivers another parable to the chief priests and elders after they question His authority.

"Listen to another parable. There was a landowner who PLANTED A VINEYARD AND PUT A WALL AROUND IT AND DUG A WINE PRESS IN IT, AND BUILT A TOWER, and rented it out to vine-growers and went on a journey. When the harvest time approached, he sent his

slaves to the vine-growers to receive his produce. The vine-growers took his slaves and beat one, and killed another, and stoned a third. Again he sent another group of slaves larger than the first; and they did the same thing to them. But afterward he sent his son to them, saying, 'They will respect my son.' But when the vine-growers saw the son, they said among themselves, 'This is the heir; come, let us kill him and seize his inheritance.' They took him, and threw him out of the vineyard and killed him. Therefore when the owner of the vineyard comes, what will he do to those vine-growers?" (Matthew 21:33–40; Jesus quotes from Isaiah 5:1, 2; cf. Mark 12:1–9; Luke 20:9–15).

Setting: The temple in Jerusalem. Jesus speaks another parable to the chief priests and elders after they question His authority.

Jesus spoke to them again in parables, saying, "The kingdom of heaven may be compared to a king who gave a wedding feast for his son. And he sent out his slaves to call those who had been invited to the wedding feast, and they were unwilling to come. Again he sent out other slaves saying, 'Tell those who have been invited, "Behold, I have prepared my dinner; my oxen and my fattened livestock are *all* butchered and everything is ready; come to the wedding feast." But they paid no attention and went their way, one to his own farm, another to his business, and the rest seized his slaves and mistreated them and killed them. But the king was enraged, and he sent his armies and destroyed those murderers and set their city on fire. Then he said to his slaves, 'The wedding is ready, but those who were invited were not worthy. 'Go therefore to the main highways, and as many as you find *there,* invite to the wedding feast.' Those slaves went out into the streets and gathered together all they found, both evil and good; and the wedding hall was filled with dinner guests. But when the king came in to look over the dinner guests, he saw a man there who was not dressed in wedding clothes, and he said to him, 'Friend, how did you come in here without wedding clothes?' And the man was speechless. Then the king said to the servants, 'Bind him hand and foot, and throw him into the outer darkness; in that place there will be weeping and gnashing of teeth.' For many are called, but few *are* chosen" (Matthew 22:1–14; cf. Matthew 8:11, 12).

Setting: The temple in Jerusalem. After the Jewish religious leaders test Him with questions, Jesus pronounces the third of eight woes on them in front of the crowds and His disciples.

"Woe to you, scribes and Pharisees, hypocrites, because you travel around on sea and land to make one proselyte; and when he becomes one, you make him twice as much a son of hell as yourselves" (Matthew 23:15).

Setting: The temple in Jerusalem. After the Jewish religious leaders test Him with questions, Jesus pronounces the eighth of eight woes upon them in front of the crowds and His disciples.

"Woe to you, scribes and Pharisees, hypocrites! For you build the tombs of the prophets and adorn the monuments of the righteous, and say, 'If we had been *living* in the days of our fathers, we would not have been partners with them in *shedding* the blood of the prophets.' So you testify against yourselves, that you are sons of those who murdered the prophets. Fill up, then, the measure *of the guilt* of you fathers. You serpents, you brood of vipers, how will you escape the sentence of hell? Therefore, behold, I am sending you prophets and wise men and scribes; some of them you will kill and crucify, and some of them you will scourge in your synagogues, and persecute from city to city, so that upon you may fall *the guilt of* all the righteous blood shed on earth, from the blood of righteous Abel to the blood of Zechariah, the son of Berechiah, whom you murdered between the temple and the altar. Truly I say to you, all these things will come upon this generation" (Matthew 23:29–36; cf. 2 Chronicles 24:21; Zechariah 1:1; Matthew 3:7; Luke 11:47–52; see Matthew 10:23).

Setting: Galilee. Early in Jesus' gospel-preaching ministry, word of His healing abilities spreads, so some friends bring a paralytic man to Him for healing.

And Jesus seeing their faith said to the paralytic, "Son, your sins are forgiven" (Mark 2:5; cf. Matthew 9:1–3; Luke 5:17–20).

Setting: The temple in Jerusalem. Having His authority questioned by the chief priests, scribes, and elders, Jesus begins to teach them in parables.

And He began to speak to them in parables: "A man PLANTED A VINEYARD AND PUT A WALL AROUND IT, AND DUG A VAT UNDER THE WINE PRESS AND BUILT A TOWER, and rented it out to vine-growers and went on a journey. At the *harvest* time he sent a slave to the vine-growers, in order to receive *some* of the produce of the vineyard from the vine-growers. They took him, and beat him and sent him away empty-handed. Again he sent them another slave, and they wounded him in the head, and treated him shamefully. And he sent another, and that one they killed; and *so with* many others, beating some and killing others. He had one more to *send*, a beloved son; he sent him last *of all* to them, saying, 'They will respect my son.' But those vine-growers said to one another, 'This is the heir; come, let us kill him, and the inheritance will be ours!' They took him, and killed him and threw him out of the vineyard. What will the owner of the vineyard do? He will come and destroy the vine-growers, and will give the vineyard to others. Have you not even read this Scripture: 'THE STONE WHICH THE BUILDERS REJECTED, THIS BECAME THE CHIEF CORNER *stone;* THIS CAME ABOUT FROM THE LORD, AND IT IS MARVELOUS IN OUR EYES'?" (Mark 12:1–11, Jesus quotes from Psalm 118:22, 23; Isaiah 5:1, 2; cf. Matthew 21:33–46; Luke 20:9–19).

Setting: The temple in Jerusalem. After commending a scribe for his nearness to the kingdom of God, Jesus teaches the crowd.

And Jesus *began* to say, as He taught in the temple, "How *is it that* the scribes say that the Christ is the son of David? David himself said in the Holy Spirit, 'THE LORD SAID TO MY LORD, SIT AT MY RIGHT HAND, UNTIL I PUT YOUR ENEMIES BENEATH YOUR FEET."' David himself calls Him 'Lord'; so in what sense is He his son?" And the large crowd enjoyed listening to Him (Mark 12:35–37, Jesus quotes from Psalm 110:1; cf. Matthew 22:41–46; Luke 20:41–44).

Setting: Galilee. The day after Jesus' transfiguration on a mountain in the area, a man from a large crowd begs Jesus to look at his demon-possessed son.

And Jesus answered and said, "You unbelieving and perverted generation, how long shall I be with you and put up with you? Bring your son here" (Luke 9:41; cf. Matthew 17:14–18; Mark 9:14–27).

Setting: On the way from Galilee to Jerusalem. After revealing to His disciples how to pray, Jesus illustrates God's benevolence in answering prayer and giving the Holy Spirit.

"Now suppose one of you fathers is asked by his son for a fish; he will not give him a snake instead of a fish, will he? Or *if* he is asked for an egg, he will not give him a scorpion, will he? If you then, being evil, know how to give good gifts to your children, how much more will *your* heavenly Father give the Holy Spirit to those who ask Him?"
(Luke 11:11–13; cf. Matthew 7:9–11).

Setting: On the way from Galilee to Jerusalem. After clarifying a parable for Peter and the crowd, Jesus conveys how a relationship with Him divides families.

"I have come to cast fire upon the earth; and how I wish it were already kindled! But I have a baptism to undergo, and how distressed I am until it is accomplished! Do you suppose that I came to grant peace on earth? I tell you, no, but rather division; for from now on five *members* in one household will be divided, three against two and two against three. They will be divided, father against son and son against father, mother against daughter, and daughter against mother, mother-in-law against daughter-in-law and daughter-in-law against mother-in-law" (Luke 12:49–53; cf. Matthew 10:34–36; see Micah 7:6; Mark 10:38).

Setting: On the way from Galilee to Jerusalem. Jesus goes into the house of a Pharisee leader on the Sabbath to eat bread. A man suffering from dropsy is sitting there.

And Jesus answered and spoke to the lawyers and Pharisees, saying, "Is it lawful to heal on the Sabbath, or not?" But they kept silent. And He took hold of him and healed him, and sent him away. And He said to them, "Which one of you will have a son or an ox fall into a well, and will not immediately pull him out on a Sabbath day?" And they could make no reply to this. (Luke 14:3–6, cf. Matthew 12:11–13).

Setting: On the way from Galilee to Jerusalem. Jesus conveys the illustration of the prodigal son because the Pharisees and scribes complain He associates with tax collectors and sinners.

And He said, "A man had two sons. The younger of them said to his father, 'Father, give me the share of the estate that falls to me.' So he divided his wealth between them. And not many days later, the younger son gathered everything together and went on a journey into a distant country, and there he squandered his estate with loose living. Now when he had spent everything, a severe famine occurred in that country, and he began to be impoverished. So he went and hired himself out to one of the citizens of that country, and he sent him into his fields to feed swine. And he would have gladly filled his stomach with the pods that the swine were eating, and no one was giving *anything* to him. But when he came to his senses, he said, 'How many of my father's hired men have more than enough bread, but I am dying here with hunger! I will get up and go to my father, and will say to him, "Father, I have sinned against heaven, and in your sight; I am no longer worthy to be called your son; make me as one of your hired men."' So he got up and came to his father. But while he was still a long way off, his father saw him and felt compassion *for him,* and ran and embraced him and kissed him. And the son said to him, "Father, I have sinned against heaven and in your sight; I am no longer worthy to be called your son.' But the father said to his slaves, 'Quickly bring out the best robe and put it on him, and put a ring on his hand and sandals on his feet; and bring the fattened calf, kill it, and let us eat and celebrate; for this son of mine was dead and has come to life again; he was lost and has been found.' And they began to celebrate. Now his older son was in the field, when he came and approached the house, he heard music and dancing. And he summoned one of the servants and *began* inquiring what these things could be. And he said to him, 'Your brother has come, and your father has killed the fattened calf because he has received him back safe and sound.' But he became angry and was not willing to go in; and his father came out and *began* pleading with him. But he answered and said to his father, 'Look! For so many years I have been serving you and I have never neglected a command of yours; and *yet* you have never given me a young goat, so that I might celebrate with my friends; but when this son of yours came, who has devoured your wealth with prostitutes, you killed the fattened calf for him.' And he said to him, 'Son, you have always been with me, and all that is mine is yours. But we had to celebrate and rejoice, for this brother of yours was dead and *has begun* to live, and was lost and has been found' " (Luke 15:11–32; see Proverb 29:2).

Setting: Jericho, on the way to Jerusalem. After taking time to heal a blind man, Jesus comments on Zaccheus's response to Him.

And Jesus said to him, "Today salvation has come to this house, because he, too, is a son of Abraham. For the Son of Man has come to seek and to save that which was lost" (Luke 19:9, 10; cf. Matthew 18:11).

Setting: The temple in Jerusalem. While ministering a few days before His crucifixion, after the chief priests and the scribes question His authority to teach and preach, Jesus conveys the Parable of the Vine-Growers to the people.

And He began to tell the people this parable: "A man planted a vineyard and rented it out to vine-growers, and went on a journey for a long time. At the *harvest* time he sent a slave to the vine-growers, so that they would give him *some* of the produce of the vineyard; but the vine-growers beat him and sent him away empty-handed. And he proceeded to send another slave; and they beat him also and treated him shamefully and sent him away empty-handed. And he proceeded to send a third; and this one also they wounded and cast out. The owner of the vineyard said, 'What shall I do? I will send my beloved son; perhaps they will respect him.' But when the vine-growers saw him, they reasoned with one another, saying, 'This is the heir; let us kill him so that the inheritance will be ours.' So they threw him out of the vineyard and killed him. What, then, will the owner of the vineyard do to them? He will come and destroy these vine-growers and will give the vineyard to others." When they heard it, they said, "May it never be!" But Jesus looked at them and said, "What then is this that is written: 'THE STONE WHICH THE BUILDERS REJECTED, THIS BECAME THE CHIEF CORNER *stone*'? Everyone who falls on that stone will be broken to pieces; but on whomever it falls, it will scatter him like dust" (Luke 20:9–18, Jesus quotes from Psalm 118:22; cf. Matthew 21:33–44; Mark 12:1–11; see Ephesians 2:20).

Setting: The temple in Jerusalem. While ministering a few days before His crucifixion, after some of the Sadducees question Him about the resurrection, Jesus poses a question to the scribes, who say He answered well.

Then He said to them, "How *is it that* they say the Christ is David's son? For David himself says in the book of Psalms, 'THE LORD SAID TO MY LORD, SIT AT MY RIGHT HAND, UNTIL I MAKE YOUR ENEMIES A FOOTSTOOL FOR YOUR FEET.' Therefore David calls Him 'Lord,' and how is He his son?" (Luke 20:41–44, Jesus quotes from Psalm 110:1; cf. Matthew 22:41–46; Mark 12:35–37).

Setting: Bethany beyond the Jordan River. After His baptism, Jesus begins His public ministry and chooses His first disciples, Andrew and Simon (Peter), who believe He is the Messiah.

He brought him to Jesus. Jesus looked at him and said, "You are Simon the son of John; you shall be called Cephas." (which is translated Peter) (John 1:42).

Setting: Cana of Galilee. After conversing with a Samaritan woman at Jacob's well, and ministering to the Samaritans for two days, Jesus encounters a royal official seeking healing for his son, sick at the point of death in Capernaum.

Jesus said to him, "Go; your son lives." The man believed the word that Jesus spoke to him and started off (John 4:50; see Matthew 8:5–13).

Setting: Cana of Galilee. After conversing with a Samaritan woman at Jacob's well, and ministering to the Samaritans for two days, Jesus encounters a royal official seeking healing for his son, sick at the point of death in Capernaum.

So the father knew that *it was* at that hour in which Jesus said to him, "Your son lives"; and he himself believed and his whole household (John 4:53).

Setting: The temple treasury in Jerusalem. After the scribes and Pharisees question His testimony about Himself, Jesus reveals to those Jews who believe in Him how He will make them free.

So Jesus was saying to those Jews who had believed Him, "If you continue in My word, *then* you are truly disciples of Mine; and you will know the truth, and the truth will make you free." They answered Him, "We are Abraham's descendants and have never yet been enslaved to anyone; how is it that You say, 'You will become free'?" Jesus answered them, "Truly, truly, I say to you, everyone who commits sin is the slave of sin. The slave does not remain in the house forever; the son does remain forever. So if the Son makes you free, you will be free indeed. I know that you are Abraham's descendants; yet you seek to kill Me, because My word has no place in you. I speak the things which I have seen with *My* Father; therefore you also do the things which you heard from *your* father" (John 8:31–38; see Romans 6:16).

Setting: Jerusalem. Before the Passover, after giving His disciples assurance that in the midst of tribulation they will have His peace, Jesus prays His high-priestly prayer.

Jesus spoke these things; and lifting up His eyes to heaven, He said, "Father, the hour has come; glorify Your Son, that the Son may glorify You, even as You gave Him authority over all flesh, that to all whom You have given Him, He may give eternal life. This is eternal life, that they may know You, the only true God, and Jesus Christ whom You have sent. I glorified You on the earth, having accomplished the work which You have given Me to do. Now, Father, glorify Me together with Yourself, with the glory which I had with You before the world was. I have manifested Your name to the men whom You gave Me out of the world; they were Yours and You gave them to Me, and they have kept Your word. Now they have come to know that everything You have given Me is from You; for the words which You gave Me I have given to them; and they received *them* and truly understood that I came forth from You, and they believed You sent Me. I ask on their behalf; I do not ask on behalf of the world, but of those whom You have given Me; for they are Yours; and all things that are Mine are Yours, and Yours are Mine; and I have been glorified in them. I am no longer in the world; and *yet* they themselves are in the world, and I come to You. Holy Father, keep them in Your name, *the name* which You have given Me, that they may be even as We *are.* While I was with them, I was keeping them in Your name which You have given Me; and I guarded them and not one of them perished but the son of perdition, so that the Scripture would be fulfilled" (John 17:1–12; see Luke 22:32; John 1:1; 3:35; 4:34; 5:44; 6:37–39, 70; 8:42; 11:41; 12:49; 13:18, 31; 16:15; Philippians 2:9).

Setting: On the Place of the Skull (Golgotha), just outside Jerusalem. While being crucified, Jesus unselfishly asks His disciple John to care for His mother.

When Jesus saw His mother, and the disciple whom He loved standing nearby, He said to His mother, "Woman, behold, your son!" Then He said to the disciple, "Behold, your mother!" From that hour the disciple took her into his own *household* (John 19:26, 27).

Setting: By the Sea of Galilee. During His third manifestation to His disciples after His resurrection from the dead in Jerusalem, Jesus quizzes Peter three times regarding the disciple's love for Him.

So when they had finished breakfast, Jesus said to Simon Peter, "Simon, *son* of John, do you love Me more than these?" He said to Him, "Yes, Lord; You know that I love You." He said to him, "Tend My lambs." He said to him again a second time, "Simon, *son* of John, do you love Me?" He said to Him, "Yes, Lord; You know that I love You." He said to him, Shepherd My sheep." He said to him the third time, "Simon, *son* of John, do you love Me?" Peter was grieved because He said to him the third time, "Do you love Me?" And he said to Him, "Lord, You know all things; You know that I love You." Jesus said to him, "Tend My sheep" (John 21:15–17; see Matthew 26:33; Mark 14:29).

SON (Jesus; SON, BELOVED is a separate entry; also see DAVID, SON OF; SON OF GOD; and SON OF MAN)
Setting: Galilee. As He teaches and preaches, after pronouncing woes against unrepentant cities, Jesus prays a thanksgiving prayer to His Father in heaven.

At that time Jesus said, "I praise You, Father, Lord of heaven and earth, that you have hidden these things from *the* wise and intelligent and have revealed them to infants. Yes, Father, for this way was well-pleasing in Your sight. All things have been handed over to Me by My Father; and no one knows the Son except the Father; nor does anyone know the Father except the Son, and anyone to whom the Son wills to reveal *Him*" (Matthew 11:25–27; cf. Luke 10:21, 22).

[SON (Son) inferred from context]
Setting: The temple in Jerusalem. Jesus delivers another parable to the chief priests and elders after they question His authority.

"Listen to another parable. There was a landowner who PLANTED A VINEYARD AND PUT A WALL AROUND IT AND DUG A WINE PRESS IN IT, AND BUILT A TOWER, and rented it out to vine-growers and went on a journey. When the harvest time approached, he sent his slaves to the vine-growers to receive his produce. The vine-growers took his slaves and beat one, and killed another, and stoned a third. Again he sent another group of slaves larger than the first; and they did the same thing to them. But afterward he sent his son to them, saying, 'They will respect my son.' But when the vine-growers saw the son, they said among themselves, 'This is the heir; come, let us kill him and seize his inheritance.' They took him, and threw him out of the vineyard and killed him. Therefore when the owner of the vineyard comes, what will he do to those vine-growers?" (Matthew 21:33–40; Jesus quotes from Isaiah 5:1, 2; cf. Mark 12:1–9; Luke 20:9–15).

[SON (Son) inferred from context]
Setting: The temple in Jerusalem. Following the Sadducees' and the Pharisees' unsuccessful attempts to test Him with questions, with the crowds listening, Jesus poses a question to some of the Pharisees.

"What do you think about the Christ, whose son is He?" They said to Him, "The *son* of David." He said to them, "Then how does David in the Spirit call Him 'Lord,' saying, 'THE LORD SAID TO MY LORD, SIT AT MY RIGHT HAND, UNTIL I PUT YOUR ENEMIES BENEATH YOUR FEET"'? "If David then calls Him 'Lord," how is He his son?" (Matthew 22:42–45; Jesus quotes from Psalm 110:1; cf. Mark 12:35–37; Luke 20:41–44; see 2 Samuel 23:2).

Setting: On the Mount of Olives, just east of Jerusalem. During His Olivet Discourse, after answering His disciples' questions as to when the temple will be destroyed and Jerusalem overrun, along with the signs of His coming and the end of the age, Jesus teaches them the Parable of the Fig Tree.

"Now learn the parable from the fig tree: when its branch has already become tender and puts forth its leaves, you know that summer is near; so, you too, when you see all these things, recognize that He is near, *right* at the door. Truly, I say to you, this generation will not pass away until all these things take place. Heaven and earth will pass away, but My words will not pass away. But of that day and hour no one knows, not even the angels of heaven, nor the Son, but the Father alone. For the coming of the Son of Man will be just like the days of Noah. For as in those days before the flood they were eating and drinking, marrying and giving in marriage, until the day that Noah entered the ark, and they did not understand until the flood came and took them all away; so will the coming of the Son of Man be. Then there will be two men in the field; one will be taken and one will be left. Two women *will be* grinding at the mill; one will be taken and one will be left" (Matthew 24:32–41; cf. Mark 13:28–32; Luke 17:34–36; 21:28–33; see Genesis 6:5; 7:7; Matthew 5:18; 10:23; James 5:9).

Setting: On a mountain in Galilee. Following His resurrection from the dead in Jerusalem, Jesus conveys the Great Commission to His eleven remaining disciples.

And Jesus came up and spoke to them, saying, "All authority has been given to Me in heaven and on earth. Go therefore and make disciples of all the nations, baptizing them in the name of the Father and the Son and the Holy Spirit, teaching them to observe all that I commanded you; and lo, I am with you always, even to the end of the age" (Matthew 28:18–20; cf. Mark 16:15; see Daniel 7:13; Matthew 28:16, 17).

[SON (Son) inferred from context]

Setting: The temple in Jerusalem. Having His authority questioned by the chief priests, scribes, and elders, Jesus begins to teach them in parables.

And He began to speak to them in parables: "A man PLANTED A VINEYARD AND PUT A WALL AROUND IT, AND DUG A VAT UNDER THE WINE PRESS AND BUILT A TOWER, and rented it out to vine-growers and went on a journey. At the *harvest* time he sent a slave to the vine-growers, in order to receive *some* of the produce of the vineyard from the vine-growers. They took him, and beat him and sent him away empty-handed. Again he sent them another slave, and they wounded him in the head, and treated him shamefully. And he sent another, and that one they killed; and *so with* many others, beating some and killing others. He had one more to *send*, a beloved son; he sent him last *of all* to them, saying, 'They will respect my son.' But those vine-growers said to one another, 'This is the heir; come, let us kill him, and the inheritance will be ours!' They took him, and killed him and threw him out of the vineyard. What will the owner of the vineyard do? He will come and destroy the vine-growers, and will give the vineyard to others. Have you not even read this Scripture: 'THE STONE WHICH THE BUILDERS REJECTED, THIS BECAME THE CHIEF CORNER *stone*; THIS CAME ABOUT FROM THE LORD, AND IT IS MARVELOUS IN OUR EYES'?" (Mark 12:1–11, Jesus quotes from Psalm 118:22, 23; Isaiah 5:1, 2; cf. Matthew 21:33–46; Luke 20:9–19).

[SON (Son) inferred from context]

Setting: The temple in Jerusalem. After commending a scribe for his nearness to the kingdom of God, Jesus teaches the crowd.

And Jesus *began* to say, as He taught in the temple, "How *is it that* the scribes say that the Christ is the son of David? David himself said in the Holy Spirit, 'THE LORD SAID TO MY LORD, SIT AT MY RIGHT HAND, UNTIL I PUT YOUR ENEMIES BENEATH YOUR FEET.'" David himself calls Him 'Lord'; so in what sense is He his son?" And the large crowd enjoyed listening to Him (Mark 12:35–37, Jesus quotes from Psalm 110:1; cf. Matthew 22:41–46; Luke 20:41–44).

Setting: On the Mount of Olives, east of the temple in Jerusalem. After prophesying the temple's destruction, Jesus responds during His Olivet Discourse to questions from Peter, James, John, and Andrew about other future events.

"Now learn the parable from the fig tree: when its branch has already become tender and puts forth its leaves, you know that summer is near. Even so, you too, when you see these things happening, recognize that He is near, *right* at the door. Truly I say to you, this generation will not pass away until all these things take place. Heaven and earth will pass away, but My words will not pass away. But of the day or hour no one knows, not even the angels in heaven, nor the Son, but the Father *alone*" (Mark 13:28–32; cf. Matthew 24:32–36; Luke 21:28–33).

Setting: On the way from Galilee to Jerusalem. The Lord responds to a report from the seventy sent out in pairs to every place He Himself will soon visit.

At that very time He rejoiced greatly in the Holy Spirit, and said, "I praise You, O Father, Lord of heaven and earth, that You have hidden these things from *the* wise and intelligent and have revealed them to infants. Yes, Father, for this way was well-pleasing in Your sight. All things have been handed over to Me by My Father, and no one knows who the Son is except the Father, and who the Father is except the Son, and anyone to whom the Son wills to reveal *Him*" (Luke 10:21, 22; cf. Matthew 11:25–27; see John 3:35; 10:15).

[SON (Son) inferred from context]
Setting: The temple in Jerusalem. While ministering a few days before His crucifixion, after some of the Sadducees question Him about the resurrection, Jesus poses a question to the scribes, who say He answered well.

Then He said to them, "How *is it that* they say the Christ is David's son? For David himself says in the book of Psalms, 'THE LORD SAID TO MY LORD, SIT AT MY RIGHT HAND, UNTIL I MAKE YOUR ENEMIES A FOOTSTOOL FOR YOUR FEET.' Therefore David calls Him 'Lord,' and how is He his son?" (Luke 20:41–44, Jesus quotes from Psalm 110:1; cf. Matthew 22:41–46; Mark 12:35–37).

Setting: Jerusalem. At the time for the Passover of the Jews, after the Lord cleanses the temple, a Pharisee, Nicodemus, asks Him by night the meaning of "born again."

"For God so loved the world, that He gave His only begotten Son, that whoever believes in Him shall not perish, but have eternal life. For God did not send the Son into the world to judge the world, but that the world might be saved through Him. He who believes in Him is not judged; he who does not believe has been judged already, because he has not believed in the name of the only begotten Son of God. This is the judgment, that the Light has come into the world, and men loved darkness rather than the Light, for their deeds were evil. For everyone who does evil hates the Light, and does not come to the Light for fear that his deeds will be exposed. But he who practices the truth comes to the Light, so that his deeds may be manifested as having been wrought in God" (John 3:16–21; see Luke 19:10; John 1:4; 1:18; 3:1–15; Romans 5:8; 1 John 1:6, 7).

Setting: By the pool of Bethesda in Jerusalem. During a feast of the Jews, Jesus responds to criticism from the Jewish religious leaders for healing a lame man on the Sabbath and for referring to God as His Father (thereby making Himself equal with God).

Therefore Jesus answered and was saying to them, "Truly, truly, I say to you, the Son can do nothing of Himself, unless *it is* something He sees the Father doing; for whatever the Father does, these things the Son also does in like manner. For the Father loves the Son, and shows Him all things that He Himself is doing; and *the Father* will show Him greater works than these, so that you will marvel. For just as the Father raises the dead and gives them life, even so the Son also gives life to whom He wishes. For not even the Father judges anyone, but He has given all judgment to the Son, so that all will honor the Son even as they honor the Father. He who does not honor the Son does not honor the Father who sent Him" (John 5:19–23; see Luke 10:16; John 3:35; 11:25; 14:12).

Setting: Jerusalem. During a feast of the Jews, Jesus responds to criticism from the Jewish religious leaders by referring to God as His Father (thereby making Himself equal with God) and prophesying His participation someday in the resurrection and judgment of men.

"Truly, truly, I say to you, an hour is coming and now is, when the dead will hear the voice of the Son of God, and those who hear will live. For just as the Father has life in Himself, even so He gave to the Son also to have life in Himself; and He gave Him authority to execute judgment, because He is *the* Son of Man. Do not marvel at this; for an hour is coming, in which all who are in the tombs will hear His voice, and will come forth; those who did the good *deeds* to a resurrection of life, those who committed the evil *deeds* to a resurrection of judgment" (John 5:25–29; see Daniel 12:2; John 1:4; 11:24).

Setting: Capernaum. The day after Jesus walks on the Sea of Galilee to join His disciples in a boat, the people He miraculously fed with a lad's five loaves and two fish ask the Lord to always give them this bread out of heaven.

Jesus said to them, "I am the bread of life; he who comes to Me will not hunger, and he who believes in Me will never thirst. But I said to you that you have seen Me, and yet do not believe. All that the Father gives Me will come to Me, and the one who comes to Me I will certainly not cast out. For I have come down from heaven, not to do My own will, but the will of Him who sent Me. This is the will of Him who sent Me, that of all that He has given Me I lose nothing, but raise it up on the last day. For this is the will of My Father, that everyone who beholds the Son and believes in Him will have eternal life, and I Myself will raise him up on the last day" (John 6:35–40; see John 3:13, 16; 4:13, 14).

Setting: The temple treasury in Jerusalem. After the scribes and Pharisees question His testimony about Himself, Jesus reveals to those Jews who believe in Him how He will make them free.

So Jesus was saying to those Jews who had believed Him, "If you continue in My word, *then* you are truly disciples of Mine; and you will know the truth, and the truth will make you free." They answered Him, "We are Abraham's descendants and have never yet been enslaved to anyone; how is it that You say, 'You will become free'?" Jesus answered them, "Truly, truly, I say to you, everyone who commits sin is the slave of sin. The slave does not remain in the house forever; the son does remain forever. So if the Son makes you free, you will be free indeed. I know that you are Abraham's descendants; yet you seek to kill Me, because My word has no place in you. I speak the things which I have seen with *My* Father; therefore you also do the things which you heard from *your* father" (John 8:31–38; see Romans 6:16).

Setting: Jerusalem. Before the Passover, after answering Thomas' question where He is going and how His disciples will know the way, Jesus responds to Philip's request for Him to show them the Father.

Jesus said to him, "Have I been so long with you, and *yet* you have not come to know Me, Philip? He who has seen Me has seen the Father; how *can* you say, 'Show us the Father'? Do you not believe that I am in the Father, and the Father is in Me? The words that I say to you I do not speak on My own initiative, but the Father abiding in Me does His works. Believe Me that I am in the Father and the Father is in Me; otherwise believe because of the works themselves. Truly, truly, I say to you, he who believes in Me, the works that I do, he will do also; and greater *works* than these he will do; because I go to the Father. Whatever you ask in My name, that will I do, so that the Father may be glorified in the Son. If you ask Me anything in My name, I will do *it*" (John 14:9–14; see Matthew 7:7; John 1:14; 5:19, 20, 36; 10:37, 38; 15:16).

Setting: Jerusalem. Before the Passover, after giving His disciples assurance that in the midst of tribulation they will have His peace, Jesus prays His high-priestly prayer.

Jesus spoke these things; and lifting up His eyes to heaven, He said, "Father, the hour has come; glorify Your Son, that the Son may glorify You, even as You gave Him authority over all flesh, that to all whom You have given Him, He may give eternal life. This is eternal life, that they may know You, the only true God, and Jesus Christ whom You have sent. I glorified You on the earth, having accomplished the work which You have given Me to do. Now, Father, glorify Me together with Yourself, with the glory which I had with You before the world was. I have manifested Your name to the men whom You gave Me out of the world; they were Yours and You gave them to Me, and they have kept Your word. Now they have come to know that everything You have given Me is from You; for the words which You gave Me I have given to them; and they received *them* and truly understood that I came forth from You, and they believed You sent Me. I ask on their behalf; I do not ask on behalf of the world, but of those whom You have given Me; for they are Yours; and all things that are Mine are Yours, and Yours are Mine; and I have been glorified in them. I am no longer in the world; and *yet* they themselves are in the world, and I come to You. Holy Father, keep them in Your name, *the name* which You have given Me, that they may be even as We *are.* While I was with them, I was keeping them in Your name which You have given Me; and I guarded them and not one of them perished but the son of perdition, so that the Scripture would be fulfilled" (John 17:1–12; see Luke 22:32; John 1:1; 3:35; 4:34; 5:44; 6:37–39, 70; 8:42; 11:41; 12:49; 13:18, 31; 16:15; Philippians 2:9).

SON, BELOVED

Setting: The temple in Jerusalem. Having His authority questioned by the chief priests, scribes, and elders, Jesus begins to teach them in parables.

And He began to speak to them in parables: "A man PLANTED A VINEYARD AND PUT A WALL AROUND IT, AND DUG A VAT UNDER THE WINE PRESS AND BUILT A TOWER, and rented it out to vine-growers and went on a journey. At the *harvest* time he sent a slave to the vine-growers, in order to receive *some* of the produce of the vineyard from the vine-growers. They took him, and beat him and sent him away empty-handed. Again he sent them another slave, and they wounded him in the head, and treated him shamefully. And he sent another, and that one they killed; and *so with* many others, beating some and killing others. He had one more to *send*, a beloved son; he sent him last *of all* to them, saying, 'They will respect my son.' But those vine-growers said to one another, 'This is the heir; come, let us kill him, and the inheritance will be ours!' They took him, and killed him and threw him out of the vineyard. What will the owner of the vineyard do? He will come and destroy the vine-growers, and will give the vineyard to others. Have you not even read this Scripture: 'THE STONE WHICH THE BUILDERS REJECTED, THIS BECAME THE CHIEF CORNER *stone;* THIS CAME ABOUT FROM THE LORD, AND IT IS MARVELOUS IN OUR EYES'?" (Mark 12:1–11, Jesus quotes from Psalm 118:22, 23; Isaiah 5:1, 2; cf. Matthew 21:33–46; Luke 20:9–19).

Setting: The temple in Jerusalem. While ministering a few days before His crucifixion, after the chief priests and the scribes question His authority to teach and preach, Jesus conveys the Parable of the Vine-Growers to the people.

And He began to tell the people this parable: "A man planted a vineyard and rented it out to vine-growers, and went on a journey for a long time. At the *harvest* time he sent a slave to the vine-growers, so that they would give him *some* of the produce of the vineyard; but the vine-growers beat him and sent him away empty-handed. And he proceeded to send another slave; and they beat him also and treated him shamefully and sent him away empty-handed. And he proceeded to send a third; and this one also they wounded and cast out. The owner of the vineyard said, 'What shall I do? I will send my beloved son; perhaps they will respect him.' But when the vine-growers saw him, they reasoned with one another, saying, 'This is the heir; let us kill him so that the inheritance will be ours.' So they threw him out of the vineyard and killed him. What, then, will the owner of the vineyard do to them? He will come and destroy these vine-growers and will give the vineyard to others." When they heard it, they said, "May it never be!" But Jesus looked at them and said, "What then is this that is written: 'THE STONE WHICH THE BUILDERS REJECTED, THIS BECAME THE CHIEF CORNER *stone*'? Everyone who falls on that stone will be broken to pieces; but on whomever it falls, it will scatter him like dust" (Luke 20:9–18, Jesus quotes from Psalm 118:22; cf. Matthew 21:33–44; Mark 12:1–11; see Ephesians 2:20).

SON, DAVID'S (Also see DAVID, SON OF)

Setting: The temple in Jerusalem. While ministering a few days before His crucifixion, after some of the Sadducees question Him about the resurrection, Jesus poses a question to the scribes, who say He answered well.

Then He said to them, "How *is it that* they say the Christ is David's son? For David himself says in the book of Psalms, 'THE LORD SAID TO MY LORD, SIT AT MY RIGHT HAND, UNTIL I MAKE YOUR ENEMIES A FOOTSTOOL FOR YOUR FEET.' Therefore David calls Him 'Lord,' and how is He his son?" (Luke 20:41–44, Jesus quotes from Psalm 110:1; cf. Matthew 22:41–46; Mark 12:35–37).

SON, OLDER (See SON, PARABLE OF THE PRODIGAL)

SON, PARABLE OF THE LOST (See SON, PARABLE OF THE PRODIGAL)

SON, PARABLE OF THE PRODIGAL

[PRODIGAL SON from traditional reference of passage]

Setting: On the way from Galilee to Jerusalem. Jesus conveys the illustration of the prodigal son because the Pharisees and scribes complain He associates with tax collectors and sinners.

And He said, "A man had two sons. The younger of them said to his father, 'Father, give me the share of the estate that falls to me.' So he divided his wealth between them. And not many days later, the younger son gathered everything together and went

on a journey into a distant country, and there he squandered his estate with loose living. Now when he had spent everything, a severe famine occurred in that country, and he began to be impoverished. So he went and hired himself out to one of the citizens of that country, and he sent him into his fields to feed swine. And he would have gladly filled his stomach with the pods that the swine were eating, and no one was giving *anything* to him. But when he came to his senses, he said, 'How many of my father's hired men have more than enough bread, but I am dying here with hunger! I will get up and go to my father, and will say to him, "Father, I have sinned against heaven, and in your sight; I am no longer worthy to be called your son; make me as one of your hired men."' So he got up and came to his father. But while he was still a long way off, his father saw him and felt compassion *for him,* and ran and embraced him and kissed him. And the son said to him, "Father, I have sinned against heaven and in your sight; I am no longer worthy to be called your son.' But the father said to his slaves, 'Quickly bring out the best robe and put it on him, and put a ring on his hand and sandals on his feet; and bring the fattened calf, kill it, and let us eat and celebrate; for this son of mine was dead and has come to life again; he was lost and has been found.' And they began to celebrate. Now his older son was in the field, when he came and approached the house, he heard music and dancing. And he summoned one of the servants and *began* inquiring what these things could be. And he said to him, 'Your brother has come, and your father has killed the fattened calf because he has received him back safe and sound.' But he became angry and was not willing to go in; and his father came out and *began* pleading with him. But he answered and said to his father, 'Look! For so many years I have been serving you and I have never neglected a command of yours; and *yet* you have never given me a young goat, so that I might celebrate with my friends; but when this son of yours came, who has devoured your wealth with prostitutes, you killed the fattened calf for him.' And he said to him, 'Son, you have always been with me, and all that is mine is yours. But we had to celebrate and rejoice, for this brother of yours was dead and *has begun* to live, and was lost and has been found' " (Luke 15:11–32; see Proverb 29:2).

SON, PRODIGAL (See SON, PARABLE OF THE PRODIGAL)

SON, YOUNGER (See SON, PARABLE OF THE PRODIGAL)

SON OF DAVID (Listed under DAVID, SON OF; also see CHRIST and MESSIAH)

SON OF GOD (Also see CHRIST, THE; JESUS; LORD; MESSIAH; and SON OF MAN)

[SON OF GOD from "Yes, I am."]

Setting: Jerusalem. After being arrested, having Peter deny Him, and being mocked and beaten, with His crucifixion imminent, Jesus appears before the Sanhedrin (Council of Elders).

"If You are the Christ, tell us." But He said to them, "If I tell you, you will not believe; and if I ask you a question, you will not answer. But from now on THE SON OF MAN WILL BE SEATED AT THE RIGHT HAND of the power OF GOD." And they all said, "Are You the Son of God, then? And He said to them, "Yes, I am" (Luke 22:67–70, Jesus quotes from Psalm 110:1; cf. Matthew 26:57–65; Mark 14:55–65).

Setting: Jerusalem. At the time for the Passover of the Jews, after the Lord cleanses the temple, a Pharisee, Nicodemus, asks Him by night the meaning of "born again."

"For God so loved the world, that He gave His only begotten Son, that whoever believes in Him shall not perish, but have eternal life. For God did not send the Son into the world to judge the world, but that the world might be saved through Him. He who believes in Him is not judged; he who does not believe has been judged already, because he has not believed in the name of the only begotten Son of God. This is the judgment, that the Light has come into the world, and men loved darkness rather than the Light, for their deeds were evil. For everyone who does evil hates the Light, and does not come to the Light for fear that his deeds will be exposed. But he who practices the truth comes to the Light, so that his deeds may be manifested as having been wrought in God" (John 3:16–21; see Luke 19:10; John 1:4; 1:18; Romans 5:8; 1 John 1:6, 7).

Setting: Jerusalem. During the Feast of the Jews, Jesus responds to criticism from the Jewish religious leaders by referring to God as His Father (thereby making Himself equal with God) and prophesying His participation in the resurrection and judgment of men.

"Truly, truly, I say to you, an hour is coming and now is, when the dead will hear the voice of the Son of God, and those who hear will live. For just as the Father has life in Himself, even so He gave to the Son also to have life in Himself; and He gave Him authority to execute judgment, because He is *the* Son of Man. Do not marvel at this; for an hour is coming, in which all who are in the tombs will hear His voice, and will come forth; those who did the good *deeds* to a resurrection of life, those who committed the evil *deeds* to a resurrection of judgment" (John 5:25–29; see Daniel 12:2; John 1:4; 11:24).

Setting: Jerusalem. At the Feast of Dedication, the Pharisees desire to stone Jesus because He claims to be equal with God when they ask Him plainly whether He is the Christ.

Jesus answered them, "Has it not been written in your Law, 'I SAID, YOU ARE GODS'? If he called them gods, to whom the word of God came (and the Scripture cannot be broken), do you say of Him, whom the Father sanctified and sent into the world, 'You are blaspheming,' because I said, 'I am the Son of God'? If I do not do the works of My Father, do not believe Me; but if I do them, though you do not believe Me, believe the works, so that you may know and understand that the Father is in Me, and I in the Father" (John 10:34–38, Jesus quotes from Psalm 82:6; see John 14:10, 20).

Setting: Beyond the Jordan. Following the Feast of Dedication and the Pharisees' desire to stone Him in Jerusalem, Jesus hears of the sickness of Lazarus of Bethany.

But when Jesus heard *this,* He said, "This sickness is not to end in death, but for the glory of God, so that the Son of God may be glorified by it" (John 11:4).

Setting: On the island of Patmos (in the Aegean Sea about fifty miles southwest of Ephesus in modern Turkey). On the Lord's Day (Sunday), about fifty years after Jesus' resurrection, the disciple John encounters the Lord Jesus Christ, who communicates a new revelation for the apostle to record for the church in Thyatira and to six other churches in Asia.

"And to the angel of the church in Thyatira write: The Son of God, who has eyes like a flame of fire, and His feet are like burnished bronze, says this: 'I know your deeds, and your love and faith and service and perseverance, and that your deeds of late are greater than at first. But I have *this* against you, that you tolerate the woman Jezebel, who calls herself a prophetess, and she teaches and leads My bond-servants astray so that they commit *acts of* immorality and eat things sacrificed to idols. I gave her time to repent, and she does not want to repent of her immorality. Behold, I will throw her on a bed *of sickness,* and those who commit adultery with her into great tribulation, unless they repent of her deeds. And I will kill her children with pestilence, and all the churches will know that I am He who searches the minds and hearts; and I will give to each one of you according to your deeds. But I say to you, the rest who are in Thyatira, who do not hold this teaching, who have not known the deep things of Satan, as they call them—I place no other burden on you. Nevertheless what you have, hold fast until I come. He who overcomes, and he who keeps My deeds until the end, TO HIM I WILL GIVE AUTHORITY OVER THE NATIONS; AND HE SHALL RULE THEM WITH A ROD OF IRON, AS THE VESSELS OF THE POTTER ARE BROKEN TO PIECES, as I also have received *authority* from My Father; and I will give him the morning star. He who has an ear, let him hear what the Spirit says to the churches' (Revelation 2:18–29; Jesus quotes from Psalm 2:8, 9; Isaiah 30:14; see 1 Kings 16:31; Psalm 7:9; Romans 2:5; 1 Corinthians 2:10; 2 Peter 3:9; Revelation 1:14; 2:7; 3:11; 17:1–20).

SON OF HELL (See HELL, SON OF)

SON OF MAN (Also see SON OF MAN, COMING OF THE)

Setting: By the Sea of Galilee. Following a time of casting out evil spirits from the demon-possessed and healing the ill in fulfillment of Isaiah 53:4, Jesus lays out to an inquiring scribe the demands of discipleship.

Then a scribe came and said to Him, "Teacher, I will follow You wherever you go." Jesus said to him, "The foxes have holes and the birds of the air *have* nests, but the Son of Man has nowhere to lay His head." Another of the disciples said to Him, "Lord, permit me first to go and bury my father." But Jesus said to him, "Follow Me, and allow the dead to bury their own dead" (Matthew 8:19–22; cf. Luke 9:57–60).

Setting: Capernaum, near the Sea of Galilee. After Jesus heals a paralytic and forgives his sins in front of crowds, some scribes accuse the Lord of blasphemy.

And they brought to Him a paralytic lying on a bed. Seeing their faith, Jesus said to the paralytic, "Take courage, son; your sins are forgiven." And some scribes said to themselves. "This *fellow* blasphemes." And Jesus knowing their thoughts said, "Why are you thinking evil in your hearts? Which is easier to say, 'Your sins are forgiven,' or to say, 'Get up, and walk'? But so that you may know that the Son of Man has authority on earth to forgive sins"—then He said to the paralytic, "Get up, pick up your bed and go home" (Matthew 9:2–6; cf. Mark 2:3–12; Luke 5:17–26).

Setting: Galilee. After His disciples observe His ministry, Jesus summons and specifically instructs them about the upcoming difficulties of their ministry to the people of Israel.

"Brother will betray brother to death, and a father *his* child; and children will rise up against parents and cause them to be put to death. You will be hated by all because of My name, but it is the one who has endured to the end who will be saved. But whenever they persecute you in one city, flee to the next; for truly I say to you, you will not finish *going through* the cities of Israel until the Son of Man comes" (Matthew 10:21–23; cf. Matthew 10:35, 36; 16:27, 28; 24:9).

Setting: Galilee. After praising John the Baptist as His forerunner, Jesus demonstrates the foolish thinking of the Jewish religious leaders by repeating what they say about John's ascetic lifestyle and ministry along with His own.

"But to what shall I compare this generation? It is like children sitting in the market places, who call out to the other *children*, and say, 'We played the flute for you, and you did not dance; we sang a dirge, and you did not mourn.' For John came neither eating nor drinking, and they say, 'He has a demon!' The Son of Man came eating and drinking, and they say, 'Behold, a gluttonous man and a drunkard, a friend of tax collectors and sinners! Yet wisdom is vindicated by her deeds" (Matthew 11:16–19; cf. Luke 7:31–35; see Matthew 9:11, 34; Luke 1:15).

Setting: Galilee. Jesus responds to the Pharisees' objection to His disciples' picking grain from the fields on the Sabbath.

But He said to them, "Have you not read what David did when he became hungry, he and his companions, how they entered the house of God, and ate the consecrated bread, which was not lawful for him to eat nor for those with him, but for the priests alone? Or, have you not read in the Law, that on the Sabbath the priests in the temple break the Sabbath and are innocent? But I say to you that something greater than the temple is here. But if you had known what this means, 'I DESIRE COMPASSION, AND NOT A SACRIFICE,' you would not have condemned the innocent. For the Son of Man is Lord of the Sabbath" (Matthew 12:3–8, Jesus quotes from Hosea 6:6; cf. Mark 2:25–28; Luke 6:3–5; see 1 Samuel 21:6).

Setting: Galilee. After Jesus heals a blind, mute, demon-possessed man, the Pharisees accuse Him in front of crowds of being a worker of Satan. The Lord warns them about the unpardonable sin.

"He who is not with Me is against Me; and he who does not gather with Me scatters. Therefore I say to you, any sin and blasphemy shall be forgiven people, but blasphemy against the Spirit shall not be forgiven. Whoever speaks a word against the Son of Man, it shall be forgiven him; but whoever speaks against the Holy Spirit, it shall not be forgiven him, either in this age or in the *age* to come" (Matthew 12:30–32; cf. Luke 12:10; see Mark 9:40).

Setting: Galilee. After Jesus warns the Pharisees about the unpardonable sin and their future judgment, some Pharisees and scribes ask Him to perform a miraculous sign for them in front of the crowds.

But He answered and said to them, "An evil and adulterous generation craves for a sign; and *yet* no sign will be given to it but the sign of Jonah the prophet; for just as JONAH WAS THREE DAYS AND THREE NIGHTS IN THE BELLY OF THE SEA MONSTER, so will the Son of Man be three days and three nights in the heart of the earth. The men of Nineveh will stand up with this generation at the

judgment, and will condemn it because they repented at the preaching of Jonah; and behold, something greater than Jonah is here. *The* Queen of *the* South will rise up with this generation at the judgment and will condemn it, because she came from the ends of the earth to hear the wisdom of Solomon; and behold, something greater than Solomon is here" (Matthew 12:39–42; Jesus quotes from Jonah 1:17; cf. 1 Kings 10:1; Jonah 3:5; Matthew 16:1, 4; 12:38; Luke 11:29).

Setting: A house near the Sea of Galilee. Jesus gives His disciples the meaning of the Parable of the Wheat and the Tares.

And He said, "The one who sows the good seed is the Son of Man, and the field is the world; and as *for* the good seed, these are the sons of the kingdom; and the tares are the sons of the evil *one;* and the enemy who sowed them is the devil, and the harvest is the end of the age; and the reapers are angels. So just as the tares are gathered up and burned with fire, so shall it be at the end of the age. The Son of Man will send forth His angels, and they will gather out of His kingdom all stumbling blocks, and those who commit lawlessness, and will throw them into the furnace of fire; in that place there will be weeping and gnashing of teeth. Then THE RIGHTEOUS WILL SHINE FORTH AS THE SUN in the kingdom of their Father. He who has ears, let him hear" (Matthew 13:37–43, Jesus quotes from Daniel 12:3; cf. Matthew 8:12; 13:50).

Setting: By the Sea of Galilee. After Jesus repeats the warning to His disciples about the teaching of the Pharisees and Sadducees, He and the disciples proceed to the district of Caesarea Philippi, where He quizzes them on who people think He is.

Now when Jesus came into the district of Caesarea Philippi, He was asking His disciples. "Who do people say that the Son of Man is?" And they said, "Some *say* John the Baptist; and others, Elijah; but still others, Jeremiah, or one of the prophets." He said to them, "But who do you say that I am?" Simon Peter answered, "You are the Christ, the Son of the living God" (Matthew 16:13–16; cf. Mark 8:27–29; Luke 9:18–21; see Matthew 14:1, 2).

Setting: Near Caesarea Philippi. After rebuking Peter for trying to forbid Him to accomplish His earthly mission of dying and being resurrected, Jesus teaches His disciples about the costs of discipleship.

Then Jesus said to His disciples, "If anyone wishes to come after Me, he must deny himself, and take up his cross and follow Me. For whoever wishes to save his life will lose it; but whoever loses his life for My sake will find it. For what will it profit a man if he gains the whole world and forfeits his soul? Or what will a man give in exchange for his soul? For the Son of Man is going to come in the glory of His Father with His angels, and WILL THEN REPAY EVERY MAN ACCORDING TO HIS DEEDS. Truly, I say to you, there are some of you who are standing here who will not taste death until they see the Son of Man coming in His kingdom" (Matthew 16:24–28, Jesus quotes from Psalm 62:12; cf. Mark 8:34–37; Luke 9:23–27; see Matthew 10:38, 39).

Setting: Descending from a high mountain immediately following the Transfiguration. Jesus instructs Peter, James, and John to keep the Transfiguration secret until after His resurrection.

As they were coming down from the mountain, Jesus commanded them, saying, "Tell the vision to no one until the Son of Man has risen from the dead" (Matthew 17:9; cf. Mark 9:9–13; Luke 9:28–36).

Setting: Descending from a high mountain immediately following the Transfiguration. Peter, James, and John ask the Lord why Elijah must come before the Messiah.

And He answered and said, "Elijah is coming and will restore all things; but I say to you that Elijah already came, and they did not recognize him, but did to him whatever they wished. So also the Son of Man is going to suffer at their hands" (Matthew 17:11, 12; cf. Mark 9:11–13).

Setting: Galilee. Following the Transfiguration, Jesus repeats to His disciples that He must suffer, die, and be raised.

And while they were gathering together in Galilee, Jesus said to them, "The Son of Man is going to be delivered into the hands of men; and they will kill Him, and He will be raised on the third day." And they were deeply grieved (Matthew 17:22, 23; cf. Matthew 16:21; Mark 9:30–32; Luke 9:44, 45).

Setting: Capernaum of Galilee. After conveying the value of little ones when His disciples ask Him about greatness in the kingdom of heaven, Jesus states His earthly mission.

["For the Son of Man has come to save that which was lost"] (Matthew 18:11; cf. Luke 19:10).

Setting: Judea beyond the Jordan (Perea). Jesus promises rewards to His disciples for their personal sacrifice and commitment to following Him.

And Jesus said to them, "Truly I say to you, that you who have followed Me, in the regeneration when the Son of Man will sit on His glorious throne, you also shall sit upon twelve thrones, judging the twelve tribes of Israel. And everyone who has left houses or brothers or sisters or father or mother or children or farms for My name's sake, will receive many times as much, and will inherit eternal life. But many *who* are first will be last; and *the* last, first" (Matthew 19:28–30; cf. Matthew 6:33; 20:15; Mark 10:29, 30; Luke 18:29, 30; 22:30).

Setting: On the road to Jerusalem. Before going to Jerusalem, Jesus again tells His disciples of His impending death and resurrection.

As Jesus was about to go up to Jerusalem, He took the twelve *disciples* aside by themselves, and on the way He said to them, "Behold, we are going up to Jerusalem; and the Son of Man will be delivered to the chief priests and scribes, and they will condemn Him to death, and will hand Him over to the Gentiles to mock and scourge and crucify *Him,* and on the third day, He will be raised up" (Matthew 20:17–19; cf. Matthew 16:21; Mark 10:32–34; Luke 18:31, 33).

Setting: On the way to Jerusalem, where Jesus will die on the cross. Jesus teaches His disciples about true greatness after the mother of disciples James and John asks Him to make her sons exalted rulers with Him in His coming kingdom.

But Jesus called them to Himself and said, "You know that the rulers of the Gentiles lord it over them, and *their* great men exercise authority over them. It is not this way among you, but whoever wishes to become great among you shall be your servant, and whoever wishes to be first among you shall be your slave; just as the Son of Man did not come to be served, but to serve, and to give His life a ransom for many" (Matthew 20:25–28; cf. Matthew 23:11; 26:28; Mark 10:42–45).

Setting: The Mount of Olives, just east of Jerusalem. During His Olivet Discourse, Jesus answers His disciples' questions as to when the temple will be destroyed and Jerusalem overrun, along with the signs of His coming and the end of the age.

"Therefore when you see the ABOMINATION OF DESOLATION which was spoken of through Daniel the prophet, standing in the holy place (let the reader understand), then those who are in Judea must flee to the mountains. Whoever is on the housetop must not go down to get the things that are in his house. Whoever is in the field must not turn back to get his cloak. But woe to those who are pregnant and to those who are nursing babies in those days! But pray that your flight will not be in the winter, or on a Sabbath. For then there will be a great tribulation, such as has not occurred since the beginning of the world until now, nor ever will. Unless those days had been cut short, no life would have been saved; but for the sake of the elect those days will be cut short. Then if anyone says to you, 'Behold, here is the Christ,' or "There *He is,*' do not believe *him.* For false Christs and false prophets will arise and will show great signs and wonders, so as to mislead, if possible, even the elect. Behold, I have told you in advance. So if they say to you, 'Behold, He is in the wilderness,' do not go out, *or,* 'Behold, He is in the inner rooms,' do not believe *them.* For just as the lightning comes from the east and flashes even to the west, so will the coming of the Son of Man be. Wherever the corpse is, there the vultures will gather" (Matthew 24:15–28, Jesus quotes from Daniel 9:27; cf. Daniel 12:1; Mark 13:14–23; Luke 17:22–31; 21:20–24; 23:29; see John 4:48).

Setting: On the Mount of Olives, just east of Jerusalem. During His discourse, after answering His disciples' questions as to when the temple will be destroyed and Jerusalem overrun, along with the signs of His coming and the end of the age, Jesus teaches them the Parable of the Fig Tree.

"Now learn the parable from the fig tree: when its branch has already become tender and puts forth its leaves, you know that summer is near; so, you too, when you see all these things, recognize that He is near, *right* at the door. Truly, I say to you, this generation will not pass away until all these things take place. Heaven and earth will pass away, but My words will not pass away. But of that day and hour no one knows, not even the angels of heaven, nor the Son, but the Father alone. For the coming of the Son of Man will be just like the days of Noah. For as in those days before the flood they were eating and drinking, marrying and giving in marriage, until the day that Noah entered the ark, and they did not understand until the flood came and took them all away; so will the coming of the Son of Man be. Then there will be two men in the field; one will be taken and one will be left. Two women *will be* grinding at the mill; one will be taken and one will be left" (Matthew 24:32–41; cf. Mark 13:28–32; Luke 17:34–36; 21:28–33; see Genesis 6:5; 7:7; Matthew 5:18; 10:23; James 5:9).

Setting: On the Mount of Olives, just east of Jerusalem. During His Olivet Discourse, after answering His disciples' questions as to when the temple will be destroyed and Jerusalem overrun, along with the signs of His coming and the end of the age, Jesus reemphasizes to His disciples that they should be on the alert for His return.

"Therefore be on the alert, for you do not know which day your Lord is coming. But be sure of this, that if the head of the house had known at what time of the night the thief was coming, he would have been on the alert and would not have allowed his house to be broken into. For this reason you also must be ready; for the Son of Man is coming at an hour when you do not think *He will.* Who then is the faithful and sensible slave whom his master put in charge of his household to give their food at the proper time? Blessed is that slave whom his master finds so doing when he comes. Truly I say to you that he will put him in charge of all his possessions. But if that evil slave says in his heart, 'My master is not coming for a long time,' and begins to beat his fellow slaves and eat and drink with drunkards; the master of that slave will come on a day when he does not expect *him* and at an hour which he does not know, and will cut him in pieces and assign him a place with the hypocrites; in that place there will be weeping and gnashing of teeth" (Matthew 24:42–51; cf. Mark 13:33–37; Luke 12:39–46; 21:34–36; see Matthew 8:11, 12; 25:21–23).

Setting: On the Mount of Olives, just east of Jerusalem. During His Olivet Discourse, after answering His disciples' questions as to when the temple will be destroyed and Jerusalem overrun, along with the signs of His coming and the end of the age, Jesus reveals the future judgments following His return.

"But when the Son of Man comes in His glory, and all the angels with Him, then He will sit on His glorious throne. All the nations will be gathered before Him; and He will separate them from one another, as the shepherd separates the sheep from the goats; and He will put the sheep on His right, and the goats on the left. Then the King will say to those on His right, 'Come, you who are blessed of My Father, inherit the kingdom prepared for you from the foundation of the world. 'For I was hungry, and you gave Me *something* to eat; I was thirsty, and you gave Me *something* to drink; I was a stranger, and you invited Me in; naked, and you clothed Me; I was sick, and you visited Me; I was in prison, and you came to Me.' Then the righteous will answer Him, 'Lord, when did we see You hungry and feed You, or thirsty, and give you *something* to drink? And when did we see You a stranger, and invite You in, or naked, and clothe You? When did we see You sick, or in prison, and come to You?' The King will answer and say to them, 'Truly I say to you, to the extent that you did it to one of these brothers of Mine, *even* the least *of them,* you did it to Me.' Then He will also say to those on His left, 'Depart from Me, accursed ones, into the eternal fire which has been prepared for the devil and his angels; for I was hungry, and you gave Me *nothing* to eat; I was thirsty, and you gave Me nothing to drink; I was a stranger, and you did not invite Me in; naked, and you did not clothe Me; sick, and in prison, and you did not visit Me.' Then they themselves also will answer, 'Lord, when did we see You hungry, or thirsty, or a stranger, or naked, or sick, or in prison, and did not take care of You?' Then He will answer them, 'Truly I say to you, to the extent that you did not do it to one of the least of these, you did not do it to Me.' These will go away into eternal punishment, but the righteous into eternal life" (Matthew 25:31–46; see Matthew 7:23; 16:27; 19:29).

Setting: On the Mount of Olives, just east of Jerusalem. During His Olivet Discourse, after answering His disciples' questions as to when the temple will be destroyed and Jerusalem overrun, along with the signs of His coming and the end of the age, Jesus prophesies His crucifixion.

When Jesus had finished all these words, He said to His disciples, "You know that after two days the Passover is coming, and the Son of Man is *to be* handed over for crucifixion" (Matthew 26:1, 2; see Mark 14:1, 2; Luke 22:1, 2).

Setting: **An upper room in Jerusalem. While celebrating the Passover meal, Jesus shocks His disciples with the revelation that one of them will soon betray Him to His enemies.**

As they were eating, He said, "Truly I say to you that one of you will betray Me." Being deeply grieved, they each one began to say to Him, 'Surely not I, Lord?' And He answered, "He who dipped his hand with Me in the bowl is the one who will betray Me. The Son of Man *is to* go, just as it is written of Him; but woe to that man by whom the Son of Man is betrayed! It would have been good for that man if he had not been born." And Judas, who was betraying Him, said, 'Surely it is not I, Rabbi?' Jesus said to him, "You have said *it* yourself" (Matthew 26:21–25; cf. Mark 14:18–21; Luke 22:21–23; John 13:21–30; see Psalm 41:9).

Setting: **An upper room in Jerusalem. After celebrating the Passover meal with His disciples, Jesus retreats to the Garden of Gethsemane on the Mount of Olives to pray prior to His betrayal by Judas.**

Then Jesus came with them to a place called Gethsemane, and said to His disciples, "Sit here while I go over there and pray." And He took with Him Peter and the two sons of Zebedee, and began to be grieved and distressed. Then He said to them, "My soul is deeply grieved, to the point of death; remain here and keep watch with Me." And He went a little beyond *them,* and fell on His face and prayed, saying, "My Father, if it is possible, let this cup pass from Me; yet not as I will, but as You will." And He came to the disciples and found them sleeping, and said to Peter, "So, you *men* could not keep watch with Me for one hour? Keep watching and praying that you may not enter into temptation; the spirit is willing, but the flesh is weak." He went away again a second time and prayed, saying, "My Father, if this cannot pass away unless I drink it, Your will be done." Again He came and found them sleeping, for their eyes were heavy. And He left them again, and went away and prayed a third time, saying the same thing once more. Then He came to the disciples and said to them, "Are you still sleeping and resting? Behold the hour is at hand and the Son of Man is being betrayed into the hands of sinners. Get up, let us be going; behold the one who betrays Me is at hand!" (Matthew 26:36–46; cf. Mark 14:32–42; Luke 22:40–46; see Matthew 20:22; John 12:27).

Setting: **Jerusalem. After being betrayed by Judas and arrested, Jesus appears before Caiaphas the high priest and the Council for interrogation aimed at entrapping Him.**

Jesus said to him, "You have said it *yourself;* nevertheless I tell you, hereafter you will see THE SON OF MAN SITTING AT THE RIGHT HAND OF POWER, AND COMING ON THE CLOUDS OF HEAVEN" (Matthew 26:64, Jesus quotes from Daniel 7:13; cf. Mark 14:62).

Setting: **Capernaum. When Jesus heals a paralytic man and forgives his sins, some scribes believe the Lord commits blasphemy.**

Immediately Jesus, aware in His spirit that they were reasoning that way within themselves, said to them, "Why are you reasoning about these things in your hearts? Which is easier, to say to the paralytic, 'Your sins are forgiven'; or to say, 'Get up, and pick up your pallet and walk'? "But so that you may know that the Son of Man has authority on earth to forgive sins"—He said to the paralytic, "I say to you, get up, pick up your pallet and go home" (Mark 2:8–11; cf. Matthew 9:4–7; Luke 5:21–24).

Setting: **Galilee. Early in His ministry, the Pharisees question Jesus why He allows His disciples to harvest grain on the Sabbath.**

And He said to them, "Have you never read what David did when he was in need and he and his companions became hungry; how he entered the house of God in the time of Abiathar *the* high priest, and ate the consecrated bread, which is not lawful for *anyone* to eat except the priests, and he also gave it to those who were with him?" Jesus said to them, "The Sabbath was made for man, and not man for the Sabbath. So the Son of Man is Lord even of the Sabbath" (Mark 2:25–28; cf. Matthew 12:1–8; Luke 6:1–5; see Exodus 23:12).

Setting: Caesarea Philippi. After rebuking Peter for desiring to thwart His mission to the cross, Jesus summons a crowd, along with His disciples, and informs them of the high costs of following Him.

And He summoned the crowd with His disciples, and said to them, "If anyone wishes to come after Me, he must deny himself, and take up his cross and follow Me. For whoever wishes to save his life will lose it, but whoever loses his life for My sake and the gospel's will save it. For what does it profit a man to gain the whole world, and forfeit his soul? For what will a man give in exchange for his soul? For whoever is ashamed of Me and My words in this adulterous and sinful generation, the Son of Man will also be ashamed of him when He comes in the glory of His Father with the holy angels" (Mark 8:34–38; cf. Matthew 16:24–28; Luke 9:23–27; see Matthew 10:33, 38, 39).

Setting: Galilee. After informing a crowd and His disciples of the hope involving the coming kingdom of God, Jesus takes Peter, James, and John to a high mountain (some think Mount Hermon), where He reveals His glory through the Transfiguration and answers their question about Elijah.

And He said to them, "Elijah does first come and restore all things. And *yet* how is it written of the Son of Man that He will suffer many things and be treated with contempt? But I say to you that Elijah has indeed come, and they did to him whatever they wished, just as it is written of him" (Mark 9:12, 13; cf. Matthew 17:1–13; Luke 9:28–36; see Malachi 4:5, 6; Matthew 16:21).

Setting: Galilee. After He casts out an unclean spirit from a young boy, Jesus teaches His disciples in secret about His coming death and resurrection.

From there they went out and *began* to go through Galilee, and He did not want anyone to know *about it.* For He was teaching His disciples and telling them, "The Son of Man is to be delivered into the hands of men, and they will kill Him; and when He has been killed, He will rise three days later." But they did not understand *this* statement, and they were afraid to ask Him (Mark 9:30–32; cf. Matthew 17:22, 23; Luke 9:43–45; see Matthew 16:21).

Setting: On the road to Jerusalem. After encouraging His disciples with a revelation of their future reward, Jesus prophesies His persecution, death, and resurrection.

They were on the road going up to Jerusalem, and Jesus was walking on ahead of them; and they were amazed, and those who followed were fearful. And again He took the twelve aside and began to tell them what was going to happen to Him, *saying,* "Behold, we are going up to Jerusalem, and the Son of Man will be delivered to the chief priests and the scribes; and they will condemn Him to death and will hand Him over to the Gentiles. They will mock Him and spit on Him, and scourge Him and kill *Him,* and three days later He will rise again" (Mark 10:32–34; cf. Matthew 20:17–19; Luke 18:31–34; see Matthew 16:21; Mark 8:31).

Setting: On the road to Jerusalem. When James and John ask Jesus for special honor and privileges in His kingdom, the other disciples become angry. The Lord uses this moment to teach them about servanthood.

Calling them to Himself, Jesus said to them, "You know that those who are recognized as rulers of the Gentiles lord it over them; and their great men exercise authority over them. But it is not this way among you, but whoever wishes to become great among you shall be your servant; and whoever wishes to be first among you shall be slave of all. For even the Son of Man did not come to be served, but to serve, and to give His life a ransom for many" (Mark 10:42–45; cf. Matthew 20:25–28).

Setting: On the Mount of Olives, east of the temple in Jerusalem. After predicting the temple's destruction, Jesus responds during His Olivet Discourse to questions from Peter, James, John, and Andrew about other future events.

"But in those days, after that tribulation, THE SUN WILL BE DARKENED AND THE MOON WILL NOT GIVE ITS LIGHT, AND THE STARS WILL BE FALLING from heaven, and the powers that are in the heavens will be shaken. Then they will see THE SON OF MAN COMING IN CLOUDS with great power and glory. And then He will send forth the angels, and will gather together His elect from the four winds, from the farthest end of the earth to the farthest end of heaven" (Mark 13:24–27. Jesus quotes from Isaiah 13:10; 34:4; Daniel 7:13; cf. Matthew 24:29–31; Luke 21:25–27).

Setting: A borrowed upper room in Jerusalem. While Jesus and His twelve disciples are eating the Passover meal, the Lord prophesies that one of them will betray Him.

As they were reclining *at the table* and eating, Jesus said, "Truly I say to you that one of you will betray Me—one who is eating with Me." They began to be grieved and to say to Him one by one, "Surely not I?" And He said to them, "*It is* one of the twelve, one who dips with Me in the bowl. For the Son of Man *is to* go just as it is written of Him; but woe to that man by whom the Son of Man is betrayed! *It would have been* good for that man if he had not been born" (Mark 14:18–21; cf. Matthew 26:21–24; Luke 22:21, 23; John 13:21, 22).

Setting: Gethsemane on the Mount of Olives, east of the temple in Jerusalem. Jesus prepares to meet Judas the betrayer, while His other disciples keep falling asleep instead of watching and praying with Him.

And He came the third time, and said to them, "Are you still sleeping and resting? It is enough; the hour has come; behold, the Son of Man is being betrayed into the hands of sinners. Get up, let us be going; behold, the one who betrays Me is at hand!" (Mark 14:41, 42; cf. Matthew 26:45, 46).

Setting: Jerusalem. Following His betrayal by Judas and His arrest, Jesus confirms He is the Christ to the high priest and all the chief priests, as they seek justification for putting Him to death.

And Jesus said, "I am; and you shall see THE SON OF MAN SITTING AT THE RIGHT HAND OF POWER, and COMING WITH THE CLOUDS OF HEAVEN" (Mark 14:62, Jesus quotes from Psalm 110:1; Daniel 7:13; cf. Matthew 26:57–68; see Luke 22:54).

Setting: Capernaum of Galilee. When Jesus heals a paralytic man and forgives his sins, some Pharisees and teachers of the law from Galilee and Judea accuse the Lord of committing blasphemy.

But Jesus, aware of their reasonings, answered and said to them, "Why are you reasoning in your hearts? Which is easier, to say, 'Your sins have been forgiven you,' or to say, 'Get up and walk'? But, so that you may know that the Son of Man has authority on earth to forgive sins,"—He said to the paralytic—"I say to you, get up, and pick up your stretcher and go home" (Luke 5:22–24; cf. Matthew 9:4–8; Mark 2:8–12; see Matthew 4:24).

Setting: Probably Galilee. As Jesus and His disciples pass through some grain fields, some of the Pharisees ask the Lord why His followers harvest grain on the Sabbath.

And Jesus answering them said, "Have you not even read what David did when he was hungry, he and those who were with him, how he entered the house of God, and took and ate the consecrated bread which is not lawful for any to eat except the priests alone, and gave it to his companions?" And He was saying to them, "The Son of Man is Lord of the Sabbath" (Luke 6:3–5; cf. Matthew 12:1–8; Mark 2:23–28; see Exodus 20:8; Leviticus 24:1–9; Deuteronomy 5:12; 1 Samuel 21:1–6).

Setting: Galilee. After selecting His twelve disciples, Jesus teaches the Beatitudes (part of the Sermon on the Mount) to those disciples and a great throng of people from Judea, Jerusalem, and the central coastal region of Tyre and Sidon.

"Blessed are you when men hate you, and ostracize you, and insult you, and scorn your name as evil, for the sake of the Son of Man. Be glad in that day and leap *for joy*, for behold, your reward is great in heaven. For in the same way their fathers used to treat the prophets" (Luke 6:22, 23; cf. Matthew 5:10–12; see 2 Chronicles 36:16).

Setting: Galilee. After praising John the Baptist to the crowds, Jesus criticizes the Pharisees and lawyers who reject God's purpose and John's message.

"To what then shall I compare the men of this generation, and what are they like? They are like children who sit in the market place and call to one another, and they say, 'We played the flute for you, and you did not dance; we sang a dirge, and you did not weep.' For John the Baptist has come eating no bread and drinking no wine, and you say, 'He has a demon!' The Son of Man has come eating and drinking, and you say, 'Behold, a gluttonous man and a drunkard, a friend of tax collectors and sinners!' Yet wisdom is vindicated by all her children" (Luke 7:31–35; cf. Matthew 11:16–19; see Luke 1:15).

Setting: Galilee. Following Peter's pronouncement that Jesus is the Christ of God, the Lord warns His disciples not to reveal His identity to anyone.

But He warned them and instructed *them* not to tell this to anyone, saying, "The Son of Man must suffer many things and be rejected by the elders and chief priests and scribes, and be killed and be raised up on the third day" (Luke 9:21, 22; cf. Matthew 16:21; Mark 8:31).

Setting: Galilee. Following Peter's pronouncement that Jesus is the Christ of God, the Lord conveys the demands of discipleship and the hope regarding the kingdom of God.

And He was saying to *them* all, "If anyone wishes to come after Me, he must deny himself, and take up his cross daily and follow Me. For whoever wishes to save his life will lose it, but whoever loses his life for My sake, he is the one who will save it. For what is a man profited if he gains the whole world, and loses or forfeits himself? For whoever is ashamed of Me and My words, the Son of Man will be ashamed of him when He comes in His glory, and *the glory* of the Father and of the holy angels. But I say to you truthfully, there are some of those standing here who will not taste death until they see the kingdom of God" (Luke 9:23–27; cf. Matthew 16:24–26, 28; Mark 8:34–37; see Matthew 10:33, 38, 39).

Setting: Galilee. After healing the demon-possessed son of a man from the crowd, the Lord prophesies His own death.

"Let these words sink into your ears; for the Son of Man is going to be delivered into the hands of men" (Luke 9:44; cf. Matthew 17:22, 23; Mark 9:31–32; see Luke 9:22).

Setting: Galilee. After clarifying who the disciples' co-laborers are, Jesus prepares to go to Jerusalem by sending messengers ahead to Samaria, where they experience rejection and seek retribution.

But He turned and rebuked them, [and said, "You do not know what kind of spirit you are of; for the Son of Man did not come to destroy men's lives, but to save them."] And they went on to another village (Luke 9:55, 56; see 2 Kings 1:9–14; Luke 13:22).

Setting: On the way from Galilee to Jerusalem. The Lord responds to someone seeking to follow Him.

And Jesus said to him, "The foxes have holes and the birds of the air *have* nests, but the Son of Man has nowhere to lay His head" (Luke 9:58; cf. Matthew 8:19–22).

Setting: On the way from Galilee to Jerusalem. After revealing a problem with exorcism and responding to a blessing from a woman in the crowd, Jesus tells the increasing crowds of the sign of Jonah.

As the crowds were increasing, He began to say, "This generation is a wicked generation; it seeks for a sign, and *yet* no sign will be given to it but the sign of Jonah. For just as Jonah became a sign to the Ninevites, so will the Son of Man be to this generation. The Queen of the South will rise up with the men of this generation at the judgment and condemn them, because she came from the ends of the earth to hear the wisdom of Solomon; and behold, something greater than Solomon is here. The men of Nineveh will stand up with this generation at the judgment and condemn it, because they repented at the preaching of Jonah; and behold, something greater than Jonah is here" (Luke 11:29–32; cf. Matthew 16:4; see 1 Kings 10:1–10; Jonah 3:4, 5).

Setting: On the way from Galilee to Jerusalem. Jesus warns His disciples of future events as the scribes and Pharisees turn hostile and question Him repeatedly in an attempt to catch Him in something He might say.

"And I say to you, everyone who confesses Me before men, the Son of Man will confess him also before the angels of God; but he who denies Me before men will be denied before the angels of God. And everyone who speaks a word against the Son of Man, it will be forgiven him; but he who blasphemes against the Holy Spirit, it will not be forgiven him. When they bring you before the synagogues and the rulers and the authorities, do not worry about how or what you are to speak in your defense, or what you are to say; for the Holy Spirit will teach you in that very hour what you ought to say" (Luke 12:8–12; cf. Matthew 10:32, 33; 12:31, 32; see Matthew 10:20).

Setting: On the way from Galilee to Jerusalem. After giving a parable about riches and greed, Jesus uses another parable to challenge the crowd and His disciples to be ready for His return.

"Be dressed in readiness, and *keep* your lamps lit. Be like men who are waiting for their master when he returns from the wedding feast, so that they may immediately open *the door* to him when he comes and knocks. Blessed are those slaves whom the master will find on the alert when he comes; truly I say to you, that he will gird himself *to serve,* and have them recline *at the table,* and will come up and wait on them. Whether he comes in the second watch, or even in the third and finds *them* so, blessed are those *slaves*. But be sure of this, that if the head of the house had known at what hour the thief was coming, he would not have allowed his house to be broken into. You too, be ready; for the Son of Man is coming at an hour that you do not expect" (Luke 12:35–40; cf. Matthew 24:42–44; see Mark 13:33; Ephesians 6:14).

Setting: On the way from Galilee to Jerusalem. After the Pharisees question Him about the coming of the kingdom of God, Jesus tells His disciples of His second coming.

And He said to the disciples, "The days will come when you will long to see one of the days of the Son of Man, and you will not see it. They will say to you, 'Look there! Look here!' Do not go away, and do not run after *them*. For just like the lightning, when it flashes out of one part of the sky, shines to the other part of the sky, so will the Son of Man be in His day. But first He must suffer many things and be rejected by this generation. And just as it happened in the days of Noah, so it will be also in the days of the Son of Man: they were eating, they were drinking, they were marrying, they were being given in marriage, until the day that Noah entered the ark, and the flood came and destroyed them all. It was the same as happened in the days of Lot: they were eating, they were drinking, they were buying, they were selling, they were planting, they were building; but on the day that Lot went out from Sodom it rained fire and brimstone from heaven and destroyed them all. It will be just the same on the day that the Son of Man is revealed. On that day, the one who is on the housetop and whose goods are in the house must not go down to take them out; and likewise the one who is in the field must not turn back. Remember Lot's wife. Whoever seeks to keep his life will lose it, and whoever loses *his life* will preserve it. I tell you, on that night there will be two in one bed; one will be taken and the other will be left. There will be two women grinding at the same place; one will be taken and the other will be left. [Two men will be in the field; one will be taken and the other will be left."] And answering they said to Him, "Where, Lord?" And He said to them, "Where the body *is*, there also the vultures will be gathered" (Luke 17:22–37; see Genesis 19; Matthew 10:39; 16:21, 27; 24:17–28, 37–41).

Setting: On the way from Galilee to Jerusalem. After telling His disciples of His second coming, Jesus instructs them about persistence in prayer.

Now He was telling them a parable to show that at all times they ought to pray and not to lose heart, saying, "In a certain city there was a judge who did not fear God and did not respect man. There was a widow in that city, and she kept coming to him, saying, 'Give me legal protection from my opponent.' For a while he was unwilling; but afterward he said to himself, 'Even though I do not fear God nor respect man, yet because this woman bothers me, I will give her legal protection, otherwise by continually coming she will wear me out.'" And the Lord said, "Hear what the unrighteous judge said; now, will not God bring about justice for His elect who cry to Him day and night, and will He delay long over them? I tell you that He will bring about justice for them quickly. However, when the Son of Man comes, will He find faith on the earth?" (Luke 18:1–8; see Luke 11:5–10).

Setting: On the way from Galilee to Jerusalem. After responding to Peter's statement about the disciples' personal sacrifice in following Him, Jesus tells them of the sacrifice He will make in Jerusalem.

Then He took the twelve aside and said to them, "Behold, we are going up to Jerusalem, and all things which are written through the prophets about the Son of Man will be accomplished. For He will be handed over to the Gentiles, and will be mocked and mistreated and spit upon, and after they have scourged Him, they will kill Him; and the third day He will rise again" (Luke 18:31–33; cf. Matthew 20:17–19; Mark 10:32–34).

Setting: Jericho, on the way to Jerusalem. After taking time to heal a blind man, Jesus comments on Zaccheus's response to Him.

And Jesus said to him, "Today salvation has come to this house, because he, too, is a son of Abraham. For the Son of Man has come to seek and to save that which was lost" (Luke 19:9, 10; cf. Matthew 18:11).

Setting: The Mount of Olives, just east of Jerusalem. After ministering in the temple a few days before His crucifixion, and giving His disciples more details regarding future events, Jesus speaks during His Olivet Discourse of His return.

"There will be signs in sun and moon and stars, and on the earth dismay among the nations, in perplexity at the roaring of the sea and the waves, men fainting from fear and the expectation of the things which are coming upon the world; for the powers of the heavens will be shaken. Then they will see THE SON OF MAN COMING IN A CLOUD with power and great glory. But when these things begin to take place, straighten up and lift up your heads, because your redemption is drawing near" (Luke 21:25–28, Jesus quotes from Daniel 7:13; cf. Matthew 24:29–31; Mark 13:24–27).

Setting: The Mount of Olives, east of the temple in Jerusalem. After ministering in the temple a few days before His crucifixion, and conveying the Parable of the Fig Tree, Jesus warns His disciples during His Olivet Discourse to keep alert regarding future events.

"Be on guard, so that your hearts will not be weighted down with dissipation and drunkenness and the worries of life, and that day will not come upon you suddenly like a trap; for it will come upon all those who dwell on the face of all the earth. But keep on the alert at all times, praying that you may have strength to escape all these things that are about to take place, and to stand before the Son of Man" (Luke 21:34–36; cf. Mark 13:33; see Matthew 24:42–44).

Setting: An upper room in Jerusalem. During the Feast of Unleavened Bread (Passover) just before His crucifixion, while celebrating the Passover meal with His disciples, Jesus institutes the Lord's Supper.

And when He had taken a cup *and* given thanks, He said, "Take this and share it among yourselves; for I say to you, I will not drink of the fruit of the vine from now on until the kingdom of God comes." And when he had taken *some* bread and given thanks, He broke it and gave it to them, saying, "This is My body which is given for you; do this in remembrance of Me." And in the same way *He took* the cup after they had eaten, saying, "This cup which is poured out for you is the new covenant in My blood. But behold, the hand of the one betraying Me is with Mine on the table. For indeed, the Son of Man is going as it has been determined; but woe to that man by whom He is betrayed!" (Luke 22:17–22; cf. Matthew 26:26–29; Mark 14:22–25; 1 Corinthians 11:23–26; see Psalm 41:9; Luke 14:15; 1 Corinthians 10:16).

Setting: Gethsemane on the Mount of Olives, east of the temple in Jerusalem. With the crucifixion imminent, after Jesus prays, with His disciples nearby, Judas betrays Him to a crowd of His enemies with a kiss.

But Jesus said to him, "Judas, are you betraying the Son of Man with a kiss?" (Luke 22:48; see Matthew 26:48, 49; Mark 14:44, 45; Luke 12:47, 49–53; John 18:2–8).

Setting: Jerusalem. After being arrested, having Peter deny Him, and being mocked and beaten, with His crucifixion imminent, Jesus appears before the Sanhedrin (Council of Elders).

"If You are the Christ, tell us." But He said to them, "If I tell you, you will not believe; and if I ask you a question, you will not answer. But from now on THE SON OF MAN WILL BE SEATED AT THE RIGHT HAND of the power OF GOD." And they all said, "Are You the Son of God, then? And He said to them, "Yes, I am" (Luke 22:67–70, Jesus quotes from Psalm 110:1; cf. Matthew 26:57–65; Mark 14:55–65).

Setting: Galilee. After beginning His public ministry and choosing His first disciples, Andrew and Simon (Peter) near Bethany beyond the Jordan, and Philip in Galilee, Jesus calls Philip's friend, Nathanael, (some believe he may have been also called Bartholomew) as His next follower.

Jesus saw Nathanael coming to Him, and said of him, "Behold, an Israelite indeed, in whom there is no deceit!" Nathanael said to Him, "How do you know me?" Jesus answered and said to him, "Before Philip called you, when you were under the fig tree, I saw you." Nathanael answered Him, "Rabbi, You are the Son of God; You are the King of Israel." Jesus answered and said to him, "Because I said to you that I saw you under the fig tree, do you believe? You will see greater things than these." And He said to him, "Truly, truly, I say to you, you will see the heavens opened and the angels of God ascending and descending on the Son of Man" (John 1:47–51).

Setting: Jerusalem. At the time for the Passover of the Jews, after the Lord cleanses the temple, a Pharisee, Nicodemus, asks Him by night the meaning of "born of the Spirit."

Jesus answered and said to him, "Are you the teacher of Israel and do not understand these things? Truly, truly, I say to you, we speak of what we know and testify of what we have seen, and you do not accept our testimony. If I told you earthly things and you do not believe, how will you believe if I tell you heavenly things? No one has ascended into heaven, but He who descended from heaven: the Son of Man. As Moses lifted up the serpent in the wilderness, even so must the Son of Man be lifted up; so that whoever believes will in Him have eternal life" (John 3:10–15; see Numbers 21:9; Proverb 30:4; John 12:34; 20:30, 31).

Setting: Jerusalem. During a feast of the Jews, Jesus responds to criticism from the Jewish religious leaders by referring to God as His Father (thereby making Himself equal with God) and prophesying His participation someday in the resurrection and judgment of men.

"Truly, truly, I say to you, an hour is coming and now is, when the dead will hear the voice of the Son of God, and those who hear will live. For just as the Father has life in Himself, even so He gave to the Son also to have life in Himself; and He gave Him authority to execute judgment, because He is *the* Son of Man. Do not marvel at this; for an hour is coming, in which all who are in the tombs will hear His voice, and will come forth; those who did the good *deeds* to a resurrection of life, those who committed the evil *deeds* to a resurrection of judgment" (John 5:25–29; see Daniel 12:2; John 1:4; 11:24).

Setting: Capernaum. The day after Jesus walks on the Sea of Galilee to join His disciples in a boat, the people He miraculously fed with a lad's five loaves and two fish ask Jesus how He crossed the water, since He had not entered the boat from land with His disciples.

Jesus answered them and said, "Truly, truly, I say to you, you seek Me, not because you saw signs, but because you ate of the loaves and were filled. Do not work for the food which perishes, but for the food which endures to eternal life, which the Son of Man will give to you, for on Him the Father, God, has set His seal" (John 6:26, 27; see John 3:33; 6:2, 14).

Setting: Capernaum of Galilee. After Jesus informs the people whom He miraculously fed with a lad's five loaves and two fish how they might receive the bread out of heaven, the Jewish religious leaders argue with one another when the Lord says He will give His flesh to the world to eat.

So Jesus said to them, "Truly, truly, I say to you, unless you eat the flesh of the Son of Man and drink His blood, you have no life in yourselves. He who eats My flesh and drinks My blood has eternal life, and I will raise him up on the last day. For My flesh is true food, and My blood is true drink. He who eats My flesh and drinks My blood abides in Me, and I in him. As the living Father sent Me, and I live because of the Father, so he who eats Me, he also will live because of Me. This is the bread which came down out of heaven; not as the fathers ate and died; he who eats this bread will live forever" (John 6:53–58; see Matthew 16:16; Luke 4:22; John 3:36; 9:16; 15:4).

Setting: The synagogue at Capernaum of Galilee. After the Jewish religious leaders argue with one another when Jesus says He will give His flesh to the world to eat, some of His disciples also express difficulty with His statements.

But, Jesus, conscious that His disciples grumbled at this, said to them, "Does this cause you to stumble? *What* then if you see the Son of Man ascending to where He was before? It is the Spirit who gives life; the flesh profits nothing; the words that I have spoken to you are spirit and are life. But there are some of you who do not believe." For Jesus knew from the beginning who they were who did not believe, and who it was that would betray Him. And He was saying, "For this reason I have said to you, that no one can come to Me unless it has been granted him from the Father" (John 6:61–65; see Matthew 11:6; 13:11; John 3:13).

Setting: The temple treasury in Jerusalem. Following the Feast of Booths and the scribes' and Pharisees' failed attempt to stone a woman for committing adultery, Jesus returns the next day to teach. They question His testimony about Himself.

So Jesus said, "When you lift up the Son of Man, then you will know that I am *He,* and I do nothing on my own initiative, but I speak these things as the Father taught Me. And He who sent Me is with Me; He has not left Me alone, for I always do the things that are pleasing to Him" (John 8:28, 29; see John 3:14).

Setting: Jerusalem. Following the Pharisees' interrogation and dismissal of the formerly blind man Jesus gave back his sight on the Sabbath, the Lord converses with him about believing in the Son of Man.

Jesus heard that they had put him out, and finding him, He said, "Do you believe in the Son of Man?" He answered, "Who is He, Lord, that I may believe in Him?" Jesus said to him, "You have both seen Him, and He is the one who is talking to you." And he said, "Lord, I believe." And he worshiped Him (John 9:35–38; see John 4:26).

Setting: Jerusalem. Just days before the Passover, with the chief priests and Pharisees plotting to seize Him, crowds welcome Jesus to Jerusalem with palm branches and praise, and some Greeks ask to meet Him.

And Jesus answered them, saying, "The hour has come for the Son of Man to be glorified. Truly, truly, I say to you, unless a grain of wheat falls into the earth and dies, it remains alone; but if it dies, it bears much fruit. He who loves his life loses it, and he who hates his life in this world will keep it to life eternal. If anyone serves Me, he must follow Me; and where I am, there My servant will be also; if anyone serves Me, the Father will honor him" (John 12:23–26; see Matthew 10:39).

Setting: Jerusalem. Just days before the Passover, with the chief priests and Pharisees plotting to seize Jesus, who is expressing anxiety about His upcoming crucifixion, the crowds ask the Lord about the identity of the Son of Man.

The crowd then answered Him, "We have heard out of the Law that the Christ is to remain forever; and how can You say, 'The Son of Man must be lifted up'? Who is this Son of Man?" So Jesus said to them, "For a little while longer the Light is among you. Walk while you have the Light, so that darkness will not overtake you; he who walks in the darkness does not know where he goes. While you have the Light, believe in the Light, so that you may become sons of Light." These things Jesus spoke, and He went away and hid Himself from them (John 12:34–36; see 1 John 1:6).

Setting: Jerusalem. Before the Passover, after revealing to His disciples that Judas will betray Him to the chief priests and Pharisees, Jesus conveys how He will soon be glorified in His death, and commands the disciples to love one another.

Therefore when he had gone out, Jesus said, "Now is the Son of Man glorified, and God is glorified in Him; if God is glorified in Him, God will also glorify Him in Himself, and will glorify Him immediately. Little children, I am with you a little while longer. You will seek Me; and as I said to the Jews, now I also say to you, 'Where I am going, you cannot come.' A new commandment I give to you, that you love one another, even as I have loved you, that you also love one another. By this all men will know that you are My disciples, if you have love for one another" (John 13:31–35; see Leviticus 19:18; John 7:33, 34; 17:1; 1 John 3:14).

SON OF MAN, COMING OF THE (Also see JESUS' RETURN; LORD, COMING OF THE; and SON OF MAN)

[COMING OF THE SON OF MAN from the Son of Man comes]

Setting: Galilee. After His disciples observe His ministry, Jesus summons and specifically instructs them about the upcoming difficulties of their ministry to the people of Israel.

"Brother will betray brother to death, and a father *his* child; and children will rise up against parents and cause them to be put to death. You will be hated by all because of My name, but it is the one who has endured to the end who will be saved. But whenever they persecute you in one city, flee to the next; for truly I say to you, you will not finish *going through* the cities of Israel until the Son of Man comes" (Matthew 10:21–23; cf. Matthew 10:35, 36; 16:27, 28; 24:9).

[COMING OF THE SON OF MAN from the Son of Man coming]

Setting: Near Caesarea Philippi. After rebuking Peter for trying to forbid Him to accomplish His earthly mission of dying and being resurrected, Jesus teaches His disciples about the costs of discipleship.

Then Jesus said to His disciples, "If anyone wishes to come after Me, he must deny himself, and take up his cross and follow Me. For whoever wishes to save his life will lose it; but whoever loses his life for My sake will find it. For what will it profit a man if he gains the whole world and forfeits his soul? Or what will a man give in exchange for his soul? For the Son of Man is going to come in the glory of His Father with His angels, and WILL THEN REPAY EVERY MAN ACCORDING TO HIS DEEDS. Truly, I say to you, there are some of you who are standing here who will not taste death until they see the Son of Man coming in His kingdom" (Matthew 16:24–28, Jesus quotes from Psalm 62:12; cf. Mark 8:34–37; Luke 9:23–27; see Matthew 10:38, 39).

Setting: The Mount of Olives, just east of Jerusalem. During His Olivet Discourse, Jesus answers His disciples' questions as to when the temple will be destroyed and Jerusalem overrun, along with the signs of His coming and the end of the age.

"Therefore when you see the ABOMINATION OF DESOLATION which was spoken of through Daniel the prophet, standing in the holy place (let the reader understand), then those who are in Judea must flee to the mountains. Whoever is on the housetop must not go down to get the things that are in his house. Whoever is in the field must not turn back to get his cloak. But woe to those who are pregnant and to those who are nursing babies in those days! But pray that your flight will not be in the winter, or on a Sabbath. For then there will be a great tribulation, such as has not occurred since the beginning of the world until now, nor ever will. Unless those days had been cut short, no life would have been saved; but for the sake of the elect those days will be cut short. Then if anyone says to you, 'Behold, here is the Christ,' or "There *He is,*' do not believe *him.* For false Christs and false prophets will arise and will show great signs and wonders, so as to mislead, if possible, even the elect. Behold, I have told you in advance. So if they say to you, 'Behold, He is in the wilderness,' do not go out, *or,* 'Behold, He is in the inner rooms,' do not believe *them.* For just as the lightning comes from the east and flashes even to the west, so will the coming of the Son of Man be. Wherever the corpse is, there the vultures will gather" (Matthew 24:15–28, Jesus quotes from Daniel 9:27; cf. Daniel 12:1; Mark 13:14–23; Luke 17:22–31; 21:20–24; 23:29; see John 4:48).

[COMING OF THE SON OF MAN from the Son of Man coming]

Setting: The Mount of Olives, just east of Jerusalem. During His Olivet Discourse, Jesus answers His disciples' questions as to when the temple will be destroyed and Jerusalem overrun, along with the signs of His coming and the end of the age.

"But immediately after the tribulation of those days THE SUN WILL BE DARKENED, AND THE MOON WILL NOT GIVE ITS LIGHT, AND THE STARS WILL FALL from the sky, and the powers of the heavens will be shaken. And then the sign of the Son of Man will appear

in the sky, and then all the tribes of the earth will mourn, and they will see the SON OF MAN COMING ON THE CLOUDS OF THE SKY with power and great glory. And He will send forth His angels with A GREAT TRUMPET and THEY WILL GATHER TOGETHER His elect from the four winds, from one end of the sky to the other" (Matthew 24:29–31, Jesus quotes from Isaiah 13:10, Daniel 7:13; Exodus 19:16; cf. Mark 13:24–27; Luke 21:25–27).

Setting: On the Mount of Olives, just east of Jerusalem. During His discourse, after answering His disciples' questions as to when the temple will be destroyed and Jerusalem overrun, along with the signs of His coming and the end of the age, Jesus teaches them the Parable of the Fig Tree.

"Now learn the parable from the fig tree: when its branch has already become tender and puts forth its leaves, you know that summer is near; so, you too, when you see all these things, recognize that He is near, *right* at the door. Truly, I say to you, this generation will not pass away until all these things take place. Heaven and earth will pass away, but My words will not pass away. But of that day and hour no one knows, not even the angels of heaven, nor the Son, but the Father alone. For the coming of the Son of Man will be just like the days of Noah. For as in those days before the flood they were eating and drinking, marrying and giving in marriage, until the day that Noah entered the ark, and they did not understand until the flood came and took them all away; so will the coming of the Son of Man be. Then there will be two men in the field; one will be taken and one will be left. Two women *will be* grinding at the mill; one will be taken and one will be left" (Matthew 24:32–41; cf. Mark 13:28–32; Luke 17:34–36; 21:28–33; see Genesis 6:5; 7:7; Matthew 5:18; 10:23; James 5:9).

[COMING OF THE SON OF MAN from the Son of Man is coming]
Setting: The Mount of Olives, just east of Jerusalem. During His Olivet Discourse, after answering His disciples' questions as to when the temple will be destroyed and Jerusalem overrun, along with the signs of His coming and the end of the age, Jesus reemphasizes to His disciples that they should be on the alert for His return.

"Therefore be on the alert, for you do not know which day your Lord is coming. But be sure of this, that if the head of the house had known at what time of the night the thief was coming, he would have been on the alert and would not have allowed his house to be broken into. For this reason you also must be ready; for the Son of Man is coming at an hour when you do not think *He will.* Who then is the faithful and sensible slave whom his master put in charge of his household to give their food at the proper time? Blessed is that slave whom his master finds so doing when he comes. Truly I say to you that he will put him in charge of all his possessions. But if that evil slave says in his heart, 'My master is not coming for a long time,' and begins to beat his fellow slaves and eat and drink with drunkards; the master of that slave will come on a day when he does not expect *him* and at an hour which he does not know, and will cut him in pieces and assign him a place with the hypocrites; in that place there will be weeping and gnashing of teeth" (Matthew 24:42–51; cf. Mark 13:33–37; Luke 12:39–46; 21:34–36; see Matthew 8:11, 12; 25:21–23).

[COMING OF THE SON OF MAN from the Son of Man comes]
Setting: The Mount of Olives, just east of Jerusalem. During His Olivet Discourse, after answering His disciples' questions as to when the temple will be destroyed and Jerusalem overrun, along with the signs of His coming and the end of the age, Jesus reveals the future judgments following His return.

"But when the Son of Man comes in His glory, and all the angels with Him, then He will sit on His glorious throne. All the nations will be gathered before Him; and He will separate them from one another, as the shepherd separates the sheep from the goats; and He will put the sheep on His right, and the goats on the left. Then the King will say to those on His right, 'Come, you who are blessed of My Father, inherit the kingdom prepared for you from the foundation of the world. 'For I was hungry, and you gave Me *something* to eat; I was thirsty, and you gave Me *something* to drink; I was a stranger, and you invited Me in; naked, and you clothed Me; I was sick, and you visited Me; I was in prison, and you came to Me.' Then the righteous will answer Him, 'Lord, when did we see You hungry and feed You, or thirsty, and give you *something* to drink? And when did we see You a stranger, and invite You in, or naked, and clothe You? When did we see You sick, or in prison, and come to You?' The King will answer and say to them, 'Truly I say to you, to the extent that you did it to one of these brothers of Mine, *even* the least *of them,* you did it to Me.' Then He will also say to those on His left, 'Depart from Me, accursed ones, into the eternal fire which has been prepared for the devil and his angels; for I was hungry, and you gave Me *nothing* to eat; I was thirsty, and you gave Me nothing to drink; I was a stranger, and you did not invite Me in; naked, and you did not clothe Me; sick, and in prison, and you did not visit Me.' Then they themselves also will answer, 'Lord, when did we see You hungry, or thirsty, or a stranger, or naked, or sick, or in prison, and did not take care of You?' Then He will answer them, 'Truly I say to you, to the extent that you did not do it to one of the least of these, you did not do it to Me.' These will go away into eternal punishment, but the righteous into eternal life" (Matthew 25:31–46; see Matthew 7:23; 16:27; 19:29).

[COMING OF THE SON OF MAN from THE SON OF MAN and COMING ON THE CLOUDS OF HEAVEN]
Setting: Jerusalem. After being betrayed by Judas and arrested, Jesus appears before Caiaphas the high priest and the Council for interrogation aimed at entrapping Him.

Jesus said to him, "You have said it *yourself;* nevertheless I tell you, hereafter you will see THE SON OF MAN SITTING AT THE RIGHT HAND OF POWER, AND COMING ON THE CLOUDS OF HEAVEN" (Matthew 26:64, Jesus quotes from Daniel 7:13; cf. Mark 14:62).

[COMING OF THE SON OF MAN from the Son of Man will also be ashamed of him when He comes in the glory of His Father with the holy angels]
Setting: Caesarea Philippi. After rebuking Peter for desiring to thwart His mission to the cross, Jesus summons a crowd, along with His disciples, and informs them of the high costs of following Him.

And He summoned the crowd with His disciples, and said to them, "If anyone wishes to come after Me, he must deny himself, and take up his cross and follow Me. For whoever wishes to save his life will lose it, but whoever loses his life for My sake and the gospel's will save it. For what does it profit a man to gain the whole world, and forfeit his soul? For what will a man give in exchange for his soul? For whoever is ashamed of Me and My words in this adulterous and sinful generation, the Son of Man will also be ashamed of him when He comes in the glory of His Father with the holy angels" (Mark 8:34–38; cf. Matthew 16:24–28; Luke 9:23–27; see Matthew 10:33, 38, 39).

[COMING OF THE SON OF MAN from the Son of Man coming]
Setting: On the Mount of Olives, east of the temple in Jerusalem. After prophesying the temple's destruction, Jesus responds during His Olivet Discourse to questions from Peter, James, John, and Andrew about other future events.

"But in those days, after that tribulation, THE SUN WILL BE DARKENED AND THE MOON WILL NOT GIVE ITS LIGHT, AND THE STARS WILL BE FALLING from heaven, and the powers that are in the heavens will be shaken. Then they will see THE SON OF MAN COMING IN CLOUDS with great power and glory. And then He will send forth the angels, and will gather together His elect from the four winds, from the farthest end of the earth to the farthest end of heaven" (Mark 13:24–27. Jesus quotes from Isaiah 13:10; 34:4; Daniel 7:13; cf. Matthew 24:29–31; Luke 21:25–27).

[COMING OF THE SON OF MAN from THE SON OF MAN and COMING WITH THE CLOUDS OF HEAVEN]
Setting: Jerusalem. Following His betrayal by Judas and His arrest, Jesus confirms that He is the Christ to the high priest and all the chief priests, as they seek justification for putting Him to death.

And Jesus said, "I am; and you shall see THE SON OF MAN SITTING AT THE RIGHT HAND OF POWER, and COMING WITH THE CLOUDS OF HEAVEN" (Mark 14:62, Jesus quotes from Psalm 110:1; Daniel 7:13; cf. Matthew 26:57–68; see Luke 22:54).

[COMING OF THE SON OF MAN from the Son of Man will be ashamed of him when He comes in His glory]
Setting: Galilee. Following Peter's pronouncement that Jesus is the Christ of God, the Lord conveys the demands of discipleship and the hope regarding the kingdom of God.

And He was saying to *them* all, "If anyone wishes to come after Me, he must deny himself, and take up his cross daily and follow Me. For whoever wishes to save his life will lose it, but whoever loses his life for My sake, he is the one who will save it. For what is a man profited if he gains the whole world, and loses or forfeits himself? For whoever is ashamed of Me and My words, the Son of Man will be ashamed of him when He comes in His glory, and *the glory* of the Father and of the holy angels. But I say to you truthfully, there are some of those standing here who will not taste death until they see the kingdom of God" (Luke 9:23–27; cf. Matthew 16:24–26, 28; Mark 8:34–37; see Matthew 10:33, 38, 39).

[COMING OF THE SON OF MAN from the Son of Man is coming]
Setting: On the way from Galilee to Jerusalem. After giving a parable about riches and greed, Jesus uses another parable to challenge the crowd and His disciples to be ready for His return.

"Be dressed in readiness, and *keep* your lamps lit. Be like men who are waiting for their master when he returns from the wedding feast, so that they may immediately open *the door* to him when he comes and knocks. Blessed are those slaves whom the master will find on the alert when he comes; truly I say to you, that he will gird himself *to serve,* and have them recline *at the table,* and will come up and wait on them. Whether he comes in the second watch, or even in the third and finds *them* so, blessed are those *slaves*. But be sure of this, that if the head of the house had known at what hour the thief was coming, he would not have allowed his house to be broken into. You too, be ready; for the Son of Man is coming at an hour that you do not expect" (Luke 12:35–40; cf. Matthew 24:42–44; see Mark 13:33; Ephesians 6:14).

[COMING OF THE SON OF MAN from the Son of Man be in His day and the Son of Man is revealed]
Setting: On the way from Galilee to Jerusalem. After the Pharisees question Him about the coming of the kingdom of God, Jesus tells His disciples of His second coming.

And He said to the disciples, "The days will come when you will long to see one of the days of the Son of Man, and you will not see it. They will say to you, 'Look there! Look here!' Do not go away, and do not run after *them*. For just like the lightning, when it flashes out of one part of the sky, shines to the other part of the sky, so will the Son of Man be in His day. But first He must suffer many things and be rejected by this generation. And just as it happened in the days of Noah, so it will be also in the days of the Son of Man: they were eating, they were drinking, they were marrying, they were being given in marriage, until the day that Noah entered the ark, and the flood came and destroyed them all. It was the same as happened in the days of Lot: they were eating, they were drinking, they were buying, they were selling, they were planting, they were building; but on the day that Lot went out from Sodom it rained fire and brimstone from heaven and destroyed them all. It will be just the same on the day that the Son of Man is revealed. On that day, the one who is on the housetop and whose goods are in the house must not go down to take them out; and likewise the one who is in the field must not turn back. Remember Lot's wife. Whoever seeks to keep his life will lose it, and whoever loses *his life* will preserve it. I tell you, on that night there will be two in one bed; one will be taken and the other will be left. There will be two women grinding at the same place; one will be taken and the other will be left. [Two men will be in the field; one will be taken and the other will be left."] And answering they said to Him, "Where, Lord?" And He said to them, "Where the body *is*, there also the vultures will be gathered" (Luke 17:22–37; see Genesis 19; Matthew 10:39; 16:21, 27; 24:17–28, 37–41).

[COMING OF THE SON OF MAN from the Son of Man comes]
Setting: On the way from Galilee to Jerusalem. After telling His disciples of His second coming, Jesus instructs them about persistence in prayer.

Now He was telling them a parable to show that at all times they ought to pray and not to lose heart, saying, "In a certain city there was a judge who did not fear God and did not respect man. There was a widow in that city, and she kept coming to him, saying, 'Give me legal protection from my opponent.' For a while he was unwilling; but afterward he said to himself, 'Even though I do not fear God nor respect man, yet because this woman bothers me, I will give her legal protection, otherwise by continually coming she will wear me out.'" And the Lord said, "Hear what the unrighteous judge said; now, will not God bring about justice for His elect who cry to Him day and night, and will He delay long over them? I tell you that He will bring about justice for them quickly. However, when the Son of Man comes, will He find faith on the earth?" (Luke 18:1–8; see Luke 11:5–10).

[COMING OF THE SON OF MAN from the Son of Man coming]
Setting: The Mount of Olives, just east of Jerusalem. After ministering in the temple a few days before His crucifixion, and giving His disciples more details regarding future events, Jesus speaks during His Olivet Discourse of His return.

"There will be signs in sun and moon and stars, and on the earth dismay among the nations, in perplexity at the roaring of the sea and the waves, men fainting from fear and the expectation of the things which are coming upon the world; for the powers of the heavens will be shaken. Then they will see THE SON OF MAN COMING IN A CLOUD with power and great glory. But when these things begin to take place, straighten up and lift up your heads, because your redemption is drawing near" (Luke 21:25–28, Jesus quotes from Daniel 7:13; cf. Matthew 24:29–31; Mark 13:24–27).

SON OF MAN, SIGN OF THE (Also see SON OF MAN, COMING OF THE)

Setting: The Mount of Olives, just east of Jerusalem. During His Olivet Discourse, Jesus answers His disciples' questions as to when the temple will be destroyed and Jerusalem overrun, along with the signs of His coming and the end of the age.

"But immediately after the tribulation of those days THE SUN WILL BE DARKENED, AND THE MOON WILL NOT GIVE ITS LIGHT, AND THE STARS WILL FALL from the sky, and the powers of the heavens will be shaken. And then the sign of the Son of Man will appear in the sky, and then all the tribes of the earth will mourn, and they will see the SON OF MAN COMING ON THE CLOUDS OF THE SKY with power and great glory. And He will send forth His angels with A GREAT TRUMPET and THEY WILL GATHER TOGETHER His elect from the four winds, from one end of the sky to the other" (Matthew 24:29–31, Jesus quotes from Isaiah 13:10, Daniel 7:13; Exodus 19:16; cf. Mark 13:24–27; Luke 21:25–27).

SONS (See other specifics following this category; ISRAEL, SONS OF; and SONS OF GOD are separate entries; also see SON)

Setting: Galilee. During the early part of His ministry, Jesus preaches the Sermon on the Mount to His disciples and the multitudes.

"You have heard that it was said, 'YOU SHALL LOVE YOUR NEIGHBOR and hate your enemy.' But I say to you, love your enemies and pray for those who persecute you, so that you may be sons of your Father who is in heaven; for He causes His sun to rise on *the* evil and *the* good, and sends rain on *the* righteous and *the* unrighteous. For if you love those who love you, what reward do you have? Do not even the tax collectors do the same? If you greet only your brothers, what more are you doing *than others?* Do not even the Gentiles do the same? Therefore, you are to be perfect, as your heavenly Father is perfect" (Matthew 5:43–48, Jesus quotes from Leviticus 19:18; cf. Leviticus 19:2; Luke 6:27–36).

Setting: Galilee. After Jesus heals a blind, mute, demon-possessed man, the Pharisees accuse the Lord in front of crowds of being a worker of Beelzebul (Satan).

And knowing their thoughts Jesus said to them, "Any kingdom divided against itself is laid waste; and any city or house divided against itself will not stand. If Satan casts out Satan, he is divided against himself; how then will his kingdom stand? If I by Beelzebul cast out demons, by whom do your sons cast *them* out? For this reason they will be your judges. But if I cast out demons by the Spirit of God, then the kingdom of God has come upon you. Or how can anyone enter the strong man's house and carry off his property, unless he first binds the strong *man?* And then he will plunder his house" (Matthew 12:25–29; cf. Matthew 9:34; Mark 3:23–27; Luke 11:17–20).

Setting: A house near the Sea of Galilee. Jesus gives the meaning of the Parable of the Wheat and the Tares to His disciples.

And He said, "The one who sows the good seed is the Son of Man, and the field is the world; and as *for* the good seed, these are the sons of the kingdom; and the tares are the sons of the evil *one;* and the enemy who sowed them is the devil, and the harvest is the end of the age; and the reapers are angels. So just as the tares are gathered up and burned with fire, so shall it be at the end of the age. The Son of Man will send forth His angels, and they will gather out of His kingdom all stumbling blocks, and those who commit lawlessness, and will throw them into the furnace of fire; in that place there will be weeping and gnashing of teeth. Then THE RIGHTEOUS WILL SHINE FORTH AS THE SUN in the kingdom of their Father. He who has ears, let him hear" (Matthew 13:37–43, Jesus quotes from Daniel 12:3; cf. Matthew 8:12; 13:50).

Setting: Capernaum of Galilee. Jesus pays the two-drachma temple tax for Peter and Himself in a miraculous manner.

He said, "Yes." And when he came into the house, Jesus spoke to him first, saying, "What do you think, Simon? From whom do the kings of the earth collect customs or poll-tax, from their sons or from strangers?" When Peter said, "From strangers," Jesus said to him, "Then the sons are exempt. However, so that we do not offend them, go to the sea and throw in a hook, and take the first fish that comes up; and when you open its mouth, you will find a shekel. Take that and give it to them for you and Me" (Matthew 17:25–27; see Exodus 30:11–16; Matthew 22:17–19; Romans 13:7).

Setting: The temple in Jerusalem. Jesus delivers a parable to the chief priests and elders after they question His authority.

"But what do you think? A man had two sons, and he came to the first and said, 'Son, go work today in the vineyard.' And he answered, 'I will not'; but afterward he regretted it and went. The man came to the second and said the same thing; and he answered, 'I *will,* sir'; but he did not go. Which of the two sons did the will of his father?" They said, "The first." Jesus said to them, "Truly, I say to you that the tax collectors and prostitutes will get into the kingdom of God before you. For John came to you in the way of righteousness and you did not believe him; but the tax collectors and prostitutes did believe him; and you, seeing *this,* did not even feel remorse afterward so as to believe him" (Matthew 21:28–32; cf. Luke 7:29, 30, 37–50).

Setting: The temple in Jerusalem. After the Jewish religious leaders test Him with questions, Jesus pronounces the eighth of eight woes upon them in front of the crowds and His disciples.

"Woe to you, scribes and Pharisees, hypocrites! For you build the tombs of the prophets and adorn the monuments of the righteous, and say, 'If we had been *living* in the days of our fathers, we would not have been partners with them in *shedding* the blood of the prophets.' So you testify against yourselves, that you are sons of those who murdered the prophets. Fill up, then, the measure *of the guilt* of you fathers. You serpents, you brood of vipers, how will you escape the sentence of hell? Therefore, behold, I am sending you prophets and wise men and scribes; some of them you will kill and crucify, and some of them you will scourge in your synagogues, and persecute from city to city, so that upon you may fall *the guilt of* all the righteous blood shed on earth, from the blood of righteous Abel to the blood of Zechariah, the son of Berechiah, whom you murdered between the temple and the altar. Truly I say to you, all these things will come upon this generation" (Matthew 23:29–36; cf. 2 Chronicles 24:21; Zechariah 1:1; Matthew 3:7; Luke 11:47–52; see Matthew 10:23).

Setting: On the way from Galilee to Jerusalem. After Jesus casts out a demon, some in the crowd test the Lord, demanding a sign from heaven.

But He knew their thoughts and said to them, "Any kingdom divided against itself is laid waste; and a house *divided* against itself falls. If Satan also is divided against himself, how will his kingdom stand? For you say that I cast out demons by Beelzebul. And if I by Beelzebul cast out demons, by whom do your sons cast them out? So they will be your judges. But if I cast out demons by the finger of God, then the kingdom of God has come upon you" (Luke 11:17–20; cf. Matthew 12:25–28; Mark 3:23–27; see Exodus 8:19; Matthew 3:2, 10:25).

Setting: On the way from Galilee to Jerusalem. Jesus conveys the illustration of the prodigal son because the Pharisees and scribes complain He associates with tax collectors and sinners.

And He said, "A man had two sons. The younger of them said to his father, 'Father, give me the share of the estate that falls to me.' So he divided his wealth between them. And not many days later, the younger son gathered everything together and went on a journey into a distant country, and there he squandered his estate with loose living. Now when he had spent everything, a severe famine occurred in that country, and he began to be impoverished. So he went and hired himself out to one of the citizens of that country, and he sent him into his fields to feed swine. And he would have gladly filled his stomach with the pods that the swine were eating, and no one was giving *anything* to him. But when he came to his senses, he said, 'How many of my father's hired men have more than enough bread, but I am dying here with hunger! I will get up and go to my father, and will say to him, "Father, I have sinned against heaven, and in your sight; I am no longer worthy to be called your son; make me as one of your hired men."' So he got up and came to his father. But while he was still a long way off, his father saw him and felt compassion *for him,* and ran and embraced him and kissed him. And the son said to him, "Father, I have sinned against heaven and in your sight; I am no longer worthy to be called your son.' But the father said to his slaves, 'Quickly bring out the best robe and put it on him, and put a ring on his hand and sandals on his feet; and bring the fattened calf, kill it, and let us eat and celebrate; for this son of mine was dead and has come to life again; he was lost and has been found.' And they began to celebrate. Now his older son was in the field, when he came and approached the house, he heard music and dancing. And he summoned one of the servants and *began* inquiring what these things could be. And he said to him, 'Your brother has come, and your father has killed the fattened calf because he has received him back safe and sound.' But he became angry and was not willing to go in; and his father came out and *began* pleading with him. But he answered and said to his father, 'Look! For so many years I have been serving you and I have never neglected a command of yours; and *yet* you have never given me a young goat, so that I might celebrate with my friends; but when this son of yours came, who has devoured your wealth with prostitutes, you killed the fattened calf for him.' And he said to him, 'Son, you have always been with me, and all that is mine is yours. But we had to celebrate and rejoice, for this brother of yours was dead and *has begun* to live, and was lost and has been found' " (Luke 15:11–32; see Proverb 29:2).

SONS, PARABLE OF THE TWO

Setting: The temple in Jerusalem. Jesus delivers a parable to the chief priests and elders after they question His authority.

[SONS, PARABLE OF THE TWO from two sons]

"But what do you think? A man had two sons, and he came to the first and said, 'Son, go work today in the vineyard.' And he answered, 'I will not'; but afterward he regretted it and went. The man came to the second and said the same thing; and he answered, 'I *will,* sir'; but he did not go. Which of the two sons did the will of his father?" They said, "The first." Jesus said to them, "Truly, I say to you that the tax collectors and prostitutes will get into the kingdom of God before you. For John came to you in the way of righteousness and you did not believe him; but the tax collectors and prostitutes did believe him; and you, seeing *this,* did not even feel remorse afterward so as to believe him" (Matthew 21:28–32; cf. Luke 7:29, 30, 37–50).

SONS, PARABLE OF TWO (Listed under SONS, PARABLE OF THE TWO)

SONS, TWO (See SON, PRODIGAL and SONS, PARABLE OF THE TWO)

SONS OF GOD

Setting: Galilee. Early in His ministry, Jesus presents the Beatitudes (part of the Sermon on the Mount) to His disciples and the gathered crowds from Galilee, Decapolis, Jerusalem, Judea, and beyond the Jordan.

"Blessed are the peacemakers, for they shall be called sons of God" (Matthew 5:9; see Matthew 5:1; 13:35).

[SONS OF GOD from sons of your Father]

Setting: Galilee. During the early part of His ministry, Jesus preaches the Sermon on the Mount to His disciples and the multitudes.

"You have heard that it was said, 'YOU SHALL LOVE YOUR NEIGHBOR and hate your enemy.' But I say to you, love your enemies and pray for those who persecute you, so that you may be sons of your Father who is in heaven; for He causes His sun to rise on *the* evil and *the* good, and sends rain on *the* righteous and *the* unrighteous. For if you love those who love you, what reward do you have? Do not even the tax collectors do the same? If you greet only your brothers, what more are you doing *than others?* Do not even the Gentiles do the same? Therefore, you are to be perfect, as your heavenly Father is perfect" (Matthew 5:43–48, Jesus quotes from Leviticus 19:18; cf. Leviticus 19:2; Luke 6:27–36).

Setting: The temple in Jerusalem. A few days before His crucifixion, after the scribes and Pharisees seek to trap Jesus by questioning Him about paying taxes to Caesar, some Sadducees (who say there is no resurrection) ask Him a question about the resurrection.

Jesus said to them, "The sons of this age marry and are given in marriage, but those who are considered worthy to attain to that age and the resurrection from the dead, neither marry nor are given in marriage; for they cannot even die anymore, because they are like angels, and are sons of God, being sons of the resurrection. But that the dead are raised, even Moses showed, in the *passage about the burning* bush, where he calls the Lord THE GOD OF ABRAHAM, AND THE GOD OF ISAAC, AND THE GOD OF JACOB. Now He is not the God of the dead but of the living; for all live to Him" (Luke 20:34–38, Jesus quotes from Exodus 3:6; cf. Matthew 22:23–32; Mark 12:18–27).

SONS OF ISRAEL (Listed under ISRAEL, SONS OF)

SONS OF LIGHT (Listed under LIGHT, SONS OF)

SONS OF MEN (Listed under MEN, SONS OF)

SONS OF THE EVIL ONE (Listed under EVIL ONE, SONS OF THE)

SONS OF THE KINGDOM (Listed under KINGDOM, SONS OF THE)

SONS OF THE MOST HIGH (Listed under MOST HIGH, SONS OF THE)

SONS OF THE RESURRECTION (Listed under RESURRECTION, SONS OF THE)

SONS OF THIS AGE (Listed under AGE, SONS OF THIS)

SONS OF YOUR FATHER (Listed under FATHER, SONS OF YOUR)

SORES

Setting: On the way from Galilee to Jerusalem. After responding to the Pharisees' scoffing at His teaching the disciples about stewardship and the permanence of the Law, Jesus conveys the story of the rich man and Lazarus.

"Now there was a rich man, and he habitually dressed in purple and fine linen, joyously living in splendor every day. And a poor man named Lazarus was laid at his gate, covered with sores, and longing to be fed with the *crumbs* which were falling from the rich man's table; besides, even the dogs were coming and licking his sores. Now the poor man died and was carried away by the angels to Abraham's bosom; and the rich man also died and was buried. In Hades he lifted up his eyes, being in torment, and saw Abraham far away and Lazarus in his bosom. And he cried out and said, 'Father Abraham, have mercy on me, and send Lazarus so that he may dip the tip of his finger in water and cool off my tongue, for I am in agony in this flame.' But Abraham said, 'Child, remember that during your life you received your good things, and likewise Lazarus bad things; but now he is being comforted here, and you are in agony. And besides all this, between us and you there is a great chasm fixed, so that those who wish to come over from here to you will not be able, and *that* none may cross over from there to us.' And he said, 'Then I beg you, father, that you send him to my father's house—for I have five brothers—in order that he may warn them, so that they will not also come to this place of torment.' But Abraham said, 'They have Moses and the Prophets; let them hear them.' But he said, 'No, father Abraham, but if someone goes to them from the dead, they will repent!' But he said to him, 'If they do not listen to Moses and the Prophets, they will not be persuaded even if someone rises from the dead.'" (Luke 16:19–31; see Luke 3:8; 6:24).

SORROW (Also see GRIEF; MOURNING; and WEEPING)

Setting: Jerusalem. Before the Passover, after warning His disciples of the persecution they will face after His departure to heaven, Jesus elaborates about the coming ministry of the Holy Spirit.

"But now I am going to Him who sent Me; and none of you asks Me, 'Where are You going?' But because I have said these things to you, sorrow has filled your heart. But I tell you the truth, it is to your advantage that I do away; for if I do not go away, the Helper will not come to you; but if I go, I will send Him to you. And He, when He comes, will convict the world concerning sin and righteousness and judgment; concerning sin, because they do not believe in Me; and concerning righteousness, because I go to the Father and you no longer see Me; and concerning judgment, because the ruler of this world has been judged" (John 16:5–11; see John 7:33; 12:31; 14:1, 16; 15:22, 24).

SOUL (Also see SOULS)

Setting: Galilee. After His disciples observe His ministry, Jesus summons and specifically instructs them about the ministry ahead involving true discipleship.

"Therefore do not fear them, for there is nothing concealed that will not be revealed, or hidden that will not be known. What I tell you in the darkness, speak in the light; and what you hear *whispered* in your ear, proclaim upon the housetops. Do not fear those who kill the body but are unable to kill the soul; but rather fear Him who is able to destroy both soul and body in hell" (Matthew 10:26–28; cf. Mark 4:22; Luke 12:3; see Hebrews 10:31).

Setting: Near Caesarea Philippi. After rebuking Peter for trying to forbid Him to accomplish His earthly mission of dying and being resurrected, Jesus teaches His disciples about the costs of following Him.

Then Jesus said to His disciples, "If anyone wishes to come after Me, he must deny himself, and take up his cross and follow Me. For whoever wishes to save his life will lose it; but whoever loses his life for My sake will find it. For what will it profit a man if he gains the whole world and forfeits his soul? Or what will a man give in exchange for his soul? For the Son of Man is going to come in the glory of His Father with His angels, and WILL THEN REPAY EVERY MAN ACCORDING TO HIS DEEDS. Truly, I say to you, there are some of you who are standing here who will not taste death until they see the Son of Man coming in His kingdom" (Matthew 16:24–28, Jesus quotes from Psalm 62:12; cf. Mark 8:34–37; Luke 9:23–27; see Matthew 10:38, 39).

Setting: The temple in Jerusalem. A Pharisee lawyer asks Jesus which is the great commandment of the Law, in order to test Him as He teaches.

And He said to him, "'YOU SHALL LOVE THE LORD YOUR GOD WITH ALL YOUR HEART, AND WITH ALL YOUR SOUL, AND WITH ALL YOUR MIND.' This is the great and foremost commandment. The second is like it,' YOU SHALL LOVE YOUR NEIGHBOR AS YOURSELF.' On these two commandments depend the whole Law and the Prophets" (Matthew 22:37–40; Jesus quotes from Leviticus 19:18; Deuteronomy 6:5; cf. Mark 12:28–34; see Matthew 7:12).

Setting: An upper room in Jerusalem. After celebrating the Passover meal with His disciples, Jesus retreats to the Garden of Gethsemane on the Mount of Olives to pray prior to His betrayal by Judas.

Then Jesus came with them to a place called Gethsemane, and said to His disciples, "Sit here while I go over there and pray." And He took with Him Peter and the two sons of Zebedee, and began to be grieved and distressed. Then He said to them, "My soul is deeply grieved, to the point of death; remain here and keep watch with Me." And He went a little beyond *them,* and fell on His face and prayed, saying, "My Father, if it is possible, let this cup pass from Me; yet not as I will, but as You will." And He came to the disciples and found them sleeping, and said to Peter, "So, you *men* could not keep watch with Me for one hour? Keep watching and praying that you may not enter into temptation; the spirit is willing, but the flesh is weak." He went away again a second time and prayed, saying, "My Father, if this cannot pass away unless I drink it, Your will be done." Again He came and found them sleeping, for their eyes were heavy. And He left them again, and went away and prayed a third time, saying the same thing once more. Then He came to the disciples and said to them, "Are you still sleeping and resting? Behold the hour is at hand and the Son of Man is being betrayed into the hands of sinners. Get up, let us be going; behold the one who betrays Me is at hand!" (Matthew 26:36–46; cf. Mark 14:32–42; Luke 22:40–46; see Matthew 20:22; John 12:27).

Setting: Caesarea Philippi. After rebuking Peter for desiring to thwart His mission to the cross, Jesus summons a crowd, along with His disciples, and informs them of the high costs of following Him.

And He summoned the crowd with His disciples, and said to them, "If anyone wishes to come after Me, he must deny himself, and take up his cross and follow Me. For whoever wishes to save his life will lose it, but whoever loses his life for My sake and the gospel's will save it. For what does it profit a man to gain the whole world, and forfeit his soul? For what will a man give in exchange for his soul? For whoever is ashamed of Me and My words in this adulterous and sinful generation, the Son of Man will also be ashamed of him when He comes in the glory of His Father with the holy angels" (Mark 8:34–38; cf. Matthew 16:24–28; Luke 9:23–27; see Matthew 10:33, 38, 39).

Setting: The temple in Jerusalem. With the Pharisees and Herodians failing to trap Jesus in a statement, one of the scribes asks Him which commandment is foremost.

Jesus answered, "The foremost is, 'HEAR, O ISRAEL! THE LORD OUR GOD IS ONE LORD; AND YOU SHALL LOVE THE LORD YOUR GOD WITH ALL YOUR HEART, AND WITH ALL YOUR SOUL, AND WITH ALL YOUR MIND AND WITH ALL YOUR STRENGTH.' The second is this, 'YOU SHALL LOVE YOUR NEIGHBOR AS YOURSELF.' There is no other commandment greater than these" (Mark 12:29–31, Jesus quotes from Deuteronomy 6:4, 5 and Leviticus 19:18; cf. Matthew 22:34–40).

Setting: Gethsemane on the Mount of Olives, just east of the temple in Jerusalem. Jesus agonizes over His impending death, disappointed His disciples keep falling asleep instead of watching and praying with Him.

They came to a place named Gethsemane; and He said to the disciples, "Sit here until I have prayed." And He took with Him Peter and James and John, and began to be very distressed and troubled. And He said to them, "My soul is deeply grieved to the point of death; remain here and keep watch." And He went a little beyond *them,* and fell to the ground and *began* to pray that if it were possible, the hour might pass Him by. And He was saying, "Abba! Father! All things are possible for You; remove this cup from Me; yet not what I will, but what You will." And He came and found them sleeping, and said to Peter, "Simon, are you asleep? Could you not keep watch for one hour? Keep watching and praying that you may not come into temptation; the spirit is willing, but the flesh is weak" (Mark 14:32–38; cf. Matthew 26:36–41; Luke 22:41–46; see Romans 8:15; Galatians 4:6).

Setting: On the way from Galilee to Jerusalem. After the scribes and Pharisees turn hostile and question Him repeatedly in an attempt to catch Him in something He might say, Jesus responds to a question from the crowd and gives a parable about riches and greed.

And He told them a parable, saying, "The land of a rich man was very productive. And he began reasoning to himself, saying, 'What shall I do, since I have no place to store my crops?' Then he said, 'This is what I will do: I will tear down my barns and build larger ones, and here I will store all my grain and my goods. And I will say to my soul, "Soul, you have many goods laid up for many years *to come;* take your ease, eat, drink *and* be merry."' But God said to him, 'You fool! This *very* night your soul is required of you; and *now* who will own what you have prepared?' So is the man who stores up treasure for himself, and is not rich toward God" (Luke 12:16–21; see Job 27:8; Psalm 39:6; Ecclesiastes 12:9; Philippians 2:3).

Setting: Jerusalem. Just days before the Passover, with the chief priests and Pharisees plotting to seize Him and crowds welcoming Him with palm branches and praise, Jesus expresses anxiety about His upcoming crucifixion.

"Now My soul has become troubled; and what shall I say, 'Father, save Me from this hour'? But for this purpose I came to this hour. Father glorify Your name." Then a voice came out of heaven: "I have glorified it, and will glorify it again." So the crowd *of people* who stood by and heard it were saying that it had thundered; others were saying, "An angel has spoken to Him." Jesus answered and said, "This voice has not come for My sake, but for your sakes. Now judgment is upon this world; now the ruler of this world will be cast out. And I, if I am lifted up from the earth, will draw all men to Myself" (John 12:27–32; see Matthew 3:17; 26:38; John 3:14; 6:44; 11:42; 14:30).

SOULS (Also see SOUL)

Setting: Galilee. After rendering a thanksgiving prayer to His Father in heaven, Jesus offers rest to all who are weary and heavy-laden as He preaches and teaches throughout the region.

"Come to Me, all who are weary and heavy-laden, and I will give you rest. Take My yoke upon you and learn from Me, for I am gentle and humble in heart, and YOU WILL FIND REST FOR YOUR SOULS. For My yoke is easy and My burden is light" (Matthew 11:28–30, Jesus quotes from Jeremiah 6:16; see Jeremiah 31:35; 1 John 5:3).

SOUTH (Also see EAST; NORTH; and WEST)

Setting: On the way from Galilee to Jerusalem. After telling how a relationship with Him will divide families, Jesus chastises the crowds for being able to discern the weather but not the present age.

And He was also saying to the crowds, "When you see a cloud rising in the west, immediately you say, 'A shower is coming,' and so it turns out. And when *you see* a south wind blowing, you say, 'It will be a hot day,' and it turns out *that way*. You hypocrites! You know how to analyze the appearance of the earth and the sky, but why do you not analyze this present time?" (Luke 12:54–56; cf. Matthew 16:2, 3).

Setting: On the way from Galilee to Jerusalem. While teaching in the cities and villages, Jesus responds to a question about who is saved.

And someone said to Him, "Lord, are here *just* a few who are being saved?" And He said to them, "Strive to enter through the narrow door; for many, I tell you, will seek to enter and will not be able. Once the head of the house gets up and shuts the door, and you begin to stand outside and knock on the door, saying, 'Lord, open up to us!' then He will answer and say to you, 'I do not know where you are from.' Then you will begin to say, 'We ate and drank in Your presence, and You taught in our streets'; and He will say, 'I tell you, I do not know where you are from; DEPART FROM ME, ALL YOU EVILDOERS.' In that place there will be weeping and gnashing of teeth when you see Abraham and Isaac and Jacob and all the prophets in the kingdom of God, but you yourselves being thrown out. And they will come from east and west and from north and south, and will recline *at the table* in the kingdom of God. And behold, *some* are last who will be first and *some* are first who will be last" (Luke 13:23–30, Jesus quotes from Psalm 6:8; cf. Matthew 7:13, 23; 8:11, 12; see Matthew 19:30; Luke 3:8).

SOUTH, QUEEN OF THE

Setting: Galilee. After Jesus warns the Pharisees about the unpardonable sin and their future judgment, some Pharisees and scribes ask Him to perform a miraculous sign for them in front of the crowds.

But He answered and said to them, "An evil and adulterous generation craves for a sign; and *yet* no sign will be given to it but the sign of Jonah the prophet; for just as JONAH WAS THREE DAYS AND THREE NIGHTS IN THE BELLY OF THE SEA MONSTER, so will the Son of Man be three days and three nights in the heart of the earth. The men of Nineveh will stand up with this generation at the judgment, and will condemn it because they repented at the preaching of Jonah; and behold, something greater than Jonah is here. *The* Queen of *the* South will rise up with this generation at the judgment and will condemn it, because she came from the ends of the earth to hear the wisdom of Solomon; and behold, something greater than Solomon is here" (Matthew 12:39–42; Jesus quotes from Jonah 1:17; cf. 1 Kings 10:1; Jonah 3:5; Matthew 16:1, 4; Luke 11:29).

Setting: On the way from Galilee to Jerusalem. After revealing a problem with exorcism and responding to a blessing from a woman in the crowd, Jesus tells the increasing crowds of the sign of Jonah.

As the crowds were increasing, He began to say, "This generation is a wicked generation; it seeks for a sign, and *yet* no sign will be given to it but the sign of Jonah. For just as Jonah became a sign to the Ninevites, so will the Son of Man be to this generation. The Queen of the South will rise up with the men of this generation at the judgment and condemn them, because she came from the ends of the earth to hear the wisdom of Solomon; and behold, something greater than Solomon is here. The men of Nineveh will stand up with this generation at the judgment and condemn it, because they repented at the preaching of Jonah; and behold, something greater than Jonah is here" (Luke 11:29–32; cf. Matthew 16:4; see 1 Kings 10:1–10; Jonah 3:4, 5).

SOWER (Also see SOWING)

Setting: By the Sea of Galilee. While teaching and preaching to the crowds from a boat, Jesus conveys the Parable of the Sower.

And He spoke many things to them in parables, saying, "Behold, the sower went out to sow; and as he sowed, some *seeds* fell beside the road, and the birds came and ate them up. Others fell on the rocky places, where they did not have much soil; and immediately they sprang up, because they had no depth of soil. But when the sun had risen, they were scorched; and because they had no root, they withered away. Others fell among the thorns, and the thorns came up and choked them out. And others fell on the good soil and yielded a crop, some a hundredfold, some sixty, and some thirty. He who has ears, let him hear" (Matthew 13:3–9; cf. Mark 4:3–9; Luke 8:4–8).

Setting: By the Sea of Galilee. With the religious leaders rejecting His message, Jesus begins to teach in parables, and gives His disciples the meaning of the Parable of the Sower.

"Hear then the parable of the sower. When anyone hears the word of the kingdom and does not understand it, the evil *one* comes and snatches away what has been sown in his heart. This is the one on whom seed was sown beside the road. The one on whom seed was sown on the rocky places, this is the man who hears the word and immediately receives it with joy; yet he has no *firm* root in himself, but is *only* temporary, and when affliction or persecution arises because of the word, immediately he falls away. And the one on whom seed was sown among the thorns, this is the man who hears the word, and the worry of the world and the deceitfulness of wealth choke the word, and it becomes unfruitful. And the one on whom seed was sown on the good soil, this is the man who hears the word and understands it; who indeed bears fruit and brings forth, some a hundredfold, some sixty, and some thirty" (Matthew 13:18–23; cf. Mark 4:13–20; Luke 8:11–15).

Setting: By the Sea of Galilee. During the early part of His ministry, just after a visit from his mother and brothers, Jesus instructs a very large crowd with the Parable of the Sower from a boat.

"Listen *to this!* Behold, the sower went out to sow; as he was sowing, some *seed* fell beside the road, and the birds came and ate it up. Other *seed* fell on the rocky *ground* where it did not have much soil; and immediately it sprang up because it had no depth of soil. And after the sun had risen, it was scorched; and because it had no root, it withered away. Other *seed* fell among the thorns, and the thorns came up and choked it, and it yielded no crop. Other *seeds* fell into the good soil, and as the grew up and increased, they yielded a crop and produced thirty, sixty, and a hundredfold." And He was saying, "He who has ears to hear, let him hear" (Mark 4:3–9; cf. Matthew 13:3–9; Luke 8:5–8).

Setting: By the Sea of Galilee. During the early part of His ministry, after presenting the Parable of the Sower from a boat to a very large crowd, Jesus gives the meaning of the parable to His disciples and other followers.

And He said to them, "Do you not understand this parable? How will you understand all the parables? The sower sows the word. These are the ones who are beside the road where the word is sown; and when they hear, immediately Satan comes and takes away the word which has been sown in them. In a similar way these are the ones on whom seed was sown on the rocky places, who, when they hear the word, immediately receive it with joy; and they have no *firm* root in themselves, but are *only* temporary; then, when affliction or persecution arises because of the word, immediately they fall away. And others are the ones on whom seed was sown among the thorns; these are the ones who have heard the word, but the worries of the world and the deceitfulness of riches, and the desires for other things enter in and choke the word, and it becomes unfruitful. And those are the ones on whom seed was sown on the good soil; and they hear the word and accept it and bear fruit, thirty, sixty, and a hundredfold" (Mark 4:13–20; cf. Matthew 13:18–23; Luke 8:11–15).

Setting: Galilee. After His visit in the home of Simon the Pharisee, Jesus goes into the villages and cities, proclaiming and preaching the kingdom of God.

When a large crowd was coming together, and those from various cities were journeying to Him, He spoke by way of a parable: "The sower went out to sow his seed; and as he sowed, some fell beside the road, and it was trampled under foot and the birds of the air ate it up. Other *seed* fell on rocky *soil,* and as soon as it grew up, it was withered away, because it had no moisture. Other *seed* fell among the thorns; and the thorns grew up with it and choked it out. Other *seed* fell into the good soil, and grew up, and produced a crop a hundred times as great." As He said these things, He would call out, "He who has ears to hear, let him hear" (Luke 8:4–8; cf. Matthew 13:2–9; Mark 4:3–9).

SOWER, EXPLANATION OF THE PARABLE OF THE (Also see SOWER, PARABLE OF THE)

Setting: By the Sea of Galilee. With the religious leaders rejecting His message, Jesus begins to teach in parables, and gives His disciples the meaning of the Parable of the Sower.

"Hear then the parable of the sower. When anyone hears the word of the kingdom and does not understand it, the evil *one* comes and snatches away what has been sown in his heart. This is the one on whom seed was sown beside the road. The one on whom seed was sown on the rocky places, this is the man who hears the word and immediately receives it with joy; yet he has no *firm* root in himself, but is *only* temporary, and when affliction or persecution arises because of the word, immediately he falls away. And the one on whom seed was sown among the thorns, this is the man who hears the word, and the worry of the world and the deceitfulness of wealth choke the word, and it becomes unfruitful. And the one on whom seed was sown on the good soil, this is the man who hears the word and understands it; who indeed bears fruit and brings forth, some a hundredfold, some sixty, and some thirty" (Matthew 13:18–23; cf. Mark 4:13–20; Luke 8:11–15).

SOWER, PARABLE OF THE (Also see SOWER, EXPLANATION OF THE PARABLE OF THE)

[PARABLE OF THE SOWER from parables and sower]

Setting: By the Sea of Galilee. While teaching and preaching to the crowds from a boat, Jesus conveys the Parable of the Sower.

And He spoke many things to them in parables, saying, "Behold, the sower went out to sow; and as he sowed, some *seeds* fell beside the road, and the birds came and ate them up. Others fell on the rocky places, where they did not have much soil; and immediately they sprang up, because they had no depth of soil. But when the sun had risen, they were scorched; and because they had no root, they withered away. Others fell among the thorns, and the thorns came up and choked them out. And others fell on the good soil and yielded a crop, some a hundredfold, some sixty, and some thirty. He who has ears, let him hear" (Matthew 13:3–9; cf. Mark 4:3–9; Luke 8:4–8).

Setting: By the Sea of Galilee. With the religious leaders rejecting His message, Jesus begins to teach in parables, and gives His disciples the meaning of the Parable of the Sower.

"Hear then the parable of the sower. When anyone hears the word of the kingdom and does not understand it, the evil *one* comes and snatches away what has been sown in his heart. This is the one on whom seed was sown beside the road. The one on whom seed was sown on the rocky places, this is the man who hears the word and immediately receives it with joy; yet he has no *firm* root in himself, but is *only* temporary, and when affliction or persecution arises because of the word, immediately he falls away. And the one on whom seed was sown among the thorns, this is the man who hears the word, and the worry of the world and the deceitfulness of wealth choke the word, and it becomes unfruitful. And the one on whom seed was sown on the good soil, this is the man who hears the word and understands it; who indeed bears fruit and brings forth, some a hundredfold, some sixty, and some thirty" (Matthew 13:18–23; cf. Mark 4:13–20; Luke 8:11–15).

[PARABLE OF THE SOWER from sower]

Setting: By the Sea of Galilee. During the early part of His ministry, just after a visit from his mother and brothers, Jesus instructs a very large crowd with the Parable of the Sower from a boat.

"Listen *to this!* Behold, the sower went out to sow; as he was sowing, some *seed* fell beside the road, and the birds came and ate it up. Other *seed* fell on the rocky *ground* where it did not have much soil; and immediately it sprang up because it had no depth of soil. And after the sun had risen, it was scorched; and because it had no root, it withered away. Other *seed* fell among the thorns, and the thorns came up and choked it, and it yielded no crop. Other *seeds* fell into the good soil, and as the grew up and increased, they yielded a crop and produced thirty, sixty, and a hundredfold." And He was saying, "He who has ears to hear, let him hear" (Mark 4:3–9; cf. Matthew 13:3–9; Luke 8:5–8).

[PARABLE OF THE SOWER from sower]
Setting: By the Sea of Galilee. During the early part of His ministry, after presenting the Parable of the Sower from a boat to a very large crowd, Jesus gives the meaning of the parable to His disciples and other followers.

And He said to them, "Do you not understand this parable? How will you understand all the parables? The sower sows the word. These are the ones who are beside the road where the word is sown; and when they hear, immediately Satan comes and takes away the word which has been sown in them. In a similar way these are the ones on whom seed was sown on the rocky places, who, when they hear the word, immediately receive it with joy; and they have no *firm* root in themselves, but are *only* temporary; then, when affliction or persecution arises because of the word, immediately they fall away. And others are the ones on whom seed was sown among the thorns; these are the ones who have heard the word, but the worries of the world and the deceitfulness of riches, and the desires for other things enter in and choke the word, and it becomes unfruitful. And those are the ones on whom seed was sown on the good soil; and they hear the word and accept it and bear fruit, thirty, sixty, and a hundredfold" (Mark 4:13–20; cf. Matthew 13:18–23; Luke 8:11–15).

[PARABLE OF THE SOWER from sower]
Setting: Galilee. After His visit in the home of Simon the Pharisee, Jesus goes into the villages and cities, proclaiming and preaching the kingdom of God.

When a large crowd was coming together, and those from various cities were journeying to Him, He spoke by way of a parable: "The sower went out to sow his seed; and as he sowed, some fell beside the road, and it was trampled under foot and the birds of the air ate it up. Other *seed* fell on rocky *soil,* and as soon as it grew up, it was withered away, because it had no moisture. Other *seed* fell among the thorns; and the thorns grew up with it and choked it out. Other *seed* fell into the good soil, and grew up, and produced a crop a hundred times as great" As He said these things, He would call out, "He who has ears to hear, let him hear" (Luke 8:4–8; cf. Matthew 13:2–9; Mark 4:3–9).

[PARABLE OF THE SOWER from parable and the seed is the word of God]
Setting: Galilee. After Jesus presents the Parable of the Sower to the crowds, His disciples ask Him to give them the parable's meaning.

And He said, "To you it has been granted to know the mysteries of the kingdom of God, but to the rest *it is* in parables, so that SEEING THEY MAY NOT SEE, AND HEARING THEY MAY NOT UNDERSTAND. Now the parable is this: the seed is the word of God. Those beside the road are those who have heard; then the devil comes and takes away the word from their heart, so that they will not believe and be saved. Those on the rocky *soil* are those who, when they hear, receive the word with joy; and these have no *firm* root; they believe for a while, and in time of temptation fall away. The *seed* which fell among the thorns, these are the ones who have heard, and as they go on their way they are choked with worries and riches and pleasures of *this* life, and bring no fruit to maturity. But the *seed* in the good soil, these are the ones who have heard the word in an honest and good heart, and hold it fast, and bear fruit with perseverance" (Luke 8:10–15, Jesus quotes from Isaiah 6:9; cf. Matthew 13:10–23; Mark 4:10–20).

SOWING (Also see GATHERING; REAPING; and SOWER)

[SOWING from sow]
Setting: Galilee. During the early part of His ministry, Jesus preaches the Sermon on the Mount to His disciples and the multitudes.

"For this reason I say to you, do not be worried about your life, *as to* what you will eat or what you will drink; nor for your body, *as to* what you will put on. Is not life more than food, and the body more than clothing? Look at the birds of the air, that they do not sow, nor reap nor gather into barns, and *yet* your heavenly Father feeds them. Are you not worth much more than they? And who of you by being worried can add a *single* hour to his life? And why are you worried about clothing? Observe how the lilies of the field grow; they do not toil nor do they spin, yet I say to you that not even Solomon in all his glory clothed himself like one of these. But if God so clothes the grass of the field, which is *alive* today and tomorrow is thrown into the furnace, *will He* not much more *clothe* you? You of little faith! Do not worry then, saying 'What will we eat?' or 'What will we drink?' or 'What will be wear for clothing?" For the Gentiles eagerly seek all these things; for your heavenly Father knows that you need all these things. But seek first His kingdom and His righteousness, and all these things will be added to you. So do not worry about tomorrow; for tomorrow will care for itself. Each day has enough trouble of its own" (Matthew 6:25–34; cf. Luke 12:22–31; see 1 Kings 10:4–7; Job 35:11; Matthew 8:26).

[SOWING from sow and sowed]
Setting: By the Sea of Galilee. While teaching and preaching to the crowds from a boat, Jesus conveys the Parable of the Sower.

And He spoke many things to them in parables, saying, "Behold, the sower went out to sow; and as he sowed, some *seeds* fell beside the road, and the birds came and ate them up. Others fell on the rocky places, where they did not have much soil; and immediately they sprang up, because they had no depth of soil. But when the sun had risen, they were scorched; and because they had no root, they withered away. Others fell among the thorns, and the thorns came up and choked them out. And others fell on the good soil and yielded a crop, some a hundredfold, some sixty, and some thirty. He who has ears, let him hear" (Matthew 13:3–9; cf. Mark 4:3–9; Luke 8:4–8).

[SOWING from sowed and sow]
Setting: By the Sea of Galilee. Because the religious leaders are rejecting His message, Jesus continues teaching the crowds with the Parable of the Wheat and the Tares.

Jesus presented another parable to them, saying, "The kingdom of heaven may be compared to a man who sowed good seed in his field. But while his men were sleeping, his enemy came and sowed tares among the wheat, and went away. But when the wheat sprouted and bore grain, then the tares became evident also. The slaves of the landowner came and said to him, 'Sir, did you not sow good seed in your field? How then does it have tares?' And he said to them, 'An enemy has done this!' The slaves said to him, 'Do you want us, then, to go and gather them up?' But he said, 'No; for while you are gathering up the tares, you may uproot the wheat with them. Allow both to grow together until the harvest; and in the time of the harvest I will say to the reapers, "First gather up the tares and bind them in bundles to burn them up; but gather the wheat into my barn" '" (Matthew 13:24–30; cf. Matthew 3:12).

[SOWING from sowed]
Setting: By the Sea of Galilee. Because the religious leaders are rejecting His message, Jesus continues teaching the crowds with the Parable of the Mustard Seed.

He presented another parable to them, saying, "The kingdom of heaven is like a mustard seed, which a man took and sowed in his field; and this is smaller than all *other* seeds, but when it is full grown, it is larger than the garden plants and becomes a tree, so that THE BIRDS OF THE AIR come and NEST IN ITS BRANCHES." (Matthew 13:31, 32, Jesus quotes from Ezekiel 17:23; cf. Mark 4:30–32; Luke 13:18, 19).

[SOWING from sows and sowed]
Setting: A house near the Sea of Galilee. Jesus gives His disciples the meaning of the Parable of the Wheat and the Tares.

And He said, "The one who sows the good seed is the Son of Man, and the field is the world; and as *for* the good seed, these are the sons of the kingdom; and the tares are the sons of the evil *one;* and the enemy who sowed them is the devil, and the harvest is the end of the age; and the reapers are angels. So just as the tares are gathered up and burned with fire, so shall it be at the end of the age. The Son of Man will send forth His angels, and they will gather out of His kingdom all stumbling blocks, and those who commit lawlessness, and will throw them into the furnace of fire; in that place there will be weeping and gnashing of teeth. Then THE RIGHTEOUS WILL SHINE FORTH AS THE SUN in the kingdom of their Father. He who has ears, let him hear" (Matthew 13:37–43, Jesus quotes from Daniel 12:3; cf. Matthew 8:12; 13:50).

[SOWING from sow]
Setting: On the Mount of Olives, just east of Jerusalem. During His Olivet Discourse, after answering His disciples' questions as to when the temple will be destroyed and Jerusalem overrun, along with the signs of His coming and the end of the age, Jesus reemphasizes to His disciples that they should be on the alert for His return.

"For *it is* just like a man *about* to go on a journey, who called his own slaves and entrusted his possessions to them. To one he gave five talents, to another, two, and to another, one, each according to his own ability; and he went on his journey. Immediately the one who had received the five talents went and traded with them, and gained five more talents. In the same manner the one who *had received* the two *talents* gained two more. But he who received the one *talent* went away, and dug a *hole* in the ground and hid his master's money. Now after a long time the master of those slaves came and settled accounts with them. The one who had received the five talents came up and brought five more talents, saying, 'Master, you entrusted five talents to me. See, I have gained five more talents.' His master said to him, 'Well done, good and faithful slave. You were faithful with a few things, I will put you in charge of many things; enter into the joy of your master.' Also the one who *had received* the two talents came up and said, 'Master, you entrusted two talents to me. See, I have gained two more talents.' His master said to him, 'Well done, good and faithful slave. You were faithful with a few things, I will put you in charge of many things; enter into the joy of your master.' And the one also who had received the one talent came up and said, 'Master, I knew you to be a hard man, reaping where you did not sow and gathering where you scattered no *seed.* And I was afraid, and went away and hid your talent in the ground. See, you have what is yours.' But his master answered and said to him, 'You wicked, lazy slave, you knew that I reap where I did not sow and gather where I scattered no *seed.* Then you ought to have put my money in the bank, and on my arrival I would have received my *money* back with interest. 'Therefore take away the talent from him, and give it to the one who has ten talents.' For to everyone who has, *more* shall be given, and he will have an abundance; but from the one who does not have, even what he does have shall be taken away. Throw out the worthless slave into the outer darkness; in that place there will be weeping and gnashing of teeth" (Matthew 25:14–30; cf. Matthew 8:12; 13:12; 24:45–47; see Matthew 18:23, 24; Luke 12:44).

Setting: By the Sea of Galilee. During the early part of His ministry, just after a visit from his mother and brothers, Jesus instructs a very large crowd with the Parable of the Sower from a boat.

"Listen *to this!* Behold, the sower went out to sow; as he was sowing, some *seed* fell beside the road, and the birds came and ate it up. Other *seed* fell on the rocky *ground* where it did not have much soil; and immediately it sprang up because it had no depth of soil. And after the sun had risen, it was scorched; and because it had no root, it withered away. Other *seed* fell among the thorns, and the thorns came up and choked it, and it yielded no crop. Other *seeds* fell into the good soil, and as the grew up and increased, they yielded a crop and produced thirty, sixty, and a hundredfold." And He was saying, "He who has ears to hear, let him hear" (Mark 4:3–9; cf. Matthew 13:3–9; Luke 8:5–8).

[SOWING from sows]
Setting: By the Sea of Galilee. During the early part of His ministry, after presenting the Parable of the Sower from a boat to a very large crowd, Jesus gives the meaning of the parable to His disciples and other followers.

And He said to them, "Do you not understand this parable? How will you understand all the parables? The sower sows the word. These are the ones who are beside the road where the word is sown; and when they hear, immediately Satan comes and takes away the word which has been sown in them. In a similar way these are the ones on whom seed was sown on the rocky places, who, when they hear the word, immediately receive it with joy; and they have no *firm* root in themselves, but are *only* temporary; then, when affliction or persecution arises because of the word, immediately they fall away. And others are the ones on whom seed was sown among the thorns; these are the ones who have heard the word, but the worries of the world and the deceitfulness of riches, and the desires for other things enter in and choke the word, and it becomes unfruitful. And those are the ones on whom seed was sown on the good soil; and they hear the word and accept it and bear fruit, thirty, sixty, and a hundredfold" (Mark 4:13–20; cf. Matthew 13:18–23; Luke 8:11–15).

[SOWING from sow and sowed]
Setting: Galilee. After His visit in the home of Simon the Pharisee, Jesus goes into the villages and cities, proclaiming and preaching the kingdom of God.

When a large crowd was coming together, and those from various cities were journeying to Him, He spoke by way of a parable: "The sower went out to sow his seed; and as he sowed, some fell beside the road, and it was trampled under foot and the birds of the air ate it up. Other *seed* fell on rocky *soil,* and as soon as it grew up, it was withered away, because it had no moisture. Other *seed* fell among the thorns; and the thorns grew up with it and choked it out. Other *seed* fell into the good soil, and grew up, and produced a crop a hundred times as great." As He said these things, He would call out, "He who has ears to hear, let him hear" (Luke 8:4–8; cf. Matthew 13:2–9; Mark 4:3–9).

[SOWING from sow]
Setting: On the way from Galilee to Jerusalem. After giving a parable about riches and greed, Jesus comforts the crowd and His disciples. The scribes and Pharisees turn hostile and question Him repeatedly in an attempt to catch Him in something He might say.

And He said to His disciples, "For this reason I say to you, do not worry about *your* life, *as to* what you will eat; nor for your body, *as to* what you will put on. For life is more than food, and the body more than clothing. Consider the ravens, for they neither sow nor reap; they have no storeroom nor barn, and *yet* God feeds them; how much more valuable you are than the birds! And which of you by worrying can add a *single* hour to his life's span? If then you cannot do even a very little thing, why do you worry about other matters? Consider the lilies, how they grow: they neither toil nor spin; but I tell you, not even Solomon in all his glory clothed himself like one of these. But if God so clothes the grass in the field, which is *alive* today and tomorrow is thrown into the furnace, how much more *will He clothe* you? You men of little faith! And do not seek what you will eat and what you will drink, and do not keep worrying. For all these things the nations of the world eagerly seek; but your Father knows that you need these things. But seek His kingdom, and these things will be added to you. Do not be afraid, little flock, for your Father has chosen gladly to give you the kingdom" (Luke 12:22–32; cf. Matthew 6:25–33; see 1 Kings 10:4–7; Job 38:41).

[SOWING from sow]
Setting: Jericho, on the way to Jerusalem. After commending Zaccheus's faith in Him, Jesus provides a parable about stewardship.

So He said, "A nobleman went to a distant country to receive a kingdom for himself, and *then* return. And he called ten of his slaves, and gave them ten minas and said to them, 'Do business *with this* until I come *back.*' But his citizens hated him and sent a delegation after him, saying, 'We do not want this man to reign over us.' When he returned, after receiving the kingdom, he ordered that these slaves, to whom he had given the money, be called to him so that he might know what business they had done. The first appeared, saying, 'Master, your mina has made ten minas more.' And he said to him, 'Well done, good slave, because you have been faithful in a very little thing, you are to be in authority over ten cities.' The second came, saying, 'Your mina, master, has made five minas.' And he said to him, also, 'And you are to be over five cities.' Another came, saying, 'Master, here is your mina, which I kept put away in a handkerchief; for I was afraid of you, because you are an exacting man; you take up what you did not lay down and reap what you did not sow.' He said to him, 'By your own words I will judge you, you worthless slave. Did you know that I am an exacting man, taking up what I did not lay down and reaping what I did not sow? Then why did you not put my money in the bank, and having come, I would have collected it with interest?' Then he said to the bystanders, 'Take the mina away from him and give it to the one who has the ten minas.' And they said to him, 'Master, he has ten minas *already.*' I tell you that to everyone who has, more shall be given, but from the one who does not have, even what he does have shall be taken away. But these enemies of mine, who did not want me to reign over them, bring them here and slay them in my presence" (Luke 19:12–27; cf. Matthew 25:14–30; see Matthew 13:12; Luke 16:10).

[SOWING from sows]
Setting: Sychar in Samaria, on the way to Galilee. After Jesus converses with a Samaritan woman at Jacob's well, the disciples return with food. They try to get Jesus to eat, but are surprised when He speaks of other food.

Jesus said to them, "My food is to do the will of Him who sent Me and to accomplish His work. Do you not say, 'There are yet four months, and *then* comes the harvest'? Behold, I say to you, lift up your eyes and look on the fields, that they are white for harvest. Already he who reaps is receiving wages and is gathering fruit for life eternal; so that he who sows and he who reaps may rejoice together. For in this *case* the saying is true, 'One sows and another reaps.' I sent you to reap that for which you have not labored; others have labored and you have entered into their labor" (John 4:34–38; see Matthew 9:37, 38 5:36).

SPAN, LIFE'S (See LIFE'S SPAN)

SPARROWS (Also see BIRDS; DOVES; and RAVENS)

Setting: Galilee. After His disciples observe His ministry, Jesus summons and specifically instructs them about their ministry ahead involving true discipleship.

"Are not two sparrows sold for a cent? And *yet* not one of them will fall to the ground apart from your Father. But the very hairs of your head are all numbered. So do not fear; you are more valuable than many sparrows" (Matthew 10:29–31; cf. Luke 12:6; see Matthew 12:12).

Setting: On the way from Galilee to Jerusalem. Jesus warns His disciples of future events, as the scribes and Pharisees turn hostile and question Him repeatedly in an attempt to catch Him in something He might say.

Under these circumstances, after so many thousands of people had gathered together that they were stepping on one another, He began saying to His disciples first *of all,* "Beware of the leaven of the Pharisees, which is hypocrisy. But there is nothing covered up that will not be revealed, and hidden that will not be known. Accordingly, whatever you have said in the dark will be heard in the light, and what you have whispered in the inner rooms will be proclaimed upon the housetops. I say to you, My friends, do not be afraid of those who kill the body and after that have no more that they can do. But I will warn you whom to fear: fear the One who, after He has killed, has authority to cast into hell; yes, I tell you, fear Him! Are not five sparrows sold for two cents? *Yet* not one of them is forgotten before God. Indeed, the very hairs of your head are all numbered. Do not fear; you are more valuable than many sparrows" (Luke 12:1–7; cf. Matthew 10:26–31; see Matthew 16:6; Hebrews 10:31).

SPEAKING EVIL (Listed under EVIL, SPEAKING)

SPECK

Setting: Galilee. During the early part of His ministry, Jesus preaches the Sermon on the Mount to His disciples and the multitudes.

"Do not judge so that you will not be judged. For in the way you judge, you will be judged; and by your standard of measure, it will be measured to you. Why do you look at the speck that is in your brother's eye, but do not notice the log that is in your own eye? Or how can you say to your brother, 'Let me take the speck out of your eye, and behold, the log is in your own eye? You hypocrite, first take the log out of your own eye, and then you will see clearly to take the speck out of your brother's eye" (Matthew 7:1–5; cf. Mark 4:24; Luke 6:37–42; Romans 2:1; 14:10, 13).

Setting: Galilee. After selecting His twelve disciples, Jesus teaches the Sermon on the Mount to those disciples and a great throng of people from Judea, Jerusalem, and the central coastal region of Tyre and Sidon.

And He also spoke a parable to them: "A blind man cannot guide a blind man, can he? Will they not both fall into a pit? A pupil is not above his teacher; but everyone, after he has been fully trained, will be like his teacher. Why do you look at the speck that is in your brother's eye, but do not notice the log that is in your own eye? Or how can you say to your brother, 'Brother, let me take out the speck that is in your eye,' when you yourself do not see the log that is in your own eye? You hypocrite, first take the log out of your own eye, and then you will see clearly to take out the speck that is in your brother's eye. For there is no good tree which produces bad fruit, nor, on the other hand, a bad tree which produces good fruit. For each tree is known by its own fruit. For men do not gather figs from thorns, nor do they pick grapes from a briar bush. The good man out of the good treasure of his heart brings forth what is good; and the evil *man* out of the evil *treasure* brings forth what is evil; for his mouth speaks from that which fills his heart" (Luke 6:39–45; cf. Matthew 7:3–6. 16, 18, 20; 12:35; see Matthew 10:24; 15:14; Luke 6:12–19).

SPEECH (Also see SLANDER; SWEARING; and WORDS)

[SPEECH from what you hear *whispered*]

Setting: Galilee. After His disciples observe His ministry, Jesus summons and specifically instructs them about their ministry ahead involving true discipleship.

"Therefore do not fear them, for there is nothing concealed that will not be revealed, or hidden that will not be known. What I tell you in the darkness, speak in the light; and what you hear *whispered* in your ear, proclaim upon the housetops. Do not fear those who kill he body but are unable to kill the soul; but rather fear Him who is able to destroy both soul and body in hell" (Matthew 10:26–28; cf. Mark 4:22; Luke 12:3; see Hebrews 10:31).

[SPEECH from the mouth speaks and by your words]

Setting: Galilee. After Jesus heals a blind, mute, demon-possessed man, the Pharisees accuse the Lord in front of crowds of being a worker of Satan.

"Either make the tree good and its fruit good, or make the tree bad and its fruit bad; for the tree is known by its fruit. You brood of vipers, how can you, being evil, speak what is good? For the mouth speaks out of that which fills the heart. The good man brings out of *his* good treasure what is good; and the evil man brings out of *his* evil treasure what is evil. But I tell you that every careless word that people speak, they shall give an accounting for it in the day of judgment. For by your words you will be justified, and by your words you will be condemned" (Matthew 12:33–37; cf. Matthew 3:7; 7:16–18).

[SPEECH from SPEAKS EVIL OF FATHER OR MOTHER]

Setting: Galilee. Pharisees and scribes from Jerusalem accuse Jesus' disciples of disobeying tradition and the commandments.

And He answered and said to them, "Why do you yourselves transgress the commandment of God for the sake of tradition? For God said, 'HONOR YOUR FATHER AND MOTHER,' and, 'HE WHO SPEAKS EVIL OF FATHER OR MOTHER IS TO BE PUT TO DEATH.' But you say, 'Whoever says to *his* father or mother, "Whatever I have that would help you has been given *to God*," he is not to honor his father or mother.' And *by this* you invalidated the word of God for the sake of your tradition. You hypocrites, rightly did Isaiah prophesy of you: 'THIS PEOPLE HONORS ME WITH THEIR LIPS, BUT THEIR HEART IS FAR AWAY FROM ME. BUT IN VAIN DO THEY WORSHIP ME, TEACHING AS DOCTRINES THE PRECEPTS OF MEN'" (Matthew 15:3–9, Jesus quotes from Exodus 20:12, 21:17, Leviticus 20:9; Isaiah 29:13; cf. Mark 7:5–7; see Colossians 2:22).

[SPEECH from what proceeds out of the mouth]

Setting: Galilee. After the Pharisees and scribes question His disciples' obedience to tradition and the commandments, Jesus instructs the crowd.

After Jesus called the crowd to Him, He said to them, "Hear and understand. *It is* not what enters into the mouth *that* defiles the man, but what proceeds out of the mouth, this defiles the man" (Matthew 15:10, 11; cf. Matthew 15:18).

[SPEECH from SPEAKS EVIL OF FATHER OR MOTHER]

Setting: Galilee. The Pharisees and some of the scribes from Jerusalem question why Jesus' disciples do not follow the tradition of ceremonial hand cleansing before eating bread.

And He said to them, "Rightly did Isaiah prophesy of you hypocrites, as it is written: 'THIS PEOPLE HONORS ME WITH THEIR LIPS, BUT THEIR HEART IS FAR AWAY FROM ME. BUT IN VAIN DO THEY WORSHIP ME, TEACHING AS DOCTRINES THE PRECEPTS OF MEN.' Neglecting the commandment of God, you hold to the tradition of men." He was also saying to them, "You are experts at setting aside the commandment of God in order to keep tradition. For Moses said, 'HONOR YOUR FATHER AND YOUR MOTHER'; and, 'HE WHO SPEAKS EVIL OF FATHER OR MOTHER, IS TO BE PUT TO DEATH'; but you say, 'If a man says to *his* father or *his* mother, whatever I have that would help you is Corban (that is to say, given *to God*),' you no longer permit him to do anything for *his* father or *his* mother; *thus*

invalidating the word of God by your tradition which you have handed down; and you do many things such as that" (Mark 7:6–13, Jesus quotes from Exodus 20:12; 21:17; Isaiah 29:13; cf. Matthew 15:1–6).

[SPEECH from his mouth speaks]

Setting: Galilee. After selecting His twelve disciples, Jesus teaches the Sermon on the Mount to those disciples and a great throng of people from Judea, Jerusalem, and the central coastal region of Tyre and Sidon.

And He also spoke a parable to them: "A blind man cannot guide a blind man, can he? Will they not both fall into a pit? A pupil is not above his teacher; but everyone, after he has been fully trained, will be like his teacher. Why do you look at the speck that is in your brother's eye, but do not notice the log that is in your own eye? Or how can you say to your brother, 'Brother, let me take out the speck that is in your eye,' when you yourself do not see the log that is in your own eye? You hypocrite, first take the log out of your own eye, and then you will see clearly to take out the speck that is in your brother's eye. For there is no good tree which produces bad fruit, nor, on the other hand, a bad tree which produces good fruit. For each tree is known by its own fruit. For men do not gather figs from thorns, nor do they pick grapes from a briar bush. The good man out of the good treasure of his heart brings forth what is good; and the evil *man* out of the evil *treasure* brings forth what is evil; for his mouth speaks from that which fills his heart" (Luke 6:39–45; cf. Matthew 7:3–6. 16, 18, 20; 12:35; see Matthew 10:24; 15:14; Luke 6:12–19).

[SPEECH from whispered in the inner rooms]

Setting: On the way from Galilee to Jerusalem. Jesus warns His disciples of future events, as the scribes and Pharisees turn hostile and question Him repeatedly in an attempt to catch Him in something He might say.

Under these circumstances, after so many thousands of people had gathered together that they were stepping on one another, He began saying to His disciples first *of all,* "Beware of the leaven of the Pharisees, which is hypocrisy. But there is nothing covered up that will not be revealed, and hidden that will not be known. Accordingly, whatever you have said in the dark will be heard in the light, and what you have whispered in the inner rooms will be proclaimed upon the housetops. I say to you, My friends, do not be afraid of those who kill the body and after that have no more that they can do. But I will warn you whom to fear: fear the One who, after He has killed, has authority to cast into hell; yes, I tell you, fear Him! Are not five sparrows sold for two cents? *Yet* not one of them is forgotten before God. Indeed, the very hairs of your head are all numbered. Do not fear; you are more valuable than many sparrows" (Luke 12:1–7; cf. Matthew 10:26–31; see Matthew 16:6; Hebrews 10:31).

[SPEECH from speaks]

Setting On the way from Galilee to Jerusalem. Jesus warns His disciples of future events, as the scribes and Pharisees turn hostile and question Him in an attempt to catch Him in something He might say.

"And I say to you, everyone who confesses Me before men, the Son of Man will confess him also before the angels of God; but he who denies Me before men will be denied before the angels of God. And everyone who speaks a word against the Son of Man, it will be forgiven him; but he who blasphemes against the Holy Spirit, it will not be forgiven him. When they bring you before the synagogues and the rulers and the authorities, do not worry about how or what you are to speak in your defense, or what you are to say; for the Holy Spirit will teach you in that very hour what you ought to say" (Luke 12:8–12; cf. Matthew 10:32, 33; 12:31, 32; see Matthew 10:20).

[SPEECH from speaks from himself]

Setting: The temple in Jerusalem. After receiving encouragement from His blood brothers in Galilee to attend the upcoming Feast of Booths in order to demonstrate His works to His disciples and the world, Jesus goes and teaches, astonishing the Jewish religious leaders.

So Jesus answered them and said, "My teaching is not Mine, but His who sent Me. If anyone is willing to do His will, he will know of the teaching, whether it is of God or *whether* I speak of Myself. He who speaks from himself seeks his own glory; but He who is seeking the glory of the One who sent Him, He is true, and there is no unrighteousness in Him" (John 7:16–18; see John 5:41).

[SPEECH from speaks]
Setting: The temple treasury in Jerusalem. After the scribes and Pharisees question His testimony about Himself, Jesus argues with them regarding their ancestry and motives.

Jesus said to them, "If God were your Father, you would love Me, for I proceeded forth and have come from God, for I have not even come on My own initiative, but He sent Me. Why do you not understand what I am saying? *It is* because you cannot hear My word. You are of *your* father the devil, and you want to do the desires of your father. He was a murderer from the beginning, and does not stand in the truth because there is no truth in him. Whenever he speaks a lie, he speaks from his own *nature,* for he is a liar and the father of lies. But because I speak the truth, you do not believe Me. Which one of you convicts Me of sin? If I speak truth, why do not believe Me? He who is of God hears the words of God; for this reason you do not hear *them,* because you are not of God" (John 8:42–47; see John 18:37; 1 John 3:8; 4:6; 5:1).

[SPEECH from speaking]
Setting: Corinth. Luke, writing in Acts, records the Lord's comforting revelation to Paul in a vision as the apostle works among the Jews and Gentiles during his second missionary journey, testifying that Jesus is the Christ (Messiah).

And the Lord said to Paul in the night by a vision, "Do not be afraid *any longer,* but go on speaking and do not be silent; for I am with you, and no man will attack you in order to harm you, for I have many people in this city" (Acts 18:9, 10).

SPEECH, FIGURES OF (See PARABLES)

SPHERE OF INFLUENCE (See INFLUENCE, PERSONAL)

SPICES – CUMMIN (See CUMMIN)

SPICES – DILL (See DILL)

SPICES – MINT (See MINT)

SPICES – RUE (See RUE)

SPIRIT (a being without a body)

Setting: Jerusalem. After rising from the tomb on the third day after being crucified and appearing to two of His followers on the road to Emmaus, Jesus appears to His disciples (except Thomas).

While they were telling these things, He Himself stood in their midst and said to them, "Peace be to you." But they were startled and frightened and thought they were seeing a spirit. And He said to them, "Why are you troubled, and why do doubts arise in your hearts? See My hands and My feet, that it is I Myself; touch Me and see, for a spirit does not have flesh and bones as you see that I have." And when He had said this, He showed them His hands and His feet. While they still could not believe *it* because of their joy and amazement. He said to them, "Have you anything to eat?" They gave Him a piece of a broiled fish; and He took it and ate *it* before them (Luke 24:36–43; see Mark 16:14; John 20:27; Acts 10:40, 41).

SPIRIT (God)

Setting: The synagogue in Jesus' hometown of Nazareth in Galilee. At the beginning of His public ministry, Jesus reads on the Sabbath from the book of the prophet Isaiah.

And the book of the prophet Isaiah was handed to Him. And He opened the book and found the place where it was written, "THE SPIRIT OF THE LORD IS UPON ME, BECAUSE HE ANOINTED ME TO PREACH THE GOSPEL TO THE POOR. HE HAS SENT ME TO PROCLAIM

RELEASE TO THE CAPTIVES, AND RECOVERY OF SIGHT TO THE BLIND, TO SET FREE THOSE WHO ARE OPPRESSED, TO PROCLAIM THE FAVORABLE YEAR OF THE LORD." And He closed the book, gave it back to the attendant and sat down; and the eyes of all in the synagogue were fixed on Him. And He began to say to them, "Today this Scripture has been fulfilled in your hearing" (Luke 4:17–21, Jesus quotes from Isaiah 61:1, 2).

[SPIRIT (Spirit) from God is spirit]
Setting: Sychar in Samaria, on the way to Galilee. Jesus interacts with a Samaritan woman at Jacob's well, while the disciples are buying food.

Jesus said to her, "Woman, believe Me, an hour is coming when neither in this mountain nor in Jerusalem will you worship the Father. You worship what you do not know; we worship what we know, for salvation is from the Jews. But an hour is coming, and now is, when the true worshipers will worship the Father in spirit and truth; for such people the Father seeks to be His worshipers. God is spirit, and those who worship Him must worship in spirit and truth" (John 4:21–24; see Isaiah 2:3; Philippians 3:3).

SPIRIT (Holy) (also see HOLY SPIRIT; SPIRIT OF GOD; SPIRIT OF THE LORD; and TRUTH, SPIRIT OF)
Setting: Galilee. After His disciples observe His ministry, Jesus summons and specifically instructs them about the upcoming hardships of their ministry to the people of Israel.

"Behold, I send you out as sheep in the midst of wolves; so be shrewd as serpents and innocent as doves. But beware of men, for they will hand you over to *the* courts and scourge you in their synagogues; and you will even be brought before governors and kings for My sake, as a testimony to them and to the Gentiles. But when they hand you over, do not worry about how or what you are to say; for it will be given you in that hour what you are to say. For it is not you who speak, but *it* is the Spirit of your Father who speaks in you" (Matthew 10:16–20; cf. Luke 10:3).

Setting: Galilee. After Jesus heals a blind, mute, demon-possessed man, the Pharisees accuse the Lord in front of crowds of being a worker of Beelzebul (Satan).

And knowing their thoughts Jesus said to them, "Any kingdom divided against itself is laid waste; and any city or house divided against itself will not stand. If Satan casts out Satan, he is divided against himself; how then will his kingdom stand? If I by Beelzebul cast out demons, by whom do your sons cast *them* out? For this reason they will be your judges. But if I cast out demons by the Spirit of God, then the kingdom of God has come upon you. Or how can anyone enter the strong man's house and carry off his property, unless he first binds the strong *man?* And then he will plunder his house" (Matthew 12:25–29; cf. Matthew 9:34; Mark 3:23–27; Luke 11:17–20).

Setting: Galilee. After Jesus heals a blind, mute, demon-possessed man, the Pharisees accuse Him in front of crowds of being a worker of Satan. The Lord warns them about the unpardonable sin.

"He who is not with Me is against Me; and he who does not gather with Me scatters. Therefore I say to you, any sin and blasphemy shall be forgiven people, but blasphemy against the Spirit shall not be forgiven. Whoever speaks a word against the Son of Man, it shall be forgiven him; but whoever speaks against the Holy Spirit, it shall not be forgiven him, either in this age or in the *age* to come" (Matthew 12:30–32; cf. Luke 12:10; see Mark 9:40).

Setting: The temple in Jerusalem. Following the Sadducees' and the Pharisees' unsuccessful attempts to test Him with questions, with the crowds listening, Jesus poses a question to some of the Pharisees.

"What do you think about the Christ, whose son is He?" They said to Him, "The *son* of David." He said to them, "Then how does David in the Spirit call Him 'Lord,' saying, 'THE LORD SAID TO MY LORD, SIT AT MY RIGHT HAND, UNTIL I PUT YOUR ENEMIES BENEATH YOUR FEET'"? "If David then calls Him 'Lord,' how is He his son?" (Matthew 22:42–45; Jesus quotes from Psalm 110:1; cf. Mark 12:35–37; Luke 20:41–44; see 2 Samuel 23:2).

Setting: Jerusalem. At the time for the Passover of the Jews, after the Lord cleanses the temple, a Pharisee, Nicodemus, asks Him by night the meaning of "born again."

Jesus answered, "Truly, truly, I say to you, unless one is born of water and the Spirit he cannot enter into the kingdom of God. That which is born of the flesh is flesh, and that which is born of the Spirit is spirit. Do not be amazed that I said to you, 'You must be born again.' The wind blows where it wishes and you hear the sound of it, but do not know where it comes from and where it is going; so is everyone who is born of the Spirit" (John 3:5–8; see Psalm 135:7; John 1:13).

Setting: The synagogue at Capernaum of Galilee. After the Jewish religious leaders argue with one another when Jesus says He will give His flesh to the world to eat, some of His disciples also express difficulty with His statements.

But, Jesus, conscious that His disciples grumbled at this, said to them, "Does this cause you to stumble? *What* then if you see the Son of Man ascending to where He was before? It is the Spirit who gives live; the flesh profits nothing; the words that I have spoken to you are spirit and are life. But there are some of you who do not believe." For Jesus knew from the beginning who they were who did not believe, and who it was that would betray Him. And He was saying, "For this reason I have said to you, that no one can come to Me unless it has been granted him from the Father" (John 6:61–65; see Matthew 11:6; 13:11; John 3:13).

Setting: Jerusalem. Before the Passover, after responding to Philip's request for Him to show His disciples the Father, Jesus conveys the upcoming role of the Holy Spirit in their lives.

"If you love Me, you will keep My commandments. I will ask the Father, and He will give you another Helper, that He may be with you forever; *that* is the Spirit of truth, whom the world cannot receive, because it does not see Him or know Him, *but* you know Him because He abides with you and will be in you" (John 14:15–17; see John 7:39; 15:26; 1 John 5:3).

Setting: Jerusalem. Before the Passover, with His departure in mind, after explaining He is the vine and His disciples are the branches, Jesus elaborates more about the future ministry of the Holy Spirit.

"When the Helper comes, whom I will send to you from the Father, *that is* the Spirit of truth who proceeds from the Father, He will testify about Me, and you *will* testify also, because you have been with Me from the beginning" (John 15:26, 27; see Luke 24:48; John 14:16).

Setting: Jerusalem. Before the Passover, after warning His disciples of the persecution they will face after His departure to heaven, Jesus elaborates about the coming ministry of the Holy Spirit.

"I have many more things to say to you, but you cannot bear *them* now. But when He, the Spirit of truth, comes, He will guide you into all the truth; for He will not speak on His own initiative, but whatever He hears, He will speak; and He will disclose to you what is to come. He will glorify Me, for He will take of Mine and will disclose *it* to you. All things that the Father has are Mine; therefore I said that He takes of Mine and will disclose *it* to you (John 16:12–15; see John 7:39; 14:17, 26; 17:10).

Setting: On the island of Patmos (in the Aegean Sea about fifty miles southwest of Ephesus in modern Turkey). On the Lord's Day (Sunday), approximately fifty years after the Resurrection, the disciple John encounters the Lord Jesus Christ, who communicates a new revelation for the apostle to record for the church in Ephesus and to six other churches in Asia.

"To the angel of the church in Ephesus write: The One who holds the seven stars in His right hand, the One who walks among the seven golden lampstands, says this: 'I know your deeds and your toil and perseverance, and that you cannot tolerate evil men, and you put to the test those who call themselves apostles, and they are not, and you found them *to be* false; and you have perseverance and have endured for My name's sake, and have not grown weary. But I have *this* against you, that you have left your first love. Therefore remember from where you have fallen, and repent and do the deeds you did at first; or else I am coming to you and will remove your lampstand out of its place—unless you repent. Yet this you do have, that you hate the deeds of the

Nicolaitans, which I also hate. He who has an ear, let him hear what the Spirit says to the churches. To him who overcomes, I will grant to eat of the tree of life which is in the Paradise of God' (Revelation 2:1–7; see Genesis 2:9; Ezekiel 28:13; 1 John 4:1; Revelation 1:10, 11, 19, 20).

Setting: On the island of Patmos (in the Aegean Sea about fifty miles southwest of Ephesus in modern Turkey). On the Lord's Day (Sunday), approximately fifty years after the Resurrection, the disciple John encounters the Lord Jesus Christ, who communicates a new revelation for the apostle to record for the church in Smyrna and to six other churches in Asia.

"And to the angel of the church in Smyrna write: The first and the last, who was dead, and has come to life, says this: 'I know your tribulation and your poverty (but you are rich), and the blasphemy by those who say they are Jews and are not, but are a synagogue of Satan. Do not fear what you are about to suffer. Behold, the devil is about to cast some of you into prison, so that you will be tested, and you will have tribulation for ten days. Be faithful until death, and I will give you the crown of life. He who has an ear, let him hear what the Spirit says to the churches. He who overcomes will not be hurt by the second death' (Revelation 2:8–11; see Isaiah 44:6; Revelation 1:9, 18; 20:6, 14).

Setting: On the island of Patmos (in the Aegean Sea about fifty miles southwest of Ephesus in modern Turkey). On the Lord's Day (Sunday), approximately fifty years after the Resurrection, the disciple John encounters the Lord Jesus Christ, who communicates a new revelation for the apostle to record for the church in Pergamum and to six other churches in Asia.

"And to the angel of the church in Pergamum write: The One who has the sharp two-edged sword says this: 'I know where you dwell, where Satan's throne is; and you hold fast My name, and did not deny My faith even in the days of Antipas, My witness, My faithful one, who was killed among you, where Satan dwells. But I have a few things against you, because you have there some who hold the teaching of Balaam, who kept teaching Balak to put a stumbling block before the sons of Israel, to eat things sacrificed to idols and to commit *acts of* immorality. So you also have some who in the same way hold the teaching of the Nicolaitans. Therefore repent; or else I am coming to you quickly, and I will make war against them with the sword of My mouth. He who has an ear, let him hear what the Spirit says to the churches. To him who overcomes, to him I will give *some* of the hidden manna, and I will give him a white stone, and a new name written on the stone which no one knows but he who receives it' (Revelation 2:12–17; see Numbers 25:1–3; Isaiah 62:2; Revelation 1:16; 2:5, 6, 16).

Setting: On the island of Patmos (in the Aegean Sea about fifty miles southwest of Ephesus in modern Turkey). On the Lord's Day (Sunday), approximately fifty years after the Resurrection, the disciple John encounters the Lord Jesus Christ, who communicates a new revelation for the apostle to record for the church in Thyatira and to six other churches in Asia.

"And to the angel of the church in Thyatira write: The Son of God, who has eyes like a flame of fire, and His feet are like burnished bronze, says this: 'I know your deeds, and your love and faith and service and perseverance, and that your deeds of late are greater than at first. But I have *this* against you, that you tolerate the woman Jezebel, who calls herself a prophetess, and she teaches and leads My bond-servants astray so that they commit *acts of* immorality and eat things sacrificed to idols. I gave her time to repent, and she does not want to repent of her immorality. Behold, I will throw her on a bed *of sickness,* and those who commit adultery with her into great tribulation, unless they repent of her deeds. And I will kill her children with pestilence, and all the churches will know that I am He who searches the minds and hearts; and I will give to each one of you according to your deeds. But I say to you, the rest who are in Thyatira, who do not hold this teaching, who have not known the deep things of Satan, as they call them—I place no other burden on you. Nevertheless what you have, hold fast until I come. He who overcomes, and he who keeps My deeds until the end, TO HIM I WILL GIVE AUTHORITY OVER THE NATIONS; AND HE SHALL RULE THEM WITH A ROD OF IRON, AS THE VESSELS OF THE POTTER ARE BROKEN TO PIECES, as I also have received *authority* from My Father; and I will give him the morning star. He who has an ear, let him hear what the Spirit says to the churches' (Revelation 2:18–29; Jesus quotes from Psalm 2:8, 9; Isaiah 30:14; see 1 Kings 16:31; Psalm 7:9; Romans 2:5; 1 Corinthians 2:10; 2 Peter 3:9; Revelation 1:14; 2:7; 3:11; 17:1–20).

Setting: On the island of Patmos (in the Aegean Sea about fifty miles southwest of Ephesus in modern Turkey). On the Lord's Day (Sunday), approximately fifty years after the Resurrection, the disciple John encounters the Lord Jesus Christ, who communicates a new revelation for the apostle to record for the church in Sardis and to six other churches in Asia.

"To the angel of the church in Sardis write: He who has the seven Spirits of God and the seven stars, says this: 'I know your deeds, that you have a name that you are alive, but you are dead. Wake up, and strengthen the things that remain, which were about to die; for I have not found your deeds completed in the sight of My God. So remember what you have received and heard; and keep *it,* and repent. Therefore if you do not wake up, I will come like a thief, and you will not know at what hour I will come to you. But you have a few people in Sardis who have not soiled their garments; and they will walk with Me in white, for they are worthy. He who overcomes will thus be clothed in white garments; and I will not erase his name from the book of life, and I will confess his name before My Father and before His angels. He who has an ear, let him hear what the Spirit says to the churches'" (Revelation 3:1–6; see Matthew 10:32; Revelation 1:16).

Setting: On the island of Patmos (in the Aegean Sea about fifty miles southwest of Ephesus in modern Turkey). On the Lord's Day (Sunday), approximately fifty years after the Resurrection, the disciple John encounters the Lord Jesus Christ, who communicates a new revelation for the apostle to record for the church in Philadelphia and to six other churches in Asia.

"And to the angel of the church in Philadelphia write: He who is holy, who is true, who has the key of David, who opens and no one will shut, and who shuts and no one opens, says this: 'I know your deeds. Behold, I have put before you an open door which no one can shut, because you have a little power, and have kept My word, and have not denied My name. Behold, I will cause *those* of the synagogue of Satan, who say that they are Jews and are not, but lie—I will make them come and bow down at your feet, and *make them* know that I have loved you. Because you have kept the word of My perseverance, I also will keep you from the hour of testing, that *hour* which is about to come upon the whole world, to test those who dwell on the earth. I am coming quickly; hold fast what you have, so that no one will take your crown. He who overcomes, I will make him a pillar in the temple of My God, and he will not go out from it anymore; and I will write on him the name of My God, and the name of the city of My God, the new Jerusalem, which comes down out of heaven from My God, and My new name. He who has an ear, let him hear what the Spirit says to the churches'" (Revelation 3:7–13; see Isaiah 22:22; Galatians 2:9; Revelation 2:9, 10, 13, 25; 14:1).

Setting: On the island of Patmos (in the Aegean Sea about fifty miles southwest of Ephesus in modern Turkey). On the Lord's Day (Sunday), approximately fifty years after the Resurrection, the disciple John encounters the Lord Jesus Christ, who communicates a new revelation for the apostle to record for the church in Laodicea and to six other churches in Asia.

"To the angel of the church in Laodicea write: The Amen, the faithful and true Witness, the Beginning of the creation of God, says this: 'I know your deeds, that you are neither cold nor hot; I wish that you were cold or hot. So because you are lukewarm, and neither hot nor cold, I will spit you out of My mouth. Because you say, "I am rich, and have become wealthy, and have need of nothing," and you do not know that you are wretched and miserable and poor and blind and naked, I advise you to buy from Me gold refined by fire so that you may become rich, and white garments so that you may clothe yourself, and *that* the shame of your nakedness will not be revealed; and eye salve to anoint your eyes so that you may see. Those whom I love, I reprove and discipline; therefore be zealous and repent. Behold, I stand at the door and knock; if anyone hears My voice and opens the door, I will come in to him and will dine with him, and he with Me. He who overcomes, I will grant to him to sit down with Me on My throne, as I also overcame and sat down with My Father on His throne. He who has an ear, let him hear what the Spirit says to the churches'" (Revelation 3:14–22; see Proverb 3:12; Hosea 12:8; John 14:23; 16:33).

SPIRIT (human)

Setting: Galilee. Early in His ministry, Jesus presents the Beatitudes (part of the Sermon on the Mount) to His disciples and the gathered crowds from Galilee, Decapolis, Jerusalem, Judea, and beyond the Jordan.

He opened His mouth and *began* to teach them, saying, "Blessed are the poor in spirit, for theirs is the kingdom of heaven" (Matthew 5:2, 3; see Matthew 13:35).

Setting: An upper room in Jerusalem. After celebrating the Passover meal with His disciples, Jesus retreats to the Garden of Gethsemane on the Mount of Olives to pray prior to His betrayal by Judas.

Then Jesus came with them to a place called Gethsemane, and said to His disciples, "Sit here while I go over there and pray." And He took with Him Peter and the two sons of Zebedee, and began to be grieved and distressed. Then He said to them, "My soul is deeply grieved, to the point of death; remain here and keep watch with Me." And He went a little beyond *them,* and fell on His face and prayed, saying, "My Father, if it is possible, let this cup pass from Me; yet not as I will, but as You will." And He came to the disciples and found them sleeping, and said to Peter, "So, you *men* could not keep watch with Me for one hour? Keep watching and praying that you may not enter into temptation; the spirit is willing, but the flesh is weak." He went away again a second time and prayed, saying, "My Father, if this cannot pass away unless I drink it, Your will be done." Again He came and found them sleeping, for their eyes were heavy. And He left them again, and went away and prayed a third time, saying the same thing once more. Then He came to the disciples and said to them, "Are you still sleeping and resting? Behold the hour is at hand and the Son of Man is being betrayed into the hands of sinners. Get up, let us be going; behold the one who betrays Me is at hand!" (Matthew 26:36–46; cf. Mark 14:32–42; Luke 22:40–46; see Matthew 20:22; John 12:27).

Setting: Gethsemane on the Mount of Olives, just east of the temple in Jerusalem. Jesus agonizes over His impending death, disappointed His disciples keep falling asleep instead of watching and praying with Him.

They came to a place named Gethsemane; and He said to the disciples, "Sit here until I have prayed." And He took with Him Peter and James and John, and began to be very distressed and troubled. And He said to them, "My soul is deeply grieved to the point of death; remain here and keep watch." And He went a little beyond *them,* and fell to the ground and *began* to pray that if it were possible, the hour might pass Him by. And He was saying, "Abba! Father! All things are possible for You; remove this cup from Me; yet not what I will, but what You will." And He came and found them sleeping, and said to Peter, "Simon, are you asleep? Could you not keep watch for one hour? Keep watching and praying that you may not come into temptation; the spirit is willing, but the flesh is weak" (Mark 14:32–38; cf. Matthew 26:36–41; Luke 22:41–46; see Romans 8:15; Galatians 4:6).

Setting: Jerusalem. At the time for the Passover of the Jews, after the Lord cleanses the temple, a Pharisee, Nicodemus, asks Him by night the meaning of "born again."

Jesus answered, "Truly, truly, I say to you, unless one is born of water and the Spirit he cannot enter into the kingdom of God. That which is born of the flesh is flesh, and that which is born of the Spirit is spirit. Do not be amazed that I said to you, 'You must be born again.' The wind blows where it wishes and you hear the sound of it, but do not know where it comes from and where it is going; so is everyone who is born of the Spirit" (John 3:5–8; see Psalm 135:7; John 1:13).

Setting: The synagogue at Capernaum of Galilee. After the Jewish religious leaders argue with one another when Jesus says He will give His flesh to the world to eat, some of His disciples also express difficulty with His statements.

But, Jesus, conscious that His disciples grumbled at this, said to them, "Does this cause you to stumble? *What* then if you see the Son of Man ascending to where He was before? It is the Spirit who gives life; the flesh profits nothing; the words that I have spoken to you are spirit and are life. But there are some of you who do not believe." For Jesus knew from the beginning who they were who did not believe, and who it was that would betray Him. And He was saying, "For this reason I have said to you, that no one can come to Me unless it has been granted him from the Father" (John 6:61–65; see Matthew 11:6; 13:11; John 3:13).

SPIRIT (Jesus')

Setting: On the hill called Golgotha (Calvary), just outside Jerusalem. Mocked and ridiculed while hanging nailed to a cross, after granting forgiveness to one of the criminals being crucified with Him who asks to be remembered in Christ's kingdom, Jesus dies.

And Jesus, crying out with a loud voice, said, "Father, INTO YOUR HANDS I COMMIT MY SPIRIT." Having said this, He breathed His last (Luke 23:46, Jesus quotes from Psalm 31:5; cf. Matthew 27:45–50; Mark 15:33–37; John 19:28–30).

SPIRIT, BAPTISM OF THE HOLY (See HOLY SPIRIT, BAPTISM OF THE)

SPIRIT, BLASPHEMY AGAINST THE (See HOLY SPIRIT, BLASPHEMY AGAINST THE)

SPIRIT, BLASPHEMY AGAINST THE HOLY (See HOLY SPIRIT, BLASPHEMY AGAINST THE)

SPIRIT, EVIL (See DEMON; DEMONS; SPIRIT, UNCLEAN; and SPIRITS, EVIL)

SPIRIT, FATHER AND THE SON AND THE HOLY (See NAME OF THE FATHER AND THE SON AND THE HOLY SPIRIT; and TRINITY)

SPIRIT, HOLY (See HOLY SPIRIT)

SPIRIT, HUMAN (See SPIRIT (human))

SPIRIT, NAME OF THE FATHER AND THE SON AND THE HOLY (See HOLY SPIRIT, NAME OF THE FATHER AND THE SON AND THE)

SPIRIT, POOR IN (Also see HUMILITY)

Setting: Galilee. Early in His ministry, Jesus presents the Beatitudes (part of the Sermon on the Mount) to His disciples and the gathered crowds from Galilee, Decapolis, Jerusalem, Judea, and beyond the Jordan.

He opened His mouth and *began* to teach them, saying, "Blessed are the poor in spirit, for theirs is the kingdom of heaven" (Matthew 5:2, 3; see Matthew 13:35).

SPIRIT, PROPHECY OF THE BAPTISM OF THE HOLY (See HOLY SPIRIT, BAPTISM OF THE)

SPIRIT, UNCLEAN (Also see DEMON; DEMONS; SPIRIT, EVIL; and SPIRITS, EVIL)

Setting: Galilee. Jesus responds to some Pharisees and scribes who ask Him for a miraculous sign as He ministers.

"Now when the unclean spirit goes out of a man, it passes through waterless places seeking rest, and does not find *it.* Then it says, 'I will return to my house from which I came'; and when it comes, it finds *it* unoccupied, swept, and put in order. Then it goes and takes along with it seven other spirits more wicked than itself, and they go in and live there; and the last state of that man becomes worse than the first. That is the way it will also be for this evil generation" (Matthew 12:43–45; cf. Luke 11:24–26; see Mark 5:9).

Setting: The country of the Gerasenes, across the Sea of Galilee from Capernaum. Jesus encounters and heals a demon-possessed man.

For He had been saying to him, "Come out of the man, you unclean spirit!" And He was asking him, "What is your name?" And he said to Him, "My name is Legion; for we are many" (Mark 5:8, 9; cf. Luke 8:30; see Matthew 8:28–32; Luke 8:26–33).

[UNCLEAN SPIRIT also from deaf and mute spirit]

Setting: Galilee. Upon returning from a high mountain [perhaps Mount Hermon] where Jesus was transfigured before Peter, James, and John, the four find the rest of the disciples arguing with some scribes.

And He asked them, "What are you discussing with them?" And one of the crowd answered Him, "Teacher, I brought You my son, possessed with a spirit which makes him mute; and whenever it seizes him, it slams him *to the ground* and he foams *at the mouth,* and grinds his teeth and stiffens out. I told Your disciples to cast it out, and they could not *do it.* And He answered them, and said, "O unbelieving generation, how long shall I be with you? How long shall I put up with you? Bring him to Me!" They brought the boy to Him. When he saw Him, immediately the spirit threw him into a convulsion, and falling to the ground, be *began* rolling around and foaming *at the mouth.* And He asked his father, "How long has this been happening to him?" And he said, "From childhood. It has often thrown him both into the fire and into the water to destroy him. But if You can do anything, take pity on us and help us!" And Jesus said to him, "'If You can?' All things are possible to him who believes." Immediately the boy's father cried out and said, "I do believe; help my unbelief." When Jesus saw that a crowd was rapidly gathering, He rebuked the unclean spirit, saying to it, "You deaf and mute spirit, I command you, come out of him and do not enter him again." After crying out and throwing him into terrible convulsions, it came out; and *the boy* became so much like a corpse that most *of them,* said, "He is dead!" But Jesus took him by the hand and raised him; and he got up. When He came into *the* house, His disciples *began* questioning Him privately, "Why could we not drive it out?" And He said to them, "This kind cannot come out by anything but prayer" (Mark 9:16–29; cf. Matthew 17:14–21; Luke 9:37–43; see Matthew 17:20).

Setting: On the way from Galilee to Jerusalem. After some in the crowd test Him, demanding a sign from heaven, Jesus illustrates His power over Satan.

"When the unclean spirit goes out of a man, it passes through waterless places seeking rest, and not finding any, it says, 'I will return to my house from which I came.' And when it comes, it finds it swept clean and put in order. Then it goes and takes *along* seven other spirits more evil than itself, and they go in and live there; and the last state of that man becomes worse than the first" (Luke 11:24–26; cf. Matthew 12:43–45).

SPIRIT, UNGODLY

[UNGODLY SPIRIT from kind of spirit you are of]

Setting: Galilee. After clarifying who the disciples' co-laborers are, Jesus prepares to go to Jerusalem by sending messengers ahead to Samaria, where they experience rejection and seek retribution.

But He turned and rebuked them, [and said, "You do not know what kind of spirit you are of; for the Son of Man did not come to destroy men's lives, but to save them."] And they went on to another village (Luke 9:55–56; see 2 Kings 1:9–14; Luke 13:22).

SPIRIT BAPTISM (See HOLY SPIRIT, BAPTISM OF THE)

SPIRIT OF GOD (Also see HOLY SPIRT; and SPIRIT (God))

Setting: Galilee. After He heals a blind, mute, demon-possessed man, the Pharisees accuse Jesus in front of crowds of being a worker of Satan.

And knowing their thoughts Jesus said to them, "Any kingdom divided against itself is laid waste; and any city or house divided against itself will not stand. If Satan casts out Satan, he is divided against himself; how then will his kingdom stand? If I by Beelzebul cast out demons, by whom do your sons cast *them* out? For this reason they will be your judges. But if I cast out demons by the Spirit of God, then the kingdom of God has come upon you. Or how can anyone enter the strong man's house and carry off his property, unless he first binds the strong *man?* And then he will plunder his house" (Matthew 12:25–29; cf. Matthew 9:34; Mark 3:23–27; Luke 11:17–20).

SPIRIT OF THE LORD (Also see HOLY SPIRIT)

Setting: The synagogue in Jesus' hometown of Nazareth in Galilee. At the beginning of His public ministry, Jesus reads on the Sabbath from the book of the prophet Isaiah.

And the book of the prophet Isaiah was handed to Him. And He opened the book and found the place where it was written, "THE SPIRIT OF THE LORD IS UPON ME, BECAUSE HE ANOINTED ME TO PREACH THE GOSPEL TO THE POOR. HE HAS SENT ME TO PROCLAIM RELEASE TO THE CAPTIVES, AND RECOVERY OF SIGHT TO THE BLIND, TO SET FREE THOSE WHO ARE OPPRESSED, TO PROCLAIM THE FAVORABLE YEAR OF THE LORD." And He closed the book, gave it back to the attendant and sat down; and the eyes of all in the synagogue were fixed on Him. And He began to say to them, "Today this Scripture has been fulfilled in your hearing" (Luke 4:17–21, Jesus quotes from Isaiah 61:1, 2).

SPIRIT OF TRUTH (Listed under TRUTH, SPIRIT OF)

SPIRITS (Also see DEMONS; and SPIRITS, UNCLEAN)

Setting: Galilee. Jesus responds to some Pharisees and scribes who ask Him for a miraculous sign as He ministers.

"Now when the unclean spirit goes out of a man, it passes through waterless places seeking rest, and does not find *it.* Then it says, 'I will return to my house from which I came'; and when it comes, it finds *it* unoccupied, swept, and put in order. Then it goes and takes along with it seven other spirits more wicked than itself, and they go in and live there; and the last state of that man becomes worse than the first. That is the way it will also be for this evil generation" (Matthew 12:43–45; cf. Luke 11:24–26; see Mark 5:9).

Setting: On the way from Galilee to Jerusalem. The Lord responds to a report from the seventy sent out in pairs to every place He Himself will soon visit.

And He said to them, "I was watching Satan fall from heaven like lightning. Behold, I have given you authority to tread on serpents and scorpions, and over all the power of the enemy, and nothing will injure you. Nevertheless do not rejoice in this, that the spirits are subject to you, but rejoice that your names are recorded in heaven" (Luke 10:18–20; see Psalm 91:13; Isaiah 14:12–14; Luke 9:1).

Setting: On the way from Galilee to Jerusalem. After some in the crowd test Him, demanding a sign from heaven, Jesus illustrates His power over Satan.

"When the unclean spirit goes out of a man, it passes through waterless places seeking rest, and not finding any, it says, 'I will return to my house from which I came.' And when it comes, it finds it swept clean and put in order. Then it goes and takes *along* seven other spirits more evil than itself, and they go in and live there; and the last state of that man becomes worse than the first" (Luke 11:24–26; cf. Matthew 12:43–45).

SPIRITS (God's)

Setting: On the island of Patmos (in the Aegean Sea about fifty miles southwest of Ephesus in modern Turkey). On the Lord's Day (Sunday), approximately fifty years after the Resurrection, the disciple John encounters the Lord Jesus Christ, who communicates a new revelation for the apostle to record for the church in Sardis and to six other churches in Asia.

"To the angel of the church in Sardis write: He who has the seven Spirits of God and the seven stars, says this: 'I know your deeds, that you have a name that you are alive, but you are dead. Wake up, and strengthen the things that remain, which were about to die; for I have not found your deeds completed in the sight of My God. So remember what you have received and heard; and keep *it,* and repent. Therefore if you do not wake up, I will come like a thief, and you will not know at what hour I will come to you. But you have a few people in Sardis who have not soiled their garments; and they will walk with Me in white, for they are worthy. He who overcomes will thus be clothed in white garments; and I will not erase his name from the book of life, and I will confess his name before My Father and before His angels. He who has an ear, let him hear what the Spirit says to the churches'" (Revelation 3:1–6; see Matthew 10:32; Revelation 1:4, 16).

SPIRITS, EVIL (See DEMON; DEMONS; SPIRIT, UNCLEAN; and SPIRITS)

SPIRITS, SEVEN (See SPIRITS (God's))

SPIRITS, UNCLEAN (See DEMONS; SPIRIT, UNCLEAN; and SPIRITS, EVIL)

SPIRITUAL BIRTH (See BORN AGAIN)

SPIRITUAL BLINDNESS (See MEN, SPIRITUALLY BLIND)

SPIRITUAL FAMILY (Listed under FAMILY, SPIRITUAL)

SPIT

Setting: On the road to Jerusalem. After encouraging His disciples with a revelation of their future reward, Jesus prophesies His persecution, death, and resurrection.

They were on the road going up to Jerusalem, and Jesus was walking on ahead of them; and they were amazed, and those who followed were fearful. And again He took the twelve aside and began to tell them what was going to happen to Him, *saying*, "Behold, we are going up to Jerusalem, and the Son of Man will be delivered to the chief priests and the scribes; and they will condemn Him to death and will hand Him over to the Gentiles. They will mock Him and spit on Him, and scourge Him and kill *Him*, and three days later He will rise again" (Mark 10:32–34; cf. Matthew 20:17–19; Luke 18:31–34; see Matthew 16:21; Mark 8:31).

Setting: On the way from Galilee to Jerusalem. After responding to Peter's statement about the disciples' personal sacrifice in following Him, Jesus tells them of the sacrifice He will make in Jerusalem.

Then He took the twelve aside and said to them, "Behold, we are going up to Jerusalem, and all things which are written through the prophets about the Son of Man will be accomplished. For He will be handed over to the Gentiles, and will be mocked and mistreated and spit upon, and after they have scourged Him, they will kill Him; and the third day He will rise again" (Luke 18:31–33; cf. Matthew 20:17–19; Mark 10:32–34).

Setting: On the island of Patmos (in the Aegean Sea about fifty miles southwest of Ephesus in modern Turkey). On the Lord's Day (Sunday), approximately fifty years after the Resurrection, the disciple John encounters the Lord Jesus Christ, who communicates a new revelation for the apostle to record for the church in Laodicea and to six other churches in Asia.

"To the angel of the church in Laodicea write: The Amen, the faithful and true Witness, the Beginning of the creation of God, says this: 'I know your deeds, that you are neither cold nor hot; I wish that you were cold or hot. So because you are lukewarm, and neither hot nor cold, I will spit you out of My mouth. Because you say, "I am rich, and have become wealthy, and have need of nothing," and you do not know that you are wretched and miserable and poor and blind and naked, I advise you to buy from Me gold refined by fire so that you may become rich, and white garments so that you may clothe yourself, and *that* the shame of your nakedness will not be revealed; and eye salve to anoint your eyes so that you may see. Those whom I love, I reprove and discipline; therefore be zealous and repent. Behold, I stand at the door and knock; if anyone hears My voice and opens the door, I will come in to him and will dine with him, and he with Me. He who overcomes, I will grant to him to sit down with Me on My throne, as I also overcame and sat down with My Father on His throne. He who has an ear, let him hear what the Spirit says to the churches'" (Revelation 3:14–22; see Proverb 3:12; Hosea 12:8; John 14:23; 16:33).

SPLENDOR

Setting: On the way from Galilee to Jerusalem. After responding to the Pharisees' scoffing at His teaching the disciples about stewardship and the permanence of the Law, Jesus conveys the story of the rich man and Lazarus.

"Now there was a rich man, and he habitually dressed in purple and fine linen, joyously living in splendor every day. And a poor man named Lazarus was laid at his gate, covered with sores, and longing to be fed with the *crumbs* which were falling from the rich man's table; besides, even the dogs were coming and licking his sores. Now the poor man died and was carried away by the angels to Abraham's bosom; and the rich man also died and was buried. In Hades he lifted up his eyes, being in torment, and saw Abraham far away and Lazarus in his bosom. And he cried out and said, 'Father Abraham, have mercy on me, and send Lazarus so that he may dip the tip of his finger in water and cool off my tongue, for I am in agony in this flame.' But Abraham said, 'Child, remember that during your life you received your good things, and likewise Lazarus bad things; but now he is being comforted here, and you are in agony. And besides all this, between us and you there is a great chasm fixed, so that those who wish to come over from here to you will not be able, and *that* none may cross over from there to us.' And he said, 'Then I beg you, father, that you send him to my father's house—for I have five brothers—in order that he may warn them, so that they will not also come to this place of torment.' But Abraham said, 'They have Moses and the Prophets; let them hear them.' But he said, 'No, father Abraham, but if someone goes to them from the dead, they will repent!' But he said to him, 'If they do not listen to Moses and the Prophets, they will not be persuaded even if someone rises from the dead'" (Luke 16:19–31; see Luke 3:8; 6:24).

STAFF (Also see ROD)

Setting: Galilee. After His twelve disciples observe His ministry, Jesus summons and specifically instructs them about their ministry to the people of Israel.

These twelve Jesus sent out after instructing them: "Do not go in *the* way of *the* Gentiles, and do not enter *any* city of the Samaritans; but rather go to the lost sheep of the house of Israel. And as you go, preach, saying, 'The kingdom of heaven is at hand.' Heal *the* sick, raise *the* dead, cleanse *the* lepers, cast out demons. Freely you received, freely give. Do not acquire gold, or silver, or copper for your money belts, or a bag for *your* journey, or even two coats, or sandals, or a staff; for the worker is worthy of his support. And whatever city or village you enter, inquire who is worthy in it, and stay at his house until you leave *that city*. As you enter the house, give it your greeting. If the house is worthy, give it your *blessing of* peace. But if it is not worthy, take back your *blessing of* peace. Whoever does not receive you, nor heed your words, as you go out of that house or that city, shake the dust off your feet. Truly I say to you, it will be more tolerable for *the* land of Sodom and Gomorrah in the day of judgment than for that city" (Matthew 10:5–15; cf. Mark 6:7–11; Luke 9:1–5; see Matthew 3:2; 11:22, 24; 15:24; Luke 22:35; 1 Corinthians 9:14).

Setting: Galilee. After raising Jairus's daughter from the dead, Jesus calls the twelve disciples together and gives them power and authority over demons, along with the ability to cure diseases.

And He said to them, "Take nothing for *your* journey, neither a staff, nor a bag, nor bread, nor money; and do not *even* have two tunics apiece. Whatever house you enter, stay there until you leave that city. And as for those who do not receive you, go out from that city, shake the dust off your feet as a testimony against them" (Luke 9:3–5; cf. Matthew 10:1–15; Mark 6:7–11; see Luke; 10:4–12).

STALL

Setting: On the way from Galilee to Jerusalem. Jesus responds to a synagogue official's anger over the Lord's healing of a woman, sick eighteen years, in the synagogue on the Sabbath.

But the Lord answered him and said, "You hypocrites, does not each of you on the Sabbath untie his ox or his donkey from the stall and lead him away to water *him?* And this woman, a daughter of Abraham as she is, whom Satan has bound for eighteen long years, should she not have been released from this bond on the Sabbath day?" (Luke 13:15, 16; see Luke 14:5).

STANDARD

Setting: Galilee. During the early part of His ministry, Jesus preaches the Sermon on the Mount to His disciples and the multitudes.

"Do not judge so that you will not be judged. For in the way you judge, you will be judged; and by your standard of measure, it will be measured to you. Why do you look at the speck that is in your brother's eye, but do not notice the log that is in your own eye? Or how can you say to your brother, 'Let me take the speck out of your eye, and behold, the log is in your own eye? You hypocrite, first take the log out of your own eye, and then you will see clearly to take the speck out of your brother's eye" (Matthew 7:1–5; cf. Mark 4:24; Luke 6:37–42; Romans 2:1; Romans 14:10, 13).

Setting: Galilee. Following His explanation of the Parable of the Sower to His disciples, Jesus informs them of personal accountability and responsibility.

And He was saying to them, "Take care what you listen to. By your standard of measure it will be measured to you; and more will be given you besides. For whoever has, to him *more* shall be given; and whoever does not have, even what he has shall be taken away from him" (Mark 4:24, 25; cf. Matthew 13:12; Luke 8:18; see Matthew 7:2).

Setting: Galilee. After selecting His twelve disciples, Jesus teaches the Sermon on the Mount to those disciples and a great throng of people from Judea, Jerusalem, and the central coastal region of Tyre and Sidon.

"Do not judge, and you will not be judged; and do not condemn, and you will not be condemned; pardon, and you will be pardoned. Give and it will be given to you. They will pour into your lap a good measure—pressed down, shaken together, *and* running over. For by your standard of measure it will be measured to you in return" (Luke 6:37, 38; cf. Matthew 7:1–5; Mark 4:24; see Luke 6:12–19).

STAR (Also see STARS)

Setting: On the island of Patmos (in the Aegean Sea about fifty miles southwest of Ephesus in modern Turkey). On the Lord's Day (Sunday), approximately fifty years after the Resurrection, the disciple John encounters the Lord Jesus Christ, who communicates a new revelation for the apostle to record for the church in Thyatira and to six other churches in Asia

"And to the angel of the church in Thyatira write: The Son of God, who has eyes like a flame of fire, and His feet are like burnished bronze, says this: 'I know your deeds, and your love and faith and service and perseverance, and that your deeds of late are greater than at first. But I have *this* against you, that you tolerate the woman Jezebel, who calls herself a prophetess, and she teaches and leads My bond-servants astray so that they commit *acts of* immorality and eat things sacrificed to idols. I gave her time to repent, and she does not want to repent of her immorality. Behold, I will throw her on a bed *of sickness,* and those who commit adultery with her into great tribulation, unless they repent of her deeds. And I will kill her children with pestilence, and all the churches will know that I am He who searches the minds and hearts; and I will give to each one of you according to your deeds. But I say to you, the rest who are in Thyatira, who do not hold this teaching, who have not known the deep things of Satan, as they call them—I place no other burden on you. Nevertheless what you have, hold fast until I come. He who overcomes, and he who keeps My deeds until the end, TO HIM I WILL GIVE AUTHORITY OVER THE NATIONS; AND HE SHALL RULE THEM WITH A ROD OF IRON, AS THE VESSELS OF THE POTTER ARE BROKEN TO PIECES, as I also have received *authority* from My Father; and I will give him the morning star. He who has an ear, let him hear what the Spirit says to the churches' (Revelation 2:18–29; Jesus quotes from Psalm 2:8, 9; Isaiah 30:14; see 1 Kings 16:31; Psalm 7:9; Romans 2:5; 1 Corinthians 2:10; 2 Peter 3:9; Revelation 1:14; 3:11; 17:1–20).

Setting: On the island of Patmos (in the Aegean Sea about fifty miles southwest of Ephesus in modern Turkey). In the final chapter of the Lord Jesus Christ's revelation via the apostle John, approximately fifty years after the Resurrection, the Lord authenticates the truthfulness of His message, along with His earthly lineage through King David.

"I, Jesus, have sent My angel to testify to you these things for the churches. I am the root and the descendant of David, the bright morning star" (Revelation 22:16).

STAR, MORNING (See STAR)

STARS (STARS, SEVEN is a separate entry; also see HEAVENS; MOON; STAR; and SUN)

Setting: The Mount of Olives, just east of Jerusalem. During His Olivet Discourse, Jesus answers His disciples' questions as to when the temple will be destroyed and Jerusalem overrun, along with the signs of His coming and the end of the age.

"But immediately after the tribulation of those days THE SUN WILL BE DARKENED, AND THE MOON WILL NOT GIVE ITS LIGHT, AND THE STARS WILL FALL from the sky, and the powers of the heavens will be shaken. And then the sign of the Son of Man will appear

in the sky, and then all the tribes of the earth will mourn, and they will see the SON OF MAN COMING ON THE CLOUDS OF THE SKY with power and great glory. And He will send forth His angels with A GREAT TRUMPET and THEY WILL GATHER TOGETHER His elect from the four winds, from one end of the sky to the other" (Matthew 24:29–31, Jesus quotes from Isaiah 13:10, Daniel 7:13; Exodus 19:16; cf. Mark 13:24–27; Luke 21:25–27).

Setting: On the Mount of Olives, east of the temple in Jerusalem. After prophesying the temple's destruction, Jesus responds during His Olivet Discourse to questions from Peter, James, John, and Andrew about other future events.

"But in those days, after that tribulation, THE SUN WILL BE DARKENED AND THE MOON WILL NOT GIVE ITS LIGHT, AND THE STARS WILL BE FALLING from heaven, and the powers that are in the heavens will be shaken. Then they will see THE SON OF MAN COMING IN CLOUDS with great power and glory. And then He will send forth the angels, and will gather together His elect from the four winds, from the farthest end of the earth to the farthest end of heaven" (Mark 13:24–27. Jesus quotes from Isaiah 13:10; 34:4; Daniel 7:13; cf. Matthew 24:29–31; Luke 21:25–27).

Setting: On the Mount of Olives, just east of Jerusalem. After ministering in the temple a few days before His crucifixion, and giving His disciples more details regarding future events, Jesus speaks during His Olivet Discourse of His return.

"There will be signs in sun and moon and stars, and on the earth dismay among the nations, in perplexity at the roaring of the sea and the waves, men fainting from fear and the expectation of the things which are coming upon the world; for the powers of the heavens will be shaken. Then they will see THE SON OF MAN COMING IN A CLOUD with power and great glory. But when these things begin to take place, straighten up and lift up your heads, because your redemption is drawing near" (Luke 21:25–28, Jesus quotes from Daniel 7:13; cf. Matthew 24:29–31; Mark 13:24–27).

STARS, SEVEN

Setting: On the island of Patmos (in the Aegean Sea about fifty miles southwest of Ephesus in modern Turkey). On the Lord's Day (Sunday), approximately fifty years after the Resurrection, the disciple John encounters the Lord Jesus Christ, who communicates new revelations for the apostle to record for the seven churches in Asia.

When I saw Him, I fell at His feet like a dead man. And He placed His right hand on me, saying, "Do not be afraid; I am the first and the last, and the living One; and I was dead, and behold, I am alive forevermore, and I have the keys of death and of Hades. Therefore write the things which you have seen, and the things which are, and the things which will take place after these things. As for the mystery of the seven stars which you saw in My right hand, and the seven golden lampstands: the seven stars are the angels of the seven churches, and the seven lampstands are the seven churches" (Revelation 1:17–20; see Isaiah 44:6; Luke 24:5; Revelation 2:8).

Setting: On the island of Patmos (in the Aegean Sea about fifty miles southwest of Ephesus in modern Turkey). On the Lord's Day (Sunday), approximately fifty years after the Resurrection, the disciple John encounters the Lord Jesus Christ, who communicates a new revelation for the apostle to record for the church in Ephesus and to six other churches in Asia.

"To the angel of the church in Ephesus write: The One who holds the seven stars in His right hand, the One who walks among the seven golden lampstands, says this: 'I know your deeds and your toil and perseverance, and that you cannot tolerate evil men, and you put to the test those who call themselves apostles, and they are not, and you found them *to be* false; and you have perseverance and have endured for My name's sake, and have not grown weary. But I have *this* against you, that you have left your first love. Therefore remember from where you have fallen, and repent and do the deeds you did at first; or else I am coming to you and will remove your lampstand out of its place—unless you repent. Yet this you do have, that you hate the deeds of the Nicolaitans, which I also hate. He who has an ear, let him hear what the Spirit says to the churches. To him who overcomes, I will grant to eat of the tree of life which is in the Paradise of God' (Revelation 2:1–7; see Genesis 2:9; Ezekiel 28:13; 1 John 4:1; Revelation 1:10, 11, 19, 20).

Setting: On the island of Patmos (in the Aegean Sea about fifty miles southwest of Ephesus in modern Turkey). On the Lord's Day (Sunday), approximately fifty years after the Resurrection, the disciple John encounters the Lord Jesus Christ, who communicates a new revelation for the apostle to record for the church in Sardis and to six other churches in Asia.

"To the angel of the church in Sardis write: He who has the seven Spirits of God and the seven stars, says this: 'I know your deeds, that you have a name that you are alive, but you are dead. Wake up, and strengthen the things that remain, which were about to die; for I have not found your deeds completed in the sight of My God. So remember what you have received and heard; and keep *it,* and repent. Therefore if you do not wake up, I will come like a thief, and you will not know at what hour I will come to you. But you have a few people in Sardis who have not soiled their garments; and they will walk with Me in white, for they are worthy. He who overcomes will thus be clothed in white garments; and I will not erase his name from the book of life, and I will confess his name before My Father and before His angels. He who has an ear, let him hear what the Spirit says to the churches'" (Revelation 3:1–6; see Matthew 10:32; Revelation 1:16).

STATE

Setting: Galilee. Jesus responds to some Pharisees and scribes who ask Him for a miraculous sign as He ministers.

"Now when the unclean spirit goes out of a man, it passes through waterless places seeking rest, and does not find *it.* Then it says, 'I will return to my house from which I came'; and when it comes, it finds *it* unoccupied, swept, and put in order. Then it goes and takes along with it seven other spirits more wicked than itself, and they go in and live there; and the last state of that man becomes worse than the first. That is the way it will also be for this evil generation" (Matthew 12:43–45; cf. Luke 11:24–26; see Mark 5:9).

Setting: On the way from Galilee to Jerusalem. After some in the crowd test Him, demanding a sign from heaven, Jesus illustrates His power over Satan.

"When the unclean spirit goes out of a man, it passes through waterless places seeking rest, and not finding any, it says, 'I will return to my house from which I came.' And when it comes, it finds it swept clean and put in order. Then it goes and takes *along* seven other spirits more evil than itself, and they go in and live there; and the last state of that man becomes worse than the first" (Luke 11:24–26; cf. Matthew 12:43–45; see Luke 11:14–16).

STATEMENT (Also see WORDS)

Setting: Galilee. During the early part of His ministry, Jesus preaches the Sermon on the Mount to His disciples and the multitudes.

"Again, you have heard that the ancients were told, 'YOU SHALL NOT MAKE FALSE VOWS, BUT SHALL FULFILL YOUR VOWS TO THE LORD.' But I say to you, make no oath at all, either by heaven, for it is the throne of God, or by the earth, for it is the footstool of His feet, or by Jerusalem, for it is THE CITY OF THE GREAT KING. Nor shall you make an oath by your head, for you cannot make one hair white or black. But let your statement be 'Yes, yes' *or* 'No, no'; anything beyond these is of evil" (Matthew 5:33–37, Jesus quotes from Leviticus 19:12, Psalm 48:2; Isaiah 66:1; cf. James 5:12).

Setting: Judea beyond the Jordan (Perea). After responding to the Pharisees' question about Moses' command regarding a certificate of divorce, Jesus answers the disciples' private question.

But He said to them, "Not all men *can* accept this statement, but *only* those to whom it has been given. For there are eunuchs who were born that way from their mother's womb; and there are eunuchs who were made eunuchs by men; and there are *also* eunuchs who made themselves eunuchs for the sake of the kingdom of heaven. He who is able to accept *this,* let him accept *it*" (Matthew 19:11, 12; cf. 1 Corinthians 7:7).

STATEMENTS, JESUS' "I AM" (See JESUS' "I AM" STATEMENTS)

STATER (See SHEKEL)

STATUS (See GREATNESS; and PRIVILEGE)

STEALING (Also see BURGLARY; ROBBER; ROBBERY; THEFT; and THIEVES)

[STEALING from steal]

Setting: Galilee. During the early part of His ministry, Jesus preaches the Sermon on the Mount to His disciples and the multitudes.

"Do not store up for yourselves treasures on earth, where moth and rust destroy, and where thieves break in and steal. But store up for yourselves treasures in heaven, where neither moth nor rust destroys, and where thieves do not break in or steal; for where your treasure is, there your heart will be also" (Matthew 6:19–21; cf. Luke 12:34; see Proverb 23:4; Matthew 19:21).

[STEALING from STEAL]

Setting: Judea beyond the Jordan (Perea). Jesus shares with a rich, young ruler how to obtain eternal life.

And He said to him, "Why are you asking Me about what is good? There is *only* One who is good; but if you wish to enter into life, keep the commandments." *Then* he said to Him, 'Which ones?' And Jesus said, "YOU SHALL NOT COMMIT MURDER; YOU SHALL NOT COMMIT ADULTERY; YOU SHALL NOT STEAL; YOU SHALL NOT BEAR FALSE WITNESS; HONOR YOUR FATHER AND MOTHER; and YOU SHALL LOVE YOUR NEIGHBOR AS YOURSELF." The young man said to Him, "All these things I have kept; what am I still lacking?" Jesus said to him, "If you wish to complete go *and* sell your possessions and give to *the* poor, and you will have treasure in heaven; and come, follow Me" (Matthew 19:16–22, Jesus quotes from Exodus 20:13–15; Leviticus 19:18; cf. Leviticus 18:5; Mark 10:17–21; Luke 10:25–28; 12:33; 18:18–24).

[STEALING from STEAL]

Setting: Judea beyond the Jordan (Perea). After demonstrating to His disciples the importance of little children, Jesus encounters a rich man seeking eternal life.

And Jesus said to him, "Why do you call Me good? No one is good except God alone. You know the commandments, 'DO NOT MURDER, DO NOT COMMIT ADULTERY, DO NOT STEAL, DO NOT BEAR FALSE WITNESS, Do not defraud, HONOR YOUR FATHER AND MOTHER.'" And he said to Him, "Teacher, I have kept all these things from my youth up." Looking at him, Jesus felt a love for him and said to him, "One thing you lack: go and sell all you possess and give to the poor, and you will have treasure in heaven; and come, follow Me" (Mark 10:18–21; Jesus quotes from Exodus 20:12–16; cf. Matthew 19:16–22; Luke 18:18–24; see Matthew 6:20).

[STEALING from STEAL]

Setting: Judea beyond the Jordan (Perea). After speaking of the importance of children, Jesus responds to a ruler's question about inheriting eternal life.

A ruler questioned Him, saying, "Good Teacher, what shall I do to inherit eternal life?" And Jesus said to him, "Why do you call Me good? No one is good except God alone. You know the commandments, 'DO NOT COMMIT ADULTERY, DO NOT MURDER, DO NOT STEAL, DO NOT BEAR FALSE WITNESS, HONOR YOUR FATHER AND MOTHER.'" And he said "All these things I have kept from *my* youth." When Jesus heard *this,* He said to him, "One thing you still lack; sell all that you possess and distribute it to the poor, and you shall have treasure in heaven; and come, follow Me" (Luke 18:18–22, Jesus quotes from Exodus 20:12–16; cf. Matthew 19:16–22; Mark 10:17–22; see Luke 10:25–28).

[STEALING from steal]

Setting: Jerusalem. Following the Pharisees' interrogation and dismissal of the formerly blind man Jesus healed on the Sabbath, the Lord conveys the Parable of the Good Shepherd to the Pharisees, using figures of speech they do not understand.

So Jesus said to them again, "Truly, truly, I say to you, I am the door of the sheep. All who came before Me are thieves and robbers, but the sheep did not hear them. I am the door; if anyone enters through Me, he will be saved, and will go in and out and find pasture. The thief comes only to steal and kill and destroy; I came that they may have life, and have *it* abundantly. I am the good shepherd; the good shepherd lays down His life for the sheep. He who is a hired hand, and not a shepherd, who is not the owner of the sheep, sees the wolf coming, and leaves the sheep and flees, and the wolf snatches them and scatters *them. He flees* because he is a hired hand and is not concerned about the sheep. I am the good shepherd, and I know My own and My own know Me, even as the Father knows Me and I know the Father; and I lay down My life for the sheep. I have other sheep, which are not of this fold; I must bring them also, and they will hear My voice; and they will become one flock *with* one shepherd. For this reason the Father loves Me, because I lay down My life so that I may take it again. No one has taken it away from Me, but I lay it down on My own initiative. I have authority to take it up again. This commandment I received from My Father" (John 10:7–18; see Isaiah 40:11; 56:8; Jeremiah 23:1; Matthew 11:27).

STERILE MAN (See CELIBACY; and EUNUCH)

STEWARD (See STEWARD, PARABLE OF THE FAITHFUL AND SENSIBLE; MANAGER; SERVANT; SERVANTS; SLAVE; and SLAVES)

STEWARD, PARABLE OF THE FAITHFUL AND SENSIBLE

[STEWARD, PARABLE OF THE FAITHFUL AND SENSIBLE from faithful and sensible slave]

Setting: On the Mount of Olives, just east of Jerusalem. During His Olivet Discourse, after answering His disciples' questions as to when the temple will be destroyed and Jerusalem overrun, along with the signs of His coming and the end of the age, Jesus reemphasizes to His disciples that they should be on the alert for His return.

"Therefore be on the alert, for you do not know which day your Lord is coming. But be sure of this, that if the head of the house had known at what time of the night the thief was coming, he would have been on the alert and would not have allowed his house to be broken into. For this reason you also must be ready; for the Son of Man is coming at an hour when you do not think *He will.* Who then is the faithful and sensible slave whom his master put in charge of his household to give their food at the proper time? Blessed is that slave whom his master finds so doing when he comes. Truly I say to you that he will put him in charge of all his possessions. But if that evil slave says in his heart, 'My master is not coming for a long time,' and begins to beat his fellow slaves and eat and drink with drunkards; the master of that slave will come on a day when he does not expect *him* and at an hour which he does not know, and will cut him in pieces and assign him a place with the hypocrites; in that place there will be weeping and gnashing of teeth" (Matthew 24:42–51; cf. Mark 13:33–37; Luke 12:39–46; 21:34–36; see Matthew 8:11, 12; 25:21–23).

Setting: On the way from Galilee to Jerusalem. After Jesus uses a parable to challenge the crowd and His disciples to be ready for His return, Peter asks Him whom He is addressing.

And the Lord said, "Who then is the faithful and sensible steward, whom his master will put in charge of his servants, to give them their rations at the proper time? Blessed is that slave whom his master finds so doing when he comes. Truly I say to you that he will put him in charge of all his possessions. But if that slave says in his heart, 'My master will be a long time in coming,' and begins to beat the slaves, *both* men and women, and to eat and drink and get drunk; the master of that slave will come on a day when he does not expect *him* and at an hour he does not know, and will cut him in pieces, and assign him a place with the unbelievers. And that slave who knew his master's will and did not get ready or act in accord with his will, will receive many lashes, but the one who did know *it,* and committed deeds worthy of flogging, will receive but few. From everyone who has been given much, much will be required; and to whom they entrusted much, of him they will ask all the more" (Luke 12:42–48; cf. Matthew 24:45–51; see Leviticus 5:17).

STEWARD, SENSIBLE (See PARABLE OF THE FAITHFUL AND SENSIBLE STEWARD)

STEWARD, UNRIGHTEOUS (See MANAGER, UNRIGHTEOUS)

STEWARDSHIP (Also see ACCOUNTING; AUTHORITY; FAITHFULNESS; MANAGER; MANAGEMENT; OFFERING; STEWARD, SENSIBLE; TALENT; TALENTS; and TITHE)

[STEWARDSHIP from For whoever has, to him *more* shall be given]

Setting: By the Sea of Galilee. Jesus responds to His disciples' questions about the Parable of the Sower, which He has just taught from a boat to a crowd.

Jesus answered them, "To you it has been granted to know the mysteries of the kingdom of heaven, but to them it has not been granted. For whoever has, to him *more* shall be given, and he will have an abundance; but whoever does not have, even what he has shall be taken away from him. Therefore, I speak to them in parables; because while seeing they do not see, and while hearing they do not hear, nor do they understand. In their case the prophecy of Isaiah is being fulfilled, which says, 'YOU WILL KEEP ON HEARING, BUT WILL NOT UNDERSTAND; YOU WILL KEEP ON SEEING, BUT WILL NOT PERCEIVE; FOR THE HEART OF THIS PEOPLE HAS BECOME DULL, WITH THEIR EARS THEY SCARCELY HEAR, AND THEY HAVE CLOSED THEIR EYES, OTHERWISE THEYWOULD SEE WITH THEIR EYES, HEAR WITH THEIR EARS, AND UNDERSTAND WITH THEIR HEART AND RETURN, AND I WOULD HEAL THEM.' But blessed are your eyes, because they see; and your ears, because they hear. For truly I say to you that many prophets and righteous men desired to see what you see, and did not see *it,* and to hear what you hear, and did not hear *it*" (Matthew 13:11–17, Jesus quotes from Isaiah 6:9, 10; cf. Matthew 25:29; Mark 4:11–13; Luke 8:10; see Deuteronomy 29:4; John 8:56).

[STEWARDSHIP from faithful and sensible slave whom his master put in charge of his household and in charge of]

Setting: On the Mount of Olives, just east of Jerusalem. During His Olivet Discourse, after answering His disciples' questions as to when the temple will be destroyed and Jerusalem overrun, along with the signs of His coming and the end of the age, Jesus reemphasizes to His disciples that they should be on the alert for His return.

"Therefore be on the alert, for you do not know which day your Lord is coming. But be sure of this, that if the head of the house had known at what time of the night the thief was coming, he would have been on the alert and would not have allowed his house to be broken into. For this reason you also must be ready; for the Son of Man is coming at an hour when you do not think *He will.* Who then is the faithful and sensible slave whom his master put in charge of his household to give their food at the proper time? Blessed is that slave whom his master finds so doing when he comes. Truly I say to you that he will put him in charge of all his possessions. But if that evil slave says in his heart, 'My master is not coming for a long time,' and begins to beat his fellow slaves and eat and drink with drunkards; the master of that slave will come on a day when he does not expect *him* and at an hour which he does not know, and will cut him in pieces and assign him a place with the hypocrites; in that place there will be weeping and gnashing of teeth" (Matthew 24:42–51; cf. Mark 13:33–37; Luke 12:39–46; 21:34–36; see Matthew 8:11, 12; Matthew 25:21–23).

[STEWARDSHIP from I will put you in charge of many things]

Setting: On the Mount of Olives, just east of Jerusalem. During His Olivet Discourse, after answering His disciples' questions as to when the temple will be destroyed and Jerusalem overrun, along with the signs of His coming and the end of the age, Jesus reemphasizes to His disciples that they should be on the alert for His return.

"For *it is* just like a man *about* to go on a journey, who called his own slaves and entrusted his possessions to them. To one he gave five talents, to another, two, and to another, one, each according to his own ability; and he went on his journey. Immediately the one who had received the five talents went and traded with them, and gained five more talents. In the same manner the one who *had received* the two *talents* gained two more. But he who received the one *talent* went away, and dug a *hole* in the ground and hid his master's money. Now after a long time the master of those slaves came and settled accounts with them. The one who had received the five talents came up and brought five more talents, saying, 'Master, you entrusted five talents to me. See, I have gained five more talents.' His master said to him, 'Well done, good and faithful slave. You were faithful with a few things, I will put you in charge of many things; enter into the joy of your master.' Also the one who *had received* the two talents came up and said, 'Master, you entrusted two talents to me. See, I have gained two more talents.' His master said to him, 'Well done, good and faithful slave. You were faithful with a few things, I will put you in charge of many things; enter into the joy of your master.' And the one also who had received the one talent came up and said, 'Master, I knew you to be a hard man, reaping where you did not sow and gathering where you scattered no *seed.* And I was afraid, and went away and hid your talent in the ground. See, you have what is yours.' But his master answered and said to him, 'You wicked, lazy slave, you knew that I reap where I did not sow and gather where I scattered no *seed.* Then you ought to have put my money in the bank, and on my arrival I would have received my *money* back with interest. 'Therefore take away the talent from him, and give it to the one who has ten talents.' For to everyone who has, *more* shall be given, and he will have an abundance; but from the one who does not have, even what he does have shall be taken away. Throw out the worthless slave into the outer darkness; in that place there will be weeping and gnashing of teeth" (Matthew 25:14–30; cf. Matthew 8:12; 13:12; 24:45–47; see Matthew 18:23, 24; Luke 12:44).

[STEWARDSHIP from For whoever has, to him *more* shall be given]
Setting: Galilee. Following His explanation of the Parable of the Sower to His disciples, Jesus informs them about personal accountability and responsibility.

And He was saying to them, "Take care what you listen to. By your standard of measure it will be measured to you; and more will be given you besides. For whoever has, to him *more* shall be given; and whoever does not have, even what he has shall be taken away from him" (Mark 4:24, 25; cf. Matthew 13:12; Luke 8:18; see Matthew 7:2).

[STEWARDSHIP from for whoever has, to him *more* shall be given]
Setting: Galilee. Following the explanation of the Parable of the Sower to His disciples, Jesus gives the Parable of the Lamp.

"Now no one after lighting a lamp covers it over with a container, or puts it under a bed; but he puts it on a lampstand, so that those who come in may see the light. For nothing is hidden that will not become evident, nor *anything* secret that will not be known and come to light. So take care how you listen; for whoever has, to him *more* shall be given; and whoever does not have, even what he thinks he has shall be taken away from him" (Luke 8:16–18; cf. Mark 4:21–23; see Matthew 5:14, 15; 10:26; 13:12).

[STEWARDSHIP from whom his master will put in charge of his servants and in charge of all his possessions]
Setting: On the way from Galilee to Jerusalem. After Jesus uses a parable to challenge the crowd and His disciples to be ready for His return, Peter asks Him whom He is addressing.

And the Lord said, "Who then is the faithful and sensible steward, whom his master will put in charge of his servants, to give them their rations at the proper time? Blessed is that slave whom his master finds so doing when he comes. Truly I say to you that he will put him in charge of all his possessions. But if that slave says in his heart, 'My master will be a long time in coming,' and begins to beat the slaves, *both* men and women, and to eat and drink and get drunk; the master of that slave will come on a day when he does not expect *him* and at an hour he does not know, and will cut him in pieces, and assign him a place with the unbelievers. And that slave who knew his master's will and did not get ready or act in accord with his will, will receive many lashes, but the one who did know *it,* and committed deeds worthy of flogging, will receive but few. From everyone who has been given much, much will be required; and to whom they entrusted much, of him they will ask all the more" (Luke 12:42–48; cf. Matthew 24:45–51; see Leviticus 5:17).

[STEWARDSHIP from Give an accounting of your management and He who is faithful in a very little thing is faithful also in much]
Setting: On the way from Galilee to Jerusalem. After giving the story of the prodigal son, the Lord teaches His disciples about stewardship.

Now He was also saying to the disciples, "There was a rich man who had a manager, and this *manager* was reported to him as squandering his possessions. And he called him and said to him, 'What is this I hear about you? Give an accounting of your management, for you can no longer be a manager.' The manager said to himself, 'What shall I do, since my master is taking the management away from me? I am not strong enough to dig; I am ashamed to beg. I know what I shall do, so that when I am removed from the management people will welcome me into their homes.' And he summoned each one of his master's debtors, and he *began* saying to the first, 'How much do you owe my master?' And he said, 'A hundred measures of oil.' And he said to him, 'Take your bill, and sit down quickly and write fifty.' Then he said to another, 'And how much do you owe?' And he said, 'A hundred measures of wheat.' He said to him, 'Take your bill, and write eighty.' And his master praised the unrighteous manager because he had acted shrewdly; for the sons of this age are more shrewd in relation to their own kind than the sons of light. And I say to you, make friends for yourselves by means of the wealth of unrighteousness, so that when it fails, they will receive you into the eternal dwellings. He who is faithful in a very little thing is faithful also in much; and he who is unrighteous in a very little thing is unrighteous also in much. Therefore if you have not been faithful in the *use of* unrighteous wealth, who will entrust the true *riches* to you? And if you have not been faithful in *the use of* that which is another's, who will give you that which is your own? No servant can serve two masters; for either he will hate the one and love the other, or else he will be devoted to one and despise the other. You cannot serve God and wealth" (Luke 16:1–13; cf. Matthew 6:24; see Matthew 25:14–30).

[STEWARDSHIP from Do business *with this* until I come *back*]

Setting: Jericho, on the way to Jerusalem. After commending Zaccheus's faith in Him, Jesus provides a parable about stewardship.

So He said, "A nobleman went to a distant country to receive a kingdom for himself, and *then* return. And he called ten of his slaves, and gave them ten minas and said to them, 'Do business *with this* until I come *back.*' But his citizens hated him and sent a delegation after him, saying, 'We do not want this man to reign over us.' When he returned, after receiving the kingdom, he ordered that these slaves, to whom he had given the money, be called to him so that he might know what business they had done. The first appeared, saying, 'Master, your mina has made ten minas more.' And he said to him, 'Well done, good slave, because you have been faithful in a very little thing, you are to be in authority over ten cities.' The second came, saying, 'Your mina, master, has made five minas.' And he said to him, also, 'And you are to be over five cities.' Another came, saying, 'Master, here is your mina, which I kept put away in a handkerchief; for I was afraid of you, because you are an exacting man; you take up what you did not lay down and reap what you did not sow.' He said to him, 'By your own words I will judge you, you worthless slave. Did you know that I am an exacting man, taking up what I did not lay down and reaping what I did not sow? Then why did you not put my money in the bank, and having come, I would have collected it with interest?' Then he said to the bystanders, 'Take the mina away from him and give it to the one who has the ten minas.' And they said to him, 'Master, he has ten minas *already.*' I tell you that to everyone who has, more shall be given, but from the one who does not have, even what he does have shall be taken away. But these enemies of mine, who did not want me to reign over them, bring them here and slay them in my presence" (Luke 19:12–27; cf. Matthew 25:14–30; see Matthew 13:12; Luke 16:10).

STOMACH (Also see BELLY)

Setting: Galilee. Jesus gives the crowd the meaning of His instruction about what defiles a man.

Peter said to Him, "Explain the parable to us." Jesus said, "Are you still lacking in understanding also? Do you not understand that everything that goes into the mouth passes into the stomach and is eliminated? But the things that proceed out of the mouth come from the heart, and those defile the man. For out of the heart come evil thoughts, murders, adulteries, fornications, thefts, false witness, slanders. These are the things which defile a man; but to eat with unwashed hands does not defile the man" (Matthew 15:15–20; cf. Mark 7:18–23; see Galatians 5:19–21).

Setting: Galilee. After the Pharisees and scribes from Jerusalem object to His disciples' lack of obedience to the tradition regarding ceremonial cleansing, Jesus speaks to a crowd and explains His teaching to the disciples.

After He called the crowd to Him again, He *began* saying to them, "Listen to Me, all of you, and understand: there is nothing outside the man which can defile him if it goes into him; but the things which proceed out of the man are what defile the man. [If anyone has ears to hear, let him hear."] When he had left the crowd *and* entered the house, His disciples questioned Him about the parable. And He said to them, "Are you so lacking in understanding also? Do you not understand that whatever goes into the man from outside cannot defile him, because it does not go into his heart, but into his stomach, and is eliminated?" (*Thus He* declared all foods clean.) And He was saying, "That which proceeds out of the man, that is what defiles the man. For from within, out of the heart of men, proceed the evil thoughts, fornications, thefts, murders, adulteries, deeds of coveting *and* wickedness, *as well* as deceit, sensuality, envy, slander, pride *and* foolishness. All these evil things proceed from within and defile the man"

(Mark 7:14–23; cf. Matthew 15:10–20).

Setting: On the way from Galilee to Jerusalem. Jesus conveys the illustration of the prodigal son because the Pharisees and scribes complain He associates with tax collectors and sinners.

And He said, "A man had two sons. The younger of them said to his father, 'Father, give me the share of the estate that falls to me.' So he divided his wealth between them. And not many days later, the younger son gathered everything together and went on a journey into a distant country, and there he squandered his estate with loose living. Now when he had spent everything, a severe famine occurred in that country, and he began to be impoverished. So he went and hired himself out to one of the citizens of that country, and he sent him into his fields to feed swine. And he would have gladly filled his stomach with the pods that the swine were eating, and no one was giving *anything* to him. But when he came to his senses, he said, 'How many of my father's hired men have more than enough bread, but I am dying here with hunger! I will get up and go to my father, and will say to him, "Father, I have sinned against heaven, and in your sight; I am no longer worthy to be called your son; make me as one of your hired men."' So he got up and came to his father. But while he was still a long way off, his father saw him and felt compassion *for him,* and ran and embraced him and kissed him. And the son said to him, "Father, I have sinned against heaven and in your sight; I am no longer worthy to be called your son.' But the father said to his slaves, 'Quickly bring out the best robe and put it on him, and put a ring on his hand and sandals on his feet; and bring the fattened calf, kill it, and let us eat and celebrate; for this son of mine was dead and has come to life again; he was lost and has been found.' And they began to celebrate. Now his older son was in the field, when he came and approached the house, he heard music and dancing. And he summoned one of the servants and *began* inquiring what these things could be. And he said to him, 'Your brother has come, and your father has killed the fattened calf because he has received him back safe and sound.' But he became angry and was not willing to go in; and his father came out and *began* pleading with him. But he answered and said to his father, 'Look! For so many years I have been serving you and I have never neglected a command of yours; and *yet* you have never given me a young goat, so that I might celebrate with my friends; but when this son of yours came, who has devoured your wealth with prostitutes, you killed the fattened calf for him.' And he said to him, 'Son, you have always been with me, and all that is mine is yours. But we had to celebrate and rejoice, for this brother of yours was dead and *has begun* to live, and was lost and has been found' " (Luke 15:11–32; see Proverb 29:2).

STONE (STONE, WHITE is a separate entry; also see CORNER STONE, CHIEF; MILLSTONE; ROCK; and STONES)

Setting: Galilee. During the early part of His ministry, Jesus preaches the Sermon on the Mount to His disciples and the multitudes.

"Ask, and it will be given to you; seek, and you will find; knock, and it will be opened to you. For everyone who asks receives, and he who seeks finds, and to him who knocks it will be opened. Or what man is there among you who, when his son asks for a loaf, will give him a stone? Or if he asks for a fish, he will not give him a snake, will he? If you then, being evil, know how to give good gifts to your children, how much more will your Father who is in heaven give what is good to those who ask Him! In everything, therefore, treat people the same way you want them to treat you, for this is the Law and the Prophets" (Matthew 7:7–12; cf. Matthew 22:40; Luke 6:31; Luke 11:9–13; see Psalm 84:11).

Setting: The temple in Jerusalem. Jesus delivers a prophecy to the chief priests and elders after they question His authority.

Jesus said to them, "Did you never read in the Scriptures, 'THE STONE WHICH THE BUILDERS REJECTED, THIS BECAME THE CHIEF CORNER *stone;* THIS CAME ABOUT FROM THE LORD, AND IT IS MARVELOUS IN OUR EYES'? Therefore I say to you, the kingdom of God will be taken away from you and given to a people, producing the fruit of it. And he who falls on this stone will be broken to pieces; but on whomever it falls, it will scatter him like dust" (Matthew 21:42–44, Jesus quotes from Psalm 118:22; cf. Isaiah 8:14, 15; Mark 12:10, 11; Luke 20:17, 18).

Setting: Jerusalem. After teaching, interacting with the religious leaders, and pronouncing woes on these same leaders just days before His crucifixion, Jesus leaves the temple and prophesies its destruction to His disciples.

Jesus came out from the temple, and was going away when His disciples came up to point out the temple buildings to Him. And He said to them, "Do you not see all these things? Truly I say to you, not one stone here will be left upon another, which will not be torn down" (Matthew 24:1, 2; cf. Mark 13:1, 2; Luke 21:5, 6; see Luke 19:43, 44).

Setting: The temple in Jerusalem. Having His authority questioned by the chief priests, scribes, and elders, Jesus begins to teach them in parables.

And He began to speak to them in parables: "A man PLANTED A VINEYARD AND PUT A WALL AROUND IT, AND DUG A VAT UNDER THE WINE PRESS AND BUILT A TOWER, and rented it out to vine-growers and went on a journey. At the *harvest* time he sent a slave to the vine-growers, in order to receive *some* of the produce of the vineyard from the vine-growers. They took him, and beat him and sent him away empty-handed. Again he sent them another slave, and they wounded him in the head, and treated him shamefully. And he sent another, and that one they killed; and *so with* many others, beating some and killing others. He had one more to *send*, a beloved son; he sent him last *of all* to them, saying, 'They will respect my son.' But those vine-growers said to one another, 'This is the heir; come, let us kill him, and the inheritance will be ours!' They took him, and killed him and threw him out of the vineyard. What will the owner of the vineyard do? He will come and destroy the vine-growers, and will give the vineyard to others. Have you not even read this Scripture: 'THE STONE WHICH THE BUILDERS REJECTED, THIS BECAME THE CHIEF CORNER *stone;* THIS CAME ABOUT FROM THE LORD, AND IT IS MARVELOUS IN OUR EYES'?" (Mark 12:1–11, Jesus quotes from Psalm 118:22, 23; Isaiah 5:1, 2; cf. Matthew 21:33–46; Luke 20:9–19).

Setting: Jerusalem. Following the teaching moment with His disciples regarding the poor widow's offering to the treasury, Jesus prophesies the destruction of the temple.

And Jesus said to him, "Do you see these great buildings? Not one stone will be left upon another which will not be torn down" (Mark 13:2; cf. Matthew 24:1, 2; Luke 21:5, 6; see Luke 19:44).

Setting: Approaching Jerusalem. After being praised by the people in a triumphal entry, the Lord weeps as He sees the city ahead of Him.

When He approached *Jerusalem,* He saw the city and wept over it, saying, "If you had known in this day, even you, the things which make for peace! But now they have been hidden from your eyes. For the days will come upon you when your enemies will throw up a barricade against you, and surround you and hem you in on every side, and they will level you to the ground and your children within you, and they will not leave in you one stone upon another, because you did not recognize the time of your visitation" (Luke 19:41–44; see Matthew 24:1, 2; Luke 13:34, 35).

Setting: The temple in Jerusalem. While ministering a few days before His crucifixion, after the chief priests and the scribes question His authority to teach and preach, Jesus conveys the Parable of the Vine-Growers to the people.

And He began to tell the people this parable: "A man planted a vineyard and rented it out to vine-growers, and went on a journey for a long time. At the *harvest* time he sent a slave to the vine-growers, so that they would give him *some* of the produce of the vineyard; but the vine-growers beat him and sent him away empty-handed. And he proceeded to send another slave; and they beat him also and treated him shamefully and sent him away empty-handed. And he proceeded to send a third; and this one also they wounded and cast out. The owner of the vineyard said, 'What shall I do? I will send my beloved son; perhaps they will respect him.' But when the vine-growers saw him, they reasoned with one another, saying, 'This is the heir; let us kill him so that the inheritance will be ours.' So they threw him out of the vineyard and killed him. What, then, will the owner of the vineyard do to them? He will come and destroy these vine-growers and will give the vineyard to others." When they heard it, they said, "May it never be!" But Jesus looked at them and said, "What then is this that is written: 'THE STONE WHICH THE BUILDERS REJECTED, THIS BECAME THE CHIEF CORNER *stone*'? Everyone who falls on that stone will be broken to pieces; but on whomever it falls, it will scatter him like dust" (Luke 20:9–18, Jesus quotes from Psalm 118:22; cf. Matthew 21:33–44; Mark 12:1–11; see Ephesians 2:20).

Setting: On the Mount of Olives, east of the temple in Jerusalem. While ministering in the temple a few days before His crucifixion, and pointing out a poor widow's sacrificial giving to the temple treasury, during His Olivet Discourse, Jesus prophesies the destruction of the temple.

"*As for* these things which you are looking at, the days will come in which there will not be left one stone upon another which will not be torn down" (Luke 21:6; cf. Matthew 24:1, 2; Mark 13:1, 2).

Setting: The temple in Jerusalem. Following the Feast of Booths, Jesus retires to the Mount of Olives, and returns the next day to teach. The scribes and Pharisees set a woman caught in adultery before Him to test whether He will follow Moses' command to stone her.

But when they persisted in asking Him, He straightened up, and said to them, "He who is without sin among you, let him *be the* first to throw a stone at her" (John 8:7; see Deuteronomy 17:2–7).

Setting: Bethany near Jerusalem. After the death of His friend Lazarus, Jesus travels with His disciples to Bethany in Judea to visit the dead man's sisters, Martha and Mary. The Lord raises Lazarus from the dead.

Jesus said, "Remove the stone." Martha, the sister of the deceased, said to Him, "Lord, by this time there will be a stench, for he has been *dead* four days." Jesus said to her, "Did I not say to you that if you believe, you will see the glory of God?" So they removed the stone. Then Jesus raised His eyes, and said, "Father, I thank You that You have heard Me. I knew that You always hear Me; but because of the people standing around I said it, so that they may believe that you sent Me." When He had said these things, He cried out with a loud voice, "Lazarus, come forth." The man who had died came forth, bound hand and foot with wrappings, and his face was wrapped around with a cloth. Jesus said to them, "Unbind him, and let him go" (John 11:39–44; see Matthew 11:25).

STONE, CHIEF CORNER (See CORNER STONE, CHIEF)

STONE, WHITE (Also see STONE)

Setting: On the island of Patmos (in the Aegean Sea about fifty miles southwest of Ephesus in modern Turkey). On the Lord's Day (Sunday), approximately fifty years after the Resurrection, the disciple John encounters the Lord Jesus Christ, who communicates a new revelation for the apostle to record for the church in Pergamum and to six other churches in Asia.

"And to the angel of the church in Pergamum write: The One who has the sharp two-edged sword says this: 'I know where you dwell, where Satan's throne is; and you hold fast My name, and did not deny My faith even in the days of Antipas, My witness, My faithful one, who was killed among you, where Satan dwells. But I have a few things against you, because you have there some who hold the teaching of Balaam, who kept teaching Balak to put a stumbling block before the sons of Israel, to eat things sacrificed to idols and to commit *acts of* immorality. So you also have some who in the same way hold the teaching of the Nicolaitans. Therefore repent; or else I am coming to you quickly, and I will make war against them with the sword of My mouth. He who has an ear, let him hear what the Spirit says to the churches. To him who overcomes, to him I will give *some* of the hidden manna, and I will give him a white stone, and a new name written on the stone which no one knows but he who receives it' (Revelation 2:12–17; see Numbers 25:1–3; Isaiah 62:2; Revelation 1:16).

STONES (Also see ROCK; and STONE)

Setting: The temple in Jerusalem. With His death on the cross just days away, Jesus laments over Jerusalem's hard-heartedness and lack of repentance.

"Jerusalem, Jerusalem, who kills the prophets and stones those who are sent to her! How often I wanted to gather your children together, the way a hen gathers her chicks under her wings, and you were unwilling. Behold, your house is being left to you desolate! For I say to you, from now on you will not see Me until you say, 'BLESSED IS HE WHO COMES IN THE NAME OF THE LORD!'"

(Matthew 23:37–39, Jesus quotes from Psalm 118:26; cf. 1 Kings 9:7; Luke 13:34, 35).

Setting: On the way from Galilee to Jerusalem. While Jesus is teaching in the cities and villages, after He responds to a question about who is saved, some Pharisees ask Him to leave, claiming Herod Antipas (tetrarch of Galilee and Perea) seeks to kill Him.

And He said to them, "Go and tell that fox, 'Behold, I cast out demons and perform cures today and tomorrow, and the third *day* I reach My goal.' Nevertheless I must journey on today and tomorrow and the next *day*; for it cannot be that a prophet would perish outside of Jerusalem. O Jerusalem, Jerusalem, *the city* that kills the prophets and stones those sent to her! How often I wanted to gather your children together, just as a hen *gathers* her brood under her wings, and you would not *have it*! Behold, your house is left to you *desolate*; and I say to you, you will not see Me until *the time* comes when you say, 'BLESSED IS HE WHO COMES IN THE NAME OF THE LORD!'" (Luke 13:32–35, Jesus quotes from Psalm 118:26; cf. Matthew 23:37).

Setting: Approaching Jerusalem. As the Lord rides a colt, His disciples and the people praise God for all the miracles they have witnessed Him performing; the Pharisees demand He rebukes His followers for such comments.

But Jesus answered, "I tell you, if these become silent, the stones will cry out!" (Luke 19:40; see Habbakkuk 2:1; Matthew 21:1–11; Mark 11:1–11; John 12:12–19).

[STONES from stoning]
Setting: Jerusalem. At the Feast of Dedication, the Pharisees desire to stone Jesus because He claims to be equal with God when they ask him plainly whether He is the Christ.

Jesus answered them, "I showed you many good works from the Father; for which of them are you stoning Me?" (John 10:32).

STOREROOM

Setting: On the way from Galilee to Jerusalem. After giving a parable about riches and greed, Jesus comforts the crowd and His disciples. The scribes and Pharisees turn hostile and question Him repeatedly in an attempt to catch Him in something He might say.

And He said to His disciples, "For this reason I say to you, do not worry about *your* life, *as to* what you will eat; nor for your body, *as to* what you will put on. For life is more than food, and the body more than clothing. Consider the ravens, for they neither sow nor reap; they have no storeroom nor barn, and *yet* God feeds them; how much more valuable you are than the birds! And which of you by worrying can add a *single* hour to his life's span? If then you cannot do even a very little thing, why do you worry about other matters? Consider the lilies, how they grow: they neither toil nor spin; but I tell you, not even Solomon in all his glory clothed himself like one of these. But if God so clothes the grass in the field, which is *alive* today and tomorrow is thrown into the furnace, how much more *will He clothe* you? You men of little faith! And do not seek what you will eat and what you will drink, and do not keep worrying. For all these things the nations of the world eagerly seek; but your Father knows that you need these things. But seek His kingdom, and these things will be added to you. Do not be afraid, little flock, for your Father has chosen gladly to give you the kingdom" (Luke 12:22–32; cf. Matthew 6:25–33; see 1 Kings 10:4–7; Job 38:41).

STORIES (See PARABLE; and PARABLES)

STORM (Also see LIGHTNING; RAIN; SEA, CALMING THE; and WEATHER)

Setting: Magadan of Galilee. Jesus' enemies, the Pharisees and the Sadducees, rejecting His message, continue to test Him by asking for a sign from heaven.

But He replied to them, "When it is evening, you say, '*It will be* fair weather, for the sky is red.' And in the morning, '*There will* be a storm today, for the sky is red and threatening.' Do you know how to discern the appearance of the sky, but cannot *discern* the signs of the times? An evil and adulterous generation seeks after a sign; and a sign will not be given it, except the sign of Jonah."

And He left them and went away (Matthew 16:2–4; cf. Matthew 12:39; Mark 8:12; Luke 12:54–56).

STORM, CALMING THE (See SEA, CALMING THE)

STORY (See PARABLE)

STRAIGHT

Setting: Damascus. Luke, writing in Acts, conveys how the Lord instructs one of His disciples, Ananias, to locate Saul of Tarsus to touch him in order to restore Saul's vision.

Now there was a disciple at Damascus named Ananias; and the Lord said to him in a vision, "Ananias." And he said, "Here I am, Lord." And the Lord *said* to him, "Get up and go to the street called Straight, and inquire at the house of Judas for a man from Tarsus named Saul, for he is praying, and he was seen in a vision a man named Ananias come in and lay his hands on him, so that he might regain his sight" (Acts 9:10–12; see Acts 22:12–14).

STRANGER (Also see STRANGERS)

Setting: On the Mount of Olives, just east of Jerusalem. During His Olivet Discourse, after answering His disciples' questions as to when the temple will be destroyed and Jerusalem overrun, along with the signs of His coming and the end of the age, Jesus reveals the future judgments following His return.

"But when the Son of Man comes in His glory, and all the angels with Him, then He will sit on His glorious throne. All the nations will be gathered before Him; and He will separate them from one another, as the shepherd separates the sheep from the goats; and He will put the sheep on His right, and the goats on the left. Then the King will say to those on His right, 'Come, you who are blessed of My Father, inherit the kingdom prepared for you from the foundation of the world. 'For I was hungry, and you gave Me *something* to eat; I was thirsty, and you gave Me *something* to drink; I was a stranger, and you invited Me in; naked, and you clothed Me; I was sick, and you visited Me; I was in prison, and you came to Me.' Then the righteous will answer Him, 'Lord, when did we see You hungry and feed You, or thirsty, and give you *something* to drink? And when did we see You a stranger, and invite You in, or naked, and clothe You? When did we see You sick, or in prison, and come to You?' The King will answer and say to them, 'Truly I say to you, to the extent that you did it to one of these brothers of Mine, *even* the least *of them,* you did it to Me.' Then He will also say to those on His left, 'Depart from Me, accursed ones, into the eternal fire which has been prepared for the devil and his angels; for I was hungry, and you gave Me *nothing* to eat; I was thirsty, and you gave Me nothing to drink; I was a stranger, and you did not invite Me in; naked, and you did not clothe Me; sick, and in prison, and you did not visit Me.' Then they themselves also will answer, 'Lord, when did we see You hungry, or thirsty, or a stranger, or naked, or sick, or in prison, and did not take care of You?' Then He will answer them, 'Truly I say to you, to the extent that you did not do it to one of the least of these, you did not do it to Me.' These will go away into eternal punishment, but the righteous into eternal life" (Matthew 25:31–46; see Matthew 7:23; 16:27; 19:29).

Setting: Jerusalem. Following the Pharisees' interrogation and dismissal of the formerly blind man Jesus healed on the Sabbath, the Lord speaks to the Pharisees, using parabolic language they do not understand.

"Truly, truly, I say to you, he who does not enter by the door into the fold of the sheep, but climbs up some other way, he is a thief and a robber. But he who enters by the door is a shepherd of the sheep. To him the doorkeeper opens, and the sheep hear his voice, and he calls his own sheep by name and leads them out. When he puts forth all his own, he goes ahead of them, and the sheep follow him because they know his voice. A stranger they simply will not follow, but will flee from him, because they do not know the voice of strangers" (John 10:1–5).

STRANGERS (Also see STRANGER)

Setting: Capernaum of Galilee. Jesus pays the two-drachma temple tax for Peter and Himself in a miraculous manner.

He said, "Yes." And when he came into the house, Jesus spoke to him first, saying, "What do you think, Simon? From whom do the kings of the earth collect customs or poll-tax, from their sons or from strangers?" When Peter said, "From strangers," Jesus said to him, "Then the sons are exempt. However, so that we do not offend them, go to the sea and throw in a hook, and take the first fish that comes up; and when you open its mouth, you will find a shekel. Take that and give it to them for you and Me" (Matthew 17:25–27; see Exodus 30:11–16; Matthew; 22:17–19; Romans 13:7).

Setting: Jerusalem. Following the Pharisees' interrogation and dismissal of the formerly blind man Jesus healed on the Sabbath, the Lord speaks to the Pharisees, using parabolic language they do not understand.

"Truly, truly, I say to you, he who does not enter by the door into the fold of the sheep, but climbs up some other way, he is a thief and a robber. But he who enters by the door is a shepherd of the sheep. To him the doorkeeper opens, and the sheep hear his voice, and he calls his own sheep by name and leads them out. When he puts forth all his own, he goes ahead of them, and the sheep follow him because they know his voice. A stranger they simply will not follow, but will flee from him, because they do not know the voice of strangers" (John 10:1–5).

STRAYING

[STRAYING from gone astray]

Setting: Capernaum of Galilee. Jesus illustrates to His disciples the value of little ones.

"What do you think? If any man has a hundred sheep, and one of them has gone astray, does he not leave the ninety-nine on the mountains and go and search for the one that is straying? If it turns out that he finds it, truly I say to you, he rejoices over it more than the ninety-nine which have not gone astray. So it is not *the* will of your Father who is in heaven that one of these little ones perish" (Matthew 18:12–14; cf. Luke 15:4–7).

STREET (Also see STREET CORNERS; and STREETS)

Setting: Galilee. During the early part of His ministry, Jesus preaches the Sermon on the Mount to His disciples and the multitudes.

"When you pray, you are not to be like the hypocrites; for they love to stand and pray in the synagogues and on the street corners so that they may be seen by men. Truly I say to you, they have their reward in full. But you, when you pray, go into your inner room, close your door and pray to your Father who is in secret, and your Father who sees *what is done* in secret will reward you" (Matthew 6:5, 6; see Mark 11:25).

Setting: Damascus. Luke, writing in Acts, conveys how the Lord instructs one of His disciples, Ananias, to locate Saul of Tarsus to touch him in order to restore Saul's vision.

Now there was a disciple at Damascus named Ananias; and the Lord said to him in a vision, "Ananias." And he said, "Here I am, Lord." And the Lord *said* to him, "Get up and go to the street called Straight, and inquire at the house of Judas for a man from Tarsus named Saul, for he is praying, and he was seen in a vision a man named Ananias come in and lay his hands on him, so that he might regain his sight" (Acts 9:10–12; see Acts 22:12–14).

STREET CORNERS (Also see STREET; and STREETS)

Setting: Galilee. During the early part of His ministry, Jesus preaches the Sermon on the Mount to His disciples and the multitudes.

"When you pray, you are not to be like the hypocrites; for they love to stand and pray in the synagogues and on the street corners so that they may be seen by men. Truly I say to you, they have their reward in full. But you, when you pray, go into your inner room, close your door and pray to your Father who is in secret, and your Father who sees *what is done* in secret will reward you" (Matthew 6:5, 6; see Mark 11:25).

STREETS (Also see HIGHWAYS, MAIN; ROADS; STREET; and STREET CORNERS)

Setting: Galilee. During the early part of His ministry, Jesus preaches the Sermon on the Mount to His disciples and the multitudes.

"So when you give to the poor, do not sound a trumpet before you, as the hypocrites do in the synagogues and in the streets, so that they may be honored by men. Truly I say to you, they have their reward in full. But when you give to the poor, do not let your left hand know what your right hand is doing, so that your giving will be in secret; and your Father who sees *what is done* in secret will reward you" (Matthew 6:2–4; see Jeremiah 17:10).

Setting: The temple in Jerusalem. Jesus speaks another parable to the chief priests and elders after they question His authority.

Jesus spoke to them again in parables, saying, "The kingdom of heaven may be compared to a king who gave a wedding feast for his son. And he sent out his slaves to call those who had been invited to the wedding feast, and they were unwilling to come. Again he sent out other slaves saying, 'Tell those who have been invited, "Behold, I have prepared my dinner; my oxen and my fattened livestock are *all* butchered and everything is ready; come to the wedding feast." But they paid no attention and went their way, one to his own farm, another to his business, and the rest seized his slaves and mistreated them and killed them. But the king was enraged, and he sent his armies and destroyed those murderers and set their city on fire. Then he said to his slaves, 'The wedding is ready, but those who were invited were not worthy. 'Go therefore to the main highways, and as many as you find *there,* invite to the wedding feast.' Those slaves went out into the streets and gathered together all they found, both evil and good; and the wedding hall was filled with dinner guests. But when the king came in to look over the dinner guests, he saw a man there who was not dressed in wedding clothes, and he said to him, 'Friend, how did you come in here without wedding clothes?' And the man was speechless. Then the king said to the servants, 'Bind him hand and foot, and throw him into the outer darkness; in that place there will be weeping and gnashing of teeth.' For many are called, but few *are* chosen" (Matthew 22:1–14; cf. Matthew 8:11, 12).

Setting: On the way from Galilee to Jerusalem. The Lord appoints seventy followers and sends them out in pairs to every place He Himself will soon visit.

And He was saying to them, "The harvest is plentiful, but the laborers are few; therefore beseech the Lord of the harvest to send out laborers into His harvest. Go; behold, I send you out as lambs in the midst of wolves. Carry no money belt, no bag, no shoes; and greet no one on the way. Whatever house you enter, first say, 'Peace be to this house.' If a man of peace is there, your peace will rest on him; but if not, it will return to you. Stay in that house, eating and drinking what they give you; for the laborer is worthy of his wages. Do not keep moving from house to house. Whatever city you enter and they receive you, eat what is set before you; and heal those in it who are sick, and say to them, 'The kingdom of God has come near to you.' But whatever city you enter and they do not receive you, go out into its streets and say, 'Even the dust of your city which clings to our feet we wipe off *in protest* against you; yet be sure of this, that the kingdom of God has come near.' I say to you, it will be more tolerable in that day for Sodom than for that city" (Luke 10:2–12; see Genesis 19:24–28; Matthew 9:37–38, 10:9–14, 16; 1 Corinthians 10:27).

Setting: On the way from Galilee to Jerusalem. While teaching in the cities and villages, Jesus responds to a question about who is saved.

And someone said to Him, "Lord, are here *just* a few who are being saved?" And He said to them, "Strive to enter through the narrow door; for many, I tell you, will seek to enter and will not be able. Once the head of the house gets up and shuts the door, and you begin to stand outside and knock on the door, saying, 'Lord, open up to us!' then He will answer and say to you, 'I do not know where you are from.' Then you will begin to say, 'We ate and drank in Your presence, and You taught in our streets'; and He will say, 'I tell you, I do not know where you are from; DEPART FROM ME, ALL YOU EVILDOERS.' In that place there will be weeping and gnashing of teeth when you see Abraham and Isaac and Jacob and all the prophets in the kingdom of God, but you yourselves being thrown out. And they will come from east and west and from north and south, and will recline *at the table* in the kingdom of God. And behold, *some* are last who will be first and *some* are first who will be last" (Luke 13:23–30, Jesus quotes from Psalm 6:8; cf. Matthew 7:13, 23; 8:11, 12; see Matthew 19:30; Luke 3:8).

Setting: On the way from Galilee to Jerusalem. After speaking a parable to the invited guests and the host at a banquet, Jesus responds to a guest's proclamation about the blessings of eating bread in the kingdom of God.

But He said to him, "A man was giving a big dinner, and he invited many; and at the dinner hour he sent his slave to say to those who had been invited, 'Come; for everything is ready now.' But they all alike began to make excuses. The first one said to him, 'I have bought a piece of land and I need to go out and look at it; please consider me excused.' Another one said, 'I have bought five yoke of oxen, and I am going to try them out; please consider me excused.' Another one said, I have married a wife, and for that reason I cannot come.' And the slave came *back* and reported this to his master. Then the head of the household became angry and said to his slave, 'Go out at once into the streets and lanes of the city and bring in here the poor and crippled and blind and lame.' And the slave said, 'Master, what you commanded has been done, and still there is room.' And the master said to the slave, 'Go out into the highways and along the hedges, and compel *them* to come in, so that my house may be filled. For I tell you, none of those men who were invited shall taste of my dinner'" (Luke 14:16–24; see Deuteronomy 24:5; Matthew 22:2–14).

STRENGTH

Setting: The temple in Jerusalem. With the Pharisees and Herodians failing to trap Jesus in a statement, one of the scribes asks Him which commandment is foremost.

Jesus answered, "The foremost is, 'HEAR, O ISRAEL! THE LORD OUR GOD IS ONE LORD; AND YOU SHALL LOVE THE LORD YOUR GOD WITH ALL YOUR HEART, AND WITH ALL YOUR SOUL, AND WITH ALL YOUR MIND AND WITH ALL YOUR STRENGTH.' The second is this, 'YOU SHALL LOVE YOUR NEIGHBOR AS YOURSELF.' There is no other commandment greater than these" (Mark 12:29–31, Jesus quotes from Deuteronomy 6:4, 5; Leviticus 19:18; cf. Matthew 22:34–40).

Setting: The Mount of Olives, east of the temple in Jerusalem. After ministering in the temple a few days before His crucifixion, and conveying the Parable of the Fig Tree, Jesus warns His disciples during His Olivet Discourse to keep alert regarding future events.

"Be on guard, so that your hearts will not be weighted down with dissipation and drunkenness and the worries of life, and that day will not come upon you suddenly like a trap; for it will come upon all those who dwell on the face of all the earth. But keep on the alert at all times, praying that you may have strength to escape all these things that are about to take place, and to stand before the Son of Man" (Luke 21:34–36; cf. Mark 13:33; see Matthew 24:42–44).

STRETCHER (Also see BED; and PALLET)

Setting: Capernaum of Galilee. When Jesus heals a paralytic man and forgives his sins, some Pharisees and teachers of the law from Galilee and Judea accuse the Lord of committing blasphemy.

But Jesus, aware of their reasonings, answered and said to them, "Why are you reasoning in your hearts? Which is easier, to say, 'Your sins have been forgiven you,' or to say, 'Get up and walk'? But, so that you may know that the Son of Man has authority on earth to forgive sins,"—He said to the paralytic—"I say to you, get up, and pick up your stretcher and go home" (Luke 5:22–24; cf. Matthew 9:4–8; Mark 2:8–12; see Matthew 4:24).

STRIFE (See DIVISION)

STRIKE (bruise)

Setting: On the way to the Mount of Olives. After celebrating the Passover meal in Jerusalem, prior to His betrayal by Judas, Jesus states that all His disciples will deny Him that very day.

Then Jesus said to them, "You will all fall away because of Me this night, for it is written, 'I WILL STRIKE DOWN THE SHEPHERD, AND THE SHEEP OF THE FLOCK SHALL BE SCATTERED.' But after I have been raised, I will go ahead of you to Galilee." But Peter said to Him, '*Even* though all may fall away because of You, I will never fall away.' Jesus said to him, "Truly I say to you that this *very* night, before a rooster crows, you will deny Me three times" (Matthew 26:31–34, Jesus quotes from Zechariah 13:7; cf. Mark 14:26–31; see Matthew 28:7, 10, 16; John 13:37).

Setting: A borrowed upper room in Jerusalem. After Jesus and His twelve disciples celebrate the Passover and the Lord's Supper, they go out to the Mount of Olives.

And Jesus said to them, "You will all fall away, because it is written, 'I WILL STRIKE DOWN THE SHEPHERD, AND THE SHEEP SHALL BE SCATTERED.' But after I have been raised, I will go ahead of you to Galilee." But Peter said to Him, "*Even* though all may fall away, yet I will not." And Jesus said to him, "Truly I say to you, that this very night, before a rooster crows twice, you yourself will deny Me three times" (Mark 14:27–30, Jesus quotes from Zechariah 13:7; cf. Matthew 26:30–34; see Mark 14:72).

Setting: Jerusalem. After Jesus is betrayed by Judas and arrested by the Roman cohort, one of the officers strikes the Lord when he believes He exhibits disrespect to the former high priest with His response to Annas's question about His disciples and teaching.

Jesus answered him, "If I have spoken wrongly, testify of the wrong; but if rightly, why do you strike Me?" (John 18:23; see Matthew 5:39).

STROKE (mark)

Setting: Galilee. During the early part of His ministry, Jesus preaches the Sermon on the Mount to His disciples and the multitudes.

"Do not think that I came to abolish the Law or the Prophets; I did not come to abolish but to fulfill. For truly I say to you, until heaven and earth pass away, not the smallest letter or stroke shall pass from the Law until all is accomplished" (Matthew 5:17, 18; cf. Matthew 24:35).

Setting: On the way from Galilee to Jerusalem. The Lord responds to the Pharisees' scoffing at His teaching His disciples about stewardship.

And He said to them, "You are those who justify yourselves in the sight of men, but God knows your hearts; for that which is highly esteemed among men is detestable in the sight of God. The Law and the Prophets *were proclaimed* until John; since that time the gospel of the kingdom of God has been preached, and everyone is forcing his way into it. But is it easier for heaven and earth to pass away than for one stroke of a letter of the Law to fail" (Luke 16:15–17; cf. Matthew 5:18; see 1 Samuel 16:7; Matthew 4:23; 11:11–14).

STRONG MAN (Listed under MAN, STRONG; also see HOUSE, STRONG MAN'S)

STRONG MAN'S HOUSE (Listed under HOUSE, STRONG MAN'S)

STUDENT (See DISCIPLE; and PUPIL)

STUMBLE (Also see OFFENSE; and STUMBLING BLOCK)

Setting: Galilee. During the early part of His ministry, Jesus preaches the Sermon on the Mount to His disciples and the multitudes.

"If your right eye makes you stumble, tear it out and throw it from you; for it is better for you to lose one of the parts of your body, than for your whole body to be thrown into hell. If your right hand makes you stumble, cut it off and throw it from you; for it is better for you to lose one of the parts of your body, than for your whole body to go into hell" (Matthew 5:29, 30; cf. Matthew 18:8, 9).

Setting: Capernaum of Galilee. Jesus answers His disciples' question about greatness, or rank, in the kingdom of heaven.

And He called a child to Himself and set him before them, and said, "Truly I say to you, unless you are converted and become like children, you will not enter the kingdom of heaven. Whoever then humbles himself as this child, he is the greatest in the kingdom of heaven. And whoever receives one such child in My name receives Me; but whoever causes one of these little ones who believe in Me to stumble, it would be better for him to have a heavy millstone hung around his neck, and to be drowned in the depth of the sea"
(Matthew 18:2–6; cf. Matthew 19:14; Mark 9:33–37, 42; Luke 9:47, 48; 17:1, 2).

Setting: Capernaum of Galilee. Jesus elaborates about stumbling blocks after His disciples' ask about greatness in the kingdom of heaven.

"Woe to the world because of *its* stumbling blocks! For it is inevitable that stumbling blocks come; but woe to that man through whom the stumbling block comes! If your hand or your foot causes you to stumble, cut if off and throw it from you; it is better for you to enter life crippled or lame, than to have two hands or two feet and be cast into the eternal fire. If your eye causes you to stumble, pluck it out and throw it from you. It is better for you to enter life with one eye, than to have two eyes and be cast into the fiery hell" (Matthew 18:7–9; cf. Matthew 5:29, 30; Mark 9:43–48; Luke 17:1).

Setting: Capernaum of Galilee. As Jesus teaches His disciples in private, they ask Him about greatness.

But Jesus said, "Do not hinder him, for there is no one who will perform a miracle in My name, and be able soon afterward to speak evil of Me. For he who is not against us is for us. For whoever gives you a cup of water to drink because of your name as *followers* of Christ, truly I say to you, he will not lose his reward. Whoever causes one of these little ones who believe to stumble, it would be better for him if, with a heavy millstone hung around his neck, he had been cast into the sea. If your hand causes you to stumble, cut it off; it is better for you to enter life crippled, than, having your two hands, to go into hell, into the unquenchable fire, [where THEIR WORM DOES NOT DIE, AND THE FIRE IS NOT QUENCHED.] If your foot causes you to stumble, cut it off; it is better for you to enter life lame, than, having your two feet, to be cast into hell, [where THEIR WORM DOES NOT DIE, AND THE FIRE IS NOT QUENCHED.] If your eye causes you to stumble, throw it out; it is better for you to enter the kingdom of God with one eye, than, having two eyes, to be cast into hell, where THEIR WORM DOES NOT DIE, AND THE FIRE IS NOT QUENCHED. For everyone will be salted with fire. Salt is good; but if the salt becomes unsalty, with what will you make it salty *again?* Have salt in yourselves, and be at peace with one another" (Mark 9:39–50; Jesus quotes from Isaiah 66:24; cf. Matthew 18:6–9; Luke 9:49, 50; see Matthew 5:13, 29, 30; Matthew 10:42; 12:30; 18:5, 6).

Setting: On the way from Galilee to Jerusalem. After conveying the story of the rich man and Lazarus, the Lord gives His disciples instruction on forgiveness.

He said to His disciples, "It is inevitable that stumbling blocks come, but woe to him through whom they come! It would be better for him if a millstone were hung around his neck and he were thrown into the sea, than that he would cause one of these little ones to stumble. Be on your guard! If your brother sins, rebuke him; and if he repents, forgive him. And if he sins against you seven times a day, and returns to you seven times, saying, 'I repent,' forgive him" (Luke 17:1–4; see Matthew 18:5–7, 15, 21, 22).

Setting: The synagogue at Capernaum of Galilee. After the Jewish religious leaders argue with one another when Jesus says He will give His flesh to the world to eat, some of His disciples also express difficulty with His statements.

But, Jesus, conscious that His disciples grumbled at this, said to them, "Does this cause you to stumble? *What* then if you see the Son of Man ascending to where He was before? It is the Spirit who gives life; the flesh profits nothing; the words that I have spoken to you are spirit and are life. But there are some of you who do not believe." For Jesus knew from the beginning who they were who did not believe, and who it was that would betray Him. And He was saying, "For this reason I have said to you, that no one can come to Me unless it has been granted him from the Father" (John 6:61–65; see Matthew 11:6; 13:11; John 3:13).

Setting: Beyond the Jordan. While He and His disciples are avoiding the Jerusalem Pharisees, Jesus receives word from Lazarus's sisters in Bethany of His friend's sickness, and decides to go there.

Then after this He said to the disciples, "Let us go to Judea again." The disciples said to Him, "Rabbi, the Jews were just now seeking to stone You, and are You going there again?" Jesus answered, "Are there not twelve hours in the day? If anyone walks in the day, he does not stumble, because he sees the light of this world. But if anyone walks in the night, he stumbles, because the light is not in him." This He said, and after that He said to them, "Our friend Lazarus has fallen asleep; but I go, so that I may awaken him out of sleep" (John 11:7–11; see John 8:59; 10:39).

[STUMBLE from stumbling]
Setting: Jerusalem. Before the Passover, after explaining He is the vine and His disciples are the branches, Jesus warns them of the persecution they will face after His departure to heaven.

"These things I have spoken to you so that you may be kept from stumbling. They will make you outcasts from the synagogue, but an hour is coming for everyone who kills you to think that he is offering service to God. These things they will do because they have not known the Father or Me. But these things I have spoken to you, so that when their hour comes, you may remember that I told you of them. These things I did not say to you at the beginning, because I was with you" (John 16:1–4; see John 8:19, 55; 9:22; 13:19; 15:18–27).

STUMBLING BLOCK (Also see STUMBLE; and STUMBLING BLOCKS)

Setting: Near Caesarea Philippi. Jesus responds to Peter for rebuking Him after He prophesies His death and resurrection.

But He turned and said to Peter, "Get behind Me, Satan! You are a stumbling block to Me; for you are not setting your mind on God's interests, but man's" (Matthew 16:23; cf. Mark 8:33; see Matthew 16:21, 22).

Setting: Capernaum of Galilee. Jesus elaborates about stumbling blocks following His disciples' question about greatness in the kingdom of heaven.

"Woe to the world because of *its* stumbling blocks! For it is inevitable that stumbling blocks come; but woe to that man through whom the stumbling block comes! If your hand or your foot causes you to stumble, cut if off and throw it from you; it is better for you to enter life crippled or lame, than to have two hands or two feet and be cast into the eternal fire. If your eye causes you to stumble, pluck it out and throw it from you. It is better for you to enter life with one eye, than to have two eyes and be cast into the fiery hell" (Matthew 18:7–9; cf. Matthew 5:29, 30; Mark 9:43–48; Luke 17:1).

Setting: On the island of Patmos (in the Aegean Sea about fifty miles southwest of Ephesus in modern Turkey). On the Lord's Day (Sunday), about fifty years after Jesus' resurrection, the disciple John encounters the Lord Jesus Christ, who communicates a new revelation for the apostle to record for the church in Pergamum and to six other churches in Asia.

"And to the angel of the church in Pergamum write: The One who has the sharp two-edged sword says this: 'I know where you dwell, where Satan's throne is; and you hold fast My name, and did not deny My faith even in the days of Antipas, My witness, My faithful one, who was killed among you, where Satan dwells. But I have a few things against you, because you have there some who hold the teaching of Balaam, who kept teaching Balak to put a stumbling block before the sons of Israel, to eat things sacrificed to idols and to commit *acts of* immorality. So you also have some who in the same way hold the teaching of the Nicolaitans. Therefore repent; or else I am coming to you quickly, and I will make war against them with the sword of My mouth. He who has an ear, let him hear what the Spirit says to the churches. To him who overcomes, to him I will give *some* of the hidden manna, and I will give him a white stone, and a new name written on the stone which no one knows but he who receives it' (Revelation 2:12–17; see Numbers 25:1–3; Isaiah 62:2; Revelation 1:16; 2:5, 6, 16).

STUMBLING BLOCKS (Also see STUMBLE; and STUMBLING BLOCK)

Setting: A house near the Sea of Galilee. Jesus explains the meaning of the Parable of the Wheat and the Tares to

His disciples.

And He said, "The one who sows the good seed is the Son of Man, and the field is the world; and as *for* the good seed, these are the sons of the kingdom; and the tares are the sons of the evil *one;* and the enemy who sowed them is the devil, and the harvest is the end of the age; and the reapers are angels. So just as the tares are gathered up and burned with fire, so shall it be at the end of the age. The Son of Man will send forth His angels, and they will gather out of His kingdom all stumbling blocks, and those who commit lawlessness, and will throw them into the furnace of fire; in that place there will be weeping and gnashing of teeth. Then THE RIGHTEOUS WILL SHINE FORTH AS THE SUN in the kingdom of their Father. He who has ears, let him hear" (Matthew 13:37–43, Jesus quotes from Daniel 12:3; cf. Matthew 8:12; 13:50; see Matthew 13:36).

Setting: Capernaum of Galilee. Jesus elaborates about stumbling blocks following His disciples' question about greatness in the kingdom of heaven.

"Woe to the world because of *its* stumbling blocks! For it is inevitable that stumbling blocks come; but woe to that man through whom the stumbling block comes! If your hand or your foot causes you to stumble, cut if off and throw it from you; it is better for you to enter life crippled or lame, than to have two hands or two feet and be cast into the eternal fire. If your eye causes you to stumble, pluck it out and throw it from you. It is better for you to enter life with one eye, than to have two eyes and be cast into the fiery hell" (Matthew 18:7–9; cf. Matthew 5:29, 30; Mark 9:43–48; Luke 17:1).

Setting: On the way from Galilee to Jerusalem. After conveying the story of the rich man and Lazarus, the Lord gives instruction to His disciples on forgiveness.

He said to His disciples, "It is inevitable that stumbling blocks come, but woe to him through whom they come! It would be better for him if a millstone were hung around his neck and he were thrown into the sea, than that he would cause one of these little ones to stumble. Be on your guard! If your brother sins, rebuke him; and if he repents, forgive him. And if he sins against you seven times a day, and returns to you seven times, saying, 'I repent,' forgive him" (Luke 17:1–4; see Matthew 18:5–7, 15, 21, 22).

SUBJECTION (Also see AUTHORITY)

[SUBJECTION from subject to you]

Setting: On the way from Galilee to Jerusalem. The Lord responds to a report from the seventy sent out in pairs to every place He Himself will soon visit.

And He said to them, "I was watching Satan fall from heaven like lightning. Behold, I have given you authority to tread on serpents and scorpions, and over all the power of the enemy, and nothing will injure you. Nevertheless do not rejoice in this, that the spirits are subject to you, but rejoice that your names are recorded in heaven" (Luke 10:18–20; see Psalm 91:13; Isaiah 14:12–14; Luke 9:1).

SUBMISSION (See OBEDIENCE; and WILL OF GOD)

SUFFERING (Also see AFFLICTION; MISTREATMENT; PERSECUTE/PERSECUTED; PERSECUTION; PERSECUTIONS and TRIBULATION)

[SUFFERING from suffer]

Setting: Galilee. Following Jesus' transfiguration, coming down the mountain, Peter, James, and John ask the Lord why Elijah must come before the Messiah.

And He answered and said, "Elijah is coming and will restore all things; but I say to you that Elijah already came, and they did not recognize him, but did to him whatever they wished. So also the Son of Man is going to suffer at their hands" (Matthew 17:11, 12; cf. Mark 9:11–13).

[SUFFERING from suffer]

Setting: Galilee. After informing a crowd and His disciples of the hope involving the coming kingdom of God,

Jesus takes Peter, James, and John to a high mountain (some think Mount Hermon), where He reveals His glory through the Transfiguration and answers their question about Elijah.

And He said to them, "Elijah does first come and restore all things. And *yet* how is it written of the Son of Man that He will suffer many things and be treated with contempt? But I say to you that Elijah has indeed come, and they did to him whatever they wished, just as it is written of him" (Mark 9:12, 13; cf. Matthew 17:1–13; Luke 9:28–36; see Malachi 4:5, 6; Matthew 16:21).

[SUFFERING from suffer]
Setting: Galilee. Following Peter's pronouncement that Jesus is the Christ of God, the Lord warns His disciples not to reveal His identity to anyone.

But He warned them and instructed *them* not to tell this to anyone, saying, "The Son of Man must suffer many things and be rejected by the elders and chief priests and scribes, and be killed and be raised up on the third day" (Luke 9:21, 22; cf. Matthew 16:21; Mark 8:31).

[SUFFERING from suffer]
Setting: On the way from Galilee to Jerusalem. After the Pharisees question Him about the coming of the kingdom of God, Jesus tells His disciples of His second coming.

And He said to the disciples, "The days will come when you will long to see one of the days of the Son of Man, and you will not see it. They will say to you, 'Look there! Look here!' Do not go away, and do not run after *them*. For just like the lightning, when it flashes out of one part of the sky, shines to the other part of the sky, so will the Son of Man be in His day. But first He must suffer many things and be rejected by this generation. And just as it happened in the days of Noah, so it will be also in the days of the Son of Man: they were eating, they were drinking, they were marrying, they were being given in marriage, until the day that Noah entered the ark, and the flood came and destroyed them all. It was the same as happened in the days of Lot: they were eating, they were drinking, they were buying, they were selling, they were planting, they were building; but on the day that Lot went out from Sodom it rained fire and brimstone from heaven and destroyed them all. It will be just the same on the day that the Son of Man is revealed. On that day, the one who is on the housetop and whose goods are in the house must not go down to take them out; and likewise the one who is in the field must not turn back. Remember Lot's wife. Whoever seeks to keep his life will lose it, and whoever loses *his life* will preserve it. I tell you, on that night there will be two in one bed; one will be taken and the other will be left. There will be two women grinding at the same place; one will be taken and the other will be left. [Two men will be in the field; one will be taken and the other will be left."] And answering they said to Him, "Where, Lord?" And He said to them, "Where the body *is*, there also the vultures will be gathered" (Luke 17:22–37; see Genesis 19; Matthew 10:39; 16:21, 27; 24:17–28, 37–41).

[SUFFERING from suffer]
Setting: Jerusalem. During the Feast of Unleavened Bread (Passover) just before Jesus' crucifixion, after Judas consents to betray Him to the chief priests and officers, during the Passover meal with His disciples, the Lord mentions His upcoming death.

And He said to them, "I have earnestly desired to eat this Passover with you before I suffer; for I say to you, I shall never again eat it until it is fulfilled in the kingdom of God" (Luke 22:15, 16; see Matthew 26:20; Luke 14:15).

[SUFFERING from suffer]
Setting: On the road to Emmaus. After rising from the tomb on the third day after being crucified, Jesus appears to two of His followers (who have heard reports the tomb is empty), and elaborates on the purpose of His coming to earth.

And He said to them, "O foolish men and slow of heart to believe in all that the prophets have spoken! Was it not necessary for the Christ to suffer these things and to enter into His glory?" (Luke 24:25, 26).

[SUFFERING from suffer]

Setting: Jerusalem. After rising from the tomb on the third day after being crucified, and appearing to two of His followers on the road to Emmaus, Jesus gives instruction to His disciples (except Thomas) about His mission on earth and the promise of future power from God.

Now He said to them, "These are My words which I spoke to you while I was still with you, that all things which are written about Me in the Law of Moses and the Prophets and the Psalms must be fulfilled." Then He opened their minds to understand the Scriptures, and He said to them, "Thus it is written, that the Christ would suffer and rise again from the dead the third day, and that repentance for forgiveness of sins would be proclaimed in His name to all the nations, beginning from Jerusalem. You are witnesses of these things. And behold, I am sending forth the promise of My Father upon you; but you are to stay in the city until you are clothed with power from on high" (Luke 24:44–49; see Matthew 28:19, 20; Acts 1:8).

[SUFFERING from suffer]

Setting: Damascus. Luke, writing in Acts, details the reluctance of Ananias, one of Jesus' followers, to locate Saul of Tarsus (a known enemy of the church), in order to restore Saul's vision.

But the Lord said to him, "Go, for he is a chosen instrument of Mine, to bear My name before the Gentiles and kings and the sons of Israel; for I will show him how much he must suffer for My name's sake" (Acts 9:15, 16; see Acts 13:2; 20:22–24).

[SUFFERING from suffer]

Setting: On the island of Patmos (in the Aegean Sea about fifty miles southwest of Ephesus in modern Turkey). On the Lord's Day (Sunday), approximately fifty years after the Resurrection, the disciple John encounters the Lord Jesus Christ, who communicates a new revelation for the apostle to record for the church in Smyrna and to six other churches in Asia.

"And to the angel of the church in Smyrna write: The first and the last, who was dead, and has come to life, says this: 'I know your tribulation and your poverty (but you are rich), and the blasphemy by those who say they are Jews and are not, but are a synagogue of Satan. Do not fear what you are about to suffer. Behold, the devil is about to cast some of you into prison, so that you will be tested, and you will have tribulation for ten days. Be faithful until death, and I will give you the crown of life. He who has an ear, let him hear what the Spirit says to the churches. He who overcomes will not be hurt by the second death' (Revelation 2:8–11; see Isaiah 44:6; Revelation 1:9, 18; 20:6, 14).

SUITCASE (See BAG)

SUMMARIZED, THE BIBLE (See COMMANDMENT, FOREMOST)

SUMMER (Also see WINTER)

Setting: On the Mount of Olives, just east of Jerusalem. During His Olivet Discourse, after answering His disciples' questions as to when the temple will be destroyed and Jerusalem overrun, along with the signs of His coming and the end of the age, Jesus teaches them the Parable of the Fig Tree.

"Now learn the parable from the fig tree: when its branch has already become tender and puts forth its leaves, you know that summer is near; so, you too, when you see all these things, recognize that He is near, *right* at the door. Truly, I say to you, this generation will not pass away until all these things take place. Heaven and earth will pass away, but My words will not pass away. But of that day and hour no one knows, not even the angels of heaven, nor the Son, but the Father alone. For the coming of the Son of Man will be just like the days of Noah. For as in those days before the flood they were eating and drinking, marrying and giving in marriage, until the day that Noah entered the ark, and they did not understand until the flood came and took them all away; so will the coming of the Son of Man be. Then there will be two men in the field; one will be taken and one will be left. Two women *will be* grinding at the mill; one will be taken and one will be left" (Matthew 24:32–41; cf. Mark 13:28–32; Luke 17:34–36;

21:28–33; see Genesis 6:5; 7:7; Matthew 5:18; 10:23; James 5:9).

Setting: On the Mount of Olives, east of the temple in Jerusalem. After prophesying the temple's destruction, Jesus responds during His Olivet Discourse to questions from Peter, James, John, and Andrew about other future events.

"Now learn the parable from the fig tree: when its branch has already become tender and puts forth its leaves, you know that summer is near. Even so, you too, when you see these things happening, recognize that He is near, *right* at the door. Truly I say to you, this generation will not pass away until all these things take place. Heaven and earth will pass away, but My words will not pass away. But of the day or hour no one knows, not even the angels in heaven, nor the Son, but the Father *alone*" (Mark 13:28–32; cf. Matthew 24:32–36; Luke 21:28–33).

Setting: On the Mount of Olives, east of the temple in Jerusalem. After ministering in the temple a few days before His crucifixion, and giving the disciples more details regarding His return, Jesus conveys the Parable of the Fig Tree during His Olivet Discourse.

Then He told them a parable: "Behold the fig tree and all the trees; as soon as they put forth *leaves,* you see it and know for yourselves that summer is now near. So you also, when you see these things happening, recognize that the kingdom of God is near. Truly, I say to you, this generation will not pass away until all things take place. Heaven and earth will pass away, but My words will not pass away" (Luke 21:29–33; cf. Matthew 24:32–35; Mark 13:28–31; see Matthew 5:18).

SUN (Also see HEAVENS; HEAT, SCORCHING; MOON; STARS; and WORLD, LIGHT OF THIS)

Setting: Galilee. During the early part of His ministry, Jesus preaches the Sermon on the Mount to His disciples and the multitudes.

"You have heard that it was said, 'YOU SHALL LOVE YOUR NEIGHBOR and hate your enemy.' But I say to you, love your enemies and pray for those who persecute you, so that you may be sons of your Father who is in heaven; for He causes His sun to rise on *the* evil and *the* good, and sends rain on *the* righteous and *the* unrighteous. For if you love those who love you, what reward do you have? Do not even the tax collectors do the same? If you greet only your brothers, what more are you doing *than others?* Do not even the Gentiles do the same? Therefore, you are to be perfect, as your heavenly Father is perfect" (Matthew 5:43–48, Jesus quotes from Leviticus 19:18; cf. Leviticus 19:2; Luke 6:27–36).

Setting: By the Sea of Galilee. While teaching and preaching to the crowds from a boat, Jesus conveys the Parable of the Sower.

And He spoke many things to them in parables, saying, "Behold, the sower went out to sow; and as he sowed, some *seeds* fell beside the road, and the birds came and ate them up. Others fell on the rocky places, where they did not have much soil; and immediately they sprang up, because they had no depth of soil. But when the sun had risen, they were scorched; and because they had no root, they withered away. Others fell among the thorns, and the thorns came up and choked them out. And others fell on the good soil and yielded a crop, some a hundredfold, some sixty, and some thirty. He who has ears, let him hear" (Matthew 13:3–9; cf. Mark 4:3–9; Luke 8:4–8).

Setting: A house near the Sea of Galilee. Jesus gives His disciples the meaning of the Parable of the Wheat and the Tares.

And He said, "The one who sows the good seed is the Son of Man, and the field is the world; and as *for* the good seed, these are the sons of the kingdom; and the tares are the sons of the evil *one;* and the enemy who sowed them is the devil, and the harvest is the end of the age; and the reapers are angels. So just as the tares are gathered up and burned with fire, so shall it be at the end of the age. The Son of Man will send forth His angels, and they will gather out of His kingdom all stumbling blocks, and those who commit lawlessness, and will throw them into the furnace of fire; in that place there will be weeping and gnashing of teeth.

Then THE RIGHTEOUS WILL SHINE FORTH AS THE SUN in the kingdom of their Father. He who has ears, let him hear" (Matthew 13:37–43, Jesus quotes from Daniel 12:3; cf. Matthew 8:12; 13:50).

Setting: The Mount of Olives, just east of Jerusalem. During His Olivet Discourse, Jesus answers His disciples' questions as to when the temple will be destroyed and Jerusalem overrun, along with the signs of His coming and the end of the age.

"But immediately after the tribulation of those days THE SUN WILL BE DARKENED, AND THE MOON WILL NOT GIVE ITS LIGHT, AND THE STARS WILL FALL from the sky, and the powers of the heavens will be shaken. And then the sign of the Son of Man will appear in the sky, and then all the tribes of the earth will mourn, and they will see the SON OF MAN COMING ON THE CLOUDS OF THE SKY with power and great glory. And He will send forth His angels with A GREAT TRUMPET and THEY WILL GATHER TOGETHER His elect from the four winds, from one end of the sky to the other" (Matthew 24:29–31, Jesus quotes from Isaiah 13:10, Daniel 7:13; Exodus 19:16; cf. Mark 13:24–27; Luke 21:25–27).

Setting: By the Sea of Galilee. During the early part of His ministry, just after a visit from his mother and brothers, Jesus instructs a very large crowd with the Parable of the Sower from a boat.

"Listen *to this!* Behold, the sower went out to sow; as he was sowing, some *seed* fell beside the road, and the birds came and ate it up. Other *seed* fell on the rocky *ground* where it did not have much soil; and immediately it sprang up because it had no depth of soil. And after the sun had risen, it was scorched; and because it had no root, it withered away. Other *seed* fell among the thorns, and the thorns came up and choked it, and it yielded no crop. Other *seeds* fell into the good soil, and as the grew up and increased, they yielded a crop and produced thirty, sixty, and a hundredfold." And He was saying, "He who has ears to hear, let him hear" (Mark 4:3–9; cf. Matthew 13:3–9; Luke 8:5–8).

Setting: On the Mount of Olives, east of the temple in Jerusalem. After prophesying the temple's destruction, Jesus responds during His Olivet Discourse to questions from Peter, James, John, and Andrew about other future events.

"But in those days, after that tribulation, THE SUN WILL BE DARKENED AND THE MOON WILL NOT GIVE ITS LIGHT, AND THE STARS WILL BE FALLING from heaven, and the powers that are in the heavens will be shaken. Then they will see THE SON OF MAN COMING IN CLOUDS with great power and glory. And then He will send forth the angels, and will gather together His elect from the four winds, from the farthest end of the earth to the farthest end of heaven" (Mark 13:24–27. Jesus quotes from Isaiah 13:10; 34:4; Daniel 7:13; cf. Matthew 24:29–31; Luke 21:25–27).

Setting: On the Mount of Olives, just east of Jerusalem. After ministering in the temple a few days before His crucifixion, and giving His disciples more details regarding future events, Jesus speaks during His Olivet Discourse of His return.

"There will be signs in sun and moon and stars, and on the earth dismay among the nations, in perplexity at the roaring of the sea and the waves, men fainting from fear and the expectation of the things which are coming upon the world; for the powers of the heavens will be shaken. Then they will see THE SON OF MAN COMING IN A CLOUD with power and great glory. But when these things begin to take place, straighten up and lift up your heads, because your redemption is drawing near" (Luke 21:25–28, Jesus quotes from Daniel 7:13; cf. Matthew 24:29–31; Mark 13:24–27).

SUPPER, LAST (See LORD'S SUPPER)

SUPPER, LORD'S (See LORD'S SUPPER)

SUPPORT

Setting: Galilee. After His twelve disciples observe His ministry, Jesus summons and specifically instructs them

about their ministry to the people of Israel.

These twelve Jesus sent out after instructing them: "Do not go in *the* way of *the* Gentiles, and do not enter *any* city of the Samaritans; but rather go to the lost sheep of the house of Israel. And as you go, preach, saying, 'The kingdom of heaven is at hand.' Heal *the* sick, raise *the* dead, cleanse *the* lepers, cast out demons. Freely you received, freely give. Do not acquire gold, or silver, or copper for your money belts, or a bag for *your* journey, or even two coats, or sandals, or a staff; for the worker is worthy of his support. And whatever city or village you enter, inquire who is worthy in it, and stay at his house until you leave *that city*. As you enter the house, give it your greeting. If the house is worthy, give it your *blessing of* peace. But if it is not worthy, take back your *blessing of* peace. Whoever does not receive you, nor heed your words, as you go out of that house or that city, shake the dust off your feet. Truly I say to you, it will be more tolerable for *the* land of Sodom and Gomorrah in the day of judgment than for that city" (Matthew 10:5–15; cf. Mark 6:7–11; Luke 9:1–5; see Matthew 3:2; 11:22, 24; 15:24; Luke 22:35; 1 Corinthians 9:14).

SUPREME COURT (Listed under COURT, SUPREME)

SURPLUS

Setting: Opposite the temple treasury in Jerusalem. Jesus focuses His disciples' attention on a widow's monetary sacrifice.

Calling His disciples to Him, He said to them, "Truly I say to you, this poor widow put in more than all the contributors to the treasury; for they all put in out of their surplus, but she, out of her poverty, put in all she owned, all she had to live on" (Mark 12:43, 44; cf. Luke 21:1–4).

Setting: The temple in Jerusalem. While ministering a few days before His crucifixion, after warning His disciples about the lifestyle of the scribes, Jesus points out a poor widow's sacrificial giving to the temple treasury.

And He said, "Truly I say to you, this poor widow put in more than all *of them;* for they all out of their surplus put into the offering; but she out of her poverty put in all that she had to live on" (Luke 21:3, 4; cf. Mark 12:41–44).

SWEARING (Also see OATHS; SPEECH; and VOWS)

[SWEARING from swears]

Setting: The temple in Jerusalem. After the Jewish religious leaders test Him with questions, Jesus pronounces the fourth of eight woes upon them in front of the crowds and His disciples.

"Woe to you, blind guides, who say, 'Whoever swears by the temple, *that* is nothing; but whoever swears by the gold of the temple is obligated.' You fools and blind men! Which is more important, the gold or the temple that sanctified the gold? And, 'Whoever swears by the altar, *that* is nothing, but whoever swears by the offering on it, he is obligated.' You blind men, which is more important, the offering, or the altar that sanctifies the offering? Therefore, whoever swears by the altar, swears *both* by the altar and by everything on it. And whoever swears by the temple, swears *both* by the temple and by Him who dwells within it. And whoever swears by heaven, swears *both* by the throne of God and by Him who sits upon it" (Matthew 23:16–22; see Exodus 29:37; 1 Kings 8:13; Isaiah 66:1; Matthew 15:14).

SWINDLERS

Setting: On the way from Galilee to Jerusalem. After instructing His disciples about persistence in prayer, Jesus conveys a parable about self-righteousness.

And He also told this parable to some people who trusted in themselves that they were righteous, and viewed others with contempt: "Two men went up into the temple to pray, one a Pharisee and the other a tax collector. The Pharisee stood and was praying this to himself: 'God, I thank You that I am not like other people: swindlers, unjust, adulterers, or even like this tax collector. I fast twice a week; I pay tithes of all that I get.' But the tax collector, standing some distance away, was even unwilling to lift up his eyes to heaven, but was beating his breast, saying, 'God, be merciful to me, the sinner!' I tell you, this man went to his house justified rather than the other; for everyone who exalts himself will be humbled, but he who humbles himself will be exalted" (Luke 18:9–14; see Ezra 9:6; Matthew 6:5, 23:12; Luke 11:42, 16:15; Romans 14:3, 10).

SWINE

Setting: Galilee. During the early part of His ministry, Jesus preaches the Sermon on the Mount to His disciples and the multitudes.

"Do not give what is holy to dogs, and do not throw your pearls before swine, or they will trample them under their feet, and turn and tear you to pieces" (Matthew 7:6; see Matthew 15:26).

Setting: On the way from Galilee to Jerusalem. Jesus conveys the illustration of the prodigal son because the Pharisees and scribes complain He associates with tax collectors and sinners.

And He said, "A man had two sons. The younger of them said to his father, 'Father, give me the share of the estate that falls to me.' So he divided his wealth between them. And not many days later, the younger son gathered everything together and went on a journey into a distant country, and there he squandered his estate with loose living. Now when he had spent everything, a severe famine occurred in that country, and he began to be impoverished. So he went and hired himself out to one of the citizens of that country, and he sent him into his fields to feed swine. And he would have gladly filled his stomach with the pods that the swine were eating, and no one was giving *anything* to him. But when he came to his senses, he said, 'How many of my father's hired men have more than enough bread, but I am dying here with hunger! I will get up and go to my father, and will say to him, "Father, I have sinned against heaven, and in your sight; I am no longer worthy to be called your son; make me as one of your hired men."' So he got up and came to his father. But while he was still a long way off, his father saw him and felt compassion *for him,* and ran and embraced him and kissed him. And the son said to him, "Father, I have sinned against heaven and in your sight; I am no longer worthy to be called your son.' But the father said to his slaves, 'Quickly bring out the best robe and put it on him, and put a ring on his hand and sandals on his feet; and bring the fattened calf, kill it, and let us eat and celebrate; for this son of mine was dead and has come to life again; he was lost and has been found.' And they began to celebrate. Now his older son was in the field, when he came and approached the house, he heard music and dancing. And he summoned one of the servants and *began* inquiring what these things could be. And he said to him, 'Your brother has come, and your father has killed the fattened calf because he has received him back safe and sound.' But he became angry and was not willing to go in; and his father came out and *began* pleading with him. But he answered and said to his father, 'Look! For so many years I have been serving you and I have never neglected a command of yours; and *yet* you have never given me a young goat, so that I might celebrate with my friends; but when this son of yours came, who has devoured your wealth with prostitutes, you killed the fattened calf for him.' And he said to him, 'Son, you have always been with me, and all that is mine is yours. But we had to celebrate and rejoice, for this brother of yours was dead and *has begun* to live, and was lost and has been found' " (Luke 15:11–32; see Proverbs 29:2).

SWORD (Also see SWORDS)

Setting: Galilee. After His disciples observe His ministry, Jesus summons and specifically instructs them about their ministry hardships ahead involving true discipleship.

"Do not think that I came to bring peace on the earth; I did not come to bring peace, but a sword. For I came to SET A MAN AGAINST HIS FATHER, AND A DAUGHTER AGAINST HER MOTHER, AND A DAUGHTER-IN-LAW AGAINST HER MOTHER-IN-LAW; and A MAN'S ENEMIES WILL BE THE MEMBERS OF HIS HOUSEHOLD" (Matthew 10:34–36; Jesus quotes from Micah 7:6; cf. Luke 12:51–53).

Setting: Gethsemane on the Mount of Olives, just east of the temple in Jerusalem. As Jesus submits to His Father's will and allows Judas to betray Him, Peter attempts to defend Him by force, but Jesus does not permit it.

Then Jesus said to him, "Put your sword back into its place; for all those who take up the sword shall perish by the sword. Or do you think that I cannot appeal to My Father, and He will at once put at My disposal more than twelve legions of angels? How then will the Scriptures be fulfilled, *which say* that it must happen this way?" (Matthew 26:52–54; cf. Mark 14:47; Luke 22:50, 51; John 18:10, 11; see Matthew 26:24).

Setting: On the Mount of Olives, east of the temple in Jerusalem. After ministering in the temple a few days before His crucifixion, and giving the disciples more details regarding future events, Jesus elaborates more during His Olivet Discourse about things to come.

"But when you see Jerusalem surrounded by armies, then recognize that her desolation is near. Then those who are in Judea must flee to the mountains, and those who are in the midst of the city must leave, and those who are in the country must not enter the city; because these are days of vengeance, so that all things which are written will be fulfilled. Woe to those who are pregnant and to those who are nursing babies in those days; for there will be a great distress upon the land and wrath to this people; and they will fall by the edge of the sword, and will be led captive into all the nations; and Jerusalem will be trampled under foot by the Gentiles until the times of the Gentiles are fulfilled" (Luke 21:20–24; see Matthew 24:15–18; Mark 13:14–16; Luke 19:43).

Setting: An upper room in Jerusalem. During the Feast of Unleavened Bread (Passover) just before Jesus' crucifixion, while celebrating the Passover meal, instituting the Lord's Supper, and prophesying Peter's denial of Him, the Lord instructs His disciples to prepare to persevere without Him.

And He said to them, "When I sent you out without money belt and bag and sandals, you did not lack anything, did you?" They said, "*No*, nothing." And He said to them, "But now, whoever has a money belt is to take it along, likewise also a bag, and whoever has no sword is to sell his coat and buy one. For I tell you that this which is written must be fulfilled in Me, 'AND HE WAS NUMBERED WITH TRANSGRESSORS'; for that which refers to Me has *its* fulfillment." They said, "Lord, look, here are two swords." And He said to them, "It is enough" (Luke 22:35–38, Jesus quotes from Isaiah 53:12; see Matthew 10:5–15; Mark 6:7–11; Luke 9:1–5; 10:1–12; 22:49; John 17:4).

Setting: A garden over the ravine of the Kidron from Jerusalem. Simon Peter attempts to defend Jesus with a sword during Judas' betrayal with a Roman cohort and officers from the chief priests and the Pharisees.

So Jesus said to Peter, "Put the sword into the sheath; the cup which the Father has given Me, shall I not drink it?" (John 18:11; see Matthew 20:22; 26:52; Luke 22:51).

Setting: On the island of Patmos (in the Aegean Sea about fifty miles southwest of Ephesus in modern Turkey). On the Lord's Day (Sunday), approximately fifty years after the Resurrection, the disciple John encounters the Lord Jesus Christ, who communicates a new revelation for the apostle to record for the church in Pergamum and to six other churches in Asia.

"And to the angel of the church in Pergamum write: The One who has the sharp two-edged sword says this: 'I know where you dwell, where Satan's throne is; and you hold fast My name, and did not deny My faith even in the days of Antipas, My witness, My faithful one, who was killed among you, where Satan dwells. But I have a few things against you, because you have there some who hold the teaching of Balaam, who kept teaching Balak to put a stumbling block before the sons of Israel, to eat things sacrificed to idols and to commit *acts of* immorality. So you also have some who in the same way hold the teaching of the Nicolaitans. Therefore repent; or else I am coming to you quickly, and I will make war against them with the sword of My mouth. He who has an ear, let him hear what the Spirit says to the churches. To him who overcomes, to him I will give *some* of the hidden manna, and I will give him a white stone, and a new name written on the stone which no one knows but he who receives it' (Revelation 2:12–17; see Numbers 25:1–3; Isaiah 62:2; Revelation 1:16).

SWORD, EDGE OF THE (See SWORD)

SWORDS (Also see CLUBS; and SWORD)

Setting: Gethsemane on the Mount of Olives, just east of the temple in Jerusalem. As He submits to His Father's will and allows Judas to betray Him, Jesus reveals that this is a fulfillment of prophecy.

At that time Jesus said to the crowds, "Have you come out with swords and clubs to arrest Me as *you would* against a robber? Every day I used to sit in the temple teaching and you did not seize Me. But all this has taken place to fulfill the Scriptures of the prophets" (Matthew 26:55, 56; cf. Mark 14:48, 49; Luke 22:52, 53; see Matthew 26:24).

Setting: Gethsemane on the Mount of Olives, just east of the temple in Jerusalem. Judas betrays Jesus with a kiss in front of a crowd from the chief priests, scribes, and elders seeking to seize the Lord with swords and clubs.

And Jesus said to them, "Have you come out with swords and clubs to arrest Me, as *you would* against a robber? Every day I was with you in the temple teaching, and you did not seize Me; but *this has taken place* to fulfill the Scriptures" (Mark 14:48, 49; cf. Matthew 26:55, 56; Luke 22:52, 53).

Setting: Gethsemane on the Mount of Olives, just east of the temple in Jerusalem. After praying for deliverance, with His crucifixion imminent, Jesus chastises the religious leaders after Judas betrays Him and the hostile crowd surrounds Him.

Then Jesus said to the chief priests and officers of the temple and elders who had come against Him, "Have you come out with swords and clubs as you would against a robber? While I was with you daily in the temple, you did not lay hands on Me; but this hour and the power of darkness are yours." (Luke 22:52, 53; cf. Matthew 26:47–56; Mark 14:43–50)

SWORDS AND CLUBS (Listed under CLUBS; and SWORDS)

SYNAGOGUE (Also see SYNAGOGUES)

Setting: Jerusalem. Before the Passover, after explaining He is the vine and His disciples are the branches, Jesus warns the disciples of the persecution they will face after His departure to heaven.

"These things I have spoken to you so that you may be kept from stumbling. They will make you outcasts from the synagogue, but an hour is coming for everyone who kills you to think that he is offering service to God. These things they will do because they have not known the Father or Me. But these things I have spoken to you, so that when their hour comes, you may remember that I told you of them. These things I did not say to you at the beginning, because I was with you" (John 16:1–4; see John 8:19, 55; 9:22; 13:19; 15:18–27).

SYNAGOGUE OF SATAN (Listed under SATAN, SYNAGOGUE OF)

SYNAGOGUES (Also see SEATS, CHIEF; and SYNAGOGUE)

Setting: Galilee. During the early part of His ministry, Jesus preaches the Sermon on the Mount to His disciples and the multitudes.

"So when you give to the poor, do not sound a trumpet before you, as the hypocrites do in the synagogues and in the streets, so that they may be honored by men. Truly I say to you, they have their reward in full. But when you give to the poor, do not let your left hand know what your right hand is doing, so that your giving will be in secret; and your Father who sees *what is done* in secret will reward you" (Matthew 6:2–4; see Jeremiah 17:10).

Setting: Galilee. During the early part of His ministry, Jesus preaches the Sermon on the Mount to His disciples and the multitudes.

"When you pray, you are not to be like the hypocrites; for they love to stand and pray in the synagogues and on the street corners so that they may be seen by men. Truly I say to you, they have their reward in full. But you, when you pray, go into your inner room, close your door and pray to your Father who is in secret, and your Father who sees *what is done* in secret will reward you" (Matthew 6:5, 6; see Mark 11:25).

Setting: Galilee. After His disciples observe His ministry, Jesus summons and specifically instructs them about the upcoming hardships of their ministry to the people of Israel.

"Behold, I send you out as sheep in the midst of wolves; so be shrewd as serpents and innocent as doves. But beware of men, for they will hand you over to *the* courts and scourge you in their synagogues; and you will even be brought before governors and kings for My sake, as a testimony to them and to the Gentiles. But when they hand you over, do not worry about how or what you are to say; for it will be given you in that hour what you are to say. For it is not you who speak, but *it* is the Spirit of your Father who speaks in you" (Matthew 10:16–20; cf. Luke 10:3).

Setting: The temple in Jerusalem. Jesus exposes the truth about Pharisaism to the crowds and His disciples after the Jewish religious leaders test Him with questions.

Then Jesus spoke to the crowds and to His disciples, saying: "The scribes and the Pharisees have seated themselves in the chair of Moses; therefore all that they tell you, do and observe, but do not do according to their deeds; for they say *things* and do not do *them.* They tie up heavy burdens and lay them on men's shoulders, but they themselves are unwilling to move them with *so much as* a finger. But they do all their deeds to be noticed by men; for they broaden their phylacteries and lengthen their tassels *of their garments.* They love the place of honor at banquets and the chief seats in the synagogues, and respectful greetings in the market places, and being called Rabbi by men. But do not be called Rabbi; for One is your Teacher, and you are all brothers. Do not call *anyone* on earth your father; for One is your Father, He who is in heaven. Do not be called leaders; for One is your Leader, *that is,* Christ. But the greatest among you shall be your servant. Whoever exalts himself shall be humbled; and whoever humbles himself shall be exalted" (Matthew 23:1–12; cf. Matthew 6:1, 5, 16; 20:26; Mark 12:38–40; Luke 11:43, 46; 14:11; 20:46, 47; see Exodus 13:9; Deuteronomy 33:3; Matthew 6:9).

Setting: The temple in Jerusalem. After the Jewish religious leaders test Him with questions, Jesus pronounces the eighth of eight woes upon them in front of the crowds and His disciples.

"Woe to you, scribes and Pharisees, hypocrites! For you build the tombs of the prophets and adorn the monuments of the righteous, and say, 'If we had been *living* in the days of our fathers, we would not have been partners with them in *shedding* the blood of the prophets.' So you testify against yourselves, that you are sons of those who murdered the prophets. Fill up, then, the measure *of the guilt* of you fathers. You serpents, you brood of vipers, how will you escape the sentence of hell? Therefore, behold, I am sending you prophets and wise men and scribes, some of them you will kill and crucify, and some of them you will scourge in your synagogues, and persecute from city to city, so that upon you may fall *the guilt of* all the righteous blood shed on earth, from the blood of righteous Abel to the blood of Zechariah, the son of Berechiah, whom you murdered between the temple and the altar. Truly I say to you, all these things will come upon this generation" (Matthew 23:29–36; cf. 2 Chronicles 24:21; Zechariah 1:1; Matthew 3:7; Luke 11:47–52; see Matthew 10:23).

Setting: The temple in Jerusalem. After commending one scribe for his nearness to the kingdom of God, Jesus warns the crowd about the rest of the scribes.

In His teaching He was saying: "Beware of the scribes who like to walk around in long robes, and *like* respectful greetings in the market places, and chief seats in the synagogues and places of honor at banquets, who devour widows' houses, and for appearance's sake offer long prayers; these will receive greater condemnation" (Mark 12:38–40; cf. Matthew 23:1–7; Luke 20:45–47).

Setting: On the Mount of Olives, east of the temple in Jerusalem. After prophesying the temple's destruction, Jesus responds during His Olivet Discourse to questions from Peter, James, John, and Andrew about other future events.

And Jesus began to say to them, "See to it that no one misleads you. Many will come in My name, saying, 'I am *He!*' and will mislead many. When you hear of wars and rumors of wars, do not be frightened; *those things* must take place; but *that is* not yet the end. For nation will rise up against nation, and kingdom against kingdom; there will be earthquakes in various places; there will *also be* famines. These things are *merely* the beginning of birth pangs. But be on your guard; for they will deliver you to *the* courts, and you will be flogged in *the* synagogues, and you will stand before governors and kings for My sake, as a testimony to them. The gospel must first be preached to all the nations. When they arrest you and hand you over, do not worry beforehand about what you are to say, but say whatever is given you in that hour; for it is not you who speak, but *it is* the Holy Spirit. Brother will betray brother to death, and a father *his* child; and children will rise up against parents and have them put to death. You will be hated by all because of My name, but the one who endures to the end, he will be saved" (Mark 13:5–13; cf. Matthew 24:4–14; Luke 21:7–19; see Matthew 10:17–22).

Setting: On the way from Galilee to Jerusalem. After speaking of how a lamp illuminates, the Lord has lunch with a Pharisee who is surprised He doesn't wash before eating.

But the Lord said to him, "Now you Pharisees clean the outside of the cup and of the platter; but inside of you, you are full of robbery and wickedness. You foolish ones, did not He who made the outside make the inside also? But give that which is within as charity, and then all things are clean for you. But woe to you Pharisees! You pay tithe of mint and rue and every *kind of* garden herb, and *yet* disregard justice and the love of God; but these are the things you should have done without neglecting the others. Woe to you Pharisees! For you love the chief seats in the synagogues and the respectful greetings in the market places. Woe to you! For you are like concealed tombs, and the people who walk over *them* are unaware *of it*" (Luke 11:39–44; cf. Matthew 23:6, 7, 23–27; see Matthew 15:2; Titus 1:15).

Setting: On the way from Galilee to Jerusalem. Jesus warns His disciples of future events, as the scribes and Pharisees turn hostile and question Him repeatedly in an attempt to catch Him in something He might say.

"And I say to you, everyone who confesses Me before men, the Son of Man will confess him also before the angels of God; but he who denies Me before men will be denied before the angels of God. And everyone who speaks a word against the Son of Man, it will be forgiven him; but he who blasphemes against the Holy Spirit, it will not be forgiven him. When they bring you before the synagogues and the rulers and the authorities, do not worry about how or what you are to speak in your defense, or what you are to say; for the Holy Spirit will teach you in that very hour what you ought to say" (Luke 12:8–12; cf. Matthew 10:32, 33; 12:31, 32; see Matthew 10:20).

Setting: The temple in Jerusalem. While ministering a few days before His crucifixion, after posing a question to the scribes, who do not answer, Jesus warns His disciples about the lifestyle of the scribes.

"Beware of the scribes, who like to walk around in long robes, and love respectful greetings in the market places, and chief seats in the synagogues and places of honor at banquets, who devour widows' houses, and for appearance's sake offer long prayers. These will receive greater condemnation" (Luke 20:46, 47; cf. Matthew 23:1–7; Mark 12:38–40; see Luke 11:43).

Setting: On the Mount of Olives, east of the temple in Jerusalem. After ministering in the temple a few days before His crucifixion, and giving His disciples more details regarding the temple's future destruction, Jesus elaborates during His Olivet Discourse about things to come.

Then He continued by saying to them, "Nation will rise against nation and kingdom against kingdom, and there will be great earthquakes, and in various places plagues and famines; and there will be terrors and great signs from heaven. But before all these things, they will lay their hands on you and will persecute you, delivering you to the synagogues and prisons, bringing you before kings and governors for My name's sake. It will lead to an opportunity for your testimony. So make up your minds not to prepare beforehand to defend yourselves; for I will give you utterance and wisdom which none of your opponents will be able to resist or refute. But you will be betrayed even by parents and brothers and relatives and friends, and they will put *some* of you to death, and you will be hated by all because of My name. Yet not a hair of your head will perish. By your endurance you will gain your lives" (Luke 21:10–19; cf. Matthew 10:19–22; 24:7–14; Mark 13:8–13).

Setting: Jerusalem. After Jesus is betrayed by Judas, and Peter denies he was His disciple, Annas, former high priest and father-in-law of the current high priest (Caiaphas), questions Jesus about His disciples and His teaching.

Jesus answered him, "I have spoken openly to the world; I always taught in synagogues and in the temple, where all the Jews come together; and I spoke nothing in secret. Why do you question Me? Question those who have heard what I spoke to them; they know what I said" (John 18:20, 21; see John 7:26).

SYRIAN

Setting: The synagogue in Jesus' hometown of Nazareth in Galilee. At the beginning of His public ministry, Jesus comments to the congregation after reading on the Sabbath from the book of the prophet Isaiah.

And He said to them, "No doubt you will quote this proverb to Me, 'Physician, heal yourself! Whatever we heard was done at Capernaum, do here in your hometown as well.'" And He said, "Truly I say to you, no prophet is welcome in his hometown. But I say to you in truth, there were many widows in Israel in the days of Elijah, when the sky was shut up for three years and six months, when a great famine came over all the land; and yet Elijah was sent to none of them, but only to Zarephath, *in the land* of Sidon, to a woman who was a widow. And there were many lepers in Israel in the time of Elisha the prophet; and none of them was cleansed, but only Naaman the Syrian" (Luke 4:23–27; Jesus refers to 1 Kings 17:1, 9; 2 Kings 5:1–14; see Matthew 13:53–58).

T

TABLE

Setting: Entering Capernaum. After the Lord gives the Sermon on the Mount and cleanses a leper, a Roman centurion implores Jesus to heal his servant.

Now when Jesus heard *this,* He marveled, and said to those who were following, "Truly I say to you, I have not found such great faith with anyone in Israel. I say to you that many will come from east and west, and recline *at the table* with Abraham, Isaac and Jacob in the kingdom of heaven; but the sons of the kingdom will be cast out into the outer darkness; in that place there will be weeping and gnashing of teeth." And Jesus said to the centurion, "Go; it shall be done for you as you have believed." And the servant was healed that *very* moment (Matthew 8:10–13; cf. Luke 7:9, 10).

Setting: On the way from Galilee to Jerusalem. After giving a parable about riches and greed, Jesus uses another parable to challenge the crowd and His disciples to be ready for His return.

"Be dressed in readiness, and *keep* your lamps lit. Be like men who are waiting for their master when he returns from the wedding feast, so that they may immediately open *the door* to him when he comes and knocks. Blessed are those slaves whom the master will find on the alert when he comes; truly I say to you, that he will gird himself *to serve,* and have them recline *at the table,* and will come up and wait on them. Whether he comes in the second watch, or even in the third and finds *them* so, blessed are those *slaves*. But be sure of this, that if the head of the house had known at what hour the thief was coming, he would not have allowed his house to be broken into. You too, be ready; for the Son of Man is coming at an hour that you do not expect" (Luke 12:35–40; cf. Matthew 24:42–44; see Mark 13:33; Ephesians 6:14).

Setting: On the way from Galilee to Jerusalem. While teaching in the cities and villages, Jesus responds to a question about who is saved.

And someone said to Him, "Lord, are here *just* a few who are being saved?" And He said to them, "Strive to enter through the narrow door; for many, I tell you, will seek to enter and will not be able. Once the head of the house gets up and shuts the door, and you begin to stand outside and knock on the door, saying, 'Lord, open up to us!' then He will answer and say to you, 'I do not know where you are from.' Then you will begin to say, 'We ate and drank in Your presence, and You taught in our streets'; and He will say, 'I tell you, I do not know where you are from; DEPART FROM ME, ALL YOU EVILDOERS.' In that place there will be weeping and gnashing of teeth when you see Abraham and Isaac and Jacob and all the prophets in the kingdom of God, but you yourselves being thrown out. And they will come from east and west and from north and south, and will recline *at the table* in the kingdom of God. And behold, *some* are last who will be first and *some* are first who will be last" (Luke 13:23–30, Jesus quotes from Psalm 6:8; cf. Matthew 7:13, 23; 8:11, 12; see Matthew 19:30; Luke 3:8).

Setting: On the way from Galilee to Jerusalem. As He observes the invited guests selecting places of honor at table in the house of a Pharisee leader on the Sabbath, Jesus speaks a parable to them.

And He *began* speaking a parable to the invited guests when He noticed how they had been picking out the places of honor *at the table,* saying to them, "When you are invited by someone to a wedding feast, do not take the place of honor, for someone more distinguished than you may have been invited by him, and he who invited you both will come and say to you, 'Give *your* place to this man, and then in disgrace you proceed to occupy the last place. But when you are invited, go and recline at the last place, so that when the one who has invited you comes, he may say to you, 'Friend, move up higher'; then you will have honor in the sight of all who are at the table with you. For everyone who exalts himself will be humbled, and he who humbles himself will be exalted" (Luke 14:7–11; see 2 Samuel 22:28; Proverb 25:6, 7; Matthew 23:6).

Setting: On the way from Galilee to Jerusalem. After responding to the Pharisees' scoffing at His teaching His disciples about stewardship and the permanence of the Law, Jesus conveys the story of the rich man and Lazarus.

"Now there was a rich man, and he habitually dressed in purple and fine linen, joyously living in splendor every day. And a poor man named Lazarus was laid at his gate, covered with sores, and longing to be fed with the *crumbs* which were falling from the rich man's table; besides, even the dogs were coming and licking his sores. Now the poor man died and was carried away by the angels to Abraham's bosom; and the rich man also died and was buried. In Hades he lifted up his eyes, being in torment, and saw Abraham far away and Lazarus in his bosom. And he cried out and said, 'Father Abraham, have mercy on me, and send Lazarus so that he may dip the tip of his finger in water and cool off my tongue, for I am in agony in this flame.' But Abraham said, 'Child, remember that during your life you received your good things, and likewise Lazarus bad things; but now he is being comforted here, and you are in agony. And besides all this, between us and you there is a great chasm fixed, so that those who wish to come over from here to you will not be able, and *that* none may cross over from there to us.' And he said, 'Then I beg you, father, that you send him to my father's house—for I have five brothers—in order that he may warn them, so that they will not also come to this place of torment.' But Abraham said, 'They have Moses and the Prophets; let them hear them.' But he said, 'No, father Abraham, but if someone goes to them from the dead, they will repent!' But he said to him, 'If they do not listen to Moses and the Prophets, they will not be persuaded even if someone rises from the dead' " (Luke 16:19–31; see Luke 3:8; 6:24; 16:1, 14).

Setting: An upper room in Jerusalem. During the Feast of Unleavened Bread (Passover) just before His crucifixion, while celebrating the Passover meal with His disciples, Jesus institutes the Lord's Supper.

And when He had taken a cup *and* given thanks, He said, "Take this and share it among yourselves; for I say to you, I will not drink of the fruit of the vine from now on until the kingdom of God comes." And when he had taken *some* bread and given thanks, He broke it and gave it to them, saying, "This is My body which is given for you; do this in remembrance of Me." And in the same way *He took* the cup after they had eaten, saying, "This cup which is poured out for you is the new covenant in My blood. But behold, the hand of the one betraying Me is with Mine on the table. For indeed, the Son of Man is going as it has been determined; but woe to that man by whom He is betrayed!" (Luke 22:17–22; cf. Matthew 26:26–29; Mark 14:22–25; 1 Corinthians 11:23–26; see Psalm 41:9; Luke 14:15; 1 Corinthians 10:16).

Setting: An upper room in Jerusalem. During the Feast of Unleavened Bread (Passover) just before His crucifixion, Jesus celebrates the Passover meal with His disciples and institutes the Lord's Supper. The disciples later argue over who is the greatest among them.

And He said to them, "The kings of the Gentiles lord it over them; and those who have authority over them are called 'Benefactors.' But *it is* not this way with you, but the one who is the greatest among you must become like the youngest, and the leader like a servant. For who is greater, the one who reclines *at the table* or the one who serves? Is it not the one who reclines *at the table?* But I am among you as the one who serves" (Luke 22:25–27; cf. Matthew 20:25–28; 23:11; Mark 10:42–45).

Setting: An upper room in Jerusalem. During the Feast of Unleavened Bread (Passover) just before His crucifixion, Jesus celebrates the Passover meal with His disciples and institutes the Lord's Supper. The disciples argue over who is the greatest among them, and the Lord details the kingdom benefits they will experience.

"You are those who have stood by Me in My trials; for just as My Father has granted Me a kingdom, I grant you that you may eat and drink at My table in My kingdom, and you will sit on thrones judging the twelve tribes of Israel" (Luke 22:28–30; cf. Matthew 19:28).

TABLE, LORD'S (See LORD'S SUPPER)

TALENT (Also see STEWARDSHIP; and TALENTS)

Setting: On the Mount of Olives, just east of Jerusalem. During His Olivet Discourse, after answering His disciples' questions as to when the temple will be destroyed and Jerusalem overrun, along with the signs of His coming and the end of the age, Jesus reemphasizes to His disciples that they should be on the alert for His return.

"For *it is* just like a man *about* to go on a journey, who called his own slaves and entrusted his possessions to them. To one he gave five talents, to another, two, and to another, one, each according to his own ability; and he went on his journey. Immediately the one who had received the five talents went and traded with them, and gained five more talents. In the same manner the one who *had received* the two *talents* gained two more. But he who received the one *talent* went away, and dug a *hole* in the ground and hid his master's money. Now after a long time the master of those slaves came and settled accounts with them. The one who had received the five talents came up and brought five more talents, saying, 'Master, you entrusted five talents to me. See, I have gained five more talents.' His master said to him, 'Well done, good and faithful slave. You were faithful with a few things, I will put you in charge of many things; enter into the joy of your master.' Also the one who *had received* the two talents came up and said, 'Master, you entrusted two talents to me. See, I have gained two more talents.' His master said to him, 'Well done, good and faithful slave. You were faithful with a few things, I will put you in charge of many things; enter into the joy of your master.' And the one also who had received the one talent came up and said, 'Master, I knew you to be a hard man, reaping where you did not sow and gathering where you scattered no *seed.* And I was afraid, and went away and hid your talent in the ground. See, you have what is yours.' But his master answered and said to him, 'You wicked, lazy slave, you knew that I reap where I did not sow and gather where I scattered no *seed.* Then you ought to have put my money in the bank, and on my arrival I would have received my *money* back with interest. 'Therefore take away the talent from him, and give it to the one who has ten talents.' For to everyone who has, *more* shall be given, and he will have an abundance; but from the one who does not have, even what he does have shall be taken away. Throw out the worthless slave into the outer darkness; in that place there will be weeping and gnashing of teeth" (Matthew 25:14–30; cf. Matthew 8:12; 13:12; 24:45–47; see Matthew 18:23, 24; Luke 12:44).

TALENTS (Also see STEWARDSHIP; and TALENT)

Setting: Capernaum of Galilee. Jesus illustrates the matter of forgiveness after Peter asks Him if forgiving someone seven times who has sinned against him is adequate.

"For this reason the kingdom of heaven may be compared to a king who wished to settle accounts with his slaves. When he had begun to settle *them,* one who owed him ten thousand talents was brought to him. But since he did not have *the means* to repay, his lord commanded him to be sold, along with his wife and children and all that he had, and repayment to be made. So the slave fell *to the ground* and prostrated himself before him, saying, 'Have patience with me and I will repay you everything.' And the lord of that slave felt compassion and released him and forgave him the debt. But that slave went out and found one of his fellow slaves who owed him a hundred denarii; and he seized him and *began* to choke *him,* saying, 'Pay back what you owe.' So his fellow slave fell *to the ground* and *began* to plead with him, saying, 'Have patience with me and I will repay you.' But he was unwilling and went and threw him in prison until he should pay back what was owed. So when his fellow slaves saw what had happened, they were deeply grieved and came and reported to their lord all that had happened. Then summoning him, his lord said to him, 'You wicked slave, I forgave you all that debt because you pleaded with me. Should you not also have had mercy on your fellow slave, in the same way that I had mercy on you?' And his lord, moved with anger, handed him over to the torturers until he should repay all that was owed him. My heavenly Father will also do the same to you, if each of you does not forgive his brother from your heart" (Matthew 18:23–35; cf. Matthew 6:12, 14, 15; Luke 7:42; see Matthew 25:19–28).

Setting: On the Mount of Olives, just east of Jerusalem. During His Olivet Discourse, after answering His disciples' questions as to when the temple will be destroyed and Jerusalem overrun, along with the signs of His coming and the end of the age, Jesus reemphasizes to His disciples that they should be on the alert for His return.

"For *it is* just like a man *about* to go on a journey, who called his own slaves and entrusted his possessions to them. To one he gave five talents, to another, two, and to another, one, each according to his own ability; and he went on his journey. Immediately the one who had received the five talents went and traded with them, and gained five more talents. In the same manner the one who *had received* the two *talents* gained two more. But he who received the one *talent* went away, and dug a *hole* in the ground and hid his master's money. Now after a long time the master of those slaves came and settled accounts with them. The one who had received the five talents came up and brought five more talents, saying, 'Master, you entrusted five talents to me. See, I have gained five more talents.' His master said to him, 'Well done, good and faithful slave. You were faithful with a few things, I will put you in charge of many things; enter into the joy of your master.' Also the one who *had received* the two talents came up and said, 'Master, you entrusted two talents to me. See, I have gained two more talents.' His master said to him, 'Well done, good and faithful slave. You were faithful with a few things, I will put you in charge of many things; enter into the joy of your master.' And the one also who had received the one talent came up and said, 'Master, I knew you to be a hard man, reaping where you did not sow and gathering where you scattered no *seed.* And I was afraid, and went away and hid your talent in the ground. See, you have what is yours.' But his master answered and said to him, 'You wicked, lazy slave, you knew that I reap where I did not sow and gather where I scattered no *seed.* Then you ought to have put my money in the bank, and on my arrival I would have received my *money* back with interest. 'Therefore take away the talent from him, and give it to the one who has ten talents.' For to everyone who has, *more* shall be given, and he will have an abundance; but from the one who does not have, even what he does have shall be taken away. Throw out the worthless slave into the outer darkness; in that place there will be weeping and gnashing of teeth" (Matthew 25:14–30; cf. Matthew 8:12; Matthew 13:12; 24:45–47; see Matthew 18:23, 24; Luke 12:44).

TALENTS, PARABLE OF THE

[PARABLE OF THE TALENTS from entrusted his possessions to them and five talents]

Setting: On the Mount of Olives, just east of Jerusalem. During His Olivet Discourse, after answering His disciples' questions as to when the temple will be destroyed and Jerusalem overrun, along with the signs of His coming and the end of the age, Jesus reemphasizes to His disciples that they should be on the alert for His return.

"For *it is* just like a man *about* to go on a journey, who called his own slaves and entrusted his possessions to them. To one he gave five talents, to another, two, and to another, one, each according to his own ability; and he went on his journey. Immediately the one who had received the five talents went and traded with them, and gained five more talents. In the same manner the one who *had received* the two *talents* gained two more. But he who received the one *talent* went away, and dug a *hole* in the ground and hid his master's money. Now after a long time the master of those slaves came and settled accounts with them. The one who had received the five talents came up and brought five more talents, saying, 'Master, you entrusted five talents to me. See, I have gained five more talents.' His master said to him, 'Well done, good and faithful slave. You were faithful with a few things, I will put you in charge of many things; enter into the joy of your master.' Also the one who *had received* the two talents came up and said, 'Master, you entrusted two talents to me. See, I have gained two more talents.' His master said to him, 'Well done, good and faithful slave. You were faithful with a few things, I will put you in charge of many things; enter into the joy of your master.' And the one also who had received the one talent came up and said, 'Master, I knew you to be a hard man, reaping where you did not sow and gathering where you scattered no *seed.* And I was afraid, and went away and hid your talent in the ground. See, you have what is yours.' But his master answered and said to him, 'You wicked, lazy slave, you knew that I reap where I did not sow and gather where I scattered no *seed.* Then you ought to have put my money in the bank, and on my arrival I would have received my *money* back with interest. 'Therefore take away the talent from him, and give it to the one who has ten talents.' For to everyone who has, *more* shall be given, and he will have an abundance; but from the one who does not have, even what he does have shall be taken away. Throw out the worthless slave into the outer darkness; in that place there will be weeping and gnashing of teeth" (Matthew 25:14–30; cf. Matthew 8:12; 13:12; 24:45–47; see Matthew 18:23, 24; Luke 12:44).

[PARABLE OF THE TALENTS from gave them ten minas]

Setting: Jericho, on the way to Jerusalem. After commending Zaccheus's faith in Him, Jesus provides a parable about stewardship.

So He said, "A nobleman went to a distant country to receive a kingdom for himself, and *then* return. And he called ten of his slaves, and gave them ten minas and said to them, 'Do business *with this* until I come *back.*' But his citizens hated him and sent a delegation after him, saying, 'We do not want this man to reign over us.' When he returned, after receiving the kingdom, he ordered that these slaves, to whom he had given the money, be called to him so that he might know what business they had done. The first appeared, saying, 'Master, your mina has made ten minas more.' And he said to him, 'Well done, good slave, because you have been faithful in a very little thing, you are to be in authority over ten cities.' The second came, saying, 'Your mina, master, has made five minas.' And he said to him, also, 'And you are to be over five cities.' Another came, saying, 'Master, here is your mina, which I kept put away in a handkerchief; for I was afraid of you, because you are an exacting man; you take up what you did not lay down and reap what you did not sow.' He said to him, 'By your own words I will judge you, you worthless slave. Did you know that I am an exacting man, taking up what I did not lay down and reaping what I did not sow? Then why did you not put my money in the bank, and having come, I would have collected it with interest?' Then he said to the bystanders, 'Take the mina away from him and give it to the one who has the ten minas.' And they said to him, 'Master, he has ten minas *already.*' I tell you that to everyone who has, more shall be given, but from the one who does not have, even what he does have shall be taken away. But these enemies of mine, who did not want me to reign over them, bring them here and slay them in my presence" (Luke 19:12–27; cf. Matthew 25:14–30; see Matthew 13:12; Luke 16:10).

TARES (Also see WHEAT)

Setting: By the Sea of Galilee. Because the religious leaders are rejecting His message, Jesus continues teaching the crowds with the Parable of the Wheat and the Tares.

Jesus presented another parable to them, saying, "The kingdom of heaven may be compared to a man who sowed good seed in his field. But while his men were sleeping, his enemy came and sowed tares among the wheat, and went away. But when the wheat sprouted and bore grain, then the tares became evident also. The slaves of the landowner came and said to him, 'Sir, did you not sow good seed in your field? How then does it have tares?' And he said to them, 'An enemy has done this!' The slaves said to him, 'Do you want us, then, to go and gather them up?' But he said, 'No; for while you are gathering up the tares, you may uproot the wheat with them. Allow both to grow together until the harvest; and in the time of the harvest I will say to the reapers, "First gather up the tares and bind them in bundles to burn them up; but gather the wheat into my barn" '" (Matthew 13:24–30; cf. Matthew 3:12).

Setting: A house near the Sea of Galilee. Jesus gives His disciples the meaning of the Parable of the Wheat and the Tares.

And He said, "The one who sows the good seed is the Son of Man, and the field is the world; and as *for* the good seed, these are the sons of the kingdom; and the tares are the sons of the evil *one;* and the enemy who sowed them is the devil, and the harvest is the end of the age; and the reapers are angels. So just as the tares are gathered up and burned with fire, so shall it be at the end of the age. The Son of Man will send forth His angels, and they will gather out of His kingdom all stumbling blocks, and those who commit lawlessness, and will throw them into the furnace of fire; in that place there will be weeping and gnashing of teeth. Then THE RIGHTEOUS WILL SHINE FORTH AS THE SUN in the kingdom of their Father. He who has ears, let him hear" (Matthew 13:37–43, Jesus quotes from Daniel 12:3; cf. Matthew 8:12; 13:50).

TARES, EXPLANATION OF THE PARABLE OF THE WHEAT AND THE (Also see TARES, PARABLE OF THE WHEAT AND THE)

Setting: A house near the Sea of Galilee. Jesus gives His disciples the meaning of the Parable of the Wheat and the Tares.

And He said, "The one who sows the good seed is the Son of Man, and the field is the world; and as *for* the good seed, these are the sons of the kingdom; and the tares are the sons of the evil *one;* and the enemy who sowed them is the devil, and the harvest is the end of the age; and the reapers are angels. So just as the tares are gathered up and burned with fire, so shall it be at the end of the age. The Son of Man will send forth His angels, and they will gather out of His kingdom all stumbling blocks, and those who commit lawlessness, and will throw them into the furnace of fire; in that place there will be weeping and gnashing of teeth. Then THE RIGHTEOUS WILL SHINE FORTH AS THE SUN in the kingdom of their Father. He who has ears, let him hear" (Matthew 13:37–43, Jesus quotes from Daniel 12:3; cf. Matthew 8:12; 13:50).

TARES, PARABLE OF THE WHEAT AND THE (Also see TARES, EXPLANATION OF THE PARABLE OF THE WHEAT AND THE)

[PARABLE OF THE WHEAT AND THE TARES from parable; wheat; and tares]

Setting: By the Sea of Galilee. Because the religious leaders are rejecting His message, Jesus continues teaching the crowds with the Parable of the Wheat and the Tares.

Jesus presented another parable to them, saying, "The kingdom of heaven may be compared to a man who sowed good seed in his field. But while his men were sleeping, his enemy came and sowed tares among the wheat, and went away. But when the wheat

sprouted and bore grain, then the tares became evident also. The slaves of the landowner came and said to him, 'Sir, did you not sow good seed in your field? How then does it have tares?' And he said to them, 'An enemy has done this!' The slaves said to him, 'Do you want us, then, to go and gather them up?' But he said, 'No; for while you are gathering up the tares, you may uproot the wheat with them. Allow both to grow together until the harvest; and in the time of the harvest I will say to the reapers, "First gather up the tares and bind them in bundles to burn them up; but gather the wheat into my barn" '" (Matthew 13:24–30; cf. Matthew 3:12).

TARSUS

Setting: Damascus. Luke, writing in Acts, conveys how the Lord instructs one of His disciples, Ananias, to locate Saul of Tarsus to touch him in order to restore Saul's vision.

Now there was a disciple at Damascus named Ananias; and the Lord said to him in a vision, "Ananias." And he said, "Here I am, Lord." And the Lord *said* to him, "Get up and go to the street called Straight, and inquire at the house of Judas for a man from Tarsus named Saul, for he is praying, and he was seen in a vision a man named Ananias come in and lay his hands on him, so that he might regain his sight" (Acts 9:10–12; see Acts 22:12–14).

TASK

Setting: On the Mount of Olives, east of the temple in Jerusalem. After prophesying the temple's destruction, Jesus responds during His Olivet Discourse to questions from Peter, James, John, and Andrew about other future events.

"Take heed, keep on the alert; for you do not know when the *appointed* time will come. *It is* like a man away on a journey, *who* upon leaving his house and putting his slaves in charge, *assigning* to each one his task, also commanded the doorkeeper to stay on the alert. Therefore, be on the alert—for you do not know when the master of the house is coming, whether in the evening, at midnight, or when the rooster crows, or in the morning—in case he should come suddenly and find you asleep. What I say to you I say to all, 'Be on the alert!' " (Mark 13:33–37; cf. Matthew 24:42, 43; Luke 21:34–36; see Luke 12:36–38; Ephesians 6:18).

TASSELS

Setting: The temple in Jerusalem. Jesus exposes the truth about Pharisaism to the crowds and His disciples after the Jewish religious leaders test Him with questions.

Then Jesus spoke to the crowds and to His disciples, saying. "The scribes and the Pharisees have seated themselves in the chair of Moses; therefore all that they tell you, do and observe, but do not do according to their deeds; for they say *things* and do not do *them.* They tie up heavy burdens and lay them on men's shoulders, but they themselves are unwilling to move them with *so much as* a finger. But they do all their deeds to be noticed by men; for they broaden their phylacteries and lengthen their tassels *of their garments.* They love the place of honor at banquets and the chief seats in the synagogues, and respectful greetings in the market places, and being called Rabbi by men. But do not be called Rabbi; for One is your Teacher, and you are all brothers. Do not call *anyone* on earth your father; for One is your Father, He who is in heaven. Do not be called leaders; for One is your Leader, *that is,* Christ. But the greatest among you shall be your servant. Whoever exalts himself shall be humbled; and whoever humbles himself shall be exalted" (Matthew 23:1–12; cf. Matthew 6:1, 5, 16; Matthew 20:26; Mark 12:38–40; Luke 11:43, 46; 14:11; 20:46, 47; see Exodus 13:9; Deuteronomy 33:3; Matthew 6:9).

TAX, POLL (See POLL-TAX)

TAX, TEMPLE (Also see TAXES)

[TEMPLE TAX from Take that and give it to them for you and Me]

Setting: Capernaum of Galilee. Jesus pays the two-drachma temple tax for Peter and Himself in a miraculous manner.

He said, "Yes." And when he came into the house, Jesus spoke to him first, saying, "What do you think, Simon? From whom do the kings of the earth collect customs or poll-tax, from their sons or from strangers?" When Peter said, "From strangers," Jesus said to him, "Then the sons are exempt. However, so that we do not offend them, go to the sea and throw in a hook, and take the first fish that comes up; and when you open its mouth, you will find a shekel. Take that and give it to them for you and Me" (Matthew 17:25–27; see Exodus 30:11–16; Matthew 22:17–19; Romans 13:7).

TAX, TWO-DRACHMA (See POLL-TAX)

TAX BOOTH (Listed under BOOTH, TAX)

TAX COLLECTOR (Also see TAX COLLECTORS; and TAXES)

Setting: Capernaum of Galilee. After conveying to His disciples the value of little ones, Jesus gives instruction about church discipline.

"If your brother sins, go and show him his fault in private; if he listens to you, you have won your brother. But if he does not listen *to you,* take one or two more with you, so that BY THE MOUTH OF TWO OR THREE WITNESSES EVERY FACT MAY BE CONFIRMED. If he refuses to listen to them, tell it to the church; and if he refuses to listen even to the church, let him be to you as a Gentile and a tax collector. Truly I say to you, whatever you bind of earth shall have been bound in heaven; and whatever you loose on earth shall have been loosed in heaven. Again, I say to you, that if two of you agree on earth about anything that they may ask, it shall be done for them by My Father who is in heaven. For there two or three have gathered together in My name, I am there in their midst" (Matthew 18:15–20. Jesus quotes from Deuteronomy 19:15; cf. Matthew 7:7; 16:19; see Leviticus 19:17; Matthew 28:20; 2 Thessalonians 3:6, 14).

Setting: On the way from Galilee to Jerusalem. After instructing His disciples about persistence in prayer, Jesus conveys a parable about self-righteousness.

And He also told this parable to some people who trusted in themselves that they were righteous, and viewed others with contempt: "Two men went up into the temple to pray, one a Pharisee and the other a tax collector. The Pharisee stood and was praying this to himself: 'God, I thank You that I am not like other people: swindlers, unjust, adulterers, or even like this tax collector. I fast twice a week; I pay tithes of all that I get.' But the tax collector, standing some distance away, was even unwilling to lift up his eyes to heaven, but was beating his breast, saying, 'God, be merciful to me, the sinner!' I tell you, this man went to his house justified rather than the other; for everyone who exalts himself will be humbled, but he who humbles himself will be exalted" (Luke 18:9–14; see Ezra 9:6; Matthew 6:5, 23:12; Luke 11:42, 16:15; Romans 14:3, 10).

TAX COLLECTORS (Also see TAX COLLECTOR; and TAXES)

Setting: Galilee. During the early part of His ministry, Jesus preaches the Sermon on the Mount to His disciples and the multitudes.

"You have heard that it was said, 'YOU SHALL LOVE YOUR NEIGHBOR and hate your enemy.' But I say to you, love your enemies and pray for those who persecute you, so that you may be sons of your Father who is in heaven; for He causes His sun to rise on *the* evil and *the* good, and sends rain on *the* righteous and *the* unrighteous. For if you love those who love you, what reward do you have? Do not even the tax collectors do the same? If you greet only your brothers, what more are you doing *than others?* Do not even the Gentiles do the same? Therefore, you are to be perfect, as your heavenly Father is perfect" (Matthew 5:43–48, Jesus quotes from Leviticus 19:18; cf. Leviticus 19:2; Luke 6:27–36).

Setting: Galilee. After praising John the Baptist as His forerunner, Jesus demonstrates the foolish thinking of the current generation of Jewish religious leaders by repeating what they say about John's ascetic lifestyle and ministry along with His own.

"But to what shall I compare this generation? It is like children sitting in the market places, who call out to the other *children,* and say, 'We played the flute for you, and you did not dance; we sang a dirge, and you did not mourn.' For John came neither eating nor drinking, and they say, 'He has a demon!' The Son of Man came eating and drinking, and they say, 'Behold, a gluttonous man and a drunkard, a friend of tax collectors and sinners! Yet wisdom is vindicated by her deeds" (Matthew 11:16–19; cf. Luke 7:31–35; see Matthew 9:11, 34; Luke 1:15).

Setting: The temple in Jerusalem. Jesus delivers a parable to the chief priests and elders after they question His authority.

"But what do you think? A man had two sons, and he came to the first and said, 'Son, go work today in the vineyard.' And he answered, 'I will not'; but afterward he regretted it and went. The man came to the second and said the same thing; and he answered, 'I *will,* sir'; but he did not go. Which of the two sons did the will of his father?" They said, "The first." Jesus said to them, "Truly, I say to you that the tax collectors and prostitutes will get into the kingdom of God before you. For John came to you in the way of righteousness and you did not believe him; but the tax collectors and prostitutes did believe him; and you, seeing *this,* did not even feel remorse afterward so as to believe him" (Matthew 21:28–32; cf. Luke 7:29, 30, 37–50).

Setting: Galilee. After praising John the Baptist to the crowds, Jesus criticizes the Pharisees and lawyers who reject God's purpose and John's message.

"To what then shall I compare the men of this generation, and what are they like? They are like children who sit in the market place and call to one another, and they say, 'We played the flute for you, and you did not dance; we sang a dirge, and you did not weep.' For John the Baptist has come eating no bread and drinking no wine, and you say, 'He has a demon!' The Son of Man has come eating and drinking, and you say, 'Behold, a gluttonous man and a drunkard, a friend of tax collectors and sinners!' Yet wisdom is vindicated by all her children" (Luke 7:31–35; cf. Matthew 11:16–19; see Luke 1:15).

TAX GATHERER (See TAX COLLECTOR)

TAX GATHERERS (See TAX COLLECTORS)

TAXES (Specific taxes such as POLL-TAX; and TAX, TEMPLE are separate entries; also see TAX COLLECTOR; and TAX COLLECTORS)

[TAXES from Take that and give it to them for you and Me]
Setting: Capernaum of Galilee. Jesus pays the two-drachma temple tax for Peter and Himself in a miraculous manner.

He said, "Yes." And when he came into the house, Jesus spoke to him first, saying, "What do you think, Simon? From whom do the kings of the earth collect customs or poll-tax, from their sons or from strangers?" When Peter said, "From strangers," Jesus said to him, "Then the sons are exempt. However, so that we do not offend them, go to the sea and throw in a hook, and take the first fish that comes up; and when you open its mouth, you will find a shekel. Take that and give it to them for you and Me" (Matthew 17:25–27; see Exodus 30:11–16; Matthew 22:17–19; Romans 13:7).

[TAXES from render to Caesar the things that are Caesar's]
Setting: The temple in Jerusalem. The Pharisees send their disciples and the Herodians to test Jesus about the poll-tax in order to trap Him.

But Jesus perceived their malice, and said, "Why are you testing Me, you hypocrites? Show Me the coin *used* for the poll-tax." And they brought Him a denarius. And He said to them, "Whose likeness and inscription is this?" They said to Him, "Caesar's." Then He said to them, "Then render to Caesar the things that are Caesar's; and to God the things that are God's" (Matthew 22:18–21; cf. Matthew 17:25; Mark 12:15–17; Luke 20:22–25).

[TAXES from Render to Caesar the things that are Caesar's]
Setting: The temple in Jerusalem. After Jesus teaches the chief priests, scribes, and elders in parables, they send some of the Pharisees and Herodians in an attempt to trap Him in a statement.

"Shall we pay or shall we not pay?" But He, knowing their hypocrisy, said to them, "Why are you testing Me? Bring Me a denarius to look at." They brought *one.* And He said to them, "Whose likeness and inscription is this?" And they said to Him, "Caesar's." And Jesus said to them, "Render to Caesar the things that are Caesar's, and to God the things that are God's." And they were amazed at Him (Mark 12:15–17; cf. Matthew 22:15–22; Luke 20:20–26).

[TAXES from render to Caesar the things that are Caesar's]
Setting: The temple in Jerusalem. While ministering a few days before His crucifixion, after Jesus gives the people the Parable of the Vine-Growers, the scribes and Pharisees seek to trap Him by questioning Him about paying taxes to Caesar.

But He detected their trickery and said to them, "Show Me a denarius. Whose likeness and inscription does it have?" They said "Caesar's." And He said to them, "Then render to Caesar the things that are Caesar's, and to God the things that are God's" (Luke 20:23–25; cf. Matthew 22:15–21; Mark 12:13–17).

TEACHER (Also see TEACHERS)

Setting: Galilee. After His disciples observe His ministry, Jesus summons and specifically instructs them about the difficulties ahead involving true discipleship.

"A disciple is not above his teacher, nor a slave above his master. It is enough for the disciple that he become like his teacher, and the slave like his master. If they have called the head of the house Beelzebul, how much more *will they malign* the members of his household!" (Matthew 10:24, 25; cf. Luke 6:40; see 2 Kings 1:2).

Setting: The temple in Jerusalem. Jesus exposes the truth about Pharisaism to the crowds and His disciples after the Jewish religious leaders test Him with questions.

Then Jesus spoke to the crowds and to His disciples, saying: "The scribes and the Pharisees have seated themselves in the chair of Moses; therefore all that they tell you, do and observe, but do not do according to their deeds; for they say *things* and do not do *them.* They tie up heavy burdens and lay them on men's shoulders, but they themselves are unwilling to move them with *so much as* a finger. But they do all their deeds to be noticed by men; for they broaden their phylacteries and lengthen their tassels *of their garments.* They love the place of honor at banquets and the chief seats in the synagogues, and respectful greetings in the market places, and being called Rabbi by men. But do not be called Rabbi; for One is your Teacher, and you are all brothers. Do not call *anyone* on earth your father; for One is your Father, He who is in heaven. Do not be called leaders; for One is your Leader, *that is,* Christ. But the greatest among you shall be your servant. Whoever exalts himself shall be humbled; and whoever humbles himself shall be exalted" (Matthew 23:1–12; cf. Matthew 20:26; Mark 12:38–40; 46; 20:46, 47; see Exodus 13:9; Deuteronomy 33:3; Matthew 6:1, 5, 6, 9, 16; Mark 14:11; Luke 11:43; 14:11).

Setting: Just outside Jerusalem. On the first day of the Feast of Unleavened Bread, just after Judas makes arrangements with the chief priests to betray Him, Jesus informs His disciples where they will celebrate the Passover.

And He said, "Go into the city to a certain man, and say to him, 'The Teacher says, "My time is near; I *am to* keep the Passover at your house with My disciples"'" (Matthew 26:18; cf. Mark 14:13–15; Luke 22:7–13).

Setting: Jerusalem. On the first day of the Feast of Unleavened Bread, when the Passover lamb is being sacrificed, Jesus responds to His disciples' question about His plans for the Passover meal.

And He sent two of His disciples and said to them, "Go into the city, and a man will meet you carrying a pitcher of water; follow him; and wherever he enters, say to the owner of the house, 'The Teacher says, "Where is My guest room in which I may eat the Passover with My disciples?"' And he himself will show you a large upper room furnished *and* ready; prepare for us there" (Mark 14:13–15; cf. Matthew 26:17–19; Luke 22:7–13).

Setting: Galilee. After selecting His twelve disciples, Jesus teaches the Sermon on the Mount to those disciples and a great throng of people from Judea, Jerusalem, and the central coastal region of Tyre and Sidon.

And He also spoke a parable to them: "A blind man cannot guide a blind man, can he? Will they not both fall into a pit? A pupil is not above his teacher; but everyone, after he has been fully trained, will be like his teacher. Why do you look at the speck that is in your brother's eye, but do not notice the log that is in your own eye? Or how can you say to your brother, 'Brother, let me take out the speck that is in your eye,' when you yourself do not see the log that is in your own eye? You hypocrite, first take the log out of your own eye, and then you will see clearly to take out the speck that is in your brother's eye. For there is no good tree which produces bad fruit, nor, on the other hand, a bad tree which produces good fruit. For each tree is known by its own fruit. For men do not gather figs from thorns, nor do they pick grapes from a briar bush. The good man out of the good treasure of his heart brings forth what is good; and the evil *man* out of the evil *treasure* brings forth what is evil; for his mouth speaks from that which fills his heart" (Luke 6:39–45; cf. Matthew 7:3–6. 16, 18, 20; 12:35; see Matthew 10:24; 15:14; Luke 6:12–19).

Setting: Just outside Jerusalem. With the Passover (Feast of Unleavened Bread) approaching, Jesus informs His disciples where they will celebrate the feast. The chief priests and scribes seek to kill Him, and Satan enters Judas Iscariot in order to betray the Lord.

And Jesus sent Peter and John, saying, "Go and prepare the Passover for us, so that we may eat it." They said to Him, "Where do You want us to prepare it?" And He said to them, "When you have entered the city, a man will meet you carrying a pitcher of water; follow him into the house that he enters. And you shall say to the owner of the house, 'The Teacher says to you, "Where is the guest room in which I may eat the Passover with My disciples?"' And he will show you a large, furnished upper room; prepare it there" (Luke 22:8–12; cf. Matthew 26:17–19; Mark 14:12–16).

Setting: Jerusalem. At the time for the Passover of the Jews, after the Lord cleanses the temple, a Pharisee, Nicodemus, asks Him by night the meaning of "born of the Spirit."

Jesus answered and said to him, "Are you the teacher of Israel and do not understand these things? Truly, truly, I say to you, we speak of what we know and testify of what we have seen, and you do not accept our testimony. If I told you earthly things and you do not believe, how will you believe if I tell you heavenly things? No one has ascended into heaven, but He who descended from heaven: the Son of Man. As Moses lifted up the serpent in the wilderness, even so must the Son of Man be lifted up; so that whoever believes will in Him have eternal life" (John 3:10–15; see Numbers 21:9; Proverb 30:4; John 12:34; 20:30, 31).

Setting: Jerusalem. Before the Passover, with His death on the cross nearing, Jesus explains the reason for His vivid example of servanthood in washing His disciples' feet.

So when He had washed their feet, and taken His garments and reclined *at the table* again, He said to them, "Do you know what I have done to you? You call Me Teacher and Lord; and you are right, for *so* I am. If I then, the Lord and the Teacher, washed your feet, you also ought to wash one another's feet. For I gave you an example that you also should do as I did to you. Truly, truly I say to you, a slave is not greater than his master, nor *is* one who is sent greater than the one who sent him. If you know these things, you are blessed if you do them. I do not speak of all of you. I know the ones I have chosen; but *it is* that the Scripture may be fulfilled, 'HE WHO EATS MY BREAD HAS LIFTED UP HIS HEEL AGAINST ME.' From now on I am telling you before *it* comes to pass, so that when it does occur, you may believe that I am *He*. Truly, truly, I say to you, he who receives whomever I send receives Me; and he who receives Me receives Him who sent Me" (John 13:12–20; Jesus quotes from Psalm 41:9; see Matthew 7:24; 10:24, 40; John 8:24; 14:29; 1 Peter 5:3).

TEACHER OF ISRAEL (Listed under ISRAEL, TEACHER OF)

TEACHERS (Also see TEACHER)

[TEACHERS from teaches others and teaches *them*]

Setting: Galilee. During the early part of His ministry, Jesus preaches the Sermon on the Mount to His disciples and the multitudes.

“Whoever then annuls one of the least of these commandments, and teaches others *to do* the same, shall be called least in the kingdom of heaven; but whoever keeps and teaches *them*, he shall be called great in the kingdom of heaven” (Matthew 5:19; cf. Matthew 11:11).

TEACHERS, FALSE (Also see APOSTLES, FALSE; CHRISTS, FALSE; DECEPTION; and PROPHETS, FALSE)

[FALSE TEACHERS from Lord, Lord, did we not prophesy in Your name, and in Your name cast out demons, and in Your name perform many miracles?' And then I will declare to them, 'I never knew you]

Setting: Galilee. During the early part of His ministry, Jesus preaches the Sermon on the Mount to His disciples and the multitudes.

“Not everyone who says to Me, ‘Lord, Lord,’ will enter the kingdom of heaven, but he who does the will of My Father who is in heaven *will enter.* Many will say to Me on that day, ‘Lord, Lord, did we not prophesy in Your name, and in Your name cast out demons, and in Your name perform many miracles?’ And then I will declare to them, ‘I never knew you, DEPART FROM ME, YOU WHO PRACTICE LAWLESSNESS’” (Matthew 7:21–23, Jesus quotes from Psalm 6:8; cf. Matthew 25:11–13; see Luke 6:46).

TEACHING (Also see DOCTRINE; LEAVEN; PREACHING; TEACHER; and TEACHERS)

[TEACHING from teaches]

Setting: Galilee. During the early part of His ministry, Jesus preaches the Sermon on the Mount to His disciples and the multitudes.

“Whoever then annuls one of the least of these commandments, and teaches others *to do* the same, shall be called least in the kingdom of heaven; but whoever keeps and teaches *them*, he shall be called great in the kingdom of heaven” (Matthew 5:19; cf. Matthew 11:11).

Setting: Galilee. Pharisees and scribes from Jerusalem accuse Jesus’ disciples of disobeying tradition and the commandments.

And He answered and said to them, “Why do you yourselves transgress the commandment of God for the sake of tradition? For God said, ‘HONOR YOUR FATHER AND MOTHER,’ and, ‘HE WHO SPEAKS EVIL OF FATHER OR MOTHER IS TO BE PUT TO DEATH.’ But you say, ‘Whoever says to *his* father or mother, “Whatever I have that would help you has been given *to God*,” he is not to honor his father or mother.’ And *by this* you invalidated the word of God for the sake of your tradition. You hypocrites, rightly did Isaiah prophesy of you: ‘THIS PEOPLE HONORS ME WITH THEIR LIPS, BUT THEIR HEART IS FAR AWAY FROM ME. BUT IN VAIN DO THEY WORSHIP ME, TEACHING AS DOCTRINES THE PRECEPTS OF MEN’” (Matthew 15:3–9, Jesus quotes from Exodus 20:12, 21:17, Leviticus 20:9; Isaiah 29:13; cf. Mark 7:5–7; see Colossians 2:22).

Setting: Gethsemane on the Mount of Olives, east of the temple in Jerusalem. As He submits to His Father’s will and allows Judas to betray Him, Jesus reveals that this is a fulfillment of prophecy.

At that time Jesus said to the crowds, “Have you come out with swords and clubs to arrest Me as *you would* against a robber? Every day I used to sit in the temple teaching and you did not seize Me. But all this has taken place to fulfill the Scriptures of the prophets” (Matthew 26:55, 56; cf. Mark 14:48, 49; Luke 22:52, 53).

Setting: On a mountain in Galilee. Following His resurrection from the dead in Jerusalem, Jesus conveys the Great Commission to His remaining eleven disciples.

And Jesus came up and spoke to them, saying, “All authority has been given to Me in heaven and on earth. Go therefore and make disciples of all the nations, baptizing them in the name of the Father and the Son and the Holy Spirit, teaching them to observe all that I commanded you; and lo, I am with you always, even to the end of the age” (Matthew 28:18–20; cf. Mark 16:15; see Daniel 7:13).

Setting: Galilee. The Pharisees and some of the scribes from Jerusalem question why Jesus' disciples do not follow the tradition of ceremonial hand cleansing before eating bread.

And He said to them, "Rightly did Isaiah prophesy of you hypocrites, as it is written: 'THIS PEOPLE HONORS ME WITH THEIR LIPS, BUT THEIR HEART IS FAR AWAY FROM ME. BUT IN VAIN DO THEY WORSHIP ME, TEACHING AS DOCTRINES THE PRECEPTS OF MEN.' Neglecting the commandment of God, you hold to the tradition of men." He was also saying to them, "You are experts at setting aside the commandment of God in order to keep tradition. For Moses said, 'HONOR YOUR FATHER AND YOUR MOTHER'; and, 'HE WHO SPEAKS EVIL OF FATHER OR MOTHER, IS TO BE PUT TO DEATH'; but you say, 'If a man says to *his* father or *his* mother, whatever I have that would help you is Corban (that is to say, given *to God*),' you no longer permit him to do anything for *his* father or *his* mother; *thus* invalidating the word of God by your tradition which you have handed down; and you do many things such as that" (Mark 7:6–13, Jesus quotes from Exodus 20:12; 21:17; Isaiah 29:13; cf. Matthew 15:1–6).

Setting: Gethsemane on the Mount of Olives, east of the temple in Jerusalem. Judas betrays Jesus with a kiss in front of a crowd from the chief priests, scribes, and elders seeking to seize the Lord with swords and clubs.

And Jesus said to them, "Have you come out with swords and clubs to arrest Me, as *you would* against a robber? Every day I was with you in the temple teaching, and you did not seize Me; but *this has taken place* to fulfill the Scriptures" (Mark 14:48, 49; cf. Matthew 26:55, 56; Luke 22:52, 53).

[TEACHING from teach]

Setting: On the way from Galilee to Jerusalem. Jesus warns His disciples of future events, as the scribes and Pharisees turn hostile and question Him repeatedly in an attempt to catch Him in something He might say.

"And I say to you, everyone who confesses Me before men, the Son of Man will confess him also before the angels of God; but he who denies Me before men will be denied before the angels of God. And everyone who speaks a word against the Son of Man, it will be forgiven him; but he who blasphemes against the Holy Spirit, it will not be forgiven him. When they bring you before the synagogues and the rulers and the authorities, do not worry about how or what you are to speak in your defense, or what you are to say; for the Holy Spirit will teach you in that very hour what you ought to say" (Luke 12:8–12; cf. Matthew 10:32, 33; 12:31, 32; see Matthew 10:20).

Setting: The temple in Jerusalem. After receiving encouragement from His blood brothers in Galilee to attend the upcoming Feast of Booths in order to demonstrate His works to His disciples and the world, Jesus goes and teaches, astonishing the Jewish religious leaders.

So Jesus answered them and said, "My teaching is not Mine, but His who sent Me. If anyone is willing to do His will, he will know of the teaching, whether it is of God or *whether* I speak of Myself. He who speaks from himself seeks his own glory; but He who is seeking the glory of the One who sent Him, He is true, and there is no unrighteousness in Him" (John 7:16–18; see John 5:41).

[TEACHING from teach]

Setting: Jerusalem. Before the Passover, after responding to Philip's request for Him to show His disciples the Father, Jesus conveys the upcoming ministry of the Holy Spirit in their lives.

These things I have spoken to you while abiding with you. But the Helper, the Holy Spirit, whom the Father will send in My name, He will teach you all things, and bring to your remembrance all that I said to you" (John 14:25, 26; see John 16:13).

Setting: On the island of Patmos (in the Aegean Sea about fifty miles southwest of Ephesus in modern Turkey). On the Lord's Day (Sunday), approximately fifty years after the Resurrection, the disciple John encounters the Lord Jesus Christ, who communicates a new revelation for the apostle to record for the church in Pergamum and to six other churches in Asia.

"And to the angel of the church in Pergamum write: The One who has the sharp two-edged sword says this: 'I know where you dwell, where Satan's throne is; and you hold fast My name, and did not deny My faith even in the days of Antipas, My witness, My faithful one, who was killed among you, where Satan dwells. But I have a few things against you, because you have there some who hold the teaching of Balaam, who kept teaching Balak to put a stumbling block before the sons of Israel, to eat things sacrificed to idols and to commit *acts of* immorality. So you also have some who in the same way hold the teaching of the Nicolaitans. Therefore repent; or else I am coming to you quickly, and I will make war against them with the sword of My mouth. He who has an ear, let him hear what the Spirit says to the churches. To him who overcomes, to him I will give *some* of the hidden manna, and I will give him a white stone, and a new name written on the stone which no one knows but he who receives it' (Revelation 2:12–17; see Numbers 25:1–3; Isaiah 62:2; Revelation 1:16; 2:5, 6, 16).

Setting: On the island of Patmos (in the Aegean Sea about fifty miles southwest of Ephesus in modern Turkey). On the Lord's Day (Sunday), approximately fifty years after the Resurrection, the disciple John encounters the Lord Jesus Christ, who communicates a new revelation for the apostle to record for the church in Thyatira and to six other churches in Asia.

"And to the angel of the church in Thyatira write: The Son of God, who has eyes like a flame of fire, and His feet are like burnished bronze, says this: 'I know your deeds, and your love and faith and service and perseverance, and that your deeds of late are greater than at first. But I have *this* against you, that you tolerate the woman Jezebel, who calls herself a prophetess, and she teaches and leads My bond-servants astray so that they commit *acts of* immorality and eat things sacrificed to idols. I gave her time to repent, and she does not want to repent of her immorality. Behold, I will throw her on a bed *of sickness,* and those who commit adultery with her into great tribulation, unless they repent of her deeds. And I will kill her children with pestilence, and all the churches will know that I am He who searches the minds and hearts; and I will give to each one of you according to your deeds. But I say to you, the rest who are in Thyatira, who do not hold this teaching, who have not known the deep things of Satan, as they call them—I place no other burden on you. Nevertheless what you have, hold fast until I come. He who overcomes, and he who keeps My deeds until the end, TO HIM I WILL GIVE AUTHORITY OVER THE NATIONS; AND HE SHALL RULE THEM WITH A ROD OF IRON, AS THE VESSELS OF THE POTTER ARE BROKEN TO PIECES, as I also have received *authority* from My Father; and I will give him the morning star. He who has an ear, let him hear what the Spirit says to the churches' (Revelation 2:18–29; Jesus quotes from Psalm 2:8, 9; Isaiah 30:14; see 1 Kings 16:31; Psalm 7:9; Romans 2:5; 1 Corinthians 2:10; 2 Peter 3:9; Revelation 1:14; 2:7; 3:11; 17:1–20).

TEACHING, FALSE (See APOSTLES, FALSE; CHRISTS, FALSE; PROPHETS, FALSE; and TEACHERS, FALSE)

TEACHING, JESUS' (See JESUS' TEACHING)

TEACHING, LEGALISTIC (See, PHARISEES, LEAVEN OF THE)

TEACHING, UNGODLY (See PHARISEES, LEAVEN OF THE)

TEACHINGS (See DOCTRINE; TEACHER; TEACHERS; and TEACHING)

TEAR (hole)

Setting: Capernaum, near the Sea of Galilee. John the Baptist's disciples ask Jesus why His disciples do not participate in fasting, even though they and the Pharisees do.

And Jesus said to them, "The attendants of the bridegroom cannot mourn as long as the bridegroom is with them, can they? But the days will come when the bridegroom is taken away from them, and then they will fast. But no one puts a patch of unshrunk cloth on an old garment; for the patch pulls away from the garment, and a worse tear results. Nor do *people* put new wine into old wineskins; otherwise the wineskins burst, and the wine pours out and the wineskins are ruined; but they put new wine into fresh wineskins, and both are preserved" (Matthew 9:15–17; cf. Mark 2:18–22; Luke 5:33–39).

Setting: Capernaum. John the Baptist's disciples and the Pharisees question why Jesus' disciples do not fast when they do.

And Jesus said to them, "While the bridegroom is with them, the attendants of the bridegroom cannot fast, can they? So long as they have the bridegroom with them, they cannot fast. But the days will come when the bridegroom is taken away from them, and then they will fast in that day. No one sews a patch of unshrunk cloth on an old garment; otherwise the patch pulls away from it, the new from the old, and a worse tear results. No one puts new wine into old wineskins; otherwise the wine will burst the skins, and the wine is lost and the skins as *well;* but *one puts* new wine into fresh wineskins" (Mark 2:19–22; cf. Matthew 9:14–17; Luke 5:33–38).

TEARS (Also see GRIEF; MOURNERS; MOURNING; SADNESS; and WEEPING)

Setting: Galilee. After Jesus praises John the Baptist to the crowds, Simon, a Pharisee, invites the Lord to dinner. A sinful woman anoints His feet with perfume, prompting Him to instruct His host about forgiveness.

Turning toward the woman, He said to Simon, "Do you see this woman? I entered your house; you gave Me no water for My feet, but she has wet My feet with her tears and wiped them with her hair. You gave Me no kiss; but she, since the time I came in, has not ceased to kiss My feet. You did not anoint My head with oil, but she anointed My feet with perfume. For this reason I say to you, her sins, which are many, have been forgiven, for she loved much; but he who is forgiven little, loves little." Then He said to her, "Your sins have been forgiven." Those who were reclining *at the table* with Him began to say to themselves, "Who is this *man* who even forgives sins?" And He said to the woman, "Your faith has saved you; go in peace" (Luke 7:44–50; see Matthew 9:2; Mark 5:34; Luke 5:21).

TEETH (See TEETH, WEEPING AND GNASHING OF; and TOOTH)

TEETH, WEEPING AND GNASHING OF

Setting: Entering Capernaum. After the Lord gives the Sermon on the Mount and cleanses a leper, a Roman centurion implores Jesus to heal his servant.

Now when Jesus heard *this,* He marveled, and said to those who were following, "Truly I say to you, I have not found such great faith with anyone in Israel. I say to you that many will come from east and west, and recline *at the table* with Abraham, Isaac and Jacob in the kingdom of heaven; but the sons of the kingdom will be cast out into the outer darkness; in that place there will be weeping and gnashing of teeth." And Jesus said to the centurion, "Go; it shall be done for you as you have believed." And the servant was healed that *very* moment (Matthew 8:10–13; cf. Luke 7:9, 10).

Setting: A house near the Sea of Galilee. Jesus gives His disciples the meaning of the Parable of the Wheat and the Tares.

And He said, "The one who sows the good seed is the Son of Man, and the field is the world; and as *for* the good seed, these are the sons of the kingdom; and the tares are the sons of the evil *one;* and the enemy who sowed them is the devil, and the harvest is the end of the age; and the reapers are angels. So just as the tares are gathered up and burned with fire, so shall it be at the end of the age. The Son of Man will send forth His angels, and they will gather out of His kingdom all stumbling blocks, and those who commit lawlessness, and will throw them into the furnace of fire; in that place there will be weeping and gnashing of teeth. Then THE RIGHTEOUS WILL SHINE FORTH AS THE SUN in the kingdom of their Father. He who has ears, let him hear" (Matthew 13:37–43, Jesus quotes from Daniel 12:3; cf. Matthew 8:12; 13:50).

Setting: By the Sea of Galilee. Because the religious leaders are rejecting His message, Jesus continues teaching His disciples with the Parable of the Dragnet.

"Again, the kingdom of heaven is like a dragnet cast into the sea, and gathering *fish* of every kind; and when it was filled, they drew it up on the beach; and they sat down and gathered the good *fish* into containers, but the bad they threw away. So it will be at the end of the age; the angels will come forth and take out the wicked from among the righteous, and will throw them into the furnace of fire; in that place there will be weeping and gnashing of teeth. Have you understood all these things?" They said to Him, "Yes" (Matthew 13:47–51).

Setting: The temple in Jerusalem. Jesus speaks another parable to the chief priests and elders after they question His authority.

Jesus spoke to them again in parables, saying, "The kingdom of heaven may be compared to a king who gave a wedding feast for his son. And he sent out his slaves to call those who had been invited to the wedding feast, and they were unwilling to come. Again he sent out other slaves saying, 'Tell those who have been invited, "Behold, I have prepared my dinner; my oxen and my fattened livestock are *all* butchered and everything is ready; come to the wedding feast." But they paid no attention and went their way, one to his own farm, another to his business, and the rest seized his slaves and mistreated them and killed them. But the king was enraged, and he sent his armies and destroyed those murderers and set their city on fire. Then he said to his slaves, 'The wedding is ready, but those who were invited were not worthy. 'Go therefore to the main highways, and as many as you find *there,* invite to the wedding feast.' Those slaves went out into the streets and gathered together all they found, both evil and good; and the wedding hall was filled with dinner guests. But when the king came in to look over the dinner guests, he saw a man there who was not dressed in wedding clothes, and he said to him, 'Friend, how did you come in here without wedding clothes?' And the man was speechless. Then the king said to the servants, 'Bind him hand and foot, and throw him into the outer darkness; in that place there will be weeping and gnashing of teeth.' For many are called, but few *are* chosen" (Matthew 22:1–14; cf. Matthew 8:11, 12).

Setting: On the Mount of Olives, just east of Jerusalem. During His Olivet Discourse, after answering His disciples' questions as to when the temple will be destroyed and Jerusalem overrun, along with the signs of His coming and the end of the age, Jesus reemphasizes to His disciples that they should be on the alert for His return.

"Therefore be on the alert, for you do not know which day your Lord is coming. But be sure of this, that if the head of the house had known at what time of the night the thief was coming, he would have been on the alert and would not have allowed his house to be broken into. For this reason you also must be ready; for the Son of Man is coming at an hour when you do not think *He will.* Who then is the faithful and sensible slave whom his master put in charge of his household to give their food at the proper time? Blessed is that slave whom his master finds so doing when he comes. Truly I say to you that he will put him in charge of all his possessions. But if that evil slave says in his heart, 'My master is not coming for a long time,' and begins to beat his fellow slaves and eat and drink with drunkards; the master of that slave will come on a day when he does not expect *him* and at an hour which he does not know, and will cut him in pieces and assign him a place with the hypocrites; in that place there will be weeping and gnashing of teeth" (Matthew 24:42–51; cf. Mark 13:33–37; Luke 12:39–46; 21:34–36; see Matthew 8:11, 12; 25:21–23).

Setting: On the Mount of Olives, just east of Jerusalem. During His Olivet Discourse, after answering His disciples' questions as to when the temple will be destroyed and Jerusalem overrun, along with the signs of His coming and the end of the age, Jesus reemphasizes to His disciples that they should be on the alert for His return.

"For *it is* just like a man *about* to go on a journey, who called his own slaves and entrusted his possessions to them. To one he gave five talents, to another, two, and to another, one, each according to his own ability; and he went on his journey. Immediately the one who had received the five talents went and traded with them, and gained five more talents. In the same manner the one who *had received* the two *talents* gained two more. But he who received the one *talent* went away, and dug a *hole* in the ground and hid his master's money. Now after a long time the master of those slaves came and settled accounts with them. The one who had received the five talents came up and brought five more talents, saying, 'Master, you entrusted five talents to me. See, I have gained five more talents.' His master said to him, 'Well done, good and faithful slave. You were faithful with a few things, I will put you in charge of many things; enter into the joy of your master.' Also the one who *had received* the two talents came up and said, 'Master, you entrusted two talents to me. See, I have gained two more talents.' His master said to him, 'Well done, good and faithful slave. You were faithful with a few things, I will put you in charge of many things; enter into the joy of your master.' And the one also who had received the one talent came up and said, 'Master, I knew you to be a hard man, reaping where you did not sow and gathering where you scattered no *seed.* And I was afraid, and went away and hid your talent in the ground. See, you have what is yours.' But his master answered and said to him, 'You wicked, lazy slave, you knew that I reap where I did not sow and gather where I scattered no *seed.* Then you ought to have put my money in the bank, and on my arrival I would have received my *money* back with interest. 'Therefore take away the talent from him, and give it to the one who has ten talents.' For to everyone who has, *more* shall be given, and he will have an abundance; but from the one who does not have, even what he does have shall be taken away. Throw out the worthless slave into the outer darkness; in that place there will be weeping and gnashing of teeth" (Matthew 25:14–30; cf. Matthew 8:12; 13:12; 24:45–47; see Matthew 18:23, 24; Luke 12:44).

Setting: On the way from Galilee to Jerusalem. While teaching in the cities and villages, Jesus responds to a question about who is saved.

And someone said to Him, "Lord, are there *just* a few who are being saved?" And He said to them, "Strive to enter through the narrow door; for many, I tell you, will seek to enter and will not be able. Once the head of the house gets up and shuts the door, and you begin to stand outside and knock on the door, saying, 'Lord, open up to us!' then He will answer and say to you, 'I do not know where you are from.' Then you will begin to say, 'We ate and drank in Your presence, and You taught in our streets'; and He will say, 'I tell you, I do not know where you are from; DEPART FROM ME, ALL YOU EVILDOERS.' In that place there will be weeping and gnashing of teeth when you see Abraham and Isaac and Jacob and all the prophets in the kingdom of God, but you yourselves being thrown out. And they will come from east and west and from north and south, and will recline *at the table* in the kingdom of God. And behold, *some* are last who will be first and *some* are first who will be last" (Luke 13:23–30, Jesus quotes from Psalm 6:8; cf. Matthew 7:13, 23; 8:11, 12; see Matthew 19:30; Luke 3:8).

TEMPLE (Also see HOUSE OF GOD; and TEMPLE (Jesus' body))

Setting: Galilee. Jesus responds to the Pharisees' objection to His disciples' picking grain from the fields on the Sabbath.

But He said to them, "Have you not read what David did when he became hungry, he and his companions, how they entered the house of God, and ate the consecrated bread, which was not lawful for him to eat nor for those with him, but for the priests alone? Or, have you not read in the Law, that on the Sabbath the priests in the temple break the Sabbath and are innocent? But I say to you that something greater than the temple is here. But if you had known what this means, 'I DESIRE COMPASSION, AND NOT A SACRIFICE,' you would not have condemned the innocent. For the Son of Man is Lord of the Sabbath" (Matthew 12:3–8, Jesus quotes from Hosea 6:6; cf. Mark 2:25–28; Luke 6:3–5; see 1 Samuel 21:6).

[TEMPLE from MY HOUSE]

Setting: Jerusalem. After being welcomed with blessings from the crowds, Jesus cleanses the temple by driving out the money changers and merchants.

And He said to them, "It is written, 'MY HOUSE SHALL BE CALLED A HOUSE OF PRAYER'; but you are making it a ROBBERS' DEN" (Matthew 21:13; Jesus quotes from Isaiah 56:7; Jeremiah 7:11; cf. Mark 11:15–18; Luke 19:46).

Setting: The temple in Jerusalem. After the Jewish religious leaders test Him with questions, Jesus pronounces the fourth of eight woes upon them in front of the crowds and His disciples.

"Woe to you, blind guides, who say, "Whoever swears by the temple, *that* is nothing; but whoever swears by the gold of the temple is obligated.' You fools and blind men! Which is more important, the gold or the temple that sanctified the gold? And, 'Whoever swears by the altar, *that* is nothing, but whoever swears by the offering on it, he is obligated.' You blind men, which is more important, the offering, or the altar that sanctifies the offering? Therefore, whoever swears by the altar, swears *both* by the altar and by everything on it. And whoever swears by the temple, swears *both* by the temple and by Him who dwells within it. And whoever swears by heaven, swears *both* by the throne of God and by Him who sits upon it" (Matthew 23:16–22; see Exodus 29:37; 1 Kings 8:13; Isaiah 66:1; Matthew 15:14).

Setting: The temple in Jerusalem. After the Jewish religious leaders test Him with questions, Jesus pronounces the eighth of eight woes upon them in front of the crowds and His disciples.

"Woe to you, scribes and Pharisees, hypocrites! For you build the tombs of the prophets and adorn the monuments of the righteous, and say, 'If we had been *living* in the days of our fathers, we would not have been partners with them in *shedding* the blood of the prophets.' So you testify against yourselves, that you are sons of those who murdered the prophets. Fill up, then, the measure *of the guilt* of you fathers. You serpents, you brood of vipers, how will you escape the sentence of hell? Therefore, behold, I am sending you prophets and wise men and scribes; some of them you will kill and crucify, and some of them you will scourge in your synagogues, and persecute from city to city, so that upon you may fall *the guilt of* all the righteous blood shed on earth, from the blood of righteous Abel to the blood of Zechariah, the son of Berechiah, whom you murdered between the temple and the altar. Truly I say to you, all these things will come upon this generation" (Matthew 23:29–36; cf. 2 Chronicles 24:21; Zechariah 1:1; Matthew 3:7; Luke 11:47–52; see Matthew 10:23).

[TEMPLE also from all these things]
Setting: Jerusalem. Just days before His crucifixion, after teaching, interacting with the religious leaders, and pronouncing woes on these same leaders, Jesus leaves the temple and prophesies its destruction to His disciples, .

Jesus came out from the temple, and was going away when His disciples came up to point out the temple buildings to Him. And He said to them, "Do you not see all these things? Truly I say to you, not one stone here will be left upon another, which will not be torn down" (Matthew 24:1, 2; cf. Mark 13:1, 2; Luke 21:5, 6; see Luke 19:43, 44).

[TEMPLE from holy place]
Setting: The Mount of Olives, just east of Jerusalem. During His Olivet Discourse, Jesus answers His disciples' questions as to when the temple will be destroyed and Jerusalem overrun, along with the signs of His coming and the end of the age.

"Therefore when you see the ABOMINATION OF DESOLATION which was spoken of through Daniel the prophet, standing in the holy place (let the reader understand), then those who are in Judea must flee to the mountains. Whoever is on the housetop must not go down to get the things that are in his house. Whoever is in the field must not turn back to get his cloak. But woe to those who are pregnant and to those who are nursing babies in those days! But pray that your flight will not be in the winter, or on a Sabbath. For then there will be a great tribulation, such as has not occurred since the beginning of the world until now, nor ever will. Unless those days had been cut short, no life would have been saved; but for the sake of the elect those days will be cut short. Then if anyone says to you, 'Behold, here is the Christ,' or "There *He is,*' do not believe *him.* For false Christs and false prophets will arise and will show great signs and wonders, so as to mislead, if possible, even the elect. Behold, I have told you in advance. So if they say to you, 'Behold, He is in the wilderness,' do not go out, *or,* 'Behold, He is in the inner rooms,' do not believe *them.* For just as the lightning comes from the east and flashes even to the west, so will the coming of the Son of Man be. Wherever the corpse is, there the vultures will gather" (Matthew 24:15–28, Jesus quotes from Daniel 9:27; cf. Daniel 12:1; Mark 13:14–23; Luke 17:22–31; 21:20–24; 23:29; see John 4:48).

Setting: Gethsemane on the Mount of Olives, east of the temple in Jerusalem. As He submits to His Father's will and allows Judas to betray Him, Jesus reveals that this is a fulfillment of prophecy.

At that time Jesus said to the crowds, "Have you come out with swords and clubs to arrest Me as *you would* against a robber? Every day I used to sit in the temple teaching and you did not seize Me. But all this has taken place to fulfill the Scriptures of the prophets" (Matthew 26:55, 56; cf. Mark 14:48, 49; Luke 22:52, 53).

[TEMPLE from house of God]
Setting: Galilee. Early in His ministry, the Pharisees question why Jesus allows His disciples to harvest grain on the Sabbath.

And He said to them, "Have you never read what David did when he was in need and he and his companions became hungry; how he entered the house of God in the time of Abiathar *the* high priest, and ate the consecrated bread, which is not lawful for *anyone* to eat except the priests, and he also gave it to those who were with him?" Jesus said to them, "The Sabbath was made for man, and not man for the Sabbath. So the Son of Man is Lord even of the Sabbath" (Mark 2:25–28; cf. Matthew 12:1–8; Luke 6:1–5; see Exodus 23:12).

[TEMPLE from MY HOUSE]
Setting: Jerusalem. Following His triumphal entry, cursing of a fig tree, and cleansing of the temple of the money changers, Jesus rebukes the Jewish religious leaders for the corrupt practices they permit in His house.

And He *began* to teach and say to them, "Is it not written, 'MY HOUSE SHALL BE CALLED A HOUSE OF PRAYER FOR ALL THE NATIONS'? But you have made it a ROBBERS' DEN" (Mark 11:17, Jesus quotes from Isaiah 56:7; Jeremiah 7:11; cf. Matthew 21:12, 13; Luke 19:45–48).

[TEMPLE from great buildings]
Setting: Jerusalem. Following a teaching moment with His disciples regarding a poor widow's offering to the treasury, Jesus prophesies the destruction of the temple.

And Jesus said to him, "Do you see these great buildings? Not one stone will be left upon another which will not be torn down" (Mark 13:2; cf. Matthew 24:1, 2; Luke 21:5, 6; Luke 19:44).

Setting: Gethsemane on the Mount of Olives, east of the temple in Jerusalem. Judas betrays Jesus with a kiss in front of a crowd from the chief priests, scribes, and elders seeking to seize the Lord with swords and clubs.

And Jesus said to them, "Have you come out with swords and clubs to arrest Me, as *you would* against a robber? Every day I was with you in the temple teaching, and you did not seize Me; but *this has taken place* to fulfill the Scriptures" (Mark 14:48, 49; cf. Matthew 26:55, 56; Luke 22:52, 53).

[TEMPLE from Father's *house*]
Setting: Jerusalem. After attending His first Passover, twelve-year-old Jesus remains at the temple interacting with the teachers. His parents return to the city after looking for Him unsuccessfully in their caravan heading back to Nazareth.

And He said to them, "Why is it that you were looking for Me? Did you not know that I had to be in My Father's *house*?" (Luke 2:49).

[TEMPLE from house of God]
Setting: Probably Galilee. As Jesus and His disciples pass through some grain fields, some of the Pharisees ask the Lord why His followers harvest grain on the Sabbath.

And Jesus answering them said, "Have you not even read what David did when he was hungry, he and those who were with him, how he entered the house of God, and took and ate the consecrated bread which is not lawful for any to eat except the priests alone, and gave it to his companions?" And He was saying to them, "The Son of Man is Lord of the Sabbath" (Luke 6:3–5; cf. Matthew 12:1–8; Mark 2:23–28; see Exodus 20:8; Leviticus 24:1–9; Deuteronomy 5:12; 1 Samuel 21:1–6).

[TEMPLE from house *of God*]
Setting: On the way from Galilee to Jerusalem. After Jesus pronounces woes upon the Pharisees, a lawyer replies that His remarks are an insult to lawyers, too.

But He said, "Woe to you lawyers as well! For you weigh men down with burdens hard to bear, while you yourselves will not even touch the burdens with one of your fingers. Woe to you! For you build the tombs of the prophets, and *it was* your fathers *who* killed them. So you are witnesses and approve the deeds of your fathers; because it was they who killed them, and you build *their tombs*. For this reason also the wisdom of God said, 'I will send them prophets and apostles, and *some* of them they will kill and *some* they will persecute, so that the blood of all the prophets, shed since the foundation of the world, may be charged against this generation, from the blood of Abel to the blood of Zechariah, who was killed between the altar and the house *of God*; yes, I tell you, it shall be charged against this generation.' Woe to you lawyers! For you have taken away the key of knowledge; you yourselves did not enter, and you hindered those who were entering" (Luke 11:46–52; cf. Matthew 23:29–32; see 2 Chronicles 24:20, 21; Matthew 23:4, 13).

Setting: On the way from Galilee to Jerusalem. After instructing His disciples about persistence in prayer, Jesus conveys a parable about self-righteousness.

And He also told this parable to some people who trusted in themselves that they were righteous, and viewed others with contempt: "Two men went up into the temple to pray, one a Pharisee and the other a tax collector. The Pharisee stood and was praying this to himself: 'God, I thank You that I am not like other people: swindlers, unjust, adulterers, or even like this tax collector. I fast twice a week; I pay tithes of all that I get.' But the tax collector, standing some distance away, was even unwilling to lift up his eyes to heaven, but was beating his breast, saying, 'God, be merciful to me, the sinner!' I tell you, this man went to his house justified rather than the other; for everyone who exalts himself will be humbled, but he who humbles himself will be exalted" (Luke 18:9–14; see Ezra 9:6; Matthew 6:5, 23:12; Luke 11:42, 16:15; Romans 14:3, 10).

[TEMPLE from MY HOUSE]
Setting: Jerusalem. After weeping as He sees the city ahead of Him, the Lord enters the temple and drives out the money changers and merchants.

Jesus entered the temple and began to drive out those who were selling, saying to them, "It is written, 'AND MY HOUSE SHALL BE A HOUSE OF PRAYER,' but you have made it a ROBBERS' DEN" (Luke 19:45, 46, Jesus quotes from Isaiah 56:7; Jeremiah 7:11; cf. Matthew 21:12, 13; Mark 11:15–17; see John 2:13–17).

[TEMPLE from one stone upon another]
Setting: The temple in Jerusalem. While ministering a few days before His crucifixion, after pointing out a poor widow's sacrificial giving to the temple treasury, Jesus prophesies the destruction of the temple.

"*As for* these things which you are looking at, the days will come in which there will not be left one stone upon another which will not be torn down" (Luke 21:6; cf. Matthew 24:1, 2; Mark 13:1, 2).

Setting: Gethsemane on the Mount of Olives, east of the temple in Jerusalem. After praying for deliverance, with His crucifixion imminent, Jesus chastises the religious leaders after Judas betrays Him and the hostile crowd surrounds Him.

Then Jesus said to the chief priests and officers of the temple and elders who had come against Him, "Have you come out with swords and clubs as you would against a robber? While I was with you daily in the temple, you did not lay hands on Me; but this hour and the power of darkness are yours" (Luke 22:52, 53; cf. Matthew 26:47–56; Mark 14:43–50).

[TEMPLE from My Father's house]
Setting: Jerusalem. After beginning His ministry in Galilee by selecting His disciples and performing a miracle at a wedding in Cana, Jesus attends the Passover of the Jews and confronts those perverting the temple for business.

And He made a scourge of cords, and drove *them* all out of the temple, with the sheep and the oxen; and He poured out the coins of the money changers and overturned their tables; and to those who were selling the doves He said, "Take these things away; stop making My Father's house a place of business" (John 2:15, 16; cf. Matthew 21:12, 13; see Deuteronomy 16:1 6).

Setting: Jerusalem. After Jesus is betrayed by Judas, and Peter denies he is the Lord's disciple, Annas, former high priest and father-in-law of the current high priest (Caiaphas), questions Jesus about His disciples and His teaching.

Jesus answered him, "I have spoken openly to the world; I always taught in synagogues and in the temple, where all the Jews come together; and I spoke nothing in secret. Why do you question Me? Question those who have heard what I spoke to them; they know what I said" (John 18:20, 21; see John 7:26).

Setting: On the island of Patmos (in the Aegean Sea about fifty miles southwest of Ephesus in modern Turkey). On the Lord's Day (Sunday), approximately fifty years after the Resurrection, the disciple John encounters the Lord

Jesus Christ, who communicates a new revelation for the apostle to record for the church in Philadelphia and to six other churches in Asia.

"And to the angel of the church in Philadelphia write: He who is holy, who is true, who has the key of David, who opens and no one will shut, and who shuts and no one opens, says this: 'I know your deeds. Behold, I have put before you an open door which no one can shut, because you have a little power, and have kept My word, and have not denied My name. Behold, I will cause *those* of the synagogue of Satan, who say that they are Jews and are not, but lie—I will make them come and bow down at your feet, and *make them* know that I have loved you. Because you have kept the word of My perseverance, I also will keep you from the hour of testing, that *hour* which is about to come upon the whole world, to test those who dwell on the earth. I am coming quickly; hold fast what you have, so that no one will take your crown. He who overcomes, I will make him a pillar in the temple of My God, and he will not go out from it anymore; and I will write on him the name of My God, and the name of the city of My God, the new Jerusalem, which comes down out of heaven from My God, and My new name. He who has an ear, let him hear what the Spirit says to the churches' " (Revelation 3:7–13; see Isaiah 22:22; Galatians 2:9; Revelation 2:9, 10, 13, 25; 14:1).

TEMPLE (Jesus' body)

[TEMPLE (as Jesus' body)]
Setting: Jerusalem. After Jesus cleanses the temple during the Passover of the Jews, the Jewish religious leaders question His authority to do these things.

Jesus answered them, "Destroy this temple, and in three days I will raise it up" (John 2:19; cf. Matthew 26:61).

TEMPLE, CLEANSING THE (Also see ROBBERS' DEN)

[CLEANSING THE TEMPLE from Take these things away]
Setting: Jerusalem. After beginning His ministry in Galilee by selecting His disciples and performing a miracle at a wedding in Cana, Jesus attends the Passover of the Jews, and confronts those perverting the temple for business.

And He made a scourge of cords, and drove *them* all out of the temple, with the sheep and the oxen; and He poured out the coins of the money changers and overturned their tables; and to those who were selling the doves He said, "Take these things away; stop making My Father's house a place of business" (John 2:15, 16; cf. Matthew 21:12, 13; see Deuteronomy 16:1–6).

TEMPLE, PROPHECY OF THE DESTRUCTION OF THE

[PROPHECY OF THE DESTRUCTION OF THE TEMPLE from your house is being left to you desolate]
Setting: The temple in Jerusalem. With His death on the cross just days away, Jesus laments over Jerusalem's hard-heartedness and lack of repentance.

"Jerusalem, Jerusalem, who kills the prophets and stones those who are sent to her! How often I wanted to gather your children together, the way a hen gathers her chicks under her wings, and you were unwilling. Behold, your house is being left to you desolate! For I say to you, from now on you will not see Me until you say, 'BLESSED IS HE WHO COMES IN THE NAME OF THE LORD!'" (Matthew 23:37–39, Jesus quotes from Psalm 118:26; cf. 1 Kings 9:7; Luke 13:34, 35).

[PROPHECY OF THE DESTRUCTION OF THE TEMPLE from not one stone here will be left upon another, which will not be torn down]
Setting: Jerusalem. Just days before His crucifixion, after teaching, interacting with the religious leaders, and pronouncing woes on these same leaders, Jesus leaves the temple and prophesies its destruction to His disciples.

Jesus came out from the temple, and was going away when His disciples came up to point out the temple buildings to Him. And He said to them, "Do you not see all these things? Truly I say to you, not one stone here will be left upon another, which will not be torn down" (Matthew 24:1, 2; cf. Mark 13:1, 2; Luke 21:5, 6; see Luke 19:43, 44).

[PROPHECY OF THE DESTRUCTION OF THE TEMPLE from Not one stone will be left upon another which will not be torn down]

Setting: Jerusalem. Following the teaching moment with His disciples regarding a poor widow's offering to the treasury, Jesus prophesies the destruction of the temple.

And Jesus said to him, "Do you see these great buildings? Not one stone will be left upon another which will not be torn down" (Mark 13:2; cf. Matthew 24:1, 2; Luke 21:5, 6; see Luke 19:44).

[PROPHECY OF THE DESTRUCTION OF THE TEMPLE from they will level you to the ground and your children within you, and they will not leave in you one stone upon another]
Setting: Approaching Jerusalem. After being praised by the people in a triumphal entry, the Lord weeps as He sees the city ahead of Him.

When He approached *Jerusalem,* He saw the city and wept over it, saying, "If you had known in this day, even you, the things which make for peace! But now they have been hidden from your eyes. For the days will come upon you when your enemies will throw up a barricade against you, and surround you and hem you in on every side, and they will level you to the ground and your children within you, and they will not leave in you one stone upon another, because you did not recognize the time of your visitation" (Luke 19:41–44; see Matthew 24:1, 2; Luke 13:34, 35).

[PROPHECY OF THE DESTRUCTION OF THE TEMPLE from there will not be left one stone upon another which will not be torn down]
Setting: Jerusalem. While ministering a few days before His crucifixion, after pointing out a poor widow's sacrificial giving to the temple treasury, Jesus prophesies the destruction of the temple.

"*As for* these things which you are looking at, the days will come in which there will not be left one stone upon another which will not be torn down" (Luke 21:6; cf. Matthew 24:1, 2; Mark 13:1, 2).

TEMPLE OF MY GOD (Listed under GOD, TEMPLE OF MY)

TEMPLE TAX (Listed under TAX, TEMPLE; also see TAXES)

TEMPORARY

Setting: By the Sea of Galilee. With the religious leaders rejecting His message, Jesus begins to teach in parables, and gives His disciples the meaning of the Parable of the Sower.

"Hear then the parable of the sower. When anyone hears the word of the kingdom and does not understand it, the evil *one* comes and snatches away what has been sown in his heart. This is the one on whom seed was sown beside the road. The one on whom seed was sown on the rocky places, this is the man who hears the word and immediately receives it with joy; yet he has no *firm* root in himself, but is *only* temporary, and when affliction or persecution arises because of the word, immediately he falls away. And the one on whom seed was sown among the thorns, this is the man who hears the word, and the worry of the world and the deceitfulness of wealth choke the word, and it becomes unfruitful. And the one on whom seed was sown on the good soil, this is the man who hears the word and understands it; who indeed bears fruit and brings forth, some a hundredfold, some sixty, and some thirty" (Matthew 13:18–23; cf. Mark 4:13–20; Luke 8:11–15).

Setting: By the Sea of Galilee. During the early part of His ministry, after presenting the Parable of the Sower from a boat to a very large crowd, Jesus gives the meaning of the parable to His disciples and other followers.

And He said to them, "Do you not understand this parable? How will you understand all the parables? The sower sows the word. These are the ones who are beside the road where the word is sown; and when they hear, immediately Satan comes and takes away the word which has been sown in them. In a similar way these are the ones on whom seed was sown on the rocky places, who, when they hear the word, immediately receive it with joy; and they have no *firm* root in themselves, but are *only* temporary; then, when affliction or persecution arises because of the word, immediately they fall away. And others are the ones on whom seed was sown among the thorns; these are the ones who have heard the word, but the worries of the world and the deceitfulness of riches, and the desires for other things enter in and choke the word, and it becomes unfruitful. And those are the ones on whom seed was sown on the good soil; and they hear the word and accept it and bear fruit, thirty, sixty, and a hundredfold" (Mark 4:13–20; cf. Matthew 13:18–23; Luke 8:11–15).

TEMPTATION (TEMPTATION OF JESUS is a separate entry; also see TEST; and TRIBULATION)

Setting: Galilee. During the early part of His ministry, Jesus gives a model prayer to His disciples and the multitudes while conveying the Sermon on the Mount.

"Pray, then, in this way: 'Our Father who is in heaven, hallowed be Your name. Your kingdom come. Your will be done, on earth as it is in heaven. Give us this day our daily bread. And forgive us our debts, as we also have forgiven our debtors. And do not lead us into temptation, but deliver us from evil. [For Yours is the kingdom and the power and the glory forever. Amen]'" (Matthew 6:9–13; cf. Luke 11:2–4; see John 17:15).

Setting: An upper room in Jerusalem. After celebrating the Passover meal with His disciples, Jesus retreats to the Garden of Gethsemane on the Mount of Olives to pray prior to His betrayal by Judas.

Then Jesus came with them to a place called Gethsemane, and said to His disciples, "Sit here while I go over there and pray." And He took with Him Peter and the two sons of Zebedee, and began to be grieved and distressed. Then He said to them, "My soul is deeply grieved, to the point of death; remain here and keep watch with Me." And He went a little beyond *them,* and fell on His face and prayed, saying, "My Father, if it is possible, let this cup pass from Me; yet not as I will, but as You will." And He came to the disciples and found them sleeping, and said to Peter, "So, you *men* could not keep watch with Me for one hour? Keep watching and praying that you may not enter into temptation; the spirit is willing, but the flesh is weak." He went away again a second time and prayed, saying, "My Father, if this cannot pass away unless I drink it, Your will be done." Again He came and found them sleeping, for their eyes were heavy. And He left them again, and went away and prayed a third time, saying the same thing once more. Then He came to the disciples and said to them, "Are you still sleeping and resting? Behold the hour is at hand and the Son of Man is being betrayed into the hands of sinners. Get up, let us be going; behold the one who betrays Me is at hand!" (Matthew 26:36–46; cf. Mark 14:32–42; Luke 22:40–46; see Matthew 20:22; John 12:27).

Setting: Gethsemane on the Mount of Olives, east of the temple in Jerusalem. Jesus agonizes over His impending death, disappointed His disciples keep falling asleep instead of watching and praying with Him.

They came to a place named Gethsemane; and He said to the disciples, "Sit here until I have prayed." And He took with Him Peter and James and John, and began to be very distressed and troubled. And He said to them, "My soul is deeply grieved to the point of death; remain here and keep watch." And He went a little beyond *them,* and fell to the ground and *began* to pray that if it were possible, the hour might pass Him by. And He was saying, "Abba! Father! All things are possible for You; remove this cup from Me; yet not what I will, but what You will." And He came and found them sleeping, and said to Peter, "Simon, are you asleep? Could you not keep watch for one hour? Keep watching and praying that you may not come into temptation; the spirit is willing, but the flesh is weak" (Mark 14:32–38; cf. Matthew 26:36–41; Luke 22:41–46; see Romans 8:15; Galatians 4:6).

Setting: Galilee. After Jesus presents the Parable of the Sower to the crowds, His disciples ask Him to give them the parable's meaning.

And He said, "To you it has been granted to know the mysteries of the kingdom of God, but to the rest *it is* in parables, so that SEEING THEY MAY NOT SEE, AND HEARING THEY MAY NOT UNDERSTAND. Now the parable is this: the seed is the word of God. Those beside the road are those who have heard; then the devil comes and takes away the word from their heart, so that they will not believe and be saved. Those on the rocky *soil* are those who, when they hear, receive the word with joy; and these have no *firm* root; they believe for a while, and in time of temptation fall away. The *seed* which fell among the thorns, these are the ones who have heard, and as they go on their way they are choked with worries and riches and pleasures of *this* life, and bring no fruit to maturity. But the *seed* in the good soil, these are the ones who have heard the word in an honest and good heart, and hold it fast, and bear fruit with perseverance" (Luke 8:10–15, Jesus quotes from Isaiah 6:9; cf. Matthew 13:10–23; Mark 4:10–20).

Setting: On the way from Galilee to Jerusalem. After Jesus visits in the home of Martha and Mary in Bethany, one of His disciples asks Him to teach them to pray.

And He said to them, "When you pray, say: 'Father, hallowed be Your name. Your kingdom come. Give us each day our daily bread. And forgive us our sins, for we ourselves also forgive everyone who is indebted to us. And lead us not into temptation'" (Luke 11:2–4; cf. Matthew 6:9–13).

Setting: An upper room in Jerusalem. After celebrating the Passover meal with His disciples and instructing them to prepare to persevere without Him, with His crucifixion imminent, Jesus proceeds to the Mount of Olives to pray.

And He came out and proceeded as was His custom to the Mount of Olives; and the disciples also followed Him. When He arrived at the place, He said to them, "Pray that you may not enter into temptation." And He withdrew from them about a stone's throw, and He knelt down and *began* to pray, saying, "Father, if You are willing, remove this cup from Me; yet not My will, but Yours be done" (Luke 22:39–42; cf. Matthew 26:36–42; Mark 14:32–49; see Luke 21:37).

Setting: An upper room in Jerusalem. After celebrating the Passover meal with His disciples and instructing them to prepare to persevere without Him, with His crucifixion imminent, Jesus proceeds to the Mount of Olives to pray.

When He rose from prayer, He came to the disciples and found them sleeping from sorrow, and said to them, "Why are you sleeping? Get up and pray that you may not enter into temptation" (Luke 22:45, 46; cf. Matthew 26:40–46; Mark 14:37–42; see Matthew 4:11; Luke 22:39–45; Hebrews 5:7).

TEMPTATION BY SATAN (See TEMPTATION OF JESUS)

TEMPTATION OF JESUS

[TEMPTATION OF JESUS from Matthew 4:1: Jesus was led up by the Spirit into the wilderness to be tempted by the devil]
Setting: Judea near the Jordan River. Following Jesus' baptism, before He begins His public ministry, the Lord is led by the Spirit into the wilderness for forty days of temptation by Satan.

But He answered and said, "It is written, 'MAN SHALL NOT LIVE ON BREAD ALONE, BUT ON EVERY WORD THAT PROCEEDS OUT OF THE MOUTH OF GOD' " (Matthew 4:4, Jesus quotes from Deuteronomy 8:3; cf. Luke 4:4; see 1 Corinthians 10:13).

[TEMPTATION OF JESUS from Matthew 4:1: Jesus was led up by the Spirit into the wilderness to be tempted by the devil]
Setting: Judea near the Jordan River. Following Jesus' baptism, before He begins His public ministry, the Lord is led by the Spirit into the wilderness for forty days of temptation by Satan.

Jesus said to him, "On the other hand, it is written, 'YOU SHALL NOT PUT THE LORD YOUR GOD TO THE TEST' " (Matthew 4:7, Jesus quotes from Deuteronomy 6:16; cf. Luke 4:12; see 1 Corinthians 10:13).

[TEMPTATION OF JESUS from Go, Satan]
Setting: Judea near the Jordan River. Following Jesus' baptism, before He begins His public ministry, the Lord is led by the Spirit into the wilderness for forty days of temptation by Satan.

Then Jesus said to him, "Go, Satan! For it is written, 'YOU SHALL WORSHIP THE LORD YOUR GOD, AND SERVE HIM ONLY'" (Matthew 4:10, Jesus quotes from Deuteronomy 6:13; cf. Luke 4:8; see 1 Corinthians 10:13).

[TEMPTATION OF JESUS from Luke 4:2: being tempted by the devil]
Setting: Judea near the Jordan River. Following Jesus' baptism, and before He begins His public ministry, the Lord is led by the Spirit into the wilderness for forty days of temptation by Satan.

And Jesus answered him, "It is written, 'MAN SHALL NOT LIVE ON BREAD ALONE'" (Luke 4:4, Jesus quotes from Deuteronomy 8:3; cf. Matthew 4:1–4; see Mark 1:12, 13; 1 Corinthians 10:13).

[TEMPTATION OF JESUS from Luke 4:2: being tempted by the devil]
Setting: Judea near the Jordan River. Following Jesus' baptism, and before He begins His public ministry, the Lord is led by the Spirit into the wilderness for forty days of temptation by Satan.

Jesus answered him, "It is written, 'YOU SHALL WORSHIP THE LORD YOUR GOD AND SERVE HIM ONLY'" (Luke 4:8, Jesus quotes from Deuteronomy 6:13; cf. Matthew 4:10; see 1 Corinthians 10:13).

[TEMPTATION OF JESUS from Luke 4:2: being tempted by the devil]
Setting: Judea near the Jordan River. Following Jesus' baptism, before He begins His public ministry, the Lord is led by the Spirit into the wilderness for forty days of temptation by Satan.

And Jesus answered and said to him, "It is said, 'YOU SHALL NOT PUT THE LORD YOUR GOD TO THE TEST'" (Luke 4:12, Jesus quotes from Deuteronomy 6:16; cf. Matthew 4:7; see 1 Corinthians 10:13).

TEN

Setting: Capernaum of Galilee. Jesus illustrates the matter of forgiveness after Peter asks Him if forgiving someone seven times who has sinned against him is adequate.

"For this reason the kingdom of heaven may be compared to a king who wished to settle accounts with his slaves. When he had begun to settle *them,* one who owed him ten thousand talents was brought to him. But since he did not have *the means* to repay, his lord commanded him to be sold, along with his wife and children and all that he had, and repayment to be made. So the slave fell *to the ground* and prostrated himself before him, saying, 'Have patience with me and I will repay you everything.' And the lord of that slave felt compassion and released him and forgave him the debt. But that slave went out and found one of his fellow slaves who owed him a hundred denarii; and he seized him and *began* to choke *him,* saying, 'Pay back what you owe.' So his fellow slave fell *to the ground* and *began* to plead with him, saying, 'Have patience with me and I will repay you.' But he was unwilling and went and threw him in prison until he should pay back what was owed. So when his fellow slaves saw what had happened, they were deeply grieved and came and reported to their lord all that had happened. Then summoning him, his lord said to him, 'You wicked slave, I forgave you all that debt because you pleaded with me. Should you not also have had mercy on your fellow slave, in the same way that I had mercy on you?' And his lord, moved with anger, handed him over to the torturers until he should repay all that was owed him. My heavenly Father will also do the same to you, if each of you does not forgive his brother from your heart" (Matthew 18:23–35; cf. Matthew 6:12, 14, 15; Luke 7:42; see Matthew 25:19–28).

Setting: On the Mount of Olives, just east of Jerusalem. During His Olivet Discourse, after answering His disciples' questions as to when the temple will be destroyed and Jerusalem overrun, along with the signs of His coming and the end of the age, Jesus reemphasizes to His disciples that they should be on the alert for His return.

"Then the kingdom of heaven will be comparable to ten virgins, who took their lamps and went out to meet the bridegroom. Five of them were foolish, and five were prudent. For when the foolish took their lamps, they took no oil with them, but the prudent took oil in flasks along with their lamps. Now while the bridegroom was delaying, they all got drowsy and *began* to sleep. But at midnight there was a shout, 'Behold, the bridegroom! Come out to meet *him.*' Then all those virgins rose and trimmed their lamps.

The foolish said to the prudent, 'Give us some of your oil, for our lamps are going out.' But the prudent answered, 'No, there will not be enough for us and you *too;* go instead to the dealers and buy *some* for yourselves.' And while they were going away to make the purchase, the bridegroom came, and those who were ready went in with him to the wedding feast; and the door was shut. Later the other virgins also came, saying, 'Lord, lord, open up for us.' But he answered, 'Truly I say to you, I do not know you.' Be on the alert then, for you do not know the day nor the hour" (Matthew 25:1–13; cf. Matthew 24:42; Luke 12:35; see Matthew 7:21, 24).

Setting: On the Mount of Olives, just east of Jerusalem. During His Olivet Discourse, after answering His disciples' questions as to when the temple will be destroyed and Jerusalem overrun, along with the signs of His coming and the end of the age, Jesus reemphasizes to His disciples that they should be on the alert for His return.

"For *it is* just like a man *about* to go on a journey, who called his own slaves and entrusted his possessions to them. To one he gave five talents, to another, two, and to another, one, each according to his own ability; and he went on his journey. Immediately the one who had received the five talents went and traded with them, and gained five more talents. In the same manner the one who *had received* the two *talents* gained two more. But he who received the one *talent* went away, and dug a *hole* in the ground and hid his master's money. Now after a long time the master of those slaves came and settled accounts with them. The one who had received the five talents came up and brought five more talents, saying, 'Master, you entrusted five talents to me. See, I have gained five more talents.' His master said to him, 'Well done, good and faithful slave. You were faithful with a few things, I will put you in charge of many things; enter into the joy of your master.' Also the one who *had received* the two talents came up and said, 'Master, you entrusted two talents to me. See, I have gained two more talents.' His master said to him, 'Well done, good and faithful slave. You were faithful with a few things, I will put you in charge of many things; enter into the joy of your master.' And the one also who had received the one talent came up and said, 'Master, I knew you to be a hard man, reaping where you did not sow and gathering where you scattered no *seed.* And I was afraid, and went away and hid your talent in the ground. See, you have what is yours.' But his master answered and said to him, 'You wicked, lazy slave, you knew that I reap where I did not sow and gather where I scattered no *seed.* Then you ought to have put my money in the bank, and on my arrival I would have received my *money* back with interest. 'Therefore take away the talent from him, and give it to the one who has ten talents.' For to everyone who has, *more* shall be given, and he will have an abundance; but from the one who does not have, even what he does have shall be taken away. Throw out the worthless slave into the outer darkness; in that place there will be weeping and gnashing of teeth" (Matthew 25:14–30; cf. Matthew 8:12; 13:12; 24:45–47; see Matthew 18:23, 24; Luke 12:44).

Setting: On the way from Galilee to Jerusalem. After He responds to a guest's proclamation about the blessings of eating bread in the kingdom of God, Jesus presents to large crowds the demands of discipleship.

Now large crowds were going along with Him; and He turned and said to them, "If anyone comes to Me, and does not hate his own father and mother and wife and children and brothers and sisters, yes, and even his own life, he cannot be My disciple. Whoever does not carry his own cross and come after Me cannot be My disciple. For which one of you, when he wants to build a tower, does not first sit down and calculate the cost to see if he has enough to complete it? Otherwise, when he has laid a foundation and is not able to finish, all who observe it begin to ridicule him, saying, 'This man began to build and was not able to finish.' Or what king, when he sets out to meet another king in battle, will not first sit down and consider whether he is strong enough with ten thousand *men* to encounter the one coming against him with twenty thousand? Or else, while the other is still far away, he sends a delegation and asks for terms of peace. So then, none of you can be My disciple who does not give up all his possessions. Therefore, salt is good; but if even salt has become tasteless, with what will it be seasoned? It is useless either for the soil or for the manure pile; it is thrown out. He who has ears to hear, let him hear" (Luke 14:25–35; cf. Matthew 5:13; 10:37–39; see Proverb 20:18; Philippians 3:7).

Setting: On the way from Galilee to Jerusalem. Jesus conveys the principles of the lost sheep and the lost coin because the Pharisees and scribes complain He associates with tax collectors and sinners.

"So He told them this parable, saying, "What man among you, if he has a hundred sheep and has lost one of them, does not leave the ninety-nine in the open pasture and go after the one which is lost until he finds it? When he has found it, he lays it on his shoulders, rejoicing. And when he comes home, he calls together his friends and his neighbors, saying to them, 'Rejoice with me, for I have found my sheep which was lost!' I tell you that in the same way, there will be more joy in heaven over one sinner who repents than over ninety-nine righteous persons who need no repentance. Or what woman, if she has ten silver coins and loses one coin, does not light a lamp and sweep the house and search carefully until she finds it? When she has found it, she calls together her friends and neighbors, saying, 'Rejoice with me, for I have found the coin which I had lost!' In the same way, I tell you, there is joy in the presence of the angels of God over one sinner who repents" (Luke 15:3–10; cf. Matthew 18:12-14; see Matthew 9:11-13).

Setting: On the way from Galilee to Jerusalem. The Lord stops to heal ten lepers who ask for cleansing.

When He saw them, He said to them, "Go and show yourselves to the priests." And as they were going, they were cleansed. Now one of them, when he saw that he had been healed, turned back, glorifying God with a loud voice, and he fell on his face at His feet, giving thanks to Him. And he was a Samaritan. Then Jesus answered and said, "Were there not ten cleansed? But the nine—where are they? Was no one found who returned to give glory to God, except this foreigner?" And He said to him, "Stand up and go; your faith has made you well." (Luke 17:14–19; see Leviticus 14:1–32).

Setting: Jericho, on the way to Jerusalem. After commending Zaccheus's faith in Him, Jesus provides a parable about stewardship.

So He said, "A nobleman went to a distant country to receive a kingdom for himself, and *then* return. And he called ten of his slaves, and gave them ten minas and said to them, 'Do business *with this* until I come *back.*' But his citizens hated him and sent a delegation after him, saying, 'We do not want this man to reign over us.' When he returned, after receiving the kingdom, he ordered that these slaves, to whom he had given the money, be called to him so that he might know what business they had done. The first appeared, saying, 'Master, your mina has made ten minas more.' And he said to him, 'Well done, good slave, because you have been faithful in a very little thing, you are to be in authority over ten cities.' The second came, saying, 'Your mina, master, has made five minas.' And he said to him, also, 'And you are to be over five cities.' Another came, saying, 'Master, here is your mina, which I kept put away in a handkerchief; for I was afraid of you, because you are an exacting man; you take up what you did not lay down and reap what you did not sow.' He said to him, 'By your own words I will judge you, you worthless slave. Did you know that I am an exacting man, taking up what I did not lay down and reaping what I did not sow? Then why did you not put my money in the bank, and having come, I would have collected it with interest?' Then he said to the bystanders, 'Take the mina away from him and give it to the one who has the ten minas.' And they said to him, 'Master, he has ten minas *already.*' I tell you that to everyone who has, more shall be given, but from the one who does not have, even what he does have shall be taken away. But these enemies of mine, who did not want me to reign over them, bring them here and slay them in my presence" (Luke 19:12–27; cf. Matthew 25:14–30; see Matthew 13:12; Luke 16:10).

Setting: On the island of Patmos (in the Aegean Sea about fifty miles southwest of Ephesus in modern Turkey). On the Lord's Day (Sunday), approximately fifty years after the Resurrection, the disciple John encounters the Lord Jesus Christ, who communicates a new revelation for the apostle to record for the church in Smyrna and to six other churches in Asia.

"And to the angel of the church in Smyrna write: The first and the last, who was dead, and has come to life, says this: 'I know your tribulation and your poverty (but you are rich), and the blasphemy by those who say they are Jews and are not, but are a synagogue of Satan. Do not fear what you are about to suffer. Behold, the devil is about to cast some of you into prison, so that you will be tested, and you will have tribulation for ten days. Be faithful until death, and I will give you the crown of life. He who has an ear, let him hear what the Spirit says to the churches. He who overcomes will not be hurt by the second death' (Revelation 2:8–11; see Isaiah 44:6; Revelation 1:9, 18; 20:6, 14).

TEN CITIES (See CITIES)

TEN COMMANDMENTS (See COMMANDMENTS)

TEN VIRGINS (Listed under VIRGINS, TEN)

TENANTS, PARABLE OF THE (See VINE-GROWERS, PARABLE OF THE)

TERMS

Setting: On the way from Galilee to Jerusalem. After responding to a guest's proclamation about the blessings of eating bread in the kingdom of God, Jesus presents to large crowds the demands of discipleship.

Now large crowds were going along with Him; and He turned and said to them, "If anyone comes to Me, and does not hate his own father and mother and wife and children and brothers and sisters, yes, and even his own life, he cannot be My disciple. Whoever does not carry his own cross and come after Me cannot be My disciple. For which one of you, when he wants to build a tower, does not first sit down and calculate the cost to see if he has enough to complete it? Otherwise, when he has laid a foundation and is not able to finish, all who observe it begin to ridicule him, saying, 'This man began to build and was not able to finish.' Or what king, when he sets out to meet another king in battle, will not first sit down and consider whether he is strong enough with ten thousand *men* to encounter the one coming against him with twenty thousand? Or else, while the other is still far away, he sends a delegation and asks for terms of peace. So then, none of you can be My disciple who does not give up all his possessions. Therefore, salt is good; but if even salt has become tasteless, with what will it be seasoned? It is useless either for the soil or for the manure pile; it is thrown out. He who has ears to hear, let him hear" (Luke 14:25–35; cf. Matthew 5:13; 10:37–39; see Proverb 20:18; Philippians 3:7).

TERRORS

Setting: On the Mount of Olives, east of the temple in Jerusalem. After ministering in the temple a few days before His crucifixion, and giving His disciples more details regarding the temple's future destruction, Jesus elaborates during His Olivet Discourse about things to come.

Then He continued by saying to them, "Nation will rise against nation and kingdom against kingdom, and there will be great earthquakes, and in various places plagues and famines; and there will be terrors and great signs from heaven. But before all these things, they will lay their hands on you and will persecute you, delivering you to the synagogues and prisons, bringing you before kings and governors for My name's sake. It will lead to an opportunity for your testimony. So make up your minds not to prepare beforehand to defend yourselves; for I will give you utterance and wisdom which none of your opponents will be able to resist or refute. But you will be betrayed even by parents and brothers and relatives and friends, and they will put *some* of you to death, and you will be hated by all because of My name. Yet not a hair of your head will perish. By your endurance you will gain your lives" (Luke 21:10–19; cf. Matthew 10:19–22; 24:7–14; Mark 13:8–13).

TEST (Also see TEMPTATION; and TRIBULATION)

Setting: Judea, near the Jordan River. Following His baptism, and before He begins His public ministry, Jesus is led by the Spirit into the wilderness for forty days of temptation by Satan.

Jesus said to him, "On the other hand, it is written, 'YOU SHALL NOT PUT THE LORD YOUR GOD TO THE TEST'" (Matthew 4:7, Jesus quotes from Deuteronomy 6:16; cf. Luke 4:12).

[TEST from testing]

Setting: The temple in Jerusalem. The Pharisees send their disciples and the Herodians to test Jesus about the poll-tax in order to trap Him.

But Jesus perceived their malice, and said, "Why are you testing Me, you hypocrites? Show Me the coin *used* for the poll-tax." And they brought Him a denarius. And He said to them, "Whose likeness and inscription is this?" They said to Him, "Caesar's." Then He said to them, "Then render to Caesar the things that are Caesar's; and to God the things that are God's" (Matthew 22:18–21; cf. Matthew 17:25; Mark 12:15–17; Luke 20:22–25).

[TEST from testing]
Setting: The temple in Jerusalem. After Jesus teaches the chief priests, scribes, and elders in parables, they send some of the Pharisees and Herodians in an attempt to trap Him in a statement.

"Shall we pay or shall we not pay?" But He, knowing their hypocrisy, said to them, "Why are you testing Me? Bring Me a denarius to look at." They brought *one.* And He said to them, "Whose likeness and inscription is this?" And they said to Him, "Caesar's." And Jesus said to them, "Render to Caesar the things that are Caesar's, and to God the things that are God's." And they were amazed at Him (Mark 12:15–17; cf. Matthew 22:15–22; Luke 20:20–26).

Setting: Judea, near the Jordan River. Following His baptism, and before He begins His public ministry, Jesus is led by the Spirit into the wilderness for forty days of temptation by Satan.

And Jesus answered and said to him, "It is said, 'YOU SHALL NOT PUT THE LORD YOUR GOD TO THE TEST'" (Luke 4:12, Jesus quotes from Deuteronomy 6:16; cf. Matthew 4:7).

Setting: On the island of Patmos (in the Aegean Sea about fifty miles southwest of Ephesus in modern Turkey). On the Lord's Day (Sunday), approximately fifty years after the Resurrection, the disciple John encounters the Lord Jesus Christ, who communicates a new revelation for the apostle to record for the church in Ephesus and to six other churches in Asia.

"To the angel of the church in Ephesus write: The One who holds the seven stars in His right hand, the One who walks among the seven golden lampstands, says this: 'I know your deeds and your toil and perseverance, and that you cannot tolerate evil men, and you put to the test those who call themselves apostles, and they are not, and you found them *to be* false; and you have perseverance and have endured for My name's sake, and have not grown weary. But I have *this* against you, that you have left your first love. Therefore remember from where you have fallen, and repent and do the deeds you did at first; or else I am coming to you and will remove your lampstand out of its place—unless you repent. Yet this you do have, that you hate the deeds of the Nicolaitans, which I also hate. He who has an ear, let him hear what the Spirit says to the churches. To him who overcomes, I will grant to eat of the tree of life which is in the Paradise of God' " (Revelation 2:1–7; see Genesis 2:9; Ezekiel 28:13; 1 John 4:1; Revelation 1:10, 11, 19, 20).

[TEST from tested]
Setting: On the island of Patmos (in the Aegean Sea about fifty miles southwest of Ephesus in modern Turkey). On the Lord's Day (Sunday), approximately fifty years after the Resurrection, the disciple John encounters the Lord Jesus Christ, who communicates a new revelation for the apostle to record for the church in Smyrna and to six other churches in Asia.

"And to the angel of the church in Smyrna write: The first and the last, who was dead, and has come to life, says this: 'I know your tribulation and your poverty (but you are rich), and the blasphemy by those who say they are Jews and are not, but are a synagogue of Satan. Do not fear what you are about to suffer. Behold, the devil is about to cast some of you into prison, so that you will be tested, and you will have tribulation for ten days. Be faithful until death, and I will give you the crown of life. He who has an ear, let him hear what the Spirit says to the churches. He who overcomes will not be hurt by the second death' (Revelation 2:8–11; see Isaiah 44:6; Revelation 1:9, 18; 20:6, 14).

[TEST from testing]
Setting: On the island of Patmos (in the Aegean Sea about fifty miles southwest of Ephesus in modern Turkey). On the Lord's Day (Sunday), approximately fifty years after the Resurrection, the disciple John encounters the Lord Jesus Christ, who communicates a new revelation for the apostle to record for the church in Philadelphia and to six other churches in Asia.

"And to the angel of the church in Philadelphia write: He who is holy, who is true, who has the key of David, who opens and no one will shut, and who shuts and no one opens, says this: 'I know your deeds. Behold, I have put before you an open door which no one can shut, because you have a little power, and have kept My word, and have not denied My name. Behold, I will cause *those* of the synagogue of Satan, who say that they are Jews and are not, but lie—I will make them come and bow down at your feet, and *make them* know that I have loved you. Because you have kept the word of My perseverance, I also will keep you from the hour of testing, that *hour* which is about to come upon the whole world, to test those who dwell on the earth. I am coming quickly; hold fast what you have, so that no one will take your crown. He who overcomes, I will make him a pillar in the temple of My God, and he will not go out from it anymore; and I will write on him the name of My God, and the name of the city of My God, the new Jerusalem, which comes down out of heaven from My God, and My new name. He who has an ear, let him hear what the Spirit says to the churches' " (Revelation 3:7–13; see Isaiah 22:22; Galatians 2:9; Revelation 2:9, 10, 13, 25; 14:1).

TESTAMENT, OLD (See OLD TESTAMENT)

TESTIFY (See TESTIMONY)

TESTIMONY (Also see JESUS, CONFESSING; LIVING, GODLY; and WITNESS)

[TESTIMONY from You are the salt of the earth]
Setting: Galilee. During the early part of His ministry, Jesus preaches the Sermon on the Mount to His disciples and the multitudes.

"You are the salt of the earth; but if the salt has become tasteless, how can it be made salty *again*? It is not longer good for anything, except to be thrown out and trampled under foot by men" (Matthew 5:13; cf. Mark 9:50).

[TESTIMONY from that they may see your good works, and glorify your Father who is in heaven]
Setting: Galilee. During the early part of His ministry, Jesus preaches the Sermon on the Mount to His disciples and the multitudes.

"You are the light of the world. A city set on a hill cannot be hidden; nor does *anyone* light a lamp and put it under a basket, but on the lampstand, and it gives light to all who are in the house. Let your light shine before men in such a way that they may see your good works, and glorify your Father who is in heaven" (Matthew 5:14–16; cf. Mark 4:21; 1 Peter 2:12).

[TESTIMONY inferred]
Setting: Galilee. During the early part of His ministry, Jesus preaches the Sermon on the Mount to His disciples and the multitudes.

"Whoever then annuls one of the least of these commandments, and teaches others *to do* the same, shall be called least in the kingdom of heaven; but whoever keeps and teaches *them*, he shall be called great in the kingdom of heaven" (Matthew 5:19; cf. Matthew 11:11).

Setting: Galilee. When Jesus comes down after preaching the Sermon on the Mount, large crowds follow Him, and a leper approaches Him asking for cleansing.

Jesus stretched out His hand and touched him, saying, "I am willing, be cleansed." And immediately his leprosy was cleansed. And Jesus said to him, "See that you tell no one; but go, show yourself to the priest and present the offering that Moses commanded, as a testimony to them" (Matthew 8:3, 4; cf. Mark 1:40–44; Luke 5:12–14).

Setting: Galilee. After His disciples observe His ministry, Jesus summons and specifically instructs them about the upcoming hardships of their ministry to the people of Israel.

"Behold, I send you out as sheep in the midst of wolves; so be shrewd as serpents and innocent as doves. But beware of men, for they will hand you over to *the* courts and scourge you in their synagogues; and you will even be brought before governors and kings for My sake, as a testimony to them and to the Gentiles. But when they hand you over, do not worry about how or what you are to say; for it will be given you in that hour what you are to say. For it is not you who speak, but *it* is the Spirit of your Father who speaks in you" (Matthew 10:16–20; cf. Luke 10:3).

[TESTIMONY from everyone who confesses Me before men]
Setting: Galilee. Jesus gives the meaning of discipleship as He commissions the Twelve for ministry.

"Therefore everyone who confesses Me before men, I will also confess him before My Father who is in heaven. But whoever denies Me before men, I will also deny him before My Father who is in heaven" (Matthew 10:32, 33; cf. Mark 8:38; Luke 12:8).

Setting: The Mount of Olives, just east of Jerusalem. During His Olivet Discourse, Jesus answers His disciples' questions as to when the temple will be destroyed and Jerusalem overrun, along with the signs of His coming and the end of the age.

And Jesus answered and said to them, "See to it that no one misleads you. For many will come in My name, saying, 'I am the Christ,' and will mislead many. You will be hearing of wars and rumors of wars. See that you are not frightened, for *those things* must take place, but *that* is not yet the end. For nation will rise against nation, and kingdom against kingdom, and in various places there will be famines and earthquakes. But all these things are *merely* the beginning of birth pangs. Then they will deliver you to tribulation, and will kill you, and you will be hated by all nations because of My name. At that time many will fall away and will betray one another and hate one another. Many false prophets will arise and will mislead many. Because lawlessness is increased, most people's love will grow cold. But the one who endures to the end, he will be saved. This gospel of the kingdom shall be preached in the whole world as a testimony to all the nations, and then the end will come" (Matthew 24:4–14; cf. Jeremiah 29:8; Matthew 7:15; Matthew 10:17, 22; Mark 13:3–13; Luke 21:7–19 Revelation 6:4).

Setting: Galilee. As Jesus preaches and casts out demons in the synagogues, a leper beseeches Him for healing.

Moved with compassion, Jesus stretched out His hand and touched him, and said to him, "I am willing; be cleansed." Immediately the leprosy left him and he was cleansed. And He sternly warned him and immediately sent him away, and He said to him, "See that you say nothing to anyone; but go, show yourself to the priest and offer for your cleansing what Moses commanded, as a testimony to them" (Mark 1:41 44; cf. Luke 5:12–14; see Leviticus 14:1–32; Matthew 8:3).

[TESTIMONY from Go home to your people and report to them what great things the Lord has done for you]
Setting: The country of the Gerasenes, on the east side of the Sea of Galilee. Jesus encounters and heals a man possessed by a legion of demons.

And He did not let him, but He said to him, "Go home to your people and report to them what great things the Lord has done for you, and *how* He had mercy on you" (Mark 5:19; cf. Luke 8:39; see Matthew 8:33, 34; Luke 8:36–38).

Setting: Jesus' hometown of Nazareth in Galilee. After encountering unbelief, Jesus sends the Twelve out in pairs with authority and instructions about ministry.

And He summoned the twelve and began to send them out in pairs, and gave them authority over the unclean spirits; and He instructed them that they should take nothing for *their* journey, except a mere staff—no bread, no bag, no money in their belt—but to wear sandals; and *He added,* "Do not put on two tunics." And He said to them, "Wherever you enter a house, stay there until you leave town. Any place that does not receive you or listen to you, as you go out from there, shake the dust off the soles of your feet for a testimony against them" (Mark 6:7–11; cf. Matthew 10:1–14; Luke 9:1–5).

Setting: On the Mount of Olives, east of the temple in Jerusalem. After prophesying the temple's destruction, Jesus responds during His Olivet Discourse to questions from Peter, James, John, and Andrew about other future events.

And Jesus began to say to them, "See to it that no one misleads you. Many will come in My name, saying, 'I am *He!*' and will mislead many. When you hear of wars and rumors of wars, do not be frightened; *those things* must take place; but *that is* not yet the end. For nation will rise up against nation, and kingdom against kingdom; there will be earthquakes in various places; there will *also be* famines. These things are *merely* the beginning of birth pangs. But be on your guard; for they will deliver you to *the* courts, and you will be flogged in *the* synagogues, and you will stand before governors and kings for My sake, as a testimony to them. The gospel must first be preached to all the nations. When they arrest you and hand you over, do not worry beforehand about what you are to say, but say whatever is given you in that hour; for it is not you who speak, but *it is* the Holy Spirit. Brother will betray brother to death, and a father *his* child; and children will rise up against parents and have them put to death. You will be hated by all because of My name, but the one who endures to the end, he will be saved" (Mark 13:5–13; cf. Matthew 24:4–14; Luke 21:7–19; see Matthew 10:17–22).

Setting: Galilee. Early in His ministry, after calling Andrew, Simon (Peter), James, and John to follow Him, Jesus heals a leper.

And He stretched out His hand and touched Him, saying, "I am willing; be cleansed." And immediately the leprosy left him. And He ordered him to tell no one, "But go and show yourself to the priest and make an offering for your cleansing, just as Moses commanded, as a testimony to them" (Luke 5:13, 14; cf. Matthew 8:2–4; Mark 1:40–45; see Leviticus 13:49).

[TESTIMONY from Return to your house and describe what great things God has done for you]
Setting: The country of the Gerasenes, to the east of Galilee. Jesus heals a demon-possessed man who then desires to join His ministry, but the Lord sends him home.

"Return to your house and describe what great things God has done for you." So he went away, proclaiming throughout the whole city what great things Jesus had done for him (Luke 8:39; cf. Matthew 8:28–34; Mark 5:1–20).

Setting: Galilee. After raising the daughter of Jairus, a synagogue official, from the dead, Jesus calls His twelve disciples together and gives them power and authority over demons, along with the ability to cure diseases.

And He said to them, "Take nothing for *your* journey, neither a staff, nor a bag, nor bread, nor money; and do not *even* have two tunics apiece. Whatever house you enter, stay there until you leave that city. And as for those who do not receive you, go out from that city, shake the dust off your feet as a testimony against them" (Luke 9:3–5; cf. Matthew 10:1–15; Mark 6:7–11; see Luke 10:4–12).

[TESTIMONY from everyone who confesses Me before men]
Setting: On the way from Galilee to Jerusalem. Jesus warns His disciples of future events, as the scribes and Pharisees turn hostile and question Him repeatedly in an attempt to catch Him in something He might say.

"And I say to you, everyone who confesses Me before men, the Son of Man will confess him also before the angels of God; but he who denies Me before men will be denied before the angels of God. And everyone who speaks a word against the Son of Man, it will be forgiven him; but he who blasphemes against the Holy Spirit, it will not be forgiven him. When they bring you before the synagogues and the rulers and the authorities, do not worry about how or what you are to speak in your defense, or what you are to say; for the Holy Spirit will teach you in that very hour what you ought to say" (Luke 12:8–12; cf. Matthew 10:32, 33; 12:31, 32; see Matthew 10:20).

Setting: On the Mount of Olives, east of the temple in Jerusalem. After ministering in the temple a few days before His crucifixion, and giving His disciples more details regarding the temple's future destruction, Jesus elaborates during His Olivet Discourse about things to come.

Then He continued by saying to them, "Nation will rise against nation and kingdom against kingdom, and there will be great earthquakes, and in various places plagues and famines; and there will be terrors and great signs from heaven. But before all these things, they will lay their hands on you and will persecute you, delivering you to the synagogues and prisons, bringing you before kings and governors for My name's sake. It will lead to an opportunity for your testimony. So make up your minds not to prepare beforehand to defend yourselves; for I will give you utterance and wisdom which none of your opponents will be able to resist or refute. But you will be betrayed even by parents and brothers and relatives and friends, and they will put *some* of you to death, and you will be hated by all because of My name. Yet not a hair of your head will perish. By your endurance you will gain your lives" (Luke 21:10–19; cf. Matthew 10:19–22; 24:7–14; Mark 13:8–13).

Setting: Jerusalem. At the time for the Passover of the Jews, after the Lord cleanses the temple, a Pharisee, Nicodemus, asks Him by night the meaning of "born of the Spirit."

Jesus answered and said to him, "Are you the teacher of Israel and do not understand these things? Truly, truly, I say to you, we speak of what we know and testify of what we have seen, and you do not accept our testimony. If I told you earthly things and you do not believe, how will you believe if I tell you heavenly things? No one has ascended into heaven, but He who descended from heaven: the Son of Man. As Moses lifted up the serpent in the wilderness, even so must the Son of Man be lifted up; so that whoever believes will in Him have eternal life" (John 3:10–15; see Numbers 21:9; Proverb 30:4; John 12:34; 20:30, 31).

Setting: Jerusalem. During a feast of the Jews, Jesus responds to criticism from the Jewish religious leaders by referring to God as His Father (thereby making Himself equal with God) and informing them that God, John the Baptist, and His works all testify to His mission.

"I can do nothing on My own initiative. As I hear, I judge; and My judgment is just, because I do not seek My own will, but the will of Him who sent Me. If I *alone* testify about Myself, My testimony is not true. There is another who testifies of Me, and I know that the testimony which He gives about Me is true. You have sent to John, and he has testified to the truth. But the testimony which I receive is not from man, but I say these things so that you may be saved. He was the lamp that was burning and was shining and you were willing to rejoice for a while in his light. But the testimony which I have is greater than the *testimony of* John; for the works which the Father has given Me to accomplish—the very works that I do—testify about Me, that the Father has sent Me. And the Father who sent Me, He has testified of Me. You have neither heard His voice at any time nor seen His form. You do not have His word abiding in you, for you do not believe Him whom He sent" (John 5:30–38; see Matthew 3:17; Mark 1:4, 5; John 1:7, 15, 32; 4:34; 8:14–16; 10:25, 37, 38).

[TESTIMONY from testify]
Setting: Jerusalem. During a feast of the Jews, Jesus responds to criticism from the Jewish religious leaders by referring to God as His Father (thereby making Himself equal with God) and informing them that God, John the Baptist, the Scriptures, and His works all testify to His mission.

"You search the Scriptures because you think that in them you have eternal life; it is these that testify about Me; and you are unwilling to come to Me so that you may have life. I do not receive glory from men; but I know you, that you do not have the love of God in yourselves. I have come in My Father's name, and you do not receive Me; if another comes in his own name, you will receive him. How can you believe, when you receive glory from one another and you do not seek the glory that is from the *one and* only God? Do not think that I will accuse you before the Father; the one who accuses you is Moses, in whom you have set your hope. For if you believed Moses, you would believe Me, for he wrote about Me. But if you do not believe his writings, how will you believe My words?" (John 5:39–47; see Matthew 24:5; Luke 16:29, 31; 24:27; John 9:28; 17:3).

[TESTIMONY from testify]
Setting: Capernaum of Galilee. Jesus' blood brothers, who do not yet believe in Him, encourage Him to attend the upcoming Feast of Booths in Jerusalem in order to demonstrate His works to His disciples and the world.

So Jesus said to them, "My time is not yet here, but your time is always opportune. The world cannot hate you, but it hates Me because I testify of it, that its deeds are evil. Go up to the feast yourselves; I do not go up to this feast because My time has not yet fully come" (John 7:6–8; see John 3:19, 20; 15:18–20).

Setting: The temple in Jerusalem. Following the Feast of Booths and the scribes' and Pharisees' failed attempt to stone a woman for adultery, Jesus returns the next day to teach. His enemies question His testimony about Himself.

Jesus answered and said to them, "Even if I testify about Myself, My testimony is true, for I know where I came from and where I am going; but you do not know where I come from or where I am going. You judge according to the flesh; I am not judging anyone. But even if I do judge, My judgment is true; for I am not alone *in it,* but I and the Father who sent Me. Even in your law it has been written that the testimony of two men is true. I am He who testifies about Myself, and the Father who sent Me testifies about Me." So they were saying to Him, "Where is Your Father?" Jesus answered, "You know neither Me nor My Father; if you knew Me, you would know My Father also" (John 8:14–19; see Deuteronomy 17:6; 19:15; Matthew 18:16; John 3:17; 5:30, 37; 7:28; 8:42).

[TESTIMONY from testify]
Setting: Jerusalem. At the Feast of Dedication, just after Jesus conveys the Parable of the Good Shepherd to the Pharisees (who do not understand it), they ask Him plainly if He is the Christ.

Jesus answered them, "I told you, and you do not believe; the works that I do in My Father's name, these testify of Me. But you do not believe because you are not of My sheep. My sheep hear My voice, and I know them, and they follow Me; and I give eternal life to them, and they will never perish; and no one will snatch them out of My hand. My Father, who has given *them* to Me, is greater than all; and no one is able to snatch *them* out of the Father's hand. I and the Father are one" (John 10:25–30; see John 8:47; 10:4; 17:1, 2, 20, 21).

[TESTIMONY from testify]
Setting: Jerusalem. Before the Passover, with His departure in mind, after explaining He is the vine and His disciples are the branches, Jesus elaborates about the future ministry of the Holy Spirit.

"When the Helper comes, whom I will send to you from the Father, *that is* the Spirit of truth who proceeds from the Father, He will testify about Me, and you *will* testify also, because you have been with Me from the beginning" (John 15:26, 27; see Luke 24:48; John 14:16).

[TESTIMONY from testify]
Setting: Jerusalem. After Jesus is betrayed by Judas and arrested by the Roman cohort, one of the officers strikes Jesus when he believes the Lord exhibits disrespect to the former high priest when He answers Annas's question about His disciples and teaching.

Jesus answered him, "If I have spoken wrongly, testify of the wrong; but if rightly, why do you strike Me?" (John 18:23; see Matthew 5:39).

[TESTIMONY from testify]
Setting: Jerusalem. After the previous and current high priests (Annas and Caiaphas) question Jesus, and Peter denies for the second and third times being the Lord's disciple, Pilate (Roman governor of Judea) questions Jesus in an attempt to determine if He is a king.

Therefore Pilate said to Him, "So You are a king?" Jesus answered, "You say *correctly* that I am a king. For this I have been born, and for this I have come into the world, to testify to the truth. Everyone who is of the truth hears my voice" (John 18:37; cf. Matthew 27:11; Mark 15:2; Luke 23:3).

Setting: Jerusalem. Luke, writing in Acts, recounts Paul's speech to a hostile Jewish crowd (after his third missionary journey), as he recalls his instructions from the Lord Jesus following his conversion on the road to Damascus.

It happened when I returned to Jerusalem and was praying in the temple, that I fell into a trance, and I saw Him saying to me, 'Make haste, and get out of Jerusalem quickly, because they will not accept your testimony about Me' (Acts 22:17, 18; see Acts 9:29).

[TESTIMONY from testify]
Setting: On the island of Patmos (in the Aegean Sea about fifty miles southwest of Ephesus in modern Turkey). In the final chapter of the Lord Jesus Christ's revelation via the apostle John, approximately fifty years after the Resurrection, the Lord authenticates the truthfulness of His message, along with His earthly lineage through King David.

"I, Jesus, have sent My angel to testify to you these things for the churches. I am the root and the descendant of David, the bright morning star" (Revelation 22:16).

TESTING (See TEST)

TESTING GOD (Listed under GOD, TESTING)

TESTING JESUS (Listed under JESUS, TESTING)

THE DEVIL AND HIS ANGELS (Listed under ANGELS, THE DEVIL AND HIS)

THEFT (Also see BURGLARY; ROBBER; ROBBERY; STEALING; THEFTS; THIEF; and THIEVES)

[THEFT from YOU SHALL NOT STEAL]
Setting: Judea beyond the Jordan (Perea). Jesus shares with a rich, young ruler how righteous believers may have treasure in heaven.

And He said to him, "Why are you asking Me about what is good? There is *only* One who is good; but if you wish to enter into life, keep the commandments." *Then* he said to Him, 'Which ones?' And Jesus said, "YOU SHALL NOT COMMIT MURDER; YOU SHALL NOT COMMIT ADULTERY; YOU SHALL NOT STEAL; YOU SHALL NOT BEAR FALSE WITNESS; HONOR YOUR FATHER AND MOTHER; and YOU SHALL LOVE YOUR NEIGHBOR AS YOURSELF." The young man said to Him, "All these things I have kept; what am I still lacking?" Jesus said to him, "If you wish to complete go *and* sell your possessions and give to *the* poor, and you will have treasure in heaven; and come, follow Me" (Matthew 19:16–22, Jesus quotes from Exodus 20:13–15; Leviticus 19:18; cf. Leviticus 18:5; Mark 10:17–21; Luke 10:25–28; 12:33; 18:18–24).

[THEFT from DO NOT STEAL]
Setting: Judea beyond the Jordan (Perea). After demonstrating to His disciples the importance of little children, Jesus encounters a rich man seeking eternal life.

And Jesus said to him, "Why do you call Me good? No one is good except God alone. You know the commandments, 'DO NOT MURDER, DO NOT COMMIT ADULTERY, DO NOT STEAL, DO NOT BEAR FALSE WITNESS, Do not defraud, HONOR YOUR FATHER AND MOTHER.'" And he said to Him, "Teacher, I have kept all these things from my youth up." Looking at him, Jesus felt a love for him and said to him, "One thing you lack: go and sell all you possess and give to the poor, and you will have treasure in heaven; and come, follow Me" (Mark 10:18–21; Jesus quotes from Exodus 20:12–16; cf. Matthew 19:16–22; Luke 18:18–24; see Matthew 6:20).

[THEFT from DO NOT STEAL]
Setting: Judea beyond the Jordan (Perea). After speaking of the importance of children, Jesus responds to a ruler's question about inheriting eternal life.

A ruler questioned Him, saying, "Good Teacher, what shall I do to inherit eternal life?" And Jesus said to him, "Why do you call Me good? No one is good except God alone. You know the commandments, 'DO NOT COMMIT ADULTERY, DO NOT MURDER, DO NOT STEAL, DO NOT BEAR FALSE WITNESS, HONOR YOUR FATHER AND MOTHER.'" And he said "All these things I have kept from *my* youth." When Jesus heard *this,* He said to him, "One thing you still lack; sell all that you possess and distribute it to the poor, and you shall have treasure in heaven; and come, follow Me" (Luke 18:18–22, Jesus quotes from Exodus 20:12–16; cf. Matthew 19:16–22; Mark 10:17–22; see Luke 10:25–28).

THEFTS (Also see BURGLARY; ROBBER; ROBBERY; STEALING; THEFT; THIEF; and THIEVES)

Setting: Galilee. Jesus gives the crowd the meaning of His instruction about what defiles a man.

Peter said to Him, "Explain the parable to us." Jesus said, "Are you still lacking in understanding also? Do you not understand that everything that goes into the mouth passes into the stomach and is eliminated? But the things that proceed out of the mouth come from the heart, and those defile the man. For out of the heart come evil thoughts, murders, adulteries, fornications, thefts, false witness, slanders. These are the things which defile a man; but to eat with unwashed hands does not defile the man" (Matthew 15:15–20; cf. Mark 7:18–23; see Galatians 5:19–21).

Setting: Galilee. After the Pharisees and scribes from Jerusalem object to His disciples' lack of obedience to the tradition regarding ceremonial cleansing, Jesus speaks to a crowd, and explains His teaching to the disciples.

After He called the crowd to Him again, He *began* saying to them, "Listen to Me, all of you, and understand: there is nothing outside the man which can defile him if it goes into him; but the things which proceed out of the man are what defile the man. [If anyone has ears to hear, let him hear."] When he had left the crowd *and* entered the house, His disciples questioned Him about the parable. And He said to them, "Are you so lacking in understanding also? Do you not understand that whatever goes into the man from outside cannot defile him, because it does not go into his heart, but into his stomach, and is eliminated?" (*Thus He* declared all foods clean.) And He was saying, "That which proceeds out of the man, that is what defiles the man. For from within, out of the heart of men, proceed the evil thoughts, fornications, thefts, murders, adulteries, deeds of coveting *and* wickedness, *as well* as deceit, sensuality, envy, slander, pride *and* foolishness. All these evil things proceed from within and defile the man" (Mark 7:14–23; cf. Matthew 15:10–20).

THESE, LEAST OF (Also see LEAST)

Setting: Galilee. During the early part of His ministry, Jesus preaches the Sermon on the Mount to His disciples and the multitudes.

"Whoever then annuls one of the least of these commandments, and teaches others *to do* the same, shall be called least in the kingdom of heaven; but whoever keeps and teaches *them*, he shall be called great in the kingdom of heaven" (Matthew 5:19; cf. Matthew 11:11).

Setting: On the Mount of Olives, just east of Jerusalem. During His Olivet Discourse, after answering His disciples' questions as to when the temple will be destroyed and Jerusalem overrun, along with the signs of His coming and the end of the age, Jesus reveals the future judgments following His return.

"But when the Son of Man comes in His glory, and all the angels with Him, then He will sit on His glorious throne. All the nations will be gathered before Him; and He will separate them from one another, as the shepherd separates the sheep from the goats; and He will put the sheep on His right, and the goats on the left. Then the King will say to those on His right, 'Come, you who are blessed of My Father, inherit the kingdom prepared for you from the foundation of the world. 'For I was hungry, and you gave Me *something* to eat; I was thirsty, and you gave Me *something* to drink; I was a stranger, and you invited Me in; naked, and you clothed Me; I was sick, and you visited Me; I was in prison, and you came to Me.' Then the righteous will answer Him, 'Lord, when did we see You hungry and feed You, or thirsty, and give you *something* to drink? And when did we see You a stranger, and invite You in, or naked, and clothe You? When did we see You sick, or in prison, and come to You?' The King will answer and say to them, 'Truly I say to you, to the extent that you did it to one of these brothers of Mine, *even* the least *of them,* you did it to Me.' Then

He will also say to those on His left, 'Depart from Me, accursed ones, into the eternal fire which has been prepared for the devil and his angels; for I was hungry, and you gave Me *nothing* to eat; I was thirsty, and you gave Me nothing to drink; I was a stranger, and you did not invite Me in; naked, and you did not clothe Me; sick, and in prison, and you did not visit Me.' Then they themselves also will answer, 'Lord, when did we see You hungry, or thirsty, or a stranger, or naked, or sick, or in prison, and did not take care of You?' Then He will answer them, 'Truly I say to you, to the extent that you did not do it to one of the least of these, you did not do it to Me.' These will go away into eternal punishment, but the righteous into eternal life" (Matthew 25:31–46; see Matthew 7:23; 16:27; 19:29).

THESE THINGS (Listed as THINGS, THESE)

THIEF (Also see BURGLARY; ROBBER; ROBBERY; STEALING; THEFT; THEFTS; and THIEVES)

Setting: On the Mount of Olives, just east of Jerusalem. During His Olivet Discourse, after answering His disciples' questions as to when the temple will be destroyed and Jerusalem overrun, along with the signs of His coming and the end of the age, Jesus reemphasizes to His disciples that they should be on the alert for His return.

"Therefore be on the alert, for you do not know which day your Lord is coming. But be sure of this, that if the head of the house had known at what time of the night the thief was coming, he would have been on the alert and would not have allowed his house to be broken into. For this reason you also must be ready; for the Son of Man is coming at an hour when you do not think *He will*. Who then is the faithful and sensible slave whom his master put in charge of his household to give their food at the proper time? Blessed is that slave whom his master finds so doing when he comes. Truly I say to you that he will put him in charge of all his possessions. But if that evil slave says in his heart, 'My master is not coming for a long time,' and begins to beat his fellow slaves and eat and drink with drunkards; the master of that slave will come on a day when he does not expect *him* and at an hour which he does not know, and will cut him in pieces and assign him a place with the hypocrites; in that place there will be weeping and gnashing of teeth" (Matthew 24:42–51; cf. Mark 13:33–37; Luke 12:39–46; 21:34–36; see Matthew 8:11, 12; 25:21–23).

Setting: On the way from Galilee to Jerusalem. After giving a parable about riches and greed, Jesus challenges the crowd and His disciples concerning godly living.

"Sell your possessions and give to charity; make yourselves money belts which do not wear out, an unfailing treasure in heaven, where no thief comes near nor moth destroys. For where your treasure is, there your heart will be also" (Luke 12:33, 34; cf. Matthew 6:19–21; 19:21).

Setting: On the way from Galilee to Jerusalem. After giving a parable about riches and greed, Jesus uses another parable to challenge the crowd and His disciples to be ready for His return.

"Be dressed in readiness, and *keep* your lamps lit. Be like men who are waiting for their master when he returns from the wedding feast, so that they may immediately open *the door* to him when he comes and knocks. Blessed are those slaves whom the master will find on the alert when he comes; truly I say to you, that he will gird himself *to serve,* and have them recline *at the table,* and will come up and wait on them. Whether he comes in the second watch, or even in the third and finds *them* so, blessed are those *slaves*. But be sure of this, that if the head of the house had known at what hour the thief was coming, he would not have allowed his house to be broken into. You too, be ready; for the Son of Man is coming at an hour that you do not expect" (Luke 12:35–40; cf. Matthew 24:42–44; see Mark 13:33; Ephesians 6:14).

Setting: Jerusalem. Following the Pharisees' interrogation and dismissal of the formerly blind man Jesus healed on the Sabbath, the Lord speaks to the Pharisees, using parabolic language they do not understand.

"Truly, truly, I say to you, he who does not enter by the door into the fold of the sheep, but climbs up some other way, he is a thief and a robber. But he who enters by the door is a shepherd of the sheep. To him the doorkeeper opens, and the sheep hear his voice, and he calls his own sheep by name and leads them out. When he puts forth all his own, he goes ahead of them, and the sheep follow him because they know his voice. A stranger they simply will not follow, but will flee from him, because they do not know the voice of strangers" (John 10:1–5).

Setting: Jerusalem. Following the Pharisees' interrogation and dismissal of the formerly blind man Jesus healed on the Sabbath, the Lord conveys to the Pharisees the Parable of the Good Shepherd, using figures of speech they do not understand.

So Jesus said to them again, "Truly, truly, I say to you, I am the door of the sheep. All who came before Me are thieves and robbers, but the sheep did not hear them. I am the door; if anyone enters through Me, he will be saved, and will go in and out and find pasture. The thief comes only to steal and kill and destroy; I came that they may have life, and have *it* abundantly. I am the good shepherd; the good shepherd lays down His life for the sheep. He who is a hired hand, and not a shepherd, who is not the owner of the sheep, sees the wolf coming, and leaves the sheep and flees, and the wolf snatches them and scatters *them. He flees* because he is a hired hand and is not concerned about the sheep. I am the good shepherd, and I know My own and My own know Me, even as the Father knows Me and I know the Father; and I lay down My life for the sheep. I have other sheep, which are not of this fold; I must bring them also, and they will hear My voice; and they will become one flock *with* one shepherd. For this reason the Father loves Me, because I lay down My life so that I may take it again. No one has taken it away from Me, but I lay it down on My own initiative. I have authority to take it up again. This commandment I received from My Father" (John 10:7–18; see Isaiah 40:11; 56:8; Jeremiah 23:1; Matthew 11:27).

Setting: On the island of Patmos (in the Aegean Sea about fifty miles southwest of Ephesus in modern Turkey). On the Lord's Day (Sunday), approximately fifty years after the Resurrection, the disciple John encounters the Lord Jesus Christ, who communicates a new revelation for the apostle to record for the church in Sardis and to six other churches in Asia.

"To the angel of the church in Sardis write: He who has the seven Spirits of God and the seven stars, says this: 'I know your deeds, that you have a name that you are alive, but you are dead. Wake up, and strengthen the things that remain, which were about to die; for I have not found your deeds completed in the sight of My God. So remember what you have received and heard; and keep *it,* and repent. Therefore if you do not wake up, I will come like a thief, and you will not know at what hour I will come to you. But you have a few people in Sardis who have not soiled their garments; and they will walk with Me in white, for they are worthy. He who overcomes will thus be clothed in white garments; and I will not erase his name from the book of life, and I will confess his name before My Father and before His angels. He who has an ear, let him hear what the Spirit says to the churches' " (Revelation 3:1–6; see Matthew 10:32; Revelation 1:16).

THIEVES (Also see BURGLARY; ROBBER; ROBBERY; STEALING; THEFT; THEFTS; and THIEF)

Setting: Galilee. During the early part of His ministry, Jesus preaches the Sermon on the Mount to His disciples and the multitudes.

"Do not store up for yourselves treasures on earth, where moth and rust destroy, and where thieves break in and steal. But store up for yourselves treasures in heaven, where neither moth nor rust destroys, and where thieves do not break in or steal; for where your treasure is, there your heart will be also" (Matthew 6:19–21; cf. Luke 12:34; see Proverb 23:4; Matthew 19:21).

Setting: Jerusalem. Following the Pharisees' interrogation and dismissal of the formerly blind man Jesus healed on the Sabbath, the Lord conveys to the Pharisees the Parable of the Good Shepherd, using figures of speech they do not understand.

So Jesus said to them again, "Truly, truly, I say to you, I am the door of the sheep. All who came before Me are thieves and robbers, but the sheep did not hear them. I am the door; if anyone enters through Me, he will be saved, and will go in and out and find pasture. The thief comes only to steal and kill and destroy; I came that they may have life, and have *it* abundantly. I am the good shepherd; the good shepherd lays down His life for the sheep. He who is a hired hand, and not a shepherd, who is not the owner of the sheep, sees the wolf coming, and leaves the sheep and flees, and the wolf snatches them and scatters *them. He*

flees because he is a hired hand and is not concerned about the sheep. I am the good shepherd, and I know My own and My own know Me, even as the Father knows Me and I know the Father; and I lay down My life for the sheep. I have other sheep, which are not of this fold; I must bring them also, and they will hear My voice; and they will become one flock *with* one shepherd. For this reason the Father loves Me, because I lay down My life so that I may take it again. No one has taken it away from Me, but I lay it down on My own initiative. I have authority to take it up again. This commandment I received from My Father" (John 10:7–18; see Isaiah 40:11; 56:8; Jeremiah 23:1; Matthew 11:27).

THING (Check for specifics such as THING, LITTLE; and THING, ONE; also see THINGS)

THING, LITTLE

Setting: On the way from Galilee to Jerusalem. After giving a parable about riches and greed, Jesus comforts the crowd and His disciples. The scribes and Pharisees turn hostile and question Him repeatedly in an attempt to catch Him in something He might say.

And He said to His disciples, "For this reason I say to you, do not worry about *your* life, *as to* what you will eat; nor for your body, *as to* what you will put on. For life is more than food, and the body more than clothing. Consider the ravens, for they neither sow nor reap; they have no storeroom nor barn, and *yet* God feeds them; how much more valuable you are than the birds! And which of you by worrying can add a *single* hour to his life's span? If then you cannot do even a very little thing, why do you worry about other matters? Consider the lilies, how they grow: they neither toil nor spin; but I tell you, not even Solomon in all his glory clothed himself like one of these. But if God so clothes the grass in the field, which is *alive* today and tomorrow is thrown into the furnace, how much more *will He clothe* you? You men of little faith! And do not seek what you will eat and what you will drink, and do not keep worrying. For all these things the nations of the world eagerly seek; but your Father knows that you need these things. But seek His kingdom, and these things will be added to you. Do not be afraid, little flock, for your Father has chosen gladly to give you the kingdom" (Luke 12:22–32; cf. Matthew 6:25–33; see 1 Kings 10:4–7; Job 38:41).

Setting: On the way from Galilee to Jerusalem. After giving the story of the prodigal son, the Lord teaches His disciples about stewardship.

Now He was also saying to the disciples, "There was a rich man who had a manager, and this *manager* was reported to him as squandering his possessions. And he called him and said to him, 'What is this I hear about you? Give an accounting of your management, for you can no longer be a manager.' The manager said to himself, 'What shall I do, since my master is taking the management away from me? I am not strong enough to dig; I am ashamed to beg. I know what I shall do, so that when I am removed from the management people will welcome me into their homes.' And he summoned each one of his master's debtors, and he *began* saying to the first, 'How much do you owe my master?' And he said, 'A hundred measures of oil.' And he said to him, 'Take your bill, and sit down quickly and write fifty.' Then he said to another, 'And how much do you owe?' And he said, 'A hundred measures of wheat.' He said to him, 'Take your bill, and write eighty.' And his master praised the unrighteous manager because he had acted shrewdly; for the sons of this age are more shrewd in relation to their own kind than the sons of light. And I say to you, make friends for yourselves by means of the wealth of unrighteousness, so that when it fails, they will receive you into the eternal dwellings. He who is faithful in a very little thing is faithful also in much; and he who is unrighteous in a very little thing is unrighteous also in much. Therefore if you have not been faithful in the *use of* unrighteous wealth, who will entrust the true *riches* to you? And if you have not been faithful in *the use of* that which is another's, who will give you that which is your own? No servant can serve two masters; for either he will hate the one and love the other, or else he will be devoted to one and despise the other. You cannot serve God and wealth" (Luke 16:1–13; cf. Matthew 6:24; see Matthew 25:14–30).

Setting: Jericho, on the way to Jerusalem. After commending Zaccheus's faith in Him, Jesus provides a parable about stewardship.

So He said, "A nobleman went to a distant country to receive a kingdom for himself, and *then* return. And he called ten of his slaves, and gave them ten minas and said to them, 'Do business *with this* until I come *back*.' But his citizens hated him and sent a delegation after him, saying, 'We do not want this man to reign over us.' When he returned, after receiving the kingdom, he ordered that these slaves, to whom he had given the money, be called to him so that he might know what business they had done. The first appeared, saying, 'Master, your mina has made ten minas more.' And he said to him, 'Well done, good slave, because you have been faithful in a very little thing, you are to be in authority over ten cities.' The second came, saying, 'Your mina, master, has made five minas.' And he said to him, also, 'And you are to be over five cities.' Another came, saying, 'Master, here is your mina, which I kept put away in a handkerchief; for I was afraid of you, because you are an exacting man; you take up what you did not lay down and reap what you did not sow.' He said to him, 'By your own words I will judge you, you worthless slave. Did you know that I am an exacting man, taking up what I did not lay down and reaping what I did not sow? Then why did you not put my money in the bank, and having come, I would have collected it with interest?' Then he said to the bystanders, 'Take the mina away from him and give it to the one who has the ten minas.' And they said to him, 'Master, he has ten minas *already*.' I tell you that to everyone who has, more shall be given, but from the one who does not have, even what he does have shall be taken away. But these enemies of mine, who did not want me to reign over them, bring them here and slay them in my presence" (Luke 19:12–27; cf. Matthew 25:14–30; see Matthew 13:12; Luke 16:10).

THING, ONE

Setting: The temple in Jerusalem. Jesus returns after spending the night in Bethany. The chief priests and elders question His authority to teach the nation.

Jesus said to them, "I will also ask you one thing, which if you tell Me, I will also tell you by what authority I do these things. The baptism of John was from what *source*, from heaven or from men?" And they *began* reasoning among themselves, saying "If we say 'From heaven,' He will say to us, 'Then why did you not believe him?' But if we say, 'From men,' we fear the people; for they all regard John as a prophet." And answering Jesus, they said, "We do not know." He also said to them, "Neither will I tell you by what authority I do these things" (Matthew 21:24–27; cf. Mark 11:29–33; Luke 20:3–8).

Setting: Judea beyond the Jordan (Perea). After demonstrating to His disciples the importance of little children, Jesus encounters a rich man seeking eternal life.

And Jesus said to him, "Why do you call Me good? No one is good except God alone. You know the commandments, 'DO NOT MURDER, DO NOT COMMIT ADULTERY, DO NOT STEAL, DO NOT BEAR FALSE WITNESS, Do not defraud, HONOR YOUR FATHER AND MOTHER.'" And he said to Him, "Teacher, I have kept all these things from my youth up." Looking at him, Jesus felt a love for him and said to him, "One thing you lack: go and sell all you possess and give to the poor, and you will have treasure in heaven; and come, follow Me" (Mark 10:18–21; Jesus quotes from Exodus 20:12–16; cf. Matthew 19:16–22; Luke 18:18–24; see Matthew 6:20).

Setting: On the way from Galilee to Jerusalem. After being tested by a lawyer, the Lord and His disciples are welcomed into the home of Martha and Mary in Bethany.

But the Lord answered and said to her, "Martha, Martha, you are worried and bothered about so many things; but *only* one thing is necessary, for Mary has chosen the good part, which shall not be taken away from her." (Luke 10:41, 42; see Matthew 6:25; Luke 10:38–40)

Setting: Judea beyond the Jordan (Perea). After speaking of the importance of children, Jesus responds to a ruler's question about inheriting eternal life.

A ruler questioned Him, saying, "Good Teacher, what shall I do to inherit eternal life?" And Jesus said to him, "Why do you call Me good? No one is good except God alone. You know the commandments, 'DO NOT COMMIT ADULTERY, DO NOT MURDER, DO NOT STEAL, DO NOT BEAR FALSE WITNESS, HONOR YOUR FATHER AND MOTHER.'" And he said "All these things I have kept from *my* youth." When Jesus heard *this*, He said to him, "One thing you still lack; sell all that you possess and distribute it to the poor, and you shall have treasure in heaven; and come, follow Me" (Luke 18:18–22, Jesus quotes from Exodus 20:12–16; cf. Matthew 19:16–22; Mark 10:17–22; see Luke 10:25–28).

THING, SAME

Setting: Judea beyond the Jordan (Perea). Jesus illustrates the kingdom of heaven to His disciples through the story of laborers in the vineyard.

"For the kingdom of heaven is like a landowner who went out early in the morning to hire laborers for his vineyard. When he had agreed with the laborers for a denarius for the day, he sent them into his vineyard. And he went out about the third hour and saw others standing idle in the market place; and to those he said,' You also go into the vineyard, and whatever is right I will give you.' And *so* they went. Again he went out about the sixth and the ninth hour, and did the same thing. And about the eleventh *hour* he went out and found others standing *around;* and he said to them, 'Why have you been standing idle here all day long?' They said to him, 'Because no one hired us.' He said to them, 'You go into the vineyard too.' When evening came, the owner of the vineyard said to his foreman, 'Call the laborers and pay them their wages, beginning with the last *group* to the first.' When those *hired* about the eleventh hour came, each one received a denarius. When those *hired* first came, they thought that they would receive more; but each of them also received a denarius. When they received it, they grumbled at the landowner, saying, 'These last men have worked *only* one hour, and you have made them equal to us who have borne the burden and the scorching heat of the day.' But he answered and said to one of them, 'Friend, I am doing you no wrong; did you not agree with me for a denarius? Take what is yours and go, but I wish to give to this last man the same as to you. It is not lawful for me to do what I wish with what is my own? Or is your eye envious because I am generous?' So the last shall be first, and the first last" (Matthew 20:1–16; cf. Matthew 19:30).

Setting: The temple in Jerusalem. Jesus delivers a parable to the chief priests and elders after they question His authority.

"But what do you think? A man had two sons, and he came to the first and said, 'Son, go work today in the vineyard.' And he answered, 'I will not'; but afterward he regretted it and went. The man came to the second and said the same thing; and he answered, 'I *will,* sir'; but he did not go. Which of the two sons did the will of his father?" They said, "The first." Jesus said to them, "Truly, I say to you that the tax collectors and prostitutes will get into the kingdom of God before you. For John came to you in the way of righteousness and you did not believe him; but the tax collectors and prostitutes did believe him; and you, seeing *this,* did not even feel remorse afterward so as to believe him" (Matthew 21:28–32; cf. Luke 7:29, 30, 37–50).

Setting: The temple in Jerusalem. Jesus delivers another parable to the chief priests and elders after they question His authority.

"Listen to another parable. There was a landowner who PLANTED A VINEYARD AND PUT A WALL AROUND IT AND DUG A WINE PRESS IN IT, AND BUILT A TOWER, and rented it out to vine-growers and went on a journey. When the harvest time approached, he sent his slaves to the vine-growers to receive his produce. The vine-growers took his slaves and beat one, and killed another, and stoned a third. Again he sent another group of slaves larger than the first; and they did the same thing to them. But afterward he sent his son to them, saying, 'They will respect my son.' But when the vine-growers saw the son, they said among themselves, 'This is the heir; come, let us kill him and seize his inheritance.' They took him, and threw him out of the vineyard and killed him. Therefore when the owner of the vineyard comes, what will he do to those vine-growers?" (Matthew 21:33–40; Jesus quotes from Isaiah 5:1, 2; cf. Mark 12:1–9; Luke 20:9–15).

THINGS (Also check for specifics such as THINGS, ALL; and THINGS, FEW; also see THING)

Setting: By the Sea of Galilee. Jesus teaches the Parable of the Head of a Household to His disciples.

And Jesus said to them, "Therefore every scribe who has become a disciple of the kingdom of heaven is like a head of a household, who brings out of his treasure things new and old" (Matthew 13:52).

Setting: Galilee. Jesus gives the crowd the meaning of His instruction about what defiles a man.

Peter said to Him, "Explain the parable to us." Jesus said, "Are you still lacking in understanding also? Do you not understand that everything that goes into the mouth passes into the stomach and is eliminated? But the things that proceed out of the mouth come from the heart, and those defile the man. For out of the heart come evil thoughts, murders, adulteries, fornications, thefts, false witness, slanders. These are the things which defile a man; but to eat with unwashed hands does not defile the man" (Matthew 15:15–20; cf. Mark 7:18–23; see Galatians 5:19–21).

Setting: The temple in Jerusalem. The Pharisees send their disciples and the Herodians to test Jesus about the poll-tax in order to trap Him.

But Jesus perceived their malice, and said, "Why are you testing Me, you hypocrites? Show Me the coin *used* for the poll-tax." And they brought Him a denarius. And He said to them, "Whose likeness and inscription is this?" They said to Him, "Caesar's." Then He said to them, "Then render to Caesar the things that are Caesar's; and to God the things that are God's" (Matthew 22:18–21; cf. Matthew 17:25; Mark 12:15–17; Luke 20:22–25).

Setting: The temple in Jerusalem. Jesus exposes the truth about Pharisaism to the crowds and His disciples after the Jewish religious leaders test Him with questions.

Then Jesus spoke to the crowds and to His disciples, saying: "The scribes and the Pharisees have seated themselves in the chair of Moses; therefore all that they tell you, do and observe, but do not do according to their deeds; for they say *things* and do not do *them.* They tie up heavy burdens and lay them on men's shoulders, but they themselves are unwilling to move them with *so much as* a finger. But they do all their deeds to be noticed by men; for they broaden their phylacteries and lengthen their tassels *of their garments.* They love the place of honor at banquets and the chief seats in the synagogues, and respectful greetings in the market places, and being called Rabbi by men. But do not be called Rabbi; for One is your Teacher, and you are all brothers. Do not call *anyone* on earth your father; for One is your Father, He who is in heaven. Do not be called leaders; for One is your Leader, *that is,* Christ. But the greatest among you shall be your servant. Whoever exalts himself shall be humbled; and whoever humbles himself shall be exalted" (Matthew 23:1–12; cf. Matthew 20:26; Mark 12:38–40; Luke 20:46, 47; see Exodus 13:9; Deuteronomy 33:3; Matthew 6:1, 5, 6, 9, 16; Mark 14:11; Luke 11:43; 14:11).

Setting: The temple in Jerusalem. After the Jewish religious leaders test Him with questions, Jesus pronounces the fifth of eight woes upon them in front of the crowds and His disciples.

"Woe to you, scribes and Pharisees, hypocrites! For you tithe mint and dill and cummin, and have neglected the weightier provisions of the law: justice and mercy and faithfulness; but these are things you should have done without neglecting the others. You blind guides, who strain out a gnat and swallow a camel!" (Matthew 23:23, 24).

Setting: The Mount of Olives, just east of Jerusalem. During His Olivet Discourse, Jesus answers His disciples' questions as to when the temple will be destroyed and Jerusalem overrun, along with the signs of His coming and the end of the age.

"Therefore when you see the ABOMINATION OF DESOLATION which was spoken of through Daniel the prophet, standing in the holy place (let the reader understand), then those who are in Judea must flee to the mountains. Whoever is on the housetop must not go down to get the things that are in his house. Whoever is in the field must not turn back to get his cloak. But woe to those who are pregnant and to those who are nursing babies in those days! But pray that your flight will not be in the winter, or on a Sabbath. For then there will be a great tribulation, such as has not occurred since the beginning of the world until now, nor ever will. Unless those days had been cut short, no life would have been saved; but for the sake of the elect those days will be cut short. Then if anyone says to you, 'Behold, here is the Christ,' or "There *He is,'* do not believe *him.* For false Christs and false prophets will arise and will show great signs and wonders, so as to mislead, if possible, even the elect. Behold, I have told you in advance. So if they say to you, 'Behold, He is in the wilderness,' do not go out, *or,* 'Behold, He is in the inner rooms,' do not believe *them.* For just as the lightning comes from the east and flashes even to the west, so will the coming of the Son of Man be. Wherever the corpse is, there the vultures will gather" (Matthew 24:15–28, Jesus quotes from Daniel 9:27; cf. Daniel 12:1; Mark 13:14–23; Luke 17:22–31; 21:20–24; 23:29; see John 4:48).

Setting: Galilee. After the Pharisees and scribes from Jerusalem object to His disciples' lack of obedience to the tradition regarding ceremonial cleansing, Jesus speaks to a crowd, and explains His teaching to the disciples.

After He called the crowd to Him again, He *began* saying to them, "Listen to Me, all of you, and understand: there is nothing outside the man which can defile him if it goes into him; but the things which proceed out of the man are what defile the man. [If anyone has ears to hear, let him hear."] When he had left the crowd *and* entered the house, His disciples questioned Him about the parable. And He said to them, "Are you so lacking in understanding also? Do you not understand that whatever goes into the man from outside cannot defile him, because it does not go into his heart, but into his stomach, and is eliminated?" (*Thus He* declared all foods clean.) And He was saying, "That which proceeds out of the man, that is what defiles the man. For from within, out of the heart of men, proceed the evil thoughts, fornications, thefts, murders, adulteries, deeds of coveting *and* wickedness, *as well* as deceit, sensuality, envy, slander, pride *and* foolishness. All these evil things proceed from within and defile the man" (Mark 7:14–23; cf. Matthew 15:10–20).

Setting: The temple in Jerusalem. After Jesus teaches the chief priests, scribes, and elders in parables, they send some of the Pharisees and Herodians in an attempt to trap Him in a statement.

"Shall we pay or shall we not pay?" But He, knowing their hypocrisy, said to them, "Why are you testing Me? Bring Me a denarius to look at." They brought *one.* And He said to them, "Whose likeness and inscription is this?" And they said to Him, "Caesar's." And Jesus said to them, "Render to Caesar the things that are Caesar's, and to God the things that are God's." And they were amazed at Him (Mark 12:15–17; cf. Matthew 22:15–22; Luke 20:20–26).

Setting: On the way from Galilee to Jerusalem. After responding to a report from the seventy sent out in pairs to every place He Himself will soon visit, the Lord addresses His disciples in private.

Turning to the disciples, He said privately, "Blessed *are* the eyes which see the things you see, for I say to you, that many prophets and kings wished to see the things you see, and did not see *them*, and to hear the things which you hear, and did not hear *them*" (Luke 10:23, 24; cf. Matthew 13:16, 17).

Setting: On the way from Galilee to Jerusalem. After speaking of how a lamp illuminates, the Lord has lunch with a Pharisee, who is surprised He doesn't wash before eating.

But the Lord said to him, "Now you Pharisees clean the outside of the cup and of the platter; but inside of you, you are full of robbery and wickedness. You foolish ones, did not He who made the outside make the inside also? But give that which is within as charity, and then all things are clean for you. But woe to you Pharisees! You pay tithe of mint and rue and every *kind of* garden herb, and *yet* disregard justice and the love of God; but these are the things you should have done without neglecting the others. Woe to you Pharisees! For you love the chief seats in the synagogues and the respectful greetings in the market places. Woe to you! For you are like concealed tombs, and the people who walk over *them* are unaware *of it*" (Luke 11:39–44; cf. Matthew 23:6, 7, 23–27; see Matthew 15:2; Titus 1:15).

Setting: On the way from Galilee to Jerusalem. After His disciples ask that their faith be increased following His instruction to them on forgiveness, the Lord illustrates with the mustard seed and an obedient slave.

And the Lord said, "If you had faith like a mustard seed, you would say to this mulberry tree, 'Be uprooted and be planted in the sea'; and it would obey you. Which of you, having a slave plowing or tending sheep, will say to him when he has come from the field, 'Come immediately and sit down to eat'? But will he not say to him, "Prepare something for me to eat, and *properly* clothe yourself and serve me while I eat and drink; and afterward you may eat and drink'? He does not thank the slave because he did the things which were commanded, does he? So you too, when you do all the things which are commanded you, say, 'We are unworthy slaves; we have done *only* that which we ought to have done'" (Luke 17:6–10; see Matthew 13:31; Luke 12:37).

Setting: On the way from Galilee to Jerusalem. After responding to a ruler's question about inheriting eternal life, Jesus replies to the disciples' conclusion about being saved.

But He said, "The things that are impossible with people are possible with God" (Luke 18:27; cf. Matthew 19:26).

Setting: Approaching Jerusalem. After being praised by the people in a triumphal entry, the Lord weeps as He sees the city ahead of Him.

When He approached *Jerusalem,* He saw the city and wept over it, saying, "If you had known in this day, even you, the things which make for peace! But now they have been hidden from your eyes. For the days will come upon you when your enemies will throw up a barricade against you, and surround you and hem you in on every side, and they will level you to the ground and your children within you, and they will not leave in you one stone upon another, because you did not recognize the time of your visitation" (Luke 19:41–44; see Matthew 24:1, 2; Luke 13:34, 35).

Setting: The temple in Jerusalem. While ministering a few days before His crucifixion, after Jesus gives the people the Parable of the Vine-Growers, the scribes and Pharisees seek to trap Him by questioning Him about paying taxes to Caesar.

But He detected their trickery and said to them, "Show Me a denarius. Whose likeness and inscription does it have?" They said "Caesar's." And He said to them, "Then render to Caesar the things that are Caesar's, and to God the things that are God's" (Luke 20:23–25; cf. Matthew 22:15–21; Mark 12:13–17).

Setting: On the Mount of Olives, just east of Jerusalem. After ministering in the temple a few days before His crucifixion, and giving His disciples more details regarding future events, Jesus speaks during His Olivet Discourse of His return.

"There will be signs in sun and moon and stars, and on the earth dismay among the nations, in perplexity at the roaring of the sea and the waves, men fainting from fear and the expectation of the things which are coming upon the world; for the powers of the heavens will be shaken. Then they will see THE SON OF MAN COMING IN A CLOUD with power and great glory. But when these things begin to take place, straighten up and lift up your heads, because your redemption is drawing near" (Luke 21:25–28, Jesus quotes from Daniel 7:13; cf. Matthew 24:29–31; Mark 13:24–27).

Setting: The temple treasury in Jerusalem. Following the Feast of Booths and the scribes' and Pharisees' failed attempt to stone a woman for adultery, Jesus returns the next day to teach. They question His testimony about Himself.

Then He said again to them, "I go away, and you will seek Me, and will die in your sin; where I am going, you cannot come." So the Jews were saying, "Surely He will not kill Himself, will He, since He says, 'Where I am going, you cannot come'?" And He was saying to them, "You are from below, I am from above; you are of this world, I am not of this world. Therefore I said to you that you will die in your sins; for unless you believe that I am *He,* you will die in your sins." So they were saying to Him, "Who are You?" Jesus said to them, "What have I been saying to you *from* the beginning? I have many things to speak and to judge concerning you, but He who sent Me is true; and the things which I heard from Him, these I speak to the world" (John 8:21–26; see John 3:31–33; 5:34, 35; 17:14, 16).

Setting: The temple treasury in Jerusalem. Following the Feast of Booths and the scribes' and Pharisees' failed attempt to stone a woman for adultery, Jesus returns the next day to teach. They question His testimony about Himself.

So Jesus said, "When you lift up the Son of Man, then you will know that I am *He,* and I do nothing on my own initiative, but I speak these things as the Father taught Me. And He who sent Me is with Me; He has not left Me alone, for I always do the things that are pleasing to Him" (John 8:28, 29; see John 3:14).

Setting: The temple treasury in Jerusalem. After the scribes and Pharisees question His testimony about Himself, Jesus reveals to those Jews who believe in Him how He will make them free.

So Jesus was saying to those Jews who had believed Him, "If you continue in My word, *then* you are truly disciples of Mine; and you will know the truth, and the truth will make you free." They answered Him, "We are Abraham's descendants and have never yet been enslaved to anyone; how is it that You say, 'You will become free'?" Jesus answered them, "Truly, truly, I say to you, everyone who commits sin is the slave of sin. The slave does not remain in the house forever; the son does remain forever. So if the Son makes you free, you will be free indeed. I know that you are Abraham's descendants; yet you seek to kill Me, because My word has no place in you. I speak the things which I have seen with *My* Father; therefore you also do the things which you heard from *your* father" (John 8:31–38; see John 8:1–30, 36, 41, 44; Romans 6:16).

Setting: Jerusalem. Just days before the Passover, with the chief priests and Pharisees plotting to seize Jesus, who is expressing anxiety about His upcoming crucifixion, some of the Jews believe in the Lord, while others are rejecting His message.

And Jesus cried out and said, "He who believes in Me, does not believe in Me but in Him who sent Me. He who sees Me sees the One who sent Me. I have come *as* Light into the world, so that everyone who believes in Me will not remain in darkness. If anyone hears My sayings and does not keep them, I do not judge him; for I did not come to judge the world, but to save the world. He who rejects Me and does not receive My sayings, has one who judges him; the word I spoke is what will judge him at the last day. For I did not speak on My own initiative, but the Father Himself who sent Me has given Me a commandment *as to* what to say and what to speak. I know that His commandment is eternal life; therefore the things I speak, I speak just as the Father as told Me" (John 12:44–50; see Matthew 10:40; Luke 10:16; John 1:4; 3:17; 5:19; 6:68; 14:9).

Setting: Caesarea. Luke, writing in Acts, gives Paul's retelling of his conversion to Christ as he appears before King Agrippa following his hearing before the Jewish Council in Jerusalem and arrest by the Roman commander (on his way to Rome after the apostle's third missionary journey).

"And when we had fallen to the ground, I heard a voice saying to me in the Hebrew dialect, 'Saul, Saul, why are you persecuting Me? It is hard for you to kick against the goads.' And I said, 'Who are You, Lord?' And the Lord said, 'I am Jesus whom you are persecuting. But get up and stand on your feet; for this purpose I have appeared to you, to appoint you a minister and a witness not only to the things which you have seen, but also to the things in which I will appear to you; rescuing you from the *Jewish* people and from the Gentiles, to whom I am sending you, to open their eyes so that they may turn from darkness to light and from the dominion of Satan to God, that they may receive forgiveness of sins and an inheritance among those who have been sanctified by faith in Me' (Acts 26.14–18, see Isaiah 35.5, Acts 21.40, 22.14).

Setting: On the island of Patmos (in the Aegean Sea about fifty miles southwest of Ephesus in modern Turkey). On the Lord's Day (Sunday), approximately fifty years after the Resurrection, the disciple John encounters the Lord Jesus Christ, who communicates new revelations for the apostle to record for the seven churches in Asia.

When I saw Him, I fell at His feet like a dead man. And He placed His right hand on me, saying, "Do not be afraid; I am the first and the last, and the living One; and I was dead, and behold, I am alive forevermore, and I have the keys of death and of Hades. Therefore write the things which you have seen, and the things which are, and the things which will take place after these things. As for the mystery of the seven stars which you saw in My right hand, and the seven golden lampstands: the seven stars are the angels of the seven churches, and the seven lampstands are the seven churches" (Revelation 1:17–20; see Isaiah 44:6; Luke 24:5; Revelation 2:8).

Setting: On the island of Patmos (in the Aegean Sea about fifty miles southwest of Ephesus in modern Turkey). On the Lord's Day (Sunday), approximately fifty years after the Resurrection, the disciple John encounters the Lord Jesus Christ, who communicates a new revelation for the apostle to record for the church in Pergamum and to six other churches in Asia.

"And to the angel of the church in Pergamum write: The One who has the sharp two-edged sword says this: 'I know where you dwell, where Satan's throne is; and you hold fast My name, and did not deny My faith even in the days of Antipas, My witness,

My faithful one, who was killed among you, where Satan dwells. But I have a few things against you, because you have there some who hold the teaching of Balaam, who kept teaching Balak to put a stumbling block before the sons of Israel, to eat things sacrificed to idols and to commit *acts of* immorality. So you also have some who in the same way hold the teaching of the Nicolaitans. Therefore repent; or else I am coming to you quickly, and I will make war against them with the sword of My mouth. He who has an ear, let him hear what the Spirit says to the churches. To him who overcomes, to him I will give *some* of the hidden manna, and I will give him a white stone, and a new name written on the stone which no one knows but he who receives it' (Revelation 2:12–17; see Numbers 25:1–3; Isaiah 62:2; Revelation 1:16).

Setting: On the island of Patmos (in the Aegean Sea about fifty miles southwest of Ephesus in modern Turkey). On the Lord's Day (Sunday), approximately fifty years after the Resurrection, the disciple John encounters the Lord Jesus Christ, who communicates a new revelation for the apostle to record for the church in Sardis and to six other churches in Asia.

"To the angel of the church in Sardis write: He who has the seven Spirits of God and the seven stars, says this: 'I know your deeds, that you have a name that you are alive, but you are dead. Wake up, and strengthen the things that remain, which were about to die; for I have not found your deeds completed in the sight of My God. So remember what you have received and heard; and keep *it,* and repent. Therefore if you do not wake up, I will come like a thief, and you will not know at what hour I will come to you. But you have a few people in Sardis who have not soiled their garments; and they will walk with Me in white, for they are worthy. He who overcomes will thus be clothed in white garments; and I will not erase his name from the book of life, and I will confess his name before My Father and before His angels. He who has an ear, let him hear what the Spirit says to the churches' " (Revelation 3:1–6; see Matthew 10:32; Revelation 1:16).

THINGS, ALL

Setting: Galilee. As He teaches and preaches, after pronouncing woes upon unrepentant cities, Jesus prays a thanksgiving prayer to His Father in heaven.

At that time Jesus said, "I praise You, Father, Lord of heaven and earth, that you have hidden these things from *the* wise and intelligent and have revealed them to infants. Yes, Father, for this way was well-pleasing in Your sight. All things have been handed over to Me by My Father; and no one knows the Son except the Father; nor does anyone know the Father except the Son, and anyone to whom the Son wills to reveal *Him*" (Matthew 11:25–27; cf. Luke 10:21, 22).

Setting: A mountain in Galilee. Following the Transfiguration, Peter, James, and John ask the Lord why Elijah must come before the Messiah.

And He answered and said, "Elijah is coming and will restore all things; but I say to you that Elijah already came, and they did not recognize him, but did to him whatever they wished. So also the Son of Man is going to suffer at their hands" (Matthew 17:11, 12; cf. Mark 9:11–13).

Setting: Judea beyond the Jordan (Perea). Jesus makes a pronouncement to His disciples following their astonishment over His statement on the difficulty of a rich man obtaining eternal life.

And looking at them, Jesus said to them, "With people this is impossible, but with God all things are possible" (Matthew 19:26; cf. Genesis 18:14; Mark 10:27; Luke 18:27).

Setting: On the way from Bethany to Jerusalem. The day after Jesus curses a fig tree (an illustration of the nation Israel), His disciples ask Him how it has so quickly withered.

And Jesus answered and said to them, "Truly I say to you, if you have faith and do not doubt, you will not only do what was done to the fig tree, but even if you say to this mountain, 'Be taken up and cast into the sea,' it will happen. And all things you ask in prayer, believing, you will receive" (Matthew 21:21, 22; cf. Matthew 7:7; Matthew 17:20; Mark 11:20–24).

Setting: Galilee. After informing a crowd and His disciples of the hope involving the coming kingdom of God, Jesus takes Peter, James, and John to a high mountain (some think Mount Hermon). The Lord reveals His glory through the Transfiguration, and answers their question about Elijah.

And He said to them, "Elijah does first come and restore all things. And *yet* how is it written of the Son of Man that He will suffer many things and be treated with contempt? But I say to you that Elijah has indeed come, and they did to him whatever they wished, just as it is written of him" (Mark 9:12, 13; cf. Matthew 17:1–13; Luke 9:28–36; see Malachi 4:5, 6; Matthew 16:21).

Setting: Galilee. After returning from a high mountain (perhaps Mount Hermon) where Jesus was transfigured in front of Peter, James, and John, the four discover the rest of the disciples arguing with some scribes.

And He asked them, "What are you discussing with them?" And one of the crowd answered Him, "Teacher, I brought You my son, possessed with a spirit which makes him mute; and whenever it seizes him, it slams him *to the ground* and he foams *at the mouth,* and grinds his teeth and stiffens out. I told Your disciples to cast it out, and they could not *do it.* And He answered them, and said, "O unbelieving generation, how long shall I be with you? How long shall I put up with you? Bring him to Me!" They brought the boy to Him. When he saw Him, immediately the spirit threw him into a convulsion, and falling to the ground, be *began* rolling around and foaming *at the mouth.* And He asked his father, "How long has this been happening to him?" And he said, "From childhood. It has often thrown him both into the fire and into the water to destroy him. But if You can do anything, take pity on us and help us!" And Jesus said to him, "'If You can?' All things are possible to him who believes." Immediately the boy's father cried out and said, "I do believe; help my unbelief." When Jesus saw that a crowd was rapidly gathering, He rebuked the unclean spirit, saying to it, "You deaf and mute spirit, I command you, come out of him and do not enter him again." After crying out and throwing him into terrible convulsions, it came out; and *the boy* became so much like a corpse that most *of them,* said, "He is dead!" But Jesus took him by the hand and raised him; and he got up. When He came into the house, His disciples *began* questioning Him privately, "Why could we not drive it out?" And He said to them, "This kind cannot come out by anything but prayer" (Mark 9:16–29; cf. Matthew 17:14–21; Luke 9:37–43; see Matthew 17:20).

Setting: Judea beyond the Jordan (Perea). After informing a rich man how righteous believers may have treasure in heaven, Jesus conveys to His disciples the difficulty the wealthy have entering the kingdom of God.

And Jesus, looking around, said to His disciples, "How hard it will be for those who are wealthy to enter the kingdom of God!" The disciples were amazed at His words. But Jesus answered again and said to them, "Children, how hard it is to enter the kingdom of God! It is easier for a camel to go through the eye of a needle than for a rich man to enter the kingdom of God." They were even more astonished and said to Him, "Then who can be saved?" Looking at them, Jesus said, "With people it is impossible, but not with God; for all things are possible with God" (Mark 10:23–27; cf. Matthew 19:23–26; Luke 18:24, 25).

Setting: Just outside Jerusalem. The day after Jesus instructs the money changers while He cleanses the temple, Peter draws the Lord's and His disciples' attention to an earlier-cursed fig tree.

And Jesus answered saying to them, "Have faith in God. Truly, I say to you, whoever says to this mountain, 'Be taken up and cast into the sea,' and does not doubt in his heart, but believes that what he says is going to happen, it will be *granted* him. Therefore I say to you, all things for which you pray and ask, believe that you have received them, and they will be *granted* you. Whenever you stand praying, forgive, if you have anything against anyone, so that your Father who is in heaven will also forgive you your transgressions. [But if you do not forgive, neither will your Father who is in heaven forgive your transgressions'] (Mark 11:22–26; cf. Matthew 21:19–22; see Matthew 6:14, 15; 7:7; 17:20).

Setting: Gethsemane on the Mount of Olives, east of the temple in Jerusalem. Jesus agonizes over His impending death, disappointed His disciples keep falling asleep instead of watching and praying with Him.

They came to a place named Gethsemane; and He said to the disciples, "Sit here until I have prayed." And He took with Him Peter and James and John, and began to be very distressed and troubled. And He said to them, "My soul is deeply grieved to the point of death; remain here and keep watch." And He went a little beyond *them,* and fell to the ground and *began* to pray that if it were possible, the hour might pass Him by. And He was saying, "Abba! Father! All things are possible for You; remove this cup from Me; yet not what I will, but what You will." And He came and found them sleeping, and said to Peter, "Simon, are you asleep? Could you not keep watch for one hour? Keep watching and praying that you may not come into temptation; the spirit is willing, but the flesh is weak" (Mark 14:32–38; cf. Matthew 26:36–41; Luke 22:41–46; see Romans 8:15; Galatians 4:6).

Setting: On the way from Galilee to Jerusalem. The Lord responds to a report from the seventy sent out in pairs to every place He Himself will soon visit.

At that very time He rejoiced greatly in the Holy Spirit, and said, "I praise You, O Father, Lord of heaven and earth, that You have hidden these things from *the* wise and intelligent and have revealed them to infants. Yes, Father, for this way was well-pleasing in Your sight. All things have been handed over to Me by My Father, and no one knows who the Son is except the Father, and who the Father is except the Son, and anyone to whom the Son wills to reveal *Him*" (Luke 10:21, 22; cf. Matthew 11:25–27; see Luke 10:1, 17; John 3:35; 10:15).

Setting: On the way from Galilee to Jerusalem. After speaking of how a lamp illuminates, the Lord has lunch with a Pharisee, who is surprised He doesn't wash before eating.

But the Lord said to him, "Now you Pharisees clean the outside of the cup and of the platter; but inside of you, you are full of robbery and wickedness. You foolish ones, did not He who made the outside make the inside also? But give that which is within as charity, and then all things are clean for you. But woe to you Pharisees! You pay tithe of mint and rue and every *kind of* garden herb, and *yet* disregard justice and the love of God; but these are the things you should have done without neglecting the others. Woe to you Pharisees! For you love the chief seats in the synagogues and the respectful greetings in the market places. Woe to you! For you are like concealed tombs, and the people who walk over *them* are unaware *of it*" (Luke 11:39–44; cf. Matthew 23:6, 7, 23–27; see Matthew 15:2; Titus 1:15).

Setting: On the way from Galilee to Jerusalem. After responding to Peter's statement about the disciples' personal sacrifice in following Him, Jesus tells them of the sacrifice He will make in Jerusalem.

Then He took the twelve aside and said to them, "Behold, we are going up to Jerusalem, and all things which are written through the prophets about the Son of Man will be accomplished. For He will be handed over to the Gentiles, and will be mocked and mistreated and spit upon, and after they have scourged Him, they will kill Him; and the third day He will rise again" (Luke 18:31–33; cf. Matthew 20:17–19; Mark 10:32–34).

Setting: On the Mount of Olives, east of the temple in Jerusalem. After ministering in the temple a few days before His crucifixion, and giving the disciples more details regarding future events, Jesus elaborates during His Olivet Discourse about things to come.

"But when you see Jerusalem surrounded by armies, then recognize that her desolation is near. Then those who are in Judea must flee to the mountains, and those who are in the midst of the city must leave, and those who are in the country must not enter the city; because these are days of vengeance, so that all things which are written will be fulfilled. Woe to those who are pregnant and to those who are nursing babies in those days; for there will be a great distress upon the land and wrath to this people; and they will fall by the edge of the sword, and will be led captive into all the nations; and Jerusalem will be trampled under foot by the Gentiles until the times of the Gentiles are fulfilled" (Luke 21:20–24; see Matthew 24:15–18; Mark 13:14–16; Luke 19:43).

Setting: On the Mount of Olives, east of the temple in Jerusalem. After ministering in the temple a few days before His crucifixion, and giving the disciples more details regarding His return, Jesus conveys the Parable of the Fig Tree during His Olivet Discourse.

Then He told them a parable: "Behold the fig tree and all the trees; as soon as they put forth *leaves,* you see it and know for yourselves that summer is now near. So you also, when you see these things happening, recognize that the kingdom of God is near.

Truly, I say to you, this generation will not pass away until all things take place. Heaven and earth will pass away, but My words will not pass away" (Luke 21:29–33; cf. Matthew 24:32–35; Mark 13:28–31; see Matthew 5:18).

Setting: Jerusalem. After rising from the tomb on the third day after being crucified, and appearing to two of His followers on the road to Emmaus, Jesus gives instruction to His disciples (except Thomas) about His mission on earth and the promise of future power from God.

Now He said to them, "These are My words which I spoke to you while I was still with you, that all things which are written about Me in the Law of Moses and the Prophets and the Psalms must be fulfilled." Then He opened their minds to understand the Scriptures, and He said to them, "Thus it is written, that the Christ would suffer and rise again from the dead the third day, and that repentance for forgiveness of sins would be proclaimed in His name to all the nations, beginning from Jerusalem. You are witnesses of these things. And behold, I am sending forth the promise of My Father upon you; but you are to stay in the city until you are clothed with power from on high" (Luke 24:44–49; see Matthew 28:19, 20; Acts 1:8).

Setting: By the pool of Bethesda in Jerusalem. During a feast of the Jews, Jesus responds to criticism from the Jewish religious leaders for healing a lame man on the Sabbath and for referring to God as His Father (thereby making Himself equal with God).

Therefore Jesus answered and was saying to them, "Truly, truly, I say to you, the Son can do nothing of Himself, unless *it is* something He sees the Father doing; for whatever the Father does, these things the Son also does in like manner. For the Father loves the Son, and shows Him all things that He Himself is doing; and *the Father* will show Him greater works than these, so that you will marvel. For just as the Father raises the dead and gives them life, even so the Son also gives life to whom He wishes. For not even the Father judges anyone, but He has given all judgment to the Son, so that all will honor the Son even as they honor the Father. He who does not honor the Son does not honor the Father who sent Him" (John 5:19–23; see Luke 10:16; John 3:35; 11:25; 14:12).

Setting: Jerusalem. Before the Passover, after responding to Philip's request for Him to show His disciples the Father, Jesus conveys the upcoming ministry of the Holy Spirit in their lives.

"These things I have spoken to you while abiding with you. But the Helper, the Holy Spirit, whom the Father will send in My name, He will teach you all things, and bring to your remembrance all that I said to you" (John 14:25, 26; see John 16:13).

Setting: Jerusalem. Before the Passover, with His departure in mind, after explaining He is the vine and His disciples are the branches, Jesus commands them to love one another.

"This is My commandment, that you love one another, just as I have loved you. Greater love has no one than this, that one lay down his life for his friends. You are My friends if you do what I command you. No longer do I call you slaves, for the slave does not know what his master is doing; but I have called you friends, for all things that I have heard from My Father I have made known to you. You did not choose Me but I chose you, and appointed you that you would go and bear fruit, and *that* your fruit would remain, so that whatever you ask of the Father in My name He may give to you. This I command you, that you love one another" (John 15:12–17; see Matthew 12:50; John 6:70; 8:26; 10:11; 13:34).

Setting: Jerusalem. Before the Passover, after warning His disciples of the persecution they will face after His departure to heaven, Jesus elaborates about the coming ministry of the Holy Spirit.

"I have many more things to say to you, but you cannot bear *them* now. But when He, the Spirit of truth, comes, He will guide you into all the truth; for He will not speak on His own initiative, but whatever He hears, He will speak; and He will disclose to you what is to come. He will glorify Me, for He will take of Mine and will disclose *it* to you. All things that the Father has are Mine; therefore I said that He takes of Mine and will disclose *it* to you (John 16:12–15; see John 7:39; 14:17, 26; 17:10).

Setting: Jerusalem. Before the Passover, after giving His disciples assurance that in the midst of tribulation they will have His peace, Jesus prays His high-priestly prayer.

Jesus spoke these things; and lifting up His eyes to heaven, He said, "Father, the hour has come; glorify Your Son, that the Son may glorify You, even as You gave Him authority over all flesh, that to all whom You have given Him, He may give eternal life. This is eternal life, that they may know You, the only true God, and Jesus Christ whom You have sent. I glorified You on the earth, having accomplished the work which You have given Me to do. Now, Father, glorify Me together with Yourself, with the glory which I had with You before the world was. I have manifested Your name to the men whom You gave Me out of the world; they were Yours and You gave them to Me, and they have kept Your word. Now they have come to know that everything You have given Me is from You; for the words which You gave Me I have given to them; and they received *them* and truly understood that I came forth from You, and they believed You sent Me. I ask on their behalf; I do not ask on behalf of the world, but of those whom You have given Me; for they are Yours; and all things that are Mine are Yours, and Yours are Mine; and I have been glorified in them. I am no longer in the world; and *yet* they themselves are in the world, and I come to You. Holy Father, keep them in Your name, *the name* which You have given Me, that they may be even as We *are.* While I was with them, I was keeping them in Your name which You have given Me; and I guarded them and not one of them perished but the son of perdition, so that the Scripture would be fulfilled" (John 17:1–12; see Luke 22:32; John 1:1; 3:35; 4:34; 5:44; 6:37–39, 70; 8:42; 11:41; 12:49; 13:18, 31; 16:15; Philippians 2:9).

THINGS, BAD (Also see THINGS, EVIL)

Setting: On the way from Galilee to Jerusalem. After responding to the Pharisees' scoffing at His teaching His disciples about stewardship and the permanence of the Law, Jesus conveys the story of the rich man and Lazarus.

"Now there was a rich man, and he habitually dressed in purple and fine linen, joyously living in splendor every day. And a poor man named Lazarus was laid at his gate, covered with sores, and longing to be fed with the *crumbs* which were falling from the rich man's table; besides, even the dogs were coming and licking his sores. Now the poor man died and was carried away by the angels to Abraham's bosom; and the rich man also died and was buried. In Hades he lifted up his eyes, being in torment, and saw Abraham far away and Lazarus in his bosom. And he cried out and said, 'Father Abraham, have mercy on me, and send Lazarus so that he may dip the tip of his finger in water and cool off my tongue, for I am in agony in this flame.' But Abraham said, 'Child, remember that during your life you received your good things, and likewise Lazarus bad things; but now he is being comforted here, and you are in agony. And besides all this, between us and you there is a great chasm fixed, so that those who wish to come over from here to you will not be able, and *that* none may cross over from there to us.' And he said, 'Then I beg you, father, that you send him to my father's house—for I have five brothers—in order that he may warn them, so that they will not also come to this place of torment.' But Abraham said, 'They have Moses and the Prophets; let them hear them.' But he said, 'No, father Abraham, but if someone goes to them from the dead, they will repent!' But he said to him, 'If they do not listen to Moses and the Prophets, they will not be persuaded even if someone rises from the dead' " (Luke 16:19–31; see Luke 3:8; 6:24; 16:1, 14).

THINGS, DEEP

Setting: On the island of Patmos (in the Aegean Sea about fifty miles southwest of Ephesus in modern Turkey). On the Lord's Day (Sunday), approximately fifty years after the Resurrection, the disciple John encounters the Lord Jesus Christ, who communicates a new revelation for the apostle to record for the church in Thyatira and to six other churches in Asia.

"And to the angel of the church in Thyatira write. The Son of God, who has eyes like a flame of fire, and His feet are like burnished bronze, says this: 'I know your deeds, and your love and faith and service and perseverance, and that your deeds of late are greater than at first. But I have *this* against you, that you tolerate the woman Jezebel, who calls herself a prophetess, and she teaches and leads My bond-servants astray so that they commit *acts of* immorality and eat things sacrificed to idols. I gave her time to repent, and she does not want to repent of her immorality. Behold, I will throw her on a bed *of sickness,* and those who commit adultery with her into great tribulation, unless they repent of her deeds. And I will kill her children with pestilence, and all the churches will know that I am He who searches the minds and hearts; and I will give to each one of you according to your deeds. But I say to you, the rest who are in Thyatira, who do not hold this teaching, who have not known the deep things of Satan, as they call them—I place no other burden on you. Nevertheless what you have, hold fast until I come. He who overcomes, and he who keeps My deeds until the end, TO HIM I WILL GIVE AUTHORITY OVER THE NATIONS; AND HE SHALL RULE THEM WITH A ROD OF IRON, AS THE VESSELS OF THE POTTER ARE BROKEN TO PIECES, as I also have received *authority* from My Father; and I will give him the morning star. He who has an ear, let him hear what the Spirit says to the churches' (Revelation 2:18–29; Jesus quotes from Psalm 2:8, 9; Isaiah 30:14; see 1 Kings 16:31; Psalm 7:9; Romans 2:5; 1 Corinthians 2:10; 2 Peter 3:9; Revelation 1:14; 2:7; 3:11; 17:1–20).

THINGS, EARTHLY

Setting: Jerusalem. At the time for the Passover of the Jews, after the Lord cleanses the temple, a Pharisee, Nicodemus, asks Him by night the meaning of "born of the Spirit."

Jesus answered and said to him, "Are you the teacher of Israel and do not understand these things? Truly, truly, I say to you, we speak of what we know and testify of what we have seen, and you do not accept our testimony. If I told you earthly things and you do not believe, how will you believe if I tell you heavenly things? No one has ascended into heaven, but He who descended from heaven: the Son of Man. As Moses lifted up the serpent in the wilderness, even so must the Son of Man be lifted up; so that whoever believes will in Him have eternal life" (John 3:10–15; see Numbers 21:9; Proverb 30:4; John 12:34; 20:30, 31).

THINGS, EVIL (Also see THINGS, BAD)

Setting: Galilee. After the Pharisees and scribes from Jerusalem object to His disciples' lack of obedience to the tradition regarding ceremonial cleansing, Jesus speaks to a crowd, and explains His teaching to the disciples.

After He called the crowd to Him again, He *began* saying to them, "Listen to Me, all of you, and understand: there is nothing outside the man which can defile him if it goes into him; but the things which proceed out of the man are what defile the man. [If anyone has ears to hear, let him hear."] When he had left the crowd *and* entered the house, His disciples questioned Him about the parable. And He said to them, "Are you so lacking in understanding also? Do you not understand that whatever goes into the man from outside cannot defile him, because it does not go into his heart, but into his stomach, and is eliminated?" (*Thus He* declared all foods clean.) And He was saying, "That which proceeds out of the man, that is what defiles the man. For from within, out of the heart of men, proceed the evil thoughts, fornications, thefts, murders, adulteries, deeds of coveting *and* wickedness, *as well* as deceit, sensuality, envy, slander, pride *and* foolishness. All these evil things proceed from within and defile the man" (Mark 7:14–23; cf. Matthew 15:10–20).

THINGS, FEW

Setting: On the Mount of Olives, just east of Jerusalem. During His Olivet Discourse, after answering His disciples' questions as to when the temple will be destroyed and Jerusalem overrun, along with the signs of His coming and the end of the age, Jesus reemphasizes to His disciples that they should be on the alert for His return.

"For *it is* just like a man *about* to go on a journey, who called his own slaves and entrusted his possessions to them. To one he gave five talents, to another, two, and to another, one, each according to his own ability; and he went on his journey. Immediately the one who had received the five talents went and traded with them, and gained five more talents. In the same manner the one who *had received* the two *talents* gained two more. But he who received the one *talent* went away, and dug a *hole* in the ground and hid his master's money. Now after a long time the master of those slaves came and settled accounts with them. The one who had received the five talents came up and brought five more talents, saying, 'Master, you entrusted five talents to me. See, I have gained five more talents.' His master said to him, 'Well done, good and faithful slave. You were faithful with a few things, I will put you in charge of many things; enter into the joy of your master.' Also the one who *had received* the two talents came up and said, 'Master, you entrusted two talents to me. See, I have gained two more talents.' His master said to him, 'Well done, good and faithful slave. You were faithful with a few things, I will put you in charge of many things; enter into the joy of your master.' And the one also who had received the one talent came up and said, 'Master, I knew you to be a hard man, reaping where you did not sow and gathering where you scattered no *seed*. And I was afraid, and went away and hid your talent in the ground. See, you have what is yours.' But his master answered and said to him, 'You wicked, lazy slave, you knew that I reap where I did not sow and gather where I scattered no *seed*. Then you ought to have put my money in the bank, and on my arrival I would have received my *money* back with interest. 'Therefore take away the talent from him, and give it to the one who has ten talents.' For to everyone who has, *more* shall be given, and he will have an abundance; but from the one who does not have, even what he does have shall be taken away. Throw out the worthless slave into the outer darkness; in that place there will be weeping and gnashing of teeth" (Matthew 25:14–30; cf. Matthew 8:12; 13:12; 24:45–47; see Matthew 18:23, 24; Luke 12:44).

Setting: On the island of Patmos (in the Aegean Sea about fifty miles southwest of Ephesus in modern Turkey). On the Lord's Day (Sunday), approximately fifty years after the Resurrection, the disciple John encounters the Lord Jesus Christ, who communicates a new revelation for the apostle to record for the church in Pergamum and to six other churches in Asia.

"And to the angel of the church in Pergamum write: The One who has the sharp two-edged sword says this: 'I know where you dwell, where Satan's throne is; and you hold fast My name, and did not deny My faith even in the days of Antipas, My witness, My faithful one, who was killed among you, where Satan dwells. But I have a few things against you, because you have there some who hold the teaching of Balaam, who kept teaching Balak to put a stumbling block before the sons of Israel, to eat things sacrificed to idols and to commit *acts of* immorality. So you also have some who in the same way hold the teaching of the Nicolaitans. Therefore repent; or else I am coming to you quickly, and I will make war against them with the sword of My mouth. He who has an ear, let him hear what the Spirit says to the churches. To him who overcomes, to him I will give *some* of the hidden manna, and I will give him a white stone, and a new name written on the stone which no one knows but he who receives it' (Revelation 2:12–17; see Numbers 25:1–3; Isaiah 62:2; Revelation 1:16; 2:5, 6, 16).

THINGS, GOD'S

[GOD'S THINGS from the things that are God's]

Setting: The temple in Jerusalem. The Pharisees send their disciples and the Herodians to test Jesus about the poll-tax in order to trap Him.

But Jesus perceived their malice, and said, "Why are you testing Me, you hypocrites? Show Me the coin *used* for the poll-tax." And they brought Him a denarius. And He said to them, "Whose likeness and inscription is this?" They said to Him, "Caesar's." Then He said to them, "Then render to Caesar the things that are Caesar's; and to God the things that are God's" (Matthew 22:18–21; cf. Matthew 17:25; Mark 12:15–17; Luke 20:22–25).

[GOD'S THINGS from the things that are God's]

Setting: The temple in Jerusalem. After Jesus teaches the chief priests, scribes, and elders in parables, they send some of the Pharisees and Herodians in an attempt to trap Him in a statement.

"Shall we pay or shall we not pay?" But He, knowing their hypocrisy, said to them, "Why are you testing Me? Bring Me a denarius to look at." They brought *one.* And He said to them, "Whose likeness and inscription is this?" And they said to Him, "Caesar's." And Jesus said to them, "Render to Caesar the things that are Caesar's, and to God the things that are God's" And they were amazed at Him (Mark 12:15–17; cf. Matthew 22:15–22; Luke 20:20–26).

[GOD'S THINGS from the things that are God's]

Setting: The temple in Jerusalem. While ministering a few days before His crucifixion, after Jesus gives the people the Parable of the Vine-Growers, the scribes and Pharisees seek to trap Him by questioning Him about paying taxes to Caesar.

But He detected their trickery and said to them, "Show Me a denarius. Whose likeness and inscription does it have?" They said "Caesar's." And He said to them, "Then render to Caesar the things that are Caesar's, and to God the things that are God's" (Luke 20:23–25; cf. Matthew 22:15–21; Mark 12:13–17).

THINGS, GOOD

Setting: On the way from Galilee to Jerusalem. After responding to the Pharisees' scoffing at His teaching His disciples about stewardship and the permanence of the Law, Jesus conveys the story of the rich man and Lazarus.

"Now there was a rich man, and he habitually dressed in purple and fine linen, joyously living in splendor every day. And a poor man named Lazarus was laid at his gate, covered with sores, and longing to be fed with the *crumbs* which were falling from the rich man's table; besides, even the dogs were coming and licking his sores. Now the poor man died and was carried away by the angels to Abraham's bosom; and the rich man also died and was buried. In Hades he lifted up his eyes, being in torment, and saw Abraham far away and Lazarus in his bosom. And he cried out and said, 'Father Abraham, have mercy on me, and send Lazarus so that he may dip the tip of his finger in water and cool off my tongue, for I am in agony in this flame.' But Abraham said, 'Child, remember that during your life you received your good things, and likewise Lazarus bad things; but now he is being comforted here, and you are in agony. And besides all this, between us and you there is a great chasm fixed, so that those who wish to come over from here to you will not be able, and *that* none may cross over from there to us.' And he said, 'Then I beg you, father, that you send him to my father's house—for I have five brothers—in order that he may warn them, so that they will not also come to this place of torment.' But Abraham said, 'They have Moses and the Prophets; let them hear them.' But he said, 'No, father Abraham, but if someone goes to them from the dead, they will repent!' But he said to him, 'If they do not listen to Moses and the Prophets, they will not be persuaded even if someone rises from the dead' " (Luke 16:19–31; see Luke 3:8; 6:24; 16:1, 14).

THINGS, GREAT

Setting: The country of the Gerasenes, on the east side of the Sea of Galilee. Jesus encounters and heals a man possessed by a legion of demons.

And He did not let him, but He said to him, "Go home to your people and report to them what great things the Lord has done for you, and *how* He had mercy on you" (Mark 5:19; cf. Luke 8:39; see Matthew 8:33, 34; Luke 8:36–38).

Setting: The country of the Gerasenes, to the east of Galilee. Jesus heals a demon-possessed man who then desires to join His ministry, but the Lord sends him home.

"Return to your house and describe what great things God has done for you." So he went away, proclaiming throughout the whole city what great things Jesus had done for him (Luke 8:39; cf. Matthew 8:28–34; Mark 5:1–20).

THINGS, GREATER (See MIRACLES; and SIGNS AND WONDERS)

Setting: Galilee. After beginning His public ministry and choosing His first disciples, Andrew and Simon (Peter) near Bethany beyond the Jordan, and Philip in Galilee, Jesus calls Philip's friend, Nathanael, (some believe he may have been also called Bartholomew) as His next follower.

Jesus saw Nathanael coming to Him, and said of him, "Behold, an Israelite indeed, in whom there is no deceit!" Nathanael said to Him, "How do you know me?" Jesus answered and said to him, "Before Philip called you, when you were under the fig tree, I saw you." Nathanael answered Him, "Rabbi, You are the Son of God; You are the King of Israel." Jesus answered and said to him, "Because I said to you that I saw you under the fig tree, do you believe? You will see greater things than these." And He said to him, "Truly, truly, I say to you, you will see the heavens opened and the angels of God ascending and descending on the Son of Man" (John 1:47–51).

THINGS, HEAVENLY

Setting: Jerusalem. At the time for the Passover of the Jews, after the Lord cleanses the temple, a Pharisee, Nicodemus, asks Him by night the meaning of "born of the Spirit."

Jesus answered and said to him, "Are you the teacher of Israel and do not understand these things? Truly, truly, I say to you, we speak of what we know and testify of what we have seen, and you do not accept our testimony. If I told you earthly things and you do not believe, how will you believe if I tell you heavenly things? No one has ascended into heaven, but He who descended from heaven: the Son of Man. As Moses lifted up the serpent in the wilderness, even so must the Son of Man be lifted up; so that whoever believes will in Him have eternal life" (John 3:10–15; see Numbers 21:9; Proverb 30:4; John 12:34; 20:30, 31).

THINGS, HIDDEN

[THINGS, HIDDEN from hidden and things]

Setting: Galilee. As He teaches and preaches, after pronouncing woes upon unrepentant cities, Jesus prays a thanksgiving prayer to His Father in heaven.

At that time Jesus said, "I praise You, Father, Lord of heaven and earth, that you have hidden these things from *the* wise and intelligent and have revealed them to infants. Yes, Father, for this way was well-pleasing in Your sight. All things have been handed over to Me by My Father; and no one knows the Son except the Father; nor does anyone know the Father except the Son, and anyone to whom the Son wills to reveal *Him*" (Matthew 11:25–27; cf. Luke 10:21, 22).

[THINGS, HIDDEN from hidden and things]

Setting: On the way from Galilee to Jerusalem. The Lord responds to a report from the seventy sent out in pairs to every place He Himself will soon visit.

At that very time He rejoiced greatly in the Holy Spirit, and said, "I praise You, O Father, Lord of heaven and earth, that You have hidden these things from *the* wise and intelligent and have revealed them to infants. Yes, Father, for this way was well-pleasing in Your sight. All things have been handed over to Me by My Father, and no one knows who the Son is except the Father, and who the Father is except the Son, and anyone to whom the Son wills to reveal *Him*" (Luke 10:21, 22; cf. Matthew 11:25–27; see Luke 10:1, 17; John 3:35; 10:15).

THINGS, MANY

Setting: On the Mount of Olives, just east of Jerusalem. During His Olivet Discourse, after answering His disciples' questions as to when the temple will be destroyed and Jerusalem overrun, along with the signs of His coming and the end of the age, Jesus reemphasizes to His disciples that they should be on the alert for His return.

"For *it is* just like a man *about* to go on a journey, who called his own slaves and entrusted his possessions to them. To one he gave five talents, to another, two, and to another, one, each according to his own ability; and he went on his journey. Immediately the one who had received the five talents went and traded with them, and gained five more talents. In the same manner the one who *had received* the two *talents* gained two more. But he who received the one *talent* went away, and dug a *hole* in the ground and hid his master's money. Now after a long time the master of those slaves came and settled accounts with them. The one who had received the five talents came up and brought five more talents, saying, 'Master, you entrusted five talents to me. See, I have gained five more talents.' His master said to him, 'Well done, good and faithful slave. You were faithful with a few things, I will put you in charge of many things; enter into the joy of your master.' Also the one who *had received* the two talents came up and said, 'Master, you entrusted two talents to me. See, I have gained two more talents.' His master said to him, 'Well done, good and faithful slave. You were faithful with a few things, I will put you in charge of many things; enter into the joy of your master.' And the one also who had received the one talent came up and said, 'Master, I knew you to be a hard man, reaping where you did not sow and gathering where you scattered no *seed.* And I was afraid, and went away and hid your talent in the ground. See, you have what is yours.' But his master answered and said to him, 'You wicked, lazy slave, you knew that I reap where I did not sow and gather where I scattered no *seed.* Then you ought to have put my money in the bank, and on my arrival I would have received my *money* back with interest. 'Therefore take away the talent from him, and give it to the one who has ten talents.' For to everyone who has, *more* shall be given, and he will have an abundance; but from the one who does not have, even what he does have shall be taken away. Throw out the worthless slave into the outer darkness; in that place there will be weeping and gnashing of teeth" (Matthew 25:14–30; cf. Matthew 8:12; 13:12; 24:45–47; see Matthew 18:23, 24; Luke 12:44).

Setting: Galilee. The Pharisees and some of the scribes from Jerusalem question why Jesus' disciples do not follow the tradition of ceremonial hand cleansing before eating bread.

And He said to them, "Rightly did Isaiah prophesy of you hypocrites, as it is written: 'THIS PEOPLE HONORS ME WITH THEIR LIPS, BUT THEIR HEART IS FAR AWAY FROM ME. BUT IN VAIN DO THEY WORSHIP ME, TEACHING AS DOCTRINES THE PRECEPTS OF MEN.' Neglecting the commandment of God, you hold to the tradition of men." He was also saying to them, "You are experts at setting aside the commandment of God in order to keep tradition. For Moses said, 'HONOR YOUR FATHER AND YOUR MOTHER'; and, 'HE WHO SPEAKS EVIL OF FATHER OR MOTHER, IS TO BE PUT TO DEATH'; but you say, 'If a man says to *his* father or *his* mother, whatever I have that would help you is Corban (that is to say, given *to God*),' you no longer permit him to do anything for *his* father or *his* mother; *thus* invalidating the word of God by your tradition which you have handed down; and you do many things such as that" (Mark 7:6–13, Jesus quotes from Exodus 20:12; 21:17; Isaiah 29:13; cf. Matthew 15:1–6).

Setting: Galilee. After informing a crowd and His disciples of the hope involving the coming kingdom of God, Jesus takes Peter, James, and John to a high mountain (some think Mount Hermon). The Lord reveals His glory through the Transfiguration, and answers their question about Elijah.

And He said to them, "Elijah does first come and restore all things. And *yet* how is it written of the Son of Man that He will suffer many things and be treated with contempt? But I say to you that Elijah has indeed come, and they did to him whatever they wished, just as it is written of him" (Mark 9:12, 13; cf. Matthew 17:1–13; Luke 9:28–36; see Malachi 4:5, 6; Matthew 16:21).

Setting: Galilee. Following Peter's pronouncement that Jesus is the Christ of God, the Lord warns His disciples not to reveal His identity to anyone.

But He warned them and instructed *them* not to tell this to anyone, saying, "The Son of Man must suffer many things and be rejected by the elders and chief priests and scribes, and be killed and be raised up on the third day" (Luke 9:21, 22; cf. Matthew 16:21; Mark 8:31).

Setting: On the way from Galilee to Jerusalem. After being tested by a lawyer, the Lord and His disciples are welcomed into the home of Martha and Mary in Bethany.

But the Lord answered and said to her, "Martha, Martha, you are worried and bothered about so many things; but *only* one thing is necessary, for Mary has chosen the good part, which shall not be taken away from her" (Luke 10:41, 42; see Matthew 6:25).

Setting: On the way from Galilee to Jerusalem. After the Pharisees question Him about the coming of the kingdom of God, Jesus tells His disciples of His second coming.

And He said to the disciples, "The days will come when you will long to see one of the days of the Son of Man, and you will not see it. They will say to you, 'Look there! Look here!' Do not go away, and do not run after *them*. For just like the lightning, when it flashes out of one part of the sky, shines to the other part of the sky, so will the Son of Man be in His day. But first He must suffer many things and be rejected by this generation. And just as it happened in the days of Noah, so it will be also in the days of the Son of Man: they were eating, they were drinking, they were marrying, they were being given in marriage, until the day that Noah entered the ark, and the flood came and destroyed them all. It was the same as happened in the days of Lot: they were eating, they were drinking, they were buying, they were selling, they were planting, they were building; but on the day that Lot went out from Sodom it rained fire and brimstone from heaven and destroyed them all. It will be just the same on the day that the Son of Man is revealed. On that day, the one who is on the housetop and whose goods are in the house must not go down to take them out; and likewise the one who is in the field must not turn back. Remember Lot's wife. Whoever seeks to keep his life will lose it, and whoever loses *his life* will preserve it. I tell you, on that night there will be two in one bed; one will be taken and the other will be left. There will be two women grinding at the same place; one will be taken and the other will be left. [Two men will be in the field; one will be taken and the other will be left."] And answering they said to Him, "Where, Lord?" And He said to them, "Where the body *is*, there also the vultures will be gathered" (Luke 17:22–37; see Genesis 19; Matthew 10:39; 16:21, 27; 24:17–28, 37–41).

Setting: The temple treasury in Jerusalem. Following the Feast of Booths and the scribes' and Pharisees' failed attempt to stone a woman for adultery, Jesus returns the next day to teach. They question His testimony about Himself.

Then He said again to them, "I go away, and you will seek Me, and will die in your sin; where I am going, you cannot come." So the Jews were saying, "Surely He will not kill Himself, will He, since He says, "Where I am going, you cannot come'?" And He was saying to them, "You are from below, I am from above; you are of this world, I am not of this world. Therefore I said to you that you will die in your sins; for unless you believe that I am *He*, you will die in your sins." So they were saying to Him, "Who are You?" Jesus said to them, "What have I been saying to you *from* the beginning? I have many things to speak and to judge concerning you, but He who sent Me is true; and the things which I heard from Him, these I speak to the world" (John 8:21–26; see John 3:31–33; 5:34, 35; 17:14, 16).

THINGS, MORE

Setting: Jerusalem. Before the Passover, after warning His disciples of the persecution they will face after His departure to heaven, Jesus elaborates about the coming ministry of the Holy Spirit.

"I have many more things to say to you, but you cannot bear *them* now. But when He, the Spirit of truth, comes, He will guide you into all the truth; for He will not speak on His own initiative, but whatever He hears, He will speak; and He will disclose to you what is to come. He will glorify Me, for He will take of Mine and will disclose *it* to you. All things that the Father has are Mine; therefore I said that He takes of Mine and will disclose *it* to you (John 16:12–15; see John 7:39; 14:17, 26; 17:10).

THINGS, OTHER

Setting: By the Sea of Galilee. During the early part of His ministry, after presenting the Parable of the Sower from a boat to a very large crowd, Jesus gives the meaning of the parable to His disciples and other followers.

And He said to them, "Do you not understand this parable? How will you understand all the parables? The sower sows the word. These are the ones who are beside the road where the word is sown; and when they hear, immediately Satan comes and takes away the word which has been sown in them. In a similar way these are the ones on whom seed was sown on the rocky places, who, when they hear the word, immediately receive it with joy; and they have no *firm* root in themselves, but are *only* temporary; then, when affliction or persecution arises because of the word, immediately they fall away. And others are the ones on whom seed was sown among the thorns; these are the ones who have heard the word, but the worries of the world and the deceitfulness of riches, and the desires for other things enter in and choke the word, and it becomes unfruitful. And those are the ones on whom seed was sown on the good soil; and they hear the word and accept it and bear fruit, thirty, sixty, and a hundredfold" (Mark 4:13–20; cf. Matthew 13:18–23; Luke 8:11–15).

THINGS, THESE

Setting: Galilee. During the early part of His ministry, Jesus preaches the Sermon on the Mount to His disciples and the multitudes.

"For this reason I say to you, do not be worried about your life, *as to* what you will eat or what you will drink; nor for your body, *as to* what you will put on. Is not life more than food, and the body more than clothing? Look at the birds of the air, that they do not sow, nor reap nor gather into barns, and *yet* your heavenly Father feeds them. Are you not worth much more than they? And who of you by being worried can add a *single* hour to his life? And why are you worried about clothing? Observe how the lilies of the field grow; they do not toil nor do they spin, yet I say to you that not even Solomon in all his glory clothed himself like one of these. But if God so clothes the grass of the field, which is *alive* today and tomorrow is thrown into the furnace, *will He* not much more *clothe* you? You of little faith! Do not worry then, saying 'What will we eat?' or 'What will we drink?' or 'What will be wear for clothing?" For the Gentiles eagerly seek all these things; for your heavenly Father knows that you need all these things. But seek first His kingdom and His righteousness, and all these things will be added to you. So do not worry about tomorrow; for tomorrow will care for itself. Each day has enough trouble of its own" (Matthew 6:25–34; cf. Luke 12:22–31; see 1 Kings 10:4–7; Job 35:11; Matthew 8:26).

Setting: Galilee. As He teaches and preaches, after pronouncing woes upon unrepentant cities, Jesus prays a thanksgiving prayer to His Father in heaven.

At that time Jesus said, "I praise You, Father, Lord of heaven and earth, that you have hidden these things from *the* wise and intelligent and have revealed them to infants. Yes, Father, for this way was well-pleasing in Your sight. All things have been handed over to Me by My Father; and no one knows the Son except the Father; nor does anyone know the Father except the Son, and anyone to whom the Son wills to reveal *Him*" (Matthew 11:25–27; cf. Luke 10:21, 22).

Setting: By the Sea of Galilee. Because the religious leaders are rejecting His message, Jesus continues teaching His disciples with the Parable of the Dragnet.

"Again, the kingdom of heaven is like a dragnet cast into the sea, and gathering *fish* of every kind, and when it was filled, they drew it up on the beach; and they sat down and gathered the good *fish* into containers, but the bad they threw away. So it will be at the end of the age; the angels will come forth and take out the wicked from among the righteous, and will throw them into the furnace of fire; in that place there will be weeping and gnashing of teeth. Have you understood all these things?" They said to Him, "Yes" (Matthew 13:47–51).

Setting: The temple in Jerusalem. Jesus returns after spending the night in Bethany. The chief priests and elders question His authority to teach the nation.

Jesus said to them, "I will also ask you one thing, which if you tell Me, I will also tell you by what authority I do these things. The baptism of John was from what *source,* from heaven or from men?" And they *began* reasoning among themselves, saying "If we say 'From heaven,' He will say to us, 'Then why did you not believe him?' But if we say, 'From men,' we fear the people; for they all regard John as a prophet." And answering Jesus, they said, "We do not know." He also said to them, "Neither will I tell you by what authority I do these things" (Matthew 21:24–27; cf. Mark 11:29–33; Luke 20:3–8).

Setting: The temple in Jerusalem. After the Jewish religious leaders test Him with questions, Jesus pronounces the eighth of eight woes upon them in front of the crowds and His disciples.

"Woe to you, scribes and Pharisees, hypocrites! For you build the tombs of the prophets and adorn the monuments of the righteous, and say, 'If we had been *living* in the days of our fathers, we would not have been partners with them in *shedding* the blood of the prophets.' So you testify against yourselves, that you are sons of those who murdered the prophets. Fill up, then, the measure *of the guilt* of you fathers. You serpents, you brood of vipers, how will you escape the sentence of hell? Therefore, behold, I am sending you prophets and wise men and scribes; some of them you will kill and crucify, and some of them you will scourge in your synagogues, and persecute from city to city, so that upon you may fall *the guilt of* all the righteous blood shed on earth, from the blood of righteous Abel to the blood of Zechariah, the son of Berechiah, whom you murdered between the temple and the altar. Truly I say to you, all these things will come upon this generation" (Matthew 23:29–36; cf. 2 Chronicles 24:21; Zechariah 1:1; Matthew 3:7; Luke 11:47–52; see Matthew 10:23)

Setting: Jerusalem. Just days before His crucifixion, after teaching, interacting with the religious leaders, and pronouncing woes upon these same leaders, Jesus leaves the temple and prophesies its destruction to His disciples.

Jesus came out from the temple, and was going away when His disciples came up to point out the temple buildings to Him. And He said to them, "Do you not see all these things? Truly I say to you, not one stone here will be left upon another, which will not be torn down" (Matthew 24:1, 2; cf. Mark 13:1, 2; Luke 21:5, 6; see Luke 19:43, 44).

Setting: The Mount of Olives, just east of Jerusalem. During His Olivet Discourse, Jesus answers His disciples' questions as to when the temple will be destroyed and Jerusalem overrun, along with the signs of His coming and the end of the age.

And Jesus answered and said to them, "See to it that no one misleads you. For many will come in My name, saying, 'I am the Christ,' and will mislead many. You will be hearing of wars and rumors of wars. See that you are not frightened, for *those things* must take place, but *that* is not yet the end. For nation will rise against nation, and kingdom against kingdom, and in various places there will be famines and earthquakes. But all these things are *merely* the beginning of birth pangs. Then they will deliver you to tribulation, and will kill you, and you will be hated by all nations because of My name. At that time many will fall away and will betray one another and hate one another. Many false prophets will arise and will mislead many. Because lawlessness is increased, most people's love will grow cold. But the one who endures to the end, he will be saved. This gospel of the kingdom shall be preached in the whole world as a testimony to all the nations, and then the end will come" (Matthew 24:4–14; cf. Jeremiah 29:8; Matthew 7:15; 10:17, 22; Mark 13:3–13; Luke 21:7–19; Revelation 6:4; see Matthew 24:3; 2 Peter 2:1).

Setting: On the Mount of Olives, just east of Jerusalem. During His Olivet Discourse, after answering His disciples' questions as to when the temple will be destroyed and Jerusalem overrun, along with the signs of His coming and the end of the age, Jesus teaches them the Parable of the Fig Tree.

"Now learn the parable from the fig tree: when its branch has already become tender and puts forth its leaves, you know that summer is near; so, you too, when you see all these things, recognize that He is near, *right* at the door. Truly, I say to you, this generation will not pass away until all these things take place. Heaven and earth will pass away, but My words will not pass away. But of that day and hour no one knows, not even the angels of heaven, nor the Son, but the Father alone. For the coming of the Son of Man will be just like the days of Noah. For as in those days before the flood they were eating and drinking, marrying and giving in marriage, until the day that Noah entered the ark, and they did not understand until the flood came and took them all away; so will the coming of the Son of Man be. Then there will be two men in the field; one will be taken and one will be left. Two women *will be* grinding at the mill; one will be taken and one will be left" (Matthew 24:32–41; cf. Mark 13:28–32; Luke 17:34–36; 21:28–33; see Genesis 6:5; 7:7; Matthew 5:18; 10:23; James 5:9).

Setting: Capernaum. When Jesus heals a paralytic man and forgives his sins, some scribes believe the Lord commits blasphemy.

Immediately Jesus, aware in His spirit that they were reasoning that way within themselves, said to them, "Why are you reasoning about these things in your hearts? Which is easier, to say to the paralytic, 'Your sins are forgiven'; or to say, 'Get up, and pick up your pallet and walk'? "But so that you may know that the Son of Man has authority on earth to forgive sins"—He said to the paralytic, "I say to you, get up, pick up your pallet and go home" (Mark 2:8–11; cf. Matthew 9:4–7; Luke 5:21–24).

Setting: The temple in Jerusalem. After Jesus teaches about faith and forgiveness, utilizing a cursed fig tree as an object lesson, His authority is questioned by the chief priests, scribes, and elders.

And Jesus said to them, "I will ask you one question, and you answer Me, and *then* I will tell you by what authority I do these things. Was the baptism of John from heaven, or from men? Answer Me." They *began* reasoning among themselves, saying, "If we say 'From heaven,' He will say, 'Then why did you not believe him?' But shall we say 'From men'?"—they were afraid of the people, for everyone considered John to have been a real prophet. Answering Jesus, they said, "We do not know." And Jesus said to them, "Nor will I tell you by what authority I do these things" (Mark 11:29–33; cf. Matthew 21:23–27; Luke 20:1–8).

Setting: On the Mount of Olives, east of the temple in Jerusalem. After prophesying the temple's destruction, Jesus responds during His Olivet Discourse to questions from Peter, James, John, and Andrew about other future events.

And Jesus began to say to them, "See to it that no one misleads you. Many will come in My name, saying, 'I am *He!*' and will mislead many. When you hear of wars and rumors of wars, do not be frightened; *those things* must take place; but *that is* not yet the end. For nation will rise up against nation, and kingdom against kingdom; there will be earthquakes in various places; there will *also be* famines. These things are *merely* the beginning of birth pangs. But be on your guard; for they will deliver you to *the* courts, and you will be flogged in *the* synagogues, and you will stand before governors and kings for My sake, as a testimony to them. The gospel must first be preached to all the nations. When they arrest you and hand you over, do not worry beforehand about what you are to say, but say whatever is given you in that hour; for it is not you who speak, but *it is* the Holy Spirit. Brother will betray brother to death, and a father *his* child; and children will rise up against parents and have them put to death. You will be hated by all because of My name, but the one who endures to the end, he will be saved" (Mark 13:5–13; cf. Matthew 24:4–14; Luke 21:7–19; see Matthew 10:17–22).

Setting: On the Mount of Olives, east of the temple in Jerusalem. After prophesying the temple's destruction, Jesus responds during His Olivet Discourse to questions from Peter, James, John, and Andrew about other future events.

"Now learn the parable from the fig tree: when its branch has already become tender and puts forth its leaves, you know that summer is near. Even so, you too, when you see these things happening, recognize that He is near, *right* at the door. Truly I say

to you, this generation will not pass away until all these things take place. Heaven and earth will pass away, but My words will not pass away. But of the day or hour no one knows, not even the angels in heaven, nor the Son, but the Father *alone*" (Mark 13:28–32; cf. Matthew 24:32–36; Luke 21:28–33).

Setting: On the way from Galilee to Jerusalem. The Lord responds to a report from the seventy sent out in pairs to every place He Himself will soon visit.

At that very time He rejoiced greatly in the Holy Spirit, and said, "I praise You, O Father, Lord of heaven and earth, that You have hidden these things from *the* wise and intelligent and have revealed them to infants. Yes, Father, for this way was well-pleasing in Your sight. All things have been handed over to Me by My Father, and no one knows who the Son is except the Father, and who the Father is except the Son, and anyone to whom the Son wills to reveal *Him*" (Luke 10:21, 22; cf. Matthew 11:25–27; see Luke 10:1, 17; John 3:35; 10:15).

Setting: On the way from Galilee to Jerusalem. After giving a parable about riches and greed, Jesus comforts the crowd and His disciples. The scribes and Pharisees turn hostile and question Him repeatedly in an attempt to catch Him in something He might say.

And He said to His disciples, "For this reason I say to you, do not worry about *your* life, *as to* what you will eat; nor for your body, *as to* what you will put on. For life is more than food, and the body more than clothing. Consider the ravens, for they neither sow nor reap; they have no storeroom nor barn, and *yet* God feeds them; how much more valuable you are than the birds! And which of you by worrying can add a *single* hour to his life's span? If then you cannot do even a very little thing, why do you worry about other matters? Consider the lilies, how they grow: they neither toil nor spin; but I tell you, not even Solomon in all his glory clothed himself like one of these. But if God so clothes the grass in the field, which is *alive* today and tomorrow is thrown into the furnace, how much more *will He clothe* you? You men of little faith! And do not seek what you will eat and what you will drink, and do not keep worrying. For all these things the nations of the world eagerly seek; but your Father knows that you need these things. But seek His kingdom, and these things will be added to you. Do not be afraid, little flock, for your Father has chosen gladly to give you the kingdom" (Luke 12:22–32; cf. Matthew 6:25–33; see 1 Kings 10:4–7; Job 38:41).

Setting: On the way from Galilee to Jerusalem. Jesus conveys the illustration of the prodigal son because the Pharisees and scribes complain He associates with tax collectors and sinners.

And He said, "A man had two sons. The younger of them said to his father, 'Father, give me the share of the estate that falls to me.' So he divided his wealth between them. And not many days later, the younger son gathered everything together and went on a journey into a distant country, and there he squandered his estate with loose living. Now when he had spent everything, a severe famine occurred in that country, and he began to be impoverished. So he went and hired himself out to one of the citizens of that country, and he sent him into his fields to feed swine. And he would have gladly filled his stomach with the pods that the swine were eating, and no one was giving *anything* to him. But when he came to his senses, he said, 'How many of my father's hired men have more than enough bread, but I am dying here with hunger! I will get up and go to my father, and will say to him, "Father, I have sinned against heaven, and in your sight; I am no longer worthy to be called your son; make me as one of your hired men."' So he got up and came to his father. But while he was still a long way off, his father saw him and felt compassion *for him,* and ran and embraced him and kissed him. And the son said to him, "Father, I have sinned against heaven and in your sight; I am no longer worthy to be called your son.' But the father said to his slaves, 'Quickly bring out the best robe and put it on him, and put a ring on his hand and sandals on his feet; and bring the fattened calf, kill it, and let us eat and celebrate; for this son of mine was dead and has come to life again; he was lost and has been found.' And they began to celebrate. Now his older son was in the field, when he came and approached the house, he heard music and dancing. And he summoned one of the servants and *began* inquiring what these things could be. And he said to him, 'Your brother has come, and your father has killed the fattened calf because he has received him back safe and sound.' But he became angry and was not willing to go in; and his father came out and *began* pleading with him. But he answered and said to his father, 'Look! For so many years I have been serving you and I have never neglected a command of yours; and *yet* you have never given me a young goat, so that I might celebrate with my friends; but when this son of yours came, who has devoured your wealth with prostitutes, you killed the fattened calf for him.' And he said to him, 'Son, you have always been with me, and all that is mine is yours. But we had to celebrate and rejoice, for this brother of yours was dead and *has begun* to live, and was lost and has been found' " (Luke 15:11–32; see Proverb 29:2).

Setting: The temple in Jerusalem. While Jesus ministers a few days before His crucifixion, with His conflict with the religious leaders of Israel escalating, the chief priests and the scribes question His authority to teach and preach.

Jesus answered and said to them, "I will also ask you a question, and you tell Me: Was the baptism of John from heaven or from men?" They reasoned among themselves, saying, "If we say, 'From heaven,' He will say, 'Why did you not believe him?' But if we say, 'From men,' all the people will stone us to death, for they are convinced that John was a prophet." So they answered that they did not know where *it came* from. And Jesus said to them, "Nor will I tell you by what authority I do these things" (Luke 20:3–8; cf. Matthew 21:23–27; Mark 11:27–33).

Setting: Jerusalem While ministering a few days before His crucifixion, after pointing out a poor widow's sacrificial giving to the temple treasury, Jesus prophesies the destruction of the temple.

"*As for* these things which you are looking at, the days will come in which there will not be left one stone upon another which will not be torn down" (Luke 21:6; cf. Matthew 24:1, 2; Mark 13:1, 2).

Setting: The temple in Jerusalem. While ministering a few days before His crucifixion, after Jesus prophesies the destruction of the temple, His disciples ask Him when this will happen.

And He said, "See to it that you are not misled; for many will come in My name, saying, "I am *He*,' and, 'The time is near.' Do not go after them. When you hear of wars and disturbances, do not be terrified; for these things must take place first, but the end *does* not *follow* immediately" (Luke 21:8, 9; cf. Matthew 24:4–8; Mark 13:5–8).

Setting: On the Mount of Olives, east of the temple in Jerusalem. After ministering in the temple a few days before His crucifixion, and giving His disciples more details regarding the temple's future destruction, Jesus elaborates during His Olivet Discourse about things to come.

Then He continued by saying to them, "Nation will rise against nation and kingdom against kingdom, and there will be great earthquakes, and in various places plagues and famines; and there will be terrors and great signs from heaven. But before all these things, they will lay their hands on you and will persecute you, delivering you to the synagogues and prisons, bringing you before kings and governors for My name's sake. It will lead to an opportunity for your testimony. So make up your minds not to prepare beforehand to defend yourselves; for I will give you utterance and wisdom which none of your opponents will be able to resist or refute. But you will be betrayed even by parents and brothers and relatives and friends, and they will put *some* of you to death, and you will be hated by all because of My name. Yet not a hair of your head will perish. By your endurance you will gain your lives" (Luke 21:10–19; cf. Matthew 10:19–22; 24:7–14; Mark 13:8–13).

Setting: On the Mount of Olives, just east of Jerusalem. After ministering in the temple a few days before His crucifixion, and giving His disciples more details regarding future events, Jesus speaks during His Olivet Discourse of His return.

"There will be signs in sun and moon and stars, and on the earth dismay among the nations, in perplexity at the roaring of the sea and the waves, men fainting from fear and the expectation of the things which are coming upon the world; for the powers of the heavens will be shaken. Then they will see THE SON OF MAN COMING IN A CLOUD with power and great glory. But when these things begin to take place, straighten up and lift up your heads, because your redemption is drawing near" (Luke 21:25–28, Jesus quotes from Daniel 7:13; cf. Matthew 24:29–31; Mark 13:24–27).

Setting: On the Mount of Olives, east of the temple in Jerusalem. After ministering in the temple a few days before His crucifixion, and giving the disciples more details regarding His return, Jesus conveys the Parable of the Fig Tree during His Olivet Discourse.

Then He told them a parable: "Behold the fig tree and all the trees; as soon as they put forth *leaves,* you see it and know for yourselves that summer is now near. So you also, when you see these things happening, recognize that the kingdom of God is near. Truly, I say to you, this generation will not pass away until all things take place. Heaven and earth will pass away, but My words will not pass away" (Luke 21:29–33; cf. Matthew 24:32–35; Mark 13:28–31; see Matthew 5:18).

Setting: The Mount of Olives, east of the temple in Jerusalem. After ministering in the temple a few days before His crucifixion, and conveying the Parable of the Fig Tree during His Olivet Discourse, Jesus warns His disciples to keep alert regarding future events.

"Be on guard, so that your hearts will not be weighted down with dissipation and drunkenness and the worries of life, and that day will not come upon you suddenly like a trap; for it will come upon all those who dwell on the face of all the earth. But keep on the alert at all times, praying that you may have strength to escape all these things that are about to take place, and to stand before the Son of Man" (Luke 21:34–36; cf. Mark 13:33; see Matthew 24:42–44).

Setting: Jerusalem. After being arrested, and appearing before the Council of Elders (Sanhedrin), Pilate (Roman governor of Judea), Herod Antipas (tetrarch of Galilee and Perea), and Pilate a second time (when the ruler bows to the crowd's pressure and grants that Jesus be crucified), the Lord prophesies to the women mourning Him regarding the coming judgment of Jerusalem.

But Jesus turning to them said, "Daughters of Jerusalem, stop weeping for Me, but weep for yourselves and for your children. For behold, the days are coming when they will say, 'Blessed are the barren, and the wombs that never bore, and the breasts that never nursed.' Then they will begin TO SAY TO THE MOUNTAINS, 'FALL ON US,' AND TO THE HILLS, 'COVER US.' For if they do these things when the tree is green, what will happen when it is dry?" (Luke 23:28–31, Jesus quotes from Hosea 10:8; see Matthew 24:19).

Setting: On the road to Emmaus. After rising from the tomb on the third day after being crucified, Jesus appears to two of His followers (who have heard reports the tomb is empty) and elaborates on the purpose of His coming to earth.

And He said to them, "O foolish men and slow of heart to believe in all that the prophets have spoken! Was it not necessary for the Christ to suffer these things and to enter into His glory?" (Luke 24:25, 26).

Setting: Jerusalem. After rising from the tomb on the third day after being crucified, and appearing to two of His followers on the road to Emmaus, Jesus gives instruction to His disciples (except Thomas) about His mission on earth and the promise of future power from God.

Now He said to them, "These are My words which I spoke to you while I was still with you, that all things which are written about Me in the Law of Moses and the Prophets and the Psalms must be fulfilled." Then He opened their minds to understand the Scriptures, and He said to them, "Thus it is written, that the Christ would suffer and rise again from the dead the third day, and that repentance for forgiveness of sins would be proclaimed in His name to all the nations, beginning from Jerusalem. You are witnesses of these things. And behold, I am sending forth the promise of My Father upon you; but you are to stay in the city until you are clothed with power from on high" (Luke 24:44–49; see Matthew 28:19, 20; Acts 1:8).

Setting: Jerusalem. After beginning His ministry in Galilee by selecting His disciples and performing a miracle at a wedding in Cana, Jesus attends the Passover of the Jews, and confronts those perverting the temple for business.

And He made a scourge of cords, and drove *them* all out of the temple, with the sheep and the oxen; and He poured out the coins of the money changers and overturned their tables; and to those who were selling the doves He said, "Take these things away; stop making My Father's house a place of business" (John 2:15, 16; cf. Matthew 21:12, 13; see Deuteronomy 16:1–6).

Setting: Jerusalem. At the time for the Passover of the Jews, after the Lord cleanses the temple, a Pharisee, Nicodemus, asks Him by night the meaning of "born of the Spirit."

Jesus answered and said to him, "Are you the teacher of Israel and do not understand these things? Truly, truly, I say to you, we speak of what we know and testify of what we have seen, and you do not accept our testimony. If I told you earthly things and you do not believe, how will you believe if I tell you heavenly things? No one has ascended into heaven, but He who descended from heaven: the Son of Man. As Moses lifted up the serpent in the wilderness, even so must the Son of Man be lifted up; so that whoever believes will in Him have eternal life" (John 3:10–15; see Numbers 21:9; Proverb 30:4; John 12:34; 20:30, 31).

Setting: By the pool of Bethesda in Jerusalem. During a feast of the Jews, Jesus responds to criticism from the Jewish religious leaders for healing a lame man on the Sabbath and for referring to God as His Father (thereby making Himself equal with God).

Therefore Jesus answered and was saying to them, "Truly, truly, I say to you, the Son can do nothing of Himself, unless *it is* something He sees the Father doing; for whatever the Father does, these things the Son also does in like manner. For the Father loves the Son, and shows Him all things that He Himself is doing; and *the Father* will show Him greater works than these, so that you will marvel. For just as the Father raises the dead and gives them life, even so the Son also gives life to whom He wishes. For not even the Father judges anyone, but He has given all judgment to the Son, so that all will honor the Son even as they honor the Father. He who does not honor the Son does not honor the Father who sent Him" (John 5:19–23; see Luke 10:16; John 3:35; 11:25; 14:12).

Setting: Jerusalem. During a feast of the Jews, Jesus responds to criticism from the Jewish religious leaders by referring to God as His Father (thereby making Himself equal with God) and informing them that God, John the Baptist, and His works all testify to His mission.

"I can do nothing on My own initiative. As I hear, I judge; and My judgment is just, because I do not seek My own will, but the will of Him who sent Me. If I *alone* testify about Myself, My testimony is not true. There is another who testifies of Me, and I know that the testimony which He gives about Me is true. You have sent to John, and he has testified to the truth. But the testimony which I receive is not from man, but I say these things so that you may be saved. He was the lamp that was burning and was shining and you were willing to rejoice for a while in his light. But the testimony which I have is greater than the *testimony of* John; for the works which the Father has given Me to accomplish—the very works that I do—testify about Me, that the Father has sent Me. And the Father who sent Me, He has testified of Me. You have neither heard His voice at any time nor seen His form. You do not have His word abiding in you, for you do not believe Him whom He sent" (John 5:30–38; see Matthew 3:17; Mark 1:4, 5; John 1:7, 15, 32; 4:34; 8:14–16; 10:25, 37, 38).

Setting: The temple treasury in Jerusalem. Following the Feast of Booths and the scribes' and Pharisees' failed attempt to stone a woman for adultery, Jesus returns the next day to teach. They question His testimony about Himself.

So Jesus said, "When you lift up the Son of Man, then you will know that I am *He,* and I do nothing on my own initiative, but I speak these things as the Father taught Me. And He who sent Me is with Me; He has not left Me alone, for I always do the things that are pleasing to Him" (John 8:28, 29; see John 3:14).

Setting: Jerusalem. Before the Passover, with His death on the cross nearing, Jesus explains the reason for His vivid example of servanthood in washing His disciples' feet.

So when He had washed their feet, and taken His garments and reclined *at the table* again, He said to them, "Do you know what I have done to you? You call Me Teacher and Lord; and you are right, for *so* I am. If I then, the Lord and the Teacher, washed your feet, you also ought to wash one another's feet. For I gave you an example that you also should do as I did to you. Truly, truly I say to you, a slave is not greater than his master, nor *is* one who is sent greater than the one who sent him. If you know these things, you are blessed if you do them. I do not speak of all of you. I know the ones I have chosen; but *it is* that the Scripture may be fulfilled, 'HE WHO EATS MY BREAD HAS LIFTED UP HIS HEEL AGAINST ME.' From now on I am telling you before *it* comes to pass, so that when it does occur, you may believe that I am *He*. Truly, truly, I say to you, he who receives whomever I send receives Me; and he who receives Me receives Him who sent Me" (John 13:12–20; Jesus quotes from Psalm 41:9; see Matthew 7:24; 10:24, 40; John 8:24; 14:29; 1 Peter 5:3).

Setting: Jerusalem. Before the Passover, after responding to Philip's request for Him to show His disciples the Father, Jesus conveys the upcoming ministry of the Holy Spirit in their lives.

"These things I have spoken to you while abiding with you. But the Helper, the Holy Spirit, whom the Father will send in My name, He will teach you all things, and bring to your remembrance all that I said to you" (John 14:25, 26; see John 16:13).

Setting: Jerusalem. Before the Passover, after conveying the upcoming ministry of the Holy Spirit in His disciples' lives with His imminent departure from them, Jesus explains He is the vine and His disciples are the branches.

"I am the true vine, and My Father is the vinedresser. Every branch in Me that does not bear fruit, He takes away; and every *branch* that bears fruit, He prunes it so that it may bear more fruit. You are already clean because of the word which I have spoken to you. Abide in Me, and I in you. As the branch cannot bear fruit of itself unless it abides in the vine, so neither *can* you unless you abide in Me. I am the vine, you are the branches; he who abides in Me and I in him, he bears much fruit, for apart from Me you can do nothing. If anyone does not abide in Me, he is thrown away as a branch and dries up; and they gather them, and cast them into the fire and they are burned. If you abide in Me, and My words abide in you, ask whatever you wish, and it will be done for you. My Father is glorified by this, that you bear much fruit, and *so* prove to be My disciples. Just as the Father has loved Me, I have also loved you; abide in My love. If you keep My commandments, you will abide in My love; just as I have kept My Father's commandments and abide in His love. These things I have spoken to you so that My joy may be in you, and *that* your joy may be made full" (John 15:1–11; see Matthew 5:16; 7:7; John 3:29, 35; 6:56; 8:29, 31; 13:10).

Setting: Jerusalem. Before the Passover, with His departure in mind, after explaining He is the vine and His disciples are the branches, Jesus prepares them for persecution from the world.

"If the world hates you, you know that it has hated Me before *it hated* you. If you were of the world, the world would love its own; but because you are not of the world, but I chose you out of the world, because of this the world hates you. Remember the word that I said to you, 'A slave is not greater than his master.' If they persecuted Me, they will also persecute you; if they kept My word, they will keep yours also. But all these things they will do to you for My name's sake, because they do not know the One who sent Me. If I had not come and spoken to them, they would not have sin, but now they have no excuse for their sin" (John 15:18–22; see Matthew 10:22; John 7:7; 8:19, 55; 9:41; 1 Corinthians 4:12).

Setting: Jerusalem. Before the Passover, after explaining He is the vine and His disciples are the branches, Jesus warns the disciples of the persecution they will face after His departure to heaven.

"These things I have spoken to you so that you may be kept from stumbling. They will make you outcasts from the synagogue, but an hour is coming for everyone who kills you to think that he is offering service to God. These things they will do because they have not known the Father or Me. But these things I have spoken to you, so that when their hour comes, you may remember that I told you of them. These things I did not say to you at the beginning, because I was with you" (John 16:1–4; see John 8:19, 55; 9:22; 13:19; 15:18–27).

Setting: Jerusalem. Before the Passover, after warning His disciples of the persecution they will face after His departure to heaven, Jesus elaborates about the coming ministry of the Holy Spirit.

"But now I am going to Him who sent Me; and none of you asks Me, 'Where are You going?' But because I have said these things to you, sorrow has filled your heart. But I tell you the truth, it is to your advantage that I go away; for if I do not go away, the Helper will not come to you; but if I go, I will send Him to you. And He, when He comes, will convict the world concerning sin and righteousness and judgment; concerning sin, because they do not believe in Me; and concerning righteousness, because I go to the Father and you no longer see Me; and concerning judgment, because the ruler of this world has been judged" (John 16:5–11; see John 7:33; 12:31; 14:1, 16; 15:22, 24).

Setting: Jerusalem. Before the Passover, after empathizing with His disciples' sadness over His prophecies and giving them the hope for the future, Jesus conveys promises about praying in His name.

"In that day you will not question Me about anything. Truly, truly, I say to you, if you ask the Father for anything in My name, He will give it to you. Until now you have asked for nothing in My name; ask and you will receive, so that your joy may be made full. These things I have spoken to you in figurative language; an hour is coming when I will no longer speak to you in figurative language, but will tell you plainly of the Father. In that day you will ask in My name, and I do not say to you that I will request of the Father on your behalf; for the Father Himself loves you, because you have loved Me and have believed that I came forth from the Father. I came forth from the Father and have come into the world; I am leaving the world again and going to the Father" (John 16:23–28; see Matthew 13:34; John 8:42; 13:1, 3; 14:14, 21, 23; 15:16).

Setting: Jerusalem. Before the Passover, after conveying promises about praying in His name, Jesus prophesies the disciples' scattering and gives them assurance that in the midst of tribulation they will have His peace.

"Jesus answered them, "Do you now believe? Behold, an hour is coming, and has *already* come, for you to be scattered, each to his own *home,* and to leave Me alone; and *yet* I am not alone, because the Father is with Me. These things I have spoken to you, so that in Me you may have peace. In the world you have tribulation, but take courage, I have overcome the world" (John 16:31–33; see Zechariah 13:7; John 8:29; 14:27; Romans 8:37).

Setting: Jerusalem. Before the Passover, after giving His disciples assurance that in the midst of tribulation they will have His peace, Jesus prays His high-priestly prayer.

Jesus spoke these things; and lifting up His eyes to heaven, He said, "Father, the hour has come; glorify Your Son, that the Son may glorify You, even as You gave Him authority over all flesh, that to all whom You have given Him, He may give eternal life. This is eternal life, that they may know You, the only true God, and Jesus Christ whom You have sent. I glorified You on the earth, having accomplished the work which You have given Me to do. Now, Father, glorify Me together with Yourself, with the glory which I had with You before the world was. I have manifested Your name to the men whom You gave Me out of the world; they were Yours and You gave them to Me, and they have kept Your word. Now they have come to know that everything You have given Me is from You; for the words which You gave Me I have given to them; and they received *them* and truly understood that I came forth from You, and they believed You sent Me. I ask on their behalf; I do not ask on behalf of the world, but of those whom You have given Me; for they are Yours; and all things that are Mine are Yours, and Yours are Mine; and I have been glorified in them. I am no longer in the world; and *yet* they themselves are in the world, and I come to You. Holy Father, keep them in Your name, *the name* which You have given Me, that they may be even as We *are.* While I was with them, I was keeping them in Your name which You have given Me; and I guarded them and not one of them perished but the son of perdition, so that the Scripture would be fulfilled" (John 17:1–12; see Luke 22:32; John 1:1; 3:35; 4:34; 5:44; 6:37–39, 70; 8:42; 11:41; 12:49; 13:18, 31; 16:15; Philippians 2:9).

Setting: Jerusalem. Before the Passover, after giving His disciples assurance that in the midst of tribulation they will have His peace, Jesus continues praying His high-priestly prayer.

"But now I come to You; and these things I speak in the world so that they may have My joy made full in themselves. I have given them Your word; and the world has hated them, because they are not of the world, even as I am not of the world. I do not ask You to take them out of the world, but to keep them from the evil *one.* They are not of the world, even as I am not of the world. Sanctify them in the truth; Your word is truth. As You sent Me into the world, I also have sent them into the world. For their sakes I sanctify Myself, that they themselves also may be sanctified in truth. I do not ask on behalf of these alone, but for those also who believe in Me through their word; that they may all be one; even as You, Father, *are* in Me and I in You, that they also maybe in Us, so that the world may believe that You sent Me" (John 17:13–21; see Matthew 10:5, 38; John 7:33; 15:3, 11, 19).

Setting: On the island of Patmos (in the Aegean Sea about fifty miles southwest of Ephesus in modern Turkey). On the Lord's Day (Sunday), approximately fifty years after the Resurrection, the disciple John encounters the Lord Jesus Christ, who communicates new revelations for the apostle to record for the seven churches in Asia.

When I saw Him, I fell at His feet like a dead man. And He placed His right hand on me, saying, "Do not be afraid; *I am* the first and the last, and the living One; and I was dead, and behold, I am alive forevermore, and I have the keys of death and of Hades. Therefore write the things which you have seen, and the things which are, and the things which will take place after these things. As for the mystery of the seven stars which you saw in My right hand, and the seven golden lampstands: the seven stars are the angels of the seven churches, and the seven lampstands are the seven churches" (Revelation 1:17–20; see Isaiah 44:6; Luke 24:5; Revelation 2:8).

Setting: On the island of Patmos (in the Aegean Sea about fifty miles southwest of Ephesus in modern Turkey). In the final chapter of the Lord Jesus Christ's revelation via the apostle John, approximately fifty years after the Resurrection, the Lord authenticates the truthfulness of His message, along with His earthly lineage through King David.

"I, Jesus, have sent My angel to testify to you these things for the churches. I am the root and the descendant of David, the bright morning star" (Revelation 22:16).

THINGS, THOSE

Setting: The Mount of Olives, just east of Jerusalem. During His Olivet Discourse, Jesus answers His disciples' questions as to when the temple will be destroyed and Jerusalem overrun, along with the signs of His coming and the end of the age.

And Jesus answered and said to them, "See to it that no one misleads you. For many will come in My name, saying, 'I am the Christ,' and will mislead many. You will be hearing of wars and rumors of wars. See that you are not frightened, for *those things* must take place, but *that* is not yet the end. For nation will rise against nation, and kingdom against kingdom, and in various places there will be famines and earthquakes. But all these things are *merely* the beginning of birth pangs. Then they will deliver you to tribulation, and will kill you, and you will be hated by all nations because of My name. At that time many will fall away and will betray one another and hate one another. Many false prophets will arise and will mislead many. Because lawlessness is increased, most people's love will grow cold. But the one who endures to the end, he will be saved. This gospel of the kingdom shall be preached in the whole world as a testimony to all the nations, and then the end will come" (Matthew 24:4–14; cf. Jeremiah 29:8; Matthew 7:15; 10:17, 22; Mark 13:3–13; Luke 21:7–19; Revelation 6:4).

Setting: On the Mount of Olives, east of the temple in Jerusalem. After predicting the temple's destruction, Jesus responds during His Olivet Discourse to questions from Peter, James, John, and Andrew about other future events.

And Jesus began to say to them, "See to it that no one misleads you. Many will come in My name, saying, 'I am *He!*' and will mislead many. When you hear of wars and rumors of wars, do not be frightened; *those things* must take place; but *that is* not yet the end. For nation will rise up against nation, and kingdom against kingdom; there will be earthquakes in various places; there will *also be* famines. These things are *merely* the beginning of birth pangs. But be on your guard; for they will deliver you to *the* courts, and you will be flogged in *the* synagogues, and you will stand before governors and kings for My sake, as a testimony to them. The gospel must first be preached to all the nations. When they arrest you and hand you over, do not worry beforehand about what you are to say, but say whatever is given you in that hour; for it is not you who speak, but *it is* the Holy Spirit. Brother will betray brother to death, and a father *his* child; and children will rise up against parents and have them put to death. You will be hated by all because of My name, but the one who endures to the end, he will be saved" (Mark 13:5–13; cf. Matthew 24:4–14; Luke 21:7–19; see Matthew 10:17–22).

THINGS, WHAT

Setting: On the road to Emmaus. After rising from the tomb on the third day after being crucified, Jesus appears to two of His followers, and asks them a question.

And He said to them, "What things?" And they said to Him, "The things about Jesus the Nazarene, who was a prophet mighty in deed and word in the sight of God and all the people, and how the chief priests and our rulers delivered Him to the sentence of death, and crucified Him (Luke 24:19, 20; see Matthew 21:11).

THIRD (DAY, THIRD is a separate entry)

Setting: Judea beyond the Jordan (Perea). Jesus illustrates the kingdom of heaven to His disciples through the story of laborers in the vineyard.

"For the kingdom of heaven is like a landowner who went out early in the morning to hire laborers for his vineyard. When he had agreed with the laborers for a denarius for the day, he sent them into his vineyard. And he went out about the third hour and saw others standing idle in the market place; and to those he said,' You also go into the vineyard, and whatever is right I will give you.' And *so* they went. Again he went out about the sixth and the ninth hour, and did the same thing. And about the eleventh *hour* he went out and found others standing *around;* and he said to them, 'Why have you been standing idle here all day long?' They said to him, 'Because no one hired us.' He said to them, 'You go into the vineyard too.' When evening came, the owner of the vineyard said to his foreman, 'Call the laborers and pay them their wages, beginning with the last *group* to the first.' When those *hired* about the eleventh hour came, each one received a denarius. When those *hired* first came, they thought that they would receive more; but each of them also received a denarius. When they received it, they grumbled at the landowner, saying, 'These last men have worked *only* one hour, and you have made them equal to us who have borne the burden and the scorching heat of the day.' But he answered and said to one of them, 'Friend, I am doing you no wrong; did you not agree with me for a denarius? Take what is yours and go, but I wish to give to this last man the same as to you. It is not lawful for me to do what I wish with what is my own? Or is your eye envious because I am generous?' So the last shall be first, and the first last" (Matthew 20:1–16; cf. Matthew 19:30)

Setting: The temple in Jerusalem. Jesus delivers another parable to the chief priests and elders after they question His authority.

"Listen to another parable. There was a landowner who PLANTED A VINEYARD AND PUT A WALL AROUND IT AND DUG A WINE PRESS IN IT, AND BUILT A TOWER, and rented it out to vine-growers and went on a journey. When the harvest time approached, he sent his slaves to the vine-growers to receive his produce. The vine-growers took his slaves and beat one, and killed another, and stoned a third. Again he sent another group of slaves larger than the first; and they did the same thing to them. But afterward he sent his son to them, saying, 'They will respect my son.' But when the vine-growers saw the son, they said among themselves, 'This is the heir; come, let us kill him and seize his inheritance.' They took him, and threw him out of the vineyard and killed him. Therefore when the owner of the vineyard comes, what will he do to those vine-growers?" (Matthew 21:33–40; Jesus quotes from Isaiah 5:1, 2; cf. Mark 12:1–9; Luke 20:9–15).

Setting: On the way from Galilee to Jerusalem. After giving a parable about riches and greed, Jesus uses another parable to challenge the crowd and His disciples to be ready for His return.

"Be dressed in readiness, and *keep* your lamps lit. Be like men who are waiting for their master when he returns from the wedding feast, so that they may immediately open *the door* to him when he comes and knocks. Blessed are those slaves whom the master will find on the alert when he comes; truly I say to you, that he will gird himself *to serve,* and have them recline *at the table,* and will come up and wait on them. Whether he comes in the second watch, or even in the third and finds *them* so, blessed are those *slaves.* But be sure of this, that if the head of the house had known at what hour the thief was coming, he would not have allowed his house to be broken into. You too, be ready; for the Son of Man is coming at an hour that you do not expect" (Luke 12:35–40; cf. Matthew 24:42–44; see Mark 13:33; Ephesians 6:14).

Setting: The temple in Jerusalem. While ministering a few days before His crucifixion, after the chief priests and the scribes question His authority to teach and preach, Jesus conveys the Parable of the Vine-Growers to the people.

And He began to tell the people this parable: "A man planted a vineyard and rented it out to vine-growers, and went on a journey for a long time. At the *harvest* time he sent a slave to the vine-growers, so that they would give him *some* of the produce of the vineyard; but the vine-growers beat him and sent him away empty-handed. And he proceeded to send another slave; and they beat him also and treated him shamefully and sent him away empty-handed. And he proceeded to send a third; and this one also they wounded and cast out. The owner of the vineyard said, 'What shall I do? I will send my beloved son; perhaps they will respect him.' But when the vine-growers saw him, they reasoned with one another, saying, 'This is the heir; let us kill him so that the inheritance will be ours.' So they threw him out of the vineyard and killed him. What, then, will the owner of the vineyard do to them? He will come and destroy these vine-growers and will give the vineyard to others." When they heard it, they said, "May it never be!" But Jesus looked at them and said, "What then is this that is written: 'THE STONE WHICH THE BUILDERS REJECTED, THIS BECAME THE CHIEF CORNER *stone*'? Everyone who falls on that stone will be broken to pieces; but on whomever it falls, it will scatter him like dust" (Luke 20:9–18, Jesus quotes from Psalm 118:22; cf. Matthew 21:33–44; Mark 12:1–11; see Ephesians 2:20).

THIRD DAY (Listed as DAY, THIRD)

THIRST (Also see DRINKING; and WATER)

Setting: Galilee. Early in His ministry, Jesus presents the Beatitudes (part of the Sermon on the Mount) to His disciples and the gathered crowds from Galilee, Decapolis, Jerusalem, Judea, and beyond the Jordan.

"Blessed are those who hunger and thirst for righteousness, for they shall be satisfied" (Matthew 5:6; see Matthew 13:35).

[THIRST from thirsty]

Setting: On the Mount of Olives, just east of Jerusalem. During His Olivet Discourse, after answering His disciples' questions as to when the temple will be destroyed and Jerusalem overrun, along with the signs of His coming and the end of the age, Jesus reveals the future judgments following His return.

"But when the Son of Man comes in His glory, and all the angels with Him, then He will sit on His glorious throne. All the nations will be gathered before Him; and He will separate them from one another, as the shepherd separates the sheep from the goats; and He will put the sheep on His right, and the goats on the left. Then the King will say to those on His right, 'Come, you who are blessed of My Father, inherit the kingdom prepared for you from the foundation of the world. 'For I was hungry, and you gave Me *something* to eat; I was thirsty, and you gave Me *something* to drink; I was a stranger, and you invited Me in; naked, and you clothed Me; I was sick, and you visited Me; I was in prison, and you came to Me.' Then the righteous will answer Him, 'Lord, when did we see You hungry and feed You, or thirsty, and give you *something* to drink? And when did we see You a stranger, and invite You in, or naked, and clothe You? When did we see You sick, or in prison, and come to You?' The King will answer and say to them, 'Truly I say to you, to the extent that you did it to one of these brothers of Mine, *even* the least *of them,* you did it to Me.' Then He will also say to those on His left, 'Depart from Me, accursed ones, into the eternal fire which has been prepared for the devil and his angels; for I was hungry, and you gave Me *nothing* to eat; I was thirsty, and you gave Me nothing to drink; I was a stranger, and you did not invite Me in; naked, and you did not clothe Me; sick, and in prison, and you did not visit Me.' Then they themselves also will answer, 'Lord, when did we see You hungry, or thirsty, or a stranger, or naked, or sick, or in prison, and did not take care of You?' Then He will answer them, 'Truly I say to you, to the extent that you did not do it to one of the least of these, you did not do it to Me.' These will go away into eternal punishment, but the righteous into eternal life" (Matthew 25:31–46; see Matthew 7:23; 16:27; 19:29).

Setting: Sychar in Samaria, on the way to Galilee. Jesus interacts with a Samaritan woman at Jacob's well, while the disciples are buying food.

Jesus answered and said to her, "Everyone who drinks of this water will thirst again; but whoever drinks of the water that I will give him shall never thirst; but the water that I will give him will become in him a well of water springing up to eternal life" (John 4:13, 14).

Setting: Capernaum. The day after Jesus walks on the Sea of Galilee to join His disciples in a boat, the people He miraculously fed with a lad's five loaves and two fish ask the Lord to always give them this bread out of heaven.

Jesus said to them, "I am the bread of life; he who comes to Me will not hunger, and he who believes in Me will never thirst. But I said to you that you have seen Me, and yet do not believe. All that the Father gives Me will come to Me, and the one who comes to Me I will certainly not cast out. For I have come down from heaven, not to do My own will, but the will of Him who sent Me. This is the will of Him who sent Me, that of all that He has given Me I lose nothing, but raise it up on the last day. For this is the will of My Father, that everyone who beholds the Son and believes in Him will have eternal life, and I Myself will raise him up on the last day" (John 6:35–40; see John 3:13, 16; 4:13, 14).

[THIRST from thirsty]
Setting: Jerusalem. On the last day of the Feast of Booths, after Jesus causes discussion about whether He is the Christ, the chief priests and Pharisees attempt to understand where it is He says He will be going soon. The Lord offers salvation and the abundant life to His hearers.

Now on the last day, the great *day* of the feast, Jesus stood and cried out, saying, "If anyone is thirsty, let him come to Me and drink. He who believes in Me, as the Scripture said, 'From his innermost being will flow rivers of living water'" (John 7:37, 38).

[THIRST from thirsty]
Setting: On a hill called Golgotha (the Place of the Skull), just outside Jerusalem. After asking His disciple John to care for His mother, in the midst of fulfilling Scripture as He dies on the cross for the sins of the world, Jesus expresses His thirst.

After this, Jesus, knowing that all things had already been accomplished, to fulfill the Scripture, said, "I am thirsty" (John 19:28; see Psalm 69:21; Matthew 27:48; Mark 15:36).

THISTLES (Also see TARES; and THORNS)
Setting: Galilee. During the early part of His ministry, Jesus preaches the Sermon on the Mount to His disciples and the multitudes.

"Beware of the false prophets, who come to you in sheep's clothing, but inwardly are ravenous wolves. You will know them by their fruits. Grapes are not gathered from *bushes* nor figs from thistles, are they? So every good tree bears good fruit, but the bad tree bears bad fruit. A good tree cannot produce bad fruit, nor can a bad tree produce good fruit. Every tree that does not bear good fruit is cut down and thrown into the fire. So then, you will know them by their fruits" (Matthew 7:15–20; cf. Matthew 3:10; Matthew 12:33, 35; Matthew 24:11, 24; Luke 6:43, 44).

THORN IN THE FLESH (Listed under FLESH, THORN IN THE)

THORNS (Also see THISTLES)
Setting: By the Sea of Galilee. While teaching and preaching to the crowds from a boat, Jesus conveys the Parable of the Sower.

And He spoke many things to them in parables, saying, "Behold, the sower went out to sow; and as he sowed, some *seeds* fell beside the road, and the birds came and ate them up. Others fell on the rocky places, where they did not have much soil; and immediately they sprang up, because they had no depth of soil. But when the sun had risen, they were scorched; and because they had no root, they withered away. Others fell among the thorns, and the thorns came up and choked them out. And others fell on the good soil and yielded a crop, some a hundredfold, some sixty, and some thirty. He who has ears, let him hear" (Matthew 13:3–9; cf. Mark 4:3–9; Luke 8:4–8).

Setting: By the Sea of Galilee. With the religious leaders rejecting His message, Jesus begins to teach in parables, and gives His disciples the meaning of the Parable of the Sower.

"Hear then the parable of the sower. When anyone hears the word of the kingdom and does not understand it, the evil *one* comes and snatches away what has been sown in his heart. This is the one on whom seed was sown beside the road. The one on whom seed was sown on the rocky places, this is the man who hears the word and immediately receives it with joy; yet he has no *firm* root in himself, but is *only* temporary, and when affliction or persecution arises because of the word, immediately he falls away. And the one on whom seed was sown among the thorns, this is the man who hears the word, and the worry of the world and the deceitfulness of wealth choke the word, and it becomes unfruitful. And the one on whom seed was sown on the good soil, this is the man who hears the word and understands it; who indeed bears fruit and brings forth, some a hundredfold, some sixty, and some thirty." (Matthew 13:18–23; cf. Mark 4:13–20; Luke 8:11–15)

Setting: By the Sea of Galilee. During the early part of His ministry, just after a visit from his mother and brothers, Jesus instructs a very large crowd with the Parable of the Sower from a boat.

"Listen *to this!* Behold, the sower went out to sow; as he was sowing, some *seed* fell beside the road, and the birds came and ate it up. Other *seed* fell on the rocky *ground* where it did not have much soil; and immediately it sprang up because it had no depth of soil. And after the sun had risen, it was scorched; and because it had no root, it withered away. Other *seed* fell among the thorns, and the thorns came up and choked it, and it yielded no crop. Other *seeds* fell into the good soil, and as the grew up and increased, they yielded a crop and produced thirty, sixty, and a hundredfold." And He was saying, "He who has ears to hear, let him hear" (Mark 4:3–9; cf. Matthew 13:3–9; Luke 8:5–8).

Setting: By the Sea of Galilee. During the early part of His ministry, after presenting the Parable of the Sower from a boat to a very large crowd, Jesus gives the meaning of the parable to His disciples and other followers.

And He said to them, "Do you not understand this parable? How will you understand all the parables? The sower sows the word. These are the ones who are beside the road where the word is sown; and when they hear, immediately Satan comes and takes away the word which has been sown in them. In a similar way these are the ones on whom seed was sown on the rocky places, who, when they hear the word, immediately receive it with joy; and they have no *firm* root in themselves, but are *only* temporary; then, when affliction or persecution arises because of the word, immediately they fall away. And others are the ones on whom seed was sown among the thorns; these are the ones who have heard the word, but the worries of the world and the deceitfulness of riches, and the desires for other things enter in and choke the word, and it becomes unfruitful. And those are the ones on whom seed was sown on the good soil; and they hear the word and accept it and bear fruit, thirty, sixty, and a hundredfold" (Mark 4:13–20; cf. Matthew 13:18–23; Luke 8:11–15).

Setting: Galilee. After selecting His twelve disciples, Jesus teaches the Sermon on the Mount to those disciples and a great throng of people from Judea, Jerusalem, and the central coastal region of Tyre and Sidon.

And He also spoke a parable to them: "A blind man cannot guide a blind man, can he? Will they not both fall into a pit? A pupil is not above his teacher; but everyone, after he has been fully trained, will be like his teacher. Why do you look at the speck that is in your brother's eye, but do not notice the log that is in your own eye? Or how can you say to your brother, 'Brother, let me take out the speck that is in your eye,' when you yourself do not see the log that is in your own eye? You hypocrite, first take the log out of your own eye, and then you will see clearly to take out the speck that is in your brother's eye. For there is no good tree which produces bad fruit, nor, on the other hand, a bad tree which produces good fruit. For each tree is known by its own fruit. For men do not gather figs from thorns, nor do they pick grapes from a briar bush. The good man out of the good treasure of his heart brings forth what is good; and the evil *man* out of the evil *treasure* brings forth what is evil; for his mouth speaks from that which fills his heart" (Luke 6:39–45; cf. Matthew 7:3–6. 16, 18, 20; 12:35; see Matthew 10:24; 15:14; Luke 6:12–19).

Setting: Galilee. After His visit in the home of Simon the Pharisee, Jesus goes into the villages and cities, proclaiming and preaching the kingdom of God.

When a large crowd was coming together, and those from various cities were journeying to Him, He spoke by way of a parable: "The sower went out to sow his seed; and as he sowed, some fell beside the road, and it was trampled under foot and the birds of the air ate it up. Other *seed* fell on rocky *soil,* and as soon as it grew up, it was withered away, because it had no moisture. Other *seed* fell among the thorns; and the thorns grew up with it and choked it out. Other *seed* fell into the good soil, and grew up, and produced a crop a hundred times as great." As He said these things, He would call out, "He who has ears to hear, let him hear" (Luke 8:4–8; cf. Matthew 13:2–9; Mark 4:3–9).

Setting: Galilee. After Jesus presents the Parable of the Sower to the crowds, His disciples ask Him to give them the parable's meaning.

And He said, "To you it has been granted to know the mysteries of the kingdom of God, but to the rest *it is* in parables, so that SEEING THEY MAY NOT SEE, AND HEARING THEY MAY NOT UNDERSTAND. Now the parable is this: the seed is the word of God. Those beside the road are those who have heard; then the devil comes and takes away the word from their heart, so that they will not believe and be saved. Those on the rocky *soil* are those who, when they hear, receive the word with joy; and these have no *firm* root; they believe for a while, and in time of temptation fall away. The *seed* which fell among the thorns, these are the ones who have heard, and as they go on their way they are choked with worries and riches and pleasures of *this* life, and bring no fruit to maturity. But the *seed* in the good soil, these are the ones who have heard the word in an honest and good heart, and hold it fast, and bear fruit with perseverance" (Luke 8:10–15, Jesus quotes from Isaiah 6:9; cf. Matthew 13:10–23; Mark 4:10–20).

THOUGHTS (Also see MEMORY; MIND; MIND READING; and REASONING)

Setting: Galilee. Jesus gives the crowd the meaning of His instruction about what defiles a man.

Peter said to Him, "Explain the parable to us." Jesus said, "Are you still lacking in understanding also? Do you not understand that everything that goes into the mouth passes into the stomach and is eliminated? But the things that proceed out of the mouth come from the heart, and those defile the man. For out of the heart come evil thoughts, murders, adulteries, fornications, thefts, false witness, slanders. These are the things which defile a man; but to eat with unwashed hands does not defile the man" (Matthew 15:15–20; cf. Mark 7:18–23; see Galatians 5:19–21).

Setting: Galilee. After the Pharisees and scribes from Jerusalem object to His disciples' lack of obedience to the tradition regarding ceremonial cleansing, Jesus speaks to a crowd, and explains His teaching to the disciples.

After He called the crowd to Him again, He *began* saying to them, "Listen to Me, all of you, and understand: there is nothing outside the man which can defile him if it goes into him; but the things which proceed out of the man are what defile the man. [If anyone has ears to hear, let him hear."] When he had left the crowd *and* entered the house, His disciples questioned Him about the parable. And He said to them, "Are you so lacking in understanding also? Do you not understand that whatever goes into the man from outside cannot defile him, because it does not go into his heart, but into his stomach, and is eliminated?" (*Thus He* declared all foods clean.) And He was saying, "That which proceeds out of the man, that is what defiles the man. For from within, out of the heart of men, proceed the evil thoughts, fornications, thefts, murders, adulteries, deeds of coveting *and* wickedness, *as well* as deceit, sensuality, envy, slander, pride *and* foolishness. All these evil things proceed from within and defile the man" (Mark 7:14–23; cf. Matthew 15:10–20).

THOUGHTS, EVIL (See THOUGHTS)

THOUSAND (See specific amount such as THOUSAND, FIVE)

THOUSAND, FIVE

Setting: By the Sea of Galilee. Jesus repeats a warning to His disciples about the teaching of the religious leaders of His time—the Pharisees and the Sadducees.

But Jesus aware of this, said, "You men of little faith, why do you discuss among yourselves that you have no bread? Do you not yet understand or remember the five loaves of the five thousand and how many baskets full you picked up? Or the seven loaves of the four thousand, and how many large baskets full you picked up? How is it that you do not understand that I did not speak to you concerning bread? But beware of the leaven of the Pharisees and Sadducees" (Matthew 16:8–11; cf. Matthew 14:17–21; Matthew 15:34–38; Mark 8:17–21).

Setting: The district of Dalmanutha. After the Pharisees argue with Jesus, seeking a sign from heaven to test Him, He and His disciples cross to the other side of the Sea of Galilee, where the disciples discuss with one another that they have no bread.

And Jesus, aware of this, said to them, "Why do you discuss *the fact* that you have no bread? Do you not yet see or understand? Do you have a hardened heart? HAVING EYES, DO YOU NOT SEE? AND HAVING EARS, DO YOU NOT HEAR? And do you not remember, when I broke the five loaves for the five thousand, how many baskets full of broken pieces you picked you? They said to Him, "Twelve." When *I broke* the seven for the four thousand, how many large baskets full of broken pieces did you pick up?" They said to Him, "Seven." And He was saying to them, "Do you not yet understand?" (Mark 8:17–21, Jesus quotes from Jeremiah 5:21; cf. Matthew 16:5–12; see Matthew 14:19, 20; Mark 6:41–44, 52).

THOUSAND, FOUR

Setting: By the Sea of Galilee. Jesus repeats a warning to His disciples about the teaching of the religious leaders of His time—the Pharisees and the Sadducees.

But Jesus aware of this, said, "You men of little faith, why do you discuss among yourselves that you have no bread? Do you not yet understand or remember the five loaves of the five thousand and how many baskets full you picked up? Or the seven loaves of the four thousand, and how many large baskets full you picked up? How is it that you do not understand that I did not speak to you concerning bread? But beware of the leaven of the Pharisees and Sadducees" (Matthew 16:8–11; cf. Matthew 14:17–21; 15:34–38; Mark 8:17–21).

Setting: The district of Dalmanutha. After the Pharisees argue with Jesus, seeking a sign from heaven to test Him, He and His disciples cross to the other side of the Sea of Galilee, where the disciples discuss with one another that they have no bread.

And Jesus, aware of this, said to them, "Why do you discuss *the fact* that you have no bread? Do you not yet see or understand? Do you have a hardened heart? HAVING EYES, DO YOU NOT SEE? AND HAVING EARS, DO YOU NOT HEAR? And do you not remember, when I broke the five loaves for the five thousand, how many baskets full of broken pieces you picked you? They said to Him, "Twelve." When *I broke* the seven for the four thousand, how many large baskets full of broken pieces did you pick up?" They said to Him, "Seven." And He was saying to them, "Do you not yet understand?" (Mark 8:17–21, Jesus quotes from Jeremiah 5:21; cf. Matthew 16:5–12; see Matthew 14:19, 20; Mark 6:41–44, 52).

THOUSAND, TEN

Setting: Capernaum of Galilee. Jesus illustrates the matter of forgiveness after Peter asks Him if forgiving someone seven times who has sinned against him is adequate.

"For this reason the kingdom of heaven may be compared to a king who wished to settle accounts with his slaves. When he had begun to settle *them,* one who owed him ten thousand talents was brought to him. But since he did not have *the means* to repay, his lord commanded him to be sold, along with his wife and children and all that he had, and repayment to be made. So the slave fell *to the ground* and prostrated himself before him, saying, 'Have patience with me and I will repay you everything.' And the lord of that slave felt compassion and released him and forgave him the debt. But that slave went out and found one of his fellow slaves who owed him a hundred denarii; and he seized him and *began* to choke *him,* saying, 'Pay back what you owe.' So his fellow slave fell *to the ground* and *began* to plead with him, saying, 'Have patience with me and I will repay you.' But he was unwilling and went and threw him in prison until he should pay back what was owed. So when his fellow slaves saw what had happened, they were deeply grieved and came and reported to their lord all that had happened. Then summoning him, his lord said to him, 'You wicked slave, I forgave you all that debt because you pleaded with me. Should you not also have had mercy on your fellow slave, in the same way that I had mercy on you?' And his lord, moved with anger, handed him over to the torturers until he should repay all that was owed him. My heavenly Father will also do the same to you, if each of you does not forgive his brother from your heart" (Matthew 18:23–35; cf. Matthew 6:12, 14, 15; Luke 7:42; see Matthew 25:19–28).

Setting: On the way from Galilee to Jerusalem. After He responds to a guest's proclamation about the blessings of eating bread in the kingdom of God, Jesus presents to large crowds the demands of discipleship.

Now large crowds were going along with Him; and He turned and said to them, "If anyone comes to Me, and does not hate his own father and mother and wife and children and brothers and sisters, yes, and even his own life, he cannot be My disciple. Whoever does not carry his own cross and come after Me cannot be My disciple. For which one of you, when he wants to build a tower, does not first sit down and calculate the cost to see if he has enough to complete it? Otherwise, when he has laid a foundation and is not able to finish, all who observe it begin to ridicule him, saying, 'This man began to build and was not able to finish.' Or what king, when he sets out to meet another king in battle, will not first sit down and consider whether he is strong enough with ten thousand *men* to encounter the one coming against him with twenty thousand? Or else, while the other is still far away, he sends a delegation and asks for terms of peace. So then, none of you can be My disciple who does not give up all his possessions. Therefore, salt is good; but if even salt has become tasteless, with what will it be seasoned? It is useless either for the soil or for the manure pile; it is thrown out. He who has ears to hear, let him hear" (Luke 14:25–35; cf. Matthew 5:13; 10:37–39; see Proverb 20:18; Philippians 3:7).

THOUSAND, TWENTY

Setting: On the way from Galilee to Jerusalem. After He responds to a guest's proclamation about the blessings of eating bread in the kingdom of God, Jesus presents to large crowds the demands of discipleship.

Now large crowds were going along with Him; and He turned and said to them, "If anyone comes to Me, and does not hate his own father and mother and wife and children and brothers and sisters, yes, and even his own life, he cannot be My disciple. Whoever does not carry his own cross and come after Me cannot be My disciple. For which one of you, when he wants to build a tower, does not first sit down and calculate the cost to see if he has enough to complete it? Otherwise, when he has laid a foundation and is not able to finish, all who observe it begin to ridicule him, saying, 'This man began to build and was not able to finish.' Or what king, when he sets out to meet another king in battle, will not first sit down and consider whether he is strong enough with ten thousand *men* to encounter the one coming against him with twenty thousand? Or else, while the other is still far away, he sends a delegation and asks for terms of peace. So then, none of you can be My disciple who does not give up all his possessions. Therefore, salt is good; but if even salt has become tasteless, with what will it be seasoned? It is useless either for the soil or for the manure pile; it is thrown out. He who has ears to hear, let him hear" (Luke 14:25–35; cf. Matthew 5:13; 10:37–39; see Proverb 20:18; Philippians 3:7).

THREE (DAYS, THREE; and NIGHTS, THREE are separate entries)

Setting: By the Sea of Galilee. Because the religious leaders are rejecting His message, Jesus continues teaching the crowds with the Parable of the Leaven.

He spoke another parable to them, "The kingdom of heaven is like leaven, which a woman took and hid in three pecks of flour until it was all leavened" (Matthew 13:33).

Setting: Capernaum of Galilee. After conveying to His disciples the value of little ones, Jesus gives instruction about church discipline.

"If your brother sins, go and show him his fault in private; if he listens to you, you have won your brother. But if he does not listen *to you,* take one or two more with you, so that BY THE MOUTH OF TWO OR THREE WITNESSES EVERY FACT MAY BE CONFIRMED. If he refuses to listen to them, tell it to the church; and if he refuses to listen even to the church, let him be to you as a Gentile and a tax collector. Truly I say to you, whatever you bind of earth shall have been bound in heaven; and whatever you loose on earth shall have been loosed in heaven. Again, I say to you, that if two of you agree on earth about anything that they may ask, it shall be done for them by My Father who is in heaven. For there two or three have gathered together in My name, I am there in their midst" (Matthew 18:15–20. Jesus quotes from Deuteronomy 19:15; cf. Matthew 7:7; Matthew 16:19; see Leviticus 19:17; Matthew 28:20; 2 Thessalonians 3:6, 14).

Setting: On the way to the Mount of Olives. After celebrating the Passover meal with His disciples in Jerusalem, prior to His betrayal by Judas, Jesus states that the disciples will all deny Him that very day.

Then Jesus said to them, "You will all fall away because of Me this night, for it is written, 'I WILL STRIKE DOWN THE SHEPHERD, AND THE SHEEP OF THE FLOCK SHALL BE SCATTERED.' But after I have been raised, I will go ahead of you to Galilee." But Peter said to Him, '*Even* though all may fall away because of You, I will never fall away.' Jesus said to him, "Truly I say to you that this *very* night, before a rooster crows, you will deny Me three times" (Matthew 26:31–34, Jesus quotes from Zechariah 13:7; cf. Mark 14:26–31; see Matthew 28:7, 10, 16; John 13:37).

Setting: Jerusalem. As Jesus appears before Caiaphas the high priest and the Council for interrogation aimed at entrapping Him, Peter, sitting in the courtyard, denies knowing Him, fulfilling the Lord's earlier prophecy.

And Peter remembered the word which Jesus had said, "Before a rooster crows, you will deny Me three times." And he went out and wept bitterly (Matthew 26:75; cf. Matthew 26:34; Mark 14:72; Luke 22:61; John 18:25–27).

Setting: A borrowed upper room in Jerusalem. After Jesus and His twelve disciples celebrate the Passover and the Lord's Supper, they go out to the Mount of Olives.

And Jesus said to them, "You will all fall away, because it is written, 'I WILL STRIKE DOWN THE SHEPHERD, AND THE SHEEP SHALL BE SCATTERED.' But after I have been raised, I will go ahead of you to Galilee." But Peter said to Him, "*Even* though all may fall away, yet I will not." And Jesus said to him, "Truly I say to you, that this very night, before a rooster crows twice, you yourself will deny Me three times" (Mark 14:27–30, Jesus quotes from Zechariah 13:7; cf. Matthew 26:30–34; see Mark 14:72).

Setting: Jerusalem. While Jesus is being falsely accused before the chief priests and the whole Council, Peter, in the courtyard of Caiaphas the high priest, denies he knows Jesus, then remembers His Lord's prophecy that Peter would deny Him three times before a rooster crowed twice.

Immediately a rooster crowed a second time. And Peter remembered how Jesus had made the remark to him, "Before a rooster crows twice, you will deny Me three times." And he began to weep (Mark 14:72; cf. Matthew 26:75; Luke 22:61; John 18:26, 27; see Mark 14:30).

Setting: The synagogue in Jesus' hometown of Nazareth in Galilee. At the beginning of His public ministry, Jesus comments to the congregation after reading from the book of the prophet Isaiah on the Sabbath.

And He said to them, "No doubt you will quote this proverb to Me, 'Physician, heal yourself! Whatever we heard was done at Capernaum, do here in your hometown as well.'" And He said, "Truly I say to you, no prophet is welcome in his hometown. But I say to you in truth, there were many widows in Israel in the days of Elijah, when the sky was shut up for three years and six months, when a great famine came over all the land; and yet Elijah was sent to none of them, but only to Zarephath, *in the land* of Sidon, to a woman who was a widow. And there were many lepers in Israel in the time of Elisha the prophet; and none of them was cleansed, but only Naaman the Syrian" (Luke 4:23–27; Jesus refers to 1 Kings 17:1, 9; 2 Kings 5:1–14; see Matthew 13:53–58).

Setting: On the way from Galilee to Jerusalem. While being tested by a lawyer, Jesus tells him the story of the good Samaritan.

Jesus replied and said, "A man was going down from Jerusalem to Jericho, and fell among robbers, and they stripped him and beat him, and went away leaving him half dead. And by chance a priest was going down on that road, and when he saw him, he passed by on the other side. Likewise a Levite also, when he came to the place and saw him, passed by on the other side. But a Samaritan, who was on a journey, came upon him; and when he saw him, he felt compassion, and came to him and bandaged up his wounds, pouring oil and wine on *them;* and he put him on his own beast, and brought him to an inn and took care of him. On the next day he took out two denarii and gave them to the innkeeper and said, 'Take care of him; and whatever more you spend, when I return I will repay you.' Which of these three do you think proved to be a neighbor to the man who fell into the robbers' *hands?*" And he said, "The one who showed mercy toward him." Then Jesus said to him, "Go and do the same" (Luke 10:30–37).

Setting: On the way from Galilee to Jerusalem. After revealing to His disciples how to pray, Jesus illustrates persistence in prayer.

Then He said to them, "Suppose one of you has a friend, and goes to him at midnight and says to him, 'Friend, lend me three loaves; for a friend of mine has come to me from a journey, and I have nothing to set before him'; and from inside he answers and says, 'Do not bother me; the door has already been shut and my children and I are in bed; I cannot get up and give you *anything.*' I tell you, even though he will not get up and give him *anything* because he is his friend, yet because of his persistence he will get up and give him as much as he needs. So I say to you, ask, and it will be given to you; seek, and you will find; knock, and it will be opened to you. For everyone who asks, receives; and he who seeks, finds; and to him who knocks, it will be opened" (Luke 11:5–10; cf. Matthew 7:7, 8; see Luke 18:1–5).

Setting: On the way from Galilee to Jerusalem. After clarifying a parable for Peter and the crowd, Jesus conveys how a relationship with Him divides families.

"I have come to cast fire upon the earth; and how I wish it were already kindled! But I have a baptism to undergo, and how distressed I am until it is accomplished! Do you suppose that I came to grant peace on earth? I tell you, no, but rather division; for from now on five *members* in one household will be divided, three against two and two against three. They will be divided, father against son and son against father, mother against daughter, and daughter against mother, mother-in-law against daughter-in-law and daughter-in-law against mother-in-law" (Luke 12:49–53; cf. Matthew 10:34–36; see Micah 7:6; Mark 10:38).

Setting: On the way from Galilee to Jerusalem. After some present report to Him about the Galileans whose blood Pilate (Roman governor of Judea) had mixed with their sacrifices, Jesus responds to their concern by calling them to repentance and illustrating His point with a parable.

And He *began* telling this parable: "A man had a fig tree which had been planted in his vineyard; and he came looking for fruit on it and did not find any. And he said to the vineyard-keeper, 'Behold, for three years I have come looking for fruit on this fig tree without finding any. Cut it down! Why does it even use up the ground?' And he answered and said to him, 'Let it alone, sir, for this year too, until I dig around it and put fertilizer; and if it bears fruit next year, *fine*; but if not, cut it down'" (Luke 13:6–9; see Matthew 3:10).

Setting: On the way from Galilee to Jerusalem. After responding to a synagogue official's anger over Jesus' healing of a woman, sick for eighteen years, in the synagogue on the Sabbath, the Lord conveys the Parable of the Mustard Seed and Parable of the Leaven.

So He was saying, "What is the kingdom of God like, and to what shall I compare it? It is like a mustard seed which a man took and threw into his own garden; and it grew and became a tree, and THE BIRDS OF THE AIR NESTED IN ITS BRANCHES." And again He said, "To what shall I compare the kingdom of God? It is like leaven, which a woman took and hid in three pecks of flour until it was all leavened" (Luke 13:18–21, Jesus quotes from Ezekiel 17:23; cf. Matthew 13:31–34; Mark 4:30–32).

Setting: An upper room in Jerusalem. During the Feast of Unleavened Bread (Passover) just before His crucifixion, Jesus celebrates the Passover meal with His disciples and institutes the Lord's Supper. The disciples later argue over who is the greatest among them, and the Lord prophesies Peter's denial of Him.

"Simon, Simon, behold, Satan has demanded *permission* to sift you like wheat; but I have prayed for you, that your faith may not fail; and you, when once you have turned again, strengthen your brothers." But he said to Him, "Lord, with You I am ready to go both to prison and to death!" And He said, "I say to you, Peter, the rooster will not crow today until you have denied three times that you know Me" (Luke 22:31–34; cf. Matthew 26:33–35; John 13:36–38; see Job 1:6–12; John 17:15).

Setting: The courtyard of the high priest in Jerusalem. After Jesus' arrest by His enemies, when the Lord turns and looks at Peter following his third denial of Jesus and the crowing of a rooster, the disciple recalls the Lord's prophecy about denying Him three times.

The Lord turned and looked at Peter. And Peter remembered the word of the Lord, how He had told him, "Before a rooster crows today, you will deny Me three times" (Luke 22:61; cf. Matthew 26:75; Luke 14:72; John 18:26, 27; see Luke 22:34).

Setting: Jerusalem. Before the Passover, after revealing to His disciples that they cannot follow Him back to heaven, Jesus takes issue with Peter's assertion that he would lay down his life for the Lord.

Simon Peter said to Him, "Lord, where are You going?" Jesus answered, "Where I go, you cannot follow Me now; but you will follow later." Peter said to Him, "Lord, why can I not follow You right now? I will lay down my life for You." Jesus answered, "Will you lay down your life for Me? Truly, truly, I say to you, a rooster will not crow until you deny Me three times" (John 13:36–38; see Matthew 26:34; Mark 14:30, 72; Luke 22:33, 34; John 13:1–35).

THREE DAYS (Listed under DAYS, THREE; also see DAY, THIRD)

THREE NIGHTS (Listed under NIGHTS, THREE)

THRONE (THRONE, GLORIOUS; THRONE, SATAN'S; and THRONE OF GOD are separate entries; also see THRONES]

Setting: On the island of Patmos (in the Aegean Sea about fifty miles southwest of Ephesus in modern Turkey). On the Lord's Day (Sunday), approximately fifty years after the Resurrection, the disciple John encounters the Lord Jesus Christ, who communicates a new revelation for the apostle to record for the church in Laodicea and to six other churches in Asia.

"To the angel of the church in Laodicea write: The Amen, the faithful and true Witness, the Beginning of the creation of God, says this: 'I know your deeds, that you are neither cold nor hot; I wish that you were cold or hot. So because you are lukewarm, and neither hot nor cold, I will spit you out of My mouth. Because you say, "I am rich, and have become wealthy, and have need of nothing," and you do not know that you are wretched and miserable and poor and blind and naked, I advise you to buy from Me gold refined by fire so that you may become rich, and white garments so that you may clothe yourself, and *that* the shame of your nakedness will not be revealed; and eye salve to anoint your eyes so that you may see. Those whom I love, I reprove and discipline; therefore be zealous and repent. Behold, I stand at the door and knock; if anyone hears My voice and opens the door, I will come in to him and will dine with him, and he with Me. He who overcomes, I will grant to him to sit down with Me on My throne, as I also overcame and sat down with My Father on His throne. He who has an ear, let him hear what the Spirit says to the churches'" (Revelation 3:14–22; see Proverb 3:12; Hosea 12:8; John 14:23; 16:33).

THRONE, GLORIOUS

Setting: Judea beyond the Jordan (Perea). Jesus promises rewards to His disciples for their personal sacrifice and commitment to following Him.

And Jesus said to them, "Truly I say to you, that you who have followed Me, in the regeneration when the Son of Man will sit on His glorious throne, you also shall sit upon twelve thrones, judging the twelve tribes of Israel. And everyone who has left houses or brothers or sisters or father or mother or children or farms for My name's sake, will receive many times as much, and will inherit eternal life. But many *who* are first will be last; and *the* last, first" (Matthew 19:28–30; cf. Matthew 6:33; 20:15; Mark 10:29, 30; Luke 18:29, 30; 22:30).

Setting: On the Mount of Olives, just east of Jerusalem. During His Olivet Discourse, after answering His disciples' questions as to when the temple will be destroyed and Jerusalem overrun, along with the signs of His coming and the end of the age, Jesus reveals the future judgments following His return.

"But when the Son of Man comes in His glory, and all the angels with Him, then He will sit on His glorious throne. All the nations will be gathered before Him; and He will separate them from one another, as the shepherd separates the sheep from the goats; and He will put the sheep on His right, and the goats on the left. Then the King will say to those on His right, 'Come, you who are blessed of My Father, inherit the kingdom prepared for you from the foundation of the world. 'For I was hungry, and you gave Me *something* to eat; I was thirsty, and you gave Me *something* to drink; I was a stranger, and you invited Me in; naked, and you clothed Me; I was sick, and you visited Me; I was in prison, and you came to Me.' Then the righteous will answer Him, 'Lord, when did we see You hungry and feed You, or thirsty, and give you *something* to drink? And when did we see You a stranger, and invite You in, or naked, and clothe You? When did we see You sick, or in prison, and come to You?' The King will answer and say to them, 'Truly I say to you, to the extent that you did it to one of these brothers of Mine, *even* the least *of them,* you did it to Me.' Then He will also say to those on His left, 'Depart from Me, accursed ones, into the eternal fire which has been prepared for the devil and his angels; for I was hungry, and you gave Me *nothing* to eat; I was thirsty, and you gave Me nothing to drink; I was a stranger, and you did not invite Me in; naked, and you did not clothe Me; sick, and in prison, and you did not visit Me.' Then they themselves also will answer, 'Lord, when did we see You hungry, or thirsty, or a stranger, or naked, or sick, or in prison, and did not take care of You?' Then He will answer them, 'Truly I say to you, to the extent that you did not do it to one of the least of these, you did not do it to Me.' These will go away into eternal punishment, but the righteous into eternal life" (Matthew 25:31–46; see Matthew 7:23; 16:27; 19:29).

THRONE, GOD'S (See THRONE OF GOD)

THRONE, SATAN'S (Also see SATAN, SYNAGOGUE OF)

Setting: On the island of Patmos (in the Aegean Sea about fifty miles southwest of Ephesus in modern Turkey). On the Lord's Day (Sunday), approximately fifty years after the Resurrection, the disciple John encounters the Lord Jesus Christ, who communicates a new revelation for the apostle to record for the church in Pergamum and to six other churches in Asia.

"And to the angel of the church in Pergamum write: The One who has the sharp two-edged sword says this: 'I know where you dwell, where Satan's throne is; and you hold fast My name, and did not deny My faith even in the days of Antipas, My witness, My faithful one, who was killed among you, where Satan dwells. But I have a few things against you, because you have there some who hold the teaching of Balaam, who kept teaching Balak to put a stumbling block before the sons of Israel, to eat things sacrificed to idols and to commit *acts of* immorality. So you also have some who in the same way hold the teaching of the Nicolaitans. Therefore repent; or else I am coming to you quickly, and I will make war against them with the sword of My mouth. He who has an ear, let him hear what the Spirit says to the churches. To him who overcomes, to him I will give *some* of the hidden manna, and I will give him a white stone, and a new name written on the stone which no one knows but he who receives it' (Revelation 2:12–17; see Numbers 25:1–3; Isaiah 62:2; Revelation 1:16).

THRONE OF GOD (Also see POWER, RIGHT HAND OF; THRONE; and THRONES)

Setting: Galilee. During the early part of His ministry, Jesus preaches the Sermon on the Mount to His disciples and the multitudes.

"Again, you have heard that the ancients were told, 'YOU SHALL NOT MAKE FALSE VOWS, BUT SHALL FULFILL YOUR VOWS TO THE LORD.' But I say to you, make no oath at all, either by heaven, for it is the throne of God, or by the earth, for it is the footstool of His feet, or by Jerusalem, for it is THE CITY OF THE GREAT KING. Nor shall you make an oath by your head, for you cannot make one hair white or black. But let your statement be 'Yes, yes' *or* 'No, no'; anything beyond these is of evil" (Matthew 5:33–37, Jesus quotes from Leviticus 19:12, Psalm 48:2; Isaiah 66:1; cf. James 5:12).

Setting: The temple in Jerusalem. After the Jewish religious leaders test Him with questions, Jesus pronounces the fourth of eight woes on them in front of the crowds and His disciples.

"Woe to you, blind guides, who say, "Whoever swears by the temple, *that* is nothing; but whoever swears by the gold of the temple is obligated.' You fools and blind men! Which is more important, the gold or the temple that sanctified the gold? And, 'Whoever swears by the altar, *that* is nothing, but whoever swears by the offering on it, he is obligated.' You blind men, which is more important, the offering, or the altar that sanctifies the offering? Therefore, whoever swears by the altar, swears *both* by the altar and by everything on it. And whoever swears by the temple, swears *both* by the temple and by Him who dwells within it. And whoever swears by heaven, swears *both* by the throne of God and by Him who sits upon it" (Matthew 23:16–22; see Exodus 29:37; 1 Kings 8:13; Isaiah 66:1; Matthew 15:14).

THRONES (Also see THRONE)

Setting: Judea beyond the Jordan (Perea). Jesus promises rewards to His disciples for their personal sacrifice and commitment to following Him.

And Jesus said to them, "Truly I say to you, that you who have followed Me, in the regeneration when the Son of Man will sit on His glorious throne, you also shall sit upon twelve thrones, judging the twelve tribes of Israel. And everyone who has left houses or brothers or sisters or father or mother or children or farms for My name's sake, will receive many times as much, and will inherit eternal life. But many *who* are first will be last; and *the* last, first" (Matthew 19:28–30; cf. Matthew 6:33; 20:15; Mark 10:29, 30; Luke 18:29, 30; Luke 22:30).

Setting: Jerusalem. During the Feast of Unleavened Bread (Passover) just before His crucifixion, Jesus celebrates the Passover meal with His disciples and institutes the Lord's Supper. The disciples argue over who is the greatest among them, and the Lord details the kingdom benefits the disciples will experience.

"You are those who have stood by Me in My trials; for just as My Father has granted Me a kingdom, I grant you that you may eat and drink at My table in My kingdom, and you will sit on thrones judging the twelve tribes of Israel" (Luke 22:28–30; cf. Matthew 19:28).

THRONES, TWELVE (See THRONES)

THYATIRA

Setting: On the island of Patmos (in the Aegean Sea about fifty miles southwest of Ephesus in modern Turkey). On the Lord's Day (Sunday), approximately fifty years after the Resurrection, the disciple John hears the voice of the Lord Jesus Christ, who communicates new revelations for the apostle to record for the seven churches in Asia.

I was in the Spirit on the Lord's day, and I heard behind me a loud voice like *the sound* of a trumpet, saying, "Write in a book what you see, and send *it* to the seven churches: to Ephesus and to Smyrna and to Pergamum and to Thyatira and to Sardis and to Philadelphia and to Laodicea" (Revelation 1:10, 11; see Revelation 4:1).

Setting: On the island of Patmos (in the Aegean Sea about fifty miles southwest of Ephesus in modern Turkey). On the Lord's Day (Sunday), approximately fifty years after the Resurrection, the disciple John encounters the Lord Jesus Christ, who communicates a new revelation for the apostle to record for the church in Thyatira and to six other churches in Asia.

"And to the angel of the church in Thyatira write: The Son of God, who has eyes like a flame of fire, and His feet are like burnished bronze, says this: 'I know your deeds, and your love and faith and service and perseverance, and that your deeds of late are greater than at first. But I have *this* against you, that you tolerate the woman Jezebel, who calls herself a prophetess, and she teaches and leads My bond-servants astray so that they commit *acts of* immorality and eat things sacrificed to idols. I gave her time to repent, and she does not want to repent of her immorality. Behold, I will throw her on a bed *of sickness,* and those who commit adultery with her into great tribulation, unless they repent of her deeds. And I will kill her children with pestilence, and all the churches will know that I am He who searches the minds and hearts; and I will give to each one of you according to your deeds. But I say to you, the rest who are in Thyatira, who do not hold this teaching, who have not known the deep things of Satan, as they call them—I place no other burden on you. Nevertheless what you have, hold fast until I come. He who overcomes, and he who keeps My deeds until the end, TO HIM I WILL GIVE AUTHORITY OVER THE NATIONS; AND HE SHALL RULE THEM WITH A ROD OF IRON, AS THE VESSELS OF THE POTTER ARE BROKEN TO PIECES, as I also have received *authority* from My Father; and I will give him the morning star. He who has an ear, let him hear what the Spirit says to the churches' (Revelation 2:18–29; Jesus quotes from Psalm 2:8, 9; Isaiah 30:14; see 1 Kings 16:31; Psalm 7:9; Romans 2:5; 1 Corinthians 2:10; 2 Peter 3:9; Revelation 1:14; 2:7; 3:11; 17:1–20).

TIBERIAS, LAKE OF (See GALILEE, SEA OF)

TIME (Specifics such as HARVEST TIME; and TIME, PROPER are separate entries; also see HOUR; and TIMES)

Setting: The Mount of Olives, just east of Jerusalem. During His Olivet Discourse, Jesus answers His disciples' questions as to when the temple will be destroyed and Jerusalem overrun, along with the signs of His coming and the end of the age.

And Jesus answered and said to them, "See to it that no one misleads you. For many will come in My name, saying, 'I am the Christ,' and will mislead many. You will be hearing of wars and rumors of wars. See that you are not frightened, for *those things* must take place, but *that* is not yet the end. For nation will rise against nation, and kingdom against kingdom, and in various places there will be famines and earthquakes. But all these things are *merely* the beginning of birth pangs. Then they will deliver you to tribulation, and will kill you, and you will be hated by all nations because of My name. At that time many will fall away and will betray one another and hate one another. Many false prophets will arise and will mislead many. Because lawlessness is increased, most people's love will grow cold. But the one who endures to the end, he will be saved. This gospel of the kingdom shall be preached in the whole world as a testimony to all the nations, and then the end will come" (Matthew 24:4–14; cf. Jeremiah 29:8; Matthew 7:15; 10:17, 22; Mark 13:3–13; Luke 21:7–19; Revelation 6:4).

Setting: On the Mount of Olives, just east of Jerusalem. During His Olivet Discourse, after answering His disciples' questions as to when the temple will be destroyed and Jerusalem overrun, along with the signs of His coming and the end of the age, Jesus reveals the future judgments following His return.

"Therefore be on the alert, for you do not know which day your Lord is coming. But be sure of this, that if the head of the house had known at what time of the night the thief was coming, he would have been on the alert and would not have allowed his house to be broken into. For this reason you also must be ready; for the Son of Man is coming at an hour when you do not think *He will.* Who then is the faithful and sensible slave whom his master put in charge of his household to give their food at the proper time? Blessed is that slave whom his master finds so doing when he comes. Truly I say to you that he will put him in charge of all his possessions. But if that evil slave says in his heart, 'My master is not coming for a long time,' and begins to beat his fellow slaves and eat and drink with drunkards; the master of that slave will come on a day when he does not expect *him* and at an hour which he does not know, and will cut him in pieces and assign him a place with the hypocrites; in that place there will be weeping and gnashing of teeth" (Matthew 24:42–51; cf. Mark 13:33–37; Luke 12:39–46; 21:34–36; see Matthew 8:11, 12; 25:21–23).

Setting: Galilee. After being baptized by John the Baptist in the Jordan River, Jesus commences His gospel-preaching ministry shortly after John is taken into custody by Herod Antipas.

Now after John had been taken into custody, Jesus came into Galilee, preaching the gospel of God, and saying, "The time is fulfilled, and the kingdom of God is at hand; repent and believe in the gospel" (Mark 1:14, 15, cf. Matthew 4:17; Galatians 4:4).

Setting: Galilee. Early in His ministry, the Pharisees question why Jesus allows His disciples to harvest grain on the Sabbath.

And He said to them, "Have you never read what David did when he was in need and he and his companions became hungry; how he entered the house of God in the time of Abiathar *the* high priest, and ate the consecrated bread, which is not lawful for *anyone* to eat except the priests, and he also gave it to those who were with him?" Jesus said to them, "The Sabbath was made for man, and not man for the Sabbath. So the Son of Man is Lord even of the Sabbath" (Mark 2:25–28; cf. Matthew 12:1–8; Luke 6:1–5; see Exodus 23:12).

Setting: On the Mount of Olives, east of the temple in Jerusalem. After prophesying the temple's destruction, Jesus responds during His Olivet Discourse to questions from Peter, James, John, and Andrew about other future events.

"But when you see the ABOMINATION OF DESOLATION standing where it should not be (let the reader understand), then those who are in Judea must flee to the mountains. The one who is on the housetop must not go down, or go in to get anything out of his house; and the one who is in the field must not turn back to get his coat. But woe to those who are pregnant and to those who are nursing babies in those days! But pray that it may not happen in winter. For those days will be a *time of* tribulation such as has not occurred since the beginning of the creation which God created until now, and never will. Unless the Lord had shortened *those* days, no life would have been saved; but for the sake of the elect, whom He chose, He shortened the days. And then if anyone says to you, 'Behold, here is the Christ'; or, 'Behold, *He is* there'; do not believe *him*; for false Christs and false prophets will arise, and will show signs and wonders, in order to lead astray, if possible, the elect. But take heed; behold, I have told you everything in advance" (Mark 13:14–23; cf. Matthew 24:15–28; Luke 21:20–24; see Daniel 9:27; 12:1; Luke 17:31).

Setting: The synagogue in Jesus' hometown of Nazareth in Galilee. At the beginning of His public ministry, Jesus comments to the congregation after reading from the book of the prophet Isaiah on the Sabbath.

And He said to them, "No doubt you will quote this proverb to Me, 'Physician, heal yourself! Whatever we heard was done at Capernaum, do here in your hometown as well.'" And He said, "Truly I say to you, no prophet is welcome in his hometown. But I say to you in truth, there were many widows in Israel in the days of Elijah, when the sky was shut up for three years and six months, when a great famine came over all the land; and yet Elijah was sent to none of them, but only to Zarephath, *in the land* of Sidon, to a woman who was a widow. And there were many lepers in Israel in the time of Elisha the prophet; and none of them was cleansed, but only Naaman the Syrian" (Luke 4:23–27; Jesus refers to 1 Kings 17:1, 9; 2 Kings 5:1–14; see Matthew 13:53–58).

Setting: Galilee. After Jesus praises John the Baptist to the crowds, Simon, a Pharisee, invites the Lord to dinner. A sinful woman anoints His feet with perfume, prompting Him to instruct His host about forgiveness.

Turning toward the woman, He said to Simon, "Do you see this woman? I entered your house; you gave Me no water for My feet, but she has wet My feet with her tears and wiped them with her hair. You gave Me no kiss; but she, since the time I came in, has not ceased to kiss My feet. You did not anoint My head with oil, but she anointed My feet with perfume. For this reason I say to you, her sins, which are many, have been forgiven, for she loved much; but he who is forgiven little, loves little." The He said to her, "Your sins have been forgiven." Those who were reclining *at the table* with Him began to say to themselves, "Who is this *man* who even forgives sins?" And He said to the woman, "Your faith has saved you; go in peace" (Luke 7:44–50; see Matthew 9:2; Mark 5:34; Luke 5:21).

Setting: Galilee. After Jesus presents the Parable of the Sower to the crowds, His disciples ask Him to give them the parable's meaning.

And He said, "To you it has been granted to know the mysteries of the kingdom of God, but to the rest *it is* in parables, so that SEEING THEY MAY NOT SEE, AND HEARING THEY MAY NOT UNDERSTAND. Now the parable is this: the seed is the word of God. Those beside the road are those who have heard; then the devil comes and takes away the word from their heart, so that they will not believe and be saved. Those on the rocky *soil* are those who, when they hear, receive the word with joy; and these have no *firm* root; they believe for a while, and in time of temptation fall away. The *seed* which fell among the thorns, these are the ones who have heard, and as they go on their way they are choked with worries and riches and pleasures of *this* life, and bring no fruit to maturity. But the *seed* in the good soil, these are the ones who have heard the word in an honest and good heart, and hold it fast, and bear fruit with perseverance" (Luke 8:10–15, Jesus quotes from Isaiah 6:9; cf. Matthew 13:10–23; Mark 4:10–20).

Setting: On the way from Galilee to Jerusalem. While teaching in the cities and villages, Jesus responds to a question about who is saved. Some Pharisees ask Him to leave, claiming Herod Antipas (tetrarch of Galilee and Perea) seeks to kill Him.

And He said to them, "Go and tell that fox, 'Behold, I cast out demons and perform cures today and tomorrow, and the third *day* I reach My goal.' Nevertheless I must journey on today and tomorrow and the next *day*; for it cannot be that a prophet would perish outside of Jerusalem. O Jerusalem, Jerusalem, *the city* that kills the prophets and stones those sent to her! How often I wanted to gather your children together, just as a hen *gathers* her brood under her wings, and you would not *have it*! Behold, your house is left to you *desolate*; and I say to you, you will not see Me until *the time* comes when you say, 'BLESSED IS HE WHO COMES IN THE NAME OF THE LORD!'" (Luke 13:32–35, Jesus quotes from Psalm 118:26; cf. Matthew 23:37).

Setting: On the way from Galilee to Jerusalem. The Lord responds to the Pharisees' scoffing at His teaching His disciples about stewardship.

And He said to them, "You are those who justify yourselves in the sight of men, but God knows your hearts; for that which is highly esteemed among men is detestable in the sight of God. The Law and the Prophets *were proclaimed* until John; since that time the gospel of the kingdom of God has been preached, and everyone is forcing his way into it. But is it easier for heaven and earth to pass away than for one stroke of a letter of the Law to fail" (Luke 16:15–17; cf. Matthew 5:18; see 1 Samuel 16:7; Matthew 4:23; 11:11–14).

Setting: Approaching Jerusalem. After being praised by the people in a triumphal entry, the Lord weeps as He sees the city ahead of Him.

When He approached *Jerusalem*, He saw the city and wept over it, saying, "If you had known in this day, even you, the things which make for peace! But now they have been hidden from your eyes. For the days will come upon you when your enemies will throw up a barricade against you, and surround you and hem you in on every side, and they will level you to the ground and your children within you, and they will not leave in you one stone upon another, because you did not recognize the time of your visitation" (Luke 19:41–44; see Matthew 24:1, 2; Luke 13:34, 35).

Setting: The temple in Jerusalem. While ministering a few days before His crucifixion, after Jesus prophesies the destruction of the temple, His disciples ask Him when this will happen.

And He said, "See to it that you are not misled; for many will come in My name, saying, "I am *He*,' and, 'The time is near.' Do not go after them. When you hear of wars and disturbances, do not be terrified; for these things must take place first, but the end *does* not *follow* immediately" (Luke 21:8, 9; cf. Matthew 24:4–8; Mark 13:5–8).

Setting: Jerusalem. During a feast of the Jews, Jesus responds to criticism from the Jewish religious leaders by referring to God as His Father (thereby making Himself equal with God) and informing them that God, John the Baptist, and His works all testify to His mission.

"I can do nothing on My own initiative. As I hear, I judge; and My judgment is just, because I do not seek My own will, but the will of Him who sent Me. If I *alone* testify about Myself, My testimony is not true. There is another who testifies of Me, and I know that the testimony which He gives about Me is true. You have sent to John, and he has testified to the truth. But the testimony which I receive is not from man, but I say these things so that you may be saved. He was the lamp that was burning and was shining and you were willing to rejoice for a while in his light. But the testimony which I have is greater than the *testimony of* John; for the works which the Father has given Me to accomplish—the very works that I do—testify about Me, that the Father has sent Me. And the Father who sent Me, He has testified of Me. You have neither heard His voice at any time nor seen His form. You do not have His word abiding in you, for you do not believe Him whom He sent" (John 5:30–38; see Matthew 3:17; Mark 1:4, 5; John 1:7, 15, 32; 4:34; 8:14–16; 10:25, 37, 38).

Setting: On the island of Patmos (in the Aegean Sea about fifty miles southwest of Ephesus in modern Turkey). On the Lord's Day (Sunday), approximately fifty years after the Resurrection, the disciple John encounters the Lord Jesus Christ, who communicates a new revelation for the apostle to record for the church in Thyatira and to six other churches in Asia.

"And to the angel of the church in Thyatira write: The Son of God, who has eyes like a flame of fire, and His feet are like burnished bronze, says this: 'I know your deeds, and your love and faith and service and perseverance, and that your deeds of late are greater than at first. But I have *this* against you, that you tolerate the woman Jezebel, who calls herself a prophetess, and she teaches and leads My bond-servants astray so that they commit *acts of* immorality and eat things sacrificed to idols. I gave her time to repent, and she does not want to repent of her immorality. Behold, I will throw her on a bed *of sickness,* and those who commit adultery with her into great tribulation, unless they repent of her deeds. And I will kill her children with pestilence, and all the churches will know that I am He who searches the minds and hearts; and I will give to each one of you according to your deeds. But I say to you, the rest who are in Thyatira, who do not hold this teaching, who have not known the deep things of Satan, as they call them—I place no other burden on you. Nevertheless what you have, hold fast until I come. He who overcomes, and he who keeps My deeds until the end, TO HIM I WILL GIVE AUTHORITY OVER THE NATIONS; AND HE SHALL RULE THEM WITH A ROD OF IRON, AS THE VESSELS OF THE POTTER ARE BROKEN TO PIECES, as I also have received *authority* from My Father; and I will give him the morning star. He who has an ear, let him hear what the Spirit says to the churches' (Revelation 2:18–29; Jesus quotes from Psalm 2:8, 9; Isaiah 30:14; see 1 Kings 16:31; Psalm 7:9; Romans 2:5; 1 Corinthians 2:10; 2 Peter 3:9; Revelation 1:14; 2:7; 3:11; 17:1–20).

TIME, APPOINTED

Setting: On the Mount of Olives, east of the temple in Jerusalem. After prophesying the temple's destruction, Jesus responds during His Olivet Discourse to questions from Peter, James, John, and Andrew about other future events.

"Take heed, keep on the alert; for you do not know when the *appointed* time will come. *It is* like a man away on a journey, *who* upon leaving his house and putting his slaves in charge, *assigning* to each one his task, also commanded the doorkeeper to stay on the alert. Therefore, be on the alert—for you do not know when the master of the house is coming, whether in the evening, at midnight, or when the rooster crows, or in the morning—in case he should come suddenly and find you asleep. What I say to you I say to all, 'Be on the alert!' " (Mark 13:33–37; cf. Matthew 24:42, 43; Luke 21:34–36; see Luke 12:36–38; Ephesians 6:18).

TIME, HARVEST (See HARVEST TIME)

TIME, LONG

Setting: On the Mount of Olives, just east of Jerusalem. During His Olivet Discourse, after answering His disciples' questions as to when the temple will be destroyed and Jerusalem overrun, along with the signs of His coming and the end of the age, Jesus reemphasizes to His disciples that they should be on the alert for His return.

"Therefore be on the alert, for you do not know which day your Lord is coming. But be sure of this, that if the head of the house had known at what time of the night the thief was coming, he would have been on the alert and would not have allowed his house to be broken into. For this reason you also must be ready; for the Son of Man is coming at an hour when you do not think *He will.* Who then is the faithful and sensible slave whom his master put in charge of his household to give their food at the proper time? Blessed is that slave whom his master finds so doing when he comes. Truly I say to you that he will put him in charge of all his possessions. But if that evil slave says in his heart, 'My master is not coming for a long time,' and begins to beat his fellow slaves and eat and drink with drunkards; the master of that slave will come on a day when he does not expect *him* and at an hour which he does not know, and will cut him in pieces and assign him a place with the hypocrites; in that place there will be weeping and gnashing of teeth" (Matthew 24:42–51; cf. Mark 13:33–37; Luke 12:39–46; 21:34–36; see Matthew 8:11, 12; 25:21–23).

Setting: On the Mount of Olives, just east of Jerusalem. During His Olivet Discourse, after answering His disciples' questions as to when the temple will be destroyed and Jerusalem overrun, along with the signs of His coming and the end of the age, Jesus reemphasizes to His disciples that they should be on the alert for His return.

"For *it is* just like a man *about* to go on a journey, who called his own slaves and entrusted his possessions to them. To one he gave five talents, to another, two, and to another, one, each according to his own ability; and he went on his journey. Immediately the one who had received the five talents went and traded with them, and gained five more talents. In the same manner the one who *had received* the two *talents* gained two more. But he who received the one *talent* went away, and dug a *hole* in the ground and hid his master's money. Now after a long time the master of those slaves came and settled accounts with them. The one who had received the five talents came up and brought five more talents, saying, 'Master, you entrusted five talents to me. See, I have gained five more talents.' His master said to him, 'Well done, good and faithful slave. You were faithful with a few things, I will put you in charge of many things; enter into the joy of your master.' Also the one who *had received* the two talents came up and said, 'Master, you entrusted two talents to me. See, I have gained two more talents.' His master said to him, 'Well done, good and faithful slave. You were faithful with a few things, I will put you in charge of many things; enter into the joy of your master.' And the one also who had received the one talent came up and said, 'Master, I knew you to be a hard man, reaping where you did not sow and gathering where you scattered no *seed.* And I was afraid, and went away and hid your talent in the ground. See, you have what is yours.' But his master answered and said to him, 'You wicked, lazy slave, you knew that I reap where I did not sow and gather where I scattered no *seed.* Then you ought to have put my money in the bank, and on my arrival I would have received my *money* back with interest. 'Therefore take away the talent from him, and give it to the one who has ten talents.' For to everyone who has, *more* shall be given, and he will have an abundance; but from the one who does not have, even what he does have shall be taken away. Throw out the worthless slave into the outer darkness; in that place there will be weeping and gnashing of teeth" (Matthew 25:14–30; cf. Matthew 8:12; 13:12; 24:45–47; see Matthew 18:23, 24; Luke 12:44).

Setting: On the way from Galilee to Jerusalem. When Jesus uses a parable to challenge the crowd and His disciples to be ready for His return, Peter asks whom He is addressing.

And the Lord said, "Who then is the faithful and sensible steward, whom his master will put in charge of his servants, to give them their rations at the proper time? Blessed is that slave whom his master finds so doing when he comes. Truly I say to you that he will put him in charge of all his possessions. But if that slave says in his heart, 'My master will be a long time in coming,' and begins to beat the slaves, *both* men and women, and to eat and drink and get drunk; the master of that slave will come on a day when he does not expect *him* and at an hour he does not know, and will cut him in pieces, and assign him a place with the unbelievers. And that slave who knew his master's will and did not get ready or act in accord with his will, will receive many lashes, but the one who did know *it,* and committed deeds worthy of flogging, will receive but few. From everyone who has been given much, much will be required; and to whom they entrusted much, of him they will ask all the more" (Luke 12:42–48; cf. Matthew 24:45–51; see Leviticus 5:17).

Setting: The temple in Jerusalem. While ministering a few days before His crucifixion, after the chief priests and the scribes question His authority to teach and preach, Jesus conveys the Parable of the Vine-Growers to the people.

And He began to tell the people this parable: "A man planted a vineyard and rented it out to vine-growers, and went on a journey for a long time. At the *harvest* time he sent a slave to the vine-growers, so that they would give him *some* of the produce of the vineyard; but the vine-growers beat him and sent him away empty-handed. And he proceeded to send another slave; and they beat him also and treated him shamefully and sent him away empty-handed. And he proceeded to send a third; and this one also they wounded and cast out. The owner of the vineyard said, 'What shall I do? I will send my beloved son; perhaps they will respect him.' But when the vine-growers saw him, they reasoned with one another, saying, 'This is the heir; let us kill him so that the inheritance will be ours.' So they threw him out of the vineyard and killed him. What, then, will the owner of the vineyard do to them? He will come and destroy these vine-growers and will give the vineyard to others." When they heard it, they said, "May it never be!" But Jesus looked at them and said, "What then is this that is written: 'THE STONE WHICH THE BUILDERS REJECTED, THIS BECAME THE CHIEF CORNER *stone*'? Everyone who falls on that stone will be broken to pieces; but on whomever it falls, it will scatter him like dust" (Luke 20:9–18, Jesus quotes from Psalm 118:22; cf. Matthew 21:33–44; Mark 12:1–11; see Ephesians 2:20).

TIME, MY (Jesus')

Setting: Jerusalem. On the first day of the Feast of Unleavened Bread, just after Judas makes arrangements with the chief priests to betray Him, Jesus informs His disciples where they will celebrate the Passover.

And He said, "Go into the city to a certain man, and say to him, 'The Teacher says, "My time is near; I *am to* keep the Passover at your house with My disciples"'" (Matthew 26:18; cf. Mark 14:13–15; Luke 22:7–13).

Setting: Capernaum of Galilee. Jesus' blood brothers, who do not yet believe in Him, encourage Him to attend the upcoming Feast of Booths in Jerusalem in order to demonstrate His works to His disciples and the world.

So Jesus said to them, "My time is not yet here, but your time is always opportune. The world cannot hate you, but it hates Me because I testify of it, that its deeds are evil. Go up to the feast yourselves; I do not go up to this feast because My time has not yet fully come" (John 7:6–8; see John 3:19, 20; 15:18–20).

TIME, PRESENT

Setting: On the way from Galilee to Jerusalem. After telling how a relationship with Him will divide families, Jesus chastises the crowds for being able to discern the weather but not the present age.

And He was also saying to the crowds, "When you see a cloud rising in the west, immediately you say, 'A shower is coming,' and so it turns out. And when *you see* a south wind blowing, you say, 'It will be a hot day,' and it turns out *that way*. You hypocrites! You know how to analyze the appearance of the earth and the sky, but why do you not analyze this present time?" (Luke 12:54–56; cf. Matthew 16:2, 3).

TIME, PROPER

Setting: On the Mount of Olives, just east of Jerusalem. During His Olivet Discourse, after answering His disciples' questions as to when the temple will be destroyed and Jerusalem overrun, along with the signs of His coming and the end of the age, Jesus reveals the future judgments following His return.

"Therefore be on the alert, for you do not know which day your Lord is coming. But be sure of this, that if the head of the house had known at what time of the night the thief was coming, he would have been on the alert and would not have allowed his house to be broken into. For this reason you also must be ready; for the Son of Man is coming at an hour when you do not think He will. Who then is the faithful and sensible slave whom his master put in charge of his household to give their food at the proper time? Blessed is that slave whom his master finds so doing when he comes. Truly I say to you that he will put him in charge of all his possessions. But if that evil slave says in his heart, 'My master is not coming for a long time,' and begins to beat his fellow slaves and eat and drink with drunkards; the master of that slave will come on a day when he does not expect him and at an hour which he does not know, and will cut him in pieces and assign him a place with the hypocrites; in that place there will be weeping and gnashing of teeth" (Matthew 24:42–51; cf. Mark 13:33–37; Luke 12:39–46; 21:34–36; see Matthew 8:11, 12; Matthew 25:21–23).

Setting: On the way from Galilee to Jerusalem. When Jesus uses a parable to challenge the crowd and His disciples to be ready for His return, Peter asks whom He is addressing.

And the Lord said, "Who then is the faithful and sensible steward, whom his master will put in charge of his servants, to give them their rations at the proper time? Blessed is that slave whom his master finds so doing when he comes. Truly I say to you that he will put him in charge of all his possessions. But if that slave says in his heart, 'My master will be a long time in coming,' and begins to beat the slaves, *both* men and women, and to eat and drink and get drunk; the master of that slave will come on a day when he does not expect *him* and at an hour he does not know, and will cut him in pieces, and assign him a place with the unbelievers. And that slave who knew his master's will and did not get ready or act in accord with his will, will receive many lashes, but the one who did not know *it,* and committed deeds worthy of flogging, will receive but few. From everyone who has been given much, much will be required; and to whom they entrusted much, of him they will ask all the more" (Luke 12:42–48; cf. Matthew 24:45–51; see Leviticus 5:17).

TIME, THIS (Also see AGE, PRESENT)

Setting: Bethany beyond the Jordan. Before being tempted by the devil and commencing His public ministry, Jesus arrives from Galilee to be baptized by John the Baptist, who questions his own worthiness to baptize the Lord.

But Jesus answering said to him, "Permit *it* at this time; for in this way it is fitting for us to fulfill all righteousness." Then he permitted Him (Matthew 3:15).

Setting: Perea, en route from Galilee to Jerusalem. After responding to His disciples' question about salvation, Jesus replies to Peter's statement about the disciples' personal sacrifice.

Peter said, "Behold, we have left our own *homes* and followed You." And He said to them, "Truly I say to you, there is no one who has left house or wife or brothers or parents or children, for the sake of the kingdom of God, who will not receive many times as much at this time and in the age to come, eternal life" (Luke 18:28–30; cf. Matthew 19:27–29; Mark 10:28–30; see Matthew 6:33; Luke 5:11).

TIME, UNDERSTANDING THE (See TIMES, SIGNS OF THE)

TIME, YOUR

Setting: Capernaum of Galilee. Jesus' blood brothers, who do not yet believe in Him, encourage Him to attend the upcoming Feast of Booths in Jerusalem in order to demonstrate His works to His disciples and the world.

So Jesus said to them, "My time is not yet here, but your time is always opportune. The world cannot hate you, but it hates Me because I testify of it, that its deeds are evil. Go up to the feast yourselves; I do not go up to this feast because My time has not yet fully come" (John 7:6–8; see John 3:19, 20; 15:18–20).

TIME OF THE NIGHT (Listed under NIGHT, TIME OF THE)

TIMES (Specifics such as GENTILES, TIMES OF THE; TIMES, SIGN OF THE; and TIMES, THREE are separate entries; also see EPOCHS; and TIME)

Setting: Jerusalem. Luke, writing in Acts, presents quotes from Jesus' post-resurrection appearances, in which He responds to His disciples' question of whether He is about to restore the kingdom to Israel.

He said to them, "It is not for you to know times or epochs which the Father has fixed by His own authority; but you will receive power when the Holy Spirit has come upon you; and you shall be My witnesses both in Jerusalem, and in all Judea and Samaria, and even to the remotest part of the earth" (Acts 1:7, 8; see Luke 24:48, 49; Acts 2:1–4).

TIMES, ALL

Setting: The Mount of Olives, east of the temple in Jerusalem. After ministering in the temple a few days before His crucifixion, and conveying the Parable of the Fig Tree during His Olivet Discourse, Jesus warns His disciples to keep alert regarding future events.

"Be on guard, so that your hearts will not be weighted down with dissipation and drunkenness and the worries of life, and that day will not come upon you suddenly like a trap; for it will come upon all those who dwell on the face of all the earth. But keep on the alert at all times, praying that you may have strength to escape all these things that are about to take place, and to stand before the Son of Man" (Luke 21:34–36; cf. Mark 13:33; see Matthew 24:42–44).

TIMES, HARD (See PERSECUTION; SUFFERING; TRIBULATION; and TROUBLE)

TIMES, HUNDRED

Setting: Judea beyond the Jordan (Perea). After informing a rich man how righteous believers may have treasure in heaven, Jesus tells His disciples about the reward of those who sacrifice in this life to follow Him.

Jesus said, "Truly I say to you, there is no one who has left house or brothers or sisters or mother or father or children or farms, for My sake and for the gospel's sake, but that he will receive a hundred times as much now in the present age, houses and brothers and sisters and mothers and children and farms, along with persecutions; and in the age to come, eternal life. But many *who are* first will be last, and the last, first" (Mark 10:29–31; cf. Matthew 19:27–30; Luke 18:28–30; see Matthew 6:33)

Setting: Galilee. After His visit in the home of Simon the Pharisee, Jesus goes into the villages and cities, proclaiming and preaching the kingdom of God.

When a large crowd was coming together, and those from various cities were journeying to Him, He spoke by way of a parable: "The sower went out to sow his seed; and as he sowed, some fell beside the road, and it was trampled under foot and the birds of the air ate it up. Other *seed* fell on rocky *soil,* and as soon as it grew up, it was withered away, because it had no moisture. Other *seed* fell among the thorns; and the thorns grew up with it and choked it out. Other *seed* fell into the good soil, and grew up, and produced a crop a hundred times as great." As He said these things, He would call out, "He who has ears to hear, let him hear" (Luke 8:4–8; cf. Matthew 13:2–9; Mark 4:3–9).

TIMES, MANY

Setting: Judea beyond the Jordan (Perea). Jesus promises rewards to His disciples for their personal sacrifice and commitment to following Him.

And Jesus said to them, "Truly I say to you, that you who have followed Me, in the regeneration when the Son of Man will sit on His glorious throne, you also shall sit upon twelve thrones, judging the twelve tribes of Israel. And everyone who has left houses or brothers or sisters or father or mother or children or farms for My name's sake, will receive many times as much, and will inherit eternal life. But many *who* are first will be last; and *the* last, first" (Matthew 19:28–30; cf. Matthew 6:33; 20:15; Mark 10:29, 30; Luke 18:29, 30; 22:30).

Setting: Perea, en route from Galilee to Jerusalem. After responding to His disciples' question about salvation, Jesus replies to Peter's statement about the disciples' personal sacrifice.

Peter said, "Behold, we have left our own *homes* and followed You." And He said to them, "Truly I say to you, there is no one who has left house or wife or brothers or parents or children, for the sake of the kingdom of God, who will not receive many times as much at this time and in the age to come, eternal life" (Luke 18:28–30; cf. Matthew 19:27–29; Mark 10:28–30; see Matthew 6:33; Luke 5:11).

TIMES, SEVEN

Setting: Capernaum of Galilee. Peter asks Jesus if forgiving someone seven times who has sinned against him is adequate.

Jesus said to him, "I do not say to you, up to seven times, but up to seventy times seven" (Matthew 18:22; see Matthew 18:21; Luke 17:3, 4).

Setting: On the way from Galilee to Jerusalem. After conveying the story of the rich man and Lazarus, the Lord gives His disciples instruction on forgiveness.

He said to His disciples, "It is inevitable that stumbling blocks come, but woe to him through whom they come! It would be better for him if a millstone were hung around his neck and he were thrown into the sea, than that he would cause one of these little ones to stumble. Be on your guard! If your brother sins, rebuke him; and if he repents, forgive him. And if he sins against you seven times a day, and returns to you seven times, saying, 'I repent,' forgive him" (Luke 17:1–4; see Matthew 18:5–7, 15, 21, 22).

TIMES, SEVENTY

Setting: Capernaum of Galilee. Peter asks Jesus if forgiving someone seven times who has sinned against him is adequate.

Jesus said to him, "I do not say to you, up to seven times, but up to seventy times seven" (Matthew 18:22; see Matthew 18:21; Luke 17:3, 4).

TIMES, SIGNS OF THE

Setting: Magadan of Galilee. Jesus' enemies, the Pharisees and the Sadducees, rejecting His message, continue to test Him by asking for a sign from heaven.

But He replied to them, "When it is evening, you say, '*It will be* fair weather, for the sky is red.' And in the morning, '*There will* be a storm today, for the sky is red and threatening.' Do you know how to discern the appearance of the sky, but cannot *discern* the signs of the times? An evil and adulterous generation seeks after a sign; and a sign will not be given it, except the sign of Jonah." And He left them and went away (Matthew 16:2–4; cf. Matthew 12:39; Mark 8:12; Luke 12:54–56).

[SIGNS OF THE TIMES inferred]
Setting: The Mount of Olives, just east of Jerusalem. During His Olivet Discourse, Jesus answers His disciples' questions as to when the temple will be destroyed and Jerusalem overrun, along with the signs of His coming and the end of the age.

And Jesus answered and said to them, "See to it that no one misleads you. For many will come in My name, saying, 'I am the Christ,' and will mislead many. You will be hearing of wars and rumors of wars. See that you are not frightened, for *those things* must take place, but *that* is not yet the end. For nation will rise against nation, and kingdom against kingdom, and in various places there will be famines and earthquakes. But all these things are *merely* the beginning of birth pangs. Then they will deliver you to tribulation, and will kill you, and you will be hated by all nations because of My name. At that time many will fall away and will betray one another and hate one another. Many false prophets will arise and will mislead many. Because lawlessness is increased, most people's love will grow cold. But the one who endures to the end, he will be saved. This gospel of the kingdom shall be preached in the whole world as a testimony to all the nations, and then the end will come" (Matthew 24:4–14; cf. Jeremiah 29:8; Matthew 7:15; 10:17, 22; Mark 13:3–13; Luke 21:7–19; Revelation 6:4).

[SIGNS OF THE TIMES inferred]
Setting: On the Mount of Olives, east of the temple in Jerusalem. After prophesying the temple's destruction, Jesus responds during His Olivet Discourse to questions from Peter, James, John, and Andrew about other future events.

And Jesus began to say to them, "See to it that no one misleads you. Many will come in My name, saying, 'I am *He!*' and will mislead many. When you hear of wars and rumors of wars, do not be frightened; *those things* must take place; but *that is* not yet the end. For nation will rise up against nation, and kingdom against kingdom; there will be earthquakes in various places; there will *also be* famines. These things are *merely* the beginning of birth pangs. But be on your guard; for they will deliver you to *the* courts, and you will be flogged in *the* synagogues, and you will stand before governors and kings for My sake, as a testimony to them. The gospel must first be preached to all the nations. When they arrest you and hand you over, do not worry beforehand about what you are to say, but say whatever is given you in that hour; for it is not you who speak, but *it is* the Holy Spirit. Brother will betray brother to death, and a father *his* child; and children will rise up against parents and have them put to death. You will be hated by all because of My name, but the one who endures to the end, he will be saved" (Mark 13:5–13; cf. Matthew 24:4–14; Luke 21:7–19; see Matthew 10:17–22).

[SIGNS OF THE TIMES from why do you not analyze this present time]
Setting: On the way from Galilee to Jerusalem. After telling how a relationship with Him will divide families, Jesus chastises the crowds for being able to discern the weather but not the present age.

And He was also saying to the crowds, "When you see a cloud rising in the west, immediately you say, 'A shower is coming,' and so it turns out. And when *you see* a south wind blowing, you say, 'It will be a hot day,' and it turns out *that way*. You hypocrites! You know how to analyze the appearance of the earth and the sky, but why do you not analyze this present time?" (Luke 12:54–56; cf. Matthew 16:2, 3).

TIMES, THREE

Setting: On the way to the Mount of Olives. After celebrating the Passover meal with His disciples in Jerusalem, prior to His betrayal by Judas, Jesus states that the disciples will all deny Him that very day.

Then Jesus said to them, "You will all fall away because of Me this night, for it is written, 'I WILL STRIKE DOWN THE SHEPHERD, AND THE SHEEP OF THE FLOCK SHALL BE SCATTERED.' But after I have been raised, I will go ahead of you to Galilee." But Peter said to Him, '*Even* though all may fall away because of You, I will never fall away.' Jesus said to him, "Truly I say to you that this *very* night, before a rooster crows, you will deny Me three times" (Matthew 26:31–34, Jesus quotes from Zechariah 13:7; cf. Mark 14:26–31; see Matthew 28:7, 10, 16; John 13:37).

Setting: Jerusalem. As Jesus appears before Caiaphas the high priest and the Council for interrogation aimed at entrapping Him, Peter, sitting in the courtyard, denies knowing Him, fulfilling the Lord's earlier prophecy.

And Peter remembered the word which Jesus had said, "Before a rooster crows, you will deny Me three times." And he went out and wept bitterly (Matthew 26:75; cf. Matthew 26:34; Mark 14:72; Luke 22:61; John 18:25–27).

Setting: A borrowed upper room in Jerusalem. After Jesus and His twelve disciples celebrate the Passover and the Lord's Supper, they go out to the Mount of Olives.

And Jesus said to them, "You will all fall away, because it is written, 'I WILL STRIKE DOWN THE SHEPHERD, AND THE SHEEP SHALL BE SCATTERED.' But after I have been raised, I will go ahead of you to Galilee." But Peter said to Him, "*Even* though all may fall away, yet I will not." And Jesus said to him, "Truly I say to you, that this very night, before a rooster crows twice, you yourself will deny Me three times" (Mark 14:27–30, Jesus quotes from Zechariah 13:7; cf. Matthew 26:30–34; see Mark 14:72).

Setting: Jerusalem. While Jesus is being falsely accused before the chief priests and the whole Council, Peter, in the courtyard of Caiaphas the high priest, denies he knows Jesus, then remembers His Lord's prophecy that Peter would deny Him three times before a rooster crowed twice.

Immediately a rooster crowed a second time. And Peter remembered how Jesus had made the remark to him, "Before a rooster crows twice, you will deny Me three times." And he began to weep (Mark 14:72; cf. Matthew 26:75; Luke 22:61; John 18:26, 27; see Mark 14:30).

Setting: An upper room in Jerusalem. During the Feast of Unleavened Bread (Passover) just before His crucifixion, Jesus celebrates the Passover meal with His disciples and institutes the Lord's Supper. The disciples later argue over who is the greatest among them, and the Lord prophesies Peter's denial of Him.

"Simon, Simon, behold, Satan has demanded *permission* to sift you like wheat; but I have prayed for you, that your faith may not fail; and you, when once you have turned again, strengthen your brothers." But he said to Him, "Lord, with You I am ready to go both to prison and to death!" And He said, "I say to you, Peter, the rooster will not crow today until you have denied three times that you know Me" (Luke 22:31–34; cf. Matthew 26:33–35; John 13:36–38; see Job 1:6–12; John 17:15).

Setting: Jerusalem. As Jesus appears before Caiaphas the high priest and the Council for interrogation aimed at entrapping Him, Peter, sitting in the courtyard, denies knowing Him, fulfilling the Lord's earlier prophecy.

The Lord turned and looked at Peter. And Peter remembered the word of the Lord, how He had told him, "Before a rooster crows today, you will deny Me three times" (Luke 22:61; cf. Matthew 26:75; Luke 14:72; John 18:26, 27; see Luke 22:34).

Setting: Jerusalem. Before the Passover, after revealing to His disciples that they cannot follow Him back to heaven, Jesus takes issue with Peter's assertion that he would lay down his life for the Lord.

Simon Peter said to Him, "Lord, where are You going?" Jesus answered, "Where I go, you cannot follow Me now; but you will follow later." Peter said to Him, "Lord, why can I not follow You right now? I will lay down my life for You." Jesus answered, "Will you lay down your life for Me? Truly, truly, I say to you, a rooster will not crow until you deny Me three times" (John 13:36–38; see Matthew 26:34; Mark 14:30, 72; Luke 22:33, 34).

TIMES, UNDERSTANDING THE (See TIMES, SIGNS OF THE)

TIMES OF THE GENTILES (Listed under GENTILES, TIMES OF THE)

TIP

Setting: On the way from Galilee to Jerusalem. After responding to the Pharisees' scoffing at His teaching His disciples about stewardship and the permanence of the Law, Jesus conveys the story of the rich man and Lazarus.

"Now there was a rich man, and he habitually dressed in purple and fine linen, joyously living in splendor every day. And a poor man named Lazarus was laid at his gate, covered with sores, and longing to be fed with the *crumbs* which were falling from the rich man's table; besides, even the dogs were coming and licking his sores. Now the poor man died and was carried away by the angels to Abraham's bosom; and the rich man also died and was buried. In Hades he lifted up his eyes, being in torment, and saw Abraham far away and Lazarus in his bosom. And he cried out and said, 'Father Abraham, have mercy on me, and send Lazarus so that he may dip the tip of his finger in water and cool off my tongue, for I am in agony in this flame.' But Abraham said, 'Child, remember that during your life you received your good things, and likewise Lazarus bad things; but now he is being comforted here, and you are in agony. And besides all this, between us and you there is a great chasm fixed, so that those who wish to come over from here to you will not be able, and *that* none may cross over from there to us.' And he said, 'Then I beg you, father, that you send him to my father's house—for I have five brothers—in order that he may warn them, so that they will not also come to this place of torment.' But Abraham said, 'They have Moses and the Prophets; let them hear them.' But he said, 'No, father Abraham, but if someone goes to them from the dead, they will repent!' But he said to him, 'If they do not listen to Moses and the Prophets, they will not be persuaded even if someone rises from the dead' " (Luke 16:19–31; see Luke 3:8; 6:24; 16:1, 14).

TITHE (Also see OFFERING; STEWARDSHIP; and TITHES)

[TITHE from render to Caesar the things that are Caesar's; and to God the things that are God's]

Setting: The temple in Jerusalem. While Jesus teaches, the Pharisees send their disciples and the Herodians to test Jesus about the poll-tax, in order to trap Him.

But Jesus perceived their malice, and said, "Why are you testing Me, you hypocrites? Show Me the coin *used* for the poll-tax." And they brought Him a denarius. And He said to them, "Whose likeness and inscription is this?" They said to Him, "Caesar's." Then He said to them, "Then render to Caesar the things that are Caesar's; and to God the things that are God's" (Matthew 22:18–21; cf. Matthew 17:25; Mark 12:15–17; Luke 20:22–25).

Setting: The temple in Jerusalem. After the Jewish religious leaders test Him with questions, Jesus pronounces the fifth of eight woes upon them in front of the crowds and His disciples.

"Woe to you, scribes and Pharisees, hypocrites! For you tithe mint and dill and cummin, and have neglected the weightier provisions of the law: justice and mercy and faithfulness; but these are things you should have done without neglecting the others. You blind guides, who strain out a gnat and swallow a camel!" (Matthew 23:23, 24).

[TITHE from "Render to Caesar the things that are Caesar's, and to God the things that are God's]

Setting: The temple in Jerusalem. After Jesus teaches the chief priests, scribes, and elders in parables, they send some of the Pharisees and Herodians in an attempt to trap Him in a statement.

"Shall we pay or shall we not pay?" But He, knowing their hypocrisy, said to them, "Why are you testing Me? Bring Me a denarius to look at." They brought *one.* And He said to them, "Whose likeness and inscription is this?" And they said to Him, "Caesar's." And Jesus said to them, "Render to Caesar the things that are Caesar's, and to God the things that are God's" And they were amazed at Him (Mark 12:15–17; cf. Matthew 22:15–22; Luke 20:20–26).

[TITHE from this poor widow put in more than all the contributors to the treasury]

Setting: Opposite the temple treasury in Jerusalem. Jesus focuses His disciples' attention on a poor widow's monetary sacrifice.

Calling His disciples to Him, He said to them, "Truly I say to you, this poor widow put in more than all the contributors to the treasury; for they all put in out of their surplus, but she, out of her poverty, put in all she owned, all she had to live on" (Mark 12:43, 44; cf. Luke 21:1–4).

Setting: On the way from Galilee to Jerusalem. After speaking of how a lamp illuminates, the Lord has lunch with a Pharisee, who is surprised He doesn't wash before eating.

But the Lord said to him, "Now you Pharisees clean the outside of the cup and of the platter; but inside of you, you are full of robbery and wickedness. You foolish ones, did not He who made the outside make the inside also? But give that which is within as charity, and then all things are clean for you. But woe to you Pharisees! You pay tithe of mint and rue and every *kind of* garden herb, and *yet* disregard justice and the love of God; but these are the things you should have done without neglecting the others. Woe to you Pharisees! For you love the chief seats in the synagogues and the respectful greetings in the market places. Woe to you! For you are like concealed tombs, and the people who walk over *them* are unaware *of it*" (Luke 11:39–44; cf. Matthew 23:6, 7, 23–27; see Matthew 15:2; Titus 1:15).

[TITHE from render to Caesar the things that are Caesar's, and to God the things that are God's]
Setting: The temple in Jerusalem. A few days before His crucifixion, after Jesus conveys the Parable of the Vine-Growers to the people, the scribes and Pharisees seek to trap Him by questioning Him about paying taxes to Caesar.

But He detected their trickery and said to them, "Show Me a denarius. Whose likeness and inscription does it have?" They said "Caesar's." And He said to them, "Then render to Caesar the things that are Caesar's, and to God the things that are God's" (Luke 20:23–25; cf. Matthew 22:15–21; Mark 12:13–17).

[TITHE from this poor widow put in more than all *of them*]
Setting: The temple in Jerusalem. While ministering a few days before His crucifixion, after warning His disciples about the lifestyle of the scribes, Jesus points out a poor widow's sacrificial giving to the temple treasury.

And He said, "Truly I say to you, this poor widow put in more than all *of them;* for they all out of their surplus put into the offering; but she out of her poverty put in all that she had to live on" (Luke 21:3, 4; cf. Mark 12:41–44).

TITHES (Also see TITHE)

Setting: On the way from Galilee to Jerusalem. After instructing His disciples about persistence in prayer, Jesus conveys a parable about self-righteousness.

And He also told this parable to some people who trusted in themselves that they were righteous, and viewed others with contempt: "Two men went up into the temple to pray, one a Pharisee and the other a tax collector. The Pharisee stood and was praying this to himself: 'God, I thank You that I am not like other people: swindlers, unjust, adulterers, or even like this tax collector. I fast twice a week; I pay tithes of all that I get.' But the tax collector, standing some distance away, was even unwilling to lift up his eyes to heaven, but was beating his breast, saying, 'God, be merciful to me, the sinner!' I tell you, this man went to his house justified rather than the other; for everyone who exalts himself will be humbled, but he who humbles himself will be exalted" (Luke 18:9–14; see Ezra 9:6; Matthew 6:5, 23:12; Luke 11:42; 16:15; Romans 14:3, 10).

TODAY (Also see TOMORROW)

Setting: Galilee. During the early part of His ministry, Jesus preaches the Sermon on the Mount to His disciples and the multitudes.

"For this reason I say to you, do not be worried about your life, *as to* what you will eat or what you will drink; nor for your body, *as to* what you will put on. Is not life more than food, and the body more than clothing? Look at the birds of the air, that they do not sow, nor reap nor gather into barns, and *yet* your heavenly Father feeds them. Are you not worth much more than they? And who of you by being worried can add a *single* hour to his life? And why are you worried about clothing? Observe how the lilies of the field grow; they do not toil nor do they spin, yet I say to you that not even Solomon in all his glory clothed himself like one of these. But if God so clothes the grass of the field, which is *alive* today and tomorrow is thrown into the furnace, *will He* not much more *clothe* you? You of little faith! Do not worry then, saying 'What will we eat?' or 'What will we drink?' or 'What will be wear for clothing?" For the Gentiles eagerly seek all these things; for your heavenly Father knows that you need all these things. But seek first His kingdom and His righteousness, and all these things will be added to you. So do not worry about tomorrow; for tomorrow will care for itself. Each day has enough trouble of its own" (Matthew 6:25–34; cf. Luke 12:22–31; see 1 Kings 10:4–7; Job 35:11; Matthew 8:26).

Setting: Magadan of Galilee. Jesus' enemies, the Pharisees and the Sadducees, rejecting His message, continue to test Him by asking for a sign from heaven.

But He replied to them, "When it is evening, you say, '*It will be* fair weather, for the sky is red.' And in the morning, '*There will* be a storm today, for the sky is red and threatening.' Do you know how to discern the appearance of the sky, but cannot *discern* the signs of the times? An evil and adulterous generation seeks after a sign; and a sign will not be given it, except the sign of Jonah." And He left them and went away (Matthew 16:2–4; cf. Matthew 12:39; Mark 8:12; Luke 12:54–56).

Setting: The temple in Jerusalem. Jesus delivers a parable to the chief priests and elders after they question His authority.

"But what do you think? A man had two sons, and he came to the first and said, 'Son, go work today in the vineyard.' And he answered, 'I will not'; but afterward he regretted it and went. The man came to the second and said the same thing; and he answered, 'I *will,* sir'; but he did not go. Which of the two sons did the will of his father?" They said, "The first." Jesus said to them, "Truly, I say to you that the tax collectors and prostitutes will get into the kingdom of God before you. For John came to you in the way of righteousness and you did not believe him; but the tax collectors and prostitutes did believe him; and you, seeing *this,* did not even feel remorse afterward so as to believe him" (Matthew 21:28–32; cf. Luke 7:29, 30, 37–50).

Setting: The synagogue in Jesus' hometown of Nazareth in Galilee. At the beginning of His public ministry, Jesus reads from the book of the prophet Isaiah on the Sabbath.

And the book of the prophet Isaiah was handed to Him. And He opened the book and found the place where it was written, "THE SPIRIT OF THE LORD IS UPON ME, BECAUSE HE ANOINTED ME TO PREACH THE GOSPEL TO THE POOR. HE HAS SENT ME TO PROCLAIM RELEASE TO THE CAPTIVES, AND RECOVERY OF SIGHT TO THE BLIND, TO SET FREE THOSE WHO ARE OPPRESSED, TO PROCLAIM THE FAVORABLE YEAR OF THE LORD." And He closed the book, gave it back to the attendant and sat down; and the eyes of all in the synagogue were fixed on Him. And He began to say to them, "Today this Scripture has been fulfilled in your hearing" (Luke 4:17–21, Jesus quotes from Isaiah 61:1, 2).

Setting: On the way from Galilee to Jerusalem. After giving a parable about riches and greed, Jesus comforts the crowd and His disciples. The scribes and Pharisees turn hostile and question Him repeatedly in an attempt to catch Him in something He might say.

And He said to His disciples, "For this reason I say to you, do not worry about *your* life, *as to* what you will eat; nor for your body, *as to* what you will put on. For life is more than food, and the body more than clothing. Consider the ravens, for they neither sow nor reap; they have no storeroom nor barn, and *yet* God feeds them; how much more valuable you are than the birds! And which of you by worrying can add a *single* hour to his life's span? If then you cannot do even a very little thing, why do you worry about other matters? Consider the lilies, how they grow: they neither toil nor spin; but I tell you, not even Solomon in all his glory clothed himself like one of these. But if God so clothes the grass in the field, which is *alive* today and tomorrow is thrown into the furnace, how much more *will He clothe* you? You men of little faith! And do not seek what you will eat and what you will drink, and

do not keep worrying. For all these things the nations of the world eagerly seek; but your Father knows that you need these things. But seek His kingdom, and these things will be added to you. Do not be afraid, little flock, for your Father has chosen gladly to give you the kingdom" (Luke 12:22–32; cf. Matthew 6:25–33; see 1 Kings 10:4–7; Job 38:41).

Setting: On the way from Galilee to Jerusalem. While teaching in the cities and villages, Jesus responds to a question about who is saved. Some Pharisees ask Him to leave, claiming Herod Antipas (tetrarch of Galilee and Perea) seeks to kill Him.

And He said to them, "Go and tell that fox, 'Behold, I cast out demons and perform cures today and tomorrow, and the third *day* I reach My goal.' Nevertheless I must journey on today and tomorrow and the next *day*; for it cannot be that a prophet would perish outside of Jerusalem. O Jerusalem, Jerusalem, *the city* that kills the prophets and stones those sent to her! How often I wanted to gather your children together, just as a hen *gathers* her brood under her wings, and you would not *have it*! Behold, your house is left to you *desolate*; and I say to you, you will not see Me until *the time* comes when you say, 'BLESSED IS HE WHO COMES IN THE NAME OF THE LORD!'" (Luke 13:32–35, Jesus quotes from Psalm 118:26; cf. Matthew 23:37).

Setting: Jericho, on the way to Jerusalem for the crucifixion. After taking time to heal a blind man, Jesus informs a curious, short tax collector observing Him and His disciples from a sycamore tree that He will stay at the man's house that night.

When Jesus came to the place, He looked up and said to him, "Zaccheus, hurry and come down, for today I must stay at your house" (Luke 19:5).

Setting: Jericho, on the way to Jerusalem. After taking time to heal a blind man, Jesus comments on Zaccheus's response to Him.

And Jesus said to him, "Today salvation has come to this house, because he, too, is a son of Abraham. For the Son of Man has come to seek and to save that which was lost" (Luke 19:9, 10; cf. Matthew 18:11).

Setting: An upper room in Jerusalem. During the Feast of Unleavened Bread (Passover) just before His crucifixion, Jesus celebrates the Passover meal with His disciples and institutes the Lord's Supper. The disciples later argue over who is the greatest among them, and the Lord prophesies Peter's denial of Him.

"Simon, Simon, behold, Satan has demanded *permission* to sift you like wheat; but I have prayed for you, that your faith may not fail; and you, when once you have turned again, strengthen your brothers." But he said to Him, "Lord, with You I am ready to go both to prison and to death!" And He said, "I say to you, Peter, the rooster will not crow today until you have denied three times that you know Me" (Luke 22:31–34; cf. Matthew 26:33–35; John 13:36–38; see Job 1:6–12; John 17:15).

Setting: Jerusalem. As Jesus appears before Caiaphas the high priest and the Council for interrogation aimed at entrapping Him, Peter, sitting in the courtyard, denies knowing Him, fulfilling the Lord's earlier prophecy.

The Lord turned and looked at Peter. And Peter remembered the word of the Lord, how He had told him, "Before a rooster crows today, you will deny Me three times" (Luke 22:61; cf. Matthew 26:75; Luke 14:72; John 18:26, 27; see Luke 22:34).

Setting: On a hill called Golgotha (Calvary), just outside Jerusalem. While Jesus is being mocked and ridiculed on the cross, one of the criminals being crucified with Him asks to be remembered in Christ's kingdom, which the Lord grants with forgiveness and entrance into Paradise.

And He said to him, "Truly I say to you, today you shall be with Me in Paradise" (Luke 23:43; see Matthew 27:39–44; Mark 15:29–32).

TOGETHER, LIVING (See LIVING TOGETHER)

TOIL (Also see WORK)

Setting: Galilee. During the early part of His ministry, Jesus preaches the Sermon on the Mount to His disciples and the multitudes.

"For this reason I say to you, do not be worried about your life, *as to* what you will eat or what you will drink; nor for your body, *as to* what you will put on. Is not life more than food, and the body more than clothing? Look at the birds of the air, that they do not sow, nor reap nor gather into barns, and *yet* your heavenly Father feeds them. Are you not worth much more than they? And who of you by being worried can add a *single* hour to his life? And why are you worried about clothing? Observe how the lilies of the field grow; they do not toil nor do they spin, yet I say to you that not even Solomon in all his glory clothed himself like one of these. But if God so clothes the grass of the field, which is *alive* today and tomorrow is thrown into the furnace, *will He* not much more *clothe* you? You of little faith! Do not worry then, saying 'What will we eat?' or 'What will we drink?' or 'What will be wear for clothing?" For the Gentiles eagerly seek all these things; for your heavenly Father knows that you need all these things. But seek first His kingdom and His righteousness, and all these things will be added to you. So do not worry about tomorrow; for tomorrow will care for itself. Each day has enough trouble of its own" (Matthew 6:25–34; cf. Luke 12:22–31; see 1 Kings 10:4–7; Job 35:11; Matthew 8:26).

Setting: On the way from Galilee to Jerusalem. After giving a parable about riches and greed, Jesus comforts the crowd and His disciples. The scribes and Pharisees turn hostile and question Him repeatedly in an attempt to catch Him in something He might say.

And He said to His disciples, "For this reason I say to you, do not worry about *your* life, *as to* what you will eat; nor for your body, *as to* what you will put on. For life is more than food, and the body more than clothing. Consider the ravens, for they neither sow nor reap; they have no storeroom nor barn, and *yet* God feeds them; how much more valuable you are than the birds! And which of you by worrying can add a *single* hour to his life's span? If then you cannot do even a very little thing, why do you worry about other matters? Consider the lilies, how they grow: they neither toil nor spin; but I tell you, not even Solomon in all his glory clothed himself like one of these. But if God so clothes the grass in the field, which is *alive* today and tomorrow is thrown into the furnace, how much more *will He clothe* you? You men of little faith! And do not seek what you will eat and what you will drink, and do not keep worrying. For all these things the nations of the world eagerly seek; but your Father knows that you need these things. But seek His kingdom, and these things will be added to you. Do not be afraid, little flock, for your Father has chosen gladly to give you the kingdom." (Luke 12:22–32; cf. Matthew 6:25–33; see 1 Kings 10:4–7; Job 38:41).

Setting: On the island of Patmos (in the Aegean Sea about fifty miles southwest of Ephesus in modern Turkey). On the Lord's Day (Sunday), approximately fifty years after the Resurrection, the disciple John encounters the Lord Jesus Christ, who communicates a new revelation for the apostle to record for the church in Ephesus and to six other churches in Asia.

"To the angel of the church in Ephesus write: The One who holds the seven stars in His right hand, the One who walks among the seven golden lampstands, says this: 'I know your deeds and your toil and perseverance, and that you cannot tolerate evil men, and you put to the test those who call themselves apostles, and they are not, and you found them *to be* false; and you have perseverance and have endured for My name's sake, and have not grown weary. But I have *this* against you, that you have left your first love. Therefore remember from where you have fallen, and repent and do the deeds you did at first; or else I am coming to you and will remove your lampstand out of its place—unless you repent. Yet this you do have, that you hate the deeds of the Nicolaitans, which I also hate. He who has an ear, let him hear what the Spirit says to the churches. To him who overcomes, I will grant to eat of the tree of life which is in the Paradise of God' " (Revelation 2:1–7; see Genesis 2:9; Ezekiel 28:13; 1 John 4:1; Revelation 1:10, 11, 19, 20).

TOMBS (PROPHETS, TOMBS OF THE; TOMBS, CONCEALED; and TOMBS, WHITEWASHED are separate entries; also see BONES, DEAD MEN'S; and DEAD)

Setting: On the way from Galilee to Jerusalem. After Jesus pronounces woes upon the Pharisees, a lawyer replies that His remarks are an insult to lawyers, too.

But He said, "Woe to you lawyers as well! For you weigh men down with burdens hard to bear, while you yourselves will not even touch the burdens with one of your fingers. Woe to you! For you build the tombs of the prophets, and *it was* your fathers *who* killed them. So you are witnesses and approve the deeds of your fathers; because it was they who killed them, and you build *their tombs*. For this reason also the wisdom of God said, 'I will send them prophets and apostles, and *some* of them they will kill and *some* they will persecute, so that the blood of all the prophets, shed since the foundation of the world, may be charged against this generation, from the blood of Abel to the blood of Zechariah, who was killed between the altar and the house *of God*; yes, I tell you, it shall be charged against this generation.' Woe to you lawyers! For you have taken away the key of knowledge; you yourselves did not enter, and you hindered those who were entering" (Luke 11:46–52; cf. Matthew 23:29–32; see 2 Chronicles 24:20, 21; Matthew 23:4, 13).

Setting: Jerusalem. During a feast of the Jews, Jesus responds to criticism from the Jewish religious leaders by referring to God as His Father (thereby making Himself equal with God) and prophesying His participation someday in the resurrection and judgment of men.

"Truly, truly, I say to you, an hour is coming and now is, when the dead will hear the voice of the Son of God, and those who hear will live. For just as the Father has life in Himself, even so He gave to the Son also to have life in Himself; and He gave Him authority to execute judgment, because He is *the* Son of Man. Do not marvel at this; for an hour is coming, in which all who are in the tombs will hear His voice, and will come forth; those who did the good *deeds* to a resurrection of life, those who committed the evil *deeds* to a resurrection of judgment" (John 5:25–29; see Daniel 12:2; John 1:4; 11:24).

TOMBS, CONCEALED

Setting: On the way from Galilee to Jerusalem. After speaking of how a lamp illuminates, the Lord has lunch with a Pharisee, who is surprised He doesn't wash before eating.

But the Lord said to him, "Now you Pharisees clean the outside of the cup and of the platter; but inside of you, you are full of robbery and wickedness. You foolish ones, did not He who made the outside make the inside also? But give that which is within as charity, and then all things are clean for you. But woe to you Pharisees! You pay tithe of mint and rue and every *kind of* garden herb, and *yet* disregard justice and the love of God; but these are the things you should have done without neglecting the others. Woe to you Pharisees! For you love the chief seats in the synagogues and the respectful greetings in the market places. Woe to you! For you are like concealed tombs, and the people who walk over *them* are unaware *of it*" (Luke 11:39–44; cf. Matthew 23:6, 7, 23–27; see Matthew 15:2; Titus 1:15).

TOMBS, WHITEWASHED (Also see BONES, DEAD MEN'S)

Setting: The temple in Jerusalem. After the Jewish religious leaders test Him with questions, Jesus pronounces the seventh of eight woes upon them in front of the crowds and His disciples.

"Woe to you, scribes and Pharisees, hypocrites! For you are like whitewashed tombs which on the outside appear beautiful, but inside they are full of dead men's bones and all uncleanness. So you, too, outwardly appear righteous to men, but inwardly you are full of hypocrisy and lawlessness" (Matthew 23:27, 28; cf. Luke 11:44).

TOMBS OF THE PROPHETS (Listed under PROPHETS, TOMBS OF THE)

TOMORROW (Also see FUTURE, PREDICTING THE; PROPHECY; and TODAY)

[TOMORROW also from tomorrow will care for itself]

Setting: Galilee. During the early part of His ministry, Jesus preaches the Sermon on the Mount to His disciples and the multitudes.

"For this reason I say to you, do not be worried about your life, *as to* what you will eat or what you will drink; nor for your body, *as to* what you will put on. Is not life more than food, and the body more than clothing? Look at the birds of the air, that they do not sow, nor reap nor gather into barns, and *yet* your heavenly Father feeds them. Are you not worth much more than they? And who of you by being worried can add a *single* hour to his life? And why are you worried about clothing? Observe how the lilies of the field grow; they do not toil nor do they spin, yet I say to you that not even Solomon in all his glory clothed himself like one of these. But if God so clothes the grass of the field, which is *alive* today and tomorrow is thrown into the furnace, *will He* not much more *clothe* you? You of little faith! Do not worry then, saying 'What will we eat?' or 'What will we drink?' or 'What will be wear for clothing?" For the Gentiles eagerly seek all these things; for your heavenly Father knows that you need all these things. But seek first His kingdom and His righteousness, and all these things will be added to you. So do not worry about tomorrow; for tomorrow will care for itself. Each day has enough trouble of its own" (Matthew 6:25–34; cf. Luke 12:22–31; see 1 Kings 10:4–7; Job 35:11; Matthew 8:26).

Setting: On the way from Galilee to Jerusalem. After giving a parable about riches and greed, Jesus comforts the crowd and His disciples. The scribes and Pharisees turn hostile and question Him repeatedly in an attempt to catch Him in something He might say.

And He said to His disciples, "For this reason I say to you, do not worry about *your* life, *as to* what you will eat; nor for your body, *as to* what you will put on. For life is more than food, and the body more than clothing. Consider the ravens, for they neither sow nor reap; they have no storeroom nor barn, and *yet* God feeds them; how much more valuable you are than the birds! And which of you by worrying can add a *single* hour to his life's span? If then you cannot do even a very little thing, why do you worry about other matters? Consider the lilies, how they grow: they neither toil nor spin; but I tell you, not even Solomon in all his glory clothed himself like one of these. But if God so clothes the grass in the field, which is *alive* today and tomorrow is thrown into the furnace, how much more *will He clothe* you? You men of little faith! And do not seek what you will eat and what you will drink, and do not keep worrying. For all these things the nations of the world eagerly seek; but your Father knows that you need these things. But seek His kingdom, and these things will be added to you. Do not be afraid, little flock, for your Father has chosen gladly to give you the kingdom." (Luke 12:22–32; cf. Matthew 6:25–33; see 1 Kings 10:4–7; Job 38:41).

Setting: On the way from Galilee to Jerusalem. While teaching in the cities and villages, Jesus responds to a question about who is saved. Some Pharisees ask Him to leave, claiming Herod Antipas (tetrarch of Galilee and Perea) seeks to kill Him.

And He said to them, "Go and tell that fox, 'Behold, I cast out demons and perform cures today and tomorrow, and the third *day* I reach My goal.' Nevertheless I must journey on today and tomorrow and the next *day*; for it cannot be that a prophet would perish outside of Jerusalem. O Jerusalem, Jerusalem, *the city* that kills the prophets and stones those sent to her! How often I wanted to gather your children together, just as a hen *gathers* her brood under her wings, and you would not *have it*! Behold, your house is left to you *desolate*; and I say to you, you will not see Me until *the time* comes when you say, 'BLESSED IS HE WHO COMES IN THE NAME OF THE LORD!'" (Luke 13:32–35, Jesus quotes from Psalm 118:26; cf. Matthew 23:37).

TONGUE (Also see MOUTH)

Setting: On the way from Galilee to Jerusalem. After responding to the Pharisees' scoffing at His teaching His disciples about stewardship and the permanence of the Law, Jesus conveys the story of the rich man and Lazarus.

"Now there was a rich man, and he habitually dressed in purple and fine linen, joyously living in splendor every day. And a poor man named Lazarus was laid at his gate, covered with sores, and longing to be fed with the *crumbs* which were falling from the rich man's table; besides, even the dogs were coming and licking his sores. Now the poor man died and was carried away by the angels to Abraham's bosom; and the rich man also died and was buried. In Hades he lifted up his eyes, being in torment, and saw Abraham far away and Lazarus in his bosom. And he cried out and said, 'Father Abraham, have mercy on me, and send Lazarus so that he may dip the tip of his finger in water and cool off my tongue, for I am in agony in this flame.' But Abraham said, 'Child, remember that during your life you received your good things, and likewise Lazarus bad things; but now he is being comforted here, and you are in agony. And besides all this, between us and you there is a great chasm fixed, so that those who wish to come over from here to you will not be able, and *that* none may cross over from there to us.' And he said, 'Then I beg you, father, that you send him to my father's house—for I have five brothers—in order that he may warn them, so that they will not also come to this place of torment.' But Abraham said, 'They have Moses and the Prophets; let them hear them.' But he said, 'No, father Abraham, but if someone goes to them from the dead, they will repent!' But he said to him, 'If they do not listen to Moses and the Prophets, they will not be persuaded even if someone rises from the dead' " (Luke 16:19–31; see Luke 3:8; 6:24; 16:1, 14).

TONGUES, NEW

Setting: Following His resurrection from the dead after being crucified, Jesus commissions His disciples to preach His gospel to the world.

And He said to them, "Go into all the world and preach the gospel to all creation. He who has believed and has been baptized shall be saved; but he who has disbelieved shall be condemned. These signs will accompany those who have believed: in My name they will cast out demons, they will speak with new tongues; they will pick up serpents, and if they drink any deadly *poison,* it will not hurt them; they will lay hands on the sick, and they will recover" (Mark 16:15–18; cf. Matthew 28:16–20; see Mark 9:38; John 3:18, 36; 1 Corinthians 15:6).

[Note: Some scholars question the authenticity of Mark 16:9–20 as these verses do not appear in some early New Testament manuscripts.]

TOOTH (Also see TEETH)

Setting: Galilee. During the early part of His ministry, Jesus preaches the Sermon on the Mount to His disciples and the multitudes.

"You have heard that it was said, 'AN EYE FOR AN EYE, AND A TOOTH FOR A TOOTH.' But I say to you, do not resist an evil person; but whoever slaps you on your right cheek, turn the other to him also" (Matthew 5:38, 39, Jesus quotes from Exodus 21:24; cf. Leviticus 24:20).

TORMENT (Also see AGONY; and TORTURERS)

Setting: On the way from Galilee to Jerusalem. After responding to the Pharisees' scoffing at His teaching His disciples about stewardship and the permanence of the Law, Jesus conveys the story of the rich man and Lazarus.

"Now there was a rich man, and he habitually dressed in purple and fine linen, joyously living in splendor every day. And a poor man named Lazarus was laid at his gate, covered with sores, and longing to be fed with the *crumbs* which were falling from the rich man's table; besides, even the dogs were coming and licking his sores. Now the poor man died and was carried away by the angels to Abraham's bosom; and the rich man also died and was buried. In Hades he lifted up his eyes, being in torment, and saw Abraham far away and Lazarus in his bosom. And he cried out and said, 'Father Abraham, have mercy on me, and send Lazarus so that he may dip the tip of his finger in water and cool off my tongue, for I am in agony in this flame.' But Abraham said, 'Child, remember that during your life you received your good things, and likewise Lazarus bad things; but now he is being comforted here, and you are in agony. And besides all this, between us and you there is a great chasm fixed, so that those who wish to come over from here to you will not be able, and *that* none may cross over from there to us.' And he said, 'Then I beg you, father, that you send him to my father's house—for I have five brothers—in order that he may warn them, so that they will not also come to this place of torment.' But Abraham said, 'They have Moses and the Prophets; let them hear them.' But he said, 'No, father Abraham, but if someone goes to them from the dead, they will repent!' But he said to him, 'If they do not listen to Moses and the Prophets, they will not be persuaded even if someone rises from the dead' " (Luke 16:19–31; see Luke 3:8; 6:24; 16:1, 14).

TORMENT, PLACE OF (See TORMENT)

TORRENT (Also see FLOOD; and FLOODS)

Setting: Galilee. After selecting His twelve disciples, Jesus teaches the Sermon on the Mount to those disciples and a great throng of people from Judea, Jerusalem, and the central coastal region of Tyre and Sidon.

"Why do you call Me, 'Lord, Lord,' and do not do what I say? Everyone who comes to Me and hears My words and acts on them, I will show you whom he is like; he is like a man building a house, who dug deep and laid a foundation on the rock; and when a flood occurred, the torrent burst against that house and could not shake it, because it had been well built. But the one who has heard and has not acted *accordingly,* is like a man who built a house on the ground without any foundation; and the torrent burst against it and immediately it collapsed, and the ruin of that house was great" (Luke 6:46–49; cf. Matthew 7:24–27; see Luke 6:12–19; James 1:22).

TORTURE (See TORMENT; and TORTURERS)

TORTURERS (Also see TORMENT)

Setting: Capernaum of Galilee. Jesus illustrates the matter of forgiveness after Peter asks Him if forgiving someone seven times who has sinned against him is adequate.

"For this reason the kingdom of heaven may be compared to a king who wished to settle accounts with his slaves. When he had begun to settle *them,* one who owed him ten thousand talents was brought to him. But since he did not have *the means* to repay, his lord commanded him to be sold, along with his wife and children and all that he had, and repayment to be made. So the slave fell *to the ground* and prostrated himself before him, saying, 'Have patience with me and I will repay you everything.' And the lord of that slave felt compassion and released him and forgave him the debt. But that slave went out and found one of his fellow slaves who owed him a hundred denarii; and he seized him and *began* to choke *him,* saying, 'Pay back what you owe.' So his fellow slave fell *to the ground* and *began* to plead with him, saying, 'Have patience with me and I will repay you.' But he was unwilling and went and threw him in prison until he should pay back what was owed. So when his fellow slaves saw what had happened, they were deeply grieved and came and reported to their lord all that had happened. Then summoning him, his lord said to him, 'You wicked slave, I forgave you all that debt because you pleaded with me. Should you not also have had mercy on your fellow slave, in the same way that I had mercy on you?' And his lord, moved with anger, handed him over to the torturers until he should repay all that was owed him. My heavenly Father will also do the same to you, if each of you does not forgive his brother from your heart" (Matthew 18:23–35; cf. Matthew 6:12, 14, 15; Luke 7:42; see Matthew 25:19–28).

TOUCH

[TOUCH from touched]

Setting: By the Sea of Galilee. After Jesus returns from ministry to the Gerasenes (to the east of Galilee), a woman who has had a hemorrhage for twelve years touches the hem of His garment in order to be healed.

Immediately Jesus, perceiving in Himself that the power *proceeding* from Him had gone forth, turned around in the crowd and said, "Who touched My garments?" (Mark 5:30; see Matthew 9:20, 21; Luke 8:43–48).

Setting: Galilee. After ministering in the country of the Gerasenes to the east of Galilee, Jesus returns, and a woman, ill for twelve years, receives healing by touching His garment.

And Jesus said, "Who is the one who touched Me?" And while they were all denying it, Peter said, "Master, the people are crowding and pressing in on You." But Jesus said, "Someone did touch Me, for I was aware, that power had gone out of Me." When the woman saw that she had not escaped notice, she came trembling and fell down before Him, and declared in the presence of all the people the reason why she had touched Him, and how she had been immediately healed. And He said to her, "Daughter, your faith has made you well; go in peace" (Luke 8:45–48; cf. Matthew 9:20; Mark 5:25–34).

Setting: On the way from Galilee to Jerusalem. After Jesus pronounces woes upon the Pharisees, a lawyer replies that His remarks are an insult to lawyers, too.

But He said, "Woe to you lawyers as well! For you weigh men down with burdens hard to bear, while you yourselves will not even touch the burdens with one of your fingers. Woe to you! For you build the tombs of the prophets, and *it was* your fathers *who* killed them. So you are witnesses and approve the deeds of your fathers; because it was they who killed them, and you build *their tombs*. For this reason also the wisdom of God said, 'I will send them prophets and apostles, and *some* of them they will kill and *some* they will persecute, so that the blood of all the prophets, shed since the foundation of the world, may be charged against this generation, from the blood of Abel to the blood of Zechariah, who was killed between the altar and the house *of God*; yes, I tell you, it shall be charged against this generation.' Woe to you lawyers! For you have taken away the key of knowledge; you yourselves did not enter, and you hindered those who were entering" (Luke 11:46–52; cf. Matthew 23:29–32; see 2 Chronicles 24:20, 21; Matthew 23:4, 13).

Setting: Jerusalem. After rising from the tomb on the third day after being crucified, and appearing to two of His followers on the road to Emmaus, Jesus appears to His disciples (except Thomas).

While they were telling these things, He Himself stood in their midst and said to them, "Peace be to you." But they were startled and frightened and thought they were seeing a spirit. And He said to them, "Why are you troubled, and why do doubts arise in your hearts? See My hands and My feet, that it is I Myself; touch Me and see, for a spirit does not have flesh and bones as you see that I have." And when He had said this, He showed them His hands and His feet. While they still could not believe *it* because of their joy and amazement. He said to them, "Have you anything to eat?" They gave Him a piece of a broiled fish; and He took it and ate *it* before them (Luke 24:36–43; see Mark 16:14; John 20:27; Acts 10:40, 41).

TOWER

Setting: The temple in Jerusalem. Jesus delivers another parable to the chief priests and elders after they question His authority.

"Listen to another parable. There was a landowner who PLANTED A VINEYARD AND PUT A WALL AROUND IT AND DUG A WINE PRESS IN IT, AND BUILT A TOWER, and rented it out to vine-growers and went on a journey. When the harvest time approached, he sent his slaves to the vine-growers to receive his produce. The vine-growers took his slaves and beat one, and killed another, and stoned a third. Again he sent another group of slaves larger than the first; and they did the same thing to them. But afterward he sent his son to them, saying, 'They will respect my son.' But when the vine-growers saw the son, they said among themselves, 'This is the heir; come, let us kill him and seize his inheritance.' They took him, and threw him out of the vineyard and killed him. Therefore when the owner of the vineyard comes, what will he do to those vine-growers?" (Matthew 21:33–40; Jesus quotes from Isaiah 5:1, 2; cf. Mark 12:1–9; Luke 20:9–15).

Setting: The temple in Jerusalem. Having His authority questioned by the chief priests, scribes, and elders, Jesus begins to teach them in parables.

And He began to speak to them in parables: "A man PLANTED A VINEYARD AND PUT A WALL AROUND IT, AND DUG A VAT UNDER THE WINE PRESS AND BUILT A TOWER, and rented it out to vine-growers and went on a journey. At the *harvest* time he sent a slave to the vine-growers, in order to receive *some* of the produce of the vineyard from the vine-growers. They took him, and beat him and sent him away empty-handed. Again he sent them another slave, and they wounded him in the head, and treated him shamefully. And he sent another, and that one they killed; and *so with* many others, beating some and killing others. He had one more to *send*, a beloved son; he sent him last *of all* to them, saying, 'They will respect my son.' But those vine-growers said to one another, 'This is the heir; come, let us kill him, and the inheritance will be ours!' They took him, and killed him and threw him out of the vineyard. What will the owner of the vineyard do? He will come and destroy the vine-growers, and will give the vineyard to others. Have you not even read this Scripture: 'THE STONE WHICH THE BUILDERS REJECTED, THIS BECAME THE CHIEF CORNER *stone*; THIS CAME ABOUT FROM THE LORD, AND IT IS MARVELOUS IN OUR EYES'?" (Mark 12:1–11, Jesus quotes from Psalm 118:22, 23; Isaiah 5:1, 2; cf. Matthew 21:33–46; Luke 20:9–19).

Setting: On the way from Galilee to Jerusalem. After some present report to Him about the Galileans whose blood Pilate (Roman governor of Judea) had mixed with their sacrifices, Jesus responds to their concern by calling them to repentance.

And Jesus said to them, "Do you suppose that these Galileans were *greater* sinners than all *other* Galileans because they suffered this *fate*? I tell you, no, but unless you repent, you will all likewise perish. Or do you suppose that those eighteen on whom the tower in Siloam fell and killed them were *worse* culprits than all the men who live in Jerusalem? I tell you, no, but unless you repent, you will all likewise perish." (Luke 13:2–5; see Luke 13:1; John 9:2, 3).

Setting: On the way from Galilee to Jerusalem. After responding to a guest's proclamation about the blessings of eating bread in the kingdom of God, Jesus presents to large crowds the demands of discipleship.

Now large crowds were going along with Him; and He turned and said to them, "If anyone comes to Me, and does not hate his own father and mother and wife and children and brothers and sisters, yes, and even his own life, he cannot be My disciple. Whoever does not carry his own cross and come after Me cannot be My disciple. For which one of you, when he wants to build a tower, does not first sit down and calculate the cost to see if he has enough to complete it? Otherwise, when he has laid a foundation and is not able to finish, all who observe it begin to ridicule him, saying, 'This man began to build and was not able to finish.' Or what king, when he sets out to meet another king in battle, will not first sit down and consider whether he is strong enough with ten thousand *men* to encounter the one coming against him with twenty thousand? Or else, while the other is still far away, he sends a delegation and asks for terms of peace. So then, none of you can be My disciple who does not give up all his possessions. Therefore, salt is good; but if even salt has become tasteless, with what will it be seasoned? It is useless either for the soil or for the manure pile; it is thrown out. He who has ears to hear, let him hear" (Luke 14:25–35; cf. Matthew 5:13; 10:37–39; see Proverb 20:18; Luke 14:1, 2; Philippians 3:7).

TOWN (Also see HOMETOWN; and TOWNS)

Setting: Jesus' hometown of Nazareth in Galilee. After encountering unbelief, Jesus sends the Twelve out in pairs with authority and instructions about ministry.

And He summoned the twelve and began to send them out in pairs, and gave them authority over the unclean spirits; and He instructed them that they should take nothing for *their* journey, except a mere staff—no bread, no bag, no money in their belt—but to wear sandals; and *He added,* "Do not put on two tunics." And He said to them, "Wherever you enter a house, stay there until you leave town. Any place that does not receive you or listen to you, as you go out from there, shake the dust off the soles of your feet for a testimony against them" (Mark 6:7–11; cf. Matthew 10:1–14; Luke 9:1–5).

TOWNS (Also see TOWN)

Setting: Capernaum in Galilee. Early in His ministry, after healing people and casting out demons, Jesus decides to take His disciples to a nearby town and preach.

He said to them, "Let us go somewhere else to the towns nearby, so that I may preach there also; for that is what I came for" (Mark 1:38; cf. Luke 4:43).

TRADITION (Also see MEN, PRECEPTS OF)

Setting: Galilee. Pharisees and scribes from Jerusalem accuse Jesus' disciples of disobeying tradition and the commandments.

And He answered and said to them, "Why do you yourselves transgress the commandment of God for the sake of tradition? For God said, 'HONOR YOUR FATHER AND MOTHER,' and, 'HE WHO SPEAKS EVIL OF FATHER OR MOTHER IS TO BE PUT TO DEATH.' But you say, 'Whoever says to *his* father or mother, "Whatever I have that would help you has been given *to God*," he is not to honor his father or mother.' And *by this* you invalidated the word of God for the sake of your tradition. You hypocrites, rightly did Isaiah prophesy of you: 'THIS PEOPLE HONORS ME WITH THEIR LIPS, BUT THEIR HEART IS FAR AWAY FROM ME. BUT IN VAIN DO THEY WORSHIP ME, TEACHING AS DOCTRINES THE PRECEPTS OF MEN'" (Matthew 15:3–9, Jesus quotes from Exodus 20:12, 21:17, Leviticus 20:9; Isaiah 29:13; cf. Mark 7:5–7; see Colossians 2:22).

Setting: Galilee. The Pharisees and some of the scribes from Jerusalem question why Jesus' disciples do not follow the tradition of ceremonial hand cleansing before eating bread.

And He said to them, "Rightly did Isaiah prophesy of you hypocrites, as it is written: 'THIS PEOPLE HONORS ME WITH THEIR LIPS, BUT THEIR HEART IS FAR AWAY FROM ME. BUT IN VAIN DO THEY WORSHIP ME, TEACHING AS DOCTRINES THE PRECEPTS OF MEN.' Neglecting the commandment of God, you hold to the tradition of men." He was also saying to them, "You are experts at setting aside the commandment of God in order to keep tradition. For Moses said, 'HONOR YOUR FATHER AND YOUR MOTHER'; and, 'HE WHO SPEAKS EVIL OF FATHER OR MOTHER, IS TO BE PUT TO DEATH'; but you say, 'If a man says to *his* father or *his* mother, whatever I have that would help you is Corban (that is to say, given *to God*),' you no longer permit him to do anything for *his* father or *his* mother; *thus* invalidating the word of God by your tradition which you have handed down; and you do many things such as that" (Mark 7:6–13, Jesus quotes from Exodus 20:12; 21:17; Isaiah 29:13; cf. Matthew 15:1–6).

TRADITION OF MEN

Setting: **Galilee. The Pharisees and some of the scribes from Jerusalem question why Jesus' disciples do not follow the tradition of ceremonial hand cleansing before eating bread.**

And He said to them, "Rightly did Isaiah prophesy of you hypocrites, as it is written: 'THIS PEOPLE HONORS ME WITH THEIR LIPS, BUT THEIR HEART IS FAR AWAY FROM ME. BUT IN VAIN DO THEY WORSHIP ME, TEACHING AS DOCTRINES THE PRECEPTS OF MEN.' Neglecting the commandment of God, you hold to the tradition of men." He was also saying to them, "You are experts at setting aside the commandment of God in order to keep tradition. For Moses said, 'HONOR YOUR FATHER AND YOUR MOTHER'; and, 'HE WHO SPEAKS EVIL OF FATHER OR MOTHER, IS TO BE PUT TO DEATH'; but you say, 'If a man says to *his* father or *his* mother, whatever I have that would help you is Corban (that is to say, given *to God*),' you no longer permit him to do anything for *his* father or *his* mother; *thus* invalidating the word of God by your tradition which you have handed down; and you do many things such as that" (Mark 7:6–13, Jesus quotes from Exodus 20:12; 21:17; Isaiah 29:13; cf. Matthew 15:1–6).

TRANSFIGURATION (Also see JESUS' GLORIFICATION)

[TRANSFIGURATION from vision]

Setting: **On a high mountain in Galilee. Jesus instructs Peter, James, and John to keep the Transfiguration, which has just occurred, secret until after His resurrection.**

As they were coming down from the mountain, Jesus commanded them, saying, "Tell the vision to no one until the Son of Man has risen from the dead" (Matthew 17:9; cf. Mark 9:9–13; Luke 9:28–36).

TRANSFIGURATION, PROPHECY OF JESUS'

[PROPHECY OF JESUS' TRANSFIGURATION from there are some of you who are standing here who will not taste death until they see the Son of Man coming in His kingdom]

Setting: **Near Caesarea Philippi. After rebuking Peter for trying to forbid Him to accomplish His earthly mission of dying and being resurrected, Jesus teaches His disciples about the costs of following Him.**

Then Jesus said to His disciples, "If anyone wishes to come after Me, he must deny himself, and take up his cross and follow Me. For whoever wishes to save his life will lose it; but whoever loses his life for My sake will find it. For what will it profit a man if he gains the whole world and forfeits his soul? Or what will a man give in exchange for his soul? For the Son of Man is going to come in the glory of His Father with His angels, and WILL THEN REPAY EVERY MAN ACCORDING TO HIS DEEDS. Truly, I say to you, there are some of you who are standing here who will not taste death until they see the Son of Man coming in His kingdom" (Matthew 16:24–28, Jesus quotes from Psalm 62:12; cf. Mark 8:34–37; Luke 9:23–27; see Matthew 10:38, 39).

[PROPHECY OF JESUS' TRANSFIGURATION from some of those standing here who will not taste death until they see the kingdom of God]

Setting: **Galilee. Following Peter's pronouncement that Jesus is the Christ of God, the Lord conveys the demands of discipleship and the hope regarding the kingdom of God.**

And He was saying to *them* all, "If anyone wishes to come after Me, he must deny himself, and take up his cross daily and follow Me. For whoever wishes to save his life will lose it, but whoever loses his life for My sake, he is the one who will save it. For what is a man profited if he gains the whole world, and loses or forfeits himself? For whoever is ashamed of Me and My words, the Son of Man will be ashamed of him when He comes in His glory, and *the glory* of the Father and of the holy angels. But I say to you truthfully, there are some of those standing here who will not taste death until they see the kingdom of God" (Luke 9:23–27; cf. Matthew 16:24–26, 28; Mark 8:34–37; see Matthew 10:33, 38, 39).

TRANSGRESSION (Also see SIN)

[TRANSGRESSION from transgress]

Setting: Galilee. Pharisees and scribes from Jerusalem question Jesus about His disciples' lack of obedience to tradition and the commandments.

And He answered and said to them, "Why do you yourselves transgress the commandment of God for the sake of tradition? For God said, 'HONOR YOUR FATHER AND MOTHER,' and, 'HE WHO SPEAKS EVIL OF FATHER OR MOTHER IS TO BE PUT TO DEATH.' But you say, 'Whoever says to *his* father or mother, "Whatever I have that would help you has been given *to God*," he is not to honor his father or mother.' And *by this* you invalidated the word of God for the sake of your tradition. You hypocrites, rightly did Isaiah prophesy of you: 'THIS PEOPLE HONORS ME WITH THEIR LIPS, BUT THEIR HEART IS FAR AWAY FROM ME. BUT IN VAIN DO THEY WORSHIP ME, TEACHING AS DOCTRINES THE PRECEPTS OF MEN' " (Matthew 15:3–9, Jesus quotes from Exodus 20:12, 21:17, Leviticus 20:9; Isaiah 29:13; cf. Mark 7:5–7; see Colossians 2:22).

TRANSGRESSIONS (Also see SINS)

Setting: Galilee. During the early part of His ministry, Jesus preaches the Sermon on the Mount to His disciples and the multitudes.

"For if you forgive others for their transgressions, your heavenly Father will also forgive you. But if you do not forgive others, then your Father will not forgive your transgressions" (Matthew 6:14, 15; cf. Matthew 18:15; see Mark 7:2).

Setting: Just outside Jerusalem. The day after Jesus instructs the money changers while He cleanses the temple, Peter draws the Lord's and His disciples' attention to an earlier-cursed fig tree.

And Jesus answered saying to them, "Have faith in God. Truly, I say to you, whoever says to this mountain, 'Be taken up and cast into the sea,' and does not doubt in his heart, but believes that what he says is going to happen, it will be *granted* him. Therefore I say to you, all things for which you pray and ask, believe that you have received them, and they will be *granted* you. Whenever you stand praying, forgive, if you have anything against anyone, so that your Father who is in heaven will also forgive you your transgressions. [But if you do not forgive, neither will your Father who is in heaven forgive your transgressions'] (Mark 11:22–26; cf. Matthew 21:19–22; see Matthew 6:14, 15; 7:7; 17:20).

TRANSGRESSORS (Also see SINNERS)

Setting: An upper room in Jerusalem. During the Feast of Unleavened Bread (Passover) just before His crucifixion, while celebrating the Passover meal, instituting the Lord's Supper, and prophesying Peter's denial of Him, Jesus instructs His disciples to prepare to persevere without Him.

And He said to them, "When I sent you out without money belt and bag and sandals, you did not lack anything, did you?" They said, "*No*, nothing." And He said to them, "But now, whoever has a money belt is to take it along, likewise also a bag, and whoever has no sword is to sell his coat and buy one. For I tell you that this which is written must be fulfilled in Me, 'AND HE WAS NUMBERED WITH TRANSGRESSORS'; for that which refers to Me has *its* fulfillment." They said, "Lord, look, here are two swords." And He said to them, "It is enough" (Luke 22:35–38, Jesus quotes from Isaiah 53:12; see Matthew 10:5–15; Mark 6:7–11; Luke 9:1–5; 10:1–12; 22:49; John 17:4).

TRAP (Also see JESUS, TESTING)

Setting: The Mount of Olives, east of the temple in Jerusalem. After ministering in the temple a few days before His crucifixion, and conveying the Parable of the Fig Tree during His Olivet Discourse, Jesus warns His disciples to keep alert regarding future events.

"Be on guard, so that your hearts will not be weighted down with dissipation and drunkenness and the worries of life, and that day will not come upon you suddenly like a trap; for it will come upon all those who dwell on the face of all the earth. But keep on the alert at all times, praying that you may have strength to escape all these things that are about to take place, and to stand before the Son of Man" (Luke 21:34–36; cf. Mark 13:33; see Matthew 24:42–44).

TRAVEL (Also see JOURNEY)

Setting: The temple in Jerusalem. After the Jewish religious leaders test Him with questions, Jesus pronounces the third of eight woes upon them in front of the crowds and His disciples.

"Woe to you, scribes and Pharisees, hypocrites, because you travel around on sea and land to make one proselyte; and when he becomes one, you make him twice as much a son of hell as yourselves" (Matthew 23:15).

TREASURE (Specifics such as TREASURE, EVIL; and TREASURE, GOOD are separate entries; also see POSSESSIONS; PRIORITIES; RICHES; TREASURE, EARTHLY; TREASURE, HEAVENLY; and TREASURES)

Setting: Galilee. During the early part of His ministry, Jesus preaches the Sermon on the Mount to His disciples and the multitudes.

"Do not store up for yourselves treasures on earth, where moth and rust destroy, and where thieves break in and steal. But store up for yourselves treasures in heaven, where neither moth nor rust destroys, and where thieves do not break in or steal; for where your treasure is, there your heart will be also" (Matthew 6:19–21; cf. Luke 12:34; see Proverb 23:4; Matthew 19:21).

Setting: By the Sea of Galilee. Because the religious leaders are rejecting His message, Jesus continues teaching the crowds with the Parable of the Hidden Treasure.

"The kingdom of heaven is like a treasure hidden in the field, which a man found and hid *again;* and from joy over it he goes and sells all that he has and buys that field" (Matthew 13:44).

Setting: By the Sea of Galilee. Jesus teaches the Parable of the Head of a Household to His disciples.

And Jesus said to them, "Therefore every scribe who has become a disciple of the kingdom of heaven is like a head of a household, who brings out of his treasure things new and old" (Matthew 13:52).

Setting: Judea beyond the Jordan (Perea). Jesus shares with a rich, young ruler how righteous believers may have treasure in heaven.

And He said to him, "Why are you asking Me about what is good? There is *only* One who is good; but if you wish to enter into life, keep the commandments." *Then* he said to Him, 'Which ones?' And Jesus said, "YOU SHALL NOT COMMIT MURDER; YOU SHALL NOT COMMIT ADULTERY; YOU SHALL NOT STEAL; YOU SHALL NOT BEAR FALSE WITNESS; HONOR YOUR FATHER AND MOTHER; and YOU SHALL LOVE YOUR NEIGHBOR AS YOURSELF." The young man said to Him, "All these things I have kept; what am I still lacking?" Jesus said to him, "If you wish to complete go *and* sell your possessions and give to *the* poor, and you will have treasure in heaven; and come, follow Me" (Matthew 19:16–22, Jesus quotes from Exodus 20:13–15; Leviticus 19:18; cf. Leviticus 18:5; Mark 10:17–21; Luke 10:25–28; 12:33; 18:18–24).

Setting: Judea beyond the Jordan (Perea). After demonstrating to His disciples the importance of little children, Jesus encounters a rich man seeking eternal life.

And Jesus said to him, "Why do you call Me good? No one is good except God alone. You know the commandments, 'DO NOT MURDER, DO NOT COMMIT ADULTERY, DO NOT STEAL, DO NOT BEAR FALSE WITNESS, Do not defraud, HONOR YOUR FATHER AND MOTHER.'" And he said to Him, "Teacher, I have kept all these things from my youth up." Looking at him, Jesus felt a love for him and said to him, "One thing you lack: go and sell all you possess and give to the poor, and you will have treasure in heaven; and come, follow Me" (Mark 10:18–21; Jesus quotes from Exodus 20:12–16; cf. Matthew 19:16–22; Luke 18:18–24; see Matthew 6:20).

Setting: On the way from Galilee to Jerusalem. After the scribes and Pharisees turn hostile and question Him repeatedly in an attempt to catch Him in something He might say, Jesus responds to a question from the crowd and gives a parable about riches and greed.

And He told them a parable, saying, "The land of a rich man was very productive. And he began reasoning to himself, saying, 'What shall I do, since I have no place to store my crops?' Then he said, 'This is what I will do: I will tear down my barns and build larger ones, and here I will store all my grain and my goods. And I will say to my soul, "Soul, you have many goods laid up for many years *to come;* take your ease, eat, drink *and* be merry."' But God said to him, 'You fool! This *very* night your soul is required of you; and *now* who will own what you have prepared?' So is the man who stores up treasure for himself, and is not rich toward God" (Luke 12:16–21; see Job 27:8; Psalm 39:6; Ecclesiastes 12:9; Philippians 2:3).

Setting: On the way from Galilee to Jerusalem. After giving a parable about riches and greed, Jesus challenges the crowd and His disciples concerning godly living.

"Sell your possessions and give to charity; make yourselves money belts which do not wear out, an unfailing treasure in heaven, where no thief comes near nor moth destroys. For where your treasure is, there your heart will be also" (Luke 12:33, 34; cf. Matthew 6:19–21; 19:21).

Setting: Judea beyond the Jordan (Perea). After speaking of the importance of children, Jesus responds to a ruler's question about inheriting eternal life.

A ruler questioned Him, saying, "Good Teacher, what shall I do to inherit eternal life?" And Jesus said to him, "Why do you call Me good? No one is good except God alone. You know the commandments, 'DO NOT COMMIT ADULTERY, DO NOT MURDER, DO NOT STEAL, DO NOT BEAR FALSE WITNESS, HONOR YOUR FATHER AND MOTHER.'" And he said "All these things I have kept from *my* youth." When Jesus heard *this,* He said to him, "One thing you still lack; sell all that you possess and distribute it to the poor, and you shall have treasure in heaven; and come, follow Me" (Luke 18:18–22, Jesus quotes from Exodus 20:12–16; cf. Matthew 19:16–22; Mark 10:17–22; see Luke 10:25–28).

TREASURE, EARTHLY (See POSSESSIONS; RICHES; TREASURE; TREASURE, HEAVENLY; TREASURES; and WEALTH)

TREASURE, EVIL (Also see TREASURE)

Setting: Galilee. After Jesus heals a blind, mute, demon-possessed man, the Pharisees accuse the Lord in front of crowds of being a worker of Satan.

"Either make the tree good and its fruit good, or make the tree bad and its fruit bad; for the tree is known by its fruit. You brood of vipers, how can you, being evil, speak what is good? For the mouth speaks out of that which fills the heart. The good man brings out of *his* good treasure what is good; and the evil man brings out of *his* evil treasure what is evil. But I tell you that every careless word that people speak, they shall give an accounting for it in the day of judgment. For by your words you will be justified, and by your words you will be condemned" (Matthew 12:33–37; cf. Matthew 3:7; 7:16–18).

Setting: Galilee. After selecting His twelve disciples, Jesus teaches the Sermon on the Mount to those disciples and a great throng of people from Judea, Jerusalem, and the central coastal region of Tyre and Sidon.

And He also spoke a parable to them: "A blind man cannot guide a blind man, can he? Will they not both fall into a pit? A pupil is not above his teacher; but everyone, after he has been fully trained, will be like his teacher. Why do you look at the speck that is in your brother's eye, but do not notice the log that is in your own eye? Or how can you say to your brother, 'Brother, let me take out the speck that is in your eye,' when you yourself do not see the log that is in your own eye? You hypocrite, first take the log out of your own eye, and then you will see clearly to take out the speck that is in your brother's eye. For there is no good tree which produces bad fruit, nor, on the other hand, a bad tree which produces good fruit. For each tree is known by its own fruit. For men do not gather figs from thorns, nor do they pick grapes from a briar bush. The good man out of the good treasure of his heart brings forth what is good; and the evil *man* out of the evil *treasure* brings forth what is evil; for his mouth speaks from that which fills his heart" (Luke 6:39–45; cf. Matthew 7:3–6. 16, 18, 20; 12:35; see Matthew 10:24; 15:14; Luke 6:12–19).

TREASURE, GOOD (Also see TREASURE)

Setting: Galilee. After Jesus heals a blind, mute, demon-possessed man, the Pharisees accuse the Lord in front of crowds of being a worker of Satan.

"Either make the tree good and its fruit good, or make the tree bad and its fruit bad; for the tree is known by its fruit. You brood of vipers, how can you, being evil, speak what is good? For the mouth speaks out of that which fills the heart. The good man brings out of *his* good treasure what is good; and the evil man brings out of *his* evil treasure what is evil. But I tell you that every careless word that people speak, they shall give an accounting for it in the day of judgment. For by your words you will be justified, and by your words you will be condemned" (Matthew 12:33–37; cf. Matthew 3:7; 7:16–18).

Setting: Galilee. After selecting His twelve disciples, Jesus teaches the Sermon on the Mount to those disciples and a great throng of people from Judea, Jerusalem, and the central coastal region of Tyre and Sidon.

And He also spoke a parable to them: "A blind man cannot guide a blind man, can he? Will they not both fall into a pit? A pupil is not above his teacher; but everyone, after he has been fully trained, will be like his teacher. Why do you look at the speck that is in your brother's eye, but do not notice the log that is in your own eye? Or how can you say to your brother, 'Brother, let me take out the speck that is in your eye,' when you yourself do not see the log that is in your own eye? You hypocrite, first take the log out of your own eye, and then you will see clearly to take out the speck that is in your brother's eye. For there is no good tree which produces bad fruit, nor, on the other hand, a bad tree which produces good fruit. For each tree is known by its own fruit. For men do not gather figs from thorns, nor do they pick grapes from a briar bush. The good man out of the good treasure of his heart brings forth what is good; and the evil *man* out of the evil *treasure* brings forth what is evil; for his mouth speaks from that which fills his heart" (Luke 6:39–45; cf. Matthew 7:3–6. 16, 18, 20; 12:35; see Matthew 10:24; 15:14; Luke 6:12–19).

TREASURE, HEAVENLY (See HEAVEN, TREASURE IN)

TREASURE, PARABLE OF THE HIDDEN

[TREASURE, PARABLE OF THE HIDDEN from treasure hidden]

Setting: By the Sea of Galilee. Because the religious leaders are rejecting His message, Jesus continues teaching the crowds with the Parable of the Hidden Treasure.

"The kingdom of heaven is like a treasure hidden in the field, which a man found and hid *again;* and from joy over it he goes and sells all that he has and buys that field" (Matthew 13:44).

TREASURE IN HEAVEN (Listed under HEAVEN, TREASURE IN)

TREASURES (Also see PRIORITIES; REWARDS; RICHES; and TREASURE)

Setting: Galilee. During the early part of His ministry, Jesus preaches the Sermon on the Mount to His disciples and the multitudes.

"Do not store up for yourselves treasures on earth, where moth and rust destroy, and where thieves break in and steal. But store up for yourselves treasures in heaven, where neither moth nor rust destroys, and where thieves do not break in or steal; for where your treasure is, there your heart will be also" (Matthew 6:19–21; cf. Luke 12:34; see Proverb 23:4; Matthew 19:21).

TREASURES, EARTHLY (See TREASURES)

TREASURY

Setting: Opposite the temple treasury in Jerusalem. Jesus focuses His disciples' attention on a poor widow's monetary sacrifice.

Calling His disciples to Him, He said to them, "Truly I say to you, this poor widow put in more than all the contributors to the treasury; for they all put in out of their surplus, but she, out of her poverty, put in all she owned, all she had to live on" (Mark 12:43, 44; cf. Luke 21:1–4).

TREE (Specifics such as TREE, BAD; TREE, FIG; and TREE, GOOD are separate entries; also see BRANCH; BRANCHES; LEAVES; ROOT; and TREES)

Setting: Galilee. During the early part of His ministry, Jesus preaches the Sermon on the Mount to His disciples and the multitudes.

"Beware of the false prophets, who come to you in sheep's clothing, but inwardly are ravenous wolves. You will know them by their fruits. Grapes are not gathered from *bushes* nor figs from thistles, are they? So every good tree bears good fruit, but the bad tree bears bad fruit. A good tree cannot produce bad fruit, nor can a bad tree produce good fruit. Every tree that does not bear good fruit is cut down and thrown into the fire. So then, you will know them by their fruits" (Matthew 7:15–20; cf. Matthew 3:10; 12:33, 35; 24:11, 24; Luke 6:43, 44; see 2 Peter 2:1).

Setting: Galilee. After Jesus heals a blind, mute, demon-possessed man, the Pharisees accuse the Lord in front of crowds of being a worker of Satan.

"Either make the tree good and its fruit good, or make the tree bad and its fruit bad; for the tree is known by its fruit. You brood of vipers, how can you, being evil, speak what is good? For the mouth speaks out of that which fills the heart. The good man brings out of *his* good treasure what is good; and the evil man brings out of *his* evil treasure what is evil. But I tell you that every careless word that people speak, they shall give an accounting for it in the day of judgment. For by your words you will be justified, and by your words you will be condemned" (Matthew 12:33–37; cf. Matthew 3:7; 7:16–18).

Setting: By the Sea of Galilee. Because the religious leaders are rejecting His message, Jesus continues teaching the crowds with the Parable of the Mustard Seed.

He presented another parable to them, saying, "The kingdom of heaven is like a mustard seed, which a man took and sowed in his field; and this is smaller than all *other* seeds, but when it is full grown, it is larger than the garden plants and becomes a tree, so that THE BIRDS OF THE AIR come and NEST IN ITS BRANCHES" (Matthew 13:31, 32, Jesus quotes from Ezekiel 17:23; cf. Mark 4:30–32; Luke 13:18, 19).

Setting: Galilee. After selecting His twelve disciples, Jesus teaches the Sermon on the Mount to those disciples and a great throng of people from Judea, Jerusalem, and the central coastal region of Tyre and Sidon.

And He also spoke a parable to them: "A blind man cannot guide a blind man, can he? Will they not both fall into a pit? A pupil is not above his teacher; but everyone, after he has been fully trained, will be like his teacher. Why do you look at the speck that is in your brother's eye, but do not notice the log that is in your own eye? Or how can you say to your brother, 'Brother, let me take out the speck that is in your eye,' when you yourself do not see the log that is in your own eye? You hypocrite, first take the log out of your own eye, and then you will see clearly to take out the speck that is in your brother's eye. For there is no good tree which produces bad fruit, nor, on the other hand, a bad tree which produces good fruit. For each tree is known by its own fruit. For men do not gather figs from thorns, nor do they pick grapes from a briar bush. The good man out of the good treasure of his heart brings forth what is good; and the evil *man* out of the evil *treasure* brings forth what is evil; for his mouth speaks from that which fills his heart" (Luke 6:39–45; cf. Matthew 7:3–6. 16, 18, 20; 12:35; see Matthew 10:24; 15:14; Luke 6:12–19).

Setting: On the way from Galilee to Jerusalem. After responding to a synagogue official's anger over His healing of a woman, sick for eighteen years, in the synagogue on the Sabbath, Jesus conveys the Parable of the Mustard Seed and the Parable of the Leaven.

So He was saying, "What is the kingdom of God like, and to what shall I compare it? It is like a mustard seed which a man took and threw into his own garden; and it grew and became a tree, and THE BIRDS OF THE AIR NESTED IN ITS BRANCHES." And again He said, "To what shall I compare the kingdom of God? It is like leaven, which a woman took and hid in three pecks of flour until it was all leavened" (Luke 13:18–21, Jesus quotes from Ezekiel 17:23; cf. Matthew 13:31–34; Mark 4:30–32).

Setting: Jerusalem. After being arrested, and appearing before the Council of Elders (Sanhedrin), Pilate (Roman governor of Judea), Herod Antipas (tetrarch of Galilee and Perea), and Pilate a second time (when the ruler bows to the crowd's pressure and grants that Jesus be crucified), the Lord prophesies to the women mourning Him regarding the coming judgment of Jerusalem.

But Jesus turning to them said, "Daughters of Jerusalem, stop weeping for Me, but weep for yourselves and for your children. For behold, the days are coming when they will say, 'Blessed are the barren, and the wombs that never bore, and the breasts that never nursed.' Then they will begin TO SAY TO THE MOUNTAINS, 'FALL ON US,' AND TO THE HILLS, 'COVER US.' For if they do these things when the tree is green, what will happen when it is dry?" (Luke 23:28–31, Jesus quotes from Hosea 10:8; see Matthew 24:19).

Setting: On the island of Patmos (in the Aegean Sea about fifty miles southwest of Ephesus in modern Turkey). On the Lord's Day (Sunday), approximately fifty years after the Resurrection, the disciple John encounters the Lord Jesus Christ, who communicates a new revelation for the apostle to record for the church in Ephesus and to six other churches in Asia.

"To the angel of the church in Ephesus write: The One who holds the seven stars in His right hand, the One who walks among the seven golden lampstands, says this: 'I know your deeds and your toil and perseverance, and that you cannot tolerate evil men, and you put to the test those who call themselves apostles, and they are not, and you found them *to be* false; and you have perseverance and have endured for My name's sake, and have not grown weary. But I have *this* against you, that you have left your first love. Therefore remember from where you have fallen, and repent and do the deeds you did at first; or else I am coming to you and will remove your lampstand out of its place—unless you repent. Yet this you do have, that you hate the deeds of the Nicolaitans, which I also hate. He who has an ear, let him hear what the Spirit says to the churches. To him who overcomes, I will grant to eat of the tree of life which is in the Paradise of God'" (Revelation 2:1–7; see Genesis 2:9; Ezekiel 28:13; 1 John 4:1; Revelation 1:10, 11, 19, 20).

TREE, BAD

Setting: Galilee. During the early part of His ministry, Jesus preaches the Sermon on the Mount to His disciples and the multitudes.

"Beware of the false prophets, who come to you in sheep's clothing, but inwardly are ravenous wolves. You will know them by their fruits. Grapes are not gathered from *bushes* nor figs from thistles, are they? So every good tree bears good fruit, but the bad tree bears bad fruit. A good tree cannot produce bad fruit, nor can a bad tree produce good fruit. Every tree that does not bear good fruit is cut down and thrown into the fire. So then, you will know them by their fruits" (Matthew 7:15–20; cf. Matthew 3:10; 12:33, 35; 24:11, 24; Luke 6:43, 44).

[BAD TREE from tree bad]
Setting: Galilee. After Jesus heals a blind, mute, demon-possessed man, the Pharisees accuse the Lord in front of crowds of being a worker of Satan.

"Either make the tree good and its fruit good, or make the tree bad and its fruit bad; for the tree is known by its fruit. You brood of vipers, how can you, being evil, speak what is good? For the mouth speaks out of that which fills the heart. The good man brings out of *his* good treasure what is good; and the evil man brings out of *his* evil treasure what is evil. But I tell you that every careless word that people speak, they shall give an accounting for it in the day of judgment. For by your words you will be justified, and by your words you will be condemned" (Matthew 12:33–37; cf. Matthew 3:7; 7:16–18).

Setting: Galilee. After selecting His twelve disciples, Jesus teaches the Sermon on the Mount to those disciples and a great throng of people from Judea, Jerusalem, and the central coastal region of Tyre and Sidon.

And He also spoke a parable to them: "A blind man cannot guide a blind man, can he? Will they not both fall into a pit? A pupil is not above his teacher; but everyone, after he has been fully trained, will be like his teacher. Why do you look at the speck that is in your brother's eye, but do not notice the log that is in your own eye? Or how can you say to your brother, 'Brother, let me take out the speck that is in your eye,' when you yourself do not see the log that is in your own eye? You hypocrite, first take the log out of your own eye, and then you will see clearly to take out the speck that is in your brother's eye. For there is no good tree which produces bad fruit, nor, on the other hand, a bad tree which produces good fruit. For each tree is known by its own fruit. For men do not gather figs from thorns, nor do they pick grapes from a briar bush. The good man out of the good treasure of his heart brings forth what is good; and the evil *man* out of the evil *treasure* brings forth what is evil; for his mouth speaks from that which fills his heart" (Luke 6:39–45; cf. Matthew 7:3–6. 16, 18, 20; 12:35; see Matthew 10:24; 15:14; Luke 6:12–19).

TREE, FIG (TREE, PARABLE OF THE FIG listed as a separate entry)

Setting: On the way from Bethany to Jerusalem. The day after Jesus curses a fig tree (an illustration of the nation Israel), His disciples ask Him how it has so quickly withered.

And Jesus answered and said to them, "Truly I say to you, if you have faith and do not doubt, you will not only do what was done to the fig tree, but even if you say to this mountain, 'Be taken up and cast into the sea,' it will happen. And all things you ask in prayer, believing, you will receive" (Matthew 21:21, 22; cf. Matthew 7:7; 17:20; Mark 11:20–24).

[FIG TREE from Mark 11:13]

Setting: Near the town of Bethany. Following His triumphal entry into Jerusalem, days before His death on the cross, Jesus curses a fig tree that has no fruit on it.

He said to it, "May no one ever eat fruit from you again!" And His disciples were listening (Mark 11:14; cf. Matthew 21:18, 19).

Setting: Galilee. After beginning His public ministry and choosing His first disciples, Andrew and Simon (Peter) near Bethany beyond the Jordan, and Philip in Galilee, Jesus calls Philip's friend, Nathanael, (some believe he may have been also called Bartholomew) as His next follower.

Jesus saw Nathanael coming to Him, and said of him, "Behold, an Israelite indeed, in whom there is no deceit!" Nathanael said to Him, "How do you know me?" Jesus answered and said to him, "Before Philip called you, when you were under the fig tree, I saw you." Nathanael answered Him, "Rabbi, You are the Son of God; You are the King of Israel." Jesus answered and said to him, "Because I said to you that I saw you under the fig tree, do you believe? You will see greater things than these." And He said to him, "Truly, truly, I say to you, you will see the heavens opened and the angels of God ascending and descending on the Son of Man" (John 1:47–51).

TREE, GOOD

Setting: Galilee. During the early part of His ministry, Jesus preaches the Sermon on the Mount to His disciples and the multitudes.

"Beware of the false prophets, who come to you in sheep's clothing, but inwardly are ravenous wolves. You will know them by their fruits. Grapes are not gathered from *bushes* nor figs from thistles, are they? So every good tree bears good fruit, but the bad tree bears bad fruit. A good tree cannot produce bad fruit, nor can a bad tree produce good fruit. Every tree that does not bear good fruit is cut down and thrown into the fire. So then, you will know them by their fruits" (Matthew 7:15–20; cf. Matthew 3:10; 12:33, 35; 24:11, 24; Luke 6:43, 44).

[GOOD TREE from tree good]

Setting: Galilee. After Jesus heals a blind, mute, demon-possessed man, the Pharisees accuse the Lord in front of crowds of being a worker of Satan.

"Either make the tree good and its fruit good, or make the tree bad and its fruit bad; for the tree is known by its fruit. You brood of vipers, how can you, being evil, speak what is good? For the mouth speaks out of that which fills the heart. The good man brings out of *his* good treasure what is good; and the evil man brings out of *his* evil treasure what is evil. But I tell you that every careless word that people speak, they shall give an accounting for it in the day of judgment. For by your words you will be justified, and by your words you will be condemned" (Matthew 12:33–37; cf. Matthew 3:7; 7:16–18).

Setting: Galilee. After selecting His twelve disciples, Jesus teaches the Sermon on the Mount to those disciples and a great throng of people from Judea, Jerusalem, and the central coastal region of Tyre and Sidon.

And He also spoke a parable to them: "A blind man cannot guide a blind man, can he? Will they not both fall into a pit? A pupil is not above his teacher; but everyone, after he has been fully trained, will be like his teacher. Why do you look at the speck that is in your brother's eye, but do not notice the log that is in your own eye? Or how can you say to your brother, 'Brother, let me take out the speck that is in your eye,' when you yourself do not see the log that is in your own eye? You hypocrite, first take the log out of your own eye, and then you will see clearly to take out the speck that is in your brother's eye. For there is no good tree which produces bad fruit, nor, on the other hand, a bad tree which produces good fruit. For each tree is known by its own fruit. For men do not gather figs from thorns, nor do they pick grapes from a briar bush. The good man out of the good treasure of his heart brings forth what is good; and the evil *man* out of the evil *treasure* brings forth what is evil; for his mouth speaks from that which fills his heart" (Luke 6:39–45; cf. Matthew 7:3–6. 16, 18, 20; 12:35; see Matthew 10:24; 15:14; Luke 6:12–19).

TREE, MULBERRY

Setting: On the way from Galilee to Jerusalem. After His disciples ask that their faith be increased following His instruction to them on forgiveness, the Lord illustrates with the mustard seed and an obedient slave.

And the Lord said, "If you had faith like a mustard seed, you would say to this mulberry tree, 'Be uprooted and be planted in the sea'; and it would obey you. Which of you, having a slave plowing or tending sheep, will say to him when he has come from the field, 'Come immediately and sit down to eat'? But will he not say to him, "Prepare something for me to eat, and *properly* clothe yourself and serve me while I eat and drink; and afterward you may eat and drink'? He does not thank the slave because he did the things which were commanded, does he? So you too, when you do all the things which are commanded you, say, 'We are unworthy slaves; we have done *only* that which we ought to have done'" (Luke 17:6–10; see Matthew 13:31; Luke 12:37).

TREE, PARABLE OF THE FIG (Also see TREE, PARABLE OF THE UNFRUITFUL FIG)

[PARABLE OF THE FIG TREE from parable from the fig tree]

Setting: On the Mount of Olives, just east of Jerusalem. During His Olivet Discourse, after answering His disciples' questions as to when the temple will be destroyed and Jerusalem overrun, along with the signs of His coming and the end of the age, Jesus teaches them the Parable of the Fig Tree.

"Now learn the parable from the fig tree: when its branch has already become tender and puts forth its leaves, you know that summer is near; so, you too, when you see all these things, recognize that He is near, *right* at the door. Truly, I say to you, this generation will not pass away until all these things take place. Heaven and earth will pass away, but My words will not pass away. But of that day and hour no one knows, not even the angels of heaven, nor the Son, but the Father alone. For the coming of the Son of Man will be just like the days of Noah. For as in those days before the flood they were eating and drinking, marrying and giving in marriage, until the day that Noah entered the ark, and they did not understand until the flood came and took them all away; so will the coming of the Son of Man be. Then there will be two men in the field; one will be taken and one will be left. Two women *will be* grinding at the mill; one will be taken and one will be left" (Matthew 24:32–41; cf. Mark 13:28–32; Luke 17:34–36; 21:28–33; see Genesis 6:5; 7:7; Matthew 5:18; 10:23; James 5:9).

[PARABLE OF THE FIG TREE from parable from the fig tree]

Setting: On the Mount of Olives, east of the temple in Jerusalem. After prophesying the temple's destruction, Jesus responds during His Olivet Discourse to questions from Peter, James, John, and Andrew about other future events.

"Now learn the parable from the fig tree: when its branch has already become tender and puts forth its leaves, you know that summer is near. Even so, you too, when you see these things happening, recognize that He is near, *right* at the door. Truly I say to you, this generation will not pass away until all these things take place. Heaven and earth will pass away, but My words will not pass away. But of the day or hour no one knows, not even the angels in heaven, nor the Son, but the Father *alone*" (Mark 13:28–32; cf. Matthew 24:32–36; Luke 21:28–33).

[PARABLE OF THE FIG TREE from parable and fig tree]
Setting: On the way from Galilee to Jerusalem. After some present report to Him about the Galileans whose blood Pilate (Roman governor of Judea) had mixed with their sacrifices, Jesus responds to their concern by calling them to repentance and illustrating His point with a parable.

And He *began* telling this parable: "A man had a fig tree which had been planted in his vineyard; and he came looking for fruit on it and did not find any. And he said to the vineyard-keeper, 'Behold, for three years I have come looking for fruit on this fig tree without finding any. Cut it down! Why does it even use up the ground?' And he answered and said to him, 'Let it alone, sir, for this year too, until I dig around it and put fertilizer; and if it bears fruit next year, *fine*; but if not, cut it down'" (Luke 13:6–9; see Matthew 3:10).

[PARABLE OF THE FIG TREE from parable and fig tree]
Setting: On the Mount of Olives, east of the temple in Jerusalem. After ministering in the temple a few days before His crucifixion, and giving the disciples more details regarding His return, Jesus conveys the Parable of the Fig Tree during His Olivet Discourse.

Then He told them a parable: "Behold the fig tree and all the trees; as soon as they put forth *leaves,* you see it and know for yourselves that summer is now near. So you also, when you see these things happening, recognize that the kingdom of God is near. Truly, I say to you, this generation will not pass away until all things take place. Heaven and earth will pass away, but My words will not pass away" (Luke 21:29–33; cf. Matthew 24:32–35; Mark 13:28–31; see Matthew 5:18).

TREE, PARABLE OF THE UNFRUITFUL FIG

[PARABLE OF THE UNFRUITFUL FIG TREE from parable; fig tree; and looking for fruit on it and did not find any]
Setting: On the way from Galilee to Jerusalem. After some present report to Him about the Galileans whose blood Pilate (Roman governor of Judea) had mixed with their sacrifices, Jesus responds to their concern by calling them to repentance and illustrating His point with a parable.

And He *began* telling this parable: "A man had a fig tree which had been planted in his vineyard; and he came looking for fruit on it and did not find any. And he said to the vineyard-keeper, 'Behold, for three years I have come looking for fruit on this fig tree without finding any. Cut it down! Why does it even use up the ground?' And he answered and said to him, 'Let it alone, sir, for this year too, until I dig around it and put fertilizer; and if it bears fruit next year, *fine*; but if not, cut it down'" (Luke 13:6–9; see Matthew 3:10).

TREE OF LIFE

Setting: On the island of Patmos (in the Aegean Sea about fifty miles southwest of Ephesus in modern Turkey). On the Lord's Day (Sunday), about fifty years after Jesus' resurrection, the disciple John encounters the Lord Jesus Christ, who communicates a new revelation for the apostle to record for the church in Ephesus and to six other churches in Asia.

"To the angel of the church in Ephesus write: The One who holds the seven stars in His right hand, the One who walks among the seven golden lampstands, says this: 'I know your deeds and your toil and perseverance, and that you cannot tolerate evil men, and you put to the test those who call themselves apostles, and they are not, and you found them *to be* false; and you have perseverance and have endured for My name's sake, and have not grown weary. But I have *this* against you, that you have left your first love. Therefore remember from where you have fallen, and repent and do the deeds you did at first; or else I am coming to you and will remove your lampstand out of its place—unless you repent. Yet this you do have, that you hate the deeds of the Nicolaitans, which I also hate. He who has an ear, let him hear what the Spirit says to the churches. To him who overcomes, I will grant to eat of the tree of life which is in the Paradise of God' " (Revelation 2:1–7; see Genesis 2:9; Ezekiel 28:13; 1 John 4:1; Revelation 1:10, 11, 19, 20).

TREES (Also see TREE)

Setting: On the Mount of Olives, east of the temple in Jerusalem. After ministering in the temple a few days before His crucifixion, and giving the disciples more details regarding His return, Jesus conveys the Parable of the Fig Tree during His Olivet Discourse.

Then He told them a parable: "Behold the fig tree and all the trees; as soon as they put forth *leaves,* you see it and know for yourselves that summer is now near. So you also, when you see these things happening, recognize that the kingdom of God is near. Truly, I say to you, this generation will not pass away until all things take place. Heaven and earth will pass away, but My words will not pass away" (Luke 21:29–33; cf. Matthew 24:32–35; Mark 13:28–31; see Matthew 5:18).

TRIALS (Also see PERSECUTION; and SUFFERING)

Setting: An upper room in Jerusalem. During the Feast of Unleavened Bread (Passover) just before His crucifixion, Jesus celebrates the Passover meal with His disciples and institutes the Lord's Supper. The disciples later argue over who is the greatest among them.

"You are those who have stood by Me in My trials; for just as My Father has granted Me a kingdom, I grant you that you may eat and drink at My table in My kingdom, and you will sit on thrones judging the twelve tribes of Israel" (Luke 22:28–30; cf. Matthew 19:28).

TRIALS, JESUS' RESPONSES AT HIS OFFICIAL

Setting: Jerusalem. After being betrayed by Judas and arrested, Jesus appears before Caiaphas the high priest and the Council for interrogation aimed at entrapping Him.

Jesus said to him, "You have said it *yourself;* nevertheless I tell you, hereafter you will see THE SON OF MAN SITTING AT THE RIGHT HAND OF POWER, AND COMING ON THE CLOUDS OF HEAVEN" (Matthew 26:64, Jesus quotes from Daniel 7:13; cf. Mark 14:62).

Setting: Jerusalem. Jesus verifies His true identity in front of the Roman governor of Judea, Pontius Pilate, prior to the crucifixion.

Now Jesus stood before the governor, and the governor questioned Him, saying, "Are You the King of the Jews?" And Jesus said to him, "*It is as* you say" (Matthew 27:11; cf. Mark 15:2, Luke 23:3; John 18:33, 34).

Setting: Jerusalem. Following His betrayal by Judas and His arrest, Jesus confirms for the high priest and all the chief priests that He is the Christ, as they seek justification for putting Him to death.

And Jesus said, "I am; and you shall see THE SON OF MAN SITTING AT THE RIGHT HAND OF POWER, and COMING WITH THE CLOUDS OF HEAVEN" (Mark 14:62, Jesus quotes from Psalm 110:1; Daniel 7:13; cf. Matthew 26:57–68; see Luke 22:54).

Setting: Jerusalem. Following Jesus' betrayal by Judas and arrest, after questioning Him, the chief priests, elders, and scribes deliver Him to Pontius Pilate (Roman governor of Judea) for further interrogation.

Pilate questioned Him, "Are You the King of the Jews?" And He answered him, "*It is as* you say" (Mark 15:2; cf. Matthew 27:2, 11–14; Luke 23:1–5; John 18:28–38).

Setting: Jerusalem. After being arrested, having Peter deny Him, and being mocked and beaten, with His crucifixion imminent, Jesus appears before the Sanhedrin (Council of Elders).

"If You are the Christ, tell us." But He said to them, "If I tell you, you will not believe; and if I ask you a question, you will not answer. But from now on THE SON OF MAN WILL BE SEATED AT THE RIGHT HAND of the power OF GOD." And they all said, "Are You the Son of God, then? And He said to them, "Yes, I am" (Luke 22:67–70, Jesus quotes from Psalm 110:1; cf. Matthew 26:57–65; Mark 14:55–65).

Setting: Jerusalem. After being arrested, mocked, and beaten, and appearing before the Council of Elders (Sanhedrin), with His crucifixion imminent, Jesus is brought before Pontius Pilate, Roman governor of Judea.

So Pilate asked Him, saying, "Are You the King of the Jews?" And He answered him and said, "*It is as* you say" (Luke 23:3; cf. Matthew 27:11–14; Mark 15:2–5; John 18:33–38; see Luke 22:70).

Setting: Jerusalem. After Jesus is betrayed by Judas, and Peter denies he is the Lord's disciple, Annas, former high priest and father-in-law of the current high priest (Caiaphas), questions Jesus about His disciples and His teaching.

Jesus answered him, "I have spoken openly to the world; I always taught in synagogues and in the temple, where all the Jews come together; and I spoke nothing in secret. Why do you question Me? Question those who have heard what I spoke to them; they know what I said" (John 18:20, 21; see John 7:26).

Setting: Jerusalem. After Jesus is betrayed by Judas and arrested by the Roman cohort, one of the officers strikes the Lord when he believes He exhibits disrespect to Annas with His response to the former high priest's question about His disciples and His teaching.

Jesus answered him, "If I have spoken wrongly, testify of the wrong; but if rightly, why do you strike Me?" (John 18:23; see Matthew 5:39).

Setting: Jerusalem. After the previous and current high priests (Annas and Caiaphas) question Jesus, and Peter denies the second and third times being the Lord's disciple, Jesus is brought before Pontius Pilate, Roman governor of Judea.

Jesus answered, "Are you saying this on your own initiative, or did others tell you about Me?" (John 18:34).

Setting: Jerusalem. After the previous and current high priests (Annas and Caiaphas) question Jesus, and Peter denies the second and third times being the Lord's disciple, Pontius Pilate (Roman governor of Judea) asks Jesus what He has done.

Jesus answered, "My kingdom is not of this world. If My kingdom were of this world, then My servants would be fighting so that I would not be handed over to the Jews; but as it is, My kingdom is not of this realm" (John 18:36; see Matthew 26:53).

Setting: Jerusalem. After the previous and current high priests (Annas and Caiaphas) question Jesus, and Peter denies the second and third times being His disciple, Pilate (Roman governor of Judea) questions the Lord in an attempt to determine if He is a king.

Therefore Pilate said to Him, "So You are a king?" Jesus answered, "You say *correctly* that I am a king. For this I have been born, and for this I have come into the world, to testify to the truth. Everyone who is of the truth hears my voice" (John 18:37; cf. Matthew 27:11; Mark 15:2; Luke 23:3).

Setting: Jerusalem. Pontius Pilate (Roman governor of Judea) continues to find no guilt in Jesus, but has Him scourged in an attempt to appease the hostile Jews. Pilate then seeks more information as to where the King of the Jews is from.

Jesus answered, "You would have no authority over Me, unless it had been given you from above; for this reason he who delivered Me to you has *the* greater sin" (John 19:11; see Romans 13:1).

TRIBES (See EARTH, TRIBES OF THE; and ISRAEL, TWELVE TRIBES OF)

TRIBES, TWELVE (See ISRAEL, TWELVE TRIBES OF)

TRIBES OF ISRAEL (See ISRAEL, TWELVE TRIBES OF)

TRIBES OF THE EARTH (Listed under EARTH, TRIBES OF THE)

TRIBULATION (GREAT TRIBULATION is a separate entry; also see PERSECUTION; and SUFFERING)

Setting: The Mount of Olives, just east of Jerusalem. During His Olivet Discourse, Jesus answers His disciples' questions as to when the temple will be destroyed and Jerusalem overrun, along with the signs of His coming and the end of the age.

And Jesus answered and said to them, "See to it that no one misleads you. For many will come in My name, saying, 'I am the Christ,' and will mislead many. You will be hearing of wars and rumors of wars. See that you are not frightened, for *those things* must take place, but *that* is not yet the end. For nation will rise against nation, and kingdom against kingdom, and in various places there will be famines and earthquakes. But all these things are *merely* the beginning of birth pangs. Then they will deliver you to tribulation, and will kill you, and you will be hated by all nations because of My name. At that time many will fall away and will betray one another and hate one another. Many false prophets will arise and will mislead many. Because lawlessness is increased, most people's love will grow cold. But the one who endures to the end, he will be saved. This gospel of the kingdom shall be preached in the whole world as a testimony to all the nations, and then the end will come" (Matthew 24:4–14; cf. Jeremiah 29:8; Matthew 7:15; 10:17, 22; Mark 13:3–13; Luke 21:7–19; Revelation 6:4).

Setting: The Mount of Olives, just east of Jerusalem. During His Olivet Discourse, Jesus answers His disciples' questions as to when the temple will be destroyed and Jerusalem overrun, along with the signs of His coming and the end of the age.

"But immediately after the tribulation of those days THE SUN WILL BE DARKENED, AND THE MOON WILL NOT GIVE ITS LIGHT, AND THE STARS WILL FALL from the sky, and the powers of the heavens will be shaken. And then the sign of the Son of Man will appear in the sky, and then all the tribes of the earth will mourn, and they will see the SON OF MAN COMING ON THE CLOUDS OF THE SKY with power and great glory. And He will send forth His angels with A GREAT TRUMPET and THEY WILL GATHER TOGETHER His elect from the four winds, from one end of the sky to the other" (Matthew 24:29–31, Jesus quotes from Isaiah 13:10, Daniel 7:13; Exodus 19:16; cf. Mark 13:24–27; Luke 21:25–27).

Setting: On the Mount of Olives, east of the temple in Jerusalem. After prophesying the temple's destruction, Jesus responds during His Olivet Discourse to questions from Peter, James, John, and Andrew about other future events.

"But when you see the ABOMINATION OF DESOLATION standing where it should not be (let the reader understand), then those who are in Judea must flee to the mountains. The one who is on the housetop must not go down, or go in to get anything out of his house; and the one who is in the field must not turn back to get his coat. But woe to those who are pregnant and to those who are nursing babies in those days! But pray that it may not happen in winter. For those days will be a *time of* tribulation such as has not occurred since the beginning of the creation which God created until now, and never will. Unless the Lord had shortened *those* days, no life would have been saved; but for the sake of the elect, whom He chose, He shortened the days. And then if anyone says to you, 'Behold, here is the Christ'; or, 'Behold, *He is* there'; do not believe *him*; for false Christs and false prophets will arise, and will show signs and wonders, in order to lead astray, if possible, the elect. But take heed; behold, I have told you everything in advance" (Mark 13:14–23; cf. Matthew 24:15–28; Luke 21:20–24; see Daniel 9:27; 12:1; Luke 17:31).

Setting: On the Mount of Olives, east of the temple in Jerusalem. After prophesying the temple's destruction, Jesus responds during His Olivet Discourse to questions from Peter, James, John, and Andrew about other future events.

"But in those days, after that tribulation, THE SUN WILL BE DARKENED AND THE MOON WILL NOT GIVE ITS LIGHT, AND THE STARS WILL BE FALLING from heaven, and the powers that are in the heavens will be shaken. Then they will see THE SON OF MAN COMING IN CLOUDS with great power and glory. And then He will send forth the angels, and will gather together His elect from the four winds, from the farthest end of the earth to the farthest end of heaven" (Mark 13:24–27. Jesus quotes from Isaiah 13:10; 34:4; Daniel 7:13; cf. Matthew 24:29–31; Luke 21:25–27).

Setting: Jerusalem. Before the Passover, after conveying promises about praying in His name, Jesus prophesies the disciples' scattering and gives them assurance that in the midst of tribulation they will have His peace.

"Jesus answered them, "Do you now believe? Behold, an hour is coming, and has *already* come, for you to be scattered, each to his own *home,* and to leave Me alone; and *yet* I am not alone, because the Father is with Me. These things I have spoken to you, so that in Me you may have peace. In the world you have tribulation, but take courage, I have overcome the world" (John 16:31–33; see Zechariah 13:7; John 8:29; 14:27; Romans 8:37).

Setting: On the island of Patmos (in the Aegean Sea about fifty miles southwest of Ephesus in modern Turkey). On the Lord's Day (Sunday), approximately fifty years after the Resurrection, the disciple John encounters the Lord Jesus Christ, who communicates a new revelation for the apostle to record for the church in Smyrna and to six other churches in Asia.

"And to the angel of the church in Smyrna write: The first and the last, who was dead, and has come to life, says this: 'I know your tribulation and your poverty (but you are rich), and the blasphemy by those who say they are Jews and are not, but are a synagogue of Satan. Do not fear what you are about to suffer. Behold, the devil is about to cast some of you into prison, so that you will be tested, and you will have tribulation for ten days. Be faithful until death, and I will give you the crown of life. He who has an ear, let him hear what the Spirit says to the churches. He who overcomes will not be hurt by the second death' (Revelation 2:8–11; see Isaiah 44:6; Revelation 1:9, 18; 20:6, 14).

TRIBULATION, GREAT (See GREAT TRIBULATION)

TRINITY

[TRINITY from the Father and the Son and the Holy Spirit]

Setting: On a mountain in Galilee. Following His resurrection from the dead in Jerusalem, Jesus conveys the Great Commission to His remaining eleven disciples.

And Jesus came up and spoke to them, saying, "All authority has been given to Me in heaven and on earth. Go therefore and make disciples of all the nations, baptizing them in the name of the Father and the Son and the Holy Spirit, teaching them to observe all that I commanded you; and lo, I am with you always, even to the end of the age" (Matthew 28:18–20; cf. Mark 16:15; see Daniel 7:13).

[TRINITY from We will come to him and make Our abode with him]

Setting: Jerusalem. Before the Passover, after conveying the upcoming ministry of the Holy Spirit in His disciples' lives, Jesus answers Judas' (not Iscariot) question about why the Lord discloses Himself to them and not to the whole world.

Jesus answered and said to him, "If anyone loves Me, he will keep My word; and My Father will love him, and We will come to him and make Our abode with him. He who does not love Me does not keep My words; and the word which you hear is not Mine, but the Father's who sent Me" (John 14:23, 24; see John 7:16; 8:51).

[TRINITY from Holy Spirit; Father; and I]
Setting: Jerusalem. Before the Passover, after responding to Philip's request for Him to show His disciples the Father, Jesus conveys the upcoming ministry of the Holy Spirit in their lives.

"These things I have spoken to you while abiding with you. But the Helper, the Holy Spirit, whom the Father will send in My name, He will teach you all things, and bring to your remembrance all that I said to you" (John 14:25, 26; see John 16:13).

[TRINITY from they may be even as We *are*]
Setting: Jerusalem. Before the Passover, after giving His disciples assurance that in the midst of tribulation they will have His peace, Jesus prays His high-priestly prayer.

Jesus spoke these things; and lifting up His eyes to heaven, He said, "Father, the hour has come; glorify Your Son, that the Son may glorify You, even as You gave Him authority over all flesh, that to all whom You have given Him, He may give eternal life. This is eternal life, that they may know You, the only true God, and Jesus Christ whom You have sent. I glorified You on the earth, having accomplished the work which You have given Me to do. Now, Father, glorify Me together with Yourself, with the glory which I had with You before the world was. I have manifested Your name to the men whom You gave Me out of the world; they were Yours and You gave them to Me, and they have kept Your word. Now they have come to know that everything You have given Me is from You; for the words which You gave Me I have given to them; and they received *them* and truly understood that I came forth from You, and they believed You sent Me. I ask on their behalf; I do not ask on behalf of the world, but of those whom You have given Me; for they are Yours; and all things that are Mine are Yours, and Yours are Mine; and I have been glorified in them. I am no longer in the world; and *yet* they themselves are in the world, and I come to You. Holy Father, keep them in Your name, *the name* which You have given Me, that they may be even as We *are.* While I was with them, I was keeping them in Your name which You have given Me; and I guarded them and not one of them perished but the son of perdition, so that the Scripture would be fulfilled" (John 17:1–12; see Luke 22:32; John 1:1; 3:35; 4:34; 5:44; 6:37–39, 70; 8:42; 11:41; 12:49; 13:18, 31; 16:15; Philippians 2:9).

[TRINITY from just as We are one]
Setting: Jerusalem. Before the Passover, after giving His disciples assurance that in the midst of tribulation they will have His peace, Jesus continues praying His high-priestly prayer.

"The glory which You have given Me I have given to them, that they may be one, just as We are one; I in them and You in Me, that they may be perfected in unity, so that the world may know that You sent Me, and loved them, even as You have loved Me. Father, I desire that they also, whom You have given Me, be with Me where I am, so that they may see My glory which You have given Me, for You loved Me before the foundation of the world. O righteous Father, although the world has not known You, yet I have known You; and these have known that You sent Me; and I have made Your name known to them, and will make it known, so that the love with which You loved Me may be in them, and I in them" (John 17:22–26; see Matthew 25:34; John 1:14; 10:38; 15:9; 16:27).

TRIP (See JOURNEY)

TRIUNE GOD (See TRINITY)

TROUBLE (Also see ADVERSITY; MINISTRY, DIFFICULTIES IN; PERSECUTION; SUFFERING; and TRIBULATION)
Setting: Galilee. During the early part of His ministry, Jesus preaches the Sermon on the Mount to His disciples and the multitudes.

"For this reason I say to you, do not be worried about your life, *as to* what you will eat or what you will drink; nor for your body, *as to* what you will put on. Is not life more than food, and the body more than clothing? Look at the birds of the air, that they do not sow, nor reap nor gather into barns, and *yet* your heavenly Father feeds them. Are you not worth much more than they? And who of you by being worried can add a *single* hour to his life? And why are you worried about clothing? Observe how the lilies of the field grow; they do not toil nor do they spin, yet I say to you that not even Solomon in all his glory clothed himself like one of these. But if God so clothes the grass of the field, which is *alive* today and tomorrow is thrown into the furnace, *will He* not much more *clothe* you? You of little faith! Do not worry then, saying 'What will we eat?' or 'What will we drink?' or 'What will be wear for clothing?" For the Gentiles eagerly seek all these things; for your heavenly Father knows that you need all these things. But seek first His kingdom and His righteousness, and all these things will be added to you. So do not worry about tomorrow; for tomorrow will care for itself. Each day has enough trouble of its own" (Matthew 6:25–34; cf. Luke 12:22–31; see 1 Kings 10:4–7; Job 35:11; Matthew 8:26),

TRUE (Also see TRUTH)

Setting: On the way from Galilee to Jerusalem. After giving the story of the prodigal son, the Lord teaches His disciples about stewardship.

Now He was also saying to the disciples, "There was a rich man who had a manager, and this *manager* was reported to him as squandering his possessions. And he called him and said to him, 'What is this I hear about you? Give an accounting of your management, for you can no longer be a manager.' The manager said to himself, 'What shall I do, since my master is taking the management away from me? I am not strong enough to dig; I am ashamed to beg. I know what I shall do, so that when I am removed from the management people will welcome me into their homes.' And he summoned each one of his master's debtors, and he *began* saying to the first, 'How much do you owe my master?' And he said, 'A hundred measures of oil.' And he said to him, 'Take your bill, and sit down quickly and write fifty.' Then he said to another, 'And how much do you owe?' And he said, 'A hundred measures of wheat.' He said to him, 'Take your bill, and write eighty.' And his master praised the unrighteous manager because he had acted shrewdly; for the sons of this age are more shrewd in relation to their own kind than the sons of light. And I say to you, make friends for yourselves by means of the wealth of unrighteousness, so that when it fails, they will receive you into the eternal dwellings. He who is faithful in a very little thing is faithful also in much; and he who is unrighteous in a very little thing is unrighteous also in much. Therefore if you have not been faithful in the *use of* unrighteous wealth, who will entrust the true *riches* to you? And if you have not been faithful in *the use of* that which is another's, who will give you that which is your own? No servant can serve two masters; for either he will hate the one and love the other, or else he will be devoted to one and despise the other. You cannot serve God and wealth" (Luke 16:1–13; cf. Matthew 6:24; see Matthew 25:14–30).

Setting: Sychar in Samaria, on the way to Galilee. Jesus interacts with a Samaritan woman at Jacob's well, while the disciples are buying food.

Jesus said to her, "Woman, believe Me, an hour is coming when neither in this mountain nor in Jerusalem will you worship the Father. You worship what you do not know; we worship what we know, for salvation is from the Jews. But an hour is coming, and now is, when the true worshipers will worship the Father in spirit and truth; for such people the Father seeks to be His worshipers. God is spirit, and those who worship Him must worship in spirit and truth" (John 4:21–24; see Isaiah 2:3; Philippians 3:3).

Setting: Sychar in Samaria, on the way to Galilee. After Jesus converses with a Samaritan woman at Jacob's well, the disciples return with food. They try to get Jesus to eat, but are surprised when He speaks of other food.

Jesus said to them, "My food is to do the will of Him who sent Me and to accomplish His work. Do you not say, 'There are yet four months, and *then* comes the harvest'? Behold, I say to you, lift up your eyes and look on the fields, that they are white for harvest. Already he who reaps is receiving wages and is gathering fruit for life eternal; so that he who sows and he who reaps may rejoice together. For in this *case* the saying is true, 'One sows and another reaps.' I sent you to reap that for which you have not labored; others have labored and you have entered into their labor" (John 4:34–38; see Matthew 9:37, 38; John 5:36).

Setting: Jerusalem. During a feast of the Jews, Jesus responds to criticism from the Jewish religious leaders by referring to God as His Father (thereby making Himself equal with God) and informing them that God, John the Baptist, and His works all testify to His mission.

"I can do nothing on My own initiative. As I hear, I judge; and My judgment is just, because I do not seek My own will, but the will of Him who sent Me. If I *alone* testify about Myself, My testimony is not true. There is another who testifies of Me, and I know that the testimony which He gives about Me is true. You have sent to John, and he has testified to the truth. But the testimony which

I receive is not from man, but I say these things so that you may be saved. He was the lamp that was burning and was shining and you were willing to rejoice for a while in his light. But the testimony which I have is greater than the *testimony of* John; for the works which the Father has given Me to accomplish—the very works that I do—testify about Me, that the Father has sent Me. And the Father who sent Me, He has testified of Me. You have neither heard His voice at any time nor seen His form. You do not have His word abiding in you, for you do not believe Him whom He sent" (John 5:30–38; see Matthew 3:17; Mark 1:4, 5; John 1:7, 15, 32; 4:34; 8:14–16; 10:25, 37, 38).

Setting: Capernaum. The day after Jesus walks on the Sea of Galilee to join His disciples in a boat, the people He miraculously fed with a lad's five loaves and two fish quiz Jesus about the signs and works He performs so they may believe in Him.

Jesus then said to them, "Truly, truly, I say to you, it is not Moses who has given you the bread out of heaven, but it is My Father who gives you the true bread out of heaven. For the bread of God is that which comes down out of heaven, and gives life to the world" (John 6:32, 33; see John 6:50).

Setting: Capernaum of Galilee. After Jesus informs the people whom He miraculously fed with a lad's five loaves and two fish how they might receive the bread out of heaven, the Jewish religious leaders argue with one another when the Lord says He will give His flesh to the world to eat.

So Jesus said to them, "Truly, truly, I say to you, unless you eat the flesh of the Son of Man and drink His blood, you have no life in yourselves. He who eats My flesh and drinks My blood has eternal life, and I will raise him up on the last day. For My flesh is true food, and My blood is true drink. He who eats My flesh and drinks My blood abides in Me, and I in him. As the living Father sent Me, and I live because of the Father, so he who eats Me, he also will live because of Me. This is the bread which came down out of heaven; not as the fathers ate and died; he who eats this bread will live forever" (John 6:53–58; see Matthew 16:16; Luke 4:22; John 3:36; 9:16; 15:4).

Setting: The temple in Jerusalem. After receiving encouragement from His blood brothers in Galilee to attend the upcoming Feast of Booths in order to demonstrate His works to His disciples and the world, Jesus goes and teaches, astonishing the Jewish religious leaders.

So Jesus answered them and said, "My teaching is not Mine, but His who sent Me. If anyone is willing to do His will, he will know of the teaching, whether it is of God or *whether* I speak of Myself. He who speaks from himself seeks his own glory; but He who is seeking the glory of the One who sent Him, He is true, and there is no unrighteousness in Him" (John 7:16–18; see John 5:41).

Setting: The temple in Jerusalem. After receiving encouragement from His blood brothers in Galilee to attend the upcoming Feast of Booths in order to demonstrate His works to His disciples and the world, Jesus goes and teaches, causing discussion about whether He is the Christ.

Then Jesus cried out in the temple, teaching and saying, "You both know Me and know where I am from; and I have not come of Myself, but He who sent Me is true, whom you do not know. I know Him, because I am from Him, and He sent Me" (John 7:28, 29; see John 3:17; 6:46; 8:42).

Setting: The temple in Jerusalem. Following the Feast of Booths and the scribes' and Pharisees' failed attempt to stone a woman for adultery, Jesus returns the next day to teach. His enemies question His testimony about Himself.

Jesus answered and said to them, "Even if I testify about Myself, My testimony is true, for I know where I came from and where I am going; but you do not know where I come from or where I am going. You judge according to the flesh; I am not judging anyone. But even if I do judge, My judgment is true; for I am not alone *in it,* but I and the Father who sent Me. Even in your law it has been written that the testimony of two men is true. I am He who testifies about Myself, and the Father who sent Me testifies about Me." So they were saying to Him, "Where is Your Father?" Jesus answered, "You know neither Me nor My Father; if you knew Me, you would know My Father also" (John 8:14–19; see Deuteronomy 17:6; 19:15; Matthew 18:16; John 3:17; 5:30, 37; 7:28; 8:42).

Setting: The temple treasury in Jerusalem. Following the Feast of Booths and the scribes' and Pharisees' failed attempt to stone a woman for adultery, Jesus returns the next day to teach. They question His testimony about Himself.

Then He said again to them, "I go away, and you will seek Me, and will die in your sin; where I am going, you cannot come." So the Jews were saying, "Surely He will not kill Himself, will He, since He says, 'Where I am going, you cannot come'?" And He was saying to them, "You are from below, I am from above; you are of this world, I am not of this world. Therefore I said to you that you will die in your sins; for unless you believe that I am *He,* you will die in your sins." So they were saying to Him, "Who are You?" Jesus said to them, "What have I been saying to you *from* the beginning? I have many things to speak and to judge concerning you, but He who sent Me is true; and the things which I heard from Him, these I speak to the world" (John 8:21–26; see John 3:31–33; 5:34, 35; 17:14, 16).

Setting: Jerusalem. Before the Passover, after He conveys the upcoming ministry of the Holy Spirit in His disciples' lives with His imminent departure from them, Jesus explains He is the vine and His disciples are the branches.

"I am the true vine, and My Father is the vinedresser. Every branch in Me that does not bear fruit, He takes away; and every *branch* that bears fruit, He prunes it so that it may bear more fruit. You are already clean because of the word which I have spoken to you. Abide in Me, and I in you. As the branch cannot bear fruit of itself unless it abides in the vine, so neither *can* you unless you abide in Me. I am the vine, you are the branches; he who abides in Me and I in him, he bears much fruit, for apart from Me you can do nothing. If anyone does not abide in Me, he is thrown away as a branch and dries up; and they gather them, and cast them into the fire and they are burned. If you abide in Me, and My words abide in you, ask whatever you wish, and it will be done for you. My Father is glorified by this, that you bear much fruit, and *so* prove to be My disciples. Just as the Father has loved Me, I have also loved you; abide in My love. If you keep My commandments, you will abide in My love; just as I have kept My Father's commandments and abide in His love. These things I have spoken to you so that My joy may be in you, and *that* your joy may be made full" (John 15:1–11; see Matthew 5:16; 7:7; John 3:29, 35; 6:56; 8:29, 31; 13:10).

Setting: Jerusalem. Before the Passover, after giving His disciples assurance that in the midst of tribulation they will have His peace, Jesus prays His high-priestly prayer.

Jesus spoke these things; and lifting up His eyes to heaven, He said, "Father, the hour has come; glorify Your Son, that the Son may glorify You, even as You gave Him authority over all flesh, that to all whom You have given Him, He may give eternal life. This is eternal life, that they may know You, the only true God, and Jesus Christ whom You have sent. I glorified You on the earth, having accomplished the work which You have given Me to do. Now, Father, glorify Me together with Yourself, with the glory which I had with You before the world was. I have manifested Your name to the men whom You gave Me out of the world; they were Yours and You gave them to Me, and they have kept Your word. Now they have come to know that everything You have given Me is from You; for the words which You gave Me I have given to them; and they received *them* and truly understood that I came forth from You, and they believed You sent Me. I ask on their behalf; I do not ask on behalf of the world, but of those whom You have given Me; for they are Yours; and all things that are Mine are Yours, and Yours are Mine; and I have been glorified in them. I am no longer in the world; and *yet* they themselves are in the world, and I come to You. Holy Father, keep them in Your name, *the name* which You have given Me, that they may be even as We *are.* While I was with them, I was keeping them in Your name which You have given Me; and I guarded them and not one of them perished but the son of perdition, so that the Scripture would be fulfilled" (John 17:1–12; see Luke 22:32; John 1:1; 3:35; 4:34; 5:44; 6:37–39, 70; 8:42; 11:41; 12:49; 13:18, 31; 16:15; Philippians 2:9).

Setting: On the island of Patmos (in the Aegean Sea about fifty miles southwest of Ephesus in modern Turkey). On the Lord's Day (Sunday), approximately fifty years after the Resurrection, the disciple John encounters the Lord Jesus Christ, who communicates a new revelation for the apostle to record for the church in Philadelphia and to six other churches in Asia.

"And to the angel of the church in Philadelphia write: He who is holy, who is true, who has the key of David, who opens and no one will shut, and who shuts and no one opens, says this: 'I know your deeds. Behold, I have put before you an open door which no one can shut, because you have a little power, and have kept My word, and have not denied My name. Behold, I will cause *those* of the synagogue of Satan, who say that they are Jews and are not, but lie—I will make them come and bow down at your feet, and *make them* know that I have loved you. Because you have kept the word of My perseverance, I also will keep you from the hour of testing, that *hour* which is about to come upon the whole world, to test those who dwell on the earth. I am coming quickly; hold fast what you have, so that no one will take your crown. He who overcomes, I will make him a pillar in the temple of My God, and he will not go out from it anymore; and I will write on him the name of My God, and the name of the city of My God, the new Jerusalem, which comes down out of heaven from My God, and My new name. He who has an ear, let him hear what the Spirit says to the churches' " (Revelation 3:7–13; see Isaiah 22:22; Galatians 2:9; Revelation 2:9, 10, 13, 25; 14:1).

Setting: On the island of Patmos (in the Aegean Sea about fifty miles southwest of Ephesus in modern Turkey). On the Lord's Day (Sunday), approximately fifty years after the Resurrection, the disciple John encounters the Lord Jesus Christ, who communicates a new revelation for the apostle to record for the church in Laodicea and to six other churches in Asia.

"To the angel of the church in Laodicea write: The Amen, the faithful and true Witness, the Beginning of the creation of God, says this: 'I know your deeds, that you are neither cold nor hot; I wish that you were cold or hot. So because you are lukewarm, and neither hot nor cold, I will spit you out of My mouth. Because you say, "I am rich, and have become wealthy, and have need of nothing," and you do not know that you are wretched and miserable and poor and blind and naked, I advise you to buy from Me gold refined by fire so that you may become rich, and white garments so that you may clothe yourself, and *that* the shame of your nakedness will not be revealed; and eye salve to anoint your eyes so that you may see. Those whom I love, I reprove and discipline; therefore be zealous and repent. Behold, I stand at the door and knock; if anyone hears My voice and opens the door, I will come in to him and will dine with him, and he with Me. He who overcomes, I will grant to him to sit down with Me on My throne, as I also overcame and sat down with My Father on His throne. He who has an ear, let him hear what the Spirit says to the churches'" (Revelation 3:14–22; see Proverb 3:12; Hosea 12:8; John 14:23; 16:33).

TRUE GOD (Listed under GOD, TRUE)

TRUE VINE (Listed under VINE, TRUE)

TRUE WITNESS (Listed under WITNESS, TRUE)

TRUMPET

Setting: Galilee. During the early part of His ministry, Jesus preaches the Sermon on the Mount to His disciples and the multitudes.

"So when you give to the poor, do not sound a trumpet before you, as the hypocrites do in the synagogues and in the streets, so that they may be honored by men. Truly I say to you, they have their reward in full. But when you give to the poor, do not let your left hand know what your right hand is doing, so that your giving will be in secret; and your Father who sees *what is done* in secret will reward you" (Matthew 6:2–4; see Jeremiah 17:10; Matthew 6:5, 16).

Setting: The Mount of Olives, just east of Jerusalem. During His Olivet Discourse, Jesus answers His disciples' questions as to when the temple will be destroyed and Jerusalem overrun, along with the signs of His coming and the end of the age.

"But immediately after the tribulation of those days THE SUN WILL BE DARKENED, AND THE MOON WILL NOT GIVE ITS LIGHT, AND THE STARS WILL FALL from the sky, and the powers of the heavens will be shaken. And then the sign of the Son of Man will appear in the sky, and then all the tribes of the earth will mourn, and they will see the SON OF MAN COMING ON THE CLOUDS OF THE SKY with power and great glory. And He will send forth His angels with A GREAT TRUMPET and THEY WILL GATHER TOGETHER His elect from the four winds, from one end of the sky to the other" (Matthew 24:29–31, Jesus quotes from Isaiah 13:10, Daniel 7:13; Exodus 19:16; cf. Mark 13:24–27; Luke 21:25–27).

TRUMPET, GREAT (See TRUMPET)

TRUSTING GOD (Listed under GOD, TRUSTING; also see FAITH)

TRUSTWORTHINESS (See FAITHFULNESS)

TRUTH (TRUTH, SPIRIT OF is a separate entry; also see TRUE)

Setting: The synagogue in Jesus' hometown of Nazareth in Galilee. At the beginning of His public ministry, Jesus comments to the congregation after reading from the book of the prophet Isaiah on the Sabbath.

And He said to them, "No doubt you will quote this proverb to Me, 'Physician, heal yourself! Whatever we heard was done at Capernaum, do here in your hometown as well.'" And He said, "Truly I say to you, no prophet is welcome in his hometown. But I say to you in truth, there were many widows in Israel in the days of Elijah, when the sky was shut up for three years and six months, when a great famine came over all the land; and yet Elijah was sent to none of them, but only to Zarephath, *in the land* of Sidon, to a woman who was a widow. And there were many lepers in Israel in the time of Elisha the prophet; and none of them was cleansed, but only Naaman the Syrian" (Luke 4:23–27; Jesus refers to 1 Kings 17:1, 9; 2 Kings 5:1–14; see Matthew 13:53–58).

Setting: Jerusalem. At the time for the Passover of the Jews, after the Lord cleanses the temple, a Pharisee, Nicodemus, asks Him by night the meaning of "born again."

"For God so loved the world, that He gave His only begotten Son, that whoever believes in Him shall not perish, but have eternal life. For God did not send the Son into the world to judge the world, but that the world might be saved through Him. He who believes in Him is not judged; he who does not believe has been judged already, because he has not believed in the name of the only begotten Son of God. This is the judgment, that the Light has come into the world, and men loved darkness rather than the Light, for their deeds were evil. For everyone who does evil hates the Light, and does not come to the Light for fear that his deeds will be exposed. But he who practices the truth comes to the Light, so that his deeds may be manifested as having been wrought in God" (John 3:16–21; see Luke 19:10; John 1:4; 1:18; Romans 5:8; 1 John 1:6, 7).

Setting: Sychar in Samaria, on the way to Galilee. Jesus interacts with a Samaritan woman at Jacob's well, while the disciples are buying food.

Jesus said to her, "Woman, believe Me, an hour is coming when neither in this mountain nor in Jerusalem will you worship the Father. You worship what you do not know; we worship what we know, for salvation is from the Jews. But an hour is coming, and now is, when the true worshipers will worship the Father in spirit and truth; for such people the Father seeks to be His worshipers. God is spirit, and those who worship Him must worship in spirit and truth" (John 4:21–24; see Isaiah 2:3; Philippians 3:3).

Setting: Jerusalem. During a feast of the Jews, Jesus responds to criticism from the Jewish religious leaders by referring to God as His Father (thereby making Himself equal with God) and informing them that God, John the Baptist, and His works all testify to His mission.

"I can do nothing on My own initiative. As I hear, I judge; and My judgment is just, because I do not seek My own will, but the will of Him who sent Me. If I *alone* testify about Myself, My testimony is not true. There is another who testifies of Me, and I know that the testimony which He gives about Me is true. You have sent to John, and he has testified to the truth. But the testimony which I receive is not from man, but I say these things so that you may be saved. He was the lamp that was burning and was shining and you were willing to rejoice for a while in his light. But the testimony which I have is greater than the *testimony of* John; for the works which the Father has given Me to accomplish—the very works that I do—testify about Me, that the Father has sent Me. And the Father who sent Me, He has testified of Me. You have neither heard His voice at any time nor seen His form. You do not have His word abiding in you, for you do not believe Him whom He sent" (John 5:30–38; see Matthew 3:17; Mark 1:4, 5; John 1:7,

15, 32; 4:34; 8:14–16; 10:25, 37, 38).

Setting: The temple treasury in Jerusalem. After the scribes and Pharisees question His testimony about Himself, Jesus reveals to those Jews who believe in Him how He will make them free.

So Jesus was saying to those Jews who had believed Him, "If you continue in My word, *then* you are truly disciples of Mine; and you will know the truth, and the truth will make you free." They answered Him, "We are Abraham's descendants and have never yet been enslaved to anyone; how is it that You say, 'You will become free'?" Jesus answered them, "Truly, truly, I say to you, everyone who commits sin is the slave of sin. The slave does not remain in the house forever; the son does remain forever. So if the Son makes you free, you will be free indeed. I know that you are Abraham's descendants; yet you seek to kill Me, because My word has no place in you. I speak the things which I have seen with *My* Father; therefore you also do the things which you heard from *your* father" (John 8:31–38; see Romans 6:16).

Setting: The temple treasury in Jerusalem. After the scribes and Pharisees question His testimony about Himself, Jesus argues with them regarding their ancestry and motives.

They answered and said to Him, "Abraham is our father." Jesus said to them, "If you are Abraham's children, do the deeds of Abraham. But as it is, you are seeking to kill Me, a man who has told you the truth, which I heard from God; this Abraham did not do. You are doing the deeds of your father." They said to Him, "We were not born of fornication; we have one Father: God" (John 8:39–41; see Romans 9:6, 7).

Setting: The temple treasury in Jerusalem. After the scribes and Pharisees question His testimony about Himself, Jesus argues with them regarding their ancestry and motives.

Jesus said to them, "If God were your Father, you would love Me, for I proceeded forth and have come from God, for I have not even come on My own initiative, but He sent Me. Why do you not understand what I am saying? *It is* because you cannot hear My word. You are of *your* father the devil, and you want to do the desires of your father. He was a murderer from the beginning, and does not stand in the truth because there is no truth in him. Whenever he speaks a lie, he speaks from his own *nature,* for he is a liar and the father of lies. But because I speak the truth, you do not believe Me. Which one of you convicts Me of sin? If I speak truth, why do you not believe Me? He who is of God hears the words of God; for this reason you do not hear *them,* because you are not of God" (John 8:42–47; see John 18:37; 1 John 3:8; 4:6; 5:1).

Setting: Jerusalem. Before the Passover, as Jesus comforts and gives hope to His disciples regarding their future after He returns to heaven, Thomas asks where the Lord is going and how they will know the way.

Jesus said to him, "I am the way, and the truth, and the life; no one comes to the Father but through Me. If you had known Me, you would have known My Father also; from now on you know Him, and have seen Him" (John 14:6, 7; see John 8:19; 10:9; 11:25).

Setting: Jerusalem. Before the Passover, after warning His disciples of the persecution they will face after His departure to heaven, Jesus elaborates about the coming ministry of the Holy Spirit.

"But now I am going to Him who sent Me; and none of you asks Me, 'Where are You going?' But because I have said these things to you, sorrow has filled your heart. But I tell you the truth, it is to your advantage that I go away; for if I do not go away, the Helper will not come to you; but if I go, I will send Him to you. And He, when He comes, will convict the world concerning sin and righteousness and judgment; concerning sin, because they do not believe in Me; and concerning righteousness, because I go to the Father and you no longer see Me; and concerning judgment, because the ruler of this world has been judged" (John 16:5–11; see John 7:33; 12:31; 14:1, 16; 15:22, 24).

Setting: Jerusalem. Before the Passover, after giving His disciples assurance that in the midst of tribulation they will have His peace, Jesus continues praying His high-priestly prayer.

"But now I come to You; and these things I speak in the world so that they may have My joy made full in themselves. I have given them Your word; and the world has hated them, because they are not of the world, even as I am not of the world. I do not ask You to take them out of the world, but to keep them from the evil *one.* They are not of the world, even as I am not of the world. Sanctify them in the truth; Your word is truth. As You sent Me into the world, I also have sent them into the world. For their sakes I sanctify Myself, that they themselves also may be sanctified in truth. I do not ask on behalf of these alone, but for those also who believe in Me through their word; that they may all be one; even as You, Father, *are* in Me and I in You, that they also maybe in Us, so that the world may believe that You sent Me" (John 17:13–21; see Matthew 10:5, 38; John 7:33; 15:3, 11, 19).

Setting: Jerusalem. After the previous and current high priests (Annas and Caiaphas) question Jesus, and Peter denies the second and third times being His disciple, Pilate (Roman governor of Judea) questions the Lord in an attempt to determine if He is a king.

Therefore Pilate said to Him, "So You are a king?" Jesus answered, "You say *correctly* that I am a king. For this I have been born, and for this I have come into the world, to testify to the truth. Everyone who is of the truth hears my voice" (John 18:37; cf. Matthew 27:11; Mark 15:2; Luke 23:3).

TRUTH, SPIRIT OF (Also see HOLY SPIRIT)

Setting: Jerusalem. Before the Passover, after responding to Philip's request for Him to show His disciples the Father, Jesus conveys the upcoming role of the Holy Spirit in their lives.

"If you love Me, you will keep My commandments. I will ask the Father, and He will give you another Helper, that He may be with you forever; *that* is the Spirit of truth, whom the world cannot receive, because it does not see Him or know Him, *but* you know Him because He abides with you and will be in you" (John 14:15–17; see John 7:39; 15:26; 1 John 5:3).

Setting: Jerusalem. Before the Passover, with His departure in mind, after explaining He is the vine and His disciples are the branches, Jesus elaborates about the future ministry of the Holy Spirit.

"When the Helper comes, whom I will send to you from the Father, *that is* the Spirit of truth who proceeds from the Father, He will testify about Me, and you *will* testify also, because you have been with Me from the beginning" (John 15:26, 27; see Luke 24:48; John 14:16).

Setting: Jerusalem. Before the Passover, after warning His disciples of the persecution they will face after His departure to heaven, Jesus elaborates about the coming ministry of the Holy Spirit.

"I have many more things to say to you, but you cannot bear *them* now. But when He, the Spirit of truth, comes, He will guide you into all the truth; for He will not speak on His own initiative, but whatever He hears, He will speak; and He will disclose to you what is to come. He will glorify Me, for He will take of Mine and will disclose *it* to you. All things that the Father has are Mine; therefore I said that He takes of Mine and will disclose *it* to you (John 16:12–15; see John 7:39; 14:17, 26; 17:10).

TRUTHFULNESS (See TRUE; and TRUTH)

TUNICS (Also see CLOTHING; and GARMENT)

Setting: Jesus' hometown of Nazareth in Galilee. After encountering unbelief, Jesus sends the Twelve out in pairs with authority and instructions about ministry.

And He summoned the twelve and began to send them out in pairs, and gave them authority over the unclean spirits; and He instructed them that they should take nothing for *their* journey, except a mere staff—no bread, no bag, no money in their belt—but to wear sandals; and *He added,* "Do not put on two tunics." And He said to them, "Wherever you enter a house, stay there until you leave town. Any place that does not receive you or listen to you, as you go out from there, shake the dust off the soles of your feet for a testimony against them" (Mark 6:7–11; cf. Matthew 10:1–14; Luke 9:1–5).

Setting: Galilee. After raising the daughter of Jairus, a synagogue official, from the dead, Jesus calls His twelve disciples together and gives them power and authority over demons, along with the ability to cure diseases.

And He said to them, "Take nothing for *your* journey, neither a staff, nor a bag, nor bread, nor money; and do not *even* have two tunics apiece. Whatever house you enter, stay there until you leave that city. And as for those who do not receive you, go out from that city, shake the dust off your feet as a testimony against them" (Luke 9:3–5; cf. Matthew 10:1–15; Mark 6:7–11; see Luke 10:4–12).

TWELVE (ISRAEL, TWELVE TRIBES OF; and THRONES, TWELVE are separate entries)

Setting: Gethsemane on the Mount of Olives, east of the temple in Jerusalem. As Jesus submits to His Father's will and allows Judas to betray Him, Peter attempts to defend Him by force, but the Lord does not permit it.

Then Jesus said to him, "Put your sword back into its place; for all those who take up the sword shall perish by the sword. Or do you think that I cannot appeal to My Father, and He will at once put at My disposal more than twelve legions of angels? How then will the Scriptures be fulfilled, *which say* that it must happen this way?" (Matthew 26:52–54; cf. Mark 14:47; Luke 22:50, 51; John 18:10, 11; see Matthew 26:24).

Setting: A borrowed upper room in Jerusalem. While Jesus and His twelve disciples are eating the Passover meal, the Lord states that one of the disciples will betray Him.

As they were reclining *at the table* and eating, Jesus said, "Truly I say to you that one of you will betray Me—one who is eating with Me." They began to be grieved and to say to Him one by one, "Surely not I?" And He said to them, "*It is* one of the twelve, one who dips with Me in the bowl. For the Son of Man *is to* go just as it is written of Him; but woe to that man by whom the Son of Man is betrayed! *It would have been* good for that man if he had not been born" (Mark 14:18–21; cf. Matthew 26:21–24; Luke 22:21–23; John 13:21, 22).

Setting: The synagogue at Capernaum of Galilee. After some of His disciples express difficulty with Jesus' statements about eating His flesh, Simon Peter responds that the Lord proclaims words of eternal life.

Jesus answered them, "Did I Myself not choose you, the twelve, and *yet* one of you is a devil?" (John 6:70; see John 15:16, 19).

Setting: Beyond the Jordan. While He and His disciples are avoiding the Jerusalem Pharisees, Jesus receives word from Lazarus's sisters in Bethany of His friend's sickness, and decides to go there.

Then after this He said to the disciples, "Let us go to Judea again." The disciples said to Him, "Rabbi, the Jews were just now seeking to stone You, and are You going there again?" Jesus answered, "Are there not twelve hours in the day? If anyone walks in the day, he does not stumble, because he sees the light of this world. But if anyone walks in the night, he stumbles, because the light is not in him." This He said, and after that He said to them, "Our friend Lazarus has fallen asleep; but I go, so that I may awaken him out of sleep" (John 11:7–11; see John 8:59; 10:39).

TWELVE THRONES (Listed under THRONES, TWELVE)

TWELVE TRIBES OF ISRAEL (Listed under ISRAEL, TWELVE TRIBES OF)

TWO (See specific entries such as SONS, TWO)

TWO SONS (Listed under SONS, TWO)

TWO TUNICS (See TUNICS)

TWO WOMEN (Listed under WOMEN, TWO)

TYRE

Setting: Galilee. After performing miracles throughout the region, Jesus pronounces woes against those cities who have not repented.

"Woe to you, Chorazin! Woe to you, Bethsaida! For if the miracles had occurred in Tyre and Sidon which occurred in you, they would have repented long ago in sackcloth and ashes. Nevertheless I say to you, it will be more tolerable for Tyre and Sidon in *the* day of judgment than for you. And you, Capernaum, will not be exalted to heaven, will you? You will descend to Hades; for if the miracles had occurred in Sodom which occurred in you, it would have remained to this day. Nevertheless, I say to you that it will be more tolerable for the land of Sodom in *the* day of judgment, than for you" (Matthew 11:21–24; cf. Matthew 10:15; Luke 10:13–15).

Setting: On the way from Galilee to Jerusalem. The Lord pronounces woes on cities who reject the gospel, as He appoints seventy followers and sends them out in pairs to every place He Himself will soon visit.

"Woe to you, Chorazin! Woe to you, Bethsaida! For if the miracles had been performed in Tyre and Sidon which occurred in you, they would have repented long ago, sitting in sackcloth and ashes. But it will be more tolerable for Tyre and Sidon in the judgment than for you. And you, Capernaum, will not be exalted to heaven, will you? You will be brought down to Hades! The one who listens to you listens to Me, and the one who rejects you rejects Me; and he who rejects Me rejects the One who sent Me" (Luke 10:13–16; cf. Matthew 11:21–23; see Matthew 10:40).

U

UNBELIEF (Also see BELIEF; DISBELIEF; DOUBT; REJECTION; and UNBELIEVERS)

[UNBELIEF from unbelieving]

Setting: Galilee. After answering Peter, James, and John about Elijah's future coming as they descend the mountain where Jesus was just transfigured, the Lord expresses dismay over His disciples' inability to heal a man's demon-possessed son.

And Jesus answered and said, "You unbelieving and perverted generation, how long shall I be with you? How long shall I put up with you? Bring him here to Me." And Jesus rebuked him, and the demon came out of him, and the boy was cured at once (Matthew 17:17, 18; cf. Mark 9:19–29; Luke 9:41–43).

[UNBELIEF from did not believe]

Setting: The temple in Jerusalem. Jesus delivers a parable to the chief priests and elders after they question His authority.

"But what do you think? A man had two sons, and he came to the first and said, 'Son, go work today in the vineyard.' And he answered, 'I will not'; but afterward he regretted it and went. The man came to the second and said the same thing; and he answered, 'I *will,* sir'; but he did not go. Which of the two sons did the will of his father?" They said, "The first." Jesus said to them, "Truly, I say to you that the tax collectors and prostitutes will get into the kingdom of God before you. For John came to you in the way of righteousness and you did not believe him; but the tax collectors and prostitutes did believe him; and you, seeing *this,* did not even feel remorse afterward so as to believe him" (Matthew 21:28–32; cf. Luke 7:29, 30, 37–50).

[UNBELIEF from do not believe]

Setting: The Mount of Olives, just east of Jerusalem. During His Olivet Discourse, Jesus answers His disciples' questions as to when the temple will be destroyed and Jerusalem overrun, along with the signs of His coming and the end of the age.

"Therefore when you see the ABOMINATION OF DESOLATION which was spoken of through Daniel the prophet, standing in the holy place (let the reader understand), then those who are in Judea must flee to the mountains. Whoever is on the housetop must not go down to get the things that are in his house. Whoever is in the field must not turn back to get his cloak. But woe to those who are pregnant and to those who are nursing babies in those days! But pray that your flight will not be in the winter, or on a Sabbath. For then there will be a great tribulation, such as has not occurred since the beginning of the world until now, nor ever will. Unless those days had been cut short, no life would have been saved; but for the sake of the elect those days will be cut short. Then if anyone says to you, 'Behold, here is the Christ,' or "There *He is,*' do not believe *him.* For false Christs and false prophets will arise and will show great signs and wonders, so as to mislead, if possible, even the elect. Behold, I have told you in advance. So if they say to you, 'Behold, He is in the wilderness,' do not go out, *or,* 'Behold, He is in the inner rooms,' do not believe *them.* For just as the lightning comes from the east and flashes even to the west, so will the coming of the Son of Man be. Wherever the corpse is, there the vultures will gather" (Matthew 24:15–28, Jesus quotes from Daniel 9:27; cf. Daniel 12:1; Mark 13:14–23; Luke 17:22–31; 21:20–24; 23:29; see John 4:48).

[UNBELIEF inferred]

Setting: The synagogue in Jesus' hometown of Nazareth. While ministering throughout the villages of Galilee, Jesus teaches in His hometown. The townspeople become offended and question His teaching, wisdom, and ability to perform miracles.

Jesus said to them, "A prophet is not without honor except in his hometown and among his *own* relatives and in his *own* household" (Mark 6:4; cf. Matthew 13:54–58).

[UNBELIEF from unbelieving]

Setting: Galilee. After returning from a high mountain (perhaps Mount Hermon) where Jesus was transfigured in front of Peter, James, and John, the four discover the rest of the disciples arguing with some scribes.

And He asked them, "What are you discussing with them?" And one of the crowd answered Him, "Teacher, I brought You my son, possessed with a spirit which makes him mute; and whenever it seizes him, it slams him *to the ground* and he foams *at the mouth,* and grinds his teeth and stiffens out. I told Your disciples to cast it out, and they could not *do it.* And He answered them, and said, "O unbelieving generation, how long shall I be with you? How long shall I put up with you? Bring him to Me!" They brought the boy to Him. When he saw Him, immediately the spirit threw him into a convulsion, and falling to the ground, be *began* rolling around and foaming *at the mouth.* And He asked his father, "How long has this been happening to him?" And he said, "From childhood. It has often thrown him both into the fire and into the water to destroy him. But if You can do anything, take pity on us and help us!" And Jesus said to him, "'If You can?' All things are possible to him who believes." Immediately the boy's father cried out and said, "I do believe; help my unbelief." When Jesus saw that a crowd was rapidly gathering, He rebuked the unclean spirit, saying to it, "You deaf and mute spirit, I command you, come out of him and do not enter him again." After crying out and throwing him into terrible convulsions, it came out; and *the boy* became so much like a corpse that most *of them,* said, "He is dead!" But Jesus took him by the hand and raised him; and he got up. When He came into *the* house, His disciples *began* questioning Him privately, "Why could we not drive it out?" And He said to them, "This kind cannot come out by anything but prayer" (Mark 9:16–29; cf. Matthew 17:14–21; Luke 9:37–43; see Matthew 17:20).

[UNBELIEF from do not believe]

Setting: On the Mount of Olives, east of the temple in Jerusalem. After prophesying the temple's destruction, Jesus responds during His Olivet Discourse to questions from Peter, James, John, and Andrew about other future events.

"But when you see the ABOMINATION OF DESOLATION standing where it should not be (let the reader understand), then those who are in Judea must flee to the mountains. The one who is on the housetop must not go down, or go in to get anything out of his house; and the one who is in the field must not turn back to get his coat. But woe to those who are pregnant and to those who are nursing babies in those days! But pray that it may not happen in winter. For those days will be a *time of* tribulation such as has not occurred since the beginning of the creation which God created until now, and never will. Unless the Lord had shortened *those* days, no life would have been saved; but for the sake of the elect, whom He chose, He shortened the days. And then if anyone says to you, 'Behold, here is the Christ'; or, 'Behold, *He is* there'; do not believe *him*; for false Christs and false prophets will arise, and will show signs and wonders, in order to lead astray, if possible, the elect. But take heed; behold, I have told you everything in advance" (Mark 13:14–23; cf. Matthew 24:15–28; Luke 21:20–24; see Daniel 9:27; 12:1; Luke 17:31).

[UNBELIEF from will not believe]

Setting: Galilee. After Jesus presents the Parable of the Sower to the crowds, His disciples ask Him to give them the parable's meaning.

And He said, "To you it has been granted to know the mysteries of the kingdom of God, but to the rest *it is* in parables, so that SEEING THEY MAY NOT SEE, AND HEARING THEY MAY NOT UNDERSTAND. Now the parable is this: the seed is the word of God. Those beside the road are those who have heard; then the devil comes and takes away the word from their heart, so that they will not believe and be saved. Those on the rocky *soil* are those who, when they hear, receive the word with joy; and these have no *firm* root; they believe for a while, and in time of temptation fall away. The *seed* which fell among the thorns, these are the ones who have heard, and as they go on their way they are choked with worries and riches and pleasures of *this* life, and bring no fruit to maturity. But the *seed* in the good soil, these are the ones who have heard the word in an honest and good heart, and hold it fast, and bear fruit with perseverance" (Luke 8:10–15, Jesus quotes from Isaiah 6:9; cf. Matthew 13:10–23; Mark 4:10–20).

[UNBELIEF from unbelieving]
Setting: Galilee. After Jesus' transfiguration on a high mountain, a man from a large crowd begs Jesus to look at his demon-possessed son.

And Jesus answered and said, "You unbelieving and perverted generation, how long shall I be with you and put up with you? Bring your son here" (Luke 9:41; cf. Matthew 17:14–18; Mark 9:14–27).

[UNBELIEF from will not believe]
Setting: Jerusalem. After being arrested, having Peter deny Him, and being mocked and beaten, with His crucifixion imminent, Jesus appears before the Sanhedrin (Council of Elders).

"If You are the Christ, tell us." But He said to them, "If I tell you, you will not believe; and if I ask you a question, you will not answer. But from now on THE SON OF MAN WILL BE SEATED AT THE RIGHT HAND of the power OF GOD." And they all said, "Are You the Son of God, then? And He said to them, "Yes, I am" (Luke 22:67–70, Jesus quotes from Psalm 110:1; cf. Matthew 26:57–65; Mark 14:55–65).

[UNBELIEF from do not believe]
Setting: Jerusalem. At the time for the Passover of the Jews, after the Lord cleanses the temple, a Pharisee, Nicodemus, asks Him by night the meaning of "born of the Spirit."

Jesus answered and said to him, "Are you the teacher of Israel and do not understand these things? Truly, truly, I say to you, we speak of what we know and testify of what we have seen, and you do not accept our testimony. If I told you earthly things and you do not believe, how will you believe if I tell you heavenly things? No one has ascended into heaven, but He who descended from heaven: the Son of Man. As Moses lifted up the serpent in the wilderness, even so must the Son of Man be lifted up; so that whoever believes will in Him have eternal life" (John 3:10–15; see Numbers 21:9; Proverb 30:4; John 12:34; 20:30, 31).

[UNBELIEF from does not believe]
Setting: Jerusalem. At the time for the Passover of the Jews, after the Lord cleanses the temple, a Pharisee, Nicodemus, asks Him by night the meaning of "born again."

"For God so loved the world, that He gave His only begotten Son, that whoever believes in Him shall not perish, but have eternal life. For God did not send the Son into the world to judge the world, but that the world might be saved through Him. He who believes in Him is not judged; he who does not believe has been judged already, because he has not believed in the name of the only begotten Son of God. This is the judgment, that the Light has come into the world, and men loved darkness rather than the Light, for their deeds were evil. For everyone who does evil hates the Light, and does not come to the Light for fear that his deeds will be exposed. But he who practices the truth comes to the Light, so that his deeds may be manifested as having been wrought in God" (John 3:16–21; see Luke 19:10; John 1:4; 1:18; Romans 5:8; 1 John 1:6, 7).

[UNBELIEF from will not believe]
Setting: Cana of Galilee. After conversing with a Samaritan woman at Jacob's well, and ministering to the Samaritans for two days, Jesus encounters a royal official seeking healing for his son, sick at the point of death in Capernaum.

So Jesus said to him, "Unless you *people* see signs and wonders, you *simply* will not believe" (John 4:48).

[UNBELIEF from do not believe]
Setting: Jerusalem. During a feast of the Jews, Jesus responds to criticism from the Jewish religious leaders by referring to God as His Father (thereby making Himself equal with God) and informing them that God, John the Baptist, and His works all testify to His mission.

"I can do nothing on My own initiative. As I hear, I judge; and My judgment is just, because I do not seek My own will, but the will of Him who sent Me. If I *alone* testify about Myself, My testimony is not true. There is another who testifies of Me, and I know that the testimony which He gives about Me is true. You have sent to John, and he has testified to the truth. But the testimony which I receive is not from man, but I say these things so that you may be saved. He was the lamp that was burning and was shining and you were willing to rejoice for a while in his light. But the testimony which I have is greater than the *testimony of* John; for the works which the Father has given Me to accomplish—the very works that I do—testify about Me, that the Father has sent Me. And the Father who sent Me, He has testified of Me. You have neither heard His voice at any time nor seen His form. You do not have His word abiding in you, for you do not believe Him whom He sent" (John 5:30–38; see Matthew 3:17; Mark 1:4–5; John 1:7, 15, 32; 4:34; 8:14–16; 10:25, 37, 38).

[UNBELIEF from do not believe]
Setting: Jerusalem. During a feast of the Jews, Jesus responds to criticism from the Jewish religious leaders by referring to God as His Father (thereby making Himself equal with God) and informing them that God, John the Baptist, the Scriptures, and His works all testify to His mission.

"You search the Scriptures because you think that in them you have eternal life; it is these that testify about Me; and you are unwilling to come to Me so that you may have life. I do not receive glory from men; but I know you, that you do not have the love of God in yourselves. I have come in My Father's name, and you do not receive Me; if another comes in his own name, you will receive him. How can you believe, when you receive glory from one another and you do not seek the glory that is from the *one and* only God? Do not think that I will accuse you before the Father; the one who accuses you is Moses, in whom you have set your hope. For if you believed Moses, you would believe Me, for he wrote about Me. But if you do not believe his writings, how will you believe My words?" (John 5:39–47; see Matthew 24:5; Luke 16:29, 31; 24:27; John 9:28; 17:3).

[UNBELIEF from do not believe]
Setting: Capernaum. The day after Jesus walks on the Sea of Galilee to join His disciples in a boat, the people He miraculously fed with a lad's five loaves and two fish ask the Lord to always give them this bread out of heaven.

Jesus said to them, "I am the bread of life; he who comes to Me will not hunger, and he who believes in Me will never thirst. But I said to you that you have seen Me, and yet do not believe. All that the Father gives Me will come to Me, and the one who comes to Me I will certainly not cast out. For I have come down from heaven, not to do My own will, but the will of Him who sent Me. This is the will of Him who sent Me, that of all that He has given Me I lose nothing, but raise it up on the last day. For this is the will of My Father, that everyone who beholds the Son and believes in Him will have eternal life, and I Myself will raise him up on the last day" (John 6:35–40; see John 3:13, 16; 4:13, 14).

[UNBELIEF from did not believe]
Setting: The synagogue at Capernaum of Galilee. After the Jewish religious leaders argue with one another when Jesus says He will give His flesh to the world to eat, some of the Lord's disciples also express difficulty with His statements.

But, Jesus, conscious that His disciples grumbled at this, said to them, "Does this cause you to stumble? *What* then if you see the Son of Man ascending to where He was before? It is the Spirit who gives life; the flesh profits nothing; the words that I have spoken to you are spirit and are life. But there are some of you who do not believe." For Jesus knew from the beginning who they were who did not believe, and who it was that would betray Him. And He was saying, "For this reason I have said to you, that no one can come to Me unless it has been granted him from the Father" (John 6:61–65; see Matthew 11:6; 13:11; John 3:13).

[UNBELIEF from you do not believe and why do you not believe Me]
Setting: The temple treasury in Jerusalem. After the scribes and Pharisees question His testimony about Himself, Jesus argues with them regarding their ancestry and motives.

Jesus said to them, "If God were your Father, you would love Me, for I proceeded forth and have come from God, for I have not even come on My own initiative, but He sent Me. Why do you not understand what I am saying? *It is* because you cannot hear My word. You are of *your* father the devil, and you want to do the desires of your father. He was a murderer from the beginning, and does not stand in the truth because there is no truth in him. Whenever he speaks a lie, he speaks from his own *nature*, for he is a liar and the father of lies. But because I speak the truth, you do not believe Me. Which one of you convicts Me of sin? If I speak truth, why do you not believe Me? He who is of God hears the words of God; for this reason you do not hear *them*, because you are not of God" (John 8:42–47; see John 18:37; 1 John 3:8; 4:6; 5:1).

[UNBELIEF from do not believe]
Setting: Jerusalem. At the Feast of Dedication, just after Jesus conveys the Parable of the Good Shepherd to the Pharisees (who do not understand it), they ask Him plainly if He is the Christ.

Jesus answered them, "I told you, and you do not believe; the works that I do in My Father's name, these testify of Me. But you do not believe because you are not of My sheep. My sheep hear My voice, and I know them, and they follow Me; and I give eternal life to them, and they will never perish; and no one will snatch them out of My hand. My Father, who has given *them* to Me, is greater than all; and no one is able to snatch *them* out of the Father's hand. I and the Father are one" (John 10:25–30; see John 8:47; 17:1, 2, 20, 21).

[UNBELIEF from do not believe]
Setting: Jerusalem. At the Feast of Dedication, the Pharisees desire to stone Jesus because He claims to be equal with God when they ask Him plainly whether He is the Christ.

Jesus answered them, "Has it not been written in your Law, 'I SAID, YOU ARE GODS'? If he called them gods, to whom the word of God came (and the Scripture cannot be broken), do you say of Him, whom the Father sanctified and sent into the world, 'You are blaspheming,' because I said, 'I am the Son of God'? If I do not do the works of My Father, do not believe Me; but if I do them, though you do not believe Me, believe the works, so that you may know and understand that the Father is in Me, and I in the Father" (John 10:34–38, Jesus quotes from Psalm 82:6; see John 14:10, 20).

[UNBELIEF from not believe]
Setting: Jerusalem. Before the Passover, after answering Thomas' question where the Lord is going and how His disciples will know the way, Jesus responds to Philip's request for Him to show them the Father.

Jesus said to him, "Have I been so long with you, and *yet* you have not come to know Me, Philip? He who has seen Me has seen the Father; how *can* you say, 'Show us the Father'? Do you not believe that I am in the Father, and the Father is in Me? The words that I say to you I do not speak on My own initiative, but the Father abiding in Me does His works. Believe Me that I am in the Father and the Father is in Me; otherwise believe because of the works themselves. Truly, truly, I say to you, he who believes in Me, the works that I do, he will do also; and greater *works* than these he will do; because I go to the Father. Whatever you ask in My name, that will I do, so that the Father may be glorified in the Son. If you ask Me anything in My name, I will do *it*" (John 14:9–14; see Matthew 7:7; John 1:14; 5:19, 20, 36; 10:37, 38; 15:16).

[UNBELIEF from do not believe]
Setting: Jerusalem. Before the Passover, after warning His disciples of the persecution they will face after His departure to heaven, Jesus elaborates about the coming ministry of the Holy Spirit.

"But now I am going to Him who sent Me; and none of you asks Me, 'Where are You going?' But because I have said these things to you, sorrow has filled your heart. But I tell you the truth, it is to your advantage that I go away; for if I do not go away, the Helper will not come to you; but if I go, I will send Him to you. And He, when He comes, will convict the world concerning sin and righteousness and judgment; concerning sin, because they do not believe in Me; and concerning righteousness, because I go to the Father and you no longer see Me; and concerning judgment, because the ruler of this world has been judged" (John 16:5–11; see John 7:33; 12:31; 14:1, 16; 15:22, 24).

[UNBELIEF from unbelieving]
Setting: Jerusalem. The risen Jesus meets with His disciple Thomas (Didymus), who has had doubts about the testimony of the other disciples claiming to have seen and spoken with the Lord eight days earlier.

After eight days His disciples were again inside, and Thomas with them. Jesus came, the doors having been shut, and stood in their midst and said, "Peace *be* with you." Then He said to Thomas, "Reach here with your finger, and see My hands; and reach here your hand and put it into My side; and do not be unbelieving, but believing." Thomas answered and said to Him, "My Lord and my God!" Jesus said to him, "Because you have seen Me, have you believed? Blessed *are* they who did not see, and *yet* believed" (John 20:26–29; see Luke 24:36, 40; 1 Peter 1:8).

UNBELIEVERS (Also see UNBELIEF)

Setting: On the way from Galilee to Jerusalem. When Jesus uses a parable to challenge the crowd and His disciples to be ready for His return, Peter asks whom He is addressing.

And the Lord said, "Who then is the faithful and sensible steward, whom his master will put in charge of his servants, to give them their rations at the proper time? Blessed is that slave whom his master finds so doing when he comes. Truly I say to you that he will put him in charge of all his possessions. But if that slave says in his heart, 'My master will be a long time in coming,' and begins to beat the slaves, *both* men and women, and to eat and drink and get drunk; the master of that slave will come on a day when he does not expect *him* and at an hour he does not know, and will cut him in pieces, and assign him a place with the unbelievers. And that slave who knew his master's will and did not get ready or act in accord with his will, will receive many lashes, but the one who did know *it,* and committed deeds worthy of flogging, will receive but few. From everyone who has been given much, much will be required; and to whom they entrusted much, of him they will ask all the more" (Luke 12:42–48; cf. Matthew 24:45–51; see Leviticus 5:17).

[UNBELIEVERS from you who do not believe]

Setting: The synagogue at Capernaum of Galilee. After the Jewish religious leaders argue with one another when Jesus says He will give His flesh to the world to eat, some of the Lord's disciples also express difficulty with His statements.

But, Jesus, conscious that His disciples grumbled at this, said to them, "Does this cause you to stumble? *What* then if you see the Son of Man ascending to where He was before? It is the Spirit who gives life; the flesh profits nothing; the words that I have spoken to you are spirit and are life. But there are some of you who do not believe." For Jesus knew from the beginning who they were who did not believe, and who it was that would betray Him. And He was saying, "For this reason I have said to you, that no one can come to Me unless it has been granted him from the Father" (John 6:61–65; see Matthew 11:6; 13:11; John 3:13).

[UNBELIEVERS from you do not believe Me and why do you not believe me]

Setting: The temple treasury in Jerusalem. After the scribes and Pharisees question His testimony about Himself, Jesus argues with them regarding their ancestry and motives.

Jesus said to them, "If God were your Father, you would love Me, for I proceeded forth and have come from God, for I have not even come on My own initiative, but He sent Me. Why do you not understand what I am saying? *It is* because you cannot hear My word. You are of *your* father the devil, and you want to do the desires of your father. He was a murderer from the beginning, and does not stand in the truth because there is no truth in him. Whenever he speaks a lie, he speaks from his own *nature,* for he is a liar and the father of lies. But because I speak the truth, you do not believe Me. Which one of you convicts Me of sin? If I speak truth, why do you not believe Me? He who is of God hears the words of God; for this reason you do not hear *them,* because you are not of God" (John 8:42–47; see John 18:37; 1 John 3:8; 4:6; 5:1).

[UNBELIEVERS from you have not come to know Him]

Setting: The temple treasury in Jerusalem. While Jesus is interacting with the scribes and Pharisees, they state their belief that Jesus is a demon-possessed Samaritan because of His statement that anyone who keeps His word will never taste death.

Jesus answered, "If I glorify Myself, My glory is nothing; it is My Father who glorifies Me, of whom you say, 'He is our God'; and you have not come to know Him, but I know Him; and if I say that I do not know Him, I will be a liar like you, but I do know Him and keep His word. Your father Abraham rejoiced to see My day, and he saw *it* and was glad" (John 8:51–56; see Matthew 13:17; John 7:29).

[UNBELIEVERS from you do not believe; the works that I do in My Father's name]
Setting: Jerusalem. At the Feast of Dedication, just after Jesus conveys the Parable of the Good Shepherd to the Pharisees (who do not understand it), they ask Him plainly if He is the Christ.

Jesus answered them, "I told you, and you do not believe; the works that I do in My Father's name, these testify of Me. But you do not believe because you are not of My sheep. My sheep hear My voice, and I know them, and they follow Me; and I give eternal life to them, and they will never perish; and no one will snatch them out of My hand. My Father, who has given *them* to Me, is greater than all; and no one is able to snatch *them* out of the Father's hand. I and the Father are one" (John 10:25–30; see John 8:47; 17:1, 2, 20, 21).

[UNBELIEVERS from you do not believe Me]
Setting: Jerusalem. At the Feast of Dedication, the Pharisees desire to stone Jesus because He claims to be equal with God when they ask Him plainly whether He is the Christ.

Jesus answered them, "Has it not been written in your Law, 'I SAID, YOU ARE GODS'? If he called them gods, to whom the word of God came (and the Scripture cannot be broken), do you say of Him, whom the Father sanctified and sent into the world, 'You are blaspheming,' because I said, 'I am the Son of God'? If I do not do the works of My Father, do not believe Me; but if I do them, though you do not believe Me, believe the works, so that you may know and understand that the Father is in Me, and I in the Father" (John 10:34–38, Jesus quotes from Psalm 82:6; see John 10:22–33, 39; 14:10, 20).

UNCHASTITY **(Also see ADULTERIES; ADULTERY; FORNICATION; and SEXUAL SIN)**
Setting: Galilee. During the early part of His ministry, Jesus preaches the Sermon on the Mount to His disciples and the multitudes.

"It was said, 'WHOEVER SENDS HIS WIFE AWAY, LET HIM GIVE HER A CERTIFICATE OF DIVORCE'; but I say to you that everyone who divorces his wife, except for *the* reason of unchastity, makes her commit adultery; and whoever marries a divorced woman commits adultery" (Matthew 5:31, 32, Jesus quotes from Deuteronomy 24:1, 3; cf. Matthew 19:9; see Romans 7:2, 3; 1 Corinthians 7:10, 39).

UNCLEANNESS **(Also see LEPERS)**
Setting: The temple in Jerusalem. After the Jewish religious leaders test Him with questions, Jesus pronounces the seventh of eight woes upon them in front of the crowds and His disciples.

"Woe to you, scribes and Pharisees, hypocrites! For you are like whitewashed tombs which on the outside appear beautiful, but inside they are full of dead men's bones and all uncleanness. So you, too, outwardly appear righteous to men, but inwardly you are full of hypocrisy and lawlessness" (Matthew 23:27, 28; cf. Luke 11:44).

UNCLEAN SPIRIT **(Listed under SPIRIT, UNCLEAN; also see DEMON; and DEMONS)**

UNDERSTANDING
[UNDERSTANDING from understand]
Setting: By the Sea of Galilee. Jesus responds to His disciples' questions about the Parable of the Sower, which He has just taught from a boat to a crowd.

Jesus answered them, "To you it has been granted to know the mysteries of the kingdom of heaven, but to them it has not been granted. For whoever has, to him *more* shall be given, and he will have an abundance; but whoever does not have, even what he has shall be taken away from him. Therefore, I speak to them in parables; because while seeing they do not see, and while hearing they do not hear, nor do they understand. In their case the prophecy of Isaiah is being fulfilled, which says, 'YOU WILL KEEP ON HEARING, BUT WILL NOT UNDERSTAND; YOU WILL KEEP ON SEEING, BUT WILL NOT PERCEIVE; FOR THE HEART OF THIS PEOPLE HAS BECOME DULL, WITH THEIR EARS THEY SCARCELY HEAR, AND THEY HAVE CLOSED THEIR EYES, OTHERWISE THEYWOULD SEE WITH THEIR EYES, HEAR WITH THEIR EARS, AND UNDERSTAND WITH THEIR HEART AND RETURN, AND I WOULD HEAL THEM.' But blessed are your eyes, because they see; and your ears, because they hear. For truly I say to you that many prophets and righteous men desired to see what you see, and did not see *it,* and to hear what you hear, and did not hear *it*" (Matthew 13:11–17, Jesus quotes from Isaiah 6:9–10; cf. Matthew 25:29; Mark 4:11–13; Luke 8:10; see Deuteronomy 29:4; John 8:56).

[UNDERSTANDING from understand and understands]
Setting: By the Sea of Galilee. With the religious leaders rejecting His message, Jesus begins to teach in parables, and gives His disciples the meaning of the Parable of the Sower.

"Hear then the parable of the sower. When anyone hears the word of the kingdom and does not understand it, the evil *one* comes and snatches away what has been sown in his heart. This is the one on whom seed was sown beside the road. The one on whom seed was sown on the rocky places, this is the man who hears the word and immediately receives it with joy; yet he has no *firm* root in himself, but is *only* temporary, and when affliction or persecution arises because of the word, immediately he falls away. And the one on whom seed was sown among the thorns, this is the man who hears the word, and the worry of the world and the deceitfulness of wealth choke the word, and it becomes unfruitful. And the one on whom seed was sown on the good soil, this is the man who hears the word and understands it; who indeed bears fruit and brings forth, some a hundredfold, some sixty, and some thirty" (Matthew 13:18–23; cf. Mark 4:13–20; Luke 8:11–15).

[UNDERSTANDING from understood]
Setting: By the Sea of Galilee. Because the religious leaders are rejecting His message, Jesus continues teaching His disciples with the Parable of the Dragnet.

"Again, the kingdom of heaven is like a dragnet cast into the sea, and gathering *fish* of every kind; and when it was filled, they drew it up on the beach; and they sat down and gathered the good *fish* into containers, but the bad they threw away. So it will be at the end of the age; the angels will come forth and take out the wicked from among the righteous, and will throw them into the furnace of fire; in that place there will be weeping and gnashing of teeth. Have you understood all these things?" They said to Him, "Yes" (Matthew 13:47–51).

[UNDERSTANDING from understand]
Setting: Galilee. After the Pharisees and scribes question His disciples' obedience to tradition and the commandments, Jesus instructs the crowd.

After Jesus called the crowd to Him, He said to them, "Hear and understand. *It is* not what enters into the mouth *that* defiles the man, but what proceeds out of the mouth, this defiles the man" (Matthew 15:10, 11).

[UNDERSTANDING from understand]
Setting: Galilee. Jesus gives the crowd the meaning of His instruction about what defiles a man.

Peter said to Him, "Explain the parable to us." Jesus said, "Are you still lacking in understanding also? Do you not understand that everything that goes into the mouth passes into the stomach and is eliminated? But the things that proceed out of the mouth come from the heart, and those defile the man. For out of the heart come evil thoughts, murders, adulteries, fornications, thefts, false witness, slanders. These are the things which defile a man; but to eat with unwashed hands does not defile the man" (Matthew 15:15–20; cf. Mark 7:18–23; see Galatians 5:19–21).

[UNDERSTANDING from understand]
Setting: By the Sea of Galilee. Jesus repeats a warning to His disciples about the teaching of the religious leaders of His time—the Pharisees and the Sadducees.

But Jesus aware of this, said, "You men of little faith, why do you discuss among yourselves that you have no bread? Do you not yet understand or remember the five loaves of the five thousand and how many baskets *full* you picked up? Or the seven loaves of the four thousand, and how many large baskets *full* you picked up? How is it that you do not understand that I did not speak to you concerning bread? But beware of the leaven of the Pharisees and Sadducees" (Matthew 16:8–11; cf. Matthew 14:17–21; 15:34–38; Mark 8:17–21).

Setting: The temple in Jerusalem. The Sadducees question Jesus about Levirate marriage (marriage to a brother-in-law), in order to test Him.

But Jesus answered and said to them, "You are mistaken, not understanding the Scriptures nor the power of God. For in the resurrection they neither marry nor are given in marriage, but are like angels in heaven. But regarding the resurrection of the dead, have you not read what was spoken to you by God: 'I AM THE GOD OF ABRAHAM, AND THE GOD OF ISAAC, AND THE GOD OF JACOB'? He is not the God of the dead but of the living" (Matthew 22:29–32, Jesus quotes from Exodus 3:6; cf. Mark 12:18–27; Luke 20:27–38; see Deuteronomy 25:5; John 20:9).

[UNDERSTANDING from understand]
Setting: On the Mount of Olives, just east of Jerusalem. During His Olivet Discourse, after answering His disciples' questions as to when the temple will be destroyed and Jerusalem overrun, along with the signs of His coming and the end of the age, Jesus teaches them the Parable of the Fig Tree.

"Now learn the parable from the fig tree: when its branch has already become tender and puts forth its leaves, you know that summer is near; so, you too, when you see all these things, recognize that He is near, *right* at the door. Truly, I say to you, this generation will not pass away until all these things take place. Heaven and earth will pass away, but My words will not pass away. But of that day and hour no one knows, not even the angels of heaven, nor the Son, but the Father alone. For the coming of the Son of Man will be just like the days of Noah. For as in those days before the flood they were eating and drinking, marrying and giving in marriage, until the day that Noah entered the ark, and they did not understand until the flood came and took them all away; so will the coming of the Son of Man be. Then there will be two men in the field; one will be taken and one will be left. Two women *will be* grinding at the mill; one will be taken and one will be left" (Matthew 24:32–41; cf. Mark 13:28–32; Luke 17:34–36; 21:28–33; see Genesis 6:5; 7:7; Matthew 5:18; 10:23; James 5:9).

[UNDERSTANDING from understand]
Setting: By the Sea of Galilee. After Jesus conveys the Parable of the Sower from a boat to a crowd, His disciples ask Him questions about it.

And He was saying to them, "To you has been given the mystery of the kingdom of God, but those who are outside get everything in parables, so that WHILE SEEING, THEY MAY SEE AND NOT PERCEIVE, AND WHILE HEARING, THEY MAY HEAR AND NOT UNDERSTAND, OTHERWISE THEY MIGHT RETURN AND BE FORGIVEN" (Mark 4:11, 12, Jesus quotes from Isaiah 6:9, 10; cf. Matthew 13:10–17).

[UNDERSTANDING from understand]
Setting: By the Sea of Galilee. During the early part of His ministry, after presenting the Parable of the Sower from a boat to a very large crowd, Jesus gives the meaning of the parable to His disciples and other followers.

And He said to them, "Do you not understand this parable? How will you understand all the parables? The sower sows the word. These are the ones who are beside the road where the word is sown; and when they hear, immediately Satan comes and takes away the word which has been sown in them. In a similar way these are the ones on whom seed was sown on the rocky places, who, when they hear the word, immediately receive it with joy; and they have no *firm* root in themselves, but are *only* temporary; then, when affliction or persecution arises because of the word, immediately they fall away. And others are the ones on whom seed was sown among the thorns; these are the ones who have heard the word, but the worries of the world and the deceitfulness of riches, and the desires for other things enter in and choke the word, and it becomes unfruitful. And those are the ones on whom seed was sown on the good soil; and they hear the word and accept it and bear fruit, thirty, sixty, and a hundredfold" (Mark 4:13–20; cf. Matthew 13:18–23; Luke 8:11–15).

Setting: Galilee. After the Pharisees and scribes from Jerusalem object to His disciples' lack of obedience to the tradition regarding ceremonial cleansing, Jesus speaks to a crowd, and explains His teaching to the disciples.

After He called the crowd to Him again, He *began* saying to them, "Listen to Me, all of you, and understand: there is nothing outside the man which can defile him if it goes into him; but the things which proceed out of the man are what defile the man. [If anyone has ears to hear, let him hear."] When he had left the crowd *and* entered the house, His disciples questioned Him about the parable. And He said to them, "Are you so lacking in understanding also? Do you not understand that whatever goes into the man from outside cannot defile him, because it does not go into his heart, but into his stomach, and is eliminated?" (*Thus He* declared all foods clean.) And He was saying, "That which proceeds out of the man, that is what defiles the man. For from within, out of the heart of men, proceed the evil thoughts, fornications, thefts, murders, adulteries, deeds of coveting *and* wickedness, *as well* as deceit, sensuality, envy, slander, pride *and* foolishness. All these evil things proceed from within and defile the man" (Mark 7:14–23; cf. Matthew 15:10–20).

[UNDERSTANDING from understand]

Setting: The district of Dalmanutha. After the Pharisees argue with Jesus, seeking a sign from heaven to test Him, the Lord and His disciples cross to the other side of the Sea of Galilee, where the disciples discuss with one another that they have no bread.

And Jesus, aware of this, said to them, "Why do you discuss *the fact* that you have no bread? Do you not yet see or understand? Do you have a hardened heart? HAVING EYES, DO YOU NOT SEE? AND HAVING EARS, DO YOU NOT HEAR? And do you not remember, when I broke the five loaves for the five thousand, how many baskets full of broken pieces you picked you? They said to Him, "Twelve." When *I broke* the seven for the four thousand, how many large baskets full of broken pieces did you pick up?" They said to Him, "Seven." And He was saying to them, "Do you not yet understand?" (Mark 8:17–21, Jesus quotes from Jeremiah 5:21; cf. Matthew 16:5–12; see Matthew 14:19, 20; Mark 6:41–44, 52).

[UNDERSTANDING from understand]

Setting: The temple in Jerusalem. After some of the Pharisees and Herodians attempt to trap Jesus in a statement, some Sadducees question Him about the status of marriage after death.

Jesus said to them, "Is this not the reason you are mistaken, that you do not understand the Scriptures or the power of God? For when they rise from the dead, they neither marry nor are given in marriage, but are like angels in heaven. But regarding the fact that the dead rise again, have you not read in the book of Moses, in the *passage* about *the burning* bush, how God spoke to him, saying, 'I AM THE GOD OF ABRAHAM, AND THE GOD OF ISAAC, and the God of Jacob?' He is not the God of the dead, but of the living; you are greatly mistaken" (Mark 12:24–27, Jesus quotes from Exodus 3:6; cf. Matthew 22:29–33; Luke 20:34–40).

[UNDERSTANDING from understand]

Setting: Galilee. After Jesus presents the Parable of the Sower to the crowds, His disciples ask Him to give them the parable's meaning.

And He said, "To you it has been granted to know the mysteries of the kingdom of God, but to the rest *it is* in parables, so that SEEING THEY MAY NOT SEE, AND HEARING THEY MAY NOT UNDERSTAND. Now the parable is this: the seed is the word of God. Those beside the road are those who have heard; then the devil comes and takes away the word from their heart, so that they will not believe and be saved. Those on the rocky *soil* are those who, when they hear, receive the word with joy; and these have no *firm* root; they believe for a while, and in time of temptation fall away. The *seed* which fell among the thorns, these are the ones who have heard, and as they go on their way they are choked with worries and riches and pleasures of *this* life, and bring no fruit to maturity. But the *seed* in the good soil, these are the ones who have heard the word in an honest and good heart, and hold it fast, and bear fruit with perseverance" (Luke 8:10–15, Jesus quotes from Isaiah 6:9; cf. Matthew 13:10–23; Mark 4:10–20).

[UNDERSTANDING from understand]

Setting: Jerusalem. At the time for the Passover of the Jews, after the Lord cleanses the temple, a Pharisee, Nicodemus, asks Him by night the meaning of "born of the Spirit."

Jesus answered and said to him, "Are you the teacher of Israel and do not understand these things? Truly, truly, I say to you, we speak of what we know and testify of what we have seen, and you do not accept our testimony. If I told you earthly things and you do not believe, how will you believe if I tell you heavenly things? No one has ascended into heaven, but He who descended from heaven: the Son of Man. As Moses lifted up the serpent in the wilderness, even so must the Son of Man be lifted up; so that whoever believes will in Him have eternal life" (John 3:10–15; see Numbers 21:9; Proverb 30:4; John 12:34; 20:30, 31).

[UNDERSTANDING from understand]
Setting: The temple treasury in Jerusalem. After the scribes and Pharisees question His testimony about Himself, Jesus argues with them regarding their ancestry and motives.

Jesus said to them, "If God were your Father, you would love Me, for I proceeded forth and have come from God, for I have not even come on My own initiative, but He sent Me. Why do you not understand what I am saying? *It is* because you cannot hear My word. You are of *your* father the devil, and you want to do the desires of your father. He was a murderer from the beginning, and does not stand in the truth because there is no truth in him. Whenever he speaks a lie, he speaks from his own *nature,* for he is a liar and the father of lies. But because I speak the truth, you do not believe Me. Which one of you convicts Me of sin? If I speak truth, why do you not believe Me? He who is of God hears the words of God; for this reason you do not hear *them,* because you are not of God" (John 8:42–47; see John 18:37; 1 John 3:8; 4:6; 5:1).

[UNDERSTANDING from understand]
Setting: Jerusalem. At the Feast of Dedication, the Pharisees desire to stone Jesus because He claims to be equal with God when they ask Him plainly whether He is the Christ.

Jesus answered them, "Has it not been written in your Law, 'I SAID, YOU ARE GODS'? If he called them gods, to whom the word of God came (and the Scripture cannot be broken), do you say of Him, whom the Father sanctified and sent into the world, 'You are blaspheming,' because I said, 'I am the Son of God'? If I do not do the works of My Father, do not believe Me; but if I do them, though you do not believe Me, believe the works, so that you may know and understand that the Father is in Me, and I in the Father" (John 10:34–38, Jesus quotes from Psalm 82:6; see John 14:10, 20).

[UNDERSTANDING from understand]
Setting: Jerusalem. Before the Passover, with His crucifixion nearing, Jesus eats supper with His disciples and assumes the role of a servant, washing His followers' feet.

Jesus answered and said to him, "What I do you do not realize now, but you will understand hereafter." Peter said to Him, "Never shall You wash my feet!" Jesus answered him, "If I do not wash you, you have no part with Me." Simon Peter said to Him, "Lord, *then wash* not only my feet, but also my hand and my head." Jesus said to him, "He who has bathed needs only to wash his feet, but is completely clean; and you are clean, but not all *of you*. For He knew the one who was betraying Him; for this reason He said, "Not all of you are clean" (John 13:7–11; see John 6:64; 15:3).

[UNDERSTANDING from understood]
Setting: Jerusalem. Before the Passover, after giving His disciples hope that in the midst of tribulation they will have His peace, Jesus prays His high-priestly prayer.

Jesus spoke these things; and lifting up His eyes to heaven, He said, "Father, the hour has come; glorify Your Son, that the Son may glorify You, even as You gave Him authority over all flesh, that to all whom You have given Him, He may give eternal life. This is eternal life, that they may know You, the only true God, and Jesus Christ whom You have sent. I glorified You on the earth, having accomplished the work which You have given Me to do. Now, Father, glorify Me together with Yourself, with the glory which I had with You before the world was. I have manifested Your name to the men whom You gave Me out of the world; they were Yours and You gave them to Me, and they have kept Your word. Now they have come to know that everything You have given Me is from You; for the words which You gave Me I have given to them; and they received *them* and truly understood that I came forth from You, and they believed You sent Me. I ask on their behalf; I do not ask on behalf of the world, but of those whom You have given

Me; for they are Yours; and all things that are Mine are Yours, and Yours are Mine; and I have been glorified in them. I am no longer in the world; and *yet* they themselves are in the world, and I come to You. Holy Father, keep them in Your name, *the name* which You have given Me, that they may be even as We *are.* While I was with them, I was keeping them in Your name which You have given Me; and I guarded them and not one of them perished but the son of perdition, so that the Scripture would be fulfilled" (John 17:1–12; see Luke 22:32; John 1:1; 3:35; 4:34; 5:44; 6:37–39, 70; 8:42; 11:41; 12:49; 13:18, 31; 16:15; Philippians 2:9).

UNDERSTANDING THE TIMES (See TIMES, SIGNS OF THE)

UNFORGIVENESS (See FORGIVENESS)

UNFORGIVABLE SIN (Listed under SIN, UNFORGIVABLE)

UNFRUITFULNESS

[UNFRUITFULNESS from unfruitful]
Setting: By the Sea of Galilee. With the religious leaders rejecting His message, Jesus begins to teach in parables, and gives His disciples the meaning of the Parable of the Sower.

"Hear then the parable of the sower. When anyone hears the word of the kingdom and does not understand it, the evil *one* comes and snatches away what has been sown in his heart. This is the one on whom seed was sown beside the road. The one on whom seed was sown on the rocky places, this is the man who hears the word and immediately receives it with joy; yet he has no *firm* root in himself, but is *only* temporary, and when affliction or persecution arises because of the word, immediately he falls away. And the one on whom seed was sown among the thorns, this is the man who hears the word, and the worry of the world and the deceitfulness of wealth choke the word, and it becomes unfruitful. And the one on whom seed was sown on the good soil, this is the man who hears the word and understands it; who indeed bears fruit and brings forth, some a hundredfold, some sixty, and some thirty" (Matthew 13:18–23; cf. Mark 4:13–20; Luke 8:11–15).

[UNFRUITFULNESS from unfruitful]
Setting: By the Sea of Galilee. During the early part of His ministry, after presenting the Parable of the Sower from a boat to a very large crowd, Jesus gives the meaning of the parable to His disciples and other followers.

And He said to them, "Do you not understand this parable? How will you understand all the parables? The sower sows the word. These are the ones who are beside the road where the word is sown; and when they hear, immediately Satan comes and takes away the word which has been sown in them. In a similar way these are the ones on whom seed was sown on the rocky places, who, when they hear the word, immediately receive it with joy; and they have no *firm* root in themselves, but are *only* temporary; then, when affliction or persecution arises because of the word, immediately they fall away. And others are the ones on whom seed was sown among the thorns; these are the ones who have heard the word, but the worries of the world and the deceitfulness of riches, and the desires for other things enter in and choke the word, and it becomes unfruitful. And those are the ones on whom seed was sown on the good soil; and they hear the word and accept it and bear fruit, thirty, sixty, and a hundredfold" (Mark 4:13–20; cf. Matthew 13:18–23; Luke 8:11–15).

UNGODLY TEACHING (Listed under TEACHING, UNGODLY)

UNITY

[UNITY from they may be even as We *are*]
Setting: Jerusalem. Before the Passover, after giving His disciples assurance that in the midst of tribulation they will have His peace, Jesus prays His high-priestly prayer.

Jesus spoke these things; and lifting up His eyes to heaven, He said, "Father, the hour has come; glorify Your Son, that the Son may glorify You, even as You gave Him authority over all flesh, that to all whom You have given Him, He may give eternal life. This is eternal life, that they may know You, the only true God, and Jesus Christ whom You have sent. I glorified You on the earth, having accomplished the work which You have given Me to do. Now, Father, glorify Me together with Yourself, with the glory which I had with You before the world was. I have manifested Your name to the men whom You gave Me out of the world; they were Yours and You gave them to Me, and they have kept Your word. Now they have come to know that everything You have given Me is from You; for the words which You gave Me I have given to them; and they received *them* and truly understood that I came forth from You, and they believed You sent Me. I ask on their behalf; I do not ask on behalf of the world, but of those whom You have given Me; for they are Yours; and all things that are Mine are Yours, and Yours are Mine; and I have been glorified in them. I am no longer in the world; and *yet* they themselves are in the world, and I come to You. Holy Father, keep them in Your name, *the name* which You have given Me, that they may be even as We *are*. While I was with them, I was keeping them in Your name which You have given Me; and I guarded them and not one of them perished but the son of perdition, so that the Scripture would be fulfilled" (John 17:1–12; see Luke 22:32; John 1:1; 3:35; 4:34; 5:44; 6:37–39, 70; 8:42; 11:41; 12:49; 13:18, 31; 16:15; Philippians 2:9).

[UNITY from that they may all be one]
Setting: Jerusalem. Before the Passover, after giving His disciples assurance that in the midst of tribulation they will have His peace, Jesus continues praying His high-priestly prayer.

"But now I come to You; and these things I speak in the world so that they may have My joy made full in themselves. I have given them Your word; and the world has hated them, because they are not of the world, even as I am not of the world. I do not ask You to take them out of the world, but to keep them from the evil *one*. They are not of the world, even as I am not of the world. Sanctify them in the truth; Your word is truth. As You sent Me into the world, I also have sent them into the world. For their sakes I sanctify Myself, that they themselves also may be sanctified in truth. I do not ask on behalf of these alone, but for those also who believe in Me through their word; that they may all be one; even as You, Father, *are* in Me and I in You, that they also maybe in Us, so that the world may believe that You sent Me" (John 17:13–21; see Matthew 10:5, 38; John 7:33; 15:3, 11, 19).

[UNITY also from that they may be one, just as We are one]
Setting: Jerusalem. Before the Passover, after giving His disciples assurance that in the midst of tribulation they will have His peace, Jesus continues praying His high-priestly prayer.

"The glory which You have given Me I have given to them, that they may be one, just as We are one; I in them and You in Me, that they may be perfected in unity, so that the world may know that you sent Me, and loved them, even as You have loved Me. Father, I desire that they also, whom You have given Me, be with Me where I am, so that they may see My glory which You have given Me, for You loved Me before the foundation of the world. O righteous Father, although the world has not known You, yet I have known You; and these have known that You sent Me; and I have made Your name known to them, and will make it known, so that the love with which You loved Me may be in them, and I in them" (John 17:22–26; see Matthew 25:34; John 1:14; 10:38; 15:9; 16:27).

UNJUST
Setting: On the way from Galilee to Jerusalem. After instructing His disciples about persistence in prayer, Jesus conveys a parable about self-righteousness.

And He also told this parable to some people who trusted in themselves that they were righteous, and viewed others with contempt: "Two men went up into the temple to pray, one a Pharisee and the other a tax collector. The Pharisee stood and was praying this to himself: 'God, I thank You that I am not like other people: swindlers, unjust, adulterers, or even like this tax collector. I fast twice a week; I pay tithes of all that I get.' But the tax collector, standing some distance away, was even unwilling to lift up his eyes to heaven, but was beating his breast, saying, 'God, be merciful to me, the sinner!' I tell you, this man went to his house justified rather than the other; for everyone who exalts himself will be humbled, but he who humbles himself will be exalted" (Luke 18:9–14; see Ezra 9:6; Matthew 6:5, 23:12; Luke 11:42; 16:15; Romans 14:3, 10).

UNLEAVENED BREAD (Listed under BREAD, UNLEAVENED)

UNPARDONABLE SIN (Listed under SIN, UNPARDONABLE)

UNREPENTANCE

[UNREPENTANCE from they would have repented]

Setting: Galilee. After performing miracles throughout the region, Jesus pronounces woes against those cities who have not repented.

"Woe to you, Chorazin! Woe to you, Bethsaida! For if the miracles had occurred in Tyre and Sidon which occurred in you, they would have repented long ago in sackcloth and ashes. Nevertheless I say to you, it will be more tolerable for Tyre and Sidon in *the* day of judgment than for you. And you, Capernaum, will not be exalted to heaven, will you? You will descend to Hades; for if the miracles had occurred in Sodom which occurred in you, it would have remained to this day. Nevertheless, I say to you that it will be more tolerable for the land of Sodom in *the* day of judgment, than for you" (Matthew 11:21–24; cf. Matthew 10:15; Luke 10:13–15).

[UNREPENTANCE from you were unwilling]

Setting: The temple in Jerusalem. With His death on the cross just days away, Jesus laments over Jerusalem's hard-heartedness and lack of repentance.

"Jerusalem, Jerusalem, who kills the prophets and stones those who are sent to her! How often I wanted to gather your children together, the way a hen gathers her chicks under her wings, and you were unwilling. Behold, your house is being left to you desolate! For I say to you, from now on you will not see Me until you say, 'BLESSED IS HE WHO COMES IN THE NAME OF THE LORD!'" (Matthew 23:37–39, Jesus quotes from Psalm 118:26; cf. 1 Kings 9:7; Luke 13:34, 35).

[UNREPENTANCE from they would have repented]

Setting: On the way from Galilee to Jerusalem. The Lord pronounces woes on cities who reject the gospel, as He appoints seventy followers and sends them out in pairs to every place He Himself will soon visit.

"Woe to you, Chorazin! Woe to you, Bethsaida! For if the miracles had been performed in Tyre and Sidon which occurred in you, they would have repented long ago, sitting in sackcloth and ashes. But it will be more tolerable for Tyre and Sidon in the judgment than for you. And you, Capernaum, will not be exalted to heaven, will you? You will be brought down to Hades! The one who listens to you listens to Me, and the one who rejects you rejects Me; and he who rejects Me rejects the One who sent Me" (Luke 10:13–16; cf. Matthew 11:21–23; see Matthew 10:40).

UNRIGHTEOUS (JUDGE, UNRIGHTEOUS is a separate entry; also see UNRIGHTEOUSNESS; and UNSAVED)

Setting: Galilee. During the early part of His ministry, Jesus preaches the Sermon on the Mount to His disciples and the multitudes.

"You have heard that it was said, 'YOU SHALL LOVE YOUR NEIGHBOR and hate your enemy.' But I say to you, love your enemies and pray for those who persecute you, so that you may be sons of your Father who is in heaven; for He causes His sun to rise on *the* evil and *the* good, and sends rain on *the* righteous and *the* unrighteous. For if you love those who love you, what reward do you have? Do not even the tax collectors do the same? If you greet only your brothers, what more are you doing *than others?* Do not even the Gentiles do the same? Therefore, you are to be perfect, as your heavenly Father is perfect" (Matthew 5:43–48, Jesus quotes from Leviticus 19:18; cf. Leviticus 19:2; Luke 6:27–36).

Setting: On the way from Galilee to Jerusalem. After giving the story of the prodigal son, the Lord teaches His disciples about stewardship.

Now He was also saying to the disciples, "There was a rich man who had a manager, and this *manager* was reported to him as squandering his possessions. And he called him and said to him, 'What is this I hear about you? Give an accounting of your management, for you can no longer be a manager.' The manager said to himself, 'What shall I do, since my master is taking the management away from me? I am not strong enough to dig; I am ashamed to beg. I know what I shall do, so that when I am removed from the management people will welcome me into their homes.' And he summoned each one of his master's debtors, and he

began saying to the first, 'How much do you owe my master?' And he said, 'A hundred measures of oil.' And he said to him, 'Take your bill, and sit down quickly and write fifty.' Then he said to another, 'And how much do you owe?' And he said, 'A hundred measures of wheat.' He said to him, 'Take your bill, and write eighty.' And his master praised the unrighteous manager because he had acted shrewdly; for the sons of this age are more shrewd in relation to their own kind than the sons of light. And I say to you, make friends for yourselves by means of the wealth of unrighteousness, so that when it fails, they will receive you into the eternal dwellings. He who is faithful in a very little thing is faithful also in much; and he who is unrighteous in a very little thing is unrighteous also in much. Therefore if you have not been faithful in the *use of* unrighteous wealth, who will entrust the true *riches* to you? And if you have not been faithful in *the use of* that which is another's, who will give you that which is your own? No servant can serve two masters; for either he will hate the one and love the other, or else he will be devoted to one and despise the other. You cannot serve God and wealth" (Luke 16:1–13; cf. Matthew 6:24; see Matthew 25:14–30).

UNRIGHTEOUS JUDGE (Listed under JUDGE, UNRIGHTEOUS)

UNRIGHTEOUS MANAGER (See MANAGER)

UNRIGHTEOUSNESS (Also see UNRIGHTEOUS)

Setting: On the way from Galilee to Jerusalem. After giving the story of the prodigal son, the Lord teaches His disciples about stewardship.

Now He was also saying to the disciples, "There was a rich man who had a manager, and this *manager* was reported to him as squandering his possessions. And he called him and said to him, 'What is this I hear about you? Give an accounting of your management, for you can no longer be a manager.' The manager said to himself, 'What shall I do, since my master is taking the management away from me? I am not strong enough to dig; I am ashamed to beg. I know what I shall do, so that when I am removed from the management people will welcome me into their homes.' And he summoned each one of his master's debtors, and he *began* saying to the first, 'How much do you owe my master?' And he said, 'A hundred measures of oil.' And he said to him, 'Take your bill, and sit down quickly and write fifty.' Then he said to another, 'And how much do you owe?' And he said, 'A hundred measures of wheat.' He said to him, 'Take your bill, and write eighty.' And his master praised the unrighteous manager because he had acted shrewdly; for the sons of this age are more shrewd in relation to their own kind than the sons of light. And I say to you, make friends for yourselves by means of the wealth of unrighteousness, so that when it fails, they will receive you into the eternal dwellings. He who is faithful in a very little thing is faithful also in much; and he who is unrighteous in a very little thing is unrighteous also in much. Therefore if you have not been faithful in the *use of* unrighteous wealth, who will entrust the true *riches* to you? And if you have not been faithful in *the use of* that which is another's, who will give you that which is your own? No servant can serve two masters; for either he will hate the one and love the other, or else he will be devoted to one and despise the other. You cannot serve God and wealth" (Luke 16:1–13; cf. Matthew 6:24; see Matthew 25:14–30).

Setting: The temple in Jerusalem. After receiving encouragement from His blood brothers in Galilee to attend the upcoming Feast of Booths in order to demonstrate His works to His disciples and the world, Jesus goes and teaches, astonishing the Jewish religious leaders.

So Jesus answered them and said, "My teaching is not Mine, but His who sent Me. If anyone is willing to do His will, he will know of the teaching, whether it is of God or *whether* I speak of Myself. He who speaks from himself seeks his own glory; but He who is seeking the glory of the One who sent Him, He is true, and there is no unrighteousness in Him" (John 7:16–18; see John 5:41).

UNSAVED (See LOST, CONCERN FOR THE; UNBELIEVING; UNBELIEVERS; and UNRIGHTEOUS)

UNSHRUNK CLOTH (Listed under CLOTH, UNSHRUNK)

UNWASHED HANDS (Listed under HANDS, UNWASHED)

UNWELCOME (Also see REJECTION; and WELCOME)

[UNWELCOME from Whoever does not receive you]

Setting: Galilee. After His twelve disciples observe His ministry, Jesus summons and specifically instructs them about their ministry to the people of Israel.

These twelve Jesus sent out after instructing them: "Do not go in *the* way of *the* Gentiles, and do not enter *any* city of the Samaritans; but rather go to the lost sheep of the house of Israel. And as you go, preach, saying, 'The kingdom of heaven is at hand.' Heal *the* sick, raise *the* dead, cleanse *the* lepers, cast out demons. Freely you received, freely give. Do not acquire gold, or silver, or copper for your money belts, or a bag for *your* journey, or even two coats, or sandals, or a staff; for the worker is worthy of his support. And whatever city or village you enter, inquire who is worthy in it, and stay at his house until you leave *that city*. As you enter the house, give it your greeting. If the house is worthy, give it your *blessing of* peace. But if it is not worthy, take back your *blessing of* peace. Whoever does not receive you, nor heed your words, as you go out of that house or that city, shake the dust off your feet. Truly I say to you, it will be more tolerable for *the* land of Sodom and Gomorrah in the day of judgment than for that city" (Matthew 10:5–15; cf. Mark 6:7–11; Luke 9:1–5; see Matthew 3:2; 11:22, 24; 15:24; Luke 22:35; 1 Corinthians 9:14).

[UNWELCOME from does not receive you or listen to you]

Setting: Jesus' hometown of Nazareth in Galilee. After encountering unbelief, Jesus sends the Twelve out in pairs with authority and instructions about ministry.

And He summoned the twelve and began to send them out in pairs, and gave them authority over the unclean spirits; and He instructed them that they should take nothing for *their* journey, except a mere staff—no bread, no bag, no money in their belt—but to wear sandals; and *He added,* "Do not put on two tunics." And He said to them, "Wherever you enter a house, stay there until you leave town. Any place that does not receive you or listen to you, as you go out from there, shake the dust off the soles of your feet for a testimony against them" (Mark 6:7–11; cf. Matthew 10:1–14; Luke 9:1–5).

[UNWELCOME from who do not receive you]

Setting: Galilee. After raising the daughter of Jairus, a synagogue official, from the dead, Jesus calls His twelve disciples together and gives them power and authority over demons, along with the ability to cure diseases.

And He said to them, "Take nothing for *your* journey, neither a staff, nor a bag, nor bread, nor money; and do not *even* have two tunics apiece. Whatever house you enter, stay there until you leave that city. And as for those who do not receive you, go out from that city, shake the dust off your feet as a testimony against them" (Luke 9:3–5; cf. Matthew 10:1–15; Mark 6:7–11; see Luke 10:4–12).

[UNWELCOME from they do not receive you]

Setting: On the way from Galilee to Jerusalem. The Lord appoints seventy followers and sends them out in pairs to every place He Himself will soon visit.

And He was saying to them, "The harvest is plentiful, but the laborers are few; therefore beseech the Lord of the harvest to send out laborers into His harvest. Go; behold, I send you out as lambs in the midst of wolves. Carry no money belt, no bag, no shoes; and greet no one on the way. Whatever house you enter, first say, 'Peace be to this house.' If a man of peace is there, your peace will rest on him; but if not, it will return to you. Stay in that house, eating and drinking what they give you; for the laborer is worthy of his wages. Do not keep moving from house to house. Whatever city you enter and they receive you, eat what is set before you; and heal those in it who are sick, and say to them, 'The kingdom of God has come near to you.' But whatever city you enter and they do not receive you, go out into its streets and say, 'Even the dust of your city which clings to our feet we wipe off *in protest* against you; yet be sure of this, that the kingdom of God has come near.' I say to you, it will be more tolerable in that day for Sodom than for that city" (Luke 10:2–12; see Genesis 19:24–28; Matthew 9:37, 38, 10:9–14, 16; 1 Corinthians 10:27).

UPPER ROOM (Listed under ROOM, UPPER)

UPPER ROOM DISCOURSE (See passages from John 13:1–16:33)

UTTERANCE

Setting: On the Mount of Olives, east of the temple in Jerusalem. After ministering in the temple a few days before His crucifixion, and giving His disciples more details regarding the temple's future destruction, Jesus elaborates during His Olivet Discourse about things to come.

Then He continued by saying to them, "Nation will rise against nation and kingdom against kingdom, and there will be great earthquakes, and in various places plagues and famines; and there will be terrors and great signs from heaven. But before all these things, they will lay their hands on you and will persecute you, delivering you to the synagogues and prisons, bringing you before kings and governors for My name's sake. It will lead to an opportunity for your testimony. So make up your minds not to prepare beforehand to defend yourselves; for I will give you utterance and wisdom which none of your opponents will be able to resist or refute. But you will be betrayed even by parents and brothers and relatives and friends, and they will put *some* of you to death, and you will be hated by all because of My name. Yet not a hair of your head will perish. By your endurance you will gain your lives" (Luke 21:10–19; cf. Matthew 10:19–22; 24:7–14; Mark 13:8–13).

V

VALUE, GREAT

Setting: By the Sea of Galilee. Jesus declares the Parable of the Pearl to the crowds.

"Again, the kingdom of heaven is like a merchant seeking fine pearls, and upon finding one pearl of great value, he went and sold all that he had and bought it" (Matthew 13:45, 46).

VALUE, HUMAN (See HUMAN VALUE)

VALUE OF MAN (See HUMAN VALUE)

VAT

Setting: The temple in Jerusalem. Having His authority questioned by the chief priests, scribes, and elders, Jesus begins to teach them in parables.

And He began to speak to them in parables: "A man PLANTED A VINEYARD AND PUT A WALL AROUND IT, AND DUG A VAT UNDER THE WINE PRESS AND BUILT A TOWER, and rented it out to vine-growers and went on a journey. At the *harvest* time he sent a slave to the vine-growers, in order to receive *some* of the produce of the vineyard from the vine-growers. They took him, and beat him and sent him away empty-handed. Again he sent them another slave, and they wounded him in the head, and treated him shamefully. And he sent another, and that one they killed; and *so with* many others, beating some and killing others. He had one more to *send*, a beloved son; he sent him last *of all* to them, saying, 'They will respect my son.' But those vine-growers said to one another, 'This is the heir; come, let us kill him, and the inheritance will be ours!' They took him, and killed him and threw him out of the vineyard. What will the owner of the vineyard do? He will come and destroy the vine-growers, and will give the vineyard to others. Have you not even read this Scripture: 'THE STONE WHICH THE BUILDERS REJECTED, THIS BECAME THE CHIEF CORNER *stone;* THIS CAME ABOUT FROM THE LORD, AND IT IS MARVELOUS IN OUR EYES'?" (Mark 12:1–11, Jesus quotes from Psalm 118:22, 23; Isaiah 5:1, 2; cf. Matthew 21:33–46; Luke 20:9–19).

VENGEANCE (Also see REVENGE)

[VENGEANCE from AN EYE FOR AN EYE, AND A TOOTH FOR A TOOTH]

Setting: Galilee. During the early part of His ministry, Jesus preaches the Sermon on the Mount to His disciples and the multitudes.

"You have heard that it was said, 'AN EYE FOR AN EYE, AND A TOOTH FOR A TOOTH.' But I say to you, do not resist an evil person; but whoever slaps you on your right cheek, turn the other to him also" (Matthew 5:38, 39, Jesus quotes from Exodus 21:24; cf. Leviticus 24:20).

Setting: On the Mount of Olives, east of the temple in Jerusalem. After ministering in the temple a few days before His crucifixion, and giving the disciples more details regarding future events, Jesus elaborates during His Olivet Discourse about things to come.

"But when you see Jerusalem surrounded by armies, then recognize that her desolation is near. Then those who are in Judea must flee to the mountains, and those who are in the midst of the city must leave, and those who are in the country must not enter the city; because these are days of vengeance, so that all things which are written will be fulfilled. Woe to those who are pregnant and to those who are nursing babies in those days; for there will be a great distress upon the land and wrath to this people; and they will fall by the edge of the sword, and will be led captive into all the nations; and Jerusalem will be trampled under foot by the Gentiles until the times of the Gentiles are fulfilled" (Luke 21:20–24; see Matthew 24:15–18; Mark 13:14–16; Luke 19:43).

VERBOSITY

[VERBOSITY from many words]

Setting: Galilee. During the early part of His ministry, Jesus preaches the Sermon on the Mount to His disciples and the multitudes.

"And when you are praying, do not use meaningless repetition as the Gentiles do, for they suppose that they will be heard for their many words. So do not be like them; for your Father knows what you need before you ask Him" (Matthew 6:7, 8; see 1 Kings 18:26–29).

VESSELS

Setting: On the island of Patmos (in the Aegean Sea about fifty miles southwest of Ephesus in modern Turkey). On the Lord's Day (Sunday), approximately fifty years after the Resurrection, the disciple John encounters the Lord Jesus Christ, who communicates a new revelation for the apostle to record for the church in Thyatira and to six other churches in Asia.

"And to the angel of the church in Thyatira write: The Son of God, who has eyes like a flame of fire, and His feet are like burnished bronze, says this: 'I know your deeds, and your love and faith and service and perseverance, and that your deeds of late are greater than at first. But I have *this* against you, that you tolerate the woman Jezebel, who calls herself a prophetess, and she teaches and leads My bond-servants astray so that they commit *acts of* immorality and eat things sacrificed to idols. I gave her time to repent, and she does not want to repent of her immorality. Behold, I will throw her on a bed *of sickness,* and those who commit adultery with her into great tribulation, unless they repent of her deeds. And I will kill her children with pestilence, and all the churches will know that I am He who searches the minds and hearts; and I will give to each one of you according to your deeds. But I say to you, the rest who are in Thyatira, who do not hold this teaching, who have not known the deep things of Satan, as they call them—I place no other burden on you. Nevertheless what you have, hold fast until I come. He who overcomes, and he who keeps My deeds until the end, TO HIM I WILL GIVE AUTHORITY OVER THE NATIONS; AND HE SHALL RULE THEM WITH A ROD OF IRON, AS THE VESSELS OF THE POTTER ARE BROKEN TO PIECES, as I also have received *authority* from My Father; and I will give him the morning star. He who has an ear, let him hear what the Spirit says to the churches' (Revelation 2:18–29; Jesus quotes from Psalm 2:8, 9; Isaiah 30:14; see 1 Kings 16:31; Psalm 7:9; Romans 2:5; 1 Corinthians 2:10; 2 Peter 3:9; Revelation 1:14; 2:7; 3:11; 17:1–20).

VICTORY

[VICTORY from I have overcome the world]

Setting: Jerusalem. Before the Passover, after conveying promises about praying in His name, Jesus prophesies the disciples' scattering and gives them assurance that in the midst of tribulation they will have His peace.

"Jesus answered them, "Do you now believe? Behold, an hour is coming, and has *already* come, for you to be scattered, each to his own *home,* and to leave Me alone; and *yet* I am not alone, because the Father is with Me. These things I have spoken to you, so that in Me you may have peace. In the world you have tribulation, but take courage, I have overcome the world" (John 16:31–33; see Zechariah 13:7; John 8:29; 14:27; Romans 8:37).

[VICTORY from To him who overcomes]

Setting: On the island of Patmos (in the Aegean Sea about fifty miles southwest of Ephesus in modern Turkey). On the Lord's Day (Sunday), approximately fifty years after the Resurrection, the disciple John encounters the Lord Jesus Christ, who communicates a new revelation for the apostle to record for the church in Ephesus and to six other churches in Asia.

"To the angel of the church in Ephesus write: The One who holds the seven stars in His right hand, the One who walks among the seven golden lampstands, says this: 'I know your deeds and your toil and perseverance, and that you cannot tolerate evil men, and you put to the test those who call themselves apostles, and they are not, and you found them *to be* false; and you have perseverance and have endured for My name's sake, and have not grown weary. But I have *this* against you, that you have left your first love. Therefore remember from where you have fallen, and repent and do the deeds you did at first; or else I am coming to you and will remove your lampstand out of its place—unless you repent. Yet this you do have, that you hate the deeds of the Nicolaitans, which I also hate. He who has an ear, let him hear what the Spirit says to the churches. To him who overcomes, I will grant to eat of the tree of life which is in the Paradise of God' " (Revelation 2:1–7; see Genesis 2:9; Ezekiel 28:13; 1 John 4:1; Revelation 1:10, 11, 19, 20).

[VICTORY from He who overcomes]
Setting: On the island of Patmos (in the Aegean Sea about fifty miles southwest of Ephesus in modern Turkey). On the Lord's Day (Sunday), approximately fifty years after the Resurrection, the disciple John encounters the Lord Jesus Christ, who communicates a new revelation for the apostle to record for the church in Smyrna and to six other churches in Asia.

"And to the angel of the church in Smyrna write: The first and the last, who was dead, and has come to life, says this: 'I know your tribulation and your poverty (but you are rich), and the blasphemy by those who say they are Jews and are not, but are a synagogue of Satan. Do not fear what you are about to suffer. Behold, the devil is about to cast some of you into prison, so that you will be tested, and you will have tribulation for ten days. Be faithful until death, and I will give you the crown of life. He who has an ear, let him hear what the Spirit says to the churches. He who overcomes will not be hurt by the second death' (Revelation 2:8–11; see Isaiah 44:6; Revelation 1:9, 18; 20:6, 14).

[VICTORY from To him who overcomes]
Setting: On the island of Patmos (in the Aegean Sea about fifty miles southwest of Ephesus in modern Turkey). On the Lord's Day (Sunday), approximately fifty years after the Resurrection, the disciple John encounters the Lord Jesus Christ, who communicates a new revelation for the apostle to record for the church in Pergamum and to six other churches in Asia.

"And to the angel of the church in Pergamum write: The One who has the sharp two-edged sword says this: 'I know where you dwell, where Satan's throne is; and you hold fast My name, and did not deny My faith even in the days of Antipas, My witness, My faithful one, who was killed among you, where Satan dwells. But I have a few things against you, because you have there some who hold the teaching of Balaam, who kept teaching Balak to put a stumbling block before the sons of Israel, to eat things sacrificed to idols and to commit *acts of* immorality. So you also have some who in the same way hold the teaching of the Nicolaitans. Therefore repent; or else I am coming to you quickly, and I will make war against them with the sword of My mouth. He who has an ear, let him hear what the Spirit says to the churches. To him who overcomes, to him I will give *some* of the hidden manna, and I will give him a white stone, and a new name written on the stone which no one knows but he who receives it' (Revelation 2:12–17; see Numbers 25:1–3; Isaiah 62:2; Revelation 1:16).

[VICTORY from He who overcomes]
Setting: On the island of Patmos (in the Aegean Sea about fifty miles southwest of Ephesus in modern Turkey). On the Lord's Day (Sunday), approximately fifty years after the Resurrection, the disciple John encounters the Lord Jesus Christ, who communicates a new revelation for the apostle to record for the church in Thyatira and to six other churches in Asia.

"And to the angel of the church in Thyatira write: The Son of God, who has eyes like a flame of fire, and His feet are like burnished bronze, says this: 'I know your deeds, and your love and faith and service and perseverance, and that your deeds of late are greater than at first. But I have *this* against you, that you tolerate the woman Jezebel, who calls herself a prophetess, and she teaches and leads My bond-servants astray so that they commit *acts of* immorality and eat things sacrificed to idols. I gave her time to repent, and she does not want to repent of her immorality. Behold, I will throw her on a bed *of sickness,* and those who commit adultery with her into great tribulation, unless they repent of her deeds. And I will kill her children with pestilence, and all the churches will know that I am He who searches the minds and hearts; and I will give to each one of you according to your deeds. But I say to you, the rest who are in Thyatira, who do not hold this teaching, who have not known the deep things of Satan, as they call them—I place no other burden on you. Nevertheless what you have, hold fast until I come. He who overcomes, and he who keeps My deeds until the end, TO HIM I WILL GIVE AUTHORITY OVER THE NATIONS; AND HE SHALL RULE THEM WITH A ROD OF IRON, AS THE VESSELS OF THE POTTER ARE BROKEN TO PIECES, as I also have received *authority* from My Father; and I will give him the morning star. He who has an ear, let him hear what the Spirit says to the churches' (Revelation 2:18–29; Jesus quotes from Psalm 2:8, 9; Isaiah 30:14; see 1 Kings 16:31; Psalm 7:9; Romans 2:5; 1 Corinthians 2:10; 2 Peter 3:9; Revelation 1:14; 2:7; 3:11; 17:1–20).

[VICTORY from He who overcomes]
Setting: On the island of Patmos (in the Aegean Sea about fifty miles southwest of Ephesus in modern Turkey). On the Lord's Day (Sunday), approximately fifty years after the Resurrection, the disciple John encounters the Lord Jesus Christ, who communicates a new revelation for the apostle to record for the church in Sardis and to six other churches in Asia.

"To the angel of the church in Sardis write: He who has the seven Spirits of God and the seven stars, says this: 'I know your deeds, that you have a name that you are alive, but you are dead. Wake up, and strengthen the things that remain, which were about to die; for I have not found your deeds completed in the sight of My God. So remember what you have received and heard; and keep *it*, and repent. Therefore if you do not wake up, I will come like a thief, and you will not know at what hour I will come to you. But you have a few people in Sardis who have not soiled their garments; and they will walk with Me in white, for they are worthy. He who overcomes will thus be clothed in white garments; and I will not erase his name from the book of life, and I will confess his name before My Father and before His angels. He who has an ear, let him hear what the Spirit says to the churches' " (Revelation 3:1–6; see Matthew 10:32; Revelation 1:16).

[VICTORY from He who overcomes]
Setting: On the island of Patmos (in the Aegean Sea about fifty miles southwest of Ephesus in modern Turkey). On the Lord's Day (Sunday), approximately fifty years after the Resurrection, the disciple John encounters the Lord Jesus Christ, who communicates a new revelation for the apostle to record for the church in Philadelphia and to six other churches in Asia.

"And to the angel of the church in Philadelphia write: He who is holy, who is true, who has the key of David, who opens and no one will shut, and who shuts and no one opens, says this: 'I know your deeds. Behold, I have put before you an open door which no one can shut, because you have a little power, and have kept My word, and have not denied My name. Behold, I will cause *those* of the synagogue of Satan, who say that they are Jews and are not, but lie—I will make them come and bow down at your feet, and *make them* know that I have loved you. Because you have kept the word of My perseverance, I also will keep you from the hour of testing, that *hour* which is about to come upon the whole world, to test those who dwell on the earth. I am coming quickly; hold fast what you have, so that no one will take your crown. He who overcomes, I will make him a pillar in the temple of My God, and he will not go out from it anymore; and I will write on him the name of My God, and the name of the city of My God, the new Jerusalem, which comes down out of heaven from My God, and My new name. He who has an ear, let him hear what the Spirit says to the churches' " (Revelation 3:7–13; see Isaiah 22:22; Galatians 2:9; Revelation 2:9, 10, 13, 25; 14:1).

[VICTORY from He who overcomes]
Setting: On the island of Patmos (in the Aegean Sea about fifty miles southwest of Ephesus in modern Turkey). On the Lord's Day (Sunday), approximately fifty years after the Resurrection, the disciple John encounters the Lord Jesus Christ, who communicates a new revelation for the apostle to record for the church in Laodicea and to six other churches in Asia.

"To the angel of the church in Laodicea write: The Amen, the faithful and true Witness, the Beginning of the creation of God, says this: 'I know your deeds, that you are neither cold nor hot; I wish that you were cold or hot. So because you are lukewarm, and neither hot nor cold, I will spit you out of My mouth. Because you say, "I am rich, and have become wealthy, and have need of nothing," and you do not know that you are wretched and miserable and poor and blind and naked, I advise you to buy from Me gold refined by fire so that you may become rich, and white garments so that you may clothe yourself, and *that* the shame of your nakedness will not be revealed; and eye salve to anoint your eyes so that you may see. Those whom I love, I reprove and discipline; therefore be zealous and repent. Behold, I stand at the door and knock; if anyone hears My voice and opens the door, I will come in to him and will dine with him, and he with Me. He who overcomes, I will grant to him to sit down with Me on My throne, as I also overcame and sat down with My Father on His throne. He who has an ear, let him hear what the Spirit says to the churches'" (Revelation 3:14–22; see Proverb 3:12; Hosea 12:8; John 14:23; 16:33).

VIGILANCE (See ALERTNESS; PREPAREDNESS; and READINESS)

VILLAGE (Also see CITY; and TOWN)

Setting: Galilee. After His twelve disciples observe His ministry, Jesus summons and specifically instructs them about their ministry to the people of Israel.

These twelve Jesus sent out after instructing them: "Do not go in *the* way of *the* Gentiles, and do not enter *any* city of the Samaritans; but rather go to the lost sheep of the house of Israel. And as you go, preach, saying, 'The kingdom of heaven is at hand.' Heal *the* sick, raise *the* dead, cleanse *the* lepers, cast out demons. Freely you received, freely give. Do not acquire gold, or silver, or copper for your money belts, or a bag for *your* journey, or even two coats, or sandals, or a staff; for the worker is worthy of his support. And whatever city or village you enter, inquire who is worthy in it, and stay at his house until you leave *that city*. As you enter the house, give it your greeting. If the house is worthy, give it your *blessing of* peace. But if it is not worthy, take back your *blessing of* peace. Whoever does not receive you, nor heed your words, as you go out of that house or that city, shake the dust off your feet. Truly I say to you, it will be more tolerable for *the* land of Sodom and Gomorrah in the day of judgment than for that city" (Matthew 10:5–15; cf. Mark 6:7–11; Luke 9:1–5; see Matthew 3:2; 11:22, 24; 15:24; Luke 22:35; 1 Corinthians 9:14).

Setting: On the way to Jerusalem for the crucifixion. After healing some blind men in Jericho, Jesus instructs two disciples as they enter Bethphage to acquire a donkey and colt to be used in His triumphal entry into the city.

When they had approached Jerusalem and had come to Bethphage, at the Mount of Olives, then Jesus sent two disciples, saying to them, "Go into the village opposite you, and immediately you will find a donkey tied *there* and a colt with her; untie them and bring them to Me. If anyone says anything to you, you shall say, 'The Lord has need of them,' and immediately he will send them" (Matthew 21:1–3; cf. Mark 11:1–3; Luke 19:29–31).

Setting: Bethsaida of Galilee. After Jesus' disciples discuss with one another that they have no bread, Jesus sends a blind man home after restoring his sight.

And He sent him to his home, saying, "Do not even enter the village" (Mark 8:26).

Setting: Bethphage, just outside Jerusalem. As He and His disciples approach Jerusalem for His impending death on the cross, the Lord instructs two of the disciples to obtain a colt for His triumphal entry into the city.

As they approached Jerusalem, at Bethphage and Bethany, near the Mount of Olives, He sent two of His disciples, and said to them, "Go into the village opposite you, and immediately as you enter it, you will find a colt tied *there,* on which no one yet has ever sat; untie it and bring it *here.* If anyone says to you, 'Why are you doing this?' you say, 'The Lord has need of it'; and immediately he will send it back here" (Mark 11:1–3; cf. Matthew 21:1–3; Luke 19:29–31; see Matthew 21:4–7; Luke 19:32–35; John 12:12–15).

Setting: Approaching Jerusalem. After Jesus provides a parable about stewardship in Jericho, He and His disciples head to the outskirts of Jerusalem to prepare for His triumphal entry into the city and His crucifixion.

When He approached Bethphage and Bethany, near the mount that is called Olivet, He sent two of the disciples, saying, "Go into the village ahead of *you;* there, as you enter, you will find a colt tied on which no one yet has ever sat; untie it and bring it *here.* If anyone asks you, 'Why are you untying it?' you shall say, 'The Lord has need of it'" (Luke 19:29–31; cf. Matthew 21:1–3; Mark 11:1–3).

VINE (Specifics such as FRUIT OF THE VINE; and VINE, TRUE are separate entries; also see BRANCHES)

VINE, FRUIT OF THE (See FRUIT OF THE VINE)

VINE, TRUE

Setting: Jerusalem. Before the Passover, after He conveys the upcoming ministry of the Holy Spirit in His disciples' lives with His imminent departure from them, Jesus explains He is the vine and His disciples are the branches.

"I am the true vine, and My Father is the vinedresser. Every branch in Me that does not bear fruit, He takes away; and every *branch* that bears fruit, He prunes it so that it may bear more fruit. You are already clean because of the word which I have spoken to you. Abide in Me, and I in you. As the branch cannot bear fruit of itself unless it abides in the vine, so neither *can* you unless you abide in Me. I am the vine, you are the branches; he who abides in Me and I in him, he bears much fruit, for apart from Me you can do nothing. If anyone does not abide in Me, he is thrown away as a branch and dries up; and they gather them, and cast them into the fire and they are burned. If you abide in Me, and My words abide in you, ask whatever you wish, and it will be done for you. My Father is glorified by this, that you bear much fruit, and *so* prove to be My disciples. Just as the Father has loved Me, I have also loved you; abide in My love. If you keep My commandments, you will abide in My love; just as I have kept My Father's commandments and abide in His love. These things I have spoken to you so that My joy may be in you, and *that* your joy may be made full" (John 15:1–11; see Matthew 5:16; 7:7; John 3:29, 35; 6:56; 8:29, 31; 13:10).

VINEDRESSER (Also see VINEYARD-KEEPER)

Setting: Jerusalem. Before the Passover, after He conveys the upcoming ministry of the Holy Spirit in His disciples' lives with His imminent departure from them, Jesus explains He is the vine and His disciples are the branches.

"I am the true vine, and My Father is the vinedresser. Every branch in Me that does not bear fruit, He takes away; and every *branch* that bears fruit, He prunes it so that it may bear more fruit. You are already clean because of the word which I have spoken to you. Abide in Me, and I in you. As the branch cannot bear fruit of itself unless it abides in the vine, so neither *can* you unless you abide in Me. I am the vine, you are the branches; he who abides in Me and I in him, he bears much fruit, for apart from Me you can do nothing. If anyone does not abide in Me, he is thrown away as a branch and dries up; and they gather them, and cast them into the fire and they are burned. If you abide in Me, and My words abide in you, ask whatever you wish, and it will be done for you. My Father is glorified by this, that you bear much fruit, and *so* prove to be My disciples. Just as the Father has loved Me, I have also loved you; abide in My love. If you keep My commandments, you will abide in My love; just as I have kept My Father's commandments and abide in His love. These things I have spoken to you so that My joy may be in you, and *that* your joy may be made full" (John 15:1–11; see Matthew 5:16; 7:7; John 3:29, 35; 6:56; 8:29, 31; 13:10).

VINE-GROWERS, PARABLE OF THE (Also see VINEDRESSER; and VINEYARD)

[PARABLE OF THE VINE-GROWERS from parable and vine-growers]

Setting: The temple in Jerusalem. Jesus delivers another parable to the chief priests and elders after they question His authority.

"Listen to another parable. There was a landowner who PLANTED A VINEYARD AND PUT A WALL AROUND IT AND DUG A WINE PRESS IN IT, AND BUILT A TOWER, and rented it out to vine-growers and went on a journey. When the harvest time approached, he sent his slaves to the vine-growers to receive his produce. The vine-growers took his slaves and beat one, and killed another, and stoned a third. Again he sent another group of slaves larger than the first; and they did the same thing to them. But afterward he sent his son to them, saying, 'They will respect my son.' But when the vine-growers saw the son, they said among themselves, 'This is the heir; come, let us kill him and seize his inheritance.' They took him, and threw him out of the vineyard and killed him. Therefore when the owner of the vineyard comes, what will he do to those vine-growers?" (Matthew 21:33–40; Jesus quotes from Isaiah 5:1, 2; cf. Mark 12:1–9; Luke 20:9–15).

[PARABLE OF THE VINE-GROWERS from parables and vine-growers]
Setting: The temple in Jerusalem. Having His authority questioned by the chief priests, scribes, and elders, Jesus begins to teach them in parables.

And He began to speak to them in parables: "A man PLANTED A VINEYARD AND PUT A WALL AROUND IT, AND DUG A VAT UNDER THE WINE PRESS AND BUILT A TOWER, and rented it out to vine-growers and went on a journey. At the *harvest* time he sent a slave to the vine-growers, in order to receive *some* of the produce of the vineyard from the vine-growers. They took him, and beat him and sent him away empty-handed. Again he sent them another slave, and they wounded him in the head, and treated him shamefully. And he sent another, and that one they killed; and *so with* many others, beating some and killing others. He had one more to *send*, a beloved son; he sent him last *of all* to them, saying, 'They will respect my son.' But those vine-growers said to one another, 'This is the heir; come, let us kill him, and the inheritance will be ours!' They took him, and killed him and threw him out of the vineyard. What will the owner of the vineyard do? He will come and destroy the vine-growers, and will give the vineyard to others. Have you not even read this Scripture: 'THE STONE WHICH THE BUILDERS REJECTED, THIS BECAME THE CHIEF CORNER *stone;* THIS CAME ABOUT FROM THE LORD, AND IT IS MARVELOUS IN OUR EYES'?" (Mark 12:1–11, Jesus quotes from Psalm 118:22, 23; Isaiah 5:1, 2; cf. Matthew 21:33–46; Luke 20:9–19).

[PARABLE OF THE VINE-GROWERS from parable and vine-growers]
Setting: The temple in Jerusalem. While ministering a few days before His crucifixion, after the chief priests and the scribes question His authority to teach and preach, Jesus conveys the Parable of the Vine-Growers to the people.

And He began to tell the people this parable: "A man planted a vineyard and rented it out to vine-growers, and went on a journey for a long time. At the *harvest* time he sent a slave to the vine-growers, so that they would give him *some* of the produce of the vineyard; but the vine-growers beat him and sent him away empty-handed. And he proceeded to send another slave; and they beat him also and treated him shamefully and sent him away empty-handed. And he proceeded to send a third; and this one also they wounded and cast out. The owner of the vineyard said, 'What shall I do? I will send my beloved son; perhaps they will respect him.' But when the vine-growers saw him, they reasoned with one another, saying, 'This is the heir; let us kill him so that the inheritance will be ours.' So they threw him out of the vineyard and killed him. What, then, will the owner of the vineyard do to them? He will come and destroy these vine-growers and will give the vineyard to others." When they heard it, they said, "May it never be!" But Jesus looked at them and said, "What then is this that is written: 'THE STONE WHICH THE BUILDERS REJECTED, THIS BECAME THE CHIEF CORNER *stone*'? Everyone who falls on that stone will be broken to pieces; but on whomever it falls, it will scatter him like dust." (Luke 20:9–18, Jesus quotes from Psalm 118:22; cf. Matthew 21:33–44; Mark 12:1–11; see Ephesians 2:20)

VINEYARD (Also see VINEDRESSER; and VINE-GROWERS, PARABLE OF THE)
Setting: Judea beyond the Jordan (Perea). Jesus illustrates the kingdom of heaven to His disciples through the story of laborers in the vineyard.

"For the kingdom of heaven is like a landowner who went out early in the morning to hire laborers for his vineyard. When he had agreed with the laborers for a denarius for the day, he sent them into his vineyard. And he went out about the third hour and saw others standing idle in the market place; and to those he said, 'You also go into the vineyard, and whatever is right I will give you.' And *so* they went. Again he went out about the sixth and the ninth hour, and did the same thing. And about the eleventh *hour* he went out and found others standing *around;* and he said to them, 'Why have you been standing idle here all day long?' They said to him, 'Because no one hired us.' He said to them, 'You go into the vineyard too.' When evening came, the owner of the vineyard said to his foreman, 'Call the laborers and pay them their wages, beginning with the last *group* to the first.' When those *hired* about the eleventh hour came, each one received a denarius. When those *hired* first came, they thought that they would receive more; but each of them also received a denarius. When they received it, they grumbled at the landowner, saying, 'These

last men have worked *only* one hour, and you have made them equal to us who have borne the burden and the scorching heat of the day.' But he answered and said to one of them, 'Friend, I am doing you no wrong; did you not agree with me for a denarius? Take what is yours and go, but I wish to give to this last man the same as to you. It is not lawful for me to do what I wish with what is my own? Or is your eye envious because I am generous?' So the last shall be first, and the first last" (Matthew 20:1–16; cf. Matthew 19:30).

Setting: The temple in Jerusalem. Jesus delivers a parable to the chief priests and elders after they question His authority.

"But what do you think? A man had two sons, and he came to the first and said, 'Son, go work today in the vineyard.' And he answered, 'I will not'; but afterward he regretted it and went. The man came to the second and said the same thing; and he answered, 'I *will*, sir'; but he did not go. Which of the two sons did the will of his father?" They said, "The first." Jesus said to them, "Truly, I say to you that the tax collectors and prostitutes will get into the kingdom of God before you. For John came to you in the way of righteousness and you did not believe him; but the tax collectors and prostitutes did believe him; and you, seeing *this*, did not even feel remorse afterward so as to believe him" (Matthew 21:28–32; cf. Luke 7:29, 30, 37–50).

Setting: On the way from Galilee to Jerusalem. After some present report to Him about the Galileans whose blood Pilate (Roman governor of Judea) had mixed with their sacrifices, Jesus responds to their concern by calling them to repentance and illustrating His point with a parable.

And He *began* telling this parable: "A man had a fig tree which had been planted in his vineyard; and he came looking for fruit on it and did not find any. And he said to the vineyard-keeper, 'Behold, for three years I have come looking for fruit on this fig tree without finding any. Cut it down! Why does it even use up the ground?' And he answered and said to him, 'Let it alone, sir, for this year too, until I dig around it and put fertilizer; and if it bears fruit next year, *fine*; but if not, cut it down'" (Luke 13:6–9; see Matthew 3:10).

Setting: The temple in Jerusalem. While ministering a few days before His crucifixion, after the chief priests and the scribes question His authority to teach and preach, Jesus conveys the Parable of the Vine-Growers to the people.

And He began to tell the people this parable: "A man planted a vineyard and rented it out to vine-growers, and went on a journey for a long time. At the *harvest* time he sent a slave to the vine-growers, so that they would give him *some* of the produce of the vineyard; but the vine-growers beat him and sent him away empty-handed. And he proceeded to send another slave; and they beat him also and treated him shamefully and sent him away empty-handed. And he proceeded to send a third; and this one also they wounded and cast out. The owner of the vineyard said, 'What shall I do? I will send my beloved son; perhaps they will respect him.' But when the vine-growers saw him, they reasoned with one another, saying, 'This is the heir; let us kill him so that the inheritance will be ours.' So they threw him out of the vineyard and killed him. What, then, will the owner of the vineyard do to them? He will come and destroy these vine-growers and will give the vineyard to others." When they heard it, they said, "May it never be!" But Jesus looked at them and said, "What then is this that is written: 'THE STONE WHICH THE BUILDERS REJECTED, THIS BECAME THE CHIEF CORNER *stone*'? Everyone who falls on that stone will be broken to pieces; but on whomever it falls, it will scatter him like dust" (Luke 20:9–18, Jesus quotes from Psalm 118:22; cf. Matthew 21:33–44; Mark 12:1–11; see Ephesians 2:20).

VINEYARD, OWNER OF THE

Setting: Judea beyond the Jordan (Perea). Jesus illustrates the kingdom of heaven to His disciples through the story of laborers in the vineyard.

"For the kingdom of heaven is like a landowner who went out early in the morning to hire laborers for his vineyard. When he had agreed with the laborers for a denarius for the day, he sent them into his vineyard. And he went out about the third hour and saw others standing idle in the market place; and to those he said,' You also go into the vineyard, and whatever is right I will give you.' And *so* they went. Again he went out about the sixth and the ninth hour, and did the same thing. And about the eleventh *hour* he went out and found others standing *around;* and he said to them, 'Why have you been standing idle here all day long?'

They said to him, 'Because no one hired us.' He said to them, 'You go into the vineyard too.' When evening came, the owner of the vineyard said to his foreman, 'Call the laborers and pay them their wages, beginning with the last *group* to the first.' When those *hired* about the eleventh hour came, each one received a denarius. When those *hired* first came, they thought that they would receive more; but each of them also received a denarius. When they received it, they grumbled at the landowner, saying, 'These last men have worked *only* one hour, and you have made them equal to us who have borne the burden and the scorching heat of the day.' But he answered and said to one of them, 'Friend, I am doing you no wrong; did you not agree with me for a denarius? Take what is yours and go, but I wish to give to this last man the same as to you. It is not lawful for me to do what I wish with what is my own? Or is your eye envious because I am generous?' So the last shall be first, and the first last" (Matthew 20:1–16; cf. Matthew 19:30).

Setting: The temple in Jerusalem. Jesus delivers another parable to the chief priests and elders after they question His authority.

"Listen to another parable. There was a landowner who PLANTED A VINEYARD AND PUT A WALL AROUND IT AND DUG A WINE PRESS IN IT, AND BUILT A TOWER, and rented it out to vine-growers and went on a journey. When the harvest time approached, he sent his slaves to the vine-growers to receive his produce. The vine-growers took his slaves and beat one, and killed another, and stoned a third. Again he sent another group of slaves larger than the first; and they did the same thing to them. But afterward he sent his son to them, saying, 'They will respect my son.' But when the vine-growers saw the son, they said among themselves, 'This is the heir; come, let us kill him and seize his inheritance.' They took him, and threw him out of the vineyard and killed him. Therefore when the owner of the vineyard comes, what will he do to those vine-growers?" (Matthew 21:33–40; Jesus quotes from Isaiah 5:1, 2; cf. Mark 12:1–9, Luke 20:9–15).

Setting: The temple in Jerusalem. Having His authority questioned by the chief priests, scribes, and elders, Jesus begins to teach them in parables.

And He began to speak to them in parables: "A man PLANTED A VINEYARD AND PUT A WALL AROUND IT, AND DUG A VAT UNDER THE WINE PRESS AND BUILT A TOWER, and rented it out to vine-growers and went on a journey. At the *harvest* time he sent a slave to the vine-growers, in order to receive *some* of the produce of the vineyard from the vine-growers. They took him, and beat him and sent him away empty-handed. Again he sent them another slave, and they wounded him in the head, and treated him shamefully. And he sent another, and that one they killed; and *so with* many others, beating some and killing others. He had one more to *send*, a beloved son; he sent him last *of all* to them, saying, 'They will respect my son.' But those vine-growers said to one another, 'This is the heir; come, let us kill him, and the inheritance will be ours!' They took him, and killed him and threw him out of the vineyard. What will the owner of the vineyard do? He will come and destroy the vine-growers, and will give the vineyard to others. Have you not even read this Scripture: 'THE STONE WHICH THE BUILDERS REJECTED, THIS BECAME THE CHIEF CORNER *stone;* THIS CAME ABOUT FROM THE LORD, AND IT IS MARVELOUS IN OUR EYES'?" (Mark 12:1–11, Jesus quotes from Psalm 118:22, 23; Isaiah 5:1, 2; cf. Matthew 21:33–46; Luke 20:9–19).

VINEYARD, PARABLE OF THE (See VINE-GROWERS, PARABLE OF THE)

VINEYARD, PARABLE OF THE LABORERS IN THE

[PARABLE OF THE LABORERS IN THE VINEYARD from hire laborers for his vineyard]

Setting: Judea beyond the Jordan (Perea). Jesus illustrates the kingdom of heaven to His disciples through the story of laborers in the vineyard.

"For the kingdom of heaven is like a landowner who went out early in the morning to hire laborers for his vineyard. When he had agreed with the laborers for a denarius for the day, he sent them into his vineyard. And he went out about the third hour and saw others standing idle in the market place; and to those he said, 'You also go into the vineyard, and whatever is right I will give you.' And *so* they went. Again he went out about the sixth and the ninth hour, and did the same thing. And about the eleventh *hour* he went out and found others standing *around;* and he said to them, 'Why have you been standing idle here all day long?' They said to him, 'Because no one hired us.' He said to them, 'You go into the vineyard too.' When evening came, the owner of the vineyard said to his foreman, 'Call the laborers and pay them their wages, beginning with the last *group* to the first.' When those *hired* about the eleventh hour came, each one received a denarius. When those *hired* first came, they thought that they would receive more; but each of them also received a denarius. When they received it, they grumbled at the landowner, saying, 'These last men have worked *only* one hour, and you have made them equal to us who have borne the burden and the scorching heat of the day.' But he answered and said to one of them, 'Friend, I am doing you no wrong; did you not agree with me for a denarius? Take what is yours and go, but I wish to give to this last man the same as to you. It is not lawful for me to do what I wish with what is my own? Or is your eye envious because I am generous?' So the last shall be first, and the first last" (Matthew 20:1–16; cf. Matthew 19:30).

VINEYARD, PARABLE OF THE WORKERS IN THE (See VINEYARD, PARABLE OF THE LABORERS IN THE)

VINEYARD-KEEPER (Also see VINEDRESSER)

Setting: On the way from Galilee to Jerusalem. After some present report to Him about the Galileans whose blood Pilate (Roman governor of Judea) had mixed with their sacrifices, Jesus responds to their concern by calling them to repentance and illustrating His point with a parable.

And He *began* telling this parable: "A man had a fig tree which had been planted in his vineyard; and he came looking for fruit on it and did not find any. And he said to the vineyard-keeper, 'Behold, for three years I have come looking for fruit on this fig tree without finding any. Cut it down! Why does it even use up the ground?' And he answered and said to him, 'Let it alone, sir, for this year too, until I dig around it and put fertilizer; and if it bears fruit next year, *fine*; but if not, cut it down'" (Luke 13:6–9; see Matthew 3:10).

VIOLENCE (Also see MEN, VIOLENT)

Setting: Galilee. While speaking to the crowds, Jesus pays tribute to the ministry of John the Baptist, but emphasizes that the one who is least in the kingdom of heaven is greater than John.

As these men were going *away,* Jesus began to speak to the crowds about John, "What did you go out into the wilderness to see? A reed shaken by the wind? But what did you go out to see? A man dressed in soft *clothing?* Those who wear soft *clothing* are in kings' palaces! But what did you go out to see? A prophet? Yes, I tell you, and the one who is more than a prophet. This is the one about whom it is written, 'BEHOLD, I SEND MY MESSENGER AHEAD OF YOU, WHO WILL PREPARE YOUR WAY BEFORE YOU.' Truly, I say to you, among those born of women there has not arisen *anyone* greater than John the Baptist! Yet the one who is least in the kingdom of heaven is greater than he. From the days of John the Baptist until now the kingdom of heaven suffers violence, and violent men take it by force. For all the prophets and the Law prophesied until John. And, if you are willing to accept *it,* John himself is Elijah who was to come. He who has ears to hear, let him hear" (Matthew 11:7–15, Jesus quotes from Malachi 3:1; cf. Malachi 4:5; Luke 7:24–28; 16:16; see Matthew 14:5).

[VIOLENCE from those who take up the sword shall perish by the sword]

Setting: Gethsemane on the Mount of Olives, east of the temple in Jerusalem. As Jesus submits to His Father's will and allows Judas to betray Him, Peter attempts to defend Him by force, but the Lord does not permit it.

Then Jesus said to him, "Put your sword back into its place; for all those who take up the sword shall perish by the sword. Or do you think that I cannot appeal to My Father, and He will at once put at My disposal more than twelve legions of angels? How then will the Scriptures be fulfilled, *which say* that it must happen this way?" (Matthew 26:52–54; cf. Mark 14:47; Luke 22:50, 51; John 18:10, 11).

VIOLENT MEN (Listed under MEN, VIOLENT; also see VIOLENCE)

VIPERS, BROOD OF (Also see SERPENTS; SNAKE; and SNAKES)

Setting: Galilee. After Jesus heals a blind, mute, demon-possessed man, the Pharisees accuse the Lord in front of crowds of being a worker of Satan.

"Either make the tree good and its fruit good, or make the tree bad and its fruit bad; for the tree is known by its fruit. You brood of vipers, how can you, being evil, speak what is good? For the mouth speaks out of that which fills the heart. The good man brings out of *his* good treasure what is good; and the evil man brings out of *his* evil treasure what is evil. But I tell you that every careless word that people speak, they shall give an accounting for it in the day of judgment. For by your words you will be justified, and by your words you will be condemned" (Matthew 12:33–37; cf. Matthew 3:7; 7:16–18; Luke 3:7).

Setting: The temple in Jerusalem. After the Jewish religious leaders test Him with questions, Jesus pronounces the eighth of eight woes upon them in front of the crowds and His disciples.

"Woe to you, scribes and Pharisees, hypocrites! For you build the tombs of the prophets and adorn the monuments of the righteous, and say, 'If we had been *living* in the days of our fathers, we would not have been partners with them in *shedding* the blood of the prophets.' So you testify against yourselves, that you are sons of those who murdered the prophets. Fill up, then, the measure *of the guilt* of you fathers. You serpents, you brood of vipers, how will you escape the sentence of hell? Therefore, behold, I am sending you prophets and wise men and scribes; some of them you will kill and crucify, and some of them you will scourge in your synagogues, and persecute from city to city, so that upon you may fall *the guilt of* all the righteous blood shed on earth, from the blood of righteous Abel to the blood of Zechariah, the son of Berechiah, whom you murdered between the temple and the altar. Truly I say to you, all these things will come upon this generation" (Matthew 23:29–36; cf. 2 Chronicles 24:21; Zechariah 1:1; Matthew 3:7; Luke 3:7; 11:47–52; see Matthew 10:23).

VIRGINS (See VIRGINS, PARABLE OF THE TEN)

VIRGINS, PARABLE OF THE TEN

[PARABLE OF THE TEN VIRGINS from comparable to ten virgins]

Setting: On the Mount of Olives, just east of Jerusalem. During His Olivet Discourse, after answering His disciples' questions as to when the temple will be destroyed and Jerusalem overrun, along with the signs of His coming and the end of the age, Jesus reemphasizes to His disciples that they should be on the alert for His return.

"Then the kingdom of heaven will be comparable to ten virgins, who took their lamps and went out to meet the bridegroom. Five of them were foolish, and five were prudent. For when the foolish took their lamps, they took no oil with them, but the prudent took oil in flasks along with their lamps. Now while the bridegroom was delaying, they all got drowsy and *began* to sleep. But at midnight there was a shout, 'Behold, the bridegroom! Come out to meet *him.*' Then all those virgins rose and trimmed their lamps. The foolish said to the prudent, 'Give us some of your oil, for our lamps are going out.' But the prudent answered, 'No, there will not be enough for us and you *too;* go instead to the dealers and buy *some* for yourselves.' And while they were going away to make the purchase, the bridegroom came, and those who were ready went in with him to the wedding feast; and the door was shut. Later the other virgins also came, saying, 'Lord, lord, open up for us.' But he answered, 'Truly I say to you, I do not know you.' Be on the alert then, for you do not know the day nor the hour" (Matthew 25:1–13; cf. Matthew 24:42; Luke 12:35; see Matthew 7:21, 24).

VISION (Also see EYE; EYES; and SIGHT)

[VISION from Do you see anything]

Setting: Bethsaida of Galilee. After His disciples discuss with one another that they have no bread, Jesus gives sight to a blind man.

Taking the blind man by the hand, He brought him out of the village; and after spitting on his eyes and laying His hands on him, He asked him, "Do you see anything?" (Mark 8:23; see Mark 8:22, 24–26).

[VISION from Go; your faith has made you well]

Setting: Passing through Jericho, on the road to Jerusalem. A blind beggar named Bartimaeus cries out to Jesus for healing.

And Jesus stopped and said, "Call him *here*." So they called the blind man, saying to him, "Take courage, stand up! He is calling for you." Throwing aside his cloak, he jumped up and came to Jesus. And answering him, Jesus said, "What do you want Me to do for you?" And the blind man said to him, "Rabboni, *I want* to regain my sight!" And Jesus said to him, "Go; your faith has made you well." Immediately he regained his sight and *began* following Him on the road (Mark 10:49–52; cf. Matthew 20:29–34; Luke 18:35–43; see Matthew 9:2, 22).

VISION (visitation from God)

Setting: **Galilee. Jesus instructs Peter, James, and John to keep the Transfiguration, which has just occurred on a high mountain, secret until after His resurrection.**

As they were coming down from the mountain, Jesus commanded them, saying, "Tell the vision to no one until the Son of Man has risen from the dead" (Matthew 17:9; cf. Mark 9:9–13; Luke 9:28–36).

Setting: **Damascus. Luke, writing in Acts, conveys how the Lord instructs one of His disciples, Ananias, to locate Saul of Tarsus to touch him in order to restore Saul's vision.**

Now there was a disciple at Damascus named Ananias; and the Lord said to him in a vision, "Ananias." And he said, "Here I am, Lord." And the Lord *said* to him, "Get up and go to the street called Straight, and inquire at the house of Judas for a man from Tarsus named Saul, for he is praying, and he was seen in a vision a man named Ananias come in and lay his hands on him, so that he might regain his sight" (Acts 9:10–12; see Acts 22:12–14).

VISITATION

Setting: **Approaching Jerusalem. After being praised by the people in a triumphal entry, the Lord weeps as He sees the city ahead of Him.**

When He approached *Jerusalem,* He saw the city and wept over it, saying, "If you had known in this day, even you, the things which make for peace! But now they have been hidden from your eyes. For the days will come upon you when your enemies will throw up a barricade against you, and surround you and hem you in on every side, and they will level you to the ground and your children within you, and they will not leave in you one stone upon another, because you did not recognize the time of your visitation" (Luke 19:41–44; see Matthew 24:1–2; Luke 13:34, 35).

VISITATION FROM GOD (See VISION)

VOICE

Setting: **Jerusalem. During a feast of the Jews, Jesus responds to criticism from the Jewish religious leaders by referring to God as His Father (thereby making Himself equal with God) and prophesying His participation someday in the resurrection and judgment of men.**

"Truly, truly, I say to you, an hour is coming and now is, when the dead will hear the voice of the Son of God, and those who hear will live. For just as the Father has life in Himself, even so He gave to the Son also to have life in Himself; and He gave Him authority to execute judgment, because He is *the* Son of Man. Do not marvel at this; for an hour is coming, in which all who are in the tombs will hear His voice, and will come forth; those who did the good *deeds* to a resurrection of life, those who committed the evil *deeds* to a resurrection of judgment" (John 5:25–29; see Daniel 12:2; John 1:4; 5:18–24; 11:24).

Setting: **Jerusalem. During a feast of the Jews, Jesus responds to criticism from the Jewish religious leaders by referring to God as His Father (thereby making Himself equal with God) and informing them that God, John the Baptist, and His works all testify to His mission.**

"I can do nothing on My own initiative. As I hear, I judge; and My judgment is just, because I do not seek My own will, but the will of Him who sent Me. If I *alone* testify about Myself, My testimony is not true. There is another who testifies of Me, and I know that the testimony which He gives about Me is true. You have sent to John, and he has testified to the truth. But the testimony which I receive is not from man, but I say these things so that you may be saved. He was the lamp that was burning and was shining and you were willing to rejoice for a while in his light. But the testimony which I have is greater than the *testimony of* John; for the works which the Father has given Me to accomplish—the very works that I do—testify about Me, that the Father has sent Me. And the Father who sent Me, He has testified of Me. You have neither heard His voice at any time nor seen His form. You do not have His word abiding in you, for you do not believe Him whom He sent" (John 5:30–38; see Matthew 3:17; Mark 1:4–5; John 1:7, 15, 32; 4:34; 8:14–16; 10:25, 37, 38).

Setting: Jerusalem. Following the Pharisees' interrogation and dismissal of the formerly blind man Jesus healed on the Sabbath, the Lord speaks to the Pharisees, using parabolic language they do not understand.

"Truly, truly, I say to you, he who does not enter by the door into the fold of the sheep, but climbs up some other way, he is a thief and a robber. But he who enters by the door is a shepherd of the sheep. To him the doorkeeper opens, and the sheep hear his voice, and he calls his own sheep by name and leads them out. When he puts forth all his own, he goes ahead of them, and the sheep follow him because they know his voice. A stranger they simply will not follow, but will flee from him, because they do not know the voice of strangers" (John 10:1–5).

Setting: Jerusalem. Following the Pharisees' interrogation and dismissal of the formerly blind man Jesus healed on the Sabbath, the Lord conveys the Parable of the Good Shepherd to the Pharisees, using figures of speech they do not understand.

So Jesus said to them again, "Truly, truly, I say to you, I am the door of the sheep. All who came before Me are thieves and robbers, but the sheep did not hear them. I am the door; if anyone enters through Me, he will be saved, and will go in and out and find pasture. The thief comes only to steal and kill and destroy; I came that they may have life, and have *it* abundantly. I am the good shepherd; the good shepherd lays down His life for the sheep. He who is a hired hand, and not a shepherd, who is not the owner of the sheep, sees the wolf coming, and leaves the sheep and flees, and the wolf snatches them and scatters *them. He flees* because he is a hired hand and is not concerned about the sheep. I am the good shepherd, and I know My own and My own know Me, even as the Father knows Me and I know the Father; and I lay down My life for the sheep. I have other sheep, which are not of this fold; I must bring them also, and they will hear My voice; and they will become one flock *with* one shepherd. For this reason the Father loves Me, because I lay down My life so that I may take it again. No one has taken it away from Me, but I lay it down on My own initiative. I have authority to take it up again. This commandment I received from My Father" (John 10:7–18; see Isaiah 40:11; 56:8; Jeremiah 23:1; Matthew 11:27).

Setting: Jerusalem. At the Feast of Dedication, just after Jesus conveys the Parable of the Good Shepherd to the Pharisees (who do not understand it), they ask Him plainly if He is the Christ.

Jesus answered them, "I told you, and you do not believe; the works that I do in My Father's name, these testify of Me. But you do not believe because you are not of My sheep. My sheep hear My voice, and I know them, and they follow Me; and I give eternal life to them, and they will never perish; and no one will snatch them out of My hand. My Father, who has given *them* to Me, is greater than all; and no one is able to snatch *them* out of the Father's hand. I and the Father are one" (John 10:25–30; see John 8:47; 17:1, 2, 20, 21).

Setting: Jerusalem. Just days before the Passover, with the chief priests and Pharisees plotting to seize Him and crowds welcoming Him with palm branches and praise, Jesus expresses anxiety about His upcoming crucifixion.

"Now My soul has become troubled; and what shall I say, 'Father, save Me from this hour'? But for this purpose I came to this hour. Father glorify Your name." Then a voice came out of heaven: "I have glorified it, and will glorify it again." So the crowd *of people* who stood by and heard it were saying that it had thundered; others were saying, "An angel has spoken to Him." Jesus answered and said, "This voice has not come for My sake, but for your sakes. Now judgment is upon this world; now the ruler of this world will be cast out. And I, if I am lifted up from the earth, will draw all men to Myself" (John 12:27–32; see Matthew 3:17; 26:38; John 3:14; 6:44; 11:42; 14:30).

Setting: Jerusalem. After the previous and current high priests (Annas and Caiaphas) question Jesus, and Peter denies the second and third times being His disciple, Pilate (Roman governor of Judea) questions the Lord in an attempt to determine if He is a king.

Therefore Pilate said to Him, "So You are a king?" Jesus answered, "You say *correctly* that I am a king. For this I have been born, and for this I have come into the world, to testify to the truth. Everyone who is of the truth hears my voice" (John 18:37; cf. Matthew 27:11; Mark 15:2; Luke 23:3).

Setting: On the island of Patmos (in the Aegean Sea about fifty miles southwest of Ephesus in modern Turkey). On the Lord's Day (Sunday), approximately fifty years after the Resurrection, the disciple John encounters the Lord Jesus Christ, who communicates a new revelation for the apostle to record for the church in Laodicea and to six other churches in Asia.

"To the angel of the church in Laodicea write: The Amen, the faithful and true Witness, the Beginning of the creation of God, says this: 'I know your deeds, that you are neither cold nor hot; I wish that you were cold or hot. So because you are lukewarm, and neither hot nor cold, I will spit you out of My mouth. Because you say, "I am rich, and have become wealthy, and have need of nothing," and you do not know that you are wretched and miserable and poor and blind and naked, I advise you to buy from Me gold refined by fire so that you may become rich, and white garments so that you may clothe yourself, and *that* the shame of your nakedness will not be revealed; and eye salve to anoint your eyes so that you may see. Those whom I love, I reprove and discipline; therefore be zealous and repent. Behold, I stand at the door and knock; if anyone hears My voice and opens the door, I will come in to him and will dine with him, and he with Me. He who overcomes, I will grant to him to sit down with Me on My throne, as I also overcame and sat down with My Father on His throne. He who has an ear, let him hear what the Spirit says to the churches'" (Revelation 3:14–22; see Proverb 3:12; Hosea 12:8; John 14:23; 16:33).

VOWS (Also see LIE; LIES; OATHS; SWEARING; and WITNESS, FALSE)

[VOWS also from FALSE VOWS]

Setting: Galilee. During the early part of His ministry, Jesus preaches the Sermon on the Mount to His disciples and the multitudes.

"Again, you have heard that the ancients were told, 'YOU SHALL NOT MAKE FALSE VOWS, BUT SHALL FULFILL YOUR VOWS TO THE LORD.' But I say to you, make no oath at all, either by heaven, for it is the throne of God, or by the earth, for it is the footstool of His feet, or by Jerusalem, for it is THE CITY OF THE GREAT KING. Nor shall you make an oath by your head, for you cannot make one hair white or black. But let your statement be 'Yes, yes' *or* 'No, no'; anything beyond these is of evil" (Matthew 5:33–37, Jesus quotes from Leviticus 19:12, Psalm 48:2; Isaiah 66:1; cf. James 5:12).

VULTURES (Also see BIRDS)

Setting: On the Mount of Olives, just east of Jerusalem. During His Olivet Discourse, Jesus answers His disciples' questions as to when the temple will be destroyed and Jerusalem overrun, along with the signs of His coming and the end of the age.

"Therefore when you see the ABOMINATION OF DESOLATION which was spoken of through Daniel the prophet, standing in the holy place (let the reader understand), then those who are in Judea must flee to the mountains. Whoever is on the housetop must not go down to get the things that are in his house. Whoever is in the field must not turn back to get his cloak. But woe to those who are pregnant and to those who are nursing babies in those days! But pray that your flight will not be in the winter, or on a Sabbath. For then there will be a great tribulation, such as has not occurred since the beginning of the world until now, nor ever will. Unless those days had been cut short, no life would have been saved; but for the sake of the elect those days will be cut short. Then if anyone says to you, 'Behold, here is the Christ,' or "There *He is*,' do not believe *him*. For false Christs and false prophets will arise and will show great signs and wonders, so as to mislead, if possible, even the elect. Behold, I have told you in advance. So if they say to you, 'Behold, He is in the wilderness,' do not go out, *or*, 'Behold, He is in the inner rooms,' do not believe *them*. For just as the lightning comes from the east and flashes even to the west, so will the coming of the Son of Man be. Wherever the corpse is, there the vultures will gather" (Matthew 24:15–28, Jesus quotes from Daniel 9:27; cf. Daniel 12:1; Mark 13:14–23; Luke 17:22–31; 21:20–24; 23:29; see John 4:48).

Setting: On the way from Galilee to Jerusalem. After the Pharisees question Him about the coming of the kingdom of God, Jesus tells His disciples of His second coming.

And He said to the disciples, "The days will come when you will long to see one of the days of the Son of Man, and you will not see it. They will say to you, 'Look there! Look here!' Do not go away, and do not run after *them*. For just like the lightning, when it flashes out of one part of the sky, shines to the other part of the sky, so will the Son of Man be in His day. But first He must suffer many things and be rejected by this generation. And just as it happened in the days of Noah, so it will be also in the days of the Son of Man: they were eating, they were drinking, they were marrying, they were being given in marriage, until the day that Noah entered the ark, and the flood came and destroyed them all. It was the same as happened in the days of Lot: they were eating, they were drinking, they were buying, they were selling, they were planting, they were building; but on the day that Lot went out from Sodom it rained fire and brimstone from heaven and destroyed them all. It will be just the same on the day that the Son of Man is revealed. On that day, the one who is on the housetop and whose goods are in the house must not go down to take them out; and likewise the one who is in the field must not turn back. Remember Lot's wife. Whoever seeks to keep his life will lose it, and whoever loses *his life* will preserve it. I tell you, on that night there will be two in one bed; one will be taken and the other will be left. There will be two women grinding at the same place; one will be taken and the other will be left. [Two men will be in the field; one will be taken and the other will be left."] And answering they said to Him, "Where, Lord?" And He said to them, "Where the body *is*, there also the vultures will be gathered" (Luke 17:22–37; see Genesis 19; Matthew 10:39; 16:21, 27; 24:17–28, 37–41).

W

WAGES (Also see COMPENSATION; and PAY)

Setting: Judea beyond the Jordan (Perea). Jesus illustrates the kingdom of heaven to His disciples through the story of laborers in the vineyard.

"For the kingdom of heaven is like a landowner who went out early in the morning to hire laborers for his vineyard. When he had agreed with the laborers for a denarius for the day, he sent them into his vineyard. And he went out about the third hour and saw others standing idle in the market place; and to those he said,' You also go into the vineyard, and whatever is right I will give you.' And *so* they went. Again he went out about the sixth and the ninth hour, and did the same thing. And about the eleventh *hour* he went out and found others standing *around;* and he said to them, 'Why have you been standing idle here all day long?' They said to him, 'Because no one hired us.' He said to them, 'You go into the vineyard too.' When evening came, the owner of the vineyard said to his foreman, 'Call the laborers and pay them their wages, beginning with the last *group* to the first.' When those *hired* about the eleventh hour came, each one received a denarius. When those *hired* first came, they thought that they would receive more; but each of them also received a denarius. When they received it, they grumbled at the landowner, saying, 'These last men have worked *only* one hour, and you have made them equal to us who have borne the burden and the scorching heat of the day.' But he answered and said to one of them, 'Friend, I am doing you no wrong; did you not agree with me for a denarius? Take what is yours and go, but I wish to give to this last man the same as to you. It is not lawful for me to do what I wish with what is my own? Or is your eye envious because I am generous?' So the last shall be first, and the first last" (Matthew 20:1–16; cf. Matthew 19:30).

Setting: On the way from Galilee to Jerusalem. The Lord appoints seventy followers and sends them out in pairs to every place He Himself will soon visit.

And He was saying to them, "The harvest is plentiful, but the laborers are few; therefore beseech the Lord of the harvest to send out laborers into His harvest. Go; behold, I send you out as lambs in the midst of wolves. Carry no money belt, no bag, no shoes; and greet no one on the way. Whatever house you enter, first say, 'Peace be to this house.' If a man of peace is there, your peace will rest on him; but if not, it will return to you. Stay in that house, eating and drinking what they give you; for the laborer is worthy of his wages. Do not keep moving from house to house. Whatever city you enter and they receive you, eat what is set before you; and heal those in it who are sick, and say to them, 'The kingdom of God has come near to you.' But whatever city you enter and they do not receive you, go out into its streets and say, 'Even the dust of your city which clings to our feet we wipe off *in protest* against you; yet be sure of this, that the kingdom of God has come near.' I say to you, it will be more tolerable in that day for Sodom than for that city" (Luke 10:2–12; see Genesis 19:24–28; Matthew 9:37, 38, 10:9–14, 16; 1 Corinthians 10:27).

Setting: Sychar in Samaria, on the way to Galilee. After Jesus converses with a Samaritan woman at Jacob's well, the disciples return with food. They try to get Jesus to eat, but are surprised when He speaks of other food.

Jesus said to them, "My food is to do the will of Him who sent Me and to accomplish His work. Do you not say, 'There are yet four months, and *then* comes the harvest'? Behold, I say to you, lift up your eyes and look on the fields, that they are white for harvest. Already he who reaps is receiving wages and is gathering fruit for life eternal; so that he who sows and he who reaps may rejoice together. For in this *case* the saying is true, 'One sows and another reaps.' I sent you to reap that for which you have not labored; others have labored and you have entered into their labor" (John 4:34–38; see Matthew 9:37, 38; John 5:36).

WALKING

[WALKING from walk]

Setting: Capernaum, near the Sea of Galilee. After Jesus heals a paralytic and forgives his sins in front of crowds, some scribes accuse the Lord of blasphemy.

And they brought to Him a paralytic lying on a bed. Seeing their faith, Jesus said to the paralytic, "Take courage, son; your sins are forgiven." And some scribes said to themselves. "This *fellow* blasphemes." And Jesus knowing their thoughts said, "Why are you thinking evil in your hearts? Which is easier to say, 'Your sins are forgiven,' or to say, 'Get up, and walk'? But so that you may know that the Son of Man has authority on earth to forgive sins"—then He said to the paralytic, "Get up, pick up your bed and go home" (Matthew 9:2–6; cf. Mark 2:3–12; Luke 5:17–26).

[WALKING from walk]
Setting: Galilee. As He teaches and preaches, Jesus responds to John the Baptist's question (posed by some of John's disciples) whether He is Israel's promised Messiah.

Jesus answered and said to them, "Go and report to John what you hear and see: *the* BLIND RECEIVE SIGHT and *the* lame walk, *the* lepers are cleansed and *the* deaf hear, *the* dead are raised up, and *the* POOR HAVE THE GOSPEL PREACHED TO THEM. And blessed is he who does not take offense at Me" (Matthew 11:4–6, Jesus quotes from Isaiah 35:5f; cf. Luke 7:22, 23).

[WALKING from walk]
Setting: Capernaum. When Jesus heals a paralytic man and forgives his sins, some scribes believe the Lord commits blasphemy.

Immediately Jesus, aware in His spirit that they were reasoning that way within themselves, said to them, "Why are you reasoning about these things in your hearts? Which is easier, to say to the paralytic, 'Your sins are forgiven'; or to say, 'Get up, and pick up your pallet and walk'? "But so that you may know that the Son of Man has authority on earth to forgive sins"—He said to the paralytic, "I say to you, get up, pick up your pallet and go home" (Mark 2:8–11; cf. Matthew 9:4–7; Luke 5:21–24).

[WALKING from walk]
Setting: The temple in Jerusalem. After commending one scribe for his nearness to the kingdom of God, Jesus warns the crowd about the rest of the scribes.

In His teaching He was saying: "Beware of the scribes who like to walk around in long robes, and *like* respectful greetings in the market places, and chief seats in the synagogues and places of honor at banquets, who devour widows' houses, and for appearance's sake offer long prayers; these will receive greater condemnation" (Mark 12:38–40; cf. Matthew 23:1–7; Luke 20:45–47).

[WALKING from walk]
Setting: Capernaum of Galilee. When Jesus heals a paralytic man and forgives his sins, some Pharisees and teachers of the law from Galilee and Judea accuse the Lord of committing blasphemy.

But Jesus, aware of their reasonings, answered and said to them, "Why are you reasoning in your hearts? Which is easier, to say, 'Your sins have been forgiven you,' or to say, 'Get up and walk'? But, so that you may know that the Son of Man has authority on earth to forgive sins,"—He said to the paralytic—"I say to you, get up, and pick up your stretcher and go home" (Luke 5:22–24; cf. Matthew 9:4–8; Mark 2:8–12; see Matthew 4:24).

[WALKING from walk]
Setting: Galilee. After Jesus raises a woman's son from the dead in Nain, the disciples of John the Baptist inquire whether He is the promised Messiah.

And He answered and said to them, "Go and report to John what you have seen and heard: *the* BLIND RECEIVE SIGHT, *the* lame walk, *the* lepers are cleansed, and *the* deaf hear, *the* dead are raised up, *the* POOR HAVE THE GOSPEL PREACHED TO THEM. Blessed is he who does not take offense at Me" (Luke 7:22, 23, Jesus quotes from Isaiah 35:5; 61:1; cf. Matthew 11:2–6).

[WALKING from walk]
Setting: On the way from Galilee to Jerusalem. After speaking of how a lamp illuminates, the Lord has lunch with a Pharisee, who is surprised He doesn't wash before eating.

But the Lord said to him, "Now you Pharisees clean the outside of the cup and of the platter; but inside of you, you are full of robbery and wickedness. You foolish ones, did not He who made the outside make the inside also? But give that which is within as charity, and then all things are clean for you. But woe to you Pharisees! You pay tithe of mint and rue and every *kind of* garden herb, and *yet* disregard justice and the love of God; but these are the things you should have done without neglecting the others. Woe to you Pharisees! For you love the chief seats in the synagogues and the respectful greetings in the market places. Woe to you! For you are like concealed tombs, and the people who walk over *them* are unaware *of it*" (Luke 11:39–44; cf. Matthew 23:6, 7, 23–27; see Matthew 15:2; Titus 1:15).

[WALKING from walk]
Setting: The temple in Jerusalem. While ministering a few days before His crucifixion, after posing a question to the scribes, who do not answer, Jesus warns His disciples about the lifestyle of the scribes.

"Beware of the scribes, who like to walk around in long robes, and love respectful greetings in the market places, and chief seats in the synagogues and places of honor at banquets, who devour widows' houses, and for appearance's sake offer long prayers. These will receive greater condemnation" (Luke 20:46, 47; cf. Matthew 23:1–7; Mark 12:38–40; see Luke 11:43).

Setting: On the road to Emmaus. After dying on the cross just outside Jerusalem the day before the Sabbath, and being buried in a tomb by Joseph of Arimathea, Jesus rises on the third day and appears to two of His followers.

And He said to them, "What are these words that you are exchanging with one another as you are walking?" And they stood still, looking sad (Luke 24:17; see Mark 16:12, 13).

[WALKING from walk]
Setting: By the pool of Bethesda in Jerusalem. After performing His second Galilean miracle by healing a royal official's son from Capernaum, Jesus returns to Jerusalem for a feast of the Jews, where He heals on the Sabbath a man who had been ill for thirty-eight years.

Jesus said to him, "Get up, pick up your pallet and walk" (John 5:8; see Matthew 9:6).

[WALKING from walk]
Setting: Jerusalem. The lame man healed by Jesus at the pool of Bethesda, upon being questioned by the Jews about why he is carrying his pallet on the Sabbath, quotes Jesus' command.

But he answered them, He who made me well was the one who said to me, 'Pick up your pallet and walk.' They asked him, "Who is the man who said to you, 'Pick up *your pallet* and walk'? (John 5:11, 12).

[WALKING from walk]
Setting: The temple in Jerusalem. Following the Feast of Booths, Jesus retires to the Mount of Olives, and returns the next day to teach. He addresses the scribes and Pharisees after their failed attempt to stone a woman caught in adultery.

Then Jesus again spoke to them, saying, "I am the Light of the world; he who follows Me will not walk in the darkness, but will have the Light of life" (John 8:12; see John 1:4).

[WALKING from Walk]
Setting: Jerusalem. Just days before the Passover, with the chief priests and Pharisees plotting to seize Jesus, who is expressing anxiety about His upcoming crucifixion, the crowds ask the Lord about the identity of the Son of Man.

The crowd then answered Him, "We have heard out of the Law that the Christ is to remain forever; and how can You say, 'The Son of Man must be lifted up'? Who is this Son of Man?" So Jesus said to them, "For a little while longer the Light is among you. Walk while you have the Light, so that darkness will not overtake you; he who walks in the darkness does not know where he goes. While you have the Light, believe in the Light, so that you may become sons of Light." These things Jesus spoke, and He went away and hid Himself from them (John 12:34–36; see John 1 John 1:6).

[WALKING from walk]
Setting: By the Sea of Galilee. During the Lord's third post-resurrection appearance to His disciples, after quizzing Peter three times regarding the disciple's love for Him, Jesus gives him details about his aging and eventual death.

"Truly, truly, I say to you, when you were younger, you used to gird yourself and walk wherever you wished; but when you grow old, you will stretch out your hands and someone else will gird you, and bring you where you do not wish to *go*." Now this He said, signifying by what kind of death he would glorify God. And when He had spoken this, He said to him, "Follow Me!" (John 21:18, 19).

[WALKING from walks]
Setting: The island of Patmos (in the Aegean Sea about fifty miles southwest of Ephesus in modern Turkey). On the Lord's Day (Sunday), about fifty years after Jesus' resurrection, the disciple John encounters the Lord Jesus Christ. Jesus communicates a new revelation for the apostle to record for the church in Ephesus and to six other churches in Asia.

"To the angel of the church in Ephesus write: The One who holds the seven stars in His right hand, the One who walks among the seven golden lampstands, says this: 'I know your deeds and your toil and perseverance, and that you cannot tolerate evil men, and you put to the test those who call themselves apostles, and they are not, and you found them *to be* false; and you have perseverance and have endured for My name's sake, and have not grown weary. But I have *this* against you, that you have left your first love. Therefore remember from where you have fallen, and repent and do the deeds you did at first; or else I am coming to you and will remove your lampstand out of its place—unless you repent. Yet this you do have, that you hate the deeds of the Nicolaitans, which I also hate. He who has an ear, let him hear what the Spirit says to the churches. To him who overcomes, I will grant to eat of the tree of life which is in the Paradise of God' " (Revelation 2:1–7; see Genesis 2:9; Ezekiel 28:13; 1 John 4:1; Revelation 1:10, 11, 19, 20).

[WALKING from walk]
Setting: On the island of Patmos (in the Aegean Sea about fifty miles southwest of Ephesus in modern Turkey). On the Lord's Day (Sunday), approximately fifty years after the Resurrection, the disciple John encounters the Lord Jesus Christ, who communicates a new revelation for the apostle to record for the church in Sardis and to six other churches in Asia.

"To the angel of the church in Sardis write: He who has the seven Spirits of God and the seven stars, says this: 'I know your deeds, that you have a name that you are alive, but you are dead. Wake up, and strengthen the things that remain, which were about to die; for I have not found your deeds completed in the sight of My God. So remember what you have received and heard; and keep *it*, and repent. Therefore if you do not wake up, I will come like a thief, and you will not know at what hour I will come to you. But you have a few people in Sardis who have not soiled their garments; and they will walk with Me in white, for they are worthy. He who overcomes will thus be clothed in white garments; and I will not erase his name from the book of life, and I will confess his name before My Father and before His angels. He who has an ear, let him hear what the Spirit says to the churches' " (Revelation 3:1–6; see Matthew 10:32; Revelation 1:16).

WALKING ON WATER (Listed under WATER, WALKING ON)

WALL
Setting: The temple in Jerusalem. Jesus delivers another parable to the chief priests and elders after they question His authority.

"Listen to another parable. There was a landowner who PLANTED A VINEYARD AND PUT A WALL AROUND IT AND DUG A WINE PRESS IN IT, AND BUILT A TOWER, and rented it out to vine-growers and went on a journey. When the harvest time approached, he sent his

slaves to the vine-growers to receive his produce. The vine-growers took his slaves and beat one, and killed another, and stoned a third. Again he sent another group of slaves larger than the first; and they did the same thing to them. But afterward he sent his son to them, saying, 'They will respect my son.' But when the vine-growers saw the son, they said among themselves, 'This is the heir; come, let us kill him and seize his inheritance.' They took him, and threw him out of the vineyard and killed him. Therefore when the owner of the vineyard comes, what will he do to those vine-growers?" (Matthew 21:33–40; Jesus quotes from Isaiah 5:1, 2; cf. Mark 12:1–9; Luke 20:9–15).

Setting: The temple in Jerusalem. Having His authority questioned by the chief priests, scribes, and elders, Jesus begins to teach them in parables.

And He began to speak to them in parables: "A man PLANTED A VINEYARD AND PUT A WALL AROUND IT, AND DUG A VAT UNDER THE WINE PRESS AND BUILT A TOWER, and rented it out to vine-growers and went on a journey. At the *harvest* time he sent a slave to the vine-growers, in order to receive *some* of the produce of the vineyard from the vine-growers. They took him, and beat him and sent him away empty-handed. Again he sent them another slave, and they wounded him in the head, and treated him shamefully. And he sent another, and that one they killed; and *so with* many others, beating some and killing others. He had one more to *send*, a beloved son; he sent him last *of all* to them, saying, 'They will respect my son.' But those vine-growers said to one another, 'This is the heir; come, let us kill him, and the inheritance will be ours!' They took him, and killed him and threw him out of the vineyard. What will the owner of the vineyard do? He will come and destroy the vine-growers, and will give the vineyard to others. Have you not even read this Scripture: 'THE STONE WHICH THE BUILDERS REJECTED, THIS BECAME THE CHIEF CORNER *stone;* THIS CAME ABOUT FROM THE LORD, AND IT IS MARVELOUS IN OUR EYES'?" (Mark 12:1–11, Jesus quotes from Psalm 118:22, 23; Isaiah 5:1, 2; cf. Matthew 21:33–46; Luke 20:9–19).

WAR (Also see WARS)

Setting: On the island of Patmos (in the Aegean Sea about fifty miles southwest of Ephesus in modern Turkey). On the Lord's Day (Sunday), approximately fifty years after the Resurrection, the disciple John encounters the Lord Jesus Christ, who communicates a new revelation for the apostle to record for the church in Pergamum and to six other churches in Asia.

"And to the angel of the church in Pergamum write: The One who has the sharp two-edged sword says this: 'I know where you dwell, where Satan's throne is; and you hold fast My name, and did not deny My faith even in the days of Antipas, My witness, My faithful one, who was killed among you, where Satan dwells. But I have a few things against you, because you have there some who hold the teaching of Balaam, who kept teaching Balak to put a stumbling block before the sons of Israel, to eat things sacrificed to idols and to commit *acts of* immorality. So you also have some who in the same way hold the teaching of the Nicolaitans. Therefore repent; or else I am coming to you quickly, and I will make war against them with the sword of My mouth. He who has an ear, let him hear what the Spirit says to the churches. To him who overcomes, to him I will give *some* of the hidden manna, and I will give him a white stone, and a new name written on the stone which no one knows but he who receives it' (Revelation 2:12–17; see Numbers 25:1–3; Isaiah 62:2; Revelation 1:16).

WARNINGS

[WARNINGS from Beware of practicing your righteousness before men to be noticed by them]
Setting: Galilee. During the early part of His ministry, Jesus preaches the Sermon on the Mount to His disciples and the multitudes.

"Beware of practicing your righteousness before men to be noticed by them; otherwise you have no reward with your Father who is in heaven" (Matthew 6:1; cf. Matthew 6:16).

[WARNINGS from Beware of the false prophets]
Setting: Galilee. During the early part of His ministry, Jesus preaches the Sermon on the Mount to His disciples and the multitudes.

"Beware of the false prophets, who come to you in sheep's clothing, but inwardly are ravenous wolves. You will know them by their fruits. Grapes are not gathered from *bushes* nor figs from thistles, are they? So every good tree bears good fruit, but the bad tree bears bad fruit. A good tree cannot produce bad fruit, nor can a bad tree produce good fruit. Every tree that does not bear good fruit is cut down and thrown into the fire. So then, you will know them by their fruits" (Matthew 7:15–20; cf. Matthew 3:10; 12:33, 35; 24:11, 24; Luke 6:43, 44).

[WARNINGS from But beware of men, for they will hand you over to *the* courts and scourge you in their synagogues]
Setting: Galilee. After His disciples observe His ministry, Jesus summons and specifically instructs them about the upcoming hardships of their ministry to the people of Israel.

"Behold, I send you out as sheep in the midst of wolves; so be shrewd as serpents and innocent as doves. But beware of men, for they will hand you over to *the* courts and scourge you in their synagogues; and you will even be brought before governors and kings for My sake, as a testimony to them and to the Gentiles. But when they hand you over, do not worry about how or what you are to say; for it will be given you in that hour what you are to say. For it is not you who speak, but *it* is the Spirit of your Father who speaks in you" (Matthew 10:16–20; cf. Luke 10:3).

[WARNINGS from Watch out and beware]
Setting: By the Sea of Galilee. Jesus warns His disciples about the teaching of some of the religious leaders of His time—the Pharisees and the Sadducees.

And Jesus said to them, "Watch out and beware of the leaven of the Pharisees and Sadducees" (Matthew 16:6; cf. Mark 8:15).

[WARNINGS from beware of the leaven of the Pharisees and Sadducees]
Setting: By the Sea of Galilee. Jesus repeats a warning to His disciples about the teaching of the religious leaders of His time—the Pharisees and the Sadducees.

But Jesus aware of this, said, "You men of little faith, why do you discuss among yourselves that you have no bread? Do you not yet understand or remember the five loaves of the five thousand and how many baskets *full* you picked up? Or the seven loaves of the four thousand, and how many large baskets *full* you picked up? How is it that you do not understand that I did not speak to you concerning bread? But beware of the leaven of the Pharisees and Sadducees" (Matthew 16:8–11; cf. Matthew 14:17–21; 15:34–38; Mark 8:17–21).

[WARNINGS from Beware of the leaven of the Pharisees and the leaven of Herod]
Setting: The district of Dalmanutha. After the Pharisees argue with Him, seeking a sign from heaven to test Him, Jesus warns His disciples about them.

And He was giving orders to them, saying, "Watch out! Beware of the leaven of the Pharisees and the leaven of Herod" (Mark 8:15; cf. Matthew 16:5–7).

[WARNINGS from Beware of the scribes]
Setting: The temple in Jerusalem. After commending one scribe for his nearness to the kingdom of God, Jesus warns the crowd about the rest of the scribes.

In His teaching He was saying: "Beware of the scribes who like to walk around in long robes, and *like* respectful greetings in the market places, and chief seats in the synagogues and places of honor at banquets, who devour widows' houses, and for appearance's sake offer long prayers; these will receive greater condemnation" (Mark 12:38–40; cf. Matthew 23:1–7; Luke 20:45–47).

[WARNINGS from Beware of the leaven of the Pharisees]
Setting: On the way from Galilee to Jerusalem. Jesus warns His disciples of future events, as the scribes and Pharisees turn hostile and question Him repeatedly in an attempt to catch Him in something He might say.

Under these circumstances, after so many thousands of people had gathered together that they were stepping on one another, He began saying to His disciples first *of all,* "Beware of the leaven of the Pharisees, which is hypocrisy. But there is nothing covered up that will not be revealed, and hidden that will not be known. Accordingly, whatever you have said in the dark will be heard in the light, and what you have whispered in the inner rooms will be proclaimed upon the housetops. I say to you, My friends, do not be afraid of those who kill the body and after that have no more that they can do. But I will warn you whom to fear: fear the One who, after He has killed, has authority to cast into hell; yes, I tell you, fear Him! Are not five sparrows sold for two cents? *Yet* not one of them is forgotten before God. Indeed, the very hairs of your head are all numbered. Do not fear; you are more valuable than many sparrows" (Luke 12:1–7; cf. Matthew 10:26–31; see Matthew 16:6; Hebrews 10:31).

[WARNINGS from Beware, and be on your guard against every form of greed]
Setting: On the way from Galilee to Jerusalem. After the scribes and Pharisees turn hostile and question Him repeatedly in an attempt to catch Him in something He might say, Jesus teaches the crowds and His disciples about greed and possessions.

But He said to him, "Man, who appointed Me a judge or arbitrator over you?" Then He said to them, "Beware, and be on your guard against every form of greed; for not *even* when one has an abundance does his life consist of his possessions" (Luke 12:14, 15; see 1 Timothy 6:6–10).

[WARNINGS from warn]
Setting: On the way from Galilee to Jerusalem. After responding to the Pharisees' scoffing at His teaching His disciples about stewardship and the permanence of the Law, Jesus conveys the story of the rich man and Lazarus.

"Now there was a rich man, and he habitually dressed in purple and fine linen, joyously living in splendor every day. And a poor man named Lazarus was laid at his gate, covered with sores, and longing to be fed with the *crumbs* which were falling from the rich man's table; besides, even the dogs were coming and licking his sores. Now the poor man died and was carried away by the angels to Abraham's bosom; and the rich man also died and was buried. In Hades he lifted up his eyes, being in torment, and saw Abraham far away and Lazarus in his bosom. And he cried out and said, 'Father Abraham, have mercy on me, and send Lazarus so that he may dip the tip of his finger in water and cool off my tongue, for I am in agony in this flame.' But Abraham said, 'Child, remember that during your life you received your good things, and likewise Lazarus bad things; but now he is being comforted here, and you are in agony. And besides all this, between us and you there is a great chasm fixed, so that those who wish to come over from here to you will not be able, and *that* none may cross over from there to us.' And he said, 'Then I beg you, father, that you send him to my father's house—for I have five brothers—in order that he may warn them, so that they will not also come to this place of torment.' But Abraham said, 'They have Moses and the Prophets; let them hear them.' But he said, 'No, father Abraham, but if someone goes to them from the dead, they will repent!' But he said to him, 'If they do not listen to Moses and the Prophets, they will not be persuaded even if someone rises from the dead' " (Luke 16:19–31; see Luke 3:8; 6:24; 16:1).

[WARNINGS from Beware of the scribes]
Setting: The temple in Jerusalem. While ministering a few days before His crucifixion, after posing a question to the scribes, who do not answer, Jesus warns His disciples about the lifestyle of the scribes.

"Beware of the scribes, who like to walk around in long robes, and love respectful greetings in the market places, and chief seats in the synagogues and places of honor at banquets, who devour widows' houses, and for appearance's sake offer long prayers. These will receive greater condemnation" (Luke 20:46, 47; cf. Matthew 23:1–7; Mark 12:38–40; see Luke 11:43).

WARS (Also see WAR; and WARS, RUMORS OF)
Setting: The Mount of Olives, just east of Jerusalem. During His Olivet Discourse, Jesus answers His disciples' questions as to when the temple will be destroyed and Jerusalem overrun, along with the signs of His coming and the end of the age.

And Jesus answered and said to them, "See to it that no one misleads you. For many will come in My name, saying, 'I am the Christ,' and will mislead many. You will be hearing of wars and rumors of wars. See that you are not frightened, for *those things* must take place, but *that* is not yet the end. For nation will rise against nation, and kingdom against kingdom, and in various places there will be famines and earthquakes. But all these things are *merely* the beginning of birth pangs. Then they will deliver you to tribulation, and will kill you, and you will be hated by all nations because of My name. At that time many will fall away and will betray one another and hate one another. Many false prophets will arise and will mislead many. Because lawlessness is increased, most people's love will grow cold. But the one who endures to the end, he will be saved. This gospel of the kingdom shall be preached in the whole world as a testimony to all the nations, and then the end will come" (Matthew 24:4–14; cf. Jeremiah 29:8; Matthew 7:15;10:17, 22; Mark 13:3–13; Luke 21:7–19; Revelation 6:4).

Setting: On the Mount of Olives, east of the temple in Jerusalem. After prophesying the temple's destruction, Jesus responds during His Olivet Discourse to questions from Peter, James, John, and Andrew about other future events.

And Jesus began to say to them, "See to it that no one misleads you. Many will come in My name, saying, 'I am *He!*' and will mislead many. When you hear of wars and rumors of wars, do not be frightened; *those things* must take place; but *that is* not yet the end. For nation will rise up against nation, and kingdom against kingdom; there will be earthquakes in various places; there will *also be* famines. These things are *merely* the beginning of birth pangs. But be on your guard; for they will deliver you to *the* courts, and you will be flogged in *the* synagogues, and you will stand before governors and kings for My sake, as a testimony to them. The gospel must first be preached to all the nations. When they arrest you and hand you over, do not worry beforehand about what you are to say, but say whatever is given you in that hour; for it is not you who speak, but *it is* the Holy Spirit. Brother will betray brother to death, and a father *his* child; and children will rise up against parents and have them put to death. You will be hated by all because of My name, but the one who endures to the end, he will be saved" (Mark 13:5–13; cf. Matthew 24:4–14; Luke 21:7–19; see Matthew 10:17–22).

Setting: The temple in Jerusalem. While ministering a few days before His crucifixion, after Jesus prophesies the destruction of the temple, His disciples ask Him when this will happen.

And He said, "See to it that you are not misled; for many will come in My name, saying, "I am *He,*' and, 'The time is near.' Do not go after them. When you hear of wars and disturbances, do not be terrified; for these things must take place first, but the end *does* not *follow* immediately" (Luke 21:8, 9; cf. Matthew 24:4–8; Mark 13:5–8).

WARS, RUMORS OF (Also see WARS)

Setting: The Mount of Olives, just east of Jerusalem. During His Olivet Discourse, Jesus answers His disciples' questions as to when the temple will be destroyed and Jerusalem overrun, along with the signs of His coming and the end of the age.

And Jesus answered and said to them, "See to it that no one misleads you. For many will come in My name, saying, 'I am the Christ,' and will mislead many. You will be hearing of wars and rumors of wars. See that you are not frightened, for *those things* must take place, but *that* is not yet the end. For nation will rise against nation, and kingdom against kingdom, and in various places there will be famines and earthquakes. But all these things are *merely* the beginning of birth pangs. Then they will deliver you to tribulation, and will kill you, and you will be hated by all nations because of My name. At that time many will fall away and will betray one another and hate one another. Many false prophets will arise and will mislead many. Because lawlessness is increased, most people's love will grow cold. But the one who endures to the end, he will be saved. This gospel of the kingdom shall be preached in the whole world as a testimony to all the nations, and then the end will come" (Matthew 24:4–14; cf. Jeremiah 29:8; Matthew 7:15; 10:17, 22; Mark 13:3–13; Luke 21:7–19; Revelation 6:4).

Setting: On the Mount of Olives, east of the temple in Jerusalem. After prophesying the temple's destruction, Jesus responds during His Olivet Discourse to questions from Peter, James, John, and Andrew about other future events.

And Jesus began to say to them, "See to it that no one misleads you. Many will come in My name, saying, 'I am *He!*' and will mislead many. When you hear of wars and rumors of wars, do not be frightened; *those things* must take place; but *that is* not yet the end. For nation will rise up against nation, and kingdom against kingdom; there will be earthquakes in various places; there will *also be* famines. These things are *merely* the beginning of birth pangs. But be on your guard; for they will deliver you to *the* courts, and you will be flogged in *the* synagogues, and you will stand before governors and kings for My sake, as a testimony to them. The gospel must first be preached to all the nations. When they arrest you and hand you over, do not worry beforehand about what you are to say, but say whatever is given you in that hour; for it is not you who speak, but *it is* the Holy Spirit. Brother will betray brother to death, and a father *his* child; and children will rise up against parents and have them put to death. You will be hated by all because of My name, but the one who endures to the end, he will be saved" (Mark 13:5–13; cf. Matthew 24:4–14; Luke 21:7–19; see Matthew 10:17–22).

WASHING (Also see BATH)

[WASHING from wash]
Setting: Galilee. During the early part of His ministry, Jesus preaches the Sermon on the Mount to His disciples and the multitudes.

"Whenever you fast, do not put on a gloomy face as the hypocrites *do,* for they neglect their appearance so that they will be noticed by men when they are fasting. Truly I say to you, they have their reward in full. But you, when you fast, anoint your head and wash your face so that your fasting will not be noticed by men, but by your Father who is in secret; and your Father who sees *what is done* in secret will reward you" (Matthew 6:16–18; see Matthew 6:4, 6).

[WASHING from wash]
Setting: The temple treasury in Jerusalem. After Jesus avoids being stoned by the scribes and Pharisees, His disciples wonder if blindness is caused by sin as the Lord heals a man born blind.

Jesus answered, "*It was* neither *that* this man sinned, nor his parents; but *it was* so that the works of God might be displayed in him. We must work the works of Him who sent Me as long as it is day; night is coming when no one can work. While I am in the world, I am the Light of the world." When He had said this, He spat on the ground, and made clay of the spittle, and applied the clay to his eyes, and said to him, "Go, wash in the pool of Siloam" (which is translated, Sent). So he went away and washed, and came *back* seeing (John 9:3–7; see John 8:12; 11:4; 12:46).

[WASHING from wash]
Setting: Jerusalem. A formerly blind man testifies to his neighbors of how Jesus gave him sight.

He answered, "The man who is called Jesus made clay, and anointed my eyes, and said to me, 'Go to Siloam and wash'; so I went away and washed, and I received sight" (John 9:11).

[WASHING from wash]
Setting: Jerusalem. Before the Passover, with His crucifixion nearing, Jesus eats supper with His disciples and assumes the role of a servant, washing His followers' feet.

Jesus answered and said to him, "What I do you do not realize now, but you will understand hereafter." Peter said to Him, "Never shall You wash my feet!" Jesus answered him, "If I do not wash you, you have no part with Me." Simon Peter said to Him, "Lord, *then wash* not only my feet, but also my hand and my head." Jesus said to him, "He who has bathed needs only to wash his feet, but is completely clean; and you are clean, but not all *of you*. For He knew the one who was betraying Him; for this reason He said, "Not all of you are clean" (John 13:7–11; see John 6:64; 15:3).

[WASHING from wash]
Setting: Jerusalem. Before the Passover, with His death on the cross nearing, Jesus explains the reason for His vivid example of servanthood in washing His disciples' feet.

So when He had washed their feet, and taken His garments and reclined *at the table* again, He said to them, "Do you know what I have done to you? You call Me Teacher and Lord; and you are right, for *so* I am. If I then, the Lord and the Teacher, washed your feet, you also ought to wash one another's feet. For I gave you an example that you also should do as I did to you. Truly, truly I say to you, a slave is not greater than his master, nor *is* one who is sent greater than the one who sent him. If you know these things, you are blessed if you do them. I do not speak of all of you. I know the ones I have chosen; but *it is* that the Scripture may be fulfilled, 'HE WHO EATS MY BREAD HAS LIFTED UP HIS HEEL AGAINST ME.' From now on I am telling you before *it* comes to pass, so that when it does occur, you may believe that I am *He*. Truly, truly, I say to you, he who receives whomever I send receives Me; and he who receives Me receives Him who sent Me" (John 13:12–20; Jesus quotes from Psalm 41:9; see Matthew 7:24; 10:24, 40; John 8:24; 14:29; 1 Peter 5:3).

WASHING, HAND (See WASHING)

WATCHFULNESS (Also see ALERTNESS; READINESS; and WARNINGS)

[WATCHFULNESS from watch]
Setting: By the Sea of Galilee. Jesus warns His disciples about the teaching of some of the religious leaders of His time—the Pharisees and the Sadducees.

And Jesus said to them, "Watch out and beware of the leaven of the Pharisees and Sadducees" (Matthew 16:6; cf. Matthew 16:12; Mark 8:15).

[WATCHFULNESS from watch]
Setting: An upper room in Jerusalem. After celebrating the Passover meal with His disciples, Jesus retreats to the Garden of Gethsemane on the Mount of Olives to pray prior to His betrayal by Judas.

Then Jesus came with them to a place called Gethsemane, and said to His disciples, "Sit here while I go over there and pray." And He took with Him Peter and the two sons of Zebedee, and began to be grieved and distressed. Then He said to them, "My soul is deeply grieved, to the point of death; remain here and keep watch with Me." And He went a little beyond *them,* and fell on His face and prayed, saying, "My Father, if it is possible, let this cup pass from Me; yet not as I will, but as You will." And He came to the disciples and found them sleeping, and said to Peter, "So, you *men* could not keep watch with Me for one hour? Keep watching and praying that you may not enter into temptation; the spirit is willing, but the flesh is weak." He went away again a second time and prayed, saying, "My Father, if this cannot pass away unless I drink it, Your will be done." Again He came and found them sleeping, for their eyes were heavy. And He left them again, and went away and prayed a third time, saying the same thing once more. Then He came to the disciples and said to them, "Are you still sleeping and resting? Behold the hour is at hand and the Son of Man is being betrayed into the hands of sinners. Get up, let us be going; behold the one who betrays Me is at hand!" (Matthew 26:36–46; cf. Mark 14:32–42; Luke 22:40–46; see Matthew 20:22; John 12:27).

[WATCHFULNESS from watch]
Setting: The district of Dalmanutha. After the Pharisees argue with Him, seeking a sign from heaven to test Him, Jesus warns His disciples about them.

And He was giving orders to them, saying, "Watch out! Beware of the leaven of the Pharisees and the leaven of Herod" (Mark 8:15; cf. Matthew 16:5–7).

[WATCHFULNESS from watch]
Setting: Gethsemane on the Mount of Olives, east of the temple in Jerusalem. Jesus agonizes over His impending death, disappointed His disciples keep falling asleep instead of watching and praying with Him.

They came to a place named Gethsemane; and He said to the disciples, "Sit here until I have prayed." And He took with Him Peter and James and John, and began to be very distressed and troubled. And He said to them, "My soul is deeply grieved to the point of death; remain here and keep watch." And He went a little beyond *them,* and fell to the ground and *began* to pray that if it were possible, the hour might pass Him by. And He was saying, "Abba! Father! All things are possible for You; remove this cup from Me; yet not what I will, but what You will." And He came and found them sleeping, and said to Peter, "Simon, are you asleep? Could you not keep watch for one hour? Keep watching and praying that you may not come into temptation; the spirit is willing, but the flesh is weak" (Mark 14:32–38; cf. Matthew 26:36–41; Luke 22:41–46; see Romans 8:15; Galatians 4:6).

[WATCHFULNESS from watch]
Setting: On the way from Galilee to Jerusalem. After telling the increasing crowds of the sign of Jonah, Jesus illustrates His point by speaking about a lamp.

"No one, after lighting a lamp, puts it away in a cellar nor under a basket, but on the lampstand, so that those who enter may see the light. The eye is the lamp of your body; when your eye is clear, your whole body also is full of light; but when it is bad, your body also is full of darkness. Then watch out that the light in you is not darkness. If therefore your whole body is full of light, with no dark part in it, it will be wholly illumined, as when the lamp illumines you with its rays" (Luke 11:33–36; cf. Matthew 5:15; 6:22, 23).

[WATCHFULNESS from watch]
Setting: On the way from Galilee to Jerusalem. After giving a parable about riches and greed, Jesus uses another parable to challenge the crowd and His disciples to be ready for His return.

"Be dressed in readiness, and *keep* your lamps lit. Be like men who are waiting for their master when he returns from the wedding feast, so that they may immediately open *the door* to him when he comes and knocks. Blessed are those slaves whom the master will find on the alert when he comes; truly I say to you, that he will gird himself *to serve,* and have them recline *at the table,* and will come up and wait on them. Whether he comes in the second watch, or even in the third and finds *them* so, blessed are those *slaves*. But be sure of this, that if the head of the house had known at what hour the thief was coming, he would not have allowed his house to be broken into. You too, be ready; for the Son of Man is coming at an hour that you do not expect" (Luke 12:35–40; cf. Matthew 24:42–44; see Mark 13:33; Ephesians 6:14).

WATER (Specifics such as WATER, DEEP; WATER, LIVING; and WATER, PITCHER OF are separate entries; also see DRINKING; MOISTURE; RAIN; WASHING; and WELL)
Setting: Galilee. After Jesus praises John the Baptist to the crowds, Simon, a Pharisee, invites the Lord to dinner. A sinful woman anoints His feet with perfume, prompting Him to instruct His host about forgiveness.

Turning toward the woman, He said to Simon, "Do you see this woman? I entered your house; you gave Me no water for My feet, but she has wet My feet with her tears and wiped them with her hair. You gave Me no kiss; but she, since the time I came in, has not ceased to kiss My feet. You did not anoint My head with oil, but she anointed My feet with perfume. For this reason I say to you, her sins, which are many, have been forgiven, for she loved much; but he who is forgiven little, loves little." Then He said to her, "Your sins have been forgiven." Those who were reclining *at the table* with Him began to say to themselves, "Who is this *man* who even forgives sins?" And He said to the woman, "Your faith has saved you; go in peace" (Luke 7:44–50; see Matthew 9:2; Mark 5:34; Luke 5:21).

Setting: On the way from Galilee to Jerusalem. Jesus responds to a synagogue official's anger over His healing of a woman, sick for eighteen years, in the synagogue on the Sabbath.

But the Lord answered him and said, "You hypocrites, does not each of you on the Sabbath untie his ox or his donkey from the stall and lead him away to water *him?* And this woman, a daughter of Abraham as she is, whom Satan has bound for eighteen long years, should she not have been released from this bond on the Sabbath day?" (Luke 13:15, 16; see Luke 14:5).

Setting: On the way from Galilee to Jerusalem. After responding to the Pharisees' scoffing at His teaching His disciples about stewardship and the permanence of the Law, Jesus conveys the story of the rich man and Lazarus.

"Now there was a rich man, and he habitually dressed in purple and fine linen, joyously living in splendor every day. And a poor man named Lazarus was laid at his gate, covered with sores, and longing to be fed with the *crumbs* which were falling from the rich man's table; besides, even the dogs were coming and licking his sores. Now the poor man died and was carried away by the angels to Abraham's bosom; and the rich man also died and was buried. In Hades he lifted up his eyes, being in torment, and saw Abraham far away and Lazarus in his bosom. And he cried out and said, 'Father Abraham, have mercy on me, and send Lazarus so that he may dip the tip of his finger in water and cool off my tongue, for I am in agony in this flame.' But Abraham said, 'Child, remember that during your life you received your good things, and likewise Lazarus bad things; but now he is being comforted here, and you are in agony. And besides all this, between us and you there is a great chasm fixed, so that those who wish to come over from here to you will not be able, and *that* none may cross over from there to us.' And he said, 'Then I beg you, father, that you send him to my father's house—for I have five brothers—in order that he may warn them, so that they will not also come to this place of torment.' But Abraham said, 'They have Moses and the Prophets; let them hear them.' But he said, 'No, father Abraham, but if someone goes to them from the dead, they will repent!' But he said to him, 'If they do not listen to Moses and the Prophets, they will not be persuaded even if someone rises from the dead' " (Luke 16:19–31; see Luke 3:8; 6:24; 16:1, 14).

Setting: Cana of Galilee. On the third day of His public ministry, after choosing Andrew, Peter, Philip, and Nathanael to be His disciples, Jesus attends a wedding. His mother prompts Him to perform His first miracle, that of turning water into wine.

Jesus said to them, "Fill the waterpots with water." So they filled them up to the brim. And He said to them, "Draw *some* out now and take it to the headwaiter." So they took it *to him* (John 2:7, 8).

Setting: Jerusalem. At the time for the Passover of the Jews, after the Lord cleanses the temple, a Pharisee, Nicodemus, asks Him by night the meaning of "born again."

Jesus answered, "Truly, truly, I say to you, unless one is born of water and the Spirit he cannot enter into the kingdom of God. That which is born of the flesh is flesh, and that which is born of the Spirit is spirit. Do not be amazed that I said to you, 'You must be born again.' The wind blows where it wishes and you hear the sound of it, but do not know where it comes from and where it is going; so is everyone who is born of the Spirit" (John 3:5–8; see Psalm 135:7; John 1:13).

Setting: Sychar in Samaria, on the way to Galilee. Jesus interacts with a Samaritan woman at Jacob's well, while the disciples are buying food.

Jesus answered and said to her, "Everyone who drinks of this water will thirst again; but whoever drinks of the water that I will give him shall never thirst; but the water that I will give him will become in him a well of water springing up to eternal life" (John 4:13, 14).

Setting: Jerusalem. Luke, writing in Acts, presents quotes from Jesus' post-resurrection appearances, in which the Lord informs and instructs His disciples about their imminent baptism with the Holy Spirit.

Gathering them together, He commanded them not to leave Jerusalem, but to wait for what the Father had promised, "Which," *He said,* "you heard of from Me; for John baptized with water, but you will be baptized with the Holy Spirit not many days from now" (Acts 1:4, 5; see Luke 24:49; John 14:16, 26; Acts 2:1–4).

Setting: Jerusalem. Luke, writing in Acts, records Peter (following a time of ministry to the Gentiles and returning) recalling the words of Jesus regarding the baptism of the Holy Spirit.

And I remembered the word of the Lord, how He used to say, "John baptized with water, but you will be baptized with the Holy Spirit" (Acts 11:16; cf. Acts 1:5).

WATER, CUP OF COLD (Also see WATER; and WATER, CUP OF)

Setting: Galilee. After His twelve disciples observe His ministry, Jesus summons and specifically instructs them about their ministry ahead that will include rewards.

"He who receives you receives Me, and he who receives Me receives Him who sent me. He who receives a prophet in the name of a prophet shall receive a prophet's reward; and he who receives a righteous man in the name of a righteous man shall receive a righteous man's reward. And whoever in the name of a disciple gives to one of these little ones even a cup of cold water to drink, truly I say to you, he shall not lose his reward" (Matthew 10:40–42; cf. Matthew 25:40, 44, 45; see Mark 9:37).

WATER, CUP OF (Also see WATER; and WATER, CUP OF COLD)

Setting: Capernaum of Galilee. As Jesus teaches His disciples in private, they ask Him about greatness.

But Jesus said, "Do not hinder him, for there is no one who will perform a miracle in My name, and be able soon afterward to speak evil of Me. For he who is not against us is for us. For whoever gives you a cup of water to drink because of your name as *followers* of Christ, truly I say to you, he will not lose his reward. Whoever causes one of these little ones who believe to stumble, it would be better for him if, with a heavy millstone hung around his neck, he had been cast into the sea. If your hand causes you to stumble, cut it off; it is better for you to enter life crippled, than, having your two hands, to go into hell, into the unquenchable fire, [where THEIR WORM DOES NOT DIE, AND THE FIRE IS NOT QUENCHED.] If your foot causes you to stumble, cut it off; it is better for you to enter life lame, than, having your two feet, to be cast into hell, [where THEIR WORM DOES NOT DIE, AND THE FIRE IS NOT QUENCHED.] If your eye causes you to stumble, throw it out; it is better for you to enter the kingdom of God with one eye, than, having two eyes, to be cast into hell, where THEIR WORM DOES NOT DIE, AND THE FIRE IS NOT QUENCHED. For everyone will be salted with fire. Salt is good; but if the salt becomes unsalty, with what will you make it salty *again?* Have salt in yourselves, and be at peace with one another" (Mark 9:39–50; Jesus quotes from Isaiah 66:24; cf. Matthew 18:6–9; Luke 9:49, 50; see Matthew 5:13, 29, 30; 10:42; 12:30; 18:5, 6).

WATER, DEEP

Setting: By the Sea of Galilee. After teaching the people from the boat of Simon (Peter), Jesus calls Simon, James, and John to follow Him. (This appears to be a permanent call, as Simon and other companions are with Him earlier, in Mark 1:35–39 and Luke 4:38, 39.)

When He had finished speaking, He said to Simon, "Put out into the deep water and let down your nets for a catch." ". . . and so also *were* James and John, sons of Zebedee, who were partners with Simon. And Jesus said to Simon, "Do not fear, from now on you will be catching men" (Luke 5:4, 10; see John 21:6).

WATER, LIVING

Setting: Sychar in Samaria, on the way to Galilee. Jesus interacts with a Samaritan woman at Jacob's well, while the disciples are buying food.

Jesus answered and said to her, "If you knew the gift of God, and who it is who says to you, 'Give Me a drink,' you would have asked Him, and He would have given you living water" (John 4:10).

Setting: Jerusalem. On the last day of the Feast of Booths, Jesus causes discussion about whether He is the Christ, while the chief priests and Pharisees attempt to understand where it is He says He will be going soon. Jesus offers salvation and the abundant life to His hearers.

Now on the last day, the great *day* of the feast, Jesus stood and cried out, saying, "If anyone is thirsty, let him come to Me and drink. He who believes in Me, as the Scripture said, 'From his innermost being will flow rivers of living water'" (John 7:37, 38; see John 7:10–15).

WATER, PITCHER OF

Setting: Jerusalem. On the first day of the Feast of Unleavened Bread, when the Passover lamb is being sacrificed, Jesus responds to His disciples' question about His plans for the Passover meal.

And He sent two of His disciples and said to them, "Go into the city, and a man will meet you carrying a pitcher of water; follow him; and wherever he enters, say to the owner of the house, 'The Teacher says, "Where is My guest room in which I may eat the

Passover with My disciples?"' And he himself will show you a large upper room furnished *and* ready; prepare for us there" (Mark 14:13–15; cf. Matthew 26:17–19; Luke 22:7–13).

Setting: Jerusalem. With the Passover (Feast of Unleavened Bread) approaching, Jesus informs His disciples where they will celebrate the feast. The chief priests and scribes seek to kill Him, and Satan enters Judas Iscariot in order to betray the Lord.

And Jesus sent Peter and John, saying, "Go and prepare the Passover for us, so that we may eat it." They said to Him, "Where do You want us to prepare it?" And He said to them, "When you have entered the city, a man will meet you carrying a pitcher of water; follow him into the house that he enters. And you shall say to the owner of the house, 'The Teacher says to you, "Where is the guest room in which I may eat the Passover with My disciples?"' And he will show you a large, furnished upper room; prepare it there" (Luke 22:8–12; cf. Matthew 26:17–19; Mark 14:12–16).

WATER, WALKING ON

[WALKING ON WATER from Matthew 14:26, When the disciples saw Him walking on the sea]

Setting: On the Sea of Galilee. Following the miraculous feeding of more than 5,000 of His countrymen, in order to take an opportunity to pray, Jesus makes His disciples get into a boat. He joins them later by walking on the water during a storm.

But immediately Jesus spoke to them, saying, "Take courage, it is I; do not be afraid." Peter said to Him, "Lord, if it is You, command me to come to You on the water." And He said, "Come!" And Peter got out of the boat, and walked on the water and came toward Jesus. But seeing the wind, he became frightened, and beginning to sink, he cried out, "Lord, save me!" Immediately Jesus stretched out His hand and took hold of him, and said to him, "You of little faith, why did you doubt?" (Matthew 14:27–31; cf. Mark 6:47–52; John 6:16–21).

[WALKING ON WATER from But when they saw Him walking on the sea]

Setting: On the Sea of Galilee. After feeding more than 5,000 people through God's miraculous provision and returning from a time of prayer on a mountain, Jesus startles His disciples by walking on the water as they head toward Bethsaida.

But when they saw Him walking on the sea, they supposed that it was a ghost, and cried out; for they all saw Him and were terrified. But immediately He spoke with them and said to them, "Take courage; it is I, do not be afraid" (Mark 6:49, 50; cf. Matthew 14:26, 27; John 6:19, 20).

[WALKING ON WATER from John 6:19, walking on the sea]

Setting: A mountain in Galilee. Perceiving the people wanting to make Him king after He miraculously feeds more than 5,000 of them, Jesus withdraws. His disciples board a boat and start across the Sea of Galilee, where He will join them by walking on water during a storm.

But He said to them, "It is I; do not be afraid" (John 6:20; cf. Matthew 14:27; Mark 6:50).

WATERPOTS

Setting: Cana of Galilee. On the third day of His public ministry, after choosing Andrew, Peter, Philip, and Nathanael to be His disciples, Jesus attends a wedding. His mother prompts Him to perform His first miracle, that of turning water into wine.

Jesus said to them, "Fill the waterpots with water." So they filled them up to the brim. And He said to them, "Draw *some* out now and take it to the headwaiter." So they took it *to him* (John 2:7, 8)

WATERLESS PLACES (Listed under PLACES, WATERLESS)

WAVES (Also see SEA)

Setting: On the Mount of Olives, just east of Jerusalem. After ministering in the temple a few days before His crucifixion, and giving His disciples more details regarding future events, Jesus speaks during His Olivet Discourse of His return.

"There will be signs in sun and moon and stars, and on the earth dismay among the nations, in perplexity at the roaring of the sea and the waves, men fainting from fear and the expectation of the things which are coming upon the world; for the powers of the heavens will be shaken. Then they will see THE SON OF MAN COMING IN A CLOUD with power and great glory. But when these things begin to take place, straighten up and lift up your heads, because your redemption is drawing near" (Luke 21:25–28, Jesus quotes from Daniel 7:13; cf. Matthew 24:29–31; Mark 13:24–27).

WAY (Specifics such as BROAD WAY; and WAY, SAME are separate entries)

Setting: Galilee. During the early part of His ministry, Jesus preaches the Sermon on the Mount to His disciples and the multitudes.

"You are the light of the world. A city set on a hill cannot be hidden; nor does *anyone* light a lamp and put it under a basket, but on the lampstand, and it gives light to all who are in the house. Let your light shine before men in such a way that they may see your good works, and glorify your Father who is in heaven" (Matthew 5:14–16; cf. Mark 4:21; 1 Peter 2:12).

Setting: Galilee. During the early part of His ministry, Jesus preaches the Sermon on the Mount to His disciples and the multitudes.

"Make friends quickly with your opponent at law while you are with him on the way, so that your opponent may not hand you over to the judge, and the judge to the officer, and you be thrown into prison. Truly I say to you, you will not come out of there until you have paid up the last cent'" (Matthew 5:25, 26; cf. Luke 12:58, 59).

Setting: Galilee. During the early part of His ministry, Jesus preaches the Sermon on the Mount to His disciples and the multitudes.

"Do not judge so that you will not be judged. For in the way you judge, you will be judged; and by your standard of measure, it will be measured to you. Why do you look at the speck that is in your brother's eye, but do not notice the log that is in your own eye? Or how can you say to your brother, 'Let me take the speck out of your eye, and behold, the log is in your own eye? You hypocrite, first take the log out of your own eye, and then you will see clearly to take the speck out of your brother's eye" (Matthew 7:1–5; cf. Mark 4:24; Luke 6:37–42; Romans 2:1; Romans 14:10, 13).

Setting: Galilee. During the early part of His ministry, Jesus preaches the Sermon on the Mount to His disciples and the multitudes.

"Enter through the narrow gate; for the gate is wide and the way is broad that leads to destruction, and there are many who enter through it. For the gate is small and the way is narrow that leads to life, and there are few who find it" (Matthew 7:13, 14; cf. Luke 13:24).

Setting: Galilee. After His twelve disciples observe His ministry, Jesus summons and specifically instructs them about their ministry to the people of Israel.

These twelve Jesus sent out after instructing them: "Do not go in *the* way of *the* Gentiles, and do not enter *any* city of the Samaritans; but rather go to the lost sheep of the house of Israel. And as you go, preach, saying, 'The kingdom of heaven is at hand.' Heal *the* sick, raise *the* dead, cleanse *the* lepers, cast out demons. Freely you received, freely give. Do not acquire gold, or silver, or copper for your money belts, or a bag for *your* journey, or even two coats, or sandals, or a staff; for the worker is worthy of his support. And whatever city or village you enter, inquire who is worthy in it, and stay at his house until you leave *that city*. As you enter the house, give it your greeting. If the house is worthy, give it your *blessing of* peace. But if it is not worthy, take back your *blessing of* peace. Whoever does not receive you, nor heed your words, as you go out of that house or that city, shake the dust off your feet. Truly I say to you, it will be more tolerable for *the* land of Sodom and Gomorrah in the day of judgment than for that city" (Matthew 10:5–15; cf. Mark 6:7–11; Luke 9:1–5; see Matthew 3:2; 11:22, 24; 15:24; Luke 22:35; 1 Corinthians 9:14).

Setting: Galilee. Jesus responds to some Pharisees and scribes who ask Him for a miraculous sign as He ministers.

"Now when the unclean spirit goes out of a man, it passes through waterless places seeking rest, and does not find *it.* Then it says, 'I will return to my house from which I came'; and when it comes, it finds *it* unoccupied, swept, and put in order. Then it goes and takes along with it seven other spirits more wicked than itself, and they go in and live there; and the last state of that man becomes worse than the first. That is the way it will also be for this evil generation" (Matthew 12:43–45; cf. Luke 11:24–26; see Mark 5:9).

Setting: Near the Sea of Galilee. After healing of demon-possession the daughter of a Canaanite woman whose faith impressed Him in the region of Tyre, Jesus feeds more than 4,000 people following Him.

And Jesus called His disciples to Him, and said, "I feel compassion for the people, because they have remained with Me now three days and have nothing to eat; and I do not want to send them away hungry, for they might faint on the way." The disciples said to Him, "Where would we get so many loaves in *this* desolate place to satisfy a large crowd?" And Jesus said to them, "How many loaves do you have?" And they said, "Seven and a few small fish" (Matthew 15:32–34; cf. Mark 8:1–9).

Setting: Judea beyond the Jordan (Perea). After responding to the Pharisees' question about Moses' command regarding a certificate of divorce, Jesus answers the disciples' private question.

But He said to them, "Not all men *can* accept this statement, but *only* those to whom it has been given. For there are eunuchs who were born that way from their mother's womb; and there are eunuchs who were made eunuchs by men; and there are *also* eunuchs who made themselves eunuchs for the sake of the kingdom of heaven. He who is able to accept *this,* let him accept *it*" (Matthew 19:11, 12; cf. 1 Corinthians 7:7).

Setting: The temple in Jerusalem. Jesus delivers a parable to the chief priests and elders after they question His authority.

"But what do you think? A man had two sons, and he came to the first and said, 'Son, go work today in the vineyard.' And he answered, 'I will not'; but afterward he regretted it and went. The man came to the second and said the same thing; and he answered, 'I *will,* sir'; but he did not go. Which of the two sons did the will of his father?" They said, "The first." Jesus said to them, "Truly, I say to you that the tax collectors and prostitutes will get into the kingdom of God before you. For John came to you in the way of righteousness and you did not believe him; but the tax collectors and prostitutes did believe him; and you, seeing *this,* did not even feel remorse afterward so as to believe him" (Matthew 21:28–32; cf. Luke 7:29, 30, 37–50).

Setting: The temple in Jerusalem. Jesus speaks another parable to the chief priests and elders after they question His authority.

Jesus spoke to them again in parables, saying, "The kingdom of heaven may be compared to a king who gave a wedding feast for his son. And he sent out his slaves to call those who had been invited to the wedding feast, and they were unwilling to come. Again he sent out other slaves saying, 'Tell those who have been invited, "Behold, I have prepared my dinner; my oxen and my fattened livestock are *all* butchered and everything is ready; come to the wedding feast." But they paid no attention and went their way, one to his own farm, another to his business, and the rest seized his slaves and mistreated them and killed them. But the king was enraged, and he sent his armies and destroyed those murderers and set their city on fire. Then he said to his slaves, 'The wedding is ready, but those who were invited were not worthy. 'Go therefore to the main highways, and as many as you find *there,* invite to the wedding feast.' Those slaves went out into the streets and gathered together all they found, both evil and good; and the wedding hall was filled with dinner guests. But when the king came in to look over the dinner guests, he saw a man there who was not dressed in wedding clothes, and he said to him, 'Friend, how did you come in here without wedding clothes?' And the man was speechless. Then the king said to the servants, 'Bind him hand and foot, and throw him into the outer darkness; in that place there will be weeping and gnashing of teeth' For many are called, but few *are* chosen" (Matthew 22:1–14; cf. Matthew 8:11, 12).

Setting: The temple in Jerusalem. With His death on the cross just days away, Jesus laments over Jerusalem's hard-heartedness and lack of repentance.

"Jerusalem, Jerusalem, who kills the prophets and stones those who are sent to her! How often I wanted to gather your children together, the way a hen gathers her chicks under her wings, and you were unwilling. Behold, your house is being left to you desolate! For I say to you, from now on you will not see Me until you say, 'BLESSED IS HE WHO COMES IN THE NAME OF THE LORD!'" (Matthew 23:37–39, Jesus quotes from Psalm 118:26; cf. 1 Kings 9:7; Luke 13:34, 35).

Setting: Decapolis, near the Sea of Galilee. Jesus miraculously feeds more than 4,000 people, primarily Gentiles, who are following Him.

In those days, when there was again a large crowd and they had nothing to eat, Jesus called His disciples and said to them, "I feel compassion for the people because they have remained with Me now three days and have nothing to eat. If I send them away hungry to their homes, they will faint on their way; and some of them have come a great distance" (Mark 8:1–3; cf. Matthew 15:32–38; see Matthew 9:36).

Setting: Capernaum of Galilee. As Jesus teaches His disciples in private, they ask Him about greatness.

They came to Capernaum; and when He was in the house, He *began* to question them, "What were you discussing on the way?" But they kept silent, for on the way they had discussed with one another which *of them* was the greatest. Sitting down, He called the twelve and said to them, "If anyone wants to be first, he shall be last of all and servant of all." Taking a child, He set him before them, and taking him in His arms, He said to them, "Whoever receives one child like this in My name receives Me; and whoever receives Me does not receive Me, but Him who sent Me" (Mark 9:33–37; cf. Matthew 18:1–5; Luke 9:46–48; see Matthew 20:26; 10:40).

Setting: Galilee. After Jesus presents the Parable of the Sower to the crowds, His disciples ask Him to give them the parable's meaning.

And He said, "To you it has been granted to know the mysteries of the kingdom of God, but to the rest *it is* in parables, so that SEEING THEY MAY NOT SEE, AND HEARING THEY MAY NOT UNDERSTAND. Now the parable is this: the seed is the word of God. Those beside the road are those who have heard; then the devil comes and takes away the word from their heart, so that they will not believe and be saved. Those on the rocky *soil* are those who, when they hear, receive the word with joy; and these have no *firm* root; they believe for a while, and in time of temptation fall away. The *seed* which fell among the thorns, these are the ones who have heard, and as they go on their way they are choked with worries and riches and pleasures of *this* life, and bring no fruit to maturity. But the *seed* in the good soil, these are the ones who have heard the word in an honest and good heart, and hold it fast, and bear fruit with perseverance" (Luke 8:10–15, Jesus quotes from Isaiah 6:9; cf. Matthew 13:10–23; Mark 4:10–20).

Setting: On the way from Galilee to Jerusalem. The Lord appoints seventy followers and sends them out in pairs to every place He Himself will soon visit.

And He was saying to them, "The harvest is plentiful, but the laborers are few; therefore beseech the Lord of the harvest to send out laborers into His harvest. Go; behold, I send you out as lambs in the midst of wolves. Carry no money belt, no bag, no shoes; and greet no one on the way. Whatever house you enter, first say, 'Peace be to this house.' If a man of peace is there, your peace will rest on him; but if not, it will return to you. Stay in that house, eating and drinking what they give you;

for the laborer is worthy of his wages. Do not keep moving from house to house. Whatever city you enter and they receive you, eat what is set before you; and heal those in it who are sick, and say to them, 'The kingdom of God has come near to you.' But whatever city you enter and they do not receive you, go out into its streets and say, 'Even the dust of your city which clings to our feet we wipe off *in protest* against you; yet be sure of this, that the kingdom of God has come near.' I say to you, it will be more tolerable in that day for Sodom than for that city" (Luke 10:2–12; see Genesis 19:24–28; Matthew 9:37, 38, 10:9–14, 16; 1 Corinthians 10:27).

Setting: On the way from Galilee to Jerusalem. After telling how a relationship with Him will divide families, Jesus chastises the crowds for being able to discern the weather but not the present age.

And He was also saying to the crowds, "When you see a cloud rising in the west, immediately you say, 'A shower is coming,' and so it turns out. And when *you see* a south wind blowing, you say, 'It will be a hot day,' and it turns out *that way*. You hypocrites! You know how to analyze the appearance of the earth and the sky, but why do you not analyze this present time?" (Luke 12:54–56; cf. Matthew 16:2, 3).

Setting: On the way from Galilee to Jerusalem. The Lord responds to the Pharisees' scoffing at His teaching His disciples about stewardship.

And He said to them, "You are those who justify yourselves in the sight of men, but God knows your hearts; for that which is highly esteemed among men is detestable in the sight of God. The Law and the Prophets *were proclaimed* until John; since that time the gospel of the kingdom of God has been preached, and everyone is forcing his way into it. But is it easier for heaven and earth to pass away than for one stroke of a letter of the Law to fail" (Luke 16:15–17; cf. Matthew 5:18; see 1 Samuel 16:7; Matthew 4:23; 11:11–14).

Setting: Jerusalem. Before the Passover, after taking issue with Peter's assertion that he would lay down his life for Him, Jesus comforts and gives hope to His disciples regarding their future after He returns to heaven.

"Do not let your heart be troubled; believe in God, believe also in Me. In My Father's house are many dwelling places; if it were not so, I would have told you; for I go to prepare a place for you. If I go and prepare a place for you, I will come again and receive you to Myself, that where I am, *there* you may be also. And you know the way where I am going" (John 14:1–4; see John 13:35; 14:27, 28).

Setting: Jerusalem. Before the Passover, as Jesus comforts and gives hope to His disciples regarding their future after He returns to heaven, Thomas asks where the Lord is going and how they will know the way.

Jesus said to him, "I am the way, and the truth, and the life; no one comes to the Father but through Me. If you had known Me, you would have known My Father also; from now on you know Him, and have seen Him" (John 14:6, 7; see John 8:19; 10:9; 11:25).

Setting: Jerusalem. After Jesus prays His high-priestly prayer on behalf of His disciples, they all go across the ravine of the Kidron to a garden where Judas waits to seize the Lord with a Roman cohort and officers from the chief priests and the Pharisees.

So Jesus, knowing all the things that were coming upon Him, went forth and said to them, "Whom do you seek?" They answered Him, "Jesus the Nazarene." He said to them, "I am *He*." And Judas also, who was betraying Him, was standing with them. So when He said to them, "I am *He*," they drew back and fell to the ground. Therefore He again asked them, "Whom do you seek?" And they said, "Jesus the Nazarene." Jesus answered, "I told you that I am *He*; so if you seek Me, let these go their way," to fulfill the word which He spoke, "Of those whom You have given Me I lost not one" (John 18:4–9; see John 6:64; 17:12).

WAY, BROAD (See **BROAD WAY**)

WAY, LONG

Setting: On the way from Galilee to Jerusalem. Jesus conveys the illustration of the prodigal son because the Pharisees and scribes complain He associates with tax collectors and sinners.

And He said, "A man had two sons. The younger of them said to his father, 'Father, give me the share of the estate that falls to me.' So he divided his wealth between them. And not many days later, the younger son gathered everything together and went on a journey into a distant country, and there he squandered his estate with loose living. Now when he had spent everything, a severe famine occurred in that country, and he began to be impoverished. So he went and hired himself out to one of the citizens of that country, and he sent him into his fields to feed swine. And he would have gladly filled his stomach with the pods that the swine were eating, and no one was giving *anything* to him. But when he came to his senses, he said, 'How many of my father's hired men have more than enough bread, but I am dying here with hunger! I will get up and go to my father, and will say to him, "Father, I have sinned against heaven, and in your sight; I am no longer worthy to be called your son; make me as one of your hired men."' So he got up and came to his father. But while he was still a long way off, his father saw him and felt compassion *for him,* and ran and embraced him and kissed him. And the son said to him, "Father, I have sinned against heaven and in your sight; I am no longer worthy to be called your son.' But the father said to his slaves, 'Quickly bring out the best robe and put it on him, and put a ring on his hand and sandals on his feet; and bring the fattened calf, kill it, and let us eat and celebrate; for this son of mine was dead and has come to life again; he was lost and has been found.' And they began to celebrate. Now his older son was in the field, when he came and approached the house, he heard music and dancing. And he summoned one of the servants and *began* inquiring what these things could be. And he said to him, 'Your brother has come, and your father has killed the fattened calf because he has received him back safe and sound.' But he became angry and was not willing to go in; and his father came out and *began* pleading with him. But he answered and said to his father, 'Look! For so many years I have been serving you and I have never neglected a command of yours; and *yet* you have never given me a young goat, so that I might celebrate with my friends; but when this son of yours came, who has devoured your wealth with prostitutes, you killed the fattened calf for him.' And he said to him, 'Son, you have always been with me, and all that is mine is yours. But we had to celebrate and rejoice, for this brother of yours was dead and *has begun* to live, and was lost and has been found' " (Luke 15:11–32; see Proverbs 29:2).

WAY, OTHER

Setting: Jerusalem. Following the Pharisees' interrogation and dismissal of the formerly blind man Jesus healed on the Sabbath, the Lord speaks to the Pharisees, using parabolic language they do not understand.

"Truly, truly, I say to you, he who does not enter by the door into the fold of the sheep, but climbs up some other way, he is a thief and a robber. But he who enters by the door is a shepherd of the sheep. To him the doorkeeper opens, and the sheep hear his voice, and he calls his own sheep by name and leads them out. When he puts forth all his own, he goes ahead of them, and the sheep follow him because they know his voice. A stranger they simply will not follow, but will flee from him, because they do not know the voice of strangers" (John 10:1–5).

WAY, SAME

Setting: Galilee. Early in His ministry, Jesus presents the Beatitudes (part of the Sermon on the Mount) to His disciples and the gathered crowds from Galilee, Decapolis, Jerusalem, Judea, and beyond the Jordan.

"Blessed are you when *people* insult you and persecute you, and falsely say all kinds of evil against you because of Me. Rejoice and be glad, for your reward in heaven is great; for in the same way they persecuted the prophets who were before you" (Matthew 5:11, 12; cf. 2 Chronicles 36:16; Luke 6:22, 23; 1 Peter 4:14; see 13:35).

Setting: Galilee. During the early part of His ministry, Jesus preaches the Sermon on the Mount to His disciples and the multitudes.

"Ask, and it will be given to you; seek, and you will find; knock, and it will be opened to you. For everyone who asks receives, and he who seeks finds, and to him who knocks it will be opened. Or what man is there among you who, when his son asks for a loaf, will give him a stone? Or if he asks for a fish, he will not give him a snake, will he? If you then, being evil, know how to give good gifts to your children, how much more will your Father who is in heaven give what is good to those who ask Him! In everything, therefore, treat people the same way you want them to treat you, for this is the Law and the Prophets" (Matthew 7:7–12; cf. Matthew 22:40; Luke 6:31; 11:9–13; see Psalm 84:11).

Setting: Capernaum of Galilee. Jesus illustrates forgiveness after Peter asks Him if forgiving someone seven times who has sinned against him is adequate.

"For this reason the kingdom of heaven may be compared to a king who wished to settle accounts with his slaves. When he had begun to settle *them,* one who owed him ten thousand talents was brought to him. But since he did not have *the means* to repay, his lord commanded him to be sold, along with his wife and children and all that he had, and repayment to be made. So the slave fell *to the ground* and prostrated himself before him, saying, 'Have patience with me and I will repay you everything.' And the lord of that slave felt compassion and released him and forgave him the debt. But that slave went out and found one of his fellow slaves who owed him a hundred denarii; and he seized him and *began* to choke *him,* saying, 'Pay back what you owe.' So his fellow slave fell *to the ground* and *began* to plead with him, saying, 'Have patience with me and I will repay you.' But he was unwilling and went and threw him in prison until he should pay back what was owed. So when his fellow slaves saw what had happened, they were deeply grieved and came and reported to their lord all that had happened. Then summoning him, his lord said to him, 'You wicked slave, I forgave you all that debt because you pleaded with me. Should you not also have had mercy on your fellow slave, in the same way that I had mercy on you?' And his lord, moved with anger, handed him over to the torturers until he should repay all that was owed him. My heavenly Father will also do the same to you, if each of you does not forgive his brother from your heart" (Matthew 18:23–35; cf. Matthew 6:12, 14, 15; Luke 7:42; see Matthew 25:19–28).

Setting: Galilee. After selecting His twelve disciples, Jesus teaches the Beatitudes (part of the Sermon on the Mount) to those disciples and a great throng of people from Judea, Jerusalem, and the central coastal region of Tyre and Sidon.

"Blessed are you when men hate you, and ostracize you, and insult you, and scorn your name as evil, for the sake of the Son of Man. Be glad in that day and leap *for joy,* for behold, your reward is great in heaven. For in the same way their fathers used to treat the prophets" (Luke 6:22, 23; cf. Matthew 5:10–12; see 2 Chronicles 36:16).

Setting: Galilee. After selecting His twelve disciples, Jesus teaches the Sermon on the Mount to those disciples and a great throng of people from Judea, Jerusalem, and the central coastal region of Tyre and Sidon.

"But I say to you who hear, love your enemies, do good to those who hate you, bless those who curse you, pray for those who mistreat you. Whoever hits you on the cheek, offer him the other also; and whoever takes away your coat, do not withhold your shirt from him either. Give to everyone who asks of you, and whoever takes away what is yours, do not demand it back. Treat others the same way you want them to treat you. If you love those who love you, what credit is *that* to you? For even sinners love those who love them. If you do good to those who do good to you, what credit is *that* to you? For even sinners do the same. If you lend to those from whom you expect to receive, what credit is *that* to you? Even sinners lend to sinners in order to receive back the same *amount.* But love your enemies, and do good, and lend, expecting nothing in return; and your reward will be great, and you will be sons of the Most High; for He Himself is kind to ungrateful and evil *men.* Be merciful, just as your Father is merciful" (Luke 6:27–36; cf. Matthew 5:9, 39–48; Matthew 7:12).

Setting: On the way from Galilee to Jerusalem. Jesus conveys the principles of the lost sheep and the lost coin because the Pharisees and scribes complain He associates with tax collectors and sinners.

"So He told them this parable, saying, "What man among you, if he has a hundred sheep and has lost one of them, does not leave the ninety-nine in the open pasture and go after the one which is lost until he finds it? When he has found it, he lays it on his shoulders, rejoicing. And when he comes home, he calls together his friends and his neighbors, saying to them, 'Rejoice with me, for I have found my sheep which was lost!' I tell you that in the same way, there will be more joy in heaven over one sinner who repents than over ninety-nine righteous persons who need no repentance. Or what woman, if she has ten silver coins and loses one coin, does not light a lamp and sweep the house and search carefully until she finds it? When she has found it, she calls together her friends and neighbors, saying, 'Rejoice with me, for I have found the coin which I had lost!' In the same way, I tell you, there is joy in the presence of the angels of God over one sinner who repents" (Luke 15:3–10; cf. Matthew 18:12-14; see Matthew 9:11-13).

Setting: On the island of Patmos (in the Aegean Sea about fifty miles southwest of Ephesus in modern Turkey). On the Lord's Day (Sunday), approximately fifty years after the Resurrection, the disciple John encounters the Lord Jesus Christ, who communicates a new revelation for the apostle to record for the church in Pergamum and to six other churches in Asia.

"And to the angel of the church in Pergamum write: The One who has the sharp two-edged sword says this: 'I know where you dwell, where Satan's throne is; and you hold fast My name, and did not deny My faith even in the days of Antipas, My witness, My faithful one, who was killed among you, where Satan dwells. But I have a few things against you, because you have there some who hold the teaching of Balaam, who kept teaching Balak to put a stumbling block before the sons of Israel, to eat things sacrificed to idols and to commit *acts of* immorality. So you also have some who in the same way hold the teaching of the Nicolaitans. Therefore repent; or else I am coming to you quickly, and I will make war against them with the sword of My mouth. He who has an ear, let him hear what the Spirit says to the churches. To him who overcomes, to him I will give *some* of the hidden manna, and I will give him a white stone, and a new name written on the stone which no one knows but he who receives it' (Revelation 2:12–17; see Numbers 25:1–3; Isaiah 62:2; Revelation 1:16).

WAY, SIMILAR

Setting: By the Sea of Galilee. During the early part of His ministry, after presenting the Parable of the Sower from a boat to a very large crowd, Jesus gives the meaning of the parable to His disciples and other followers.

And He said to them, "Do you not understand this parable? How will you understand all the parables? The sower sows the word. These are the ones who are beside the road where the word is sown; and when they hear, immediately Satan comes and takes away the word which has been sown in them. In a similar way these are the ones on whom seed was sown on the rocky places, who, when they hear the word, immediately receive it with joy; and they have no *firm* root in themselves, but are *only* temporary; then, when affliction or persecution arises because of the word, immediately they fall away. And others are the ones on whom seed was sown among the thorns; these are the ones who have heard the word, but the worries of the world and the deceitfulness of riches, and the desires for other things enter in and choke the word, and it becomes unfruitful. And those are the ones on whom seed was sown on the good soil; and they hear the word and accept it and bear fruit, thirty, sixty, and a hundredfold" (Mark 4:13–20; cf. Matthew 13:18–23; Luke 8:11–15).

WAY, THIS

Setting: Bethany beyond the Jordan. Before being tempted by the devil and commencing His public ministry, Jesus arrives from Galilee to be baptized by John the Baptist, who questions his own worthiness to baptize the Lord.

But Jesus answering said to him, "Permit *it* at this time; for in this way it is fitting for us to fulfill all righteousness." Then he permitted Him (Matthew 3:15).

Setting: Galilee. During the early part of His ministry, Jesus gives a model prayer to His disciples and the multitudes while conveying the Sermon on the Mount.

"Pray, then, in this way: 'Our Father who is in heaven, hallowed be Your name. Your kingdom come. Your will be done, on earth as it is in heaven. Give us this day our daily bread. And forgive us our debts, as we also have forgiven our debtors. And do not lead us into temptation, but deliver us from evil. [For Yours is the kingdom and the power and the glory forever. Amen]'" (Matthew 6:9–13; cf. Luke 11:2–4; see John 17:15).

Setting: Galilee. After pronouncing woes against unrepentant cities as He teaches and preaches, Jesus prays a thanksgiving prayer to His Father in heaven.

At that time Jesus said, "I praise You, Father, Lord of heaven and earth, that you have hidden these things from *the* wise and intelligent and have revealed them to infants. Yes, Father, for this way was well-pleasing in Your sight. All things have been handed over to Me by My Father; and no one knows the Son except the Father; nor does anyone know the Father except the Son, and anyone to whom the Son wills to reveal *Him*" (Matthew 11:25–27; cf. Luke 10:21, 22).

Setting: Judea beyond the Jordan (Perea). Jesus responds to the Pharisees' follow-up question in front of a large crowd about Moses' command regarding a certificate of divorce.

He said to them. "Because of your hardness of heart Moses permitted you to divorce your wives; but from the beginning it has not been this way. And I say to you, whoever divorces his wife, except for immorality, and marries another woman commits adultery" (Matthew 19:8, 9; cf. Deuteronomy 24:1–4; Matthew 5:32; 19:7; Mark 10:1–12; see Romans 7:2, 3; 1 Corinthians 7:10, 39).

Setting: On the way to Jerusalem, where Jesus will die on the cross. Jesus teaches His disciples about true greatness after the mother of James and John, the sons of Zebedee, asks Him to make her sons exalted rulers with Him in His coming kingdom.

But Jesus called them to Himself and said, "You know that the rulers of the Gentiles lord it over them, and *their* great men exercise authority over them. It is not this way among you, but whoever wishes to become great among you shall be your servant, and whoever wishes to be first among you shall be your slave; just as the Son of Man did not come to be served, but to serve, and to give His life a ransom for many" (Matthew 20:25–28; cf. Matthew 23:11; 26:28; Mark 10:42–45).

Setting: Gethsemane on the Mount of Olives, east of the temple in Jerusalem. As Jesus submits to His Father's will and allows Judas to betray Him, Peter attempts to defend Him by force, but the Lord does not permit it.

Then Jesus said to him, "Put your sword back into its place; for all those who take up the sword shall perish by the sword. Or do you think that I cannot appeal to My Father, and He will at once put at My disposal more than twelve legions of angels? How then will the Scriptures be fulfilled, *which say* that it must happen this way?" (Matthew 26:52–54; cf. Mark 14:47; Luke 22:50–51; John 18:10, 11; see Matthew 26:24).

Setting: On the road to Jerusalem. When James and John ask Jesus for special honor and privileges in His kingdom, the other disciples become angry. The Lord uses this moment to teach them about servanthood.

Calling them to Himself, Jesus said to them, "You know that those who are recognized as rulers of the Gentiles lord it over them; and their great men exercise authority over them. But it is not this way among you, but whoever wishes to become great among you shall be your servant; and whoever wishes to be first among you shall be slave of all. For even the Son of Man did not come to be served, but to serve, and to give His life a ransom for many" (Mark 10:42–45; cf. Matthew 20:25–28).

Setting: On the way from Galilee to Jerusalem. The Lord responds to a report from the seventy sent out in pairs to every place He Himself will soon visit.

At that very time He rejoiced greatly in the Holy Spirit, and said, "I praise You, O Father, Lord of heaven and earth, that You have hidden these things from *the* wise and intelligent and have revealed them to infants. Yes, Father, for this way was well-pleasing in Your sight. All things have been handed over to Me by My Father, and no one knows who the Son is except the Father, and who the Father is except the Son, and anyone to whom the Son wills to reveal *Him*" (Luke 10:21, 22; cf. Matthew 11:25–27; see Luke 10:1; John 3:35; 10:15).

Setting: An upper room in Jerusalem. During the Feast of Unleavened Bread (Passover) just before His crucifixion, Jesus celebrates the Passover meal with His disciples and institutes the Lord's Supper. The disciples later argue over who is the greatest among them.

And He said to them, "The kings of the Gentiles lord it over them; and those who have authority over them are called 'Benefactors.' But *it is* not this way with you, but the one who is the greatest among you must become like the youngest, and the leader like a servant. For who is greater, the one who reclines *at the table* or the one who serves? Is it not the one who reclines *at the table?* But I am among you as the one who serves" (Luke 22:25–27; cf. Matthew 20:25–28; 23:11; Mark 10:42–45).

WAY, YOUR

Setting: Galilee. While speaking to the crowds, Jesus pays tribute to the ministry of John the Baptist, but emphasizes that the one who is least in the kingdom of heaven is greater than John.

As these men were going *away,* Jesus began to speak to the crowds about John, "What did you go out into the wilderness to see? A reed shaken by the wind? But what did you go out to see? A man dressed in soft *clothing?* Those who wear soft *clothing* are in kings' palaces! But what did you go out to see? A prophet? Yes, I tell you, and the one who is more than a prophet. This is the one about whom it is written, 'BEHOLD, I SEND MY MESSENGER AHEAD OF YOU, WHO WILL PREPARE YOUR WAY BEFORE YOU.' Truly, I say to you, among those born of women there has not arisen *anyone* greater than John the Baptist! Yet the one who is least in the kingdom of heaven is greater than he. From the days of John the Baptist until now the kingdom of heaven suffers violence, and violent men take it by force. For all the prophets and the Law prophesied until John. And, if you are willing to accept *it,* John himself is Elijah who was to come. He who has ears to hear, let him hear" (Matthew 11:7–15, Jesus quotes from Malachi 3:1; cf. Malachi 4:5; Luke 7:24–28; Luke 16:16; see Matthew 14:5).

Setting: Galilee. After Jesus responds to the disciples of John the Baptist about whether He is the promised Messiah, the Lord speaks to the crowds about John.

When the messengers of John had left, He began to speak to the crowds about John, "What did you go out into the wilderness to see? A reed shaken by the wind? But what did you go out to see? A man dressed in soft clothing? Those who are splendidly clothed and live in luxury are *found* in royal palaces! But what did you go out to see? A prophet? Yes, I say to you, and one who is more than a prophet. This is the one about whom it is written, 'BEHOLD, I SEND MY MESSENGER AHEAD OF YOU, WHO WILL PREPARE YOUR WAY BEFORE YOU.' I say to you, among those born of women there is no one greater than John; yet he who is least in the kingdom of God is greater than he" (Luke 7:24–28, Jesus quotes from Malachi 3:1; cf. Matthew 11:7–11).

Setting: On the way from Galilee to Jerusalem. After chastising the crowds for being able to discern the weather but not the present age, Jesus exhorts them to settle any financial disputes outside of court.

"And why do you not even on your own initiative judge what is right? For while you are going with your opponent to appear before the magistrate, on *your* way *there* make an effort to settle with him, so that he may not drag you before the judge, and the judge turn you over to the officer, and the officer throw you into prison. I say to you, you will not get out of there until you have paid the very last cent" (Luke 12:57–59; cf. Matthew 5:25, 26).

WAY OF RIGHTEOUSNESS (Listed under RIGHTEOUSNESS, WAY OF)

WAYWARDNESS

[WAYWARDNESS from one of them has gone astray]

Setting: Capernaum of Galilee. Jesus illustrates to His disciples the value of little ones.

"What do you think? If any man has a hundred sheep, and one of them has gone astray, does he not leave the ninety-nine on the mountains and go and search for the one that is straying? If it turns out that he finds it, truly I say to you, he rejoices over it more than the ninety-nine which have not gone astray. So it is not *the* will of your Father who is in heaven that one of these little ones perish" (Matthew 18:12–14; cf. Luke 15:4–7).

WEAKNESS

Setting: During his third missionary journey, writing from Macedonia a second letter to the church at Corinth, the apostle Paul recounts the Lord's response to his three petitions asking God to remove the affliction caused by the thorn in his flesh from Satan.

And He has said to me, "My grace is sufficient for you, for power is perfected in weakness." Most gladly, therefore, I will rather boast about my weaknesses, so that the power of Christ may dwell in me (2 Corinthians 12:9; see 1 Corinthians 2:1–5).

WEALTH (Also see COIN; MAN, RICH; MATERIALISM; MONEY; POSSESSIONS; RICH; STEWARD; STEWARDSHIP; TREASURE; and WEALTHY)

Setting: Galilee. During the early part of His ministry, Jesus preaches the Sermon on the Mount to His disciples and the multitudes.

"No one can serve two masters; for either he will hate the one and love the other, or he will be devoted to one and despise the other. You cannot serve God and wealth (Matthew 6:24).

Setting: By the Sea of Galilee. With the religious leaders rejecting His message, Jesus begins to teach in parables, and gives His disciples the meaning of the Parable of the Sower.

"Hear then the parable of the sower. When anyone hears the word of the kingdom and does not understand it, the evil *one* comes and snatches away what has been sown in his heart. This is the one on whom seed was sown beside the road. The one on whom seed was sown on the rocky places, this is the man who hears the word and immediately receives it with joy; yet he has no *firm* root in himself, but is *only* temporary, and when affliction or persecution arises because of the word, immediately he falls away. And the one on whom seed was sown among the thorns, this is the man who hears the word, and the worry of the world and the deceitfulness of wealth choke the word, and it becomes unfruitful. And the one on whom seed was sown on the good soil, this is the man who hears the word and understands it; who indeed bears fruit and brings forth, some a hundredfold, some sixty, and some thirty" (Matthew 13:18–23; cf. Mark 4:13–20; Luke 8:11–15; see Matthew 13:8).

[WEALTH from For what will it profit a man if he gains the whole world and forfeits his soul]

Setting: Near Caesarea Philippi. After rebuking Peter for trying to forbid Him to accomplish His earthly mission of dying and being resurrected, Jesus teaches His disciples about the costs of following Him.

Then Jesus said to His disciples, "If anyone wishes to come after Me, he must deny himself, and take up his cross and follow Me. For whoever wishes to save his life will lose it; but whoever loses his life for My sake will find it. For what will it profit a man if he gains the whole world and forfeits his soul? Or what will a man give in exchange for his soul? For the Son of Man is going to come in the glory of His Father with His angels, and WILL THEN REPAY EVERY MAN ACCORDING TO HIS DEEDS. Truly, I say to you, there are some of you who are standing here who will not taste death until they see the Son of Man coming in His kingdom" (Matthew 16:24–28, Jesus quotes from Psalm 62:12; cf. Mark 8:34–37; Luke 9:23–27; see Matthew 10:38, 39).

[WEALTH from For what does it profit a man to gain the whole world, and forfeit his soul]

Setting: Caesarea Philippi. After rebuking Peter for desiring to thwart His mission to the cross, Jesus summons a crowd, along with His disciples, and informs them of the high costs of following Him.

And He summoned the crowd with His disciples, and said to them, "If anyone wishes to come after Me, he must deny himself, and take up his cross and follow Me. For whoever wishes to save his life will lose it, but whoever loses his life for My sake and the gospel's will save it. For what does it profit a man to gain the whole world, and forfeit his soul? For what will a man give in exchange for his soul? For whoever is ashamed of Me and My words in this adulterous and sinful generation, the Son of Man will also be ashamed of him when He comes in the glory of His Father with the holy angels" (Mark 8:34–38; cf. Matthew 16:24–28; Luke 9:23–27; see Matthew 10:33, 38, 39).

[WEALTH from For what is a man profited if he gains the whole world, and loses or forfeits himself]

Setting: Galilee. Following Peter's pronouncement that Jesus is the Christ of God, the Lord conveys the demands of discipleship and the hope regarding the kingdom of God.

And He was saying to *them* all, "If anyone wishes to come after Me, he must deny himself, and take up his cross daily and follow Me. For whoever wishes to save his life will lose it, but whoever loses his life for My sake, he is the one who will save it. For what is a man profited if he gains the whole world, and loses or forfeits himself? For whoever is ashamed of Me and My words, the Son of Man will be ashamed of him when He comes in His glory, and *the glory* of the Father and of the holy angels. But I say to you truthfully, there are some of those standing here who will not taste death until they see the kingdom of God" (Luke 9:23–27; cf. Matthew 16:24–26, 28; Mark 8:34–37; see Matthew 10:33, 38, 39).

Setting: On the way from Galilee to Jerusalem. Jesus conveys the illustration of the prodigal son because the Pharisees and scribes complain He associates with tax collectors and sinners.

And He said, "A man had two sons. The younger of them said to his father, 'Father, give me the share of the estate that falls to me.' So he divided his wealth between them. And not many days later, the younger son gathered everything together and went on a journey into a distant country, and there he squandered his estate with loose living. Now when he had spent everything, a severe famine occurred in that country, and he began to be impoverished. So he went and hired himself out to one of the citizens of that country, and he sent him into his fields to feed swine. And he would have gladly filled his stomach with the pods that the swine were eating, and no one was giving *anything* to him. But when he came to his senses, he said, 'How many of my father's hired men have more than enough bread, but I am dying here with hunger! I will get up and go to my father, and will say to him, "Father, I have sinned against heaven, and in your sight; I am no longer worthy to be called your son; make me as one of your hired men."' So he got up and came to his father. But while he was still a long way off, his father saw him and felt compassion *for him,* and ran and embraced him and kissed him. And the son said to him, "Father, I have sinned against heaven and in your sight; I am no longer worthy to be called your son.' But the father said to his slaves, 'Quickly bring out the best robe and put it on him, and put a ring on his hand and sandals on his feet; and bring the fattened calf, kill it, and let us eat and celebrate; for this son of mine was dead and has come to life again; he was lost and has been found.' And they began to celebrate. Now his older son was in the field, when he came and approached the house, he heard music and dancing. And he summoned one of the servants and *began* inquiring what these things could be. And he said to him, 'Your brother has come, and your father has killed the fattened calf because he has received him back safe and sound.' But he became angry and was not willing to go in; and his father came out and *began* pleading with him. But he answered and said to his father, 'Look! For so many years I have been serving you and I have never neglected a command of yours; and *yet* you have never given me a young goat, so that I might celebrate with my friends; but when this son of yours came, who has devoured your wealth with prostitutes, you killed the fattened calf for him.' And he said to him, 'Son, you have always been with me, and all that is mine is yours. But we had to celebrate and rejoice, for this brother of yours was dead and *has begun* to live, and was lost and has been found' " (Luke 15:11–32; see Proverb 29:2).

Setting: On the way from Galilee to Jerusalem. After giving the story of the prodigal son, the Lord teaches His disciples about stewardship.

Now He was also saying to the disciples, "There was a rich man who had a manager, and this *manager* was reported to him as squandering his possessions. And he called him and said to him, 'What is this I hear about you? Give an accounting of your management, for you can no longer be a manager.' The manager said to himself, 'What shall I do, since my master is taking the management away from me? I am not strong enough to dig; I am ashamed to beg. I know what I shall do, so that when I am removed from the management people will welcome me into their homes.' And he summoned each one of his master's debtors, and he *began* saying to the first, 'How much do you owe my master?' And he said, 'A hundred measures of oil.' And he said to him, 'Take your bill, and sit down quickly and write fifty.' Then he said to another, 'And how much do you owe?' And he said, 'A hundred measures of wheat.' He said to him, 'Take your bill, and write eighty.' And his master praised the unrighteous manager because he had acted shrewdly; for the sons of this age are more shrewd in relation to their own kind than the sons of light. And I say to you, make friends for yourselves by means of the wealth of unrighteousness, so that when it fails, they will receive you into the eternal dwellings. He who is faithful in a very little thing is faithful also in much; and he who is unrighteous in a very little thing is unrighteous also in much. Therefore if you have not been faithful in the *use of* unrighteous wealth, who will entrust the true *riches* to you? And if you have not been faithful in *the use of* that which is another's, who will give you that which is your own? No servant can serve two masters; for either he will hate the one and love the other, or else he will be devoted to one and despise the other. You cannot serve God and wealth" (Luke 16:1–13; cf. Matthew 6:24; 25:14–30).

WEALTHY (See MAN, RICH; MATERIALISM; POSSESSIONS; and RICH)

Setting: Judea beyond the Jordan (Perea). After informing a rich man how righteous believers may have treasure in heaven, Jesus conveys to His disciples the difficulty the wealthy have entering the kingdom of God.

And Jesus, looking around, said to His disciples, "How hard it will be for those who are wealthy to enter the kingdom of God!" The disciples were amazed at His words. But Jesus answered again and said to them, "Children, how hard it is to enter the kingdom of God! It is easier for a camel to go through the eye of a needle than for a rich man to enter the kingdom of God." They were even more astonished and said to Him, "Then who can be saved?" Looking at them, Jesus said, "With people it is impossible, but not with God; for all things are possible with God" (Mark 10:23–27; cf. Matthew 19:23–26; Luke 18:24, 25).

Setting: Perea, en route from Galilee to Jerusalem. After responding to a ruler's question about inheriting eternal life, Jesus comments to him about the challenge of being wealthy and saved.

And Jesus looked at him and said, "How hard it is for those who are wealthy to enter the kingdom of God! For it is easier for a camel to go through the eye of a needle than for a rich man to enter the kingdom of God" (Luke 18:24, 25; cf. Matthew 19:23, 24; Mark 10:25).

Setting: On the island of Patmos (in the Aegean Sea about fifty miles southwest of Ephesus in modern Turkey). On the Lord's Day (Sunday), approximately fifty years after the Resurrection, the disciple John encounters the Lord Jesus Christ, who communicates a new revelation for the apostle to record for the church in Laodicea and to six other churches in Asia.

"To the angel of the church in Laodicea write: The Amen, the faithful and true Witness, the Beginning of the creation of God, says this: 'I know your deeds, that you are neither cold nor hot; I wish that you were cold or hot. So because you are lukewarm, and neither hot nor cold, I will spit you out of My mouth. Because you say, "I am rich, and have become wealthy, and have need of nothing," and you do not know that you are wretched and miserable and poor and blind and naked, I advise you to buy from Me gold refined by fire so that you may become rich, and white garments so that you may clothe yourself, and *that* the shame of your nakedness will not be revealed; and eye salve to anoint your eyes so that you may see. Those whom I love, I reprove and discipline; therefore be zealous and repent. Behold, I stand at the door and knock; if anyone hears My voice and opens the door, I will come in to him and will dine with him, and he with Me. He who overcomes, I will grant to him to sit down with Me on My throne, as I also overcame and sat down with My Father on His throne. He who has an ear, let him hear what the Spirit says to the churches'" (Revelation 3:14–22; see Proverb 3:12; Hosea 12:8; John 14:23; 16:33).

WEARINESS

[WEARINESS from weary and heavy-laden]

Setting: Galilee. After rendering a thanksgiving prayer to His Father in heaven, Jesus offers rest to all who are weary and heavy-laden as He preaches and teaches throughout the region.

"Come to Me, all who are weary and heavy-laden, and I will give you rest. Take My yoke upon you and learn from Me, for I am gentle and humble in heart, and YOU WILL FIND REST FOR YOUR SOULS. For My yoke is easy and My burden is light" (Matthew 11:28–30, Jesus quotes from Jeremiah 6:16; see Jeremiah 31:35; 1 John 5:3).

[WEARINESS from weary]

Setting: On the island of Patmos (in the Aegean Sea about fifty miles southwest of Ephesus in modern Turkey). On the Lord's Day (Sunday), approximately fifty years after the Resurrection, the disciple John encounters the Lord Jesus Christ, who communicates a new revelation for the apostle to record for the church in Ephesus and to six other churches in Asia.

"To the angel of the church in Ephesus write: The One who holds the seven stars in His right hand, the One who walks among the seven golden lampstands, says this: 'I know your deeds and your toil and perseverance, and that you cannot tolerate evil men, and you put to the test those who call themselves apostles, and they are not, and you found them *to be* false; and you have perseverance and have endured for My name's sake, and have not grown weary. But I have *this* against you, that you have left your first love. Therefore remember from where you have fallen, and repent and do the deeds you did at first; or else I am coming to you and will remove your lampstand out of its place—unless you repent. Yet this you do have, that you hate the deeds of the

Nicolaitans, which I also hate. He who has an ear, let him hear what the Spirit says to the churches. To him who overcomes, I will grant to eat of the tree of life which is in the Paradise of God' " (Revelation 2:1–7; see Genesis 2:9; Ezekiel 28:13; 1 John 4:1; Revelation 1:10, 11, 19, 20).

WEATHER (Also see specifics such as CLOUDS; LIGHTNING; RAIN; SHOWER; STORM; WIND; and WINDS)

Setting: Magadan of Galilee. Jesus' enemies, the Pharisees and the Sadducees, rejecting His message, continue to test Him by asking for a sign from heaven.

But He replied to them, "When it is evening, you say, '*It will be* fair weather, for the sky is red.' And in the morning, '*There will* be a storm today, for the sky is red and threatening.' Do you know how to discern the appearance of the sky, but cannot *discern* the signs of the times? An evil and adulterous generation seeks after a sign; and a sign will not be given it, except the sign of Jonah." And He left them and went away (Matthew 16:2–4; cf. Matthew 12:39; Mark 8:12; Luke 12:54–56).

[WEATHER from the winds and the water]

Setting: On the Sea of Galilee. After conveying who His true relatives are while ministering in Galilee, Jesus and His disciples set sail, and the Lord calms a storm.

And He said to them, "Where is your faith?" They were fearful and amazed, saying to one another, "Who then is this, that He commands even the winds and the water, and they obey Him?" (Luke 8:25; cf. Matthew 8:23–27; Mark 4:35–41).

[WEATHER from the appearance of the earth and the sky]

Setting: On the way from Galilee to Jerusalem. After telling how a relationship with Him will divide families, Jesus chastises the crowds for being able to discern the weather but not the present age.

And He was also saying to the crowds, "When you see a cloud rising in the west, immediately you say, 'A shower is coming,' and so it turns out. And when *you see* a south wind blowing, you say, 'It will be a hot day,' and it turns out *that way*. You hypocrites! You know how to analyze the appearance of the earth and the sky, but why do you not analyze this present time?" (Luke 12:54–56; cf. Matthew 16:2, 3).

WEDDING (Also see CLOTHES, WEDDING; WEDDING, FEAST; and WEDDING, HALL)

Setting: The temple in Jerusalem. Jesus speaks another parable to the chief priests and elders after they question His authority.

Jesus spoke to them again in parables, saying, "The kingdom of heaven may be compared to a king who gave a wedding feast for his son. And he sent out his slaves to call those who had been invited to the wedding feast, and they were unwilling to come. Again he sent out other slaves saying, 'Tell those who have been invited, "Behold, I have prepared my dinner; my oxen and my fattened livestock are *all* butchered and everything is ready; come to the wedding feast." But they paid no attention and went their way, one to his own farm, another to his business, and the rest seized his slaves and mistreated them and killed them. But the king was enraged, and he sent his armies and destroyed those murderers and set their city on fire. Then he said to his slaves, 'The wedding is ready, but those who were invited were not worthy. 'Go therefore to the main highways, and as many as you find *there,* invite to the wedding feast.' Those slaves went out into the streets and gathered together all they found, both evil and good; and the wedding hall was filled with dinner guests. But when the king came in to look over the dinner guests, he saw a man there who was not dressed in wedding clothes, and he said to him, 'Friend, how did you come in here without wedding clothes?' And the man was speechless. Then the king said to the servants, 'Bind him hand and foot, and throw him into the outer darkness; in that place there will be weeping and gnashing of teeth.' For many are called, but few *are* chosen" (Matthew 22:1–14; cf. Matthew 8:11, 12).

WEDDING BANQUET (See FEAST, WEDDING)

WEDDING CLOTHES (Listed under CLOTHES, WEDDING)

WEDDING FEAST (Listed under FEAST, WEDDING)

WEDDING HALL (Listed under HALL, WEDDING)

WEEDS (See TARES; THISTLES; and THORNS)

WEEK

Setting: On the way from Galilee to Jerusalem. After instructing His disciples about persistence in prayer, Jesus conveys a parable about self-righteousness.

And He also told this parable to some people who trusted in themselves that they were righteous, and viewed others with contempt: "Two men went up into the temple to pray, one a Pharisee and the other a tax collector. The Pharisee stood and was praying this to himself: 'God, I thank You that I am not like other people: swindlers, unjust, adulterers, or even like this tax collector. I fast twice a week; I pay tithes of all that I get.' But the tax collector, standing some distance away, was even unwilling to lift up his eyes to heaven, but was beating his breast, saying, 'God, be merciful to me, the sinner!' I tell you, this man went to his house justified rather than the other; for everyone who exalts himself will be humbled, but he who humbles himself will be exalted" (Luke 18:9–14; see Ezra 9:6; Matthew 6:5, 23:12; Luke 11:42; 16:15; Romans 14:3, 10).

WEEPING (TEETH, WEEPING AND GNASHING is a separate entry; also see GRIEF; LAMENT; MOURNING; and SORROW)

[WEEPING from weep]

Setting: The home of Jairus, a synagogue official in Capernaum, by the Sea of Galilee. Jesus assures those present that Jairus's daughter has not died, but is only asleep.

And entering in, He said to them, "Why make a commotion and weep? The child has not died, but is asleep" (Mark 5:39; cf. Matthew 9:24; Luke 8:52).

[WEEPING from weep]

Setting: Galilee. After selecting His twelve disciples, Jesus teaches the Beatitudes (part of the Sermon on the Mount) to those disciples and a great throng of people from Judea, Jerusalem, and the central coastal region of Tyre and Sidon.

"Blessed *are* you who hunger now, for you shall be satisfied. Blessed *are* you who weep now, for you shall laugh" (Luke 6:21; cf. Matthew 5:4, 6).

[WEEPING from weep]

Setting: Galilee. After selecting His twelve disciples, Jesus teaches the Beatitudes (part of the Sermon on the Mount) to those disciples and a great throng of people from Judea, Jerusalem, and the central coastal region of Tyre and Sidon.

"Woe to you who are well-fed now, for you shall be hungry. Woe *to you* who laugh now, for you shall mourn and weep" (Luke 6:25; cf. Matthew 5:4).

[WEEPING from weep]

Setting: Galilee. Following His healing of a Roman centurion's slave from a distance in Capernaum, Jesus travels to Nain, where He raises a young man from the dead.

When the Lord saw her, He felt compassion for her and said to her, "Do not weep." And He came up and touched the coffin; and the bearers came to a halt. And He said, "Young man, I say to you, arise!" (Luke 7:13, 14).

[WEEPING from weep]

Setting: Galilee. After praising John the Baptist to the crowds, Jesus criticizes the Pharisees and lawyers who reject God's purpose and John's message.

"To what then shall I compare the men of this generation, and what are they like? They are like children who sit in the market place and call to one another, and they say, 'We played the flute for you, and you did not dance; we sang a dirge, and you did not weep.' For John the Baptist has come eating no bread and drinking no wine, and you say, 'He has a demon!' The Son of Man has come eating and drinking, and you say, 'Behold, a gluttonous man and a drunkard, a friend of tax collectors and sinners!' Yet wisdom is vindicated by all her children" (Luke 7:31–35; cf. Matthew 11:16–19; see Luke 1:15).

Setting: Galilee. After healing a woman who has been ill for twelve years, Jesus receives word that the daughter of a Galilee synagogue official has died.

But when Jesus heard *this,* He answered him, "Do not be afraid *any longer;* only believe and she will be made well." When He came to the house, He did not allow anyone to enter with Him except Peter and John and James and the girl's father and mother. Now they were all weeping and lamenting for her; but He said, "Stop weeping; for she has not died, but is asleep." And they *began* laughing at Him, knowing that she had died. He, however, took her by the hand and called, saying, "Child, arise!" And her spirit returned, and she got up immediately; and He gave orders for *something* to be given her to eat (Luke 8:50–55; cf. Matthew 9:18, 19, 23–26; Mark 5:21–24, 35–43).

Setting: Jerusalem. After being arrested, and appearing before the Council of Elders (Sanhedrin), Pilate (Roman governor of Judea), Herod Antipas (tetrarch of Galilee and Perea), and Pilate a second time (when the ruler bows to the crowd's pressure and grants that Jesus be crucified), the Lord prophesies to the women mourning Him regarding the coming judgment of Jerusalem.

But Jesus turning to them said, "Daughters of Jerusalem, stop weeping for Me, but weep for yourselves and for your children. For behold, the days are coming when they will say, 'Blessed are the barren, and the wombs that never bore, and the breasts that never nursed.' Then they will begin TO SAY TO THE MOUNTAINS, 'FALL ON US,' AND TO THE HILLS, 'COVER US.' For it they do these things when the tree is green, what will happen when it is dry?" (Luke 23:28–31, Jesus quotes from Hosea 10:8; see Matthew 24:19).

[WEEPING from weep]

Setting: Jerusalem. Before the Passover, after warning His disciples of the persecution they will face after His departure to heaven, empathizing with their sadness over His prophecies, Jesus gives them the hope for the future.

"A little while, and you will no longer see Me; and again a little while, and you will see Me." *Some* of His disciples then said to one another, "What is this thing He is telling us, 'A little while, and you will not see Me; and again a little while, and you will see Me'; and, 'because I go to the Father'?" So they were saying, "What is this that He says, 'A little while'? We do not know what He is talking about." Jesus knew that they wished to question Him, and He said to them, "Are you deliberating together about this, that I said, 'A little while, and you will not see Me, and again a little while, and you will see Me'? Truly, truly, I say to you, that you will weep and lament, but the world will rejoice; you will grieve, but your grief will be turned into joy. Whenever a woman is in labor she has pain, because her hour has come; but when she gives birth to the child, she no longer remembers the anguish because of the joy that a child has been born into the world. Therefore you too have grief now; but I will see you again, and your heart will rejoice, and no one *will* take your joy away from you" (John 16:16–22; see Mark 9:32; Luke 23:27; John 14:18–24; 20:20).

Setting: Jerusalem. The risen Jesus first appears to Mary Magdalene after she tells Simon Peter and John about the empty tomb where Jesus had been the day before the Sabbath, after dying on a cross for the sins of the world.

Jesus said to her, "Woman, why are you weeping? Whom are you seeking?" Supposing Him to be the gardener, she said to Him, "Sir, if you have carried Him away, tell me where you have laid Him, and I will take Him away." Jesus said to her, "Mary!" She turned and said to Him in Hebrew "Rabboni!" (which means, Teacher). Jesus said to her, "Stop clinging to Me, for I have not yet ascended to the Father; but go to My brethren and say to them, 'I ascend to My Father and your Father, and My God and Your God'" (John 20:15–17; see Mark 16:9–11; John 7:33; 19:31–42).

WEEPING AND GNASHING OF TEETH (Listed under TEETH, WEEPING AND GNASHING OF)

WELCOME (Also see HOSPITALITY; and UNWELCOME)

[WELCOME from He who receives you receives Me, and he who receives Me receives Him who sent me]

Setting: Galilee. After His twelve disciples observe His ministry, Jesus summons and specifically instructs them about their ministry ahead that will include rewards.

"He who receives you receives Me, and he who receives Me receives Him who sent me. He who receives a prophet in the name of a prophet shall receive a prophet's reward; and he who receives a righteous man in the name of a righteous man shall receive a righteous man's reward. And whoever in the name of a disciple gives to one of these little ones even a cup of cold water to drink, truly I say to you, he shall not lose his reward" (Matthew 10:40–42; cf. Matthew 25:40, 44, 45; see Mark 9:37).

[WELCOME from Any place that does not receive you or listen to you]

Setting: Jesus' hometown of Nazareth in Galilee. After encountering unbelief, Jesus sends the Twelve out in pairs with authority and instructions about ministry.

And He summoned the twelve and began to send them out in pairs, and gave them authority over the unclean spirits; and He instructed them that they should take nothing for *their* journey, except a mere staff—no bread, no bag, no money in their belt—but to wear sandals; and *He added,* "Do not put on two tunics." And He said to them, "Wherever you enter a house, stay there until you leave town. Any place that does not receive you or listen to you, as you go out from there, shake the dust off the soles of your feet for a testimony against them" (Mark 6:7–11; cf. Matthew 10:1–14; Luke 9:1–5).

Setting: The synagogue in Jesus' hometown of Nazareth in Galilee. At the beginning of His public ministry, Jesus comments to the congregation after reading from the book of the prophet Isaiah on the Sabbath.

And He said to them, "No doubt you will quote this proverb to Me, 'Physician, heal yourself! Whatever we heard was done at Capernaum, do here in your hometown as well.'" And He said, "Truly I say to you, no prophet is welcome in his hometown. But I say to you in truth, there were many widows in Israel in the days of Elijah, when the sky was shut up for three years and six months, when a great famine came over all the land; and yet Elijah was sent to none of them, but only to Zarephath, *in the land* of Sidon, to a woman who was a widow. And there were many lepers in Israel in the time of Elisha the prophet; and none of them was cleansed, but only Naaman the Syrian" (Luke 4:23–27; Jesus refers to 1 Kings 17:1, 9; 2 Kings 5:1–14; see Matthew 13:53–58).

[WELCOME from whoever receives Me receives Him who sent Me]

Setting: Galilee. After Jesus prophesies His death, an argument arises among His disciples as to who is the greatest. The Lord resolves the matter by using a child as a teaching illustration.

But Jesus, knowing what they were thinking in their heart, took a child and stood him by His side, and said to them, "Whoever receives this child in My name receives Me, and whoever receives Me receives Him who sent Me; for the one who is least among all of you, this is the one who is great" (Luke 9:47, 48; cf. Matthew 18:1–5; Mark 9:33–47; see Matthew 10:40; Luke 22:24).

[WELCOME from they receive you, eat what is set before you]

Setting: On the way from Galilee to Jerusalem. The Lord appoints seventy followers and sends them out in pairs to every place He Himself will soon visit.

And He was saying to them, "The harvest is plentiful, but the laborers are few; therefore beseech the Lord of the harvest to send out laborers into His harvest. Go; behold, I send you out as lambs in the midst of wolves. Carry no money belt, no bag, no shoes; and greet no one on the way. Whatever house you enter, first say, 'Peace be to this house.' If a man of peace is there, your peace will rest on him; but if not, it will return to you. Stay in that house, eating and drinking what they give you; for the laborer is worthy of his wages. Do not keep moving from house to house. Whatever city you enter and they receive you, eat what is set before you; and heal those in it who are sick, and say to them, 'The kingdom of God has come near to you.' But whatever city you enter and they do not receive you, go out into its streets and say, 'Even the dust of your city which clings to our feet we wipe off *in protest* against you; yet be sure of this, that the kingdom of God has come near.' I say to you, it will be more tolerable in that day for Sodom than for that city" (Luke 10:2–12; see Genesis 19:24–28; Matthew 9:37, 38, 10:9–14, 16; 1 Corinthians 10:27).

Setting: On the way from Galilee to Jerusalem. After giving the story of the prodigal son, the Lord teaches His disciples about stewardship.

Now He was also saying to the disciples, "There was a rich man who had a manager, and this *manager* was reported to him as squandering his possessions. And he called him and said to him, 'What is this I hear about you? Give an accounting of your management, for you can no longer be a manager.' The manager said to himself, 'What shall I do, since my master is taking the management away from me? I am not strong enough to dig; I am ashamed to beg. I know what I shall do, so that when I am removed from the management people will welcome me into their homes.' And he summoned each one of his master's debtors, and he *began* saying to the first, 'How much do you owe my master?' And he said, 'A hundred measures of oil.' And he said to him, 'Take your bill, and sit down quickly and write fifty.' Then he said to another, 'And how much do you owe?' And he said, 'A hundred measures of wheat.' He said to him, 'Take your bill, and write eighty.' And his master praised the unrighteous manager because he had acted shrewdly; for the sons of this age are more shrewd in relation to their own kind than the sons of light. And I say to you, make friends for yourselves by means of the wealth of unrighteousness, so that when it fails, they will receive you into the eternal dwellings. He who is faithful in a very little thing is faithful also in much; and he who is unrighteous in a very little thing is unrighteous also in much. Therefore if you have not been faithful in the *use of* unrighteous wealth, who will entrust the true *riches* to you? And if you have not been faithful in *the use of* that which is another's, who will give you that which is your own? No servant can serve two masters; for either he will hate the one and love the other, or else he will be devoted to one and despise the other. You cannot serve God and wealth" (Luke 16:1–13; cf. Matthew 6:24; see Matthew 25:14–30).

[WELCOME from he who receives whomever I send receives Me]
Setting: Jerusalem. Before the Passover, with His death on the cross nearing, Jesus explains the reason for His vivid example of servanthood in washing His disciples' feet.

So when He had washed their feet, and taken His garments and reclined *at the table* again, He said to them, "Do you know what I have done to you? You call Me Teacher and Lord; and you are right, for so I am. If I then, the Lord and the Teacher, washed your feet, you also ought to wash one another's feet. For I gave you an example that you also should do as I did to you. Truly, truly I say to you, a slave is not greater than his master, nor *is* one who is sent greater than the one who sent him. If you know these things, you are blessed if you do them. I do not speak of all of you. I know the ones I have chosen; but *it is* that the Scripture may be fulfilled, 'HE WHO EATS MY BREAD HAS LIFTED UP HIS HEEL AGAINST ME.' From now on I am telling you before *it* comes to pass, so that when it does occur, you may believe that I am *He*. Truly, truly, I say to you, he who receives whomever I send receives Me; and he who receives Me receives Him who sent Me" (John 13:12–20; Jesus quotes from Psalm 41:9; see Matthew 7:24; 10:24, 40; John 8:24; 14:29; 1 Peter 5:3).

WELL (water; also see DRINKING; and WATER)

Setting: On the way from Galilee to Jerusalem. Jesus goes into the house of a Pharisee leader on the Sabbath to eat bread. A man suffering from dropsy is sitting there.

And Jesus answered and spoke to the lawyers and Pharisees, saying, "Is it lawful to heal on the Sabbath, or not?" But they kept silent. And He took hold of him and healed him, and sent him away. And He said to them, "Which one of you will have a son or an ox fall into a well, and will not immediately pull him out on a Sabbath day?" And they could make no reply to this. (Luke 14:3–6, cf. Matthew 12:11–13).

Setting: Sychar in Samaria, on the way to Galilee. Jesus interacts with a Samaritan woman at Jacob's well, while the disciples are buying food.

Jesus answered and said to her, "Everyone who drinks of this water will thirst again; but whoever drinks of the water that I will give him shall never thirst; but the water that I will give him will become in him a well of water springing up to eternal life" (John 4:13, 14).

WELLNESS (Also see HEALING; and HEALTH)

[WELLNESS from well]

Setting: Capernaum, near the Sea of Galilee. Jesus heals a woman suffering with internal bleeding for twelve years.

But Jesus turning and seeing her said, "Daughter, take courage; your faith has made you well." At once the woman was made well (Matthew 9:22; cf. Mark 5:34; Luke 8:48).

[WELLNESS from well]

Setting: By the Sea of Galilee. After Jesus returns from ministry to the Gerasenes (to the east of Galilee), a woman who has had a hemorrhage for twelve years touches Jesus in order to be healed.

And He said to her, "Daughter, your faith has made you well; go in peace and be healed of your affliction" (Mark 5:34; cf. Matthew 9:22; Luke 8:48; see Luke 7:50).

[WELLNESS from well]

Setting: Jericho, on the road to Jerusalem. As Jesus and His disciples pass through the city, a blind beggar named Bartimaeus cries out to the Lord for healing.

And Jesus stopped and said, "Call him *here*." So they called the blind man, saying to him, "Take courage, stand up! He is calling for you." Throwing aside his cloak, he jumped up and came to Jesus. And answering him, Jesus said, "What do you want Me to do for you?" And the blind man said to him, "Rabboni, *I want* to regain my sight!" And Jesus said to him, "Go; your faith has made you well." Immediately he regained his sight and *began* following Him on the road (Mark 10:49–52; cf. Matthew 20:29–34; Luke 18:35–43; see Matthew 9:2, 22).

[WELLNESS from well]

Setting: The house of Levi (Matthew) in Capernaum. At a reception for Jesus, after He calls Levi to become His disciple, the Pharisees and their scribes question why the Lord associates with tax collectors and sinners.

And Jesus answered and said to them, "*It is* not those who are well who need a physician, but those who are sick. I have not come to call the righteous but sinners to repentance" (Luke 5:31, 32; cf. Matthew 9:10–13; Mark 2:15–17).

[WELLNESS from well]

Setting: Galilee. After ministering in the country of the Gerasenes, to the east of Galilee, Jesus returns, and a woman, ill for twelve years, receives healing by touching His garment.

And Jesus said, "Who is the one who touched Me?" And while they were all denying it, Peter said, "Master, the people are crowding and pressing in on You." But Jesus said, "Someone did touch Me, for I was aware, that power had gone out of Me." When the woman saw that she had not escaped notice, she came trembling and fell down before Him, and declared in the presence of all the people the reason why she had touched Him, and how she had been immediately healed. And He said to her, "Daughter, your faith has made you well; go in peace" (Luke 8:45–48; cf. Matthew 9:20; Mark 5:25–34).

[WELLNESS from well]

Setting: Galilee. After healing a woman, ill for twelve years, Jesus receives word that the daughter of a Galilee synagogue official has died.

But when Jesus heard *this,* He answered him, "Do not be afraid *any longer;* only believe and she will be made well." When He came to the house, He did not allow anyone to enter with Him except Peter and John and James and the girl's father and mother. Now they were all weeping and lamenting for her; but He said, "Stop weeping; for she has not died, but is asleep." And they *began* laughing at Him, knowing that she had died. He, however, took her by the hand and called, saying, "Child, arise!" And her spirit returned, and she got up immediately; and He gave orders for *something* to be given her to eat (Luke 8:50–55; cf. Matthew 9:18, 19, 23–26; Mark 5:21–24, 35–43).

[WELLNESS from well]
Setting: On the way from Galilee to Jerusalem. The Lord stops to heal ten lepers who ask for cleansing.

When He saw them, He said to them, "Go and show yourselves to the priests." And as they were going, they were cleansed. Now one of them, when he saw that he had been healed, turned back, glorifying God with a loud voice, and he fell on his face at His feet, giving thanks to Him. And he was a Samaritan. Then Jesus answered and said, "Were there not ten cleansed? But the nine—where are they? Was no one found who returned to give glory to God, except this foreigner?" And He said to him, "Stand up and go; your faith has made you well" (Luke 17:14–19; see Leviticus 14:1–32).

[WELLNESS from well]
Setting: On the way from Galilee to Jerusalem. After telling the disciples of the upcoming sacrifice He will make in Jerusalem, while approaching Jericho, Jesus takes time to heal a blind man.

And Jesus stopped and commanded that he be brought to Him; and when he came near, He questioned him, "What do you want Me to do for you?" And he said, "Lord, *I want* to regain my sight!" And Jesus said to him, "Receive your sight; your faith has made you well" (Luke 18:40–42; cf. Matthew 20:29–34; Mark 10:46–52).

[WELLNESS from well]
Setting: The pool of Bethesda in Jerusalem. After performing His second Galilean miracle by healing a royal official's son from Capernaum, Jesus returns for a feast of the Jews, where He offers healing on the Sabbath to a man who has been ill for thirty-eight years.

When Jesus saw him lying *there,* and knew that he had already been a long time *in that condition,* He said to him, "Do you wish to get well?" (John 5:6).

[WELLNESS from well]
Setting: The temple in Jerusalem. During a feast of the Jews, Jesus addresses the former lame man He healed earlier on the Sabbath at the pool of Bethesda.

Afterward Jesus found him in the temple and tells him, "Behold, you have become well; do not sin anymore, so that nothing worse happens to you" (John 5:14).

[WELLNESS from well]
Setting: The temple in Jerusalem. After receiving encouragement from His blood brothers in Galilee to attend the upcoming Feast of Booths in order to demonstrate His works to His disciples and the world, Jesus goes and teaches, astonishing the Jewish religious leaders.

Jesus answered them, "I did one deed, and you all marvel. For this reason Moses has given you circumcision (not because it is from Moses, but from the fathers), and on *the* Sabbath you circumcise a man. If a man receives circumcision on *the* Sabbath so that the Law of Moses will not be broken, are you angry with Me because I made an entire man well on *the* Sabbath? Do not judge according to appearance, but judge with righteous judgment" (John 7:21–24; see Genesis 17:10–14; Leviticus 12:3; 19:15; Matthew 12:2; John 5:2–16; 7–20).

WEST (Also see EAST; NORTH; and SOUTH)

Setting: Entering Capernaum. After the Lord gives the Sermon on the Mount and cleanses a leper, a Roman centurion implores Jesus to heal his servant.

Now when Jesus heard *this,* He marveled, and said to those who were following, "Truly I say to you, I have not found such great faith with anyone in Israel. I say to you that many will come from east and west, and recline *at the table* with Abraham, Isaac and Jacob in the kingdom of heaven; but the sons of the kingdom will be cast out into the outer darkness; in that place there will be weeping and gnashing of teeth." And Jesus said to the centurion, "Go; it shall be done for you as you have believed." And the servant was healed that *very* moment (Matthew 8:10–13; cf. Luke 7:9, 10).

Setting: The Mount of Olives, just east of Jerusalem. During His Olivet Discourse, Jesus answers His disciples' questions as to when the temple will be destroyed and Jerusalem overrun, along with the signs of His coming and the end of the age.

"Therefore when you see the ABOMINATION OF DESOLATION which was spoken of through Daniel the prophet, standing in the holy place (let the reader understand), then those who are in Judea must flee to the mountains. Whoever is on the housetop must not go down to get the things that are in his house. Whoever is in the field must not turn back to get his cloak. But woe to those who are pregnant and to those who are nursing babies in those days! But pray that your flight will not be in the winter, or on a Sabbath. For then there will be a great tribulation, such as has not occurred since the beginning of the world until now, nor ever will. Unless those days had been cut short, no life would have been saved; but for the sake of the elect those days will be cut short. Then if anyone says to you, 'Behold, here is the Christ,' or "There *He is,'* do not believe *him.* For false Christs and false prophets will arise and will show great signs and wonders, so as to mislead, if possible, even the elect. Behold, I have told you in advance. So if they say to you, 'Behold, He is in the wilderness,' do not go out, *or,* 'Behold, He is in the inner rooms,' do not believe *them.* For just as the lightning comes from the east and flashes even to the west, so will the coming of the Son of Man be. Wherever the corpse is, there the vultures will gather" (Matthew 24:15–28, Jesus quotes from Daniel 9:27; cf. Daniel 12:1; Mark 13:14–23; Luke 17:22–31; 21:20–24; 23:29; see John 4:48).

Setting: On the way from Galilee to Jerusalem. After telling how a relationship with Him will divide families, Jesus chastises the crowds for being able to discern the weather but not the present age.

And He was also saying to the crowds, "When you see a cloud rising in the west, immediately you say, 'A shower is coming,' and so it turns out. And when *you see* a south wind blowing, you say, 'It will be a hot day,' and it turns out *that way*. You hypocrites! You know how to analyze the appearance of the earth and the sky, but why do you not analyze this present time?" (Luke 12:54–56; cf. Matthew 16:2, 3).

Setting: On the way from Galilee to Jerusalem. While teaching in the cities and villages, Jesus responds to a question about who is saved.

And someone said to Him, "Lord, are here *just* a few who are being saved?" And He said to them, "Strive to enter through the narrow door; for many, I tell you, will seek to enter and will not be able. Once the head of the house gets up and shuts the door, and you begin to stand outside and knock on the door, saying, 'Lord, open up to us!' then He will answer and say to you, 'I do not know where you are from.' Then you will begin to say, 'We ate and drank in Your presence, and You taught in our streets'; and He will say, 'I tell you, I do not know where you are from; DEPART FROM ME, ALL YOU EVILDOERS.' In that place there will be weeping and gnashing of teeth when you see Abraham and Isaac and Jacob and all the prophets in the kingdom of God, but you yourselves being thrown out. And they will come from east and west and from north and south, and will recline *at the table* in the kingdom of God. And behold, *some* are last who will be first and *some* are first who will be last" (Luke 13:23–30, Jesus quotes from Psalm 6:8; cf. Matthew 7:13, 23; 8:11, 12; see Matthew 19:30; Luke 3:8).

WHEAT (Also see BLADE; BREAD; CROP; CROPS; FLOUR; GRAIN; and TARES)

Setting: By the Sea of Galilee. Because the religious leaders are rejecting His message, Jesus continues teaching the crowds with the Parable of the Wheat and the Tares.

Jesus presented another parable to them, saying, "The kingdom of heaven may be compared to a man who sowed good seed in his field. But while his men were sleeping, his enemy came and sowed tares among the wheat, and went away. But when the wheat

sprouted and bore grain, then the tares became evident also. The slaves of the landowner came and said to him, 'Sir, did you not sow good seed in your field? How then does it have tares?' And he said to them, 'An enemy has done this!' The slaves said to him, 'Do you want us, then, to go and gather them up?' But he said, 'No; for while you are gathering up the tares, you may uproot the wheat with them. Allow both to grow together until the harvest; and in the time of the harvest I will say to the reapers, "First gather up the tares and bind them in bundles to burn them up; but gather the wheat into my barn" '" (Matthew 13:24–30; cf. Matthew 3:12).

Setting: On the way from Galilee to Jerusalem. After giving the story of the prodigal son, the Lord teaches His disciples about stewardship.

Now He was also saying to the disciples, "There was a rich man who had a manager, and this *manager* was reported to him as squandering his possessions. And he called him and said to him, 'What is this I hear about you? Give an accounting of your management, for you can no longer be a manager.' The manager said to himself, 'What shall I do, since my master is taking the management away from me? I am not strong enough to dig; I am ashamed to beg. I know what I shall do, so that when I am removed from the management people will welcome me into their homes.' And he summoned each one of his master's debtors, and he *began* saying to the first, 'How much do you owe my master?' And he said, 'A hundred measures of oil.' And he said to him, 'Take your bill, and sit down quickly and write fifty.' Then he said to another, 'And how much do you owe?' And he said, 'A hundred measures of wheat.' He said to him, 'Take your bill, and write eighty.' And his master praised the unrighteous manager because he had acted shrewdly; for the sons of this age are more shrewd in relation to their own kind than the sons of light. And I say to you, make friends for yourselves by means of the wealth of unrighteousness, so that when it fails, they will receive you into the eternal dwellings. He who is faithful in a very little thing is faithful also in much; and he who is unrighteous in a very little thing is unrighteous also in much. Therefore if you have not been faithful in the *use of* unrighteous wealth, who will entrust the true *riches* to you? And if you have not been faithful in *the use of* that which is another's, who will give you that which is your own? No servant can serve two masters; for either he will hate the one and love the other, or else he will be devoted to one and despise the other. You cannot serve God and wealth" (Luke 16:1–13; cf. Matthew 6:24; see Matthew 25:14–30).

Setting: An upper room in Jerusalem. During the Feast of Unleavened Bread (Passover) just before His crucifixion, Jesus celebrates the Passover meal with His disciples and institutes the Lord's Supper. The disciples later argue over who is the greatest among them, and the Lord prophesies Peter's denial of Him.

"Simon, Simon, behold, Satan has demanded *permission* to sift you like wheat; but I have prayed for you, that your faith may not fail; and you, when once you have turned again, strengthen your brothers." But he said to Him, "Lord, with You I am ready to go both to prison and to death!" And He said, "I say to you, Peter, the rooster will not crow today until you have denied three times that you know Me" (Luke 22:31–34; cf. Matthew 26:33–35; John 13:36–38; see Job 1:6–12; John 17:15).

Setting: Jerusalem. Just days before the Passover, with the chief priests and Pharisees plotting to seize Him, crowds welcome Jesus with palm branches and praise, and some Greeks ask to meet Him.

And Jesus answered them, saying, "The hour has come for the Son of Man to be glorified. Truly, truly, I say to you, unless a grain of wheat falls into the earth and dies, it remains alone; but if it dies, it bears much fruit. He who loves his life loses it, and he who hates his life in this world will keep it to life eternal. If anyone serves Me, he must follow Me; and where I am, there My servant will be also; if anyone serves Me, the Father will honor him" (John 12:23–26; see Matthew 10:39).

WHEAT, PARABLE OF THE TARES AMONG (See TARES, PARABLE OF THE WHEAT AND THE)

WHISPER

[WHISPER from *whispered*]
Setting: Galilee. After His disciples observe His ministry, Jesus summons and specifically instructs them about their ministry ahead involving true discipleship.

"Therefore do not fear them, for there is nothing concealed that will not be revealed, or hidden that will not be known. What I tell you in the darkness, speak in the light; and what you hear *whispered* in your ear, proclaim upon the housetops. Do not fear those who kill he body but are unable to kill the soul; but rather fear Him who is able to destroy both soul and body in hell" (Matthew 10:26–28; cf. Mark 4:22; Luke 12:3; see Hebrews 10:31).

[WHISPER from whispered]

Setting: On the way from Galilee to Jerusalem. Jesus warns His disciples of future events, as the scribes and Pharisees turn hostile and question Him repeatedly in an attempt to catch Him in something He might say.

Under these circumstances, after so many thousands of people had gathered together that they were stepping on one another, He began saying to His disciples first *of all,* "Beware of the leaven of the Pharisees, which is hypocrisy. But there is nothing covered up that will not be revealed, and hidden that will not be known. Accordingly, whatever you have said in the dark will be heard in the light, and what you have whispered in the inner rooms will be proclaimed upon the housetops. I say to you, My friends, do not be afraid of those who kill the body and after that have no more that they can do. But I will warn you whom to fear: fear the One who, after He has killed, has authority to cast into hell; yes, I tell you, fear Him! Are not five sparrows sold for two cents? *Yet* not one of them is forgotten before God. Indeed, the very hairs of your head are all numbered. Do not fear; you are more valuable than many sparrows" (Luke 12:1–7; cf. Matthew 10:26–31; see Matthew 16:6; Hebrews 10:31).

WHITE (STONE, WHITE is a separate entry]

Setting: Galilee. During the early part of His ministry, Jesus preaches the Sermon on the Mount to His disciples and the multitudes.

"Again, you have heard that the ancients were told, 'YOU SHALL NOT MAKE FALSE VOWS, BUT SHALL FULFILL YOUR VOWS TO THE LORD.' But I say to you, make no oath at all, either by heaven, for it is the throne of God, or by the earth, for it is the footstool of His feet, or by Jerusalem, for it is THE CITY OF THE GREAT KING. Nor shall you make an oath by your head, for you cannot make one hair white or black. But let your statement be 'Yes, yes' *or* 'No, no'; anything beyond these is of evil" (Matthew 5:33–37, Jesus quotes from Leviticus 19:12, Psalm 48:2; Isaiah 66:1; cf. James 5:12).

Setting: Sychar in Samaria, on the way to Galilee. After Jesus converses with a Samaritan woman at Jacob's well, the disciples return with food. They try to get Jesus to eat, but are surprised when He speaks of other food.

Jesus said to them, "My food is to do the will of Him who sent Me and to accomplish His work. Do you not say, 'There are yet four months, and *then* comes the harvest'? Behold, I say to you, lift up your eyes and look on the fields, that they are white for harvest. Already he who reaps is receiving wages and is gathering fruit for life eternal; so that he who sows and he who reaps may rejoice together. For in this *case* the saying is true, 'One sows and another reaps.' I sent you to reap that for which you have not labored; others have labored and you have entered into their labor" (John 4:34–38; see Matthew 9:37, 38; John 5:36).

Setting: On the island of Patmos (in the Aegean Sea about fifty miles southwest of Ephesus in modern Turkey). On the Lord's Day (Sunday), approximately fifty years after the Resurrection, the disciple John encounters the Lord Jesus Christ, who communicates a new revelation for the apostle to record for the church in Sardis and to six other churches in Asia.

"To the angel of the church in Sardis write: He who has the seven Spirits of God and the seven stars, says this: 'I know your deeds, that you have a name that you are alive, but you are dead. Wake up, and strengthen the things that remain, which were about to die; for I have not found your deeds completed in the sight of My God. So remember what you have received and heard; and keep *it,* and repent. Therefore if you do not wake up, I will come like a thief, and you will not know at what hour I will come to you. But you have a few people in Sardis who have not soiled their garments; and they will walk with Me in white, for they are worthy. He who overcomes will thus be clothed in white garments; and I will not erase his name from the book of life, and I will confess his name before My Father and before His angels. He who has an ear, let him hear what the Spirit says to the churches'" (Revelation 3:1–6; see Matthew 10:32; Revelation 1:16).

WHITEWASHED TOMBS **(Listed under TOMBS, WHITEWASHED)**

WHITE STONE **(Listed under STONE, WHITE)**

WHOLE WORLD **(Listed under WORLD, WHOLE)**

WICKED **(GENERATION, WICKED is a separate entry; also see EVILDOERS; and WICKEDNESS)**
Setting: Galilee. Jesus responds to some Pharisees and scribes who ask Him for a miraculous sign as He ministers.

"Now when the unclean spirit goes out of a man, it passes through waterless places seeking rest, and does not find *it*. Then it says, 'I will return to my house from which I came'; and when it comes, it finds *it* unoccupied, swept, and put in order. Then it goes and takes along with it seven other spirits more wicked than itself, and they go in and live there; and the last state of that man becomes worse than the first. That is the way it will also be for this evil generation" (Matthew 12:43–45; cf. Luke 11:24–26; Mark 5:9).

Setting: By the Sea of Galilee. Because the religious leaders are rejecting His message, Jesus continues teaching His disciples with the Parable of the Dragnet.

"Again, the kingdom of heaven is like a dragnet cast into the sea, and gathering *fish* of every kind; and when it was filled, they drew it up on the beach; and they sat down and gathered the good *fish* into containers, but the bad they threw away. So it will be at the end of the age; the angels will come forth and take out the wicked from among the righteous, and will throw them into the furnace of fire; in that place there will be weeping and gnashing of teeth. Have you understood all these things?" They said to Him, "Yes" (Matthew 13:47–51).

WICKED AND LAZY SLAVE **(Listed under SLAVE, WICKED AND LAZY)**

WICKED GENERATION **(See GENERATION, WICKED)**

WICKED SLAVE **(Listed under SLAVE, WICKED)**

WICKEDNESS **(Also see EVILDOERS; and WICKED)**
Setting: Galilee. After the Pharisees and scribes from Jerusalem object to His disciples' lack of obedience to the tradition regarding ceremonial cleansing, Jesus speaks to a crowd, and explains His teaching to the disciples.

After He called the crowd to Him again, He *began* saying to them, "Listen to Me, all of you, and understand: there is nothing outside the man which can defile him if it goes into him; but the things which proceed out of the man are what defile the man. [If anyone has ears to hear, let him hear."] When he had left the crowd *and* entered the house, His disciples questioned Him about the parable. And He said to them, "Are you so lacking in understanding also? Do you not understand that whatever goes into the man from outside cannot defile him, because it does not go into his heart, but into his stomach, and is eliminated?" (*Thus He* declared all foods clean.) And He was saying, "That which proceeds out of the man, that is what defiles the man. For from within, out of the heart of men, proceed the evil thoughts, fornications, thefts, murders, adulteries, deeds of coveting *and* wickedness, *as well* as deceit, sensuality, envy, slander, pride *and* foolishness. All these evil things proceed from within and defile the man" (Mark 7:14–23; cf. Matthew 15:10–20).

Setting: On the way from Galilee to Jerusalem. After speaking of how a lamp illuminates, the Lord has lunch with a Pharisee, who is surprised He doesn't wash before eating.

But the Lord said to him, "Now you Pharisees clean the outside of the cup and of the platter; but inside of you, you are full of robbery and wickedness. You foolish ones, did not He who made the outside make the inside also? But give that which is within as charity, and then all things are clean for you. But woe to you Pharisees! You pay tithe of mint and rue and every *kind of* garden herb, and *yet* disregard justice and the love of God; but these are the things you should have done without neglecting the others. Woe to you Pharisees! For you love the chief seats in the synagogues and the respectful greetings in the market places. Woe to you! For you are like concealed tombs, and the people who walk over *them* are unaware *of it*" (Luke 11:39–44; cf. Matthew 23:6, 7, 23–27; see Matthew 15:2; Titus 1:15).

WIDOW (WIDOW, POOR is a separate entry; also see WIDOWS)

Setting: The synagogue in Jesus' hometown of Nazareth in Galilee. At the beginning of His public ministry, Jesus comments to the congregation after reading from the book of the prophet Isaiah on the Sabbath.

And He said to them, "No doubt you will quote this proverb to Me, 'Physician, heal yourself! Whatever we heard was done at Capernaum, do here in your hometown as well.'" And He said, "Truly I say to you, no prophet is welcome in his hometown. But I say to you in truth, there were many widows in Israel in the days of Elijah, when the sky was shut up for three years and six months, when a great famine came over all the land; and yet Elijah was sent to none of them, but only to Zarephath, *in the land* of Sidon, to a woman who was a widow. And there were many lepers in Israel in the time of Elisha the prophet; and none of them was cleansed, but only Naaman the Syrian" (Luke 4:23–27; Jesus refers to 1 Kings 17:1, 9; 2 Kings 5:1–14; see Matthew 13:53–58).

Setting: On the way from Galilee to Jerusalem. After telling His disciples of His second coming, Jesus instructs them about persistence in prayer.

Now He was telling them a parable to show that at all times they ought to pray and not to lose heart, saying, "In a certain city there was a judge who did not fear God and did not respect man. There was a widow in that city, and she kept coming to him, saying, 'Give me legal protection from my opponent.' For a while he was unwilling; but afterward he said to himself, 'Even though I do not fear God nor respect man, yet because this woman bothers me, I will give her legal protection, otherwise by continually coming she will wear me out.'" And the Lord said, "Hear what the unrighteous judge said; now, will not God bring about justice for His elect who cry to Him day and night, and will He delay long over them? I tell you that He will bring about justice for them quickly. However, when the Son of Man comes, will He find faith on the earth?" (Luke 18:1–8; see Luke 11:5–10).

WIDOW, PARABLE OF THE PERSISTENT (See JUDGE, PARABLE OF THE UNRIGHTEOUS)

WIDOW, POOR

Setting: Opposite the temple treasury in Jerusalem. Jesus focuses His disciples' attention on a poor widow's monetary sacrifice.

Calling His disciples to Him, He said to them, "Truly I say to you, this poor widow put in more than all the contributors to the treasury; for they all put in out of their surplus, but she, out of her poverty, put in all she owned, all she had to live on" (Mark 12:43, 44; cf. Luke 21:1–4).

Setting: The temple in Jerusalem. While ministering a few days before His crucifixion, after warning His disciples about the lifestyle of the scribes, Jesus points out a poor widow's sacrificial giving to the temple treasury.

And He said, "Truly I say to you, this poor widow put in more than all *of them;* for they all out of their surplus put into the offering; but she out of her poverty put in all that she had to live on" (Luke 21:3, 4; cf. Mark 12:41–44).

WIDOW'S MITE (Listed under MITE, WIDOW'S)

WIDOWS (Also see WIDOW)

Setting: The synagogue in Jesus' hometown of Nazareth in Galilee. At the beginning of His public ministry, Jesus comments to the congregation after reading from the book of the prophet Isaiah on the Sabbath.

And He said to them, "No doubt you will quote this proverb to Me, 'Physician, heal yourself! Whatever we heard was done at Capernaum, do here in your hometown as well.'" And He said, "Truly I say to you, no prophet is welcome in his hometown. But I say to you in truth, there were many widows in Israel in the days of Elijah, when the sky was shut up for three years and six months, when a great famine came over all the land; and yet Elijah was sent to none of them, but only to Zarephath, *in the land* of Sidon, to a woman who was a widow. And there were many lepers in Israel in the time of Elisha the prophet; and none of them was cleansed, but only Naaman the Syrian" (Luke 4:23–27; Jesus refers to 1 Kings 17:1, 9; 2 Kings 5:1–14; see Matthew 13:53–58).

WIDOWS' HOUSES (Listed under HOUSES, WIDOWS')

WIFE (WIFE, LOT'S is a separate entry; also see HUSBAND; MARRIAGE; WIVES; WOMAN; and WOMEN)

Setting: Galilee. During the early part of His ministry, Jesus preaches the Sermon on the Mount to His disciples and the multitudes.

"It was said, 'WHOEVER SENDS HIS WIFE AWAY, LET HIM GIVE HER A CERTIFICATE OF DIVORCE'; but I say to you that everyone who divorces his wife, except for *the* reason of unchastity, makes her commit adultery; and whoever marries a divorced woman commits adultery" (Matthew 5:31, 32, Jesus quotes from Deuteronomy 24: 1, 3; cf. Matthew 19:9; see Romans 7:2, 3; 1 Corinthians 7:10, 39).

Setting: Capernaum of Galilee. Jesus illustrates the matter of forgiveness after Peter asks Him if forgiving someone seven times who has sinned against him is adequate.

"For this reason the kingdom of heaven may be compared to a king who wished to settle accounts with his slaves. When he had begun to settle *them,* one who owed him ten thousand talents was brought to him. But since he did not have *the means* to repay, his lord commanded him to be sold, along with his wife and children and all that he had, and repayment to be made. So the slave fell *to the ground* and prostrated himself before him, saying, 'Have patience with me and I will repay you everything.' And the lord of that slave felt compassion and released him and forgave him the debt. But that slave went out and found one of his fellow slaves who owed him a hundred denarii; and he seized him and *began* to choke *him,* saying, 'Pay back what you owe.' So his fellow slave fell *to the ground* and *began* to plead with him, saying, 'Have patience with me and I will repay you.' But he was unwilling and went and threw him in prison until he should pay back what was owed. So when his fellow slaves saw what had happened, they were deeply grieved and came and reported to their lord all that had happened. Then summoning him, his lord said to him, 'You wicked slave; I forgave you all that debt because you pleaded with me. Should you not also have had mercy on your fellow slave, in the same way that I had mercy on you?' And his lord, moved with anger, handed him over to the torturers until he should repay all that was owed him. My heavenly Father will also do the same to you, if each of you does not forgive his brother from your heart" (Matthew 18:23–35; cf. Matthew 6:12, 14, 15; Luke 7:42; see Matthew 25:19–28).

Setting: Judea beyond the Jordan (Perea). After Jesus replies to Peter's question about forgiveness, in front of a large crowd the Pharisees test the Lord with a question about divorce.

And He answered and said, "Have you not read that He who created *them* from the beginning MADE THEM MALE AND FEMALE, and said, 'FOR THIS REASON A MAN SHALL LEAVE HIS FATHER AND MOTHER AND BE JOINED TO HIS WIFE, AND THE TWO SHALL BECOME ONE FLESH'? So they are no longer two, but one flesh. What therefore God has joined together, let no man separate" (Matthew 19:4–6, Jesus quotes from Genesis 1:27; 2:24; cf. Mark 10:5–9).

Setting: Judea beyond the Jordan (Perea). In front of a large crowd, Jesus responds to the Pharisees' follow-up question about Moses' command regarding a certificate of divorce.

He said to them. "Because of your hardness of heart Moses permitted you to divorce your wives; but from the beginning it has not been this way. And I say to you, whoever divorces his wife, except for immorality, and marries another woman commits adultery" (Matthew 19:8, 9; cf. Deuteronomy 24:1–4; Matthew 5:32; 19:7; Mark 10:1–12; see Romans 7:2, 3; 1 Corinthians 7:10, 39).

Setting: Judea beyond the Jordan (Perea). Jesus teaches the crowds gathered around Him about divorce after the Pharisees test and question Him on the subject.

And He answered and said to them, "What did Moses command you?" They said, "Moses permitted a *man* TO WRITE A CERTIFICATE OF DIVORCE AND SEND *her* AWAY." But Jesus said to them, "Because of your hardness of heart he wrote you this commandment. But from the beginning of creation, *God* MADE THEM MALE AND FEMALE. FOR THIS REASON A MAN SHALL LEAVE HIS FATHER AND MOTHER, AND THE TWO SHALL BECOME ONE FLESH; so they are no longer two, but one flesh. What therefore God has joined together, let no man separate. In the house the disciples *began* questioning Him about this again. And He said to them, "Whoever divorces his wife and marries another woman commits adultery against her; and if she herself divorces her husband and marries another man, she is committing adultery" (Mark 10:3–12, Jesus quotes from Genesis 1:27; 2:24; cf. Matthew 19:1–9; see Deuteronomy 24:1–3; Matthew 5:32; Mark 10:1, 2; see Romans 7:2, 3; 1 Corinthians 7:10, 11, 13, 39).

Setting: On the way from Galilee to Jerusalem. After speaking a parable to the invited guests and the host at a banquet, Jesus responds to a guest's proclamation about the blessings of eating bread in the kingdom of God.

But He said to him, "A man was giving a big dinner, and he invited many; and at the dinner hour he sent his slave to say to those who had been invited, 'Come; for everything is ready now.' But they all alike began to make excuses. The first one said to him, 'I have bought a piece of land and I need to go out and look at it; please consider me excused.' Another one said, 'I have bought five yoke of oxen, and I am going to try them out; please consider me excused.' Another one said, I have married a wife, and for that reason I cannot come.' And the slave came *back* and reported this to his master. Then the head of the household became angry and said to his slave, 'Go out at once into the streets and lanes of the city and bring in here the poor and crippled and blind and lame.' And the slave said, 'Master, what you commanded has been done, and still there is room.' And the master said to the slave, 'Go out into the highways and along the hedges, and compel *them* to come in, so that my house may be filled. For I tell you, none of those men who were invited shall taste of my dinner'" (Luke 14:16–24; see Deuteronomy 24:5; Matthew 22:2–14; Luke 14:1, 2, 15).

Setting: On the way from Galilee to Jerusalem. After He responds to a guest's proclamation about the blessings of eating bread in the kingdom of God, Jesus presents to large crowds the demands of discipleship.

Now large crowds were going along with Him; and He turned and said to them, "If anyone comes to Me, and does not hate his own father and mother and wife and children and brothers and sisters, yes, and even his own life, he cannot be My disciple. Whoever does not carry his own cross and come after Me cannot be My disciple. For which one of you, when he wants to build a tower, does not first sit down and calculate the cost to see if he has enough to complete it? Otherwise, when he has laid a foundation and is not able to finish, all who observe it begin to ridicule him, saying, 'This man began to build and was not able to finish.' Or what king, when he sets out to meet another king in battle, will not first sit down and consider whether he is strong enough with ten thousand *men* to encounter the one coming against him with twenty thousand? Or else, while the other is still far away, he sends a delegation and asks for terms of peace. So then, none of you can be My disciple who does not give up all his possessions. Therefore, salt is good; but if even salt has become tasteless, with what will it be seasoned? It is useless either for the soil or for the manure pile; it is thrown out. He who has ears to hear, let him hear" (Luke 14:25–35; cf. Matthew 5:13; 10:37–39; see Proverb 20:18; Luke 14:1, 2; Philippians 3:7).

Setting: On the way from Galilee to Jerusalem. The Lord responds to the Pharisees' scoffing at His teaching His disciples about stewardship with an illustration of the earthly commitment of marriage.

"Everyone who divorces his wife and marries another commits adultery, and he who marries one who is divorced from a husband commits adultery" (Luke 16:18; cf. Matthew 5:31, 32; 19:9; Mark 10:11, 12; see Romans 7:2, 3; 1 Corinthians 7:10, 39).

Setting: Perea, en route from Galilee to Jerusalem. After responding to His disciples' question about salvation, Jesus replies to Peter's statement about the disciples' personal sacrifice.

Peter said, "Behold, we have left our own *homes* and followed You." And He said to them, "Truly I say to you, there is no one who has left house or wife or brothers or parents or children, for the sake of the kingdom of God, who will not receive many times as much at this time and in the age to come, eternal life" (Luke 18:28–30; cf. Matthew 19:27–29; Mark 10:28–30; see Matthew 6:33; Luke 5:11).

WIFE, LOT'S

Setting: On the way from Galilee to Jerusalem. After the Pharisees question Him about the coming of the kingdom of God, Jesus tells His disciples of His second coming.

And He said to the disciples, "The days will come when you will long to see one of the days of the Son of Man, and you will not see it. They will say to you, 'Look there! Look here!' Do not go away, and do not run after *them*. For just like the lightning, when it flashes out of one part of the sky, shines to the other part of the sky, so will the Son of Man be in His day. But first He must suffer many things and be rejected by this generation. And just as it happened in the days of Noah, so it will be also in the days of the Son of Man: they were eating, they were drinking, they were marrying, they were being given in marriage, until the day that Noah entered the ark, and the flood came and destroyed them all. It was the same as happened in the days of Lot: they were eating, they were drinking, they were buying, they were selling, they were planting, they were building; but on the day that Lot went out from Sodom it rained fire and brimstone from heaven and destroyed them all. It will be just the same on the day that the Son of Man is revealed. On that day, the one who is on the housetop and whose goods are in the house must not go down to take them out; and likewise the one who is in the field must not turn back. Remember Lot's wife. Whoever seeks to keep his life will lose it, and whoever loses *his life* will preserve it. I tell you, on that night there will be two in one bed; one will be taken and the other will be left. There will be two women grinding at the same place; one will be taken and the other will be left. [Two men will be in the field; one will be taken and the other will be left."] And answering they said to Him, "Where, Lord?" And He said to them, "Where the body *is*, there also the vultures will be gathered" (Luke 17:22–37; see Genesis 19; Matthew 10:39; 16:21, 27; 24:17–28, 37–41).

WILDERNESS

Setting: Galilee. While speaking to the crowds, Jesus pays tribute to the ministry of John the Baptist, but emphasizes that the one who is least in the kingdom of heaven is greater than John.

As these men were going *away,* Jesus began to speak to the crowds about John, "What did you go out into the wilderness to see? A reed shaken by the wind? But what did you go out to see? A man dressed in soft *clothing?* Those who wear soft *clothing* are in kings' palaces! But what did you go out to see? A prophet? Yes, I tell you, and the one who is more than a prophet. This is the one about whom it is written, 'BEHOLD, I SEND MY MESSENGER AHEAD OF YOU, WHO WILL PREPARE YOUR WAY BEFORE YOU.' Truly, I say to you, among those born of women there has not arisen *anyone* greater than John the Baptist! Yet the one who is least in the kingdom of heaven is greater than he. From the days of John the Baptist until now the kingdom of heaven suffers violence, and violent men take it by force. For all the prophets and the Law prophesied until John. And, if you are willing to accept *it,* John himself is Elijah who was to come. He who has ears to hear, let him hear" (Matthew 11:7–15, Jesus quotes from Malachi 3:1; cf. Malachi 4:5; Luke 7:24–28; Luke 16:16; see Matthew 14:5).

Setting: The Mount of Olives, just east of Jerusalem. During His Olivet Discourse, Jesus answers His disciples' questions as to when the temple will be destroyed and Jerusalem overrun, along with the signs of His coming and the end of the age.

"Therefore when you see the ABOMINATION OF DESOLATION which was spoken of through Daniel the prophet, standing in the holy place (let the reader understand), then those who are in Judea must flee to the mountains. Whoever is on the housetop must not go down to get the things that are in his house. Whoever is in the field must not turn back to get his cloak. But woe to those who are pregnant and to those who are nursing babies in those days! But pray that your flight will not be in the winter, or on a Sabbath. For then there will be a great tribulation, such as has not occurred since the beginning of the world until now, nor ever will. Unless those days had been cut short, no life would have been saved; but for the sake of the elect those days will be cut short. Then if anyone says to you, 'Behold, here is the Christ,' or "There *He is,*' do not believe *him.* For false Christs and false prophets will arise and will show great signs and wonders, so as to mislead, if possible, even the elect. Behold, I have told you in advance. So if they say to you, 'Behold, He is in the wilderness,' do not go out, *or,* 'Behold, He is in the inner rooms,' do not

believe *them.* For just as the lightning comes from the east and flashes even to the west, so will the coming of the Son of Man be. Wherever the corpse is, there the vultures will gather" (Matthew 24:15–28, Jesus quotes from Daniel 9:27; cf. Daniel 12:1; Mark 13:14–23; Luke 17:22–31; 21:20–24; 23:29; see John 4:48).

Setting: Galilee. After Jesus responds to the disciples of John the Baptist whether He is the promised Messiah, the Lord speaks to the crowds about John.

When the messengers of John had left, He began to speak to the crowds about John, "What did you go out into the wilderness to see? A reed shaken by the wind? But what did you go out to see? A man dressed in soft clothing? Those who are splendidly clothed and live in luxury are *found* in royal palaces! But what did you go out to see? A prophet? Yes, I say to you, and one who is more than a prophet. This is the one about whom it is written, 'BEHOLD, I SEND MY MESSENGER AHEAD OF YOU, WHO WILL PREPARE YOUR WAY BEFORE YOU.' I say to you, among those born of women there is no one greater than John; yet he who is least in the kingdom of God is greater than he" (Luke 7:24–28, Jesus quotes from Malachi 3:1; cf. Matthew 11:7–11).

Setting: Jerusalem. At the time for the Passover of the Jews, after the Lord cleanses the temple, a Pharisee, Nicodemus, asks Him by night the meaning of "born of the Spirit."

Jesus answered and said to him, "Are you the teacher of Israel and do not understand these things? Truly, truly, I say to you, we speak of what we know and testify of what we have seen, and you do not accept our testimony. If I told you earthly things and you do not believe, how will you believe if I tell you heavenly things? No one has ascended into heaven, but He who descended from heaven: the Son of Man. As Moses lifted up the serpent in the wilderness, even so must the Son of Man be lifted up; so that whoever believes will in Him have eternal life" (John 3:10–15; see Numbers 21:9; Proverb 30:4; John 12:34; 20:30, 31).

Setting: Capernaum of Galilee. After Jesus informs the people whom He miraculously fed with a lad's five loaves and two fish how they might receive the bread out of heaven, the Jewish religious leaders grumble when the Lord claims that He came down out of heaven.

Therefore the Jews were grumbling about Him, because He said, "I am the bread that came down out of heaven." They were saying, "Is not this Jesus, the son of Joseph, whose father and mother we know? How does He now say, 'I have come down out of heaven'?" Jesus answered and said to them, "Do not grumble among yourselves. No one can come to Me unless the Father who sent Me draws him; and I will raise him up on the last day. It is written in the prophets, 'AND THEY SHALL ALL BE TAUGHT OF GOD.' Everyone who has heard and learned from the Father, comes to Me. Not that anyone has seen the Father, except the One who is from God; He has seen the Father. Truly, truly, I say to you, he who believes has eternal life. I am the bread of life. Your fathers ate the manna in the wilderness, and they died. This is the bread which comes down out of heaven, so that one may eat of it and not die. I am the living bread that came down out of heaven; if anyone eats of this bread, he will live forever; and the bread also which I will give for the life of the world is My flesh" (John 6:41–51, Jesus quotes from Isaiah 54:13; see John 1:18, 29; 3:36; 7:27).

WILDERNESS TEMPTATION (See TEMPTATION OF JESUS)

WILL (See FATHER, WILL OF HIS (human); FATHER, WILL OF MY; FATHER, WILL OF YOUR; WILL, MASTER'S; and WILL OF GOD)

WILL, FATHER'S (See FATHER, WILL OF MY; FATHER, WILL OF YOUR; and WILL OF GOD)

WILL, GOD'S (See FATHER, WILL OF MY; FATHER, WILL OF YOUR; and WILL OF GOD)

WILL, MASTER'S

Setting: On the way from Galilee to Jerusalem. When Jesus uses a parable to challenge the crowd and His disciples to be ready for His return, Peter asks whom He is addressing.

And the Lord said, "Who then is the faithful and sensible steward, whom his master will put in charge of his servants, to give them their rations at the proper time? Blessed is that slave whom his master finds so doing when he comes. Truly I say to you that he will put him in charge of all his possessions. But if that slave says in his heart, 'My master will be a long time in coming,' and begins to beat the slaves, *both* men and women, and to eat and drink and get drunk; the master of that slave will come on a day when he does not expect *him* and at an hour he does not know, and will cut him in pieces, and assign him a place with the unbelievers. And that slave who knew his master's will and did not get ready or act in accord with his will, will receive many lashes, but the one who did know *it,* and committed deeds worthy of flogging, will receive but few. From everyone who has been given much, much will be required; and to whom they entrusted much, of him they will ask all the more" (Luke 12:42–48; cf. Matthew 24:45–51; see Leviticus 5:17).

WILL OF GOD (Also see FATHER, WILL OF MY; FATHER, WILL OF YOUR; and OBEDIENCE)

[WILL OF GOD from Your will be done]
Setting: Galilee. During the early part of His ministry, Jesus gives a model prayer to His disciples and the multitudes while conveying The Sermon on the Mount.

"Pray, then, in this way: 'Our Father who is in heaven, hallowed be Your name. Your kingdom come. Your will be done, on earth as it is in heaven. Give us this day our daily bread. And forgive us our debts, as we also have forgiven our debtors. And do not lead us into temptation, but deliver us from evil. [For Yours is the kingdom and the power and the glory forever. Amen]'" (Matthew 6:9–13; cf. Luke 11:2–4; see John 17:15).

[WILL OF GOD from not as I will, but as You will and Your will be done]
Setting: Jerusalem. After celebrating the Passover meal with His disciples, Jesus retreats to the Garden of Gethsemane on the Mount of Olives to pray prior to His betrayal by Judas.

Then Jesus came with them to a place called Gethsemane, and said to His disciples, "Sit here while I go over there and pray." And He took with Him Peter and the two sons of Zebedee, and began to be grieved and distressed. Then He said to them, "My soul is deeply grieved, to the point of death; remain here and keep watch with Me." And He went a little beyond *them,* and fell on His face and prayed, saying, "My Father, if it is possible, let this cup pass from Me; yet not as I will, but as You will." And He came to the disciples and found them sleeping, and said to Peter, "So, you *men* could not keep watch with Me for one hour? Keep watching and praying that you may not enter into temptation; the spirit is willing, but the flesh is weak." He went away again a second time and prayed, saying, "My Father, if this cannot pass away unless I drink it, Your will be done." Again He came and found them sleeping, for their eyes were heavy. And He left them again, and went away and prayed a third time, saying the same thing once more. Then He came to the disciples and said to them, "Are you still sleeping and resting? Behold the hour is at hand and the Son of Man is being betrayed into the hands of sinners. Get up, let us be going; behold the one who betrays Me is at hand!" (Matthew 26:36–46; cf. Mark 14:32–42; Luke 22:40–46; see Matthew 20:22; John 12:27).

Setting: Galilee. During the early part of His ministry, just after selecting the Twelve, Jesus explains to the crowd who His true relatives are after being informed His mother and brothers are waiting to see Him.

Answering them, He said, "Who are My mother and My brothers?" Looking about at those who were sitting around Him, He said, "Behold My mother and My brothers! For whoever does the will of God, he is My brother and sister and mother" (Mark 3:33–35; cf. Matthew 12:46–50; Luke 8:19–21).

[WILL OF GOD from not My will, but Yours be done]
Setting: Jerusalem. After celebrating the Passover meal and instructing His disciples to prepare to persevere without Him, with His crucifixion imminent, Jesus proceeds to the Mount of Olives to pray.

And He came out and proceeded as was His custom to the Mount of Olives; and the disciples also followed Him. When He arrived at the place, He said to them, "Pray that you may not enter into temptation." And He withdrew from them about a stone's throw, and He knelt down and *began* to pray, saying, "Father, if You are willing, remove this cup from Me; yet not My will, but Yours be done" (Luke 22:39–42; cf. Matthew 26:36–42; Mark 14:32–49; see Luke 21:37).

WILL OF MY FATHER (Listed under FATHER, WILL OF MY; also see WILL OF GOD)

WIND (WIND, SOUTH is a separate entry; also see WINDS)

Setting: Galilee. While speaking to the crowds, Jesus pays tribute to the ministry of John the Baptist, but emphasizes that the one who is least in the kingdom of heaven is greater than John.

As these men were going *away,* Jesus began to speak to the crowds about John, "What did you go out into the wilderness to see? A reed shaken by the wind? But what did you go out to see? A man dressed in soft *clothing?* Those who wear soft *clothing* are in kings' palaces! But what did you go out to see? A prophet? Yes, I tell you, and the one who is more than a prophet. This is the one about whom it is written, 'BEHOLD, I SEND MY MESSENGER AHEAD OF YOU, WHO WILL PREPARE YOUR WAY BEFORE YOU.' Truly, I say to you, among those born of women there has not arisen *anyone* greater than John the Baptist! Yet the one who is least in the kingdom of heaven is greater than he. From the days of John the Baptist until now the kingdom of heaven suffers violence, and violent men take it by force. For all the prophets and the Law prophesied until John. And, if you are willing to accept *it,* John himself is Elijah who was to come. He who has ears to hear, let him hear" (Matthew 11:7–15, Jesus quotes from Malachi 3:1; cf. Malachi 4:5; Luke 7:24–28; 16:16; see Matthew 14:5).

Setting: Galilee. After Jesus responds to the disciples of John the Baptist about whether He is the promised Messiah, the Lord speaks to the crowds about John.

When the messengers of John had left, He began to speak to the crowds about John, "What did you go out into the wilderness to see? A reed shaken by the wind? But what did you go out to see? A man dressed in soft clothing? Those who are splendidly clothed and live in luxury are *found* in royal palaces! But what did you go out to see? A prophet? Yes, I say to you, and one who is more than a prophet. This is the one about whom it is written, 'BEHOLD, I SEND MY MESSENGER AHEAD OF YOU, WHO WILL PREPARE YOUR WAY BEFORE YOU.' I say to you, among those born of women there is no one greater than John; yet he who is least in the kingdom of God is greater than he" (Luke 7:24–28, Jesus quotes from Malachi 3:1; cf. Matthew 11:7–11).

Setting: Jerusalem. At the time for the Passover of the Jews, after the Lord cleanses the temple, a Pharisee, Nicodemus, asks Him by night the meaning of "born again."

Jesus answered, "Truly, truly, I say to you, unless one is born of water and the Spirit he cannot enter into the kingdom of God. That which is born of the flesh is flesh, and that which is born of the Spirit is spirit. Do not be amazed that I said to you, 'You must be born again.' The wind blows where it wishes and you hear the sound of it, but do not know where it comes from and where it is going; so is everyone who is born of the Spirit" (John 3:5–8; see Psalm 135:7; John 1:13).

WIND, SOUTH (Also see WIND)

Setting: On the way from Galilee to Jerusalem. After telling how a relationship with Him will divide families, Jesus chastises the crowds for being able to discern the weather but not the present age.

And He was also saying to the crowds, "When you see a cloud rising in the west, immediately you say, 'A shower is coming,' and so it turns out. And when *you see* a south wind blowing, you say, 'It will be a hot day,' and it turns out *that way.* You hypocrites! You know how to analyze the appearance of the earth and the sky, but why do you not analyze this present time?" (Luke 12:54–56; cf. Matthew 16:2, 3).

WINDS (Also see WEATHER; and WIND)

Setting: Galilee. During the early part of His ministry, Jesus preaches the Sermon on the Mount to His disciples and the multitudes.

"Therefore everyone who hears these words of Mine and acts on them, may be compared to a wise man who built his house on the rock. And the rain fell, and the floods came, and the winds blew and slammed against that house; and *yet* it did not fall, for it had been founded on the rock. Everyone who hears these words of Mine and does not act on them, will be like a foolish man who built his house on the sand. The rain fell, and the floods came, and the winds blew and slammed against that house; and it fell—and great was its fall" (Matthew 7:24–28; cf. Luke 6:47–49).

Setting: The Mount of Olives, just east of Jerusalem. During His Olivet Discourse, Jesus answers His disciples' questions as to when the temple will be destroyed and Jerusalem overrun, along with the signs of His coming and the end of the age.

"But immediately after the tribulation of those days THE SUN WILL BE DARKENED, AND THE MOON WILL NOT GIVE ITS LIGHT, AND THE STARS WILL FALL from the sky, and the powers of the heavens will be shaken. And then the sign of the Son of Man will appear in the sky, and then all the tribes of the earth will mourn, and they will see the SON OF MAN COMING ON THE CLOUDS OF THE SKY with power and great glory. And He will send forth His angels with A GREAT TRUMPET and THEY WILL GATHER TOGETHER His elect from the four winds, from one end of the sky to the other" (Matthew 24:29–31, Jesus quotes from Isaiah 13:10, Daniel 7:13; Exodus 19:16; cf. Mark 13:24–27; Luke 21:25–27).

Setting: On the Mount of Olives, east of the temple in Jerusalem. After prophesying the temple's destruction, Jesus responds during His Olivet Discourse to questions from Peter, James, John, and Andrew about other future events.

"But in those days, after that tribulation, THE SUN WILL BE DARKENED AND THE MOON WILL NOT GIVE ITS LIGHT, AND THE STARS WILL BE FALLING from heaven, and the powers that are in the heavens will be shaken. Then they will see THE SON OF MAN COMING IN CLOUDS with great power and glory. And then He will send forth the angels, and will gather together His elect from the four winds, from the farthest end of the earth to the farthest end of heaven" (Mark 13:24–27. Jesus quotes from Isaiah 13:10; 34:4; Daniel 7:13; cf. Matthew 24:29–31; Luke 21:25–27).

WINDS, FOUR (See WINDS)

WINE (WINE, NEW; WINE, OLD; and WINE PRESS are separate entries; also see DRINKING; FRUIT OF THE VINE; and WINESKINS)

Setting: Capernaum, near the Sea of Galilee. John the Baptist's disciples ask Jesus why His disciples do not participate in fasting, while they and the Pharisees do.

And Jesus said to them, "The attendants of the bridegroom cannot mourn as long as the bridegroom is with them, can they? But the days will come when the bridegroom is taken away from them, and then they will fast. But no one puts a patch of unshrunk cloth on an old garment; for the patch pulls away from the garment, and a worse tear results. Nor do *people* put new wine into old wineskins; otherwise the wineskins burst, and the wine pours out and the wineskins are ruined; but they put new wine into fresh wineskins, and both are preserved" (Matthew 9:15–17; cf. Mark 2:18–22; Luke 5:33–39).

Setting: Capernaum. John the Baptist's disciples and the Pharisees question why Jesus' disciples do not fast when they do.

And Jesus said to them, "While the bridegroom is with them, the attendants of the bridegroom cannot fast, can they? So long as they have the bridegroom with them, they cannot fast. But the days will come when the bridegroom is taken away from them, and then they will fast in that day. No one sews a patch of unshrunk cloth on an old garment; otherwise the patch pulls away from it, the new from the old, and a worse tear results. No one puts new wine into old wineskins; otherwise the wine will burst the skins, and the wine is lost and the skins as *well;* but *one puts* new wine into fresh wineskins" (Mark 2:19–22; cf. Matthew 9:14–17; Luke 5:33–38).

Setting: Galilee. After praising John the Baptist to the crowds, Jesus criticizes the Pharisees and lawyers who reject God's purpose and John's message.

"To what then shall I compare the men of this generation, and what are they like? They are like children who sit in the market place and call to one another, and they say, 'We played the flute for you, and you did not dance; we sang a dirge, and you did not weep.' For John the Baptist has come eating no bread and drinking no wine, and you say, 'He has a demon!' The Son of Man has come eating and drinking, and you say, 'Behold, a gluttonous man and a drunkard, a friend of tax collectors and sinners!' Yet wisdom is vindicated by all her children" (Luke 7:31–35; cf. Matthew 11:16–19; see Luke 1:15).

Setting: On the way from Galilee to Jerusalem. While being tested by a lawyer, Jesus tells him the story of the good Samaritan.

Jesus replied and said, "A man was going down from Jerusalem to Jericho, and fell among robbers, and they stripped him and beat him, and went away leaving him half dead. And by chance a priest was going down on that road, and when he saw him, he passed by on the other side. Likewise a Levite also, when he came to the place and saw him, passed by on the other side. But a Samaritan, who was on a journey, came upon him; and when he saw him, he felt compassion, and came to him and bandaged up his wounds, pouring oil and wine on *them;* and he put him on his own beast, and brought him to an inn and took care of him. On the next day he took out two denarii and gave them to the innkeeper and said, 'Take care of him; and whatever more you spend, when I return I will repay you.' Which of these three do you think proved to be a neighbor to the man who fell into the robbers' *hands?*" And he said, "The one who showed mercy toward him" Then Jesus said to him, "Go and do the same" (Luke 10:30–37).

[WINE from draw some out]
Setting: Cana of Galilee. On the third day of His public ministry, after choosing Andrew, Peter, Philip, and Nathanael to be His disciples, Jesus attends a wedding. His mother prompts Him to perform His first miracle, that of turning water into wine.

Jesus said to them, "Fill the waterpots with water." So they filled them up to the brim. And He said to them, "Draw *some* out now and take it to the headwaiter." So they took it *to him* (John 2:7, 8).

WINE, NEW (Also see WINE)

Setting: Capernaum, near the Sea of Galilee. John the Baptist's disciples ask Jesus why His disciples do not participate in fasting, while they and the Pharisees do.

And Jesus said to them, "The attendants of the bridegroom cannot mourn as long as the bridegroom is with them, can they? But the days will come when the bridegroom is taken away from them, and then they will fast. But no one puts a patch of unshrunk cloth on an old garment; for the patch pulls away from the garment, and a worse tear results. Nor do *people* put new wine into old wineskins; otherwise the wineskins burst, and the wine pours out and the wineskins are ruined; but they put new wine into fresh wineskins, and both are preserved" (Matthew 9:15–17; cf. Mark 2:18–22; Luke 5:33–39).

Setting: Capernaum. John the Baptist's disciples and the Pharisees question why Jesus' disciples do not fast when they do.

And Jesus said to them, "While the bridegroom is with them, the attendants of the bridegroom cannot fast, can they? So long as they have the bridegroom with them, they cannot fast. But the days will come when the bridegroom is taken away from them, and then they will fast in that day. No one sews a patch of unshrunk cloth on an old garment; otherwise the patch pulls away from it, the new from the old, and a worse tear results. No one puts new wine into old wineskins; otherwise the wine will burst the skins, and the wine is lost and the skins as *well;* but *one puts* new wine into fresh wineskins" (Mark 2:19–22; cf. Matthew 9:14–17; Luke 5:33–38).

Setting: The home of Levi (Matthew) in Capernaum. At a reception for Jesus following Levi's call to be a disciple, the Lord tells a parable to the Pharisees and their scribes, who question His association with tax collectors and sinners.

And He was also telling them a parable: "No one tears a piece of cloth from a new garment and puts it on an old garment; otherwise he will both tear the new, and the piece from the new will not match the old. And no one puts new wine into old wineskins; otherwise the new wine will burst the skins and it will be spilled out, and the skins will be ruined. But new wine must be put into fresh wineskins. And no one, after drinking old *wine* wishes for new; for he says, 'The old is good *enough*'" (Luke 5:36–39; cf. Matthew 9:16, 17; Mark 2:21, 22).

WINE, OLD

Setting: The home of Levi (Matthew) in Capernaum. At a reception for Jesus following Levi's call to be a disciple, the Lord tells a parable to the Pharisees and their scribes, who question His association with tax collectors and sinners.

And He was also telling them a parable: "No one tears a piece of cloth from a new garment and puts it on an old garment; otherwise he will both tear the new, and the piece from the new will not match the old. And no one puts new wine into old wineskins; otherwise the new wine will burst the skins and it will be spilled out, and the skins will be ruined. But new wine must be put into fresh wineskins. And no one, after drinking old *wine* wishes for new; for he says, 'The old is good *enough*'" (Luke 5:36–39; cf. Matthew 9:16, 17; Mark 2:21, 22).

WINE, TURNING WATER INTO (See HEADWAITER)

WINE PRESS (Also see WINE)

Setting: The temple in Jerusalem. Jesus delivers another parable to the chief priests and elders after they question His authority.

"Listen to another parable. There was a landowner who PLANTED A VINEYARD AND PUT A WALL AROUND IT AND DUG A WINE PRESS IN IT, AND BUILT A TOWER, and rented it out to vine-growers and went on a journey. When the harvest time approached, he sent his slaves to the vine-growers to receive his produce. The vine-growers took his slaves and beat one, and killed another, and stoned a third. Again he sent another group of slaves larger than the first; and they did the same thing to them. But afterward he sent his son to them, saying, 'They will respect my son.' But when the vine-growers saw the son, they said among themselves, 'This is the heir; come, let us kill him and seize his inheritance.' They took him, and threw him out of the vineyard and killed him. Therefore when the owner of the vineyard comes, what will he do to those vine-growers?" (Matthew 21:33–40; Jesus quotes from Isaiah 5:1, 2; cf. Mark 12:1–9; Luke 20:9–15).

Setting: The temple in Jerusalem. Having His authority questioned by the chief priests, scribes, and elders, Jesus begins to teach them in parables.

And He began to speak to them in parables: "A man PLANTED A VINEYARD AND PUT A WALL AROUND IT, AND DUG A VAT UNDER THE WINE PRESS AND BUILT A TOWER, and rented it out to vine-growers and went on a journey. At the *harvest* time he sent a slave to the vine-growers, in order to receive *some* of the produce of the vineyard from the vine-growers. They took him, and beat him and sent him away empty-handed. Again he sent them another slave, and they wounded him in the head, and treated him shamefully. And he sent another, and that one they killed; and *so with* many others, beating some and killing others. He had one more to *send*, a beloved son; he sent him last *of all* to them, saying, 'They will respect my son.' But those vine-growers said to one another, 'This is the heir; come, let us kill him, and the inheritance will be ours!' They took him, and killed him and threw him out of the vineyard. What will the owner of the vineyard do? He will come and destroy the vine-growers, and will give the vineyard to others. Have you not even read this Scripture: 'THE STONE WHICH THE BUILDERS REJECTED, THIS BECAME THE CHIEF CORNER *stone;* THIS CAME ABOUT FROM THE LORD, AND IT IS MARVELOUS IN OUR EYES'?" (Mark 12:1–11, Jesus quotes from Psalm 118:22, 23; Isaiah 5:1, 2; cf. Matthew 21:33–46; Luke 20:9–19).

WINESKINS, PARABLE OF THE NEW WINE IN OLD (Also see WINE)

WINESKINS, PARABLE OF THE NEW WINE IN OLD from new wine and old wineskins]

Setting: Capernaum, near the Sea of Galilee. John the Baptist's disciples ask Jesus why His disciples do not participate in fasting, while they and the Pharisees do.

And Jesus said to them, "The attendants of the bridegroom cannot mourn as long as the bridegroom is with them, can they? But the days will come when the bridegroom is taken away from them, and then they will fast. But no one puts a patch of unshrunk cloth on an old garment; for the patch pulls away from the garment, and a worse tear results. Nor do *people* put new wine into old wineskins; otherwise the wineskins burst, and the wine pours out and the wineskins are ruined; but they put new wine into fresh wineskins, and both are preserved" (Matthew 9:15–17; cf. Mark 2:18–22; Luke 5:33–39).

[WINESKINS, PARABLE OF THE NEW WINE IN OLD from new wine and old wineskins]
Setting: Capernaum. John the Baptist's disciples and the Pharisees question why Jesus' disciples do not fast when they do.

And Jesus said to them, "While the bridegroom is with them, the attendants of the bridegroom cannot fast, can they? So long as they have the bridegroom with them, they cannot fast. But the days will come when the bridegroom is taken away from them, and then they will fast in that day. No one sews a patch of unshrunk cloth on an old garment; otherwise the patch pulls away from it, the new from the old, and a worse tear results. No one puts new wine into old wineskins; otherwise the wine will burst the skins, and the wine is lost and the skins as *well;* but *one puts* new wine into fresh wineskins" (Mark 2:19–22; cf. Matthew 9:14–17; Luke 5:33–38).

[WINESKINS, PARABLE OF THE NEW WINE IN OLD from new wine and old wineskins]
Setting: The home of Levi (Matthew) in Capernaum. At a reception for Jesus following Levi's call to be a disciple, the Lord tells a parable to the Pharisees and their scribes, who question His association with tax collectors and sinners.

And He was also telling them a parable: "No one tears a piece of cloth from a new garment and puts it on an old garment; otherwise he will both tear the new, and the piece from the new will not match the old. And no one puts new wine into old wineskins; otherwise the new wine will burst the skins and it will be spilled out, and the skins will be ruined. But new wine must be put into fresh wineskins. And no one, after drinking old *wine* wishes for new; for he says, 'The old is good *enough*'" (Luke 5:36–39; cf. Matthew 9:16, 17; Mark 2:21, 22).

WINGS

Setting: The temple in Jerusalem. With His death on the cross just days away, Jesus laments over Jerusalem's hard-heartedness and lack of repentance.

"Jerusalem, Jerusalem, who kills the prophets and stones those who are sent to her! How often I wanted to gather your children together, the way a hen gathers her chicks under her wings, and you were unwilling. Behold, your house is being left to you desolate! For I say to you, from now on you will not see Me until you say, 'BLESSED IS HE WHO COMES IN THE NAME OF THE LORD!'" (Matthew 23:37–39, Jesus quotes from Psalm 118:26; cf. 1 Kings 9:7; Luke 13:34, 35).

Setting: On the way from Galilee to Jerusalem. While teaching in the cities and villages, Jesus responds to a question about who is saved. Some Pharisees ask Him to leave, claiming Herod Antipas (tetrarch of Galilee and Perea) seeks to kill Him.

And He said to them, "Go and tell that fox, 'Behold, I cast out demons and perform cures today and tomorrow, and the third *day* I reach My goal.' Nevertheless I must journey on today and tomorrow and the next *day*; for it cannot be that a prophet would perish outside of Jerusalem. O Jerusalem, Jerusalem, *the city* that kills the prophets and stones those sent to her! How often I wanted to gather your children together, just as a hen *gathers* her brood under her wings, and you would not *have it*! Behold, your house is left to you *desolate*; and I say to you, you will not see Me until *the time* comes when you say, 'BLESSED IS HE WHO COMES IN THE NAME OF THE LORD!'" (Luke 13:32–35, Jesus quotes from Psalm 118:26; cf. Matthew 23:37).

WINTER (Also see SUMMER)

Setting: The Mount of Olives, just east of Jerusalem. During His Olivet Discourse, Jesus answers His disciples' questions as to when the temple will be destroyed and Jerusalem overrun, along with the signs of His coming and the end of the age.

"Therefore when you see the ABOMINATION OF DESOLATION which was spoken of through Daniel the prophet, standing in the holy place (let the reader understand), then those who are in Judea must flee to the mountains. Whoever is on the housetop must not go down to get the things that are in his house. Whoever is in the field must not turn back to get his cloak. But woe to those who are pregnant and to those who are nursing babies in those days! But pray that your flight will not be in the winter, or on a Sabbath. For then there will be a great tribulation, such as has not occurred since the beginning of the world until now, nor ever will. Unless those days had been cut short, no life would have been saved; but for the sake of the elect those days will be cut short. Then if anyone says to you, 'Behold, here is the Christ,' or "There *He is,*' do not believe *him.* For false Christs and false prophets will arise and will show great signs and wonders, so as to mislead, if possible, even the elect. Behold, I have told you in advance. So if they say to you, 'Behold, He is in the wilderness,' do not go out, *or,* 'Behold, He is in the inner rooms,' do not believe *them.* For just as the lightning comes from the east and flashes even to the west, so will the coming of the Son of Man be. Wherever the corpse is, there the vultures will gather" (Matthew 24:15–28, Jesus quotes from Daniel 9:27; cf. Daniel 12:1; Mark 13:14–23; Luke 17:22–31; 21:20–24; 23:29; see John 4:48).

Setting: On the Mount of Olives, east of the temple in Jerusalem. After prophesying the temple's destruction, Jesus responds during His Olivet Discourse to questions from Peter, James, John, and Andrew about other future events.

"But when you see the ABOMINATION OF DESOLATION standing where it should not be (let the reader understand), then those who are in Judea must flee to the mountains. The one who is on the housetop must not go down, or go in to get anything out of his house; and the one who is in the field must not turn back to get his coat. But woe to those who are pregnant and to those who are nursing babies in those days! But pray that it may not happen in winter. For those days will be a *time of* tribulation such as has not occurred since the beginning of the creation which God created until now, and never will. Unless the Lord had shortened *those* days, no life would have been saved; but for the sake of the elect, whom He chose, He shortened the days. And then if anyone says to you, 'Behold, here is the Christ'; or, 'Behold, *He is* there'; do not believe *him*; for false Christs and false prophets will arise, and will show signs and wonders, in order to lead astray, if possible, the elect. But take heed; behold, I have told you everything in advance" (Mark 13:14–23; cf. Matthew 24:15–28; Luke 21:20–24; see Daniel 9:27; 12:1; Luke 17:31).

WISDOM (Also see DISCERNMENT; and WISE)

Setting: Galilee. After praising John the Baptist as His forerunner, Jesus demonstrates the foolish thinking of the Jewish religious leaders by repeating what they say about John's ascetic lifestyle and ministry along with His own.

"But to what shall I compare this generation? It is like children sitting in the market places, who call out to the other *children,* and say, 'We played the flute for you, and you did not dance; we sang a dirge, and you did not mourn.' For John came neither eating nor drinking, and they say, 'He has a demon!' The Son of Man came eating and drinking, and they say, 'Behold, a gluttonous man and a drunkard, a friend of tax collectors and sinners! Yet wisdom is vindicated by her deeds" (Matthew 11:16–19; cf. Luke 7:31–35; see Matthew 9:11, 34; Luke 1:15).

Setting: Galilee. After praising John the Baptist to the crowds, Jesus criticizes the Pharisees and lawyers who reject God's purpose and John's message.

"To what then shall I compare the men of this generation, and what are they like? They are like children who sit in the market place and call to one another, and they say, 'We played the flute for you, and you did not dance; we sang a dirge, and you did not weep.' For John the Baptist has come eating no bread and drinking no wine, and you say, 'He has a demon!' The Son of Man has come eating and drinking, and you say, 'Behold, a gluttonous man and a drunkard, a friend of tax collectors and sinners!' Yet wisdom is vindicated by all her children" (Luke 7:31–35; cf. Matthew 11:16–19; see Luke 1:15).

Setting: On the Mount of Olives, east of the temple in Jerusalem. After ministering in the temple a few days before His crucifixion, and giving His disciples more details regarding the temple's future destruction, Jesus elaborates during His Olivet Discourse about things to come.

Then He continued by saying to them, "Nation will rise against nation and kingdom against kingdom, and there will be great earthquakes, and in various places plagues and famines; and there will be terrors and great signs from heaven. But before all these things, they will lay their hands on you and will persecute you, delivering you to the synagogues and prisons, bringing you before kings and governors for My name's sake. It will lead to an opportunity for your testimony. So make up your minds not to prepare beforehand to defend yourselves; for I will give you utterance and wisdom which none of your opponents will be able to resist or refute. But you will be betrayed even by parents and brothers and relatives and friends, and they will put *some* of you to death, and you will be hated by all because of My name. Yet not a hair of your head will perish. By your endurance you will gain your lives" (Luke 21:10–19; cf. Matthew 10:19–22; 24:7–14; Mark 13:8–13).

WISDOM OF GOD (Listed under GOD, WISDOM OF)

WISDOM OF SOLOMON (See SOLOMON)

WISE (MAN, WISE; and MEN, WISE are separate entries; also see WISDOM)

Setting: Galilee. As He teaches and preaches, after pronouncing woes upon unrepentant cities, Jesus prays a thanksgiving prayer to His Father in heaven.

At that time Jesus said, "I praise You, Father, Lord of heaven and earth, that you have hidden these things from *the* wise and intelligent and have revealed them to infants. Yes, Father, for this way was well-pleasing in Your sight. All things have been handed over to Me by My Father; and no one knows the Son except the Father; nor does anyone know the Father except the Son, and anyone to whom the Son wills to reveal *Him*" (Matthew 11:25–27; cf. Luke 10:21, 22).

Setting: On the way from Galilee to Jerusalem. The Lord responds to a report from the seventy sent out in pairs to every place He Himself will soon visit.

At that very time He rejoiced greatly in the Holy Spirit, and said, "I praise You, O Father, Lord of heaven and earth, that You have hidden these things from *the* wise and intelligent and have revealed them to infants. Yes, Father, for this way was well-pleasing in Your sight. All things have been handed over to Me by My Father, and no one knows who the Son is except the Father, and who the Father is except the Son, and anyone to whom the Son wills to reveal *Him*" (Luke 10:21, 22; cf. Matthew 11:25–27; see Luke 10:1, 17; John 3:35; John 10:15).

WISE MAN (Listed under MAN, WISE; also see MEN, WISE)

WISE MEN (Listed under MEN, WISE; also see MAN, WISE)

WISH (Also see ASKING; BESEECH; and REQUEST)

Setting: The district of Tyre and Sidon. A Canaanite woman appeals to Jesus to heal her demon-possessed daughter.

But He answered and said, "I was sent only to the lost sheep of the house of Israel." But she came and *began* to bow down before Him, saying, "Lord, help me!" And He answered and said, "It is not good to take the children's bread and throw it to the dogs." But she said, "Yes, Lord; but even the dogs feed from the crumbs which fall from their masters' table." Then Jesus said to her, "O woman, your faith is great; it shall be done for you as you wish." And her daughter was healed at once (Matthew 15:24–28; cf. Mark 7: 24–30; see Matthew 9:22; 10:5, 6).

[WISH from wished]

Setting: A mountain in Galilee. Following the Transfiguration, coming down the mountain, Peter, James, and John ask the Lord why Elijah must come before the Messiah.

And He answered and said, "Elijah is coming and will restore all things; but I say to you that Elijah already came, and they did not recognize him, but did to him whatever they wished. So also the Son of Man is going to suffer at their hands" (Matthew 17:11, 12; cf. Mark 9:11–13).

[WISH from wished]

Setting: Capernaum of Galilee. Jesus illustrates the matter of forgiveness after Peter asks Him if forgiving someone seven times who has sinned against him is adequate.

"For this reason the kingdom of heaven may be compared to a king who wished to settle accounts with his slaves. When he had begun to settle *them,* one who owed him ten thousand talents was brought to him. But since he did not have *the means* to repay, his lord commanded him to be sold, along with his wife and children and all that he had, and repayment to be made. So the slave fell *to the ground* and prostrated himself before him, saying, 'Have patience with me and I will repay you everything.' And the lord of that slave felt compassion and released him and forgave him the debt. But that slave went out and found one of his fellow slaves who owed him a hundred denarii; and he seized him and *began* to choke *him,* saying, 'Pay back what you owe.' So his fellow slave fell *to the ground* and *began* to plead with him, saying, 'Have patience with me and I will repay you.' But he was unwilling and went and threw him in prison until he should pay back what was owed. So when his fellow slaves saw what had happened, they were deeply grieved and came and reported to their lord all that had happened. Then summoning him, his lord said to him, 'You wicked slave, I forgave you all that debt because you pleaded with me. Should you not also have had mercy on your fellow slave, in the same way that I had mercy on you?' And his lord, moved with anger, handed him over to the torturers until he should repay all that was owed him. My heavenly Father will also do the same to you, if each of you does not forgive his brother from your heart" (Matthew 18:23–35; cf. Matthew 6:12, 14, 15; Luke 7:42; see Matthew 25:19–28).

Setting: Judea beyond the Jordan (Perea). Jesus shares with a rich, young ruler how righteous believers may have treasure in heaven.

And He said to him, "Why are you asking Me about what is good? There is *only* One who is good; but if you wish to enter into life, keep the commandments." *Then* he said to Him, 'Which ones?' And Jesus said, "YOU SHALL NOT COMMIT MURDER; YOU SHALL NOT COMMIT ADULTERY; YOU SHALL NOT STEAL; YOU SHALL NOT BEAR FALSE WITNESS; HONOR YOUR FATHER AND MOTHER; and YOU SHALL LOVE YOUR NEIGHBOR AS YOURSELF." The young man said to Him, "All these things I have kept; what am I still lacking?" Jesus said to him, "If you wish to complete go *and* sell your possessions and give to *the* poor, and you will have treasure in heaven; and come, follow Me" (Matthew 19:16–22, Jesus quotes from Exodus 20:13–15; Leviticus 19:18; cf. Leviticus 18:5; Mark 10:17–21; Luke 10:25–28; 12:33; 18:18–24).

Setting: Judea beyond the Jordan (Perea). Jesus illustrates the kingdom of heaven to His disciples through the story of laborers in the vineyard.

"For the kingdom of heaven is like a landowner who went out early in the morning to hire laborers for his vineyard. When he had agreed with the laborers for a denarius for the day, he sent them into his vineyard. And he went out about the third hour and saw others standing idle in the market place; and to those he said,' You also go into the vineyard, and whatever is right I will give you.' And *so* they went. Again he went out about the sixth and the ninth hour, and did the same thing. And about the eleventh *hour* he went out and found others standing *around;* and he said to them, 'Why have you been standing idle here all day long?' They said to him, 'Because no one hired us.' He said to them, 'You go into the vineyard too.' When evening came, the owner of the vineyard said to his foreman, 'Call the laborers and pay them their wages, beginning with the last *group* to the first.' When those *hired* about the eleventh hour came, each one received a denarius. When those *hired* first came, they thought that they would receive more; but each of them also received a denarius. When they received it, they grumbled at the landowner, saying, 'These last men have worked *only* one hour, and you have made them equal to us who have borne the burden and the scorching heat of the day.' But he answered and said to one of them, 'Friend, I am doing you no wrong; did you not agree with me for a denarius? Take what is yours and go, but I wish to give to this last man the same as to you. It is not lawful for me to do what I wish with what is my own? Or is your eye envious because I am generous?' So the last shall be first, and the first last" (Matthew 20:1–16; cf. Matthew 19:30).

Setting: On the way to Jerusalem. The mother of James and John, the sons of Zebedee, asks Jesus to make her sons exalted rulers with Him in His coming kingdom.

And He said to her, "What do you wish?" She said to Him, 'Command that in Your kingdom these two sons of mine may sit one on Your right and one on Your left.' But Jesus answered, "You do not know what you are asking. Are you able to drink the cup that I am about to drink?" They said to Him, 'We are able.' He said to them, "My cup you shall drink; but to sit on My right and on *My* left, this is not Mine to give, but it is for those for whom it has been prepared by My Father" (Matthew 20:21–23; cf. Mark 10:35–40; see Matthew 19:28; Acts 12:2).

[WISH from wished]

Setting: Galilee. After informing a crowd and His disciples of the hope involving the coming kingdom of God, Jesus takes Peter, James, and John to a high mountain (some think Mount Hermon). The Lord reveals His glory through the Transfiguration, and answers their question about Elijah.

And He said to them, "Elijah does first come and restore all things. And *yet* how is it written of the Son of Man that He will suffer many things and be treated with contempt? But I say to you that Elijah has indeed come, and they did to him whatever they wished, just as it is written of him" (Mark 9:12, 13; cf. Matthew 17:1–13; Luke 9:28–36; see Malachi 4:5, 6; Matthew 16:21).

Setting: The home of Simon the leper in Bethany. Two days before the Feast of Unleavened Bread (Passover), Jesus commends a woman who anoints His head with costly perfume, which some there think should have been sold and the proceeds given to the poor.

But Jesus said, "Let her alone; why do you bother her? She has done a good deed to Me. For you always have the poor with you, and whenever you wish you can do good to them; but you do not always have Me. She has done what she could; she has anointed My body beforehand for the burial. Truly I say to you, wherever the gospel is preached in the whole world, what this woman has done will also be spoken of in memory of her" (Mark 14:6–9; cf. Matthew 26:6–13; John 12:2–8; see Deuteronomy 15:11).

[WISH from wished]

Setting: On the way from Galilee to Jerusalem. After responding to a report from the seventy sent out in pairs to every place He Himself will soon visit, the Lord addresses His disciples in private.

Turning to the disciples, He said privately, "Blessed *are* the eyes which see the things you see, for I say to you, that many prophets and kings wished to see the things you see, and did not see *them*, and to hear the things which you hear, and did not hear *them*" (Luke 10:23, 24; cf. Matthew 13:16, 17).

Setting: On the way from Galilee to Jerusalem. After clarifying a parable for Peter and the crowd, Jesus conveys how a relationship with Him divides families.

"I have come to cast fire upon the earth; and how I wish it were already kindled! But I have a baptism to undergo, and how distressed I am until it is accomplished! Do you suppose that I came to grant peace on earth? I tell you, no, but rather division; for from now on five *members* in one household will be divided, three against two and two against three. They will be divided, father against son and son against father, mother against daughter, and daughter against mother, mother-in-law against daughter-in-law and daughter-in-law against mother-in-law" (Luke 12:49–53; cf. Matthew 10:34–36; see Micah 7:6; Mark 10:38).

Setting: On the way from Galilee to Jerusalem. After responding to the Pharisees' scoffing at His teaching His disciples about stewardship and the permanence of the Law, Jesus conveys the story of the rich man and Lazarus.

"Now there was a rich man, and he habitually dressed in purple and fine linen, joyously living in splendor every day. And a poor man named Lazarus was laid at his gate, covered with sores, and longing to be fed with the *crumbs* which were falling from the rich man's table; besides, even the dogs were coming and licking his sores. Now the poor man died and was carried away by the angels to Abraham's bosom; and the rich man also died and was buried. In Hades he lifted up his eyes, being in torment, and saw Abraham far away and Lazarus in his bosom. And he cried out and said, 'Father Abraham, have mercy on me, and send Lazarus so that he may dip the tip of his finger in water and cool off my tongue, for I am in agony in this flame.' But Abraham said, 'Child, remember that during your life you received your good things, and likewise Lazarus bad things; but now he is being comforted here, and you are in agony. And besides all this, between us and you there is a great chasm fixed, so that those who wish to come over from here to you will not be able, and *that* none may cross over from there to us.' And he said, 'Then I beg you, father, that you send him to my father's house—for I have five brothers—in order that he may warn them, so that they will not also come to this place of torment.' But Abraham said, 'They have Moses and the Prophets; let them hear them.' But he said, 'No, father Abraham, but if someone goes to them from the dead, they will repent!' But he said to him, 'If they do not listen to Moses and the Prophets, they will not be persuaded even if someone rises from the dead' " (Luke 16:19–31; see Luke 3:8; 6:24; 16:1, 14).

Setting: By the pool of Bethesda in Jerusalem. After performing His second Galilean miracle by healing the son of a royal official from Capernaum, Jesus returns for a feast of the Jews, where, on the Sabbath, He heals a man who has been ill for thirty-eight years.

When Jesus saw him lying *there,* and knew that he had already been a long time *in that condition,* He said to him, "Do you wish to get well?" (John 5:6).

Setting: Jerusalem. Before the Passover, after He conveys the upcoming ministry of the Holy Spirit in His disciples' lives with His imminent departure from them, Jesus explains He is the vine and His disciples are the branches.

"I am the true vine, and My Father is the vinedresser. Every branch in Me that does not bear fruit, He takes away; and every *branch* that bears fruit, He prunes it so that it may bear more fruit. You are already clean because of the word which I have spoken to you. Abide in Me, and I in you. As the branch cannot bear fruit of itself unless it abides in the vine, so neither *can* you unless you abide in Me. I am the vine, you are the branches; he who abides in Me and I in him, he bears much fruit, for apart from Me you can do nothing. If anyone does not abide in Me, he is thrown away as a branch and dries up; and they gather them, and cast them into the fire and they are burned. If you abide in Me, and My words abide in you, ask whatever you wish, and it will be done for you. My Father is glorified by this, that you bear much fruit, and *so* prove to be My disciples. Just as the Father has loved Me, I have also loved you; abide in My love. If you keep My commandments, you will abide in My love; just as I have kept My Father's commandments and abide in His love. These things I have spoken to you so that My joy may be in you, and *that* your joy may be made full" (John 15:1–11; see Matthew 5:16; 7:7; John 3:29, 35; 6:56; 8:29, 31; 13:10).

Setting: By the Sea of Galilee. During the Lord's third post-resurrection appearance to His disciples, after quizzing Peter three times regarding the disciple's love for Him, Jesus gives him details about his aging and eventual death.

"Truly, truly, I say to you, when you were younger, you used to gird yourself and walk wherever you wished; but when you grow old, you will stretch out your hands and someone else will gird you, and bring you where you do not wish to *go*." Now this He said, signifying by what kind of death he would glorify God. And when He had spoken this, He said to him, "Follow Me!" (John 21:18, 19).

Setting: On the island of Patmos (in the Aegean Sea about fifty miles southwest of Ephesus in modern Turkey). On the Lord's Day (Sunday), approximately fifty years after the Resurrection, the disciple John encounters the Lord Jesus Christ, who communicates a new revelation for the apostle to record for the church in Laodicea and to six other churches in Asia.

"To the angel of the church in Laodicea write: The Amen, the faithful and true Witness, the Beginning of the creation of God, says this: 'I know your deeds, that you are neither cold nor hot; I wish that you were cold or hot. So because you are lukewarm, and neither hot nor cold, I will spit you out of My mouth. Because you say, "I am rich, and have become wealthy, and have need of nothing," and you do not know that you are wretched and miserable and poor and blind and naked, I advise you to buy from Me gold refined by fire so that you may become rich, and white garments so that you may clothe yourself, and *that* the shame of your nakedness will not be revealed; and eye salve to anoint your eyes so that you may see. Those whom I love, I reprove and discipline; therefore be zealous and repent. Behold, I stand at the door and knock; if anyone hears My voice and opens the door, I will come in to him and will dine with him, and he with Me. He who overcomes, I will grant to him to sit down with Me on My throne, as I also overcame and sat down with My Father on His throne. He who has an ear, let him hear what the Spirit says to the churches'" (Revelation 3:14–22; see Proverb 3:12; Hosea 12:8; John 14:23; 16:33).

WITNESS (WITNESS, FALSE; WITNESS, MY; and WITNESS, TRUE are separate entries; also see EVANGELISM; TESTIMONY; and WITNESSES)

Setting: Jerusalem. Luke, writing in Acts, presents Jesus' encouraging words in an appearance to Paul in the Roman barracks following his hearing before the Jewish Council in Jerusalem and arrest by the Roman commander (after his third missionary journey).

But on the night *immediately* following, the Lord stood at his side and said, "Take courage; for as you have solemnly witnessed to My cause at Jerusalem, so you must witness at Rome also" (Acts 23:11; see Acts 19:21).

Setting: Caesarea. Luke, writing in Acts, gives Paul's retelling of his conversion to Christ as he appears before King Agrippa following his hearing before the Jewish Council in Jerusalem and arrest by the Roman commander (on his way to Rome after the apostle's third missionary journey).

"And when we had fallen to the ground, I heard a voice saying to me in the Hebrew dialect, 'Saul, Saul, why are you persecuting Me? It is hard for you to kick against the goads.' And I said, 'Who are You, Lord?' And the Lord said, 'I am Jesus whom you are persecuting. But get up and stand on your feet; for this purpose I have appeared to you, to appoint you a minister and a witness not only to the things which you have seen, but also to the things in which I will appear to you; rescuing you from the *Jewish* people and from the Gentiles, to whom I am sending you, to open their eyes so that they may turn from darkness to light and from the dominion of Satan to God, that they may receive forgiveness of sins and an inheritance among those who have been sanctified by faith in Me' (Acts 26:14–18; see Isaiah 35:5; Acts 21:40; 22:14).

WITNESS, FALSE (See LIE; LIES; VOWS; and WITNESS, TRUE)

Setting: Galilee. Jesus gives the crowd the meaning of His instruction about what defiles a man.

Peter said to Him, "Explain the parable to us." Jesus said, "Are you still lacking in understanding also? Do you not understand that everything that goes into the mouth passes into the stomach and is eliminated? But the things that proceed out of the mouth come from the heart, and those defile the man. For out of the heart come evil thoughts, murders, adulteries, fornications, thefts, false witness, slanders. These are the things which defile a man; but to eat with unwashed hands does not defile the man" (Matthew 15:15–20; cf. Mark 7:18–23; see Galatians 5:19–21).

Setting: Judea beyond the Jordan (Perea). Jesus shares with a rich, young ruler how righteous believers may have treasure in heaven.

And He said to him, "Why are you asking Me about what is good? There is *only* One who is good; but if you wish to enter into life, keep the commandments." *Then* he said to Him, 'Which ones?' And Jesus said, "YOU SHALL NOT COMMIT MURDER; YOU SHALL NOT COMMIT ADULTERY; YOU SHALL NOT STEAL; YOU SHALL NOT BEAR FALSE WITNESS; HONOR YOUR FATHER AND MOTHER; and YOU SHALL LOVE YOUR NEIGHBOR AS YOURSELF." The young man said to Him, "All these things I have kept; what am I still lacking?" Jesus said to him, "If you wish to complete go *and* sell your possessions and give to *the* poor, and you will have treasure in heaven; and come, follow Me" (Matthew 19:16–22, Jesus quotes from Exodus 20:13–15 and Leviticus 19:18; cf. Leviticus 18:5; Mark 10:17–21; Luke 10:25–28; 12:33; 18:18–24).

Setting: Judea beyond the Jordan (Perea). After demonstrating to His disciples the importance of little children, Jesus encounters a rich man seeking eternal life.

And Jesus said to him, "Why do you call Me good? No one is good except God alone. You know the commandments, 'DO NOT MURDER, DO NOT COMMIT ADULTERY, DO NOT STEAL, DO NOT BEAR FALSE WITNESS, Do not defraud, HONOR YOUR FATHER AND MOTHER.'" And he said to Him, "Teacher, I have kept all these things from my youth up." Looking at him, Jesus felt a love for him and said to him, "One thing you lack: go and sell all you possess and give to the poor, and you will have treasure in heaven; and come, follow Me" (Mark 10:18–21; Jesus quotes from Exodus 20:12–16; cf. Matthew 19:16–22; Luke 18:18–24; see Matthew 6:20).

Setting: Judea beyond the Jordan (Perea). After speaking of the importance of children, Jesus responds to a ruler's question about inheriting eternal life.

A ruler questioned Him, saying, "Good Teacher, what shall I do to inherit eternal life?" And Jesus said to him, "Why do you call Me good? No one is good except God alone. You know the commandments, 'DO NOT COMMIT ADULTERY, DO NOT MURDER, DO NOT STEAL, DO NOT BEAR FALSE WITNESS, HONOR YOUR FATHER AND MOTHER.'" And he said "All these things I have kept from *my* youth." When Jesus heard *this,* He said to him, "One thing you still lack; sell all that you possess and distribute it to the poor, and you shall have treasure in heaven; and come, follow Me" (Luke 18:18–22, Jesus quotes from Exodus 20:12–16; cf. Matthew 19:16–22; Mark 10:17–22; see Luke 10:25–28).

WITNESS, MY (Also see WITNESSES, MY)

Setting: On the island of Patmos (in the Aegean Sea about fifty miles southwest of Ephesus in modern Turkey). On the Lord's Day (Sunday), approximately fifty years after the Resurrection, the disciple John encounters the Lord Jesus Christ, who communicates a new revelation for the apostle to record for the church in Pergamum and to six other churches in Asia.

"And to the angel of the church in Pergamum write: The One who has the sharp two-edged sword says this: 'I know where you dwell, where Satan's throne is; and you hold fast My name, and did not deny My faith even in the days of Antipas, My witness, My faithful one, who was killed among you, where Satan dwells. But I have a few things against you, because you have there some who hold the teaching of Balaam, who kept teaching Balak to put a stumbling block before the sons of Israel, to eat things sacrificed to idols and to commit *acts of* immorality. So you also have some who in the same way hold the teaching of the Nicolaitans. Therefore repent; or else I am coming to you quickly, and I will make war against them with the sword of My mouth. He who has an ear, let him hear what the Spirit says to the churches. To him who overcomes, to him I will give *some* of the hidden manna, and I will give him a white stone, and a new name written on the stone which no one knows but he who receives it' (Revelation 2:12–17; see Numbers 25:1–3; Isaiah 62:2; Revelation 1:16; 2:5, 6, 16).

WITNESS, TRUE

Setting: On the island of Patmos (in the Aegean Sea about fifty miles southwest of Ephesus in modern Turkey). On the Lord's Day (Sunday), approximately fifty years after the Resurrection, the disciple John encounters the Lord Jesus Christ, who communicates a new revelation for the apostle to record for the church in Laodicea and to six other churches in Asia.

"To the angel of the church in Laodicea write: The Amen, the faithful and true Witness, the Beginning of the creation of God, says this: 'I know your deeds, that you are neither cold nor hot; I wish that you were cold or hot. So because you are lukewarm, and neither hot nor cold, I will spit you out of My mouth. Because you say, "I am rich, and have become wealthy, and have need of nothing," and you do not know that you are wretched and miserable and poor and blind and naked, I advise you to buy from Me gold refined by fire so that you may become rich, and white garments so that you may clothe yourself, and *that* the shame of your nakedness will not be revealed; and eye salve to anoint your eyes so that you may see. Those whom I love, I reprove and discipline; therefore be zealous and repent. Behold, I stand at the door and knock; if anyone hears My voice and opens the door, I will come in to him and will dine with him, and he with Me. He who overcomes, I will grant to him to sit down with Me on My throne, as I also overcame and sat down with My Father on His throne. He who has an ear, let him hear what the Spirit says to the churches'" (Revelation 3:14–22; see Proverb 3:12; Hosea 12:8; John 14:23; 16:33).

WITNESSES (WITNESSES, MY; and WITNESSES, THREE are separate entries; also see WITNESS)

Setting: On the way from Galilee to Jerusalem. After Jesus pronounces woes upon the Pharisees, a lawyer replies that His remarks are an insult to lawyers, too.

But He said, "Woe to you lawyers as well! For you weigh men down with burdens hard to bear, while you yourselves will not even touch the burdens with one of your fingers. Woe to you! For you build the tombs of the prophets, and *it was* your fathers *who* killed them. So you are witnesses and approve the deeds of your fathers; because it was they who killed them, and you build *their tombs*. For this reason also the wisdom of God said, 'I will send them prophets and apostles, and *some* of them they will kill and *some* they will persecute, so that the blood of all the prophets, shed since the foundation of the world, may be charged against this generation, from the blood of Abel to the blood of Zechariah, who was killed between the altar and the house *of God*; yes, I tell you, it shall be charged against this generation.' Woe to you lawyers! For you have taken away the key of knowledge; you yourselves did not enter, and you hindered those who were entering" (Luke 11:46–52; cf. Matthew 23:29–32; see 2 Chronicles 24:20, 21; Matthew 23:4, 13).

Setting: Jerusalem. After rising from the tomb on the third day after being crucified, and appearing to two of His followers on the road to Emmaus, Jesus gives instruction to His disciples (except Thomas) about His mission on earth and the promise of future power from God.

Now He said to them, "These are My words which I spoke to you while I was still with you, that all things which are written about Me in the Law of Moses and the Prophets and the Psalms must be fulfilled." Then He opened their minds to understand the Scriptures, and He said to them, "Thus it is written, that the Christ would suffer and rise again from the dead the third day, and that repentance for forgiveness of sins would be proclaimed in His name to all the nations, beginning from Jerusalem. You are witnesses of these things. And behold, I am sending forth the promise of My Father upon you; but you are to stay in the city until you are clothed with power from on high" (Luke 24:44–49; see Matthew 28:19, 20; Acts 1:8).

WITNESSES, MY (Also see WITNESS, MY)

Setting: Jerusalem. Luke, writing in Acts, presents quotes from Jesus' post-resurrection appearances, in which He responds to His disciples' question of whether He is about to restore the kingdom to Israel.

He said to them, "It is not for you to know times or epochs which the Father has fixed by His own authority; but you will receive power when the Holy Spirit has come upon you; and you shall be My witnesses both in Jerusalem, and in all Judea and Samaria, and even to the remotest part of the earth" (Acts 1:7, 8; see Luke 24:48, 49; Acts 2:1–4).

WITNESSES, THREE

Setting: Capernaum of Galilee. After conveying to His disciples the value of little ones, Jesus gives instruction about church discipline.

"If your brother sins, go and show him his fault in private; if he listens to you, you have won your brother. But if he does not listen *to you,* take one or two more with you, so that BY THE MOUTH OF TWO OR THREE WITNESSES EVERY FACT MAY BE CONFIRMED. If he refuses to listen to them, tell it to the church; and if he refuses to listen even to the church, let him be to you as a Gentile and a tax collector. Truly I say to you, whatever you bind of earth shall have been bound in heaven; and whatever you loose on earth shall have been loosed in heaven. Again, I say to you, that if two of you agree on earth about anything that they may ask, it shall be done for them by My Father who is in heaven. For there two or three have gathered together in My name, I am there in their midst" (Matthew 18:15–20. Jesus quotes from Deuteronomy 19:15; cf. Matthew 7:7; 16:19; see Leviticus 19:17; Matthew 28:20; 2 Thessalonians 3:6, 14).

WIVES (Also see WIFE; WOMAN; and WOMEN)

Setting: Judea beyond the Jordan (Perea). Jesus responds to the Pharisees' follow-up question in front of a large crowd about Moses' command regarding a certificate of divorce.

He said to them. "Because of your hardness of heart Moses permitted you to divorce your wives; but from the beginning it has not been this way. And I say to you, whoever divorces his wife, except for immorality, and marries another woman commits adultery" (Matthew 19:8, 9; cf. Deuteronomy 24:1–4; Matthew 5:32; 19:7; Mark 10:1–12; see Romans 7:2, 3; 1 Corinthians 7:10, 39).

WOE (Also see LEADERS, WOES TO THE RELIGIOUS)

Setting: Galilee. After performing miracles throughout the region, Jesus pronounces woes against those cities who have not repented.

"Woe to you, Chorazin! Woe to you, Bethsaida! For if the miracles had occurred in Tyre and Sidon which occurred in you, they would have repented long ago in sackcloth and ashes. Nevertheless I say to you, it will be more tolerable for Tyre and Sidon in *the* day of judgment than for you. And you, Capernaum, will not be exalted to heaven, will you? You will descend to Hades; for if the miracles had occurred in Sodom which occurred in you, it would have remained to this day. Nevertheless, I say to you that it will be more tolerable for the land of Sodom in *the* day of judgment, than for you" (Matthew 11:21–24; cf. Matthew 10:15; Luke 10:13–15).

Setting: Capernaum of Galilee. When His disciples ask about greatness in the kingdom of heaven, Jesus elaborates about stumbling blocks.

"Woe to the world because of *its* stumbling blocks! For it is inevitable that stumbling blocks come; but woe to that man through whom the stumbling block comes! If your hand or your foot causes you to stumble, cut if off and throw it from you; it is better for you to enter life crippled or lame, than to have two hands or two feet and be cast into the eternal fire. If your eye causes you to stumble, pluck it out and throw it from you. It is better for you to enter life with one eye, than to have two eyes and be cast into the fiery hell" (Matthew 18:7–9; cf. Matthew 5:29, 30; Mark 9:43–48; Luke 17:1).

Setting: The temple in Jerusalem. After the Jewish religious leaders test Him with questions, Jesus pronounces the first of eight woes upon them in front of the crowds and His disciples.

"But woe to you, scribes and Pharisees, hypocrites, because you shut off the kingdom of heaven from people; for you do not enter in yourselves, nor do you allow those who are entering to go in (Matthew 23:13; cf. Luke 11:52).

Setting: The temple in Jerusalem. After the Jewish religious leaders test Him with questions, Jesus pronounces the second of eight woes upon them in front of the crowds and His disciples.

["Woe to you, scribes and Pharisees, hypocrites, because you devour widows' houses, and for a pretense you make long prayers; therefore you will receive greater condemnation] (Matthew 23:14; cf. Mark 12:40; Luke 20:47).

Setting: The temple in Jerusalem. After the Jewish religious leaders test Him with questions, Jesus pronounces the third of eight woes upon them in front of the crowds and His disciples.

"Woe to you, scribes and Pharisees, hypocrites, because you travel around on sea and land to make one proselyte; and when he becomes one, you make him twice as much a son of hell as yourselves" (Matthew 23:15).

Setting: The temple in Jerusalem. After the Jewish religious leaders test Him with questions, Jesus pronounces the fourth of eight woes upon them in front of the crowds and His disciples.

"Woe to you, blind guides, who say, "Whoever swears by the temple, *that* is nothing; but whoever swears by the gold of the temple is obligated.' You fools and blind men! Which is more important, the gold or the temple that sanctified the gold? And, 'Whoever swears by the altar, *that* is nothing, but whoever swears by the offering on it, he is obligated.' You blind men, which is more important, the offering, or the altar that sanctifies the offering? Therefore, whoever swears by the altar, swears *both* by the altar and by everything on it. And whoever swears by the temple, swears *both* by the temple and by Him who dwells within it. And whoever swears by heaven, swears *both* by the throne of God and by Him who sits upon it" (Matthew 23:16–22; see Exodus 29:37; 1 Kings 8:13; Isaiah 66:1; Matthew 15:14).

Setting: The temple in Jerusalem. After the Jewish religious leaders test Him with questions, Jesus pronounces the fifth of eight woes upon them in front of the crowds and His disciples.

"Woe to you, scribes and Pharisees, hypocrites! For you tithe mint and dill and cummin, and have neglected the weightier provisions of the law: justice and mercy and faithfulness; but these are things you should have done without neglecting the others. You blind guides, who strain out a gnat and swallow a camel!" (Matthew 23:23, 24).

Setting: The temple in Jerusalem. After the Jewish religious leaders test Him with questions, Jesus pronounces the sixth of eight woes upon them in front of the crowds and His disciples.

"Woe to you, scribes and Pharisees, hypocrites! For you clean the outside of the cup and of the dish, but inside they are full of robbery and self-indulgence. You blind Pharisee, first clean the inside of the cup and of the dish, so that the outside of it may become clean also" (Matthew 23:25, 26; see Mark 7:4).

Setting: The temple in Jerusalem. After the Jewish religious leaders test Him with questions, Jesus pronounces the seventh of eight woes upon them in front of the crowds and His disciples.

"Woe to you, scribes and Pharisees, hypocrites! For you are like whitewashed tombs which on the outside appear beautiful, but inside they are full of dead men's bones and all uncleanness. So you, too, outwardly appear righteous to men, but inwardly you are full of hypocrisy and lawlessness" (Matthew 23:27, 28; cf. Luke 11:44).

Setting: The temple in Jerusalem. After the Jewish religious leaders test Him with questions, Jesus pronounces the eighth of eight woes upon them in front of the crowds and His disciples.

"Woe to you, scribes and Pharisees, hypocrites! For you build the tombs of the prophets and adorn the monuments of the righteous, and say, 'If we had been *living* in the days of our fathers, we would not have been partners with them in *shedding* the blood of the prophets.' So you testify against yourselves, that you are sons of those who murdered the prophets. Fill up, then, the measure *of the guilt* of you fathers. You serpents, you brood of vipers, how will you escape the sentence of hell? Therefore, behold, I am sending you prophets and wise men and scribes; some of them you will kill and crucify, and some of them you will scourge in your synagogues, and persecute from city to city, so that upon you may fall *the guilt of* all the righteous blood shed on earth, from the blood of righteous Abel to the blood of Zechariah, the son of Berechiah, whom you murdered between the temple and the altar. Truly I say to you, all these things will come upon this generation" (Matthew 23:29–36; cf. 2 Chronicles 24:21; Zechariah 1:1; Matthew 3:7; Luke 11:47–52; see Matthew 10:23).

Setting: The Mount of Olives, just east of Jerusalem. During His Olivet Discourse, Jesus answers His disciples' questions as to when the temple will be destroyed and Jerusalem overrun, along with the signs of His coming and the end of the age.

"Therefore when you see the ABOMINATION OF DESOLATION which was spoken of through Daniel the prophet, standing in the holy place (let the reader understand), then those who are in Judea must flee to the mountains. Whoever is on the housetop must not go down to get the things that are in his house. Whoever is in the field must not turn back to get his cloak. But woe to those who are pregnant and to those who are nursing babies in those days! But pray that your flight will not be in the winter, or on a Sabbath. For then there will be a great tribulation, such as has not occurred since the beginning of the world until now, nor ever will. Unless those days had been cut short, no life would have been saved; but for the sake of the elect those days will be cut short. Then if anyone says to you, 'Behold, here is the Christ,' or "There *He is*,' do not believe *him*. For false Christs and false prophets will arise and will show great signs and wonders, so as to mislead, if possible, even the elect. Behold, I have told you in advance. So if they say to you, 'Behold, He is in the wilderness,' do not go out, *or*, 'Behold, He is in the inner rooms,' do not believe *them*. For just as the lightning comes from the east and flashes even to the west, so will the coming of the Son of Man be. Wherever the corpse is, there the vultures will gather" (Matthew 24:15–28, Jesus quotes from Daniel 9:27; cf. Daniel 12:1; Mark 13:14–23; Luke 17:22–31; Luke 21:20–24; Luke 23:29; see John 4:48).

Setting: An upper room in Jerusalem. While celebrating the Passover meal, Jesus shocks His disciples with the revelation that one of them will soon betray Him to His enemies.

As they were eating, He said, "Truly I say to you that one of you will betray Me." Being deeply grieved, they each one began to say to Him, 'Surely not I, Lord?' And He answered, "He who dipped his hand with Me in the bowl is the one who will betray Me. The Son of Man *is to* go, just as it is written of Him; but woe to that man by whom the Son of Man is betrayed! It would have been good for that man if he had not been born." And Judas, who was betraying Him, said, 'Surely it is not I, Rabbi?' Jesus said to him, "You have said *it* yourself" (Matthew 26:21–25; cf. Mark 14:18–21; Luke 22:21, 23; John 13:21–30; see Psalm 41:9).

Setting: On the Mount of Olives, east of the temple in Jerusalem. After prophesying the temple's destruction, Jesus responds during His Olivet Discourse to questions from Peter, James, John, and Andrew about other future events.

"But when you see the ABOMINATION OF DESOLATION standing where it should not be (let the reader understand), then those who are in Judea must flee to the mountains. The one who is on the housetop must not go down, or go in to get anything out of his house; and the one who is in the field must not turn back to get his coat. But woe to those who are pregnant and to those who are nursing babies in those days! But pray that it may not happen in winter. For those days will be a *time of* tribulation such as has not occurred since the beginning of the creation which God created until now, and never will. Unless the Lord had shortened *those* days, no life would have been saved; but for the sake of the elect, whom He chose, He shortened the days. And then if anyone says to you, 'Behold, here is the Christ'; or, 'Behold, *He is* there'; do not believe *him*; for false Christs and false prophets will arise, and will show signs and wonders, in order to lead astray, if possible, the elect. But take heed; behold, I have told you everything in advance" (Mark 13:14–23; cf. Matthew 24:15–28; Luke 21:20–24; see Daniel 9:27; 12:1; Luke 17:31).

Setting: A borrowed upper room in Jerusalem. While Jesus and His twelve disciples are eating the Passover meal, the Lord states that one of them will betray Him.

As they were reclining *at the table* and eating, Jesus said, "Truly I say to you that one of you will betray Me—one who is eating with Me." They began to be grieved and to say to Him one by one, "Surely not I?" And He said to them, "*It is* one of the twelve, one who dips with Me in the bowl. For the Son of Man *is to* go just as it is written of Him; but woe to that man by whom the Son of Man is betrayed! *It would have been* good for that man if he had not been born" (Mark 14:18–21; cf. Matthew 26:21–24; Luke 22:21–23; John 13:21, 22).

Setting: Galilee. After selecting His twelve disciples, Jesus teaches the Beatitudes (part of the Sermon on the Mount) to those disciples and a great throng of people from Judea, Jerusalem, and the central coastal region of Tyre and Sidon.

"But woe to you who are rich, for you are receiving your comfort in full" (Luke 6:24).

Setting: Galilee. After selecting His twelve disciples, Jesus teaches the Beatitudes (part of the Sermon on the Mount) to those disciples and a great throng of people from Judea, Jerusalem, and the central coastal region of Tyre and Sidon.

"Woe to you who are well-fed now, for you shall be hungry. Woe *to you* who laugh now, for you shall mourn and weep" (Luke 6:25; cf. Matthew 5:4)

Setting: Galilee. After selecting His twelve disciples, Jesus teaches the Beatitudes (part of the Sermon on the Mount) to those disciples and a great throng of people from Judea, Jerusalem, and the central coastal region of Tyre and Sidon.

"Woe *to you* when all men speak well of you, for their fathers used to treat the false prophets in the same way" (Luke 6:26; see Matthew 7:15; 24:11, 24).

Setting: On the way from Galilee to Jerusalem. The Lord pronounces woes upon cities who reject the gospel, as He appoints seventy followers and sends them out in pairs to every place He Himself will soon visit.

"Woe to you, Chorazin! Woe to you, Bethsaida! For if the miracles had been performed in Tyre and Sidon which occurred in you, they would have repented long ago, sitting in sackcloth and ashes. But it will be more tolerable for Tyre and Sidon in the judgment than for you. And you, Capernaum, will not be exalted to heaven, will you? You will be brought down to Hades! The one who listens to you listens to Me, and the one who rejects you rejects Me; and he who rejects Me rejects the One who sent Me" (Luke 10:13–16; cf. Matthew 11:21–23; see Matthew 10:40; Luke 10:1).

Setting: On the way from Galilee to Jerusalem. After speaking of how a lamp illuminates, the Lord has lunch with a Pharisee, who is surprised He doesn't wash before eating.

But the Lord said to him, "Now you Pharisees clean the outside of the cup and of the platter; but inside of you, you are full of robbery and wickedness. You foolish ones, did not He who made the outside make the inside also? But give that which is within as charity, and then all things are clean for you. But woe to you Pharisees! You pay tithe of mint and rue and every *kind of* garden herb, and *yet* disregard justice and the love of God; but these are the things you should have done without neglecting the others. Woe to you Pharisees! For you love the chief seats in the synagogues and the respectful greetings in the market places. Woe to you! For you are like concealed tombs, and the people who walk over *them* are unaware *of it*" (Luke 11:39–44; cf. Matthew 23:6, 7, 23–27; see Matthew 15:2; Titus 1:15).

Setting: On the way from Galilee to Jerusalem. After Jesus pronounces woes upon the Pharisees, a lawyer replies that His remarks are an insult to lawyers, too.

But He said, "Woe to you lawyers as well! For you weigh men down with burdens hard to bear, while you yourselves will not even touch the burdens with one of your fingers. Woe to you! For you build the tombs of the prophets, and *it was* your fathers *who* killed them. So you are witnesses and approve the deeds of your fathers; because it was they who killed them, and you build *their tombs*. For this reason also the wisdom of God said, 'I will send them prophets and apostles, and *some* of them they will kill and *some* they will persecute, so that the blood of all the prophets, shed since the foundation of the world, may be charged against this generation, from the blood of Abel to the blood of Zechariah, who was killed between the altar and the house *of God*; yes, I tell you, it shall be charged against this generation.' Woe to you lawyers! For you have taken away the key of knowledge; you yourselves did not enter, and you hindered those who were entering" (Luke 11:46–52; cf. Matthew 23:29–32; see 2 Chronicles 24:20, 21; Matthew 23:4, 13).

Setting: On the way from Galilee to Jerusalem. After conveying the story of the rich man and Lazarus, the Lord gives His disciples instruction on forgiveness.

He said to His disciples, "It is inevitable that stumbling blocks come, but woe to him through whom they come! It would be better for him if a millstone were hung around his neck and he were thrown into the sea, than that he would cause one of these little ones to stumble. Be on your guard! If your brother sins, rebuke him; and if he repents, forgive him. And if he sins against you seven times a day, and returns to you seven times, saying, 'I repent,' forgive him" (Luke 17:1–4; see Matthew 18:5–7, 15, 21, 22).

Setting: On the Mount of Olives, east of the temple in Jerusalem. After ministering in the temple a few days before His crucifixion, and giving the disciples more details regarding future events, Jesus elaborates during His Olivet Discourse about things to come.

"But when you see Jerusalem surrounded by armies, then recognize that her desolation is near. Then those who are in Judea must flee to the mountains, and those who are in the midst of the city must leave, and those who are in the country must not enter the city; because these are days of vengeance, so that all things which are written will be fulfilled. Woe to those who are pregnant and to those who are nursing babies in those days; for there will be a great distress upon the land and wrath to this people; and they will fall by the edge of the sword, and will be led captive into all the nations; and Jerusalem will be trampled under foot by the Gentiles until the times of the Gentiles are fulfilled" (Luke 21:20–24; see Matthew 24:15–18; Mark 13:14–16; Luke 19:43).

Setting: An upper room in Jerusalem. During the Feast of Unleavened Bread (Passover) just before His crucifixion, while celebrating the Passover meal with His disciples, Jesus institutes the Lord's Supper.

And when He had taken a cup *and* given thanks, He said, "Take this and share it among yourselves; for I say to you, I will not drink of the fruit of the vine from now on until the kingdom of God comes." And when he had taken *some* bread and given thanks, He broke it and gave it to them, saying, "This is My body which is given for you; do this in remembrance of Me." And in the same way *He took* the cup after they had eaten, saying, "This cup which is poured out for you is the new covenant in My blood. But behold, the hand of the one betraying Me is with Mine on the table. For indeed, the Son of Man is going as it has been determined; but woe to that man by whom He is betrayed!" (Luke 22:17–22; cf. Matthew 26:26–29; Mark 14:22–25; 1 Corinthians 11:23–26; see Psalm 41:9; Luke 14:15; 1 Corinthians 10:16).

WOES TO THE RELIGIOUS LEADERS (Listed under LEADERS, WOES TO THE RELIGIOUS; also see CONDEMNATION; and JUDGMENT)

WOLF (Also see WOLVES)

Setting: Jerusalem. Following the Pharisees' interrogation and dismissal of the formerly blind man Jesus healed on the Sabbath, the Lord conveys the Parable of the Good Shepherd to the Pharisees, using figures of speech they do not understand.

So Jesus said to them again, "Truly, truly, I say to you, I am the door of the sheep. All who came before Me are thieves and robbers, but the sheep did not hear them. I am the door; if anyone enters through Me, he will be saved, and will go in and out and find pasture. The thief comes only to steal and kill and destroy; I came that they may have life, and have *it* abundantly. I am the good shepherd; the good shepherd lays down His life for the sheep. He who is a hired hand, and not a shepherd, who is not the owner of the sheep, sees the wolf coming, and leaves the sheep and flees, and the wolf snatches them and scatters *them. He flees* because he is a hired hand and is not concerned about the sheep. I am the good shepherd, and I know My own and My own know Me, even as the Father knows Me and I know the Father; and I lay down My life for the sheep. I have other sheep, which are not of this fold; I must bring them also, and they will hear My voice; and they will become one flock *with* one shepherd. For this reason the Father loves Me, because I lay down My life so that I may take it again. No one has taken it away from Me, but I lay it down on My own initiative. I have authority to take it up again. This commandment I received from My Father" (John 10:7–18; see Isaiah 40:11; 56:8; Jeremiah 23:1; Matthew 11:27).

WOLVES (Also see WOLF)

Setting: Galilee. During the early part of His ministry, Jesus preaches the Sermon on the Mount to His disciples and the multitudes.

"Beware of the false prophets, who come to you in sheep's clothing, but inwardly are ravenous wolves. You will know them by their fruits. Grapes are not gathered from *bushes* nor figs from thistles, are they? So every good tree bears good fruit, but the bad tree bears bad fruit. A good tree cannot produce bad fruit, nor can a bad tree produce good fruit. Every tree that does not bear good fruit is cut down and thrown into the fire. So then, you will know them by their fruits" (Matthew 7:15–20; cf. Matthew 3:10; Matthew 12:33, 35; 24:11, 24; Luke 6:43, 44).

Setting: Galilee. After His disciples observe His ministry, Jesus summons and specifically instructs them about the upcoming hardships of their ministry to the people of Israel.

"Behold, I send you out as sheep in the midst of wolves; so be shrewd as serpents and innocent as doves. But beware of men, for they will hand you over to *the* courts and scourge you in their synagogues; and you will even be brought before governors and kings for My sake, as a testimony to them and to the Gentiles. But when they hand you over, do not worry about how or what you are to say; for it will be given you in that hour what you are to say. For it is not you who speak, but *it* is the Spirit of your Father who speaks in you" (Matthew 10:16–20; cf. Luke 10:3).

Setting: On the way from Galilee to Jerusalem. The Lord appoints seventy followers and sends them out in pairs to every place He Himself will soon visit.

And He was saying to them, "The harvest is plentiful, but the laborers are few; therefore beseech the Lord of the harvest to send out laborers into His harvest. Go; behold, I send you out as lambs in the midst of wolves. Carry no money belt, no bag, no shoes; and greet no one on the way. Whatever house you enter, first say, 'Peace be to this house.' If a man of peace is there, your peace will rest on him; but if not, it will return to you. Stay in that house, eating and drinking what they give you; for the laborer is worthy of his wages. Do not keep moving from house to house. Whatever city you enter and they receive you, eat what is set before you; and heal those in it who are sick, and say to them, 'The kingdom of God has come near to you.' But whatever city you enter and they do not receive you, go out into its streets and say, 'Even the dust of your city which clings to our feet we wipe off *in protest* against you; yet be sure of this, that the kingdom of God has come near.' I say to you, it will be more tolerable in that day for Sodom than for that city" (Luke 10:2–12; see Genesis 19:24–28; Matthew 9:37, 38, 10:9–14, 16; 1 Corinthians 10:27).

WOLVES, RAVENOUS (See WOLVES)

WOMAN (Also see FEMALE; WIFE; WIVES; and WOMEN)

Setting: Galilee. During the early part of His ministry, Jesus preaches the Sermon on the Mount to His disciples and the multitudes.

"You have heard that it was said, 'YOU SHALL NOT COMMIT ADULTERY'; but I say to you that everyone who looks at a woman with lust for her has already committed adultery with her in his heart" (Matthew 5:27, 28, Jesus quotes from Exodus 20:14; see 2 Samuel 11:2–5).

Setting: Galilee. During the early part of His ministry, Jesus preaches the Sermon on the Mount to His disciples and the multitudes.

"It was said, 'WHOEVER SENDS HIS WIFE AWAY, LET HIM GIVE HER A CERTIFICATE OF DIVORCE'; but I say to you that everyone who divorces his wife, except for *the* reason of unchastity, makes her commit adultery; and whoever marries a divorced woman commits adultery" (Matthew 5:31, 32, Jesus quotes from Deuteronomy 24: 1, 3; cf. Matthew 19:9; see Romans 7:2, 3; 1 Corinthians 7:10, 39).

Setting: Capernaum, near the Sea of Galilee. Jesus heals a woman suffering with internal bleeding for twelve years.

But Jesus turning and seeing her said, "Daughter, take courage; your faith has made you well." At once the woman was made well (Matthew 9:22; cf. Mark 5:34; Luke 8:48).

Setting: By the Sea of Galilee. Because the religious leaders are rejecting His message, Jesus continues teaching the crowds with the Parable of the Leaven.

He spoke another parable to them, "The kingdom of heaven is like leaven, which a woman took and hid in three pecks of flour until it was all leavened" (Matthew 13:33).

Setting: The district of Tyre and Sidon. A Canaanite woman appeals to Jesus to heal her demon-possessed daughter.

But He answered and said, "I was sent only to the lost sheep of the house of Israel." But she came and *began* to bow down before Him, saying, "Lord, help me!" And He answered and said, "It is not good to take the children's bread and throw it to the dogs." But she said, "Yes, Lord; but even the dogs feed from the crumbs which fall from their masters' table." Then Jesus said to her, "O woman, your faith is great; it shall be done for you as you wish." And her daughter was healed at once (Matthew 15:24–28; cf. Mark 7: 24–30; see Matthew 9:22; 10:5, 6).

Setting: Judea beyond the Jordan (Perea). Jesus responds to the Pharisees' follow-up question in front of a large crowd about Moses' command regarding a certificate of divorce.

He said to them. "Because of your hardness of heart Moses permitted you to divorce your wives; but from the beginning it has not been this way. And I say to you, whoever divorces his wife, except for immorality, and marries another woman commits adultery" (Matthew 19:8, 9; cf. Deuteronomy 24:1–4; Matthew 5:32; Mark 10:1–12; see Romans 7:2, 3; 1 Corinthians 7:10, 39).

Setting: The home of Simon the leper in Bethany. Jesus rebukes His disciples after they criticize a woman for pouring a costly vial of perfume on His head in preparation for His burial.

But Jesus, aware of this, said to them, "Why do you bother the woman? For she has done a good deed to Me. For you always have the poor with you; but you do not always have Me. For when she poured this perfume on My body, she did it to prepare Me for burial. Truly I say to you, wherever this gospel is preached in the whole world, what this woman has done will also be spoken of in memory of her" (Matthew 26:10–13; cf. Mark 14:3–9; Luke 7:37–39; John 12:2–8; see Deuteronomy 15:11).

Setting: Judea beyond the Jordan (Perea). Jesus teaches the crowds gathered around Him about divorce after the Pharisees test and question Him on the subject.

And He answered and said to them, "What did Moses command you?" They said, "Moses permitted a *man* TO WRITE A CERTIFICATE OF DIVORCE AND SEND *her* AWAY." But Jesus said to them, "Because of your hardness of heart he wrote you this commandment. But from the beginning of creation, *God* MADE THEM MALE AND FEMALE. FOR THIS REASON A MAN SHALL LEAVE HIS FATHER AND MOTHER, AND THE TWO SHALL BECOME ONE FLESH; so they are no longer two, but one flesh. What therefore God has joined together, let no man separate. In the house the disciples *began* questioning Him about this again. And He said to them, "Whoever divorces his wife and marries another woman commits adultery against her; and if she herself divorces her husband and marries another man, she is committing adultery" (Mark 10:3–12, Jesus quotes from Genesis 1:27; 2:24; cf. Matthew 19:1–9; see Deuteronomy 24:1–3; Matthew 5:32; see Romans 7:2, 3; 1 Corinthians 7:10, 11, 13, 39; 1 Timothy 2:14).

Setting: The home of Simon the leper in Bethany. Two days before the Feast of Unleavened Bread (Passover), Jesus commends a woman who anoints His head with costly perfume, which some there think should have been sold and the proceeds given to the poor.

But Jesus said, "Let her alone; why do you bother her? She has done a good deed to Me. For you always have the poor with you, and whenever you wish you can do good to them; but you do not always have Me. She has done what she could; she has anointed My body beforehand for the burial. Truly I say to you, wherever the gospel is preached in the whole world, what this woman has done will also be spoken of in memory of her" (Mark 14:6–9; cf. Matthew 26:6–13; John 12:2–8; see Deuteronomy 15:11).

Setting: The synagogue in Jesus' hometown of Nazareth in Galilee. At the beginning of His public ministry, Jesus comments to the congregation after reading from the book of the prophet Isaiah on the Sabbath.

And He said to them, "No doubt you will quote this proverb to Me, 'Physician, heal yourself! Whatever we heard was done at Capernaum, do here in your hometown as well.'" And He said, "Truly I say to you, no prophet is welcome in his hometown. But I say to you in truth, there were many widows in Israel in the days of Elijah, when the sky was shut up for three years and six months, when a great famine came over all the land; and yet Elijah was sent to none of them, but only to Zarephath, *in the land* of Sidon, to a woman who was a widow. And there were many lepers in Israel in the time of Elisha the prophet; and none of them was cleansed, but only Naaman the Syrian" (Luke 4:23–27; Jesus refers to 1 Kings 17:1, 9; 2 Kings 5:1–14; see Matthew 13:53–58).

Setting: Galilee. After Jesus praises John the Baptist to the crowds, Simon, a Pharisee, invites the Lord to dinner. A sinful woman anoints His feet with perfume, prompting Him to instruct His host about forgiveness.

Turning toward the woman, He said to Simon, "Do you see this woman? I entered your house; you gave Me no water for My feet, but she has wet My feet with her tears and wiped them with her hair. You gave Me no kiss; but she, since the time I came in, has not ceased to kiss My feet. You did not anoint My head with oil, but she anointed My feet with perfume. For this reason I say to you, her sins, which are many, have been forgiven, for she loved much; but he who is forgiven little, loves little." The He said to her, "Your sins have been forgiven." Those who were reclining *at the table* with Him began to say to themselves, "Who is this *man* who even forgives sins?" And He said to the woman, "Your faith has saved you; go in peace" (Luke 7:44–50; see Matthew 9:2; Mark 5:34; Luke 5:21).

Setting: On the way from Galilee to Jerusalem. Jesus teaches in the synagogue on the Sabbath, where a woman who has been sick for eighteen years seeks healing.

When Jesus saw her, He called her over and said to her, "Woman, you are freed from your sickness" (Luke 13:12).

Setting: On the way from Galilee to Jerusalem. Jesus responds to a synagogue official's anger over His healing of a woman, sick for eighteen years, in the synagogue on the Sabbath.

But the Lord answered him and said, "You hypocrites, does not each of you on the Sabbath untie his ox or his donkey from the stall and lead him away to water *him?* And this woman, a daughter of Abraham as she is, whom Satan has bound for eighteen long years, should she not have been released from this bond on the Sabbath day?" (Luke 13:15, 16; see Luke 14:5).

Setting: On the way from Galilee to Jerusalem. After responding to a synagogue official's anger over His healing of a woman, sick for eighteen years, in the synagogue on the Sabbath, Jesus conveys the Parable of the Mustard Seed and the Parable of the Leaven.

So He was saying, "What is the kingdom of God like, and to what shall I compare it? It is like a mustard seed which a man took and threw into his own garden; and it grew and became a tree, and THE BIRDS OF THE AIR NESTED IN ITS BRANCHES." And again He said, "To what shall I compare the kingdom of God? It is like leaven, which a woman took and hid in three pecks of flour until it was all leavened" (Luke 13:18–21, Jesus quotes from Ezekiel 17:23; cf. Matthew 13:31–34; Mark 4:30–32).

Setting: On the way from Galilee to Jerusalem. Jesus conveys the principles of the lost sheep and the lost coin because the Pharisees and scribes complain He associates with tax collectors and sinners.

"So He told them this parable, saying, "What man among you, if he has a hundred sheep and has lost one of them, does not leave the ninety-nine in the open pasture and go after the one which is lost until he finds it? When he has found it, he lays it on his shoulders, rejoicing. And when he comes home, he calls together his friends and his neighbors, saying to them, 'Rejoice with me, for I have found my sheep which was lost!' I tell you that in the same way, there will be more joy in heaven over one sinner who repents than over ninety-nine righteous persons who need no repentance. Or what woman, if she has ten silver coins and loses one coin, does not light a lamp and sweep the house and search carefully until she finds it? When she has found it, she calls together her friends and neighbors, saying, 'Rejoice with me, for I have found the coin which I had lost!' In the same way, I tell you, there is joy in the presence of the angels of God over one sinner who repents" (Luke 15:3–10; cf. Matthew 18:12-14; see Matthew 9:11-13).

Setting: On the way from Galilee to Jerusalem. After telling His disciples of His second coming, Jesus instructs them about persistence in prayer.

Now He was telling them a parable to show that at all times they ought to pray and not to lose heart, saying, "In a certain city there was a judge who did not fear God and did not respect man. There was a widow in that city, and she kept coming to him, saying, 'Give me legal protection from my opponent.' For a while he was unwilling; but afterward he said to himself, 'Even though I do not fear God nor respect man, yet because this woman bothers me, I will give her legal protection, otherwise by continually coming she will wear me out.'" And the Lord said, "Hear what the unrighteous judge said; now, will not God bring about justice for His elect who cry to Him day and night, and will He delay long over them? I tell you that He will bring about justice for them quickly. However, when the Son of Man comes, will He find faith on the earth?" (Luke 18:1–8; see Luke 11:5–10).

Setting: Cana of Galilee. On the third day of His public ministry, after choosing Andrew, Peter, Philip, and Nathanael to be His disciples, Jesus attends a wedding. His mother prompts Him to perform His first miracle, that of turning water into wine.

And Jesus said to her, "Woman, what does that have to do with us? My hour has not yet come" (John 2:4).

Setting: Sychar in Samaria, on the way to Galilee. Jesus interacts with a Samaritan woman at Jacob's well, while the disciples are buying food.

Jesus said to her, "Woman, believe Me, an hour is coming when neither in this mountain nor in Jerusalem will you worship the Father. You worship what you do not know; we worship what we know, for salvation is from the Jews. But an hour is coming, and now is, when the true worshipers will worship the Father in spirit and truth; for such people the Father seeks to be His worshipers. God is spirit, and those who worship Him must worship in spirit and truth" (John 4:21–24; see Isaiah 2:3; Philippians 3:3).

Setting: The temple in Jerusalem. Following the Feast of Booths, Jesus retires to the Mount of Olives, and returns the next day to teach. The scribes and Pharisees set a woman caught in adultery before Him to test whether He will follow Moses' command to stone her.

Straightening up, Jesus said to her, "Woman, where are they? Did no one condemn you?" She said, "No one, Lord." And Jesus said, "I do not condemn you either. Go. From now on sin no more" (John 8:10, 11; see John 3:17).

Setting: Jerusalem. Before the Passover, after warning His disciples of the persecution they will face after His departure to heaven, empathizing with their sadness over His prophecies, Jesus gives them the hope for the future.

"A little while, and you will no longer see Me; and again a little while, and you will see Me." *Some* of His disciples then said to one another, "What is this thing He is telling us, 'A little while, and you will not see Me; and again a little while, and you will see Me'; and, 'because I go to the Father'?" So they were saying, "What is this that He says, 'A little while'? We do not know what He is talking about." Jesus knew that they wished to question Him, and He said to them, "Are you deliberating together about this, that I said, 'A little while, and you will not see Me, and again a little while, and you will see Me'? Truly, truly, I say to you, that you will weep and lament, but the world will rejoice; you will grieve, but your grief will be turned into joy. Whenever a woman is in labor she has pain, because her hour has come; but when she gives birth to the child, she no longer remembers the anguish because of the joy that a child has been born into the world. Therefore you too have grief now; but I will see you again, and your heart will rejoice, and no one *will* take your joy away from you" (John 16:16–22; see Mark 9:32; Luke 23:27; John 14:18–24; 20:20).

Setting: On the Place of the Skull (Golgotha), just outside Jerusalem. While being crucified, Jesus unselfishly asks His disciple John to care for His mother, Mary.

When Jesus saw His mother, and the disciple whom He loved standing nearby, He said to His mother, "Woman, behold, your son!" Then He said to the disciple, "Behold, your mother!" From that hour the disciple took her into his own *household* (John 19:26, 27).

Setting: Jerusalem. The risen Jesus first appears to Mary Magdalene after she tells Simon Peter and John about the empty tomb where Jesus had been the day before the Sabbath, after dying on the cross for the sins of the world.

Jesus said to her, "Woman, why are you weeping? Whom are you seeking?" Supposing Him to be the gardener, she said to Him, "Sir, if you have carried Him away, tell me where you have laid Him, and I will take Him away." Jesus said to her, "Mary!" She turned and said to Him in Hebrew "Rabboni!" (which means, Teacher). Jesus said to her, "Stop clinging to Me, for I have not yet ascended to the Father; but go to My brethren and say to them, 'I ascend to My Father and your Father, and My God and Your God'" (John 20:15–17; see Mark 16:9–11; John 7:33; 19:31–42).

Setting: On the island of Patmos (in the Aegean Sea about fifty miles southwest of Ephesus in modern Turkey). On the Lord's Day (Sunday), approximately fifty years after the Resurrection, the disciple John encounters the Lord Jesus Christ, who communicates a new revelation for the apostle to record for the church in Thyatira and to six other churches in Asia.

"And to the angel of the church in Thyatira write: The Son of God, who has eyes like a flame of fire, and His feet are like burnished bronze, says this: 'I know your deeds, and your love and faith and service and perseverance, and that your deeds of late are greater than at first. But I have *this* against you, that you tolerate the woman Jezebel, who calls herself a prophetess, and she teaches and leads My bond-servants astray so that they commit *acts of* immorality and eat things sacrificed to idols. I gave her time to repent, and she does not want to repent of her immorality. Behold, I will throw her on a bed *of sickness,* and those who commit adultery with her into great tribulation, unless they repent of her deeds. And I will kill her children with pestilence, and all the churches will know that I am He who searches the minds and hearts; and I will give to each one of you according to your deeds. But I say to you, the rest who are in Thyatira, who do not hold this teaching, who have not known the deep things of Satan, as they call them—I place no other burden on you. Nevertheless what you have, hold fast until I come. He who overcomes, and he who keeps My deeds until the end, TO HIM I WILL GIVE AUTHORITY OVER THE NATIONS; AND HE SHALL RULE THEM WITH A ROD OF IRON, AS THE VESSELS OF THE POTTER ARE BROKEN TO PIECES, as I also have received *authority* from My Father; and I will give him the morning star. He who has an ear, let him hear what the Spirit says to the churches' (Revelation 2:18–29; Jesus quotes from Psalm 2:8, 9; Isaiah 30:14; see 1 Kings 16:31; Psalm 7:9; Romans 2:5; 1 Corinthians 2:10; 2 Peter 3:9; Revelation 1:14; 2:7; 3:11; 17:1–20).

WOMB (See WOMB, MOTHER'S)

WOMB, MOTHER'S (also see WOMBS)

Setting: Judea beyond the Jordan (Perea). After responding to the Pharisees' question about Moses' command regarding a certificate of divorce, Jesus answers the disciples' private question.

But He said to them, "Not all men *can* accept this statement, but *only* those to whom it has been given. For there are eunuchs who were born that way from their mother's womb; and there are eunuchs who were made eunuchs by men; and there are *also* eunuchs who made themselves eunuchs for the sake of the kingdom of heaven. He who is able to accept *this,* let him accept *it*" (Matthew 19:11, 12; cf. 1 Corinthians 7:7).

WOMBS (Also see WOMB)

Setting: Jerusalem. After being arrested, and appearing before the Council of Elders (Sanhedrin), Pilate (Roman governor of Judea), Herod Antipas (tetrarch of Galilee and Perea), and Pilate a second time (when the ruler bows to the crowd's pressure and grants that Jesus be crucified), the Lord prophesies to the women mourning Him regarding the coming judgment of Jerusalem.

But Jesus turning to them said, "Daughters of Jerusalem, stop weeping for Me, but weep for yourselves and for your children. For behold, the days are coming when they will say, 'Blessed are the barren, and the wombs that never bore, and the breasts that never nursed.' Then they will begin TO SAY TO THE MOUNTAINS, 'FALL ON US,' AND TO THE HILLS, 'COVER US.' For it they do these things when the tree is green, what will happen when it is dry?" (Luke 23:28–31, Jesus quotes from Hosea 10:8; see Matthew 24:19).

WOMEN (WOMEN, TWO is a separate entry; also see FEMALE; WIFE; WIVES; and WOMAN)

Setting: Galilee. While speaking to the crowds, Jesus pays tribute to the ministry of John the Baptist, but emphasizes that the one who is least in the kingdom of heaven is greater than John.

As these men were going *away,* Jesus began to speak to the crowds about John, "What did you go out into the wilderness to see? A reed shaken by the wind? But what did you go out to see? A man dressed in soft *clothing?* Those who wear soft *clothing* are in kings' palaces! But what did you go out to see? A prophet? Yes, I tell you, and the one who is more than a prophet. This is the one about whom it is written, 'BEHOLD, I SEND MY MESSENGER AHEAD OF YOU, WHO WILL PREPARE YOUR WAY BEFORE YOU.' Truly, I say to you, among those born of women there has not arisen *anyone* greater than John the Baptist! Yet the one who is least in the kingdom of heaven is greater than he. From the days of John the Baptist until now the kingdom of heaven suffers violence, and violent men take it by force. For all the prophets and the Law prophesied until John. And, if you are willing to accept *it,* John himself is Elijah who was to come. He who has ears to hear, let him hear" (Matthew 11:7–15, Jesus quotes from Malachi 3:1; cf. Malachi 4:5; Luke 7:24–28; 16:16; see Matthew 14:5).

Setting: Galilee. After Jesus responds to the disciples of John the Baptist about whether He is the promised Messiah, the Lord speaks to the crowds about John.

When the messengers of John had left, He began to speak to the crowds about John, "What did you go out into the wilderness to see? A reed shaken by the wind? But what did you go out to see? A man dressed in soft clothing? Those who are splendidly clothed and live in luxury are *found* in royal palaces! But what did you go out to see? A prophet? Yes, I say to you, and one who is more than a prophet. This is the one about whom it is written, 'BEHOLD, I SEND MY MESSENGER AHEAD OF YOU, WHO WILL PREPARE YOUR WAY BEFORE YOU.' I say to you, among those born of women there is no one greater than John; yet he who is least in the kingdom of God is greater than he" (Luke 7:24–28, Jesus quotes from Malachi 3:1; cf. Matthew 11:7–11).

Setting: On the way from Galilee to Jerusalem. When Jesus uses a parable to challenge the crowd and His disciples to be ready for His return, Peter asks whom He is addressing.

And the Lord said, "Who then is the faithful and sensible steward, whom his master will put in charge of his servants, to give them their rations at the proper time? Blessed is that slave whom his master finds so doing when he comes. Truly I say to you that he will put him in charge of all his possessions. But if that slave says in his heart, 'My master will be a long time in coming,' and begins to beat the slaves, *both* men and women, and to eat and drink and get drunk; the master of that slave will come on a day when he does not expect *him* and at an hour he does not know, and will cut him in pieces, and assign him a place with the unbelievers. And that slave who knew his master's will and did not get ready or act in accord with his will, will receive many lashes, but the one who did know *it*, and committed deeds worthy of flogging, will receive but few. From everyone who has been given much, much will be required; and to whom they entrusted much, of him they will ask all the more" (Luke 12:42–48; cf. Matthew 24:45–51; see Leviticus 5:17).

WOMEN, TWO (Also see WOMEN)

Setting: On the Mount of Olives, just east of Jerusalem. During His Olivet Discourse, after answering His disciples' questions as to when the temple will be destroyed and Jerusalem overrun, along with the signs of His coming and the end of the age, Jesus teaches them the Parable of the Fig Tree.

"Now learn the parable from the fig tree: when its branch has already become tender and puts forth its leaves, you know that summer is near; so, you too, when you see all these things, recognize that He is near, *right* at the door. Truly, I say to you, this generation will not pass away until all these things take place. Heaven and earth will pass away, but My words will not pass away. But of that day and hour no one knows, not even the angels of heaven, nor the Son, but the Father alone. For the coming of the Son of Man will be just like the days of Noah. For as in those days before the flood they were eating and drinking, marrying and giving in marriage, until the day that Noah entered the ark, and they did not understand until the flood came and took them all away; so will the coming of the Son of Man be. Then there will be two men in the field; one will be taken and one will be left. Two women *will be* grinding at the mill; one will be taken and one will be left" (Matthew 24:32–41; cf. Mark 13:28–32; Luke 17:34–36; 21:28–33; see Genesis 6:5; 7:7; Matthew 5:18; 10:23; James 5:9).

Setting: On the way from Galilee to Jerusalem. After the Pharisees question Him about the coming of the kingdom of God, Jesus tells His disciples of His second coming.

And He said to the disciples, "The days will come when you will long to see one of the days of the Son of Man, and you will not see it. They will say to you, 'Look there! Look here!' Do not go away, and do not run after *them*. For just like the lightning, when it flashes out of one part of the sky, shines to the other part of the sky, so will the Son of Man be in His day. But first He must suffer many things and be rejected by this generation. And just as it happened in the days of Noah, so it will be also in the days of the Son of Man: they were eating, they were drinking, they were marrying, they were being given in marriage, until the day that Noah entered the ark, and the flood came and destroyed them all. It was the same as happened in the days of Lot: they were eating, they were drinking, they were buying, they were selling, they were planting, they were building; but on the day that Lot went out from Sodom it rained fire and brimstone from heaven and destroyed them all. It will be just the same on the day that the Son of Man is revealed. On that day, the one who is on the housetop and whose goods are in the house must not go down to take them out; and likewise the one who is in the field must not turn back. Remember Lot's wife. Whoever seeks to keep his life will lose it, and whoever loses *his life* will preserve it. I tell you, on that night there will be two in one bed; one will be taken and the other will be left. There will be two women grinding at the same place; one will be taken and the other will be left. [Two men will be in the field; one will be taken and the other will be left."] And answering they said to Him, "Where, Lord?" And He said to them, "Where the body *is*, there also the vultures will be gathered" (Luke 17:22–37; see Genesis 19; Matthew 10:39; 16:21, 27; 24:17–28, 37–41).

WONDERS, SIGNS AND (See SIGNS AND WONDERS)

WORD (Specifics such as WORD, HIS; WORD, MY; WORD, YOUR; and WORD OF GOD are separate entries; also see WORDS)

Setting: Judea, near the Jordan River. Following His baptism, and before He begins His public ministry, Jesus is led by the Spirit into the wilderness to be tempted by Satan for forty days.

But He answered and said, "It is written, 'MAN SHALL NOT LIVE ON BREAD ALONE, BUT ON EVERY WORD THAT PROCEEDS OUT OF THE MOUTH OF GOD'" (Matthew 4:4, Jesus quotes from Deuteronomy 8:3; cf. Luke 4:4).

Setting: Galilee. After Jesus heals a blind, mute, demon-possessed man, the Pharisees accuse Him in front of crowds of being a worker of Satan. The Lord warns them about the unpardonable sin.

"He who is not with Me is against Me; and he who does not gather with Me scatters. Therefore I say to you, any sin and blasphemy shall be forgiven people, but blasphemy against the Spirit shall not be forgiven. Whoever speaks a word against the Son of Man, it shall be forgiven him; but whoever speaks against the Holy Spirit, it shall not be forgiven him, either in this age or in the *age* to come" (Matthew 12:30–32; cf. Luke 12:10; see Mark 9:40).

Setting: By the Sea of Galilee. With the religious leaders rejecting His message, Jesus begins to teach in parables, and gives His disciples the meaning of the Parable of the Sower.

"Hear then the parable of the sower. When anyone hears the word of the kingdom and does not understand it, the evil *one* comes and snatches away what has been sown in his heart. This is the one on whom seed was sown beside the road. The one on whom seed was sown on the rocky places, this is the man who hears the word and immediately receives it with joy; yet he has no *firm* root in himself, but is *only* temporary, and when affliction or persecution arises because of the word, immediately he falls away. And the one on whom seed was sown among the thorns, this is the man who hears the word, and the worry of the world and the deceitfulness of wealth choke the word, and it becomes unfruitful. And the one on whom seed was sown on the good soil, this is the man who hears the word and understands it; who indeed bears fruit and brings forth, some a hundredfold, some sixty, and some thirty" (Matthew 13:18–23; cf. Mark 4:13–20; Luke 8:11–15; see Matthew 13:8).

Setting: Jerusalem. The day after the Sabbath, after rising from the dead, Jesus appears to Mary Magdalene and the other Mary with instructions for His disciples.

Then Jesus said to them, "Do not be afraid; go and take word to My brethren to leave for Galilee, and there they will see Me" (Matthew 28:10; see John 20:17).

Setting: By the Sea of Galilee. During the early part of His ministry, after presenting the Parable of the Sower from a boat to a very large crowd, Jesus gives the meaning of the parable to His disciples and other followers.

And He said to them, "Do you not understand this parable? How will you understand all the parables? The sower sows the word. These are the ones who are beside the road where the word is sown; and when they hear, immediately Satan comes and takes away the word which has been sown in them. In a similar way these are the ones on whom seed was sown on the rocky places, who, when they hear the word, immediately receive it with joy; and they have no *firm* root in themselves, but are *only* temporary; then, when affliction or persecution arises because of the word, immediately they fall away. And others are the ones on whom seed was sown among the thorns; these are the ones who have heard the word, but the worries of the world and the deceitfulness of riches, and the desires for other things enter in and choke the word, and it becomes unfruitful. And those are the ones on whom seed was sown on the good soil; and they hear the word and accept it and bear fruit, thirty, sixty, and a hundredfold" (Mark 4:13–20; cf. Matthew 13:18–23; Luke 8:11–15).

Setting: Galilee. After Jesus presents the Parable of the Sower to the crowds, His disciples ask Him to give them the parable's meaning.

And He said, "To you it has been granted to know the mysteries of the kingdom of God, but to the rest *it is* in parables, so that SEEING THEY MAY NOT SEE, AND HEARING THEY MAY NOT UNDERSTAND. Now the parable is this: the seed is the word of God. Those beside the road are those who have heard; then the devil comes and takes away the word from their heart, so that they will not believe and be saved. Those on the rocky *soil* are those who, when they hear, receive the word with joy; and these have no *firm* root; they believe for a while, and in time of temptation fall away. The *seed* which fell among the thorns, these are the ones who have heard, and as they go on their way they are choked with worries and riches and pleasures of *this* life, and bring no fruit to maturity. But the *seed* in the good soil, these are the ones who have heard the word in an honest and good heart, and hold it fast, and bear fruit with perseverance" (Luke 8:10–15, Jesus quotes from Isaiah 6:9; cf. Matthew 13:10–23; Mark 4:10–20).

Setting: On the way from Galilee to Jerusalem. Jesus warns His disciples of future events, as the scribes and Pharisees turn hostile and question Him repeatedly in an attempt to catch Him in something He might say.

"And I say to you, everyone who confesses Me before men, the Son of Man will confess him also before the angels of God; but he who denies Me before men will be denied before the angels of God. And everyone who speaks a word against the Son of Man, it will be forgiven him; but he who blasphemes against the Holy Spirit, it will not be forgiven him. When they bring you before the synagogues and the rulers and the authorities, do not worry about how or what you are to speak in your defense, or what you are to say; for the Holy Spirit will teach you in that very hour what you ought to say" (Luke 12:8–12; cf. Matthew 10:32, 33; 12:31, 32; see Matthew 10:20).

Setting: Jerusalem. Just days before the Passover, with the chief priests and Pharisees plotting to seize Jesus, who is expressing anxiety about His upcoming crucifixion, some of the Jews believe in the Lord, while others are rejecting His message.

And Jesus cried out and said, "He who believes in Me, does not believe in Me but in Him who sent Me. He who sees Me sees the One who sent Me. I have come *as* Light into the world, so that everyone who believes in Me will not remain in darkness. If anyone hears My sayings and does not keep them, I do not judge him; for I did not come to judge the world, but to save the world. He who rejects Me and does not receive My sayings, has one who judges him; the word I spoke is what will judge him at the last day. For I did not speak on My own initiative, but the Father Himself who sent Me has given Me a commandment *as to* what to say and what to speak. I know that His commandment is eternal life; therefore the things I speak, I speak just as the Father as told Me" (John 12:44–50; see Matthew 10:40; Luke 10:16; John 1:4; 3:17; 5:19; 6:68; 14:9).

Setting: Jerusalem. Before the Passover, after conveying the upcoming ministry of the Holy Spirit in His disciples' lives, Jesus answers Judas' (not Iscariot) question about why He discloses Himself to them and not to the whole world.

Jesus answered and said to him, "If anyone loves Me, he will keep My word; and My Father will love him, and We will come to him and make Our abode with him. He who does not love Me does not keep My words; and the word which you hear is not Mine, but the Father's who sent Me" (John 14:23, 24; see John 7:16; 8:51).

Setting: Jerusalem. Before the Passover, after He conveys the upcoming ministry of the Holy Spirit in His disciples' lives with His imminent departure from them, Jesus explains He is the vine and His disciples are the branches.

"I am the true vine, and My Father is the vinedresser. Every branch in Me that does not bear fruit, He takes away; and every *branch* that bears fruit, He prunes it so that it may bear more fruit. You are already clean because of the word which I have spoken to you. Abide in Me, and I in you. As the branch cannot bear fruit of itself unless it abides in the vine, so neither *can* you unless you abide in Me. I am the vine, you are the branches; he who abides in Me and I in him, he bears much fruit, for apart from Me you can do nothing. If anyone does not abide in Me, he is thrown away as a branch and dries up; and they gather them, and cast them into the fire and they are burned. If you abide in Me, and My words abide in you, ask whatever you wish, and it will be done for you. My Father is glorified by this, that you bear much fruit, and *so* prove to be My disciples. Just as the Father has loved Me, I have also loved you; abide in My love. If you keep My commandments, you will abide in My love; just as I have kept My Father's commandments and abide in His love. These things I have spoken to you so that My joy may be in you, and *that* your joy may be made full" (John 15:1–11; see Matthew 5:16; 7:7; John 3:29, 35; 6:56; 8:29, 31; 13:10).

Setting: Jerusalem. Before the Passover, with His departure in mind, after explaining He is the vine and His disciples are the branches, Jesus prepares them for persecution from the world.

"If the world hates you, you know that it has hated Me before *it hated* you. If you were of the world, the world would love its own; but because you are not of the world, but I chose you out of the world, because of this the world hates you. Remember the word that I said to you, 'A slave is not greater than his master.' If they persecuted Me, they will also persecute you; if they kept My word, they will keep yours also. But all these things they will do to you for My name's sake, because they do not know the One who sent Me. If I had not come and spoken to them, they would not have sin, but now they have no excuse for their sin" (John 15:18–22; see Matthew 10:22; John 7:7; 8:19, 55; 9:41; 1 Corinthians 4:12).

Setting: Jerusalem. Before the Passover, with His upcoming departure in mind, after explaining He is the vine and His disciples are the branches, Jesus prepares them for hatred by the world.

"He who hates Me hates My Father also. If I had not done among them the works which no one else did, they would not have sin; but now they have both seen and hated Me and My Father as well. But *they have done this* to fulfill the word that is written in their Law, 'THEY HATED ME WITHOUT A CAUSE'" (John 15:23–25, Jesus quotes from Psalm 35:19; see John 9:41).

Setting: Jerusalem. Before the Passover, after giving His disciples assurance that in the midst of tribulation they will have His peace, Jesus continues praying His high-priestly prayer.

"But now I come to You; and these things I speak in the world so that they may have My joy made full in themselves. I have given them Your word; and the world has hated them, because they are not of the world, even as I am not of the world. I do not ask You to take them out of the world, but to keep them from the evil *one.* They are not of the world, even as I am not of the world. Sanctify them in the truth; Your word is truth. As You sent Me into the world, I also have sent them into the world. For their sakes I sanctify Myself, that they themselves also may be sanctified in truth. I do not ask on behalf of these alone, but for those also who believe in Me through their word; that they may all be one; even as You, Father, *are* in Me and I in You, that they also maybe in Us, so that the world may believe that You sent Me" (John 17:13–21; see Matthew 10:5, 38; John 7:33; 15:3, 11, 19).

Setting: On the island of Patmos (in the Aegean Sea about fifty miles southwest of Ephesus in modern Turkey). On the Lord's Day (Sunday), approximately fifty years after the Resurrection, the disciple John encounters the Lord Jesus Christ, who communicates a new revelation for the apostle to record for the church in Philadelphia and to six other churches in Asia.

"And to the angel of the church in Philadelphia write: He who is holy, who is true, who has the key of David, who opens and no one will shut, and who shuts and no one opens, says this: 'I know your deeds. Behold, I have put before you an open door which no one can shut, because you have a little power, and have kept My word, and have not denied My name. Behold, I will cause *those* of the synagogue of Satan, who say that they are Jews and are not, but lie—I will make them come and bow down at your feet, and *make them* know that I have loved you. Because you have kept the word of My perseverance, I also will keep you from the hour of testing, that *hour* which is about to come upon the whole world, to test those who dwell on the earth. I am coming quickly; hold fast what you have, so that no one will take your crown. He who overcomes, I will make him a pillar in the temple of My God, and he will not go out from it anymore; and I will write on him the name of My God, and the name of the city of My God, the new Jerusalem, which comes down out of heaven from My God, and My new name. He who has an ear, let him hear what the Spirit says to the churches' " (Revelation 3:7–13; see Isaiah 22:22; Galatians 2:9; Revelation 2:9, 10, 13, 25; 14:1).

WORD, CARELESS

Setting: Galilee. After Jesus heals a blind, mute, demon-possessed man, the Pharisees accuse the Lord in front of crowds of being a worker of Satan.

"Either make the tree good and its fruit good, or make the tree bad and its fruit bad; for the tree is known by its fruit. You brood of vipers, how can you, being evil, speak what is good? For the mouth speaks out of that which fills the heart. The good man brings out of *his* good treasure what is good; and the evil man brings out of *his* evil treasure what is evil. But I tell you that every careless word that people speak, they shall give an accounting for it in the day of judgment. For by your words you will be justified, and by your words you will be condemned" (Matthew 12:33–37; cf. Matthew 3:7; 7:16–18).

WORD, GOD'S (See WORD OF GOD; also see BIBLE; OLD TESTAMENT; SCRIPTURE; and SCRIPTURES)

WORD, HIS (God's)

Setting: Jerusalem. During a feast of the Jews, Jesus responds to criticism from the Jewish religious leaders by referring to God as His Father (thereby making Himself equal with God) and informing them that God, John the Baptist, and His works all testify to His mission.

"I can do nothing on My own initiative. As I hear, I judge; and My judgment is just, because I do not seek My own will, but the will of Him who sent Me. If I *alone* testify about Myself, My testimony is not true. There is another who testifies of Me, and I know that the testimony which He gives about Me is true. You have sent to John, and he has testified to the truth. But the testimony which I receive is not from man, but I say these things so that you may be saved. He was the lamp that was burning and was shining and you were willing to rejoice for a while in his light. But the testimony which I have is greater than the *testimony of* John; for the works which the Father has given Me to accomplish—the very works that I do—testify about Me, that the Father has sent Me. And the Father who sent Me, He has testified of Me. You have neither heard His voice at any time nor seen His form. You do not have His word abiding in you, for you do not believe Him whom He sent" (John 5:30–38; see Matthew 3:17; Mark 1:4, 5; John 1:7, 15, 32; 4:34; 8:14–16; 10:25, 37, 38).

Setting: The temple treasury in Jerusalem. While Jesus is interacting with the scribes and Pharisees, they state their belief that Jesus is a demon-possessed Samaritan because of His statement that anyone who keeps His word will never taste death.

Jesus answered, "If I glorify Myself, My glory is nothing; it is My Father who glorifies Me, of whom you say, 'He is our God'; and you have not come to know Him, but I know Him; and if I say that I do not know Him, I will be a liar like you, but I do know Him and keep His word. Your father Abraham rejoiced to see My day, and he saw *it* and was glad" (John 8:54–56; see Matthew 13:17; John 7:29).

WORD, MY (Jesus'; also see WORDS, MY)

Setting: By the pool of Bethesda in Jerusalem. During a feast of the Jews, Jesus responds to criticism from the Jewish religious leaders for healing a lame man on the Sabbath and for referring to God as His Father (thereby making Himself equal with God).

"Truly, truly, I say to you, he who hears My word, and believes Him who sent Me, has eternal life, and does not come into judgment, but has passed out of death into life" (John 5:24; see John 3:18; 12:44).

Setting: The temple treasury in Jerusalem. After the scribes and Pharisees question His testimony about Himself, Jesus reveals to those Jews who believe in Him how He will make them free.

So Jesus was saying to those Jews who had believed Him, "If you continue in My word, *then* you are truly disciples of Mine; and you will know the truth, and the truth will make you free." They answered Him, "We are Abraham's descendants and have never yet been enslaved to anyone; how is it that You say, 'You will become free'?" Jesus answered them, "Truly, truly, I say to you, everyone who commits sin is the slave of sin. The slave does not remain in the house forever; the son does remain forever. So if the Son makes you free, you will be free indeed. I know that you are Abraham's descendants; yet you seek to kill Me, because My word has no place in you. I speak the things which I have seen with *My* Father; therefore you also do the things which you heard from *your* father" (John 8:31–38; see Romans 6:16).

Setting: The temple treasury in Jerusalem. After the scribes and Pharisees question His testimony about Himself, Jesus argues with them regarding their ancestry and motives.

Jesus said to them, "If God were your Father, you would love Me, for I proceeded forth and have come from God, for I have not even come on My own initiative, but He sent Me. Why do you not understand what I am saying? *It is* because you cannot hear My word. You are of *your* father the devil, and you want to do the desires of your father. He was a murderer from the beginning, and does not stand in the truth because there is no truth in him. Whenever he speaks a lie, he speaks from his own *nature,* for he is a liar and the father of lies. But because I speak the truth, you do not believe Me. Which one of you convicts Me of sin? If I speak truth, why do you not believe Me? He who is of God hears the words of God; for this reason you do not hear *them,* because you are not of God" (John 8:42–47; see John 18:37; 1 John 3:8; 4:6; 5:1).

Setting: The temple treasury in Jerusalem. While Jesus is interacting with the scribes and Pharisees about His testimony, their ancestry, and their motives, they state their belief that Jesus is a demon-possessed Samaritan.

Jesus answered, "I do not have a demon; but I honor My Father, and you dishonor Me. But I do not seek My glory; there is One who seeks and judges. Truly, truly, I say to you, if anyone keeps My word he will never see death" (John 8:49–51; see Matthew 16:28; John 5:41; 7:20).

Setting: The temple treasury in Jerusalem. While Jesus is interacting with the scribes and Pharisees, they state their belief that Jesus is a demon-possessed Samaritan because of His statement that anyone who keeps His word will never taste death.

The Jews said to Him, "Now we know that You have a demon. Abraham died, and the prophets *also;* and You say, 'If anyone keeps My word, he will never taste of death'" (John 8:52).

Setting: Jerusalem. Before the Passover, after conveying the upcoming ministry of the Holy Spirit in His disciples' lives, Jesus answers Judas' (not Iscariot) question about why He discloses Himself to them and not to the whole world.

Jesus answered and said to him, "If anyone loves Me, he will keep My word; and My Father will love him, and We will come to him and make Our abode with him. He who does not love Me does not keep My words; and the word which you hear is not Mine, but the Father's who sent Me" (John 14:23, 24; see John 7:16; 8:51).

Setting: Jerusalem. Before the Passover, with His departure in mind, after explaining He is the vine and His disciples are the branches, Jesus prepares them for persecution from the world.

"If the world hates you, you know that it has hated Me before *it hated* you. If you were of the world, the world would love its own; but because you are not of the world, but I chose you out of the world, because of this the world hates you. Remember the word that I said to you, 'A slave is not greater than his master.' If they persecuted Me, they will also persecute you; if they kept My word, they will keep yours also. But all these things they will do to you for My name's sake, because they do not know the One who sent Me. If I had not come and spoken to them, they would not have sin, but now they have no excuse for their sin" (John 15:18–22; see Matthew 10:22; John 7:7; 8:19, 55; 9:41; 1 Corinthians 4:12).

Setting: On the island of Patmos (in the Aegean Sea about fifty miles southwest of Ephesus in modern Turkey). On the Lord's Day (Sunday), approximately fifty years after the Resurrection, the disciple John encounters the Lord Jesus Christ, who communicates a new revelation for the apostle to record for the church in Philadelphia and to six other churches in Asia.

"And to the angel of the church in Philadelphia write: He who is holy, who is true, who has the key of David, who opens and no one will shut, and who shuts and no one opens, says this: 'I know your deeds. Behold, I have put before you an open door which no one can shut, because you have a little power, and have kept My word, and have not denied My name. Behold, I will cause *those* of the synagogue of Satan, who say that they are Jews and are not, but lie—I will make them come and bow down at your feet, and *make them* know that I have loved you. Because you have kept the word of My perseverance, I also will keep you from the hour of testing, that *hour* which is about to come upon the whole world, to test those who dwell on the earth. I am coming quickly; hold fast what you have, so that no one will take your crown. He who overcomes, I will make him a pillar in the temple of My God, and he will not go out from it anymore; and I will write on him the name of My God, and the name of the city of My God, the new Jerusalem, which comes down out of heaven from My God, and My new name. He who has an ear, let him hear what the Spirit says to the churches' " (Revelation 3:7–13; see Isaiah 22:22; Galatians 2:9; Revelation 2:9, 10, 13, 25; 14:1).

WORD, YOUR (God's; also see SCRIPTURE; and SCRIPTURES)

Setting: Jerusalem. Before the Passover, after giving His disciples assurance that in the midst of tribulation they will have His peace, Jesus prays His high-priestly prayer.

Jesus spoke these things; and lifting up His eyes to heaven, He said, "Father, the hour has come; glorify Your Son, that the Son may glorify You, even as You gave Him authority over all flesh, that to all whom You have given Him, He may give eternal life. This is eternal life, that they may know You, the only true God, and Jesus Christ whom You have sent. I glorified You on the earth, having accomplished the work which You have given Me to do. Now, Father, glorify Me together with Yourself, with the glory which I had with You before the world was. I have manifested Your name to the men whom You gave Me out of the world; they were Yours and You gave them to Me, and they have kept Your word. Now they have come to know that everything You have given Me is from You; for the words which You gave Me I have given to them; and they received *them* and truly understood that I came forth from You, and they believed You sent Me. I ask on their behalf; I do not ask on behalf of the world, but of those whom You have given Me; for they are Yours; and all things that are Mine are Yours, and Yours are Mine; and I have been glorified in them. I am no longer in the world; and *yet* they themselves are in the world, and I come to You. Holy Father, keep them in Your name, *the name* which You have given Me, that they may be even as We *are*. While I was with them, I was keeping them in Your name which You have given Me; and I guarded them and not one of them perished but the son of perdition, so that the Scripture would be fulfilled" (John 17:1–12; see Luke 22:32; John 1:1; 3:35; 4:34; 5:44; 6:37–39, 70; 8:42; 11:41; 12:49; 13:18, 31; 16:15; Philippians 2:9).

Setting: Jerusalem. Before the Passover, after giving His disciples assurance that in the midst of tribulation they will have His peace, Jesus continues praying His high-priestly prayer.

"But now I come to You; and these things I speak in the world so that they may have My joy made full in themselves. I have given them Your word; and the world has hated them, because they are not of the world, even as I am not of the world. I do not ask You to take them out of the world, but to keep them from the evil *one*. They are not of the world, even as I am not of the world. Sanctify them in the truth; Your word is truth. As You sent Me into the world, I also have sent them into the world. For their sakes I sanctify Myself, that they themselves also may be sanctified in truth. I do not ask on behalf of these alone, but for those also who believe in Me through their word; that they may all be one; even as You, Father, *are* in Me and I in You, that they also maybe in Us, so that the world may believe that You sent Me" (John 17:13–21; see Matthew 10:5, 38; John 7:33; 15:3, 11, 19).

WORD OF GOD (Also see BIBLE; OLD TESTAMENT; SCRIPTURES; WORD, MY; and WORD, YOUR)

[WORD OF GOD from WORD]

Setting: Judea, near the Jordan River. Following His baptism, and before He begins His public ministry, Jesus is led by the Spirit into the wilderness for forty days of temptation by Satan.

But He answered and said, "It is written, 'MAN SHALL NOT LIVE ON BREAD ALONE, BUT ON EVERY WORD THAT PROCEEDS OUT OF THE MOUTH OF GOD' " (Matthew 4:4, Jesus quotes from Deuteronomy 8:3; cf. Luke 4:4).

Setting: Galilee. Pharisees and scribes from Jerusalem question Jesus about His disciples' lack of obedience to tradition and the commandments.

And He answered and said to them, "Why do you yourselves transgress the commandment of God for the sake of tradition? For God said, 'HONOR YOUR FATHER AND MOTHER,' and, 'HE WHO SPEAKS EVIL OF FATHER OR MOTHER IS TO BE PUT TO DEATH.' But you say, 'Whoever says to *his* father or mother, "Whatever I have that would help you has been given *to God*," he is not to honor his father or mother.' And *by this* you invalidated the word of God for the sake of your tradition. You hypocrites, rightly did Isaiah prophesy of you: 'THIS PEOPLE HONORS ME WITH THEIR LIPS, BUT THEIR HEART IS FAR AWAY FROM ME. BUT IN VAIN DO THEY WORSHIP ME, TEACHING AS DOCTRINES THE PRECEPTS OF MEN' " (Matthew 15:3–9, Jesus quotes from Exodus 20:12, 21:17, Leviticus 20:9; Isaiah 29:13; cf. Mark 7:5–7; see Matthew 15:1, 2; Colossians 2:22).

Setting: Galilee. The Pharisees and some of the scribes from Jerusalem question why Jesus' disciples do not follow the tradition of ceremonial hand cleansing before eating bread.

And He said to them, "Rightly did Isaiah prophesy of you hypocrites, as it is written: 'THIS PEOPLE HONORS ME WITH THEIR LIPS, BUT THEIR HEART IS FAR AWAY FROM ME. BUT IN VAIN DO THEY WORSHIP ME, TEACHING AS DOCTRINES THE PRECEPTS OF MEN.' Neglecting the commandment of God, you hold to the tradition of men." He was also saying to them, "You are experts at setting aside the commandment of God in order to keep tradition. For Moses said, 'HONOR YOUR FATHER AND YOUR MOTHER'; and, 'HE WHO SPEAKS EVIL OF FATHER OR MOTHER, IS TO BE PUT TO DEATH'; but you say, 'If a man says to *his* father or *his* mother, whatever I have that would help you is Corban (that is to say, given *to God*),' you no longer permit him to do anything for *his* father or *his* mother; *thus* invalidating the word of God by your tradition which you have handed down; and you do many things such as that" (Mark 7:6–13, Jesus quotes from Exodus 20:12; 21:17; Isaiah 29:13; cf. Matthew 15:1–6).

Setting: Galilee. After Jesus presents the Parable of the Sower to the crowds, His disciples ask Him to give them the parable's meaning.

And He said, "To you it has been granted to know the mysteries of the kingdom of God, but to the rest *it is* in parables, so that SEEING THEY MAY NOT SEE, AND HEARING THEY MAY NOT UNDERSTAND. Now the parable is this: the seed is the word of God. Those beside the road are those who have heard; then the devil comes and takes away the word from their heart, so that they will not believe and be saved. Those on the rocky *soil* are those who, when they hear, receive the word with joy; and these have no *firm* root; they believe for a while, and in time of temptation fall away. The *seed* which fell among the thorns, these are the ones who have heard, and as they go on their way they are choked with worries and riches and pleasures of *this* life, and bring no fruit to maturity. But the *seed* in the good soil, these are the ones who have heard the word in an honest and good heart, and hold it fast, and bear fruit with perseverance" (Luke 8:10–15, Jesus quotes from Isaiah 6:9; cf. Matthew 13:10–23; Mark 4:10–20).

Setting: Galilee. After giving the Parable of the Lamp to His disciples, Jesus conveys who His true relatives are after being informed His mother and brothers are seeking Him.

But He answered and said to them, "My mother and My brothers are these who hear the word of God and do it" (Luke 8:21; cf. Matthew 12:26–50; Mark 3:31–35).

Setting: On the way from Galilee to Jerusalem. After revealing a problem with exorcism, Jesus responds to a blessing from a woman in the crowd.

But He said, "On the contrary, blessed are those who hear the word of God and observe it" (Luke 11:28).

Setting: Jerusalem. At the Feast of Dedication, the Pharisees desire to stone Jesus because He claims to be equal with God when they ask Him plainly whether He is the Christ.

Jesus answered them, "Has it not been written in your Law, 'I SAID, YOU ARE GODS'? If he called them gods, to whom the word of God came (and the Scripture cannot be broken), do you say of Him, whom the Father sanctified and sent into the world, 'You are blaspheming,' because I said, 'I am the Son of God'? If I do not do the works of My Father, do not believe Me; but if I do them, though you do not believe Me, believe the works, so that you may know and understand that the Father is in Me, and I in the Father" (John 10:34–38, Jesus quotes from Psalm 82:6; see John 14:10, 20).

WORD OF THE KINGDOM (Listed under, KINGDOM, WORD OF THE)

WORDS (Specifics such as WORDS, MY; and WORDS OF GOD are separate entries; also see SPEECH; VERBOSITY; and WORD)

Setting: Galilee. After His twelve disciples observe His ministry, Jesus summons and specifically instructs them about their ministry to the people of Israel.

These twelve Jesus sent out after instructing them: "Do not go in *the* way of *the* Gentiles, and do not enter *any* city of the Samaritans; but rather go to the lost sheep of the house of Israel. And as you go, preach, saying, 'The kingdom of heaven is at hand.' Heal *the* sick, raise *the* dead, cleanse *the* lepers, cast out demons. Freely you received, freely give. Do not acquire gold, or silver, or copper for your money belts, or a bag for *your* journey, or even two coats, or sandals, or a staff; for the worker is worthy of his support. And whatever city or village you enter, inquire who is worthy in it, and stay at his house until you leave *that city*. As you enter the house, give it your greeting. If the house is worthy, give it your *blessing of* peace. But if it is not worthy, take back your *blessing of* peace. Whoever does not receive you, nor heed your words, as you go out of that house or that city, shake the dust off your feet. Truly I say to you, it will be more tolerable for *the* land of Sodom and Gomorrah in the day of judgment than for that city" (Matthew 10:5–15; cf. Mark 6:7–11; Luke 9:1–5; see Matthew 3:2; 11:22, 24; 15:24; Luke 22:35; 1 Corinthians 9:14).

Setting: Galilee. After Jesus heals a blind, mute, demon-possessed man, the Pharisees accuse the Lord in front of crowds of being a worker of Satan.

"Either make the tree good and its fruit good, or make the tree bad and its fruit bad; for the tree is known by its fruit. You brood of vipers, how can you, being evil, speak what is good? For the mouth speaks out of that which fills the heart. The good man brings out of *his* good treasure what is good; and the evil man brings out of *his* evil treasure what is evil. But I tell you that every careless word that people speak, they shall give an accounting for it in the day of judgment. For by your words you will be justified, and by your words you will be condemned" (Matthew 12:33–37; cf. Matthew 3:7; 7:16–18).

Setting: Galilee. After healing the demon-possessed son of a man in the crowd, Jesus prophesies His own death.

"Let these words sink into your ears; for the Son of Man is going to be delivered into the hands of men" (Luke 9:44; cf. Matthew 17:22, 23; Mark 9:31, 32).

Setting: Jericho, on the way to Jerusalem. After commending Zaccheus's faith in Him, Jesus provides a parable about stewardship.

So He said, "A nobleman went to a distant country to receive a kingdom for himself, and *then* return. And he called ten of his slaves, and gave them ten minas and said to them, 'Do business *with this* until I come *back*.' But his citizens hated him and sent a delegation after him, saying, 'We do not want this man to reign over us.' When he returned, after receiving the kingdom, he ordered that these slaves, to whom he had given the money, be called to him so that he might know what business they had done. The first appeared, saying, 'Master, your mina has made ten minas more.' And he said to him, 'Well done, good slave, because you have been faithful in a very little thing, you are to be in authority over ten cities.' The second came, saying, 'Your mina, master, has made five minas.' And he said to him, also, 'And you are to be over five cities.' Another came, saying, 'Master, here is your mina, which I kept put away in a handkerchief; for I was afraid of you, because you are an exacting man; you take up what you did not lay down and reap what you did not sow.' He said to him, 'By your own words I will judge you, you worthless slave. Did you know that I am an exacting man, taking up what I did not lay down and reaping what I did not sow? Then why did you not put my money in the bank, and having come, I would have collected it with interest?' Then he said to the bystanders, 'Take the mina away from him and give it to the one who has the ten minas.' And they said to him, 'Master, he has ten minas *already.*' I tell you that to everyone who has, more shall be given, but from the one who does not have, even what he does have shall be taken away. But these enemies of mine, who did not want me to reign over them, bring them here and slay them in my presence" (Luke 19:12–27; cf. Matthew 25:14–30; see Matthew 13:12; Luke 16:10).

Setting: On the road to Emmaus. After dying on the cross just outside Jerusalem the day before the Sabbath, and being buried in a tomb by Joseph of Arimathea, Jesus rises on the third day and appears to two of His followers.

And He said to them, "What are these words that you are exchanging with one another as you are walking?" And they stood still, looking sad (Luke 24:17; see Mark 16:12, 13).

Setting: The synagogue at Capernaum of Galilee. After the Jewish religious leaders argue with one another when Jesus says He will give His flesh to the world to eat, some of the Lord's disciples also express difficulty with His statements.

But, Jesus, conscious that His disciples grumbled at this, said to them, "Does this cause you to stumble? *What* then if you see the Son of Man ascending to where He was before? It is the Spirit who gives life; the flesh profits nothing; the words that I have spoken to you are spirit and are life. But there are some of you who do not believe." For Jesus knew from the beginning who they were who did not believe, and who it was that would betray Him. And He was saying, "For this reason I have said to you, that no one can come to Me unless it has been granted him from the Father" (John 6:61–65; see Matthew 11:6; 13:11; John 3:13).

Setting: Jerusalem. Before the Passover, after answering Thomas' question about where the Lord is going and how His disciples will know the way, Jesus responds to Philip's request for Him to show them the Father.

Jesus said to him, "Have I been so long with you, and *yet* you have not come to know Me, Philip? He who has seen Me has seen the Father; how *can* you say, 'Show us the Father'? Do you not believe that I am in the Father, and the Father is in Me? The words that I say to you I do not speak on My own initiative, but the Father abiding in Me does His works. Believe Me that I am in the Father and the Father is in Me; otherwise believe because of the works themselves. Truly, truly, I say to you, he who believes in Me, the works that I do, he will do also; and greater *works* than these he will do; because I go to the Father. Whatever you ask in My name, that will I do, so that the Father may be glorified in the Son. If you ask Me anything in My name, I will do *it*" (John 14:9–14; see Matthew 7:7; John 1:14; 5:19, 20, 36; 10:37, 38; 15:16).

Setting: Jerusalem. Before the Passover, after giving His disciples assurance that in the midst of tribulation they will have His peace, Jesus prays His high-priestly prayer.

Jesus spoke these things; and lifting up His eyes to heaven, He said, "Father, the hour has come; glorify Your Son, that the Son may glorify You, even as You gave Him authority over all flesh, that to all whom You have given Him, He may give eternal life. This is eternal life, that they may know You, the only true God, and Jesus Christ whom You have sent. I glorified You on the earth, having accomplished the work which You have given Me to do. Now, Father, glorify Me together with Yourself, with the glory which I had with You before the world was. I have manifested Your name to the men whom You gave Me out of the world; they were Yours and You gave them to Me, and they have kept Your word. Now they have come to know that everything You have given Me is from You; for the words which You gave Me I have given to them; and they received *them* and truly understood that I came forth from You, and they believed You sent Me. I ask on their behalf; I do not ask on behalf of the world, but of those whom You have given Me; for they are Yours; and all things that are Mine are Yours, and Yours are Mine; and I have been glorified in them. I am no longer in the world; and *yet* they themselves are in the world, and I come to You. Holy Father, keep them in Your name, *the name* which You have given Me, that they may be even as We *are.* While I was with them, I was keeping them in Your name which You have given Me; and I guarded them and not one of them perished but the son of perdition, so that the Scripture would be fulfilled" (John 17:1–12; see Luke 22:32; John 1:1; 3:35; 4:34; 5:44; 6:37–39, 70; 8:42; 11:41; 12:49; 13:18, 31; 16:15; Philippians 2:9).

Setting: On the island of Patmos (in the Aegean Sea about fifty miles southwest of Ephesus in modern Turkey). In the final chapter of the Lord Jesus Christ's revelation via the apostle John, approximately fifty years after the Resurrection, the Lord reveals His upcoming return and the blessing to those who heed the words of the prophecy of this book.

"And behold, I am coming quickly. Blessed is he who heeds the words of the prophecy of this book" (Revelation 22:7; see Revelation 1:3).

WORDS, JESUS' (See WORD, MY; and WORDS, MY)

WORDS, JESUS' DYING (See JESUS' LAST WORDS)

WORDS, JESUS' LAST (See JESUS' LAST WORDS)

WORDS, MY (Jesus'; also see SAYINGS; and WORD, MY)

[MY WORDS from these words of Mine]

Setting: Galilee. During the early part of His ministry, Jesus preaches the Sermon on the Mount to His disciples and the multitudes.

"Therefore everyone who hears these words of Mine and acts on them, may be compared to a wise man who built his house on the rock. And the rain fell, and the floods came, and the winds blew and slammed against that house; and *yet* it did not fall, for it had been founded on the rock. Everyone who hears these words of Mine and does not act on them, will be like a foolish man who built his house on the sand. The rain fell, and the floods came, and the winds blew and slammed against that house; and it fell—and great was its fall" (Matthew 7:24–28; cf. Luke 6:47–49).

Setting: On the Mount of Olives, just east of Jerusalem. During His Olivet Discourse, after answering His disciples' questions as to when the temple will be destroyed and Jerusalem overrun, along with the signs of His coming and the end of the age, Jesus teaches them the Parable of the Fig Tree.

"Now learn the parable from the fig tree: when its branch has already become tender and puts forth its leaves, you know that summer is near; so, you too, when you see all these things, recognize that He is near, *right* at the door. Truly, I say to you, this generation will not pass away until all these things take place. Heaven and earth will pass away, but My words will not pass away. But of that day and hour no one knows, not even the angels of heaven, nor the Son, but the Father alone. For the coming of the Son of Man will be just like the days of Noah. For as in those days before the flood they were eating and drinking, marrying and giving in marriage, until the day that Noah entered the ark, and they did not understand until the flood came and took them all away; so will the coming of the Son of Man be. Then there will be two men in the field; one will be taken and one will be left. Two women *will be* grinding at the mill; one will be taken and one will be left" (Matthew 24:32–41; cf. Mark 13:28–32; Luke 17:34–36; 21:28–33; see Genesis 6:5; 7:7; Matthew 5:18; 10:23; James 5:9).

Setting: Caesarea Philippi. After rebuking Peter for desiring to thwart His mission to the cross, Jesus summons a crowd, along with His disciples, and informs them of the high costs of following Him.

And He summoned the crowd with His disciples, and said to them, "If anyone wishes to come after Me, he must deny himself, and take up his cross and follow Me. For whoever wishes to save his life will lose it, but whoever loses his life for My sake and the gospel's will save it. For what does it profit a man to gain the whole world, and forfeit his soul? For what will a man give in exchange for his soul? For whoever is ashamed of Me and My words in this adulterous and sinful generation, the Son of Man will also be ashamed of him when He comes in the glory of His Father with the holy angels" (Mark 8:34–38; cf. Matthew 16:24–28; Luke 9:23–27; see Matthew 10:33, 38, 39).

Setting: On the Mount of Olives, east of the temple in Jerusalem. After prophesying the temple's destruction, Jesus responds during His Olivet Discourse to questions from Peter, James, John, and Andrew about other future events.

"Now learn the parable from the fig tree: when its branch has already become tender and puts forth its leaves, you know that summer is near. Even so, you too, when you see these things happening, recognize that He is near, *right* at the door. Truly I say to you, this generation will not pass away until all these things take place. Heaven and earth will pass away, but My words will not pass away. But of the day or hour no one knows, not even the angels in heaven, nor the Son, but the Father *alone*" (Mark 13:28–32; cf. Matthew 24:32–36; Luke 21:28–33).

Setting: Galilee. After selecting His twelve disciples, Jesus teaches the Sermon on the Mount to those disciples and a great throng of people from Judea, Jerusalem, and the central coastal region of Tyre and Sidon.

"Why do you call Me, 'Lord, Lord,' and do not do what I say? Everyone who comes to Me and hears My words and acts on them, I will show you whom he is like; he is like a man building a house, who dug deep and laid a foundation on the rock; and when a flood occurred, the torrent burst against that house and could not shake it, because it had been well built. But the one who has heard and has not acted *accordingly,* is like a man who built a house on the ground without any foundation; and the torrent burst against it and immediately it collapsed, and the ruin of that house was great" (Luke 6:46–49; cf. Matthew 7:24–27; see Luke 6:12–19; James 1:22).

Setting: Galilee. Following Peter's pronouncement that Jesus is the Christ of God, the Lord conveys the demands of discipleship and the hope regarding the kingdom of God.

And He was saying to *them* all, "If anyone wishes to come after Me, he must deny himself, and take up his cross daily and follow Me. For whoever wishes to save his life will lose it, but whoever loses his life for My sake, he is the one who will save it. For what is a man profited if he gains the whole world, and loses or forfeits himself? For whoever is ashamed of Me and My words, the Son of Man will be ashamed of him when He comes in His glory, and *the glory* of the Father and of the holy angels. But I say to you truthfully, there are some of those standing here who will not taste death until they see the kingdom of God" (Luke 9:23–27; cf. Matthew 16:24–26, 28; Mark 8:34–37; see Matthew 10:33, 38, 39).

Setting: On the Mount of Olives, east of the temple in Jerusalem. After ministering in the temple a few days before His crucifixion, and giving the disciples more details regarding His return, Jesus conveys the Parable of the Fig Tree during His Olivet Discourse.

Then He told them a parable: "Behold the fig tree and all the trees; as soon as they put forth *leaves,* you see it and know for yourselves that summer is now near. So you also, when you see these things happening, recognize that the kingdom of God is near. Truly, I say to you, this generation will not pass away until all things take place. Heaven and earth will pass away, but My words will not pass away" (Luke 21:29–33; cf. Matthew 24:32–35; Mark 13:28–31; see Matthew 5:18).

Setting: Jerusalem. After rising from the tomb on the third day after being crucified, and appearing to two of His followers on the road to Emmaus, Jesus gives instruction to His disciples (except Thomas) about His mission on earth and the promise of future power from God.

Now He said to them, "These are My words which I spoke to you while I was still with you, that all things which are written about Me in the Law of Moses and the Prophets and the Psalms must be fulfilled." Then He opened their minds to understand the Scriptures, and He said to them, "Thus it is written, that the Christ would suffer and rise again from the dead the third day, and that repentance for forgiveness of sins would be proclaimed in His name to all the nations, beginning from Jerusalem. You are witnesses of these things. And behold, I am sending forth the promise of My Father upon you; but you are to stay in the city until you are clothed with power from on high" (Luke 24:44–49; see Matthew 28:19, 20; Acts 1:8).

Setting: Jerusalem. During a feast of the Jews, Jesus responds to criticism from the Jewish religious leaders by referring to God as His Father (thereby making Himself equal with God) and informing them that God, John the Baptist, the Scriptures, and His works all testify to His mission.

"You search the Scriptures because you think that in them you have eternal life; it is these that testify about Me; and you are unwilling to come to Me so that you may have life. I do not receive glory from men; but I know you, that you do not have the love of God in yourselves. I have come in My Father's name, and you do not receive Me; if another comes in his own name, you will receive him. How can you believe, when you receive glory from one another and you do not seek the glory that is from the *one and* only God? Do not think that I will accuse you before the Father; the one who accuses you is Moses, in whom you have set your hope. For if you believed Moses, you would believe Me, for he wrote about Me. But if you do not believe his writings, how will you believe My words?" (John 5:39–47; see Matthew 24:5; Luke 16:29, 31; 24:27; John 9:28; 17:3).

Setting: Jerusalem. Before the Passover, after conveying the upcoming ministry of the Holy Spirit in His disciples' lives, Jesus answers Judas' (not Iscariot) question about why He discloses Himself to them and not to the whole world.

Jesus answered and said to him, "If anyone loves Me, he will keep My word; and My Father will love him, and We will come to him and make Our abode with him. He who does not love Me does not keep My words; and the word which you hear is not Mine, but the Father's who sent Me" (John 14:23, 24; see John 7:16; 8:51).

Setting: Jerusalem. Before the Passover, after He conveys the upcoming ministry of the Holy Spirit in His disciples' lives with His imminent departure from them, Jesus explains He is the vine and His disciples are the branches.

"I am the true vine, and My Father is the vinedresser. Every branch in Me that does not bear fruit, He takes away; and every *branch* that bears fruit, He prunes it so that it may bear more fruit. You are already clean because of the word which I have spoken to you. Abide in Me, and I in you. As the branch cannot bear fruit of itself unless it abides in the vine, so neither *can* you unless you abide in Me. I am the vine, you are the branches; he who abides in Me and I in him, he bears much fruit, for apart from Me you can do nothing. If anyone does not abide in Me, he is thrown away as a branch and dries up; and they gather them, and cast them into the fire and they are burned. If you abide in Me, and My words abide in you, ask whatever you wish, and it will be done for you. My Father is glorified by this, that you bear much fruit, and *so* prove to be My disciples. Just as the Father has loved Me, I have also loved you; abide in My love. If you keep My commandments, you will abide in My love; just as I have kept My Father's commandments and abide in His love. These things I have spoken to you so that My joy may be in you, and *that* your joy may be made full" (John 15:1–11; see Matthew 5:16; 7:7; John 3:29, 35; 6:56; 8:29, 31; 13:10).

WORDS OF GOD (Also see WORD, MY; WORD OF GOD; WORD, YOUR; and WORDS, MY)

[WORDS OF GOD from what was spoken to you by God]

Setting: The temple in Jerusalem. The Sadducees question Jesus about Levirate marriage (marriage to a brother-in-law), in order to test Him.

But Jesus answered and said to them, "You are mistaken, not understanding the Scriptures nor the power of God. For in the resurrection they neither marry nor are given in marriage, but are like angels in heaven. But regarding the resurrection of the dead, have you not read what was spoken to you by God: 'I AM THE GOD OF ABRAHAM, AND THE GOD OF ISAAC, AND THE GOD OF JACOB'? He is not the God of the dead but of the living" (Matthew 22:29–32, Jesus quotes from Exodus 3:6; cf. Mark 12:18–27; Luke 20:27–38; see Deuteronomy 25:5; John 20:9).

Setting: The temple treasury in Jerusalem. After the scribes and Pharisees question His testimony about Himself, Jesus interacts with them regarding their ancestry and motives.

Jesus said to them, "If God were your Father, you would love Me, for I proceeded forth and have come from God, for I have not even come on My own initiative, but He sent Me. Why do you not understand what I am saying? *It is* because you cannot hear My word. You are of *your* father the devil, and you want to do the desires of your father. He was a murderer from the beginning, and does not stand in the truth because there is no truth in him. Whenever he speaks a lie, he speaks from his own *nature,* for he is a liar and the father of lies. But because I speak the truth, you do not believe Me. Which one of you convicts Me of sin? If I speak truth, why do not believe Me? He who is of God hears the words of God; for this reason you do not hear *them,* because you are not of God" (John 8:42–47; see John 18:37; 1 John 3:8; 4:6; 5:1).

WORK **(Also see FATHER, WORK OF MY; FOREMAN; GOD, WORK OF; JESUS' WORK; LABOR; LABORERS; LANDOWNER; WORKERS; and WORKS)**
[WORK from worked]
Setting: Judea beyond the Jordan (Perea). Jesus illustrates the kingdom of heaven to His disciples through the story of laborers in the vineyard.

"For the kingdom of heaven is like a landowner who went out early in the morning to hire laborers for his vineyard. When he had agreed with the laborers for a denarius for the day, he sent them into his vineyard. And he went out about the third hour and saw others standing idle in the market place; and to those he said,' You also go into the vineyard, and whatever is right I will give you.' And *so* they went. Again he went out about the sixth and the ninth hour, and did the same thing. And about the eleventh *hour* he went out and found others standing *around;* and he said to them, 'Why have you been standing idle here all day long?' They said to him, 'Because no one hired us.' He said to them, 'You go into the vineyard too.' When evening came, the owner of the vineyard said to his foreman, 'Call the laborers and pay them their wages, beginning with the last *group* to the first.' When those *hired* about the eleventh hour came, each one received a denarius. When those *hired* first came, they thought that they would receive more; but each of them also received a denarius. When they received it, they grumbled at the landowner, saying, 'These last men have worked *only* one hour, and you have made them equal to us who have borne the burden and the scorching heat of the day.' But he answered and said to one of them, 'Friend, I am doing you no wrong; did you not agree with me for a denarius? Take what is yours and go, but I wish to give to this last man the same as to you. It is not lawful for me to do what I wish with what is my own? Or is your eye envious because I am generous?' So the last shall be first, and the first last" (Matthew 20:1–16; cf. Matthew 19:30).

Setting: The temple in Jerusalem. Jesus delivers a parable to the chief priests and elders after they question His authority.

"But what do you think? A man had two sons, and he came to the first and said, 'Son, go work today in the vineyard.' And he answered, 'I will not'; but afterward he regretted it and went. The man came to the second and said the same thing; and he answered, 'I *will,* sir'; but he did not go. Which of the two sons did the will of his father?" They said, "The first." Jesus said to them, "Truly, I say to you that the tax collectors and prostitutes will get into the kingdom of God before you. For John came to you in the way of righteousness and you did not believe him; but the tax collectors and prostitutes did believe him; and you, seeing *this,* did not even feel remorse afterward so as to believe him" (Matthew 21:28–32; cf. Luke 7:29, 30, 37–50).

Setting: Capernaum. The day after Jesus walks on the Sea of Galilee to join His disciples in a boat, the people He miraculously fed with a lad's five loaves and two fish ask the Lord how He crossed the water, since He had not entered the boat from land with His disciples.

Jesus answered them and said, "Truly, truly, I say to you, you seek Me, not because you saw signs, but because you ate of the loaves and were filled. Do not work for the food which perishes, but for the food which endures to eternal life, which the Son of Man will give to you, for on Him the Father, God, has set His seal" (John 6:26, 27; see John 3:33).

Setting: The temple treasury in Jerusalem. After Jesus avoids being stoned by the scribes and Pharisees, His disciples wonder if blindness is caused by sin as the Lord heals a man born blind.

Jesus answered, "*It was* neither *that* this man sinned, nor his parents; but *it was* so that the works of God might be displayed in him. We must work the works of Him who sent Me as long as it is day; night is coming when no one can work. While I am in the world, I am the Light of the world." When He had said this, He spat on the ground, and made clay of the spittle, and applied the clay to his eyes, and said to him, "Go, wash in the pool of Siloam" (which is translated, Sent). So he went away and washed, and came *back* seeing
(John 9:3–7; see John 8:12; 11:4; 12:46).

WORK, GOD'S **(See FATHER, WORKS OF MY; GOD, WORK OF; and JESUS' WORK)**

WORK, JESUS' (See JESUS' WORK)

WORK OF GOD (Listed under GOD, WORK OF)

WORKER (Also see WORKERS)

Setting: Galilee. After His twelve disciples observe His ministry, Jesus summons and specifically instructs them about their ministry to the people of Israel.

These twelve Jesus sent out after instructing them: "Do not go in *the* way of *the* Gentiles, and do not enter *any* city of the Samaritans; but rather go to the lost sheep of the house of Israel. And as you go, preach, saying, 'The kingdom of heaven is at hand.' Heal *the* sick, raise *the* dead, cleanse *the* lepers, cast out demons. Freely you received, freely give. Do not acquire gold, or silver, or copper for your money belts, or a bag for *your* journey, or even two coats, or sandals, or a staff; for the worker is worthy of his support. And whatever city or village you enter, inquire who is worthy in it, and stay at his house until you leave *that city*. As you enter the house, give it your greeting. If the house is worthy, give it your *blessing of* peace. But if it is not worthy, take back your *blessing of* peace. Whoever does not receive you, nor heed your words, as you go out of that house or that city, shake the dust off your feet. Truly I say to you, it will be more tolerable for *the* land of Sodom and Gomorrah in the day of judgment than for that city" (Matthew 10:5–15; cf. Mark 6:7–11; Luke 9:1–5; see Matthew 3:2; 11:22, 24; 15:24; Luke 22:35; 1 Corinthians 9:14).

WORKERS (Also see FOREMAN; LABORERS; LANDOWNER; WORK; and WORKER)

Setting: The villages and cities of Galilee. While healing the sick, raising the dead, and casting out demons, Jesus comments on the enormity of the task and the need to ask the Lord of the harvest for additional workers.

Then He said to His disciples, "The harvest is plentiful, but the workers are few. Therefore beseech the Lord of the harvest to send out workers into His harvest" (Matthew 9:37, 38; cf. Luke 10:2).

WORKS (Specifics such as FATHER, WORKS OF MY; WORKS, GOOD; and WORKS, GREATER are separate entries; also see DEEDS; FRUIT; JESUS' WORK; MIRACLES; SIGNS AND WONDERS; and WORK)

Setting: The temple treasury in Jerusalem. After Jesus avoids being stoned by the scribes and Pharisees, His disciples wonder if blindness is caused by sin as the Lord heals a man born blind.

Jesus answered, "*It was* neither *that* this man sinned, nor his parents; but *it was* so that the works of God might be displayed in him. We must work the works of Him who sent Me as long as it is day; night is coming when no one can work. While I am in the world, I am the Light of the world." When He had said this, He spat on the ground, and made clay of the spittle, and applied the clay to his eyes, and said to him, "Go, wash in the pool of Siloam" (which is translated, Sent). So he went away and washed, and came *back* seeing (John 9:3–7; see John 8:12; 11:4; 12:46).

Setting: Jerusalem. At the Feast of Dedication, the Pharisees desire to stone Jesus because He claims to be equal with God when they ask Him plainly whether He is the Christ.

Jesus answered them, "Has it not been written in your Law, 'I SAID, YOU ARE GODS'? If he called them gods, to whom the word of God came (and the Scripture cannot be broken), do you say of Him, whom the Father sanctified and sent into the world, 'You are blaspheming,' because I said, 'I am the Son of God'? If I do not do the works of My Father, do not believe Me; but if I do them, though you do not believe Me, believe the works, so that you may know and understand that the Father is in Me, and I in the Father" (John 10:34–38, Jesus quotes from Psalm 82:6; see John 14:10, 20).

Setting: Jerusalem. Before the Passover, after answering Thomas' question where the Lord is going and how His disciples will know the way, Jesus responds to Philip's request for Him to show them the Father.

Jesus said to him, "Have I been so long with you, and *yet* you have not come to know Me, Philip? He who has seen Me has seen the Father; how *can* you say, 'Show us the Father'? Do you not believe that I am in the Father, and the Father is in Me? The words that I say to you I do not speak on My own initiative, but the Father abiding in Me does His works. Believe Me that I am in the Father and the Father is in Me; otherwise believe because of the works themselves. Truly, truly, I say to you, he who believes in Me, the works that I do, he will do also; and greater *works* than these he will do; because I go to the Father. Whatever you ask in My name, that will I do, so that the Father may be glorified in the Son. If you ask Me anything in My name, I will do *it*" (John 14:9–14; see Matthew 7:7; John 1:14; 5:19, 20, 36; 10:37, 38; 15:16).

Setting: Jerusalem. Before the Passover, with His upcoming departure in mind, after explaining He is the vine and His disciples are the branches, Jesus prepares them for hatred by the world.

"He who hates Me hates My Father also. If I had not done among them the works which no one else did, they would not have sin; but now they have both seen and hated Me and My Father as well. But *they have done this* to fulfill the word that is written in their Law, 'THEY HATED ME WITHOUT A CAUSE'" (John 15:23–25, Jesus quotes from Psalm 35:19; see John 9:41).

WORKS, GOOD (Also see DEED, GOOD; DEEDS, GOOD; GOOD, DOING; POOR, GIVING TO THE; and SERVING GOD)

Setting: Galilee. During the early part of His ministry, Jesus preaches the Sermon on the Mount to His disciples and the multitudes.

"You are the light of the world. A city set on a hill cannot be hidden; nor does *anyone* light a lamp and put it under a basket, but on the lampstand, and it gives light to all who are in the house. Let your light shine before men in such a way that they may see your good works, and glorify your Father who is in heaven" (Matthew 5:14–16; cf. Mark 4:21; 1 Peter 2:12).

[GOOD WORKS from who does the will of My Father]

Setting: Galilee. During the early part of His ministry, Jesus preaches the Sermon on the Mount to His disciples and the multitudes.

"Not everyone who says to Me, 'Lord, Lord,' will enter the kingdom of heaven, but he who does the will of My Father who is in heaven *will enter.* Many will say to Me on that day, 'Lord, Lord, did we not prophesy in Your name, and in Your name cast out demons, and in Your name perform many miracles?' And then I will declare to them, 'I never knew you; DEPART FROM ME, YOU WHO PRACTICE LAWLESSNESS'" (Matthew 7:21–23, Jesus quotes from Psalm 6:8; cf. Matthew 25:11–13; see Luke 6:46).

Setting: Jerusalem. At the Feast of Dedication, the Pharisees desire to stone Jesus because He claims to be equal with God when they ask Him plainly whether He is the Christ.

Jesus answered them, "I showed you many good works from the Father; for which of them are you stoning Me?" (John 10:32).

WORKS, GREATER

Setting: By the pool of Bethesda in Jerusalem. During a feast of the Jews, Jesus responds to criticism from the Jewish religious leaders for healing a lame man on the Sabbath and for referring to God as His Father (thereby making Himself equal with God).

Therefore Jesus answered and was saying to them, "Truly, truly, I say to you, the Son can do nothing of Himself, unless *it is* something He sees the Father doing; for whatever the Father does, these things the Son also does in like manner. For the Father loves the Son, and shows Him all things that He Himself is doing; and *the Father* will show Him greater works than these, so that you will marvel. For just as the Father raises the dead and gives them life, even so the Son also gives life to whom He wishes. For not even the Father judges anyone, but He has given all judgment to the Son, so that all will honor the Son even as they honor the Father. He who does not honor the Son does not honor the Father who sent Him" (John 5:19–23; see Luke 10:16; John 3:35; 11:25; 14:12).

Setting: Jerusalem. Before the Passover, after answering Thomas' question where the Lord is going and how His disciples will know the way, Jesus responds to Philip's request for Him to show them the Father.

Jesus said to him, "Have I been so long with you, and *yet* you have not come to know Me, Philip? He who has seen Me has seen the Father; how *can* you say, 'Show us the Father'? Do you not believe that I am in the Father, and the Father is in Me? The words that I say to you I do not speak on My own initiative, but the Father abiding in Me does His works. Believe Me that I am in the Father and the Father is in Me; otherwise believe because of the works themselves. Truly, truly, I say to you, he who believes in Me, the works that I do, he will do also; and greater *works* than these he will do; because I go to the Father. Whatever you ask in My name, that will I do, so that the Father may be glorified in the Son. If you ask Me anything in My name, I will do *it*" (John 14:9–14; see Matthew 7:7; John 1:14; 5:19, 20, 36; 10:37, 38; 15:16).

WORKS, JESUS' (See JESUS' WORK; MIRACLES; and SIGNS AND WONDERS)

WORKS OF GOD (Listed under GOD, WORKS OF; also see FATHER, WORKS OF MY)

WORLD (Specifics such as WORLD, LIGHT OF THE; and WORLD, WHOLE are separate entries)

Setting: A house near the Sea of Galilee. Jesus gives His disciples the meaning of the Parable of the Wheat and the Tares.

And He said, "The one who sows the good seed is the Son of Man, and the field is the world; and as *for* the good seed, these are the sons of the kingdom; and the tares are the sons of the evil *one;* and the enemy who sowed them is the devil, and the harvest is the end of the age; and the reapers are angels. So just as the tares are gathered up and burned with fire, so shall it be at the end of the age. The Son of Man will send forth His angels, and they will gather out of His kingdom all stumbling blocks, and those who commit lawlessness, and will throw them into the furnace of fire; in that place there will be weeping and gnashing of teeth. Then THE RIGHTEOUS WILL SHINE FORTH AS THE SUN in the kingdom of their Father. He who has ears, let him hear" (Matthew 13:37–43, Jesus quotes from Daniel 12:3; cf. Matthew 8:12; 13:50).

Setting: Capernaum of Galilee. After His disciples ask about greatness in the kingdom of heaven, Jesus elaborates about stumbling blocks.

"Woe to the world because of *its* stumbling blocks! For it is inevitable that stumbling blocks come; but woe to that man through whom the stumbling block comes! If your hand or your foot causes you to stumble, cut it off and throw it from you; it is better for you to enter life crippled or lame, than to have two hands or two feet and be cast into the eternal fire. If your eye causes you to stumble, pluck it out and throw it from you. It is better for you to enter life with one eye, than to have two eyes and be cast into the fiery hell" (Matthew 18:7–9; cf. Matthew 5:29, 30; Mark 9:43–48; Luke 17:1).

Setting: Following His resurrection from the dead after being crucified, Jesus commissions His disciples to preach His gospel to the world.

And He said to them, "Go into all the world and preach the gospel to all creation. He who has believed and has been baptized shall be saved; but he who has disbelieved shall be condemned. These signs will accompany those who have believed: in My name they will cast out demons, they will speak with new tongues; they will pick up serpents, and if they drink any deadly *poison,* it will not hurt them; they will lay hands on the sick, and they will recover" (Mark 16:15–18; cf. Matthew 28:16–20; see Mark 9:38; John 3:18, 36; 1 Corinthians 15:6).

[Note: Some scholars question the authenticity of Mark 16:9–20 as these verses do not appear in some early New Testament manuscripts.]

Setting: On the Mount of Olives, just east of Jerusalem. After ministering in the temple a few days before His crucifixion, and giving His disciples more details regarding future events, Jesus speaks during His Olivet Discourse of His return.

"There will be signs in sun and moon and stars, and on the earth dismay among the nations, in perplexity at the roaring of the sea and the waves, men fainting from fear and the expectation of the things which are coming upon the world; for the powers of the heavens will be shaken. Then they will see THE SON OF MAN COMING IN A CLOUD with power and great glory. But when these things begin to take place, straighten up and lift up your heads, because your redemption is drawing near" (Luke 21:25–28, Jesus quotes from Daniel 7:13; cf. Matthew 24:29–31; Mark 13:24–27).

Setting: Jerusalem. At the time for the Passover of the Jews, after the Lord cleanses the temple, a Pharisee, Nicodemus, asks Him by night the meaning of "born again."

"For God so loved the world, that He gave His only begotten Son, that whoever believes in Him shall not perish, but have eternal life. For God did not send the Son into the world to judge the world, but that the world might be saved through Him. He who believes in Him is not judged; he who does not believe has been judged already, because he has not believed in the name of the only begotten Son of God. This is the judgment, that the Light has come into the world, and men loved darkness rather than the Light, for their deeds were evil. For everyone who does evil hates the Light, and does not come to the Light for fear that his deeds will be exposed. But he who practices the truth comes to the Light, so that his deeds may be manifested as having been wrought in God" (John 3:16–21; see Luke 19:10; John 1:4; 1:18; 3:1–15; Romans 5:8; 1 John 1:6, 7).

Setting: Capernaum. The day after Jesus walks on the Sea of Galilee to join His disciples in a boat, the people He miraculously fed with a lad's five loaves and two fish quiz Jesus about the signs and works He performs so they may believe in Him.

Jesus then said to them, "Truly, truly, I say to you, it is not Moses who has given you the bread out of heaven, but it is My Father who gives you the true bread out of heaven. For the bread of God is that which comes down out of heaven, and gives life to the world" (John 6:32, 33; see John 6:50).

Setting: Capernaum of Galilee. After Jesus informs the people whom He miraculously fed with a lad's five loaves and two fish how they might receive the bread out of heaven, the Jewish religious leaders grumble when the Lord claims that He came down out of heaven.

Therefore the Jews were grumbling about Him, because He said, "I am the bread that came down out of heaven." They were saying, "Is not this Jesus, the son of Joseph, whose father and mother we know? How does He now say, 'I have come down out of heaven'?" Jesus answered and said to them, "Do not grumble among yourselves. No one can come to Me unless the Father who sent Me draws him; and I will raise him up on the last day. It is written in the prophets, 'AND THEY SHALL ALL BE TAUGHT OF GOD.' Everyone who has heard and learned from the Father, comes to Me. Not that anyone has seen the Father, except the One who is from God; He has seen the Father. Truly, truly, I say to you, he who believes has eternal life. I am the bread of life. Your fathers ate the manna in the wilderness, and they died. This is the bread which comes down out of heaven, so that one may eat of it and not die. I am the living bread that came down out of heaven; if anyone eats of this bread, he will live forever; and the bread also which I will give for the life of the world is My flesh" (John 6:41–51, Jesus quotes from Isaiah 54:13; see John 1:18, 29; 3:36; 7:27).

Setting: Capernaum of Galilee. Jesus' blood brothers, who do not yet believe in Him, encourage Him to attend the upcoming Feast of Booths in Jerusalem in order to demonstrate His works to His disciples and the world.

So Jesus said to them, "My time is not yet here, but your time is always opportune. The world cannot hate you, but it hates Me because I testify of it, that its deeds are evil. Go up to the feast yourselves; I do not go up to this feast because My time has not yet fully come" (John 7:6–8; see John 3:19, 20; 15:18–20).

Setting: The temple treasury in Jerusalem. Following the Feast of Booths and the scribes' and Pharisees' failed attempt to stone a woman for adultery, Jesus returns the next day to teach. They question His testimony about Himself.

Then He said again to them, "I go away, and you will seek Me, and will die in your sin; where I am going, you cannot come." So the Jews were saying, "Surely He will not kill Himself, will He, since He says, "Where I am going, you cannot come'?" And He was saying to them, "You are from below, I am from above; you are of this world, I am not of this world. Therefore I said to you that you will die in your sins; for unless you believe that I am *He,* you will die in your sins." So they were saying to Him, "Who are You?" Jesus said to them, "What have I been saying to you *from* the beginning? I have many things to speak and to judge concerning you, but He who sent Me is true; and the things which I heard from Him, these I speak to the world" (John 8:21–26; see John 3:31–33; 5:34, 35; 17:14, 16).

Setting: The temple treasury in Jerusalem. After Jesus avoids being stoned by the scribes and Pharisees, His disciples wonder if blindness is caused by sin as the Lord heals a man born blind.

Jesus answered, "*It was* neither *that* this man sinned, nor his parents; but *it was* so that the works of God might be displayed in him. We must work the works of Him who sent Me as long as it is day; night is coming when no one can work. While I am in the world, I am the Light of the world." When He had said this, He spat on the ground, and made clay of the spittle, and applied the clay to his eyes, and said to him, "Go, wash in the pool of Siloam" (which is translated, Sent). So he went away and washed, and came *back* seeing (John 9:3–7; see John 8:12; 11:4; 12:46).

Setting: Jerusalem. Following the Pharisees' interrogation and dismissal of the formerly blind man Jesus healed on the Sabbath, the Lord addresses the Pharisees about His mission in this world.

And Jesus said, "For judgment I came into this world, so that those who do not see may see, and that those who see may become blind" (John 9:39; see Luke 4:18; John 5:22, 27).

Setting: Jerusalem. At the Feast of Dedication, the Pharisees desire to stone Jesus because He claims to be equal with God when they ask Him plainly whether He is the Christ.

Jesus answered them, "Has it not been written in your Law, 'I SAID, YOU ARE GODS'? If he called them gods, to whom the word of God came (and the Scripture cannot be broken), do you say of Him, whom the Father sanctified and sent into the world, 'You are blaspheming,' because I said, 'I am the Son of God'? If I do not do the works of My Father, do not believe Me; but if I do them, though you do not believe Me, believe the works, so that you may know and understand that the Father is in Me, and I in the Father" (John 10:34–38, Jesus quotes from Psalm 82:6; see John 14:10, 20).

Setting: Jerusalem. Just days before the Passover, with the chief priests and Pharisees plotting to seize Him, crowds welcome Jesus with palm branches and praise, and some Greeks ask to meet Him.

And Jesus answered them, saying, "The hour has come for the Son of Man to be glorified. Truly, truly, I say to you, unless a grain of wheat falls into the earth and dies, it remains alone; but if it dies, it bears much fruit. He who loves his life loses it, and he who hates his life in this world will keep it to life eternal. If anyone serves Me, he must follow Me; and where I am, there My servant will be also; if anyone serves Me, the Father will honor him" (John 12:23–26; see Matthew 10:39).

Setting: Jerusalem. Just days before the Passover, with the chief priests and Pharisees plotting to seize Him and crowds welcoming Him with palm branches and praise, Jesus expresses anxiety about His upcoming crucifixion.

"Now My soul has become troubled; and what shall I say, 'Father, save Me from this hour'? But for this purpose I came to this hour. Father glorify Your name." Then a voice came out of heaven: "I have glorified it, and will glorify it again." So the crowd *of people* who stood by and heard it were saying that it had thundered; others were saying, "An angel has spoken to Him." Jesus answered and said, "This voice has not come for My sake, but for your sakes. Now judgment is upon this world; now the ruler of this world will be cast out. And I, if I am lifted up from the earth, will draw all men to Myself" (John 12:27–32; see Matthew 3:17; 26:38; John 3:14; 6:44; 11:42; 14:30).

Setting: Jerusalem. Just days before the Passover, with the chief priests and Pharisees plotting to seize Jesus, who is expressing anxiety about His upcoming crucifixion, some of the Jews believe in the Lord, while others are rejecting His message.

And Jesus cried out and said, "He who believes in Me, does not believe in Me but in Him who sent Me. He who sees Me sees the

One who sent Me. I have come *as* Light into the world, so that everyone who believes in Me will not remain in darkness. If anyone hears My sayings and does not keep them, I do not judge him; for I did not come to judge the world, but to save the world. He who rejects Me and does not receive My sayings, has one who judges him; the word I spoke is what will judge him at the last day. For I did not speak on My own initiative, but the Father Himself who sent Me has given Me a commandment *as to* what to say and what to speak. I know that His commandment is eternal life; therefore the things I speak, I speak just as the Father as told Me" (John 12:44–50; see Matthew 10:40; Luke 10:16; John 1:4; 3:17; 5:19; 6:68; 14:9).

Setting: Jerusalem. Before the Passover, after responding to Philip's request for Him to show His disciples the Father, Jesus conveys the upcoming role of the Holy Spirit in their lives.

"If you love Me, you will keep My commandments. I will ask the Father, and He will give you another Helper, that He may be with you forever; *that* is the Spirit of truth, whom the world cannot receive, because it does not see Him or know Him, *but* you know Him because He abides with you and will be in you" (John 14:15–17; see John 7:39; 15:26; 1 John 5:3).

Setting: Jerusalem. Before the Passover, after responding to Philip's request for Him to show His disciples the Father, Jesus conveys the upcoming role of the Holy Spirit in their lives.

"I will not leave you as orphans; I will come to you. After a little while the world will no longer see Me, but you *will* see Me; because I live, you will live also. In that day you will know that I am in the Father, and you in Me, and I in you. He who has My commandments and keeps them is the one who loves Me; and he who loves Me will be loved by My Father, and I will love him and will disclose Myself to him" (John 14:18–21; see John 6:57; 10:37, 38; 16:16, 22).

Setting: Jerusalem. Before the Passover, after He conveys the upcoming ministry of the Holy Spirit in His disciples' lives, Jesus again relates peace, hope, and comfort to them regarding His return to the Father.

"Peace I leave with you; My peace I give to you; not as the world gives do I give to you. Do not let your heart be troubled, nor let it be fearful. You heard that I said to you, 'I go away, and I will come to you,' If you loved Me, you would have rejoiced because I go to the Father, for the Father is greater than I. Now I have told you before it happens, so that when it happens, you may believe. I will not speak much more with you, for the ruler of the world is coming, and he has nothing in Me; but so that the world may know that I love the Father, I do exactly as the Father commanded Me. Get up, let us go from here" (John 14:27–31; see John 10:18, 29; 12:31; 13:19; 16:33).

Setting: Jerusalem. Before the Passover, with His departure in mind, after explaining He is the vine and His disciples are the branches, Jesus prepares them for persecution from the world.

"If the world hates you, you know that it has hated Me before *it hated* you. If you were of the world, the world would love its own; but because you are not of the world, but I chose you out of the world, because of this the world hates you. Remember the word that I said to you, 'A slave is not greater than his master.' If they persecuted Me, they will also persecute you; if they kept My word, they will keep yours also. But all these things they will do to you for My name's sake, because they do not know the One who sent Me. If I had not come and spoken to them, they would not have sin, but now they have no excuse for their sin" (John 15:18–22; see Matthew 10:22; John 7:7; 8:19, 55; 9:41; 1 Corinthians 4:12).

Setting: Jerusalem. Before the Passover, after warning His disciples of the persecution they will face after His departure to heaven, Jesus elaborates about the coming ministry of the Holy Spirit.

"But now I am going to Him who sent Me; and none of you asks Me, 'Where are You going?' But because I have said these things to you, sorrow has filled your heart. But I tell you the truth, it is to your advantage that I go away; for if I do not go away, the Helper will not come to you; but if I go, I will send Him to you. And He, when He comes, will convict the world concerning sin and righteousness and judgment; concerning sin, because they do not believe in Me; and concerning righteousness, because I go to the Father and you no longer see Me; and concerning judgment, because the ruler of this world has been judged" (John 16:5–11; see

John 7:33; 12:31; 14:1, 16; 15:22, 24).

Setting: Jerusalem. Before the Passover, after warning His disciples of the persecution they will face after His departure to heaven, empathizing with their sadness over His prophecies, Jesus gives them the hope for the future.

"A little while, and you will no longer see Me; and again a little while, and you will see Me." *Some* of His disciples then said to one another, "What is this thing He is telling us, 'A little while, and you will not see Me; and again a little while, and you will see Me'; and, 'because I go to the Father'?" So they were saying, "What is this that He says, 'A little while'? We do not know what He is talking about." Jesus knew that they wished to question Him, and He said to them, "Are you deliberating together about this, that I said, 'A little while, and you will not see Me, and again a little while, and you will see Me'? Truly, truly, I say to you, that you will weep and lament, but the world will rejoice; you will grieve, but your grief will be turned into joy. Whenever a woman is in labor she has pain, because her hour has come; but when she gives birth to the child, she no longer remembers the anguish because of the joy that a child has been born into the world. Therefore you too have grief now; but I will see you again, and your heart will rejoice, and no one *will* take your joy away from you" (John 16:16–22; see Mark 9:32; Luke 23:27; John 14:18–24; 20:20).

Setting: Jerusalem. Before the Passover, after empathizing with His disciples' sadness over His prophecies and giving them the hope for the future, Jesus conveys promises about praying in His name.

"In that day you will not question Me about anything. Truly, truly, I say to you, if you ask the Father for anything in My name, He will give it to you. Until now you have asked for nothing in My name; ask and you will receive, so that your joy may be made full. These things I have spoken to you in figurative language; an hour is coming when I will no longer speak to you in figurative language, but will tell you plainly of the Father. In that day you will ask in My name, and I do not say to you that I will request of the Father on your behalf; for the Father Himself loves you, because you have loved Me and have believed that I came forth from the Father. I came forth from the Father and have come into the world; I am leaving the world again and going to the Father" (John 16:23–28; see Matthew 13:34; John 8:42; 13:1, 3; 14:14, 21, 23; 15:16).

Setting: Jerusalem. Before the Passover, after conveying promises about praying in His name, Jesus prophesies the disciples' scattering and gives them assurance that in the midst of tribulation they will have His peace.

"Jesus answered them, "Do you now believe? Behold, an hour is coming, and has *already* come, for you to be scattered, each to his own *home,* and to leave Me alone; and *yet* I am not alone, because the Father is with Me. These things I have spoken to you, so that in Me you may have peace. In the world you have tribulation, but take courage, I have overcome the world" (John 16:31–33; see Zechariah 13:7; John 8:29; 14:27; Romans 8:37).

Setting: Jerusalem. Before the Passover, after giving His disciples assurance that in the midst of tribulation they will have His peace, Jesus prays His high-priestly prayer.

Jesus spoke these things; and lifting up His eyes to heaven, He said, "Father, the hour has come; glorify Your Son, that the Son may glorify You, even as You gave Him authority over all flesh, that to all whom You have given Him, He may give eternal life. This is eternal life, that they may know You, the only true God, and Jesus Christ whom You have sent. I glorified You on the earth, having accomplished the work which You have given Me to do. Now, Father, glorify Me together with Yourself, with the glory which I had with You before the world was. I have manifested Your name to the men whom You gave Me out of the world; they were Yours and You gave them to Me, and they have kept Your word. Now they have come to know that everything You have given Me is from You; for the words which You gave Me I have given to them; and they received *them* and truly understood that I came forth from You, and they believed You sent Me. I ask on their behalf; I do not ask on behalf of the world, but of those whom You have given Me; for they are Yours; and all things that are Mine are Yours, and Yours are Mine; and I have been glorified in them. I am no longer in the world; and *yet* they themselves are in the world, and I come to You. Holy Father, keep them in Your name, *the name* which You have given Me, that they may be even as We *are.* While I was with them, I was keeping them in Your name which You have given Me; and I guarded them and not one of them perished but the son of perdition, so that the Scripture would be fulfilled" (John 17:1–12; see Luke 22:32; John 1:1; 3:35; 4:34; 5:44; 6:37–39, 70; 8:42; 11:41; 12:49; 13:18, 31; 16:15; Philippians 2:9).

Setting: Jerusalem. Before the Passover, after giving His disciples assurance that in the midst of tribulation they will have His peace, Jesus continues praying His high-priestly prayer.

"But now I come to You; and these things I speak in the world so that they may have My joy made full in themselves. I have given them Your word; and the world has hated them, because they are not of the world, even as I am not of the world. I do not ask You to take them out of the world, but to keep them from the evil *one.* They are not of the world, even as I am not of the world. Sanctify them in the truth; Your word is truth. As You sent Me into the world, I also have sent them into the world. For their sakes I sanctify Myself, that they themselves also may be sanctified in truth. I do not ask on behalf of these alone, but for those also who believe in Me through their word; that they may all be one; even as You, Father, *are* in Me and I in You, that they also maybe in Us, so that the world may believe that You sent Me" (John 17:13–21; see Matthew 10:5, 38; John 7:33; 15:3, 11, 19).

Setting: Jerusalem. Before the Passover, after giving His disciples assurance that in the midst of tribulation they will have His peace, Jesus continues praying His high-priestly prayer.

"The glory which You have given Me I have given to them, that they may be one, just as We are one; I in them and You in Me, that they may be perfected in unity, so that the world may know that you sent Me, and loved them, even as You have loved Me. Father, I desire that they also, whom You have given Me, be with Me where I am, so that they may see My glory which You have given Me, for You loved Me before the foundation of the world. O righteous Father, although the world has not known You, yet I have known You; and these have known that You sent Me; and I have made Your name known to them, and will make it known, so that the love with which You loved Me may be in them, and I in them" (John 17:22–26; see Matthew 25:34; John 1:14; 10:38; 15:9; 16:27).

Setting: Jerusalem. After Jesus is betrayed by Judas, and Peter denies he is the Lord's disciple, Annas, former high priest and father-in-law of the current high priest (Caiaphas), questions Jesus about His disciples and His teaching.

Jesus answered him, "I have spoken openly to the world; I always taught in synagogues and in the temple, where all the Jews come together; and I spoke nothing in secret. Why do you question Me? Question those who have heard what I spoke to them; they know what I said" (John 18:20, 21; see John 7:26).

Setting: Jerusalem. After the previous and current high priests (Annas and Caiaphas) question Jesus, and Peter denies the second and third times being the Lord's disciple, Pilate (Roman governor of Judea) asks Jesus what He has done.

Jesus answered, "My kingdom is not of this world. If My kingdom were of this world, then My servants would be fighting so that I would not be handed over to the Jews; but as it is, My kingdom is not of this realm" (John 18:36; see Matthew 26:53).

Setting: Jerusalem. After the previous and current high priests (Annas and Caiaphas) question Jesus, and Peter denies the second and third times being His disciple, Pilate (Roman governor of Judea) questions the Lord in an attempt to determine if He is a king.

Therefore Pilate said to Him, "So You are a king?" Jesus answered, "You say *correctly* that I am a king. For this I have been born, and for this I have come into the world, to testify to the truth. Everyone who is of the truth hears my voice" (John 18:37; cf. Matthew 27:11; Mark 15:2; Luke 23:3).

WORLD, BEGINNING OF THE **(Also see CREATION; CREATION, BEGINNING OF; CREATION, BEGINNING OF THE; CREATOR; and WORLD, FOUNDATION OF THE)**

Setting: The Mount of Olives, just east of Jerusalem. During His Olivet Discourse, Jesus answers His disciples' questions as to when the temple will be destroyed and Jerusalem overrun, along with the signs of His coming and the end of the age.

"Therefore when you see the ABOMINATION OF DESOLATION which was spoken of through Daniel the prophet, standing in the holy place (let the reader understand), then those who are in Judea must flee to the mountains. Whoever is on the housetop must not go down to get the things that are in his house. Whoever is in the field must not turn back to get his cloak. But woe to those who are pregnant and to those who are nursing babies in those days! But pray that your flight will not be in the winter, or on a Sabbath. For then there will be a great tribulation, such as has not occurred since the beginning of the world until now, nor ever will. Unless those days had been cut short, no life would have been saved; but for the sake of the elect those days will be cut short. Then if anyone says to you, 'Behold, here is the Christ,' or "There *He is*,' do not believe *him*. For false Christs and false prophets will arise and will show great signs and wonders, so as to mislead, if possible, even the elect. Behold, I have told you in advance. So if they say to you, 'Behold, He is in the wilderness,' do not go out, *or*, 'Behold, He is in the inner rooms,' do not believe *them*. For just as the lightning comes from the east and flashes even to the west, so will the coming of the Son of Man be. Wherever the corpse is, there the vultures will gather" (Matthew 24:15–28, Jesus quotes from Daniel 9:27; cf. Daniel 12:1; Mark 13:14–23; Luke 17:22–31; 21:20–24; 23:29; see John 4:48).

WORLD, FOUNDATION OF THE (Also see CREATION; CREATION, BEGINNING OF; CREATION, BEGINNING OF THE; CREATOR; and WORLD, BEGINNING OF THE)

Setting: On the Mount of Olives, just east of Jerusalem. During His Olivet Discourse, after answering His disciples' questions as to when the temple will be destroyed and Jerusalem overrun, along with the signs of His coming and the end of the age, Jesus reveals the future judgments following His return.

"But when the Son of Man comes in His glory, and all the angels with Him, then He will sit on His glorious throne. All the nations will be gathered before Him; and He will separate them from one another, as the shepherd separates the sheep from the goats; and He will put the sheep on His right, and the goats on the left. Then the King will say to those on His right, 'Come, you who are blessed of My Father, inherit the kingdom prepared for you from the foundation of the world. 'For I was hungry, and you gave Me *something* to eat; I was thirsty, and you gave Me *something* to drink; I was a stranger, and you invited Me in; naked, and you clothed Me; I was sick, and you visited Me; I was in prison, and you came to Me.' Then the righteous will answer Him, 'Lord, when did we see You hungry and feed You, or thirsty, and give you *something* to drink? And when did we see You a stranger, and invite You in, or naked, and clothe You? When did we see You sick, or in prison, and come to You?' The King will answer and say to them, 'Truly I say to you, to the extent that you did it to one of these brothers of Mine, *even* the least *of them,* you did it to Me.' Then He will also say to those on His left, 'Depart from Me, accursed ones, into the eternal fire which has been prepared for the devil and his angels; for I was hungry, and you gave Me *nothing* to eat; I was thirsty, and you gave Me nothing to drink; I was a stranger, and you did not invite Me in; naked, and you did not clothe Me; sick, and in prison, and you did not visit Me.' Then they themselves also will answer, 'Lord, when did we see You hungry, or thirsty, or a stranger, or naked, or sick, or in prison, and did not take care of You?' Then He will answer them, 'Truly I say to you, to the extent that you did not do it to one of the least of these, you did not do it to Me.' These will go away into eternal punishment, but the righteous into eternal life" (Matthew 25:31–46; see Matthew 7:23; 16:27; 19:29).

Setting: On the way from Galilee to Jerusalem. After Jesus pronounces woes upon the Pharisees, a lawyer replies that His remarks are an insult to lawyers, too.

But He said, "Woe to you lawyers as well! For you weigh men down with burdens hard to bear, while you yourselves will not even touch the burdens with one of your fingers. Woe to you! For you build the tombs of the prophets, and *it was* your fathers *who* killed them. So you are witnesses and approve the deeds of your fathers; because it was they who killed them, and you build *their tombs*. For this reason also the wisdom of God said, 'I will send them prophets and apostles, and *some* of them they will kill and *some* they will persecute, so that the blood of all the prophets, shed since the foundation of the world, may be charged against this generation, from the blood of Abel to the blood of Zechariah, who was killed between the altar and the house *of God*; yes, I tell you, it shall be charged against this generation.' Woe to you lawyers! For you have taken away the key of knowledge; you yourselves did not enter, and you hindered those who were entering" (Luke 11:46–52; cf. Matthew 23:29–32; see 2 Chronicles 24:20, 21; Matthew 23:4, 13).

Setting: Jerusalem. Before the Passover, after giving His disciples assurance that in the midst of tribulation they will have His peace, Jesus continues praying His high-priestly prayer.

"The glory which You have given Me I have given to them, that they may be one, just as We are one; I in them and You in Me, that they may be perfected in unity, so that the world may know that you sent Me, and loved them, even as You have loved Me. Father, I desire that they also, whom You have given Me, be with Me where I am, so that they may see My glory which You have given Me, for You loved Me before the foundation of the world. O righteous Father, although the world has not known You, yet I have known You; and these have known that You sent Me; and I have made Your name known to them, and will make it known, so that the love with which You loved Me may be in them, and I in them" (John 17:22–26; see Matthew 25:34; John 1:14; 10:38; 15:9; 16:27; 17:1–21).

WORLD, LIGHT INTO THE

Setting: Jerusalem. Just days before the Passover, with the chief priests and Pharisees plotting to seize Jesus, who is expressing anxiety about His upcoming crucifixion, some of the Jews believe in the Lord, while others are rejecting His message.

And Jesus cried out and said, "He who believes in Me, does not believe in Me but in Him who sent Me. He who sees Me sees the One who sent Me. I have come *as* Light into the world, so that everyone who believes in Me will not remain in darkness. If anyone hears My sayings and does not keep them, I do not judge him; for I did not come to judge the world, but to save the world. He who rejects Me and does not receive My sayings, has one who judges him; the word I spoke is what will judge him at the last day. For I did not speak on My own initiative, but the Father Himself who sent Me has given Me a commandment *as to* what to say and what to speak. I know that His commandment is eternal life; therefore the things I speak, I speak just as the Father as told Me" (John 12:44–50; see Matthew 10:40; Luke 10:16; John 1:4; 3:17; 5:19; 6:68; 14:9).

WORLD, LIGHT OF THE (Also see WORLD, LIGHT OF THIS)

Setting: Galilee. During the early part of His ministry, Jesus preaches the Sermon on the Mount to His disciples and the multitudes.

"You are the light of the world. A city set on a hill cannot be hidden; nor does *anyone* light a lamp and put it under a basket, but on the lampstand, and it gives light to all who are in the house. Let your light shine before men in such a way that they may see your good works, and glorify your Father who is in heaven" (Matthew 5:14–16; cf. Mark 4:21; 1 Peter 2:12).

Setting: The temple in Jerusalem. Following the Feast of Booths, Jesus retires to the Mount of Olives, and returns the next day to teach. He addresses the scribes and Pharisees after their failed attempt to stone a woman caught in adultery.

Then Jesus again spoke to them, saying, "I am the Light of the world; he who follows Me will not walk in the darkness, but will have the Light of life" (John 8:12; see John 1:4).

Setting: The temple treasury in Jerusalem. After Jesus avoids being stoned by the scribes and Pharisees, His disciples wonder if blindness is caused by sin as the Lord heals a man born blind.

Jesus answered, "*It was* neither *that* this man sinned, nor his parents; but *it was* so that the works of God might be displayed in him. We must work the works of Him who sent Me as long as it is day; night is coming when no one can work. While I am in the world, I am the Light of the world." When He had said this, He spat on the ground, and made clay of the spittle, and applied the clay to his eyes, and said to him, "Go, wash in the pool of Siloam" (which is translated, Sent). So he went away and washed, and came *back* seeing (John 9:3–7; see John 8:12; 11:4; 12:46).

WORLD, LIGHT OF THIS (Also see SUN; and WORLD, LIGHT OF THE)

Setting: Beyond the Jordan. While He and His disciples are avoiding the Jerusalem Pharisees, Jesus receives word from Lazarus's sisters in Bethany of His friend's sickness, and decides to go there.

Then after this He said to the disciples, "Let us go to Judea again." The disciples said to Him, "Rabbi, the Jews were just now seeking to stone You, and are You going there again?" Jesus answered, "Are there not twelve hours in the day? If anyone walks in the day, he does not stumble, because he sees the light of this world. But if anyone walks in the night, he stumbles, because the light is not in him." This He said, and after that He said to them, "Our friend Lazarus has fallen asleep; but I go, so that I may awaken him out of sleep" (John 11:7–11; see John 8:59; 10:39).

WORLD, NATIONS OF THE

Setting: On the way from Galilee to Jerusalem. After giving a parable about riches and greed, Jesus comforts the crowd and His disciples. The scribes and Pharisees turn hostile and question Him repeatedly in an attempt to catch Him in something He might say.

And He said to His disciples, "For this reason I say to you, do not worry about *your* life, *as to* what you will eat; nor for your body, *as to* what you will put on. For life is more than food, and the body more than clothing. Consider the ravens, for they neither sow nor reap; they have no storeroom nor barn, and *yet* God feeds them; how much more valuable you are than the birds! And which of you by worrying can add a *single* hour to his life's span? If then you cannot do even a very little thing, why do you worry about other matters? Consider the lilies, how they grow: they neither toil nor spin; but I tell you, not even Solomon in all his glory clothed himself like one of these. But if God so clothes the grass in the field, which is *alive* today and tomorrow is thrown into the furnace, how much more *will He clothe* you? You men of little faith! And do not seek what you will eat and what you will drink, and do not keep worrying. For all these things the nations of the world eagerly seek; but your Father knows that you need these things. But seek His kingdom, and these things will be added to you. Do not be afraid, little flock, for your Father has chosen gladly to give you the kingdom" (Luke 12:22–32; cf. Matthew 6:25–33; see 1 Kings 10:4–7; Job 38:41).

WORLD, OVERCOMING THE (See VICTORY)

WORLD, RULER OF THE (Also see SATAN; and WORLD, RULER OF THIS)

Setting: Jerusalem. Before the Passover, after He conveys the upcoming ministry of the Holy Spirit in His disciples' lives, Jesus again relates peace, hope, and comfort to them regarding His return to the Father.

"Peace I leave with you; My peace I give to you; not as the world gives do I give to you. Do not let your heart be troubled, nor let it be fearful. You heard that I said to you, 'I go away, and I will come to you.' If you loved Me, you would have rejoiced because I go to the Father, for the Father is greater than I. Now I have told you before it happens, so that when it happens, you may believe. I will not speak much more with you, for the ruler of the world is coming, and he has nothing in Me; but so that the world may know that I love the Father, I do exactly as the Father commanded Me. Get up, let us go from here" (John 14:27–31; see John 10:18, 29; 12:31; 13:19; 16:33).

WORLD, RULER OF THIS (Also see SATAN; and WORLD, RULER OF THE)

Setting: Jerusalem. Just days before the Passover, with the chief priests and Pharisees plotting to seize Him and crowds welcoming Him with palm branches and praise, Jesus expresses anxiety about His upcoming crucifixion.

"Now My soul has become troubled; and what shall I say, 'Father, save Me from this hour'? But for this purpose I came to this hour. Father glorify Your name." Then a voice came out of heaven: "I have glorified it, and will glorify it again." So the crowd *of people* who stood by and heard it were saying that it had thundered; others were saying, "An angel has spoken to Him." Jesus answered and said, "This voice has not come for My sake, but for your sakes. Now judgment is upon this world; now the ruler of this world will be cast out. And I, if I am lifted up from the earth, will draw all men to Myself" (John 12:27–32; see Matthew 3:17; 26:38; John 3:14; 6:44; 11:42; 14:30).

Setting: Jerusalem. Before the Passover, after warning His disciples of the persecution they will face after His departure to heaven, Jesus elaborates about the coming ministry of the Holy Spirit.

"But now I am going to Him who sent Me; and none of you asks Me, 'Where are You going?' But because I have said these things to you, sorrow has filled your heart. But I tell you the truth, it is to your advantage that I go away; for if I do not go away, the Helper will not come to you; but if I go, I will send Him to you. And He, when He comes, will convict the world concerning sin and righteousness and judgment; concerning sin, because they do not believe in Me; and concerning righteousness, because I go to the Father and you no longer see Me; and concerning judgment, because the ruler of this world has been judged" (John 16:5–11; see John 7:33; 12:31; 14:1, 16; 15:22, 24).

WORLD, WHOLE

Setting: Near Caesarea Philippi. After rebuking Peter for trying to forbid Him to accomplish His earthly mission of dying and being resurrected, Jesus teaches His disciples about the costs of following Him.

Then Jesus said to His disciples, "If anyone wishes to come after Me, he must deny himself, and take up his cross and follow Me. For whoever wishes to save his life will lose it; but whoever loses his life for My sake will find it. For what will it profit a man if he gains the whole world and forfeits his soul? Or what will a man give in exchange for his soul? For the Son of Man is going to come in the glory of His Father with His angels, and WILL THEN REPAY EVERY MAN ACCORDING TO HIS DEEDS. Truly, I say to you, there are some of you who are standing here who will not taste death until they see the Son of Man coming in His kingdom" (Matthew 16:24–28, Jesus quotes from Psalm 62:12; cf. Mark 8:34–37; Luke 9:23–27; see Matthew 10:38, 39).

Setting: The Mount of Olives, just east of Jerusalem. During His Olivet Discourse, Jesus answers His disciples' questions as to when the temple will be destroyed and Jerusalem overrun, along with the signs of His coming and the end of the age.

And Jesus answered and said to them, "See to it that no one misleads you. For many will come in My name, saying, 'I am the Christ,' and will mislead many. You will be hearing of wars and rumors of wars. See that you are not frightened, for *those things* must take place, but *that* is not yet the end. For nation will rise against nation, and kingdom against kingdom, and in various places there will be famines and earthquakes. But all these things are *merely* the beginning of birth pangs. Then they will deliver you to tribulation, and will kill you, and you will be hated by all nations because of My name. At that time many will fall away and will betray one another and hate one another. Many false prophets will arise and will mislead many. Because lawlessness is increased, most people's love will grow cold. But the one who endures to the end, he will be saved. This gospel of the kingdom shall be preached in the whole world as a testimony to all the nations, and then the end will come" (Matthew 24:4–14; cf. Jeremiah 29:8; Matthew 7:15; 10:17, 22; Mark 13:3–13; Luke 21:7–19; Revelation 6:4).

Setting: The home of Simon the leper in Bethany. Jesus rebukes His disciples after they criticize a woman for pouring a costly vial of perfume on His head in preparation for His burial.

But Jesus, aware of this, said to them, "Why do you bother the woman? For she has done a good deed to Me. For you always have the poor with you; but you do not always have Me. For when she poured this perfume on My body, she did it to prepare Me for burial. Truly I say to you, wherever this gospel is preached in the whole world, what this woman has done will also be spoken of in memory of her" (Matthew 26:10–13; cf. Mark 14:3–9; Luke 7:37–39; John 12:2–8; see Deuteronomy 15:11).

Setting: Caesarea Philippi. After rebuking Peter for desiring to thwart His mission to the cross, Jesus summons a crowd, along with His disciples, and informs them of the high costs of following Him.

And He summoned the crowd with His disciples, and said to them, "If anyone wishes to come after Me, he must deny himself, and take up his cross and follow Me. For whoever wishes to save his life will lose it, but whoever loses his life for My sake and the gospel's will save it. For what does it profit a man to gain the whole world, and forfeit his soul? For what will a man give in exchange for his soul? For whoever is ashamed of Me and My words in this adulterous and sinful generation, the Son of Man will also be ashamed of him when He comes in the glory of His Father with the holy angels" (Mark 8:34–38; cf. Matthew 16:24–28; Luke 9:23–27; see Matthew 10:33, 38, 39).

Setting: The home of Simon the leper in Bethany. Two days before the Feast of Unleavened Bread (Passover), Jesus commends a woman who anoints His head with costly perfume, which some there think should have been sold and the proceeds given to the poor.

But Jesus said, "Let her alone; why do you bother her? She has done a good deed to Me. For you always have the poor with you, and whenever you wish you can do good to them; but you do not always have Me. She has done what she could; she has anointed My body beforehand for the burial. Truly I say to you, wherever the gospel is preached in the whole world, what this woman has done will also be spoken of in memory of her" (Mark 14:6–9; cf. Matthew 26:6–13; John 12:2–8; see Deuteronomy 15:11).

Setting: Galilee. Following Peter's pronouncement that Jesus is the Christ of God, the Lord conveys the demands of discipleship and the hope regarding the kingdom of God.

And He was saying to *them* all, "If anyone wishes to come after Me, he must deny himself, and take up his cross daily and follow Me. For whoever wishes to save his life will lose it, but whoever loses his life for My sake, he is the one who will save it. For what is a man profited if he gains the whole world, and loses or forfeits himself? For whoever is ashamed of Me and My words, the Son of Man will be ashamed of him when He comes in His glory, and *the glory* of the Father and of the holy angels. But I say to you truthfully, there are some of those standing here who will not taste death until they see the kingdom of God" (Luke 9:23–27; cf. Matthew 16:24–26, 28; Mark 8:34–37; see Matthew 10:33, 38, 39).

Setting: On the island of Patmos (in the Aegean Sea about fifty miles southwest of Ephesus in modern Turkey). On the Lord's Day (Sunday), approximately fifty years after the Resurrection, the disciple John encounters the Lord Jesus Christ, who communicates a new revelation for the apostle to record for the church in Philadelphia and to six other churches in Asia.

"And to the angel of the church in Philadelphia write: He who is holy, who is true, who has the key of David, who opens and no one will shut, and who shuts and no one opens, says this: 'I know your deeds. Behold, I have put before you an open door which no one can shut, because you have a little power, and have kept My word, and have not denied My name. Behold, I will cause *those* of the synagogue of Satan, who say that they are Jews and are not, but lie—I will make them come and bow down at your feet, and *make them* know that I have loved you. Because you have kept the word of My perseverance, I also will keep you from the hour of testing, that *hour* which is about to come upon the whole world, to test those who dwell on the earth. I am coming quickly; hold fast what you have, so that no one will take your crown. He who overcomes, I will make him a pillar in the temple of My God, and he will not go out from it anymore; and I will write on him the name of My God, and the name of the city of My God, the new Jerusalem, which comes down out of heaven from My God, and My new name. He who has an ear, let him hear what the Spirit says to the churches' " (Revelation 3:7–13; see Isaiah 22:22; Galatians 2:9; Revelation 2:9, 10, 13, 25; 14:1).

WORLD, WORRIES OF THE (Also see WORRIES; and WORRY)

Setting: By the Sea of Galilee. With the religious leaders rejecting His message, Jesus begins to teach in parables, and gives His disciples the meaning of the Parable of the Sower.

"Hear then the parable of the sower. When anyone hears the word of the kingdom and does not understand it, the evil *one* comes and snatches away what has been sown in his heart. This is the one on whom seed was sown beside the road. The one on whom seed was sown on the rocky places, this is the man who hears the word and immediately receives it with joy; yet he has no *firm* root in himself, but is *only* temporary, and when affliction or persecution arises because of the word, immediately he falls away. And the one on whom seed was sown among the thorns, this is the man who hears the word, and the worry of the world and the deceitfulness of wealth choke the word, and it becomes unfruitful. And the one on whom seed was sown on the good soil, this is the man who hears the word and understands it; who indeed bears fruit and brings forth, some a hundredfold, some sixty, and some thirty" (Matthew 13:18–23; cf. Mark 4:13–20; Luke 8:11–15).

Setting: By the Sea of Galilee. During the early part of His ministry, after presenting the Parable of the Sower from a boat to a very large crowd, Jesus gives the meaning of the parable to His disciples and other followers.

And He said to them, "Do you not understand this parable? How will you understand all the parables? The sower sows the word. These are the ones who are beside the road where the word is sown; and when they hear, immediately Satan comes and takes away the word which has been sown in them. In a similar way these are the ones on whom seed was sown on the rocky places, who, when they hear the word, immediately receive it with joy; and they have no *firm* root in themselves, but are *only* temporary; then, when affliction or persecution arises because of the word, immediately they fall away. And others are the ones on whom seed was sown among the thorns; these are the ones who have heard the word, but the worries of the world and the deceitfulness of riches, and the desires for other things enter in and choke the word, and it becomes unfruitful. And those are the ones on whom seed was sown on the good soil; and they hear the word and accept it and bear fruit, thirty, sixty, and a hundredfold"

(Mark 4:13–20; cf. Matthew 13:18–23; Luke 8:11–15).

WORM

Setting: Capernaum of Galilee. As Jesus teaches His disciples in private, they ask Him about greatness.

But Jesus said, "Do not hinder him, for there is no one who will perform a miracle in My name, and be able soon afterward to speak evil of Me. For he who is not against us is for us. For whoever gives you a cup of water to drink because of your name as *followers* of Christ, truly I say to you, he will not lose his reward. Whoever causes one of these little ones who believe to stumble, it would be better for him if, with a heavy millstone hung around his neck, he had been cast into the sea. If your hand causes you to stumble, cut it off; it is better for you to enter life crippled, than, having your two hands, to go into hell, into the unquenchable fire, [where THEIR WORM DOES NOT DIE, AND THE FIRE IS NOT QUENCHED.] If your foot causes you to stumble, cut it off; it is better for you to enter life lame, than, having your two feet, to be cast into hell, [where THEIR WORM DOES NOT DIE, AND THE FIRE IS NOT QUENCHED.] If your eye causes you to stumble, throw it out; it is better for you to enter the kingdom of God with one eye, than, having two eyes, to be cast into hell, where THEIR WORM DOES NOT DIE, AND THE FIRE IS NOT QUENCHED. For everyone will be salted with fire. Salt is good; but if the salt becomes unsalty, with what will you make it salty *again?* Have salt in yourselves, and be at peace with one another" (Mark 9:39–50; Jesus quotes from Isaiah 66:24; cf. Matthew 18:6–9; Luke 9:49, 50; see Matthew 5:13, 29, 30; 10:42; 12:30; 18:5, 6).

WORRIES (WORLD, WORRIES OF THE is a separate entry; also see WORRY)

[WORRIES from do not be worried about your life and Do not worry]

Setting: Galilee. During the early part of His ministry, Jesus preaches the Sermon on the Mount to His disciples and the multitudes.

"For this reason I say to you, do not be worried about your life, *as to* what you will eat or what you will drink; nor for your body, *as to* what you will put on. Is not life more than food, and the body more than clothing? Look at the birds of the air, that they do not sow, nor reap nor gather into barns, and *yet* your heavenly Father feeds them. Are you not worth much more than they? And who of you by being worried can add a *single* hour to his life? And why are you worried about clothing? Observe how the lilies of the field grow; they do not toil nor do they spin, yet I say to you that not even Solomon in all his glory clothed himself like one of these. But if God so clothes the grass of the field, which is *alive* today and tomorrow is thrown into the furnace, *will He* not much more *clothe* you? You of little faith! Do not worry then, saying 'What will we eat?' or 'What will we drink?' or 'What will be wear for clothing?" For the Gentiles eagerly seek all these things; for your heavenly Father knows that you need all these things. But seek first His kingdom and His righteousness, and all these things will be added to you. So do not worry about tomorrow; for tomorrow will care for itself. Each day has enough trouble of its own" (Matthew 6:25–34; cf. Luke 12:22–31; see 1 Kings 10:4–7; Job 35:11; Matthew 8:26).

Setting: Galilee. After Jesus presents the Parable of the Sower to the crowds, His disciples ask Him to give them the parable's meaning.

And He said, "To you it has been granted to know the mysteries of the kingdom of God, but to the rest *it is* in parables, so that SEEING THEY MAY NOT SEE, AND HEARING THEY MAY NOT UNDERSTAND. Now the parable is this: the seed is the word of God. Those beside the road are those who have heard; then the devil comes and takes away the word from their heart, so that they will not believe and be saved. Those on the rocky *soil* are those who, when they hear, receive the word with joy; and these have no *firm* root; they believe for a while, and in time of temptation fall away. The *seed* which fell among the thorns, these are the ones who have heard, and as they go on their way they are choked with worries and riches and pleasures of *this* life, and bring no fruit to maturity. But the *seed* in the good soil, these are the ones who have heard the word in an honest and good heart, and hold it fast, and bear fruit with perseverance" (Luke 8:10–15, Jesus quotes from Isaiah 6:9; cf. Matthew 13:10–23; Mark 4:10–20).

Setting: The Mount of Olives, east of the temple in Jerusalem. After ministering in the temple a few days before His crucifixion, and conveying the Parable of the Fig Tree during His Olivet Discourse, Jesus warns His disciples to keep alert regarding future events.

"Be on guard, so that your hearts will not be weighted down with dissipation and drunkenness and the worries of life, and that day will not come upon you suddenly like a trap; for it will come upon all those who dwell on the face of all the earth. But keep on the alert at all times, praying that you may have strength to escape all these things that are about to take place, and to stand before the Son of Man" (Luke 21:34–36; cf. Mark 13:33; see Matthew 24:42–44).

WORRY (Also see ANGUISH; ANXIETY; DESPAIR; FEAR; and WORRIES)

Setting: Galilee. During the early part of His ministry, Jesus preaches the Sermon on the Mount to His disciples and the multitudes.

"For this reason I say to you, do not be worried about your life, *as to* what you will eat or what you will drink; nor for your body, *as to* what you will put on. Is not life more than food, and the body more than clothing? Look at the birds of the air, that they do not sow, nor reap nor gather into barns, and *yet* your heavenly Father feeds them. Are you not worth much more than they? And who of you by being worried can add a *single* hour to his life? And why are you worried about clothing? Observe how the lilies of the field grow; they do not toil nor do they spin, yet I say to you that not even Solomon in all his glory clothed himself like one of these. But if God so clothes the grass of the field, which is *alive* today and tomorrow is thrown into the furnace, *will He* not much more *clothe* you? You of little faith! Do not worry then, saying 'What will we eat?' or 'What will we drink?' or 'What will be wear for clothing?" For the Gentiles eagerly seek all these things; for your heavenly Father knows that you need all these things. But seek first His kingdom and His righteousness, and all these things will be added to you. So do not worry about tomorrow; for tomorrow will care for itself. Each day has enough trouble of its own" (Matthew 6:25–34; cf. Luke 12:22–31; see 1 Kings 10:4–7; Job 35:11; Matthew 8:26).

Setting: Galilee. After His disciples observe His ministry, Jesus summons and specifically instructs them about the upcoming hardships of their ministry to the people of Israel.

"Behold, I send you out as sheep in the midst of wolves; so be shrewd as serpents and innocent as doves. But beware of men, for they will hand you over to *the* courts and scourge you in their synagogues; and you will even be brought before governors and kings for My sake, as a testimony to them and to the Gentiles. But when they hand you over, do not worry about how or what you are to say; for it will be given you in that hour what you are to say. For it is not you who speak, but *it* is the Spirit of your Father who speaks in you" (Matthew 10:16–20; cf. Luke 10:3).

Setting: By the Sea of Galilee. With the religious leaders rejecting His message, Jesus begins to teach in parables, and gives His disciples the meaning of the Parable of the Sower.

"Hear then the parable of the sower. When anyone hears the word of the kingdom and does not understand it, the evil *one* comes and snatches away what has been sown in his heart. This is the one on whom seed was sown beside the road. The one on whom seed was sown on the rocky places, this is the man who hears the word and immediately receives it with joy; yet he has no *firm* root in himself, but is *only* temporary, and when affliction or persecution arises because of the word, immediately he falls away. And the one on whom seed was sown among the thorns, this is the man who hears the word, and the worry of the world and the deceitfulness of wealth choke the word, and it becomes unfruitful. And the one on whom seed was sown on the good soil, this is the man who hears the word and understands it; who indeed bears fruit and brings forth, some a hundredfold, some sixty, and some thirty" (Matthew 13:18–23; cf. Mark 4:13–20; Luke 8:11–15; see Matthew 13:8).

Setting: On the Mount of Olives, east of the temple in Jerusalem. After prophesying the temple's destruction, Jesus responds during His Olivet Discourse to questions from Peter, James, John, and Andrew about other future events.

And Jesus began to say to them, "See to it that no one misleads you. Many will come in My name, saying, 'I am *He!*' and will mislead many. When you hear of wars and rumors of wars, do not be frightened; *those things* must take place; but *that is* not yet the end. For nation will rise up against nation, and kingdom against kingdom; there will be earthquakes in various places; there will *also be* famines. These things are *merely* the beginning of birth pangs. But be on your guard; for they will deliver you to *the* courts, and you will be flogged in *the* synagogues, and you will stand before governors and kings for My sake, as a testimony to them. The gospel must first be preached to all the nations. When they arrest you and hand you over, do not worry beforehand about what you are to say, but say whatever is given you in that hour; for it is not you who speak, but *it is* the Holy Spirit. Brother will betray brother to death, and a father *his* child; and children will rise up against parents and have them put to death. You will be hated by all because of My name, but the one who endures to the end, he will be saved" (Mark 13:5–13; cf. Matthew 24:4–14; Luke 21:7–19; see Matthew 10:17–22).

[WORRY from worried and bothered]

Setting: On the way from Galilee to Jerusalem. After being tested by a lawyer, the Lord and His disciples are welcomed into the home of Martha and Mary in Bethany.

But the Lord answered and said to her, "Martha, Martha, you are worried and bothered about so many things; but *only* one thing is necessary, for Mary has chosen the good part, which shall not be taken away from her" (Luke 10:41, 42; see Matthew 6:25).

Setting: On the way from Galilee to Jerusalem. Jesus warns His disciples of future events, as the scribes and Pharisees turn hostile and question Him repeatedly in an attempt to catch Him in something He might say.

"And I say to you, everyone who confesses Me before men, the Son of Man will confess him also before the angels of God; but he who denies Me before men will be denied before the angels of God. And everyone who speaks a word against the Son of Man, it will be forgiven him; but he who blasphemes against the Holy Spirit, it will not be forgiven him. When they bring you before the synagogues and the rulers and the authorities, do not worry about how or what you are to speak in your defense, or what you are to say; for the Holy Spirit will teach you in that very hour what you ought to say" (Luke 12:8–12; cf. Matthew 10:32, 33; 12:31, 32; see Matthew 10:20).

Setting: On the way from Galilee to Jerusalem. After giving a parable about riches and greed, Jesus comforts the crowd and His disciples. The scribes and Pharisees turn hostile and question Him repeatedly in an attempt to catch Him in something He might say.

And He said to His disciples, "For this reason I say to you, do not worry about *your* life, *as to* what you will eat; nor for your body, *as to* what you will put on. For life is more than food, and the body more than clothing. Consider the ravens, for they neither sow nor reap; they have no storeroom nor barn, and *yet* God feeds them; how much more valuable you are than the birds! And which of you by worrying can add a *single* hour to his life's span? If then you cannot do even a very little thing, why do you worry about other matters? Consider the lilies, how they grow: they neither toil nor spin; but I tell you, not even Solomon in all his glory clothed himself like one of these. But if God so clothes the grass in the field, which is *alive* today and tomorrow is thrown into the furnace, how much more *will He clothe* you? You men of little faith! And do not seek what you will eat and what you will drink, and do not keep worrying. For all these things the nations of the world eagerly seek; but your Father knows that you need these things. But seek His kingdom, and these things will be added to you. Do not be afraid, little flock, for your Father has chosen gladly to give you the kingdom" (Luke 12:22–32; cf. Matthew 6:25–33; see 1 Kings 10:4–7; Job 38:41).

WORSHIP (Also see OFFERING; PRAISE; SERVING GOD; and TITHE)

Setting: Judea, near the Jordan River. Following His baptism, and before He begins His public ministry, Jesus is led by the Spirit into the wilderness for forty days of temptation by Satan.

Then Jesus said to him, "Go, Satan! For it is written, 'YOU SHALL WORSHIP THE LORD YOUR GOD, AND SERVE HIM ONLY'" (Matthew 4:10, Jesus quotes from Deuteronomy 6:13; cf. Luke 4:8).

Setting: Galilee. Pharisees and scribes from Jerusalem accuse Jesus' disciples of disobeying tradition and the commandments.

And He answered and said to them, "Why do you yourselves transgress the commandment of God for the sake of tradition? For God said, 'HONOR YOUR FATHER AND MOTHER,' and, 'HE WHO SPEAKS EVIL OF FATHER OR MOTHER IS TO BE PUT TO DEATH.' But you say, 'Whoever says to *his* father or mother, "Whatever I have that would help you has been given *to God*," he is not to honor his father or mother.' And *by this* you invalidated the word of God for the sake of your tradition. You hypocrites, rightly did Isaiah prophesy of you: 'THIS PEOPLE HONORS ME WITH THEIR LIPS, BUT THEIR HEART IS FAR AWAY FROM ME. BUT IN VAIN DO THEY WORSHIP ME, TEACHING AS DOCTRINES THE PRECEPTS OF MEN'" (Matthew 15:3–9, Jesus quotes from Exodus 20:12, 21:17, Leviticus 20:9; Isaiah 29:13; cf. Mark 7:5–7; see Colossians 2:22).

Setting: Galilee. The Pharisees and some of the scribes from Jerusalem question why Jesus' disciples do not follow the tradition of ceremonial hand cleansing before eating bread.

And He said to them, "Rightly did Isaiah prophesy of you hypocrites, as it is written: 'THIS PEOPLE HONORS ME WITH THEIR LIPS, BUT THEIR HEART IS FAR AWAY FROM ME. BUT IN VAIN DO THEY WORSHIP ME, TEACHING AS DOCTRINES THE PRECEPTS OF MEN.' Neglecting the commandment of God, you hold to the tradition of men." He was also saying to them, "You are experts at setting aside the commandment of God in order to keep tradition. For Moses said, 'HONOR YOUR FATHER AND YOUR MOTHER'; and, 'HE WHO SPEAKS EVIL OF FATHER OR MOTHER, IS TO BE PUT TO DEATH'; but you say, 'If a man says to *his* father or *his* mother, whatever I have that would help you is Corban (that is to say, given *to God*),' you no longer permit him to do anything for *his* father or *his* mother; *thus* invalidating the word of God by your tradition which you have handed down; and you do many things such as that" (Mark 7:6–13, Jesus quotes from Exodus 20:12; 21:17; Isaiah 29:13; cf. Matthew 15:1–6).

Setting: Judea, near the Jordan River. Following His baptism, and before He begins His public ministry, Jesus is led by the Spirit into the wilderness for forty days of temptation by Satan.

Jesus answered him, "It is written, 'YOU SHALL WORSHIP THE LORD YOUR GOD AND SERVE HIM ONLY'" (Luke 4:8, Jesus quotes from Deuteronomy 6:13; cf. Matthew 4:10).

Setting: Sychar in Samaria, on the way to Galilee. Jesus interacts with a Samaritan woman at Jacob's well, while the disciples are buying food.

Jesus said to her, "Woman, believe Me, an hour is coming when neither in this mountain nor in Jerusalem will you worship the Father. You worship what you do not know; we worship what we know, for salvation is from the Jews. But an hour is coming, and now is, when the true worshipers will worship the Father in spirit and truth; for such people the Father seeks to be His worshipers. God is spirit, and those who worship Him must worship in spirit and truth" (John 4:21–24; see Isaiah 2:3; Philippians 3:3).

WORSHIPERS

Setting: Sychar in Samaria, on the way to Galilee. Jesus interacts with a Samaritan woman at Jacob's well, while the disciples are buying food.

Jesus said to her, "Woman, believe Me, an hour is coming when neither in this mountain nor in Jerusalem will you worship the Father. You worship what you do not know; we worship what we know, for salvation is from the Jews. But an hour is coming, and now is, when the true worshipers will worship the Father in spirit and truth; for such people the Father seeks to be His worshipers. God is spirit, and those who worship Him must worship in spirit and truth" (John 4:21–24; see Isaiah 2:3; Philippians 3:3).

WORSHIPING GOD (Listed under WORSHIP; also see SERVING GOD)

WORTH, HUMAN (See HUMAN VALUE)

WORTHLESS SLAVE (Listed under SLAVE, WORTHLESS)

WORTHINESS

[WORTHINESS from worthy]

Setting: Galilee. After His twelve disciples observe His ministry, Jesus summons and specifically instructs them

about their ministry to the people of Israel.

These twelve Jesus sent out after instructing them: "Do not go in *the* way of *the* Gentiles, and do not enter *any* city of the Samaritans; but rather go to the lost sheep of the house of Israel. And as you go, preach, saying, 'The kingdom of heaven is at hand.' Heal *the* sick, raise *the* dead, cleanse *the* lepers, cast out demons. Freely you received, freely give. Do not acquire gold, or silver, or copper for your money belts, or a bag for *your* journey, or even two coats, or sandals, or a staff; for the worker is worthy of his support. And whatever city or village you enter, inquire who is worthy in it, and stay at his house until you leave *that city*. As you enter the house, give it your greeting. If the house is worthy, give it your *blessing of* peace. But if it is not worthy, take back your *blessing of* peace. Whoever does not receive you, nor heed your words, as you go out of that house or that city, shake the dust off your feet. Truly I say to you, it will be more tolerable for *the* land of Sodom and Gomorrah in the day of judgment than for that city" (Matthew 10:5–15; cf. Mark 6:7–11; Luke 9:1–5; see Matthew 3:2; 11:22, 24; 15:24; Luke 22:35; 1 Corinthians 9:14).

[WORTHINESS from worthy]
Setting: Galilee. After His twelve disciples observe His ministry, Jesus summons and specifically instructs them about their ministry ahead involving true discipleship.

"He who loves father or mother more than Me is not worthy of Me; and he who loves son or daughter more than Me is not worthy of Me. And he who does not take his cross and follow after Me is not worthy of Me. He who has found his life will lose it, and he who has lost his life for My sake will find it" (Matthew 10:37–39; cf. Matthew 16:24, 25).

[WORTHINESS from worthy]
Setting: The temple in Jerusalem. Jesus speaks another parable to the chief priests and elders after they question His authority.

Jesus spoke to them again in parables, saying, "The kingdom of heaven may be compared to a king who gave a wedding feast for his son. And he sent out his slaves to call those who had been invited to the wedding feast, and they were unwilling to come. Again he sent out other slaves saying, 'Tell those who have been invited, "Behold, I have prepared my dinner; my oxen and my fattened livestock are *all* butchered and everything is ready; come to the wedding feast." But they paid no attention and went their way, one to his own farm, another to his business, and the rest seized his slaves and mistreated them and killed them. But the king was enraged, and he sent his armies and destroyed those murderers and set their city on fire. Then he said to his slaves, 'The wedding is ready, but those who were invited were not worthy. 'Go therefore to the main highways, and as many as you find *there,* invite to the wedding feast.' Those slaves went out into the streets and gathered together all they found, both evil and good; and the wedding hall was filled with dinner guests. But when the king came in to look over the dinner guests, he saw a man there who was not dressed in wedding clothes, and he said to him, 'Friend, how did you come in here without wedding clothes?' And the man was speechless. Then the king said to the servants, 'Bind him hand and foot, and throw him into the outer darkness; in that place there will be weeping and gnashing of teeth.' For many are called, but few *are* chosen" (Matthew 22:1–14; cf. Matthew 8:11, 12).

[WORTHINESS from worthy]
Setting: On the way from Galilee to Jerusalem. The Lord appoints seventy followers and sends them out in pairs to every place He Himself will soon visit.

And He was saying to them, "The harvest is plentiful, but the laborers are few; therefore beseech the Lord of the harvest to send out laborers into His harvest. Go; behold, I send you out as lambs in the midst of wolves. Carry no money belt, no bag, no shoes; and greet no one on the way. Whatever house you enter, first say, 'Peace be to this house.' If a man of peace is there, your peace will rest on him; but if not, it will return to you. Stay in that house, eating and drinking what they give you; for the laborer is worthy of his wages. Do not keep moving from house to house. Whatever city you enter and they receive you, eat what is set before you; and heal those in it who are sick, and say to them, 'The kingdom of God has come near to you.' But whatever city you enter and they do not receive you, go out into its streets and say, 'Even the dust of your city which clings to our feet we wipe off *in protest* against you; yet be sure of this, that the kingdom of God has come near.' I say to you, it will be more tolerable in that day for Sodom than for that city" (Luke 10:2–12; see Genesis 19:24–28; Matthew 9:37, 38, 10:9–14, 16; 1 Corinthians 10:27).

[WORTHINESS from worthy]
Setting: On the way from Galilee to Jerusalem. When Jesus uses a parable to challenge the crowd and His disciples to be ready for His return, Peter asks whom He is addressing.

And the Lord said, "Who then is the faithful and sensible steward, whom his master will put in charge of his servants, to give them their rations at the proper time? Blessed is that slave whom his master finds so doing when he comes. Truly I say to you that he will put him in charge of all his possessions. But if that slave says in his heart, 'My master will be a long time in coming,' and begins to beat the slaves, *both* men and women, and to eat and drink and get drunk; the master of that slave will come on a day when he does not expect *him* and at an hour he does not know, and will cut him in pieces, and assign him a place with the unbelievers. And that slave who knew his master's will and did not get ready or act in accord with his will, will receive many lashes, but the one who did know *it*, and committed deeds worthy of flogging, will receive but few. From everyone who has been given much, much will be required; and to whom they entrusted much, of him they will ask all the more" (Luke 12:42–48; cf. Matthew 24:45–51; see Leviticus 5:17).

[WORTHINESS from worthy]
Setting: On the way from Galilee to Jerusalem. Jesus conveys the illustration of the prodigal son because the Pharisees and scribes complain He associates with tax collectors and sinners.

And He said, "A man had two sons. The younger of them said to his father, 'Father, give me the share of the estate that falls to me.' So he divided his wealth between them. And not many days later, the younger son gathered everything together and went on a journey into a distant country, and there he squandered his estate with loose living. Now when he had spent everything, a severe famine occurred in that country, and he began to be impoverished. So he went and hired himself out to one of the citizens of that country, and he sent him into his fields to feed swine. And he would have gladly filled his stomach with the pods that the swine were eating, and no one was giving *anything* to him. But when he came to his senses, he said, 'How many of my father's hired men have more than enough bread, but I am dying here with hunger! I will get up and go to my father, and will say to him, "Father, I have sinned against heaven, and in your sight; I am no longer worthy to be called your son; make me as one of your hired men."' So he got up and came to his father. But while he was still a long way off, his father saw him and felt compassion *for him,* and ran and embraced him and kissed him. And the son said to him, "Father, I have sinned against heaven and in your sight; I am no longer worthy to be called your son.' But the father said to his slaves, 'Quickly bring out the best robe and put it on him, and put a ring on his hand and sandals on his feet; and bring the fattened calf, kill it, and let us eat and celebrate; for this son of mine was dead and has come to life again; he was lost and has been found.' And they began to celebrate. Now his older son was in the field, when he came and approached the house, he heard music and dancing. And he summoned one of the servants and *began* inquiring what these things could be. And he said to him, 'Your brother has come, and your father has killed the fattened calf because he has received him back safe and sound.' But he became angry and was not willing to go in; and his father came out and *began* pleading with him. But he answered and said to his father, 'Look! For so many years I have been serving you and I have never neglected a command of yours; and *yet* you have never given me a young goat, so that I might celebrate with my friends; but when this son of yours came, who has devoured your wealth with prostitutes, you killed the fattened calf for him.' And he said to him, 'Son, you have always been with me, and all that is mine is yours. But we had to celebrate and rejoice, for this brother of yours was dead and *has begun* to live, and was lost and has been found' " (Luke 15:11–32; see Proverb 29:2).

[WORTHINESS from worthy]
Setting: The temple in Jerusalem. While ministering a few days before His crucifixion, after the scribes and Pharisees seek to trap Jesus by questioning Him about paying taxes to Caesar, some Sadducees (who say that there is no resurrection) ask the Lord a question about the resurrection.

Jesus said to them, "The sons of this age marry and are given in marriage, but those who are considered worthy to attain to that age and the resurrection from the dead, neither marry nor are given in marriage; for they cannot even die anymore, because they are like angels, and are sons of God, being sons of the resurrection. But that the dead are raised, even Moses showed, in the *pas-*

sage about the burning bush, where he calls the Lord THE GOD OF ABRAHAM, AND THE GOD OF ISAAC, AND THE GOD OF JACOB. Now He is not the God of the dead but of the living; for all live to Him" (Luke 20:34–38, Jesus quotes from Exodus 3:6; cf. Matthew 22:23–32; Mark 12:18–27).

[WORTHINESS from worthy]
Setting: On the island of Patmos (in the Aegean Sea about fifty miles southwest of Ephesus in modern Turkey). On the Lord's Day (Sunday), approximately fifty years after the Resurrection, the disciple John encounters the Lord Jesus Christ, who communicates a new revelation for the apostle to record for the church in Sardis and to six other churches in Asia.

"To the angel of the church in Sardis write: He who has the seven Spirits of God and the seven stars, says this: 'I know your deeds, that you have a name that you are alive, but you are dead. Wake up, and strengthen the things that remain, which were about to die; for I have not found your deeds completed in the sight of My God. So remember what you have received and heard; and keep *it,* and repent. Therefore if you do not wake up, I will come like a thief, and you will not know at what hour I will come to you. But you have a few people in Sardis who have not soiled their garments; and they will walk with Me in white, for they are worthy. He who overcomes will thus be clothed in white garments; and I will not erase his name from the book of life, and I will confess his name before My Father and before His angels. He who has an ear, let him hear what the Spirit says to the churches' " (Revelation 3:1–6; see Matthew 10:32; Revelation 1:16).

WOUNDS

Setting: On the way from Galilee to Jerusalem. While being tested by a lawyer, Jesus tells him the story of the good Samaritan.

Jesus replied and said, "A man was going down from Jerusalem to Jericho, and fell among robbers, and they stripped him and beat him, and went away leaving him half dead. And by chance a priest was going down on that road, and when he saw him, he passed by on the other side. Likewise a Levite also, when he came to the place and saw him, passed by on the other side. But a Samaritan, who was on a journey, came upon him; and when he saw him, he felt compassion, and came to him and bandaged up his wounds, pouring oil and wine on *them;* and he put him on his own beast, and brought him to an inn and took care of him. On the next day he took out two denarii and gave them to the innkeeper and said, 'Take care of him; and whatever more you spend, when I return I will repay you.' Which of these three do you think proved to be a neighbor to the man who fell into the robbers' *hands?*" And he said, "The one who showed mercy toward him." Then Jesus said to him, "Go and do the same" (Luke 10:30–37).

WRATH

Setting: On the Mount of Olives, east of the temple in Jerusalem. After ministering in the temple a few days before His crucifixion, and giving the disciples more details regarding future events, Jesus elaborates during His Olivet Discourse about things to come.

"But when you see Jerusalem surrounded by armies, then recognize that her desolation is near. Then those who are in Judea must flee to the mountains, and those who are in the midst of the city must leave, and those who are in the country must not enter the city; because these are days of vengeance, so that all things which are written will be fulfilled. Woe to those who are pregnant and to those who are nursing babies in those days; for there will be a great distress upon the land and wrath to this people; and they will fall by the edge of the sword, and will be led captive into all the nations; and Jerusalem will be trampled under foot by the Gentiles until the times of the Gentiles are fulfilled" (Luke 21:20–24; see Matthew 24:15–18; Mark 13:14–16; Luke 19:43).

WRETCHEDNESS

[WRETCHEDNESS from wretched]
Setting: On the island of Patmos (in the Aegean Sea about fifty miles southwest of Ephesus in modern Turkey). On the Lord's Day (Sunday), approximately fifty years after the Resurrection, the disciple John encounters the Lord Jesus Christ, who communicates a new revelation for the apostle to record for the church in Laodicea and to six other churches in Asia.

"To the angel of the church in Laodicea write: The Amen, the faithful and true Witness, the Beginning of the creation of God, says this: 'I know your deeds, that you are neither cold nor hot; I wish that you were cold or hot. So because you are lukewarm, and neither hot nor cold, I will spit you out of My mouth. Because you say, "I am rich, and have become wealthy, and have need of nothing," and you do not know that you are wretched and miserable and poor and blind and naked, I advise you to buy from Me gold refined by fire so that you may become rich, and white garments so that you may clothe yourself, and *that* the shame of your nakedness will not be revealed; and eye salve to anoint your eyes so that you may see. Those whom I love, I reprove and discipline; therefore be zealous and repent. Behold, I stand at the door and knock; if anyone hears My voice and opens the door, I will come in to him and will dine with him, and he with Me. He who overcomes, I will grant to him to sit down with Me on My throne, as I also overcame and sat down with My Father on His throne. He who has an ear, let him hear what the Spirit says to the churches'" (Revelation 3:14–22; see Proverb 3:12; Hosea 12:8; John 14:23; 16:33).

WRITINGS (Also see OLD TESTAMENT; PROPHECY; SCRIPTURE; and SCRIPTURES)

[WRITINGS from written]

Setting: Judea, near the Jordan River. Following His baptism, and before He begins His public ministry, Jesus is led by the Spirit into the wilderness to be tempted by Satan for forty days.

But He answered and said, "It is written, 'MAN SHALL NOT LIVE ON BREAD ALONE, BUT ON EVERY WORD THAT PROCEEDS OUT OF THE MOUTH OF GOD'" (Matthew 4:4, Jesus quotes from Deuteronomy 8:3; cf. Luke 4:4).

[WRITINGS from written]

Setting: Judea, near the Jordan River. Following His baptism, and before He begins His public ministry, Jesus is led by the Spirit into the wilderness to be tempted by Satan for forty days.

Jesus said to him, "On the other hand, it is written, 'YOU SHALL NOT PUT THE LORD YOUR GOD TO THE TEST'" (Matthew 4:7, Jesus quotes from Deuteronomy 6:16; cf. Luke 4:12).

[WRITINGS from written]

Setting: Judea, near the Jordan River. Following His baptism, and before He begins His public ministry, Jesus is led by the Spirit into the wilderness to be tempted by Satan for forty days.

Then Jesus said to him, "Go, Satan! For it is written, 'YOU SHALL WORSHIP THE LORD YOUR GOD, AND SERVE HIM ONLY'" (Matthew 4:10, Jesus quotes from Deuteronomy 6:13; cf. Luke 4:8).

[WRITINGS from written]

Setting: Galilee. While speaking to the crowds, Jesus pays tribute to the ministry of John the Baptist, but emphasizes that the one who is least in the kingdom of heaven is greater than John.

As these men were going *away,* Jesus began to speak to the crowds about John, "What did you go out into the wilderness to see? A reed shaken by the wind? But what did you go out to see? A man dressed in soft *clothing?* Those who wear soft *clothing* are in kings' palaces! But what did you go out to see? A prophet? Yes, I tell you, and the one who is more than a prophet. This is the one about whom it is written, 'BEHOLD, I SEND MY MESSENGER AHEAD OF YOU, WHO WILL PREPARE YOUR WAY BEFORE YOU.' Truly, I say to you, among those born of women there has not arisen *anyone* greater than John the Baptist! Yet the one who is least in the kingdom of heaven is greater than he. From the days of John the Baptist until now the kingdom of heaven suffers violence, and violent men take it by force. For all the prophets and the Law prophesied until John. And, if you are willing to accept *it,* John himself is Elijah who was to come. He who has ears to hear, let him hear" (Matthew 11:7–15, Jesus quotes from Malachi 3:1; cf. Malachi 4:5; Luke 7:24–28; Luke 16:16; see Matthew 14:5).

[WRITINGS from written]

Setting: Jerusalem. After being welcomed with blessings from the crowds, Jesus cleanses the temple by driving out the money changers and merchants.

And He said to them, "It is written, 'MY HOUSE SHALL BE CALLED A HOUSE OF PRAYER'; but you are making it a ROBBERS' DEN" (Matthew 21:13; Jesus quotes from Isaiah 56:7; Jeremiah 7:11; cf. Mark 11:15–18; Luke 19:46).

[WRITINGS from written]
Setting: An upper room in Jerusalem. While celebrating the Passover meal, Jesus shocks His disciples with the revelation that one of them will soon betray Him to His enemies.

As they were eating, He said, "Truly I say to you that one of you will betray Me." Being deeply grieved, they each one began to say to Him, 'Surely not I, Lord?' And He answered, "He who dipped his hand with Me in the bowl is the one who will betray Me. The Son of Man *is to* go, just as it is written of Him; but woe to that man by whom the Son of Man is betrayed! It would have been good for that man if he had not been born." And Judas, who was betraying Him, said, 'Surely it is not I, Rabbi?' Jesus said to him, "You have said *it* yourself" (Matthew 26:21–25; cf. Mark 14:18–21; Luke 22:21–23; John 13:21–30; see Psalm 41:9).

[WRITINGS from written]
Setting: On the way to the Mount of Olives. After celebrating the Passover meal in Jerusalem, prior to His betrayal by Judas, Jesus states that the disciples will all deny Him that very day.

Then Jesus said to them, "You will all fall away because of Me this night, for it is written, 'I WILL STRIKE DOWN THE SHEPHERD, AND THE SHEEP OF THE FLOCK SHALL BE SCATTERED.' But after I have been raised, I will go ahead of you to Galilee." But Peter said to Him, '*Even* though all may fall away because of You, I will never fall away.' Jesus said to him, "Truly I say to you that this *very* night, before a rooster crows, you will deny Me three times" (Matthew 26:31–34, Jesus quotes from Zechariah 13:7; cf. Mark 14:26–31; see Matthew 28:7, 10, 16; John 13:37).

[WRITINGS from written]
Setting: Galilee. The Pharisees and some of the scribes from Jerusalem question why Jesus' disciples do not follow the tradition of ceremonial hand cleansing before eating bread.

And He said to them, "Rightly did Isaiah prophesy of you hypocrites, as it is written: 'THIS PEOPLE HONORS ME WITH THEIR LIPS, BUT THEIR HEART IS FAR AWAY FROM ME. BUT IN VAIN DO THEY WORSHIP ME, TEACHING AS DOCTRINES THE PRECEPTS OF MEN.' Neglecting the commandment of God, you hold to the tradition of men." He was also saying to them, "You are experts at setting aside the commandment of God in order to keep tradition. For Moses said, 'HONOR YOUR FATHER AND YOUR MOTHER'; and, 'HE WHO SPEAKS EVIL OF FATHER OR MOTHER, IS TO BE PUT TO DEATH'; but you say, 'If a man says to *his* father or *his* mother, whatever I have that would help you is Corban (that is to say, given *to God*),' you no longer permit him to do anything for *his* father or *his* mother; *thus* invalidating the word of God by your tradition which you have handed down; and you do many things such as that" (Mark 7:6–13, Jesus quotes from Exodus 20:12; 21:17; Isaiah 29:13; cf. Matthew 15:1–6).

[WRITINGS from written]
Setting: Galilee. After informing a crowd and His disciples of the hope involving the coming kingdom of God, Jesus takes Peter, James, and John to a high mountain (some think Mount Hermon). The Lord reveals His glory through the Transfiguration, and answers their question about Elijah.

And He said to them, "Elijah does first come and restore all things. And *yet* how is it written of the Son of Man that He will suffer many things and be treated with contempt? But I say to you that Elijah has indeed come, and they did to him whatever they wished, just as it is written of him" (Mark 9:12, 13; cf. Matthew 17:1–13; Luke 9:28–36; see Malachi 4:5, 6; Matthew 16:21).

[WRITINGS from written]
Setting: Jerusalem. Following His triumphal entry, cursing of a fig tree, and cleansing of the temple of the money changers, Jesus rebukes the Jewish religious leaders for the corrupt practices they permit in His house.

And He *began* to teach and say to them, "Is it not written, 'MY HOUSE SHALL BE CALLED A HOUSE OF PRAYER FOR ALL THE NATIONS'? But you have made it a ROBBERS' DEN" (Mark 11:17, Jesus quotes from Isaiah 56:7; Jeremiah 7:11; cf. Matthew 21:12, 13; Luke 19:45–48).

[WRITINGS from written]
Setting: A borrowed upper room in Jerusalem. While Jesus and His twelve disciples are eating the Passover meal, the Lord states that one of them will betray Him.

As they were reclining *at the table* and eating, Jesus said, "Truly I say to you that one of you will betray Me—one who is eating with Me." They began to be grieved and to say to Him one by one, "Surely not I?" And He said to them, "*It is* one of the twelve, one who dips with Me in the bowl. For the Son of Man *is to* go just as it is written of Him; but woe to that man by whom the Son of Man is betrayed! *It would have been* good for that man if he had not been born" (Mark 14:18–21; cf. Matthew 26:21–24; Luke 22:21–23; John 13:21, 22).

[WRITINGS from written]
Setting: A borrowed upper room in Jerusalem. After Jesus and His twelve disciples celebrate the Passover and the Lord's Supper, they go out to the Mount of Olives.

And Jesus said to them, "You will all fall away, because it is written, 'I WILL STRIKE DOWN THE SHEPHERD, AND THE SHEEP SHALL BE SCATTERED.' But after I have been raised, I will go ahead of you to Galilee." But Peter said to Him, "*Even* though all may fall away, yet I will not." And Jesus said to him, "Truly I say to you, that this very night, before a rooster crows twice, you yourself will deny Me three times" (Mark 14:27–30, Jesus quotes from Zechariah 13:7; cf. Matthew 26:30–34; see Mark 14:72).

[WRITINGS from written]
Setting: Judea, near the Jordan River. Following His baptism, and before He begins His public ministry, Jesus is led by the Spirit into the wilderness to be tempted by Satan for forty days.

And Jesus answered him, "It is written, 'MAN SHALL NOT LIVE ON BREAD ALONE'" (Luke 4:4, Jesus quotes from Deuteronomy 8:3; cf. Matthew 4:1–4; see Mark 1:12, 13).

[WRITINGS from written]
Setting: Judea, near the Jordan River. Following His baptism, and before He begins His public ministry, Jesus is led by the Spirit into the wilderness to be tempted by Satan for forty days.

Jesus answered him, "It is written, 'YOU SHALL WORSHIP THE LORD YOUR GOD AND SERVE HIM ONLY'" (Luke 4:8, Jesus quotes from Deuteronomy 6:13; cf. Matthew 4:10).

[WRITINGS from written]
Setting: Galilee. After Jesus responds to the disciples of John the Baptist about whether He is the promised Messiah, the Lord speaks to the crowds about John.

When the messengers of John had left, He began to speak to the crowds about John, "What did you go out into the wilderness to see? A reed shaken by the wind? But what did you go out to see? A man dressed in soft clothing? Those who are splendidly clothed and live in luxury are *found* in royal palaces! But what did you go out to see? A prophet? Yes, I say to you, and one who is more than a prophet. This is the one about whom it is written, 'BEHOLD, I SEND MY MESSENGER AHEAD OF YOU, WHO WILL PREPARE YOUR WAY BEFORE YOU.' I say to you, among those born of women there is no one greater than John; yet he who is least in the kingdom of God is greater than he" (Luke 7:24–28, Jesus quotes from Malachi 3:1; cf. Matthew 11:7–11).

[WRITINGS from written]

Setting: On the way from Galilee to Jerusalem. After Jesus tells His disciples in private the privilege they are experiencing by living in the time of the Messiah, a lawyer tests Him.

And a lawyer stood up and put Him to the test, saying, "Teacher, what shall I do to inherit eternal life?" And He said to him, "What is written in the Law? How does it read to you?" And he answered, "YOU SHALL LOVE THE LORD YOUR GOD WITH ALL YOUR HEART, AND WITH ALL YOUR SOUL, AND WITH ALL YOUR STRENGTH, AND WITH ALL YOUR MIND; AND YOUR NEIGHBOR AS YOURSELF." And He said to him, "You have answered correctly; DO THIS AND YOU WILL LIVE" (Luke 10:25–28, Jesus quotes from Leviticus 18:5; see Deuteronomy 6:5; Matthew 19:16–19).

[WRITINGS from written]
Setting: On the way from Galilee to Jerusalem. After responding to Peter's statement about the disciples' personal sacrifice in following Him, Jesus tells them of the sacrifice He will make in Jerusalem.

Then He took the twelve aside and said to them, "Behold, we are going up to Jerusalem, and all things which are written through the prophets about the Son of Man will be accomplished. For He will be handed over to the Gentiles, and will be mocked and mistreated and spit upon, and after they have scourged Him, they will kill Him; and the third day He will rise again" (Luke 18:31–33; cf. Matthew 20:17–19; Mark 10:32–34).

[WRITINGS from written]
Setting: Jerusalem. After weeping over Jerusalem as He sees the city ahead of Him, the Lord enters the temple and drives out the money changers and the merchants.

Jesus entered the temple and began to drive out those who were selling, saying to them, "It is written, 'AND MY HOUSE SHALL BE A HOUSE OF PRAYER,' but you have made it a ROBBERS' DEN" (Luke 19:45, 46, Jesus quotes from Isaiah 56:7; Jeremiah 7:11; cf. Matthew 21:12, 13; Mark 11:15–17; see John 2:13–17).

[WRITINGS from written]
Setting: The temple in Jerusalem. While ministering a few days before His crucifixion, after the chief priests and the scribes question His authority to teach and preach, Jesus conveys the Parable of the Vine-Growers to the people.

And He began to tell the people this parable: "A man planted a vineyard and rented it out to vine-growers, and went on a journey for a long time. At the *harvest* time he sent a slave to the vine-growers, so that they would give him *some* of the produce of the vineyard; but the vine-growers beat him and sent him away empty-handed. And he proceeded to send another slave; and they beat him also and treated him shamefully and sent him away empty-handed. And he proceeded to send a third; and this one also they wounded and cast out. The owner of the vineyard said, 'What shall I do? I will send my beloved son; perhaps they will respect him.' But when the vine-growers saw him, they reasoned with one another, saying, 'This is the heir; let us kill him so that the inheritance will be ours.' So they threw him out of the vineyard and killed him. What, then, will the owner of the vineyard do to them? He will come and destroy these vine-growers and will give the vineyard to others." When they heard it, they said, "May it never be!" But Jesus looked at them and said, "What then is this that is written: 'THE STONE WHICH THE BUILDERS REJECTED, THIS BECAME THE CHIEF CORNER *stone*'? Everyone who falls on that stone will be broken to pieces; but on whomever it falls, it will scatter him like dust" (Luke 20:9–18, Jesus quotes from Psalm 118:22; cf. Matthew 21:33–44; Mark 12:1–11; see Ephesians 2:20).

[WRITINGS from written]
Setting: On the Mount of Olives, east of the temple in Jerusalem. After ministering in the temple a few days before His crucifixion, and giving the disciples more details regarding future events, Jesus elaborates during His Olivet Discourse about things to come.

"But when you see Jerusalem surrounded by armies, then recognize that her desolation is near. Then those who are in Judea must flee to the mountains, and those who are in the midst of the city must leave, and those who are in the country must not enter the city; because these are days of vengeance, so that all things which are written will be fulfilled. Woe to those who are pregnant and to those who are nursing babies in those days; for there will be a great distress upon the land and wrath to this people; and they will fall by the edge of the sword, and will be led captive into all the nations; and Jerusalem will be trampled under foot by the Gentiles until the times of the Gentiles are fulfilled" (Luke 21:20–24; see Matthew 24:15–18; Mark 13:14–16; Luke 19:43).

[WRITINGS from written]
Setting: Jerusalem. During the Feast of Unleavened Bread (Passover) just before His crucifixion, while celebrating the Passover meal, instituting the Lord's Supper, and prophesying Peter's denial of Him, Jesus instructs His disciples to prepare to persevere without Him.

And He said to them, "When I sent you out without money belt and bag and sandals, you did not lack anything, did you?" They said, "*No*, nothing." And He said to them, "But now, whoever has a money belt is to take it along, likewise also a bag, and whoever has no sword is to sell his coat and buy one. For I tell you that this which is written must be fulfilled in Me, 'AND HE WAS NUMBERED WITH TRANSGRESSORS'; for that which refers to Me has *its* fulfillment." They said, "Lord, look, here are two swords." And He said to them, "It is enough" (Luke 22:35–38, Jesus quotes from Isaiah 53:12; see Matthew 10:5–15; Mark 6:7–11; Luke 9:1–5; 10:1–12; 22:49; John 17:4).

[WRITINGS from written]
Setting: Jerusalem. After rising from the tomb on the third day after being crucified, and appearing to two of His followers on the road to Emmaus, Jesus gives instruction to His disciples (except Thomas) about His mission on earth and the promise of future power from God.

Now He said to them, "These are My words which I spoke to you while I was still with you, that all things which are written about Me in the Law of Moses and the Prophets and the Psalms must be fulfilled." Then He opened their minds to understand the Scriptures, and He said to them, "Thus it is written, that the Christ would suffer and rise again from the dead the third day, and that repentance for forgiveness of sins would be proclaimed in His name to all the nations, beginning from Jerusalem. You are witnesses of these things. And behold, I am sending forth the promise of My Father upon you; but you are to stay in the city until you are clothed with power from on high" (Luke 24:44–49; see Matthew 28:19, 20; Acts 1:8).

Setting: Jerusalem. During a feast of the Jews, Jesus responds to criticism from the Jewish religious leaders by referring to God as His Father (thereby making Himself equal with God) and informing them that God, John the Baptist, the Scriptures, and His works all testify to His mission.

"You search the Scriptures because you think that in them you have eternal life; it is these that testify about Me; and you are unwilling to come to Me so that you may have life. I do not receive glory from men; but I know you, that you do not have the love of God in yourselves. I have come in My Father's name, and you do not receive Me; if another comes in his own name, you will receive him. How can you believe, when you receive glory from one another and you do not seek the glory that is from the *one and* only God? Do not think that I will accuse you before the Father; the one who accuses you is Moses, in whom you have set your hope. For if you believed Moses, you would believe Me, for he wrote about Me. But if you do not believe his writings, how will you believe My words?" (John 5:39–47; see Matthew 24:5; Luke 16:29, 31; 24:27; 9:28; 17:3).

[WRITINGS from written]
Setting: Capernaum of Galilee. After Jesus informs the people whom He miraculously fed with a lad's five loaves and two fish how they might receive the bread out of heaven, the Jewish religious leaders grumble when the Lord claims that He came down out of heaven.

Therefore the Jews were grumbling about Him, because He said, "I am the bread that came down out of heaven." They were saying, "Is not this Jesus, the son of Joseph, whose father and mother we know? How does He now say, 'I have come down out of heaven'?" Jesus answered and said to them, "Do not grumble among yourselves. No one can come to Me unless the Father who sent Me draws him; and I will raise him up on the last day. It is written in the prophets, 'AND THEY SHALL ALL BE TAUGHT OF GOD.' Everyone who has heard and learned from the Father, comes to Me. Not that anyone has seen the Father, except the One who is from God; He has seen the Father. Truly, truly, I say to you, he who believes has eternal life. I am the bread of life. Your fathers ate the manna in the wilderness, and they died. This is the bread which comes down out of heaven, so that one may eat of it and not die. I am the living bread that came down out of heaven; if anyone eats of this bread, he will live forever; and the bread also which I will give for the life of the world is My flesh" (John 6:41–51, Jesus quotes from Isaiah 54:13; see John 1:18, 29; 3:36; 7:27).

[WRITINGS from written]
Setting: The temple in Jerusalem. Following the Feast of Booths and the scribes' and Pharisees' failed attempt to stone a woman for adultery, Jesus returns the next day to teach. His enemies question His testimony about Himself.

Jesus answered and said to them, "Even if I testify about Myself, My testimony is true, for I know where I came from and where I am going; but you do not know where I come from or where I am going. You judge according to the flesh; I am not judging anyone. But even if I do judge, My judgment is true; for I am not alone *in it,* but I and the Father who sent Me. Even in your law it has been written that the testimony of two men is true. I am He who testifies about Myself, and the Father who sent Me testifies about Me." So they were saying to Him, "Where is Your Father?" Jesus answered, "You know neither Me nor My Father; if you knew Me, you would know My Father also" (John 8:14–19; see Deuteronomy 17:6; 19:15; Matthew 18:16; John 3:17; 5:30, 37; 7:28; 8:42).

[WRITINGS from written]
Setting: Jerusalem. At the Feast of Dedication, the Pharisees desire to stone Jesus because He claims to be equal with God when they ask Him plainly whether He is the Christ.

Jesus answered them, "Has it not been written in your Law, 'I SAID, YOU ARE GODS'? If he called them gods, to whom the word of God came (and the Scripture cannot be broken), do you say of Him, whom the Father sanctified and sent into the world, 'You are blaspheming,' because I said, 'I am the Son of God'? If I do not do the works of My Father, do not believe Me; but if I do them, though you do not believe Me, believe the works, so that you may know and understand that the Father is in Me, and I in the Father" (John 10:34–38, Jesus quotes from Psalm 82:6; see John 14:10, 20).

[WRITINGS from written]
Setting: Jerusalem. Before the Passover, with His upcoming departure in mind, after explaining He is the vine and His disciples are the branches, Jesus prepares them for hatred by the world.

"He who hates Me hates My Father also. If I had not done among them the works which no one else did, they would not have sin; but now they have both seen and hated Me and My Father as well. But *they have done this* to fulfill the word that is written in their Law, 'THEY HATED ME WITHOUT A CAUSE'" (John 15:23–25, Jesus quotes from Psalm 35:19; see John 9:41).

[WRITINGS from Write]
Setting: On the island of Patmos (in the Aegean Sea about fifty miles southwest of Ephesus in modern Turkey). On the Lord's Day (Sunday), approximately fifty years after the Resurrection, the disciple John hears the voice of the Lord Jesus Christ, who communicates new revelations for the apostle to record for the seven churches in Asia.

I was in the Spirit on the Lord's day, and I heard behind me a loud voice like *the sound* of a trumpet, saying, "Write in a book what you see, and send *it* to the seven churches: to Ephesus and to Smyrna and to Pergamum and to Thyatira and to Sardis and to Philadelphia and to Laodicea" (Revelation 1:10, 11).

[WRITINGS from write]
Setting: On the island of Patmos (in the Aegean Sea about fifty miles southwest of Ephesus in modern Turkey). On the Lord's Day (Sunday), approximately fifty years after the Resurrection, the disciple John encounters the Lord Jesus Christ, who communicates new revelations for the apostle to record for the seven churches in Asia.

When I saw Him, I fell at His feet like a dead man. And He placed His right hand on me, saying, "Do not be afraid; I am the first and the last, and the living One; and I was dead, and behold, I am alive forevermore, and I have the keys of death and of Hades. Therefore write the things which you have seen, and the things which are, and the things which will take place after these things. As for the mystery of the seven stars which you saw in My right hand, and the seven golden lampstands: the seven stars are the angels of the seven churches, and the seven lampstands are the seven churches" (Revelation 1:17–20; see Isaiah 44:6; Luke 24:5; Revelation 2:8).

[WRITINGS from write]
Setting: On the island of Patmos (in the Aegean Sea about fifty miles southwest of Ephesus in modern Turkey). On the Lord's Day (Sunday), approximately fifty years after the Resurrection, the disciple John encounters the Lord Jesus Christ, who communicates a new revelation for the apostle to record for the church in Ephesus and to six other churches in Asia.

"To the angel of the church in Ephesus write: The One who holds the seven stars in His right hand, the One who walks among the seven golden lampstands, says this: 'I know your deeds and your toil and perseverance, and that you cannot tolerate evil men, and you put to the test those who call themselves apostles, and they are not, and you found them *to be* false; and you have perseverance and have endured for My name's sake, and have not grown weary. But I have *this* against you, that you have left your first love. Therefore remember from where you have fallen, and repent and do the deeds you did at first; or else I am coming to you and will remove your lampstand out of its place—unless you repent. Yet this you do have, that you hate the deeds of the Nicolaitans, which I also hate. He who has an ear, let him hear what the Spirit says to the churches. To him who overcomes, I will grant to eat of the tree of life which is in the Paradise of God' " (Revelation 2:1–7; see Genesis 2:9; Ezekiel 28:13; 1 John 4:1; Revelation 1:10, 11, 19, 20).

[WRITINGS from write]
Setting: On the island of Patmos (in the Aegean Sea about fifty miles southwest of Ephesus in modern Turkey). On the Lord's Day (Sunday), approximately fifty years after the Resurrection, the disciple John encounters the Lord Jesus Christ, who communicates a new revelation for the apostle to record for the church in Smyrna and to six other churches in Asia.

"And to the angel of the church in Smyrna write: The first and the last, who was dead, and has come to life, says this: 'I know your tribulation and your poverty (but you are rich), and the blasphemy by those who say they are Jews and are not, but are a synagogue of Satan. Do not fear what you are about to suffer. Behold, the devil is about to cast some of you into prison, so that you will be tested, and you will have tribulation for ten days. Be faithful until death, and I will give you the crown of life. He who has an ear, let him hear what the Spirit says to the churches. He who overcomes will not be hurt by the second death' (Revelation 2:8–11; see Isaiah 44:6; Revelation 1:9, 18; 20:6, 14).

[WRITINGS from write]
Setting: On the island of Patmos (in the Aegean Sea about fifty miles southwest of Ephesus in modern Turkey). On the Lord's Day (Sunday), approximately fifty years after the Resurrection, the disciple John encounters the Lord Jesus Christ, who communicates a new revelation for the apostle to record for the church in Pergamum and to six other churches in Asia.

"And to the angel of the church in Pergamum write: The One who has the sharp two-edged sword says this: 'I know where you dwell, where Satan's throne is; and you hold fast My name, and did not deny My faith even in the days of Antipas, My witness, My faithful one, who was killed among you, where Satan dwells. But I have a few things against you, because you have there some who hold the teaching of Balaam, who kept teaching Balak to put a stumbling block before the sons of Israel, to eat things sacrificed to idols and to commit *acts of* immorality. So you also have some who in the same way hold the teaching of the Nicolaitans. Therefore repent; or else I am coming to you quickly, and I will make war against them with the sword of My mouth. He who has an ear, let him hear what the Spirit says to the churches. To him who overcomes, to him I will give *some* of the hidden manna, and I will give him a white stone, and a new name written on the stone which no one knows but he who receives it' (Revelation 2:12–17; see Numbers 25:1–3; Isaiah 62:2; Revelation 1:16).

[WRITINGS from write]
Setting: On the island of Patmos (in the Aegean Sea about fifty miles southwest of Ephesus in modern Turkey). On the Lord's Day (Sunday), approximately fifty years after the Resurrection, the disciple John encounters the Lord Jesus Christ, who communicates a new revelation for the apostle to record for the church in Thyatira and to six other churches in Asia.

"And to the angel of the church in Thyatira write: The Son of God, who has eyes like a flame of fire, and His feet are like burnished bronze, says this: 'I know your deeds, and your love and faith and service and perseverance, and that your deeds of late are greater than at first. But I have *this* against you, that you tolerate the woman Jezebel, who calls herself a prophetess, and she teaches and leads My bond-servants astray so that they commit *acts of* immorality and eat things sacrificed to idols. I gave her time to repent, and she does not want to repent of her immorality. Behold, I will throw her on a bed *of sickness,* and those who commit adultery with her into great tribulation, unless they repent of her deeds. And I will kill her children with pestilence, and all the churches will know that I am He who searches the minds and hearts; and I will give to each one of you according to your deeds. But I say to you, the rest who are in Thyatira, who do not hold this teaching, who have not known the deep things of Satan, as they call them—I place no other burden on you. Nevertheless what you have, hold fast until I come. He who overcomes, and he who keeps My deeds until the end, TO HIM I WILL GIVE AUTHORITY OVER THE NATIONS; AND HE SHALL RULE THEM WITH A ROD OF IRON, AS THE VESSELS OF THE POTTER ARE BROKEN TO PIECES, as I also have received *authority* from My Father; and I will give him the morning star. He who has an ear, let him hear what the Spirit says to the churches' (Revelation 2:18–29; Jesus quotes from Psalm 2:8, 9; Isaiah 30:14; see 1 Kings 16:31; Psalm 7:9; Romans 2:5; 1 Corinthians 2:10; 2 Peter 3:9; Revelation 1:14; 2:7; 3:11; 17:1–20).

[WRITINGS from write]
Setting: On the island of Patmos (in the Aegean Sea about fifty miles southwest of Ephesus in modern Turkey). On the Lord's Day (Sunday), approximately fifty years after the Resurrection, the disciple John encounters the Lord Jesus Christ, who communicates a new revelation for the apostle to record for the church in Sardis and to six other churches in Asia.

"To the angel of the church in Sardis write: He who has the seven Spirits of God and the seven stars, says this: 'I know your deeds, that you have a name that you are alive, but you are dead. Wake up, and strengthen the things that remain, which were about to die; for I have not found your deeds completed in the sight of My God. So remember what you have received and heard; and keep *it,* and repent. Therefore if you do not wake up, I will come like a thief, and you will not know at what hour I will come to you. But you have a few people in Sardis who have not soiled their garments; and they will walk with Me in white, for they are worthy. He who overcomes will thus be clothed in white garments; and I will not erase his name from the book of life, and I will confess his name before My Father and before His angels. He who has an ear, let him hear what the Spirit says to the churches' " (Revelation 3:1–6; see Matthew 10:32; Revelation 1:16).

[WRITINGS from write]
Setting: On the island of Patmos (in the Aegean Sea about fifty miles southwest of Ephesus in modern Turkey). On the Lord's Day (Sunday), approximately fifty years after the Resurrection, the disciple John encounters the Lord Jesus Christ, who communicates a new revelation for the apostle to record for the church in Philadelphia and to six other churches in Asia.

"And to the angel of the church in Philadelphia write: He who is holy, who is true, who has the key of David, who opens and no one will shut, and who shuts and no one opens, says this: 'I know your deeds. Behold, I have put before you an open door which no one can shut, because you have a little power, and have kept My word, and have not denied My name. Behold, I will cause *those* of the synagogue of Satan, who say that they are Jews and are not, but lie—I will make them come and bow down at your feet, and *make them* know that I have loved you. Because you have kept the word of My perseverance, I also will keep you from the hour of testing, that *hour* which is about to come upon the whole world, to test those who dwell on the earth. I am coming quickly; hold fast what you have, so that no one will take your crown. He who overcomes, I will make him a pillar in the temple of My God, and he will not go out from it anymore; and I will write on him the name of My God, and the name of the city of My God, the new Jerusalem, which comes down out of heaven from My God, and My new name. He who has an ear, let him hear what the Spirit says to the churches' " (Revelation 3:7–13; see Isaiah 22:22; Galatians 2:9; Revelation 2:9, 10, 13, 25; 14:1).

[WRITINGS from write]

Setting: On the island of Patmos (in the Aegean Sea about fifty miles southwest of Ephesus in modern Turkey). On the Lord's Day (Sunday), approximately fifty years after the Resurrection, the disciple John encounters the Lord Jesus Christ, who communicates a new revelation for the apostle to record for the church in Laodicea and to six other churches in Asia.

"To the angel of the church in Laodicea write: The Amen, the faithful and true Witness, the Beginning of the creation of God, says this: 'I know your deeds, that you are neither cold nor hot; I wish that you were cold or hot. So because you are lukewarm, and neither hot nor cold, I will spit you out of My mouth. Because you say, "I am rich, and have become wealthy, and have need of nothing," and you do not know that you are wretched and miserable and poor and blind and naked, I advise you to buy from Me gold refined by fire so that you may become rich, and white garments so that you may clothe yourself, and *that* the shame of your nakedness will not be revealed; and eye salve to anoint your eyes so that you may see. Those whom I love, I reprove and discipline; therefore be zealous and repent. Behold, I stand at the door and knock; if anyone hears My voice and opens the door, I will come in to him and will dine with him, and he with Me. He who overcomes, I will grant to him to sit down with Me on My throne, as I also overcame and sat down with My Father on His throne. He who has an ear, let him hear what the Spirit says to the churches'" (Revelation 3:14–22; see Proverb 3:12; Hosea 12:8; John 14:23; 16:33).

WRONG

Setting: Judea beyond the Jordan (Perea). Jesus illustrates the kingdom of heaven to His disciples through the story of laborers in the vineyard.

"For the kingdom of heaven is like a landowner who went out early in the morning to hire laborers for his vineyard. When he had agreed with the laborers for a denarius for the day, he sent them into his vineyard. And he went out about the third hour and saw others standing idle in the market place; and to those he said,' You also go into the vineyard, and whatever is right I will give you.' And *so* they went. Again he went out about the sixth and the ninth hour, and did the same thing. And about the eleventh *hour* he went out and found others standing *around;* and he said to them, 'Why have you been standing idle here all day long?' They said to him, 'Because no one hired us.' He said to them, 'You go into the vineyard too.' When evening came, the owner of the vineyard said to his foreman, 'Call the laborers and pay them their wages, beginning with the last *group* to the first.' When those *hired* about the eleventh hour came, each one received a denarius. When those *hired* first came, they thought that they would receive more; but each of them also received a denarius. When they received it, they grumbled at the landowner, saying, 'These last men have worked *only* one hour, and you have made them equal to us who have borne the burden and the scorching heat of the day.' But he answered and said to one of them, 'Friend, I am doing you no wrong; did you not agree with me for a denarius? Take what is yours and go, but I wish to give to this last man the same as to you. It is not lawful for me to do what I wish with what is my own? Or is your eye envious because I am generous?' So the last shall be first, and the first last" (Matthew 20:1–16; cf. Matthew 19:30).

Setting: Jerusalem. After being betrayed by Judas and arrested by the Roman cohort, one of the officers strikes Jesus when he believes the Lord exhibits disrespect to Annas with His response to the former high priest's question about His disciples and His teaching.

Jesus answered him, "If I have spoken wrongly, testify of the wrong; but if rightly, why do you strike Me?" (John 18:23; see Matthew 5:39).

Y

YEAR (Also see YEARS)

Setting: The synagogue in Jesus' hometown of Nazareth in Galilee. At the beginning of His public ministry, Jesus reads from the book of the prophet Isaiah on the Sabbath.

And the book of the prophet Isaiah was handed to Him. And He opened the book and found the place where it was written, "THE SPIRIT OF THE LORD IS UPON ME, BECAUSE HE ANOINTED ME TO PREACH THE GOSPEL TO THE POOR. HE HAS SENT ME TO PROCLAIM RELEASE TO THE CAPTIVES, AND RECOVERY OF SIGHT TO THE BLIND, TO SET FREE THOSE WHO ARE OPPRESSED, TO PROCLAIM THE FAVORABLE YEAR OF THE LORD." And He closed the book, gave it back to the attendant and sat down; and the eyes of all in the synagogue were fixed on Him. And He began to say to them, "Today this Scripture has been fulfilled in your hearing" (Luke 4:17–21, Jesus quotes from Isaiah 61:1, 2).

Setting: On the way from Galilee to Jerusalem. After some present report to Him about the Galileans whose blood Pilate (Roman governor of Judea) had mixed with their sacrifices, Jesus responds to their concern by calling them to repentance and illustrating His point with a parable.

And He *began* telling this parable: "A man had a fig tree which had been planted in his vineyard; and he came looking for fruit on it and did not find any. And he said to the vineyard-keeper, 'Behold, for three years I have come looking for fruit on this fig tree without finding any. Cut it down! Why does it even use up the ground?' And he answered and said to him, 'Let it alone, sir, for this year too, until I dig around it and put fertilizer; and if it bears fruit next year, *fine*; but if not, cut it down'"(Luke 13:6–9; see Matthew 3:10).

YEAR OF THE LORD

Setting: The synagogue in Jesus' hometown of Nazareth in Galilee. At the beginning of His public ministry, Jesus reads on the Sabbath from the book of the prophet Isaiah.

And the book of the prophet Isaiah was handed to Him. And He opened the book and found the place where it was written, "THE SPIRIT OF THE LORD IS UPON ME, BECAUSE HE ANOINTED ME TO PREACH THE GOSPEL TO THE POOR. HE HAS SENT ME TO PROCLAIM RELEASE TO THE CAPTIVES, AND RECOVERY OF SIGHT TO THE BLIND, TO SET FREE THOSE WHO ARE OPPRESSED, TO PROCLAIM THE FAVORABLE YEAR OF THE LORD." And He closed the book, gave it back to the attendant and sat down; and the eyes of all in the synagogue were fixed on Him. And He began to say to them, "Today this Scripture has been fulfilled in your hearing" (Luke 4:17–21, Jesus quotes from Isaiah 61:1, 2).

YEARS (Also see YEAR)

Setting: The synagogue in Jesus' hometown of Nazareth in Galilee. At the beginning of His public ministry, Jesus comments to the congregation after reading from the book of the prophet Isaiah on the Sabbath.

And He said to them, "No doubt you will quote this proverb to Me, 'Physician, heal yourself! Whatever we heard was done at Capernaum, do here in your hometown as well.'" And He said, "Truly I say to you, no prophet is welcome in his hometown. But I say to you in truth, there were many widows in Israel in the days of Elijah, when the sky was shut up for three years and six months, when a great famine came over all the land; and yet Elijah was sent to none of them, but only to Zarephath, *in the land* of Sidon, to a woman who was a widow. And there were many lepers in Israel in the time of Elisha the prophet; and none of them was cleansed, but only Naaman the Syrian" (Luke 4:23–27; Jesus refers to 1 Kings 17:1, 9; 2 Kings 5:1–14; see Matthew 13:53–58).

Setting: On the way from Galilee to Jerusalem. As the scribes and Pharisees turn hostile and question Him repeatedly in an attempt to catch Him in something He might say, Jesus responds to a question from the crowd and gives a parable about riches and greed.

And He told them a parable, saying, "The land of a rich man was very productive. And he began reasoning to himself, saying, 'What shall I do, since I have no place to store my crops?' Then he said, 'This is what I will do: I will tear down my barns and build larger ones, and here I will store all my grain and my goods. And I will say to my soul, "Soul, you have many goods laid up for many years *to come;* take your ease, eat, drink *and* be merry."' But God said to him, 'You fool! This *very* night your soul is required of you; and *now* who will own what you have prepared?' So is the man who stores up treasure for himself, and is not rich toward God" (Luke 12:16–21; see Job 27:8; Psalm 39:6; Ecclesiastes 12:9; Philippians 2:3).

Setting: On the way from Galilee to Jerusalem. After some present report to Him about the Galileans whose blood Pilate (Roman governor of Judea) had mixed with their sacrifices, Jesus responds to their concern by calling them to repentance and illustrating His point with a parable.

And He *began* telling this parable: "A man had a fig tree which had been planted in his vineyard; and he came looking for fruit on it and did not find any. And he said to the vineyard-keeper, 'Behold, for three years I have come looking for fruit on this fig tree without finding any. Cut it down! Why does it even use up the ground?' And he answered and said to him, 'Let it alone, sir, for this year too, until I dig around it and put fertilizer; and if it bears fruit next year, *fine*; but if not, cut it down'"(Luke 13:6–9; see Matthew 3:10).

Setting: On the way from Galilee to Jerusalem. Jesus responds to a synagogue official's anger over His healing of a woman, sick for eighteen years, in the synagogue on the Sabbath.

But the Lord answered him and said, "You hypocrites, does not each of you on the Sabbath untie his ox or his donkey from the stall and lead him away to water *him?* And this woman, a daughter of Abraham as she is, whom Satan has bound for eighteen long years, should she not have been released from this bond on the Sabbath day?" (Luke 13:15, 16; see Luke 14:5).

Setting: On the way from Galilee to Jerusalem. Jesus conveys the illustration of the prodigal son because the Pharisees and scribes complain He associates with tax collectors and sinners.

And He said, "A man had two sons. The younger of them said to his father, 'Father, give me the share of the estate that falls to me.' So he divided his wealth between them. And not many days later, the younger son gathered everything together and went on a journey into a distant country, and there he squandered his estate with loose living. Now when he had spent everything, a severe famine occurred in that country, and he began to be impoverished. So he went and hired himself out to one of the citizens of that country, and he sent him into his fields to feed swine. And he would have gladly filled his stomach with the pods that the swine were eating, and no one was giving *anything* to him. But when he came to his senses, he said, 'How many of my father's hired men have more than enough bread, but I am dying here with hunger! I will get up and go to my father, and will say to him, "Father, I have sinned against heaven, and in your sight; I am no longer worthy to be called your son; make me as one of your hired men."' So he got up and came to his father. But while he was still a long way off, his father saw him and felt compassion *for him,* and ran and embraced him and kissed him. And the son said to him, "Father, I have sinned against heaven and in your sight; I am no longer worthy to be called your son.' But the father said to his slaves, 'Quickly bring out the best robe and put it on him, and put a ring on his hand and sandals on his feet; and bring the fattened calf, kill it, and let us eat and celebrate; for this son of mine was dead and has come to life again; he was lost and has been found.' And they began to celebrate. Now his older son was in the field, when he came and approached the house, he heard music and dancing. And he summoned one of the servants and *began* inquiring what these things could be. And he said to him, 'Your brother has come, and your father has killed the fattened calf because he has received him back safe and sound.' But he became angry and was not willing to go in; and his father came out and *began* pleading with him. But he answered and said to his father, 'Look! For so many years I have been serving you and I have never neglected a command of yours; and *yet* you have never given me a young goat, so that I might celebrate with my friends; but when this son of yours came, who has devoured your wealth with prostitutes, you killed the fattened calf for him.' And he said to him, 'Son, you have always been with me, and all that is mine is yours. But we had to celebrate and rejoice, for this brother of yours was dead and *has begun* to live, and was lost and has been found' " (Luke 15:11–32; see Proverb 29:2).

YEARS, THREE (See YEARS)

YEAST (See LEAVEN)

YEAST, PARABLE OF THE (See LEAVEN, PARABLE OF THE)

YOKE

Setting: Galilee. After rendering a thanksgiving prayer to His Father in heaven, Jesus offers rest to all who are weary and heavy-laden as He preaches and teaches throughout the region.

"Come to Me, all who are weary and heavy-laden, and I will give you rest. Take My yoke upon you and learn from Me, for I am gentle and humble in heart, and YOU WILL FIND REST FOR YOUR SOULS. For My yoke is easy and My burden is light" (Matthew 11:28–30, Jesus quotes from Jeremiah 6:16; see Jeremiah 31:35; 1 John 5:3).

Setting: On the way from Galilee to Jerusalem. After speaking a parable to the invited guests and the host at a banquet, Jesus responds to a guest's proclamation about the blessings of eating bread in the kingdom of God.

But He said to him, "A man was giving a big dinner, and he invited many; and at the dinner hour he sent his slave to say to those who had been invited, 'Come; for everything is ready now.' But they all alike began to make excuses. The first one said to him, 'I have bought a piece of land and I need to go out and look at it; please consider me excused.' Another one said, 'I have bought five yoke of oxen, and I am going to try them out; please consider me excused.' Another one said, I have married a wife, and for that reason I cannot come.' And the slave came *back* and reported this to his master. Then the head of the household became angry and said to his slave, 'Go out at once into the streets and lanes of the city and bring in here the poor and crippled and blind and lame.' And the slave said, 'Master, what you commanded has been done, and still there is room.' And the master said to the slave, 'Go out into the highways and along the hedges, and compel *them* to come in, so that my house may be filled. For I tell you, none of those men who were invited shall taste of my dinner'" (Luke 14:16–24; see Deuteronomy 24:5; Matthew 22:2–14).

YOUNG MAN (Listed under MAN, YOUNG)

YOUNGER (Also see YOUNGEST)

Setting: On the way from Galilee to Jerusalem. Jesus conveys the illustration of the prodigal son because the Pharisees and scribes complain He associates with tax collectors and sinners.

And He said, "A man had two sons. The younger of them said to his father, 'Father, give me the share of the estate that falls to me.' So he divided his wealth between them. And not many days later, the younger son gathered everything together and went on a journey into a distant country, and there he squandered his estate with loose living. Now when he had spent everything, a severe famine occurred in that country, and he began to be impoverished. So he went and hired himself out to one of the citizens of that country, and he sent him into his fields to feed swine. And he would have gladly filled his stomach with the pods that the swine were eating, and no one was giving *anything* to him. But when he came to his senses, he said, 'How many of my father's hired men have more than enough bread, but I am dying here with hunger! I will get up and go to my father, and will say to him, "Father, I have sinned against heaven, and in your sight; I am no longer worthy to be called your son; make me as one of your hired men."' So he got up and came to his father. But while he was still a long way off, his father saw him and felt compassion *for him,* and ran and embraced him and kissed him. And the son said to him, "Father, I have sinned against heaven and in your sight; I am no longer worthy to be called your son.' But the father said to his slaves, 'Quickly bring out the best robe and put it on him, and put a ring on his hand and sandals on his feet; and bring the fattened calf, kill it, and let us eat and celebrate; for this son of mine was dead and has come to life again; he was lost and has been found.' And they began to celebrate. Now his older son was in the field, when he came and approached the house, he heard music and dancing. And he summoned one of the servants and *began* inquiring what these things could be. And he said to him, 'Your brother has come, and your father has killed the fattened calf because he has received him back safe and sound.' But he became angry and was not willing to go in; and his father came out and *began* pleading with him. But he answered and said to his father, 'Look! For so many years I have been serving you and I have never neglected a command of yours; and *yet* you have never given me a young goat, so that I might celebrate with my friends; but when this son of yours came, who has devoured your wealth with prostitutes, you killed the fattened calf for him.' And he said to him, 'Son, you have always been with me, and all that is mine is yours. But we had to celebrate and rejoice, for this brother of yours was dead and *has begun* to live, and was lost and has been found' " (Luke 15:11–32; see Proverb 29:2).

Setting: By the Sea of Galilee. During the Lord's third post-resurrection appearance to His disciples, after quizzing Peter three times regarding the disciple's love for Him, Jesus gives him details about his aging and eventual death.

"Truly, truly, I say to you, when you were younger, you used to gird yourself and walk wherever you wished; but when you grow old, you will stretch out your hands and someone else will gird you, and bring you where you do not wish to *go*." Now this He said, signifying by what kind of death he would glorify God. And when He had spoken this, He said to him, "Follow Me!" (John 21:18, 19).

YOUNGEST (Also see YOUNGER)

Setting: An upper room in Jerusalem. During the Feast of Unleavened Bread (Passover) just before His crucifixion, Jesus celebrates the Passover meal with His disciples and institutes the Lord's Supper. The disciples later argue over who is the greatest among them.

And He said to them, "The kings of the Gentiles lord it over them; and those who have authority over them are called 'Benefactors.' But *it is* not this way with you, but the one who is the greatest among you must become like the youngest, and the leader like a servant. For who is greater, the one who reclines *at the table* or the one who serves? Is it not the one who reclines *at the table?* But I am among you as the one who serves" (Luke 22:25–27; cf. Matthew 20:25–28; 23:11; Mark 10:42–45).

YOURSELF (Also see YOURSELVES)

Setting: Galilee. When Jesus comes down after preaching the Sermon on the Mount, large crowds follow Him, and a leper approaches Him asking for cleansing.

Jesus stretched out His hand and touched him, saying, "I am willing, be cleansed." And immediately his leprosy was cleansed. And Jesus said to him, "See that you tell no one; but go, show yourself to the priest and present the offering that Moses commanded, as a testimony to them" (Matthew 8:3, 4; cf. Mark 1:40–44; Luke 5:12–14; see Matthew 8:1, 2).

Setting: Judea beyond the Jordan (Perea). Jesus shares with a rich, young ruler how righteous believers may have treasure in heaven.

And He said to him, "Why are you asking Me about what is good? There is *only* One who is good; but if you wish to enter into life, keep the commandments." *Then* he said to Him, 'Which ones?' And Jesus said, "YOU SHALL NOT COMMIT MURDER; YOU SHALL NOT COMMIT ADULTERY; YOU SHALL NOT STEAL; YOU SHALL NOT BEAR FALSE WITNESS; HONOR YOUR FATHER AND MOTHER; and YOU SHALL LOVE YOUR NEIGHBOR AS YOURSELF." The young man said to Him, "All these things I have kept; what am I still lacking?" Jesus said to him, "If you wish to complete go *and* sell your possessions and give to *the* poor, and you will have treasure in heaven; and come, follow Me" (Matthew 19:16–22, Jesus quotes from Exodus 20:13–15; Leviticus 19:18; cf. Leviticus 18:5; Mark 10:17–21; Luke 10:25–28; 12:33; 18:18–24).

Setting: The temple in Jerusalem. After cleansing the temple by driving out the money changers and merchants, Jesus comments to the indignant chief priests and scribes about the praises the children render unto Him.

But when the chief priests and the scribes saw the wonderful things that He had done, and the children who were shouting in the temple, "Hosanna to the Son of David," they became indignant and said to Him, "Do You hear what these *children* are saying?"

And Jesus said to them, "Yes, have you never read, 'OUT OF THE MOUTH OF INFANTS AND NURSING BABIES YOU HAVE PREPARED PRAISE FOR YOURSELF'?" (Matthew 21:15, 16, Jesus quotes from Psalm 8:2; see Matthew 9:27).

Setting: The temple in Jerusalem. A Pharisee lawyer asks Jesus which is the great commandment of the Law, in order to test Him as He teaches.

And He said to him, " 'YOU SHALL LOVE THE LORD YOUR GOD WITH ALL YOUR HEART, AND WITH ALL YOUR SOUL, AND WITH ALL YOUR MIND.' This is the great and foremost commandment. The second is like it,' YOU SHALL LOVE YOUR NEIGHBOR AS YOURSELF.' On these two commandments depend the whole Law and the Prophets" (Matthew 22:37–40; Jesus quotes from Leviticus 19:18; Deuteronomy 6:5; cf. Mark 12:28–34; see Matthew 7:12).

Setting: An upper room in Jerusalem. While celebrating the Passover meal, Jesus shocks His disciples with the revelation that one of them will soon betray Him to His enemies.

As they were eating, He said, "Truly I say to you that one of you will betray Me." Being deeply grieved, they each one began to say to Him, 'Surely not I, Lord?' And He answered, "He who dipped his hand with Me in the bowl is the one who will betray Me. The Son of Man *is to* go, just as it is written of Him; but woe to that man by whom the Son of Man is betrayed! It would have been good for that man if he had not been born." And Judas, who was betraying Him, said, 'Surely it is not I, Rabbi?' Jesus said to him, "You have said *it* yourself" (Matthew 26:21–25; cf. Mark 14:18–21; Luke 22:21–23; John 13:21–30; see Psalm 41:9).

Setting: Jerusalem. After being betrayed by Judas and arrested, Jesus appears before Caiaphas (the high priest) and the Council for interrogation in an attempt to entrap Him.

Jesus said to him, "You have said it *yourself;* nevertheless I tell you, hereafter you will see THE SON OF MAN SITTING AT THE RIGHT HAND OF POWER, AND COMING ON THE CLOUDS OF HEAVEN" (Matthew 26:64, Jesus quotes from Daniel 7:13; cf. Mark 14:62).

Setting: Galilee. Early in His ministry, as Jesus preaches and casts out demons in the synagogues, a leper beseeches Him for healing.

Moved with compassion, Jesus stretched out His hand and touched him, and said to him, "I am willing; be cleansed." Immediately the leprosy left him and he was cleansed. And He sternly warned him and immediately sent him away, and He said to him, "See that you say nothing to anyone; but go, show yourself to the priest and offer for your cleansing what Moses commanded, as a testimony to them" (Mark 1:41–44; cf. Luke 5:12–14; see Leviticus 14:1–32; Matthew 8:3).

Setting: The temple in Jerusalem. With the Pharisees and Herodians failing to trap Jesus in a statement, one of the scribes asks Him which commandment is foremost.

Jesus answered, "The foremost is, 'HEAR, O ISRAEL! THE LORD OUR GOD IS ONE LORD; AND YOU SHALL LOVE THE LORD YOUR GOD WITH ALL YOUR HEART, AND WITH ALL YOUR SOUL, AND WITH ALL YOUR MIND AND WITH ALL YOUR STRENGTH.' The second is this, 'YOU SHALL LOVE YOUR NEIGHBOR AS YOURSELF.' There is no other commandment greater than these" (Mark 12:29–31, Jesus quotes from Deuteronomy 6:4–5; Leviticus 19:18; cf. Matthew 22:34–40; see Mark 12:28).

Setting: A borrowed upper room in Jerusalem. After Jesus and His twelve disciples celebrate the Passover and the Lord's Supper, they go out to the Mount of Olives.

And Jesus said to them, "You will all fall away, because it is written, 'I WILL STRIKE DOWN THE SHEPHERD, AND THE SHEEP SHALL BE SCATTERED.' But after I have been raised, I will go ahead of you to Galilee." But Peter said to Him, "*Even* though all may fall away, yet I will not." And Jesus said to him, "Truly I say to you, that this very night, before a rooster crows twice, you yourself will deny Me three times" (Mark 14:27–30, Jesus quotes from Zechariah 13:7; cf. Matthew 26:30–34; see Mark 14:31, 72).

Setting: The synagogue in Jesus' hometown of Nazareth in Galilee. At the beginning of His public ministry, Jesus comments to the congregation after reading from the book of the prophet Isaiah on the Sabbath.

And He said to them, "No doubt you will quote this proverb to Me, 'Physician, heal yourself! Whatever we heard was done at Capernaum, do here in your hometown as well.'" And He said, "Truly I say to you, no prophet is welcome in his hometown. But I say to you in truth, there were many widows in Israel in the days of Elijah, when the sky was shut up for three years and six months, when a great famine came over all the land; and yet Elijah was sent to none of them, but only to Zarephath, *in the land* of Sidon, to a woman who was a widow. And there were many lepers in Israel in the time of Elisha the prophet; and none of them was cleansed, but only Naaman the Syrian" (Luke 4:23–27; Jesus refers to 1 Kings 17:1, 9; 2 Kings 5:1–14; see Matthew 13:53–58).

Setting: Galilee. Early in His ministry, after calling Andrew, Simon (Peter), James, and John to follow Him, Jesus heals a leper.

And He stretched out His hand and touched Him, saying, "I am willing; be cleansed." And immediately the leprosy left him. And He ordered him to tell no one, "But go and show yourself to the priest and make an offering for your cleansing, just as Moses commanded, as a testimony to them" (Luke 5:13, 14; cf. Matthew 8:2–4; Mark 1:40–45; see Leviticus 13:49).

Setting: Galilee. After selecting His twelve disciples, Jesus teaches the Sermon on the Mount to those disciples and a great throng of people from Judea, Jerusalem, and the central coastal region of Tyre and Sidon.

And He also spoke a parable to them: "A blind man cannot guide a blind man, can he? Will they not both fall into a pit? A pupil is not above his teacher; but everyone, after he has been fully trained, will be like his teacher. Why do you look at the speck that is in your brother's eye, but do not notice the log that is in your own eye? Or how can you say to your brother, 'Brother, let me take out the speck that is in your eye,' when you yourself do not see the log that is in your own eye? You hypocrite, first take the log out of your own eye, and then you will see clearly to take out the speck that is in your brother's eye. For there is no good tree which produces bad fruit, nor, on the other hand, a bad tree which produces good fruit. For each tree is known by its own fruit. For men do not gather figs from thorns, nor do they pick grapes from a briar bush. The good man out of the good treasure of his heart brings forth what is good; and the evil *man* out of the evil *treasure* brings forth what is evil; for his mouth speaks from that which fills his heart" (Luke 6:39–45; cf. Matthew 7:3–6. 16, 18, 20; 12:35; see Matthew 10:24; 15:14; Luke 6:12–19).

Setting: On the way from Galilee to Jerusalem. After Jesus tells His disciples in private the privilege they are experiencing by living in the time of the Messiah, a lawyer tests Him.

And a lawyer stood up and put Him to the test, saying, "Teacher, what shall I do to inherit eternal life?" And He said to him, "What is written in the Law? How does it read to you?" And he answered, "YOU SHALL LOVE THE LORD YOUR GOD WITH ALL YOUR HEART, AND WITH ALL YOUR SOUL, AND WITH ALL YOUR STRENGTH, AND WITH ALL YOUR MIND; AND YOUR NEIGHBOR AS YOURSELF." And He said to him, "You have answered correctly; DO THIS AND YOU WILL LIVE" (Luke 10:25–28, Jesus quotes from Leviticus 18:5; see Deuteronomy 6:5; Matthew 19:16–19).

Setting: On the way from Galilee to Jerusalem. After His disciples ask that their faith be increased following His instruction to them on forgiveness, the Lord illustrates with the mustard seed and an obedient slave.

And the Lord said, "If you had faith like a mustard seed, you would say to this mulberry tree, 'Be uprooted and be planted in the sea'; and it would obey you. Which of you, having a slave plowing or tending sheep, will say to him when he has come from the field, 'Come immediately and sit down to eat'? But will he not say to him, 'Prepare something for me to eat, and *properly* clothe yourself and serve me while I eat and drink; and afterward you may eat and drink'? He does not thank the slave because he did the things which were commanded, does he? So you too, when you do all the things which are commanded you, say, 'We are unworthy slaves; we have done *only* that which we ought to have done'" (Luke 17:6–10; see Matthew 13:31; Luke 12:37).

Setting: Jerusalem. Before the Passover, after giving His disciples hope that in the midst of tribulation they will have His peace, Jesus prays His high-priestly prayer.

Jesus spoke these things; and lifting up His eyes to heaven, He said, "Father, the hour has come; glorify Your Son, that the Son may glorify You, even as You gave Him authority over all flesh, that to all whom You have given Him, He may give eternal life. This is eternal life, that they may know You, the only true God, and Jesus Christ whom You have sent. I glorified You on the earth, having accomplished the work which You have given Me to do. Now, Father, glorify Me together with Yourself, with the glory which I had with You before the world was. I have manifested Your name to the men whom You gave Me out of the world; they were Yours and You gave them to Me, and they have kept Your word. Now they have come to know that everything You have given Me is from You; for the words which You gave Me I have given to them; and they received *them* and truly understood that I came forth from You, and they believed You sent Me. I ask on their behalf; I do not ask on behalf of the world, but of those whom You have given Me; for they are Yours; and all things that are Mine are Yours, and Yours are Mine; and I have been glorified in them. I am no longer in the world; and *yet* they themselves are in the world, and I come to You. Holy Father, keep them in Your name, *the name* which You have given Me, that they may be even as We *are.* While I was with them, I was keeping them in Your name which You have given Me; and I guarded them and not one of them perished but the son of perdition, so that the Scripture would be fulfilled" (John 17:1–12; see Luke 22:32; John 1:1; 3:35; 4:34; 5:44; 6:37–39, 70; 8:42; 11:41; 12:49; 13:18, 31; 16:15; Philippians 2:9).

Setting: By the Sea of Galilee. During the Lord's third post-resurrection appearance to His disciples, after quizzing Peter three times regarding the disciple's love for Him, Jesus gives him details about his aging and eventual death.

"Truly, truly, I say to you, when you were younger, you used to gird yourself and walk wherever you wished; but when you grow old, you will stretch out your hands and someone else will gird you, and bring you where you do not wish to *go.*" Now this He said, signifying by what kind of death he would glorify God. And when He had spoken this, He said to him, "Follow Me!" (John 21:18, 19).

Setting: On the island of Patmos (in the Aegean Sea about fifty miles southwest of Ephesus in modern Turkey). On the Lord's Day (Sunday), approximately fifty years after the Resurrection, the disciple John encounters the Lord Jesus Christ, who communicates a new revelation for the apostle to record for the church in Laodicea and to six other churches in Asia.

"To the angel of the church in Laodicea write: The Amen, the faithful and true Witness, the Beginning of the creation of God, says this: 'I know your deeds, that you are neither cold nor hot; I wish that you were cold or hot. So because you are lukewarm, and neither hot nor cold, I will spit you out of My mouth. Because you say, "I am rich, and have become wealthy, and have need of nothing," and you do not know that you are wretched and miserable and poor and blind and naked, I advise you to buy from Me gold refined by fire so that you may become rich, and white garments so that you may clothe yourself, and *that* the shame of your nakedness will not be revealed; and eye salve to anoint your eyes so that you may see. Those whom I love, I reprove and discipline; therefore be zealous and repent. Behold, I stand at the door and knock; if anyone hears My voice and opens the door, I will come in to him and will dine with him, and he with Me. He who overcomes, I will grant to him to sit down with Me on My throne, as I also overcame and sat down with My Father on His throne. He who has an ear, let him hear what the Spirit says to the churches'" (Revelation 3:14–22; see Proverb 3:12; Hosea 12:8; John 14:23; 16:33).

YOURSELVES (Also see YOURSELF)

Setting: Galilee. During the early part of His ministry, Jesus preaches the Sermon on the Mount to His disciples and the multitudes.

"Do not store up for yourselves treasures on earth, where moth and rust destroy, and where thieves break in and steal. But store up for yourselves treasures in heaven, where neither moth nor rust destroys, and where thieves do not break in or steal; for where your treasure is, there your heart will be also" (Matthew 6:19–21; cf. Luke 12:34; see Proverb 23:4; Matthew 19:21).

Setting: Galilee. Pharisees and scribes from Jerusalem accuse Jesus' disciples of disobeying tradition and the commandments.

And He answered and said to them, "Why do you yourselves transgress the commandment of God for the sake of tradition? For God said, 'HONOR YOUR FATHER AND MOTHER,' and, 'HE WHO SPEAKS EVIL OF FATHER OR MOTHER IS TO BE PUT TO DEATH.' But you say, 'Whoever says to *his* father or mother, "Whatever I have that would help you has been given *to God*," he is not to honor his father or mother.' And *by this* you invalidated the word of God for the sake of your tradition. You hypocrites, rightly did Isaiah prophesy of you: 'THIS PEOPLE HONORS ME WITH THEIR LIPS, BUT THEIR HEART IS FAR AWAY FROM ME. BUT IN VAIN DO THEY WORSHIP ME, TEACHING AS DOCTRINES THE PRECEPTS OF MEN'" (Matthew 15:3–9, Jesus quotes from Exodus 20:12, 21:17, Leviticus 20:9; Isaiah 29:13; cf. Mark 7:5–7; see Colossians 2:22).

Setting: By the Sea of Galilee. Jesus repeats a warning to His disciples about the teaching of the religious leaders of His time—the Pharisees and the Sadducees.

But Jesus aware of this, said, "You men of little faith, why do you discuss among yourselves that you have no bread? Do you not yet understand or remember the five loaves of the five thousand and how many baskets *full* you picked up? Or the seven loaves of the four thousand, and how many large baskets *full* you picked up? How is it that you do not understand that I did not speak to you concerning bread? But beware of the leaven of the Pharisees and Sadducees" (Matthew 16:8–11; cf. Matthew 14:17–21; 15:34–38; Mark 8:17–21).

Setting: The temple in Jerusalem. After the Jewish religious leaders test Him with questions, Jesus pronounces the first of eight woes upon them in front of the crowds and His disciples.

"But woe to you, scribes and Pharisees, hypocrites, because you shut off the kingdom of heaven from people; for you do not enter in yourselves, nor do you allow those who are entering to go in" (Matthew 23:13; cf. Luke 11:52).

Setting: The temple in Jerusalem. After the Jewish religious leaders test Him with questions, Jesus pronounces the third of eight woes upon them in front of the crowds and His disciples.

"Woe to you, scribes and Pharisees, hypocrites, because you travel around on sea and land to make one proselyte; and when he becomes one, you make him twice as much a son of hell as yourselves" (Matthew 23:15).

Setting: The temple in Jerusalem. After the Jewish religious leaders test Him with questions, Jesus pronounces the eighth of eight woes upon them in front of the crowds and His disciples.

"Woe to you, scribes and Pharisees, hypocrites! For you build the tombs of the prophets and adorn the monuments of the righteous, and say, 'If we had been *living* in the days of our fathers, we would not have been partners with them in *shedding* the blood of the prophets.' So you testify against yourselves, that you are sons of those who murdered the prophets. Fill up, then, the measure *of the guilt* of you fathers. You serpents, you brood of vipers, how will you escape the sentence of hell? Therefore, behold, I am sending you prophets and wise men and scribes; some of them you will kill and crucify, and some of them you will scourge in your synagogues, and persecute from city to city, so that upon you may fall *the guilt of* all the righteous blood shed on earth, from the blood of righteous Abel to the blood of Zechariah, the son of Berechiah, whom you murdered between the temple and the altar. Truly I say to you, all these things will come upon this generation" (Matthew 23:29–36; cf. 2 Chronicles 24:21; Zechariah 1:1; Matthew 3:7; Luke 11:47–52; see Matthew 10:23).

Setting: The Mount of Olives, just east of Jerusalem. During His discourse, after answering His disciples' questions as to when the temple will be destroyed and Jerusalem overrun, along with the signs of His coming and the end of the age, Jesus reemphasizes to His disciples that they should be on the alert for His return.

"Then the kingdom of heaven will be comparable to ten virgins, who took their lamps and went out to meet the bridegroom. Five of them were foolish, and five were prudent. For when the foolish took their lamps, they took no oil with them, but the prudent took oil in flasks along with their lamps. Now while the bridegroom was delaying, they all got drowsy and *began* to sleep. But at midnight there was a shout, 'Behold, the bridegroom! Come out to meet *him*.' Then all those virgins rose and trimmed their lamps.

The foolish said to the prudent, 'Give us some of your oil, for our lamps are going out.' But the prudent answered, 'No, there will not be enough for us and you *too;* go instead to the dealers and buy *some* for yourselves.' And while they were going away to make the purchase, the bridegroom came, and those who were ready went in with him to the wedding feast; and the door was shut. Later the other virgins also came, saying, 'Lord, lord, open up for us.' But he answered, 'Truly I say to you, I do not know you.' Be on the alert then, for you do not know the day nor the hour" (Matthew 25:1–13; cf. Matthew 24:42; Luke 12:35; see Matthew 7:21, 24).

Setting: Galilee. After Jesus' disciples report to Him about their ministry in the cities and villages, He instructs them to rest.

And He said to them, "Come away by yourselves to a secluded place and rest a while." (For there were many *people* coming and going, and they did not even have time to eat.) (Mark 6:31; see Mark 3:20).

Setting: Capernaum of Galilee. As Jesus teaches His disciples in private, they ask Him about greatness.

But Jesus said, "Do not hinder him, for there is no one who will perform a miracle in My name, and be able soon afterward to speak evil of Me. For he who is not against us is for us. For whoever gives you a cup of water to drink because of your name as *followers* of Christ, truly I say to you, he will not lose his reward. Whoever causes one of these little ones who believe to stumble, it would be better for him if, with a heavy millstone hung around his neck, he had been cast into the sea. If your hand causes you to stumble, cut it off; it is better for you to enter life crippled, than, having your two hands, to go into hell, into the unquenchable fire, [where THEIR WORM DOES NOT DIE, AND THE FIRE IS NOT QUENCHED.] If your foot causes you to stumble, cut it off; it is better for you to enter life lame, than, having your two feet, to be cast into hell, [where THEIR WORM DOES NOT DIE, AND THE FIRE IS NOT QUENCHED.] If your eye causes you to stumble, throw it out; it is better for you to enter the kingdom of God with one eye, than, having two eyes, to be cast into hell, where THEIR WORM DOES NOT DIE, AND THE FIRE IS NOT QUENCHED. For everyone will be salted with fire. Salt is good; but if the salt becomes unsalty, with what will you make it salty *again?* Have salt in yourselves, and be at peace with one another" (Mark 9:39–50; Jesus quotes from Isaiah 66:24; cf. Matthew 18:6–9; Luke 9:49, 50; see Matthew 5:13, 29, 30; 10:42; 12:30; 18:5, 6).

Setting: On the way from Galilee to Jerusalem. After Jesus pronounces woes upon the Pharisees, a lawyer replies that His remarks are an insult to lawyers, too.

But He said, "Woe to you lawyers as well! For you weigh men down with burdens hard to bear, while you yourselves will not even touch the burdens with one of your fingers. Woe to you! For you build the tombs of the prophets, and *it was* your fathers *who* killed them. So you are witnesses and approve the deeds of your fathers; because it was they who killed them, and you build *their tombs*. For this reason also the wisdom of God said, 'I will send them prophets and apostles, and *some* of them they will kill and *some* they will persecute, so that the blood of all the prophets, shed since the foundation of the world, may be charged against this generation, from the blood of Abel to the blood of Zechariah, who was killed between the altar and the house *of God*; yes, I tell you, it shall be charged against this generation.' Woe to you lawyers! For you have taken away the key of knowledge; you yourselves did not enter, and you hindered those who were entering" (Luke 11:46–52; cf. Matthew 23:29–32; see 2 Chronicles 24:20, 21; Matthew 23:4, 13).

Setting: On the way from Galilee to Jerusalem. After giving a parable about riches and greed, Jesus challenges the crowd and His disciples concerning godly living.

"Sell your possessions and give to charity; make yourselves money belts which do not wear out, an unfailing treasure in heaven, where no thief comes near nor moth destroys. For where your treasure is, there your heart will be also" (Luke 12:33, 34; cf. Matthew 6:19–21; 19:21).

Setting: On the way from Galilee to Jerusalem. While teaching in the cities and villages, Jesus responds to a question about who is saved.

And someone said to Him, "Lord, are here *just* a few who are being saved?" And He said to them, "Strive to enter through the narrow door; for many, I tell you, will seek to enter and will not be able. Once the head of the house gets up and shuts the door, and you begin to stand outside and knock on the door, saying, 'Lord, open up to us!' then He will answer and say to you, 'I do not know where you are from.' Then you will begin to say, 'We ate and drank in Your presence, and You taught in our streets'; and He will say, 'I tell you, I do not know where you are from; DEPART FROM ME, ALL YOU EVILDOERS.' In that place there will be weeping and gnashing of teeth when you see Abraham and Isaac and Jacob and all the prophets in the kingdom of God, but you yourselves being thrown out. And they will come from east and west and from north and south, and will recline *at the table* in the kingdom of God. And behold, *some* are last who will be first and *some* are first who will be last" (Luke 13:23–30, Jesus quotes from Psalm 6:8; cf. Matthew 7:13, 23; 8:11, 12; see Matthew 19:30; Luke 3:8).

Setting: On the way from Galilee to Jerusalem. After giving the story of the prodigal son, the Lord teaches His disciples about stewardship.

Now He was also saying to the disciples, "There was a rich man who had a manager, and this *manager* was reported to him as squandering his possessions. And he called him and said to him, 'What is this I hear about you? Give an accounting of your management, for you can no longer be a manager.' The manager said to himself, 'What shall I do, since my master is taking the management away from me? I am not strong enough to dig; I am ashamed to beg. I know what I shall do, so that when I am removed from the management people will welcome me into their homes.' And he summoned each one of his master's debtors, and he *began* saying to the first, 'How much do you owe my master?' And he said, 'A hundred measures of oil.' And he said to him, 'Take your bill, and sit down quickly and write fifty.' Then he said to another, 'And how much do you owe?' And he said, 'A hundred measures of wheat.' He said to him, 'Take your bill, and write eighty.' And his master praised the unrighteous manager because he had acted shrewdly; for the sons of this age are more shrewd in relation to their own kind than the sons of light. And I say to you, make friends for yourselves by means of the wealth of unrighteousness, so that when it fails, they will receive you into the eternal dwellings. He who is faithful in a very little thing is faithful also in much; and he who is unrighteous in a very little thing is unrighteous also in much. Therefore if you have not been faithful in the *use of* unrighteous wealth, who will entrust the true *riches* to you? And if you have not been faithful in *the use of* that which is another's, who will give you that which is your own? No servant can serve two masters; for either he will hate the one and love the other, or else he will be devoted to one and despise the other. You cannot serve God and wealth" (Luke 16:1–13; cf. Matthew 6:24; see Matthew 25:14–30).

Setting: On the way from Galilee to Jerusalem. The Lord responds to the Pharisees' scoffing at His teaching His disciples about stewardship.

And He said to them, "You are those who justify yourselves in the sight of men, but God knows your hearts; for that which is highly esteemed among men is detestable in the sight of God. The Law and the Prophets *were proclaimed* until John; since that time the gospel of the kingdom of God has been preached, and everyone is forcing his way into it. But is it easier for heaven and earth to pass away than for one stroke of a letter of the Law to fail" (Luke 16:15–17; cf. Matthew 5:18; see 1 Samuel 16:7; Matthew 4:23; 11:11–14).

Setting: On the way from Galilee to Jerusalem. The Lord stops to heal ten lepers who ask for cleansing.

When He saw them, He said to them, "Go and show yourselves to the priests." And as they were going, they were cleansed. Now one of them, when he saw that he had been healed, turned back, glorifying God with a loud voice, and he fell on his face at His feet, giving thanks to Him. And he was a Samaritan. Then Jesus answered and said, "Were there not ten cleansed? But the nine—where are they? Was no one found who returned to give glory to God, except this foreigner?" And He said to him, "Stand up and go; your faith has made you well" (Luke 17:14–19; see Leviticus 14:1–32).

Setting: On the Mount of Olives, east of the temple in Jerusalem. After ministering in the temple a few days before His crucifixion, and giving His disciples more details regarding the temple's future destruction, Jesus elaborates during His Olivet Discourse about things to come.

Then He continued by saying to them, "Nation will rise against nation and kingdom against kingdom, and there will be great earthquakes, and in various places plagues and famines; and there will be terrors and great signs from heaven. But before all these things, they will lay their hands on you and will persecute you, delivering you to the synagogues and prisons, bringing you before kings and governors for My name's sake. It will lead to an opportunity for your testimony. So make up your minds not to prepare beforehand to defend yourselves; for I will give you utterance and wisdom which none of your opponents will be able to resist or refute. But you will be betrayed even by parents and brothers and relatives and friends, and they will put *some* of you to death, and you will be hated by all because of My name. Yet not a hair of your head will perish. By your endurance you will gain your lives" (Luke 21:10–19; cf. Matthew 10:19–22; 24:7–14; Mark 13:8–13).

Setting: On the Mount of Olives, east of the temple in Jerusalem. After ministering in the temple a few days before His crucifixion, and giving the disciples more details regarding His return, Jesus conveys the Parable of the Fig Tree during His Olivet Discourse.

Then He told them a parable: "Behold the fig tree and all the trees; as soon as they put forth *leaves,* you see it and know for yourselves that summer is now near. So you also, when you see these things happening, recognize that the kingdom of God is near. Truly, I say to you, this generation will not pass away until all things take place. Heaven and earth will pass away, but My words will not pass away" (Luke 21:29–33; cf. Matthew 24:32–35; Mark 13:28–31; see Matthew 5:18).

Setting: An upper room in Jerusalem. During the Feast of Unleavened Bread (Passover) just before His crucifixion, while celebrating the Passover meal with His disciples, Jesus institutes the Lord's Supper.

And when He had taken a cup *and* given thanks, He said, "Take this and share it among yourselves; for I say to you, I will not drink of the fruit of the vine from now on until the kingdom of God comes." And when he had taken *some* bread and given thanks, He broke it and gave it to them, saying, "This is My body which is given for you; do this in remembrance of Me." And in the same way *He took* the cup after they had eaten, saying, "This cup which is poured out for you is the new covenant in My blood. But behold, the hand of the one betraying Me is with Mine on the table. For indeed, the Son of Man is going as it has been determined; but woe to that man by whom He is betrayed!" (Luke 22:17–22; cf. Matthew 26:26–29; Mark 14:22–25; 1 Corinthians 11:23–26; see Psalm 41:9; Luke 14:15; 1 Corinthians 10:16).

Setting: Jerusalem. After being arrested, and appearing before the Council of Elders (Sanhedrin), Pilate (Roman governor of Judea), Herod Antipas (tetrarch of Galilee and Perea), and Pilate a second time (when the ruler bows to the crowd's pressure and grants that Jesus be crucified), the Lord prophesies to the women mourning Him regarding the coming judgment of Jerusalem.

But Jesus turning to them said, "Daughters of Jerusalem, stop weeping for Me, but weep for yourselves and for your children. For behold, the days are coming when they will say, 'Blessed are the barren, and the wombs that never bore, and the breasts that never nursed.' Then they will begin TO SAY TO THE MOUNTAINS, 'FALL ON US,' AND TO THE HILLS, 'COVER US.' For it they do these things when the tree is green, what will happen when it is dry?" (Luke 23:28–31, Jesus quotes from Hosea 10:8; see Matthew 24:19).

Setting: Jerusalem. During a feast of the Jews, Jesus responds to criticism from the Jewish religious leaders by referring to God as His Father (thereby making Himself equal with God) and informing them that God, John the Baptist, the Scriptures, and His works all testify to His mission.

"You search the Scriptures because you think that in them you have eternal life; it is these that testify about Me; and you are unwilling to come to Me so that you may have life. I do not receive glory from men; but I know you, that you do not have the love of God in yourselves. I have come in My Father's name, and you do not receive Me; if another comes in his own name, you will receive him. How can you believe, when you receive glory from one another and you do not seek the glory that is from the *one and* only God? Do not think that I will accuse you before the Father; the one who accuses you is Moses, in whom you have set your hope. For if you believed Moses, you would believe Me, for he wrote about Me. But if you do not believe his writings, how will you believe My words?" (John 5:39–47; see Matthew 24:5; Luke 16:29, 31; 24:27; John 9:28; 17:3).

Setting: Capernaum of Galilee. After Jesus informs the people whom He miraculously fed with a lad's five loaves and two fish how they might receive the bread out of heaven, the Jewish religious leaders grumble when the Lord claims that He came down out of heaven.

Therefore the Jews were grumbling about Him, because He said, "I am the bread that came down out of heaven." They were saying, "Is not this Jesus, the son of Joseph, whose father and mother we know? How does He now say, 'I have come down out of heaven'?" Jesus answered and said to them, "Do not grumble among yourselves. No one can come to Me unless the Father who sent Me draws him; and I will raise him up on the last day. It is written in the prophets, 'AND THEY SHALL ALL BE TAUGHT OF GOD.' Everyone who has heard and learned from the Father, comes to Me. Not that anyone has seen the Father, except the One who is from God; He has seen the Father. Truly, truly, I say to you, he who believes has eternal life. I am the bread of life. Your fathers ate the manna in the wilderness, and they died. This is the bread which comes down out of heaven, so that one may eat of it and not die. I am the living bread that came down out of heaven; if anyone eats of this bread, he will live forever; and the bread also which I will give for the life of the world is My flesh" (John 6:41–51, Jesus quotes from Isaiah 54:13; see John 1:18, 29; 3:36; 7:27).

Setting: Capernaum of Galilee. After Jesus informs the people whom He miraculously fed with a lad's five loaves and two fish how they might receive the bread out of heaven, the Jewish religious leaders argue with one another when the Lord says He will give His flesh to the world to eat.

So Jesus said to them, "Truly, truly, I say to you, unless you eat the flesh of the Son of Man and drink His blood, you have no life in yourselves. He who eats My flesh and drinks My blood has eternal life, and I will raise him up on the last day. For My flesh is true food, and My blood is true drink. He who eats My flesh and drinks My blood abides in Me, and I in him. As the living Father sent Me, and I live because of the Father, so he who eats Me, he also will live because of Me. This is the bread which came down out of heaven; not as the fathers ate and died; he who eats this bread will live forever" (John 6:53–58; see Matthew 16:16; Luke 4:22; John 3:36; 9:16; 15:4).

Setting: Capernaum of Galilee. Jesus' blood brothers, who do not yet believe in Him, encourage Him to attend the upcoming Feast of Booths in Jerusalem in order to demonstrate His works to His disciples and the world.

So Jesus said to them, "My time is not yet here, but your time is always opportune. The world cannot hate you, but it hates Me because I testify of it, that its deeds are evil. Go up to the feast yourselves; I do not go up to this feast because My time has not yet fully come" (John 7:6–8; see John 3:19, 20; 15:18–20).

Z

ZACCHEUS

Setting: Jericho, en route to Jerusalem for the crucifixion. After taking time to heal a blind man, Jesus informs a curious, short tax collector observing Him and His disciples from a sycamore tree that He will stay at the man's house that night.

When Jesus came to the place, He looked up and said to him, "Zaccheus, hurry and come down, for today I must stay at your house" (Luke 19:5).

[ZACCHEUS from he, too, is a son of Abraham]

Setting: Jericho, on the way to Jerusalem. After taking time to heal a blind man, Jesus comments on Zaccheus's response to Him.

And Jesus said to him, "Today salvation has come to this house, because he, too, is a son of Abraham. For the Son of Man has come to seek and to save that which was lost" (Luke 19:9, 10; cf. Matthew 18:11).

ZAREPHATH

Setting: The synagogue in Jesus' hometown of Nazareth in Galilee. At the beginning of His public ministry, Jesus comments to the congregation after reading from the book of the prophet Isaiah on the Sabbath.

And He said to them, "No doubt you will quote this proverb to Me, 'Physician, heal yourself! Whatever we heard was done at Capernaum, do here in your hometown as well.'" And He said, "Truly I say to you, no prophet is welcome in his hometown. But I say to you in truth, there were many widows in Israel in the days of Elijah, when the sky was shut up for three years and six months, when a great famine came over all the land; and yet Elijah was sent to none of them, but only to Zarephath, *in the land* of Sidon, to a woman who was a widow. And there were many lepers in Israel in the time of Elisha the prophet; and none of them was cleansed, but only Naaman the Syrian" (Luke 4:23–27; Jesus refers to 1 Kings 17:1, 9; 2 Kings 5:1–14; see Matthew 13:53–58).

ZEALOUS

Setting: On the island of Patmos (in the Aegean Sea about fifty miles southwest of Ephesus in modern Turkey). On the Lord's Day (Sunday), approximately fifty years after the Resurrection, the disciple John encounters the Lord Jesus Christ, who communicates a new revelation for the apostle to record for the church in Laodicea and to six other churches in Asia.

"To the angel of the church in Laodicea write: The Amen, the faithful and true Witness, the Beginning of the creation of God, says this: 'I know your deeds, that you are neither cold nor hot; I wish that you were cold or hot. So because you are lukewarm, and neither hot nor cold, I will spit you out of My mouth. Because you say, "I am rich, and have become wealthy, and have need of nothing," and you do not know that you are wretched and miserable and poor and blind and naked, I advise you to buy from Me gold refined by fire so that you may become rich, and white garments so that you may clothe yourself, and *that* the shame of your nakedness will not be revealed; and eye salve to anoint your eyes so that you may see. Those whom I love, I reprove and discipline; therefore be zealous and repent. Behold, I stand at the door and knock; if anyone hears My voice and opens the door, I will come in to him and will dine with him, and he with Me. He who overcomes, I will grant to him to sit down with Me on My throne, as I also overcame and sat down with My Father on His throne. He who has an ear, let him hear what the Spirit says to the churches'" (Revelation 3:14–22; see Proverb 3:12; Hosea 12:8; John 14:23; 16:33).

ZECHARIAH (Also see PROPHET; and PROPHETS)

Setting: The temple in Jerusalem. After the Jewish religious leaders test Him with questions, Jesus pronounces the eighth of eight woes upon them in front of the crowds and His disciples.

"Woe to you, scribes and Pharisees, hypocrites! For you build the tombs of the prophets and adorn the monuments of the righteous, and say, 'If we had been *living* in the days of our fathers, we would not have been partners with them in *shedding* the blood of the prophets.' So you testify against yourselves, that you are sons of those who murdered the prophets. Fill up, then, the measure *of the guilt* of you fathers. You serpents, you brood of vipers, how will you escape the sentence of hell? Therefore, behold, I am sending you prophets and wise men and scribes; some of them you will kill and crucify, and some of them you will scourge in your synagogues, and persecute from city to city, so that upon you may fall *the guilt of* all the righteous blood shed on earth, from the blood of righteous Abel to the blood of Zechariah, the son of Berechiah, whom you murdered between the temple and the altar. Truly I say to you, all these things will come upon this generation" (Matthew 23:29–36; cf. 2 Chronicles 24:21; Zechariah 1:1; Matthew 3:7; Luke 11:47–52; see Matthew 10:23).

Setting: On the way from Galilee to Jerusalem. After Jesus pronounces woes upon the Pharisees, a lawyer replies that His remarks are an insult to lawyers, too.

But He said, "Woe to you lawyers as well! For you weigh men down with burdens hard to bear, while you yourselves will not even touch the burdens with one of your fingers. Woe to you! For you build the tombs of the prophets, and *it was* your fathers *who* killed them. So you are witnesses and approve the deeds of your fathers; because it was they who killed them, and you build *their tombs*. For this reason also the wisdom of God said, 'I will send them prophets and apostles, and *some* of them they will kill and *some* they will persecute, so that the blood of all the prophets, shed since the foundation of the world, may be charged against this generation, from the blood of Abel to the blood of Zechariah, who was killed between the altar and the house *of God*; yes, I tell you, it shall be charged against this generation.' Woe to you lawyers! For you have taken away the key of knowledge; you yourselves did not enter, and you hindered those who were entering" (Luke 11:46–52; cf. Matthew 23:29–32; see 2 Chronicles 24:20, 21; Matthew 23:4, 13).

And there are also many other things which Jesus did, which if they were written in detail, I suppose that even the world itself would not contain the books that would be written (John 21:25).

Appendix A

How to Personally Know Jesus

So What?

Usually, the last chapter of a book is the *So What?* chapter. With this volume being a reference work, you may be wondering the purpose of this book. Why was it written? A lot of time and effort go into most books, including this one.

By now, you have probably perused some of the categorized subjects. Out of curiosity, you thought about checking out the appendixes. As the Preface conveys, this work, though large, only scratches the surface of the incredible life and teachings of the Lord Jesus Christ in the New Testament. Yet, if God gives you a better comprehension and application to your life of the truths of Jesus through this book, your time and expense in using it will be well spent.

Hopefully, this book brings you the words of Christ in the New Testament in a few areas you have never seen before. Did you know this same Jesus desires a personal relationship with you? Do you know Him? To you, is He a friend? A stranger? Or, just a figure from history? Four types of people will examine this book:

1. Non-Christians, or unbelievers, curious about the title, or Christianity itself, along with some skeptics.
2. People who believe they are Christians, but aren't truly saved.
3. Christians who are saved, but are not absolutely, positively sure they are right with God.
4. Christians who are absolutely, positively 100 percent sure they are saved and have a personal relationship with Jesus.

The Bad News and the Good News

Whatever category you find yourself in, the God of the universe has revealed Himself to you through His Word, the Bible, and through His Son, Jesus Christ. God desires for all human beings to come to a saving knowledge of His Son. He does not wish for any person to spend an eternity separated from Him in hell, or the lake of fire. Yet, the Lord allows men and women to reject His free offer of eternal life. Since souls of humans were created to exist forever, if someone chooses to go their own way without God, He has provided a place for them to suffer the consequences of this foolish decision. This is bad news, but—there is good news.

The good news is that as long as you are alive on earth, you have the opportunity to receive the gift of salvation that God offers through believing in, or trusting, Jesus Christ, and Him alone, as your Savior. Those who believe in, or trust, Jesus to forgive them of their sins are forgiven and will live forever in fellowship and blessing with their Creator in heaven.

The next paragraphs are directed especially to individuals in categories 1, 2, and 3: unbelievers, people who believe they are saved but aren't, and people who believe they are Christians, but aren't 100 percent sure they are right with God.

Some people know they are not saved. Others may think they are saved and aren't. You may even be offended that anyone would even include a category such as number 2 above. But, here's a question to you: Is it possible to be a disciple of Jesus Christ and not be saved? According to the Bible, absolutely. Take for example, Judas. He was chosen as one of Jesus' twelve disciples. He spent years listening to Christ's teaching and even ministering alongside Him. Yet, at the end of Jesus' earthly ministry, he betrayed the Lord. So, indeed, some people think they are Christians, or disciples of Christ, and aren't. Though unpleasant, this reality is true. Furthermore, remember the words of the Lord regarding Judgment Day in Matthew 7:21–23:

> "Not everyone who says to Me, 'Lord, Lord,' will enter the kingdom of heaven, but he who does the will of My Father who is in heaven *will enter.* Many will say to Me on that day, 'Lord, Lord, did we not prophesy in Your name, and in Your name cast out demons, and in Your name perform many miracles?' And then I will declare to them, "I never knew you; DEPART FROM ME, YOU WHO PRACTICE LAWLESSNESS.'"

But, perhaps you are wondering, what must I do be saved, or to become a true Christian? Some believe you must try to be a good person or follow a system of do's and don'ts. Others advocate keeping the Ten Commandments or following some prescribed religious ritual(s) or discipline(s). Still many may believe that attending a church or other house of worship is the answer. According to the Bible, God's Word, it's impossible to work your way to heaven. Heaven is a free gift offered by God through the finished work that His Son, Jesus, performed on the cross. Ephesians 2:8, 9 states:

> For by grace you have been saved through faith; and that not of yourselves, *it is* the gift of God; not as a result of works, so that no one may boast.

Hopefully, you will not get the idea from these verses that everyone is saved. Again, as previously stated, God *does* desire for everyone to be saved. Note the words of the apostle Peter in 2 Peter 3:9:

> The Lord is not slow about His promise, as some count slowness, but is patient toward you, not wishing for any to perish, but for all to come to repentance.

The Biblical word *repentance* comes from *repent,* meaning a *change of mind*[1]. If you currently believe that you can do anything yourself to earn your way to heaven, you must repent, or have a change of mind about that viewpoint, and, instead, believe the truths of the gospel of Jesus Christ from the Bible. The apostle Paul provides a summary of these truths in 1 Corinthians 15:3–5:

> For I delivered to you as of first importance what I also received, that Christ died for our sins according to the Scriptures, and that He was buried, and that He was raised on the third day according to the Scriptures, and that He appeared to Cephas, then to the twelve.

In the verses above, Paul uses the name *Cephas* to refer to the apostle Peter. Jesus, Himself, utilizes this same term for this disciple that is translated as Peter in John 1:42.

Since "*What does* Jesus *say about . . .*" allows the words of Christ to speak for themselves, let the words of God address this important issue. According to the Bible, how does one become saved, or receive eternal life?

Most of you probably have some type of life insurance to provide for your loved ones when you die. Life insurance is helpful, but you or someone else must pay the premiums in order for your policy to stay in force. The Lord Jesus Christ offers an even better deal. It's called eternal life insurance. And, instead of you having to pay the premiums, Christ has paid the policy in full for you. How does one receive this eternal life insurance? Again, you don't have to pay any premiums, but there are certain requirements:

1. *Acknowledge* that you are a sinner and are in need of a Savior, as you cannot save yourself on the basis of going to church, being baptized, or doing any kind of good works or deeds.

   If we say that we have no sin, we are deceiving ourselves and the truth is not in us (1 John 1:8).

   . . . for all have sinned and fall short of the glory of God (Romans 3:23).

   For the wages of sin is death, but the free gift of God is eternal life in Christ Jesus our Lord (Romans 6:23).

2. *Affirm* that Jesus is God, the Savior of the world, and the only way *to* God.

   But God demonstrates His own love toward us, in that while we were yet sinners, Christ died for us (Romans 5:8).

   Jesus in His own words states:

   ". . . I am the way, and the truth, and the life; no one comes to the Father but through Me" (John 14:6).

   John, an apostle of the Lord Jesus, elaborates in 1 John 5:11–13 on the eternal life Jesus offers:

   And the testimony is this, that God has given us eternal life, and this life is in His Son. He who has the Son has the life; he who does not have the Son of God does not have the life. These things I have written to you who believe in the name of the Son of God, so that you may know that you have eternal life.

3. *Believe,* or trust, or place your faith for this eternal life insurance and the forgiveness of your sins in the Lord Jesus Christ, and Him alone, based on His death on the cross and resurrection from the dead.

Again, God makes it clear in the writings of the apostle Paul that one's faith must be in the Lord Jesus Christ:

But what does it say? THE WORD IS NEAR YOU, IN YOUR MOUTH AND IN YOUR HEART"—that is, the word of faith which we are preaching, that if you confess with your mouth Jesus as Lord, and believe in your heart that God raised Him from the dead, you will be saved; for with the heart a person believes, resulting in righteousness, and with the mouth he confesses, resulting in salvation (Romans 10:8–10).

Being Different

We all want to be unique. Everyone desires to be accepted and at the same time be the distinct individual God created.

You may recall some of the past television commercials for Apple computers and Dodge trucks. These advertisements stand out because they reach the part of us that longs to break away from the crowd.

A few years ago, The Barna Group did a study indicating that nearly half (43 percent) of all Americans who accept Jesus Christ as their Savior do so before reaching their 13th birthday.[2] Two out of three make their commitment to Christ prior to their 18th birthday.[3] Around 13 percent make their faith profession in Christ between the age of 18 and 21.[4] And, less than one out of every four born-again Christians come to trust Christ after their 21st birthday.[5]

In all likelihood, you are over 18 years old. If you haven't trusted Jesus Christ as your personal Savior, break the trend! Be different! Don't follow the pack. Recall the words of Christ:

> "Enter through the narrow gate; for the gate is wide and the way is broad that leads to destruction, and there are many who enter through it. For the gate is small and the way is narrow that leads to life, and there are few who find it" (Matthew 7:13, 14).

No matter who you are or what you've done, the God of the universe, the Creator of all things, desires a relationship with you. He desires to be your Friend and spend time with you. The relationship you begin with Him on earth will last forever.

You cannot depend on who you are or what you have or have not done to win God's approval. All things, except what Jesus offers, fall short. Salvation comes only by faith alone in Christ alone.

Only a decision to trust Christ as your personal Savior prior to when you will eventually face God will change your destiny. As long as you are alive on this earth, it is not too late. Ask yourself today, as you finish reading these words, where do you stand in relation to God? If you were to die tonight are you absolutely certain that you would go to heaven? If you were to stand before God and He were to ask you, "What right do you have to enter heaven?" what would you say? The only appropriate response would be that you are trusting in His Son, Jesus, and His finished work on the cross alone that opened the way for forgiveness of all your sins and eternal life forever with Him.

No doubt, this appendix contains a lot of Scripture to digest. However, if you sense that you would like to believe in, or trust, Christ as your Savior, to forgive you of your sins and give you eternal life, you may do so right now. Your next question may be, "How do I make Jesus my Savior?" God knows your heart. Speak to God right now. Communicate your desire for salvation to Him. Perhaps you might want to express yourself to Him with a prayer like this:

> "Dear God, I know that I am a sinner. I have broken Your laws. I have done so many wrong things. Today, I have to be honest, I am not sure of my salvation. If I were to die tonight, I do not know if I would be with You. Lord Jesus, I know You love me. I believe the truths of the Bible that You paid the price for my sins by dying on the cross and that God accepted Your sacrifice by raising You from the dead on the third day. Right now, I put my faith in You and You alone for my salvation. Jesus, I call upon You to save me. I believe You and receive You as my personal Savior. I put the eternal destiny of my life in Your hands alone. Amen."

Did you pray this prayer or something similar? Remember—it's not the prayer that saves you, it's the Person you are trusting, or believing in, who saves you. Do you believe the truths of the gospel of the Lord Jesus Christ? If so, you are now a child of God, a believer, a true Christian. Welcome to the family of God! To receive some helpful information on how to grow as a Christian and to locate a Bible-honoring church, please contact one of the following ministries:

Back To The Bible
PO Box 82808
Lincoln, NE 68501
402-464-7200
www.backtothebible.org

Dallas Theological Seminary
3909 Swiss Avenue
Dallas, TX 75204
800-387-9673
www.dts.edu

RBC Ministries
PO Box 2222
Grand Rapids, MI 49501
616-974-2210
www.rbc.org

Walk Thru the Bible Ministries
4201 North Peachtree Road
Atlanta, GA 30341
866-710-5320
www.walkthru.org

Hopefully, these pages have shown you a wonderful aspect of God. If not, I pray that He will take the veil off your eyes so that you may see Him as He is. May you catch a glimpse of His love, power, and grace. And, may you believe the truths of the gospel of the Lord Jesus Christ.

Being Obedient

Finally, a few parting words to those in category 4: Christians, believers in the Lord Jesus Christ who are 100 percent sure they are saved and will spend eternity with their God. If the Lord Jesus Christ is your personal Savior, may the truths of this book excite your heart! Remember that He loves you every day, in every way. At all times, He is working in your life and making you more like Him. You are His and He is yours! There is nothing you could do that would change one inch of the depth of His love.

Please respond to His love today. Tell Him how you feel. Perhaps you might consider praying this prayer:

> "Lord, Jesus, I worship You. I love You and I want to serve You. Thank You for the privilege of being known and loved by You. Revive me today. Let me catch the excitement of knowing You and living with You moment by moment. I want my life, my time, my abilities, and my resources, along with whatever I do, to count for You. I desire to do whatever Your will demands. In Your name, I pray. Amen."

As you open your eyes—without fear, but with joy, confidence, and excitement—look at the blessings and the world He provides! In God's eyes, the two most important things are His Word in the Bible and the souls of men and women. If you love God, and seek to obey Him, you must be concerned about the things that are of immense importance to Him.

For believers, the mission field is not always overseas. Our mission fields may be next door, down the street, or across town, as well as in distant lands.[6]

Again the words of Jesus are appropriate:

And He was saying to them, "The harvest is plentiful, but the laborers are few; therefore beseech the Lord of the harvest to send out laborers into His harvest" (Luke 10:2).

A Few Final Verses to Encourage Everyone

"For God so loved the world, that He gave His only begotten Son, that whoever believes in Him shall not perish, but have eternal life" (John 3:16).

Jesus said to her, "I am the resurrection and the life; he who believes in Me will live even if he dies, and everyone who lives and believes in Me will never die. Do you believe this?" (John 11:25, 26).

Therefore many other signs Jesus also performed in the presence of the disciples, which are not written in this book; but these have been written so that you may believe that Jesus is the Christ, the Son of God; and that believing you may have life in His name (John 20:30, 31).

Notes

1. *Zondervan NASB Exhaustive Concordance* (Grand Rapids, MI: Zondervan, 2000), 1547.
2. "Evangelism Is Most Effective Among Kids," www.barna.org, 11 October 2004.
3. Ibid.
4. Ibid.
5. Ibid.
6. Susan R. Garrett, "Matthew 10:24–33," *Interpretation* 47 (April 1993), 167.

Appendix B

Resources for Additional Study

In researching previously published books, I discovered a number of helpful works covering the life and teachings of Jesus on various topics, including:

Ankerberg, John and Dillon Burroughs. *What's the Big Deal About Jesus?: Why All the Controversy? Is He Relevant? Doe It Matter to Me?* Eugene, OR: Harvest House Publishers, 2007.

Bock, Darrell L. *Jesus According to Scripture: Restoring the Portrait from the Gospels.* Grand Rapids, MI: Baker Academic, 2002.

———. *Jesus in Context: Background Readings For Gospel Study.* Grand Rapids, MI: Baker Academic, 2005.

———, ed. *The Bible Knowledge Key Word Study: The Gospels.* Colorado Springs, CO: Cook Communications Ministries, 2002.

Coffey, Brian R. *The Life of Jesus.* Wheaton, IL: Tyndale House Publishers, 2002.

Following Jesus. Torrance, CA: Rose Publishing, 2005.

Green, Michael. *Who Is This Jesus?* Eastbourne, England: Kingsway Communications, 1990.

Littleton, Mark. *Jesus: Everything You Need to Know to Figure Him Out.* Louisville, KY: Westminster John Knox Press, 2001.

Lockyer, Herbert. *All the Teachings of Jesus.* Peabody, MA: Hendrickson Publishers, 1991.

Lutzer, Erwin W. *Christ Among Other gods.* Chicago: Moody Press, 1994.

Pentecost, J. Dwight. *The Words & Works of Jesus Christ.* Grand Rapids, MI: Zondervan Publishing House, 1981.

Rhodes, Ron. *What Did Jesus Mean?* Eugene, OR: Harvest House Publishers, 1999.

Richards, Larry. *Every Teaching of Jesus in the Bible.* Nashville: Thomas Nelson Publishers, 2001.

Strauss, Mark L. *Four Portraits, One Jesus: An Introduction to Jesus and the Gospels.* Grand Rapids, MI: Zondervan, 2007.

Strobel, Lee. *The Case For The Real Jesus: A Journalist Investigates Current Attacks on the Identity of Christ.* Grand Rapids, MI: Zondervan, 2007.

Thomas, Robert L. *A Harmony of the Gospels: New American Standard Edition.* San Francisco: Harper & Row, 1986.

Walvoord, John F. and Roy B. Zuck. *The Bible Knowledge Commentary.* Colorado Springs, CO: Cook Communications Ministries, 2004.

Zondervan NASB Exhaustive Concordance. Grand Rapids, MI: Zondervan, 2000.

Appendix C

Map of the Ministry of Jesus

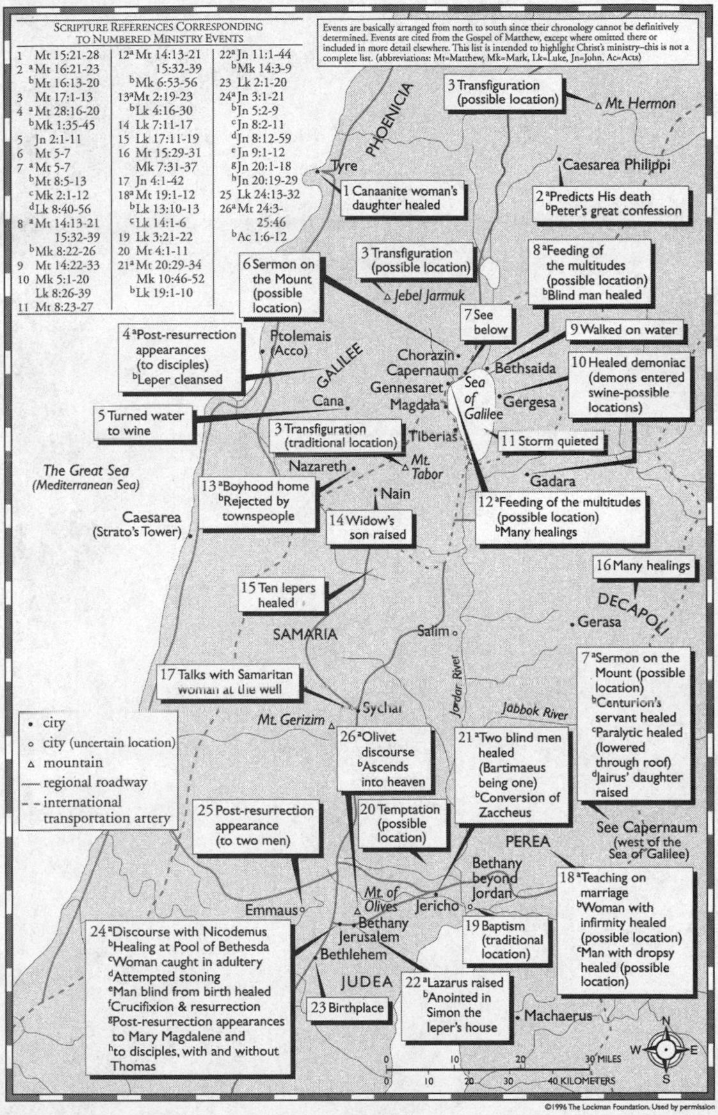